THE AUTHORITY SINCE 1868

THE WORLD ALMANAC & BOOK OF FACTS 1981

NEA

Published Annually by
NEWSPAPER ENTERPRISE ASSOCIATION, INC.
New York

THE WORLD ALMANAC & BOOK OF FACTS 1981

Publisher: Jane D. Flatt
Editor: Hana Umlauf Lane

Managing Editor: Vincent P. Bannan
Associate Editors: Henry H. Doering
Juliana N. Mace

Assistant Editors: June Foley,
Thomas J. McGuire
Senior Assistant: Lon Hill
Assistant to the Publisher: Patricia Fisher

Canadian Editor: John Filion

Paperback cover design: Barbara Wilhelm, Elke Raedisch

The editors acknowledge with thanks the many letters of helpful comment and criticism from users of THE WORLD ALMANAC, and invite further suggestions and observations. Because of the volume of mail directed to the editorial offices, it is not possible personally to reply to each letter writer. However, every communication is read by the editors and all comments and suggestions receive careful attention. Inquiries regarding contents should be sent to: The World Almanac, 200 Park Avenue, New York, NY 10166.

THE WORLD ALMANAC is published annually in November. Purchase orders should be sent to: Newspaper Enterprise Association, Inc., 1100 Central Trust Tower, Cincinnati, OH 45202

THE WORLD ALMANAC does not decide wagers.

The first edition of THE WORLD ALMANAC, a 120-page volume with 12 pages of advertising, was published by the New York World in 1868, 112 years ago. Annual publication was suspended in 1876. Joseph Pulitzer, publisher of the New York World, revived THE WORLD ALMANAC in 1886 with the goal of making it a "compendium of universal knowledge." It has been published annually since then. In 1931, it was acquired by the Scripps-Howard Newspapers; until 1951, it bore the imprint of the New York World-Telegram and thereafter, until 1967, that of the New York World-Telegram and Sun. It is now published in paper and clothbound editions by Newspaper Enterprise Association, Inc., a Scripps-Howard company.

THE WORLD ALMANAC & BOOK OF FACTS 1981

Library of Congress Catalog Card Number 4-3781
International Standard Serial Number (ISSN) 0084-1382
Newspaper Enterprise Association, Inc. (softcover) ISBN 0-911818-17-0
Newspaper Enterprise Association Inc. (hardcover) ISBN 0-911818-18-9
Doubleday and Co., Inc. ISBN 0-385-17323-7
Ballantine Books ISBN 0-345-29176-X
Windward/W.H. Smith & Son Ltd. ISBN 0-7112-0068-8
Microfilm Edition since 1868: Bell and Howell Co.
Printed in the United States of America
The Ballantine paperback edition distributed in the United States by Ballantine Books, a division of Random House, Inc. and in Canada by Random House of Canada, Ltd.

NEWSPAPER ENTERPRISE ASSOCIATION, INC.
200 Park Avenue, New York, NY 10166

ALL NEW THIS YEAR

GENERAL INDEX

— M —

—N—

—O—

— P —

— S —

—T—

Addenda, Late News, Changes

Aerospace (pp. 209-215)

Manned Space Flights: Soviet astronauts Leonid Popov and Valery Ryumin broke the 175-day, 36-minute record for space endurance Oct. 1 during their Soyuz 35 mission (pp. 209-210).

Education (pp. 240-272)

Ellen V. Fuller assumed the post of acting president of **Barnard College,** July 21 (p. 241).

The new president of the **University of Pennsylvania** is Sheldon Hackney (p. 250).

The new president of **West Coast University** is Barnard F. Cohlan (p. 254).

U.S. Judiciary (pp. 301-304)

U.S. Courts of Appeals: Congressional legislation split the existing 5th federal judicial circuit into 2 circuits, a new **5th Circuit,** consisting of Alabama, Florida, and Georgia, and an **11th Circuit,** consisting of Louisiana, Mississippi, Texas, and the Canal Zone (pp. 302-303).

Religious Information (pp. 334-345)

Roman Catholic Hierarchy: Sergio Cardinal Pignedoli, president of the Secretariet for Non-Christians, died June 15. His successor to the post is Archbishop Jean Jadot (p. 345).

Noted Personalities (pp. 346-390)

Entertainment Personalities: Peggy should read **Polly Holliday** (p. 373).

Awards (pp. 391-403)

Nobel Prize in Physics: James W. Cronin and Val. L.

Fitch, both U.S., to share $212,000 for discoveries concerning the symmetry of subatomic particles (p. 391).

Nobel Prize in Chemistry: Paul Berg, U.S., and jointly to Walter Gilbert, U.S. and Frederick Sanger, U.K., $212,000 for the development of methods that make it possible to map in detail the structure and function of DNA (p. 391).

Nobel Prize in Medicine or Physiology: Baruj Benacerraf and George Snell, U.S., and Jean Dausset, France, $211,000 for their work in making tissue typing possible and shedding new light on the body's immune system. (pp. 391-392).

Nobel Prize in Literature: Czeslaw Milosz, Polish emigre poet and novelist who is now an American citizen: $210,000 (p. 392).

Nobel Peace Prize: Adolfo Perez Esquivel, an Argentine, the leader of an organization promoting human rights in Latin America: $211,000 (pp. 392-393).

Nobel Memorial Prize in Economics: Lawrence R. Klein, U.S., $212,000, for research dealing with the construction and analysis of empirical models of business fluctuations (p. 393).

Journalism Awards (pp. 399-400):

Maria Moors Cabot Prizes for distinguished journalistic contributions to the advancement of inter-American understanding, administered by Columbia University, $1,000: Guido Fernández, La Nacíon, San José, Costa Rica; Penny Lernoux, Los Angeles, Alan Riding, The New York Times Mexico City bureau; posthumous citations: Bill Stewart, ABC News; Richard T. Baker, Columbia University.

Gavel Awards for coverage of the justice system, by the American Bar Assn.: newspapers: Gloucester County Times (Woodbury, N.J.); Clarion-Ledger (Jackson, Miss.); Village Voice (N.Y., N.Y.); Philadelphia Inquirer; Miami (Fla.) Herald; California Living Magazine (San Francisco Examiner). Magazines: Angolite (Angola, L.A.); Washington (D.C.) Monthly; New West Magazine; Better Homes and Gardens. Other media: Associated Press, "Juris Prudent"; Warner Bros. TV, "Dummy." Books: Russell Sage Foundation, "The Process is the Punishment"; Congressional Quarterly, Inc., "Guide to the U.S. Supreme Court."

Broadcasting and Theater (p. 400):

Emmy Awards, by Academy of Television Arts and Sciences, for nighttime programs, 1979-80: Dramatic series: Lou Grant; actor: Ed Asner, Lou Grant; actress: Barbara Bel Geddes, Dallas; supporting actor: Stuart Margolin, The Rockford Files; supporting actress: Nancy Marchand, Lou Grant; director: Roger Grant, Lou Grant; writer: Seth Freeman, Lou Grant. Comedy series: Taxi; actor: Richard Mulligan, Soap; actress: Cathryn Damon, Soap; supporting actor: Harry Morgan, M*A*S*H; supporting actress: Loretta Swit, M*A*S*H; director: James Burrows, Taxi; writer: Bob Colleary, Barney Miller. Limited series or specials: Edward and Mrs. Simpson; actor: Powers Boothe, Guyana Tragedy; actress: Patty Duke Astin, The Miracle Worker; supporting actor: George Grizzard, The Oldest Living Graduate; supporting actress: Mare Winningham, Amber Waves; director: Marvin Chomsky, Attica; writer: David Chase, Off the Minnesota Strip. Specials: drama: The Miracle Worker; information: The Body Human: the Magic Sense; variety or music: Baryshnikov on Broadway; classical performing arts: Live from Studio 8H: A Tribute to Toscanini (p. 400).

Arts and Media (pp. 404-416)

Symphony Orchestras of the U.S. and Canada: Eugene Ormandy retired as music director of the **Philadelphia Orchestra** Aug. 23. The new music director is Riccardo Muti (p. 405).

Susan Powell, of Elk City, Oklahoma, was chosen **Miss America 1981** (p. 409).

Nations of the World (pp. 513-597)

Argentina: Roberto Eduardo Viola, b. Oct. 13, 1924, was named by the ruling junta, Oct. 3, to succeed Jorge Rafael Videla as president March, 1981 (p. 515).

People's Republic of China: The new prime minister is Zhao Ziyang, b. 1919, elected Sept. 10 (p. 525).

Guyana: Under a new constitution, Prime Min. Linden Forbes Burnham also became president, Oct. 6 (p. 541).

Iran: The new prime minister is Mohammed Ali Rajai, approved by the Iranian parliament Aug. 11 (pp. 545-546).

Italy: The new prime minister is Arnaldo Forlani, in office Oct. 22 (p. 549).

Jamaica: The new prime minister is Edward P.G. Seaga, in office Oct. 31 (p. 550).

Jordan: The new prime minister is Mudar Badran, b. 1934, in office Aug. 28 (p. 551).

So. Korea: The new president is Chun Doo Hwan, in office Sept. 1; the new prime minister is Nam Duck Woo, approved by the National Assembly Sept. 22 (pp. 552-553).

Lebanon: The new prime minister is Shafig al-Wazan, in office Oct. 26 (p. 554).

Libya and Syria: The 2 nations proclaimed, Sept. 10, that they were a unified state (pp. 555 and 581).

Poland: The new prime minister is Jozef Pinkowski, in office Aug. 24; the new head of the Communist Party is Stanislaw Kania, b. Mar. 8, 1927, in office Sept. 6 (p. 569).

St. Vincent and the Grenadines was admitted as the 153d member of the United Nations Sept. 1980 (p. 598).

San Marino: The new prime minister captain regent is Giordano Bruno Reffi, in office Oct. 1 (p. 573).

Suriname: Pres. Johan Ferrier was deposed in a coup, Aug. 14, and replaced by Prime Minister Chin A Sen (p. 579).

Turkey: The National Security Council, headed by Gen. Kenan Evren, b. 1918, seized power in a bloodless military coup, Sept. 12. The Council named Bulent Ulusu prime minister, Sept. 20 (p.584).

Uganda: The Uganda People's Congress of former Pres. Milton Obote took full control of the nation, Sept. 17 (p. 585).

USSR: The new prime minister is Nikolai A. Tikhonov, b. May 1, 1905 (p. 586).

Vanuatu: The former condominium of **New Hebrides,** jointly administered by France and UK, became independent as the nation **Vanuatu** (pp. 537 and 591).

Yugoslavia: The new president of the Communist Party's ruling Presidium is Lazar Mojsov, elected Oct. 20 (p. 595).

Zaire: Nguza Karl-i-Bond was named prime minister Aug. 27 (p. 596).

Zimbabwe was admitted as the 154th member of the United Nations Sept. 1980 (p. 598).

Non-permanent members of the **United Nations Security Council** elected Oct. 1980 to serve 1981-1982 were: Ireland, Japan, Spain, and Uganda. Costa Rica and Nicaragua were deadlocked for the final vacant seat (p. 599).

Ambassadors and Envoys (pp. 600-601):

The new **U.S. ambassador to Argentine** is Harry W. Schlaudeman.

The new **U.S. ambassador to Colombia** is Thomas Boyatt.

The new **U.S. ambassador to Honduras** is Jack R. Binns.

The new **U.S. ambassador to Malaysia** is Barbara M. Watson.

The new **U.S. ambassador to Paraguay** is Lyle F. Lane.

The new **U.S. ambassador to Peru** is Edwin G. Corr.

Robert S. Gershenson has been nominated **U.S. ambassador to Uruguay.**

North American Cities (pp. 608-676)

The editor of the **Albuquerque,** New Mexico, **Tribune** is now William Tanner (p. 608).

Arnold Rosenfeld was named executive editor and John Black was named vice president for administration and community affairs of the **Dayton,** Ohio, **Journal Herald** (p. 619).

The editor of the **Denver,** Colorado, **Rocky Mountain News** is now Ralph Looney (p. 620).

Sports (pp. 801-896)

World Track and Field Records: Men's Records, Running - Metric Distances: Steve Ovett of Great Britain set a new record in running 1,500 meters in 3 minutes, 31.4 seconds, Aug. 27, in Koblenz, W. Germany (p. 857).

113th ANNIVERSARY EDITION

The World Almanac

and Book of Facts for 1981

The Top 10 News Stories of 1980

Mounting anguish and suspense over the fate of the American hostages held by Iranian militants dominated the thoughts of the nation as the imposition of sanctions, economic and political, by the U.S. and the European Economic Community, UN efforts to mediate, and an aborted rescue mission failed to bring the hostages home.

A severe drop in industrial output, the lowest in 5 years and a soaring jobless rate, aggravated by the government's anti-inflationary tight money policy, plunged the nation's economy into a recession by late spring. By the end of the 3d quarter, the economy showed signs of coming out of the recession, but inflation continued to rise, a bad indicator during an economic comeback.

To denounce the Soviet Union for its invasion of Afghanistan, the U.S. Olympic Committee, in response to a plea from Pres. Jimmy Carter and a large segment of the U.S. people, voted to boycott the Summer Olympics in Moscow. Earlier, the U.S. government had placed an embargo on the sale of grain and high technology to the USSR and deferred new cultural and economic exchanges; the UN Security Council and General Assembly had condemned the invasion and demanded immediate withdrawal of Soviet troops from Afghanistan.

Three candidates, the Democratic incumbent, Pres. Jimmy Carter, the former Republican governor of California, Ronald Reagan, and the Republican Congressman from Illinois running as an independent, John Anderson, battled, often acrimoniously, for the presidency, but, by the end of the campaign, all had fallen short of igniting the electorate, as most voters went to the polls disenchanted with their alternatives.

Halting 60 percent of the world's oil traffic, a 10-month skirmish between Iraq and Iran over the Shatt-al Arab waterway broke into open warfare when Iraq attacked Iranian oil and air fields and Iran retaliated. As the two nations attempted to cripple each other's economies, stiff resolve on both sides soon stalemated the situation, though by the end of October Iraq held claim to the port city of Khuramshahr in Iran's oil-rich province of Khuzistan.

Embittered Polish workers at the Lenin shipyard in Gdansk went on strike, culminating 2 months of labor turmoil, and, in a political development unprecedented in the Soviet bloc, won the right to form independent trade unions, the right to strike, the release of all political prisoners, and the abolition of government censorship. After granting the concessions, veteran Communist party head Edward Gierek was replaced, ostensibly due to poor health, by security affairs chief Stanislaw Kania.

Waiting was the watchword for Cuban refugees after Castro's sudden decision to allow those persons who wanted to leave Cuba to do so: first in the Peruvian embassy in Havana, then to be picked up in boats in the harbor at Mariel, and finally in processing centers in the U.S. Their arrival in the U.S. was greeted with hostility by many Americans who feared further strain on the already battered economy and job market. Many of the refugees, frustrated and disillusioned by the slow-moving processing apparatus, rioted in protest in the refugee centers.

Ferociously hurling ash and steam some 60,000 feet into the sky in a giant blast, Mount St. Helens erupted, claiming more than 26 lives and wreaking general devastation on the surrounding area in southwestern Washington, forcing President Carter to declare the state a major disaster area.

Legislative corruption, uncovered by the surreptitious Abscam investigative operation conducted by the FBI, was linked to 31 public officials, and led to the first expulsion of a Congressman from the House of Representatives in the history of the U.S. Public disdain over political hanky-panky was roused again when Billy Carter registered as an agent of Libya, but Senate investigation revealed no illegality on his or the administration's part, but only the exercise of poor judgment.

Other top news stories included the declaration of a state of emergency at Love Canal (an area in New York state contaminated by toxic waste), the emergence of Zimbabwe as an independent state led by a former guerrilla leader, the passage and signing of a funding bill for draft registration in peacetime, and the unprecedented price of gold, reaching over $800 an ounce in the early part of the year.

Reagan Landslide Victor, as Democratic Coalition Collapses; Republicans Capture Senate

Though the outcome of the 1980 presidential election had been called too close to predict by political observers and pollsters, Republican Ronald Wilson Reagan, former governor of California, swept to a landslide victory over Pres. Jimmy Carter **Nov. 4,** marking the first time since 1932 that an incumbent elected President had not been retained in office.

In becoming the nation's 40th (and oldest) President, conservative Reagan, 69, won 43 states, garnering 483 electoral votes, well over the 270 needed for election. The president won in only 6 states and the Distict of Columbia, with a total of 49 electoral votes. Independent candidate Rep. John B. Anderson (R, Ill.) won no electoral votes, and finished far back in the popular vote totals with 7% of the vote.

The swift and stunning Republican victory extended to the U.S. Congress, where, for the first time since 1954, they gained control of the Senate. The split in the Senate will be 53 Republicans and 47 Democrats. (Virginia Sen. Harry F. Byrd, Jr. runs as an independent, but votes with the Democrats in the Senate.) Though the House of Representatives remained under Democratic control, the majority party lost more than two dozen seats to the GOP, making the split 250-245 seats.

Carter's defeat came on a day of heavier-than-expected voter turnout in most areas of the country, traditionally a good sign for Democratic candidates. But the time-honored Democratic coalition of blue collar workers, labor, and various ethnic and minority groups failed to materialize around the president, as they had in 1976. Carter fared no better regionally, winning only his home state of Georgia in the South, and the border states of West Virginia and Maryland, in addition to the District of Columbia. As expected, Reagan made a clean sweep of the Southwest and Far Western states (except Hawaii, which was solidly for Carter). Reagan also scored impressive victories in the Midwest, and his early victories in Michigan, Ohio, and Illinois, three states crucial to Carter's strategy, spelled disaster for the president.

Most surprising was Reagan's strong showing in the northeast, where he captured New York (thought to be a Carter state) Pennsylvania, New Jersey, Massachusetts, and Connecticut. Carter won only Rhode Island and Delaware.

When Carter appeared before cheering supporters in Washington to concede the election at 9:50 p.m. EST, he made the earliest concession speech of any major candidate for the presidency since Alton Parker acknowledged defeat to Theodore Roosevelt in 1904. With his wife, Rosalynn, and daughter, Amy, at his side, a somber Carter admitted his defeat "hurt," but pledged an orderly transition to a Reagan presidency. "We must come together as a united and unified people." said Carter, "and join in a sincere and fruitful effort" to make Reagan's presidency productive.

Seesaw Battle for Votes

The 1980 campaign was always close, a seesaw battle between the two major contenders. Since both Reagan and Carter had easy first-ballot victories at their respective nominating conventions, Election Day was a somewhat exciting climax to a campaign that many voters had found lackluster.

Carter and Reagan remained close in the polls all during the campaign, which began in earnest **Sept. 1.** Reagan hammered away at Carter's record, portraying him as a weak and vacillating leader responsible for economic chaos at home and loss of American power and prestige abroad. Carter, for his part, decried Reagan's conservative stands on defense and social issues, and criticized GOP plans for economic recovery as unrealistic.

The League of Women Voters attempted to sponsor a three-way debate between the presidential candidates, but Carter refused to participate if Anderson was included. Reagan and Anderson debated **Sept. 21.** Reagan and Carter finally met face-to-face in Cleveland on **Oct. 28,** in another debate sponsored by the league, without Anderson present.

The debate, which failed to have the decisive effect that both sides had hoped for, centered on the candidates' positions on nuclear weapons and energy, the economy, foreign affairs, and the cities. Each candidate claimed victory in the contest, but polls showed large blocs of voters still undecided as election time drew near. A renewal of interest in the Iran hostage crisis at the end of October, without a successful resolution of the problem, apparently adversely affected the president's strength with the electorate.

Liberal Senators Fall

The move was to the right in both houses of Congress, particularly in the Senate, where several prominent liberals were defeated in reelection bids. Sen. Birch Bayh, (D, Ind.), George McGovern (D, S.D.), Frank Church (D, Id.), John Culver (D. (a.) were all defeated by conservative Republican challengers. Those senators, along with Sen. Thomas Eagleton (D, Mo.) and Sen. Alan Cranston (D, Calif.), were targeted for defeat in a million-dollar advertising campaign waged by the National Conservative Political Action Committee (NCPAC). Eagleton and Cranston successfully fought off their opponents to remain in the Senate.

House Majority Whip John D. Brademas of Indiana, another favorite target of conservatives, was defeated in his bid for another term by 27-year-old John Hiler, a LaPorte businessman. House Ways and Means Committee Chairman Al Ullman, in a fight for his political life, lost to Republican Denny Smith, in a close race in Oregon.

Scandals claimed their share of incumbents in both houses of Congress. Convicted ABSCAM Reps.Michael Myers (D, Pa.) and John Jenrette (D, S.C.) were resoundingly defeated, as were New York Rep. John Murphy and New Jersey Rep. Frank Thompson, both under indictment in the ABSCAM case. Rep. Robert Bauman (R, Md.), a prominent House conservative, was accused of soliciting sex from a teenage boy and was ousted in his election contest.

In the Senate, Georgia's Democratic Sen. Herman Talmadge lost a close race to Republican challenger Mack Mattingly. Talmadge had been "denounced" by Senate colleagues for financial misconduct earlier in the year.

In a major upset, Republican unknown Alfonse D'Amato narrowly defeated Democratic Congresswoman Elizabeth Holtzmann and veteran Senator Jacob Javits in a bitterly contested race for Javits' seat.

Thirteen Governorships Contested

With 13 governorships at stake, Republicans scored a major upset in Arkansas, where Democratic Governor Bill Clinton, the nation's youngest governor, was defeated for reelection by Republican Frank White.

The GOP also captured the governorships in Missouri and North Dakota, in addition to keeping their two incumbents in Delaware and Vermont.

Issues Show Trends

The conservative trend also manifested itself in a number of local ballot issues. Tax reforms, many patterned on the successfuly Proposition 13, drew a mixed response. Constitutional change held property tax increases to 10% per year in Arkansas, Massachusetts voters passed Proposition 2-1/2, which reduced property taxes 40% to 2.5% of property value. And in Missouri, voters decided to keep tax revenues from rising faster than the economic indicators.

Arizona, Michigan, Nevada, South Dakota, Oregon, and Utah, on the other hand, turned down similar measures that would slash property taxes, apparently heeding warnings from government officials about sharp cutbacks in service.

In a non-binding vote, residents of eight Nevada localities said that they did not want the MX missile placed in their state. District of Columbia voters started the long process to become the 51st state. In California, Proposition 10, restricting smoking in public places, was also defeated by voters.

The 1980 Conventions

The Republicans

In a convention that held few surprises after a rough and tumble primary campaign that saw as many as 7 candidates seeking nomination, Republicans, meeting in Detroit, Mich., **July 16,** nominated Ronald W. Reagan, former California governor, for president.

Reagan soared to a first-ballot victory with 1,939 votes (1,130 needed to nominate) in the climax of his quest for the nomination that had survived his 1976 convention defeat at the hands of former Pres. Gerald R. Ford, Rep. John B. Anderson (Ill.), the only one of Reagan's competitors still running for the nomination at convention time (as an independent), received 37 votes.

The convention's major drama came in the selection of George H. Bush as Reagan's running mate. Bush, former congressman and UN ambassador, had been Reagan's most successful foe in the primary campaign. Though he garnered 1,832 of a possible 1,993 votes in his nomination July 17, Bush's selection was somewhat of a surprise to the delegates, who believed that a highly-touted "dream ticket" of Reagan and Ford was imminent.

Breaking tradition by coming to the convention hall before his acceptance speech, Reagan announced Bush's selection to the delegates after negotiations failed to produce an agreement for Ford to join the ticket. Reportedly, Ford asked for (and got) promises of extraordinary vice-presidential authority. However, after a day of meetings and speculation, Ford decided (in Reagan's words) "he can be of more value campaigning his heart out as a former President . . . than as a member of the ticket."

The GOP platform, adopted July 15, provided controversy with its planks withdrawing 40 years of support for the Equal Rights Amendment and calling for a constitutional ban on abortion and the appointment of judges who favored such an amendment. Party co-chairperson Mary D. Crisp expressed the dismay of some Republican women when she resigned, citing the anti-ERA plank as a major reason for her departure, saying the party was "burying the rights of over 100 million women under a heap of platitudes."

In the area of the economy, the platform supported the Kemp-Roth tax bill, which provided for across-the-board cuts of 10% a year for three years. The economic plank also sought a lesser role for government in American business, a federal spending limit based on a fixed percentage of the GNP, and a balanced budget.

The longest platform section dealt with national security and foreign affairs. Characterizing the Carter foreign policy as aimless, the platform warned of Soviet expansionism and endorsed development of such new weapons as the controversial MX ballistic missile system. In addition, opposition was expressed to the SALT II treaty and peacetime draft registration, and called for a build-up of conventional military forces.

Other planks: attainment of energy self-sufficiency by decontrol of domestic oil and gas prices and a repeal of portions of the windfall profits tax; mandatory sentences for crimes committed with firearms, the death penalty, voluntary prayer in public schools, repeal of campaign spending limits, and an end of grain embargo against the Soviet Union.

In his acceptance speech, Reagan, **July 17,** called on voters to create a "new consensus of common values . . . embodied in the[se] words; family, work, neighborhood, peace, and freedom." He pledged a "great national crusade to make America great again," by making the nation stronger militarily and economically.

Though Reagan was long-favored to win the party's endorsement, challenges by Bush had added some excitement to the race. At the Iowa precinct caucuses **July 21,** the first step in delegate selection in the nation, Bush upset Reagan, capturing 32% of the voters polled to the Californian's 29%. Bush also won the Puerto Rico primary (the nation's first), **Feb. 17,** with a victory over Sen. Howard H. Baker (Tenn.); and tied Anderson in the Massachusetts primary, **Mar. 4.**

It was in New Hampshire that Reagan scored his first decisive victory; he garnered 50% of the vote Feb. 26, trouncing Bush by greater than 2-1, although the race was thought to be a toss-up, Reagan went on to win big in Florida, Georgia, Alabama, (all Mar. 11), Illinois, (Mar. 18), New York (Mar. 25), and Wisconsin (Apr. 1).

One by one, challengers dropped out of the race: Baker withdrew **Mar. 5.** He was followed by John B. Connally of Texas (**Mar. 9**), Sen. Robert Dole of Kansas (**Mar. 15**), Rep. Philip M. Crane of Illinois (**Apr. 17**) and Anderson (**Apr. 24**), who announced he would run as an independent to provide voters with a more clear-cut choice in November.

Bush scored another upset of Reagan in Pennsylvania Apr. 22, gaining 53% of the votes to the front-runner's 46%, but by **May 6** the process was all but over, with Reagan having 871 of the 998 delegates needed to nominate, and the Bush camp conceding that their candidate would probably not catch up. Bush did win Michigan's May 20 primary, but Reagan had gained enough votes by then to put him within 5 votes of victory. Bush ended his campaign May 26, pledging to ask delegates committed to him to switch their votes to Reagan.

The Democrats

After failing to win a key rules battle, Sen. Edward M. Kennedy (Mass.) ended his campaign for the Democratic nomination for President Aug. 11 when the party convention in New York City was but a few hours old, paving the way for a first-ballot renomination of Pres. Jimmy Carter and V. Pres. Walter F. Mondale **Aug. 14.**

Carter received 2,219 votes, well over the 1,666 votes needed to win. Kennedy received 1,146 votes, although he had released his delegates to "vote their consciences" on the first ballot.

The President's victory was assured when the convention voted 1,396.4 to 1,390.6 to retain the disputed Rule F3(c). The rule, adopted after the 1976 Democratic convention, stated that all delegates "shall be bound to vote for the Presidential candidate whom they were elected to support for at least the first . . . ballot, unless released in writing by the . . . candidate." Kennedy supporters had sought to have delegates vote as they pleased on the first ballot.

Though Kennedy lost the nomination, his influence was widely felt during the convention. A dramatic and rousing speech by the senator to the delegates on Aug. 12 (marking the first time since William Jennings Bryan in 1896 that a potential Presidential candidate made a major address to the convention before the nomination) sparked some 35 minutes of cheering, placard waving, and cavorting in the aisles. Kennedy exhorted delegates to renew the Democrats' traditional committment to economic justice for all, unite, and "march" ahead to victory in November.

A Kennedy victory was scored on the Democratic platform, with the adoption of a plank called for $12 billion jobs program, which was opposed by Carter forces. Other Kennedy planks adopted included a pledge not to support any program that would increase unemployment, and a promise that jobs would be the party's "single highest domestic priority."

Among other planks in the Democratic platform: strong support for the ERA and a commitment to cut off campaign funding for any Democratic candidates who did not favor the amendment; endorsement of federal funding for abortions; a pledge to seek a reduction in states' burdens in welfare; objection to a proposed law giving the federal government power to override state and local environmental protection laws.

Carter indicated his acceptance of most of the platform Aug. 12, under a rule that the nominee must state objections to the platform in writing. He stopped short of formally endorsing Kennedy's jobs plank, but agreed to "accept and support the intent behind the plank" without committing to a specific program or dollar amount.

"We have made mistakes, and we have learned from them," the President said. "But we have built the foundation now for a better future."

Carter and Kennedy both won major victories during the primary campaign, but Calif. Gov. Jerry Brown's candidacy (he dropped out of the race Apr. 1 after his campaign failed to ignite much voter interest) appeared to have little effect.

Carter did not personally appear on the campaign trail until late in the primary season, citing the crises in Iran and Afghanistan, as well as domestic economic problems, as reasons for staying close to the White House. Kennedy assailed Carter's "Rose Garden" campaign, and urged the President to debate him on the issues, which Carter declined to do.

In the Iowa caucusas **Jan. 21,** Carter defeated Kennedy by a 2-1 margin. Carter also solidly defeated Kennedy in the New Hampshire primary **Feb. 26,** by a 49% to 38% margin.

The senator's major victories came in the Massachusetts primary Mar. 4 and the New York and Connecticut primaries Mar. 25. Kennedy scored an impressive upset of Carter in New York, defeating the President by 59% to 41%. Since Kennedy had suffered a huge loss in the Illinois primary **Mar. 19** (Carter receiving 65% of the vote to Kennedy's 30%), the New York win was seen by the Kennedy camp as a hopeful sign that he could overtake the President.

Once Carter dropped his ban on campaigning Apr. 30, however, Kennedy was never able to catch up. Even though Kennedy won 5 primaries on June 3 (California, New Jersey, New Mexico, Rhode Island, and South Dakota), his best showing of the campaign, Carter, on that same day, achieved a clear majority of delegates, in effect ending the race.

Laws Passed During 96th Congress, Second Session, 1980

The 96th Congress convened its Second Session Jan. 22, 1980, and it was quickly overwhelmed by a scandal. Details of an FBI investigation called "Abscam" because agents in the investigation had posed as businessmen from Abdul Enterprises Ltd., first surfaced on the NBC-TV evening news, Feb. 2. It was reported that a senator and 7 representatives were linked in the investigation to bribery and corruption. The ethics committees of both houses of Congress immediately set up their own investigations. Six of the representatives were later indicted by grand juries and 2 were convicted. Following the conviction of Rep. Michael Myers (D, Pa.) the House of Representatives, which had seen videotapes of Myers taking a bribe, expelled him by a vote of 376 to 30, the first expulsion of a member of the House since 1861.

Bills passed and signed and other major actions during the Second Session included:

China's Trade Status. Approved (Jan. 24) most-favored-nation trade status for China, putting into effect a bilateral trade agreement signed in July 1979.

Olympics resolution. The Senate (Jan. 29) and the House (Jan. 24) passed resolutions backing Pres. Jimmy Carter's call for an international boycott of the 1980 Summer Olympics in Moscow after the Soviet invasion of Afghanistan.

Gratitude to Canada. After the Canadian government helped 6 U.S. diplomats escape from Iran, the Senate and the House approved (Jan. 30) separate resolutions expressing the U.S. government's gratitude for the Canadian action.

Refugee Bill. Approved the Refugee Act of 1980 (signed March 17), which established new procedures for admitting refugees and for resettling them in the U.S., raised the limit of the number admitted each year to 50,000 (with provisions for additional emergency admissions), and established the office of U.S. Coordinator for Refugee Affairs.

Windfall Oil Profits Tax. Approved a windfall profits tax on oil companies (signed April 2). Proposed by Pres. Carter in April 1979, the tax was designed to complement the decontrol of oil prices, which was expected to bring producers an extra $1 trillion by the end of the decade. The tax was expected to bring the government more than $227 billion by 1990.

Banking, Railroads

Banking Deregulation. Approved the Depository Institutions Deregulation and Monetary Control Act of 1980 (signed March 31). The act established a universal system of banking reserves, raised the ceiling on interest paid to small savers, authorized the payment of interest on checking accounts, and increased to $100,000 from $40,000 the amount of bank savings insured by the federal government.

Railroad Aid. Approved legislation to improve service on the high-speed Northeast Corridor railroads and to prevent the breakdown of services on the bankrupt Chicago, Rock Island & Pacific Railroad (signed May 30).

Oil Import Fee Barred. Approved a resolution, over Pres. Carter's veto, to block an oil import fee that would have levied a 10-cent-a-gallon duty at the gasoline pump to discourage energy consumption.

Representative Censured. The House (June 10) censured Rep. Charles H. Wilson (D, Calif.) for violating House rules by converting campaign funds to his own use and for accepting money from a person with a direct interest in legislation. He was the 3d member of Congress to be censured in the 20th century.

1981 Balanced Budget. Approved (June 12) a budget resolution for fiscal 1981 that called for $613.6 billion in spending and a surplus of $200 million. Also approved the final 1980 budget of $572.6 billion, with a deficit of $47 billion.

NRC Authorization. Approved, by the House (June 10) and the Senate (June 16), a $426 million fiscal authorization bill for the Nuclear Regulatory Commission which also stiffened rules relating to nuclear safety. The new rules would site nuclear reactors away from population centers and would allow the issue of licenses for operation only if emergency plans for responding to an accident existed.

Synthetic Fuels Corp. Created. Approved, by the House (June 26) and the Senate (June 19), legislation to create the U.S. Synthetic Fuels Corp. to speed development of alternate energy sources. The bill also created a solar-energy bank and authorized a $1.45 billion alcohol fuel production program.

Draft, Hostages

Draft Registration Funded. Approved $13.3 million in funds to put the draft registration program into effect (signed June 27).

American Hostages in Iran. The Senate adopted a resolution (June 18) deploring any actions by private citizens to engage in negotiations affecting the American hostages in Iran. The action followed the return, June 15, of former Attorney General Ramsey Clark to the U.S. from Iran June 15, after attending, with 9 other Americans, a conference on "Crimes of America."

Trucking Decontrol. Approved, by the House (June 19) and the Senate (June 20), a truck-decontrol bill which made the entry of new companies into trucking easier, eased regulations that restricted service, and gave companies more freedom in setting rates.

Emergency Appropriations. Approved a $16.9 billion fiscal 1980 supplemental appropriations bill (signed July 8). The measure included $75 million in aid to Nicaragua, $1.5 billion in loan guarantees for Chrysler Corp., $1.5 billion to aid auto, steel, and other workers laid off because of foreign imports, funds for Mount St. Helens volcano victims, resettlement money for Cuban and Haitian immigrants and aid for Cambodian refugees.

Major Decisions of the U.S. Supreme Court, 1979-80

Among the notable actions in 1979-80, the Supreme Court:

Ruled, 6-3, that a warrant to search a particular place does not automatically authorize the police to search anyone who happens to be there (Nov. 28, 1979).

Refused to review, therefore let stand, a $75,000 libel award against a novelist and her publisher, won in a suit brought by the self-described real-life model for one of the fictional characters in the novel (Dec. 3, 1979).

Affirmed an appeals court ruling that a parent union was not liable for the losses caused by a wildcat strike in the absence of evidence that it "instigated, supported, ratified or encouraged" the unauthorized work stoppage (Dec. 10, 1979).

Ordered dismissal of a suit by 24 members of Congress which challenged Pres. Jimmy Carter's termination of the defense treaty with Taiwan (Dec. 13, 1979).

Ruled, 8-0, that real estate agents who charge identical commissions in a given geographical area may be sued for price-fixing under the Federal antitrust laws (Jan. 8, 1980).

Voted, unanimously, that states may constitutionally give their parole officials absolute immunity from liability for their decisions to release prisoners on parole (Jan. 15, 1980).

Voted, 6-2, that escaped prisoners who do not turn themselves in promptly are not entitled to an opportunity to persuade a jury that intolerable prison conditions justified their escape (Jan. 21, 1980).

Faculty Unions

Voted, 5-4, that most of the faculty unions at private colleges and universities were not protected by federal labor law, asserting that the members of most faculties at private universities were, in effect, "managerial employees" (Feb. 20, 1980).

Ruled unanimously that workers have the right, under certain circumstances, to refuse to perform tasks they believe pose a danger of death or serious injury (Feb. 26, 1980).

Ruled, 6-3, that an agreement requiring that employees of the Central Intelligence Agency not publish "any information" about the agency without specific prior approval is a judicially enforceable contract that applies to nonclassified as well as classified information (Feb. 19, 1980).

Ruled unanimously that husbands or wives may, if they choose, testify against their spouses in Federal criminal trials (Feb. 27, 1980).

Voted, 5-2, to reverse 2 lower federal courts and ruled that once former Secretary of State Henry Kissinger removed transcripts of his telephone conversations from the State Department, he in effect removed them from the reach of the Freedom of Information Act as well. The information act, the court ruled, does not require a government agency to retrieve documents it no longer has (March 3, 1980).

8th Amendment Interpreted

Ruled, 5-4, that a mandatory life sentence imposed on a Texas man convicted of stealing $120.75, his third felony conviction, did not violate the constitutional prohibition against cruel and unusual punishment (March 18, 1980).

Voted, 6-3, that trading securities on the basis of "inside," or non-public, information violates the anti-fraud provisions only if the trader breaches a pre-existing relationship of trust with the other party to the transaction (March 18, 1980).

Ruled, 7-2, that state legislators facing Federal prosecution are not entitled to bar introduction of their "legislative acts" as evidence (March 19, 1980).

Ruled, 6-1, that a state could tax foreign dividends earned by a U.S. company doing business in that state, even if the company was headquartered elsewhere (March 19, 1980).

Ruled unanimously that the victim of a crime should be allowed to identify the accused at trial even if the accused is found to have been arrested illegally (March 25, 1980).

Found, 6-3, that public employees cannot ordinarily be dismissed solely on the basis of their party affiliation (March 31, 1980).

Upheld unanimously the federal campaign law that bars private fund-raising by a Presidential nominee who accepts public financing for his campaign (April 14, 1980).

Need for Warrant Broadened

Ruled, 6-3, that the police need a warrant before entering a suspect's home to make a routine arrest (April 15, 1980).

Voted, 5-4, that local governments are not entitled to base their defenses against private civil rights suits on the ground that their employees acted in good faith or committed the civil rights violations unintentionally (April 16, 1980).

Ruled, 7-2, that the Eighth Amendment's prohibition against cruel and unusual punishment gives federal prisoners or their survivors a direct right to bring suits for demages against prison officials on charges of mistreatment (April 22, 1980).

Overturned, on a 6-3 vote, a finding by 2 lower courts that the at-large system for electing city commissioners in Mobile, Ala., unconstitutionally diluted the voting strength of the city's black population. An opinion signed by 4 of the majority justices said that the Constitution "does not protect any 'political group,' however defined, from electoral defeat." (April 22, 1980).

Interrogation Rights Defined

Held, by a 6-3 vote, that an offhand remark by a police officer did not violate a murder suspect's rights even though the remark led the suspect to incriminate himself (May 12, 1980).

Ruled unanimously that a state court that issues rules governing the behavior of lawyers is acting like a legislature and is entitled to the same absolute immunity from lawsuits that is accorded to individual legislators (June 2, 1980).

Voted, unanimously, that states can require privately-owned shopping centers to provide access to citizens wishing to circulate petitions (June 9, 1980).

Voted, 7-2, that a defendant who chooses to testify in court can be questioned about his failure to turn himself in or to talk to the police before his arrest (June 10, 1980).

Ruled, unanimously, that a zoning ordinance that limits development in the name of conservation does not necessarily violate the constitutional rights of affected property owners (June 10, 1980).

Ruled unanimously that a state could base its corporate income tax on a corporation's entire income, not just on its earnings from local operations (June 10, 1980).

Patent of Biological Organisms

Ruled, 5-4, that biological organisms could be patented under federal law (June 16, 1980).

Ruled unanimously that farmers in California's Imperial Valley are entitled to federally subsidized irrigation water regardless of the size of their farms (June 16, 1980).

Voted, 6-3, that federal agents had violated a robbery suspect's constitutional right to the assistance of counsel by instructing a paid informer who shared the man's cellblock to report back on any incriminating statements the man made (June 16, 1980).

Held that utilities cannot be prevented from expressing their views or promoting their products (June 20, 1980).

Ruled, 5-4, that a judge can delegate important pretrial duties to a magistrate without violating the constitutional rights of a criminal defendant who asks instead to be heard by a federal judge (June 23, 1980).

Extended Civil Rights Act

Voted, 6-3, that the Civil Rights Act of 1871 provided a ground for private citizens to sue state officials whenever a state policy violates a federal law (June 25, 1980).

Overruled, 7-2, a 20-year precedent and held that a person charged with illegal possession is entitled to challenge the legality of a search only if he can demonstrate "an expectation of privacy in the premises searched" (June 25, 1980).

Ruled, 5-4, that Congress may refuse to finance most abortions for poor women, even those for whom the procedure is medically necessary (June 30, 1980).

Affirmed, 8-1, a ruling that the federal government must pay an additional $105 million to 8 tribes of Sioux Indians in compensation for its illegal seizure of the Black Hills of South Dakota in 1877 (June 30, 1980).

Upheld, 8-1, the constitutionality of a federal water pollution law that requires polluters to report oil spills and subjects them to fines for causing the spills (June 27, 1980).

Racial Quotas in Federal Contracts

Held, 6-3, that Congress could award federal funds on the basis of race when the purpose of the preference—in this case, a public works program that set aside 10 percent of the money for minority contractors—was to redress racial discrimination (July 2, 1980).

Ruled, 7-1, that "absent an overriding interest," judges were forbidden from barring the public and press from criminal trials (July 2, 1980).

Voted, 5-4, to uphold a lower court decision that voided the federal government's work safety standard on exposure to the chemical benzene (July 2, 1980).

Refused to grant a stay of a federal appeals court decision allowing the 3 commercial television networks to copy and broadcast the videotapes that were used as evidence in the first Abscam trial (Oct. 14, 1980).

Presidential Election Statistics

Popular and Electoral Vote, 1976 and 1980

	1976				1980				
	Electoral Vote		Democrat	Republican	Electoral Vote		Democrat	Republican	Indep.
States	Carter	Ford	Carter	Ford	Carter	Reagan	Carter	Reagan	Anderson
Ala. . . .	9		659,170	504,070	0	9	625,759	639,294	15,521
Alas. . .		3	44,058	71,555	0	3	31,408	66,874	8,091
Ariz. . . .		6	295,602	418,642	0	6	243,498	523,124	75,805
Ark. . . .	6		498,604	267,903	0	6	388,570	391,356	22,166
Cal. . . .		45	3,742,284	3,882,244	0	45	3,040,680	4,447,266	10,727,872
Col. . . .		7	460,353	584,367	0	7	367,895	649,389	130,360
Conn. . .		8	647,895	719,261	0	8	537,407	672,648	168,260
Del. . . .	3		122,596	109,831	0	3	106,650	111,631	16,344
D.C. . . .	3		137,818	27,873	3	0	124,376	21,765	14,971
Fla. . . .	17		1,636,000	1,469,531	0	17	1,359,237	1,923,973	177,321
Ga. . . .	12		979,409	483,743	12	0	969,335	629,575	33,734
Ha. . . .	4		147,375	140,003	4	0	135,879	130,112	32,921
Ida. . . .		4	126,549	204,151	0	4	109,410	290,087	27,096
Ill.		26	2,271,295	2,364,269	0	26	1,949,511	2,342,399	344,563
Ind. . . .		13	1,014,714	1,185,958	0	13	834,787	1,229,129	126,773
Ia.		8	619,931	632,863	0	8	507,826	675,299	114,305
Kan. . .		7	430,421	502,752	0	7	322,186	557,487	66,883
Ky. . . .	9		615,717	531,852	0	9	609,687	625,823	29,843
La. . . .	10		661,365	587,446	0	10	707,981	795,240	26,190
Me. . . .		4	232,279	236,320	0	4	220,387	238,156	53,458
Md. . . .	10		759,612	672,661	10	0	706,327	656,255	113,452
Mass. . .	14		1,429,475	1,030,276	0	14	1,048,391	1,054,390	382,044
Mich. . .		21	1,696,714	1,893,742	0	21	1,351,190	1,752,701	250,570
Minn. . .	10		1,070,440	819,395	10	0	892,536	823,502	165,553
Miss. . .	7		381,309	366,846	0	7	429,115	440,712	11,611
Mo. . . .	12		999,163	928,808	0	12	916,245	1,053,489	76,365
Mon. . .		4	149,259	173,703	0	4	108,453	188,252	27,157
Neb. . .		5	233,287	359,219	0	5	164,270	413,336	44,024
Nev. . .		3	92,479	101,273	0	3	66,468	154,570	17,580
N.H.. . .		4	147,645	185,935	0	4	109,859	221,198	49,295
N.J. . . .		17	1,444,653	1,509,688	0	17	1,111,983	1,425,522	221,884
N.M. . .		4	201,148	211,419	0	4	164,913	245,537	28,403
N.Y. . . .	41		3,389,558	3,100,791	0	41	2,627,959	2,790,498	441,863
N.C. . . .	13		927,365	741,960	0	13	876,105	914,975	52,368
N.D.. . .		3	136,078	153,470	0	3	68,963	165,632	21,166
Oh. . . .	25		2,011,621	2,000,505	0	25	1,744,254	2,282,256	255,555
Okla. . .		8	532,442	545,708	0	8	394,403	673,030	37,063
Ore. . . .		6	490,407	492,120	0	6	445,627	554,545	139,256
Pa. . . .	27		2,328,677	2,205,604	0	27	1,931,549	2,249,971	
R.I. . . .	4		227,636	181,249	4	0	185,126	145,423	58,091
S.C. . . .	8		450,807	346,149	0	8	422,029	445,364	14,876
S.D. . . .		4	147,068	151,505	0	4	103,909	190,102	21,342
Tenn. . .	10		825,879	633,969	0	10	762,624	767,952	35,892
Tex. . . .	26		2,082,319	1,953,300	0	26	1,769,598	2,418,893	132,936
Ut. . . .		4	182,110	337,908	0	4	123,447	435,839	33,191
Vt.		3	78,789	100,387	0	3	80,384	92,555	31,242
Va. . . .		12	813,896	836,554	0	12	743,788	975,461	91,637
Wash. .		8*	717,323	777,732	0	9	582,498	762,025	165,068
W.Va. . .	6		435,864	314,726	5	0	353,508	326,545	30,499
Wis. . . .	11		1,040,232	1,004,987	0	11	985,255	1,089,750	159,793
Wyo. . .		3	62,239	92,717	0	3	49,102	110,707	12,072
Total . .	**297**	**240**	**40,828,929**	**39,148,940**	**49**	**489**	**34,434,100**	**42,797,153**	**5,533,927**

*One elector in Washington for Reagan. In 1976, McCarthy (Independent) received 739,256 votes; McBride (Libertarian) received 171,818 votes.

Presidential Election Returns by Counties

Compiled from official returns by The World Almanac.

Alabama

County	1976 Carter (D)	1976 Ford (R)	1980 Carter (D)	1980 Reagan (R)	1980 Anderson (I)
Autauga	4,640	4,512	4,295	6,292	125
Baldwin	9,191	13,256	8,384	18,774	395
Barbour	4,730	3,758	4,458	4,171	65
Bibb	2,850	1,591	3,097	2,491	22
Blount	6,645	4,233	5,657	6,819	74
Bullock	3,536	1,482	3,514	1,233	26
Butler	4,271	2,909	4,157	3,806	58
Calhoun	20,466	11,763	16,739	17,658	433
Chambers	6,164	5,488	6,649	4,864	122
Cherokee	4,668	1,492	3,925	2,474	57
Chilton	5,550	4,725	4,703	6,610	60
Choctaw	3,911	3,033	3,680	2,859	22
Clarke	4,737	4,126	5,247	5,058	48
Clay	2,946	1,883	2,858	2,764	34
Cleburne	2,490	1,436	2,050	2,389	34
Coffee	7,844	4,683	6,140	6,760	189
Colbert	11,996	4,471	12,250	6,408	206
Conecuh	3,086	1,812	2,873	2,813	29
Coosa	2,533	1,196	2,383	1,714	19
Covington	7,081	4,977	6,205	7,014	110
Crenshaw	3,372	1,801	2,558	2,394	41
Cullman	12,961	6,899	11,531	10,214	210
Dale	6,346	4,996	4,937	7,247	141
Dallas	8,866	7,144	9,770	7,647	131
DeKalb	9,759	6,597	8,711	9,611	105
Elmore	6,646	6,551	5,947	8,688	171
Escambia	5,957	4,934	5,148	6,513	87
Etowah	25,020	10,333	20,790	16,168	357
Fayette	4,076	2,165	3,429	3,321	44
Franklin	6,279	3,345	6,126	4,448	48
Geneva	5,983	2,663	4,703	4,747	67
Greene	2,900	903	3,474	1,034	16
Hale	3,236	2,034	3,683	2,074	56
Henry	3,144	2,052	2,973	2,813	18
Houston	8,787	10,672	7,708	11,924	178
Jackson	10,989	3,913	8,809	4,868	156
Jefferson	99,531	113,590	108,786	129,844	3,425
Lamar	3,860	1,739	3,366	2,778	16
Lauderdale	15,549	7,226	14,548	8,933	352
Lawrence	6,810	1,415	6,112	2,456	64
Lee	8,427	9,884	9,606	10,982	643
Limestone	8,803	2,997	9,120	5,574	192
Lowndes	3,732	1,621	3,577	1,524	50
Macon	5,915	1,387	7,028	1,259	35
Madison	35,497	20,959	30,451	30,405	2,132
Marengo	4,731	3,841	4,879	3,858	34
Marion	6,244	3,036	5,450	5,182	58
Marshall	13,696	6,006	10,854	8,161	283
Mobile	50,264	53,835	44,483	63,220	1,161
Monroe	3,669	3,476	4,262	4,615	38
Montgomery	24,641	29,360	27,955	35,745	977
Morgan	16,547	9,058	14,629	13,371	541
Perry	4,486	2,164	4,208	2,242	21
Pickens	3,776	2,969	4,413	3,440	56
Pike	5,387	4,363	4,312	5,289	85
Randolph	3,539	2,286	3,378	3,279	58
Russell	8,077	4,150	8,122	4,483	137
St. Clair	5,653	4,877	5,233	7,964	121
Shelby	7,197	9,035	7,308	14,676	224
Sumter	3,457	2,191	5,015	2,104	45
Talladega	10,577	6,425	9,835	9,273	205
Tallapoosa	7,614	5,237	6,802	5,511	0
Tuscaloosa	20,275	16,021	19,603	19,750	789
Walker	16,232	7,389	13,198	8,703	80
Washington	3,471	2,171	3,420	3,045	39
Wilcox	3,723	1,824	4,886	2,280	11
Winston	4,134	3,710	3,368	4,981	39
Totals	**659,170**	**504,070**	**627,808**	**641,609**	**15,855**

Alabama Vote Since 1932

1932 (Pres.), Roosevelt, Dem., 207,910; Hoover, Rep., 34,675; Foster, Com., 406; Thomas, Soc. 2,030; Upshaw, Proh., 13.

1936 (Pres.), Roosevelt, Dem., 238,195; Landon, Rep., 35,358; Colvin, Proh., 719; Browder, Com., 679; Lemke, Union, 549; Thomas, Soc., 242.

1940 (Pres.), Roosevelt, Dem., 250,726; Willkie, Rep., 42,174; Babson, Proh., 698; Browder, Com., 509; Thomas, Soc., 100.

1944 (Pres.), Roosevelt, Dem., 198,918; Dewey, Rep., 44,540; Watson, Proh., 1,095; Thomas, Soc., 190.

1948 (Pres.), Thurmond, States' Rights, 171,443; Dewey, Rep., 40,930; Wallace, Prog., 1,522; Watson, Proh., 1,085.

1952 (Pres.), Eisenhower, Rep., 149,231; Stevenson, Dem., 275,075; Hamblen, Proh., 1,814.

1956 (Pres.), Stevenson, Dem., 290,844; Eisenhower, Rep. 195,694; Independent electors, 20,323.

1960 (Pres.), Kennedy, Dem., 324,050; Nixon, Rep., 237,981; Faubus, States' Rights, 4,367; Decker, Proh., 2,106; King, Afro-Americans, 1,485; scattering, 236.

1964 (Pres.), Dem. 209,848 (electors unpledged); Goldwater, Rep., 479,085; scattering, 105.

1968 (Pres.), Nixon, Rep., 146,923; Humphrey, Dem., 196,579; Wallace, 3d party, 691,425; Munn, Proh., 4,022.

1972 (Pres.), Nixon, Rep., 728,701; McGovern, Dem., 219,108 plus 37,815 Natl. Demo. Party of Alabama; Schmitz, Conservative, 11,918; Munn., Proh., 8,551.

1976 (Pres.), Carter, Dem., 659,170; Ford, Rep., 504,070; Maddox, Am. Ind., 9,198; Bubar, Proh., 6,669; Hall, Com., 1,954; MacBride, Libertarian, 1,481.

Alaska

Election District	1976 Carter (D)	1976 Ford (R)	1980 Carter (D)	1980 Reagan (R)	1980 Anderson (I)
No. 1	1,983	2,994	...	N/A	...
No. 2	1,022	1,423	...	N/A	...
No. 3	1,152	1,710	...	N/A	...
No. 4	3,214	5,252	...	N/A	...
No. 5	1,307	2,071	...	N/A	...
No. 6	1,486	2,882	...	N/A	...
No. 7	2,935	4,105	...	N/A	...
No. 8	3,368	5,412	...	N/A	...
No. 9	1,726	2,561	...	N/A	...
No. 10	2,839	6,837	...	N/A	...
No. 11	3,568	6,588	...	N/A	...
No. 12	2,700	6,381	...	N/A	...
No. 13	2,099	4,057	...	N/A	...
No. 14	856	1,380	...	N/A	...
No. 15	538	746	...	N/A	...
No. 16	876	1,063	...	N/A	...
No. 17	1,149	1,074	...	N/A	...
No. 18	804	942	...	N/A	...
No. 19	1,415	1,893	...	N/A	...
No. 20	6,706	10,306	...	N/A	...
No. 21	1,229	749	...	N/A	...
No. 22	1,086	1,129	...	N/A	...
Totals	**44,058**	**71,555**	...	...	...

Alaska Vote Since 1960

1960 (Pres.), Kennedy, Dem., 29,809; Nixon, Rep. 30,953.

1964 (Pres.), Johnson, Dem., 44,329; Goldwater, Rep., 22,930.

1968 (Pres.), Nixon, Rep., 37,600; Humphrey, Dem., 35,411; Wallace, 3d party, 10,024.

1972 (Pres.), Nixon, Rep., 55,349; McGovern, Dem., 32,967; Schmitz, American, 6,906.

1976 (Pres.), Carter, Dem., 44,058; Ford, Rep., 71,555; MacBride, Libertarian, 6,785.

Arizona

County	1976 Carter (D)	1976 Ford (R)	1980 Carter (D)	1980 Reagan (R)	1980 Anderson (I)
Apache	6,583	3,447	3,876	5,944	488
Cochise	9,281	9,921	7,028	13,351	1,656
Coconino	9,450	11,036	7,806	14,582	2,812
Gila	6,440	5,136	4,986	7,281	647
Graham	3,050	3,659	2,799	4,761	268
Greenlee	2,601	1,532	2,043	1,537	150
Maricopa	144,613	258,262	119,586	315,764	38,917
Mohave	6,504	7,601	4,900	13,809	998
Navajo	7,323	6,796	5,614	10,448	691
Pima	71,214	77,264	61,511	87,606	24,250
Pinal	10,595	9,354	9,267	12,195	1,346
Santa Cruz	2,265	2,312	2,079	2,662	479
Yavapai	7,685	12,998	6,664	19,821	1,754
Yuma	7,998	9,324	5,999	13,365	1,369
Totals	**295,602**	**418,642**	**243,498**	**523,124**	**75,805**

Arizona Vote Since 1932

1932 (Pres.), Roosevelt, Dem., 79,264; Hoover, Rep., 36,104; Thomas, Soc., 2,030; Foster, Com., 406.

1936 (Pres.), Roosevelt, Dem., 86,722; Landon, Rep., 33,433; Lemke, Union, 3,307; Colvin, Proh., 384; Thomas, Soc., 317.

1940 (Pres.), Roosevelt, Dem., 95,267; Willkie, Rep., 54,030; Babson, Proh., 742.

1944 (Pres.), Roosevelt, Dem., 80,826; Dewey, Rep., 56,287; Watson, Proh., 421.

1948 (Pres.), Truman, Dem., 95,251; Dewey, Rep., 77,597; Wallace, Prog., 3,310; Watson, Proh., 786; Teichert, Soc. Labor, 121.

1952 (Pres.), Eisenhower, Rep., 152,042; Stevenson, Dem., 108,528.

1956 (Pres.), Eisenhower, Rep., 176,990; Stevenson, Dem., 112,880; Andrews, Ind. 303.

1960 (Pres.), Kennedy, Dem., 176,781; Nixon, Rep., 221,241; Hass, Soc. Labor, 469.

1964 (Pres.), Johnson, Dem., 237,753; Goldwater, Rep., 242,535; Hass, Soc. Labor, 482.

1968 (Pres.), Nixon, Rep., 266,721; Humphrey, Dem., 170,514; Wallace, 3d party, 46,573; McCarthy, New Party, 2,751; Halstead, Soc. Worker, 85; Cleaver, Peace and Freedom, 217; Blomen, Soc. Labor, 75.

1972 (Pres.), Nixon, Rep., 402,812; McGovern, Dem., 198,540; Schmitz, Amer., 21,208; Soc. Workers, 30,945. (Due to ballot peculiarities in 3 counties (particularly Pima), thousands of voters cast ballots for the Socialist Workers Party *and* one of the major candidates. Court ordered both votes counted as official.

1976 (Pres.), Carter, Dem., 295,602; Ford, Rep., 418,642; McCarthy, Ind., 19,229; MacBride, Libertarian, 7,647; Camejo, Soc. Workers, 928; Anderson, Amer., 564; Maddox, Am. Ind., 85.

Arkansas

	1976		1980		
County	Carter (D)	Ford (R)	Carter (D)	Reagan (R)	Anderson (I)
Arkansas	5,640	2,480	4,303	3,408	181
Ashley	5,253	3,092	4,552	3,960	130
Baxter	5,766	5,885	4,789	9,684	483
Benton	11,289	12,670	9,190	18,724	1,050
Boone	5,388	3,959	4,576	6,778	429
Bradley	3,567	1,134	3,139	1,650	66
Calhoun	2,014	495	1,438	896	52
Carroll	3,791	2,804	2,977	4,273	298
Chicot	3,868	1,621	3,445	2,239	26
Clark	6,641	1,816	6,122	2,743	215
Clay	5,664	1,893	3,985	3,091	121
Cleburne	5,726	1,992	4,021	4,042	204
Cleveland	2,320	646	1,856	1,124	36
Columbia	4,708	4,287	4,445	5,259	107
Conway	6,443	2,177	4,698	4,145	232
Craighead	13,840	6,213	9,231	11,010	708
Crawford	5,946	4,764	3,948	8,542	245
Crittenden	8,249	5,202	7,022	6,248	185
Cross	4,198	1,909	3,471	2,895	89
Dallas	3,266	1,012	2,838	1,596	67
Desha	4,228	1,372	3,747	2,057	77
Drew	3,750	1,730	3,747	2,272	117
Faulkner	11,423	3,904	8,528	7,539	771
Franklin	3,703	1,973	2,716	3,448	197
Fulton	2,670	1,038	2,037	2,101	83
Garland	15,707	10,394	12,515	15,739	1,042
Grant	3,797	1,047	3,078	2,007	102
Greene	7,495	2,690	5,996	4,514	219
Hempstead	5,397	2,859	4,526	3,828	71
Hot Spring	7,809	2,187	6,897	3,561	244
Howard	3,207	1,575	2,564	2,386	63
Independence	7,116	2,878	5,683	5,076	276
Izard	3,328	1,394	2,750	2,260	160
Jackson	6,456	1,783	4,651	3,191	174
Jefferson	21,001	8,034	17,114	10,698	796
Johnson	5,044	2,173	3,709	3,619	187
Lafayette	2,342	1,467	1,947	1,756	47
Lawrence	5,167	1,708	3,547	3,245	117
Lee	3,463	1,574	3,103	1,711	47
Lincoln	3,045	699	2,517	1,243	56
Little River	3,142	1,431	2,631	2,272	41
Logan	5,313	2,909	4,098	4,511	164
Lonoke	7,761	2,522	5,605	5,619	246
Madison	2,926	2,502	2,434	3,180	126
Marion	2,979	2,045	2,046	3,059	158
Miller	6,821	4,737	5,982	6,770	16
Mississippi	10,292	6,009	9,074	7,297	222
Monroe	3,556	1,285	2,445	2,027	280
Montgomery	2,420	924	1,878	1,685	86
Nevada	3,101	1,163	2,637	1,701	53
Newton	**1,840**	**1,641**	**1,436**	**1,701**	**53**
Ouachita	8,946	2,753	7,152	4,329	248
Perry	2,310	832	1,606	1,459	73
Phillips	7,774	3,342	6,642	4,270	163
Pike	2,822	1,234	2,096	1,916	69
Poinsett	6,835	2,726	4,994	4,040	153
Polk	3,505	2,432	2,617	3,944	138
Pope	8,355	4,348	6,369	7,216	450
Prairie	2,836	813	1,909	1,821	63
Pulaski	63,541	37,690	55,227	52,149	4,662
Randolph	4,551	1,571	3,070	2,579	125
St. Francis	6,851	3,639	5,816	4,485	132
Saline	12,008	4,123	10,368	8,330	643
Scott	2,880	1,427	2,236	2,228	92
Searcy	2,067	1,767	1,556	2,459	101
Sebastian	15,698	17,665	10,074	23,403	1,023
Sevier	3,391	1,468	2,854	2,502	97
Sharp	3,532	2,151	2,774	3,420	160
Stone	2,718	1,014	1,968	1,793	133
Union	8,257	7,918	6,846	9,401	313
Van Buren	4,004	1,624	2,968	3,090	158
Washington	15,610	14,132	12,279	20,540	235
White	11,412	4,756	8,750	8,079	309
Woodruff	3,040	848	2,452	1,204	74
Yell	5,785	1,932	3,702	3,187	181
Totals	**498,604**	**267,903**	**397,919**	**402,945**	**21,057**

Arkansas Vote Since 1932

1932 (Pres.), Roosevelt, Dem., 189,602; Hoover, Rep. 28,467; Thomas, Soc., 1,269; Harvey, Ind., 1,049; Foster Com., 175.

1936 (Pres.), Roosevelt, Dem. 146,765; Landon, Rep. 32,039; Thomas, Soc., 446; Browder, Com., 164; Lemke Union, 4.

1940 (Pres.), Roosevelt, Dem., 158,622; Willkie, Rep 42,121; Babson, Proh., 793; Thomas, Soc., 305.

1944 (Pres.), Roosevelt, Dem., 148,965; Dewey, Rep 63,551; Thomas, Soc. 438.

1948 (Pres.), Truman, Dem., 149,659; Dewey, Rep., 50,959 Thurmond, States' Rights, 40,068; Thomas, Soc., 1,037 Wallace, Prog., 751; Watson, Proh., 1.

1952 (Pres.), Eisenhower, Rep., 177,155; Stevenson, Dem 226,300; Hamblen, Proh., 886; MacArthur, Christian Nationalist, 458; Hass, Soc. Labor, 1.

1956 (Pres.), Stevenson, Dem., 213,277; Eisenhower, Rep 186,287; Andrews, Ind., 7,008.

1960 (Pres.), Kennedy, Dem., 215,049; Nixon, Rep 184,508; Nat'l. States' Rights, 28,952.

1964 (Pres.), Johnson, Dem., 314,197; Goldwater, Rep. 243,264; Kasper, Nat'l. States Rights, 2,965.

1968 (Pres.), Nixon, Rep., 189,062; Humphrey, Dem 184,901; Wallace, 3d party, 235,627.

1972 (Pres.), Nixon, Rep., 445,751; McGovern, Dem 198,899; Schmitz, Amer. , 3,016.

1976 (Pres.), Carter, Dem., 498,604; Ford, Rep., 267,903 McCarthy, Ind., 639; Anderson, Amer., 389.

California

	1976		1980		
County	Carter (D)	Ford (R)	Carter (D)	Reagan (R)	Anderso (I)
Alameda	235,988	155,280	200,104	157,102	40,5[illegible]
Alpine	189	255	133	254	50
Amador	4,037	3,699	3,191	5,401	788
Butte	24,203	28,400	19,266	37,703	6,046
Calaveras	3,607	3,695	3,068	6,035	762
Colusa	2,340	2,733	1,591	2,889	316
Contra Costa	123,742	126,598	107,059	143,556	28,109
Del Norte	2,789	2,481	2,356	4,020	486
El Dorado	12,763	12,472	10,667	21,045	3,252
Fresno	74,958	72,533	64,350	81,244	10,581
Glenn	3,501	4,094	2,227	5,380	537
Humboldt	23,500	18,034	17,043	23,923	5,420
Imperial	10,244	10,618	8,160	12,467	1,221
Inyo	2,635	3,905	2,059	5,176	511
Kern	50,567	58,023	39,874	70,532	5,621
Kings	8,061	8,263	7,299	10,531	901
Lake	6,374	5,462	5,915	8,779	1,146
Lassen	3,801	3,007	2,941	4,462	542
Los Angeles	1,221,893	1,174,926	961,874	1,196,358	171,496
Madera	7,625	6,844	7,691	10,562	1,014
Marin	43,590	53,425	38,907	49,170	13,666
Mariposa	2,093	2,012	1,916	3,075	456
Mendocino	10,653	9,784	10,612	12,263	2,702
Merced	16,637	14,842	15,886	18,077	2,315
Modoc	1,733	1,917	1,046	2,579	293
Mono	1,025	1,600	865	2,132	302
Monterey	36,849	40,896	28,880	47,057	7,954

	1976 (D)	1976 (R)	1980 (D)	1980 (R)	1980 (I)
Napa	18,048	20,839	14,631	23,149	4,119
Nevada	7,926	8,170	7,605	15,207	2,235
Orange	232,246	408,632	173,932	520,549	54,364
Placer	21,026	18,154	17,147	27,004	4,314
Plumas	3,429	2,884	2,911	4,172	783
Riverside	96,228	97,774	75,946	143,458	16,137
Sacramento	144,203	123,110	128,504	151,762	29,308
San Benito	3,122	3,398	2,766	4,055	535
San Bernardino	109,636	113,265	90,941	172,065	18,982
San Diego	263,654	353,302	191,181	424,490	65,975
San Francisco	133,733	103,561	131,103	78,962	28,880
San Joaquin	48,733	50,277	41,315	64,358	8,365
San Luis Obispo	24,926	27,785	20,294	38,197	8,315
San Mateo	102,896	117,338	86,755	115,888	27,893
Santa Barbara	55,018	60,922	40,174	68,660	14,636
Santa Clara	208,023	219,188	163,222	222,114	63,732
Santa Cruz	37,772	31,872	32,175	37,067	10,546
Shasta	19,200	17,273	15,364	27,547	3,220
Sierra	841	680	651	855	156
Siskiyou	7,060	7,070	5,664	9,331	1,269
Solano	33,682	26,136	30,785	40,647	6,680
Sonoma	50,353	50,555	45,008	59,944	13,901
Stanislaus	38,448	32,937	33,642	41,207	7,094
Sutter	6,966	8,745	4,779	10,964	998
Tehama	6,990	6,110	4,832	9,137	1,014
Trinity	2,172	1,989	1,730	3,046	506
Tulare	25,551	31,864	25,046	41,081	3,231
Tuolumne	6,492	6,104	5,432	8,781	1,388
Ventura	68,529	82,670	55,758	113,543	14,755
Yolo	23,533	18,376	21,438	19,446	6,650
Yuba	6,451	5,496	4,889	7,918	877
Totals	**3,742,284**	**3,882,244**	**3,040,600**	**4,447,266**	**727,871**

California Vote Since 1932

1932 (Pres.), Roosevelt, Dem., 1,324,157; Hoover, Rep., 847,902; Thomas, Soc., 63,299; Upshaw, Proh., 20,637; Harvey, Liberty, 9,827; Foster, Com., 1,023.

1936 (Pres.), Roosevelt, Dem., 1,766,836; Landon, Rep., 836,431; Colvin, Proh., 12,917; Thomas, Soc., 11,325; Browder, Com., 10,877.

1940 (Pres.), Roosevelt, Dem., 1,877,618; Willkie, Rep., 1,351,419; Thomas, Prog., 16,506; Browder, Com., 13,586; Babson, Proh., 9,400.

1944 (Pres.), Roosevelt, Dem., 1,988,564; Dewey, Rep., 1,512,965; Watson, Proh., 14,770; Thomas, Soc., 3,923; Teichert, Soc. Labor, 327.

1948 (Pres.), Truman, Dem., 1,913,134; Dewey, Rep., 1,895,269; Wallace, Prog., 190,381; Watson, Proh., 16,926; Thomas, Soc., 3,459; Thurmond, States' Rights, 1,228; Teichert, Soc. Labor, 195; Dobbs, Soc. Workers, 133.

1952 (Pres.), Eisenhower, Rep., 2,897,310; Stevenson, Dem., 2,197,548; Hallinan, Prog., 24,106; Hamblen, Proh., 15,653; MacArthur, (Tenny Ticket), 3,326; (Kellems Ticket) 178; Hass, Soc. Labor, 273; Hoopes, Soc., 206; scattered, 3,249.

1956 (Pres.), Eisenhower, Rep., 3,027,668; Stevenson, Dem., 2,420,136; Holtwick, Proh., 11,119; Andrews, Constitution, 6,087; Hass, Soc. Labor, 300; Hoopes, Soc., 123; Dobbs, Soc. Workers, 96; Smith, Christian Nat'l., 8.

1960 (Pres.), Kennedy, Dem., 3,224,099; Nixon, Rep., 3,259,722; Decker, Proh., 21,706; Hass, Soc. Labor, 1,051.

1964 (Pres.), Johnson, Dem., 4,171,877; Goldwater, Rep., 2,879,108; Hass, Soc. Labor, 489; DeBerry, Soc. Worker, 378; Munn, Proh., 305; Hensley, Universal, 19.

1968 (Pres.), Nixon, Rep., 3,467,664; Humphrey, Dem., 3,244,318; Wallace, 3d party, 487,270; Peace and Freedom party, 27,707; McCarthy, Alternative, 20,721; Gregory, write-in, 3,230; Mitchell, Com., 260; Munn, Proh., 59; Blomen, Soc. Labor, 341; Soeters, Defense, 17.

1972 (Pres.), Nixon, Rep., 4,602,096; McGovern, Dem., 3,475,847; Schmitz, Amer., 232,554; Spock, Peace and Freedom, 55,167; Hall, Com., 373; Hospers, Libertarian, 980; Munn, Proh., 53; Fisher, Soc. Labor, 197; Jenness, Soc. Workers, 574; Green, Universal, 21.

1976 (Pres.), Carter, Dem., 3,742,284; Ford, Rep., 3,882,244; MacBride, Libertarian, 56,388; Maddox, Am. Ind., 51,098; Wright, People's, 41,731; Camejo, Soc. Workers, 17,259; Hall, Com., 12,766; write-in, McCarthy, 58,412; other write-in, 4,935.

Colorado

County	1976 Carter (D)	1976 Ford (R)	1980 Carter (D)	1980 Reagan (R)	1980 Anderson (I)
Adams	40,551	35,392	31,357	42,916	8,342
Alamosa	2,052	2,599	1,821	2,606	289
Arapahoe	33,685	63,154	29,797	78,457	15,165
Archuleta	632	768	532	1,252	83
Baca	1,164	1,303	551	1,999	106
Bent	1,268	1,156	930	1,206	164
Boulder	33,284	42,830	28,398	40,657	13,708
Chaffee	2,064	2,925	1,581	3,327	432
Cheyenne	625	610	322	816	76
Clear Creek	1,069	1,477	837	1,783	402
Conejos	1,698	1,426	1,523	1,607	84
Costilla	1,033	392	1,036	489	38
Crowley	667	834	472	926	57
Custer	259	491	231	674	59
Delta	3,232	4,980	2,347	6,175	454
Denver	112,229	105,960	85,956	88,569	28,603
Dolores	374	343	157	615	32
Douglas	2,459	5,078	2,108	7,626	1,058
Eagle	1,502	2,963	1,607	3,064	906
Elbert	1,068	1,279	698	2,112	238
El Paso	32,911	50,929	27,463	66,193	7,886
Fremont	4,886	5,647	3,952	7,162	731
Garfield	2,852	4,699	2,589	5,416	978
Gilpin	563	451	441	694	175
Grand	910	1,703	820	2,133	413
Gunnison	1,250	2,568	1,296	2,751	704
Hinsdale	83	189	76	232	13
Huerfano	1,932	1,182	1,574	1,263	146
Jackson	279	455	283	673	80
Jefferson	52,782	87,080	41,521	96,998	19,529
Kiowa	529	598	331	754	61
Kit Carson	1,647	1,888	790	2,622	185
Lake	1,549	1,575	1,212	1,374	289
La Plata	3,843	6,228	3,034	7,289	1,537
Larimer	19,005	32,169	17,061	36,496	8,987
Las Animas	4,459	2,615	4,111	2,917	278
Lincoln	1,059	1,276	602	1,533	175
Logan	3,543	4,256	2,332	5,238	588
Mesa	8,807	17,924	7,549	22,686	2,004
Mineral	167	235	125	271	41
Moffat	1,451	2,099	1,079	3,344	328
Montezuma	1,993	3,002	1,467	4,120	275
Montrose	3,164	4,838	2,232	6,484	635
Morgan	3,798	4,603	2,466	5,209	693
Otero	4,118	4,597	3,294	4,801	572
Ouray	333	645	237	813	129
Park	741	1,034	674	1,623	293
Philips	1,173	1,142	640	1,488	193
Pitkin	2,194	2,955	1,760	2,153	1,128
Prowers	2,861	2,578	1,733	3,054	340
Pueblo	25,841	18,518	21,875	20,767	3,102
Rio Blanco	627	1,439	462	1,971	143
Rio Grande	1,475	2,627	1,370	2,844	185
Routt	2,130	2,822	1,995	3,615	950
Saguache	1,059	1,094	893	1,124	71
San Juan	167	221	146	268	94
San Miguel	674	622	651	774	297
Sedgwick	773	902	438	1,151	100
Summit	1,087	1,826	1,208	2,027	840
Teller	986	1,410	802	2,457	322
Washington	1,211	1,440	568	2,007	160
Weld	16,501	21,976	11,433	23,901	4,309
Yuma	2,025	2,350	1,043	3,220	319
Total	**460,353**	**58,367**	**367,966**	**650,786**	**130,579**

Colorado Vote Since 1932

1932 (Pres.), Roosevelt, Dem., 250,877; Hoover, Rep., 189,617; Thomas, Soc., 14,018; Upshaw, Proh., 1,928

1936 (Pres.), Roosevelt, Dem., 295,081; Landon, Rep., 181,267; Lemke, Union, 9,962; Thomas, Soc., 1,593; Browder, Com., 497; Aiken, Soc. Labor, 336.

1940 (Pres.), Roosevelt, Dem., 265,554; Willkie, Rep., 279,576; Thomas, Soc., 1,899; Babson, Proh., 1,597; Browder, Com., 378.

1944 (Pres.), Roosevelt, Dem., 234,331; Dewey, Rep., 268,731; Thomas, Soc., 1,977.

1948 (Pres.), Truman, Dem., 267,288; Dewey, Rep., 239,714; Wallace, Prog., 6,115; Thomas, Soc., 1,678; Dobbs, Soc. Workers, 228; Teichert, Soc. Labor, 214.

1952 (Pres.), Eisenhower, Rep., 379,782; Stevenson, Dem., 245,504; MacArthur, Constitution, 2,181; Hallinan, Prog., 1,919; Hoopes, Soc., 365; Hass, Soc. Labor, 352.

1956 (Pres.), Eisenhower, Rep., 394,479; Stevenson, Dem., 263,997; Hass, Soc. Lab., 3,308; Andrews, Ind., 759; Hoopes, Soc., 531.

1960 (Pres.), Kennedy, Dem., 330,629; Nixon, Rep., 402,242; Hass, Soc. Labor, 2,803; Dobbs, Soc. Workers, 572.

1964 (Pres.), Johnson, Dem., 476,024; Goldwater, Rep., 296,767; Hass, Soc. Labor, 302; DeBerry, Soc. Worker, 2,537; Munn, Proh., 1,356.

1968 (Pres.), Nixon, Rep., 409,345; Humphrey, Dem., 335,174; Wallace, 3d party, 60,813; Blomen, Soc. Labor, 3,016; Gregory, New-party, 1,393; Munn, Proh., 275; Halstead, Soc. Worker, 235.

1972 (Pres.), Nixon, Rep., 597,189; McGovern, Dem., 329,980; Fisher, Soc. Labor, 4,361; Hospers, Libertarian, 1,111; Hall, Com., 432; Jenness, Soc. Workers, 555; Munn, Proh., 467; Schmitz, Amer., 17,269; Spock, Peoples, 2,403.

1976 (Pres.), Carter, Dem., 460,353; Ford, Rep., 584,367; McCarthy, Ind., 26,107; MacBride, Libertarian, 5,330; Bubar, Proh., 2,882.

Connecticut

County	1976 Carter (D)	1976 Ford (R)	1980 Carter (D)	1980 Reagan (R)	1980 Anderson (I)
Fairfield	148,353	209,458	. . .	N/A	. . .
Hartford	191,257	175,064	. . .	N/A	. . .
Litchfield	32,419	40,705	. . .	N/A	. . .
Middlesex	29,097	31,115	. . .	N/A	. . .
New Haven	157,402	174,342	. . .	N/A	. . .
New London	45,908	47,231	. . .	N/A	. . .
Tolland	23,079	23,703	. . .	N/A	. . .
Windham	20,380	17,643	. . .	N/A	. . .
Totals	**647,895**	**719,261**	. . .	. . .	. . .

Connecticut Vote Since 1932

1932 (Pres.), Roosevelt, Dem., 281,632; Hoover, Rep., 288,420; Thomas, Soc., 22,767.

1936 (Pres.), Roosevelt, Dem., 382,129; Landon, Rep., 278,685; Lemke, Union, 21,805; Thomas, Soc., 5,683; Browder, Com., 1,193.

1940 (Pres.), Roosevelt, Dem., 417,621; Willkie, Rep., 361,021; Browder, Com., 1,091; Aiken, Soc. Labor, 971; Willkie, Union, 798.

1944 (Pres.), Roosevelt, Dem., 435,146; Dewey, Rep., 390,527; Thomas, Soc., 5,097; Teichert, Soc. Labor, 1,220.

1948 (Pres.), Truman, Dem., 423,297; Dewey, Rep., 437,754; Wallace, Prog., 13,713; Thomas, Soc., 6,964; Teichert, Soc. Labor, 1,184; Dobbs, Soc. Workers, 606.

1952 (Pres.), Eisenhower, Rep., 611,012; Stevenson, Dem., 481,649; Hoopes, Soc., 2,244; Hallinan, Peoples, 1,466; Hass, Soc. Labor, 535; write-in, 5.

1956 (Pres.), Eisenhower, Rep., 711,837; Stevenson, Dem., 405,079; scattered, 205.

1960 (Pres.), Kennedy, Dem., 657,055; Nixon, Rep., 565,813.

1964 (Pres.), Johnson, Dem., 826,269; Goldwater, Rep., 390,996; scattered, 1,313.

1968 (Pres.), Nixon, Rep., 556,721; Humphrey, Dem., 621,561; Wallace, 3d party, 76,650; scattered, 1,300.

1972 (Pres.), Nixon, Rep., 810,763; McGovern, Dem., 555,498; Schmitz, Amer., 17,239; scattered, 777.

1976 (Pres.), Carter, Dem., 647,895; Ford, Rep., 719,261; Maddox, George Wallace Party, 7,101; LaRouche, U.S. Labor, 1,789.

Delaware

County	1976 Carter (D)	1976 Ford (R)	1980 Carter (D)	1980 Reagan (R)	1980 Anderson (I)
Kent	16,523	12,604	12,884	14,662	1,835
New Castle	87,521	80,074	77,793	77,497	12,880
Sussex	18,552	17,153	15,973	19,472	1,629
Totals	**122,596**	**109,831**	**106,650**	**111,631**	**16,344**

Delaware Vote Since 1932

1932 (Pres.), Hoover, Rep., 57,074; Roosevelt, Dem., 54,319; Thomas, Soc., 1,376; Foster, Com., 133.

1936 (Pres.), Roosevelt, Dem., 69,702; Landon, Rep. 54,014; Lemke, Union, 442; Thomas, Soc., 179; Browder, Com., 52.

1940 (Pres.), Roosevelt, Dem., 74,559; Willkie, Rep., 61,440; Babson, Proh., 220; Thomas, Soc., 115.

1944 (Pres.), Roosevelt, Dem., 68,166; Dewey, Rep., 56,747; Watson, Proh., 294; Thomas, Soc., 154.

1948 (Pres.), Truman, Dem., 67,813; Dewey, Rep., 69,688; Wallace, Prog., 1,050; Watson, Proh., 343; Thomas, Soc., 250; Teichert, Soc. Labor, 29.

1952 (Pres.), Eisenhower, Rep., 90,059; Stevenson, Dem., 83,315; Hass, Soc. Labor, 242; Hamblen, Proh., 234; Hallinan, Prog., 155; Hoopes, Soc., 20.

1956 (Pres.), Eisenhower, Rep., 98,057; Stevenson, Dem., 79,421; Oltwick, Proh., 400; Hass, Soc. Labor, 110.

1960 (Pres.), Kennedy, Dem., 99,590; Nixon, Rep., 96,373; Faubus, States' Rights, 354; Decker, Proh., 284; Hass, Soc. Labor, 82.

1964 (Pres.), Johnson, Dem., 122,704; Goldwater, Rep., 78,078; Hass, Soc. Labor, 113; Munn, Proh., 425.

1968 (Pres.), Nixon, Rep., 96,714; Humphrey, Dem., 89,194; Wallace, 3d party, 28,459.

1972 (Pres.), Nixon, Rep., 140,357; McGovern, Dem., 92,283; Schmitz, Amer., 2,638; Munn, Proh., 238.

1976 (Pres.), Carter, Dem., 122,596; Ford, Rep., 109,831; McCarthy, non-partisan, 2,437; Anderson, Amer., 645; LaRouche, U.S. Labor, 136; Bubar, Proh., 103; Levin, Soc. Labor, 86.

District of Columbia

County	1976 Carter (D)	1976 Ford (R)	1980 Carter (D)	1980 Reagan (R)	1980 Anderson (I)
Totals	**137,818**	**27,873**	**124,376**	**21,765**	**14,971**

District of Columbia Vote Since 1964

1964 (Pres.), Johnson, Dem., 169,796; Goldwater, Rep., 28,801.

1968 (Pres.), Nixon, Rep., 31,012; Humphrey, Dem., 139,566.

1972 (Pres.), Nixon, Rep., 35,226; McGovern, Dem., 127,627; Reed, Soc. Workers, 316; Hall, Com., 252.

1976 (Pres.), Carter, Dem., 137,818; Ford, Rep., 27,873; Camejo, Soc. Workers, 545; MacBride, Libertarian, 274; Hall, Com., 219; LaRouche, U.S. Labor, 157.

Florida

County	1976 Carter (D)	1976 Ford (R)	1980 Carter (D)	1980 Reagan (R)	1980 Anderson (I)
Alachua	27,895	15,546	25,461	18,238	3,878
Baker	2,985	1,058	2,606	2,271	56
Bay	14,858	14,208	11,376	18,671	573
Bradford	3,868	1,680	3,340	2,771	89
Brevard	46,421	44,470	36,460	63,438	5,239
Broward	176,491	161,411	140,655	217,247	29,847
Calhoun	2,487	1,153	2,295	1,504	52
Charlotte	10,300	12,703	9,148	18,850	1,088
Citrus	9,438	7,973	8,566	13,184	709
Clay	8,410	8,468	7,110	13,866	557
Collier	8,764	14,643	7,735	23,878	1,675
Columbia	6,683	3,947	5,434	5,347	232
Dade	303,047	211,148	202,063	251,081	42,014
De Soto	2,715	2,000	2,534	3,108	144
Dixie	2,169	558	2,007	1,098	45
Duval	105,912	74,997	86,649	91,023	4,582
Escambia	38,279	41,471	31,556	45,867	2,143
Flagler	2,086	1,262	2,328	2,668	133
Franklin	1,859	1,054	1,667	1,352	53
Gadsden	6,798	3,531	7,777	3,438	184
Gilchrist	1,807	528	1,502	1,010	54
Glades	1,311	624	1,203	1,096	61
Gulf	2,641	1,584	2,506	1,958	34
Hamilton	2,053	794	1,776	1,176	26
Hardee	2,670	2,189	2,432	2,423	77
Hendry	2,337	1,843	2,540	2,696	130
Hernando	7,717	5,793	8,835	12,100	852
Highlands	7,218	8,317	6,418	11,282	483
Hillsborough	94,589	78,504	85,097	99,793	8,316
Holmes	3,256	1,850	2,670	3,064	66
Indian River	3,316	9,818	7,357	14,191	1,070
Jackson	7,687	4,795	7,194	5,898	144
Jefferson	2,310	1,361	2,253	1,521	88
Lafayette	1,126	523	1,050	802	22
Lake	14,369	19,976	12,456	25,017	1,127
Lee	30,567	38,038	28,007	60,717	4,191
Leon	28,729	23,739	26,898	22,994	2,904

	1976		1980		
	(D)	(R)	(D)	(R)	(I)
Levy	4,025	1,965	3,988	2,969	155
Liberty	1,137	620	1,111	895	24
Madison	3,218	1,761	3,129	2,275	59
Manatee	24,342	29,300	21,660	40,506	2,921
Marion	16,963	16,163	15,369	23,671	1,177
Martin	8,785	11,682	7,507	18,658	1,201
Monroe	11,079	8,232	7,198	10,161	1,729
Nassau	5,896	3,136	4,806	5,085	147
Okaloosa	14,210	18,598	9,755	24,049	867
Okeechobee	3,184	1,598	2,997	2,568	145
Orange	58,442	70,451	6,542	81,697	4,891
Osceola	6,893	7,062	6,276	10,181	529
Palm Beach	96,705	98,236	91,929	143,487	15,178
Pasco	33,710	28,306	32,809	47,757	3,364
Pinellas	141,879	150,003	138,307	185,482	17,789
Polk	47,286	44,238	41,827	56,269	2,331
Putnam	9,597	5,040	8,456	7,664	374
St. Johns	7,412	6,660	6,535	10,297	483
St. Lucie	12,386	11,502	10,341	18,107	1,109
Santa Rosa	8,020	9,122	6,964	13,802	606
Sarasota	26,293	44,157	23,911	62,486	4,267
Seminole	19,609	26,655	17,431	39,970	2,451
Sumter	4,721	2,212	4,211	3,464	13[illegible]
Suwannee	4,718	2,405	4,345	3,894	112
Taylor	3,370	1,983	2,955	2,772	78
Union	1,480	544	1,117	1,033	42
Volusia	49,161	37,523	41,794	49,090	3,030
Wakulla	2,353	1,580	1,977	1,887	105
Walton	5,196	2,927	4,016	4,209	172
Washington	3,566	2,313	2,896	2,966	78
Totals	**1,636,000**	**1,469,531**	**1,369,120**	**1,943,989**	**178,483**

Florida Vote Since 1932

1932 (Pres.), Roosevelt, Dem., 206,307; Hoover, Rep., 69,170; Thomas, Soc., 775.

1936 (Pres.), Roosevelt, Dem., 249,117; Landon, Rep., 78,248.

1940 (Pres.), Roosevelt, Dem., 359,334; Willkie, Rep., 126,158.

1944 (Pres.), Roosevelt, Dem., 339,377; Dewey, Rep., 143,215.

1948 (Pres.), Truman, Dem., 281,988; Dewey, Rep., 194,280; Thurmond, States' Rights, 89,755; Wallace, Prog., 11,620.

1952 (Pres.), Eisenhower, Rep., 544,036; Stevenson, Dem., 444,950; scattered, 351.

1956 (Pres.), Eisenhower, Rep., 643,849; Stevenson, Dem., 480,371.

1960 (Pres.), Kennedy, Dem., 748,700; Nixon, Rep., 795,476.

1964 (Pres.), Johnson, Dem., 948,540; Goldwater, Rep., 905,941.

1968 (Pres.), Nixon, Rep., 886,804; Humphrey, Dem., 676,794; Wallace, 3d party, 624,207.

1972 (Pres.), Nixon, Rep., 1,857,759; McGovern, Dem., 718,117; scattered, 7,407.

1976 (Pres.), Carter, Dem., 1,636,000; Ford, Rep., 1,469,531; McCarthy, Ind., 23,643; Anderson, Amer., 21,325.

Georgia

	1976		1980		
County	Carter (D)	Ford (R)	Carter (D)	Reagan (R)	Anderson (I)
Appling	3,585	961	2,985	1,961	41
Atkinson	1,560	347	1,449	747	16
Bacon	2,395	594	1,622	1,427	32
Baker	1,162	305	1,035	1,427	32
Baldwin	4,674	3,612	4,368	3,639	230
Banks	2,387	330	2,091	746	18
Barrow	4,756	1,364	3,876	2,284	99
Bartow	8,166	1,876	7,490	3,145	134
Ben Hill	2,449	814	2,541	1,469	41
Berrien	3,394	555	2,869	1,487	24
Bibb	31,902	12,819	31,770	15,175	847
Bleckley	2,605	972	2,014	1,261	47
Brantley	2,294	358	2,066	882	17
Brooks	2,653	1,102	2,227	1,546	39
Bryan	2,045	761	1,974	1,212	40
Bulloch	5,199	3,156	5,130	3,973	174
Burke	3,014	1,565	3,122	1,799	47
Butts	2,898	819	2,572	1,207	37
Calhoun	1,394	436	1,414	652	16
Camden	2,962	995	2,924	1,439	62
Candler	1,388	646	1,359	1,030	24
Carroll	10,050	3,640	8,202	5,815	294
Catoosa	6,020	3,799	4,918	5,962	121
Charlton	1,750	452	1,469	779	26
Chatham	32,075	24,160	28,635	26,499	1,244
Chattahoochee	506	178	476	256	16
Chattooga	4,686	1,087	4,279	1,946	61
Cherokee	6,539	2,609	6,020	5,250	230
Clarke	11,342	6,610	10,519	8,094	1,060
Clay	947	295	909	316	9
Clayton	21,432	12,905	17,540	19,160	923
Clinch	1,414	383	1,325	513	18
Cobb	45,002	34,324	39,157	51,977	3,229
Coffee	4,601	1,417	4,038	2,499	58
Colquitt	6,928	2,181	5,353	3,593	80
Columbia	4,674	3,423	5,335	6,293	248
Cook	2,882	670	2,461	1,188	25
Coweta	6,195	3,044	5,697	4,480	161
Crawford	1,842	378	1,673	642	35
Crisp	3,747	1,328	3,403	1,843	54
Dade	2,263	1,388	1,735	2,114	62
Dawson	1,884	370	1,072	729	23
Decatur	3,736	2,500	3,242	2,919	54
DeKalb	86,872	67,160	75,379	66,190	6,332
Dodge	5,267	848	4,635	1,719	56
Dooly	2,441	655	2,364	1,083	32
Dougherty	11,461	9,337	13,430	12,726	320
Douglas	7,805	3,959	6,807	6,945	304
Early	2,405	1,157	2,110	1,538	23
Echols	585	111	515	259	8
Effingham	2,906	1,654	2,777	2,528	30
Elbert	4,730	961	4,014	1,967	50
Emanuel	4,603	1,493	3,971	2,199	45
Evans	1,631	746	1,456	1,090	20
Fannin	3,402	2,646	2,291	2,909	58
Fayette	3,718	2,837	3,630	5,971	249
Floyd	15,151	7,713	13,232	8,765	359
Forsyth	4,693	1,443	4,325	3,157	160
Franklin	4,192	687	3,528	1,387	20
Fulton	129,849	61,552	118,729	64,933	6,718
Gilmer	2,499	1,261	2,246	2,170	72
Glascock	704	371	614	460	7
Glynn	9,459	5,403	7,540	7,214	296
Gordon	6,052	1,698	5,199	3,107	141
Grady	3,758	1,209	3,023	2,018	56
Greene	2,534	652	2,349	896	26
Gwinnett	20,838	13,912	23,281	27,981	1,560
Habersham	5,120	1,315	4,394	2,224	102
Hall	12,804	5,093	12,189	7,760	423
Hancock	2,117	651	2,205	573	23
Haralson	4,550	1,301	3,606	2,229	62
Harris	2,861	1,544	2,807	2,001	100
Hart	4,605	860	4,538	1,575	59
Heard	1,593	433	1,348	875	34
Henry	5,717	2,622	5,635	5,326	163
Houston	13,164	5,404	10,915	9,005	536
Irwin	2,012	561	1,555	1,056	11
Jackson	5,931	1,239	4,591	2,209	99
Jasper	1,852	689	1,546	879	38
Jeff Davis	2,405	622	2,059	1,191	39
Jefferson	3,115	1,309	3,305	1,605	44
Jenkins	1,820	563	1,632	824	24
Johnson	2,210	698	1,854	1,123	29
Jones	3,471	1,317	3,239	1,828	112
Lamar	2,785	847	2,453	1,298	42
Lanier	1,269	207	1,116	470	9
Laurens	8,617	3,281	7,860	4,392	147
Lee	1,727	1,110	1,670	1,942	26
Liberty	3,328	979	3,099	1,507	49
Lincoln	1,583	576	1,617	806	10
Long	1,243	222	1,202	514	23
Lowndes	8,830	4,512	5,989	6,622	214
Lumpkin	2,301	547	1,951	1,024	83
Macon	3,013	638	3,025	894	39
Madison	3,367	1,115	2,980	2,330	59
Marion	1,314	291	1,174	567	16
McDuffie	3,024	1,694	2,667	1,928	59
McIntosh	1,978	535	1,973	805	31
Meriwether	4,830	1,450	3,876	1,838	52
Miller	1,536	476	1,127	900	19
Mitchell	4,495	1,572	3,566	2,231	40
Monroe	2,962	1,078	2,542	1,242	41
Montgomery	1,610	626	1,663	948	23
Morgan	2,274	904	2,276	1,323	57
Murray	3,511	889	3,094	1,538	42
Muscogee	24,092	13,496	23,272	15,263	811
Newton	6,294	2,137	5,611	3,205	150
Oconee	2,228	1,184	2,141	2,065	106
Oglethorpe	1,854	811	1,631	1,187	42
Paulding	5,420	1,432	4,686	2,845	97
Peach	3,989	1,163	3,415	1,642	68
Pickens	2,571	973	2,358	1,612	73
Pierce	2,628	544	1,918	1,027	21
Pike	1,903	776	1,775	1,271	45
Polk	6,115	1,944	5,431	2,956	111
Pulaski	2,318	485	1,997	1,153	54
Putnam	2,040	835	1,951	1,166	35
Quitman	677	313	589	240	2
Rabun	2,398	591	2,327	1,070	67
Randolph	2,186	747	1,861	879	1
Richmond	24,042	17,893	24,104	19,619	887
Rockdale	4,640	2,974	4,395	5,296	147
Schley	783	268	613	453	9
Screven	2,168	1,176	2,117	1,490	36
Seminole	2,074	681	1,7794	1,117	16

	1976 (D)	1976 (R)	1980 (D)	1980 (R)	1980 (I)
Spalding	7,593	3,739	7,176	4,809	248
Stephens	5,560	1,340	4,523	2,040	71
Stewart	1,632	433	1,440	611	23
Sumter	5,328	2,053	4,955	2,957	111
Talbot	1,634	459	1,635	572	20
Taliaferro	748	236	670	270	8
Tattnall	3,556	1,326	2,864	2,082	37
Taylor	1,962	504	1,845	815	19
Telfair	3,534	637	2,700	1,173	41
Terrell	2,348	1,168	1,895	1,262	20
Thomas	6,147	3,263	5,695	4,294	117
Tift	5,185	2,162	4,572	3,280	99
Toombs	4,047	2,126	3,255	3,835	68
Towns	1,786	1,175	1,177	1,241	45
Treutlen	1,567	465	1,307	668	21
Troup	7,699	4,422	7,716	5,398	191
Turner	2,265	416	1,990	904	16
Twiggs	2,515	513	2,213	747	8
Union	2,795	1,154	1,701	1,547	43
Upson	4,219	2,897	4,713	2,788	77
Walker	8,007	4,807	6,808	7,088	171
Walton	5,402	1,687	4,525	2,618	112
Ware	7,719	2,661	6,307	3,715	77
Warren	1,335	720	1,509	831	20
Washington	3,865	1,657	3,452	1,822	60
Wayne	4,489	1,499	3,843	2,213	52
Webster	622	165	608	312	8
Wheeler	1,378	344	797	364	10
White	2,125	625	2,017	1,175	58
Whitfield	10,475	4,498	9,691	6,404	229
Wilcox	2,153	346	1,780	827	13
Wilkes	2,461	1,067	2,350	1,212	31
Wilkinson	2,652	837	2,365	1,116	31
Worth	2,790	1,156	2,567	2,073	31
Totals	**979,409**	**483,743**	**882,785**	**644,691**	**34,912**

Georgia Vote Since 1932

1932 (Pres.), Roosevelt, Dem., 234,118; Hoover, Rep., 19,863; Upshaw, Proh., 1,125; Thomas, Soc., 461; Foster, Com., 23.

1936 (Pres.), Roosevelt, Dem., 255,364; Landon, Rep., 36,942; Colvin, Proh., 660; Lemke, Union, 141; Thomas, Soc., 68.

1940 (Pres.), Roosevelt, Dem., 265,194; Willkie, Rep., 23,934; Ind. Dem., 22,428; total, 46,362; Babson, Proh., 983.

1944 (Pres.), Roosevelt, Dem., 268,187; Dewey, Rep., 56,506; Watson, Proh., 36.

1948 (Pres.), Truman, Dem., 254,646; Dewey, Rep., 76,691; Thurmond, States' Rights, 85,055; Wallace, Prog., 1,636; Watson, Proh., 732.

1952 (Pres.), Eisenhower, Rep., 198,979; Stevenson, Dem., 456,823; Liberty Party, 1.

1956 (Pres.), Stevenson, Dem., 444,388; Eisenhower, Rep., 222,778; Andrews, Ind., write-in, 1,754.

1960 (Pres.), Kennedy, Dem., 458,638; Nixon, Rep., 274,472; write-in, 239.

1964 (Pres.), Johnson, Dem., 522,557; Goldwater, Rep., 616,600.

1968 (Pres.), Nixon, Rep., 380,111; Humphrey, Dem., 334,440; Wallace, 3d party, 535,550; write-in, 162.

1972 (Pres.), Nixon, Rep., 881,496; McGovern, Dem., 289,529; Schmitz, Amer., 2,288; scattered.

1976 (Pres.), Carter, Dem., 979,409; Ford, Rep., 483,743; write-in, 4,306.

Hawaii

County	1976 Carter (D)	1976 Ford (R)	1980 Carter (D)	1980 Reagan (R)	1980 Anderson (I)
Hawaii	091	15,960	15,366	17,630	14,247
Honolulu	111,389	108,041	96,494	99,623	25,341
Kauai	8,105	6,278	9,081	5,883	1,352
Maui	11,921	10,318	12,674	10,359	2,237
Totals	**147,375**	**140,003**	...	...	...

Hawaii Vote Since 1960

1960 (Pres.), Kennedy, Dem., 92,410; Nixon, Rep., 92,295.

1964 (Pres.), Johnson, Dem., 163,249; Goldwater, Rep., 44,022.

1968 (Pres.), Nixon, Rep., 91,425; Humphrey, Dem., 141,324; Wallace, 3d party, 3,469.

1972 (Pres.), Nixon, Rep., 168,865; McGovern, Dem., 101,409.

1976 (Pres.), Carter, Dem., 147,375; Ford, Rep., 140,003; MacBride, Libertarian, 3,923.

Idaho

County	1976 Carter (D)	1976 Ford (R)	1980 Carter (D)	1980 Reagan (R)	1980 Anderso[n] (I)
Ada	21,125	41,135	21,415	55,442	8,031
Adams	639	809	590	1,189	88
Bannock	10,261	13,172	8,639	18,476	1,896
Bear Lake	960	2,094	508	2,941	63
Benewah	1,549	1,458	1,362	2,111	286
Bingham	4,347	7,327	2,933	11,781	489
Blaine	1,604	2,176	1,839	2,716	776
Boise	433	684	518	1,134	86
Bonner	4,065	4,549	4,060	6,728	880
Bonneville	7,230	15,793	5,052	24,710	1,353
Boundary	1,217	1,458	945	2,000	225
Butte	663	751	424	1,275	35
Camas	160	288	145	360	16
Canyon	9,460	17,263	9,172	24,375	1,798
Caribou	1,110	2,253	481	3,234	106
Cassias	1,881	4,575	1,369	6,511	212
Clark	169	334	87	379	11
Clearwater	1,752	1,469	1,699	2,178	291
Custer	516	850	398	1,398	64
Elmore	2,164	2,808	1,760	3,694	310
Franklin	1,157	2,720	511	3,669	61
Freemont	1,445	2,581	926	4,158	99
Gem	1,978	2,401	1,613	3,766	218
Gooding	1,923	2,909	1,443	3,822	387
Idaho	2,323	3,185	2,078	4,425	409
Jefferson	1,745	3,599	833	5,860	135
Jerome	1,800	3,188	1,368	4,962	179
Kootenai	7,225	10,493	7,521	17,022	1,808
Latah	5,314	6,846	5,038	6,966	2,464
Lemhi	1,159	1,685	794	2,646	167
Lewis	898	824	784	1,088	154
Lincoln	615	909	462	1,294	83
Madison	1,320	4,190	728	6,555	64
Minidoka	2,441	3,600	1,689	6,035	260
Nez Perce	6,324	6,151	6,565	7,495	1,344
Oneida	637	1,065	434	1,461	50
Owyhee	1,054	1,519	732	2,257	91
Payette	2,195	3,115	1,828	4,508	253
Power	1,286	1,374	732	2,235	119
Shoshone	3,216	3,570	2,393	3,323	352
Teton	514	904	360	1,227	67
Twin Falls	6,085	12,659	4,835	17,427	949
Valley	897	1,374	926	2,041	241
Washington	1,693	2,044	1,421	2,915	172
Totals	**126,549**	**204,151**	**109,410**	**289,789**	**27,142**

Idaho Vote Since 1932

1932 (Pres.), Roosevelt, Dem., 109,479; Hoover, Rep. 71,312; Harvey, Lib., 4,712; Thomas, Soc., 526; Foster Com., 491.

1936 (Pres.), Roosevelt, Dem., 125,683; Landon, Rep. 66,256; Lemke, Union, 7,684.

1940 (Pres.), Roosevelt, Dem., 127,842; Willkie, Rep. 106,553; Thomas, Soc., 497; Browder, Com., 276.

1944 (Pres.), Roosevelt, Dem., 107,399; Dewey, Rep. 100,137; Watson, Proh., 503; Thomas, Soc., 282.

1948 (Pres.), Truman, Dem., 107,370; Dewey, Rep. 101,514; Wallace, Prog., 4,972; Watson, Proh., 628 Thomas, Soc., 332.

1952 (Pres.), Eisenhower, Rep., 180,707; Stevenson Dem. 95,081; Hallinan, Prog., 443; write-in, 23.

1956 (Pres.), Eisenhower, Rep., 166,979; Stevenson, Dem 105,868; Andrews, Ind., 126; write-in, 16.

1960 (Pres.), Kennedy, Dem., 138,853; Nixon, Rep 161,597.

1964 (Pres.), Johnson, Dem., 148,920; Goldwater, Rep. 143,557.

1968 (Pres.), Nixon, Rep., 165,369; Humphrey, Dem 89,273; Wallace, 3d party, 36,541.

1972 (Pres.), Nixon, Rep., 199,384; McGovern, Dem. 80,826; Schmitz, Amer., 28,869; Spock, Peoples, 903.

1976 (Pres.), Carter, Dem., 126,549; Ford, Rep., 204,151 Maddox, Amer., 5,935; MacBride, Libertarian, 3,558 LaRouche, U.S. Labor, 739.

Illinois

County	1976 Carter (D)	1976 Ford (R)	1980 Carter (D)	1980 Reagan (R)	1980 Anderson (I)
Adams	11,926	18,189	10,506	19,842	1,202
Alexander	3,246	2,349	2,925	2,650	74
Bond	3,682	3,716	2,834	4,398	244
Boone	4,458	6,470	3,175	5,597	1,573
Brown	1,533	1,519	950	1,660	59
Bureau	7,566	10,854	6,741	11,461	1,091
Calhoun	1,549	1,364	1,208	1,591	76
Carroll	3,372	5,059	2,154	5,084	705
Cass	3,589	3,524	2,543	3,965	199
Champaign	26,858	34,546	21,017	33,329	9,972
Christian	9,306	7,445	5,625	8,770	499
Clark	4,071	4,506	2,855	5,476	0
Clay	3,837	3,860	2,587	4,447	187
Clinton	6,275	7,245	4,470	8,500	528
Coles	8,639	11,021	6,743	11,994	1,726
Cook	1,180,814	987,498	1,093,548	836,299	144,677
Crawford	5,007	5,522	2,740	4,723	280
Cumberland	2,752	2,518	1,892	3,159	190
DeKalb	11,535	18,193	8,913	15,370	4,526
DeWitt	3,477	4,137	2,262	4,548	368
Douglas	3,826	4,635	2,564	5,330	344
DuPage	72,137	175,055	68,375	180,601	29,568
Edgar	5,058	5,842	3,394	6,639	400
Edwards	1,648	2,379	1,041	2,556	107
Effingham	5,952	7,194	4,229	9,104	393
Fayette	383	6,523	328	5,059	
Ford	2,690	4,801	1,803	5,024	328
Franklin	12,818	7,420	9,425	9,731	558
Fulton	9,314	9,588	7,437	10,250	835
Gallatin	2,611	1,499	1,678	1,700	78
Greene	4,057	3,706	2,507	4,224	220
Grundy	5,534	7,581	3,970	8,397	701
Hamilton	3,036	2,433	1,990	3,254	171
Hancock	4,730	6,043	3,522	6,597	383
Hardin	1,602	1,393	1,314	1,721	56
Henderson	2,152	2,210	1,509	2,443	143
Henry	9,822	12,849	7,077	14,505	1,440
Iroquois	5,167	10,129	3,362	11,247	592
Jackson	12,940	10,152	10,291	10,505	2,526
Jasper	2,772	2,794	1,846	3,548	157
Jefferson	8,989	7,422	6,751	8,972	506
Jersey	4,625	4,273	3,394	5,266	314
JoDaviess	3,979	5,478	2,617	5,142	982
Johnson	2,182	2,417	1,586	3,200	84
Kane	34,057	59,275	29,015	54,105	9,179
Kankakee	18,394	23,003	14,544	23,861	1,642
Kendall	4,202	9,011	3,143	10,023	979
Knox	11,525	14,123	8,999	15,149	2,104
Lake	57,741	92,231	48,287	96,350	17,726
LaSalle	23,105	25,114	16,818	27,323	3,041
Lawrence	4,044	4,345	3,029	4,450	293
Lee	6,076	8,674	3,170	11,373	781
Livingston	5,174	10,097	4,112	11,541	980
Logan	5,686	8,623	3,916	9,681	550
Macon	28,243	24,893	22,325	28,298	2,804
Macoupin	11,910	10,242	9,116	12,131	901
Madison	56,457	44,183	43,404	50,739	4,151
Marion	9,834	8,729	6,990	10,969	567
Marshall	2,570	4,017	1,903	4,349	336
Mason	3,947	3,847	2,680	4,644	267
Massac	3,666	3,226	2,821	4,284	124
McDonough	5,464	9,683	4,093	8,795	1,207
McHenry	16,799	37,115	14,617	40,315	5,921
McLean	16,601	28,493	13,587	30,095	4,961
Menard	2,301	3,137	1,589	3,622	274
Mercer	4,090	4,816	3,361	5,144	540
Monroe	3,984	5,602	3,121	5,25	405
Montgomery	8,322	7,379	5,721	8,947	611
Morgan	7,403	8,885	5,483	10,406	900
Moultrie	3,332	2,803	2,332	3,405	380
Ogle	6,463	11,073	4,067	12,533	2,042
Peoria	34,606	46,526	28,221	47,704	6,145
Perry	5,976	5,286	4,337	5,888	319
Piatt	3,509	4,442	2,417	4,858	444
Pike	5,006	4,975	3,695	5,301	303
Pope	1,070	1,187	881	1,501	58
Pulaski	2,489	1,836	1,955	2,083	48
Putnam	1,344	1,572	1,158	1,959	235
Randolph	8,693	8,190	5,044	8,793	513
Richland	3,485	4,434	2,471	5,240	558
Rock Island	35,994	34,007	33,286	36,191	7,502
St. Clair	59,177	40,333	49,783	45,922	3,849
Saline	7,472	5,970	5,162	5,572	271
Sangamon	38,017	43,309	29,354	49,372	5,439
Schuyler	2,014	5,234	1,445	2,799	155
Scott	1,424	1,789	941	1,990	80
Shelby	61,172	2,191	3,988	5,441	381
Stark	1,146	2,191	806	2,358	147
Stephenson	7,192	11,678	8,315	11,231	3,275
Tazewell	22,821	28,951	16,924	36,481	3,206
Union	5,003	3,531	3,781	4,289	2,191
Vermilion	18,438	19,751	14,498	22,579	2,110
Wabash	2,781	3,388	1,975	3,571	230
Warren	3,808	5,822	2,754	5,567	489
Washington	3,222	4,485	2,212	5,435	163
Wayne	4,303	5,211	3,258	5,013	222
White	5,306	4,600	3,463	5,279	274
Whiteside	11,255	14,308	7,190	17,390	1,243
Will	51,103	61,784	41,975	59,310	7,855
Williamson	13,600	10,703	10,542	14,486	908
Winnebago	42,399	52,736	32,384	48,825	22,596
Woodford	4819	8,899	3,552	10,791	711
Totals	**2,271,295**	**2,364,269**	**1,951,073**	**2,335,806**	**344,836**

Illinois Vote Since 1932

1932 (Pres.), Roosevelt, Dem., 1,882,304; Hoover, Rep., 1,432,756; Thomas, Soc., 67,258; Foster, Com., 15,582; Upshaw, Proh., 6,388; Reynolds, Soc. Labor, 3,638.

1936 (Pres.), Roosevelt, Dem., 2,282,999; Landon, Rep., 1,570,393; Lemke, Union, 89,439; Thomas, Soc., 7,530; Colvin, Proh., 3,439; Aiken, Soc. Labor, 1,921.

1940 (Pres.), Roosevelt, Dem., 2,149,934; Willkie, Rep., 2,047,240; Thomas, Soc., 10,914; Babson, Proh., 9,190.

1944 (Pres.), Roosevelt, Dem., 2,079,479; Dewey, Rep., 1,939,314; Teichert, Soc. Labor, 9,677; Watson, Proh., 7,411; Thomas, Soc., 180.

1948 (Pres.), Truman, Dem., 1,994,715; Dewey, Rep., 1,961,103; Watson, Proh., 11,959; Thomas, Soc., 11,522; Teichert, Soc. Labor, 3,118.

1952 (Pres.), Eisenhower, Rep., 2,457,327; Stevenson, Dem., 2,013,920; Hass, Soc. Labor, 9,363; write-in, 448.

1956 (Pres.), Eisenhower, Rep., 2,623,327; Stevenson, Dem., 1,775,682; Hass, Soc. Labor, 8,342; write-in, 56.

1960 (Pres.), Kennedy, Dem., 2,377,846; Nixon, Rep., 2,368,988; Hass, Soc. Labor, 10,560; write-in, 15.

1964 (Pres.), Johnson, Dem., 2,796,833; Goldwater, Rep., 1,905,946; write-in, 62.

1968 (Pres.), Nixon, Rep., 2,174,774; Humphrey, Dem., 2,039,814; Wallace, 3d party, 390,958; Blomen, Soc. Labor, 13,878; write-in, 325.

1972 (Pres.), Nixon, Rep. 2,788,179; McGovern, Dem., 1,913,472; Fisher, Soc. Labor, 12,344; Schmitz, Amer., 2,471; Hall, Com., 4,541; others, 2,229.

1976 (Pres.), Carter, Dem., 2,271,295; Ford, Rep., 2,364,269; McCarthy, Ind., 55,939; Hall, Com., 9,250; MacBride, Libertarian, 8,057; Camejo, Soc. Workers, 3,615; Blomen, Soc. Labor, 2,422; LaRouche, U.S. Labor, 2,018; write-in, 1,968.

Indiana

County	1976 Carter (D)	1976 Ford (R)	1980 Carter (D)	1980 Reagan (R)	1980 Anderson (I)
Adams	4,908	6,280	4,673	6,368	767
Allen	44,744	71,321	35,966	64,068	9,202
Bartholomew	11,203	14,771	9,250	15,801	1,604
Benton	2,071	3,093	1,520	31,89	187
Blackford	3,174	2,886	2,431	3,168	258
Boone	5,686	9,214	4,535	10,484	681
Brown	2,381	2,466	2,014	2,884	237
Carroll	3,606	4,797	3,072	5,226	331
Cass	7,610	10,342	5,838	11,500	697
Clark	16,670	12,732	14,137	15,508	1,102
Clay	5,433	5,674	4,363	6,980	311
Clinton	6,662	8,199	5,258	8,158	427
Crawford	2,721	2,181	2,130	2,654	124
Daviess	4,952	6,829	4,057	7,022	345
Dearborn	6,348	6,176	5,133	7,467	433
Decatur	4,365	5,555	3,546	5,819	377
Dekalb	6,151	7,860	4,911	7,886	883
Delaware	25,151	26,417	20,923	28,342	2,743
Dubois	7,385	6,383	6,700	6,775	578
Elkhart	17,581	27,291	14,883	30,081	3,255
Fayette	5,519	5,704	4,304	6,004	293
Floyd	12,744	11,259	11,543	12,456	1,047
Fountain	4,089	4,903	2,845	5,289	280
Franklin	3,234	3,557	2,834	4,551	234
Fulton	3,488	5,083	2,795	5,458	312
Gibson	8,430	7,105	6,834	7,643	591
Grant	13,468	16,847	9,305	17,022	974
Greene	7,263	6,442	6,027	7,452	299
Hamilton	7,857	21,828	7,036	25,218	1,736
Hancock	6,191	10,072	5,124	12,093	746
Harrison	5,685	4,911	4,865	6,287	341
Hendricks	9,066	16,725	7,412	19,365	1,048
Henry	10,137	11,620	7,626	12,724	562
Howard	14,815	19,571	12,916	21,272	1,325
Huntington	6,515	9,182	5,415	9,497	824
Jackson	7,610	7,615	6,425	8,903	430
Jasper	3,286	5,398	2,544	5,316	283
Jay	4,124	4,606	3,256	6,351	484
Jefferson	6,139	5,573	5,496	6,831	477
Jennings	4,430	4,505	3,931	5,372	281

	1976 (D)	1976 (R)	1980 (D)	1980 (R)	1980 (I)
Johnson	10,075	16,414	8,445	20,018	1,348
Knox	9,612	9,100	7,829	10,083	617
Kosciusko	7,328	14,505	5,684	15,633	1,164
LaGrange	2,835	3,876	2,095	4,259	377
Lake	120,700	90,119	101,145	95,408	8,275
LaPorte	18,217	21,989	15,387	22,424	2,080
Lawrence	7,908	9,278	5,813	10,824	377
Madison	29,811	32,437	23,550	35,585	2,388
Marion	145,274	177,767	117,159	155,150	13,589
Marshall	6,424	9,707	5,149	10,209	836
Martin	2,827	2,702	2,479	3,082	149
Miami	6,257	8,263	4,927	8,672	508
Monroe	16,609	18,938	13,316	18,233	3,921
Montgomery	5,320	9,509	4,158	9,936	622
Morgan	7,181	10,983	5,439	13,321	498
Newton	2,236	3,204	1,649	3,850	194
Noble	5,875	6,885	4,721	7,624	750
Ohio	1,300	1,027	1,074	1,261	57
Orange	4,031	4,399	3,228	5,073	181
Owen	3,103	2,896	2,325	3,6342	188
Parke	3,158	3,929	2,432	4,595	194
Perry	5,620	4,088	4,540	4,350	443
Pike	3,938	3,138	3,346	3,343	190
Porter	16,468	25,489	12,869	30,055	3,061
Posey	5,298	5,136	4,465	6,096	667
Pulaski	2,813	3,586	2,092	3,915	175
Putnam	5,116	6,063	3,996	7,090	501
Randolph	5,330	6,891	4,025	7,762	426
Ripley	4,792	5,293	4,030	5,775	295
Rush	3,052	4,723	2,388	4,829	224
St. Joseph	49,156	50,358	43,680	49,359	6,406
Scott	4,229	2,657	3,694	3,432	139
Shelby	7,098	8,918	5,861	10,496	614
Spencer	4,796	4,166	4,153	5,284	195
Starke	4,753	4,354	3,615	5,035	297
Steuben	3,323	5,079	2,606	5,670	602
Sullivan	5,198	3,747	4,335	4,465	212
Switzerland	2,150	1,329	1,704	1,584	38
Tippecanoe	17,850	29,186	14,636	27,589	5,141
Tipton	3,428	4,776	2,547	5,150	285
Union	1,160	1,631	898	1,766	92
Vanderburgh	34,911	37,975	30,086	35,917	4,199
Vermillion	4,791	3,674	3,793	4,195	269
Vigo	24,684	23,555	19,261	24,133	2,484
Wabash	5,704	8,534	4,620	8,738	797
Warren	1,906	2,377	1,287	2,655	145
Warrick	7,804	7,200	8,845	8,681	890
Washington	4,409	3,794	3,663	5,234	191
Wayne	12,306	16,697	9,599	18,981	1,174
Wells	4,250	5,596	3,760	5,864	717
White	3,963	6,287	3,217	6,000	466
Whitley	5,445	6,761	4,592	7,041	928
Totals	**1,014,714**	**1,185,958**	**832,213**	**1,232,764**	**107,729**

Indiana Vote Since 1932

1932 (Pres.), Roosevelt, Dem., 862,054; Hoover, Rep., 677,184; Thomas, Soc., 21,388; Upshaw, Proh., 10,399; Foster, Com., 2,187; Reynolds, Soc. Labor, 2,070.

1936 (Pres.), Roosevelt, Dem., 943,974; Landon, Rep., 691,570; Lemke, Union, 19,407; Thomas, Soc., 3,856; Browder, Com., 1,090.

1940 (Pres.), Roosevelt, Dem., 874,063; Willkie, Rep., 899,466; Babson, Proh., 6,437; Thomas, Soc., 2,075; Aiken, Soc. Labor, 706.

1944 (Pres.), Roosevelt, Dem., 781,403; Dewey, Rep., 875,891; Watson, Proh., 12,574; Thomas, Soc., 2,223.

1948 (Pres.), Truman, Dem., 807,833; Dewey, Rep., 821,079; Watson, Proh., 14,711; Wallace, Prog., 9,649; Thomas, Soc., 2,179; Teichert, Soc. Labor, 763.

1952 (Pres.), Eisenhower, Rep., 1,136,259; Stevenson, Dem., 801,530; Hamblen, Proh., 15,335; Hallinan, Prog., 1,222; Hass, Soc. Labor, 979.

1956 (Pres.), Eisenhower, Rep., 1,182,811; Stevenson, Dem., 783,908; Holtwick, Proh., 6,554; Hass, Soc. Labor, 1,334.

1960 (Pres.), Kennedy, Dem., 952,358; Nixon, Rep., 1,175,120; Decker, Proh., 6,746; Hass, Soc. Labor, 1,136.

1964 (Pres.), Johnson, Dem. 1,170,848; Goldwater, Rep., 911,118; Munn, Proh., 8,266; Hass, Soc. Labor, 1,374.

1968 (Pres.), Nixon, Rep., 1,067,885; Humphrey, Dem., 806,659; Wallace, 3d party, 243,108; Munn, Proh., 4,616; Halstead, Soc. Worker, 1,293; Gregory, write-in, 36.

1972 (Pres.), Nixon, Rep., 1,405,154; McGovern, Dem., 708,568; Reed, Soc. Workers, 5,575; Fisher, Soc. Labor, 1,688; Spock, Peace & Freedom, 4,544.

1976 (Pres.), Carter, Dem., 1,014,714; Ford, Rep., 1,185,958; Anderson, Amer., 14,048; Camejo, Soc. Workers, 5,695; LaRouche, U.S. Labor, 1,947.

Iowa

County	1976 Carter (D)	1976 Ford (R)	1980 Carter (D)	1980 Reagan (R)	1980 Anderson (I)
Adair	2,294	2,326	1,454	2,822	356
Adams	1,507	1,388	940	1,779	211
Allamakee	2,568	3,648	2,149	3,990	343
Appanoose	3,424	3,036	2,769	3,544	339
Audubon	2,104	1,978	1,555	2,523	251
Benton	5,514	5,014	4,223	5,329	948
Black Hawk	29,508	30,994	27,456	29,635	5,813
Boone	6,595	5,413	5,126	5,421	1,067
Bremer	4,203	6,252	3,527	6,705	970
Buchanan	4,258	4,794	3,605	5,041	689
Buena Vista	4,227	5,126	3,445	5,254	766
Butler	2,503	4,207	1,990	4,730	392
Calhoun	3,001	3,215	2,150	3,685	407
Carroll	5,333	4,094	3,885	5,010	733
Cass	2,866	4,589	2,176	5,391	423
Cedar	3,354	4,308	2,489	4,395	680
Cerro Gordo	11,189	10,604	9,356	11,251	2,029
Cherokee	3,358	3,993	2,718	4,085	600
Chickasaw	3,503	3,432	2,934	3,929	476
Clarke	2,333	1,737	1,619	2,417	310
Clay	3,776	4,548	3,179	4,478	991
Clayton	3,804	4,826	3,462	5,112	654
Clinton	11,746	12,401	9,696	13,018	2,131
Crawford	3,903	3,879	2,500	4,883	496
Dallas	6,722	5,308	5,130	6,292	1,200
Davis	2,426	1,631	1,689	2,003	201
Decatur	2,698	1,932	2,048	2,212	318
Delaware	3,168	4,161	2,671	4,327	720
Des Moines	11,268	9,023	9,952	9,100	1,040
Dickinson	3,074		2,620	4,028	687
Dubuque	20,548	17,459	18,684	18,645	3,718
Emmet	2,720	2,872	2,153	3,062	456
Fayette	5,220	6,618	4,376	6,445	626
Floyd	4,646	4,361	3,632	4,658	723
Franklin	2,682	3,056	1,914	3,296	390
Fremont	1,964	2,163	1,201	2,692	151
Greene	3,094	2,811	2,210	3,154	510
Grundy	2,410	4,173	1,869	4,644	440
Guthrie	2,873	2,644	1,863	3,182	367
Hamilton	3,953	3,932	2,741	4,545	679
Hancock	2,975	3,127	1,918	3,681	462
Hardin	4,479	4,682	3,757	5,339	730
Harrison	3,228	3,489	2,152	4,502	302
Henry	3,882	3,848	3,316	4,430	629
Howard	2,917	2,618	2,212	2,979	286
Humboldt	2,677	3,075	1,840	3,575	231
Ida	1,868	2,590	1,235	2,824	236
Iowa	3,367	3,926	2,606	4,153	667
Jackson	4,467	4,221	3,518	4,479	622
Jasper	8,783	7,728	7,256	8,285	1,169
Jefferson	3,377	3,746	2,577	4,099	505
Johnson	20,208	16,090	20,114	13,630	8,252
Jones	4,245	4,463	3,436	4,406	759
Keokuk	3,482	2,920	2,388	3,145	369
Kossuth	5,190	4,653	3,802	5,563	712
Lee	9,017	8,195	8,200	8,788	1,036
Linn	38,252	36,513	32,162	36,250	8,729
Louisa	2,089	2,284	1,699	2,528	291
Lucas	2,733	2,071	1,989	2,593	291
Lyon	1,870	3,558	1,426	4,332	372
Madison	3,109	2,681	2,494	3,319	502
Mahaska	4,838	5,267	3,968	5,650	603
Marion	6,226	5,429	5,483	6,655	1,232
Marshall	8,695	9,562	7,098	10,706	1,540
Mills	1,908	2,722	1,244	3,579	278
Mitchell	2,906	2,887	2,040	3,398	361
Monona	2,661	2,636	1,660	3,262	275
Monroe	2,360	1,581	1,866	2,223	246
Montgomery	2,229	3,673	1,564	4,113	223
Muscatine	6,567	7,697	5,586	8,190	1,619
O'Brien	2,732	4,643	2,210	4,937	475
Osceola	1,309	1,955	1,051	2,177	234
Page	2,865	5,343	1,774	5,617	420
Palo Alto	3,182	2,623	2,463	3,025	412
Plymouth	4,284	5,590	2,962	6,514	711
Pocahontas	3,055	2,700	1,959	3,195	397
Polk	71,917	62,316	61,668	64,063	15,648
Pottawattamie	14,754	17,264	10,705	20,155	1,792
Poweshiek	4,360	4,194	3,525	4,995	799
Ringgold	1,739	1,543	1,149	1,884	191
Sac	2,996	3,347	1,976	3,752	458
Scott	29,771	35,021	26,361	34,680	5,509
Shelby	2,851	3,301	1,892	4,047	369
Sioux	3,322	9,448	2,698	10,768	610
Story	15,717	18,394	14,122	16,612	7,506
Tama	4,580	4,379	3,049	4,840	593
Taylor	1,947	2,059	1,226	2,715	193
Union	2,955	2,873	2,182	3,371	368
Van Buren	1,807	1,804	1,307	2,138	183
Wapello	10,249	6,786	8,896	7,475	1,039
Warren	7,653	6,099	6,632	7,337	1,285
Washington	3,448	4,218	2,877	3,967	700
Wayne	2,145	1,781	1,627	2,221	218
Webster	10,543	9,068	8,999	10,431	1,359
Winnebago	2,950	3,315	2,201	3,807	417
Winneshiek	4,158	4,765	3,201	4,933	938

	1976 (D)	1976 (R)	1980 (D)	1980 (R)	1980 (I)
Woodbury	19,664	22,853	15,715	23,549	3,164
Worth	2,399	1,964	1,721	2,247	301
Wright	3,637	3,544	2,645	3,936	497
Total	**619,931**	**632,863**	**508,735**	**676,556**	**114,589**

Iowa Vote Since 1932

1932 (Pres.), Roosevelt, Dem., 598,019; Hoover, Rep., 414,433; Thomas, Soc., 20,467; Upshaw, Proh., 2,111; Coxey, Farm-Lab., 1,094; Foster, Com., 559.

1936 (Pres.), Roosevelt, Dem., 621,756; Landon, Rep., 487,977; Lemke, Union, 29,687; Thomas, Soc., 1,373; Colvin, Proh., 1,182; Browder, Com., 506; Aiken, Soc. Labor, 252.

1940 (Pres.), Roosevelt, Dem., 578,800; Willkie, Rep., 632,370; Babson, Proh., 2,284; Browder, Com., 1,524; Aiken, Soc. Labor, 452.

1944 (Pres.), Roosevelt, Dem., 499,876; Dewey, Rep., 547,267; Watson, Proh., 3,752; Thomas, Soc., 1,511; Teichert, Soc. Labor, 193.

1948 (Pres.), Truman, Dem., 522,380; Dewey, Rep., 494,018; Wallace, Prog., 12,125; Teichert, Soc. Labor, 4,274; Watson, Proh., 3,382; Thomas, Soc., 1,829; Dobbs, Soc. Workers, 26.

1952 (Pres.), Eisenhower, Rep., 808,906; Stevenson, Dem., 451,513; Hallinan, Prog., 5,085; Hamblen, Proh., 2,882; Hoopes, Soc., 219; Hass, Soc. Labor, 139; scattering 29.

1956 (Pres.), Eisenhower, Rep., 729,187; Stevenson, Dem., 501,858; Andrews (A.C.P. of Iowa), 3,202; Hoopes, Soc., 192; Hass, Soc. Labor, 125.

1960 (Pres.), Kennedy, Dem., 550,565; Nixon, Rep., 722,381; Hass, Soc. Labor, 230; write-in, 634.

1964 (Pres.), Johnson, Dem., 733,030; Goldwater, Rep., 449,148; Hass, Soc. Labor, 182; DeBerry, Soc. Worker, 159; Munn, Proh., 1,902.

1968 (Pres.), Nixon, Rep., 619,106; Humphrey, Dem., 476,699; Wallace, 3d party, 66,422; Munn, Proh., 362; Halstead, Soc. Worker, 3,377; Cleaver, Peace and Freedom, 1,332; Blomen, Soc. Labor, 241.

1972 (Pres.), Nixon, Rep., 706,207; McGovern, Dem., 496,206; Schmitz, Amer., 22,056; Jenness, Soc. Workers, 488; Fisher, Soc. Labor, 195; Hall, Com. 272; Green, Universal, 199; scattered, 321.

1976 (Pres.), Carter, Dem., 619,931; Ford, Rep., 632,863; McCarthy, Ind., 20,051; Anderson, Amer., 3,040; MacBride, Libertarian, 1,452.

Kansas

County	1976 Carter (D)	1976 Ford (R)	1980 Carter (D)	1980 Reagan (R)	1980 Anderson (I)
Allen	2,746	3,269	2,009	3,811	340
Anderson	1,886	1,872	1,170	2,363	184
Atchison	4,108	4,030	3,063	4,084	345
Barber	1,494	1,568	914	1,871	170
Barton	5,497	7,311	3,399	8,510	699
Bourbon	3,237	3,589	2,605	4,262	251
Brown	1,745	3,407	1,269	3,598	276
Butler	8,540	8,390	6,875	10,110	1,015
Chase	643	922	413	1,072	92
Chautauqua	866	1,159	543	1,565	57
Cherokee	5,154	3,957	1,231	5,290	962
Cheyenne	758	1,008	358	1,330	81
Clark	680	761	430	901	67
Clay	1,610	3,085	932	3,448	217
Cloud	2,976	2,954	1,793	3,581	344
Coffey	1,549	2,145	1,038	2,488	127
Comanche	630	719	393	877	50
Cowley	7,095	7,513	5,468	8,749	866
Crawford	9,021	7,225	7,658	8,058	847
Decatur	1,011	1,232	618	1,642	140
Dickinson	3,672	4,759	2,108	5,654	469
Doniphan	1,428	2,649	1,006	2,523	146
Douglas	11,922	14,277	9,360	14,106	4,770
Edwards	1,304	1,001	616	1,409	121
Elk	865	1,087	482	1,280	55
Ellis	6,280	4,719	3,930	5,634	923
Ellsworth	1,573	1,618	886	2,155	167
Finney	3,813	3,711	2,689	4,830	531
Ford	4,934	4,679	3,194	5,686	622
Franklin	3,607	4,760	2,724	5,525	432
Geary	2,843	3,230	2,375	3,534	329
Gove	848	860	396	1,263	103
Graham	936	1,112	473	1,450	98
Grant	1,151	1,226	683	1,713	150
Gray	1,111	837	583	1,310	123
Greeley	479	389	235	600	84
Greenwood	1,737	2,319	1,241	2,685	170
Hamilton	746	560	402	899	66
Harper	1,681	1,777	990	2,254	182
Harvey	6,003	6,624	4,172	7,044	1,355
Haskell	676	761	374	1,014	84
Hodgeman	697	576	339	831	69
Jackson	2,129	2,725	1,537	3,211	234
Jefferson	2,470	3,225	1,776	4,046	364
Jewell	1,111	1,592	578	2,074	153
Johnson	35,605	75,798	33,039	77,422	10,854
Keamy	658	674	375	924	62
Kingman	2,142	1,839	1,133	2,617	282
Kiowa	764	1,180	438	1,433	88
Labette	5,294	4,640	3,946	5,243	572
Lane	646	651	321	924	100
Leavenworth	8,022	8,407	6,354	9,157	955
Lincoln	985	1,225	528	1,685	96
Linn	1,681	1,873	1,157	2,407	103
Logan	694	957	357	1,261	66
Lyon	5,634	7,062	4,680	8,481	1,216
Marion	2,483	3,519	1,569	3,965	488
Marshall	3,004	3,226	1,555	4,127	316
McPherson	5,366	6,187	3,340	6,843	1,222
Meade	526	983	482	1,618	121
Miami	4,000	3,999	3,071	4,740	368
Mitchell	1,700	2,095	876	2,821	197
Montgomery	7,157	8,864	5,282	10,856	488
Morris	1,337	1,698	810	1,933	166
Morton	735	738	414	1,157	71
Nemaha	2,586	2,759	1,600	3,445	243
Neosho	3,842	4,038	2,923	4,613	397
Ness	1,106	1,016	616	1,657	136
Norton	1,337	2,201	666	2,625	151
Osage	2,755	2,945	2,088	3,807	330
Osborne	1,190	1,574	620	2,188	124
Ottawa	1,393	1,629	630	2,050	150
Pawnee	1,959	1,692	1,184	2,170	281
Phillips	1,264	2,317	748	2,731	143
Pottawatomie	2,316	3,483	1,723	3,894	444
Pratt	2,307	2,427	1,369	2,866	329
Rawlins	903	1,148	427	1,524	87
Reno	14,620	11,212	9,615	14,266	2,230
Republic	1,617	2,294	850	3,029	183
Rice	3,056	2,584	1,847	3,211	426
Riley	6,540	9,518	5,399	9,077	2,443
Rooks	1,412	1,664	725	2,275	144
Rush	1,359	1,170	557	1,840	144
Russell	1,453	3,165	910	3,241	229
Saline	8,476	11,218	6,022	11,997	1,556
Scott	919	1,195	456	1,829	99
Sedgwick	63,989	69,828	55,234	75,236	10,291
Seward	1,907	3,604	1,460	4,385	250
Shawnee	28,578	37,101	23,976	34,556	5,220
Sheridan	793	838	391	1,206	68
Sherman	1,573	1,671	779	2,310	215
Smith	1,333	2,009	719	2,415	180
Stafford	1,659	1,430	871	1,865	177
Stanton	489	510	231	672	62
Stevens	901	1,262	478	1,502	67
Summer	5,385	4,645	3,761	6,040	486
Thomas	1,802	2,246	1,048	2,789	269
Trego	1,003	1,025	523	1,340	138
Wabaunsee	1,354	1,921	810	2,122	162
Wallace	486	600	167	811	36
Washington	1,564	2,543	784	3,055	195
Wichita	614	593	303	880	60
Wilson	2,047	2,682	1,204	3,325	208
Woodson	904	1,104	646	1,435	89
Wyandotte	37,478	23,141	32,562	22,609	3,012
Totals	**430,421**	**502,752**	**324,974**	**562,848**	**67,535**

Kansas Vote Since 1932

1932 (Pres.), Roosevelt, Dem., 424,204; Hoover, Rep., 349,498; Thomas, Soc., 18,276.

1936 (Pres.), Roosevelt, Dem., 464,520; Landon, Rep., 397,727; Thomas, Soc., 2,766; Lemke, Union, 494.

1940 (Pres.), Roosevelt, Dem., 364,725; Willkie, Rep., 489,169; Babson, Proh., 4,056; Thomas, Soc., 2,347.

1944 (Pres.), Roosevelt, Dem., 287,458; Dewey, Rep., 442,096; Watson, Proh., 2,609; Thomas, Soc., 1,613.

1948 (Pres.), Truman, Dem., 351,902; Dewey, Rep., 423,039; Watson, Proh., 6,468; Wallace, Prog., 4,603; Thomas, Soc., 2,807.

1952 (Pres.), Eisenhower, Rep., 616,302; Stevenson, Dem., 273,296; Hamblen, Proh., 6,038; Hoopes, Soc., 530.

1956 (Pres.), Eisenhower, Rep., 566,878; Stevenson. Dem., 296,317; Holtwick, Proh., 3,048.

1960 (Pres.), Kennedy, Dem., 363,213; Nixon, Rep., 561,474; Decker, Proh., 4,138.

1964 (Pres.), Johnson, Dem., 464,028; Goldwater, Rep., 386,579; Munn, Proh., 5,393; Hass, Soc. Labor, 1,901.

1968 (Pres.), Nixon, Rep., 478,674; Humphrey, Dem., 302,996; Wallace, 3d, 88,921; Munn, Proh., 2,192.

1972 (Pres.), Nixon, Rep., 619,812; McGovern, Dem., 270,287; Schmitz, Cons., 21,808; Munn, Proh., 4,188.

1976 (Pres.), Carter, Dem., 430,421; Ford, Rep., 502,752; McCarthy, Ind., 13,185; Anderson, Amer., 4,724; MacBride, Libertarian, 3,242; Maddox, Cons., 2,118; Bubar, Proh., 1,403.

Kentucky

	1976		1980		
County	Carter (D)	Ford (R)	Carter (D)	Reagan (R)	Anderson (I)
Adair	2,366	3,201	2,285	4,051	22
Allen	2,231	2,508	2,010	3,186	54
Anderson	2,388	1,682	2,567	2,052	88
Ballard	2,794	649	2,583	1,190	23
Barren	5,878	3,797	5,285	6,405	164
Bath	2,113	938	2,174	1,463	42
Bell	5,284	5,035	6,362	5,433	150
Boone	5,602	5,602	5,374	8,263	383
Bourbon	3,504	2,260	3,641	2,475	153
Boyd	11,150	9,106	10,642	10,367	496
Boyle	4,095	3,511	4,429	3,848	256
Bracken	1,577	879	1,420	1,146	36
Breathitt	3,544	1,014	3,884	1,514	67
Breckinridge	3,347	2,698	3,163	3,629	72
Bullitt	5,623	3,639	5,884	6,364	202
Butler	1,588	2,363	1,274	3,129	28
Caldwell	3,016	1,808	2,924	2,609	66
Calloway	8,141	3,171	6,809	4,498	318
Campbell	12,423	15,798	6,823	10,489	627
Carlisle	1,985	435	1,542	975	8
Carroll	2,251	815	2,127	1,076	82
Carter	3,915	3,185	3,782	3,934	86
Casey	1,602	3,379	1,298	4,239	38
Christian	7,845	4,964	7,048	8,209	190
Clark	4,575	3,114	5,071	4,302	242
Clay	1,674	3,652	2,131	4,594	30
Clinton	987	2,354	1,001	3,539	34
Crittenden	1,715	1,596	1,508	2,219	28
Cumberland	853	1,653	821	2,216	27
Daviess	14,114	12,826	14,902	14,643	752
Edmonson	1,418	1,976	1,252	2,913	28
Elliott	1,987	455	1,668	551	15
Estill	2,034	2,250	1,965	2,818	45
Fayette	28,012	35,170	26,809	30,202	4,257
Fleming	2,317	1,647	2,051	2,189	54
Floyd	10,151	3,108	10,978	4,179	175
Franklin	10,475	5,536	11,193	6,455	610
Fulton	2,370	1,060	2,016	1,462	31
Gallatin	1,164	436	988	684	20
Garrard	1,887	2,045	1,774	2,585	62
Grant	2,336	1,212	2,292	1,779	76
Graves	8,982	3,195	6,999	6,556	135
Grayson	3,064	3,658	2,788	5,084	78
Green	2,085	2,397	1,758	2,775	39
Greenup	6,880	5,062	71,26	6,857	220
Hancock	1,562	1,124	1,530	1,367	110
Hardin	7,977	6,965	8,339	9,779	452
Harlan	7,300	4,624	8,798	5,328	131
Harrison	3,582	1,911	3,319	2,184	107
Hart	3,189	2,013	3,005	3,129	42
Henderson	7,916	4,053	8,347	5,271	380
Henry	2,985	1,192	2,999	1,723	69
Hickman	2,035	585	1,456	1,143	28
Hopkins	7,749	5,115	8,810	6,238	213
Jackson	680	2,766	702	3,379	29
Jefferson	122,731	130,262	123,228	123,052	9,029
Jessamine	2,795	3,081	1,459	2,466	140
Johnson	3,683	4,891	3,142	5,039	96
Kenton	18,833	22,087	4,799	6,998	383
Knott	4,762	962	5,405	1,602	25
Knox	3,642	4,931	3,543	5,539	113
Larue	2,207	1,409	2,183	2,000	43
Laurel	3,813	6,186	3,972	8,868	104
Lawrence	2,402	1,838	2,362	2,564	32
Lee	1,091	1,449	1,017	1,640	41
Leslie	1,478	3,770	1,327	3,536	40
Letcher	4,590	3,122	274	135	76
Lewis	1,929	2,383	1,543	2,802	34
Lincoln	3,198	2,694	2,991	3,304	46
Livingston	2,497	878	2,287	1,670	30
Logan	4,850	2,430	4,264	3,366	85
Lyon	1,606	585	1,496	968	26
McCracken	14,956	6,997	13,368	10,201	369
McCreary	1,827	3,272	1,377	3,786	40
McLean	2,346	1,212	2,147	1,497	44
Madison	7,299	6,581	8,041	8,252	744
Magoffin	2,451	1,793	2,986	2,265	25
Marion	3,520	1,723	3,577	2,126	87
Marshall	6,906	2,578	6,231	4,403	96
Martin	1,267	2,120	1,518	2,792	51
Mason	3,397	2,529	3,181	2,926	127
Meade	3,030	1,755	3,205	2,740	90
Menifee	1,041	304	966	547	11
Mercer	3,411	2,451	3,528	3,275	92
Metcalfe	1,877	1,356	1,628	2,013	38
Monroe	1,412	3,352	1,156	4,592	47
Montgomery	3,141	2,032	3,391	2,869	117
Morgan	2,897	973	2,698	1,450	15
Muhlenberg	7,058	4,292	6,616	4,893	148
Nelson	4,454	2,804	5,514	3,349	162
Nicholas	1,582	738	1,351	915	56
Ohio	3,508	3,764	3,486	5,272	103
Oldham	2,819	3,695	3,487	5,586	351
Owen	2,332	676	2,323	944	43
Owsley	305	1,053	437	1,250	7
Pendleton	2,147	1,230	1,992	1,757	609
Perry	5,633	4,434	6,031	4,266	72
Pike	14,320	9,178	14,758	10,530	204
Powell	1,859	1,148	2,006	1,716	33
Pulaski	5,752	9,226	6,570	12,970	257
Robertson	546	275	562	463	14
Rockcastle	1,408	2,583	1,335	3,547	35
Rowen	3,541	2,244	2,975	2,758	185
Russell	1,803	2,882	1,693	3,804	29
Scott	3,118	2,408	3,531	2,868	197
Shelby	3,841	2,916	4,129	3,423	178
Simpson	2,782	1,481	2,713	2,020	59
Spencer	1,209	742	1,216	935	27
Taylor	3,456	3,337	3,400	4,243	84
Todd	2,436	1,095	1,956	19,45	44
Trigg	2,727	991	2,619	1,913	56
Trimble	1,568	517	1,478	824	49
Union	3,540	1,716	3,479	1,847	68
Warren	9,657	9,439	9,592	12,181	602
Washington	2,376	1,765	2,147	2,008	43
Wayne	2,537	3,243	2,673	3,972	50
Webster	3,523	1,402	3,506	1,939	51
Whitley	4,212	6,100	3,889	7,007	125
Wolfe	1,777	659	1,814	951	19
Woodford	2,689	2,646	3,122	31,05	213
Totals	**615,717**	**531,852**	**609,687**	**625,820**	**29,843**

Kentucky Vote Since 1932

1932 (Pres.), Roosevelt, Dem., 580,574; Hoover, Rep., 394,716; Upshaw, Proh., 2,252; Thomas, Soc., 3,853; Reynolds, Soc. Labor, 1,396; Foster, Com., 272.

1936 (Pres.), Roosevelt, Dem., 541,944; Landon, Rep., 369,702; Lemke, Union, 12,501; Colvin, Proh., 929; Thomas, Soc., 627; Aiken, Soc. Labor, 294; Browder, Com., 204.

1940 (Pres.), Roosevelt, Dem., 557,222; Willkie, Rep., 410,384; Babson, Proh., 1,443; Thomas, Soc., 1,014.

1944 (Pres.), Roosevelt, Dem., 472,589; Dewey, Rep., 392,448; Watson, Proh., 2,023; Thomas, Soc., 535; Teichert, Soc. Labor, 326.

1948 (Pres.), Truman, Dem., 466,756; Dewey, Rep., 341,210; Thurmond, States' Rights, 10,411; Wallace, Prog., 1,567; Thomas, Soc., 1,284; Watson, Proh., 1,245; Teichert, Soc. Labor, 185.

1952 (Pres.), Eisenhower, Rep., 495,029; Stevenson, Dem., 495,729; Hamblen, Proh., 1,161; Hass, Soc. Labor, 893; Hallinan, Proh., 336.

1956 (Pres.), Eisenhower, Rep., 572,192; Stevenson, Dem., 476,453; Byrd, States' Rights, 2,657; Holtwick, Proh., 2,145; Hass, Soc. Labor, 358.

1960 (Pres.), Kennedy, Dem., 521,855; Nixon, Rep., 602,607.

1964 (Pres.), Johnson, Dem., 669,659; Goldwater, Rep., 372,977; John Kasper, Nat'l. States Rights, 3,469.

1968 (Pres.), Nixon, Rep., 462,411; Humphrey, Dem., 397,547; Wallace, 3d p., 193,098; Halstead, Soc. Worker, 2,843.

1972 (Pres.), Nixon, Rep., 676,446; McGovern, Dem., 371,159; Schmitz, Amer., 17,627; Jenness, Soc. Workers, 685; Hall, Com., 464; Spock, Peoples, 1,118.

1976 (Pres.), Carter, Dem., 615,717; Ford, Rep., 531,852; Anderson, Amer., 8,308; McCarthy, Ind., 6,837; Maddox, Amer. Ind., 2,328; MacBride, Libertarian, 814.

Louisiana

	1976		1980		
Parish	Carter (D)	Ford (R)	Carter (D)	Reagan (R)	Anderson (I)
Acadia	10,814	6,296	9,948	11,533	416
Allen	5,373	2,080	6,057	3,328	110
Ascension	9,100	4,435	12,381	7,237	286
Assumption	4,401	3,117	4,679	4,001	153

	1976		1980		
	(D)	(R)	(D)	(R)	(I)
Avoyelles	8,104	4,574	7,174	8,216	190
Beauregard	5,322	3,196	5,556	5,248	144
Bienville	3,402	2,499	4,123	3,508	51
Bossier	8,062	12,132	9,377	16,515	327
Caddo	30,593	42,627	36,422	56,097	1,110
Calcasieu	33,980	17,485	33,438	27,600	1,236
Caldwell	1,830	1,890	1,786	2,653	43
Cameron	2,432	819	2,221	1,449	82
Catahoula	2,547	2,086	2,412	2,930	34
Claiborne	2,891	3,216	3,443	3,538	52
Concordia	3,892	3,849	3,956	4,933	52
DeSoto	4,630	3,601	5,861	4,349	49
E. Baton Rouge	49,956	51,655	57,013	71,253	3,310
East Carroll	2,367	1,681	2,283	1,867	24
East Feliciana	3,485	1,668	4,033	2,650	53
Evangeline	7,578	3,715	6,722	7,416	100
Franklin	3,824	3,947	4,167	5,301	65
Grant	3,670	2,280	3,290	3,611	77
Iberia	9,984	10,392	9,681	14,273	410
Iberville	7,254	3,822	9,397	4,552	172
Jackson	3,605	3,310	3,639	3,922	56
Jefferson	53,257	71,787	51,176	99,915	3,567
Jefferson Davis	6,376	3,603	6,140	5,667	201
Lafayette	19,918	22,805	19,916	30,816	1,247
Lafourche	14,131	11,434	14,222	14,951	675
LaSalle	2,961	3,161	2,655	3,792	61
Lincoln	4,971	6,828	5,598	7,515	169
Livingston	9,875	5,555	11,310	10,666	287
Madison	4,933	2,096	3,264	2,531	16
Morehouse	4,017	5,418	4,856	7,149	65
Natchitoches	6,692	5,248	7,101	6,668	158
Orleans	93,130	70,925	106,398	73,729	4,237
Ouachita	15,738	24,082	16,392	29,701	495
Plaquemines	2,614	6,052	4,618	5,489	155
Pointe Coupee	5,147	2,567	6,395	3,667	105
Rapides	20,851	17,766	19,118	24,861	497
Red River	1,906	1,728	2,796	2,137	29
Richland	3,495	3,630	3,745	4,772	48
Sabine	4,555	3,531	5,098	4,263	74
St. Bernard	12,969	12,707	11,357	19,410	616
St. Charles	6,872	4,270	7,898	6,779	284
St. Helen	2,622	1,046	3,283	1,531	42
St. James	4,531	2,751	6,206	3,429	113
St. John	5,700	3,597	7,647	5,819	256
St. Landry	15,631	9,956	17,032	14,781	328
St. Martin	7,992	4,112	7,760	6,701	295
St. Mary	9,401	8,919	10,506	10,378	339
St. Tammany	14,691	15,822	14,063	27,214	870
Tangipahoa	14,432	9,242	15,274	15,178	491
Tensas	2,081	1,553	2,046	1,645	25
Terrebonne	10,627	12,895	10,804	16,644	559
Unien	3,600	4,139	3,805	5,130	60
Vermillion	11,246	6,133	9,540	10,481	473
Vernon	6,202	3,970	7,313	5,869	163
Washington	10,000	5,677	10,413	8,681	170
Webster	7,286	7,550	8,568	8,865	119
W. Baton Rouge	3,809	1,913	4,739	2,828	115
West Carroll	2,595	2,407	2,118	3,430	35
West Feliciana	1,890	990	2,341	1,2137	40
Winn	3,543	3,209	3,411	3,944	57
Totals	**661,365**	**587,446**	**707,981**	**796,240**	**26,198**

Louisiana Vote Since 1932

1932 (Pres.), Roosevelt, Dem., 249,418; Hoover, Rep., 18,863.

1936 (Pres.), Roosevelt, Dem., 292,894; Landon, Rep., 36,791.

1940 (Pres.), Roosevelt, Dem., 319,751; Willkie, Rep., 52,446.

1944 (Pres.), Roosevelt, Dem., 281,564; Dewey, Rep., 67,750.

1948 (Pres.), Thurmond, States' Rights, 204,290; Truman, Dem., 136,344; Dewey, Rep., 72,657; Wallace, Prog., 3,035.

1952 (Pres.), Eisenhower, Rep., 306,925, Stevenson, Dem., 345,027.

1956 (Pres.), Eisenhower, Rep., 329,047; Stevenson, Dem., 243,977; Andrews, States' Rights, 44,520.

1960 (Pres.), Kennedy, Dem., 407,339; Nixon, Rep., 230,890; States' Rights (unpledged) 169,572.

1964 (Pres.), Johnson, Dem., 387,068; Goldwater, Rep., 509,225.

1968 (Pres.), Nixon, Rep., 257,535; Humphrey, Dem., 309,615; Wallace, 3d party, 530,300.

1972 (Pres.), Nixon, Rep., 686,852; McGovern, Dem., 298,142; Schmitz, Amer., 52,099; Jenness, Soc. Workers, 14,398.

1976 (Pres.), Carter, Dem., 661,365; Ford, Rep., 587,446; Maddox, Amer., 10,058; Hall, Com., 7,417; McCarthy, Ind., 6,588; MacBride, Libertarian, 3,325.

Maine

	1976		1980		
County	Carter (D)	Ford (R)	Carter (D)	Reagan (R)	Anderson (I)
Androscoggin	26,484	16,330	20,327	15,809	3,882
Aroostook	15,484	15,550	...	...	...
Cumberland	47,007	48,959	...	...	...
Franklin	5,140	5,799	4,961	5,680	1,205
Hancock	6,725	12,,064	...	...	...
Kennebec	23,473	22,534	...	...	...
Knox	5,922	8,315	...	...	...
Lincoln	4,818	7,554	...	...	...
Oxford	10,340	10,551	9,914	11,041	2,063
Penobscot	24,672	29,016	...	...	...
Piscataquis	3,727	4,084	...	...	...
Sagadahoc	5,529	5,988	...	...	...
Somerset	9,465	8,868	...	...	...
Waldo	4,853	6,289	...	...	...
Washington	6,644	7,039	...	...	...
York	31,996	27,380	...	...	...
Totals	**232,279**	**236,320**	...	...	...

Maine Vote Since 1932

1932 (Pres.), Roosevelt, Dem., 128,907; Hoover, Rep., 166,631; Thomas, Soc., 2,439; Reynolds, Soc. Labor, 255; Foster, Com., 162.

1936 (Pres.), Landon, Rep., 168,823; Roosevelt, Dem., 126,333; Lemke, Union, 7,581; Thomas, Soc., 783; Colvin, Proh., 334; Browder, Com., 257; Aiken, Soc. Labor, 129.

1940 (Pres.), Roosevelt, Dem., 156,478; Willkie, Rep., 165,951; Browder, Com., 411.

1944 (Pres.), Roosevelt, Dem., 140,631; Dewey, Rep., 155,434; Teichert, Soc. Labor, 335.

1948 (Pres.), Truman, Dem., 111,916; Dewey, Rep., 150,234; Wallace, Prog., 1,884; Thomas, Soc., 547; Teichert, Soc. Labor, 206.

1952 (Pres.), Eisenhower, Rep., 232,353; Stevenson, Dem., 118,806; Hallinan, Prog., 332; Hass, Soc. Labor, 156; Hoopes, Soc., 138; scattered, 1.

1956 (Pres.), Eisenhower, Rep., 249,238; Stevenson, Dem., 102,468.

1960 (Pres.), Kennedy, Dem., 181,159; Nixon, Rep., 240,608.

1964 (Pres.), Johnson, Dem., 262,264; Goldwater, Rep., 118,701.

1968 (Pres.), Nixon, Rep., 169,254; Humphrey, Dem., 217,312; Wallace, 3d party, 6,370.

1972 (Pres.), Nixon, Rep., 256,458; McGovern, Dem., 160,584; scattered, 229.

1976 (Pres.), Carter, Dem., 232,279; Ford, Rep., 236,320; McCarthy, Ind., 10,874; Bubar, Proh., 3,495.

Maryland

	1976		1980		
County	Carter (D)	Ford (R)	Carter (D)	Reagan (R)	Anderson (I)
Allegany	15,967	15,435	11,741	16,827	1,352
Anne Arundel	54,351	61,353	49,402	67,056	9,461
Baltimore	118,505	143,293	118,190	128,643	21,934
Calvert	4,626	3,439	4,644	5,300	551
Caroline	3,017	3,114	2,742	3,480	269
Carroll	9,940	15,661	10,136	19,392	2,133
Cecil	8,950	7,833	7,707	9,331	957
Charles	9,525	7,792	8,778	11,418	1,077
Dorchester	4,528	4,768	4,784	5,013	337
Frederick	14,542	17,941	12,925	21,131	2,702
Garrett	3,332	4,640	2,602	5,281	248
Harford	19,890	24,309	23,042	26,713	3,761
Howard	20,533	21,200	19,940	23,309	5,696
Kent	3,211	2,821	2,889	2,784	344
Montgomery	131,098	122,674	99,847	118,474	29,873
Prince George	111,743	81,027	96,552	76,241	13,801
Queen Anne	3,457	3,479	3,717	4,581	452
St. Mary's	7,227	5,640	6,578	7,966	811
Somerset	3,472	3,254	3,247	3,188	205
Talbot	3,715	5,848	3,954	5,755	516
Washington	15,902	20,194	13,635	22,163	1,521
Wicomico	9,412	10,537	9,116	10,765	992
Worcester	4,076	4,647	3,987	5,081	518
BALTIMORE CITY	178,593	81,762	189,172	56,363	13,941
Totals	**759,612**	**672,661**	**706,327**	**656,253**	**113,452**

Maryland Vote Since 1932

1932 (Pres.), Roosevelt, Dem., 314,314; Hoover, Rep., 184,184; Thomas, Soc., 10,489; Reynolds, Soc. Labor,

1,036; Foster, Com., 1,031.

1936 (Pres.), Roosevelt, Dem., 389,612; Landon, Rep., 231,435; Thomas, Soc., 1,629; Aiken, Soc. Labor, 1,305; Browder, Com., 915.

1940 (Pres.), Roosevelt, Dem., 384,546; Willkie, Rep., 269,534; Thomas, Soc., 4,093; Browder, Com., 1,274; Aiken, Soc. Labor, 657.

1944 (Pres.), Roosevelt, Dem., 315,490; Dewey, Rep., 292,949.

1948 (Pres.), Truman, Dem., 286,521; Dewey, Rep., 294,814; Wallace, Prog., 9,983; Thomas, Soc., 2,941; Thurmond, States' Rights, 2,476; Wright, write-in, 2,294.

1952 (Pres.), Eisenhower, Rep., 499,424; Stevenson, Dem., 395,337; Hallinan, Prog., 7,313.

1956 (Pres.), Eisenhower, Rep., 559,738; Stevenson, Dem., 372,613.

1960 (Pres.), Kennedy, Dem., 565,800; Nixon, Rep., 489,538.

1964 (Pres.), Johnson, Dem., 730,912; Goldwater, Rep., 385,495; write-in, 50.

1968 (Pres.), Nixon, Rep., 517,995; Humphrey, Dem., 538,310; Wallace, 3d party, 178,734.

1972 (Pres.), Nixon, Rep., 829,305; McGovern, Dem., 505,781; Schmitz, Amer., 18,726.

1976 (Pres.), Carter, Dem., 759,612; Ford, Rep., 672,661.

Massachusetts

County	1976 Carter (D)	Ford (R)	1980 Carter (D)	Reagan (R)	Anderson (I)
Barnstable	31,268	39,295	...	N/A	...
Berkshire	39,337	27,462	...	N/A	...
Bristol	116,318	69,957	...	N/A	...
Dukes	2,513	2,365	...	N/A	...
Essex	165,710	125,538	...	N/A	...
Franklin	14,985	14,837	...	N/A	...
Hampden	110,028	70,008	...	N/A	...
Hampshire	34,947	22,219	...	N/A	...
Middlesex	359,919	260,044	...	N/A	...
Nantucket	1,115	1,399	...	N/A	...
Norfolk	155,342	136,628	...	N/A	...
Plymouth	83,663	74,684	...	N/A	...
Suffolk	142,010	80,623	...	N/A	...
Worcester	172,320	105,217	...	N/A	...
Totals	**1,429,475**	**1,030,276**	...	...	...

Massachusetts Vote Since 1932

1932 (Pres.), Roosevelt, Dem., 800,148; Hoover, Rep., 736,959; Thomas, Soc., 34,305; Foster, Com., 4,821; Reynolds, Soc. Labor, 2,668; Upshaw, Proh., 1,142.

1936 (Pres.), Roosevelt, Dem., 942,716; Landon, Rep., 768,613; Lemke, Union, 118,639; Thomas, Soc., 5,111; Browder, Com., 2,930; Aiken, Soc. Labor, 1,305; Colvin, Proh., 1,032.

1940 (Pres.), Roosevelt, Dem., 1,076,522; Willkie, Rep., 939,700; Thomas, Soc., 4,091; Browder, Com., 3,806; Aiken, Soc. Labor, 1,492; Babson, Proh., 1,370.

1944 (Pres.), Roosevelt, Dem., 1,035,296; Dewey, Rep., 921,350; Teichert, Soc. Labor, 2,780; Watson, Proh., 973.

1948 (Pres.), Truman, Dem., 1,151,788; Dewey, Rep., 909,370; Wallace, Prog., 38,157; Teichert, Soc. Labor, 5,535; Watson, Proh., 1,663.

1952 (Pres.), Eisenhower, Rep., 1,292,325; Stevenson, Dem., 1,083,525; Hallinan, Prog., 4,636; Hass, Soc. Labor, 1,957; Hamblen, Proh., 886; scattered, 69; blanks, 41,150.

1956 (Pres.), Eisenhower, Rep., 1,393,197; Stevenson, Dem., 948,190; Hass, Soc. Labor, 5,573; Holtwick, Proh., 1,205; others, 341.

1960 (Pres.), Kennedy, Dem., 1,487,174; Nixon, Rep., 976,750; Hass, Soc. Labor, 3,892; Decker, Proh., 1,633; others, 31; blank and void, 26,024.

1964 (Pres.), Johnson, Dem., 1,786,422; Goldwater, Rep., 549,727; Hass, Soc. Labor, 4,755; Munn, Proh., 3,735; scattered, 159; blank, 48,104.

1968 (Pres.), Nixon, Rep., 766,844; Humphrey, Dem., 1,469,218; Wallace, 3d party, 87,088; Blomen, Soc. Labor, 6,180; Munn, Proh., 2,369; scattered, 53; blanks, 25,394.

1972 (Pres.), Nixon, Rep., 1,112,078; McGovern, Dem., 1,332,540; Jenness, Soc. Workers, 10,600; Fisher, Soc. Labor, 129; Schmitz, Amer., 2,877; Spock, Peoples, 101; Hall, Com., 46; Hospers, Libertarian, 43; scattered, 342.

1976 (Pres.), Carter, Dem., 1,429,475; Ford, Rep., 1,030,276; McCarthy, Ind., 65,637; Camejo, Soc. Workers, 8,138; Anderson, Amer., 7,555; La Rouche, U.S. Labor, 4,922; MacBride, Libertarian, 135.

Michigan

County	1976 Carter (D)	Ford (R)	1980 Carter (D)	Reagan (R)	Anderson (I)
Alcona	2,038	2,328	1,857	2,905	247
Alger	2,379	1,722	2,237	2,059	263
Allegan	9,794	19,330	9,848	20,468	1,973
Alpena	6,310	6,380	5,866	6,956	917
Antrim	3,032	4,369	2,909	4,706	602
Arenac	2,695	2,687	2,342	3,311	285
Baraga	1,778	1,788	1,609	2,046	201
Barry	6,967	11,178	6,857	12,006	1,399
Bay	25,958	23,174	24,577	24,297	3,906
Benzie	1,891	3,085	1,842	3,054	455
Berrien	25,163	40,835	22,456	39,872	3,331
Branch	6,301	8,251	4,635	10,224	1,102
Calhoun	25,229	30,390	23,077	30,909	4,349
Cass	7,843	9,893	6,894	10,977	1,140
Charlevoix	3,953	5,145	3,805	5,053	816
Cheboygan	3,880	4,894	3,938	5,417	638
Chippewa	6,022	7,025	5,258	6,991	883
Clare	4,153	4,879	4,165	5,722	665
Clinton	7,549	13,475	7,539	14,967	1,736
Crawford	1,889	2,359	1,826	2,652	390
Delta	9,027	7,809	8,586	7,987	849
Dickinson	6,134	5,922	5,065	5,849	523
Eaton	12,083	22,120	12,755	22,991	3,533
Emmet	4,013	5,910	3,724	5,930	1,134
Genesee	88,967	80,004	90,393	78,572	12,274
Gladwin	3,719	3,794	3,733	4,509	428
Gogebic	6,341	3,953	5,362	4,517	485
Grand Traverse	7,263	13,505	7,045	14,372	2,552
Gratiot	5,429	9,526	4,918	9,294	1,193
Hillsdale	5,427	9,307	4,375	10,951	874
Houghton	7,352	8,049	6,858	7,926	1,374
Huron	5,721	9,297	4,434	10,553	565
Ingham	47,890	66,729	48,278	56,777	17,139
Ionia	6,820	11,737	7,039	12,041	1,529
Iosco	4,875	5,500	4,256	6,886	739
Iron	4,401	3,224	3,732	3,516	332
Isabella	7,281	10,577	7,293	10,407	2,518
Jackson	24,726	32,873	23,873	35,377	3,587
Kalamazoo	33,411	51,462	35,028	48,669	10,833
Kalkaska	1,957	2,280	1,691	2,776	263
Kent	59,000	126,805	72,744	112,169	17,846
Keweenaw	658	606	570	583	87
Lake	2,179	1,598	2,041	1,730	187
Lapeer	9,503	12,349	9,671	15,997	1,868
Leelanau	2,437	4,240	2,348	4,585	805
Lenawee	14,610	18,397	12,960	20,265	2,330
Livingston	12,415	19,437	12,626	25,008	3,247
Luce	1,099	1,379	992	1,659	177
Mackinac	2,452	3,107	2,141	3,021	334
Macomb	121,176	132,499	121,982	156,808	19,085
Manistee	4,479	5,532	4,164	5,661	671
Marquette	12,837	12,984	13,166	13,061	2,460
Mason	4,541	6,812	4,134	7,137	825
Mecosta	4,725	7,287	5,228	7,764	1,321
Menominee	5,596	5,633	4,962	6,170	658
Midland	11,959	17,631	11,389	17,101	3,051
Missaukee	1,688	2,943	1,563	3,221	230
Monroe	23,290	20,676	20,608	25,608	3,111
Montcalm	6,684	10,439	6,738	10,921	1,306
Montmorency	1,684	1,882	1,654	2,400	191
Muskegon	27,013	35,548	26,667	36,501	4,045
Newaygo	5,622	8,258	5,236	8,918	862
Oakland	164,266	244,271	164,864	252,771	38,112
Oceana	3,427	5,236	3,386	5,465	270
Ogemaw	3,545	3,212	3,427	4,169	409
Ontonagon	3,104	2,462	2,374	2,565	227
Osceola	2,603	4,467	2,543	4,861	432
Oscoda	1,108	1,541	1,325	1,915	183
Otsego	2,724	3,155	2,571	3,666	483
Ottawa	16,381	49,196	18,439	51,260	4,852
Presque Isle	3,334	3,545	2,952	3,486	382
Roscommon	3,691	4,608	3,763	5,280	508
Saginaw	36,280	46,765	41.461	45,078	5,659
St. Clair	22,734	26,311	18,899	31,081	3,617
St. Joseph	7,306	11,784	6,318	13,631	1,269
Sanilac	6,042	10,597	5,492	12,158	846
Schoolcraft	2,158	1,933	1,963	2,098	243
Shiawassee	12,202	15,113	11,982	15,756	2,043
Tuscola	7,932	12,059	7,491	13,231	1,321
Van Buren	10,366	13,615	9,498	14,420	1,730
Washtenaw	50,917	56,807	51,012	48,698	13,463
Wayne	548,767	348,588	519,549	315,163	43,428
Wexford	4,519	5,670	4,339	6,027	752
Totals	**1,696,714**	**1,893,742**	**1,659,208**	**1,914,559**	**272,948**

Michigan Vote Since 1932

1932 (Pres.), Roosevelt, Dem., 871,700; Hoover, Rep., 739,894; Thomas, Soc., 39,025; Foster, Com., 9,318; Upshaw, Proh., 2,893; Reynolds, Soc. Labor, 1,041; Harvey, Lib., 217.

1936 (Pres.), Roosevelt, Dem., 1,016,794; Landon, Rep., 699,733; Lemke, Union, 75,795; Thomas, Soc., 8,208; Browder, Com., 3,384; Aiken, Soc. Labor, 600; Colvin, Proh., 579.

1940 (Pres.), Roosevelt, Dem., 1,032,991; Willkie, Rep., 1,039,917; Thomas, Soc., 7,593; Browder, Com., 2,834; Babson, Proh., 1,795; Aiken, Soc. Labor, 795.

1944 (Pres.), Roosevelt, Dem., 1,106,899; Dewey, Rep., 1,084,423; Watson, Proh., 6,503; Thomas, Soc., 4,598; Smith, America First, 1,530; Teichert, Soc. Labor, 1,264.

1948 (Pres.), Truman, Dem., 1,003,448; Dewey, Rep., 1,038,595; Wallace, Prog., 46,515; Watson, Proh., 13,052; Thomas, Soc. 6,063; Teichert, Soc. Labor, 1,263; Dobbs, Soc. Workers, 672.

1952 (Pres.), Eisenhower, Rep., 1,551,529; Stevenson, Dem., 1,230,657; Hamblen, Proh., 10,331; Hallinan, Prog., 3,922; Hass, Soc. Labor, 1,495; Dobbs, Soc. Workers, 655; scattered, 3.

1956 (Pres.), Eisenhower, Rep., 1,713,647; Stevenson, Dem., 1,359,898; Holtwick, Proh., 6,923.

1960 (Pres.), Kennedy, Dem., 1,687,269; Nixon, Rep., 1,620,428; Dobbs, Soc. Workers, 4,347; Decker, Proh., 2,029; Daly, Tax Cut, 1,767; Hass, Soc. Labor, 1,718; Ind. American, 539.

1964 (Pres.), Johnson, Dem., 2,136,615; Goldwater, Rep., 1,060,152; DeBerry, Soc. Workers, 3,817; Hass, Soc. Labor, 1,704; Proh. (no candidate listed), 699, scattering, 145.

1968 (Pres.), Nixon, Rep., 1,370,665; Humphrey, Dem., 1,593,082; Wallace, 3d party, 331,968; Halstead, Soc. Worker, 4,099; Blomen, Soc. Labor, 1,762; Cleaver, New Politics, 4,585; Munn, Proh., 60; scattering, 29.

1972 (Pres.), Nixon, Rep., 1,961,721; McGovern, Dem., 1,459,435; Schmitz, Amer., 63,321; Fisher, Soc. Labor, 2,437; Jenness, Soc. Workers, 1,603; Hall, Com., 1,210.

1976 (Pres.), Carter, Dem., 1,696,714; Ford, Rep., 1,893,742; McCarthy, Ind., 47,905; MacBride, Libertarian, 5,406; Wright, People's, 3,504, Camejo, Soc. Workers, 1,804; LaRouche, U.S. Labor, 1,366; Levin, Soc. Labor, 1,148; scattering, 2,160.

Minnesota

County	1976 Carter (D)	1976 Ford (R)	1980 Carter (D)	1980 Reagan (R)	1980 Anderson (I)
Aitkin	4,308	2,476	3,677	3,390	374
Anoka	48,173	27,863	43,178	30,935	6,503
Becker	6,597	5,611	5,221	6,848	866
Beltrami	7,540	5,214	7,432	6,491	1,238
Benton	6,235	4,099	5,269	5,513	674
Big Stone	2,581	1,332	1,814	1,950	249
Blue Earth	12,930	11,998	10,689	11,658	2,645
Brown	5,792	7,479	4,845	5,514	842
Carlton	9,247	4,371	8,822	4,760	883
Carver	7,574	8,199	6,621	9,909	1,496
Cass	5,424	4,443	4,717	6,119	434
Chippewa	4,648	3,254	3,154	4,252	532
Chisago	6,625	3,874	6,240	5,017	939
Clay	10,876	10,317	8,639	10,004	2,689
Clearwater	2,437	1,374	1,955	1,919	185
Cook	1,018	1,034	871	1,147	182
Cottonwood	3,813	3,906	2,958	4,258	535
Crow Wing	10,653	8,072	9,323	10,1844	1,046
Dakota	44,253	37,542	42,488	40,280	8,469
Dodge	3,009	3,446	2,698	3,900	367
Douglas	7,097	5,910	5,530	7,778	844
Faribault	5,049	5,577	3,824	6,508	548
Fillmore	4,758	5,984	4,010	6,452	645
Freeborn	9,470	8,220	8,202	8,475	798
Goodhue	8,926	9,967	8,566	9,329	1,964
Grant	2,624	1,635	1,822	2,054	333
Hennepin	257,380	211,892	215,960	172,498	52,072
Houston	3,861	4,853	3,218	5,582	477
Hubbard	3,196	2,985	2,840	4,172	365
Isanti	6,013	3,159	5,457	4,480	641
Itasca	12,979	6,646	12,131	8,368	1,073
Jackson	4,311	2,870	3,062	3,391	463
Kanabec	3,188	1,943	2,654	2,500	269
Kandiyohi	9,992	6,664	8,098	8,480	1,244
Kittson	2,008	1,555	1,407	1,875	243
Koochiching	4,846	2,893	4,181	3,433	398
LacQuiParle	3,647	2,292	2,457	2,981	334
Lake	3,973	2,313	3,864	2,414	443
Lake O'Woods	1,105	757	763	1,052	91
Le Sueur	6,556	4,565	5,161	5,478	731
Lincoln	2,594	1,599	1,640	2,022	295
Lyon	7,122	5,036	5,628	5,851	1,129
McLeod	6,249	6,519	4,987	7,817	852
Mahnomen	1,590	905	1,175	1,275	153
Marshall	3,744	2,605	2,636	3,638	397
Martin	5,672	6,484	4,396	6,956	712
Meeker	5,295	4,097	4,238	5,032	668
Mille Lacs	5,172	3,212	4,443	3,860	550
Morrison	8,176	4,590	6,932	6,297	559
Mower	12,837	8,163	10,528	8,298	1,565
Murray	3,685	2,605	2,714	3,004	369
Nicollet	5,777	6,071	5,400	5,436	1,579
Nobles	6,034	4,503	4,703	4,706	657
Norman	2,946	1,983	2,253	2,192	371
Olmsted	14,676	24,030	13,834	22,383	3,551
Otter Tail	11,881	12,113	8,708	15,091	1,515
Pennington	3,787	3,023	3,101	3,715	472
Pine	5,442	3,057	5,121	3,900	467
Pipestone	3,272	3,018	2,392	3,207	561
Polk	9,078	6,522	7,151	9,036	1,207
Pope	3,746	2,251	2,527	3,169	357
Ramsey	133,682	86,480	124,611	78,872	23,331
Red Lake	1,748	737	1,318	1,223	116
Redwood	4,525	4,926	2,952	5,993	548
Renville	5,762	4,482	4,058	5,544	643
Rice	10,590	8,311	9,531	8,168	2,414
Rock	2,769	2,892	2,089	3,164	397
Roseau	3,215	2,382	2,626	3,358	259
St. Louis	75,040	35,331	68,243	33,128	8,659
Scott	9,912	7,154	9,117	9,018	1,475
Sherburne	6,678	4,361	6,229	6,035	985
Sibley	3,752	3,871	2,521	4,458	509
Stearns	25,027	19,574	21,856	24,887	3,555
Steele	6,263	7,053	5,096	7,805	1,087
Stevens	3,171	2,484	2,563	3,283	616
Swift	4,428	2,190	3,245	3,045	511
Todd	6,530	4,278	4,975	6,461	451
Traverse	2,020	1,130	1,256	1,574	169
Wabasha	4,286	4,484	3,712	4,986	549
Wadena	3,164	3,048	2,308	3,474	226
Waseca	4,002	4,582	3,525	4,801	777
Washington	26,454	20,716	25,634	22,718	5,050
Watonwan	3,177	3,351	2,442	3,629	409
Wilkin	2,103	1,882	1,496	2,224	316
Winona	10,939	10,436	9,814	10,332	1,780
Wright	13,379	9,314	12,383	12,293	1,672
Yellow Med	4,337	2,946	2,833	4,003	456

Minnesota Vote Since 1932

1932 (Pres.), Roosevelt, Dem., 600,806; Hoover, Rep., 363,959; Thomas, Soc., 25,476; Foster, Com., 6,101; Coxey, Farm.-Lab., 5,731; Reynolds, Ind., 770.

1936 (Pres.), Roosevelt, Dem., 698,811; Landon, Rep., 350,461; Lemke, Union, 74,296; Thomas, Soc., 2,872; Browder, Com., 2,574; Aiken, Soc. Labor, 961.

1940 (Pres.), Roosevelt, Dem., 644,196; Willkie, Rep., 596,274; Thomas, Soc., 5,454; Browder, Com., 2,711; Aiken, Ind., 2,553.

1944 (Pres.), Roosevelt, Dem., 589,864; Dewey, Rep., 527,416; Thomas, Soc., 5,073; Teichert, Ind. Gov't., 3,176.

1948 (Pres.), Truman, Dem., 692,966; Dewey, Rep., 483,617; Wallace, Prog., 27,866; Thomas, Soc., 4,646; Teichert, Soc. Labor, 2,525; Dobbs, Soc. Workers, 606.

1952 (Pres.), Eisenhower, Rep., 763,211; Stevenson, Dem., 608,458; Hallinan, Prog., 2,666; Hass, Soc. Labor, 2,383; Hamblen, Proh., 2,147; Dobbs, Soc. Workers, 618.

1956 (Pres.), Eisenhower, Rep., 719,302; Stevenson, Dem., 617,525; Hass, Soc. Labor (Ind. Gov.), 2,080; Dobbs, Soc. Workers, 1,098.

1960 (Pres.), Kennedy, Dem., 779,933; Nixon, Rep., 757,915; Dobbs, Soc. Workers, 3,077; Industrial Gov., 962.

1964 (Pres.), Johnson, Dem., 991,117; Goldwater, Rep., 559,624; DeBerry, Soc. Workers, 1,177; Hass, Industrial Gov., 2,544.

1968 (Pres.), Nixon, Rep., 658,643; Humphrey, Dem., 857,738; Wallace, 3d party, 68,931; scattered, 2,443; Halstead, Soc. Worker, 808; Blomen, Ind. Gov't., 285; Mitchell, Com., 415; Cleaver, Peace, 935; McCarthy, write-in, 585; scattered, 170.

1972 (Pres.), Nixon, Rep., 898,269; McGovern, Dem., 802,346; Schmitz, Amer., 31,407; Spock, Peoples, 2,805; Fisher, Soc. Labor, 4,261; Jenness, Soc. Workers, 940;

Hall, Com., 662; scattered, 962.

1976 (Pres.), Carter, Dem., 1,070,440; Ford, Rep., 819,395; McCarthy, Ind., 35,490; Anderson, Amer., 13,592; Camejo, Soc. Workers, 4,149; MacBride, Libertarian, 3,529; Hall, Com., 1,092.

Mississippi

County	1976 Carter (D)	1976 Ford (R)	1980 Carter (D)	1980 Reagan (R)	1980 Anderson (I)
Adams	6,619	6,431	7,213	7,494	151
Alcorn	6,995	3,430	6,222	5,196	898
Amite	2,574	2,256	3,113	2,602	42
Attala	4,068	3,146	4,913	3,973	120
Benton	2,375	790	2,037	1,075	31
Bolivar	7,561	5,136	8,889	5,168	301
Calhoun	2,724	1,892	3,295	2,579	58
Carroll	1,566	1,561	2,035	2,050	20
Chickasaw	2,891	2,581	3,625	2,544	70
Choctaw	1,520	1,562	1,725	1,919	24
Claiborne	2,657	1,078	3,027	1,128	22
Clarke	2,816	2,935	3,303	3,303	41
Clay	3,514	3,017	4,202	3,398	81
Coahoma	6,412	4,269	7,207	4,573	255
Copiah	4,267	4,108	5,546	4,461	78
Covington	2,862	2,591	3,956	3,437	41
DeSoto	7,756	6,240	6,344	9,655	237
Forrest	7,914	10,770	8,274	12,656	275
Franklin	1,578	1,719	1,796	1,923	22
George	3,072	1,957	2,957	3,052	64
Greene	2,127	1,538	1,717	2,146	21
Grenada	3,263	3,569	4,182	3,993	59
Hancock	3,855	3,765	3,544	5,088	159
Harrison	16,569	19,207	16,256	25,078	818
Hinds	28,748	45,803	39,142	48,135	1,414
Holmes	4,616	2,438	5,457	2,692	57
Humphreys	2,172	1,445	2,980	1,839	69
Issaquena	567	325	598	349	5
Itawamba	4,480	2,153	4,851	2,816	0
Jackson	12,533	17,177	12,226	22,498	653
Jasper	3,109	2,356	3,798	2,777	0
Jefferson	2,562	782	2,871	751	38
Jefferson Davis	2,747	1,868	3,829	2,277	22
Jones	10,139	11,098	11,007	12,842	159
Kemper	2,436	1,680	2,601	1,822	12
Lafayette	4,375	3,735	4,794	4,313	241
Lamar	3,109	4,056	3,005	5,395	84
Lauderdale	9,813	14,273	10,015	14,768	910
Lawrence	2,242	2,109	2,702	2,785	60
Leake	3,415	2,952	3,533	3,757	0
Lee	8,504	7,366	10,485	8,308	321
Leflore	6,135	5,872	7,528	5,790	184
Lincoln	4,043	6,084	5,173	7,248	75
Lowndes	6,181	8,003	6,121	9,890	130
Madison	6,240	4,838	7,415	5,987	264
Marion	5,283	5,300	5,343	5,184	0
Marshall	6,769	2,242	7,137	3,481	129
Monroe	6,097	4,737	5,998	4,793	177
Montgomery	2,410	2,278	2,736	2,390	43
Neshoba	3,891	3,859	3,870	5,326	68
Newton	2,741	3,813	3,455	4,317	81
Noxubee	2,121	1,860	3,093	1,875	45
Oktibbeha	4,339	5,194	6,057	6,308	271
Panola	5,517	3,341	6,178	4,219	143
Pearl River	5,024	4,332	5,030	6,719	118
Perry	1,965	1,527	1,955	2,218	25
Pike	5,749	5,659	6,685	6,646	129
Pontotoc	4,066	2,245	4,499	3,189	61
Prentiss	4,431	2,362	4,830	3,260	45
Quitman	2,621	1,287	2,926	1,690	82
Rankin	6,937	11,507	7,996	16,555	286
Scott	3,643	3,649	4,063	4,644	68
Sharkey	1,283	1,024	1,957	996	28
Simpson	3,600	4,291	4,015	5,190	70
Smith	2,434	3,147	2,474	3,772	46
Stone	1,648	1,575	1,821	1,888	53
Sunflower	4,322	3,456	5,035	3,785	82
Tallahatchie	2,991	2,146	3,465	2,211	45
Tate	3,747	2,497	3,892	3,352	94
Tippah	4,260	1,887	3,847	3,273	0
Tishomingo	3,734	1,969	4,595	2,487	79
Tunica	1,695	951	2,198	954	24
Union	5,021	2,507	5,102	3,542	93
Walthall	2,650	2,110	2,966	2,732	34
Warren	6,299	8,699	7,393	10,099	274
Washington	9,650	7,474	10,683	8,948	183
Wayne	3,306	3,022	3,494	3,844	26
Webster	2,218	1,943	2,132	2,358	73
Wilkinson	2,514	1,273	2,981	1,442	25
Winston	3,956	3,659	4,416	3,998	65
Yalobusha	2,603	1,808	3,432	2,224	78
Yazoo	4,053	4,255	5,455	4,806	99
Totals	**381,309**	**366,846**	**429,713**	**440,245**	**11,826**

Mississippi Vote Since 1932

1932 (Pres.), Roosevelt, Dem., 140,168; Hoover, Rep., 5,180; Thomas, Soc., 686.

1936 (Pres.), Roosevelt, Dem., 157,318; Landon, Rep., Howard faction, 2,760; Rowlands faction, 1,675 total 4,435; Thomas, Soc., 329.

1940 (Pres.), Roosevelt, Dem., 168,252; Willkie, Ind. Rep., 4,550; Rep., 2,814; total, 7,364; Thomas, Soc., 103.

1944 (Pres.), Roosevelt, Dem., 158,515; Dewey, Rep., 3,742; Reg. Dem., 9,964; Ind. Rep., 7,859.

1948 (Pres.), Thurmond, States' Rights, 167,538; Truman, Dem., 19,384; Dewey, Rep., 5,043; Wallace, Prog., 225.

1952 (Pres.), Eisenhower, Ind. vote pledged to Rep. candidate, 112,966; Stevenson, Dem., 172,566.

1956 (Pres.), Stevenson, Dem., 144,498; Eisenhower, Rep., 56,372; Black and Tan Grand Old Party, 4,313; total, 60,685; Byrd, Ind., 42,966.

1960 (Pres.), Democratic unpledged electors, 116,248; Kennedy, Dem., 108,362; Nixon, Rep., 73,561. Mississippi's victorious slate of 8 unpledged Democratic electors cast their votes for Sen. Harry F. Byrd (D-Va.).

1964 (Pres.), Johnson, Dem., 52,618; Goldwater, Rep., 356,528.

1968 (Pres.), Nixon, Rep., 88,516; Humphrey, Dem., 150,644; Wallace, 3d party, 415,349.

1972 (Pres.), Nixon, Rep., 505,125; McGovern, Dem., 126,782; Schmitz, Amer., 11,598; Jenness, Soc. Workers, 2,458.

1976 (Pres.), Carter, Dem., 381,309; Ford, Rep., 366,846; Anderson, Amer., 6,678; McCarthy, Ind., 4,074; Maddox, Ind., 4,049; Camejo, Soc. Workers, 2,805; MacBride, Libertarian, 2,609.

Missouri

County	1976 Carter (D)	1976 Ford (R)	1980 Carter (D)	1980 Reagan (R)	1980 Anderson (I)
Adair	3,684	5,249	3,507	5,513	414
Andrew	3,042	3,130	2,585	3,690	245
Atchison	1,126	1,960	1,273	2,095	151
Audrain	5,600	5,378	5,168	6,362	233
Barry	5,046	5,053	4,193	7,038	150
Barton	2,326	2,708	1,901	3,337	115
Bates	4,288	3,350	3,302	4,056	114
Benton	2,684	2,875	2,241	3,451	126
Bollinger	2,740	2,113	2,170	2,863	56
Boone	17,674	16,373	18,516	16,308	3,518
Buchanan	17,427	16,446	16,967	16,551	1,301
Butler	6,759	5,669	6,001	8,797	186
Caldwell	2,113	2,094	1,541	2,551	108
Callaway	4,843	5,115	5,560	6,755	420
Camden	3,975	4,469	3,437	6,590	218
Cape Girardeau	10,440	12,607	8,625	14,861	873
Carroll	3,114	2,936	2,130	3,291	115
Carter	1,154	842	1,088	1,218	37
Cass	9,008	7,182	8,109	10,105	607
Cedar	2,192	2,752	1,832	3,599	94
Chariton	3,055	2,128	2,250	2,641	63
Christian	3,830	4,553	3,502	6,487	205
Clark	1,679	1,582	1,494	2,041	56
Clay	26,609	24,962	24,268	28,508	2,708
Clinton	3,424	2,807	3,001	3,599	184
Cole	7,949	14,370	9,210	16,373	691
Cooper	3,087	3,694	2,687	3,996	110
Crawford	3,565	3,224	2,710	4,081	170
Dade	1,681	2,015	1,283	2,410	15
Dallas	2,453	2,430	2,011	3,297	114
Daviess	2,250	1,919	1,770	2,125	61
DeKalb	2,023	1,739	1,677	2,064	110
Dent	2,931	2,433	2,530	3,117	86
Douglas	1,981	2,652	1,677	3,440	91
Dunklin	7,107	3,314	6,120	5,253	127
Franklin	11,695	12,242	10,480	15,210	863
Gasconade	1,702	3,925	1,550	4,481	136
Gentry	2,249	1,772	1,720	2,005	116
Greene	33,824	37,691	21,071	30,309	2,303
Grundy	2,597	2,646	2,064	2,890	110
Harrison	2,304	2,478	1,732	2,734	140
Henry	5,282	4,168	4,648	4,807	238
Hickory	1,398	1,403	1,248	1,893	48
Holt	1,529	1,777	1,119	1,993	60
Howard	2,769	1,690	2,243	2,179	114
Howell	5,265	4,692	4,472	7,149	214
Iron	2,646	1,765	2,532	2,215	94
Jackson	130,120	101,401	135,805	106,156	12,260
Jasper	14,910	17,086	11,952	21,676	780
Jefferson	25,159	18,261	24,042	28,445	1,745

	1976		1980		
	(D)	(R)	(D)	(R)	(I)
Johnson	5,551	5,513	5,441	6,449	571
Knox	1,319	1,216	1,187	1,475	36
Laclede	4,381	4,067	1,892	3,163	93
Lafayette	6,410	6,823	5,793	7,274	338
Lawrence	5,315	5,784	2,829	4,716	105
Lewis	2,486	1,983	2,204	2,343	73
Lincoln	4,473	3,581	4,110	4,963	182
Linn	4,092	3,114	3,467	3,582	139
Livingston	3,819	3,010	3,368	3,654	204
McDonald	3,111	2,949	2,485	4,114	124
Macon	4,296	3,360	3,578	4,430	135
Madison	2,229	1,739	2,231	2,618	139
Maries	1,796	1,485	1,732	1,985	39
Marion	6,124	5,501	5,890	6,063	192
Mercer	1,177	1,025	821	1,191	54
Miller	2,739	4,095	2,469	5,479	114
Mississippi	3,366	1,733	3,030	2,459	64
Moniteau	2,462	3,077	2,284	3,430	98
Monroe	3,039	1,585	2,445	2,006	51
Montgomery	2,535	2,665	2,007	3,062	121
Morgan	2,738	2,831	2,460	3,577	114
New Madrid	5,319	2,798	4,171	4,041	64
Newton	7,045	7,142	6,793	10,535	339
Nodaway	4,875	4,558	4,257	4,544	414
Oregon	2,564	1,122	2,326	1,523	26
Osage	2,015	3,224	2,045	3,679	72
Ozark	1,341	1,754	1,242	2,435	62
Pemiscot	4,681	2,541	4,140	3,519	52
Perry	2,801	4,086	2,416	5,053	178
Pettis	7,887	7,344	6,475	8,833	435
Phelps	6,261	6,153	5,410	7,366	620
Pike	3,770	3,355	3,454	3,932	158
Platte	8,651	8,103	7,193	9,779	1,051
Polk	3,663	3,893	3,326	4,862	135
Pulaski	4,370	2,865	3,707	3,998	122
Putnam	1,097	1,444	971	1,722	44
Ralls	2,318	1,334	2,069	1,968	75
Randolph	5,839	3,594	4,851	5,100	213
Ray	5,535	2,853	4,518	4,774	215
Reynolds	2,143	879	1,919	1,271	44
Ripley	2,577	1,640	2,156	2,524	61
St. Charles	22,063	26,105	20,438	35,690	2,473
St. Clair	2,271	1,808	1,706	2,439	60
St. Francois	8,852	7,002	7,475	8,907	396
Ste. Genevieve	3,091	2,241	3,324	2,768	151
St. Louis	196,915	246,988	192,889	264,025	25,084
Saline	5,890	4,883	4,943	5,218	353
Schuyler	1,417	1,193	1,114	1,385	48
Scotland	1,449	1,286	1,200	1,592	63
Scott	8,075	5,473	6,854	8,204	194
Shannon	1,960	989	1,818	1,523	40
Shelby	2,227	1,453	1,849	2,151	70
Stoddard	6,097	3,989	5,128	6,167	100
Stone	2,358	3,457	2,210	4,800	180
Sullivan	2,313	2,141	1,834	2,412	54
Taney	3,626	4,696	3,389	6,230	195
Texas	4,638	3,338	4,261	4,879	125
Vernon	4,921	3,715	3,705	4,391	277
Warren	2,164	3,214	2,132	4,366	191
Washington	3,543	2,526	2,883	3,351	87
Wayne	2,987	1,963	2,549	2,813	40
Webster	3,759	3,510	3,429	5,143	149
Worth	969	771	760	833	47
Wright	2,781	3,397	2,182	4,421	56
ST. LOUIS CITY	118,703	58,367	111,326	49,547	5,530
Write-in Vote	1,576	1,365			
Totals	**999,163**	**928,808**	**917,663**	**1,055,355**	**76,488**

Missouri Vote Since 1932

1932 (Pres.), Roosevelt, Dem., 1,025,406; Hoover, Rep., 564,713; Thomas, Soc., 16,374; Upshaw, Proh., 2,429; Foster, Com., 568; Reynolds, Soc. Labor, 404.

1936 (Pres.), Roosevelt, Dem., 1,111,403; Landon, Rep., 697,891; Lemke, Union, 14,630; Thomas, Soc., 3,454; Colvin, Proh., 908; Browder, Com., 417; Aiken, Soc. Labor, 292.

1940 (Pres.), Roosevelt, Dem., 958,476; Willkie, Rep., 871,009; Thomas, Soc., 2,226; Babson, Proh., 1,809; Aiken, Soc. Labor, 209.

1944 (Pres.), Roosevelt, Dem., 807,357; Dewey, Rep., 761,175; Thomas, Soc., 1,750; Watson, Proh., 1,175; Teichert, Soc. Labor, 221.

1948 (Pres.), Truman, Dem., 917,315; Dewey, Rep., 655,039; Wallace, Prog., 3,998; Thomas, Soc., 2,222.

1952 (Pres.), Eisenhower, Rep., 959,429; Stevenson, Dem., 929,830; Hallinan, Prog., 987; Hamblen, Proh., 885; MacArthur, Christian Nationalist, 302; America First, 233; Hoopes, Soc., 227; Hass, Soc. Labor, 169.

1956 (Pres.), Stevenson, Dem., 918,273; Eisenhower, Rep., 914,299.

1960 (Pres.), Kennedy, Dem., 972,201; Nixon, Rep., 962,221.

1964 (Pres.), Johnson, Dem., 1,164,344; Goldwater, Rep., 653,535.

1968 (Pres.), Nixon, Rep., 811,932; Humphrey, Dem., 791,444; Wallace, 3d party, 206,126.

1972 (Pres.), Nixon, Rep., 1,154,058; McGovern, Dem., 698,531.

1976 (Pres.), Carter, Dem., 999,163; Ford, Rep., 928,808; McCarthy, Ind., 24,329.

Montana

	1976		1980		
	Carter	Ford	Carter	Reagan	Anderson
County	(D)	(R)	(D)	(R)	(I)
Beaverhead	1,013	2,461	842	2,956	205
Big Horn	1,962	1,615	1,644	1,730	308
Blaine	1,356	1,349	1,157	1,686	163
Broadwater	557	820	311	1,052	69
Carbon	1,853	2,121	1,468	2,471	331
Carter	344	558	232	766	39
Cascade	14,678	15,289	9,991	15,781	2,456
Chouteau	1,568	1,814	853	2,448	216
Custer	2,425	3,120	1,812	3,516	366
Daniels	797	816	483	1,086	77
Dawson	2,201	2,639	1,544	3,046	425
Deer Lodge	3,859	2,197	3,148	1,905	474
Fallon	847	934	512	2,286	94
Fergus	2,470	3,556	1,510	3,605	316
Flathead	7,827	10,494	6,341	15,010	
Gallatin	6,215	11,062	5,720	670	2,410
Garfield	273	625	169	760	29
Glacier	1,755	1,892	1,399	2,283	277
Golden Valley	255	302	155	362	28
Granite	509	746	439	811	76
Hill	3,878	3,274	2,872	4,413	604
Jefferson	1,210	1,387	1,055	1,841	216
Judith Basin	772	809	480	1,030	93
Lake	3,253	3,809	2,613	5,080	573
Lewis & Clark	8,118	10,155	6,829	12,138	1,792
Liberty	506	638	283	872	71
Lincoln	3,146	3,017	2,427	4,202	485
Madison	870	1,688	182	507	43
McCone	749	730	349	1,000	86
Meagher	364	565	247	689	41
Mineral	819	679	660	800	138
Missoula	15,099	16,350	16,422	12,907	3,238
Musselshell	922	1,117	784	1,279	106
Park	2,364	3,281	1,633	3,887	452
Petroleum	110	211	90	225	15
Phillips	1,117	1,347	745	1,723	146
Pondera	1,413	1,666	897	2,269	207
Powder River	429	683	336	985	103
Powell	1,302	1,610	883	1,770	198
Prairie	415	597	283	580	57
Ravalli	3,504	4,894	3,061	7,339	743
Richland	1,961	2,189	1,262	3,348	343
Roosevelt	2,061	1,822	1,584	2,288	304
Rosebud	1,413	1,538	1,180	1,862	265
Sanders	1,725	1,738	1,395	2,194	291
Sheridan	1,560	1,114	1,003	1,610	242
Silver Bow	11,377	7,506	9,622	7,254	1,739
Stillwater	1,143	1,446	919	1,828	121
Sweet Grass	502	1,135	440	1,169	98
Teton	1,506	1,730	902	2,415	186
Toole	1,080	1,469	634	1,997	154
Treasure	239	315	181	321	34
Valley	2,352	2,520	1,567	3,242	264
Wheatland	535	755	381	742	88
Wibaux	352	308	219	450	45
Yellowstone	18,329	25,201	14,037	23,754	4,329
Totals	**149,259**	**173,703**	**149,259**	**173,703**	**112,137**

Montana Vote Since 1932

1932 (Pres.), Roosevelt, Dem., 127,286; Hoover, Rep., 78,078; Thomas, Soc., 7,891; Foster, Com., 1,775; Harvey, Lib., 1,449.

1936 (Pres.), Roosevelt, Dem., 159,690; Landon, Rep., 63,598; Lemke, Union, 5,549; Thomas, Soc., 1,066; Browder, Com., 385; Colvin, Proh., 224.

1940 (Pres.), Roosevelt, Dem., 145,698; Willkie, Rep., 99,579; Thomas, Soc., 1,443; Babson, Proh., 664; Browder, Com., 489.

1944 (Pres.), Roosevelt, Dem., 112,556; Dewey, Rep., 93,163; Thomas, Soc., 1,296; Watson, Proh., 340.

1948 (Pres.), Truman, Dem., 119,071; Dewey, Rep., 96,770; Wallace, Prog., 7,313; Thomas, Soc., 695; Watson, Proh., 429.

1952 (Pres.), Eisenhower, Rep., 157,394; Stevenson, Dem., 106,213; Hallinan, Prog., 723; Hamblen, Proh., 548;

Hoopes, Soc., 159.

1956 (Pres.), Eisenhower, Rep., 154,933; Stevenson, Dem., 116,238.

1960 (Pres.), Kennedy, Dem., 134,891; Nixon, Rep., 141,841; Decker, Proh., 456; Dobbs, Soc. Workers, 391.

1964 (Pres.), Johnson, Dem., 164,246; Goldwater, Rep., 113,032; Kasper, Nat'l States Rights, 519; Munn, Proh., 499; DeBerry, Soc. Worker, 332.

1968 (Pres.), Nixon, Rep., 138,835; Humphrey, Dem., 114,117; Wallace, 3d party, 20,015; Halstead, Soc. Worker, 457; Munn, Proh., 510; Caton, New Reform, 470.

1972 (Pres.), Nixon, Rep., 183,976; McGovern, Dem., 120,197; Schmitz, Amer., 13,430.

1976 (Pres.), Carter, Dem., 149,259; Ford, Rep., 173,703; Anderson, Amer., 5,772.

Nebraska

	1976		1980		
County	Carter (D)	Ford (R)	Carter (D)	Reagan (R)	Anderson (I)
Adams	4,949	7,612	3,320	8,387	863
Antelope	1,325	2,488	651	3,176	149
Arthur	64	193	56	239	9
Banner	210	281	32	477	14
Blaine	133	281	63	351	15
Boone	1,329	2,035	751	2,509	173
Box Butte	1,516	2,956	1,197	3,871	303
Boyd	792	1,004	353	1,195	55
Brown	557	1,239	336	1,598	94
Buffalo	4,296	8,083	3,141	9,592	1,021
Burt	1,373	2,507	810	2,789	231
Butler	2,336	1,808	1,099	2,576	159
Cass	3,202	3,800	2,004	5,193	568
Cedar	2,225	2,415	1,245	3,242	269
Chase	724	1,146	320	1,583	88
Cherry	906	2,197	484	2,490	99
Cheyenne	1,663	2,285	774	3,056	193
Clay	1,369	2,254	835	2,716	190
Colfax	1,666	2,363	889	3,235	224
Cuming	1,367	3,298	741	3,714	243
Custer	1,985	3,935	1,041	4,542	276
Dakota	2,290	2,629	1,924	3,153	315
Dawes	1,278	2,435	697	3,261	225
Dawson	2,393	5,411	1,401	6,387	333
Deuel	398	775	192	936	60
Dixon	1,286	1,981	818	2,320	197
Dodge	5,276	8,972	3,561	9,527	984
Douglas	61,692	92,980	50,612	94,949	12,828
Dundy	457	774	155	1,054	52
Fillmore	1,483	2,098	1,014	2,424	216
Franklin	941	1,170	439	1,665	109
Frontier	588	994	260	1,338	70
Furnas	1,126	1,884	521	2,360	102
Gage	4,506	5,199	2,245	6,045	717
Garden	445	928	199	1,288	60
Garfield	343	726	236	808	40
Gosper	332	654	181	773	46
Grant	116	313	74	371	12
Greeley	877	787	491	1,023	77
Hall	6,077	10,931	4,471	12,058	949
Hamilton	1,337	2,737	741	3,044	225
Harlan	879	1,325	482	1,684	107
Hayes	267	411	81	608	20
Hitchcock	786	898	326	1,466	114
Holt	1,751	3,389	1,002	4,438	235
Hooker	98	326	63	383	17
Howard	1,316	1,362	782	1,946	168
Jefferson	2,067	2,628	1,110	3,063	295
Johnson	1,115	1,298	618	1,703	176
Kearney	1,218	1,827	748	2,566	240
Keith	1,139	2,485	706	3,353	196
Keya Paha	245	405	117	518	28
Kimball	696	1,257	377	1,590	95
Knox	1,922	2,610	994	3,257	229
Lancaster	28,193	38,937	917	38,487	9,183
Lincoln	5,352	7,074	3,717	9,525	822
Logan	195	283	69	435	17
Loup	140	299	72	366	21
McPherson	104	221	49	284	5
Madison	3,433	7,844	1,908	9,672	542
Merrick	1,360	2,229	707	2,688	208
Morrill	971	1,351	511	2,371	94
Nance	936	1,119	558	1,423	98
Nemaha	1,404	2,092	924	2,682	217
Nuckolls	1,424	1,752	859	2,056	148
Otoe	2,436	3,715	1,468	1,593	150
Pawnee	845	990	430	1,411	121
Perkins	622	981	303	1,331	79
Phelps	1,166	3,209	702	3,246	181
Pierce	1,004	2,172	590	2,916	155
Platte	3,681	7,206	2,282	8,383	502
Polk	1,190	1,795	534	2,195	149
Red Willow	1,722	2,978	896	4,043	255
Richardson	2,415	3,117	1,267	3,433	236
Rock	255	732	136	807	36
Saline	3,205	2,330	1,842	2,831	464
Sarpy	7,384	11,912	5,563	15,286	1,646
Saunders	3,504	3,840	2,014	5,177	508
Scotts Bluff	4,297	6,885	2,828	9,385	652
Seward	2,609	3,215	1,797	3,522	526
Sheridan	810	2,003	363	2,737	120
Sherman	1,078	935	571	1,246	114
Sioux	329	532	117	753	33
Stanton	763	1,462	359	1,941	118
Thayer	1,315	1,994	916	2,499	171
Thomas	103	343	64	304	26
Thurston	1,020	1,290	725	1,448	139
Valley	1,042	1,587	650	2,093	122
Washington	2,233	3,792	1,443	4,533	366
Wayne	1,089	2,521	699	2,747	284
Webster	1,130	1,267	516	1,590	127
Wheeler	146	274	93	367	22
York	1,655	4,202	1,037	4,694	295
Totals	**233,287**	**359,219**	**164,276**	**413,401**	**44,025**

Nebraska Vote Since 1932

1932 (Pres.), Roosevelt, Dem., 359,082; Hoover, Rep., 201,177; Thomas, Soc., 9,876.

1936 (Pres.), Roosevelt, Dem., 347,454; Landon, Rep., 248,731; Lemke, Union, 12,847.

1940 (Pres.), Roosevelt, Dem., 263,677; Willkie, Rep., 352,201.

1944 (Pres.), Roosevelt, Dem., 233,246; Dewey, Rep., 329,880.

1948 (Pres.), Truman, Dem., 224,165; Dewey, Rep., 264,774.

1952 (Pres.), Eisenhower, Rep., 421,603; Stevenson Dem., 188,057.

1956 (Pres.), Eisenhower, Rep., 378,108; Stevenson, Dem., 199,029.

1960 (Pres.), Kennedy, Dem., 232,542; Nixon, Rep., 380,553.

1964 (Pres.), Johnson, Dem., 307,307; Goldwater, Rep., 276,847.

1968 (Pres.), Nixon, Rep., 321,163; Humphrey, Dem., 170,784; Wallace, 3d party, 44,904.

1972 (Pres.), Nixon, Rep., 406,298; McGovern, Dem., 169,991; scattered 817.

1976 (Pres.), Carter, Dem., 233,287; Ford, Rep., 359,219; McCarthy, Ind., 9,383; Maddox, Amer. Ind., 3,378; MacBride, Libertarian, 1,476.

Nevada

	1976		1980		
County	Carter (D)	Ford (R)	Carter (D)	Reagan (R)	Anderson (I)
Churchill	1,800	2,358	1,055	3,841	257
Clark	51,178	48,236	38,240	76,071	8,685
Douglas	1,934	3,095	1,352	5,254	511
Elko	1,955	3,293	1,296	4,393	301
Esmeralda	214	181	110	311	29
Eureka	163	272	103	430	13
Humboldt	1,074	1,380	684	1,950	128
Lander	518	561	361	935	64
Lincoln	642	700	396	1,087	38
Lyon	1,866	2,068	1,288	3,709	271
Mineral	1,361	1,104	631	1,628	147
Nye	1,261	1,027	973	2,387	204
Pershing	633	635	311	877	60
Storey	310	274	222	460	62
Washoe	21,687	29,264	15,544	40,952	5,651
White Pine	2,009	1,543	1,133	8,389	964
CARSON CITY	3,874	5,282			
Totals	**92,479**	**101,273**	**66,468**	**154,570**	**17,580**

Nevada Vote Since 1932

1932 (Pres.), Roosevelt, Dem., 28,756; Hoover, Rep., 12,674.

1936 (Pres.), Roosevelt, Dem., 31,925; Landon, Rep., 11,923.

1940 (Pres.), Roosevelt, Dem., 31,945; Willkie, Rep., 21,229.

1944 (Pres.), Roosevelt, Dem., 29,623; Dewey, Rep., 24,611.

1948 (Pres.), Truman, Dem., 31,291; Dewey, Rep., 29,357; Wallace, Prog., 1,469.

1952 (Pres.), Eisenhower, Rep., 50,502; Stevenson, Dem., 31,688.

1956 (Pres.), Eisenhower, Rep., 56,049; Stevenson, Dem.,

40,640.

1960 (Pres.), Kennedy, Dem., 54,880; Nixon, Rep., 52,387.

1964 (Pres.), Johnson, Dem., 79,339; Goldwater, Rep., 56,094.

1968 (Pres.), Nixon, Rep., 73,188; Humphrey, Dem., 60,598; Wallace, 3d party, 20,432.

1972 (Pres.), Nixon, Rep., 115,750; McGovern, Dem. 66,016.

1976 (Pres.), Carter Dem., 92,479; Ford, Rep., 101,273; MacBride, Libertarian, 1,519; Maddox, Amer. Ind., 1,497; scattered 5,108.

New Hampshire

County	1976 Carter (D)	1976 Ford (R)	1980 Carter (D)	1980 Reagan (R)	Anderson (I)
Belknap	6,143	9,876	...	N/A	...
Carroll	3,374	8,561	...	N/A	...
Cheshire	10,388	12,554	...	N/A	...
Coos	7,385	7,094	...	N/A	...
Grafton	8,996	14,430	...	N/A	...
Hillsborough	45,554	53,581	...	N/A	...
Merrimack	14,865	21,853	...	N/A	...
Rockingham	30,051	36,738	...	N/A	...
Strafford	14,566	14,569	...	N/A	...
Sullivan	6,323	6,679	...	N/A	...
Totals	**147,645**	**185,935**	**...**	**...**	**...**

New Hampshire Vote Since 1932

1932 (Pres.), Roosevelt, Dem., 100,680; Hoover, Rep., 103,629; Thomas, Soc., 947; Foster, Com., 264.

1936 (Pres.), Roosevelt, Dem., 108,640; Landon, Rep., 104,642; Lemke, Union, 4,819; Browder, Com., 193.

1940 (Pres.), Roosevelt, Dem., 125,292; Willkie, Rep., 110,127.

1944 (Pres.), Roosevelt, Dem., 119,663; Dewey, Rep., 109,916; Thomas, Soc., 46.

1948 (Pres.), Truman, Dem., 107,995; Dewey, Rep., 121,299; Wallace, Prog., 1,970; Thomas, Soc., 86; Teichert, Soc. Labor, 83; Thurmond, States' Rights, 7.

1952 (Pres.), Eisenhower, Rep., 166,287; Stevenson, Dem., 106,663.

1956 (Pres.), Eisenhower, Rep., 176,519; Stevenson, Dem., 90,364; Andrews, Const., 111.

1960 (Pres.), Kennedy, Dem., 137,772; Nixon, Rep., 157,989.

1964 (Pres.), Johnson, Dem., 182,065; Goldwater, Rep., 104,029.

1968 (Pres.), Nixon, Rep., 154,903; Humphrey, Dem., 130,589; Wallace, 3d party, 11,173; New Party, 421; Halstead, Soc. Worker, 104.

1972 (Pres.), Nixon, Rep., 213,724; McGovern, Dem., 116,435; Schmitz, Amer., 3,386; Jenness, Soc. Workers, 368; scattered, 142.

1976 (Pres.), Carter, Dem., 147,645; Ford, Rep., 185,935; McCarthy, Ind., 4,095; MacBride, Libertarian, 936; Reagan, write-in, 388; La Rouche, U.S. Labor, 186; Camejo, Soc. Workers, 161, Levin, Soc. Labor, 66; scattered, 215.

New Jersey

County	1976 Carter (D)	1976 Ford (R)	1980 Carter (D)	1980 Reagan (R)	Anderson (I)
Atlantic	41,965	36,733	30,762	36,475	5,078
Bergen	180,738	237,331	133,872	223,164	35,285
Burlington	63,309	60,960	49,421	67,354	11,080
Camden	108,854	82,801	8,414	85,642	15,454
Cape May	16,489	19,498	12,018	21,205	2,341
Cumberland	29.165	20,535	19,268	23,280	3,215
Essex	174,434	133,911	139,062	111,787	19,775
Gloucester	38,726	34,888	29,804	40,306	7,333
Hudson	116,241	92,636	92,493	87,394	8,287
Hunterdon	12,592	19,616	10,569	22,743	3,817
Mercer	69,621	58,453	60,721	53,934	11,581
Middlesex	122,859	113,539	97,404	121,899	17,478
Monmouth	88,956	110,104	71,541	121,871	17,326
Morris	63,749	105,921	49,970	104,889	16,997
Ocean	56,413	77,875	45,560	94,585	9,449
Passaic	76,194	85,102	61,701	82,697	9,532
Salem	12,826	11,639	10,209	13,000	1,800
Somerset	36,258	51,260	29,470	52,591	8,346
Sussex	14,759	23,613	10,535	27,063	27,063
Union	106,267	118,019	76,122	97,624	12,975
Warren	14,238	15,254	10,510	16,934	2,828
Totals	**1,444,653**	**1,509,688**	**1,119,576**	**1,506,437**	**224,173**

New Jersey Vote Since 1932

1932 (Pres.), Roosevelt, Dem., 806,630; Hoover, Rep., 775,684; Thomas, Soc., 42,998; Foster, Com., 2,915; Reynolds, Soc. Labor, 1,062; Upshaw, Proh., 774.

1936 (Pres.), Roosevelt, Dem., 1,083,549; Landon, Rep., 719,421; Lemke, Union, 9,405; Thomas, Soc., 3,895; Browder, Com., 1,590; Colvin, Proh., 916; Aiken, Soc. Labor, 346.

1940 (Pres.), Roosevelt, Dem., 1,016,404; Willkie, Rep., 944,876; Browder, Com., 8,814; Thomas, Soc., 2,823; Babson, Proh., 851; Aiken, Soc. Labor, 446.

1944 (Pres.), Roosevelt, Dem., 987,874; Dewey, Rep., 961,335; Teichert, Soc. Labor, 6,939; Watson, Nat'l. Proh., 4,255; Thomas, Soc., 3,385.

1948 (Pres.), Truman, Dem., 895,455; Dewey, Rep., 981,124; Wallace, Prog., 42,683; Watson, Proh., 10,593; Thomas, Soc., 10,521; Dobbs, Soc. Workers, 5,825; Teichert, Soc. Labor, 3,354.

1952 (Pres.), Eisenhower, Rep., 1,373,613; Stevenson, Dem., 1,015,902; Hoopes, Soc., 8,593; Hass, Soc. Labor, 5,815; Hallinan, Prog., 5,589; Krajewski, Poor Man's, 4,203; Dobbs, Soc. Workers, 3,850; Hamblen, Proh., 989.

1956 (Pres.), Eisenhower, Rep., 1,606,942; Stevenson Dem., 850,337; Holtwick, Proh., 9,147; Hass, Soc. Labor, 6,736; Andrews, Conservative, 5,317; Dobbs, Soc. Workers, 4,004; Krajewski, American Third Party, 1,829.

1960 (Pres.), Kennedy, Dem., 1,385,415; Nixon, Rep., 1,363,324; Dobbs, Soc. Workers, 11,402; Lee, Conservative, 8,708; Hass, Soc. Labor, 4,262.

1964 (Pres.), Johnson, Dem., 1,867,671; Goldwater, Rep., 963,843; DeBerry, Soc. Workers, 8,181; Hass, Soc. Labor, 7,075.

1968 (Pres.), Nixon, Rep., 1,325,467; Humphrey, Dem., 1,264,206; Wallace, 3d party, 262,187; Halstead, Soc. Worker, 8,667; Gregory, Peace Freedom, 8,084; Blomen, Soc. Labor, 6,784.

1972 (Pres.), Nixon, Rep., 1,845,502; McGovern, Dem., 1,102,211; Schmitz, Amer., 34,378; Spock, Peoples, 5,355; Fisher, Soc. Labor, 4,544; Jenness, Soc. Workers, 2,233; Mahalchik, Amer. First, 1,743; Hall, Com., 1,263.

1976 (Pres.), Carter, Dem., 1,444,653; Ford, Rep., 1,509,688; McCarthy, Ind., 32,717; MacBride, Libertarian, 9,449; Maddox, Amer., 7,716; Levin, Soc. Labor, 3,686; Hall, Com., 1,662; LaRouche, U.S. Labor, 1,650; Camejo, Soc. Workers, 1,184; Wright, People's, 1,044; Bubar, Proh., 554; Zeidler, Soc., 469.

New Mexico

County	1976 Carter (D)	1976 Ford (R)	1980 Carter (D)	1980 Reagan (R)	Anderson (I)
Bernalillo	63,949	76,614	...	N/A	...
Catron	517	602	...	N/A	...
Chaves	7,139	10,631	...	N/A	...
Colfax	2,718	2,259	...	N/A	...
Curry	5,004	6,232	...	N/A	...
De Bacat	597	556	...	N/A	...
Dona Ana	12,036	13,888	...	N/A	...
Eddy	9,073	7,698	...	N/A	...
Grant	5,176	4,095	...	N/A	...
Guadalupe	1,379	1,047	...	N/A	...
Harding	285	387	...	N/A	...
Hidalgo	938	891	...	N/A	...
Lea	6,533	8,773	...	N/A	...
Lincoln	1,415	2,320	...	N/A	...
Los Alamos	2,890	5,383	...	N/A	...
Luna	2,872	2,966	...	N/A	...
McKinley	6,856	4,617	...	N/A	...
Mora	1,438	904	...	N/A	...
Otero	5,333	5,914	...	N/A	...
Quay	2,095	2,059	...	N/A	...
Rio Arriba	7,125	3,213	...	N/A	...
Roosevelt	3,111	3,269	...	N/A	...
Sandoval	5,072	4,110	...	N/A	...
San Juan	8,615	10,852	...	N/A	...
San Miguel	5,204	3,162	...	N/A	...
Santa Fe	14,127	11,576	...	N/A	...
Sierra	1,564	1,665	...	N/A	...
Socorro	2,606	2,265	...	N/A	...

	1976 (D)	1976 (R)	1980 (D)	1980 (R)	1980 (I)
Taos	4,414	3,012	...	N/A	...
Torrance	1,526	1,462	...	N/A	...
Union	975	1,146	...	N/A	...
Valencia	8,566	7,851	...	N/A	...
Totals	**201,148**	**211,419**	...	...	...

New Mexico Vote Since 1932

1932 (Pres.), Roosevelt, Dem., 95,089; Hoover, Rep., 54,217; Thomas, Soc., 11,776; Harvey, Lib., 389; Foster, Com., 135.

1936 (Pres.), Roosevelt, Dem., 105,838; Landon, Rep., 61,710; Lemke, Union, 942; Thomas, Soc., 343; Browder, Com., 43.

1940 (Pres.), Roosevelt, Dem., 103,699; Willkie, Rep., 79,315.

1944 (Pres.), Roosevelt, Dem., 81,389; Dewey, Rep., 70,688; Watson, Proh., 148.

1948 (Pres.), Truman, Dem., 105,464; Dewey, Rep., 80,303; Wallace, Prog., 1,037; Watson, Proh., 127; Thomas, Soc., 83; Teichert, Soc. Labor, 49.

1952 (Pres.), Eisenhower, Rep., 132,170; Stevenson, Dem., 105,661; Hamblen, Proh., 297; Hallinan, Ind. Prog., 225; MacArthur, Christian National, 220; Hass, Soc. Labor, 35.

1956 (Pres.), Eisenhower, Rep., 146,788; Stevenson, Dem., 106,098; Holtwick, Proh., 607; Andrews, Ind., 364; Hass, Soc. Labor, 69.

1960 (Pres.), Kennedy, Dem., 156,027; Nixon, Rep., 153,733; Decker, Proh., 777; Hass, Soc. Labor, 570.

1964 (Pres.), Johnson, Dem., 194,017; Goldwater, Rep., 131,838; Hass, Soc. Labor, 1,217; Munn, Proh., 543.

1968 (Pres.), Nixon, Rep., 169,692; Humphrey, Dem., 130,081; Wallace, 3d party, 25,737; Chavez, 1,519; Halstead, Soc. Worker, 252.

1972 (Pres.), Nixon, Rep., 235,606; McGovern, Dem., 141,084; Schmitz, Amer., 8,767; Jenness, Soc. Workers, 474.

1976 (Pres.), Carter, Dem., 201,148; Ford, Rep., 211,419; Camejo, Soc. Workers, 2,462; MacBride, Libertarian, 1,110; Zeidler, Soc., 240; Bubar, Proh., 211.

New York

County	1976 Carter (D-L*)	1976 Ford (R-C**)	1980 Carter (D)	1980 Reagan (R)	1980 Anderson (I)
Albany	71,616	69,592	73,427	51,321	13,747
Allegany	6,134	11,769	5,626	9,839	975
Broome	39,827	50,340	35,726	37,155	10,602
Cattaraugus	13,768	19,469	12,159	16,271	1,651
Cayuga	13,348	19,775	11,534	17,979	2,482
Chautauqua	27,447	33,730	21,575	28,429	4,403
Chemung	17,207	20,640	13,395	18,441	2,154
Chenango	7,356	12,384	6,488	9,791	1,595
Clinton	11,555	15,433	11,363	13,020	1,968
Columbia	10,514	15,871	9,517	13,935	2,072
Cortland	6,947	11,222	5,842	9,445	1,459
Delaware	7,254	12,443	6,299	10,627	1,941
Dutchess	37,531	51,312	28,142	52,795	6,530
Erie	229,397	220,310	209,312	164,066	28,436
Essex	6,556	10,194	6,040	8,293	1,858
Franklin	7,248	8,846	7,633	7,435	1,020
Fulton	9,323	12,161	8,027	11,281	1,526
Genesee	10,803	14,567	10,631	11,435	1,618
Greene	7,740	11,370	5,532	10,564	902
Hamilton	1,052	2,306	921	2,031	176
Herkimer	12,875	15,362	11,343	13,888	1,741
Jefferson	13,503	20,401	12,464	15,748	2,537
Lewis	3,764	5,840	3,954	4,915	707
Livingston	9,629	14,044	8,785	11,086	1,610
Madison	8,822	15,674	7,774	13,247	2,097
Monroe	134,739	167,303	135,561	123,516	27,093
Montgomery	11,271	13,281	5,833	5,928	1,133
Niagara	43,667	46,101	39,511	36,983	5,576
Oneida	47,779	57,655	40,841	47,975	5,108
Onondaga	76,097	115,474	70,293	94,685	16,985
Ontario	14,044	21,118	6,300	8,068	1,405
Orange	40,362	49,685	29,335	45,311	7,004
Orleans	5,927	8,994	5,703	7,379	969
Oswego	16,332	23,949	4,675	21,595	3,059
Otsego	9,787	14,796	8,585	11,629	2,553
Putnam	11,963	18,523	8,101	19,401	2,001
Rensselaer	28,979	40,229	28,407	30,195	5,996
Rockland	48,673	52,087	34,400	57,551	8,381
St. Lawrence	17,503	16,173	17,563	3,373	
Saratoga	23,768	38,296	22,829	32,929	5,987
Schenectady	31,838	40,789	29,548	31,670	5,836
Schoharie	5,250	7,154	4,519	6,139	865
Schuyler	2,885	4,267	2,435	3,727	443
Seneca	5,745	7,659	4,899	7,111	1,195
Steuben	14,685	23,164	12,721	22,056	2,180
Sullivan	14,189	13,709	9,619	15,646	2,086
Tioga	6,969	11,824	6,674	10,277	1,839
Tompkins	12,808	15,463	11,351	11,987	3,716
Ulster	30,190	35,353	20,729	35,159	5,482
Warren	7,264	14,548	6,841	13,089	1,711
Washington	7,262	13,946	6,831	11,975	1,340
Wayne	12,061	19,324	12,370	15,894	2,367
Wyoming	5,737	9,726	5,108	8,047	942
Yates	2,903	5,796	2,820	4,693	680
Outside N.Y. Metro Area	**1,281,893**	**1,607,517**	**1,127,911**	**1,375,216**	**225,286**
Nassau	302,869	329,176	206,590	330,927	44,192
Suffolk	208,263	248,908	137,402	247,900	32,911
Westchester	173,153	208,527	112,246	176,618	25,333
N.Y. Suburban	**648,285**	**786,611**	**456,238**	**745,445**	**102,436**
Bronx	238,786	96,842	177,674	86,599	11,509
Kings	419,382	190,728	295,839	199,568	24,370
New York	337,438	117,702	269,830	114,877	39,305
Queens	379,907	244,396	266,795	249,843	32,238
Richmond	47,867	56,995	35,724	62,721	6,695
N.Y. City	**1,423,380**	**706,633**	**1,045,862**	**713,608**	**114,117**
N.Y. Metro Area	**2,107,665**	**1,493,274**	**1,502,100**	**1,465,053**	**216,553**
D/R Total	**3,244,165**	**2,825,913**	-	-	-
2d party (Lib/Con)	**145,393**	**274,878**	-	-	-
Totals	**3,389,558**	**3,100,791**	**2,627,781**	**2,790,269**	**441,839**

*Democratic and Liberal **Republican and Conservative

New York Vote Since 1932

1932 (Pres.), Roosevelt, Dem., 2,534,959; Hoover, Rep., 1,937,963; Thomas, Soc., 177,397; Foster, Com., 27,956; Reynolds, Soc. Labor, 10,339.

1936 (Pres.), Roosevelt, Dem., 3,018,298; American Lab., 274,924; total 3,293,222; Landon, Rep., 2,180,670; Thomas, Soc., 86,879; Browder, Com., 35,609.

1940 (Pres.), Roosevelt, Dem., 2,834,500; American Lab., 417,418; total, 3,251,918; Willkie, Rep., 3,027,478; Thomas, Soc., 18,950; Babson, Proh., 3,250.

1944 (Pres.), Roosevelt, Dem., 2,478,598; American Lab., 496,405; Liberal, 329,325; total, 3,304,238; Dewey, Rep., 2,987,647; Teichert, Ind. Gov't., 14,352; Thomas, Soc., 10,553.

1948 (Pres.), Truman, Dem., 2,557,642; Liberal, 222,562; total, 2,780,204; Dewey, Rep., 2,841,163; Wallace, Amer. Lab., 509,559; Thomas, Soc., 40,879; Teichert, Ind. Gov't., 2,729; Dobbs, Soc. Workers, 2,675.

1952 (Pres.), Eisenhower, Rep., 3,952,815; Stevenson, Dem., 2,687,890, Liberal, 416,711; total, 3,104,601; Hallinan, American Lab., 64,211; Hoopes, Soc., 2,664; Dobbs, Soc. Workers, 2,212; Hass, Ind. Gov't., 1,560; scattering, 178; blank and void, 87,813.

1956 (Pres.), Eisenhower, Rep., 4,340,340; Stevenson, Dem., 2,458,212; Liberal, 292,557; total, 2,750,769; write-in votes for Andrews, 1,027; Werdel, 492; Hass, 150; Hoopes, 82; others, 476.

1960 (Pres.), Kennedy, Dem., 3,423,909; Liberal, 406,176; total, 3,830,085; Nixon, Rep., 3,446,419; Dobbs, Soc. Workers, 14,319; scattering, 256; blank and void, 88,896.

1964 (Pres.), Johnson, Dem., 4,913,156; Goldwater, Rep., 2,243,559; Hass, Soc. Labor, 6,085; DeBerry, Soc. Workers, 3,215; scattering, 188; blank and void, 151,383.

1968 (Pres.), Nixon, Rep., 3,007,932; Humphrey, Dem., 3,378,470; Wallace, 3d party, 358,864; Blomen, Soc. Labor, 8,432; Halstead, Soc. Worker, 11,851; Gregory, Freedom and Peace, 24,517; blank, void, and scattering, 171,624.

1972 (Pres.), Nixon, Rep., 3,824,642; Conservative, 368,136; McGovern, Dem., 2,767,956; Liberal, 183,128; Reed, Soc. Workers, 7,797; Fisher, Soc. Labor, 4,530; Hall, Com., 5,641; blank, void, or scattered, 161,641.

1976 (Pres.), Carter, Dem., 3,389,558; Ford, Rep., 3,100,791; MacBride, Libertarian, 12,197; Hall, Com., 10,270; Camejo, Soc. Workers, 6,996; LaRouche, U.S. Labor, 5,413; blank, void, or scattered, 143,037.

North Carolina

County	1976 Carter (D)	1976 Ford (R)	1980 Carter (D)	1980 Reagan (R)	1980 Anderson (I)
Alamance	17,371	12,680	15,042	18,072	750
Alexander	5,287	4,661	4,525	6,349	130
Alleghany	2,550	1,532	2,305	1,999	91
Anson	4,796	1,608	4,969	1,965	110
Ashe	5,193	4,937	3,876	5,267	134
Avery	1,869	3,085	1,521	3,463	116
Beaufort	5,728	4,677	6,026	6,772	187
Bertie	4,117	1,332	3,863	1,695	45
Bladen	6,009	1,546	6,102	2,745	64
Brunswick	7,377	3,636	6,761	5,890	246
Buncombe	26,633	22,461	24,837	26,124	2,153
Burke	14,254	10,070	11,679	12,962	565
Cabarrus	12,049	12,455	9,768	15,144	562
Caldwell	11,894	9,872	8,741	12,965	403
Camden	1,231	562	1,212	813	45
Carteret	7,080	5,786	6,451	7,707	452
Caswell	3,707	1,761	3,529	2,156	66
Catawba	16,862	18,696	13,873	22,873	856
Chatham	6,397	4,279	7,144	5,414	481
Cherokee	3,571	3,210	3,114	3,849	80
Chowan	1,862	1,019	2,146	1,424	71
Clay	1,569	1,428	1,324	2,136	51
Cleveland	14,406	8,106	12,218	10,825	320
Columbus	11,148	3,184	10,311	5,423	148
Craven	7,553	5,881	7,781	8,554	356
Cumberland	24,297	14,226	21,029	21,208	1,176
Currituck	1,999	954	1,985	1,668	91
Dare	2,191	1,680	2,497	2,794	256
Davidson	17,859	18,813	14,586	22,794	679
Davie	3,635	4,772	3,289	6,302	223
Duplin	7,696	3,912	7,521	5,403	109
Durham	22,425	18,945	24,809	19,286	3,016
Edgecombe	8,001	4,850	7,945	5,916	148
Forsyth	39,561	38,886	38,740	42,130	2,873
Franklin	5,405	2,630	5,427	3,508	104
Gaston	22,878	19,727	19,016	25,134	791
Gates	2,291	722	2,435	958	61
Graham	1,791	1,621	1,666	2,020	133
Granville	5,244	2,955	5,556	3,513	133
Greene	2,740	1,356	2,835	2,221	34
Guilford	46,826	45,441	44,516	53,291	4,019
Halifax	7,892	5,257	8,583	6,175	214
Harnett	8,992	5,935	8,781	7,265	147
Haywood	10,692	5,885	9,813	7,216	349
Henderson	8,155	10,830	7,572	13,569	901
Hertford	3,986	1,517	4,101	1,853	80
Hoke	3,186	920	3,376	1,168	56
Hyde	1,084	623	1,221	807	35
Iredell	13,295	11,573	11,976	14,920	624
Jackson	5,223	3,536	4,846	4,140	246
Johnston	10,301	8,511	9,595	10,462	267
Jones	2,016	948	2,193	1,396	18
Lee	5,104	3,691	5,426	4,847	251
Lenoir	7,650	7,715	7,545	9,833	263
Lincoln	9,462	6,682	7,796	9,009	299
Macon	4,406	3,673	4,105	4,727	153
Madison	3,433	2,446	3,202	2,629	106
Martin	4,518	1,931	4,750	2,564	80
McDowell	6,246	4,450	4,703	5,683	141
Mecklenburg	63,198	61,715	67,281	68,658	6,591
Mitchell	2,031	3,728	1,765	4,322	146
Montgomery	4,308	2,872	4,136	3,589	104
Moore	7,373	7,577	8,083	10,158	554
Nash	8,937	8,477	8,209	11,097	274
New Hanover	14,504	13,687	13,615	17,153	1,107
Northampton	5,118	1,238	4,940	1,846	62
Onslow	7,954	5,953	7,315	8,785	395
Orange	15,755	9,302	15,230	9,261	3,364
Pamlico	2,113	1,068	2,219	1,502	50
Pasquotank	4,302	2,651	4,128	3,340	179
Pender	4,422	2,063	4,382	3,018	102
Perquimans	1,666	909	1,560	1,210	63
Person	3,977	3,038	4,133	3,278	104
Pitt	11,636	9,532	12,480	12,705	814
Polk	3,155	2,605	2,375	3,020	160
Randolph	12,714	14,337	10,134	19,858	563
Richmond	8,793	2,848	7,410	3,911	211
Robeson	20,695	4,907	17,513	6,971	325
Rockingham	13,413	9,362	11,647	11,143	436
Rowan	15,363	14,644	11,671	18,566	707
Rutherford	10,361	6,718	8,312	8,360	203
Sampson	8,869	6,968	9,087	8,095	308
Scotland	4,430	1,932	4,436	2,123	155
Stanly	9,262	8,845	7,784	9,834	248
Stokes	6,647	6,029	5,764	7,203	151
Surry	10,024	7,403	10,985	10,058	259
Swain	2,141	1,608	1,987	1,457	70
Transylvania	4,636	4,089	3,997	4,808	273
Tyrrell	900	403	887	466	14
Union	10,578	6,184	10,073	9,012	487
Vance	5,620	3,813	5,417	4,217	101
Wake	44,005	44,291	49,001	49,756	5,453
Warren	3,185	1,427	3,751	1,582	74
Washington	2,840	1,486	3,009	1,944	68
Watauga	5,358	5,400	4,835	6,153	645
Wayne	9,265	9,607	9,586	12,860	322
Wilkes	10,176	11,768	8,814	14,462	282
Wilson	8,209	6,795	8,042	8,329	243
Yadkin	4,497	5,916	3,848	7,530	136
Yancey	3,932	2,688	4,010	3,363	100
Totals	**927,365**	**741,960**	**875,776**	**913,898**	**52,364**

North Carolina Vote Since 1932

1932 (Pres.), Roosevelt, Dem., 497,566; Hoover, Rep., 208,344; Thomas, Soc., 5,591.

1936 (Pres.), Roosevelt, Dem., 616,141; Landon, Rep., 223,283; Thomas, Soc., 21; Browder, Com., 11; Lemke, Union 2.

1940 (Pres.), Roosevelt, Dem., 609,015; Willkie, Rep., 213,633.

1944 (Pres.), Roosevelt, Dem., 527,399; Dewey, Rep., 263,155.

1948 (Pres.), Truman, Dem., 459,070; Dewey, Rep., 258,572; Thurmond, States' Rights, 69,652; Wallace, Prog., 3,915.

1952 (Pres.), Eisenhower, Rep., 558,107; Stevenson, Dem., 652,803.

1956 (Pres.), Eisenhower, Rep., 575,062; Stevenson, Dem., 590,530.

1960 (Pres.), Kennedy, Dem., 713,136; Nixon, Rep., 655,420.

1964 (Pres.), Johnson, Dem., 800,139; Goldwater Rep., 624,844.

1968 (Pres.), Nixon, Rep., 627,192; Humphrey, Dem., 464,113; Wallace, 3d party, 496,188.

1972 (Pres.), Nixon, Rep., 1,054,889; McGovern, Dem., 438,705; Schmitz, Amer., 25,018.

1976 (Pres.), Dem., 927,365; Ford, Rep., 741,960; Anderson, Amer., 5,607; MacBride, Libertarian, 2,219; LaRouche, U.S. Labor, 755.

North Dakota

County	1976 Carter (D)	1976 Ford (R)	1980 Carter (D)	1980 Reagan (R)	1980 Anderson (I)
Adams	959	940	469	1,344	100
Barnes	3,321	4,011	2,124	4,379	680
Benson	1,973	1,689	1,112	2,139	260
Billings	285	351	122	521	33
Bottineau	1,987	2,638	1,099	3,386	265
Bowman	911	1,033	454	1,505	142
Burke	899	1,087	418	1,441	82
Burleigh	9,188	13,680	6,103	18,344	2,093
Cass	17,879	22,583	12,980	22,983	5,251
Cavalier	2,178	2,046	1,096	2,560	236
Dickey	1,612	2,027	912	2,452	161
Divide	1,057	881	504	1,264	109
Dunn	1,051	1,041	529	1,689	109
Eddy	1,123	890	537	1,151	144
Emmons	1,459	1,370	502	2,374	137
Foster	1,147	1,120	605	1,534	152
Golden Valley	479	663	259	1,003	61
Grand Forks	11,545	13,820	5,849	12,167	2,533
Grant	952	1,205	315	1,887	109
Griggs	1,122	1,086	635	1,328	156
Hettinger	1,095	1,135	433	1,693	98
Kidder	936	954	325	1,474	70
La Moure	1,718	1,735	847	2,132	254
Logan	809	944	283	1,358	31
McHenry	1,994	2,043	932	2,924	190
McIntosh	912	1,785	307	2,465	64
McKenzie	1,335	1,595	866	2,261	188
McLean	2,815	2,729	1,613	4,229	317
Mercer	1,298	1,982	1,239	3,330	204
Morton	5,241	4,921	2,853	7,644	741
Mountrail	2,189	1,430	1,171	2,146	181
Nelson	1,610	1,336	724	1,600	226
Oliver	529	575	268	962	36
Pembina	2,274	2,810	1,238	3,092	295
Pierce	1,434	1,396	516	2,271	167
Ramsey	3,096	3,293	1,602	4,068	512
Ransom	1,715	1,696	979	1,878	236
Renville	1,008	812	688	1,154	98
Richland	4,592	4,991	2,672	5,649	739
Rolette	2,531	1,094	1,659	1,594	265
Sargent	1,644	1,344	1,048	1,562	173
Sheridan	569	935	208	1,323	59
Sioux	697	354	386	615	66
Slope	347	355	128	461	45
Stark	4,076	4,374	2,061	6,303	707
Steele	1,066	835	617	998	228
Stutsman	4,883	5,653	2,565	6,532	683
Towner	1,216	993	566	1,373	151
Traill	2,352	2,800	1,425	3,080	409
Walsh	3,555	3,518	1,848	4,385	483

	1976 (D)	1976 (R)	1980 (D)	1980 (R)	1980 (I)
Ward	9,484	12,751	5,546	14,969	1,225
Wells	1,742	1,941	501	1,761	0
Williams	4,189	4,230	1,905	4,747	436
Totals	**136,078**	**153,470**	**76,533**	**187,483**	**22,390**

North Dakota Vote Since 1932

1932 (Pres.), Roosevelt, Dem., 178,350; Hoover, Rep., 71,772; Harvey, Lib., 1,817; Thomas, Soc., 3,521; Foster, Com., 830.

1936 (Pres.), Roosevelt, Dem., 163,148; Landon, Rep., 72,751; Lemke, Union, 36,708; Thomas, Soc., 552; Browder, Com., 360; Colvin, Proh., 197.

1940 (Pres.), Roosevelt, Dem., 124,036; Willkie, Rep., 154,590; Thomas, Soc., 1,279; Knutson, Com., 545; Babson, Proh., 325.

1944 (Pres.), Roosevelt, Dem., 100,144; Dewey, Rep., 118,535; Thomas, Soc., 943, Watson, Proh., 549.

1948 (Pres.), Truman, Dem., 95,812; Dewey, Rep., 115,139; Wallace, Prog., 8,391; Thomas, Soc., 1,000, Thurmond, States' Rights, 374.

1952 (Pres.), Eisenhower, Rep., 191,712; Stevenson, Dem., 76,694; MacArthur, Christian Nationalist, 1,075; Hallinan, Prog., 344; Hamblen, Proh., 302.

1956 (Pres.), Eisenhower, Rep., 156,766; Stevenson, Dem., 96,742; Andrews, Amer., 483.

1960 (Pres.), Kennedy, Dem., 123,963; Nixon, Rep., 154,310; Dobbs, Soc. Workers, 158.

1964 (Pres.), Johnson, Dem., 149,784; Goldwater, Rep., 108,207; DeBerry, Soc. Worker, 224; Munn, Proh., 174.

1968 (Pres.), Nixon, Rep., 138,669; Humphrey, Dem., 94,769; Wallace, 3d party, 14,244; Halstead, Soc. Worker, 128; Munn, Prohibition, 38; Troxell, Ind., 34.

1972 (Pres.), Nixon, Rep., 174,109; McGovern, Dem., 100,384; Jenness, Soc. Workers, 288; Hall, Com., 87; Schmitz, Amer., 5,646.

1976 (Pres.), Carter, Dem., 136,078; Ford, Rep., 153,470; Anderson, Amer., 3,698; McCarthy, Ind., 2,952; Maddox, Amer. Ind., 269; MacBride. Libertarian, 256; scattering, 371.

Ohio

County	1976 Carter (D)	1976 Ford (R)	1980 Carter (D)	1980 Reagan (R)	1980 Anderson (I)
Adams	4,450	4,197	3,767	4,989	269
Allen	14,627	23,721	13,140	29,070	1,439
Ashland	7,205	9,761	5,141	11,565	1,105
Ashtabula	20,883	16,885	17,362	19,836	2,481
Athens	9,896	8,387	9,437	8,097	1,528
Auglaize	5,840	9,772	5,022	11,536	784
Belmont	21,162	13,550	16,650	13,597	1,433
Brown	5,432	4,549	4,700	6,050	339
Butler	35,123	49,625	31,795	61,227	4,717
Carroll	5,006	5,091	3,476	5,806	406
Champaign	4,748	6,526	4,109	7,356	596
Clark	26,135	26,745	22,376	27,039	3,375
Clermont	14,850	19,616	13,199	26,674	1,697
Clinton	4,959	6,597	3,967	7,675	608
Columbiana	23,096	22,318	17,455	20,795	2,322
Coshocton	5,827	6,361	4,615	8,059	523
Crawford	7,553	10,801	6,058	12,424	915
Cuyahoga	349,186	255,594	306,405	253,890	41,138
Darke	9,901	11,580	7,635	12,773	1,198
Defiance	5,850	7,526	5,100	9,363	897
Delaware	7,058	12,285	6,418	14,738	1,278
Erie	13,843	14,742	12,323	15,629	1,908
Fairfield	13,361	19,098	13,137	24,073	1,687
Fayette	4,477	5,719	2,811	5,826	327
Franklin	141,624	189,645	38,570	200,369	21,660
Fulton	4,850	7,891	3,972	9,519	1,026
Gallia	4,971	5,198	4,400	6,430	400
Geauga	10,449	15,004	9,437	17,761	2,359
Greene	20,245	22,598	20,068	24,922	3,160
Guemsey	7,573	7,746	5,119	8,179	604
Hamilton	135,605	211,267	128,975	206,854	17,880
Hancock	8,548	15,983	6,949	18,262	1,467
Hardin	4,650	6,076	3,857	7,457	520
Harrison	4,070	3,509	2,844	3,634	341
Henry	4,592	7,656	3,059	7,584	691
Highland	6,327	6,853	4,361	7,356	454
Hocking	5,126	4,114	3,762	4,580	312
Holmes	2,242	2,870	2,093	3,859	329
Huron	7,742	9,386	6,537	11,173	1,110
Jackson	6,699	5,987	4,381	5,876	274
Jefferson	22,318	14,839	20,382	15,777	1,796
Knox	7,361	9,290	6,594	10,371	982
Lake	40,734	36,390	35,159	43,437	6,220
Lawrence	12,072	10,668	11,359	13,794	813
Licking	19,247	23,518	17,176	28,450	2,425
Logan	5,949	9,092	4,312	9,726	717
Lorain	52,387	39,459	40,082	50,083	7,017
Lucas	103,658	76,069	85,221	86,578	16,737
Madison	4,885	7,074	3,530	7,044	436
Mahoning	75,837	46,314	64,159	50,154	9,757
Marion	10,962	13,141	9,419	14,605	1,255
Medina	16,251	19,066	13,565	24,705	2,964
Meigs	5,262	4,942	3,828	4,909	294
Mercer	6,724	7,678	5,506	8,673	941
Miami	13,074	18,686	12,893	19,928	2,429
Monroe	4,296	2,728	3,166	2,869	266
Montgomery	106,468	100,223	104,850	101,232	13,778
Morgan	2,727	2,971	1,875	3,236	156
Morrow	4,870	5,814	3,239	,179	383
Muskingum	14,178	15,358	12,584	17,913	1,332
Noble	2,612	3,007	1,944	3,025	208
Ottawa	9,646	8,241	6,753	8,638	1,281
Paulding	3,229	3,593	2,778	4,971	550
Perry	6,268	5,637	4,385	5,711	373
Pickaway	5,907	7,695	5,068	9,289	518
Pike	5,734	3,729	4,937	4,426	257
Portage	24,417	17,927	20,564	22,827	3,798
Preble	5,850	6,654	5,417	8,375	686
Putnam	5,035	7,332	3,742	9,752	533
Richland	23,065	24,310	18,253	29,198	2,586
Ross	10,743	11,477	9,354	13,251	812
Sandusky	11,202	13,074	8,482	13,420	1,851
Scioto	18,019	13,021	15,412	15,716	898
Seneca	10,074	11,730	7,303	14,170	1,415
Shelby	6,414	8,011	6,423	8,987	895
Stark	70,012	72,607	58,961	87,695	8,022
Summit	123,711	80,415	102,366	92,206	14,997
Trumbull	53,828	36,469	44,352	41,036	6,279
Tuscarawas	16,880	14,279	12,118	15,707	1,777
Union	4,377	7,464	3,037	7,574	421
Van Wert	5,689	8,344	4,070	7,866	741
Vinton	2,629	2,148	2,381	2,484	138
Warren	13,349	16,115	11,303	22,429	1,348
Washington	8,914	11,513	7,936	14,310	1,121
Wayne	13,087	16,976	12,124	18,955	2,311
Williams	4,920	7,596	4,015	9,146	872
Wood	16,926	19,331	14,185	23,307	4,154
Wyandot	4,043	5,661	2,784	5,827	424
Totals	**2,011,621**	**2,000,505**	**1,743,829**	**2,201,864**	**255,521**

Ohio Vote Since 1932

1932 (Pres.), Roosevelt, Dem., 1,301,695; Hoover, Rep., 1,227,679; Thomas, Soc., 64,094; Upshaw, Proh., 7,421; Foster, Com., 7,221; Reynolds, Soc. Labor, 1,968.

1936 (Pres.), Roosevelt, Dem., 1,747,122; Landon, Rep., 1,127,709; Lemke, Union, 132,212; Browder, Com., 5,251; Thomas, Soc., 117; Aiken, Soc. Labor, 14.

1940 (Pres.), Roosevelt, Dem., 1,733,139; Willkie, Rep., 1,586,773.

1944 (Pres.), Roosevelt, Dem., 1,570,763; Dewey, Rep., 1,582,293.

1948 (Pres.), Truman, Dem., 1,452,791; Dewey, Rep., 1,445,684; Wallace, Prog., 37,596.

1952 (Pres.), Eisenhower, Rep., 2,100,391; Stevenson, Dem., 1,600,367.

1956 (Pres.), Eisenhower, Rep., 2,262,610; Stevenson, Dem., 1,439,655.

1960 (Pres.), Kennedy, Dem., 1,944,248; Nixon, Rep., 2,217,611.

1964 (Pres.), Johnson, Dem., 2,498,331; Goldwater, Rep., 1,470,865.

1968 (Pres.), Nixon, Rep., 1,791,014; Humphrey, Dem., 1,700,586; Wallace, 3d party, 467,495; Gregory, 372; Munn, Proh., 19; Blomen, Soc. Labor, 120; Halstead, Soc. Worker, 69; Mitchell, Com., 23.

1972 (Pres.), Nixon, Rep., 2,441,827; McGovern, Dem., 1,558,889; Fisher, Soc. Labor, 7,107; Hall, Com., 6,437; Schmitz, Amer., 80,067; Wallace, Ind., 460.

1976 (Pres.), Carter, Dem., 2,011,621; Ford, Rep., 2,000,505; McCarthy, Ind., 58,258; Maddox, Amer. Ind., 15,529; MacBride, Libertarian, 8,961; Hall, Com., 7,817; Camejo, Soc. Workers, 4,717; LaRouche, U.S. Labor, 4,335; scattered, 130.

Oklahoma

County	1976 Carter (D)	1976 Ford (R)	1980 Carter (D)	1980 Reagan (R)	1980 Anderson (I)
Adair	3,183	3,013	...	N/A	...
Alfalfa	1,725	2,113	...	N/A	...
Atoka	3,276	1,098	...	N/A	...
Beaver	1,213	1,801	...	N/A	...
Beckham	4,530	2,351	...	N/A	...
Blaine	2,297	2,682	...	N/A	...
Bryan	7,410	2,848	...	N/A	...
Caddo	7,382	3,854	...	N/A	...
Canadian	7,288	9,766	...	N/A	...
Carter	8,319	6,668	...	N/A	...
Cherokee	6,006	4,443	...	N/A	...
Choctaw	4,269	1,821	...	N/A	...
Cimarron	962	872	...	N/A	...
Cleveland	20,054	22,098	...	N/A	...
Coal	1,774	769	...	N/A	...
Comanche	12,910	13,163	...	N/A	...
Cotton	1,911	1,127	...	N/A	...
Craig	3,577	2,540	...	N/A	...
Creek	8,964	8,458	...	N/A	...
Custer	4,597	4,847	...	N/A	...
Delaware	4,924	3,642	...	N/A	...
Dewey	1,540	1,230	...	N/A	...
Ellis	1,256	1,429	...	N/A	...
Garfield	8,969	14,202	...	N/A	...
Garvin	6,797	3,905	...	N/A	...
Grady	7,155	4,686	...	N/A	...
Grant	1,853	1,685	...	N/A	...
Greer	2,113	1,164	...	N/A	...
Harmon	1,371	666	...	N/A	...
Harper	978	1,303	...	N/A	...
Haskell	3,388	1,401	...	N/A	...
Hughes	4,185	1,715	...	N/A	...
Jackson	4,914	3,189	...	N/A	...
Jefferson	2,303	956	...	N/A	...
Johnston	2,765	1,127	...	N/A	...
Kay	9,371	12,441	...	N/A	...
Kingfisher	2,372	3,443	...	N/A	...
Kiowa	3,403	1,971	...	N/A	...
Latimer	2,661	1,312	...	N/A	...
Le Flore	8,033	4,907	...	N/A	...
Lincoln	4,988	4,429	...	N/A	...
Logan	4,594	4,382	...	N/A	...
Love	1,923	846	...	N/A	...
McClain	4,048	2,444	...	N/A	...
McCurtain	7,560	3,423	...	N/A	...
McIntosh	4,145	1,822	...	N/A	...
Major	1,357	2,282	...	N/A	...
Marshall	2,939	1,358	...	N/A	...
Mayes	6,298	5,040	...	N/A	...
Murray	2,932	1,563	...	N/A	...
Muskogee	14,678	10,287	...	N/A	...
Noble	2,278	2,634	...	N/A	...
Nowata	2,195	2,077	...	N/A	...
Okfuskee	2,663	1,630	...	N/A	...
Oklahoma	87,185	119,120	...	N/A	...
Okmulgee	8,449	5,333	...	N/A	...
Osage	6,832	6,398	...	N/A	...
Ottawa	7,446	4,985	...	N/A	...
Pawnee	3,031	3,111	...	N/A	...
Payne	9,987	13,481	...	N/A	...
Pittsburg	10,743	4,807	...	N/A	...
Pontotoc	7,466	4,895	...	N/A	...
Pottawatomie	11,255	9,090	...	N/A	...
Pushmataha	2,987	1,360	...	N/A	...
Roger Mills	1,346	873	...	N/A	...
Rogers	7,368	7,318	...	N/A	...
Seminole	5,874	4,237	...	N/A	...
Sequoyah	5,873	3,938	...	N/A	...
Stephens	9,795	7,099	...	N/A	...
Texas	2,591	3,919	...	N/A	...
Tillman	2,852	1,802	...	N/A	...
Tulsa	65,298	108,653	...	N/A	...
Wagoner	5,879	5,071	...	N/A	...
Washington	6,898	14,560	...	N/A	...
Washita	3,304	2,165	...	N/A	...
Woods	2,530	2,788	...	N/A	...
Woodward	2,807	3,782	...	N/A	...
Totals	**532,442**	**545,708**	...	...	...

Oklahoma Vote Since 1932

1932 (Pres.), Roosevelt, Dem., 515,468; Hoover, Rep., 188,165.

1936 (Pres.), Roosevelt, Dem., 501,069; Landon, Rep., 245,122; Thomas, Soc., 2,221; Colvin, Proh., 1,328.

1940 (Pres.), Roosevelt, Dem., 474,313; Willkie, Rep., 348,872; Babson, Proh., 3,027.

1944 (Pres.), Roosevelt, Dem., 401,549; Dewey, Rep., 319,424; Watson, Proh., 1,663.

1948 (Pres.), Truman, Dem., 452,782; Dewey, Rep., 268,817.

1952 (Pres.), Eisenhower, Rep., 518,045; Stevenson, Dem., 430,939.

1956 (Pres.), Eisenhower, Rep., 473,769; Stevenson, Dem., 385,581.

1960 (Pres.), Kennedy, Dem., 370,111; Nixon, Rep., 533,039.

1964 (Pres.), Johnson, Dem., 519,834; Goldwater, Rep. 412,665.

1968 (Pres.), Nixon, Rep., 449,697; Humphrey, Dem., 301,658; Wallace, 3d party, 191,731.

1972 (Pres.), Nixon, Rep. 759,025; McGovern, Dem., 247,147; Schmitz, Amer., 23,728.

1976 (Pres.), Carter, Dem., 532,442; Ford, Rep., 545,708; McCarthy, Ind., 14,101.

Oregon

County	1976 Carter (D)	1976 Ford (R)	1980 Carter (D)	1980 Reagan (R)	1980 Anderson (I)
Baker	3,306	3,340	...	N/A	...
Benton	11,887	15,555	...	N/A	...
Clackamas	42,504	47,671	...	N/A	...
Clatsop	6,690	6,178	...	N/A	...
Columbia	8,005	5,226	...	N/A	...
Coos	14,168	9,481	...	N/A	...
Crook	2,536	2,093	...	N/A	...
Curry	3,227	2,962	...	N/A	...
Deschutes	9,480	9,054	...	N/A	...
Douglas	14,965	16,500	...	N/A	...
Gilliam	508	612	...	N/A	...
Grant	1,393	1,640	...	N/A	...
Harney	1,567	1,652	...	N/A	...
Hood River	3,114	3,210	...	N/A	...
Jackson	23,384	24,237	...	N/A	...
Jefferson	1,769	1,810	...	N/A	...
Josephine	9,061	10,726	...	N/A	...
Klamath	9,659	11,649	...	N/A	...
Lake	1,381	1,575	...	N/A	...
Lane	56,479	46,245	...	N/A	...
Lincoln	6,685	5,755	...	N/A	...
Linn	15,776	14,128	...	N/A	...
Malheur	3,507	5,682	...	N/A	...
Marion	33,781	35,497	...	N/A	...
Morrow	1,162	1,091	...	N/A	...
Multnomah	129,060	112,400	...	N/A	...
Polk	8,141	8,528	...	N/A	...
Sherman	491	567	...	N/A	...
Tillamook	4,456	4,033	...	N/A	...
Umatilla	7,985	9,345	...	N/A	...
Union	4,280	5,111	...	N/A	...
Wallowa	1,310	1,693	...	N/A	...
Wasco	4,560	4,258	...	N/A	...
Washington	34,847	52,376	...	N/A	...
Wheeler	402	355	...	N/A	...
Yamhill	8,881	9,885	...	N/A	...
Totals	**490,407**	**492,120**	...	...	...

Oregon Vote Since 1932

1932 (Pres.), Roosevelt, Dem., 213,871; Hoover, Rep., 136,019; Thomas, Soc., 15,450; Reynolds, Soc. Labor, 1,730; Foster, Com., 1,681.

1936 (Pres.), Roosevelt, Dem., 266,733; Landon, Rep., 122,706; Lemke, Union, 21,831; Thomas, Soc., 2,143; Aiken, Soc. Labor, 500; Browder, Com., 104; Colvin, Proh., 4.

1940 (Pres.), Roosevelt, Dem., 258,415; Willkie, Rep., 219,555; Aiken, Soc. Labor, 2,487; Thomas, Soc., 398; Browder, Com., 191; Babson, Proh., 154.

1944 (Pres.), Roosevelt, Dem., 248,635; Dewey, Rep., 225,365; Thomas, Soc., 3,785; Watson, Proh., 2,362.

1948 (Pres.), Truman, Dem., 243,147; Dewey, Rep., 260,904; Wallace, Prog., 14,978; Thomas, Soc., 5,051.

1952 (Pres.), Eisenhower, Rep., 420,815; Stevenson, Dem., 270,579; Hallinan, Ind., 3,665.

1956 (Pres.), Eisenhower, Rep., 406,393; Stevenson, Dem., 329,204.

1960 (Pres.), Kennedy, Dem., 367,402; Nixon, Rep., 408,060.

1964 (Pres.), Johnson, Dem., 501,017; Goldwater, Rep., 282,779; write-in, 2,509.

1968 (Pres.), Nixon, Rep., 408,433; Humphrey, Dem., 358,866; Wallace, 3d party, 49,683; write-in, McCarthy, 1,496; N. Rockefeller, 69; others, 1,075.

1972 (Pres.), Nixon, Rep., 486,686; McGovern, Dem., 392,760, Schmitz, Amer., 46,211; write-in, 2,289.

1976 (Pres.), Carter, Dem., 490,407; Ford, Rep., 492,120;

McCarthy, Ind., 40,207; write-in, 7,142.

Pennsylvania

County	1976 Carter (D)	1976 Ford (R)	1980 Carter (D)	1980 Reagan (R)	1980 Anderson (I)
Adams	8,771	12,133	7,266	13,760	1,108
Allegheny	328,343	303,127	295,219	270,402	38,818
Armstrong	15,179	13,378	12,719	12,953	1,067
Beaver	46,117	33,593	43,989	31,034	4,431
Bedford	6,652	9,355	5,142	10,888	405
Berks	50,994	54,452	36,441	60,571	10,081
Blair	18,397	28,290	15,008	28,877	2,002
Bradford	7,913	12,851	6,439	13,138	1,055
Bucks	79,838	85,628	59,081	100,163	18,083
Butler	22,611	26,366	19,709	28,821	3,446
Cambria	38,797	32,469	36,274	33,113	2,394
Cameron	1,319	1,616	1,102	1,795	92
Carbon	10,791	8,883	7,986	9,998	937
Centre	17,867	21,177	042	20,636	5,222
Chester	42,712	67,686	32,701	70,825	10,429
Clarion	6,585	8,360	5,475	8,796	670
Clearfield	13,714	13,626	11,738	15,078	929
Clinton	6,532	5,858	4,787	6,283	730
Columbia	12,051	11,508	9,431	12,431	1,189
Crawford	14,712	15,301	11,717	16,321	2,087
Cumberland	23,008	39,950	19,791	40,148	5,438
Dauphin	34,342	46,819	27,313	44,052	6,026
Delaware	117,252	148,679	86,882	142,894	18,383
Elk	6,713	6,159	5,580	6,912	54
Erie	55,385	49,641	46,456	49,724	6,425
Fayette	32,232	20,021	27,906	19,178	1,336
Forest	1,017	1,135	819	1,206	91
Franklin	14,643	20,009	12,150	22,699	1,625
Fulton	1,737	2,219	1,342	2,740	109
Greene	8,769	5,293	8,196	5,333	454
Huntingdon	5,410	7,843	5,090	8,128	568
Indiana	14,650	15,786	13,825	15,606	1,649
Jefferson	7,456	9,437	6,437	9,672	677
Juniata	3,105	3,991	2,696	4,139	280
Lackawanna	57,685	43,354	45,265	43,777	4,094
Lancaster	35,533	72,106	30,142	79,437	7,349
Lawrence	23,337	18,546	19,411	18,314	1,903
Lebanon	11,785	20,880	8,278	24,468	2,271
Lehigh	46,620	46,895	34,747	50,664	8,852
Luzerne	74,655	60,058	59,421	67,868	4,706
Lycoming	18,635	22,648	14,323	22,746	1,921
McKean	6,424	10,305	5,147	9,270	648
Mercer	25,041	22,469	19,563	22,395	3,000
Mifflin	6,210	7,698	5,224	7,548	573
Monroe	9,544	10,228	7,428	12,320	1,973
Montgomery	112,644	155,480	83,792	156,279	25,888
Montour	2,727	3,259	2,271	3,395	390
Northampton	42,514	32,926	31,821	35,635	6,715
Northumberland	18,939	19,283	13,734	20,566	1,471
Perry	4,605	7,454	3,675	8,014	813
Philadelphia	494,579	239,000	419,645	242,078	42,682
Pike	2,775	4,241	2,067	5,069	426
Potter	2,983	3,828	2,293	4,062	222
Schuykill	33,905	31,944	24,809	36,346	3,123
Snyder	3,097	6,557	2,423	7,638	446
Somerset	13,452	15,960	11,564	17,718	806
Sullivan	1,347	1,584	1,074	1,576	130
Susquehanna	6,075	8,331	4,642	8,971	776
Tioga	5,795	8,417	4,269	8,843	647
Union	3,405	6,309	2,686	6,795	623
Venango	8,653	12,270	7,791	11,529	1,013
Warren	7,412	8,508	5,533	9,483	910
Washington	49,317	32,827	46,950	32,821	3,375
Wayne	4,244	7,811	3,359	8,437	482
Westmoreland	74,217	59,172	68,585	62,864	5,9651
Wyoming	3,628	5,705	2,715	5,752	381
York	41,281	56,912	33,323	60,945	5,738
Totals	**2,328,677**	**2,205,604**	**1,930,719**	**2,251,937**	**288,588**

Pennsylvania Vote Since 1932

1932 (Pres.), Roosevelt, Dem., 1,295,948; Hoover, Rep., 1,453,540; Thomas, Soc., 91,119; Upshaw, Proh., 11,319; Foster, Com., 5,658; Cox, Jobless, 725; Reynolds, Indust., 659.

1936 (Pres.), Roosevelt, Dem., 2,353,788; Landon, Rep., 1,690,300; Lemke, Royal Oak, 67,467; Thomas, Soc., 14,375; Colvin, Proh., 6,691; Browder, Com., 4,060; Aiken, Ind. Lab., 1,424.

1940 (Pres.), Roosevelt, Dem., 2,171,035; Willkie, Rep., 1,889,848; Thomas, Soc., 10,967; Browder, Com., 4,519; Aiken, Ind. Gov., 1,518.

1944 (Pres.), Roosevelt, Dem., 1,940,479; Dewey, Rep., 1,835,054; Thomas, Soc., 11,721; Watson, Proh., 5,750; Teichert, Ind. Gov., 1,789.

1948 (Pres.), Truman, Dem., 1,752,426; Dewey, Rep., 1,902,197; Wallace, Prog., 55,161; Thomas, Soc., 11,325; Watson, Proh., 10,338; Dobbs, Militant Workers, 2,133; Teichert, Ind. Gov., 1,461.

1952 (Pres.), Eisenhower, Rep., 2,415,789; Stevenson, Dem., 2,146,269; Hamblen, Proh., 8,771; Hallinan, Prog., 4,200; Hoopes, Soc., 2,684; Dobbs, Militant Workers, 1,502; Hass, Ind. Gov., 1,347; scattered, 155.

1956 (Pres.), Eisenhower, Rep., 2,585,252; Stevenson, Dem., 1,981,769; Hass, Soc. Labor, 7,447; Dobbs, Militant Workers, 2,035.

1960 (Pres.), Kennedy, Dem., 2,556,282; Nixon, Rep., 2,439,956; Hass, Soc. Labor, 7,185; Dobbs, Soc. Workers, 2,678; scattering, 440.

1964 (Pres.), Johnson, Dem., 3,130,954; Goldwater, Rep., 1,673,657; DeBerry, Soc. Workers, 10,456; Hass, Soc. Labor, 5,092; scattering, 2,531.

1968 (Pres.), Nixon, Rep., 2,090,017; Humphrey, Dem., 2,259,405; Wallace, 3d party, 378,582; Blomen, Soc. Labor, 4,977; Halstead, Soc. Workers, 4,862; Gregory, 7,821; others, 2,264.

1972 (Pres.), Nixon, Rep., 2,714,521; McGovern, Dem., 1,796,951; Schmitz, Amer., 70,593; Jenness, Soc. Workers, 4,639; Hall, Com., 2,686; others, 2,715.

1976 (Pres.), Carter, Dem., 2,328,677; Ford, Rep., 2,205,604; McCarthy, Ind., 50,584; Maddox, Constitution, 25,344; Camejo, Soc. Workers, 3,009; LaRouche, U.S. Labor, 2,744; Hall, Com., 1,891; others, 2,934.

Rhode Island

County	1976 Carter (D)	1976 Ford (R)	1980 Carter (D)	1980 Reagan (R)	1980 Anderson (I)
Bristol	11,228	10,131	...	N/A	...
Kent	35,855	34,131	...	N/A	...
Newport	17,768	15,155	...	N/A	...
Providence	144,805	103,976	...	N/A	...
Washington	17,980	17,856	...	N/A	...
Totals	**227,636**	**181,249**	...	...	...

Rhode Island Vote Since 1932

1932 (Pres.), Roosevelt, Dem., 146,604; Hoover, Rep., 115,266; Thomas, Soc., 3,138; Foster, Com., 546; Reynolds, Soc. Labor, 433; Upshaw, Proh., 183.

1936 (Pres.), Roosevelt, Dem., 165,238; Landon, Rep., 125,031; Lemke, Union, 19,569; Aiken, Soc. Labor, 929; Browder, Com., 411.

1940 (Pres.), Roosevelt, Dem., 182,182; Willkie, Rep., 138,653; Browder, Com., 239; Babson, Proh., 74.

1944 (Pres.), Roosevelt, Dem., 175,356; Dewey, Rep., 123,487; Watson, Proh., 433.

1948 (Pres.), Truman, Dem., 188,736; Dewey, Rep., 135,787; Wallace, Prog., 2,619; Thomas, Soc., 429; Teichert, Soc. Labor, 131.

1952 (Pres.), Eisenhower, Rep., 210,935; Stevenson, Dem., 203,293; Hallinan, Prog., 187; Hass, Soc. Labor, 83.

1956 (Pres.), Eisenhower, Rep., 225,819; Stevenson, Dem., 161,790.

1960 (Pres.), Kennedy, Dem., 258,032; Nixon, Rep., 147,502.

1964 (Pres.), Johnson, Dem., 315,463; Goldwater, Rep., 74,615.

1968 (Pres.), Nixon, Rep., 122,359; Humphrey, Dem., 246,518; Wallace, 3d party, 15,678; Halstead, Soc. Worker, 383.

1972 (Pres.), Nixon, Rep., 220,383; McGovern, Dem., 194,645; Jenness, Soc. Workers, 729.

1976 (Pres.), Carter, Dem., 227,636; Ford, Rep., 181,249; MacBride, Libertarian, 715; Camejo, Soc. Workers, 462; Hall, Com., 334; Levin, Soc. Labor, 188.

South Carolina

County	1976 Carter (D)	1976 Ford (R)	1980 Carter (D)	1980 Reagan (R)	1980 Anderson (I)
Abbeville	4,700	1,791	4,049	2,261	111
Aiken	14,927	16,011	12,973	18,528	599
Allendale	2,634	1,064	3,024	1,181	17
Anderson	19,002	9,496	15,642	13,353	384
Bamberg	3,330	1,849	3,208	2,099	17
Barnwell	4,083	2,569	3,399	3,228	64

	1976		1980		
	(D)	(R)	(D)	(R)	(I)
Beaufort	6,049	5,935	7,404	8,603	511
Berkeley	9,741	6,981	9,842	12,510	292
Calhoun	2,055	1,382	1,964	1,767	31
Charleston	34,328	34,010	32,012	38,322	2,182
Cherokee	7,765	3,931	6,887	5,378	85
Chester	5,200	2,982	5,154	3,105	87
Chesterfield	7,687	2,537	6,378	3,459	63
Clarendon	5,489	3,040	5,985	4,163	28
Colleton	5,134	3,324	5,745	4,719	56
Darlington	10,165	6,678	9,151	8,765	211
Dillon	5,089	2,527	4,520	3,385	59
Dorchester	8,046	6,695	4,653	3,227	19
Edgefield	3,216	1,878	3,464	2,460	31
Fairfield	4,155	1,817	4,153	2,098	34
Florence	16,294	13,539	15,937	16,564	289
Georgetown	7,169	4,068	6,609	5,147	151
Greenville	35,923	39,099	32,135	46,168	1,600
Greenwood	9,976	5,974	9,280	7,284	230
Hampton	3,923	1,773	3,390	1,630	33
Horry	15,720	9,339	13,860	14,364	267
Jasper	2,903	1,221	3,312	1,618	33
Kershaw	6,211	6,126	5,103	6,652	145
Lancaster	8,324	4,997	8,158	6,343	331
Laurens	7,440	5,300	7,827	6,010	148
Lee	3,869	2,357	4,706	2,935	18
Lexington	14,339	21,442	12,309	28,271	762
Marion	5,927	3,076	1,760	763	24
Marlboro	5,409	1,961	4,855	2,965	40
McCormick	1,774	640	5,360	2,592	69
Newberry	5,034	4,931	4,825	5,568	80
Oconee	8,447	3,805	4,079	2,036	90
Orangeburg	13,652	8,794	16,128	11,304	141
Pickens	8,505	8,029	7,759	9,517	400
Richland	36,855	32,727	33,766	36,351	1,898
Saluda	2,715	2,085	2,647	2,449	38
Spartanburg	27,925	20,456	28,387	29,939	1,403
Sumter	10,471	9,332	9,223	10,665	252
Union	6,363	3,463	6,274	4,035	93
Williamsburg	8,745	5,275	8,110	5,099	44
York	14,099	9,843	12,056	11,228	535
Totals	**450,807**	**346,149**	**417,633**	**421,117**	**13,990**

South Carolina Vote Since 1932

1932 (Pres.), Roosevelt, Dem., 102,347; Hoover, Rep., 1,978; Thomas, Soc., 82.

1936 (Pres.), Roosevelt, Dem., 113,791; Landon, Rep., Tolbert faction 953, Hambright faction 693, total, 1,646.

1940 (Pres.), Roosevelt, Dem., 95,470; Willkie, Rep., 1,727.

1944 (Pres.), Roosevelt, Dem., 90,601; Dewey, Rep., 4,547; Southern Democrats, 7,799; Watson, Proh., 365; Rep. Tolbert faction, 63.

1948 (Pres.), Thurmond, States' Rights, 102,607; Truman, Dem., 34,423; Dewey, Rep., 5,386; Wallace, Prog., 154; Thomas, Soc., 1.

1952 (Pres.), Eisenhower ran on two tickets. Under state law vote cast for two Eisenhower slates of electors could not be combined. Eisenhower, Ind., 158,289; Rep., 9,793; total, 168,082; Stevenson, Dem., 173,004; Hamblen, Proh., 1.

1956 (Pres.), Stevenson, Dem., 136,372; Byrd, Ind., 88,509; Eisenhower, Rep., 75,700; Andrews, Ind., 2.

1960 (Pres.), Kennedy, Dem., 198,129; Nixon, Rep., 188,558; write-in, 1.

1964 (Pres.), Johnson, Dem., 215,700; Goldwater, Rep., 309,048; write-ins: Nixon, 1, Wallace, 5; Powell, 1; Thurmond, 1.

1968 (Pres.), Nixon, Rep., 254,062; Humphrey, Dem., 197,486; Wallace, 3d party, 215,430.

1972 (Pres.), Nixon, Rep., 477,044; McGovern, Dem., 184,559, United Citizens, 2,265; Schmitz, Amer., 10,075; write-in, 17.

1976 (Pres.), Carter, Dem., 450,807; Ford, Rep., 346,149; Anderson, Amer., 2,996; Maddox, Amer. Ind., 1,950; write-in, 681.

South Dakota

	1976		1980		
	Carter	Ford	Carter	Reagan	Anderson
County	(D)	(R)	(D)	(R)	(I)
Aurora	1,269	831	709	1,241	125
Beadle	4,846	4,758	3,521	5,921	545
Bennett	481	610	345	918	12
Bon Homme	2,154	1,897	1,175	2,725	199
Brookings	4,685	5,278	3,935	5,728	1,171
Brown	8,888	7,609	6,048	10,370	1,143
Brule	1,534	1,175	925	1,674	153
Buffalo	240	194	147	272	26
Butte	1,366	2,055	843	2,850	150
Campbell	489	897	182	1,271	39
Chas. Mix	2,593	1,779	1,741	2,508	203
Clark	1,376	1,449	774	1,963	151
Clay	2,593	2,647	2,271	3,004	906
Codington	4,680	4,504	3,353	5,903	538
Corson	967	846	522	1,233	82
Custer	995	1,373	708	2,057	129
Davison	4,510	3,688	3,076	4,723	529
Day	2,610	1,617	1,720	2,507	259
Deuel	1,465	1,177	891	1,687	157
Dewey	706	820	600	1,045	109
Douglas	975	1,315	508	1,855	91
Edmunds	1,629	1,294	883	1,881	121
Fall River	1,537	2,046	982	2,838	184
Faulk	1,063	868	520	1,300	110
Grant	2,398	2,051	1,502	2,591	251
Gregory	1,658	1,475	883	2,283	121
Haakon	477	812	255	1,152	38
Hamlin	1,402	1,452	903	1,885	197
Hand	1,477	1,510	803	2,066	159
Hanson	1,005	693	598	1,015	93
Harding	459	470	205	727	28
Hughes	2,506	3,997	1,751	4,652	554
Hutchinson	2,062	2,822	1,145	3,789	228
Hyde	572	687	273	864	60
Jackson	313	532	354	929	50
Jerauld	845	821	596	1,019	103
Jones	374	515	189	689	37
Kingsbury	1,762	1,844	1,133	2,377	258
Lake	2,930	2,530	2,212	3,093	499
Lawrence	3,102	4,206	2,259	5,306	574
Lincoln	2,957	3,105	2,261	3,848	524
Lyman	831	892	486	1,256	106
Marshall	1,721	1,233	1,120	1,710	137
McCook	1,822	1,744	1,223	2,014	269
McPherson	693	1,662	287	2,056	54
Meade	2,478	3,096	1,721	5,349	340
Mellette	429	508	279	524	46
Miner	1,289	839	833	1,172	148
Minnehaha	22,068	23,286	20,008	26,256	4,658
Moody	1,942	1,475	1,364	1,807	279
Pennington	10,058	13,352	7,135	18,990	1,651
Perkins	1,262	1,298	595	1,931	92
Potter	908	1,136	434	1,633	81
Roberts	2,890	1,915	1,823	2,904	235
Sanborn	1,025	881	628	1,178	107
Shannon	756	301	1,132	438	91
Spink	2,650	2,003	1,572	2,915	294
Stanley	548	637	339	892	56
Sully	505	630	220	862	50
Todd	826	583	972	803	112
Tripp	1,822	1,980	947	2,669	130
Turner	1,906	2,694	1,459	3,343	281
Union	2,540	2,297	1,830	2,788	360
Walworth	1,516	2,187	753	2,675	139
Washabaugh	276	229			
Yankton	3,987	4,029	2,698	5,355	553
Ziebach	370	369	246	523	27
Totals	**147,068**	**151,505**	**103,909**	**198,102**	**21,342**

South Dakota Vote Since 1932

1932 (Pres.), Roosevelt, Dem., 183,515; Hoover, Rep., 99,212; Harvey, Lib., 3,333; Thomas, Soc., 1,551; Upshaw, Proh., 463; Foster, Com., 364.

1936 (Pres.), Roosevelt, Dem., 160,137; Landon, Rep., 125,977; Lemke, Union, 10,338.

1940 (Pres.), Roosevelt, Dem., 131,862; Willkie, Rep., 177,065.

1944 (Pres.), Roosevelt, Dem., 96,711; Dewey, Rep., 135,365.

1948 (Pres.), Truman, Dem., 117,653; Dewey, Rep., 129,651; Wallace, Prog., 2,801.

1952 (Pres.), Eisenhower, Rep., 203,857; Stevenson, Dem., 90,426.

1956 (Pres.), Eisenhower, Rep., 171,569; Stevenson, Dem., 122,288.

1960 (Pres.), Kennedy, Dem., 128,070; Nixon, Rep., 178,417.

1964 (Pres.), Johnson, Dem., 163,010; Goldwater, Rep., 130,108.

1968 (Pres.), Nixon, Rep., 149,841; Humphrey, Dem., 118,023; Wallace, 3d party, 13,400.

1972 (Pres.), Nixon, Rep., 166,476; McGovern, Dem., 139,945; Jenness, Soc. Workers, 994.

1976 (Pres.), Carter, Dem., 147,068; Ford, Rep., 151,505; MacBride, Libertarian, 1,619; Hall, Com., 318; Camejo, Soc. Workers, 168.

Tennessee

County	1976 Carter (D)	1976 Ford (R)	1980 Carter (D)	1980 Reagan (R)	1980 Anderson (I)
Anderson	13,455	10,494	10,235	14,135	1,161
Bedford	7,228	3,023	5,988	3,377	159
Benton	4,088	1,678	3,775	2,303	73
Bledsoe	1,757	1,620	1,585	1,970	1,161
Blount	12,096	13,851	9,399	17,959	606
Bradley	8,776	9,136	8,014	12,404	338
Campbell	5,206	4,277	4,752	5,540	115
Cannon	2,463	908	2,351	1,373	39
Carroll	5,581	4,031	5,277	5,681	122
Carter	7,443	8,934	6,006	11,848	326
Cheatham	4,225	1,376	3,790	2,314	90
Chester	2,532	1,949	2,123	2,741	52
Claiborne	3,461	3,227	2,844	4,289	94
Clay	1,671	982	1,376	1,344	27
Cocke	3,141	5,004	1,239	6,585	139
Coffee	8,017	3,848	7,621	5,449	239
Crockett	2,963	1,694	2,341	2,024	25
Cumberland	4,543	4,119	3,770	6,351	230
Davidson	99,007	60,662	103,559	66,147	4,826
Decatur	2,432	1,637	2,139	2,095	35
De Kalb	3,222	1,443	2,948	1,841	48
Dickson	6,551	2,285	6,498	3,559	135
Dyer	5,937	4,391	5,688	5,404	153
Fayette	3,853	2,133	4,141	2,944	75
Fentress	1,953	1,767	1,543	2,493	51
Franklin	6,788	2,619	6,760	3,995	248
Gibson	10,356	5,563	9,964	6,784	247
Giles	5,225	1,952	4,699	2,769	89
Grainger	2,018	2,805	1,395	3,254	66
Greene	7,070	8,664	5,822	10,704	338
Grundy	2,850	850	2,835	1,137	30
Hamblen	7,504	6,989	5,889	9,741	336
Hamilton	45,348	47,969	4,913	57,575	2,087
Hancock	764	1,309	702	1,734	33
Hardeman	3,934	2,254	4,153	2,931	73
Hardin	3,438	3,362	3,159	4,184	78
Hawkins	5,931	6,407	5,172	7,775	308
Haywood	3,681	1,952	3,445	2,435	49
Henderson	3,366	4,152	2,702	5,108	75
Henry	7,162	2,585	6,600	4,301	200
Hickman	3,590	1,154	3,223	1,899	79
Houston	1,990	407	1,757	738	31
Humphreys	4,021	1,338	3,972	1,897	74
Jackson	2,959	591	2,471	1,026	26
Jefferson	3,995	5,459	3,180	6,944	201
Johnson	1,464	2,986	1,141	3,705	66
Knox	53,034	56,013	45,078	64,838	4,832
Lake	1,933	591	1,718	823	11
Lauderdale	4,747	2,105	4,318	2,817	73
Lawrence	7,140	4,967	6,082	6,532	212
Lewis	2,391	617	2,190	1,076	33
Lincoln	5,732	1,724	5,386	2,854	115
Loudon	4,683	4,458	3,700	6,382	235
McMinn	7,020	6,638	5,460	7,825	200
McNairy	4,293	3,388	3,801	4,603	76
Macon	1,951	2,063	1,947	2,925	63
Madison	12,989	11,364	12,884	13,666	363
Marion	4,615	2,965	4,623	3,902	92
Marshall	4,457	1,674	4,276	2,283	76
Maury	8,747	5,327	8,157	6,635	199
Meigs	1,254	975	999	1,278	30
Monroe	5,368	5,335	4,612	6,246	125
Montgomery	12,310	5,923	11,573	8,503	492
Moore	1,101	331	993	551	34
Morgan	2,953	1,949	2,088	2,836	73
Obion	7,204	2,986	5,756	5,396	146
Overton	3,897	1,115	3,341	1,869	37
Perry	1,660	520	1,401	783	31
Pickett	948	986	746	1,319	12
Polk	3,284	1,835	2,383	2,364	44
Putnam	8,485	4,079	8,078	6,232	342
Rhea	3,735	3,449	3,099	4,689	93
Roane	9,216	7,121	6,473	11,096	481
Robertson	7,547	2,505	7,381	3,560	126
Rutherford	14,854	7,921	15,212	11,208	703
Scott	2,260	2,432	1,521	3,010	63
Sequatchie	1,733	1,065	1,509	1,512	23
Sevier	3,993	7,608	3,531	10,577	327
Shelby	147,893	128,646	159,246	140,113	7,167
Smith	3,753	1,332	3,674	1,755	69
Stewart	2,442	510	2,274	985	42
Sullivan	23,353	22,087	22,341	26,085	1,873
Sumner	13,848	7,946	14,150	11,876	540
Tipton	5,667	3,329	4,933	4,338	106
Trousdale	1,385	332	1,674	627	30
Unicoi	2,526	3,211	1,880	3,828	97
Union	1,631	1,801	1,435	2,453	44
Van Buren	1,085	346	896	602	14
Warren	6,666	2,364	6,021	3,680	148
Washington	13,951	14,770	11,588	17,447	934
Wayne	1,891	2,597	1,633	3,317	49
Weakley	6,605	2,875	5,911	5,668	136
White	3,874	1,382	3,434	2,099	64
Williamson	8,183	7,880	8,913	11,903	548
Wilson	10,537	4,696	11,238	7,582	380
Totals	**825,879**	**633,969**	**782,624**	**787,962**	**35,892**

Tennessee Vote Since 1932

1932 (Pres.), Roosevelt, Dem., 259,817; Hoover, Rep., 126,806; Upshaw, Proh., 1,995; Thomas, Soc., 1,786; Foster, Com., 234.

1936 (Pres.), Roosevelt, Dem., 327,083; Landon, Rep., 146,516; Thomas, Soc., 685; Colvin, Proh., 632; Browder, Com., 319; Lemke, Union, 296.

1940 (Pres.), Roosevelt, Dem., 351,601; Willkie, Rep., 169,153; Babson, Proh., 1,606; Thomas, Soc., 463.

1944 (Pres.), Roosevelt, Dem., 308,707; Dewey, Rep., 200,311; Watson, Proh., 882; Thomas, Soc., 892.

1948 (Pres.), Truman, Dem., 270,402; Dewey, Rep., 202,914; Thurmond, States' Rights, 73,815; Wallace, Prog., 1,864; Thomas, Soc., 1,288.

1952 (Pres.), Eisenhower, Rep., 446,147; Stevenson, Dem., 443,710; Hamblen, Proh., 1,432; Hallinan, Prog., 885; MacArthur, Christian Nationalist, 379.

1956 (Pres.), Eisenhower, Rep., 462,288; Stevenson, Dem., 456,507; Andrews, Ind., 19,820; Holtwick, Proh., 789.

1960 (Pres.), Kennedy, Dem., 481,453; Nixon, Rep., 556,577; Faubus, States' Rights, 11,304; Decker, Proh., 2,458.

1964 (Pres.), Johnson, Dem. 635,047; Goldwater, Rep., 508,965; write-in, 34.

1968 (Pres.), Nixon, Rep., 472,592; Humphrey, Dem., 351,233; Wallace, 3d party, 424,792.

1972 (Pres.), Nixon, Rep., 813,147; McGovern, Dem., 357,293; Schmitz, Amer., 30,373; write-in, 369.

1976 (Pres.), Carter, Dem., 825,879; Ford, Rep., 633,969; Anderson, Amer., 5,769; McCarthy, Ind., 5,004; Maddox, Am. Ind., 2,303; MacBride, Libertarian, 1,375; Hall, Com., 547; LaRouche, U.S. Labor, 512; Bubar, Proh., 442; Miller, Ind., 316; write-in, 230.

Texas

County	1976 Carter (D)	1976 Ford (R)	1980 Carter (D)	1980 Reagan (R)	1980 Anderson (I)
Anderson	5,499	4,172	5,163	5,970	137
Andrews	1,777	2,127	1,155	2,800	
Angelina	9,750	7,223	10,140	9,900	
Aransas	2,136	1,985	1,800	3,081	134
Archer	1,577	966	1,444	1,804	30
Armstrong	513	506	333	709	9
Atascosa	4,565	2,415	3,980	4,364	93
Austin	2,313	2,686	1,893	3,734	87
Bailey	1,356	1,255	772	1,805	26
Bandera	1,183	1,554	894	2,373	64
Bastrop	4,788	2,383	4,716	3,767	182
Baylor	1,335	783	1,183	1,098	14
Bee	3,690	2,953	3,606	4,171	125
Bell	17,499	15,126	15,823	20,732	934
Bexar	146,581	121,176	137,729	148,126	9,467
Blanco	923	1,015	794	1,434	52
Borden	234	150	131	279	3
Bosque	2,954	1,912	2,431	2,932	62
Bowie	12,445	9,590	11,399	13,942	244
Brazoria	21,711	19,475	18,253	27,614	1,205
Brazos	10,628	15,685	9,856	17,798	1,453
Brewster	1,227	1,368	1,271	1,496	89
Briscoe	823	285	561	562	13
Brooks	2,782	641	2,488	780	43
Brown	5,577	4,483	4,867	6,515	99
Burleson	2,924	1,142	2,615	1,943	33
Burnet	3,818	2,777	3,155	3,364	123
Caldwell	3,647	2,235	3,155	2,879	109
Calhoun	3,642	2,377	3,034	3,312	136
Callahan	2,241	1,581	2,002	2,284	29
Cameron	25,310	16,448	23,209	22,041	804
Camp	2,146	1,133	2,052	1,531	19
Carson	1,542	1,269	1,006	1,888	26
Cass	5,134	3,712	5,578	4,993	60
Castro	2,033	1,007	1,199	1,955	44
Chambers	2,927	1,835	2,517	3,140	96
Cherokee	6,509	3,921	5,592	5,619	91
Childress	1,578	1,043	1,222	1,443	33
Clay	2,568	1,200	2,231	1,824	40
Cochran	1,031	701	513	1,064	23
Coke	844	517	815	706	10
Coleman	2,264	1,669	1,719	2,228	33
Collin	14,039	21,608	15,189	36,559	1,559
Collingsworth	1,169	629	798	1,020	18
Colorado	3,028	2,991	2,377	3,520	58
Comal	4,068	6,377	3,548	9,743	323
Comanche	3,414	1,297	2,550	1,982	39
Concho	715	474	702	700	8
Cooke	4,483	4,804	3,842	6,750	124
Coryell	4,710	4,140	4,097	5,494	228
Cottle	1,047	311	732	511	9

	1976 (D)	1976 (R)	1980 (D)	1980 (R)	1980 (I)
Crane	664	963	607	1,310	23
Crockett	804	802	595	885	10
Crosby	2,176	897	1,393	1,353	17
Culberson	407	373	423	541	7
Dallam	1,029	936	632	1,335	33
Dallas	196,303	263,081	166,328	359,518	12,893
Dawson	2,162	2,474	1,806	3,228	55
Deaf Smith	2,613	2,776	1,666	4,073	77
Delta	1,563	421	1,285	762	18
Denton	18,887	20,440	17,381	29,908	1,953
DeWitt	2,540	2,754	2,044	3,450	69
Dickens	1,222	343	912	554	13
Dimmit	1,721	890	2,102	1,173	25
Donley	1,095	704	741	1,098	22
Duval	4,267	661	3,706	1,012	28
Eastland	4,320	2,340	3,346	3,442	37
Ector	10,802	18,973	8,943	25,846	629
Edwards	258	412	237	575	11
Ellis	9,991	6,996	9,218	10,050	211
El Paso	45,477	42,697	40,082	53,276	5,096
Erath	4,821	2,925	4,141	3,949	83
Falls	4,277	2,261	3,328	2,602	51
Fannin	5,845	2,102	4,895	2,965	71
Fayette	3,428	3,030	2,590	4,104	77
Fisher	1,993	573	1,564	838	23
Floyd	1,991	1,402	1,477	2,043	24
Foard	706	240	617	349	7
Fort Bend	11,264	17,354	11,564	24,914	1,005
Franklin	1,636	758	1,487	1,105	14
Freestone	2,679	1,674	2,649	2,468	34
Frio	2,598	1,280	2,849	1,753	47
Gaines	1,880	1,643	1,182	2,390	46
Galveston	37,873	25,251	30,778	29,527	1,955
Garza	957	755	677	1,188	22
Gillespie	1,260	3,541	1,170	4,736	90
Glasscock	190	218	116	416	2
Goliad	875	846	1,010	1,169	22
Gonzales	3,219	1,789	2,896	2,931	47
Gray	3,872	6,010	2,785	7,187	103
Grayson	17,015	11,981	13,807	16,811	532
Gregg	9,827	17,582	10,219	23,399	311
Grimes	2,656	1,473	2,440	2,087	60
Guadalupe	6,054	6,766	5,049	9,901	407
Hale	5,580	5,390	3,610	7,277	123
Hall	1,633	671	1,057	1,141	13
Hamilton	1,981	1,176	1,556	1,683	30
Hansford	983	1,401	518	2,046	17
Hardeman	1,403	805	1,171	1,056	28
Hardin	6,558	4,046	7,358	6,087	199
Harris	321,897	357,336	272,630	416,965	22,819
Harrison	7,796	7,787	7,746	9,328	125
Hartley	774	811	535	1,248	28
Haskell	2,512	838	1,951	1,447	22
Hays	7,005	5,714	6,013	6,517	590
Hemphill	707	858	592	1,162	21
Henderson	8,245	4,658	8,199	7,903	152
Hidalgo	35,021	19,199	34,152	25,499	1,042
Hill	5,327	2,680	4,688	4,114	71
Hockley	3,949	3,137	2,447	4,599	90
Hood	3,181	1,857	2,237	2,404	75
Hopkins	4,992	2,556	4,344	3,832	193
Houston	3,179	2,229	4,179	2,889	46
Howard	6,984	4,899	4,451	6,658	158
Hudspeth	479	395	394	471	14
Hunt	8,543	6,676	8,652	8,868	322
Hutchinson	3,691	6,137	2,940	7,440	170
Irion	297	302	239	427	2
Jack	1,814	1,049	1,349	1,482	29
Jackson	2,524	1,884	1,826	2,540	66
Jasper	5,422	3,167	5,637	4,015	89
Jeff Davis	309	288	300	409	10
Jefferson	47,581	32,451	45,642	36,763	1,664
Jim Hogg	1,645	429	796	298	16
Jim Wells	7,961	3,547	7,267	4,706	107
Johnson	10,864	7,194	10,137	11,411	333
Jones	3,318	2,072	3,043	2,777	45
Karnes	2,996	1,675	2,299	2,702	51
Kaufman	6,302	3,867	5,618	5,081	99
Kendall	1,190	2,543	1,075	3,890	88
Kenedy	139	65	106	76	0
Kent	474	171	351	339	0
Kerr	3,767	6,021	3,376	9,090	259
Kimble	759	846	608	1,011	22
King	100	96	55	144	5
Kinney	516	318	472	543	23
Kleberg	5,803	3,771	5,125	4,608	331
Knox	1,498	551	1,163	783	17
Lamar	8,601	4,443	6,965	5,964	151
Lamb	3,374	2,413	2,132	3,723	51
Lampasas	2,376	1,563	1,979	2,323	56
LaSalle	1,294	677	1,442	703	19
Lavaca	3,458	2,466	2,678	3,254	54
Lee	1,937	1,348	1,276	1,242	40
Leon	2,085	1,161	2,190	1,768	19
Liberty	7,086	4,552	6,810	7,470	163
Limestone	3,825	2,045	3,408	2,835	45
Lipscomb	644	911	338	1,343	28
Live Oak	1,656	1,287	1,380	2,191	32
Llano	2,361	1,947	2,130	2,866	72
Loving	35	47	21	50	0
Lubbock	24,797	38,478	18,732	46,711	1,952
Lynn	1,575	1,166	1,236	1,603	28
Madison	1,885	1,062	1,583	1,389	32
Marion	1,860	1,291	2,015	1,646	28
Martin	907	698	605	1,095	15
Mason	814	805	630	967	17
Matagorda	4,971	3,679	4,685	5,545	146
Maverick	2,840	924	2,932	1,370	39
McCulloch	1,888	1,300	1,755	1,572	24
McLennan	30,091	25,370	25,371	30,026	857
McMullen	194	217	122	271	4
Medina	3,681	3,252	3,034	4,742	84
Menard	543	441	489	548	11
Midland	7,725	19,178	6,859	25,027	586
Milam	4,871	2,404	4,230	3,251	111
Mills	1,012	684	1,028	985	24
Mitchell	1,730	1,058	1,279	1,263	12
Montague	4,087	2,182	3,233	3,143	59
Montgomery	13,718	15,739	12,593	26,237	819
Moore	2,767	2,759	1,743	3,736	67
Morris	3,071	1,843	3,105	2,133	27
Motley	522	428	341	573	7
Nacogdoches	6,697	7,315	5,981	8,626	422
Navarro	6,995	4,012	6,609	4,791	108
Newton	3,468	1,011	3,237	1,310	24
Nolan	3,094	2,431	2,796	2,781	87
Nueces	52,755	32,797	42,030	37,276	1,810
Ochiltree	1,084	2,471	594	3,022	52
Oldham	554	354	290	557	9
Orange	15,177	9,147	14,936	12,489	395
Palo Pinto	5,170	2,684	4,244	4,068	98
Panola	3,731	3,218	3,637	4,022	58
Parker	8,186	4,692	7,336	8,663	189
Parmer	1,914	1,487	707	2,640	30
Pecos	1,971	2,234	1,602	2,723	37
Polk	4,384	2,529	4,213	3,771	80
Potter	11,917	13,819	9,633	16,327	545
Presidio	1,232	687	1,039	723	22
Rains	1,339	510	1,174	813	19
Randall	9,074	17,115	7,323	23,136	677
Reagan	563	666	414	917	14
Real	510	448	603	832	14
Red River	3,670	1,852	3,491	2,225	31
Reeves	2,613	1,711	21,138	2,315	52
Refugio	2,218	1,537	2,232	1,944	57
Roberts	202	350	138	477	4
Robertson	3,741	1,244	3,572	1,661	33
Rockwall	1,828	2,087	1,985	4,036	113
Runnels	2,068	2,203	1,658	2,552	36
Rusk	6,063	6,800	5,582	8,705	116
Sabine	2,391	904	1,983	1,387	15
San Augustine	1,817	1,047	1,678	1,397	14
San Jacinto	2,406	1,094	1,928	3,158	45
San Patricio	9,469	5,853	8,249	7,662	274
San Saba	1,408	582	1,256	908	23
Schleicher	468	516	444	672	6
Scurry	2,639	2,797	2,003	3,745	53
Shackelford	764	748	606	959	9
Shelby	4,680	2,695	4,215	3,500	69
Sherman	718	679	286	1,128	28
Smith	16,856	22,238	14,838	28,236	414
Somervell	1,054	332	1,015	792	21
Starr	4,646	664	4,782	1,389	50
Stephens	1,796	1,621	1,372	2,161	34
Sterling	174	202	218	364	2
Stonewall	812	252	719	488	6
Sutton	768	831	485	1,000	13
Swisher	2,811	753	1,854	1,450	50
Tarrant	122,287	124,433	121,068	173,466	7,818
Taylor	14,453	19,822	13,244	22,943	620
Terrell	321	317	260	411	4
Terry	2,859	2,113	1,932	3,177	44
Throckmorton	658	356	455	444	7
Titus	4,205	2,603	3,872	3,747	44
Tom Green	11,064	12,316	9,716	15,840	627
Travis	78,585	71,031	75,028	73,151	9,796
Trinity	2,100	1,042	2,510	1,503	32
Tyler	3,322	1,965	3,540	2,545	70
Upshur	4,902	3,272	4,894	4,836	78
Upton	686	869	475	1,150	13
Uvalde	2,299	3,103	2,402	3,887	62
Val Verde	4,603	3,476	3,829	4,768	145
Van Zandt	6,449	3,385	5,707	5,495	81
Victoria	7,326	9,594	7,382	13,392	303
Walker	5,105	4,974	4,804	5,630	274
Waller	2,828	1,992	2,276	2,965	76
Ward	2,046	2,123	1,405	2,912	50
Washington	2,635	3,820	2,518	4,821	95
Webb	10,362	4,222	11,856	5,421	242
Wharton	5,914	4,682	5,142	6,598	160
Wheeler	1,598	1,273	1,090	1,626	16
Wichita	22,017	19,024	17,657	22,884	847
Wilbarger	3,280	2,145	2,347	3,031	48
Willacy	2,984	1,542	2,954	1,942	38
Williamson	9,355	7,481	10,429	15,032	946
Wilson	3,973	1,926	3,097	3,443	74
Winkler	1,382	1,842	1,021	2,160	35
Wise	5,133	2,856	4,646	4,338	116
Wood	4,107	3,076	4,033	4,515	74
Yoakum	1,181	1,477	715	1,937	28

	1976 (D)	1976 (R)	1980 (D)	1980 (R)	1980 (I)
Young	3,473	2,652	2,740	4,227	84
Zapata	1,216	462	1,220	871	19
Zavala	1,822	735	2,621	831	69
Totals	**2,082,319**	**1,953,300**	**1,845,114**	**2,541,519**	**109,747**

Texas Vote Since 1932

1932 (Pres.), Roosevelt, Dem., 760,348; Hoover, Rep., 97,959; Thomas, Soc., 4,450; Harvey, Lib., 324; Foster, Com., 207; Jackson Party, 104.

1936 (Pres.), Roosevelt, Dem., 734,485; Landon, Rep., 103,874; Lemke, Union, 3,281; Thomas, Soc., 1,075; Colvin, Proh., 514; Browder, Com., 253.

1940 (Pres.), Roosevelt, Dem., 840,151; Willkie, Rep., 199,152; Babson, Proh., 925; Thomas, Soc., 728; Browder, Com., 212.

1944 (Pres.), Roosevelt, Dem., 821,605; Dewey, Rep., 191,425; Texas Regulars, 135,439; Watson, Proh., 1,017; Thomas, Soc., 594; America First, 250.

1948 (Pres.), Truman, Dem., 750,700; Dewey, Rep., 282,240; Thurmond, States' Rights, 106,909; Wallace, Prog., 3,764; Watson, Proh., 2,758; Thomas, Soc., 874.

1952 (Pres.), Eisenhower, Rep., 1,102,878; Stevenson, Dem., 969,228; Hamblen, Proh., 1,983; MacArthur, Christian Nationalist, 833; MacArthur, Constitution, 730; Hallinan, Prog., 294.

1956 (Pres.), Eisenhower, Rep., 1,080,619; Stevenson, Dem., 859,958; Andrews, Ind., 14,591.

1960 (Pres.), Kennedy, Dem., 1,167,932; Nixon, Rep., 1,121,699; Sullivan, Constitution, 18,169; Decker, Proh., 3,870; write-in, 15.

1964 (Pres.), Johnson, Dem., 1,663,185; Goldwater, Rep., 958,566; Lightburn, Constitution, 5,060.

1968 (Pres.), Nixon, Rep., 1,227,844; Humphrey, Dem., 1,266,804; Wallace, 3d party, 584,269; write-in, 489.

1972 (Pres.), Nixon, Rep., 2,298,896; McGovern, Dem., 1,154,289; Schmitz, Amer., 6,039; Jenness, Soc. Workers, 8,664; others, 3,393.

1976 (Pres.), Carter, Dem., 2,082,319; Ford, Rep., 1,953,300; McCarthy, Ind., 20,118; Anderson, Amer., 11,442; Camejo, Soc. Workers, 1,723; write-in, 2,982.

Utah

County	1976 Carter (D)	1976 Ford (R)	1980 Carter (D)	1980 Reagan (R)	1980 Anderson (I)
Beaver	963	1,088	619	1,472	43
Box Elder	3,353	9,319	2,138	12,379	296
Cache	5,430	16,636	3,629	20,166	1,488
Carbon	5,157	3,360	4,151	3,752	275
Daggett	131	217	109	288	9
Davis	14,084	31,216	9,030	45,441	2,237
Duchesne	1,110	2,619	845	3,778	82
Emery	1,771	1,717	1,304	3,109	88
Garfield	539	1,163	366	1,548	43
Grand	931	1,781	699	2,360	193
Iron	1,700	4,757	1,236	6,188	238
Juab	1,091	1,290	720	1,869	43
Kane	330	1,094	256	1,483	57
Millard	1,224	2,484	795	3,620	72
Morgan	701	1,356	373	1,985	42
Piute	265	377	157	551	5
Rich	248	541	143	762	18
Salt Lake	86,659	144,100	58,119	167,760	19,4033
San Juan	1,182	1,856	762	2,767	72
Sanpete	1,925	3,683	1,259	5,244	116
Sevier	1,564	3,686	1,110	5,457	126
Summit	1,282	2,316	1,179	3,317	478
Tooele	4,371	4,657	3,122	6,024	392
Unitah	1,342	4,017	1,045	6,020	154
Utah	18,327	49,328	12,131	71,235	1,239
Wasatch	1,092	1,940	917	2,607	297
Washington	1,893	5,944	1,673	10,144	185
Wayne	334	555	225	833	0
Weber	23,111	34,811	15,335	43,685	2,502
Totals	**182,110**	**337,908**	**123,447**	**435,839**	**30,191**

Utah Vote Since 1932

1932 (Pres.), Roosevelt, Dem., 116,750; Hoover, Rep., 84,795; Thomas, Soc., 4,087; Foster, Com., 947.

1936 (Pres.), Roosevelt, Dem., 150,246; Landon, Rep., 64,555; Lemke, Union, 1,121; Thomas, Soc., 432; Browder, Com., 280; Colvin, Proh., 43.

1940 (Pres.), Roosevelt, Dem., 154,277; Willkie, Rep., 93,151; Thomas, Soc., 200; Browder, Com., 191.

1944 (Pres.), Roosevelt, Dem., 150,088; Dewey, Rep., 97,891; Thomas, Soc., 340.

1948 (Pres.), Truman, Dem., 149,151; Dewey, Rep., 124,402; Wallace, Prog., 2,679; Dobbs, Soc. Workers, 73.

1952 (Pres.), Eisenhower, Rep., 194,190; Stevenson, Dem., 135,364.

1956 (Pres.), Eisenhower, Rep., 215,631; Stevenson, Dem., 118,364.

1960 (Pres.), Kennedy, Dem., 169,248; Nixon, Rep., 205,361; Dobbs, Soc. Workers, 100.

1964 (Pres.), Johnson, Dem., 219,628; Goldwater, Rep., 181,785.

1968 (Pres.), Nixon, Rep., 238,728; Humphrey, Dem., 156,665; Wallace, 3d party, 26,906; Halstead, Soc. Worker, 89; Peace and Freedom, 180.

1972 (Pres.), Nixon, Rep., 323,643; McGovern, Dem., 126,284; Schmitz, Amer., 28,549.

1976 (Pres.), Carter, Dem., 182,110; Ford, Rep., 337,908; Anderson, Amer., 13,304; McCarthy, Ind., 3,907; MacBride, Libertarian, 2,438; Maddox, Am. Ind., 1,162; Camejo, Soc. Workers, 268; Hall, Com., 121.

Vermont

County	1976 Carter (D)	1976 Ford (R)	1980 Carter (D)	1980 Reagan (R)	1980 Anderson (I)
Addison	4,164	5,726	...	N/A	...
Bennington	5,443	6,712	...	N/A	...
Caledonia	3,511	5,488	...	N/A	...
Chittenden	17,992	22,013	...	N/A	...
Essex	1,002	1,161	...	N/A	...
Franklin	5,610	6,190	...	N/A	...
Grand Isle	866	1,004	...	N/A	...
Lamoille	2,016	3,535	...	N/A	...
Orange	3,171	4,768	...	N/A	...
Orleans	3,561	4,075	...	N/A	...
Rutland	7,613	9,867	...	N/A	...
Washington	8,764	10,919	...	N/A	...
Windham	6,794	7,928	...	N/A	...
Windsor	8,282	11,001	...	N/A	...
Totals	**78,789**	**100,387**	**...**	**...**	**...**

Vermont Vote Since 1932

1932 (Pres.), Roosevelt, Dem., 56,266; Hoover, Rep., 78,984; Thomas, Soc., 1,533; Foster, Com., 195.

1936 (Pres.), Landon, Rep., 81,023; Roosevelt, Dem., 62,124; Browder, Com., 405.

1940 (Pres.), Roosevelt, Dem., 64,269; Willkie, Rep., 78,371; Browder, Com., 411.

1944 (Pres.), Roosevelt, Dem., 53,820; Dewey, Rep., 71,527.

1948 (Pres.), Truman, Dem., 45,557; Dewey, Rep., 75,926; Wallace, Prog., 1,279; Thomas, Soc., 585.

1952 (Pres.), Eisenhower, Rep., 109,717; Stevenson, Dem., 43,355; Hallinan, Prog., 282; Hoopes, Soc., 185.

1956 (Pres.), Eisenhower, Rep., 110,390; Stevenson, Dem., 42,549; scattered, 39.

1960 (Pres.), Kennedy, Dem., 69,186; Nixon, Rep., 98,131.

1964 (Pres.), Johnson, Dem., 107,674; Goldwater, Rep., 54,868.

1968 (Pres.), Nixon, Rep., 85,142; Humphrey, Dem., 70,255; Wallace, 3d party, 5,104; Halstead, Soc. Worker, 295; Gregory, New Party, 579.

1972 (Pres.), Nixon, Rep., 117,149; McGovern, Dem., 68,174; Spock, Liberty Union, 1,010; Jenness, Soc. Workers, 296; scattered, 318.

1976 (Pres.), Carter, Dem., 77,798; Carter, Ind. Vermonter, 991; Ford, Rep., 100,387; McCarthy, Ind., 4,001; Camejo, Soc. Workers, 430; LaRouche, U.S. Labor, 196; scattered, 99.

Virginia

County	1976 Carter (D)	1976 Ford (R)	1980 Carter (D)	1980 Reagan (R)	1980 Anderson (I)
Accomack	4,807	4,494	4,863	5,342	265
Albemarle	7,310	9,084	7,293	10,424	1,435
Alleghany	2,462	1,756	2,411	2,185	116
Amelia	1,715	1,634	1,643	1,969	52
Amherst	3,675	3,956	3,476	5,088	208

	1976 (D)	1976 (R)	1980 (D)	1980 (R)	1980 (I)
Appomattox	1,702	1,964	1,492	2,549	85
Arlington	32,536	30,972	26,501	30,804	8,042
Augusta	5,626	8,452	5,202	11,011	539
Bath	1,029	888	999	921	70
Bedford	4,766	4,189	4,719	6,605	337
Bland	961	1,047	1,004	1,278	35
Botetourt	4,021	3,343	3,690	4,400	296
Brunswick	3,071	2,387	3,422	2,309	71
Buchanan	5,791	3,850	5,767	4,554	95
Buckingham	2,179	1,487	1,933	1,864	77
Campbell	4,354	7,442	4,473	9,592	396
Caroline	3,064	1,648	2,924	2,071	116
Carroll	4,010	4,820	3,435	5,896	183
Charles City	1,455	439	1,564	506	27
Charlotte	2,312	2,023	2,108	2,322	58
Chesterfield	14,126	27,812	9,828	24,730	1,239
Clarke	1,276	1,440	1,156	1,876	177
Craig	1,103	546	946	768	41
Culpeper	2,892	3,659	2,519	4,312	231
Cumberland	1,302	1,284	1,355	1,515	51
Dickenson	4,583	3,471	3,406	3,083	57
Dinwiddie	3,873	2,413	3,475	3,369	104
Essex	1,306	1,380	1,280	1,581	76
Fairfax	92,037	110,424	34,545	67,154	11,258
Fauquier	4,002	4,715	4,129	6,782	548
Floyd	1,728	2,071	1,642	2,447	126
Fluvanna	1,415	1,296	1,424	1,685	108
Franklin	6,439	3,532	5,685	4,993	304
Frederick	3,389	5,162	2,948	7,298	455
Giles	3,779	2,731	3,689	2,979	211
Gloucester	3,156	3,025	3,138	4,261	354
Goochland	2,259	2,104	2,290	2,423	113
Grayson	3,146	3,021	2,875	3,494	106
Greene	895	1,095	925	1,702	104
Greensville	2,413	1,137	3,092	1,583	39
Halifax	4,352	4,045	4,528	5,088	125
Hanover	6,069	11,559	5,383	14,262	589
Henrico	21,729	45,405	21,023	50,505	2,956
Henry	9,680	5,612	8,900	8,257	355
Highland	493	629	487	741	25
Isle of Wight	4,145	2,718	3,951	3,521	197
James City	3,000	3,186	3,069	4,291	544
King George	1,513	1,383	1,318	1,784	185
King and Queen	1,111	778	1,126	944	42
King William	1,501	1,597	1,446	2,036	89
Lancaster	1,581	2,381	1,567	2,750	106
Lee	5,415	4,679	4,754	4,413	130
Loudoun	7,995	9,192	6,695	12,075	1,311
Louisa	2,857	2,151	2,792	2,612	156
Lunenburg	1,739	1,816	1,958	2,045	122
Madison	1,466	1,710	1,351	1,959	156
Mathews	1,309	1,908	1,300	2,204	148
Mecklenburg	4,076	4,423	3,790	4,853	144
Middlesex	1,312	1,608	1,395	1,810	90
Montgomery	7,539	7,971	7,450	8,217	1,399
Nelson	2,426	1,516	2,410	1,866	143
New Kent	1,338	1,259	1,203	1,739	68
Northampton	2,459	2,043	2,362	2,165	114
Northumberland	1,814	2,167	1,551	2,598	111
Nottoway	2,558	2,486	2,593	2,813	113
Orange	2,309	2,549	2,420	3,381	295
Page	3,401	3,780	2,607	4,297	161
Patrick	2,740	2,349	2,382	3,436	105
Pittsylvania	7,929	9,173	7,645	12,012	249
Powhatan	1,528	2,010	1,484	2,933	98
Prince Edward	2,448	2,734	2,553	2,774	137
Prince George	2,630	2,254	2,308	3,388	130
Prince William	15,215	15,446	12,739	22,997	2,749
Pulaski	5,546	4,764	5,769	5,747	341
Rappahannock	1,071	881	1,055	1,177	99
Richmond	864	1,391	854	1,567	49
Roanoke	13,120	13,587	12,111	17,182	1,286
Rockbridge	2,525	2,157	2,475	2,784	296
Rockingham	5,349	9,768	5,441	11,215	701
Russell	6,014	4,287	5,658	4,750	106
Scott	4,496	4,313	4,273	4,696	108
Shenandoah	3,364	6,296	3,137	7,517	385
Smyth	5,246	5,032	5,335	6,033	224
Southampton	3,399	2,366	3,347	2,997	163
Spotsylvania	4,210	3,210	4,039	5,385	454
Stafford	4,900	4,451	2,961	5,276	477
Surry	1,829	929	1,756	967	63
Sussex	2,497	1,360	2,447	1,664	86
Tazewell	7,565	5,565	7,001	7,019	230
Warren	3,221	2,985	2,597	3,861	297
Washington	6,547	6,865	6,440	8,402	375
Westmoreland	2,355	1,909	2,272	2,510	133
Wise	7,134	5,691	6,778	5,765	198
Wythe	3,578	4,231	3,677	4,758	164
York	4,736	5,603	4,532	6,744	723
Total	**489,208**	**540,351**	...	...	...
CITIES					
Alexandria	19,858	16,880	17,131	17,865	4,546
Bedford	1,122	1,043	1,149	1,145	75
Bristol	3,343	2,943	2,889	3,432	160
Buena Vista	993	771	1,031	942	59
Charlottesville	6,846	6,673	6,866	5,907	1,377
Chesapeake	17,651	12,851	17,152	17,888	1,189
Clifton Forge	993	770	1,102	723	69
Colonial Heights	2,409	4,291	1,652	5,012	219
Covington	1,820	1,173	1,807	1,187	101
Danville	6,425	10,235	6,138	10,665	296
Emporia	899	1,055	855	988	41
Fairfax	3,464	4,174	2,614	4,475	800
Falls Church	2,202	2,323	1,703	2,483	497
Franklin	1,116	1,127	1,324	1,045	62
Fredericksburg	2,550	2,527	2,174	2,502	245
Galax	1,218	1,128	1,061	1,188	31
Hampton	19,202	15,021	18,597	17,051	1,598
Harrisonburg	1,803	3,376	1,845	3,388	403
Hopewell	3,691	3,764	3,102	4,423	178
Lexington	945	1,027	963	960	129
Lynchburg	8,227	14,564	6,475	11,600	654
Manassas	1,646	1,992	1,565	3,009	318
Manassas Park	709	444	447	729	52
Martinsville	3,491	3,147	3,337	3,433	162
Newport News	23,058	20,914	21,758	22,425	2,069
Norfolk	39,295	28,099	35,281	27,504	3,436
Norton	811	577	762	572	42
Petersburg	7,852	5,041	7,931	5,001	254
Poquoson	1,140	1,461	877	2,338	158
Portsmouth	22,837	12,872	20,899	13,656	1,123
Radford	2,240	1,844	2,225	1,964	233
Richmond	44,687	37,176	47,939	34,583	3,496
Roanoke	20,696	14,738	18,139	15,164	1,350
Salem	4,404	4,196	4,091	4,862	359
South Boston	1,001	1,389	971	1,615	51
Staunton	2,951	4,681	2,658	4,819	311
Suffolk	9,246	6,066	9,064	7,299	358
Virginia Beach	25,824	34,593	22,042	43,623	4,393
Waynesboro	2,209	3,528	1,926	3,697	255
Williamsburg	1,468	1,654	1,199	1,344	340
Winchester	2,346	4,075	2,006	4,240	320
Total	**324,688**	**296,203**	...	...	...
Aggregate	**813,896**	**836,554**	**743,780**	**975,461**	**91,637**

Virginia Vote Since 1932

1932 (Pres.), Roosevelt, Dem., 203,979; Hoover, Rep., 89,637; Thomas, Soc., 2,382; Upshaw, Proh., 1,843; Foster, Com., 86; Cox, Ind. 15.

1936 (Pres.), Roosevelt, Dem., 234,980; Landon, Rep., 98,366; Colvin, Proh., 594; Thomas, Soc., 313; Lemke, Union, 233; Browder, Com., 98.

1940 (Pres.), Roosevelt, Dem., 235,961; Willkie, Rep., 109,363; Babson, Proh., 882; Thomas, Soc., 282; Browder, Com., 71; Aiken, Soc. Labor, 48.

1944 (Pres.), Roosevelt, Dem., 242,276; Dewey, Rep., 145,243; Watson, Proh., 459; Thomas, Soc., 417; Teichert, Soc. Labor, 90.

1948 (Pres.), Truman, Dem., 200,786; Dewey, Rep., 172,070; Thurmond, States' Rights, 43,393; Wallace, Prog., 2,047; Thomas, Soc., 726; Teichert, Soc. Labor, 234.

1952 (Pres.), Eisenhower, Rep., 349,037; Stevenson, Dem., 268,677; Hass, Soc. Labor, 1,160; Hoopes, Social Dem., 504; Hallinan, Prog., 311.

1956 (Pres.), Eisenhower, Rep., 386,459; Stevenson, Dem., 267,760; Andrews, States' Rights, 42,964; Hoopes, Soc. Dem., 444; Hass, Soc. Labor, 351.

1960 (Pres.), Kennedy, Dem., 362,327; Nixon, Rep., 404,521; Coiner, Conservative, 4,204; Hass, Soc. Labor, 397.

1964 (Pres.), Johnson, Dem., 558,038; Goldwater, Rep., 481,334; Hass, Soc. Labor, 2,895.

1968 (Pres.), Nixon, Rep., 590,319; Humphrey, Dem., 442,387; Wallace, 3d party, *320,272; Blomen, Soc. Labor, 4,671; Munn, Proh., 601; Gregory, Peace and Freedom, 1,680.

*10,561 votes for Wallace were omitted in the count.

1972 (Pres.), Nixon, Rep., 988,493; McGovern, Dem., 438,887; Schmitz, Amer., 19,721; Fisher, Soc. Labor, 9,918.

1976 (Pres.), Carter, Dem., 813,896; Ford, Rep., 836,554; Camejo, Soc. Workers, 17,802; Anderson, Amer., 16,686; LaRouche, U.S. Labor, 7,508; MacBride, Libertarian, 4,648.

Washington

County	1976 Carter (D)	1976 Ford (R)	1980 Carter (D)	1980 Reagan (R)	1980 Anderson (I)
Adams	1,790	2,795	1,079	2,726	213
Asotin	2,898	2,752	2,620	3,163	522
Benton	11,306	22,135	10,131	25,584	2,896

	1976 (D)	1976 (R)	1980 (D)	1980 (R)	1980 (I)
Chelan	7,623	10,492	5,581	9,534	1,338
Clallam	8,268	9,132	7,079	9,942	1,909
Clark	31,080	27,938	29,610	32,022	6,117
Columbia	829	1,153	575	1,324	113
Cowlitz	14,958	12,531	11,177	11,686	2,314
Douglas	3,809	4,547	2,475	4,545	474
Ferry	814	776	718	974	113
Franklin	4,369	5,671	3,149	6,291	582
Garfield	616	892	399	680	91
Grant	7,777	9,192	4,886	9,540	900
Grays Harbor	13,478	9,464	10,230	8,852	3,155
Island	5,859	7,804	4,697	9,050	1,542
Jefferson	2,913	2,794	2,512	2,722	708
King	248,743	279,382	214,656	245,196	69,225
Kitsap	25,701	23,124	18,034	25,098	7,444
Kittitas	4,858	4,765	3,659	4,651	938
Klickitat	2,890	2,573	2,297	2,715	359
Lewis	9,026	10,933	6,170	12,034	1,376
Lincoln	1,978	2,925	1,378	2,860	287
Mason	6,060	4,758	4,581	5,730	1,163
Okanogan	5,543	5,455	4,384	6,159	948
Pacific	4,278	2,781	3,655	3,076	916
Pend Oreille	1,533	1,516	1,155	1,807	168
Pierce	78,238	74,668	52,129	71,160	14,695
San Juan	1,467	1,998	1,300	1,770	542
Skagit	12,718	13,060	9,954	13,668	2,498
Skamania	1,436	1,102	1,267	1,263	181
Snohomish	55,623	55,375	49,189	62,434	13,621
Spokane	55,660	68,290	44,439	69,599	10,015
Stevens	3,824	4,719	3,083	6,092	502
Thurston	21,247	21,000	18,784	24,042	5,451
Wahkiakum	942	704	670	753	138
Walla Walla	7,012	10,883	5,471	10,564	1,488
Whatcom	19,739	20,007	16,044	18,241	4,341
Whitman	6,197	8,168	5,569	8,405	2,259
Yakima	24,223	29,478	18,810	28,441	3,902
Totals	**717,323**	**777,732**	**583,596**	**764,393**	**165,443**

Washington Vote Since 1932

1932 (Pres.), Roosevelt, Dem., 353,260; Hoover, Rep., 208,645; Harvey, Lib., 30,308; Thomas, Soc., 17,080; Foster, Com., 2,972; Upshaw, Proh., 1,540; Reynolds, Soc. Labor, 1,009.

1936 (Pres.), Roosevelt, Dem., 459,579; Landon, Rep., 206,892; Lemke, Union, 17,463; Thomas, Soc., 3,496; Browder, Com., 1,907; Pellsy, Christian, 1,598; Colvin, Proh., 1,041; Aiken, Soc. Labor, 362.

1940 (Pres.), Roosevelt, Dem., 462,145; Willkie, Rep., 322,123; Thomas, Soc., 4,586; Browder, Com., 2,626; Babson, Proh., 1,686; Aiken, Soc. Labor, 667.

1944 (Pres.), Roosevelt, Dem., 486,774; Dewey, Rep., 361,689; Thomas, Soc., 3,824; Watson, Proh., 2,396; Teichert, Soc. Labor, 1,645.

1948 (Pres.), Truman, Dem., 476,165; Dewey, Rep., 386,315; Wallace, Prog., 31,692; Watson, Proh., 6,117; Thomas, Soc., 3,534; Teichert, Soc. Labor, 1,133; Dobbs, Soc. Workers, 103.

1952 (Pres.), Eisenhower, Rep., 599,107; Stevenson, Dem., 492,845; MacArthur, Christian Nationalist, 7,290; Hallinan, Prog., 2,460; Hass, Soc. Labor, 633; Hoopes, Soc., 254; Dobbs, Soc. Workers, 119.

1956 (Pres.), Eisenhower, Rep., 620,430; Stevenson, Dem., 523,002; Hass, Soc. Labor, 7,457.

1960 (Pres.), Kennedy, Dem., 599,298; Nixon, Rep., 629,273; Hass, Soc. Labor, 10,895; Curtis, Constitution, 1,401; Dobbs, Soc. Workers, 705.

1964 (Pres.), Johnson, Dem., 779,699; Goldwater, Rep., 470,366; Hass, Soc. Labor, 7,772; DeBerry, Freedom Soc., 537.

1968 (Pres.), Nixon, Rep., 588,510; Humphrey, Dem., 616,037; Wallace, 3d party, 96,990; Blomen, Soc. Labor, 488; Cleaver, Peace and Freedom, 1,609; Halstead, Soc. Worker, 270; Mitchell, Free Ballot, 377.

1972 (Pres.), Nixon, Rep., 837,135; McGovern, Dem., 568,334; Schmitz, Amer., 58,906; Spock, Ind., 2,644; Fisher, Soc. Labor, 1,102; Jenness, Soc. Worker, 623; Hall, Com., 566; Hospers, Libertarian, 1,537.

1976 (Pres.), Carter, Dem., 717,323; Ford, Rep., 777,732; McCarthy, Ind., 36,986; Maddox, Amer. Ind., 8,585; Anderson, Amer., 5,046; MacBride, Libertarian, 5,042; Wright, People's, 1,124; Camejo, Soc. Workers, 905; LaRouche, U.S. Labor, 903; Hall, Com., 817; Levin, Soc. Labor, 713; Zeidler, Soc., 358.

West Virginia

County	1976 Carter (D)	1976 Ford (R)	1980 Carter (D)	1980 Reagan (R)	1980 Anderson (I)
Barbour	3,647	3,235	3,444	3,306	287
Berkeley	8,216	8,935	6,761	9,912	617
Boone	8,528	3,072	7,463	4,136	266
Braxton	4,012	1,912	3,770	2,392	171
Brooke	8,197	4,792	6,425	4,618	633
Cabell	20,811	19,644	17,005	18,368	2,006
Calhoun	2,173	1,283	1,709	1,593	92
Clay	2,662	1,282	2,179	1,448	102
Doddridge	1,245	1,804	1,040	1,862	107
Fayette	15,496	5,459	1,357	557	58
Gilmer	2,245	1,371	1,850	1,451	153
Grant	1,323	2,976	1,041	3,452	87
Greenbrier	8,291	5,862	7,125	6,219	545
Hampshire	3,104	2,097	2,522	2,882	157
Hancock	10,627	6,771	8,483	6,677	846
Hardy	2,993	1,858	2,050	2,329	99
Harrison	21,467	15,172	18,777	14,223	1,339
Jackson	5,334	5,360	4,105	6,027	351
Jefferson	5,166	3,864	4,471	4,425	568
Kanawha	53,602	42,213	42,510	42,102	5,733
Lewis	3,960	3,736	3,419	3,727	319
Lincoln	5,260	2,997	5,239	3,741	134
Logan	13,122	4,021	11,829	4,881	377
Marion	17,800	10,391	14,125	10,910	1,176
Marshall	8,641	6,705	7,773	7,202	717
Mason	6,769	5,205	5,642	6,018	302
McDowell	10,557	4,107	9,752	3,852	196
Mercer	14,761	10,791	11,764	12,238	560
Mineral	5,898	5,130	4,653	6,104	385
Mingo	8,655	3,010	9,964	3,715	208
Monongalia	16,163	11,827	12,797	11,879	2,725
Monroe	3,297	2,750	2,845	2,993	165
Morgan	1,929	2,369	1,577	2,808	169
Nicholas	6,235	3,462	5,232	3,858	319
Ohio	11,817	12,476	10,936	11,382	1,329
Pendleton	2,104	1,554	1,724	1,677	80
Pleasants	1,699	1,608	1,494	1,854	84
Pocahontas	2,330	1,740	2,190	2,011	138
Preston	5,595	5,719	4,303	5,793	498
Putnam	8,226	6,334	6,409	7,561	632
Raleigh	19,768	10,637	16,836	10,643	1,028
Randolph	7,265	4,822	5,920	4,260	515
Ritchie	1,941	2,874	1,450	3,080	128
Roane	3,519	3,216	2,496	3,217	184
Summers	3,943	2,254	3,110	2,426	200
Taylor	3,905	2,891	3,212	3,004	232
Tucker	2,323	1,396	1,861	1,797	153
Tyler	1,817	2,514	1,478	2,707	162
Upshur	3,513	4,789	2,860	4,731	415
Wayne	9,958	6,009	8,692	7,504	443
Webster	2,931	971	2,576	1,260	116
Wetzel	5,042	3,793	4,021	3,681	327
Wirt	1,182	1,031	1,058	1,173	33
Wood	17,025	18,348	13,569	20,025	1,529
Wyoming	7,775	4,286	6,615	5,054	304
Totals	**435,864**	**314,726**	**353,508**	**326,645**	**30,499**

West Virginia Vote Since 1932

1932 (Pres.), Roosevelt, Dem., 405,124; Hoover, Rep., 330,731; Thomas, Soc., 5,133; Upshaw, Proh., 2,342; Foster, Com., 444.

1936 (Pres.), Roosevelt, Dem., 502,582; Landon, Rep., 325,358; Colvin, Prog., 1,173; Thomas, Soc., 832.

1940 (Pres.), Roosevelt, Dem., 495,662; Willkie, Rep., 372,414.

1944 (Pres.), Roosevelt, Dem., 392,777; Dewey, Rep., 322,819.

1948 (Pres.), Truman, Dem., 429,188; Dewey, Rep., 316,251; Wallace, Prog., 3,311.

1952 (Pres.), Eisenhower, Rep., 419,970; Stevenson, Dem., 453,578.

1956 (Pres.), Eisenhower, Rep., 449,297; Stevenson, Dem., 381,534.

1960 (Pres.), Kennedy, Dem., 441,786; Nixon, Rep., 395,995.

1964 (Pres.), Johnson, Dem., 538,087; Goldwater, Rep., 253,953.

1968 (Pres.), Nixon, Rep., 307,555; Humphrey, Dem., 374,091; Wallace, 3d party, 72,560.

1972 (Pres.), Nixon, Rep., 484,964; McGovern, Dem., 277,435.

1976 (Pres.), Carter, Dem., 435,864; Ford, Rep., 314,726.

Wisconsin

County	1976 Carter (D)	1976 Ford (R)	1980 Carter (D)	1980 Reagan (R)	1980 Anderson (I)
Adams	3,089	2,377	2,713	3,304	318
Ashland	4,688	3,045	4,360	3,282	625
Barron	8,678	7,393	8,647	8,788	883
Bayfield	3,885	2,624	3,717	3,304	541
Brown	33,572	36,571	29,782	46,967	4,680
Buffalo	3,448	2,844	3,276	3,569	404
Burnett	3,720	2,573	3,197	3,0267	389
Calumet	6,241	6,589	5,306	7,885	1,064
Chippewa	11,538	8,137	9,841	10,5231	1,160
Clark	7,238	6,095	6,091	7,923	682
Columbia	9,457	10,075	8,7156	10,477	1,373
Crawford	3,629	3,393	4,392	3,939	342
Dane	82,321	63,466	85,560	57,446	19,772
Dodge	13,643	17,335	11,972	19,370	1,693
Door	4,553	6,557	4,960	7,170	655
Douglas	13,478	6,999	11,703	7,558	1,700
Dunn	7,882	6,751	7,843	7,428	1,565
Eau Claire	18,263	16,388	17,527	17,304	3,486
Florence	965	922	948	1,187	86
Fond duLac	16,571	22,226	15,300	24,216	2,192
Forest	2,574	1,604	2,402	2,070	141
Grant	9,639	12,016	8,40:6	13,297	1,681
Green	5,632	7,085	5,336	7,714	941
Green Lake	3,411	5,020	2,857	5,873	368
Iowa	4,252	4,195	4,145	4,068	546
Iron	2,399	1,340	1,946	1,811	219
Jackson	3,735	3,406	3,629	4,328	413
Jefferson	12,577	15,528	11,332	16,213	1,925
Juneau	4,512	4,242	3,884	5,591	463
Kenosha	27,585	22,349	26,732	24,481	3,802
Kewaunee	4,607	4,447	3,706	5,577	318
La Crosse	16,674	24,188	17,304	23,427	3,509
La Fayette	3,839	4,131	3,578	4,421	450
Langlade	4,134	4,630	4,477	4,865	369
Lincoln	5,800	5,672	5,438	6,473	530
Manitowoc	19,819	16,039	17,330	18,592	2,012
Marathon	24,934	21,898	23,275	25,867	3,219
Marinette	8,482	8,591	7,717	10,445	683
Marquette	2,516	2,607	2,180	3,166	270
Menominee	766	324	544	302	35
Milwaukee	249,739	192,008	245,536	183,667	34,428
Monroe	6,465	7,242	6,520	8,135	769
Oconto	6,541	6,232	5,351	8,292	440
Oneida	7,216	7,347	7,012	8,602	832
Outagamie	23,079	28,363	21,215	31,551	5,610
Ozaukee	11,271	19,817	10,779	21,371	2,463
Pepin	1,955	1,312	1,673	1,541	183
Pierce	8,039	5,676	7,317	6,209	1,652
Polk	8,485	6,159	7,607	7,207	1,102
Portage	15,912	9,520	15,617	9,904	2,662
Price	4,028	3,204	3,595	4,028	349
Racine	36,740	37,088	33,574	39,682	5,093
Richland	3,634	4,466	3,413	4,601	404
Rock	28,048	28,325	24,751	30,960	4,408
Rusk	4,050	2,724	3,594	3,704	340
St. Croix	10,601	7,685	10,202	9,265	1,867
Sauk	9,204	9,577	8,476	10,093	1,405
Sawyer	3,055	2,720	3,065	3,504	311
Shawano	6,751	8,505	5,411	9,911	652
Sheboygan	24,226	22,332	20,980	23,036	3,859
Taylor	4,101	3,591	3,739	4,596	403
Trempealeau	6,218	5,341	5,390	5,992	491
Vernon	5,534	6,132	5,503	6,533	494
Vilas	3,209	4,929	3,293	6,304	429
Walworth	12,418	18,091	11,390	19,244	2,456
Washburn	3,503	2,787	3,172	3,193	355
Washington	14,422	18,798	12,944	23,213	2,654
Waukesha	47,487	70,418	16,601	26,701	2,772
Waupaca	6,857	10,849	6,402	12,538	1,084
Waushara	3,485	4,449	2,990	5,576	335
Winnebago	24,485	32,149	24,203	34,286	4,799
Wood	14,728	15,479	15,133	19,287	2,022
Totals	**1,040,232**	**1,004,987**	**988,255**	**1,089,750**	**159,793**

Wisconsin Vote Since 1932

1932 (Pres.), Roosevelt, Dem., 707,410; Hoover, Rep., 347,741; Thomas, Soc. 53,379; Foster, Com., 3,112; Upshaw Proh., 2,672; Reynolds, Soc. Labor, 494.

1936 (Pres.), Roosevelt, Dem., 802,984; Landon, Rep., 380,828; Lemke, Union, 60,297; Thomas, Soc., 10,626; Browder, Com., 2,197; Colvin, Proh., 1,071; Aiken, Soc. Labor, 557.

1940 (Pres.), Roosevelt, Dem., 704,821; Willkie, Rep., 679,260; Thomas, Soc., 15,071; Browder, Com., 2,394; Babson, Proh., 2,148; Aiken, Soc. Labor, 1,882.

1944 (Pres.), Roosevelt, Dem., 650,413; Dewey, Rep., 674,532; Thomas, Soc., 13,205; Teichert, Soc. Labor, 1,002.

1948 (Pres.), Truman, Dem., 647,310; Dewey, Rep., 590,959; Wallace, Prog., 25,282; Thomas, Soc., 12,547; Teichert, Soc. Labor, 399; Dobbs, Soc. Workers, 303.

1952 (Pres.), Eisenhower, Rep., 979,744; Stevenson, Dem., 622,175; Hallinan, Ind., 2,174; Dobbs, Ind., 1,350; Hoopes, Ind., 1,157; Hass, Ind., 770.

1956 (Pres.), Eisenhower, Rep., 954,844; Stevenson, Dem., 586,768; Andrews, Ind., 6,918; Hoopes, Soc., 754; Hass, Soc. Labor, 710; Dobbs, Soc. Workers, 564.

1960 (Pres.), Kennedy, Dem., 830,805; Nixon, Rep., 895,175; Dobbs, Soc. Workers, 1,792; Hass, Soc. Labor, 1,310.

1964 (Pres.), Johnson, Dem., 1,050,424; Goldwater, Rep., 638,495; DeBerry, Soc. Worker, 1,692; Hass, Soc. Labor, 1,204.

1968 (Pres.), Nixon, Rep., 809,997; Humphrey, Dem., 748,804; Wallace, 3d party, 127,835; Blomen, Soc. Labor, 1,338; Halstead, Soc. Worker, 1,222; scattered, 2,342.

1972 (Pres.) Nixon, Rep., 989,430; McGovern, Dem., 810,174; Schmitz, Amer., 47,525; Spock, Ind., 2,701; Fisher, Soc. Labor, 998; Hall, Com., 663; Reed, Ind., 506; scattered, 893.

1976 (Pres.), Carter, Dem., 1,040,232; Ford, Rep., 1,004,987; McCarthy, Ind., 34,943; Maddox, Amer. Ind., 8,552; Zeidler, Soc., 4,298; MacBride, Libertarian, 3,814; Camejo, Soc. Workers, 1,691; Wright, People's, 943; Hall, Com., 749; LaRouche, U.S. Lab., 738; Levin, Soc. Labor, 389; scattered, 2,839.

Wyoming

County	1976 Carter (D)	1976 Ford (R)	1980 Carter (D)	1980 Reagan (R)	1980 Anderson (I)
Albany	4,663	6,734	...	N/A	...
Big Horn	1,618	3,117	...	N/A	...
Campbell	1,620	3,306	...	N/A	...
Carbon	3,010	3,556	...	N/A	...
Converse	1,150	2,188	...	N/A	...
Crook	653	1,438	...	N/A	...
Fremont	4,423	6,584	...	N/A	...
Goshen	2,262	2,764	...	N/A	...
Hot Springs	958	1,413	...	N/A	...
Johnson	797	2,042	...	N/A	...
Laramie	12,040	14,061	...	N/A	...
Lincoln	1,555	2,464	...	N/A	...
Natrona	8,640	13,761	...	N/A	...
Niobrara	427	1,042	...	N/A	...
Park	2,656	5,878	...	N/A	...
Platte	1,593	1,844	...	N/A	...
Sheridan	3,206	5,382	...	N/A	...
Sublette	528	1,284	...	N/A	...
Sweetwater	5,575	4,937	...	N/A	...
Teton	1,204	2,667	...	N/A	...
Uinta	1,559	2,124	...	N/A	...
Washakie	1,168	2,361	...	N/A	...
Weston	934	1,770	...	N/A	...
Totals	**62,239**	**92,717**	**...**	**...**	**...**

Wyoming Vote Since 1932

1932 (Pres.), Roosevelt, Dem., 54,370; Hoover, Rep., 39,583; Thomas, Soc. 2,829; Foster, Com., 180.

1936 (Pres.), Roosevelt, Dem., 62,624; Landon, Rep., 38,739; Lemke, Union, 1,653; Thomas, Soc., 200; Browder, Com., 91; Colvin, Proh., 75.

1940 (Pres.), Roosevelt, Dem., 59,287; Willkie, Rep., 52,633; Babson, Proh., 172; Thomas, Soc., 148.

1944 (Pres.), Roosevelt, Dem., 49,419; Dewey, Rep., 51,921.

1948 (Pres.), Truman, Dem., 52,354; Dewey, Rep., 47,947; Wallace, Prog., 931; Thomas, Soc., 137; Teichert, Soc. Labor, 56.

1952 (Pres.), Eisenhower, Rep., 81,047; Stevenson, Dem., 47,934; Hamblen, Proh., 194; Hoopes, Soc., 40; Haas, Soc. Labor, 36.

1956 (Pres.), Eisenhower, Rep., 74,573; Stevenson, Dem., 49,554.

1960 (Pres.), Kennedy, Dem., 63,331; Nixon, Rep., 77,451.

1964 (Pres.), Johnson, Dem., 80,718; Goldwater, Rep., 61,998.

1968 (Pres.), Nixon, Rep., 70,927; Humphrey, Dem., 45,173; Wallace, 3d party, 11,105.

1972 (Pres.), Nixon, Rep., 100,464; McGovern, Dem., 44,358; Schmitz, Amer., 748.

1976 (Pres.), Carter, Dem., 62,239; Ford, Rep., 92,717; McCarthy, Ind., 624; Reagan, Ind., 307; Anderson, Amer., 290; MacBride, Libertarian, 89; Brown, Ind., 47; Maddox, Amer. Ind., 30.

The Ninety-Seventh Congress

With 1980 Election Results

The Senate

Terms are for 6 years and end Jan. 3 of the year preceding name. Annual salary $60,662.50. To be eligible for the U.S. Senate a person must be at least 30 years of age, a citizen of the United States for at least 9 years, and a resident of the state from which he is chosen. The Congress must meet annually on Jan. 3, unless it has, by law, appointed a different day.

Address: Washington, DC 20510

Senate officials (96th Congress): President Pro Tempore Warren G. Magnuson; Majority Leader Robert C. Byrd; Majority Whip Alan Cranston; Minority Leader Howard H. Baker Jr.; Minority Whip Ted Stevens.

Rep., 53; Dem., 46; Indep., 1; Total, 100. *Designates senior senator.
Preliminary returns.

Term ends	Senator (Party, home)	1980 Election
	Alabama	
1985	Howell Heflin* (D, Tuscumbia)	
1987	Jeremiah Denton (R, Mobile)	637,733
	Jim Folsom Jr. (D, Cullman)	602,953
	Alaska	
1985	Ted Stevens* (R, Anchorage)	
1987	Frank H. Murkowski (R, Anchorage)	65,924
	Clark S. Gruening (D, Anchorage)	53,674
	Arizona	
1983	Dennis DeConcini (D, Tucson)	
1987	Barry M. Goldwater* (R, Scottsdale)	426,171
	Bill Schulz (D, Scottsdale)	418,371
	Arkansas	
1985	David Pryor (D, Little Rock)	
1987	Dale Bumpers* (D, Charleston)	466,001
	Bill Clark (R, Little Rock)	324,621
	California	
1983	S.I. (Sam) Hayakawa (R, Mill Valley)	
1987	Alan Cranston* (D, Palm Springs)	4,638,448
	Paul Gann (R, Carmichael)	3,038,180
	Colorado	
1985	William L. Armstrong (R, Aurora)	
1987	Gary Hart* (D, Denver)	585,047
	Mary Estill Buchanan (R, Boulder)	563,752
	Connecticut	
1983	Lowell P. Weicker Jr.* (R, Greenwich)	
1987	Christopher J. Dodd (D, Norwich)	765,126
	James L. Buckley (R, Sharon)	575,644
	Delaware	
1983	William V. Roth Jr.* (R, Wilmington)	
1985	Joseph R. Biden Jr. (D, Wilmington)	
	Florida	
1983	Lawton Chiles* (D, Lakeland)	
1987	Paula Hawkins (R, Winter Park)	1,721,375
	Bill Gunter (D, Tallahassee)	1,634,800
	Georgia	
1985	Sam Nunn (D, Perry)	
1987	Mack Mattingly (R, St. Simons Is.)	771,774
	Herman E. Talmadge* (D, Lovejoy)	757,505
	Hawaii	
1983	Spark M. Matsunaga (D, Honolulu)	
1987	Daniel K. Inouye (D, Honolulu)	224,485
	Cooper Brown (R, Honolulu)	53,068
	Idaho	
1985	James A. McClure* (R, Payette)	
1987	Steven D. Symms (R, Boise)	218,793
	Frank Church (D, Boise)	214,351
	Illinois	
1985	Charles H. Percy* (R, Wilmette)	
1987	Alan Dixon (D, Belleville)	2,493,085
	Dave O'Neal (R, Belleville)	1,924,063
	Indiana	
1983	Richard G. Luger* (R, Indianapolis)	
1987	Dan Quayle (R, Huntington)	1,162,509
	Birch Bayh (D, W. Terre Haute)	998,772
	Iowa	
1985	Roger W. Jepsen* (R, Davenport)	
1987	Charles E. Grassley (R, New Hartford)	683,747
	John C. Culver (D, Cedar Rapids)	580,298
	Kansas	
1985	Nancy Landon Kassebaum (R, Wichita)	
1987	Robert J. Dole* (R, Russell)	589,806
	John Simpson (D, Salina)	334,657
	Kentucky	
1985	Walter D. Huddleston* (D, Elizabethtown	
1987	Wendell H. Ford (D, Owensboro)	719,679
	Mary Louise Foust (R, Shelbyville)	382,434
	Louisiana	
1985	J. Johnston Jr. (D, Shreveport	
1987	Russell B. Long* (D, Baton Rouge)	Unopposed
	Maine	
1983	George J. Mitchell (D, Waterville)	
1985	William S. Cohen* (R, Bangor)	
	Maryland	
1983	Paul S. Sarbanes (D, Baltimore)	
1987	Charles McC. Mathias Jr.* (R, Frederick)	811,925
	Edward T. Conroy (D, Bowie)	423,879
	Massachusetts	
1983	Edward M. Kennedy* (D, Boston)	
1985	Paul E. Tsongas (D, Lowell)	
	Michigan	
1983	Donald W. Riegle Jr.* (D, Flint)	
1985	Carl Levin (D, Detroit)	
	Minnesota	
1983	David Durenberger* (R, Minneapolis)	
1985	Rudolph E. Boschwitz (R, Wayzata)	

Term ends	Senator (Party, home)	1980 Election
	Mississippi	
1983	John C. Stennis* (D, DeKalb)	
1985	Thad Cochran (R, Jackson)	
	Missouri	
1983	John C. Danforth (R, Jefferson City)	
1987	Thomas F. Eagleton* (D, St. Louis)	1,059,041
	Gene McNary (R, Sunset Hills)	965,316
	Montana	
1983	John Melcher* (D, Forsyth)	
1985	Max Baucus (D, Missoula)	
	Nebraska	
1983	Edward Zorinsky* (D, Omaha)	
1985	J. James Exon (D, Lincoln	
	Nevada	
1983	Howard W. Cannon* (D, Las Vegas)	
1987	Paul Laxalt (R, Carson City)	143,781
	Mary Gojack (D, Reno)	92,203
	New Hampshire	
1985	Gordon J. Humphrey* (R, Swapee)	
1987	Warren Rudman (R, Nashua)	195,053
	John A. Durkin (D, Manchester)	178,943
	New Jersey	
1983	Harrison A. Williams Jr.* (D, Bedminster)	
1985	Bill Bradley (D, Denville)	
	New Mexico	
1983	Harrison "Jack" Schmitt (R, Silver City)	
1985	Pete V. Domenici* (R, Albuquerque)	
	New York	
1983	Daniel Patrick Moynihan* (D, New York)	
1987	Alphonse D'Amato (R, Island Park)	2,627,458
	Elizabeth Holtzman (D, Brooklyn)	2,538,921
	Jacob K. Javits (L, New York)	629,468
	North Carolina	
1985	Jesse A. Helms* (R, Raleigh)	
1987	John P. East (R, Greenville)	891,373
	Robert Morgan (D, Lillington)	884,640
	North Dakota	
1983	Quentin N. Burdick* (D, Fargo)	
1987	Mark Andrews (R, Mapleton)	187,221
	Kent Johanneson (D, Bismarck)	77,205
	Ohio	
1983	Howard M. Metzenbaum (D, Shaker Heights)	
1987	John Glenn* (D, Grandview Hts.)	2,731,088
	James E. Betts (R, Rocky River)	1,129,003
	Oklahoma	
1985	David Lyle Boren* (D, Okla. City)	
1987	Don Nickles (R, Ponca City)	573,339
	Andy Coats (D, Okla. City)	471,914

Term ends	Senator (Party, home)	1980 Election
	Oregon	
1985	Mark O. Hatfield* (R, Salem)	
1987	Robert W. Packwood (R, Lake Oswego)	575,515
	Ted Kulongoski (D, Eugene)	490,511
	Pennsylvania	
1983	H. John Heinz III* (R, Pittsburgh)	
1987	Arlen Specter (R, Philadelphia)	2,237,729
	Peter Flaherty (D, Pittsburgh)	2,102,525
	Rhode Island	
1983	John H. Chafee (R, Warwick)	
1985	Claiborne Pell* (D, Newport)	
	South Carolina	
1985	Strom Thurmond* (R, Aiken)	
1987	Ernest F. Hollings (D, Columbia)	595,210
	Marshall T. Mays (R, Greenwood)	233,052
	South Dakota	
1985	Larry Pressler* (R, Humboldt)	
1987	James Abnor (R, Mitchell)	190,726
	George McGovern (D, Mitchell)	128,956
	Tennessee	
1983	James R. Sasser (D, Nashville)	
1985	Howard H. Baker Jr.* (R, Huntsville)	
	Texas	
1983	Lloyd Bentsen (D, Houston)	
1985	John G. Tower* (R, Wichita Falls)	
	Utah	
1983	Orrin G. Hatch (R, Salt Lake City)	
1987	Jake Garn* (R, Salt Lake City)	433,943
	Dan Berman (D, Salt Lake City)	150,495
	Vermont	
1983	Robert T. Stafford* (R, Rutland)	
1987	Patrick J. Leahy (D, Burlington)	101,721
	Stewart Ledbetter (R, Montpelier)	99,455
	Virginia	
1983	Harry F. Byrd Jr.* (I, Winchester)	
1985	John William Warner (R, Middleburg)	
	Washington	
1983	Henry M. Jackson* (D, Everett)	
1987	Slade Gorton (R, Olympia)	831,099
	Warren G. Magnuson (D, Seattle)	701,079
	West Virginia	
1983	Robert C. Byrd* (D, Sophia)	
1985	Jennings Randolph (D, Charleston)	
	Wisconsin	
1983	William Proxmire* (D, Madison)	
1987	Robert W. Kasten (R, Thiensville)	1,101,669
	Gaylord A. Nelson (D, Madison)	1,061,899
	Wyoming	
1983	Malcolm Wallop* (R, Big Horn)	
1985	Alan Kooi Simpson (R, Cody)	

The House of Representatives

Members' terms to Jan. 3, 1983. Annual salary $60,662.50; house speaker $79,125. To be eligible for membership, a person must be at least 25, a U.S. citizen for at least 7 years, and a resident of the state from which he is chosen.

Address: Washington, DC 20515

House Officials (96th Congress): Speaker Thomas P. O'Neill; Majority Leader James Wright; Majority Whip John Brademas; Minority Leader John J. Rhodes; Minority Whip Robert H. Michel.

C-Conservative; D-Democratic; DFL-Democrat Farmer-Labor; I-Independent; L-Liberal; LIBERT- Libertarian; R-Republican; S-Statesmen's Party.

Democrats, 277, Republicans, 158. Total 435.

(Those marked * served in the 96th Congress.)

Bold face denotes the winner.

Preliminary returns.

Dist.	Representative (Party, Home)	1980 Election
	Alabama	
1.	**Jack Edwards*** (R, Mobile)	**104,395**
	Steve Smith (Libert, Birmingham)	14,537
2.	**William L. Dickenson*** (R, Montgomery)	**103,636**
	Cecil Wyatt (D, Ramer)	62,979
3.	**Bill Nichols*** (D, Sylacauga)	**Unopposed**
4.	**Tom Bevill*** (D, Jasper)	**130,754**
	A.J. Killingsworth (S, Leeds)	3,734
5.	**Ronnie G. Flippo*** (D, Florence)	**115,101**
	Betty T. Benson (Libert, Madison)	7,309
6.	**Albert Lee Smith Jr.** (R, Birmingham)	**89,613**
	W. B. (Pete) Clifford (D, Birmingham)	80,738
7.	**Richard C. Shelby*** (D, Tuscaloosa)	**119,359**
	James E. Bacon (R, Hueytown)	42,619
	Alaska At Large	
	Don Young* (R, Anchorage)	**87,403**
	Kevin "Pat" Parnell (D, Anchorage)	30,428
	Arizona	
1.	**John J. Rhodes*** (R, Mesa)	**136,781**
	Steve Jancek (R, Mesa)	40,000
2.	**Morris K. Udall*** (D, Tucson)	**122,710**
	Richard H. Huff (R, Tucson)	84,362
3.	**Bob Stump*** (D, Tolleson)	**141,280**
	Bob Croft (R, Munds Park)	66,311
	Sharon Hayse (write-in) (Libert, Sedona)	12,512
4.	**Eldon Rudd*** (R, Scottsdale)	**135,816**
	Les Miller (D, Phoenix)	82,840
	Arkansas	
1.	**Bill Alexander*** (D, Osceola)	**Unopposed**
2.	**Ed Bethune** (R, Searcy)	**157,407**
	James G. Reid (D, Jacksonville)	41,976
3.	**John Paul Hammerschmidt*** (R, Harrison)	**Unopposed**
4.	**Beryl Anthony Jr.*** (D, El Dorado)	**Unopposed**
	California	
1.	**Eugene A. Chappie** (R, Roseville)	**144,702**
	Harold T. Johnson* (D, Roseville)	107,388
2.	**Don H. Clausen** (R, Del Norte County)	**139,825**
	Norma K. Bork (D, Angwin)	108,423
3.	**Robert T. Matsui*** (D, Sacramento)	**163,682**
	Joseph Murphy (R, Sacramento)	63,359
4.	**Vic Fazio*** (D, Sacramento)	**132,420**
	Albert Dehr (R, Sacramento)	59,983
5.	**John L. Burton*** (D, San Francisco)	**100,066**
	Dennis McQuaid (R, Novato)	88,287
6.	**Phillip Burton*** (D, San Francisco)	**91,810**
	Tom Spinosa (R, San Franciso)	33,423
7.	**George Miller*** (D, Martinez)	**141,565**
	Giles St. Clair (R, Alaino)	70,203
8.	**Ronald V. Dellums*** (D, Berkeley)	**107,554**
	Charles V. Hughes (R, Berkeley)	75,972
9.	**Fortney H. (Pete) Stark*** (D, Oakland)	**89,589**
	William J. Kennedy (R, Pleasanton)	66,580
10.	**Don Edwards*** (D, San Jose)	**100,901**
	John M. Lutton (R, San Jose)	45,234
11.	**Tom Lantos** (D, Hillsborough)	**85,203**
	Bill Royer* (R, Redwood City)	79,586
12.	**Paul N. McCloskey Jr.*** (R, Menlo Park)	**139,737**
	Kirsten Olsen (D, Atherton)	36,162
13.	**Norman Y. Mineta*** (D, San Jose)	**129,188**
	W. E. (Ted) Gagne (R, Saratoga)	77,576
14.	**Norman D. Shumway*** (R, Stockton)	**132,516**
	Ann Cerney (D, Lodi)	79,260
15.	**Tony Coelho** (D, Hilmar)	**106,793**
	Ron Schwartz (R, Fresno)	37,423
16.	**Leon E. Panetta*** (D, Carmel Valley)	**157,230**
	W. A. (Jack) Roth (R, Pacific Grove)	54,192
17.	**Charles (Chip) Pashayan Jr.** (R, Fresno)	**127,939**
	Willard H. Johnson (D, Selma)	53,320
18.	**William M. Thomas*** (R, Bakersfield)	**122,639**
	Mary "Pat" Timmermans (D, Bakersfield)	50,029
19.	**Robert J. Lagomarsino** (R, Ventura)	**160,893**
	Carmen Lodise (D, Isla Vista)	36,601
20.	**Barry M. Goldwater** (R, Burbank)	**195,789**
	Matt Miller (D, Camarillo)	42,375
21.	**Bobbi Fiedler** (R, Northridge)	**73,152**
	James C. Corman* (R, (D, Van Guys)	72,152
22.	**Carlos J. Moorhead*** (R, Glendale)	**112,533**
	Pierce O'Donnell (D, Altadena)	56,407
23.	**Anthony C. Beilenson*** (D, Los Angeles)	**123,038**
	Robert Winckler (R, Woodland Hills)	61,009
24.	**Henry A. Waxman*** (D, Los Angeles)	**91,568**
	Roland Cayard (R, Los Angeles)	38,631
25.	**Edward R. Roybal*** (D, Los Angeles)	**48,283**
	Richard L. Ferraro Jr. (R, Los Angeles)	20,665
26.	**John H. Rousselot*** (R, Sau Marino)	**113,991**
	Joseph L. Lisoni (D, Arcadia)	39,375
27.	**Robert K. Dornan*** (R, Redondo Beach)	**106,342**
	Carey Peck (D, Santa Monica)	97,663
28.	**Julian C. Dixon*** (D, Los Angeles)	**106,975**
	Robert Reid (R, Culver City)	22,638
29.	**Augustus F. Hawkins*** (D, Los Angeles)	**79,100**
	Michael A. Hirt (R, Los Angeles)	70,094
30.	**George E. Danielson*** (D, Monterey Park)	**72,995**
	J. Arthur Platten (R, El Monte)	23,683
31.	**Mervyn M. Dymally** (D, Lynwood)	**68,160**
	Don Grimshaw (R, Lawndale)	37,447
32.	**Glenn M. Anderson*** (D, Harbor City)	**82,436**
	John R. Adler (R, Torrance)	38,250
33.	**Wayne Grisham*** (R, La Mirada)	**120,421**

Dist.	Representative (Party, Home)	1980 Election
	Fred L. Anderson (D, Whittier)	49,664
34.	**Dan Lungren*** (R, Long Beach)	**135,253**
	Simone (D, Los Alamitos)	45,386
35.	**David Dreier** (R, La Verre)	**99,134**
	Jim Lloyd* (D, West Covina)	86,728
36.	**George E. Brown Jr.*** (D, Riverside)	**87,895**
	John Paul Stark (R, San Bernardino)	73,096
37.	**Jerry Lewis)** (R, Highland)	**164,663**
	Donald M. Rusk (D, Redlands)	57,815
38.	**Jerry M. Patterson*** (D, Buena Park)	**90,647**
	Art Jacobson (R, Los Alamitos)	65,340
39.	**William L. Dannemeyer*** (R, Fullerton)	**172,029**
	Leonard L. Lahtinen (D, Anaheim)	35,738
40.	**Robert E. Badham*** (R, Newport Beach)	**209,775**
	Michael E. Dow (D, Balboa Island)	69,388
41.	**Bill Lowery** (R, San Diego)	**120,617**
	Bob Wilson (D, La Mesa)	99,102
42.	**Lionel Van Deerlin*** (D, Chula Vista)	**77,819**
	Duncan L. Hunter (R, Coronado)	68,354
43.	**Clair W. Burgener*** (R, La Jolla)	**292,039**
	Tom Metzer (D, Fallbrook)	45,623
	Colorado	
1.	**Patricia Schroeder*** (D, Denver)	**107,332**
	Naomi Bradford (R, Denver)	67,811
2.	**Timothy E. Wirth*** (D, Lakewood)	**153,568**
	John McElderry (R, Wheatridge)	111,792
3.	**Ray Kogovsek*** (D, Pueblo)	**105,054**
	Harold McCormick (R, Canon City)	84,054
4.	**Hank Brown** (R, Greeley)	**178,158**
	Polly Baca Barragan (D, Thornton)	77,054
5.	**Ken Kramer*** (R, Colorado Springs)	**176,726**
	Ed Scheiber (D, Greenwood Village)	61,898
	Connecticut	
1.	**William R. Cotter*** (D, Hartford)	**137,477**
	Marjorie D. Anderson (R, West Hartford)	80,873
2.	**Samuel Gejdenson** (D, Bozrah)	**118,893**
	Tony Guglielmo (R, Stafford Springs)	102,859
3.	**Lawrence J. DeNardis** (R, Hamden)	**108,213**
	Joseph I. Lieberman (D, New Haven)	97,119
4.	**Stewart B. McKinney*** (R, Fairfield)	**121,926**
	John A. Phillips (D, Norwalk)	73,719
5.	**William R. Ratchford** (D, Danbury)	**116,265**
	Edward M Donahue (R, Shelton)	114,376
6.	**Toby Moffett*** (D, Litchfield)	**142,980**
	Nicholas Schaus (R, Farmington)	98,349
	Delaware At Large	
	Thomas B. Evans Jr.* (R, Wilmington)	**133,557**
	Robert L. Maxwell (D, Wilmington)	81,805
	Florida	
1.	**Earl Hutto*** (D, Panama City)	**109,541**
	Warren Briggs (R, Pensacola)	66,896
2.	**Don Fuqua*** (D, Tallahassee)	**128,674**
	John R. LaCapra (R, Tallahassee)	52,987
3.	**Charles E. Bennett*** (D, Jacksonville)	**98,385**
	Harry Radcliff (R, Jacksonville)	28,776
4.	**Bill Chappell Jr.*** (D, Ocala)	**136,301**
	Barney E. Dillard Jr. (R, Altoona)	71,308
5.	**Bill McCollum** (R, Altamonte Springs)	**172,107**
	David Best (D, Crystal River)	137,136
6.	**C. W. Bill Young** (R, St. Petersburg)	**Unopposed**
7.	**Sam Gibbons*** (D, Tampa)	**126,686**
	Charles P. Jones (R, Tampa)	48,982
8.	**Andy Ireland*** (D, Winter Haven)	**144,200**
	Scott Nicholson (R, Bradenton)	56,079
9.	**Bill Nelson*** (D, Melbourne)	**130,498**
	Stan Dowiat (R, Melbourne Beach)	53,330
10.	**L. A. (Skip) Bafalis*** (R, Fort Myers Beach)	**260,214**
	Richard D. Sparkman (D, Naples)	69,674
11.	**Dan Mica*** (D, West Palm Beach)	**198,477**
	Al Coogler (R, West Palm Beach)	134,433
12.	**Clay Shaw** (R, Ft. Lauderdale)	**121,465**
	Alan S. Becker (D, Plantation	103,090
13.	**William Lehman*** (D, N. Miami Beach)	**122,555**
	Alvin E. Entin (R, Miami)	40,825
14.	**Claude Pepper*** (D, Miami)	**91,096**
	Evelio S. Estrella (R, Miami)	30,675
15.	**Dante B. Fascell*** (D, Miami)	**125,205**
	Herbert J. Hoodwin (R, Miami)	65,122
	Georgia	
1.	**Bo Ginn*** (D, Millen)	**Unopposed**
2.	**Charles F. Hatcher** (D, Albany)	**89,723**
	Jack E. Harrell Jr. (R, Quitman)	32,270
3.	**Jack Brinkley*** (D, Columbus)	**Unopposed**
4.	**Elliot H. Levitas** (D, Atlanta)	**98,565**
	Barry E. Billington (R, Decatur)	43,013
5.	**Wyche Fowler Jr.*** (D, Atlanta)	**101,613**
	F. William Dowda (R, Atlanta)	35,664
6.	**Newt Gingrich*** (R, Carrollton	**95,550**
	Dock H. Davis (D, Franklin	66,474
7.	**Larry P. McDonald*** (D, Marietta)	**112,988**
	Richard L. Castellucis (R, Marietta)	53,002
8.	**Billy Lee Evans*** (D, Macon)	**87,160**
	Darwin Carter (R, Alma)	30,898
9.	**Ed Jenkins*** (D, Jasper)	**114,803**
	David G. Ashworth (R, Canton)	55,579
10.	**Doug Barnard*** (D, Augusta)	**101,046**
	Bruce J. Neubauer (R, Athens)	24,888
	Hawaii	
1.	**Cecil Heftel*** (D, Honolulu)	**98,256**
	Aloma Keen Noble (R, Honolulu)	19,819
2.	**Daniel K. Akaka*** (D, Honolulu)	**141,477**
	Don G. Smith (Libert, Kaneohe)	15,903
	Idaho	
1.	**Larry Craig** (R, Midvale)	**116,977**
	Glenn W. Nichols (D, Boise)	100,870
2.	**George Hansen* (R, Pocatello)**	**116,123**
	Diane Bilyeu (D, Pocatello)	81,364
	Illinois	
1.	**Harold Washington** (D, Chicago)	**115,617**
	George Williams (R, Chicago)	6,471
2.	**Gus Savage** (D, Chicago)	**118,148**
	Marsha A. Harris (R, Chicago)	16,305
3.	**Marty Russo*** (D, South Holland)	**131,683**
	Lawrence C. Sarsoun (R, Midlothian)	58,888
4.	**Edward J. Derwinski** (R, Flossmoor)	**146,299**
	Richard S. Jalovec (D, Burr Ridge)	70,022
5.	**John G. Fary*** (D, Chicago)	**99,704**
	Robert V. Kotowski (R, Chicago)	26,242
6.	**Henry J. Hyde** (R, Bensenville)	**116,782**
	Mario Raymond Reda (D, River Forest)	58,378
7.	**Cardiss Collins*** (D, Chicago)	**75,135**
	Ruth R. Hooper (R, Chicago)	13,233
8.	**Dan Rostenkowski*** (D, Chicago)	**91,719**
	Walter F. Zilke (R, Chicago)	89,069
9.	**Sidney R. Yates*** (D, Chicago)	**98,098**
	John D. Andrica (D, Chicago)	36,025
10.	**John E. Porter (R, Evanston)**	**132,032**
	Robert A. Weinberger (D, Glencoe)	85,716
11.	**Frank Annunzio*** (D, Chicago)	**116,317**
	Michael R. Zanillo (R, Chicago)	51,236
12.	**Philip M. Crane*** (R, Mt. Prospect)	**177,594**
	David McCartney (D, Kildeer)	61,859
13.	**Robert McClory***Reese (R, Lake Bluff)	**131,750**
	Michael Reese (D, Elgin)	52,086
14.	**John N. Erienborn*** (R, Glen Ellyn)	**200,934**
	LeRoy E. Kennel (D, Lombard)	60,702
15.	**Tom Corcoran*** (R, Ottowa)	**150,897**
	John P. Quillin (D, Seneca)	45,722

Dist.	Representative (Party, Home)	1980 Election
16.	**Lynn M. Martin (R, Rockford)**	**133,533**
	Douglas R. Aurand (D, Rockford)	64,480
17.	**George M. O'Brien*** (R, Joliet)	**131,719**
	Michael A. Murer (D, Joliet)	64,869
18.	**Robert H. Michel*** (R. Peoria)	**125,644**
	John L. Knuppel (D, Havana)	76,689
19.	**Tom Railsback*** (R, Moline)	**143,260**
	Thomas J. Hand (D, Fulton)	51,248
20.	**Paul Findley*** (R, Pittsfield)	**132,174**
	David L. Robinson (D, Springfield)	96,590
21.	**Edward R. Madigan*** (R, Lincoln)	**132,124**
	Penny L. Severns (D, Decator)	63,474
22.	**Daniel B. Crane*** (R, Danville)	**144,586**
	Peter M. Voelz (D, Paris)	65,481
23.	**Melvin Price*** (D, East St. Louis)	**107,106**
	Ronald L. Davinroy (R, O'Fallon)	59,617
24.	**Paul Simon*** (D, Carbondale)	**110,389**
	John T. Anderson (R, Marion)	108,112

Indiana

Dist.	Representative (Party, Home)	1980 Election
1.	**Adam Benjamin Jr.*** (D, Hobart)	**112,016**
	Joseph D. Harkin (R, Highland)	43,537
2.	**Floyd Fithian*** (D, Lafayette)	**122,192**
	Ernest Niemeyer (R, Lowell)	105,918
3.	**John P. Hiler** (R, LaPorte)	**100,106**
	John Brademas* (D, South Bend)	83,140
4.	**Daniel R. Coates** (R, Fort Wayne)	**115,357**
	John D. Walda (D, Fort Wayne)	75,112
5.	**Elwood Hills** (R, Kokamo)	**127,235**
	Nels J. Ackerson (D, Noblesville)	79,606
6.	**David W. Evans*** (D, Indianapolis)	**95,999**
	David G. Crane (R, Martinsville)	94,804
7.	**John T. Myers*** (R, Covington)	**132,137**
	Patrick D. Carroll (R, Bloomington)	67,619
8.	**H. Joel Deckard** (R, Evansville)	**119,667**
	Kenneth C. Snider (D, Decker)	96,963
9.	**Lee H. Hamilton*** (D, Columbus)	**136,205**
	George Meyer Jr. (R, Jeffersonville)	76,708
10.	**Phil Sharp*** (D, Muncie)	**102,696**
	William G. Frazier (R, Muncie)	88,896
11.	**Andy Jacobs Jr.*** (D, Indianapolis)	**96,225**
	Sheila Suess (R, Indianapolis)	71,771

Iowa

Dist.	Representative (Party, Home)	1980 Election
1.	**Jim Leach*** (R, Davenport)	**134,248**
	Jim Larew (D, Iowa City)	72,438
2.	**Tom Tauke** (R, Dubuque)	**116,829**
	Steve Sovern, (D, Marion)	87,223
3.	**Cooper Evans** (R, Grundy Center)	**107,830**
	Lynn G. Cutler (D, Waterloo)	101,639
4.	**Neal Smith*** (D, Altoona)	**117,716**
	Donald C. Young (R, Des Moines)	100,162
5.	**Tom Harkin*** (D, Ames)	**128,687**
	Cal Hultman (R,)	85,868
6.	**Berkley Bedell*** (D, Spirit Lake)	**128,009**
	Clarence S. Carney (R, Sioux City)	72,049

Kansas

Dist.	Representative (Party, Home)	1980 Election
1.	**Pat Roberts** (R, Dodge City)	**119,688**
	Phil Martin (D, Larned)	73,402
2.	**Jim Jeffries*** (R, Atchison)	**90,452**
	Sam Keys (D, Manhattan)	77,464
3.	**Larry Winn Jr.** (R, Overland Park)	**109,277**
	Dan Watkins (D, Lawrence)	82,109
4.	**Dan Gluckman*** (D, Wichita)	**123,940**
	Clay Hunter (R, Wichita)	56,189
5.	**Bob Whittaker** (R, Augusta)	**140,501**
	David L. Miller (D, Parsons)	45,283

Kentucky

Dist.	Representative (Party, Home)	1980 Election
1.	**Carroll Hubbard Jr.*** (D, Mayfield)	**Unopposed**
2.	**William H. Natcher*** (D, Bowling Green)	**99,682**
	Mark T. Watson (R, Elizabethtown)	52,123
3.	**Romano L. Mazzoli*** (D, Louisville)	**84,091**
	Richard Cesler (R, Louisville)	45,676
4.	**Gene Snyder** (R, Brownsboro Farms)	**122,794**
	Phil M. McGary (D, Louisville)	60,831
5.	**Harold Rogers** (R, Somerset)	**111,779**
	Ted R. Marcum (D, Richmond)	53,716
6.	**Larry J. Hopkins** (R, Lexington)	**103,271**
	Tom Easterly (D, Frankfort)	70,999
7.	**Carl D. Perkins*** (D, Hindman)	**Unopposed**

Louisiana

Dist.	Representative (Party, Home)	1980 Election
1.	**Robert L. Livingston*** (R, New Orleans)	**Unopposed**
2.	**Lindy Boggs*** (D, New Orleans)	**Unopposed**
3.	**W. J. (Billy) Tauzin** (D, Thibodaux)	**Unopposed**
4.	**Buddy Roemer** (D, Bossier City)	**103,511**
	Claude (Buddy) Leach (D, Leesville)	58,641
5.	**Jerry Huckaby*** (D, Ringgold)	**Unopposed**
6.	**W. Henson Moore*** (R, Baton Rouge)	**Unopposed**
7.	**John B. Breaux*** (D, Crowley)	**Unopposed**
8.	**Gillis W. Long*** (D, Alexandria)	Unopposed

Maine

Dist.	Representative (Party, Home)	1980 Election
1.	**David F. Emery*** (R, Rockland)	**184,943**
	Harold C. Pachios (D, Cape Elizabeth)	86,719
2.	**Olympia J. Snowe*** (R, Auburn)	**186,083**
	Harold L. Silverman (D, Calais)	50,228

Maryland

Dist.	Representative (Party, Home)	1980 Election
1.	**Roy Dyson** (D, Great Mills)	**96,394**
	Robert E. Bauman (R, Easton)	88,736
2.	**Clarence D. Long*** (D, Ruxton)	**115,846**
	Helen D. Bentley (R, Lutherville)	22,490
3.	**Barbara A. Mikulski*** (D, Baltimore)	**100,677**
	Russell T. Schaffer (R, Towson)	31,346
4.	**Majorie S. Holt*** (R, Severna Park)	**116,162**
	James J. Riley (D, Severna Park)	45,869
5.	**Gladys Noon Spellman*** (D, Laurel)	**103,150**
	Kevin R. Igoe (R, East Riverdale)	24,728
6.	**Beverly B. Byron** (D, Frederick)	**130,172**
	Raymond E. Beck (R, Westminster)	50,619
7.	**Parren J. Mitchell*** (D, Baltimore)	**76,014**
	Victor Clark Jr. (R, Baltimore)	12,257
8.	**Michael D. Barnes** (D, Kensington)	**140,214**
	Newton I. Steers Jr.* (R, Bethesda)	94,714

Massachusetts

Dist.	Representative (Party, Home)	1980 Election
1.	**Silvio O. Conte*** (R, Pittsfield)	**156,167**
	Helen Poppy Doyle (D, Ashfield)	52,438
2.	**Edward P. Boland*** (D, Springfield)	**120,511**
	Thomas P. Swank (R, West Brookfield)	38,675
3.	**Joseph D. Early*** (D, Worcester)	**140,632**
	David G. Skehan (R, Milford)	54,409
4.	**Barney Frank** (D, Newton)	**102,461**
	Richard A. Jones (R, Harvard)	95,895
5.	**James M. Shannon** (D, Lawrence)	**136,711**
	William C. Sawyer (R, Acton)	70,578
6.	**Nicholas Mavroules** (D, Peabody)	**111,344**
	Thomas H. Trimarco (R, Beverly)	103,120
7.	**Edward J. Markey*** (D, Malden)	**Unopposed**
8.	**Thomas P. O'Neill Jr.*** (D, Cambridge)	**126,425**
	William A. Barnstead (R, Arlington)	35,802
9.	**Joe Moakley*** (D, Boston)	**Unopposed**
10.	**Margaret M. Heckler*** (R, Wellesley Hills)	**131,600**
	Robert E. McCarthy (D, East Bridgewater)	83,557
11.	**Brian J. Donnelly** (D, Dorchester)	**Unopposed**
12.	**Gerry E. Studds*** (D, Cohasset)	**195,294**
	Paul V. Doane (R, Harwich)	71,468

Michigan

Dist.	Representative (Party, Home)	1980 Election
1.	**John Conyers Jr.*** (D, Detroit)	**95,400**
	William M. Bell (R, Detroit)	5,016
2.	**Carl D. Pursell*** (R, Plymouth)	**114,537**
	Kathleen F. O'Reilly (D, Plymouth)	83,430

Dist.	Representative (Party, Home)	1980 Election
3.	**Howard Wolpe*** (D, Lansing)	**112,547**
	James S. Gilmore (R, Kalamazoo)	101,988
4.	**Dave Stockman** (R, St. Joseph)	**136,028**
	Lyndon G. Furst (D, Berrien Springs)	47,656
5.	**Dale R. Sprik** (D, Grand Rapids)	**117,855**
	Howard S. Sawyer (R, Rockford)	101,664
6.	**Jim Dunn** (R, East Lansing)	**113,316**
	Bob Carr* (D, East Lansing)	109,563
7.	**Dale E. Kildee*** (D, Flint)	**146,416**
	Dennis L. Berry (R, Burton)	11,393
8.	**Bob Traxler*** (D, Bay City)	**123,803**
	Norman R. Hughes (R, Metamora)	77,066
9.	**Guy Vander Jagt*** (R, Luther)	**160,303**
	Marshall A. Tufts (Am I, Fruitport)	5,383
10.	**Don Albosta** (D, St. Charles)	**123,544**
	Richard J. Allen (R, Ithaca)	107,104
11.	**Robert W. Davis** (R, Gaulord)	**114,833**
	Dan Dorrity (D, Saulte Ste. Marie)	73,881
12.	**David E. Bonior*** (D, Mt. Clemens)	**95,913**
	Kirk Walsh (R, St. Clair Shores)	81,621
13.	**George W. Crockett Jr.** (D, Detroit)	**63,561**
	M. Michael Hurd (R, Detroit)	5,348
14.	**Dennis M. Hertel** (D, Detroit)	**69,267**
	Vic Caputo (R, Grosse Pointe)	61,788
15.	**William D. Ford*** (D, Taylor)	**114,454**
	Gerald R. Carlson (R, Dearborn)	53,570
16.	**John D. Dingell*** (D, Trenton)	**101,186**
	Pamella A. Seay (R, Trenton)	41,843
17.	**William M. Brodhead*** (D, Detroit)	**104,131**
	Alfred L. Patterson (R, Detroit)	40,472
18.	**James J. Blanchard*** (D, Pleasant Ridge)	**96,732**
	Betty J. Suida (R, Royal Oak)	43,966
19.	**William S. Broomfield*** (R, Birmingham)	**110,555**
	Wayne E. Daniels (D, Union Lake	38,883

Minnesota

Dist.	Representative (Party, Home)	1980 Election
1.	**Arlen Erdahl*** (R, West St. Paul)	**163,289**
	Russell V. Smith (D, Rochester)	62,777
2.	**Tom Hagedorn*** (R, Truman)	**151,247**
	Harold J.Bergquist (D, Burnsville)	98,875
3.	**Bill Frenzel*** (R, Golden Valley)	**128,672**
	Joel Alexander Saliterman (D, St. Louis Park)	44,844
4.	**Bruce F. Vento*** (D, St. Paul)	**116,946**
	John Berg (R, St. Paul)	80,664
5.	**Martin Olav Sabo*** (D, Minneapolis)	**121,201**
	John Doherty (R, Minneapolis)	46,060
6.	**Vin Weber** (R, Elbow Lake)	**129,708**
	Archie Baumann (D, Redwood Falls)	112,617
7.	**Arlan Strangeland*** (R, Barnsville)	**130,350**
	Gene Wenstrom (D, Elbow Lake)	120,770
8.	**James L. Oberstar*** (D, Chisholm)	**165,783**
	Edward Fiore (R, Anoka)	64,994

Mississippi

Dist.	Representative (Party, Home)	1980 Election
1.	**Jamie L. Whitten*** (D, Charleston)	**109,988**
	Terrill K. Moffett (R, Oxford)	61,175
2.	**David R. Bowen*** (D, Cleveland)	**84,669**
	Frank Drake (R, Durant)	41,783
3.	**G. V. (Sonny) Montgomery*** (D, Meridian)	**Unopposed**
4.	**Jon C. Hinson*** (R, Tylertown)	**69,517**
	Britt R. Singletary (D, Jackson)	52,827
	Leslie B. McLemore (I, Jackson)	53,288
5.	**Trent Lott*** (R, Pascagoula)	**130,422**
	Jimmy McVeay (D, Ocean Springs)	46,363

Missouri

Dist.	Representative (Party, Home)	1980 Election
1.	**William Clay*** (D, St. Louis)	**89,890**
	Bill White (R, Rock Hill)	38,463
2.	**Robert A. Young*** (D, St. Ann)	**148,620**
	John O. Shields (R, St. Louis)	82,563
3.	**Richard A. Gephardt*** (D, St. Louis)	**141,221**
	Robert A. Cedarburg (R, St. Louis)	40,714
4.	**Ike Skelton*** (D, Lexington)	**151,455**
	Bill Baker (R, Lee's Summit)	71,868
5.	**Richard Bolling*** (D, Kansas City)	**110,952**
	Vincent E. Baker (R, Kansas City)	47,309
6.	**E. Thomas Coleman*** (R, Kansas City)	**144,821**
	Vernon King (D, Excelsior Springs)	61,955
7.	**Gene Taylor*** (R, Sarcoxie)	**140,843**
	Ken Young (D, Point Lookout)	65,651
8.	**Wendell Bailey** (R, Willow Springs)	**127,668**
	Steve Gardner (D, Ellisville)	95,744
9.	**Harold L. Volkmer*** (D, Hannibal)	**135,601**
	John W. Turner (R, St. Louis)	107,803
10.	**Bill Emerson** (R, DeSoto)	**116,715**
	Bill D. Burlison* (D, Cape Girardeau)	95,198

Montana

Dist.	Representative (Party, Home)	1980 Election
1.	**Pat Williams*** (D, Helena)	
	John K. McDonald (R, Lakeside)	
2.	**Ron Marlenee*** (R, Scobey)	**82,966**
	Tom Monahan (D, Billings)	58,440

Nebraska

Dist.	Representative (Party, Home)	1980 Election
1.	**Douglas K. Bereuter*** (R, Utica)	**158,740**
	Rex S. Story (D, Lincoln)	43,131
2.	**Harold J. Daub** (R, Omaha)	
	Richard M. Fellman (D, Omaha)	
3.	**Virginia Smith*** (R, Chappell)	**120,469**
	Stan Ditus (D, McCook)	34,691

Nevada At Large

Dist.	Representative (Party, Home)	1980 Election
	Jim Santini* (D, Las Vegas)	164,714
	Vince Saunders (R, Las Vegas)	62,920

New Hampshire

Dist.	Representative (Party, Home)	1980 Election
1.	**Norman E. D'Amours*** (D, Manchester)	**113,840**
	Marshall W. Cobleigh (R, Manchester)	72,982
2.	**Judd Gregg** (R, Greenfield)	**113,090**
	Maurice L. Arel (D, Nashua)	63,182

New Jersey

Dist.	Representative (Party, Home)	1980 Election
1.	**James J. Florio*** (D, Camden)	**145,717**
	Scott L. Sibert (R, Woodbury)	41,493
2.	**William J. Hughes*** (D, Ocean City)	**131,527**
	Beech N. Fox (R, Cape May Courthouse)	93,835
3.	**James J. Howard*** (D, Spring Lake Heights)	**101,193**
	Marie Sheehan Muhler (R, Marlboro)	99,377
4.	**Christopher H. Smith** (R, Trenton)	**88,680**
	Frank Thompson Jr.* (D, Trenton)	71,741
5.	**Millicent Fenwick*** (R, Bernardsville)	**153,942**
	Kieran E. Pillion Jr. (D, Millington)	40,690
6.	**Edwin B. Forsythe*** (R, Moorestown)	**120,930**
	Lewis M. Weinstein (D, Cherry Hill)	90,233
7.	**Margaret S. Roukema** (R, Ridgewood)	**104,033**
	Andrew Maguire* (D, Ridgewood)	95,089
8.	**Robert A. Roe*** (Paterson)	**96,351**
	William R. Cleveland (R, Pompton Lakes)	44,166
9.	**Harold C. Hollenbeck*** (R, East Rutherford)	**110,864**
	Gabriel Ambrosio (D, Lyndhurst)	72,687
10.	**Peter W. Rodino Jr.*** (D, Newark)	**72,472**
	Everett J. Jennings (R, East Orange)	11,310
11.	**Joseph G. Minish*** (D, West Orange)	**100,990**
	Robert A. Davis (R, Verona)	55,162
12.	**Matthew J. Rinaldo*** (R, Union)	**117,840**
	Rose Zeidwerg Monyek (D, Rahway)	83,193
13.	**Jim Courter*** (R, Hackettstown)	**152,019**
	Dave Stickle (D, Pompton Plains)	55,553
14.	**Frank J. Guarini*** (D, Jersey City)	**75,707**
	Dennis E. Teti (R, Weehawken)	38,464
15.	**Bernard J. Dwyer** (D, Edison)	**91,349**
	William J. O'Sullivan Jr. (R, Sayreville)	74,989

New Mexico

Dist.	Representative (Party, Home)	1980 Election
1.	**Manuel Lujan Jr.*** (R, Albuquerque)	**123,049**
	Bill Richardson (D, Santa Fe)	117,152
2.	**David King** (D, Pie Town)	**Unopposed**

New York

Dist.	Representative (Party, Home)	1980 Election
1.	**William Carney*** (R, Hauppaugh)	**107,661**
	Thomas A. Twomey (D, East Hampton)	81,695
2.	**Thomas J. Downey*** (D, W. Islip)	**78,651**
	Louis J. Modica (R, Brightwaters)	62,681
3.	**Gregory W. Carman** (R, C, Farmington)	**86,842**
	Jerome A. Ambro* (D, East Northport)	73,385
4.	**Norman F. Lent** (R, C, East Rockaway)	**116,931**
	Charles F. Brennan (D, Baldwin)	58,146
5.	**Raymond J. McGrath** (R, Valley Stream)	**104,668**
	Karen S. Burstein (D, Woodmere)	76,927
6.	**John LeBoutillier** (R, Westbury)	**90,008**
	Lester L. Wolff* (D, L, Great Neck)	79,701
7.	**Joseph P. Addabbo*** (D, R, L, Ozone Park)	**94,025**
	Francis A. Lees (C, East Meadow)	4,700
8.	**Benjamin S. Rosenthal*** (D, L, Flushing)	**93,445**
	Albert Lemishow (R, Flushing)	21,976
9.	**Geraldine A. Ferraro*** (D, Forest Hills)	**63,015**
	Vito P. Battista (R, Brooklyn)	44,086
10.	**Mario Biaggi*** (D, R, L, Bronx)	**93,451**
	Joseph P. Cavanna (C, Bronx)	3,986
11.	**James H. Scheuer*** (D, L, Neponsit)	**70,703**
	Andrew E. Carlan (R, Nassau)	25,173
12.	**Shirley Chisholm*** (D, L, Brooklyn)	**34,431**
	Charles Gibbs (R, Brooklyn)	3,540
13.	**Stephen J. Solarz** (D, L, Brooklyn)	**80,379**
	Harry DeMell (R, C, Brooklyn)	19,582
14.	**Fred Richmond*** (D, L, Brooklyn)	**44,469**
	Christopher Lovell (R, C, Brooklyn)	8,423
15.	**Leo C. Zeferetti*** (D, Brooklyn)	**48,303**
	Paul M. Atanasio (R, Brooklyn)	46,107
16.	**Charles E. Schumer** (D, L, Brooklyn)	**66,841**
	Theodore Silverman (R, C, Brooklyn)	16,840
17.	**Guy V. Molinari** (R, C, Staten Island)	**67,663**
	John M. Murphy*)D, Staten Island)	49,164
18.	**S. William Green** (R, New York)	**87,540**
	Mark J Green* (D, L, New York)	67,724
19.	**Charles B. Rangel*** (D, R, L, New York)	**83,507**
	Marjorie Garvey (C, New York)	2,915
20.	**Ted Weiss*** (D, L, New York)	**84,661**
	James E. Greene (R, New York)	15,147
21.	**Robert Garcia*** (D, R, L, Bronx)	**31,839**
	Gina A. Aceto (C, Bronx)	274
22.	**Jonathan B. Bingham*** (D, L, Bronx)	**64,914**
	Robert S. Black (R, Bronx)	9,919
23.	**Peter A. Peyser*** (D, Irvington)	**67,847**
	Andrew Albanese (R, C, Scarsdale)	56,110
24.	**Richard L. Ottinger*** (D, Pleasantville)	
	Joseph W. Christiana (R, C, Mt. Vernon)	37,429
25.	**Hamilton Fish Jr.*** (R, C, Poughkeepsie)	**149,666**
	Gunars Ozols (D, Wappingers)	
26.	**Benjamin A. Gilman*** (R, Middletown)	**133,508**
	Eugene Victor (D, L, Goshen)	38,177
27.	**Matthew F. McHugh*** (D, Ithaca)	**100,099**
	Neil T. Wallace (R, C, Ithaca)	80,126
28.	**Samuel S. Stratton*** (D, Amsterdam)	**163,453**
	Frank Wicks (R, Schenectady)	38,823
29.	**Gerald B. Solomon*** (R, C, Glens Falls)	**134,612**
	Roger L. Hurley (D, L, Granville)	67,808
30.	**David O'B. Martin** (R, C, Canton)	**107,379**
	Mary Anne Krupsak (D, L, Canajoharie)	55,905
31.	**Donald J. Mitchell*** (R, Herkimer)	**127,319**
	Irving A. Schwartz (D, L, Utica)	36,884
32.	**George Wortley** (R, C, Fayetteville)	**102,983**
	Jeffery S. Brooks (D, Green)	53,557
33.	**Gary A. Lee*** (R, C, Ithaca)	**129,222**
	Dolores M. Reed (D, C, L, Syracuse)	39,240
34.	**Frank Horton** (R, Rochester)	**125,198**
	James Toole (D, Rochester)	35,351
35.	**Barbara B. Conable Jr.** (R, Rochester)	**112,819**
	John M. Owens (D, C, Rochester)	40,055
36.	**John J. LaFalce*** (D, L, Tonawanda)	**118,966**
	H. William Feder (R, C, Niagara Falls)	47,626
37.	**Henry J. Nowak*** (D, L, Buffalo)	**91,033**
	Roger Heymanowski (R, C, Buffalo)	16,245
38.	**Jack F. Kemp*** (R, C, Buffalo)	**161,899**
	Gale A. Denn (D, L, Eden)	37,932
39.	**Stanley N. Lundine*** (D, Jamestown)	**93,123**
	James Abdella (R, C, Jamestown)	74,173

North Carolina

Dist.	Representative (Party, Home)	1980 Election
1.	**Walter B. Jones*** (D, Farmville)	**Unopposed**
2.	**L. H. Fountain*** (D, Tarboro)	**89,878**
	Barry L. Gardner (R, Rocky Mount)	36,286
3.	**Charles Whitley*** (D, Mt. Olive)	**84,824**
	Larry J. Parker (R, Erwin)	40,332
4.	**Ike F. Andrews*** (D, Siler City)	**97,590**
	Thurman Hogan (R, Asheboro)	84,695
5.	**Stephen L. Neal*** (D, Winston-Salem)	**98,674**
	Anne Bagnal (R, Winston-Salem)	94,135
6.	**Eugene Johnston** (R, Greensboro)	**80,263**
	Richardson Preyer (D, Greensboro)	76,916
7.	**Charles Rose***87,904 (D, Fayetteville)	
	Vivian S. Wright (R, Wilmington)	40,068
8.	**W. G. (Bill) Hefner*** (D, Concord)	**94,101**
	L. E. (Larry) Harris (R, Kannapolis)	66,356
9.	**James G. Martin*** (R, Charlotte)	**98,288**
	Randall R. Kincaid (D, Davidson)	70,479
10.	**James T. Broyhill*** (R, Lenoir)	**120,747**
	James O. Icenhour (D, Hickory)	52,517
11.	**William M. Hendon** (R, Asheville)	**103,215**
	Lamar Gudger* (D, Asheville)	89,330

North Dakota At Large

Dist.	Representative (Party, Home)	1980 Election
	Byron L. Dorgan (D, Bismarck)	**144,499**
	Jim Smykowski (R, Cayuga)	106,700

Ohio

Dist.	Representative (Party, Home)	1980 Election
1.	**Bill Gradison*** (R, Cincinnati)	**123,806**
	Donald J. Zwick (D, Cincinnati)	38,451
2.	**Thomas A. Luken*** (D, Cincinnati)	**103,366**
	Tom Atkins (R, Cincinnati)	72,721
3.	**Tony P. Hall*** (D, Dayton)	**95,426**
	Albert H. Sealy (R, Dayton)	66,590
4.	**Tennyson Guyer*** (R, Findlay)	**133,781**
	Geraldine Tebben (D, Lima	51,329
5.	**Delbert L. Latta** (R, Bowling Green)	**136,459**
	James R. Sherck (D, Fremont	57,790
6.	**Bob McEwen** (R, Hillsboro)	**101,226**
	Ted Strickland (D, Lucasville)	84,231
7.	**Clarence J. Brown*** (R, Urbana)	**123,817**
	Donald Hollister (D, Yellow Springs)	38,964
8.	**Thomas N. Kindness*** (R, Hamilton)	**139,354**
	John W. Griffen (D, Miamisburg)	44,049
9.	**Ed Weber** (R, Toledo)	**96,960**
	Thomas L. Ashley* (D, Maumee)	68,753
10.	**Clarence E. Miller*** (R, Lancaster	**143,092**
	Jack E. Stecker (D, Zanesville)	49,350
11.	**J. William Stanton*** (R, Painesville)	**125,965**
	Patrick J. Donlin (D, Hubbard)	50,550

Dist.	Representative (Party, Home)	1980 Election
12.	**Robert N. Shamansky** (D, Columbus)	**108,598**
	Samuel L. Devine* (R, Columbus)	97,618
13.	**Don J. Pease*** (D, Oberlin)	**111,953**
	David E. Armstrong (R, North Ridgeville)	63,304
14.	**John F. Seiberling*** (D, Akron)	**102,829**
	Louis A. Mangels (R, Akron)	55,707
15.	**Chalmers P. Wylie*** (R, Columbus)	**128,333**
	Terry Freeman (D, Columbus)	48,561
16.	**Ralph S. Regula*** R, Navarre)	**149,799**
	Larry V. Slagle (D, Massillon)	34,194
17.	**John M. Ashbrook*** (R, Johnstown)	**128,974**
	Donald E. Yunker (D, Galion)	48,486
18.	**Douglas Applegate*** (D, Steubenville)	**134,650**
	Gary L. Hammersley (R, Bolivar)	42,301
19.	**Lyle Williams*** (R, Niles)	**103,866**
	Harry Meshel (D, Youngstown)	76,444
20.	**Mary Rose Oakar*** (D, Cleveland)	**Unopposed**
21.	**Louis Stokes*** (D, Warrensville Heights)	**82,288**
	Robert L. Woodall (R, Cleveland)	11,136
22.	**Dennis E. Eckart** (D, Euclid)	**102,356**
	Joseph J. Nahra (R, Cleveland Heights)	80,385
23.	**Ronald M. Mottl*** (D, Parma)	**Unopposed**

Oklahoma

Dist.	Representative (Party, Home)	1980 Election
1.	**James R. Jones*** (D, Tulsa)	**115,381**
	Richard C. Freeman (R, Tulsa)	82,293
2.	**Mike Synar*** (D, Muskogee)	**95,736**
	Gary Richardson (R, Muskogee)	80,490
3.	**Wesley Wade Watkins*** (D, Ada)	**Unopposed**
4.	**Dave McCurdy** (D, Norman)	**94,707**
	Howard Rutledge (R, Norman)	73,363
5.	**Mickey Edwards*** (R, Oklahoma City)	**86,518**
	David C. Hood (D, Oklahoma City)	35,500
6.	**Glenn English*** (D, Cordell)	**110,180**
	Carol McCurley (R, Oklahoma City)	59,592

Oregon

Dist.	Representative (Party, Home)	1980 Election
1.	**Les AuCoin*** (D, Portland)	**196,011**
	Lynn Engdahl (R, Portland)	100,343
2.	**Al Ullman*** (D, Baker)	**139,618**
	Denny Smith (R, Salem)	136,104
3.	**Ron Wyden** (D, Portland)	**149,323**
	Darrell R. Conger (R, Portland)	59,246
4.	**James Weaver*** (D, Eugene)	**158,172**
	Michael Fitzgerald (R, Brookings)	130,287

Pennsylvania

Dist.	Representative (Party, Home)	1980 Election
1.	**Thomas Foglietta** (I,)	**56,529**
	Michael (Ozzie) Meyers (D, Philadelphia)	51,770
	Robert R. Burke (R, Philadelphia)	36,919
2.	**William H. Gray III*** (D, Philadelphia)	**123,020**
	James L. Buckman (I, Philadelphia)	2,217
3.	**Raymond F. Lederer*** (D, Philadelphia)	**67,660**
	William J. Phillips (R, Philadelphia)	40,294
4.	**Charles E. Dougherty*** (R, Philadelphia)	**124,904**
	Thomas J. Magrann (D, Philadelphia)	73,892
5.	**Richard T. Schulze*** (R, West Chester)	**157,473**
	Grady G. Brickhouse (R, (D, Spring)	47,108
6.	**Gus Yatron*** (D, Reading)	**117,559**
	George Hulshart (R, Laureldale)	58,038
7.	**Robert W. Edgar*** (D, Broomall)	**98,083**
	Dennis J. Rochford (R, Springfield)	87,618
8.	**James K. Coyne** (R, Newtown)	**103,557**
	Peter H. Kostmayer* (D, New Hope)	99,588
9.	**Bud Shuster*** (R, D, Everett)	**Unopposed**
10.	**Joseph M. McDade*** (R, Clarks Summit)	**144,230**
	Gene Bosalyga (D, Olyphant)	42,881
11.	**James L. Nelligan** (R, Forty-Fort)	**93,439**
	Raphael Musto* (D, Pittston)	86,386
12.	**John P. Murtha*** (D, Johnstown)	**107,933**
	Charles A. Getty (R, Johnstown)	72,903
13.	**Lawrence Coughlin*** (R, Norristown)	**137,563**
	Peter Slawek (D, Lafayette Hill)	57,558
14.	**William J. Coyne** (D, Pittsburgh)	**101,308**
	Stan Thomas (R, Pittsburgh)	43,429
15.	**Donald L. Ritter*** R, Coopersburg)	**99,062**
	Jeanette Reibman (D, Easton)	68,324
16.	**Robert S. Walker** (R, E. Petersburg)	**130,584**
	James A. Woodcock (D, Lancaster)	37,318
17.	**Allen E. Ertel*** (D, Montoursville)	**96,950**
	Daniel S. Seiverling (R, Hershey)	63,278
18.	**Doug Walgren*** (D, Pittsburgh)	**127,154**
	Steven R. Snyder (R, Sewickley)	58,965
19.	**William F. Goodling* (R, York)**	**135,255**
	Richard P. Noll (D, York)	41,544
20.	**Joseph M. Gaydos*** (D, McKeesport)	**121,260**
	Kathleen M. Meyer (R, Pittsburgh)	46,659
21.	**Donald A. Bailey*** (D, Greensburg)	**112,144**
	Dirk Matson (R, Ligonier)	51,834
22.	**Austin J. Murphy** (D, Monongahela)	**114,501**
	Marilyn C. Ecoff (R, Pittsburgh)	49,579
23.	**William E. Clinger Jr.*** (R, Warren)	**123,171**
	Peter Atigan (D, Kane)	41,079
24.	**Marc L. Marks*** (R, Sharon)	**86,578**
	David C. DiCario (D, Erie)	86,293
25.	**Eugene V. Atkinson*** (D, Aliquippa)	**119,338**
	Robert H. Morris (R, New Castle)	58,708

Rhode Island

Dist.	Representative (Party, Home)	1980 Election
1.	**Fernand J. St Germain*** (D, Woonsocket)	**116,149**
	William P. Montgomery (R, Central Falls)	55,559
2.	**Claudine Camarada Schneider** (R, Narragansett)	**110,175**
	Edward P. Beard* (D, Cranston)	88,158

South Carolina

Dist.	Representative (Party, Home)	1980 Election
1.	**Thomas F. Daschle*** (R, Charleston)	**69,893**
	Charles D. (Pug) Ravenel (D, Charleston)	67,212
2.	**Floyd Spence** (R, Lexington)	**92,295**
	Tom Turnipseed (D, Columbia)	73,143
3.	**Butler Derrick*** (D, Edgefield)	**86,619**
	Marshall Parker (R, Clemson)	53,431
4.	**Carroll A. Campbell Jr.*** (R, Fountain Inn)	**91,391**
	Thomas Waldenfels (LIBERT, Landrum)	6,984
5.	**Ken Holland*** (D, Rock Hill)	**99,296**
	Thomas Campbell (LIBERT, Blacksburg)	**14,188**
6.	**John L. Napier** (R, Bennettsville)	**76,307**
	John W. Jenrette Jr. (D, N. Myrtle Beach)	71,781

South Dakota

Dist.	Representative (Party, Home)	1980 Election
1.	**Thomas A. Daschle*** (D, Aberdeen)	**109,918**
	Bart Kull (R, Sioux Falls)	57,140
2.	**Clint 6 Stofferahn** (R, Presho)	**87,932**
	Kenneth D. Stofferahn (D, Pierre)	63,415

Tennessee

Dist.	Representative (Party, Home)	1980 Election
1.	**James H. Quillen*** (R, Kingsport)	**Unopposed**
2.	**Dave Dunaway** (D, La Follette)	**146,983**
	John J. Duncan (R, Knoxville)	46,320
3.	**Marilyn Lloyd Bouquard*** (D, Chattanooga)	**117,722**
	Glen M. Byers (R, Cleveland)	75,073
4.	**Albert Gore Jr.*** (D, Carthage)	**136,732**
	James Beau Seigneur (R, Shelbyville)	35,539

Dist.	Representative (Party, Home)	1980 Election
5.	**William Hill Boner*** (D, Nashville)	**118,627**
	Mike Adams (R, Nashville)	62,715
6.	**Robin L. Beard Jr.*** (R, Memphis)	**Unopposed**
7.	**Ed Jones*** (D, Yorkville)	**133,348**
	Daniel Campbell (R, Memphis)	39,522
8.	**Harold E. Ford*** (D, Memphis)	**Unopposed**

Texas

Dist.	Representative (Party, Home)	1980 Election
1.	**Sam B. Hall Jr.*** (D, Marshall)	**Unopposed**
2.	**Charles Wilson*** (D, Lufkin)	**138,341**
	F. H. Pannill Sr. (R, Huntsville)	59,001
3.	**Earle S. Porter** (R, Dallas)	**2202,128**
	James M. Collins* (R, Dallas)	47,433
4.	**Ralph M. Hall** (D, Rockwall)	**95,941**
	John H. Wright (R, Tyler)	86,768
5.	**Jim Mattox*** (D, Dallas)	**69,523**
	Tom Pauken (R, Mesquite)	66,739
6.	**Phil Gramm** (D, College Station)	**133,527**
	Dave (Buster) Haskins (R, Fort Worth)	57,472
7.	**Bill Archer*** (R, Houston)	**222,697**
	Robert L. Hutchings (D, Houston)	46,519
8.	**Jack Fields** (R, Humble)	**68,653**
	Bob Eckhardt* (D, Houston)	65,736
9.	**Jack Brooks*** (D, Beaumont)	**Unopposed**
10.	**J. J. Pickle** (D, Austin)	**131,738**
	John Biggar (R, Austin)	86,436
11.	**Marvin Leath** (D, Marlin)	**Unopposed**
12.	**Jim Wright*** (D, Fort Worth)	**109,125**
	Jim Bradshaw (R, Fort Worth)	67,225
13.	**Jack Hightower*** (D, Vernon)	**98,564**
	Ron Slover (R, Amarillo)	80,789
14.	**William N. Patman** (D, Ganacio)	**89,058**
	Charles L. Concklin (R, Corpus Christi)	67,540
15.	**E. (Kika) de la Garza*** (D, Mission)	**102,204**
	Lendy McDonald (R, Pt. Isabel)	42,926
16.	**Richard C. White*** (D, Bethesda)	**104,549**
	Catherine A. McDivitt (Libert, El Paso)	18,983
17.	**Charles W. Stenholm** (D, Stenholm)	**Unopposed**
18.	**Mickey Leland** (D, Houston)	**71,986**
	C. L. Kennedy (R, Houston)	16,128
19.	**Kent Hance** (D, Lubbock)	**124,419**
	J. D. Webster (Libert, Midland)	8,737
20.	**Henry B. Gonzalez*** (D, San Antonio)	**37,301**
	Merle W. Nash (R, San Antonio)	7,422
21.	**Tom Loeffler** (R, Hunt)	**94,263**
	Joe Sullivan (D, San Antonio)	30,748
22.	**Mike Andrews** (R, Lake Jackson)	**106,766**
	Mike Andrews (D, Houston)	101,081
23.	**Abraham Kazen Jr.*** (D, Laredo)	**91,148**
	Bobby Locke (R, San Antonio)	37,109
24.	**Martin Frost** (D, Dallas)	**91,000**
	Clay Smothers (R, Fort Worth)	55,564

Utah

Dist.	Representative (Party, Home)	1980 Election
1.	**James V. Hansen**211 (R, Farmington)	**1**
	Gunn McKay* (D, Huntsville)	143,049
2.	**Dan Marriott*** (R, Salt Lake City)	**193,120**
	Arthur L. Monson (D, Salt Lake City)	87,459

Vermont At Large

Dist.	Representative (Party, Home)	1980 Election
1.	**James M. Jeffords*** (R, Montpelier)	**151,608**
	Robin Lloyd (Cit, Burlington)	24,665

Virginia

Dist.	Representative (Party, Home)	1980 Election
1.	**Paul S. Trible Jr.*** (R, Tappahannock)	**130,583**
	Sharon D. Grant (I, Newport News)	13,585
2.	**G. William Whitehurst*** (R, Virginia Beach)	**95,913**
	Kenneth P. Morrison (I, Norfolk)	10,820
3.	**Thomas J. Bliley** (R, Richmond)	**96,870**
	John A. Mapp (D, Richmond)	61,127
4.	**Robert W. Daniel Jr.*** (R, Spring Grove)	**92,444**
	Cecil Y. Jenkins Jr.* (D, Chesapeake	59,476
5.	**Dan Daniel*** (D, Danville)	**Unopposed**
6.	**M. Caldwell Butler*** (R, Roanoke)	**Unopposed**
7.	**J. Kenneth Robinson*** (R, Winchester)	**Unopposed**
8.	**Stanford E. Parris** (R, Woodbridge)	**95,556**
	Herbert E. Harris II* (D, Alexandria)	94,391
9.	**William C. Wampler*** (R, Bristol)	**116,089**
	Roosevelt C. Ferguson (D, Lebanon)	51,471
10.	**Frank R. Wolf** (R, Vienna)	**105,606**
	Joseph L. Fisher* (D, Arlington)	98,673

Washington

Dist.	Representative (Party, Home)	1980 Election
1.	**Joel Pritchard*** (R, Seattle)	**162,298**
	Robin Drake (D, Seattle)	38,542
2.	**Al Swift** (D, Bellingham)	**146,847**
	Neal Snider (R, Bellingham)	73,688
3.	**Don Bonker*** (D, Olympia)	**136,744**
	Rod Culp (R, Montesano)	80,122
4.	**Sid Morrison** (R, Zillah)	**119,585**
	Mike McCormack* D, Richland	90,133
5.	**Thomas S. Foley*** (D, Spokane)	**108,520**
	John Sonneland (R, Spokane)	101,106
6.	**Norman D. Dicks*** (D, Bremerton)	**101,214**
	Jim Beaver (R, Tacoma)	86,653
7.	**Mike Lowry** (D, Mercer Island)	**101,439**
	Ron Dunlap (R, Bellevue)	74,650

West Virginia

Dist.	Representative (Party, Home)	1980 Election
1.	**Robert H. Mollohan*** (D, Fairmont)	**107,119**
	Joe Bartlett (R, Lost Creek)	61,273
2.	**Cleve Benedict** (R, Lewisburg)	**96,479**
	Pat R. Hamilton (D, Oak Hill)	69,377
3.	**Mick Staton** (R, South Charleston)	**94,084**
	John G. Hutchinson (D, Charleston)	84,096
4.	**Nick J. Rahall*** (D, Beckley)	**115,938**
	Winton G. Covey Jr. (R, Lerona)	35,405

Wisconsin

Dist.	Representative (Party, Home)	1980 Election
1.	**Les Aspin*** (D, East Troy)	**126,331**
	Kathryn H. Canary (R, Delavan)	45,960
2.	**Robert W. Kastenmeier*** (D, Sun Prairie)	**142,031**
	James A. Wright (R, Baraboo)	119,435
3.	**Steven Gunderson** (R, Osseo)	**131,581**
	Alvin Baldus* (D, Menomonie)	126,797
4.	**Clement J. Zablocki*** (D, Milwaukee)	**149,572**
	Elroy C. Honadel (R, Oak Creek)	60,578
5.	**Henry S. Reuss*** (D, Milwaukee)	**129,509**
	David Bathke (R, Milwaukee)	366
6.	**Thomas E. Petri** (R, Fond du Lac)	**143,992**
	Gary R. Goyke (D, Oshkosh)	98,716
7.	**David R. Obey*** (D, Wausau)	**162,010**
	Vinton A. Vesta* (R, Hayward)	89,134
8.	**Toby Roth** (R, Appleton)	**169,296**
	Michael R. Monfils (D, Green Bay)	81,474
9.	**F. James Sensenbrenner** (R, Shorewood)	**204,972**
	Gary C. Benedict (D, New Berlin)	56,040

Wyoming At Large

Dist.	Representative (Party, Home)	1980 Election
	Richard B. Cheney (R, Casper	115,692
	Jim Rogers (D, Lyman)	53,309

Non-Voting Delegates

District of Columbia	Walter E. Fauntroy* (D, D.C.)
	Robert J. Roehr (R, D.C.)
Guam	Antonio Borja Wo Pat* (D, Agana)
	Antonio M. Palomo (R, Agana)
Virgin Islands	Ron deLugo (D, St. Thomas)
	Melvin Evans (R, St. Croix)

Political Divisions of the U.S. Senate and House of Representatives From 1857 (35th Cong.) to 1981-1983 (97th Cong.)

Source: Clerk of the House of Representatives

All figures reflect immediate result of elections.

		Senate					House of Representatives				
Congress	Years	Number of Senators	Democrats	Republicans	Other parties	Vacant	Number of Representatives	Democrats	Republicans	Other parties	Vacant
35th. . . .	1857-59	64	39	20	5		237	131	92	14	
36th. . . .	1859-61	66	38	26	2		237	101	113	23	
37th. . . .	1861-63	50	11	31	7	1	178	42	106	28	2
38th. . . .	1863-65	51	12	39			183	80	103		
39th. . . .	1865-67	52	10	42			191	46	145		
40th. . . .	1867-69	53	11	42			193	49	143		1
41st. . . .	1869-71	74	11	61		2	243	73	170		
42d	1871-73	74	17	57			243	104	139		
43d	1873-75	74	19	54		1	293	88	203		2
44th. . . .	1875-77	76	29	46		1	293	181	107	3	2
45th. . . .	1877-79	76	36	39	1		293	156	137		
46th. . . .	1879-81	76	43	33			293	150	128	14	1
47th. . . .	1881-83	76	37	37	2		293	130	152	11	
48th. . . .	1883-85	76	36	40			325	200	119	6	
49th. . . .	1885-87	76	34	41		1	325	182	140	2	1
50th. . . .	1887-89	76	37	39			325	170	151	4	
51st. . . .	1889-91	84	37	47			330	156	173	1	
52d	1891-93	88	39	47	2		333	231	88	14	
53d	1893-95	88	44	38	3	3	356	220	126	10	
54th. . . .	1895-97	88	39	44	5		357	104	246	7	
55th. . . .	1897-99	90	34	46	10		357	134	206	16	1
56th. . . .	1899-1901	90	26	53	11		357	163	185	9	
57th. . . .	1901-03	90	29	56	3	2	357	153	198	5	1
58th. . . .	1903-05	90	32	58			386	178	207		1
59th. . . .	1905-07	90	32	58			386	136	250		
60th. . . .	1907-09	92	29	61		2	386	164	222		
61st. . . .	1909-11	92	32	59		1	391	172	219		
62d	1911-13	92	42	49		1	391	228	162	1	
63d	1913-15	96	51	44	1		435	290	127	18	
64th. . . .	1915-17	96	56	39	1		435	231	193	8	3
65th. . . .	1917-19	96	53	42	1		435	[1]210	216	9	
66th. . . .	1919-21	96	47	48	1		435	191	237	7	
67th. . . .	1921-23	96	37	59			435	132	300	1	2
68th. . . .	1923-25	96	43	51	2		435	207	225	3	
69th. . . .	1925-27	96	40	54	1	1	435	183	247	5	
70th. . . .	1927-29	96	47	48	1		435	195	237	3	
71st. . . .	1929-31	96	39	56	1		435	163	267	1	4
72d	1931-33	96	47	48	1		435	[2]216	218	1	
73d	1933-35	96	59	36	1		435	313	117	5	
74th. . . .	1935-37	96	69	25	2		435	322	103	10	
75th. . . .	1937-39	96	75	17	4		435	333	89	13	
76th. . . .	1939-41	96	69	23	4		435	262	169	4	
77th. . . .	1941-43	96	66	28	2		435	267	162	6	
78th. . . .	1943-45	96	57	38	1		435	222	209	4	
79th. . . .	1945-47	96	57	38	1		435	243	190	2	
80th. . . .	1947-49	96	45	51			435	188	246	1	
81st. . . .	1949-51	96	54	42			435	263	171	1	
82d	1951-53	96	48	47	1		435	234	199	2	
83d	1953-55	96	46	48	2		435	213	221	1	
84th. . . .	1955-57	96	48	47	1		435	232	203		
85th. . . .	1957-59	96	49	47			435	234	201		
86th. . . .	1959-61	98	64	34			[3]436	283	153		
87th. . . .	1961-63	100	64	36			[4]437	262	175		
88th. . . .	1963-65	100	67	33			435	258	176		1
89th. . . .	1965-67	100	68	32			435	295	140		
90th. . . .	1967-69	100	64	36			435	248	187		
91st. . . .	1969-71	100	58	42			435	243	192		
92d	1971-73	100	54	44	2		435	255	180		
93d	1973-75	100	56	42	2		435	242	192	1	
94th. . . .	1975-77	100	61	37	2		435	291	144		
95th. . . .	1977-79	100	61	38	1		435	292	143		
96th. . . .	1979-81	100	58	41	1		435	277	158		
97th. . . .	1981-83	100	53	46	1		435[5]	242	192		

(1) Democrats organized House with help of other parties. (2) Democrats organized House due to Republican deaths. (3) Proclamation declaring Alaska a State issued Jan. 3, 1959. (4) Proclamation declaring Hawaii a State issued Aug. 21, 1959. (5) One seat undecided.

Governors of States and Possessions

Reflecting Nov. 4, 1980 election

State	Capital	Governor	Party	Term years	Term expires	Annua salar
Alabama	Montgomery	Forrest "Fob" James	Dem.	4	Jan. 1983	$50,00
Alaska	Juneau	Jay Hammond	Rep.	4	Dec. 1982	70,00
Arizona	Phoenix	Bruce E. Babbitt	Dem.	4	Jan. 1983	50,00
Arkansas	Little Rock	Frank White	Rep.	2	Jan. 1983	35,00
California	Sacramento	Edmund G. Brown Jr.	Dem.	4	Jan. 1983	49,10
Colorado	Denver	Richard D. Lamm	Dem.	4	Jan. 1983	40,00
Connecticut	Hartford	Ella T. Grasso	Dem.	4	Jan. 1983	42,00
Delaware	Dover	Pierre S. du Pont 4th	Rep.	4	Jan. 1985	35,00
Florida	Tallahassee	Robert Graham	Dem.	4	Jan. 1983	56,01
Georgia	Atlanta	George Busbee	Dem.	4	Jan. 1983	50,00
Hawaii	Honolulu	George R. Ariyoshi	Dem.	4	Dec. 1982	50,00
Idaho	Boise	John V. Evans	Dem.	4	Jan. 1983	40,00
Illinois	Springfield	James R. Thompson	Rep.	4	Jan. 1983	50,00
Indiana	Indianapolis	Robert Orr	Rep.	4	Jan. 1985	36,00
Iowa	Des Moines	Robert D. Ray	Rep.	4	Jan. 1983	55,00
Kansas	Topeka	John Carlin	Dem.	4	Jan. 1983	45,00
Kentucky	Frankfort	John Y. Brown Jr.	Dem.	4	Dec. 1983	45,00
Louisiana	Baton Rouge	David C. Treen	Rep.	4	May 1984	52,40
Maine	Augusta	Joseph E. Brennan	Dem.	4	Jan. 1983	35,00
Maryland	Annapolis	Harry Hughes	Dem.	4	Jan. 1983	60,00
Massachusetts	Boston	Edward J. King	Dem.	4	Jan. 1983	40,00
Michigan	Lansing	William G. Milliken	Rep.	4	Jan. 1983	58,00
Minnesota	St. Paul	Albert H. Quie	Rep.	4	Jan. 1983	58,00
Mississippi	Jackson	William Winter	Dem.	4	Jan. 1984	43,00
Missouri	Jefferson City	Christopher S. Bond	Rep.	4	Jan. 1985	37,50
Montana	Helena	Ted Schwinden	Dem.	4	Jan. 1985	37,50
Nebraska	Lincoln	Charles Thone	Rep.	4	Jan. 1983	40,00
Nevada	Carson City	Robert List	Rep.	4	Jan. 1983	50,00
New Hampshire	Concord	Hugh Gallen	Dem.	2	Jan. 1983	42,00
New Jersey	Trenton	Brendan T. Byrne	Dem.	4	Jan. 1982	65,00
New Mexico	Sante Fe	Bruce King	Dem.	4	Jan. 1983	40,00
New York	Albany	Hugh L. Carey	Dem.	4	Jan. 1983	85,00
North Carolina	Raleigh	James B. Hunt Jr.	Dem.	4	Jan. 1985	50,08
North Dakota	Bismarck	Allen Olsen	Rep.	4	Jan. 1985	27,50
Ohio	Columbus	James A. Rhodes	Rep	4	Jan. 1983	50,00
Oklahoma	Oklahoma City	George Nigh	Dem.	4	Jan. 1983	42,50
Oregon	Salem	Victor Atiyeh	Rep.	4	Jan. 1983	47,97
Pennsylvania	Harrisburg	Richard Thornburgh	Rep.	4	Jan. 1983	66,00
Rhode Island	Providence	J. Joseph Garrahy	Dem.	2	Jan. 1983	42,50
South Carolina	Columbia	Richard Riley	Dem.	4	Jan. 1983	39,00
South Dakota	Pierre	William Janklow	Rep.	4	Jan. 1983	37,00
Tennessee	Nashville	Lamar Alexander	Rep.	4	Jan. 1983	65,00
Texas	Austin	William P. Clements Jr.	Rep.	4	Jan. 1983	71,40
Utah	Salt Lake City	Scott M. Matheson	Dem.	4	Jan. 1985	48,00
Vermont	Montpelier	Richard A. Snelling	Rep.	2	Jan. 1983	39,00
Virginia	Richmond	John Dalton	Rep.	4	Jan. 1982	60,00
Washington	Olympia	John Spellman	Rep.	4	Jan. 1985	63,00
West Virginia	Charleston	John D. Rockefeller 4th	Dem.	4	Jan. 1985	50,00
Wisconsin	Madison	Lee Dreyfus	Rep.	4	Jan. 1983	44,92
Wyoming	Cheyenne	Ed Herschler	Dem.	4	Jan. 1983	55,00
Possessions						
Amer. Samoa	Pago Pago	Peter Coleman	Rep.	4	Jan. 1985	–
Guam	Agana	Paul Calvo	Rep.	4	Jan. 1985	35,00
N. Mariana Isls.	Saipan	Carlos Camacho	Dem.	4	Jan. 1982	20,00
Puerto Rico	San Juan	Carlos Romero Barcelo	N.P.	4	Jan. 1985	36,20
Virgin Isls.	Charlotte Amalie	Juan Luis	Ind.	4	Jan. 1983	35,50

The Races for Governor

State	Democrats	Vote	Republicans	Vote
Arkansas	Bill Clinton	394,746	Frank White	425,37
Delaware	William J. Gorcy	64,933	Pierre S. du Pont	159,77
Indiana	Robert D. Orr	1,231,213	John A. Hillenbrand 2d	988,42
Missouri	Joseph P. Teasdale	967,117	Christopher S. Bond	1,076,72
Montana	Ted Schwinden	184,577	Jack Ramirez	148,40
New Hampshire	Hugh Gallen	226,285	Meldrim Thomson Jr.	155,71
No. Carolina	James B. Hunt Jr.	1,178,507	I. Beverly Lake Jr.	686,97
No. Dakota	Arthur A. Link	126,086	Allen I. Olson	144,38
Rhode Island	J. Joseph Garrahy	283,995	Vincent A. Cianci	99,37
Utah	Scott A. Matheson	327,886	Bob Wright	264,52
Vermont	M. Jerome Diamond	75,456	Richard A. Snelling	128,43
Washington	James A. McDermott	669,337	John Spellman	868,23
West Virginia	John D. Rockefeller 4th	387,269	Arch A. Moore	328,91

Mayors and City Managers of Larger North American Cities

Reflecting Nov. 4, 1980 elections

*Asterisk before name denotes city manager. All others are mayors. For mayors, dates are those of next election; for city ıanagers, they are dates of appointment.

D, Democrat; R, Republican; N-P, Non-Partisan

City	Name	Term
bilene, Tex.	*Fred Sandlin	**1974, May**
bington, Pa.	*Albert Herrmann	**1978, May**
kron, Oh.	Roy L. Ray, R	**1983, Nov.**
lameda, Cal.	*J. Bruce Rupp	**1980, Jan.**
lbany, Ga.	James H. Gray, D	**1981, Nov.**
lbany, N.Y.	Erastus Corning 2d, D	**1983, Nov.**
lbuquerque, N.M.	David Rusk, D	**1981, Oct.**
lexandria, La.	Carroll E. Lanier, D	**1982, Oct.**
lexandria, Va.	*Douglas Harman	**1976, Jan.**
lhambra, Cal.	*Andrew Lazzaretto Jr.	**1980, Jan.**
llen Park, Mich.	Frank J. Lada, D	**1981, Nov.**
llentown, Pa.	Frank Fischl Jr., D	**1981, Nov.**
lton, Ill.	Paul A. Lenz, N-P	**1981, Apr.**
ltoona, Pa.	Alan Hancock, R	**1983, Nov.**
marillo, Tex.	*John S. Stiff	**1963, Sept.**
mes, La.	*John Elwell	**1980, May**
naheim, Cal.	*William O. Talley	**1976, July**
nchorage, Alas.	George M. Sullivan, R	**1981, Nov.**
nderson, Ind.	Thomas McMahan, R	**1983, Nov.**
nderson, S.C.	*Richard Burnette	**1976, Sept.**
nn Arbor, Mich.	*Terry V. Sprenkel	**1979, Dec.**
ppleton, Wis.	Dorothy Johnson, N-P	**1984, Apr.**
rcadia, Cal.	*Lyle W. Alberg	**1978, Jan.**
rlington, Mass.	*Donald R. Marquis	**1966, Nov.**
rlington, Tex.	S.J. Stovall, D	**1981, Apr.**
rlington, Va.	*W.V. Ford	**1976, Mar.**
rlington Hts., Ill.	*L.A. Hanson	**1958, Oct.**
rvada, Col.	*Craig Kocian	**1977, Mar.**
sheville, N.C.	*K.M. Michalove	**1977, May**
tlanta, Ga.	Maynard Jackson, D	**1981, Nov.**
tlantic City, N.J.	Joseph Lazarow, R	**1984, May**
uburn, N.Y.	*Bruce Clifford	**1966, Aug.**
ugusta, Ga.	Lewis A. Newman, N-P	**1981, Nov.**
urora, Col.	*Robert E. Brown	**1978, July**
urora, Ill.	Jack Hill, N-P	**1981, Apr.**
ustin, Tex.	*Dan H. Davidson	**1972, Aug.**
akersfield, Cal.	*Harold E. Bergen	**1966, July**
aldwin Park, Cal.	*Philip R. Sexton	**1977, Dec.**
altimore, Md.	William Schaefer, D	**1983, Nov.**
angor, Me.	*John W. Flynn	**1977, Feb.**
aton Rouge, La.	Pat Screen, D	**1984, Nov.**
attle Creek, Mich.	*Gordon Jaeger	**1976, Mar.**
ay City, Mich.	*David D. Barnes	**1979, May**
ayonne, N.J.	Dennis Collins, D	**1982, May**
aytown, Tex.	*Fritz Lanham	**1972, May**
eaumont, Tex.	*Ray A. Riley	**1978, Apr.**
elleville, Ill.	Richard Brauer, N-P	**1981, Apr.**
ellevue, Wash.	*William Parness	**1978, Sept.**
ellflower, Cal.	*Jack Simpson	**1980, July**
eloit, Wis.	*H. Herbert Holt	**1971, Mar.**
erkeley, Cal.	*Wise E. Allen	**1980, Feb.**
essemer, Ala.	Ed Porter, D	**1982, Sept.**
ethlehem, Pa.	Paul M. Marcincin, D	**1981, Nov.**
everly Hills, Cal.	*Edward Kreins	**1979, Oct.**
illings, Mont.	William Fox, D	**1983, May**
iloxi, Miss.	Jerry O'Keefe, D	**1981, May**
inghamton, N.Y.	Alfred J. Libous, R	**1981, Nov.**
irmingham, Ala.	Richard Arrington Jr., D	**1983, Oct.**
ismarck, N.D.	Bus Leary, N-P	**1982, Apr.**
loomfield, Minn.	*John Pidgeon	**1967, Sept.**
loomington, Ill.	*William Vail	**1976, Oct.**
loomington, Ind.	Francis X. McCloskey, D	**1983, Nov.**
loomington, Minn.	*John Pidgeon	**1967, Dec.**
oise, Ida.	Dick Eardley, N-P	**1981, Nov.**
ossier City, La.	Marvin E. Anding, D	**1981, Apr.**
oston, Mass.	Kevin White, D	**1981, Nov.**
oulder, Col.	Ruth Correll, N-P	**1981, Nov.**
owie, Md.	Audrey E. Scott, N-P	**1982, Apr.**
owling Green, Ky.	*Charles W. Coates	**1977, Feb.**
ridgeport, Conn.	John Mandanici, D	**1981, Nov.**
ristol, Conn.	Michael Werner, R	**1981, Nov.**
rockton, Mass.	David E. Crosby, D	**1981, Nov.**
rookline, Mass.	Board of Selectmen	
rooklyn Center, Minn.	*Gerald G. Splinter	**1977, Oct.**
ryan, Tex.	*Ernest R. Clark	**1979, Feb.**
uffalo, N.Y.	James D. Griffen, D	**1981, Nov.**
urbank, Cal.	Leland Ayers, N-P	**1981, Apr.**
Burlington, Vt.	Gordon H. Paquette, D	**1981, Mar.**
Calumet City, Ill.	Robert C. Stefaniak, D	**1981, Apr.**
Cambridge, Mass.	*James L. Sullivan	**1975, Apr.**
Camden, N.J.	Angelo Errichetti, D	**1981, May**
Canton, Oh.	Stanley A. Cmich, R	**1983, Nov.**
Cape Girardeau, Mo.	Paul Stehr, N-P	**1981, Apr.**
Carson, Cal.	*E. Frederick Bien	**1968, May**
Casper, Wyo.	*Kenneth Erickson	**1969, Oct.**
Cedar Rapids, Ia.	Donald J. Canney, N-P	**1981, Nov.**
Champaign, Ill.	*V. Eugene Miller	**1974, Sept.**
Charleston, S.C.	Joseph P. Riley Jr., D	**1983, Nov.**
Charleston, W. Va.	Joe F. Smith, D	**1983, Apr.**
Charlotte, N.C.	*David A. Burkhalter	**1971, Jan.**
Charlottesville, Va.	*Cole Hendrix	**1971, Jan.**
Chattanooga, Tenn.	Charles A. Rose, N-P	**1983, Apr.**
Chesapeake, Va.	*John T. Maxwell	**1978, Sept.**
Chester, Pa.	Joseph Battle, R	**1983, Nov.**
Cheyenne, Wyo.	Donald Erickson, R	**1984, Nov.**
Chicago, Ill.	Jane M. Byrne, D	**1983, Apr.**
Chicago Hts., Ill.	Charles Panici, R	**1983, Apr.**
Chicopee, Mass.	Robert Kumor Jr.	**1981, Nov.**
Chula Vista, Cal.	*Lane F. Cole	**1975, Feb.**
Cincinnati, Oh.	*Sylvester Murray	**1979, Sept.**
Clarksville, Tenn.	Ted Crozier, N-P	**1982, Nov.**
Clearwater, Fla.	*Anthony Shoemaker	**1977, June**
Cleveland, Oh.	George Voinovich, R	**1981, Nov.**
Cleveland Hgts., Oh.	*Richard Robinson	**1978, July**
Clifton, N.J.	*William Holster	**1957, Jan.**
Col. Spgs., Col.	*George H. Fellows	**1966, July**
Columbia, Mo.	*Vacant	
Columbia, S.C.	*Graydon V. Olive Jr.	**1970, Mar.**
Columbus, Ga.	Harry Jackson, D	**1982, Nov.**
Columbus, Oh.	Tom Moody, R	**1983, Nov.**
Commerce, Cal.	*Robert Hinderliter	**1973, Aug.**
Compton, Cal.	*Allen Parker	**1975, Dec.**
Concord, Cal.	*Farrel A. Stewart	**1960, Apr.**
Coon Rapids., Minn.	*Richard Thistle	**1979, July**
Coral Gables, Fla.	*J. Martin Gainer	**1975, Jan.**
Corpus Christi, Tex.	*R. Marvin Townsend	**1968, Jan.**
Corvallis, Ore.	*Gary F. Pokorny	**1978, Nov.**
Costa Mesa, Cal.	*Fred Sorsabel	**1970**
Council Bluffs, Ia.	*Michael G. Miller	**1978, Aug.**
Covington, Ky.	Bernard Moorman, N-P	**1983, Nov.**
Cranston, R.I.	Edward DiPrefe, R	**1981, Nov.**
Crystal, Minn.	*John Irving	**1963, Jan.**
Culver City, Cal.	*Dale Jones	**1969, Aug.**
Cuyahoga Falls, Oh.	Robert Quirk, D	**1981, Nov.**
Dallas, Tex.	*George Schrader	**1972, Dec.**
Daly City, Cal.	*David R. Rowe	**1969, Aug.**
Danbury, Conn.	James Dyer, D	**1981, Nov.**
Danville, Ill.	David S. Palmer, N-P	**1983, Apr.**
Danville, Va.	*James W. Lord	**1971, Nov.**
Dayton, Oh.	*Earl Sterzer	**1979, Feb.**
Daytona Bch., Fla.	*Howard D. Tipton	**1978, Oct.**
Dearborn, Mich.	John O'Reilly, N-P	**1981, Nov.**
Decatur, Ala.	Bill Dukes, D	**1984, July**
Decatur, Ill.	*Leslie T. Allen	**1972, Sept.**
Denver, Col.	William H. McNichols, D	**1983, May**
Des Moines, Ia.	*Richard Wilkey	**1974, Mar.**
Des Plaines, Ill.	H.H. Volberding Sr., N-P	**1981, Apr.**
Detroit, Mich.	Coleman A. Young, N-P	**1981, Nov.**
Dotham, Ala.	James W. Grant 3d, N-P	**1981, Sept.**
Dover, Del.	*John P. Mogan	**1979, Mar.**
Downers Grove, Ill.	*James R. Griesemer	**1972, Sept.**
Downey, Cal.	*Charles W. Thompson	**1970, Apr.**
Dubuque, Ia.	*W. Kenneth Gearhart	**1979, July**
Duluth, Minn.	John Fedo, D	**1983, Nov.**
Durham, N.C.	*Barry Del Castilho	**1980, Oct.**
E. Chicago, Ind.	Robert A. Pastrick, D	**1983, Nov.**
E. Cleveland, Oh.	*Frank Wise	**1978, Jan.**
E. Detroit, Mich.	*J. Scott Miller	**1979, Oct.**
E. Hartford, Conn.	George Dagon, D	**1981, Nov.**
E. Lansing, Mich.	*Jerry Coffman	**1977, Jan.**
E. Orange, N.J.	Thomas H. Cooke Jr., D	**1981, Nov.**
E. Providence, R.I.	Edward B. Langton, N-P	**1982, Nov.**
E. St. Louis, Ill.	Carl E. Officer, D	**1983, Apr.**

City	Name	Term
Eau Claire, Wis.	*Stephen Atkins	**1978, Sept.**
Edina, Minn.	*Kenneth Rosland	**1977, Nov.**
Edison, N.J.	Anthony Yelencsics, D	**1981, Nov.**
El Cajon, Cal.	*Robert Applegate	**1958, Sept.**
El Monte, Cal.	*J.R. Castner	**1978, July**
El Paso, Tex.	Thomas Westfall, D	**1981, Apr.**
Elgin, Ill.	*Leo Wilson	**1972, Dec.**
Elizabeth, N.J.	Thomas G. Dunn, D	**1984, Nov.**
Elmhurst, Ill.	*Robert T. Palmer	**1953, June**
Elmira, N.Y.	*Joseph E. Sartori	**1972, June**
Elyria, Oh.	Michael Keys, D	**1983, Nov.**
Enfield, Conn.	*Robert F. Ledger Jr.	**1977, Mar.**
Enid, Okla.	*Lyle Smith	**1979, Feb.**
Erie, Pa.	Louis J. Tullio, D	**1981, Nov.**
Escondido, Cal.	*Ray Windsor	**1980, Jan.**
Euclid, Oh.	Anthony Giunta, D	**1983, Nov.**
Eugene, Ore.	*Charles T. Henry	**1975, July**
Evanston, Ill.	*Edward A. Martin	**1971, Apr.**
Evansville, Ind.	Michael Vandiver, D	**1983, Nov.**
Everett, Mass.	Edward Connolly, D.	**1981, Nov.**
Everett, Wash.	Bill Moore, N-P	**1981, Sept.**
Fairborn, Oh.	*William Burns	**1977, Feb.**
Fairfield, Cal.	*B. Gale Wilson	**1956, Mar.**
Fairfield, Conn.	John J. Sullivan, D.	**1981, Nov.**
Fair Lawn, N.J.	*Frank Peruggi	**1977, July**
Fall River, Mass.	Carlton Viveiros, D	**1981, Nov.**
Fargo, N.D.	Jon Lindgren, D	**1982, Apr.**
Fayetteville, Ark.	*Donald Grimes	**1972, Apr.**
Fayetteville, N.C.	*William G. Thomas 3d	**1976, Sept.**
Fitchburg, Mass.	David Gilmartin, D	**1981, Nov.**
Flagstaff, Ariz.	Paul Babbitt Jr., N-P	**1982, Apr.**
Flint, Mich.	*Nanette Lynn	**1978, July**
Florissant, Mo.	James J. Eagan, N-P	**1983, Apr.**
Fond du Lac, Wis.	*Myron J. Medin Jr.	**1967, Nov.**
Ft. Collins, Col.	*John Arnold	**1977, Oct.**
Ft. Lauderdale, Fla.	*Constance Hoffmann, Act.	**1980, Aug.**
Ft. Lee, N.J.	Nicholas Corbiscello, R	**1984, Nov.**
Ft. Smith, Ark.	Jack Freeze, N-P	**1982, Dec.**
Ft. Wayne, Ind.	Wilfred Moses, D	**1983, Nov.**
Ft. Worth, Tex.	*Robert Herchert	**1978, Aug.**
Fremont, Cal.	*Allen Sprague, Act.	**1980, Aug.**
Fresno, Cal.	*Gerald E. Newfarmer	**1978, Sept.**
Fullerton, Cal.	*William C. Winter	**1979, Oct.**
Gadsden, Ala.	Steve Means, D.	**1982, Aug.**
Gainesville, Fla.	*Orville Powell	**1980, Jan.**
Galesburg, Ill.	*Lawrence Asaro	**1979, Sept.**
Galveston, Tex.	*Stephen Huffman	**1980, Apr.**
Gardena, Cal.	*John Sheehan	**1979, Oct.**
Garden Grove, Cal.	*Delbert L. Powers	**1980, July**
Garfield Hts., Oh.	Theodore Holtz, D.	**1981, Nov.**
Garland, Tex.	*Fred Greene	**1979, Sept.**
Gary, Ind.	Richard G. Hatcher, D	**1983, Nov.**
Gastonia, N.C.	*Gary Hicks	**1973, Dec.**
Glendale, Ariz.	*S.F. Van de Putte	**1960, Aug.**
Glendale, Cal.	Carroll Parcher, N-P	**1981 Apr.**
Grand Forks, N.D.	H.C. Wessman, R	**1982, Apr.**
Gr. Island, Neb.	Robert L. Kriz, N-P	**1982, Nov.**
Gr. Prairie, Tex.	*Clifford Johnson	**1962, Sept.**
Gr. Rapids, Mich.	*Joseph G. Zainea	**1976, Oct.**
Great Falls, Mont.	*Richard D. Thomas	**1973, May**
Greeley, Col.	*Peter Morrell	**1973, Dec.**
Green Bay, Wis.	Samuel Halloin, N-P.	**1983, Apr.**
Greensboro, N.C.	*T.Z. Osborne	**1973, Feb.**
Greensville, S.C.	*John J. Dullea	**1971, Oct.**
Greenville, Miss.	William Burnley Jr., D	**1984, Oct.**
Greenwich, Conn.	Ruth L. Sims, D	**1981, Nov.**
Groton, Conn.	Donald Sweet, R	**1981, May**
Gulfport, Miss.	Jack Barnett, D	**1981, June**
Hackensack, N.J.	*Joseph J. Squillace	**1964, Oct.**
Hagerstown, Md.	Varner L. Paddack, R	**1981, Mar.**
Hamden, Conn.	Richard Harris, D	**1981, Nov.**
Hamilton, Oh.	*Jack Kirsch	**1975, Dec.**
Hammond, Ind.	Edward J. Raskosky, D.	**1983, May**
Hampton, Va.	*C.E. Johnson	**1958, May**
Harlingen, Tex.	*Harry Savio	**1979, Feb.**
Harrisburg, Pa.	Paul Doutrich, R	**1981, Nov.**
Hartford, Conn.	*W. Wilson Gaitor	**1980, July**
Harvey, Ill.	James A. Haines, R	**1983, Apr.**
Hattiesburg, Miss.	Bobby L. Chain, D.	**1981, May**
Haverhill, Mass.	Thomas Vathally, D	**1981, Nov.**
Hawthorne, Cal.	*R. Kenneth Jue	**1977, Jan.**
Hayward, Cal.	*Donald Blubaugh	**1979, Nov.**
Hempstead, N.Y.	Dalton R. Miller, R	**1981, Apr.**
Hialeah, Fla.	Dale Bennett, D	**1981, Nov.**
High Point, N.C.	*Cyrus L. Books	**1976, Aug.**
Highland Pk., Ill.	Robert Buhai, N-P	**1983, Apr.**
Hoboken, N.J.	Steve Cappiello, D	**1981, May**
Holyoke, Mass.	Ernest Proulx, D	**1981, Nov.**
Hollywood, Fla.	*James Chandler	**1976, Nov.**
Honolulu, Ha.	Eileen Anderson, D	**1984, Nov.**
Hot Springs, Ark.	Tom Ellsworth, N-P	**1982, Nov.**
Houston, Tex.	James McConn, N-P	**1981, Nov.**
Huntington, W. Va.	*Richard Barton	**1978, Feb.**
Huntington Beach, Cal.	*Floyd Belsito	**1976, June**
Huntsville, Ala.	Joe W. Davis, N-P	**1984, July**
Hutchinson, Kan.	*George Pyle	**1967, Sept.**
Independence, Mo.	*Keith Wilson Jr.	**1980, July**
Indianapolis, Ind.	William Hudnut, R	**1983, Nov.**
Inglewood, Cal.	*Douglas W. Ayres	**1968, Apr.**
Inkster, Mich.	William Daniels, D	**1983, Nov.**
Iowa City, Ia.	*Neal Berlin	**1975, Mar.**
Irving, Tex.	*Jack Huffman	**1974, Jan.**
Irvington, N.J.	Robert Miller, D	**1982, Apr.**
Jackson, Mich.	*S.W. McAllister Jr.	**1974, Mar.**
Jackson, Miss.	Dale Danks, D	**1981, July**
Jackson, Tenn.	Bob Conger, D	**1983, May**
Jacksonville, Fla.	Jake Godbold, D.	**1983, May**
Jamestown, N.Y.	Steve Carlson, D	**1981, Nov.**
Janesville, Wis.	*Philip L. Deaton	**1976, Mar.**
Jefferson City, Mo.	George Hartsfield, D	**1983, Apr.**
Jersey City, N.J.	Thomas F.X. Smith, D.	**1981, May**
Johnson City, Tenn.	*Charles Tyson	**1979, Jan.**
Johnstown, Pa.	Charles Tomljanovic, D	**1981, Nov.**
Joliet, Ill.	*Robert H. Oldland	**1977, July**
Joplin, Mo.	*James P. Berzina	**1968, Mar.**
Kalamazoo, Mich.	*Robert C. Bobb	**1976, Nov.**
Kansas City, Kan.	John Reardon, D	**1983, Apr.**
Kansas City, Mo.	*Robert A. Kipp	**1974, Jan.**
Kettering, Oh.	Charles Horn, R	**1981, Nov.**
Key West, Fla.	*Robert Sanders	**1980, Aug.**
Killeen, Tex.	*Mike Eastland	**1974, Apr.**
Knoxville, Tenn.	Randell L. Tyree, D	**1983, Oct.**
Kokomo, Ind.	Stephen Daily, D	**1983, Dec.**
LaCrosse, Wis.	Patrick Zielke, N-P	**1981, Apr.**
La Habra, Cal.	*Lee Risner	**1970, Nov.**
La Mesa, Cal.	*Ronald Bradley	**1980, May**
La Mirada, Cal.	*Claude J. Klug	**1971, Aug.**
Lafayette, Ind.	James Riehle, D.	**1983, Apr.**
Lake Charles, La.	William E. Boyer, D	**1981, June**
Lakeland, Fla.	*Robert V. Youkey	**1960, Jan.**
Lakewood, Cal.	*Howard L. Chambers	**1976, Mar.**
Lakewood, Col.	*Bill Kirchhoff	**1980, Nov.**
Lakewood, Oh.	Anthony Sinagra, R	**1983, Nov.**
Lancaster, Pa.	Arthur E. Morris, R	**1981, Nov.**
Lansing, Mich.	Gerald Graves, N-P	**1981, Nov.**
Laredo, Tex.	Aldo Tatangelo, D.	**1982, Apr.**
Las Cruces, N.M.	*Clifford W. O'Key	**1979, Aug.**
Las Vegas, Nev.	*Russell Dorn	**1978, Jan.**
Lawrence, Kan.	*Buford M. Watson Jr.	**1970, Jan.**
Lawton, Okla.	*Robert Metzinger	**1977, Jan.**
Lewiston, Me.	Paul Dionne, D.	**1981, Nov.**
Lexington, Ky.	James Amato, N-P	**1981, Nov.**
Lima, Oh.	Harry Moyer, N-P	**1981, Nov.**
Lincoln, Neb.	Helen Boosalis, D	**1983, May**
Linden, N.J.	John Gregorio, D	**1982, Nov.**
Little Rock, Ark.	*Mahlon Martin	**1980, July**
Livermore, Cal.	Dale Turner, N-P	**1982, Apr.**
Lombard, Ill.	Mardyth Pollard, N-P	**1981, May**
Long Beach, Cal.	*John Dever	**1977, Jan.**
Long Beach, N.Y.	*William McKenney	**1978, Jan.**
Longview, Tex.	*C. Ray Jackson	**1980, Apr.**
Lorain, Oh.	William Parker, R	**1983, Nov.**
Los Angeles, Cal.	Thomas Bradley, D	**1981, June**
Louisville, Ky.	William Stansbury, D	**1981, Nov.**
Lowell, Mass.	*B. Joseph Tully	**1979, June**
L. Merion, Pa.	*Thomas B. Fulweiler	**1968, Jan.**
Lubbock, Tex.	*Larry Cunningham	**1976, Sept.**
Lynchburg, Va.	*E. Allen Culverhouse	**1979, June**
Lynn, Mass.	Antonio J. Marino, D.	**1981, Nov.**
Lynwood, Cal.	*Tommy Davis	**1979, Nov.**
Macon, Ga.	George Israel, R.	**1983, Nov.**
Madison, Wis.	Joel Skornicka, N-P	**1981, Apr.**
Malden, Mass.	James Conway, D.	**1981, Nov.**
Manchester, Conn.	Stephen Penny, D.	**1981, Nov.**

City	Name	Term
Manchester, N.H.	Charles Stanton, D	**1981, Nov.**
Manitowoc, Wis.	Anthony V. Dufek, D	**1981, Apr.**
Mansfield, Oh.	Edward Meehan, R	**1983, Nov.**
Marion, Ind.	Fred Weagley, R	**1983, Nov.**
Marion, Oh.	Ronald Malone, D	**1983, Nov.**
McAllen, Tex.	Othal Brand, N-P	**1981, Apr.**
McKeesport, Pa.	Lou Washowich, D	**1983, May**
Medford, Mass.	*Carroll P. Sheehan	**1980, Aug.**
Melbourne, Fla.	*Samuel Halter	**1978, May**
Memphis, Tenn.	Wyeth Chandler, N-P	**1983, Nov.**
Mentor, Oh.	*Edward Podojil	**1977, Nov.**
Meridian, Miss.	*Joel W. Forrester	**1959, July**
Mesa, Ariz.	*C.K. Luster	**1979, June**
Mesquite, Tex.	B. J. Smith, N-P	**1981, Apr.**
Miami, Fla.	*Richard Fosmoen	**1980, Sept.**
Miami Beach, Fla.	Murray Meyerson, N-P	**1981, Nov.**
Middletown, Oh.	*Dale F. Helsel	**1970, Oct.**
Midland, Tex.	G. Thane Akins, N-P	**1981, Apr.**
Midwest City, Okla.	*Irving P. Frank	**1978, Apr.**
Milwaukee, Wis.	Henry W. Maier, D	**1984, Apr.**
Minneapolis, Minn.	Donald Fraser, D	**1981, Nov.**
Minnetonka, Minn.	*Carsten D. Leikvold	**1973, Dec.**
Minot, N.D.	*R.A. Schempp	**1977, Nov.**
Mobile, Ala.	Robert Doyle Jr., N-P	**1981, July**
Modesto, Cal.	Peggy Mensinger, N-P	**1983, Mar.**
Moline, Ill.	Lawrence Lorenson, D	**1981, Apr.**
Monroe, La.	Robert Powell, D	**1984, May**
Montclair, N.J.	*Bertrand Kendall	**1980, Sept.**
Montebello, Cal.	*Joseph Goeden	**1980, May**
Monterey Park, Cal.	*Lloyd de Llamas	**1976, Sept.**
Montgomery, Ala.	Emory Folmar, R	**1983, Nov.**
Mt. Prospect, Ill.	*Terrance Burghard	**1978, Oct.**
Mt. Vernon, N.Y.	Thomas E. Sharpe, D	**1983, Nov.**
Mountain View, Cal.	*Bruce Liedstrand	**1976, Aug.**
Muncie, Ind.	Alan K. Wilson, R	**1983, Nov.**
Mundelein, Ill.	Colin McRae, N-P	**1981, May**
Muskegon, Mich.	*William Gleason	**1979, June**
Muskogee, Okla.	Coleman Fite, D	**1982, Apr.**
Napa, Cal.	Phyllis Moore, R	**1984, Apr.**
Nashua, N.H.	Morris Arel, D	**1983, Nov.**
Nashville, Tenn.	Richard Fulton, D	**1984, Sept.**
National City, Cal.	*Tom McCabe	**1979, Feb.**
New Bedford, Mass.	John Markey, N-P	**1981, Nov.**
New Britain, Conn.	William J. McNamara, D	**1981, Nov.**
New Brunswick, N.J.	John Lynch, D	**1982, Nov.**
New Castle, Pa.	Angelo Sands, D	**1983, Nov.**
New Haven, Conn.	Biagio DiLieto, D	**1981, Nov.**
New Kensington, Pa.	Verle N. Bevan, D	**1981, Nov.**
New London, Conn.	*C.F. Driscoll	**1969, May**
New Orleans, La.	Ernest Morial, D	**1982, Apr.**
New Rochelle, N.Y.	*C. Samuel Kissinger	**1975, Apr.**
New York, N.Y.	Edward Koch, D	**1981, Nov.**
Newark, N.J.	Kenneth Gibson, D	**1982, July**
Newark, Oh.	Mary M. Lusk, D	**1983, Nov.**
Newport, R.I.	*Paul Steinbrenner	**1976, May**
Newport Beach, Cal.	*Robert L. Wynn	**1971, Aug.**
Newport News, Va.	*Frank Smiley	**1976, Oct.**
Newton, Mass.	Theodore Mann, R	**1981, Nov.**
Niagara Falls, N.Y.	*William Sdao	**1980, Mar.**
Niles, Ill.	Nicholas B. Blase, D	**1981, Apr.**
Norfolk, Va.	*Julian Hirst	**1975, Apr.**
Norman, Okla.	*James D. Crosby	**1976, Feb.**
Norristown, Pa.	*John Plonski	**1979, Apr.**
No. Charleston, S.C.	John Bourne, R	**1982, June**
North Chicago, Ill.	Leo F. Kukla, D	**1981, Apr.**
No. Little Rock, Ark.	Reed Thompson, N-P	**1984, Nov.**
Norwalk, Cal.	*William H. Kraus	**1973, May**
Norwalk, Conn.	William A. Collins, D	**1981, Nov.**
Norwich, Conn.	*Charles Whitty	**1973, June**
Novato, Cal.	*Phillip J. Brown	**1974, May**
Oak Lawn, Ill.	*Richard E. O'Neill	**1976, Sept.**
Oak Park, Ill.	*Jack Gruber	**1976, Oct.**
Oak Park, Mich.	*Vacant	
Oak Ridge, Tenn.	*M. Lyle Lacy 3d	**1978, July**
Oakland, Cal.	*David A. Self	**1978, July**
Oceanside, Cal.	*Robert Bourcier	**1978, June**
Odessa, Tex.	*Kerry R. Sweatt	**1978, Jan.**
Ogden, Ut.	*L. D. Hunter	**1977, Sept.**
Oklahoma City, Okla.	*James Cook	**1976, Apr.**
Omaha, Neb.	Al Veys, N-P	**1981, May**
Ontario, Cal.	*Roger Hughbanks	**1975, July**
Orange, Cal.	*Joseph Baker	**1978, Dec.**
Orange, N.J.	Joel Shain, D	**1984, May**
Orlando, Fla.	Bill Frederick, D	**1984, Sept.**
Oshkosh, Wis.	*W. O. Frueh	**1976, Aug.**
Overland Park, Kan.	*Donald Pipes	**1977, June**
Owensboro, Ky.	*Max Rhoads	**1956, Sept.**
Oxnard, Cal.	*Stephen Cook	**1979**
Pacifica, Cal.	*Albert St. Cyr	**1978, July**
Palm Springs, Cal.	*Norman R. King	**1979, Nov.**
Palo Alto, Cal.	*William Zaner	**1979, Sept.**
Parkersburg, W. Va.	Alvin K. Smith, D	**1981, Nov.**
Pasadena, Cal.	*Donald F. McIntyre	**1973, June**
Pasadena, Tex.	Jim Clark, D	**1981, Apr.**
Passaic, N.J.	Robert Hare, N-P	**1981, May**
Paterson, N.J.	Lawrence Kramer, R	**1982, May**
Pawtucket, R.I.	Dennis Lynch, D	**1981, Nov.**
Pekin, Ill.	Willard Birkmeier, D	**1983, Apr.**
Pensacola, Fla.	*Steve Garman	**1978, June**
Peoria, Ill.	*James B. Daken	**1979, Jan.**
Perth Amboy, N.J.	George J. Otlowski, D	**1984, May**
Philadelphia, Pa.	William Green, D	**1983, Nov.**
Phoenix, Ariz.	*Marvin Andrews	**1976, Oct.**
Pico Rivera, Cal.	*John Donlevy	**1977, May**
Pine Bluff, Ark.	D.W. Wallis, D	**1984, Nov.**
Pittsburgh, Pa.	Richard S. Caliguiri, D	**1981, Nov.**
Pittsfield, Mass.	Charles Smith, D	**1981, Nov.**
Plainfield, N.J.	Paul O'Keefe, R	**1981, Nov.**
Pocatello, Ida.	*Charles W. Moss	**1970, Sept.**
Pomona, Cal.	*Ora E. Lampman	**1978, July**
Pompano Bch., Fla.	*John Schoeberlein	**1975, May**
Pontiac, Mich.	*Joseph Neipling	**1979, May**
Port Arthur, Tex.	*George Dibrell	**1962, Oct.**
Port Huron, Mich.	*Gerald R. Bouchard	**1965, June**
Portage, Mich.	*Donald Ziemke	**1974, Aug.**
Portland, Me.	*A. J. Wilson	**1977, Apr.**
Portland, Ore.	Frank Ivancie, N-P	**1984, Nov.**
Portsmouth, Oh.	*Barry Feldman	**1977, Jan.**
Portsmouth, Va.	*Robert T. Williams	**1975, Apr.**
Poughkeepsie, N.Y.	*Daniel Fitzpatrick	**1979, Feb.**
Providence, R.I.	Vincent Cianci Jr., R	**1982, Nov.**
Provo, Ut.	Jim Ferguson, N-P	**1981, Nov.**
Pueblo, Col.	*Fred E. Weisbroad	**1967, Feb.**
Quincy, Ill.	C. David Neussen, R	**1981, Apr.**
Quincy, Mass.	Arthur H. Tobin, D	**1981, Nov.**
Racine, Wis.	Stephen Olson, N-P	**1981, Apr.**
Raleigh, N.C.	*Lawrence P. Zachery Jr.	**1973, Nov.**
Rapid City, S.D.	Arthur La Croix, R	**1981, Apr.**
Reading, Pa.	Karen Miller, D	**1983, Nov.**
Redlands, Cal.	*Chris Christiansen	**1978, Nov.**
Redondo Beach, Cal.	*David Dolter	**1978, Dec.**
Redwood City, Cal.	*James M. Fales Jr.	**1971, Aug.**
Reno, Nev.	*Chris Cherches	**1980, Nov.**
Revere, Mass.	George V. Colella, D	**1981, Nov.**
Richardson, Tex.	Raymond Noah, N-P	**1981, Apr.**
Richfield, Minn.	*Karl Nollenberger	**1979, July**
Richmond, Cal.	*Joseph Salvato	**1980, July**
Richmond, Ind.	Clifford Dickman, R	**1983, Nov.**
Richmond, Va.	*Manuel Deese	**1979, Feb.**
Riverside, Cal.	*Douglas Weiford	**1980, Mar.**
Roanoke, Va.	*H. Bern Ewert	**1978, Jan.**
Rochester, Minn.	*Steven Kvenvold	**1979, June**
Rochester, N.Y.	*L. Joe Miller	**1979, Feb.**
Rock Hill, S.C.	*Max Holland	**1965, Mar.**
Rock Island, Ill.	James R. Davis, N-P	**1981, Apr.**
Rockford, Ill.	Robert McGaw, D	**1981, May**
Rockville, Md.	*Larry N. Blick	**1972, Nov.**
Rome, N.Y.	Carl Eilenberg, R	**1983, Nov.**
Rosemead, Cal.	*Frank Tripepi	**1974, Oct.**
Roseville, Mich.	*B. J. Nardelli	**1975, Nov.**
Roseville, Minn.	*James Andre	**1974, May**
Rosewell, N.M.	*Robert Owen	**1973, Oct.**
Royal Oak, Mich.	*William Baldridge	**1975, Sept.**
Sacramento, Cal.	*Walter Slipe	**1976, Mar.**
Saginaw, Mich.	*Thomas Dalton	**1978, Nov.**
St. Clair Shores, Mich.	*Robert James	**1979, July**
St. Cloud, Minn.	Robert Huston, N-P	**1982, Apr.**
St. Joseph, Mo.	Gordon Weiser, R	**1982, Apr.**
St. Louis, Mo.	James F. Conway, D	**1981, Apr.**
St. Louis Pk., Minn.	*John Elwell	**1977, Oct.**
St. Paul, Minn.	George Latimer, D	**1982, Apr.**
St. Petersburg, Fla.	Corinne Freeman, N-P	**1981, Apr.**
Salem, Mass.	Jean Levesque, D	**1981, Nov.**
Salem, Ore.	*Ralph Hanley	**1978, June**
Salina, Kan.	*Rufus L. Nye	**1979, May**
Salinas, Cal.	*Robert Christofferson	**1972, Dec.**
Salt Lake City, Ut.	Ted Wilson, D	**1983, Nov.**

City	Name	Term
San Angelo, Tex.	*H. D. Howard	**1958**
San Antonio, Tex.	*Thomas Huebner	**1977, Jan.**
San Bernardino, Cal.	W. R. Holcomb, R.	**1981, May**
San Diego, Cal.	*Hugh McKinley	**1975, Apr.**
San Francisco, Cal.	Dianne Feinstein, D	**1983, Nov.**
San Jose, Cal.	*Francis T. Fox	**1980, May**
San Leandro, Cal.	*Lee Riordan	**1976, Apr.**
San Mateo, Cal.	*Richard Delong	**1976, Sept.**
San Rafael, Cal.	*Vacant	
Sandusky, Oh.	*Frank Link	**1972, Jan.**
Santa Ana, Cal.	*A. J. Wilson	**1980, July**
Santa Barbara, Cal.	*Richard Thomas	**1977, Jan.**
Santa Cruz, Cal.	*David Koester	**1962, Oct.**
Santa Fe, N.M.	Arthur Trujillo, D	**1982, Mar.**
Santa Maria, Cal.	*Robert Grogan	**1963, Jan.**
Santa Monica, Cal.	*Charles McClain	**1979, Jan.**
Santa Rosa, Cal.	Jerry Wilhelm, N-P	**1981, Apr.**
Sarasota, Fla.	*Kenneth Thompson	**1950, Feb.**
Savannah, Ga.	*Arthur A. Mendonsa	**1971, Sept.**
Schenectady, N.Y.	Frank J. Duci, R	**1983, Nov.**
Scottsdale, Ariz.	*Roy Pederson	**1980, Mar.**
Scranton, Pa.	Eugene Hickey, D	**1981, Nov.**
Seattle, Wash.	Charles Royer, N-P	**1981, Nov.**
Shaker Heights, Oh.	Walter C. Kelley, N-P	**1983, Nov.**
Sheboygan, Wis.	Richard Suscha, N-P	**1981, Apr.**
Shreveport, La.	W. T. (Billy) Hanna Jr., D	**1982, Nov.**
Simi Valley, Cal.	*Lin Koester	**1979, June**
Sioux City, Ia.	*Paul Flynn	**1979, May**
Sioux Falls, S.D.	Rick Knobe, R	**1984, Apr.**
Skokie, Ill.	*Robert Eppley	**1979, Jan.**
Somerville, Mass.	Eugene Brune, D	**1981, Nov.**
South Bend, Ind.	Roger Parent, D	**1983, Nov.**
So. Gate, Cal.	*Carl Zeise	**1966, Oct.**
So. S.F., Cal.	*C. W. Birkelo	**1978**
Southfield, Mich.	*Del Borgsdorf	**1980, June**
Spartanburg, S.C.	*W. H. Carstarphen	**1975, Mar.**
Spokane, Wash.	*Terry Novak	**1978, July**
Springfield, Ill.	J. Michael Houston, R.	**1983, Apr.**
Springfield, Mass	Theodore Dimauro, D.	**1981, Nov.**
Springfield, Mo.	*Don G. Busch	**1971, Oct.**
Springfield, Oh.	*Thomas M. Bay	**1978, Sept.**
Stamford, Conn.	Louis A. Clapes, R	**1981, Nov.**
Sterling Hts., Mich.	*Leonard Hendricks	**1968, Aug.**
Stillwater, Okla.	*Lawrence Gish	**1966, Aug.**
Stockton, Cal.	*John B. Wentz	**1979, July**
Stratford, Conn.	*Michael Brown	**1978, May**
Sunnyvale, Cal.	*Lee Ayres	**1977, Mar.**
Syracuse, N.Y.	Lee Alexander, D	**1981, Nov.**
Tacoma, Wash.	*Erling O. Mork	**1975, June**
Tallahassee, Fla.	*Daniel A. Kleman	**1974, Aug.**
Tampa, Fla.	Bob Martinez, N-P	**1981, Oct.**
Taunton, Mass.	Joseph Amaral, D	**1981, Nov.**
Taylor, Mich.	Donald L. Zub, D	**1981, Nov.**
Teaneck, N.J.	*Werner H. Schmid	**1959, Mar.**
Tempe, Ariz.	Harry E. Mitchell, D	**1982, Mar.**
Temple, Tex.	*Barney Knight	**1978, Dec.**
Terre Haute, Ind.	P. Pete Chalos, D	**1983, Nov.**
Thousand Oaks, Cal.	*Grant Brimhall	**1978, Jan.**
Titusville, Fla.	*Norman Hickey	**1974, June**
Toledo, Oh.	*J. Michael Porter	**1979, Feb.**
Topeka, Kan.	William McCormick, N-P	**1981, Apr.**
Torrance, Cal.	*Edward J. Ferraro	**1964, Aug.**
Trenton, N.J.	Arthur Holland, D	**1982, June**
Troy, Mich.	*Frank Gerstenecker	**1970, Feb.**
Troy, N.Y.	*John P. Buckley	**1972, June**
Tucson, Ariz.	*Joel Valdez	**1974, May**
Tulsa, Okla.	James M. Inhofe, R	**1982, Apr.**
Tuscaloosa, Ala.	Ernest Collins, N-P	**1981, Oct.**
Tyler, Tex.	*Ed Wagoner	**1977, June**
Union City, N.J.	William Musto, D.	**1982, May**
Univ. City, Mo.	*Frank Ollendorff	**1980, Mar.**
Upland, Cal.	*S. Lee Travers	**1974, June**
Upper Arlington, Oh.	*H. W. Hyrne	**1968, May**
Urbana, Ill.	Jeffrey Markland, R.	**1981, Apr.**
Utica, N.Y.	Stephen Pawlinga, D	**1981, Nov.**
Vallejo, Cal.	*Ted McDonell	**1978, Sept.**
Vancouver, Wash.	*Alan Harvey	**1969, May**
Ventura, Cal.	*Edward E. McCombs	**1970, Mar.**
Victoria, Tex.	*John F. Lee	**1959, Sept.**
Vineland, N.J.	Patrick R. Fiorilli, N-P	**1984, May**
Virginia Beach, Va.	*George L. Hanbury	**1974, Nov.**
Waco, Tex.	*David F. Smith Jr.	**1970, Sept.**
Walnut Creek, Cal.	*Thomas Dunne	**1972, May**
Waltham, Mass.	Arthur J. Clark, N-P	**1981, Nov.**
Warren, Mich.	Daniel Sferra, D	**1983, Nov.**
Warwick, R.I.	Joseph Walsh, D	**1982, Nov.**
Wash, D.C.	Marion Barry, D	**1982, Nov.**
Waterbury, Conn.	Edward Bergin, D	**1981, Nov.**
Waterloo, Ia.	Leo Rooff, N-P	**1981, Nov.**
Waukegan, Ill.	Bill Morris, D	**1981, Apr.**
Waukesha, Wis.	Joseph Laporte, N-P	**1982, Apr.**
Wausau, Wis.	John Kannenberg, N-P	**1984, Apr.**
Wauwatosa, Wis.	James A. Benz, N-P	**1984, Apr.**
W. Allis, Wis.	Jack Barlich, N-P	**1984, Feb.**
W. Covina, Cal.	*Herman Fast	**1976, Aug.**
W. Hartford, Conn.	*William Brady	**1977, Sept.**
W. Haven, Conn.	Robert A. Johnson, D	**1981, Nov.**
W. New York, N.J.	Anthony DeFino, D	**1983, May**
W. Palm Beach, Fla.	*Richard Simmons	**1969, Nov.**
Westland, Mich.	Thomas F. Taylor, N-P	**1981, Nov.**
Westminster, Cal.	*Carl Berry	**1977, Mar.**
Weymouth, Mass.	Board of Selectmen	
Wheaton, Ill.	Ralph Barger, R	**1983, Apr.**
Wheeling, W. Va.	*Jack Maloney	**1977, Aug.**
White Plains, N.Y.	Alfred Del Vecchio, R	**1981, Nov.**
Whittier, Cal.	*Tom Mauk	**1980, Sept.**
Wichita, Kan.	*E. H. Denton	**1976, July**
Wichita Falls, Tex.	*Stuart A. Bach	**1980, Oct.**
Wilkes-Barre, Pa.	Thomas McLaughlin, D	**1983, Nov.**
Williamsport, Pa.	Stephen Lucasi, R	**1983, Nov.**
Wilmington, Del.	William T. McLaughlin, D	**1984, Nov.**
Wilmington, N.C.	*Robert Cobb	**1977, Dec.**
Winston-Salem, N.C.	*Bryce A. Stuart	**1980, Jan.**
Woonsocket, R.I.	Gerard Bouley, D	**1981, Nov.**
Worcester, Mass.	*Francis J. McGrath	**1948, May**
Wyandotte, Mich.	James Wagner, N-P	**1981, Apr.**
Wyoming, Mich.	*James Sheeran	**1976, Nov.**
Yakima, Wash.	*Richard Zais Jr.	**1978, Nov.**
Yonkers, N.Y.	*Eugene J. Fox	**1980, June**
York, Pa.	Elizabeth Marshall, D	**1981, Nov.**
Youngstown, Oh.	George Vukovich, D.	**1981, Nov.**
Zanesville, Oh.	Cameron R. Agin, N-P	**1983, Nov.**

Canadian Cities

(as of Nov. 5, 1980)

City	Name	Term
Calgary, Alta.	Ralph Klein	**1983, Oct.**
Charlottetown, P.E.I.	Frank Moran	**1980, Nov.**
Edmonton, Alta.	Cec Purves	**1983, Oct.**
Fredericton, N.B.	Elbridge Wilkins	**1983, May**
Guelph, Ont.	Norman Jary	**1980, Nov.**
Halifax, N.S.	Ron Hanson	**1981, Oct.**
Hamilton, Ont.	Jack MacDonald	**1980, Nov.**
Hull, Que.	Gilles Rocheleau	**1980, Nov.**
Kingston, Ont.	Ken Keyes	**1980, Nov.**
Kitchener, Ont.	Morley Rosenberg	**1980, Nov.**
London, Ont.	Al Gleeson	**1980, Nov.**
Moncton, N.B.	Dennis Cochrane	**1983, May**
Montreal, Que.	Jean Drapeau	**1982, Nov.**
North York, Ont.	Mel Lastman	**1980, Nov.**
Oshawa, Ont.	James Potticary	**1980, Nov.**
Ottawa, Ont.	Mrs. Marion Dewar	**1980, Nov.**
Peterborough, Ont.	Cameron Wasson	**1980, Nov.**
Quebec, Que.	Jean Pelletier	**1981, Nov.**
Regina, Sask.	Larry Schneider	**1982, Oct.**
Saint John, N.B.	Bob Lockhart	**1983, May**
St. John's, Nfld.	Mrs. Dorothy Wyatt	**1981, Nov.**
Saskatoon, Sask.	Clifford Wright	**1982, Oct.**
Sault Ste. Marie, Ont.	Nicholas Trbovich	**1980, Nov.**
Sherbrooke, Que.	Jacques O'Bready	**1982, Nov.**
Sudbury, Ont.	Jim Gordon	**1980, Nov.**
Toronto, Ont.	John Sewell	**1980, Nov.**
Vancouver, B.C.	Jack Volrich	**1980, Nov.**
Victoria, B.C.	Bill Tindall	**1981, Nov.**
Waterloo, Ont.	Marjorie Carroll	**1982, Nov.**
Windsor, Ont.	Bert Weeks	**1980, Nov.**
Winnipeg, Man.	Bill Norrie	**1983, Oct.**

UNITED STATES POPULATION

1980 Census May Approach 224 Million

By Vincent P. Barabba
Director, U.S. Bureau of the Census

The United States took a human inventory in 1980, just as it has at the start of each decade beginning with 1790. The event was the 1980 census, the 20th in an unbroken string of such canvasses mandated by the Constitution.

While the primary purpose of the census remains the same as in 1790—to make sure that seats in the House of Representatives reflect the distribution of the population—many aspects of the 1980 census were unprecedented: its size and scope, its importance, and the controversy it generated.

When the questionnaires arrived in the mail at every home in the nation on March 28, they had been preceded by 6 years of increasingly intensive preparatory work. A series of public meetings across the nation had given the people an opportunity to say what they felt should be asked in the census. The questionnaire was then honed during a 4-year long series of test and dress rehearsal censuses, and reviewed by Congress and the Office of Management and Budget.

Census Questions Reflect New National Concerns

Although the 1980 questionnaire resembled that of 1970, changes reflected new national concerns. New questions were aimed at collecting more information about race and ethnicity, energy use, the overall cost of housing, the disabled population and additional data on commuting patterns.

Many questions provide data either directly or indirectly required by law. Others provide basic information about the population which is widely used by both the public and private sectors in making decisions important to everyone.

Every household received its form in the mail, and every household was asked to fill out its own form. Some 90 percent were requested to mail the form back on April 1; the remainder—mostly in rural areas—were instructed to hold onto the completed form until it was picked up by a census taker.

Approximately 4 out of 5 households received a short version of the questionnaire, containing 19 questions. The remaining households were requested to fill out a longer form, which, in addition to the basic 19 questions, had 46 additional queries. This sampling technique allows detailed social and economic characteristics to be developed without having to ask all questions of all households.

Census Creates Temporary Work Force

The Census Bureau estimated that there were some 86 million households in the United States on April 1, 1980, and those were estimated to contain some 222 million people. The size and complexity of the population meant that some 275,000 temporary employees were needed to take the census, working out of 409 temporary district offices. These workers picked up forms in rural areas, checked questionnaires for completeness, called on households which did not mail back a questionnaire, and performed the wide range of clerical tasks required to avoid duplication, omission, and other potential errors.

It was expected that about 80 percent of households which had been asked to mail in their forms would do so voluntarily. However, the actual figure was 86 percent, greatly reducing the number of followup calls which had to be made.

The followup work was divided into two phases. Between the two, the Census Bureau sent working field counts to the highest elected officials in jurisdictions where these officials were willing, asking that they review the figures and point out areas in which households might have been missed.

The release of these numbers in the Local Review Program generated controversy in some quarters, especially among mayors of towns and cities that did not grow or lost population during the decade.

Housing Units Up, Size of Households Down

These early figures reflected one of the key demographic events of the 1970's: the rapid growth in housing units and the corresponding drop in the average size of households. Estimates show that the average household size fell 11.5 percent, from 3.14 persons in 1970 to 2.78 in 1979. This meant that an average community would have to show at least a 10 percent increase in the number of households over 1970 just to keep the same population it had that year.

The 1980 census employed a number of techniques aimed at improving the accuracy of the count. One element was a massive publicity campaign. Every media channel was utilized, from network TV to subway car cards to census reminders on bills to flyers hand delivered by Boy Scouts across the country. The media campaign alone resulted in an estimated $38 million in time and space donated by the nation's media outlets. The saturation was such that every person in the country was exposed to an estimated average of 100 census advertising messages between January and June 1980.

Efforts aimed at obtaining cooperation from the nation's minority populations were greatly stepped up for the 1980 census. Some 200 specially trained Census Bureau employees worked with community organizations at the local level to underline the importance of every person being counted in the census.

Other technical innovations were employed to create a more accurate master address list and to verify that housing units were truly vacant—both aimed at making sure every household was reached.

1980 Results Bring Surprises

The results are proving to be a surprise. The 1980 census found some two million more households than had been estimated. This meant more work, time, and money to take the census, but it also indicated that the 1980 techniques were an improvement over those used in 1970.

Early estimates by the Bureau indicated that the population total would probably be closer to 224 million than the expected 222 million. If this proves to be the case, it may mean a large reduction in the undercount—that estimated portion of the population which was not reached or counted by the census. In 1970, the undercount was estimated at 2.5 percent of the total population (about 5.3 million people). The early estimate of the 1980 undercount shows a probable improvement to a level of not more than 1.4 percent.

As the year drew to a close, the Census Bureau was continuing to tabulate results to meet its legal deadlines for reporting results of the census. The law requires that population totals for each state must be given to the President by December 31, 1980, so that reapportionment of seats in the House of Representatives can occur. New this time is a requirement that totals for all political jurisdictions in each state must be ready for the 50 governors by April 1, 1981 for use in state and local redistricting.

South and West to Gain House Seats

Estimates in 1979 showed that 14 seats would probably change hands in the House of Representatives as a result of population shifts during the decade. The estimates show the West and the South gaining representation at the expense of the Northeast and North Central regions.

Political representation, while the underlying reason for taking a census, is just one of the uses of census data—uses which have grown in number and importance since 1970. An estimated $50 billion each year is now allocated to state and local jurisdictions from the Federal government in a wide variety of programs, based on census data.

This use of census data to determine dollar amounts flowing to the nation's cities—many of them plagued with chronic fiscal problems—has thrust the results of the 1980 census into the limelight as never before.

When the census was only one day old—April 2, 1980—the city of Detroit had filed suit, asking that the court order the Census Bureau to adjust its population by the amount of the estimated undercount *before* reporting the official results. Other suits also dealt with adjusting the actual headcounts, and still others questioned the procedures used by the Census Bureau to count the population in certain areas.

Adjustment of Results Under Debate

As the taking and tabulating of the census continued, and the suits were heard, the Census Bureau was moving toward the culmination of more than a year's examination of the issues involved in possible adjustment of the actual count. The Secretary of Commerce had instructed the Director of the Census Bureau to make a decision whether or not to adjust the results, and the Bureau's position was that such a decision was within the law with regard to uses such as funding allocation but not for political reapportionment.

Data from the 1980 census will be available for a wider range of geographic areas than any previous census—some 3,200 counties, 20,000 incorporated places, 45,000 census tracts, and 2,500,000 city blocks, in the U.S. as well as Puerto Rico, the Virgin Islands, Guam, American Samoa, and the Trust Territories of the Pacific Islands.

The Decennial Census of Population and Housing is a unique undertaking—the only function of government which attempts to touch every person living in the country at one time. From its relatively simple beginning in 1790, the census has become the largest single statistical enterprise in the country—a highly visible, extremely important tool used by decisionmakers in all walks of life.

Population of the U.S., 1960-1970

				1970			Rank	
Region, division, and state	1970 Census	1960 Census	Pct. + or −	Urban	Rural	Pct. urban	1970	1960
United States	**203,235,298**	**179,323,175**	**13.3**	**149,324,930**	**53,886,996**	**73.5**	...	...
Regions:								
Northeast	49,050,525	44,677,819	9.7	39,449,818	9,590,885	80.4	...	...
North Central	56,577,067	51,619,139	9.6	40,480,760	16,090,903	71.6	...	...
South	62,798,347	54,973,113	14.2	40,539,961	22,255,406	64.6	...	...
West	34,809,359	28,053,104	24.1	28,854,391	5,949,802	82.9	...	...
New England	**11,847,186**	**10,509,367**	**12.7**	**9,043,517**	**2,798,146**	**76.4**	...	...
Maine	993,663	969,265	2.5	504,157	487,891	50.8	38	36
New Hampshire	737,681	606,921	21.5	416,040	321,641	56.4	42	45
Vermont	444,732	389,881	14.1	142,889	301,441	32.2	49	47
Massachusetts	5,689,170	5,148,578	10.5	4,810,449	878,721	84.6	10	9
Rhode Island	949,723	859,488	10.5	824,930	121,795	87.1	39	39
Connecticut	3,032,217	2,535,234	19.6	2,345,052	686,657	77.4	24	25
Middle Atlantic	**37,203,339**	**34,168,452**	**8.7**	**30,406,301**	**6,792,739**	**81.7**	...	...
New York	18,241,266	16,782,304	8.4	15,602,486	2,634,481	85.6	2	1
New Jersey	7,168,164	6,066,782	18.2	6,373,405	794,759	88.9	8	8
Pennsylvania	11,793,909	11,319,366	4.2	8,430,410	3,363,499	71.5	3	3
East North Central	**40,252,678**	**36,225,024**	**11.1**	**30,091,847**	**10,160,629**	**74.8**	...	...
Ohio	10,652,017	9,706,397	9.7	8,025,775	2,625,242	75.3	6	5
Indiana	5,913,669	4,662,498	11.4	3,372,060	1,821,609	64.9	11	11
Illinois	11,113,976	10,081,158	10.2	9,229,821	1,884,155	83.0	5	4
Michigan	8,875,083	7,823,194	13.4	6,553,773	2,321,310	73.8	7	7
Wisconsin	4,417,933	3,951,777	11.8	2,910,418	1,507,313	65.9	16	15
West North Central	**16,324,389**	**15,394,115**	**6.0**	**10,388,913**	**5,930,274**	**63.7**	...	...
Minnesota	3,805,069	3,413,864	11.5	2,527,308	1,277,663	66.4	19	18
Iowa	2,825,041	2,757,537	2.4	1,616,405	1,207,971	57.2	25	24
Missouri	4,677,399	4,319,813	8.3	3,277,662	1,398,839	70.1	13	13
North Dakota	617,761	632,446	-2.3	273,442	344,319	44.3	46	44
South Dakota	666,257	680,514	-2.1	296,628	368,879	44.6	45	40
Nebraska	1,483,791	1,411,330	5.1	912,598	570,895	61.5	35	34
Kansas	2,249,071	2,178,611	3.2	1,484,870	761,708	66.1	28	28
South Atlantic	**30,671,337**	**25,971,732**	**18.1**	**19,523,920**	**11,147,417**	**63.7**	...	...
Delaware	548,104	446,292	22.8	395,569	152,535	72.2	47	46
Maryland	3,922,399	3,100,689	26.5	3,003,935	918,464	76.6	18	21
District of Columbia	756,510	763,956	-1.0	756,510	...	100.0	41	...
Virginia	4,648,494	3,966,949	17.2	2,934,841	1,713,653	63.1	14	14
West Virginia	1,744,237	1,860,421	-6.2	679,491	1,064,746	39.0	34	30
North Carolina	5,082,059	4,556,155	11.5	2,285,168	2,796,891	45.0	12	12
South Carolina	2,590,516	2,382,594	8.7	1,232,195	1,358,321	47.6	26	26
Georgia	4,589,575	3,943,116	16.4	2,768,074	1,821,501	60.3	15	16
Florida	6,789,443	4,951,560	37.1	5,468,137	1,321,306	80.5	9	10
East South Central	**12,804,552**	**12,050,126**	**6.3**	**6,987,943**	**5,815,527**	**54.6**	...	...
Kentucky	3,219,311	3,038,156	6.0	1,684,053	1,534,653	52.3	23	22
Tennessee	3,924,164	3,567,089	10.0	2,305,307	1,618,380	58.7	17	17
Alabama	3,444,165	3,266,740	5.4	2,011,941	1,432,224	58.4	21	19
Mississippi	2,216,912	2,178,141	1.8	986,642	1,230,270	44.5	29	29
West South Central	**19,322,458**	**16,951,255**	**14.0**	**14,028,098**	**5,292,462**	**72.6**	...	...
Arkansas	1,923,295	1,786,272	7.7	960,865	962,430	50.0	32	31
Louisiana	3,643,180	3,257,022	11.9	2,406,150	1,235,156	66.1	20	20
Oklahoma	2,559,253	2,328,284	9.9	1,740,137	819,092	68.0	27	27
Texas	11,196,730	9,579,677	16.9	8,920,946	2,275,784	79.7	4	6
Mountain	**8,283,585**	**6,855,060**	**20.8**	**6,054,979**	**2,226,583**	**73.1**	...	...
Montana	694,409	674,767	2.9	370,676	323,733	53.4	44	41
Idaho	713,008	667,191	6.9	385,434	327,133	54.1	43	42
Wyoming	332,416	330,066	0.7	201,111	131,305	60.5	50	48
Colorado	2,207,259	1,753,947	25.8	1,733,311	473,948	78.5	30	33
New Mexico	1,016,000	951,023	6.8	708,775	307,225	69.8	37	37
Arizona	1,772,482	1,302,161	36.1	1,408,864	362,036	79.6	33	35
Utah	1,059,273	890,627	18.9	851,472	207,801	80.4	36	38
Nevada	488,738	285,278	71.3	395,336	93,402	80.9	48	49
Pacific	**26,525,774**	**21,198,044**	**25.1**	**22,799,412**	**3,723,219**	**86.0**	...	...
Washington	3,409,169	2,853,214	19.5	2,476,468	932,701	72.6	22	23
Oregon	2,091,385	1,768,687	18.2	1,402,704	688,681	67.1	31	32
California	19,953,134	15,717,204	27.0	18,136,045	1,817,089	90.9	1	2
Alaska	302,173	226,167	33.6	145,512	154,870	48.4	51	50
Hawaii	769,913	632,772	21.7	638,683	129,878	83.1	40	43

Urban and rural figures do not equal total 1970 population because of errors discovered by Census Bureau after tabulation.

U.S. Area and Population: 1790 to 1970

Source: U.S. Bureau of the Census

Area figures represent area on indicated date including in some cases considerable areas not then organized or settled, and not covered by the census. Area figures have been adjusted to bring them into agreement with remeasurements made in 1940.

Census date	Area (square miles) Gross	Land	Water	Population Number	Per sq. mile of land	Increase over preceding census Number	%
1790 (Aug. 2)	888,811	864,746	24,065	3,929,214	4.5	(X)	(X)
1800 (Aug. 4)	888,811	864,746	24,065	5,308,483	6.1	1,379,269	35.1
1810 (Aug. 6)	1,716,003	1,681,828	34,175	7,239,881	4.3	1,931,398	36.4
1820 (Aug. 7)	1,788,006	1,749,462	38,544	9,638,453	5.5	2,398,572	33.1
1830 (June 1)	1,788,006	1,749,462	38,544	12,866,020	7.4	3,227,567	33.5
1840 (June 1)	1,788,006	1,749,462	38,544	17,069,453	9.8	4,203,433	32.7
1850 (June 1)	2,992,747	2,940,042	52,705	23,191,876	7.9	6,122,423	35.9
1860 (June 1)	3,022,387	2,969,640	52,747	31,443,321	10.6	8,251,445	35.6
1870 (June 1)	3,022,387	2,969,640	52,747	[1]39,818,449	[1]13.4	8,375,128	26.6
1880 (June 1)	3,022,387	2,969,640	52,747	50,155,783	16.9	10,337,334	26.0
1890 (June 1)	3,022,387	2,969,640	52,747	62,947,714	21.2	12,791,931	25.5
1900 (June 1)	3,022,387	2,969,834	52,553	75,994,575	25.6	13,046,861	20.7
1910 (Apr. 15)	3,022,387	2,969,565	52,822	91,972,266	31.0	15,977,691	21.0
1920 (Jan. 1)	3,022,387	2,969,451	52,936	105,710,620	35.6	13,738,354	14.9
1930 (Apr. 1)	3,022,387	2,977,128	45,259	122,775,046	41.2	17,064,426	16.1
1940 (Apr. 1)	3,022,387	2,977,128	45,259	131,669,275	44.2	8,894,229	7.2
1950 (Apr. 1)[2]	3,615,211	3,552,206	63,005	151,325,798	42.6	19,161,229	14.5
1960 (Apr. 1)[2]	3,615,123	3,540,911	74,212	179,323,175	50.6	27,997,377	18.5
1970 (Apr. 1)[2]	[3]3,618,467	[3]3,540,023	[3]78,444	[4]203,211,926	57.4	23,888,751	13.3

(X) Not applicable. (1) Revised to include adjustments for underenumeration in Southern States; unrevised number is 38,558,371. (2) Includes Alaska and Hawaii. (3) Figures corrected after final reports were issued. (4) The official 1970 resident population count is 203,235,298; the difference of 23,372 is due to errors found after tabulations were completed.

Population, Urban and Rural, by Race: 1960 and 1970

Source: U.S. Bureau of the Census

An urbanized area comprises at least one city of 50,000 inhabitants (central city) plus contiguous, closely settled areas (urban fringe). (thousands)

Year and area	1960 Total	1960 White	1960 Negro and other	1970 Total	1970 White	1970 Negro and other
Population, total	**179,323**	**158,832**	**20,491**	**[1]203,212**	**177,749**	**25,463**
Urban	125,269	110,428	14,840	149,325	128,773	20,552
Inside urbanized areas	95,848	83,770	12,070	118,447	100,952	17,495
Central cities	57,975	47,627	10,348	63,922	49,547	14,375
Urban fringe	37,873	36,143	1,731	54,525	51,405	3,120
Outside urbanized areas	29,420	26,658	2,762	30,878	27,822	3,057
Rural	54,054	48,403	5,651	53,887	48,976	4,911

(1) See footnote 4 above.

Congressional Apportionment

	1970	1960		1970	1960		1970	1960		1970	1960		1970	1960
Ala.	7	8	Ida.	2	2	Minn.	8	8	N. D.	1	2	Vt.	1	1
Alas.	1	1	Ill.	24	24	Miss.	5	5	Oh.	23	24	Va.	10	10
Ariz.	4	3	Ind.	11	11	Mo.	10	10	Okla.	6	6	Wash.	7	7
Ark.	4	4	Ia.	6	7	Mon.	2	2	Ore.	4	4	W. Va.	4	5
Cal.	43	38	Kan.	5	5	Neb.	3	3	Pa.	25	27	Wis.	9	10
Col.	5	4	Ky.	7	7	Nev.	1	1	R. I.	2	2	Wy.	1	1
Conn.	6	6	La.	8	8	N. H.	2	2	S. C.	6	6			
Del.	1	1	Me.	2	2	N. J.	15	15	S. D.	2	2	**Totals.**	**435**	**435**
Fla.	15	12	Md.	8	8	N. M.	2	2	Tenn.	8	9			
Ga.	10	10	Mass.	12	12	N. Y.	39	41	Tex.	24	23			
Ha.	2	2	Mich.	19	19	N. C.	11	11	Ut.	2	2			

The chief reason the Constitution provided for a census of the population every 10 years was to give a basis for apportionment of representatives among the states. This apportionment largely determines the number of electoral votes allotted to each state.

The number of representatives of each state in Congress is determined by the state's population, but each state is entitled to one representative regardless of population. A Congressional apportionment has been made after each decennial census except that of 1920.

Under provisions of a law that became effective Nov. 15, 1941, apportionment of representatives is made by the method of equal proportions. In the application of this method, the apportionment is made so that the average population per representative has the least possible variation between one state and any other. The first House of Representatives, in 1790, had 65 members, or one representative for each 30,000 of the estimated population, as provided by the Constitution. As the population grew, the number of representatives was increased but the total membership has been fixed at 435 since 1912.

U.S. Population by Official

(Members of the Armed Forces overseas or

State	1790	1800	1810	1820	1830	1840	1850	1860	1870	1880
Ala.	....	1,250	9,046	127,901	309,527	590,756	771,623	964,201	996,992	1,262,505
Alas.	....	....	....	....	....	....	....	....	....	....
Ariz.	....	....	....	....	....	....	....	....	9,658	40,440
Ark.	....	....	1,062	14,273	30,388	97,574	209,897	435,450	484,471	802,525
Cal.	....	....	....	....	....	....	92,597	379,994	560,247	864,694
Col.	....	....	....	....	....	....	....	34,277	39,864	194,327
Conn.	237,946	251,002	261,942	275,248	297,675	309,978	370,792	460,147	537,454	622,700
Del.	59,096	64,273	72,674	72,749	76,748	78,085	91,532	112,216	125,015	146,608
D.C.	....	14,023	24,023	33,039	39,834	43,712	51,687	75,080	131,700	177,624
Fla.	....	....	....	....	34,730	54,477	87,445	140,424	187,748	269,493
Ga.	82,548	162,686	252,433	340,989	516,823	691,392	906,185	1,057,286	1,184,109	1,542,180
Ha.	....	....	....	....	....	....	....	....	....	....
Ida.	....	....	....	....	....	....	....	....	14,999	32,610
Ill.	....	....	12,282	55,211	157,445	476,183	851,470	1,711,951	2,539,891	3,077,871
Ind.	....	5,641	24,520	147,178	343,031	685,866	988,416	1,350,428	1,680,637	1,978,301
Ia.	....	....	....	....	....	43,112	192,214	674,913	1,194,020	1,624,615
Kan.	....	....	....	....	....	....	....	107,206	364,399	996,096
Ky.	73,677	220,995	406,511	564,317	687,917	779,828	982,405	1,155,684	1,321,011	1,648,690
La.	....	....	76,556	153,407	215,739	352,411	517,762	708,002	726,915	939,946
Me.	96,540	151,719	228,705	298,335	399,455	501,793	583,169	628,279	626,915	648,936
Md.	319,728	341,548	380,546	407,350	447,040	470,019	583,034	687,049	780,894	934,943
Mass.	378,787	422,845	472,040	523,287	610,408	737,699	994,514	1,231,066	1,457,351	1,783,085
Mich.	....	....	4,762	8,896	31,639	212,267	397,654	749,113	1,184,059	1,636,937
Minn.	....	....	....	....	....	....	6,077	172,023	439,706	780,773
Miss.	....	8,850	40,352	75,448	136,621	375,651	606,526	791,305	827,922	1,131,597
Mo.	....	....	19,783	66,586	140,455	383,702	682,044	1,182,012	1,721,295	2,168,380
Mon.	....	....	....	....	....	....	....	....	20,595	39,159
Neb.	....	....	....	....	....	....	....	28,841	122,993	452,402
Nev.	....	....	....	....	....	....	....	6,857	42,491	62,266
N.H.	141,885	183,858	214,460	244,161	269,328	284,574	317,976	326,073	318,300	346,991
N.J.	184,139	211,149	245,562	277,575	320,823	373,306	489,555	672,035	906,096	1,131,116
N.M.	....	....	....	....	....	....	61,547	93,516	91,874	119,565
N.Y.	340,120	589,051	959,049	1,372,812	1,918,608	2,428,921	3,097,394	3,880,735	4,382,759	5,082,871
N.C.	393,751	478,103	555,500	638,829	737,987	753,419	869,039	992,622	1,071,361	1,399,750
N.D.	....	....	....	....	....	....	....	....	*2,405	36,909
Oh.	....	45,365	230,760	581,434	937,903	1,519,467	1,980,329	2,339,511	2,665,260	3,198,062
Okla.	....	....	....	....	....	....	....	....	....	....
Ore.	....	....	....	....	....	....	13,294	52,465	90,923	174,768
Pa.	434,373	602,365	810,091	1,049,458	1,348,233	1,724,033	2,311,786	2,906,215	3,521,951	4,282,891
R.I.	68,825	69,122	76,931	83,059	97,199	108,830	147,545	174,620	217,353	276,531
S.C.	249,073	345,591	415,115	502,741	581,185	594,398	668,507	703,708	705,606	995,577
S.D.	....	....	....	....	....	....	....	*4,837	*11,776	98,268
Tenn.	35,691	105,602	261,727	422,823	681,904	829,210	1,002,717	1,109,801	1,258,520	1,542,359
Tex.	....	....	....	....	....	....	212,592	604,215	818,579	1,591,749
Ut.	....	....	....	....	....	....	11,380	40,273	86,786	143,963
Vt.	85,425	154,465	217,895	235,981	280,652	291,948	314,120	315,098	330,551	332,286
Va.	821,287	880,200	974,600	1,065,366	1,211,405	1,239,797	1,421,661	1,596,318	1,225,163	1,512,565
Wash.	....	....	....	....	....	....	1,201	11,594	23,955	75,116
W. Va.	....	....	....	....	....	....	....	....	442,014	618,457
Wis.	....	....	....	....	....	30,945	305,391	775,881	1,054,670	1,315,497
Wy.	....	....	....	....	....	....	....	....	9,118	20,789
U.S.	**3,929,214**	**5,308,483**	**7,239,881**	**9,638,453**	**12,866,020**	**17,069,453**	**23,191,876**	**31,443,321**	**38,558,371**	**50,155,783**

*1860 figure is for Dakota Territory; 1870 figures are for parts of Dakota Territory. (1) U.S. total includes persons (5,318 in 1830 and 6,100 in 1840) on public ships in the service of the United States not credited to any region, division, or state.

Density of Population by States

(Per square mile, land area only)

State	1920	1960	1970	State	1920	1960	1970	State	1920	1960	1970
Ala.	45.8	64.2	67.9	Ky.	60.1	76.2	81.2	N. D.	9.2	9.1	8.9
Alas.*	0.1	0.4	0.5	La.	39.6	72.2	81.0	Oh.	141.4	236.6	260.0
Ariz.	2.9	11.5	15.6	Me.	25.7	31.3	32.1	Okla.	29.2	33.8	37.2
Ark.	33.4	34.2	37.0	Md.	145.8	313.5	396.6	Ore.	8.2	18.4	21.7
Cal.	22.0	100.4	127.6	Mass.	479.2	657.3	727.0	Pa.	194.5	251.4	262.3
Col.	9.1	16.9	21.3	Mich.	63.8	137.6	156.2	R. I.	566.4	819.3	905.5
Conn.	286.4	520.6	623.7	Minn.	29.5	43.0	48.0	S. C.	55.2	78.7	85.7
Del.	113.5	225.2	276.5	Miss.	38.6	46.0	46.9	S. D.	8.3	9.0	8.8
D. C.	7,292.9	12,523.9	12,401.8	Mo.	49.5	62.6	67.8	Tenn.	56.1	86.2	94.9
Fla.	17.7	91.5	125.5	Mon.	3.8	4.6	4.8	Tex.	17.8	36.4	42.7
Ga.	49.3	67.8	79.0	Neb.	16.9	18.4	19.4	Ut.	5.5	10.8	12.9
Ha.*	39.9	98.5	119.8	Nev.	.7	2.6	4.4	Vt.	38.6	42.0	47.9
Ida.	5.2	8.1	8.6	N. H.	49.1	67.2	81.7	Va.	57.4	99.5	116.9
Ill.	115.7	180.4	199.4	N. J.	420.0	805.5	953.1	Wash.	20.3	42.8	51.2
Ind.	81.3	128.8	143.9	N. M.	2.9	7.8	8.4	W. Va.	60.9	77.2	72.5
Ia.	43.2	49.2	50.5	N. Y.	217.9	350.6	381.3	Wis.	47.6	72.6	81.1
Kan.	21.6	26.6	27.5	N. C.	52.5	93.2	104.1	Wy.	2.0	3.4	3.4
								U.S.	***29.9**	**50.6**	**57.5**

*For purposes of comparison, Alaska and Hawaii included in above tabulation for 1920, even though not states then.

Census from 1790 to 1980

other U.S. nationals overseas are not included.)

1890	1900	1910	1920	1930	1940	1950	1960	1970	1980[1]
1,513,401	1,828,697	2,138,093	2,348,174	2,646,248	2,832,961	3,061,743	3,266,740	3,444,165	*3,742,000*
....	....	....	....	....	....	....	226,167	302,173	*403,000*
88,243	122,931	204,354	334,162	435,573	499,261	749,587	1,302,161	1,772,482	*2,354,000*
1,128,211	1,311,564	1,574,449	1,752,204	1,854,482	1,949,387	1,909,511	1,786,272	1,923,295	*2,186,000*
1,213,398	1,485,053	2,377,549	3,426,861	5,677,251	6,907,387	10,586,223	15,717,204	19,953,134	*22,294,000*
413,249	539,700	799,024	939,629	1,035,791	1,123,296	1,325,089	1,753,947	2,207,259	*2,670,000*
746,258	908,420	1,114,756	1,380,631	1,606,903	1,709,242	2,007,280	2,535,234	3,032,217	3,096,951
168,493	184,735	202,322	223,003	238,380	266,505	318,085	446,292	548,104	594,711
230,392	278,718	331,069	437,571	486,869	663,091	802,178	763,956	756,510	*673,600*
391,422	528,542	752,619	968,470	1,468,211	1,897,414	2,771,305	4,951,560	6,789,443	*8,594,000*
1,837,353	2,216,331	2,609,121	2,895,832	2,908,506	3,123,723	3,444,578	3,943,116	4,589,575	*5,084,000*
....	....	....	....	....	....	....	632,772	769,913	*897,000*
88,548	161,772	325,594	431,866	445,032	524,873	588,637	667,191	713,008	*878,000*
3,826,352	4,821,550	5,638,591	6,485,280	7,630,654	7,897,241	8,712,176	10,081,158	11,113,976	*11,243,000*
2,192,404	2,516,462	2,700,876	2,930,390	3,238,503	3,427,796	3,934,224	4,662,498	5,193,669	*5,374,000*
1,912,297	2,231,853	2,224,771	2,404,021	2,470,939	2,538,268	2,621,073	2,757,537	2,825,041	*2,896,000*
1,428,108	1,470,495	1,690,949	1,769,257	1,880,999	1,801,028	1,905,299	2,178,611	2,249,071	*2,348,000*
1,858,635	2,147,174	2,289,905	2,416,630	2,614,589	2,845,627	2,944,806	3,038,156	3,219,311	*3,498,000*
1,118,588	1,381,625	1,656,388	1,798,509	2,101,593	2,363,880	2,683,516	3,257,022	3,643,180	*3,966,000*
661,086	694,466	742,371	768,014	797,423	847,226	913,774	969,265	993,663	1,123,560
1,042,390	1,188,044	1,295,346	1,449,661	1,631,526	1,821,244	2,343,001	3,100,689	3,922,399	*4,143,000*
2,238,947	2,805,346	3,366,416	3,852,356	4,249,614	4,316,721	4,690,514	5,148,578	5,689,170	5,725,983
2,093,890	2,420,982	2,810,173	3,668,412	4,842,325	5,256,106	6,371,766	7,823,194	8,875,083	*9,189,000*
1,310,283	1,751,394	2,075,708	2,387,125	2,563,953	2,792,300	2,982,483	3,413,864	3,805,069	*4,008,000*
1,289,600	1,551,270	1,797,114	1,790,618	2,009,821	2,183,796	2,178,914	2,178,141	2,216,912	*2,404,000*
2,679,185	3,106,665	3,293,335	3,404,055	3,629,367	3,784,664	3,954,653	4,319,813	4,677,399	*4,860,000*
142,924	243,329	376,053	548,889	537,606	559,456	591,024	674,767	694,409	783,647
1,062,656	1,066,300	1,192,214	1,296,372	1,377,963	1,315,834	1,325,510	1,411,330	1,483,791	*1,565,000*
47,355	42,335	81,875	77,407	91,058	110,247	160,083	285,278	488,738	*663,000*
376,530	411,588	430,572	443,083	465,293	491,524	533,242	606,921	737,681	918,959
1,444,933	1,883,669	2,537,167	3,155,900	4,041,334	4,160,165	4,835,329	6,066,782	7,168,164	*7,327,000*
160,282	195,310	327,301	360,350	423,317	531,818	681,187	951,023	1,016,000	*1,212,000*
6,003,174	7,268,894	9,113,614	10,385,227	12,588,066	13,479,142	14,830,192	16,782,304	18,241,266	*17,748,000*
1,617,949	1,893,810	2,206,287	2,559,123	3,170,276	3,571,623	4,061,929	4,556,155	5,082,059	*5,577,000*
190,983	319,146	577,056	646,872	680,845	641,935	619,636	632,446	617,761	652,222
3,672,329	4,157,545	4,767,121	5,759,394	6,646,697	6,907,612	7,946,627	9,706,397	10,652,017	*10,749,000*
258,657	790,391	1,657,155	2,028,283	2,396,040	2,336,434	2,233,351	2,328,284	2,559,253	*2,880,000*
317,704	413,536	672,765	783,389	953,786	1,089,684	1,521,341	1,768,687	2,091,385	*2,444,000*
5,258,113	6,302,115	7,665,111	8,720,017	9,631,350	9,900,180	10,498,012	11,319,366	11,793,909	*11,750,000*
345,506	428,556	542,610	604,397	687,497	713,346	791,896	859,488	949,723	945,761
1,151,149	1,340,316	1,515,400	1,683,724	1,738,765	1,899,804	2,117,027	2,382,594	2,590,516	*2,918,000*
348,600	401,570	583,888	636,547	692,849	642,961	652,740	680,514	666,257	687,643
1,767,518	2,020,616	2,184,789	2,337,885	2,616,556	2,915,841	3,291,718	3,567,089	3,924,164	*4,357,000*
2,235,527	3,048,710	3,896,542	4,663,228	5,824,715	6,414,824	7,711,194	9,579,677	11,196,730	*13,014,000*
210,779	276,749	373,351	449,396	507,847	550,310	688,862	890,627	1,059,273	1,454,630
332,422	343,641	355,956	352,428	359,611	359,231	377,747	389,881	444,732	511,297
1,655,980	1,854,184	2,061,612	2,309,187	2,421,851	2,677,773	3,318,680	3,966,949	4,648,494	*5,148,000*
357,232	518,103	1,141,990	1,356,621	1,563,396	1,736,191	2,378,962	2,853,214	3,409,169	*3,774,000*
762,794	958,800	1,221,119	1,463,701	1,729,205	1,901,974	2,005,553	1,860,421	1,744,237	*1,860,000*
1,693,330	2,069,042	2,333,860	2,632,067	2,939,006	3,137,587	3,434,575	3,951,777	4,417,933	*4,679,000*
62,555	92,531	145,965	194,402	225,565	250,742	290,529	330,066	332,416	468,909
62,947,714	**75,994,575**	**91,972,266**	**105,710,620**	**122,775,046**	**131,669,275**	**150,697,361**	**179,323,175**	**203,235,298**	**223,889,000**[2]

(1) Non-italic figures listed below represent preliminary 1980 census results; italic figures are 1978 Census Bureau estimates. (2) This is the Census Bureau estimate based on preliminary 1980 census results; an estimated undercount of 3,111,000 could raise this figure to an estimated 227,000,000.

U.S. Center of Population, 1790-1970

Center of Population is that point which may be considered as center of population gravity of the U.S. or that point upon which the U.S. would balance if it were a rigid plane without weight and the population distributed thereon with each individual being assumed to have equal weight and to exert an influence on a central point proportional to his distance from that point.

Year	N. Lat. °	'	"	W.Long. °	'	"	Approximate location
1790	39	16	30	76	11	12	23 miles east of Baltimore, Md.
1800	39	16	6	76	56	30	18 miles west of Baltimore, Md.
1810	39	11	30	77	37	12	40 miles northwest by west of Washington, D.C. (in Va.)
1820	39	5	42	78	33	0	16 miles east of Moorefield, W. Va.[1]
1830	38	57	54	79	16	54	19 miles west-southwest of Moorefield, W. Va.[1]
1840	39	2	0	80	18	0	16 miles south of Clarksburg, W. Va.[1]
1850	38	59	0	81	19	0	23 miles southeast of Parkersburg, W. Va.[1]
1860	39	0	24	82	48	48	20 miles south by east of Chillicothe, Oh.
1870	39	12	0	83	35	42	48 miles east by north of Cincinnati, Oh.
1880	39	4	8	84	39	40	8 miles west by south of Cincinnati, Oh. (in Ky.)
1890	39	11	56	85	32	53	20 miles east of Columbus, Ind.
1900	39	9	36	85	48	54	6 miles southeast of Columbus, Ind.
1910	39	10	12	86	32	20	In the city of Bloomington, Ind.
1920	39	10	21	86	43	15	8 miles south-southeast of Spencer, Owen County, Ind.
1930	39	3	45	87	8	6	3 miles northeast of Linton, Greene County, Ind.
1940	38	56	54	87	22	35	2 miles southeast by east of Carlisle, Haddon township, Sullivan County, Ind.
1950 (Inc. Alaska & Hawaii)	38	48	15	88	22	8	3 miles northeast of Louisville, Clay County, Ill.
1960	38	35	58	89	12	35	6 1/2 miles northwest of Centralia, Ill.
1970	38	27	47	89	42	22	5 miles east southeast of Mascoutah, St. Clair County, Ill.

(1) West Viginia was set off from Virginia Dec. 31, 1862, and admitted as a state June 20, 1863.

Rankings of U.S. Standard Metropolitan Statistical Areas

Source: U.S. Bureau of the Census

Metropolitan areas are ranked by 1978 provisional population size based on new SMSA definitions and compared with a ranking of areas as defined in the 1970 census. Included are 264 of the 281 Standard Metropolitan Statistical Areas (SMSAs) as defined through June 30, 1979 by the Office of Federal Statistical Policy and Standards, excluding 4 areas in Puerto Rico not covered in the report.

Asterisk (*) indicates 13 New England County Metropolitan Areas comprised of 26 New England SMSAs.

SMSA	1978 (P) Rank	1978 (P) Pop.	1970 Rank	1970 Pop.
New York, N.Y.-N.J.	1	9,221,800	1	9,973,716
Los Angeles-Long Beach, Cal.	2	7,080,900	2	7,041,980
Chicago, Ill.	3	7,029,600	3	6,977,267
Philadelphia, Pa.-N.J.	4	4,770,400	4	4,824,110
Detroit, Mich.	5	4,386,400	5	4,435,051
Boston-Lowell-Brockton-Lawrence-Haverhill, Mass.-N.H.*	6	3,887,800	6	3,848,593
San Francisco-Oakland, Cal.	7	3,183,800	7	3,109,247
Washington, D.C.-Md.-Va.	8	3,016,900	8	2,910,111
Dallas-Ft. Worth, Tex.[3]	9	2,719,900	12	2,377,623
Nassau-Suffolk, N.Y.[1]	10	2,690,000	9	2,555,868
Houston, Tex.	11	2,595,400	16	1,999,316
St. Louis, Mo.-Ill.	12	2,385,900	10	2,410,884
Pittsburgh, Pa.	13	2,277,300	11	2,401,362
Baltimore, Md.	14	2,145,200	13	2,071,016
Minneapolis-St.Paul, Minn.-Wis.	15	2,063,000	17	1,965,391
Newark, N.J.	16	1,951,300	15	2,057,468
Cleveland, Oh.	17	1,938,900	14	2,063,729
Atlanta, Ga.	18	1,851,500	18	1,595,517
Anaheim-Santa Ana-Garden Grove, Cal.	19	1,833,000	20	1,421,233
San Diego, Cal.	20	1,743,600	23	1,357,854
Denver-Boulder, Col.[1]	21	1,504,700	27	1,239,545
Seattle-Everett, Wash.	22	1,467,600	19	1,424,605
Miami, Fla.	23	1,451,200	26	1,267,792
Milwaukee, Wis.	24	1,417,200	21	1,403,884
Tampa-St. Petersburg, Fla.	25	1,396,300	30	1,088,549
Cincinnati, Oh.-Ky.-Ind.	26	1,389,100	22	1,387,287
Riverside-San Bernadino-Ontario, Cal.	27	1,385,400	28	1,139,149
Kansas City, Mo.-Kan.	28	1,324,600	25	1,273,926
Buffalo, N.Y.	29	1,303,000	24	1,349,211
Phoenix, Ariz.	30	1,293,200	36	971,228
San Jose, Cal.	31	1,232,200	31	1,065,313
Indianapolis, Ind.	32	1,156,200	29	1,111,352
New Orleans, La.	33	1,141,100	32	1,046,470
Portland, Oreg.-Wash.	34	1,140,100	35	1,007,130
Columbus, Oh.	35	1,088,900	34	1,017,847
Hartford-New Britain-Bristol, Conn.*	36	1,045,300	33	1,035,195
San Antonio, Tex.	37	1,037,800	38	888,179
Rochester, N.Y.	38	969,800	37	961,516
Sacramento, Cal.	39	951,000	43	803,793
Memphis, Tenn.-Ark.-Miss.	40	888,800	42	834,103
Louisville, Ky.-Ind.	41	887,300	39	867,330
Fort Lauderdale-Hollywood, Fla.	42	881,900	61	620,100
Providence-Warwick-Pawtucket, R.I.*	43	852,800	40	855,495
Salt Lake City-Ogden, Ut.[3]	44	842,500	51	705,458
Dayton, Oh.	45	834,200	41	852,531
Birmingham, Ala.	46	818,200	46	767,230
Bridgeport-Stamford-Norwalk-Danbury, Conn.*	47	808,400	44	792,814
Norfolk-Virginia Beach-Portsmouth, Va.-N.C.	48	800,100	49	732,600
Albany-Schenectady-Troy, N.Y.	49	792,300	45	777,977
Oklahoma City, Okla.	50	789,400	53	699,092
Nashville-Davidson, Tenn.	51	786,000	52	699,271
Greensboro-Winston-Salem-High Point, N.C.	52	779,300	50	724,129
Toledo, Ohio-Mich.	53	775,800	47	762,658
New Haven-West Haven-Waterbury, Meriden, Conn.*	54	754,600	48	744,948
Honolulu, Ha.	55	719,600	58	630,528
Jacksonville, Fla.	56	701,500	60	621,827
Akron, Oh.	57	657,000	54	679,239
Syracuse, N.Y.	58	649,600	56	636,596
Gary-Hammond-East Chicago, Ind.	59	648,400	57	633,367
Worcester-Fitchburg-Leominster, Mass.*	60	645,100	55	637,037
Northeast Pennsylvania	61	629,200	59	621,882
Tulsa, Okla.	62	628,500	67	549,154
Allentown-Bethlehem-Easton, Pa.-N.J.	63	625,700	63	594,382
Richmond, Va.	64	611,700	68	547,542
Orlando, Fla.	65	609,900	77	453,270
Charlotte-Gastonia, N.C.[3]	66	605,900	66	557,785
New Brunswick-Perth Amboy-Sayreville, N.J.[1]	67	591,100	64	583,813
Springfield-Chicopee-Holyoke, Mass.*	68	587,200	65	583,031
Grand Rapids, Mich.	69	585,100	70	539,225
Omaha, Neb.-Ia.	70	581,700	69	542,646
Jersey City, N.J.	71	554,000	62	607,839
Youngstown-Warren, Oh.	72	545,800	71	537,124
Greenville-Spartanburg, S.C.	73	541,100	74	473,454
Flint, Mich.	74	521,300	72	508,664
Wilmington, Del-N.J.-Md.	75	515,500	73	499,493
Long Branch-Asbury Park, N.J.[1]	76	499,900	75	461,849
Raleigh-Durham, N.C.[3]	77	493,600	80	419,254
West Palm Beach-Boca Raton, Fla.	78	486,700	97	348,993
Oxnard-Simi Valley-Ventura, Cal.	79	484,500	87	378,497
Fresno, Cal.	80	479,000	81	413,329
Austin, Tex.	81	477,900	94	360,463
New Bedford-Fall River, Mass.*	82	472,100	78	444,301
Tucson, Ariz.	83	461,700	96	351,667
Lansing-East Lansing, Mich.	84	457,700	79	424,271
Knoxville, Tenn.	85	455,700	84	409,409
Paterson-Clifton-Passaic, N.J.	86	444,700	76	460,782
Baton Rouge, La.	87	444,600	89	375,628
El Paso, Tex.	88	443,400	95	359,291
Tacoma, Wash.	89	436,900	82	412,344
Mobile, Ala.	90	435,300	88	376,690
Harrisburg, Pa.	91	429,800	83	410,505
Johnson City-Kingsport-Bristol, Tenn.-Va.[1]	92	411,300	90	373,591
Albuquerque, N.M.	93	408,800	103	333,266
Canton, Oh.	94	403,700	85	393,789
Chattanooga, Tenn.-Ga.	95	400,900	91	370,857
Wichita, Kan.	96	397,500	86	389,352
Charleston-North Charleston, S.C.	97	389,000	101	336,036
Columbia, S.C.	98	380,000	108	322,880
Las Vegas, Nev.	99	376,800	124	273,288
Little Rock-North Little Rock, Ark.	100	376,400	107	323,296
Fort Wayne, Ind.	101	375,700	93	361,984
Davenport-Rock Island-Moline, Ia.-Ill.	102	374,200	92	362,638
Bakersfield, Cal.	103	365,300	105	330,234
Beaumont-Port Arthur-Orange, Tex.	104	364,300	98	347,568
Newport News-Hampton, Va.	105	361,400	104	333,140
Peoria, Ill.	106	360,600	99	341,979
Shreveport, La.	107	356,200	102	333,826
York, Pa.	108	355,700	106	329,540
Lancaster, Pa.	109	351,200	109	320,079
Des Moines, Ia.	110	334,100	110	313,562
Utica-Rome, N.Y.	111	325,500	100	340,477
Spokane, Wash.	112	319,600	116	287,487
Madison, Wis.	113	319,000	115	290,272
Trenton, N.J.	114	317,200	111	304,116
Stockton, Cal.	115	313,100	114	291,073
Reading, Pa.	116	305,500	113	296,382
Binghamton, N.Y.-Pa.	117	303,400	112	302,672
Corpus Christi, Tex.	118	302,100	119	284,832
Vallejo-Fairfield-Napa, Cal.	119	301,100	135	251,129
Huntington-Ashland, W.Va.-Ky.-Oh.	120	299,900	117	286,935

SMSA	1978 (P) Rank	1978 (P) Pop.	1970 Rank	1970 Pop.
Lexington-Fayette, Ky.	121	299,800	126	266,701
Jackson, Miss.	122	298,700	131	258,906
Evansville, Ind.-Ky.	123	294,800	118	284,959
Huntsville, Ala.	124	292,700	120	282,450
Santa Barbara-Santa Maria-Lompoc, Calif.	125	292,000	128	264,324
Colorado Springs, Colo.	126	291,400	138	239,288
Augusta, Ga.-S.C.	127	290,900	123	275,787
Appleton-Oshkosh, Wis.	128	290,600	122	276,948
South Bend, Ind.	129	280,800	121	279,813
Lakeland-Winter Haven, Fla.[1]	130	278,200	143	228,515
Salinas-Seaside-Monterey, Calif.	131	275,800	136	247,450
Pensacola, Fla.	132	275,500	137	243,075
Santa Rosa, Calif.	133	274,200	155	204,885
Lorain-Elyria, Ohio	134	271,200	134	256,843
Kalamazoo-Portage, Mich.	135	270,300	132	257,723
Erie, Pa.	136	269,400	129	263,654
Rockford, Ill.	137	269,300	125	272,063
Duluth-Superior, Minn.-Wis.	138	265,700	127	265,350
Johnstown, Pa.	139	264,900	130	262,822
Charlestown, W. Va.	140	261,000	133	257,140
Manchester-Nashua, N.H.*	141	260,000	147	223,941
Montgomery, Ala.	142	258,200	146	225,911
Eugene-Springfield, Oreg.	143	257,700	151	215,401
Hamilton-Middletown, Ohio	144	256,400	145	226,207
Ann Arbor, Mich.	145	254,500	140	234,103
Modesto, Calif.	146	246,100	157	194,506
New London-Norwich, Conn.*	147	244,500	141	230,654
Macon, Ga.	148	243,100	144	226,782
McAllen-Pharr-Edinburg, Tex.	149	235,800	161	181,535
Melbourne-Titusville-Cocoa, Fla.[1]	150	234,400	142	230,006
Portland, Maine*	151	233,500	150	215,980
Poughkeepsie, N.Y.[1]	152	233,300	148	222,295
Fayetteville, N.C.	153	233,200	152	212,042
Columbus, Ga.-Ala.	154	228,200	139	238,584
Saginaw, Mich.	155	227,700	149	219,743
Salem, Oreg.	156	225,900	159	186,658
Savannah, Ga.	157	218,500	154	207,987
Daytona Beach, Fla.[1]	158	217,900	171	169,487
Lima, Ohio	159	211,600	153	210,074
Roanoke, Va.	160	210,800	156	203,153
Killeen-Temple, Tex.[1]	161	209,100	180	159,794
Springfield, Mo.	162	204,800	172	168,053
Lubbock, Tex.	163	200,000	164	179,295
Galveston-Texas City, Tex.	164	198,000	170	169,812
Fort Smith, Ark.-Okla.	165	190,400	178	160,421
Atlantic City, N.J.	166	190,000	167	175,043
Topeka, Kans.	167	186,600	162	180,619
Lincoln, Nebr.	168	186,200	173	167,972
Provo-Orem, Utah	169	185,400	191	137,776
Springfield, Ill.	170	184,600	168	171,020
Battle Creek, Mich.	171	183,600	163	180,129
Fort Myers-Cape Coral, Fla.[1]	172	183,400	230	105,216
Springfield, Ohio	173	183,200	158	187,606
Wheeling, W. Va.-Ohio	174	181,100	160	181,954
Muskegon-Norton Shores-Muskegon Heights, Mich.	175	179,800	165	175,410
Anchorage, Alaska	176	179,800	204	126,385
Green Bay, Wis.	177	178,000	181	158,244
Brownsville-Harlingen-San Benito, Tex.	178	177,400	189	140,368
Racine, Wis.	179	177,100	169	170,838
Biloxi-Gulfport, Miss.	180	175,600	179	160,070
Sarasota, Fla.[1]	181	174,400	211	120,413
Terre Haute, Ind.	182	173,900	166	175,143
Santa Cruz, Calif.[1]	183	173,300	206	123,790
Asheville, N.C.	184	171,600	177	161,059
Cedar Rapids, Iowa	185	166,500	176	163,213
Champaign-Urbana-Rantoul, Ill.	186	164,200	175	163,281
Reno, Nev.	187	163,200	209	121,068
Steubenville-Weirton, Ohio-W. Va.	188	162,000	174	166,385
Waco, Tex.	189	160,900	184	147,553
St. Cloud, Minn.[1]	190	160,500	194	134,585
Fayetteville-Springdale, Ark.	191	160,500	202	127,846
Yakima, Wash.[1]	192	159,300	186	145,212
Amarillo, Tex.	193	158,100	187	144,396
Lake Charles, La.	194	157,700	185	145,415
Parkersburg-Marietta, W. Va.-Ohio[2]	195	157,700	183	148,132
Boise City, Idaho	196	152,700	224	112,230
Jackson, Mich.	197	150,200	188	143,274
Lynchburg, Va.	198	147,900	193	134,744
Clarksville-Hopkinsville, Tenn.-Ky.[1]	199	147,700	213	118,945
Pittsfield, Mass.*	200	143,700	182	149,402
Alexandria, La.[2]	201	140,100	197	131,749
Tallahassee, Fla.	202	140,000	227	109,355
Waterloo-Cedar Falls, Iowa	203	138,800	195	132,916
Anderson, Ind.	204	138,100	190	138,522
Elkhart, Ind.	205	135,700	203	126,529
Janesville-Beloit, Wis.	206	134,400	196	131,970
Lafayette, La.	207	134,200	225	111,643
Altoona, Pa.	208	134,100	192	135,356
Longview-Marshall, Tex.	209	133,600	210	120,770
Fargo-Moorhead, N. Dak.-Minn.	210	132,300	212	120,261
Abilene, Tex.	211	131,600	207	122,164
Fort Collins, Colo.[1]	212	130,900	249	89,900
Monroe, La.	213	130,700	220	115,387
Wilmington, N.C.	214	130,400	229	107,219
Mansfield, Ohio	215	130,300	198	129,997
Vineland-Millville-Bridgeton, N.J.	216	130,200	208	121,374
Gainesville, Fla.	217	129,700	231	104,764
Bradenton, Fla.[1]	218	129,200	238	97,115
Wichita Falls, Tex.	219	128,900	201	128,642
Richland-Kennewick-Pasco, Wash.[1]	220	128,000	245	93,356
Decatur, Ill.	221	127,800	205	125,010
Muncie, Ind.	222	127,700	199	129,219
Petersburg-Colonial Heights-Hopewell, Va.	223	127,600	200	128,809
Florence, Ala.[1]	224	127,100	216	117,743
Tuscaloosa, Ala.	225	126,300	219	116,029
Eau Claire, Wis.[1]	226	125,600	221	114,936
Kenosha, Wis.	227	123,600	215	117,917
Bay City, Mich.	228	121,600	217	117,339
Pueblo, Colo.	229	121,500	214	118,238
Lawton, Okla.	230	119,900	228	108,144
Sioux City, Iowa-Nebr.	231	119,500	218	116,189
Texarkana, Tex.-Texarkana, Ark.	232	118,700	222	113,488
Bloomington-Normal, Ill.	233	118,600	232	104,389
Pascagoula-Moss Point, Miss.[1]	234	117,800	251	87,975
Anniston, Ala.[1]	235	116,700	233	103,092
Lafayette-West Lafayette, Ind.	236	115,000	226	109,378
Tyler, Tex.	237	113,800	239	97,096
Williamsport, Pa.[1]	238	113,300	223	113,296
Greeley, Colo.[1]	239	110,300	250	89,297
Odessa, Tex.	240	105,500	246	92,660
Albany, Ga.	241	105,400	240	96,683
Billings, Mont.	242	104,000	252	87,367
Kokomo, Ind.[1]	243	103,700	235	99,848
Sioux Falls, S. Dak.	244	103,100	243	95,209
St. Joseph, Mo.	245	100,100	236	98,828
Grand Forks, N. Dak.-Minn.[1]	246	100,100	242	95,537
Gadsden, Ala.	247	98,600	244	94,144
Elmira, N.Y.[1]	248	98,300	234	101,537
Burlington, N.C.[1]	249	98,000	241	96,502
Kankakee, Ill.[1]	250	96,600	237	97,250
Lewiston-Auburn, Maine*	251	95,700	247	91,279
Dubuque, Iowa	252	92,900	248	90,609
Rochester, Minn.[1]	253	92,300	255	84,104
Bloomington, Ind.	254	92,200	254	85,221
Panama City, Fla.[1]	255	92,100	262	75,283
Columbia, Mo.[1]	256	90,600	258	80,935
Rapid City, S. Dak.	257	90,500	261	76,369
La Crosse, Wis.[1]	258	89,800	259	80,468
Great Falls, Mont.	259	86,400	257	81,804
Pine Bluff, Ark.	260	85,900	253	85,329
Laredo, Tex.	261	85,800	263	72,859
Sherman-Denison, Tex.	262	84,500	256	83,225
Owensboro, Ky.[1]	263	81,100	260	79,486
San Angelo, Tex.	264	77,300	264	71,047

(1) New SMSA established since 1970 census.
(2) New SMSA established in Nov. 1971, and area definition changed in Apr. 1973.
(3) Merger of 2 existing SMSAs since 1970 census; rank and population given for 1970 refer to the merger of the 2 SMSAs.

How the Cities Grew

Source: U.S. Bureau of the Census

(cities over 100,000 ranked by 1978 population estimates)

Rank	City	1978	1970	1960	1950	1900	1850	1790
1	New York, N.Y.	7,134,542	7,895,563	7,781,984	7,891,957	3,437,202	[1]696,115	[1]49,401
2	Chicago, Ill.	3,049,479	3,369,357	3,550,404	3,620,962	1,698,575	29,963	...
3	Los Angeles, Cal.	2,787,176	2,811,801	2,479,015	1,970,358	102,479	1,610	...
4	Philadelphia, Pa.	1,754,829	1,949,996	2,002,512	2,071,605	1,293,697	121,376	28,522
5	Houston, Tex.	1,572,981	1,282,443	938,219	596,163	44,633	2,396	...
6	Detroit, Mich.	1,257,879	1,514,063	1,670,144	1,849,568	285,704	21,019	...
7	Dallas, Tex.	847,420	844,621	679,684	434,462	42,638	...	...
8	San Diego, Cal.	816,659	697,471	573,224	334,387	17,700	...	...
9	San Antonio, Tex.	798,195	708,582	587,718	408,442	53,321	3,488	...
10	Baltimore, Md.	791,857	905,787	939,024	949,708	508,957	169,054	13,603
11	Honolulu Co., Ha.	722,689	630,528	294,194	248,034	39,306	...	...
12	Indianapolis, Ind.	704,045	740,000	476,258	427,173	169,164	8,091	...
13	Phoenix, Ariz.	681,355	589,016	439,170	106,818	5,544	...	...
14	Washington, D.C.	671,001	756,668	763,956	802,178	278,718	40,001	...
15	Memphis, Tenn.	663,769	657,007	497,524	396,000	102,320	8,841	...
16	San Francisco, Cal.	649,315	715,674	740,316	775,357	342,782	[2]34,776	...
17	Milwaukee, Wis.	633,220	717,372	741,324	637,392	285,315	20,061	...
18	Boston, Mass.	597,254	641,071	697,197	801,444	560,892	136,881	18,320
19	Cleveland, Oh.	594,529	750,879	876,050	914,808	381,768	17,034	...
20	San Jose, Cal.	592,773	461,212	204,196	95,280	21,500	...	...
21	New Orleans, La.	556,428	593,471	627,525	570,445	287,104	116,375	...
22	Jacksonville, Fla.	529,787	528,865	201,030	204,517	28,429	1,045	...
23	Columbus, Oh.	524,304	540,025	471,316	375,901	125,560	17,832	...
24	St. Louis, Mo.	508,496	622,236	750,026	856,796	575,238	77,860	...
25	Seattle, Wash.	485,487	530,831	557,087	467,591	80,671	...	...
26	Denver, Col.	474,595	514,678	493,887	415,786	133,859	...	...
27	Kansas City, Mo.	456,907	507,330	475,539	456,622	163,752	...	...
28	Pittsburgh, Pa.	432,723	520,089	604,332	676,806	321,616	46,601	...
29	Nashville-Davidson, Tenn.[3]	425,424	447,877	170,874	174,307	80,865	10,165	...
30	Atlanta, Ga.	405,437	495,039	487,455	331,314	89,872	2,572	...
31	El Paso, Tex.	400,741	322,261	276,687	130,435	15,906	...	...
32	Cincinnati, Oh.	399,072	453,514	502,550	503,998	325,902	115,435	...
33	Buffalo, N.Y.	378,617	462,768	532,759	580,132	352,387	42,261	...
34	Oklahoma City, Okla.	372,690	368,164	324,253	243,504	10,037	...	...
35	Omaha, Neb.	368,347	358,452	301,598	251,117	102,555	...	...
36	Fort Worth, Tex.	367,432	393,455	356,263	278,778	26,688	...	...
37	Portland, Ore.	364,735	382,352	372,676	373,628	90,426	...	...
38	Minneapolis, Minn.	353,992	434,400	482,872	521,718	202,718	...	...
39	Toledo, Oh.	351,686	383,062	318,003	303,616	131,822	3,829	...
40	Miami, Fla.	347,862	334,859	291,688	249,276	1,681	...	...
41	Long Beach, Cal.	339,629	361,427	344,168	250,767	2,252	...	...
42	Oakland, Cal.	332,247	361,561	367,548	384,575	66,960	...	...
43	Tulsa, Okla.	328,684	330,350	261,685	182,740	1,390	...	...
44	Austin, Tex.	319,194	255,869	186,545	132,459	22,258	629	...
45	Louisville, Ky.	317,503	361,706	390,639	369,129	204,731	43,194	200
46	Newark, N.J.	314,412	381,930	405,220	438,776	246,070	38,894	...
47	Baton Rouge, La.	311,053	271,064	152,419	125,629	11,269	3,905	...
48	Tucson, Ariz.	301,875	267,464	212,892	45,454	7,531	...	...
49	Charlotte, N.C.	299,444	274,640	201,564	134,042	18,091	1,065	...
50	Albuquerque, N.M.	295,150	243,751	201,189	96,815	6,238	...	...
51	Norfolk, Va.	280,568	307,951	304,869	213,513	46,624	14,326	2,959
52	Birmingham, Ala.	280,413	310,904	340,887	326,037	38,415	...	...
53	Wichita, Kan.	267,748	276,554	254,698	168,279	24,671	...	...
54	Tampa, Fla.	264,325	277,714	274,970	124,681	15,839	...	...
55	Sacramento, Cal.	264,219	257,105	191,667	137,572	29,282	6,820	...
56	St. Paul, Minn.	263,147	309,866	313,411	311,349	163,065	1,112	...
57	Rochester, N.Y.	252,491	295,011	318,611	332,488	162,608	36,403	...
58	Virginia Beach, Va.	245,076	172,106	8,091	5,390	...	...	...
59	Akron, Oh.	239,229	275,425	290,351	274,605	42,728	3,266	...
60	St. Petersburg, Fla.	230,965	216,159	181,298	96,738	1,575	...	...
61	Jersey City, N.J.	225,957	260,350	276,101	299,017	206,433	6,856	...
62	Richmond, Va.	219,596	249,431	219,958	230,310	85,050	27,570	3,761
63	Corpus Christi, Tex.	214,647	204,525	167,690	108,287	4,703	...	...
64	Colorado Springs, Col.	211,844	141,207	70,194	45,472	21,038	...	...
65	Mobile, Ala.	207,741	190,026	194,856	129,009	38,469	20,515	...
66	Anaheim, Cal.	207,007	166,408	104,184	14,566	1,456	...	...
67	Shreveport, La.	201,920	182,064	164,372	127,206	16,013	1,728	...
68	Fresno, Cal.	199,273	167,427	133,929	91,699	12,470	...	...
69	Dayton, Oh.	194,861	244,564	262,332	243,872	85,333	10,977	...
70	Des Moines, Ia.	192,526	201,404	208,982	177,965	62,139	...	...
71	Jackson, Miss.	190,791	180,814	144,422	98,271	7,816	1,881	...
72	Lexington-Fayette, Ky.[5]	190,686	174,323	62,810	55,534	26,369	8,159	834
73	Yonkers, N.Y.	190,240	204,297	190,634	152,798	47,931	...	...
74	Knoxville, Tenn.	185,236	174,587	111,827	124,769	32,637	2,076	...
75	Santa Ana, Cal.	185,155	155,710	100,350	45,533	4,933	...	...
76	Grand Rapids, Mich.	183,917	197,649	177,313	176,515	87,565	2,686	...
77	Fort Wayne, Ind.	181,066	184,853	161,776	133,607	45,115	4,282	...
78	Anchorage, Alas.	180,255	126,385	44,237	11,254	...	...	...
79	Spokane, Wash.	177,019	170,516	181,608	161,721	36,848	...	...
80	Syracuse, N.Y.	174,899	197,297	216,038	220,583	103,374	22,271	...
81	Madison, Wis.	170,382	171,809	126,706	96,056	19,164	1,525	...
82	Las Vegas, Nev.	168,932	125,787	64,405	24,624	...	...	...
83	Lubbock, Tex.	168,127	149,101	128,691	71,747	...	...	...

Rank	City	1978	1970	1960	1950	1900	1850	1790
84	Huntington Beach, Cal.	167,897	115,960	11,492	5,237	...	...	...
85	Warren, Mich.	167,237	179,260	89,246	727	350	...	...
86	Lincoln, Neb.	166,311	152,639	128,521	98,884	40,159	...	...
87	Salt Lake City, Ut.	164,379	175,885	189,454	182,121	53,531	...	...
88	Kansas City, Kan.	164,250	178,885	121,901	129,553	51,418	...	...
89	Columbus, Ga.	163,837	167,377	116,779	79,611	17,614	5,942	...
90	Worcester, Mass.	163,523	176,572	186,587	203,486	118,421	17,049	2,095
91	Greensboro, N.C.	163,493	147,948	119,574	74,389	10,035	...	...
92	Chattanooga, Tenn.	162,778	167,838	130,009	131,041	30,154	...	...
93	Flint, Mich.	162,707	193,317	196,940	163,143	13,103	...	...
94	Springfield, Mass.	161,889	163,905	174,463	162,399	62,059	11,766	1,574
95	Montgomery, Ala.	158,724	140,102	134,393	106,525	30,346	8,728	...
96	Providence, R.I.	157,222	179,116	207,493	248,674	175,597	41,513	6,380
97	Riverside, Cal.	157,087	140,089	84,332	46,764	7,973	...	...
98	Tacoma, Wash.	156,625	154,407	147,979	143,673	37,714	...	...
99	Gary, Ind.	156,056	188,398	178,320	133,911	...	...	...
100	Little Rock, Ark.	151,756	132,483	107,813	102,213	38,307	2,167	...
101	Fort Lauderdale, Fla.	149,408	139,590	83,648	36,328	...	...	...
102	Paterson, N.J.	145,426	144,824	143,663	139,336	105,171	11,334	...
103	Newport News, Va.	144,023	138,177	113,662	42,358	19,635	...	...
104	Amarillo, Tex.	143,665	127,010	137,969	74,246	1,442	...	...
105	Huntsville, Ala.	143,580	139,282	72,365	16,437	8,068	2,863	...
106	Aurora, Col.	141,548	76,477	48,548	11,421	202	...	...
107	Winston-Salem, N.C.[4]	140,438	133,683	111,135	87,811	13,650	...	...
108	Rockford, Ill.	139,999	147,370	126,706	92,927	31,051	...	...
109	Springfield, Mo.	138,833	120,096	95,865	66,731	23,267	415	...
110	Raleigh, N.C.	138,410	122,830	93,931	65,679	13,643	4,518	...
111	Savannah, Ga.	135,896	118,349	149,245	119,638	54,244	15,312	...
112	Bridgeport, Conn.	134,439	156,542	156,748	158,809	70,996	6,080	...
113	Evansville, Ind.	134,388	138,764	141,543	128,635	59,007	3,235	...
114	Arlington, Tex.	132,932	90,229	44,775	7,692	1,079	...	...
115	Glendale, Cal.	132,235	132,664	119,442	95,702	...	...	...
116	Garland, Tex.	131,263	81,437	38,501	10,571	819	...	...
117	Youngstown, Oh.	128,538	140,909	166,689	168,330	44,885	...	...
118	Torrance, Cal.	128,254	134,968	100,991	22,241	...	...	...
119	Hartford, Conn.	127,053	158,017	162,178	177,397	72,850	13,555	2,683
120	Lakewood, Col.	126,469	92,743	...	...	...	...	...
121	Stockton, Cal.	125,526	109,963	86,321	70,853	17,506	...	...
122	Hialeah, Fla.	125,365	102,452	66,972	19,676	...	...	...
123	Lansing, Mich.	125,229	131,403	107,807	92,129	16,485	...	...
124	Hampton, Va.	125,116	120,779	89,258	5,966	2,764	...	...
125	Peoria, Ill.	122,981	126,963	103,162	111,856	56,100	5,095	...
126	Garden Grove, Cal.	122,749	121,155	84,238	...	...	...	...
127	Erie, Pa.	122,152	129,265	138,440	130,803	52,733	5,858	...
128	Topeka, Kan.	122,100	125,011	119,484	76,791	33,608	...	...
129	Fremont, Cal.	122,028	100,869	43,790	...	...	...	...
130	Macon, Ga.	121,122	122,423	69,764	70,252	23,272	5,720	...
131	New Haven, Conn.	120,561	137,707	152,048	164,443	108,027	20,345	4,487
132	Orlando, Fla.	120,181	100,081	88,135	52,367	2,481	...	...
133	Mesa, Ariz.	117,840	62,853	33,772	16,790	...	...	...
134	Beaumont, Tex.	117,764	117,548	119,175	94,014	9,427	...	...
135	Hollywood, Fla.	114,943	106,873	35,237	14,351	...	...	...
136	Boise City, Ida.	114,033	74,990	34,481	34,393	...	...	...
137	Chesapeake, Va.	113,965	89,580	73,637	110,371	...	...	...
138	South Bend, Ind.	113,147	127,328	132,445	115,911	35,999	1,652	...
139	Independence, Mo.	112,544	112,766	62,328	36,963	6,974	...	...
140	Berkeley, Cal.	109,898	114,091	111,268	113,805	13,214	...	...
141	Portsmouth, Va.	108,297	110,963	114,773	80,039	17,427	8,626	...
142	Columbia, S.C.	108,216	113,542	97,433	86,914	21,103	6,060	...
143	Cedar Rapids, Ia.	107,071	110,642	92,035	72,296	25,656	...	...
144	Pasadena, Cal.	106,208	112,951	116,407	104,577	3,117	...	...
145	Sunnyvale, Cal.	106,162	95,976	52,898	9,829	...	...	...
146	Albany, N.Y.	105,688	115,781	129,726	134,995	94,151	50,763	3,498
147	Ann Arbor, Mich.	105,213	100,035	67,340	48,251	14,509	...	...
148	Irving, Tex.	105,101	98,961	45,985	2,621	...	...	...
149	Durham, N.C.	105,060	95,438	78,302	71,311	6,679	...	...
150	Livonia, Mich.	105,054	110,109	66,702	17,534	...	...	...
151	Stamford, Conn.	104,718	108,798	92,713	74,293	15,997	...	...
152	Pasadena, Tex.	104,385	89,277	58,737	22,483	...	...	...
153	Alexandria, Va.	104,085	110,927	91,023	61,787	14,528	8,734	2,748
154	San Bernardino, Cal.	103,982	109,203	91,992	63,058	6,150	...	...
155	Waterbury, Conn.	103,810	108,033	107,130	104,477	45,859	...	...
156	Waco, Tex.	103,768	95,326	97,808	84,706	...	...	...
157	Sterling Heights, Mich.	103,083	61,365	...	...	...	...	...
158	Elizabeth, N.J.	102,669	112,654	107,698	112,817	52,130	5,583	...
159	Eugene, Ore.	102,591	80,607	50,977	35,879	3,236	...	...
160	Pueblo, Col.	102,356	99,978	91,181	63,685	28,157	...	...
161	Allentown, Pa.	102,077	109,871	108,347	106,756	35,416	3,779	...
162	Davenport, Ia.	101,478	98,469	88,981	74,549	...	...	...
163	Hammond, Ind.	101,076	107,983	111,698	87,594	12,376	...	...
164	Fullerton, Cal.	100,844	85,987	56,180	13,958	...	...	...

(1) Population shown for years prior to 1900 is for New York and its boroughs as constituted under the act of consolidation in 1898. (2) Population shown is for 1862 as given in State census for that year; 1850 returns for San Francisco were destroyed by fire. (3) Figure for 1970 is for the Metropolitan Government of Nashville and Davidson County (consolidated 1963); figures for previous years are for Nashville city. (4) Winston city and Salem town consolidated as Winston-Salem city between 1910 and 1920. Figure for 1900 represents combined population of Winston and Salem. (5) Lexington city and Fayette county governments consolidated in 1974. Figure for 1970 is for combined populations; figures for previous years are for Lexington city.

Jewish Population by Countries and Cities

Source: American Jewish Year Book 1979.

Europe (including Asiatic USSR and Turkey)	4,163,370
America, North, Central, and South	6,698,070
Asia	3,172,410
Africa	177,770
Australia and New Zealand	75,000
Total	**14,286,620**

Europe

Albania	300
Austria	13,000
Belgium	41,000
Bulgaria	7,000
Czechoslovakia	13,000
Denmark	7,500
Finland	1,320
France	650,000
Germany	34,000
Gibraltar	650
Great Britain	410,000
Greece	6,000
Hungary	80,000
Ireland	4,000
Italy	39,000
Luxembourg	1,000
Malta	50
Netherlands	30,000
Norway	950
Poland	6,000
Portugal	600
Romania	60,000
Spain	10,000
Sweden	16,000
Switzerland	21,000
Turkey	27,000
USSR	2,678,000
Yugoslavia	6,000

North America

Canada	305,000
Mexico	37,500
United States	5,781,000

Central America and West Indies

Barbados	70
Costa Rica	2,500
Cuba	1,500
Curaçao	700
Dominican Republic	200
El Salvador	350
Guatemala	2,000
Haiti	150
Honduras	200
Jamaica	500
Nicaragua	200
Panama	2,000
Trinidad	300

South America

Argentina	300,000
Bolivia	2,000
Brazil	150,000
Chile	27,000
Colombia	12,000
Ecuador	1,000
Paraguay	1,200
Peru	5,200
Surinam	500
Uruguay	50,000
Venezuela	15,000

Asia

Afghanistan	200
Burma	200
China	30
Cyprus	30
Hong Kong	250
India	8,000
Indonesia	100
Iran	80,000
Iraq	350
Israel	3,076,000
Japan	400
Lebanon	400
Pakistan	250
Philippines	200
Singapore	500
Syria	4,500
Yemen	1,000

Australia and New Zealand

Australia	70,000
New Zealand	5,000

Africa

Algeria	1,000
Egypt	400
Ethiopia	28,000
Kenya	400
Libya	20
Morocco	18,000
Rep. of South Africa	118,000
Rhodesia	3,800
Tunisia	7,000
Zaire	750
Zambia	400

World Cities

Adelaide	1,600
Amsterdam	20,000
Antwerp	13,000
Athens	2,800
Auckland	1,500
Basel	2,300
Belgrade	1,500
Berlin (both sectors)	6,000
Bogota	5,500
Bombay (and district)	6,970
Bordeaux	6,400
Brisbane	1,500
Brussels	24,500
Bucharest	40,000
Budapest	65,000
Cape Town	25,650
Copenhagen	7,000
Durban	5,990
Geneva	3,250
Glasgow	13,000
Goteborg	4,000
Guatemala City	1,500
Haifa	210,000
Istanbul	23,000
Izmir	2,500
Jerusalem	266,000
Johannesburg	57,500
Kiev	170,000
Leeds	18,000
Leningrad	165,000
Lima	5,000
Liverpool	6,500
London (greater)	280,000
Lyons	20,000
Madrid	3,000
Malmo	4,000
Manchester (greater)	35,000
Marseilles	65,000
Melbourne	34,000
Mexico, D. F.	32,500
Milan	9,000
Montevideo	48,000
Montreal	115,000
Moscow	285,000
Nice	20,000
Ottawa	7,500
Paris	300,000
Perth	3,200
Porto Alegre	12,000
Prague	3,000
Rabat	2,500
Recife	3,000
Rio de Janeiro	55,000
Rome	10,000
Salisbury	2,000
San-Jose	2,500
Sao Paulo	75,000
Sofia	4,000
Stockholm	8,000
Strasbourg	12,000
Sydney	28,500
Teheran	50,000
Tel Aviv-Jaffa	394,000
Toronto	115,000
Toulouse	18,000
Vancouver	12,000
Valparaiso	4,000
Vienna	9,000
Wellington	1,500
Warsaw	4,500
Winnipeg	20,000
Zurich	6,150

U.S. Cities and Counties

Alameda and Contra Costa Co., Cal.	28,000
Albany, NY	13,500
Alexandria, Va. (area)	30,000
Atlanta, Ga.	22,000
Atlantic City, NJ	11,800
Baltimore, Md.	92,000
Bergen Co., NJ.	100,000
Boston (inc. Brockton)	170,000
Bridgeport, Conn.	14,500
Buffalo, NY	22,000
Camden, NJ	26,000
Chicago Metro Area	253,000
Cincinnati, Oh.	30,000
Cleveland, Oh.	80,000
Columbus, Oh.	13,000
Dallas, Tex.	20,000
Denver, Col.	30,000
Detroit, Mich.	80,000
Essex Co., NJ	95,000
Fort Lauderdale, Fla.	50,000
Framingham, Mass.	16,000
Hartford (inc. New Britain)	23,500
Hollywood, Fla.	30,000
Houston, Tex.	27,000
Indianapolis, Ind.	11,000
Kansas City, Mo.	19,000
Las Vegas, Nev.	13,500
Long Beach, Cal.	12,500
Los Angeles Metro	455,000
Lynn, Mass.	19,000
Miami, Fla.	225,000
Milwaukee, Wis.	23,900
Minneapolis, Minn.	22,090
Montgomery Co., Md.	70,000
Monmouth Co., NJ.	30,000
Morris Co., NJ	15,000
New Haven, Conn.	20,000
New Orleans, La.	10,600
New York, (greater)	1,998,000
New York City	1,228,000
Manhattan	171,000
Brooklyn	514,000
Bronx	143,000
Queens	379,000
Staten Island	21,000
Nassau-Suffolk	605,000
Westchester	165,000
Ocean Co., NJ	12,000
Orange Co., Cal.	35,000
Palm Beach Co., Fla.	40,000
Philadelphia Metro.	295,000
Phoenix, Ariz.	25,000
Pittsburgh, Pa.	51,000
Prince George's Co., Md.	20,000
Raritan Valley, NJ	18,000
Richmond, Va.	10,000
Rochester, NY	21,500
Rockland Co., NY	25,000
San Diego, Cal.	23,000
San Francisco, Cal.	75,000
San Jose, Cal.	14,500
Seattle, Wash.	13,000
Springfield, Mass.	11,000
Stamford, Conn.	11,000
St. Louis, Mo.	60,000
Syracuse, NY	11,000
Union Co., NJ	39,500
Washington, DC (greater)	160,000
Worcester, Mass.	10,000

Black Population by States

Source: U.S. Bureau of the Census (estimated July 1, 1975)

Ala.	919,900
Alas.[1]	8,911
Ariz.	67,400
Ark.	356,100
Cal.	1,601,100
Col.	86,800
Conn.	187,900
Del.	85,300
D.C.	511,400
Fla.	1,179,000
Ga.	1,288,100
Ha.[1]	7,573
Ida.[1]	2,130
Ill.	1,534,300
Ind.	388,600
Ia.	40,300
Kan.	107,700
Ky.	244,300
La.	1,134,000
Me.[1]	2,800
Md.	828,500
Mass.	211,200
Mich.	1,080,300
Minn.	39,900
Miss.	840,500
Mo.	507,300
Mon.[1]	1,995
Neb.	46,300
Nev.	35,600
N.H.[1]	2,505
N.J.	870,500
N.M.[1]	19,555
N.Y.	2,382,200
N.C.	1,193,300
N.D.[1]	2,494
Oh.	1,033,600
Okla.	191,400
Ore.	30,700
Pa.	1,049,200
R.I.	27,600
S.C.	867,000
S.D.[1]	1,627
Tenn.	651,200
Tex.	1,529,600
Ut.[1]	6,617
Vt.[1]	761
Va.	930,800
Wash.	80,400
W.Va.	64,400
Wis.	143,500
Wy.[1]	2,568
Total	24,426,736

(1) 1970 census figures.

PERSONAL FINANCE

Using the Consumer Price Index

Beginning in January 1978, the Bureau of Labor Statistics introduced a revised consumer price index for urban wage earners and clerical workers — about 40% of the population. The revised index (CPI-W) is based on a new, larger market basket of goods priced in 85 areas (29 more areas than for the old CPI). The new market basket includes TV and sound equipment and repairs, additional children's clothes, luggage, automotive body work, medical supplies such as crutches, and a variety of other goods and services which were not included in the old CPI.

In addition to the revised CPI, the Bureau also began to publish a completely new index for all urban dwellers, including the unemployed, the retired, and professional and managerial workers — about 80% of the U.S. population. This new urban index (CPI-U) takes into account the different ways price changes affect the purchasing habits of the poor and the moderately rich.

Both the CPI-W and the CPI-U use the same base year as the old CPI (1967=100) and were dovetailed into the old CPI. However, because of the many changes in sampling procedures, neither of the new indexes are strictly comparable with the old index.

Which Index For You?

Which index should you use to calculate the impact of inflation on your life? If your income is near the poverty level, or if you are retired on a moderate income, you should probably use the new CPI-U. Otherwise, even if you are moderately rich, the CPI-W will probably be the best indicator for you.

The CPI (W and U) emerges each month as single numbers. At the end of the year an average is computed from the monthly figures. (Averaging does away with fluctuations caused by special situations that have nothing to do with inflation.)

For example, the average CPI for 1979 was 217.7. This means that the value of goods and services, which was set at 100% in 1967, cost 117.7% more in 1979.

Changes in prices and how they affect you can be calculated by comparing the CPI of one period against another. The 1979 CPI reading of 217.7 can be compared to the 1978 reading of 195.3. Dividing 217.7 by 195.3, the excess over 1 is the percentage increase for the year 1979; in this case,

Consumer Price Indexes, 1980

Source: Bureau of Labor Statistics, U.S. Labor Department

	December 1979		January		March		May	
(1967=100)	CPI-U	CPI-W	CPI-U	CPI-W	CPI-U	CPI-W	CPI-U	CPI-W
All Items	229.2	230.0	232.2	233.2	239.8	239.9	244.9	245.1
Food, beverages	235.5	235.7	237.5	237.8	241.0	241.2	244.1	244.7
Housing	243.6	243.6	247.3	247.3	254.5	254.4	261.7	261.7
Apparel, upkeep	172.2	171.4	171.0	169.8	176.0	175.1	177.5	176.8
Transportation	227.7	228.3	233.5	234.1	243.7	244.3	249.0	249.9
Medical care	250.7	251.7	253.9	254.9	260.2	260.9	263.4	264.9
Entertainment	193.4	192.3	195.3	193.9	200.6	199.5	204.0	202.4
Other goods, services	204.2	203.0	206.3	206.0	208.9	208.3	211.2	210.6
Services	249.3	249.6	253.1	253.6	261.3	261.7	269.2	269.9
Rent, for home	182.9	182.7	184.1	183.9	186.6	309.6	188.9	188.7
Household, less rent	289.2	291.1	295.1	297.2	307.3	186.4	319.6	322.2
Transportation	224.2	224.0	226.8	226.6	233.4	232.7	241.5	249.9
Medical care	270.7	271.8	274.4	275.6	281.5	282.2	284.7	264.9
Other services	207.1	207.4	209.0	209.3	212.9	213.5	215.9	216.5
All items less food	226.4	226.4	229.9	230.0	237.1	237.3	242.6	242.9
Commodities	219.4	219.4	222.2	222.3	228.0	228.1	231.4	231.7
Commodities less food	207.2	207.1	210.4	210.3	216.7	216.9	222.0	220.5
Nondurables	228.2	229.0	232.0	232.9	240.3	241.4	243.2	244.6
Energy	313.7	317.0	327.9	331.5	255.0	359.6	363.2	367.3
All items less energy	223.6	223.0	225.9	225.3	230.8	230.0	235.7	235.1

Average Consumer Price Indexes

Source: Bureau of Labor Statistics, U.S. Labor Department

The Consumer Price Index (CPI-W) measures the average change in prices of goods and services purchased by urban wage earners and clerical workers. (1967 = 100)

	1973		1974		1975		1976		1977		1978		1979	
	Index	%+	Index	%+	Index	%+	Index	%+	Index	%+	Index	%+	Index	%+
All items	133.1	6.2	147.7	11.0	161.2	9.1	170.5	5.8	181.5	6.5	195.3	7.6	217.7	11.5
Food, drink	139.5	13.2	158.7	13.8	172.1	8.4	177.4	3.1	188.0	6.0	206.2	9.7	228.7	10.9
Housing	133.7	4.4	148.8	11.3	164.5	10.6	174.6	6.1	186.5	6.8	202.6	8.6	227.5	12.3
Apparel, upkeep	126.8	3.7	136.2	7.4	142.3	4.5	147.6	3.7	154.2	4.5	159.5	3.4	166.4	4.3
Transportation	123.8	3.3	137.7	11.2	150.6	9.4	165.5	9.9	177.2	7.1	185.8	4.9	212.8	14.5
Medical care	137.7	3.9	150.5	9.3	168.6	12.0	184.7	9.5	202.4	9.6	219.4	8.4	240.1	9.4
Entertainment	130.0	2.8	139.8	7.5	152.2	8.9	159.8	5.0	167.7	4.9	176.2	5.1	187.7	6.5
Other	132.5	3.9	142.0	7.2	153.9	8.4	162.7	5.7	172.2	5.8	183.2	6.4	196.3	7.2

11.5%.

Did your income increase by enough to keep up with this inflation? To make the comparison, dig out your old W-2 or income tax return forms, or find your old paycheck stubs. Both gross and takehome pay comparisons will be of interest to you, but take care to compare equals. Overtime pay should not be counted. Also, watch out for changes in deductions such as those for tax exemptions, credit union payments, payroll bonds, and the like. These have nothing to do with inflation and should be added back to your take home pay.

Measuring Your Paycheck

A. To compare year-to-year earnings in percent form, divide your 1979 earnings by those of 1978 and express the result as a percentage. For example, if you earned the gross wages of the average U.S. worker, your paychecks in 1978 showed about $203.70 per week as compared with $219.30 per week in 1979, an increase of 7.66%. Since prices rose by only 11.5% during 1979, the average worker had a loss of 3.84% in real gross income that year. You can do the same kind of calculation on your total 1978 and 1979 earnings by using your total annual income figures in place of weekly earnings figures.

B. Another way to handle the same figures takes a dollar form. For this calculation, assume your wage was $203.70 at the end of 1978. During 1979, prices increased by 11.5% To match that price increase, your wages should have gone up to $227.13 (203.70 times 1.115) by the end of 1979.

While readings on a monthly basis may be misleading, you may want a rough idea of how much you are being affected by inflation right now. For example, if you had weekly earnings of $205.77 in May of 1980, compared to earnings of $199.47 in December, 1979, your income went up 3.16% (The difference, $6.30, divided by 199.47). The CPI-W went from 233.3 to 245.1 during the same period, a gain of 5.58%. This means you had a loss on inflation in the first 5 months of 1980. You can make the same calculation for any month by using the latest CPI figures as they are issued by the Department of Labor and published in your local newspaper.

Consumer Price Index by Cities

(1967=100, except Anchorage and Miami)

City[1]	1977 avg.	1978 (2)	February, 1980		March, 1980		April, 1980		May, 1980	
			CPI-U	CPI-W	CPI-U	CPI-W	CPI-U	CPI-W	CPI-U	CPI-W
Anchorage, Alas. (10/67 = 100)	—	194.7(11)	—	—	223.5	220.2	—	—	226.5	223.1
Atlanta, Ga.	184.5	198.8	230.3	233.5	—	—	235.3	239.3	—	—
Baltimore, Md.	190.7	203.0(11)	—	—	245.0	243.9	—	—	249.1	247.8
Boston, Mass.	185.7	199.7(11)	—	—	234.2	234.2	—	—	236.9	236.8
Buffalo, N.Y.	185.1	199.7	227.9	227.9	—	—	233.7	233.3	—	—
Chicago, Ill.-Northwest Ind.	180.0	198.6	232.7	232.5	235.5	235.2	240.1	239.8	243.1	243.0
Cincinnati, Ohio-Ky.-Ind.	186.7	207.0(11)	—	—	247.8	249.7	—	—	251.6	252.9
Cleveland, Ohio	184.4	205.7	243.5	244.1	—	—	247.3	248.4	—	—
Dallas-Ft. Worth, Tex.	183.8	201.6	241.7	240.9	—	—	251.4	249.6	—	—
Denver-Boulder, Col.	—	211.4(11)	255.2	—	255.2	259.4	—	—	258.0	262.4
Detroit, Mich.	184.4	202.2	240.4	239.9	242.9	242.4	248.2	248.0	248.4	248.9
Honolulu, Ha.	174.9	191.3	220.9	221.3	—	—	227.4	228.4	—	—
Houston, Tex.	192.7	219.7	255.9	251.9	—	—	260.8	257.3	—	—
Kansas City, Mo-Kan.	182.7	198.8	238.7	236.6	—	—	243.8	242.2	—	—
Los Angeles-Long Beach, Anaheim, Cal.	184.4	197.1	237.6	240.0	241.3	243.9	244.6	247.8	249.1	252.6
Miami, Fla. (11/77 = 100)	—	107.4(11)	—	—	127.7	128.8	—	—	129.7	130.9
Milwaukee, Wis.	186.6	199.0(11)	—	—	242.7	247.8	—	—	250.3	255.2
Minneapolis-St. Paul, Minn.-Wis.	187.0	208.6	237.9	239.6	—	—	244.3	245.7	—	—
New York, N.Y.-Northeast N.J.	188.8	201.5	228.0	227.7	231.2	230.8	233.1	232.4	234.5	234.1
Northeast Pa. (Scranton)	182.8	190.0	—	—	229.0	231.3	—	—	232.5	235.8
Philadelphia, Pa.-N.J.	186.9	201.1	231.1	231.6	234.6	235.1	237.4	237.9	239.4	239.9
Pittsburgh, Pa.	183.5	205.2	235.5	235.9	—	—	240.9	240.9	—	—
Portland, Ore.-Wash.	183.8	207.1(11)	—	—	253.6	251.7	—	—	240.9	255.9
St. Louis, Mo.-Ill.	180.6	199.3(11)	—	—	238.1	238.5	—	—	241.8	242.6
San Diego, Cal.	186.6	209.8(11)	—	—	258.3	255.6	—	—	269.7	264.8
San Francisco-Oakland, Cal.	187.3	200.8	240.7	240.0	—	—	243.5	242.8	—	—
Seattle-Everett, Wash.	182.5	202.6(11)	—	—	243.8	241.3	—	—	249.6	246.8
Washington, D.C.-Md.-Va.	188.1	203.9(11)	—	—	238.8	239.2	—	—	241.2	242.0

(1) The area listed includes the entire Standard Metropolitan Statistical Area, except New York and Chicago which include the Standard Consolidated Area. (2) Latest month in 1978: usually Dec., except (11) = Nov.

Annual Average Purchasing Power of the Dollar

Source: Bureau of Labor Statistics, U.S. Labor Department

Obtained by dividing the index for 1967 (100.00) by the index for the given period and expressing the result in dollars and cents. Beginning 1961, wholesale prices include data for Alaska and Hawaii; beginning 1964, consumer prices include them.

Year	As measured by— Wholesale prices	Consumer prices	Year	Wholesale prices	Consumer prices	Year	Wholesale prices	Consumer prices
1940	$2.469	$2.381	1968	$ .976	$ .960	1974	$ .625	$ .677
1950	1.222	1.387	1969	.939	.911	1975	.572	.620
1955	1.139	1.247	1970	.906	.860	1976	.546	.587
1960	1.054	1.127	1971	.878	.824	1977	.515	.551
1965	1.035	1.058	1972	.840	.799	1978	.478	.493
1967	1.000	1.000	1973	.744	.752	1979	.463	.461
						1980, July	.406	.404

Consumer Price Index (CPI-U) by Region and City Size

Source: Bureau of Labor Statistics, U.S. Labor Department

(City sizes: A=1.25 million or more; B=385,000 to 1.25 million; C=75,000 to 385,000; D=75,000 or less.)

April, 1980 (Dec. 1977 = 100)	All items	Food and beverages	Housing	Apparel, upkeep	Transportation	Medical care	Entertainment	Other goods and services
Northeast								
Size A	125.0	124.5	126.1	112.5	133.8	122.4	116.7	114.7
Size B	129.0	127.1	130.0	111.1	140.8	122.4	117.9	117.5
Size C	132.7	128.8	140.2	112.7	136.2	122.5	115.7	119.6
Size D	127.4	125.2	127.9	113.0	138.1	122.7	121.5	116.0
North Central								
Size A	133.2	126.8	141.1	109.2	138.1	125.3	118.9	116.2
Size B	130.9	124.9	135.8	111.2	137.6	125.0	114.0	121.5
Size C	128.9	127.0	130.4	110.7	139.3	125.7	118.7	116.7
Size D	128.7	128.9	129.1	113.6	137.4	127.4	116.1	119.8
South								
Size A	130.7	126.4	133.9	116.4	139.7	121.9	115.7	119.3
Size B	131.7	127.0	136.7	112.9	138.4	123.3	119.8	118.1
Size C	131.3	127.8	136.6	108.2	137.2	126.4	118.3	118.8
Size D	128.3	126.2	129.7	104.7	136.5	131.2	124.4	121.9
West								
Size A	132.8	126.5	136.3	115.7	141.2	128.8	117.8	121.2
Size B	134.1	128.8	139.1	115.8	139.2	126.9	123.1	121.5
Size C	131.4	125.7	134.8	107.7	141.2	126.7	121.0	117.7
Size D	130.4	128.0	129.7	121.8	139.6	128.9	127.5	122.5

The Northeast region includes cities from Bostom to Pittsburgh; the North Central, cities from Cleveland to Grand Island, Neb. and from Minneapolis to St. Louis and Cincinnati; the South, cities from Baltimore to Dallas; the West, cities from Alamogordo, N. Mex., to Butte, Mont. Anchorage, and Honolulu.

Annual Percent Change in Productivity and Related Data, 1969-79

Source: Bureau of Labor Statistics, U.S. Labor Department

Item	1969	1970	1971	1972	1973	1974	1975	1976	1977	1978	1979
Private business sector:											
Output per hour of all persons	0.2	0.7	3.4	3.5	1.9	-3.0	2.1	3.5	1.6	0.3	-0.8
Real compensation per hour	1.4	1.1	2.4	2.9	1.9	-1.7	0.7	2.8	1.6	1.5	-1.7
Unit labor cost	6.6	6.4	3.2	2.8	6.2	12.5	7.7	5.0	6.4	9.0	10.3
Unit nonlabor payments	1.0	1.2	6.8	5.2	5.0	4.4	15.3	5.2	4.2	4.3	5.8
Implicit price deflator	4.7	4.7	4.4	3.6	5.8	9.8	10.1	5.1	5.7	7.5	8.9
Nonfarm business sector:											
Output per hour of all persons	-0.3	0.2	3.1	3.7	1.7	-3.1	1.9	3.5	1.3	0.5	-1.1
Real compensation per hour	0.9	0.7	2.3	3.1	1.5	-1.7	0.7	2.5	1.5	1.5	-2.1
Unit labor cost	6.6	6.5	3.5	2.8	6.0	12.6	7.8	4.7	6.7	8.8	10.2
Unit nonlabor payments	0.4	1.6	6.7	3.8	0.3	5.9	17.1	6.9	4.3	3.3	5.1
Implicit price deflator	4.5	4.9	4.5	3.1	4.1	10.5	10.6	5.4	5.9	7.0	8.6
Manufacturing:											
Output per hour of all persons	1.1	-0.3	5.3	5.1	2.7	-5.2	4.9	4.3	2.4	2.5	0.8
Real compensation per hour	1.0	0.9	1.9	2.1	0.9	-0.8	2.4	2.4	2.2	1.8	-2.0
Unit labor cost	5.2	7.2	0.9	0.4	4.3	16.1	6.6	3.9	6.3	6.9	8.2
Unit nonlabor payments	-4.4	-3.2	9.2	2.3	-1.0	-0.7	21.6	8.5	3.3	NA	NA
Implicit price deflator	2.3	4.2	3.1	1.0	2.8	11.5	10.2	5.1	5.5	NA	NA

Average Weekly Earnings of Production Workers[1]

Source: Bureau of Labor Statistics, U.S. Labor Department

Year and month	Private nonagricultural workers: Gross average weekly earnings, Current dollars	Gross average weekly earnings, 1967 dollars	Spendable average weekly earnings[2]: Worker with no dependents, Current dollars	Worker with no dependents, 1967 dollars	Worker with 3 dependents, Current dollars	Worker with 3 dependents, 1967 dollars	Manufacturing workers: Gross average weekly earnings, Current dollars	Gross average weekly earnings, 1967 dollars	Spendable average weekly earnings[2]: Worker with no dependents, Current dollars	Worker with no dependents, 1967 dollars	Worker with 3 dependents, Current dollars	Worker with 3 dependents, 1967 dollars
1973	145.39	109.23	117.51	88.29	127.38	95.70	166.46	125.06	132.57	99.60	143.50	107.81
1974	154.76	104.78	124.37	84.20	134.61	91.14	176.80	119.70	140.19	94.92	151.56	102.61
1975	163.53	101.45	132.49	82.19	145.65	90.35	190.79	118.36	151.61	94.05	166.29	103.16
1976	175.45	102.90	143.30	84.05	155.87	91.42	209.32	122.77	167.83	98.43	181.32	106.35
1977	189.00	104.13	155.19	85.50	169.93	93.63	228.90	126.12	183.80	101.27	200.06	110.23
1978	203.70	104.30	165.39	84.69	180.71	92.53	249.27	127.63	197.40	101.08	214.87	110.02
1979	219.30	100.73	177.55	81.56	194.35	89.27	268.94	123.54	212.43	97.58	232.07	106.60
1980 Jan.	225.34	96.59	181.96	77.99	199.00	85.30	277.01	118.74	217.91	93.40	238.20	102.10
Feb.	226.75	95.88	182.98	77.37	200.07	84.60	278.60	117.80	218.99	92.60	239.40	101.23
Mar.	229.15	95.52	184.67	76.98	201.89	84.16	280.99	95.52	220.61	76.98	241.22	84.16
Apr.	228.55	94.21	184.25	75.95	201.43	83:03	279.35	115.15	219.49	90.47	239.97	98.92
May	229.95	93.82	185.23	75.57	202.49	82.62	280.21	114.32	220.08	89.79	240.63	98.18
June[p]	233.99	94.43	188.05	75.89	205.56	82.95	283.19	114.48	222.43	89.76	243.26	98.17

(1) Data relate to production workers in mining and manufacturing; to construction workers in contract construction; and to nonsupervisory workers in transportation and public utilities; wholesale and retail trade; finance, insurance, and real estate; and services. (2) Spendable average weekly earnings are based on gross average weekly earnings less the estimated amount of the worker's Federal, social security, and income taxes. (p)—preliminary.

Federal Individual Income Tax

Source: Internal Revenue Service, U.S. Treasury Department.

Who Must File

Every individual under 65 years of age who resided in the United States and had a gross income of $3,300 or more during the year must file a federal income tax return. Anyone 65 or older on the last day of the tax year is not required to file a return unless he had gross income of $4,300 or more during the year. A married couple both 65 or older, need not file unless their gross income is $7,400 or more.

A taxpayer with gross income of less than $3,300 (or less than $4,300 if 65 or older) should file a return to claim the refund of any taxes withheld, even if he is listed as a dependent by another taxpayer.

Forms to Use

A taxpayer may, at his election, use form 1040 or Form 1040A. However, those taxpayers who choose to itemize deductions must use the longer form 1040.

Deductions

A taxpayer may either itemize deductions or choose the zero bracket amount. For single taxpayers the zero bracket amount is $2,300. For married taxpayers filing a joint return it is $3,400. For married taxpayers filing separate returns the deduction is $1,700 each.

Dates for Filing Returns

For individuals using the calendar year, Apr. 15 is final date (unless it falls on a Saturday, Sunday, or a legal holiday) for filing income tax returns and for payment of any tax due, and the first quarterly installment of the estimated tax. Other installments of estimated tax to be paid June 15, Sept. 15, and Jan. 15.

Apr. 15 is final date for filing declaration of estimated tax. Amended declarations may be filed June 15, Sept. 15, and Jan. 15.

Instead of paying the 4th installment a final income return may be filed by Jan. 31. Farmers may file a final return by Mar. 1 to satisfy estimated tax requirements.

Joint Return

A husband and wife may make a return jointly, even if one has no income personally.

One provision stipulates that if one spouse dies, the survivor may compute his tax using joint return rates for the first two taxable years following, provided he or she was also entitled to file a joint return the year of the death, and furnishes over half the cost of maintaining in his household a home for a dependent child or stepchild. If the taxpayer remarries before the end of the taxable year these privileges are lost but he is permitted to file a joint return with his new spouse.

Estimated Tax

If total tax exceeds withheld tax by at least $100, declarations of estimated tax are required from (1) single individuals, heads of a household or surviving spouses, or a married person entitled to file a joint return whose spouse does not receive wages, who expects a gross income over $20,000; (2) married individuals with over $10,000 where both spouses receive wages; (3) married individuals with over $5,000 not entitled to file a joint return; and (4) individuals whose gross income can reasonably be expected to include more than $500 from sources other than wages subject to withholdings.

Exemptions

Personal exemption is $1,000.

Every individual has an exemption of $1,000, to be deducted from gross income. A husband and a wife are each entitled to a $1,000 exemption. A taxpayer 65 or over on the last day of the year gets another exemption of $1,000. A person blind on the last day of the year gets another exemption of $1,000.

Exemption for dependents, over one-half of whose total support comes from the taxpayer and for whom the other dependency tests have been met, is $1,000. This applies to a child, stepchild, or adopted child as well as certain other relatives with less than $1,000 gross income; also to a child, stepchild, or adopted child of the taxpayer who is under 19 at the end of the year or was a full-time student during 5 months of the year even if he makes $1,000 or more. A dependent can be a non-relative if a member of the taxpayer's household and living there all year.

Taxpayer gets the exemption for his child who is a student regardless of the student's age or earnings, provided the taxpayer provides over half of the student's total support. If the student gets a scholarship, this is not counted as support.

Child and Disabled Dependent Care

To qualify, a taxpayer must be employed and provide over one-half the cost of maintaining a household for a dependent child under 15, a disabled dependent of any age, or a disabled spouse.

Taxpayers may be allowed a credit of an amount equal to 20% of employment related expenses.

For further information consult your local IRS office or the instructional material attached to your return form.

Life Insurance

Life insurance paid to survivors is not taxed as income. Interest on life insurance left with the insurance company and paid to survivors at intervals is taxable when available. Surviving spouse has an exclusion of the prorata amount of principal payable at death plus up to $1,000 per year of interest earned when life insurance proceeds are payable in installments.

Regular payments under the Railroad Retirement Act, and those received as social security, are exempt.

Dividends

The first $100 in dividends can be excluded from income. If husband and wife both receive $100 on their joint return they can exclude $200.

The exclusion does not apply to dividends from tax-exempt corporations, mutual savings banks, building and loan associations, and several others.

Dividends paid in stock or in stock rights are generally exempt from tax, except when paid in place of preferred stock dividends of the current or preceding year, or when the stockholder has an option to take stock or property or when the stock distribution is disproportionate.

Deductible Medical Expenses

Expenses for medical care, not compensated for by insurance or other payment for taxpayer, spouse, and dependents, in excess of 3% of adjusted gross income are deductible.

There is no limit to the maximum amount of medical expenses that can be deducted.

Medical care includes diagnosis, treatment and prevention of disease or for the purpose of affecting any structure or function of the body, and amounts paid for insurance to reimburse for hospitalization, surgical fees and other medical expenses.

Only medicine and drugs in excess of 1% of adjusted gross income may be deducted.

One-half the cost of medical care insurance premiums up to $150 can be deducted without regard to the 3% limitation. The other half plus any excess over $150 is included with other medical expenses subject to the 3% limit.

Medical expenses for a decedent paid by his estate within one year after his death may be treated as expenses of the decedent taxpayer.

Medical and hospital benefits provided by the employer may be exempt from individual income tax.

Disability income payments are excludable only if the payee is totally and permanently disabled and under age 65 at the end of the tax year. Up to $5,200 can be excluded but must be reduced by income above certain limits.

Deductions for Contributions

Deductions up to 50% of taxpayers' adjusted gross income may be taken for contribution to most publicly supported charitable organizations, including churches or associations of churches, tax-exempt educational institutions, tax-exempt hospitals, and medical research organizations associated with a hospital. The deduction is generally limited to 20% for such organizations as private nonoperating foundations, and certain organizations that do not qualify for the 50% limitation.

Taxpayers also are permitted to carry over for five years certain contributions, generally to publicly supported organizations, which exceed the 50% allowable deduction the year the contribution was made.

Also permissible is the deduction as a charitable contribution of unreimbursed amounts up to $50 a school month spent to maintain an elementary or high school student, other than a dependent or relative, in taxpayer's home. There must be a written agreement between you and a qualified organization.

Deductions for Interest Paid

Interest paid by the taxpayer is deductible.

To deduct interest on a debt, you must be legally liable for that debt. No deduction will be allowed for payments you make for another person if you were not legally liable to make them.

Prizes and Awards

All prizes and awards must be reported in gross income, except when received without action by the recipient. To be exempt, awards must be received primarily in recognition of religious, charitable, scientific, educational, artistic, literary, or civic achievement. (Nobel and Pulitzer prizes exempt.)

Deductions for Employees

An employee may use the zero bracket amount and deduct as well the following if in connection with his employment: transportation, except commuting; automobile expense, including gas, oil, and depreciation; however, meals and lodging are deductible as traveling expense only if the employee is away from home overnight.

An outside salesman—a salesman who works fulltime outside the office, using the latter only for incidentals—may use the zero bracket amount and deduct all his business expenses

An employee who is reimbursed and is required to account to his employer for his business expenses will not be required to report either the reimbursement or the expenses on his tax return. Any allowance to the employee in excess of his expenses must be included in gross income. If he claims a deduction for an excess of expenses over reimbursement he will have to report the reimbursement and claim actual expenses.

An employee who is not required to account to his employer must report on his return the total amounts of reimbursements and expenses for travel, transportation, entertainment, etc., that he incurs under a reimbursement arrangement with his employer.

The expense of moving to a new place of employment may be deducted under certain circumstances regardless of whether the taxpayer is a new or continuing employee, or whether he pays his own expenses or is reimbursed by his employer. Reimbursement must be reported as income.

Tax Credit for the Elderly

Subject to certain rules or exclusions, taxpayers 65 or older may claim a credit which varies according to filing status. Taxpayers should read IRS instructions carefully for full details. You may also be eligible for a credit if you are under age 65 and receive a taxable pension from a public retirement system.

The credit is limited to 15% of $2,500 for single taxpayers; 15% of $2,500 for married taxpayers filing a joint return when only one taxpayer is 65 or older; 15% of $3,750 for married taxpayers both 65 or older filing a joint return; and 15% of $1,875 for a married taxpayer filing a separate return.

Net Capital Losses

An individual taxpayer may deduct capital losses up to $3,000 against his ordinary income. However, it takes $2 of net long-term capital loss to get $1 of offset against other income. He may carry the rest over to subsequent years at the same rate, no legal limit on the number of years.

Income Averaging

Individuals with large fluctuations in their annual income may be able to take advantage of averaging provisions available to taxpayers whose income for a particular year exceeds 120% of their average income for the prior 4 years, if the excess is more than $3,000.

Returns with Itemized Deductions for 1978

Size of adjusted gross income	Total deductions		Zero bracket amount		Itemized deductions		
	No. of returns	Amount (thousands)	No. of returns	Amount (thousands)	No. of returns	%[1]	Amount (thousands)
Total, all returns	**89,889,669**	**$303,871,125**	**59,777,260**	**$140,063,830**	**25,774,779**	**2.9**	**$163,807,295**
(thousands)							
under $2	9,048,077	3,539,229	5,130,440	3,317,438	135,003	1.5	221,791
$2 under 4	9,260,108	15,875,309	8,586,505	15,493,028	177,290	1.9	382,281
4 under 6	8,400,764	19,135,357	8,001,625	17,869,920	342,686	4.0	1,265,437

Size of adjusted gross income	Total deductions		Zero bracket amount		Itemized deductions		
	No. of returns	Amount (thousands)	No. of returns	Amount (thousands)	No. of returns	%[1]	Amount (thousands)
6 under 8	8,263,096	21,177,876	7,720,276	18,942,626	540,639	6.5	2,235,250
8 under 10	6,943,938	18,996,563	6,128,201	15,555,001	815,708	11.7	3,441,562
10 under 12	6,096,515	17,922,145	5,083,435	13,470,303	1,013,080	16.6	4,451,842
12 under 14	5,603,534	17,481,290	4,423,419	12,095,009	1,180,115	21.1	5,386,281
14 under 16	5,016,424	16,748,856	3,566,848	10,004,231	1,449,576	28.9	6,744,625
16 under 18	4,682,500	17,090,464	2,907,594	8,376,021	1,774,906	37.9	8,714,443
18 under 20	4,277,380	16,851,073	2,268,349	6,721,312	2,009,031	47.0	10,129,761
20 under 25	8,554,843	37,989,909	3,409,297	10,311,251	5,145,546	60.1	27,678,658
25 under 30	5,384,966	27,749,503	1,493,945	4,619,162	3,891,021	72.3	23,130,341
30 under 50	6,534,412	44,325,312	948,201	2,954,085	5,586,211	85.5	41,371,227
50 under 100	1,468,912	17,374,761	97,905	299,743	1,371,007	93.3	17,075,018
100 under 200	285,161	6,511,085	10,028	31,006	275,133	96.5	6,480,079
200 under 500	60,075	3,093,774	1,118	3,421	58,957	98.1	3,090,353
500 under 1,000	6,872	1,009,788	74	217	6,798	98.9	1,009,571
1,000 or more	2,092	998,832	20	57	2,072	99.0	998,775

Size of adjusted gross income	Medical and dental			Taxes paid			Contributions		
	No. of returns	Amount (thousands)	Avg.	No. of returns	Amount (thousands)	Avg.	No. of returns	Amount (thousands)	Avg.
Total, all returns	**17,907,909**	**$12,175,406**	**$680**	**25,636,926**	**$59,530,486**	**$2,322**	**23,977,430**	**$19,684,306**	**$821**
(thousands)									
under $2	34,835	35,936	1,032	92,139	54,438	591	52,234	36,975	708
$2 under 4	67,254	108,958	1,620	126,148	95,494	757	75,109	18,836	251
4 under 6	268,482	353,992	1,318	336,275	311,143	925	255,350	108,400	425
6 under 8	439,279	618,792	1,409	529,818	507,710	958	441,903	258,135	584
8 under 10	659,990	767,163	1,162	813,002	926,149	1,139	711,223	365,795	514
10 under 12	816,212	874,297	1,071	1,008,368	1,150,878	1,141	903,203	471,818	522
12 under 14	909,535	912,889	1,004	1,177,132	1,477,562	1,255	1,067,297	594,440	557
14 under 16	1,106,443	1,106,443	1,000	1,444,603	1,994,226	1,380	1,331,329	682,400	513
16 under 18	1,304,310	857,236	657	1,774,875	2,716,628	1,531	1,624,506	825,875	508
18 under 20	1,375,688	903,773	657	2,009,031	3,306,135	1,646	1,867,542	1,060,493	568
20 under 25	3,582,041	2,011,077	561	5,140,009	9,642,284	1,876	4,835,027	2,757,363	570
25 under 30	2,579,705	1,284,838	498	3,891,020	8,735,379	2,245	3,713,241	2,390,717	644
30 under 50	3,738,719	1,879,515	503	5,583,309	16,789,858	3,007	5,436,447	4,724,100	869
50 under 100	850,395	568,043	668	1,368,843	7,267,566	5,309	1,329,532	2,426,069	1,825
100 under 200	140,214	135,022	963	274,620	2,746,580	10,001	267,404	1,250,490	4,676
200 under 500	30,134	43,964	1,459	58,883	1,182,346	20,080	57,379	850,775	14,827
500 under 1,000	3,557	6,986	1,964	6,781	335,722	49,509	6,663	379,131	56,901
1,000 or more	1,116	1,592	1,427	2,070	290,388	140,284	2,041	482,492	236,400

Size of adjusted gross income	Interest paid			Miscellaneous deductions			Total tax as % of taxable income
	No. of returns	Amount (thousands)	Avg.	No. of returns	Amount (thousands)	Avg.	
Total, all returns	**23,572,476**	**$60,199,082**	**$2,554**	**21,912,742**	**$12,218,014**	**$558**	**17.6**
(thousands)							
under $2	24,607	47,433	1,928	73,718	47,010	638	0.4
$2 under 4	73,611	100,275	1,362	105,950	58,718	554	0.9
4 under 6	232,941	400,544	1,720	262,542	91,357	348	0.5
6 under 8	416,237	737,584	1,772	380,955	113,028	297	7.2
8 under 10	657,592	1,158,352	1,762	627,370	224,102	357	9.4
10 under 12	870,199	1,621,802	1,864	819,379	333,047	406	10.9
12 under 14	1,054,510	1,969,632	1,868	966,099	431,758	447	12.2
14 under 16	1,354,282	2,699,586	1,993	1,210,523	557,080	460	13.2
16 under 18	1,662,242	3,597,900	2,164	1,530,457	716,804	468	14.0
18 under 20	1,902,222	4,087,700	2,149	1,748,012	771,660	441	14.8
20 under 25	4,919,987	11,218,721	2,280	4,503,365	2,049,213	455	16.0
25 under 30	3,696,955	9,079,166	2,456	3,420,683	1,640,240	480	18.0
30 under 50	5,212,326	15,011,397	2,880	4,839,644	2,966,357	613	21.5
50 under 100	1,206,305	5,531,220	4,585	1,128,653	1,282,120	1,136	30.3
100 under 200	232,951	1,847,937	7,933	235,486	500,051	2,123	40.7
200 under 500	48,285	747,441	15,480	51,825	265,827	5,129	49.3
500 under 1,000	5,530	197,328	35,683	6,184	90,404	14,619	56.4
1,000 or more	1,694	145,064	85,634	1,897	79,240	41,771	61.6

(1) Percent of returns in each income category which are itemized.

Individual Income Tax Returns for 1978

Source: Internal Revenue Service, U.S. Treasury Department

Size of adjusted gross income	All returns				Taxable returns		
	Returns		Adjusted gross income less deficit		Returns		Adjusted gross income less deficit
	Number	Percent of total	Amount ($000)	Average (dollars)	Number	Percent of total	Amount ($000)
Total	**89,889,669**	**100.0**	**1,304,188,847**	**14,509**	**68,805,961**	**100.0**	**1,242,436,934**
No adjusted gross income	506,017	0.6	−6,329,580	−12,509	13,284	(1)	−480,830
$1 under $1,000	3,509,421	3.9	2,037,534	581	2,346	(1)	710
$1,000 under $2,000	5,032,639	5.6	7,521,594	1,495	138,398	0.2	213,206
$2,000 under $3,000	4,684,163	5.2	11,709,712	2,500	139,895	0.2	358,964
$3,000 under $4,000	4,575,945	5.1	15,987,007	3,494	2,282,488	3.3	8,186,010
$4,000 under $5,000	3,990,373	4.4	17,937,631	4,495	2,571,709	3.7	11,601,562
$5,000 under $6,000	4,410,391	4.9	24,354,756	5,522	3,060,375	4.4	16,904,671
$6,000 under $7,000	4,391,512	4.9	28,538,388	6,499	3,389,991	4.9	22,066,055
$7,000 under $8,000	3,871,584	4.3	29,040,229	7,501	3,396,778	4.9	25,498,493
$8,000 under $9,000	3,701,698	4.1	31,386,245	8,479	3,456,339	5.0	29,311,111
$9,000 under $10,000	3,242,240	3.6	30,759,872	9,487	3,065,012	4.5	29,072,985
$10,000 under $11,000	3,156,654	3.5	33,135,913	10,497	3,006,172	4.4	31,556,142
$11,000 under $12,000	2,939,861	3.3	33,813,408	11,502	2,829,426	4.1	32,552,076
$12,000 under $13,000	2,928,858	3.3	36,590,126	12,493	2,869,143	4.2	35,844,896
$13,000 under $14,000	2,674,676	3.0	36,080,789	13,490	2,623,623	3.8	35,393,888
$14,000 under $15,000	2,560,594	2.8	37,151,846	14,509	2,516,250	3.7	36,511,022
$15,000 under $20,000	11,415,710	12.7	198,904,499	17,424	11,287,720	16.4	196,716,046
$20,000 under $25,000	8,554,843	9.5	190,968,905	22,323	8,496,442	12.3	189,667,995
$25,000 under $30,000	5,384,966	6.0	146,793,790	27,260	5,351,190	7.8	145,874,988
$30,000 under $50,000	6,534,412	7.3	238,845,792	36,552	6,498,889	9.4	237,511,649
$50,000 under $100,000	1,468,912	1.6	96,004,790	65,358	1,457,339	2.1	95,267,136
$100,000 under $200,000	285,161	0.3	37,471,450	131,405	284,197	0.4	37,349,418
$200,000 under $500,000	60,075	0.1	16,726,346	278,424	60,004	0.1	16,706,268
$500,000 under $1,000,000	6,872	(1)	4,572,184	665,335	8,954	(1)	4,567,156
$1,000,000 or more	2,092	(1)	4,185,621	2,000,775	**	(1)	4,183,317

Size of adjusted gross income	Taxable returns—continued					
	Taxable income	Income tax after credits		Total income tax		
	Amount ($000)	Number of returns	Amount ($000)	Amount ($000)	Percent of adjusted gross income	Average (dollars)
Total	**1,028,686,777**	**68,736,839**	**187,172,925**	**188,577,186**	**15.2**	**2,741**
No adjusted gross income	—	*28	*82	50,797	(1)	3,824
$1 under $1,000	*21	*2,137	*5,291	6,055	(1)	2,581
$1,000 under $2,000	393,165	137,997	8,415	9,043	4.2	65
$2,000 under $3,000	375,285	139,446	11,553	12,734	3.5	91
$3,000 under $4,000	6,525,919	2,281,424	144,645	146,723	1.8	64
$4,000 under $5,000	9,348,948	2,566,543	460,602	463,966	4.0	180
$5,000 under $6,000	14,035,215	3,056,284	954,625	959,631	5.7	314
$6,000 under $7,000	18,272,300	3,389,469	1,442,621	1,425,324	6.5	420
$7,000 under $8,000	20,756,787	3,393,897	1,758,641	1,761,545	6.9	519
$8,000 under $9,000	23,966,410	3,453,294	2,239,391	2,243,615	7.7	649
$9,000 under $10,000	23,794,422	3,064,664	2,426,149	2,429,346	8.4	793
$10,000 under $11,000	25,954,083	3,005,079	2,833,680	2,837,300	9.0	944
$11,000 under $12,000	26,758,578	2,828,126	3,063,307	3,065,189	9.4	1,083
$12,000 under $13,000	29,605,292	2,868,197	3,572,174	3,574,864	10.0	1,246
$13,000 under $14,000	29,345,154	2,622,354	3,686,331	3,690,141	10.4	1,407
$14,000 under $15,000	30,429,464	2,515,148	3,982,522	3,988,264	10.9	1,585
$15,000 under $20,000	163,342,052	11,280,887	23,410,856	23,440,513	11.9	2,077
$20,000 under $25,000	157,098,589	8,489,121	25,305,645	25,332,749	13.4	2,982
$25,000 under $30,000	121,424,158	5,348,744	21,914,906	21,961,430	15.1	4,104
$30,000 under $50,000	197,169,079	6,490,191	42,588,467	42,782,289	18.0	6,583
$50,000 under $100,000	78,719,319	1,452,092	24,021,669	24,343,970	25.6	16,704
$100,000 under $200,000	30,962,777	283,102	12,646,521	12,908,164	34.6	45,420
$200,000 under $500,000	13,653,105	59,726	6,734,932	6,944,938	41.6	115,741
$500,000 under $1,000,000	3,566,230	6,816	2,013,449	2,112,475	46.3	307,762
$1,000,000 or more	3,190,426	2,073	1,966,451	2,086,121	49.9	998,144

(1) Less than 0.05 per cent. *Estimate based on very small sample. **Sample too small for usage data.

Social Security Programs

Source: Social Security Administration, U.S. Department of Health, Education, and Welfare

Old-Age, Survivors, and Disability Insurance; Medicare; Supplemental Security Income

Old-Age, Survivors, and Disability Insurance

Old-age, survivors, and disability insurance covers almost all jobs in which people work for wages or salaries, as well as most work of self-employed persons, whether in a city job, or in business, or on a farm.

Old-age, survivors, and disability insurance is paid for by a tax on earnings (for 1979 up to $22,900 and for 1980 up to $25,900; the taxable earnings base is now subject to adjustment when cost-of-living benefit increases have been made). The employed worker and his employer share the tax equally (cash tips count as covered wages if they amount to $20 or more from one place of employment. The worker reports them to his employer, who includes them in his social security tax reports, but only the worker pays contributions on the amount of the tips).

The employer deducts the tax each payday and sends it, with an equal amount as his own share, to the District Director of Internal Revenue. The collected taxes are deposited in the Federal Old-Age and Survivors Insurance Trust Fund and the Federal Disability Insurance Trust Fund; they can be used only to pay benefits, the cost of rehabilitation services, and administrative expenses.

H.E.W. Reorganized

Under a March 1977 reorganization of the Department of Health, Education, and Welfare, the federal-state assistance program of aid to families with dependent children became the responsibility of the Social Security Administration. The reorganization placed the Medicare program under the newly created Health Care Financing Administration, which also now administers Medicaid, the federal-state medical assistance program. The Social Security Administration continues to provide services, such as those relating to contributions and premiums and maintenance of beneficiary records, for the Medicare program.

In Medicare, following the required annual review of hospital costs under the program, increases were made in the hospital insurance deductible amount (what the patient must pay for hospital services before reimbursement can begin) and in the cost-sharing for days above the number specified in the law.

The Commissioner of Social Security is Stanford G. Ross. There are 632 district offices with 682 branch offices, and 30 teleservice centers where the public may obtain information about benefit rights.

Benefit Increase, June 1979

Social Security checks delivered to beneficiaries in the first week of July 1979 reflected the fifth automatic cost-of-living increase in cash benefits under legislation enacted in 1972 and 1973. The 9.9-percent increase, which became effective in June, applied to benefits for all persons on the social security benefit rolls at the end of May.

Automatic increases are initiated whenever the Consumer Price Index (CPI) of the Bureau of Labor Statistics for the first calendar quarter of a year exceeds by at least 3 percent the CPI for the base quarter, which is either the first calendar quarter of the preceding year or the quarter in which an increase was legislated by Congress. In this case, the base quarter was the first quarter of 1978. The size of the benefit increase is determined by the actual percentage rise of the CPI during the quarters measured.

As a result of the benefit increase, average monthly benefits payable to retired workers were $323.43 for men (up $29.20) and $254.26 for women ($22.98 more). Average amounts for disabled workers rose to $349.97 for men and $257.13 for women, increases of $31.75 and $23.30, respectively. Average increases for entitled dependents of these workers ranged from $8.63 for children of disabled workers to $13.31 for wives and husbands of retired workers. Among survivors of deceased workers, average benefit increases were highest for nondisabled widows and widowers ($24.22) and lowest for disabled widows and widowers ($16.40), resulting in average benefits of $268.04, and $181.29, respectively.

Social security benefits are based on a worker's primary insurance amount (PIA), which is related by law to the average monthly earnings (AME) on which social security contributions have been paid. The full PIA is payable to a retired worker who becomes entitled to benefits at age 65 and to an entitled disabled worker at any age. Spouses and children of retired or disabled workers and survivors of deceased workers receive set proportions of the PIA subject to a family maximum amount. The PIA is calculated by applying varying percentages to succeeding parts of the AME. Whenever a cost-of-living benefit increase is implemented, these percentages are changed to reflect the percentage increase in benefits.

Medicare

Under Medicare, protection against the costs of hospital care is provided for social security and railroad retirement beneficiaries aged 65 and over (beginning July 1966) and, effective July 1973, for persons entitled for 24 months to receive a social security disability benefit, certain persons with chronic kidney disease and their dependents, and, on a voluntary basis with payment of a special premium, persons aged 65 and over not otherwise eligible for hospital benefits; all those eligible for hospital benefits may enroll for medical benefits and pay a monthly premium and so may persons aged 65 and over who are not eligible for hospital benefits.

Persons eligible for both hospital and medical insurance or for medical insurance only may choose to have their covered services provided through a Health Maintenance Organization (a prepaid group health or other capitation plan that meets prescribed standards).

Hospital insurance.—In the 11th year of operation (July 1976-June 1977) about $58.7 billion was withdrawn from the hospital insurance trust fund for hospital and related benefits. About 25,316,000 persons were enrolled under the program as of July 1976—2,392,000 of them disabled beneficiaries under age 65.

The hospital insurance program pays the cost of covered services for hospital and posthospital care as follows:

- Up to 90 days of hospital care during a benefit period (spell of illness) starting the first day that care as a bed-patient is received in a hospital or skilled-nursing facility and ending when the individual has not been a bed-patient for 60 consecutive days. For the first 60 days, the hospital insurance pays for all but the first $144 of expenses; for the 61st day to 90th day, the program pays all but $36 a day for covered services. In addition, each person has a 60-day lifetime reserve that can be used after the 90 days of hospital care in a benefit period are exhausted, and all but $72 a day of expenses during the reserve days are paid. Once used, the reserve days are not replaced. (Payment for care in a mental hospital is limited to 190 days.)
- Up to 100 days' care in a skilled-nursing facility (skilled-nursing home) in each benefit period. Hospital insurance pays for all covered services for the first 20 days and all but $18 daily for the next 80 days. At least 3 days' hospital stay must precede these services, and the skilled-nursing facility must be entered within 14 days after leaving the hospital. (The 1972 law permits more than 14 days in certain circumstances.)
- Up to 100 visits by nurses or other health workers (not doctors) from a home health agency in the 365 days after release from a hospital or extended-care facility.

Money to pay these benefits comes from special contributions paid by workers, their employers, and the self-employed.

Medical insurance. Aged persons can receive benefits under this supplementary program only if they sign up for them and agree to a monthly premium ($8.70 beginning July 1979). The federal government pays the rest of the cost. In December of each year the Secretary of Health, Education, and Welfare announces the premium payable starting in July of the following year. The premiums are to be increased only when there is a general benefit increase in the year and it will rise no more than the percent by which the cash benefits have been increased since the last premium increase.

About 140 million bills were reimbursed under the medical insurance program from Jan. 1976 to July 1977 for a total of $7.5 billion. As of July 1976, 24,614,400 persons were enrolled — 2,168,500 of them disabled persons under age 65.

The medical insurance program pays 80% of the reasonable charges (after the first $60 in each calendar year) for the following services:

- Physicians' and surgeons' services, whether in the doctor's office, a clinic, or hospital or at home (but physician's charges for X-ray or clinical laboratory services for hospital bed-patients are paid in full and without meeting the deductible).
- Other medical and health services, such as diagnostic tests, surgical dressings and splints, and rental or purchase of medical equipment. Services of a physical therapist in independent practice, furnished in his office or the patient's home. A hospital or extended-care facility may provide covered outpatient physical therapy services under the medical insurance program to its patients who have exhausted their hospital insurance coverage.
- Physical therapy services furnished under the supervision of a practicing hospital, clinic, skilled nursing facility, or agency.
- Certain services by podiatrists.
- All outpatient services of a participating hospital (including diagnostic tests).
- Outpatient speech pathology services, under the same requirements as physical therapy.
- Services of licensed chiropractors who meet uniform standards, but only for treatment by means of manual manipulation of the spine and treatment of subluxation of the spine demonstrated by X-ray.
- Supplies related to colostomies are considered prosthetic devices and payable under the program.
- Home health services even without a hospital stay (up to 100 visits a year) are paid up to 100%.

To get medical insurance protection, persons approaching age 65 may enroll in the 7-month period that includes 3 months before the 65th birthday, the month of the birthday, and 3 months after the birthday, but if they wish coverage to begin in the month they reach 65 they must enroll in the 3 months **before** their birthday. Persons not enrolling within their first enrollment period may enroll later, during the first 3 months of each year but their premium is 10% higher for each 12-month period elapsed since they first could have enrolled.

The monthly premium is deducted from the cash benefit for persons receiving social security, railroad retirement, or civil service retirement benefits. Income from the medical premiums and the federal matching payments are put in a Supplementary Medical Insurance Trust Fund, from which benefits and administrative expenses are paid.

Medicare card. Persons qualifying for hospital insurance under social security receive a health insurance card similar to cards now used by Blue Cross and other health agencies. The card indicates whether the individual has taken out medical insurance protection. It is to be shown to the hospital, skilled nursing facility, home health agency, doctor, or whoever provides the covered services.

Payments are made only in the 50 states, Puerto Rico, the Virgin Islands, Guam, and American Samoa, except that hospital services may be provided in border areas immediately outside the U.S. if comparable services are not accessible in the U.S. for a beneficiary who becomes ill or is injured in the U.S.

Amount of Work Required

To qualify for benefits for himself and his family, the worker must have been in covered employment long enough to become insured. Just how long depends on his date of birth (or if he dies or becomes disabled, the date of his death or disability).

A person is fully covered if he has one quarter of coverage for every year after 1950 (or year he reaches age 21) up to but not including the year in which he reaches age 62 or dies.

Certain provisions in the law permit special monthly payments under the social security program to persons aged 72 and over who are not eligible for regular social security benefits since they had little or no opportunity to earn social security work credits during their working lifetime.

To get disability benefits, the worker must also have credit for 5 out of 10 years before he becomes disabled. Persons disabled before age 31 can qualify with a briefer period of coverage.

Work Years Required

The following table shows the number of work years required to be fully insured for old-age or survivors benefits, according to the year worker reaches retirement age or dies.

Work credit for retirement benefits

If you reach 62 in	Years you need	If you reach 62 in	Years you need
1974	6*	1979	7
1975	6	1981	7½
1976	6¼	1983	8
1977	6½	1987	9
1978	6¾	1991 or later	10

*For 1974 a woman needs only 5¾ years.

Deceased's work credit for survivor's benefits

Born after 1929, die at	Born before 1930, die before age 62	Years needed
28 or younger		1½
30		2
32		2½
34		3
36		3½
38		4
40		4½
42		5
44	1973	5½
45	1974	5¾
46	1975	6
48	1977	6½
50	1979	7
52	1981	7½
54	1983	8
56	1985	8½
58	1987	9
60	1989	9½
62 or older	1991 or later	10

Tax-rate schedule under old and new law
[Percent of covered earnings]

Year	Total Old law	Total New law	OASDI Old law	OASDI New law	HI Old law	HI New law
	Employees and employers, each					
1977	5.85	5.85	4.95	4.95	0.90	0.90
1978	6.05	6.05	4.95	5.05	1.10	1.00
1979-80	6.05	6.13	4.95	5.08	1.10	1.05
1981	6.30	6.65	4.95	5.35	1.35	1.30
1982-84	6.30	6.70	4.95	5.40	1.35	1.30
1985	6.30	7.05	4.95	5.70	1.35	1.35
1986-89	6.45	7.15	4.95	5.70	1.50	1.45
1990-2010	6.45	7.65	4.95	6.20	1.50	1.45
2011 and after	7.45	7.65	5.95	6.20	1.50	1.45
	Self-employed					
1977	7.90	7.90	7.00	7.00	0.90	0.90
1978	8.10	8.10	7.00	7.10	1.10	1.00
1979-80	8.10	8.10	7.00	7.05	1.10	1.05
1981	8.35	9.30	7.00	8.00	1.35	1.30
1982-84	8.35	9.35	7.00	8.05	1.35	1.30
1985	8.35	9.90	7.00	8.55	1.35	1.35
1986-89	8.50	10.00	7.00	8.55	1.50	1.45
1990-2010	8.50	10.75	7.00	9.30	1.50	1.45
2011 and after	8.50	10.75	7.00	9.30	1.50	1.45

What Aged Workers Get

When a person has enough work in covered employment and reaches retirement age (65 for full benefit, 62 for reduced benefit), he may retire and get monthly old-age benefits. If he continues to work and has earnings of more than $5,000 in 1980, $1 in benefits will be withheld for every $2 above $5,000. The amount that can be earned in a month without loss of any benefits is $270. The annual exempt amount and the monthly test are raised automatically or according to the rise in general earnings levels. The eligible worker who is 72 receives the full amount of benefit regardless of earnings.

A worker's benefit will be raised by 1% for each year after 1970 for which the worker between 65 and 72 did not receive benefits because of earnings from work. No increases are to be paid to the worker's dependents or survivors under this provision.

A special minimum benefit is payable to persons who worked 20 or more years under social security as an alternative to the regular minimum ($114.30 in June 1977) if a higher amount results. The highest minimum under this provision would be $252.80 a month, effective June 1979, for a person with 30 or more years of coverage.

When a person receives old-age benefits, payments can also be made to certain of his dependents, including a wife 62 or over, dependent children under 18 or who became totally disabled before age 22 or who are full-time students not yet aged 22, a wife (regardless of age) if caring for an eligible child, and a dependent husband 62 or over.

The special benefit for persons aged 72 or over who do not meet the regular coverage requirements is $78.40 a month ($117.60 for a couple if both members are eligible). Like the monthly benefits, these payments are now subject to cost-of-living increases. The special payment is not made to persons on the public assistance or supplemental security income rolls.

Social Security benefits are not subject to income taxes.

A woman worker is eligible for a full old-age benefit at age 65, but she may retire at 62 and get 80% of her full benefit for the rest of her life; the nearer she is to 65 when she begins collecting her benefit, the larger it will be. (Benefits for men retiring before 65 are reduced at the same rate as benefits for women retiring before 65.)

A child can get benefits based on his mother's earnings on the same conditions as those entitling a child to benefits based on his father's earnings record.

OASDI	July 1979	July 1978	June 1977
Monthly beneficiaries, total (in thousands)	**34,673**	**34,106**	**33,333**
Aged 65 and over, total	22,858	22,154	21,447
Retired workers	16,729	16,126	15,549
Survivors and dependents	6,010	5,885	5,725
Special age-72 beneficiaries	120	143	173
Under age 65, total	11,815	11,952	11,886
Retired workers	1,924	1,901	1,831
Disabled workers	2,881	2,871	2,755
Survivors and dependents	7,010	7,180	7,300
Total monthly benefits (in millions)	**$8,871**	**$7,739**	**$6,933**

Benefits for Worker's Spouse

The wife of a man who is getting social security retirement or disability payments may become entitled to wife's insurance benefits in a reduced amount when she reaches 62, or she may wait until she reaches 65 and get the entire amount of the wife's benefit, which is one-half of the husband's benefit. Benefits are also payable to the divorced wife of an insured worker if she was married to him for at least 20 years (10 years eff. Jan. 1979) and he was contributing to or was ordered by a court to contribute to her support.

If a woman worker entitled to an old-age benefit has a dependent husband aged 65 or over, he may draw a benefit similar to a wife's benefit at 65 (or a reduced benefit at age 62).

Benefits for Children of Retired or Disabled Workers

If a worker has children under 18 when he retires for age or disability they will get a benefit that is half his benefit, and so will his wife, even if she is under 62. Total benefits paid on a worker's earnings record are subject to a maximum and if the total paid to a family exceed that maximum, the individual dependents' benefits are adjusted downward. (Total benefits paid to the family of a worker who retired in 1975 at age 65 with average monthly earnings of $1,175 can be no higher than $1,098.)

When his children reach 18, their benefits will stop, except that a child permanently and totally disabled before 22 may get a benefit as long as his disability meets the definition in the law. In addition, child's benefits are payable until the child reaches his 22nd birthday if he is attending school as a full-time student. Benefits may now be paid to a grandchild or step-grandchild of a worker or of his spouse, in special circumstances.

What Disabled Workers Get

If a worker becomes so severely disabled that he is unable to work, he may be eligible to receive a monthly disability benefit that is the same amount he would receive as an old-age benefit if he were 65 at the start of his disability. When he reaches 65, his disability benefit becomes an old-age benefit.

Benefits like those provided for dependents of retired-worker beneficiaries may be paid to dependents of disabled beneficiaries.

Survivor Benefits

If a worker should die while insured, one or more types of benefits would be payable to survivors.

1. A cash payment to cover burial expenses that amounts to 3 times the basic benefit but not more than $255, paid at the death of every insured worker.

2. A benefit for each child until the child reaches 18 (or up to age 22, if he is attending school). The monthly benefit of each child of a worker who has died is three-quarters of the amount the worker would have received if he had lived and drawn retirement benefits. A child with a permanent disability that began before age 22 may receive his benefit after that age.

3. A mother's benefit for the widow, if children under 18 are left in her care. Her benefit is 75% of the basic benefit and she draws it until the youngest child reaches 18. Payments stop then even if the child's benefit continues because he is attending school. They will start again when she is 62 (or 60), unless she marries. If she marries and the marriage is ended, she regains benefit rights. If she has a disabled child beneficiary aged 18 or over in her care, her benefits also continue.

Disabled widows and widowers qualify for benefits at age 50 at reduced rates that depend on age at entitlement. The widow or widower must have become totally disabled before or within 7 years after the spouse's death.

4. If there are no children entitled to receive benefits, the widow will receive a benefit that is 100% of the husband's basic amount, if it is first payable when she is 65. She may choose to get her benefit when she is 60; her benefit is then reduced by 19/40 of 1% for each month it is paid before she is 65. However, for widows aged 62 and over whose husbands claimed their benefits before 65, the benefit is the reduced amount he would be getting if he were alive but not less than 82 1/2% of his basic benefit. Dependent widowers aged 60 or over are entitled to survivor benefits on same basis as widows.

5. Dependent parents may be eligible for benefits, if they have been receiving at least half their support from the worker before his death, have reached age 62, and (except in certain circumstances) have not remarried since the worker's death. Each parent gets 75% of the basic benefit except that if only one parent survives the benefit is 82 1/2%.

"The survivors of a woman worker receive benefits on the same basis as those of men workers. (Beginning March 1975, widowed father's benefits are payable on same basis as widowed mother's benefits).

Maximum Benefits Payable

The illustrative table on page 108 shows a column heading for average monthly earnings of $1,475, but the benefit amounts shown in the column are not in general payable yet, since it will be some time before workers can have an average that high (years when the maximum creditable amount of earnings was lower than $17,700 — the 1978 maximum — must currently be included when the average is figured). Benefit amounts larger than those shown in the table will eventually be payable to persons who raise their average yearly earnings for social security purposes by earning, for a sufficient period, the highest creditable amount in years with the higher maximums specified in the law —$17,700 in 1978 and $22,900 in 1979 (higher amounts in the future whenever the base is raised under the automatic adjustment procedure).

Contribution and benefit base under old and new law

Calendar year	Old law[1]	New law[2]
1977	$16,500	$16,500
1978	17,700	17,700
1979	18,900	22,900
1980	20,400	25,900
1981	21,900	29,700
1982	23,400	31,800

(1) Estimated under automatic-adjustment provisions for 1979-82. (2) Stated in law for 1979-81. Estimated under automatic adjustment-provisions for 1982.

Self-Employed

A self-employed person who has earnings of $400 or more in a year must report his earnings for income tax and social security tax purposes. If he is not a farmer he reports only net returns from his business. He need not add income from real estate, savings, dividends, loans, pensions or insurance policies if these are not part of his business.

A self-employed person who has net earnings of $400 or more in a year gets 4 quarters of coverage for that year. If his earnings are less than $400 in a year they do not count toward social security credits. The nonfarm self-employed person must make estimated payments of his social security taxes, on a quarterly basis, for taxable years after 1966, if combined estimated income tax and social security tax amount to at least $40.

The self-employed now have the option, comparable to that for farm workers, of reporting their earnings as ⅔ of their gross income from self-employment but not more than $1,600 a year. This option can be used only if actual net earnings from self-employment income is less than $1,600 and less than ⅔ of gross income and may be used only 5 times.

When a person has both taxable wages and earnings from self-employment, only as much of the self-employment income as will bring total earnings up to the current taxable maximum is subject to tax for social security purposes. A self-employed person pays the tax at a lower rate than the combined rate for an employee and his employer — about 1 ½ times what the employee alone pays.

Farm Owners and Workers

Self-employed farmers whose gross annual earnings from farming are under $2,400 may report ⅔ of their gross earnings instead of net earnings for social security purposes. Cash or crop shares received from a tenant or share farmer count if the owner participated materially in production or management. The self-employed farmer pays contributions at the same rate as other self-employed, but he may make his tax returns annually.

Farm workers. Earnings from farm work count toward benefits (1) if the employer pays $150 or more in cash during the year; (2) if the employee works on 20 or more days for cash pay figured on a time basis. Under these rules a person gets credit for one calendar quarter for each $250 in cash pay in a year but no more than four quarters in any one year.

Foreign farm workers admitted to the United States on a temporary basis are not covered.

Household Workers

Anyone working as maid, cook, laundress, nursemaid, baby-sitter, chauffeur, gardener and at other household tasks in the house of another, is covered by social security if he or she earns $50 or more in cash in three months from any one employer. Room and board do not count, but carfare counts if paid in cash. The job does not have to be regular or fulltime. The employee should get a card at the social security office and show it to the employer.

The employer deducts the amount of the social security tax from the worker's pay, adds an identical amount as his own tax and sends the total amount to the federal government, with the number of the employee's social security card.

Supplemental Security Income

On Jan. 1, 1974, the supplemental security income program established by the 1972 Social Security Act amendments replaced the former federal grants to states for aid to the needy aged, blind, and disabled in the 50 states and the District of Columbia. The program provides both for federal payments based on uniform national standards and eligibility requirements and for state supplementary payments varying from state to state. The Social Security Administration administers the federal payments financed from general funds of the Treasury—and the state supplements as well, if the state elects to have its supplementary program federally administered. The states may supplement the federal payment for all recipients and must supplement it for persons otherwise adversely affected by the transition from the former public assistance programs. In July 1979, the number of persons receiving federal payments and federally administered state payments was 4,165,600, and the amount of these payments was $587.4 million. The average amount of combined federal payments and federally administered state payments was $141 for that month.

As a result of the 9.9 percent cost-of-living increase in social security benefits in June, 1979, the federal SSI payment levels were raised in July, 1979, from $189.40 per month for an individual and $284.10 for a couple to $208.20 and $312.30 respectively.

Minimum and maximum monthly retired-worker benefits payable to individuals who retired at age 65, 1940—79

Year of attainment of age 65[1]	Minimum benefit		Maximum benefit			
	Payment at the time of retirement	Payable effective June 1979	Payable at the time of retirement		Payable effective June 1979	
			Men[2]	Women	Men[2]	Women
1940 . . .	$10.00	$133.90	$41.20	. . .	$259.00	. . .
1941 . . .	10.00	133.90	41.60	. . .	259.00	. . .
1942 . . .	10.00	133.90	42.00	. . .	262.20	. . .
1943 . . .	10.00	133.90	42.40	. . .	262.20	. . .
1944 . . .	10.00	133.90	42.80	. . .	265.00	. . .
1945 . . .	10.00	133.90	43.20	. . .	265.00	. . .
1946 . . .	10.00	133.90	43.60	. . .	268.20	. . .
1947 . . .	10.00	133.90	44.00	. . .	270.70	. . .
1948 . . .	10.00	133.90	44.40	. . .	270.70	. . .
1949 . . .	10.00	133.90	44.80	. . .	273.40	. . .
1950 . . .	10.00	133.90	45.20	. . .	276.80	. . .
1951 . . .	20.00	133.90	68.50	. . .	276.80	. . .
1952 . . .	20.00	133.90	68.50	. . .	276.80	. . .
1953 . . .	25.00	133.90	85.00	. . .	305.70	. . .
1954 . . .	25.00	133.90	85.00	. . .	305.70	. . .
1955 . . .	30.00	133.90	98.50	. . .	305.70	. . .
1956 . . .	30.00	133.90	103.50	. . .	322.90	. . .
1957 . . .	30.00	133.90	108.50	. . .	337.60	. . .
1958 . . .	30.00	133.90	108.50	. . .	337.60	. . .
1959 . . .	33.00	133.90	116.00	. . .	337.60	. . .
1960 . . .	33.00	133.90	119.00	. . .	346.10	. . .
1961 . . .	33.00	133.90	120.00	. . .	348.80	. . .
1962 . . .	40.00	133.90	121.00	$123.00	351.90	$357.90-
1963 . . .	40.00	133.90	122.00	125.00	354.90	363.30
1964 . . .	40.00	133.90	123.00	127.00	357.90	369.30
1965 . . .	44.00	133.90	131.70	135.90	357.90	369.30
1966 . . .	44.00	133.90	132.70	135.90	360.50	369.30
1967 . . .	44.00	133.90	135.90	140.00	369.30	380.30
1968 . . .	55.00[3]	133.90	156.00[3]	161.60[3]	374.90	388.20
1969 . . .	55.00	133.90	160.50	167.30	385.90	402.20
1970 . . .	64.00	133.90	189.80	196.40	396.60	410.50
1971 . . .	70.40	133.90	213.10	220.40	404.80	418.40
1972 . . .	70.40	133.90	216.10	224.70	410.50	426.70
1973 . . .	84.50	133.90	266.10	276.40	421.10	437.50
1974 . . .	84.50	133.90	274.60	284.90	434.50	450.90
1975 . . .	93.80	133.90	316.30	333.70	450.90	475.60
1976 . . .	101.40	133.90	364.00	378.80	480.20	499.80
1977 . . .	107.90	133.90	412.70	422.40	511.70	523.70
1978 . . .	114.30	133.90	459.80	459.80	538.20	538.20
1979 . . .	121.80	133.90	503.40	503.40	553.30	553.30

(1) Assumes retirement at beginning of year. (2) Represents benefit for both men and women until 1962. (3) Effective for February 1968.

Examples of OASDI Monthly Cash Benefits
(under the Social Security Act, effective June 1979)

Beneficiary family	Average monthly earnings of insured worker								
	$76 or less	$200	$400	$550	$750	$900	$1,100	$1,275	$1,475
Retired worker claiming benefits at age 65, or disabled worker:									
Worker alone	$133.90	$244.50	$369.30	$456.50	$560.60	$608.20	$668.50	$716.00	$764.30
Worker with spouse claiming benefits at—									
Age 65 or over	200.90	366.80	554.00	684.80	840.90	912.30	1,002.80	1,074.00	1,146.50
Age 62	184.20	336.30	507.90	627.80	770.90	836.30	919.30	984.50	1,051.00
Worker, spouse, and 1 child	200.90	366.80	673.40	826.10	981.10	1,064.20	1,169.40	1,252.90	1,337.40
Retired worker claiming benefits at age 62:									
Worker alone	107.20	195.60	295.50	365.20	448.50	486.60	534.80	572.80	611.50
Worker with spouse claiming benefits at—									
Age 65 or over	174.20	317.90	480.20	593.50	728.80	790.70	869.10	930.80	993.70
Age 62	157.50	287.40	434.10	536.50	658.80	714.70	785.60	841.30	898.20
Widow or widower claiming benefits at—									
Age 65 or over[1]	133.90	244.50	369.30	456.50	560.60	608.20	668.50	716.00	764.30
Age 60	95.80	174.90	264.10	326.40	400.90	434.90	478.00	512.00	546.50
Disabled widow or widower claiming benefits at age 50	67.10	122.40	184.80	228.30	280.40	304.20	334.30	358.10	382.20
1 surviving child	[2]133.90	183.40	277.00	342.40	420.50	456.20	501.40	537.00	573.30
Widow or widower aged 65 and over and 1 child[1]	200.90	366.80	646.30	798.90	981.10	1,064.20	1,169.40	1,252.90	1,337.40
Widowed mother or father and 1 child	200.90	366.80	554.00	684.80	841.00	912.40	1,002.80	1,074.00	1,146.60
Widowed mother or father and 2 children	200.90	366.80	673.40	826.10	981.10	1,064.20	1,169.40	1,252.90	1,337.40
Maximum family benefits	200.90	366.80	673.40	826.10	981.10	1,064.20	1,169.40	1,252.90	1,337.40

(1) Widow's or widower's benefit limited to amount spouse would have been receiving if still living but not less than 82½ percent of the PIA. (2) Sole survivor. **NOTE:** The higher monthly earnings shown in column headings on the right are not, in general, possible now, since earnings in some of the earlier years—when the maximum amount creditable was lower—must be included in the average. Therefore, the benefit amounts shown in these columns are not generally currently payable. (Effective June 1979, the highest average monthly earnings possible for a worker retiring at age 65 is $727).

Social Security Trust Funds

Old-Age, Survivors, and Disability Insurance Trust Funds, 1937-1979
(thousands)

Fiscal year:	Receipts: Net contrib. inc., transfers, and reimb. from gen'l rev.	Receipts: Net interest received	Expenditures: Cash benefit payments and rehab. services	Expenditures: Transfers to R.R. ret. acct.	Expenditures: Administrative expenses	Total assets at end of period
1937	$ 265,000	$ 2,262	$ 27	$...	$ 26,840	$ 267,235
1940	550,000	42,489	15,805	...	12,288	1,744,698
1950	2,109,912	256,778	727,266	...	56,841	12,892,612
1955	5,087,154	438,029	4,333,147	-9,551	103,202	21,141,001
1960	10,829,664	564,040	10,798,013	573,606	234,291	22,995,939
1965	17,032,456	648,372	16,618,084	459,253	379,145	22,187,184
1970	34,554,182	1,572,375	29,062,772	589,257	623,055	37,719,951
1975	63,872,883	2,803,838	62,547,281	1,010,299	1,100,693	48,138,321
1976	67,867,099	2,815,197	71,462,416	1,238,669	1,200,326	44,919,209
1976 (July-Sept.)[1]	18,264,899	93,726	19,459,572	...	304,448	43,513,811
1977	78,511,213	2,658,629	82,490,402	1,207,523	1,370,386	39,615,344
1978	87,192,105	2,403,128	90,828,787	1,618,461	1,413,414	35,349,916
1979 (Oct. '78-June '79)	72,919,080	2,072,954	73,866,540	1,477,438	1,111,725	33,886,245
Cum. 1937-June '79)	**852,718,813**	**36,049,844**	**824,072,561**	**14,922,643**	**15,885,923**	**33,886,245**

(1) Transitional quarter. Beginning Oct. 1976, federal fiscal year begins Oct. 1.

Hospital Insurance Trust Fund, 1966-79
(thousands)

Fiscal year:	Receipts: Net contribution income[1]	Receipts: Transfers from general revenues[2]	Receipts: Transfers from railroad retirement account[3]	Receipts: Net interest[4]	Expenditures: Net hospital and related service benefits[5]	Expenditures: Administrative expenses[6]	Total assets
1966	$908,797	...	...	$5,970	...	$63,564	$851,204
1967	2,688,684	$337,850	$16,200	45,903	$2,507,773	88,848	1,343,221
1970	4,784,789	628,262	61,307	139,423	4,804,242	148,660	2,677,401
1973	7,663,119	429,415	61,222	197,844	6,648,819	192,839	4,368,666
1974	10,606,551	498,780	96,163	408,273	7,785,596	258,066	7,934,772
1975	11,296,773	529,353	126,749	614,989	10,355,390	256,134	9,870,039
1976	12,039,194	658,430	130,904	715,744	12,270,382	308,215	10,835,714
1976 (July-Sept.)[7]	3,367,940	...	135,863	11,951	3,315,251	88,408	10,947,810
1977	13,659,042	944,000	...	770,966	14,912,370	294,762	11,114,685
1978	16,689,361	830,938	196,506	797,209	17,415,132	417,537	11,796,031
1979 (Oct. '78-June '79)	14,444,121	874,849	175,600	873,215	14,764,472	302,400	13,096,943
Cum. July '66-June '79)	**116,209,516**	**8,211,676**	**1,224,940**	**5,111,773**	**114,742,926**	**2,918,046**	**13,096,943**

(1)Represents amounts appropriated (estimated tax collections with suitable subsequent adjustments), after deductions for refund of estimated amount of employee-tax overpayment. (2)Represents Federal Government transfers from general funds appropriations to meet costs of benefits for persons not insured for cash benefits under OASDHI or railroad retirement and for costs of benefits arising from military wage credits. (3)Represents receipts under the financial interchange with railroad retirement account with respect to contributions for hospital insurance coverage of railroad workers. (4)Represents interest and profit on investments after transfers of interest on administrative expenses reimbursed to the OASI trust fund and on amounts transferred from railroad accounts. (5)Represents (1) payment vouchers on letters of credit issued to fiscal intermediaries under sec. 1816 and (2) direct payments to providers of services under sec. 1815 of the Social Security Act. (6)Subject to subsequent adjustment among all 4 social security trust funds, for allocated cost of each operation. (7)Transitional quarter. Beginning Oct. 1976, federal fiscal year begins Oct. 1.

Supplementary Medical Insurance Trust Fund, 1967-79

(thousands)

	Receipts			Expenditures		
Fiscal year:	Premium income[1]	Transfers from general revenues[2]	Net interest[3]	Net medical service benefits[4]	Administrative expenses[5]	Total assets
1967	$646,682	$623,000	$14,052	$664,261	$133,682	$485,791
1970	936,000	928,151	11,536	1,979,287	216,993	57,181
1974	1,703,189	2,028,926	75,924	2,869,132	409,146	1,275,483
1975	1,886,962	2,329,590	105,539	3,765,397	404,458	1,424,413
1976	1,951,221	2,939,338	103,645	4,671,847	528,214	1,218,555
1976 (July-Sept.)[6]	538,648	878,000	4,420	1,269,038	132,077	1,238,508
1977	2,192,903	5,052,944	136,710	5,866,922	474,717	2,279,426
1978	2,431,133	6,385,503	228,848	6,852,252	504,234	3,968,425
1979 (Oct. '78-June '79)	1,952,405	5,096,780	352,803	6,078,129	411,911	4,880,371
Cum. July '67-June '79.	**19,861,206**	**31,921,545**	**1,168,930**	**43,736,547**	**4,334,962**	**4,880,371**

(1) Represents voluntary premium payments from and in behalf of insured persons. (2) Represents Federal Government transfers from general funds appropriations to match aggregate premiums paid. (3) Represents interest and profit on investments after transfer of interest on administrative expenses reimbursed to the OASI trust fund (see footnote 5). (4) Represents payment vouchers on letters of credit issued to carriers under section 1842 of the Social Security Act. (5) Subject to subsequent adjustment among all 4 social security trust funds for allocated cost of each operation. (6) Transitional quarter. Beginning Oct. 1976, federal fiscal year begins Oct. 1.

Employment and Training Services and Unemployment Insurance

Source: Employment and Training Administration, U.S. Labor Department

Employment Service

The Federal-State Employment Service consists of the U.S. Employment Service and affiliated state employment services with their network of about 2,500 local offices. During fiscal year 1978, these offices made 6.6 million placements, 6.2 million in nonagricultural and 385,000 in agricultural industries. Overall, 4.6 million different individuals were placed in employment.

The employment service works to refer employable applicants to job openings that use their highest skills and helps the unemployed obtain services or training to make them employable. It also provides special attention to help older workers, youth, minorities, the poor, handicapped workers, migrants, seasonal farmworkers, and workers who lose their jobs because of foreign trade competition.

Veterans receive special services and absolute preference in placements at all employment service offices. During fiscal year 1978, these offices placed over 766,000 veterans in jobs.

Comprehensive Employment and Training Services

The Comprehensive Employment and Training Act (CETA) of 1973 sets up a community system to give people training and job-related services and place them in jobs. Under this system all states and cities, counties, and combinations of local units with populations of 100,000 or more receive federal grants to plan and run comprehensive employment and training programs and provide public service jobs in their localities. Under the new Private Sector Initiative Program, every program sponsor sets up a Private Industry Council to help involve businesses in hiring and training economically disadvantaged workers. A major inducement for employers to hire certain disadvantaged workers is the targeted jobs tax credit, amounting to $3,000 for each eligible worker paid $6,000 or more for the first year of employment.

Besides operating comprehensive programs, local governments plan and provide public service jobs for unemployed workers.

National Activities

The federal role under CETA is to provide support and technical assistance to local programs, insure proper use of federal money, and serve groups with special job disadvantages.

In addition to continuing programs for Indians and migrant and seasonal farmworkers, there are new and expanded efforts for youth. These efforts include the Young Adult Conservation Corps, which hires unemployed young people to work on public lands; Youth Incentive Entitlement Pilot Projects, providing part-time jobs and training to youth attending school; Youth Community Conservation and Improvement Projects, which give unemployed youth paid work in community betterment; and Youth Employment and Training Programs to improve young people's job prospects. In addition, Job Corps, which was training disadvantaged youth at 90 residential centers at the end of fiscal year 1979, plans continued expansion so that it can serve 44,000 youth at any one time. The Summer Program for Economically Disadvantaged Youth supported over a million part-time jobs in 1978. The Employment and Training Administration also has programs to promote apprenticeship and to help employable people on Aid to Families with Dependent Children find jobs.

Unemployment Insurance

Unlike old-age and survivors insurance, entirely a federal program, the unemployment insurance program is a Federal-State system that provides insured wage earners with partial replacement of wages lost during involuntary unemployment. The program protects most workers in industry. During calendar year 1978, an estimated 86.2 million jobs in commerce, industry, agriculture, and government, including the armed forces, were covered under the Federal-State system. In addition, an estimated 500,000 railroad workers were insured against unemployment by the Railroad Retirement Board.

Each state, as well as the District of Columbia, Puerto Rico, and the Virgin Islands, has its own law and operates its own program. The amount and duration of the weekly benefits are determined by state laws, based on prior wages and length of employment. States are required to extend the duration of benefits when unemployment rises to and remains above specified state or national levels; costs of extended benefits are shared by the state and federal governments.

Under the Federal Unemployment Tax Act, as amended in 1976, the tax rate is 3.4% on the first $6,000 paid to each employee of employers with one or more employees in 20 weeks of the year or a quarterly payroll of $1,500. A credit of up to 2.7% is allowed for taxes paid under state unemployment insurance laws that meet certain criteria, leaving the federal share at 0.7% of taxable wages.

Social Security Requirement

The Social Security Act requires, as a condition of such grants, prompt payment of due benefits. The Federal Unemployment Tax Act provides safeguards for workers' right to benefits if they refuse jobs that fail to meet certain labor standards. Through the Unemployment Insurance Service of the Employment and Training Administration, the Secretary of Labor determines whether states qualify for grants and for tax offset credit for employers.

Benefits are financed solely by employer contributions, except in Alaska, Alabama, and New Jersey, where employees also contribute. Benefits are paid through the public employment offices, at which unemployed workers must register for work and to which they must report regularly for referral to a possible job during the time when they are drawing weekly benefit payments. During the 1978 calendar year, $7.7 billion in benefits was paid under state unemployment insurance programs to 7,566,000 beneficiaries, representing compensation for 128,723,700 weeks of unemployment. They received an average weekly payment of $83.67 for total unemployment for an average of 13.3 weeks.

Federal Worker Benefits

Title 5, chapter 85 of the U.S. Code provided unemployment insurance protection during calendar year 1978 to about 2,922,600 federal civilian employees and about 2,167,800 members of the armed forces. Benefits for unemployed federal workers and ex-servicemen are financed through direct federal appropriations but are paid by the state agencies as agents of the federal government.

During calendar year 1978, a total of $175,498,200 was paid to 96,900 unemployed federal civilian workers for a total of 1,793,400 weeks of unemployment. The average weekly payment was $86.06 and was paid for an average of 16.5 weeks. A total of $277,681,690 was paid to 175,300 unemployed ex-servicemen for 2,863,400 weeks of unemployment. The average weekly benefit was $89.69 and was paid for an average of 15.8 weeks.

Employment Security

Selected unemployment insurance data by state. Calendar year 1978, state programs only.

	Insured claimants[1] (1,000)	Beneficiaries[2] (1,000)	Exhaustions[3] (1,000)	Initial claims[4] (1,000)	Benefits paid[5] (1,000)	Avg. weekly benefit for total unemployment[p]	Funds available for benefits Dec. 31, 1978[6] (millions)	Employers subject to state law Dec. 31, 1978 (1,000)
Alabama	160	153	36	297	$101,255	$70.18	$88	64
Alaska	43	43	15	80	76,387	85.01	58	10
Arizona	55	37	11	115	31,854	73.82	138	47
Arkansas	129	81	17	220	54,482	72.00	34	48
California	1,553	1,134	275	2,513	962,998	75.84	1,756	515
Colorado	68	52	15	147	49,902	92.59	98	66
Connecticut	190	159	31	367	138,351	89.43	76	76
Delaware	30	25	6	63	30,068	93.56	16	13
District of Columbia	33	28	12	40	50,531	106.66	9	17
Florida	191	150	65	364	111,848	63.68	403	185
Georgia	248	181	48	367	104,077	73.39	347	96
Hawaii	37	28	9	57	37,392	93.29	38	20
Idaho	38	33	7	97	25,192	84.30	81	22
Illinois	390	370	124	768	608,959	97.68	−604	231
Indiana	203	137	38	352	95,081	75.75	358	90
Iowa	96	81	14	152	106,423	103.96	94	65
Kansas	60	45	12	90	47,335	84.47	200	54
Kentucky	153	120	26	253	101,259	79.30	166	62
Louisiana	139	97	32	208	123,472	91.62	124	72
Maine	66	62	17	173	40,737	73.33	25	29
Maryland	141	112	22	264	98,455	76.40	121	72
Massachusetts	264	234	66	550	263,381	84.00	215	115
Michigan	434	420	125	1,015	392,904	92.85	617	157
Minnesota	128	105	33	182	116,634	96.66	164	83
Mississippi	85	58	13	154	37,411	60.37	180	40
Missouri	222	169	49	436	125,883	75.62	211	108
Montana	40	29	7	63	26,696	84.14	15	22
Nebraska	45	31	9	58	24,487	79.54	66	36
Nevada	32	29	8	77	29,651	83.54	60	18
New Hampshire	38	27	1	52	14,389	74.35	60	21
New Jersey	432	338	134	739	515,675	87.68	148	159
New Mexico	27	20	5	62	19,047	68.71	55	27
New York	812	617	206	1,736	881,247	83.74	31	392
North Carolina	267	165	26	507	99,358	71.65	404	124
North Dakota	19	18	4	35	20,286	87.40	17	18
Ohio	353	266	58	682	336,028	100.32	452	192
Oklahoma	56	38	13	106	30,775	75.91	119	56
Oregon	120	93	18	274	86,718	81.18	194	63
Pennsylvania	679	599	110	1,390	730,759	97.83	193	208
Puerto Rico	112	127	47	244	73,108	45.53	36	46
Rhode Island	84	100	20	263	65,456	76.79	−88	24
South Carolina	120	77	21	247	58,711	73.31	136	50
South Dakota	13	13	3	34	8,807	78.35	14	18
Tennessee	236	139	33	401	98,617	66.16	243	72
Texas	233	173	64	409	137,519	68.18	346	242
Utah	42	34	7	67	31,720	88.70	49	28
Vermont	25	19	4	43	16,909	76.10	16	14
Virginia	156	99	26	228	90,998	83.51	96	90
Virgin Islands	4	3	1	6	3,534	63.46[p]	2	2
Washington	152	129	33	440	134,482	86.80	104	90
West Virginia	208	94	12	154	74,517	75.22	57	32
Wisconsin	248	168	49	360	168,097	94.36	362	94
Wyoming	11	7	1	15	7,309	88.03	59	14
Total	**9,718**	**7,566**	**2,039**	**18,013**	**$7,717,173**	**$83.67[p]**	**$8,258**	**4,512**

(p.) Preliminary. (1) Claimants whose base-period earnings or whose employment — covered by the unemployment insurance program — was sufficient to make them eligible for unemployment insurance benefits as provided by state law. (2) Based on number of first payments. (3) Based on final payments. Some claimants shown, therefore, actually experienced their final week of compensable unemployment toward the end of the previous calendar year but received their final payments in the current calendar year. Similarly, some claimants who served their last week of compensable unemployment toward the end of the current calendar year did not receive their final payment in this calendar year and hence are not shown. A final week of compensable unemployment in a benefit year results in the exhaustion of benefit rights for the benefit year. Claimants who exhaust their benefit rights in one benefit year may be entitled to further benefits in the following benefit year. (4) Excludes intrastate transitional claims to reflect more nearly instances of new unemployment. Includes claims filed by interstate claimants in the Virgin Islands. (5) Adjusted for voided benefit checks and transfers under interstate combined wage plan. (6) Sum of balance in state clearing accounts, benefit payment accounts, and unemployment trust fund accounts maintained in the U.S. Treasury.

Canadian Income Tax Rates

Source: Revenue Canada

1980 Rates of Federal Income Tax

Taxable income	Tax			
$ 903 or less		6%		
903	$ 54	+	16% on next	$ 903
1,806	199	+	17% on next	1,806
3,612	506	+	18% on next	1,806
5,418	831	+	19% on next	3,612
9,030	1,517	+	21% on next	3,612
12,642	2,276	+	23% on next	3,612
16,254	3,106	+	25% on next	3,612
19,866	4,009	+	28% on next	5,418
25,284	5,526	+	32% on next	18,060
43,344	11,306	+	36% on next	27,090
70,434	21,058	+	39% on next	37,926
108,360	35,849	+	43% on remainder	

1980 Rates of Provincial Income Tax[1]

Newfoundland	58%
Prince Edward Island	50%
Nova Scotia	52.5%
New Brunswick	55.5%
Ontario	44%[2]
Manitoba	54%[3]
Saskatchewan	53%[4]
Alberta	38.5%
British Columbia	44%

(1) Rates are applied to basic federal tax payable. (2) No provincial tax payable if taxable income is $1,812 or less. (3) No provincial tax payable if basic federal tax is $200 or less. (4) No provincial tax payable if basic taxable income is $2,411 or less.

Canada: Taxable Returns by Income, 1977

Source: Revenue Canada Taxation Statistics

Total income in dollars	Number	Per-cent	Total income (millions)	Per-cent	Taxed income (millions)	Federal tax (millions)	Per-cent	Effective-rate on total income
0-1,500	821,402	6.53	394.5	.41	2.1	—	—	—
1,500-2,000	445,749	3.54	787.0	.56	2.4	—	—	—
2,000-3,000	752,685	5.98	1,877.9	1.34	53.5	.1	—	.01%
3,000-4,000	757,298	6.02	2,641.7	1.89	420.7	.5	—	.02%
4,000-5,000	730,978	5.80	3,282.7	2.34	880.8	9.7	.08	.3%
5,000-10,000	3,312,027	26.32	24,685.6	17.62	11,907.3	1,048.3	7.79	4.2%
10,000-15,000	2,503,400	19.89	30,942.6	22.1	19,216.3	2,553.9	18.97	8.3%
15,000-20,000	1,691,205	13.44	29,140.3	20.8	19,685.0	3,072.6	22.83	10.5%
20,000-25,000	815,223	6.47	18,068.2	12.91	12,758.1	2,184.9	16.24	12.1%
25,000-50,000	667,409	5.31	20,973.7	14.97	15,359.0	3,035.4	22.55	14.5%
50,000-100,000	75,119	.59	4,887.3	3.49	3,890.2	988.5	7.35	20.2%
100,000-200,000	11,099	.09	1,438.1	1.03	1,185.5	359.0	2.67	24.9%
200,000 and over	2,297	.02	759.5	.54	610.3	205.1	1.52	27.0%

Average Canadian Income and Taxes by Occupation, 1977

Source: Revenue Canada Taxation Statistics

Occupation	Number[1]	Average income[2]	Average federal tax
Self-employed doctors and surgeons	27,274	$50,548	$10,275
Self-employed dentists	7,263	42,602	8,373
Self-employed lawyers and notaries	14,412	41,372	8,099
Self-employed accountants	8,297	33,748	5,951
Self-employed engineers and architects	3,448	32,990	6,047
Teachers and professors	296,294	17,574	1,987
Armed Forces employees	79,752	15,118	1,567
Federal government employees	375,208	14,892	1,573
Other self-employed professionals	28,807	14,642	1,842
Provincial government employees	491,224	14,289	1,502
Municipal government employees	510,261	12,921	1,244
Business employees	6,591,475	11,906	1,200
Self-employed salesmen	32,262	11,688	1,204
Investors	540,057	11,212	957
Property owners	103,907	10,567	1,079
Employees of institutions	766,217	10,531	884
Business proprietors	442,957	10,366	916
Farmers	245,902	10,036	625
Fishermen	26,626	9,861	829
Unclassified employees	258,942	7,060	476
Self-employed entertainers and artists	13,450	6,944	498
Pensioners	996,624	5,000	138
Unclassified	725,232	3,950	135
Total	**12,585,891**	**11,114**	**1,069**

(1) Based on number of tax returns. (2) Average total income after business expense deductions but before personal deductions.

Average Income in Selected Canadian Cities, 1977

Source: Revenue Canada Taxation Statistics

City	Average income[1]	Rank	No. of tax returns
Oakville, Ont.	$13,954	1	39,563
Sept-Iles, Que.	13,553	2	15,499
Burlington, Ont.	13,551	3	58,473
Alberni, B.C.	13,234	4	13,811
Brossard, Que.	13,201	5	19,537
Prince George, B.C.	12,932	6	36,718
Sarnia, Ont.	12,890	7	46,547
Repentigny, Que.	12,761	8	14,317
Mississauga, Ont.	12,751	9	143,410
Pickering, Ont.	12,466	10	16,180
Calgary, Alta.	12,450	11	295,143
Ottawa, Ont.	12,446	12	300,662
Edmonton, Alta.	12,425	13	340,059
Bramalea, Ont.	12,372	14	25,813
Kamloops, B.C.	12,237	15	32,353
Milton, Ont.	12,225	16	13,485
Vancouver, B.C.	12,189	17	641,211
Langley, B.C.	12,157	18	26,218
Nanaimo, B.C.	$12,073	19	22,649
Whitby, Ont.	12,022	20	16,805
Regina, Sask.	11,859	23	88,425
Oshawa, Ont.	11,736	24	64,910
Quebec City, Que.	11,609	27	215,155
Victoria, B.C.	11,526	30	139,412
Montreal, Que.	11,422	35	1,102,025
Toronto, Ont.	11,377	37	1,477,384
Windsor, Ont.	11,363	39	149,361
Halifax, N.S.	11,021	48	82,242
London, Ont.	10,712	57	160,897
Hamilton, Ont.	10,703	59	231,436
St. John's, Nfld.	10,693	60	57,718
Fredericton, N.B.	10,666	62	30,811
Kitchener, Ont.	10,665	63	117,034
Winnipeg, Man.	9,932	84	368,639
Charlottetown, P.E.I.	9,743	91	14,643
Pembroke, Ont.	8,831	100	14,271

(1) Average total income after business expense deductions but before personal deductions.

State Individual Income Taxes: Rates, Exemptions

Source: Tax Foundation, Inc. Data as of Sept. 1, 1980
Footnotes at end of table.

State	Taxable income	Percentage rates	Taxable income	Percentage rates	Personal exemp. Single	Personal exemp. Married family head	Credit per depend.
Alabama[1]	First $1,000	1.5	$3,001-$5,000	4.5	$1,500	$3,000	$300
	1,001-3,000	3	Over 5,000	5			
Alaska	Rates range from 3% on first $4,000 to 14.5% over $400,000				Federal exemptions		
Arizona[1,2,4]	First 1,000	2	3,001-4,000	5	1,000	2,000	600
	1,001-2,000	3	4,001-5,000	6			
	2,001-3,000	4	5,001-6,000	7	Over 6,000	8	
Arkansas[3]	First 2,999	1	9,000-14,999	4.5	17.50	35	6
	3,000-5,999	2.5	15,000-24,999	6	(tax credit)		
	6,000-8,999	3.5	25,000 and over	7			
California[1,2,4,6]	First 2,000	1	8,001-9,500	6	(tax credit)		
	2,001-3,500	2	9,501-11,000	7	25	50	8
	3,501-5,000	3	11,001-12,500	8	Heads of households have slightly lower tax rates.		
	5,001-6,500	4	12,501-14,000	9			
	6,501-8,000	5	14,001-15,500	10	Over 15,500	11	
Colorado[1,4,6]	First 1,000	3	6,001-7,000	6	850	1,700	850
	1,001-2,000	3.5	7,001-8,000	6.5			
	2,001-3,000	4	8,001-9,000	7	Surtax on intangible income over $15,000, 2%. A credit equal to 1/2 of 1% of net taxable income is allowed for income under $9,000.		
	3,001-4,000	4.5	9,001-10,000	7.5			
	4,001-5,000	5	Over 10,000	8			
	5,001-6,000	5.5					
Connecticut	7% capital gains tax; tax on dividends earned if federal adjusted gross income is greater than or equal to $20,000; tax ranges from 1% on $20,000 through 9% on $100,000 and over.				100	200	
Delaware[3] (Effective 1/1/80)	First 1,000	1.4	10,001-15,000	8.2	Exemptions apply only to adjusted gross incomes of more than $20,000 and net capital gains more than $100 (or $200 on joint returns).		
	1,001-2,000	2.0	15,001-20,000	8.4			
	2,001-3,000	3.0	20,001-25,000	8.8			
	3,001-4,000	4.2	25,001-30,000	9.4			
	4,001-5,000	5.2	30,001-40,000	11.0	600	1,200	600
	5,001-6,000	6.2	40,001-50,000	12.2			
	6,001-8,000	7.2	Over 50,000	13.5			
	8,001-10,000	8.0					
Dist. of Col.[1,4]	First 1,000	2	5,001-10,000	7	Federal exemptions		
	1,001-2,000	3	10,001-13,000	8			
	2,001-3,000	4	13,001-17,000	9			
	3,001-4,000	5	17,001-25,000	10			
	4,001-5,000	6	Over 25,000	11			
Georgia[3,5]	First 1,000	1	7,000-10,000	5	1,500	3,000	700
	1,001-2,999	2	Over 10,000	6	For married persons filing separately, rates range from 1% on the first $500 to 6% on $5,000 or more. For married couples filing jointly and heads of households, rates range from 1% on the first $1,000 to 6% on $10,000 or more.		
	3,000-4,999	3					
	5,000-6,999	4					
Hawaii[1]	First 500	2.25	3,001-5,000	7.5	750	1,500	750
	501-1,000	3.25	5,001-10,000	8.5	Special tax rates for heads of households.		
	1,001-1,500	4.5	10,001-14,000	9.5			
	1,501-2,000	5	14,001-20,000	10			
	2,001-3,000	6.5	20,001-30,000	10.5	Over 30,000	11	
Idaho[2,3,4]	First 1,000	2	3,001-4,000	5.5	Federal exemptions		
	1,001-2,000	4	4,001-5,000	6.5	Each person (husband and wife filing jointly are deemed one person) filing return pays additional $10.		
	2,001-3,000	4.5	Over 5,000	7.5			
Illinois	Total net income	2.5			1,000	2,000	1,000
Indiana[4]	Adjusted gross	1.9			1,000	*2,000	500
	*Lesser of $1,000 or adjusted gross income of each spouse, but not less than $500.						
Iowa[3,6]	First 1,000	0.5	3,001-4,000	3.5	(tax credit) 15	30	10
	1,001-2,000	1.25	4,001-7,000	5	Net incomes $5,000 or less are not taxable.		
	2,001-3,000	2.75	7,001-9,000	6	On up to 13% over $75,000		
Kansas[2,4]	First 2,000	2	5,001-7,000	5	1,000	2,000	1,000
	2,001-3,000	3.5	7,001-10,000	6.5	20,001-25,000	8.5	
	3,001-5,000	4	10,001-20,000	7.5	Over 25,000	9.0	
Kentucky[3]	First 3,000	2	4,001-5,000	4			
	3,001-4,000	3	5,001-8,000	5	(tax credit)		
			Over 8,000	6	20	40	20

State	Taxable income	Percentage rates	Taxable income	Percentage rates	Personal exemp.: Single	Personal exemp.: Married family head	Personal exemp.: Credit per depend.
Louisiana[1,2]	First 10,000	2	Over 50,000	6	2,500	5,000	400
	10,001-50,000	4					
Credits are allowed new income which is taxed at 2%; additional $1,000 exemp. for blindness allowed for dependents.							
Maine[1,3]	First 2,000	1	8,001-10,000	7	1,000	2,000	1,000
	2,001-4,000	2	10,001-15,000	8			
	4,001-6,000	3	15,001-25,000	9.2			
	6,001-8,000	6	Over 25,000	10			
Maryland[1,3,4]	First 1,000	2	2,001-3,000	4	800	1,600	800
	1,001-2,000	3	Over 3,000	5			
An additional exemption of $800 is allowed for each dependent 65 or over.							
Massachusetts	Earned and business income:	5*			2,000	2,600-4,600	600
	Interest, divs., capital gains on intangibles:	10*					
The exemptions shown are those allowed against business income, including salaries and wages. A specific exemption of $2,000 is allowed for each taxpayer. In addition, a dependency exemption of $600 is allowed for a dependent spouse who has income from all sources of less than $2,000. In the case of a joint return, the exemption is the smaller of (1) $4,600 or (2) $2,600 plus the income of the spouse having the smaller income. *Plus 7.5% surtax.							
Michigan[4]	All taxable income	4.6			1,500	3,000	1,500
Minnesota[1,3,4,6]	First 500	1.6	5,001- 7,000	10.2	60	120	60
	501-1,000	2.2	7,001- 9,000	11.5			
	1,001-2,000	3.5	9,001-12,500	12.8			
	2,001-3,000	5.8	12,501-20,000	14			
	3,001-4,000	7.3	20,001-27,500	15			
	4,001-5,000	8.8	Over 27,500	16			
An additional tax credit of $60 is allowed for each unmarried taxpayer aged 65 or older.							
Mississippi[3]	First 5,000	3	Over 5,000	4	5,250	8,000	1,500
Missouri[4]	First 1,000	1.5	5,001- 6,000	4	1,200	2,400	400
	1,001-2,000	2	6,001- 7,000	4.5			
	2,001-3,000	2.5	7,001- 8,000	5			
	3,001-4,000	3	8,001-9,000	5.5			
	4,001-5,000	3.5	Over 9,000	6			
An additional $800 exemption is allowed unmarried head of household.							
Montana[3]	First 1,000	2	8,001-10,000	7	800	1,600	800
	1,001-2,000	3	10,001-14,000	8			
	2,001-4,000	4	14,001-20,000	9			
	4,001-6,000	5	20,001-35,000	10			
	6,001-8,000	6	Over 35,000	11			
Additional surtax of 10% on tax liability.							
Nebraska[3,4]					Federal exemptions		
The tax is imposed as a % of the taxpayer's Fed. income tax liability (not including surtax) before credits, with limited adjustments. For the year 1980 the rate was set at 17% by State Board of Equalization and Assessment.							
New Hampshire	Interest and dividends (except interest on savings accounts).	5	4% commuter tax		$600 of each income is exempt; additional $600 exemptions are allowed to persons who are 65 or older, blind or handicapped and unable to work.		
New Jersey[3]	First 20,000	2			1,000	2,000	1,000
	Over 20,000	2.5					
Additional credit of $1,000 allowed for the elderly, and disabled. Commuter tax from 2% on net income under $1,000 to 14% on income over $23,000. (Will cease after 12/31/80)							
New Mexico[2,3,4]	First 2,000	.8	12,001-14,000	4.2	Federal exemptions		
	2,001-3,000	.9	14,001-16,000	4.9			
	3,001-4,000	1.1	16,001-18,000	5.6			
	4,001-5,000	1.3	18,001-20,000	6.3			
	5,001-6,000	1.5	20,001-25,000	7.0			
	6,001-7,000	1.8	25,001-35,000	7.5			
	7,001-8,000	2.3	35,001-50,000	8.0			
	8,001-10,000	2.9	50,001-100,000	8.5			
	10,000-12,000	3.5	Over 100,000	9.0			
The income classes reported are for individuals. For joint returns and heads of households, a separate rate schedule is provided. A credit is allowed for state and local taxes for gross income of less than $9,000							
New York[1,4]	First 1,000	2	13,001-15,000	9	750	1,500	750
	1,001-3,000	3	15,001-17,000	10			
	3,001-5,000	4	17,001-19,000	11			
	5,001-7,000	5	19,001-21,000	12			
	7,001-9,000	6	21,001-23,000	13			
	9,001-11,000	7	Over 23,000	14			
	11,001-13,000	8					
Income from unincorporated business is taxed at 4%. The following credit is allowed: $100 tax or less, full amount; $100 to $200 difference between $200.00 and amount of tax; $200 or more, no credit.							

State	Taxable income	Percentage rates	Taxable income	Percentage rates	Personal exemp. Single	Personal exemp. Married family head	Credit per depend.
North Carolina[3,4]	First 2,000	3	6,001-10,000	6	1,100	2,200*	700
	2,001-4,000	4	Over 10,000	7			
	4,001-6,000	5					
	*An additional exemption of $1,000 is allowed the spouse having the lower income; joint returns are not permitted.						
North Dakota[3]	First 3,000	1	12,001-30,000	5			
	3,001-5,000	2	Over 30,000	7.5	Federal exemptions		
	5,001-8,000	3			A credit of 25% of income tax liability is allowed up to a maximum of $100.		
	8,001-12,000	4					
Ohio[4]	First 5,000	0.5	15,001-20,000	2.5	650	1,300	650
	5,001-10,000	1	20,001-40,000	3			
	10,001-15,000	2	over 40,000	3.5			
	Taxpayers age 65 or older are allowed a $25 credit, or if they have received a lump sum distribution from a pension, retirement or profit sharing plan during the tax year, they are allowed a credit equal to $25 times the taxpayer's expected remaining life. Credit may not exceed tax otherwise due. Credit is also allowed for an amount paid during the school year for elementary and secondary education or instruction or training of dependents who do not have a high school diploma.						
Oklahoma[1,4]	First 1,000	0.5	5,001-6,250	4	750	1,500	750
	1,001-2,500	1	6,251-7,500	5	For joint returns and heads of households the rates shown apply to income classes twice as large.		
	2,501-3,750	2	Over 7,500	6			
	3,751-5,000	3					
	Non-resident aliens are taxed at a flat rate of 6% of Oklahoma taxable income.						
Oregon[3,4]	First 500	4	3,001-4,000	8	750	1,500	750
	501-1,000	5	4,001-5,000	9	A credit is provided in an amount and equal to 25% of the federal retirement income tax credit to the extent that such a credit is based on Oregon taxable income.		
	1,001-2,000	6	Over 5,000	10			
	2,001-3,000	7					
Pennsylvania	2.2% of specified classes of taxable income						
Rhode Island	19% of modified federal income tax liability				Federal Exemptions		
South Carolina[1]	First 2,000	2	6,001-8,000	5	800	1,600	800
	2,001-4,000	3	8,001-10,000	6			
	4,001-6,000	4	Over 10,000	7			
Tennessee	Interest and dividends	6	Dividends from corporations, 75% of whose property is taxable in Tenn., are taxed at 4%.				
Utah[1]	First 750	2.25	2,251-3,000	5.25	Federal exemptions		
	751-1,500	3.25	3,001-3,750	6.25	Over 4,500	7.75	
	1,501-2,250	4.25	3,751-4,500	7.25			
Vermont[4]	Federal exemptions. The tax is imposed at a rate of 23% of the fed. income tax liability of the taxpayer for the taxable year after certain credits (retirement income, investment, foreign tax, child and dependent care, and tax-free covenant bonds) but before any surtax on fed. liability, reduced by a % equal to the % of the taxpayer's adjusted gross income for the taxable year which is not Vermont income.						
Virginia[3]	First 3,000	2	5,001-12,000	5	600	1,200	600
	3,001-5,000	3	Over 12,000	5.75			
West Virginia[1,3]	First 2,000	2.1	26,001-32,000	6.5	600	1,200	600
	2,001-4,000	2.3	32,001-38,000	6.8			
	4,001-6,000	2.8	38,001-44,000	7.2			
	6,001-8,000	3.2	44,001-50,000	7.5			
	8,001-10,000	3.5	50,001-60,000	7.9			
	10,001-12,000	4	60,001-70,000	8.2			
	12,001-14,000	4.6	70,001-80,000	8.6			
	14,001-16,000	4.9	80,001-90,000	8.8			
	16,001-18,000	5.3	90,001-100,000	9.1			
	18,001-20,000	5.4	100,001-150,000	9.3	For joint returns and a return of a surviving spouse, a separate rate schedule is provided.		
	20,001-22,000	6	150,001-200,000	9.5			
	22,001-26,000	6.1	Over 200,000	9.6			
Wisconsin[1,4]	First 3,000	3.4	15,001-20,000	9.1	(Tax Credit)		
	3,001-6,000	5.2	20,001-40,000	9.5	20	40	20
	6,001-9,000	7.0	Over 40,000	10.0			
	9,001-12,000	8.2					
	12.001-15.000	8.7					

(1) A standard deduction and optional tax table are provided. In Louisiana, standard deduction is incorporated in tax tables.

(2) Community property state in which, in general, one-half of the community income is taxable to each spouse.

(3) A standard deduction is allowed.

(4) A limited general tax credit for taxpayers filing joint returns and a credit for home improvements is allowed in Ohio; a limited tax credit is allowed for sales taxes in Colorado, Massachusetts, Nebraska, and Vermont; for property taxes and city

income taxes in Michigan; for personal property taxes in Maryland and Wisconsin; for property taxes in D.C. if household income is less than $10,000, and in N.Y. if household income is less than $12,000; for installation of solar energy devices in Arizona, California, Kansas, New Mexico, North Carolina, and Oregon; for property taxes paid on pollution control property in Colorado; for installation of insulation in residences in Idaho; and for making an existing building accessible to the handicapped in Kansas.

(5) Tax credits are allowed: $15 for single person or married person filing separately if AGI is $3,000 or less. (For each dollar by which the federal AGI exceeds $3,000 the credit is reduced by $1 until no credit is allowed if federal AGI is $3,015 or more.) $30 for heads of households or married persons filing jointly with $6,000 or less AGI. (For each dollar by which federal AGI exceeds $6,000, credit is reduced by $1 until no credit is allowed if federal AGI is $6,030 or more.)

(6) Tax bracket adjusted for inflation.

State Retail Sales Taxes: Types and Rates

State	Tangible personal property	Admissions	Selected service: Rest. meals	Selected service: Transient lodging	Selected service: Public utilities	Rates on other services and nonretail business
Alabama[2]	4%[3]	4%	4%	4%	...	Gross rcpts of amus't operators, 4%, agric., mining and mfg. mach., 1.5%
Arizona[2]	4	4	4	3	4	Timbering, 1.5%; storage, apt., office rental, 3%.
Arkansas[2]	3	3	3	3	3	Printing, photographic services; rcpts. from coin-operated dev.; repair services incl. auto and elect., 3%.
California[2]	4.75[5]	...	4.75	...	[14]	Renting, leasing, producing, fabricating, processing, pringting, 4.75%
Colorado[2]	3	...	3	3[10]	3	
Connecticut	7.5	...	7[7]	7[10]	7[13]	Storing for use or consumption of personal property items, 7%.
D. of C.	6	5	6	6	5	Duplicating, mailing, addressing and public stenographic services, 5%; sales of food for off-premise consumption, nonprescription medicines, 2%.
Florida	4	4	4	4	...	Rental income of amus't mach., 4%.
Georgia	3	3	3	3 3		Levies on amus's dev., 3%.
Hawaii[1]	4	4	4	4	...	Sugar processors, pineapple farmers and selected businesses, 0.5%; insur. solicitors, 2% contractors, sales rep., professions, radio stations, 4%.
Idaho[6]	3	3	3	3	...	Closed circuit TV boxing, wrestling, 5%.
Illinois[2]	4	...	4	...	...	Property sold in connection with a sale of service, 4%, remodeling repairing and reconditioning of tangible personal property, 4%.
Indiana	4	...	4	4	4	
Iowa	3	3	3	3	3	Laundry, dry cleaning, automobile and cold storage, photography, printing, repairs, barber and beauty parlor services, advt., dry cleaning equip. rentals and gross rcpts. from amus't dev., 3%.
Kansas[2]	3	3	3	3	3	Gross rcpts. from operation of coin-operated devices; commer. amus't, 3%.
Kentucky[2]	5	5	5	5	5	Storage, sewer services, photog. and photo fin., 5%; ticket sales to boxing or wrestling on closed circuit TV, 5% of gross rcpts; tax also applies to pay'ts for right to broadcast matches.
Louisana[2]	3	3	3	3	...	Food and prescpt'n. drugs, exempt.
Maine	5	...	5	5	5	Proceeds from closed circuit TV, 5%.
Maryland[2]	5[3]	[11]	5[7]	5	5	Farm equip., 2%; mfg. equip., including that used in generation of electricity or in R.&S. sold to mfrs., 2%; watercraft, 3%
Mass.	5	...	[7]	5.7[9]	...	
Michigan	4	...	4	4	4	
Minnesota[2]	4[3]	4	4	4	4	Food, medicines and clothing are exempt; coin-operated vending mach., 3% of gross sales.
Mississippi[1]	5[3]	...	5	5	5	Wholesaling, 0.125% (0.5% on sales of meat for human consumption; 5% on beer, alc. bevs., soft drinks and motor fuel); extracting or mining of minerals, specified miscellaneous bus. incl. bowling, pool halls, warehouses, laundry and dry cleaning, pest control services, specified repair services, 5%; cotton ginning, 15c per bale; sales of materials to railroads for use in track structures, 3%; tractors, indust. fuel and mfg. mach. sales over $500, 1%.
Missouri[2]	3.125	3.125	3.125	3.125	3.125	
Nebraska[2]	3	3	3	3	3	

State	Tangible personal property	Admissions	Selected service			Rates on other services and nonretail business
			Rest. meals	Transient lodging	Public utilities	
Nevada[2]	3[10]	...	3	...	...	
New Jersey[1 2]	5	5[11]	5	5[9]	...	
New Mexico[1 2]	3.75[3]	3.75	3.75	3.75	3.75	
New York[2]	4	4[11]	4[7]	4[9]	4	Safe deposit rentals, 4%.
North Carolina[2]	3[3]	...	3	3	...	Farm and industrial machinery, 1% ($80 max.); airplanes, boats and locomotives, 2% ($120 max.); sales of horses and mules, 1%.
North Dakota	3[3]	3	3	3	3	Severance of sand or gravel from the soil, 3%.
Ohio[2]	4	...	4	4	...	
Oklahoma[2]	2[3]	2	2	2	2	Advert. (exclusive of newspapers, periodicals, billboards), printing, auto storage, gross proceeds from amusement dev., 2%.
Pennsylvania[2]	6	...	6[7]	6	6	Cleaning, polishing, lubr. and insp. motor vehicles, rental income of coin-operated amuse. dev., 6%.
Rhode Island	6	...	6	6	6	
South Carolina	4	...	4	4	4	
South Dakota[1 2]	5	4	4	3	3	Farm mach. and agric. irrigation equip., 2%; gross rcpts. from professions (other than medical), 4%.
Tennessee[2]	4.5	...	4.5	4.5	4.5	Vending machines, 1.5% (except tobacco products, 2.5%); industrial, farm equipment and machinery, 1%.
Texas[2]	4[3]	...	4	...	4	
Utah[2]	4	4	4	4	4	
Vermont	3	3	[12]	[12]	3	
Virginia[2]	3[3]	...	3	3	...	
Washington[1 2]	4.5	4.5	4.5	4.5	...	Rentals, auto, parking, other specified services, amusements, recreations, 4.5% (unless subject to county or city adm. taxes, when they remain taxable under the state business, occupation levy, 1%).
West Virginia[1]	3[3]	3	3	3	...	All services except public util. and personal and professional services, 3%.
Wisconsin[2]	4	4[11]	4	4	4	
Wyoming[2]	3	3	3	3	3	

(1) All but a few states levy sales taxes of the single-stage retail type. Ha. and Miss. levy multiple-stage sales taxes. The N.M. and S.D. taxes have broad bases with respect to taxable services but they are not multiple-stage taxes. Wash. and W.Va. levy gross receipts taxes on all business, distinct from their sales taxes. Alaska also levies a gross receipts tax on businesses. The rates applicable to retailers, with exceptions, under these gross receipts taxes are as follows: Alaska 0.5% on gross receipts of $20,000-$100,000 and 0.25% on gross receipts in excess of $100,000; Wash., 0.44%, plus a 6% surtax; and W.Va., 0.55%. N.J. imposes a tax of 0.05% on retail stores with income in excess of $150,000, and an unincorporated business tax at the rate of 0.25% of 1% if gross receipts exceed $5,000.

(2) In addition to the State tax, sales taxes are also levied by certain cities and/or counties.

(3) Motor vehicles are taxed at the general sales tax rates with the following exceptions: Ala., 1.5%; Miss., 3%; and N.C., 2% ($120 maximum). Motor vehicles are exempt from the general sales and use taxes but are taxed under motor vehicle tax laws in Md., 4%; Minn., 4%; N.M., 2%; N.D. 4%; Okla., 2%; S.D. and W.Va., 3%; Tex., 4%; Va., 2%; and the D.C., 4%.

(4)Ariz. and Miss. also tax the transportation of oil and gas by pipeline. Ga., Mo., Okla., and Utah do not tax transportation of property. Miss. taxes taxicab transportation at the rate of 2%. Okla. does not tax fares of 15¢ or less on local transportation. Utah does not tax street railway fares.

(5) "Lease" excludes the use of tangible personal property for a period of less than one day for a charge of less than $10 when the privilege of using the property is restricted to use on the premises or at a business location of the grantor.

(6) A limited credit (or refund) in the form of a flat dollar amount per personal exemption is allowed against the personal income tax to compensate for (1) sales taxes paid on food in Col., D.C., and Neb.; and (2) all sales taxes paid in Ida., Mass., and Vt. Low-income taxpayers (adjusted gross income not over $6,000) are allowed a credit against D.C. tax liability ranging from $2 to $6 per personal exemption, depending on taxpayer's income bracket. A refund is allowed if credit exceeds tax liability.

(7) Restaurant meals below a specified price are exempt: Conn. and Md. less than $1; N.Y. less than $1 (when alcoholic beverages are sold, meals are taxable regardless of price); and Pa., 50¢ or less. In Mass., restaurant meals ($1 or more) which are taxed at 8% under the meals excise tax are exempt.

(8) Conn., exempts clothing for children under 10 years of age. Pa. and Wisc. exempt clothing with certain exceptions.

(9) In Col. and Conn., the first 30 consecutive days of rental or occupancy of rooms is taxable. Over 30 days is exempt. In Mass., transient lodging (in excess of $2 a day) is subject to a 5.7% (5% plus 14% surtax) room occupancy excise tax. In N.J. and N.Y., rooms which rent for $2 a day or less are exempt.

(10) Includes a statewide mandatory 1% county sales tax collected by the state and paid to the counties for support of local school districts.

(11) Md. taxes at 0.5% gross receipts derived from charges for rentals of sporting or recreational equipment, and admis-

sions, cover charges for tables, services or merchandise at any roof garden or cabaret. In N.J., admissions to a place of amusement are taxable if the charge is in excess of 75¢. N.Y. taxes admissions when the charge is over 10¢; exempt are participating sports (such as bowling and swimming), motion picture theaters, race tracks, boxing, wrestling, and live dramatic or musical performances. In Wis., sales of admissions to motion picture theaters costing 75¢ or less are exempt.

(12) Meals and rooms are exempt from sales tax, but are subject to a special excise tax of 5%.

(13) Gas, water, electricity, telephone and telegraph services provided to consumers through mains, lines or pipes are exempt. Gas and electric energy used for domestic heating are exempt. Interstate telephone calls are exempt, as are calls from coin-operated telephones.

(14) Beginning Jan. 1, 1975, a surcharge for efficiency is imposed at the rate of 1/10th mill ($0.0001) per kwh.

State Estate Tax Rates and Exemptions

Source: Compiled by Tax Foundation from Commerce Clearing House data

As of Sept. 1, 1980. *See index for state inheritance tax rates and exemptions.*

State (a)	Rates (on net estate after exemptions) (b)	Maximum rate applies above	Exemption
Alabama	Maximum federal credit (c, d)	$10,040,000	$60,000
Alaska	Maximum federal credit (c, d)	10,040,000	60,000
Arizona	0.8% on first $50,000 to 16% (e)	10,000,000	100,000 (f, g)
Arkansas	Maximum federal credit (c, d)	10,040,000	60,000 (g)
Colorado	Maximum federal credit	10,040,000	60,000
Florida	Maximum federal credit (c, d)	10,040,000	60,000
Georgia	Maximum federal credit (c, d)	10,040,000	60,000
Massachusetts	5% on first $50,000 to 16%	4,000,000	30,000 (h)
Minnesota	7% on first $100,000 to 12% (e)	1,000,000	200,000 (g)
Mississippi	1% on first $60,000 to 16%	10,000,000	147,333 (f, g)
New Mexico	Maximum federal credit (c, d)	10,040,000	60,000
New York	2% on first $50,000 to 21% (e,i)	10,100,000	(f,g,i)
North Dakota	Maximum federal credit (c, d)	10,040,000	60,000 (g)
Ohio	2% on first $40,000 to 7% (e)	500,000	5,000 (g, k)
Oklahoma	1% on first $10,000 to 10% (e)	10,000,000	60,000 (g,l,m)
South Carolina	5% on first $40,000 to 7%	100,000	120,000 (g)
Utah	Maximum federal credit (c, d)	10,400,000	60,000 (g)
Vermont	Maximum federal credit (e, n)	10,040,000	60,000 (g)
Virginia	Maximum federal credit	10,040,000	60,000

(a) Excludes states shown in table on page 118 which levy an estate tax, in addition to their inheritance taxes, to assure full absorption of the federal credit.

(b) The rates generally are in addition to graduated absolute amounts.

(c) Maximum federal credit allowed under the 1954 code for state estate taxes paid is expressed as a percentage of the taxable estate (after $60,000 exemption) in excess of $40,000, plus a graduated absolute amount.

(d) A tax on nonresident estates is imposed on the proportionate share of the net estate which the property located in the state bears to the entire estate wherever situated.

(e) An additional estate tax is imposed to assure full absorption of the federal credit.

(f) Insurance receives special treatment.

(g) Transfers to religious, charitable, educational, and municipal corporations are fully exempt. Limited in Mississippi to those located in U.S. or its possessions.

(h) Applies to net estates above $60,000.

(i) On net estate before exemption.

(j) The specific exemptions ($20,000 of the net estate transferred to spouse and $5,000 to lineal ancestors and descendants and certain other named relatives) are allowed in an amount equal to 2% of the first $50,000 and 3% of the next $100,000.

(k) Property is exempt to the extent transferred to surviving spouse not exceeding $30,000; for a child under 18, $7,000, and for each child 18 or over, $3,000.

(l) An estate valued at $100 or less is exempt.

(m) Exemption is a total aggregate of $60,000 for father, mother, child, and other named relatives.

(n) The tax is 30% of the federal estate tax liability. Taxes on estates of decedents dying after 12/31/76, but before 1/1/79, are reduced by the percentage that $120,000 is of the amount of the federal taxable estate; after 12/31/78, $240,000. The reduction shall not be more than 100%.

City Income Tax in U.S. Cities over 50,000

Compiled by Tax Foundation from Commerce Clearing House data and other sources.

City	Rates % 1980	Rates % Orig.	Year began
Cities with 500,000 or more inhabitants			
Baltimore, Md.	(50% of state tax)	1.0	1966
Cleveland, Oh.	1.5	0.5	1967
Columbus, Oh.	1.5	0.5	1947
Detroit, Mich.	2.0	1.0	1965
Kansas City, Mo.	1.0	0.5	1964
New York, N.Y.	.9-4.3	0.4-2.0	1966
Philadelphia, Pa.	4.3125	1.5	1939
Pittsburgh, Pa.	1.25	1.0	1954
St. Louis, Mo.	1.0	.25	1948
Cities with 100,000 to 499,999 inhabitants			
Akron, Oh.	1.5	1.0	1962
Allentown, Pa.	1.0	1.0	1958
Birmingham, Ala.	1.0	1.0	1970
Canton, Oh.	1.5	0.6	1954
Cincinnati, Oh.	2.0	1.0	1954
Dayton, Oh.	1.75	0.5	1949
Erie, Pa.	1.0	1.0	1948
Flint, Mich.	1.0	1.0	1965
Grand Rapids, Mich.	1.0	1.0	1967
Lansing, Mich.	1.0	1.0	1968
Lexington, Ky.	2.0	1.0	1952
Louisville, Ky.	1.45	0.75	1948
Parma, Oh.	1.5	0.5	1967
Scranton, Pa.	1.6	1.0	1948
Toledo, Oh.	1.5	1.0	1946
Youngstown, Oh.	1.5	0.3	1948
Cities with 50,000 to 99,999 Inhabitants			
Altoona, Pa.	1.0	1.0	1948
Bethlehem, Pa.	1.0	1.0	1957
Chester, Pa.	1.0	1.0	1956
Covington, Ky.	2.5	1.0	1956
Euclid, Oh.	1.0	0.5	1967
Gadsden, Ala.	2.0	1.0	1956
Hamilton, Oh.	1.5	0.8	1960
Harrisburg, Pa.	1.0	1.0	1966
Lakewood, Oh.	1.0	1.0	1968
Lancaster, Pa.	0.5	0.5	1959
Lima, Oh.	1.0	.75	1959
Lorain, Oh.	1.0	0.5	1967
Pontiac, Mich.	1.0	1.0	1968
Reading, Pa.	1.0	1.0	1969
Saginaw, Mich.	1.0	1.0	1965
Springfield, Oh.	2.0	1.0	1948
Warren, Oh.	1.0	0.5	1952
Wilkes-Barre, Pa.	1.0	1.0	1966
Wilmington, Del.	1.0	0.5	1970
York, Pa.	1.0	1.0	1965

State Inheritance Tax Rates and Exemptions

Source: Compiled by Tax Foundation from Commerce Clearing House data.
As of Sept. 1, 1980

State (a)	Rates (b) (percent) Spouse, child, or parent	Brother or sister	Other than relative	Max. rate applies above ($1,000)	Exemptions (c) ($1,000) Spouse	Child or parent	Brother or sister	Other than relative
California	3-14	6-20	10-24	$400	$60(d)	$5(e)	$2	$0.3
Connecticut (f)	3-8	4-10	8-14	1,000	100	20	6	1
Delaware	1-6	5-10	10-16	200	70	3	1	None
District of Columbia	1-8	5-23	5-23	1,000	5	5	1	1
Hawaii	2-7	3-8	3-10	200	100	50	5	5
Idaho	2-15	4-20	8-30	500	30(d)	20(e)	10	10
Illinois	2-14	2-14	10-30	500	20	20	10	0.1
Indiana	1-10	7-15	10-20	1,500(g)	exempt	2(e)	0.5	0.1
Iowa	1-8	5-10	10-15	150	80	10(e)	None	None
Kansas	0.5-5	3-12.5	10-15	500	250	30	5	0.2 (h)
Kentucky	2-10	4-16	6-16	500(u)	50	5(e)	1	0.5
Louisiana	2-3	5-7	5-10	25	5(d)	5	1	0.5
Maine	5-10	8-14	14-18	(g)	50	25	1	1
Maryland (j)	1	10	10	(k)	.15 (h)	.15 (h)	0.15 (h)	0.15 (h)
Michigan	2-10 (l)	2-10 (l)	12-17 (l)	750	65(e)	10	10	None
Missouri	1-6	3-18	5-30	400	20(m)	5(e)	0.5	0.1 (h)
Montana	2-8	4-16	8-32	100	40	7(e)	1.0	None
Nebraska	1	1	6-18	60	10	10	10	0.5
New Hampshire	(n)	15	15	(k)	(n)	(n)	None	None
New Jersey	2-16	11-16	15-16	3,200	15	15	0.5 (h)	0.5 (h)
North Carolina	1-12	4-16	8-17	3,000	10	2(e)	None	None
Oregon	12	12	12	70(q)	54(p)	None	None	None
Pennsylvania	6	15	15	(k)	None(q)	None(q)	None	None
Rhode Island	2-9	3-10	8-15	1,000(r)	10	10	5	1
South Dakota (a)	(s)	4-16	6-24	100	80(s)	3(e)	0.5	0.1
Tennessee	5.5-9.5	6.5-16	6.5-16	440	120	120	10	10
Texas	1-6	3-10	5-20	1,000	200(t)	200(t)	10	0.5
Washington	1-10	3-20	10-25	500	5(d)	5	1	None
West Virginia	3-13	4-18	10-30	1,000	30	10	10	None
Wisconsin	1.25-12.5	5-25	10-30(u)	500	50	4	1	0.5
Wyoming	2	2	6	(k)	60	10	10	None

(a) In addition to an inheritance tax, all states listed also levy an estate tax, generally to assure full absorption of the federal credit. Exception is S.D.

(b) Rates generally apply to excess above graduated absolute amounts.

(c) Generally, transfers to governments or to solely charitable, educational, scientific, religious, literary, public, and other similar organizations in the U.S. are wholly exempt. Some states grant additional exemptions either for insurance, homestead, joint deposits, support allowance, disinherited minor children, orphaned, incompetent or blind children, and for previously or later taxed transfers. In many states, exemptions are deducted from the first bracket only.

(d) Community property state in which, in general, either all community property to the surviving spouse is exempt, or only one-half of the community property is taxable on the death of either spouse.

(e) Exemption for child (in thousands); $30 in Iowa; and $30 in S.D. Exemption for minor child is (in thousands): $12 in Cal.; $30 in Idaho; $5 in Ind.; $10 in Ky.; $15 in Mon.; $5 in N.C. In Mo. the exemption for an insane, blind or otherwise incapacitated lineal descendant is (thousands) $15. In Mich. a widow receives $5,000 for every minor child to whom no property is transferred in addition to the normal exemption for a spouse.

(f) On estates an additional inheritance tax equal to 30% of the basic tax is imposed.

(g) Maximum rate for brother or sister and any other than relative in Indiana is $1 million. In Maine the maximum rate for any other than relative is $150 thousand.

(h) No exemption if share exceeds amount stated.

(i) Estates over $3 million are not subject to the inheritance tax but are subject to an estate tax equal to the amount of the federal credit.

(j) Where property of a decedent subject to administration in Md. is $5,000 or less, no inheritance taxes are due.

(k) Rate applies to entire share.

(l) There is no tax on the share of any beneficiary if the value of the share is less than $100. In addition each county collects an additional 0.5% of the tax collected.

(m) In addition, an exemption of 1/2 of the decedent's estate, or 1/3 if decedent is survived by lineal descendents.

(n) Spouses, children, parents, and adopted children in the decedent's line of succession are exempt.

(o) Net taxable estates are allowed an exemption of $50,000 if the decedent died in 1978, $70,000 if death occurs in 1979 or 1980, $100,000 if death occurs in 1981 or 1982, $200,000 if death occurs in 1983 or 1984 and $500,000 if death occurs in 1985 or 1986.

(p) Credit is allowed to surviving spouse, child or stepchild under 18 years or child who is incapable of self support. The credit is $54,000 in 1978, $51,000 in 1979 and 1980, $48,000 in 1981 and 1982, $36,000 in 1983 and 1984 and zero thereafter. Estates of descendants dying on or after 1/1/87 are not subject to inheritance tax.

(q) However, the $2,000 family exemption is specifically allowed as a deduction.

(r) Beneficiaries of estates worth more than $250,000 are liable for their share of the additional estate tax.

(s) The rates range from 3-6% for a spouse and child and from 3-12% for parents. Effective 7/1/79, exemption for spouse is $100,000.

(t) Increased to $250,000 from 1/1/82 through 8/31/85 and to $300,000 beginning 9/1/85. When more than one beneficiary (spouse, child or parent) receives property, and when the total exceeds the amount of the exemption, the exemption is divided proportionally.

(u) Maximum rate applies above $50,000.

Federal Estate and Gift Tax

Source: Tax Foundation, Inc.

As a result of sweeping changes introduced by the Tax Reform Act of 1976, the federal government now taxes estates and gifts on an entirely different basis than previously applied. The major changes include the unification of estate and gift rates, the substitution of a unified credit for the previous estate and gift tax exemptions, and a new tax on generation-skipping.

Estate Tax

Instead of the specific exemptions which were subtracted from the total estate (previously $60,000) or the lifetime gift total (previously $30,000), the new law provides for a unified credit against combined estate and gift taxes. For estates of decedents who die in 1977, the unified credit is $30,000; in 1978, $34,000; in 1979, $38,000; in 1980, $42,500; in 1981 and thereafter $47,000. The 1977 credit is in general equivalent to an exemption of $120,660; by 1981, to $175,625.

Estate taxes are computed by applying the unified rate schedule, shown below, to the total estate (minus allowable deductions) plus taxable gifts made after 1976. Gift taxes paid are subtracted from tax due, and credit also may be taken for state death taxes. The amount of the state tax credit is determined by the schedule shown in the table below or the actual state taxes paid, whichever is less. No state tax credit is available to an adjusted taxable estate (i.e., taxable estate minus $60,000) smaller than $40,000.

Deductions may be taken from the gross estate for funeral expenses, administration expenses, debts, charitable contributions, and, within limitations, bequests to the surviving spouse. A special deduction is allowed for estates passing to orphans, up to $5,000 per child multiplied by the number of years by which 21 exceeds the child's age. For instance, two orphaned children aged 7 and 9 would be entitled to a deduction of $130,000.

The marital deduction for small and medium-sized estates is increased to the larger of 50 percent of the adjusted gross estate or $250,000. A fractional interest rule eliminates the previous requirement for a consideration-furnished test. In general, each spouse's interest will be one-half, where property is jointly held with rights of survivorship and joint tenancy is created by a transfer subject to gift tax provisions.

The new law provides for real property passed on to family members for use in a closely held business, such as farming, to be valued on basis of such use, rather than fair market value on basis of highest and best use. In no case may this special valuation reduce the gross estate by more than $500,000.

Generation-skipping transfers which occur after April 30, 1976, in general are now subject to taxes substantially equivalent to those which would have been imposed had the property been transferred outright to each successive generation. However, an exclusion is provided for transfers to grandchildren up to $250,000 for each child of the decedent who serves as a conduit for the transfer (not for each grandchild).

A return must be filed for the estate of every U.S. citizen or resident whose gross estate exceeds $120,000 ($60,000 if the decedent dies before 1977; $36,000 for the estate of a nonresident not a citizen). The return is due nine months after death unless an extension is granted.

Gift Tax

Any citizen or resident alien whose gifts to any one person exceed $3,000 within a calendar year will be liable for payment of a gift tax, at rates determined under the unified estate and gift tax schedule. Gift tax returns are filed on a quarterly basis and ordinarily are due a month and a half following any quarter in which a taxable gift was made (i.e., May 15, August 15, November 15, and February 15). After 1976, however, quarterly filing is not required until cumulative taxable gifts during the year exceed $25,000.

Gifts made by husband and wife to a third party may be considered as having been made one-half by each, provided both spouses consent to such division. For gifts between spouses, there is an unlimited deduction for the first $100,000 of lifetime gifts.

Unified Rate Schedule for Estate and Gift Tax

If the amount with respect to which the tentative tax to be computed is:	The tentative tax is:		
Not over $10,000	18 percent of such amount.		
Over $10,000 but not over $20,000	$1,800, plus 20%	of the excess over	$10,000.
Over $20,000 but not over $40,000	$3,800, plus 22%	of the excess over	$20,000.
Over $40,000 but not over $60,000	$8,200, plus 24%	of the excess over	$40,000.
Over $60,000 but not over $80,000	$13,000, plus 26%	of the excess over	$60,000.
Over $80,000 but not over $100,000	$18,200, plus 28%	of the excess over	$80,000.
Over $100,000 but not over $150,000	$23,800, plus 30%	of the excess over	$100,000.
Over $150,000 but not over $250,000	$38,800, plus 32%	of the excess over	$150,000.
Over $250,000 but not over $500,000	$70,800, plus 34%	of the excess over	$250,000.
Over $500,000 but not over $750,000	$155,800, plus 37%	of the excess over	$500,000.
Over $750,000 but not over $1,000,000	$248,300, plus 39%	of the excess over	$750,000.
Over $1,000,000 but not over $1,250,000	$345,800, plus 41%	of the excess over	$1,000,000.
Over $1,250,000 but not over $1,500,000	$448,300, plus 43%	of the excess over	$1,250,000.
Over $1,500,000 but not over $2,000,000	$555,800, plus 45%	of the excess over	$1,500,000.
Over $2,000,000 but not over $2,500,000	$780,800, plus 49%	of the excess over	$2,000,000.
Over $2,500,000 but not over $3,000,000	$1,025,800, plus 53%	of the excess over	$2,500,000.
Over $3,000,000 but not over $3,500,000	$1,290,800, plus 57%	of the excess over	$3,000,000.
Over $3,500,000 but not over $4,000,000	$1,575,800, plus 61%	of the excess over	$3,500,000.
Over $4,000,000 but not over $4,500,000	$1,880,800, plus 65%	of the excess over	$4,000,000.
Over $4,500,000 but not over $5,000,000	$2,205,800, plus 69%	of the excess over	$4,500,000.
Over $5,000,000	$2,550,800, plus 70%	of the excess over	$5,000,000.

State Death Tax Credit for Estate Tax

Adjusted taxable estate from	to	Credit=+	%	Of excess over
$ 0	$ 40,000	0	0	$ 0
40,000	90,000	0	.8	40,000
90,000	140,000	400	1.6	90,000
140,000	240,000	1,200	2.4	140,000
240,000	440,000	3,600	3.2	240,000
440,000	640,000	10,000	4	440,000
640,000	840,000	18,000	4.8	640,000
840,000	1,040,000	27,600	5.6	840,000
1,040,000	1,540,000	38,800	6.4	1,040,000
1,540,000	2,040,000	70,800	7.2	1,540,000
2,040,000	2,540,000	106,800	8	2,040,000

Adjusted taxable estate from	to	Credit=+	%	Of excess over
2,540,000	3,040,000	146,800	8.8	2,540,000
3,040,000	3,540,000	190,800	9.6	3,040,000
3,540,000	4,040,000	238,800	10.4	3,540,000
4,040,000	5,040,000	290,800	11.2	4,040,000
5,040,000	6,040,000	402,800	12	5,040,000
6,040,000	7,040,000	522,800	12.8	6,040,000
7,040,000	8,040,000	650,800	13.6	7,040,000
8,040,000	9,040,000	786,800	14.4	8,040,000
9,040,000	10,040,000	930,800	15.2	9,040,000
10,040,000		1,082,800	16	10,040,000

(1) The adjusted taxable estate equals the taxable estate minus $60,000.

Savings by Individuals in the U.S.

Source: Federal Reserve System

(billions of dollars).

	1969	1970	1975	1976	1977	1978	1979
Increase in financial assets	64.6	78.6	167.2	208.1	241.4	275.3	291.6
Currency and demand deposits	−2.5	8.9	4.0	14.9	22.7	18.3	14.2
Savings accounts	9.1	43.6	84.0	109.3	109.2	105.2	81.0
Money market fund shares	—	—	1.3	—	.2	6.9	34.4
Securities	32.4	−3.1	23.4	11.6	18.5	37.3	54.4
U.S. Savings Bonds	−.1	.3	4.0	4.7	4.7	3.9	−0.8
Other U.S. Treasury securities	11.1	−11.3	15.7	1.5	5.6	13.3	33.6
U.S. Govt. agency securities	5.0	4.6	−3.0	3.3	5.4	9.7	20.0
State & local obligations	9.3	−.9	6.2	2.5	2.6	3.3	−2.4
Corporation & foreign bonds	5.4	9.4	8.4	5.8	−3.3	−1.4	12.2
Open market paper	5.3	−3.8	−4.4	−3.1	9.6	14.6	3.8
Investment company shares	4.9	2.8	−.1	−1.0	−.9	−1.0	−2.1
Other corporate equities	−8.5	−4.3	−3.5	−2.2	−5.2	−5.2	−9.8
Private life insurance reserves	4.9	5.4	8.5	8.2	11.4	11.7	12.3
Private insured pension reserves	3.2	2.8	8.1	15.3	13.9	19.5	16.2
Private noninsured pension reserves	6.3	6.9	11.8	11.2	17.7	19.6	21.1
Government ins. & pension reserves	7.1	8.9	15.1	17.9	22.4	27.1	25.1
Miscellaneous financial assets	4.0	5.4	11.0	19.7	25.5	29.7	32.9
Gross investment in tangible assets	144.4	142.4	215.0	257.0	308.6	352.2	376.5
Owner-occupied homes	26.3	24.5	43.0	57.5	76.3	92.0	95.6
Other fixed assets	31.6	32.6	39.7	43.0	50.7	57.3	66.7
Consumer durables	85.5	84.9	132.6	157.4	178.8	200.3	213.0
Inventories	1.0	.4	−.3	−.8	2.7	2.6	1.1
Capital consumption allowances	92.6	100.8	167.8	184.5	203.8	228.7	257.7
Owner-occupied homes	12.1	12.8	22.2	24.4	28.2	32.8	40.0
Other fixed assets	21.3	23.2	39.6	43.2	47.6	53.0	57.3
Consumer durables	59.2	64.7	106.0	116.8	128.0	142.8	160.5
Net investment in tangible assets	51.8	41.6	47.2	72.6	104.9	123.5	118.7
Owner-occupied homes	14.2	11.7	20.8	33.1	48.1	59.2	55.6
Other fixed assets	10.3	9.4	.1	−.2	3.2	4.3	9.4
Consumer durables	26.2	20.2	26.6	40.6	50.9	57.5	52.6
Inventories	1.0	.4	−.3	−.8	2.7	2.6	1.1
Net increase in debt	42.2	34.3	64.2	116.3	173.5	200.6	211.6
Mortgage debt on nonfarm homes	18.5	14.1	38.1	61.3	93.2	103.8	110.2
Other mortgage debt	6.7	8.5	7.4	10.8	18.9	21.0	25.5
Consumer credit	10.8	5.4	9.7	25.6	40.6	50.6	44.2
Security credit	−3.4	−1.8	.7	4.8	3.1	1.4	0.8
Policy loans	2.6	2.3	1.6	1.4	1.7	2.6	4.7
Other debt	6.9	5.8	6.7	12.5	16.0	21.2	26.3
Individuals' saving	74.3	85.9	150.2	164.4	172.8	198.2	198.8
Less Govt. ins. & pen. reserves	7.1	8.9	15.1	17.9	22.4	27.1	25.1
Net inv. in consumer durables	26.2	20.2	26.6	40.6	50.9	57.5	52.6
Capital gains dividends from invest. cos.	2.5	.9	.2	.5	.6	.7	0.9
Net savings by farm corps.	—	−.1	.2	—	−.2	−0.8	−0.8
Equals pers. saving, F/F basis	38.4	56.0	108.3	106.0	99.7	113.8	121.0
Personal saving, NIA basis	35.1	50.6	83.6	68.6	65.0	72.0	73.8
Difference	3.3	5.4	24.7	37.5	34.8	41.8	47.2

Major Federal Tax Expenditures (Loopholes)

Source: Office of Management and Budget

(Estimates for fiscal year 1980)

Income tax provisions resulting in tax expenditures are defined as exceptions to the "normal structure" of individual and corporate income tax. They reduce tax liabilities for particular groups of taxpayers. The normal structure is nowhere defined in the tax code. Existing rates are accepted as "normal"; when the rate structure is changed, for whatever reason, the new rate structure becomes the new norm.

The following features of the tax system are defined as part of the normal tax structure and therefore **do not result in tax expenditures**: progressive rate schedules for individual income tax; personal exemptions and the minimum standard deduction; separate schedules for single and married persons, married persons filing separately, and heads of households, deduction of business expenses; exclusion of unrealized capital gains and losses; exclusion of gifts and bequests received; exclusion of the value of government services received in kind (e.g., food stamps); foreign tax credits; treatment of individuals and corporations as separate tax paying entities.

Item	Amount (in millions) Individual	Corporate
Capital gains, lower tax on	$22,270	$1,010
State and local tax deduction	17,655	—
Investment tax credit	3,090	15,370
Exclusion, employer's pension cont.	12,925	—
Deduction of charitable contrib.	7,955	1,015
Exclusion, employer contributions for medical insurance premiums	9,595	—
Exclusion, interest on state and local debt	3,045	4,695
Surtax exemption	—	135
Exclusion, social security benefits	6,430	—
Deduction, medical expenses	3,120	—
Employers tax credit for wages paid under work incentive program	—	215
Asset depreciation	150	2,880

Item	Amount (in millions) Individual	Corporate
Exclusion, interest on life insurance savings	2,720	—
Exclusion, untaxed unemployment insurance benefits	1,935	—
Exclusion, self-employed pension contribution	2,205	—
Energy exploration and development	505	1,160
Research and development expend.	35	1,745
Additional exemption for elderly	1,855	—
Exclusion, armed forces personnel benefits	1,470	—
Maximum tax on personal service inc.	1,625	—
Parental personal exemption for student, age 19 or over	1,020	—
Exclusion of income earned abroad	555	—

Directory of Federal Consumer and Information Offices

Source: Office of Consumer Affairs, U.S. Department of Health, Education, and Welfare

Advertising:
Office of the Secretary, Federal Trade Commission, Washington, DC 20580; (202) 523-3598.

Aging:
Director, National Clearinghouse on Aging, Department of Health, Education, and Welfare, Washington, DC 20201; (202) 245-2158.

Air travel:
Routes and services
Bureau of Consumer Protection, Civil Aeronautics Board, Washington, DC 20428; (202) 673-6047.
Safety
Public Information Center, Federal Aviation Administration, APA-430, Department of Transportation, Washington, DC 20591; (202) 426-8058 or Chief, Community and Consumer Liaison Division, Federal Aviation Administration, APA-100, Department of Transportation; (202) 426-1960.

Alcohol and Alcoholism:
Director, National Clearinghouse for Alcohol Information, P.O. Box 2345, Rockville, MD 20852; (301) 468-2600.

Appliances:
Energy Efficiency
Office of the Secretary, Federal Trade Commission, Washington, DC 20580; (202) 523-3600.
Product Safety
Director, Office of Communications, Consumer Product Safety Commission, Washington, DC 20207; (800) 638-8326; (800) 492-8363 in Maryland; (800) 638-8333 in Puerto Rico, Virgin Islands, Alaska.
Radiation
Director, Technical Information Staff (HFX-25), Bureau of Radiological Health, Food and Drug Administration, Department of Health, Education and Welfare, 5600 Fishers Lane, Rockville, MD 20857; (301) 443-3434.
Warranties
Office of the Secretary, Federal Trade Commission, Washington, DC 20580; (202) 523-3600.

Automobiles:
Safety and Recalls
Administrator, National Highway Traffic Safety Administration, Department of Transportation, Washington, DC 20590; (800) 424-9393; (202) 426-0123 in Washington, DC.

Banks:
Federally Chartered Banks
Director, Consumer, Community, and Fair Lending, Examinations Division, Comptroller of the Currency, Department of the Treasury, Washington, DC 20219; (202) 447-1600.
State Chartered Banks/Members of Federal Reserve System
Director, Division of Consumer Affairs, Board of Governors of Federal Reserve System, Washington, DC 20551; (202) 452-3000.

Business:
Director, Consumer Affairs Office, Department of Commerce, Washington, DC 20230; (202) 377-5001.
Director, Office of the Ombudsman, Department of Commerce, Washington, DC 20230; (202) 377-3176.

Children, Youth, and Families:
Chief, Office of Public Information, Administration for Children, Youth, and Families, Department of Health, Education, and Welfare, Washington, DC 20201; (202) 755-7724.
Runaway children
Free, confidential advisory services to runaways and parents are provided 24 hours a day by National Runaway Hotline; (800) 621-4000; (800) 972-6004 in Illinois.
Operation Peace of Mind is a confidential, 24-hour message relay service which provides referral information on medical assistance and shelter; (800) 231-6946; (800) 392-3352 in Texas; (800) 231-6762 in Alaska, Hawaii.

Consumer information:
For a copy of the free Consumer Information Catalog, a listing of more than 200 selected Federal consumer publications on such topics as automobiles, health, energy, housing, food and health care, send a postcard to Consumer Information Center, Pueblo, CO 81009. An annual listing of Federal consumer publications in Spanish can also be obtained from the same address.

Copyrights:
Information and Publication Section, Copyright Office, Library of Congress, Washington, DC 20559; (703) 557-8700.

Cosmetics:
Director, Consumer Communications; HFJ-10, Food and Drug Administration, Department of Health, Education, and Welfare, 5600 Fishers Lane, Rockville, MD 20857; (301) 443-3170.

Drugs, Drug Abuse:
Abuse
Director, Office of Communications and Public Affairs, Alcohol, Drug Abuse, and Mental Health Administration, Department of Health, Education, and Welfare, 5600 Fishers Lane, Rockville, MD 20857; (301) 443-3783 or (301) 443-6500.
Effectiveness and Safety
Director, Consumer Communications; HFJ-10, Food and Drug Administration, Department of Health, Education, and Welfare, 5600 Fishers Lane, Rockville, MD 20857 or (301) 443-3170.
Enforcement
Director of Compliance and Regulatory Affairs, Drug Enforcement Administration, Washington, DC 20537; (202) 633-1000.

Education:
Discrimination
Director, Office of Civil Rights, Department of Health, Education, and Welfare, 330 Independence Avenue, S.W., Washington, DC 20201; (202) 245-6671.
Grants and Loans
Director, Office of Public Affairs, Office of Education, Department of Health, Education, and Welfare, Washington, DC 20202; (800) 638-6700; (800) 492-6602 in Maryland.
Handicapped
Director, Bureau of Education for the Handicapped, Department of Health, Education, and Welfare, Washington, DC 20201; (202) 245-9815.

Employment:
Discrimination
Director, Equal Employment Opportunity Commission, Washington, DC 20506; (202) 634-6930.
Safety and Health
Director, Office of Information, Occupational Safety and Health Administration, Department of Labor, Washington, DC 20210; (202) 523-8151.
Training
For information on employment and training programs, such as the Comprehensive Employment and Training Act (CETA) programs, most of which are handled by state and local governments, check with state or local employment services listed in the white pages of the phone book, or your mayor's office. General information can be

obtained from the Director, Employment and Training Administration, Department of Labor, Washington, DC 20213; (202) 376-6905.

Women

Director, Women's Bureau, Department of Labor, Washington, DC 20210; (202) 523-6652.

Energy:

Director, Office of Consumer Affairs, Department of Energy, Washington, DC 20585.

Complaints

Administrator, Economic Regulatory Administration, 2000 M Street, N.W., Washington, DC 20461; (800) 424-9246; (202) 254-5474 in Washington, DC.

Nuclear regulation

Office of Public Affairs, Nuclear Regulatory Commission, Washington, DC 20555; (202) 492-7715.

Solar Energy

Director, National Solar Heating and Cooling Information Center, P.O. Box 1607, Rockville, MD 20850.

Environment:

Consumer Complaints

James Keys, Public Information Center (PM-215), Environmental Protection Agency, Washington, DC 20460; (202) 755-0707.

Federal Regulations:

For information on federal regulations and proposals, the Office of the Federal Register (OFR) is offering, among other services, recorded "Dial-a-Reg" phone messages. "Dial-a-Reg" gives advance information on significant documents to be published in the Federal Register the following work day. The service is currently available in Washington, DC at (202) 523-5033; Chicago at (312) 663-0884; and Los Angeles at (213) 688-6694.

The *Federal Register*, published five days a week, informs the public about proposed and new government regulations. It includes Presidential proclamations, Executive Orders, and other Presidential documents. It may be ordered from the Superintendent of Documents, U.S. Government Printing Office, Washington, DC 20402 for $.75 per copy, $5.00 per month, or $50.00 per year. Contact the Director, Office of the *Federal Register*, National Archives and Record Services, Washington, DC 20408; (202) 523-5240.

Food:

Consumer information

Information Division, Food Safety and Quality Service, Department of Agriculture, Washington, DC 20250; (202) 447-9113.

Safety and quality

Director, Consumer Communications, Food and Drug Administration, Department of Health, Education, and Welfare, 5600 Fishers Lane, Rockville, MD 20857; (301) 443-3170.

Food Stamps and Food Assistance Programs

Contact local or state Welfare Office, local health department, or the Administrator, Food and Nutrition Service, Department of Agriculture, Washington, DC 20250; (202) 447-8384.

Nutrition:

Food and Nutrition Information and Educational Resources Center, Technical Information Systems, SEA/USDA, Natl. Agricultural Library Building, Beltsville, MD 20705, (301) 344-3719.

Handicapped:

Chief, Clearinghouse on the Handicapped, Office for Handicapped Individuals, Department of Health, Education, and Welfare, Washington, DC 20201; (202) 245-1961.

Architectural barriers

Director, Architectural Transportation Barriers Compliance Board, 330 C Street, S.W., Washington, DC 20201; (202) 245-1591.

Reading Material for the blind and physically handicapped

Director, National Library Service for the Blind and Physically Handicapped, 1291 Taylor Street, N.W., Washington, DC 20542; (202) 882-5500.

Health:

Diseases

Public Inquiries, Center for Disease Control, Public Health Service, Atlanta, GA 30333; (404) 329-3534.

Mental Health

Director, National Clearinghouse for Mental Health Information, Department of Health, Education, and Welfare, 5600 Fishers Lane, Rockville, MD 20852. (301) 443-4513.

Research

Director, Division of Public Information, National Institutes of Health, 9000 Rockville Pike, Bethesda, MD 20014.

Housing:

Office of Consumer Affairs, Assistant Secretary for Neighborhoods, Voluntary Associations and Consumer Protection, Department of Housing and Urban Development, Washington, DC 20410; (202) 755-6860.

Insurance:

Crime Insurance

Federal Insurance Administrator, Federal Emergency Management Agency, Washington, DC 20410; (800) 638-8780; (202) 652-2637 in Washington, DC.

Flood Insurance

Federal Insurance Administrator, above address; (800) 424-8872, 8873; (202) 472-2381 in Washington, DC.

Immigration and Naturalization:

Assistant Commissioner, Information Services Division, Immigration and Naturalization Service, Department of Justice, 425 Eye Street, N.W., Washington, DC 20536; (202) 633-2989.

Legal Assistance

The Federal Communications Bar Association has instituted a Legal Aid Program for indigent individuals and groups. In addition, there are several public interest communications law firms throughout the country. For a list of possible sources of legal assistance, contact the Chief, Consumer Assistance Office, Federal Communications Commission, Washington, DC 20554; (202) 632-7000.

Mail:

Fraud

Check with your local postal inspector, or the Chief Postal Inspector, U.S. Postal Service, Rm. 3517, Washington, DC 20260; (202) 245-5445.

Mail Orders

Federal Trade Commission, Office of the Secretary, Washington, DC 20580; (202) 523-3600.

Unordered merchandise

Check with your local postmaster, or the Chief Postal Inspector, above.

Unsolicited mail

Those who want to stop most advertising mail from coming to their homes should contact the Director, Mail Marketing Association, 6 East 43rd Street, N.Y., N.Y. 10017. This organization will remove their names from the mailing lists of all its members.

Maps:

National Cartographic Information Center, U.S. Geological Survey, 507 National Center, Reston, VA 22092; (703) 860-6045.

Medicare:

Contact your local Social Security Office, or your area Medicare carrier, by looking under Medicare in the local telephone directory.

Medicaid:

Contact your local welfare office of State Medicaid Office, or the Director, Consumer Affairs Staff, Health Care Financing Administration, Department of Health, Education, and Welfare, Washington, DC 20201; (202) 245-6575.

Moving and Movers:
Consumer Assistance Office, Interstate Commerce Commission, Washington, DC 20423; (800) 424-9312; (800) 432-4537 in Florida; (202) 275-0860 in Washington, DC.

Parks and recreation areas:
National forests
Director, Information Office, Forest Service, Department of Agriculture, Washington, DC 20250; (202) 447-3760.
National parks and historic sites
Director, Office of Public Inquiry, National Park Service, Department of the Interior, Washington, DC; (202) 343-7394.

Passports:
For passport information check with your local post office or contact the Office of Passport Services, Bureau of Consular Affairs, Department of State, 1425 K Street, N.W., Washington, DC 20524; (202) 783-8170.

Patents and Trademarks:
Commissioner of Patents and Trademarks, Washington, DC 20231; (703) 557-3080.

Pensions:
Pension Benefit Guaranty Corp., 2020 K Street, N.W., Washington, DC 20006; (202) 254-4817.
PBGC Field Office, Federal Office Building, Rm. 4033, 300 North Los Angeles Street, Los Angeles, CA 90012; (213) 688-6428.

Product Safety:
Director, Office of Communications, Consumer Product Safety Commission, Washington, DC 20207; (800) 638-8326; (800) 492-8363 in Maryland; (800) 638-8333 in Puerto Rico, Virgin Islands, Alaska, Hawaii.

Social Security
Director, Office of Public Inquiries, Social Security Administration, 6401 Security Blvd., Baltimore, MD; (301) 594-7705.

Stocks and Bonds
Director, Office of Consumer Affairs, Securities and Exchange Commission, 500 N. Capitol Street, N.W., Washington, DC 20549; (202) 523-3952.

Taxes
The Internal Revenue Service (IRS) has 58 district offices which provide tax assistance by toll-free telephone. Toll-free numbers are listed in IRS tax packages and in local telephone directories. Taxpayers may also use the toll-free network to clarify bills and notices, and to contact the Problem Resolution Officer for problems and complaints unresolved through normal channels.

Train travel
Amtrak, Office of Consumer Relations, P.O. Box 2709, Washington, DC 20013; (202) 383-2121.
Director, Public Information Office, Interstate Commerce Commission, Washington, DC 20423; (800) 424-9312.
Consumer Affairs Officer, Federal Railroad Administration, Department of Transportation, Washington, DC 20590; (202) 426-0881.

Veterans:
Veterans Administration, Washington, DC 20420; (202) 393-4120.

Warranties:
Federal Trade Commission, Office of the Secretary, Washington, DC 20580; (202) 523-3600.

Canadian Consumer Associations

Automobile Protection Association

The Automobile Protection Association (APA) is a non-profit, independently-financed consumer group founded in 1969 to advise motorists on the quality of automotive products and services, to publicize and encourage legal action against what it considers dishonest or dangerous practices in the automobile industry, and to press federal and provincial governments for protective legislation. For a $15 annual fee members receive periodic APA bulletins as well as free legal consultation when needed. Accredited garage service including a free annual check-up of your car is provided in Montreal and Ottawa. Headquarters are at 292 St-Joseph West, Montreal, Quebec H2V 2N7. Branch office at 255 Argyle, Ottawa, Ont. K2P 1B8.

Consumers' Association of Canada

The Consumers' Association of Canada (CAC) is a voluntary, non-profit organization founded in 1947 to represent consumer interests. It also provides members with information on consumer legislation and the results of its research and tests on consumer goods and services. The national office is at 200 First Avenue, Ottawa, Ontario K1S 2G6; branch offices are in each province and territory. CAC publishes bi-monthly, bilingual magazines, *Canadian Consumer* and *Le Consommateur Canadien* (circulation 140,000). Annual membership fee is $10.

Consumer Installment Credit

Source: Federal Reserve System (amounts outstanding, millions of dollars)

		By holder					By type			
End of year or month	Total	Commercial banks	Finance companies	Credit unions	Retailers	Savings and loans and others	Automobile	Mobile homes	Revolving	All other
1974	164,594	80,054	36,087	21,895	18,114	8,444	54,266	14,642	13,681	82,005
1975	172,353	82,936	35,995	25,666	18,201	9,555	57,242	14,434	15,019	85,658
1976	193,977	93,728	38,919	31,169	19,260	10,901	67,707	14,573	17,189	94,508
1977	230,829	112,373	44,868	37,605	23,490	12,493	82,911	15,141	39,274	93,503
1978	275,629	136,189	54,298	45,939	24,876	14,327	102,468	16,042	47,051	110,068
1979, June	291,856	144,035	60,996	47,478	23,672	15,675	110,930	16,607	47,458	116,861
1979, Nov.	307,641	149,057	67,164	48,673	25,732	17,015	115,121	17,349	52,060	123,111

Interest Laws and Consumer Finance Loan Rates

Source: Revised by Christian T. Jones. Editor Consumer Finance Law Bulletin, Prospect Heights, Ill.

Most states have laws regulating interest rates. These laws fix a legal or conventional rate which applies when there is no contract for interest. They also fix a general maximum contract rate, but in many states there are so many exceptions that the general contract maximum actually applies only to exceptional cases. Also, federal law has preempted state limits on first home mortgages and, over $25,000, business and agricultural credit.

Legal rate of interest. The legal or conventional rate of interest applies to money obligations when no interest rate is contracted for and also to judgments. The rate is usually 6% a year; 5% or 7% in some states.

General maximum contract rates. General interest laws in most states set the maximum rate between 8% and 12% per year. The general maximum is fixed by the state constitution rather than by statute at 10% per year in Arkansas. Loans to corporations are frequently exempted or subject to a higher maximum. In recent years, it has also been common to provide special rates for home mortgage loans and variable rates that change quarterly by rule.

Specific enabling acts. In many states special statutes permit industrial loan companies, second mortgage lenders, and banks to charge 1.5% a month or more. Laws regulating revolving loans, charge accounts and credit cards generally limit charges to 1.5% per month. Rates for installment sales contracts in most states are somewhat higher. Credit unions may generally charge 1% to 1½% a month. Pawnbrokers' rates vary widely. Building and loan associations, and loans insured by the Federal Housing Administration, are also specially regulated.

Consumer finance loan statutes. Most consumer finance loan statutes are based on early models drafted by the Russell Sage Foundation (1916-42) to provide small loans to wage earners under license and other protective regulations. Since 1969, however, the model has frequently been the Uniform Consumer Credit Code which applies to credit sales and loans for consumer purposes up to $25,000. In general, licensed lenders may charge 2.5% or 3% a month for $300 or less and reduced rates for additional amounts up to $2,000 or more. A number of states permit add-on rates of 17% to 20% ($17 to $20 per $100) a year of the original principal for $300 and lower rates for additional amounts. An add-on of 17% ($17 per $100) per year yields about 2.5% per month when the loan is paid in equal monthly installments. In the table below unless otherwise stated, monthly and annual rates are based on reducing principal balances, annual add-on rates are based on the original principal for the full term, and two or more rates apply to different portions of balance or original principal.

States with consumer finance loan laws and the rates of charge as of Oct. 1, 1980:

Maximum monthly rates computed on unpaid balances, unless otherwise stated.

Ala. . . Annual add-on: 15% to $750, 10% to $2,000, 8% over $2,000 (min. 1.5% on unpaid balances). Higher rates for loans up to $749. To 12/31/81, no limit over $5,000.

Alas. . . 3% to $500, 2% to $5,000; or equivalent flat rate. 1.5% to $25,000.

Ariz. . . Up to $1,000: 3% to $300, 2% to $600, 1.5% to $1,500, 1% to $2,500. Over $1,000: 2.5% to $300, 2% to $1,000, 1.5% to $1,500, 1% to $10,000; (1.625%) (min.)

Cal. . . 2.5% to $225, 2% to $625, 1.5% to $1,650, 1% to $10,000 (1.5% min.). No max. over $10,000.

Colo. . . 36% per year to $300, 21% to $1,000, 15% to $25,000 (18% min.).

Conn. . Annual Add-on: 17% to $600, 11% to $5,000; 11% over $1,800 to $5,000 for certain secured loans.

Del. . . Annual Discount: 9% for 1st 36 mos., 6% for remaining months; plus 2% fee.

Fla. . . 30% per year to $500, 24% to $1,000, 18% to $2,500; 18% per year on any amount over $2,500 to $25,000.

Ga. . . 10% per year (8% after 7/1/81) discount for 18 months, add-on to 36½ months; 8% fee to $600, 4% on excess plus $2 per month; max. $3,000.

Ha. . . 3.5% to $100, 2.5% to $300; 2% on entire balance over $300 (temporary rate to 7/1/85).

Ida. . . 36% per year to $660, 21% to $2,200, 15% to $55,000 (18% min.).

Ill. . . 2.5% to $300, 2% to $600, 1.5% to $1,500; or equivalent flat rate. Approx. 1.5% to $10,000.

Ind. . . 36% per year to $540, 21% to $1,800, 15% to $45,000 (18% min.).

Ia. . . 3% to $500, 2% to $1,200, 1.5% to $2,000; or equivalent flat rate.

Kan. . . 36% per year to $420, 21% to $1,400, 14.45% to $25,000 (18% min.).

Ky. . . 3% to $600, 2% to $1,500, 1.5% to $2,000.

La. . . 36% per year to $1,400, 27% to $4,000, 24% to $7,000, 21% over $7,000.

Me. . . 30% per year to $540, 21% to $1,800, 15% to $45,000 (18% min.).

Md. . . 2.75% to $300, 2% to $500, 1.25% to $1,200; 1.75% to $3,500; 1.5% to $5,000; 1.35% to $6,000.

Mass. . 23% per year plus $20 fee to $6,000.

Mich. . . 31% per year to $500, 13% to $3,000 (18% min.).

Minn. . . 2.75% to $300, 1.5% to $600, 1.25% to $1,200 plus fee of $1 per $100.

Miss. . . 36% per year to $800, 33% to $1,800, 24% to $4,500, 12% over $4,500.

Mo. . . 2.218% to $800, 1.25% to $2,500, 10% per year over $2,500.

Mont. . Annual add-on; 20% to $300, 16% to $500, 12% to $1,000, 10% to $7,500. 1½% per mo. over $7,500 to $25,000.

Neb. . . 24% to $1,000, 18% to $5,000, 16% to $7,000.

Nev. . . 36% per year to $300, 21% to $1,000, 15% to $10,000 (1.5% min.).

N.H. . . 2% to $600, 1.5% to $1,500; 1.5% on entire amount over $1,500 to $5,000.

N.J. . . 24% per year to $500, 22% to $1,500, 18% to $5,000.

N.M. . . 3% to $150, 2.5% to $300, 1.5% to $1,000, 1.25 to $2,500 (temporary rate to 7/1/82).

N.Y. . . 2.5% to $100, 2% to $300, 1.5% to $900, 1.25% to $2,500.

N.C. . . 3% to $300, 1.5% to $3,000.

N.D. . . 2.5% to $250, 2% to $500, 1.75% to $750, 1.5% to $1,000; 1.5% on entire amount over $1,000 to $7,500.

Ohio . . Annual add-on: 16% to $750, 11% to $1,500, 9% to $3,000; or equivalent simple interest rate. 18% per year on unpaid balances over $3,000.

Okla. . . 30% per annum to $480, 21% to $1,600, 15% to $40,000. (18% min.). Special rates to $100.

Ore. . . 3% to $500, 1.75% to $2,000, 1.25% to $5,000. Over $5,000, 19.5% per year.

Pa. . . 9.5% per year discount to 36 months, 6% for remaining time plus 2% fee (min. 2%) to $5,000.

P.R. . . Annual Add-on: 20% to $300, 7% to $600.

R.I. . . 3% to $300, 2.5% for loans between $300 and $800; 2% for larger loans to $2,500.

S.C. . . 36% per year to $390, 21% to $1,300, 15% to $32,500 (18% min.). Special rate to $150.

S.D. . . 2.5% to $500, 2% to $1,200, 1.5% to $2,000, 1% to $2,500. Over $2,500, 19.5% per year.

Tenn. . . 7.5% per year discount plus fees; no size limit (max. 18% per year on unpaid balances).

Texas . Annual add-on: 18% to $300, 8% to $2,500. Special rates to $100.

Utah . . 36% per year to $600, 21% to $2,200, 15% to $55,000 (18% min.).

Vt. . . 2% to $1,000, 1% to $3,000 (min. 1.5%).

Va. . . 2.5% to $750, 1.6% to $2,300; annual add-on of 17% to $750, $14 to $1,250, $12 to $2,300.

Wash. . 2.5% to $500, 1.5% to $1,000, 1% to $2,500.

W.Va. . 36% per year to $200, 24% to $1,200, 18% to $1,500.

Wis. . . Annual discount: 9.5% on first $2,000, 8% to $3,000 up to 36 months; 19% per year for larger loans. (temporary rate to 10/31/81).

Wyo. . . 36% per year to $300, 21% to $1,000, 15% to $25,000 (18% min.).

Business Directory

Source: World Almanac Questionnaire

Listed below are major U.S. corporations, and major foreign corporations with their U.S. headquarters, **whose operations—products and services—directly concern the American consumer.** At the end of each listing is a **representative sample** of some of the company's subsidiaries or holdings.

Should you, as a dissatisfied consumer, wish to register a complaint beyond the local level, address your correspondence to the attention of the Consumer Complaint Office of the individual company. Be as specific as possible about the dealer's name and address, purchase date or date of service, price, name and serial number (if any) of the product, and places you may have sought relief, with dates. Include copies of receipts and guarantees and/or warranties. Don't forget your name and complete address and telephone number with area code.

Company. . .Address. . .Chief executive officer. . .Business. . .Subsidiaries, products/ *Parent Co.*

AMF Inc.. . .777 Westchester Ave., White Plains, NY 10604. . .Ray A. Tritten. . .producer leisure time, industrial prods.. . .AMF Bowling Products; AMF Harley-Davidson.

AM International, Inc.. . .1900 Ave. of the Stars, Los Angeles, CA 90067. . .Roy L. Ash. . .communications information management.

A-T-O Inc.. . .4420 Sherwin Rd., Willoughby, OH 44094. . .Harry E. Figgie Jr.. . .fire-fighting equip., recreational, industrial, technical prods.. . .Rawlings Sporting Goods; "Automatic" Sprinkler Corp., Fred Ferry Sportswear, Thermometer Corp. of America.

Admiral Group. . .1701 E. Woodfield Rd., Schaumberg, IL 60172. . .John J. Henry. . .electronic prods.

Alberto-Culver Co.. . .2525 Armitage Ave., Melrose Park, IL 60160. . .Leonard H. Lavin. . .mfg. & sales of toiletries.

Allegheny Ludlum Industries, Inc.. . .2 Oliver Plaza, Pittsburgh, PA 15222. . .Robert J. Buckley. . .steel specialty metals & materials, consumer products.

Ethan Allen, Inc.. . . Ethan Allen Dr., Danbury, CT 06810. . .Nathan S. Ancell. . .furniture.

Allied Chemical Corp.. . . Columbia Rd. & Park Ave., Morristown, NJ 07960. . .Edward L. Hennessy Jr.. . .oil, gas, chemicals, fibers & plastics, electrical products, auto safety restraints.

Allied Stores Corp.. . .1114 Ave. of the Americas, N.Y., NY 10036. . .Thomas M. Macioce. . .dept. stores, shopping centers. . .Bon Marche; Jordan Marsh, Joske's, Maas Bros.

Allied Van Lines, Inc.. . .P.O. Box 4403, Chicago, IL 60680. . .Don J. Storseth. . .moving, storage.

Allis Chalmers Corp.. . .1205 S. 70th St., Milwaukee, WI 53201. . .David C. Scott. . .technology in solids, liquids, gases, agricultural equip., electrical prods., material handling equip., outdoor power equip.

Aluminum Co. of America. . .1501 Alcoa Bldg., Pittsburgh, PA 15219. . .W.H. Krome George. . .mining, refining, & processing of aluminum.

Amana Refrigeration, Inc.. . . Amana, IA 52403. . .Alex A. Meyer. . .appliance mfg.. . .*Raytheon.*

Amerada Hess Corp.. . .1185 Ave. of the Americas, N.Y., NY 10036. . .Leon Hess. . .integrated petroleum co.

American Airlines. . .P.O. Box 61616, Dallas/Ft.Worth Airport, TX 75261. . .Albert V. Casey. . .air transport.

American Bakeries Co.. . .10 Riverside Plaza, Chicago, IL 60606. . .G.P. Turci. . .wholesale bakery goods.

American Brands, Inc.. . .245 Park Ave., N.Y., NY 10017. . .John F. Walrath. . .tobacco, food prods., office supplies, toiletries, golf, industrial rubber prods., locks, wholesaling & retailing businesses, distilled beverages. . .American Cigar; American Tobacco Co.; James B. Beam Distilling Co.; Duffy-Mott Co.; Andrew Jergens Co.; Sunshine Biscuits; Swingline.

American Broadcasting Companies Inc.. . .1330 Ave. of the Americas, N.Y., NY 10019. . .Elton H. Rule. . .broadcasting, recordings, publication, operation of outdoor attractions.

American Can Co.. . . American Lane, Greenwich, CT 06830. . .William S. Woodside. . .packaging consumer prods.

American Cigar. . .245 Park Ave., N.Y., NY 10017. . .Felipe Silva. . .cigars, smoking tobacco. . .*American Brands, Inc.*

American Cyanamid Co.. . .859 Berdan Ave., Wayne, NJ 07470. . .J.G. Affleck. . .medical, agricultural prods., specialty chemicals. . .Formica Corp.; Shulton.

American Express Co.. . . American Express Plaza, N.Y., N.Y. 10004. . .Alva O. Way. . .travel, insurance services, international banking. . .Fireman's Fund Insurance.

American Greetings Corp.. . .10500 American Rd., Cleveland, OH 44144. . .Irving I. Stone. . .greeting cards.

American Hoechst Corp.. . . Rte. 202-206 North, Somerville, NJ 08876. . .John G. Brookhuis. . .chemicals, plastics, fibers, sunglasses, pharmaceuticals. . .Foster Grant Co./ *Hoechst AG.*

American Hoist & Derrick Co.. . .63 S. Robert, St. Paul, MN 55107. . .Robert P. Fox. . .material handling equip.

American Home Products Corp.. . .685 3d Ave., N.Y., NY 10017. . .William F. LaPorte. . .household prods., housewares, drugs, foods, candy.

American Honda Motor Co., Inc.. . .100 W. Almdra Blvd., Gardena, CA 90247. . .passenger vehicles.

American Motors Corp.. . .2777 Franklin Rd., Southfield, MI 48034. . .Roy D. Chapin. . .passenger vehicles, service parts. . .Jeep Corp.

American Petrofina, Inc.. . .8350 N. Central Exp., Dallas, TX 75206. . .R.I. Galland. . .petroleum, petrochemicals.

American Standard Inc.. . .40 W. 40th St., N.Y., NY 10018. . .William A. Marquard. . .building, transportation, industrial, security, and graphic prods., construction and mining equipment.

American Stores Co.. . . One Rollins Pl., Wilmington, DE 19803. . .William R. Delley. . .retail food markets, dept. & drug stores, restaurants. . .Acme Markets.

American Telephone & Telegraph Co.. . .195 Broadway, N.Y., NY 10007. . .Charles L. Brown. . .communications. . .Western Electric.

American Tobacco Co.. . .245 Park Ave., N.Y., NY 10017. . .Robert K. Heimann. . .cigarettes. . .*American Brands.*

Amstar Corp.. . .1251 Ave. of Americas, N.Y., NY 10020. . .Robert T. Quittmeyer. . .sweeteners.

Anaconda Co.. . .555 17th St., Denver CO 80202. . .James S. Morrison Jr.. . .copper, aluminum, uranium. . .*Atlantic Richfield.*

Anchor Hocking Corp.. . .109 N. Broad, Lancaster, OH 43130. . .J. R. Topper. . .glass containers, metal and plastic closures.

Anheuser-Busch, Inc.. . .721 Pestalozzi St., St. Louis, MO 63118. . .Dennis P. Longnow. . .brewing. . .St. Louis Cardinals baseball club.

Armour & Co.. . . Greyhound Tower, Phoenix, AZ 85077. . .Gerald H. Trautman. . .food and consumer products. . .*Greyhound.*

Armstrong World Industries. . .P.O. Box 3001, Lancaster, PA 17604. . .Harry A. Jensen. . .interior furnishings.

Armstrong Rubber Co.. . .500 Sargent Dr., New Haven, CT 06507. . .James A. Walsh. . .tires.

Arrow Co.. . .530 5th Ave., N.Y., NY 10036. . .John Currier. . .apparel. . .*Cluett, Peabody.*

Arvin Industries, Inc.. . .1531 13th St., Columbus, IN 47201. . .Eugene I. Anderson. . .auto parts, record players.

Ashland Oil, Inc.. . .P.O. Box 391, Ashland, KY 41101. . .Orin E. Atkins. . .petroleum, chemicals, coal.

Associates Corp. of North America. . .2 Gulf & Western Plaza, New York, N.Y. 10023. . .Reese Overcash. . .financial services. . .*Gulf & Western.*

Atlantic Richfield Co.. . .515 S. Flower St., Los Angeles, CA 90071. . .Robert O. Anderson. . .petroleum. . .Anaconda.

Avco Embassy Pictures Corp.. . .6601 Romaine St., Los Angeles, CA 90038. . .William E. Chaikin. . .film distributor. . .*Avco Corp.*

Avco Financial Services, Inc.. . .620 Newport Center Dr., Newport Beach, CA 92660. . .H. Wallace Merryman. . .financial services, insurance. . .*Avco Corp.*

Avery International Corp.. . .415 Huntington Dr., San Marino, CA 91108. . .Charles D. Miller. . .labels.

Avis, Inc.. . .1114 Ave. of the Americas, N.Y., NY 10036. . .James F. Calvano. . .car, truck rental/leasing. . .*Norton Simon.*

Avon Products, Inc.. . .9 West 57th St., N.Y., NY 10019. . .David W. Mitchell. . .cosmetics. . .Tiffany.

Babcock & Wilcox Co.. . .1010 Common St., P.O. Box 60035, New Orleans, LA 70160.. . .George G. Zipf. . .steam generating systems, air pollution control. . .*J. Ray McDermott.*

Bali Co.. . .260 Executive Park Blvd., Winston-Salem, NC 27103. . .Terry L. Johnson. . .bras, swimwear. . .*Hanes.*

Ball Corp.. . .345 S. High St., Muncie, IN 47302. . .J.W. Fisher. . .glass & metal containers, computer equip., aerospace instruments.

Bausch & Lomb. . .One Lincoln First Square, Rochester, NY 14601. . .Daniel G. Schuman. . .vision care products, instruments.
Baxter Travenol Labs Inc.. . .One Baxter Pky., Deerfield, IL. 60015. . .Vernon R. Loucks Jr.. . .medical care.
James B. Beam Distilling Co.. . .500 N. Michigan Ave., Chicago, IL 60611. . .Julian J. McShane Jr.. . .distilled beverages. . .*American Brands.*
Beatrice Foods Co.. . .2 La Salle St., Chicago, IL 60602. . .James L. Dutt. . .foods. . .Buxton; Charmglow; Dannon; Royal Crown; Samsonite; Louis Sherry; Stiffel; Tropicana.
Beech Aircraft Corp.. . .Wichita, KS 67201. . .Mrs. O. A. Beech. . .aircraft mfg.. . .*Raytheon Co.*
Beech-Nut Foods Corp.. . .1035 Virginia Dr., Ft. Washington, PA 19034. . .Frank C. Nicholas. . .food processing. . .*Nestle.*
Bell & Howell Co.. . .7100 McCormick Rd., Lincolnwood, IL 60645.. . .Donald N. Frey. . .audio-visual instruments.
Bendix Corp.. . .The Bendix Center, Southfield, MI 48076. . .W. P. Panney. . .automotive, aerospace, electronics, forest prods.
Beneficial Personal Finance Co. Ltd.. . .Beneficial Bldg., Wilmington, DE 19899. . .F.M.W. Caspersen. . .financial services. . .*Beneficial Corp.*
Bethlehem Steel Corp.. . .8th & Eaton Ave., Bethlehem, PA 18016. . .Lewis W. Foy. . .steel & steel prods.
Betty Crocker.. . .9200 Wayzata Blvd., Minneapolis, MN 55440. . .Donald L. Knutzen. . .dessert mixes. . .*General Mills.*
Bic Pen Corp.. . .One Wiley St., Milford, CT 06460. . .Robert P. Adler. . .pens, lighters, shavers.
Binney & Smith Inc.. . .1100 Church La., Easton, PA 18042. . .Russell J. McChesney. . .art material and supplies. . .Crayola crayons, Liquitex artists colors.
Black & Decker Mfg. Co.. . .701 E. Joppa Rd., Towson, MD 21204. . .Francis P. Lucier. . .power tools.
H & R Block, Inc.. . .4410 Main St., Kansas City, MO 64111. . .Henry W. Block. . .tax preparation.
Boeing Company. . .7755 E. Marginal Way So., Seattle, WA 98108. . .T.A. Wilson. . .aerospace.
Boise Cascade Corp.. . .P.O. Box 50, Boise, ID 83728. . .Jon H. Miller. . .timber, paper, wood prod.
Borden, Inc.. . .277 Park Ave., N.Y., NY 10017. . .Augustine R. Marusi. . .food, industrial and consumer prods.
Borg-Warner Corp.. . .200 S. Michigan Ave., Chicago, IL 60604. . .Robert O. Bass. . .air conditioning, plastics, vehicle components, financial & protective services.
Braniff Airways, Inc.. . .Braniff Blvd., Dallas-Ft. Worth Airport, TX 75261. . .Harding L. Lawrence. . .air transportation.
Braun North America. . .Prudential Tower Bldg., Boston, MA 02199. . .Richard S. Rohe. . .consumer prods.. . .*Gillette.*
Brink's, Inc.. . .234 E. 24th St., Chicago, IL 60616. . .N.T. Camicia. . .armored car security. . .*Pittston.*
Bristol-Myers Co.. . .345 Park Ave., N.Y., NY 10022. . .Richard L. Gelb. . .toiletries, cosmetics, household prods., pharmaceuticals. . .Clairol; Drackett; Mead Johnson.
Brown & Williamson Tobacco Co.. . .1600 West Hill St., Louisville, KY 40210. . .John Alar. . .tobacco. . .*Brown & Williamson Industries Inc.*
Brunswick Corp.. . .One Brunswick Plaza, Skokie, IL 60075. . .Jack F. Reichert. . .marine, medical, recreation prods.
Bucyrus-Erie Co.. . .P.O. Box 56, S. Milwaukee, WI 53172. . .W. B. Winter. . .mining, construction equip.
Bulova Watch Co., Inc.. . .Bulova Park, Flushing, NY 11370. . .Andrew H. Tisch. . .watch mfg. and sales.
Burger King Corp.. . .P.O. Box 520783, Miami, FL 33152. . .Donald N. Smith. . .fast-food restaurants. . .*Pillsbury.*
Burlington Industries, Inc.. . .3330 W. Friendly Ave., Greensboro, N.C.. . .W. A. Klopman. . .textile mfg.
Burlington Northern Inc.. . .176 E. 5th St., St. Paul, MN 55101. . .N.M. Lorentzsen. . .transportation, natural resources.
Buxton, Inc.. . .265 Main St., Agawan, MA 01001. . .C. William Crain. . .leather goods. . .*Beatrice Foods.*

CBS Inc.. . .51 W. 52d St., N.Y., NY 10019. . .John D. Backe. . .broadcasting, publishing, recorded music, leisure prods.
CNA Financial Corp.. . .CNA Plaza, Chicago, IL 60685. . .Laurence A. Tisch. . .insurance services.. . .*Loews Corp.*
CPC International, Inc.. . .International Plaza, Englewood Cliffs, NJ 07632. . .J.W. McKee Jr.. . .branded food items, corn wet milling prods.. . .Best Foods; Knorr Soups; S.B. Thomas.
Cadbury Schweppes USA Inc.. . .1200 High Ridge Rd., Stamford, CT 06905. . .Robert E. Ix. . .chocolate bars, carbonated beverages, cocktail mixers. . .*Cadbury Schweppes Ltd.*
Caloric Corp.. . .Washington & Heffner Sts., Topton, PA 19562. . .Kenneth J. Haas. . .major appliances. . .*Raytheon Co.*
Campbell Soup Co.. . .Campbell Pl., Camden, NJ 08101. . .Harold A. Shaub. . .convenience foods. . .Godiva Chocolates; Pepperidge Farm; Vlasic Foods; Swanson Frozen Foods; Franco-American; V-8 vegetable juice; Hanover Trail restaurants.
Campbell Taggart, Inc.. . .6211 Lemmon Ave., Dallas, TX 75209. . .C.B. Lane. . .bakeries, food prods., Mexican restaurants.
Canada Dry Corp.. . .100 Park Ave., N.Y., NY 10017. . .Richard Armstrong. . .soft drinks. . .*Norton Simon.*
Cannon Mills Co.. . .P.O. Box 107, Kannapolis, NC 28081. . .Harold P. Hornaday. . .textile mfg. and marketing.
Carborundum Co.. . .P.O. Box 156, Niagara Falls, NY 14302. . .Paul W. Joy. . .abrasives, air & water pollution control equip., refractories, insulation. . .*Kennecott Copper.*
Carnation Co.. . .5045 Wilshire Blvd., Los Angeles, CA 90036. . .H.E. Olson. . .food prods.. . .Contadina.
Carrier Corp.. . .P.O. Box 4800, Syracuse, NY 13221. . .Melvin Holm. . .air conditioning, refrigeration, chemical specialties. . .*United Technologies.*
Carte Blanche Corp.. . .3460 Wilshire Blvd., Los Angeles, CA 90010. . .P.K. Dunsire. . .travel, entertainment credit card. . .*Avco Corp.*
Castle & Cooke, Inc.. . .Financial Plaza of the Pacific, P.O. Box 2990, Honolulu, HI 96802. . .D.J. Kirchhoff. . .food processing. . .Dole, Bumble Bee.
Caterpillar Tractor Co.. . .100 N.E. Adams St., Peoria, IL 61629. . .Robert E. Gilmore. . .heavy duty earth-moving equip., diesel engines.
Celanese Corp.. . .1211 Ave. of the Americas, N.Y., NY 10036. . .John D. Macomber. . .chemicals, fibers, plastics, and specialties.
Cessna Aircraft Co.. . .P.O. Box 1521, Wichita, KS 67201. . .Russell W. Meyer Jr.. . .aircraft, propellers, fluid power systems.
Champion Home Builders Co.. . .5573 North St., Dryden, MI 48428. . .Joseph J. Morris. . .mobile homes, commuter vans & buses; delivery trucks.
Champion Spark Plug Co.. . .P.O. Box 910, Toledo, OH 43661. . .R.A. Stranahan Jr.. . .spark plugs.
Chap Stick Co.. . .1000 Robins Rd., Lynchburg, VA 24505. . .D.E. French. . .drugs, cosmetics, household prods.. . .*A.H. Robins.*
Chesebrough-Pond's Inc.. . .33 Benedict Pl., Greenwich, CT 06830. . .Ralph E. Ward. . .cosmetics, toiletries, clothing, food prods., footwear. . .Adolph's Ltd.; G.H. Bass; Health-tex; Prince Matchabelli; Ragu.
Chicago Pneumatic Tool Co.. . .6 E. 44th St., N.Y., NY 10017. . .T.P. Latimer. . .compressors, pneumatic tools, automotive service tools, rotary water wells, blast hole drills.
Chris Craft Industries, Inc.. . .600 Madison Ave., N.Y., NY 10022. . .Herbert J. Siegel. . .pleasure boats, TV broadcasting, mail order sales.
Chromalloy American Corp.. . .120 S. Central Ave., St. Louis, MO 63105. . .Wesley J. Barta. . .agricultural equip., consumer prods., financial services, textiles and apparel, marine and land transport.
Chrysler Corp.. . .P.O. Box 1919, Detroit, MI 48231. . .Lee Iacocca. . .cars, trucks.
Cities Service Co.. . .P.O. Box 300, Tulsa, OK 74102. . .Charles J. Waidezich. . .industrial chemicals, oil.
Clorox Co.. . .1221 Broadway, Oakland, CA 94612. . .Edwin H. Shutt Jr.. . .retail consumer prods.
Coastal Corp.. . .9 Greenway Plaza, Houston, TX 77046. . .O. S. Wyatt Jr.. . .petroleum products, coal, and natural gas.
Coats & Clark Inc.. . .72 Cummings Point Rd., Stamford, CT 06902. . .R.G. Laidlaw. . .thread, yarn, slide fasteners.
Coca-Cola Co.. . .310 North Ave., Atlanta, GA 30301. . .J. Paul Austin. . .soft drink syrups, citrus and fruit juices, wines, plastics. . .Taylor Wine.
Colgate-Palmolive Co.. . .300 Park Ave., N.Y., NY 10022. . .Keith Crane. . .laundry, cleaning, personal, and health care prods., sports prods., foods. . .Kendall Co.; Riviani Foods; Marisa Christina.
Collins & Aikman Corp.. . .210 Madison Ave., N.Y., NY 10016. . .Donald F. McCullough. . .textiles.
Columbia Pictures Industries, Inc.. . .711 5th Ave., N.Y., NY 10022. . .Francis T. Vincent Jr.. . .entertainment.
Commonwealth Oil Refining Co., Inc.. . .8626 Tesoro Dr., San Antonio, TX 78217. . .C. Howard Hardesty Jr. . .oil refining and petrochemicals.
Conagra, Inc.. . .Kiewit Plaza, Omaha, NE 68131. . .Charles M. Harper. . .grain processing & merchandising, poultry products.
Consolidated Foods Corp.. . .135 S. La Salle, Chicago, IL 60603. . .John H. Bryan Jr.. . .foods, identification prods.,

housewares, appliances, clothing. . .Electrolux; Fuller Brush; Hanes; Gant; Popsicle; Sara Lee; Shasta; Tyco.

Consolidated Rail Corp. (Conrail). . .6 Penn Center Plaza, Phila., PA 19104. . .Edward G. Jordan. . .railroads.

Continental Air Lines, Inc.. . .7300 World Way West, Los Angeles, CA 90009. . .A. L. Feldman. . .commercial air carrier.

The Continental Group, Inc.. . . One Harbor Plaza, Stamford, CT 06902. . .R. S. Hatfield. . .natural resources, financial services, packaging; Continental Can.

Continental Oil Co.. . . High Ridge Park, Stamford, CT 06904. . .H.W. Blauvelt. . .oil, natural gas, plastics.

Control Data Corp.. . .P.O. Box 0, Minneapolis, MN 55440. . .Wm. C. Norris. . .computing, financial services.

Converse. . .55 Fordham Rd., Wilmington, MA 01887. . .J.P. O'Neil. . .athletic, recreational, and leisure footwear. . .*Eltra.*

Thomas Cook, Inc.. . .380 Madison Ave., N.Y., NY 10017. . .David Lorretto. . .travel.

Adolph Coors Company. . . East of Town, Golden, CO 80401. . .Joe Coors. . .brewery.

Corning Glass Works. . . Houghton Park, Corning, NY 14830. . .Amory Houghton Jr.. . .glass mfg.

Crane Co.. . .300 Park Ave., N.Y., NY 10022. . .Thomas M. Evans. . .fluid & pollution controls, steel, cement, building prods.

Crown Cork & Seal Co.. . .9300 Ashton Rd., Phila., PA 19136. . .J.F. Connelly. . .cans, packaging machinery & equip.

Crown Zellerbach Corp.. . . One Bush St., San Francisco, CA 94102. . .C.R. Dahl. . .pulp and paper products; forest products.

Dairylea Cooperative Inc.. . . One Blue Hill Plaza, Pearl River, NY 10965. . .Richard E. Richmond. . .dairy prods.

Dan River Inc.. . .P.O. Box 6126, Greenville, SC 29606. . .Robert S. Small. . .textiles.

Dana Corp.. . .4500 Dorr St., Toledo, OH 43697. . .Gerald B. Mitchell. . .truck and auto parts supplies.

Deere & Company. . . John Deere Rd., Moline, IL 61265. . .William A. Hewitt. . .farm, industrial, and outdoor power equip.

Del Monte Corp.. . .P.O. Box 3575, San Francisco, CA 94119. . .R.G. Landis. . .food prods.

Delta Air Lines, Inc.. . . Hartsfield Atlanta Intl. Airport, Atlanta, GA 30320. . .David C. Garrett Jr.. . .air transportation.

Diamond International Corp.. . .733 3d Ave., N.Y., NY 10017. . .William J. Koslo. . .mfg. lumber, matches, woodenware, machinery, pulp & paper, packaging, specialty printing.

Diamond Shamrock Corp.. . .2300 Southland Ctr., Dallas, TX 75201. . .W.H. Bricker. . .energy, technology, and chemicals.

DiGiorgio Corp.. . . One Maritime Plaza, San Francisco, CA 94111. . .Robert C. McCracken. . .consumer and forest prods. distributor. . .TreeSweet; Carando; White Rose.

Digital Equipment Corp.. . .146 Main St., Maynard, MA 01754. . .Kenneth H. Olsen. . .computers.

Walt Disney Productions. . .500 S. Buena Vista St., Burbank, CA 91521. . .E. Cardon Walker. . .motion pictures, amusement parks. . .Disneyland, Walt Disney World.

Dr Pepper Co.. . .5523 E. Mockingbird Lane, Dallas, TX 75265. . .W.W. Clements. . .soft drinks.

Dow Chemical Co.. . .2020 Dow Center, Midland, MI 48640. . .P.F. Oreffice. . .chemicals.

Duffy-Mott Co., Inc.. . .370 Lexington Ave., N.Y., NY 10017. . .Raymond M. Anrig. . .fruit prods.. . .*American Brands.*

Dunlop Tire & Rubber Corporation. . .P.O. Box 1109, Buffalo, NY 14240. . .A. Neville Procter. . .tires, sporting goods.

E.I. du Pont de Nemours & Co.. . .1007 Market St., Wilmington, DE 19898. . .I. S. Shapiro. . .chemical mfg.

Durkee Foods. . .900 Union Commerce Bldg., Cleveland, OH 44115. . .R.E. Dorfmeyer. . .foods, food services. . .*SCM.*

Dutch Boy Inc.. . .500 Central Ave., Northfield, IL 60093. . .Peter R. Harvey. . .lighting, metal, plastic prods., paints & coatings.

Eastern Air Lines Inc.. . . Miami International Airport, Miami, FL 33148. . .Frank Borman. . .air transportation.

Eastman Kodak Co.. . .343 State, Rochester, NY 14650. . .Walter A. Fallon. . .photographic materials & equip.

Electrolux. . .2777 Summer St., Stamford, CT 06905. . .Charles A. McKee. . .household cleaning equip.. . .*Consolidated Foods.*

Elizabeth Arden, Inc.. . .1345 Ave. of the Americas, N.Y., NY 10019. . .J. Richard Zapapas. . .cosmetics. . .*Eli Lilly.*

Emerson Electric Co.. . .8100 W. Florissant Ave., St. Louis, MO 63136. . .C.F. Knight. . .electrical/electronics products.

Emery Air Freight Corp.. . . Old Danbury Rd., Wilton, CT 06897. . .John C. Emery Jr.. . .air freight forwarder.

Envirotech Corp.. . .3000 Sand Hill Rd., Menlo Park, CA 94025. . .Robert L. Chambers. . .supplier of equipment and technology for air and water pollution control.

Esmark, Inc.. . .55 E. Monroe St., Chicago, IL 60603. . .Donald P. Kelley. . .holding co.. . .International Playtex; Estech; Vickers Energy; STP.

Ethyl Corp.. . .330 S. 4th St., Richmond, VA 23217. . .Floyd D. Gottwald Jr.. . .petroleum and industrial chemicals, plastics, aluminum, energy development.

Ex-Cell-O Corporation. . .2855 Coolidge Rd., Troy, MI 48084. . .E. Paul Casey. . .industrial tools, automotive & aerospace components, ordnance, abrasives.

Exxon Corp.. . .1251 Ave. of the Americas, N.Y., NY 10020. . .C.C. Garvin Jr.. . .chemical, oil, exploration prods.

Fabergé, Inc.. . .1345 Ave. of the Americas, N.Y., NY 10019. . .George Barrie. . .cosmetics, toiletries. . .Brut.

Max Factor & Co.. . .1655 N. McCadden Pl., Hollywood, CA 90028. . .Robert Kamerschen. . .cosmetics. . .*Norton Simon.*

Fairmont Foods Co.. . .P.O. Box 19683, Houston, TX 77024. . .E.W. Kelley. . .convenience stores, dairies, snacks.

Farberware. . .1500 Bassett Ave., Bronx, NY 10461. . .Fred R. Sullivan. . .electrical appliances, cookware. . .*Walter Kidde.*

Fedders Corp.. . . Woodbridge Ave., Edison, NJ 08817. . .Salvatore Giordano Jr.. . .air conditioners, appliances. . .Norge.

Federal Company. . .1755-D Lynnfield, Suite 149, Memphis, TN 38138. . .L.K. McKee. . .food prods.

Federated Department Stores, Inc.. . .7 W. 7th St., Cincinnati, OH 45202. . .Harold Krensky. . .dept. stores. . .Abraham & Straus; Bloomingdale's; Boston Store; Bullock's; Burdines; Filene's; Foley's; Goldsmith's; Lazarus; Levy's; I. Magnin; Rich's; Rike's; Sanger-Harris; Shillito's.

Fiat Motors of North America, Inc.. . .155 Chestnut Ridge Rd., Montvale, NJ 07645. . .Claudio Ferrari. . .automobiles.

Fieldcrest Mills, Inc.. . . Eden, NC 27288. . .William C. Battle. . .textiles. . .Karastan Rugs.

Firestone Tire & Rubber Co.. . .1200 Firestone Pkwy., Akron, OH 44317. . .Richard A. Riley. . .tires, rubber and metal prods.

Fleetwood Enterprises, Inc.. . .3125 Myers St., Riverside, CA 92523. . .John C. Crean. . .mobile, motor homes, trailers.

Ford Motor Co.. . . The American Rd., Dearborn, MI 48121. . .Philip Caldwell. . .motor vehicles. . .Ford Tractor; Lincoln-Mercury.

Foster Grant Co., Inc.. . . Rte. 202-206, Somerville North, NJ 08876. . .D. Markowitz. . .sunglasses. . .*American Hoechst.*

Franklin Mint Corp.. . . Franklin Center, PA 19091. . .Charles L. Andes. . .coins, medals, sculpture, crystal, and porcelain collectibles.

R.T. French Co.. . . One Mustard St., Rochester, NY 14609. . .Robert Silkett. . .mustard, sauces.

Frigidaire. . .300 Taylor St., Dayton, OH 45442. . .Emmett B. Lewis Jr.. . .major electrical appliances. . .*General Motors.*

Fuller Brush Co.. . . Westport Addition, P.O. Box 729, Great Bend, KS 67530. . .Nat Zivin. . .housewares, personal care prods.. . .*Consolidated Foods.*

GAF Corp.. . .140 W. 51st St., New York, NY 10020. . .Dr. Jesse Werner. . .chemicals, bldg. materials, photographic and reprographic products.

Gant Incorporated. . .689 5th Ave., N.Y., NY 10022. . .William R. Keegan. . .shirts, sportswear. . .Palm Beach Inc./*Consolidated Foods.*

General Dynamics Corp.. . . Pierre Laclede Ctr., St. Louis, MO 63105. . .D. S. Lewis. . .aerospace, shipping, telecommunications, coal, tactical missiles.

General Electric Co.. . .3135 Easton Ave., Fairfield, CT 06431. . .R.H. Jones. . .electrical, electronic, atomic prods.

General Foods Corp.. . .250 North, White Plains, NY 10625. . .J.L. Ferguson. . .grocery prods., fast-food restaurants. . .Burger Chef.

General Host Corp.. . .22 Gate House Rd., Stamford, CT 06902. . .Harris J. Ashton. . .foods, agricultural prods.. . .Van de Kamp's; Cudahy.

General Mills, Inc.. . .9200 Wayzata Blvd., Minneapolis, MN 55440 . . .E. Robert Kinney. . .foods, toys, restaurants, fashion and specialty retailing. . .Kenner Products; Parker Brothers; Monet; Ship 'N Shore; The Talbots.

General Motors Corp.. . . Gen. Motors Bldg., Detroit, MI 48202. . .Thomas A. Murphy. . .motor vehicles, household appliances. . .AC Spark Plug; Buick; Cadillac; Chevrolet; Delco; Frigidaire; G.M. Acceptance Corp.

General Telephone & Electronics Corp.. . . One Stamford Forum, Stamford, CT 06904. . .Theodore F. Brophy. . .utilities. . .Sylvania Lighting.

General Tire & Rubber Co.. . . One General St., Akron, OH 44329. . .M.G. O'Neil. . .tires, rubber prods.

Genesco Inc.. . . Genesco Park, Nashville, TN 37202. . .John L. Hannigan. . .footwear and men's clothing. . .Hardy Amies; Jarman; Flagg Bros.; Bell Bros.; MALE; Greif; Johnston & Murphy.

Georgia-Pacific Corp.. . .900 S.W. 5th Ave., Portland, OR 97204. . .Robert F. Flowerree. . .wood and gypsum building prods., pulp, paper, chemicals.

Gerber Products Co.. . .445 State St., Fremont, MI 49412. . .Arthur J. Frens. . .baby foods, clothing, nursery accessories.

Getty Oil Co.. . .3810 Wilshire Blvd., Los Angeles, CA 90010. . .Sidney R. Petersen. . .petroleum exploration & production.

Gillette Co.. . . Prudential Tower Bldg., Boston, MA 02199. . .Colman M. Mockler Jr.. . .razors, pens, toiletries, appliances. . .Paper Mate; Ship 'N Shore.

Gimbel Brothers, Inc.. . .1275 Broadway, N.Y., NY. . .A.R. Johnson. . .dept. store. . .*Brown & Williamson Tobacco Corp.*

B.F. Goodrich Company. . .500 S. Main St., Akron, OH 44318. . .John D. Ong. . .rubber, chemical, plastic prods.

Goodyear Tire & Rubber Co.. . .1144 E. Market St., Akron, OH 44316. . .Charles J. Pilliod Jr.. . .tires, rubber prods.. . .Kelly-Springfield.

Gould Inc.. . .10 Gould Center, Rolling Meadows, IL 60008. . .Daniel T. Carroll. . .electrical and industrial prods.

W.R. Grace & Co.. . . Grace Plaza, 1114 Ave. of the Americas, N.Y., NY 10036. . .J. Peter Grace. . .chemicals, natural resources, consumer prods. and services, restaurants.. . .Baker & Taylor; Channel Home Centers; Herman's World of Sporting Goods.

Grand Union Co.. . .100 Broadway, Elmwood Park, NJ 07407. . .James Wood. . .retail supermarket chain. . .*Cavenham Ltd.*

Great Atlantic & Pacific Tea Co.. . .2 Paragon Dr., Montvale, NJ 07645. . .Jonathan L. Scott. . .retail food stores.

Great Western United Corp.. . .716 Metro Bank Bldg., Denver, CO 80202. . .W.H. Hunt. . .sugar refining, real estate, restaurants. . .Shakey's.

Green Giant Co.. . . Hazeltine Gates, Chaska, MN 55318. . .John M. Stafford. . .restaurants, food processing. . .*Pillsbury.*

Greyhound Corp.. . .111 W. Clarendon, Phoenix, AZ 85013. . .Gerald H. Trautman. . .meat and poultry packer, bus transportation, soap prods., food, financial services. . .Armour; Bucilla; Carey Transportation.

Grumman Corp.. . .1111 Stewart, Bethpage, NY 11714. . .John C. Bierwirth. . .aerospace, buses, truck bodies, data computing services.

Gulf Oil Corp.. . .439 7th Ave., Pittsburgh, PA 15219. . .Jerry McAfee. . .production and marketing of petroleum and related products.

Gulf & Western Industries, Inc.. . . One Gulf & Western Plaza, N.Y., NY 10023. . .David N. Judelson. . .diversified manufacturer. . .Consolidated Cigar; Schrafft Candy; Kayser-Roth; Associates Corp. of No. Amer.; Paramount Pictures; Simon & Schuster, Madison Square Garden; Simmons; A.P.S., Inc.

Hamilton Beach. . . Scovill Sq., Waterbury, CT 06720. . .John J. Flaherty. . .electric housewares. . .*Scovill.*

Hanes Corp.. . .2000 W. 1st St., Winston-Salem, NC 27101. . .Robert E. Elberson. . .consumer packaged goods. . .*Consolidated Foods.*

Hart Schaffner & Marx. . .36 S. Franklin St., Chicago, IL 60606. . .Jerome S. Gore. . .apparel manufacturer and retailer. . .Hickey-Freeman.

Hartz Mountain Corp.. . .700 S. 4th St., Harrison, NJ 07029. . .David D. Lovitz. . .pet supplies.

Havatampa Corp.. . .P.O. Box 1909, Tampa, FL 33601. . .Doyle E. Carlton. . .cigars.

Health-tex Inc.. . .1411 Broadway, N.Y., NY 10018. . .Ralph E. Ward. . .children's apparel. . .*Chesebrough-Pond's.*

H.J. Heinz Co.. . .P.O. Box 57, Pittsburgh, PA 15230. . .Anthony J.F. O'Reilly. . .foods. . .Ore-Ida; Star-Kist; Weight Watchers Intl.

Helene Curtis Industries, Inc.. . .4401 W. North Ave., Chicago, IL 60639. . .Gerald Gidwitz. . .beauty products for hair care.

Hershey Food Corp.. . .100 Mansion Rd., Hershey, PA 17033. . .William Dearden. . .chocolate & confectionery prods. & services. . .San Giorgio Macaroni; Friendly Ice Cream.

Hertz Corp.. . .660 Madison Ave., N.Y., NY 10021. . .Frank A. Olson. . .car, truck, equipment renting and leasing. . .*RCA.*

Heublein, Inc.. . . Farmington, CT 06032. . .Hicks B. Waldron. . .alcoholic beverages, foods. . .Smirnoff, Kentucky Fried Chicken.

Hewlett-Packard Co.. . .1501 Page Mill Rd., Palo Alto, CA 94304. . .John A. Young. . .electronics equip.

Hilton Hotels Corp.. . .9880 Wilshire Blvd., Beverly Hills, CA 90210. . .Barron Hilton. . .hotels. . .*Trans World Corp.*

Hobart Corp.. . . World Headquarters, Troy, OH 45374. . .David B. Meeker. . .food equip., appliances. . .KitchenAid.

Holiday Inns, Inc.. . .3742 Lamar Ave., Memphis, TN 38195. . .Roy E. Winegardner. . .hotels, restaurants, casinos, steamships.

Honda Motor Co., Inc., American. . .100 W. Alondra Blvd., Gardena, CA 90247. . .K. Yoshibawa. . .distributor, autos, motorcycles, power prods.

Honda Motor Co., Ltd.. . .P.O. Box 50-100, Gardena, CA 90247. . .Kiyoshi Kawashima. . .mfg. motorcycles, cars, power prods.

Honeywell, Inc.. . . Honeywell Plaza, Minneapolis, MN 55408. . .E.W. Spencer. . .information and control systems.

H.P. Hood Inc.. . .500 Rutherford Ave., Boston, MA 02129. . .Edward Gelsthorpe. . .dairy and food prods.

Hoover Ball & Bearing Co.. . .P.O. Box 1003, Ann Arbor, MI 41806. . .J.F. Daly. . .aluminum, steel, plastic prods.

Hoover Co.. . .101 E. Maple St., No. Canton, OH 44720. . .M. R. Rawson. . .electrical floorcare and laundry prods.

Geo. A. Hormel & Co.. . .501 16th Ave. N.E., Austin, MN 55912. . .I.J. Holton. . .meat packaging, pork and beef prods.

Household Finance Corp.. . .2700 Sanders Rd., Prospect Heights, IL 60106. . .G.R. Ellis. . .financial and insurance services, merchandising, manufacturing, transportation. . .King-Seeley Thermos; National Car Rental; City Products Corp.

Howard Johnson Co.. . . One Howard Johnson Plaza, Boston, MA 02125. . .Howard B. Johnson. . .restaurants, motor lodges.

Hughes Tool Co.. . .P.O. Box 2539, Houston, TX 77001. . .supplier of products and services to the oil, gas, & mining industries; mfg. of rock drilling bits & tool joints.

Hunt-Wesson Foods, Inc.. . .1645 W. Valencia Dr.. . .Fullerton, CA 92634. . .William K. Hood. . .food prods.. . .*Norton Simon.*

IC Industries, Inc. . . One Illinois Ctr., 111 E. Wacker Dr., Chicago, IL 60601. . .William B. Johnson. . .diversified prods. and services. . .Bubble-Up; Dad's Root Beer; Midas International Corp.; Pepsi-Cola Bottlers; Pet Inc.

Ideal Toy Corp.. . .184-10 Jamaica Ave., Hollis, NY 11423. . .Lionel A. Weintraub. . .toys.

Ingredient Technology Corp.. . .245 Park Ave., N.Y., NY 10017. . .Rudolph Eberstadt Jr.. . .manufacturer, food ingredients.

Insilco Corp.. . .1000 Research Pkwy., Meriden, CT 06450. . .Durand B. Blatz. . .diversified manufacturer. . .International Silver; Red Devil Paints and Chemicals; Rolodex.

Interco Incorporated. . .P.O. Box 8777, St. Louis, MO 63102. . .John K. Riedy. . .apparel, footwear mfg., general retail.

International Business Machines Corp.. . . Old Orchard Rd., Armonk, NY 10504. . .Frank T. Cary. . .information handling systems, equipment, services.

International Harvester Co.. . .401 N. Michigan Ave., Chicago, IL 60611. . .Warren J. Hayford. . .trucks, agricultural, construction equipment, turbomachinery.

International Paper Co.. . .220 E. 42d St., N.Y., NY 10017. . .J. Stanford Smith. . .paper, wood prods.

International Telephone and Telegraph Corp.. . .320 Park Ave., N.Y., NY 10022. . .R.V. Araskog. . .communication systems, multi-prods.. . .Sheraton Corp., Hartford Insurance.

Iroquois Brands, Ltd.. . .41 W. Putnam Ave., Greenwich, CT 06830. . .Terence J. Fox. . .beverages, nutritional and specialty food prods.. . .All World Brands; Champale; Yoo-Hoo Chocolate Beverage; Leeds-Dixon Laboratories; Magic Mountain Herb Tea.

Jeep Corp.. . .27777 Franklin Rd., Southfield, MI 48034. . .W. Paul Tippett Jr.. . .vehicles. . .*American Motors.*

Andrew Jergens Co.. . .2535 Spring Grove Ave., Cincinnati, OH 45214. . .Thomas C. Hays. . .toiletries, cosmetics. . .*American Brands.*

Johns-Manville Corp.. . .P.O. Box 5108, Denver, CO 80217. . .Fred L. Punsack. . .insulations, pipe systems, building prods.

Johnson & Johnson. . .501 George St., New Brunswick, NJ 08903. . .James E. Burke. . .surgical dressings, pharmaceuticals, health and baby prods.

Jonathan Logan, Inc.. . .P.O. Box 122, Midtown Sta., N.Y., NY 10018. . .Richard J. Schwartz. . .apparel. . .Act III; Butte Knitting Mills; Etienne Aigner; Misty Harbor.

Kaiser Aluminum & Chemical. . .300 Lakeside Dr., Oakland, CA 94643. . .Cornell C. Maier. . .aluminum, chemicals, real estate, refractories, international trading.

Kaiser Steel Corp.. . .P.O. Box 58, Oakland, CA 94604. . .Edgar F. Kaiser Jr.. . .iron, steel, and associated prods.

Kane-Miller Corp.. . .P.O. Box 7, Tarrytown, NY 10591. . .Stanley B. Kane. . .food processing. . .American Meat Packing.

Keebler Co.. . . One Hollow Tree Lane, Elmhurst, IL 60126. . .Thomas M. Garvin. . .cookies, crackers.

Kellogg Co.. . .235 Porter, Battle Creek, MI 49016. . .William E. LaMothe. . .ready to eat cereal & other food prods.. . .Mrs. Smith's Pie Co.; Salada Foods; Fearn International.

Kentucky Fried Chicken-Retail Stores. . . Box 92092, Los Angeles, CA 90009. . .Chet Rondinella. . .fast food restaurants. . .*Heublin.*

Kerr-McGee Corp.. . .123 Robert S. Kerr Ave., Oklahoma City, OK 73102. . .Dean A. McGee. . .natural resources

Walter Kidde & Co., Inc.. . .9 Brighton Rd., Clifton, NJ 07015. . .Fred R. Sullivan. . .mfgr. safety, security, protection, industrial, commercial, consumer and recreation prods. and services. . .E.J. Burke Security; Farberware; Lucien Piccard.

Kimberly-Clark Corp.. . .N. Lake St., Neenah, WI 54956. . .Darwin E. Smith. . .paper and lumber prods.

K mart Corp.. . .3100 W. Big Beaver Rd., Troy, MI 48084. . .R.E. Dewar. . .retail stores.

Kraft, Inc.. . . Kraft Ct., Glenview, IL 60025. . .John M. Richman. . .processed, packaged food prods.

Kroger Co.. . .1014 Vine St., Cincinnati, OH 45201. . .Lyle Everingham. . .supermarkets, drugstores, food prods.

LTV Corporation. . .P.O. Box 225003, Dallas, TX 75265. . .Paul Thayer. . .steel, aerospace, meat & food prods., shipping, energy-oriented prods.. . .Vought Helicopters; Wilson Foods.

Land O'Lakes Inc.. . .614 McKinley Pl., Minneapolis, MN 55413. . .Ralph Hofstad. . .agri-business, food prods. and marketing.

Lever Brothers Co.. . .390 Park Ave., N.Y., NY 10022. . .Thomas S. Carroll. . .soaps, detergents, dentifrices, foods.

Levi Strauss & Co.. . .2 Embarcadero Center, San Francisco, CA 94106. . .Robert T. Graham. . .apparel.

Levitz Furniture Corp.. . .1317 NW 167th St., Miami, FL 33169. . .Robert M. Elliott. . .retail furniture stores.

Libbey-Owens-Ford Co.. . .811 Madison Ave., Toledo, OH 43695. . .Don T. Mc Kone. . .glass and plastic prods.

Libby, McNeil & Libby, Inc.. . .200 S. Michigan Ave., Chicago, IL 60604. . .Ian W. Murray. . .food processor. . .*Nestle.*

Liggett Group Inc.. . .100 Paragon Dr., Montvale, NJ 07645. . .Raymond J. Mulligan. . .soft drinks, tobacco prods., spirits and wines, pet foods, home care prods., sporting goods. . .Austin, Nichols; L & M Tobacco; Pinkerton Tobacco; Allen Products (Alpo); Pepsi-Cola; National Oats.

Eli Lilly & Company. . .P.O. Box 618, Indianapolis, IN 46206. . .Richard D. Wood. . .mfg. human health, agricultural, cosmetic prods.. . .Elizabeth Arden; Cardiac Pacemakers.

Thomas J. Lipton Inc.. . .800 Sylvan Ave., Englewood Cliffs, NJ 07632. . .H.M. Tibbetts. . .importer of teas, mfg. food prods.. . .Good Humor; Knox.

Litton Industries, Inc.. . .360 N. Crescent, Beverly Hills, CA 90210. . .Charles B. Thornton. . .commercial, consumer, industrial, and defense related products.

Lockheed Corp.. . .2555 N. Hollywood Way, Burbank, CA 91520. . .Lawrence O. Kitchen. . .aerospace.

Loews Corp.. . .666 5th Ave., N.Y., NY 10019. . .Laurence A. Tisch. . .tobacco prods., motion picture theaters, hotels. . .CNA Financial Corp.; Loew's Theatres; Lorillard Int'l. Sales.

Longines-Wittnauer, Inc.. . .145 Huguenot St., New Rochelle, NY 10810. . .R.E. Kirby. . .watches. . .*Westinghouse Electric.*

M. Lowenstein & Sons, Inc.. . .1430 Broadway, N.Y., NY 10018. . .L. Terrell Sovey Jr.. . .textiles. . .Wamsutta Fabrics.

Lucky Stores, Inc.. . .630 Clark Ave., Dublin, CA 94566. . .Wayne H. Fisher. . .supermarkets, restaurants, dept., fabric, and automotive stores.

MCA Inc.. . .100 Universal City Plaza, Universal City, CA 91608. . .Lew R. Wasserman. . .motion pictures, television; recreation services; record, music, book publishing; savings and loan. . .Columbia Savings & Loan; G.P. Putnam's Sons; Berkley Books; DisoVision; Spencer Gifts; Universal City Studios.

M E I Corp.. . .733 Marquette Ave., Minneapolis, MN 55402. . .Donald E. Benson. . .soft drink bottler, distributor.

Magic Chef, Inc.. . .740 King Edward Ave. S.E., Cleveland, TN 37311. . .S.B. Rymer Jr.. . .major household appliances, heating and air conditioning equip., soft drink vending machines. . .Admiral; Norge; Gaffers & Sattler; Johnson; Dixie-Narco.

Magnavox Consumer Electronics. . .1700 Magnavox Way, Ft. Wayne, IN 48804. . .Kenneth C. Meinken. . .electrical, electronic components. . .*North American Philips.*

Marmon Group, Inc.. . .39 S. La Salle St., Chicago, IL 60603. . .Robert A. Pritzker. . .metal prods., mining equip., automobile seat belts. . .Hammond Organ Co.; Kangol Headwear.

Marriott Corp.. . .5161 River Rd., Wash., DC 20016. . .J. Willard Marriott Jr.. . .food service, lodging and leisure time.

Martin Marietta Corp.. . .6801 Rockledge Dr., Bethesda, MD 20034. . .F. Donald Rauth. . .diversified manufacturer, Martin Marietta Aluminum Inc.

Masonite Corp.. . .29 N. Wacker Dr., Chicago, IL 60606. . .Samuel S. Greeley. . .building materials.

Massey-Ferguson Inc.. . .1901 Bell Ave., Des Moines, IA 50315. . .D.G. Kettering. . .farm machinery. . .*Massey-Ferguson Ltd.*

Matsushita Electric Corp. of America. . . One Panasonic Way, Secaucus, NJ 07094. . .T. Mizutani. . .consumer, industrial electronic prods.. . .Panasonic; Quasar Electronics.

Mattel, Inc.. . .5150 Rosecrans Ave., Hawthorne, CA 90250. . .Robert E. Anderson. . .toys, hobbies, publishing, entertainment. . .Ringling Bros.-Barnum & Bailey; Western Publishing.

Maxell Corp. of America. . .60 Oxford Dr., Moonachie, NJ 07074. . .Mr. T. Okada. . .recording media prods. for audio, video and digital, and batteries.

Maytag Co.. . .403 W. 4th St. N., Newton, IA 50208. . .Daniel J. Krumm. . .appliances.

Thom McAn Shoe Co.. . .67 Millbrook St., Worcester, MA 01606. . .Lawrence McGourty. . .retail shoe chain. . .*Melville.*

McCall Pattern Co.. . .230 Park Ave., N.Y., NY 10017. . .Earle K. Angstadt Jr.. . .patterns. . .*Norton Simon.*

McDonald's Corp.. . . McDonald's Plaza, Oak Brook, IL 60521. . .Edward H. Schmitt. . .fast service restaurants.

McDonnell Douglas Corp.. . .P.O. Box 516, St. Louis, MO 63166. . .Sanford N. McDonnell. . .aerospace.

McGraw-Edison Co.. . .333 W. River Rd., Elgin, IL 60120. . .E.J. Williams. . .electrical equip.

Mead Corp.. . . Courthouse Plaza N.E., Dayton, OH 45463. . .Warren L. Batts. . .pulp, paper, school and office prods., furniture.

Melville Corp.. . .3000 Westchester Ave., Harrison, NY 10528. . .Francis C. Rooney Jr.. . .shoe stores, apparel, health and beauty aids. . .Foxmoor Casuals; Thom McAn; Chess King.

Memorex Corp.. . . San Tomas at Central Exp., Santa Clara, CA 95052. . .C.W. Spangle. . .computer, communication prods.

Mercedes-Benz of North America, Inc.. . . One Mercedes Dr., Montvale, NJ 07645. . .Karlfried Nordmann. . .cars, trucks, diesel engines.

Merck & Co., Inc.. . .P.O. Box 2000, Rahway, NJ 07065. . .John L. Huck. . .pharmaceuticals. . .Calgon.

Miles Laboratories, Inc.. . .1127 Myrtle St., Elkhart, IN 46515. . .T.H. Heinrichs. . .pharmaceuticals, chemicals, foods.

Miller Brewing Co.. . .3939 W. Highland Blvd., Milwaukee, WI 53208. . .John A. Murphy. . .beer. . .*Philip Morris, Inc.*

Milton Bradley Co.. . .1500 Main St., Springfield, MA 01101. . .James J. Shea Jr.. . .toys, educational materials, games, leisure time prods.. . .Playskool.

Mobil Corp.. . .150 E. 42d St., N.Y., NY 10017. . .Rawleigh Warner Jr.. . .integrated energy co.;. . .Mobil Oil Corp.; Montgomery Ward; Container Corp. of Amer.

Mohasco Corp.. . .57 Lyon St., Amsterdam, NY 12010. . .Herbert L. Shuttleworth 2d. . .home furnishings. . .Mohawk Carpet Mills.

Monet Jewelers, Inc.. . .16 E. 34th St., N.Y., NY 10016. . .Norman Gatof. . .jewelry. . .*General Mills.*

Monsanto Company. . .800 N. Lindbergh Blvd., St. Louis, MO 63166. . .John W. Hanley. . .chemicals, plastics, agricultural prods., man-made fibers, electronics.

Montgomery Ward & Co.. . .535 W. Chicago Ave., Chicago, IL 60671. . .Edward S. Donnell. . .retailing. . .*Mobil.*

Morton Norwich. . .110 N. Wacker Dr., Chicago, IL 60606. . .Charles S. Locke. . .pharmaceuticals, household prods., salt & specialty chemicals. . .Morton Salt; Pepto-Bismol.

Motorola, Inc.. . .1303 E. Algonquin Rd., Schaumburg, IL 60196. . .William J. Weiss. . .electronic equipment and components.

NCR Corp.. . .1700 S. Patterson Blvd., Dayton, OH 45479. . .Charles E. Exley Jr.. . .computers, electronic business equip.

NL Industries. . .1230 Ave. of the Americas, New York, NY 10020. . .Ray C. Adam. . .petroleum services & equipment, specialty chemicals, fabricated metal products.
Nabisco, Inc.. . . DeForest Ave., E. Hanover, NJ 07936. . .Robert M. Schaeberle. . .foods, pharmaceuticals, toys, games.
National Airlines, Inc.. . .P.O. Box 592055, Miami, FL 33159. . .E.F. Dolansky. . .air transportation.
National Broadcasting Co., Inc.. . .30 Rockefeller Plaza, N.Y., NY 10021. . .Fred Silverman. . .broadcasting. . .*RCA.*
National Car Rental System, Inc.. . .5501 Green Valley Dr., Minneapolis, MN 55437. . .J. W. James. . .vehicle transportation services. . .*Household Finance.*
National Distillers & Chemical Corp.. . .99 Park Ave., N.Y., NY 10016. . .Drummond C. Bell. . .wines and liquors, chemicals, textiles, metals, insurance. . .Almaden Vineyards.
National Semiconductor Corp.. . .2900 Semiconductor Dr., Santa Clara, CA 95051. . .Charles E. Sporck. . .semiconductors.
Nestle Co., Inc.. . .100 Bloomingdale Rd., White Plains, NY 10605. . .D.E. Guerrant. . .food products.
A.C. Nielson Co.. . . Nielson Plaza, Northbrook, IL 60062. . .Arthur C. Nielson Jr.. . .market research.
North American Philips Corp.. . .100 E. 42d St., N.Y., NY 10017. . .Cees Bruynes. . .consumer prods., electrical, electronic components, professional equip., chemicals, animal health prods.. . .Magnavox; Norelco.
Northrop Corp.. . .1800 Century Park E., Los Angeles, CA 90067. . .Thomas V. Jones. . .aircraft, electronics.
Northwest Airlines, Inc.. . . Minneapolis-St. Paul Intl. Airport, St. Paul, MN 55111. . .M. J. Lapensky. . .air transportation.
Northwest Industries, Inc.. . .6300 Sears Tower, Chicago, IL 60606. . .Ben W. Heineman. . .tubular steel, ingot moulds, batteries, soft drinks, alcoholic beverages, specialty pesticides, apparel. . .Fruit of the Loom; B.V.D.
Norton Simon Inc.. . .277 Park Ave., N.Y., NY 10017. . .David J. Mahoney. . .foods, beverages, fashion & cosmetics packaging, car rental. . .Avis; Canada Dry; Max Factor; Halston; Hunt-Wesson Foods; McCall Pattern.

Occidental Petroleum Corp.. . .10889 Wilshire Blvd., Los Angeles, CA 90024. . .Dr. Armand Hammer. . .oil, gas, chemicals, coal.
Olin Corp.. . .120 Long Ridge Rd., Stamford, CT 06904. . .John M. Henske. . .chemicals, metals, paper.
Oneida Ltd.. . . Oneida, NY 13421. . .P.T. Noyes. . .tableware, wire and cable, cookware, emblematic jewelry.
Oscar Mayer & Co., Inc.. . .P.O. Box 7188, Madison, WI 53707. . .P. Goff Beach. . .meat packing, food prods.. . .Claussen Pickle.
Oster Div.. . .5055 N. Lydell Ave., Milwaukee, WI 53217. . .L.S. Mattson. . .small electric appliances. . .*Sunbeam.*
Outboard Marine Corp.. . .100 Sea Horse Dr., Waukegan, IL 60085. . .C.D. Strang. . .outboard motors, power equip.. . .Johnson Outboards.
Owens-Corning Fiberglas Corp.. . . Fiberglas Tower, Toledo, OH 43659. . .W.W. Boeschenstein. . .glass fiber materials.
Owens-Illinois, Inc.. . .P.O. Box 1035, Toledo, OH 43666. . .Edwin D. Dodd. . .glass, corrugated, and plastic containers.

Pabst Brewing Co.. . .917 W. Juneau Ave., Milwaukee, WI 53201. . .Frank C. DeGuire. . .brewery.
Pan American World Airways. . . Pan Am Bldg., 200 Park Ave., N.Y., NY 10017. . .William T. Seawell. . .air transportation.
Panasonic Co.. . . One Panasonic Way, Secaucus, NJ 07094. . .T. Mizutani. . .consumer & industrial electronic prods.. . .*Matsushita Electric.*
Paper Mate. . . Prudential Tower Bldg., Boston, MA 02199. . .William H. Holtsnider. . .pens. . .*Gillette.*
Paramount Pictures Corp.. . . One Gulf & Western Plaza, N.Y., NY 10023. . .Michael D. Eisner. . .motion pictures, television. . .*Gulf & Western.*
Parker Pen Co.. . .219 E. Court St., Janesville, WI 53545. . .E. William Swanson. . .writing instruments, recreational equip.
Peavey Co.. . .730 2d Ave. So., Minneapolis, MN 55402. . .William G. Stocks. . .food and specialty retailing, crafts.
Penn Dixie Industries, Inc.. . .1345 Ave. of the Americas, N.Y., NY 10019. . .William J. Scharffenberger. . .steel, cement mfg.
J.C. Penney Co., Inc.. . .1301 Ave. of the Americas, N.Y., NY 10019. . .Donald V. Seibert. . .dept. stores, catalog sales, food, drugs, insurance.
Pennwalt Corp.. . . Pennwalt Bldg., 3 Pkwy., Phila., PA 19102. . .Edwin E. Tuttle. . .chemicals, health prods., precision equip.
Pepperidge Farm Inc.. . .P.O. Box 5500, Norwalk, CT 06856. . .R.G. McGovern. . .bakery prods.. . .*Campbell Soup.*
PepsiCo, Inc.. . . Anderson Hill Rd., Purchase, NY 10577. . .Andrall E. Pearson. . .soft drinks, snack foods, transportation, sporting goods.. . .Frito-Lay; Pepsi-Cola; PepsiCo Transportation; Wilson Sporting Goods.
Pet Inc.. . .400 S. 4th St., St. Louis, MO 63102. . .Boyd F. Schenk. . .food prods., store environments and distribution services, specialty retailing, consumer services. . .Whitman's Chocolates, Stuckey's, Old El Paso/*IC Industries.*
Pfizer Inc.. . .235 E. 42d St., N.Y., NY 10017. . .E.T. Pratt Jr.. . .pharmaceutical, hospital, agricultural, chemical prods.
Philip Morris Inc.. . .100 Park Ave., N.Y., NY 10017. . .George Weissman. . .cigarettes (Marlboro, Benson & Hedges 100's, Merit, Virginia Slims, Parliament Lights); beer (Miller High Life, Lite; Lowenbrau brands); soft drinks (Seven-up); specialty chemicals, paper, packaging materials, land development.
Pillsbury Co.. . .608 2d Ave. So., Minneapolis, MN 55402.. . .Winston R. Wallin. . .food. . .Burger King; Green Giant; Steak and Ale Restaurants.
Pitney Bowes, Inc.. . . Walter H. Wheeler Dr., Stamford, CT 06926. . .Fred T. Allen. . .mfg. and marketing of office equipment and retail systems.
Playtex, Intl.. . .700 Fairfield Ave., Stamford, CT 06902. . .Joel E. Smilow. . .personal prods.. . .*Esmark.*
Polaroid Corp.. . .549 Technology Sq., Cambridge, MA 02139. . .William J. McCune Jr.. . .photographic equip., supplies and optical goods.
Potlatch Corp.. . .P.O. Box 3591, San Francisco, CA 94119. . .Roderick M. Steele. . .lumber, paper prods.
Procter & Gamble Co.. . .301 E. 6th St., Cincinnati, OH 45202. . .E.G. Harness. . .household, personal care, food prods.. . .Charmin; Folger Coffee.
Pullman Inc.. . .200 S. Michigan Ave., Chicago, IL 60604. . .Clark P. Lattin Jr.. . .manufacture, leasing, and financing of transportation equip., engineering, construction.
Purex Corp.. . .5101 Clark Ave., Lakewood, CA 90712. . .William R. Tincher. . .household cleaning prods., drugs, toiletries, foods, chemicals.

Quaker Oats Co.. . . Merchandise Mart Plaza, Chicago, IL 60654. . .Robert D. Stuart, Jr.. . .foods, pet foods, toys, chemicals, needlecraft kits, restaurants.
Quaker State Oil Refining Corp.. . .P.O. Box 989, Oil City, PA 16301. . .Q.E. Wood. . .refining, marketing petroleum prods., filters, mining & marketing coal.
Quasar Electronics Co.. . .9401 W. Grand Ave., Franklin Park, IL 60131. . .R.T. Bloomberg. . .electrical prods.. . .*Matsushita Electric.*
Questor Corp.. . . One John Goerlich Sq., Toledo, OH 43691. . .P.M. Grieve. . .home environmental, automotive, juvenile, recreation prods.. . .Tinkertoy; Spalding.

RCA Corp.. . . Rockefeller Plaza, N.Y., NY 10020. . .Edgar H. Griffiths. . .electronics, communications, broadcasting, financial services, vehicle renting, diversified businesses.. . .Banquet Foods; Coronet Industries; Hertz; NBC; C.I.T. Financial.
Radio Shack. . . One Tandy Center, Ft. Worth, TX 76102. . .Lewis F. Kornfeld. . .consumer electronics stores, computer centers. . .*Tandy Corp.*
Ralston Purina Co.. . .835 S. 8th St., St. Louis, MO 63188. . .R. Hal Dean. . .feeds and grocery prods.
Ramada Inns, Inc.. . .3838 E. Van Buren, Phoenix, AZ 85008. . .M. William Isbell.. . .hotel operation.
Rath Packing Co.. . .P.O. Box 330, Waterloo, IA 50704. . .Emmet A. McGuire. . .meat processing, food distribution.
Raytheon Company. . .141 Spring St., Lexington, MA 02173. . .Thomas L. Phillips. . .electronics, aviation, appliances. . .Amana Refrigeration; Beech Aircraft; Caedmon Records; Caloric.
Red Devil Paints & Chemicals. . .30 Northwest St., Mt. Vernon, NY 10550. . .Arthur R. Brown. . .paints, stains. . .*Insilco.*
Revere Copper & Brass Inc.. . .605 3d Ave., N.Y., NY 10016. . .William F. Collins. . .metal fabricators.
Revlon, Inc.. . .767 5th Ave., N.Y., NY 10022. . .Michael C. Ber-

gerac. . .cosmetics, pharmaceuticals.
Reynolds Metals Co.. . .P.O. Box 27003, Richmond, VA 23261. . .John E. Bloomquist. . .aluminum prods.
R.J. Reynolds Industries, Inc.. . .401 N. Main St., Winston-Salem, NC 27102. . .Colin Stokes. . .crude oil, petroleum, transportation, tobacco, food, and beverage prods.
Richardson-Merrell Inc.. . .10 Westport Rd., Wilton, CT 06897. . .J.S. Scott. . .health and personal care prods., drugs.
Robertshaw Controls Co.. . .P.O. Box 26544, Richmond, VA 23261. . .Ralph S. Thomas. . .controls, control systems.
A.H. Robins Co., Inc.. . .1407 Cummings Dr., Richmond, VA 23220. . .E.C. Robins Jr.. . .health care, consumer prods.
Rockwell Intl. Corp.. . .600 Grant St., Pittsburgh, PA 15219. . .Robert Anderson. . .aerospace, electronics, automotive.
Roper Corp.. . .1905 W. Court St., Kankakee, IL 60901. . .C.M. Hoover. . .appliances, home and lawn prods.
Rubbermaid Inc.. . .1147 Akron Rd., Wooster, OH 44691. . .Donald E. Noble. . .rubber and plastic prods.
Helena Rubenstein, Inc.. . .300 Park Ave., N.Y., NY 10022. . .William S. Shanahan. . .cosmetics. . .*Colgate-Palmolive.*

SCM Corp.. . .299 Park Ave., N.Y., NY 10017. . .Paul H. Elicker. . .diversified manufacturer. . .Smith Corona; Durkee Foods.
Safeway Stores, Inc.. . . Oakland, CA 94660. . .Dale L. Lynch. . .retail food stores.
St. Regis Paper Co.. . .150 E. 42d St., N.Y., NY 10017. . .William R. Haselton. . .pulp and paper machinery, building prods.
Santa Fe Industries, Inc.. . .224 S. Michigan Ave., Chicago, IL 60604. . .D.G. Ruegg. . .transport, real estate, construction, natural resources. . .Atchison, Topeka and Santa Fe Railway.
Sara Lee, Kitchens of. . .500 Waukegan Rd., Deerfield, IL 60015. . .William P. Mahoney. . .frozen bakery prods.. . .*Consolidated Foods.*
Schering-Plough Corp.. . .1000 Galloping Hill Rd., Kenilworth, NJ 07033. . .Richard J. Bennett. . .ethical and proprietary drugs.
Schick, Inc.. . .33 Riverside Ave., Westport, CT 06880. . .James W. Hart. . .personal care appliances.
Jos. Schlitz Brewing Co.. . .235 W. Galena St., Milwaukee, WI 53212. . .Frank Sellinger. . .brewery.
Schlumberger Ltd.. . .277 Park Ave., New York, NY 10017. . .Jean Riboud. . .oilfield services, electronics, measurement and control.
Scott Paper Co.. . . Scott Plaza, Phila., PA 19113. . .Charles D. Dickey Jr.. . .paper prods.
Scovill Inc.. . .500 Chase Pkwy., Waterbury, CT 06708. . .Malcolm Baldrige. . .automotive, automation, security and housing prods., small appliances.
Joseph E. Seagram & Sons, Inc.. . .375 Park Ave., N.Y., NY 10022. . .Philip E. Beekman. . .distilled spirits & wine. . .*Seagram Co. Ltd.*
G.D. Searle & Co.. . .P.O. Box 1045, Skokie, IL 60076. . .Donald Rumsfeld. . .pharmaceutical/consumer, medical, optical prods. Pearle Vision Centers.
Sears Roebuck & Co.. . . Sears Tower, Chicago, IL 60684. . .Edward R. Telling. . .merchandising. . .Allstate Insurance.
Seven-up Company. . .121 S. Meramec, St. Louis, MO 63105. . .Edward W. Frantel. . .soft drinks, food colors & flavors, lemon & lime prods., freeze-dried foods. . .*Philip Morris.*
Shasta Beverages. . .26901 Industrial Blvd., Hayward, CA 94545. . .Fred Schmid. . .soft drinks. . .*Consolidated Foods.*
Shell Oil Co.. . .P.O. Box 2463, Houston, TX 77001. . .John F. Bookout. . .oil, gas, chemicals.
Sheller-Globe Corp.. . .P.O. Box 962. . .Toledo, OH 43297. . .Chester Devenow. . .auto, industrial & consumer products.
Sheraton Corporation. . .60 State St., Boston, MA 02109. . .Howard P. James. . .hotels. . .*Intl. Telephone and Telegraph.*
Sherwin-Williams Co.. . .101 Prospect Ave. N.W., Cleveland, OH 44115. . .John G. Breen. . .paints and related prods.
Ship 'N Shore, Inc.. . . Bridgewater Rd., Aston, PA 19014. . .George B. Stephan. . .apparel. . .*General Mills.*
Simmons U.S.A.. . .P.O. Box 105032, Atlanta, GA 30348. . .R.A. Magnusson. . .bedding, furniture. . .*Gulf & Western.*
Singer Co.. . .30 Rockefeller Plaza, N.Y., NY 10020. . .Joseph B. Flavin. . .sewing prods., furniture, power tools.
Skyline Corp.. . .2520 By-Pass Rd., Elkhart, IN 46514. . .Arthur J. Decio. . .mfg. housing and recreational vehicles.
A.O. Smith. . .3533 N. 27th. . .Milwaukee, WI 53216. . .L.B. Smith. . .water heating equip., agricultural feed storage/handling systems, computer services, agricultural financing.
Smith Corona. . .65 Locust Ave., New Canaan, CT 06840. . .P.J. Uebbing. . .typewriters. . .*SCM Corp.*
SmithKline Corp.. . .1500 Spring Garden, Phila., PA 19101. . .Henry Wendt. . .pharmaceuticals, animal health prods., diagnostic instruments. . .Sea & Ski.
Sony Corp. of America. . .9 W. 57th St., N.Y., NY 10019. . .Kazuo Iwama. . .electronics.
Southern Pacific Co.. . . One Market Plaza, San Francisco, CA 94105. . .B.F. Biaggini. . .transportation, leasing, communications, land management, title insurance.
Spencer Foods, Inc.. . .P.O. Box 1228, Spencer, IA 51301. . .Gerald L. Pearson. . .beef processing.
Sperry Corp.. . .1290 Ave. of the Americas, N.Y., NY 10019. . .J. Paul Lyet. . .computers and data processing equip.
Sperry and Hutchinson Co.. . .S & H Bldg., 330 Madison Ave., N.Y., NY 10017. . .J.T. Mills. . .S & H stamps, carpeting, furniture, insurance.
Spiegel, Inc.. . .1515 W. 22d St., Oak Brook, IL 60521. . .Henry A. Johnson. . .catalog merchandising. . .*Beneficial Corp.*
Spring Mills, Inc.. . . Executive Office Bldg., Ft. Mill, SC 29715. . .Peter G. Scotese. . .textiles, frozen foods. . .Seabrook Foods.
Squibb Corp.. . .40 W. 57th St., N.Y., NY 10019. . .Richard M. Furlaud. . .drugs, confectionery, household prods.. . .Lanvin-Charles of the Ritz; Life Savers.
A.E. Staley Manufacturing Co.. . .2200 E. Eldorado, Decatur, IL 62525. . .Donald E. Nordlund. . .corn and soybean processing.
Standard Brands Incorporated. 625 Madison Ave., N.Y., NY 10022. . .F. Ross Johnson. . .foods, related prods.. . .Julius Wile Sons & Co.; All Brand Importers; Fleishmann's; Planters; Curtiss Candy.
Standard Oil Co. of California. . .225 Bush, San Francisco, CA 94104. . .H.J. Haynes. . .petroleum.
Standard Oil Co. (Indiana). . .200 E. Randolph Dr., Chicago, IL 60601. . .John E. Swearinger. . .petroleum and petroleum products.
Standard Oil Co. (Ohio). . . Midland Bldg., Cleveland, OH 44115. . .Alton W. Whitehouse Jr.. . .petroleum.
Stanley Home Products, Inc.. . .333 Western Ave., Westfield, MA 01085. . .H.L. Tower. . .household and personal prods.
Stanley Works. . .195 Lake, New Britain, CT 06050. . .D.W. Davis. . .hand tools, hardware, door opening equipment.
Star-Kist Foods, Inc.. . .582 Tuna St., Terminal Island, CA 90731. . .John J. Real. . .canned fish. . .*H.J. Heinz.*
Sterling Drug Inc.. . .90 Park Ave., N.Y., NY 10016. . .W. Clarke Wescoe. . .pharmaceuticals, cosmetics & toiletries, household, proprietary prods., chemicals, environmental control. . .Bayer Aspirin, Lysol, Dorothy Gray, Parfums Givenchy.
J.P. Stevens & Co., Inc.. . .1185 Ave. of the Americas, N.Y., NY 10036. . .James D. Finley. . .fabrics, carpets, other textile home furnishings.
Stokely-Van Camp, Inc.. . .941 N. Meridian, Indianapolis, IN 46206. . .A.J. Stokley. . .canned fruits, vegetables, and frozen foods.
Studebaker-Worthington, Inc.. . . One Dag Hammarskjold Plaza, N.Y., NY 10017. . .Derald H. Ruttenberg. . .manuf. process equipment and other industrial prods.
Subaru of America, Inc.. . .7040 Central Hwy., Pennsauken, NJ 08109. . .Harvey Lamm. . .auto importer.
Sunbeam Corp.. . .5400 W. Roosevelt Rd., Chicago, IL 60650. . .manuf. of small appliances, industrial/commercial products.
Sun Company, Inc.. . .100 Matsonford Rd., Radnor, PA 19087. . .T. A. Burtis. . .petroleum.
Sunshine Biscuits, Inc.. . .245 Park Ave., N.Y., NY 10017. . .Edward J. Jennings Jr.. . .biscuits, crackers, snacks. . .*American Brands.*
Swift & Co.. . .115 W. Jackson, Chicago, IL 60604. . .William S. Watchman Jr.. . .food.
Swingline, Inc.. . .32-00 Skillman Ave., Long Island City, NY 11101. . .Ernest M. Raasch. . .staplers, cutlery, fasteners, automotive chemicals, lighting prods.. . .*American Brands.*
Sylvania Lighting Products. . .100 Endicott St., Danvers, MA 01923. . .John C. Avallon. . .lighting prods.. . .*General Telephone & Electronics.*

Talbots, Inc., The. . .175 Beal St., Hingham, MA 02043. . .William A. DeJonge. . .clothing mail order and retail stores. . .*General Mills.*
Talley Industries, Inc.. . .P.O. Box 849, Mesa, AZ 85201. . .B. Paul Barnes. . .diversified manufacturing. . .Seth Thomas; Westclox.
Tandy Corp.. . .1900 One Tandy Center, Fort Worth, TX 76102. . .Phil R. North. . .consumer electronics retailing & mfg.. . .Radio Shack.

Tappan Co.. . . Tappan Park, Mansfield, OH 44901. . .D.C. Blasius. . .major kitchen appliances, microwave ovens, kitchen cabinets, bathroom vanities.
Teledyne, Inc.. . .1901 Ave. of the Stars, Los Angeles, CA 90067. . .George Roberts. . .electronics, aerospace prods.
Texaco Inc.. . .2000 Westchester Ave., White Plains, NY 10650. . .Maurice F. Granville. . .petroleum and petroleum prods.
Texas Instruments Inc.. . .13500 North Central, Dallas, TX 75265. . .Mark Shepherd Jr.. . .electronics mfg.
Textron Inc.. . .40 Westminster St., Providence, RI 02903. . .Robert P. Straetz. . .aerospace, consumer, industrial, metal prods., creative capital. . .Gorham; Speidel; Talon.
3M. . .3M Center, St. Paul, MN 55101. . .Lewis W. Lehr. . .abrasives, adhesives, building services & chemicals, electrical, health care, photographic, printing, recording materials.
Trane Co., The. . .3600 Pammel Creek Rd., La Crosse, WI 54601. . .Richard J. Campbell. . .air conditioning and heat transfer equip.
Transamerica Corp.. . .600 Montgomery St., San Francisco, CA 94111. . .John R. Beckett. . .diversified services: insurance, financial, leisure, business. . .Budget Rent-A-Car; Occidental Life Insurance; United Artists.
Trans World Corp.. . .605 3d Ave., N.Y., NY 10158. . .L. Edwin Smart. . .holding co.. . .Trans World Airlines; Hilton International; Canteen Corp.; Spartan Food Systems; Century 21 Real Estate Corp.
Tropicana Products, Inc.. . .P.O. Box 338, Bradenton, FL 33506. . .Kenneth A. Barnebey. . .citrus processing. . .*Beatrice Foods.*
Tupperware. . .N. Highway 441, Kissimmee, FL 32741. . .Thomas P. Mullaney. . .food containers, toys. . .*Dart Industries.*
Twentieth Century-Fox Film Corp.. . .P.O. Box 900, Beverly Hills, CA 90213. . .Dennis C. Stanfill. . .motion pictures, leisure time.

Union Carbide Corp.. . .270 Park Ave., N.Y. NY 10017. . .William S. Sneath. . .chemicals.
Union Pacific Corp.. . .345 Park Ave., N.Y., NY 10022. . .J.H. Evans. . .transportation, petroleum, mining.
Uniroyal, Inc.. . . World Headquarters, Middlebury, CT 06749. . .Joseph P. Flannery. . .chemical, rubber, plastic prods.
United Air Lines, Inc.. . .P.O. Box 66100, Chicago, IL 60666. . .Richard J. Ferris. . .air transportation. . .*UAL.*
United Brands Co.. . .1271 Ave. of the Americas, N.Y., NY 10020. . .Seymour Milstein. . .foods, telecommunications, restaurants. . .Chiquita; John Morrell.
United Merchants and Manufacturers, Inc.. . .1407 Broadway, N.Y., NY 10018. . .Z.B. Lane Jr.. . .textiles, plastics, chemicals.
United Parcel Service. . . Greenwich Office Park #5, Greenwich, CT 06830. . .Harold Oberkotter. . .parcel delivery.
United States Steel Corp.. . .600 Grant St., Pittsburgh, PA 15230. . .David M. Roderick. . .steel, chemicals, transportation.
United States Tobacco Co.. . .100 W. Putnam Ave., Greenwich, CT 06830. . .L.F. Bantle. . .smokeless, pipe tobacco, cigars, pet foods, wines, pens and pencils.
United Technologies. . . United Technologies Bldg., Hartford, CT 06101. . .Harry J. Gray. . .high-technology prods.. . .Carrier Corp.; Otis Elevator; Pratt & Whitney, Sikorsky Aircraft.
Universal Leaf Tobacco Co., Inc.. . .P.O. Box 25099, Richmond, VA 23260. . .Gordon L. Crenshaw. . .leaf tobacco.
Upjohn Co.. . .7000 Portage Rd., Kalamazoo, MI 49001. . .R.T. Parfet Jr.. . .pharmaceuticals, chemicals, agricultural prods., health care services.
USAir . . .Washington National Airport, Wash., DC 20001. . .Edwin I. Colodny. . .transportation.

VF Corp.. . .P.O. Box 1022, Reading, PA 19610. . .M.O. Lee. . .apparel. . .Vanity Fair; Kay Windsor.
Volkswagen of America, Inc.. . .27621 Parkview Blvd., Warren, MI 48077. . .James W. McLernon. . .auto mfg.
Volvo of America Corporation. . . Volvo Dr., Rockleigh, NJ 07647. . .Bjorn Ahlstrom. . .automobiles.

Walgreen Co.. . .200 Wilmot Rd., Deerfield, IL 60015. . .Charles R. Walgreen 3d. . .retail drug chain.
Ward Foods, Inc.. . .2 Penn Plaza, N.Y., NY 10001. . .Joseph A. Marshall Jr.. . .foods. . .Plymouth Rock; Quinlan Pretzel.
Warnaco Inc.. . .350 Lafayette, Bridgeport, CT 06602. . .James C. Walker. . .apparel. . .Hathaway, Warner's; White Stag.
Warner Communications Inc.. . .75 Rockefeller Plaza, N.Y., NY 10019. . .Steven J. Ross. . .entertainment, communications. . .Warner Books; Warner Bros.; Atlantic Records; Atari; Cosmos soccer; Warner Amex Cable Comm.
Warner-Lambert Co.. . .201 Tabor Rd., Morris Plains, NJ 07950. . .Ward S. Hagan. . .health care prods., baked goods, hospital prods., shaving systems & blades, optical prods.. . .American Chicle; DuBarry; Good & Plenty; American Optical; Parke-Davis.
Wear-Ever Aluminum, Inc.. . .1089 Eastern Ave., Chillicothe, OH 45601. . .W.H. Krome George. . .aluminum. . .*Aluminum Co. of America.*
Weight Watchers International. . .800 Community Dr., Manhasset, N.Y. 11030. . .Charles Berger. . .weight control programs and prods.. . .*H.J. Heinz.*
West Bend Co.. . .400 W. Washington, West Bend, WI 53095. . .E.M. Davis. . .cookware, electric housewares, humidifiers. . .*Dart Industries.*
Western Airlines, Inc.. . .6060 Avion Dr., Los Angeles, CA 90045. . .Dominic P. Renda. . .air transportation.
Western Union Corp.. . . One Lake St., Upper Saddle River, NJ 07458. . .Robert M. Flanagan. . .telecommunications. . .Western Union Telegraph Co.
Westinghouse Broadcasting Co., Inc.. . .90 Park Ave., N.Y., NY 10016. . .R.E. Kirby. . .Radio, TV broadcasting, CATV. . .*Westinghouse Electric.*
Westinghouse Electric Corp.. . . Westinghouse Bldg., Gateway Center, Pittsburgh, PA 15222. . .R.E. Kirby. . .products that generate, transmit, distribute, and use electricity. . .Westinghouse Broadcasting.
West Point-Pepperell—Consumer Prods.. . .1221 Ave. of the Americas, N.Y., NY 10020. . .C.J. Kjorlien. . .towels, sheets, blankets, carpets and rugs.
Weyerhaeuser Co.. . . Tacoma, WA 98477. . .George H. Weyerhaeuser. . .manuf., distribution forest prods., including bldg. materials, pulp, paper, newsprint.
Whirlpool Corp.. . . Administrative Center, Benton Harbor, MI 49022. . .John H. Platts. . .major home appliances.
White Consolidated Industries, Inc.. . .11770 Berea Rd., Cleveland, OH 44111. . .R.H. Holdt. . .major home appliances and machinery, industrial equip.
White Motor Corp.. . .34500 Grand River Ave., Farmington Hills, MI 48024. . .Cruse W. Moss. . .heavy duty trucks, farm equip.
Willamette Industries, Inc.. . .1300 S.W. 5th Ave., Portland, OR 97201. . .Gene D. Knudson. . .lumber prods.
Wilson Sporting Goods Co.. . .2233 West St., River Grove, IL 60171. . .Gordon Hollywood. . .sports equip.. . .*PepsiCo.*
Winn-Dixie Stores, Inc.. . .5050 Edgewood Ct., Jacksonville, FL 32203. . .B.L. Thomas. . .retail grocery chain.
Winnebago Industries, Inc.. . . Junction 9 and 69, Forest City, IA 50436. . .John K. Hanson. . .recreational vehicles.
F.W. Woolworth Co.. . .233 Broadway, N.Y., NY 10007. . .Edward F. Gibbons. . .general merchandise. . .Kinney Shoes.
Wm. Wrigley Jr. Co.. . .410 N. Michigan Ave., Chicago, IL 60611. . .William Wrigley. . .chewing gum.

Xerox Corporation. . . Stamford, CT 06904. . .C. Peter McColough. . .copiers, duplicators, computer related equip., textbook publishing.

Yashica, Inc.—U.S.A.. . .411 Sette Dr., Paramus, NJ 07652. . .Mr. T. Kakutani. . .cameras, photographic supplies.
Yoo-Hoo Chocolate Beverage Corp.. . .600 Commercial Ave., Carlstadt, NJ 07072. . .Edward L. Cott. . .soft drinks. . .*Iroquois Brands.*

Zale Corp.. . .3000 Diamond Park, Dallas TX 75247. . .Bruce A. Lipshy. . .jewelry, footware, catalog sales, sporting goods.
Zenith Radio Corp.. . .1000 Milwaukee Ave., Glenview, IL 60025. . .John J. Nevin. . .electronic home entertainment prods.

Poverty by Family Status, Sex, and Race

Source: U.S. Bureau of the Census
(In 1978, according to poverty level defined in table below. Thousands)

	1978		1977		1976		1975	
	No.	%*	No.	%*	No.	%*	No.	%*
Total poor	**24,497**	**11.4**	**24,720**	**11.6**	**24,975**	**11.8**	**25,877**	**12.3**
In families	19,062	10.0	19,505	10.2	19,632	10.3	20,789	10.9
Head	5,280	9.1	5,311	9.3	5,311	9.4	5,450	9.7
Related children	9,722	15.7	10,028	16.0	10,081	15.8	10,882	16.8
Other relatives	4,059	5.7	4,165	5.9	4,240	6.0	4,457	6.4
Unrelated individuals	5,435	22.1	5,216	22.6	5,344	24.9	5,088	25.1
In male-head families	**9,793**	**5.9**	**10,300**	**6.2**	**10,603**	**6.4**	**11,943**	**7.1**
Head	2,626	5.3	2,701	5.5	2,768	5.6	3,020	6.2
Related children	4,035	7.9	4,371	8.5	4,497	8.5	5,284	9.8
Other relatives	3,131	4.8	3,228	5.0	3,337	5.2	3,638	5.7
Unrelated male individuals	1,824	17.1	1,796	18.0	1,787	19.7	1,667	19.9
In female-head families	**9,269**	**35.6**	**9,205**	**36.2**	**9,029**	**37.3**	**8,846**	**37.5**
Head	2,654	31.4	2,610	31.7	2,543	33.0	2,430	32.5
Related children	5,687	50.6	5,658	50.3	5,583	52.0	5,597	52.7
Other relatives	928	14.6	938	15.8	903	15.7	819	15.0
Unrelated female individuals	3,611	26.0	3,419	26.1	3,557	28.7	3,422	28.9
Total white poor	**16,259**	**8.7**	**16,416**	**8.9**	**16,713**	**9.1**	**17,770**	**9.7**
In families	12,050	7.3	12,364	7.5	12,500	7.5	13,799	8.3
Head	3,523	6.9	3,540	7.0	3,560	7.1	3,838	7.7
Female	1,391	23.5	1,400	24.0	1,379	25.2	1,394	25.9
Related children	5,674	11.0	5,943	11.4	6,034	11.3	6,748	12.5
Other relatives	2,852	4.5	2,882	4.6	2,906	4.7	3,213	5.2
Unrelated individuals	4,209	19.8	4,051	20.4	4,213	22.7	3,972	22.7
Total black poor	**7,625**	**30.6**	**7,726**	**31.3**	**7,595**	**31.1**	**7,545**	**31.3**
In families	6,493	29.5	6,667	30.5	6,576	30.1	6,533	30.1
Head	1,622	27.5	1,637	28.2	1,617	27.9	1,513	27.1
Female	1,208	50.6	1,162	51.0	1,122	52.2	1,004	50.1
Related children	3,781	41.2	3,850	41.6	3,758	40.4	3,884	41.4
Other relatives	1,094	15.7	1,181	17.4	1,201	17.8	1,136	16.9
Unrelated individuals	1,132	38.6	1,059	37.0	1,019	39.8	1,011	42.1

*Percent of total population in that general category who fell below poverty level. For example, of all black female heads of households in 1978, 50.6% were poor.

Estimated Poverty Level, 1979, by Family Size and Sex of Head

		Non-Farm			Farm		
Number of family members	**Total**	**Total**	**Male**	**Female**	**Total**	**Male**	**Female**
1 member	$3,670	$3,680	$3,850	$3,560	$3,110	$3,220	$2,990
Under 65 yrs.	3,770	3,770	3,910	3,620	3,240	3,320	3,080
65 yrs. and over	3,470	3,480	3,510	3,470	2,960	2,990	2,950
2 members	4,700	4,730	4,740	4,680	3,980	3,990	3,890
Head under 65 yrs	4,850	4,880	4,900	4,770	4,150	4,160	4,020
Head 65 yrs. and over	4,360	4,390	4,390	4,360	3,730	3,730	3,690
3 members	5,760	5,790	5,820	5,640	4,910	4,930	4,690
4 members	7,370	7,410	7,420	7,380	6,320	6,320	6,250
5 members	8,710	8,770	8,780	8,680	7,470	7,470	7,450
6 members	9,820	9,890	9,900	9,850	8,390	8,390	8,300
7 members or more	12,160	12,240	12,280	11,980	10,430	10,440	9,810

Poverty Level, 1978

		Non-Farm			Farm		
Numbers of family members	**Total**	**Total**	**Male**	**Female**	**Total**	**Male**	**Female**
1 member	$3,302	$3,311	$3,460	$3,196	$2,795	$2,898	$2,690
Under 65 yrs.	3,386	3,392	3,516	3,253	2,913	2,987	2,764
65 years and over	3,116	3,127	3,159	3,118	2,661	2,685	2,650
2 members	4,225	4,249	4,258	4,206	3,578	3,582	3,497
Head under 65 yrs.	4,363	4,383	4,407	4,286	3,731	3,737	3,614
Head 65 years and over	3,917	3,944	3,948	3,923	3,352	3,354	3,313
3 members	5,178	5,201	5,231	5,065	4,413	4,430	4,216
4 members	6,628	6,662	6,665	6,632	5,681	5,683	5,622
5 members	7,833	7,880	7,888	7,806	6,714	6,714	6,700
6 members	8,825	8,891	8,895	8,852	7,541	7,543	7,462
7 members or more	10,926	11,002	11,038	10,765	9,373	9,386	8,813

Income Distribution by Population Fifths

Source: U.S. Bureau of the Census

Families, 1978	Top income of each fifth				Average	Percent distribution of total income					
	Lowest	Second	Third	Fourth	Top 5%	Lowest fifth	Second fifth	Third fifth	Fourth fifth	Highest fifth	Top 5%
Total	$8,720	$14,700	$20,600	$28,632	$44,878	5.2	11.6	17.5	24.1	41.5	15.6
White	9,500	15,443	21,284	29,332	46,272	5.6	12.0	17.6	23.9	41.0	15.5
Black and other	4,879	9,081	14,665	22,195	35,416	4.2	9.6	16.3	25.1	44.7	15.9
Black	4,536	8,438	13,800	20,984	32,958	4.3	9.7	16.3	25.3	44.0	15.4

Aid to Families with Dependent Children

Source: Office of Research and Statistics, Social Security Administration

December, 1979 State	No. of families	Number of recipients Total[1]	Children	Payments to recipients Total amount	Average per-family	Average per-recipient	% change from Dec., 1978 No. of recip.	Amount
Alabama	62,118	179,086	129,197	$6,903,917	$111.14	$38.55	2.7	4.1
Alaska	6,214	15,101	10,441	1,972,524	317.43	130.62	16.3	18.3
Arizona	17,777	49,946	36,945	3,004,098	168.99	60.15	-0.3	14.0
Arkansas	29,203	84,673	62,149	4,407,145	150.91	52.05	-2.4	1.7
California	468,971	1,360,301	918,592	172,444,632	367.71	126.77	-1.1	15.1
Colorado	26,889	74,465	51,669	6,446,328	239.74	86.57	-4.4	3.5
Connecticut	46,650	135,767	94,708	15,964,851	342.23	117.59	-0.5	6.4
Delaware	11,663	32,579	22,689	2,659,782	228.05	81.64	5.8	14.5
Dist. of Columbia	30,897	86,427	59,669	8,017,363	259.49	92.76	-4.3	7.0
Florida	89,967	247,791	178,456	15,719,171	174.72	63.44	7.0	28.1
Georgia	82,038	215,389	157,254	10,201,480	124.35	47.36	3.3	20.5
Guam	1,312	4,725	3,506	273,597	208.53	57.90	4.4	9.1
Hawaii	19,317	60,050	39,964	7,455,403	385.95	124.15	1.0	1.8
Idaho	7,482	20,507	13,983	2,005,513	268.05	97.80	5.0	10.9
Illinois	209,330	661,292	466,892	58,016,574	277.15	87.73	-3.3	-0.2
Indiana	52,840	152,302	107,749	10,004,662	189.34	65.69	3.1	5.0
Iowa	35,830	97,921	66,061	10,892,205	304.00	111.23	6.2	14.3
Kansas	24,494	64,651	47,103	6,550,691	267.44	101.32	2.0	17.0
Kentucky	61,310	164,119	115,963	10,184,961	166.12	62.06	-0.2	1.2
Louisiana	67,207	210,310	155,277	9,451,306	140.63	44.94	3.9	14.6
Maine	21,247	60,819	40,370	4,997,787	235.22	82.17	1.9	9.9
Maryland	75,874	209,728	143,829	16,424,334	216.47	78.31	2.0	13.1
Massachusetts	123,989	352,228	230,223	40,867,254	329.60	116.03	-3.1	3.9
Michigan	213,168	646,424	439,295	79,371,856	372.34	122.79	4.3	10.6
Minnesota	48,254	130,113	87,986	15,490,159	321.01	119.05	1.1	10.1
Mississippi	56,727	171,415	127,551	4,967,262	87.56	28.98	1.7	14.9
Missouri	64,764	191,029	130,657	13,538,652	209.05	70.87	-1.1	8.7
Montana	6,613	18,297	12,756	1,470,627	222.38	80.38	3.8	16.3
Nebraska	12,005	33,941	23,858	3,116,556	259.60	91.82	-4.3	-1.3
Nevada	4,019	11,158	7,829	807,529	200.93	72.37	19.9	30.2
New Hampshire	7,813	21,557	14,384	2,027,759	259.54	94.06	1.5	15.6
New Jersey	146,494	456,032	316,231	44,137,506	301.29	96.79	-0.3	3.7
New Mexico	17,771	52,072	36,285	3,040,208	171.08	58.38	2.7	11.8
New York	360,208	1,095,400	757,839	134,156,863	372.44	122.47	-2.6	1.1
North Carolina	75,335	193,423	138,507	12,330,295	163.67	63.75	1.1	8.4
North Dakota	4,657	12,702	8,829	1,286,641	276.28	101.29	-4.8	8.1
Ohio	172,240	489,433	334,257	43,067,557	250.04	87.99	2.3	15.9
Oklahoma	29,239	87,158	63,828	7,407,795	253.35	84.99	1.6	18.4
Oregon	37,057	98,180	63,027	12,185,325	328.83	124.11	-17.7	1.6
Pennsylvania	212,044	621,277	428,086	59,336,447	279.83	95.51	-3.4	-1.7
Puerto Rico[2]	45,984	174,780	124,449	2,448,560	53.25	14.01	3.7	23.5
Rhode Island	17,376	50,285	34,474	7,002,593	403.00	139.26	2.4	31.6
South Carolina	54,016	149,334	106,965	5,490,323	101.64	36.77	4.8	20.5
South Dakota	7,455	20,183	14,744	1,583,952	212.47	78.48	-1.8	5.6
Tennessee	59,087	157,763	113,113	6,726,175	113.84	42.63	-1.2	0.9
Texas	100,177	306,084	224,693	10,988,338	109.69	35.90	6.3	10.6
Utah	11,306	34,729	22,072	3,366,205	297.74	96.93	-5.8	-1.2
Vermont	7,155	21,139	13,665	2,342,897	327.45	110.83	8.0	14.4
Virgin Islands[2]	996	3,038	2,458	145,039	145.62	47.74	-4.6	13.0
Virginia	59,292	163,231	114,382	12,161,545	205.11	74.51	1.5	3.5
Washington	51,336	143,318	91,607	18,424,310	358.90	128.56	3.5	18.2
West Virginia	26,942	77,041	58,130	4,707,596	174.73	61.11	15.1	7.1
Wisconsin	74,908	201,385	137,887	25,272,175	337.38	125.49	6.5	13.4
Wyoming	2,584	6,581	4,710	664,919	257.32	101.04	10.6	28.6
Total	**3,559,641**	**10,378,679**	**7,207,243**	**$963,929,242**	**$270.79**	**$92.88**	**.3**	**8.1**

(e) Estimated. (1) Includes as recipients the children and one or both parents or one caretaker relative other than a parent in families in which the requirements of such adults were considered in determining the amount of assistance. (2) Incomplete. Data for foster care not reported by Puerto Rico and the Virgin Islands.

Welfare Recipients and Payments, 1955-1979

Category		1955, Dec.	1965, Dec.	1970, Dec.	1975, Dec. (b)	1977, Dec.	1978, Dec.	1979, Dec.
Old age:	Recipients	2,538,000	2,087,000	2,082,000	2,333,685	2,050,921	1,967,900	1,871,716
	Total amt.	$127,003,000	$131,674,000	$161,642,000	$217,002,000	$198,166,000	$197,630,000	$229,613,000
	Avg. amt.	$50.05	$63.10	$77.65	$92.99	$96.62	$100.43	$122.67
	(a)Avg. real $	$62.41	$66.75	$66.78	$57.65	$53.23	$49.47	$53.50
AFDC:	Recipients	2,192,000	4,396,000	9,659,000	11,389,000	10,760,521	10,325,000	10,378,679
	Total amt.	$51,472,000	$144,355,000	$485,877,000	$824,648,000	$855,012,135	$891,399,000	$963,929,242
	Avg. amt.	$23.50	$32.85	$50.30	$72.40	$79.46	$86.33	$92.88
	(a)Avg. real $	$29.30	$34.76	$43.26	$44.89	$43.78	$46.49	$45.58
Blind:	Recipients	104,000	85,100	81,000	75,315	77,362	77,135	77,250
	Total amt.	$5,803,000	$6,922,000	$8,446,000	$11,220,000	$12,316,000	$12,681,000	$16,398,000
	Avg. amt.	$55.55	$81.35	$104.35	$148.97	$159.20	$164.40	$212.27
	(a)Avg. real $	$69.27	$86.07	$89.74	$92.36	$87.72	$88.34	$92.25
Disabled:	Recipients	241,000	557,000	935,000	1,950,625	2,109,409	2,171,890	2,200,609
	Total amt.	$11,750,000	$37,035,000	$91,325,000	$279,073,000	$317,176,000	$336,256,000	$399,879,000
	Avg. amt.	$48.75	$66.50	$97.65	$143.07	$150.36	$154.82	$181.71
	(a)Avg. real $	$60.79	$70.36	$83.98	$88.70	$82.85	$83.19	$79.35

(a) Dollar amounts adjusted to represent actual purchasing power in terms of average value of dollar during 1967. (b) Administration of the public assistance programs of Old-age Assistance, Aid to the Blind, and Aid to the Disabled was transferred to the Social Security Administration by Public Law 92-603 effective 1/1/74.

Labor Union Directory

Source: Bureau of Labor Statistics; World Almanac Questionnaire
(*) Independent union; all others affiliated with AFL-CIO.

Actors and Artistes of America, Associated (AAAA), 165 W. 46th St., New York, NY 10036; founded 1919; Frederick O'-Neal, Pres. (since 1971); no individual members, 9 affiliates.

Air Line Pilots Association, 1625 Massachusetts Ave. NW, Washington, DC 20036. John J. O'Donnell, Pres.; 27,707 members, 105 locals.

Aluminum Workers International Union (AWIU), Paul Brown Bldg., St. Louis, MO 63101; founded 1953; Lawrence A. Holly, Pres. (since 1977); 35,000 members, 100 locals.

***Automobile, Aerospace & Agricultural Implement Workers of America; International Union, United (UAW),** 8000 E. Jefferson Ave., Detroit, MI 48214; founded 1935; Douglas Fraser, Pres. (since 1977); 1,800,000 members, 1,575 locals.

Bakery, Confectionery & Tobacco Workers International Union (BC&T), 1828 L St., Suite 900, Washington, DC 20036; founded 1886; John DeConcini, Pres. (since 1978); 170,000 members, 234 locals.

Barbers, Beauticians, and Allied Industries, International Association, 7050 West Washington St., Indianapolis, IN 46214; Richard Plumb, Pres.; 41,000 members, 702 locals.

Boilermakers, Iron Shipbuilders, Blacksmiths, Forgers and Helpers, International Brotherhood of (BSF), 570 New Brotherhood Bldg., Kansas City, KS 66101; founded 1880; Harold J. Buoy, Pres. (since 1973); 150,000 members, 400 locals.

Bricklayers and Allied Craftsmen, International Union of, 815 15th St. NW, Washington, DC 20005; Thomas F. Murphy, Pres.; 147,715 members, 758 locals.

Carpenters and Joiners of America, United Brotherhood of, 101 Constitution Ave. NW, Washington, DC 20001; William Sidell, Pres.; 820,000 members, 2,301 locals.

Cement, Lime and Gypsum Workers International Union, United (U.C.L.G.W.I.U.), 7830 West Lawrence Ave., Chicago, IL 60656; founded 1939; Thomas F. Miechur, Pres. (since 1970); 37,500 members, 312 locals.

Chemical Workers Union, International (ICWU), 1655 West Market St., Akron, OH 44313; founded 1944; Frank D. Martino, Pres. (since 1975); 70,000 members, 400 locals.

Clothing and Textile Workers Union, Amalgamated (ACTWU), 770 Broadway, New York, NY 10003; founded 1914; Murray H. Finley, Pres. (since 1972); 510,000 members, 900 locals.

Communications Workers of America, 1925 K St. NW, Washington, DC 20006; Glenn E. Watts, Pres.; 498,743 members, 874 locals.

Distillery, Wine & Allied Workers International Union (DWU), 66 Grand Ave., Englewood, NJ 07631; founded 1940; George J. Oneto, Pres. (since 1974); 28,000 members, 73 locals.

***Distributive Workers of America,** 13 Astor Place, New York, NY 10003; Cleveland Robinson, Pres.; 50,000 members, 40 locals.

***Education Association, National,** 1201 16th St. NW, Washington, DC 20036; John E. Ryor, Pres.; 1,470,212 members, 9,815 affiliates.

Electrical, Radio and Machine Workers, International Union of (IUE), 1126 16th St. NW, Washington, DC 20036; founded 1949; David J. Fitzmaurice, Pres. (since 1976); 250,000 members, 640 locals.

***Electrical, Radio & Machine Workers of America, United (UE),** 11 E. 51st St. New York, NY 10022; founded 1936; Denis Glavin, Gen. Pres. (since 1978); 165,000 members, 200 locals.

Electrical Workers, International Brotherhood of (IBEW), 1125 15th St., NW, Washington, DC 20005; founded 1891; Charles H. Pillard, Pres. (since 1970); 1,000,000 members, 1,479 locals.

Farm Workers of America, United (UFW), La Paz, Keene, CA 93531; founded 1962; Cesar E. Chavez, Pres. (since 1973); 100,000 members.

***Federal Employees, National Federation of (NFFE),** 1016 16th St. NW, Washington, DC 20036; founded 1917; James M. Peirce Jr., Pres. (since 1976); 150,000 members, 600 locals.

Fire Fighters, International Association of, 1750 New York Ave. NW, Washington, DC 20006; William McClennan, Pres.; 171,674 members, 1,798 locals.

Firemen and Oilers, International Brotherhood of, VFM Bldg., 200 Maryland Ave. NE, Washington, DC 20002; John J. McNamara, Pres.; 40,000 members.

Furniture Workers of America, United, 700 Broadway, New York, NY 10003; Carl Scarbrough, Pres.; 29,967 members, 106 locals.

Garment Workers of America, United (UGWA), 200 Park Ave. So., New York, NY 10003; founded 1891; William O'Donnell, Gen. Pres. (since 1977); 25,000 members, 155 locals.

Glass Bottle Blowers Association (GBBA), 608 E. Baltimore Pike, Media, PA 19063; founded 1842; James Hatfield, Pres.; 85,000 members, 251 locals.

Glass and Ceramic Workers of North America, United, 556 E. Town St., Columbus, OH 43215; Joseph Roman, Pres.; 38,500 members, 197 locals.

Glass Workers Union of North America, American Flint (AFGWU), 1440 So. Byrne Rd., Toledo, OH 43614; founded 1878; George M. Parker, Pres. (since 1961); 31,000 members, 238 locals.

Government Employees, American Federation of (AFGE), 1325 Massachusetts Ave. NW, Washington, DC 20005; founded 1932; Kenneth T. Blaylock, Natl. Pres. (since 1976); 300,000 members, 1,500 locals.

Grain Millers, American Federation of (AFGM), 4949 Olson Memorial Hwy., Minneapolis, MN 55422; founded 1948; Frank Hoese, Gen. Pres. (since 1979); 35,000 members, 204 locals.

Graphic Arts International Union (GAIU), 1900 L St., NW, Washington, DC 20036; founded 1882; Kenneth J. Brown, Pres. (since 1959); 120,000 members, 220 locals.

Hotel and Restaurant Employees and Bartenders International Union, 120 E. 4th St., Cincinnati, OH 45202; Edward T. Hanley, Pres.; 451,989 members, 386 locals.

Industrial Workers of America, International Union, Allied (AIW), 3520 W. Oklahoma Ave., Milwaukee, WI 53215; founded 1935; Dominick D'Ambrosio, Intl. Pres. (since 1975); 100,000 members, 438 locals.

Iron Workers, International Association of Bridge and Structural, 1750 New York Ave. NW, Washington, DC 20006; John H. Lyons, Pres.; 181, 647 members, 322 locals.

Laborers' International Union of North America (LIUNA), 905 16th St. NW, Washington, DC 20006; founded 1903; Angelo Fosco, Gen. Pres. (since 1976); 650,000 members, 820 locals.

Ladies Garment Workers Union, International (ILGWU), 1710 Broadway, New York, NY 10019; founded 1900; Sol C. Chaikin, Pres. (since 1975); 340,936 members, 454 locals.

Leather Goods, Plastic and Novelty Workers' Union, International, 265 W. 14th St., New York, NY 10011; Frank Casale, Pres.; 40,000 members, 97 locals.

Letter Carriers, National Association of (NALC), 100 Indiana Ave. NW, Washington, DC 20001; founded 1889; Vincent R. Sombrotto, Pres. (since 1980); 233,000 members, 4,800 locals.

***Locomotive Engineers, Brotherhood of (BLE),** 1365 Ontario Ave., Cleveland, OH 44114; founded 1863; John F. Sytsma, Pres. (since 1976); 62,500 members, 750 locals.

Longshoremen's Association, International, 17 Battery Pl., New York, NY 10004; Thomas W. Gleason, Pres.; 76,579 members, 367 locals.

***Longshoremen's & Warehousemen's Union, International (ILWU),** 1188 Franklin St., San Francisco, CA 94109; founded 1937; James R. Herman, Pres. (since 1977); 58,000 members, 78 locals.

Machinists and Aerospace Workers, International Association of, 1300 Connecticut Ave. NW, Washington, DC 20036; William W. Winpisinger, Pres.; 943,280 members, 1,904 locals.

Maintenance of Way Employes, Brotherhood of, 12050 Woodward Ave., Detroit, MI 48203; Harold C. Crotty, Pres.; 119,184 members, 1,040 locals.

Marine & Shipbuilding Workers of America, Industrial Union of (IUMSWA), 8121 Georgia Ave., Silver Springs, MD 20910; founded 1934; Frank Derwin, Pres. (since 1971); 25,000 members, 40 locals.

Maritime Union of America, National, 346 W. 17th St., New York NY 10011; Shannon Wall, Pres.; 35,000 members.

Meat Cutters and Butcher Workmen of North America, Amalgamated, 2800 North Sheridan Rd., Chicago, IL 60657; Harry Poole, Pres.; 525,000 members, 461 locals.

Mechanics Educational Society of America, 1421 First National Bldg., Detroit, MI 48226; Alfred J. Smith, Pres.; 25,000 members, 29 locals.

***Mine Workers of America, United (UMWA),** 900 15th St. NW, Washington, DC 20005; founded 1890; Sam Church Jr.,

Pres.; 250,000 members, 910 locals.

Molders' and Allied Workers' Union, International, 1225 E. McMillan St., Cincinnati, OH 45206; Carl W. Studenroth, Pres.; 75,000 members, 247 locals.

Musicians of the United States and Canada, American Federation of (AF of M), 1500 Broadway, New York, NY 10036; founded 1896; Victor W. Fuentealba, Pres. (since 1978); 300,000 members, 605 locals.

Newspaper Guild, The (TNG), 1125 15th St. NW, Washington, DC; founded 1933; Charles A. Perlik Jr., Pres. (since 1969); 33,500 members, 80 locals.

***Nurses Association, American,** 2420 Pershing Rd., Kansas City, MO 64108; Anne Zimmerman, Pres.; 196,499 members, 53 affiliates.

Office and Professional Employees International Union, 265 W. 14th St., New York, NY 10011; Howard Coughlin, Pres.; 89,468 members, 245 locals.

Oil, Chemical and Atomic Workers International Union, PO Box 2812, 1636 Champa St., Denver, CO 80201, A.F. Grospiron, Pres.; 177,433 members, 617 locals.

Operating Engineers, International Union of (IUOE), 1125 17th St. NW, Washington, DC 20036; founded 1896; J.C. Turner, Gen. Pres.; 421,395 members, 230 locals.

Painters and Allied Trades, International Brotherhood of (IBPAT), 1750 New York Ave. NW, Washington, DC 20006; founded 1887; S. Frank Raftery, Gen. Pres. (since 1965); 192,170 members, 809 locals.

Paperworkers International Union, United (UPIU), 163-03 Horace Harding Expressway, Flushing, NY 11365; founded 1884; Wayne E. Glenn, Pres. (since 1978); 324,842 members, 1,347 locals.

***Plant Guard Workers of America; International Union, United (UPGWA),** 25510 Kelly Rd., Roseville, MI 48066; founded 1948; James C. McGahey, Pres. (since 1948); 29,000 members, 154 locals.

Plasterers' and Cement Mason's International Association of the United States & Canada; Operative, 1125 17th St. NW, Washington, DC 20036; Joseph T. Power, Pres.; 65,000 members, 450 locals.

Plumbing and Pipe Fitting Industry of the United States and Canada, United Association of Journeymen and Apprentices of the, 901 Massachusetts Ave. NW, Washington, DC 20001; Martin Ward, Pres.; 228,000 members.

***Police, Fraternal Order of,** G-3136 W. Pasadena Ave., Flint, MI 48504; Robert H. Stark, Pres.; 147,000 members, 1,036 affiliates.

***Postal Supervisors, National Association of,** PO Box 23456, L'Enfant Plaza Station, Washington, DC 20024; Donald N. Ledbetter, Pres.; 35,000 members, 450 locals.

Postal Workers Union, American (APWU), 817 14th St. NW, Washington, DC 20005; founded 1971; Emmet Andrews, Gen. Pres. (since 1977); 260,000 members, 5,000 locals.

Printing and Graphic Communications Union, International, 1730 Rhode Island Ave. NW, Washington, DC 20036; Sol Fishko, Pres.; 128,714 members, 785 locals.

Railway, Airline and Steamship Clerks, Freight Handlers, Express and Station Employees; Brotherhood of, O'Hare International Transportation Center, 6300 River Rd., Rosemont, IL 60018; Fred J. Kroll, Pres.; 235,000 members, 980 locals.

Railway Carmen of the United States and Canada, Brotherhood, 4929 Main St., Kansas City, MO 64112; founded 1890; O.W. Jacobson, Gen. Pres.; 96,500 members, 621 locals.

Retail Clerks International Union, 1775 K St. NW, Washington, DC 20006; William Wynn, Pres.; 650,876 members, 208 locals.

Retail, Wholesale and Department Store Union, 101 W. 31st St., New York, NY 10001; Alvin E. Heaps, Pres.; 180,000 members, 315 locals.

Roofers, Damp and Waterproof Workers Association, United Slate, Tile and Composition, 1125 17th St. NW, Washington, DC 20036; Roy Johnson, Pres.; 28,000 members, 205 locals.

Rubber, Cork, Linoleum and Plastic Workers of America, United, 87 South High St., Akron, OH 44308; Peter Bommarito, Pres.; 190,523 members, 565 locals.

***Rural Letter Carriers' Association, National,** 1750 Pennsylvania Ave. NW, Washington, DC 20006; Clifford Edwards, Pres.; 49,135 members.

Seafarers International Union of North America (SIUNA), 675 4th Ave., Brooklyn, NY 11232; founded 1938; Frank Drozak, Pres. (act.); 90,000 members.

Service Employees International Union (SEIU), 2020 K St. NW, Washington, DC 20006; founded 1921; George Hardy, Pres. (since 1971); 650,000 members, 321 locals.

Sheet Metal Workers' International Association (SMWIA), 1750 New York Ave. NW, Washington, DC 20006; founded 1888; Edward J. Carlough, Gen. Pres. (since 1970); 160,000 members, 394 locals.

Shoe Workers of America, United, 120 Boylston St., Boston, MA 02116; George O. Fecteau, Pres.; 35,000 members, 125 locals.

State, County and Municipal Employees, American Federation of, 1625 L St. NW, Washington, DC 20036; Jerry Wurf, Pres.; 648,160 members, 2,570 locals.

Steelworkers of America, United (USWA), 5 Gateway Center, Pittsburgh, PA 15222; founded 1936; Lloyd McBride, Pres. (since 1977); 1,400,000 members, 5,200 locals.

Teachers, American Federation of (AFT), 11 Dupont Circle NW, Washington, DC 20036; founded 1916; Albert Shanker, Pres. (since 1974); 550,000 members, 2,010 locals.

***Teamsters, Chauffeurs, Warehousemen and Helpers of America, International Brotherhood of (IBT),** 25 Louisiana Ave. NW, Washington, DC 20001; founded 1903; Frank E. Fitzsimmons, Gen. Pres. (since 1971); 2,000,000 members, 759 locals.

Textile Workers of America, United (UTWA), 420 Common St., Lawrence, MA 01840; founded 1901; Francis Schaufenbil, Intl. Pres. (since 1972); 50,000 members, 221 locals.

Theatrical Stage Employees and Moving Picture Operators of the United States and Canada, International Alliance of, 1515 Broadway, New York, NY 10036; Walter Diehl, Pres.; 61,471 members, 870 locals.

Toys, Playthings, Novelties and Allied Products of the United States and Canada, International Union of Dolls, 147 E. 26th St., New York, NY 10010; Julius Isaacson, Pres.; 31,000 members, 23 locals.

Transit Union, Amalgamated (ATU), 5025 Wisconsin Ave. NW, Washington, DC 20016; founded 1892; Dan V. Maroney Jr., Intl. Pres. (since 1973); 160,000 members, 354 locals.

Transport Workers Union of America, 1980 Broadway, New York, NY 10023; Matthew Guinan, Pres.; 150,000 members, 105 locals.

Transportation Union, United (UTU), 14600 Detroit Ave., Cleveland, OH 44107; founded 1969; Fred A. Hardin, Pres. (since 1979); 245,000 members.

***Treasury Employees Union, National (NTEU),** 1730 K St. NW, Washington, DC 20006; founded 1938; Vincent L. Connery, Natl. Pres. (since 1966); 115,000 members, 201 chapters.

Typographical Union, International (ITU), PO Box 157, Colorado Springs, CO 80901; founded 1852; Joe Bingel, Pres. (since 1978); 88,200 members, 568 locals.

***University Professors, American Association of (AAUP),** 1 Dupont Circle, Washington, DC 20036; founded 1915; Martha Friedman, Pres.; 70,000 members, 1,300 locals.

Upholsterers' International Union of North America (UIU), 25 N. 4th St., Philadelphia, PA 19106; founded 1882; Sal B. Hoffmann, Pres. (since 1937); 46,755 members, 152 locals.

Utility Workers Union of America (UWUA), 815 16th St. NW, Washington, DC 20006; founded 1946; Valentine P. Murphy, Natl. Pres. (since 1979); 60,000 members, 220 locals.

Woodworkers of America, International (IWA), 1622 N. Lombard St., Portland, OR 97217; founded 1937; Keith Johnson, Intl. Pres. (since 1973); 120,000 members, 212 locals.

Canadian Unions

Source: Labour Canada

Independent Unions (1980)

Nurses' Association, Ontario	27,000
Quebec Govt. Employees' Union	36,000
Teaching Congress, Quebec	81,033
Teachers' Federation, British Columbia	28,866
Teachers' Federation, Ontario Secondary School	36,073

Confederation of National Trade Unions (CNTU) (1980)

Public Service Employees Inc., Federation of	25,000
Social Affairs Federation	70,000

Canadian Labor Congress (CLC) (1980)

Automobile, Aerospace and Agricultural Implement Workers of America, International Union, United	130,000
Communication Workers of Canada	27,000
Paperworkers Union, Canadian	61,500
Postal Workers, Canadian Union of	24,500
Provincial Govt. Employees, National Union of	195,754
Public Employees, Canadian Union of	257,180
Public Service Alliance of Canada	155,731
Railway, Transport and General Workers, Canadian Brotherhood of	40,638

VITAL STATISTICS

Source: National Center for Health Statistics, U.S. Department of Health and Human Services

January-June 1980

Births

During the first half of 1980 there were 1,720,000 live births, an increase of 4% over the first half of 1979. The birth rate increased 3% to 15.6, and the fertility rate increased 2% to 66.9.

Marriages

For the first half of 1980 a total of 1,112,000 marriages was reported, yielding a marriage rate of 10.1 per 1,000 population. The number of marriages and the marriage rate were 2 and 1% higher, respectively, than the corresponding figures for the first 6 months of 1979.

Divorces

In the 6 months from January through June, a cumulative total of 583,000 divorces was reported, and the divorce rate for the period was 5.3 per 1,000 population. For both the number and rate this was an increase of 2% over the level recorded in the first 6 months of 1979.

Deaths

For June 1980 the provisional count of deaths totaled 153,000, amounting to a rate of 8.4 deaths per 1,000 population. This rate was the same as the rate for June 1979. Among the 153,000 deaths for June 1980 were 3,700 deaths at ages under 1 year, yielding an infant mortality rate of 12.7 deaths per 1,000 live births. This rate was 1.6% lower than the rate of 12.9 for June 1979.

The provisional death rate for the 12 months ending with May 1980, 8.8 deaths per 1,000 population, was 2.3% higher than the rate for the 12 months ending with May 1979, 8.6 deaths per 1,000 population.

Provisional Statistics

12 months ending with June

	Number		Rate*	
	1980	1979	1980	1979
Live births	3,543,000	3,384,000	16.0	15.6
Deaths	1,954,000	1,887,000	8.8	8.6
Natural increase	1,589,000	1,497,000	7.2	6.9
Marriages	2,343,000	2,276,000	10.6	10.4
Divorces	1,184,000	1,143,000	5.4	5.2
Infant deaths	45,300	44,900	12.8	13.3
Population base (in millions)			221.2	219.0

*Per 1,000 population

Annual Report for the Year 1979 (Provisional Statistics)

Births

During 1979 an estimated 3,473,000 live births occurred in the United States, 4% more than in 1978. The birth rate was 15.8 live births per 1,000 population and the fertility rate was 68.0 live births per 1,000 women aged 15–44 years. These rates were 3 and 2% higher, respectively, than in 1978.

The increase in the number of births and the birth rate in 1979 is a result of the growth in the number of women in the childbearing ages as well as the increase in the rate of childbearing. The number of women in the childbearing ages increased 2% between 1978 and 1979.

As a result of natural increase, the excess of births over deaths, 1,567,000 persons were added to the population during 1979. The rate of natural increase was 7.1 persons per 1,000 population compared with 6.5 for 1978. This increase was due both to the increase in the birth rate and to the decrease in the death rate.

Deaths

The provisional count of deaths in the United States during 1979 totaled 1,906,000, resulting in a rate of 8.7 deaths per 1,000 population. This rate was 1.1% lower than the provisional rate of 8.8 for 1978.

Among these deaths were 45,000 deaths at ages under 1 year yielding an infant mortality rate of 13.0 deaths per 1,000 live births. This rate was 4.4% lower than the provisional infant mortality rate for 1978, 13.6 deaths per 1,000 live births.

Marriages and Divorces

According to provisional reports, there were 2,317,000 marriages in 1979. This represented an increase of 3% over the provisional total for 1978 and the 4th consecutive increase in the annual marriage total. The 1979 provisional marriage total was the largest annual number of marriages ever recorded in the United States, exceeding by about 26,000 the previous peak of 2,291,045 recorded in 1946.

In 1979 the provisional marriage rate was 10.5 per 1,000 population. This rate was 2% higher than the provisional rate for 1978. After a steady decline in the period from 1972 to 1976, the marriage rate has increased each year since 1976.

An estimated 1,170,000 divorces were granted in 1979. This was 42,000 (4%) more than the provisional total for 1978 and almost 3 times more than the final total recorded for 1959.

In 1979 the provisional divorce rate increased to 5.3 per 1,000 population, up 2% over the provisional rate of 5.2 for 1978. The 1979 provisional rate represents the 2d consecutive increase in the annual divorce rate since 1977, when the final rate remained unchanged from 1976 at 5.0 per 1,000 population.

Births and Deaths in the U.S.

Refers only to events occurring within the U.S., including Alaska and Hawaii beginning in 1960. Excludes fetal deaths. Rates per 1,000 population enumerated as of April 1 for 1960, and 1970; estimated as of July 1 for all other years. (p) provisional. (NA) not available. Beginning 1970 excludes births and deaths occurring to nonresidents of the U.S.

	Births				Deaths			
Year	Males	Females	Total number	Rate	Males	Females	Total number	Rate
1955	2,073,719	1,973,576	4,047,295	24.6	872,638	656,079	1,528,717	9.3
1960	2,179,708	2,078,142	4,257,850	23.7	975,648	736,334	1,711,982	9.5
1965	1,927,054	1,833,304	3,760,358	19.4	1,035,200	792,936	1,828,136	9.4
1970	1,915,378	1,816,008	3,731,386	18.4	1,078,478	842,553	1,921,031	9.5
1975	1,613,135	1,531,063	3,144,198	14.8	1,050,819	842,060	1,892,879	8.9
1977	1,705,916	1,620,716	3,326,632	15.4	1,046,243	853,354	1,899,597	8.8
1978	1,709,394	1,623,885	3,333,279	15.3	1,055,290	872,498	1,927,788	8.8
1979(p)	NA	NA	3,473,000	15.8	NA	NA	1,906,000	8.7

Births and Deaths by States

Source: National Center for Health Statistics, U.S. Department of Health and Human Services

State	Births 1979p	Births 1978	Deaths 1979p	Deaths 1978
Alabama	60,628	58,738	34,304	34,458
Alaska	8,912	8,761	1,639	1,762
Arizona	45,707	43,004	20,385	19,623
Arkansas	35,008	33,445	21,554	21,555
California	363,463	356,190	169,954	172,077
Colorado	47,813	44,387	19,057	18,944
Connecticut	36,959	35,695	26,124	26,104
Delaware	9,123	8,945	5,048	5,095
Dist. of Col.	17,339	19,054	9,042	8,737
Florida	120,839	112,987	100,757	97,791
Georgia	89,446	83,784	42,646	43,416
Hawaii	17,429	16,650	6,061	6,168
Idaho	19,686	18,751	5,128	4,853
Illinois	181,218	174,212	100,218	100,363
Indiana	87,452	83,595	47,153	47,451
Iowa	47,083	45,071	26,237	27,203
Kansas	37,100	34,747	20,552	21,001
Kentucky	60,182	58,359	32,552	33,108
Louisiana	79,413	75,659	34,918	35,649
Maine	15,755	14,584	10,367	10,139
Maryland	50,043	47,987	32,002	32,390
Massachusetts	73,104	69,078	52,624	53,860
Michigan	142,127	136,449	72,480	73,911
Minnesota	64,997	62,356	32,592	33,956
Mississippi	45,913	45,583	22,720	22,919
Missouri	78,505	77,072	48,558	51,786
Montana	13,803	13,176	6,407	6,401
Nebraska	26,093	25,216	14,116	14,510
Nevada	11,830	10,868	5,842	5,245
New Hampshire	12,829	12,330	7,287	7,190
New Jersey	91,896	89,778	64,126	64,353
New Mexico	25,570	21,988	8,596	8,488
New York	231,787	229,782	160,937	164,635
North Carolina	84,388	82,583	47,168	47,640
North Dakota	12,769	12,112	5,566	5,720
Ohio	164,111	161,813	93,197	97,928
Oklahoma	47,214	43,735	27,204	26,924
Oregon	42,984	39,940	21,071	21,031
Pennsylvania	157,783	153,238	117,269	119,812
Rhode Island	12,235	11,766	9,295	9,095
South Carolina	49,956	47,198	23,736	23,577
South Dakota	12,623	12,037	6,236	6,359
Tennessee	72,261	70,431	41,264	41,289
Texas	265,066	236,699	107,493	102,707
Utah	42,304	40,051	8,546	8,180
Vermont	7,396	7,114	4,364	4,587
Virginia	73,812	70,418	40,183	40,242
Washington	55,077	57,681	24,496	30,068
West Virginia	30,263	31,357	19,140	20,112
Wisconsin	72,818	68,129	38,873	40,625
Wyoming	8,946	8,102	2,929	3,029
Total	**3,473,000**	**3,329,000**	**1,906,000**	**1,924,000**

(p) provisional

Marriages and Divorces by States

Source: National Center for Health Statistics, U.S. Department of Health and Human Services

1979 provisional figures; divorces include reported annulments.

State	Marriages	Divorces
Alabama	48,807	26,900
Alaska	5,071	3,513
Arizona	29,549	19,917
Arkansas	24,947	19,337
California	159,172	137,714
Colorado	31,889	16,688
Connecticut	24,675	12,780
Delaware	4,418	3,166
Dist. of Col.	4,974	4,173
Florida	103,406	70,155
Georgia	65,898	32,842
Hawaii	11,658	5,035
Idaho	13,568	6,519
Illinois	108,443	53,842
Indiana	59,613	NA
Iowa	27,731	11,403
Kansas	24,867	13,017
Kentucky	36,513	16,913
Louisiana	41,816	NA
Maine	11,944	6,110
Maryland	45,903	15,541
Massachusetts	42,652	17,405
Michigan	86,660	45,951
Minnesota	35,758	14,526
Mississippi	26,718	12,901
Missouri	52,336	28,467
Montana	8,246	5,159
Nebraska	14,032	6,021
Nevada	121,874	10,465
New Hampshire	9,189	5,056
New Jersey	54,844	24,667
New Mexico	16,785	9,329
New York	141,350	59,898
North Carolina	45,233	27,523
North Dakota	5,997	2,076
Ohio	102,539	60,108
Oklahoma	44,452	22,823
Oregon	21,907	17,709
Pennsylvania	89,417	39,689
Rhode Island	7,350	3,599
South Carolina	53,968	13,965
South Dakota	9,098	2,635
Tennessee	59,407	32,349
Texas	174,743	91,454
Utah	16,823	7,542
Vermont	5,228	2,296
Virginia	58,739	23,648
Washington	45,809	26,802
West Virginia	17,733	10,066
Wisconsin	39,551	16,880
Wyoming	6,032	3,654
Total	**2,317,000**	**1,120,228**

(NA) not available.

Marriages, Divorces, and Rates in the U.S.

Source: National Center for Health Statistics, Public Health Service

Data refer only to events occurring within the United States, including Alaska and Hawaii beginning with 1960. Rates per 1,000 population.

Year	Marriages[1] No.	Marriages[1] Rate	Divorces[2] No.	Divorces[2] Rate
1890	570,000	**9.0**	33,461	**0.5**
1895	620,000	**8.9**	40,387	**0.6**
1900	709,000	**9.3**	55,751	**0.7**
1905	842,000	**10.0**	67,976	**0.8**
1910	948,166	**10.3**	83,045	**0.9**
1915	1,007,595	**10.0**	104,298	**1.0**
1920	1,274,476	**12.0**	170,505	**1.6**
1925	1,188,334	**10.3**	175,449	**1.5**
1930	1,126,856	**9.2**	195,961	**1.6**
1935	1,327,000	**10.4**	218,000	**1.7**
1940	1,595,879	**12.1**	264,000	**2.0**
1945	1,612,992	**12.2**	485,000	[3]**3.5**
1950	1,667,231	**11.1**	385,144	**2.6**
1955	1,531,000	**9.3**	377,000	**2.3**
1960	1,523,000	**8.5**	393,000	**2.2**
1965	1,800,000	**9.3**	479,000	**2.5**
1970	2,158,802	**10.6**	708,000	**3.5**
1975	2,152,662	**10.1**	1,036,000	**4.9**
1978	2,282,272	**10.5**	1,130,000	**5.2**
1979(p)	2,359,000	**10.7**	1,170,000	**5.3**

(1) Includes estimates and marriage licenses for some states for all years. (2) Includes reported annulments. (3) Divorce rates for 1945 based on population including armed forces overseas. (p) provisional.

Wedding Anniversaries

The traditional names for wedding anniversaries go back many years in social usage. As such names as wooden, crystal, silver, and golden were applied it was considered proper to present the married pair with gifts made of these products or of something related. The traditional list follows, with a few allowable revisions in parentheses.

1st—Paper
2d—Cotton
3d—Leather
4th—Linen (silk)
5th—Wood
6th—Iron
7th—Wool (copper)
8th—Bronze
9th—Pottery (china)
10th—Tin (aluminum)
11th—Steel
12th—Silk
13th—Lace
14th—Ivory
15th—Crystal
20th—China
25th—Silver
30th—Pearl
35th—Coral (jade)
40th—Ruby
45th—Sapphire
50th—Gold
55th—Emerald
60th—Diamond
75th—Diamond

Deaths and Death Rates for Selected Causes

Source: National Center for Health Statistics, U.S. Department of Health and Human Services

1978 Cause of death	Number	Rate[1]
All causes	**1,927,788**	**883.4**
Enteritis and other diarrheal diseases	1,874	0.9
Tuberculosis, all forms	2,914	1.3
Septicemia	7,800	3.6
Syphilis and its sequelae	169	0.1
Other infective and parasitic diseases	4,813	2.2
Malignant neoplasms, including neoplasms of lymphatic and hematopoietic tissues	396,992	181.9
Diabetes mellitus	33,841	15.5
Meningitis	1,560	0.7
Major cardiovascular diseases	996,120	442.7
Diseases of heart	729,510	334.3
Active rheumatic fever and chronic rheumatic heart disease	13,402	6.1
Hypertensive heart disease and renal disease	3,249	1.5
Ischemic heart disease	642,270	294.3
Chronic disease of endocardium and other myocardial insufficiency	4,072	1.9
All other forms of heart disease	59,430	27.2
Hypertension	5,490	2.5
Cerebrovascular diseases	175,629	80.5
Arteriosclerosis	28,940	13.3
Other diseases of arteries, arterioles, and capillaries	26,551	12.2
Acute bronchitis and bronchiolitis	756	0.3
Influenza and pneumonia	58,319	26.7
Influenza	4,052	1.9
Pneumonia	54,267	24.9
Bronchitis, emphysema, and asthma	21,875	10.0
Chronic and unqualified bronchitis	4,376	2.0
Emphysema	15,627	7.2
Asthma	1,872	0.9
Peptic ulcer	5,545	2.5
Hernia and intestinal obstruction	5,568	2.6
Cirrhosis of liver	30,066	13.8
Cholelithiasis, cholecystitis, and cholangitis	2,941	1.3
Nephritis and nephrosis	8,868	4.1
Infections of kidney	3,096	1.4
Hyperplasia of prostate	854	0.4
Congenital anomalies	12,968	5.9
Certain causes of mortality in early infancy	22,033	10.1
Symptoms and ill-defined conditions	31,324	14.4
All other diseases	137,396	63.0
Accidents	105,561	48.4
Motor vehicle accidents	52,411	24.0
Suicide	27,294	12.5
Homicide	20,432	9.4
All other external causes	4,163	1.9

Due to rounding estimates of death, figures may not add to total. Data based on a 10% sampling of all death certificates for a 12-month (Jan.-Dec.) period. (1) Rates per 100,000 population.

Principal Types of Accidental Deaths

Source: National Center for Health Statistics, U.S. Department of Health and Human Services

Year	All types	Motor vehicle	Falls	Burns	Drowning	Firearms	Machinery	Poison gases	Other poisons
1960	93,806	38,137	19,023	7,645	5,232	2,334	1,951	1,253	1,679
1965	108,004	49,163	19,984	7,347	5,485	2,344	2,054	1,526	2,110
1970	114,638	54,633	16,926	6,718	6,391	2,406	...	1,620	3,679
1975	103,030	45,853	14,896	6,071	6,640	2,380	...	1,577	4,694
1978	105,561	52,411	13,690	6,163	5,784	1,806	...	1,737	3,035
Death rates per 100,000 population									
1960	52.1	21.2	10.6	4.3	2.9	1.3	1.1	0.7	0.9
1965	55.8	25.4	10.3	3.8	2.8	1.2	1.1	0.8	1.1
1970	56.4	26.9	8.3	3.3	3.1	1.2	...	0.8	1.8
1975	48.4	21.5	7.0	2.8	3.1	1.1	...	0.7	2.2
1978	48.4	24.0	6.3	2.8	2.7	0.8	...	0.8	1.4

Deaths in Civil Aviation Accidents

Source: National Safety Council

(includes only U.S. carriers)

Year	Total deaths[1]	Passenger deaths in scheduled flights — Domestic No.	Domestic Rate[2]	International No.	International Rate[2]	General aviation deaths — Total	Pleasure flying
1960	1,286	297	0.93	10	0.12	787	NA
1965	1,279	205	0.38	21	0.12	1,029	590
1970	1,454	0	0.00	2	0.01	1,310	726
1975	1,446	113	0.09	0	0.00	1,345	863
1979p	1,664	262	0.12	59	0.11	1,311	NA

(1) Includes some deaths not shown separately—crew members in scheduled operations and persons not in planes killed in airplane accidents. Excludes deaths in military plane accidents. (2) Rates are the number of deaths per 100,000,000 passenger miles. (p) preliminary. NA—not available.

Accidental Injuries by Severity of Injury

Source: National Safety Council

1979 Severity of injury	Total*	Motor vehicle	Work	Home	Public[1]
Deaths*	103,500	51,900	13,200	22,000	21,000
Disabling injuries*	10,000,000	2,000,000	2,300,000	3,300,000	2,600,000
Permanent impairments	360,000	150,000	80,000	90,000	60,000
Temporary total disabilities	9,600,000	1,850,000	2,200,000	3,200,000	2,500,000
Certain Costs of Accidental Injuries, 1979 ($ billions)					
Total*	**$75.7**	**$35.8**	**$27.3**	**$8.1**	**$6.0**
Wage loss	20.9	10.8	4.7	3.2	3.4
Medical expense	9.2	3.1	2.8	2.0	1.6
Insurance administration	15.1	9.8	5.1	0.1	0.1

*Duplication between motor vehicle, work, and home are eliminated in the total column. (1) Excludes motor vehicle and work accidents in public places.

Motor Vehicle Traffic Deaths by State

Source: National Safety Council

Place of accidents	Number 1979	Number 1978	Death rate* 1979	Death rate* 1978
Total U.S.†	**51,900**	**51,500**	**3.4**	**3.3**
Alabama	1,020	1,169	3.7	3.9
Alaska	90	127	3.3	4.6
Arizona	1,030	1,027	5.1	5.3
Arkansas	548	571	3.5	3.5
California	5,503	5,296	3.4	3.3
Colorado	691	713	3.4	3.6
Connecticut	576	461	2.9	2.4
Delaware	121	126	3.1	3.0
Dist. of Col.	50	51	1.6	1.4
Florida	2,637	2,305	3.5	3.2
Georgia	1,523	1,498	3.3	3.4
Hawaii	205	195	4.0	4.1
Idaho	333	330	4.4	4.3
Illinois	2,048	2,166	3.1	3.3
Indiana	1,309	1,316	3.0	3.1
Iowa	654	650	3.1	3.3
Kansas	520	572	3.4	3.4
Kentucky	905	893	3.2	3.2
Louisiana	1,187	1,092	4.8	4.8
Maine	241	241	3.3	3.0
Maryland	700	730	2.4	2.6
Massachusetts	920	864	2.8	2.5
Michigan	1,847	2,076	2.9	3.1
Minnesota	881	980	3.0	3.4
Mississippi	716	784	4.3	4.7
Missouri	1,162	1,224	3.4	3.5
Montana	332	271	4.9	3.9
Nebraska	330	350	2.7	2.8
Nevada	365	312	6.3	5.4
New Hampshire	184	171	3.0	2.6
New Jersey	1,141	1,122	2.1	2.2
New Mexico	650	661	5.6	5.7
New York	2,377	2,551	3.8	3.4
North Carolina	1,522	1,515	3.6	3.6
North Dakota	127	185	2.5	3.5
Ohio	2,281	2,048	3.1	2.8
Oklahoma	869	920	3.3	3.4
Oregon	675	722	3.5	3.6
Pennsylvania	2,204	2,137	3.0	2.9
Rhode Island	125	108	1.9	1.8
South Carolina	900	898	3.8	3.7
South Dakota	211	194	3.8	3.3
Tennessee	1,236	1,270	3.2	3.3
Texas	4,229	3,980	4.1	3.6
Utah	330	376	3.5	3.8
Vermont	163	127	4.4	3.4
Virginia	1,014	1,080	2.6	2.7
Washington	1,032	1,006	3.5	3.4
West Virginia	532	467	4.8	4.1
Wisconsin	997	998	3.0	2.9
Wyoming	244	241	5.3	5.0
Puerto Rico††	...	565	...	7.0

*The death rate is the number of deaths per 100 million vehicle miles. †Includes both traffic and nontraffic motor-vehicle deaths. ††Not included in Total U.S.

Transportation Accident Passenger Death Rates, 1979

Source: National Safety Council

Kind of transportation	Passenger miles (billions)	Passenger deaths	Rate per 100,000,000 pass. miles	1977-1979 aver. death rate
Passenger automobiles and taxis(1)	2,220.0	29,100	1.31	1.30
Passenger automobiles on turnpikes	46.8	340	0.73	0.69
Buses	80.4	120	0.15	0.15
Intercity buses(2)	17.3	3	0.02	0.02
Railroad passenger trains	11.3	6	0.05	0.07
Scheduled air transport planes (domestic)	223.8	262	0.12	0.06

(1) Drivers of passenger automobiles are considered passengers. (2) Class 1 only, representing 65 per cent of total intercity bus passenger mileage.

Home Accident Deaths

Source: National Safety Council

Year	Total home	Falls	Fires, burns(2)	Suffo., ingested object	Suffo., mechanical	Poison (solid, liquid)	Poison by gas	Firearms	Other
1950	29,000	14,800	5,000	(1)	1,600	1,300	1,250	950	4,100
1955	28,500	14,100	5,400	(1)	1,250	1,150	900	1,100	4,600
1960	28,000	12,300	6,350	1,850	1,500	1,350	900	1,200	2,550
1965	28,500	11,700	6,100	1,300*	1,200	1,700	1,100	1,300	4,100
1970	27,000	9,700	5,600	1,800	1,100	3,000	1,100	1,400	3,300
1975	25,000	8,000	5,000	1,800	800	3,700	1,000	1,300	3,400
1979	22,000	7,000	4,700	2,000	500	2,600	1,000	1,000	3,200

*Data for this year and subsequent years not comparable with previous years due to classification changes. (1) Included in Other. (2) Includes deaths resulting from conflagration, regardless of nature of injury.

Accidental Deaths by Age, Sex, and Type, 1977

Source: National Safety Council

	All types	Motor vehicle	Falls	Drowning	Fires, burns	Ingest. of food, object	Firearms	Poison (solid, liquid)	Poison by gas	% Male all types
All ages	**103,202**	**49,510**	**13,773**	**7,126**	**6,357**	**3,037**	**1,982**	**3,374**	**1,596**	**70**
Under 5	4,470	1,472	175	716	767	443	48	94	35	59
5 to 14	6,305	3,142	122	1,110	550	79	344	40	59	68
15 to 24	25,619	18,092	518	2,150	612	195	665	709	425	78
25 to 34	14,593	8,600	445	1,100	594	181	346	875	276	81
35 to 44	8,867	4,431	511	590	487	211	189	474	217	76
45 to 54	9,427	4,148	904	520	676	303	155	432	201	73
55 to 64	9,740	3,852	1,341	420	805	455	130	357	161	70
65 to 74	9,006	3,060	1,995	280	843	447	71	207	121	62
75 & over	15,175	2,713	7,762	240	1,023	723	34	186	101	46
Sex										
Male	71,935	35,804	7,226	6,006	3,866	1,764	1,675	2,204	1,204	
Female	31,267	13,706	6,547	1,120	2,491	1,273	307	1,350	392	
Percent male	70%	72%	52%	84%	61%	58%	85%	60%	75%	

Average Lifetime in the U.S.

Source: National Center for Health Statistics, U.S. Department of Health and Human Services

1979p Age interval	Number living[1]	Avg. life expect.[2]	1979p Age interval	Number living[1]	Avg. life expect.[2]
0-1	100,000	73.8	40-45	94,740	36.8
1-5	98,696	73.8	45-50	93,414	32.3
5-10	98,451	69.9	50-55	91,356	28.0
10-15	98,289	65.0	55-60	88,087	23.9
15-20	98,108	60.2	60-65	83,397	20.1
20-25	97,610	55.5	65-70	76,550	16.7
25-30	96,949	50.8	70-75	67,879	13.5
30-35	96,282	46.2	75-80	56,547	10.6
35-40	95,606	41.5	80-85	41,923	8.5
			85 and over	26,925	6.8

(1) Of 100,000 born alive, number living at beginning of age interval. (2) Average number of years of life remaining at beginning of age interval.

Years of Life Expected at Birth

Year	Total pop.	Male	Female	Year	Total pop.	Male	Female
1979p	73.8	69.9	77.8	1950	68.2	65.6	71.1
1978	73.3	69.5	77.2	1940	62.9	60.8	65.2
1975	72.5	68.7	76.5	1930	59.7	58.1	61.6
1970	70.8	67.1	74.7	1920[1]	54.1	53.6	54.6
1965	70.2	66.8	73.8	1910[1]	50.0	48.4	51.8
1960	69.7	66.6	73.1	1900[1]	47.3	46.3	48.3

(p) Provisional (1) Based on data for death registration states only.

Ownership of Life Insurance in the U.S. and Assets of U.S. Life Insurance Companies

Source: American Council of Life Insurance

Legal Reserve Life Insurance Companies (millions of dollars)

	Purchases of life insurance				Insurance in force					
Year	Ordinary	Group	Industrial	Total	Ordinary	Group	Industrial	Credit	Total	Assets
1940	7,022	747	3,318	11,087	79,346	14,938	20,866	380	115,530	30,802
1950	18,260	6,237	5,492	29,989	149,116	47,793	33,415	3,844	234,168	64,020
1960	56,183	15,328	6,906	78,417	341,881	175,903	39,563	29,101	586,448	119,576
1965	89,643	52,867*	7,302	149,812*	499,638	308,078	39,818	53,020	900,554	158,884
1970	134,802	65,381*	6,612	206,795*	734,730	551,357	38,644	77,392	1,402,123	207,254
1975	207,052	102,659*	6,741	316,452*	1,083,421	904,695	39,423	112,032	2,139,571	289,304
1977	247,453	115,839	6,504	369,796	1,289,321	1,115,047	39,045	139,402	2,582,815	351,722
1978	283,067	125,129	6,015	414,211	1,425,095	1,243,994	38,080	163,081	2,870,250	389,924
1979	323,640	159,998	5,165	488,803	1,585,878	1,419,418	37,794	179,250	3,222,340	432,282

*Includes Servicemen's Group Life Insurance $27.4 billion in 1965, $16.8 billion in 1970, and $1.7 billion in 1975.

Accidental Deaths by Month and Type, 1977 and 1979

Source: National Safety Council

		1977 details by type								
Month	1979 totals	All types	Motor vehicle	Falls	Drowning†	Fires, burns*	Ingest. of food, object	Firearms	Poison (solid, liquid)	Poison by gas
Total	**103,500**	**103,202**	**49,510**	**13,773**	**7,126**	**6,357**	**3,037**	**1,982**	**3,374**	**1,596**
January	7,700	7,792	2,909	1,273	186	1,032	300	194	344	299
February	6,700	6,957	2,973	1,058	250	736	213	140	239	194
March	7,900	7,726	3,600	1,150	370	611	280	132	295	125
April	8,050	8,106	3,873	1,119	540	519	235	142	290	81
May	9,100	8,890	4,270	1,130	960	584	211	139	322	78
June	9,600	9,299	4,457	1,144	1,170	330	244	132	262	110
July	9,500	10,625	5,075	1,189	1,570	285	263	158	284	71
August	9,100	9,302	4,759	1,093	870	283	258	142	267	50
September	8,650	8,314	4,417	1,080	480	260	232	145	268	62
October	9,350	8,850	4,728	1,169	320	411	253	217	266	143
November	8,750	8,265	4,240	1,116	220	511	279	243	240	166
December	9,100	8,796	4,209	1,252	190	795	269	198	297	217
Average	**8,625**	**8,600**	**4,126**	**1,148**	**594**	**530**	**253**	**165**	**281**	**133**

*Includes deaths resulting from conflagration regardless of nature of injury. †Includes drowning in water transport accidents. Some totals partly estimated.

Pedalcycle Accidents

Since 1935, the National Safety Council reports the number of pedalcycle motor vehicle deaths has more than doubled to 1,000 in 1979. The number of pedalcycles in use, 98.5 million (including sidewalk pedalcycles), is 28 times the number in 1935; so the death rate in 1979 was one-twelfth the rate in 1935. The proportion of deaths occurring to young adults and adults has steadily increased since 1960. Persons 15 years of age and older accounted for more than one-half the deaths in 1979 compared to about one-fifth in 1960.

Physical Growth Range for Children from 2 to 18 Years

Source: National Center for Health Statistics, U.S. Department of Health and Human Services

Boys

Age	Height in centimeters: Shortest 5%	Median height	Tallest 5%	Weight in kilograms: Lightest 5%	Median weight	Heaviest 5%
2	82.5	86.8	94.4	10.49	12.34	15.50
3	89.0	94.9	102.0	12.05	14.62	17.77
4	95.8	102.9	109.9	13.64	16.69	20.27
5	102.0	109.9	117.0	15.27	18.67	23.09
6	107.7	116.1	123.5	16.93	20.69	26.34
7	113.0	121.7	129.7	18.64	22.85	30.12
8	118.1	127.0	135.7	20.40	25.30	34.51
9	122.9	132.2	141.8	22.25	28.30	39.58
10	127.7	137.5	148.1	24.33	31.44	45.27
11	132.6	143.3	154.9	26.80	35.30	51.47
12	137.6	149.7	162.3	29.85	39.78	58.09
13	142.9	156.5	169.8	33.64	44.95	65.02
14	148.8	163.1	176.7	38.22	50.77	72.13
15	155.2	169.0	181.9	43.11	56.71	79.12
16	161.1	173.5	185.4	47.74	62.10	85.62
17	164.9	176.2	187.3	51.50	66.31	91.31
18	165.7	176.8	187.6	53.97	68.88	95.76

Girls

Age	Height in centimeters: Shortest 5%	Median height	Tallest 5%	Weight in kilograms: Lightest 5%	Median weight	Heaviest 5%
2	81.6	86.8	93.6	9.95	11.80	14.15
3	88.3	94.1	100.6	11.61	14.10	17.22
4	95.0	101.6	108.3	13.11	15.96	19.91
5	101.1	108.4	115.6	14.55	17.66	22.62
6	106.6	114.6	122.7	16.05	19.52	25.75
7	111.8	120.6	129.5	17.71	21.84	29.68
8	116.9	126.4	136.2	19.62	24.84	34.71
9	122.1	132.2	142.9	21.82	28.46	40.64
10	127.5	138.3	149.5	24.36	32.55	47.17
11	133.5	144.8	156.2	27.24	36.95	54.00
12	139.8	151.5	162.7	30.52	41.53	60.81
13	145.2	157.1	168.1	34.14	46.10	67.30
14	148.7	160.4	171.3	37.76	50.28	73.08
15	150.5	161.8	172.8	40.99	53.68	77.78
16	151.6	162.4	173.3	43.41	55.89	80.99
17	152.7	163.1	173.5	44.74	56.69	82.46
18	153.6	163.7	173.6	45.26	56.62	82.47

This table simply gives a general picture for American children at specific age/dates (not the entire age range). When used as a standard, the individual variation in children's growth should not be overlooked. In most cases the height-weight relationship is probably a more valid index of weight status than a weight-for-age assessment.

Average Weight of Americans by Height and Age

Source: Society of Actuaries; from the *1979 Build and Blood Pressure Study*

The figures represent weights in ordinary indoor clothing and shoes, and heights with shoes.

Men: Height	20-24	25-29	30-39	40-49	50-59	60-69	Women: Height	20-24	25-29	30-39	40-49	50-59	60-69
5'2"	130	134	138	140	141	140	4'10". . . .	105	110	113	118	121	123
5'3"	136	140	143	144	145	144	4'11". . . .	110	112	115	121	125	127
5'4"	139	143	147	149	150	149	5'0"	112	114	118	123	127	130
5'5"	143	147	151	154	155	153	5'1"	116	119	121	127	131	133
5'6"	148	152	156	158	159	158	5'2"	120	121	124	129	133	136
5'7"	153	156	160	163	164	163	5'3"	124	125	128	133	137	140
5'8"	157	161	165	167	168	167	5'4"	127	128	131	136	141	143
5'9"	163	166	170	172	173	172	5'5"	130	132	134	139	144	147
5'10". . . .	167	171	174	176	177	176	5'6"	133	134	137	143	147	150
5'11". . . .	171	175	179	181	182	181	5'7"	137	138	141	147	152	155
6'0"	176	181	184	186	187	186	5'8"	141	142	145	150	156	158
6'1"	182	186	190	192	193	191	5'9"	146	148	150	155	159	161
6'2"	187	191	195	197	198	196	5'10". . . .	149	150	153	158	162	163
6'3"	193	197	201	203	204	200	5'11". . . .	155	156	159	162	166	167
6'4"	198	202	206	208	209	207	6'0"	157	159	164	168	171	172

How to Obtain Birth, Marriage, Death Records

The United States government has published a series of inexpensive booklets entitled: Where to Write for Birth & Death Records; Where to Write for Marriage Records; Where to Write for Divorce Records; Where to Write for Birth and Death Records of U. S. Citizens Who were Born or Died Outside of the U. S.; Birth Certifications for Alien Children Adopted by U. S. Citizens; You May Save Time Proving Your Age and Other Birth Facts. They tell where to write to get a certified copy of an original vital record. Supt. of Documents, Government Printing Office, Washington, DC 20402.

The Nation's Hospitals

Source: American Hospital Association

In 1979, there were 6,988 hospitals in the United States registered by the American Hospital Association. These institutions had about 1.36 million beds and reported admitting some 37.8 million inpatients. About $79.8 billion was spent to provide services for both inpatients and outpatients.

State	Hospitals		Beds		Average daily census		Admissions		Expenses ($1,000)	
	Fed.	Non-fed.	Fed.	Non-fed.	Fed.	Non-fed.	Fed.	Non-fed.	Fed.	Non-fed.
Alabama	8	139	2,555	22,790	2,028	17,135	43,086	727,600	138,682	1,084,346
Alaska	9	17	571	1,120	299	672	16,552	37,824	44,296	105,609
Arizona	16	64	1,844	9,876	1,316	7,203	54,632	339,752	145,235	706,207
Arkansas	4	92	1,866	10,880	1,514	7,468	25,105	416,735	83,978	486,310
California	30	578	9,762	104,592	7,321	72,732	215,098	3,120,977	788,299	8,158,237
Colorado	6	93	1,762	13,264	1,436	8,933	41,878	424,920	160,655	787,725
Connecticut	5	61	960	17,484	657	13,971	18,848	440,474	66,271	1,103,503
Delaware	2	13	426	3,794	321	3,220	6,529	78,720	21,500	194,353
Dist. of Columbia	3	14	3,620	4,943	3,451	3,839	42,547	156,890	282,704	502,731
Florida	13	238	3,881	52,615	3,127	38,041	102,040	1,585,207	275,043	2,922,928
Georgia	9	180	2,792	28,290	2,168	20,115	56,291	921,033	218,092	1,388,407
Hawaii	1	26	547	3,341	430	2,574	18,320	98,832	53,155	216,609
Idaho	2	49	182	3,567	111	2,379	4,905	129,480	15,309	174,906
Illinois	10	275	5,824	67,711	4,464	51,745	72,601	1,979,208	302,285	4,546,418
Indiana	4	130	1,973	30,362	1,469	23,897	19,476	890,120	80,615	1,581,048
Iowa	3	138	1,558	19,918	1,104	13,575	19,436	557,362	76,496	875,096
Kansas	7	157	1,906	16,493	1,419	11,682	26,535	425,186	91,387	770,249
Kentucky	5	116	1,834	16,747	1,296	13,002	35,531	632,065	116,354	822,318
Louisiana	8	150	2,498	22,651	1,717	15,875	42,474	749,688	134,343	1,159,669
Maine	1	51	642	6,447	533	4,809	6,938	175,786	26,200	337,325
Maryland	9	75	2,997	22,178	2,302	18,301	48,011	525,081	225,064	1,347,651
Massachusetts	7	179	3,699	40,759	2,970	33,177	31,570	908,516	168,158	2,797,561
Michigan	8	231	2,289	47,966	1,746	37,674	36,618	1,456,308	137,061	3,408,348
Minnesota	5	178	1,683	28,949	1,347	20,924	23,519	686,125	91,287	1,302,251
Mississippi	5	111	1,764	14,719	1,466	10,970	30,935	468,435	99,603	571,342
Missouri	7	157	2,985	31,782	2,181	23,769	50,441	912,737	237,383	1,734,925
Montana	6	61	396	4,926	245	3,167	10,062	130,025	23,930	182,685
Nebraska	5	104	883	11,022	665	7,382	20,178	290,153	52,370	478,018
Nevada	4	21	263	2,989	193	2,025	7,257	112,157	23,623	236,435
New Hampshire	2	31	322	4,358	292	3,175	6,797	130,970	22,523	213,086
New Jersey	4	131	2,591	41,152	2,032	33,955	27,432	1,051,988	127,331	2,239,970
New Mexico	11	43	895	5,209	618	3,703	33,397	164,106	74,978	281,689
New York	16	342	9,762	121,678	8,100	105,316	105,525	2,656,801	498,578	7,755,744
North Carolina	9	150	2,889	30,485	2,280	23,312	50,809	889,046	151,066	1,384,203
North Dakota	5	55	414	5,506	273	3,724	11,918	134,505	23,400	204,347
Ohio	5	234	4,045	59,530	3,173	46,590	43,045	1,821,880	221,985	3,631,462
Oklahoma	12	130	1,103	16,472	802	11,328	41,971	485,741	89,108	778,354
Oregon	2	83	958	10,670	720	7,464	15,831	367,505	54,570	662,338
Pennsylvania	11	303	6,020	80,340	4,879	63,585	46,199	1,956,557	265,592	4,497,442
Rhode Island	2	19	399	5,759	307	5,002	10,515	136,452	31,798	370,362
South Carolina	7	82	1,619	15,258	1,095	11,744	40,351	440,306	108,312	637,550
South Dakota	10	59	1,146	4,448	837	2,751	20,266	123,541	55,762	156,783
Tennessee	5	162	2,807	28,564	2,254	21,977	39,412	934,382	140,029	1,361,616
Texas	24	544	8,514	71,569	6,965	50,142	178,253	2,341,653	587,166	3,596,526
Utah	2	39	487	4,634	356	3,378	12,791	197,444	35,223	294,568
Vermont	1	18	224	2,717	191	2,010	3,693	75,068	16,511	126,997
Virginia	9	125	3,115	28,744	2,451	22,250	68,688	741,890	234,845	1,351,882
Washington	11	114	2,319	13,640	1,782	9,513	51,495	543,477	151,258	884,587
West Virginia	5	73	1,134	12,971	934	9,955	18,967	394,659	65,737	582,082
Wisconsin	3	164	2,090	26,624	1,713	19,395	23,996	759,675	107,301	1,450,782
Wyoming	3	28	533	1,998	443	1,132	6,563	64,487	23,304	83,052
Total U.S.	**361**	**6,627**	**117,348**	**1,245,501**	**91,793**	**951,657**	**1,985,597**	**35,816,529**	**7,265,755**	**72,530,632**

Selected Statistics on State and County Mental Hospitals

Source: National Institute of Mental Health

Year	Total admitted	Net releases	Deaths in hospital	Residents end of year	Expense per patient
1955	178,003	NA	44,384	558,922	$1,116.59
1960	234,791	NA	49,748	535,540	1,702.41
1970	393,174	394,627	30,804	338,592	5,435.38
1973	377,020*	386,962	19,899	248,562	9,207.92
1975	376,156	391,345	13,401	193,436	13,634.53
1977	414,703	408,667	9,961	159,405	NA

*Includes estimates. NA-not available. (1) Per average daily resident patient population.

Patients' Expenditures in Mental Hospitals

Source: National Institute of Mental Health

Based on reports of 298 state and county hospitals on the Jan., 1978, Inventory of Mental Health Facilities.

State	No. patients	Tot. expend. ($000)	State	No. patients	Tot. expend. ($000)	State	No. patients	Tot. expend. ($000)	State	No. patients	Tot. expend. ($000)
U.S.	**159,405**	**3,329,351**	Ariz.	642	19,143	Col.	1,151	36,303	D.C.	2,344	89,107
Ala.	2,196	37,549	Ark.	351	13,936	Conn.	2,709	50,218	Fla.	6,108	78,611
Alas.	102	6,439	Cal.	6,981	163,386	Del.	688	18,535	Ga.	5,432	113,505

State	No. patients	Tot. expend. ($000)	State	No. patients	Tot. expend. ($000)	State	No. patients	Tot. expend. ($000)	State	No. patients	Tot. expend. ($000)
Ha. . .	135	6,265	Mass. .	4,270	71,767	N.M.. .	312	9,275	S.D . .	625	7,995
Ida. . .	190	5,235	Mich. .	4,680	150,047	N.Y. . .	30,122	692,574	Tenn. .	3,694	55,465
Ill. . . .	6,049	174,511	Minn. .	2,353	41,102	N.C. . .	4,062	79,453	Tex. . .	5,578	108,310
Ind. . .	4,019	67,193	Miss. .	2,407	20,845	N.D. . .	615	9,381	Ut. . . .	337	5,930
Ia. . . .	1,180	24,918	Mo. . .	3,904	77,413	Oh. . .	6,868	153,285	Vt. . . .	356	7,954
Kan. . .	1,253	28,563	Mon. .	490	13,878	Okla. .	2,087	34,078	Va. . .	5,793	67,090
Ky. . .	886	20,141	Neb. . .	692	20,912	Ore. . .	1,467	27,205	Wash. .	1,203	20,658
La. . .	2,099	38,290	Nev. . .	206	7,431	Pa. . .	12,235	291,355	W. Va.	2,376	20,788
Me. . .	663	12,201	N.H. . .	784	19,689	R.I. . .	1,354	23,291	Wis. . .	747	35,587
Md. . .	4,012	67,028	N.J. . .	6,799	140,629	S.C. . .	3,527	39,022	Wy. . .	276	5,865

Patient Care Episodes in Mental Health Facilities

Source: National Institute of Mental Health

Year	Total all facilities[1]	Inpatient services: State & county mental hospitals	Private mental[2] hospitals	Gen. hosp. psychiatric service (non-VA)	VA psychiatric inpatient services	Federally assisted comm. men. health cen.	Outpatient services: Federally assisted comm. men. health cen.	Other
1977	6,392,979	574,226	184,189	571,725	217,507	268,966	1,741,729	2,834,637
1975	6,409,477	598,993	165,327	565,696	214,264	246,891	1,584,968	3,033,308
1969	3,572,822	767,115	123,850	535,493	186,913	65,000	291,148	1,603,303
1965	2,636,525	804,926	125,428	519,328	115,843	—	—	1,071,000
1955	1,675,352	818,832	123,231	265,934	88,355	—	—	379,000

(1) In order to present trends on the same set of facilities over this interval, it has been necessary to exclude from this table the following: private psychiatric office practice; psychiatric service modes of all types in hospitals or outpatient clinics of federal agencies other than the VA (e.g., Public Health Service, Indian Health Service, Department of Defense Bureau of Prisons, etc.); inpatient service modes of multiservice facilities not shown in this table; all partial care episodes, and outpatient episodes of VA hospitals. (2) Includes estimates of episodes of care in residential treatment centers for emotionally disturbed children.

U.S. Health Expenditures

Source: Health Care Financing Administration, U.S. Department of Health and Human Services

	1950	1960	1965	1970	1975	1977	1979[1]
Total (billions)	**$12.7**	**$26.9**	**$43.0**	**$74.7**	**$132.1**	**$170.0**	**$212.2**
Type of expenditure				Percent distribution			
Health services and supplies	92.4	93.6	92.0	92.9	93.7	94.9	95.3
Hospital care	30.4	33.8	32.4	37.2	39.5	40.0	40.2
Physician services	21.7	21.1	19.7	19.2	18.9	18.4	19.1
Dentist services	7.6	7.4	6.5	6.4	6.2	6.9	6.4
Nursing home care.	1.5	2.0	4.8	6.3	7.6	7.9	8.4
Other professional services.	3.1	3.2	2.4	2.1	2.0	2.2	2.2
Drugs and drug sundries	13.6	13.6	13.4	11.3	8.9	8.1	8.0
Eyeglasses and appliances	3.9	2.9	4.3	2.8	2.3	2.0	2.1
Expenses for prepayment.	3.6	4.1	3.4	3.1	3.1	4.6	3.6
Gov. public health activities	2.9	1.5	1.9	1.9	2.4	2.5	2.8
Other health services	4.2	4.1	3.0	2.8	2.8	2.4	2.4
Research and construction.	7.6	6.4	8.1	7.1	6.3	5.2	4.7
Research	0.9	2.5	3.4	2.5	2.5	2.2	2.2
Construction	6.7	3.9	4.7	4.6	3.8	3.0	2.5

(1) Preliminary estimate.

Legal Abortions in the U.S.

Source: Center for Disease Control, U.S. Department of Health and Human Services

Legal abortions, according to selected characteristics of the patient.

	1972	1973	1974	1975	1976	1977	1978
Number	586,760	615,831	763,476	854,853	988,267	1,079,430	1,157,776
Age Characteristic				Percent distribution			
Under 20 years.	32.6	32.7	32.7	33.1	32.1	30.8	30.0
20-24 years.	32.5	32.0	31.8	31.9	33.3	34.5	35.0
25 years and over	34.9	35.3	35.6	35.0	34.6	34.7	34.9
Color							
White	77.0	72.5	69.7	67.8	66.6	66.4	67.0
All other.	23.0	27.5	30.3	32.2	33.4	33.6	33.0
Marital status							
Married	29.7	27.4	27.4	26.1	24.6	24.3	26.4
Unmarried.	70.3	72.6	72.6	73.9	75.4	75.7	73.6
Number of living children							
0	49.4	48.6	47.8	47.1	47.7	53.4	56.6
1	18.2	18.8	19.6	20.2	20.7	19.1	19.2
2	13.3	14.2	14.8	15.5	15.4	14.4	14.1
3	8.7	8.7	8.7	8.7	8.3	7.0	5.9
4	5.0	4.8	4.5	4.4	4.1	3.3	4.2*
5 or more	5.4	4.9	4.5	4.2	3.8	2.9	—
Location of abortion facility							
In state of residence	56.2	74.8	86.6	89.2	90.0	90.0	93.8
Out of state of residence	43.8	25.2	13.4	10.8	10.0	10.0	6.2
Period of gestation							
Under 9 weeks	34.0	36.1	42.6	44.6	47.0	51.2	53.2
9-10 weeks	30.7	29.4	28.7	28.4	28.0	27.2	26.9
11-12 weeks	17.5	17.9	15.4	14.9	14.4	13.1	12.3
13-15 weeks	8.4	6.9	5.5	5.0	4.5	3.4	4.0
16-20 weeks	8.2	8.0	6.5	6.1	5.1	4.3	3.7
21 weeks and over.	1.3	1.7	1.2	1.0	0.9	0.9	0.9

*Beginning with 1978, 4 or more.

The Nation's Handicapped

Source: National Center for Health Statistics, U.S. Department of Health and Human Services

1978 Acitivity limitation, sex, and age	Number of persons limited in activity	Chronic condition: Arthritis, rheumatism	Heart conditions	Hypertension w/o heart involvement	Diabetes	Mental, nervous conditions	Asthma	Impairments of back/spine	Impairments of lower extremities, hips	Visual impairments	Hearing impairments
All degrees of activity limitation		Percent of persons limited in activity because of specified condition									
Both sexes, all ages	**30,175,062**	**16.8**	**15.7**	**6.9**	**5.1**	**4.9**	**4.8**	**7.5**	**6.1**	**5.4**	**2.5**
Under 17 years	2,266,695	*1.0	2.4	*0.3	*1.0	6.7	20.1	3.2	6.9	3.7	5.2
17-44	7,512,474	6.8	4.8	3.4	2.3	5.9	5.9	13.9	8.0	4.2	2.7
45-64	10,504,689	19.6	19.0	9.0	6.8	5.7	3.4	7.9	5.6	4.0	1.9
65 and over	9,891,204	24.9	23.4	8.9	6.3	3.0	2.1	3.3	5.0	8.2	2.4
Male, all ages	**14,564,509**	**11.4**	**16.7**	**4.8**	**4.8**	**4.4**	**4.9**	**7.2**	**6.7**	**5.7**	**2.8**
Under 17 years	1,279,389	*0.4	*2.5	*0.4	*1.1	8.1	21.2	*1.5	7.4	3.8	5.2
17-44	3,777,280	4.9	3.9	2.4	1.8	5.5	5.3	13.3	10.2	5.7	3.2
45-64	5,182,145	14.9	22.2	6.8	6.9	4.7	2.7	8.0	6.3	4.8	2.6
65 and over	4,325,695	16.3	25.3	6.1	6.2	2.0	2.2	2.7	4.0	7.6	2.0
Female, all ages	**15,610,553**	**21.7**	**14.8**	**8.9**	**5.2**	**5.4**	**4.8**	**7.9**	**5.5**	**5.0**	**2.2**
Under 17 years	987,306	*1.9	*2.2	*0.2	*0.9	5.0	18.6	5.4	6.2	3.6	5.1
17-44	3,735,194	8.8	5.7	4.5	2.7	6.3	6.5	14.5	5.8	2.6	2.1
45-64	5,322,544	24.2	15.9	11.1	6.7	6.6	4.0	7.9	4.9	3.2	1.2
65 and over	5,565,509	31.6	22.0	11.1	6.4	3.8	2.0	3.8	5.7	8.6	2.7
Limited but not in major activity											
Both sexes, all ages	**7,495,791**	**13.0**	**6.7**	**5.2**	**3.2**	**3.4**	**7.2**	**8.0**	**8.2**	**6.1**	**4.6**
Under 17 years	1,087,587	*1.3	*3.0	*0.5	*1.4	6.1	19.1	5.4	9.3	4.3	5.6
17-44	2,843,947	7.2	3.1	2.9	2.4	3.7	8.2	12.2	10.8	5.6	4.1
45-64	2,264,578	18.4	8.8	7.8	4.9	2.6	3.8	6.9	6.5	4.7	4.2
65 and over	1,299,679	25.7	14.0	9.6	3.4	*1.6	*0.9	3.0	4.9	11.2	5.6
Limited in amount or kind of major activity											
Both sexes, all ages	**15,210,160**	**18.3**	**16.3**	**7.8**	**5.0**	**4.7**	**4.6**	**8.8**	**5.3**	**4.2**	**1.8**
Under 17 years	1,058,928	*0.7	*1.9	*0.2	*0.7	7.5	22.6	*0.7	4.2	*1.7	4.9
17-44	3,721,693	6.8	5.4	4.0	2.3	5.4	4.7	16.5	6.6	3.2	1.8
45-64	5,671,034	20.7	19.9	9.5	6.9	5.3	3.4	9.3	4.8	3.2	1.2
65 and over	4,758,505	28.4	23.9	10.5	5.9	2.9	1.9	4.1	5.0	6.5	1.7
Unable to carry on major activity											
Both sexes, all ages	**7,469,111**	**17.5**	**23.4**	**6.8**	**7.0**	**7.0**	**3.0**	**4.4**	**5.6**	**7.2**	**1.9**
Under 17 years	120,180	*1.7	*1.4	*-	*-	*5.7	*7.1	*4.2	*9.0	*15.1	*3.2
17-44	946,834	5.8	7.5	*2.7	*1.9	14.5	*3.7	8.4	5.3	3.7	*1.8
45-64	2,569,077	18.2	26.2	8.7	8.1	9.1	2.9	5.8	6.5	5.0	1.4
65 and over	3,833,020	20.4	26.1	6.8	7.7	3.6	2.7	2.5	5.0	9.2	2.2

*Figure does not meet standards of reliability or precision.

Personal Health Care Costs Per Capita in the U.S.

Source: Public Health Service, U.S. Department of Health and Human Services

Age, fiscal year	Total expenditures	Source of payment: Direct payment	Third-party payment: Total	Private health insurance	Philanthropy and industry	Government
		Percent distribution				
All ages						
1970	$289.76	40.4	59.6	24.0	1.5	34.2
1971	320.84	39.1	60.9	24.9	1.4	34.6
1972	353.00	37.6	62.4	24.9	1.4	36.1
1973	386.84	36.8	63.2	25.4	1.4	36.4
1974[1]	425.15	36.1	63.9	25.2	1.3	37.3
1975[1]	488.23	33.6	66.4	25.4	1.3	39.7
1976[2,3]	551.50	32.5	67.5	26.0	1.3	40.2
1977[2,3]	646.11	30.3	69.7	27.6	2.0	40.1
Under 65 years						
1970	232.50	43.3	56.7	31.0	1.9	23.9
1971	255.09	41.1	58.9	32.6	1.8	24.5
1972	278.23	38.4	61.6	33.0	1.5	26.8
1973	309.45	38.3	61.7	33.2	1.7	26.8
1974[1]	347.87	39.0	61.0	32.3	1.7	27.0
1975[1]	390.79	36.5	63.5	33.3	1.6	28.6
1976[2,3]	437.83	34.9	65.1	34.5	1.7	29.0
1977[2,3]	514.25	31.9	68.1	36.4	2.6	29.1
65 years and over						
1970	828.31	32.6	67.4	5.5	0.5	61.4
1971	925.98	34.2	65.8	5.4	0.5	60.0
1972	1,033.51	35.5	64.5	5.2	0.4	58.9
1973	1,081.35	33.0	67.0	5.4	0.4	61.1
1974[1]	1,109.54	28.0	72.0	5.7	0.5	65.9
1975[1]	1,335.72	26.3	73.7	5.4	0.4	68.0
1976[2,3]	1,521.36	26.5	73.5	5.4	0.4	67.0
1977[2,3]	1,745.17	26.5	73.5	5.8	0.7	67.0

(1) Revised estimates. (2) Preliminary estimates. (3) Data for fiscal year ending Sept. 30; all other data for fiscal year ending June 30.

Active Federal and Non-Federal Doctors (M.D.s) by State

Source: Division of Health Manpower and Facilities Statistics, U.S. Department of Health and Human Services (1978)

	Total	Non-fed.	Fed.
All areas	**401,364**	**381,122**	**20,242**
United States	**396,445**	**377,492**	**18,953**
Alabama	4,562	4,363	199
Alaska	558	445	113
Arizona	4,569	4,229	340
Arkansas	2,548	2,423	125
California	50,850	47,891	2,959
Colorado	5,671	5,248	423
Connecticut	7,403	7,222	181
Delaware	951	911	40
D.C.	3,944	3,322	622
Florida	16,224	15,456	768
Georgia	7,471	6,925	546
Hawaii	1,892	1,670	222
Idaho	973	928	45
Illinois	20,327	19,704	623
Indiana	6,659	6,549	110
Iowa	3,524	3,424	100
Kansas	3,548	3,385	163
Kentucky	4,641	4,455	186
Louisiana	5,958	5,675	283
Maine	1,631	1,562	69
Maryland	11,687	9,851	1,836
Mass.	14,732	14,149	583
Michigan	13,742	13,513	229
Minnesota	7,437	7,212	225
Mississippi	2,630	2,436	194
Missouri	7,679	7,448	231
Montana	1,027	965	62
Nebraska	2,277	2,198	79
Nevada	911	860	51
N.H.	1,418	1,376	42
New Jersey	13,216	12,870	346
New Mexico	1,855	1,696	159
New York	45,570	44,458	1,112
North Carolina	8,350	7,934	416
North Dakota	835	780	55
Ohio	16,792	16,366	426
Oklahoma	3,651	3,453	198
Oregon	4,327	4,192	135
Pennsylvania	21,315	20,831	484
Rhode Island	1,921	1,850	71
South Carolina	3,914	3,640	274
South Dakota	753	677	76
Tennessee	6,736	6,498	238
Texas	20,570	19,101	1,469
Utah	2,188	2,107	81
Vermont	999	970	29
Virginia	8,965	8,114	851
Washington	7,020	6,460	560
West Virginia	2,533	2,419	114
Wisconsin	7,017	6,841	176
Wyoming	474	440	34
Puerto Rico	3,577	3,424	153
Outlying areas	1,342	206	1,136

(1) Excludes 8,858 physicians with addresses unknown.

Canadian General and Allied Special Hospitals

Source: Health and Welfare Canada

	Hospitals			Beds			Admissions[2]			Expenses ($1,000)
1979[1]	**Public**	**Private**	**Fed.**	**Public**	**Private**	**Fed.**	**Public**	**Private**	**Fed.**	**Public**
Newfoundland	47	—	—	3,298	—	—	91,563	—	—	145,892
Prince Edward Is.	10	—	1	753	—	14	26,107	—	n.a.	24,308
Nova Scotia	48	—	3	5,549	—	162	143,915	—	2,399	236,781
New Brunswick	34	—	1	4,286	—	10	120,705	—	n.a.	179,436
Quebec	194	38	11	48,018	2,361	1,266	763,766	5,038	1,924	2,110,778
Ontario	232	36	17	49,502	731	615	1,277,756	5,136	9,231	2,363,693
Manitoba	80	—	23	6,302	—	703	161,380	—	3,958	265,161
Saskatchewan	139	—	3	7,954	—	76	204,874	—	967	253,825
Alberta	147	—	9	14,604	—	848	366,236	—	12,160	544,477
British Columbia	120	2	15	18,314	7	107	410,858	261	1,304	710,715
Yukon	—	—	6	—	—	161	—	—	3,892	—
N.W.T.	3	—	43	162	—	288	5,122	—	3,943	5,000
Canada	**1,054**	**76**	**132**	**158,742**	**3,099**	**4,250**	**3,572,282**	**10,435**	**39,778**	**6,840,066**

(1) as of March 31. (2) Preliminary data.

Canadian Active Civilian Doctors

Source: Health and Welfare Canada (Dec. 31, 1979)

Province	Number[1]	Population per physician[1]
Newfoundland	822	702
Prince Edward Island	153	810
Nova Scotia	1,572	541
New Brunswick	767	919
Quebec	11,981	525
Ontario	16,309	524
Manitoba	1,839	558
Saskatchewan	1,433	674
Alberta	3,241	633
British Columbia	5,011	521
Yukon	27	807
Northwest Territories	37	1,165
Canada	**43,192**	**551**

(1) Includes interns and residents.

Patients in Canadian Mental Hospitals

Source: Statistics Canada

Average patients per day, 1977

	Canada	Nfld.	P.E.I.	N.S.	N.B.	Que.	Ont.	Man.	Sask.	Alta.	B.C.
Public hospitals:											
Mental	11,763	365	238	236	918	1,137	5,320	894	304	1,066	1,285
Psychiatric	1,011	—	—	449	—	—	476	35	31	—	20
Retardates	—	—	—	—	—	—	—	—	—	—	—
Emotionally disturbed children	—	—	—	—	—	—	—	—	—	—	—
Other	1,076	—	—	—	—	87	133	—	—	45	808
Total private	**421**	—	—	—	—	—	421	—	—	—	—
Total mental hospitals	**14,268**	**365**	**238**	**685**	**918**	**1,224**	**6,350**	**929**	**335**	**1,111**	**2,113**

Heart Disease

Warning Signs

Source: American Heart Association

Of Heart Attack

- Prolonged, oppressive pain or unusual discomfort in the center of the chest
- Pain may radiate to the shoulder, arm, neck or jaw
- Sweating may accompany pain or discomfort
- Nausea and vomiting may also occur
- Shortness of breath may accompany other signs

The American Heart Association advises immediate action at the onset of these symptoms. The Association points out that over half of heart attack victims die before they reach the hospital and that the average victim waits 3 hours before seeking help.

Of Stroke

- Sudden temporary weakness or numbness of face or limbs on one side of the body
- Temporary loss of speech, or trouble speaking or understanding speech
- Temporary dimness or loss of vision, particularly in one eye
- An episode of double vision
- Unexplained dizziness or unsteadiness
- Change in personality, mental ability
- New or unusual pattern of headaches

Major Risk Factors

Blood pressure— systolic pressure under 120 is normal; systolic pressure over 150
= 2 times the risk of heart attack
= 4 times the risk of stroke

Cholesterol— level under 194 is normal;
level of 250 or over
= 3 times the risk of heart attack or stroke

Cigarettes— with non-smoking considered normal;
smoking one pack a day
= 2 times the risk of heart attack
= 4 times the risk of stroke

U. S. Deaths Due to Cardiovascular Diseases by Major Type of Disorder, 1976

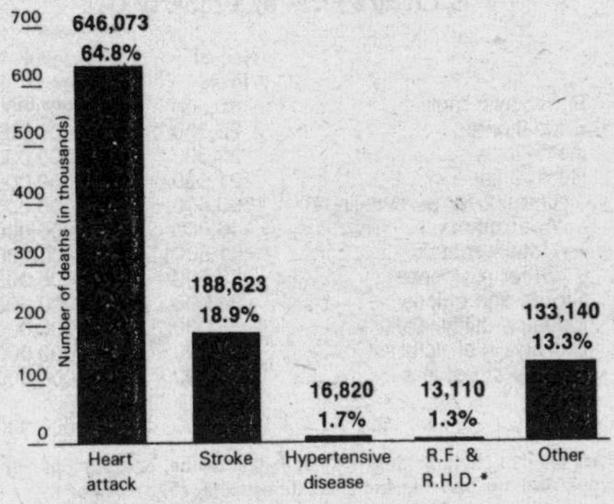

*Rheumatic fever and Rheumatic heart disease
Source: National Center for Health Statistics, U.S. Department of Health, Education, and Welfare

Estimated Economic Costs in Billions of Dollars of Cardiovascular Diseases by Type of Expenditure, 1979

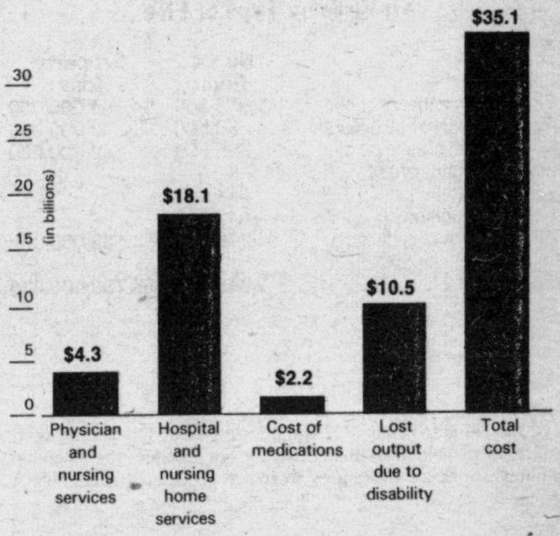

Source: American Heart Association

Cardiovascular Disease Statistical Summary

Cost — 35.1 billion (AHA est.) in 1979.

Prevalence — 40,120,000 Americans have some form of heart and blood vessel disease.

- hypertension — 33,740,000 (one in 6 adults).
- coronary heart disease — 4,190,000.
- rheumatic heart disease — 1,800,000.
- stroke — 1,950,000.

Mortality — 997,766 in 1976 (52% of all deaths). 1979 (AHA est.): 980,900 (51%).

- one-fourth of all persons killed by CVD are under age 65.

Congenital or inborn heart defects — 35 recognizable types of defects.

- about 25,000 babies are born every year with heart defects.
- post-natal mortality from heart defects had been reduced to 6,279 in 1976.

Heart attack — caused 646,073 deaths in 1976.

- 4,190,000 alive today have history of heart attack and/or angina pectoris.
- 350,000 a year die of heart attack before they reach hospital.
- Over 1,000,000 Americans will have a heart attack this year and about 650,000 of them will die.

Stroke — killed 188,623 in 1976; afflicts 1,950,000.

CCU — most of the 7,000 general hospitals in U.S. have coronary care capability.

- 1,800 have separate CCUs; 3,000 have combined intensive care and coronary care facilities.

Hypertension (high blood pressure) — 33,740,000 adults.

- easily detected and usually controllable, but only a minority have it under adequate control.

Rheumatic heart disease — 100,000 children; 1,700,000 adults.

- killed 13,110 in 1976. Modern antibiotic therapy has sharply reduced mortality in 5-24 age group.

Suicide Rates

Source: National Center for Health Statistics, U.S. Department of Health and Human Services

(Rates per 100,000 population) (1978)

Age group	Total	Male	Female	White			All other		
				Total	Male	Female	Total	Male	Female
Total	**12.5**	**19.0**	**6.3**	**13.4**	**20.2**	**6.9**	**6.9**	**11.1**	**3.1**
10-14 years	0.8	1.2	0.4	0.9	1.4	0.4	0.5	0.6	0.5
15-19 years	8.0	12.8	3.1	8.7	13.8	3.4	4.5	7.5	1.6
20-24 years	16.9	27.4	6.4	17.5	28.1	6.7	13.8	23.3	5.0
25-29 years	17.6	27.5	7.9	17.9	27.6	8.3	15.4	26.6	5.8
30-34 years	15.7	23.4	8.3	16.2	23.8	8.7	12.2	20.2	5.5
35-39 years	15.6	22.3	9.3	16.2	22.7	9.8	11.9	19.5	5.7
40-44 years	16.1	21.4	11.0	17.2	22.4	12.2	8.4	14.2	3.7
45-49 years	16.7	22.5	11.1	17.8	23.6	12.2	8.7	14.5	3.7
50-54 years	17.6	24.3	11.3	18.7	25.8	12.1	8.4	11.8	5.6
55-59 years	17.8	25.4	10.8	19.1	27.1	11.6	6.4	9.4	3.8
60-64 years	18.6	30.1	8.4	19.7	32.0	8.8	7.6	11.9	3.9
65-69 years	18.0	30.2	8.3	19.4	32.5	9.0	6.2	10.9	2.5
70-74 years	20.0	37.2	7.4	21.1	39.6	7.8	7.5	13.1	3.0
75-79 years	23.1	45.9	8.4	24.3	48.9	8.7	8.8	14.5	4.3
80-84 years	21.8	50.6	6.0	23.2	54.4	6.3	6.9	13.2	2.9
85+ years	18.6	48.3	5.1	20.0	53.1	5.2	6.3	10.3	4.1

U.S. Fires

Source: National Fire Protection Assn.

Fires attended by the public fire service (1979 estimates)

All Fires by Type of Fire

	No. of fires	Property loss
Fires in structures	1,036,500	$4,964,000,000
Fires outside of structures[1]	80,500	38,000,000
Fires in vehicles[2]	495,500	682,000,000
Fires in brush, grass, wildland[3]	614,500	*
Fires in rubbish[4]	342,000	*
All other fires	276,500	66,000,000
Total[6]	**2,845,500**	**$5,750,000,000**

Structure Fires by Property Use

	No. of fires	Property loss
Public assembly	30,500	$284,000,000
Educational	22,500	79,000,000
Institutional	29,500	34,000,000
Residential	721,500	2,529,000,000
One-/2-family dwellings[5]	550,500	2,304,000,000
Apartments	146,000	343,000,000
Hotels, motels	11,500	100,000,000
Other residential	13,500	52,000,000
Stores and offices	64,000	457,000,000
Industry, utility, defense[6]	58,000	966,000,000
Storage in structures[6]	64,500	507,000,000
Special structures	46,000	108,000,000
Total[6]	**1,036,500**	**$4,964,000,000**

*No value involved. (1) Includes outside storage, crops, timber, etc. (2) Includes highway vehicles, trains, boats, ships, aircraft, farm vehicles, and construction vehicles. (3) Excludes crops and timber. (4) Includes dumpsters. (5) Includes mobile homes. (6) Since some fires were not reported to the NFPA, the results presented represent only a portion of the total U.S. fires.

Annual Fire Losses in the U.S.

Source: Insurance Services Office

Year	Loss	Year	Loss	Year	Loss	Year	Loss
1940	$285,878,697	1955	$885,218,000	1970	$2,264,000,000	1977	$3,764,000,000
1945	484,274,000	1960	1,107,824,000	1975	3,560,000,000	1978	4,008,000,000
1950	648,909,000	1965	1,455,631,000	1976	3,558,000,000	1979	4,851,000,000

Fire Fighters: Deaths and Injuries

Source: International Association of Fire Fighters

U.S. and Canadian professional fire fighters

Year	In line of duty		Occupational diseases[1]		Year	In line of duty		Occupational diseases[1]	
	Deaths	Injuries	Deaths	Retirement		Deaths	Injuries	Deaths	Retirement
1970	115	38,583	233	465	1975	108	51,312	88	721
1972	100	62,682	133	695	1976	79	49,819	79	673
1973	90	62,619	111	702	1977	79	55,562	84	828
1974	100	56,296	107	604	1978	74	46,668	61	391

(1) Includes: heart and cardiovascular diseases; lung and respiratory diseases; and other occupational diseases.

Marriage Information

Source: Compiled by William E. Mariano, Council on Marriage Relations, Inc., 110 E. 42d St., New York, NY 10017 (as of Jan. 1, 1980)

Marriageable age, by states, for both males and females with and without consent of parents or guardians. But in most states, the court has authority, in an emergency, to marry young couples below the ordinary age of consent, where due regard for their morals and welfare so requires. In many states, under special circumstances, blood test and waiting period may be waived.

State	With consent		Without consent		Blood test		Wait for license	Wait after license
	Men	Women	Men	Women	Required	Other state accepted*		
Alabama(b)	14	14	18	18	Yes	Yes	none	none
Alaska	16	16	18	18	Yes	No	3 days	none
Arizona	16(i)	16	18	18	Yes	Yes	none	none
Arkansas	17	16(j)	18	18	Yes	No	3 days	none
California	18(i)	18	18	18	Yes	Yes	none	none
Colorado	16	16	18	18	Yes	...	none	none
Connecticut	16	16(l)	18	18	Yes	Yes	4 days	none
Delaware	18	16(o)	18	18	Yes	Yes	none	24 hrs. (c)
District of Columbia	16	16	18	18	Yes	Yes	3 days	none
Florida	18	18	18	18	Yes	Yes	3 days	none
Georgia	16	16	18	18	Yes	Yes	none (k)	none
Hawaii	16	16	18	18	Yes	Yes	none	none
Idaho	16	16	18	18	Yes (n)	Yes	none (k)	none
Illinois (a)	16	16	18	18	Yes	Yes	none	1 day
Indiana	17(o)	17(o)	18	18	Yes (p)	No	3 days	none
Iowa	16(o)	16(o)	18	18	Yes	Yes	3 days	none
Kansas	14	12	18	18	Yes	Yes	3 days	none
Kentucky	18(o)	18(o)	18	18	Yes	No	3 days	none
Louisiana (a)	18(o)	16(j)	18	18	Yes	No	none	72 hours
Maine	16(j)	16(j)	18	18	Yes	No	5 days	none
Maryland	16	16	18	18	none	none	48 hours	none
Massachusetts	—(o)	—(o)	18	18	Yes	Yes	3 days	none
Michigan (a)	18	16	18	18	Yes	No	3 days	none
Minnesota	—	16(e)	18	18	none	...	5 days	none
Mississippi (b)	17	15	21	21	Yes	...	3 days	none
Missouri	15	15	18	18	Yes	Yes	3 days	none
Montana	15	15	18	18	Yes	Yes	3 days	none
Nebraska	17	17	18	18	Yes (n)	Yes	2 days	none
Nevada	16	16	18	18	none	none	none	none
New Hampshire (a)	14(e)	13(e)	18	18	Yes	Yes	5 days	none
New Jersey (a)	—	12	18	18	Yes	Yes	72 hours	none
New Mexico	16	16	18	18	Yes	Yes	none	none
New York	16	14	18	18	Yes	No	none	24 hrs.(g)
North Carolina (a)	16	16	18	18	Yes	Yes	none	none
North Dakota (a)	16	16	18	18	Yes	...	none	none
Ohio (a)	18	16	18	18	Yes	Yes	5 days	none
Oklahoma	16	16	18	18	Yes	No	none (f)(h)	none
Oregon	17	17	17	17	Yes	No	7 days	none
Pennsylvania	16	16	18	18	Yes	Yes	3 days	none
Rhode Island (a) (b)	18	16	18	18	Yes	No	none	none
South Carolina	16	14	18	18	none	none	24 hrs.	none
South Dakota	16	16	18	18	Yes	Yes	none	none
Tennessee (b)	16	16	18	18	Yes	Yes	3 days	none
Texas	14	14	18	18	Yes	Yes	none	none
Utah (a)	14	14	16	16	Yes	Yes	none	none
Vermont (a)	18	16	18	18	Yes	...	none	5 days
Virginia (a)	16	16	18	18	Yes	Yes (m)	none	none
Washington	17	17	18	18	(d)	...	3 days	none
West Virginia	(o)	(o)	18	16	Yes	No	3 days	none
Wisconsin	16	16	18	18	Yes	Yes	5 days	none
Wyoming	16	16	19	19	Yes	Yes	none	none
Puerto Rico	18	16	21	21	(f)	none	none	none
Virgin Islands	16	14	18	18	none	none	8 days	none

***Many states have additional special requirements; contact individual state.** (a) Special laws applicable to non-residents. (b) Special laws applicable to those under 21 years; Ala., bond required if male is under 18, female under 18. (c) 24 hours if one or both parties resident of state; 96 hours if both parties are non-residents. (d) None, but both must file affidavit. (e) Parental consent plus court's consent required. (f) None, but a medical certificate is required. (g) Marriage may not be solemnized within 10 days from date of blood test. (h) If either under 18, 72 hrs. (i) Statute provides for obtaining license with parental or court consent with no state minimum age. (j) Under 16, with parental and court consent. (k) If either under 18, wait 3 full days. (l) If under stated age, court consent required. (m) Va. blood test form must be used. (n) Applicant must also supply a certificate of immunity against German measles (rubella). (o) If under 18, parental and/or court consent required. (p) Statement whether person is carrier of sickle-cell anemia may be required.

Grounds for Divorce

Source: Compiled by William E. Mariano, Council on Marriage Relations, Inc., 110 E. 42d St., New York, NY 10017 (as of Jan. 1, 1980)

Persons contemplating divorce should study latest decisions or secure legal advice before initiating proceedings since different interpretations or exceptions in each case can change the conclusion reached.

State	Breakdown of marriage/incompatibility	Cruelty	Desertion	Non-support	Alcohol &/or drug addiction	Felony	Impotency	Insanity[1]	Living separate and apart	Other grounds	Residence time	Time between interlocut'y and final decrees
Alabama	X	X	X	X	X	X	X	X	2 yrs.	A-E	6 mos.	none-M
Alaska	X	X	X	...	X	X	X	X		C	1 yr.	none
Arizona	X	...	...	...	...	...	...	...			90 days	none
Arkansas	...	X	X	X	X	X	X	X	3 yrs.	C	3 mos.	none
California[2]	X	...	...	...	...	...	...	X			6 mos.	6 mos.
Colorado	X	...	...	...	...	...	...	...			90 days	none
Connecticut	X	X	X	X	X	X	...	X	18 mos.	B	1 yr.	none
Delaware	X[4]	...	...	...	...	...	...	...	6 mos.		6 mos.	none
Dist. of Columbia	...	...	...	...	...	...	...	...	6 mos.-1 yr.		6 mos.	none
Florida	X	...	...	...	...	...	...	X			6 mos.	none
Georgia	X	X	X	...	X	X	X	X		A-B-D	6 mos.	L
Hawaii	X	...	...	...	...	...	...	...	2 yrs.	K	6 mos.	none
Idaho	X	X	X	X	X	X	...	X	5 yrs.		6 wks.	none
Illinois	...	X	X	...	X	X	X	...			3 mos.	none
Indiana	X	...	...	...	...	X	X	X			6 mos.	none
Iowa	X	...	...	...	...	...	...	...			1 yr.	none-N
Kansas	X	X	X	...	X	X	X	X		H	60 days	none-M
Kentucky	X	...	...	...	...	...	...	...			180 days	none
Louisiana	...	...	...	...	...	X	...	...	2 yrs.	K	2 yrs.	none-N
Maine	X	X	X	X	X	...	X	X			6 mos.	none
Maryland	...	X	X	...	...	X	X	X	1-3 yrs.		1 yr.	none
Massachusetts	X[4]	X	X	X	X	X	X	...	6 mos.-1 yr.		1 yr.	6 mos.
Michigan	X	...	...	...	...	...	...	...			1 yr.	none
Minnesota	X[4]	...	...	...	...	...	...	...		K	180 days	none-O
Mississippi	X[4]	X	X	...	X	X	X	X		A-D-I	6 mos.	none-P
Missouri	X[4]	...	...	...	...	...	...	...			3 mos.	none
Montana	X	...	...	...	...	...	...	...			3 mos.	none
Nebraska	X	...	...	...	...	...	...	...			1 yr.	6 mos.
Nevada	X	...	...	...	...	...	...	X	1 yr.		6 wks.	none
New Hampshire[3]	X	X	X	X	X	X	X	...		K	1 yr.	none
New Jersey	...	X	X	...	X	X	...	X	18 mos.	E-K	1 yr.	none
New Mexico	X	X	X	...	...	...	...	...			6 mos.	none
New York	...	X	X	...	...	X	...	...	1 yr.	K	1 yr.	none
North Carolina	...	...	...	...	...	...	X	X	1 yr.	A-E	6 mos.	none
North Dakota	X	X	X	X	X	X	X	X		K	1 yr.	none
Ohio	X	X	X	...	X	X	X	...	2 yrs.	B-G-H-I	6 mos.	none
Oklahoma	X	X	X	X	X	X	X	X		A-B-G-H	6 mos.	none
Oregon	X	...	...	...	...	...	...	...			6 mos.	90 days
Pennsylvania	...	X	X	...	...	X	X	X		B-C-D-I	1 yr.	none
Rhode Island	X	X	X	X	X	X	X	...	3 yrs.		1 yr.	6 mos.
South Carolina	...	X	X	...	X	...	...	...	1 yr.		1 yr.	none
South Dakota	...	X	X	X	X	X	...	...			none	none
Tennessee	X	X	X	X	X	X	X	...		A-I-J-K	6 mos.	none
Texas	X	X	X	...	...	X	...	X	3 yrs.		6 mos.	none-O
Utah	...	X	X	X	X	X	X	X		K	3 mos.	none
Vermont	...	X	X	X	...	X	...	X	6 mos.		6 mos.	3 mos.
Virginia	...	X	...	...	...	X	...	...	1 yr.		6 mos.	none-P
Washington	X	...	...	...	...	...	...	...	2 yrs.		1 yr.	none-R
West Virginia	X	X	X	...	X	X	...	X	1 yr.	T	actual	none
Wisconsin	X[4]	...	...	...	...	...	...	...	1 yr.	K	6 mos.	none-O
Wyoming	X	...	...	...	...	...	...	X	2 yrs.		60 days	none

Adultery is either grounds for divorce or evidence of irreconcilable differences and a breakdown of the marriage in all states. The plaintiff can invariably remarry in the same state where he or she procured a decree of divorce or annulment. Not so the defendant, who is barred in certain states for some offenses. After a period of time has elapsed even the offender can apply for permission.

(1) Generally 5 yrs. insanity but: permanent insanity in Ut.; incurable insanity in Col.; 1 yr. Wis.; 18 mos. Alas.; 2 yrs. Ga., Ha., Ind., Nev., N.J., Ore., Wash., Wy.; 3 yrs. Ark., Cal., Fla., Kan., Md., Minn., Miss., N.C., Tex., W. Va.; 6 yrs. Ida. (2) Cal. has a procedure whereby if the couple has been married less than 2 years, have no children, no real estate, little personal property, and few debts they can get a divorce without an attorney and without appearing in court. (3) Other grounds existing only in N.H. are: Joining a religious order disbelieving in marriage, treatment which injures health or endangers reason, wife without the state for 10 years, and wife in state 2 yrs. husband never in state and intends to become a citizen of a foreign country. (4) Provable only by fault grounds, separation for some period, generally a year, proof of marital discord or commitment for mental illness. (A) Pregnancy at marriage. (B) Fraudulent contract. (C) Indignities. (D) Consanguinity. (E) Crime against nature. (F) Mental incapacity at time of marriage. (G) Procurement of out-of-state divorce. (H) Gross neglect of duty. (I) Bigamy. (J) Attempted homocide. (K) Separation by decree in Conn.; after decree: one yr. in La., N.Y., Wis.; 18 mos. in N.H.; 2 yrs. in Ala., Ha., Minn., N.C. Tenn.; 3 yrs. in Ut.; 4 yrs. in N.J., N.D.; 5 yrs. in Md. (L) Determined by court order. (M) 60 days to remarry. (N) One yr. to remarry except Ha. one yr. with minor child; La. 90 days. (O) 6 mos. to remarry. (P) Adultery cases, remarriage in court's discretion. (Q) Plaintiff, 6 mos.; defendant 2 yrs. to remarry. (R) No remarriage if an appeal is pending. (S) Actual domicile in adultery cases. **Enoch Arden Laws:** disappearance and unknown to be alive - Conn., 7 yrs. absence, N.H., 2 yrs., N.Y. 5 yrs. (called dissolution), Vt. 7 yrs.

N.B. Grounds not recognized for divorce may be recognized for separation or annulment. Local laws should be consulted.

Canadian Marriage Information

Source: Compiled from information provided by the various provincial government departments and agencies concerned.

Marriageable age, by provinces, for both males and females with and without consent of parents or guardians. In some provinces, the court has authority, given special circumstances, to marry young couples below the minimum age. Most provinces waive the blood test requirement and the waiting period varies across the provinces.

Province	With consent		Without consent		Blood test other province		Wait for license	Wait after license
	Men	Women	Men	Women	Required	Accepted		
Newfoundland	16	16	19	19	None	None	4 days	4 days
Prince Edward Island	16	16	18	18	Yes	Yes	5 days	None
Nova Scotia	(1)	(1)	19	19	None	None	5 days	None
New Brunswick	16	14	18	18	None	None	5 days	None
Quebec	14	12	18	18	None	—	—	None
Ontario	16	16	18	18	None	—	None[2]	3 days
Manitoba	16	16	18	18	Yes	Yes	None	24 hours
Saskatchewan	15	15	18	18	Yes	Yes	5 days	None
Alberta	16[8]	16[8]	18	18	Yes[3]	Yes[4]	None[5]	None
British Columbia	16[6]	16[6]	19	19	None	None	2 days[7]	None
Yukon Territory	15	15	19	19	None	None	None	24 hours
Northwest Territories	15	15	19	19	None	Yes	None	None

(1) There is no statutory minimum age in the province. Anyone under the age of 19 years must have consent for marriage and no person under the age of 16 may be married without authorization of a Family Court judge and in addition must have the necessary consent of the parent or guardian. (2) Special requirements applicable to nonresidents. (3) Applies only to applicants under 60 years of age. (4) This is upon filing of negative lab report indicating blood test was taken within 14 days preceding date of application for license. (5) Exception where consent is required by mail; depending receipt of divorce documents, etc. (6) Persons under 16 years of age (no minimum age specified) may also be married if they have obtained, in addition to the usual consent from parents or guardian, an order from a judge of the Supreme or County Court in this province. (7) Including day of application, e.g., a license applied for on a Monday cannot be issued until Wednesday. (8) Under 16 allowed if pregnant or the mother of a living child.

Grounds for Divorce in Canada

Source: Government of Canada Divorce Act

The grounds for divorce in Canada are the same for all the provinces and its territories. There are two categories of offense:

A. Marital Offense:
- Adultery
- Sodomy
- Bestiality
- Rape
- Homosexual act
- Subsequent marriage
- Physical cruelty
- Mental cruelty

B. Marriage breakdown by reason of:
- Imprisonment for aggregate period of not less than 3 years
- Imprisonment for not less than 2 years on sentence of death or sentence of 10 years or more
- Addiction to alcohol
- Addiction to narcotics
- Whereabouts of spouse unknown
- Non-consummation
- Separation for not less than 3 years
- Desertion by petitioner for not less than 5 years

Residence time: Domicile in Canada. Time between interlocutory and final decree: normally 3 months before final can be applied for.

Canadian Motor Vehicle Traffic Deaths

Source: Statistics Canada

Province	Number 1978	Number 1977
Newfoundland	74	86
Prince Edward Island	30	51
Nova Scotia	228	183
New Brunswick	224	212
Quebec	1,766	1,556
Ontario	1,450	1,420
Manitoba	198	183
Saskatchewan	296	183
Alberta	503	576
British Columbia	636	716
Yukon	16	4
Northwest Territories	6	2
Total	**5,426**	**5,253**

Birthstones

Source: Jewelry Industry Council

Month	Ancient	Modern
January	Garnet	Garnet
February	Amethyst	Amethyst
March	Jasper	Bloodstone or Aquamarine
April	Sapphire	Diamond
May	Agate	Emerald
June	Emerald	Pearl, Moonstone, or Alexandrite
July	Onyx	Ruby
August	Carnelian	Sardonyx or Peridot
September	Chrysolite	Sapphire
October	Aquamarine	Opal or Tourmaline
November	Topaz	Topaz
December	Ruby	Turquoise or Zircon

Federal Bureau of Investigation

The Federal Bureau of Investigation (FBI) is the investigative arm of the Department of Justice, and is located at 9th St. and Pennsylvania Ave., Washington, DC 20535. It investigates all violations of federal laws except those specifically assigned to some other agency by legislative action, such violations including counterfeiting, and internal revenue, postal, and customs violations. It also investigates espionage, sabotage, treason, and other matters affecting internal security, as well as kidnaping, transportation of stolen goods across state lines, and violations of the federal bank and atomic energy laws.

The Identification Division has about 195 million fingerprint cards on file. While this division is of great usefulness in detecting criminals, it serves a wider purpose in recording the fingerprints of many other citizens who voluntarily make this record.

The FBI has 59 field divisions in the principal cities of the country. *Consult telephone directories for location and phone numbers.*

An applicant for the position of Special Agent of the FBI must be a citizen of the U.S. at least 23 and under 35 years old and graduate of a state-accredited resident law school or from a resident 4-year college with a major in accounting with at least one year of practical accounting and/or auditing experience. In addition, applicants with a 4-year resident college degree with a major in certain areas or 3 years specialized experience of a professional, executive, or complex investigative nature are presently being considered on a limited basis. An agent gets 15 weeks of training.

William H. Webster, a federal appeals court judge from St. Louis, was confirmed as FBI Director for a 10-year term on Feb. 9, 1978. He replaced Clarence Kelley.

U.S. Crime Reports

Source: Federal Bureau of Investigation

Offense	Number 1978 est.	% change over[1] 1977	% change over[1] 1974
Murder	19,560	+2.3	− 5.6
Rape	67,130	+6.5	+21.2
Robbery	417,040	+3.0	− 5.7
Aggravated assault	588,100	+6.8	+22.3
Burglary	3,104,500	+1.7	+ 2.1
Larceny-theft	5,983,400	+1.3	+13.7
Auto theft	991,600	+2.4	+ 1.5

[1]Percent by which the rate of crime per 100,000 population changed in 1978 as compared with 1977 and 1974.

U.S. Crime Rate Up 1.1% in 1978

The rate of crime per 100,000 population increased by 1.1% in 1978 as compared to 1977, according to the Crime Index offenses measured by the FBI. All offenses within the Index increased in volume. Violent crime rates were up 4.4%, with a 5.8% increase in the rate of reported rape and 6.0% increase in the aggravated assault rate. The robbery rate rose 2.2% and the murder rate 1.6%. Property crime rates rose .7%, with the larceny rate up .5%, burglary up .9%, and auto theft up 2.3%.

Reported Crime, 1977-78, by Size of Place

Source: 1978 Uniform Crime Reports, Federal Bureau of Investigation

Population group	Crime Index total	Violent crime	Property crime	Murder and non-negligent man-slaughter	Forcible rape	Robbery	Aggravated assault	Burglary	Larceny–theft
Total all agencies: 12,023 agencies; total population 207,768,000:									
1977	10,579,458	979,452	9,600,006	18,530	61,187	397,925	501,810	2,947,664	5,708,758
1978	10,719,993	1,029,645	9,690,348	18,745	65,084	410,224	535,592	2,982,398	5,748,209
Percent change	+1.3	+5.1	+.9	+1.2	+6.4	+3.1	+6.7	+1.2	+.7
Total cities: 8,465 cities; total population 144,413,000:									
1977	8,559,513	812,423	7,747,090	14,062	47,496	361,768	389,097	2,268,762	4,677,864
1978	8,660,232	854,495	7,805,737	14,252	50,984	372,194	417,065	2,297,954	4,698,189
Percent change	+1.2	+5.2	+.8	+1.4	+7.3	+2.9	+7.2	+1.3	+.4
57 cities, 250,000 and over; population 41,342,000:									
1977	3,278,585	449,895	2,828,690	8,198	25,089	245,276	171,332	921,135	1,501,155
1978	3,258,118	463,341	2,794,777	8,384	26,709	248,567	179,681	915,678	1,483,889
Percent change	−.6	+3.0	−1.2	+2.3	+6.5	+1.3	+4.9	−.6	−1.2
117 cities, 100,000 to 249,999; population 16,863,000:									
1977	1,190,643	97,642	1,093,001	1,841	6,776	38,660	50,365	324,182	669,000
1978	1,210,859	105,712	1,105,147	1,736	7,388	41,195	55,393	330,678	669,281
Percent change	+1.7	+8.3	+1.1	−5.7	+9.0	+6.6	+10.0	+2.0	...
276 cities, 50,000 to 99,999; population 18,889,000:									
1977	1,118,150	83,402	1,034,748	1,204	5,374	30,286	46,538	296,726	644,718
1978	1,145,897	90,918	1,054,979	1,294	5,714	32,799	51,111	307,002	649,384
Percent change	+2.5	+9.0	+2.0	+7.5	+6.3	+8.3	+9.8	+3.5	+.7
649 cities, 25,000 to 49,999; population 22,203,000:									
1977	1,160,047	75,011	1,085,036	1,088	4,544	24,137	45,242	289,824	706,247
1978	1,182,703	80,610	1,102,093	1,088	4,947	24,720	49,855	298,574	712,214
Percent change	+2.0	+7.5	+1.6	...	+8.9	+2.4	+10.2	+3.0	+.8
1,550 cities, 10,000 to 24,999; population 24,101,000:									
1977	1,033,818	60,840	972,978	974	3,290	15,444	41,132	250,294	653,418
1978	1,057,560	65,159	992,401	1,011	3,665	16,424	44,059	257,459	661,956
Percent change	+2.3	+7.1	+2.0	+3.8	+11.4	+6.3	+7.1	+2.9	+1.3
5,816 cities under 10,000; population 21,016,000:									
1977	778,270	45,633	732,637	757	2,423	7,965	34,488	186,601	503,326
1978	805,095	48,755	756,340	739	2,561	8,489	36,966	188,563	521,465
Percent change	+3.4	+6.8	+3.2	−2.4	+5.7	+6.6	+7.2	+1.1	+3.6
Suburban area 5,072 agencies; population 75,913,000:									
1977	3,266,216	226,657	3,039,559	3,726	16,024	62,911	143,996	910,791	1,878,853
1978	3,329,009	239,605	3,089,404	3,875	16,824	65,897	153,009	926,838	1,902,837
Percent change	+1.9	+5.7	+1.6	+4.0	+5.0	+4.7	+6.3	+1.8	+1.3
Rural area 2,651 agencies; population 28,648,000:									
1977	572,855	48,053	524,802	2,141	3,917	5,692	36,303	217,162	274,579
1978	580,732	49,993	530,739	2,077	4,013	5,792	38,111	214,926	280,276
Percent change	+1.4	+4.0	+1.1	−3.0	+2.5	+1.8	+5.0	−1.0	+2.1

Reported Crime in Metropolitan Areas, 1978

Source: 1978 Uniform Crime Reports, Federal Bureau of Investigation

The 28 Standard Metropolitan Statistical Areas listed below are those which appear most frequently among the top 30 cities in per capita reported crime rate for each of 7 kinds of major crime: the 5 listed below plus aggravated assault and auto theft.

The rates are for reported crimes only; they are not an accurate index of crimes actually committed. In many metropolitan areas an unknown number of crimes go unreported by victims. This is especially true of the crimes of rape, burglary, and larceny. Additionally, figures are often distorted for political reasons.

The number in parentheses following the city name indicates the number of categories (including auto theft and aggravated assault) in which the city appears among the top 30.

The numbers in parentheses following crime rate figures give that city's rank in that category of crime. If no number appears, the city is not among the top 30 in that category. The cities are listed in order of the diversity and violence of criminal activity.

	Rate per 100,000 population							
Metropolitan areas	**Total**[1]	**Violent**[2]	**Property**[3]	**Murder**[4]	**Rape**	**Robbery**	**Burglary**	**Larceny**
Las Vegas, Nev. (7)	9,417.4 (1)	978.0 (5)	8,439.4 (2)	17.9 (9)	67.7 (3)	470.5 (2)	3,266.3 (1)	4,462.3(14)
Los Angeles-Long Beach, Cal. (6)	7,341.7(22)	1,082.8 (3)	6,258.9	17.4(11)	66.9 (4)	467.1 (3)	2,333.9(12)	2,938.1
Stockton, Cal. (6)	7,868.4(15)	667.9	7,200.5	17.5(10)	56.4(14)	270.7(22)	2,286.9(17)	4,205.9(27)
Houston, Tex. (5)	7,212.6(27)	570.4	6,642.2(22)	23.5 (2)	57.8(12)	336.6(12)	2,072.0	3,655.0
Lubbock, Tex. (5)	7,843.1(17)	556.6	7,286.6(13)	18.9 (7)	62.6 (5)	153.8	2,289.5(16)	4,550.3(11)
New York, N.Y. (5)	7,089.9	1,370.6 (1)	5,719.3	16.8(14)	43.8	819.0 (1)	2,005.2	2,723.7
Reno, Nev. (5)	8,612.5 (4)	594.3	8,018.3 (4)	15.7(18)	51.4(25)	331.6(13)	2,405.5 (8)	5,020.9 (3)
Fresno, Cal. (5)	8,473.8 (5)	781.3(18)	7,692.5 (6)	15.3(19)	47.3	321.8(15)	2,873.5 (3)	4,087.6
Miami, Fla. (5)	8,406.5 (7)	1,274.6 (2)	7,131.9(17)	17.0(13)	44.8	445.9 (5)	2,224.5(23)	4,318.5(19)
Sacramento, Cal. (5)	8,310.5 (9)	729.4(22)	7,581.1 (7)	11.5	50.3(28)	310.0(16)	2,409.7 (7)	4,508.0(12)
Gainesville, Fla. (5)	8,230.8(10)	788.9(16)	7,441.9 (9)	7.7	62.2 (6)	185.0	2,318.4(13)	4,801.1 (5)
Little Rock-N. Lit. Rock, Ark. (4)	7,145.8	801.3(13)	6,344.5	12.7	61.3 (7)	269.5	2,061.9	3,799.2
Bakersfield, Cal. (4)	7,962.0(13)	716.9(27)	7,245.1(15)	16.8(14)	44.8	222.4	2,374.6(10)	4,283.2(20)
Tallahassee, Fla. (4)	7,755.5(18)	729.0(23)	7,026.4(18)	7.3	75.1 (1)	132.0	2,139.0(24)	4,565.9(10)
Daytona Beach, Fla. (4)	9,344.8 (2)	728.1(24)	8,616.7 (1)	9.1	57.8(13)	237.1(28)	2,779.1 (4)	5,330.2 (1)
San Francisco, Cal. (4)	8,046.8(12)	819.7(11)	7,227.1(16)	11.2	53.0(20)	414.4 (7)	2,249.0(21)	4,279.2(21)
Phoenix, Ariz. (4)	8,716.3 (3)	621.1	8,095.2 (3)	10.0	52.9(21)	208.6	2,374.0(11)	5,187.5 (2)
Savannah, Ga. (3)	7,199.0(28)	940.2 (7)	6,258.8	16.2(16)	62.6 (5)	214.8	1,961.6	3,912.1
Dallas-Ft. Worth, Tex. (3)	7,221.5(26)	606.0	6,615.5(24)	15.3(19)	51.2(26)	221.4	2,021.1	4,106.1
Pensacola, Fla. (3)	7,402.6(20)	713.0(29)	6,689.6(21)	13.0	59.0(10)	170.6	2,078.6(26)	4,130.5
Lakeland-Winter Haven, Fla. (3)	7,631.9(19)	1,033.6 (4)	6,598.4(27)	7.7	55.0(16)	137.6	1,914.5	4,269.3(23)
Columbia, S.C. (3)	7,256.2(25)	879.4(10)	6,376.8(30)	11.4	55.1(15)	185.7	2,299.4(14)	3,606.0
Orlando, Fla. (3)	8,435.4 (6)	897.7 (8)	7,537.7 (8)	11.1	61.7 (7)	187.4	2,453.9 (5)	4,668.2 (7)
Atlantic City, N.J. (3)	7,165.6(29)	558.0	6,607.6(26)	8.5	39.1	236.2(29)	2,267.0(19)	3,736.1
West Palm Beach-Boca Raton, Fla. (3)	8,093.8(11)	789.6(15)	7,304.2(12)	10.3	41.4	197.1	2,296.5(15)	4,590.8 (9)
Riverside-San Bernardino-Ontario, Cal. (2)	7,299.1(24)	687.4	6,611.6(25)	13.2	53.4(19)	210.7	2,438.8 (6)	3,636.1
Baton Rouge, La. (2)	7,352.0(21)	713.9(28)	6,638.1(23)	11.2	43.6	119.7	1,922.5	4,277.1(22)
Springfield, Ill. (2)	7,858.1(16)	591.2	7,264.9(14)	10.3	24.4	241.1(27)	3,002.0 (2)	3,840.8

(1) Other metro areas among the top 30 in total reported crime (predominantly property crime): Modesto, Cal. (23); Honolulu, Ha. (30).

(2) Violent crime includes murder and non-negligent manslaughter, forcible rape, robbery, and aggravated assault. Other metro areas in the top 30 in violent crime are: New Orleans, La. (6); Charleston-N. Charleston, S.C. (9); Pueblo, Col. (12); Flint, Mich. (14); Fayetteville, N.C. (17); Detroit, Mich. (19); Mansfield, Oh. (20); Jacksonville, Fla. (21); Albuquerque, New Mex. (25); Atlanta, Ga. (26); Memphis, Tenn. (30); Tampa, Fla. (30).

(3) Property crime includes burglary, larceny and auto theft. Other metro areas in the top 30 are: Tucson, Ariz. (5); Denver, Col. (10); Ft. Lauderdale, Fla. (11); Honolulu, Ha. (19); Modesto, Cal. (20); Yakima, Wash. (28); Springfield, Mo. (29).

(4) Of the top 30 cities in murder, all but 8 are in the South (14) or in Texas (8). New Orleans, La. is the no. 1 murder city, with a rate of 23.8.

Crime Rates by State

Source: 1978 Uniform Crime Reports, Federal Bureau of Investigation

(Rates per 100,000 population)

State	**Total**	**Violent**	**Property**	**Murder**	**Rape**	**Robbery**	**Assault**	**Burglary**	**Larceny**	**Auto theft**
Alabama	3,938.8	419.1	3,519.7	13.3	25.5	99.1	281.2	1,229.3	1,987.9	302.5
Alaska	6,046.2	441.9	5,604.2	12.9	55.6	91.3	282.1	1,339.2	3,603.5	661.5
Arizona	7,603.8	552.1	7,051.7	9.4	44.2	162.9	335.6	2,082.5	4,504.8	464.4
Arkansas	3,461.7	344.1	3,117.6	9.1	23.1	80.0	231.9	967.1	1,950.9	199.6
California	7,116.2	742.9	6,373.3	11.7	50.8	306.1	374.4	2,193.3	3,488.8	691.3
Colorado	6,832.4	498.0	6,334.5	7.3	49.6	159.2	281.9	1,869.6	3,977.0	487.9
Connecticut	4,929.5	315.0	4,614.5	4.2	17.2	154.8	138.8	1,362.0	2,597.6	654.9
Delaware	6,353.9	440.7	5,913.2	6.7	20.4	145.5	268.1	1,623.7	3,792.6	496.9
Florida	7,069.5	765.6	6,303.9	11.0	46.1	206.0	502.5	1,978.8	3,936.5	388.6
Georgia	4,771.3	482.8	4,288.5	14.4	37.9	166.3	264.2	1,475.6	2,456.3	356.5
Hawaii	7,136.1	270.1	6,866.0	6.7	25.9	173.6	64.0	1,937.7	4,357.5	570.8
Idaho	4,014.8	236.4	3,778.4	5.4	19.2	40.0	171.9	1,038.4	2,496.2	243.7
Illinois	5,018.2	465.7	4,552.5	9.9	23.8	205.0	227.1	1,139.2	2,902.0	511.2
Indiana	4,338.5	323.5	4,015.1	6.2	27.0	121.4	168.8	1,108.3	2,495.7	411.1
Iowa	3,980.1	161.4	3,818.7	2.6	10.4	46.9	101.6	870.6	2,712.9	235.1
Kansas	4,544.1	318.2	4,225.9	5.7	25.0	93.7	193.8	1,286.8	2,691.4	247.7
Kentucky	3,023.0	223.2	2,799.9	9.0	20.7	81.3	112.1	884.6	1,664.7	250.6
Louisiana	4,792.3	584.9	4,207.4	15.8	34.8	173.7	360.7	1,275.5	2,570.3	361.6

State	Total	Violent	Property	Murder	Rape	Robbery	Assault	Burglary	Larceny	Auto theft
Maine	4,138.5	207.7	3,930.8	2.7	11.1	32.9	161.0	1,241.2	2,436.2	253.3
Maryland	5,813.6	732.0	5,081.6	8.2	35.6	309.6	378.6	1,421.8	3,235.0	424.8
Massachusetts	5,350.4	462.0	4,888.5	3.7	22.6	172.3	263.3	1,515.1	2,277.8	1,095.6
Michigan	5,594.1	577.2	5,016.9	10.6	39.6	219.3	307.7	1,444.3	3,046.7	525.9
Minnesota	4,144.1	189.6	3,954.5	2.0	19.9	85.1	82.6	1,093.7	2,536.1	324.7
Mississippi	2,554.9	321.2	2,233.7	12.6	21.8	70.2	216.6	846.3	1,235.6	151.8
Missouri	4,527.4	467.9	4,059.5	10.4	28.0	184.0	245.5	1,345.2	2,345.5	268.8
Montana	3,915.8	237.6	3,678.2	4.8	15.8	36.8	180.1	786.0	2,585.1	307.1
Nebraska	3,441.3	190.5	3,250.7	3.0	18.3	64.9	104.4	746.8	2,287.2	216.8
Nevada	8,286.8	780.8	7,506.1	15.5	53.9	359.5	351.8	2,659.2	4,245.2	601.7
New Hampshire	4,067.5	118.8	3,948.7	1.4	9.4	26.3	81.7	1,159.7	2,483.4	305.6
New Jersey	5,207.2	423.5	4,783.7	5.4	23.6	192.6	201.9	1,456.3	2,766.8	560.6
New Mexico	5,180.4	528.2	4,652.1	10.2	42.7	111.6	363.8	1,335.6	3,002.7	313.8
New York	5,792.2	841.0	4,951.2	10.3	29.1	472.1	329.5	1,650.6	2,628.6	672.0
North Carolina	3,882.1	413.4	3,468.7	10.8	18.4	65.9	318.4	1,184.0	2,083.4	201.3
North Dakota	2,405.4	67.0	2,338.3	1.2	8.9	15.6	41.3	423.0	1,767.2	148.2
Ohio	4,658.8	412.7	4,246.2	6.9	27.4	182.6	195.8	1,214.5	2,629.7	402.0
Oklahoma	4,129.8	353.0	3,776.9	8.5	31.0	88.3	225.2	1,299.8	2,125.8	351.4
Oregon	6,075.4	502.4	5,573.0	5.0	41.2	131.1	325.0	1,617.1	3,561.1	394.8
Pennsylvania	3,184.7	301.1	2,883.6	6.2	18.7	136.7	139.5	899.9	1,643.0	340.7
Rhode Island	5,262.2	348.1	4,914.1	4.0	11.0	98.2	235.0	1,392.6	2,714.3	807.2
South Carolina	4,895.9	637.6	4,258.4	11.5	35.4	101.3	489.4	1,498.6	2,483.6	276.1
South Dakota	2,689.3	163.5	2,525.8	1.9	10.9	15.9	134.8	599.7	1,766.1	160.0
Tennessee	3,690.4	382.6	3,307.8	9.4	30.6	152.4	190.2	1,213.6	1,766.1	328.1
Texas	5,556.8	435.3	5,121.5	14.2	37.9	164.4	218.8	1,611.9	3,065.3	444.3
Utah	4,978.9	271.8	4,707.1	3.7	22.9	66.5	178.7	1,187.1	3,186.1	333.9
Vermont	3,806.6	166.3	3,640.2	3.3	14.6	14.4	134.1	1.261.2	2,164.9	214.2
Virginia	4,073.0	286.4	3,786.6	8.8	22.7	97.1	157.8	990.8	2,566.8	229.0
Washington	6,115.6	405.3	5,710.3	4.6	41.2	125.0	234.4	1,766.6	3,548.8	394.9
West Virginia	2,270.1	167.7	2,102.4	6.8	14.7	46.3	99.9	648.3	1,278.3	175.8
Wisconsin	3,880.2	132.2	3,748.1	2.5	14.5	49.9	65.2	846.3	2,672.3	229.5
Wyoming	4,494.6	280.4	4,214.2	7.1	23.6	48.1	201.7	836.1	3,035.6	342.5

Total Arrest Trends by Sex, 1978

Source: 1978 Uniform Crime Reports, Federal Bureau of Investigation

	Males				Females			
	Total		Under 18		Total		Under 18	
	1978	Percent change 1977-78	1978	Percent change 1977-78	1978	Percent change 1977-78	1978	Percent change 1977-78
Total[1]	**6,755,387**	**+ 1.5**	**1,507,287**	**− 1.5**	**1,318,348**	**+ 1.7**	**410,628**	**− 4.3**
Murder and non-negligent manslaughter	12,736	+ 1.4	1,197	− 9.4	2,234	− .3	149	+10.4
Forcible rape	22,608	+ 2.4	3,526	− 2.5	186	−19.5	58	−31.0
Robbery	88,928	+ .9	27,272	− .1	6,911	− 3.8	1,985	− 7.4
Aggravated assault	172,849	+ 6.8	26,452	+ 3.1	25,033	+ 6.3	4,618	+ 1.5
Burglary	376,982	+ .2	199,105	+ .2	24,977	+ 2.1	13,070	+ 2.4
Larceny-theft	636,550	+ 1.7	285,416	− .9	299,371	+ 2.7	112,794	− .5
Motor vehicle theft	107,690	+ 4.1	56,121	− .5	10,430	+ 9.8	6,331	+ 9.2
Other assaults	332,081	+ 4.3	56,607	+ .8	53,266	+ 4.0	14,359	− 1.2
Arson	13,400	+ 1.3	6,866	+ .2	1,786	+ 9.1	719	+ 3.5
Forgery and counterfeiting	42,682	− .2	5,734	+ 5.5	18,626	+ 4.0	2,520	+15.0
Fraud	122,039	+ 7.9	3,941	− .5	83,087	+19.2	1,681	+ 8.4
Embezzlement	4,951	+ 5.4	574	− .3	1,693	+24.0	207	+30.2
Stolen property; buying, receiving, possessing	79,367	− 1.5	27,762	− .4	10,276	+ 3.3	2,819	+ 4.1
Vandalism	178,336	+ 7.0	104,265	+ 2.3	16,287	+ 6.0	8,533	+ 2.2
Weapons; carrying, possessing, etc.	115,927	+ 3.2	18,727	+ .9	9,978	− .2	1,190	− 6.2
Prostitution and commercialized vice	21,967	+13.4	891	− .4	46,812	+ 2.3	2,031	+ 2.2
Sex offenses (except forcible rape and prostitution)	47,825	− .4	8,953	− 2.6	4,116	−11.7	897	−14.8
Drug abuse violations	426,682	− .9	101,855	+ .8	69,347	− .1	20,774	+ 3.4
Gambling	37,566	− 4.7	1,547	−11.9	3,782	− 4.9	74	−25.3
Offenses against family and children	45,127	− 2.3	1,711	− 9.3	5,169	− .9	953	−15.7
Driving under the influence	993,468	+ 6.8	22,789	+ 8.6	92,076	+ 8.9	2,432	+15.0
Liquor laws	272,604	+ 4.4	89,991	− .8	47,291	+ 3.9	25,392	+ 1.3
Drunkenness	919,200	− 8.8	33,949	−14.5	74,897	− 7.0	5,381	−15.1
Disorderly conduct	518,816	+ 6.8	93,452	+ 3.1	99,505	+ 1.3	19,582	− 7.5
Vagrancy	17,954	−10.8	3,849	− 9.2	7,092	+15.3	808	−19.4
All other offenses (except traffic)	1,023,489	+ 3.7	201,172	− 3.7	198,449	+ .6	55,600	− 6.8

(1) Totals will not add due to deletion of several minor arrest categories.

Police Roster

Source: Uniform Crime Reports

Police officers and civilian employees in large cities as of Oct. 31, 1978

City	Officer	Civilian	City	Officer	Civilian	City	Officer	Civilian
Anchorage, Alas.	220	78	Indianapolis, Ind.	1,046	313	Phoenix, Ariz.	1,528	523
Atlanta, Ga.	1,018	261	Jacksonville, Fla.	958	650	Pittsburgh, Pa.	1,400	31
Baltimore, Md.	3,337	575	Kansas City, Mo.	1,192	465	Portland, Ore.	699	191
Birmingham, Ala.	702	180	Little Rock, Ark.	262	58	Rochester, N.Y.	617	140
Boston, Mass.	3,002	832	Los Angeles, Cal.	6,979	1,670	Sacramento, Cal.	492	161
Bridgeport, Conn.	3,892	33	Louisville, Ky.	716	200	St. Louis, Mo.	1,997	591
Buffalo, N.Y.	1,092	117	Memphis, Tenn.	1,240	414	St. Petersburg, Fla.	435	214
Chicago, Ill.	130,290	1,304	Miami, Fla.	698	314	San Antonio, Tex.	1,100	286
Cincinnati, Oh.	888	166	Milwaukee, Wis.	2,028	236	San Diego, Cal.	1,193	364
Cleveland, Oh.	1,906	155	Minneapolis, Minn.	765	105	San Francisco, Cal.	1,658	228
Columbus, Oh.	883	1,047	Newark, N.J.	1,453	269	San Jose, Cal.	787	189
Dallas, Tex.	1,997	577	New Orleans, La.	1,532	366	Santa Ana, Cal.	306	106
Denver, Col.	1,390	276	New York, N.Y.	24,408	5,035	Seattle, Wash.	970	318
Detroit, Mich.	5,688	683	Norfolk, Va.	601	107	Stockton, Cal.	231	63
Ft. Worth, Tex.	684	195	Oakland, Cal.	642	233	Tampa, Fla.	588	51
Fresno, Cal.	329	91	Oklahoma City, Okl.	693	180	Toledo, Oh.	564	103
Hartford, Conn.	394	68	Omaha, Neb.	550	127	Tucson, Ariz.	538	168
Honolulu, Ha.	1,472	366	Pasadena, Cal.	191	140	Washington, D.C.	5,078	573
Houston, Tex.	2,988	885	Philadelphia Pa.	8,209	1,046	Wichita, Kan.	397	117

1,123 Law Enforcement Officers Killed 1969-1978

Responding to disturbance calls	178	Handling, transporting, custody of prisoners	52
Burglaries in progress or pursuing suspect	76	Investigating suspicious persons and circumstances	88
Robberies in progress or pursuing suspect	211	Ambush	104
Attempting other arrests	242	Mentally deranged	30
Civil disorders	7	Traffic stops	135

Geographically for the period of 1969-1978 the 1,123 officers who were slain in the line of duty were divided in this fashion: Northeast 161; North Central 260; South 482; and West 188. Another 32 officers were killed in outlying territories.

Crime Index Trends by Geographic Region 1978 over 1977

(rates per 100,000 population)

Region	Total	Violent	Property	Murder	Rape	Robbery	Assault	Burglary	Larceny	Auto theft
Northeast	+1	−3	−2	—	+1	+2	+6	−2	−2	−3
North Central	—	+1	−1	−1	+3	−6	+8	+1	−1	−1
South	+4	+6	+3	+3	+10	+7	+5	+3	+3	+9
West	+2	+6	+1	+2	+5	+7	+5	+1	+1	+5

— means no significant change

Canada: Criminal Offenses and Crime Rate

Source: Statistics Canada

	1978		1979[1]		Percent change in rate
	Actual offenses	Rate[2]	Actual offenses	Rate[2]	
Total criminal code	**1,714,297**	**7300.29**	**1,855,376**	**7838.02**	**+ 7.4**
Total homicide	**1,400**	**5.96**	**1,385**	**5.85**	**− 1.8**
Murder, 1st degree	211	0.90	234	0.99	+10.0
Murder, 2nd degree	379	1.61	353	1.49	− 7.5
Manslaughter	57	0.24	39	0.16	−33.3
Infanticide	11	0.05	5	0.02	−60.0
Attempted murder	742	3.16	754	3.19	+ 1.0
Total sexual offenses	**11,598**	**49.39**	**12,332**	**52.10**	**+ 5.5**
Rape	2,014	8.58	2,291	9.68	+12.8
Indecent assault on female	5,724	24.38	6,087	25.71	+ 5.5
Indecent assault on male	1,223	5.21	1,375	5.81	+11.5
Other sexual offenses	2,637	11.23	2,579	10.90	− 2.9
Total crimes of violence	**138,972**	**591.81**	**147,528**	**623.23**	**+ 5.3**
Assaults (not indecent)	106,301	452.68	112,912	477.00	+ 5.4
Robbery	19,673	83.78	20,899	88.29	+ 5.4
Total property crimes	**1,097,242**	**4672.57**	**1,186,650**	**5012.99**	**+ 7.3**
Breaking and entering	278,480	1185.90	296,424	1252.24	+ 5.6
Theft, motor vehicle	83,130	354.01	91,447	386.32	+ 9.1
Theft, over $200	130,024	553.70	169,953	717.96	+29.7
Theft, $200 and under	497,336	2117.89	516,190	2180.64	+ 3.0
Having stolen goods	19,715	83.96	20,952	88.51	+ 5.4
Fraud	88,557	377.12	91,684	387.32	+ 2.7
Total other crimes	**478,083**	**2035.90**	**521,198**	**2201.80**	**+ 8.1**
Prostitution	1,808	7.70	1,283	5.42	−29.6
Gaming and betting	2,781	11.84	3,060	12.93	+ 9.2
Offensive weapons	16,113	68.62	15,458	65.30	− 4.8
Other criminal code	457,381	1947.74	501,397	2118.15	+ 8.7
Federal statutes-drugs	60,747	258.69	64,920	274.25	+ 6.0
Federal statutes-other	73,284	312.08	57,634	243.47	−22.0
Provincial statutes (3)	398,324	1696.25	438,204	1851.19	+ 9.1
Municipal by-laws (3)	59,313	252.58	69,593	293.99	+16.4
Total-all offenses	**2,305,965**	**9819.89**	**2,485,727**	**10,500.93**	**+ 6.9**

(1) Preliminary. (2) Rate per 100,000 population. (3) Excluding traffic offenses.

POSTAL INFORMATION

U.S. Postal Service

The Postal Reorganization Act, creating a government-owned postal service under the executive branch and replacing the old Post Office Department, was signed into law by President Nixon on Aug. 12, 1970. The service officially came into being on July 1, 1971.

The new U.S. Postal Service is governed by an 11-man Board of Governors. Nine members are appointed to 9-year terms by the president with Senate approval. These 9, in turn, choose a postmaster general, who is no longer a member of the president's cabinet. The board and the new postmaster general choose the 11th member, who serves as deputy postmaster general. A new Postal Rate Commission of 5 members, appointed by the president, recommends postal rates to the governors for their approval.

The first postmaster general under the new system was Winton M. Blount. He resigned Oct. 29, 1971, and was replaced by his deputy, E. T. Klassen, Dec. 7, 1971. Benjamin F. Bailar succeeded him Feb. 16, 1975, and was succeeded by William F. Bolger on March 15, 1978.

As of Oct. 5, 1979, there was a total of 30,499 post offices throughout the U.S. and possessions.

U.S. Domestic Rates (in effect Sept. 1, 1980)

Domestic includes the U.S., territories and possessions, APO and FPO.

First Class

Letters written, and matter sealed against inspection, 15¢ for 1st ounce or fraction, 13¢ for each additional ounce or fraction.

U.S. Postal cards; single 10¢; double 20¢; private postcards, same.

First class includes written matter, namely letters, postal cards, postcards (private mailing cards) and all other matter wholly or partly in writing, whether sealed or unsealed, except manuscripts for books, periodical articles and music, manuscript copy accompanying proofsheets or corrected proofsheets of the same and the writing authorized by law on matter of other classes. Also matter sealed or closed against inspection, bills and statements of accounts.

Greeting Cards

May be sent first class or single piece third class.

Express Mail

Express Mail Service is available for any mailable article up to 70 pounds, and guarantees delivery between major U.S. cities or your money back.

Articles received by 5 p.m. at a postal facility offering Express Mail will be delivered by 3 p.m. the next day or, if you prefer, your shipment can be picked up as early as 10 a.m. the next business day. Rates include insurance, Shipment Receipt, and Record of Delivery at the destination post office.

Consult Postmaster for other Express Mail Services and rates. (The Postal Service will refund, upon application to originating office, the postage for any Express Mail shipments not meeting the service standard except for those delayed by strike or work stoppage.)

Second Class

Single copy mailings by general public 10¢ for first 2 ounces and 6¢ for each additional ounce or the 4th class rate, whichever is lower. There are special rates for publications, newspapers, and bulk mailing, consult local postmasters for rates and permit.

Third Class

Third class (limit up to but not including 16 ounces): Mailable matter not in 1st and 2d classes.

Single mailing: Greeting cards (sealed or unsealed), small parcels, printed matter, booklets and catalogs. 20¢ the first 2 ounces plus 20¢ for the next 2 ounces, plus 13¢ for each additional 2 ounces through 15.9 ounces.

Bulk material: books, catalogs of 24 pages or more, seeds, cuttings, bulbs, roots, scions, and plants. 36¢ per pound, 8.4¢ minimum per price.

Other matter: newsletters, shoppers' guides, advertising circulars. 41¢ per pound, 8.4¢ minimum per piece. Separate rates for some nonprofit organizations. Bulk mailing fee, $40 per calendar year. Apply to postmaster for permit. One-time fee for permit imprint, $30.

Parcel Post—Fourth Class

Fourth class or parcel post (16 ounces and over): merchandise, printed matter, etc., may be sealed, subject to inspection.

On parcels weighing less than 15 lbs. and measuring more than 84 inches, but not more than 100 inches in length and girth combined, the minimum postal charge shall be the zone charge applicable to a 15-pound parcel.

Priority Mail

First class mail of more than 12 ounces can be sent "Priority Mail (Heavy Pieces)" service. The most expeditious handling and transportation available will be used for fastest delivery.

Forwarding Addresses

The mailer, in order to obtain a forwarding address, must endorse the envelope or cover "Address Correction Requested." The destination post office then will determine whether a forwarding address has been left on file and provide if for a fee of 25¢.

Priority Mail

Packages weighing up to 70 pounds and exceeding 100 inches in length and girth combined, including written and other material of the first class, whether sealed or unsealed, fractions of a pound being charged as a full pound, except in the 1 to 5 pound weight category where half-pound weight increments apply.

Rates according to zone apply between the U.S. and Puerto Rico and Virgin Islands.

Parcels weighing less than 15 pounds, measuring over 84 inches but not exceeding 100 inches in length and girth combined are chargeable with a minimum rate equal to that for a 15 pound parcel for the zone to which addressed.

Zones	To 1 lb.	1½	2	2½	3	3½	4	4½	5*
1, 2, 3,	$1.71	$1.86	$1.99	$2.11	$2.23	$2.35	$2.47	$2.59	$2.72
4	1.81	1.96	2.12	2.27	2.42	2.58	2.73	2.89	3.04
5	1.88	2.07	2.27	2.46	2.65	2.84	3.03	3.22	3.42
6	1.97	2.21	2.44	2.68	2.91	3.15	3.38	3.62	3.85
7	2.06	2.34	2.61	2.89	3.17	3.45	3.73	4.01	4.29
8	2.25	2.50	2.83	3.16	3.50	3.83	4.16	4.50	4.83

*Consult postmaster for parcels over 5 lbs.

Special Handling

Third and fourth class parcels will be handled and delivered as expeditiously as practicable (but not special delivery) upon payment, in addition to the regular postage: up to 10 lbs., 70¢; over 10 lbs., $1.25. Such parcels must be endorsed, Special Handling.

Special Delivery

First class mail up to 2 lbs. $2.00, over 2 lbs. and up to 10 lbs., $2.25; over 10 lbs. $2.85. All other classes up to 2 lbs. $2.25, over 2 and up to 10 lbs., $2.85, over 10 lbs. $3.25.

Individual Piece Mailings
(Fourth class catalogs)

Weight lbs.	Local	Zones 1&2	3	4	5	6	7	8
1.5	.69	.92	.94	.97	1.02	1.08	1.16	1.19
2	.69	.93	.95	.99	1.06	1.14	1.25	1.28
2.5	.69	.93	.96	1.01	1.10	1.20	1.33	1.38
3	.69	.94	.97	1.03	1.14	1.25	1.41	1.47
3.5	.69	.94	.98	1.05	1.17	1.31	1.50	1.56
4	.69	.95	.99	1.07	1.21	1.37	1.58	1.66
4.5	.69	.95	1.00	1.09	1.25	1.42	1.67	1.75
5	.70	.96	1.02	1.12	1.29	1.48	1.75	1.85
6	.70	.96	1.04	1.16	1.36	1.59	1.92	2.03
7	.70	.97	1.06	1.20	1.44	1.71	2.09	2.22
8	.70	.98	1.08	1.24	1.51	1.82	2.25	2.41
9	.70	.99	1.10	1.28	1.59	1.94	2.42	2.59
10	.70	1.00	1.12	1.32	1.66	2.05	2.59	2.78

Zone Mileage

1. . Up to 50	3. . 150-300	5. . . 600-1,000	7. 1,400-1,800
2. . . 50-150	4. . 300-600	6. . 1,000-1,400	8 . over 1,800

Domestic Mail Special Services

Registry — all mailable matter prepaid with postage at the first-class or airmail rate may be registered. The mailer is required to declare the value of mail presented for registration.

Registered Mail

Indemnity to $100	$3.00
100.01 to 200	3.30
200.01 to 400	3.70
400.01 to 600	4.10
600.01 to 800	4.50
800.01 to 1,000	4.90
1,000.01 to 2,000	5.30
2,000.01 to 3,000	5.70
3,000.01 to 4,000	6.10
4,000.01 to 5,000	6.50
5,000.01 to 6,000	6.90
6,000.01 to 7,000	7.30
7,000.01 to 8,000	7.70
8,000.01 to 9,000	8.10
9,000.01 to 10,000	8.50

Consult postmaster for registry rates above $10,000.

Insurance — is applicable to 3d and 4th class matter. Matter for sale addressed to prospective purchasers who have not ordered it or authorized its sending will not be insured.

Insured Mail

$0.01 to $15	$0.50
15.01 to 50	0.85
50.01 to 100	1.10
100.01 to 150	1.40
150.01 to 200	1.75
200.01 to 300	2.25
300.01 to 400	2.75

Liability for insured mail is limited to $400.

C.O.D.: Unregistered — is applicable to 3d and 4th class matter and sealed domestic mail of any class bearing postage at the 1st class rate. Such mail must be based on bona fide orders or be in conformity with agreements between senders and addressees. **Registered** — for details consult postmaster.

Certified mail — service is available for any matter having no intrinsic value on which 1st class or air mail postage is paid. Receipt is furnished at time of mailing and evidence of delivery obtained. The fee is 80¢ in addition to postage. Return receipt, restricted delivery, and special delivery are available upon payment of additional fees. No indemnity.

Special Fourth Class Rate
(limit 70 lbs.)

First pound or fraction, 59¢ (52¢ if 500 pieces or more of special rate matter are presorted to 5 digit ZIP code or 55¢ if 2,000 pieces or more are presorted to both 3 and 5 digits); each additional pound or fraction through 7 pounds, 22¢; each additional pound, 13¢. Only following specific articles: books 24 pages or more, at least 22 of which are printed consisting wholly of reading matter or scholarly bibliography containing no advertisement other than incidental announcements of books; 16 millimeter films in final form (except when mailed to or from commercial theaters); printed music in bound or sheet form; printed objective test materials; sound recordings, playscripts, and manuscripts for books, periodicals, and music; printed educational reference charts; loose-leaf pages and binders therefor consisting of medical information for distribution to doctors, hospitals, medical schools, and medical students. Package must be marked "Special 4th Class Rate" stating item contained.

Library Rate (limit 70 lbs.)

First pound 17¢, each additional pound through 7 pounds, 6¢; each additional pound, 5¢. Books when loaned or exchanged between schools, colleges, public libraries, and certain non-profit organizations; books, printed music, bound academic theses, periodicals, sound recordings, other library materials, museum materials (specimens, collections), scientific or mathematical kits, instruments or other devices; also catalogs, guides or scripts for some of these materials. Must be marked "Library Rate".

Postal Union Mail Special Services

Registration — available to practically all countries. Fee $3.00. The maximum indemnity payable — generally only in case of complete loss (of both contents and wrapper) — is $15.76. To Canada only the fees are $3.00 and $3.30, providing indemnity for loss up to $100 to $200, respectively.

Parcel Post Rate Schedule

1 lb., not exceeding	Local	Zones 1 & 2	3	4	5	6	7	8
2	1.15	1.35	1.39	1.56	1.72	1.84	1.98	2.22
3	1.23	1.45	1.53	1.73	1.86	2.04	2.24	2.61
4	1.29	1.56	1.65	1.82	2.00	2.23	2.50	3.00
5	1.36	1.66	1.77	1.92	2.14	2.43	2.77	3.39
6	1.42	1.71	1.84	2.01	2.28	2.62	3.03	3.78
7	1.47	1.76	1.90	2.11	2.41	2.82	3.29	4.17
8	1.51	1.80	1.97	2.20	2.55	3.02	3.56	4.56
9	1.54	1.85	2.03	2.29	2.69	3.21	3.82	4.95
10	1.57	1.89	2.10	2.39	2.83	3.41	4.08	5.34
11	1.60	1.94	2.17	2.50	3.00	3.65	4.42	5.73
12	1.64	1.98	2.22	2.56	3.09	3.77	4.57	6.12
13	1.67	2.02	2.27	2.63	3.17	3.89	4.72	6.41
14	1.70	2.05	2.32	2.69	3.25	3.99	4.86	6.62
15	1.73	2.09	2.36	2.74	3.33	4.09	4.99	6.30
16	1.76	2.13	2.41	2.80	3.40	4.19	5.11	6.98
17	1.79	2.16	2.45	2.85	3.47	4.28	5.23	7.15
18	1.82	2.20	2.49	2.91	3.54	4.37	5.34	7.31
19	1.86	2.23	2.53	2.96	3.61	4.46	5.45	7.47
20	1.89	2.27	2.58	3.01	3.67	4.54	5.55	7.62

Consult postmaster for parcels over 20 pounds or measuring more than 84 inches, length and girth.

Return receipt —fee is 45¢.

Special delivery — Available to most countries. Consult post office. Fees: for post cards, letter mail, and airmail "other articles," $2.00 up to 2 pounds; over 2 to 10 pounds, $2.25; over 10 pounds, $2.85. For surface "other articles," $2.25, $2.85, and $3.25, respectively.

Marking — an article intended for special delivery service must have affixed to the cover near the name of the country of destination "EXPRESS" (special delivery) label, obtainable at the post office, or it may be marked on the cover boldly in red "EXPRESS" (special delivery).

Special handling — entitles AO surface packages to priority handling between mailing point and U.S. point of dispatch. Fees: 70¢ for packages to 10 pounds, and $1.25 for packages over 10 pounds.

Airmail — there is daily air service to practically all countries.

Prepayment of replies from other countries — a mailer who wishes to prepay a reply by letter from another country may do so by sending his correspondent one or more international reply coupons, which may be purchased at United States post offices. One coupon should be accepted in any country in exchange for stamps to prepay a surface letter of the first unit of weight to the U.S.

Post Office-Authorized 2-Letter State Abbreviations

The abbreviations below are approved by the U.S. Postal Service for use in addresses only. They do not replace the traditional abbreviations in other contexts. The official list follows, including the District of Columbia, Guam, Puerto Rico, the Canal Zone, and the Virgin Islands (all capital letters are used):

Alabama	AL	Idaho	ID	Montana	MT	Rhode Island	RI
Alaska	AK	Illinois	IL	Nebraska	NE	South Carolina	SC
Arizona	AZ	Indiana	IN	Nevada	NV	South Dakota	SD
Arkansas	AR	Iowa	IA	New Hampshire	NH	Tennessee	TN
California	CA	Kansas	KS	New Jersey	NJ	Texas	TX
Canal Zone	CZ	Kentucky	KY	New Mexico	NM	Utah	UT
Colorado	CO	Louisiana	LA	New York	NY	Vermont	VT
Connecticut	CT	Maine	ME	North Carolina	NC	Virginia	VA
Delaware	DE	Maryland	MD	North Dakota	ND	Virgin Islands	VI
Dist. of Col.	DC	Massachusetts	MA	Ohio	OH	Washington	WA
Florida	FL	Michigan	MI	Oklahoma	OK	West Virginia	WV
Georgia	GA	Minnesota	MN	Oregon	OR	Wisconsin	WI
Guam	GU	Mississippi	MS	Pennsylvania	PA	Wyoming	WY
Hawaii	HI	Missouri	MO	Puerto Rico	PR		

Also approved for use in addressing mail are the following abbreviations:

Alley	Aly	Court	Ct	Grove	Grv	Rural	R
Arcade	Arc	Courts	Cts	Heights	Hts	Square	Sq
Boulevard	Blvd	Crescent	Cres	Highway	Hwy	Street	St
Branch	Br	Drive	Dr	Lane	Ln	Terrace	Ter
Bypass	Byp	Expressway	Expy	Manor	Mnr	Trail	Trl
Causeway	Cswy	Extended	Ext	Place	Pl	Turnpike	Tpke
Center	Ctr	Extension	Ext	Plaza	Plz	Viaduct	Via
Circle	Cir	Freeway	Fwy	Point	Pt	Vista	Vis
		Gardens	Gdns	Road	Rd		

Commemorative Stamps and Regular Postal Issues 1980

Date	Commemorative stamp	Value	From
Jan. 29	W.C. Fields	15¢	Beverly Hills, CA
Feb. 1	Winter Olympics (4 stamps)	15¢	Lake Placid, NY
Feb. 7	Windmill booklet (10 stamps)	15¢	Lubbock, TX
Feb. 15	Benjamin Banneker	15¢	Annapolis, MD
Feb. 25	Letter Writing (6 stamps)	15¢	Washington, DC
Mar. 6	Quill Pen coil	1¢	New York, NY
Apr. 10	Frances Perkins	15¢	Washington, DC
May 20	Dolley Madison	15¢	Washington, DC
May 31	Emily Bissell	15¢	Wilmington, DE
June 23	Nonprofit coil	3.5¢	Williamsburg, PA
June 27	Helen Keller/Anne Sullivan	15¢	Tuscumbia, AL
July 21	Veterans Administration	15¢	Washington, DC
July 23	Gen. Bernardo de Galvez	15¢	New Orleans, LA
Aug. 26	Coral Reefs (4 stamps)	15¢	Charlotte Amalie, St. Thomas, VI
Sept. 1	Organized Labor	15¢	Washington, DC
Sept. 5	Edith Wharton	15¢	New Haven, CT
Sept. 12	American Education	15¢	Franklin, MA
Sept. 25	Northwest Indian Masks (4 stamps)	15¢	Spokane, WA
Oct. 9	Architecture (4 stamps)	15¢	New York, NY
Oct. 13	Philip Mazzei International Airmail	40¢	Washington, DC
Oct. 31	Christmas (masterpiece)	15¢	Washington, DC
Oct. 31	Christmas (contemporary)	15¢	Christmas, MI

Postal Receipts at Large Cities

Fiscal year	Boston	Chicago	Detroit	L.A.	New York	Phila.	St. Louis	Wash., D.C.
1974	$123,164,661	$347,561,637	$87,784,811	$176,847,940	$409,392,651	$130,655,216	$79,412,843	$133,458,807
1975	136,453,079	365,378,795	84,338,282	193,229,077	453,905,277	134,571,376	85,591,774	115,489,343
1976	151,642,227	384,380,826	95,527,250	203,413,409	484,180,727	147,650,431	96,844,188	125,997,649
1977	173,933,702	424,045,237	102,018,571	232,293,590	528,545,213	168,521,442	107,379,762	138,050,517
1978	185,983,338	451,745,664	112,884,557	251,481,356	559,199,325	180,365,543	115,610,668	156,623,025
1979	211,082,724	506,395,438	120,690,772	273,563,824	627,445,984	211,571,818	126,031,314	175,467,893

Other cities for fiscal year 1979: Atlanta, $190,508,405; Baltimore, $104,346,301; Cincinnati, $79,520,084; Cleveland, $124,793,361; Columbus, $107,595,868; Dallas, $199,111,891; Denver, $105,981,308; Houston, $165,662,500; Indianapolis, $109,787,250; Kansas City, $93,593,169; Minneapolis, $138,953,790; Pittsburgh, $98,991,275; San Francisco, $151,822,109; Seattle, $94,814,291.

Air Mail, Parcel Post International Rates

Aerogrammes — 22¢ each to all countries.
Air mail postcards (single) - 21¢ to all countries except Canada and Mexico (14¢)

Country	Misc. rates (see below)	Air parcel post rates: First 4 oz.	Air parcel post rates: Each add'l. 4 oz. or fraction
Afghanistan	G	3.14	1.20
Albania	E	3.33	.79
Algeria	F	2.71	.80
Andorra	F	2.79	.70
Angola	G	2.93	1.01
Anguilla	A	1.78	.36
Antigua	A	1.78	.36
Argentina	F	2.46	1.07
Aruba	C	2.08	.45
Ascension Is.	E	(4)	—
Australia[3]	I	2.62	1.21
Austria	F	2.70	.74
Azores	F	1.95	.56
Bahamas	C	2.19	.27
Bahrain	G	2.42	1.03
Bangladesh	G	3.46	1.22
Barbados	A	1.90	.51
Barbuda	A	1.78	.36
Belgium	F	2.41	.66
Belize	C	1.89	.48
Benin	I	2.36	.85
Bermuda	B	1.77	.35
Bhutan	*	(4)	—
Bolivia[3]	F	2.47	.69
Bonaire	C	2.08	.45
Botswana	G	2.66	1.27
Brazil	F	2.94	.79
Br. Virgin Is.	A	1.78	.36
Brunei	G	3.01	1.47
Bulgaria	E	2.15	.75
Burma[3]	G	3.30	1.43
Burundi	G	2.76	1.07
Cameroon	G	2.79	.92
Canada[3]	*	(6)	—
Canary, Balearic Is.[1]	F	2.79	.70
Cape Verde	G	2.72	.81
Cayman	A	2.36	.33
Cen. African Emp.	I	2.76	1.07
Chad	I	2.76	1.07
Chile[3]	E	2.92	.89
China, People's Rep.[7]	E	3.08	1.37
China. Rep. of	E	2.46	1.05
Colombia[3]	D	2.86	.50
Comoro	I	3.13	1.43
Congo	I	2.76	1.07
Corsica	F	2.98	.66
Costa Rica	C	2.06	.43
Crete	F	2.62	.84
Cuba	*	(4)	—
Curacao	C	2.08	.45
Cyprus	F	2.88	.85
Czechoslovakia	F	2.17	.76
Denmark	F	2.14	.72
Djibouti	I	2.89	1.03
Dominica	A	2.39	.48
Dominican Rep.	C	2.24	.36
East Timor	G	3.64	1.72
Ecuador	F	2.78	.48
Egypt	F	2.32	.92
El Salvador	C	2.21	.44
Equatorial Guinea	I	2.82	1.22
Estonia[2]	I	2.84	.95
Ethiopia	I	2.83	1.10
Falkland Is.	E	2.99	.85
Fiji	G	2.79	.90
Finland	F	2.17	.79
France	F	2.98	.66
French Guiana	F	2.19	.56
Fr. Polynesia	I	2.70	.76
Gabon	I	2.76	1.07
Gambia	G	2.39	.76
Germany, Fed. Rep. (West)	F	2.10	.70
Germany (East)	E	2.10	.70
Ghana	G	2.92	.92
Gilbraltar	E	2.16	.75
Great Britain	F	2.08	.66
Greece	F	2.62	.84
Greenland	F	2.35	.93

Country	Misc. rates (see below)	Air parcel post rates: First 4 oz.	Air parcel post rates: Each add'l. 4 oz. or fraction
Grenada	A	2.39	.48
Guadeloupe	C	2.00	.36
Guatemala	C	2.51	.46
Guinea, Rep. of	I	2.46	.96
Guinea-Bissau	G	2.93	1.01
Guyana	E	2.42	.50
Haiti	C	2.25	.35
Honduras[1]	C	2.14	.46
Hong Kong	G	2.65	1.24
Hungary	F	2.16	.76
Iceland	F	2.66	.56
India[1]	I	2.67	1.27
Indonesia	G	3.48	1.52
Iran	I	2.67	.96
Iraq	I	2.98	.95
Ireland	E	2.06	.66
Israel	H	2.93	.91
Italy	F	2.63	.79
Ivory Coast	I	2.46	.95
Jamaica	A	2.36	.33
Japan	G	2.19	.80
Jordan	G	2.72	.90
Kampuchea (Cambodia)	*	(4)	—
Kenya	G	2.93	1.10
Kiribati (Gilbert Is.)	I	2.66	1.00
Korea (Rep. of)	G	2.25	.85
No. Korea[1]	*	(4)	—
Kuwait	I	2.39	1.00
Laos	G	3.35	1.37
Latvia[2]	I	2.84	.95
Lebanon[1]	I	2.72	.90
Leeward Is.	A	1.78	.36
Lesotho	G	2.66	1.27
Liberia	G	2.24	.84
Libya	F	2.70	.85
Liechtenstein	F	2.39	.67
Lithuania[2]	I	2.84	.95
Luxembourg	F	2.47	.65
Macao	G	3.20	1.24
Madagascar	I	3.09	1.22
Madeira Is.	E	2.10	.72
Malawi	G	2.66	1.24
Malaysia	G	3.23	1.42
Maldives	G	3.59	1.29
Mali	I	3.46	.82
Malta	E	2.61	.79
Martinique	C	2.00	.36
Mauritania	I	2.36	.79
Mauritius	G	3.01	1.29
Mexico	*	1.77	.35
Monaco	F	2.98	.66
Mongolia	*	(4)	—
Montserrat	C	1.78	.36
Morocco	F	2.63	.79
Mozambique	G	3.43	1.28
Namibia (SW Africa)	G	2.66	1.27
Nauru	G	2.62	1.21
Nepal	G	2.66	1.27
Netherlands	F	2.36	.66
Neth. Antilles	C	2.08	.45
Nevis	A	1.78	.36
New Caledonia	I	2.81	.93
New Zealand	G	2.98	1.07
Nicaragua	C	2.08	.43
Niger	I	3.45	.80
Nigeria	G	3.14	.93
Norway	F	2.14	.72
Oman	G	2.42	1.03
Pakistan	G	3.46	1.22
Panama	*	2.50	.45
Papua New Guinea	G	2.72	1.32
Paraguay	F	2.47	.67
Peru	F	2.88	.60
Philippines[1]	I	3.03	1.17
Pitcairn	G	2.89	1.03
Poland	F	2.61	.75
Portugal	E	2.05	.64
Qatar	G	2.42	1.03

Country	Misc. rates (see below)	Air parcel post rates: First 4 oz.	Air parcel post rates: Each add'l. 4 oz. or fraction
Reunion	I	2.89	1.27
Romania	E	2.42	.79
Rwanda	G	2.76	1.07
Saba	C	2.08	.45
St. Christopher	A	2.39	.48
St. Eustatius	C	2.08	.45
St. Helena	G	3.01	1.22
St. Lucia	A	2.39	.48
St. Pierre, Miquelon	C	1.72	.35
St. Vincent	A	2.39	.48
Samoa	G	2.71	.80
San Marino	F	2.63	.79
Santa Cruz Is.	G	3.10	1.39
Sao Tome & Principe	G	2.93	1.01
Saudi Arabia	G	3.10	1.00
Senegal	I	2.34	.75
Seychelles	G	2.53	1.12
Sierra Leone	G	3.09	.81
Singapore	G	3.23	1.42
Solomon Is.	G	3.12	1.39
Somalia	G	3.23	1.13
South Africa	G	2.66	1.27
Spain[1]	F	2.79	.70
Sri Lanka (Ceylon)	G	3.33	1.28
Sudan	G	3.13	1.01
Surinam	F	2.24	.53
Swaziland	G	2.66	1.27
Sweden	F	2.14	.72

Country	Misc. rates (see below)	Air parcel post rates: First 4 oz.	Air parcel post rates: Each add'l. 4 oz. or fraction
Switzerland	F	2.39	.67
Syria[1]	I	2.47	.92
Tanzania	G	2.99	1.15
Thailand	G	3.28	1.17
Togo	I	2.57	.95
Tonga	G	2.34	.93
Trinidad & Tobago	A	2.37	.45
Tristan da Cunha	G	2.83	1.21
Tunisia	F	2.62	.75
Turkey	F	2.26	.85
Turks & Caicos	A	2.25	.33
Tuvalu (Ellice)	G	2.66	1.00
Uganda	G	2.93	1.10
USSR[2]	I	2.84	.95
United Arab Emir	G	2.42	1.03
Upper Volta	I	2.72	.89
Uruguay	F	2.93	.90
Vanuatu (New Hebrides)	I	2.65	.93
Vatican City	F	2.42	.74
Venezuela	D	2.71	.43
Vietnam[1]	*	(4)	—
Windward Is.	A	2.39	.48
Yemen (Aden)	I	2.81	1.10
Yemen (Sanaa)	I	3.04	1.55
Yugoslavia	F	2.17	.79
Zaire	I	2.76	1.07
Zambia	G	2.66	1.24
Zimbabwe (Rhodesia)	G	2.66	1.24

Miscellaneous Rates

Group or country	Air service: Letters and letter pkgs.: per 1/2 oz. thru 2 oz.	Air service: Letters and letter pkgs.: per 1/2 oz. over 2 oz.	Air service: Other articles: First 2 oz.	Air service: Other articles: Each add'l. 2 oz. or fraction	Surface parcel post: First 2 lbs.	Surface parcel post: Each add'l. pound or fraction	Max. wt. for parcel post (surface or air) lbs.
A	.25	.21	.60	.16	2.19	.52	22
B	.25	.21	.60	.16	2.19	.52	33
C	.25	.21	.60	.16	2.19	.52	44
D	.25	.21	.60	.16	2.34	.59	44
E	.31	.26	.73	.29	2.34	.59	22
F	.31	.26	.73	.29	2.34	.59	44
G	.31	.26	.86	.42	2.34	.59	22
H	.31	.26	.86	.42	2.34	.59	33
I	.31	.26	.86	.42	2.34	.59	44
* *Exceptions:*							
Bhutan	.31	.26	.86	.42	...	...	(5)
Cambodia	.31	.26	(1)	...	...	...	(5)
Canada[3]	(oz.) .15	(addl. oz.) .13	(6)	...	2.19	.52	35
Cuba	.25	.21	.60	.16	...	...	(5)
Korea, No.[1]	.31	.26	.86	.42	...	...	(5)
Mexico	(oz.) .15	(addl. oz.) .13	.60	.16	2.19	.52	44
Mongolia	.31	.26	.86	.42	...	...	(5)
Panama	.25	.21	.60	.16	2.19	.52	'70
Vietnam[1]	.31	.26	.86	.42	...	...	(5)

(1) Restrictions apply; consult post office. (2) To facilitate distribution and delivery, include "Union of Soviet Socialist Republics" or "USSR" as part of the address. (3) Small packets weight limit one pound. (4) No air parcel post service. (5) No surface parcel post service. (6) No airmail AO or parcel post to Canada; prepare and prepay all airmail packages as letter mail. (7) The continental China postal authorities will not deliver articles unless addressed to show name of the country as "People's Republic of China"; also, only acceptable spelling of capital is "Beijing."

International Mails

Weight and Dimensional Limits and Surface Rates

For air rates and parcel post see pages 159-160

Letters and letter packages: all written matter or correspondence recordings, must be sent as letter mail. Weight limit: 4 lbs. to all countries except Canada, which is 60 lbs. **Surface rates:** Canada and Mexico, 15¢ first ounce; 13¢ each additional ounce or fraction through 12 ounces; eighth-zone priority rates for heavier weights. Countries other than Canada and Mexico, 1 ounce, 20¢; over 1 to 2 ounces, 36¢; over 2 to 4 ounces, 42¢; over 4 to 8 ounces, 96¢; over 8 ounces to 1 pound, $1.84; over 1 to 2 pounds, $3.20; and over 2 to 4 pounds, $5.20. **Air rates:** Canada and Mexico, 15¢ first ounce; 13¢ each additional ounce or fraction. Central America, Colombia, Venezuela, the Caribbean Islands, Bahamas, Bermuda, and St. Pierre and Miquelon, 25¢ per half ounce up to and including 2 ounces; 21¢ each additional half ounce or fraction. All other countries, 31¢ per half ounce up to and including 2 ounces; 26¢ each additional half ounce or fraction. Aerogrammes, which can be folded into the form of an envelope and sent by air to all countries, are available at post offices for 22¢ each.

Note. Mail to Canada and Mexico bearing postage paid at the surface letter rate will receive first class service in the U.S. and airmail service in Canada and Mexico during the Postal Service First Class Mail Service Improvement Program.

Postcards. Surface rates to Canada and Mexico, 10¢; to all other countries, 14¢. By air, Canada and Mexico, 10¢; to all other countries, 21¢. Maximum size permitted, 6 x 4¼ in.; minimum, 5½ x 3½.

Printed matter. To Canada and Mexico, 20¢ the first 2 ounces, 20¢ for the next two ounces, plus 13¢ each add'l. 2 ounces or fraction through 1 pound; $1.26 for 1 to 2 pounds, $1.68 for 2 to 4 pounds. To other countries, 20¢ the first 2 ounces, 40¢ 2 to 4 ounces, 66¢ 4 to 8 ounces, $1.05 8 to 16 ounces, $1.26 1 to 2 pounds, $1.68 2 to 4 pounds. To countries admitting regular prints over 4 lbs. 84¢ for each additional 2 lbs. or fraction. (Consult post office for rates and conditions applying to certain publications mailed by the publishers or by registered news agents.) Book weight limit for most countries is 11 lbs; for exceptions see below. Consult post office for book rates.

Exceptional weight limits for printed matter. Printed matter may weigh up to 22 lbs. to Argentina, Bolivia, Brazil, Chile, Colombia, Costa Rica, Cuba, Dominican Republic, Ecuador, El Salvador, Guatemala, Haiti, Honduras, Mexico, Nicaragua, Panama, Paraguay, Peru, Spain (including Baleraic Islands, and Canary Islands) Surinam, Uruguay, and Venezuela. For other countries, limit for books is 11 lbs., all other prints, 4 lbs.

Matter for the blind. Surface rate free; air service to Canada for matter prepared as letters/letter packages is at the letter rate. (For all other countries, consult postmaster.) Weight limit 15 lbs.

Small packets. Postage rates for small items of merchandise and samples are lower than for letter packages or parcel post; consult post office for weight limits and requirements for customs declarations. Surface rates: Canada and Mexico, 20¢ the first 2 oz.; 40¢ for the next 2 oz.; plus 13¢ for each add'l 2 oz. or fraction. All other countries, 20¢ the first 2 oz.; 40¢ for the next 2 oz.; 4 to 8 oz. 66¢; 8oz. to 1 lb. $1.05; 1 to 2 lbs. $1.26. For other rates, see schedule "Air Service Other Articles" under heading of International Rates for Air Mail and Surface Parcel Post, pages 159-160.

International Parcel Post

For rates see pages 159-160

General dimensional limits — greatest length, 3½ feet; greatest length and girth combined, 6 feet.

Prohibited articles. Before sending goods abroad the mailer should consult the post office that they will not be confiscated or returned because their importation is prohibited or restricted by the country of address.

Packing. Parcels for transmission overseas should be even more carefully packed than those intended for delivery within the continental U.S. Containers should be used which will be strong enough to protect the contents from the weight of other mail, from pressure and friction, climatic changes, and repeated handlings.

Sealing. Registered or insured parcels must be sealed. To some countries the sealing of ordinary (unregistered and uninsured) parcels is optional, and to others compulsory. Consult post office.

Customs declarations and other forms. At least one customs declaration is required for parcel post packages (surface or air) mailed to another country. In addition, to some countries, a dispatch note is required. The forms may be obtained at post offices.

United Nations Postage Stamps Issued in 1980

UN stamps in U. S. denominations, valid for postage only on mail deposited at UN Headquarters, New York, UN stamps in Swiss denominations, valid for postage only on mail deposited at the UN Office, Geneva, and UN stamps in Austrian denominations, valid for postage only on mail deposited at the Vienna International Centre, are available at face value from the UN Postal Administration in New York, Geneva, and Vienna, and through sales agencies around the world. They may be obtained by mail or automatically through the Customer Deposit Account Service, both in New York and Geneva. Revenue from the sale of UN stamps for postage purposes goes to the U.S. Postal Service, the Swiss PTT, and the Austrian PTT respectively; from philatelic sales, revenue goes to the UN.

Date	Stamp	Value
11 Jan.	New International Economic Order	15¢, 31¢
7 Mar.	UN Decade for Women	15¢, 20¢
16 May	UN Peace-keeping Operations	15¢, 31¢
26 June	35th Anniversary of the UN	15¢, 31¢ 46¢ souvenir sheet
26 Sept.	UN Flag Series (16 stamps)	15¢ each
21 Nov.	Economic and Social Council	15¢, 20¢

Canadian Postal Rates

(in effect July 1, 1980)

First class letter mail and postcards. Up to 30 grams 17¢, over 30g and up to 50g 26¢, over 50g and up to 100g 38¢, over 100g and up to 150g 56¢, over 150g and up to 200g 74¢, over 200g and up to 250g 91¢, over 250g and up to 300g $1.09, over 300g and up to 350g $1.27, over 350g and up to 400g $1.44, over 400g and up to 450g $1.62, over 450g and up to 500g $1.80.

Parcels (over 500g). **First class** (maximum 30kg) receive priority air service. **Fourth class** (maximum 16kg) receive surface transmission.

The charges given below are for local (short haul) deliveries. A chart showing the cost for deliveries to all other postal zones may be obtained from your local postmaster.

Over/up to	500g/1kg-	1kg/1.5	1.5/2	2/2.5	2.5/3	3/3.5	3.5/4	4/6	6/8	8/10	10/12	12/14
1st class	$1.85	2.05	2.25	2.45	2.65	2.85	3.05	3.35	3.65	4.25	4.55	4.85
4th class	.85	1.00	1.10	1.25	1.35	1.50	1.60	1.80	2.00	2.20	2.40	2.60

Third class. Standard addressed rates (includes greeting cards). Up to 50g 15¢ plus 8¢for each additional 50g up to a maximum of 500g.

Premium services. Certified mail (proof of delivery service) 90¢ plus postage. Special delivery first class postage plus $1 per item. Money order fee (maximum $200) - 40¢.

To U.S.A., Territories and Possessions

Airmail letters and postcards, up to and including 30g 17¢, from 30g to 50g 30¢ plus approximately 25¢ for each additional 50g up to 500g. Over 500g up to and including 1kg $3.90 with increases up to $52.69 for 30kg.

Surface parcel post. Up to and including 1kg $1.90 plus 55¢ for each additional 500g up to a maximum of 16kg.

ECONOMICS

U.S. Budget Receipts and Outlays—1977-1980

Source: Treasury Department; Office of Management and Budget.
(Fiscal years end Sept. 30)
(thousands of dollars)

Classification	Fiscal 1977	Fiscal 1978	Fiscal 1979	Fiscal 1980[1]
Net Receipts				
Individual income taxes	156,725,183	180,987,773	217,840,966	240,700,000
Corporation income taxes	54,892,364	59,951,865	65,676,588	65,500,000
Social insurance taxes and contributions:				
Federal old-age and survivors insurance	68,031,809	73,140,779	83,409,910	NA
Federal disability insurance	8,785,502	12,250,395	14,583,743	NA
Federal hospital insurance	13,484,042	16,679,867	19,890,684	NA
Railroad retirement taxes	1,908,494	1,822,006	2,189,887	NA
Total employment taxes and contributions	**92,209,847**	**103,893,048**	**120,074,224**	**NA**
Other insurance and retirement:				
Unemployment	11,311,506	13,849,597	15,386,733	NA
Federal supplementary medical insurance	2,192,903	2,431,133	2,636,005	NA
Federal employees retirement	2,909,697	3,174,262	3,428,322	NA
Civil service retirement and disability	58,923	62,323	66,042	NA
Total social insurance taxes and contributions	**108,682,876**	**123,410,366**	**141,591,326**	**160,500,000**
Excise taxes	17,547,715	18,376,183	18,744,953	25,400,000
Estate and gift taxes	7,326,877	5,285,401	5,410,556	6,100,000
Customs duties	5,150,151	6,572,717	7,438,533	7,000,000
Deposits of earnings-Federal Reserve Banks	5,908,214	6,641,091	8,326,930	NA
All other miscellaneous receipts	640,568	771,976	910,317	NA
Net Budget Receipts	**356,861,331**	**401,997,000**	**465,940,168**	**517,900,000**
Net Outlays				
Legislative Branch	976,492	1,048,776	1,077,101	1,300,000
The Judiciary	391,839	435,124	479,665	600,000
Executive Office of the President:				
The White House Office	17,236	16,571	16,159	NA
Office of Management and Budget	26,536	29,299	29,788	NA
Total Executive Office	**73,386**	**74,566**	**79,589**	**100,000**
Funds appropriated to the President:				
Appalachian regional development	248,868	261,674	304,337	NA
Disaster relief	294,016	470,290	284,220	NA
Foreign assistance-security	347,287	2,019,665	1,786,014	NA
Foreign assistance-development-bilateral	507,098	434,972	593,058	NA
Int. narcotics control assistance	NA	34,987	46,702	NA
Total funds appropriated to the President	**2,497,204**	**4,475,091**	**2,536,618**	**7,600,000**
Agriculture Department:				
Food stamp program	5,398,795	5,498,774	6,821,746	NA
Child Nutrition Program	2,635,039	2,526,732	2,879,668	NA
Total Agriculture Department	**16,737,730**	**20,368,401**	**20,633,725**	**25,700,000**
Commerce Department	2,606,804	5,252,159	4,071,765	3,800,000
Defense Department:				
Military personnel	25,714,935	27,075,347	28,407,171	NA
Retired military personnel	8,216,429	9,171,474	10,279,058	NA
Operation and maintenance	30,688,742	33,577,970	36,424,304	NA
Procurement	18,178,230	19,975,553	25,404,254	NA
Research and development	9,795,166	10,507,963	11,152,177	NA
Military construction	1,913,804	1,931,504	2,079,987	NA
Family housing	1,357,866	1,404,772	1,467,517	NA
Corps of Engineers and civil functions	2,279,998	2,611,625	2,886,226	NA
Total Defense Department	**98,031,451**	**105,677,084**	**117,921,453**	**135,600,000**
Energy Department	5,020,477	6,429,745	7,888,792	6,500,000
Health, Education and Welfare Department:				
Food and Drug Administration	NA	275,971	299,834	NA
National Institutes of Health	2,253,040	2,675,703	2,869,565	NA
Public Health Service	NA	6,757,527	6,928,528	NA
Old-age and survivors benefits	73,478,596	81,205,460	87,591,968	NA
Social Security Administration	NA	108,221,236	118,041,422	NA
Education Division	7,783,479	8,763,618	10,713,037	NA
Human Development Services	NA	5,252,264	5,718,598	NA
Total HEW	**147,455,436**	**162,809,429**	**181,185,638**	**NA**
Housing and Urban Development Department	5,832,430	7,760,944	9,218,091	12,600,000
Interior Department	3,085,260	3,677,605	4,087,007	4,000,000
Justice Department:				
Federal Bureau of Investigation	520,218	552,001	585,991	NA
Total Justice Department	**2,349,726**	**2,397,372**	**2,521,715**	**2,700,000**
Labor Department:				
Unemployment Trust Fund	14,102,958	11,169,127	11,172,982	NA
Total Labor Department	**22,374,056**	**22,902,043**	**22,650,336**	**29,600,000**
State Department	1,131,820	1,251,536	1,548,046	1,900,000
Transportation Department	12,513,984	13,451,791	15,485,569	18,600,000
Treasury Department:				
Internal Revenue Service	2,265,183	3,325,766	3,422,178	NA
Interest on the public debt	41,899,720	48,694,855	59,837,203	NA
General revenue sharing	6,760,092	6,854,924	6,847,709	NA
Total Treasury Department	**49,560,182**	**56,309,144**	**64,595,923**	**76,500,000**
Environmental Protection Agency	4,364,808	4,071,472	4,799,768	5,700,000

Classification	Fiscal 1977	Fiscal 1978	Fiscal 1979	Fiscal 1980[1]
Net Outlays (cont'd)				
General Services Administration	−31,100	117,042	172,761	NA
National Aeronautics and Space Administration	3,943,817	3,980,022	4,187,232	4,900,000
Veterans Administration	18,019,353	18,962,152	19,887,171	20,800,000
Independent agencies:				
ACTION	186,296	203,163	211,325	NA
Arms Control and Disarmament Agency	11,863	13,990	14,653	NA
Board for International Broadcasting	57,837	65,451	82,692	NA
Civil Aeronautics Board	102,707	101,359	99,336	NA
Commission on Civil Rights	9,476	10,464	10,257	NA
Community Services Administration	639,363	767,918	778,894	NA
Consumer Product Safety Commission	39,867	40,058	39,270	NA
Corporation for Public Broadcasting	103,000	119,200	120,200	NA
District of Columbia	315,717	370,968	393,151	NA
Equal Employment Opportunity Commission	71,729	74,160	92,453	NA
Export-Import Bank of the United States	NA	−105,904	200,052	NA
Federal Communications Commission	55,776	64,065	69,542	NA
Federal Deposit Insurance Corporation	−851,645	−566,610	−1,218,370	NA
Federal Emergency Management Agency	NA	259,290	417,422	NA
Federal Home Loan Bank Board	1,913,355	−403,045	−488,357	NA
Federal Trade Commission	51,703	58,815	62,605	NA
Intergovernmental Agencies	292,403	153,247	88,911	NA
International Communications Agency	NA	352,116	373,463	NA
Interstate Commerce Commission	60,602	64,899	54,797	NA
Legal Services Corporation	125,004	157,429	254,307	NA
Merit Systems Protection Board	NA	NA	6,476	NA
National Foundation on the Arts and Humanities	192,753	247,261	283,630	NA
National Labor Relations Board	80,546	90,414	97,190	NA
National Science Foundation	752,035	802,783	869,647	NA
National Transportation Safety Board	NA	15,513	15,515	NA
Nuclear Regulatory Commission	230,547	270,862	309,475	NA
Office of Personnel Management	NA	10,962,658	12,654,562	NA
Postal Service	2,267,449	1,778,240	1,786,509	NA
Railroad Retirement Board	3,858,848	4,074,556	4,365,399	NA
Securities and Exchange Commission	53,635	61,302	65,978	NA
Small Business Administration	699,974	2,766,028	1,631,142	NA
Smithsonian Institution	114,988	125,239	132,182	NA
Tennessee Valley Authority	1,099,559	1,412,228	1,884,141	NA
U.S. Railway Association	735,500	753,725	737,150	NA
Other independent agencies	85,569	177,152	186,299	NA
Total independent agencies	**20,014,438**	**25,078,715**	**26,681,897**	**NA**
Undistributed offsetting receipts	−15,053,215	−15,772,226	−18,488,845	−21,900,000
Net Budget Outlays	**401,896,376**	**450,758,000**	**493,221,018**	**578,800,000**
Less net receipts	356,861,331	401,997,000	465,940,168	517,900,000
Deficit	**−45,035,045**	**−48,761,000**	**−27,280,850**	**−60,900,000**

(1) Estimate. (NA) Not available.

U.S. Net Receipts and Outlays

Source: Treasury Department; annual statements for year ending June 30[1] (thousands of dollars)

Yearly average	Receipts	Expenditures	Yearly average	Receipts	Expenditures	Yearly average	Receipts	Expenditures
1789-1800[1]	5,717	5,776	1871-1875	336,830	287,460	1916-1920[6]	3,483,652	8,065,333
1801-1810[2]	13,056	9,086	1876-1880	288,124	255,598	1921-1925	4,306,673	3,578,989
1811-1820[2]	21,032	23,943	1881-1885	366,961	257,691	1926-1930	4,069,138	3,182,807
1821-1830[2]	21,928	16,162	1886-1890	375,448	279,134	1931-1935[4]	2,770,973	5,214,874
1831-1840[2]	30,461	24,495	1891-1895	352,891	363,599	1936-1940[4]	4,960,614	10,192,367
1841-1850[2]	28,545	34,097	1896-1900	434,877	457,451	1941-1945[4]	25,951,137	66,037,928
1851-1860	60,237	60,163	1901-1905	559,481	535,559	1946-1950[5 7]	39,047,243	42,334,534
1861-1865	160,907	683,785	1906-1910	628,507	639,178			
1866-1870	447,301	377,642	1911-1915	710,227	720,252			

Fiscal year	Receipts	Expenditures	Fiscal year	Receipts	Expenditures	Fiscal year	Receipts	Expenditures
1955	60,389,744	64,569,973	1970	193,843,791	194,968,258	1976	300,005,077	365,610,129
1960	77,763,460	76,539,413	1971	188,332,129	210,652,667	1976 Trans[3]	81,772,766	94,472,996
1963	86,357,020	92,589,764	1972[8]	215,262,639	238,285,907	1977[3]	356,861,331	401,896,376
1964	89,458,664	97,684,375	1973	232,191,842	246,603,359	1978	401,997,000	450,758,000
1965	93,071,797	96,506,904	1974	264,847,484	268,342,952	1979	465,940,168	493,221,018
1968[9]	153,675,705	172,803,186	1975	281,037,466	324,641,586	1980[10]	517,900,000	578,800,000

(1) Average for period March 4, 1789, to Dec. 31, 1800. (2) Years ended Dec. 31, 1801 to 1842; average for 1841-1850 is for the period Jan. 1, 1841, to June 30, 1850. (3) Effective fiscal year 1977, fiscal year is reckoned Oct. 1-Sept. 30; transition quarter covers July 1, 1976-Sept. 30, 1976. (4) Expenditures for years 1932 through 1946 have been revised to include Government corps. (wholly owned) etc. (net). (5) Effective January 3, 1949, amounts refunded by the Government, principally for the overpayment of taxes, are being reported as deductions from total receipts rather than as expenditures. Also, effective July 1, 1948, payments to the Treasury, principally by wholly owned Government corporations for retirement of capital stock and for disposition of earnings, are excluded in reporting both budget receipts and expenditures. Neither of these changes affects the size of the budget surplus or deficit. Beginning 1931 figures in each case have been adjusted accordingly for comparative purposes. (6) Figures for 1918 through 1946 are revised to exclude statutory debt retirement (sinking fund, etc.). (7) Excludes $3 billion transferred to Foreign Economics Corporation Trust Fund, and includes $3 billion representing expenditures made from the FEC Trust Fund. (8) Effective fiscal year 1972 loan repayments and loan disbursements will be netted against expenditures and known as outlays. (9) From 1968, figures include trust funds (e.g. Social Security). (10) Estimate.

Summary of U.S. Receipts by Source and Outlays by Function

Source: U.S. Treasury Department, and the Office of Management and Budget

(in millions)

Net Receipts	**Fiscal 1977**	**Fiscal 1978**	**Fiscal 1979**	**Fiscal 1980**[1]
Individual income taxes	$156,725	$180,988	$217,800	$240,700
Corporation income taxes	54,892	59,952	65,700	65,500
Social insurance taxes and contributions	108,689	117,743	141,600	160,500
Excise taxes	17,548	18,376	18,700	25,400
Estate and gift taxes	7,327	5,285	5,400	6,100
Customs duties	5,150	6,572	7,400	7,000
Miscellaneous receipts	6,531	7,400	9,200	12,700
Total	**356,861**	**401,997**	**465,900**	**517,900**
Net outlays				
National defense	97,501	105,200	117,700	135,600
International affairs	4,831	5,900	6,100	10,900
General science, space, and technology	4,677	4,700	5,000	5,700
Energy	4,172	5,900	6,900	6,500
Natural resources and environment	10,000	10,900	12,100	13,700
Agriculture	5,526	7,700	6,200	5,800
Commerce and housing credit	−31	3,300	2,600	8,300
Transportation	14,636	15,400	17,500	20,800
Community and regional development	6,283	11,000	9,500	9,500
Education, training, employment and social services	20,985	26,500	29,700	29,900
Health	38,785	43,700	49,600	56,900
Income security	137,004	146,200	160,200	193,500
Veterans benefits and services	18,038	19,000	19,900	20,900
Administration of justice	3,600	3,800	4,200	4,600
General government	3,357	3,800	4,200	5,000
General purpose fiscal assistance	9,499	9,600	8,400	8,600
Interest	38,092	44,000	52,600	64,300
Undistributed offsetting receipts	−15,053	−15,800	−18,500	−21,900
Total	**401,902**	**450,800**	**493,700**	**578,800**

(1) Estimate

U.S. Direct Investment Abroad, Countries and Industries

Source: Bureau of Economic Analysis, U.S. Commerce Department

(millions of dollars)

	Direct investment position		Equity and intercompany account outflows (inflows (−))		Reinvested earnings		Interest, dividends, and earnings of unincorp. affiliates		Income	
	1978	1979	1978	1979	1978	1979	1978	1979	1978	1979
Total all areas	167,804	192,648	4,877	5,904	11,469	18,414	13,696	19,400	25,165	37,815
Petroleum	33,790	41,553	412	2,730	1,355	4,979	4,352	8,243	5,707	13,222
Manufacturing	74,080	83,564	1,587	1,236	6,152	8,139	4,422	5,507	10,573	13,646
Other	59,934	67,531	2,878	1,938	3,962	5,296	4,922	5,650	8,885	10,947
Developed countries	120,471	137,927	2,227	2,542	8,573	14,509	7,417	9,919	15,990	24,428
Canada	37,071	41,033	-600	915	1,724	2,884	1,615	2,455	3,339	5,339
Petroleum	8,246	9,168	-437	5	564	828	419	826	983	1,654
Manufacturing	17,477	19,237	41	380	679	1,320	710	871	1,389	2,190
Other	11,348	12,628	-204	530	481	736	486	758	967	1,495
Europe	69,553	81,463	2,447	1,246	5,665	10,522	4,610	6,233	10,275	16,756
Petroleum	15,122	18,555	728	439	213	2,947	816	1,583	1,029	4,530
Manufacturing	36,304	41,246	937	-119	3,572	5,039	2,561	3,148	6,133	8,187
Other	18,127	21,662	782	926	1,880	2,536	1,233	1,502	3,113	4,039
Other	13,847	15,431	380	381	1,184	1,103	1,192	1,231	2,376	2,333
Petroleum	3,503	4,098	-66	293	252	323	233	301	486	624
Manufacturing	6,077	6,883	106	287	582	499	450	482	1,032	982
Other	4,267	4,450	340	-199	350	281	509	448	858	727
Developing countries	40,399	47,841	2,864	3,749	2,864	3,573	6,100	9,162	8,964	12,735
Latin America	32,662	36,834	2,204	1,454	2,096	2,589	2,797	3,706	4,893	6,295
Petroleum	3,892	4,568	218	38	187	623	363	749	549	1,372
Manufacturing	11,712	13,220	432	621	1,119	918	543	835	1,661	1,752
Other	17,058	19,046	1,554	795	790	1,048	1,891	2,122	2,683	3,171
Other	7,737	11,007	660	2,295	768	984	3,303	5,456	4,071	6,440
Petroleum	469	2,663	336	2,050	210	220	2,458	4,586	2,668	4,806
Manufacturing	2,511	2,978	71	67	200	363	157	171	358	535
Other	4,757	5,366	253	178	357	401	688	699	1,045	1,099
International and unallocated	6,934	6,880	-215	-387	31	332	180	319	211	651

State Finances

Revenues, Expenditures, Debts, Taxes, U.S. Aid, Military Contracts

Sources: Bureau of the Census, U.S. Commerce and Treasury Departments

For fiscal 1979 (year ending June 30, 1978, except: New York, Mar. 31; Texas, Aug. 31, Alabama and Michigan, Sept. 30). Taxes are state income and sales (or gross receipts) taxes, and vehicle, etc., fees. *Military prime contracts.

State	Revenues (thousands)	Expenditures (thousands)	Total debt (thousands)	Per cap. debt	Per cap. taxes	Per cap. U.S. aid	*Military contracts (thousands)
Alabama	$3,770,597	$3,558,214	$1,053,409	$279.49	$463.61	$363	$499,288
Alaska	1,699,416	1,466,388	1,362,526	3,355.98	2,011.60	957	214,971
Arizona	2,817,319	2,287,937	96,170	39.25	618.70	330	692,937
Arkansas	1,967,915	1,896,527	244,251	112.04	456.22	388	71,675
California	31,057,817	28,319,385	7,676,120	338.24	720.54	363	11,674,320
Colorado	3,050,254	2,517,894	426,200	153.75	519.78	340	411,917
Connecticut	3,173,689	2,966,712	3,590,955	1,152.79	551.56	345	3,777,393
Delaware	869,002	762,291	854,958	1,469.00	845.20	400	85,763
Florida	7,286,206	6,461,600	2,670,982	301.47	484.31	271	1,760,926
Georgia	4,604,977	4,346,541	1,370,711	267.87	478.43	426	668,449
Hawaii	1,670,028	1,524,074	1,696,853	1,854.48	957.33	446	307,041
Idaho	994,768	891,351	220,856	244.04	515.33	373	21,861
Illinois	11,201,903	10,418,099	5,717,915	509.21	563.07	337	752,432
Indiana	4,612,299	4,088,514	580,456	107.49	494.18	258	1,107,185
Iowa	3,056,164	3,010,871	372,753	128.45	540.78	302	258,257
Kansas	2,177,882	2,012,395	459,143	193.81	501.34	305	590,057
Kentucky	3,841,847	3,880,372	2,810,488	796.85	588.53	382	168,231
Louisiana	4,588,980	4,123,067	2,636,921	656.28	557.55	377	274,213
Maine	1,233,664	1,182,604	695,558	634.05	505.36	462	407,061
Maryland	4,976,732	4,678,333	3,690,228	889.64	638.18	380	1,509,298
Massachusetts	6,824,373	6,377,089	5,414,472	938.55	626.82	473	2,982,783
Michigan	11,449,101	10,507,367	2,505,461	272.13	653.60	388	1,493,592
Minnesota	5,316,208	4,778,526	1,873,723	461.51	771.86	373	896,470
Mississippi	2,597,642	2,367,447	843,131	347.11	492.58	431	703,188
Missouri	3,821,220	3,337,485	711,594	146.21	413.61	311	3,283,929
Montana	1,006,125	900,928	146,999	187.02	509.61	553	48,020
Nebraska	1,333,812	1,249,578	52,672	33.46	471.77	302	85,746
Nevada	1,059,485	861,520	374,059	532.85	658.95	400	66,849
New Hampshire	839,724	784,231	738,576	832.67	297.75	332	236,372
New Jersey	7,881,329	7,718,083	5,382,459	734.11	508.63	372	1,300,060
New Mexico	1,847,066	1,578,199	513,904	414.10	681.22	504	259,297
New York	25,180,984	22,707,937	22,982,754	1,302.29	659.21	504	4,542,368
North Carolina	5,537,119	5,249,076	1,107,365	197.53	519.97	325	568,817
North Dakota	823,043	777,270	130,792	199.07	494.35	457	63,378
Ohio	11,434,729	9,761,512	3,745,220	349.01	430.52	287	1,275,273
Oklahoma	2,966,194	2,732,959	1,510,966	522.46	524.18	332	316,713
Oregon	3,499,397	2,906,342	3,808,764	1,507.23	547.88	424	147,104
Pennsylvania	12,757,488	11,574,943	6,448,112	549.66	578.11	350	1,877,706
Rhode Island	1,210,642	1,171,144	1,177,900	1,267.92	578.93	446	192,259
South Carolina	3,169,069	3,007,347	1,590,110	542.33	519.43	344	290,778
South Dakota	655,604	641,812	579,796	841.50	356.36	463	21,210
Tennessee	3,614,601	3,360,630	1,388,633	317.04	420.98	346	473,642
Texas	11,049,147	9,665,072	2,316,852	173.16	428.88	271	4,235,790
Utah	1,604,561	1,464,340	393,057	287.53	508.34	334	226,425
Vermont	639,571	612,297	510,620	1,035.74	542.54	491	100,017
Virginia	5,135,929	4,875,996	1,662,758	319.95	493.31	337	2,747,036
Washington	5,659,976	4,859,997	1,514,826	385.84	692.38	336	1,539,568
West Virginia	2,394,764	2,423,711	1,636,887	871.61	612.38	411	61,578
Wisconsin	6,255,349	5,381,001	2,233,958	473.30	690.77	366	372,998
Wyoming	788,572	633,197	216,070	480.16	761.83	544	51,874
Total or average	**247,059,033**	**224,656,926**	**111,739,943**	**509.20**	**569.46**	**393**	**55,714,114**

U.S. Customs and Internal Revenue Receipts

Source: Treasury Department

Gross. Not reduced by appropriations to Federal old-age and survivors insurance trust fund or refunds or receipts.

Fiscal year	Customs	Internal Revenue	Fiscal year	Customs	Internal Revenue	Fiscal year	Customs	Internal Revenue
1930	$587,000,903	$3,039,295,014	1955	$606,396,634	$66,288,691,586	1976	$4,074,176,000	$302,520,000,000
1935	343,353,034	3,277,690,028	1960	1,123,037,579	91,774,802,823	T.Q.[1]	1,212,173,000	75,463,000,000
1940	348,590,635	5,303,133,988	1965	1,477,548,820	114,428,991,753	1977	5,150,151,000	358,139,000,000
1945	354,775,542	43,902,001,929	1970	2,429,799,000	195,700,000,000	1978	6,728,612,000	399,776,000,000
1950	422,650,329	39,448,607,109	1975	3,675,532,000	293,800,000,000	1979	7,639,620,000	460,412,185,000

(1) Transitional quarter; July 1, 1976 through Sept. 30, 1976. Through 1976 the fiscal year ended June 30. From 1977 on, fiscal year ends Sept. 30.

U.S. Business Indexes

Source: Federal Reserve System; F.W. Dodge Div., McGraw-Hill; U.S. Labor Department; U.S. Commerce Department

(1967=100, except as noted)

Period	Industrial production: Total	Market: Total	Products: Total	Final: Consumer goods	Final: Equipment	Intermediate	Materials	Industry: Manufacturing	Capacity utilization in mfg.[1]	Construction contracts	Nonagricultural employment Total[2]	Manufacturing: Employment[3]	Manufacturing: Payrolls	Total retail sales[4]	Prices[4]: Consumer	Prices[4]: Producer finished goods
1963	76.5	76.4	75.5	81.3	67.5	79.9	76.7	75.8	83.5	86.1	86.1	87.7	76.0	79	91.8	93.8
1965	89.8	88.2	87.6	92.6	80.7	90.6	92.4	89.7	89.5	93.2	92.3	93.9	88.1	90	94.5	95.7
1970	107.8	106.9	105.3	109.0	100.1	112.9	109.2	106.4	79.3	123.1	107.7	98.0	114.1	119	116.3	110.3
1975	117.8	119.3	118.2	124.0	110.2	123.1	115.5	116.3	72.9	162.3	116.9	91.3	157.3	185	161.2	163.4
1976	130.5	129.7	127.6	137.1	114.6	137.2	131.7	130.3	79.5	190.2	120.7	95.3	177.0	204	170.5	170.3
1977	138.2	137.9	135.9	145.3	123.0	145.1	138.6	138.4	81.9	160.5	125.0	98.6	198.3	224	181.5	180.6
1978	146.1	144.8	142.2	149.1	132.8	154.1	148.3	146.8	84.4	174.3	130.3	102.1	222.4	248	195.4	194.6
1979	152.5	150.0	147.2	150.8	142.2	160.5	156.4	153.6	85.7	183.0	136.0	104.9	246.8	282	217.4	216.1
1980[5]	140.5	142.3	141.7	141.7	141.6	144.4	137.8	138.9	74.5	148.0	136.9	96.8	251.5	304	247.8	249.0

(1) Percent of capacity; based on output and capacity indexes, 1967=100. (2) Employees only; excludes personnel in the Armed Forces. (3) Production workers only. (4) FR index based on Census Bureau figures. (5) Seasonally adjusted indexes except for prices. Figures shown are for Aug. 1980 except for construction contracts and consumer prices which are for July 1980.

Producer Price Indexes

Source: Bureau of Labor Statistics, U.S. Labor Department

Producer Price Indexes measure average changes in prices received in primary markets of the U.S. by producers of commodities in all stages of processing.

Commodity group (1967 = 100)	Annual Avg. 1978	1979 June	1979 Dec.	1980 Jan.	1980 June
All commodities	**209.3**	**233.5**	**249.7**	**254.9**	**265.2**
Farm products, processed foods, and feeds	**206.6**	**229.0**	**234.6**	**231.9**	**234.2**
Farm products	212.5	242.8	242.5	236.4	233.4
Processed foods and feeds	202.6	220.6	229.3	228.5	233.8
Industrial commodities	**209.4**	**234.0**	**253.1**	**260.6**	**273.0**
Textile products and apparel	159.8	168.4	173.1	175.2	182.4
Hides, skins, leathers, and related products	200.0	268.0	249.2	255.7	241.0
Fuels and related products and power	322.5	393.7	487.9	508.0	574.8
Chemicals and allied products	198.8	219.2	238.2	246.0	261.7
Rubber and plastic products	174.8	193.1	205.9	207.8	217.1
Lumber and wood products	276.0	299.8	290.1	290.0	279.8
Pulp, paper, and allied products	195.6	216.6	231.7	237.4	251.3
Metals and metal products	227.1	258.2	273.6	284.6	282.4
Machinery and equipment	196.1	212.4	223.4	227.6	238.8
Furniture and household durables	160.4	170.2	177.9	183.4	185.3
Nonmetallic mineral products	222.8	246.9	259.6	268.4	283.2
Transportation equipment (Dec. 1968 = 100)	173.5	187.5	195.6	198.7	202.2
Miscellaneous products	184.3	205.2	227.4	242.9	257.4

Indexes of Manufacturing, Industrial Countries

Source: Bureau of Labor Statistics, U.S. Labor Department (1967=100)

Output per hour

Country	1960	1965	1970	1973	1974	1975	1976	1977	1978
United States	78.9	98.3	104.5	118.8	112.6	118.2	123.2	126.1	129.2
10 Foreign countries	67.5	89.6	124.7	150.0	154.6	154.2	164.5	170.5	178.6
Canada	75.1	93.7	114.7	134.3	136.6	133.3	139.4	146.1	152.2
Japan	52.6	79.1	146.5	181.2	181.7	174.6	188.7	199.2	215.7
Belgium	69.9	87.5	129.5	168.8	178.8	186.9	205.0	217.7	N.A.
Denmark	66.6	86.7	129.3	159.8	165.1	178.0	191.4	195.4	200.8
France	68.7	88.5	121.2	142.5	146.5	150.3	164.0	172.6	181.2
W. Germany	67.8	90.7	116.1	136.6	145.0	151.3	160.3	169.0	175.3
Italy	61.2	88.5	121.7	151.7	159.7	152.9	165.9	167.8	172.7
Netherlands	67.5	87.8	134.0	170.2	184.3	181.1	199.1	206.0	N.A.
Sweden	64.1	88.8	123.5	148.9	153.9	151.9	152.9	151.9	160.2
United Kingdom	77.0	92.5	108.8	127.6	127.7	124.2	127.9	126.5	128.6
8 European countries	68.8	90.9	119.7	143.3	149.0	150.5	160.5	165.1	170.7
Original EEC	68.2	91.1	120.7	144.5	151.2	154.4	165.3	172.5	179.1

Unit labor costs in U.S. dollars

Country	1960	1965	1970	1973	1974	1975	1976	1977	1978
United States	97.7	92.6	116.5	123.2	143.1	152.4	158.4	168.3	179.9
10 Foreign countries	82.4	97.4	112.4	174.1	198.3	238.7	234.4	259.9	311.4
Canada	106.9	92.0	111.7	127.0	147.7	166.6	187.4	183.7	175.8
Japan	82.5	102.5	113.2	195.2	237.3	284.8	285.3	326.5	412.0
Belgium	74.9	94.3	101.4	152.0	173.8	212.3	204.5	230.6	N.A.
Denmark	74.7	91.8	104.4	147.6	170.3	199.2	195.8	212.7	248.1
France	81.5	98.2	96.7	146.4	157.8	206.7	194.5	206.4	244.4
W. Germany	76.5	94.4	125.7	211.7	236.2	268.5	265.4	299.4	358.3
Italy	76.5	97.1	119.2	172.5	182.6	245.1	212.5	234.9	270.4
Netherlands	65.4	91.8	108.7	174.0	198.3	245.4	238.8	268.7	N.A.
Sweden	79.2	93.0	105.0	145.8	161.4	212.2	239.4	262.5	278.2
United Kingdom	85.5	98.6	104.8	130.2	154.7	196.2	182.9	196.9	249.0
8 European countries	78.7	95.9	113.6	175.5	195.2	236.1	228.3	252.7	301.5
Original EEC	77.1	95.7	116.0	185.5	204.5	245.0	235.7	262.0	312.4

Gross National Product, National Income, and Personal Income

Source: Bureau of Economic Analysis, U.S. Commerce Department
includes Alaska and Hawaii beginning in 1960 (millions of dollars)

	1950	1960	1970	1975	1978	1979
Gross national product	**286,172**	**505,978**	**982,419**	**1,528,833**	**2,127,560**	**2,368,818**
Less: Capital consumption allowances	23,853	47,712	90,827	161,954	216,888	242,953
Equals: Net national product	**262,319**	**458,266**	**894,592**	**1,366,879**	**1,910,672**	**2,125,865**
Less: Indirect business tax and nontax liability	23,422	45,389	94,027	139,246	178,065	189,490
Business transfer payments	778	1,974	3,983	7,599	9,158	10,175
Statistical discrepancy	2,030	−683	−2,076	7,371	3,315	3,720
Plus: Subsidies minus current surplus of government enterprises	114	422	2,716	2,339	4,197	2,334
Equals: National income	**236,203**	**412,008**	**798,374**	**1,215,002**	**1,724,331**	**1,924,814**
Less: Corporate profits and inventory valuation adjustment	2,272	9,760	37,549	95,902	167,673	178,158
Net interest	...	...	...	78,615	109,455	129,741
Contributions for social insurance	7,058	21,058	58,712	110,579	164,117	189,816
Wage accruals less disbursement	24	0	0	0	221	−181
Plus: Government transfer payment to persons	14,404	26,966	75,898	170,567	214,935	241,866
Personal interest income	8,929	23,284	64,284	115,529	163,277	192,117
Dividends	8,803	12,890	22,884	31,885	47,164	52,735
Business transfer payments	778	1,974	3,983	7,599	9,158	10,175
Equals: Personal income	**226,102**	**399,724**	**801,271**	**1,255,486**	**1,717,399**	**1,924,173**

National Income by Type of Income

(millions of dollars)

	1960	1965	1970	1975	1978	1979
Compensation of employees	**294,932**	**396,543**	**609,150**	**931,079**	**1,304,515**	**1,459,234**
Wages and salaries	271,932	362,005	546,453	805,872	1,103,494	1,227,397
Private	222,782	292,145	430,481	630,431	885,502	993,910
Government	49,150	69,860	115,972	175,441	217,992	233,487
Supplements to wages, salary	23,000	34,538	62,697	125,207	201,021	231,837
Employer contrib. for social insurance	11,780	16,698	30,680	60,079	94,562	109,147
Other labor income	11,220	17,840	32,017	65,128	106,459	122,690
Proprietors' income	**46,978**	**56,674**	**65,140**	**86,980**	**116,789**	**130,775**
Business and professional	35,558	44,106	51,208	63,509	89,091	97,965
Inventory valuation adj.	91	-198	-506	-1,164	-2,062	-2,974
Farm	11,420	12,568	13,932	23,471	27,698	32,810
Rental income of persons	**13,758**	**17,117**	**18,644**	**22,426**	**25,899**	**26,908**
Corp. prof., with inv. adjust.	**46,580**	**77,096**	**67,891**	**95,902**	**167,673**	**178,158**
Corp. profits before tax	48,540	75,209	71,485	120,378	206,023	236,638
Corp. profits tax liability	22,696	30,876	34,477	49,811	84,518	92,531
Corp. profits after tax	25,844	44,333	37,008	70,567	121,505	144,107
Dividends	12,890	19,120	22,884	31,885	47,164	52,735
Undistributed profits	12,954	25,213	14,124	38,682	74,341	91,372
Inventory valuation adj.	327	-1,865	-5,067	-12,432	-25,218	-41,769
Net interest	**9,760**	**18,529**	**37,549**	**78,615**	**109,455**	**129,741**
National income	**412,008**	**565,959**	**798,374**	**1,215,002**	**1,724,331**	**1,924,814**

Appropriations by the Federal Government

Source: U.S. Treasury Department (fiscal year)

Year	Appropriations	Year	Appropriations	Year	Appropriations	Year	Appropriations
1890	$395,430,284.26	1940	$13,349,202,681.73	1958	$77,145,934,082.25	1971	$247,623,820,964.75
1895	492,477,759.97	1944	118,411,173,965.24	1959	82,055,863,758.58	1972	247,638,104,722.57
1900	698,912,982.83	1945	73,067,712,071.39	1960	80,169,728,902.87	1973	275,554,945,383.88
1905	781,288,215.95	1950	52,867,672,466.21	1961	89,229,575,129.94	1974	311,728,034,120.95
1910	1,044,433,622.64	1952	127,788,153,262.97	1962	91,447,827,731.00	1975	374,124,469,875.62
1915	1,122,471,919.12	1953	94,916,821,231.67	1963	102,149,886,566.52	1976	403,740,395,600.61
1920	6,454,596,649.56	1954	74,744,844,304.88	1965	107,555,087,622.62	T.Q.[1]	111,767,892,878.83
1925	3,748,651,750.35	1955	54,761,172,461.58	1967	140,861,235,376.56	1977	466,559,809,964.06
1930	4,665,236,678.04	1956	63,857,731,203.86	1969	203,049,351,090.91	1978	507,782,291,489.99
1935	7,527,559,327.66	1957	70,717,305,080.55	1970	222,200,021,901.52	1979	563,960,833,788.25

(1) Transitional Quarter; July 1, 1976 through Sept. 30, 1976. Through 1976 the fiscal year ended June 30. From 1977 on, fiscal year ends Sept. 30.

Public Debt of the U.S.

Source: U.S. Treasury Department

Fiscal year	Gross debt	Per cap.	Fiscal year	Gross debt	Per cap.	Fiscal year	Gross debt	Per cap.
1870	$2,436,453,269	$61.06	1930	$16,185,309,831	$131.51	1975	$533,188,976,772	$2,496.90
1880	2,090,908,872	41.60	1940	42,967,531,038	325.23	1976	620,432,971,265	2,883.83
1890	1,132,396,584	17.80	1950	256,087,352,351	1,688.30	T.Q.[1]	634,701,954,322	2,950.15
1900	1,263,416,913	16.60	1960	284,092,760,848	1,572.31	1977	698,839,928,356	3,215.59
1910	1,146,939,969	12.41	1965	313,818,898,984	1,612.70	1978	771,544,478,952	3,521.78
1920	24,299,321,467	228.23	1970	370,093,706,950	1,807.09	1979	826,519,096,841	p3,739.92

(p) Preliminary. (1) Transitional Quarter; July 1, 1976 through Sept. 30, 1976. Through 1976 the fiscal year ended June 30. From 1977 on, fiscal year ends Sept. 30.

National Income by Industry

Source: Bureau of Economic Analysis, U.S. Commerce Department
(millions of dollars)

	1960	1965	1970	1975	1977	1978	1979
Agricul., forestry, fisheries	**17,468**	**20,366**	**24,455**	**42,827**	**43,345**	**54,723**	**63,985**
Farms	16,452	18,805	22,191	39,379	38,488	48,823	NA
Agri. services, forestry, fisheries	1,016	1,561	2,264	3,448	4,857	5,900	NA
Mining	**5,613**	**6,013**	**7,810**	**18,149**	**22,445**	**26,470**	**32,165**
Metal mining	807	856	1,179	1,635	1,963	2,287	NA
Coal mining	1,286	1,372	2,231	6,228	6,550	6,930	NA
Crude petroleum, natural gas	2,606	2,670	3,099	8,075	11,428	14,298	NA
Nonmetallic min. & quar.	914	1,115	1,301	2,211	2,504	2,955	NA
Contract construction	**20,972**	**29,840**	**43,821**	**61,795**	**76,276**	**87,593**	**100,433**
Manufacturing	**125,448**	**170,361**	**215,388**	**312,467**	**409,404**	**459,502**	**510,332**
Nondurable goods	**51,818**	**65,416**	**88,088**	**127,942**	**161,629**	**175,998**	**199,176**
Food, kindred products	12,150	14,232	19,579	30,020	32,611	34,513	NA
Tobacco manufactures	1,020	1,096	1,696	2,155	2,849	3,208	NA
Textile mill products	4,484	5,872	7,525	8,754	11,852	12,906	NA
Apparel, other fabric prod.	4,933	6,494	8,722	10,773	13,603	14,896	NA
Paper, allied products	4,706	6,005	7,968	11,833	15,677	17,094	NA
Printing, pub., allied industry	6,666	8,725	11,883	16,672	20,987	23,715	NA
Chemicals, allied products	9,106	12,398	16,042	23,820	30,100	30,694	NA
Petroleum and coal products	4,396	4,811	6,632	12,893	18,739	20,303	NA
Rubber, misc. plastic products	2,751	3,939	5,804	8,661	12,441	13,745	NA
Leather, leather products	1,606	1,844	2,237	2,361	2,770	2,924	NA
Durable goods	**73,630**	**104,945**	**127,300**	**184,525**	**247,775**	**283,504**	**311,156**
Lumber, wood, except furn.	3,362	4,534	5,537	8,936	13,645	16,230	NA
Furniture and fixtures	2,098	2,904	3,715	4,588	6,053	6,924	NA
Stone, clay, glass products	4,620	5,654	6,891	9,858	13,071	15,445	NA
Primary metal industries	11,066	14,491	15,757	24,231	28,673	33,396	NA
Fabricated metal products	8,124	11,475	14,812	24,300	31,365	35,252	NA
Machinery, except electrical	11,919	18,239	24,353	36,801	47,554	55,100	NA
Electric and electronic equipment	10,496	14,855	20,132	26,646	35,258	41,037	NA
Transport equip. exc. autos	8,266	11,330	14,480	15,715	18,492	21,317	NA
Motor vehicles and equipment	8,399	14,455	12,086	19,045	34,622	37,236	NA
Instruments	2,948	4,128	5,797	9,006	12,036	13,668	NA
Misc. manufacturing	2,332	2,880	3,740	5,399	7,006	7,898	NA
Transportation	**18,141**	**23,069**	**30,308**	**44,455**	**58,779**	**68,175**	**78,370**
Railroad	6,710	7,016	7,612	9,987	12,882	14,217	NA
Local; interurban passenger transit	1,619	1,897	2,308	2,933	3,520	3,771	NA
Motor freight trans., warehousing	5,886	8,396	11,830	18,935	24,387	28,508	NA
Water transportation	1,635	1,982	2,503	3,323	3,914	4,673	NA
Air transportation	1,370	2,636	4,358	7,062	10,031	12,054	NA
Pipeline transportation	350	390	528	820	1,054	1,336	NA
Transportation service	571	752	1,169	1,935	2,991	3,616	NA
Communication	**8,228**	**11,497**	**17,600**	**27,066**	**35,192**	**40,533**	**44,941**
Telephone and telegraph	7,293	10,255	15,887	24,358	31,113	35,792	NA
Radio broadcasting, television	935	1,242	1,713	2,708	4,079	4,741	NA
Electric, gas, sanitary services	**8,923**	**11,442**	**14,864**	**24,302**	**31,127**	**34,912**	**36,979**
Wholesale and retail trade	**64,737**	**84,662**	**122,213**	**194,227**	**234,471**	**261,780**	**291,407**
Wholesale trade	23,420	30,469	44,860	80,564	96,041	106,950	NA
Retail trade	41,317	54,193	77,353	113,663	138,430	154,830	NA
Finance, ins. and real estate	**48,608**	**63,987**	**92,625**	**140,375**	**184,437**	**210,735**	**238,652**
Banking	7,255	8,943	16,448	20,109	23,368	24,649	NA
Credit agencies, other than banks	−1,076	−1,617	−1,981	−4,729	−4,261	−4,164	NA
Security, commodity brokers	1,219	1,942	2,733	4,144	4,576	5,428	NA
Insurance carriers	4,816	5,880	9,269	12,751	18,903	22,616	NA
Insurance agents, brokers, service	2,070	2,957	4,223	6,704	9,605	11,182	NA
Real estate	33,940	45,741	61,812	100,078	130,258	148,858	NA
Holding and other investment cos.	384	141	121	1,318	1,988	2,166	NA
Services	**44,648**	**64,142**	**103,304**	**168,516**	**213,379**	**245,246**	**277,864**
Hotels, other lodging places	2,114	2,964	4,659	6,952	8,722	10,372	NA
Personal services	4,608	5,965	7,436	8,329	10,058	11,284	NA
Misc. business services	5,091	8,399	14,051	23,928	31,989	38,311	NA
Automobile repair, serv., garages	1,746	2,402	3,616	5,944	7,863	9,451	NA
Misc. repair services	1,094	1,494	2,149	3,478	4,414	5,188	NA
Motion pictures	891	1,201	1,581	1,842	2,761	3,347	NA
Amusement, recreation services	1,662	2,201	3,321	5,268	6,846	7,973	NA
Medical, other health services	10,636	15,790	29,472	54,075	68,762	77,784	NA
Legal services	2,695	4,197	6,691	11,828	14,379	16,232	NA
Education services	2,419	4,145	6,688	10,014	12,402	13,808	NA
Social Services	—	—	—	5,003	6,449	7,420	NA
Nonprofit membership org.	4,176	5,787	8,912	11,016	12,638	13,858	NA
Misc. professional services	3,719	5,629	9,673	15,030	19,254	22,688	NA
Private households	3,797	3,968	5,055	5,809	6,842	7,530	NA
Government, government enterprises	**52,707**	**75,374**	**127,421**	**199,875**	**235,048**	**256,570**	**227,438**
Federal	25,303	33,303	53,093	72,007	81,295	87,858	NA
General Government	21,676	28,298	44,723	58,976	66,409	71,814	NA
Government enterprises	3,627	5,005	8,370	13,031	14,886	16,044	NA
State & local	27,404	42,071	74,328	127,868	153,753	168,712	NA
General Government	25,470	39,294	69,964	119,641	143,730	157,763	NA
Government enterprises	1,934	2,777	4,364	8,227	10,023	10,949	NA
Domestic income	**415,493**	**560,753**	**799,809**	**1,234,054**	**1,543,903**	**1,746,239**	**1,952,566**
Rest of the world	**2,477**	**4,681**	**4,616**	**10,534**	**17,813**	**20,547**	**25,275**
All industries, total	**417,970**	**565,434**	**804,425**	**1,244,588**	**1,561,716**	**1,766,786**	**1,977,841**

U.S. Currency and Coin — June 30, 1980

Source: U.S. Treasury Department

Amounts in Circulation and Outstanding

	Amounts in circulation	Add amounts held by: United States Treasury	Add amounts held by: Federal Reserve Banks	Amounts outstanding
Currency[1]				
Federal Reserve Notes	$114,499,889,325	$1,669,601	$18,359,909,211	$132,861,468,137
United States Notes	310,027,067	12,511,933	16	322,539,016
Currency No Longer Issued	277,397,595	213,929	45,362	277,656,886
Total	**115,087,313,987**	**14,395,463**	**18,359,954,589**	**133,461,664,039**
Coin[2]				
Dollars[3]	$1,474,282,841	$374,951,251	$164,017,806	[3]$2,013,251,898
Fractional Coin	10,535,595,320	130,674,997	243,685,683	10,909,956,000
Total	**12,009,878,161**	**505,626,248**	**407,703,489**	**12,923,207,898**
Total currency and coin	**127,097,192,148**	**520,021,711**	**18,767,658,078**	**146,384,871,937**

Currency in Circulation by Denominations

Denomination	Total currency in circulation	Federal Reserve Notes[4]	United States Notes	Currency no longer issued
1 Dollar	$3,245,932,445	$3,091,086,643	$143,486	$154,702,316
2 Dollars	668,326,860	533,647,582	134,666,066	13,212
5 Dollars	4,312,899,760	4,157,664,060	114,613,205	40,622,495
10 Dollars	11,119,971,830	11,093,964,000	5,940	26,001,890
20 Dollars	37,777,864,240	37,757,474,740	3,380	20,386,120
50 Dollars	12,737,958,850	12,726,010,000	.....	11,948,850
100 Dollars	44,865,818,400	44,782,059,300	60,594,900	23,164,200
500 Dollars	163,423,000	163,227,000	.....	196,000
1,000 Dollars	189,798,000	189,586,000	.....	212,000
5,000 Dollars	1,830,000	1,780,000	.....	50,000
10,000 Dollars	3,490,000	3,390,000	.....	100,000
Fractional parts	487	...	.....	487
Partial notes[5]	115	...	90	25
Total currency	**115,087,313,987**	**114,499,889,325**	**310,027,067**	**277,397,595**

Comparative Totals of Money in Circulation — Selected Dates

Date	Amounts (in millions)	Per capita[6]	Date	Amounts (in millions)	Per capita[6]	Date	Amounts (in millions)	Per capita[6]
June 30, 1980	$127,097.2[7]	$570.51	June 30, 1955	$30,229.3	$182.90	June 30, 1930	$4,522.0	$36.74
June 30, 1975	81,196.4	380.08	June 30, 1950	27,156.3	179.03	June 30, 1925	4,815.2	41.56
June 30, 1970	54,351.0	265.39	June 30, 1945	26,746.4	191.14	June 30, 1920	5,467.6	51.36
June 30, 1965	39,719.8	204.14	June 30, 1940	7,847.5	59.40	June 30, 1915	3,319.6	33.01
June 30, 1960	32,064.6	177.47	June 30, 1935	5,567.1	43.75	June 30, 1910	3,148.7	34.07

(1) Excludes gold certificates, 1934 Series — $1,277,800, at 6/30/74 which are issued only to Federal Reserve banks and do not appear in circulation. (2) Excludes coin sold to collectors at premium prices. (3) Includes $481,781,898 in standard silver dollars. (4) Issued on and after July 1, 1929. (5) Represents value of certain partial denominations not presented for redemption. (6) Based on Bureau of the Census estimates of population. (7) Highest amount to date.

The requirement for a gold reserve against U.S. notes was repealed by Public Law 90-269 approved Mar. 18, 1968. Silver certificates issued on and after July 1, 1929 became redeemable from the general fund on June 24, 1968. The amount of security after those dates has been reduced accordingly.

U.S. Money in Circulation, by Denominations

Source: Fiscal Service, Bureau of Government Financial Operations, U.S. Treasury Department

Outside Treasury and Federal Reserve Banks. (millions of dollars)

End of year	Total in circulation	Coin and small denomination: Total	Coin	$1	$2	$5	$10	$20	Large denomination currency: Total	$50	$100	$500	$1,000	$5,000	$10,000
1950	27,741	19,305	1,554	1,113	64	2,049	5,998	8,529	8,438	2,422	5,043	368	588	4	12
1960	32,869	23,521	2,427	1,533	88	2,246	6,691	10,536	9,348	2,815	5,954	249	316	3	10
1970	57,093	39,639	6,281	2,310	136	3,161	9,170	18,581	17,454	4,896	12,084	215	252	3	4
1975	86,547	54,866	8,959	2,809	135	3,841	10,777	28,344	31,681	8,157	23,139	175	204	2	4
1977	103,811	62,543	10,071	3,038	650	4,190	11,361	33,233	41,269	10,079	30,818	169	197	2	4
1978	114,645	66,693	10,739	3,194	661	4,393	11,661	36,045	47,952	11,279	36,306	167	194	2	4
1979	125,600	70,693	11,658	3,308	671	4,549	11,894	38,613	54,907	12,585	41,960	164	192	2	4

Seigniorage on Coin and Silver Bullion

Source: Fiscal Service, U.S. Treasury Department

Seigniorage is the profit from coining money; it is the difference between the monetary value of coins and their cost, including the manufacturing expense.

Fiscal year	Total	Fiscal year	Total
Jan. 1, 1935-June 30, 1965, cumulative	$2,525,927,763.84	1974	$320,706,638.49
1968	383,141,339.00[1]	1975	660,898,070.69
1970	274,217,884.01	1976	769,722,066.00
1971	399,652,811.18	1977	407,022,950.00
1972	580,586,683.00	1978	367,156,260.25
1973	399,799,682.00	1979	991,909,496.55
		Cumulative Jan. 1, 1935-Sept. 30, 1979	9,816,450,287.49

(1) Revised to include seigniorage on clad coins.

Bureau of the Mint

Source: Bureau of the Mint, U.S. Treasury Department

The first United States Mint was established in Philadelphia, Pa., then the nation's capital, by the Act of April 2, 1792, which provided for gold, silver, and copper coinage. Originally, supervision of the Mint was a function of the secretary of state, but it became (1799) an independent agency reporting directly to the president. When the Coinage Act of 1873 was passed, all mint and assay office activities were placed under a newly organized Bureau of the Mint in the Department of the Treasury.

The Bureau of the Mint manufactures all U.S. coins and distributes them through the Federal Reserve banks and branches. The Mint also maintains physical custody of the Treasury's monetary stocks of gold and silver, and refines and processes gold and silver bullion. Functions performed by the Mint on a reimbursable basis include: the manufacture and sale of medals of a national character, the production and sale of numismatic coins and coin sets, and, as scheduling permits, the manufacture of foreign coins.

Amendments to the Coinage Act of 1965 (Public Law 19-607, Dec. 31, 1970) authorized the production of dollar coins and provided that the dollar and half dollar coins for general circulation be of the same nonsilver clad composition as the quarter dollars and dimes. The cladding is an alloy of 75 percent copper and 25 percent nickel, bonded to a core of pure copper. The coins were first minted in calendar year 1971. The legislation authorized the secretary of the treasury to mint and issue not more than 150 million one dollar pieces containing 40-percent silver for sale to the public at premium prices. The dollar coins which bore the likeness of President Eisenhower and a reverse design emblematic of the Apollo 11 moon landing were minted and issued from 1971 until early in 1975.

Public Law 93-127, Oct. 18, 1973, authorized the minting for issue after July 4, 1975, of dollar, half dollar, and quarter dollar coins with reverse designs emblematic of the Bicentennial and the obverse dates 1776-1976, for general issue; and the production of 45 million numismatic 40-percent silver coins of the same designs and denominations to be sold to the public at premium prices. Although the production of Bicentennial-design coins was terminated on Dec. 31, 1976, 40-percent silver coin sets continued to be packaged and sold after that date.

Public Law 95-447, Oct. 10, 1978, amended the Coinage Act of 1965 to provide for changes in the design, weight, and size of the $1 coin. From Jan. 1979, the $1 coins bore the likeness of Susan B. Anthony on the obverse and the Apollo 11 Moon landing on the reverse; these cupronickel clad coins weigh 8.1 grams and have a diameter of 26.5 mms.

The composition of the five cent coin continues to be 75 percent copper, 25 percent nickel, while the one cent coins are 95 percent copper and 5 percent zinc.

Calendar year 1979 coinage production follows:

Domestic Coinage Executed During Calendar Year 1979

Denomination	Philadelphia	Denver	San Francisco	Total value	Total pieces
Dollars — non-silver					
1979	$360,222,000.00	$288,015,744.00	$109,576,000.00	$757,813,744.00	757,813,744
Total dollars	**$360,222,000.00**	**$288,015,744.00**	**$109,576,000.00**	**$757,813,744.00**	**757,813,744**
Subsidiary					
Half dollars - 1979	$34,156,000.00	$7,907,711.00	-0-	$42,063,711.00	84,127,422
Quarters - 1979[1]	128,927,000.00	122,447,445.00	-0-	251,374,445.00	1,005,497,780[1]
Dimes	31,544,000.00	39,092,118.40	-0-	70,636,118.40	706,361,184
Total Subsidiary	**$194,627,000.00**	**$169,447,274.40**	**-0-**	**$364,074,274.40**	**1,795,986,386**
Minor					
Five-cent pieces	$23,159,400.00	$16,293,383.60	-0-	$39,452,783.60	789,055,672
One-cent pieces[2]	52,667,900.00	41,393,572.54	$7,517,250.00	101,578,722.54	10,157,872,254[2]
Total minor	**$75,827,300.00**	**$57,686,956.14**	**$7,517,250.00**	**$141,031,506.14**	**10,946,927,926**
Total domestic coinage	**$630,676,300.00**	**$515,149,974.54**	**$117,093,250.00**	**$1,262,919,524.54**	**13,500,728,056**

Delivered at San Francisco Assay Office

1979 Proof sets	3,677,175
Bicentennial 40% silver proof sets	146,237
Bicentennial 40% silver uncirc. sets	166,031

Coinage executed for foreign governments

Country	No. of Pieces
Panama	13,000,000
Dominican Republic	530,090
Haiti	2,000,000
Total	**15,530,090**

(1) Manufactured at West Point Depository - $5,668,000.00 (22,672,000 pieces)
(2) Manufactured at West Point Depository - $17,058,500.00 (1,705,850,000 pieces)

Portraits on U.S. Treasury Bills, Bonds, Notes and Savings Bonds

Denomination	Savings bonds	Treas. bills	Treas. bonds	Treas. notes
25	Washington			
50	Jefferson		Jefferson	
75	Kennedy			
100	Cleveland		Jackson	
200	F.D. Roosevelt			
500	Wilson		Washington	
1,000	Lincoln	H. McCulloch	Lincoln	Lincoln
5,000		J.G. Carlisle	Monroe	Monroe
10,000	T. Roosevelt	J. Sherman	Cleveland	Cleveland
50,000		C. Glass		
100,000		A Gallatin	Grant	Grant
1,000,000		O. Wolcott	T. Roosevelt	T. Roosevelt
100,000,000				Madison
500,000,000				McKinley

Large Denominations of U.S. Currency Discontinued

The largest denomination of United States currency now being issued is the $100 bill. Issuance of currency in denominations of $500, $1000, $5,000 and $10,000 has been discontinued because their use has declined sharply over the past two decades.

As large denomination bills reach the Federal Reserve Bank they are removed from circulation.

Because some of the discontinued currency is expected to be in the hands of holders for many years, the description of the various denominations below is continued:

Amt.	Portrait	Embellishment on back
$ 1	Washington	Great Seal of U.S.
2	Jefferson	Signers of Declaration
5	Lincoln	Lincoln Memorial
10	Hamilton	U.S. Treasury
20	Jackson	White House
50	Grant	U.S. Capitol
$ 100	Franklin	Independence Hall
500*	McKinley	Ornate denominational marking
1,000*	Cleveland	Ornate denominational marking
5,000*	Madison	Ornate denominational marking
10,000*	Chase	Ornate denominational marking
100,000*	Wilson	Ornate denominational marking

*For use only in transactions between Federal Reserve System and Treasury Department.

Gold Reserves of Central Banks and Governments

Source: IMF, *International Financial Statistics*
(Million fine troy ounces)

Year end	All countries[1]	Int'l Monetary Fund	United States	Canada	Japan	Belgium	France	Fed. Rep. of Germany	Italy	Netherlands	Switzerland	United Kingdom
1964	1,156.84	62.26	442.03	29.31	8.69	41.46	106.54	121.37	60.19	48.23	77.86	61.04
1965	1,186.52	53.40	401.86	32.88	9.37	44.52	134.46	126.00	68.68	50.19	86.91	64.72
1966	1,165.02	75.77	378.14	29.87	9.40	43.56	149.66	122.62	68.97	49.45	81.17	55.44
1967	1,125.52	76.63	344.71	29.00	9.66	42.26	149.54	120.79	68.57	48.91	88.26	36.89
1968	1,106.56	65.37	311.20	24.66	10.17	43.53	110.77	129.69	83.52	48.51	74.97	42.10
1969	1,112.05	66.00	338.83	24.92	11.80	43.40	101.34	116.56	84.46	49.16	75.49	42.03
1970	1,056.83	123.97	316.34	22.59	15.20	42.01	100.91	113.70	82.48	51.06	78.03	38.54
1971	1,026.12	135.20	291.60	22.69	19.43	44.12	100.66	116.47	82.40	54.53	83.11	22.15
1972	1,017.41	153.43	275.97	21.95	21.11	43.08	100.69	117.36	82.37	54.17	83.11	21.05
1973	1,017.45	153.43	275.97	21.95	21.11	42.17	100.91	117.61	82.48	54.33	83.20	21.03
1974	1,015.96	153.40	275.97	21.95	21.11	42.17	100.93	117.61	82.48	54.33	83.20	21.03
1975	1,014.82	153.43	274.71	21.95	21.11	42.17	100.93	117.61	82.48	54.33	83.20	21.03
1976	1,009.90	149.51	274.68	21.62	21.11	42.17	101.02	117.61	82.48	54.33	83.28	21.03
1977	1,011.74	131.57	277.55	22.01	21.62	42.45	101.67	118.30	82.91	54.63	83.28	22.22
1978	1,018.53	118.20	276.41	22.13	23.97	42.59	101.99	118.64	83.12	54.78	83.28	22.82
1979	929.96	106.83	264.60	22.18	24.23	34.21	81.92	95.25	66.71	43.97	83.28	18.25

(1) Covers IMF members with reported gold holdings, Switzerland and Netherlands Antilles. For countries not listed above, see *International Financial Statistics*, a monthly publication of the International Monetary Fund.

World Gold Production

Source: Bureau of Mines, U.S. Interior Department (in ounces)

Year	Estimated world prod.	Africa: South Africa	Africa: Ghana	Africa: Zaire	North and South America: United States	North and South America: Canada	North and South America: Mexico	North and South America: Nicaragua	North and South America: Colombia	Other: Australia	Other: India	Other: Japan	Other: Philippines	Other: All other
1970	47,522,342	32,164,107	707,900	180,590	1,743,322	2,408,574	198,241	115,173	201,519	619,922	104,200	225,189	602,715	8,220,890
1971	46,494,837	31,388,631	697,517	171,685	1,495,108	2,243,000	150,915	121,134	188,847	672,106	118,569	255,255	637,048	8,355,022
1972	44,843,374	29,245,273	724,051	140,724	1,449,943	2,078,567	146,061	112,340	188,137	754,866	105,776	243,027	606,730	9,047,879
1973	43,296,755	27,494,603	722,531	133,642	1,175,750	1,954,340	132,557	85,051	215,876	554,278	105,390	188,274	572,250	9,962,213
1974	39,941,080	24,388,203	566,617	130,603	1,126,886	1,698,392	134,454	82,639	265,195	522,127	101,114	139,727	536,338	10,248,785
1975	38,574,162	22,937,820	523,889	103,217	1,052,252	1,674,000	132,236	70,281	299,366	514,186	91,437	143,489	501,776	10,530,213
1976	39,233,798	22,935,988	532,473	91,093	1,048,037	1,691,806	162,811	75,841	300,307	502,741	100,696	137,669	501,210	11,152,852
1977	39,121,056	22,501,886	480,884	80,418	1,100,347	1,733,609	212,709	65,764	263,437	630,155	96,902	149,018	558,235	11,247,692
1978p	39,303,757	22,648,558	402,034	76,077	998,832	1,735,077	202,003	65,800	257,632	647,580	87,579	145,225	586,598	11,450,762
1979p	39,238,343	22,616,656	482,300	75,000	919,783	1,581,013	188,000	60,000	290,000	588,359	84,749	132,879	546,536	11,673,068

(p) preliminary.

U.S. and World Silver Production

Source: Bureau of Mines, U.S. Interior Department

Largest production of silver in the United States in 1915—74,961,075 fine ounces.

Year (Cal.)	United States: Fine ozs.	United States: Value	World Fine ozs.	Year (Cal.)	United States: Fine ozs.	United States: Value	World Fine ozs.
1930	50,748,127	$19,538,000	248,708,426	1960. . . .	36,000,000	$33,305,858	241,300,000
1935	45,924,454	33,008,000	220,704,231	1965. . . .	39,806,033	51,469,201	257,415,000
1940	69,585,734	49,483,000	275,387,000	1970. . . .	45,006,000	79,697,000	310,891,000
1945	29,063,255	20,667,200	162,000,000	1975. . . .	34,938,000	154,424,000	303,112,000
1950	43,308,739	38,291,545	203,300,000	1978. . . .	39,385,000	212,681,000	344,657,000
1955	36,469,610	33,006,839	224,000,000	1979p . . .	38,055,000	422,032,000	344,457,000

(p) preliminary (NA) not available.

50 Stocks Most Widely Held by Insurance Cos., Mutual Funds, and Banks

Source: Vickers Associates, Inc.

Publicly-held issues throughout the U.S. in order of number of institutions, etc., which held shares, as of Aug. 30, 1980.

Intl. Bus. Machines
Amer. Tel. & Tel.
Exxon Corp.
General Electric
Eastman Kodak
General Motors
Atlantic Richfield
Xerox Corp.
Mobil Corp.
Texaco Inc.
Standard Oil, Ind.
Schlumberger, Ltd.
Merck & Co.
Minn. Mng./Mfg.
Standard Oil of Cal.
Dow Chemical
Phillips Petroleum
Amer. Home Products
Halliburton Co.
Caterpillar Tractor
Sears, Roebuck & Co.
Philip Morris
Gulf Oil
Conoco Inc.
E.I. Du Pont
Procter & Gamble
K mart
Citicorp
General Tel. & El.
Tenneco, Inc.
Union Carbide
Coca-Cola Co.
Johnson & Johnson
Pfizer, Inc.
R.J. Reynolds Ind.
Burroughs Corp.
Bristol-Myers
Union Oil of Cal.
Avon Products
Texas Utilities
Union Pacific
Eli Lilly & Co.
Intl. Tel. & Tel.
Digital Equipment
PepsiCo Inc.
Standard Oil, Ohio
Warner-Lambert
Abbott Laboratories
Ford Motor
Weyerhaeuser Co.

Corporations and Stocks

Stock Exchanges Trade 10.9 Billion Shares in U.S. Firms

The Securities and Exchange Commission reported in 1980 that 10.9 billion shares of stock were traded on the New York, American, and other U.S. stock exchanges in 1979, valued at $300 billion.

The N.Y. Stock Exchange listed 2,210 issues of 1,565 companies for a total of 32.3 billion shares, valued on July 31, 1980, at $1.1 trillion. Average daily trading was 42.4 million through July 31, 1980, compared to 29.9 million in 1979.

The American Stock Exchange listed 1,029 issues of 931 companies. Average daily volume through July 31, 1980, was 5.86 million shares.

A 1975 count indicated that 25.3 million persons owned shares in American corporations. More recent counts are not available.

N.Y. Stock Exchange Transactions and Seat Prices

Source: New York Stock Exchange

Year	Yearly volumes: Stock shares	Yearly volumes: Bonds par values	Seat price: High	Seat price: Low
1900	138,981,000	$579,293,000	$47,500	$37,500
1905	260,569,000	1,026,254,000	85,000	72,000
1910	163,705,000	634,863,000	94,000	65,000
1915	172,497,000	961,700,000	74,000	38,000
1920	227,636,000	3,868,422,000	115,000	85,000
1925	459,717,623	3,427,042,210	150,000	99,000
1929	1,124,800,410	2,996,398,000	625,000	550,000
1930	810,632,546	2,720,301,800	480,000	205,000
1935	381,635,752	3,339,458,000	140,000	65,000
1940	207,599,749	$1,669,438,000	$60,000	$33,000
1950	524,799,621	1,112,425,170	54,000	46,000
1960	766,693,818	1,346,419,750	162,000	135,000
1970	2,937,359,448	4,494,864,600	320,000	130,000
1975	4,693,427,000	5,178,300,000	138,000	55,000
1977	5,273,767,000	4,646,354,000	95,000	35,000
1978	7,205,059,000	4,554,013,000	105,000	46,000
1979	*8,155,914,000	4,087,890,000	210,000	82,000

*Record high for trading in stocks.

American Stock Exchange Transactions and Seat Prices

Source: American Stock Exchange

Year	Yearly volumes: Stock shares	Yearly volumes: Bonds par values	Seat price: High	Seat price: Low
1929	476,140,375	$513,551,000	$254,000	$150,000
1930	222,270,065	863,541,000	225,000	70,000
1940	42,928,337	303,902,000	7,250	6,900
1945	143,309,392	167,333,000	32,000	12,000
1950	107,792,340	47,549,000	11,000	6,500
1960	286,039,982	$32,670,000	$60,000	$51,000
1970	843,116,260	641,270,000	180,000	70,000
1975	457,610,360	259,128,000	72,000	34,000
1978	988,559,026	265,514,000	65,000	25,000
1979	1,100,263,500	225,892,000	90,000	45,000

50 U.S. Industrials with Largest Annual Sales and Income

Source: Reprinted by permission from The Fortune Directory; © 1980 Time Inc.

Company	Sales (thousands)	Income (or loss) (thousands)
Exxon	$79,106,471	$4,295,243
General Motors	66,311,200	2,892,700
Mobil	44,720,908	2,007,158
Ford Motor	43,513,700	1,169,300
Texaco	38,350,370	1,759,069
Standard Oil of California	29,947,554	1,784,694
Gulf Oil	23,910,000	1,322,000
International Business Machines	22,862,776	3,011,259
General Electric	22,460,600	1,408,800
Standard Oil (Ind.)	18,610,347	1,506,618
International Telephone & Telegraph	17,197,423	380,685
Atlantic Richfield	16,233,959	1,165,894
Shell Oil	14,431,211	1,125,561
U.S. Steel	12,929,100	(293,000)
Conoco	12,647,998	815,360
E.I. du Pont de Nemours	12,571,800	938,900
Chrysler	12,001,900	(1,097,300)
Tenneco	11,209,000	571,000
Western Electric	10,964,075	635,898
Sun	10,666,000	699,900
Occidental Petroleum	9,554,795	561,646
Phillips Petroleum	9,502,775	891,121
Procter & Gamble	9,329,306	577,331
Dow Chemical	9,255,387	783,898
Union Carbide	$9,176,500	$556,200
United Technologies	9,053,358	325,608
International Harvester	8,392,042	369,562
Goodyear Tire & Rubber	8,238,676	146,184
Boeing	8,131,000	505,400
Eastman Kodak	8,028,231	1,000,764
LTV	7,996,809	173,527
Standard Oil (Ohio)	7,916,023	1,186,116
Caterpillar Tractor	7,613,200	491,600
Union Oil of California	7,567,698	500,604
Beatrice Foods	7,468,373	261,010
RCA	7,454,600	283,800
Westinghouse Electric	7,332,000	(73,900)
Bethlehem Steel	7,137,200	275,700
R.J. Reynolds Industries	7,133,100	550,900
Xerox	7,027,000	563,100
Amerada Hess	6,769,941	507,116
Esmark	6,743,167	92,423
Marathon Oil	6,680,597	323,222
Ashland Oil	6,473,867	526,253
Rockwell International	6,466,100	261,100
Kraft	6,432,900	188,100
Cities Service	6,276,500	347,500
Monsanto	6,192,600	331,000
Philip Morris	6,144,091	507,881
General Foods	5,472,456	232,149

30 Largest Industrials Outside the U.S.

Source: Reprinted by permission from The Fortune Directory; © 1980 Time Inc.

Company	Sales (thousands)	Income (or loss) (thousands)
Royal Dutch/Shell Group, N-B	$59,416,560	$6,474,283
British Petroleum, B	38,713,496	3,439,582
Unilever, B-N	21,748,583	920,320
ENI, It	18,984,960	89,040
Fiat, It	18,300,000	NA
Française des Pétroles, F	17,305,220	1,137,282
Peugeot-Citroën, F	17,270,104	254,318
Volkswagenwerk, G	16,765,683	371,534
Philips' Gloeilampenfabrieken, N	16,576,123	308,701
Renault, F	16,117,376	241,520
Siemens, G	15,069,575	361,938
Daimler-Benz, G	14,942,324	347,794
Hoechst, G	14,785,464	141,684
Bayer, G	14,196,027	239,376
BASF, G	14,138,872	338,040

Company	Sales (thousands)	Income (or loss) (thousands)
Petróleos de Venezuela, V	$14,115,899	$2,907,291
Toyota Motor, J	14,012,345	510,290
Thyssen, G	13,636,918	87,262
Elf Aquitaine, F	13,385,876	1,310,132
Nestlé, S	13,016,940	490,865
Nissan Motor, J	12,652,060	331,206
Hitachi, J	12,632,844	484,190
Nippon Steel, J	12,595,259	243,562
Mitsubishi Heavy Industries, J	11,959,912	111,616
Imperial Chemical Industries, B	11,391,003	880,638
Matsushita Electric Industrial, J	11,127,658	463,177
Petrobrás, Br	10,278,517	756,773
B.A.T. Industries, B	9,478,860	398,940
Ruhrkohle, G	8,856,975	3,249
St.-Gobain-Pont-à-Mousson, F	8,354,964	154,350

National headquarters: B, Britain; Br, Brazil; F, France; G, West Germany; Ir, Iran; It, Italy; J, Japan; N, Netherlands; S, Switzerland; V, Venezuela. NA—not available.

All Banks in U.S.—Number, Deposits

Source: Federal Reserve System

Comprises all national banks in the United States and all state commercial banks, trust companies, mutual stock savings banks, private and industrial banks, and special types of institutions that are treated as banks by the federal bank supervisory agencies.

Year	Number of banks						Total deposits (millions of dollars)					
		F.R.S. members			Nonmembers			F.R.S. members			Nonmembers	
(As of June 30)	Total all banks	Total	Nat'l	State	Mutual savings	Other	Total all banks	Total	Nat'l	State	Mutual savings	Other
1925	**26,479**	9,538	8,066	1,472	621	18,320	**51,641**	32,457	19,912	12,546	7,089	12,095
1930	**23,855**	8,315	7,247	1,068	604	14,936	**59,828**	38,069	23,235	14,834	9,117	12,642
1935	**16,047**	6,410	5,425	985	569	9,068	**51,149**	34,938	22,477	12,461	9,830	6,381
1940	**14,955**	6,398	5,164	1,234	551	8,008	**70,770**	51,729	33,014	18,715	10,631	8,410
1945	**14,542**	6,840	5,015	1,825	539	7,163	**151,033**	118,378	76,534	41,844	14,413	18,242
1950	**14,674**	6,885	4,971	1,914	527	7,262	**163,770**	122,707	82,430	40,277	19,927	21,137
1955	**14,309**	6,611	4,744	1,867	525	7,173	**208,850**	154,670	98,636	56,034	27,310	26,870
1960	**14,006**	6,217	4,542	1,675	513	7,276	**249,163**	179,519	116,178	63,341	35,316	34,328
1965	**14,295**	6,235	4,803	1,432	504	7,556	**362,611**	259,743	171,528	88,215	50,980	51,889
1970	**14,167**	5,803	4,637	1,166	496	7,868	**502,658**	346,229	254,261	91,967	69,285	87,145
1975, Dec. 31	**15,108**	5,787	4,741	1,046	475	8,846	**897,101**	590,999	447,590	143,409	110,569	195,533
1977, Dec. 31	**15,174**	5,668	4,654	1,014	467	9,039	**1,074,426**	683,611	520,167	163,443	134,916	255,898
1978, Dec. 31	**14,712**	5,564	4,564	1,000	465	8,848	**1,176,247**	737,127	559,284	177,843	143,684	295,436

Bank Rates on Short-term Business Loans

Source: Federal Reserve System

Percent per annum. Short-term loans mature within one year.

		All size loans							Size of loan in $1,000				
		Ave. 35 cities	N.Y. C.	7 Other N.E.	8 No. Cent.	7 S.E.	8 S.W.	4 West	1-9	10-99	100 to 499	500 to 999	1,000 and over
1967	Aug. 1-15	5.95	5.66	6.29	5.92	5.92	6.01	6.02	6.58	6.46	6.16	5.89	5.72
1970	Aug. 1-15	8.50	8.24	8.89	8.47	8.49	8.53	8.54	9.15	9.07	8.75	8.46	8.25
1974	May	11.15	11.08	11.65	11.09	10.88	10.82	11.19	10.50	11.06	11.41	11.32	11.06
1975	May	8.16	7.88	8.37	8.00	8.70	8.34	8.33	9.57	9.10	8.52	8.18	7.90
1976	Aug.	7.80	7.48	8.18	7.70	7.95	7.75	8.15	8.85	9.41	8.65	9.33	9.26
	Nov.	7.28	6.88	7.62	7.28	7.51	7.33	7.52	8.56	9.22	8.45	9.13	8.69

		Size of Loan in $1,000[1]						
		All sizes	1-24	25-49	50-99	100-499	500-999	1,000 and over
1977	Feb.	7.50	9.03	8.46	8.47	7.67	7.17	6.58
	May	7.40	9.09	8.43	8.07	7.60	7.13	6.67
1978	Feb.	8.90	9.65	9.45	9.29	9.05	8.79	8.34
	May	8.96	9.81	9.63	9.40	9.08	8.90	8.53
1979	Feb.	12.27	12.14	12.01	12.83	12.55	12.63	11.99
	May	12.34	12.30	12.69	13.02	12.61	12.68	12.07
1980	Feb.	15.67	15.06	15.54	15.91	16.23	16.34	15.50
	May	17.75	17.90	18.78	18.95	18.49	19.13	17.10

(1) In Feb. 1977, The Quarterly Interest Rate Survey was replaced by the Survey of Terms of Bank Lending (STBL). The STBL is conducted in the middle month of each quarter at about 340 member and nonmember banks. The regional breakdown was discontinued at that time. The last previous revision began with the survey period of Feb. 1971. It incorporated a number of technical changes in coverage, sampling, and interest rate calculations.

Federal Reserve System

The Federal Reserve System, central banking system of the U.S., was established Dec. 23, 1913, by an Act of Congress to give the country an elastic currency, to provide facilities for discounting commercial paper, and to improve supervision of banking. Today it is generally recognized that the primary function of the system is to foster a flow of credit and money that will facilitate orderly economic growth, a stable dollar, and a long-run balance in international payments.

The Federal Reserve System consists of the (1) Board of Governors of the Federal Reserve System; (2) Federal Open Market Committee; (3) 12 Fed. Reserve Banks and 25 branches; (4) member banks; (5) Fed. Advisory Council, and (6) the Consumer Advisory Council.

The 7 members of the Board of Governors in Washington are appointed by the President with the advice and consent of the Senate; Paul A. Volcker is chairman. The Board's principal function is in the area of monetary policy. Under the Monetary Control Act of 1980, uniform reserve requirements, set by the Federal Reserve Board, are applied to the transaction accounts and non-personal time deposits of all depository institutions; extends access to Federal Reserve discount and borrowing privileges and other services to nonmember depository institutions; and requires the Federal Reserve to set a schedule of fees for Federal Reserve services. The Depository Institutions Deregulation Committee (DIDC) was established by this act to provide for the orderly phase-out and the ultimate elimination of the limitations on the maximum rates of interest and dividends which may be paid on deposits and accounts by commercial banks, mutual savings banks, and savings and loan associations. Credit unions are not subject to the Act. Congress intended that the phase-out be completed by March 31, 1986. The DIDC consists of the Secretary of the Treasury, the Chairman of the Board of Governors of the Federal Reserve System, the Chairman of the Board of Directors of the Federal Deposit Insurance Corporation, the Chairman of the Federal Home Loan Bank Board, and the Chairman of the National Credit Union Administration Board, each of whom has one vote, and the Comptroller of the Currency who is a nonvoting member. The Board has authority to approve changes in discount rates, and to set margin requirements for certain kinds of stock transactions. Another important duty of the Board relates to supervision of state chartered member banks, and bank holding companies. The Federal Reserve has also been given responsibility by the Congress for rule writing and enforcement of a number of consumer credit protection laws.

Expenses of the Board of Governors are paid out of assessments upon the Reserve Banks.

The Federal Open Market Committee is composed of the 7 members of the Board of Governors, the president of the Federal Reserve Bank of New York, and 4 other Federal Reserve Bank presidents elected annually. The Committee establishes System open market policy for the purchases and sales of securities and for operations in foreign currencies.

Under policy adopted by the Board in 1964 all net earnings of the System (about $9 billion in 1979) are paid to the U.S. Treasury.

The Federal Advisory Council is composed of representatives of the banking industry from the 12 Federal Reserve Districts. The Council is required by law to meet with the Board at least 4 times yearly, to consult with and advise the Board on all matters within the Board's jurisdiction.

Congress established the Consumer Advisory Council in 1976. It consults with the Board at least 4 times a year on consumer-related matters. The Council has an authorized membership of 30, appointed by the Board for terms of 3 years. Members have a wide range of experience in the area of consumer credit.

Rather than having one central bank in the political capital, as in central banking systems of most countries, the Federal Reserve System is divided into 12 districts, each with a Federal Reserve Bank—in Boston, New York, Philadelphia, Cleveland, Richmond, Atlanta, Chicago, St. Louis, Minneapolis, Kansas City, Dallas, and San Francisco. The Federal Reserve Board is the policy-making organ of the System. The Board supervises the budgets and operations of the Reserve Banks, approves appointment of their presidents and first vice presidents and appoints 3 of each district bank's directors, including the chairman and vice chairman of each Reserve Bank's board. Reserve Banks are operated for public service. By statute, their stock is held entirely by member banks, which include all national banks and such state banks and trust companies as have elected to be members. Ownership of Reserve Bank stock is in the nature of an obligation incident to membership in the System and does not carry with it the attributes of control and financial interest ordinarily attached to stock ownership in corporations that are operated for profit. The amount of stock that member banks own is specified by law and dividends are limited to 6% per annum. In case of the liquidation of any Reserve Bank, its surplus would be paid entirely to the U.S. Each Reserve Bank has 9 directors, 6 of whom are chosen by member banks and 3 by the Board of Governors, including the chairman of the Reserve Bank board.

Largest Bank in Each of 48 Foreign Countries

Source: 500 Largest Banks in the Free World, compiled by the American Banker, New York. (Copyright 1980) Based on deposits Dec. 31, 1979, or nearest fiscal year-end. For Canada, see Index.

(thousands)

Country, bank	Deposits in U.S. $
Argentina, Banco de la Nacion	$ 6,844,865
Australia, Commonwealth Bkng. Corp.	14,685,740
Austria, Creditanstalt-Bankverein	16,017,842
Belgium, Societe Generale de Banque	30,182,815
Brazil, Banco do Brasil	16,058,652
Denmark, Danske Bank	5,705,985
Egypt, National Bank of Egypt	3,620,070
Finland, Kansallis-Osake Pankki	5,145,426
France, Banque Nationale de Paris	85,747,164
Germany, Deutsche Bank	85,132,855
Ghana, Ghana Commercial Bank	1,114,716
Greece, National Bank of Greece	10,081,817
Hong Kong, Hongkong & Shanghai	19,776,737
India, State Bank of India	13,332,637
Indonesia, Bank Dagang Negara	2,160,110
Iran, Bank Melli Iran	10,249,150
Iraq, Rafidain Bank	7,835,355
Ireland, Allied Irish Banks, Ltd.	5,863,462
Israel, Bank Leumi le-Israel	12,378,909
Italy, Banca Nazionale del Lavoro	39,866,800
Japan, Dai-Ichi Kangyo Bank Ltd.	51,859,807
Jordan, Arab Bank, Ltd.	4,026,016
Korea, Bank of Seoul & Trust Co.	4,198,421
Kuwait, National Bank of	3,322,391
Luxembourg, Cie, Luxembourgeoise	9,596,561
Malaysia, Bank Bumiputra Malaysia Berhad	2,774,829
Mexico, Bancomer	9,151,037
Netherlands, Rabobank Nederland	43,536,529
New Zealand, Bank of	2,561,392
Nigeria, First Bank of	2,868,550
Norway, Norske Creditbank	3,728,027
Pakistan, Habib Bank	2,344,723
Peru, Banco de la Nacion	2,316,690
Philippines, Philippine National Bank	1,916,999
Portugal, Banco Portugues Do Atlantico	2,266,180
Saudi Arabia, National Commercial Bank	7,177,925
Singapore, United Overseas Bank Ltd.	1,730,704
South Africa, Barclays Nat'l Bank Ltd.	5,426,809
Spain, Banco Central	16,855,775
Sweden, Post-Och Kreditbanken	15,633,342
Switzerland, Swiss Bank Corp.	37,874,213
Taiwan, Bank of	5,751,151
Thailand, Bangkok Bank Ltd.	3,294,200
Turkey, Turkiye Is Bankasi	3,048,084
United Arab Emirates, Nat'l Bank of Abu Dhabi	4,516,841
United Kingdom, National Westminster Bank	59,055,950
Venezuela, Banco Union	1,735,077
Yugoslavia, Udruzena Beogradska Banka	8,688,904

100 Largest U.S. Commercial Banks

Source: 300 Largest Commercial Banks in U.S., compiled by the American Banker, New York. (Copyright 1980) Based on deposits June 30, 1980.

Rank	Bank	Deposits
1	Bank of America NT&SA, San Francisco	$85,069,944,000
2	Citibank NA, New York	72,429,528,000
3	Chase Manhattan Bank NA, New York	56,173,381,000
4	Manufacturers Hanover Trust Co. New York	39,000,618,000
5	Morgan Guaranty Trust Co., New York	35,485,994,000
6	Chemical Bank, New York	30,521,757,000
7	Continental Illinois National Bank & Trust Co., Chicago	25,566,850,000
8	Bankers Trust Co., New York	22,121,919,000
9	First National Bank, Chicago	20,784,969,000
10	Security Pacific National Bank, Los Angeles	19,590,575,898
11	Wells Fargo Bank NA, San Francisco	16,153,222,000
12	Marine Midland Bank NA, Buffalo, NY	13,418,696,000
13	Crocker National Bank, San Francisco	12,989,763,000
14	United California Bank, Los Angeles	11,351,080,000
15	Mellon Bank NA, Pittsburgh	11,341,341,000
16	Irving Trust Co., New York	11,117,347,000
17	First National Bank, Boston	9,189,275,000
18	Bank of New York	7,990,304,303
19	National Bank of Detroit	6,866,871,000
20	Seattle First National Bank	6,674,777,000
21	Republic National Bank, Dallas	5,968,133,183
22	First National Bank, Dallas	5,703,883,000
23	First City National Bank, Houston	4,799,288,809
24	North Carolina National Bank, Charlotte	4,654,681,000
25	Union Bank, Los Angeles	4,578,524,000
26	Harris Trust & Savings Bank, Chicago	4,536,100,334
27	Valley National Bank, Phoenix	4,490,585,000
28	National Bank of North America, New York	4,265,985,000
29	Republic National Bank, New York	4,190,031,824
30	Texas Commerce Bank NA, Houston	4,045,414,000
31	Pittsburgh National Bank	3,943,321,026
32	Northern Trust Co., Chicago	3,912,677,000
33	Philadelphia National Bank	3,875,088,000
34	Wachovia Bank & Trust Co. NA, Winston-Salem, N.C.	3,755,788,141
35	First Pennsylvania Bank NA, Philadelphia	3,686,497,000
36	BancOhio National Bank, Columbus	3,623,171,886
37	Rainier National Bank, Seattle	3,596,677,000
38	First National Bank of Oregon, Portland	3,583,299,000
39	United States National Bank of Oregon, Portland	3,443,582,000
40	AmeriTrust Co., Cleveland	3,434,256,000
41	Citizens & Southern National Bank, Atlanta	3,320,758,000
42	European American Bank & Trust Co. New York	3,264,552,000
43	Manufacturers National Bank, Detroit	3,177,467,000
44	Detroit Bank & Trust Co.	3,142,553,000
45	Bank of Tokyo Trust Co., New York	3,127,449,766
46	California First Bank of San Francisco	2,967,404,000
47	First National Bank of Arizona, Phoenix	2,945,239,000
48	Maryland National Bank, Baltimore	2,882,531,000
49	Girard Bank, Philadelphia	2,807,592,000
50	United Virginia Bank, Richmond	2,666,910,000
51	Northwestern National Bank, Minneapolis	2,660,919,000
52	National City Bank, Cleveland	2,402,379,000
53	Lincoln First Bank NA, Rochester, N.Y.	2,362,018,475
54	Riggs National Bank, Washington, D.C.	2,328,020,000
55	Connecticut Bank & Trust Co., Hartford	2,269,488,392
56	Lloyds Bank California, Los Angeles	2,265,630,016
57	Bank of California NA, San Francisco	2,263,756,000
58	Industrial National Bank of Rhode Island, Providence	2,248,013,000
59	First Union National Bank of North Carolina, Charlotte	2,241,638,000
60	Southeast First National Bank, Miami	2,195,645,000
61	Citibank (New York State) NA, Buffalo	2,175,663,000
62	First National Bank, Minneapolis	2,130,276,000
63	Fidelity Bank, Philadelphia	2,115,233,000
64	Equibank, Pittsburgh	2,074,084,000
65	Virginia National Bank, Norfolk	2,073,759,000
66	First Wisconsin National Bank, Milwaukee	2,058,886,000
67	Huntington National Bank, Columbus, Ohio	2,029,701,155
68	Banco Popular de Puerto Rico, San Juan	1,983,564,256
69	American Security Bank NA, Washington, D.C.	1,925,046,000
70	First National Bank, Atlanta	1,916,421,000
71	Mercantile National Bank, Dallas	1,911,307,000
72	Bank of Hawaii, Honolulu	1,858,401,000
73	Central National Bank, Cleveland	1,822,703,000
74	American National Bank & Trust Co., Chicago	1,767,301,401
75	New England Merchants National Bank, Boston	1,765,956,030
76	Provident National Bank, Philadelphia	1,741,963,000
77	Hartford National Bank & Trust Co., Conn.	1,724,139,000
78	First National Bank, Baltimore	1,714,993,000
79	First & Merchants National Bank, Richmond, Va.	1,693,517,000
80	American Fletcher National Bank & Trust Co., Indianapolis	1,678,955,000
81	Mercantile Trust Co. NA, St. Louis	1,650,015,000
82	Bank of Virginia, Richmond	1,640,089,255
83	Sumitomo Bank of California, San Francisco	1,628,460,900
84	First National Bank, St. Louis	1,626,534,000
85	American Bank & Trust Co., Reading, Pa.	1,609,246,000
86	Indiana National Bank, Indianapolis	1,606,206,779
87	Arizona Bank, Phoenix	1,604,820,169
88	Equitable Trust Co., Baltimore	1,558,679,775
89	Shawmut Bank of Boston NA	1,538,088,000
90	First National Bank of Nevada, Reno	1,533,096,000
91	J. Henry Schroder Bank & Trust Co., New York	1,518,304,000
92	Hamilton Bank, Lancaster, Pa.	1,491,852,000
93	State Street Bank & Trust Co., Boston	1,481,139,000
94	First National State Bank of New Jersey, Newark	1,462,086,000
95	Northwestern Bank, North Wilkesboro, N.C.	1,445,378,578
96	First National Bank, St. Paul, Minn.	1,442,767,000
97	Idaho First National Bank, Boise	1,432,075,569
98	Bank Leumi Trust Co. of New York	1,431,957,779
99	First Hawaiian Bank, Honolulu	1,403,338,000
100	United States Trust Co., New York	1,390,112,672

Bank Suspensions

Source: Federal Deposit Insurance Corp. Deposits in thousands of dollars. The figures represent banks which, during the periods shown, closed temporarily or permanently on account of financial difficulties; does not include banks whose deposit liabilities were assumed by other banks.

Year	Susp.	Deposits	Year	Susp.	Deposits	Year	Susp.	Deposits	Year	Susp.	Deposits
1929	659	230,643	1937	50	14,960	1961	5	8,936	1971	5	74,605
1930	1,352	853,363	1938	50	10,296	1963	2	23,444	1972	1	20,482
1931	2,294	1,690,669	1939	32	32,738	1964	7	23,438	1973	3	25,811
1932	1,456	715,626	1940	19	5,657	1965	3	42,889	1975	1	18,248
1933*	4,004	3,598,975	1955(a)	4	6,503	1966	1	774	1976	3	18,859
1934	9	1,968	1958	3	4,156	1967	4	10,878	1978	1	1,284
1935	24	9,091	1959	3	2,593	1969	4	9,011	1979	3	12,795
1936	42	11,241	1960	1	6,930	1970	4	34,040			

*Figures for 1933 comprise 628 banks with deposits of $360,413,000 suspended before or after the banking holiday (the holiday began March 6 and closed March 15) or placed in receivership during the holiday; 2,124 banks with deposits of $2,520,391,000 which were not licensed following the banking holiday and were placed in liquidation or receivership; and 1,252 banks with deposits of $718,171,000 which had not been licensed by June 20, 1933. (a) No suspensions in years 1945-1954, 1962, 1968, 1974, 1977.

Civilian Employment of the Federal Government

Source: Workforce Analysis and Statistics Division, U.S. Office of Personnel Management as of June 30, 1979

Agency	All areas	United States			Outside United States		
		Total	Full-time	Part-time & intermittent	Total	Territories	Foreign countries
Total, all agencies[1]	**2,956,426**	**2,824,320**	**2,562,665**	**261,655**	**132,106**	**35,485**	**96,621**
Percent distribution	100	96	87	9	4	1	3
Legislative branch	**41,114**	**41,041**	**39,690**	**1,351**	**73**	**13**	**60**
Congress	19,970	19,970	19,969	1	...	...	...
Senate	7,527	7,527	7,527	...	...	...	...
House of Representatives	12,431	12,431	12,431	...	...	...	...
Comm. on Security and Coop. in Europe	12	12	11	1	...	...	...
Architect of the Capitol	2,368	2,368	1,730	638	...	...	...
General Accounting Office	5,437	5,374	5,208	166	63	13	50
Government Printing Office	7,342	7,342	7,175	167	...	...	...
Library of Congress	5,318	5,308	4,961	347	10	...	10
Tax Court	216	216	213	3	...	...	...
Other	463	463	434	29	...	...	...
Judicial branch	**13,276**	**13,107**	**12,541**	**566**	**169**	**169**	**...**
United States Courts	12,956	12,787	12,248	539	169	169	...
Supreme Court	320	320	293	27	...	...	...
Executive branch	**2,902,036**	**2,770,172**	**2,510,434**	**259,738**	**131,864**	**35,303**	**96,561**
Executive Office of the President	1,731	1,731	1,583	148	...	...	...
White House Office	404	404	372	32	...	...	...
Office of the Vice President	25	25	24	1	...	...	...
Office of Management and Budget	643	643	613	30	...	...	...
Council of Economic Advisors	34	34	32	2	...	...	...
Council on Environmental Quality	69	69	56	13	...	...	...
Council on Wage and Price Stability	46	46	42	4	...	...	...
Domestic Council	60	60	56	4	...	...	...
Executive Mansions and Grounds	85	85	85	...	...	...	...
Office of Administration	185	185	158	27	...	...	...
Office of Special Representatives Trade Negotiations	67	67	54	13	...	...	...
Office of Science and Technology Policy	43	43	30	13	...	...	...
National Security Council	70	70	61	9	...	...	...
Executive departments	**1,790,579**	**1,685,863**	**1,592,982**	**92,881**	**104,716**	**14,317**	**90,399**
State[2]	30,351	10,849	10,178	671	19,502	...	19,502
Treasury	130,990	129,968	124,638	5,330	1,022	624	398
Defense	985,727	906,569	891,434	15,135	79,158	10,374	68,784
Department of the Army	357,050	321,645	315,128	6,517	35,405	3,698	31,707
Department of the Navy	313,164	291,581	286,658	4,923	21,583	4,909	16,674
Department of the Air Force	237,785	225,361	222,406	2,955	12,424	1,573	10,851
Defense Logistics Agency	47,541	47,116	46,754	362	425	62	363
Other Defense Activities	30,187	20,866	20,488	378	9,321	132	9,189
Justice	55,305	54,411	52,898	1,513	894	407	487
Interior	89,418	89,060	78,872	10,188	358	289	69
Agriculture	137,669	136,153	107,597	28,556	1,516	755	761
Commerce	52,865	52,621	38,073	14,548	244	89	155
Labor	24,122	24,017	22,993	1,024	105	64	41
Health, Education, and Welfare	169,553	168,658	155,627	13,031	895	847	48
Housing and Urban Development	19,263	19,074	18,165	909	189	189	...
Transportation	74,908	74,087	72,896	1,191	821	678	143
Department of Energy	20,408	20,396	19,611	785	12	1	11
Independent agencies	**1,109,726**	**1,082,578**	**915,869**	**166,709**	**27,148**	**20,986**	**6,162**
Action	1,969	1,436	1,371	65	533	24	509
Board of Governors, Fed. Res. System	1,494	1,494	1,455	39	...	...	...
Canal Zone Government	3,210	...	...	...	3,210	3,210	...
Community Service Admin.	1,118	1,118	1,094	24	...	...	...
Environmental Protection Agency	13,962	13,951	12,226	1,725	11	11	...
Federal Communications Comm.	2,241	2,233	2,191	42	8	8	...
Federal Trade Commission	1,953	1,953	1,767	186	...	...	...
General Services Admin.	38,949	38,828	36,496	2,332	121	106	15
International Communications Agency	8,405	3,417	3,329	88	4,988	...	4,988
Interstate Commerce Commission	2,130	2,130	2,073	57	...	...	...
National Aeronautics and Space Admin.	24,449	24,426	24,272	154	23	1	22
National Labor Relations Board	3,054	3,030	2,987	43	24	24	...
Nuclear Regulatory Comm.	3,160	3,160	3,025	135	...	...	...
Office of Personnel Mgmt.	8,405	8,384	6,425	1,959	21	21	...
Panama Canal Company	12,368	76	75	1	12,292	12,292	...
Securities and Exchange Comm.	2,007	2,007	1,969	38	...	...	...
Selective Service System	70	70	70	...	...	...	...
Small Business Admin.	5,993	5,890	5,779	111	103	103	...
Tennessee Valley Authority	48,353	48,349	48,074	275	4	...	4
U. S. Postal Service	665,980	663,156	533,026	130,130	2,824	2,824	...
Veterans Administration	233,153	230,696	203,025	27,671	2,457	2,213	244
All other agencies	27,303	26,774	25,140	1,634	529	149	380

(1) Excludes employees of Central Intelligence Agency, National Security Agency (not reported to the Office of Personnel Management) and uncompensated employees. June 1979 total includes 41,792 employees exempted from personnel ceilings in the Youth Programs and Worker Trainee Opportunities Program. (2) Includes 6,263 employees in Agency for International Development (2,712 in the Washington, D.C. metropolitan area); employees in foreign countries include 381 paid from local currency trust funds established by foreign governments.

U.S. Labor Force, Employment and Unemployment

Source: Bureau of Labor Statistics, U.S. Labor Department

(numbers in thousands; seasonally adjusted)

Labor force	Annual average			1980				
	1977	1978[1]	1979	Jan.	Feb.	Mar.	Apr.	May
Civilian labor force	97,401	100,420	102,908	104,229	104,260	104,094	104,419	104,542
Employed	90,546	94,373	96,945	97,804	97,953	97,656	97,154	96,537
Agriculture	3,244	3,342	3,297	3,270	3,326	3,358	3,242	3,191
Nonagricultural industries	87,302	91,031	93,648	94,534	94,626	94,298	93,912	93,346
Unemployed	6,855	6,047	5,963	6,425	6,307	6,438	7,265	8,006
Long term, 15 weeks and over	1,911	1,379	1,202	1,334	1,286	1,363	1,629	1,766
Unemployment rates (unemployment in each group as a percent of the groups' civilian labor force)								
Total, 16 years and over	7.0	6.0	5.8	6.2	6.0	6.2	7.0	7.7
Men, 20 years and over	5.2	4.2	4.1	4.7	4.6	4.9	5.9	6.7
Women, 20 years and over	7.0	6.0	5.7	5.8	5.7	5.7	6.3	6.5
Both sexes, 16 to 19 years	17.7	16.3	16.1	16.3	16.5	15.9	16.2	18.5
White, total	6.2	5.2	5.1	5.4	5.3	5.4	6.2	6.8
Men, 20 years and over	4.6	3.7	3.6	4.1	4.0	4.4	5.3	6.0
Women, 20 years and over	6.2	5.2	5.0	5.1	5.2	4.9	5.5	5.8
Both sexes, 16 to 19 years	15.4	13.9	13.9	14.0	13.8	13.8	14.6	14.6
Black and other, total	13.1	11.9	11.3	11.8	11.5	11.8	12.6	13.6
Men, 20 years and over	10.0	8.6	8.4	9.6	9.2	9.3	10.9	12.6
Women, 20 years and over	11.7	10.6	10.1	10.0	9.0	10.5	11.4	10.9
Both sexes, 16 to 19 years	38.3	36.3	33.5	34.6	37.9	33.0	29.8	36.3
Married men, spouse present	3.6	2.8	2.7	3.4	3.1	3.4	4.1	4.9
Married women, spouse present	6.5	5.5	5.1	5.2	5.4	5.3	5.7	6.1
Women who head families	9.3	8.5	8.3	9.2	8.5	8.7	9.3	8.4
Full-time workers	6.5	5.5	5.3	5.7	5.6	5.8	6.6	7.4
Part-time workers	9.8	9.0	8.7	8.7	8.9	8.3	8.9	8.8
White-collar workers	4.3	3.5	3.3	3.4	3.4	3.3	3.7	3.7
Blue-collar workers	8.1	6.9	6.9	8.0	7.7	8.0	9.7	11.5
Service workers	8.2	7.4	7.1	6.9	6.9	7.1	8.0	8.1
Farm workers	4.6	3.8	3.8	4.4	3.9	4.0	5.0	4.2
Nonagricultural private wage and salary workers[2]	7.0	5.9	5.7	6.2	6.0	6.2	7.1	8.3
Construction	12.7	10.6	10.2	10.8	10.5	13.0	15.1	16.5
Manufacturing	6.7	5.5	5.5	6.7	6.4	6.5	7.9	9.9
Durable goods	6.2	4.9	5.0	6.7	6.3	6.4	8.3	11.2
Nondurable goods	7.4	6.3	6.4	6.8	6.7	6.7	7.4	8.0
Wholesale and retail trade	8.0	6.9	6.5	6.6	6.4	6.3	7.0	8.0
Finance and service industries	6.0	5.1	4.9	4.6	4.6	4.9	5.1	5.7
Government workers	4.2	3.9	3.7	3.8	4.0	4.2	4.4	3.5

(1) Data for periods prior to 1978 are not strictly comparable with current data because of an expansion in the sample and revisions in the estimation procedures. (2) Includes mining, not shown separately.

Employed Persons by Major Occupational Groups and Sex

Annual averages 1978 Occupational group	Thousands of persons			Percent distribution		
	Both sexes	Males	Females	Both sexes	Males	Females
Total employed	94,773	55,491	38,882	100.0	100.0	100.0
White-collar workers	47,205	22,633	24,572	50.0	40.8	63.2
Professional and technical	14,245	8,163	6,082	15.1	14.7	15.6
Managers and administrators, except farm	10,105	7,744	2,361	10.7	14.0	6.1
Sales workers	5,951	3,285	2,666	6.3	5.9	6.9
Clerical workers	16,904	3,442	13,463	17.9	6.2	34.6
Blue-collar workers	31,531	25,765	5,766	33.4	46.4	14.8
Craft and kindred workers	12,386	11,689	697	13.1	21.1	1.8
Operatives, except transport	10,875	6,554	4,321	11.5	11.8	11.1
Transport equipment operatives	3,541	3,284	257	3.8	5.9	.7
Nonfarm laborers	4,729	4,238	491	5.0	7.6	1.3
Service workers	12,839	4,804	8,035	13.6	8.7	20.7
Private household workers	1,162	27	1,135	1.2	(1)	2.9
Other service workers	11,677	4,277	6,900	12.4	8.6	17.7
Farm workers	2,798	2,289	509	3.0	4.1	1.3
Farmers and farm managers	1,480	1,349	131	1.6	2.4	.3
Farm laborers and supervisors	1,318	940	377	1.4	1.7	1.0

(1) Less than 0.05 percent.

Employment and Unemployment in the U.S.

Civilian labor force, persons 16 years of age and over (in thousands)

Year	Civilian labor force	Employed	Unem-ployed	Year	Civilian labor force	Employed	Unem-ployed
1940	52,705	45,070	7,635	1974	91,011	85,936	5,076
1950	62,208	58,918	3,288	1975	92,613	84,783	7,830
1960	69,628	65,778	3,852	1976	94,773	87,485	7,288
1965	74,455	71,088	3,366	1977	97,401	90,546	6,855
1970	82,715	78,627	4,088	1978	100,420	94,373	6,047
1973	88,714	84,409	4,304	1979	102,908	96,945	5,963

Average Salaries of Full-time Federal Civilian Employees

Source: Office of Personnel Management, Oct. 31, 1978

Occupation	Total no. of employees	Men: No. of employees	Men: Average salary	Women: No. of employees	Women: Average salary
Blue-Collar					
Baker	279	259	$15,683	20	$13,865
Barber	36	35	15,817	1	17,326
Beautician	11	—	—	11	17,130
Boiler operator	7,290	7,277	17,080	13	15,705
Carpenter	8,562	8,520	16,908	42	14,694
Cook	5,892	4,552	16,593	1,340	14,873
Electrician	13,462	13,308	17,660	154	14,159
Elevator operator	758	503	14,199	255	12,325
Forklift operator	2,077	2,036	14,227	41	13,583
Janitor	24,733	18,138	12,305	6,595	12,086
Laborer	26,084	24,060	12,778	2,024	12,670
Locksmith	395	390	16,594	5	16,267
Machinist	14,920	14,756	17,814	164	14,131
Mechanic, A/C	5,459	5,445	17,385	14	13,238
Mechanic, aircraft	16,383	16,179	17,984	204	15,087
Mechanic, general	5,399	5,357	17,670	42	14,605
Painter	9,579	9,396	16,700	183	14,672
Pipefitter	11,016	10,975	17,654	41	13,365
Plumber	2,591	2,582	16,620	9	14,165
Pressman	2,763	2,509	17,171	254	15,988
Sheet metal	12,546	12,143	17,609	403	15,638
Store clerk	4,567	3,716	13,818	851	13,190
Toolmaker	1,071	1,065	20,027	6	15,614
Trainman	251	249	16,132	2	21,393
Tractor operator	2,301	2,284	14,218	17	14,773
Vehicle operator	18,930	18,678	15,331	252	14,055
Warehouseman	21,702	20,169	14,805	1,533	13,533
Welder	6,535	6,458	17,287	77	14,853
White-Collar					
Accountant	1,693	1,188	28,356	505	23,753
Architect	1,645	1,566	26,386	79	22,810
Attorney	15,532	13,035	32,581	2,497	27,388
Chaplain	518	512	25,969	6	11,871
Chemist	8,256	6,890	27,864	1,366	22,349
Clerk/Typist	69,525	3,344	9,464	66,181	9,434
Dental assistant	2,849	216	11,151	2,633	10,820
Dietitian	1,185	31	22,950	1,154	20,228
Editor/Writer	2,178	973	24,025	1,205	19,309
Editor, technical	1,708	1,163	23,666	545	20,006
Engineer, civil	15,708	15,515	27,361	193	19,659
Engineer, electrical	4,587	4,543	26,546	44	22,310
Engineer, mechanical	10,106	10,043	27,128	63	21,126
Law clerk	643	346	18,654	297	18,504
Librarian	3,379	1,122	25,185	2,257	22,000
Messenger	785	688	8,800	97	9,094
Nurse	34,438	2,204	16,631	32,234	17,859
Paralegal	1,291	603	22,970	688	18,362
Personnel management	26,064	16,540	26,441	9,524	21,052
Pharmacist	2,158	1,793	21,938	365	19,640
Public relations	2,798	1,899	29,501	899	21,802
Purchasing	4,304	1,138	14,100	3,166	12,997
Secretary	63,296	416	13,410	62,880	13,505
Social work	19,148	14,639	28,958	4,509	23,437
Statistician	2,802	2,106	27,667	696	22,350
Technician, medical	4,141	1,346	16,172	2,795	15,809
Therapist, occupational	680	96	17,924	584	17,514
Therapist, physical	744	284	18,946	460	17,319

Average Salaries of Federal Employees by Pay System and Area

as of March 31, 1979
Source: Office of Personnel Management

Pay System	No. of employees	% of work force	Pay: Mean annual	Pay: Median annual
General Schedule	1,396,947	71.3	$18,175	$16,035
Wage Systems	457,186	23.3	$16,926	$16,631
Postal Service[1]	66	0.0	$27,859	$23,500
All other	105,498	5.4	$22,383	$18,723
Totals	**1,959,697**	**100.0**	**$18,496**	**$16,386**

(1) Includes Postal Rate Commission employees only; Postal Service not included.

NOTE: The highest average salary for General Schedule employees is $22,047, paid in the District of Columbia; the lowest, $15,858, is paid in Kentucky. Alaska pays Wage System employees the highest average salary ($28,071); Rhode Island pays the lowest ($13,965).

U.S. Government Pay Systems

Source: Office of Personnel Management

The major Congressionally-mandated pay systems for U. S. government employees are:

The General Schedule (GS) covers most "white-collar" employees and consists of 18 job grades based on responsibility and difficulty of position, with 9 or 10 "steps" of salary advancement based on length of service and/or merit.

The Federal Wage Systems cover employees in "blue-collar" jobs, including trade, craft, and labor occupations; pay is set in accordance with local rates.

The Executive Schedule covers top officials in the Executive Branch, above the grade GS-18.

The Administratively-Determined Pay Systems are those which Congress has authorized individual agencies to set on their own, for certain positions.

Per Capita Personal Income, by States and Regions

Source: Bureau of Economic Analysis, U.S. Commerce Department (dollars)

State and Region	1970	1975	1977	1978	1979
nited States	**3,893**	**5,861**	**7,043**	**7,854**	**8,773**
New England	**4,245**	**6,030**	**7,163**	**7,956**	**8,910**
Connecticut	4,871	6,779	8,044	8,973	10,129
Maine	3,250	4,766	5,748	6,334	7,039
Massachusetts	4,276	6,077	7,201	7,952	8,893
New Hampshire	3,720	5,417	6,646	7,483	8,351
Rhode Island	3,878	5,709	6,790	7,628	8,510
Vermont	3,447	4,924	5,837	6,609	7,329
Mideast	**4,384**	**6,380**	**7,431**	**8,206**	**9,112**
Delaware	4,468	6,547	7,651	8,427	9,327
District of Columbia	4,644	7,262	8,721	9,513	10,570
Maryland	4,267	6,403	7,612	8,514	9,331
New Jersey	4,684	6,794	7,927	8,792	9,747
New York	4,605	6,519	7,433	8,192	9,104
Pennsylvania	3,879	5,841	6,969	7,669	8,558
Great Lakes	**4,050**	**6,047**	**7,417**	**8,224**	**9,118**
Illinois	4,446	6,735	8,049	8,887	9,799
Indiana	3,709	5,609	6,940	7,701	8,570
Michigan	4,041	5,991	7,604	8,514	9,403
Ohio	3,949	5,778	7,091	7,836	8,715
Wisconsin	3,712	5,616	6,823	7,555	8,484
Plains	**3,657**	**5,719**	**6,796**	**7,637**	**8,628**
Iowa	3,643	5,894	6,899	7,905	8,772
Kansas	3,725	5,958	7,110	7,975	9,233
Minnesota	3,819	5,779	7,106	7,858	8,865
Missouri	3,654	5,476	6,617	7,341	8,251
Nebraska	3,657	5,882	6,661	7,491	8,684
North Dakota	3,077	5,888	5,947	7,642	8,231
South Dakota	3,108	5,009	5,868	6,580	7,455

State and Region	1970	1975	1977	1978	1979
Southeast	**3,208**	**5,028**	**6,090**	**6,836**	**7,624**
Alabama	2,892	4,635	5,651	6,347	6,962
Arkansas	2,791	4,510	5,450	6,236	6,933
Florida	3,698	5,631	6,740	7,605	8,546
Georgia	3,300	5,029	6,030	6,830	7,630
Kentucky	3,076	4,887	5,968	6,618	7,390
Louisiana	3,023	4,803	5,985	6,748	7,583
Mississippi	2,547	4,047	5,027	5,582	6,178
North Carolina	3,200	4,940	5,941	6,693	7,385
South Carolina	2,951	4,665	5,676	6,344	7,057
Tennessee	3,079	4,804	5,848	6,602	7,343
Virginia	3,677	5,772	6,951	7,670	8,587
West Virginia	3,038	4,962	6,011	6,593	7,372
Southwest	**3,465**	**5,469**	**6,733**	**7,608**	**8,627**
Arizona	3,614	5,391	6,520	7,411	8,423
New Mexico	3,045	4,843	5,919	6,733	7,560
Oklahoma	3,341	5,280	6,455	7,376	8,509
Texas	3,507	5,584	6,908	7,776	8,788
Rocky Mountain	**3,540**	**5,571**	**6,659**	**7,512**	**8,357**
Colorado	3,838	5,987	7,184	8,070	9,122
Idaho	3,243	5,179	6,180	6,995	7,571
Montana	3,395	5,388	6,020	7,067	7,684
Utah	3,169	4,900	5,964	6,600	7,197
Wyoming	3,672	6,123	7,647	8,668	9,922
Far West	**4,310**	**6,474**	**7,866**	**8,807**	**9,901**
California	4,423	6,575	7,975	8,900	10,047
Nevada	4,583	6,625	8,276	9,529	10,521
Oregon	3,677	5,769	7,190	8,112	8,938
Washington	3,997	6,298	7,585	8,581	9,565
Alaska	4,638	9,636	10,417	10,485	11,219
Hawaii	4,599	6,708	7,712	8,438	9,223

Real After-Tax Income Per Capita
Adjusted for Taxes and Relative Living Costs

Source: Alan Reynolds, First Chicago World Report, May-June, 1979
(Estimated on the basis of 1977 income and tax figures)

	Per capita personal income	Per capita federal taxes	Per capita state and local taxes[1]	After-tax per capita income	Adjusted per capita income[2]
labama	5,622	1,163	507	3,952	4,357
laska	10,586	2,516	2,296	5,774	4,246
rkansas	5,540	1,382	494	3,664	4,103
rizona	6,509	1,143	827	4,539	4,728
alifornia	7,911	1,756	1,089	5,066	5,102
olorado	7,160	1,557	824	4,779	4,957
onnecticut	8,061	2,040	885	5,136	4,796
elaware	7,697	1,964	829	4,904	5,004
lorida	6,684	1,530	628	4,526	4,957
eorgia	6,014	1,298	609	4,107	4,543
awaii	7,677	1,749	974	4,954	4,271
daho	5,980	1,255	639	4,085	4,475
linois	7,768	1,903	860	5,005	4,960
ndiana	6,921	1,541	652	4,728	4,889
owa	6,878	1,643	749	4,486	4,798
ansas	7,134	1,627	728	4,779	5,068
entucky	5,945	1,258	601	4,086	4,315
ouisiana	5,913	1,260	636	4,017	4,424
aine	5,734	1,246	658	3,830	3,785
aryland	7,572	1,858	892	4,822	5,049
ass.	7,258	1,709	1,002	4,547	3,954
ichigan	7,619	1,666	878	5,075	5,111
innesota	7,129	1,549	906	4,674	4,869
ississippi	5,030	987	527	3,516	3,968
issouri	6,654	1,472	609	4,573	4,804
ontana	6,125	1,402	766	3,957	4,301

	Per capita personal income	Per capita federal taxes	Per capita state and local taxes[1]	After-tax per capita income	Adjusted per capita income[2]
Nebraska	6,720	1,670	774	4,276	4,539
Nevada	7,988	1,903	892	5,193	5,376
New Hamp.	6,536	1,467	618	4,451	4,372
New Jersey	7,994	1,992	931	5,071	4,528
New Mexico	5,857	1,217	625	4,015	4,491
New York	7,537	1,848	1,252	4,437	3,979
No. Carolina	5,935	1,275	593	4,067	4,509
North Dakota	6,190	1,395	682	4,113	4,404
Ohio	7,084	1,599	641	4,844	5,004
Oklahoma	6,346	1,389	598	4,359	4,790
Oregon	7,007	1,554	793	4,660	4,736
Pennsylvania	7,011	1,653	770	4,588	4,740
Rhode Island	6,775	1,626	793	4,356	4,056
So. Carolina	5,628	1,167	549	3,912	4,327
South Dakota	5,957	1,308	629	4,020	4,341
Tennessee	5,785	1,339	564	3,882	4,243
Texas	6,803	1,485	637	4,681	5,061
Utah	5,923	1,227	652	4,044	4,199
Vermont	5,823	1,293	810	3,720	3,720
Virginia	6,865	1,536	675	4,654	4,773
Washington	7,528	1,722	821	4,985	4,980
West Virginia	5,986	1,271	622	4,093	4,568
Wisconsin	6,890	1,521	870	4,499	4,591
Wyoming	7,562	1,707	988	4,867	5,407
Dist. of Col.	8,999	2,073	1,071	5,855	5,684
U.S. Ave.	**7,019**	**1,600**	**813**	**4,606**	**4,606**

(1) Tax Foundation, Inc. (2) After-tax per capita income adjusted by the Bureau of Labor Statistics index of comparative costs, 4-person family, intermediate budget less personal income taxes (weighted by percentage of state's population in metropolitan areas).

Federal Deposit Insurance Corporation (FDIC)

The primary purpose of the Federal Deposit Insurance Corporation (FDIC) is to insure deposits in all banks approved for insurance coverage benefits under the Federal Deposit Insurance Act. The major functions of the FDIC are to pay off depositors of insured banks closed without adequate provision having been made to pay depositors' claims, to act as receiver for all national banks placed in receivership and for state banks placed in receivership when appointed receiver by state authorities, and to prevent the continuance or development of unsafe and unsound banking practices. The FDIC's entire income consists of assessments on insured banks and income from investments; it receives no appropriations from Congress. It may borrow from the U.S. Treasury not to exceed $3 billion outstanding, but has made no such borrowings since it was organized in 1933. The FDIC surplus (Deposit Insurance Fund) as of Dec. 31, 1979 was $9.8 billion.

U.S. Balance of International Payments

Source: Bureau of Economic Analysis, U.S. Commerce Department
(millions of dollars)

	1955	1960	1965	1970	1975	1977	1978	1979
Exports of goods and services	**19,948**	**28,861**	**41,086**	**65,673**	**155,729**	**184,705**	**221,036**	**286,508**
Merchandise, adjusted	14,424	19,650	26,461	42,469	107,088	120,816	142,054	182,055
Transfers under U.S. military agency sales contracts	200	335	830	1,501	4,049	7,451	8,240	7,194
Receipts of income on U.S. investments abroad	2,817	4,616	7,436	11,746	25,351	32,587	42,972	65,970
Other services	2,507	4,261	6,359	9,957	19,242	23,852	27,772	31,289
Imports of goods and services	**−17,795**	**−23,729**	**−32,801**	**−60,050**	**−132,836**	**−194,169**	**−230,240**	**−281,630**
Merchandise, adjusted	−11,527	−14,758	−21,510	−39,866	−98,041	−151,689	−175,813	−211,524
Direct defense expenditures	−2,901	−3,087	−2,952	−4,855	−4,795	−5,823	−7,354	−8,469
Payments of income on foreign investments in the U.S.	−520	−1,237	−2,088	−5,516	−12,564	−14,598	−22,073	−33,460
Other services	−2,847	−4,646	−6,251	−9,815	−17,436	−22,059	−25,001	−28,178
Unilateral transfers, net	−2,498	−2,308	−2,854	−3,294	−4,613	−4,605	−5,055	−5,666
U.S. official reserve assets, net	182	2,145	1,225	2,481	−849	−375	732	−1,107
U.S. Government assets, other than official reserve assets, net	−310	−1,100	−1,605	−1,589	−3,474	−3,693	−4,644	−3,783
U.S. private assets, net	−1,255	−5,144	−5,335	−10,228	−35,380	−31,725	−57,279	−56,858
Foreign official assets in the U.S., net	1,357	1,473	134	6,908	7,027	36,575	33,293	−14,271
Other foreign assets in the U.S., net		821	607	−550	8,643	14,167	30,804	51,845
Allocations of special drawing rights	—	—	—	867	—	—	—	1,139
Statistical discrepancy	371	−1,019	−458	−219	5,753	−880	11,354	23,822
Memoranda:								
Balance on merchandise trade	2,897	4,892	4,951	2,603	9,047	−30,873	−33,759	−29,469
Balance on goods and services	2,153	5,132	8,284	5,624	22,893	−9,464	−9,204	4,878
Balance on goods, services, and remittances	1,556	4,496	7,238	4,066	21,175	−11,293	−11,088	2,736
Balance on current account	−345	2,824	5,431	2,330	18,280	−14,068	−14,259	−788

Note.—Details may not add to totals because of rounding.

Average Weekly Canadian Wages and Salaries, by Province

Source: Canadian Statistical Review, May 1980 (Canadian dollars)

Year & month	Canada[1]	Nfld.	P.E.I.	N.S.	N.B.	Que.	Ont.	Man.	Sask.	Alta.	B.C.
1970	126.82	117.70	83.82	104.21	104.01	122.38	131.52	115.88	114.87	128.15	137.97
1975	203.34	196.50	149.84	172.40	182.40	199.22	204.86	186.01	188.31	207.39	229.97
1976	228.03	221.63	170.88	193.21	202.56	222.41	228.72	208.55	214.87	236.89	259.52
1977	249.95	242.43	187.73	212.09	223.34	244.77	249.46	226.28	235.61	261.96	284.13
1978	265.37	248.36	196.72	223.72	232.89	262.82	264.04	239.71	250.44	276.32	301.26
1979	288.25	271.64	209.77	245.23	256.49	284.35	285.57	259.00	275.79	306.79	327.14
1980 Jan.	299.72	282.89	218.47	258.09	270.96	296.80	294.66	268.44	288.12	321.74	340.52

(1) Includes Yukon and Northwest Territories.

Canadian Labor Force

Source: Statistics Canada; March, 1980, seasonally adjusted (thousands of persons)

	Can.	Nfld.	P.E.I.	N.S.	N.B.	Que.	Ont.	Man.	Sask.	Alta.	B.C.
Labor force	11,472	211	54	358	289	2,914	4,364	483	440	1,059	1,269
Employed	10,618	183	48	324	257	2,662	4,065	456	423	1,022	1,171
Unemployed	854	28	6	34	32	279	299	27	17	37	98
Percent unemployed	7.4	13.3	10.5	9.5	11.1	9.5	6.9	5.6	3.9	3.5	7.7

Canadian Labor Force Characteristics

Source: Statistics Canada (thousands of workers)

		Employed						
		All workers[1]			Paid workers			
Year	Labor force	Total	Agri-culture	Non-agri-culture	Total	Non-agri-culture	Unem-ployed	Unem-ployed %
1950	5,163	4,976	1,018	3,958	3,522	3,411	186	3.6
1955	5,610	5,364	819	4,546	4,133	4,027	245	4.4
1960	6,411	5,965	683	5,282	4,843	4,732	446	7.0
1965	7,141	6,862	594	6,268	5,760	5,655	280	3.9
1970	8,374	7,879	511	7,368	6,839	6,740	495	5.9
1975	9,974	9,284	497	8,787	8,951	8,814	690	6.9
1977	10,498	9,648	482	9,166	9,438	9,295	850	8.1
1978	10,882	9,972	494	9,478	9,740	9,608	911	8.4
1979	11,207	10,369	504	9,865	10,032	9,871	838	7.5

(1) Including self-employed.

Foreign Direct Investment in the U.S.

Source: Bureau of Economic Analysis, U.S. Commerce Department

(millions of dollars)

Country	Position at yearend 1978	Position at yearend 1979	Equity and intercompany account inflows (outflows (-))[1] 1978	Equity and intercompany account inflows (outflows (-))[1] 1979	Reinvested earnings of incorporated affiliates[2] 1978	Reinvested earnings of incorporated affiliates[2] 1979	Income[3] 1978	Income[3] 1979	Interest, dividends, and earnings of unincorporated affiliates[4] 1978	Interest, dividends, and earnings of unincorporated affiliates[4] 1979
Total	**42,471**	**52,260**	**5,313**	**5,984**	**2,583**	**3,729**	**4,211**	**6,033**	**1,628**	**2,303**
By country:										
Canada	6,180	6,974	449	356	231	402	354	590	123	188
Europe	29,180	35,999	3,350	4,201	1,866	2,600	3,038	4,246	1,172	1,646
Belgium and Luxembourg	1,303	1,658	8	95	168	260	174	267	6	7
France	1,978	2,214	101	117	79	106	163	222	84	115
Germany	3,654	5,004	1,010	1,246	96	162	194	256	98	94
Italy	243	212	−41	−38	4	6	16	28	12	22
Netherlands	10,078	12,462	979	699	967	1,622	1,392	2,240	425	618
Denmark and Ireland	125	142	6	18	6	−1	8	1	2	1
United Kingdom	7,638	9,391	799	1,424	521	314	813	783	292	469
Sweden	893	1,150	165	155	33	106	73	165	40	59
Switzerland	2,879	3,290	237	430	−34	−9	177	242	210	251
Other	388	476	87	55	26	33	29	41	3	8
Japan	2,749	3,441	770	287	217	405	301	510	84	105
Australia, New Zealand, and South Africa	128	199	76	60	2	(*)	22	35	20	35
Latin America	3,603	4,878	459	967	254	304	407	525	153	221
Panama	495	573	14	25	42	53	45	56	3	2
Other Latin America	65	185	−52	138	−9	−17	16	44	25	60
Other Western Hemisphere	3,043	4,119	497	804	222	267	346	426	125	158
Middle East	415	474	142	45	7	14	37	59	30	45
Israel	105	139	44	31	3	4	10	14	7	10
Other	311	335	98	14	4	10	27	45	23	35
Other Africa, Asia, and Pacific	217	295	67	68	6	5	52	68	46	63
Memorandum: OPEC[5]	366	401	107	24	4	11	27	52	23	41
By industry:										
Petroleum	7,762	9,903	303	526	940	1,615	1,239	2,003	299	388
Manufacturing	17,202	20,029	2,537	1,914	660	910	1,146	1,512	490	603
Trade	9,161	11,167	1,430	1,386	488	620	805	1,082	317	462
Finance	2,458	3,701	52	1,012	171	231	445	638	274	407
Insurance	2,773	3,454	268	482	270	188	445	528	175	341
Real Estate	1,161	1,566	262	350	−20	−8	41	73	61	81
Other	1,954	2,439	461	313	74	173	86	195	12	21

* Less than $500,000 (±). (1) Foreign parents' shares in net changes in capital stock and intercompany accounts with incorporated U.S. affiliates, and in equity in unincorporated U.S. affiliates. (2) Foreign parents' shares in the earnings of incorporated U.S. affiliates (net of U.S. income taxes), less their shares in the gross dividends of these affiliates. (3) Foreign parents' shares in the earnings of U.S. affiliates (net of U.S. income taxes), plus net interest paid on intercompany debt, less withholding taxes on dividends and interest. Also equals interest, dividends, and earnings of unincorporated affiliates plus reinvested earnings of incorporated affiliates. (4) Dividends and interest on intercompany debt credited to foreign parents by affiliates, less interest credited by foreign parents to affiliates, exclusive of withholding taxes; plus foreign parents' shares in the earnings of unincorporated U.S. affiliates. (5) Countries in the Organization of Petroleum Exporting Countries (OPEC) are: Algeria, Ecuador, Gabon, Indonesia, Iran, Iraq, Kuwait, Libya, Nigeria, Qatar, Saudi Arabia, Venezuela, and United Arab Emirates.

Canadian Unemployment Insurance Commission

Source: Canadian Statistical Review, Apr. 1980
(Canadian dollars)

Year	Claims data: Beneficiaries[1,2] (000)	Claims data: Claims received (000)	Claims data: Weeks paid	Benefits paid: Total paid (thousands of dollars)	Benefits paid: Regular	Benefits paid: Sickness	Benefits paid: Maternity	Benefits paid: Retirement	Benefits paid: Fishing
1976	701	2,675	36,189	3,342,246	3,019,686	129,802	139,624	18,048	28,881
1977	750	2,807	38,701	3,909,045	3,485,080	155,828	172,228	13,543	48,400
1978	803	2,809	41,355	4,536,910	4,006,868	157,405	195,297	14,831	63,434
1979	711	2,602	36,896	4,008,002	3,431,216	145,183	207,649	15,055	70,897

(1) Refer to the number of persons receiving $1.00 or more in unemployment insurance benefits during a specific week each month. (2) Annual figures are average of 12 months.

Canadian Provincial Unemployment Rates

Source: Statistics Canada

Year	Can.	Nfld.	P.E.I.	N.S.	N.B.	Que.	Ont.	Man.	Sask.	Alta.	B.C.
1975	6.9	12.2	...	7.8	9.9	8.1	6.3	4.5	2.9	4.1	8.5
1976	7.1	13.6	9.8	9.6	11.1	8.7	6.2	4.7	4.0	3.9	8.6
1977	8.1	15.9	10.0	10.7	13.4	10.3	7.0	5.9	4.5	4.4	8.5
1978	8.4	16.4	9.9	10.6	12.6	10.9	7.2	6.5	4.9	4.7	8.3
1979	7.5	15.4	11.3	10.2	11.1	9.6	6.5	5.4	4.2	3.9	7.7

Total Value of Canadian Construction Work

Source: Statistics Canada (thousands of Canadian dollars)

Province	1978 New	1978 Repair	1978 Total	1979 New	1979 Repair	1979 Total
Newfoundland	533,695	109,147	642,842	689,681	117,981	807,662
Prince Edward Island	127,965	37,642	165,607	133,996	30,402	164,398
Nova Scotia	783,221	215,478	998,699	896,876	225,486	1,122,362
New Brunswick	793,281	134,455	927,736	916,539	161,571	1,078,110
Quebec	7,015,539	1,512,120	8,527,659	7,743,384	1,651,354	9,394,738
Ontario	8,914,240	2,065,227	10,979,467	9,212,925	2,325,540	11,538,465
Manitoba	1,269,727	232,697	1,502,424	1,155,072	296,700	1,451,772
Saskatchewan	1,349,607	303,610	1,653,217	1,695,050	351,841	2,046,891
Alberta	6,549,933	860,426	7,410,359	8,161,652	889,592	9,051,194
British Columbia	4,573,179	808,993	5,382,172	4,865,455	849,606	5,715,061
Total	**31,910,387**	**6,279,795**	**38,190,182**	**35,470,630**	**6,900,023**	**42,370,653**

Canadian Pulpwood, Wood Pulp, and Newsprint

Source: Canadian Statistical Review, April 1980 (thousands of metric tons)

Year	Pulpwood production (thousand units[1])	Wood pulp production[2] Total	Mechanical	Chemical	Wood pulp exports[3]	Newsprint production	Newsprint shipments Total	Domestic	Exports[4]
1976	15,093	17,590.2	6,843.4	10,687.2	6,742	8,915	8,712	885	7,827
1977	15,603	17,772.2	6,830.1	10,916.8	6,715	8,988	9,005	909	8,096
1978	16,048	19,185.6	7,480.2	11,671.0	7,320	8,811	8,883	908	7,975
1979	17,210	19,530.0	7,392.6	12,111.5	7,816	8,710	8,730	948	7,781

(1) 100 cu. ft. of solid wood; pulpwood produced for domestic use and excluding exports, but including receipts of purchased roundwood. (2) Total pulp production covers "screenings" which are already included in exports. "Screenings" are excluded throughout from mechanical and chemical pulp. (3) Customs exports. (4) Mill shipments destined for export.

Telephones in North American Cities

Source: American Telephone and Telegraph Co., and Trans-Canada Telephone Systems (Jan. 1, 1979)

City	Number	City	Number	City	Number	City	Number
Akron, Oh.	340,478	Erie, Pa.	140,323	Memphis, Tenn.	599,060	Royal Oaks, Mich.	207,057
Albany, N.Y.	170,643	Eugene-Spring-		Mexico City (area)	1,671,950	Sacramento, Cal.	512,670
Albuquerque, N.M.	279,531	field, Ore.	147,957	Miami, Fla.	1,019,014	Saginaw, Mich.	132,147
Alexandria, Va.	241,865	Evansville, Ind.	128,398	Milwaukee, Wis.	848,381	St. Louis, Mo.	573,529
Allentown, Pa.	147,262	Fayetteville, N.C.	141,266	Minn.-St. Paul, Minn.	1,580,900	St. Petersburg, Fla.	289,355
Amarillo, Tex.	135,088	Flint, Mich.	228,836	Mobile, Ala.	231,811	Salt Lake City, Ut.	488,412
Anaheim, Cal.	215,734	Ft. Lauderdale, Fla.	390,906	Modesto, Cal.	117,751	San Antonio, Tex.	413,492
Anchorage, Alas.	122,066	Fort Wayne, Ind.	175,461	Monterey, Mex.	211,565	San Diego, Cal. (area)	1,043,695
Ann Arbor, Mich.	123,422	Fort Worth, Tex.	347,138	Montgomery, Ala.	153,817	San Francisco, Cal.	815,520
Atlanta, Ga.	887,476	Fremont City, Cal.	126,979	Montreal, Que.	1,244,494	San Jose, Cal.	601,580
Augusta, Ga.	145,361	Fresno, Cal.	254,272	Mt. Vernon, N.Y.	123,444	San Mateo, Cal.	127,389
Austin, Tex.	276,984	Gary, Ind.	128,459	Nashville, Tenn.	405,791	Santa Ana, Cal.	449,260
Bakersfield, Cal.	170,554	Grand Rapids, Mich.	300,823	New Haven, Conn.	268,541	Santa Barbara, Cal.	136,197
Baltimore, Md.	1,353,051	Greensboro, N.C.	198,397	New Orleans, La.	727,051	Savannah, Ga.	145,196
Baton Rouge, La.	284,331	Greenville, S.C.	173,244	New York, N.Y.	5,936,829	Schenectady, N.Y.	131,925
Birmingham, Ala.	450,540	Guadalajara, Mex.	231,665	Newark, N.J.	322,523	Seattle, Wash.	633,972
Boise, Ida.	124,657	Halifax, N.S.	151,836	Newport Beach, Cal.	121,137	Shreveport, La.	210,292
Boston, Mass.	509,534	Hamilton, Ont.	219,215	Newport News, Va.	208,625	Skokie, Ill.	145,306
Bridgeport, Conn.	181,444	Harrisburg, Pa.	206,752	Norfolk (Area), Va.	453,912	South Bend, Ind.	139,876
Buffalo, N.Y.	424,880	Hartford, Conn.	321,387	Oak Lawn, Ill.	122,299	Southfield, Mich.	114,441
Calgary, Alta.	447,649	Hayward, Cal.	142,399	Oklahoma City, Okla.	616,070	Spokane, Wash.	222,829
Cambridge, Mass.	111,498	Hollywood, Fla.	216,671	Omaha, Neb.	454,800	Springfield, Ill.	152,939
Canton, Oh.	126,750	Honolulu, Ha.	361,901	Orange, Cal.	116,293	Springfield, Mass.	154,908
Cedar Rapids, Ia.	125,900	Houston, Tex.	1,359,494	Orlando, Fla.	247,532	Springfield, Mo.	125,517
Champaign, Ill.	109,886	Huntington Beach, Cal.	137,054	Ottawa, Ont.	463,327	Stamford, Conn.	113,574
Charleston, S.C.	204,475	Huntsville, Ala.	145,724	Overland Pk., Kan.	131,630	Stockton, Cal.	142,591
Charleston, W. Va.	174,296	Indianapolis, Ind.	670,039	Palo Alto, Cal.	156,381	Sunnyvale, Cal.	114,824
Charlotte, N.C.	351,982	Jackson, Miss.	205,315	Passaic, N.J.	141,904	Syracuse, N.Y.	258,611
Chattanooga, Tenn.	244,797	Jacksonville, Fla.	418,919	Paterson, N.J.	127,387	Tacoma, Wash.	254,491
Chicago, Ill.	2,610,000	Jersey City, N.J.	183,048	Pensacola, Fla.	147,013	Tampa, Fla.	387,000
Cincinnati, Oh.	740,074	Kalamazoo, Mich.	151,553	Peoria, Ill.	197,631	Toledo, Oh.	306,704
Clearwater, Fla.	200,181	Kansas City, Kan.	170,627	Philadelphia, Pa.	1,683,341	Topeka, Kan.	121,820
Cleveland, Oh.	911,182	Kansas City, Mo.	342,558	Phoenix, Ariz.	942,847	Toronto, Ont.	1,741,760
Colorado Springs, Col.	210,816	Kitchener, Ont.	131,878	Pittsburgh, Pa.	810,193	Tucson, Ariz.	309,266
Columbia, S.C.	271,618	Knoxville, Tenn.	214,420	Pomona, Cal.	197,128	Tulsa, Okla.	401,445
Columbus, Ga.	140,291	Lancaster, Pa.	110,089	Pompano Beach, Fla.	177,894	Union City, N.J.	130,536
Columbus, Oh.	473,954	Lansing, Mich.	225,661	Pontiac, Mich.	123,454	Vancouver, B.C.	445,671
Corpus Christi, Tex.	147,287	Las Vegas, Nev.	369,811	Portland, Ore.	493,172	Victoria, B.C.	146,193
Covington, Ky.	120,423	Lexington, Ky.	163,114	Providence, R.I.	277,826	Warren, Mich.	313,496
Dallas, Tex.	809,921	Lincoln, Neb.	160,900	Quebec City	285,622	Washington, D.C.	1,038,376
Davenport, Ia.	117,100	Little Rock, Ark.	222,619	Raleigh, N.C.	199,119	West Palm Beach, Fla.	284,551
Dayton, Oh.	371,496	Livonia, Mich.	177,722	Reading, Pa.	162,804	Wichita, Kan.	237,310
Denver, Col.	1,186,519	London, Ont.	142,495	Regina, Sask.	124,322	Wilmington, Del.	199,127
Des Moines, Ia.	274,000	Los Angeles, Cal.		Reno, Nev.	139,218	Windsor, Ont.	135,078
Detroit, Mich.	1,510,543	(Area)	5,861,543	Richmond, Va.	388,196	Winnipeg, Man.	421,158
Durham, N.C.	111,443	Louisville, Ky.	563,848	Riverside, Cal.	164,987	Winston-Salem, N.C.	172,291
East Orange, N.J.	133,530	Lubbock, Tex.	161,860	Roanoke, Va.	129,910	Winter Park, Fla.	132,329
Edmonton, Alta.	405,139	Macon, Ga.	117,716	Rochester, N.Y.	360,819	Worcester, Mass.	141,817
El Paso, Tex.	262,710	Madison, Wis.	196,310	Rockford, Ill.	190,401	Youngstown, Oh.	187,225

ENERGY

Nuclear Power Reactors in U.S.

Source: Technical Information Center, U.S. Energy Department

State	Site	Plant name	Capacity (kilowatts)	Utility	Commercial operation
Alabama	Decatur	Browns Ferry Unit 1	1,065,000	Tennessee Valley Authority	1974
	Decatur	Browns Ferry Unit 2	1,065,000	Tennessee Valley Authority	1975
	Decatur	Browns Ferry Unit 3	1,065,000	Tennessee Valley Authority	1977
	Dothan	Joseph M. Farley Unit 1	829,000	Alabama Power Co.	1977
Arkansas	Russellville	Arkansas Unit 1	850,000	Ark. Power & Light Co.	1974
	Russellville	Arkansas Unit 2	912,000	Ark. Power & Light Co.	1979
California	Eureka	Humboldt Bay Unit 3	63,000	Pacific Gas & Electric Co.	1963
	San Clemente	San Onofre Unit 1	430,000	So. Calif. Ed. & San Diego Gas & El. Co.	1968
	Diablo Canyon	Diablo Canyon Unit 1	1,084,000	Pacific Gas & Electric Co.	1979
	Diablo Canyon	Diablo Canyon Unit 2	1,106,000	Pacific Gas & Electric Co.	1979
	Clay Station	Rancho Seco Station	918,000	Sacramento Munic. Utility District	1975
Colorado	Platteville	Ft. St. Vrain Station	330,000	Public Service Co. of Colorado	1978
Connecticut	Haddam Neck	Haddam Neck	575,000	Conn. Yankee Atomic Power Co.	1968
	Waterford	Millstone Unit 1	660,000	Northeast Nuclear Energy Co.	1971
	Waterford	Millstone Unit 2	830,000	Northeast Nuclear Energy Co.	1975
Florida	Florida City	Turkey Point Unit 3	693,000	Fla. Power & Light Co.	1972
	Florida City	Turkey Point Unit 4	693,000	Fla. Power & Light Co.	1973
	Red Level	Crystal River Unit 3	825,000	Florida Power Corp.	1977
	Ft. Pierce	St. Lucie Unit 1	802,000	Fla. Power & Light Co.	1976
Georgia	Baxley	Edwin I. Hatch Unit 1	786,000	Georgia Power Co.	1975
	Baxley	Edwin 1. Hatch Unit 2	795,000	Georgia Power Co.	1978
Illinois	Morris	Dresden Unit 1	200,000	Commonwealth Edison Co.	1960
	Morris	Dresden Unit 2	794,000	Commonwealth Edison Co.	1970
	Morris	Dresden Unit 3	794,000	Commonwealth Edison Co.	1971
	Zion	Zion Unit 1	1,040,000	Commonwealth Edison Co.	1973
	Zion	Zion Unit 2	1,040,000	Commonwealth Edison Co.	1974
	Cordova	Quad-Cities Unit 1	789,000	Comm. Ed. Co.-Ia.-Ill. Gas & Elec. Co.	1973
	Cordova	Quad-Cities Unit 2	789,000	Comm. Ed. Co.-Ia.-Ill. Gas & Elec. Co.	1973
	Seneca	LaSalle County Unit 1	1,078,000	Commonwealth Edison Co.	1979
Iowa	Palo	Duane Arnold Unit 1	538,000	Iowa Electric Light and Power Co.	1975
Maine	Wiscasset	Maine Yankee	790,000	Me. Yankee Atomic Power Co.	1972
Maryland	Lusby	Calvert Cliffs Unit 1	845,000	Baltimore Gas & Electric Co.	1975
	Lusby	Calvert Cliffs Unit 2	845,000	Baltimore Gas & Electric Co.	1977
Massachusetts	Rowe	Yankee Station	175,000	Yankee Atomic Electric Co.	1961
	Plymouth	Pilgrim Unit 1	655,000	Boston Edison Co.	1972
Michigan	Big Rock Point	Big Rock Point	72,000	Consumers Power Co.	1963
	South Haven	Palisades Station	805,000	Consumers Power Co.	1971
	Bridgman	Donald C. Cook Unit 1	1,054,000	Ind. & Michigan Electric Co.	1975
	Bridgman	Donald C. Cook Unit 2	1,100,000	Ind. & Michigan Electric Co.	1978
Minnesota	Monticello	Monticello	545,000	Northern States Power Co.	1971
	Red Wing	Prairie Island Unit 1	530,000	Northern States Power Co.	1973
	Red Wing	Prairie Island Unit 2	530,000	Northern States Power Co.	1974
Nebraska	Fort Calhoun	Ft. Calhoun Unit 1	457,000	Omaha Public Power District	1973
	Brownville	Cooper Station	778,000	Neb. Pub. Power Dist.-Ia. Power & Light Co.	1974
New Jersey	Toms River	Oyster Creek Unit 1	650,000	Jersey Central Power & Light Co.	1969
	Salem	Salem Unit 1	1,090,000	Public Service Electric & Gas, N.J.	1977
	Salem	Salem Unit 2	1,115,000	Public Service Electric & Gas, N.J.	1979
New York	Buchanan	Indian Point Unit 1	265,000	Consolidated Edison Co.	1962
	Buchanan	Indian Point Unit 2	873,000	Consolidated Edison Co.	1973
	Buchanan	Indian Point Unit 3	965,000	Power Authority of State of N.Y.	1976
	Ontario	R.E. Ginna Unit 1	490,000	Rochester Gas & Electric Co.	1970
	Scriba	James A. FitzPatrick	821,000	Power Authority of State of N.Y.	1975
North Carolina	Southport	Brunswick Steam Unit 1	821,000	Carolina Power & Light Co.	1977
	Southport	Brunswick Steam Unit 2	821,000	Carolina Power & Light Co.	1975
	Cowans Ford Dam	Wm. B. McGuire Unit 1	1,180,000	Duke Power Co.	1979
Ohio	Oak Harbor	Davis-Besse Unit 1	906,000	Toledo Edison-Cleveland El. Illum. Co.	1977
Oregon	Prescott	Trojan Unit 1	1,130,000	Portland Gen. Electric Co.	1976
Pennsylvania	Peach Bottom	Peach Bottom Unit 2	1,065,000	Philadelphia Electric Co.	1974
	Peach Bottom	Peach Bottom Unit 3	1,065,000	Philadelphia Electric Co.	1974
	Shippingport	Shippingport Station	60,000	U.S. Energy Department	1957
	Shippingport	Beaver Valley Unit 1	852,000	Duquesne Light Co.-Ohio Edison Co.	1976
	Middletown	Three Mile Island Unit 1	819,000	Metropolitan Edison Co.	1974
	Middletown	Three Mile Island Unit 2	906,000	Jersey Central Power & Light Co.	1978
South Carolina	Hartsville	H. B. Robinson Unit 2	700,000	Carolina Power & Light Co.	1971
	Seneca	Oconee Unit 1	887,000	Duke Power Co.	1973
	Seneca	Oconee Unit 2	887,000	Duke Power Co.	1974
	Seneca	Oconee Unit 3	887,000	Duke Power Co.	1974
	Broad River	Virgil C. Summer Station	900,000	So. Carolina Electric & Gas Co.	1980
Tennessee	Daisy	Sequoyah Unit 1	1,148,000	Tennessee Valley Authority	1979
	Daisy	Sequoyah Unit 2	1,148,000	Tennessee Valley Authority	1980
	Spring City	Watts Bar Unit 1	1,177,000	Tennessee Valley Authority	1979
Vermont	Vernon	Vermont Yankee Station	514,000	Vt. Yankee Nuclear Power Corp.	1972
Virginia	Gravel Neck	Surry Unit 1	822,000	Va. Electric & Power Co.	1972
	Gravel Neck	Surry Unit 2	822,000	Va. Electric & Power Co.	1973
	Mineral	North Anna Unit 1	907,000	Va. Electric & Power Co.	1978
	Mineral	North Anna Unit 2	907,000	Va. Electric & Power Co.	1979
Washington	Richland	N-Reactor/WPPSS Steam	850,000	U.S. Energy Department	1966
	Richland	WPPSS Nuclear No. 2	1,100,000	Washington Public Power Supply System	1980
Wisconsin	La Crosse	Genoa Station	50,000	Dairyland Power Cooperative	1969
	Two Creeks	Point Beach Unit 1	497,000	Wis. Mich. Power Co.	1970
	Two Creeks	Point Beach Unit 2	497,000	Wis. Mich. Power Co.	1972
	Carlton	Kewaunee Unit 1	535,000	Wis. Public Service Corp.	1974

Nuclear plant capacity (kilowatts): operable 51,527,000; being built 100,824,400; planned 33,076,000; Total 190,449,400.

World Nuclear Power

Source: Energy Information Agency, U.S. Energy Department

Country	Operational reactors	Capacity[1]	Generation[2] 1979	Country	Operational reactors	Capacity[1]	Generation[2] 1979
Argentina	1	360	2.7	Netherlands	2	520	3.5
Belgium	3	1,740	11.4	Pakistan	1	140	0
Canada	8	5,590	38.4	South Korea	1	590	3.2
Finland	2	1,150	6.7	Spain	3	1,120	6.7
France	15	7,800	39.9	Sweden	6	3,850	21.0
Germany, W.	10	7,050	40.4	Switzerland	3	1,060	11.8
Great Britain	33	9,040	38.6	Taiwan	2	1,270	6.3
India	3	620	2.9	U.S.	71	54,180	270.7
Italy	4	1,490	2.6	**Total[3]**	**189**	**110,410[4]**	**568.8**
Japan	20	12,840	62.0				

(1) Thousand kilowatts. (2) Billion kilowatt hours. (3) Non-Communist countries. (4) Total may not equal sum of components due to independent rounding.

World Electricity Production

Source: UN Monthly Bulletin of Statistics, July 1980 (1979 production, in million kilowatt-hours.)

U.S.	2,247,652	Italy	180,522	Sweden	92,398	Romania[4]	59,856
USSR[1]	1,239,998	China[2]	121,000	Australia	93,701	Mexico[4]	50,052
Japan	512,070	Poland	117,460	South Africa[3]	84,384	Yugoslavia	54,879
W. Germany	374,219	Spain	105,411	Norway	89,008	Belgium	52,254
Canada	352,303	E. Germany	95,952[3]	Czechoslovakia	67,897	Switzerland	42,710
United Kingdom	299,960	India	106,060	Netherlands	64,457	Austria	40,463
France	241,124	Brazil[1]	99,864[4]				

(1) Estimated figures for Jan., March. (2) 1975 estimate. (3) 1978. (4) 1977.

Production of Electricity in the U.S. by Source

Source: Energy Information Administration, U.S. Energy Department
Amounts include both privately-owned and publicly-owned utilities.

Calendar Year	Net production million kwh	Percentage produced by source: Coal	Oil	Gas	Nuclear	Hydro	Other[1]	Fuel Consumption: Coal 1,000 sht. tns.	Oil 1,000 bbls.	Gas million cu. ft.
1971	1,612,593	44.3	13.6	23.2	2.4	16.5	0.05	327,887	396,468	3,975,971
1974	1,867,103	44.5	16.0	17.2	6.1	16.1	0.1	392,423	536,245	3,443,293
1975	1,917,638	44.5	15.1	15.6	9.0	15.6	0.2	406,029	506,128	3,157,584
1976	2,037,775	46.4	15.7	14.4	9.4	13.9	0.2	448,456	555,937	3,081,286
1977	2,124,580	46.4	16.8	14.4	11.8	10.4	0.2	477,229	623,742	3,191,948
1978	2,206,515	44.2	16.5	13.8	12.5	12.7	0.2	481,254	635,600	3,188,306
1979	2,247,372	47.8	13.5	14.7	11.4	12.4	0.2	527,051	523,565	3,490,523

(1) Includes electricity produced from geothermal power, wood, and waste.

U.S. Petroleum Imports by Source

Source: Department of Energy
(in thousands of barrels per day)

Nation	1975	1976	1977	1978	1979
Algeria	288.2	438.3	565.2	632.1	630.5
Indonesia	437.7	569.4	576.2	538.2	416.9
Iran	524.8	546.5	786.4	544.7	303.2
Libya	329.3	529.3	837.7	641.1	654.0
Nigeria	837.8	1,119.2	1,229.6	904.7	1,077.6
Saudi Arabia	891.6	1,365.8	1,523.8	1,137.2	1,346.8
United Arab Emirates	154.2	323.2	446.3	378.4	279.7
Venezuela	1,030.1	972.2	908.8	633.5	691.1
Other OPEC[1]	259.3	216.0	378.1	224.0	212.2
Total OPEC	**4,753.0**	**6,079.9**	**7,252.2**	**5,636.9**	**5,612.0**
Arab OPEC Members	1,790.1	2,773.0	3,636.5	2,920.8	3,037.4
Bahamas	152.0	116.5	168.0	158.4	147.7
Canada	845.2	599.3	502.8	468.6	532.5
Neth'lands Antilles	323.6	274.6	218.3	317.8	231.3
Puerto Rico	89.7	88.1	102.8	230.1	91.8
Trinidad/Tobago	240.9	272.6	286.0	89.4	186.3
Virgin Islands	406.5	422.3	468.7	251.0	431.5
Mexico	71.4	87.1	179.3	426.8	434.1
Other non-OPEC	306.1	373.5	657.1	649.9	744.0
Total non-OPEC	**2,435.4**	**2,234.0**	**2,583.0**	**2,591.5**	**2,799.1**
Total imports (avg.)	**6,056.0**	**7,313.0**	**8,714.0**	**10,843.7**	**NA**

(1) Ecuador, Gabon, Iraq, Kuwait, Qatar. (2) Imports do not add to totals because OPEC figures include petroleum transshipped through, and usually refined in, other countries and counted again as imports from those countries. NA-Not available.

World Production of Crude Oil

Twenty Leading Nations

(thousands of barrels)
Source: Energy Information Administration, U.S. Energy Dept.

Nation	1978 Production	1978 % of total world production
1. USSR	4,093,475	18.5%
2. United States[1]	3,175,927	14.3
3. Saudi Arabia	3,113,470	14.0
4. Iran	1,900,555	8.6
5. Iraq	959,585	4.3
6. Venezuela	790,418	3.6
7. People's Republic of China	731,825	3.3
8. Libya	727,445	3.3
9. Nigeria	697,150	3.2
10. Kuwait	680,725	3.1
11. United Arab Emirates	668,680	3.0
12. Indonesia	597,505	2.7
13. Canada[1]	483,260	2.2
14. Algeria[1]	447,125	2.0
15. Mexico[1]	440,555	2.0
16. United Kingdom	394,930	1.8
17. Qatar	176,537	0.8
18. Neutral Zone	170,090	0.8
19. Egypt	169,360	0.8
20. Argentina	165,195	0.8
Total World	**22,158,251**	**100.0**

Nation	1979 Production	1979 % of total world production
1. USSR	4,186,550	18.6%
2. Saudi Arabia	3,374,425	14.7
3. United States[1]	3,111,625	13.7
4. Iraq	1,253,775	5.5
5. Iran	1,107,775	5.0
6. Venezuela	859,575	3.8
7. Nigeria	841,325	3.7
8. Kuwait	808,475	3.5
9. People's Republic of China	773,800	3.4
10. Libya	753,725	3.3
11. United Arab Emirates	669,775	2.9
12. Indonesia	580,350	2.5
13. United Kingdom	573,050	2.5
14. Canada[1]	545,675	2.4
15. Mexico[1]	532,900	2.3
16. Algeria[1]	414,275	1.8
17. Neutral Zone	206,225	0.9
18. Egypt	186,150	0.8
19. Qatar	184,325	0.8
20. Brunei-Malaysia	182,500	0.8
Total World	**22,765,050**	**100.0**

(1) Includes lease condensate

World Oil Supply and Demand Projections

Source: Central Intelligence Agency
(million barrels per day)

	1976	1977	1978	1979	1980	1985
Demand (non-Communist)	**48.4**	**49.8-50.5**	**51.2-52.2**	**52.5-54.1**	**54.9-56.7**	**68.3-72.6**
United States	16.7	17.8-18.3	18.2-19.0	18.4-19.7	19.3-20.7	22.2-25.6
West Europe	13.6	13.9-14.3	13.8-14.2	13.7-14.4	13.7-14.7	15.8-18.2
Japan	5.2	5.3-5.4	5.5-5.8	5.9-6.2	6.2-6.6	8.1-8.8
Canada	2.0	2.0-2.1	2.1-2.2	2.2-2.3	2.2-2.4	2.9-3.5
Other developed[1]	1.2	1.2	1.3	1.3	1.4	1.9
Non-OPEC LDCs[2]	6.7	7.1	7.5	7.8	8.5	12.0
OPEC[3] countries	2.1	2.3	2.5	2.8	3.0	4.0
Other demand[4]	0.9	0	0	0	0	0
Non-OPEC supply[5]	**17.5**	**18.5**	**20.1**	**21.2**	**22.0**	**20.4-22.4**
United States	9.7	9.6	10.2	10.2	10.0	10.0-11.0
West Europe	0.9	1.8	2.5	3.1	3.7	4.0-5.0
Japan	0	0	0	0	0	0.1
Canada	1.6	1.6	1.5	1.5	1.5	1.3-1.5
Other developed[1]	0.5	0.5	0.5	0.5	0.5	0.4
Non-OPEC LDCs	3.7	4.1	4.6	5.3	6.1	8.0-9.0
Net Communist trade[6]						
USSR-East Europe	0.9	0.7	0.5	0.2	−0.3	−3.5−4.5
China	0.2	0.2	0.3	0.4	0.5	0
Required OPEC production[7]	**30.9**	**31.3-32.0**	**31.1-32.1**	**31.3-32.9**	**32.9-34.7**	**46.7-51.2**

(1) Australia, Israel, New Zealand, South Africa. (2) LDCs: less developed countries. (3) OPEC: Organization of Petroleum Exporting Countries. (4) Including stock changes and statistical discrepancy. (5) Including natural gas liquids. (6) Difference of Communist countries' exports and imports; minus sign indicates net Communist imports. (7) OPEC production capacity will reach 27.5-29.4 million barrels per day by 1985, exclusive of Saudi Arabia; Saudi projections are uncertain.

U.S. Dependence on Petroleum Imports

Source: Department of Energy
(million barrels per day average)

Source	1974	1975	1976	1977	1978	1979	1980 (1st Qtr.)
Arab nations	0.75	1.38	2.42	3.18	2.96	3.04	2.96
All OPEC	3.28	3.60	5.07	6.19	5.64	5.61	4.89
All nations	6.11	6.06	7.31	8.81	8.23	8.41	7.79
U.S. production	16.65	16.32	17.46	18.43	18.82	18.43	18.12

U.S. Crude Oil Reserves

Source: American Petroleum Institute

Estimates of proved reserves, which can be recovered under present economic relationships and known technology. Improved technology or higher world prices would increase estimates of reserves. Cumulative production for all years through Dec. 31, 1978 was 117,766,214 thousand barrels.

(thousands of 42-gallon barrels)

Year	Discoveries, revisions, extensions	Production	Proved reserves at end of year	Change from previous year[1]
1947	2,464,570	1,850,445	21,487,685	614,125
1948	3,795,207	2,002,448	23,280,444	1,792,759
1949	3,187,845	1,818,800	24,649,489	1,369,045
1950	2,562,685	1,943,776	25,268,398	618,909
1951	4,413,954	2,214,321	27,468,031	2,199,633
1952	2,749,288	2,256,765	27,960,554	492,523
1953	3,296,130	2,311,856	28,944,828	984,274
1954	2,873,037	2,257,119	29,560,746	615,918
1955	2,870,724	2,419,300	30,012,170	451,424
1956	2,974,336	2,551,857	30,434,649	422,479
1957	2,424,800	2,559,044	30,300,405	(134,244)
1958	2,608,242	2,372,730	30,535,917	235,512
1959	3,666,745	2,483,315	31,719,347	1,183,430
1960	2,365,328	2,471,464	31,613,211	(106,136)
1961	2,657,567	2,512,273	31,758,505	145,294
1962	2,180,896	2,550,178	31,389,223	(369,282)
1963	2,174,110	2,593,343	30,969,990	(419,233)
1964	2,664,767	2,644,247	30,990,510	20,520
1965	3,048,079	2,686,198	31,352,391	361,881
1966	2,963,978	2,864,242	31,452,127	99,736
1967	2,962,122	3,037,579	31,376,670	(75,457)
1968	2,454,635	3,124,188	30,707,117	(669,553)
1969	2,120,036	3,195,291	29,631,862	(1,075,255)
1970	12,688,918	3,319,445	39,001,335	9,369,473
1971	2,317,732	3,256,110	38,062,957	(938,378)
1972	1,557,848	3,281,397	36,339,408	(1,723,549)
1973	2,145,831	3,185,400	35,299,839	(1,039,569)
1974	1,993,573	3,043,456	34,249,956	(1,049,883)
1975	1,318,463	2,886,292	32,682,127	(1,567,829)
1976	1,085,291	2,825,252	30,942,166	(1,739,961)
1977	1,403,780	2,859,544	29,486,402	(1,455,764)
1978	1,347,265	3,029,898	27,803,760	(1,682,642)
1979	2,205,673	2,958,144	27,051,289	(752,471)

(1) Parenthesis indicate decline.

U.S. Crude Petroleum Production by Chief States

Source: Energy Information Administration, U.S. Energy Department (thousands of 42-gallon barrels)

Year	Alas.	Cal.	Col.	Fla.	Kan.	La.	Miss.	N.M.	Okla.	Tex.	Wyo.
1950	0	327,607	23,303	487	107,586	208,965	38,236	47,367	164,599	829,874	61,631
1960	559	305,352	47,469	369	113,453	400,832	51,673	107,380	192,913	927,479	133,910
1965	11,128	316,428	33,511	1,462	104,733	594,853	56,183	119,166	203,441	1,000,749	138,314
1970	83,616	372,191	24,723	12,999	84,853	906,907	65,119	128,184	223,574	1,249,697	160,345
1972	72,893	347,022	32,015	16,897	73,744	891,827	61,100	110,525	207,633	1,301,685	140,011
1974	70,603	323,003	37,508	36,351	61,691	737,324	50,779	98,695	177,785	1,262,126	139,997
1975	69,834	322,199	38,089	41,877	59,106	650,840	46,614	95,063	163,123	1,221,929	135,943
1976	63,398	326,021	38,992	44,460	58,714	606,501	46,072	92,130	161,426	1,189,523	134,149
1977	169,201	349,609	39,460	46,641	57,496	562,905	43,022	87,223	156,382	1,137,880	136,472
1978	448,620	347,181	36,797	47,536	56,586	532,740	39,494	83,365	150,456	1,074,050	137,385
1979	511,538	352,465	32,251	47,170	56,995	494,462	38,286	79,379	143,642	1,013,255	124,553

U.S. Petroleum and Natural Gas Production

Source: Energy Information Administration, U.S. Energy Department

Year	Crude oil		Natural gas liquids		Total oil & N.G.L.	Natural gas	
	Production 1,000 bbls.	Value $1,000	Production 1,000 bbls.	Value $1,000	1,000 bbls.	Marketed mil. cu. ft.	Value $1,000
1945	1,713,655	2,094,250	112,004	187,564	1,828,539	3,944,021	191,006
1950	1,973,574	4,963,380	181,961	419,605	2,155,693	6,282,060	408,521
1955	2,484,428	6,870,380	281,371	619,006	2,766,325	9,405,351	978,357
1960	2,574,933	7,420,181	340,157	808,385	2,915,365	12,771,038	1,789,970
1965	2,848,514	8,158,298	441,556	911,603	3,290,083	16,042,753	2,494,542
1970	3,517,450	11,173,726	605,916	1,275,112	4,123,366	21,920,642	3,745,680
1975	3,056,779	23,116,059	595,958	2,772,588	3,652,737	20,108,661	8,945,062
1976	2,976,180	24,229,540	587,045	3,284,089	3,563,225	19,952,438	11,571,776
1977	2,986,710	25,397,307	584,900	4,386,750	3,571,610	19,924,671	15,522,658
1978	3,178,216	28,476,815	572,320	NA	3,578,892	19,690,000	18,095,009

Average Consumer Cost of Fuels

Source: Department of Energy
(1972 constant dollars)

Fuel	1974	1975	1976	1977	1978	1979	1980/1st qtr.
Leaded regular gasoline (cent/gal)	44.8	43.7	43.1	43.2	41.0	49.8	61.5
Residential heating oil (cent/gal)	29.4	29.3	30.2	31.2	31.7	40.8	49.8
Residential natural gas (cent/Mcf)	123.4	132.8	145.4	162.2	163.5	185.3	190.8
Residential electricity (cent/kWh)	2.63	2.73	2.77	2.81	2.76	2.66	NA

Mcf=million cubic feet; kWh=million kilowatt hours.
NA-Not available

U.S. Total Fuel Supply and Demand

Source: Energy Information Administration, U.S. Energy Department

(thousands of 42-gallon barrels)

Year	Gasoline[1] Production	Gasoline[1] Total demand	Kerosene[2] Production	Kerosene[2] Total demand	Distillate fuel oil Production	Distillate fuel oil Total demand	Residual fuel oil Production	Residual fuel oil Total demand
1950[3] . . .	1,024,181	1,019,011	118,512	119,922	398,912	75,435	425,217	570,021
1960. . . .	1,522,497	1,525,126	136,842	133,188	667,050	695,165	332,147	577,934
1965. . . .	1,733,258	1,756,419	201,788	219,932	765,430	779,644	268,567	601,893
1970. . . .	2,135,838	2,165,598	313,544	358,146	897,097	928,109	257,510	824,073
1971. . . .	2,231,157	2,246,025	306,847	365,308	912,097	974,077	274,684	851,262
1972. . . .	2,352,310	2,384,734	313,554	379,984	963,625	1,067,321	292,519	937,707
1974. . . .	2,371,004	2,436,681	290,780	346,706	974,025	1,076,771	390,491	968,185
1975. . . .	2,420,962	2,479,857	308,034	347,399	968,650	1,040,838	450,957	903,914
1976. . . .	2,549,627	2,597,305	323,114	350,565	1,070,209	1,146,695	503,953	1,025,148
1977. . . .	2,565,950	2,625,080	355,145	376,680	1,192,090	1,213,990	635,100	1,111,425
1978. . . .	2,612,670	2,702,095	354,415	386,900	1,153,765	1,242,825	615,390	1,103,395
1979. . . .	2,494,655	2,566,128	368,707	391,650	1,148,778	1,207,278	614,806	1,029,913

Demand usually exceeds the production; the difference is made up by dipping into stocks or by imports. (1) Includes special naphtha production. (2) Includes kerosene type jet fuel. (3) 1950 figures are on a 48-state basis.

U.S. Natural Gas Reserves

Source: American Gas Association

Estimates of proved reserves, which can be recovered under existing economic and operating conditions.

Year	Natural gas (millions of cu. ft.) Discoveries, revisions and extensions	Change in underground storage[1]	Production[4]	Proved reserves at end of year	Natural gas liquids (1,000 42-gallon barrels) Discoveries, revisions and extensions	Production[4]	Proved reserves at end of year
1946	17,632,864	(2)	4,915,774	159,703,813	(2)	129,262	3,163,219
1947	10,921,187	(2)	5,599,235	165,025,765	251,538	160,782	3,253,975
1948	13,823,090	51,202	5,975,001	172,925,056	470,557	183,749	3,540,783
1949	12,605,615	82,146	6,211,124	179,401,693	386,776	198,547	3,729,012
1950	11,985,361	52,935	6,855,244	184,584,745	766,062	227,411	4,267,663
1951	15,965,808	132,030	7,923,673	192,758,910	723,991	267,052	4,724,602
1952	14,267,606	197,766	8,592,716	198,631,566	556,838	284,789	4,996,651
1953	20,341,933	513,629[3]	9,188,365	210,298,763	743,969	302,698	5,437,922
1954	9,547,074	90,408	9,375,314	210,560,931	107,350	300,815	5,244,457
1955	21,897,616	87,164	10,063,167	222,482,544	514,508	320,400	5,438,565
1956	24,716,115	133,241	10,848,685	236,483,215	809,820	346,053	5,902,332
1957	20,008,051	178,761	11,439,890	245,230,137	137,392	352,364	5,687,360
1958	18,896,724	57,582	11,422,651	252,761,792	858,206	341,548	6,204,018
1959	20,621,249	160,453	12,373,063	261,170,431	703,444	385,154	6,522,308
1960	13,893,978	281,273	13,019,356	262,326,326	725,130	431,379	6,816,059
1961	17,166,421	159,544	13,378,649	266,273,642	694,686	461,649	7,049,096
1962	19,483,958	159,231	13,637,973	272,278,858	732,549	470,128	7,311,517
1963	18,164,667	253,733	14,546,025	276,151,233	878,120	515,659	7,673,978
1964	20,252,139	195,110	15,347,028	281,251,454	608,744	536,090	7,746,632
1965	21,319,279	150,483	16,252,293	286,468,923	832,312	555,410	8,023,534
1966	20,220,432	134,523	17,491,073	289,332,805	894,116	588,684	8,328,966
1967	21,804,333	151,403	18,380,838	292,907,703	929,758	644,493	8,614,231
1968	13,697,008	118,568	19,373,427	287,349,852	685,659	701,782	8,598,108
1969	8,375,004	107,169	20,723,190	275,108,835	281,028	735,962	8,143,174
1970	37,196,359	402,018	21,960,804	290,746,408	307,579	747,812	7,702,941
1971	9,825,421	310,301	22,076,512	278,805,618	347,720	746,434	7,304,227
1972	9,634,563	156,563	22,511,898	266,084,846	238,273	755,941	6,786,559
1973	6,825,049	(354,282)	22,605,406	249,950,207	408,979	740,831	6,454,707
1974	8,679,184	(178,424)	21,318,470	237,132,497	619,841	724,099	6,350,449
1975	10,483,688	302,561	19,718,570	228,200,176	618,504	701,123	6,267,830
1976	7,555,468	(187,550)	19,542,020	216,026,074	834,766	700,629	6,401,967
1977	11,851,924	446,930	19,447,050	208,877,878	291,171	698,773	5,994,365
1978	10,586,144	148,733	19,311,048	200,301,707	595,666	664,179	5,925,852
1979	14,285,947	293,323	19,910,353	194,916,624	389,805	660,334	5,655,323

(1) Parentheses indicate decline. (2) Not estimated. (3) All native gas in storage reservoirs formerly classified as proved reserves is included in this figure. (4) Preliminary net production.

U.S. Energy Consumption per GNP Dollar

Source: Department of Energy
(Average thousand Btu per 1972 constant dollar)

1973	60.4	**1978**/1st qtr	63.1	**1979**/1st qtr	62.8	**1980**/1st qtr	59.3
1974	59.7	2nd qtr	52.4	2nd qtr	51.6		
1975	58.8	3rd qtr	52.1	3rd qtr	50.7		
1976	58.5	4th qtr	56.1	4th qtr	55.2		
1977	56.0	Average	55.9	Average	55.0		

U.S. Motor Fuel Supply and Demand

Source: Energy Information Administration, U.S. Energy Department

(thousands of 42-gallon barrels)

Year	Supply: Production	Supply: Daily average	Demand: Domestic	Demand: Export
1945	793,431	2,174	696,333	88,059
1950	1,024,481	2,806	994,290	24,721
1955	1,373,950	3,764	1,329,788	34,521
1960[2]	1,522,497	4,171	1,511,670	13,456
1965	1,733,258	4,749	1,750,028	6,391
1970	2,135,838	5,852	2,162,642	2,956
1971	2,231,157	6,113	2,242,921	3,104
1972	2,352,310	6,445	2,382,569	2,165
1973	2,434,943	6,671	2,484,262	3,318
1974	2,371,004	6,496	2,434,368	2,313
1975	2,420,962	6,633	2,477,786	2,071
1976	2,549,627	6,966	2,597,305	3,807
1977	2,566,315	7,031	2,619,605	2,155
1978	2,615,955	7,167	2,706,840	1,250
1979	2,513,937	7,030	2,580,080	NA[3]

(1) Includes special naphtha. (2) Beginning with 1960 Alaska and Hawaii are included. (3) Not available.

U.S. Passenger Car Efficiency

Source: Department of Energy

Year	Average fuel consumed per car: Gal.	Average fuel consumed per car: Index	Average miles traveled per car: Miles	Average miles traveled per car: Index	Average miles per gallon: Miles	Average miles per gallon: Index
1968	698	102.0	9,627	101.0	13.79	99.0
1969	718	105.0	9,782	102.6	13.63	97.8
1970	735	107.5	9,978	104.7	13.57	97.4
1971	746	109.1	10,121	106.2	13.57	97.4
1973	763	111.5	9,992	104.8	13.10	94.0
1974	704	102.9	9,448	99.1	13.43	96.4
1975	712	104.1	9,634	101.1	13.53	97.1
1976	711	103.9	9,763	102.4	13.72	98.5
1977	706	103.2	9,839	103.2	13.94	100.1
1978	715	104.5	10,046	105.4	14.06	100.9

Fuel Economy in 1981 Autos; Comparative Miles per Gallon

Source: U.S. Environmental Protection Agency

The mileage numbers and rankings below refer to testing completed through August 29, 1980. The testing of several major model types has not been completed when these data were released.

Make, model	Cu. in. displcmt.	Cylinders	Trans.[1]	Mileage
Alfa Romeo Spider	120	4	m	20
AMC Concord	258	6	a	19
AMC Spirit	258	6	a	20
Audi 4000	97	4	m	26
Audi 5000	131	5	a	19
BMW 320	108	4	m	25
BMW 528	170	6	m	18
BMW 633 CSI	196	6	m	16
BMW 733 I	196	6	a	16
Buick Century	231	6	a	21
Buick Electra	252	6	a	18
Buick LeSabre	252	6	a	18
Buick Regal	231	6	a	19
Buick Riviera	350	8	a	20
Buick Skyhawk	231	6	a	19
Buick Skylark	173	6	a	21
Cadillac Deville/ Brougham	350	8	a	21
Cadillac Eldorado, Seville	350	8	a	20
Chevrolet Camaro	229	6	a	19
Chevrolet Chevette	98	4	a	26
Chevrolet Citation	173	6	a	21
Chevrolet Impala/ Caprice	229	6	a	19
Chevrolet Corvette	350	8	a	15
Chevrolet Malibu	229	6	a	19
Chevrolet Monte Carlo	229	6	a	19
Chrysler Cordoba/300	225	6	a	18
Chrysler LeBaron	225	6	a	18
Chrysler Newport-N.Y.	225	6	a	17
Datsun 2-Seater 280zx	168	6	a	21
Datsun 210	85	4	m	36
Datsun 200SX	119	4	a	26
Datsun 310	91	4	m	32
Datsun 510	119	4	a	27
Datsun 810	146	6	m	23
Dodge Aries	135	4	m	25
Dodge Aspen	225	6	a	17
Dodge Challenger	156	4	a	21
Dodge Colt	98	4	a	28
Dodge DeTomaso	105	4	m	27
Dodge Diplomat	225	6	a	18
Dodge Miranda	225	6	a	18
Dodge St. Regis	225	6	a	17
Dodge Omni	104	4	m	28
Fiat Brava	122	4	a	24
Fiat Spider 2000	122	4	a	22
Fiat Strada	91	4	a	26
Ford Escort	98	4	m	30
Ford Fairmont	200	6	a	20
Ford Granada	200	6	a	19
Ford LTD	302	8	a	16
Ford Mustang	200	6	a	20
Ford Thunderbird	302	8	a	16
Honda Accord, Prelude	107	4	m	27
Honda Civic	91	4	m	35
Jaguar XJ	258	6	a	14
Mazda GLC	91	4	a	30
Mazda Rx7	70	2	a	16
Mercury Capri	200	6	a	20
Merc. Cougar XR7	302	8	a	16
Mercury Lynx	98	4	m	30
Mercury Marquis	302	8	a	16
Mercury Zephyr	200	6	a	20
Olds. Cutlass	231	6	a	21
Olds. Cutlass Sup.	260	8	a	19
Oldsmobile Delta 88	231	6	a	19
Oldsmobile 98	307	8	a	17
Oldsmobile Omega	151	4	a	23
Oldsmobile Toronado	252	6	m	17
Plymouth Champ	86	4	m	37
Plymouth Gran Fury	318	8	a	16
Plymouth Horizon/ Tourismo	105	4	a	25
Plymouth Reliant	135	4	m	25
Plym. Sapporo	156	4	a	21
Pontiac Cat.-Bonne	231	6	a	19
Pontiac Firebird	231	6	a	19
Pontiac Grand Prix	231	6	a	21
Pontiac LeMans	231	6	a	21
Pontiac Phoenix	173	6	a	21
Porsche 924	121	4	m	20
Porsche 928	273	8	m	16
Renault 181	100	4	m	24
Subaru	109	4	m	28
Toyota Celica	144	4	m	25
Toy. Cel. Supra	168	6	m	21
Toyota Corolla	108	4	a	27
Toyota Corona	144	4	a	25
Toyota Cressida	168	6	a	22
Toyota Starlet	79	4	m	39
Toyota Tercel	89	4	a	29
Volkswgn Diesl Rabt.	97	4	m	42
Volkswgn Jetta	105	4	m	25
Volkswgn Rabbit	105	4	a	25
Volkswgn Scirocco	105	4	a	25

(1) Type of transmission: a=automatic; m=manual.

Measuring Energy

Source: Energy Information Administration, U.S. Energy Dept.

The following tables of equivalents contain those figures commonly used to compare different types of energy sources and their various measurements.

Btu - a British thermal unit — the amount of heat required to raise one pound of water one degree Fahrenheit. Equivalent to 1,055 joules or about 252 gram calories. A **therm** is usually 100,000 Btu but is sometimes used to refer to other units.

Calorie - the amount of heat required to raise one gram of water one degree Centigrade; abbreviated cal.; equivalent to about .003968 Btu. More common is the kilogram calorie, also called a **kilocalorie** and abbreviated Cal. or Kcal; equivalent to about 3.97 Btu. (One Kcal is equivalent to one food calorie.)

Btu Values of Energy Sources

(These are conventional or average values, not precise equivalents.)

Coal (per 2,000 lb. ton):
- Anthracite = 23.0×10^6 Btu
- Bituminous = 22.1×10^6

Average heating value of coal used to generate electricity in 1979 was 21.1×10^6 Btu.

Natural gas (per cubic foot):
- Dry = 1,025 Btu
- Liquid (avg.) = 3,925

Electricity — 1 kwh = 3,412 Btu

Petroleum (per barrel):
- Crude oil = 5.80×10^6 Btu
- Residual fuel oil = 6.29×10^6
- Distillate fuel oil = 5.83×10^6
- Gasoline (including av gas) = 5.25×10^6
- Jet fuel (kerosene) = 5.67×10^6
- Jet fuel (naphtha) = 5.36×10^6
- Kerosene = 5.67×10^6

Nuclear — (per kilowatt-hour) = 10,769

The Btu and calorie, being small amounts of energy, are usually expressed as follows when large numbers are involved.

- 1×10^3 Btu = 1,000
- 1×10^6 = 1,000,000
- 1×10^9 = 1,000,000,000
- 1×10^{12} = 1 trillion
- 1×10^{15} = 1 quadrillion
- 1×10^{18} = 1 quintillion or 1 Q unit
- One Q unit = 38.46 billions tons of coal
  = 172.4 billion tons of oil
  = 968.9 trillion cubic ft. of natural gas

Other Conversion Factors

Electricity — 1 kwh. = 0.88 lbs. of coal
= 0.076 gallon of oil
= 10.4 cu. ft. of natural gas

Natural gas — 1 tcf (trillion cubic feet) = 39.3×10^6 tons of coal
= 184×10^6 barrels of oil

Coal — 1 mtce (million tons of coal equivalent) = 4.48×10^6 barrels of oil
= 667,000 tons of oil
= 25.19×10^{12} cu. ft. of natural gas

Oil — 1 million tons (6.65×10^6 barrels)
= 4×10^9 kwh of electricity (when used to generate power)
= 12×10^9 kwh uncoverted
= 1.5×10^6 tons of coal
= 41.2×10^9 cu. ft. of natural gas

Approximate Conversion Factors for Oils

To convert	Barrels to metric tons	Metric tons to barrels	Barrels/ days to tons/ year	Tons/year to barrels day
	Multiply by —			
Crude oil[1] . .	.136	7.33	49.8	.0201
Gasoline . .	.118	8.45	43.2	.0232
Kerosene . .	.128	7.80	46.8	.0214
Diesel fuel .	.133	7.50	48.7	.0205
Fuel oil . . .	.149	6.70	54.5	.0184

(1) Based on world average gravity (excluding natural gas liquids).

Coal and Coke Production in the U.S.

Source: Energy Information Administration, U.S. Energy Department

Year	Penn. anthracite Production 1,000 net tons	Penn. anthracite Value $1,000	Bituminous Production 1,000 net tons	Bituminous Value $1,000
1945	54,934	323,944	577,617	1,768,204
1950	44,077	392,398	516,311	2,500,374
1955	26,205	206,097	464,633	2,092,383
1960	18,817	147,116	415,512	1,950,421
1962	16,894	134,094	422,149	1,891,555
1963	18,267	153,503	458,928	2,013,390
1964	17,184	148,648	486,998	2,165,582
1965	14,866	122,021	512,088	2,276,022
1966	12,941	100,663	533,881	2,421,293
1967	12,256	96,160	552,026	2,555,377
1968	11,461	97,245	545,245	2,546,340
1969	10,473	100,769	560,505	2,795,509
1970	9,729	105,341	602,932	3,772,662
1971	8,727	103,469	552,192	3,901,496
1972	7,106	85,251	595,386	4,561,983
1973	6,830	90,260	591,738	5,049,612
1974	6,617	144,695	603,406	9,502,347
1975	6,203	198,481	648,438	12,472,486
1976	6,228	209,234	678,685	13,189,481
1977	5,861	202,373	691,300	13,700,000
1978	5,370	352,260	665,127	14,500,000
1979 est. . . .	5,750	375,000	770,000	18,095,000

Coke production (1,000 net tons—value in $1,000)—(1968) 63,653, $1,157,359; (1969) 64,757, $1,355,260; (1970) 66,525, $1,849,160; (1971) 57,436, $1,745,693; (1972) 60,507, $2,012,486; (1973) 64,325, $2,442,151; (1974) 61,581, $4,510,150; (1975) 57,207, $4,835,654; (1976) 58,333, $5,021,616; (1977) 53,510, $4,652,776; (1978) 49,010, $5,608,138.

Coke exports (short tons)—(1968) 791,909; (1969) 1,629,000; (1970) 2,478,338; (1971) 1,508,639; (1972) 1,231,633; (1973) 1,394,980; (1974) 1,277,681; (1975) 1,272,906; (1976) 1,314,725; (1977) 1,240,577. **Imports** —(1968) 94,085; (1969) 173,052; (1970) 152,879; (1971) 173,914; (1972) 185,023; (1973) 1,077,737; (1974) 3,540,326; (1975) 1,818,981; (1976) 1,311,472; (1977) 1,240,000; (1978) 69,000; (1979 est.) 1,440,000.

Anthracite exports (net tons)—(1966) 766,025; (1967) 594,797; (1968) 518,159; (1969) 627,492; (1970) 789,499; (1971) 671,024; (1972) 743,451; (1973) 716,546; (1974) 735,173; (1975) 639,601; (1976) 615,167; (1977) 624,908; (1978) 866,000; (1979) 1,233,000.

World's Largest Hydroelectric Generating Plants

Source: Water and Power Resources Service, U.S. Interior Dept.

Existing dams	Present megawatts	Ultimate megawatts	Year of initial operation
Grand Coulee, U.S.A.	6,263	10,080	1941
Krasnoyarsk, USSR	6,096	6,096	1968
Churchill Falls, Canada	5,225	5,225	1971
Bratsk, USSR	4,100	4,600	1964
Ilha Solteira, Brazil	2,650	2,650	1973
Volgograd 22d Congress, USSR	2,560	2,560	1958
Volga-VI Lenin (Kuibishev), USSR	2,300	2,300	1955
Iron Gates I, Romania/Yugoslavia	2,300	2,300	1970
Foz Do Areia, Brazil	2,250	2,250	—
John Day, U.S.A.	2,160	2,700	1968
W.A.C. Bennett, Canada	2,116	2,416	1969
Raul Leoni, Venezuela	2,100	10,100	1968
High Aswan (Sadd-el-Aali), Egypt	2,100	2,100	1967
Cabora Bassa, Mozambique	2,075	4,150	1975
Robert Moses-Niagara, U.S.A.	1,950	1,950	1961
Ludington, U.S.A.	1,872	1,872	1973
St. Lawrence Power Dam, U.S.A./Canada	1,824	1,824	1958
The Dalles, U.S.A.	1,807	1,807	1957
Paulo Afonso, Brazil	1,524	3,409	1955
Chief Joseph, U.S.A.	1,879	2,069	1956
Ust-Ipimsk, USSR	720	4,320	1974
Tarbela, Pakistan	700	2,100	1977
Guri, Venezuela	524	7,300	1967
Inga I, Zaire	360	2,820	1974
Salto Grande, Argentina/Uruguay	135	1,890	1979

Dams under construction	Present megawatts	Ultimate megawatts	Year of initial operation
Itaipu, Brazil/Paraguay	—	12,870	—
Sayanskaya, USSR	—	6,400	—
La Grande #2, Canada	—	5,328	1980
Sukhovo, USSR	—	4,500	—
Tucurui, Brazil	—	3,960	—
Rogunsky, USSR	—	3,600	—
Revelstoke, Canada	—	2,760	1983
Gezhouba, Peoples Republic of China	—	2,710	1986
Nurek, USSR	—	2,700	—
Sao Simao, Brazil	—	2,680	—
La Grande #4, Canada	—	2,637	1984
Yacyreta, Brazil/Paraguay	—	2,560	1985
Itaparica, Brazil	—	2,500	—
Attaturk, Turkey	—	2,400	1990
Chicoasen, Mexico	—	2,400	1980
La Grande #3, Canada	—	2,304	1982
Itumbiara, Brazil	—	2,124	—
Bath County, U.S.A.	—	2,100	—
Salto Santiago, Brazil	—	2,031	—
Dinorwic, Great Britain	—	1,880	1981
Karakaya, Turkey	—	1,800	1985
Grand Maison, France	—	1,800	1984

Non-Federal Hydroelectric Plants in U.S.

Capacities of 150,000 Kilowatts or More as of Jan 1, 1980

Source: Energy Information Administration, U.S. Energy Department

Auxiliary and pumped storage units are not included in hydroelectric capacities.

Plant	State	Owner	Kilowatts
Robert Moses, (Niagara)	New York	Power Authority State of New York	1,950,000
Rocky Reach	Washington	Chelan County PUD[2]	1,213,100
Robert Moses, (Massena)	New York	Power Authority State of New York	912,000
Wanapum	Washington	Grant County PUD No. 2	831,250
Priest Rapids	Washington	Grant County PUD No. 2	788,500
Wells	Washington	Douglas County PUD No. 1	774,250
Boundary	Washington	Seattle Department of Lighting	551,000
Conowingo	Maryland	Susquehanna Pow. Co., Phila. Elec. Pow. Co.	474,480
Hells Canyon	Oregon	Idaho Power Company	391,500
Brownlee	Idaho	Idaho Power Company	360,400
Ross	Washington	Seattle Department of Lighting Company	360,000
Edward G. Hyatt	California	California Department of Water Resources	351,000
Cowans Ford	North Carolina	Duke Power Company	350,000
Smith Mt.	Virginia	Appalachian Power Company	300,200
Mossyrock	Washington	City of Tacoma	300,000
New Colgate	California	Yuba County Water Agency	284,400
Noxon Rapids	Montana	The Washington Water Power Company	282,880
Round Butte	Oregon	Portland General Electric Company	247,050
Safe Harbor	Pennsylvania	Safe Harbor Water Power Corporation	226,500
Walter Bouldin[1]	Alabama	Alabama Power Company	225,000
Rock Island	Washington	Chelan County PUD No. 1	212,100
Swift No. 1	Washington	Pacific Power and Light Company	204,000
Cabinet Gorge	Idaho	The Washington Water Power Company	200,000
Saluda	South Carolina	South Carolina Electric and Gas Company	197,500
Oxbow	Oregon	Idaho Power Company	190,000
White Rock	California	Sacramento Municipal Utility District	190,000
Caribou No. 1 & 2	California	Pacific Gas and Electric Company	184,800
Gaston	North Carolina	Virginia Electric and Power Company	177,920
Lay Dam	Alabama	Alabama Power Company	177,000
Osage	Missouri	Union Electric Company of Missouri	172,000
Kerr	Montana	The Montana Power Company	168,000
King's River	California	King's River Conservation District	165,000
Lewis Smith	Alabama	Alabama Power Company	157,500
Keowee	South Carolina	Duke Power Company	157,500
James B. Black	California	Pacific Gas and Electric Company	154,800
Martin Dam	Alabama	Alabama Power Company	154,200

(1) Units out of service Feb. 1975 in dam failure. (2) Public utility district.

MANUFACTURES AND MINERALS

General Statistics for Major Industry Groups

Source: Bureau of the Census

The estimates for 1977 in the following table are based upon reports from a representative sample of about 70,000 manufacturing establishments.

Industry	All employees		Production workers			Value added by mfr.
	Number (1,000)	Payroll (millions)	Number (1,000)	Manhours (millions)	Wages (millions)	(millions)
Food & kindred products	1,515.4	$ 18,523.1	1,065.6	2,104.7	$ 11,714.0	$ 56,232.8
Tobacco mfg.	60.6	750.8	50.4	92.5	570.6	4,342.5
Textile mill prods.	870.2	7,849.1	759.4	1,514.6	6,148.4	15,965.2
Apparel and other textile prods.	1,331.6	9,648.3	1,151.8	2,032.2	7,223.5	19,448.1
Lumber & wood prods.	689.9	7,401.0	588.3	1,143.3	5,778.8	16,168.0
Furniture & fixtures	460.1	4,401.9	379.5	729.9	3,158.1	8,797.5
Paper & allied prods.	625.5	8,913.2	483.4	980.5	6,300.5	21,699.4
Printing & publishing	1,087.8	13,974.2	614.4	1,146.8	7,277.6	31,543.6
Chemicals & allied prods.	877.9	13,764.4	540.5	1,085.3	7,412.0	56,522.5
Petroleum & coal prods.	147.6	2,712.0	101.8	209.1	1,776.7	16,223.7
Rubber & plastic prods.	718.2	8,504.7	560.7	1,106.4	5,823.1	19,834.3
Leather & leather prods.	238.9	1,834.1	208.6	375.5	1,391.9	3,650.5
Stone, clay & glass prods.	607.0	7,840.8	477.2	949.0	5,692.9	18,800.1
Primary metal industries	1,117.6	18,794.8	887.7	1,749.3	14,096.3	37,298.2
Fabricated metal prods.	1,540.4	20,846.4	1,177.3	2,348.5	14,305.4	44,943.0
Machinery, except electric	2,082.2	30,583.3	1,407.3	2,794.5	18,266.4	67,406.0
Electric, electronic equip.	1,707.5	22,305.1	1,180.5	2,286.4	12,835.9	49,708.3
Transportation equip.	1,763.3	30,588.4	1,280.8	2,604.4	20,232.7	64,166.4
Instruments & related prods.	555.4	7,476.8	344.1	673.4	3,719.6	18,692.1
Misc. mfg. industries	435.7	4,348.1	333.0	620.4	2,724.1	10,197.7
Administrative & auxiliary[1]	1,073.0	21,960.1	—	—	—	—
All industries total	**19,505.8**	**263,020.6**	**13,592.3**	**26,546.7**	**156,440.5**	**581,640.9**

(1) In addition to the employment and payroll for operating manufacturing establishments, manufacturing concerns reported separately for central administrative offices or auxiliary units (e.g., research laboratories, storage warehouses, power plants, garages, repair shops, etc.) which serve the manufacturing establishments of a company rather than the public.

Manufacturing Production Worker Statistics

Source: Bureau of Labor Statistics, U.S. Labor Department (p — preliminary)

Year	All employees	Production workers	Payroll index 1967=100	Avg. weekly earnings	Avg. hourly earnings	Avg. hrs. per wk.
1955	16,882,000	13,288,000	61.1	$75.30	$1.85	40.7
1960	16,796,000	12,586,000	68.9	89.72	2.26	39.7
1965	18,062,000	13,434,000	88.1	107.53	2.61	41.2
1970	19,367,000	14,044,000	114.3	133.33	3.35	39.8
1973	20,154,000	14,834,000	150.5	166.46	4.09	40.7
1974	20,077,000	14,638,000	158.1	176.80	4.42	40.0
1975	18,323,000	13,043,000	151.6	190.79	4.83	39.5
1976	18,997,000	13,638,000	174.1	209.32	5.22	40.1
1977	19,647,000	14,110,000	197.1	228.90	5.68	40.3
1978	20,476,000	14,714,000	222.1	249.27	6.17	40.4
1979	20,972,000	15,010,000	234.7	268.94	6.69	40.2
1980, Jan.	20,699,000	14,674,000	245.3	277.01	6.96	39.8
Feb.	20,648,000	14,615,000	248.1	278.20	6.99	39.8
Mar.	20,709,000	14,662,000	250.1	280.99	7.06	39.8
Apr.p	20,448,000	14,398,000	252.3	278.95	7.08	39.4
Mayp	20,256,000	14,175,000	254.3	280.53	7.12	39.4

Personal Consumption Expenditures for the U.S.

Source: Bureau of Economic Analysis, U.S. Commerce Department (millions of dollars)

Product	1950	1955	1960	1965	1970	1975	1978	1979
Food and tobacco	58,120	72,236	87,979	106,966	147,140	224,319	289,581	321,263
Clothing accessories and jewelry	23,709	27,982	32,219	40,304	55,619	81,971	107,642	117,479
Personal care	2,438	3,162	5,242	7,617	10,920	14,228	18,569	20,264
Housing	21,286	34,339	48,117	65,469	93,986	150,151	212,153	241,463
Household operation	29,086	36,890	46,126	61,322	87,793	142,265	195,022	219,466
Medical care	9,104	13,206	20,002	30,053	49,853	89,155	131,026	146,837
Personal business	6,556	9,524	14,233	18,049	31,336	51,558	71,097	82,223
Transportation	25,415	34,583	42,391	58,205	78,032	125,493	191,327	212,221
Recreation	11,147	14,979	17,855	25,907	40,999	66,527	91,244	101,046
Private educ. and research	1,685	2,677	3,746	5,684	9,874	15,459	20,770	23,546
Religious and welfare activities	2,340	3,323	4,872	6,055	8,539	12,979	17,157	19,221
Foreign travel and other—net	655	1,619	2,121	2,858	4,705	4,965	5,177	4,770
Total personal consumption expenditures	**191,966**	**253,665**	**324,903**	**430,154**	**618,796**	**979,070**	**1,350,765**	**1,509,799**

General Manufacturing Statistics for States

Source: Bureau of the Census, U.S. Commerce Department

1977 States	All employees Number (1,000)	All employees Payroll (millions)	Production workers Number (1,000)	Production workers Man-hrs. (millions)	Production workers Wages (millions)	Value added by mfr. (millions)	Value of shipments (millions)	Capital expend. (millions)
U.S. total	**19,505.8**	**$263,020.6**	**13,593.0**	**26,547.7**	**$156,446.2**	**$581,660.3**	**$1,354,375.5**	**$47,688.4**
Alabama	340.3	3,769.8	271.9	223.5	2,693.5	8,100.7	20,949.5	1,338.7
Alaska	11.4	177.1	9.3	16.9	122.8	479.3	1,232.1	179.0
Arizona	110.7	1,463.3	69.8	136.2	783.9	3,387.6	7,103.4	220.4
Arkansas	194.3	1,911.8	158.3	309.6	1,388.7	4,865.0	12,253.6	467.2
California	1,770.0	24,811.0	1,142.9	2,234.9	13,185.7	55,452.3	121,384.5	3,470.0
Colorado	151.9	2,119.9	97.9	191.9	1,149.3	4,551.8	10,329.8	447.4
Connecticut	413.1	5,880.0	254.9	511.4	2,901.3	10,998.9	19,984.2	570.7
Delaware	68.1	1,178.9	33.0	64.1	414.5	1,618.0	5,298.7	154.0
Dist. of Columbia	18.6	297.5	7.0	12.5	101.2	612.2	990.6	31.1
Florida	357.6	4,128.5	246.8	483.7	2,321.9	9,332.1	21,928.3	752.0
Georgia	484.4	5,091.0	375.8	741.6	3,404.0	12,499.7	32,812.2	1,146.0
Hawaii	25.1	276.4	17.2	31.3	160.3	790.9	1,976.8	53.0
Idaho	51.7	625.0	39.6	76.4	430.9	1,418.5	3,655.5	154.5
Illinois	1,286.9	18,739.0	857.9	1,680.0	10,772.1	40,277.2	93,215.3	2,685.0
Indiana	704.9	10,427.1	520.9	1,024.7	7,039.1	22,593.7	52,052.7	2,130.0
Iowa	239.9	3,375.4	170.0	331.3	2,189.1	8,715.8	23,509.1	689.4
Kansas	172.0	2,147.1	121.8	242.4	1,375.5	5,385.3	16,047.3	349.3
Kentucky	277.0	3,445.6	208.3	398.9	2,295.1	9,440.1	22,739.2	713.7
Louisiana	194.2	2,673.7	143.7	291.3	1,782.8	9,503.1	29,491.2	2,167.0
Maine	103.1	1,075.3	84.3	163.7	781.4	2,346.6	5,145.9	223.3
Maryland	241.9	3,407.1	161.8	310.0	1,958.1	7,108.7	15,950.1	517.4
Massachusetts	627.1	8,051.1	407.9	793.3	4,197.8	16,895.4	30,662.8	978.2
Michigan	1,119.2	20,072.4	790.9	1,632.3	12,732.2	37,480.4	93,679.5	3,698.7
Minnesota	330.3	4,677.0	209.7	403.3	2,398.9	9,245.3	22,182.3	578.9
Mississippi	219.2	2,060.0	177.3	346.7	1,474.0	5,598.5	12,749.7	467.6
Missouri	435.8	5,733.2	300.5	576.9	3,432.0	12,813.5	33,083.2	885.8
Montana	24.0	314.9	18.7	37.1	238.2	860.3	2,846.5	97.5
Nebraska	90.0	1,107.9	61.4	121.4	665.0	2,821.8	8,653.2	176.5
Nevada	15.2	186.6	9.8	19.3	113.2	497.8	950.8	47.2
New Hampshire	94.9	1,026.9	71.6	138.0	647.4	2,172.8	4,028.9	160.9
New Jersey	783.7	10,961.4	491.3	962.4	5,576.4	23,197.1	50,176.8	1,489.9
New Mexico	30.4	309.3	23.7	42.5	191.6	790.0	2,051.3	100.8
New York	1,550.5	21,473.0	985.1	1,882.4	10,579.1	44,676.9	87,101.7	2,715.6
North Carolina	763.9	7,500.2	609.6	1,184.1	5,073.4	18,105.6	40,763.3	1,349.7
North Dakota	14.2	162.8	9.2	17.8	97.0	474.6	1,314.0	52.9
Ohio	1,345.8	20,615.3	923.1	1,840.1	12,887.7	43,294.0	95,849.9	2,789.6
Oklahoma	168.1	2,100.9	110.3	214.4	1,168.3	4,650.7	12,563.6	497.7
Oregon	203.9	2,784.7	153.9	292.1	1,896.3	6,255.7	14,471.8	584.9
Pennsylvania	1,346.7	18,245.1	937.9	1,784.2	10,960.5	35,997.6	80,034.3	2,103.2
Rhode Island	125.7	1,330.4	99.8	179.2	826.8	2,764.8	5,410.5	160.1
South Carolina	375.3	3,815.9	300.6	596.2	2,649.0	8,095.4	18,781.2	792.7
South Dakota	22.2	247.8	16.4	31.6	166.4	608.5	1,783.5	36.0
Tennessee	488.1	5,200.9	373.1	777.4	3,456.3	12,635.0	28,753.2	963.2
Texas	889.2	11,689.4	597.8	1,187.7	6,603.6	32,922.9	92,533.5	5,553.8
Utah	74.2	883.5	48.2	94.9	525.8	1,971.5	5,154.2	395.8
Vermont	42.8	499.1	29.0	56.3	283.8	1,050.0	2,204.0	93.3
Virginia	394.5	4,454.1	302.4	582.6	2,926.4	10,765.4	23,938.4	955.9
Washington	265.7	4,065.2	181.0	341.7	2,383.8	8,628.9	21,607.9	980.5
West Virginia	118.9	1,637.9	90.5	173.6	1,138.3	3,908.1	8,751.0	370.1
Wisconsin	541.7	7,394.5	383.3	751.3	4,737.7	16,761.5	39,060.0	1,189.2
Wyoming	8.9	115.1	6.3	12.6	76.5	380.7	1,315.1	51.7

Employees in Non-Agricultural Establishments

Source: Bureau of Labor Statistics, U.S. Labor Department

(thousands)

Annual Average by Industry Division

Year	Total	Mining	Contr./construction	Manufacturing	Trans. and public utilities	Whole., retail trade	Finance, insur., real estate	Service, miscellaneous	Government
1955	50,641	792	2,839	16,882	4,141	10,535	2,298	6,240	6,914
1960	54,189	712	2,926	16,796	4,004	11,391	2,629	7,378	8,353
1965	60,765	632	3,232	18,062	4,036	12,716	2,977	9,036	10,074
1970	70,880	623	3,588	19,367	4,515	15,040	3,645	11,548	12,554
1975	76,945	752	3,525	18,323	4,542	17,060	4,165	13,892	14,686
1976	79,382	779	3,576	18,997	4,582	17,755	4,271	14,551	14,871
1977	82,256	809	3,833	19,647	4,696	18,492	4,452	15,249	15,079
1978	86,697	851	4,229	20,505	4,923	19,542	4,724	16,252	15,672
1979	89,886	960	4,483	21,062	5,141	20,269	4,974	17,078	15,920

Profits of Manufacturing Corporations by Industry Groups

Source: Federal Trade Commission

Industry Group (Amounts estimated in millions of dollars)	Before Income Taxes	Pct. of sales		Profits After Taxes	Pct. of sales	
	1978	1978	1977	1978	1978	1977
Durable goods	**69,563**	**9.1**	**8.8**	**41,821**	**5.5**	**5.3**
Transportation equipment	14,189	7.7	8.5	8,585	4.7	5.0
Motor vehicles and equipment[1]	10,109	8.0	9.2	6,211	4.9	5.5
Electrical and electronic equipment	11,177	9.8	9.4	6,500	5.7	5.3
Machinery, except electrical	17,600	12.6	12.4	10,746	7.7	7.6
Fabricated metal products	6,484	7.9	8.2	3,815	4.7	4.8
Primary iron and steel	3,470	4.9	1.9	2,124	3.0	1.5
Primary nonferrous metal	2,174	7.0	4.8	1,362	4.4	3.4
Stone, clay, and glass products	3,776	10.0	8.6	2,353	6.2	5.2
Instruments and related products	5,382	15.7	15.0	3,175	9.3	9.0
Other durable goods	5,311	7.7	7.3	3,164	4.6	4.4
Nondurable goods	**62,983**	**8.4**	**8.3**	**39,364**	**5.2**	**5.2**
Food and kindred products	10,228	5.3	5.1	6,213	3.2	3.1
Tobacco manufactures	2,465	14.9	13.7	1,412	8.6	7.5
Textile mill products	2,120	5.7	4.6	1,170	3.1	2.4
Paper and allied products	4,036	8.2	7.9	2,598	5.3	5.2
Printing and publishing	5,894	11.0	10.3	3,311	6.2	5.7
Chemicals and allied products	14,343	11.5	11.6	9,117	7.3	7.2
Petroleum and coal products	19,166	10.1	10.4	12,842	6.8	7.1
Rubber and miscellaneous plastic products	2,008	5.2	6.8	1,195	3.1	3.9
Other nondurable products	2,723	5.7	5.5	1,507	3.2	2.9
All Manufacturing Corps	**132,547**	**8.8**	**8.6**	**81,185**	**5.4**	**5.2**

(1) Included in major industry above.

Annual Rates of Profit on Stockholders' Equity

Source: Federal Trade Commission

(Each rate is the arithmetic mean of 4 quarterly rates, each on an annual basis.)

By industry after taxes: by percent	1950	1960	1965	1970[1]	1974[2]	1975	1977	1978
All manufacturing corporations, except newspapers	15.4	9.2	13.0	9.3	14.9	11.6	14.2	15.0
Durable goods industries	16.8	8.6	13.8	8.3	12.6	10.3	14.5	15.9
Metals and metal fabricating industries	16.9	8.6	14.2	*	*	*	*	*
Transportation equipment	21.5	11.7	18.5	6.3	8.0	7.5	17.4	16.5
Motor vehicles and equipment	25.2	13.5	19.5	6.1	6.9	6.2	18.7	16.9
Aircraft and parts	*	7.4	15.1	6.8	10.6	11.0	15.0	15.6
Electrical machinery, equipment and supplies	20.8	9.5	13.5	9.1	11.1	9.0	15.2	16.7
Machinery, except electrical	14.0	7.6	14.1	9.9	13.2	13.7	16.7	17.6
Metalworking machinery and equipment	*	5.3	14.4	8.3	*	*	*	*
Other fabricated metal products	15.9	5.6	13.2	8.6	16.6	13.2	15.7	16.0
Primary metal industries	14.5	7.2	10.6	7.0	16.4	8.6	4.7	9.3
Blast furnaces, steel works and foundries	14.3	7.2	9.8	4.3	16.8	10.9	3.6	8.9
Nonferrous metals	15.0	7.1	11.9	10.7	15.8	5.0	7.0	10.0
Other durable goods industries	16.3	8.6	12.2	*	*	*	*	*
Lumber and wood products, except furniture	17.4	3.6	10.0	5.9	*	*	*	*
Furniture and fixtures	15.1	6.5	13.3	7.9	*	*	*	*
Stone, clay and glass products	17.6	9.9	10.2	6.9	10.6	8.3	13.3	16.6
Instruments and related products	16.7	11.6	17.5	14.2	16.1	13.5	16.9	17.9
Miscellaneous manufacturing and ordnance	12.2	9.2	10.7	10.0	*	*	*	*
Nondurable goods industries	14.0	9.8	12.2	10.3	17.2	12.9	13.9	14.2
Chemicals: petroleum, rubber, and plastics	15.4	10.8	13.0	*	*	*	*	*
Chemicals and allied products	17.8	12.2	15.2	11.5	18.2	15.2	15.1	15.6
Basic chemicals and related products	*	11.1	14.3	8.5	17.4	13.3	13.5	14.5
Drugs	*	16.8	20.3	17.6	18.8	17.8	18.2	19.1
Petroleum refining and related industries	13.8	10.1	11.8	11.0	21.0	12.5	13.6	13.3
Petroleum refining	*	10.1	11.8	11.0	*	*	*	*
Rubber and miscellaneous plastics products	16.7	9.1	11.7	7.1	14.4	8.0	12.1	10.1
Other nondurable goods industries	12.8	8.5	11.1	*	*	*	*	*
Food and kindred products	12.3	8.7	10.7	10.8	14.0	14.4	13.3	13.8
Dairy products	*	*	10.6	10.2	*	*	*	*
Bakery products	*	*	9.3	8.8	*	*	*	*
Alcoholic beverages	*	7.1	9.3	10.5	*	*	*	*
Tobacco manufactures	11.5	13.4	13.5	15.7	15.6	15.9	17.5	18.1
Textile mill products	12.6	5.8	10.8	5.1	8.2	4.2	8.6	11.5
Apparel and other fabricated textile products	10.1	7.7	12.6	11.9	*	*	*	*
Paper and allied products	16.1	8.5	9.4	7.0	17.8	12.6	12.4	12.9
Printing and publishing, except newspapers	11.5	10.6	14.1	11.2	13.2	12.8	17.4	18.4
Leather and leather products	10.9	6.3	11.6	9.4	*	*	*	*

*—Not available. (1) Includes newspapers for the first time. (2) Profits for 1974 include equity in earnings (net of taxes) of nonconsolidated subsidiaries. In prior years this component was included in adjustment to earned surplus.

Retail Store Sales

Source: Bureau of the Census, U.S. Commerce Department (millions of dollars)

Kind of business	1978	1979
All retail stores	**798,818**	**886,047**
Durable goods stores	**277,916**	**308,156**
Automotive group	163,668	177,714
Motor vehicle, other automotive dealers	149,675	161,277
Tire, battery, accessory dealers	13,993	16,437
Furniture and appliance group	37,430	41,868
Furniture, home furnishings stores	22,719	26,726
Household appliance, radio TV stores	10,991	12,119
Lumber, building, hardware group	44,125	52,239
Lumber, building materials dealers	29,991	35,102
Hardware stores	6,881	8,993

Kind of business	1978	1979
Nondurable goods stores	**520,902**	**577,891**
Apparel group	37,828	43,028
Men's and boys' wear stores	7,353	8,772
Women's apparel, accessory stores	14,660	15,802
Shoe stores	6,593	7,127
Food group	174,458	191,326
Grocery stores	161,527	177,703
General merchandise group with stores	99,505	110,233
Department stores	79,732	[1]89,127
Mail order (catalog sales)	7,073	—
Variety stores	7,809	7,914
Eating and drinking places	70,083	75,139
Gasoline service stations	60,884	71,894
Drug and proprietary stores	25,337	27,174
Liquor stores	13,616	15,595

(1) After Feb. 1979, includes some mail order.

Total retail stores sales (millions of dollars) — (1955) 183,851; (1958) 200,353; (1959) 215,413; (1960) 219,529; (1961) 218,992; (1962) 235,563; (1963) 246,666; (1964) 261,870; (1965) 284,128; (1966) 303,956; (1967) 292,956; (1968) 324,358; (1969) 346,717; (1970) 368,403; (1971) 406,234; (1972) 449,069; (1973) 503,332; (1974) 536,309; (1975) 584,776; (1976) 655,163; (1977) 725,220.

Cotton, Wool, Silk, and Man-Made Fibers Production

Source: Economics, Statistics, and Cooperatives Service, U.S. Agriculture Department

Cotton and wool from reports of the Agriculture Department; silk, rayon, and non-cellulosic man-made fibers from Textile Organon, a publication of the Textile Economics Bureau, Inc.

Year	Cotton[1] (million bales)[5]		Wool[2] (million pounds)		Silk	Man-made fibers[3] (million pounds)			
						Cellulosic		Non-cellulosic[4]	
	U.S.	World	U.S.	World	World (mil. lbs.)	U.S.	World	U.S.[4]	World[6]
1940	12.6	31.2	434.0	4,180	130	471.2	2,485.3	4.6	4.6
1950	10.0	30.6	249.3	4,000	42	1,259.4	3,552.8	145.9	177.4
1960	14.2	46.2	298.9	5,615	68	1,028.5	5,749.1	854.2	1,779.1
1965	15.0	55.0	224.8	5,731	72	1,527.0	7,359.4	2,062.4	4,928.9
1969	10.0	53.2	182.8	6,131	86	1,576.2	7,835.1	4,029.3	9,211.4
1970	10.2	53.6	176.8	6,107	90	1,373.2	7,573.9	4,053.5	10,361.7
1971	10.5	59.8	172.2	5,972	90	1,390.9	7,617.1	4,761.0	12,366.0
1972	13.7	62.9	168.2	5,560	93	1,394.3	7,846.0	5,927.3	14,057.8
1973	13.0	63.3	151.7	5,474	95	1,357.0	8,069.4	6,997.4	16,842.0
1974	11.5	64.3	137.1	5,769	99	1,198.8	7,786.7	6,906.5	16,505.2
1975	8.3	54.0	124.8	5,911	104	749.0	6,523.2	6,432.2	16,209.6
1976	10.6	57.4	114.8	5,672	106	840.9	7,075.9	7,302.6	18,962.7
1977	14.4	63.9	108.9	5,683	107	887.7	7,232.7	8,114.6	20,170.7
1978	10.9	60.0	101.8	5,811	113	904.5	7,314.4	8,706.3	22,119.6
1979	14.6	65.0	103.1	5,966	116	929.8	7,451.7	9,448.5	23,399.4

(1) Year beginning Aug. 1. (2) Grease basis. (3) Includes filament yarn and staple and tow fiber. (4) Includes textile glass fiber. (5) 480-pound net weight bales, U.S. beginning 1960 and world beginning 1965. (6) 1966 to date, excludes Olefin.

Work Stoppages (Strikes) in the U.S.

Source: Bureau of Labor Statistics, U.S. Labor Department

	Number stoppages	Workers involved (thousands)	Man days idle (thousands)
Average 1935-1939	2,862	1,130	16,900
War Period Dec. 8, 1941-Aug. 14, 1945	14,371	6,744	36,300
Year			
1950	4,843	2,410	38,800
1952	5,117	3,540	59,100
1953	5,091	2,400	28,300
1954	3,468	1,530	22,600
1955	4,320	2,650	28,200
1956	3,825	1,900	33,100
1957	3,673	1,390	16,500
1958	3,694	2,060	23,900
1959	3,708	1,880	69,000
1960	3,333	1,320	19,100
1961	3,367	1,450	16,300
1962	3,614	1,230	18,600
1963	3,362	941	16,100
1964	3,655	1,640	22,900

	Number stoppages	Workers involved (thousands)	Man days idle (thousands)
1965	3,963	1,550	23,300
1966	4,405	1,960	25,400
1967	4,595	2,870	42,100
1968	5,045	2,649	49,018
1969	5,700	2,481	42,869
1970	5,716	3,305	66,414
1971	5,138	3,280	47,589
1972	5,010	1,714	27,066
1973	5,353	2,251	27,948
1974	6,074	2,778	47,991
1975	5,031	1,746	31,237
1976	5,648	2,420	37,859
1977	5,506	2,040	35,822
1978	4,230	1,623	36,922
1979p	4,951	1,840	32,776
1980 Jan.p	352	207	3,142
Feb.p	354	114	3,025
Mar.p	396	123	2,705
Apr.p	425	116	2,786
Mayp	505	139	2,464

(p) Preliminary

Employment Status of Civilian Labor Force

Source: Bureau of Labor Statistics, U.S. Labor Department (thousands)

Employment status	Annual average 1978	Annual average 1979	1979 Nov.	1979 Dec.	1980 Jan.	1980 Feb.	1980 Mar.	1980 Apr.	1980 May
Total noninstitutional population	161,058	163,620	164,682	164,898	165,101	165,298	165,506	165,693	166,105
Total labor force	102,537	104,996	105,744	106,088	106,310	106,346	106,184	106,511	106,634
Civilian noninstitutional population	158,941	161,532	162,589	162,809	163,020	163,211	163,416	163,601	164,013
Civilian labor force	100,420	102,908	103,652	103,999	104,229	104,260	104,094	104,419	104,542
Employed	94,373	96,945	97,608	97,912	97,804	97,953	97,656	97,154	96,537
Agriculture	3,342	3,297	3,385	3,359	3,270	3,326	3,358	3,242	3,191
Nonagricultural industries	91,031	93,648	94,223	94,553	94,534	94,626	94,298	93,912	93,346
Unemployed	6,047	5,963	6,044	6,087	6,425	6,307	6,438	7,265	8,006
Unemployment rate	6.0	5.8	5.8	5.9	6.2	6.0	6.2	7.0	7.7
Not in labor force	58,521	58,623	58,937	58,810	58,791	58,951	59,322	59,182	59,471
Men, 20 years and over									
Civilian noninstitutional population	67,006	68,293	68,804	68,940	69,047	69,140	69,238	69,329	69,532
Civilian labor force	53,464	54,486	54,709	54,781	54,855	55,038	54,996	55,114	55,220
Employed	51,212	52,264	52,374	52,478	52,279	52,531	52,300	51,868	51,510
Agriculture	2,361	2,350	2,438	2,427	2,387	2,435	2,394	2,320	2,270
Nonagricultural industries	48,852	49,913	49,936	50,051	49,892	50,096	49,906	49,548	49,240
Unemployed	2,252	2,223	2,335	2,303	2,577	2,507	2,696	3,246	3,710
Unemployment rate	4.2	4.1	4.3	4.2	4.7	4.6	4.9	5.9	6.7
Not in labor force	13,541	13,807	14,095	14,159	14,192	14,102	14,242	14,215	14,312
Women, 20 years and over									
Civilian noninstitutional population	75,489	76,860	77,426	77,542	77,656	77,766	77,876	77,981	78,211
Civilian labor force	37,416	38,910	39,445	39,659	39,878	39,857	39,751	40,137	40,125
Employed	35,180	36,698	37,248	37,402	37,574	37,604	37,496	37,602	37,530
Agriculture	586	591	612	582	540	567	582	552	541
Nonagricultural industries	34,593	36,107	36,636	36,820	37,034	37,037	36,914	37,051	36,989
Unemployed	2,236	2,213	2,197	2,257	2,304	2,254	2,255	2,534	2,596
Unemployment rate	6.0	5.7	5.6	5.7	5.8	5.7	5.7	6.3	6.5
Not in labor force	38,073	37,949	37,981	37,883	37,778	37,909	38,125	37,844	38,086

Industrial Minerals: Distribution, Resources, Reserves

Source: Organization for Economic Cooperation and Development

(Resource and reserve figures are based on average conservative estimates.)

Minerals	Distribution of reserves, 1974 (% of world total)	Resources[1] 1975/76 (million metric tons)	Reserves[2] 1975/76 (million metric tons)	Ratio of reserves to 1975 demand in years[3]	Ratio of reserves to total demand 1974-2000[4]
Iron	USSR(31.1) Brazil(16.6) Canada(11.7) Australia(10.2) India(6.4)	195,000	90,500	177	4.5
Copper	U.S.(18.4) Chilie(18.4) USSR(7.9) Canada(6.8) Peru(6.5) Zambia(6.3) Zaire(5.6)	1,500	408.2	62	1.3
Lead	U.S.(35.6) Canada(11.5) USSR(10.9) Australia(10.9) Mexico(3.0)	300	150.0	49	1.2
Tin	China(23.6) Thailand(15.0) Malaysia(12.2) Bolivia(9.9) Indonesia(8.3) Brazil(6.0)	37	10.2	44	1.3
Zinc	Canada(22.8) U.S.(20.1) Australia(12.1) USSR(8.1) Ireland(5.4)	245	135.0	41	1.1
Aluminum	Australia(26.0) Guinea(26.0) Brazil(15.6) Jamaica(6.1) Greece(4.4) Cameroon(3.9)	5,700	3,483	over 200	4.0
Titanium	Brazil(65.9) India(21.7) Australia(5.4) U.S.(3.5) Sierra Leone(1.7) Canada(1.6)	1,234	340.1	over 300	4.4
Chromium	S. Africa(73.9) Rhodesia(19.7) USSR(2.9) Finland(1.2) India(0.5) Madagascar(0.4) Philippines(0.4) Turkey(0.4) Brazil(0.3)	1,049	523.2	over 200	5.7
Cobalt	Zaire(27.7) New Caledonia(27.1) Zambia(14.2) Cuba(13.8) USSR(8.3)	4.3	2.4	78	2.1
Niobium	Brazil(75.8) Canada(7.6) USSR(6.3) Zaire(3.8) Uganda(2.9) Nigeria(2.7)	14.6	10.0	over 800	over 10
Manganese	S. Africa(45.0) USSR(37.5) Australia(8.0) Gabon(5.0) Brazil(2.2)	3,265	1,814	197	4.9
Molybdenum	U.S.(49.5) USSR(15.2) Canada(14.4) Chile(13.6) China(3.8)	28.6	6.0	65	1.4
Nickel	New Caledonia(43.7) Canada(16.1) USSR(9.6) Australia(9.2) Indonesia(8.4) Cuba(5.7)	129.7	55.3	77	2.1
Tantulum	Zaire(55.0) Nigeria(11.0) USSR(6.7) Thailand(6.7) Malaysia(5.4) Canada(4.8) Brazil(4.4)	0.26	0.07	49	1.1
Tungsten	China(53.6) Canada(12.1) USSR(8.9) N. Korea(6.4) U.S.(6.1)	5.2	1.8	46	1.2
Vanadium	USSR(74.7) S. Africa(18.7) Australia(1.4) Chilie(1.4) U.S.(1.1)	56.2	9.7	over 300	7.5
Bismuth	Japan(25.6) Australia(19.5) U.S.(13.3) Mexico(6.2) Peru(5.1)	0.13	0.06	22	0.5
Mercury	Spain(40.6) USSR(10.1) Yugoslavia(10.1) China(10.1) U.S.(9.1) Italy(8.1)	17,510	4,930	21	0.7
Silver	USSR(26.7) U.S.(25.0) Mexico(13.3) Canada(11.7) Peru(10.0) Australia(3.3)	0.70	0.19	16	0.4
Platinum	S. Africa(71.3) USSR(26.7) Canada(1.8) U.S.(0.2) Colombia(0.2)	0.026	0.009	110	3.1
Asbestos	Canada(45.2) USSR(24.8) S. Africa(6.9) Australia(3.6) U.S.(3.0)	249.4	145.1	35	0.9

(1) Seabed deposits not included; these are (in million metric tons): cobalt, 583; manganese, 36,425; nickel, 1,305; molybdenum, 78; vanadium, 107. Other minerals for which resource estimates are considerably increased if seabed deposits are included are titanium, aluminum, lead, copper, and to a smaller extent zinc, iron, and chromium. (2) Reserves are defined as that portion of the identified resources from which useable material can be economically and legally extracted at the time of determination. (3) Ie., iron will last 177 years if used at the 1975 rate. (4) Ie., there is 4.5 times more iron than total estimated demand between 1974 and 2000.

U.S. Mineral Production

Source: Bureau of Mines, U.S. Interior Department

Production as measured by mine shipments, sales, or marketable production (including consumption by producers)

Non metals (except fuels)		1978 Quantity	1978 Value (thousands)	1979[p] Quantity	1979[p] Value (thousands)
Abrasive stones[2]	short tons	487	1,283	1,944	1,714
Asbestos	short tons	93,108	26,987	102,903	28,925
Asphalt and related bitumens (native)					
Bituminous limestone & sandstone & gilsonite	short tons	1,697,300	19,283	1,614,500	25,622
Barite	thousand short tons	2,112	43,981	1,937	48,024
Boron minerals	thousand short tons	1,554	279,927	1,590	310,211
Bromine	thousand pounds	446,543	100,003	497,000	114,500
Calcium chloride	short tons	773,138	53,869	719,709	51,884
Carbon dioxide, natural	thousand cubic feet	2,014,914	2,568	2,028,045	3,243
Cement: Portland	thousand short tons	80,010	3,239,580	78,978	3,650,436
Masonry	thousand short tons	4,123	208,566	3,748	204,797
Natural and slag	thousand short tons	—	—	—	—
Clays	thousand short tons	56,822	717,274	54,689	846,089
Diatomite	short tons	651,000	72,429	717,000	90,323
Feldspar	short tons	734,870	18,185	740,472	21,474
Fluorspar	short tons	129,428	13,262	109,299	12,162
Garnet (abrasive)	short tons	29,732	2,335	21,240	1,975
Gem stones (e)		NA	8,930	NA	8,230
Gypsum	thousand short tons	14,891	92,726	14,630	99,868
Helium: Crude	million cubic feet	549	6,582	611	7,327
High purity	million cubic feet	1,001	25,276	1,062	26,847
Lime	thousand short tons	20,443	749,667	20,945	862,459
Magnesium compounds from sea water and brime					
(except for metals)	short tons, MgO equivalent	W	W	W	W
Mica Scrap	thousand short tons	182	8,035	175	7,814
Sheet	pounds	W	W	NA	NA
Peat	thousand short tons	750	12,988	798	15,517
Perlite	short tons	641,000	13,740	660,000	16,435
Phosphate rock	thousand metric tons	50,037	928,820	51,611	1,045,655
Potassium salts	thousand metric tons K_2O equivalent	2,307	226,468	2,388	279,199
Pumice	thousand short tons	4,757	14,455	4,414	15,961
Pyrites	thousand metric tons	768	12,169	1,049	17,087
Salt	thousand short tons	42,869	499,345	45,793	538,352
Sand and gravel	thousand short tons	996,200	2,302,000	979,000	2,427,000
Sodium carbonate (natural)	thousand short tons	6,790	371,255	W	W
Sodium sulfate (natural)	thousand short tons	605	27,866	533	29,689
Stone[3]	thousand short tons	1,050,960	2,885,689	1,098,617	3,398,968
Sulfur: Frasch process mines	thousand metric tons	5,736	279,918	7,507	449,433
Talc, soapstone, and pyrophyllite	short tons	1,383,752	15,767	1,452,733	20,364
Tripoli	short tons	118,671	756	116,009	6,279
Vermiculite	thousand short tons	337	19,734	346	21,955
Value of items that cannot be disclosed: Aplite, brucite, emery, graphite, iodine, kyanite, lithium minerals, magnesite, greensand marl, olivine, staurolite, wollastonite, and values of nonmetal items indicated by symbol W:		XX	222,567	XX	740,520
Total nonmetals		**XX**	**13,524,000**	**XX**	**15,446,000**

Metals		1978 Quantity	1978 Value (thousands)	1979[p] Quantity	1979[p] Value (thousands)
Antimony ore concentrate, antimony content	short tons	W	W	W	W
Bauxite	thousand metric tons, dried equivalent	1,669	23,186	1,821	24,875
Beryllium concentrate	short tons, gross weight	W	W	W	W
Copper (recoverable content of ores, etc.)	metric tons	1,357,587	1,990,323	1,441,148	2,955,737
Gold (recoverable content of ores, etc.)	troy ounces	998,832	193,325	919,783	282,833
Iron ore (excluding iron sinter)	thousand long tons, gr. wgt.	82,826	2,387,965	86,130	2,811,574
Lead (recoverable content of ores, etc.)	metric tons	529,661	393,516	525,569	609,929
Manganese ore (35% or more Mn)	short tons, gross wgt.	—	—	—	—
Manganiferous ore (5 to 35% Mn)	short tons, gross wgt.	312,124	3,074	240,696	2,902
Mercury	76-pound flasks	24,163	3,705	29,519	8,299
Molybdenum (content of concentrate)	thousand pounds	130,694	607,950	143,504	871,067
Nickel (content of ore and concentrate)	short tons	13,509	W	15,065	W
Rare-earth metal concentrates	short tons	W	W	W	W
Silver (recoverable content of ores, etc.)	thousand troy ozs.	39,385	212,681	38,055	422,032
Titanium concentrate, ilmenite	short tons, gross weight	580,878	25,629	646,399	32,965
Tungsten ore and concentrate	thousand pounds	6,901	56,691	6,466	55,785
Uranium (recoverable content U_3O_8)	thousand pounds	NA	NA	NA	NA
Vanadium (recoverable in ore and concentrate)	short tons	4,272	56,776	5,520	73,892
Zinc (recoverable content of ores, etc.)	metric tons	302,669	206,854	267,341	219,841
Value of items that cannot be disclosed: symbol W		XX	133,849	XX	144,962
Total metals		**XX**	**6,296,000**	**XX**	**8,517,000**

(e) Estimate. (NA) Not available. (W) Withheld to avoid disclosing individual company confidential data: included with "Value of items that cannot be disclosed." (XX) Not applicable. (p) Preliminary.
(1) Includes a small quantity of anthracite mined in states other than Pennsylvania.
(2) Grindstones, pulpstones, grinding pebbles, sharpening stones, and tube mill liners.
(3) Excludes abrasive stone, bituminous limestone, bituminous sandstone, and soapstone, all included elsewhere.

U.S. Mineral Production—Leading States

Source: Bureau of Mines, U.S. Interior Department

State 1977	Value (thousands)	Percent of U.S. total	Principal minerals, in order of value
Texas	$19,519,631	25.32	Petroleum, natural gas, natural gas liquids, cement.
Louisiana	10,911,885	14.16	Natural gas petroleum, natural gas liquids, sulfur.
West Virginia	3,208,068	4.16	Coal, natural gas, petroleum, natural gas liquids.
California	4,311,824	5.59	Petroleum, cement, natural gas, sand and gravel.
Pennsylvania	3,043,964	3.95	Coal, cement, stone, natural gas.
Kentucky	3,217,860	4.17	Coal, stone, petroleum, natural gas.
Oklahoma	3,497,447	4.54	Petroleum, natural gas, natural gas liquids, coal.
New Mexico	2,910,804	3.78	Natural gas, petroleum, natural gas liquids, uranium.
Wyoming	2,331,349	3.02	Petroleum, coal, sodium compounds, natural gas.
Illinois	1,663,280	2.15	Coal, petroleum, stone, sand and gravel.

Value of U.S. Mineral Production

(millons of dollars)

Production as measured by mine shipments sales or marketable production.

Year[1]	Fuels	Nonmetallic	Metals	Total[2]	Year[1]	Fuels	Nonmetallic	Metals	Total[2]
1930	2,500	973	501	3,980	1972	22,061	6,482	3,642	32,185
1940	2,662	784	752	4,198	1973	24,949	7,476	4,362	36,787
1950	8,689	1,882	1,351	11,862	1974	40,889	8,687	5,501	55,077
1960	12,142	3,868	2,022	18,032	1975	47,505	9,570	5,191	62,266
1965	14,047	4,933	2,544	21,524	1976	52,484	10,616	6,086	69,186
1969	17,965	5,624	3,333	26,921	1977	59,575	11,701	5,810	77,086
1970	20,152	5,712	3,928	29,792	1978	NA	13,524	6,296	NA
1971	21,247	6,058	3,406	30,711	1979[p]	NA	15,446	8,517	NA

(1) Excludes Alaska and Hawaii, 1930-53. (2) Data may not add to total because of rounding figures. (P) Preliminary.

U.S. Pig Iron and Steel Output

Source: American Iron and Steel Institute (net tons)

Year	Total pig iron	Pig iron and ferro-alloys	Raw steel	Year	Total pig iron	Pig iron and ferro-alloys	Raw steel
1940	46,071,666	47,398,529	66,982,686	1973	100,837,000	103,089,000	150,799,000
1945	53,223,169	54,919,029	79,701,648	1974	95,909,000	98,332,000	145,720,000
1950	64,586,907	66,400,311	96,836,075	1975	101,208,000	103,345,000	116,642,000
1955	76,857,417	79,263,865	117,036,085	1976	86,870,000	88,780,000	128,000,000
1960	66,480,648	68,566,384	99,281,601	1977	81,328,000	83,082,000	125,333,000
1965	88,184,901	90,918,040	131,461,601	1978	87,679,000	89,351,000	137,031,000
1970	91,435,000	93,851,000	131,514,000	1979	87,003,000	89,011,000	136,341,000

Steel figures include only that portion of the capacity and production of steel for castings used by foundries which were operated by companies producing steel ingots.

Raw Steel Production

(thousands of net tons)

State	1977	1978	1979	State	1977	1978	1979
New York	3,958	4,203	4,035	Illinois	10,872	12,443	11,729
Pennsylvania	25,737	28,070	28,213	Michigan	10,051	10,789	10,922
R.I., Conn., N.J., Del., Md.	5,306	6,350	6,638	Minn., Mo., Okla., Texas	6,753	7,845	8,260
Va., W.Va., Ga., Fla., N.C., S.C.,	5,484	6,444	6,788	Ariz., Colo., Utah, Wash., Ore., Ha.	4,758	4,968	5,165
Kentucky	2,289	2,523	2,438	California	3,224	3,472	3,672
Ala., Tenn., Miss., Ark.	3,963	4,305	4,487	**Total**	**125,333**	**137,031**	**136,341**
Ohio	21,466	21,268	21,082				
Indiana	21,472	24,351	22,912				

U.S. Copper, Lead, and Zinc Production

Source: Bureau of Mines, U.S. Interior Department

Year	Copper		Lead[1]		Zinc	
	Mil. lbs.	$1,000	Short tons	$1,000	Short tons	Mil. dol.
1950	1,823	379,122	418,809	113,078	591,454	167
1960	2,286	733,708	228,899	53,562	334,101	87
1965	2,703	957,028	301,147	93,959	611,153	178
1970	3,439	1,984,484	571,767	178,609	534,136	164
1973	3,436	2,044,346	603,024	196,465	478,850	198

Year	Copper		Lead[1]		Zinc	
	Mil. lbs.	$1,000	Metric tons	$1,000	Metric tons	Mil. dol.
1975	2,827	1,814,763	563,783	267,230	425,792	366
1977	3,008	2,009,297	537,499	363,789	407,889	309
1978	2,993	1,990,323	529,661	393,516	302,669	207
1979	3,182	2,960,676	525,569	609,929	267,341	220

(1) Production from domestic ores.

TRADE AND TRANSPORTATION

Notable Steamships and Motorships

Source: Lloyd's Register of Shipping as of May 2, 1980

Gross tonnage is a measurement of enclosed space (1 gross ton = 100 cu. ft.) Deadweight tonnage is the weight (long tons) of cargo, fuel, etc., which a vessel is designed to carry safely.

Oil Tankers

Name, registry	Dwght. ton.	Lgth. ft.	Bdth. ft.
Pierre Guillaumat, Fr.	555,031	1359	206
Prairial, Fr.	554,000	1359	206
Bellamya, Fr.	553,662	1359	206
Batillus, Fr.	550,000	1358	206
Esso Atlantic, Liber.	516,893	1333	233
Esso Pacific, Liber.	516,423	1333	233
Nanny, Swed.	498,995	1194	259
Nissei Maru, Jap.	484,337	1243	203
Globtik London, Liber.	483,939	1243	203
Globtik Tokyo, Liber.	483,664	1243	203
Burmah Enterprise, Br.	457,927	1241	224
Burmah Endeavour, Br.	447,000	1241	223
Esso Mediterranean, Liber.	446,500	1241	223
Berge Emperor, Nor.	423,700	1285	223
Berge Empress, Nor.	423,700	1252	223
Hilda Knudsen, Nor.	423,639	1240	226
Esso Deutschland, W. Ger.	421,678	1240	226
Al Rekkah, Kuw.	414,366	1200	229
Jinko Maru, Jap.	413,549	1200	229
Chevron So. America, Liber.	413,159	1200	229
David Packard, Liber.	413,115	1200	229
Aiko Maru, Jap.	413,012	1200	229
Chevron No. America, Liber.	412,612	1200	229
Oppama, Liber.	412,000	1236	209
World Petrobras, Liber.	411,508	1187	229
Robinson, Liber.	410,590	1236	226
Coraggio, It.	409,500	1240	226
Nai Genova, It.	409,400	1253	207
Nai Superba, It.	409,400	1253	207
Esso Japan, Liber.	406,640	1187	229
Esso Tokyo, Liber.	406,258	1187	229

Bulk, Ore, Bulk Oil, & Ore Oil Carriers

Name, registry	Dwght. ton.	Lgth. ft.	Bdth. ft.
World Gala, Liber.	282,462	1109	179
Brazilian Wealth, Liber.	278,734	1099	170
Docecanyon, Liber.	271,235	1113	180
Licorne Pacifique, Fr.	271,000	1111	176
Jose Bonifacio, Braz.	270,358	1106	179
Rhine Ore, Liber.	265,000	1099	170
Mary F. Koch, Liber.	265,000	1099	170
Usa Maru, Jap.	264,523	1105	179
Nordic Conqueror, Liber.	264,485	1101	176
Lauderdale, Br.	260,424	1101	176
Licorne Atlantique, Fr.	258,268	1101	176
Seiko Maru, Jap.	248,300	1069	170
World Truth, Liber.	245,288	1069	170
Hoegh Hood, Nor.	244,677	1069	170
Hoegh Hill, Nor.	241,447	1069	170
Konkar Dinos, Gr.	231,045	1075	160
Berge Adria, Nor.	227,561	1030	164
Berge Brioni, Nor.	227,557	1030	165
Andros Antares, Liber.	227,480	1061	158
San Giusto, It.	227,408	1091	149
World Recovery, Liber.	227,406	1075	161
Ambrosiana, It.	227,400	1091	149
Konkar Theodoros, Liber.	225,000	1091	164
Andros Atlas, Gr.	224,074	1061	158
Andros Aries, Gr.	223,808	1061	158
Ruhr Ore, Liber.	223,500	1096	149
Alva Bay, Br.	222,331	1091	149
Alva Sea, Br.	221,457	1090	149
World Era, Liber.	215,500	1075	164
Tantalus, Br.	214,592	1075	164
Atsuta Maru, Jap.	214,017	1075	164
Tsurumi Maru, Jap.	213,842	1075	164

World's Largest Passenger Ships

Name, registry	Dwght. ton.	Lgth. ft.	Bdth. ft.
Norway, Nor.	69,379	1035	110
Queen Elizabeth 2, Br.	67,140	963	105
Canberra, Br.	44,807	818	102
Oriana, Br.	41,910	804	97
United States, U.S.	38,216	990	101
Rotterdam, Neth. Antil.	37,783	748	94
Leonardo Da Vinci, It.	33,340	767	92
Eugenio C., It.	30,567	713	96

Container, Liquefied Gas, Misc. Ships

Name, registry	Dwght. ton.	Lgth. ft.	Bdth. ft.
Hoegh Gandria, Nor.	95,683	943	142
Golar Freeze, Liber.	85,158	943	142
Gimi, Liber.	84,855	963	136
Hilli, Liber.	84,855	961	136
Khamnur, Liber.	84,855	963	136
LNG Taurus, U.S.	83,729	936	149
LNG Gemini, U.S.	83,608	936	149
LNG Capricorn, U.S.	83,608	936	149
LNG Libra, U.S.	83,607	936	149
LNG Leo, U.S.	83,601	936	149
LNG Virgo, U.S.	83,601	936	149
LNG Aquarius, U.S.	83,102	936	143
LNG Aries, U.S.	83,102	936	143
Mostefa Ben-Boulaid, Alger.	82,243	914	134
Larbi Ben M'Hidi, Alger.	80,328	924	136
Chihani Bachir, Alger.	80,328	924	136
Ben Franklin, Fr.	80,071	894	134
Nestor, Berm.	78,915	902	138
Edovard L.D., Fr.	78,212	902	138
Methania, Belg.	78,056	918	136
Pollenger, Br.	76,496	857	131
LNG Challenger, Br.	76,496	857	131
Norman Lady, Br.	76,416	818	131
El Paso Howard Boyd, U.S.	74,016	948	135
El Paso Savannah, U.S.	72,000	931	140
El Paso Southern, U.S.	69,472	948	135
El Paso Arzew, U.S.	69,470	948	135
Gastor, Pan.	68,247	902	138
El Paso Paul Kayser, Liber.	66,808	920	136
El Paso Consolidated, Liber.	66,808	920	136
El Paso Sonatrach, Liber.	66,807	920	136
Palace Tokyo, Jap.	64,378	807	131
Kurama Maru, Jap.	59,294	898	105
Cardigan Bay, Br.	58,899	950	106
Tokyo Bay, Br.	58,889	950	106
Kowloon Bay, Br.	58,889	950	106
Liverpool Bay, Br.	58,889	950	106
Kowloon Bay, Br.	58,889	950	106
Osaka Bay, Br.	58,889	950	106
Nedlloyd Delft, Neth.	58,716	941	106
Nedlloyd Dejima, Neth.	58,716	941	106
Benavon, Br.	58,440	950	106
Benalder, Br.	58,440	950	106
City of Edinburgh, Br.	58,440	950	106
Hamburg Express, W. Ger.	58,088	943	105
Tokio Express, W. Ger.	58,082	943	105
Bremen Express, W. Ger.	57,535	941	106
Hongkong Express, W. Ger.	57,525	941	106
Kasuga Maru, Jap.	57,500	948	105
Korrigan, Fr.	57,249	946	105
Esso Fuji, Pan.	55,896	807	131
Esso Westernport, Liber.	54,057	838	116
City of Durban, Br.	53,790	848	106
Barcelona, Br.	53,784	848	106
Geomitra, Br.	53,128	849	114
Genota, Br.	53,128	849	113
S.A. Winterberg, So. Afr.	53,050	848	106
S.A. Waterberg, So. Afr.	53,050	848	106
S.A. Helderberg, So. Afr.	53,023	848	106
S.A. Secterberg, So. Afr.	53,023	848	106
Transvaal, W. Germ.	52,608	848	105
Nedlloyd Hontman, Neth.	52,562	848	106
Nedlloyd Hooru, Neth.	52,553	848	106
Ortelius, Belg.	52,444	848	106
Toyama, Nor.	52,196	902	106
Elbe Maru, Jap.	51,623	882	105
Kitano Maru, Jap.	51,159	856	105
Kamakura Maru, Jap.	51,139	856	105
Rhine Maru, Jap.	51,085	856	105

Nuclear Powered Merchant Ships

Name, registry	Dwght. ton.	Lgth. ft.	Bdth. ft.
Arktika, USSR	18,172	485	98
Sibir, USSR	18,171	485	98
Savannah, U.S.	15,585	595	78
Lenin, USSR	14,067	439	90
Mutsu, Jap.	8,214	428	62

Merchant Fleets of the World

Source: Maritime Administration, U.S. Commerce Department

Oceangoing steam and motor ships of 1,000 gross tons and over as of Dec. 31, 1978, excludes ships operating exclusively on the Great Lakes and inland waterways and special types such as channel ships, icebreakers, cable ships, etc., and merchant ships owned by any military force. Tonnage is in thousands. Gross tonnage is a volume measurement; each cargo gross ton represents 100 cubic ft. of enclosed space. Deadweight tonnage is the carrying capacity of a ship in long tons (2,240 lbs.).

Country of registry	Total no.	Gross tons	Dwt. tons	Bulk carriers		Freighters		Tankers	
				No.	Dwt.	No.	Dwt.	No.	Dwt.
Total-All Countries	24,641	380,312	647,378	4,821	181,956	14,000	117,289	5,265	325,624
United States[1]	879	14,681	21,926	22	638	481	6,872	302	23,924
Privately owned	584	12,158	18,981	22	638	278	4,702	278	13,591
Government owned	295	2,523	2,945	—	—	203	2,170	24	333
Algeria	69	1,133	1,774	9	154	37	254	23	1,366
Argentina	188	1,842	2,210	26	683	104	970	56	1,053
Australia	80	1,401	2,173	34	1,334	32	378	14	461
Bangladesh	27	236	342	1	93	21	200	4	43
Belgium	68	1,547	2,421	23	1,318	32	474	12	614
Brazil	285	3,679	6,071	39	2,069	178	1,446	62	2,550
British Colonies	175	2,865	4,483	57	1,086	89	733	27	1,258
*Bulgaria	112	1,058	1,530	33	573	56	391	19	595
Canada	130	1,119	1,676	52	1,199	27	127	46	348
Chile	48	529	837	7	326	34	393	6	116
China (Taiwan)	149	1,744	2,813	34	1,329	95	774	13	655
*China (People's Rep.)	559	5,385	8,078	71	2,163	398	4,077	78	1,775
Colombia	41	271	352	—	—	35	283	3	42
Cuba	86	658	871	7	83	65	660	11	111
Cyprus	483	2,236	3,088	28	321	421	2,457	26	274
*Czechoslovakia	15	151	226	5	163	10	63	—	—
Denmark	340	5,061	8,472	40	1,137	217	1,690	74	5,631
Ecuador	24	195	271	—	—	12	108	11	151
Egypt	82	428	585	—	—	60	336	14	201
Finland	181	2,081	3,309	87	803	99	559	40	1,941
France	383	11,020	19,704	50	2,702	199	2,217	129	14,763
Gabon	1	374	138	—	—	—	—	1	138
Germany (West)	592	8,759	14,289	68	3,639	441	4,148	81	6,497
*Germany (East)	155	1,288	1,798	19	378	124	941	9	463
Ghana	23	137	186	—	—	23	186	—	—
Greece	2,693	33,744	52,146	762	23,164	1,507	14,016	366	19,744
India	364	5,570	9,044	101	4,318	221	2,632	33	2,047
Indonesia	219	900	1,234	11	150	161	864	22	131
Iran	57	1,053	1,734	—	—	42	538	15	1,196
*Iraq	36	1,228	2,257	—	—	15	129	21	2,128
Ireland	25	156	241	7	197	14	30	4	14
Israel	37	406	542	10	314	27	228	—	—
Italy	609	11,007	18,606	153	2,528	203	1,462	226	9,487
Ivory Coast	21	192	250	—	—	21	250	—	—
Japan	1,781	35,126	59,947	540	22,100	761	6,696	474	31,129
Korea (South)	301	2,856	4,778	72	1,502	183	1,167	46	2,109
Kuwait	88	2,174	3,677	2	18	73	1,305	13	2,354
Lebanon	66	197	264	2	3	63	254	—	—
Liberia	2,439	79,389	154,180	934	43,034	607	6,716	884	104,317
Libya	26	835	1,531	—	—	12	45	14	1,486
Malaysia	54	519	782	12	484	35	201	3	89
Maldives	30	86	110	1	3	28	102	—	—
Mexico	52	550	850	3	60	19	158	30	632
Morocco	46	320	521	3	99	27	213	16	309
Netherlands	443	4,777	7,701	37	1,006	339	2,346	64	4,333
New Zealand	26	210	256	8	38	15	136	3	82
Nigeria	23	302	492	—	—	22	227	1	265
Norway	884	27,889	49,875	287	16,711	254	2,360	313	30,735
Pakistan	48	424	570	1	17	41	500	—	—
Panama	2,170	19,895	32,606	334	7,899	1,545	11,783	252	12,672
Peru	43	427	655	9	259	24	258	10	138
Philippines	178	1,060	1,564	14	387	116	645	31	500
Poland	310	3,121	4,912	26	2,237	214	1,673	14	985
Portugal	85	1,086	1,767	5	123	58	412	24	1,211
Qatar	2	80	144	—	—	1	8	1	136
*Romania	163	1,546	2,324	41	1,073	112	667	8	577
Saudi Arabia	61	1,197	2,115	3	91	28	137	28	1,882
Singapore	634	7,342	12,051	26	2,646	426	3,679	116	5,646
Somalia	16	91	130	—	—	15	114	1	16
South Africa	15	575	746	6	281	27	404	2	61
Spain	495	7,175	12,733	67	2,012	283	1,328	131	9,340
Sweden	265	6,245	10,819	54	3,274	133	1,245	76	6,294
Switzerland	27	235	354	6	195	18	150	3	9
Thailand	48	265	405	1	2	32	222	15	181
Tunisia	19	105	144	2	32	12	46	4	63
Turkey	154	1,179	1,801	20	671	95	524	28	580
United Arab Emirates	14	112	201	1	2	10	53	1	135
United Kingdom	1,228	28,122	46,921	278	12,462	568	5,977	370	28,409
Uruguay	14	150	247	—	—	9	53	5	194
*USSR[2]	2,501	16,209	21,411	145	2,702	1,814	11,150	476	7,377
Venezuela	74	727	1,045	4	24	51	441	19	580
Vietnam	34	170	258	2	23	28	185	4	50
Yugoslavia	245	2,279	3,475	49	1,475	175	1,607	13	352
Zaire	9	86	129	—	—	8	114	—	—

*Source material limited. (1) Excludes 38 non-merchant ships currently in the National Defense Reserve Fleet. (2) Includes U.S. government-owned ships transferred to USSR under lend-lease agreements, 2 of which are still under that registry.

U.S. Foreign Trade with Leading Countries

Source: Office of Planning and Research, U.S. Commerce Department

(millions of dollars)

Exports from the U.S. to the following areas and countries and imports into the U.S. from those areas and countries:	Exports			Imports		
	1977	1978	1979	1977	1978	1979
Total	**$121,212**	**$143,663**	**$181,802**	**$147,685**	**$171,978**	**$206,327**
Western Hemisphere	**43,751**	**50,394**	**61,533**	**50,697**	**56,473**	**68,582**
Canada	25,788	28,374	33,096	29,599	33,525	38,099
19 American Republics	16,371	20,185	26,257	16,450	18,556	24,782
Central American Common Market	1,478	1,571	1,655	1,580	1,478	1,895
Dominican Republic	424	473	610	637	537	667
Panama	346	438	528	159	153	191
Bahamas	224	284	334	1,058	977	1,589
Jamaica	293	313	330	349	390	380
Netherlands Antilles	304	377	412	1,292	1,262	1,830
Trinidad and Tobago	306	330	462	1,677	1,425	1,560
Europe	**37,304**	**43,608**	**60,014**	**28,801**	**37,985**	**43,549**
OECD countries (excludes depend. and Yugo.)	34,346	39,405	53,502	27,310	36,072	41,275
Western Europe	34,760	39,929	54,331	27,669	36,483	41,684
European Economic Community	27,092	32,048	42,582	22,209	29,006	33,295
Belgium and Luxembourg	3,138	3,653	5,186	1,453	1,762	1,741
Denmark	532	585	732	583	694	707
France	3,503	4,166	5,587	3,032	4,051	4,771
Germany, Federal Republic of	5,989	6,957	8,482	7,238	9,962	10,955
Ireland	378	527	695	236	320	323
Italy	2,790	3,361	4,359	3,037	4,102	4,918
Netherlands	4,812	5,683	6,907	1,488	1,602	1,852
United Kingdom	5,951	7,116	10,635	5,141	6,514	8,029
European Free Trade Association	...	...	...	...	...	...
Austria	245	260	312	281	407	380
Finland	195	215	337	280	368	449
Iceland	36	39	48	159	174	225
Norway	541	558	688	766	1,190	1,266
Portugal	551	525	691	146	180	244
Sweden	1,101	1,091	1,513	998	1,328	1,652
Switzerland	1,749	1,728	3,660	1,180	1,820	2,076
Greece	539	699	812	174	167	183
Spain	1,875	1,884	2,507	971	1,257	1,304
Turkey	424	358	354	148	175	201
Yugoslavia	357	475	757	347	395	389
Eastern Europe	2,544	3,679	5,683	1,132	1,502	1,865
USSR	1,628	2,252	3,607	453	539	872
Asia	**31,436**	**39,630**	**48,771**	**49,312**	**58,264**	**66,740**
Near East	**10,039**	**12,412**	**11,030**	**12,849**	**11,814**	**14,988**
Iran	2,731	3,684	1,019	2,802	2,877	2,784
Iraq	211	317	442	381	243	618
Israel	1,447	1,925	1,857	572	720	749
Jordan	302	235	334	3	1	4
Kuwait	548	745	765	215	50	87
Lebanon	124	142	227	42	15	15
Saudi Arabia	3,575	4,370	4,875	6,347	5,307	7,983
Syria	134	143	229	16	37	165
Japan	**10,529**	**12,885**	**17,579**	**18,550**	**24,458**	**26,243**
East and South Asia	**10,869**	**14,331**	**20,161**	**17,910**	**21,999**	**25,505**
Bangladesh	156	170	204	57	79	88
China, People's Republic of	171	822	1,724	201	324	591
China, Republic of	1,798	2,342	3,271	3,666	5,170	5,901
Hong Kong	1,292	1,625	2,083	2,894	3,474	4,006
India	779	948	1,167	776	979	1,038
Indonesia	763	751	982	3,475	3,607	3,621
Korea, Republic of	2,371	3,160	4,191	2,883	3,746	4,047
Malaysia	561	728	932	1,318	1,519	2,146
Pakistan	293	496	529	56	84	120
Philippines	876	1,041	1,570	1,110	1,207	1,489
Singapore	1,172	1,462	2,331	883	1,068	1,467
Thailand	510	629	961	346	439	600
Oceania	**2,877**	**3,464**	**4,319**	**1,728**	**2,350**	**3,072**
Australia	2,356	2,912	3,617	1,185	1,659	2,164
New Zealand and Samoa	405	409	533	357	528	710
Africa	**5,546**	**5,886**	**6,299**	**17,120**	**16,904**	**24,377**
Algeria	527	374	404	3,104	3,482	4,940
Canary Islands	85	91	113	46	12	6
Egypt	982	1,134	1,433	170	105	381
Gabon	30	97	33	229	184	320
Ghana	146	126	91	214	215	225
Ivory Coast	89	93	128	300	415	363
Kenya	77	138	61	92	51	50
Liberia	91	108	108	106	133	136
Libya	314	425	468	3,817	3,779	5,256
Morocco	372	406	271	22	44	40
Nigeria	958	985	632	6,152	4,709	8,162
South Africa, Rep. of	1,054	1,080	1,413	1,261	2,259	2,617
Sudan	87	157	103	18	14	16
Tunisia	111	83	175	11	21	95
Zaire	114	83	113	173	225	286

U.S. Exports and Imports of Leading Commodities

Source: Office of Planning and Research, U.S. Commerce Department (millions of dollars)

Commodity	Exports			Imports		
	1979	1978	1977	1979	1978	1977
Food and live animals	**22,245**	**18,311**	**14,116**	**15,171**	**13,522**	**12,558**
Cattle, except for breeding	...	...	...	236	250	186
Meat and preparations	1,127	958	797	2,539	1,856	1,276
Cheese	...	...	...	293	270	218
Dairy products and eggs	161	190	189	...	...	...
Fish	1,027	837	476	2,639	2,212	2,056
Grains and preparations	14,450	11,634	8,755	178	155	149
Wheat, including flour	5,491	4,532	2,882	...	...	...
Rice	850	929	730	...	...	...
Grains and animal feed	2,317	1,921	1,573	120	92	100
Fruits and nuts	1,525	1,335	1,080	1,324	1,126	957
Vegetables	605	554	518	737	711	593
Sugar	...	...	...	974	723	1,076
Coffee, green	...	...	...	3,820	3,728	3,910
Cocoa or cacao beans	...	...	...	555	667	482
Tea	...	...	...	126	115	176
Spices	...	...	...	139	144	139
Beverages and Tobacco	**2,337**	**2,293**	**1,847**	**2,566**	**2,221**	**1,669**
Alcoholic beverages	...	...	...	2,013	1,744	1,287
Tobacco and manufactures	2,093	2,107	1,709	436	396	322
Beverages and other tobacco	244	186	138	117	81	60
Crude materials, inedible, except fuels	**20,755**	**15,555**	**13,086**	**10,651**	**9,294**	**8,464**
Hides and skins	992	695	578	322	248	219
Soybeans, oilseeds, peanuts	6,379	5,864	4,798	...	...	...
Synthetic rubber	579	369	327	...	...	...
Rubber, including latex	...	...	...	1,058	840	783
Lumber and rough wood	2,770	1,828	1,622	2,910	2,736	2,096
Wood pulp	1,104	817	875	1,506	1,125	1,213
Textile fibers and wastes	3,047	2,302	1,899	231	248	222
Ores and metal scrap	3,325	1,839	1,290	3,247	2,813	2,732
Mineral fuels and related mat'ls	**5,616**	**3,881**	**4,184**	**60,061**	**42,096**	**44,537**
Coal	3,394	2,046	2,655	...	...	...
Petroleum and products	1,914	1,564	1,280	56,046	39,104	42,368
Natural gas	180	194	173	2,765	2,000	1,941
Animal and vegetable oils and fats	**1,845**	**1,521**	**1,309**	**740**	**511**	**531**
Chemicals	**17,306**	**12,623**	**10,812**	**7,485**	**6,430**	**4,970**
Medicines and pharmaceuticals	1,591	1,404	1,081	441	449	313
Fertilizers, manufactured	1,404	1,091	704	976	869	829
Plastic materials and resins	3,241	2,088	1,838	626	518	410
Machinery and transport equip.	**70,491**	**59,268**	**50,248**	**53,678**	**47,590**	**36,407**
Machinery	45,914	38,105	32,630	28,530	24,752	18,836
Aircraft engines and parts	1,423	1,142	939	328	285	136
Auto engines and parts	1,631	1,364	990	1,949	2,090	1,607
Agricultural machinery	1,088	844	716	698	489	499
Tractors and parts	597	493	868	1,205	848	626
Office machines	6,475	5,006	3,885	2,500	2,254	1,568
Transport equipment	24,577	21,163	17,619	25,148	22,838	17,571
Road motor vehicles and parts	13,904	12,148	10,887	22,053	20,579	15,844
Aircraft and parts except engines	9,719	8,203	5,874	1,078	602	603
Other manufactured goods	**28,879**	**22,644**	**19,091**	**51,071**	**46,296**	**35,176**
Tires and tubes	353	280	286	1,135	923	851
Wood and manufactures, exc. furniture	448	356	356	1,370	1,219	1,032
Paper and manufactures	1,967	1,597	1,517	3,356	2,923	2,402
Glassware and pottery	658	574	489	1,097	1,048	786
Diamonds, excl. industrial	623	457	336	1,862	1,973	1,452
Nonmetallic mineral manuf.	1,949	1,597	1,275	...	...	...
Metals and manufactures	7,505	5,856	6,045	17,457	15,712	12,278
Pig iron and ferroalloys	...	...	...	702	573	528
Iron and steel-mill products	2,227	1,646	2,608	6,764	6,681	5,302
Platinum group metals	...	...	...	800	430	252
Nonferrous base metals	1,609	1,048	1,059	4,678	4,367	3,380
Other manuf. of metals	3,431	3,107	2,399	3,671	3,333	2,500
Textiles, other than clothing	3,189	2,225	1,970	2,216	2,200	1,736
Clothing	919	650	572	5,876	5,657	4,100
Footwear	...	...	...	2,859	2,585	1,806
Furniture	385	348	258	1,035	875	670
Scientific and photo equip., photo supplies	5,422	4,350	3,435	1,912	1,739	1,256
Printed matter	956	812	668	529	479	340
Clocks and watches	...	...	...	946	947	722
Toys, games, sporting goods	882	669	491	1,591	1,274	1,155
Artworks and antiques	...	...	...	1,487	1,312	720
Other transactions	**9,103**	**5,030**	**4,314**	**4,905**	**4,018**	**3,358**
Total	**181,802**	**143,663**	**121,212**	**206,327**	**171,978**	**147,685**

U.S. Merchandise Exports and Imports, by Continent

Source: Office of Planning and Research, U.S. Commerce Department (millions of dollars)

Year	Exports: Western Hemis.	Exports: Europe	Exports: Asia & Oceania	Exports: Africa	General imports: Western Hemis.	General imports: Europe	General imports: Asia & Oceania	General imports: Africa
1965	9,932	9,397	7,129	1,071	9,257	6,292	4,999	867
1970	15,611	14,817	11,294	1,502	16,928	11,395	10,515	1,090
1973	25,033	23,160	20,388	2,081	27,322	19,812	19,745	2,557
1974	35,746	30,070	28,937	3,204	40,332	24,410	28,943	6,551
1975	38,843	32,732	31,246	4,266	37,773	21,465	28,590	8,277
1976	41,074	35,900	33,229	4,396	43,356	23,645	41,131	12,522
1977	43,751	37,304	35,295	4,564	50,697	28,801	51,210	16,950
1978	50,394	43,608	44,228	4,752	56,473	37,985	60,719	16,799
1979	61,553	60,014	54,523	4,866	68,582	43,549	70,193	23,996

Value of U.S. Exports, Imports, and Merchandise Balance

(millions of dollars)

Year	Principal Census trade totals: U.S. exports and reexports excluding military grant-aid	U.S. general imports f.a.s. transaction values[1]	U.S. merchandise balance f.a.s.[1]	U.S. general imports c.i.f.	U.S. balance exports f.a.s. imports c.i.f.	Other Census totals: Military grant-aid shipments	Exports of domestic merchandise	Re-exports
1950	9,997	8,954	1,043	—	—	282	10,146	133
1955	14,298	11,566	2,732	—	—	1,256	15,426	128
1960	19,659	15,073	4,586	—	—	949	20,408	201
1965	26,742	21,427	5,315	—	—	773	27,178	343
1970[2]	42,664	40,114	2,550	42,591	73	565	42,590	634
1975[2]	107,589	96,570	11,019	103,843	3,746	461	106,561	1,489
1979[2]	181,637	206,326	−24,689	218,927	−37,290	165	178,578	3,224

Note: Export values include both commercially-financed shipments and shipments under government-financed programs such as AID and PL-480. (1) Prior to 1974, imports are customs values, i.e. generally at prices in principal foreign markets. (2) Beginning 1970, includes nonmonetary gold valued as follows in millions of dollars in 1970-79 respectively: Exports - 4, 24, 28, 50, 89, 459, 348, 1,079, 1,123, and 4,929; imports - 162, 221, 358, 356, 397, 457, 331, 649, 898, and 1,461.

U.S. Foreign Trade, by Economic Classes

(millions of dollars)

Economic class	1965	1970	1975	1976	1977	1978	1979
Exports, total	**29,128**	**45,114**	**106,102**	**113,318**	**117,966**	**141,154**	**178,578**
Excluding military grant-aid	...	...	**105,641**	**113,133**	**117,899**	**141,069**	**178,413**
Crude foods	2,587	2,748	11,804	11,420	9,438	12,723	15,782
Manufactured foods	1,590	1,921	4,221	4,764	5,356	6,690	7,652
Crude materials	2,887	4,492	10,883	11,805	13,976	15,603	20,030
Agricultural	1,942	2,524	5,747	6,765	8,804	12,090	15,025
Semimanufactures	4,114	6,866	12,815	13,969	14,107	18,904	30,844
Finished manufactures	16,008	26,563	66,379	71,365	75,084	87,234	104,296
Excluding military grant-aid	...	...	65,918	71,175	75,022	87,149	104,131
Imports, total[1]	**22,293**	**40,748**	**96,902**	**121,795**	**147,848**	**173,290**	**207,131**
Crude foods	2,008	2,579	3,642	5,225	7,065	7,241	7,748
Manufactured foods	1,877	3,519	5,953	6,277	6,755	8,127	9,615
Crude materials	3,709	4,126	23,570	32,080	40,822	41,141	57,674
Agricultural	864	797	1,280	1,620	1,732	1,956	2,377
Semimanufactures	4,964	7,263	17,326	20,495	24,182	27,575	31,767
Finished manufactures	8,871	22,464	46,411	57,716	69,025	89,204	100,327

(1) Customs values are shown for imports.

Total Exports and Exports Financed by Foreign Aid

(millions of dollars)

	1965	1970	1975	1976	1977	1978	1979
Exports, total	**27,530**	**43,224**	**107,592**	**114,992**	**120,163**	**143,663**	**181,802**
Agricultural commodities	6,306	7,349	22,097	23,281	24,234	29,777	35,209
Nonagricultural commodities	20,445	35,310	85,094	91,522	95,867	113,801	146,428
Manufactured goods (domestic)	17,439	29,343	70,950	77,241	80,453	94,535	116,676
Military grant—aid	779	565	461	190	62	85	165
Export financed under P.L.-480	1,323	1,021	1,181	1,078	1,074	1,144	1,159
Sales for foreign currency	899	276	—	—	—	—	—
Donations, including disaster relief	253	255	257	307	368	350	341
Long-term dollar credit sales	152	490	924	771	706	794	818
AID expend. for U.S. goods for export	—	—	665	671	802	988	709

Value of Principal Agricultural Exports

(millions of dollars)

Commodity	Avg. 1961-65	Avg. 1966-70	1965	1970	1975	1977	1978	1979
Wheat and wheat products	1,268	1,197	1,214	1,144	5,292	2,932	4,602	5,586
Feed grains	841	1,082	1,162	1,099	5,492	4,862	5,853	7,739
Rice	178	311	244	314	858	698	932	854
Fodders and feeds	179	386	278	496	987	592	609	838
Oilseeds and products	774	1,182	1,029	1,642	NA	6,630	8,175	8,886
Cotton, raw	639	408	495	377	991	1,529	1,740	2,198

Shortest Navigable Distances Between Ports

Source: Distances Between Ports. Defense Mapping Agency Hydrographic/Topographic Center

Distances shown are in nautical miles (1,852 meters or about 6,076.115 feet) To get statute miles, multiply by 1.15.

TO FROM	New York	Montreal	Colon[1]
Algiers, Algeria	3,617	3,600	4,745
Amsterdam, Netherlands	3,438	3,162	4,825
Baltimore, Md.	417	1,769	1,901
Barcelona, Spain	3,714	3,697	4,842
Boston, Mass.	386	1,308	2,157
Buenos Aires, Argentina	5,817	6,455	5,472
Cape Town, S. Africa[2]	6,786	7,118	6,494
Cherbourg, France	3,154	2,878	4,541
Cobh, Ireland	2,901	2,603	4,308
Copenhagen, Denmark	3,846	3,570	5,233
Dakar, Senegal	3,335	3,566	3,694
Galveston, Tex.	1,882	3,165	1,492
Gibraltar[3]	3,204	3,187	4,332
Glasgow, Scotland	3,086	2,691	4,508
Halifax, N.S.	600	895	2,295
Hamburg, W. Germany	3,674	3,398	5,061
Hamilton, Bermuda	697	1,572	1,659
Havana, Cuba	1,186	2,473	998
Helsinki, Finland	4,309	4,033	5,696
Istanbul, Turkey	5,001	4,984	6,129
Kingston, Jamaica	1,474	2,690	551
Lagos, Nigeria	4,883	5,130	5,049
Lisbon, Portugal	2,972	2,943	4,152
Marseille, France	3,891	3,874	5,019
Montreal, Quebec	1,460		3,126
Naples, Italy	4,181	4,164	5,309
Nassau, Bahamas	962	2,274	1,166
New Orleans, La.	1,708	2,991	1,389
New York, N.Y.		1,460	1,974
Norfolk, Va.	294	1,700	1,779
Oslo, Norway	3,827	3,165	5,053
Piraeus, Greece	4,688	4,671	5,816
Port Said, Egypt	5,123	5,106	6,251
Rio de Janeiro, Brazil	4,770	5,354	4,367
St. John's, Nfld.	1,093	1,043	2,695
San Juan, Puerto Rico	1,399	2,445	993
Southampton, England	3,189	2,913	4,576

TO FROM	San. Fran.	Vancouver	Panama[1]
Acapulco, Mexico	1,833	2,613	1,426
Anchorage, Alas.	1,872	1,444	5,093
Bombay, India	9,794	9,578	12,962
Calcutta, India	8,991	8,728	12,154
Colon, Panama[1]	3,298	4,076	44
Jakarta, Indonesia	7,641	7,360	10,637
Haiphong, Vietnam	6,496	6,231	9,673
Hong Kong	6,044	5,777	9,195
Honolulu, Hawaii	2,091	2,423	4,685
Los Angeles, Cal.	371	1,161	2,913
Manila, Philippines	6,221	5,976	9,347
Melbourne, Australia	6,970	7,343	7,928
Pusan, S. Korea	4,914	4,623	8,074
Ho Chi Min City, Vietnam	6,878	6,664	10,017
San Francisco, Cal.		812	3,245
Seattle, Wash.	807	126	4,020
Shanghai, China	5,396	5,110	8,566
Singapore	7,353	7,078	10,505
Suva, Fiji	4,749	5,183	6,325
Valparaiso, Chile	5,140	5,915	2,616
Vancouver, B.C.	812		4,032
Vladivostok, USSR	4,563	4,378	7,741
Yokohama, Japan	4,536	4,262	7,682

TO FROM	Port Said	Cape Town[2]	Singapore
Bombay, India	3,049	4,616	2,441
Calcutta, India	4,695	5,638	1,649
Dar es Salaam, Tanzania	3,238	2,365	4,042
Jakarta, Indonesia	5,293	5,276	525
Hong Kong	6,462	7,006	1,454
Kuwait	3,360	5,176	3,833
Manila, Philippines	6,348	6,777	1,330
Melbourne, Australia	7,842	5,963	3,844
Ho Chi Min City, Vietnam	5,667	6,263	649
Singapore	5,018	5,614	
Yokohama, Japan	7,907	8,503	2,889

(1) Colon on the Atlantic is 44 nautical miles from Panama (port) on the Pacific. (2) Cape Town is 35 nautical miles northwest of the Cape of Good Hope. (3) Gibraltar (port) is 24 nautical miles east of the Strait of Gibraltar.

Notable Ocean Passages by Ships

Compiled by N.R.P. Bonsor

Date	Ship		From	To	Nautical miles	Time D. H. M	Speed (knots)
			Sailing Vessels				
1846	Yorkshire		Liverpool	New York	3150	16. 0. 0	8.46†
1853	Northern Light		San Francisco	Boston	—	76. 6. 0	—
1854	James Baines		Boston Light	Light Rock	—	12. 6. 0	—
1854	Flying Cloud		New York	San Francisco	15091	89. 0. 0	7.07†
1868-9	Thermopylae		Liverpool	Melbourne	—	63.18.15	—
—	Red Jacket		New York	Liverpool	3150	13. 1.25	10.05†
—	Starr King		50 S. Lat	Golden Gate	—	36. 0. 0	—
—	Golden Fleece		Equator	San Francisco	—	12.12. 0	—
1905	Atlantic		Sandy Hook	England	3013	12. 4. 0	10.32
			Atlantic Crossing by Passenger Steamships				
1819 (5/22 - 6/20)	Savannah (a)	US	Savannah	Liverpool	—	29. 4. 0	—
1838 (5/7 - 5/22)	Great Western	Br	New York	Avonmouth	3218	14.15.59	9.14
1840 (8/4 - 8/14)	Britannia	Br	Halifax	Liverpool	2610	9.21.44	10.98†
1854 (6/28 - 7/7)	Baltic	US	Liverpool	New York	3037	9.16.52	13.04
1856 (8/6 - 8/15)	Persia	Br	Sandy Hook	Liverpool	3046	8.23.19	14.15†
1876 (12/16-12/24)	Britannic	Br	Sandy Hook	Queenstown	2882	7.12.41	15.94
1895 (5/18 - 5/24)	Lucania	Br	Sandy Hook	Queenstown	2897	5.11.40	22.00
1898 (3/30 - 4/5)	Kaiser Wilhelm der Grosse	Ger	Needles	Sandy Hook	3120	5.20. 0	22.29
1901 (7/10 - 7/17)	Deutschland	Ger	Sandy Hook	Eddystone	3082	5.11. 5	23.51
1907 (10/6 - 10/10)	Lusitania	Br	Queenstown	Sandy Hook	2780	4.19.52	23.99
1924 (8/20 - 8/25)	Mauretania	Br	Ambrose	Cherbourg	3198	5. 1.49	26.25
1929 (7/17 - 7/22)	Bremen*	Ger	Cherbourg	Ambrose	3164	4.17.42	27.83
1933 (6/27 - 7/2)	Europa	Ger	Cherbourg	Ambrose	3149	4.16.48	27.92
1933 (8/11 - 8/16)	Rex	It	Gibraltar	Ambrose	3181	4.13.58	28.92
1935 (5/30 - 6/3)	Normandie*	Fr	Bishop Rock	Ambrose	2971	4. 3. 2	29.98
1938 (8/10 - 8/14)	Queen Mary	Br	Ambrose	Bishop Rock	2938	3.20.42	31.69
1952 (7/11 - 7/15)	United States	US	Bishop Rock	Ambrose	2906	3.12.12	34.51
1952 (7/3 - 7/7)	United States* (e)	US	Ambrose	Bishop Rock	2942	3.10.40	35.59
			Other Ocean Passages				
1928 (June)	USS Lexington		San Pedro	Honolulu	2226	3. 0.36	30.66
1944 (Jul-Sep)	St. Roch (c) (Can)		Halifax	Vancouver	7295	86. 0. 0	—
1945 (7/16-7/19)	USS Indianapolis (d)		San Francisco	Oahu, Hawaii	2091	3. 2.20	28.07
1945 (11/26)	USS Lake Champlain		Gibraltar	Newport News	3360	4. 8.51	32.04
1950 (Jul-Aug)	USS Boxer		Japan	San Francisco	5000	7.18.36	26.80†

(continued)

Date	Ship	From	To	Nautical miles	Time D. H. M	Speed (knots)
1951 (6/1-6/9)	USS Philippine Sea	Yokohama	Alameda	5000	7.13. 0	27.62†
1958 (2/25-3/4)	USS Skate (f)	Nantucket	Portland, Eng	3161	8.11. 0	15.57
1958 (3/23-3/29)	USS Skate (f)	Lizard, Eng	Nantucket	—	7. 5. 0	—
1958 (7/23-8/7)	USS Nautilus (g)	Pearl Harbor	Iceland (via N. Pole)	—	15. 0. 0	—
1960 (2/16-5/10)	USS Triton (h)	New London	Rehoboth, Del	41500	84. 0. 0	20.59†
1960 (8/15-8/20)	USS Seadragon (i)	Baffin Bay	NW Passage, Pac	850	6. 0. 0	—
1962 (10/30-11/11)	African Comet* (US)	New York	Cape Town	6786	12.16.22	22.03
1973 (8/20)	Sea-Land Exchange (k) (US)	Bishop Rock	Ambrose	2912	3.11.24	34.92
1973 (8/24)	Sea-Land Trade (US)	Kobe	Race Rock, BC	4126	5. 6. 0	32.75

† The time taken and/or distance covered is approximate and so, therefore, is the average speed.

* Maiden voyage. (a) The Savannah, a fully rigged sailing vessel with steam auxiliary (over 300 tons, 98.5 ft. long, beam 25.8 ft., depth 12.9 ft.) was launched in the East River in 1818. It was the first ship to use steam in crossing any ocean. It was supplied with engines and detachable iron paddle wheels. On its famous voyage it used steam 105 hours. (b) First Cunard liner. (c) First ship to complete NW Passage in one season. (d) Carried Hiroshima atomic bomb in World War II. (e) Set world speed record; average speed eastbound on maiden voyage 35.59 knots (about 41 m.p.h.). (f) First atomic submarine to cross Atlantic both ways submerged. (g) World's first atomic submarine also first to make undersea voyage under polar ice cap, 1,830 mi. from Point Barrow, Alaska, to Atlantic Ocean, Aug. 1-4, 1958, reaching North Pole Aug. 3. Second undersea transit of the North Pole made by submarine USS Skate Aug. 11, 1958, during trip from New London, Conn., and return. (h) World's largest submarine. Nuclear-powered Triton was submerged during nearly all its voyage around the globe. It duplicated the route of Ferdinand Magellan's circuit (1519-1522) 30,708 mi., starting from St. Paul Rocks off the NE coast of Brazil, Feb. 24-Apr. 25, 1960, then sailed to Cadiz, Spain, before returning home. (i) First underwater transit of Northwest Passage. (k) Fastest freighter crossing of Atlantic.

Commerce at Principal North American Ports

Handling 1,000,000 tons or more per year

Source: Corps of Engineers, Department of the Army; Statistics Canada

1978 (short tons)

Major Ports

Port of New York, N.Y. & N.J.	185,292,125
New Orleans, La.	162,991,985
Houston, Tex.	104,291,267
Baton Rouge, La.	70,008,229
Philadelphia Harbor, Pa.	49,710,565
Beaumont, Tex.	48,918,843
Corpus Christi, Tex.	46,871,695
Tampa Harbor, Fla.	45,619,951
Baltimore Harbor and Channels, Md.	44,756,359
Norfolk Harbor, Va.	43,862,200
Vancouver, B.C.	42,973,946
Mobile Harbor, Ala.	35,943,893
Texas City, Tex.	33,583,596
Long Beach, Cal.	32,985,424
Los Angeles Harbor, Cal.	31,325,506
Port Arthur, Tex.	30,753,732
Marcus Hook, Pa. and vicinity	29,780,434
Paulsboro, N.J. and vicinity	27,014,723
Boston, Mass.	25,975,275
Lake Charles, La.	25,401,265
Sept-Isles, Que.	24,963,214
Port Cartier, Que.	23,954,821
Pascagoula Harbor, Miss.	23,832,891
Richmond Harbor, Cal.	23,823,508
Port of Metropolitan St. Louis	22,478,309
Thunder Bay, Ont.	21,789,749
Portland, Ore.	21,400,262
Portland Harbor, Me.	18,326,110
Montreal, Que.	17,518,979
Huntington, W.Va.	17,126,958
Seattle Harbor, Wash.	16,432,876
Freeport Harbor, Tex.	15,332,518
Jacksonville Harbor, Fla.	15,108,032
Quebec, Que.	15,039,690
Hamilton, Ont.	14,389,877
St. John, N.B.	13,088,237
Halifax, N.S.	12,034,052
Memphis, Tenn.	11,894,972
Port Everglades Harbor, Fla.	11,828,434
New Haven Harbor, Conn.	11,119,383
New Castle, Del. and vicinity	10,994,355
Tacoma Harbor, Wash.	10,699,337
Cincinnati, Oh.	10,355,854
Charleston Harbor, S.C.	10,327,659

Other U.S. Ports

Savannah Harbor, Ga.	9,875,678
Port of Albany, N.Y.	9,591,325
Clairton-Elizabeth, Pa.	9,567,313
Galveston, Tex.	9,563,626
Port of Wilmington, N.C.	9,504,953
Harbor Island, Tex.	9,308,303
El Segundo, Cal.	9,271,831
Louisville, Ky.	9,006,440
Anacortes Harbor, Wash.	8,968,313
Port of Newport News, Va.	8,730,346
Providence River and Harbor, R.I.	8,624,315
Longview, Wash.	8,169,386
Coos Bay, Ore.	7,599,421
Pittsburgh, Pa.	7,545,645
Camden-Gloucester, N.J.	7,170,923
Oakland Harbor, Cal.	6,828,938
St. Paul, Minn.	6,809,376
Aliquippa-Rochester, Pa.	5,346,909
Penn Manor, Pa. and vicinity	5,311,156
Fall River Harbor, Mass.	5,285,473
Everett Harbor, Wash.	4,589,002
Port Jefferson Harbor, N.Y.	4,484,081
Matagorda Ship Channel, Port Lavaca, Tex.	3,894,810
Mount Vernon, Ind.	3,677,285
Helena, Ark.	3,510,229
Miami Harbor, Fla.	3,504,543
Portsmouth Harbor, N.H.	3,499,854
Bridgeport Harbor, Conn.	3,495,140
Nashville, Tenn.	3,332,947
Port Angeles Harbor, Wash.	3,283,012
Vicksburg, Miss.	3,107,608
Pensacola Harbor, Fla.	3,105,287
Greenville, Miss.	3,036,199
Wilmington Harbor, Del.	2,917,774
Morehead City Harbor, N.C.	2,874,828
Vancouver, Wash.	2,832,673
Canaveral Harbor, Fla.	2,807,463
New London Harbor, Conn.	2,649,757
Grays Harbor and Chehalis River, Wash.	2,646,192
Astoria, Ore.	2,628,963
Victoria, Tex.	2,564,684
Minneapolis, Minn.	2,513,142
Charlotte Harbor, Fla.	2,472,973
San Diego Harbor, Cal.	2,264,445
Moss Landing Harbor, Cal.	2,204,350
Brownsville, Tex.	2,130,440
Kansas City, Mo.	1,955,825
San Francisco Harbor, Cal.	1,931,693
Brunswick Harbor, Ga.	1,744,797
Chattanooga, Tenn.	1,738,241
Bellingham Bay and Harbor, Wash.	1,718,417
Salem Harbor, Mass.	1,648,636
Humboldt Harbor and Bay, Cal.	1,644,573
Port of Richmond, Va.	1,584,253
Washington Harbor, D.C.	1,537,085
Stockton, Cal.	1,520,991
Hempstead Harbor, N.Y.	1,502,662
Searsport Harbor, Me.	1,497,184
Ventura Harbor, Cal.	1,458,529
Panama City Harbor, Fla.	1,393,065
Georgetown Harbor, S.C.	1,380,577
Port Townsend Harbor, Wash.	1,262,736
Trenton Harbor, N.J.	1,248,079
Weedon Island, Fla.	1,210,932
Port of Hopewell, Va.	1,111,457
Gulfport Harbor, Miss.	1,094,796
Hammersley Inlet, Wash.	1,073,781
Guntersville, Ala.	1,050,871
Orange, Tex.	1,003,331

Alaska, Hawaii, Puerto Rico

San Juan Harbor, P.R.	9,400,996
Honolulu Harbor, Ha.	6,881,556
Barbers Point, Ha.	6,630,994
Anchorage, Alas.	2,267,081
Ketchikan Harbor, Alas.	1,965,726
Kahului Harbor, Ha.	1,301,095
Skagway Harbor, Alas.	1,026,448
Hilo Harbor, Ha.	1,013,430

Commerce at Great Lakes Ports

Port of Chicago, Ill.	36,136,148
Duluth-Superior Harbor, Minn. and Wis.	33,419,210
Port of Detroit, Mich.	25,092,847
Toledo Harbor, Oh.	23,275,707
Cleveland Harbor, Oh.	16,103,781
Indiana Harbor, Ind.	15,958,303
Conneaut Harbor, Oh.	15,146,627
Calcite, Mich.	11,985,201
Ashtabula Harbor, Oh.	11,632,975
Escanaba, Mich.	9,506,126
Port of Buffalo, N.Y.	8,696,209
Gary Harbor, Ind.	8,072,538
Stoneport, Mich.	7,991,640
Lorain Harbor, Oh.	6,286,913
Presque Isle Harbor, Mich.	5,215,296
Silver Bay, Minn.	4,908,728
St. Clair, Mich.	4,586,145
Sandusky Harbor, Oh.	4,314,377
Taconite Harbor, Minn.	4,155,476
Milwaukee Harbor, Wis.	3,946,382
Port Dolomite, Mich.	3,798,652
Port Inland, Mich.	3,469,169
Alpena Harbor, Mich.	3,004,934
Green Bay Harbor, Wis.	2,476,718
Ludington Harbor, Mich.	2,448,983
Fairport Harbor, Oh.	2,199,262
Buffington Harbor, Ind.	2,181,630
Drummond Island, Mich.	2,131,597
Marblehead, Oh.	2,011,134
Huron Harbor, Oh.	1,933,192
Muskegon Harbor, Mich.	1,912,425
Oswego Harbor, N.Y.	1,346,112

Commerce on U.S. Inland Waterways

Source: Corps of Engineers, Department of the Army 1977

Mississippi River System and Gulf Intracoastal Waterway

Waterway	Tons
Mississippi River System	536,826,836
Mississippi River, Minneapolis to the Gulf	396,771,216
Mississippi River, Minneapolis to St. Louis	67,218,142
Mississippi River, St. Louis to Cairo	74,512,050
Mississippi River, Cairo to Baton Rouge	124,061,787
Mississippi River, Baton Rouge to New Orleans	274,110,997
Mississippi River, New Orleans to Gulf	266,473,540
Gulf Intracoastal Waterway	104,934,179

Ton-Mileage of Freight Carried on Inland Waterways

System	Ton-miles
Atlantic Coast Waterways	30,381,926
Gulf Coast Waterways	37,571,386
Pacific Coast Waterways	12,774,038
Mississippi River System, including Ohio River and Tributaries	196,853,367
Great Lakes System, U.S. Commerce Only	90,694,592
Total:	**368,275,309**

Important Waterways and Canals

The St. Lawrence & Great Lakes Waterway, the largest inland navigation system on the continent, extends from the Atlantic Ocean to Duluth at the western end of Lake Superior, a distance of 2,342 miles. With the deepening of channels and locks to 27 ft., ocean carriers are able to penetrate to ports in the Canadian interior and the American midwest.

The major canals are those of the St. Lawrence Great Lakes waterway — the 3 new canals of the St. Lawrence Seaway, with their 7 locks, providing navigation for vessels of 26-foot draught from Montreal to Lake Ontario; the Welland Ship Canal by-passing the Niagara River between Lake Ontario and Lake Erie with its 8 locks, and the Sault Ste. Marie Canal and lock between Lake Huron and Lake Superior. These 16 locks overcome a drop of 580 ft. from the head of the lakes to Montreal. From Montreal to Lake Ontario the former bottleneck of narrow, shallow canals and of slow passage through 22 locks has been overcome, giving faster and safer movement for larger vessels. The new locks and linking channels now accommodate all but the largest ocean-going vessels and the upper St. Lawrence and Great Lakes are open to 80% of the world's saltwater fleet.

Subsidiary Canadian canals or branches include the St. Peters Canal between Bras d'Or Lakes and the Atlantic Ocean in Nova Scotia; the St. Ours and Chambly Canals on the Richelieu River, Quebec; the Ste. Anne and Carillon Canals on the Ottawa River; the Rideau Canal between the Ottawa River and Lake Ontario, the Trent and Murrary Canals between Lake Ontario and Georgian Bay in Ontario and the St. Andrew's Canal on the Red River. The commercial value of these canals is not great but they are maintained to control water levels and permit the passage of small vessels and pleasure craft. The Canso Canal, completed 1957, permits shipping to pass through the causeway connecting Cape Breton Island with the Nova Scotia mainland.

The 1978 navigation season began on April 3 and ended when the last commercial vessel cleared the St. Lawrence Seaway system on December 22.

Cargo tonnage on the Montreal - Lake Ontario Section of the Seaway was 62.8 million tons, second only to 1977 when 63.3 million tons of cargo moved through the Seaway. Bulk cargo for the 1978 season reached 57.7 million tons, setting a Seaway record, with an increase of 34.3% in the shipment of grains largely responsible for the record-setting tonnage.

Addresses: St. Lawrence Seaway Development Corporation (U.S.), P.O. Box 520, Massena, N.Y., David W. Oberlin, Administrator, and St. Lawrence Seaway Authority (Canada), Ottawa, Ont., Mr. Paul D. Normandeau, president.

The Welland Canal overcomes the 326-ft. drop of Niagara Falls and the rapids of the Niagara River. It has 8 locks, each 859 ft. long, 80 ft. wide and 30 ft. deep. Regulations permit ships of 730-ft. length and 75-ft. beam to transit.

Panama Canal

The Panama Canal is a lock and lake canal, crossing the Isthmus of Panama from the Caribbean Sea in a southeasterly direction to the Bay of Panama of the Pacific Ocean. It is 50 mi. long from deep water to deep water, at least 500 ft. wide at the bottom of excavated channels, 110 ft. wide in lock chambers, which have a usable length of 1,000 ft. Depth varies, but is not less than 40 ft. Time in transit is about 8 hours.

Gatun Dam blocks the Chagres River near its Atlantic mouth, creating Gatun Lake, 23 3/4 mi. long, 85 ft. above sea level, about 45 ft. deep. Ships ascend to the lake by locks and then pass through Gaillard (formerly Culebra) Cut, 8 mi. long.

Cargo tonnage on the Panama Canal in fiscal 1977 amounted to 123.1 million compared with 117.4 million tons in 1976. Transit of oceangoing ships in fiscal 1977 totaled 11,997 compared with 12,280 in fiscal 1976. Toll collections in fiscal 1977 were $164.6 million, $135.0 million in 1976.

Improvements have included the widening of the 8-mile long channel through Gaillard Cut from 300 to 500 ft., costing $60 million; illumination of Gaillard Cut and installation of new towing locomotives at the locks costing $8 million.

Thatcher Ferry Bridge, opened 1962, spans Panama Canal 201 ft. above the water level near Balboa. It is a steel-arch bridge, about one mi. long, with 3 spans and 4 lanes. It cost $20 million authorized by the U.S. Congress in 1956.

Fastest Scheduled Train Runs in U.S. and Canada

Source: Donald M. Steffee; figures are based on 1980 timetables

Electric Traction-passenger-(75 mph and over)

Railroad	Train	From	To	Dis.	Time	Speed
Amtrak	Chesapeake	Perryville	Elkton	14.6	10	87.6
Amtrak	Chesapeake	Elkton	Perryville	14.6	11	79.7
Conrail	Jersey Arrow	Princeton Jct.	Newark	38.4	29	79.4
Amtrak	Chesapeake	Edmondson	Odenton	15.3	12	76.5
Amtrak	Metroliners(9)	Eilmington	Baltimore	68.4	54	76.0

Diesel Traction—Passenger—(75 mph and over)

Railroad	Train	From	To	Dis.	Time	Speed
VIA Rail Canada	Turbotrain	Kingston	Guildwood	145.1	101	86.2
VIA Rail Canada	Rapido	Cornwall	Kingston	108.1	78	83.2
VIA Rail Canada	Turbotrain	Kingston	Dorval	165.8	120	82.9
VIA Rail Canada	Turbotrain	Dorval	Kingston	165.8	121	82.2
Amtrak	Southwest Limited	Garden City	Lamar	99.9	73	82.1
VIA Rail Canada	Turbotrain	Guildwood	Kingston	145.1	106	82.1
Amtrak	Southwest Limited	Dodge City	Hutchinson	120.1	90	80.1
Amtrak	Southwest Limited	Marceline	Carrollton	39.1	30	78.2
Amtrak	Southwest Limited	Lamar	Garden City	99.9	77	77.8
VIA Rail Canada	Rapidos(2)	Dorval	Kingston	165.8	128	77.7
VIA Rail Canada	Rapidos(2)	Guildwood	Kingston	145.1	113	77.0
Amtrak	San Francisco Zephyr	Akron	McCook	142.9	112	76.5
VIA Rail Canada	Rapido	Kingston	Cornwall	108.1	85	76.3

Diesel Traction—Freight—(62 mph and over)

Railroad	Train	From	To	Dis.	Time	Speed
Union Pacific	BASV	North Platte	Cheyenne	225.4	205	66.0
Union Pacific	Super Van	North Platte	Cheyenne	225.4	215	62.9
Santa Fe	6 trains	Gallup	Winslow	125.8	120	62.9
Santa Fe	No. 991	Winslow	Gallup	125.8	120	62.9
Santa Fe	No. 198	Kingman	Seligman	88.1	85	62.2

Fastest Scheduled Passenger Train Runs in Japan and European Countries

Country	Train	From	To	Dis.	Time	Speed
Japan	Hikari train	Nagoya	Shizouka	108.4	59	110.2
Great Britain	High speed trains(2)	Stevenage	Peterborough	48.8	27½	106.5
France	Etendard	St. Pierre des Corps	Poitiers	62.7	37	101.5
West Germany	3 trains	Uelzen	Celle	32.5	21	92.8
Sweden	No. 142	Skvode	Laxa	52.2	41	77.4
Italy	Rapido 904	Rome	Chiusi	91.9	72	76.6

Passenger Car Production, U.S. Plants

Source: Motor Vehicle Manufacturers Association of the U.S., Inc.

	1978	1979	1980 6 mos.
American Motors Corp.			
Spirit/AMX (Gremlin)	37,466	64,363	32,392
Concord	106,697	88,580	35,151
Pacer	15,386	5,729	—
Eagle (Matador)	4,803	25,964	26,367
Total American Motors Corp.	**164,352**	**184,636**	**93,910**
Chrysler Corp.			
Horizon	162,011	169,981	84,774
Voyager	10,673	6,312	—
Volare	221,761	183,486	51,224
Caravelle	4,493	9,213	3,959
Gran Fury (Fury)	49,176	5,412	13,148
Total Plymouth	**448,114**	**374,404**	**153,105**
LeBaron	150,908	103,678	34,369
Chrysler	85,596	77,749	10,669
Total Chrysler-Plymouth	**684,618**	**555,831**	**198,143**
Omni	126,225	148,125	73,753
Sportsman	33,220	23,124	—
Aspen	162,651	132,610	36,537
Monaco	28,246	—	—
Diplomat	75,755	50,610	16,466
St. Regis	15,453	25,846	10,505
Total Dodge	**441,550**	**380,315**	**137,261**
Total Chrysler Corp.	**1,126,168**	**936,146**	**335,404**
Ford Motor Co.			
LTD (Ford)	278,949	167,170	50,512
LTD II	134,608	22,667	—
Thunderbird	326,873	264,451	74,836
Club Wagon	45,309	36,177	—
Granada	246,407	139,402	49,370
Fairmont	286,046	213,761	143,534
Pinto	185,091	172,619	61,571
Mustang	240,162	365,357	139,893
Total Ford	**1,743,445**	**1,381,604**	**519,716**
Marquis (Mercury)	152,149	100,937	27,522
Cougar	38,460	1,919	—
Cougar XR-7	179,648	133,479	23,697
Monarch	89,974	59,810	16,445
Zephyr	88,254	62,837	45,835
Bobcat	38,601	43,374	11,311
Capri	37,143	107,094	40,151
Lincoln	98,119	71,783	7,028
Mark VI/V	75,845	68,313	9,366
Versailles	15,559	11,864	1,866
Total Lincoln-Mercury	**813,752**	**661,410**	**183,221**
Total Ford Motor Co.	**2,557,197**	**2,043,014**	**702,937**
General Motors Corp.			
Chevrolet	524,094	447,343	70,004
Corvette	48,972	48,568	23,337
Monte Carlo	325,809	227,043	57,197
Malibu	373,454	322,764	125,885
Camaro	281,735	257,872	70,563
Citation/Nova	309,941	343,821	251,296
Monza	166,951	157,979	91,027
Chevette	301,614	413,648	241,270
Acadian	13,585	17,133	13,107
Total Chevrolet	**2,346,155**	**2,236,171**	**943,776**
Pontiac	184,327	144,486	36,372
Grand Prix	206,605	93,158	34,336
LeMans	124,035	88,652	34,670
Firebird	195,378	194,033	46,709
Phoenix	67,951	88,184	74,198
Sunbird	88,714	105,998	80,099
Total Pontiac	**867,010**	**714,511**	**306,384**
Oldsmobile	400,714	365,327	132,318
Toronado	28,251	53,552	22,279
Cutlass	416,458	509,726	220,303
Omega	47,279	58,032	64,614
Starfire	17,547	21,609	—
Total Oldsmobile	**910,249**	**1,008,246**	**439,514**
Buick	300,677	252,220	83,230
Riviera	25,179	58,029	25,818
Century/Regal	352,212	330,560	217,860
Skylark	107,276	121,625	122,159
Skyhawk	24,980	24,715	—
Total Buick	**810,324**	**787,149**	**449,067**
Cadillac	244,355	230,958	65,050
Eldorado	46,612	66,565	29,840
Seville	59,794	48,308	19,546
Total Cadillac	**350,761**	**345,831**	**114,436**
Total General Motors Corp.	**5,284,499**	**5,091,908**	**2,253,177**
Checker Motors Corp.	**4,225**	**4,765**	**1,630**
Volkswagen of America	**40,194**	**173,192**	**109,128**
Total Passenger Cars	**9,176,635**	**8,433,662**	**3,496,186**

Automobile Factory Sales

Source: Motor Vehicle Manufacturers Association, Detroit, Mich.—wholesale values

Year	Passenger cars		Motor trucks, buses		Total	
	Number	Value	Number	Value	Number	Value
1900	4,192	$4,899,433	...	...	4,190	$4,899,443
1910	181,000	215,340,000	6,000	9,660,000	187,000	225,000,000
1920	1,905,560	1,809,170,963	321,789	423,249,410	2,227,349	2,232,420,373
1930	2,787,456	1,644,083,152	575,364	390,752,061	3,362,820	2,034,853,213
1940	3,717,385	2,370,654,083	754,901	567,820,414	4,472,286	2,938,474,497
1950	6,665,863	8,468,137,000	1,337,193	1,707,748,000	8,003,056	10,175,885,000
1960	6,674,796	12,164,234,000	1,194,475	2,350,680,000	7,869,271	14,514,914,000
1970	6,546,817	14,630,217,000	1,692,440	4,819,752,000	8,239,257	19,449,969,000
1979	8,419,226	NA	3,036,706	NA	11,455,932	NA

After July 1, 1964 all tactical vehicles are excluded. Federal excise taxes are excluded in all years.

Trucking: Employees, Payroll, Registration, Taxes

Source: American Trucking Assns.

1977	Trucks registered	Employment in trucking	Wages and salaries ($1,000)	Payments of federal and state highway users taxes ($1,000)	1977	Trucks registered	Employment in trucking	Wages and salaries ($1,000)	Payments of federal and state highway users taxes ($1,000)
Ala.	639,455	163,600	1,803,199	187,275	Mon.	265,956	51,100	541,813	64,847
Alas.	88,924	15,200	300,246	26,245	Neb.	352,459	92,300	970,811	96,477
Ariz.	415,748	116,000	1,393,624	139,850	Nev.	131,744	42,700	531,017	42,814
Ark.	459,808	135,400	1,311,349	125,353	N.H.	81,523	28,700	305,368	26,617
Cal.	3,113,478	1,197,900	16,644,821	888,707	N.J.	358,039	212,500	2,852,388	170,758
Col.	525,214	146,900	1,771,026	120,963	N.M.	297,832	57,100	643,917	81,935
Conn.	142,222	127,700	1,662,016	55,678	N.Y.	837,704	408,500	5,734,523	285,663
Del.	62,576	29,900	390,434	26,170	N.C.	873,157	314,300	3,215,603	266,626
Dist. of Col.	11,873	10,900	176,297	7,715	N.D.	227,974	37,600	384,460	42,207
Fla.	982,872	283,900	3,233,905	305,428	Oh.	1,084,523	334,900	4,350,016	399,934
Ga.	718,471	217,200	2,433,943	181,876	Okla.	715,867	168,400	1,862,167	169,225
Ha.	71,531	21,200	255,926	17,407	Ore.	371,235	121,000	1,471,965	126,444
Ida.	256,968	49,700	529,603	68,397	Pa.	1,137,856	453,200	5,682,675	423,586
Ill.	1,081,335	341,600	4,652,934	379,921	R.I.	76,231	35,900	394,074	21,829
Ind.	812,456	321,700	4,020,607	276,365	S.C.	370,695	145,600	1,471,142	106,885
Ia.	550,553	165,600	1,854,554	172,301	S.D.	196,606	38,400	369,293	43,247
Kan.	560,091	149,500	1,572,441	143,010	Tenn.	653,202	143,700	1,538,309	203,298
Ky.	650,986	154,500	1,733,490	214,000	Tex.	2,375,716	685,000	7,854,895	754,078
La.	655,515	168,100	1,916,340	169,628	Ut.	274,577	60,400	679,983	63,010
Me.	149,223	55,700	554,159	46,294	Vt.	61,085	18,800	198,622	25,075
Md.	370,762	123,400	1,537,193	142,601	Va.	457,740	182,000	2,087,176	211,395
Mass.	359,773	168,000	2,040,024	103,832	Wash.	735,764	195,500	2,553,621	243,807
Mich.	973,831	318,300	4,620,443	357,439	W. Va.	348,875	88,400	1,065,927	116,059
Minn.	667,358	192,100	2,271,583	185,337	Wis.	423,072	157,400	1,881,087	149,981
Miss.	407,435	106,700	1,023,680	115,466	Wy.	147,516	25,600	302,131	54,299
Mo.	726,547	241,800	2,882,014	201,744	**U.S. Total**	**28,311,953**	**9,121,500**	**111,528,835**	**8,849,098**

Car, Truck, and Bus Drivers in the U.S.

Source: Federal Highway Administration, estimated total licenses in force during 1979. (thousands)

State	No. of drivers	State	No. of drivers	State	No. of drivers	State	No. of drivers
Alabama	2,181	Illinois	7,065	Montana	569	Rhode Island	589
Alaska	223	Indiana	3,588	Nebraska	1,079	South Carolina	1,829
Arizona	1,560	Iowa	2,057	Nevada	490	South Dakota	476
Arkansas	1,384	Kansas	1,808	New Hampshire	609	Tennessee	2,730
California	15,157	Kentucky	2,069	New Jersey	4,610	Texas	8,701
Colorado	2,035	Louisiana	2,294	New Mexico	805	Utah	772
Connecticut	2,089	Maine	700	New York	9,487	Vermont	332
Delaware	405	Maryland	2,604	North Carolina	3,663	Virginia	3,340
Dist. of Col.	369	Massachusetts	3,784	North Dakota	413	Washington	2,471
Florida	6,858	Michigan	6,359	Ohio	8,327	West Virginia	1,457
Georgia	3,270	Minnesota	2,282	Oklahoma	1,881	Wisconsin	2,954
Hawaii	540	Mississippi	1,621	Oregon	1,830	Wyoming	312
Idaho	585	Missouri	3,209	Pennsylvania	7,270	**Total**	**143,092**

Minimum Legal Age for Purchase of Alcoholic Beverages

In the U.S. and Canada

	Years		Years		Years		Years		Years
Alabama	19	Hawaii	18	Minnesota	19	North Dakota	21	South Dakota (a)	21
Alaska	19	Idaho	19	Mississippi (e)	21	Northwest Terr.	19	Tennessee	19
Alberta	18	Illinois	21	Missouri	21	Nova Scotia	19	Texas	18
Arizona	19	Indiana	21	Montana	19	Ohio (a)	21	Utah	21
Arkansas	21	Iowa	19	Nebraska	20	Oklahoma	21	Vermont	18
British Columbia	19	Kansas (a)	21	Nevada	21	Oregon	21	Virginia (f)	21
California	21	Kentucky	21	New Brunswick	19	Ontario	18	Washington	21
Colorado (a)	21	Louisiana	18	Newfoundland	19	Pennsylvania	21	West Virginia	18
Connecticut	18	Maine	20	New Hampshire	20	Prince Edward Isl.	18	Wisconsin	18
Delaware	20	Manitoba	18	New Jersey	19	Quebec	18	Wyoming	19
Dist. of Col. (b)	21	Maryland (b)	21	New Mexico	21	Rhode Island (c)	19	Yukon Territory	19
Florida	19	Massachusetts	20	New York	18	Saskatchewan	19		
Georgia	19	Michigan	21	North Carolina (b)	21	South Carolina (d)	21		

(a) 3.2 beer 18. (b) Light wine, beer 18. (c) effective July 1, 1981; 20. (d) Wine, beer 18. (e) Beer not over 4% by wgt. and wine 18. (f) Beer 18.

Motor Vehicle Registrations, Taxes, Motor Fuel, Drivers' Ages

Source: Federal Highway Adm.

State, 1979	Driver's age Jan. 1, 1980 (1) Regular	Driver's age Jan. 1, 1980 (2) Juvenile	Registered autos, buses & trucks (1,000)	State gas tax per gal. cents	Motor fuel adjusted net total tax receipts $1,000	Motor fuel consumption: Highway 1,000 gallons	Motor fuel consumption: Non-highway 1,000 gallons	Motor fuel consumption: Total 1,000 gallons
Alabama	16		2,863	7	168,224	2,341,058	65,435	2,406,493
Alaska	16		268	8	18,989	229,745	6,274	236,019
Arizona	16		1,776	8	123,458	1,536,522	42,334	1,578,856
Arkansas	16		1,502	9.5	134,731	1,471,801	39,910	1,511,711
California	16/18	14	15,973	7	832,000	12,226,316	356,951	12,583,267
Colorado	21	16	2,694	7	123,000	1,708,829	48,171	1,757,000
Connecticut	16/18		2,229	11	154,988	1,451,219	42,986	1,494,205
Delaware	16/18		396	9	30,219	316,037	9,372	325,409
Dist. of Col.	18	16	229	10	20,589	227,680	6,701	234,381
Florida	16/18		7,191	8	402,827	5,056,227	147,891	5,204,118
Georgia	16		3,789	7.5	252,225	3,363,915	93,439	3,457,354
Hawaii	15		548	8.5	27,162	328,848	9,975	338,823
Idaho	16	14	796	9.5	54,379	602,558	16,911	619,469
Illinois	16/18		7,353	7.5	437,630	6,087,498	176,085	6,263,583
Indiana	16/18		3,878	8	256,332	3,240,162	90,150	3,330,312
Iowa	16/18	14	2,425	10	180,108	1,914,036	54,820	1,968,856
Kansas	16	14	1,978	8	120,675	1,531,483	43,620	1,575,103
Kentucky	16		2,648	9	190,045	2,048,992	58,242	2,107,234
Louisiana	15/17	15	2,678	8	184,572	2,295,147	64,919	2,360,066
Maine	15/17	15	726	9	53,936	607,754	17,581	625,335
Maryland	16/18	15¾	2,789	9	185,266	2,065,414	61,279	2,126,693
Massachusetts	17/18	16½	3,744	8.5	206,072	2,480,434	73,972	2,554,406
Michigan	16/18	14	6,488	11	551,135	5,081,801	150,309	5,232,110
Minnesota	16/18	15	2,754	9	210,221	2,430,253	69,240	2,499,493
Mississippi	15		1,648	9	132,565	1,433,648	39,905	1,473,553
Missouri	16		3,238	7	215,157	3,129,145	88,396	3,217,541
Montana	15/16		902	9	55,638	629,251	16,725	645,976
Nebraska	16	14	1,242	10.5	103,940	1,047,831	28,766	1,076,597
Nevada	16	16	631	6	32,921	550,732	15,291	566,023
New Hampshire	16/18	16	682	11	41,923	451,975	13,661	465,636
New Jersey	17	16	4,762	8	298,195	3,635,210	105,268	3,740,478
New Mexico	15/16		1,048	7	65,707	936,048	24,652	960,700
New York	17/18	16	8,350	8	500,733	6,173,530	186,074	6,359,604
North Carolina	16/18	16	4,489	9	306,964	3,447,132	97,775	3,544,907
North Dakota	16	14	617	8	37,104	503,080	14,035	517,115
Ohio	16/18	14	8,141	7	367,895	5,914,245	165,323	6,079,568
Oklahoma	16		2,542	6.58	136,813	2,152,455	60,135	2,212,590
Oregon	16	14	1,996	7	96,169	1,567,761	42,237	1,609,998
Pennsylvania	17/18	16	6,898	11	570,296	5,695,687	156,570	5,852,257
Rhode Island	16/18		674	10	40,156	395,704	11,899	407,603
South Carolina	16	15	1,984	10	168,686	1,814,939	51,741	1,866,680
South Dakota	16	14	599	9	46,179	529,392	14,896	544,288
Tennessee	16	14	3,021	7	199,388	2,825,406	77,494	2,902,900
Texas	16/18	15	10,681	5	468,436	9,318,406	261,939	9,580,345
Utah	16/18		1,004	9	56,981	813,932	22,859	836,791
Vermont	18	16	377	9	24,076	291,954	8,076	300,030
Virginia	16/18		3,516	9	273,237	3,015,173	85,840	3,101,013
Washington	16/18		3,113	12	245,450	2,130,644	61,217	2,191,861
West Virginia	16/18	16	1,208	10.5	85,927	961,876	27,195	989,071
Wisconsin	16/18	14	2,898	7	180,825	2,600,254	73,453	2,673,707
Wyoming	16	14	436	8	36,635	468,940	11,660	480,600
Total			**154,412**		**9,706,779**	**123,078,079**	**3,509,649**	**126,587,728**

(1) Unrestricted operation of private passenger car. When 2 ages are shown, license is issued at lower age upon completion of approved driver education course. (2) Juvenile license issued with consent of parent or guardian.

Auto Registrations, Taxes, Motor Fuel, Drivers' Ages in Canada

Source: Statistics Canada

Province	Driver's age Minimum (1978)	Driver's age Minor (1978)	Registered[1] road motor vehicles (1978)	Province gas tax per gal. (1979)[2]	Fuel consumption on roads and highways 1978[3]: Gasoline 1,000 gallons	Diesel 1,000 gallons	Liquified petroleum 1,000 gallons
Newfoundland	17	—	188,357	27	131,916	20,325	179
Prince Edward Island	16	—	65,501	21	40,473	2,771	17
Nova Scotia	16	—	413,034	21	258,791	34,016	291
New Brunswick	18	16	340,777	20	234,009	29,388	54
Quebec	18	16	3,042,726	19	1,910,033	338,935	985
Ontario	16	—	4,496,105	21	2,774,047	368,228	898
Manitoba	16	—	628,427	18	312,961	40,461	594
Saskatchewan	16	—	722,643	19	323,979	48,872	667
Alberta	16	14	1,413,173	—	258,500[4]	43,702[4]	649
British Columbia	19	16	1,633,739	17	836,038	113,750	1,489
Yukon and N.W.T.	16	—	30,967	14	18,311	15,525	9
Total			**12,975,449**		**7,099,058**	**1,055,974**	**5,832**

(1) Registrations include: passenger automobiles (including taxis and for-hire cars) 9,744,994; trucks and truck tractors 2,717,832; buses 52,966; motorcycles 341,381; registered mopeds 56,772; other road vehicles (ambulances, fire trucks, etc.) 61,504. (2) As of July. (3) Net sales of gasoline, diesel fuel and liquified petroleum gas at road-use tax rates. (4) Represents sales only up to April 1/78 when road-use tax in Alberta was removed.

Memorable Manned Space Flights

Sources: National Aeronautics and Space Administration and The World Almanac.

Crew, date	Mission name	Orbits[1]	Duration	Remarks
Yuri A. Gagarin (4/12/61)	Vostok 1	1	1h 48m	First manned orbital flight.
Alan B. Shepard Jr. (5/5/61)	Mercury-Redstone 3	(2)	15m 22s	First American in space.
Virgil I. Grissom (7/21/61)	Mercury-Redstone 4	(2)	15m 37s	Spacecraft sank. Grissom rescued.
Gherman S. Titov (8/6-7/61)	Vostok 2	16	25h 18m	First space flight of more than 24 hrs.
John H. Glenn Jr. (2/20/62)	Mercury-Atlas 6	3	4h 55m 23s	First American in orbit.
M. Scott Carpenter (5/24/62)	Mercury-Atlas 7	3	4h 56m 05s	Manual retrofire error caused 250 mi. landing overshoot.
Andrian G. Nikolayev (8/11-15/62)	Vostok 3	64	94h 22m	Vostok 3 and 4 made first group flight.
Pavel R. Popovich (8/12-15/62)	Vostok 4	48	70h 57m	On first orbit it came within 3 miles of Vostok 3.
Walter M. Schirra Jr. (10/3/62)	Mercury-Atlas 8	6	9h 13m 11s	Closest splashdown to target to date (4.5 mi.).
L. Gordon Cooper (5/15-16/63)	Mercury-Atlas 9	22	34h 19m 49s	First U.S. evaluation of effects on man of one day in space.
Valery F. Bykovsky (6/14-6/19/63)	Vostok 5	81	119h 06m	Vostok 5 and 6 made 2d group flight.
Valentina V. Tereshkova (6/16-19/63)	Vostok 6	48	70h 50m	First woman in space.
Vladimir M. Komarov, Konstantin P. Feoktistov, Boris B. Yegorov (10/12/64)	Voskhod 1	16	24h 17m	First 3-man orbital flight: first without space suits.
Pavel I. Belyayev, Aleksei A. Leonov (3/18/65)	Voskhod 2	17	26h 02m	Leonov made first "space walk" (10 min.)
Virgil I. Grissom, John W. Young (3/23/65)	Gemini-Titan 3	3	4h 53m 00s	First manned spacecraft to change its orbital path.
James A. McDivitt, Edward H. White 2d, (6/3-7/65)	Gemini-Titan 4	62	97h 56m 11s	White was first American to "walk in space" (20 min.).
L. Gordon Cooper Jr., Charles Conrad Jr. (8/21-29/65)	Gemini-Titan 5	120	190h 55m 14s	First use of fuel cells for electric power; evaluated guidance and navigation system.
Frank Borman, James A. Lovell Jr. (12/4-18/65)	Gemini-Titan 7	206	330h 35m 31s	Longest duration Gemini flight
Walter M. Schirra Jr., Thomas P. Stafford (12/15-16/65)	Gemini-Titan 6-A	16	25h 51m 24s	Completed world's first space rendezvous with Gemini 7.
Neil A. Armstrong, David R. Scott (3/16-17/66)	Gemini-Titan 8	6.5	10h 41m 26s	First docking of one space vehicle with another; mission aborted, control malfunction.
John W. Young, Michael Collins (7/18-21/66)	Gemini-Titan 10	43	70h 46m 39s	First use of Agena target vehicle's propulsion systems; rendezvoused with Gemini 8.
Charles Conrad Jr., Richard F. Gordon Jr. (9/12-15/66)	Gemini-Titan 11	44	71h 17m 08s	Docked, made 2 revolutions of earth tethered; set Gemini altitude record (739.2 mi.).
James A. Lovell Jr., Edwin E. Aldrin Jr. (11/11-15/66)	Gemini-Titan 12	59	94h 34m 31s	Final Gemini mission; record 5½ hrs. of extravehicular activity.
Vladimir M. Komarov (4/23/67)	Soyuz 1	17	26h 40m	Crashed after re-entry killing Komarov.
Walter M. Schirra Jr., Donn F. Eisele, R. Walter Cunningham (10/11-22/68)	Apollo-Saturn 7	163	260h 09m 03s	First manned flight of Apollo spacecraft command-service module only.
Georgi T. Beregovoi (10/26-30/68)	Soyuz 3	64	94h 51m	Made rendezvous with unmanned Soyuz 2.
Frank Borman, James A. Lovell Jr., William A. Anders (12/21-27/68)	Apollo-Saturn 8	10[3]	147h 00m 42s	First flight to moon (command-service module only); views of lunar surface televised to earth.
Vladimir A. Shatalov (1/14-17/69)	Soyuz 4	45	71h 14m	Docked with Soyuz 5.
Boris V. Volyanov, Aleksei S. Yeliseyev, Yevgeny V. Khrunov (1/15-18/69)	Soyuz 5	46	72h 46m	Docked with Soyuz 4; Yeliseyev and Khrunov transferred to Soyuz 4.
James A. McDivitt, David R. Scott, Russell L. Schweickart (3/3-13/69)	Apollo-Saturn 9	151	241h 00m 54s	First manned flight of lunar module.

(continued)

Crew, date	Mission name	Orbits[1]	Duration	Remarks
Thomas P. Stafford, Eugene A. Cernan, John W. Young (5/18-26/69)	Apollo-Saturn 10	31[4]	192h 03m 23s	First lunar module orbit of moon.
Neil A. Armstrong, Edwin E. Aldrin Jr., Michael Collins (7/16-24/69)	Apollo-Saturn 11	30[3]	195h 18m 35s	First lunar landing made by Armstrong and Aldrin; collected 48.5 lbs. of soil, rock samples; lunar stay time 21 h, 36m, 21 s.
Georgi S. Shonin, Valery N. Kubasov (10/11-16/69)	Soyuz 6	79	118h 42m	First welding of metals in space.
Anatoly V. Filipchenko, Vladislav N. Volkov, Viktor V. Gorbatko (10/12-17/69)	Soyuz 7	79	118h 41m	Space lab construction tests made; Soyuz 6, 7 and 8 — first time 3 spacecraft 7 crew orbited earth at once.
Vladimir A. Shatalov, Aleksei S. Yeliseyev (10/13-18/69)	Soyuz 8	79	118h 41m	Orbiting space laboratory construction tests were made.
Charles Conrad Jr., Richard F. Gordon, Alan L. Bean (11/14-24/69)	Apollo-Saturn 12	45[3]	244h 36m 25s	Conrad and Bean made 2d moon landing; collected 74.7 lbs. of samples, lunar stay time 31 h, 31 m.
James A. Lovell Jr., Fred W. Haise Jr., John L. Swigart Jr. (4/11-17/70)	Apollo-Saturn 13	...	142h 54m 41s	Aborted after service module oxygen tank ruptured; crew returned safely using lunar module oxygen and power.
Alan B. Shepard Jr., Stuart A. Roosa, Edgar D. Mitchell (1/31-2/9/71)	Apollo-Saturn 14	34[3]	216h 01m 57s	Shepard and Mitchell made 3d moon landing, collected 96 lbs. of lunar samples; lunar stay 33 h, 31 m.
Vladimir A. Shatalov, Aleksei S. Yeliseyev, Nikolai Rukavishnikov (4/22-24/71)	Soyuz 10	32	47h 46m	Docked with prototype Salyut orbiting space station for 5½ hrs. then mission was aborted.
Georgi T. Dobrovolsky, Vladislav N. Volkov, Viktor I. Patsayev (6/6-30/71)	Soyuz 11	360	569h 40m	Docked with Salyut space station; and orbited in Salyut for 23 days; crew died during re-entry from loss of pressurization.
David R. Scott, Alfred M. Worden, James B. Irwin (7/26-8/7/71)	Apollo-Saturn 15	74[3]	295h 11m 53s	Scott and Irwin made 4th moon landing; first lunar rover use; first deep space walk; 170 lbs. of samples; 66 h, 55 m, stay.
Charles M. Duke Jr., Thomas K. Mattingly, John W. Young (4/16-27/72)	Apollo-Saturn 16	64[3]	265h 51m 05s	Young and Duke made 5th moon landing; collected 213 lbs. of lunar samples; lunar stay line 71 h, 2 m.
Eugene A. Cernan, Ronald E. Evans, Harrison H. Schmitt (12/7-19/72)	Apollo-Saturn 17	75[3]	301h 51m 59s	Cernan and Schmitt made 6th manned lunar landing; collected 243 lbs. of samples; record lunar stay of 75 h.
Charles Conrad Jr., Joseph P. Kerwin, Paul J. Weitz (5/25-6/22/73)	Skylab 2	...	672h 49m 49s	First American manned orbiting space station; made long-flights tests, crew repaired damage caused during boost.
Alan L. Bean, Jack R. Lousma, Owen K. Garriott (7/28-9/25/73)	Skylab 3	...	1,427h 09m 04s	Crew systems and operational tests, exceeded pre-mission plans for scientific activities; space walk total 13h, 44 m.
Gerald P. Carr, Edward G. Gibson, William Pogue (11/16/73-2/8/74)	Skylab 4	...	2,017h 16m 30s	Final Skylab mission; record space walk of 7 h, 1 m., record space walks total for a mission 22 h, 21 m.
Alexi Leonov, Valeri Kubason (7/15-7/21/75)	Soyuz 19	96	143h 31m	
Vance Brand, Thomas P. Stafford, Donald K. Slayton (7/15-7/24/75)	Apollo 18	136	217h 30m	U.S.-USSR joint flight. Crews linked-up in space, conducted experiments, shared meals, and held a joint news conference.
Boris Yolynov, Vitaly Zhobovov (7/26-8/24/76)	Soyuz 21	...	50 days	Conducted experiments aboard Salyut 5.
Viktor Gorbatko, Yuri Glazkov (2/7-2/25/77)	Soyuz 24	...	18 days	Docked with Salyut 5.
Georgi Grechko, Yuri Romanenko (12/10/77-3/16/78)	Soyuz 26	...	96 days	Docked with Salyut 6. Conducted scientific experiments.
Vladimir Lyakhov, Varery Ryumin (2/26-8/19/79)	Soyuz 34	...	175 days	Docked with Salyut 6. Set new space endurance record.

(1) The Americans measure orbital flights in revolutions while the Soviets use "orbits." (2) Suborbital. (3) Moon orbits in command module. (4) Moon orbits.

Fire aboard spacecraft Apollo I on the ground at Cape Kennedy, Fla. killed Virgil I. Grissom, Edward H. White and Roger B. Chaffee on Jan. 27, 1967. They were the only U.S. astronauts killed in space tests.

Notable Ocean and Intercontinental Flights

(Certified by the Federation Aeronautique Internationale as of Jan., 1980)

	From	To	Miles	Time	Date
		Dirigible Balloons			
British R-34(1)	East Fortune, Scot.	Mineola, N.Y.	.....	108 hrs.	July 2-6, 1919
	Mineola, N.Y.	Pulham, Eng.	.....	75 hrs.	July 9-13, 1919
Amundsen-Ellsworth-Nobile expedition	Spitsbergen	Teller, Alas.	.....	80 hrs.	May 11-14, 1926
Graf Zeppelin	Friedrichshafen	Lakehurst, N.J.	6,630	4d 15h 46m	Oct. 11-15, 1928
Hindenburg Zeppelin	Germany	Lakehurst, N.J.	.....	51h 17m	June 30-July 2, 1936
	Lakehurst, N.J.	Frankfort, Ger.	.....	42h 53m	Aug. 9-11, 1936
USN ZPG-2 Blimp	S. Weymouth, Mass.	Africa			
	Africa	Key West, Fla.	7,000	275h	Mar. 4-16, 1957
		Airplanes			
USN NC-4	Rockaway, N.Y.	Lisbon, Port.	.....	....	May 8-27, 1919
John Alcock-A.W. Brown (2)	St. John's, Nfld.	Clifden, Ireland	1,960	16h 12m	June 14-15, 1919
Richard E. Byrd (3)	Spitsbergen	North Pole	1,545	15h 30m	May 9, 1926
Charles Lindbergh (4)	Mineola, N.Y.	Paris	3,610	33h 29m 30s	May 20-21, 1927
C. Levin-	Roosevelt Field, N.Y.				
C. Chamberlin (5)	Mineola, N.Y.	Isleben, Germany	3,911	42h 31m	June 4-6, 1927
Baron G. von Huenefeld, crew (6)	Dublin	Greenly Isl., Lab.	.....	37 hrs.	Apr. 12-13, 1928
Sir Hubert Wilkins (9)	Point Barrow, Alaska	Spitsbergen	.....	....	Apr. 16, 1928
Sir Chas. Kingsford-Smith, crew (7)	Oakland, Cal.	Brisbane, Aust.	.....	....	May 31-June 8, 1928
Amelia Earhart Putnam, W. Stultz, L. Gordon	Trepassy, Nfld.	Burry Port, Wales	.....	20h 40m	June 17-18, 1928
Richard E. Byrd (8)	Bay of Whales	South Pole	.....	....	Nov. 28-29, 1929
D. Coste-M. Bellonte	Paris	Valley Stream, N.Y.	4,100	37h 18m 30s	Sept. 1-2, 1930
Wiley Post-Harold Gatty	Harbor Grace, Nfld.	England	2,200	16h 17m	June 23-24, 1931
Clyde Pangborn-Hugh Herndon Jr. (10)	Tokyo	Wenatchee, Wash.	4,458	41h 34m	Oct. 3-5, 1931
Amelia Earhart Putnam (11)	Harbor Grace, Nfld.	Ireland	2,026	14h 56m	May 20-21, 1932
James A. Mollison (12)	Portmarnock, Ire.	Pennfield, N.B.	.....	....	Aug. 18, 1932
China Clipper (Pan	San Francisco	Manila, P.I.	.....	....	Nov. 22-28, 1935
Am. Airways) (13)	Manila, P.I.	San Francisco	.....	....	Dec. 1-6, 1935
Gromoff, Yumasheff, Danilin (USSR)	Moscow, USSR	San Jacinto, Cal.	6,262	62h 02m	July 12-14, 1937
Douglas C. Corrigan	New York	Dublin, Ire.	.....	28h 13m	July 17-18, 1938
B-29 (C.J. Miller)	Honolulu	Washington, D.C.	4,640	17h 21m	Sept. 1, 1945
C-54 (Maj. G.E. Cain)	Tokyo	Washington, D.C.		31h 24m	Sept. 3, 1945
Col. David C. Schilling, USAF (14)	England	Limestone, Me.	3,300	10h 01m	Sept. 22, 1950
Chas. F. Blair Jr.	New York	London	3,500	7h 48m	Jan 31, 1951
Chas. F. Blair Jr. (15)	Bardufoss, Norway	Fairbanks, Alas.	3,300	10h 29m	May 29, 1951
Chas. F. Blair Jr.	Fairbanks, Alaska	New York	3,450	9h 31m	May 30, 1950
Canberra Bomber	England	Australia	.....	20h 20m	Mar. 16, 1952
Two U.S. S-55 Helicopters (16)	Westover AFB, Mass.	Prestwick, Scotland	3,410	42h 30m	July 15-31, 1952
Canberra Bomber (17)	Aldergrove, N.Ire.	Gander, Nfld.	2,073	4h 34m	Aug. 26, 1952
	Gander, Nfld.	Aldergrove, N.Ire.	2,073	3h 25m	Aug. 26, 1952
British Comet	London-Tokyo	Tokyo-London	20,400	74h 52m	Apr. 3-7, 1953
British Comet	London	Rio de Janeiro	6,000	12h 30m	Sept. 13-14, 1953
Max Conrad (solo)	New York	Paris	.....	22h 23m	Nov. 7, 1954
Canberra Bomber	London (round trip)	New York	6,920	14h 21m 45.4s	Aug. 23, 1955
Capt. William F. Judd	New York	Paris	.....	24h 11m	Jan. 29-30, 1956
Three USAF F-100Cs	London	Los Angeles	6,710	14h 5m	May 13, 1957
Spirit of St. Louis II (USAF F-100F jet)	McGuire AFB, N.J.	Le Bourget, Paris	.....	6h 38m	May 21, 1957
USAF KC-135	Tokyo	Lajes AFB, Azores	10,230	18h 48m	Apr. 7-8, 1958
Max Conrad (solo)	New York	Palermo, Sicily	4,440	32h 55m	June 22-23, 1958
USAF KC-135	Yokota AB, Japan	Washington, D.C.	7,100	12h 28m	Sept. 12, 1958
Max Conrad (solo)	Chicago	Rome	5,000	34h 3m	Mar. 5-6, 1959
Max Conrad (solo)	Casablanca, Mor.	Los Angeles	7,700	58h 36m	June 2-4, 1959
USSR TU-114 (18)	Moscow	New York	5,092	11h 6m	June 28, 1959
Boeing 707 airliner	San Francisco	Sydney, Australia	7,630	16h 10m	July 2, 1959
Boeing 707-320	New York	Moscow	c.5,090	8h 54m	July 23, 1959
Max Conrad (solo)	Casablanca, Mor.	El Paso, Tex.	6,911	56h 26m	Nov. 22-26, 1959
Col. J.B. Swindal	Washington, D.C.	Moscow	5,004	8h 39m 02.2s	May 19, 1963
Concorde GB	London	Washington, D.C.	3,662	3h 34m 48s	May 29, 1976
Concorde	Paris	Washington, D.C.	3,840	3h 35m 15s	Aug. 18, 1978
Concorde	Paris	New York	3,636	3h 30m 11s	Aug. 22, 1978

Notable first flights: (1) Atlantic aerial round trip. (2) Non-stop transatlantic flight. (3) Polar flight. (4) Solo transatlantic flight in the Ryan monoplane the "Spirit of St. Louis." (5) Transatlantic passenger flight. (6) East-West transatlantic crossing. (7) U.S. to Australia flight. (8) South Pole flight. (9) Trans-Arctic flight. (10) Non-stop Pacific flight. (11) Woman's transoceanic solo flight. (12) Westbound transatlantic solo flight. (13) Pacific airmail and U.S. to Philippines crossing. (14) Non-stop jet transatlantic flight. (15) Solo across North Pole. (16) Transatlantic helicopter flight. (17) Transatlantic round trip on same day. (18) Non-stop between Moscow and New York.

International Aeronautical Records

Source: The National Aeronautic Association, 806 15th St. NW, Washington, DC 20005, representative in the United States of the Federation Aeronautique Internationale, certifying agency for world aviation and space records. The International Aeronautical Federation was formed in 1905 by representatives from Belgium, France, Germany, Great Britain, Spain, Italy, Switzerland, and the United States, with headquarters in Paris. Regulations for the control of official records were signed Oct. 14, 1905. World records are defined as maximum performance, regardless of class or type of aircraft used. Records to May, 1980.

World Air Records—Maximum Performance in Any Class

Speed over a straight course — 3,529.56 kph. (2,193.16 mph) — Capt. Elden W. Joersz, USAF, Lockheed SR-71; Beale AFB, Cal., July 28, 1976.

Speed over a closed circuit — 3,367.221 kph. (2,092.294 mph) — Maj. Adolphus H. Bledsoe Jr., USAF, Lockheed SR-71; Beale AFB, Cal., July 27, 1976.

Distance in a straight line — 20,168.78 kms (12,532.28 mi.) — Maj. Clyde P. Evely, USAF, Boeing B52-H; Kadena, Okinawa to Madrid, Spain, Jan. 11, 1962.

Distance over a closed circuit — 18,245.05 kms (11,336.92 mi.) — Capt. William Stevenson, USAF, Boeing B52-H; Seymour-Johnson, N.C., June 6-7, 1962.

Altitude — 37,650 meters (123,523.58 feet) — Alexander Fedotov, USSR, E-266M; Podmoskovnoye, USSR, Aug. 31, 1977.

Altitude in horizontal flight — 25,929.031 meters (85,068.997 ft.) — Capt. Robert C. Helt, USAF, Lockheed SR-71; Beale AFB, Cal., July 28, 1976.

Manned Space Craft

Duration — 175 days — Vladimir Lyakhov & Valery Ryumin, USSR, Salyut 6, Feb. 26—Aug. 19, 1979.

Altitude — 377,668.9 kms (234,672.5 mi.) — Frank Borman, James A. Lovell Jr., William Anders, Apollo 8; Dec. 21-27, 1968.

Greatest mass lifted — 127,980 kgs. (282,197 lbs.) — Frank Borman, James S. Lovell Jr., William Anders, Apollo 8; Dec. 21-27, 1968.

Distance — 55,474,039 kms. (34,469,970 mi.) — Gerald P. Carr, Edward G. Gibson, William R. Pogue, U.S.; Skylab 3; Nov. 16, 1973-Feb. 8, 1974.

World "Class" Records

All other records, international in scope, are termed World "Class" records and are divided into classes: airships, free balloons, airplanes, seaplanes, amphibians, gliders, and rotorplanes. Airplanes (Class C) are sub-divided into four groups: Group I — piston engine aircraft, Group II — turboprop aircraft, Group III — jet aircraft, Group IV — rocket powered aircraft. A partial listing of world records follows:

Airplanes (Class C, Group I—piston engine)

Distance, closed circuit — 14,441.26 kms (8,974 mi.) — James R. Bede, U.S.; BD-2, Columbus, Oh. to Kansas City course, Nov. 7-9, 1969.

Distance, straight line — 18,081.99 kms. (11,235.6 miles) — Cmdr. Thomas D. Davies, USN; Cmdr. Eugene P. Rankin, USN; Cmdr. Walter S. Reid, USN, and Lt. Cmdr. Ray A. Tabeling, USN; Lockheed P2V-1; from Pearce Field, Perth, Australia, to Port Columbus, Oh., Sept. 29-Oct. 1, 1946.

Speed over 3-kilometer measured course — 803.138 kph. (499.04 mph) — Steve Hinton; P-51D; Tonopah, Nev., Aug. 14, 1979.

Speed for 100 kilometers (62.137 miles) without payload — 755.668 kph. (469.549 mph.) — Jacqueline Cochran, U.S.; North American P-51; Coachella Valley, Cal., Dec. 10, 1947.

Speed for 1,000 kilometers (621.369 miles) without payload — 693.78 kph. (431.09 mph.) — Jacqueline Cochran, U.S.; North American P-51; Santa Rosasummit, Cal. — Flagstaff, Ariz. course, May 24, 1948.

Speed for 5,000 kilometers (3,106.849 miles) without payload — 544.59 kph. (338.39 mph.) — Capt. James Bauer, USAF, Boeing B-29; Dayton, Oh., June 28, 1946.

Speed around the world — 327.73 kph (203.64 mph) — D.N. Dalton, Australia; Beechcraft Duke; Brisbane, Aust., July 20-25, 1975. Time: 5 days, 2 hours, 19 min., 57 sec.

Light Airplanes—(Class C-1.d)

Distance in a straight line — 12,341.26 kms. (7,668.48 miles) — Max Conrad, U.S.; Piper Comanche; Casablanca, Morocco to Los Angeles, June 2-4, 1959.

Speed for 100 kilometers — (62,137 miles) in a closed circuit — 519.480 kph. (322.780 mph.) — Ms. R. M. Sharpe, Great Britain; Vickers Supermarine Spitfire 5-B; Wolverhampton, June 17, 1950.

Helicopters (Class E-1)

Distance in a straight line — 3,561.55 kms. (2,213.04 miles) — Robert G. Ferry, U.S.; Hughes YOH-6A helicopter; Culver City, Cal., to Ormond Beach, Fla., Apr. 6-7, 1966.

Speed over 3-km. course — 348.971 kph. (216.839 mph.) — Byron Graham, U.S.; Sikorsky S-67 helicopter; Windsor Locks, Conn., Dec. 14, 1970.

Gliders (Class D—single place)

Distance, straight line — 1,460.8 kms. (907.7 miles) — Hans Werner Grosse, West Germany; ASK12 sailplane; Luebeck to Biarritz, Apr. 25, 1972.

Altitude above sea level — 14,102 meters (46,267 feet) — Paul F. Bikle, U.S.; Sailplane Schweizer SGS-123-E; Mojave, Lancaster, Cal., Feb. 25, 1961.

Airplanes (Class C, Group II—Turboprop)

Distance in a straight line — 14,052.95 kms. (8,732.09 miles) — Lt. Col. Edgar L. Allison Jr., USAF, Lockheed HC-130 Hercules aircraft; Taiwan to Scott AFB, Ill.; Feb. 20, 1972.

Altitude — 15,549 meters (51,014 ft.) — Donald R. Wilson, U.S.; LTV L450F aircraft; Greenville, Tex., Mar. 27, 1972.

Speed for 1,000 kilometers (621.369 miles) without payload — 871.38 kph. (541.449 mph.) — Ivan Soukhomline, USSR; TU-114 aircraft; Sternberg, USSR; Mar. 24, 1960.

Speed for 5,000 kilometers (3,106.849 miles) without payload — 877.212 kph. (545.072 mph.) — Ivan Soukhomline, USSR; TU-114 aircraft, Sternberg, USSR; Apr. 9, 1960.

Airplanes (Class C-1, Group III—Jet-powered)

Distance in a straight line — 20,168.78 kms. (12,532.28 mi.) — Maj. Clyde P. Evely, USAF, Boeing B-52-H, Kadena, Okinawa, to Madrid, Spain, Jan. 10-11, 1962.

Distance in a closed circuit — 18,245.05 kms. (11,336.92 miles) — Capt. William Stevenson, USAF, Boeing B-52-H, Seymour-Johnson, N.C., June 6-7, 1962.

Altitude — 36,650 meters (123,523.58 ft.) — Alexander Fedotov, USSR; E-226M airplane; Podmoskovnoye, USSR, Aug. 31, 1977.

Speed over a 3-kilometer course — 1,590.45 kph (988.26 mph) — Darryl G. Greenamyer, U.S.; F-104; Tonopah, Nev., Oct. 24, 1977.

Speed for 100 kilometers in a closed circuit — 2,605 kph. (1,618.7 mph.) — Alexander Fedotov, USSR; E-266 airplane, Apr. 8, 1973.

Speed for 500 kilometers in a closed circuit — 2,981.5 kph. (1,852.61 mph.) — Mikhail Komarov, USSR; E-266 airplane, Oct. 5, 1967.

Speed for 1,000 kilometers in a closed circuit — 3,367.221 kph (2,092.294 mph) — Maj. Adolphus H. Bledsoe Jr., USAF; Lockheed SR-71; Beale AFB, Cal., July 27, 1976.

Speed for 2,000 kilometers in closed circuit — 1,708.817 kph. (1,061.808 mph.) — Maj. H. J. Deutschendorf Jr., U.S.; Convair B-58 Hustler Bomber; Edwards AFB, Cal., Jan. 12, 1961.

Free Balloons (Sub-Class A-10, over 4,000 cubic meters)

Altitude — 34,668 meters (113,739.9 feet) — Cmdr. Malcolm D. Ross, USNR; Lee Lewis Memorial Winzen Research Balloon; Gulf of Mexico, May 4, 1961.

FAI Course Records

Los Angeles to New York — 1,954.79 kph (1,214.65 mph) — Capt. Robert G. Sowers, USAF; Convair B-58 Hustler; elapsed time: 2 hrs. 58.71 sec., Mar. 5, 1962.

New York to Los Angeles — 1,741 kph (1,081.80 mph) — Capt. Robert G. Sowers, USAF; Convair B-58 Hustler; elapsed time: 2 hrs. 15 min. 50.08 sec., Mar. 5, 1962.

New York to Paris — 1,753.068 kph (1,089.36 mph) — Maj. W. R. Payne, U.S.; Convair B-58 Hustler; elapsed time: 3 hrs 19 min. 44 sec., May 26, 1961.

London to New York — 945.423 kph (587.457 mph) — Maj. Burl Davenport, USAF; Boeing KC-135; elapsed time: 5 hrs. 53 min. 12.77 sec.; June 27, 1958.

Baltimore to Moscow, USSR — 906.64 kph (563.36 mph) — Col. James B. Swindal, USAF; Boeing VC-137 (707); elapsed time: 8 hrs. 33 min. 45.4 sec., May 19, 1963.

Belfast to Gander, Newfoundland — 774.25 kph (481.099 mph) — Wing Commander R. P. Beamont, Great Britain; Canberra bomber, Aug. 31, 1951; elapsed time: 4 hrs. 18 min. 24.4 sec.

New York to London — 2,908.026 kph (1,806.964 mph) — Maj. James V. Sullivan, USAF; Lockheed SR-71; elapsed time 1 hr. 54 min. 56.4 sec., Sept. 1, 1974.

London to Los Angeles — 2,310.353 kph (1,435.587 mph) — Capt. Harold B. Adams, USAF; Lockheed SR-71; elapsed time: 3 hrs. 47 min. 39 sec., Sept. 13, 1974.

Aviation Hall of Fame

The Aviation Hall of Fame at Dayton, Oh., is dedicated to honoring aviation's outstanding pioneers.

Allen, William M.
Armstrong, Neil A.
Arnold, Henry "Hap"
Balchen, Bernt
Baldwin, Thomas S.
Beachey, Lincoln
Beech, Walter H.
Bell, Alexander Graham
Bell, Lawrence D.
Boeing, William E.
Byrd, Richard E.
Cessna, Clyde V.
Chamberlin, Clarence D.
Chanute, Octave
Chennault, Claire L.
Cunningham, Alfred A.
Curtiss, Glenn H.
deSeversky, Alexander P.
Doolittle, James H.
Douglas, Donald W.
Eaker, Ira C.
Earhart, (Putnam), Amelia
Ellyson, Theodore G.
Ely, Eugene B.
Fairchild, Sherman M.
Fleet, Reuben H.
Foulois, Benjamin D.
Gabreski, Francis
Glenn Jr., John H.
Goddard, George W.
Goddard, Robert H.
Gross, Robert E.
Grumman, Leroy R.
Guggenheim, Harry F.
Hegenberger, Albert F.
Hughes, Howard R.
Johnson, Clarence L.
Kenney, George C.
Kettering, Charles F.
Kindelberger, James H.
Knabenshue, A. Roy
Lahm, Frank P.
Langley, Samuel P.
Lear, William P. Sr.
LeMay, Curtis E.
LeVier, Anthony W.
Lindbergh, Anne M.
Lindbergh, Charles A.
Link, Edwin A.
Loening, Grover C.
Luke Jr., Frank
Macready, John A.
Martin, Glenn L.
McDonnell, James S.
Mitchell, William "Billy"
Montgomery, John J.
Moss, Sanford A.
Northrop, John K.
Odlum, Jacqueline Cochran
Patterson, William A.
Post, Wiley H.
Read, Albert C.
Reeve, Robert C.
Richardson, Holden C.
Rickenbacker, Edward V.
Rodgers, Calbraith P.
Rogers, "Will"
Ryan, T. Claude
Selfridge, Thomas E.
Shepard Jr., Alan B.
Sikorsky, Igor I.
Smith, C.R.
Spaatz, Carl A.
Sperry Sr., Elmer A.
Taylor, Charles E.
Towers, John H.
Trippe, Juan T.
Turner, Roscoe
Twining, Nathan F.
Wade, Leigh
Walden, Henry W.
Wright, Orville
Wright, Wilbur
Yeager, Charles E.

The Busiest Airports, 1979

(Total take-offs and landings)

United States

Source: Federal Aviation Administration

Chicago O'Hare International	732,701
Long Beach	679,337
Santa Ana	630,556
Van Nuys	600,953
Atlanta International	599,138
Los Angeles International	543,545
Opa Locka (Miami, Fla.)	528,259
Oakland International	516,338
Denver Stapleton	486,527
Tamiami, Fla.	451,560
Dallas, Ft. Worth	446,145
San Jose Municipal	445,011

Canada

Source: Aviation Statistics Centre, Statistics Canada

St. Hubert, Que.	312,542
Pitt Meadows, B.C.	287,862
Vancouver International, B.C.	276,012
Toronto International	262,957
Springbank, Alta.	241,422
Calgary, Alta.	226,223
Buttonville, Ont.	225,846
Hamilton City, Ont.	221,374
St. Andrews, Man.	221,297
Ottawa International, Ont.	219,135
Victoria International, B.C.	202,624
Edmonton Municipal, Alta.	202,037

Notable Trips Around the World

(Certified by Federation Aeronautique Internationale as of Jan., 1980)

Fast circuits of the earth have been a subject of wide interest since Jules Verne, French novelist, described an imaginary trip by Phileas Fogg in Around the World in 80 Days, assertedly occurring Oct. 2 to Dec. 20, 1872.

	Terminal	Miles	Time	Date
Nellie Bly	New York, N.Y.		72d 06h 11m	1889
George Francis Train	New York, N.Y.		67d 12h 03m	1890
Charles Fitzmorris	Chicago		60d 13h 29m	1901
J. W. Willis Sayre	Seattle		54d 09h 42m	1903
Col. Burnlay-Campbell			40d 19h 30m	1907
Andre Jaeger-Schmidt			39d 19h 42m 38s	1911
John Henry Mears			35d 21h 36m	1913
Two U.S. Army airplanes	Seattle (57 hops, 21 countries)	26,103	35d 01h 11m	1924
Edward S. Evans and Linton Wells (New York World) (1)	New York	18,400	28d 14h 36m 05s	June 16-July 14, 1926
John H. Mears and Capt. C.B.D. Collyer	New York		23d 15h 21m 03s	June 29-July 22, 1928
Graf Zeppelin	Friedrichshafen, Ger. via Tokyo, Los Angeles, Lakehurst, N.J.	21,700	20d 04h	Aug. 14-Sept. 4, 1929
Wiley Post and Harold Gatty (Monoplane Winnie Mae)	Roosevelt Field, N.Y. via Arctic Circle	15,474	8d 15h 51m	June 23-July 1, 1931
Wiley Post (Monoplane Winnie Mae) (2)	Floyd Bennett Field, N.Y. via Arctic Circle	15,596	115h 36m 30s	July 15-22, 1933
H. R. Ekins (Scripps-Howard Newspapers in race) (Zeppelin Hindenburg to Germany air planes from Frankfurt)	Lakehurst, N.J., via Frankfurt, Germany	25,654	18d 11h 14m 33s	Sept, 30-Oct. 19, 1936
Howard Hughes and 4 assistants	New York, Paris, Moscow, Siberia, Fairbanks	14,824	3d 19h 08m 10s	July 10-13, 1938
Mrs. Clara Adams (Pan American Clipper)	Port Washington, N.Y., return Newark, N.J.		16d 19h 04m	June 28-July 15, 1939
Globester, U.S. Air Transport Command	Washington, D.C.	23,279	149h 44m	Sept. 28-Oct. 4, 1945
Capt. William P. Odom (A-26 Reynolds Bombshell)	New York, via Paris, Cairo, Tokyo, Alaska	20,000	78h 55m 12s	Apr. 12-16, 1947
America, Pan American 4-engine Lockheed Constellation (3)	New York	22,219	101h 32m	June 17-30, 1947
Col. Edward Eagan	New York	20,559	147h 15m	Dec. 13, 1948
USAF B-50 Lucky Lady II (Capt. James Gallagher) (4)	Fort Worth, Tex.	23,452	94h 01m	Feb. 26-Mar. 2, 1949
Jean-Marie Audibert	Paris		4d 19h 38m	Dec. 11-15, 1952
Pamela Martin	Midway Airport, Chicago		90h 59m	Dec. 5-8, 1953
Three USAF B-52 Stratofortresses (5)	Merced, Cal., via Nfld., Morocco, Saudi Arabia, India, Ceylon, P.I., Guam	24,325	45h 19m	Jan. 15-18, 1957
Joseph Cavoli	Cleveland, Oh.		89h 13m 37s	Jan. 31-Feb. 4, 1958
Peter Gluckmann (solo)	San Francisco	22,800	29d	Aug. 22-Sept. 20, 1959
Milton Reynolds	San Francisco		51h 45m 22s	Jan. 12-14, 1960
Sue Snyder	Chicago	21,219	62h 59m	June 22-24, 1960
Max Conrad (solo)	Miami, Fla.	25,946	8d 18h 35m 57s	Feb. 28-Mar. 8, 1961
Sam Miller & Louis Fodor	New York		46h 28m	Aug. 3-4, 1963
Robert & Joan Wallick	Manila, Philippines	23,129	5d 6h 17m 10s	June 2-7, 1966
Arthur Godfrey, Richard Merrill Fred Austin, Karl Keller	New York	23,333	86h 9m 01s	June 4-7, 1966
Trevor K. Brougham	Darwin, Australia	24,800	5d 05h 57m	Aug. 5-10, 1972
Walter H. Mullikin, Albert Frink, Lyman Watt, Frank Cassaniti, Edward Shields	New York	23,137	1d 22h 50s	May 1-3,1976
Arnold Palmer	Denver, Col.	22,985	57h 25m 42s	May 17-19, 1976
Boeing 747 (6)	San Francisco. . . . San Francisco	26,382	54h 7m 12s	Oct. 28-31, 1977

(1) Mileage by train and auto, 4,110; by plane, 6,300; by steamship, 8,000. (2) First to fly solo around northern circumference of the world, also first to fly twice around the world. (3) Inception of regular commercial global air service. (4) First non-stop round-the-world flight, refueled 4 times in flight. (5) First non-stop global flight by jet planes; refueled in flight by KC-97 aerial tankers; average speed approx. 525 mph. (6) Speed record around the world over both the earth's poles.

U.S. Scheduled Airline Traffic

Source: Air Transport Association of America (thousands)

	1977	1978	1979
Passenger traffic			
Revenue passengers enplaned	240,326	274,716	316,683
Revenue passenger miles	193,218,837	226,781,182	261,979,204
Available seat miles	345,566,005	368,750,719	416,044,986
Cargo traffic (ton miles)	6,573,871	6,987,425	7,170,130
Freight	5,385,130	5,763,214	5,907,640
Express	41,417	56,494	56,192
U.S. Mail	1,147,324	1,167,717	1,206,298
Overall traffic and service			
Nonscheduled traffic—total ton miles	1,674,174	1,415,774	1,157,893
Total revenue ton miles—all services	27,582,944	31,095,184	34,538,856
Total available ton miles—all services	54,789,420	56,869,894	62,541,587

Air Line Distances Between Selected Cities of the World

Source: Defense Mapping Agency Aerospace Center (statute miles)
Point-to-point measurements are usually from City Hall

	Bangkok	Berlin	Cairo	Cape-town	Caracas	Chicago	Hong Kong	Hono-lulu	Lima	London
Bangkok	....	5,352	4,523	6,300	10,555	8,570	1,077	6,609	12,244	5,944
Berlin	5,352	....	1,797	5,961	5,238	4,414	5,443	7,320	6,896	583
Cairo	4,523	1,797	....	4,480	6,342	6,141	5,066	8,848	7,726	2,185
Capetown	6,300	5,961	4,480	....	6,366	8,491	7,376	11,535	6,072	5,989
Caracas	10,555	5,238	6,342	6,366	....	2,495	10,165	6,021	1,707	4,655
Chicago	8,570	4,414	6,141	8,491	2,495	....	7,797	4,256	3,775	3,958
Hong Kong	1,077	5,443	5,066	7,376	10,165	7,797	....	5,556	11,418	5,990
Honolulu	6,609	7,320	8,848	11,535	6,021	4,256	5,556	....	5,947	7,240
London	5,944	583	2,185	5,989	4,655	3,958	5,990	7,240	6,316	....
Madrid	6,337	1,165	2,087	5,308	4,346	4,189	6,558	7,872	5,907	785
Melbourne	4,568	9,918	8,675	6,425	9,717	9,673	4,595	5,505	8,059	10,500
Mexico City	9,793	6,056	7,700	8,519	2,234	1,690	8,788	3,789	2,639	5,558
Montreal	8,338	3,740	5,427	7,922	2,438	745	7,736	4,918	3,970	3,254
Moscow	4,389	1,006	1,803	6,279	6,177	4,987	4,437	7,047	7,862	1,564
New Delhi	1,813	3,598	2,758	5,769	8,833	7,486	2,339	7,412	10,432	4,181
New York	8,669	3,979	5,619	7,803	2,120	714	8,060	4,969	3,639	3,469
Paris	5,877	548	1,998	5,786	4,732	4,143	5,990	7,449	6,370	214
Peking	2,046	4,584	4,698	8,044	8,950	6,604	1,217	5,077	10,349	5,074
Rio de Janeiro	9,994	6,209	6,143	3,781	2,804	5,282	11,009	8,288	2,342	5,750
Rome	5,494	737	1,326	5,231	5,195	4,824	5,774	8,040	6,750	895
San Francisco	7,931	5,672	7,466	10,248	3,902	1,859	6,905	2,398	4,518	5,367
Singapore	883	6,164	5,137	6,008	11,402	9,372	1,605	6,726	11,689	6,747
Stockholm	5,089	528	2,096	6,423	5,471	4,331	5,063	6,875	7,166	942
Tokyo	2,865	5,557	5,958	9,154	8,808	6,314	1,791	3,859	9,631	5,959
Warsaw	5,033	322	1,619	5,935	5,559	4,679	5,147	7,366	7,215	905
Washington, D.C.	8,807	4,181	5,822	7,895	2,047	596	8,155	4,838	3,509	3,674

	Madrid	Mel-bourne	Mexico City	Mon-treal	Mos-cow	Nai-robi	New Delhi	New York	Paris	Peking
Bangkok	6,337	4,568	9,793	8,338	4,389	4,483	1,813	8,669	5,877	2,046
Berlin	1,165	9,918	6,056	3,740	1,006	3,949	3,598	3,979	548	4,584
Cairo	2,087	8,675	7,700	5,427	1,803	2,186	2,758	5,619	1,998	4,698
Capetown	5,308	6,425	8,519	7,922	6,279	2,542	5,769	7,803	5,786	8,044
Caracas	4,346	9,717	2,234	2,438	6,177	7,178	8,833	2,120	4,732	8,950
Chicago	4,189	9,673	1,690	745	4,987	8,011	7,486	714	4,143	6,604
Hong Kong	6,558	4,595	8,788	7,736	4,437	5,449	2,339	8,060	5,990	1,217
Honolulu	7,872	5,505	3,789	4,918	7,047	10,741	7,412	4,969	7,449	5,077
London	785	10,500	5,558	3,254	1,564	4,231	4,181	3,469	214	5,074
Madrid	....	10,758	5,643	3,448	2,147	3,841	4,530	3,593	655	5,745
Melbourne	10,758	....	8,426	10,395	8,950	7,153	6,329	10,359	10,430	5,643
Mexico City	5,643	8,426	....	2,317	6,676	9,219	9,120	2,090	5,725	7,753
Montreal	3,448	10,395	2,317	....	4,401	7,267	7,012	331	3,432	6,519
Moscow	2,147	8,950	6,676	4,401	....	3,930	2,698	4,683	1,554	3,607
New Delhi	4,530	6,329	9,120	7,012	2,698	3,374	....	7,318	4,102	2,353
New York	3,593	10,359	2,090	331	4,683	7,364	7,318	....	3,636	6,844
Paris	655	10,430	5,725	3,432	1,554	4,022	4,102	3,636	....	5,120
Peking	5,745	5,643	7,753	6,519	3,607	5,727	2,353	6,844	5,120	....
Rio de Janeiro	5,045	8,226	4,764	5,078	7,170	5,560	8,753	4,801	5,684	10,768
Rome	851	9,929	6,377	4,104	1,483	3,339	3,684	4,293	690	5,063
San Francisco	5,803	7,856	1,887	2,543	5,885	9,597	7,691	2,572	5,577	5,918
Singapore	7,080	3,759	10,327	9,203	5,228	4,638	2,571	9,534	6,673	2,771
Stockholm	1,653	9,630	6,012	3,714	716	4,281	3,414	3,986	1,003	4,133
Tokyo	6,706	5,062	7,035	6,471	4,660	6,999	3,638	6,757	6,053	1,307
Warsaw	1,427	9,598	6,337	4,022	721	3,801	3,277	4,270	852	4,325
Washington, D.C.	3,792	10,180	1,885	489	4,876	7,551	7,500	205	3,840	6,942

	Rio de Janiero	Rome	San Fran-cisco	Singa-pore	Stock holm	Teheran	Tokyo	Vienna	Warsaw	Wash., D.C.
Bangkok	9,994	5,494	7,931	883	5,089	3,391	2,865	5,252	5,033	8,807
Berlin	6,209	737	5,672	6,164	528	2,185	5,557	326	322	4,181
Cairo	6,143	1,326	7,466	5,137	2,096	1,234	5,958	1,481	1,619	5,822
Capetown	3,781	5,231	10,248	6,008	6,423	5,241	9,154	5,656	5,935	7,895
Caracas	2,804	5,195	3,902	11,402	5,471	7,320	8,808	5,372	5,559	2,047
Chicago	5,282	4,824	1,859	9,372	4,331	6,502	6,314	4,698	4,679	596
Hong Kong	11,009	5,774	6,905	1,605	5,063	3,843	1,791	5,431	5,147	8,155
Honolulu	8,288	8,040	2,398	6,726	6,875	8,070	3,859	7,632	7,366	4,838
London	5,750	895	5,367	6,747	942	2,743	5,959	771	905	3,674
Madrid	5,045	851	5,803	7,080	1,653	2,978	6,706	1,128	1,427	3,792
Melbourne	8,226	9,929	7,856	3,759	9,630	7,826	5,062	9,790	9,598	10,180
Mexico City	4,764	6,377	1,887	10,327	6,012	8,184	7,035	6,320	6,337	1,885
Montreal	5,078	4,104	2,543	9,203	3,714	5,880	6,471	4,009	4,022	489
Moscow	7,170	1,483	5,885	5,228	716	1,532	4,660	1,043	721	4,876
New Delhi	8,753	3,684	7,691	2,571	3,414	1,583	3,638	3,465	3,277	7,500
New York	4,801	4,293	2,572	9,534	3,986	6,141	6,757	4,234	4,270	205
Paris	5,684	690	5,577	6,673	1,003	2,625	6,053	645	852	3,840
Peking	10,768	5,063	5,918	2,771	4,133	3,490	1,307	4,648	4,325	6,942
Rio de Janeiro	....	5,707	6,613	9,785	6,683	7,374	11,532	6,127	6,455	4,779
Rome	5,707	....	6,259	6,229	1,245	2,127	6,142	477	820	4,497
San Francisco	6,613	6,259	....	8,448	5,399	7,362	5,150	5,994	5,854	2,441
Singapore	9,785	6,229	8,448	....	5,936	4,103	3,300	6,035	5,843	9,662
Stockholm	6,683	1,245	5,399	5,936	....	2,173	5,053	780	494	4,183
Tokyo	11,532	6,142	5,150	3,300	5,053	4,775	....	5,689	5,347	6,791
Warsaw	6,455	820	5,854	5,843	494	1,879	5,689	347	....	4,472
Washington, D.C.	4,779	4,497	2,441	9,662	4,183	6,341	6,791	4,438	4,472	....

AGRICULTURE

World and Regional Food Production, 1973 to 1978

Source: UN Food and Agriculture Organization

Region	1974	1975	1976	1977	1978	1979[1]	Change 1978 to 1979	Annual rate of change 1970-79
	(1969-71 = 100)							
Food Production								
Developing market economies[2]	109	114	116	121	125	125	0	2.4
Africa	107	117	110	108	112	115	+ 3	1.5
Far East	106	114	114	122	127	124	− 3	2.3
Latin America	113	115	118	124	129	132	+ 3	3.1
Near East	113	118	125	123	129	128	− 1	3.0
Asian centrally planned economies	114	118	122	121	126	133	+ 7	3.2
Total Developing Countries	**110**	**115**	**118**	**121**	**126**	**127**	**+ 1**	**2.6**
Developed market economies[2]	109	111	112	115	118	120	+ 2	2.1
North America	106	113	117	122	120	125	+ 5	2.8
Oceania	104	113	119	115	128	124	− 4	2.4
Western Europe	111	110	109	111	116	118	+ 2	1.8
Eastern Europe and the USSR	113	112	115	117	125	120	− 5	2.0
Total Developed Countries	**110**	**111**	**113**	**116**	**120**	**120**	**0**	**2.1**
World	**110**	**113**	**115**	**118**	**123**	**123**	**0**	**2.3**

Note: Food production covers crops and livestock only. (1) Preliminary. (2) Including countries in other regions not specified.

Food Production Per Capita in Developing Regions, 1973-78

Source: UN Food and Agriculture Organization

Region	1974	1975	1976	1977	1978	1979[1]	Change 1978 to 1979	Annual rate of change 1970-79
	(1969-71 = 100)							
Developing market economies[2]	98	100	100	101	102	99	−3	−0.2
Africa	95	93	93	89	89	89	—	−1.2
Far East	96	101	99	103	105	100	−5	−0.1
Latin America	102	101	101	103	105	104	−1	0.3
Near East	102	104	107	102	104	100	−4	0.2
Total developing countries	**101**	**103**	**103**	**103**	**105**	**104**	**−1**	**0.3**

(1) Preliminary. (2) Including countries in other regions not specified.

Food Intake Below Critical Minimum Limit in Developing Regions

Source: UN Food and Agriculture Organization

(Estimated)

The critical minimum limit for food intake is 1.2 times the Basal Metabolic Rate (BMR).

Region	Total Population (millions)		Percentage below 1.2 BMR		Total number below 1.2 BMR (millions)	
	1969-71	1972-74	1969-71	1972-74	1969-71	1972-74
Africa	278	301	25	28	70	83
Far East	968	1,042	25	29	256	297
Latin America	279	302	16	15	44	46
Near East	167	182	18	16	31	29
MSA[1]	954	1,027	27	30	255	307
Other developing market economies	738	800	20	18	146	148
Total developing market economies	1,692	1,827	24	25	401	455

(1) Countries most severely affected by food shortages.

World Daily Dietary Energy Supply in Relation to Requirements

Source: UN Food and Agriculture Organization

Region	Dietary energy[1]				Supply as percent of requirement[2]			
	1966-68	1969-71	1972-74	1975-77	1966-68	1969-71	1972-74	1975-77
Developing market economies	2,122	2,206	2,193	2,219	81	85	84	85
Africa	2,136	2,194	2,174	2,208	82	84	84	85
Latin America	2,511	2,531	2,518	2,552	97	97	97	98
Near East	2,413	2,431	2,498	2,657	93	94	96	102
Far East	1,959	2,079	2,053	2,053	75	80	80	80
Others	2,268	2,326	2,371	2,345	87	89	91	90
Asian centrally planned econ.	2,087	2,224	2,317	2,420	80	86	89	93
Total developing countries	**2,110**	**2,211**	**2,233**	**2,282**	**81**	**85**	**86**	**88**
Developed market economies	3,200	3,275	3,323	3,329	123	126	128	128
North America	3,384	3,467	3,493	3,519	130	133	134	135
Western Europe	3,256	3,333	3,389	3,378	125	128	130	130
Oceania	3,288	3,360	3,365	3,418	126	129	129	131
Others	2,701	2,769	2,852	2,872	104	107	110	110
Eastern Europe and the U.S.S.R.	3,300	3,379	3,413	3,465	127	130	131	133
Total developed countries	**3,232**	**3,309**	**3,353**	**3,373**	**124**	**127**	**129**	**130**
World	**2,457**	**2,541**	**2,559**	**2,590**	**95**	**98**	**98**	**99**

(1) Calories per capita per day. (2) Daily calorie requirement is 3,000 for men, 2,200 for women.

Grain, Hay, Potato, Cotton, Soybean, Tobacco Production

Source: Statistical Reporting Service: U.S. Agriculture Department

1979 State	Barley 1,000 bushels	Corn, grain 1,000 bushels	Cotton lint 1,000 bales[1]	All hay 1,000 tons	Oats 1,000 bushels	Potatoes 1,000 cwt.	Soybeans 1,000 bushels	Tobacco 1,000 pounds	All wheat 1,000 bushels
Alabama	—	30,622	320	1,134	1,025	2,552	56,250	825	2,470
Alaska	—	—	—	—	—	—	—	—	—
Arizona	3,225	5,175	1,420	1,397	—	1,302	—	—	9,540
Arkansas	—	2,100	610	1,552	2,080	—	144,200	—	14,700
California	47,400	30,420	3,380	7,295	4,675	20,911	—	—	58,200
Colorado	20,010	92,075	—	3,216	2,500	13,353	—	—	70,183
Connecticut	—	—	—	175	—	418	—	4,868	—
Delaware	1,125	17,034	—	52	—	1,056	7,950	—	1,020
Florida	—	19,080	4	494	—	6,008	13,137	22,575	—
Georgia	—	100,750	155	1,170	3,186	—	58,800	100,965	5,600
Hawaii	—	—	—	—	—	—	—	—	—
Idaho	49,300	3,608	—	4,126	2,288	88,200	—	—	74,140
Illinois	329	1,358,080	—	3,766	16,200	447	374,220	—	55,900
Indiana	—	664,160	—	2,150	8,845	1,359	159,120	13,000	44,415
Iowa	—	1,625,600	—	8,271	63,000	231	310,460	—	2,664
Kansas	2,700	171,990	—	5,716	3,740	—	41,340	—	410,400
Kentucky	1,250	132,600	—	3,134	328	—	53,950	347,040	11,020
Louisiana	—	2,214	690	827	—	147	89,600	56	756
Maine	—	—	—	385	2,418	28,750	—	—	—
Maryland	4,312	58,905	—	606	1,210	248	11,550	26,400	4,218
Massachusetts	—	—	—	278	—	748	—	1,539	—
Michigan	799	237,500	—	3,833	16,470	9,548	28,615	—	33,755
Minnesota	40,810	606,000	—	9,030	84,930	14,716	167,360	—	90,384
Mississippi	—	5,720	1,450	1,287	—	—	118,900	—	3,680
Missouri	—	228,660	159	6,070	2,025	—	186,795	5,520	70,400
Montana	40,560	385	—	4,291	5,460	1,800	—	—	116,475
Nebraska	1,204	793,500	—	7,618	20,140	1,752	54,740	—	86,700
Nevada	1,320	—	2	979	—	4,950	—	—	1,610
New Hampshire	—	—	—	188	—	—	—	—	—
New Jersey	918	7,380	—	339	400	2,125	6,750	—	1,476
New Mexico	1,566	8,066	112	1,158	—	1,210	—	—	8,756
New York	528	55,250	—	5,539	17,980	12,894	598	—	6,560
North Carolina	3,111	128,440	44	589	5,320	2,729	45,825	622,605	7,560
North Dakota	75,900	22,040	—	5,780	36,960	18,240	5,562	—	252,235
Ohio	468	417,450	—	3,606	23,800	2,694	145,080	16,405	63,360
Oklahoma	2,530	8,250	520	4,030	4,560	—	7,590	—	216,600
Oregon	8,000	1,100	—	2,409	4,160	25,310	—	—	57,310
Pennsylvania	5,405	115,425	—	4,293	18,425	6,000	2,624	22,100	8,122
Rhode Island	—	—	—	18	—	897	—	—	—
South Carolina	1,104	40,720	115	452	3,186	—	39,840	117,705	3,597
South Dakota	20,000	210,900	—	7,915	98,500	1,203	20,955	—	60,060
Tennessee	598	51,460	172	2,022	1,107	387	70,740	105,392	10,030
Texas	2,300	132,300	5,721	6,147	16,800	3,752	20,930	—	138,000
Utah	9,039	1,504	—	2,026	708	1,300	—	—	6,680
Vermont	—	—	—	850	—	147	—	—	—
Virginia	5,200	51,045	0.2	1,775	1,715	3,185	14,136	113,400	6,300
Washington	17,010	12,257	—	2,459	1,749	48,925	—	—	118,000
West Virginia	410	4,543	—	749	612	—	—	1,820	340
Wisconsin	1,176	306,940	—	12,555	55,860	17,010	10,030	25,140	2,162
Wyoming	8,460	2,523	—	2,127	2,024	1,144	—	—	6,354
Total U.S.	**378,067**	**7,763,771**	**14,873**	**145,878**	**534,386**	**347,648**	**2,267,647**	**1,547,355**	**2,141,732**

(1) Equiv. to 480 lbs.

Agricultural Products — U.S. and World Production and Exports

Source: Foreign Agricultural Service, U.S. Agriculture Department

1979/80 Commodity	Unit	Production U.S.	Production World	Production % U.S.	Exports[6] U.S.	Exports[6] World	Exports[6] % U.S.
Wheat	MMT	[1] 58	[2] 419	14	[3] 37	[3] 83	45
Oats	MMT	[1] 8	[2] 45	18	[1] .058	[2] 1	6
Corn	MMT	[4] 197	[2] 412	48	[4] 62	[2] 74	84
Barley	MMT	[1] 8	[2] 157	5	[1] 1	[2] 16	6
Rice[5]	MMT	6	313	2	[5] 3	[7] 11	28
Soybeans	MMT	62	[8] 94	66	23	28	82
Lard	1,000 MT	445	3,644	12	110	591	19
Tallow & Grease	1,000 MT	3,125	5,888	53	1,180	2,170	54
Tobacco, unmtd.[9]	1,000 MT	[10] 703	[10] 5,381	13	259	1,373	19
Edible, Veg. Oils	MMT	13	42	31	[8,11] 5.9	[8,11,12] 15.3	39
Cotton[5,13]	Mil. Bales	15	66	23	9	22	41

(1) Year beginning with June 1. (2) Year beginning with July 1. (3) Includes wheat flour in grain. (4) Year beginning with Oct. 1. (5) Year beginning Aug. 1. (6) Preliminary (7) Calendar year 1980. (8) Year beginning Sept. 1. (9) Calendar Year 1979. (10) Farm sales weight basis. (11) Includes oil equivalent of exported oilseed. (12) Exports from producing countries. (13) Bales of 480 lbs. net weight.

Production of Chief U.S. Crops

Source: Economics, Statistics, and Cooperatives Service: U.S. Agriculture Department

Year	Corn grain	Oats	Barley	Sorghums for grain	All wheat	Rye	Flax-seed	Cotton lint	Cotton seed
	1,000 bushels	1,000 bushels	1,000 bushels	1,000 bushels	1,000 bushels	1,000 bushels	1,000 bushels	1,000 bales	1,000 tons
1970 . .	4,152,243	915,236	416,091	683,179	1,351,558	36,840	29,416	10,192	4,068
1974 . .	4,701,402	600,655	298,669	622,711	1,781,918	17,506	14,083	11,540	4,510
1975 . .	5,828,961	642,042	374,386	753,046	2,122,459	15,958	15,553	8,302	3,218
1976 . .	6,266,359	546,315	372,461	719,817	2,142,362	14,951	7,820	10,581	4,122
1977 . .	6,425,457	750,901	420,159	792,983	2,036,318	17,312	15,105	14,389	5,521
1978 . .	7,086,666	595,882	449,177	747,790	1,797,528	26,160	10,404	10,856	4,269
1979 . .	7,763,771	534,386	378,067	814,308	2,141,732	24,549	13,539	14,873	5,796

Year	Tobacco	All hay	Beans dry edible	Peas dry edible	Peanuts	Soy-beans	Pota-toes	Sweet pota-toes
	1,000 lbs.	1,000 tons	1,000 cwt.	1,000 cwt.	1,000 lbs.	1,000 bushels	1,000 cwt.	1,000 cwt.
1970	1,906,453	126,969	17,399	3,315	2,983,121	1,127,100	325,716	13,164
1974	1,989,728	126,384	20,330	3,228	3,667,604	1,216,287	342,395	13,339
1975	2,181,775	132,210	17,442	2,731	3,857,122	1,547,383	322,254	13,225
1976	2,135,829	120,006	17,786	2,150	3,750,890	1,287,560	357,674	13,432
1977	1,912,759	131,313	16,610	1,023	3,726,015	1,761,755	354,576	12,395
1978	2,024,369	142,209	19,040	3,601	3,988,624	1,870,181	365,249	14,301
1979	1,547,355	145,878	20,665	2,039	3,976,140	2,267,647	347,648	14,421

Year	Five seed crops*	Sugar and seed	Sugar beets	Pecans	Al-monds	Wal-nuts	Fil-berts	Oranges and tan-gerines**	Grape-fruit**
	1,000 lbs.	1,000 tons	1,000 tons	1,000 tons	1,000 tons	1,000 tons	1,000 tons	1,000 boxes	1,000 boxes
1970	251,934	23,996	26,378	77.6	124.0	111.8	9.3	189,970	53,910
1974	179,918	25,140	22,123	68.7	189.0	156.5	6.7	221,050	65,500
1975	161,609	28,344	29,704	124.2	160.0	199.3	12.1	243,060	61,610
1976	143,006	28,120	29,386	51.6	142.0	183.7	7.2	248,140	70,080
1977	139,101	26,830	25,007	118.3	156.5	192.5	11.8	248,720	74,600
1978	155,694	25,997	25,725	125.3	90.5	160.0	14.1	225,320	74,660
1979	159,908	27,681	21,996	110.5	185.0	205.0	12.5	215,900	67,020

*Five seed crops include alfalfa, red clover, ladino clover, lespedeza, and timothy. ** Crop year ending in year cited.

Production of Principal Field Crops in Canada

Source: Statistics Canada

1979	Wheats	Oats	Barley	Ryes	Flaxseed
	1,000 bushels	1,000 bushels	1,000 bushels	1,000 bushels	1,000 bushels
Canada[1]	**652,050**	**193,093**	**388,573**	**20,657**	**32,900**
Prince Edward Island	484	2,916	2,276	—	—
Nova Scotia	189	788	253	—	—
New Brunswick	316	1,940	420	—	—
Quebec	4,255	26,877	3,826	327	—
Ontario	27,806	23,272	18,998	1,950	—
Manitoba	77,000	20,000	58,000	3,150	18,500
Saskatchewan	389,000	41,000	90,000	8,000	10,200
Alberta	150,000	73,000	209,000	6,900	4,200
British Columbia	3,000	3,300	5,800	330	—

	Mixed grains	Corn grains	Soybeans	Rapeseed	Potatoes
	1,000 bushels	1,000 bushels	1,000 bushels	1,000 bushels	1,000 c.w.t.
Canada[1]	**81,911**	**195,398**	**24,680**	**157,000**	**59,644**
Prince Edward Island	3,638	—	—	—	15,195
Nova Scotia	293	—	—	—	710
New Brunswick	399	—	—	—	12,578
Quebec	5,649	18,389	—	—	9,015
Ontario	49,532	169,209	24,680	—	9,225
Manitoba	5,900	7,800	—	29,000	6,216
Saskatchewan	3,300	—	—	56,500	316
Alberta	13,000	—	—	65,500	3,825
British Columbia	200	—	—	6,000	2,444

	Mustard seed	Sunflower seed	Tame hay	Fodder corn	Sugar beets
	1,000 pounds	1,000 pounds	1,000 tons	1,000 tons	1,000 tons
Canada[1]	**117,500**	**487,000**	**29,168**	**16,178**	**950**
Prince Edward Island	—	—	280	135	—
Nova Scotia	—	—	423	138	—
New Brunswick	—	—	365	88	—
Quebec	—	—	5,851	3,890	124
Ontario	—	—	7,849	10,487	—
Manitoba	21,000	460,000	2,600	360	276
Saskatchewan	66,500	27,000	3,000	—	—
Alberta	30,000	—	6,900	530	551
British Columbia	—	—	1,900	550	—

(1) Excluding Newfoundland.

U.S. Farms by State—Number, Acreage, and Value

Source: U.S. Bureau of the Census

State 1974	Farms (Number)	Average size of farm (acres)	Value of land and buildings (per acre)	Farms: 2000 acres or more	Farms: 10-49 acres	Land in farms (acres)
Alabama	56,678	209	$ 364	643	15,475	11,852,946
Alaska	291	5,612	42	37	40	1,633,070
Arizona	5,803	6,539	111	877	1,253	37,944,191
Arkansas	50,959	287	419	787	8,537	14,641,677
California	67,674	493	653	2,813	24,162	33,385,619
Colorado	25,501	1,408	188	4,061	2,800	35,902,165
Connecticut	3,421	129	1,525	6	888	440,056
Delaware	3,400	185	971	17	783	630,605
Florida	32,466	407	685	1,006	10,940	13,199,365
Georgia	54,911	253	474	723	11,118	13,878,294
Hawaii	3,020	702	485	70	812	2,118,976
Idaho	23,680	603	339	1,246	4,251	14,274,258
Illinois	111,049	262	846	229	13,420	29,094,794
Indiana	87,915	191	720	125	17,325	16,785,208
Iowa	126,104	262	719	150	9,841	33,044,768
Kansas	79,188	605	296	3,819	5,127	47,945,722
Kentucky	102,053	141	427	159	20,945	14,431,713
Louisiana	33,240	275	512	594	9,233	9,133,275
Maine	6,436	237	341	28	728	1,523,696
Maryland	15,163	174	1,060	57	3,399	2,634,395
Massachusetts	4,497	134	961	9	1,185	601,734
Michigan	64,094	169	553	62	12,233	10,832,234
Minnesota	98,537	280	429	443	6,846	27,605,228
Mississippi	53,620	267	379	938	10,351	14,300,498
Missouri	115,711	258	396	509	13,919	29,801,127
Montana	23,324	2,665	112	7,411	1,550	62,158,351
Nebraska	67,597	683	282	3,719	3,384	46,172,012
Nevada	2,076	5,209	85	342	317	10,813,610
New Hampshire	2,412	210	564	5	360	506,464
New Jersey	7,409	130	1,807	18	2,215	961,395
New Mexico	11,282	4,170	78	2,610	1,694	47,046,388
New York	43,682	215	510	67	5,093	9,410,706
North Carolina	91,280	123	590	237	30,195	11,243,933
North Dakota	42,710	992	195	3,789	773	42,387,424
Ohio	92,158	170	706	76	16,163	15,668,238
Oklahoma	69,719	475	302	2,191	6,001	33,082,848
Oregon	26,753	682	250	1,731	8,292	18,241,445
Pennsylvania	53,171	154	734	45	8,368	8,186,378
Rhode Island	597	102	1,500	2	177	61,068
South Carolina	29,275	211	467	312	7,677	6,177,024
South Dakota	42,825	1,074	145	4,444	1,549	45,977,776
Tennessee	93,659	140	467	233	24,759	13,103,224
Texas	174,068	771	243	10,038	20,951	134,185,289
Utah	12,184	871	188	822	2,948	10,610,050
Vermont	5,906	282	462	14	402	1,667,561
Virginia	52,699	184	558	264	11,521	9,678,307
Washington	29,410	567	350	1,657	8,739	16,661,902
West Virginia	16,909	207	300	60	2,160	3,496,606
Wisconsin	89,479	197	434	118	8,176	17,624,826
Wyoming	8,018	4,274	80	2,607	403	34,271,918
Total	**2,314,013**	**440**	**336**	**62,225**	**379,543**	**1,017,030,357**

Livestock on Farms in the U.S.

Source: Economics, Statistics, and Cooperatives Service: U.S. Agriculture Department (thousands)

Year (On Jan. 1)	All cattle	Milk cows	All sheep	Hogs	Horses* and mules
1890	60,014	15,000	44,518	48,130	18,054
1900	59,739	16,544	48,105	51,055	21,004
1910	58,993	19,450	50,239	48,072	24,211
1920	70,400	21,455	40,743	60,159	25,742
1925	63,373	22,575	38,543	55,770	22,569
1930	61,003	23,032	51,565	55,705	19,124
1935	68,846	26,082	51,808	39,066	16,683
1940	68,039	24,940	52,107	61,165	14,478
1945	85,573	27,770	46,520	59,373	11,950
1950	77,963	23,853	29,826	58,937	7,781
1955	96,592	23,462	31,582	50,474	4,309
1960	96,236	19,527	33,170	59,026	3,089

Year (On Jan. 1)	All cattle	Milk cows	All sheep	Hogs
1965	109,000	[2]15,380	25,127	57,030
1970	112,369	12,091	20,423	[3]57,046
1971	114,578	11,909	19,731	[3]67,285
1972	117,862	11,776	18,739	[3]62,412
1973	121,539	11,622	17,641	[3]59,017
1974	127,788	11,297	16,310	60,614
1975	132,028	11,220	14,515	[3]54,693
1976	127,980	11,087	13,311	[3]49,267
1977	122,810	11,035	12,766	[3]54,934
1978	116,375	10,939	12,348	[3]56,539
1979	110,864	10,839	12,220	[3]60,100
1980[1]	110,961	10,810	12,513	[3]66,950

*Discontinued in 1960. (1) Total estimated value on farms as of Jan. 1, 1980, was as follows (avg. value per head in parentheses): cattle and calves $55,702,422 ($502); sheep and lambs $974,762,700 ($77.90); hogs and pigs $3,769,285,000 ($56.30). (2) New series, milk cows and heifers that have calved, beginning 1965. (3) As of Dec. 1 of preceding year.

Harvested Acreage of Principal U.S. Crops

Source: Economics, Statistics, and Cooperatives Service: U.S. Agriculture Department (thousands of acres)

State	1977	1978	1979
Alabama	3,497	3,919	4,161
Arizona	1,183	1,213	1,207
Arkansas	8,190	7,907	8,343
California	6,134	6,426	6,510
Colorado	5,832	5,871	6,107
Connecticut	140	143	140
Delaware	514	511	530
Florida	1,358	1,487	1,520
Georgia	3,777	4,868	5,348
Hawaii	104	106	109
Idaho	4,326	4,507	4,493
Illinois	23,441	22,709	23,442
Indiana	12,664	12,211	12,515
Iowa	24,559	24,438	24,984
Kansas	22,490	20,596	21,009
Kentucky	5,098	5,056	5,231
Louisiana	4,564	4,723	4,974
Maine	476	418	415
Maryland	1,469	1,526	1,572
Massachusetts	160	161	159
Michigan	6,582	6,536	6,907
Minnesota	21,748	21,057	21,863
Mississippi	6,196	6,167	6,389
Missouri	14,171	13,384	14,345
Montana	9,021	8,990	8,828
Nebraska	18,285	17,353	17,858
Nevada	489	509	530
New Hampshire	113	114	116
New Jersey	531	542	556
New Mexico	1,325	1,185	1,305
New York	4,233	4,271	4,309
North Carolina	4,734	4,918	5,243
North Dakota	20,264	20,452	20,881
Ohio	10,837	10,701	10,995
Oklahoma	9,873	9,110	9,600
Oregon	2,647	2,653	2,641
Pennsylvania	4,383	4,366	4,454
Rhode Island	16	16	17
South Carolina	2,750	2,745	2,871
South Dakota	14,937	15,175	15,491
Tennessee	5,064	5,093	5,276
Texas	23,305	20,498	22,421
Utah	1,008	1,079	1,100
Vermont	543	549	556
Virginia	2,794	2,768	2,827
Washington	4,668	4,644	4,561
West Virginia	714	719	714
Wisconsin	9,387	9,181	9,376
Wyoming	1,773	1,856	1,844
Total U.S.	**332,367**	**325,427**	**336,643**

Crop acreages included are corn, sorghum, oats, barley, wheat, rice, rye, soybeans, flaxseed, peanuts, sunflower, popcorn, cotton, all hay, dry edible beans, dry edible peas, potatoes, sweet potatoes, tobacco, sugarcane and sugar beets.

Harvested Acreage of Principal Canadian Crops

Source: Statistics Canada (thousands of acres)

Province	1976	1977	1978	1979
Prince Edward Island	373	372	376	382
Nova Scotia	228	230	228	233
New Brunswick	308	306	311	308
Quebec	4,035	3,890	4,003	4,073
Ontario	8,228	8,186	8,296	8,483
Manitoba	9,353	9,545	10,036	10,009
Saskatchewan	25,851	26,228	27,350	27,302
Alberta	18,115	17,741	18,581	18,962
British Columbia	1,078	1,130	1,186	1,260
Total	**67,569**	**67,627**	**70,667**(1)	**71,014**(1)

Crops included are winter wheat, spring wheat, oats, barley, fall rye, spring rye, flaxseed, mixed grains, corn for grain, buckwheat, peas, dry beans, soybeans, rapeseed, potatoes, mustard seed, sunflower seed, tame hay, fodder corn, and sugar beets. (1) Totals include Newfoundland potatoes (1978) 1,120 acres, (1979) 940 acres.

Wool Production

Source: Economics, Statistics, and Cooperatives Service: U.S. Agriculture Department

	Sheep shorn (1,000)	Shorn wool (1,000 lbs.)	Value ($1,000)	Price per lb. (cents)	Pulled wool (1,000 lbs.)	Total wool (1,000 lbs)
1970	19,163	161,587	57,162	35.4	15,200	176,787
1971	19,036	160,156	31,416	19.6	12,000	172,156
1972	18,770	158,506	55,496	35.0	9,700	168,206
1973	17,425	143,738	118,839	82.7	8,000	151,738
1974	15,956	131,382	77,788	59.2	5,700	137,082
1975	14,403	119,535	53,505	44.7	5,300	124,835
1976	13,669	110,817	73,148	65.7	4,000	114,817
1977	13,214	107,159	77,147	72.0	1,700	108,859
1978	12,609	101,874	75,883	74.5	550	102,424
1979	12,826	102,803	88,719	86.3	260	103,063

Egg Production in the U.S.

Source: Economics, Statistics, and Cooperatives Service: U.S. Agriculture Department (millions of eggs)

State	1976	1977	1978	1979
Ala.	2,919	3,183	3,329	3,300
Alas.	6.0	6.2	4.5	6.4
Ariz.	143	140	124	109
Ark.	3,752	3,812	4,002	4,123
Cal.	8,635	8,345	8,412	8,713
Col.	505	508	533	481
Conn.	803	863	897	938
Del.	129	128	129	130
Fla.	2,846	2,998	2,954	3,189
Ga.	5,591	5,468	5,662	6,067
Ha.	218	218	218	229
Ida.	192	192	206	192
Ill.	1,398	1,389	1,380	1,347
Ind.	3,091	3,128	3,447	3,536
Ia.	2,040	2,004	1,914	1,849
Kan.	564	548	511	483
Ky.	541	566	553	583
La.	671	598	603	601
Me.	1,791	1,849	1,916	1,926
Md.	327	308	313	327
Mass.	343	355	341	339
Mich.	1,520	1,530	1,497	1,491
Minn.	2,238	2,120	2,189	2,183
Miss.	1,719	1,775	1,696	1,653
Mo.	1,193	1,199	1,320	1,376
Mon.	185	179	193	178
Neb.	737	739	780	802
Nev.	5.2	3.1	2.3	1.8
N.H.	237	210	222	218
N.J.	548	446	375	342
N.M.	270	288	359	368
N.Y.	1,903	1,805	1,845	1,767
N.C.	2,756	2,846	3,081	3,155
N.D.	120	99	95	89
Oh.	1,994	1,941	2,140	2,199
Okla.	458	487	612	754
Ore.	532	525	555	590
Pa.	2,701	2,960	3,436	3,836
R.I.	51.5	50.7	51.0	59.2
S.C.	1,282	1,248	1,409	1,561
S.D.	620	579	565	512
Tenn.	974	993	974	998
Tex.	2,357	2,436	2,630	2,795
Ut.	283	335	395	385
Vt.	114	121	120	111
Va.	800	819	885	939
Wash.	1,058	1,063	1,121	1,172
W.Vir.	230	192	154	178
Wis.	1,094	981	973	911
Wy.	26.4	23.7	17.5	14.3
Total U.S.	**64,511**	**64,600**	**67,140**	**69,107**

Note: The egg and chicken production year runs from Dec. 1 of the previous year through Nov. 30.

Egg Production in Canada

Source: Statistics Canada
(thousand dozens)

Province	1977	1978	1979
Newfoundland	7,135	7,115	7,222
Prince Edward Island	2,625	2,645	2,716
Nova Scotia	17,531	16,330	16,687
New Brunswick	9,141	8,768	8,964
Quebec	75,200	73,800	74,867
Ontario	178,569	180,381	180,250
Manitoba	50,270	49,377	48,358
Saskatchewan	19,522	20,851	20,566
Alberta	40,403	41,646	43,924
British Columbia	58,107	58,280	59,077
Total	**458,503**	**459,203**	**462,631**

Gross farm value of eggs (1976) $308,342,000; (1977) $313,398,000; (1978) $317,613,000; (1979) $354,069,000. Average price of eggs sold for consumption (1976) $.64; (1977) $.65; (1978) $.64; (1979) $.72. Number and value of chicken and fowl (1976) 251,734,000 - $353,404,000; (1977) 259,556,000 - $365,480,000; (1978) 277,434,000 - $415,504,000; (1979) 309,331,000 - $501,278,000. Gross farm income from eggs, chicken and fowl (1976) $661,746,000; (1977) $678,878,000; (1978) $733,117,000; (1979) $855,347,000.

Grain Receipts at U.S. Grain Centers

Source: Chicago Board of Trade (thousands bushels)

1978	Wheat	Corn	Oats	Rye	Barley	Soybeans	Total
Chicago	7,600	111,243	134	—	—	27,585	146,562
Duluth	—	—	—	—	—	—	—
Enid	63,472	2	—	—	—	—	63,474
Hutchinson	—	—	—	—	—	—	—
Kansas City	56,997	36,004	368	—	6	11,376	104,751
Milwaukee	560	46,391	354	—	22,161	2,040	71,506
Minneapolis	114	92	95	2	333	4	640
Omaha	19,183	53,085	1,330	—	—	5,918	79,516
Peoria	105	16,727	50	84	—	63	17,029
Sioux City	822	1,272	3,390	—	18	368	5,870
St. Joseph	2,016	7,336	2,288	—	—	1,726	13,366
St. Louis	2,301	301	172	—	—	1,904	4,678
Toledo	—	—	—	—	—	—	—
Wichita	22,900	230	—	—	148	3,654	26,932
Total	**176,070**	**272,683**	**8,181**	**86**	**22,666**	**54,638**	**534,324**

Grain Storage Capacity at Principal Grain Centers in U.S.

Source: Chicago Board of Trade
(bushels)

Cities	Capacity
Atlantic Coast	36,800,000
Great Lakes	
Toledo	4,330,000
Buffalo	8,200,000
Chicago	48,835,000
Milwaukee	9,100,000
Duluth	75,800,000
River Points	
Minneapolis	124,200,000
Peoria	6,600,000
St. Louis	25,500,000
Sioux City	11,600,000
Omaha-Council Bluffs	35,300,000
Atchinson	24,500,000
St. Joseph	20,600,000
Kansas City	72,400,000
Southwest	
Forth Worth	57,600,000

Cities	Capacity
Texas High Plains	76,800,000
Enid	66,100,000
Gulf Points	
South Mississippi	43,600,000
North Texas Gulf	28,200,000
South Texas Gulf	14,000,000
Plains	
Wichita	60,300,000
Topeka	61,600,000
Salina	45,000,000
Hutchinson	42,000,000
Hastings-Grand Island	24,100,000
Lincoln	39,600,000
Pacific N.W.	
Puget Sound	9,500,000
Portland	24,900,000
California Ports	14,300,000

Atlantic Coast — Albany, N.Y., Philadelphia, Pa., Baltimore, Md., Norfolk, Va., North Charleston, S.C. **Gulf Points** — New Orleans, Baton Rouge, Ama. Belle Chase, La., Mobile, Ala., Pascagoula, Miss. **North Texas Gulf** — Houston, Galveston, Beaumont, Port Arthur, Texas. **South Texas Gulf** — Corpus Christi, Brownsville, Texas. **Pacific N.W.** — Seattle, Tacoma, Wash., Portland, Oreg., Columbia River **Calif. Ports** — San Francisco, Stockton, Sacramento, Los Angeles. **Texas High Plains** — Amarillo, Lubbock, Hereford, Plainview, Texas.

U.S. Meat and Lard Production and Consumption

Source: Economics, Statistics, and Cooperatives Service: U.S. Agriculture Department (million lbs.)

	Beef		Veal		Lamb and mutton		Pork (exclud. lard)		All meats		Lard	
Year	Production	Consumption	Production	Consumption	Production	Consumption	Production	Consumption	Production	Consumption	Production	Consumption
1940	7,175	7,257	981	981	876	873	10,044	9,701	19,076	18,812	2,288	1,901
1950	9,534	9,529	1,230	1,206	597	596	10,714	10,390	22,075	21,721	2,631	1,891
1960	14,753	15,147	1,109	1,093	768	852	13,905	13,838	30,535	30,930	2,562	1,358
1965	18,727	19,060	1,020	992	651	716	12,781	12,870	33,179	33,638	2,045	1,225
1970	21,685	22,926	588	581	551	657	14,699	14,661	37,523	38,825	1,913	939
1975	23,976	25,398	873	876	410	430	11,779	11,852	37,038	38,556	1,012	632
1978	24,242	25,999	632	646	309	342	13,393	13,293	38,576	40,280	1,006	497

Net Income per Farm by States

Source: Economics, Statistics, and Cooperatives Service, U.S. Agriculture Department (dollars)

State	1970	1972	1973	1974	1975	1976	1977	1978
Alabama	2,744	4,232	6,732	4,886	5,118	5,505	4,347	7,636
Alaska	4,306	3,690	4,561	3,942	10,590	8,800	9,923	9,971
Arizona	18,295	25,480	40,104	65,828	30,390	60,101	48,449	56,706
Arkansas	4,570	5,609	11,798	12,402	11,039	7,744	8,186	14,220
California	15,520	23,384	38,940	44,093	33,834	33,177	33,670	41,762
Colorado	7,946	10,629	16,476	15,916	15,713	7,724	5,561	9,688
Connecticut	9,728	8,675	12,420	11,906	8,032	7,076	12,445	8,300
Delaware	6,974	11,954	28,550	21,619	26,146	23,560	16,114	33,511
Florida	10,824	19,266	25,197	23,579	25,134	22,464	20,810	34,354
Georgia	4,310	5,637	10,240	8,390	7,640	7,326	3,158	9,075
Hawaii	11,017	17,164	16,317	80,944	34,821	19,981	22,389	24,997
Idaho	7,269	9,752	16,584	21,615	11,493	6,254	3,497	12,594
Illinois	4,788	6,366	13,131	11,490	17,571	8,489	10,550	10,359
Indiana	3,262	4,257	11,225	5,976	10,232	9,592	7,133	6,940
Iowa	7,434	9,085	19,068	10,497	12,172	6,264	7,564	14,903
Kansas	6,208	10,546	16,962	10,955	7,969	5,541	5,398	9,366
Kentucky	2,843	3,811	4,461	5,150	3,944	4,719	4,850	4,576
Louisiana	4,242	5,825	10,724	12,131	7,576	8,197	8,101	8,901
Maine	6,093	6,081	18,166	23,478	7,534	16,630	9,767	10,214
Maryland	5,667	6,621	11,523	7,729	10,180	8,672	4,444	11,773
Massachusetts	6,438	6,215	7,890	7,182	6,193	8,701	1,563	9,758
Michigan	3,261	4,466	6,262	7,022	6,446	4,284	5,704	7,695
Minnesota	6,772	7,798	19,173	13,151	9,444	4,796	14,094	14,474
Mississippi	3,557	4,889	7,307	5,214	3,644	4,508	5,461	6,480
Missouri	2,955	4,345	7,865	4,005	4,476	2,630	6,045	7,494
Montana	9,168	13,835	22,829	14,829	14,015	6,689	55	12,536
Nebraska	6,442	10,096	17,798	8,169	14,565	5,433	7,089	12,768
Nevada	11,483	17,563	27,070	13,285	11,769	10,356	5,591	12,088
New Hampshire	4,924	6,901	9,209	6,416	5,036	6,110	4,445	4,506
New Jersey	6,671	5,451	10,592	11,402	6,354	7,223	7,268	10,634
New Mexico	9,158	10,403	16,247	10,900	13,201	9,695	9,009	15,395
New York	5,794	4,915	7,043	5,880	4,192	5,146	2,614	5,947
North Carolina	3,813	4,926	8,297	7,838	8,558	8,781	6,440	12,248
North Dakota	5,440	13,943	35,692	24,840	16,966	7,637	2,811	16,054
Ohio	3,224	3,823	5,355	6,216	6,413	5,964	5,715	5,422
Oklahoma	3,291	4,013	8,320	4,339	3,460	2,130	1,377	3,249
Oregon	4,080	5,751	10,628	12,648	8,086	7,054	3,983	9,111
Pennsylvania	4,187	4,036	6,034	5,553	4,154	5,031	4,833	8,229
Rhode Island	8,837	7,866	5,676	8,453	9,504	11,426	8,439	12,243
South Carolina	2,769	3,750	5,668	6,593	4,590	3,586	2,378	5,567
South Dakota	6,941	11,641	23,151	12,964	9,937	3,117	11,287	13,786
Tennessee	1,781	2,261	3,464	2,195	1,863	2,714	2,042	3,114
Texas	4,249	4,795	10,211	4,339	5,113	4,438	5,731	5,242
Utah	4,353	6,145	10,634	6,421	4,182	5,389	5,704	8,919
Vermont	6,792	8,658	9,241	7,044	7,564	9,918	8,087	15,316
Virginia	2,266	2,952	4,831	3,888	3,938	2,695	2,295	6,045
Washington	5,611	10,763	19,203	20,264	21,266	14,447	12,838	24,990
West Virginia	641	956	1,484	1,076	578	41	248	811
Wisconsin	5,273	6,403	8,637	6,910	7,376	5,743	11,746	11,726
Wyoming	5,895	11,675	14,788	6,751	2,317	256	110	8,213
Total U.S.	**4,790**	**6,504**	**11,727**	**9,232**	**8,845**	**6,823**	**7,302**	**10,434**

Farm Income—Cash Receipts from Marketings

Source: Economics, Statistics, and Cooperatives Service: U.S. Agriculture Department

($1,000)

1977 State	Crops	Live-stock	Gov't pay'ts	Total
Alabama	615,604	926,143	29,662	1,571,409
Alaska	7,210	4,525	127	11,862
Arizona	659,257	505,991	4,713	1,169,961
Arkansas	1,233,412	1,175,920	53,527	2,462,859
California	6,388,994	2,952,259	75,157	9,416,410
Colorado	563,164	1,505,549	65,404	2,134,117
Connecticut	94,533	129,641	379	224,553
Delaware	79,980	180,137	419	260,536
Florida	1,882,512	748,555	20,750	2,651,817
Georgia	969,703	1,226,470	51,166	2,247,339
Hawaii	260,233	64,949	24,693	349,875
Idaho	686,632	476,529	42,859	1,206,020
Illinois	3,849,130	1,874,015	32,082	5,755,227
Indiana	2,114,162	1,262,129	21,821	3,398,112
Iowa	2,641,386	4,244,825	28,901	6,915,112
Kansas	1,642,315	2,216,165	236,689	4,095,169
Kentucky	999,353	730,639	7,192	1,737,184
Louisiana	830,642	406,100	44,390	1,281,132
Maine	154,874	263,120	2,099	420,093
Maryland	228,728	428,383	3,398	660,509
Massachusetts	118,699	105,056	575	224,330
Michigan	1,042,682	836,967	21,195	1,900,844
Minnesota	2,039,884	2,228,343	82,484	4,351,075
Mississippi	896,789	793,650	23,853	1,714,292
Missouri	1,244,321	1,667,339	51,183	2,962,843
Montana	470,943	494,453	61,443	1,026,839
Nebraska	1,711,363	2,254,856	92,939	4,059,158
Nevada	45,531	101,353	2,590	149,474
New Hampshire	24,446	55,100	621	80,167
New Jersey	250,556	98,237	1,116	349,909
New Mexico	221,492	569,334	15,112	805,938
New York	517,231	1,200,517	8,576	1,726,324
North Carolina	1,570,709	1,052,802	21,645	2,645,156
North Dakota	1,125,985	472,560	122,603	1,721,148
Ohio	1,731,758	1,144,795	33,102	2,909,655
Oklahoma	705,154	1,159,684	84,132	1,948,970
Oregon	695,735	356,461	23,532	1,075,728
Pennsylvania	590,973	1,302,575	7,476	1,901,024
Rhode Island	15,385	11,162	63	26,610
South Carolina	515,374	278,555	15,712	809,641
South Dakota	417,586	1,111,433	94,858	1,623,877
Tennessee	705,224	675,422	12,370	1,393,016
Texas	3,135,826	3,524,564	157,993	6,818,383
Utah	104,487	264,606	18,565	387,658
Vermont	21,913	244,106	2,026	268,045
Virginia	451,198	558,043	17,108	1,026,349
Washington	1,248,213	508,937	58,844	1,815,994
West Virginia	41,115	105,663	4,507	151,285
Wisconsin	586,319	2,551,497	26,338	3,164,154
Wyoming	73,540	381,892	10,526	465,958
Total	**48,222,255**	**47,432,006**	**1,818,879**	**97,473,140**

Average Prices Received by U.S. Farmers

Source: Economics, Statistics, and Cooperatives Service: U.S. Agriculture Department

The figures represent dollars per 100 lbs. for hogs, beef cattle, veal calves, sheep, lamb, and milk (wholesale), dollars per head for milk cows; cents per lb. for milk fat (in cream), chickens, broilers, turkeys, and wool; cents for eggs per dozen.

Weighted calendar year prices for livestock and livestock products other than wool. 1943 through 1963, wool prices are weighted on marketing year basis. The marketing year has been changed (1964) from a calendar year to a Dec.-Nov. basis for hogs, chickens, broilers and eggs.

Year	Hogs	Cattle (beef)	Calves (veal)	Sheep	Lambs	Cows (milk)	Milk (wholesale)	Milk fat (in cream)	Chickens (excl. broilers)	Broilers	Turkeys	Eggs	Wool
1930	8.84	7.71	9.68	4.74	7.76	74.20	2.21	34.5	...	...	20.2	23.7	19.5
1940	5.39	7.56	8.83	3.95	8.10	61.00	1.82	28.0	13.0	17.3	15.2	18.0	28.4
1950	18.00	23.30	26.30	11.60	25.10	198.00	3.89	62.0	22.0	27.4	32.9	36.3	62.1
1960	15.30	20.40	22.90	5.61	17.90	223.00	4.21	60.5	12.2	16.9	25.4	36.1	42.0
1970	22.70	27.10	34.50	7.51	26.40	332.00	5.71	70.0	9.1	13.6	22.6	39.1	35.5
1973	38.40	42.80	56.60	12.70	35.10	496.00	7.14	67.2	15.1	24.0	38.2	52.5	82.7
1974	34.20	35.60	35.20	11.30	37.00	500.00	8.33	63.5	9.7	21.5	28.0	53.3	59.1
1975	46.10	32.30	27.20	11.20	42.10	412.00	8.75	71.0	9.9	26.3	34.8	52.5	44.7
1976	43.30	33.70	34.10	13.20	46.90	477.00	9.66	83.4	12.9	23.6	31.7	58.4	65.7
1977	39.40	34.40	36.90	13.40	51.30	504.00	9.72	92.0	12.1	23.6	35.5	55.6	72.0
1978	46.60	48.50	59.10	21.70	62.70	675.00	10.60	102.0	12.4	26.3	43.6	52.2	74.5
1979	41.80	66.00	88.80	26.30	66.70	1,040.00	12.00	119.0	14.4	25.9	41.1	58.3	86.3

The figures represent cents per lb. for cotton, apples, and peanuts; dollars per bushel for oats, wheat, corn, barley, and soybeans; dollars per 100 lbs. for rice, sorghum, and potatoes; dollars per ton for cottonseed and baled hay.

Weighted crop year prices. Crop years are as follows: apples, June-May; wheat, oats, barley, hay and potatoes, July-June; cotton, rice, peanuts and cottonseed, August-July; soybeans, September-August; and corn and sorghum grain, October-September.

Crop year	Corn	Wheat	Upland cotton[1]	Oats	Barley	Rice	Soybeans	Sorghum	Peanuts	Cotton-seed	Hay	Potatoes	Apples
1930	.663	.550	9.46	0.31	.420	1.74	1.34	1.02	3.46	22.00	11.00	1.47	...
1940	.674	.601	9.83	0.30	.393	1.80	.892	.873	3.33	21.70	9.78	.850	...
1950	2.00	1.52	39.90	0.79	1.19	5.09	2.47	1.88	10.9	86.60	21.10	1.50	...
1960	1.74	.997	30.08	0.60	.838	4.55	2.13	1.49	10.0	42.50	21.70	2.00	4.79
1970	1.33	1.33	22.81	0.62	.973	5.17	2.85	2.04	12.8	56.50	26.10	1.21	6.97
1973	2.55	3.95	44.40	1.18	2.14	13.80	5.68	3.82	16.2	100.00	41.60	4.89	10.70
1974	3.02	4.09	42.70	1.53	2.81	11.20	6.64	4.95	17.9	136.0	50.90	4.01	11.10
1975	2.54	3.56	51.10	1.46	2.42	8.35	4.92	4.23	19.6	97.00	52.20	4.48	8.80
1976	2.15	2.73	63.80	1.56	2.25	7.02	6.81	3.63	20.0	103.00	60.30	3.59	11.50
1977	2.02	2.33	52.10	1.10	1.78	9.49	5.88	3.25	21.0	70.30	54.00	3.55	13.80
1978	2.25	2.98	58.10	1.20	1.92	8.16	6.66	3.61	21.1	114.00	49.80	3.38	13.90
1979	2.41	3.82	62.30	1.36	2.31	11.00	6.19	4.16	20.7	122.00	59.70	3.47	13.90

(1) Beginning 1964, 480 lb. net weight bales.

Index Numbers of Prices Received by Farmers

Source: Economics, Statistics, and Cooperatives Service; U.S. Agriculture Department (index 1910-14=100 per cent)

Year	All farm products	All crops	Livestock	Food grains	Feed grains and hay	Cotton	Tobacco	Oil-bearing crops	Fruit	Commercial vegetables	Potatoes sweetpot[1]	Meat animals	Dairy products	Poultry and eggs
1910	104	105	102	109	96	118	84	120	100	...	83	101	100	104
1920	211	235	190	249	202	262	233	208	188	...	294	171	202	222
1930	125	115	134	93	106	104	140	111	149	128	162	133	142	128
1940	100	90	109	84	85	83	134	103	81	122	89	108	120	98
1950	258	233	280	224	193	282	402	276	194	211	166	340	249	186
1960	239	222	253	203	152	254	500	214	244	230	203	296	259	160
1965	245	230	260	163	174	245	513	265	240	262	293	315	260	144
1970	274	225	325	162	179	183	604	265	217	292	218	405	350	147
1975	463	452	474	426	400	348	899	529	313	458	400	567	537	235
1978	524	456	595	336	320	466	1,061	608	508	522	379	757	647	242
1979	603	502	708	403	360	490	1,148	670	545	548	333	938	736	252

(1) Including dry edible beans.

Ratio of prices received to prices paid by farmers

Year	ratio
1967	100
1968	99
1969	100
1970	98
1971	96
1972	101
1973	124
1974	117
1975	103
1978	96
1979	97

Farm Employment—Annual Averages

Source: Economics, Statistics, and Cooperatives Service: U.S. Agriculture Department (Index 1910-14=100 per cent)

Year	Total: Aver. no. (1,000)	Total: Index %	Family: Aver. no. (1,000)	Family: Index %	Hired: Aver. no. (1,000)	Hired: Index %
1920	13,432	99	10,041	99	3,391	100
1930	12,497	92	9,307	92	3,190	94
1940	10,979	82	8,300	81	2,679	79
1950	9,926	75	7,597	73	2,329	69
1960	7,057	52	5,172	52	1,885	55
1970	4,523	34	3,348	33	1,175	35
1978	3,957	29	2,689	26	1,268	37
1979	3,774	28	2,501	25	1,273	37

Canadian Farm Cash Receipts

Source: Statistics Canada
(millions of Canadian Dollars)

Cash receipts from farming operations excluding supplementary payments. Excludes Newfoundland

Crops

Year	Total cash receipts	Total crops	Wheat	Barley	C.W.B. advance payments[1]	Deferred grain receipts	Other grains[2]	Potatoes	Fruits	Vegetables	Floriculture and nursery	Tobacco	Other crops[3]
1975	10,026.8	4,773.8	1,699.2	465.7	990.3	−69.6	626.6	159.1	130.5	242.6	141.8	195.9	191.7
1976	10,005.1	4,609.4	1,642.8	451.3	526.4	149.2	639.5	199.6	147.1	243.7	170.4	233.8	205.6
1977	10,098.7	4,343.6	1,650.3	319.8	252.9	112.2	843.9	173.8	164.3	238.5	184.4	182.1	230.4
1978	11,880.3	4,968.4	1,674.7	398.2	349.6	83.8	1,100.4	151.8	206.7	280.7	201.1	267.5	253.9
1979	13,970.9	5,861.3	1,914.3	497.4	711.2	−55.3	1,348.6	158.8	180.2	310.1	218.4	289.7	287.9

Livestock and Products

Year	Total	Cattle and calves	Hogs	Dairy products	Poultry	Eggs	Other products[4]	Forest and maple products	Provincial income stabilization payments	Dairy Supplementary payments	Deficiency[5] payments
1975	5,253.0	1,873.9	878.9	1,347.3	411.8	269.8	94.5	44.6	49.8	259.9	22.6
1976	5,395.7	1,940.9	829.1	1,331.3	477.2	295.6	100.8	54.2	82.9	258.9	24.8
1977	5,755.1	2,101.5	837.9	1,413.8	484.5	299.1	125.4	55.3	119.5	269.4	48.7
1978	6,911.9	2,868.8	1,156.2	1,508.5	541.7	303.5	154.8	61.7	31.6	242.5	42.6
1979	8,109.6	3,523.1	1,300.5	1,722.9	658.4	339.6	179.6	73.1	9.7	246.1	56.6

(1) Represents participation payments made by the Canadian Wheat Board direct to producers on crops delivered in previous years. (2) Includes oats, rye, flaxseed, rapeseed, soybeans, and corn. (3) Includes sugar beets, clover and grass seed, hay, clover, mustard seed, sunflower seed, dry beans and dry peas, net non-grain cash advances, and miscellaneous products. (4) Including sheep and lambs. (5) Made under the authority of the Agricultural Stabilization Act.

Canadian Farm Cash Receipts by Province

Source: Statistics Canada
(thousands of Canadian dollars)

Province	1974	1975	1976	1977	1978	1979
Prince Edward Island	85,527	84,901	103,455	89,932	100,711	120,281
Nova Scotia	102,737	113,847	126,413	133,155	155,931	175,262
New Brunswick	103,248	98,954	113,087	109,643	122,395	137,952
Quebec	1,137,568	1,341,098	1,370,065	1,420,753	1,661,695	1,924,788
Ontario	2,511,014	2,684,429	2,780,354	2,845,791	3,398,181	3,951,020
Manitoba	827,057	931,958	885,100	892,819	1,125,316	1,288,200
Saskatchewan	2,077,854	2,469,503	2,304,476	2,135,978	2,471,439	2,905,193
Alberta	1,702,716	1,879,823	1,841,813	1,950,463	2,263,022	2,835,669
British Columbia	406,250	422,241	480,347	520,203	581,655	632,547
Total	**8,953,971**	**10,026,754**	**10,005,110**	**10,098,737**	**11,880,345**	**13,970,912**

Canadian Production of Sawn Lumber

Source: Canadian Statistical Review
(million feet, board measure)

Year	Canada[1]	N.S.	N.B.	Que.	Ont.	Sask.	Alta.	B.C.
1976 . . .	15,431	159	321	2,364	1,175	156	511	10,745
1977. . .	17,582	194	308	2,700	1,412	218	620	12,038
1978. . .	18,884	178	394	3,209	1,622	221	611	12,545
1979. . .	19,066	215	399	3,330	1,620	195	695	12,511

(1) Excludes Newfoundland, P.E.I., Manitoba, the Yukon, and the Northwest Territories which, together, account for less than 1% of the total.

Average Farm Wages

Source: Economics, Statistics, and Cooperatives Service, U.S. Agriculture Department

(dollars per hour)

Method of pay:	1977	1978	1979
All hired farm workers	2.87	3.09	3.39
Paid by piece-rate	3.48	3.76	4.07
Paid by other than piece-rate	2.82	3.04	3.34
Paid by hour only[1]	2.84	3.08	3.38
Paid cash wages only[2]	3.06	3.22	3.58
Paid by hour cash wages only[3]	2.90	3.10	3.41
Type of work performed:			
Field and livestock workers	2.65	2.81	3.11
Packinghouse workers	2.97	3.18	3.39

	1977	1978	1979
Machine operators	2.92	3.13	3.44
Maintenance and bookkeeping	(5)	(5)	(5)
Supervisors	4.63	4.95	5.22
Other agricultural workers	3.37	3.60	3.82
Indexes[4]			
(1910-14=100)	1,904	2,044	2,242
(1967=100)	225	241	265

(1) May include perquisites such as room and board, includes only those paid by the hour. (2) Does not include perquisites, includes all methods of pay. (3) Does not include perquisites, includes only those paid by the hour. (4) Indexes are based on all hired farm workers and are adjusted for seasonal variation. (5) Maintainance and bookkeeping included with other workers in 1977, 1978, and 1979.

Government Payments by Programs, by States

Source: Economics, Statistics, and Cooperatives Service: U.S. Agriculture Department ($1,000)

1979 State	Conservation[1]	Feed grain program	Wheat program	Cotton program	Rice program	Drought & flood program	Misc. program[3]	Total
Alabama	4,955	1,137	31	1,274	—	4	4,671	12,072
Alaska	266	—	—	—	—	—	4	270
Arizona	5,249	751	277	1,609	—	—	1,186	9,072
Arkansas	3,187	1,550	750	7,068	15,240	166	4,603	32,564
California	11,173	2,987	2,452	27,340	11,794	184	5,398	61,328
Colorado	5,214	11,810	8,936	—	—	103	11,233	37,296
Connecticut	329	14	—	—	—	—	76	419
Delaware	182	157	5	—	—	—	23	367
Florida	3,463	1,149	2	19	—	—	1,144	5,777
Georgia	4,115	7,145	169	848	—	—	5,668	17,945
Hawaii	726	—	—	—	—	—	15	741
Idaho	2,350	4,597	3,098	—	—	—	11,014	21,059
Illinois	7,421	17,273	515	—	—	33	7,968	33,210
Indiana	4,262	11,543	220	—	—	—	2,562	18,587
Iowa	6,557	37,993	63	—	—	136	24,440	69,189
Kansas	5,151	81,234	21,639	—	—	124	17,690	125,838
Kentucky	3,910	2,456	65	—	—	—	228	6,659
Louisiana	3,163	211	34	1,680	13,225	—	1,876	20,189
Maine	1,777	93	—	—	—	27	3,643	5,540
Maryland	767	1,144	66	—	—	—	150	2,127
Massachusetts	433	44	—	—	—	—	115	592
Michigan	3,753	9,115	200	—	—	36	2,489	15,593
Minnesota	4,897	21,071	2,277	—	—	151	40,040	68,436
Mississippi	4,026	333	91	3,944	1,552	18	2,923	12,887
Missouri	6,632	19,197	1,627	1,269	87	—	2,528	31,340
Montana	6,131	4,769	10,059	—	—	341	12,697	33,997
Nebraska	4,755	71,914	8,262	—	—	54	47,711	132,696
Nevada	803	77	9	—	—	—	448	1,337
New Hampshire	468	6	—	—	—	3	140	617
New Jersey	565	186	12	—	—	—	43	806
New Mexico	2,658	8,814	2,250	3,108	—	—	4,511	21,341
New York	4,127	3,399	28	—	—	—	1,482	9,036
North Carolina	3,757	2,791	51	307	—	1	1,399	8,306
North Dakota	3,326	7,729	8,227	—	—	—	27,237	46,519
Ohio	3,934	4,613	325	—	—	—	1,730	10,602
Oklahoma	4,702	10,397	6,287	3,272	9	31	16,978	41,676
Oregon	3,116	487	1,240	—	—	59	3,570	8,472
Pennsylvania	3,372	2,113	87	—	—	—	464	6,036
Rhode Island	67	1	—	—	—	—	10	78
South Carolina	2,150	1,847	37	453	—	—	1,970	6,457
South Dakota	3,164	14,531	16,032	—	—	30	20,930	54,687
Tennessee	4,630	992	485	1,357	—	147	821	8,432
Texas	16,736	104,808	10,765	131,398	16,844	817	25,731	307,099
Utah	1,601	489	780	—	—	—	2,362	5,232
Vermont	987	41	1	—	—	—	186	1,215
Virginia	2,520	1,854	70	3	—	2	1,498	5,947
Washington	3,633	1,224	5,129	—	—	28	6,659	16,673
West Virginia	1,531	77	—	—	—	—	431	2,039
Wisconsin	4,439	17,438	94	—	—	344	6,158	28,473
Wyoming	2,186	352	795	—	—	149	4,801	8,283
Total	**179,316**	**493,953**	**113,542**	**184,949**	**58,751**	**2,988**	**341,654**	**1,375,153**

(1) Includes amounts paid under Agricultural and Conservation Programs. (2) Includes Sugar Act, National Wool Act, Milk Indemnity Program, Beekeepers Indemnity Program, Hay and Cattle Transportation Program, Cropland Adjustment Program, Forest Incentive Program, Water Bank Program, Emergency Livestock Feed Program, Great Plains and other miscellaneous programs.

Food Stamps—Costs and Benefits

Fiscal year	Average persons participating per month	Value per year: Total purchase	Value per year: Bonus	Avg. bonus per participant per month: Current $	Avg. bonus per participant per month: 1967 $
1962	142,817	$ 35,202,266	$ 13,152,695	7.67	8.47
1965	424,652	85,471,989	32,505,096	6.38	6.75
1970	4,340,030	1,089,960,761	549,663,811	10.55	9.07
1974	12,861,526	4,727,450,579	2,718,296,427	17.61	11.87
1975	17,064,196	7,265,641,706	4,385,501,248	21.41	13.62
1976	18,548,715	8,700,208,987	5,326,505,192	23.93	—
1977p	17,057,598	8,339,804,533	5,057,723,608	24.71	—
1978p	16,043,861	8,310,918,211	5,165,208,676	26.83	—
1979p	17,130,000	4,265,501,319	3,520,279,189	29.36	—

(p) preliminary. The Food Stamp Program enables low-income families to buy more food of greater variety to improve their diets. If a household meets eligibility requirements it receives food stamps based on its net income and the number of people in the household. Major reform measures went into effect Jan. 1, 1979, to lower the net income eligibility standards to the official poverty level ($6,500 for a family of four for fiscal year 1978); change the allowable deductions; eliminate the food stamp purchase requirement; streamline administration; and reduce the potential for fraud or abuse. County and city welfare departments administer the program locally.

Federal Food Program Costs

Source: Food and Nutrition Service, U.S. Agriculture Department (millions of dollars)

Calendar year	Food stamps			Food distribution[3]			Child nutrition					Total costs
	Total value	Bonus[1]	WIC[2]	Needy persons[4]	Schools	Institutions	School lunch	School bkfst.	Child care	Summer food	Special milk	
1971	3,105	1,699[1]	—	331	296	26	647	22	14	20	92	3,147
1975	8,325	5,073[1]	119	37	364	15	1,385	99	57	65	133	7,347
1976	8,613	5,262[1]	177	41	407	16	1,543	113	94	140	150	7,943
1977	8,272	5,014	289	50	503	19	1,700	154	117	122	151	8,119
1978	8,347	5,260	346	43	576	34	1,864	186	—	114	138	8,561

(1) Includes Food Certificate Program. (2) Special Supplemental Food Program for Women, Infants, and Children. (3) Cost of food delivered to state distribution centers. (4) Represents cost of the Needy Family Program, Supplemental Food Program, and the Nutrition Program for the Elderly.

Civilian Consumption of Major Food Commodities per Person

Source: Economics, Statistics, and Cooperatives Service: U.S. Agriculture Department

Commodity[1]	1960	1970	1979[2]
Meats	134.1	151.4	147.2
Beef	64.3	84.1	79.6
Veal	5.2	2.4	1.7
Lamb and mutton	4.3	2.9	1.3
Pork	60.3	62.0	64.6
Fish (edible weight)	10.3	11.8	13.3
Poultry products:			
Eggs	42.4	39.5	35.9
Chicken (ready-to-cook)	27.8	40.5	51.5
Turkey (ready-to-cook)	6.2	8.0	10.1
Dairy products:			
Cheese	8.3	11.5	17.7
Condensed and evaporated milk	13.7	7.1	4.4
Fluid milk and cream (product weight)	321.0	296.0	283.0
Ice cream (product weight)	18.3	17.7	17.6
Fats and Oils—Total fat content	45.3	53.0	57.7
Butter (actual weight)	7.5	5.3	4.6
Margarine (actual weight)	9.4	11.0	11.5
Lard	7.6	4.7	2.6
Shortening	12.6	17.3	18.9
Other edible fats and oils	11.5	17.9	22.4
Fruits:			
Fresh	90.0	79.4	81.3
Citrus	32.5	28.0	24.0
Noncitrus	57.5	51.4	57.3

Commodity[1]	1960	1970	1979[2]
Processed:			
Canned fruit	22.6	23.3	19.5
Canned juice	12.9	14.5	17.3
Frozen (including juices)	9.2	9.3	12.3
Chilled citrus juices	2.1	4.7	5.6
Dried	3.1	2.7	3.1
Vegetables:			
Fresh[3]	96.0	91.1	94.3
Canned (excluding potatoes and sweet potatoes)	43.4	51.1	53.5
Frozen (excluding potatoes)	7.0	9.6	11.5
Potatoes[4]	105.0	115.2	120.7
Sweet potatoes[4]	6.5	5.3	5.2
Grains:			
Wheat flour[5]	118	110	117
Rice	6.1	6.7	9.2
Other:			
Coffee	11.6	10.4	8.6
Tea	.6	.7	.7
Cocoa	2.9	3.1	2.6
Peanuts (shelled)	4.9	5.9	7.1
Dry edible beans	7.3	5.9	6.4
Melons	23.2	21.2	19.5
Sugar (refined)	97.3	101.8	91.1

(1) Quantity in pounds, retail weight unless otherwise shown. Data on calendar year basis except for dried fruits, fresh citrus fruits, peanuts, and rice which are on a crop-year basis. (2) Preliminary. (3) Commercial production for sale as fresh produce. (4) Including fresh equivalent of processed. (5) White, whole wheat, and semolina flour including use in bakery products.

U.S. Farm Marketing, Supply, Related Service Cooperatives

Source: Economics, Statistics, and Cooperatives Service, U.S. Agriculture Department

Marketing season 1976-77[1]; a marketing season includes the period during which the farm products of a specified year are moved into the channels of trade. Marketing seasons overlap.

State	Number of cooperatives	Memberships	Net business
Alabama	100	109,589	535,435
Alaska	1	18	[2]
Arizona	21	92,489	339,801
Arkansas	117	98,218	834,214
California	271	83,865	[3]3,784,016
Colorado	79	44,765	477,249
Connecticut	7	5,147	101,591
Delaware	7	12,915	52,024
Florida	89	61,391	1,018,003
Georgia	93	161,866	759,520
Hawaii	16	2,278	28,667
Idaho	60	38,593	351,861
Illinois	270	287,358	3,048,424
Indiana	105	331,591	1,715,703
Iowa	402	304,596	3,441,800
Kansas	257	209,429	1,754,552
Kentucky	77	251,393	449,978
Louisiana	91	17,749	390,272
Maine	10	7,490	117,758
Maryland	33	52,285	378,360
Massachusetts	16	10,805	175,837
Michigan	141	138,858	1,117,706
Minnesota	768	573,147	3,087,482
Mississippi	130	119,246	668,738
Missouri	154	266,281	1,523,517
Montana	156	61,937	343,875
Nebraska	316	209,729	1,481,739
Nevada	3	197	22,530
New Hampshire	7	6,456	69,205
New Jersey	33	14,993	181,000
New Mexico	22	5,519	84,897
New York	256	141,843	1,447,899
North Carolina	39	142,693	454,817
North Dakota	455	195,274	1,294,569
Ohio	194	204,807	1,618,488
Oklahoma	149	97,532	796,241
Oregon	65	55,000	593,702
Pennsylvania	95	72,547	1,085,518
Rhode Island	1	868	23,319
South Carolina	24	65,145	163,314
South Dakota	244	169,380	675,079
Tennessee	100	156,938	469,460
Texas	424	143,585	1,920,600
Utah	38	21,571	245,397
Vermont	9	6,967	251,436
Virginia	109	182,684	551,904
Washington	135	74,338	1,111,025
West Virginia	71	72,291	90,257
Wisconsin	451	364,687	2,297,135
Wyoming	25	9,092	46,010
Foreign	—	293	112,229
Total	**6,736**	**5,757,728**	**43,584,153**

(1) Preliminary. (2) Included in dollar volume of California. (3) The volume of a sugar cooperative located in Hawaii but headquartered in California is included in California.

Farm-Real Estate Debt Outstanding by Lender Groups

Source: Economics, Statistics, and Cooperatives Service, U.S. Agriculture Department

	Total farm-real estate debt[1]	Federal land banks[1]	Amounts held by principal lender groups: Farmers Home Administration[2]	Life insurance companies[3]	All commercial banks	Other[4]
	$1,000	$1,000	$1,000	$1,000	$1,000	$1,000
1952	6,662,327	1,026,906	290,529	1,541,874	1,017,360	2,785,658
1953	7,240,937	1,095,257	330,087	1,716,022	1,069,398	3,030,173
1954	7,930,931	1,187,046	352,199	1,892,773	1,091,949	3,215,964
1955	8,245,278	1,279,787	378,108	2,051,784	1,161,308	3,374,291
1956	9,012,016	1,480,204	412,670	2,271,784	1,275,429	3,571,929
1957	9,821,525	1,722,381	462,942	2,476,543	1,298,113	3,861,546
1958	10,382,475	1,897,187	540,762	2,578,958	1,315,530	4,050,038
1959	11,091,390	2,065,372	608,101	2,661,229	1,407,548	4,349,140
1960	12,082,409	2,335,124	676,224	2,819,542	1,523,051	4,728,468
1961	12,820,304	2,539,044	722,870	2,974,609	1,591,762	4,992,019
1962	13,899,105	2,803,103	948,346	3,161,757	1,640,790	5,345,109
1963	15,167,821	3,024,013	1,057,923	3,391,183	1,870,216	5,824,486
1964	16,803,505	3,281,797	1,171,373	3,780,537	2,136,571	6,433,227
1965	18,894,240	3,686,755	1,284,913	4,287,671	2,416,634	7,218,267
1966	21,186,886	4,240,227	1,497,313	4,801,677	2,607,404	8,040,265
1967	23,077,186	4,914,522	1,663,067	5,213,587	2,770,010	8,516,000
1968	25,142,401	5,563,204	1,844,046	5,539,600	3,060,551	9,135,000
1969	27,397,370	6,081,229	2,054,382	5,763,500	3,333,259	10,165,000
1970	29,182,766	6,671,222	2,279,620	5,733,900	3,545,024	10,953,000
1971	30,346,083	7,145,363	2,440,043	5,610,300	3,772,377	11,378,000
1972	32,207,666	6,879,753	2,618,131	5,564,300	4,218,482	11,927,000
1973	35,757,754	9,050,067	2,835,202	5,643,300	4,792,185	13,437,000
1974	41,252,870	10,901,352	3,013,440	5,964,800	5,458,278	15,915,000
1975	46,288,419	13,402,441	3,214,657	6,297,400	5,966,282	17,407,639
1976	51,068,946	15,949,720	3,368,747	6,726,000	6,296,286	18,728,193
1977	56,559,645	18,454,578	3,657,467	7,400,200	6,781,410	20,265,990
1978	63,641,566	21,391,162	3,982,054	8,819,400	7,780,261	21,668,689
1979	70,832,666	24,619,174	4,121,038	10,478,200	8,556,539	23,057,715
1980	82,123,242	29,641,784	6,556,271	12,165,379	8,623,281	25,136,527

(1) Includes data for joint stock land banks and Federal Farm Mortgage Corporations. (2) Includes loans made directly by FmHA for farm ownership, soil and water loans to individuals, recreation loans to individuals, Indian tribe land acquisition, grazing associations, and irrigation drainage and soil conservation associations. Also includes loans for rural housing on farm tracts and labor housing. (3) Taken from Life Insurance Institute Tally sheet. (4) Estimated by ESCS, USDA.

Giant Trees of the U.S.

Source: The American Forestry Association

There are approximately 1,180 different species of trees native to the continental U.S., including a few imports that have become naturalized to the extent of reproducing themselves in the wild state.

The oldest living trees in the world are reputed to be the bristlecone pines, the majority of which are found growing on the arid crags of California's White Mts. Some of them are estimated to be more than 4,600 years old. The largest known bristlecone pine is the "Patriarch," believed to be 1,500 years old. The oldest known redwoods are about 3,500 years old.

Recognition as the National Champion of each species is determined by total mass of each tree, based on this formula: the circumference in inches as measured at a point 4 1/2 feet above the ground plus the total height of the tree, plus 1/4 of the average crown spread in feet. Trunk circumference is the most significant factor and in case of a tie the champion is determined on the basis of circumference. The Giant Sequoia champion has the largest circumference, 83 ft. 2 in., Gallberry Holly the smallest, 5 in. Following is a small selection of the 661 trees registered with the American Forestry Assn.

(Figure in parentheses is year of most recent measurement)

Species	Height (ft.)	Location
Acacia, Koa (1969)	140	Kau, Ha.
Ailanthus, Tree-of-Heaven (1972)	60	Long Island, N.Y.
Alder, European (1974)	68	Princeton, Ill.
Apple, Southern Crab (1976)	46	Williamsburg, Va.
Ash, Blue (1970)	86	Danville, Ky.
Aspen, Bigtooth (1979)	92	Rocky, Md.
Bald Cypress, Common (1977)	122	Sharon, Tenn.
Basswood, American (1971)	115	Grand Traverse Co. Mich.
Bayberry, Pacific (1972)	38	Siuslaw Natl. Forest, Ore.
Beech, American (1976)	161	Three Oaks, Mich.
Birch, River (1974)	95	Cumberland For., Va.
Birch, Yellow (1979)	107	Huron Mtn. Club, Mich.
Birch, Yellow (1973)	114	Gould City, Mich.
Blackbead, Catclaw (1976)	88	Sarasota, Fla.
Blackhaw, Rusty (1961)	25	nr. Washington, Ark.
Bladdernut, American (1972)	36	nr. Utica, Mich.
Boxelder (1976)	110	Lenawee Co., Mich.
Buckeye, Painted (1972)	144	Union County, Ga.
Buckthorn, Cascara (1977)	37	Seaside, Ore.
Buckwheat tree (1967)	30	nr. Crooked Creek, Fla.
Buffaloberry, Silver (1975)	22	Malheur Co., Ore.
Bumelia, Gum (1977)	80	Robertson Co., Tex.
Butternut (1973)	102	Portland, Ore.
Buttonbush, Common (1977)	23	nr. High Springs, Fla.
Button-Mangrove (1974)	52	Palm Beach, Fla.
Cajeput (1975)	66	Sarasota, Fla.
Camphor-tree (1977)	72	Hardee Co., Fla.
Casuarina, Horsetail (1968)	89	Olowalo, Maui, Ha.
Catalpa, Northern (1972)	94	Lansing, Mich.
Cedar, Port-Orford (1972)	219	Siskiyou Natl. Forest, Ore.
Cercocarpus, Birchleaf (1972)	34	Central Point, Ore.
Cherry, Black (1980)	132	Washtenow Co., Mich.
Chestnut, American (1979)	82	Oregon City, Ore.
Chinaberry (1967)	75	Koahe, So. Kuona, Ha.
Chinkapin, Golden (1979)	75	Cottage Grove, Ore.
Chokecherry, Common (1972)	66	Ada, Mich.
Coconut (1978)	67	Ft. Myers, Fla.
Coffeetree, Kentucky (1976)	110	Van Buren Co., Mich.

(continued)

Species	Height (ft.)	Location
Cottonwood, Black (1969)	147	Unionvalle, Ore.
Cypress, Monterey (1975)	97	Brookings, Ore.
Dahoon (1975)	72	Osceola For., Fla.
Desert Willow (1976)	56	Gila Co., Ariz.
Devil's-walkingstick (1976)	51	San Felasco Hammock, Fla.
Devilwood (1972)	37	Mayo, Fla.
Dogwood, Pacific (1975)	50	nr. Clatskanie, Ore.
Douglas Fir (1972)	221	Olympic Natl. Pk., Wash.
Doveplum (1965)	45	Miami, Fla.
Elder, Blackbead (1972)	42	nr. Prescott, Ore.
False-Mastic (1975)	70	Lignumvitae Key, Fla.
Fig, Florida Strangler (1973)	80	Old Cutler Hammock, Fla.
Fir, Noble (1972)	278	Gifford Pinchot Natl. Forest, Wash.
Gumbo-limbo (1973)	50	Homestead, Fla.
Hackberry, Common (1972)	118	Allegany Co., Mich.
Hawthorn (1967)	50	Glenview, Ill.
Hemlock, Western (1979)	195	Tillamock, Ore.
Hercules-club (1961)	38	Little Rock, Ark.
Hickory, Pignut (1972)	125	nr. Brunswick, Ga.
Holly, American (1979)	99	Congaree Swamp, S.C.
Honeylocust, Thornless (1976)	130	Washtenaw Co., Mich.
Hophornbeam, Eastern (1976)	73	Traverse Co., Mich.
Hoptree, Common (1972)	31	Ada, Mich.
Hornbeam, American (1975)	65	Milton, N.Y.
Joshua-tree (1967)	32	San Bernardino Natl. Forest, Cal.
Juniper, Western (1954)	87	Stanislaus Natl. Forest, Cal.
Larch, Western (1980)	175	Libby, Mont.
Laurelcherry, Carolina (1972)	44	Dellwood, Fla.
Lebbek (1968)	65	Lahaina, Maui, Ha.
Loblolly-Bay (1972)	84	Ocala Natl. Forest, Fla.
Locust, Black (1974)	96	Dansville, N.Y.
Lysiloma, Bahama (1973)	79	Homestead, Fla.
Madrone, Pacific (1974)	79	Humboldt Co., Cal.
Magnolia, Cucumber tree (1979)	94	North Canton, Oh.
Mangrove, Red (1975)	75	Everglades Natl. Pk., Fla.
Maple, Red (1972)	125	nr. Armada, Mich.
Mesquite, Velvet (1972)	55	Coronado Natl. Forest, Ariz.
Mountain-Ash, Showy (1972)	58	nr. Gould City, Mich.
Mountain-Laurel (1972)	20	Chattahoochee Natl. Forest, Ga.
Mulberry, White (1976)	82	Battle Creek, Mich.
Oak, Pin (1979)	134	Smithland, Ky.
Oak, Scarlet (1979)	150	Maud, Ala.
Osage-Orange (1972)	51	Charlotte Co., Va.
Palmetto, Cabbage (1978)	90	Highlands Hammock State Pk., Fla.
Paloverde, Blue (1976)	53	Riverside Co., Cal.
Paulownia, Royal (1969)	105	Philadelphia, Pa.
Pawpaw, Blue (1972)	41	nr. Smith Mills, Ky.
Pear (1976)	57	Clawson, Mich.
Pecan (1980)	143	Cocke Co., Tenn.
Peppertree (1973)	47	San Juan Capistrano, Cal.
Pinckneya (1972)	21	nr. Mt. Pleasant, Fla.
Pine, Ponderosa (1974)	223	Plumas, Cal.
Plum, American (1972)	35	Oakland Co., Mich.
Poison Sumac (1972)	20	Robin's Island, N.Y.
Pondcypress (1972)	135	nr. Newton, Ga.
Poplar, Balsam (1976)	128	Champion, Mich.
Possumhaw (1976)	30	Congaree Swamp, S.C.
Redbay (1972)	58	Randolph Co., Ga.
Redwood, Coast (1972)	362	Humboldt Redwoods State Park, Cal.
Royalpalm, Florida (1973)	80	Homestead, Fla.
Sassafras (1972)	100	Owensboro, Ky.
Seagrape (1972)	57	Miami, Fla.
Sequoia, Giant (1975)	275	Sequoia Natl. Pk., Cal.
Serviceberry, Downy (1975)	50	Gnadenhutten, Oh.
Silktree (1971)	41	Gilmer, Tex.
Silverbell, Two-wing (1971)	55	Tallahassee, Fla.
Smoketree, American (1974)	47	Lewiston, Ida.
Soapberry, Western (1972)	67	Newton County, Tex.
Sourwood (1972)	118	nr. Robbinsville, N.C.
Sparkleberry Tree (1977)	30	Pensacola, Fla.
Spruce, Sitka (1973)	216	Seaside, Ore.
Sugarberry (1976)	78	Society Hill, S.C.
Sumac, Shining (1974)	55	Grenada Co., Miss.
Sweetleaf, Common (1972)	55	Tallahassee, Fla.
Sycamore, Cal. (1945)	116	nr. Santa Barbara, Cal.
Tamarack (1972)	95	Jay, Me.
Tamarisk, Five-Stamen (1972)	37	Albuquerque, N.M.
Tesota (1972)	32	nr. Quartzsite, Ariz.
Torreya, Cal. (1945)	141	nr. Mendocino, Cal.
Trifoliate-Orange (1968)	26	Harrisburg, Pa.
Tupelo, Black (1969)	117	Harrison Co., Tex.
(1969)	139	nr. Houston, Tex.
Walnut, Cal. (1973)	116	Santa Rosa, Cal.
Willow, Crack (1972)	112	nr. Utica, Mich.
Winterberry, Common (1971)	40	Wildwood, Fla.
Witch Hazel, Common (1976)	43	Muskegon, Mich.
Yaupon (1972)	45	nr. Devers, Tex.
Yellow-Poplar (1972)	124	Bedford, Va.
Yellowwood (1967)	58	Morrisville, Pa.
Yew, Pacific (1969)	60	nr. Mineral, Wash.
Yucca, Aloe (1972)	15	Lakeland, Fla.

Giant Trees of Canada

Source: Native Trees of Canada by R.C. Hosie; Canadian Forestry Service, Dept. of Fisheries & Forestry

There are nearly 140 species of trees native to Canada on which information is easily available. A "native" tree is defined as a single-stemmed perennial woody plant growing to a height of more than 10 feet, and which is indigenous to Canada. Most of the "giant" trees in Canada are to be found in the forest regions. These regions reflect differences caused by terrain, soil, and climate. The 9 forest regions are: The Grassland, Boreal, Great Lakes-St. Lawrence, Columbia, Deciduous, Coast, Subalpine, Acadian, and Montane.

It is difficult to obtain precise records of single trees of outstanding heights. Given below are several common species of trees native to Canada showing the usual or normal height of the species. But many exceptions have been noted. For example, the Douglas Fir, whose average range in height is given at 150 to 200 ft. with diameters of up to 9 ft., occasionally may attain heights above 300 ft. and diameters of 15 ft. or more. The Sitka Spruce is also known to have reached heights of at least 280 ft., and the Western White Pine is recorded as having attained 200 ft.

Species	Height (ft.)	Forest region
Alpine Fir	65-100	Subalpine; N. W. Boreal
Amabilis Fir.	80-125	Coast & coastal parts of Subalpine
Balsam Poplar	60-80	Boreal, Great Lakes-St. Lawrence & Acadian
Black Cottonwood	80-125	Throughout B.C. and western Alberta
Black Maple	80-90	Ontario to Montreal Is.
Douglas Fir	150-200	Coast
Eastern Cottonwood	75-100	Gt. Lakes-St. Lawrence
Eastern White Pine	100-175	Through east Canada
Engelmann Spruce	100-120	Southern Subalpine
Grand Fir	100-125	S. Coast & Columbia
Mockernut Hickory	75-90	Deciduous
Silver Maple	80-90	S.E. parts of G. Lakes-St. Lawrence
Sitka Spruce	125-175	Coast
Sugar Maple	80-90	Gt. Lakes-St. Lawrence
Sycamore	Up to 150	Deciduous
Western Hemlock	120-160	Coast & Columbia
Western Larch	100-180	Southern part of Columbia & Montane, B.C.
Western Red Cedar	150-200	Coast & Columbia
Western White Pine	90-110	S. Coast & Columbia
White Birch	Med.-80	Throughout Canada
White Elm	60-80	G. Lakes-St. Lawrence & Acadian
White Oak	Med.-100	Southern Ontario
White Spruce	80-120	Boreal
Yellow Cypress	60-80	Coast & in coastal parts of Subalpine

Food and Nutrition

Food contains proteins, carbohydrates, fats, water, vitamins and minerals. Nutrition is the way your body takes in and uses these ingredients to maintain proper functioning. If you aren't eating foods that your body needs, you suffer from poor nutrition and, sooner or later, your health will deteriorate.

Protein

Proteins are composed of amino acids and are indispensable in the diet. They build, maintain, and repair the body. Best sources: eggs, milk, soybeans, nuts, fish, meat, poultry. No one of these foods will supply all the necessary proteins.

Fats

Fats provide energy by furnishing calories to the body, and by carrying vitamins A, D, E, and K. They are the most concentrated source of energy in the diet. Best sources: butter, margarine, salad oils, nuts, cream, eggs, most cheeses, lard, meat.

Carbohydrates

Carbohydrates provide energy for body function and activity by supplying immediate calories. The 3 forms of carbohydrates are sugars, starches, and cellulose. Best sources: wheats and cereals, legumes, nuts, potatoes (with skin), fruits, honey.

Water

Water dissolves and transports other nutrients throughout the body aiding the process of digestion, absorption, circulation, and excretion. It also helps regulate body temperature. We get water from all foods.

Vitamins

Vitamin A—promotes good eyesight and helps keep the skin and mucous membranes resistant to infection. Best sources: liver, carrots, sweet potatoes, kale, collard greens, turnips, whole milk.

Vitamin B_1 (thiamine)—essential to the nervous system, heart, liver. Best sources: meat, fish, poultry, wheat germ, brewers' yeast, brown rice, whole grain cereals.

Vitamin B_2 (riboflavin)—an aid to healthy eyes. Best sources: liver, almonds, wheat germ, mushrooms, turnip greens, whole milk, milk products.

Vitamin B_6 (pyridoxine)—important in the regulation of the central nervous system. Best sources: whole grains, meats, nuts, brewers' yeast.

Vitamin B_{12} (cobalamin)—necessary for the formation of red blood cells. Best sources: meat, fish, eggs, soybeans.

Niacin—maintains the health of skin, tongue, and digestive system. Best sources: poultry, peanuts, fish, organ meats, milk and milk products, eggs.

Other B vitamins are—biotin, choline, folic acid (folacin), inositol, PABA (para-aminobenzoic acid), and pantothenic acid.

Vitamin C (ascorbic acid)—maintains collagen, a protein necessary for the formation of skin, ligaments, and bones. It helps heal wounds and mend fractures, and aids in resisting some types of virus and bacterial infections. Best sources: citrus fruits and juices, turnips, broccoli, Brussels sprouts, potatoes and sweet potatoes, tomatoes, cabbage.

Vitamin D—important for bone development. Best sources: sunlight, fortified milk and milk products, fish, egg yolks, organ meats.

Vitamin E (tocopherol)—helps protect red blood cells. May aid the circulatory system and counteract the aging process. Best sources: wheat germ, whole grains, eggs, peanuts, organ meats, margarine, vegetable oils, green leafy vegetables.

Vitamin K—necessary for formation of prothrombin, which helps blood to clot. Best sources: green leafy vegetables, tomatoes, egg yolks, oats, wheat, rye.

Minerals

Calcium—the most abundant mineral in the body, works with phosphorus in building and maintaining bones and teeth. Best sources: whole sesame seeds, cheese, milk and milk products, and blackstrap molasses.

Phosphorus—the 2d most abundant mineral, performs more functions than any other mineral, and plays a part in nearly every chemical reaction in the body. Best source: wheat germ, brewers' yeast, powdered skim milk.

Iron—the 2d most essential trace element in the body, it is necessary for the formation of myoglobin, which transports oxygen to muscle tissue, and hemoglobin, which transports oxygen in the blood. Best sources: organ meats, molasses, beans, green leafy vegetables, and shellfish.

Other minerals—chromium, cobalt, copper, fluorine, iodine, magnesium, manganese, molybdenum, potassium, selenium, sodium, sulfur, and zinc.

Recommended Daily Dietary Allowances

Source: Food and Nutrition Board, National Academy of Sciences—National Research Council (Revised 1980)

The allowances are amounts of nutrients recommended as adequate for maintenance of good nutrition in almost all healthy persons in the U.S. Diets should be based on a variety of common foods in order to provide other nutrients for which human requirements have been less well defined.

				Fat soluble Vitamins			Water soluble Vitamins							Minerals					
	Age (years)	Weight (lbs.)	Protein (grams)	Vitamin A[1]	Vitamin D[2]	Vitamin E[3]	Vitamin C (mg.)	Thiamin (mg.)	Riboflavin (mg.)	Niacin (mg.)[4]	Vitamin B_6 (mg.)	Folacin (micrograms)	Vitamin B_{12} (micrograms)	Calcium (mg.)	Phosphorus (mg.)	Magnesium (mg.)	Iron (mg.)	Zinc (mg.)	Iodine (micrograms)
Infants. . .	to 6 mos.	13	kg × 2.2	420	10	3	35	0.3	0.4	6	0.3	30	0.5	360	240	50	10	3	40
	to 1 yr.	20	kg × 2.0	400	10	4	35	0.5	0.6	8	0.6	45	1.5	540	360	70	15	5	50
Children. .	1-3	29	23	400	10	5	45	0.7	0.8	9	0.9	100	2.0	800	800	150	15	10	70
	4-6	44	30	500	10	6	45	0.9	1.0	11	1.3	200	2.5	800	800	200	10	10	90
	7-10	62	34	700	10	7	45	1.2	1.4	16	1.6	300	3.0	800	800	250	10	10	120
Males . . .	11-14	99	45	1000	10	8	50	1.4	1.6	18	1.8	400	3.0	1200	1200	350	18	15	150
	15-18	145	56	1000	10	10	60	1.4	1.7	18	2.0	400	3.0	1200	1200	400	18	15	150
	19-22	154	56	1000	7.5	10	60	1.5	1.7	19	2.2	400	3.0	800	800	350	10	15	150
	23-50	154	56	1000	5	10	60	1.4	1.6	18	2.2	400	3.0	800	800	350	10	15	150
	51+	154	56	1000	5	10	60	1.2	1.4	16	2.2	400	3.0	800	800	350	10	15	150
Females .	11-14	101	46	800	10	8	50	1.1	1.3	15	1.8	400	3.0	1200	1200	300	18	15	150
	15-18	120	46	800	10	8	60	1.1	1.3	14	2.0	400	3.0	1200	1200	300	18	15	150
	19-22	120	44	800	7.5	8	60	1.1	1.3	14	2.0	400	3.0	800	800	300	18	15	150
	23-50	120	44	800	5	8	60	1.0	1.2	13	2.0	400	3.0	800	800	300	18	15	150
	51+	120	44	800	5	8	60	1.0	1.2	13	2.0	400	3.0	800	800	300	10	15	150
Pregnant			+30	+200	+5	+2	+20	+0.4	+0.3	+2	+0.6	+400	+1.0	+400	+400	+150	[5]	+5	+25
Lactating			+20	+400	+5	+3	+40	+0.5	+0.5	+5	+0.5	+100	+1.0	+400	+400	+150	[5]	+10	+50

(1) Retinol equivalents. (2) Micrograms of cholecalciferol. (3) Milligrams alpha-tocopherol equivalents. (4) Niacin equivalents. (5) The use of 30-60 milligrams of supplemental iron is recommended.

Nutritive Value of Food (Calories, Proteins, etc.)

Source: Home and Garden Bulletin No. 72 (revised Sept. 1978), U.S. Agriculture Department

Available from Supt. of Documents, U. S. Government Printing Office, Washington, DC 20402

Food	Measure	Food Energy (calories)	Protein (grams)	Fat (grams)	Saturated fats (grams)	Carbohydrate (grams)	Calcium (milligrams)	Iron (milligrams)	Vitamin A (I.U.)	Thiamin (milligrams)	Riboflavin (milligrams)	Niacin (milligrams)	Ascorbic acid (milligrams)
Dairy products													
Cheese, cheddar	1 oz.	115	7	9	6.1	T	204	.2	300	.01	.11	T	0
Cheese, cottage, small curd	1 cup	220	26	9	6.0	6	126	.3	340	.04	.34	.3	T
Cheese, cream	1 oz.	100	2	10	6.2	1	23	.3	400	T	.06	T	0
Cheese, Swiss	1 oz.	105	8	8	5.0	1	272	T	240	.01	.10	T	0
Cheese, pasteurized process spread, American	1 oz.	82	5	6	3.8	2	159	.1	220	.01	.12	T	0
Half-and-Half	1 tbsp.	20	T	2	1.1	1	16	T	20	.01	.02	T	T
Cream, sour	1 tbsp.	25	T	3	1.6	1	14	T	90	T	.02	T	T
Milk, whole	1 cup	150	8	8	5.1	11	291	.1	310	.09	.40	.2	2
Milk, nonfat (skim)	1 cup	85	8	T	.3	12	302	.1	500	.09	.37	.2	2
Buttermilk	1 cup	100	8	2	1.3	12	285	.1	80	.08	.38	.1	2
Milkshake, chocolate	10.6 oz.	355	9	8	5.0	63	396	.9	260	.14	.67	.4	0
Ice Cream, hardened	1 cup	270	5	14	8.9	32	176	.1	540	.05	.33	.1	1
Sherbet	1 cup	270	2	4	2.4	59	103	.3	190	.03	.09	.1	4
Yogurt, fruit-flavored	8 oz.	230	10	3	1.8	42	343	.2	120	.08	.40	.2	1
Eggs													
Fried in butter	1	85	5	6	2.4	1	26	.9	290	.03	.13	T	0
Hard-cooked	1	80	6	6	1.7	1	28	1.0	260	.04	.14	T	0
Scrambled in butter (milk added)	1	95	6	7	2.8	1	47	.9	310	.04	.16	T	0
Fats & oils													
Butter	1 tbsp.	100	T	12	7.2	T	3	T	430	T	T	T	0
Margarine	1 tbsp.	100	T	12	2.1	T	3	T	470	T	T	T	0
Salad dressing, blue cheese	1 tbsp.	75	1	8	1.6	1	12	T	30	T	.02	T	T
Salad dressing, French	1 tbsp.	65	T	6	1.1	3	2	1	-	-	-	-	-
Salad dressing, Italian	1 tbsp.	85	T	9	1.6	1	2	T	T	T	T	T	-
Mayonnaise	1 tbsp.	100	T	11	2.0	T	3	.1	40	T	.01	T	-
Meat, poultry, fish													
Bluefish, baked with butter or margarine	3 oz.	135	22	4	-	0	25	0.6	40	.09	.08	1.6	-
Clams, raw, meat only	3 oz.	65	11	1	-	2	59	5.2	90	.08	.15	1.1	8
Crabmeat, white or king, canned	1 cup	135	24	3	.6	1	61	1.1	-	.11	.11	2.6	-
Fish sticks, breaded, cooked, frozen	1 oz.	50	5	3	-	2	3	.1	0	.01	.02	.5	-
Salmon, pink, canned	3 oz.	120	17	5	.9	0	167	.7	60	.03	.16	6.8	-
Sardines, Atlantic, canned in oil	3 oz.	175	20	9	3.0	0	372	2.5	190	.02	.17	4.6	-
Shrimp, French fried	3 oz.	190	17	9	2.3	9	61	1.7	-	.03	.07	2.3	-
Tuna, canned in oil	3 oz.	170	24	7	1.7	0	7	1.6	70	.04	.10	10.1	
Bacon, broiled or fried crisp	2 slices	85	4	8	2.5	T	2	.5	0	.08	.05	.8	-
Ground beef, broiled, 10% fat	3 oz.	185	23	10	4.0	0	10	3.0	20	.08	.20	5.1	-
Roast beef, relatively lean	3 oz.	165	25	7	2.8	0	11	3.2	10	.06	.19	4.5	-
Beef steak, lean and fat	3 oz.	330	20	27	11.3	0	9	2.5	50	.05	.15	4.0	-
Beef & vegetable stew	1 cup	220	16	11	4.9	15	29	2.9	2,400	.15	.17	4.7	17
Lamb, chop, lean and fat	3.1 oz.	360	18	32	14.8	0	8	1.0	-	.11	.19	4.1	-
Ham, light cure, lean and fat	3 oz.	245	18	19	6.8	0	8	2.2	0	.40	.15	3.1	-
Pork, chop, lean and fat	2.7 oz	305	19	25	8.9	0	9	2.7	0	.75	.22	4.5	-
Bologna	1 slice	85	3	8	3.0	T	2	.5	-	.05	.06	.7	-
Frankfurter, cooked	1	170	7	15	5.6	1	3	.8	-	.08	.11	1.4	-
Sausage, pork link, cooked	1 link	60	2	6	2.1	T	1	.3	0	.10	.04	.5	-
Veal, cutlet, braised or boiled	3 oz.	185	23	9	4.0	0	9	2.7	-	.06	.21	4.6	-
Chicken, drumstick, fried, bones removed	1.3 oz.	90	12	4	1.1	T	6	.9	50	.03	.15	2.7	-
Chicken, half broiler, broiled, bones removed	6.2 oz.	240	42	7	2.2	0	16	3.0	160	.09	.34	15.5	-
Chicken a la king	1 cup	470	27	34	12.7	12	127	2.5	1,130	.10	.42	5.4	12
Chicken potpie, baked, 1/3 of 9 in. diam. pie	1 piece	545	23	31	11.3	42	70	3.0	3,090	.34	.31	5.5	5
Fruits & products													
Apple, raw, 2-3/4 in. diam.	1	80	T	1	-	20	10	.4	120	.04	.03	.1	6
Applejuice	1 cup	120	T	T	-	30	15	1.5	-	.02	.05	.2	2
Applesauce, canned, sweetened	1 cup	230	1	T	-	61	10	1.3	100	.05	.03	.1	3
Banana, raw	1	100	1	T	-	26	10	.8	230	.06	.07	.8	12
Cherries, sweet, raw	10	45	1	T	-	12	15	.3	70	.03	.04	.3	7
Fruit cocktail, canned, in heavy syrup	1 cup	195	1	T	-	50	23	1.0	360	.05	.03	1.0	5
Grapefruit, raw, medium, white	1/2	45	1	T	-	12	19	.5	10	.05	.02	.2	44
Grapes, Thompson seedless	10	35	T	T	-	9	6	.2	50	.03	.02	.2	2
Lemonade, frozen, diluted	1 cup	105	T	T	-	28	2	.1	10	.01	.02	.2	17
Cantaloupe, 5-in. diam.	1/2	80	2	T	-	20	38	1.1	9,240	.11	.08	1.6	90
Orange, 2-5/8 in. diam.	1	65	1	T	-	16	54	.5	260	.13	.05	.5	66
Orange juice, frozen, diluted	1 cup	120	2	T	-	29	25	.2	540	.23	.03	.9	120
Peach, raw, 2-1/2 in. diam.	1	40	1	T	-	10	9	.5	1,330	.02	.05	1.0	7
Peaches, canned in syrup	1 cup	200	1	T	-	51	10	.8	1.100	.03	.05	1.5	8
Pear, raw, Bartlett, 2-1/2 in. diam.	1	100	1	1	-	25	13	.5	30	.03	.07	.2	7
Pineapple, heavy syrup pack, crushed, chunks	1 cup	190	1	T	-	49	28	.8	130	.20	.05	.5	18
Raisins, seedless	1 cup	420	4	T	-	112	90	5.1	30	.16	.12	.7	1
Strawberries, whole	1 cup	55	1	1	-	13	31	1.5	90	.04	.10	.9	88
Watermelon, 4 by 8 in. wedge	1 wedge	110	2	1	-	27	30	2.1	2,510	.13	.13	.9	30
Grain products													
Bagel, egg	1	165	6	2	.5	28	9	1.2	30	.14	.10	1.2	0
Biscuit, 2 in. diam., from home recipe	1	105	2	5	1.2	13	34	.4	T	.08	.08	.7	T
Bread, raisin	1 slice	65	2	1	.2	13	18	.6	T	.09	.06	.6	T
Bread, white, enriched, soft-crumb	1 slice	70	2	1	.2	13	21	.6	T	.10	.06	.8	T
Bread, whole wheat, soft-crumb	1 slice	65	3	1	.1	14	24	.8	T	.09	.03	.8	T
Oatmeal or rolled oats	1 cup	130	5	2	.4	23	22	1.4	0	.19	.05	.2	0
Bran flakes (40% bran), added sugar, salt, iron, vitamins	1 cup	105	4	1	-	28	19	12.4	1,650	.41	.49	4.1	12
Corn flakes, added sugar, salt, iron, vitamins	1 cup	95	2	T	-	21	*	0.6	1,180	.29	.35	2.9	9
Rice, puffed, added iron, thiamin, niacin	1 cup	60	1	T	-	13	3	.3	0	.07	.01	.7	0

(continued)

(continued)

Food	Measure	Food Energy (calories)	Protein (grams)	Fat (grams)	Saturated fats (grams)	Carbohydrate (grams)	Calcium (milligrams)	Iron (milligrams)	Vitamin A (I.U.)	Thiamin (milligrams)	Riboflavin (milligrams)	Niacin (milligrams)	Ascorbic acid (milligrams)
Wheat, shredded, plain, 1 biscuit or 1/2 cup	1 serving	90	2	1	-	20	11	.9	0	.06	.03	1.1	0
Cake, angel food, 1/12 of cake	1	135	3	T	-	32	50	.2	0	.03	.08	.3	0
Coffeecake, 1/6 cake	1	230	5	7	2.0	38	44	1.2	120	.14	.15	1.3	T
Cupcake, 2-1/2 in. diam., with chocolate icing	1	130	2	5	2.0	21	47	.4	60	.05	.06	.4	T
Boston cream pie with custard filling, 1/12 of cake	1	210	3	6	1.9	34	46	.7	140	.09	.11	.8	T
Fruitcake, dark, 1/30 of loaf	1	55	1	2	.5	9	11	.4	20	.02	.02	.2	T
Cake, pound, 1/17 of loaf	1	160	2	10	2.5	16	6	.5	80	.05	.06	.4	0
Brownies, with nuts, from commercial recipe	1	85	1	4	.9	13	9	.4	20	.03	.02	.2	T
Cookies, chocolate chip, from home recipe	4	205	2	12	3.5	24	14	.8	40	.06	.06	.5	T
Vanilla wafers	10	185	2	6	-	30	16	.6	50	.10	.09	.8	0
Crackers, graham	2	55	1	1	.3	10	6	.5	0	.02	.08	.5	0
Crackers, saltines	4	50	1	1	.3	8	2	.5	0	.05	.05	.4	0
Danish pastry, round piece	1	275	5	15	4.7	30	33	1.2	200	.18	.19	1.7	T
Doughnut, cake type	1	100	1	5	1.2	13	10	.4	20	.05	.05	.4	T
Macaroni and cheese, from home recipe	1 cup	430	17	22	8.9	40	362	1.8	860	.20	.40	1.8	T
Muffin, corn	1	125	3	4	1.2	19	42	.7	120	.10	.10	.7	T
Noodles, enriched, cooked	1 cup	200	7	2	-	37	16	1.4	110	.22	.13	1.9	0
Pancake, plain, from home recipe	1	60	2	2	.5	9	27	.4	30	.06	.07	.5	T
Pie, apple, 1/7 of pie	1	345	3	15	3.9	51	11	.9	40	.15	.11	1.3	2
Pie, banana cream, 1/7 of pie	1	285	6	12	3.8	40	86	1.0	330	.11	.22	1.0	1
Pie, cherry, 1/7 of pie	1	350	4	15	4.0	52	19	.9	590	.16	.12	1.4	T
Pie, lemon meringue, 1/7 of pie	1	305	4	12	3.7	45	17	1.0	200	.09	.12	.7	4
Pie, pecan, 1/7 of pie	1	495	6	27	4.0	61	55	3.7	190	.26	.14	1.0	T
Pie, pumpkin, 1/7 of pie	1	275	5	15	5.4	32	66	1.0	3,210	.11	.18	1.0	T
Pizza, cheese, 1/8 of 12 in. diam. pie	1	145	6	4	1.7	22	86	1.1	230	.16	.18	1.6	4
Popcorn, popped, plain	1 cup	25	1	T	T	5	1	.2	-	-	.01	.1	0
Pretzels, stick	10	10	T	T	-	2	1	T	0	.01	.01	.1	0
Rice, white, enriched, instant, cooked	1 cup	180	4	T	T	40	5	1.3	0	.21	**	1.7	0
Rolls, enriched, brown & serve	1	85	2	2	.4	14	20	.5	T	.10	.06	.9	T
Rolls, frankfurter & hamburger	1	120	3	2	.5	21	30	.8	T	.16	.10	1.3	T
Spaghetti with meat balls & tomato sauce, from home recipe	1 cup	330	19	12	3.3	39	124	3.7	1,590	.25	.30	4.0	22
Legumes, nuts, seeds													
Beans, Great Northern, cooked	1 cup	210	14	1	-	38	90	4.9	0	.25	.13	1.3	0
Peanuts, roasted in oil, salted	1 cup	840	37	72	13.7	27	107	3.0	-	.46	.19	24.8	0
Peanut butter	1 tbsp.	95	4	8	1.5	3	9	.3	-	.02	.02	2.4	0
Sunflower seeds	1 cup	810	35	69	8.2	29	174	10.3	70	2.84	.33	7.8	-
Sugars & sweets													
Candy, caramels	1 oz.	115	1	3	1.6	22	42	.4	T	.01	.05	.1	T
Candy, milk chocolate	1 oz.	145	2	9	5.5	16	65	.3	80	.02	.10	.1	T
Fudge, chocolate	1 oz.	115	1	3	1.3	21	22	.3	T	.01	.03	.1	T
Candy, hard	1 oz.	110	0	T	-	28	6	.5	0	0	0	0	0
Honey	1 tbsp.	65	T	0	0	17	1	.1	0	T	.01	.1	T
Jams & Preserves	1 tbsp.	55	T	T	-	14	4	.2	T	T	.01	T	T
Sugar, white, granulated	1 tbsp.	45	0	0	0	12	0	T	0	0	0	0	0
Vegetables													
Asparagus, canned, spears	4 spears	15	2	T	-	3	15	1.5	640	.05	.08	.6	12
Beans, lima, thick-seeded	1 cup	170	10	T	-	32	34	2.9	390	.12	.09	1.7	29
Beans, green, from frozen, cuts	1 cup	35	2	T	-	8	54	.9	780	.09	.12	.5	7
Beets, canned, diced or sliced	1 cup	65	2	T	-	15	32	1.2	30	.02	.05	.2	5
Broccoli, cooked	1 stalk	45	6	1	-	8	158	1.4	4,500	.16	.36	1.4	162
Cabbage, raw, coarsely shredded or sliced	1 cup	15	1	T	-	4	34	.3	90	.04	.04	.02	33
Carrots, raw, 7-1/2 by 1-1/8 in.	1	30	1	T	-	7	27	.5	7,930	.04	.04	.4	6
Cauliflower, raw	1 cup	31	3	T	-	6	29	1.3	70	.13	.12	.8	90
Celery, raw	1 stalk	5	T	T	-	2	16	.1	110	.01	.01	.1	4
Collards, cooked	1 cup	65	7	1	-	10	357	1.5	14,820	.21	.38	2.3	144
Corn, sweet, cooked	1 ear	70	2	1	-	16	2	.5	310	.09	.08	1.1	7
Corn, cream style	1 cup	210	5	2	-	51	8	1.5	840	.08	.13	2.6	13
Cucumber, with peel	6-8 slices	5	T	T	-	1	7	.3	70	.01	.01	.1	3
Lettuce, Iceberg, chopped	1 cup	5	T	T	-	2	11	.3	180	.03	.03	.2	3
Mushrooms, raw	1 cup	20	2	T	-	3	4	.6	T	.07	.32	2.9	2
Onions, raw, chopped	1 cup	65	3	T	-	15	46	.9	T	.05	.07	.3	17
Peas, frozen, cooked	1 cup	110	8	T	-	19	30	3.0	960	.43	.14	2.7	21
Potatoes, baked, peeled	1	145	4	T	-	33	14	1.1	T	.15	.07	2.7	31
Potatoes, mashed, milk added	1 cup	135	4	2	.7	27	50	.8	40	.17	.11	2.1	21
Potato chips	10	115	1	8	2.1	10	8	.4	T	.04	.01	1.0	3
Potato salad	1 cup	250	7	7	2.0	41	80	1.5	350	.20	.18	2.8	28
Sauerkraut, canned	1 cup	40	2	T	-	9	85	1.2	120	.07	.09	.5	33
Spinach, chopped, from frozen	1 cup	45	6	1	-	8	232	4.3	16,200	.14	.31	.8	39
Squash, summer, cooked	1 cup	30	2	T	-	7	53	.8	820	.11	.17	1.7	21
Sweet potatoes, baked in skin, peeled	1	160	2	1	-	37	46	1.0	9,230	.10	.08	.8	25
Tomatoes, raw	1	25	1	T	-	6	16	.6	1,110	.07	.05	.9	28
Tomato catsup	1 tbsp.	15	T	T	-	4	3	.1	210	.01	.01	.2	2
Tomato juice	1 cup	45	2	T	-	10	17	2.2	1,940	.12	.07	1.9	39
Miscellaneous													
Beer	12 fl. oz.	150	1	0	0	14	18	T	-	.01	.11	2.2	-
Gin, rum, vodka, whisky, 86 proof	1-1/2 fl. oz.	105	-	-	0	T	-	-	-	-	-	-	-
Wine, table	3-1/2 fl. oz.	85	T	0	0	4	9	.4	-	T	.01	.1	-
Cola-type beverage	12 fl. oz.	145	0	0	0	37	-	-	0	0	0	0	0
Ginger ale	12 fl. oz	115	0	0	0	29	-	-	0	0	0	0	0
Gelatin dessert	1 cup	140	4	0	0	34	-	-	-	-	-	-	-
Mustard, prepared	1 tsp.	5	T	T	-	T	4	.1	-	-	-	-	-
Olives, pickled, green	4 medium	15	T	2	.2	T	8	.2	40	-	-	-	-
Pickles, dill, whole	1	5	T	T	-	1	17	.7	70	T	.01	T	4
Popsicle, 3 fl. oz.	1	70	0	0	0	18	0	T	0	0	0	0	0
Soup, cream of chicken, prepared with milk	1 cup	180	7	10	4.2	15	172	.5	610	.05	.27	.7	2
Soup, cream of mushroom, prepared with milk	1 cup	215	7	14	5.4	16	191	.5	250	.05	.34	.7	1
Soup, tomato, prepared with water	1 cup	90	2	3	.5	16	15	.7	1,000	.05	.05	1.2	12

T — Indicates trace * — Varies by brand

Estimated Total Pollution Control Expenditures

Source: Council on Environmental Quality (billions of 1978 dollars). Does not include research, conservation, and enhancement programs.

Pollutant/source	1978 O&M[1]	1978 Capital costs[2]	1978 Total annual costs[3]	1987 O&M[1]	1987 Capital costs[2]	1987 Total annual costs[3]	Cumulative 1978-87 O&M[1]	Cumulative 1978-87 Capital costs[2]	Cumulative 1978-87 Total costs[3]
Air pollution									
Public	1.3	0.4	1.7	2.8	1.2	4.0	19.6	7.8	27.4
Private									
Mobile[5]	4.3	3.3	7.6	5.1	9.3	14.4	45.0	66.4	111.4
Industrial	2.8	3.4	6.2	4.8	6.5	11.3	36.0	51.4	87.4
Utilities	2.2	1.6	3.8	7.5	5.5	13.0	45.5	34.0	79.5
Subtotal	**10.6**	**8.7**	**19.3**	**20.2**	**22.5**	**42.7**	**146.1**	**159.6**	**305.7**
Water pollution									
Public	2.8	10.3	13.1	3.8	16.1	19.9	32.8	131.7	164.5
Private									
Industrial	2.7	2.0	4.7	6.8	5.2	12.0	48.5	36.8	85.3
Utilities	1.5	.9	2.4	2.4	1.5	3.9	19.9	12.2	32.1
Subtotal	**7.0**	**13.2**	**20.2**	**13.0**	**22.8**	**35.8**	**101.2**	**180.7**	**281.9**
Solid Waste									
Public	1.6	.3	1.9	2.5	.7	3.2	21.5	5.5	27.0
Private	3.9	.6	4.5	6.5	1.4	7.9	54.6	11.7	66.3
Subtotal	**5.5**	**.9**	**6.4**	**9.0**	**2.1**	**11.1**	**76.1**	**17.2**	**93.3**
Toxic Substances[5]	0.1	NA	0.1	0.3	NA	0.3	2.2	NA	2.2
Drinking Water	0.3	0.3	0.6	0.8	0.8	1.6	6.4	6.1	12.5
Noise[5]	(4)	(4)	(4)	0.6	1.0	1.6	2.5	4.1	6.6
Pesticides	(4)	(4)	(4)	0.1	(4)	0.1	0.5	(4)	0.5
Land Reclamation	0.1	NA	0.1	1.0	NA	1.0	8.0	NA	8.0
Total	**23.6**	**23.1**	**46.7**	**45.0**	**49.2**	**94.2**	**343.0**	**367.7**	**710.7**

(1) Operating and maintenance costs. (2) Interest and depreciation. (3) O&M plus capital costs. (4) Less than 0.05. (5) Incremental and total costs are assumed to be the same. (NA) Not available.

Investment for Pollution Control by U.S. Industries

Source: Bureau of Economic Analysis, U.S. Commerce Department (millions of dollars)

	1979 Pollution abatement Air	1979 Water	1979 Solid waste	1979 Total	1979 Percent of investment[2]	1980[1] Pollution abatement Air	1980[1] Water	1980[1] Solid waste	1980[1] Total	1980[1] Percent of investment[2]
All industries[3]	**3,915**	**2,664**	**564**	**7,143**	**4.04**	**4,530**	**2,604**	**566**	**7,699**	**3.93**
Manufacturing	**2,103**	**1,493**	**381**	**3,976**	**5.08**	**2,515**	**1,642**	**383**	**4,540**	**5.07**
Durable goods	936	540	109	1,585	4.18	1,192	628	137	1,956	4.47
Primary metals	558	227	26	811	12.40	688	289	32	1,010	13.43
Blast furnaces, steel works	351	154	5	510	17.62	435	197	6	638	18.99
Nonferrous metals	142	59	13	213	8.09	187	75	23	285	9.54
Electrical machinery	27	82	6	114	2.26	46	73	7	126	2.08
Machinery, except electrical	36	39	13	88	1.08	45	44	8	97	1.01
Transportation equipment	122	97	42	261	3.35	181	119	50	350	3.98
Motor vehicles	106	83	34	223	4.15	168	100	43	311	5.40
Aircraft	13	12	8	33	1.54	11	16	7	34	1.23
Stone, clay, and glass	116	22	7	145	5.04	130	33	13	176	5.34
Other durables	78	72	16	166	2.22	101	70	28	199	2.35
Nondurable goods	1,167	953	272	2,391	5.92	1,323	1,014	246	2,583	5.65
Food including beverage	51	84	13	148	2.91	51	83	15	150	2.77
Textiles	21	10	1	31	3.01	23	12	1	36	3.05
Paper	133	124	40	297	6.14	135	125	40	300	5.04
Chemicals	203	184	53	440	5.23	218	205	53	476	5.24
Petroleum	708	530	147	1,385	8.41	844	565	127	1,536	8.06
Rubber	38	12	12	62	3.34	39	14	6	58	2.86
Other nondurables	13	9	6	29	1.07	13	10	5	27	0.89
Nonmanufacturing	**1,812**	**1,171**	**183**	**3,166**	**3.23**	**2,015**	**962**	**183**	**3,160**	**2.98**
Mining	59	105	23	187	3.38	63	71	37	171	2.65
Railroad	2	17	1	20	0.51	9	22	1	32	0.73
Air Transportation	7	5	1	12	0.36	11	2	1	13	0.38
Other transportation	11	11	2	24	0.81	20	15	5	40	1.17
Public utilities	1,653	975	135	2,763	8.33	1,817	781	104	2,702	7.86
Electric	1,636	950	129	2,715	9.63	1,795	761	102	2,658	9.09
Gas and other	18	25	6	49	0.98	22	20	2	44	0.85
Communication, commercial, and other	79	59	22	160	0.33	96	70	36	203	0.38

(1) Planned. (2) Pollution control as a percent of total plant and equipment investment. (3) Excludes agricultural business; real estate operators; medical, legal, educational, and cultural services; and nonprofit organizations. (4) Includes trade, service, construction, finance, and insurance.

Environmental Quality Index

Source: National Wildlife Federation.
Adapted from the Feb.-Mar., 1980 issue of *National Wildlife Magazine.*

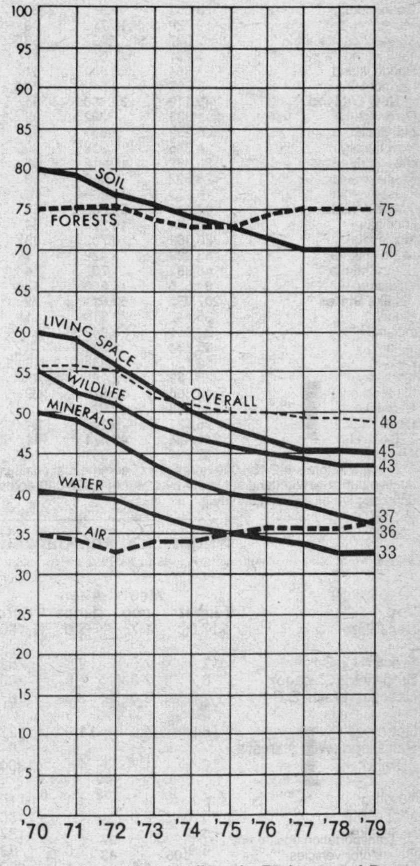

In 1969, the National Wildlife Federation began to record an index of environmental quality which measures progress or decline in 7 environmental areas. The index represents the judgment of environmental protection experts and advocates influenced by very high standards of environmental quality.

Wildlife: In general, wildlife did well in 1979. Fish returned to some rivers—such as the Merrimac and the Connecticut—and some endangered species continued to come back, including bald eagles, peregrine falcons and alligators. The International Whaling Commission tightened regulations on the killing of sperm whales and the U.S. and Canada agreed to protect the habitat of a Porcupine caribou herd of 100,000 animals. In Congress, however, the Tennessee Valley Authority's controversial Tellico Dam was approved, even though it would kill off the snail darter. Energy pressures also led to the Interior Department's approval of oil exploration on the Georges Bank off Cape Cod, one of the world's most productive fisheries.

Air: As the nation's inflation worsened, clean air standards and the cost of complying with them came under increasing criticism and threatened to halt progress against air pollution. The Environmental Protection Agency granted automakers their 6th delay in meeting the goals of the 1970 Clean Air Act. The agency also increased by half the amount of smog considered "safe" for people to breathe. In his energy message, Pres. Carter asked utilities to cut their oil consumption in half mainly by switching to coal, which would increase sulfur pollution. A positive development was the redesigning of the 3M Company's manufacturing processes, which reduced air pollution in the St. Paul, Minn. area by some 75,000 tons a year.

Minerals: 1979 was the year the American public began at last to take the energy crisis seriously. The year of Three Mile Island, new gasoline lines and doubled fuel prices produced the first drop in gasoline demand due to a decrease in driving and improved auto mileage. As the conservation ethic has spread, half of all American homeowners have added at least some insulation. Energy efficiency in homes and apartments increased as much as 10 percent since 1973. However, Pres. Carter's 1979 energy program emphasized a massive and enormously expensive program to increase domestic production of oil, develop "synthetic" fossil fuels, and create an "energy mobilization board." In non-energy developments, 2 more states passed initiatives for recycling bottles and several others are likely to do so.

Water: U.S. Steel's 1979 decision to spend $400 million to clean up air and water around its plants was a breakthrough. It was reported that parts of the Willamette River in Oregon improved as much as 90 percent since paper mills began controlling their discharges. In Washington, D.C., a new sewage treatment plant reduced bacteria in the Potomac River by 90 percent. And during the summer, a U.S.-Canadian task force reported that pollution in most of the Great Lakes had "bottomed out." Despite some successes in curbing industrial and municipal pollution, general contamination from rain runoff and waste disposal continued to be a monumental water pollution problem.

Forests: The total U.S. timber harvest last year was about the same as in other recent years: between 11 and 13 billion cubic feet. During the year, the U.S. Forest Service proposed to set aside more than 15 million additional acres as inviolable wilderness, and to open up another 36 million acres to timber and other kinds of development. The Forest Service also announced a new 5-year management plan that may lessen the old conflicts between developers and environmentalists by providing for more public say-so on how forests are run. In addition, the plan gives higher priority to watershed protection, wildlife habitat, and recreation. In a move applauded by environmentalists, the Environmental Protection Agency banned 2 of the most commonly used herbicides, 2,4,5-T and Silvex.

Soil: The Department of Agriculture, which had previously estimated that top soil was being eroded away at an average rate of 9 tons per acre annually, revised that estimate downward to less than 5 tons. This was good news because organic matter and crop residues can replace the 5 tons each year on some soils. A new strategy called integrated pest management promised to reduce the contamination of the soil by pesticides. On the negative side, the conversion of cropland to suburbs continued unabated.

Living Space: The relentless growth of the population (it passed 220 million in 1979) continued to put a strain on living space. Higher gasoline prices and uncertainty over supply, however, may slow the exurban tide and encourage the economic rebirth of central cities. During 1979, Congress passed an Omnibus Parks bill which designated 2 million acres as wilderness, protected 8 river segments from development, established 5 new national trails and added 12 new units to the National Park System.

U.S. Forest Land by State and Region

Source: Forest Service, U.S. Agriculture Department, 1979.

State or region	Land area (1,000 acres)	Area forested (1,000 acres)	Percent forested
Connecticut	3,081	1,861	60
Maine	19,729	17,718	90
Massachusetts	5,007	2,952	59
New Hampshire	5,731	5,013	87
Rhode Island	664	404	61
Vermont	5,907	4,512	76
New England	**40,119**	**32,460**	**81**
Delaware	1,233	392	32
Maryland	6,289	2,653	42
New Jersey	4,775	1,928	40
New York	30,357	17,218	57
Pennsylvania	28,592	16,826	59
West Virginia	15,334	11,669	76
Mid Atlantic	**87,813**	**50,686**	**58**
Michigan	30,634	19,270	63
Minnesota	50,382	16,709	33
North Dakota	43,939	422	1
South Dakota	48,381	1,702	4
Wisconsin	34,616	14,908	43
Lake States	**207,952**	**53,011**	**25**
Illinois	35,442	3,810	11
Indiana	22,951	3,943	17
Iowa	35,634	1,561	4
Kansas	52,127	1,344	3
Kentucky	25,282	12,161	48
Missouri	43,868	12,876	29
Nebraska	48,828	1,029	2
Ohio	26,121	6,147	24
Central	**241,425**	**42,871**	**18**
Alabama	32,231	21,361	66
Arkansas	33,091	18,282	55
Florida	33,994	17,040	50
Georgia	36,796	25,256	69
Louisiana	28,409	14,558	51
Mississippi	29,930	16,716	56
North Carolina	30,956	20,043	65
Oklahoma	43,728	8,513	19
South Carolina	19,143	12,249	64
Tennessee	26,290	13,161	50
Texas	167,283	23,279	14
Virginia	25,286	16,417	65
South	**474,906**	**185,514**	**39**
Alaska	362,485	119,145	33
California	99,847	40,152	48
Hawaii	4,109	1,986	40
Oregon	61,356	29,810	49
Washington	42,456	23,181	55
Pacific Coast	**570,253**	**214,274**	**38**
Arizona	72,580	18,494	25
Colorado	66,283	22,271	34
Idaho	52,676	21,726	41
Montana	92,826	22,559	24
Nevada	70,295	7,683	11
New Mexico	77,669	18,060	23
Utah	52,505	15,557	30
Wyoming	62,055	10,028	16
Rocky Mountain	**546,959**	**136,378**	**25**
Total U.S.	**2,169,427**	**[1]715,194**	**33**

(1) Of this total, 482,486,000 acres are of commercial quality (137 million acres are government owned); 20,664,000 acres are productive but reserved (land set aside by statute); 4,626,000 acres are deferred for possible reserve status; and 228,782,000 acres are unproductive or awaiting survey.

Major U.S. and Canadian Public Zoological Parks

Source: World Almanac questionnaire. Figures are for 1980; budget, metro population, and attendance are in millions. (A) designates Park has not provided up-to-date information. (e) estimate

Zoo	Budget	Metro pop.	Attendance	Acres	Species	Major Attractions
San Diego	$17.0	1.7	3.0	100	875	Loalas, pygmy chimps, Skyfari aerial tramway, parrots.
Bronx (N.Y.C.)	12.0	7.0	2.0	252	550	Wild Asia, Aquatic Birds bldg., Reptile House.
Brookfield (Chicago)	8.7	7.8	1.8	200	650	Porpoise show, tropic world, baboon island.
National (Wash. D.C.)	7.0	3.0	3.0	167	550	Lion/Tiger complex, Beaver Valley, Great Flight Cage.
Detroit	6.8	4.5	1.0	122	451	Penguinarium, walk-through aviary bldg.
San Diego (Wild Animal Park)	6.4	1.7	1.1	1800	320	New canine show, bird and elephant show, monorail.
Toronto	6.2	2.1	1.1	710	407	Canadian Domain ride, exotic plants and birds.
Minnesota	5.3	2.0	1.1	480	280	Sky, ocean, tropics and discovery trails.
Milwaukee	5.3	1.0	1.1	187	646	Predator/prey exhibits, Dall sheep exhibit.
St. Louis	5.0	1.8	2.0	83	625	Big cat country, herpetarium, primate house.
Detroit (A)	4.7	4.5	1.1	122	487	Penguinarium, great ape house.
Philadelphia (A)	4.5	4.8e	1.2	42	523	Reptiles, African plains, great apes, monorail.
Lincoln Park (Chicago)	3.0	7.0	4.0	35	780	Great ape collection, farm in the zoo.
Cincinnati	3.0	1.5	1.0	63	703	White tigers, insect world, outdoor gorilla display.
Los Angeles	3.0	8.0	1.5	113	500	California Condor, Mountain Tapir, Monkey-eating eagle.
Buffalo	2.4	0.4	0.4	23	297	Rhino yard, outside bear exhibit, children's zoo.
Oklahoma City	2.4	0.6	0.6	500	500	African plains, Patagonian cliffs, Galapagos Isl.
San Antonio	2.1	1.0	0.9	49	700	Whooping cranes, snow leopards, African safari trail.
Arizona-Sonora Desert Museum (Tucson)	2.0	0.4	0.5	10	200	Earth science center, Sonoran Desert animals.
Washington Park (Portland)	2.0	2.0	0.6	62	131	Insect zoo, children's zoo, waterfowl pond.
Houston	2.0	2.5	1.8	43	600	Gorilla habitat, tropical bird house.
Denver	2.0e	1.6	0.8	76	348	Bird world, Bighorn and Dall sheep exhibit.
Cleveland	1.9	2.0	0.5	125	226	Primate and cat bldg., waterfowl collection.
Columbus	1.9	0.9	0.5	95	609	New herbivore, canivore, giraffe complex.
Phoenix	1.8	1.8	0.6	125	270	Arabian oryx herd, children's zoo, Arizona exhibit.
Calgary	1.8	0.6	0.8	220	300	Northern Canadian mammals and birds.
Baltimore	1.8	1.5	0.3	142	259	Insectarium and Amphibian zoo, reptile house.
Woodland Park (Seattle)	1.6	1.2	0.7	90	290	Only nocturnal house west of the Mississippi.
Dallas	1.6	2.9	0.6	50	600	Reptile, hoofed animals exhibit.
Pittsburgh	1.5	1.3	0.5	75	374	Twilight zoo, AquaZoo, Children's zoo train.
Louisville	1.4	0.9	0.4	58	164	Siberian tiger exhibit, miniature train ride.

Mammals: Orders and Major Families

Subclass Theria
Infraclass Placentalia

Family	Superfamily / Infraorder / Suborder	Order
Canidae: wolf, dog, jackal, fox	Canoidea; Fissipedia (toe-footed)	Carnivora
Ursidae: bear, giant panda	Canoidea; Fissipedia (toe-footed)	Carnivora
Procyonidae: coati, racoon, lesser panda	Canoidea; Fissipedia (toe-footed)	Carnivora
Mustelidae: badger, weasel, skunk, otter	Canoidea; Fissipedia (toe-footed)	Carnivora
Felidae: cat, leopard, lion, tiger, cheetah	Feloidea; Fissipedia (toe-footed)	Carnivora
Hyaenidae: hyena, aardwolf	Feloidea; Fissipedia (toe-footed)	Carnivora
Viverridae: mongoose, civet	Feloidea; Fissipedia (toe-footed)	Carnivora
Otariidae: eared seals, sea lion	Pinnipedia (fin-footed)	Carnivora
Odobenidae: walrus	Pinnipedia (fin-footed)	Carnivora
Phocidae: earless seals	Pinnipedia (fin-footed)	Carnivora
Suidae: pig	Suina; Suiformes	Artiodactyla
Tayassuidae: peccary	Suina; Suiformes	Artiodactyla
Hippopotamidae: hippopotamus	Ancodonta; Suiformes	Artiodactyla
Camelidae: camel, llama	Tylopoda	Artiodactyla
Giraffidae: giraffe, okapi	Ruminantia	Artiodactyla
Cervidae: deer, moose, reindeer, wapiti (elk)	Ruminantia	Artiodactyla
Antilocapridae: pronghorn	Bovoidea; Ruminantia	Artiodactyla
Family Bovidae — **Subfamily** **Bovinae:** cattle, eland, kudu, bison, yak; **Hippotraginae:** sable, oryx, waterbuck; **Acelaphinae:** hartebeest, wildebeest (gnu); **Antilopinae:** gazelle, springbok, saiga; **Caprinae:** sheep, goat, musk ox	Bovoidea; Ruminantia	Artiodactyla
Equidae: horse, donkey zebra	Hippomorpha	Perissodactyla
Tapiridae: tapir	Ceratomorpha	Perissodactyla
Rhinocerotidae: rhinoceros	Ceratomorpha	Perissodactyla
Aplodontidae: mountain beaver	Sciuromorpha	Rodentia
Sciuridae: chipmunk, squirrel, marmot	Sciuromorpha	Rodentia
Cricetidae: field mice, lemming, muskrat, hamster, gerbil	Myomorpha	Rodentia
Muridae: rat, Old World mice	Myomorpha	Rodentia
Heteromyidae: New World mice	Myomorpha	Rodentia
Geomyidae: gopher	Myomorpha	Rodentia
Dipodidae: jerboa	Myomorpha	Rodentia
Chinchillidae: chinchilla	Caviomorpha	Rodentia
Dasyproctidae: agouti, paca	Caviomorpha	Rodentia
Erethizontidae: New World porcupine	Caviomorpha	Rodentia
Hystricidae: Old World porcupine		Rodentia
Castoridae: beaver		Rodentia
Bats - various familes		Chiroptera
Leporidae: rabbit, hare		Lagomorpha
Ochotonidae: pika		Lagomorpha
Manidae: pangolin		Pholidata
Erinaceidae: hedgehog		Insectivora
Talpidae: mole		Insectivora
Saricidae: some shrews		Insectivora
Dasypodidae: armadillo	Loricata	Edentate (toothless)
Bradypodidae: sloth	Pilosa	Edentate (toothless)
Myrmecophagidae: hairy anteater	Vermilingua	Edentate (toothless)
Physeteridae: sperm whale	Odontoceti (toothed)	Cetacea
Monodontidae: narwhal, beluga	Odontoceti (toothed)	Cetacea
Phocoenidae: porpoise	Odontoceti (toothed)	Cetacea
Delphinidae: dolphin, killer whale	Odontoceti (toothed)	Cetacea
Eschrichtiidae: gray whale	Mysticeti (baleen)	Cetacea
Balaenidae: right whale	Mysticeti (baleen)	Cetacea
Balaenopteridae: humpback whale	Mysticeti (baleen)	Cetacea
Manatee, dugong		Sirenea
Elephantidae: elephant		Proboscidea
Tupaiidae: tree shrew	Prosimii	Primates
Lemuridae: lemur	Prosimii	Primates
Daubentoniidae: aye-aye	Prosimii	Primates
Lorisidae: loris, potto	Prosimii	Primates
Tarsiidae: tarsier	Prosimii	Primates
Callitrichidae: marmoset	Anthropoidea	Primates
Cebidae: New World monkeys (flat-nosed)	Anthropoidea	Primates
Cercopithecidae: baboon, Old World monkeys (long-nosed, bare buttocks)	Anthropoidea	Primates
Hylobatidae: gibbon	Anthropoidea	Primates
Pongidae (great apes): gorilla, chimpanzee, orangutan	Anthropoidea	Primates
Hominidae: human	Anthropoidea	Primates

Canoids have long snouts and unretractable claws.

Feloids have retractable claws.

Most carnivora also eat some plants and insects.

The artiodactyla have an even number of toes.

All ruminants have 4-chamber stomachs and chew cuds.

The perissodactyla have an odd number of toes.

Rodent suborders are distinguished by the placement of a major jaw muscle.

Rodents are the most numerous of all mammals.

The prosimians usually have longer snouts than anthropoids.

Most primates have opposable thumbs; all but man have opposable big toes.

Infraclass Marsupialia

Family	Superfamily	Order
Dasyuridae: mouse- and ratlike, Tasmanian devil	Dasyuroidea	Marsupicanivora
Notoryctidae: molelike	Dasyuroidea	Marsupicanivora
Thylacinidae: wolflike	Dasyuroidea	Marsupicanivora
Didelphidae: American opossums	Didelphoidea	Marsupicanivora
Caenolestidae: ratlike So. America only		Paucituberculata
Peramelidae: bandicoot		Peramalina
Burramyidae: mouse- and squirrellike	Phalangeroidea	Diprodonta
Macropodidae: kangaroo, wallaby	Phalangeroidea	Diprodonta
Petauridae: squirrellike, some Australian possums	Phalangeroidea	Diprodonta
Phalangeridae: cuscus, some Australian possums	Phalangeroidea	Diprodonta
Tarsipedidae: honey possum	Tarsipedoidea	Diprodonta
Vombatidae: wombat	Vombatoidea	Diprodonta
Phascolarctidae: koala	Vombatoidea	Diprodonta

Subclass Prototheria

Family		Order
Ornithorhynchidae: duck-billed platypus		Monotremata
Tachyglossidae: echidna (spiny anteater)		Monotremata

Some Endangered Species in North America

Source: U.S. Fish and Wildlife Service, U.S. Interior Department

Common name	Scientific name	Range
Mammals		
Virginia big-eared bat	Plecotus townsendii virginiarnus	U.S. (Ky., W.V., Va., In., Il.)
Columbian white-tailed deer	Odocoileus virginianus leucurus	U.S. (Wa., Or.)
San Joaquin kit fox	Vulpes macrotis mutica	U.S. (Cal.)
Jaguar	Panthera onca	U.S. (Tx., N.M., Az.)
Margay	Felis wiedii	U.S. (N.M., Az.)
Salt marsh harvest mouse	Reithrodontomys raviventris	U.S. (Cal.)
Florida panther	Felis concolor coryi	U.S. (Southeast)
Utah prairie dog	Cynomys parvidens	U.S. (Ut.)
Morro Bay kangaroo rat	Dipodomy heermanni	U.S. (Cal.)
Delmarva Peninsula fox squirrel	Scuiris niger cinereus	U.S. (Pa.)
Birds		
Masked bobwhite (quail)	Colinus virginianus ridgwayi	U.S. (Ariz.), Mexico
California condor	Gymnogyps californianus	U.S. (Cal., Or.)
Whooping crane	Grus americana	U.S., Canada
Eskimo curlew	Numenius borealis	Canada to Argentina
Bald eagle	Haliaeetus leucocephalus	U.S. (most states), Canada
American peregrine falcon	Falco peregrinus anatum	Canada to Mexico
Arctic peregrine falcon	Falco peregrinus tundrius	Canada to Mexico
Aleutian Canada goose	Branta canadensis leucopareia	U.S., Japan
Brown pelican	Pelecanus occidentalis	U.S. to South America
Attwater's greater prairie chicken	Tympanuchus cupido attwateri	U.S. (Tex.)
Bachman's warbler (wood)	Vermivora bachmanii	U.S., Cuba
Kirtland's warbler (wood)	Dendroica Kirtlandii	U.S., Bahamas
Ivory-billed woodpecker	Campephilus principalis	U.S., Cuba
Reptiles		
American alligator	Alligator mississippiensis	U.S. (Southeast)
American crocodile	Crocodylus acutus	U.S. (Fla.) to So. Amer.
Island night lizard	Klauberina riversiana	U.S. (Cal.)
Eastern indigo snake	Drymarchon corais couperi	U.S. (Al., Fl., Ga., Ms., S.C.)

Some Other Endangered Species in the World

Source: U.S. Fish and Wildlife Service, U.S. Interior Department

Common name	Scientific name	Range
Mammals		
Giant sable antelope	Hippotragus niger variani	Angola
African elephant	Loxoconta africana	Africa
Saudi Arabian gazelle	Gazella dorcas saudiya	Israel, Iraq, Jordan, Saudi Arabia
Brown hyena	Hyaena brunnea	Southern Africa
Red kangaroo	Megaleia rufa	Australia
Leopard	Panthera pardus	Africa, India, SE Asia
Black howler monkey	Alouatta pigra	Mexico, Guatamala
Ocelot	Felis pardalis	C. and S. America
Thin-spined porcupine	Chaetomys subspinosus	Brazil
Tiger	Panthera tigris	Asia
Banded hare wallaby	Lagostrophus fasciatus	Australia
Gray whale	Eschrichtius robustus	N. Pacific Ocean
Wild yak	Bos grunniens mutus	China, India
Mountain zebra	Equus zebra	South Africa
Birds		
Indigo macaw	Anodorhynchus leari	Brazil
West African ostrich	Struthio camelus spatzi	Spanish Sahara
Anjouan scops owl	Otus rutilus capnodes	Indian Ocean
Golden parakeet	Aratinga guarouba	Brazil
Australian parrot	Geopsittacus occidentalis	Australia

A Collection of Animal Collectives

The English language boasts an abundance of names to describe groups of things, particularly pairs or aggregations of animals. Some of these words have fallen into comparative disuse, but many of them are still in service, helping to enrich the vocabularies of those who like their language to be precise, who tire of hearing a group referred to as "a bunch of," or who enjoy the sound of words that aren't overworked.

band of gorillas
bed of clams, oysters
bevy of quail, swans
brace of ducks
brood of chicks
cast of hawks
cete of badgers
charm of goldfinches
chattering of choughs
cloud of gnats
clowder of cats
clutch of chicks
clutter of cats
colony of ants
congregation of plovers
covey of quail, partridge
cry of hounds
down of hares
drift of swine
drove of cattle, sheep
exaltation of larks
flight of birds
flock of sheep, geese
gaggle of geese
gam of whales
gang of elks
grist of bees
herd of elephants
hive of bees
horde of gnats
husk of hares
kindle or **kendle** of kittens
knot of toads
leap of leopards
leash of greyhounds, foxes
litter of pigs

mob of kangaroos
murder of crows
muster of peacocks
mute of hounds
nest of vipers
nest, nide of pheasants
pack of hounds, wolves
pair of horses
pod of whales, seals
pride of lions
school of fish
sedge or **siege** of cranes
shoal of fish, pilchards
skein of geese
skulk of foxes
sleuth of bears
sounder of boars, swine
span of mules
spring of teals
swarm of bees
team of ducks, horses
tribe or **trip** of goats
troop of kangaroos, monkeys
volery of birds
watch of nightingales
wing of plovers
yoke of oxen

Young of Animals Have Special Names

The young of many animals, birds and fish have come to be called by special names. A young eel, for example, is an elver. Many young animals, of course, are often referred to simply as infants, babies, younglets, or younglings.

bunny: rabbit.
calf: cattle, elephant, antelope, rhino, hippo, whale, etc.
cheeper: grouse, partridge, quail.
chick, chicken: fowl.
cockerel: rooster.
codling, sprag: codfish.
colt: horse (male).
cub: lion, bear, shark, fox, etc.
cygnet: swan.
duckling: duck.
eaglet: eagle.
elver: eel.
eyas: hawk, others.
fawn: deer.
filly: horse (female).
fingerling: fish generally.
flapper: wild fowl.
fledgling: birds generally.
foal: horse, zebra, others.
fry: fish generally.
gosling: goose.
heifer: cow.
joey: kangaroo, others.
kid: goat.
kit: fox, beaver, rabbit, cat.
kitten, kitty, catling: cats, other fur-bearers.
lamb, lambkin, cosset, hog: sheep.
leveret: hare.
nestling: birds generally.
owlet: owl.
parr, smolt, grilse: salmon.
piglet, shoat, farrow, suckling: pig.
polliwog, tadpole: frog.
poult: turkey.
pullet: hen.
pup: dog, seal, sea lion, fox.
puss, pussy: cat.
spike, blinker, tinker: mackerel.
squab: pigeon.
squeaker: pigeon, others.
whelp: dog, tiger, beasts of prey.
yearling: cattle, sheep, horse, etc.

Speeds of Animals

Source: Natural History magazine, March 1974.
Copyright © The American Museum of Natural History, 1974.

Animal	Mph	Animal	Mph	Animal	Mph
Cheetah	70	Mongolian wild ass	40	Human	27.89
Pronghorn antelope	61	Greyhound	39.35	Elephant	25
Wildebeest	50	Whippet	35.50	Black mamba snake	20
Lion	50	Rabbit (domestic)	35	Six-lined race runner	18
Thomson's gazelle	50	Mule deer	35	Wild turkey	15
Quarterhorse	47.5	Jackal	35	Squirrel	12
Elk	45	Reindeer	32	Pig (domestic)	11
Cape hunting dog	45	Giraffe	32	Chicken	9
Coyote	43	White-tailed deer	30	Spider (Tegenaria atrica)	1.17
Gray fox	42	Wart hog	30	Giant tortoise	0.17
Hyena	40	Grizzly bear	30	Three-toed sloth	0.15
Zebra	40	Cat (domestic)	30	Garden snail	0.03

Most of these measurements are for maximum speeds over approximate quarter-mile distances. Exceptions are the lion and elephant, whose speeds were clocked in the act of charging; the whippet, which was timed over a 200-yard course; the cheetah over a 100-yard distance; man for a 15-yard segment of a 100-yard run (of 13.6 seconds); and the black mamba, six-lined race runner, spider, giant tortoise, three-toed sloth, and garden snail, which were measured over various small distances.

Gestation, Longevity, and Incubation of Animals

Longevity figures were supplied by Ronald T. Reuther. They refer to animals in captivity; the potential life span of animals is rarely attained in nature. Maximum longevity figures are from the Biology Data Book, 1972. Figures on gestation and incubation are averages based on estimates by leading authorities.

Animal	Gestation (day)	Average longevity (years)	Maximun longevity (yrs., mos.)
Ass	365	12	35-10
Baboon	187	20	35-7
Bear: Black	219	18	36-10
Grizzly	225	25	—
Polar	240	20	34-8
Beaver	122	5	20-6
Buffalo (American)	278	15	—
Bactrian camel	406	12	29-5
Cat (domestic)	63	12	28
Chimpanzee	231	20	44-6
Chipmunk	31	6	8
Cow	284	15	30
Deer (white-tailed)	201	8	17-6
Dog (domestic)	61	12	20
Elephant (African)	—	35	60
Elephant (Asian)	645	40	70
Elk	250	15	26-6
Fox (red)	52	7	14
Giraffe	425	10	33-7
Goat (domestic)	151	8	18
Gorilla	257	20	39-4
Guinea pig	68	4	7-6
Hippopotamus	238	25	—
Horse	330	20	46
Kangaroo	42	7	—

Animal	Gestation (day)	Average longevity (years)	Maximum longevity (yrs., mos.)
Leopard	98	12	19-4
Lion	100	15	25-1
Monkey (rhesus)	164	15	—
Moose	240	12	—
Mouse (meadow)	21	3	—
Mouse (dom. white)	19	3	3-6
Opossum (American)	14-17	1	—
Pig (domestic)	112	10	27
Puma	90	12	19
Rabbit (domestic)	31	5	13
Rhinoceros (black)	450	15	—
Rhinoceros (white)	—	20	—
Sea lion (California)	350	12	28
Sheep (domestic)	154	12	20
Squirrel (gray)	44	10	—
Tiger	105	16	26-3
Wolf (maned)	63	5	—
Zebra (Grant's)	365	15	—

Incubation time (days)

Chicken	21
Duck	30
Goose	30
Pigeon	18
Turkey	26

Major Venomous Animals

Snakes

Coral snake - 2 to 4 ft. long, in Americas south of Canada; bite is nearly painless; very slow onset of paralysis, difficulty breathing; mortality high without anti-venin.

Rattlesnake - 2 to 8 ft. long, throughout W. Hemisphere. Rapid onset of symptoms of severe pain, swelling; mortality low, but amputation of affected limb is sometimes necessary; anti-venin. Probably high mortality for Mojave rattler.

Cottonmouth water moccasin - less than 6 ft. long, wetlands of southern U.S. from Virginia to Texas. Rapid onset of symptoms of severe pain, swelling; mortality low, but tissue destruction, caused by the venom's effect on the blood, can be extensive; anti-venin.

Copperhead - less than 4 ft. long, from New England to Texas; pain and swelling; very seldom fatal.

Fer-de-lance - up to 7 ft. long, Martinique only; venom attacks nerves and blood; probably high mortality.

Bushmaster - up to 9 ft. long, jungles of C. and S. America; few bites recorded; probably low mortality.

Yellow-beard - up to 7 ft. long, from tropical Mexico to Brazil; severe tissue damage common; low mortality; anti-venin.

Asian pit vipers - from 2 to 5 ft. long throughout Asia; reactions and mortality vary but most bites cause tissue damage and mortality is generally low.

Sharp-nosed pit viper - up to 5 ft. long, in eastern China and Indo-China; the most toxic of Asian pit vipers; very rapid onset of swelling and tissue damage, internal bleeding; moderate mortality; anti-venin.

Boomslang - under 6 ft. long, in African savannahs; rapid onset of nausea and dizziness, often followed by slight recovery and then sudden death from internal hemorrhaging; bites rare, mortality high; anti-venin.

European vipers - from 1 to 3 ft. long; bleeding and tissue damage; mortality low; anti-venins.

Puff adder - up to 5 ft. long, fat; south of the Sahara and throughout the Middle East; rapid large swelling, great pain, dizziness; moderate mortality often from internal bleeding; anti-venin.

Gaboon viper - over 6 ft. long, fat; 2-inch fangs; south of the Sahara; massive tissue damage, internal bleeding; mortality rate not clear.

Saw-scaled or carpet viper - up to 2 ft. long, in dry areas from India to Africa; severe bleeding, fever; high mortality, venom 3 times more toxic than common cobra's; anti-venin.

Desert horned viper - in dry areas of Africa and western Asia; swelling and tissue damage; low mortality; anti-venin.

Russel's viper or tic-palonga - over 5 ft. long, throughout Asia; internal bleeding; mortality rate not clear; bite reports common; anti-venin.

Black mamba - up to 14 ft. long, fast-moving; S. and C. Africa; rapid onset of dizziness, difficulty breathing, erratic heart-beat; mortality high, nears 100% without anti-venin.

Kraits - in S. Asia; rapid onset of sleepiness; numbness; kraits are among the most lethal snakes in the world with up to 50% mortality even with anti-venin treatment.

Common or Asian cobra - 4 to 8 ft. long, throughout S. Asia; considerable tissue damage, sometimes paralysis; mortality probably not more than 10%; anti-venin.

King cobra - up to 16 ft. long, large hood; throughout S. Asia; rapid swelling, dizziness, loss of consciousness, difficulty breathing, erratic heart-beat; mortality varies sharply with amount of venom involved, most bites involve non-fatal amounts; anti-venin.

Yellow or Cape cobra - 7 ft. long, in southern Africa; most toxic venom of any cobra; rapid onset of swelling, breathing and cardiac difficulties; mortality high without treatment; anti-venin.

Ringhals, or spitting, cobra - 5 ft. and 7 ft. long; southern Africa; squirt venom through holes in front of fangs as a defense; venom is severely irritating and can cause blindness.

Australian brown snakes - very slow onset of symptoms of cardiac or respiratory distress; moderate mortality; anti-venin.

Tiger snake - 2 to 6 ft. long, S. Australia; pain, numbness, mental disturbances with rapid onset of paralysis; may be the most deadly of all land snakes though anti-venin is quite effective.

Death adder - less than 3 ft. long, Australia; rapid onset of faintness, cardiac and respiratory distress; at least 50% mortality without anti-venin.

Taipan - up to 11 ft. long, in Australia and New Guinea; rapid paralysis with severe breathing difficulty; mortality nears 100% without anti-venin.

Sea snakes - throughout Pacific and Indian oceans except NE Pacific; almost painless bite, variety of muscle pain, paralysis; mortality rate about 15%, many bites are not envenomed; some anti-venins.

Notes: Not all snake bites by venomous snakes are actually envenomed; for a variety of reasons, the snake may be temporarily lacking in venom or fail to inject it. Any animal bite, however, carries the danger of tetanus and no bite by a venomous snake should go untreated. Anti-venins are not certain cures; they are only an aid in the treatment of bites. Mortality rates above are for envenomed bites; low mortality, up to 5% result in death; moderate, up to 15%; high, over 15%. Even in cases in which the victim recovers fully, prolonged hospitalization and extensive, continuous medical procedures are usually required.

Lizards

Gila monster - up to 30 inches long with heavy body and tail, in high desert in southwest U.S. and N. Mexico; immediate severe pain followed by vomiting, thirst, difficulty swallowing, weakness approaching paralysis; mortality very low with medical treatment, otherwise high; anti-venin.

Mexican beaded lizard - similar to Gila monster, Mexican west-coast; reaction and mortality rate similar to Gila monster; anti-venin.

Insects

Ants, bees, wasps, hornets, etc. All have global distribution. Usual reaction is piercing pain in area of sting. Never directly fatal, except in cases of massive multiple stings. Many people suffer allergic reactions - swelling, rashes, partial paralysis –and a few may die within minutes from severe sensitivity to the venom (anaphylactic shock).

Spiders, scorpions

Black widow - small, round-bodied with hour-glass marking; the widow and its relatives are found around the world in tropical and temperate zones; sharp pain, weakness, clammy skin, muscular rigidity, breathing difficulty and, in small children, convulsions; low mortality.

Brown recluse or fiddleback - small, oblong body; can be found anywhere in U.S. today; slow onset of pain and severe ulceration at place of bite; in severe cases fever, nausea, and stomach cramps; ulceration may last months; very low mortality.

***Atrax* spiders** - several varieties, often large, found in Australia; slow onset of breathing and circulation difficulties; low mortality.

Tarantulas - large, hairy spiders found around the world; American tarantulas, and probably all others, are **harmless,** though their bite may cause some pain and swelling.

Scorpions - crab-like body with stinger in tail, various sizes, many varieties throughout tropical and subtropical areas; various symptoms may include severe pain spreading from the wound, numbness, severe emotional agitation, cramps; severe reactions include vomiting, diarrhea, respiratory failure; moderate, perhaps high, mortality, particularly in children; anti-venins.

Sea Life

Sea wasps - jellyfish, with tentacles up to 30 ft. long, in the South Pacific; very rapid onset of circulatory problems; high mortality largely because of the speed of toxic reaction; anti-venin.

Portuguese man-of-war - jellyfish-like, with tentacles up to 70 ft. long, in most warm water areas; immediate severe pain; not fatal, though shock may cause death in a rare case.

Octopi - global distribution, usually in warm waters; all varieties produce venom but only a few can cause death; rapid onset of paralysis with breathing difficulty.

Stingrays - several varieties of differing sizes, found in tropical and temperate seas and some fresh water; severe pain, rapid onset of nausea, vomiting, breathing difficulties; wound area may ulcerate, gangrene may appear; seldom fatal.

Stonefish - brownish fish which lies motionless as a rock on bottom in shallow water; throughout S. Pacific and Indian oceans; extraordinary pain, rapid paralysis; low mortality.

Cone-shells - molluscs in small, beautiful shells in the S. Pacific and Indian oceans; shoot barbs into victims; paralysis; low mortality.

American Kennel Club Registrations

	Rank	1979	1978
Poodles	1	94,950	101,100
Doberman Pinschers	2	80,363	81,964
Cocker Spaniels	3	65,685	58,719
German Shepherd Dogs	4	57,683	61,783
Labrador Retrievers	5	46,077	43,500
Golden Retrievers	6	38,060	34,249
Beagles	7	35,374	36,920
Dachshunds	8	32,777	33,660
Miniature Schnauzers	9	32,666	33,534
Shetland Sheepdogs	10	25,943	24,668
Lhasa Apsos	11	22,714	22,330
Yorkshire Terriers	12	22,458	21,913
Collies	13	21,210	22,032
Irish Setters	14	20,912	30,839
English Springer Spaniels	15	20,071	19,131
Siberian Huskies	16	19,876	20,650
Pekingese	17	17,992	18,892
Brittany Spaniels	18	17,038	18,418
Pomeranians	19	16,184	15,870
Shih Tzu	20	16,042	14,894
Chihuahuas	21	15,512	15,206
Great Danes	22	15,322	16,600
Basset Hounds	23	14,930	14,264
Boxers	24	13,250	13,248
Old English Sheepdogs	25	12,018	12,997
Chow Chows	26	11,739	9,368
Boston Terriers	27	11,125	10,811
German Shorthaired Pointers	28	10,579	11,517
Samoyeds	29	8,653	9,222
St. Bernards	30	7,444	9,727
Alaskan Malamutes	31	7,377	7,861
Afghan Hounds	32	6,833	7,878
Maltese	33	6,806	6,504
Airedale Terriers	34	6,594	6,601
Bulldogs	35	6,566	6,413
Scottish Terriers	36	6,343	6,430
Cairn Terriers	37	6,262	6,369
West Highland White Terriers	38	6,210	5,984
Keeshonden	39	5,850	5,923
Norwegian Elkhounds	40	5,794	6,364
Dalmations	41	5,558	5,924
Pugs	42	5,497	5,716
Weimaraners	43	4,605	5,004
Fox Terriers	44	3,762	3,960
Chesapeake Bay Retrievers	45	3,460	3,059
Rottweilers	46	3,286	2,439
Silky Terriers	47	2,565	2,557
Newfoundlands	48	2,345	2,092
Welsh Corgis (Pembroke)	49	2,216	2,349
Bichons Frises	50	2,146	1,829
Akitas	51	1,878	1,531
Vizslas	52	1,737	1,845
Bloodhounds	53	1,671	1,586
Miniature Pinschers	54	1,428	1,361
Basenjis	55	1,393	1,455
Schipperkes	56	1,353	1,346
Bouviers des Flandres	57	1,345	1,301
Great Pyrenees	57	1,345	1,397
Whippets	59	1,296	1,259
Borzois	60	1,283	1,408
English Setters	61	1,263	1,477
Irish Wolfhounds	62	1,189	1,270
English Cocker Spaniels	63	1,156	1,134
Gordon Setters	64	1,140	1,293
Mastiffs	65	1,097	948
American Staffordshire Terriers	66	1,072	1,014
Bull Terriers	67	1,042	1,103
Rhodesian Ridgebacks	68	1,029	946
German Wirehaired Pointers	69	978	1,077
Bullmastiffs	70	804	826
Soft-Coated Wheaten Terriers	71	797	798
Australian Terriers	72	784	857
Welsh Terriers	73	691	676
Standard Schnauzers	74	687	770
Salukis	75	619	656
Bearded Collies	76	588	472
Belgian Sheepdogs	77	584	617
Papillons	78	576	574
Manchester Terriers	79	534	484
Italian Greyhounds	80	515	596
Kerry Blue Terriers	81	499	563
Giant Schnauzers	82	496	459
Belgian Tervuren	83	452	445
Japanese Chin	84	411	399
Pointers	85	398	399
Tibetan Terriers	86	343	269
Pulik	87	341	435
Welsh Corgis (Cardigan)	87	341	339
Bernese Mountain Dogs	89	318	238
Irish Terriers	90	316	262
Bedlington Terriers	91	311	387
Black And Tan Coonhounds	92	302	332
American Water Spaniels	93	282	289
Staffordshire Bull Terriers	94	257	268
Briards	95	246	232
Welsh Springer Spaniels	96	224	117
Norwich Terriers	97	205	319
Flat Coated Retrievers	98	200	122
Dandie Dinmont Terriers	99	192	208
Lakeland Terriers	99	192	201
Skye Terriers	101	190	191
Kuvaszok	102	180	206
Scottish Deerhounds	103	174	129
Border Terriers	104	163	136
Greyhounds	105	157	144
Brussels Griffons	106	156	203
French Bulldogs	106	156	187
Wirehaired Pointing Griffons	108	131	145
Sealyham Terriers	109	112	105
Irish Water Spaniels	110	110	86
Norfolk Terriers	111	106	—
Ibizan Hounds	112	102	568
Komondorok	112	102	87
Affenpinschers	114	87	109
Clumber Spaniels	115	76	55
English Toy Spaniels	116	71	56
Foxhounds (American)	117	70	50
Belgian Malinois	118	60	14
Otter Hounds	119	30	22
Curly-Coated Retrievers	120	27	76
Field Spaniels	120	27	39
Harriers	122	21	34
Sussex Spaniels	123	14	10
Foxhounds (English)	124	6	5
Total Registrations		**965,250**	**980,299**

Dogs registered by groups	1979	1978
Sporting breeds	234,250	232,600
Hound breeds	105,050	108,950
Working breeds	287,850	297,949
Terrier breeds	69,300	70,450
Toy breeds	106,300	104,850
Non-sporting breeds	162,500	165,500
	965,250	980,299

Cat Breeds

There are 27 cat breeds recognized: abyssinian, american shorthair, balinese, birman, bombay, burmese, colorpoint shorthair, egyptian mau, exotic shorthair, havana brown, himalayan, japanese bobtail, korat, leopard cat, lilac foreign shorthair, maine coon cat, manx, ocicat, oriental shorthair, persian, rex, russian blue, scottish fold, siamese, sphynx, turkish angora, wirehair shorthair.

EDUCATION

American Colleges and Universities

Student and Faculty Figures for Spring Term, 1980

Source: World Almanac questionnaires and U.S. Office of Education

(For Canadian Colleges and Universities, see Index)

All coeducational unless followed by (M) for men only, or (W) for women only. Even though marked (M) or (W) some are coeducational at graduate level and in evening and summer divisions. Asterisk (*) denotes landgrant college.

Governing official is president unless otherwise designated. Year is that of founding. The word college is part of the name unless another designation is given.

Affiliation: C-county; D-religious denomination; Di-district; F-federal; Mu-municipal; P-private; S-state; T-territorial govt.

Each institution listed has an enrollment of at least 200 students of college grade. Number of teachers is the total number of individuals on teaching staff. Enrollment and faculty in italics includes all branches and campuses.

(A) Designates colleges that have not provided up-to-date information.

(See Index for typical tuition fees)

Senior Colleges

Name, address	Year	Governing official and affiliation		Students	Teachers
Abilene Christian, Abilene, TX 79601	1906	John C. Stevens	P	4,372	175
Adams, State, Alamosa, CO 81102	1921	Milton Byrd	S	2,000	104
Adelphi Univ. (A), Garden City, NY 11530	1896	Timothy Costello	P	10,500	360
Adrian, Adrian, MI 49221	1859	Donald S. Stanton	P	945	61
Agnes Scott (W), Decatur, GA 30030	1889	Marvin Perry Jr	P	561	67
Akron, Univ. of, Akron, OH 44325	1870	Dominic J. Guzzetta	S	*23,400*	*674*
Alabama A&M Univ, Normal, AL 35762	1875	Richard D. Morrison	S	4,431	255
Alabama State Univ., Montgomery, AL 36101	1874	Levi Watkins	S	4,096	202
Alabama, Univ. of, University, AL 35486	1831	David Mathews	S	16,870	820
at Birmingham, Birmingham, AL 35294	1966	S.R. Hill Jr	S	13,799	1,417
at Huntsville, Huntsville, AL 35807	1950	John C. Wright	S	*4,702*	*217*
Alaska, Univ. of* (A), Fairbanks, AK 99701	1917	Robert W. Hiatt	S	*7,773*	*400*
Albany Coll. of Pharmacy, Albany, NY 12208	1881	Dean Walter Singer	P	590	27
Albany State, Albany, GA 31705	1903	Charles Hays	S	2,000	135
Albertus Magnus (W), New Haven, CT 06511	1925	Sr. Francis Heffernan	D	561	37
Albion, Albion, MI 49224	1835	Bernard Tagg Lomas	P	1,807	116
Albright, Reading, PA 19603	1856	Dr. David G. Ruffer	P	1,672	83
Albuquerque, Univ. of, Albuquerque, NM 87140	1920	Clifford Smith	D	2,000	75
Alcorn State Univ., Lorman, MS 39096	1871	Walter Washington	S	2,294	136
Alderson-Broaddus, Philippi, WV 26416	1871	Richard E. Shearer	D	1,000	80
Alfred Univ., Alfred, NY 14802	1836	Howard R. Neville	P	2,146	147
Allegheny, Meadville, PA 16335	1815	David B. Harned	D	1,936	127
Allen Univ., Columbia, SC 29204	1870	Alvis V. Adair	D	342	36
Alma, Alma, MI 48801	1886	Robert D. Swanson	D	1,250	75
Alvernia, Reading, PA 19607	1958	Sister Mary Victorine	D	600	45
Alverno (W), Milwaukee, WI 53215	1936	Sister Joel Read	D	1,364	111
American Cons. of Music, Chicago, IL 60603	1886	Leo Heim	P	393	13
American International, Springfield, MA 01109	1885	Harry J. Courniotes	P	2,200	90
American Univ., Washington DC 20016	1893	Richard Berendzen	D	12,500	444
Amherst, Amherst, MA 01002	1821	John William Ward	P	1,475	150
Anderson, Anderson, IN 46011	1917	Robert H. Reardon	D	2,041	95
Andrews Univ., Berrien Springs, MI 49104	1874	Joseph Smoot	D	2,983	232
Angelo State Univ., San Angelo, TX 76901	1928	Lloyd Vincent	S	5,637	187
Anna Maria, Paxton, MA 01612	1946	Bernadette Madore	P	1,288	125
Annhurst, Woodstock, CT 06281	1940	Paul Buchanan	P	300	30
Antioch, Yellow Spgs., OH 45387	1852	Dr. Wm. Birenbaum	P	*6,000*	*200*
Appalachian Bible, Bradley, WV 25818	1950	Lester E. Pipkin	D	223	12
Appalachian State Univ., Boone, NC 28607	1899	John E. Thomas, Chan	S	9,334	550
Aquinas, Grand Rapids, MI 49506	1922	Norbert J. Hruby	P	2,172	78
Arizona, State Univ., Tempe, AZ 85281	1885	John W. Schwada	S	37,755	1,303
Arizona, Univ. of* (A), Tucson, AZ 85721	1885	John Paul Schaefer	S	29,062	1,525
Arkansas, Batesville, AR 72501	1872	Dan C. West	D	496	28
Arkansas Tech, Russellville, AR 72801	1909	Kenneth Kersh	S	3,000	146
Arkansas State Univ., State Univ., AR 72467	1909	Eugene Smith	S	8,649	353
Arkansas, Univ. of*, Fayetteville, AR 72701	1871	James E. Martin	S	15,119	820
at Little Rock, Little Rock, AR 72204	1927	G. Robert Ross, Chan.	S	10,038	406
at Pine Bluff, Pine Bluff, AR 71601	1873	Herman Smith Jr., Chan.	S	2,848	168
Armstrong State, Savannah, GA 31406	1937	Henry L. Ashmore	S	2,873	117
Art Academy, Cincinnati, OH 45202	1887	Roger Williams, Dir.	P	200	21
Art Center Coll. of Design, Pasadena, CA 91103	1930	Donald R. Kubly	P	1,140	141
Art Inst. of Chicago, Chicago, IL 60603	1866	Donald Irving, Dir.	P	1,850	95
Asbury, Wilmore, KY 40390	1890	Dennis F. Kinlaw	P	1,145	91
Ashland, Ashland, OH 44805	1878	Dr. Arthur Schultz	D	2,598	104
Assumption, Worcester, MA 01609	1904	Joseph H. Hagan	D	1,700	75
Athens State, Athens AL 35611	1822	Sidney Sandridge	S	1,305	48
Atlanta College of Art, Atlanta, GA 30309	1928	William Voos	P	471	23
Atlantic Christian, Wilson, NC 27893	1902	Harold C. Doster	P	1,600	95
Atlantic Union, So. Lancaster, MA 01561	1882	R. Dale McCune	M	689	51
Auburn Univ.*, Auburn, AL 36830	1856	Harry Philpott	S	*22,500*	*1,000*
Augsburg, Minneapolis, MN 55454	1869	Oscar A. Anderson	D	1,625	85
Augusta, Augusta, GA 30904	1925	George A. Christenberry	S	3,719	156
Augustana, Rock Island, IL 61201	1860	J. Thomas Tredway	D	2,041	117
Augustana, Sioux Falls, SD 57102	1860	William Nelson	D	2,243	136
Aurora, Aurora, IL 60507	1893	Alan J. Stone	D	1,050	54
Austin, Sherman, TX 75090	1849	Dr. Harry E. Smith	D	1,119	101
Austin Peay State Univ., Clarksville, TN 37040	1928	Robert O. Riggs	S	5,500	225
Averett, Danville, VA 24541	1859	Howard W. Lee	D	954	47
Avila, Kansas City, MO 64145	1940	Sister Olive Louise	D	2,005	74
Azusa Pacific, Azusa CA 91702	1899	Paul Sago	P	2,268	94
Babson, Babson Park, MA 02157	1919	Ralph Z. Sorenson	P	2,800	89
Baker Univ., Baldwin City, KS 66006	1858	Ralph Tanner	D	977	67

Name, address	Year	Governing official and affiliation		Students	Teachers
Baldwin-Wallace, Berea, OH 44017	1845	A.B. Bonds Jr.	D	3,407	128
Ball State Univ., Muncie, IN 47306	1918	Jerry M. Anderson	S	17,012	926
Baltimore, Univ. of, Baltimore, MD 21201	1925	H. Mebane Turner	S	5,474	115
Baptist Bible, Springfield, MO 65802	1950	William E. Dowell,	D	1,963	62
Baptist Bible College of Pa., Clarks Summit, PA 18411	1932	Dr. Mark Jackson	D	896	35
Baptist Coll. at Charleston, Charleston, SC 29411	1960	John Hamrick	D	2,400	80
Barat (W), Lake Forest, IL 60045	1858	Sr. Judith Cagney	D	737	48
Barber-Scotia, Concord, NC 28025	1867	Mable McLean	D	351	33
Bard, Annandale-on-Hudson, NY 12504	1860	Leon Botstein	P	700	75
Barnard (W), New York, NY 10027	1889	Vacant	P	2,441	165
Barrington, Barrington, RI 02806	1900	David G. Horner	P	455	25
Barry, Miami, FL 33161	1940	Sister M. Trinita Flood	P	2,050	150
Bates, Lewiston, ME 04240	1855	Thomas H. Reynolds	P	1,432	114
Baylor Univ., Waco, TX 76703	1845	Abner V. McCall	D	*9,594*	*471*
Beaver, Glenside, PA 19038	1853	Edward D. Gates	P	1,994	90
Belhaven, Jackson, MS 39202	1883	Howard J. Cleland	D	611	44
Bellarmine, Louisville, KY 40205	1950	Eugene Petrick	P	2,095	62
Bellevue, Bellevue, NE 68005	1966	Richard Winchell	P	2,272	29
Belmont, Nashville, TN 37203	1951	Herbert C. Gabhart	D	1,313	70
Belmont Abbey, Belmont, NC 28012	1876	Rev. Neil W. Tobin	D	668	56
Beloit, Beloit, WI 53511	1846	Martha Peterson	P	987	81
Bemidji State, Bemidji, MN 56601	1919	Rebecca Stafford	S	5,534	200
Benedict, Columbia, SC 29204	1870	Henry Ponder	P	1,613	106
Benedictine, Atchison KS 66002	1858	Rev. Gerard Senecal	D	1,100	90
Benjamin Franklin Univ., Washington, DC 20036	1907	Mrs. Clephane Kennedy	P	1,000	40
Bennett (W), Greensboro, NC 27420	1873	Isaac H. Miller	D	617	67
Bennington, Bennington, VT 05201	1925	Joseph S. Murphy	P	589	57
Bentley, Waltham, MA 02154	1917	Gregory Adamian	P	6,282	120
Berea (A), Berea, KY 40404	1855	W.D. Weatherford	P	1,434	113
Berry, Mount Berry, GA 30149	1902	John R. Bertrand	P	1,562	88
Bethany, Lindsborg, KS 67456	1881	Arvin Hahn	D	805	50
Bethany, Bethany, WV 26032	1840	William Tucker	P	1,000	65
Bethany Bible, Santa Cruz, CA 95060	1919	Richard B. Foth	D	489	20
Bethany Nazarene, Bethany, OK 73008	1899	John Knight	D	1,279	72
Bethel, North Newton, KS 67117	1888	Harold Schultz	D,P	638	42
Bethel, McKenzie, TN 38201	1842	William L. Odom	D	360	20
Bethel, Mishawaka, IN 46544	1947	Albert J. Beutler	D	464	18
Bethel, St. Paul, MN 55112	1871	Carl Lundquist	D	1,989	90
Bethune-Cookman, Daytona Beach, FL 32015	1904	O.P. Bronson	D	1,657	110
Biola, La Mirada, CA 90639	1908	J. Richard Chase	D	2,400	171
Birmingham-Southern, Birmingham, AL 35204	1856	Neal R. Berte	D	1,400	75
Biscayne (A), Miami, FL 33054	1962	Rev. John McDonnell	D	2,329	150
Bishop, Dallas, TX 75241	1881	Harry S. Wright	P	926	48
Black Hills State, Spearfish, SD 57783	1883	Dr. J. Gilbert Hause	S	2,054	91
Blackburn, Carlinville, IL 62626	1837	John Alberti	D	542	39
Bloomfield, Bloomfield, NJ 07003	1868	Merle F. Allshouse	P	2,500	180
Bloomsburg State, Bloomsburg, PA 17815	1839	James McCormick	S	6,532	321
Blue Mountain (W), Blue Mountain, MS 38610	1873	E. Harold Fisher	D	371	24
Bluefield, Bluefield, VA 24605	1922	Dr. Chas. Tyer	P,D	345	30
Bluefield State, Bluefield, WV 24701	1895	Ben Martin	S	2,400	75
Bluffton, Bluffton, OH 45817	1900	Dr. Elmer Neufeld	P	640	60
Bob Jones Univ., Greenville, SC 29614	1927	Dr. Bob Jones	D	4,870	210
Boise State, Boise, ID 83725	1932	Dr. John Keiser	S	10,000	425
Boston, Chestnut Hill, MA 02167	1863	Rev. Donald J. Monan	P	*13,977*	*540*
Boston State, Boston, MA 02115	1852	Kermit C. Morrissey	S	11,000	328
Boston Conserv. of Music, Boston, MA 02215	1867	Mr. Dale A. DuVall	P	505	101
Boston Univ., Boston, MA 02215	1869	John Silber	P	25,528	2,449
Bowdoin, Brunswick, ME 04011	1794	Willard Enteman	P	1,362	99
Bowie State*, Bowie, MD 20715	1865	Dr. Rufus L. Barfield	S	2,664	137
Bowling Green State Univ., Bowling Green, OH 43403	1910	Hollis A. Moore Jr.	S	*18,047*	*752*
Bradford, Bradford, MA 01830	1803	Inge Heckel	P	350	24
Bradley Univ., Peoria, IL 61625	1897	Martin G. Abegg	P	5,249	328
Brandeis Univ., Waltham, MA 02254	1948	Marver Bernstein	P	3,515	317
Brenau, Gainesville, GA 30501	1878	James T. Rogers	P	775	60
Brescia, Owensboro, KY 42301	1950	Sister Geo. Ann Cecil	D	844	50
Briar Cliff, Sioux City, IA 51104	1930	Chas. Bensman	D	1,258	57
Bridgeport Engineering Inst., Bridgeport, CT 06606	1924	William J. Owens	P	*639*	*72*
Bridgeport, Univ. of, Bridgeport, CT 06602	1927	Leland Miles	P	7,700	250
Bridgewater, Bridgewater, VA 22812	1880	Dr. Wayne F. Geisert	P	850	51
Bridgewater State (A), Bridgewater, MA 02324	1840	Adrian Rondileau	S	8,000	260
Brigham Young Univ., Provo, UT 84601	1875	Dallin U. Oaks	D	28,000	1,250
Brooks Inst., Santa Barbara, CA 93108	1945	Ernest Brooks II	P	791	41
Brown Univ., Providence, RI 02912	1764	Howard R. Swearer	P	6,500	450
Bryan, Dayton, TN 37321	1930	Theodore Mercer	P	601	33
Bryant, Smithfield RI 02917	1863	William O'Hara	P	5,400	86
Bryn Mawr (W), Bryn Mawr, PA 19010	1885	Mary Patterson McPherson	P	1,722	130
Bucknell Univ., Lewisburg, PA 17837	1846	Dennis O'Brien	P	3,212	230
Buena Vista, Storm Lake, IA 50588	1891	Keith G. Briscoe	D	949	47
Butler Univ., Indianapolis, IN 46208	1855	John G. Johnson	P	*3,737*	216
Cabrini, Radnor, PA 19087	1957	Sr. Mary Sullivan	D	577	29
Caldwell, Caldwell, NJ 07006	1939	Sr. Edith Magdalen Visic	D,P	663	33
California Baptist, Riverside, CA 92504	1950	James R. Staples	D	740	37
Cal. Coll. of Arts and Crafts, Oakland, CA 94618	1907	Harry Xavier Ford	P	1,100	130
Cal. College of Podiatric Med., San Francisco, CA 94120	1914	Richard Allen	P	396	32
Cal. Inst. of the Arts, Valencia, CA 91355	1961	Robert Fitzpatrick	P	750	75
Cal. Inst. of Tech., Pasadena, CA 91125	1890	Marvin L. Goldberger	P	1,700	339
Cal. Lutheran, Thousand Oaks, CA 91360	1959	Mark Mathews	P	1,290	80
Cal. Maritime Academy, Vallejo, CA 94590	1929	R. Adm. Joseph Rizza	S	468	27
Cal. Polytechnic State Univ., San Luis Obispo, CA 93407	1901	Warren J. Baker	S	16,000	850
Cal. State, Bakersfield, CA 93309	1970	Jacob Frankel	S	3,100	200
Cal. State, California, PA 15419	1852	John P. Watkins	S	4,900	305
Cal. State, Dominguez Hills, CA 90747	1960	Donald Gerth	S	7,000	300
Cal. State (A), Rohnert Park, CA 94928	1960	P. Diamandopoulos	S	6,024	424
Cal. State, San Bernardino, CA 92407	1965	John Pfau	S	3,800	160
Cal. State Stanislaus, Turlock, CA 95380	1957	Walter Olson	S	3,650	160
Cal. State Polytechnic Univ., Pomona, CA 91768	1938	Hugh La Bounty Jr.	S	14,445	601
Cal. State Univ., Chico, CA 95929	1887	Stanford Cazier	S	13,135	665
Cal. State Univ., Fresno, CA 93740	1911	Norman Baxter	S	14,717	720

Name, address	Year	Governing official and affiliation		Students	Teachers
Cal. State Univ., Fullerton, CA 92634	1959	L. Donald Shields	S	21,272	800
Cal. State Univ., Hayward, CA 94542	1958	Ellis McCune	S	10,000	460
Cal. State Univ., Long Beach, CA 90840	1949	Stephen Horn	S	31,157	1,601
Cal. State Univ., Los Angeles, CA 90032	1947	James M. Rosser	S	25,000	895
Cal. State Univ., Northridge, CA 91330	1958	James W. Cleary	S	26,877	820
Cal. State Univ., Sacramento, CA 95819	1947	Dr. W. Lloyd Johns	S	21,222	1,032
Cal. State Univ. (A), San Francisco, CA 94132	1899	Paul F. Romberg	S	23,273	828
Cal., Univ. of* (A), Berkeley, CA 94720	1868	David S. Saxon	S	*128,478*	*7,000*
Berkeley Campus (A), Berkeley, CA 94720	1873	Ira Michael Heyman, Chan.	S	30,445	1,494
Davis Campus, Davis, CA 95616	1905	James Meyer, Chan.	S	17,511	1,207
Irvine Campus, Irvine, CA 92717	1960	D.G. Aldrich, Chan.	S	10,033	731
Los Angeles Campus, Los Angeles, CA 90024	1919	Charles Young, Chan.	S	31,743	2,700
Riverside Campus (A), Riverside, CA 92502	1907	Ivan Hinderaker, Chan.	S	5,058	766
San Diego Campus (A), La Jolla, CA 92093	1912	William D. McElroy, Chan.	S	8,875	946
San Francisco Campus (A), San Francisco, CA 94122	1873	F. A. Sooy, Chan.	S	3,295	1,414
Santa Barbara Campus, Santa Barbara, CA 93106	1898	Robert A. Huttenback, Chan.	S	14,231	1,051
Santa Cruz Campus, Santa Cruz, CA 95064	1965	R.L. Sinsheimer, Chan.	S	5,880	346
Calumet, Whiting, IN 46394	1951	Rev. James McCabe	P	1,392	47
Calvin, Grand Rapids, MI 49506	1876	Anthony Dickema	D	4,024	200
Cameron, Lawton, OK 73505	1908	Richard Murray, (act.)	S	4,714	197
Campbell, Buies Creek, NC 27506	1887	Norman A. Wiggins	D	*2,571*	*137*
Campbellsville, Campbellsville, KY 42718	1906	William R. Davenport	P	674	45
Canisius, Buffalo, NY 14208	1870	Rev. James Demske	P	3,071	155
Capital Univ., Columbus, OH 43209	1850	Harvey A. Stegemoeller	P	2,544	155
Capitol Inst. of Tech., Kensington, MD 20795	1964	G.W. Troxler	P	630	12
Cardinal Stritch, Milwaukee, WI 53217	1937	Sister M. Kliebhan	D	1,130	41
Carleton, Northfield, MN 55057	1865	Robert Edwards	P	1,842	165
Carlow (W), Pittsburgh, PA 15213	1929	Sister Jane Scully	D,P	959	45
Carnegie-Mellon, Univ., Pittsburgh, PA 15213	1900	Richard M. Cyert	P	4,772	417
Carroll, Helena, MT 59601	1909	Francis Kerins	D	1,342	110
Carroll, Waukesha, WI 53186	1846	Robert V. Cramer	P	1,340	80
Carson-Newman, Jefferson City, TN 37760	1851	J. Cordell Maddox	D	1,616	91
Carthage, Kenosha, WI 53141	1847	Erno Dahl	D	1,014	83
Case Western Reserve Univ., Cleveland OH 44106	1826	L.A. Toepfer	P	7,865	1,291
Castleton State, Castleton, VT 05735	1787	Thomas K. Meier	S	1,982	110
Catawba, Salisbury, NC 28144	1851	M.L. Shotzberger	D	947	57
Cathedral (M), Douglaston, NY 11362	1914	Rev. Thomas Gradilone	D	135	31
Catholic Univ. of America, Washington, DC 20064	1887	Dr. Edmund D. Pellegrino	D,P	7,749	386
Cath. Univ. of Puerto Rico, Ponce, PR 00731	1948	F.J. Carreras	D	*8,959*	*380*
Cedar Crest, Allentown, PA 18104	1867	Dr. Gene S. Cesari	P	992	57
Cedarville, Cedarville, OH 45314	1887	James Jeremiah	D,P	1,185	68
Centenary (W), Hackettstown, NJ 07840	1873	Charles Dick	P	750	50
Centenary Coll. of La, Shreveport, LA 71104	1825	Donald Webb	D	950	107
Central Bible, Springfield, MO 65802	1922	Rev. Philip Crouch	D,P	1,135	38
Central, Pella, IA 50219	1853	Kenneth J. Weller	P	*1,498*	*70*
Central Connecticut State, New Britain, CT 06050	1849	F. Don James	S	12,061	646
Central Florida, Univ. of, Orlando FL 32816	1963	Dr. Trevor Colbourn	S	12,022	455
Central Methodist, Fayette, MO 65248	1884	Dr. Joe Howell	D	618	65
Central Mich. Univ., Mt. Pleasant, MI 48859	1892	Harold Abel	S	16,281	728
Central Missouri St. Univ., Warrensburg, MO 64093	1871	James Horner	S	9,905	456
Central New England, Worcester, MA 01610	1888	Edward Mattar III	P	1,200	78
Central State Univ., Edmond, OK 73034	1890	Bill Lillard	S	10,333	321
Central State Univ., Wilberforce, OH 45384	1887	Lionel H. Newsom	S	2,414	110
Central Washington State, Ellensburg, WA 98926	1891	Donald L. Garrity	S	7,909	332
Central Wesleyan, Central, SC 29630	1906	John Newby	D	400	34
Centre Coll. of Ky. Danville, KY 40422	1819	Thomas Spragens	P	760	65
Chadron State, Chadron, NE 69337	1911	Edwin Nelson	S	1,954	90
Chaminade Univ. of Honolulu, Honolulu, HI 96816	1955	Rev. D. Schuyler	D,P	2,242	144
Chapman, Orange, CA 92666	1861	G.T. Smith	P	4,917	271
Charleston, Coll. of, Charleston, SC 29401	1770	Edward M. Collins Jr.	S	4,741	198
Charleston, Univ. of, Charleston, WV 25304	1891	Thomas G. Voss	P	1,857	81
Chatham (W), Pittsburgh, PA 15232	1869	Alberta Arthurs	P	617	86
Chestnut Hill (W), Philadelphia, PA 19118	1924	Sister Mary Xavier	D	750	90
Cheyney State, Cheyney, PA 19319	1837	Wade Wilson	S	2,262	202
Chicago Coll. of Osteopathic, Chicago, IL 60615	1900	Thaddeus Kawalek	P	400	291
Chicago State Univ., Chicago, IL 60628	1867	Benjamin Alexander	S	7,334	259
Chicago, Univ. of Chicago, IL 60637	1890	Hanna Gray	P	9,236	1,035
Christian Brothers, Memphis, TN 38104	1871	Bro. Bernard LoCoco, F.S.C.	D	1,292	75
Christopher Newport, Newport News, Va 23606	1960	John E. Anderson	S	4,100	160
Cincinnati, Univ. of, Cincinnati, OH 45221	1819	Henry Winkler	S	*33,479*	*2,354*
Citadel, The, Charleston, SC 29409	1843	V. Adm. James Stockdale	S	3,277	155
Claflin, Orangeburg, SC 29115	1869	Hubert V. Manning	D	872	60
Claremont Men's, Claremont, CA 91711	1946	Jack Lee Stark	P	849	99
Clarion State, Clarion, PA 16214	1867	Charles D. Leach, Act.	S	*5,262*	*312*
Clark, Atlanta, GA 30314	1869	Elias Blake Jr.	P	1,876	116
Clark Univ., Worcester, MA 01610	1887	Mortimer Appley	P	3,053	213
Clarke (W), Dubuque, IA 52001	1843	Meneve Dunham	D	620	52
Clarkson, Potsdam, NY 13676	1896	Robert A. Plane	P	3,406	179
Cleary, Ypsilanti, MI 48197	1883	Gilbert Bursley	P	526	12
Clemson Univ.*, Clemson, SC 29631	1889	Robert C. Edwards	S	11,030	640
Cleveland Inst. of Art, Cleveland, OH 44106	1882	Joseph McCullough	P	760	103
Cleveland Inst. of Music, Cleveland, OH 44106	1920	Grant Johannesen	P	300	120
Cleveland State Univ., Cleveland, OH 44115	1964	Walter Waetjen	S	17,500	540
Coe, Cedar Rapids, IA 52402	1851	Leo Nussbaum	P	1,320	80
Coker, Hartsville, SC 29550	1908	C.H. Womble	P	409	36
Colby, Waterville, ME 04901	1813	William R. Cotter	P	1,625	140
Colby-Sawyer, New London, NH 03257	1837	H. Nicholas Muller	P	700	69
Colgate Univ., Hamilton, NY 13346	1819	George D. Langdon, Jr.	P	2,415	182
Colorado, Colo. Spgs., CO 80903	1874	Lloyd E. Worner	P	1,850	135
Colorado Sch. of Mines, Golden, CO 80401	1876	Guy McBride Jr.	S	2,543	176
Colorado State Univ.*, Fort Collins, CO 80523	1870	C.O. Neidt	S	*16,476*	*986*
Colorado, Univ. of, Boulder, CO 80302	1876	Arnold Weber	S	20,167	950
Colorado Springs, Colorado Springs, CO 80907	1965	Donald Schwartz, Chan.	S	*4,500*	*130*
Colorado Women's (W), Denver, CO 80220	1909	Sherry Manning	P	467	42
Columbia (W), Columbia, SC 29203	1854	Ralph Mirse	Mu	960	60
Columbia, Columbia, MO 65216	1851	Bruce B. Kelly	P	1,100	74
Columbia Bible, Columbia, SC 29230	1923	J. Robertson McQuilkin	P	787	27
Columbia Union, Takoma Park, MD 20012	1904	Colin Standish	D	914	69

Name, address	Year	Governing official and affiliation		Students	Teachers
Columbia Univ., New York, NY 10027	1754	Michael I. Sovern	P	17,861	1,666
Teachers College, New York, NY 10027	1887	L.A. Cremin	P	4,500	300
Columbus, Columbus, GA 31907	1958	William Lenoir (Act).	S	4,665	198
Columbus Coll. of Art & Design, Columbus, OH 43215	1879	Joseph Canzani	P	1,008	67
Concord, Athens, WV 24712	1872	Meredith Freeman	S	1,730	90
Concordia, Ann Arbor, MI 48105	1963	M.S. Pohl	D	552	49
Concordia, Bronxville, NY 10708	1881	Ralph Schultz	D	423	56
Concordia, Moorhead, MN 56560	1891	Paul Dovre	D	2,407	147
Concordia, Portland, OR 97211	1905	E.P. Weber	D	318	26
Concordia, River Forest, IL 60305	1864	Paul A. Zimmerman	D	1,129	100
Concordia, St. Paul, MN 55104	1893	Gerhardt Hyatt	P	650	54
Concordia Teachers, Seward, NE 68434	1894	M.J. Stelmachowicz	P	1,164	110
Connecticut, New London, CT 06320	1911	Oakes Ames	P	1,945	148
Connecticut, Univ. of, Storrs, CT 06268	1881	Edward V. Gant, Act.	S	*21,349*	*1,157*
Converse (W), Spartanburg, SC 29302	1889	Robert T. Coleman, Jr.	P	780	71
Cooper Union, New York, NY 10003	1859	John White	P	889	49
Coppin State, Baltimore, MD 21216	1900	Calvin Burnett	S	2,873	137
Cornell, Mt. Vernon, IA 52314	1853	Philip Secor	P	898	71
Cornell Univ.*, Ithaca, NY 14853	1865	Frank Rhodes	P	*18,000*	*1,800*
Covenant, Lookout Mt., TN 37350	1955	Martin Essenburg	P	494	32
Creighton Univ., Omaha, NE 68178	1878	Rev. Matthew E. Creighton	P	5,420	428
Culver-Stockton, Canton, MO 63435	1853	Robert W. Brown	P	500	40
Cumberland, Williamsburg, KY 40769	1889	Jim Taylor	D	2,081	94
Curry, Milton, MA 02186	1869	William L. Boyle, Jr.	P	1,132	65
Daemen, Amherst, NY 14226	1947	R.S. Marshall	P	1,436	81
Dakota State, Madison, SD 57042	1881	Carleton M. Opgaard	S	895	47
Dakota Wesleyan Univ., Mitchell, SD 57301	1885	Donald E. Messer	D	526	60
Dallas Baptist, Dallas, TX 75211	1963	W. Marvin Watson	D	931	44
Dallas, Univ. of, Irving, TX 75061	1956	John R. Sommerfeldt	D	2,030	141
Dana, Blair, NE 68008	1884	James Kallas	D	503	33
Daniel Webster, Nashua, NH 03063	1965	Louis D'Allesandro	P	900	15
Dartmouth, Hanover, NH 03755	1769	John George Kemeny	P	4,115	291
David Lipscomb, Nashville, TN 37203	1891	G. Williard Collins	P	2,293	109
Davidson, Davidson, NC 28036	1837	Samuel R. Spencer Jr.	D	1,370	101
Davis & Elkins, Elkins, WV 26241	1904	Gordon E. Hermanson	D	1,098	51
Dayton, Univ. of, Dayton, OH 45469	1850	Bro. Raymond Fitz	D	9,816	349
Defiance, Defiance, OH 43512	1850	Marvin J. Ludwig	D	746	50
Delaware State*, Dover, DE 19901	1890	Luna I. Mishoe	S	2,047	110
Delaware, Univ. of*, Newark, DE 19711	1833	E.A. Trabant	S	19,000	840
Del. Valley Coll. of S&A, Doylestown, PA 18901	1896	Joshua Feldstein	P	1,647	78
Delta State Univ., Cleveland, MS 38733	1924	Kent Wyatt	S	2,693	156
Denison Univ., Granville, OH 43023	1831	Robert C. Good	P	2,050	148
Denver, Univ. of, Denver, CO 80208	1864	Ross Pritchard	P	7,800	350
DePaul Univ., Chicago, IL 60604	1898	Rev. J.R. Cortelyou	D	12,857	365
DePauw Univ., Greencastle, IN 46135	1837	Richard Rosser	D	2,354	150
Desert, Coll. of the, Palm Desert, CA 92260	1958	F.D. Stout	Di	10,000	103
Detroit Coll. of Business, Dearborn, MI 48126	1936	Frank Paone	P	2,198	19
Detroit Coll. of Law, Detroit, MI 48201	1891	G. Cameron Buchanan	P	948	20
Detroit Inst. of Tech., Detroit, MI 48201	1877	H. Thompson	P	1,443	31
Detroit, Univ. of, Detroit, MI 48221	1877	Rev. M. Carron	P	*8,091*	*284*
Dickinson (A), Carlisle, PA 17013	1773	Samuel Banks	P	1,758	115
Dickinson School of Law (A), Carlisle, PA 17013	1834	Dale F. Shughart	P	445	32
Dickinson State (A), Dickinson, ND 58601	1918	R.C. Gillund	S	1,100	70
Dillard Univ., New Orleans, LA 70122	1869	Samuel Cook	D,F	1,217	81
District of Columbia, Univ. of (A), Washington, DC 20009	1851	Wendell Russell	Mu	*1,310*	*132*
Van Ness Campus, Washington, DC 20008	1977	Lisle C. Carter, Jr.	S	*13,647*	*851*
Doane, Crete, NE 68333	1872	Philip C. Heckman	P	650	53
Dr. Martin Luther, New Ulm, MN 56073	1884	Lloyd Hueber	D	850	70
Dominican Coll. of Blauvelt, Blauvelt, NY 10962	1952	Sr. Eileen O'Brien	D	1,230	39
Dominican Coll. of San Rafael, San Rafael, CA 94901	1890	Barbara Bundy	P	650	113
Dordt (A), Sioux Center, IA 51250	1955	B.J. Haan	D	990	50
Dowling, Oakdale, NY 11769	1968	V.P. Meskill	P	2,270	67
Drake Univ., Des Moines, IA 50311	1881	Wilbur C. Miller	P	6,025	344
Drew Univ. (A), Madison, NJ 07940	1866	Paul Hardin	P	2,112	173
Drexel Univ., Philadelphia, PA 19104	1891	William W. Hagerty	P	14,142	630
Drury, Springfield, MO 65802	1873	John Bartholomy	P	2,368	62
Dubuque, Univ. of, Dubuque, IA 52001	1852	Walter F. Peterson	D	1,039	45
Duke Univ., Durham, NC 27706	1838	Terry Sanford	P	*9,900*	*1,385*
Duquesne Univ., Pittsburgh, PA 15219	1878	Fr. Henry J. McAnulty	D	6,825	277
Dyke, Cleveland, OH 44114	1848	John Corfias	P	1,416	74
D'Youville, Buffalo, NY 14201	1908	Sister Denise Roche	P	1,500	90
Earlham, Richmond, IN 47374	1847	Franklin Wallin	D	989	96
East Carolina Univ., Greenville, NC 27834	1907	Dr. Thomas B. Brewer, Chan.	S	*12,874*	*744*
East Central Univ., Ada, OK 74820	1909	Stanley Wagner	S	3,882	193
East Stroudsburg State, E. Stroudsburg, PA 18301	1893	Darrell Holmes	S	3,875	189
East Tennessee State Univ., Johnson City, TN 37601	1911	Arthur H. DeRosier, Jr.	S	*10,195*	*525*
East Texas Baptist, Marshall, TX 75670	1912	Jerry Dawson	D	858	44
East Texas State Univ., Commerce, TX 75428	1889	F.H. McDowell	S	*8,752*	*347*
Eastern, St. Davids, PA 19087	1952	Daniel E. Weiss	D	710	37
Eastern Conn. State, Willimantic, CT 06226	1889	Charles Richard Webb	S	2,700	130
Eastern Illinois Univ., Charleston, IL 61920	1895	Daniel Marvin	S	10,536	429
Eastern Kentucky Univ., Richmond, KY 40475	1906	Julius Powell	S	13,714	650
Eastern Maine Voc. Tech Inst., Bangor, ME 04401	1968	Alan R. Campbell, Dir.	S	1,500	60
Eastern Mennonite, Harrisonburg, VA 22801	1917	Myron S. Augsburger	D	1,042	102
Eastern Michigan Univ. (A), Ypsilanti, MI 48197	1849	James Brickley	S	18,931	752
Eastern Montana, Billings MT 59101	1928	J. Van de Wetering	S	3,415	144
Eastern Nazarene, Quincy, MA 02170	1918	Donald Irwin	D,P	759	51
Eastern New Mexico Univ., Portales, NM 88130	1934	Warren Armstrong	S	3,707	143
Eastern Oregon State, LaGrande, OR 97850	1929	Rodney A. Briggs	S	1,625	84
Eastern Washington State, Cheney, WA 99004	1882	H.G. Frederickson	S	7,729	350
Eckerd, St. Petersburg, FL 33733	1958	Peter Armacost	P	1,060	65
Edgecliff, Cincinnati, OH 45206	1935	Sr. M. Molitor	D	841	42
Edgewood, Madison, WI 53711	1927	Sister Alice O'Rourke	D	630	44
Edinboro State, Edinboro, PA 16444	1857	Foster F. Diebold	S	5,596	384
Edward Waters, Jacksonville, FL 32209	1866	Cecil Wayne Cone	P	703	35
Eisenhower, Seneca Falls, NY 13148	1965	Joseph D. Coffee, Jr.	P	500	51
Elizabeth City State Univ., Eliz. City, NC 27909	1891	Marion Thorpe, Chan.	S	1,560	114

Name, address	Year	Governing official and affiliation		Stu-dents	Teach-ers
Elizabethtown, Elizabethtown, PA 17022	1899	Mark C. Ebersole	D	1,423	98
Elmhurst, Elmhurst, IL 60126	1871	Ivan Frick	P,D	3,031	95
Elmira, Elmira, NY 14901	1855	Leonard Grant	P	2,760	70
Elon, Elon College, NC 27244	1889	J.F. Young	D	2,267	85
Embry Riddle Aero. Univ., Daytona Beach, FL 32014	1926	Jack R. Hunt	P	*7,315*	*280*
Emerson, Boston, MA 02116	1880	Allan Koenig	P	1,814	85
Emmanuel (W), Boston, MA 02115	1919	Sister Janet Eisner, Act.	D	*1,068*	*56*
Emmanuel, Franklin Springs, GA 30639	1919	C.Y. Melton	D	335	23
Emory & Henry, Emory, VA 24327	1836	Thomas F. Chilcote	D	800	55
Emory Univ., Atlanta, GA 30322	1836	James T. Laney	D	*7,346*	*965*
Emporia State, Emporia, KS 66801	1863	John Visser	S	6,200	245
Erskine, Due West, SC 29639	1839	M.S. Bell	D	621	45
Eureka, Eureka, IL 61530	1855	Daniel Gilbert	P	438	32
Evangel, Springfield, MO 65802	1955	Robert Spence	P,D	1,612	65
Evansville, Univ. of, Evansville, IN 47702	1854	Wallace B. Graves	D	*4,898*	*299*
Evergreen State, Olympia, WA 98505	1967	Daniel Evans	S	2,514	130
Fairfield Univ., Fairfield, CT 06430	1942	Rev. Aloysius P. Kelly	P	4,713	171
Fairleigh Dickinson Univ., Rutherford, NJ 07070	1942	Jerome Pollack	P	*19,796*	*1,574*
Fairmont State, Fairmont, WV 26554	1867	Wendell G. Hardway	S	4,848	185
Faith Baptist Bible, Ankeny, IA 50021	1924	David Nettleton	P	526	30
Fayetteville St. Univ., Fayetteville, NC 28301	1877	Charles Lyons Jr.	S	*3,052*	*141*
Felician, Lodi, NJ 07644	1942	Sr. M. Hiltrude Koba	P,D	659	52
Ferris State (A), Big Rapids, MI 49507	1884	Robert Ewigleben	S	9,934	535
Ferrum, Ferrum, VA 24088	1913	Joseph T. Hart	D	1,600	70
Findlay, Findlay, OH 45840	1882	Glen R. Rasmussen	P	1,041	57
Fisk Univ. (A), Nashville, TN 37203	1867	Walter Leonard	P	1,281	79
Fitchburg State, Fitchburg, MA 01420	1894	Vincent J. Mara	S	5,896	208
Flagler, St. Augustine, FL 32084	1967	William L. Proctor	P	750	32
Florida A.&M. Univ.* (A), Tallahassee, FL 32307	1887	Benjamin Luther Perry Jr.	S	5,725	384
Florida Atlantic Univ., Boca Raton, FL 33431	1961	Glenwood L. Creech	S	7,100	300
Florida Inst. of Tech., Melbourne, FL 32901	1958	Jerome P. Keuper	P	*3,899*	*180*
Florida Memorial, Miami, FL 33054	1879	Willie Robinson	Mu	820	40
Florida Southern (A), Lakeland, FL 33802	1885	Robert Davis	D	17,000	90
Florida State Univ., Tallahassee, FL 32306	1857	Bernard Sliger	S	21,531	1,180
Florida Tech. Univ., Orlando, FL 32816	1963	Trevor Colbourn	S	10,605	397
Florida Univ. of*, Gainesville, FL 32611	1853	Robert Marston	S	31,133	2,079
Fontbonne, St. Louis, MO 63105	1917	Sister Jane Hassett	D	781	61
Fordham Univ., Bronx, NY 10458	1841	Rev. James C. Finlay	P	*14,676*	*475*
Ft. Hays State, Hays, KS 67601	1902	Gerald W. Tomanek	S	5,644	268
Ft. Lauderdale, Ft. Lauderdale, FL 33301	1940	Douglas Devaux	P	*1,011*	*40*
Fort Lewis, Durango, CO 81301	1912	Rexer Berndt	S	3,020	145
Fort Valley State*, Fort Valley, GA 31030	1895	Cleveland W. Pettigrew	S	1,727	153
Fort Wayne Bible, Fort Wayne, IN 46807	1904	Timothy Warner	M	522	28
Fort Wright, Spokane, WA 99204	1907	Sr. Katherine Gray	P	405	58
Framingham State, Framingham, MA 01701	1839	D. Justin McCarthy	S	3,125	160
Francis Marion, Florence, SC 29501	1970	Walter D. Smith	S	2,818	104
Franklin (A), Franklin, IN 46131	1834	Edwin A. Penn	P	603	50
Franklin Univ., Columbus, OH 43215	1902	Frederick J. Bunte	P	4,904	201
Franklin and Marshall, Lancaster, PA 17604	1787	Keith Spalding	P	1,986	132
Franklin Pierce, Rindge, NH 03461	1962	Walter Peterson	P	900	55
Freed-Hardeman, Henderson, TN 38340	1869	E. Claude Gardner	D	1,451	70
Free Will Baptist Bible, Nashville, TN 37205	1942	Charles A. Thigpen	D	600	26
Fresno Pacific, Fresno, CA 93702	1944	Edmund Janzen	D	727	44
Friends, Univ., Wichita, KS 67213	1898	Harold C. Cope	P	908	47
Frostburg State, Frostburg, MD 21532	1898	Nelson Guild	S	3,651	189
Furman Univ., Greenville, SC 29613	1826	John Johns	D	2,822	141
Gallaudet (A), Washington, DC 20002	1864	Edward C. Merrill Jr.	P	943	126
Gannon, Erie, PA 16541	1944	Dr. Joseph P. Scottino	D	3,786	122
Gardner-Webb, Boiling Springs, NC 28017	1905	Dr. Craven E. Williams	D	1,450	80
General Motors Inst., Flint, MI 48502	1919	W. Cottingham	P	2,241	148
Geneva, Beaver Falls, PA 15010	1848	Edwin C. Clarke	D	1,291	64
George Fox, Newberg, OR 97132	1891	David Le Shana	D	734	44
George Mason Univ., Fairfax, VA 22030	1956	George W. Johnson	S	*12,249*	*441*
Geo. Washington Univ., Washington, DC 20052	1821	Lloyd H. Elliott	P	11,971	1,063
George Williams, Downers Grove, IL 60515	1890	Richard E. Hamlin	P	1,682	66
Georgetown, Georgetown, KY 40324	1829	Ben M. Elrod	D	1,100	60
Georgetown Univ. (A), Washington, DC 20057	1789	Rev. Timothy Healy	D	11,043	1,013
Georgia, Milledgeville, GA 31061	1889	J. Whitney Bunting	S	3,400	172
Georgia Inst. Of Tech.* (A), Atlanta, GA 30332	1885	Joseph M. Pettit	S	*10,741*	*755*
Georgia Southern, Statesboro, GA 30460	1906	Pope A. Duncan	S	6,725	302
Georgia Southwestern, Americus, GA 31709	1908	William H. Capitan	S	2,101	117
Georgia State Univ., Atlanta, GA 30303	1913	Noah N. Langdale Jr.	S	20,338	856
Georgia, Univ. of*, Athens, GA 30602	1785	Fred C. Davison	S	21,711	1,916
Georgian Court, Lakewood, NJ 08701	1908	Sister Maria Cordis	D	1,258	47
Gettysburg, Gettysburg, PA 17325	1832	Chas. Glassick	D	1,900	135
Glassboro State (A), Glassboro, NJ 08028	1923	Mark Chamberlain	S	10,331	403
Glenville State, Glenville, WV 26351	1872	Wm. Simmons	S	1,640	87
Goddard, Plainfield, VT 05667	1938	John Hall	P	1,400	53
Golden Gate Univ., San Francisco, CA 94105	1901	Otto Butz	P	*9,600*	*300*
Gonzaga Univ., Spokane, WA 99258	1887	Rev. Bernard Coughlin	D	3,340	150
Gordon, Wenham, MA 01984	1889	Richard Gross	P	1,000	55
Goshen, Goshen, IN 46526	1894	J. Lawrence Burkholder	D	1,262	72
Goucher (W), Towson, MD 21204	1885	Rhoda Dorsey	P	1,009	83
Governors State Univ., Park Forest South, IL 60466	1969	L. Goodman-Malamuth II	S	4,403	145
Grace, Winona Lake, IN 46590	1948	Homer Kent	D	804	34
Grace Coll. of the Bible, Omaha, NE 68108	1943	Robert Benton	P,D	458	28
Graceland, Lamoni, IA 50140	1895	Franklin Hough	P	1,343	83
Grambling State Univ., Grambling, LA 71245	1901	Dr. Joseph B. Johnson	S	3,285	211
Grand Canyon, Phoenix, AZ 85061	1949	Bill Williams	D	1,267	52
Grand Valley State, Allendale, MI 49401	1963	Arend D. Lubbers	S	7,065	258
Grand View, Des Moines, IA 50316	1896	Karl F. Langrock	D	1,149	70
Great Falls, Coll. of, Great Falls, MT 59405	1932	Dr. Wm. A. Shields	P,D	1,137	40
Green Mountain, Poultney, VT 05764	1834	James Pollock	P	462	30
Greensboro, Greensboro, NC 27420	1838	H.C. Wilkinson	P	650	32
Greenville, Greenville, IL 62246	1892	Dr. W. Richard Stephens	P	879	68
Grinnell, Grinnell, IA 50112	1846	A. Richard Turner	P	1,243	105

Name, address	Year	Governing official and affiliation		Students	Teachers
Grove City, Grove City, PA 16127	1876	Charles S. MacKenzie	D	2,186	95
Guilford, Greensboro, NC 27410	1837	William R. Rogers	D	1,600	83
Gulf Coast Bible, Houston, TX 77008	1953	John W. Conley	D	351	19
Gustavus Adolphus, St. Peter, MN 56082	1862	Edward Lindell	D,P	2,216	141
Gwynedd-Mercy (A), Gwynedd Valley, PA 19437	1948	Sister Isabelle Keiss	D,P	1,092	113
Hahnemann Medical, Philadelphia, PA 19102	1848	William Likoff	P	1,784	485
Hamilton, Clinton, NY 13323	1812	J.M. Carovano	P	1,600	145
Hamline Univ., St. Paul, MN 55104	1854	Jerry E. Hudson	P	1,666	140
Hampden-Sydney (M), Hampden-Sydney, VA 23943	1776	Josiah Bunting III	P	730	53
Hampton Institute, Hampton, VA 23668	1868	Dr. Wm. R. Harvey	P	3,010	208
Hanover, Hanover, IN 47243	1827	John E. Horner	D,P	901	72
Hardin-Simmons Univ., Abilene, TX 79698	1891	Dr. Jesse C. Fletcher	D	1,830	86
Harding Univ., Searcy, AR 72143	1924	Clinton L. Ganus Jr.	D	*3,250*	*135*
Harris-Stowe State, St. Louis, MO 63103	1857	Henry Givens, Jr.	S	837	31
Hartford, Univ. of, W. Hartford, CT 06117	1957	S. Trachtenberg	P	9,300	240
Hartwick, Oneonta, NY 13820	1928	Philip S. Wilder Jr.	P	1,418	103
Harvard Univ.**, Cambridge, MA 02139	1636	Derek Curtis Bok	P	22,643	3,019
Harvey Mudd, Claremont, CA 91711	1955	D. Kenneth Baker	P	473	53
Hastings, Hastings, NE 68901	1882	Clyde B. Matters	P,D	730	54
Haverford, Haverford, PA 19041	1833	Robert B. Stevens	P	995	60
Hawaii, Univ. of, Honolulu, HI 96822	1907	Fujio Matsuda	S	*67,000*	*4,742*
Heald Engineering (A), San Francisco, CA 94109	1863	James Dietz	P	1,000	70
Heidelberg, Tiffin, OH 44883	1850	Leslie H. Fishel Jr.	P	943	73
Henderson State Univ. (A), Arkadelphia, AR 71923	1890	Martin Garrison	S	*3,333*	*175*
Hendrix, Conway, AR 72032	1876	Roy Schilling, Jr.	D,P	1,004	51
High Point, High Point, NC 27262	1924	Wendell M. Patton	D	1,067	64
Hillsdale, Hillsdale, MI 49242	1844	George C. Roche III	P	1,000	70
Hiram, Hiram, OH 44234	1850	Elmer Jagow	P,D	1,109	77
Hobart & William Smith, Geneva, NY 14456	1822	Allan A. Kuusisto	P	1,793	131
Hofstra Univ., Hempstead, NY 11550	1935	James Shuart	P	5,700	350
Hollins (W), Hollins Coll., VA 24020	1842	Carroll Brewster	P	927	79
Holy Cross (A), Coll. of the, Worcester, MA 01610	1843	Rev. John Brooks	D	2,565	195
Holy Family, Philadelphia, PA 19114	1954	Sister Mary Lillian	D	1,185	38
Holy Names, Oakland, CA 94619	1868	Sister Irene Woodward	D	654	48
Hood (A), Frederick, MD 21701	1893	Martha Church	P,D	1,506	117
Hope, Holland, MI 49423	1862	Gordon Van Wylen	P	2,355	145
Houghton, Houghton, NY 14744	1883	D.R. Chamberlain	D	*1,215*	*80*
Houston Baptist Univ., Houston, TX 77074	1960	William Hinton	P	1,875	95
Houston, Univ. of, Houston, TX 77004	1927	Philip G. Hoffman	S	*40,500*	*1,652*
Downtown College, Houston, TX 77002	1974	Allen Commander (Act. Chan.)	S	4,737	105
Howard Payne Univ., Brownwood, TX 76801	1889	Ralph Phelps Jr.	P	1,150	75
Howard Univ., Washington, DC 20059	1867	James E. Cheek	P	10,709	1,098
Humboldt State Univ., Arcata, CA 95521	1913	Alistair McCrone	S	7,500	400
Huntingdon, Montgomery, AL 36106	1854	Allen Jackson	P	602	55
Huntington, Huntington, IN 46750	1897	E. DeWitt Baker	D	525	35
Huron, Huron, SD 57350	1883	Wendell Jahnke	P	303	26
Husson, Bangor, ME 04401	1898	Delmont Merrill	P	1,299	56
Huston-Tillotson, Austin, TX 78702	1876	John T. King	D	606	34
Idaho, Coll. of, Caldwell, ID 83605	1891	Vacant	P	750	47
Idaho State Univ. (A), Pocatello, ID 83209	1901	Myron Coulter	S	9,843	499
Idaho, Univ. of.*, Moscow, ID 83843	1889	Richard D. Gibb	S	7,931	430
Illinois, Jacksonville, IL 62650	1829	Donald Mundinger	D	800	45
Illinois Benedictine, Lisle, IL 60532	1887	Richard Becker	D	1,663	85
Illinois Coll. of Optometry, Chicago, IL 60616	1872	Alfred Rosenbloom	P	574	65
Illinois Coll. of Pod. Med, Chicago, IL 60610	1912	Vacant	P	646	70
Illinois Inst. of Technology, Chicago, IL 60616	1892	Thomas L. Martin Jr.	P	7,058	280
Illinois State Univ., Normal, IL 61761	1857	Lloyd I. Watkins	S	20,412	1,089
Illinois, Univ. of*, Urbana, IL 61801	1867	Stanley Ikenberry	S	*59,584*	*4,854*
Chicago Circle*, Chicago, IL 60680	1965	Donald Riddle, Chan.	S	20,285	1,500
Medical Center*, Chicago, IL 60680	1896	Joseph Begando, Chan.	S	*4,923*	*729*
Urbana-Champaign*, Urbana, IL 61801	1867	John E. Cribbet, Chan.	S	*34,376*	*2,714*
Illinois Wesleyan Univ., Bloomington, IL 61701	1850	Robert Eckley	P	1,625	122
Immaculata, Immaculata, PA 19345	1920	Sister Marie Antoine	D	752	69
Immaculate Heart, Los Angeles, CA 90027	1916	Nancy Heer	P	701	40
Incarnate Word, San Antonio, TX 78209	1881	Sr. Margaret Slattery	D,P	1,370	77
Indiana Central Univ., Indianapolis, IN 46227	1902	Gene Sease	P,D	3,145	201
Indiana State Univ., Terre Haute, IN 47809	1865	Richard Landini	S	*12,056*	*667*
Indiana Univ., Bloomington, IN 47401	1820	John W. Ryan	S	*76,394*	*3,267*
Indiana Univ. of Pa., Indiana, PA 15705	1875	John Worthern	S	*12,145*	*606*
Insurance, Coll. of., New York, NY 10038	1962	A. Leslie Leonard	P	1,857	230
Inter Amer. Univ. of P.R. San German PR 00753	1912	Ramon A. Cruz	P	32,000	570
Iona (A), New Rochelle, NY 10801	1940	John Driscoll	P,D	4,926	256
Iowa State Univ.*, Ames, IA 50011	1858	W. Robert Parks	S	23,486	1,816
Iowa, Univ. of., Iowa City, IA 52242	1847	Willard L. Boyd	S	23,349	1,502
Iowa Wesleyan, Mt. Pleasant, IA 52641	1842	Louis Haselmayer	P	645	49
Ithaca, Ithaca, NY 14850	1892	James J. Whalen	P	4,738	286
Jackson State Univ. (A), Jackson, MS 39217	1877	John A. Peoples Jr.	S	7,928	882
Jacksonville State Univ., Jacksonville, AL 36265	1883	Ernest Stone	S	7,018	340
Jacksonville Univ., Jacksonville, FL 32211	1934	Frances Bartlett Kinne	P	2,217	149
James Madison Univ., Harrisonburg, VA 22807	1908	Ronald Carrier	S	8,387	419
Jamestown, Jamestown, ND 58401	1883	J.N. Anderson	D	542	37
Jarvis Christian, Hawkins, TX 75765	1912	C.A. Berry	P	569	45
Jersey City State, Jersey City, NJ 07305	1929	William Maxwell	S	8,753	305
John Brown Univ., Siloam Springs, AR 72761	1919	John E. Brown Jr.	P	742	52
John Carroll Univ., Cleveland, OH 44118	1886	Rev. Thomas P. O'Malley	D	4,170	174
John F. Kennedy Univ., Orinda, CA 94563	1954	Robert Fisher	P	1,212	4
John Marshall Law School, Chicago, IL 60604	1899	Fred F. Herzog	P	1,500	80
John Wesley, Owosso, MI 48867	1909	William H. Reid	P	204	16
Johns Hopkins Univ., Baltimore, MD 21218	1876	Steven Muller	P	*9,647*	*1,222*
Johnson C. Smith Univ., Charlotte, NC 28216	1867	Wilbert Greenfield	P	1,473	68
Johnson State, Johnson, VT 05656	1828	E. Elmendorf	S	1,020	62
Johnson & Wales, Providence, RI 02903	1914	Morris J. Gaebe	P	6,000	75
Jones, Jacksonville, FL 32211	1918	Donald C. Jones	P	1,188	20
at Orlando, Orlando, FL 32803	1953	Donald C. Jones	P	*1,332*	*35*
Judson, Elgin, IL 60120	1963	Harm A. Weber	D	486	22

**Oldest college in the United States

Name, address	Year	Governing official and affiliation		Students	Teachers
Judson, Marion, AL 36756	1838	N. McCrummen	D	413	28
Juilliard School, The, New York, NY 10023	1905	Peter Mennin	P	1,000	300
Juniata, Huntingdon, PA 16652	1876	Frederick M. Binder	P	1,140	71
Kalamazoo, Kalamazoo, MI 49007	1833	George N. Rainsford	P	1,450	90
Kan. City Art Inst., Kansas City, MO 64111	1885	John W. Lottes	P	600	47
Kan. City Coll. of Osteop. Med., Kansas City, MO 64124	1916	Rudolph Bremen	P	617	57
Kansas Newman, Wichita, KS 67213	1933	Rev. Roman S. Galiardi	D,P	650	50
Kansas State Univ.*, Manhattan, KS 66506	1863	Duane Acker	S	16,244	1,017
Kansas, Univ. of., Lawrence, KS 66045	1866	Archie R. Dykes, Chan.	S	*25,480*	*1,389*
Kansas Wesleyan, Salina, KS 67401	1896	Daniel Bratton	D	500	40
Kean Coll. of New Jersey, Union, NJ 07083	1855	Nathan Weiss	S	13,800	370
Kearney State, Kearney, NE 68847	1905	Brendan McDonald	S	6,256	238
Keene State, Keene, NH 03431	1909	William E. Whybrew	S	3,375	150
Kendall, Evanston, IL 60201	1934	Andrew Cothran	P	425	28
Kennesaw, Marietta, GA 30061	1963	Horace W. Sturgis	S	4,132	133
Kent State Univ., Kent, OH 44242	1910	Brage Golding	S	*17,800*	*1,050*
Kentucky State Univ.*, Frankfort, KY 40601	1886	W.A. Butts	S	2,195	144
Kentucky, Univ. of*, Lexington, KY 40506	1865	Otis A. Singletary	S	22,489	1,216
Kentucky Wesleyan, Owensboro, KY 42301	1858	Luther W. White III	D	916	50
Kenyon, Gambier, OH 43022	1824	Philip Jordan Jr.	P	1,440	108
Keuka (W), Keuka Park, NY 14478	1890	Elizabeth Woods Shaw	P	549	42
King, Bristol, TN 37620	1867	Donald R. Mitchell	D	221	22
King's, Briarcliff Manor, NY 10510	1938	Robert A. Cook	P,D	862	45
King's, Wilkes-Barre, PA 18711	1946	Rev. Charles Sherrer	D	2,040	131
Kirksville Coll. of Osteop. Med., Kirksville, MO 63501	1894	H.C. Moore	P	490	62
Knox, Galesburg, IL 61401	1837	E. Inman Fox	P	1,042	76
Knoxville, Knoxville, TN 37921	1875	Rutherford Adkins	D	731	54
Kutztown State, Kutztown, PA 19530	1966	Lawrence M. Stratton	S	5,169	265
Lafayette, Easton, PA 18042	1826	David W. Ellis	P	2,000	175
LaGrange, LaGrange, GA 30240	1831	Dr. Charles L. Hagood	D	839	51
Lake Erie (W), Painesville, OH 44077	1856	Charles E.P. Simmons	P	1,010	101
Lake Forest, Lake Forest, IL 60045	1857	Eugene Hotchkiss III	Mu	1,010	83
Lakeland, Sheboygan, WI 53081	1862	Dr. Richard E. Hill	D	530	35
Lake Superior State, Sault Ste. Marie, MI 49783	1946	Kenneth Shouldice	S	2,309	107
Lamar Univ., Beaumont, TX 77710	1923	Dr. C. Robert Kemble	S	*11,951*	*441*
Lambuth, Jackson, TN 38301	1843	James S. Wilder Jr.	D	807	56
Lander, Greenwood, SC 29646	1872	Larry Jackson	S	1,581	83
Lane, Jackson, TN 38301	1882	Herman Stone Jr.	P	670	36
Langston Univ.*, Langston, OK 73050	1897	Dr. Ernest L. Holloway	S	1,046	68
LaRoche, Pittsburgh, PA 15237	1963	Sr. Mary J. Coultas	P	1,283	35
La Salle, Philadelphia, PA 19141	1863	Bro. Patrick Ellis	D	7,000	195
La Verne, La Verne, CA 91750	1891	Armen Sarafian	P	3,800	253
Lawrence Inst. of Tech., Southfield, MI 48075	1932	Richard E. Marburger	P	4,991	220
Lawrence Univ., Appleton, WI 54912	1847	Richard Warch	P	1,200	115
Lebanon Valley, Annville, PA 17003	1866	Frederick P. Sample	D	1,000	85
Lee, Cleveland, TN 37311	1918	Charles Conn	D	1,434	55
Lehigh Univ., Bethlehem, PA 18015	1865	W. Deming Lewis	P	5,326	396
Le Moyne, Syracuse, NY 13214	1946	W. O'Halloran	P	1,838	100
Le Moyne-Owen, Memphis, TN 38126	1870	Walter L. Walker	P	1,100	58
Lenoir-Rhyne (A), Hickory, NC 28601	1891	Albert Anderson	D,P	1,139	96
Lesley (W), Cambridge, MA 02238	1909	Don A. Orton	P	1,650	64
LeTourneau, Longview, TX 75607	1946	Richard H. LeTourneau	P	965	62
Lewis Univ., Romeoville, IL 60441	1930	Dr. Paul A. Whelan	D	2,790	109
Lewis & Clark, Portland, OR 97219	1867	John R. Howard	D	3,030	144
Limestone, Gaffney, SC 29340	1845	Jack Jones Early	P	1,124	33
Lincoln Christian, Lincoln, IL 62656	1944	Robert Phillips	D	636	18
Lincoln Memorial Univ., Harrogate, TN 37752	1897	Frank W. Welch	P	1,085	45
Lincoln Univ. (A), Jefferson City, MO 65101	1866	James Frank	S	2,400	165
Lincoln Univ., Lincoln Univ., PA 19352	1854	Herman Branson	S	1,100	70
Lincoln Univ., San Francisco, CA 94118	1919	E. Barbara Jorss	P	532	69
Lindenwood, St. Charles, MO 63301	1827	Robert Johns	P	*1,700*	*51*
Linfield, McMinnville, OR 97128	1849	Charles Walker	P	1,109	72
Livingston Univ., Livingston, AL 35470	1835	Asa Green	S	1,194	74
Livingstone, Salisbury, NC 28144	1879	F. George Shipman	D,P	921	49
Lock Haven State, Lock Haven, PA 17745	1870	Francis Hamblin	S	2,244	168
Loma Linda Univ., Loma Linda, CA 92354	1905	V. Norskov Olsen	P	*5,283*	*1,680*
Long Island Univ., Brooklyn, NY 11201	1926	Edward Clark	P	7,500	340
C.W. Post, Greenvale, NY 11548	1954	Edward Cook	P	10,803	331
Longwood (A), Farmville, VA 23901	1839	Henry I. Willett Jr.	S	2,320	150
Loras, Dubuque, IA 52001	1839	P. Di Pasquale Jr.	D	1,771	137
Loretto Heights, Denver, CO 80236	1918	F. Adele Phelan	P	820	110
Los Angeles Baptist, Newhall, CA 91322	1927	John Dunkin	D	392	34
Louisiana, Pineville, LA 71360	1906	Robert Lynn	D	1,404	63
Louisiana St. Univ.*, Baton Rouge, LA 70803	1860	Martin Woodin	S	*48,049*	*2,241*
A & M, Baton Rouge, LA 70803	1860	Paul Murrill, Chan.	S	25,000	900
Law Center, Baton Rouge, LA 70803	1906	Dr. William D. Hawkland, Chan.	S	876	27
Medical Center, New Orleans, LA 70112	1931	Allen Copping, Chan.	S	2,391	637
New Orleans Campus (A), New Orleans, LA 70122	1956	Homer L. Hitt, Chan.	S	14,161	461
Shreveport Campus, Shreveport, LA 71115	1965	A.J. Howell, Act. Chan.	S	3,337	122
Louisiana Tech. Univ., Ruston, LA 71272	1894	F. Jay Taylor	S	*9,363*	470
Louisville, Univ. of, Louisville, KY 40929	1798	James G. Miller	S	19,155	1,003
Lowell, Univ. of, Lowell, MA 01854	1894	John B. Duff	S	13,252	825
Loyola, Baltimore, MD 21210	1852	Rev. J.A. Sellinger	D	5,217	120
Loyola Univ., Chicago, IL 60611	1870	Rev. R.C. Baumhart	D	*14,909*	*677*
Loyola Univ., New Orleans, LA 70118	1904	Rev. James Carter	D	4,535	291
Loyola Marymount Univ., Los Angeles, CA 90045	1911	Rev. D.P. Merrifield	D	*6,051*	*221*
Lubbock Christian, Lubbock, TX 79407	1957	H.M. Pruitt	D	1,241	59
Luther, Decorah, IA 52101	1861	Elwin D. Farwell	P	2,014	126
Lycoming, Williamsport, PA 17701	1812	F. Blumer	P	1,071	72
Lynchburg, Lynchburg, VA 24501	1903	Carey Brewer	D	2,412	113
Lyndon State, Lyndonville, VT 05851	1911	Janet Gorman Murphy	S	1,025	59
Macalester, St. Paul, MN 55105	1874	John B. Davis Jr.	M	1,685	127
MacMurray, Jacksonville, IL 62650	1846	John Wittich	D	700	55
Madonna, Livonia, MI 48150	1947	Sr. Mary Francilene	D	3,106	108
Maine Maritime Academy, Castine, ME 04421	1941	E.A. Rodgers, Supt.	S	624	45
Maine System, Univ. of* (A), Bangor, ME 04401	1865	P. McCarthy, Chan.	S	*26,750*	*1,136*
at Augusta, Augusta, ME 04330	1965	Donald W. Beattie	S	3,602	205

Name, address	Year	Governing official and affiliation		Students	Teachers
at Farmington, Farmington, ME 04938	1863	Einar Olsen	S	2,100	83
at Ft. Kent, Ft. Kent, ME 04743	1878	Richard J. Spath	S	650	30
at Machias, Machias, ME 04654	1909	Arthur Buswell	S	729	35
at Orono*, Orono, ME 04469	1865	Kenneth W. Allen, Act.	S	11,574	611
at Portland-Gorham (A), Portland, ME 04103	1878	N.E. Miller	S	*7,602*	*544*
at Presque Isle, Presque Isle, ME 04769	1903	Stanley F. Salwak	S	1,359	52
Malone, Canton, OH 44709	1892	Lon D. Randall	D	772	36
Manchester, N. Manchester, IN 46962	1889	Alfred B. Helman	D	1,152	64
Manhattan, Riverdale, NY 10471	1853	Brother J.S. Sullivan	P	3,973	219
Manhattan Sch. of Music, New York, NY 10027	1917	John O. Crosby	P	650	179
Manhattanville, Purchase, NY 10577	1841	Barbara K. Debs	P	2,130	79
Mankato State Univ., Mankato, MN 56001	1868	Dr. Margaret R. Preska	S	11,801	463
Mannes Coll. of Music, New York, NY 10021	1916	Charles Kaufman	P	550	110
Mansfield State, Mansfield, PA 16933	1857	Janet L. Travis	S	2,581	207
Marian, Indianapolis, IN 46222	1851	Louis C. Gatto	D,P	759	53
Marian Coll. of Fond du Lac, Fond du Lac, WI 54935	1936	Leo V. Krzywkowski	P	450	48
Marietta, Marietta, OH 45750	1835	Sherrill Cleland	P	1,250	98
Marion, Marion, IN 46952	1920	Robert Luckey	D	1,019	57
Marist, Poughkeepsie, NY 12601	1946	Dennis J. Murray	P	2,400	80
Marlboro, Marlboro, VT 05344	1946	Thomas B. Ragle	P	222	35
Marquette Univ., Milwaukee, WI 53233	1881	Rev. J.P. Raynor	P	13,932	535
Mars Hill, Mars Hill, NC 28754	1856	Fred Blake Bentley	P	1,808	100
Marshall Univ., Huntington, WV 25701	1837	Robert B. Hayes	S	11,144	381
Mary Baldwin, Staunton, VA 24401	1842	Virginia Lester	D	817	60
Mary Hardin Baylor, Univ. of, Belton, TX 76513	1845	Bobby E. Parker	D	1,077	65
Mary Washington, Fredericksburg, VA 22401	1908	Prince B. Woodard	S	2,292	130
Marycrest, Davenport, IA 52804	1939	Ron Van Ryswyk	D	1,300	90
Marygrove, Detroit, MI 48221	1910	Wade Ellis, Act.	M,D	668	48
Maryland Inst. of Art, Baltimore, MD 21217	1826	Fred Lazarus IV	P	1,650	169
Maryland, Univ. of*, Adelphi, MD 20783	1807	John S. Toll	S	76,209	6,026
Eastern Shore, Princess Anne, MD 21853	1881	William P. Hytche, Chan.	S	1,200	89
Marylhurst, Marylhurst, OR 97036	1893	Sr. V.A. Baxter	P	740	22
Marymount (W)., Tarrytown, NY 10591	1907	Robert Christin	P	978	63
Marymount Coll. of Ks., Salina, KS 67401	1922	Sr. Mary Buser	P	787	45
Marymount Coll. of Va., Arlington, VA 22207	1950	Sr. M. Majella Berg	F	1,020	60
Marymount Manhattan, New York, NY 10021	1961	Colette Mahoney	P	2,300	48
Maryville (A), Maryville, TN 37801	1819	Wayne Anderson	D,P	580	50
Maryville, St. Louis, MO 63141	1872	C. Pritchard	P	1,351	58
Marywood (W), Scranton, PA 18509	1915	Sister M. Coleman Nee	D	3,020	143
Massachusetts Coll. Of Art, Boston, MA 02215	1873	John Nolan	S	3,040	64
Mass. Coll. of Pharmacy, Boston, MA 02115	1823	Raymond A. Gosselin	P	*1,250*	*77*
Mass. Institute of Tech.* (A), Cambridge, MA 02139	1861	Jerome Wiesner	P	7,972	972
Mass. Maritime Academy, Buzzards Bay, MA 02532	1891	Lee Harrington	S	864	75
Massachusetts, Univ. of*, Boston, MA 02108	1863	Robert C. Wood	S	*31,905*	*1,859*
Amherst Campus, Amherst, MA 01003	1863	Henry Koffler, Chan.	S	24,900	1,500
Harbor Campus, Boston, MA 02125	1965	Robert A. Corrigan, Chan.	S	6,600	500
Mayville State, Mayville, ND 58257	1889	James Schobel	S	746	49
McKendree, Lebanon, IL 62254	1828	Adolph Unruh	D	747	45
McMurry, Abilene, TX 79605	1923	Tom K. Kim	D	1,327	56
McNeese State Univ., Lake Charles, LA 70609	1939	Thomas S. Leary	S	4,912	263
McPherson, McPherson, KS 67460	1887	Paul Hoffman	P	480	37
Medaille, Buffalo, NY 14214	1937	Dr. Leo R. Downey	P	636	37
Medical Coll. of Ga. (A), Augusta, GA 30902	1828	William Moretz	S	2,224	440
Medical Coll. of Pa. (A), Philadelphia, PA 19129	1850	Robert J. Slater	P	836	423
Medical Univ. of S.C. (A), Charleston, SC 29401	1824	William McCord	S	2,020	630
Med. & Dentistry of NJ, Newark, NJ 07103	1956	S.S. Bergen Jr.	S	*1,340*	*612*
Meharry Medical, Nashville, TN 37208	1876	Lloyd C. Elam	P	1,038	335
Memphis Acad. of Arts, Memphis, TN 38112	1936	Jameson M. Jones	P	219	17
Memphis State Univ., Memphis, TN 38152	1912	Jerry Boone, Act.	S	21,248	757
Menlo, Menlo Park, CA 94025	1927	Richard O'Brien	P	617	60
Mercer Univ., Macon, GA 31207	1833	R. Kirk Godsey	P	*4,527*	*250*
Mercy, Dobbs Ferry, NY 10522	1950	Donald Grunewald	P	*8,147*	*139*
Mercy Coll. of Detroit, Detroit, MI 48219	1941	Sister Agnes Mary Mansour	P	2,376	120
Mercyhurst (A), Erie, PA 16501	1926	Marion Shane	P	1,426	104
Meredith (W) Raleigh, NC 27611	1891	John Edgar Weems	D	1,463	72
Merrimack, No. Andover, MA 01845	1947	Rev. John A. Coughlan	D	3,288	175
Mesa, Grand Junction, CO 81501	1925	John Tomlinson	S	3,900	109
Messiah, Grantham, PA 17027	1909	D. Ray Hostetter	P	*1,200*	*61*
Methodist, Fayetteville, NC 28301	1956	Richard Pearce	D	843	44
Metropolitan State, Denver, CO 80204	1963	Donald J. MacIntyre	S	12,351	279
Miami Univ., Oxford, OH 45056	1809	Phillip R. Shriver	S	*18,000*	*800*
Miami, Univ. of, Coral Gables, FL 33124	1925	Henry K. Stanford	P	*18,489*	*1,187*
Michigan State Univ., East Lansing, MI 48824	1855	Cecil Mackey	S	44,576	3,514
Michigan Tech Univ., Houghton, MI 49931	1885	Dale F. Stein	S	7,371	52
Michigan, Univ. of, Ann Arbor, MI 48109	1817	Harold T. Shapiro	S	*46,680*	*2,462*
Mid-America Nazarene, Olathe, KS 66061	1966	R. Curtis Smith	D	1,292	60
Middle Tenn. State Univ., Murfreesboro, TN 37132	1911	Sam H. Ingram	S	10,880	430
Middlebury, Middlebury, VT 05753	1800	Olin Robinson	P	1,870	145
Midland Lutheran, Fremont, NE 68025	1883	L. Dale Lund	D	802	60
Midwestern State Univ., Wichita Falls, TX 76308	1922	John Barker	S	4,222	140
Miles, Birmingham, AL 35208	1905	W. Clyde Williams	P	1,058	69
Millersville State, Millersville, PA 17551	1855	William Duncan	S	4,400	350
Milligan, Milligan Coll., TN 37682	1881	Jess W. Johnson	D	772	48
Millikin Univ., Decatur, IL 62522	1901	J. Roger Miller	D	1,568	128
Mills (W), Oakland, CA 94613	1852	Barbara White	P	973	87
Millsaps, Jackson, MS 39210	1890	George M. Harmon	D	972	57
Milton, Milton, WI 53563	1844	Ronald J. Dickman	P	540	35
Milwaukee Sch. of Eng., Milwaukee, WI 53201	1903	Robert R. Spitzer	P	2,564	133
Mpls. Coll. of Art & Design, Minneapolis, MN 55404	1886	Jerome J. Hausman	P	600	42
Minnesota, Univ. of*, Minneapolis, MN 55414	1851	C.P. Magrath	S	*74,203*	9,386
Duluth Campus*, Duluth, MN 55812	1902	Robt. Heller(Prov.)	S	9,060	575
Morris Campus*, Morris, MN 56267	1959	John Imholte (Prov.)	S	1,743	82
Minot State, Minot, ND 58701	1913	Gordon Olson	S	2,100	110
Misericordia, Dallas, PA 18612	1924	Joseph R. Fink	P	835	67
Mississippi, Clinton, MS 39058	1826	Lewis Nobles	P	3,110	115
Mississippi Industrial (A), Holly Springs, MS 38635	1905	E.E. Rankin	D,P	400	24
Miss. Univ. for Women (W), Columbus, MS 39701	1884	James Strobel	S	2,307	161
Mississippi State Univ.*, Miss. State, MS 39762	1878	James McComas	S	12,000	802

Name, address	Year	Governing official and affiliation		Students	Teachers
Mississippi, Univ. of, University, MS 38677	1848	P.L. Fortune Jr., Chan.	S	*11,987*	*805*
Mississippi Valley State Univ. (A), Itta Bena, MS 38941	1950	E.A. Boykins	S	3,228	140
Missouri Baptist, St. Louis, MO 63141	1968	R. Sutherland	D	434	22
Missouri Inst. of Tech., Kansas City, MO 64114	1931	C.R. LeValley	P	953	19
Missouri Southern State, Joplin, MO 64801	1938	Donald C. Darnton	S	3,900	175
Missouri, Univ. of*, Columbia, MO 65211	1839	James Olson	S	*51,829*	*2,183*
at Columbia*, Columbia, MO 65211	1839	Barbara Uehling, Chan.	S	23,545	1,065
at Kansas City*, Kansas City, MO 64110	1933	George Russell, Chan.	S	10,824	480
at Rolla*, Rolla, MO 65401	1870	James M. Marchello, Chan.	S	6,103	296
at St. Louis*, St. Louis, MO 63121	1963	A. Grobman, Chan.	S	11,357	342
Missouri Valley, Marshall, MO 65340	1889	Alton E. Harris, Act.	P	343	29
Missouri Western State, St. Joseph, MO 64507	1915	Marvin Looney	S	3,777	182
Mobile, Mobile, AL 36613	1963	William K. Weaver Jr.	D	1,044	52
Molloy, Rockville Ctre, NY 11580	1955	Sister Janet Fitzgerald	D	1,527	111
Monmouth, Monmouth, IL 61462	1853	Bruce Haywood	P	650	50
Monmouth, W. Long Branch, NJ 07764	1933	Samuel H. Magill	P	2,848	200
Montana Coll. of Mineral Science & Tech., Butte, MT 59701	1893	Fred W. DeMoney	S	1,393	65
Montana State Univ., Bozeman, MT 59717	1893	Wm. Tietz Jr.	S	9,920	498
Montana, Univ. of, Missoula, MT 59812	1893	Richard Bowers	S	8,574	400
Montclair State, Upper Montclair, NJ 07043	1908	David W.D. Dickson	S	15,000	489
Monterey Inst. of International Studies, Monterey, CA 93940	1955	Jack Kolbert	P	470	29
Montevallo, Univ. of, Montevallo, AL 35115	1896	James Vickrey	S	2,812	149
Moody Bible Institute, Chicago, IL 60610	1886	George Sweeting	P	3,313	88
Moore Coll. of Art (W), Philadelphia, PA 19103	1844	H.J. Burgart	P	959	77
Moorhead State, Moorhead, MN 56560	1887	Roland Dille	S	6,998	332
Moravian, Bethlehem, PA 18018	1742	Herman E. Collier Jr.	D	1,786	85
Morehead State Univ , Morehead, KY 40351	1922	Morris Norfleet	S	7,029	294
Morehouse (M), Atlanta, GA 30314	1867	Hugh Gloster	P	1,678	105
Morgan State, Baltimore, MD 21239	1867	Andrew Billingsley	S	5,294	276
Morningside, Sioux City, IA 51106	1894	Miles Tommeraasen	P	1,365	70
Morris, Sumter, SC 29150	1908	Luns C. Richardson	D,P	626	48
Morris Brown, Atlanta, GA 30314	1881	Robert Threatt	D	1,660	119
Morris Harvey, Charleston, WV 25304	1888	Thomas Voss	P	2,156	80
Mount Holyoke (W), S. Hadley, MA 01075	1837	Elizabeth Kennan	P	1,850	168
Mt. Marty, Yankton, SD 57078	1936	William Tucker	D	590	55
Mt. Mary (W), Milwaukee, WI 53222	1913	Sister Ellen Lorenz	D	1,126	80
Mt. Mercy, Cedar Rapids, IA 52402	1928	Thomas R. Feld	D	1,052	52
Mt. St. Clare, Clinton, IA 52732	1918	Dan C. Johnson	D	322	7
Mt. St. Joseph (W), Mt. St. Joseph, OH 45051	1920	Jean Patrice Harrington	P	1,355	55
Mt. St. Mary, Newburgh, NY 12550	1959	Sr. Ann Sakac	P	1,046	56
Mt. St. Mary's, Los Angeles, CA 90049	1925	Sr. Magdalen Coughlin	D	*1,108*	*74*
Mt. St. Mary's, Emmitsburg, MD 21727	1808	Robt. Wickenheiser	D,P	1,352	70
Mt. St. Vincent, Coll. of, Riverdale, NY 10471	1847	Sister Doris Smith	P	1,274	101
Mt. Senario, Ladysmith, WI 54848	1962	Robert E. Lovett	P	478	30
Mt. Union, Alliance, OH 44601	1846	Ronald Weber	D	1,067	74
Mt. Vernon, Washington, DC 20007	1875	Victoria Schuck	P	2,500	32
Mt. Vernon Nazarene, Mount Vernon, OH 43050	1968	L. Guy Nees	D	1,005	51
Muhlenberg, Allentown, PA 18104	1848	John H. Morey	D	1,940	150
Multnomah Sch. of the Bible, Portland, OR 97220	1936	Joseph C. Aldrich	P	712	40
Mundelein, Chicago, IL 60660	1929	Sr. Susan Rink	D	1,500	83
Murray State Univ., Murray, KY 42071	1923	C. Curris	S	*8,158*	*360*
Muskingum, New Concord, OH 43762	1837	Arthur J. DeJong	P	850	68
Nasson, Springvale, ME 04083	1912	William Cole	P	500	42
Nathaniel Hawthorne, Antrim, NH 03440	1962	Kenneth F. McLaughlin	P	1,200	50
National Coll. of Business, Rapid City, SD 57709	1941	John Hauer	P	1,128	30
National Coll. of Chiropractic, Lombard, IL 60148	1906	Joseph Janse	P	1,008	70
National Coll. of Education, Evanston, IL 60201	1886	Orley R. Herron	P	*3,524*	*57*
Nazareth Coll. at Kalamazoo, Nazareth, MI 49074	1924	John E. Hopkins	D	540	59
Nazareth Coll. of Rochester, Rochester, NY 14610	1924	Robert Kidera	P	2,594	174
Nebraska, Univ. of*, Lincoln, NE 68583	1869	Roy A. Young, Chan.	S	22,755	1,250
at Omaha, Omaha, NE 68182	1908	D. Weber, Chan.	S	15,000	500
Nebraska Wesleyan Univ., Lincoln, NE 68504	1887	John White Jr.	P	1,189	80
Nevada, Univ. of*, Reno, NV 89557	1864	Joseph Crowley	S	8,642	335
at Las Vegas, Las Vegas, NV 89154	1957	Leonard E. Goodall	S	9,164	294
Newberry, Newberry, SC 29108	1856	Glen E. Whitesides	P	883	52
New England, Henniker, NH 03242	1946	J.K. Cummiskey	P	*1,770*	*141*
New England Cons. of Music, Boston, MA 02115	1867	J.S. Ballinger	P	750	145
New Hampshire, Manchester, NH 03104	1932	Edward Shapiro	P	4,200	115
New Hampshire, Univ. of*, Durham, NH 03824	1963	Evelyn E. Handler	S	11,666	494
New Haven, Univ. of*, New Haven, CT 06516	1920	Phillip Kaplan	P	7,000	149
New Jersey Inst. of Tech., Newark, NJ 07102	1881	Saul K. Fenster	S	6,021	270
New Mexico Highlands Univ., Las Vegas, NM 87701	1893	John Aragon	S	2,000	150
N. Mexico Inst. of Min. & Tech., Socorro, NM 87801	1889	Kenneth Ford	S	1,100	80
New Mexico State Univ.*, Las Cruces, NM 88003	1888	Gerald W. Thomas	S	*15,095*	*601*
New Mexico, Univ. of*, Albuquerque, NM 87131	1889	William Davis	S	23,500	988
New Orleans, Univ. of, New Orleans, LA 70122	1958	Homer Hitt, Chan.	S	14,431	459
Newport-Salve Regina, Newport, RI 02840	1947	Lucille McKillop	D	1,700	120
New Rochelle, Coll. of (W), New Rochelle, NY 10801	1904	Sister Dorothy Ann Kelly	P	*4,613*	*90*
New School for Soc. Research, New York, NY 10011	1919	John R. Everett	P	25,000	1,500
New York City, Univ. of, New York, NY 10021	1847	Robert J. Kibbee, Chan.	Mu	*164,398*	*6,764*
Bernard M. Baruch, New York, NY 10010	1919	Joel Segall	Mu,S	11,813	431
Brooklyn, Brooklyn, NY 11210	1930	Robert L. Hess	Mu	14,627	959
City, New York, NY 10031	1847	Arthur Tiedemann, Act.	Mu	12,000	720
Medgar Evers, Brooklyn, NY 11225	1969	Richard D. Trent	Mu	3,014	107
Hunter, New York, NY 10021	1870	Donna E. Shalala	Mu	17,989	1,246
John Jay Coll. of Criminal Just., New York, NY 10019	1964	Gerald Lynch	Mu,S	6,394	260
Herbert H. Lehman, Bronx, NY 10468	1931	Leonard Lief	Mu	9,521	487
Queens, Flushing, NY 11367	1937	Saul B. Cohen	Mu	17,458	783
Staten Island, Staten Island, NY 10301	1976	Edmond Volpe	Mu,S	10,500	400
York, Jamaica, NY 11451	1966	Milton G. Bassin	Mu,S	3,293	184
N.Y. Inst. of Technology, Old Westbury, NY 11568	1955	Alexander Schure	P	*14,000*	*200*
New York Law School, New York, NY 10013	1891	E. Donald Shapiro, Dean	P	1,236	166
New York Medical, Valhalla, NY 10590	1860	Joseph A. Cimino	P	756	560
New York, State Univ. of, Albany, NY 12210	1948	C.R. Wharton Jr., Chan.	S	*348,361*	*14,138*
State Univ., Albany, NY 12222	1844	V.J. O'Leary	S	15,391	654
" " Buffalo, NY 14214	1846	Robert Ketter	S	*25,000*	*1,450*
" " Binghamton, NY 13901	1946	Clifford D. Clark	S	10,636	477
" " Stony Brook, NY 11790	1957	Richard F. Schmidt, Act.	S	16,000	1,200

Name, address	Year	Governing official and affiliation		Students	Teachers
State Univ. Colleges, Brockport, NY 14420	1867	Albert W. Brown	S	9,000	450
" " Buffalo, NY 14222	1867	D. Bruce Johnstone	S	10,909	499
" " Cortland, NY 13045	1866	James M. Clark	S	5,875	296
" " Fredonia, NY 14063	1867	Dallas K. Beal	S	5,262	264
" " Geneseo, NY 14454	1867	E. B. Jakubauskas	S	5,551	316
" " New Paltz, NY 12561	1885	Alice Chandler	S	4,982	350
" " Oneonta, NY 13820	1887	Clifford Craven	S	6,204	337
" " Oswego, NY 13126	1861	Virginia Radley	S	7,283	413
" " Old Westbury, NY 11568	1965	John Maguire	S	2,850	125
" " Plattsburgh, NY 12901	1889	Joseph C. Burke	S	6,155	302
" " Potsdam, NY 13676	1867	James H. Young	S	4,682	291
" " Purchase, NY, 10577	1965	Michael Hammond	S	3,241	131
" " College of Tech., Utica, NY 13502	1966	William Kunsela	S	3,100	70
" " Empire State, Saratoga Spgs., NY 12866	1971	James Hall	S	3,300	120
Agri. & Tech. Coll., Farmingdale, NY 11735	1948	Frank A. Cipriani	S	13,591	400
Buffalo Health Sciences Ctr., Buffalo, NY 14214	1846	F.C. Pannill, V.P.	S	2,968	354
College of Ceramics, Alfred, NY 14802	1900	W.G. Lawrence, Dean	S	680	40
Env'm't'l. Sci. & Forestry, Syracuse, NY 13210	1911	Edward Palmer	S	1,891	107
Downstate Medical Center, Brooklyn, NY 11203	1858	Stanley L. Lee, Act.	S	1,446	717
Health Sciences Center, Stony Brook, NY 11790	1957	James H. Oaks, V.P.	S	1,329	175
Maritime, Bronx, NY 10465	1874	Sheldon Kinney	S	1,100	70
Upstate Medical Center, Syracuse, NY 13210	1834	Richard P. Schmidt	S	878	274
New York Univ., New York, NY 10012	1831	John Sawhill	P	32,537	5,300
Niagara Univ., Niagara Univ., NY 14109	1856	V. Rev. G. Mahoney	D	4,565	165
Nicholls State Univ., Thibodaux, LA 70301	1948	Vernon Galliano	S	7,016	226
Nichols, Dudley, MA 01570	1815	Lowell Smith	P	960	33
Norfolk State, Norfolk, VA 23540	1935	Lyman Brooks	S	6,260	405
North Adams State, North Adams, MA 01247	1894	William P Hass	S	2,800	148
North Carolina Central U., Durham, NC 27707	1910	A. Whiting, Chan.	S	4,810	340
North Carolina, Univ. of (A), Chapel Hill, NC 27514	1972	William Friday	S	*104,786*	*6,325*
A&T State Univ., Greensboro, NC 27411	1891	Lewis Dowdy, Chan.	S	5,385	340
at Asheville, Asheville, NC 28814	1927	William Highsmith, Chan.	S	1,893	76
at Chapel Hill (A), Chapel Hill, NC 27514	1776	N.F. Taylor, Chan.	S	20,293	1,730
at Charlotte, Charlotte, NC 28223	1946	E.K. Fretwell, Jr., Chan.	S	8,945	417
at Greensboro, Greensboro, NC 27412	1892	William E. Moran, Chan.	S	9,925	541
at Wilmington, Wilmington, NC 28406	1947	Wm. H. Wagoner, Chan.	S	4,300	250
N.C. School of the Arts, Winston-Salem, NC 27107	1965	R. Suderburg, Chan.	S	650	75
N.C. State Univ. at Raleigh, NC 27650	1887	Joab Thomas	S	18,300	1,235
North Carolina Wesleyan, Rocky Mount, NC 27801	1956	S. Bruce Petteway	P	850	45
North Central Bible, Minneapolis, MN 55404	1930	E.M. Clark	P	607	25
North Central, Naperville, IL 60540	1861	Gael D. Swing	D	1,111	52
North Dakota State Univ. (A), Fargo, ND 58102	1890	L.D. Loftsgard	S	*6,600*	*475*
North Dakota, Univ. of*, Grand Forks, ND 58202	1883	Thomas Clifford	S	9,708	584
North Florida, Univ. of, Jacksonville, FL 32216	1965	Thos. Carpenter	S	4,039	205
North Georgia, Dahlonega, GA 30533	1873	John H. Owen	S	1,850	100
North Park, Chicago, IL 60625	1891	Lloyd Ahlem	D	1,092	77
North Texas State Univ., Denton, TX 76203	1890	C.C. Nolen	S	17,300	729
Northeast Louisiana Univ., Monroe, LA 71209	1931	Dwight Vines	S	9,175	312
Northeast Missouri State Univ., Kirksville, MO 63501	1867	Charles T. McClain	S	5,659	276
Northeastern Illinois Univ., Chicago, IL 60625	1867	Ronald Williams	S	10,061	480
Northeastern Okla. State (A), Tahlequah, OK 74464	1909	Robert Collier	S	5,469	226
Northeastern Univ., Boston, MA 02115	1898	Kenneth Ryder	P	*42,437*	*739*
Northern Arizona Univ., Flagstaff, AZ 86011	1899	Eugene M. Hughes	S	12,300	520
Northern Colorado, Univ. of, Greeley, CO 80639	1890	Richard R. Bond	S	10,794	620
Northern Illinois Univ., DeKalb, Il 60115	1899	Wm. Monat	S	25,259	1,011
Northern Iowa, Univ. of, Cedar Falls, IA 50613	1876	John Kamerick	S	11,056	569
Northern Kentucky Univ., Highland Hts., KY 41076	1968	A.D. Albright	S	7,032	200
Northern Michigan Univ., Marquette, MI 49855	1899	John X. Jamrich	S	9,171	350
Northern Montana, Havre, MT 59501	1929	James H.M. Erickson	S	1,233	69
Northern State, Aberdeen, SD 57401	1901	Joseph McFadden	S	2,459	115
Northland, Ashland, WI 54806	1892	Malcolm McLean	D	700	46
Northrop Univ., Inglewood, CA 90306	1942	B.J. Shell	P	2,200	123
Northwest Bible, Minot, ND 58701	1934	Laud Vaught	D	212	11
Northwest Christian, Eugene, OR 97401	1895	William E. Hays	D	247	14
Northwest Col. of the Assemblies of God, Kirkland, WA 98033	1934	D.V. Hurst	D	787	21
Northwest Missouri State Univ., Maryville, MO 64468	1905	B.D. Owens	S	4,400	250
Northwest Nazarene, Nampa, ID 83651	1913	Kenneth Pearsall	D	1,332	52
Northwestern, Orange City, IA 51041	1882	Friedhelm Radandt, Act.	P	802	52
Northwestern State Univ., Natchitoches, LA 71457	1884	René Bienvenu	S	*6,358*	*283*
Northwestern Okla. St. Univ., Alva, OK 73717	1897	Joe Struckle	S	2,160	76
Northwestern Univ., Evanston, IL 60201	1851	Robert Henry Strotz	P	*15,117*	*1,309*
Norwich Univ., Northfield, VT 05663	1819	Loring Hart	P	*1,913*	*57*
Northwood Inst., Midland, MI 48640	1959	T.J. Brown, Chan.	P	*2,400*	*80*
Notre Dame, Coll of, Belmont, CA 94002	1851	Sr. Catharine Cunningham	D	1,368	63
Notre Dame, Manchester, NH 03104	1950	Sr. Jeannette Vezeau	D	700	70
Notre Dame Coll. of Oh (W), Cleveland, OH 44121	1922	Sister Mary Marthe Reinhard	D	600	34
Notre Dame of Maryland, Baltimore, MD 21210	1873	Sister Kathleen Feeley	D	507	54
Notre Dame, Univ. of, Notre Dame, IN 46556	1842	Rev. T.M. Hesburgh	D	8,768	680
Nova Univ., Ft. Lauderdale, FL 33314	1964	Abraham Fischler	P	*8,171*	*125*
Nyack, Nyack, NY 10960	1882	Thomas Bailey	D,P	823	78
Oakland City, Oakland City, IN 47660	1885	J.W. Murray	D	520	30
Oakland Univ., Rochester, MI 48063	1957	George T. Matthews	S	11,729	450
Oakwood, Huntsville, AL 35806	1896	C.B. Rock	D	1,300	64
Oberlin, Oberlin, OH 44074	1833	E. Danenberg	P	2,750	226
Occidental, Los Angeles, CA 90041	1887	Richard C. Gilman	P	1,652	125
Oglethorpe Univ., Atlanta, GA 30319	1835	Manning Pattillo Jr.	P	864	32
Ohio Dominican, Columbus, OH 43219	1911	Sister M. Andrew Matesich	D	849	45
Ohio Coll. of Podiatric Med., Cleveland, OH 44106	1916	Abe Rubin	P	585	28
Ohio Inst. of Technology, Columbus, OH 43209	1952	Richard A. Czerniak	P	2,978	102
Ohio Northern Univ., Ada, OH 45810	1871	R.B. Loeschner	P	2,661	160
Ohio State Univ.*, Columbus, OH 43210	1870	Harold L. Enarson	S	*54,579*	*3,533*
Ohio Univ., Athens, OH 45701	1804	Charles J. Ping	S	19,154	797
Ohio Wesleyan Univ., Delaware, OH 43015	1842	Thomas Wenzlau	D,P	2,214	167
Oklahoma Baptist Univ., Shawnee, OK 74801	1910	E. Eugene Hall	D,P	1,531	100
Oklahoma Christian, Oklahoma City, OK 73111	1950	J. Johnson	P	1,635	49
Oklahoma City Southwestern, Oklahoma City, OK 73127	1946	Scott T. Muse, Jr.	D,P	693	25
Oklahoma City Univ., Oklahoma City, OK 73106	1904	Jerald C. Walker	D	2,335	86
Okla. Coll. of Liberal Arts (A), Chickasha, OK 73018	1908	Roy Troutt	S	1,200	58

Name, address	Year	Governing official and affiliation		Students	Teachers
Oklahoma Panhandle St. Univ. (A), Goodwell, OK 73939	1909	Thomas L. Palmer	S	1,115	74
Oklahoma State Univ.*, Stillwater, OK 74074	1890	Lawrence Boger	S	*22,003*	*1,041*
Oklahoma, Univ. of, Norman, OK 73019	1890	William S. Banowsky	S	*21,090*	*756*
Okla. Univ. of Science & Arts, Chickasha, OK 73018	1908	Roy Troutt	S	1,344	53
Old Dominion Univ., Norfolk, VA 23508	1930	A.B. Rollins Jr.	S	14,647	583
Olivet, Olivet, MI 49076	1844	Donald A. Morris	P,D	630	48
Olivet Nazarene, Kankakee, IL 60901	1907	Leslie Parrott	P,D	2,002	96
Oral Roberts Univ., Tulsa, OK 74171	1963	Granville Oral Roberts	P	3,800	300
Orangeburg-Calhoun Tech (A), Orangeburg, SC 29115	1968	M. Rudy Groomes	S	1,400	51
Oregon College of Educ., Monmouth, OR 97361	1856	G. Leinwand	S	3,200	175
Oregon Inst. of Tech., Klamath Falls, OR 97601	1947	Kenneth Light	S	2,450	135
Oregon State Univ.*, Corvallis, OR 97331	1868	R. MacVicar	S	16,666	1,582
Oregon, Univ. of, Eugene, OR 97403	1876	William Boyd	S	16,916	1200
Osteopathic Med. & Sur., Coll. of, Des Moines, IA 50312	1898	J.L. Azneer	P	539	50
Otis Art Inst., Los Angeles, CA 90057	1918	Peter Clothier, Act. Dir.	C	460	19
Ottawa Univ., Ottawa, KS 66067	1865	Robert Shaw	D	*535*	*52*
Otterbein, Westerville, OH 43081	1847	Thomas Jefferson Kerr	P	1,687	88
Ouachita Baptist Univ., Arkadelphia, AR 71923	1886	Daniel R. Grant	D	1,614	96
Our Lady of Angels, Aston, PA 19014	1965	Sr. Marie Cunningham	D	668	31
Our Lady of Elms, Col. of (W), Chicopee, MA 01013	1928	Sr. Mary Dooley	D	514	48
Our Lady of the Lake Univ., San Antonio, TX 78285	1911	Sr. Eliz. Sueltenfuss	P	1,744	95
Ozarks, Coll. of the, Clarksville, AR 72830	1834	J. Robert Campbell, Act.	P	564	30
Ozarks, School of the, Pt. Lookout, MO 65726	1906	M. Graham Clark	P	1,200	81
Pace Univ., New York, NY 10038	1906	Edward J. Mortola	P	*21,523*	*373*
Pacific Christian, Fullerton, CA 92631	1928	Medford Jones	D,P	600	20
Pacific Lutheran Univ., Tacoma, WA 98447	1890	William Rieke	P	3,376	202
Pacific States Univ., Los Angeles, CA 90006	1928	Steven Kase	P	700	25
Pacific Union, Angwin, CA 94508	1882	J.W. Cassel, Jr.	D,P	2,000	126
Pacific Univ., Forest Grove, OR 97116	1849	James Miller	P	1,100	76
Pacific, Univ. of the, Stockton, CA 95211	1851	Stanley McCaffrey	P	5,900	367
Paine, Augusta, GA 30910	1882	J.S. Scott Jr.	D,P	750	60
Palm Beach Atlantic, W. Palm Beach, FL 33401	1968	George Borders	D	576	28
Pan American Univ. (A), Edinburg, TX 78539	1927	Ralph Schilling	S	*7,183*	*321*
Park, Parkville, MO 64152	1875	Harold Condit	D	*868*	*44*
Parsons School of Design (A), New York, NY 10011	1896	John R. Everett	P	3,000	250
Paul Quinn, Waco, TX 76704	1872	William D. Watley	D,P	381	31
Peabody Cons. of Music, Baltimore, MD 21202	1857	Elliott W. Galkin	P	527	48
Pembroke St. Univ., Pembroke, NC 28372	1887	English E. Jones	S	2,158	125
Penn Col. of Optometry (A), Philadelphia, PA 19141	1919	Norman F. Wallis	P	545	90
Penn. Col. of Podiatric Med., Phila., PA 19107	1963	James Bates	P	451	34
Penn., Medical Col. of, Philadelphia, PA 19129	1850	Maurice Clifford	P	425	213
Penn. State Univ.*, University Park, PA 16802	1855	John W. Oswald	S	*59,541*	*2,613*
Pennsylvania, Univ. of, Philadelphia, PA 19104	1740	Martin Meyerson	P	18,500	3,000
Pepperdine Univ., Malibu, CA 90265	1937	Howard A. White	P	*7,298*	*427*
Peru State, Peru, NE 68421	1867	Larry Tangeman	S	765	52
Pfeiffer, Misenheimer, NC 28109	1885	Cameron West	D	844	52
Phila. College of Art, Philadelphia, PA 19102	1876	Thomas Schutte	P	1,138	73
Phila. Coll. of Bible, Langhorne, PA 19047	1913	W. Sherrill Babb	P	526	29
Phila. Coll. of Osteopathic Med., Philadelphia, PA 19131	1899	Thomas Rowland Jr.	P	822	94
Phila. Coll. of Pharm. & Science, Philadelphia, PA 19104	1821	William Thawley, Act.	P	1,100	68
Phila. Coll. of Textiles & Science, Philadelphia, PA 19144	1884	D.B. Partridge	P	2,600	85
Philander Smith, Little Rock, AR 72203	1877	Walter Hazzard	D,P	631	38
Phillips Univ., Enid, OK 73701	1907	Samuel Curl	P	1,439	78
Piedmont, Demorest, GA 30535	1897	James E. Walker	P	489	33
Piedmont Bible, Winston-Salem, NC 27101	1945	Donald Drake	D	447	19
Pikeville, Pikeville, KY 41501	1889	Jackson Hall	P	615	42
Pine Manor (W), Chestnut Hill, MA 02167	1911	Rosemary Ashby	P	516	30
Pittsburg State U., Pittsburg, KS 66762	1903	James Appleberry	S	5,560	225
Pittsburgh, Univ. of, Pittsburgh, PA 15260	1787	Wesley W. Posvar	S	*35,188*	*4,316*
Pitzer, Claremont, CA 91711	1963	Robert Atwell	P	750	60
Plymouth State, Plymouth, NH 03264	1870	Kasper Marking	S	3,351	138
Point Loma, San Diego, CA 92106	1902	Bill D. Draper	D,P	1,781	97
Point Park, Pittsburgh, PA 15222	1960	John Hopkins	P	2,077	147
Polytechnic Institute, Brooklyn, NY 11201	1854	George Bugliarello	P	*4,583*	*226*
Pomona, Claremont, CA 91711	1887	David Alexander	P	1,342	130
Portland State Univ., Portland, OR 97207	1946	Joseph Blumel	S	16,841	508
Portland, Univ. of, Portland, OR 97203	1901	Bro. Raphael Wilson	D	2,831	111
Prairie View A & M Univ., Prairie View, TX 77445	1878	Alvin Thomas	S	5,125	306
Pratt Institute, Brooklyn, NY 11205	1887	Richardson Pratt Jr.	P	4,422	295
Presbyterian, Clinton, SC 29325	1880	Kenneth B. Orr	D	925	52
Princeton Univ., Princeton, NJ 08540	1746	William G. Bowen	P	*5,931*	*810*
Principia, Elsah, IL 62028	1932	David K. Andrews	P	876	72
Providence, Providence, RI 02918	1917	Rev. T.R. Peterson	P	4,100	258
Puerto Rico, Univ. of*, San Juan, PR 00931	1903	Ismael Almodovar	S	21,794	1185
Puget Sound, Univ. of, Tacoma, WA 98416	1888	Philip M. Phibbs	P	3,300	191
Purdue Univ.*, W. Lafayette, IN 47907	1869	Arthur G. Hansen	S	41,948	2,349
Queens (W), Charlotte, NC 28274	1857	Billy Wireman	P	641	37
Quincy, Quincy, IL 62301	1860	Rev. G. Brinkman	D,P	1,648	82
Quinnipiac, Hamden, CT 06518	1929	Richard A. Terry	P	3,778	158
Radcliffe (W), Cambridge, MA 02138	1879	Matina Souretia Horner	P	2,161	(a)
Radford, Radford, VA 24142	1910	Donald N. Dedmon	S	5,693	300
Ramapo Coll. of N.J., Mahwah, NJ 07430	1969	George T. Potter	S	4,318	153
Randolph-Macon, Ashland, VA 23005	1830	Ladell Payne	P,D	921	57
Randolph-Macon Woman's (W), Lynchburg, VA 24503	1891	Robert Spivey	D	751	63
Redlands, Univ. of, Redlands, CA 92373	1907	Douglas R. Moore	P	2,621	119
Reed, Portland, OR 97202	1909	Paul Bragdon	P	1,156	78
Regis, Denver, CO 80221	1877	Rev. David M. Clarke	D,P	986	75
Regis (W), Weston, MA 02193	1927	Sister Therese Higgins	P	1,270	55
Rensselaer Poly. Inst., Troy, NY 12181	1824	George M. Low	P	6,031	355
Rhode Island, Providence, RI 02908	1854	David E. Sweet	S	9,223	439
R.I. School of Design, Providence, RI 02903	1877	Ms. Lee Hall	P	1,477	92
Rhode Island, Univ. of*, Kingston, RI 02881	1892	Frank Newman	S	*14,316*	*900*
Rice Univ., Houston, TX 77001	1891	Norman Hackerman	P	3,610	375
Richmond, Univ. of, Richmond, VA 23173	1830	E. Bruce Heilman	P,D	4,404	188
Rider, Lawrenceville, NJ 08648	1865	Frank N. Elliott	P	5,583	188

(a) Radcliffe students are taught by the Harvard faculty.

Name, address	Year	Governing official and affiliation		Stu-dents	Teach-ers
Rio Grande, Rio Grande, OH 45674	1876	Paul Hayes	P	1,083	45
Ripon, Ripon, WI 54971	1851	Bernard S. Adams	P	925	74
Rivier, Nashua, NH 03060	1933	Sister Doris Benoit	P	1,687	49
Roanoke, Salem, VA 24153	1842	Norman Fintel	P	1,357	67
Robert Morris, Coraopolis, PA 15108	1921	Charles Sewall	P	4,133	88
Roberts Wesleyan, Rochester, NY 14624	1866	Paul L. Adams	D,P	630	49
Rochester Inst. of Tech., Rochester, NY 14623	1829	M. Richard Rose	P	13,999	545
Rochester, Univ. of, Rochester, NY 14627	1850	Robert Sproull	P	*8,268*	*1,107*
Rockford, Rockford, IL 61101	1847	Norman L. Stewart	P	1,100	60
Rockhurst, Kansas City, MO 64110	1910	Rev. Robert Weiss	P	3,688	231
Rocky Mountain, Billings, MT 59102	1878	B. Alton	P	517	45
Roger Williams, Bristol, RI 02809	1948	Wm. Rizzini	P	3,613	254
Rollins, Winter Park, FL 32789	1885	Thaddeus Seymour	P	1,233	96
Roosevelt Univ., Chicago, IL 60605	1945	Rolf A. Weil	P	6,782	248
Rosary, River Forest, IL 60305	1918	Sister Candida Lund	P	1,575	61
Rosary Hill (A), Buffalo, NY 14226	1948	Robert S. Marshall	P	1,200	115
Rose-Hulman Inst. of Tech., (M) Terre Haute, IN 47803	1874	S.F. Hulbert	P	1,170	70
Rosemont, Rosemont, PA 19010	1921	Dorothy Brown	D,P	585	79
Russell Sage, Troy, NY 12180	1916	William Kahl	P	*2,400*	*165*
Rust, Holly Spgs., MS 38635	1866	W.A. McMillan	D	634	36
Rutgers Univ.*, New Brunswick, NJ 08903	1766	Edward J. Bloustein	S	*49,131*	*2,476*
Sacred Heart, Univ. of the, Santurce, PR 00914	1935	Pedro Gonzalez-Ramos	D	6,213	81
Sacred Heart Univ. (A), Bridgeport, CT 06606	1963	Robert Kidera	P	2,481	139
Saginaw Valley State, Univ. Center, MI 48710	1963	Jack Ryder	S	3,855	169
St. Ambrose, Davenport, LA 52803	1882	William Bakrow	Mu	1,818	54
St. Andrews Presbyterian, Laurinburg, NC 28352	1958	A.P. Perkinson Jr.	P	647	51
St. Anselm's, Manchester, NH 03102	1889	Rev. Joseph Gerry, Chan.	P	1,613	103
St. Augustine's, Raleigh, NC 27610	1867	Prezell R. Robinson	P	1,765	74
St. Benedict, Coll. of (W), St. Joseph, MN 56374	1913	Beverly Miller	D,P	*1,599*	*92*
St. Bernard (A), St. Bernard, AL 35138	1891	Robert Kaffer	D	450	52
St. Bonaventure Univ., St. Bonaventure, NY 14778	1856	V. Rev. Mathias Doyle	P	2,800	170
St. Catherine, Coll. of (W), St. Paul, MN 55105	1905	Catherine McNamee	D	2,057	130
St. Cloud State Univ., St. Cloud, MN 56301	1869	Charles J. Graham	S	11,591	600
St. Edward's Univ., Austin, TX 78704	1885	Stephen Walsh	P	2,119	84
St. Elizabeth, Coll. of (W), Convent Station, NJ 07961	1899	Sister Eliz. Ann Maloney	P	675	83
St. Francis, Fort Wayne, IN 46808	1890	Sister M. Jo Ellen Scheetz	D	1,350	36
St. Francis, Brooklyn, NY 11201	1884	Bro. Donald Sullivan	P	3,100	65
St. Francis, Loretto, PA 15940	1847	Rev. Christian Oravec	D	1,754	88
St. Francis, Coll. of, Joliet, IL 60435	1930	John Orr	P	2,927	135
St. John Fisher, Rochester, NY 14625	1948	Rev. C.J. Lavery	P	1,750	157
St. John's, Annapolis, MD 21404	1696	Richard D. Weigle	P	*651*	*79*
St. John's Univ., Collegeville, MN 56321	1857	Rev. Jerome Theisen	D	1,925	120
St. John's Univ., Jamaica, NY 11439	1870	V. Rev. Joseph T. Cahill	D	*17,812*	*515*
St. Joseph, West Hartford, CT 06117	1932	Sr. Mary O'Connor	P	1,289	66
St. Joseph's, Rensselaer, IN 47978	1889	Rev. Charles Banet	D	950	47
St. Joseph's, Brooklyn, NY 11205	1916	Sr. G.A. O'Connor	P	*1,864*	*155*
St. Joseph's, North Windham, ME 04062	1912	Anthony Sandoro	D	500	50
St. Joseph's, Philadelphia, PA 19131	1852	Rev. Donald MacLean	P	5,400	127
St. Lawrence Univ., Canton, NY 13617	1856	Frank Peter Piskor	P	2,400	165
St. Leo, St. Leo, FL 33574	1889	Thomas Southard	D	1,070	48
St. Louis Coll. of Pharmacy, St. Louis, MO 63110	1864	Charles C. Rabe	P	709	32
St. Louis Univ., St. Louis, MO 63103	1818	Rev. Thomas R. Fitzgerald	D	*10,496*	*852*
Parks, Cahokia, IL 62206	1927	Leon Z. Seltzer (Dean)	D	958	50
St. Martin's, Lacey WA 98503	1895	Fr. John C. Scott	D,P	655	32
St. Mary, Coll. of, Omaha, NE 68124	1923	John Richert	D	612	45
St. Mary (W), Leavenworth, KS 66048	1923	Sr. Mary J. McGilley	D	798	40
St. Mary of the Plains Coll., Dodge City, KS 67801	1952	Michael McCarthy	D	661	48
St. Mary-of-the Woods (W), St. Mary-of-the-Woods, IN 47876	1840	Sister Jeanne Knoerle	D,P	350	50
St. Mary's (W), Notre Dame, IN 46556	1844	John Duggan	P	1,710	113
St. Mary's, Winona, MN 55987	1912	Peter Clifford	P	1,354	71
St. Mary's, Moraga, CA 94575	1863	Bro. Mel Anderson	D	2,519	243
St. Mary's Coll. of Maryland, St. Mary's City, MD 20686	1839	J. Renwick Jackson Jr.	S	1,318	69
St. Mary's Dominican (W), New Orleans, LA 70118	1910	Sr. Mary Gerald Shea	D	860	32
St. Mary's Univ., San Antonio, TX 78284	1852	Rev. James Young	D	3,072	150
St. Michael's, Winooski, VT 05404	1904	Edward L. Henry	D	1,575	90
St. Norbert, DePere, WI 54115	1898	Neil Webb	D	1,628	80
St. Olaf, Northfield, MN 55057	1874	Harlan Foss	D	3,024	190
St. Paul Bible, Bible College, MN 55375	1916	Francis W. Grubbs	D	656	26
St. Paul's, Lawrenceville, VA 23868	1888	James Alvin Russell Jr.	D	650	41
St. Peter's, Jersey City, NJ 07306	1872	Rev. Edward Glynn	D	*3,973*	*121*
St. Rose, Coll. of, Albany, NY 12203	1920	Thomas Manion	P	2,750	92
St. Scholastica, Coll. of, Duluth, MN 55811	1912	Bruce Stender	D	1,162	75
St. Teresa, Coll. of (W), Winona, MN 55987	1907	Thomas Hamilton	P	800	85
St. Thomas Aquinas, Sparkill, NY 10976	1952	Donald McNelis	P	1,388	85
St. Thomas, Coll. of, St. Paul, MN 55105	1885	Msgr. Terrence Murphy	D	4,140	136
St. Thomas, Univ. of, Houston, TX 77006	1947	Rev. William J. Young	D	1,760	110
St. Vincent (M), Latrobe, PA 15650	1846	Rev. Cecil Diethrich	P	817	75
St. Xavier (A), Chicago, IL 60655	1847	Sr. M. Chekouras	P	2,100	107
Salem (W), Winston-Salem, NC 27108	1772	Richard Morrill	D	528	60
Salem, Salem, WV 26426	1888	James C. Stam	P	*1,300*	*65*
Salem State, Salem, MA 01970	1854	James T. Amsler	S	8,821	443
Salisbury State, Salisbury, MD 21801	1925	A.N. Page (Act.)	S	4,140	185
Sam Houston State Univ., Huntsville, TX 77340	1879	E.T. Bowers	S	10,548	402
Samford Univ., Birmingham, AL 35209	1841	Leslie S. Wright	P	3,674	218
San Diego, Univ. Of, San Diego, CA 92110	1949	Author E. Hughes	D	3,750	175
San Diego State Univ., San Diego, CA 92182	1897	Thomas Day	S	*30,463*	*1,029*
San Francisco Art Inst., San Francisco, CA 94133	1874	Stephen Goldstine	P	480	30
San Francisco, Univ. of, San Francisco, CA 94117	1855	Rev. J. LoSchiavo	D	6,500	264
Sangamon State Univ. (A), Springfield, IL 62708	1969	Robert Spencer	S	3,792	185
San Jose State Univ., San Jose, CA 95192	1857	Gail P. Fullerton	S	26,951	1,677
Santa Clara, Univ. of, Santa Clara, CA 95053	1850	William Rewak	D	6,718	351
Sante Fe, Coll. of, Sante Fe, NM 87501	1947	Bro. Cyprian Luke	P	1,188	53
Sarah Lawrence, Bronxville, NY 10708	1926	Charles DeCarlo	P	1,036	69
Savannah State, Savannah, GA 31404	1890	Clyde Hall, Act.	S	1,960	136
Scranton, Univ. of, Scranton, PA 18510	1888	Rev. William Byron	D	4,196	157
Scripps (W), Claremont, CA 91711	1926	John Chandler	P	550	63
Seattle Pacific Univ., Seattle, WA 98119	1891	David L. McKenna	D	*2,265*	*131*

Name, address	Year	Governing official and affiliation		Students	Teachers
Seattle Univ., Seattle, WA 98122	1891	Rev. William Sullivan	D	4,150	176
Selma Univ., Selma, AL 36701	1878	M.C. Cleveland Jr.	D	525	32
Seton Hall Univ., S. Orange, NJ 07079	1856	Rev. Laurence Murphy	P	9,762	426
Seton Hill (W), Greensburg, PA 15601	1883	Eileen Farrell	D	877	49
Shaw Coll. at Detroit, Detroit, MI 48202	1936	Romallus Murphy	P	895	41
Shaw Univ., Raleigh, NC 27611	1865	Stanley Smith	P	1,389	57
Sheldon Jackson, Sitka, AK 99835	1878	Hugh H. Holloway	P	200	23
Shenandoah Coll. of Music, Winchester, VA 22601	1875	Robert P. Parker	D	717	125
Shepherd, Shepherdstown, WV 25443	1871	James Butcher	S	3,000	124
Shippensburg State, Shippensburg, PA 17257	1871	Gilmore B. Seavers	S	5,891	348
Shorter, Rome, GA 30161	1873	Randall H. Minor	D	830	50
Siena, Loudonville, NY 12211	1937	Rev. Hugh F. Hines	P	2,300	143
Siena Heights, Adrian, MI 49221	1919	Louis Vaccaro	D	1,500	100
Simmons (W), Boston, MA 02115	1899	William J. Holmes	P	1,800	250
Simpson, Indianola, IA 50125	1860	Robert McBride	P	830	59
Simpson, San Francisco, CA 94134	1921	Mark W. Lee	D	225	23
Sioux Falls, Sioux Falls, SD 57101	1883	Owen Halleen	D	677	45
Skidmore, Saratoga Spgs., NY 12866	1922	Joseph C. Palamountian Jr.	P	*2,349*	*157*
Slippery Rock State, Slippery Rock, PA 16057	1889	Herb Reinhard Jr.	S	5,600	350
Smith (W), Northampton, MA 01060	1875	Jill Kerr Conway	P	2,518	240
Sonoma State Univ., Rohnert Park, CA 94928	1960	Peter Diamandopoulos	S	5,600	400
South, Univ. of the, Sewanee, TN 37375	1857	Robert Ayres Jr.	D	1,278	136
South Alabama, Univ. of, Mobile, AL 36688	1963	Frederick Whiddon	S	6,968	392
South Carolina St.*, Orangeburg, SC 29117	1896	M.M. Nance Jr.	S	3,314	242
South Carolina, Univ. of*, Columbia, SC 29208	1804	James B. Holderman	S	*35,748*	*1,622*
S.D. Sch. of Mines & Tech., Rapid City, SD 57701	1885	Richard Schleusener	S	2,158	96
South Dakota State Univ.*, Brookings, SD 57007	1881	Sherwood Berg	S	6,464	700
South Dakota, Univ. of, Vermillion, SD 57069	1862	Charles D. Lein	S	5,936	522
South Florida, Univ. of, Tampa, FL 33620	1956	John Lott Brown	S	*23,581*	*1,050*
South Texas Coll. of Law, Houston, TX 77002	1923	G.R. Walker	P	1,196	19
Southeast Missouri St. Univ., Cape Girardeau, MO 63701	1873	Robert Leestamper	S	8,804	432
Southeastern, Lakeland, FL 33801	1935	Cyril Homer	D	1,208	41
Southeastern Louisiana Univ., Hammond, LA 70402	1925	Clea E. Parker	S	7,300	250
Southeastern Mass. Univ., N. Dartmouth, MA 02747	1895	Donald E. Walker	S	7,235	355
Southeastern Okla. St. Univ., Durant, OK 74701	1909	Leon Hibbs	S	*4,470*	*165*
Southeastern Univ., Washington, DC 20024	1879	Barkev Kibarian	P	1,125	120
Southern Arkansas Univ., Magnolia, AR 71753	1909	Harold Brinson	S	*2,954*	*152*
Southern California, Costa Mesa, CA 92626	1920	Wayne Kraiss	D	660	30
Southern Cal., Univ. of, Los Angeles, CA 90007	1880	John R. Hubbard	P	27,879	1,679
Southern Coll. of Optometry, Memphis, TN 38104	1932	Spurgeon B. Eure	P	600	60
Southern Colorado, Univ. of, Pueblo, CO 81001	1933	Richard Pesqueira	S	6,000	285
Southern Conn. State, New Haven, CT 06515	1893	Manson Van B. Jennings	S	11,720	396
Southern Illinois Univ., Edwardsville, IL 62026	1965	Kenneth Shaw	S	12,060	610
Southern Illinois Univ., Carbondale, IL 62901	1869	Hiram Lesar (Act.)	S	*22,788*	*2,200*
Southern Methodist Univ., Dallas, TX 75275	1911	J. Zumberge	P	8,923	448
Southern Missionary, Collegedale, TN 37315	1892	Frank Knittel	D,P	*1,800*	*126*
Southern Miss., Univ. of, Hattiesburg, MS 39401	1910	Aubrey Lucas	S	*12,042*	*542*
Southern Oregon State, Ashland, OR 97520	1926	Natale Sicuro	S	4,500	210
Southern State (A), Magnolia, AR 71753	1909	Harold T. Brinson	S	*2,325*	*200*
Southern Tech. Inst., Marietta, GA 30060	1948	Vacant	S	2,300	88
Southern Univ., Baton Rouge, LA 70813	1880	Jesse Stone Jr.	S	8,311	381
Southern Utah State, Cedar City, UT 84720	1897	Orville D. Carnahan	S	2,000	250
Southwest Baptist, Bolivar, MO 65613	1878	James L. Sells (Chan.)	D	*1,265*	*70*
Southwest St. Univ., Marshall, MN 56258	1963	Jon Wefald	S	2,042	104
Southwest Mo. St. Univ., Springfield, MO 65802	1905	Duane Meyer	S	*14,473*	*520*
Southwest Texas St. Univ., San Marcos, TX 78666	1903	Lee Smith	S	15,924	564
Southwestern, Winfield, KS 67156	1885	Donald Ruthenberg	P	683	43
Southwestern La., Univ. of, Lafayette, LA 70504	1898	Ray Authement	S	13,311	594
Southwestern at Memphis, Memphis, TN 38112	1848	James Daughdrill Jr.	D	1,006	85
Southwestern Okla. St. Univ., Weatherford, OK 73096	1901	Leonard Campbell	S	4,320	204
Southwestern Adventist, Keene, TX 76059	1893	Donald McAdams	D	731	46
Southwestern Univ., Georgetown, TX 78626	1840	Durwood Fleming	P	1,001	60
Spalding, Louisville, KY 40203	1814	Sister Eileen Egan	D	1,010	58
Spelman (W), Atlanta, GA 30314	1881	Donald Stewart	P	1,250	97
Spring Arbor, Spring Arbor, MI 49283	1873	Kenneth Coffman	D	948	39
Spring Garden, Philadelphia, PA 19118	1851	Daniel DeLucca	P	1,013	52
Spring Hill, Mobile, AL 36608	1830	Rev. Paul S. Tipton	D	904	52
Springfield, Springfield, MA 01109	1885	Wilbert Locklin	P	2,365	131
Stanford Univ., Stanford, CA 94305	1885	Donald Kennedy	P	11,727	1,653
Stephen F. Austin State Univ., Nacogdoches, TX 75962	1923	William Johnson	S	9,472	415
Stephens (W), Columbia, MO 65243	1833	Arland Christ-Janer	P	1,450	118
Sterling, Sterling, KS 67579	1887	Charles Schoenherr	P	486	38
Stetson Univ., De Land, FL 32720	1883	Pope A. Duncan	D,P	*2,839*	*130*
Steubenville Coll. of, Steubenville, OH 43952	1946	Rev. M. Scanlon	P	900	46
Stevens Inst. of Tech., Hoboken, NJ 07030	1870	Kenneth C. Rogers	P	2,500	140
Stillman, Tuscaloosa, AL 35403	1876	Harold N. Stinson	D	633	35
Stockton State, Pomona, NJ 08240	1966	Peter Mitchell	S	4,600	163
Stonehill, N. Easton, MA 02356	1948	Rev. Bartley MacPhaidin	D	2,600	120
Strayer, Washington, DC 20005	1904	Murray Donoho III	P	1,800	50
Suffolk Univ., Boston, MA 02114	1906	Thomas Fulham	P	4,607	257
Sul Ross State Univ., Alpine, TX 79830	1917	C.R. Richardson	S	*2,161*	*81*
Susquehanna Univ., Selinsgrove, PA 17870	1858	Jonathan Messerli	P	1,457	103
Swarthmore, Swarthmore, PA 19081	1864	Theodore Friend	P	1,314	136
Sweet Briar, Sweet Briar, VA 24595	1901	Harold B. Whiteman Jr.	P	674	71
Syracuse Univ., Syracuse, NY 13210	1870	M.A. Eggers	P	20,233	891
Tabor, Hillsboro, KS 67063	1908	Vernon Janzen	P	445	30
Talladega, Talladega, AL 35160	1867	Joseph Gayles	P	698	46
Tampa, Tampa, FL 33609	1890	Donald C. Jones	P	*1,110*	*22*
Tampa, Univ. of, Tampa, FL 33606	1931	Richard Cheshire	P	*2,423*	*90*
Tarkio, Tarkio, MO 64491	1883	Frank Bretz	D	610	62
Tarleton State Univ., Stephenville, TX 76402	1899	Wm. Trogdon	S	3,138	140
Taylor Univ., Upland, IN 46989	1846	Milo Rediger	D,P	1587	82
Technical Career Inst., New York, NY 10001	1909	Meyer Dolinko	P	2,400	75
Temple Univ., Philadelphia, PA 19122	1884	Marvin Wachman	S	*28,434*	*1,783*
Tennessee State Univ.*, Nashville, TN 37203	1912	F. Humphries	S	5,545	270
Tennessee System, Univ. of*, Knoxville, TN 37916	1794	Edward Boling	S	*49,485*	*2,040*
Ctr. for Health Sci.*, Memphis, TN 38103	1911	T. Farmer, Chan.	S	2,152	171
at Chattanooga*, Chattanooga, TN 37401	1886	James Drinnon Jr., Chan.	S	7,106	306

Name, address	Year	Governing official	and affiliation	Students	Teachers
at Knoxville*, Knoxville, TN 37916	1794	Jack Reese, Chan.	S	29,720	1,288
at Martin*, Martin, TN 38238	1927	Larry T. McGehee, Chan.	S	4,518	216
at Nashville*, Nashville, TN 37203	1947	Charles Smith, Act. Chan.	S	5,419	120
Tennessee Tech. Univ., Cookeville, TN 38501	1915	Arliss Roaden	S	7,473	587
Tennessee Temple, Chattanooga, TN 37404	1946	Lee Roberson, Chan.	P	4,004	140
Tennessee Wesleyan, Athens, TN 37303	1857	George Naff Jr.	D	451	30
Texas (A), Tyler, TX 75701	1894	Allen C. Hancock	P	592	37
Texas A & I Univ., Kingsville, TX 78363	1925	Duane Leach	S	*6,043*	*284*
Texas A & M Univ.* (A), College Station, TX 77843	1876	Jack K. Williams	S	*28,000*	*2,000*
Prairie View A. & M. Univ. (A), Prairie View, TX 77445	1876	Alvin Thomas	S	5,007	716
Tarleton State Univ. (A), Stephenville, TX 76402	1899	William O. Trogdon	S	2,983	150
Texas Christian Univ., Fort Worth, TX 76129	1873	William Tucker, Chan.	P,D	5,800	316
Texas Eastern Univ., Tyler, TX 75701	1971	James Stewart Jr.	S	1,938	78
Texas Lutheran, Seguin, TX 78155	1891	Chas. Oestreich	D	1,034	59
Texas Southern Univ. (A), Houston, TX 77004	1947	Granville Sawyer	S	9,147	453
Texas System, Univ. of, Austin, TX 78701	1881	E. Don Walker	S	*105,328*	*6,571*
at Arlington, Arlington, TX 76019	1895	Wendell Nedderman	S	19,135	829
at Austin, Austin, TX 78712	1881	Peter Flawn	S	44,103	2,278
at Dallas, Richardson, TX 75080	1969	Bryce Jordan	S	5,644	205
at El Paso, El Paso, TX 79968	1913	Haskell Monroe	S	15,752	443
Health Science Center, Dallas, TX 75235	1943	Charles Sprague	S	*1,403*	*461*
at Houston, Houston, TX 77025	1905	Roger J. Bulger	S	*2,442*	*626*
at San Antonio, San Antonio, TX 78284	1959	Frank Harrison	S	2,018	490
Medical Branch, Galveston, TX 77550	1881	William Levin	S	1,553	503
at Permian Basin, Odessa, TX 79762	1969	V.R. Cardozier	S	1,597	71
at San Antonio, San Antonio, TX 78285	1969	James Wagener	S	9,453	296
at Tyler, Tyler, TX 75701	1971	James Stewart	S	1,854	78
Texas Tech. Univ., Lubbock, TX 79409	1923	M. Cecil Mackey Jr.	S	22,696	1,097
Texas Wesleyan, Fort Worth, TX 76105	1891	Jon Fleming	D	1,580	79
Texas Woman's Univ. (W), Denton, TX 76204	1901	Mary B. Huey	S	7,752	485
Thiel, Greenville, PA 16125	1866	Louis Almen	P	1,023	64
Thomas, Waterville, ME 04901	1894	Ford Grani, Acting	P	1,000	25
Thomas A. Edison Col. of N.J., Trenton, NJ 08625	1972	Larraine Matusak	S	NA	NA
Thomas Jefferson Univ. (A), Philadelphia, PA 19107	1824	Geo. Norwood Jr., Act.	P	1,700	1,400
Thomas More, Ft. Mitchell, KY 41017	1921	Robert J. Giroux	P,D	1,350	85
Tiffin Univ., Tiffin, OH 44883	1918	Richard Pfeiffer	P	390	12
Tift, Forsyth, GA 31029	1847	Robert W. Jackson	P,D	800	35
Toccoa Falls, Toccoa Falls, GA 30598	1907	Paul L. Alford	D	582	33
Toledo, Univ. of, Toledo, OH 43606	1872	Glen R. Driscoll	S	18,246	*650*
Tougaloo, Tougaloo, MS 39174	1869	George A. Owens	P	832	67
Towson State Univ., Baltimore, MD 21204	1866	Hoke Smith	S	15,283	488
Transylvania Univ., Lexington, KY 40508	1780	William Kelly	P	810	63
Trenton State, Trenton, NJ 08625	1855	Harold Eickhoff	S	10,584	373
Trevecca Nazarene, Nashville, TN 37210	1901	Homer Adams	P,D	1,033	35
Trinity, Hartford, CT 06106	1823	Theodore Lockwood	P	1,885	135
Trinity, Deerfield, IL 60015	1897	Harry Evans	P	805	38
Trinity, Burlington, VT 05401	1925	Catherine McNamee	D	450	32
Trinity, Washington, DC 20017	1897	Sr. Rose Anne Fleming	D,P	832	79
Trinity Univ., San Antonio, TX 78284	1869	Robert Calgaard	P	3,112	226
Tri-State Univ., Angola, IN 46703	1884	Carl Elliott	P	1,295	77
Troy State Univ. System, Troy, AL 36081	1887	Ralph W. Adams	S	12,141	303
Tufts Univ., Medford, MA 02155	1852	Jean Mayer	P	6,830	505
Tulane Univ., New Orleans, LA 70118	1834	Sheldon Hackney	P	9,326	683
Tulsa, Univ. of, Tulsa, OK 74104	1894	J. Paschal Twyman	P	*6,000*	*300*
Tusculum, Greenville, TN 37743	1794	Earl R. Mezoff	P	475	29
Tuskegee Institute, Tuskegee Inst., AL 36088	1881	Luther H. Foster	P	3,500	278
Union, Barbourville, KY 40906	1879	Mahlon A. Miller	P	1,239	50
Union, Lincoln, NE 68506	1891	Myrl O. Manley	D	*923*	*53*
Union, Schenectady, NY 12308	1795	John Morris	P	3,318	140
Union Univ., Jackson, TN 38301	1825	Robert E. Craig	D	1,092	82
U.S. Air Force Academy (A), Col. Springs, CO 80840	1955	Lt. Gen. J. Allen, Supt.	F	4,000	550
U.S. Coast Guard Acad., New London, CT 06320	1876	R. Adm. Malcolm Clark, Supt.	F	852	127
U.S. International Univ., San Diego, CA 92131	1952	William Rust	P	2,893	91
U.S. Merch. Marine Acad., Kings Point, NY 11024	1938	Rear Adm. A. Engel, Supt.	F	1,102	84
U.S. Military Academy, West Point, NY 10996	1802	Lt. Gen. A. Goodpaster,	F	4,067	636
U.S. Naval Academy, Annapolis, MD 21402	1845	William Lawrence, Supt.	F	4,400	550
Unity, Unity, ME 04988	1966	Ralph Wendell Conant	P	427	35
Upper Iowa Univ., Fayette, IA 52142	1857	Darcy C. Coyle	P	520	29
Upsala, E. Orange, NJ 07019	1893	Rodney Felder	P	1,264	67
Urbana, Urbana, OH 43078	1850	Roland Patzer	D	617	24
Ursinus, Collegeville, PA 19426	1869	Richard Richter	P	1,870	80
Ursuline, Cleveland, OH 44124	1871	Sister M. Kenan Dulzer	P	997	43
Utah State Univ.*, Logan, UT 84322	1890	Stanford Cazier	S	9,266	800
Utah, Univ. of, Salt Lake City, UT 84112	1850	David P. Gardner	S	21,992	3,564
Valdosta State, Valdosta, GA 31601	1906	Hugh C. Bailey	S	4,862	250
Valley City State, Valley City, ND 58072	1889	Ted De Vries	S	1,145	54
Valparaiso Univ., Valparaiso, IN 46383	1859	Robert V. Schnabel	P,D	4,206	320
Vanderbilt Univ. (A), Nashville, TN 37240	1873	Alexander Heard, Chan.	P	6,833	1,687
Vassar, Poughkeepsie, NY 12601	1861	Virginia Smith	P	2,260	189
Vermont, Univ. of*, Burlington, VT 05405	1791	Lattie Coor	S	10,954	716
Villa Maria (W), Erie, PA 16505	1925	Sr. M. Lawrence Antoun	P	545	52
Villanova Univ., Villanova, PA 19085	1842	Rev. John M. Driscoll	D,P	9,800	385
Virgin Islands, Coll. of the, St. Thomas, VI 00801	1962	Arthur A. Richards, Act.	T	1,996	60
Virginia Commonwealth Univ., Richmond, VA 23284	1838	Edmund Ackell	S	*19,428*	*1,469*
Virginia Intermont, Bristol, VA 24201	1884	Floyd Turner	P	*811*	*48*
Virginia Military Inst. (M), Lexington, VA 24450	1839	Lt. Gen. R. Irby	S	1,313	91
Virginia Poly. Inst. & State Univ.*, Blacksburg, VA 24061	1872	William Lavery	S	19,648	1,505
Virginia State*, Petersburg, VA 23803	1882	Thomas Law	S	4,310	236
Virginia Union Univ., Richmond, VA 23220	1865	David Shannon	P	1,178	85
Virginia, Univ. of, Charlottesville, VA 22903	1819	F. Hereford Jr.	S	15,900	1,279
Virginia Wesleyan, Norfolk, VA 23502	1961	Lambuth M. Clarke	P	804	43
Viterbo, La Crosse, WI 54601	1890	Robert Gibbons	P	1,074	80
Voorhees, Denmark, SC 29042	1897	George B. Thomas	D,P	709	51
Wabash (M), Crawfordsville, IN 47933	1832	Lewis S. Salter	P	800	73
Wagner, Staten Island NY 10301	1883	John Satterfield	P	2,539	97
Wake Forest Univ., Winston-Salem, NC 27109	1834	James R. Scales	D	*4,630*	*549*
Walla Walla, College Place, WA 99324	1892	N.C. Sorensen	D	2,010	125

Name, address	Year	Governing official and affiliation		Students	Teachers
Walsh, North Canton, OH 44720	1958	Francis Blovin	D	732	27
Walsh Coll. of Accounting, Troy, MI 48084	1922	Jeffrey Barry	P	1,393	75
Warner Pacific, Portland, OR 97215	1937	Milo L. Chapman	D	370	36
Warren Wilson, Swannanoa, NC 28778	1894	Reuben H. Holden	P	488	50
Wartburg, Waverly, IA 50677	1852	W. Jellema	P,D	1,079	79
Washburn Univ. of Topeka, Topeka, KS 66621	1865	John W. Henderson	Mu	5,763	177
Washington, Chestertown, MD 21620	1782	Joseph McLain	P	857	59
Washington and Jefferson, Washington, PA 15301	1781	Howard J. Burnett	P	1,105	101
Washington and Lee Univ., Lexington, VA 24450	1749	Robert Huntley	P	1,742	145
Washington State Univ., Pullman, WA 99164	1890	Glenn Terrell	S	16,992	1,092
Washington Univ., St. Louis, MO 63130	1853	W.H. Danforth, Chan.	P	*10,691*	*1,278*
Washington, Univ. of*, Seattle, WA 98195	1861	John R. Hogness	S	36,249	2,154
Way Coll. of Emporia, The, Emporia, KS 66801	1882	V.P. Wierwille	P	548	80
Wayland Baptist, Plainview, TX 79072	1908	Roy C. McClung	D	1,333	56
Wayne State, Wayne, NE 68787	1921	Lyle Seymour	S	2,419	91
Wayne State Univ., Detroit, MI 48202	1868	Thomas N. Bonner	S	34,337	1,545
Waynesburg, Waynesburg, PA 15370	1849	Joseph Marsh	P	850	59
Weber State, Ogden, UT 84408	1889	Rodney H. Brady	S	10,800	450
Webster, St. Louis, MO 63119	1915	Leigh Gerdine	P	*3,658*	*586*
Wellesley (W), Wellesley, MA 02181	1875	Carol J. Johns, Act.	P	2,134	220
Wells (W), Aurora, NY 13026	1868	Vacant	P	500	53
Wesleyan (W)(A), Macon, GA 31201	1836	W. Earl Strickland	D	570	53
Wesleyan Univ., Middletown, CT 06457	1831	Colin G. Campbell	P	2,471	261
West Chester State, West Chester, PA 19380	1871	Charles Mayo	S	8,374	512
West Coast Univ., Los Angeles, CA 90020	1909	Victor Elconin	P	*1,400*	*250*
West Florida, Univ. of, Pensacola, FL 32504	1967	James Robinson	S	*5,150*	*256*
West Georgia, Carrollton, GA 30118	1933	Maurice Townsend	S	5,119	250
West Liberty State, West Liberty, WV 26074	1837	James L. Chapman	S	2,631	148
West Texas State Univ., Canyon, TX 79016	1909	Max Sherman	S	6,469	217
W. Va. Inst. of Tech., Montgomery, WV 25136	1895	Leonard C. Nelson	S	3,237	165
West Virginia State, Institute, WV 25112	1890	Harold M. McNeill	S	4,000	135
West Virginia Univ.*, Morgantown, WV 26506	1867	Gene Budig	S	*22,376*	*1,384*
W. Virginia Wesleyan, Buckhannon, WV 26201	1890	Fred Earl Harris	Mu	1,671	120
Western Baptist, Salem, OR 97302	1935	W.T. Younger	D,P	436	20
Western Carolina Univ., Cullowhee, NC 28723	1889	H.F. Robinson, Chan.	S	6,274	311
Western Conn. State, Danbury, CT 06810	1903	Robert Bersi	S	*5,454*	*168*
Western Illinois Univ., Macomb, IL 61455	1899	L. Malpass	S	13,006	702
Western Kentucky Univ., Bowling Green, KY 42101	1906	Donald Zacharias	S	12,779	604
Western Maryland, Westminster, MD 21157	1868	Ralph C. John	P	2,140	106
Western Mich. Univ., Kalamazoo, MI 49008	1903	John T. Bernhard	S	20,689	1,040
Western Montana, Dillon, MT 59725	1893	Robert Thomas	S	837	38
Western New England, Springfield, MA 01119	1919	Beverly Miller	P	*5,181*	*317*
Western New Mexico Univ, Silver City, NM 88061	1893	John Snedeker	S	1,567	95
Western State Col. of Colo., Gunnison, CO 81230	1911	John Mellon	S	3,200	136
Western Washington Univ., Bellingham, WA 98225	1899	Paul Olscamp	S	10,104	435
Westfield State, Westfield, MA 01085	1838	Francis J. Pilecki	S	4,500	175
Westmar, Le Mars, IA 51031	1890	John F. Courter	D	650	38
Westminster, Fulton, MO 65251	1851	J.H. Saunders	P	625	51
Westminster, New Wilmington, PA 16142	1852	Earland I. Carlson	P	1,857	109
Westminster, Salt Lake City, UT 84105	1875	C. David Cornell	P	1,176	53
Westminster Choir, Princeton, NJ 08540	1926	Ray E. Robinson	P	470	38
Westmont, Santa Barbara, CA 93108	1940	David Winter	P	1,043	55
Wheaton, Wheaton, IL 60187	1860	Hudson T. Armerding	P	2,358	133
Wheaton (W), Norton, MA 02766	1834	Alice F. Emerson	P	1,140	84
Wheeling, Wheeling, WV 26003	1954	Rev. Charles Currie	D	1,196	65
Wheelock, Boston, MA 02215	1888	Gordon L. Marshall	P	1,001	44
White Plains, Coll. of (A), White Plains, NY 10603	1923	Edward Mortola	P	800	55
Whitman, Walla Walla, WA 99362	1859	Robert Skotheim	P	1,138	79
Whittier, Whittier, CA 90608	1901	Eugene Mills	P	*1,450*	*95*
Whitworth, Spokane, WA 99251	1890	Edward B. Lindaman	P	1,701	69
Wichita State Univ., Wichita, KS 67208	1895	Clark Ahlberg	S	16,649	516
Widener, Chester, PA 19013	1821	Clarence R. Moll	P	*6,401*	*273*
Wilberforce Univ., Wilberforce, OH 45384	1856	Charles Taylor	P	1,115	50
Wiley, Marshall, TX 75670	1873	Robert Hayes Sr.	D,P	603	34
Wilkes, Wilkes-Barre, PA 18766	1933	Robert Capin	P	2,900	157
Willamette Univ., Salem, OR 97301	1842	Robert Lisensky	P	1,830	110
William Carey, Hattiesburg, MS 39401	1906	J. Ralph Noonkester	D	*2,631*	*52*
William Jewell, Liberty, MO 64068	1849	J. Gordon Kingsley	D	1,601	85
Wm. and Mary, Coll. of, Williamsburg, VA 23185	1693	Thomas A. Graves Jr.	S	6,387	389
Wm. Mitchell Coll. of Law, St. Paul, MN 55105	1900	Bruce Barton, Dean.	P	1,127	26
Wm. Paterson, Wayne, NJ 07470	1855	Seymour C. Hyman	S	12,555	379
William Penn, Oskaloosa, IA 52577	1873	Gus Turbeville	D	585	35
William Woods (W), Fulton, MO 65251	1870	Randall B. Cutlip	P	1,000	96
Williams, Williamstown, MA 01267	1793	John W. Chandler	P	1,900	212
Wilmington, New Castle, DE 19720	1967	Audrey K. Doberstein	P	866	12
Wilmington, Wilmington, OH 45177	1870	Robert E. Lucas	D	1,125	55
Wilson (W), Chambersburg, PA 17201	1869	Donald Bletz	P,D	127	22
Wingate, Wingate, NC 28174	1896	Thomas Corts	P,D	1,520	63
Winona State Univ., Winona, MN 55987	1858	Robt. Hanson	S	4,747	185
Winston-Salem St. Univ., Winston-Salem, NC 27102	1892	H. Douglas Covington	S	2,224	155
Winthrop, Rock Hill, SC 29733	1886	Charles Vail	S	5,006	266
Wisconsin, Univ. of*, Madison, WI 53706	1971	Edwin Young	S	*150,629*	*7,036*
Eau Claire, Eau Claire, WI 54701	1916	Leonard Haas	S	10,494	499
Green Bay (A), Green Bay, WI 54302	1969	Edward W. Weidner, Chan.	S	3,641	160
La Crosse, La Crosse, WI 54601	1908	Noel Richards, Chan.	S	9,000	500
Madison, Madison, WI 53706	1849	Irving Shain, Chan.	S	39,000	2,300
Milwaukee (A), Milwaukee, WI 53201	1885	Werner Baum, Chan.	S	24,686	846
Oshkosh, Oshkosh, WI 54901	1871	Edward Penson, Chan.	S	10,368	550
Parkside (A), Kenosha, WI 53141	1969	Alan Guskin, Chan.	S	5,300	180
Platteville, Platteville, WI 53818	1866	Warren Carrier, Chan.	S	4,632	309
River Falls (A), River Falls, WI 54022	1874	George Field, Chan.	S	4,873	238
Stevens Point, Stevens Point, WI 54481	1894	Philip R. Marshall, Chan.	S	8,942	430
Stout, Menomonie, WI 54751	1893	Robert Swanson, Chan.	S	7,096	334
Superior, Superior, WI 54880	1893	Karl W. Meyer, Chan.	S	2,149	145
Whitewater, Whitewater, WI 53190	1868	James Connor, Chan.	S	9,601	505
Wittenberg Univ., Springfield, OH 45501	1845	W.A. Kinnison	D	2,318	136
Wofford, Spartanburg, SC 29301	1854	J.M. Lesesne Jr.	P,D	950	52
Woodbury, Los Angeles, CA 90017	1884	Wayne Miller	P	1,435	61

Name, address	Year	Governing official and affiliation		Students	Teachers
Wooster, Coll. of, Wooster, OH 44691	1866	Henry Copeland	P	1,776	134
Worcester Polytechnic Inst., Worcester, MA 01609	1865	Edmund T. Cranch	P	3,034	184
Worcester State, Worcester, MA 01602	1874	Joseph Orze	S	5,580	184
Wright State Univ., Dayton, OH 45431	1964	R.J. Kegerreis	S	*14,261*	*777*
Wyoming, Univ. of*, Laramie, WY 82071	1886	Edward H. Jennings	S	9,000	850
Xavier Univ. of La., New Orleans, LA 70125	1925	Norman C. Francis	D	1,700	158
Xavier Univ., Cincinnati, OH 45207	1831	Rev. Robert Mulligan	P	6,418	169
Yale Univ., New Haven, CT 06520	1701	A.B. Giamatti	P	9,526	1,580
Yankton, Yankton, SD 57078	1881	Orlan Mitchell	P	300	31
Yeshiva Univ., New York, NY 10033	1886	Norman Lamm	P	*6,819*	*1,200*
York College of Pa., York, PA 17405	1776	R.V. Iosue	P	3,168	95
Youngstown State Univ., Youngstown, OH 44555	1908	John J. Coffelt	S	15,303	799

Community and Junior Colleges

Enrollment and faculty figures in italics includes all branches and campuses

Name, address	Year	Governing official and affiliation		Students	Teachers
Abraham Baldwin Agric. Tifton, GA 31794	1908	Stanley R. Anderson	S	2,372	101
Adirondacks Community (A), Glens Falls, NY 12801	1960	Charles R. Eisenhart	S	2,037	65
Aeronautics, Academy of, Flushing, NY 11371	1932	Walter M. Hartung	P	1,800	57
Aims Comm., Greeley, CO 80632	1967	Jerry Kiefer, Act.	Di	4,850	89
Air Force, Comm. Coll. of the, Maxwell AFB, AL 36112	1972	Col. Lyle Kaapke	F	*96,845*	N/A
Alabama Christian, Montgomery, AL 36109	1942	E.R. Brannan	D	*1,200*	*77*
Alameda, Coll. of (A), Alameda, CA 94501	1970	Jeanette Poore	C,S	7,337	241
Albany Junior, Albany, GA 31707	1963	B.R. Tilley	S	1,790	67
Albany, Junior Coll. of (A), Albany, NY 12208	1957	William Kahl	P	1,045	42
Albemarle, Coll. of the, Elizabeth City, NC 27909	1960	J.P. Chesson Jr.	S	1,118	43
Alexander City State Jr., Alexander City, AL 35010	1965	W. Byron Causey	S	*1,236*	*44*
Allen Co. Comm. Jr., Iola, KS 66749	1923	Bill R. Spencer	S	985	28
Allan Hancock, Santa Maria, CA 93454	1920	Gary Edelbrock	Di	*10,500*	*130*
Allegany Community, Cumberland, MD 21502	1961	W. Ardell Haines	C,S	1,650	95
Allegheny Co., Comm. Coll. of, Pittsburgh, PA 15668	1966	Lawrence V. Lauth	C	71,420	349
Alpena Community, Alpena, MI 49707	1952	Charles Donnelly	S	1,659	50
Alvin Comm., Alvin, TX 77511	1948	A.R. Allbright	S	4,114	84
Amarillo, Amarillo, TX 79178	1929	John C. Manot	Mu	4,300	232
American Academy of Art, Chicago, IL 60604	1923	I. Shapiro	P	894	23
American Inter., Springfield, MA 01109	1885	Harry J. Courniotes	P	1,474	108
American River, Sacramento, CA 95841	1955	Robert D. Jensen	S	*24,151*	*298*
Anderson, Anderson, SC 29621	1911	Ray P. Rust	D	1,158	46
Andrew, Cuthbert, GA 31740	1854	Walter Murphy	P	350	21
Angelina, Lufkin, TX 75901	1968	Jack W. Hudgins	S,C	1,949	79
Anne Arundel Comm., Arnold, MD 21012	1961	Thomas E. Florestano	C,Mu	*6,600*	*180*
Anoka-Ramsey Comm., Coon Rapids, MN 55433	1965	Neil Christenson	S	3,645	92
Anson Tech. Inst., Ansonville, NC 28007	1963	H.B. Monroe	S	*1,000*	*50*
Antelope Valley, Lancaster, CA 93534	1929	Clinton Stine	Di	4,665	200
Aquinas Junior, (W) Milton, MA 02186	1956	Sr. Mary Morgan	D	389	21
Aquinas Junior, Nashville, TN 37205	1961	Sister Robert Ann Britton	D	325	20
Arapahoe Community (A), Littleton, CO 80120	1966	Joseph K. Bailey	S	5,100	300
Arizona Western, Yuma, AZ 85364	1963	Kenneth E. Borland	S	1,952	66
Art Academy of Cincinnati, Cincinnati, OH 45202	1887	Roger Williams, Dir.	P	171	9
Asheville Buncombe Tech., Asheville, NC 28801	1959	Harvey Haynes	S	2,500	130
Ashland Community, Ashland, KY 41101	1937	Robert Goodpaster	S	1,480	50
Atlantic Comm., Mays Landing, NJ 08330	1964	L.R. Winchell Jr.	C,S	3,767	120
Austin Comm., Austin, MN 55912	1940	Arlan Burmeister	S	700	43
Bacone, Muskogee, OK 74401	1880	Dean Chavers	D	453	44
Bakersfield, Bakersfield, CA 93305	1913	John J. Collins	S	*14,000*	*450*
Baltimore, Comm. Col. of, Baltimore, MD 21215	1947	Rafael L. Cortada	Mu	*10,865*	*250*
Barstow, Barstow, CA 92311	1959	J.W. Edwin Spear	S	1,475	42
Barton County Comm., Great Bend, KS 67530	1965	Jimmie Downing	C	2,632	52
Bay de Noc Comm., Escanaba, MI 49829	1963	Edwin E. Wuehle	S	1,591	41
Bay Path Junior, Longmeadow, MA 01106	1897	Jeanette T. Wright	P	639	24
Beal, Bangor, ME 04401	1891	David Tibbetts	P	437	50
Beaufort Co. Comm. Washington, NC 27889	1967	James P. Blanton	S	1,000	35
Beaver Co., Comm. Col. of, Monaca, PA 15061	1966	Richard Adams	S,Di	2,000	55
Becker Junior, Worcester, MA 01609	1784	Lloyd H. Van Buskirk	P	*1,200*	*45*
Beckley, Beckley, WV 25801	1933	John Saunders	P	1,154	15
Bee County, Beeville, TX 78102	1965	Grady C. Hogue	C	1,927	76
Belleville Area, Belleville, IL 62221	1946	William Keel	S	11,583	145
Bellevue Community, Bellevue, WA 98007	1966	Thos. O'Connell	S	10,582	114
Belmont Technical, St. Clairsville, OH 43950	1969	Paul R. Ohm	S	563	20
Bergen Community, Paramus, NJ 07652	1965	Alban E. Reid	C	10,600	350
Berkeley School, The, Little Falls, NJ 07424	1931	Larry L. Luing	P	465	18
Berkshire Community, Pittsfield, MA 01201	1960	Jonathan M. Daube	S	2,896	180
Big Bend Community, Moses Lake, WA 98837	1962	Peter DeVries	S	2,000	45
Bismarck Junior, Bismarck, ND 58501	1939	Kermit Lidstrom	Mu	3,100	90
Black Hawk, Moline, IL 61265	1946	Richard J. Puffer	Di	*4,500*	*136*
Blackhawk Technical Inst., Janesville, WI 53545	1968	O.L. Johnson (Dir.)	S	1,886	85
Bladen Tech. Inst., Dublin, NC 28332	1967	Geo. Resseguie	S	380	18
Blinn, Brenham, TX 77833	1883	James H. Atkinson	C,S	2,477	61
Bliss, Columbus, OH 43214	1899	Gerald J. Wickham	P	450	16
Bluefield (A), Bluefield, VA 24605	1922	Charles L. Tyer	D	634	33
Blue Mountain Comm., Pendleton, OR 97801	1962	Ronald L. Daniels	S	*2,500*	*355*
Blue Ridge Comm., Weyers Cave, VA 24486	1965	James A. Armstrong	S	2,086	48
Boca Raton, Coll. of, Boca Raton, FL 33431	1963	Donald E. Ross	P	500	12
Brainerd Comm., Brainerd, MN 56401	1938	Curtis Murton Jr.	S	700	29
Brandywine, Wilmington, DE 19803	1966	C.R. Moll	D	*1,223*	*885*
Brazosport, Lake Jackson, TX 77566	1968	W.A. Bass	Di	4,500	79
Brevard, Brevard, NC 28712	1853	J.C. Martinson Jr.	D	700	47
Brevard Comm., Cocoa, FL 32922	1960	Maxwell King	Di	*9,200*	*302*
Brewton-Parker, Mt. Vernon, GA 30445	1904	William S. Miller	D	783	21
Bristol Community, Fall River, MA 02720	1965	Eileen T. Farley	S	6,114	86
Brookdale Comm., Lincroft, NJ 07738	1967	Donald H. Smith	C	9,791	140
Broome Community, Binghamton, NY 13902	1946	Vacant	C	5,556	155
Broward Community (A), Ft. Lauderdale, FL 33301	1960	Hugh Adams	S	*16,000*	*275*
Brunswick Junior, Brunswick, GA 31520	1961	John W. Teel	S	1,109	56
Bucks County Comm., Newtown, PA 18940	1964	Charles Rollins	C,S	8,100	190

Name, address	Year	Governing official and affiliation		Students	Teachers
Butler County Comm., Butler, PA 16001	1965	Thomas Ten Hoeve Jr.	C	2,319	69
Butler County Comm. Jr., El Dorado, KS 67042	1927	Carl Heinrich	C	1,760	60
Butte Community (A), Oroville, CA 95965	1967	Albert Schlueter	S	7,716	350
Cabrillo Comm. Coll., Aptos, CA 95003	1959	John C. Petersen	Di	8,720	158
Caldwell Comm. Coll. & Tech. Inst. (A), Lenoir, NC 28645	1964	H. Edwin Beam	C,S	*1,300*	*120*
Camden County, Blackwood, NJ 08012	1967	Otto R. Mauke	C,S	*7,466*	*335*
Canada, Redwood City, CA 94061	1968	Samuel Ferguson	C	8,600	114
Canyons, Coll. of the, Valencia, CA 91355	1969	L.D. Newcomer	C	3,438	157
Cape Cod Comm., W. Barnstable, MA 02668	1960	James F. Hall	S	4,377	86
Cape Fear Tech. Inst., Wilmington, NC 28401	1959	M.J. McLeod	S,C	1,450	61
Carl Albert Junior, Poteau, OK 74953	1934	Joe E. White	S	1,710	60
Carl Sandburg, Galesburg, IL 61401	1966	William Anderson	S	3,500	150
Carteret Tech. Inst., Morehead City, NC 28557	1963	Donald Bryant	S	759	28
Casper, Casper, WY 82601	1945	Tilghman Aley	S	4,146	117
Catawba Valley Tech. Inst., Hickory, NC 28601	1957	Robert E. Paap	S	2,084	69
Catonsville Comm., Baltimore, MD 21228	1957	Robert Barringer	C	*10,000*	*200*
Cayuga Co. Comm. (A), Auburn, NY 13021	1953	John Anthony	S	2,829	84
Cazenovia (W), Cazenovia, NY 13035	1824	Stephen Schneeweiss	P	483	25
Cecil Community, North East, MD 21901	1968	Robert L. Gell	S	1,200	27
Central Arizona, Coolidge, AZ 85228	1969	Mel Everingham	C	*6,028*	*50*
Central Carolina Tech. Inst., Sanford, NC 27330	1962	James F. Hockaday	S,C	1,884	95
Central, McPherson, KS 67460	1884	Bruce L. Kline	D	280	20
Central Florida Comm. (A), Ocala, FL 32670	1957	Henry E. Goodlett	S	2,357	185
Central Oregon Comm., Bend, OR 97701	1949	Frederick Boyle	Di	1,896	69
Central Piedmont Comm., Charlotte, NC 28204	1963	Richard H. Hagemeyer	S,C	28,220	260
Central Nebr. Tech. Comm. (A), Grand Island, NE 68801	1966	Chester Guasman	C	*16,072*	*132*
Central Texas (A), Killeen, TX 76541	1967	L.M. Morton Jr.	S	*5,000*	*125*
Central Virginia Comm., Lynchburg, VA 24502	1966	Donald Puyear	S	3,417	73
Central Wyoming, Riverton, WY 82501	1966	William Day	Di	1,946	36
Central YMCA Comm., Chicago, IL 60606	1960	Ralph H. Lee	P	3,189	83
Centralia, Centralia, WA 98531	1925	Nels W. Hanson	S	6,544	60
Cerritos, Norwalk, CA 90650	1955	Wilford Michael	Di	21,928	411
Cerro Coso Comm., Ridgecrest, CA 93555	1973	Richard Meyers	S	4,527	68
Chabot, Hayward, CA 94545	1961	Reed L. Buffington	Di	18,886	800
Chaffey (A), Alta Loma, CA 91701	1883	K.C. Hinrichsen	S	11,644	461
Champlain, Burlington, VT 05401	1878	Robert A. Skiff	P	1,170	71
Charles Co. Comm., La Plata, MD 20646	1958	J.N. Carsey	C	4,579	39
Charles S. Mott Comm., Flint, MI 48503	1923	Charles Pappas	C	8,457	220
Chattanooga St. Tech. Comm., Chattanooga, TN 37406	1963	Charles W. Branch	S	4,602	164
Chemeketa Comm., Salem, OR 97303	1969	Arthur A. Binnie	Di	4,330	231
Chesapeake, Wye Mills, MD 21679	1967	Robert Schleiger	C	2,564	30
Chicago, City Colleges of, Chicago, IL 60601	1911	Oscar Shabat, Chan.	Mu	*96,477*	*1,340*
Daley, Chicago, IL 60652	1960	Virginia R. Keehan	S	5,765	150
Kennedy-King, Chicago, IL 60621	1934	Ewen Akin	S	8,999	300
Loop, Chicago, IL 60601	1962	David H. Heller	S	7,143	250
Malcolm X., Chicago, IL 60612	1911	James C. Griggs	S	6,381	175
Olive-Harvey, Chicago, IL 60628	1957	Eugene T. Speller	S	5,775	175
Truman, Chicago, IL 60640	1956	Wallace B. Appelson	S	8,032	175
Wright, Chicago, IL 60634	1934	Ernest Clements	S	8,120	250
Chipola Junior (A), Marianna, FL 32446	1947	Raymond M. Deming	S	999	47
Chowan, Murfreesboro, NC 27855	1848	Bruce E. Whitaker	D	1,124	55
Cisco Junior, Cisco, TX 76437	1909	Norman Wallace	S	1,500	62
Citrus, Azusa, CA 91702	1915	Robert Haugh	Di	10,000	150
Clackamas Comm., Oregon City, OR 97045	1966	John Hakanson	S	9,500	137
Claremore, Claremore, OK 74017	1971	Richard Mosier	S	1,918	48
Clarendon, Clarendon, TX 79226	1898	Kenneth D. Vaughan	S	772	23
Clark, Vancouver, WA 98663	1933	Richard A. Jones	S	4,256	129
Clark Co. Comm., N. Las Vegas, NV 89030	1971	Judith Eaton	S	*9,100*	*432*
Clark Tech. (A), Springfield, OH 45501	1962	Richard Brinkman	S	2,010	110
Clatsop Community, Astoria, OR 97103	1958	Philip Bainer	C	*7,110*	*271*
Clayton Junior, Morrow, GA 30260	1969	Harry S. Downs	S	2,669	88
Cleveland Tech., Shelby, NC 28150	1965	James Petty	S	1,050	51
Cleveland State Comm., Cleveland, TN 37311	1967	L. Quentin Lane	S	4,260	93
Clinton Community, Clinton, IA 52732	1946	Chuck Spence	S,Di	702	35
Clinton Community (A), Plattsburgh, NY 12901	1966	Albert B. Light	S	1,400	31
Cloud County Comm., Concordia, KS 66901	1965	James P. Ihrig	C,S	2,123	42
Coahoma Junior, Clarksdale, MS 38614	1949	McKinley C. Martin	S,C	1,521	64
Coastal Carolina Comm., Jacksonville, NC 28540	1965	James Henderson Jr.	S	2,157	70
Cochise Comm., Douglas, AZ 85607	1962	Vacant	S	*4,209*	*68*
Coffeyville Comm. Jr., Coffeyville, KS 67337	1923	Russell Graham	S	775	51
Colby Comm., Colby, KS 67701	1964	James Tangeman	C,S	*1,200*	*60*
Colorado Mountain, Glenwood Spgs., CO 81601	1967	F. Dean Lillie	Di	*21,066*	*410*
Colorado Northwestern Comm., Rangely, CO 81648	1962	James H. Bos	Di	2,680	32
Columbia Basin, Pasco, WA 99301	1955	Fred L. Esvelt	S	10,000	382
Columbia Greene Comm. (A), Hudson, NY 12534	1966	Edward J. Owen	S	1,218	37
Columbia Junior, Columbia, CA 95310	1968	Harvey Rhodes	S	2,263	36
Columbia State Comm., Columbia, TN 38401	1966	Harold S. Pryor	S	2,201	61
Columbus Tech. Inst. (A), Columbus, OH 43215	1963	Clarence Schauer	S	4,966	264
Compton Comm. (A), Compton, CA 90221	1927	Abel B. Sykes Jr.	S	6,832	268
Concordia, Milwaukee, WI 53208	1881	Ronald L. Berg	D,P	*400*	*25*
Connors State (A), Warner, OK 74469	1908	Melvin Self	S	1,800	64
Contra Costa, San Pablo, CA 94806	1950	H. Rex Craig	Di	8,652	156
Cooke County, Gainesville, TX 76240	1924	Alton Laird	S	1,437	59
Coplah-Lincoln Junior (A), Wesson, MS 39191	1928	Billy Thames	C	*1,365*	*98*
Corning Community, Corning, NY 14830	1957	Donald H. Hangen	S	3,068	104
Cottey (W), Nevada, MO 64772	1884	Evelyn Milam	P	327	30
Cowley County Comm., Arkansas City, KS 67005	1922	Owen Nelson	C	1,419	48
Crafton Hills (A), Yucaipa, CA 92399	1972	Wm. Moore	S	3,416	167
Craven Comm., New Bern, NC 28560	1965	Thurman E. Brock	S	1,455	50
Crowder, Neosho, MO 64850	1963	Dell Reed	Di	1,100	39
Cuesta, San Luis Obispo, CA 93406	1964	Frank Martinez	Di	6,280	91
Cumberland, Lebanon, TN 37087	1842	Ernest Stockton	P	470	22
Cumberland County, Vineland, NJ 08360	1965	Philip Phelan	C,S	2,013	51
Curry (A), Milton, MA 02186	1879	John S. Hafer	P	1,027	54
Cuyahoga, Community, Cleveland, OH 44115	1962	Nolen Ellison, Chan.	C,S	*25,594*	*420*
Cuyamaca, El Cajon, CA 92020	1977	Wallace F. Cohen	Di	2,740	108
Cypress, Cypress, CA 90630	1966	Jack A. Scott	Di	*12,000*	*210*

Name, address	Year	Governing official and affiliation		Students	Teachers
Dabney S. Lancaster, Comm., Clifton Forge, VA 24422	1964	John F. Backels	S	1,100	37
Dallas Co. Comm. Col. System (A), Dallas, TX 75202	1965	Bill J. Priest	C	*32,790*	*2,412*
Dalton Jr., Dalton, GA 30720	1963	Derrell Roberts	S	1,450	75
Danville Junior, Danville, IL 61832	1946	Joseph A. Borgen	S	3,200	80
Davenport Coll. of Business (A), Grand Rapids, MI 49502	1866	Robert W. Sneden	P	1,311	46
Davidson County Comm., Lexington, NC 27292	1958	Grady Love	C	2,360	103
Davis Jr. Coll. of Business, Toledo, OH 43604	1858	Ruth L. Davis	P	450	35
Dawson Comm. (A), Glendive, MT 59330	1940	James Hoffman	C	730	43
Daytona Beach Comm., Daytona Beach, FL 32015	1958	Charles Polk	S	*32,634*	*160*
Dean Junior, Franklin, MA 02038	1865	Richard Crockford	P	1,606	51
DeAnza Comm., Cupertino, CA 95014	1967	Thomas H. Clements	Di	22,033	324
DeKalb Community, Clarkston, GA 30021	1964	W.W. Scott	C	18,333	280
Delgado, New Orleans, LA 70122	1921	Harry J. Bayer	S	8,771	178
Del Mar, Corpus Christi, TX 78404	1935	Jean Richardson	S	13,155	309
Delaware County Comm., Media, PA 19063	1967	Richard D. DeCosmo	S,Di	5,880	100
Delaware Tech. Comm., Dover, DE 19901	1967	John R. Kotula	S	*7,022*	*195*
Delta, University Ctr., MI 48710	1958	Donald Carlyon	C	12,500	205
Denver, Comm. Coll. of, Denver, CO 80218	1968	Robert E. Lahti	S	*14,308*	*304*
Des Moines Area Comm., Ankeny, IA 50021	1967	Paul Lowery	S	*6,535*	*300+*
Desert, Coll. of the, Palm Desert, CA 92260	1958	F.D. Stout	Di	10,000	103
Diablo Valley, Pleasant Hill, CA 94523	1949	William P. Niland	Di	18,742	580
District One Tech. Inst., Eau Claire, WI 54701	1911	Norbert Wurtzel, Dir.	S,Di	*2,800*	*142*
Dixie, St. George, UT 84770	1911	Wm. Kerr	S	1,585	72
Dodge City Community, Dodge City, KS 67801	1935	Charles M. Barnes	C	1,420	50
Donnelly, Kansas City, KS 66102	1949	Rev. Raymond Davern	D	978	35
Dundalk Community (A), Baltimore, MD 21222	1969	John E. Ravekes	C	2,200	65
Du Page, Coll. of, Glen Ellyn, IL 60137	1966	Harold D. McAninch	S,Di	*22,230*	*220*
Durham Tech. Inst. (A), Durham, NC 27703	1965	John Crumpton Jr.	S,C	2,000	130
Dutchess Community (A), Poughkeepsie, NY 12601	1957	John J. Connolly	S	5,975	132
Dyersburg State Comm., Dyersburg, TN 38024	1969	Edward Eller	S	1,042	31
East Central Junior, Decatur, MS 39327	1928	Charles V. Wright	S	806	53
East Central Junior, Union, MO 63084	1968	Donald D. Shook	Di	1,723	47
East Los Angeles, Monterey Park, CA 91754	1945	Arthur D. Avila, Act	Di	16,226	680
East Mississippi Jr., Scooba, MS 39358	1927	C. Cheatham	S	*1,554*	*47*
Eastern Arizona, Thatcher, AZ 85552	1888	W.M. McGrath	S	3,643	85
Eastern Iowa Comm., Davenport, IA 52803	1966	Michael E. Crawford, Supt.	S	*2,900*	*155*
Eastern Maine Voc. Tech. (A), Bangor, ME 04401	1965	Francis Sprague, Dir.	S	2,280	100
Eastern Oklahoma State, Wilburton, OK 74578	1909	James Miller	S	*1,622*	*69*
Eastern Utah, Coll. Of, Price, UT 84501	1937	Dean McDonald	S	*1,250*	*35*
Eastern Wyoming, Torrington, WY 82240	1948	Charles Rogers	S,Di	776	27
Eastfield, Mesquite, TX 75210	1970	Eleanor Ott	C,Di	*7,525*	*130*
Edgecombe Tech. Inst., Tarboro, NC 27886	1968	Charles McIntyre	S	*1,200*	*40*
Edison Community, Ft. Myers, FL 33907	1962	David G. Robinson	S	*4,383*	*67*
Edmonds Community, Lynnwood, WA 98036	1967	Thomas C. Nielsen	S	8,011	84
Edward Williams, Hackensack, NJ 07601	1964	Jerome Pollack	P	398	9
Eisenhower, Seneca Falls, NY 13148	1965	Joseph D. Coffee, Jr.	S	500	50
El Camino, Torrance, CA 90506	1947	Stuart E. Marsee	Di	27,624	637
El Centro, Dallas, TX 75202	1966	Ruby H. Herd	C	6,089	161
El Paso Community, El Paso, TX 79998	1969	Robert E. Shepack	S	*16,567*	*221*
El Reno Jr., El Reno, OK 73036	1938	Bill S. Cole	S	1,116	35
Elgin Community, Elgin, IL 60120	1949	Dwight Link, Act.	S	5,500	100
Elizabeth Seton (A), Yonkers, NY 10701	1960	Sr. Mary Ellen Brosnan	P	989	81
Elizabethtown Comm., Elizabethtown, KY 42701	1964	James Owen, Dir.	S	1,641	40
Ellsworth Comm., Iowa Falls, IA 50126	1890	Duane R. Lloyd, Dean	S	850	60
Emmanuel, Franklin Spgs., GA 30639	1919	C.Y. Melton	D	376	21
Endicott Junior (W), Beverly, MA 01915	1939	Eleanor Tupper	P	891	43
Enterprise State Junior, Enterprise AL 36331	1965	Benjamin A. Forrester	S	1,525	43
Erie Community (A), Buffalo, NY 14221	1946	Oscar Smuckler, Act.	S	10,296	325
Essex Community, Baltimore, MD 21237	1957	Vernon Wanty	C,S	2,273	204
Essex County (A), Newark, NJ 07102	1968	J. Harry Smith	C	6,749	257
Everett Comm. (A), Everett, WA 98201	1941	Nina Haynes, Act.	S	7,900	150
Fashion Inst. of Tech. (A), New York, NY 10001	1944	Marvin J. Feldman	S	8,444	164
Faulkner State Jr., Bay Minette, AL 36507	1965	L. Sibert	S	1,532	36
Fayetteville Tech. Inst., Fayetteville, NC 28303	1961	Howard Boudreau	S	4,860	218
Feather River, Quincy, CA 95971	1968	Lyndell D. Cheeves	Di	1,500	60
Fergus Falls Comm., Fergus Falls, MN 56537	1960	W.A. Waage	S	521	38
Finger Lakes, Comm. Coll. of, Canandaigua, NY 14424	1965	Charles Meder	C	2,800	85
Fisher Junior (A), Boston, MA 02116	1903	Scott Fisher	P	*2,115*	*97*
Flathead Valley Comm. (A), Kalispell, MT 59901	1967	R.C. Mattson, Act.	S,C	1,407	100
Florida, Temple Terrace, FL 33617	1946	James R. Cope	P	475	28
Florida Jr., Jacksonville, FL 32202	1966	Benjamin R. Wygal	S	*38,524*	*335*
Florida Keys Comm., Key West, FL 33040	1963	William A. Seeker	S	1,678	32
Florissant Valley Comm. (A), St. Louis, MO 63135	1962	Raymond J. Stith	Di	6,869	350
Floyd Junior, Rome, GA 30161	1970	David McCorkle	S	1,445	55
Foothill, Los Altos Hills, CA 94022	1957	Thomas W. Fryer Jr.	S	39,117	472
Forest Park Comm. (A), St. Louis, MO 63110	1962	Ralph H. Lee	Di	8,704	367
Forsyth Sch for Dental Hygienists, Boston, MA 02115	1916	Ralph R. Lobene, Dean	P	201	11
Forsyth Tech. Inst., Winston-Salem, NC 27103	1960	Harley Affeldt	S,C	2,660	103
Ft. Scott Comm. Junior, Ft. Scott, KS 66701	1912	Wayne McElroy	S,C	1,181	31
Ft. Steilacoom Comm., Tacoma, WA 98498	1967	Robert H. Stauffer	S	4,723	98
Fox Valley Tech. Inst., Appleton, WI 54913	1967	William Sirek, Dir.	Di,S	*31,838*	*187*
Franklin Inst., Boston, MA 02116	1908	Michael Mazzola	P	1,040	75
Fresno City, Fresno, CA 93741	1910	Clyde McCully	Di,S	13,501	232
Fullerton, Fullerton, CA 92634	1913	Philip W. Borst	S	19,500	300
Fulton-Montgomery Comm. (A), Johnstown, NY 12095	1963	Hadley S. DePuy	S	1,565	57
Gadsden State Junior, Gadsden, AL 35999	1965	Arthur W. Dennis	S	3,538	107
Gainesville Junior, Gainesville, GA 30503	1965	Hugh Mills Jr.	S	1,303	47
Galveston (A), Galveston, TX 77550	1967	Melvin M. Plexco	S	*2,203*	*80*
Garden City Comm. Jr., Garden City, KS 67846	1919	Thomas F. Saffell	S	1,800	63
Gaston, Dallas, NC 28034	1963	Robert Howard	S	3,049	98
Gateway Tech. Inst., Kenosha, WI 53141	1911	Keith Stoehr, Dir.	Di	*10,437*	*200*
Gavilan, Gilroy, CA 95020	1963	Rudy Melone	S	*2,400*	*83*
Genesee Community, Batavia, NY 14020	1966	Stuart Steiner	S	2,069	72
George C. Wallace St. Comm. (A), Dothan, AL 36301	1965	Phillip J. Hamm	S	2,239	96
Germanna Comm., Locust Grove, VA 22508	1970	Arnold E. Wirtala	S	1,266	28
Glen Oaks Comm. (A), Centreville, MI 49032	1965	Justus Sundermann	S	900	66
Glendale Comm., Glendale AZ 85032	1965	John Waltrip	C	12,291	180

Name, address	Year	Governing official and affiliation		Students	Teachers
Glendale Comm., Glendale, CA 91208	1927	John Grande	Di	8,594	275
Gloucester County (A), Sewell, NJ 08080	1966	William Apetz	C	2,500	114
Gogebic Community, Ironwood, MI 49938	1932	R. Ernest Dear	Di	1,300	50
Golden West, Huntgtn. Bch., CA 92647	1966	Lee A. Stevens	S	20,000	670
Goldey Beacom, Wilmington, DE 19808	1886	William R. Baldt	P	1,460	23
Gordon Junior, Barnesville, GA 30204	1852	Jerry M. Williamson	S	1,506	40
Grahm Junior, Boston, MA 02215	1950	Robert B. Vail	P	541	59
Grand Rapids Junior (A), Grand Rapids, MI 49502	1914	Richard Calkins	Mu	7,301	230
Grand View (A), Des Moines, IA 50316	1896	K.F. Langrock	P	858	40
Grays Harbor, Aberdeen, WA 98520	1930	Joseph Malik	S	1,340	60
Grayson County Junior, Denison, TX 75020	1964	Truman Wester	S	4,037	115
Greater Hartford Comm., Hartford, CT 06105	1967	Arthur C. Banks Jr.	S	2,715	46
Green River Comm., Auburn, WA 98002	1965	Melvin Lindbloom	S	7,793	348
Greenfield Comm., Greenfield, MA 01301	1962	Nancy L. Goodwin	S	2,111	116
Greenville Tech., Greenville, SC 29606	1962	Thomas Barton, Jr.	S	23,369	460
Grossmont, El Cajon, CA 92020	1961	Erv. F. Metzgar	Di	*15,674*	*217*
Guilford Tech. Inst., Jamestown, NC 27282	1958	Ray Lane (Act)	S	3,730	236
Gulf Coast Comm., Panama City, FL 32401	1957	Lawrence Tyree	S	3,700	76
Hagerstown Junior, Hagerstown, MD 21740	1946	Atlee Kepler	C	2,074	60
Halifax Comm., Weldon, NC 27890	1967	Phillip W. Taylor	S	1,000	48
Harcum Junior, Bryn Mawr, PA 19010	1915	Michael A. Duzy	P	949	30
Harrisburg Area Comm., Harrisburg, PA 17110	1964	James Odom Jr.	Di	5,050	125
Harford Community, Bel Air, MD 21014	1957	A.C. O'Connell	S	6,700	282
Hartford State Tech., Hartford, CT 06106	1946	L. Barrell	S	1,423	46
Hartnell Comm., Salinas, CA 93901	1920	Gibb R. Madsen	Di	6,300	96
Haskell Indian Junior (A), Lawrence, KS 66044	1884	Wallace Galluzzi	F	1,086	81
Hawkeye Inst. of Tech., Waterloo, IA 50704	1966	John Hawse	Di	20,252	125
Haywood Tech. Inst. (A), Clyde, NC 28721	1965	J.H. Nanney	S	1,600	160
Hazard Community, Hazard, KY 41701	1968	J. Marvin Jolly, Dir.	S	315	12
Henderson Community, Henderson, KY 42420	1960	Marshall Arnold, Dir.	S	800	39
Henderson County, Athens, TX 75751	1946	William J. Campion	Di	2,400	80
Henry Ford Comm. (A), Dearborn, MI 48128	1938	Stuart M. Bundy	Mu	14,856	609
Herkimer Co. Comm., Herkimer, NY 13350	1966	Robert McLaughlin	C	2,059	95
Hesston, Hesston, KS 67062	1909	Laban Peachey	D	675	44
Hibbing Comm., Hibbing, MN 55746	1916	Jennis Bapst	S	628	33
Highland Comm., Freeport, IL 61032	1961	Howard Sims	Di	1,630	47
Highland Comm., Highland, KS 66035	1858	Jack D. Nutt	S,C	1,648	28
Highland Park Comm., Highland Park, MI 48203	1918	Comer Heath III	S	2440	78
Highline Comm. (A), Midway, WA 98031	1961	Shirley Gordon	S	7,095	356
Hilbert, Hamburg, NY 14075	1957	Sr. Edmunette	P	540	17
Hill Junior, Hillsboro, TX 76645	1922	Elbert C. Hutchins	Di	1,150	45
Hillsborough Comm., Tampa, FL 33622	1968	F. Scaglione	S	*11,556*	*196*
Hinds Junior, Raymond, MS 39154	1917	Clyde Muse	C,S,F	*6,281*	*280*
Hiwassee, Madisonville, TN 37354	1849	Horace N. Barker	Mu	574	34
Hocking Technical, Nelsonville, OH 45764	1968	John J. Light	S	2,621	135
Holding Tech. Inst. (A), Raleigh, NC 27603	1963	R. LeMay Jr.	S	1,362	83
Holmes Junior (A), Goodman, MS 39079	1925	Frank Branch	S	1,338	68
Holy Cross Jr., Notre Dame, IN 46556	1966	Br. John Driscoll	D	265	20
Holyoke Community, Holyoke, MA 01040	1946	David Bartley	S	4,900	250
Honolulu Comm., Honolulu, HI 96817	1968	C. Yoshioka	S	4,600	220
Hopkinsville Comm. (A), Hopkinsville, KY 42240	1965	Thomas Riley	S	1,345	65
Horry-Georgetown Tech., Conway, SC 29526	1966	W.F. Anderson	S	*1,350*	*47*
Housatonic Comm., Bridgeport, CT 06608	1966	Vincent Darnowski	S	2,693	60
Houston Comm. Coll., Houston, TX 77007	1971	J.B. Whiteley	Di	*30,011*	*265*
Howard Community, Columbia, MD 21044	1969	Alfred Smith Jr.	S	2,682	42
Howard, Big Spring, TX 79720	1945	Charles Hays	S,C	1,047	33
Hudson Valley Comm. (A), Troy, NY 12180	1953	J. Fitzgibbons	S	6,932	240
Humphreys, Stockton, CA 95207	1896	Robert G. Humphreys	P	300	26
Hutchinson Comm. Jr., Hutchinson, KS 67501	1928	David Cothrun	S	1,800	120
Illinois Central, E. Peoria, IL 61635	1967	Leon Perley	Di	12,050	84
Illinois Eastern Comm., Olney, IL 62450	1968	James S. Spencer	S	*9,314*	*140*
Illinois Valley Comm. (A), Oglesby, IL 61348	1924	Alfred Wisgoski	S	3,100	143
Imperial Valley (A), Imperial, CA 92251	1922	Terrell Spencer	S	4,565	213
Independence Comm. Jr., Independence, KS 67301	1925	Neil Edds	Di	850	30
Indian Hills Comm. (A), Ottumwa, IA 52501	1966	Lyle A. Hellyer	S	1,550	161
Indian Hills Comm. (A), Centerville, IA 52544	1930	Lyle Hellyer	S	1,228	96
Indian River Comm., Ft. Pierce, FL 33450	1959	Herman Heise	S	21,250	107
Indian Valley, Novato, CA 94947	1971	Constance M. Carroll	S	3,550	126
Indiana Vocational Tech., Indianapolis, IN 46206	1963	Glenn W. Sample	S	*18,946*	*391*
International Business, Ft. Wayne, IN 46804	1889	Anthony Conti	P	600	25
Inver Hills Comm., Inver Grove Hts., MN 55075	1970	Wallace A. Simpson	S	3,500	64
Iowa Central Comm., Ft. Dodge, IA 50501	1966	Edwin Barbour	S	2,513	117
Iowa Lakes Comm., Estherville, IA 51334	1967	Richard Blacker, Supt.	S	*1,605*	*85*
Iowa Western Comm., Council Bluffs, IA 51501	1967	Robert Looft	S	*4,000*	*140*
Isothermal Comm., Spindale, NC 28160	1965	Ben E. Fountain Jr.	S	1,785	39
Itasca Comm., Grand Rapids, MN 55744	1922	Philip J. Anderson	S	1,046	35
Itawamba Junior, Fulton, MS 38843	1948	W.O. Benjamin	Di	*3,710*	*123*
Jackson Comm., Jackson, MI 49201	1928	Harold Sheffer	C	9,742	107
Jackson State Comm., Jackson, TN 38301	1967	W.L. Nelms	S	2,729	73
Jamestown Community, Jamestown, NY 14701	1950	David W. Petty, Act.	S	3,607	105
Jefferson Davis State Jr., Brewton, AL 36426	1965	George McCormick	S	842	25
Jefferson, Hillsboro, MO 63050	1964	Ray Henry	Di	4,650	152
Jefferson Community, Louisville, KY 40201	1968	Ronald Horvath, Dir.	S	*4,205*	*132*
Jefferson Community, Watertown, NY 13601	1961	John Henderson	C	1,578	93
Jefferson State Jr., Birmingham, AL 35215	1965	Judy Merritt	S	*6,324*	*169*
John A. Logan, Carterville, IL 62918	1967	Robert Tarvin	S	1,800	48
John C. Calhoun St. Comm., Decatur, AL 35602	1965	J.R. Chasteen	S	5,000	134
John Tyler Comm., Chester, VA 23831	1967	Freddie W. Nicholas	S	3,335	80
Johnson County Comm., Overland Park, KS 66210	1968	John E. Cleek	C,S	5,544	118
Joliet Junior, Joliet, IL 60436	1901	Derek N. Nunney	S	2,160	279
Jones County Junior, Ellisville, MS 39437	1927	Thos. Terrell Tisdale	S,Di	2,231	119
Kalamazoo Valley Comm., Kalamazoo, MI 49009	1966	Dale B. Lake	Di	6,814	94
Kankakee Comm., Kankakee, IL 60901	1968	L.H. Horton	S	4,039	56
Kan. City Kan. Comm., Kansas City, KS 66112	1923	A.L. Davies	S	3,300	95
Kapiolani Comm., Honolulu, HI 96814	1965	J.S. Tsunoda, Prov.	S	*4,160*	*102*
Kaskaskia, Centralia, IL 62801	1966	Paul Blowers	Di	*2,820*	*52*

Name, address	Year	Governing official and affiliation		Students	Teachers
Katharine Gibbs School (A), New York, NY 10017	1917	Miss Edith Foster	P	1,000	25
Kauai Community (A), Lihue, HI 96766	1965	Edward White, Provost	S	1,256	75
Kellogg Community, Battle Creek, MI 49016	1956	Richard F. Whitmore	Di	8,000	96
Kendall (A), Evanston, IL 60204	1934	Andrew Cothran	D	400	25
Kettering Coll. of Med. Arts, Kettering, OH 45429	1967	Winton Beaven, Dean	P	399	50
Keystone Junior, La Plume, PA 18440	1868	John B. Hibbard	P	900	40
Kilgore, Kilgore, TX 75662	1935	Stewart McLaurin	S,Di	5,000	150
King's, Charlotte, NC 28204	1901	Richard Poyner	P	375	14
Kirtland Comm., Roscommon, MI 48653	1968	Raymond D. Homer	S	1,800	93
Kirkwood Comm., Cedar Rapids, IA 52406	1966	Bill F. Stewart	S	3,938	222
Kishwaukee, Malta, IL 60150	1968	Norman Jenkins	S,Di	3,600	68
Labette Comm., Parsons, KS 67357	1923	Jerry L. Gallentine	C	1,566	33
Lackawanna Jr., Scranton, PA 18503	1894	John X. McConkey	P	*1,115*	*25*
Lake City Comm., Lake City, FL 32055	1962	Herbert E. Phillips	S	2,900	72
Lake County, Coll. of, Grayslake, IL 60030	1968	John O. Hunter	S	11,060	163
Lake Land, Mattoon, IL 61938	1966	Robert D. Webb	S	3,500	94
Lakeland Comm., Mentor, OH 44060	1967	Wayne Rodehorst	S	6,158	100
Lake Michigan, Benton Harbor, MI 49022	1946	Walter Browe	Di	3,400	56
Lake Region Jr., Devils Lake, ND 58301	1941	Dennis Michaelis	S	468	41
Lake-Sumter Comm., Leesburg, FL 32748	1962	Paul P. Williams	Di	1,979	44
Lakeshore Tech Inst., Cleveland, WI 53015	1912	Frederick Nierode	Di	3,000	108
Lakewood Comm. (A), White Bear Lake, MN 55110	1967	N. Christenson, Act.	S	2,474	93
Lamar Community, Lamar, CO 81052	1937	Gordon Snowbarger	S	484	20
Lane Community, Eugene, OR 97405	1964	Eldon G. Schafer	Di	16,280	232
Laney, Oakland, CA 94607	1953	Lawrence A. Davis	S,Di	12,500	220
Lansing Community, Lansing, MI 48901	1957	Philip Gannon	S	20,129	197
Laramie County Comm., Cheyenne, WY 82001	1969	Harlan L. Heglar	S,C	4,295	96
Laredo Junior, Laredo, TX 78040	1946	Domingo Arechiga	Mu	2,981	102
Lasell Junior (W), Newton, MA 02166	1851	Arthur Griffin	P	650	44
Lassen Comm. (A), Susanville, CA 96130	1925	Robert Theiler	Di	3,100	215
Latter-Day Saints Bus., Salt Lake City, UT 84111	1886	R.F. Kirkham	D	1,000	15
Lawson State Comm., Birmingham, AL 35020	1949	Jesse Lewis	S	1,740	84
Lee, Baytown, TX 77520	1934	Robert Cloud	S	4,307	114
Lees Junior, Jackson, KY 41339	1883	Troy R. Eslinger	P	260	22
Lees-McRae, Banner Elk, NC 28604	1900	H.C. Evans Jr.	P	714	36
Lehigh County Comm., Schnecksville, PA 18078	1966	John G. Berrier	Di	2,940	69
Leicester Jr. (A), Leicester, MA 01524	1784	L. Van Burkirk	P	209	26
Lenoir Comm., Kinston, NC 28501	1958	Jesse L. McDaniel	S	1,817	70
Lewis and Clark Comm., Godfrey, IL 62035	1971	Wilbur R.L. Trimpe	Di	4,803	89
Lexington Technical Inst., Lexington, KY 40506	1965	William Price	S	2,074	60
Lima Technical, Lima, OH 45804	1971	James S. Biddle	S	1,493	50
Lincoln Land Comm., Springfield, IL 62708	1967	Robert L. Poorman	S	5,790	125
Lincoln, Lincoln, IL 62656	1865	Dale Brummet	P	553	34
Lincoln Trail (A), Robinson, IL 62454	1969	Joseph Piland	S	2,000	103
Linn Benton Comm., Albany, OR 97321	1968	Raymond J. Needham	Di	13,500	150
Long Beach City (A), Long Beach, CA 90808	1927	Frank Pearce	Mu	*31,065*	*1,187*
Longview Community, Lee's Summit, MO 64063	1969	Aldo Leker	Di	4,027	60
Lorain County Comm., Elyria, OH 44035	1963	Omar Olson	C	6,051	110
Los Angeles City, Los Angeles, CA 90029	1929	Stelle Feuers	Di	20,000	800
Los Angeles Harbor, Wilmington, CA 90744	1949	Edward R. Robings	Di	11,894	200
Los Angeles Pierce (A), Woodland Hills, CA 91364	1947	Edward Liston	S	23,500	750
Los Angeles Southwest, Los Angeles, CA 90047	1967	Walter C. McIntosh	S	7,450	125
L.A. Trade Technical, Los Angeles, CA 90015	1949	Thomas L. Stevens Jr.	Di	18,000	600
Los Angeles Valley, Van Nuys, CA 91401	1949	Alice Thurston	Di	22,000	600
Louisburg (A), Louisburg, NC 27549	1787	J. Allen Norris Jr.	D	576	39
Louisiana State Univ.					
at Alexandria, Alexandria, LA 71301	1960	Sam H. Frank, Chan.	S	1,609	96
at Eunice, Eunice, LA 70535	1967	Anthony Mumphrey, Chan.	S	1,342	60
Lower Columbia, Longview, WA 98632	1934	David Story	S	4,242	78
Lurleen B. Wallace St. Jr. (A), Andalusia, AL 36420	1969	W.H. McWhorter	S	1,072	50
Luzerne County Comm., Nanticoke, PA 18634	1966	Byron Rinehimer	C	6,200	200
Macomb County Comm., Warren, MI 48093	1954	Frank Blackford	C	*26,032*	*345*
MacCormac Junior, Chicago, IL 60604	1904	Gordon Borchardt	P	*520*	*25*
Macon Junior, Macon, GA 31206	1968	William Wright	S	2,382	77
Madison Area Technical, Madison, WI 53703	1912	Norman P. Mitby, Dir.	Di	*42,700*	*325*
Madison Business, Madison, WI 53703	1856	Stuart E. Sears	P	285	11
Maine, Univ of					
at Augusta, ME 04330	1965	Donald W. Beattie	S	3,409	52
Mainland, Coll. of the, Texas City, TX 77590	1967	Fred Taylor	Di	2,419	86
Malcolm X (A), Chicago, IL 60612	1911	Samuel Huffman	Mu	6,830	215
Manatee Junior, Bradenton, FL 33507	1957	W. Wetzler	S	3,500	110
Manchester Comm. (A), Manchester, CT 06040	1963	Ronald Denison	S	5,000	110
Manor Junior, Jenkintown, PA 19046	1947	Sr. Miriam Clare	P	357	37
Maple Woods Comm., Kansas City, MO 64156	1969	Stephen R. Brainard	Mu	2,200	37
Maria, Albany, NY 12208	1958	Sr. L. Fitzgerald	P	490	52
Maria Regina, Syracuse, NY 13208	1963	Sr. Stella M. Zuccolillo	D	416	42
Maricopa Tech. Comm. (A), Phoenix, AZ 85004	1968	N. Bruemmer, Dean	C	5,196	366
Marin, Coll. of, Kentfield, CA 94904	1926	I.P. Diamond	S	6,950	162
Marion Institute, Marion, AL 36756	1842	Maj. Gen. Barfield	P	220	19
Marshalltown Comm., Marshalltown, IA 50158	1927	Paul Kegel	Di	1,089	45
Martin, Pulaski, TN 38478	1870	Bill Starnes	D	210	17
Martin Comm., Williamston, NC 27892	1968	C. Neill McLeod	S	585	30
Martin Tech. Inst. (A), Williamston, NC 27892	1968	Joseph B. Carter	S,C	1,250	65
Mary Holmes, West Point, MS 39773	1892	Joseph A. Gore	D	472	31
Marymount Palos Verdes, Rancho Palos Verdes, CA 90274	1932	Thomas D. Wood	P	368	17
Mass. Bay Comm. (A), Watertown, MA 02181	1961	John McKenzie	S	4,096	248
Massasoit Comm., Brockton, MA 02402	1966	George E. Ayers	S	*5,642*	*207*
Mattatuck Comm., Waterbury, CT 06708	1967	Charles B. Kinney	S	3,003	75
Maui Community, Kahului, HI 96732	1965	Sanae Moikeha, Provost	S	1,757	85
Mayland Technical, Spruce Pine, NC 28777	1971	O.M. Blake Jr.	S	572	25
Maysville Comm., Maysville, KY 41056	1968	James C. Shires, Dir.	S	418	25
McCook Comm., McCook, NE 69001	1926	Elmer Kuntz	S	605	25
McDowell Tech. Inst., Marion, NC 28752	1964	John Price	S	544	30
McHenry County, Crystal Lake, IL 60014	1968	Robert G. Harris	Di,S	3,895	50
McLennan Comm., Waco, TX 76708	1965	Wilbur Ball	Di	4,050	120
Meramec Community (A), St. Louis, MO 63122	1962	Glynn E. Clark	Di	7,070	378
Merced, Merced, CA 95340	1962	W.C. Martineson	Di	7,744	125

Name, address	Year	Governing official and affiliation		Students	Teachers
Mercer County Comm., Trenton, NJ 08690	1966	John P. Hanley	C	*7,293*	*125*
Mercy (A), Dobbs Ferry, NY 10522	1950	Donald Grunewald	P	4,300	275
Meridian Jr. (A), Meridian, MS 39301	1937	William F. Scaggs	Mu	2,857	221
Merritt (A), Oakland, CA 94619	1964	Donald Godbold	Di	10,500	350
Mesa Comm., Mesa, AZ 85202	1965	Theo Heap	C	12,169	187
Mesabi Comm., Virginia, MN 55792	1918	Gilbert Staupe	S	679	32
Metropolitan Comm., Minneapolis, MN 55403	1965	Curtis W. Johnson	S	2,450	66
Metropolitan Comm., Kansas City, MO 64111	1964	William D. Hatley, Chan.	S	*11,750*	*241*
Miami-Dade Comm., Miami, FL 33176	1960	Robert H. McCabe, Act.	S	*43,822*	*909*
Miami-Jacobs Jr. Coll. of Bus., Dayton, OH 45401	1860	Charles P. Harbottle	P	595	18
Michael J. Owens Tech. (A), Perrysburg, OH 43551	1967	Jacob H. See	S	2,991	63
Michigan Christian, Rochester, MI 48063	1959	Walter L. Gilfilen	P	300	13
Mid Michigan Comm., Harrison, MI 48625	1965	Eugene W. Gillaspy	S,Di	2,800	81
Mid-Plains Comm., No. Platte, NE 69101	1965	Kenneth L. Aten	S	1,721	58
Mid-State Tech. Inst., Wis. Rapids, WI 54494	1967	Earl F. Jaeger	Di	*12,000*	*100*
Middle Georgia, Cochran, GA 31014	1884	Louis C. Alderman Jr.	S	1,527	85
Middlesex Comm., Middletown, CT 06457	1966	Robert A. Chapman	S	2,500	47
Middlesex County, Edison, NJ 08817	1964	Rose M. Channing	C	10,894	264
Midland, Midland, TX 79701	1972	Al G. Langford	C	2,550	70
Midlands Tech., Columbia, SC 29202	1974	Robert Grigsby Jr.	C	*5,431*	*183*
Miles Comm., Miles City, MT 59301	1939	Judson H. Flower	Di,S,C	613	40
Milwaukee Area Tech., Milwaukee, WI 53203	1912	William Ramsey	Di	*68,863*	*662*
Mineral Area (A), Flat River, MO 63601	1922	Richard Caster	Di	917	53
Mira Costa (A), Oceanside, CA 92054	1934	John MacDonald	S	5,400	190
Mississippi Delta Jr., Moorhead, MS 38761	1926	J.T. Hall	S,C	1,541	122
Mississippi Gulf Coast Jr., Perkinston, MS 39573	1925	J.J. Hayden Jr.	Di	*5,789*	*267*
Mitchell, New London, CT 06320	1938	Robert C. Weller	P	743	23
Mitchell Comm., Statesville, NC 28677	1852	Charles Poindexter	S	1,221	55
Moberly Junior, Moberly, MO 65270	1927	Andrew Komar Jr.	S,Di	851	25
Modesto Junior, Modesto, CA 95350	1921	Kenneth Griffin	S	*15,038*	*221*
Mohawk Valley Comm., Utica, NY 13501	1946	G.H. Robertson	S,C	6,800	175
Mohegan Comm., Norwich, Ct 06360	1969	Roland W. Wright, Act.	S	2,100	36
Monroe Comm., Rochester, NY 14623	1961	Moses Koch	C	10,234	285
Monroe County Comm., Monroe, MI 48161	1964	Ronald Campbell	C,S	1,700	50
Montcalm Comm., Sidney, MI 48885	1965	Herbert N. Stoutenburg	C	1,300	26
Monterey Peninsula (A), Monterey, CA 93940	1947	George J. Faul	S	*8,000*	*425*
Montgomery Comm., Rockville, MD 20850	1946	Robert E. Parilla	Di	16,075	355
Montgomery Co. Comm., Blue Bell, PA 19422	1964	Leroy Brendlinger	S,C	7,200	150
Montreat-Anderson, Montreat, NC 28757	1917	Silas M. Vaughn	P	425	22
Moorpark, Moorpark, CA 93021	1963	W. Ray Hearon	C	8,298	115
Morame Valley Comm. (A), Palos Hills, IL 60465	1968	James Koeller	S	10,516	379
Morgan Comm., Ft. Morgan, CO 80701	1970	Robert F. Datteri	S	325	13
Morris, County Coll. of, Randolph, NJ 07869	1965	Sherman H. Masten	C,S	10,858	188
Morristown, (A) Morristown, TN 37814	1881	Raymond White	D	233	18
Motlow State Comm., Tullahoma, TN 37388	1969	Harry D. Wagner	S	2,300	43
Mt. Aloysius Junior (A), Cresson, PA 16630	1939	J.P. Gallagher	P	489	35
Mt. Hood Comm., Gresham, OR 97030	1966	R.S. Nicholson	S	7,997	171
Mt. Ida Junior, Newton Centre, MA 02159	1899	B.E. Carlson	P	1,000	75
Mt. Olive, Mt. Olive, NC 28365	1951	Williams B. Raper	D	380	25
Mt. San Antonio, Walnut, CA 91789	1946	John D. Randall	S	18,133	264
Mt. San Jacinto, San Jacinto, CA 92383	1962	Milo P. Johnson	S	2,700	41
Mt. Wachusett Comm., Gardner, MA 01440	1963	Arthur F. Haley	S	3,471	77
Mountain View (A), Dallas, TX 75211	1970	David Sims	S	*6,500*	*250*
Murray State (A), Tishomingo, OK 73460	1908	Clyde Kindell	S	1,357	49
Muskegon Business, Muskegon, MI 49442	1885	Robert Jewell	P	1,001	18
Muskegon Comm. (A), Muskegon, MI 49442	1926	J.G. Thompson	C	4,762	200
Napa, Napa, CA 94558	1941	Andrew J. Fox	C	5,532	82
Nash Tech. Inst. (A), Rocky Mount, NC 27801	1968	Jack D. Ballard	S	813	35
Nassau Community (A), Garden City, NY 11530	1959	George Chambers	C	17,595	474
National Business College, Roanoke, VA 24009	1890	Francis H. Birchfield	P	*716*	*18*
Navarro, Corsicana, TX 75110	1946	Kenneth Walker	C	1,500	50
Nebraska Western, Scottsbluff, NE 69361	1926	John Harms	Mu	1,096	45
Neosho County Comm. Jr., Chanute, KS 66720	1936	J.C. Sanders	C	851	28
New Hampshire Tech. Inst., Concord, NH 03301	1965	D. Larrabee Sr.	S	1,850	80
New Hampshire Voc. Tech., Portsmouth, NH 03102	1943	R.E. Mandeville, Dir.	S	850	48
New Mexico Junior, Hobbs, NM 88240	1965	Robert A. Anderson, Jr.	Di	1,416	44
New Mexico Military Inst. (M), Roswell, NM 88201	1891	Maj. Gen. G. Childress	S	1,250	74
New River Community, Dublin, VA 24084	1966	H.R. Edwards	S	2,284	86
New York City, Univ. of, New York, NY 10021	1847	Robert Kibbee	C	*164,398*	*6,764*
Bronx Comm., Bronx, NY 10453	1957	Roscoe C. Brown Jr.	Mu	7,546	300
Hostos Comm., Bronx, NY 10451	1968	Flora Mancuso Edwards	C	2,506	103
Kingsborough Comm., Brooklyn, NY 11235	1963	Leon M. Goldstein	Mu	8,000	320
LaGuardia Comm., Long Is. City, NY 11101	1968	Joseph Shenker	Mu	6,117	178
Manhattan Comm., New York, NY 10019	1963	Joshua Smith	Mu	5,805	440
New York City Comm., Brooklyn, NY 11201	1947	Ursula Schwerin	Mu	13,500	435
Queensborough Comm., Bayside, NY 11364	1958	Kurt R. Schmeller	C	11,603	384
New York, State Univ. of					
Agric. & Tech. Inst. (A), Alfred, NY 14802	1908	David H. Huntington	S	4,138	221
" " " Canton, NY 13617	1907	Earl MacArthur	S	2,329	302
" " " (A), Cobleskill, NY 12043	1911	Walton A. Brown	S	2,683	145
" " " Delhi, NY 13753	1913	Seldon M. Kruger	S	2,381	137
" " " (A), Farmingdale, NY 11735	1912	F.A. Cipriani	S	13,049	314
" " " (A), Morrisville, NY 13408	1908	Royson N. Whipple	S	2,997	144
Niagara County Comm. (A), Sanborn, NY 14132	1962	Jack C. Watson	S	3,835	123
Normandale Comm., Bloomington, MN 55431	1968	Dale A. Lorenz	S	4,869	250
North Central Michigan (A), Petoskey, MI 49770	1958	A.D. Shankland	S,C	1,569	90
North Central Tech. Inst., Wausau, WI 54401	1912	Dwight E. Davis	Di,S	*14,000*	*135*
North County Comm. (A), Saranac Lake, NY 12983	1967	P.J. Cayan	S	1,376	48
N. Dak. St. Sch. of Science, Wahpeton, ND 58075	1903	Clair T. Blikre	S	3,500	181
North Florida Junior, Madison, FL 32340	1958	Gary P. Sims	S	1,985	36
North Greenville, Tigerville, SC 29688	1892	George Silver	D	534	29
North Harris County, Houston, TX 77073	1972	W.W. Thorne	S	5,444	130
North Hennepin Comm., Brooklyn Pk., MN 55445	1966	John F. Helling	S	4,103	94
North Idaho, Coeur d'Alene, ID 83814	1933	Barry Schuler	Di	2,904	95
North Iowa Area Comm., Mason City, LA 50401	1918	David R. Pierce	Di	1,929	90
North Shore Community, Beverly, MA 01915	1965	George Traicoff	S	2,321	110
Northampton Co. Area Comm., Bethlehem, PA 18017	1966	Robert J. Kopecek	C	1,332	90
Northeast Alabama State Jr., Rainsville, AL 35986	1965	E.R. Knox	S	1,374	25

Name, address	Year	Governing official and affiliation		Students	Teachers
Northeast Miss. Junior, Booneville, MS 38829	1948	Harold T. White	Di	1,467	101
Northeast Neb. Tech. Comm., Norfolk, NE 68701	1973	Robert P. Cox	S	1,500	110
Northeast Wisc. Tech. Inst. (A), Green Bay, WI 54303	1916	K.W. Hanbenschild, Dir.	Di	*3,050*	*650*
Northeastern Junior, Sterling, CO 80751	1941	Marvin W. Weiss	C	2,111	69
Northeastern Okla. A&M, Miami, OK 74354	1919	D.D. Creech	S	2,786	115
Northern Essex Comm., Haverhill, MA 01830	1961	J.R. Dimitry	S	6,182	120
Northern Oklahoma, Tonkawa, OK 74653	1901	Edwin Vineyard	S	1,668	49
Northern Virginia Comm., Annandale, VA 22003	1965	Richard Ernst	S	*31,327*	*1,446*
Northland Comm., Thief River Falls, MN 56701	1965	Alex Easton	S	560	19
Northwest Community, Powell, WY 82435	1946	Sinclair Orendorff	C	1,650	60
Northwest Miss. Junior (A), Senotobia, MS 38668	1927	Henry B. Koon	S	*2,743*	*130*
Northwestern Conn. Comm., Winsted, CT 06098	1965	Regina Duffy	S	2,500	50
Northwestern Michigan, Traverse City, MI 49684	1951	William J. Yankee	C	2,971	97
Norwalk Community, Norwalk, CT 06854	1961	E.I.L. Baker	S	2,980	60
Norwalk State Tech., Norwalk, CT 06854	1961	P.A. Marino	S	1,481	46
Oakland Comm., Bloomfield Hills, MI 48013	1964	Robert F. Roelofs	S	19,995	291
Oakton Comm., Morton Grove, IL 60053	1969	William Koehnline	S	5,795	144
Ocean County, Toms River, NJ 08753	1964	Andrews S. Moreland	C	5,317	246
Odessa, Odessa, TX 79760	1946	Philip Speegle	Di	4,080	131
Ohlone, Fremont, CA 94538	1966	Peter Blomerly	Di	7,326	256
Okaloosa-Walton Jr., Niceville, FL 32578	1964	J.E. McCracken	S	5,249	74
Oklahoma Sch. of Business, Acctg., Law & Finance, Tulsa, OK 74103	1919	H. Everett Pope Jr.	P	287	5
Olney Central (A), Olney, IL 62450	1963	Paul Thompson	S	1,576	63
Olympic, Bremerton, WA 98310	1946	Henry Milander	S	7,633	111
Onondaga Comm., Syracuse, NY 13215	1962	A. Paloumpis	C	7,000	212
Orangeburg-Calhoun Tech., Orangeburg, SC 29115	1968	M. Rudy Groomes	S	1,369	125
Orange Coast, Costa Mesa, CA 92626	1947	Robert Moore	S	30,300	504
Orange County Comm. (A), Middletown, NY 10940	1950	Robert T. Novak	S	4,988	138
Oscar Rose Junior, Midwest City, OK 73110	1970	Joe Packnett, Act.	S	7,841	148
Otero Junior, La Junta, CO 81050	1941	William L. McDivitt	S	749	43
Ottumwa Heights (A), Ottumwa, IA 52501	1925	Sr. Bernadine Pieper	P	310	27
Paducah Comm., Paducah, KY 42201	1932	Donald J. Clemens, Dir.	S	1,406	55
Palm Beach Junior, Lake Worth, FL 33461	1933	Harold C. Manor	S	10,586	172
Palomar Comm., San Marcos, CA 92069	1946	Omar H. Scheidt	S	15,241	243
Palo Verde Comm., Blythe, CA 92225	1947	George W. Pennell	S	584	17
Panola Junior, Carthage, TX 75633	1947	Arthur Johnson	S	971	31
Paris Junior, Paris, TX 75460	1924	Louis B. Williams	S	2,042	79
Parkersburg Comm., Parkersburg, WV 26101	1971	Byron N. McClenney	S	3,288	80
Parkland, Champaign, IL 61820	1966	William M. Staerkel	S	7,000	318
Pasadena City, Pasadena, CA 91106	1924	Richard S. Meyers	S	19,115	408
Pasco-Hernando Comm. (A), Dade City, FL 33525	1972	Milton O. Jones	S	1,700	174
Passaic Co. Comm., Paterson, NJ 07509	1970	Gustavo Mellander	C	3,118	34
Patrick Henry State Jr., Monroeville, AL 36460	1965	Cecil Murphy	S	596	26
Paul D. Camp Comm., Franklin, VA 23851	1968	Perry Adams	S	1,094	36
Paul Smith's Coll. of Arts & Sci., Paul Smiths, NY 12970	1946	T.N. Stainback	P	1,045	72
Peace (W), Raleigh, NC 27604	1857	S. David Frazier	D	484	27
Pearl River Junior (A), Poplarville, MS 39470	1921	M.R. White	S	2,500	106
Peirce Junior (A), Philadelphia, PA 19102	1865	Thomas M. Peirce III	P	1,407	71
Peninsula, Port Angeles, WA 98362	1961	Paul G. Cornaby	S	1,200	60
Penn Valley Comm., Kansas City, MO 64111	1915	Dorothy M. Wright	Di	5,033	105
Pensacola Jr., Pensacola, FL 32504	1948	T. Felton Harrison	S	*12,453*	*278*
Peralta Comm., Oakland, CA 94610	1964	Max R. Tadlock, Chan.	Di	*30,484*	*560*
Philadelphia, Comm., Coll. of, Philadelphia, PA 19107	1964	Allen T. Bonnell	C	13,637	384
Phillips County Comm., Helena, AR 72342	1965	John Easley	S,C	2,415	51
Phoenix, Phoenix, AZ 85013	1920	William Berry	C	13,143	187
Piedmont Tech., Greenwood, SC 29646	1966	Lex Walters	S,C	1,725	58
Piedmont Tech. Inst. (A), Roxboro, NC 27573	1970	Edward W. Cox	S	*877*	*59*
Piedmont Virginia Comm., Charlottesville, VA 22901	1972	George B. Vaughan	S	3,400	49
Pikes Peak Comm., Colorado Springs, CO 80906	1969	Donald McInnis	S	4,280	213
Pima Comm. (A), Tucson, AZ 85709	1970	Irwin Spector	S	*19,996*	*998*
Pine Manor Junior (W)(A), Chestnut Hill, MA 02167	1911	Rosemary Ashby	P	377	47
Pitt Comm., Greenville, NC 27834	1961	W.E. Fulford Jr.	S	2,050	70
Polk Comm., Winter Haven, FL 33880	1964	Frederick T. Lenfestey	S	5,600	150
Porterville, Porterville, CA 93257	1927	Paul D. Alcantra	S	*2,500*	*73*
Portland Comm., Portland, OR 97219	1961	Amo De Bernardis	Di	29,826	333
Post Junior, Waterbury, CT 06708	1890	Harold Harlow	P	1,446	42
Potomac State, Keyser, WV 26726	1902	J.L. McBee, Exec. Dean	S	1,087	40
Prairie State, Chicago Hts., IL 60411	1958	Richard Creal	S	5,434	98
Pratt Community, Pratt, KS 67124	1938	Norman Myers	C,S	1,325	95
Presentation, Aberdeen, SD 57401	1951	Sr. Lynn Marie Welbig	D	294	24
Prestonburg Comm., Prestonburg, KY	1964	Henry A. Campbell	S	623	27
Prince George's Comm. (A), Largo, MD 20870	1958	Robert Bickford	C	11,830	569
Puerto Rico Jr. (A), Rio Piedras, PR 00928	1949	Federico J. Modesto	P	*5,691*	*218*
Quincy Jr., Quincy, MA 02169	1958	Edward Pierce	Mu	3,780	40
Quinebaug Valley Comm., Danielson, CT 06239	1971	Robert E. Miller	S	900	11
Quinsigamond Comm., Worcester, MA 01606	1963	Donald J. Donato	S	5,094	86
Randolph Tech., Asheboro, NC 27203	1962	M.H. Branson	S	1,400	52
Ranger Junior, Ranger, TX 76470	1926	Jack Elsom	S	722	32
Reading Area Comm. (A), Reading, PA 19603	1971	Lewis Ogle	S	887	74
Redwoods, Coll. of the, Eureka, CA 95501	1964	Donald Weichert	S	*8,500*	*125*
Reedley, Reedley, CA 93654	1926	R.A. Cattant	S	3,314	91
Reinhardt, Waleska, GA 30183	1883	Allen O. Jernigan	D	486	20
Rend Lake, Ina, IL 62846	1967	Harry J. Braun	S	4,000	67
Rhode Island Jr., Warwick, RI 02886	1964	Edward J. Liston	S	*10,105*	*300*
Richard J. Daley (A), Chicago, IL 60652	1960	Virginia Keehan	C	7,766	185
Richland (A), Dallas, TX 75243	1972	E. Biggerstaff Jr.	C	11,200	428
Richland Comm., Decatur, IL 62523	1972	James L. Becker	Di	2,643	37
Richmond Tech. Inst., Hamlet, NC 28345	1964	R. Kenneth Meliun	S	950	36
Ricks, Rexburg, ID 83440	1888	Bruce C. Hafen	D	6,403	235
Rio Hondo, Comm. (A), Whittier, CA 90608	1960	L.A. Grandy	C,S	13,656	555
Rio Salado Comm., Phoenix, AZ 85004	1978	Walter Morrison	C	8,328	NA
Riverside City, Riverside, CA 92506	1916	Charles A. Kane	Di	13,589	191
Roanoke-Chowan Tech. Inst., Ahoskie, NC 27910	1967	J.W. Young	S	989	50
Robeson Tech. Inst., Lumberton, NC 28358	1965	R. Craig Allen	S	1,134	40
Rochester Comm., Rochester, MN 55901	1915	Charles Hill	S	2,911	145

Name, address	Year	Governing official and affiliation		Students	Teachers
Rockland Comm., Suffern, NY 10901	1959	Seymour Eskow	S	7,456	125
Rock Valley, Rockford, IL 61101	1964	Karl Jacobs	Di	4,970	126
Rockingham Comm., Wentworth, NC 27375	1966	Gerald B. James	S,C	3,086	128
Rogue Comm., Grants Pass. OR 97526	1970	Henry O. Pete	S	3,000	60
Sacramento City, Sacramento, CA 95822	1916	Douglas Burris	S	13,080	450
Saddleback (A), Mission Viejo, CA 92675	1967	R.A. Lombardi	S	13,773	683
St. Clair County Comm. (A), Pt. Huron, MI 48060	1923	Richard L. Norris	C	3,316	176
St. Gregory's, Shawnee, OK 74801	1875	Rev. Michael Roethler	P	313	12
St. John's, Winfield KS 67156	1893	Gordon Beckler	D	249	21
St. John's River Comm., Palatka, FL 32077	1958	Robert L. McLendon Jr.	S	1,404	50
St. Louis Community, St. Louis, MO 63110	1962	Richard Greenfield, Chan.	S	*25,147*	*625*
at Florissant Valley, St. Louis, MO 63135	1962	David Harris	Di	8,500	200
at Forest Park, St. Louis, MO 63110	1963	Philip Carlock, Act.	C	6,639	180
at Meramec (A), St. Louis, MO 63122	1962	Glynn Clark	Di	9,040	433
St. Mary's Jr., Minneapolis, MN 55454	1964	Sr. Anne Joachim Moore	D	770	100
St. Mary's (W), Raleigh, NC 27611	1842	John T. Rice	D	510	32
St. Petersburg Junior, St. Petersburg, FL 33733	1927	Carl M. Kuttler, Jr.	Di	14,499	303
Salem Community, Penns Grove, NJ 08069	1972	William Bryan	C	1,172	35
Sampson Tech. Inst., Clinton, NC 28328	1967	Vacant	S	737	42
San Antonio, San Antonio, TX 78284	1925	Jerome Weynand	S,Di	20,668	495
San Bernardino Valley, San Bernardino, CA 92410	1926	Arthur Jensen	S,Di	*16,000*	*227*
San Diego City, San Diego, CA 92101	1914	Allen Repashy	S	4,436	165
San Diego, Mesa, San Diego, CA 92111	1963	Ellis Benson	S	18,000	235
San Francisco, City Coll. of, San Francisco, CA 94112	1935	K.S. Washington	C	26,313	520
San Jacinto, Pasadena, TX 77505	1961	Thomas M. Spencer	S	12,000	300
San Joaquin Delta Comm. (A), Stockton, CA 95207	1935	Dale Parnell	S,Di	20,710	549
San Jose City, San Jose, CA 95128	1921	Theodore Murguia	Di	14,000	150
San Luis Obispo Co. Comm. (A), San Luis Obispo, CA 93406	1965	Merlin Eisenbise	C	5,504	200
San Mateo, Coll. of, San Mateo, CA 94402	1923	Lois A. Callahan	C,S	14,616	666
Sandhills Comm., Carthage, NC 28387	1965	Raymond A. Stone	S	1,700	87
Santa Ana (A), Santa Ana, CA 92706	1915	John E. Johnson	S	23,288	784
Santa Barbara City (A), Santa Barbara, CA 93109	1908	Glenn Gooder	Di,S	8,613	243
Santa Fe Community (A), Gainesville, FL 32602	1965	Alan Robertson	S	6,056	326
Santa Monica, Santa Monica, CA 90405	1929	Richard Moore	S	18,286	205
Santa Rosa Junior, Santa Rosa, CA 95401	1928	Roy Mikalson	C	18,788	188
Sauk Valley (A), Dixon, IL 61021	1965	George Cole	S	3,261	150
Schenectady Co. Comm., Schenectady, NY 12305	1968	Karl Zopf	S	2,120	69
Schoolcraft, Livonia, MI 48152	1961	C. Nelson Grote	S	9,742	160
Schreiner, Kerrville, TX 78028	1923	Sam Junkin	D	298	21
Scottsdale Comm., Scottsdale, AZ 85251	1970	Arthur W. DeCabooter	C,Di	6,383	96
S.D. Bishop State Jr. (A), Mobile, AL 36603	1965	Sanford Bishop	S	1,650	75
Seattle Central Comm., Seattle, WA 98122	1966	Robert Terry	S	*8,771*	*418*
Selma Univ. (A), Selma, AL 36701	1878	M.C. Cleveland Jr.	D,P	620	28
Seminole Comm., Sanford, FL 32771	1966	E.S. Weldon	S	4,066	105
Sequoias, Coll. of the (A), Visalia, CA 93277	1925	Ivan Crookshanks	Di	6,592	331
Seward County Comm., Liberal, KS 67901	1967	James Hooper	C,S	1,402	32
Shasta (A), Redding, CA 96001	1950	Dale Miller	C	12,800	482
Shelby State Comm. (A), Memphis, TN 38104	1972	Jess Parrish	S	*4,326*	*236*
Sheldon Jackson, Sitka, AK 99835	1878	H.H. Holloway	D	297	28
Sheridan, Sheridan, WY 82801	1948	Gordon Ward	S	1,172	42
Shoreline Comm. (A), Seattle, WA 98133	1964	Richard S. White	S	8,000	320
Sierra, Rocklin, CA 95677	1914	G.C. Angove	C	6,890	136
Sinclair Comm., Dayton, OH 45402	1887	David Ponitz	C,S	14,300	300
Siskiyous, Coll. of the, Weed, CA 96094	1957	Eugene Schumacher	S	2,423	87
Skagit Valley (A), Mt. Vernon, WA 98273	1926	Norwood Cole	S	*15,662*	*371*
Skyline, San Bruno, CA 94066	1969	Glenn P. Smith, Chan.	Di	6,886	120
Snead State Jr., Boaz, AL 35957	1935	William H. Osborn	S	850	35
Snow, Ephraim, UT 84627	1888	J.M. Higbee	S	1,000	68
Solano Comm., Suisun City, CA 94585	1945	William Wilson	Di	8,919	128
Somerset Comm., Somerset, KY 42501	1965	Roscoe Kelley	S	900	45
Somerset County, Somerville, NJ 08876	1966	Joseph Fink	C,S	4,200	108
South Florida Jr., Avon Park, FL 33825	1965	William Stallard	S	938	28
South Georgia, Douglas, GA 31533	1906	Denton Coker	S	1,252	50
South Oklahoma City, Oklahoma City, OK 73159	1970	Dale L. Gibson	S	6,819	140
South Plains, Levelland, TX 79336	1958	Marvin L. Baker	C	2,531	104
Southeast Comm., Fairbury, NE 68352	1941	Daniel Gerber, Dir.	C,S	430	25
Southeast Comm., Cumberland, KY 40823	1960	Larry Stanley	S	600	21
Southeastern Comm., Burlington, IA 52655	1966	C.A. Callison, Supt.	S	*2,068*	*92*
Southeastern Comm., Keokuk, IA 52632	1953	C.A. Callison	S	350	27
Southeastern Comm., Whiteville, NC 28472	1964	W.R. McCarter	S	2,241	52
Southeastern Illinois, Harrisburg, IL 62946	1960	Harry Abell	S	2,400	65
Southern Baptist, Walnut Ridge, AR 72476	1941	D.J. Nicholas	P,D	550	25
Southern Idaho, Coll. of, Twin Falls, ID 83301	1964	James L. Taylor	S	4,923	123
Southern Ohio, Cincinnati, OH 45202	1927	H.W. Nagel	P	*1,600*	*60*
Southern Seminary Jr., Buena Vista, VA 24416	1867	Bill J. Elkins	P	237	20
Southern Union State Jr., Wadley, AL 36276	1922	Ray Jones	S	*1,413*	*31*
Southwest Mississippi Jr., Summit, MS 39666	1918	Horace Holmes	S	1,234	46
Southwest Texas Junior, Uvalde, TX 78801	1946	Wayne Matthews	S	2,211	54
Southwest Virginia Comm., Richlands, VA 24641	1966	Charles King	S	2,106	83
Southwestern, Chula Vista, CA 92010	1960	C.S. DeVore	S	11,596	171
Southwestern (A), Okla. City, OK 73127	1946	Hugh Morgan	D	1,500	75
Southwestern Comm., Creston, IA 50801	1966	John A. Smith	S	535	41
Southwestern Michigan, Dowagiac, MI 49047	1964	R.M. Owens	Di	2,400	40
Southwestern Oregon Comm., Coos Bay, OR 97420	1961	Jack E. Brookins	Di	4,808	61
Spartanburg Methodist, Spartanburg, SC 29301	1911	George D. Fields, Jr.	Mu	1,035	40
Spartanburg Tech. (A), Spartanburg, SC 29303	1963	Joe D. Gault	S	3,097	217
Spokane Comm. (A), Spokane, WA 99202	1963	Lloyd Stannard	S	*3,600*	*343*
Spokane Falls Comm., Spokane, WA 99204	1967	Gerald Saling	S	6,500	137
Spoon River, Canton, IL 61520	1959	Paul C. Gianini, Jr.	Di	2,200	40
Springfield Tech. Comm., Springfield, MA 01105	1967	Robert Geitz	S	6,601	163
Springfield Coll. in Illinois, Springfield, IL 62702	1929	Sr. Francis M. Thrailkill	P	517	26
State Fair Comm., Sedalia, MO 65301	1966	Fred E. Davis	Di	1,342	57
State Tech Inst., Memphis, TN 38134	1967	Charles Whitehead	S	5,649	154
Sue Bennett, London, KY 40741	1897	Earl F. Hays	D,P	295	15
Suffolk County Comm., Selden, NY 11784	1960	Albert M. Ammerman	S	21,000	600
Sullivan County Comm. (A), Loch Sheldrake, NY 12759	1962	Richard F. Grego	S	1,740	71
Sumter Area Tech, Sumter, SC 29150	1963	L.E. Terrell Jr., Act.	S	*2,000*	*110*
Suomi (A), Hancock, MI 49930	1896	Ralph J. Jalkanen	P,D	371	30

Name, address	Year	Governing official and affiliation		Students	Teachers
Surry Community, Dobson, NC 27017	1965	Swanson Richards	S	1,723	62
Tacoma Comm., Tacoma, WA 98465	1965	Larry P. Stevens	S	7,114	84
Taft, Taft, CA 93268	1922	Wendell Reeder	Di	1,279	66
Tallahassee Comm., Tallahassee, FL 32304	1965	Marm Harris	C	3,303	126
Tarrant County Junior, Ft. Worth, TX 76102	1965	Joe B. Rushing	C,S	*18,000*	*500*
Technical Career Inst., New York, NY 10001	1909	Samuel Steinman	P	1,900	90
Tech. Inst. of Alamance (A), Burlington, NC 27215	1958	William Taylor	S	9,783	2,207
Temple Junior, Temple, TX 76501	1926	Marvin Felder	S	2,257	80
Texarkana Comm., Texarkana, TX 75501	1927	Carl M. Nelson	S	2,876	193
Texas Southmost, Brownsville, TX 78520	1926	Albert A. Besteiro	Mu	4,072	133
Thames Valley State Tech., Norwich, CT 06360	1963	Donald Welter	S	1,850	77
Thomas Nelson Comm. (A), Hampton, VA 23670	1968	Gerald O. Cannon	S	4,662	194
Thornton Comm., So. Holland, IL 60473	1927	Nathan A. Ivey	S	10,000	136
Three Rivers Comm., Poplar Bluff, MO 63901	1966	J.L. Bottenfield	Di	1,520	54
Tidewater Comm., Portsmouth, VA 23703	1968	George Pass	S	*15,000*	*250*
Tomkins-Courtland Comm. (A), Groton, NY 13053	1967	Hushang Bahar	S	2,793	48
Treasure Valley Comm., Ontario, OR 97914	1962	Emery Skinner	Di,S	1,301	57
Tri-County Tech. Pendleton, SC 29670	1962	Don Garrison	S	*2,080*	*79*
Trident Tech, Charleston, SC 29405	1964	Charles F. Ward	S	*5,400*	*170*
Trinidad State Junior, Trinidad, CO 81082	1925	Thomas Sullivan	S	1,200	121
Triton, River Grove, IL 60171	1964	Brent Knight	S	23,547	230
Trocaire, Buffalo, NY 14220	1958	Sr. M. Carmina Coppola	P	911	35
Truett McConnell, Cleveland, GA 30528	1946	Ronald Weitman	D	*625*	*20*
Tulsa Junior, Tulsa, OK 74119	1969	A.M. Philips	S	*10,505*	*146*
Tunxis Comm., Farmington, CT 06032	1970	Benjamin G. Davis	S	*2,672*	*143*
Tyler Junior, Tyler, TX 75711	1926	Harry E. Jenkins	S	15,893	248
Ulster County Comm. (A), Stone Ridge, NY 12484	1961	Robert T. Brown	S	2,681	87
Umpqua Comm., Roseburg, OR 97470	1964	I.S. Hakanson	S	1,730	60
Union, Cranford, NJ 07016	1933	Saul Orkin	P	5,900	100
Union County Voc.-Tech., Scotch Plains, NJ 07076	1960	Myron Corman, Act.	C	1,760	94
Utica Junior, Utica, MS 39175	1903	J. Louis Stokes	S	950	61
Valencia Comm., Orlando, FL 32802	1967	James F. Gollattscheck	S	*5,101*	*145*
Ventura, Ventura, CA 93003	1925	Richard A. Glenn	S	12,612	178
Vermillion Comm., Ely, MN 55731	1922	Ralph R. Doty	S	450	30
Vermont, Comm. Coll. of, Montpelier, VT 05602	1970	Peter Smith	S	2,000	455
Vermont Technical, Randolph Center, VT 05061	1962	Ned Herrin Jr.	S	750	50
Victor Valley, Victorville, CA 92392	1961	B.W. Wadsworth	Di	3,024	72
Victoria, Victoria, TX 77901	1925	Roland E. Bing	S	2,231	60
Villa Julie, Stevenson, MD 21153	1952	Carolyn Manuszak	P	606	80
Vincennes Univ., Vincennes, IN 47591	1806	Isaac K. Beckes	S	*4,445*	*203*
Virginia Highlands Comm., Abingdon, VA 24210	1967	Emma Schulken	S	1,445	50
Virginia Western Comm., Roanoke, VA 24015	1966	Harold H. Hopper	S	*4,167*	*134*
Wabash Valley, Mt. Carmel, IL 62863	1959	John Gwaltney	Di	1,500	59
Wake Tech. Inst., Raleigh, NC 27603	1963	Robert LeMay Jr.	P	1,164	89
Waldorf, Forest City, IA 50436	1903	Arndt Bratten	D	500	35
Walker, Jasper, AL 35501	1938	David J. Rowland	P	719	45
Walla Walla Comm., Walla Walla, WA 99362	1967	Eldon Dietrich	S	2,693	105
Walters State Comm., Morristown, TN 37814	1970	Jack E. Campbell	S	3,870	70
Washington State Comm., Spokane, WA 92207	1963	Max M. Synder	S	*26,729*	*378*
Washtenaw Comm., Ann Arbor, MI 48106	1965	Gunder Myran	C	7,465	159
Waterbury State Tech, Waterbury, CT 06708	1964	Kenneth E. DeRego	S	1,567	61
Waubonsee Comm., Sugar Grove, IL 60554	1966	F.D. Etheredge	S,Di	4,910	250
Waukesha Co. Tech. Inst., Pewaukee, WI 53072	1920	R. Anderson, Dist. Dir.	Di	*30,000*	*125*
Wayne Community, Goldsboro, NC 27530	1957	Clyde Erwin Jr.	S,C	2,232	98
Wayne County Comm., Detroit, MI 48201	1967	Reginald Wilson	S	*19,737*	*186*
Weatherford Jr. (A), Weatherford, TX 76086	1869	E.W. Mince	C	*1,453*	*74*
Wenatchee Valley, Wenatchee, WA 98801	1939	James R. Davis	S	3,939	92
Wentworth Institute of Technology, Boston, MA 02115	1904	Edward I. Kirkpatrick	P	2,250	137
Wesley, Dover, DE 19901	1873	R.J. Cooke	D	1,127	47
West Hills, Coalinga, CA 93210	1932	Robert A. Annand	S,C	2,300	158
West Los Angeles, Culver City, CA 90230	1968	M. Fujimoto	Di	10,041	400
West Valley, Saratoga, CA 95070	1963	Melvin F. Tuscher	Di	18,000	200
West Virginia North, Comm., Wheeling, WV 26003	1972	Daniel B. Crowder	S	*3,946*	*63*
Westark Comm., Ft. Smith, AR 72901	1928	James Kraby	S	3,252	98
Westbrook, Portland, ME 04103	1831	Thomas B. Courtice	P	900	37
Westchester Comm., Valhalla, NY 10595	1946	Joseph N. Hankin	C,S	7,000	300
Western Okla. State, Altus, OK 73521	1926	W.C. Burris	S	1,818	65
Western Piedmount Comm., Morganton, NC 28655	1964	H.D. Moretz, Act.	S	1,500	53
Western Wisc. Tech. Inst., LaCrosse, WI 54601	1912	Charles Richardson, Dir.	S	5,467	369
Wharton County Junior, Wharton, TX 77488	1946	Theodore Nicksick Jr.	S	1,850	120
Wilkes Community, Wilkesboro, NC 28697	1965	David E. Daniel	S	2,900	110
William Rainey Harper (A), Palatine, IL 60067	1965	Robert E. Lahti	S	19,575	933
Williamsport Area Comm., Williamsport, PA 17701	1965	William Fedderson	Di	*3,093*	*173*
Willmar Comm., Willmar, MN 56201	1961	John Torgelson	S	840	35
Wilson Co. Tech. Inst., Wilson, NC 27893	1958	Ernest B. Parry	S	2,500	43
Wisconsin Center, Univ. of	1973	Edward Fort	S	*8,382*	*347*
at Barron, Rice Lake, WI 54868	1966	John Meggers, Dean	S	334	26
at Fond du Lac, Fond du Lac, WI 54935	1968	Willard J. Henken, Dean	S	564	26
at Fox Valley, Menasha, WI 54952	1960	Rue C. Johnson	S	851	42
at Manitowoc, Manitowoc, WI 54220	1933	C. Natunewicz, Dean	S	360	22
at Marathon (A), Wausau, WI 54401	1947	W.R. Peters, Dean	S	840	35
at Marshfield/Wood, Marshfield, WI 54449	1964	Norbert Koopman, Dean	S	638	30
at Medford, Medford, WI 54451	1968	Darwin A. Slocum, Dean	S	138	17
at Richland (A), Richland Ctr., WI 53581	1967	Marjorie Wallace, Dean	S	326	9
at Rock County, Janesville, WI 53545	1966	Thomas Walterman, Dean	S	650	40
at Sheboygan, Sheboygan, WI 53081	1933	K.M. Bailey, Dean	S	616	35
at Waukesha, Waukesha, WI 53186	1966	Kenneth D. Oliver, Dean	S	1,700	90
at Washington, West Bend, WI 53095	1968	R.O. Thompson, Dean	S	616	37
Wood Junior, Mathiston, MS 39752	1886	Felix Sutphin	D	233	14
Worthington Comm., Worthington, MN 56187	1936	Frederick A. Voda	S	800	30
Yakima Valley, Yakima, WA 98907	1928	William Russell	S	6,600	122
Yavapai, Prescott, AZ 86301	1966	Joseph Russo	S	*5,206*	*85*
York, York, NE 68467	1890	Gary Bartholomew	D	324	19
York Technical, Rock Hill, SC 29730	1964	Baxter Hood	S,C	1,504	64
Young Harris, Young Harris, GA 30582	1866	Ray Farley	D	500	25
Yuba Comm., Marysville, CA 95901	1927	Daniel G. Walker	S	8,000	142

Canadian Colleges and Universities

Source: Statistics Canada

Each institution listed has an enrollment of at least 200 students of college grade. Enrollment and faculty include all branches and campuses for the 1978-79 academic year. Number of full-time teachers is the total number of individuals on teaching staff. Governing official is the president unless otherwise designated. All institutions are co-educational.

Name	Location	Established	Governing official	Students	Teachers
Acadia Univ.	Wolfville, N.S.	1838	A.M. Sinclair	2,701	198
Alberta, Univ. of	Edmonton, Alta.	1906	M. Horowitz	18,467	1,583
Bishop's Univ.	Lennoxville, Que.	1843	Christopher Nicholl	817	71(1)
Brandon Univ.	Brandon, Man.	1899	H.J. Perkins	1,162	124
British Columbia, Univ. of	Vancouver, B.C.	1908	Douglas T. Kenny	19,324	1,988
Brock Univ.	St. Catharines, Ont.	1964	A.J. Earp	2,188	216
Calgary, Univ. of	Calgary, Alta.	1945	Norman E. Wagner	10,644	1,061
Carleton Univ.	Ottawa, Ont.	1942	William Beckel	8,298	628
Concordia Univ.	Montreal, Que.	1974	John O'Brien, Rector	10,205	674(1)
Dalhousie Univ.	Halifax, N.S.	1818	Henry D. Hicks	7,015	798(1)
Guelph, Univ. of	Guelph, Ont.	1964	Donald F. Forster	8,934	786
King's Coll., Univ. of	Halifax, N.S.	1789	John F. Godfrey	349	8
Lakehead Univ.	Thunder Bay, Ont.	1965	G.A. Harrower	2,217	252
Laurentian Univ.	Sudbury, Ont.	1960	Henry B.M. Best	2,809	348
Laval Universite	Quebec, Que.	1852	Jean-Guy Paquet, Rector	17,203	1,422(1)
Lethbridge, Univ. of	Lethbridge, Alta.	1967	John Woods	1,441	165
Manitoba, Univ. of	Winnipeg, Man.	1877	Ralph Campbell	13,063	1,302
McGill Univ.	Montreal, Que.	1821	David Johnston	18,796	1,296(1)
McMaster Univ.	Hamilton, Ont.	1887	A.N. Bourns	10,027	903
Mem. Univ. of Newfoundland	St. John's, Nfld.	1925	M.O. Morgan	6,161	812
Moncton, Univ. de	Moncton, N.B.	1963	Jean Cadieux, Rector	2,954	328
Montreal, Univ. de	Montreal, Que.	1920	Paul Lacoste, Rector	14,147	1,696(1)
Mount Allison Univ.	Sackville, N.B.	1840	Guy MacLean	1,333	130
Mount St. Vincent Univ.	Halifax, N.S.	1925	Margaret Fulton	1,466	109
New Brunswick, Univ. of	Fredericton, N.B.	1785	T.J. Condon	5,886	551
Nova Scotia Coll. of Arts & Design	Halifax, N.S.	1887	Garry Neill Kennedy	390	42
Nova Scotia Technical	Halifax, N.S.	1907	Clair Callaghan	702	67
Ontario Inst. for Studies in Education	Toronto, Ont.	1965	Clifford C. Pitt	624	155
Ottawa, Univ. of	Ottawa, Ont.	1848	Roger Guindon	10,826	953
Prince Edward Island, Univ. of	Charlottetown, P.E.I.	1969	Peter Meincke	1,390	120
Quebec, Univ. of	Ste-Foy, Que.	1969	Gilles Boulet	14,607	1,360(1)
Queen's Univ.	Kingston, Ont.	1841	R.L. Watts	10,429	916
Regina, Univ. of	Regina, Sask.	1974	Lloyd I. Barber	3,340	386
Royal Military Coll. of Can.	Kingston, Ont.	1876	Donald Tilley	665	133
Ryerson Polytechnical Inst.	Toronto, Ont.	1948	Walter G. Pitman	9,171	649
Sainte-Anne Univ.	Church Point, N.S.	1890	Charles J. Gaudet, Rector	207	25
Saint Paul Univ.	Ottawa, Ont.	1866	Rev. Henri Goudreault	202	48
St. Francis Xavier Univ.	Antigonish, N.S.	1853	Rev. G.A. MacKinnon	2,175	159
St. Mary's Univ.	Halifax, N.S.	1802	Kenneth L. Ozmon	2,207	178
Saskatchewan, Univ. of	Saskatoon, Sask.	1907	R.W. Begg	10,140	968
Sherbrooke, Univ. of	Sherbrooke, Que.	1954	Yves Martin	6,592	618(1)
Simon Fraser Univ.	Burnaby, B.C.	1965	George Pederson	5,448	466
Toronto, Univ. of	Toronto, Ont.	1827	James M. Ham	31,420	2,545
Trent Univ.	Peterborough, Ont.	1963	T.E.W. Nind	2,175	176
Victoria, Univ. of	Victoria, B.C.	1963	H.E. Petch	5,267	458
Waterloo, Univ. of	Waterloo, Ont.	1957	B.C. Mathews	14,273	815
Western Ontario, Univ. of	London, Ont.	1878	George E. Connell	16,511	1,420
Wilfrid Laurier Univ.	Waterloo, Ont.	1973	N.H. Tayler	3,278	216
Windsor, Univ. of	Windsor, Ont.	1857	Mervyn Franklin	6,077	526
Winnipeg, Univ. of	Winnipeg, Man.	1871	Henry E. Duckworth	2,602	205
York Univ.	Downsview, Ont.	1959	H. Ian MacDonald	11,717	1,044

(1) Estimate.

Typical Tuition Fees at Canadian Colleges and Universities

Source: Statistics Canada

Undergraduate tuition fees at universities and colleges with enrollment of 5,000 full day-time students or more. Fee is for 1979-80 academic year.

Institution	Tuition
Alberta, University of	$550-825
British Columbia, Univ. of	536-838
Calgary, University of	275-550(1)
Carleton University, Ottawa	715-780
Concordia University	450-540
Dalhousie University	840-960
Guelph, University of	338-403(1)
Laval Université	225-300(3)
Manitoba, University of	570-1020
Montréal, Université de	270-370(3)
Memorial University of Newfoundland	600-900
McGill University	570-719
McMaster University	460(1)-780
New Brunswick, University of	790
Ottawa, University of	$698-877
Queen's University of Kingston	715-870
Québec, Université du	250(2)
Ryerson Polytechnical Institute	484
Saskatchewan, University of	655-945
Sherbrooke, University of	233-325(3)
Simon Fraser University	270(1)
Toronto, University of	720-945
Victoria, University of	585-713
Waterloo, University of	761-955
Western Ontario, University of	720-920
Windsor, University of	715-780
York University	863

(1) Per semester. (2) Per session. (3) Per trimester.
(4) Most universities in Alberta, Ontario, Quebec and the Maritime provinces have differential fees for foreign students.

Tuition Fees at Selected U.S. Colleges and Universities

Source: World Almanac Questionnaire

The College Entrance Examination Board has estimated that the average cost in a private college in the fall of 1979 was $6,082 a 10.3% increase over the previous year. The cost at a public college averaged $3,409, an 8.1% increase.

Fees for tuition charged per year by colleges and universities for courses, use of libraries, laboratories and other facilities are a major part of student expenses. Tuition varies considerably, depending on the type of institution, its control and location. The lowest tuition fees are those of state-controlled or other public-controlled institutions for residents of their state, city, etc. Students from other states or areas have to pay more. In the following list, such state or other public institutions are shown with two figures. The lower one is the tuition fee for residents, the higher one the tuition fee for students from other states or areas.

(*Tuition does not include room, board, or other expenses.*)

School	Tuition
Abilene Christian	$2,080
Adams State	680-2,000
Agnes Scott	3,500
Akron, Univ. of	840-1,800
Alabama State	525-870
Alabama, Univ. of	722-1,543
Albion	3,728
Albright	4,180
Allegheny	4,300
Alma	4,144
Amherst	4,620
Appalachian State Univ.	614-2,334
Arizona, Univ. of	550-2,100
Arkansas, Univ. of	600-1,230
Auburn	600-1,200
Augusta	496-1,210
Austin	3,100
Austin Peay State Univ.	550-1,600
Avila	2,400
Baldwin-Wallace	4,131
Ball State	840-1,800
Barat	3,250
Baylor	1,920
Bemidji State Univ.	585-1,164
Blue Mountain	1,640
Bob Jones	1,449
Boston	4,530
Bowdoin	5,100
Brandeis Univ.	5,075
Brown	6,140
Bryan	2,250
Buena Vista	3,100
Cabrini	3,012
Cal. Inst. of Tech.	4,302
Cal. Lutheran	3,600
Canisius	2,850
Cardinal Stritch	2,500
Carnegie-Mellon	4,100
Case Western Reserve Univ.	3,900
Catholic Univ. of America	3,750
Charleston, Univ. of	2,150
Chicago State Univ.	590-1,530
Clemson Univ.	850-1,800
Colorado, Univ. of	$892-3,388
Daemen	3,430
Dakota Wesleyan Univ.	2,065
Dayton, Univ. of	2,600
Delaware, Univ. of	990-2,400
Delta State Univ.	280
Detroit Inst. of Tech.	1,363-1,463
Drake	4,060
East Carolina Univ.	578-2,298
East Texas State	360-1,210
Eastern New Mexico Univ.	717-1,596
Fairfield Univ.	3,900
Fordham Univ.	3,400
Fort Lewis	445-1,959
Framingham State	600-1,200
Georgetown	2,200-2,300
George Washington Univ.	3,550
Goucher	4,650
Green Mountain	4,050
Hastings	2,580
Hawaii, Univ. of	450-1,125
Hope	3,430
Idaho, College of	3,150
Indiana State Univ.	930-2,015
Iowa State Univ.	816-1,881
Ithaca	4,052
Jacksonville State Univ.	600
John Brown Univ.	2,100
John Carroll Univ.	3,200
Juilliard School	3,600
Kalamazoo	4,194
Kentucky, Univ. of	562-1,812
Kutztown State	950-1,780
Lock Haven State	950-1,780
Lowell, Univ. of	700-2,300
Marquette Univ.	3,620
Memphis State Univ.	516-1,600
Miami Univ.	890-1,690
Montclair State	704-1,408
Montana, Univ. of	625-1,993
Muskingum	4,337
Nazareth	3,100
Nebr. Wesleyan Univ.	3,050
New England	$4,680
New Mexico, Univ. of	312-936
New Orleans, Univ. of	524-1,454
New York Univ.	4,150-5,355
Notre Dame, Univ. of	4,630
Oberlin	4,483
Occidental	5,350
Ohio Univ.	1,056-2,400
Oklahoma, Univ. of	574-1,518
Old Dominion Univ.	816-1,416
Pace Univ.	2,976
Paine	2,010
Pennsylvania State Univ.	1,368-2,748
Peru State	570-1,020
Pfeiffer	2,345
Portland State Univ.	858-2,982
Quinnipiac	2,940
Radcliffe	5,265
Redlands, Univ. of	4,100
Reed	5,560
Rhode Island, Univ. of	872-2,508
Richmond, Univ. of	4,100
Rutgers Univ.	1,087-1,919
St. Bonaventure Univ.	3,300
St. Louis Univ.	3,700
St. Olaf	3,795
St. Paul Bible	1,100
Selma Univ.	2,300
Southern Methodist Univ.	4,340
Tabor	2,560
Tampa, Univ. of	6,460
Temple Univ.	1,810-3,374
Tennessee, Univ. of	512-1,448
Tiffin Univ.	1,800
Utah, Univ. of	630-1,635
Vermont, Univ. of	1,500-4,150
Virginia State	904-1,479
Washington, Univ. of	687-2,394
West Virginia Inst. of Tech.	371-1,311
Worcester State	637-1,500
Wyoming, Univ. of	592-1,878
Yankton	3,260

Federal Funds for Education, 1979

Source: National Center for Education Statistics, U.S. Health, Education, and Welfare Department

Includes grants, loans, and directly administered services. Estimated. (thousands of dollars)

Type of support, level, and program	
Elementary-secondary education	**$6,485,096**
School asst.—federally affected areas	780,500
Educationally deprived/Economic Opportunity Programs	3,891,837
Supporting services	368,461
Teacher corps	11,776
Vocational education	371,490
Dependents' schools abroad	372,116
Public lands revenue for schools	286,579
Assistance in special areas	88,554
Veterans' education	65,600
Emergency school asst.	225,134
Other	28,049
Higher education	**9,085,451**
Basic research	2,070,000
Research facilities	452,300
Training grants, fellowships, and traineeships	1,100,790
Facilities and equipment	102,127
Other institutional support	573,338
Other student assistance	4,786,896
Vocational-tech. and continuing ed.	**6,348,299**
Vocational-technical education	$5,687,000
Veterans' education	391,100
General continuing education	211,851
Training, federal, state, and local personnel	58,348
Grants, total	**22,018,846**
Loans, total	**1,099,561**
Student loan program, Nat. Def. Ed. Act.	1,018,546
College facilities loans	81,015
Total grants and loans	**23,118,407**
Other federal funds, total	**7,781,212**
Applied research and development	2,920,600
School lunch and milk programs	2,699,167
Training of federal personnel	881,423
U.S. academies	336,974
Professional training, military	544,449
Library services	**254,961**
Grants to public libraries	61,247
National library services	193,714
International education	**159,242**
Educational exchange program	47,493
AID projects	96,525
ACTION (previously Peace Corps)	13,124

(Continued)

(Continued)

Other international educ. and training	2,100	Educational television facilities	137,400
Other	**865,819**	Education in federal correctional inst.	11,676
Agricultural extension service	251,611	Other education; property transfers	465,132

Fall Enrollment and Teachers in Full-time Day Schools

Public Elementary and Secondary Day Schools, Fall 1978

Source: National Center for Education Statistics, U.S. Health, Education and Welfare Dept.

State	Local school systems Total	Operating	Nonoperating	Enrollment Total	Elementary	Secondary	Classroom teachers
United States	15,992	15,705	287	[1]42,559,000	[1]25,030,000	[1]17,529,000	[1]2,199,000
Alabama	127	127	—	761,666	382,562	379,104	40,771
Alaska	51	51	—	90,728	49,895	40,833	5,057
Arizona	226	211	15	509,830	349,695	160,135	25,654
Arkansas	382	381	1	456,698	241,178	215,520	23,112
California	1,034	1,034	—	4,187,967	2,728,637	1,459,330	207,000
Colorado	181	181	—	558,285	307,001	251,284	29,461
Connecticut	165	165	—	593,757	396,975	196,782	35,739
Delaware	16	16	—	111,034	53,041	57,993	6,014
Florida	67	67	—	1,513,819	776,607	737,212	71,853
Georgia	188	188	—	(2)	(2)	(2)	(2)
Hawaii	1	1	—	170,761	89,630	81,131	7,940
Idaho	115	115	—	203,022	108,744	94,278	9,830
Illinois	1,013	1,011	2	2,039,430	1,365,164	674,266	112,904
Indiana	305	304	1	1,113,331	720,671	392,660	53,657
Iowa	447	447	—	568,540	295,748	272,792	33,511
Kansas	307	307	—	433,547	227,325	206,222	26,812
Kentucky	181	181	—	692,999	441,712	251,287	32,835
Louisiana	66	66	—	816,669	565,844	250,825	41,756
Maine	280	224	56	240,016	161,797	78,219	13,878
Maryland	24	24	—	809,933	402,609	407,324	42,543
Massachusetts	398	356	42	1,081,464	544,746	536,718	59,138
Michigan	577	576	1	1,920,465	969,830	950,635	87,622
Minnesota	440	440	—	807,716	390,437	417,279	44,488
Mississippi	153	153	—	493,710	274,173	219,537	25,685
Missouri	555	555	—	900,002	489,283	410,719	48,800
Montana	583	564	19	164,326	109,463	54,863	9,682
Nebraska	1,115	1,077	38	297,796	156,662	141,134	17,731
Nevada	17	17	—	146,281	74,644	71,637	6,294
New Hampshire	168	157	11	172,389	117,241	55,148	8,874
New Jersey	606	587	19	1,337,327	827,978	509,349	78,000
New Mexico	88	88	—	279,249	143,927	135,322	13,909
New York	723	717	6	3,093,885	1,520,552	1,573,333	158,146
North Carolina	145	145	—	1,162,810	800,807	362,003	55,309
North Dakota	338	304	34	122,021	57,902	64,119	7,381
Ohio	615	615	—	2,102,440	1,246,513	855,927	102,645
Oklahoma	621	621	—	588,870	321,187	267,683	32,136
Oregon	330	328	2	471,374	276,905	194,469	24,579
Pennsylvania	504	504	—	2,046,746	1,008,664	1,038,082	110,833
Rhode Island	40	40	—	160,656	85,771	74,885	9,314
South Carolina	92	92	—	624,931	428,682	196,249	30,022
South Dakota	194	186	8	138,228	90,437	47,791	8,179
Tennessee	147	147	—	873,036	616,060	256,976	41,220
Texas	1,086	1,084	2	2,867,254	1,999,905	867,349	154,913
Utah	40	40	—	325,026	182,924	142,102	13,235
Vermont	271	245	26	101,292	57,625	43,667	6,480
Virginia	139	135	4	1,055,238	642,590	412,648	56,739
Washington	299	299	—	769,246	395,560	373,686	34,893
West Virginia	55	55	—	395,722	269,979	125,743	19,765
Wisconsin	427	427	—	886,419	486,599	399,820	47,677
Wyoming	49	49	—	94,328	51,300	43,028	5,806
District of Columbia	1	1	—	113,858	61,361	52,497	5,964

[1]Includes an estimate for the nonreporting state. [2]Data not reported.

National Spelling Bee Champions

The National Spelling Bee, conducted by Scripps-Howard Newspapers and other newspapers since 1939, was instituted by the Louisville (Ky.) Courier-Journal in 1925. Children under 16 years of age sponsored by participating newspapers are eligible to compete for the cash prizes and prize trips.

In the 1980 spelldown, the runner-up missed "glitch" (which means an unwanted brief surge of electric power). The winner spelled it correctly, and also the final word, "elucubrate." **Recent winners are:**

1979 — 1. Katie Kerwin, 13, Denver (Denver Rocky Mountain News). 2. Julie Won, 14, Mechanicsburg, Pa. (Harrisburg Patriot and Evening News). 3. Donna Marie Allmon, 12, Newport News, Va. (Newport News Times-Herald).

1980 — 1. Jacques Bailly, 14, (Denver Rocky Mountain News). 2. Paige Pipkin (El Paso Herald-Post). 3. Rosalind Dambaugh (Pittsburgh Press).

Public School Attendance, Teachers, Expenditures

Source: National Center for Education Statistics, U.S. Health, Education and Welfare Department

School year	Pop. 5 to 17 yrs.	Pupils		Teachers[1]				Total expend.
		Enrolled	Av. daily attend.	Male	Female	Total	Salary[2]	
1900	21,404,322	15,503,110	**10,632,772**	126,588	296,474	**423,062**	$325	**$214,964,618**
1910	24,239,948	17,813,852	**12,827,307**	110,481	412,729	**523,210**	485	**426,250,434**
1920	27,728,788	21,578,316	**16,150,035**	95,654	583,648	**679,302**	871	**1,036,151,209**
1930	31,571,322	25,678,015	**21,264,886**	141,771	712,492	**854,263**	1,420	**2,316,790,384**
1940	29,805,259	25,433,542	**22,042,151**	194,725	680,752	**875,477**	1,441	**2,344,048,927**
1950	30,788,000	25,111,427	**22,283,845**	194,968	718,703	**913,671**	3,010	**5,837,643,000**
1960	43,881,000	36,086,771	**32,477,440**	392,700	962,300	**1,355,000**	5,174	**15,613,255,000**
1970 (Fall).	52,435,000	45,909,088	**42,495,346**	649,250	1,411,865	**2,061,115**	9,570	**44,423,865,000**
1971 (Fall).	52,133,000	46,081,000	**42,544,000**	668,000	1,395,000	**2,063,000**	10,100	**48,513,986,000**
1972 (Fall).	51,637,000	45,744,000	**42,408,000**	702,000	1,400,000	**2,102,000**	10,608	**51,905,025,000**
1974 (Fall).	51,485,000	46,441,189	**41,438,054**	722,868	1,432,580	**2,155,448**	11,185	**56,970,355,000**
1975 (Fall).	50,372,000	44,790,946	**41,269,720**	741,000	1,455,000	**2,196,000**	*12,448	**70,629,000,000**
1976 (Fall).	49,853,000	44,317,000	**40,832,000**	*741,000	*1,445,000	**2,186,000**	*13,397	**75,014,000,000**
1977 (Fall).	49,008,000	43,730,964	***40,201,000**	*747,000	*1,450,000	**2,197,000**	*14,244	***81,097,000,000**

* Estimated. (1) Prior to 1954 includes other nonsupervisory instructional staff (librarians and guidance and psychological personnel). (2) Average annual salary per member of instructional staff, including supervisors and principals. Beginning in 1975, data are for classroom teachers only.

Cost per Pupil by State

Source: National Center for Education Statistics, U. S. Health, Education and Welfare Department

Expenditures per pupil in average daily attendance in public elementary and secondary day schools, 1976-77.

State	Expenditure per pupil			
	Total	Current	Capital outlay	Interest on school debt
United States . .	**$1,816**	**$1,638**	**$131**	**$48**
Alabama.	1,327	1,230	87	10
Alaska	3,890	3,389	347	154
Arizona.	1,944	1,572	311	61
Arkansas	1,218	1,090	97	31
California	1,802	1,668	108	26
Colorado.	1,950	1,653	232	64
Connecticut	1,851	1,739	68	44
Delaware	2,108	1,924	94	90
District of Columbia.	2,467	2,467	. . .	. . .
Florida	1,572	1,390	147	34
Georgia	1,467	1,299	148	20
Hawaii	2,079	1,835	240	4
Idaho.	1,348	1,180	137	31
Illinois	2,075	1,759	257	60
Indiana.	1,552	1,353	144	55
Iowa	1,820	1,677	111	32
Kansas.	1,731	1,541	156	35
Kentucky.	1,233	1,130	59	44
Louisiana	1,433	1,285	113	35
Maine	1,467	1,305	116	45
Maryland	2,181	1,900	237	45
Massachusetts . . .	2,230	2,071	86	72
Michigan.	2,035	1,814	137	84
Minnesota	2,012	1,805	149	59
Mississippi	1,225	1,128	85	12
Missouri	1,484	1,375	77	32
Montana	1,950	1,784	143	23
Nebraska	1,685	1,614	31	39
Nevada	1,707	1,449	160	99
New Hampshire. . .	1,562	1,416	103	44
New Jersey	2,285	2,153	66	66
New Mexico	1,634	1,415	196	23
New York	2,645	2,496	69	80
North Carolina . . .	1,389	1,246	130	12
North Dakota	1,632	1,453	128	21
Ohio	1,554	1,435	86	34
Oklahoma	1,463	1,321	130	15
Oregon.	2,195	1,920	235	40
Pennsylvania	2,074	1,852	127	95
Rhode Island	1,860	1,795	12	52
South Carolina . . .	1,375	1,212	134	29
South Dakota	1,499	1,334	144	21
Tennessee.	1,334	1,200	119	14
Texas	1,606	1,368	171	67
Utah	1,632	1,286	306	39
Vermont	1,631	1,536	50	46
Virginia.	1,635	1,445	140	50
Washington	1,835	1,679	122	34
West Virginia	1,528	1,358	152	18
Wisconsin	1,917	1,776	94	47
Wyoming.	2,220	1,784	368	68
Outlying areas				
American Samoa . .	773	773	. . .	. . .
Canal Zone	1,737	1,689	47	. . .
Guam	1,857	1,579	277	. . .
Puerto Rico	687	687	. . .	. . .
Virgin Islands	1,765	1,459	407	. . .

Canadian Fall Enrollment, Teachers, Expenditures in Day Schools

Full-time Public Elementary and Secondary Day Schools—1978-79

Source: Statistics Canada

	Enrollment			Teachers			School Board expenditure per pupil[4] 1977 (calendar year) (e)
	Elementary Kdgn.-Gr. 8	Secondary Gr. 9 and up	Total	Elementary Kdgn.-Gr. 8	Secondary Gr. 9 and up	Total	
Canada.	**3,580,368**	**2,232,526**	**5,812,894**	**122,092**(2)	**71,504**(2)	**256,996**	**1,921**
Nfld.	118,714	34,851	153,565	5,606	2,054	7,660	1,389
P.E.I.	18,841	9,012	27,853	895	523	1,418	1,559
N.S.	138,226	58,585	196,811	7,162	3,623	10,785	1,498
N.B.	107,856	52,817	160,673	4,861	2,853	7,714	1,433
Que.	903,711	924,393	1,828,104	(1)	(1)	63,400(3)	2,063
Ont.	1,300,589	681,389	1,981,978	58,617	35,743	94,360	2,005
Man.	160,637	71,833	232,470	7,384	4,187	11,571	1,762
Sask.	151,808	69,171	220,979	7,648	3,184	10,832	1,723
Alta.	299,766	147,483	447,249	14,566	7,415	21,981	1,820
B.C.	365,233	179,829	545,062	14,584	11,756	26,340	1,965
Yukon	3,909	1,338	5,247	219	49	268	2,540
N.W.T.	11,078	1,825	12,903	550	117	667	3,043

(e) estimate. (1) Data not available. (2) Excludes Quebec. (3) Source: Advance Statistics of Education, 1978-79. (4) Includes provincial expenditures made on behalf of school boards.

Public Libraries in Selected North American Cities

Source: World Almanac questionnaire (1979)

First figure in parentheses denotes number of branches-2d figure indicates number of bookmobiles. (*) indicates county library system; (†) indicates state library system; (C) Canadian dollars; (A) library has not provided up-to-date information.

City	No. bound volumes	Circulation	Cost of operation
Akron, Oh.* (18-2)	940,184	2,091,196	$ 3,873,938
Albuquerque, N.M. (7-2)	327,392	1,384,732	1,874,367
Atlanta, Ga. (27-3)	979,195	2,248,313	4,999,958
Austin, Tex. (15-0)	635,072	2,205,537	3,808,265
Baltimore, Md. (33-2)	2,001,953	2,410,374	9,783,204
Birmingham, Ala. (18-3)	1,017,570	2,095,156	3,600,000
Boston, Mass. (28-1)	4,472,684	2,098,042	10,983,108
Buffalo, N.Y.* (52-4)	3,205,191	5,455,117	11,131,972
Calgary, Alta. (13-3)	748,539	3,457,461	C6,519,390
Charlotte, N.C.* (15-0)	680,656	1,785,669	2,752,080
Chicago, Ill. (89-0)	6,164,605	6,608,290	35,304,274
Cincinnati, Oh.* (37-2)	3,242,497	5,654,005	8,763,052
Cleveland, Oh. (34-2)	2,541,876	1,060,681	12,153,389
Columbus, Oh.* (21-3)	1,214,890	3,084,857	3,201,055
Dallas, Tex. (17-3)	1,883,091	3,573,391	7,910,782
Dayton, Oh.* (19-1)	1,354,488	4,441,967	4,237,413
Denver, Col. (21-1)	1,732,225	2,862,488	8,855,185
Des Moines, Ia. (5-1)	427,445	1,139,141	1,636,863
Detroit, Mich. (26-4)	2,507,495	2,022,007	15,528,248
Edmonton, Alta. (11-3)	785,768	3,139,889	C7,073,000
El Paso, Tex. (9-4)	428,161	988,100	2,108,000
Ft. Worth, Tex. (7-2)	759,351	2,259,338	2,517,510
Hamilton, Ont. (10-2)	767,663	1,813,581	C4,926,000
Honolulu, Ha.† (45-8)	1,945,399	5,004,477	7,967,229
Houston, Tex. (26-4)	2,282,945	5,503,313	11,688,241
Indianapolis, Ind.* (23-2)	1,345,816	3,495,641	6,769,489
Jacksonville, Fla. (11-3)	848,264	1,747,943	2,991,352
Jersey City, N.J. (10-1)	696,085	379,422	2,593,131
Kansas City, Mo. (13-0)	1,204,000	700,000	2,936,444
Kitchener, Ont. (2-4)	402,118	1,205,000	C2,034,000
London, Ont. (10-2)	536,806	1,801,992	C3,834,135
Long Beach, Cal. (11-0)	734,009	1,814,607	4,420,823
Los Angeles, Cal. (66-5)	5,364,882	12,009,014	17,543,199
Los Angeles, Cal.* (91-7)	4,700,000	10,500,500	21,700,000
Louisville, Ky. (24-4)	995,170	1,894,736	5,204,073
Memphis, Tenn.* (21-3)	1,341,727	2,568,506	6,186,527
Miami, Fla.* (24-5)	1,615,240	3,000,000	11,510,460
Milwaukee, Wis. (12-5)	2,322,979	2,790,124	9,521,651
Minneapolis, Minn. (14-1)	1,520,085	2,288,991	7,680,422
Mobile, Ala. (5-1)	372,943	789,421	1,958,846
Montreal, Que. (18-1)	1,279,229	1,536,269	C7,500,000
Nashville, Tenn.* (13-3)	506,670	1,753,700	3,309,871
Newark, N.J. (13-1)	1,187,479	1,767,083	$ 4,353,280
New Haven, Conn. (8-0)	553,014	440,936	1,104,603
New Orleans, La. (11-0)	713,474	1,099,425	3,061,308
New York City (research)	4,950,955	None	21,051,000
N.Y.C. branches (83-0)	6,900,222	9,164,151	29,929,000
Brooklyn* (58-0)	3,573,673	6,915,959	17,193,018
Queens* (55-0)	3,853,469	6,128,948	17,530,584
Norfolk, Va. (11-2)	634,455	1,111,188	2,347,331
Oakland, Cal. (18-2)	784,438	1,571,202	3,785,053
Okla. City, Okla.* (10-4)	613,845	1,689,737	2,353,357
Omaha, Neb. (9-1)	543,627	1,578,152	2,458,383
Ottawa, Ont. (7-2)	631,324	2,073,424	C4,880,634
Philadelphia, Pa. (51-0)	2,913,935	4,840,059	19,360,053
Phoenix, Ariz. (9-1)	1,155,407	3,207,648	5,283,439
Pittsburgh, Pa. (21-4)	1,984,239	2,942,141	7,975,808
Portland, Ore.* (16-3)	1,110,186	2,945,611	4,447,391
Richmond, Va. (6-2)	614,981	1,047,915	1,551,241
Rochester, N.Y. (11-1)	885,214	1,495,655	4,602,552
Sacramento, Cal. (26-3)	1,108,226	3,970,303	6,072,786
St. Louis, Mo.* (13-22)	1,549,811	7,269,432	5,890,779
St. Paul, Minn. (10-1)	760,009	1,727,639	3,031,353
St. Petersburg, Fla. (2-3)	415,671	1,203,157	1,156,661
San Antonio, Tex. (9-7)	1,065,347	2,244,943	2,770,203
San Diego, Cal. (29-1)	1,531,362	3,936,594	5,505,501
San Francisco, Cal. (28-1)A	1,642,482	2,494,858	7,027,873
San Jose, Cal. (16-1)	1,031,581	2,579,274	3,868,000
Saskatoon, Sask. (5-3)	353,828	1,221,588	C2,558,712
Seattle, Wash. (22-3)	1,515,680	4,270,187	8,247,835
Tampa, Fla.* (13-1)	619,616	1,985,474	4,549,057
Toledo, Oh.* (17-2)	1,121,437	3,170,478	6,428,507
Toronto, Ont. (27-1)	1,216,248	4,807,573	C12,028,880
Tucson, Ariz. (15-2)	750,000	3,000,000	4,990,000
Tulsa, Okla.* (20-2)	809,546	1,672,242	2,987,626
Vancouver, B.C. (18-1)	876,494	4,480,203	C8,238,937
Washington, D.C.* (24-0)	1,371,084	1,413,275	9,856,700
Wichita, Kan. (11-0)	414,133	1,025,873	1,803,061
Windsor, Ont. (6-0)	463,427	997,522	3,122,127
Winnipeg, Man. (20-5)	1,187,128	3,038,261	C4,306,321
Yonkers, N.Y. (4-2)	352,825	782,299	2,319,177

Major U.S. Academic Libraries

Source: World Almanac questionnaire (1979)

(A) library has not provided up-to-date information.

Institution	No. bound volumes	Microfilm units	Enrollment	Staff		Annual acquisition expense
				Prof.	Total	
U. of California, Berkeley	5,597,154	1,440,011	29,115	141	602	$3,164,447
U. of California, Los Angeles (A)	4,051,290	1,688,908	32,130	162	537	2,766,000
U. of Chicago	4,182,938	692,540	7,937	70	304	1,700,385
U. of Colorado, Boulder	1,800,000	1,900,000	20,157	42	178	1,026,000
Columbia U.	5,000,000	2,000,000	17,000	140	515	2,370,000
Cornell U.	4,207,146	1,977,023	16,676	124	483	2,694,849
Duke U.	3,022,839	318,222	9,362	86	323	1,801,479
U. of Florida	2,079,344	1,200,148	26,562	79	287	4,106,569
Harvard U.	9,913,992	1,937,315	16,816	263	913	4,262,774
U. of Illinois, Urbana-Champaign	5,759,666	1,377,970	34,376	138	398	2,982,339
Indiana U., Bloomington	3,735,523	898,879	76,394	121	471	2,433,500
U. of Iowa	2,216,970	1,383,829	23,349	77	251	2,303,656
Johns Hopkins U.	2,214,282	343,821	6,319	50	176	1,199,583
U. of Kansas	1,900,000	727,000	22,000	56	152	1,445,000
U. of Michigan, Ann Arbor (A)	5,049,501	1,403,096	35,824	155	576	2,212,803
Michigan State U.	2,525,000	106,000	44,756	76	225	1,663,282
U. of Minnesota	3,702,599	1,126,011	47,000	129	434	2,250,000
U. of Missouri, Columbia	1,984,632	2,040,615	21,084	55	208	1,404,436
New York U.	2,700,201	1,366,699	40,869	75	319	1,804,831
U. of No. Carolina, Chapel Hill	2,487,122	1,329,557	21,060	107	355	2,640,430
Northwestern U.	3,032,938	825,982	12,787	97	314	1,652,746
Ohio State U.	3,315,029	1,296,153	52,863	85	324	1,676,993
U. of Pennsylvania	2,900,000	1,400,000	21,900	88	242	1,471,368
U. of Pittsburgh	2,375,542	1,128,925	26,024	148	349	1,566,108
Princeton U.	3,172,238	1,210,189	5,930	42	382	2,199,875
Rutgers U.	2,166,200	1,334,430	50,000	116	329	2,713,000
Stanford U.	4,557,827	1,981,748	11,865	130	512	3,682,000
U. of Texas, Austin	4,406,193	1,990,097	41,963	126	525	4,207,995
U. of Virginia	2,351,842	2,206,241	15,912	78	271	2,525,724
U. of Washington, Seattle	3,778,788	2,665,263	36,034	121	488	2,598,693
U. of Wisconsin, Madison	3,475,184	1,720,218	39,554	121	480	2,834,724
Yale U.	7,246,195	1,190,959	9,941	172	523	2,868,230

107 Years of Public Schools

Source: National Center for Education Statistics, U.S. Health, Education and Welfare Department

Pupils and teachers (thousands)	1869-70	1899-1900	1909-10	1919-20	1929-30	1939-40	1949-50	1959-60	1969-70	1975-76
Total U.S. population	39,818	75,995	90,492	104,512	121,770	130,880	148,665	179,323	203,212	213,051
Population 5-17 years of age	12,055	21,573	24,009	27,556	31,417	30,150	30,168	43,881	52,490	50,372
Percent aged 5-17 years	30.3	28.4	26.5	26.4	25.8	23.0	20.3	24.5	25.8	23.6
Enrollment (thousands)										
Elementary and secondary	6,872	15,503	17,814	21,578	25,678	25,434	25,111	36,087	45,619	44,791
Percent pop. 5-17 enrolled	57.0	71.9	74.2	78.3	81.7	84.4	83.2	82.2	86.9	88.9
Percent in high schools	1.2	3.3	5.1	10.2	17.1	26.0	22.7	23.5	28.5	31.9
High school graduates	....	62	111	231	592	1,143	1,063	1,627	2,589	2,837
Average school term (in days)	132.2	144.3	157.5	161.9	172.7	175.0	177.9	178.0	178.9	178.3
Total instructional staff	....	....	....	678	880	912	962	1,464	2,253	2,476
Teachers, librarians: Men	78	127	110	93	140	195	195	402	691	789
Women	123	296	413	565	703	681	719	985	1,440	1,549
Percent men	38.7	29.9	21.1	14.1	16.6	22.2	21.3	29.0	33.4	33.7
Receipts & expenditures (millions)										
Total receipts	....	$219	$433	$970	$2,088	$2,260	$5,437	$14,746	$40,267	$71,206
Total expenditures	$63	214	426	1,036	2,316	2,344	5,837	15,613[1]	40,683	70,629
Current elem. and secondary	....	179	356	861	1,843	1,941	4,687	12,329	34,218	62,083
Capital outlay	....	35	69	153	370	257	1,014	2,661	4,659	6,146
Interest on school debt	....	....	....	18	92	130	100	489	1,171	1,846
Other	....	....	....	3	9	13	35	132	636	554
Salaries and pupil cost				(Data in unadjusted dollars)						
Average annual teacher salary[2]	$189	$325	$485	$2,130	$3,869	$3,894	$5,928	$8,213	$10,917	$13,021[4]
Expenditure per capita total pop.	1.59	2.83	4.71	24.24	51.85	48.40	77.34	138.21	247.23	332.00
Current expenditure per pupil ADA[3]	....	16.67	27.85	130.41	236.25	238.05	411.29	595.50	1,007.65	1,504.00

(1) Because of a modification of the scope, "current expenditures for elementary and secondary schools" data for 1959-60 and later years are not entirely comparable with data for prior years. (2) Includes supervisors, principals, teachers and other non-supervisory instructional staff. (3) "ADA" means average daily attendance in elementary and secondary day schools. (4) Estimated.

Family Income, 1970-78, in Constant 1978 Dollars

Source: U.S. Bureau of the Census

All Races	1978	1977	1976	1975	1974	1973	1972	1970
Number (000)	**57,804**	**57,215**	**56,710**	**56,245**	**55,698**	**55,053**	**54,373**	**52,227**
Percent	100.0	100.0	100.0	100.0	100.0	100.0	100.0	100.0
Under $3,000	3.3	3.3	3.2	3.4	3.3	3.0	3.3	3.9
$3,000 to $4,999	4.9	5.0	5.0	5.1	4.7	4.7	4.2	4.9
$5,000 to $6,999	6.0	6.5	6.4	6.8	6.2	6.0	6.1	6.1
$7,000 to $9,999	9.8	10.2	10.4	10.6	10.0	9.6	9.7	9.8
$10,000 to $11,999	6.8	6.7	6.9	7.0	6.8	6.7	6.9	7.3
$12,000 to $14,999	9.9	10.3	10.6	11.2	11.3	10.4	10.7	11.8
$15,000 to $24,999	31.4	31.7	32.6	32.3	32.3	34.2	33.3	33.5
$25,000 and over	27.9	26.2	24.8	23.6	25.5	25.4	25.2	22.7
Median income (78 dollars)	**17,640**	**17,226**	**17,134**	**16,621**	**17,060**	**17,683**	**17,326**	**16,569**
Median income(current dollars)	**17,640**	**16,009**	**14,958**	**13,719**	**12,902**	**12,051**	**11,116**	**9,867**
White								
Number (000)	**50,910**	**50,530**	**50,083**	**49,873**	**49,440**	**48,919**	**48,477**	**46,535**
Percent	100.0	100.0	100.0	100.0	100.0	100.0	100.0	100.0
Under $3,000	2.6	2.6	2.6	2.8	2.6	2.4	2.6	3.2
$3,000 to $4,999	3.9	4.1	4.0	4.3	3.8	3.9	4.1	4.2
$5,000 to $6,999	5.6	5.8	5.8	6.2	5.5	5.3	5.5	5.6
$7,000 to $9,999	9.3	9.7	9.9	10.2	9.5	8.9	9.1	9.2
$10,000 to $11,999	6.6	6.6	6.8	6.8	6.7	6.5	6.7	7.1
$12,000 to $14,999	10.0	10.3	10.7	11.2	11.4	10.4	10.7	11.9
$15,000 to $24,999	32.5	32.9	33.6	33.4	33.4	35.5	34.5	34.8
$25,000 and over	29.5	28.0	26.5	25.1	27.1	27.1	26.7	24.0
Median income(78 dollars)	**18,368**	**18,013**	**17,797**	**17,286**	**17,729**	**18,481**	**18,001**	**17,189**
Median income(current dollars)	**18,368**	**16,740**	**15,537**	**14,268**	**13,408**	**12,595**	**11,549**	**10,236**
Black								
Number (000)	**5,906**	**5,806**	**5,804**	**5,586**	**5,491**	**5,440**	**5,265**	**4,928**
Percent	100.0	100.0	100.0	100.0	100.0	100.0	100.0	100.0
Under $3,000	9.0	9.1	8.2	9.0	8.8	8.6	8.9	9.9
$3,000 to $4,999	13.4	12.8	13.5	12.4	12.2	11.7	12.1	11.2
$5,000 to $6,999	9.8	12.2	11.4	12.1	11.7	12.0	11.6	10.9
$7,000 to $9,999	14.0	14.8	14.7	14.0	14.9	14.7	14.6	15.5
$10,000 to $11,999	7.7	8.3	7.6	8.2	8.2	9.0	8.7	9.2
$12,000 to $14,999	10.0	10.0	9.8	11.8	10.8	10.5	10.3	11.4
$15,000 to $24,999	22.7	21.8	24.1	22.7	22.6	23.4	22.6	22.2
$25,000 and over	13.4	11.1	10.7	9.9	10.8	10.1	11.1	9.7
Median income(78 dollars)	**10,879**	**10,290**	**10,586**	**10,636**	**10,586**	**10,666**	**10,699**	**10,544**
Median income(current dollars)	**10,879**	**9,563**	**9,242**	**8,779**	**8,006**	**7,269**	**6,864**	**6,279**

Median income means that one half of American families had more income than that shown, and one half had less. Income figures here refer to gross income before taxes. The figures show that while incomes of white families have improved by 6.9% in the last 8 years, the incomes of black families have improved by 3.1%. The disparity is particularly marked in 1972-1973, when white family median income in constant dollars exceeded 1970 income by over $1,000, while black family income in 1972 barely exceeded 1970 income and fell even lower in 1973. The figures also tend to suggest, however, that all families have experienced slight increases in income since 1968, particularly those in the top and bottom income groups.

Educational Attainment by Age, Race, and Sex

Source: U.S. Bureau of the Census (Number of persons in thousands)

Race, age, and sex	Years of school completed					Percent				
	All persons	Less than high school, 4 years	High school, 4 years	College, 1 to 3 years	College, 4 years or more	All persons	Less than high school, 4 years	High school, 4 years	College, 1 to 3 years	College, 4 years or more
March 1979										
All races										
18 to 24 years	28,050	6,226	12,875	7,012	1,936	100.0	22.2	45.9	25.0	6.9
25 years and over	125,295	40,408	45,915	18,392	20,579	100.0	32.3	36.6	14.7	16.4
25 to 34 years	34,053	5,203	13,338	7,414	8,096	100.0	15.3	39.2	21.8	23.8
35 to 44 years	24,611	5,632	10,344	3,822	4,813	100.0	22.9	42.0	15.5	19.6
45 to 54 years	22,826	7,424	9,145	2,833	3,424	100.0	32.5	40.1	12.4	15.0
55 to 64 years	20,631	8,263	7,693	2,398	2,277	100.0	40.1	37.3	11.6	11.0
65 years and over	23,175	13,886	5,395	1,925	1,968	100.0	59.9	23.3	8.3	8.5
Male, 25 years and over	58,986	18,610	19,250	9,099	12,025	100.0	31.5	32.6	15.4	20.4
Female, 25 years and over	66,309	21,799	26,665	9,293	8,554	100.0	32.9	40.2	14.0	12.9
White										
18 to 24 years	23,984	4,945	11,141	6,129	1,768	100.0	20.6	46.5	25.6	7.4
25 years and over	110,798	33,531	41,612	16,632	19,023	100.0	30.3	37.6	15.0	17.2
25 to 34 years	29,573	4,102	11,564	6,557	7,350	100.0	13.9	39.1	22.2	24.9
35 to 44 years	21,534	4,500	9,221	3,386	4,427	100.0	20.9	42.8	15.7	20.6
45 to 54 years	20,145	5,974	8,427	2,554	3,189	100.0	29.7	41.8	12.7	15.8
55 to 64 years	18,595	6,869	7,263	2,300	2,163	100.0	36.9	39.1	12.4	11.6
65 years and over	20,950	12,085	5,136	1,834	1,894	100.0	57.7	24.5	8.8	9.0
Male, 25 years and over	52,504	15,576	17,382	8,295	11,250	100.0	29.7	33.1	15.8	21.4
Female, 25 years and over	58,294	17,954	24,230	8,337	7,773	100.0	30.8	41.6	14.3	13.3
Black										
18 to 24 years	3,500	1,183	1,485	708	124	100.0	33.8	42.4	20.2	3.5
25 years and over	12,227	6,190	3,670	1,404	964	100.0	50.6	30.0	11.5	7.9
25 to 34 years	3,644	970	1,534	674	466	100.0	26.6	42.1	18.5	12.8
35 to 44 years	2,577	1,026	982	362	206	100.0	39.8	38.1	14.0	8.0
45 to 54 years	2,277	1,305	589	219	164	100.0	57.3	25.9	9.6	7.2
55 to 64 years	1,776	1,267	346	83	80	100.0	71.3	19.5	4.7	4.5
65 years and over	1,954	1,621	219	66	48	100.0	83.0	11.2	3.4	2.5
Male, 25 years and over	5,393	2,741	1,590	613	450	100.0	50.8	29.5	11.4	8.3
Female, 25 years and over	6,834	3,449	2,080	791	514	100.0	50.5	30.4	11.6	7.5
Spanish Origin[1]										
18 to 24 years	1,699	727	653	278	40	100.0	42.8	38.4	16.4	2.4
25 years and over	5,367	3,112	1,374	521	359	100.0	58.0	25.6	9.7	6.7
25 to 34 years	1,926	878	600	294	151	100.0	45.6	31.2	15.3	7.8
35 to 44 years	1,367	759	387	118	104	100.0	55.5	28.3	8.6	7.6
45 to 54 years	961	609	239	60	52	100.0	63.4	24.9	6.2	5.4
55 to 64 years	574	412	100	32	30	100.0	71.8	17.4	5.6	5.2
65 years and over	539	454	48	17	20	100.0	84.2	8.9	3.2	3.7
Male, 25 years and over	2,534	1,462	581	283	208	100.0	57.7	22.9	11.2	8.2
Female, 25 years and over	2,833	1,652	793	238	151	100.0	58.3	28.0	8.4	5.3
March 1970										
All races										
18 to 24 years	22,494	5,732	9,996	5,392	1,374	100.0	25.5	44.4	24.0	6.1
25 years and over	109,310	48,948	37,134	11,164	12,063	100.0	44.8	34.0	10.2	11.0
25 to 34 years	24,865	6,517	10,929	3,491	3,926	100.0	26.2	44.0	14.0	15.8
35 to 44 years	23,021	8,216	9,325	2,523	2,958	100.0	35.7	40.5	11.0	12.8
45 to 54 years	23,298	9,735	8,875	2,352	2,336	100.0	41.8	38.1	10.1	10.0
55 to 64 years	18,413	10,347	4,905	1,567	1,594	100.0	56.2	26.6	8.5	8.7
65 years and over	19,713	14,134	3,100	1,230	1,249	100.0	71.7	15.7	6.2	6.3
Male, 25 years and over	51,784	23,311	15,571	5,580	7,321	100.0	45.0	30.1	10.8	14.1
Female, 25 years and over	57,527	25,638	21,563	5,584	4,743	100.0	44.6	37.5	9.7	8.2
White										
18 to 24 years	19,536	4,496	8,865	4,886	1,289	100.0	23.0	45.4	25.0	6.6
25 years and over	98,112	41,789	34,493	10,452	11,380	100.0	42.6	35.2	10.7	11.6
25 to 34 years	21,887	5,222	9,828	3,204	3,633	100.0	23.9	44.9	14.6	16.6
35 to 44 years	20,392	6,756	8,541	2,319	2,776	100.0	33.1	41.9	11.4	13.6
45 to 54 years	20,961	8,134	8,392	2,209	2,227	100.0	38.8	40.0	10.5	10.6
55 to 64 years	16,731	8,960	4,719	1,526	1,527	100.0	53.6	28.2	9.1	9.1
65 years and over	18,141	12,716	3,013	1,193	1,218	100.0	70.1	16.6	6.6	6.7
Male, 25 years and over	46,606	19,963	14,410	5,259	6,972	100.0	42.8	30.9	11.3	15.0
Female, 25 years and over	51,506	21,825	20,083	5,191	4,408	100.0	42.4	39.0	10.1	8.6
Black										
18 to 24 years	2,713	1,158	1,076	419	61	100.0	42.7	39.7	15.4	2.2
25 years and over	10,089	6,686	2,358	592	452	100.0	66.3	23.4	5.9	4.5
25 to 34 years	2,651	1,237	1,018	237	161	100.0	46.7	38.4	8.9	6.1
35 to 44 years	2,347	1,372	690	164	122	100.0	58.5	29.4	7.0	5.2
45 to 54 years	2,128	1,509	422	117	81	100.0	70.9	19.8	5.5	3.8
55 to 64 years	1,545	1,284	165	38	59	100.0	83.1	10.7	2.5	3.8
65 years and over	1,417	1,290	64	35	28	100.0	91.0	4.5	2.5	2.0
Male, 25 years and over	4,619	3,120	1,025	261	212	100.0	67.5	22.2	5.7	4.6
Female, 25 years and over	5,470	3,565	1,333	330	240	100.0	65.2	24.4	6.0	4.4

(1) Persons of Spanish origin may be of any race.

Median Income by Sex, Age, Education, Occupation, and Race

Source: U.S. Bureau of the Census

(B-base less than 75,000; — represents zero or rounds to zero; . . .-not applicable. Median income means that half the working population made more than that and half made less.)

Selected Characteristics	All persons: 1978 No. (000)	All persons: 1978 Median income ($)	All persons: 1977 Median income ($)	All persons: % Change 79$	All persons: % Change 78$	Year-round full-time workers: 1978 No. (000)	Year-round full-time workers: 1978 Median income ($)	Year-round full-time workers: 1977 Median income ($)	Year-round full-time workers: % Change 79$	Year-round full-time workers: % Change 78$
All males	**75,609**	**10,935**	**10,123**	**8.0**	**0.4**	**41,044**	**16,062**	**15,070**	**6.6**	**−0.9**
Race										
White	67,273	11,453	10,603	8.0	0.4	37,218	16,360	15,378	6.4	−1.1
Black	6,971	6,861	6,292	9.0	1.3	3,098	12,530	10,602	8.2	9.8
Hispanic	3,447	8,380	7,797	7.5	−0.1	1,878	11,943	10,935	9.2	1.5
Age										
14-19	7,806	1,315	1,129	16.5	8.2	661	7,079	6,042	17.2	8.9
20-24	9,355	7,059	6,288	12.3	4.3	4,073	10,410	9,800	6.2	−1.3
25-34	16,508	13,410	12,361	8.5	0.8	11,811	15,376	14,129	8.8	1.1
35-44	11,852	16,572	15,604	6.2	−1.3	9,303	18,046	16,863	7.0	−0.5
45-54	10,929	16,574	15,331	8.1	0.5	8,490	18,684	17,029	9.7	2.0
55-64	9,658	13,624	12,243	11.3	3.4	5,876	17,292	15,669	10.4	2.6
65 & over	9,501	5,966	5,526	8.0	0.3	830	14,315	13,815	3.6	−3.7
Occupation of longest job										
White collar	**24,902**	**16,066**	**15,112**	**6.3**	**−1.2**	**19,266**	**18,270**	**17,095**	**7.5**	**−0.1**
Professional, technical	9,124	17,391	16,212	7.3	−0.3	7,121	19,729	18,224	8.3	0.6
Managers	8,186	18,234	16,850	8.2	0.6	7,128	19,633	18,086	8.6	0.9
Sales	3,830	12,061	11,685	3.2	−4.1	2,456	16,839	16,067	4.8	−2.6
Clerical	3,762	11,909	10,822	10.0	2.3	2,561	15,289	13,966	9.5	1.7
Blue collar	**29,289**	**11,096**	**10,202**	**8.8**	**1.1**	**17,469**	**14,698**	**13,228**	**11.1**	**3.3**
Craftsmen	12,770	13,583	12,313	10.3	2.5	8,768	15,776	14,517	8.7	1.0
Operatives	11,035	10,980	10,066	9.1	1.4	6,827	13,660	12,612	8.3	0.7
Laborers	5,484	4,476	4,566	−2.0	−8.9	1,873	12,031	13,180	6.8	−0.8
Service	**6,132**	**5,505**	**4,961**	**11.0**	**3.1**	**2,821**	**11,057**	**10,332**	**7.0**	**−0.5**
Private household	45	(B)	573	...	...	9	(B)	(B)	...	...
Other	6,088	5,563	5,077	9.6	1.8	2,813	11,076	10,338	7.1	−0.4
Farm	**2,579**	**4,475**	**2,985**	**49.9**	**39.3**	**1,480**	**7,948**	**6,412**	**24.0**	**15.2**
Education (workers age 25 or over)	**58,448**	**13,377**	**12,375**	**8.1**	**0.5**	**36,310**	**16,882**	**15,726**	**7.4**	**−0.2**
Elementary	10,814	6,520	6,134	6.3	−1.2	3,706	11,765	10,509	12.0	4.0
High School: 1-3 years	7,510	10,419	10,023	4.0	−3.4	4,029	14,199	13,120	8.2	0.6
4 years	19,119	14,341	13,207	8.6	0.9	12,964	16,396	15,434	6.2	−1.3
College: 1-3 years	9,046	15,459	14,247	8.5	0.8	6,454	17,411	16,235	7.2	−0.3
4 years	6,384	18,774	17,391	8.0	0.3	4,937	20,941	19,603	6.8	−0.7
5 or more yrs.	5,574	21,428	20,108	6.6	−1.0	4,220	23,578	21,941	7.5	−0.1
All females	**71,864**	**4,068**	**3,941**	**7.7**	**0.1**	**20,992**	**9,641**	**8,814**	**9.4**	**1.7**
Race										
White	62,695	4,117	4,001	7.6	—	18,043	9,732	8,870	9.7	2.0
Black	7,959	3,707	3,455	8.7	1.1	2,499	9,020	8,290	8.8	1.1
Hispanic	2,949	3,788	3,669	5.0	−2.4	859	8,331	7,599	9.6	1.9
Age										
14-19	7,159	1,118	948	19.2	10.8	457	5,928	5,632	5.3	−2.2
20-24	8,907	4,588	4,107	11.8	3.9	3,121	8,116	7,497	8.3	0.6
25-34	14,282	5,839	5,902	4.5	−2.9	5,836	10,148	9,543	6.3	−1.2
35-44	10,243	5,804	5,538	9.8	2.0	4,257	10,200	9,282	9.9	2.1
45-54	9,306	5,672	5,670	4.9	−2.5	4,090	10,004	9,142	9.4	1.7
55-64	8,758	4,473	4,533	6.4	−1.1	2,871	10,101	8,846	14.2	6.1
65 & over	13,208	3,360	3,088	8.2	0.6	360	10,187	7,838	30.0	20.8
Occupation of longest job										
White collar	**29,793**	**6,797**	**6,218**	**9.2**	**1.4**	**15,004**	**10,137**	**9,467**	**7.1**	**−0.5**
Professional, technical	7,434	9,909	9,161	8.6	1.0	3,977	12,647	11,995	5.4	−2.0
Managers	2,786	8,598	7,817	9.5	1.7	1,836	10,689	9,799	9.1	1.4
Sales	3,438	2,840	2,425	16.2	8.0	880	7,644	6,825	12.0	4.1
Clerical	16,135	6,470	6,053	6.1	−1.4	8,311	9,158	8,601	6.5	−1.0
Blue collar	**7,172**	**5,411**	**5,028**	**9.7**	**1.9**	**3,120**	**8,140**	**7,524**	**8.2**	**0.5**
Craftsmen	791	6,617	5,600	25.6	16.7	390	9,584	8,902	7.7	0.1
Operatives	5,709	5,490	5,109	8.9	1.2	2,530	8,005	7,350	8.9	1.2
Laborers	672	3,146	2,857	10.0	2.2	199	7,452	7,441	0.1	−6.9
Service	**10,940**	**2,200**	**1,971**	**12.9**	**5.0**	**2,699**	**6,832**	**6,108**	**11.9**	**3.9**
Private household	1,860	780	736	3.1	−4.2	166	2,830	2,714	4.3	−3.1
Other	9,080	2,770	2,463	13.6	5.6	2,533	7,010	6,330	10.7	2.9
Education (workers age 25 or over)	**55,797**	**4,636**	**4,556**	**6.1**	**−1.4**	**17,414**	**10,121**	**9,257**	**9.3**	**1.6**
Elementary	10,092	2,882	2,769	6.4	−1.2	1,209	7,079	6,283	12.7	4.7
High School: 1-3 years	7,918	3,701	3,679	1.3	−5.8	1,828	7,996	7,387	8.2	0.6
4 years	21,904	5,221	5,276	4.4	−3.0	8,032	9,769	8,894	9.8	2.1
College: 1-3 years	8,071	6,204	6,239	1.6	−5.6	2,991	10,634	10,157	4.7	−2.7
4 years	4,812	8,090	8,077	5.3	−2.1	1,907	12,347	11,605	6.4	−1.1
5 or more yrs.	3,001	11,365	11,081	5.7	−1.7	1,447	15,310	14,338	6.8	−0.8

The Principal Languages of the World

Source: Sidney S. Culbert, Assoc. Professor of Psychology, University of Washington

Total number of speakers of languages spoken by at least one million persons (midyear 1980)

Language	Millions
Achinese (Indonesia)	2
Afrikaans (S. Africa)	8
Albanian	4
Amharic (Ethiopia)	9
Arabic	147
Armenian	4
Assamese[1] (India)	14
Aymara (Bolivia; Peru)	1
Azerbaijani (USSR; Iran)	8
Bahasa (see Malay-Indonesian)	
Balinese	3
Baluchi (Pakistan; Iran)	3
Batak (Indonesia)	2
Bemba (S. Central Africa)	2
Bengali[1] (Bangladesh; India)	144
Berber[2] (N. Africa)	
Bhili (India)	4
Bihari (India)	17
Bikol (Philippines)	2
Bisaya (see Cebuano, Panay-Hiligaynon, and Samar-Leyte)	
Bugi (Indonesia)	2
Bulgarian	9
Burmese	25
Byelorussian (mainly USSR)	9
Cambodian (see Khmer)	
Canarese (see Kannada)	
Cantonese (China)	52
Catalan (Spain; France; Andorra)	6
Cebuano (Philippines)	9
Chinese[3]	
Chuang[7] (China)	
Chuvash (USSR)	2
Czech	11
Danish	5
Dayak (Borneo)	1
Dutch (see Netherlandish)	
Edo (W. Africa)	1
Efik	3
English	386
Esperanto	1
Estonian	1
Ewe (W. Africa)	3
Fang-Bulu (W. Africa)	2
Finnish	5
Flemish (see Netherlandish)	
French	103
Fula (W. Africa)	9
Galician (Spain)	3
Galla (see Oromo)	
Ganda (or Luganda)(E. Africa)	3
Georgian (USSR)	4
German	119
Gilaki (Iran)	2
Gondi (India)	2
Greek	10
Guarani (mainly Paraguay)	3
Gujarati[1] (India)	33
Hakka (China)	23
Hausa (W. and Central Africa)	21
Hebrew	3
Hindi[1,4]	237
Hindustani[4]	
Hungarian (or Magyar)	13
Ibibio (see Efik)	
Ibo (or Igbo)(W. Africa)	11
Ijaw (W. Africa)	2
Ilocano (Philippines)	4
Iloko (see Ilocano)	
Indonesian (see Malay-Indonesian)	
Italian	61
Japanese	117
Javanese	47
Kamba (E. Africa)	1
Kanarese (see Kannada)	
Kannada[1] (India)	31
Kanuri (W. and Central Africa)	3
Kashmiri[1]	3
Kazakh (USSR)	6
Khalkha (Mongolia)	2
Khmer (Kampuchea)	6
Kikongo (see Kongo)	
Kikuyu (or Gekoyo)(Kenya)	3
Kimbundu (see Mbundu-Kimbundu)	
Kirghiz (USSR)	2
Kituba (Congo River)	3
Kongo (Congo River)	2
Konkani (India)	2
Korean	58
Kurdish (S.W. of Caspian Sea)	7
Kurukh (or Oraon)(India)	1
Lao[5] (Laos, Asia)	3
Latvian (or Lettish)	2
Lingala (see Ngala)	
Lithuanian	3
Luba-Lulua (Zaire)	3
Luganda (see Ganda)	
Luhya (or Luhia)(Kenya)	1
Luo (Kenya)	2
Luri (Iran)	2
Macedonian (Yugoslavia)	2
Madurese (Indonesia)	8
Makua (S.E. Africa)	3
Malagasy (Madagascar)	8
Malay-Indonesian	109
Malayalam[1] (India)	29
Malinke-Bambara-Dyula (Africa)	7
Mandarin (China)	701
Marathi[1] (India)	55
Mazandarani (Iran)	2
Mbundu (Umbundu group)(S.Angola)	3
Mbundu (Kimbundu group)(Angola)	2
Mende (Sierra Leone)	1
Meo (see Miao)	
Miao (and Meo)(S.E.Asia)	3
Min (China)	41
Minankabau (Indonesia)	4
Moldavian (inc. with Romanian)	
Mongolian (see Khalkha)	
Mordvin (USSR)	1
Moré (see Mossi)	
Mossi (or Moré)(W. Africa)	3
Ndongo (see Mbundu-Kimbundu)	
Nepali (Nepal; India)	11
Netherlandish (Dutch and Flemish)	20
Ngala (or Lingala)(Africa)	3
Norwegian	5
Nyamwezi-Sukuma (S.E. Africa)	2
Nyanja (S.E. Africa)	3
Oraon (see Kurukh)	
Oriya[1] (India)	26
Oromo (Ethiopia)	7
Panay-Hiligaynon (Philippines)	4
Panjabi (see Punjabi)	
Pashto (see Pushtu)	
Pedi (see Sotho, Northern)	
Persian	27
Polish	38
Portuguese	145
Provencal (Southern France)	5
Punjabi[1] (India; Pakistan)	63
Pushtu (mainly Afghanistan)	18
Quechua (S. America)	7
Rajasthani (India)	16
Romanian	23
Ruanda (S. Central Africa)	7
Rundi (S. Central Africa)	4
Russian (Great Russian only)	265
Samar-Leyte (Philippines)	2
Sango (Central Africa)	2
Santali (India)	4
Sepedi (see Sotho, Northern)	
Serbo-Croatian (Yugoslavia)	19
Shan (Burma)	2
Shona (S.E. Africa)	5
Siamese (see Thai)	
Sindhi[1] (India; Pakistan)	10
Sinhalese (Sri Lanka)	11
Slovak	5
Slovene (Yugoslavia)	2
Somali (E. Africa)	5
Sotho, Northern (S. Africa)	2
Sotho, Southern (S. Africa)	3
Spanish	245
Sundanese (Indonesia)	16
Swahili (E. Africa)	29
Swedish	10
Tagalog (Philippines)	24
Tajiki (USSR)	3
Tamil[1] (India; Sri Lanka)	57
Tatar (or Kazan-Turkic)(USSR)	7
Telugu[1] (India)	57
Thai[5]	37
Thonga (S.E. Africa)	1
Tibetan	6
Tigrinya (Ethiopia)	4
Tiv (E. Central Nigeria)	2
Tswana (S. Africa)	3
Tulu (India)	1
Turkish	43
Turkoman (USSR)	2
Twi-Fante (or Akan)(W.Africa)	5
Uighur (Sinkiang, China)	5
Ukrainian (mainly USSR)	42
Umbundu (see Mbundu)	
Urdu[1] (Pakistan; India)	68
Uzbek (USSR)	10
Vietnamese	42
Visayan (see Cebuano, Panay-Hiligaynon, and Samar-Leyte)	
White Russian (see Byelorussian)	
Wolof (W. Africa)	3
Wu (China)	46
Xhosa (S. Africa)	5
Yi (China)	4
Yiddish[6]	3
Yoruba (W. Africa)	14
Zhuang[7] (China)	
Zulu (S. Africa)	6

(1) One of the fifteen languages of the Constitution of India. (2) Here considered a group of dialects. (3) See Mandarin, Cantonese, Wu, Min and Hakka. The "national language" (Guoyu) or "common speech" (Putonghua) is a standardized form of Mandarin as spoken in the area of Peking. (4) Hindi and Urdu are essentially the same language, Hindustani. As the official language of India it is written in the Devanagari script and called Hindi. As the official language of Pakistan it is written in a modified Arabic script and called Urdu. (5) Thai includes Central, Southwestern, Northern and Northeastern Thai. The distinction between Northeastern Thai and Lao is political rather than linguistic. (6) Yiddish is usually considered a variant of German, though it has its own standard grammar, dictionaries, a highly developed literature, and is written in Hebrew characters. (7) A group of Thai-like dialects with about 9 million speakers.

Heroes of Young America: A National Poll

Who are the heroes of today's youth? Without question, entertainers and sports figures capture the imaginations of young Americans, according to a national survey conducted by The World Almanac. And first among them is Burt Reynolds, the sexy, handsome actor whose movies range from the intense "macho" drama of *Deliverance* to the light-hearted fast-paced comedy of *Smokey and the Bandit*.

In fact, the final list of the top 30 heroes (actually 32, due to 2 ties) chosen by some 2,000 eighth graders across the country does not include any government officials, politicians, business leaders or scientists. The only non-entertainment or sports figures on the list are ex-astronaut Neil Armstrong, writers Alex Haley and Judy Blume, and cartoonist Charles Schulz. And the latter, the creator of the "Peanuts" gang, might be considered an entertainer by many.

In the World Almanac survey, a geographic cross-section of students in the U.S., most of them 13 and 14 years old, was asked to name the "famous or important living" person they admired most. The base for the survey was 58 junior high schools, both inner-city and suburban, which were approached to participate in the poll through representatives of World Almanac co-sponsoring newspapers. Economic and racial characteristics of the participants closely approximated that of the 13-14 age group throughout the country: about 18 percent black, and mostly middle class with a few students from wealthier families and many more from poorer families. The participants were slightly more likely to be among the brighter students in their age group.

A look at the final results points to some interesting observations about today's youth. Even though the students polled were almost evenly divided between male and female, only 6 of the top heroes are women. Boys, in fact, voted far less frequently for women than girls did for men. Kristy McNichol, the top female on the list, made it to the 6th spot with 4 times as many female as male votes. As disturbing as it may be to many women, it is apparent that America's youth still thinks male when asked whom they admire most.

A look at the vital statistics of the top 30 heroes shows that across the board they're young. None are over 60, only 4 are 50 or older, only 9 are over 40, and 9 are under 30. Although the survey does show that America's youth trusts and looks up to people over 30, it's an unmistakable fact that their heroes have young, active images. It is interesting to note, however, that George Burns, the 84-year-old comedian and actor, although he did not make the top 30, made a strong showing, coming in 23rd among the boys.

Among the 18 entertainers, the field ran strongly toward comedians and both TV and film actors associated with light entertainment. The top 30 include Steve Martin, Alan Alda, Scott Baio, John Belushi, Robin Williams, Bill Cosby, and Gilda Radner, all either out-and-out comics or regulars in situation comedy. America's youth, indeed, seems to admire those who make them laugh and poke fun at the world around them.

Among the 10 sports figures in the top 30, no sport has the winning edge. The top sports vote-getter, Eric Heiden, coming off his stunning 5-gold medal victories in speed skating at the Winter Olympics, received high votes of admiration from both boys and girls. In general, the sports heroes, like Pete Rose, Willy Stargell, Terry Bradshaw, Julius Erving, Kareem Abdul-Jabbar, have been solid performers over many years.

Here they are, the heroes of young America:

1. **Burt Reynolds,** actor, popular TV "talk show" personality, has starred in many movies, including *Smokey and the Bandit, Semi-Tough,* and *The Longest Yard.*
2. **Steve Martin,** TV and movie comedian, starred in *The Jerk* and authored the best-selling book *Cruel Shoes.*
3. **Eric Heiden,** speed skater, won 5 gold medals in the 1980 Winter Olympics at Lake Placid, N.Y.
4. **Erik Estrada,** TV actor, stars in the top-rated show, *CHiPs.*
5. **Alan Alda,** TV and movie actor, is best known for his role as "Hawkeye" Pierce on the TV series *M*A*S*H.*
6. **Kristy McNichol,** TV and movie actress, plays "Buddy" on the popular TV series *Family.*
7. **"Sugar Ray" Leonard,** boxer, won a gold medal in the 1976 Summer Olympics and held the WBC welter-weight boxing title in 1979-1980.
8. **Scott Baio,** TV actor, plays "Chachi Arcola" on *Happy Days.*
9. **John Belushi,** TV and movie comedian, was one of the original *Saturday Night Live* cast and has appeared in the films *Animal House* and *The Blues Brothers.*
   Robin Williams, TV comedian/actor, plays "Mork" from the planet Ork on the top-rated series *Mork and Mindy.*
10. **Kurt Thomas,** gymnast, won the Sullivan Award for best amateur athlete of the year in 1979.
11. **Terry Bradshaw,** quarterback for the Pittsburgh Steelers, led his team to Super Bowl titles in 1975, 1976, 1979, and 1980.
    Sylvester Stallone, actor, author, shot to stardom in the title role of the film *Rocky.*
12. **Julius Erving,** basketball player, called "Dr. J" by his fans, led the ABA in scoring in 1973, 1974, and 1976 and was selected a NBA All-Star in 1977, 1978, and 1980.
13. **Earl Campbell,** running back for the Houston Oilers, won the Heisman Trophy in 1977, the NFL Rookie-of-the-Year and MVP in 1978, and MVP again in 1979.
14. **Bill Cosby,** actor/comedian, was the first black to star in a TV series, *I Spy,* 1966-68.
15. **Olivia Newton-John,** singer, starred in the movie *Grease.*
16. **John Ritter,** actor, stars in the popular TV series *Three's Company.*
17. **Sally Field,** actress, recently won the best actress Oscar for the movie *Norma Rae.*
18. **Charles Schulz,** cartoonist, draws the comic strip "Peanuts," starring Charlie Brown, Snoopy, Lucy et al.
19. **Gilda Radner,** comedienne, starred in *Saturday Night Live* and had a one-woman show on Broadway.
20. **Kareem Abdul-Jabbar,** basketball player with the Los Angeles Lakers, has won the NBA MVP title 6 times and was the NBC leading scorer in 1971 and 1972.
21. **Neil Armstrong,** former astronaut and currently a professor of aerospace engineering, was the first man to walk on the moon.
22. **Muhammad Ali,** boxer, poet, has held the world heavyweight title 3 times during his career.
23. **Willy Stargell,** first baseman and leading spirit of the Pittsburgh Pirates, was National League and World Series MVP in 1979.
24. **Judy Blume,** author, has written numerous books for young adults including *Forever* and *Are You There God?. . .*, as well as the adult bestseller *Wifey.*
25. **Pete Rose,** baseball player, controversial star of the Cincinnati Reds and Philadelphia Phillies, hit safely in 44 games for a National League record.
26. **Alex Haley,** author, wrote the best-selling book *Roots* which broke records as a television series.
27. **Dustin Hoffman,** actor, recently won the best actor Oscar for his role in *Kramer vs. Kramer.*
28. **Barbra Streisand,** singer/actress, won best actress Oscar in 1968 for *Funny Girl* and has also starred in *The Way We Were,* and *A Star Is Born.*
29. **Johnny Carson,** host of TV's *Tonight Show,* has dominated the late night talk show circuit since the early 1960s.
30. **Paul McCartney,** singer/composer, was one of the original Beatles and now leads the group Wings.

Population by Age — States: 1978

Source: U.S. Bureau of the Census (thousands)

State	Total	Under 5 years	5-17 years	18-44 years	45-64 years	65 yrs. and over	14 yrs. and over	21 yrs. and over
United States	**218,059**	**15,361**	**48,015**	**86,783**	**43,845**	**24,054**	**171,319**	**141,930**
New England	**12,256**	**721**	**2,668**	**4,861**	**2,554**	**1,451**	**9,806**	**8,141**
Maine	1,091	76	248	412	223	133	854	703
New Hampshire	871	58	197	351	169	96	684	566
Vermont	487	34	111	199	88	55	380	311
Massachusetts	5,774	326	1,242	2,308	1,198	700	4,646	3,853
Rhode Island	935	54	201	356	203	120	749	626
Connecticut	3,099	173	669	1,235	674	347	2,493	2,083
Middle Atlantic	**36,825**	**2,262**	**7,875**	**14,116**	**8,193**	**4,380**	**29,419**	**24,693**
New York	17,748	1,096	3,795	6,890	3,873	2,095	14,167	11,892
New Jersey	7,327	452	1,603	2,800	1,648	824	5,831	4,890
Pennsylvania	11,750	715	2,477	4,426	2,672	1,461	9,422	7,911
East North Central	**41,233**	**2,901**	**9,364**	**16,482**	**8,178**	**4,308**	**32,188**	**26,509**
Ohio	10,749	743	2,416	4,292	2,173	1,125	8,411	6,949
Indiana	5,374	393	1,230	2,143	1,044	564	4,171	3,431
Illinois	11,243	801	2,504	4,448	2,283	1,206	8,801	7,287
Michigan	9,189	649	2,151	3,751	1,771	867	7,120	5,828
Wisconsin	4,679	315	1,063	1,848	907	546	3,686	3,014
West North Central	**17,018**	**1,183**	**3,733**	**6,652**	**3,312**	**2,138**	**13,442**	**11,074**
Minnesota	4,008	274	911	1,625	735	463	3,150	2,573
Iowa	2,896	198	643	1,097	580	378	2,287	1,888
Missouri	4,860	330	1,042	1,898	961	629	3,857	3,202
North Dakota	652	50	148	247	128	78	509	412
South Dakota	690	54	155	252	139	89	537	437
Nebraska	1,565	113	343	606	301	202	1,233	1,014
Kansas	2,348	164	491	928	469	297	1,869	1,548
South Atlantic	**34,579**	**2,396**	**7,486**	**13,839**	**6,879**	**3,978**	**27,270**	**22,667**
Delaware	583	39	130	243	115	55	458	376
Maryland	4,143	252	930	1,756	834	370	3,287	2,707
District of Columbia	674	41	135	295	129	73	541	452
Virginia	5,148	344	1,124	2,197	1,014	468	4,073	3,349
West Virginia	1,860	139	400	690	408	223	1,456	1,225
North Carolina	5,577	401	1,238	2,295	1,093	550	4,355	3,602
South Carolina	2,918	233	685	1,202	539	258	2,232	1,817
Georgia	5,084	397	1,181	2,109	924	473	3,896	3,201
Florida	8,594	549	1,662	3,050	1,823	1,510	6,972	5,939
East South Central	**14,001**	**1,076**	**3,194**	**5,475**	**2,713**	**1,543**	**10,824**	**8,924**
Kentucky	3,498	267	784	1,379	680	388	2,717	2,243
Tennessee	4,357	312	956	1,735	876	478	3,418	2,844
Alabama	3,742	283	857	1,461	732	408	2,895	2,385
Mississippi	2,404	213	596	900	425	269	1,794	1,452
West South Central	**22,046**	**1,787**	**5,032**	**8,797**	**4,145**	**2,285**	**16,939**	**13,919**
Arkansas	2,186	169	484	812	428	293	1,702	1,417
Louisiana	3,966	332	969	1,574	721	370	2,997	2,420
Oklahoma	2,880	215	608	1,126	574	357	2,269	1,891
Texas	13,014	1,071	2,971	5,286	2,422	1,264	9,972	8,191
Mountain	**10,289**	**912**	**2,357**	**4,149**	**1,906**	**966**	**7,838**	**6,383**
Montana	785	61	179	304	159	81	611	498
Idaho	878	84	203	338	166	87	661	539
Wyoming	424	37	94	169	87	36	325	267
Colorado	2,670	205	582	1,167	484	232	2,088	1,710
New Mexico	1,212	107	297	482	222	104	913	729
Arizona	2,354	205	531	906	443	269	1,800	1,481
Utah	1,307	161	323	517	205	102	925	736
Nevada	660	50	148	267	139	55	514	424
Pacific	**29,811**	**2,124**	**6,307**	**12,411**	**5,964**	**3,005**	**23,593**	**19,620**
Washington	3,774	263	816	1,572	721	401	2,982	2,470
Oregon	2,444	178	511	977	493	285	1,935	1,620
California	22,294	1,568	4,677	9,285	4,522	2,243	17,693	14,742
Alaska	403	41	104	191	57	10	293	227
Hawaii	897	75	200	385	171	66	691	560

Immigration by Country of Last Residence 1820-1978

Source: U.S. Immigration and Naturalization Service (thousands)

Country	1820-1978, total	1951-1960, total	1961-1970, total	1974	1975	1976	1977	1978	Percent 1820-1978	Percent 1961-1970	Percent 1971-1978
All countries	**48,563**	**2,515.5**	**3,321.7**	**394.9**	**386.2**	**398.6**	**462.3**	**602.6**	**100.0**	**100.0**	**100.0**
Europe	**36,184**	**1,325.6**	**1,123.4**	**80.4**	**72.8**	**73.0**	**74.0**	**76.2**	**74.5**	**33.8**	**19.3**
Austria[1]	4,315	67.1	20.6	0.7	0.5	0.5	0.5	0.5	8.9	0.6	0.2
Hungary		36.6	5.4	0.9	0.6	0.6	0.5	0.6		0.2	0.1
Belgium	203	18.6	9.2	0.4	0.4	0.5	0.5	0.6	0.4	0.3	0.1
Czechoslovakia	137	.9	3.3	0.4	0.3	0.3	0.3	0.4	0.3	0.1	0.1
Denmark	364	11.0	9.2	0.5	0.3	0.4	0.4	0.4	0.7	0.3	0.1
Finland	33	4.9	4.2	0.2	0.2	0.2	0.2	0.3	0.1	0.1	0.1
France	750	51.1	45.2	2.2	1.8	2.0	2.7	2.7	1.5	1.4	0.6
Germany[1]	6,976	477.8	190.8	7.2	5.9	6.6	7.4	7.6	14.4	5.7	1.7
Great Britain[2]	4,895	195.5	210.0	11.7	12.2	13.0	14.0	16.4	10.1	6.3	2.9
Greece	653	47.6	86.0	10.6	9.8	8.6	7.8	7.0	1.3	2.6	2.3
Ireland[3]	4,723	57.3	37.5	1.3	1.1	1.0	1.0	0.9	9.7	1.1	0.4
Italy	5,292	185.5	214.1	15.0	11.0	8.0	7.4	7.0	10.9	6.4	3.4
Netherlands	359	52.3	30.6	1.0	0.8	0.9	1.0	1.2	0.7	0.9	0.2
Norway	856	22.9	15.5	0.4	0.4	0.3	0.3	0.4	1.8	0.5	0.1
Poland[1]	515	10.0	53.5	3.5	3.5	3.2	3.3	4.5	1.1	1.6	0.8
Portugal	443	19.6	76.1	10.7	11.3	11.0	10.0	10.5	0.9	2.3	2.5
Spain	258	7.9	44.7	4.7	2.6	2.8	5.6	4.3	0.5	1.3	1.0
Sweden	1,272	21.7	17.1	0.6	0.5	0.6	0.6	0.6	2.6	0.5	0.1
Switzerland	349	17.7	18.5	0.7	0.7	0.8	0.8	0.9	0.7	0.6	0.2
USSR[1,4]	3,372	.6	2.3	0.9	4.7	7.4	5.4	4.7	6.9	0.1	0.7
Yugoslavia	113	8.2	20.4	5.0	2.9	2.3	2.3	2.2	0.2	0.6	0.8
Other Europe	306	10.8	9.2	1.8	1.3	2.0	2.0	2.5	0.6	0.3	0.7
Asia	**2,817**	**153.3**	**427.8**	**127.0**	**129.2**	**146.7**	**150.8**	**243.6**	**5.8**	**12.9**	**33.3**
China[5]	524	9.7	34.8	10.0	9.2	9.9	12.5	14.5	1.1	1.0	2.4
Hong Kong	[6]180	15.5	75.0	10.7	12.5	13.7	12.3	11.1	0.4	2.3	2.6
India	159	2.0	27.2	11.7	14.3	16.1	16.8	19.1	0.3	0.8	3.5
Iran	[6]39	3.4	10.3	2.5	2.2	2.6	4.2	5.9	0.1	0.3	0.7
Israel	[6]84	25.5	29.6	2.9	3.5	5.2	4.4	4.5	0.2	0.9	0.8
Japan	405	46.3	40.0	5.4	4.8	4.8	4.5	4.5	0.8	1.2	1.2
Jordan	[6]37	5.8	11.7	2.5	2.3	2.4	2.9	3.2	0.1	0.3	0.6
Korea	[6]240	6.2	34.5	27.5	28.1	30.6	30.7	28.8	0.5	1.0	5.9
Lebanon	[6]51	4.5	15.2	3.0	4.0	5.0	5.5	4.8	0.1	0.5	0.9
Philippines	[7]380	19.3	98.4	32.5	31.3	36.8	38.5	36.6	0.8	3.0	7.7
Turkey	385	3.5	10.1	1.4	1.1	1.0	1.0	1.0	0.8	0.3	0.3
Vietnam	[8]114	2.7	4.2	3.1	2.7	2.4	3.4	87.6	0.2	0.1	3.2
Other Asia	219	9.0	36.7	13.8	13.2	16.2	14.1	22.0	0.5	1.2	3.4
America	**9,006**	**996.9**	**1,716.4**	**178.8**	**174.7**	**169.2**	**223.2**	**266.5**	**18.5**	**51.7**	**45.2**
Argentina	[9]93	19.5	49.7	2.9	2.8	2.7	3.1	4.1	0.2	1.5	0.7
Brazil	[9]57	13.8	29.3	1.6	1.4	1.4	1.9	2.2	0.1	0.9	0.4
Canada	4,101	378.0	413.3	12.3	11.2	11.4	18.0	23.5	8.4	12.4	3.9
Colombia	[9]144	18.0	72.0	5.9	6.4	5.7	8.2	10.9	0.3	2.2	1.6
Cuba	[10]518	78.9	208.5	17.4	25.6	28.4	66.1	27.5	1.1	6.3	6.7
Dominican Rep.	[9]213	9.9	93.3	15.7	14.1	12.5	11.6	19.5	0.4	2.8	3.3
Ecuador	[9]86	9.8	36.8	4.8	4.7	4.5	5.2	5.7	0.2	1.1	1.1
El Salvador	[9]44	5.9	15.0	2.3	2.4	2.4	4.4	5.9	0.1	0.4	0.7
Guatemala	[9]40	4.7	15.9	1.6	1.9	2.0	3.7	4.1	0.1	0.5	0.6
Haiti	[10]82	4.4	34.5	3.8	5.0	5.3	5.2	6.1	0.2	1.0	1.2
Honduras	[9]34	6.0	15.7	1.4	1.4	1.3	1.6	2.7	0.1	0.5	0.4
Mexico	2,108	299.8	453.9	71.9	62.6	58.4	44.6	92.7	4.3	13.7	15.1
Panama	[9]46	11.7	19.4	1.7	1.7	1.8	2.5	3.3	0.1	0.6	0.5
Peru	[9]47	7.4	19.1	2.0	2.3	2.6	3.9	5.1	0.1	0.6	0.6
West Indies	719	29.8	133.9	24.4	22.3	19.6	27.1	34.6	1.5	4.0	5.9
Other America	676	99.2	106.2	9.1	8.9	9.2	16.1	18.6	1.4	3.2	2.6
Africa	**131**	**14.1**	**29.0**	**5.2**	**5.9**	**5.7**	**9.6**	**11.5**	**0.3**	**0.9**	**1.6**
Australia and New Zealand	**119**	**11.5**	**19.6**	**2.0**	**1.8**	**2.1**	**2.5**	**2.7**	**0.2**	**0.6**	**0.5**
Other Oceania	**306**	**14.0**	**5.7**	**1.4**	**1.8**	**1.8**	**2.1**	**2.2**	**0.6**	**0.2**	**0.4**

(1) 1938-1945, Austria included with Germany; 1899-1919, Poland included with Austria-Hungary, Germany, and USSR. (2) Beginning 1952, includes data for United Kingdom not specified, formerly included with "Other Europe". (3) Comprises Eire and Northern Ireland. (4) Europe and Asia. (5) Beginning 1957, includes Taiwan. (6) Prior to 1951, included with "Other Asia". (7) Prior to 1951, Philippines included with "All other". (8) Prior to 1953, data for Vietnam not available. (9) Prior to 1951, included with "Other America". (10) Prior to 1951, included with "West Indies".

Women 1980: Discouraged But Not Defeated

By June Foley

It was a discouraging year for women.

On June 18 the Illinois House of Representatives failed to ratify the proposed equal rights amendment. The vote fell five short of the majority needed for approval, despite a major effort on behalf of ratification by the National Organization for Women, and the support of Pres. Carter, Illinois Gov. James R. Thompson Jr., and Chicago Mayor Jane M. Byrne. Illinois is the only northern industrial state that has not ratified the ERA. Thirty-five states have already ratified, but three more must do so by June 30, 1982 for the proposal to become part of the Constitution.

Another setback came on July 9 when the Republican National Convention's platform committee dropped its 40-year-long endorsement of the ERA. The 1980 platform on the ERA states only the following: "We acknowledge the legitimate efforts of those who support or oppose ratification of the equal rights amendment." Mary D. Crisp, the party's co-chairman, resigned, in part because of the change. She said the new platform position "would bury the rights of over 100 million women under a heap of platitudes," and warned that it "could prevent the party from electing the next President of the United States." Party chairman Bill Brock and leading Republican pollster Robert M. Teeter disagreed, contending that the ERA issue would not affect many votes. They also stated that Ronald Reagan, the Republican Presidential candidate, would continue to oppose the ERA no matter what the platform said.

For many women, a major defeat was the June 30 Supreme Court ruling upholding the constitutionality of the Hyde Amendment. From 1976 to January 1980, the Hyde Amendment (an amendment to an appropriations bill) allowed poor women's abortions to be financed by Medicaid only in those very few cases when a woman's life was in danger or her pregnancy the result of rape or incest that was promptly reported. This had cut off funds from an estimated 250,000 to 300,000 women a year who had wanted but could not afford abortions. Then in January, 1980 a Federal district judge in Brooklyn ruled that the Amendment violated the constitutional rights of poor women who needed abortions. But the latest decision of the Supreme Court overruled that decision, 5-4.

Individual Achievement

The year did see a number of notable achivements by individual women. Mother Teresa, Calcutta's "Saint of the Gutters," became the sixth woman to be awarded the Nobel Peace Prize. The 69-year-old Roman Catholic nun said she would use the $192,000 prize money to build homes for lepers. In the field of government, Shirley Hufstedler was named to head the new U.S. Dept. of Education, with about 17,000 employees and a budget of $14.2 billion. In industry, Sherry Lansing, 35, was named president of 20th Century Fox Productions, with a three-year contract that will bring her a minimum of $300,000 a year, but could include more than a million dollars in bonuses. She is the first woman to head production at a major motion picture studio, and one of the highest-paid female executives in any industry.

One Supreme Court decision was favorable: the court ruled unanimously on June 25 that a provision of the Social Security Act was unconstitutional because it provided benefits to families with unemployed fathers, while denying similar benefits to families whose mothers were out of work. The decision concerned the program Aid to Families with Dependent Children, Unemployed Father (AFDC-UF), which has assisted about 300,000 children in 26 states since 1968. The court voted to end the discrimination against women by extending benefits to any family with an unemployed parent.

In another step forward, women graduated for the first time from U.S. military academies—61 from West Point, 55 from Annapolis, 97 from the Air Force Academy, and 14 from the Coast Guard Academy. Also, some 15,000 women who served in the Army Auxiliary Corps in World War II, but did not stay on duty with its successor, the Women's Army Corps, received formal recognition from the Pentagon as full-fledged military veterans, and became eligible for veterans' benefits.

Pres. Carter's Feb. 7th plan for draft registration called for the registration of both women and men. Most women's leaders opposed registration of either sex, but said if registration took place women should not be exempted. House and Senate subcommittees opposed registration of women, however, and on April 22, the House rejected by a voice vote an amendment to provide enough money to register women. On June 10, the Senate rejected by a 51-40 vote an amendment by Sen. Nancy Kassebaum (R, Kan.) to include women in the registration plan. The American Civil Liberties Union filed suit June 26 to halt registration, charging that the plan was unconstitutional because it applied only to men. Nevertheless, in July registration began.

A New Decade

A new decade began in 1980, and with it came an accounting of the major accomplishments of the 1970s.

1970: The Senate held the first ERA hearings since 1956; the House held the first subcommittee hearings on sex discrimination in education; the Dept. of Justice filed the first Title VII suit of sex discrimination in employment; the first women generals were commissioned.

1971: The first affirmative action program began at the Univ. of Michigan; girls were admitted to the Boy Scout Explorer program for the first time; Billie Jean King became the first woman athlete to earn more than $100,000 a year.

1972: Congress passed the ERA, first introduced in 1923, and Hawaii became the first state to ratify it; the Equal Employment Opportunity Act of 1972 empowered the Equal Employment Opportunity Commission to go to court with discrimination cases; Title IX of the Education Amendments of 1972 prohibited sex discrimination in most federally-assisted educational programs; Congresswoman Shirley Chisholm (D, N.Y.) ran for president; Democrat Frances T. Farenthold was the first woman nominated for vice president at a major party convention; Jean Westwood became the first woman chair of the Democratic National Committee.

1973: The Supreme Court legalized abortion; the Supreme Court outlawed classified ads specifying gender; the American Stock Exchange created an affirmative action plan; the Federal Home Loan Bank Board barred sex bias by savings and loan institutions.

1974: Coverage under minimum wage requirements was extended to more than 1.5 million domestic workers; the Supreme Court outlawed forced maternity leave for teachers; the Natl. Little League agreed to admit women; the Housing and Community Development Act outlawed sex bias in housing; Ella Grasso became the first woman governor elected in her own right; the Equal Credit Opportunity Act prohibited discrimination in credit on the basis of sex or marital status; at the Univ. of Texas, Lorene Rogers became the first woman president of a major university.

1975: Congress required the service academies to admit women; the Pentagon outlawed the automatic discharge of pregnant servicewomen; federal court decisions gave federal employees the right to sue for sex discrimination; The First Women's Bank opened in New York City; Carla Hills was named U.S. Secretary of Housing and Urban Development.

1976: The Supreme Court required federal agencies to end sex discrimination in the industries they regulate; the

Electoral Votes for President, 1960-76

The Constitution, Article 2, Section 1 (consult index), provides for the appointment of electors, the counting of the electoral ballots and the procedure in the event of a tie. (*see Electoral College.*)

State	1960		1964		1968			1972		1976	
	R.	D.	R.	D.	R.	D.	3d	R.	D.	R.	D.
Ala.	...	[1]5	10	...	...	...	10	9	...	...	9
Alas.	[2]3	...	...	3	3	...	...	3	...	3	...
Ariz.	4	...	5	...	5	...	...	6	...	6	...
Ark.	...	8	...	6	...	...	6	6	...	...	6
Cal.	32	...	...	40	40	...	...	45	...	45	...
Col.	6	...	...	6	6	...	...	7	...	7	...
Conn.	...	8	...	8	...	8	...	8	...	8	...
Del.	...	3	...	3	3	...	...	3	...	...	3
D.C.	...	...	...	[2]3	...	3	...	...	3	...	3
Fla.	10	...	...	14	14	...	...	17	...	...	17
Ga.	...	12	12	...	...	...	12	12	...	...	12
Ha.	...	[2]3	...	4	...	4	...	4	...	...	4
Ida.	4	...	...	4	4	...	...	4	...	4	...
Ill.	...	27	...	26	26	...	...	26	...	26	...
Ind.	13	...	...	13	13	...	...	13	...	13	...
Ia.	10	...	...	9	9	...	...	8	...	8	...
Kan.	8	...	...	7	7	...	...	7	...	7	...
Ky.	10	...	...	9	9	...	...	9	...	...	9
La.	...	10	10	...	...	...	10	10	...	...	10
Me.	5	...	...	4	...	4	...	4	...	4	...
Md.	...	9	...	10	...	10	...	10	...	...	10
Mass.	...	16	...	14	...	14	...	...	14	...	14
Mich.	...	20	...	21	...	21	...	21	...	21	...
Minn.	...	11	...	10	...	10	...	10	...	...	10
Miss.	...	([1])	7	...	...	...	7	7	...	...	7
Mo.	...	13	...	12	12	...	...	12	...	...	12
Mon.	4	...	...	4	4	...	...	4	...	4	...
Neb.	6	...	...	5	5	...	...	5	...	5	...
Nev.	...	3	...	3	3	...	...	3	...	3	...
N.H.	4	...	...	4	4	...	...	4	...	4	...
N.J.	...	16	...	17	17	...	...	17	...	17	...
N.M.	...	4	...	4	4	...	...	4	...	4	...
N.Y.	...	45	...	43	...	43	...	41	...	...	41
N.C.	...	14	...	13	12	...	([3])	13	...	...	13
N.D.	4	...	...	4	4	...	...	3	...	3	...
Oh.	25	...	...	26	26	...	...	25	...	...	25
Okla.	[1]7	...	...	8	8	...	...	8	...	8	...
Ore.	6	...	...	6	6	...	...	6	...	6	...
Pa.	...	32	...	29	...	29	...	27	...	...	27
R.I.	...	4	...	4	...	4	...	4	...	...	4
S.C.	...	8	8	...	8	...	...	8	...	...	8
S.D.	4	...	...	4	4	...	...	4	...	4	...
Tenn.	11	...	...	11	11	...	...	10	...	...	10
Tex.	...	24	...	25	...	25	...	26	...	...	26
Ut.	4	...	...	4	4	...	...	4	...	4	...
Vt.	3	...	...	3	3	...	...	3	...	3	...
Va.	12	...	...	12	12	...	...	[4]11	...	12	...
Wash.	9	...	...	9	...	9	...	9	...	[5]8	...
W.Va.	...	8	...	7	...	7	...	6	...	...	6
Wis.	12	...	...	12	12	...	...	11	...	...	11
Wy.	3	...	...	3	3	...	...	3	...	3	...
Totals	**219**	**303**	**52**	**486**	**301**	**191**	**46**	**520**	**17**	**240**	**297**
Plurality	...	**[1]84**	...	**434**	**[3]110**	...	...	**[4]503**	...	...	**[5]57**

(1) In 1960 Sen. Harry F. Byrd (D-Va.) got 15 electoral votes including those of 8 unpledged Miss. Dem. electors, 6 unpledged Ala. Dem., and one Okla. Rep. (2) First Presidential election. (3) In 1968 in N. C. one Rep. elector cast his ballot for Wallace. (4) In 1972 one Rep. elector in Va. cast his ballot for John Hospers. (5) In 1976 one Rep. elector in Wash. cast his ballot for Reagan.

Voter Turnout in Presidential Elections

Source: League of Women Voters

National average of voting age population voting: 1960—63%; 1964—62%; 1968—60%; 1972—55.4%; 1976—56.5%. The sharp drop in 1972 reflects the expansion of eligibility with the enfranchisement of 18 to 21 year olds.

State	1976 Registered voters voting	1976 Voting age population voting	1972 Voting age population voting
Ala.	63%	47%	44%
Alas.	59	53	48
Ariz.	78	49	52
Ark.	71	48	49
Cal.	79	51	60
Col.	81	61	61
Conn.	84	64	66
Del.	78	58	64
D.C.	59	31	32
Fla.	77	50	51
Ga.	64	43	38
Ha.	85	52	51
Ida.	68	63	65
Ill.	76	61	63
Ind.	76	61	61
Ia.	n/a	64	64
Kan.	86	59	59
Ky.	68	49	48
La.	69	50	45
Me.	n/a	66	63
Md.	74	50	50
Mass.	82	62	62
Mich.	72	59	59
Minn.	77	73	68
Miss.	70	50	46
Mo.	82	58	57
Mon.	75	66	69
Neb.	74	58	56
Nev.	82	49	52
N.H.	71	59	64
N.J.	79	58	60
N.M.	81	55	61
N.Y.	78	52	56
N.C.	66	44	44
N.D.	*	71	70
Oh.	89	56	57
Okla.	n/a	57	57
Ore.	78	62	62
Pa.	80	55	56
R.I.	77	63	62
S.C.	72	52	40
S.D.	71	64	71
Tenn.	69	50	44
Tex.	64	48	45
Ut.	78	70	70
Vt.	73	64	61
Va.	81	49	46
Wash.	77	62	62
W.Va.	69	59	65
Wis.	n/a	65	63
Wy.	82	60	65

*No statewide registration. n/a—not available.

Party Nominees for President and Vice President

Asterisk (*) denotes winning ticket

Year	Democratic President	Democratic Vice President	Republican President	Republican Vice President
1916	Woodrow Wilson*	Thomas R. Marshall	Charles E. Hughes	Charles W. Fairbanks
1920	James M. Cox	Franklin D. Roosevelt	Warren G. Harding*	Calvin Coolidge
1924	John W. Davis	Charles W. Bryan	Calvin Coolidge*	Charles G. Dawes
1928	Alfred E. Smith	Joseph T. Robinson	Herbert Hoover*	Charles Curtis
1932	Franklin D. Roosevelt*	John N. Garner	Herbert Hoover	Charles Curtis
1936	Franklin D. Roosevelt*	John N. Garner	Alfred M. Landon	Frank Knox
1940	Franklin D. Roosevelt*	Henry A. Wallace	Wendell L. Willkie	Charles McNary
1944	Franklin D. Roosevelt*	Harry S. Truman	Thomas E. Dewey	John W. Bricker
1948	Harry S. Truman*	Alben W. Barkley	Thomas E. Dewey	Earl Warren
1952	Adlai E. Stevenson	John J. Sparkman	Dwight D. Eisenhower*	Richard M. Nixon
1956	Adlai E. Stevenson	Estes Kefauver	Dwight D. Eisenhower*	Richard M. Nixon
1960	John F. Kennedy*	Lyndon B. Johnson	Richard M. Nixon	Henry Cabot Lodge
1964	Lyndon B. Johnson*	Hubert H. Humphrey	Barry M. Goldwater	William E. Miller
1968	Hubert H. Humphrey	Edmund S. Muskie	Richard M. Nixon*	Spiro T. Agnew
1972	George S. McGovern	R. Sargent Shriver Jr.	Richard M. Nixon*	Spiro T. Agnew
1976	Jimmy Carter*	Walter F. Mondale	Gerald R. Ford	Robert J. Dole

Presidents of the U.S.

No.	Name	Politics	Born	in	Inaug.	at age	Died	at age
1	George Washington	Fed.	1732, Feb. 22	Va.	1789	57	1799, Dec. 14	67
2	John Adams	Fed.	1735, Oct. 30	Mass.	1797	61	1826, July 4	90
3	Thomas Jefferson	Dem.-Rep.	1743, Apr. 13	Va.	1801	57	1826, July 4	83
4	James Madison	Dem.-Rep.	1751, Mar. 16	Va.	1809	57	1836, June 28	85
5	James Monroe	Dem.-Rep.	1758, Apr. 28	Va.	1817	58	1831, July 4	73
6	John Quincy Adams	Dem.-Rep.	1767, July 11	Mass.	1825	57	1848, Feb. 23	80
7	Andrew Jackson	Dem.	1767, Mar. 15	S.C.	1829	61	1845, June 8	78
8	Martin Van Buren	Dem.	1782, Dec. 5	N.Y.	1837	54	1862, July 24	79
9	William Henry Harrison	Whig	1773, Feb. 9	Va.	1841	68	1841, Apr. 4	68
10	John Tyler	Whig	1790, Mar. 29	Va.	1841	51	1862, Jan. 18	71
11	James Knox Polk	Dem.	1795, Nov. 2	N.C.	1845	49	1849, June 15	53
12	Zachary Taylor	Whig	1784, Nov. 24	Va.	1849	64	1850, July 9	65
13	Millard Fillmore	Whig	1800, Jan. 7	N.Y.	1850	50	1874, Mar. 8	74
14	Franklin Pierce	Dem.	1804, Nov. 23	N.H.	1853	48	1869, Oct. 8	64
15	James Buchanan	Dem.	1791, Apr. 23	Pa.	1857	65	1868, June 1	77
16	Abraham Lincoln	Rep.	1809, Feb. 12	Ky.	1861	52	1865, Apr. 15	56
17	Andrew Johnson	(1)	1808, Dec. 29	N.C.	1865	56	1875, July 31	66
18	Ulysses Simpson Grant	Rep.	1822, Apr. 27	Oh.	1869	46	1885, July 23	63
19	Rutherford Birchard Hayes	Rep.	1822, Oct. 4	Oh.	1877	54	1893, Jan. 17	70
20	James Abram Garfield	Rep.	1831, Nov. 19	Oh.	1881	49	1881, Sept. 19	49
21	Chester Alan Arthur	Rep.	1829, Oct. 5	Vt.	1881	50	1886, Nov. 18	57
22	Grover Cleveland	Dem.	1837, Mar. 18	N.J.	1885	47	1908, June 24	71
23	Benjamin Harrison	Rep.	1833, Aug. 20	Oh.	1889	55	1901, Mar. 13	67
24	Grover Cleveland	Dem.	1837, Mar. 18	N.J.	1893	55	1908, June 24	71
25	William McKinley	Rep.	1843, Jan. 29	Oh.	1897	54	1901, Sept. 14	58
26	Theodore Roosevelt	Rep.	1858, Oct. 27	N.Y.	1901	42	1919, Jan. 6	60
27	William Howard Taft	Rep.	1857, Sept. 15	Oh.	1909	51	1930, Mar. 8	72
28	Woodrow Wilson	Dem.	1856, Dec. 28	Va.	1913	56	1924, Feb. 3	67
29	Warren Gamaliel Harding	Rep.	1865, Nov. 2	Oh.	1921	55	1923, Aug. 2	57
30	Calvin Coolidge	Rep.	1872, July 4	Vt.	1923	51	1933, Jan. 5	60
31	Herbert Clark Hoover	Rep.	1874, Aug. 10	Ia.	1929	54	1964, Oct. 20	90
32	Franklin Delano Roosevelt	Dem.	1882, Jan. 30	N.Y.	1933	51	1945, Apr. 12	63
33	Harry S. Truman	Dem.	1884, May 8	Mo.	1945	60	1972, Dec. 26	88
34	Dwight David Eisenhower	Rep.	1890, Oct. 14	Tex.	1953	62	1969, Mar. 28	78
35	John Fitzgerald Kennedy	Dem.	1917, May 29	Mass.	1961	43	1963, Nov. 22	46
36	Lyndon Baines Johnson	Dem.	1908, Aug. 27	Tex.	1963	55	1973, Jan. 22	64
37	Richard Milhous Nixon (2)	Rep.	1913, Jan. 9	Cal.	1969	56		
38	Gerald Rudolph Ford	Rep.	1913, July 14	Neb.	1974	61		
39	Jimmy (James Earl) Carter	Dem.	1924, Oct. 1	Ga.	1977	52		

(1) Andrew Johnson — a Democrat, nominated vice president by Republicans and elected with Lincoln on National Union ticket. (2) Resigned Aug. 9, 1974.

Presidents, Vice Presidents, Congresses

	President	Service		Vice President	Congress
1	George Washington	Apr. 30, 1789—Mar. 3, 1797	1	John Adams	1, 2, 3, 4
2	John Adams	Mar. 4, 1797—Mar. 3, 1801	2	Thomas Jefferson	5, 6
3	Thomas Jefferson	Mar. 4, 1801—Mar. 3, 1805	3	Aaron Burr	7, 8
	"	Mar. 4, 1805—Mar. 3, 1809	4	George Clinton	9, 10
4	James Madison	Mar. 4, 1809—Mar. 3, 1813		"(1)	11, 12
	"	Mar. 4, 1813—Mar. 3, 1817	5	Elbridge Gerry (2)	13, 14
5	James Monroe	Mar. 4, 1817—Mar. 3, 1825	6	Daniel D. Tompkins	15, 16, 17, 18
6	John Quincy Adams	Mar. 4, 1825—Mar. 3, 1829	7	John C. Calhoun	19, 20
7	Andrew Jackson	Mar. 4, 1829—Mar. 3, 1833		"(3)	21, 22
	"	Mar. 4, 1833—Mar. 3, 1837	8	Martin Van Buren	23, 24
8	Martin Van Buren	Mar. 4, 1837—Mar. 3, 1841	9	Richard M. Johnson	25, 26
9	William Henry Harrison (4)	Mar. 4, 1841—Apr. 4, 1841	10	John Tyler	27
10	John Tyler	Apr. 6, 1841—Mar. 3, 1845			27, 28
11	James K. Polk	Mar. 4, 1845—Mar. 3, 1849	11	George M. Dallas	29, 30
12	Zachary Taylor (4)	Mar. 5, 1849—July 9, 1850	12	Millard Fillmore	31
13	Millard Fillmore	July 10, 1850—Mar. 3, 1853			31, 32
14	Franklin Pierce	Mar. 4, 1853—Mar. 3, 1857	13	William R. King (5)	33, 34
15	James Buchanan	Mar. 4, 1857—Mar. 3, 1861	14	John C. Breckinridge	35, 36
16	Abraham Lincoln	Mar. 4, 1861—Mar. 3, 1865	15	Hannibal Hamlin	37, 38
	"(4)	Mar. 4, 1865—Apr. 15, 1865	16	Andrew Johnson	39
17	Andrew Johnson	Apr. 15, 1865—Mar. 3, 1869			39, 40
18	Ulysses S. Grant	Mar. 4, 1869—Mar. 3, 1873	17	Schuyler Colfax	41, 42
	"	Mar. 4, 1873—Mar. 3, 1877	18	Henry Wilson (6)	43, 44
19	Rutherford B. Hayes	Mar. 4, 1877—Mar. 3, 1881	19	William A. Wheeler	45, 46
20	James A. Garfield (4)	Mar. 4, 1881—Sept. 19, 1881	20	Chester A. Arthur	47
21	Chester A. Arthur	Sept. 20, 1881—Mar. 3, 1885			47, 48
22	Grover Cleveland (7)	Mar. 4, 1885—Mar. 3, 1889	21	Thomas A. Hendricks (8)	49, 50
23	Benjamin Harrison	Mar. 4, 1889—Mar. 3, 1893	22	Levi P. Morton	51, 52
24	Grover Cleveland (7)	Mar. 4, 1893—Mar. 3, 1897	23	Adlai E. Stevenson	53, 54
25	William McKinley	Mar. 4, 1897—Mar. 3, 1901	24	Garret A. Hobart (9)	55, 56
	"(4)	Mar. 4, 1901—Sept. 14, 1901	25	Theodore Roosevelt	57
26	Theodore Roosevelt	Sept. 14, 1901—Mar. 3, 1905			57, 58
	"	Mar. 4, 1905—Mar. 3, 1909	26	Charles W. Fairbanks	59, 60

President	Service	Vice President	Congress
27 William H. Taft	Mar. 4, 1909—Mar. 3, 1913	27 James S. Sherman (10)	61, 62
28 Woodrow Wilson	Mar. 4, 1913—Mar. 3, 1921	28 Thomas R. Marshall	63, 64, 65, 66
29 Warren G. Harding (4)	Mar. 4, 1921—Aug. 2, 1923	29 Calvin Coolidge	67
30 Calvin Coolidge	Aug. 3, 1923—Mar. 3, 1925		68
"	Mar. 4, 1925—Mar. 3, 1929	30 Charles G. Dawes	69, 70
31 Herbert C. Hoover	Mar. 4, 1929—Mar. 3, 1933	31 Charles Curtis	71, 72
32 Franklin D. Roosevelt (16)	Mar. 4, 1933—Jan. 20, 1941	32 John N. Garner	73, 74, 75, 76
"	Jan. 20, 1941—Jan. 20, 1945	33 Henry A. Wallace	77, 78
"(4)	Jan. 20, 1945—Apr. 12, 1945	34 Harry S. Truman	79
33 Harry S. Truman	Apr. 12, 1945—Jan. 20, 1949		79, 80
"	Jan. 20, 1949—Jan. 20, 1953	35 Alben W. Barkley	81, 82
34 Dwight D. Eisenhower	Jan. 20, 1953—Jan. 20, 1961	36 Richard M. Nixon	83, 84, 85, 86
35 John F. Kennedy (4)	Jan. 20, 1961—Nov. 22, 1963	37 Lyndon B. Johnson	87, 88
36 Lyndon B. Johnson	Nov. 22, 1963—Jan. 20, 1965		88
"	Jan. 20, 1965—Jan. 20, 1969	38 Hubert H. Humphrey	89, 90
37 Richard M. Nixon	Jan. 20, 1969—Jan. 20, 1973	39 Spiro T. Agnew (11)	91, 92, 93
"(12)	Jan. 20, 1973—Aug. 9, 1974	40 Gerald R. Ford (13)	93
38 Gerald R. Ford (14)	Aug. 9, 1974—Jan. 20, 1977	41 Nelson A. Rockefeller (15)	93, 94
39 Jimmy (James Earl) Carter	Jan. 20, 1977—	42 Walter F. Mondale	95, 96

(1) Died Apr. 20, 1812. (2) Died Nov. 23, 1814. (3) Resigned Dec. 28, 1832, to become U.S. Senator. (4) Died in office. (5) Died Apr. 18, 1853. (6) Died Nov. 22, 1875. (7) Terms not consecutive. (8) Died Nov. 25, 1885. (9) Died Nov. 21, 1899. (10) Died Oct. 30, 1912. (11) Resigned Oct. 10, 1973. (12) Resigned Aug. 9, 1974. (13) First non-elected vice president, chosen under 25th Amendment procedure. (14) First non-elected president. (15) 2d non-elected vice president, sworn in Dec. 19, 1974. (16) First president to be inaugurated under 20th Amendment, Jan. 20, 1937.

Vice Presidents of the U.S.

The numerals given vice presidents do not coincide with those given presidents, because some presidents had none and some had more than one.

Name	Birthplace	Year	Residence	Inaug.	Politics	Place of death	Year	Age
1 John Adams	Quincy, Mass.	1735	Mass.	1789	Fed.	Quincy, Mass.	1826	90
2 Thomas Jefferson	Shadwell, Va.	1743	Va.	1797	Rep.	Monticello, Va.	1826	83
3 Aaron Burr	Newark, N.J.	1756	N.Y.	1801	Rep.	Staten Island, N.Y.	1836	80
4 George Clinton	Ulster Co., N.Y.	1739	N.Y.	1805	Rep.	Washington, D.C.	1812	73
5 Elbridge Gerry	Marblehead, Mass.	1744	Mass.	1813	Rep.	Washington, D.C.	1814	70
6 Daniel D. Tompkins	Scarsdale, N.Y.	1774	N.Y.	1817	Rep.	Staten Island, N.Y.	1825	51
7 John C. Calhoun (1)	Abbeville, S.C.	1782	S.C.	1825	Rep.	Washington, D.C.	1850	68
8 Martin Van Buren	Kinderhook, N.Y.	1782	N.Y.	1833	Dem.	Kinderhook, N.Y.	1862	79
9 Richard M. Johnson	Louisville, Ky.	1780	Ky.	1837	Dem.	Frankfort, Ky.	1850	70
10 John Tyler	Greenway, Va.	1790	Va.	1841	Whig.	Richmond, Va.	1862	71
11 George M. Dallas	Philadelphia, Pa.	1792	Pa.	1845	Dem.	Philadelphia, Pa.	1864	72
12 Millard Fillmore	Summerhill, N.Y.	1800	N.Y.	1849	Whig.	Buffalo, N.Y.	1874	74
13 William R. King	Sampson Co., N.C.	1786	Ala.	1853	Dem.	Dallas Co., Ala.	1853	67
14 John C. Breckinridge	Lexington, Ky.	1821	Ky.	1857	Dem.	Lexington, Ky.	1875	54
15 Hannibal Hamlin	Paris, Me.	1809	Me.	1861	Rep.	Bangor, Me.	1891	81
16 Andrew Johnson	Raleigh, N.C.	1808	Tenn.	1865	(2)	Carter Co., Tenn.	1875	66
17 Schuyler Colfax	New York City, N.Y.	1823	Ind.	1869	Rep.	Mankato, Minn.	1885	62
18 Henry Wilson	Farmington, N.H.	1812	Mass.	1873	Rep.	Washington, D.C.	1875	63
19 William A. Wheeler	Malone, N.Y.	1819	N.Y.	1877	Rep.	Malone, N.Y.	1887	68
20 Chester A. Arthur	Fairfield, Vt.	1830	N.Y.	1881	Rep.	New York City, N.Y.	1886	56
21 Thomas A. Hendricks	Muskingum Co., Oh.	1819	Ind.	1885	Dem.	Indianapolis, Ind.	1885	66
22 Levi P. Morton	Shoreham, Vt.	1824	N.Y.	1889	Rep.	Rhinebeck, N.Y.	1920	96
23 Adlai E. Stevenson (3)	Christian Co., Ky.	1835	Ill.	1893	Dem.	Chicago, Ill.	1914	78
24 Garret A. Hobart	Long Branch, N.J.	1844	N.J.	1897	Rep.	Paterson, N.J.	1899	55
25 Theodore Roosevelt	New York City, N.Y.	1858	N.Y.	1901	Rep.	Oyster Bay, N.Y.	1919	60
26 Charles W. Fairbanks	Unionville Centre, Oh.	1852	Ind.	1905	Rep.	Indianapolis, Ind.	1918	66
27 James S. Sherman	Utica, N.Y.	1855	N.Y.	1909	Rep.	Utica, N.Y.	1912	57
28 Thomas R. Marshall	N. Manchester, Ind.	1854	Ind.	1913	Dem.	Washington, D.C.	1925	71
29 Calvin Coolidge	Plymouth, Vt.	1872	Mass.	1921	Rep.	Northampton, Mass.	1933	60
30 Charles G. Dawes	Marietta, Oh.	1865	Ill.	1925	Rep.	Evanston, Ill.	1951	85
31 Charles Curtis	Topeka, Kan.	1860	Kan.	1929	Rep.	Washington, D.C.	1936	76
32 John Nance Garner	Red River Co., Tex.	1868	Tex.	1933	Dem.	Uvalde, Tex.	1967	98
33 Henry Agard Wallace	Adair County, Ia.	1888	Iowa	1941	Dem.	Danbury, Conn.	1965	77
34 Harry S. Truman	Lamar, Mo.	1884	Mo.	1945	Dem.	Kansas City, Mo.	1972	88
35 Alben W. Barkley	Graves County, Ky.	1877	Ky.	1949	Dem.	Lexington, Va.	1956	78
36 Richard M. Nixon	Yorba Linda, Cal.	1913	Cal.	1953	Rep.			
37 Lyndon B. Johnson	Johnson City, Tex.	1908	Tex.	1961	Dem.	San Antonio, Tex.	1973	64
38 Hubert H. Humphrey	Wallace, S.D.	1911	Minn.	1965	Dem.	Waverly, Minn.	1978	66
39 Spiro T. Agnew	Baltimore, Md.	1918	Md.	1969	Rep.			
40 Gerald R. Ford	Omaha, Neb.	1913	Mich.	1973	Rep.			
41 Nelson A. Rockefeller	Bar Harbor, Me.	1908	N.Y.	1974	Rep.	New York, N.Y.	1979	70
42 Walter F. Mondale	Ceylon, Minn.	1928	Minn.	1977	Dem.			

(1) John C. Calhoun resigned Dec. 28, 1832, having been elected to the Senate to fill a vacancy. (2) Andrew Johnson — a Democrat nominated by Republicans and elected with Lincoln on the National Union Ticket. (3) Adlai E. Stevenson, 23d vice president, was grandfather of Democratic candidate for president, 1952 and 1956.

The Continental Congress: Meetings, Presidents

Meeting places	Dates of meetings	Congress presidents	Date elected
Philadelphia	Sept. 5 to Oct. 26, 1774	Peyton Randolph, Va. (1)	Sept. 5, 1774
"	"	Henry Middleton, S.C.	Oct. 22, 1774
Philadelphia	May 10, 1775 to Dec. 12, 1776	Peyton Randolph, Va.	May 10, 1775
"	"	John Hancock, Mass.	May 24, 1775
Baltimore	Dec. 20, 1776 to Mar. 4, 1777	"	
Philadelphia	Mar. 5 to Sept. 18, 1777	"	
Lancaster, Pa.	Sept. 27, 1777 (one day)	"	
York, Pa.	Sept. 30, 1777 to June 27, 1778	Henry Laurens, S.C.	Nov. 1, 1777(4)
Philadelphia	July 2, 1778 to June 21, 1783	John Jay, N.Y.	Dec. 10, 1778
"	"	Samuel Huntington, Conn.	Sept. 28, 1779
"	"	Thomas McKean, Del.	July 10, 1781
"	"	John Hanson, Md. (2)	Nov. 5, 1781
"	"	Elias Boudinot, N.J.	Nov. 4, 1782
Princeton, N.J.	June 30 to Nov. 4, 1783	Thomas Mifflin, Pa.	Nov. 3, 1783
Annapolis, Md.	Nov. 26, 1783 to June 3, 1784	"	
Trenton, N.J.	Nov. 1 to Dec. 24, 1784	Richard Henry Lee, Va.	Nov. 30, 1784
New York City	Jan. 11 to Nov. 4, 1785	"	
"	Nov. 7, 1785 to Nov. 3, 1786	John Hancock, Mass. (3)	Nov. 23, 1785
"	"	Nathaniel Gorman, Mass.	June 6, 1786
"	Nov. 6, 1786 to Oct. 30, 1787	Arthur St. Clair, Pa.	Feb. 2, 1787
"	Nov. 5, 1787 to Oct. 21, 1788	Cyrus Griffin, Va.	Jan. 22, 1788
"	Nov. 3, 1788 to Mar. 2, 1789	"	

(1) Resigned Oct. 22, 1774. (2) Titled "President of the United States in Congress Assembled," John Hanson is considered by some to be the first U.S. President as he was the first to serve under the Articles of Confederation. He was, however, little more than presiding officer of the Congress, which retained full executive power. He could be considered the head of government, but not head of state. (3) Resigned May 29, 1786, without serving, because of illness. (4) Articles of Confederation agreed upon, Nov. 15, 1777; last ratification from Maryland, Mar. 1, 1781.

Cabinets of the U. S.

Secretaries of State

The Department of Foreign Affairs was created by act of Congress July 27, 1789, and the name changed to Department of State on Sept. 15.

President	Secretary	Home	Apptd.
Washington	Thomas Jefferson	Va.	1789
"	Edmund Randolph	"	1794
"	Timothy Pickering	Pa.	1795
Adams, J.	"	"	1797
"	John Marshall	Va.	1800
Jefferson	James Madison	"	1801
Madison	Robert Smith	Md.	1809
"	James Monroe	Va.	1811
Monroe	John Quincy Adams	Mass.	1817
Adams, J.Q.	Henry Clay	Ky.	1825
Jackson	Martin Van Buren	N.Y.	1829
"	Edward Livingston	La.	1831
"	Louis McLane	Del.	1833
"	John Forsyth	Ga.	1834
Van Buren	"	"	1837
Harrison, W.H.	Daniel Webster	Mass.	1841
Tyler	"	"	1841
"	Abel P. Upshur	Va.	1843
"	John C. Calhoun	S.C.	1844
Polk	"	"	1845
"	James Buchanan	Pa.	1845
Taylor	"	"	1849
"	John M. Clayton	Del.	1849
Fillmore	"	"	1850
"	Daniel Webster	Mass.	1850
"	Edward Everett	"	1852
Pierce	William L. Marcy	N.Y.	1853
Buchanan	"	"	1857
"	Lewis Cass	Mich.	1857
"	Jeremiah S. Black	Pa.	1860
Lincoln	"	"	1861
"	William H. Seward	N.Y.	1861
Johnson, A.	"	"	1865
Grant	Elihu B. Washburne	Ill.	1869
"	Hamilton Fish	N.Y.	1869
Hayes	"	"	1877
"	William M. Evarts	"	1877
Garfield	"	"	1881
"	James G. Blaine	Me.	1881
Arthur	"	"	1881
"	F.T. Frelinghuysen	N.J.	1881

President	Secretary	Home	Apptd.
Cleveland	"	"	1885
"	Thomas F. Bayard	Del.	1885
Harrison, B.	"	"	1889
"	James G. Blaine	Me.	1889
"	John W. Foster	Ind.	1892
Cleveland	Walter Q. Gresham	Ill.	1893
"	Richard Olney	Mass.	1895
McKinley	"	"	1897
"	John Sherman	Oh.	1897
"	William R. Day	"	1898
"	John Hay	D.C.	1898
Roosevelt, T.	"	"	1901
"	Elihu Root	N.Y.	1905
"	Robert Bacon	"	1909
Taft	"	"	1909
"	Philander C. Knox	Pa.	1909
Wilson	"	"	1913
"	William J. Bryan	Neb.	1913
"	Robert Lansing	N.Y.	1915
"	Bainbridge Colby	"	1920
Harding	Charles E. Hughes	"	1921
Coolidge	"	"	1923
"	Frank B. Kellogg	Minn.	1925
Hoover	"	"	1929
"	Henry L. Stimson	N.Y.	1929
Roosevelt, F.D.	Cordell Hull	Tenn.	1933
"	E.R. Stettinius Jr.	Va.	1944
Truman	"	"	1945
"	James F. Byrnes	S.C.	1945
"	George C. Marshall	Pa.	1947
"	Dean G. Acheson	Conn.	1949
Eisenhower	John Foster Dulles	N.Y.	1953
"	Christian A. Herter	Mass.	1959
Kennedy	Dean Rusk	N.Y.	1961
Johnson, L.B.	"	"	1963
Nixon	William P. Rogers	N.Y.	1969
"	Henry A. Kissinger	D.C.	1973
Ford	"	"	1974
Carter	Cyrus R. Vance	N.Y.	1977
"	Edmund Muskie	Me.	1980

Secretaries of the Treasury

The Treasury Department was organized by act of Congress Sept. 2, 1789.

President	Secretary	Home	Apptd.
Washington	Alexander Hamilton	N.Y.	1789
"	Oliver Wolcott	Conn.	1795
Adams, J.	"	"	1797
"	Samuel Dexter	Mass.	1801
Jefferson	"	"	1801
"	Albert Gallatin	Pa.	1801
Madison	"	Pa	1809
"	George W. Campbell	Tenn.	1814
"	Alexander J. Dallas	Pa.	1814
"	William H. Crawford	Ga.	1816
Monroe	"	"	1817
Adams, J.Q.	Richard Rush	Pa.	1825
Jackson	Samuel D. Ingham	"	1829
"	Louis McLane	Del.	1831
"	William J. Duane	Pa.	1833
"	Roger B. Taney	Md.	1833
"	Levi Woodbury	N.H.	1834
Van Buren	"	"	1837
Harrison, W.H.	Thomas Ewing	Oh.	1841
Tyler	"	"	1841
"	Walter Forward	Pa.	1841
"	John C. Spencer	N.Y.	1843
Tyler	George M. Bibb	Ky.	1844
Polk	Robert J. Walker	Miss.	1845
Taylor	William M. Meredith	Pa.	1849
Fillmore	Thomas Corwin	Oh.	1850
Pierce	James Guthrie	Ky.	1853
Buchanan	Howell Cobb	Ga.	1857
"	Phillip F. Thomas	Md.	1860
"	John A. Dix	N.Y.	1861
Lincoln	Salmon P. Chase	Oh.	1861
"	William P. Fessenden	Me.	1864
"	Hugh McCulloch	Ind.	1865
Johnson, A.	"	"	1865
Grant	George S. Boutwell	Mass.	1869
"	William A. Richardson	Mass.	1873
"	Benjamin H. Bristow	Ky.	1874
"	Lot M. Morrill	Me.	1876
Hayes	John Sherman	Oh.	1877
Garfield	William Windom	Minn.	1881
Arthur	Charles J. Folger	N.Y.	1881
"	Walter Q. Gresham	Ind.	1884
"	Hugh McCulloch	"	1884
Cleveland	Daniel Manning	N.Y.	1885
Cleveland	Charles S. Fairchild	"	1887
Harrison, B.	William Windom	Minn.	1889
"	Charles Foster	Oh.	1891
Cleveland	John G. Carlisle	Ky.	1893
McKinley	Lyman J. Gage	Ill.	1897
Roosevelt, T.	"	"	1901
"	Leslie M. Shaw	Ia.	1902
"	George B. Cortelyou	N.Y.	1907
Taft	Franklin MacVeagh	Ill.	1909
Wilson	William G. McAdoo	N.Y.	1913
"	Carter Glass	Va.	1918
"	David F. Houston	Mo.	1920
Harding	Andrew W. Mellon	Pa.	1921
Coolidge	"	"	1923
Hoover	"	"	1929
"	Ogden L. Mills	N.Y.	1932
Roosevelt, F.D.	William H. Woodin	"	1933
"	Henry Morgenthau, Jr.	"	1934
Truman	Fred M. Vinson	Ky.	1945
"	John W. Snyder	Mo.	1946
Eisenhower	George M. Humphrey	Oh.	1953
"	Robert B. Anderson	Conn.	1957
Kennedy	C. Douglas Dillon	N.J.	1961
Johnson, L.B.	"	"	1963
"	Henry H. Fowler	Va.	1965
"	Joseph W. Barr	Ind.	1968
Nixon	David M. Kennedy	Ill.	1969
"	John B. Connally	Tex.	1971
"	George P. Shultz	Ill.	1972
"	William E. Simon	N.J.	1974
Ford	"	"	1974
Carter	W. Michael Blumenthal	Mich.	1977
"	G. William Miller	R.I.	1979

Secretaries of Defense

The Department of Defense, originally designated the National Military Establishment, was created Sept. 18, 1947. It is headed by the secretary of defense, who is a member of the president's cabinet.

The departments of the army, of the navy, and of the air force function within the Department of Defense, and their respective secretaries are no longer members of the president's cabinet.

President	Secretary	Home	Apptd.
Truman	James V. Forrestal	N.Y.	1947
"	Louis A. Johnson	W.Va.	1949
"	George C. Marshall	Pa.	1950
"	Robert A. Lovett	N.Y.	1951
Eisenhower	Charles E. Wilson	Mich.	1953
"	Neil H. McElroy	Oh.	1957
"	Thomas S. Gates Jr.	Pa.	1959
Kennedy	Robert S. McNamara	Mich.	1961
Johnson, L.B.	Robert S. McNamara	Mich.	1963
"	Clark M. Clifford	Md.	1968
Nixon	Melvin R. Laird	Wis.	1969
"	Elliot L. Richardson	Mass.	1973
"	James R. Schlesinger	Va.	1973
Ford	"	"	1974
"	Donald H. Rumsfeld	Ill.	1975
Carter	Harold Brown	Cal.	1977

Secretaries of the Armed Services

Not members of the president's Cabinet

The Department of Defense; created Sept. 18, 1947, consolidated the navy, army, air force into a single department.

Secretary of the Air Force	Appointed
W. Stuart Symington	Sept. 18, 1947
Thomas K. Finletter	Apr. 24, 1950
Harold E. Talbot	Feb. 4, 1953
Donald A. Quarles	Aug. 12, 1965
James H. Douglas	Mar. 26, 1957
Dudley C. Sharpe	Dec. 10, 1959
Eugene M. Zuckert	Jan. 23, 1961
Dr. Harold Brown	July 10, 1965
Robert C. Seamans Jr.	Jan. 20, 1969
John L. McLucas	July 19, 1973
Thomas C. Reed	Jan. 2, 1976
John C. Stetson	Apr. 6, 1977
Hans M. Mark	July 11, 1979

Secretary of the Army	Appointed
Kenneth C. Royall	Sept. 18, 1947
Gordon Gray*	June 20, 1949
Frank Pace Jr.	Apr. 12, 1950
Earl D. Johnson (acting)	Jan. 20, 1953
Robert T. Stevens	Feb. 4, 1953
Wilber M. Brucker	July 21, 1955
Elvis J. Stahr Jr.	Jan. 23, 1961
Cyrus R. Vance	May 21, 1962
Stephen Ailes	Jan. 20, 1964
Stanley R. Resor	June 17, 1965
Robert F. Froehlke	June 15, 1971
Howard H. Callaway	May 2, 1973
Norman R. Augustine (acting)	July 3, 1975
Martin R. Hoffman	Aug. 5, 1975
Clifford L. Alexander Jr.	Jan. 19, 1977

*In addition, Gordon Gray was acting secretary of the army from Apr. 28, 1949, and under secretary from May 25, 1949, until

June 20, 1949.

Secretary of the Navy	Appointed
John L. Sullivan	Sept. 18, 1947
Francis P. Matthews	May 25, 1949
Dan A. Kimball	July 31, 1951
Robert B. Anderson	Feb. 4, 1953
Charles S. Thomas	May 3, 1954
Thomas S. Gates Jr.	Apr. 1, 1957
William B. Franke	June 1, 1958
John B. Connally Jr.	Jan. 23, 1961
Fred Korth	Dec. 11, 1961
Paul H. Nitze	Oct. 14, 1963
John T. McNaughton	June 6, 1967
Paul R. Ignatius	Aug. 4, 1967
John H. Chafee	Jan. 20, 1969
John W. Warner	Apr. 7, 1972
J. William Middendorf 2d	June 10, 1974
W. Graham Claytor Jr.	Jan. 19, 1977
Edward Hidalgo	Oct. 19, 1979

Secretaries of War

The War (and Navy) Department was created by act of Congress Aug. 7, 1789, and Gen. Henry Knox was commissioned secretary of war under that act Sept. 12, 1789.

President	Secretary	Home	Apptd.
Washington	Henry Knox	Mass.	1789
"	Timothy Pickering	Pa.	1795
"	James McHenry	Md.	1796
Adams, J.	"	"	1797
"	Samuel Dexter	Mass.	1800
Jefferson	Henry Dearborn	"	1801
Madison	William Eustis	Mass.	1809
"	John Armstrong	N.Y.	1813
Madison	James Monroe	Va.	1814
"	William H. Crawford	Ga.	1815
Monroe	John C. Calhoun	S.C.	1817
Adams, J.Q.	James Barbour	Va.	1825
"	Peter B. Porter	N.Y.	1828
Jackson	John H. Eaton	Tenn.	1829
"	Lewis Cass	Oh.	1831
"	Benjamin F. Butler	N.Y.	1837
Van Buren	Joel R. Poinsett	S.C.	1837
Harrison, W.H.	John Bell	Tenn.	1841
Tyler	"	"	1841
Tyler	John C. Spencer	N.Y.	1841
"	James M. Porter	Pa.	1843
"	William Wilkins	"	1844
Polk	William L. Marcy	N.Y.	1845
Taylor	George W. Crawford	Ga.	1849
Fillmore	Charles M. Conrad	La.	1850
Pierce	Jefferson Davis	Miss.	1853
Buchanan	John B. Floyd	Va.	1857
"	Joseph Holt	Ky.	1861
Lincoln	Simon Cameron	Pa.	1861
"	Edwin M. Stanton	Pa.	1862
Johnson, A.	"	"	1865
"	John M. Schofield	Ill.	1868
Grant	John A. Rawlins	Ill.	1869
"	William T. Sherman	Oh.	1869
"	William W. Belknap	Ia.	1869
"	Alphonso Taft	Oh.	1876
Grant	James D. Cameron	Pa.	1876
Hayes	George W. McCrary	Ia.	1877
"	Alexander Ramsey	Minn.	1879
Garfield	Robert T. Lincoln	Ill.	1881
Arthur	"	"	1881
Cleveland	William C. Endicott	Mass.	1885
Harrison, B.	Redfield Proctor	Vt.	1889
"	Stephen B. Elkins	W.Va.	1891
Cleveland	Daniel S. Lamont	N.Y.	1893
McKinley	Russel A. Alger	Mich.	1897
"	Elihu Root	N.Y.	1899
Roosevelt, T.	"	"	1901
"	William H. Taft	Oh.	1904
"	Luke E. Wright	Tenn.	1908
Taft	Jacob M. Dickinson	"	1909
"	Henry L. Stimson	N.Y.	1911
Wilson	Lindley M. Garrison	N.J.	1913
"	Newton D. Baker	Oh.	1916
Harding	John W. Weeks	Mass.	1921
Coolidge	"	"	1923
"	Dwight F. Davis	Mo.	1925
Hoover	James W. Good	Ill.	1929
Hoover	Patrick J. Hurley	Okla.	1929
Roosevelt, F.D.	George H. Dern	Ut.	1933
"	Harry H. Woodring	Kan.	1937
Roosevelt, F.D.	Henry L. Stimson	N.Y.	1940
Truman	Robert P. Patterson	N.Y.	1945
"	*Kenneth C. Royall	N.C.	1947

Secretaries of the Navy

The Navy Department was created by act of Congress Apr. 30, 1798.

President	Secretary	Home	Apptd.
Adams, J.	Benjamin Stoddert	Md.	1798
Jefferson	"	"	1801
"	Robert Smith	"	1801
Madison	Paul Hamilton	S.C.	1809
"	William Jones	Pa.	1813
"	Benjamin Williams Crowninshield	Mass.	1814
Monroe	"	"	1817
"	Smith Thompson	N.Y.	1818
"	Samuel L. Southard	N.J.	1823
Adams, J.Q.	"	"	1825
Jackson	John Branch	N.C.	1829
"	Levi Woodbury	N.H.	1831
"	Mahlon Dickerson	N.J.	1834
Van Buren	"	"	1837
"	James K. Paulding	N.Y.	1838
Harrison, W.H.	George E. Badger	N.C.	1841
Tyler	"	"	1841
"	Abel P. Upshur	Va.	1841
"	David Henshaw	Mass.	1843
"	Thomas W. Gilmer	Va.	1844
"	John Y. Mason	"	1844
Polk	George Bancroft	Mass.	1845
"	John Y. Mason	Va.	1846
Taylor	William B. Preston	"	1849
Fillmore	William A. Graham	N.C.	1850
"	John P. Kennedy	Md.	1852
Pierce	James C. Dobbin	N.C.	1853
Buchanan	Isaac Toucey	Conn.	1857
Lincoln	Gideon Welles	Conn.	1861
Johnson, A.	"	"	1865
Grant	Adolph E. Borie	Pa.	1869
"	George M. Robeson	N.J.	1869
Hayes	Richard W. Thompson	Ind.	1877
"	Nathan Goff Jr.	W.Va.	1881
Garfield	William H. Hunt	La.	1881
Arthur	William E. Chandler	N.H.	1882
Cleveland	William C. Whitney	N.Y.	1885
Harrison, B.	Benjamin F. Tracy	N.Y.	1889
Cleveland	Hilary A. Herbert	Ala.	1893
McKinley	John D. Long	Mass.	1897
Roosevelt, T.	"	"	1901
"	William H. Moody	"	1902
"	Paul Morton	Ill.	1904
"	Charles J. Bonaparte	Md.	1905
"	Victor H. Metcalf	Cal.	1906
"	Truman H. Newberry	Mich.	1908
Taft	George von L. Meyer	Mass.	1909
Wilson	Josephus Daniels	N.C.	1913
Harding	Edwin Denby	Mich.	1921
Coolidge	"	"	1923
"	Curtis D. Wilbur	Cal.	1924
Hoover	Charles Francis Adams	Mass.	1929
Roosevelt, F.D.	Claude A. Swanson	Va.	1933
"	Charles Edison	N.J.	1940
"	Frank Knox	Ill.	1940
"	*James V. Forrestal	N.Y.	1944
Truman	"	"	1945

*Last members of Cabinet. The War Department became the Department of the Army and it and the Navy Department became branches of the Department of Defense, created Sept. 18, 1947.

Attorneys General

The office of attorney general was organized by act of Congress Sept. 24, 1789. The Department of Justice was created June 22, 1870.

President	Attorney General	Home	Apptd.
Washington	Edmund Randolph	Va.	1789
"	William Bradford	Pa.	1794
"	Charles Lee	Va.	1795
Adams, J.	"	"	1797
Jefferson	Levi Lincoln	Mass.	1801
"	John Breckenridge	Ky.	1805
Jefferson	Caesar A. Rodney	Del.	1807
Madison	"	"	1809
"	William Pinkney	Md.	1811
"	Richard Rush	Pa.	1814
Monroe	"	"	1817
"	William Wirt	Va.	1817
Adams, J.Q.	"	"	1825
Jackson	John M. Berrien	Ga.	1829
"	Roger B. Taney	Md.	1831
"	Benjamin F. Butler	N.Y.	1833
Van Buren	"	"	1837
"	Felix Grundy	Tenn.	1838
"	Henry D. Gilpin	Pa.	1840
Harrison, W.H.	John J. Crittenden	Ky.	1841
Tyler	"	"	1841
"	Hugh S. Legare	S.C.	1841
"	John Nelson	Md.	1843
Polk	John Y. Mason	Va.	1845
"	Nathan Clifford	Me.	1846
"	Isaac Toucey	Conn.	1848
Taylor	Reverdy Johnson	Md.	1849
Fillmore	John J. Crittenden	Ky.	1850
Pierce	Caleb Cushing	Mass.	1853
Buchanan	Jeremiah S. Black	Pa.	1857
"	Edwin M. Stanton	Pa.	1860
Lincoln	Edward Bates	Mo.	1861
"	James Speed	Ky.	1864
Johnson, A.	"	"	1865
"	Henry Stanbery	Oh.	1866
"	William M. Evarts	N.Y.	1868
Grant	Ebenezer R. Hoar	Mass.	1869
"	Amos T. Akerman	Ga.	1870
"	George H. Williams	Ore.	1871
"	Edwards Pierrepont	N.Y.	1875
"	Alphonso Taft	Oh.	1876
Hayes	Charles Devens	Mass.	1877

President	Attorney General	Home	Apptd.
Garfield	Wayne MacVeagh	Pa.	1881
Arthur	Benjamin H. Brewster	"	1881
Cleveland	Augustus Garland	Ark.	1885
Harrison, B.	William H. H. Miller	Ind.	1889
Cleveland	Richard Olney	Mass.	1893
"	Judson Harmon	Oh.	1895
McKinley	Joseph McKenna	Cal.	1897
"	John W. Griggs	N.J.	1898
"	Philander C. Knox	Pa.	1901
Roosevelt, T.	"	"	1901
"	William H. Moody	Mass.	1904
"	Charles J. Bonaparte	Md.	1906
Taft	George W. Wickersham	N.Y.	1909
Wilson	J.C. McReynolds	Tenn.	1913
"	Thomas W. Gregory	Tex.	1914
"	A. Mitchell Palmer	Pa.	1919
Harding	Harry M. Daugherty	Oh.	1921
Coolidge	"	"	1923
"	Harlan F. Stone	N.Y.	1924
"	John G. Sargent	Vt.	1925
Hoover	William D. Mitchell	Minn.	1929
Roosevelt, F.D.	Homer S. Cummings	Conn.	1933
"	Frank Murphy	Mich.	1939
"	Robert H. Jackson	N.Y.	1940
"	Francis Biddle	Pa.	1941
Truman	Thomas C. Clark	Tex.	1945
"	J. Howard McGrath	R.I.	1949
"	J.P. McGranery	Pa.	1952
Eisenhower	Herbert Brownell Jr.	N.Y.	1953
"	William P. Rogers	Md.	1957
Kennedy	Robert F. Kennedy	Mass.	1961
Johnson, L.B.	"	"	1963
"	N. de B. Katzenbach	Ill.	1964
"	Ramsey Clark	Tex.	1967
Nixon	John N. Mitchell	N.Y.	1969
"	Richard G. Kleindienst	Ariz.	1972
"	Elliot L. Richardson	Mass.	1973
"	William B. Saxbe	Oh.	1974
Ford	"	"	1974
"	Edward H. Levi	Ill.	1975
Carter	Griffin B. Bell	Ga.	1977
"	Benjamin R. Civiletti	Md.	1979

Secretaries of the Interior

The Department of Interior was created by act of Congress Mar. 3, 1849

President	Secretary	Home	Apptd.
Taylor	Thomas Ewing	Oh.	1849
Fillmore	Thomas M. T. McKennan	Pa.	1850
Fillmore	Alex H. H. Stuart	Va.	1850
Pierce	Robert McClelland	Mich.	1853
Buchanan	Jacob Thompson	Miss.	1857
Lincoln	Caleb B. Smith	Ind.	1861
"	John P. Usher	"	1863
Johnson, A.	"	"	1865
"	James Harlan	Ia.	1865
"	Orville H. Browning	Ill.	1866
Grant	Jacob D. Cox	Oh.	1869
"	Columbus Delano	"	1870
"	Zachariah Chandler	Mich.	1875
Hayes	Carl Schurz	Mo.	1877
Garfield	Samuel J. Kirkwood	Ia.	1881
Arthur	Henry M. Teller	Col.	1882
Cleveland	Lucius Q.C. Lamar	Miss.	1885
"	William F. Vilas	Wis.	1888
Harrison, B.	John W. Noble	Mo.	1889
Cleveland	Hoke Smith	Ga.	1893
"	David R. Francis	Mo.	1896
McKinley	Cornelius N. Bliss	N.Y.	1897
"	Ethan A. Hitchcock	Mo.	1898
Roosevelt, T.	"	"	1901

President	Secretary	Home	Apptd.
"	James R. Garfield	Oh.	1907
Taft	Richard A. Ballinger	Wash.	1909
"	Walter L. Fisher	Ill.	1911
Wilson	Franklin K. Lane	Cal.	1913
"	John B. Payne	Ill.	1920
Harding	Albert B. Fall	N.M.	1921
"	Hubert Work	Col.	1923
Coolidge	"	"	1923
"	Roy O. West	Ill.	1929
Hoover	Ray Lyman Wilbur	Cal.	1929
Roosevelt, F.D.	Harold L. Ickes	Ill.	1933
Truman	"	"	1945
"	Julius A. Krug	Wis.	1946
"	Oscar L. Chapman	Col.	1949
Eisenhower	Douglas McKay	Ore.	1953
"	Fred A Seaton	Neb.	1956
Kennedy	Stewart L. Udall	Ariz.	1961
Johnson, L.B.	"	"	1963
Nixon	Walter J. Hickel	Alas.	1969
"	Rogers C.B. Morton	Md.	1971
Ford	"	"	1974
"	Stanley K. Hathaway	Wyo.	1975
"	Thomas S. Kleppe	N.D.	1975
Carter	Cecil D. Andrus	Ida.	1977

Secretaries of Agriculture

The Department of Agriculture was created by act of Congress May 15, 1862. On Feb. 8, 1889, its commissioner was renamed secretary of agriculture and became a member of the cabinet.

President	Secretary	Home	Apptd.
Cleveland	Norman J. Colman	Mo.	1889
Harrison, B.	Jeremiah M. Rusk	Wis.	1889
Cleveland	J. Sterling Morton	Neb.	1893
McKinley	James Wilson	Ia.	1897
Roosevelt, T.	"	"	1901
Taft	"	"	1909

President	Secretary	Home	Apptd.
Wilson	David F. Houston	Mo.	1913
"	Edwin T. Meredith	Ia.	1920
Harding	Henry C. Wallace	Ia.	1921
Coolidge	"	"	1923
"	Howard M. Gore	W.Va.	1924
"	William M. Jardine	Kan.	1925

President	Secretary	Home	Apptd.
Hoover	Arthur M. Hyde	Mo.	1929
Roosevelt, F.D.	Henry A. Wallace	Ia.	1933
"	Claude R. Wickard	Ind.	1940
Truman	Clinton P. Anderson	N.M.	1945
"	Charles F. Brannan	Col.	1948
Eisenhower	Ezra Taft Benson	Ut.	1953
Kennedy	Orville L. Freeman	Minn.	1961
Johnson, L.B.	"	"	1963
Nixon	Clifford M. Hardin	Ind.	1969
"	Earl L. Butz	Ind.	1971
Ford	"	"	1974
"	John A. Knebel	Va.	1976
Carter	Bob Bergland	Minn.	1977

Secretaries of Commerce and Labor

The Department of Commerce and Labor, created by Congress Feb. 14, 1903, was divided by Congress Mar. 4, 1913, into separate departments of Commerce and Labor. The secretary of each was made a cabinet member.

President	Secretary	Home	Apptd.
	Secretaries of Commerce and Labor		
Roosevelt, T.	George B. Cortelyou	N.Y.	1903
"	Victor H. Metcalf	Cal.	1904
"	Oscar S. Straus	N.Y.	1906
Taft	Charles Nagel	Mo.	1909
	Secretaries of Labor		
Wilson	William B. Wilson	Pa.	1913
Harding	James J. Davis	Pa.	1921
Coolidge	"	"	1923
Hoover	"	"	1929
"	William N. Doak	Va.	1930
Roosevelt, F.D.	Frances Perkins	N.Y.	1933
Truman	L.B. Schwellenbach	Wash.	1945
"	Maurice J. Tobin	Mass.	1949
Eisenhower	Martin P. Durkin	Ill.	1953
"	James P. Mitchell	N.J.	1953
Kennedy	Arthur J. Goldberg	Ill.	1961
"	W. Willard Wirtz	Ill.	1962
Johnson, L.B.	"	Ill.	1963
Nixon	George P. Shultz	Ill.	1969
"	James D. Hodgson	Cal.	1970
	Peter J. Brennan	N.Y.	1973
Ford	"	"	1974
"	John T. Dunlop	Cal.	1975
"	W.J. Usery Jr.	Ga.	1976
Carter	F. Ray Marshall	Tex.	1977
	Secretaries of Commerce		
Wilson	William C. Redfield	N.Y.	1913
"	Joshua W. Alexander	Mo.	1919
Harding	Herbert C. Hoover	Cal.	1921
Coolidge	"	"	1923
"	William F. Whiting	Mass.	1928
Hoover	Robert P. Lamont	Ill.	1929
"	Roy D. Chapin	Mich.	1932
Roosevelt, F.D.	Daniel C. Roper	S.C.	1933
"	Harry L. Hopkins	N.Y.	1939
"	Jesse Jones	Tex.	1940
"	Henry A. Wallace	Ia.	1945
Truman	"	"	1945
"	W. Averell Harriman	N.Y.	1947
"	Charles Sawyer	Oh.	1948
Eisenhower	Sinclair Weeks	Mass.	1953
"	Lewis L. Strauss	N.Y.	1958
"	Frederick H. Mueller	Mich.	1959
Kennedy	Luther H. Hodges	N.C.	1961
Johnson, L.B.	"	"	1963
"	John T. Connor	N.J.	1965
"	Alex B. Trowbridge	N.J.	1967
"	Cyrus R. Smith	N.Y.	1968
Nixon	Maurice H. Stans	Minn.	1969
"	Peter G. Peterson	Ill.	1972
"	Frederick B. Dent	S.C.	1973
Ford	"	"	1974
"	Rogers C.B. Morton	Md.	1975
"	Elliot L. Richardson	Mass.	1975
Carter	Juanita M. Kreps	N.C.	1977
"	Philip M. Klutznick	Ill.	1979

Secretaries of Education, and Health and Human Services

The Department of Health, Education and Welfare, created by Congress Apr. 11, 1953, was divided by Congress Sept. 27, 1979, into separate departments of Education, and Health and Human Services. The secretary of each is a cabinet member.

President	Secretary	Home	Apptd.
	Secretaries of Health, Education, and Welfare		
Eisenhower	Oveta Culp Hobby	Tex.	1953
"	Marion B. Folsom	N.Y.	1955
"	Arthur S. Flemming	Oh.	1958
Kennedy	Abraham A. Ribicoff	Conn.	1961
"	Anthony J. Celebrezze	Oh.	1962
Johnson, L.B.	"	"	1963
"	John W. Gardner	N.Y.	1965
Johnson, L.B.	Wilbur J. Cohen	Mich.	1968
Nixon	Robert H. Finch	Cal.	1969
"	Elliot L. Richardson	Mass.	1970
"	Caspar W. Weinberger	Cal.	1973
Ford	"	"	1974
"	Forrest D. Mathews	Ala.	1975
Carter	Joseph A. Califano, Jr.	D.C.	1977
"	Patricia Roberts Harris	D.C.	1979
	Secretaries of Health and Human Services		
Carter	Patricia Roberts Harris	D.C.	1979
	Secretaries of Education		
Carter	Shirley Hufstedler	Cal.	1979

Secretaries of Housing and Urban Development

The Department of Housing and Urban Development was created by act of Congress Sept. 9, 1965.

President	Secretary	Home	Apptd.
Johnson, L.B.	Robert C. Weaver	Wash.	1966
"	Robert C. Wood	Mass.	1969
Nixon	George W. Romney	Mich.	1969
"	James T. Lynn	Oh.	1973
Ford	"	"	1974
"	Carla Anderson Hills	Cal.	1975
Carter	Patricia Roberts Harris	D.C.	1977
"	Moon Landrieu	La.	1979

Secretaries of Transportation

The Department of Transportation was created by act of Congress Oct. 15, 1966.

President	Secretary	Home	Apptd.
Johnson, L.B.	Alan S. Boyd	Fla.	1966
Nixon	John A. Volpe	Mass.	1969
"	Claude S. Brinegar	Cal.	1973
Ford	Claude S. Brinegar	Cal.	1974
"	William T. Coleman Jr.	Pa.	1975
Carter	Brock Adams	Wash.	1977
"	Neil E. Goldschmidt	Ore.	1979

Secretaries of Energy

The Department of Energy was created by federal law Aug. 4, 1977.

President	Secretary	Home	Apptd.
Carter	James R. Schlesinger	Va.	1977
"	Robert W. Duncan Jr.	Wyo.	1979

Postmasters General

Congress established the Post Office Department as a branch of the Treasury Sept. 22, 1789. The postmaster general was made a member of the Cabinet Mar. 9, 1829. The Postal Reorganization Act of 1970 replaced the department with the U.S. Postal Service, an independent federal agency. Its head, the postmaster general, is not a member of the Cabinet.

President	Postmaster General	Home	Apptd.
Washington	Samuel Osgood	Mass.	1789
"	Timothy Pickering	Pa.	1791
"	Joseph Habersham	Ga.	1795
Adams, J.	"	"	1797
Jefferson	"	"	1801
"	Gideon Granger	Conn.	1801
Madison	"	"	1809
"	Return J. Meigs Jr.	Ohio	1814
Monroe	"	"	1817
"	John McLean	"	1823
Adams, J.Q.	"	"	1825
Jackson	William T. Barry	Ky.	1829
"	Amos Kendall	"	1835
Van Buren	"	"	1837
"	John M. Niles	Conn.	1840
Harrison, W.H.	Francis Granger	N.Y.	1841
Tyler	"	N.Y.	1841
"	Charles A. Wickliffe	Ky.	1841
Polk	Cave Johnson	Tenn.	1845
Taylor	Jacob Collamer	Vt.	1849
Fillmore	Nathan K. Hall	N.Y.	1850
"	Samuel D. Hubbard	Conn.	1852
Pierce	James Campbell	Pa.	1853
Buchanan	Aaron V. Brown	Tenn.	1857
"	Joseph Holt	Ky.	1859
"	Horatio King	Me.	1861
Lincoln	Montgomery Blair	D.C.	1861
"	William Dennison	Oh.	1864
Johnson, A.	"	"	1865
"	Alex W. Randall	Wis.	1866
Grant	John A.J. Creswell	Md.	1869
"	James W. Marshall	Va.	1874
"	Marshall Jewell	Conn.	1874
"	James N. Tyner	Ind.	1876
Hayes	David McK. Key	Tenn.	1877
"	Horace Maynard	Tenn.	1880
Garfield	Thomas L. James	N.Y.	1881
Arthur	Timothy O. Howe	Wis.	1881
"	Walter Q. Gresham	Ind.	1883
"	Frank Hatton	Ia.	1884
Cleveland	William F. Vilas	Wis.	1885
"	Don M. Dickinson	Mich.	1888
Harrison, B.	John Wanamaker	Pa.	1889
Cleveland	Wilson S. Bissel	N.Y.	1893
"	William L. Wilson	W.Va.	1895
McKinley	James A. Gary	Md.	1897
"	Charles E. Smith	Pa.	1898
Roosevelt, T.	"	"	1901
"	Henry C. Payne	Wis.	1902
"	Robert J. Wynne	Pa.	1904
"	George B. Cortelyou	N.Y.	1905
"	George von L. Meyer	Mass.	1907
Taft	Frank H. Hitchcock	"	1909
Wilson	Albert S. Burleson	Tex.	1913
Harding	Will H. Hays	Ind.	1921
"	Hubert Work	Col.	1922
"	Harry S. New	Ind.	1923
Coolidge	"	"	1923
Hoover	Walter F. Brown	Oh.	1929
Roosevelt, F.D.	James A. Farley	N.Y.	1933
"	Frank C. Walker	Pa.	1940
Truman	Robert E. Hannegan	Mo.	1945
"	Jesse M. Donaldson	Mo.	1947
Eisenhower	A.E. Summerfield	Mich.	1953
Kennedy	J. Edward Day	Cal.	1961
"	John A. Gronouski	Wis.	1963
Johnson, L.B.	"	"	1963
"	Lawrence F. O'Brien	Mass.	1965
"	W. Marvin Watson	Tex.	1968
Nixon	Winton M. Blount	Ala.	1969
(1)	Elmer T. Klassen	Md.	1971
"	Benjamin F. Bailar	D.C.	1975
"	William F. Bolger	Conn.	1978

(1) Appointed by Postal Service Board of Governors.

Law on Succession to the Presidency

If by reason of death, resignation, removal from office, inability, or failure to qualify there is neither a president nor vice president to discharge the powers and duties of the office of president, then the speaker of the House of Representatives shall upon his resignation as speaker and as representative, act as president. The same rule shall apply in the case of the death, resignation, removal from office, or inability of an individual acting as president.

If at the time when a speaker is to begin the discharge of the powers and duties of the office of president there is no speaker, or the speaker fails to qualify as acting president, then the president pro tempore of the Senate, upon his resignation as president pro tempore and as senator, shall act as president.

An individual acting as president shall continue to act until the expiration of the then current presidential term, except that (1) if his discharge of the powers and duties of the office is founded in whole or in part in the failure of both the president-elect and the vice president-elect to qualify, then he shall act only until a president or vice president qualifies, and (2) if his discharge of the powers and duties of the office is founded in whole or in part on the inability of the president or vice president, then he shall act only until the removal of the disability of one of such individuals.

If, by reason of death, resignation, removal from office, or failure to qualify, there is no president pro tempore to act as president, then the officer of the United States who is highest on the following list, and who is not under disability to discharge the powers and duties of president, shall act as president; the secretaries of state, treasury, defense, attorney general; secretaries of interior, agriculture, commerce, labor, health and human services, housing and urban development, transportation, energy, education.

(Legislation approved July 18, 1947; amended Sept. 9, 1965, Oct. 15, 1966, Aug. 4, 1977, and Sept. 27, 1979. (See also Constitutional Amendment XXV.)

Burial Places of the Presidents

Washington	Mt. Vernon, Va.
J. Adams	Quincy, Mass.
Jefferson	Charlottesville, Va.
Madison	Montpelier Station, Va.
Monroe	Richmond, Va.
J.Q. Adams	Quincy, Mass.
Jackson	Nashville, Tenn.
Van Buren	Kinderhook, N.Y.
W.H. Harrison	North Bend, Oh.
Tyler	Richmond, Va.
Polk	Nashville, Tenn.
Taylor	Louisville, Ky.
Fillmore	Buffalo, N.Y.
Pierce	Concord, N.H.
Buchanan	Lancaster, Pa.
Lincoln	Springfield, Ill.
A. Johnson	Greeneville, Tenn.
Grant	New York City
Hayes	Fremont, Oh.
Garfield	Cleveland, Oh.
Arthur	Albany, N.Y.
Cleveland	Princeton, N.J.
B. Harrison	Indianapolis, Ind.
McKinley	Canton, Oh.
T. Roosevelt	Oyster Bay, N.Y.
Taft	Arlington Nat'l. Cem'y.
Wilson	Washington Cathedral
Harding	Marion, Oh.
Coolidge	Plymouth, Vt.
Hoover	West Branch, Ia.
F.D. Roosevelt	Hyde Park, N.Y.
Truman	Independence, Mo.
Eisenhower	Abilene, Kan.
Kennedy	Arlington Nat'l. Cem'y.
L.B. Johnson	Stonewall, Tex.

BIOGRAPHIES OF U.S. PRESIDENTS

George Washington

George Washington, first president, was born Feb. 22, 1732 (Feb. 11, 1731, old style), the son of Augustine Washington and Mary Ball, at Wakefield on Pope's Creek, Westmoreland Co., Va. His early childhood was spent on the Ferry farm, near Fredericksburg. His father died when George was 11. He studied mathematics and surveying and when 16 went to live with his half brother Lawrence, who built and named Mount Vernon. George surveyed the lands of William Fairfax in the Shenandoah Valley, keeping a diary. He accompanied Lawrence to Barbados, West Indies, contracted small pox, and was deeply scarred. Lawrence died in 1752 and George acquired his property by inheritance. He valued land and when he died owned 70,000 acres in Virginia and 40,000 acres in what is now West Virginia.

Washington's military service began in 1753 when Gov. Dinwiddie of Virginia sent him on missions deep into Ohio country. He clashed with the French and had to surrender Fort Necessity July 3, 1754. He was an aide to Braddock and at his side when the army was ambushed and defeated on a march to Ft. Duquesne, July 9, 1755. He helped take Fort Duquesne from the French in 1758.

After his marriage to Martha Dandridge Custis, a widow, in 1759, Washington managed his family estate at Mount Vernon. Although not at first for independence, he opposed British exactions and took charge of the Virginia troops before war broke out. He was made commander-in-chief by the Continental Congress June 15, 1775.

The successful issue of a war filled with hardships was due to his leadership. He was resourceful, a stern disciplinarian, and the one strong, dependable force for unity. He favored a federal government and became chairman of the Constitutional Convention of 1787. He helped get the Constitution ratified and was unanimously elected president by the electoral college and inaugurated, Apr. 30, 1789, on the balcony of New York's Federal Hall.

He was reelected 1792, but refused to consider a 3d term and retired to Mount Vernon. He suffered acute laryngitis after a ride in snow and rain around his estate, was bled profusely, and died Dec. 14, 1799.

John Adams

John Adams, 2d president, Federalist, was born in Braintree (Quincy), Mass., Oct. 30, 1735 (Oct. 19, o. s.), the son of John Adams, a farmer, and Susanna Boylston. He was a great-grandson of Henry Adams who came from England in 1636. He was graduated from Harvard, 1755, taught school, studied law. In 1765 he argued against taxation without representation before the royal governor. In 1770 he defended the British soldiers who fired on civilians in the "Boston Massacre." He was a delegate to the first Continental Congress, and signed the Declaration of Independence. He was a commissioner to France, 1778, with Benjamin Franklin and Arthur Lee; won recognition of the U.S. by The Hague, 1782; was first American minister to England, 1785-1788, and was elected vice president, 1788 and 1792.

In 1796 Adams was chosen president by the electors. Intense antagonism to America by France caused agitation for war, led by Alexander Hamilton. Adams, breaking with Hamilton, opposed war.

To fight alien influence and muzzle criticism Adams supported the Alien and Sedition laws of 1798, which led to his defeat for reelection. He died July 4, 1826, on the same day as Jefferson (the 50th anniversary of the Declaration of Independence).

Thomas Jefferson

Thomas Jefferson, 3d president, was born Apr. 13, 1743 (Apr. 2, o. s.), at Shadwell, Va., the son of Peter Jefferson, a civil engineer of Welsh descent who raised tobacco, and Jane Randolph. His father died when he was 14, leaving him 2,750 acres and his slaves. Jefferson attended the College of William and Mary, 1760-1762, read classics in Greek and Latin and played the violin. In 1769 he was elected to the House of Burgesses. In 1770 he began building Monticello, near Charlottesville. He was a member of the Virginia Committee of Correspondence and the Continental Congress. Named a member of the committee to draw up a Declaration of Independence, he wrote the basic draft. He was a member of the Virginia House of Delegates, 1776-79, elected governor to succeed Patrick Henry, 1779, reelected 1780, resigned June 1781, amid charges of ineffectual military preparation. During his term he wrote the statute on religious freedom. In the Continental Congress, 1783, he drew up an ordinance for the Northwest Territory, forbidding slavery after 1800; its terms were put into the Ordinance of 1787. He was sent to Paris with Benjamin Franklin and John Adams to negotiate commercial treaties, 1784; made minister to France, 1785.

Washington appointed him secretary of state, 1789. Jefferson's strong faith in the consent of the governed, as opposed to executive control favored by Hamilton, secretary of the treasury, often led to conflict: Dec. 31, 1793, he resigned. He was the Republican candidate for president in 1796; beaten by John Adams, he became vice president. In 1800, Jefferson and Aaron Burr received equal electoral college votes for president. The House of Representatives elected Jefferson. Major events of his administration were the Louisiana Purchase, 1803, and the Lewis and Clark Expedition. He established the Univ. of Virginia and designed its buildings. He died July 4, 1826, on the same day as John Adams.

James Madison

James Madison, 4th president, Republican, was born Mar. 16, 1751 (Mar. 5, 1750, o. s.) at Port Conway, King George Co., Va., eldest son of James Madison and Eleanor Rose Conway. Madison was graduated from Princeton, 1771; studied theology, 1772; sat in the Virginia Constitutional Convention, 1776. He was a member of the Continental Congress. He was chief recorder at the Constitutional Convention in 1787, and supported ratification in the Federalist Papers, written with Alexander Hamilton and John Jay. He was elected to the House of Representatives in 1789, helped frame the Bill of Rights and fought the Alien and Sedition Acts. He became Jefferson's secretary of state, 1801.

Elected president in 1808, Madison was a "strict constructionist," opposed to the free interpretation of the Constitution by the Federalists. He was reelected in 1812 by the votes of the agrarian South and recently admitted western states. Caught between British and French maritime restrictions, the U.S. drifted into war, declared June 18, 1812. The war ended in a stalemate. He retired in 1817 to his estate at Montpelier. There he edited his famous papers on the Constitutional Convention. He became rector of the Univ. of Virginia, 1826. He died June 28, 1836.

James Monroe

James Monroe, 5th president, Republican, was born Apr. 28, 1758, in Westmoreland Co., Va., the son of Spence Monroe and Eliza Jones, who were of Scottish and Welsh descent, respectively. He attended the College of William and Mary, fought in the 3d Virginia Regiment at White Plains, Brandywine, Monmouth, and was wounded at Trenton. He studied law with Thomas Jefferson, 1780, was a member of the Virginia House of Delegates and of Congress, 1783-86. He opposed ratification of the Constitution because it lacked a bill of rights; was U.S. senator, 1790; minister to France, 1794-96; governor of Virginia, 1799-1802, and 1811. Jefferson sent him to France as minister, 1803. He helped R. Livingston negotiate the Louisiana Purchase, 1803. He ran against Madison for president in 1808. He was elected to the Virginia Assembly, 1810-1811; was secretary of state under Madison, 1811-1817.

In 1816 Monroe was elected president; in 1820 reelected

with all but one electoral college vote. Monroe's administration became the "Era of Good Feeling." He obtained Florida from Spain; settled boundaries with Canada, and eliminated border forts. He supported the anti-slavery position that led to the Missouri Compromise. His most significant contribution was the "Monroe Doctrine," which became a cornerstone of U.S. foreign policy. Monroe retired to Oak Hill, Va. Financial problems forced him to sell his property. He moved to New York City to live with a daughter. He died there July 4, 1831.

John Quincy Adams

John Quincy Adams, 6th president, independent Federalist, was born July 11, 1767, at Braintree (Quincy), Mass., the son of John and Abigail Adams. His father was the 2d president. He was educated in Paris, Leyden, and Harvard, graduating in 1787. He served as American minister in various European capitals, and helped draft the War of 1812 peace treaty. He was U.S. Senator, 1803-08. President Monroe made him secretary of state, 1817, and he negotiated the cession of the Floridas from Spain, supported exclusion of slavery in the Missouri Compromise, and helped formulate the Monroe Doctrine. In 1824 he was elected president by the House after he failed to win an electoral college majority. His expansion of executive powers was strongly opposed and he was beaten in 1828 by Jackson. In 1831 he entered Congress and served 17 years with distinction. He opposed slavery, the annexation of Texas, and the Mexican War. He helped establish the Smithsonian Institution. He had a stroke in the House and died in the Speaker's Room, Feb. 23, 1848.

Andrew Jackson

Andrew Jackson, 7th president, was a Jeffersonian-Republican, later a Democrat. He was born in the Waxhaws district, New Lancaster Co., S.C., Mar. 15, 1767, the posthumous son of Andrew Jackson and Elizabeth Hutchinson, who were Irish immigrants. At 13, he joined the militia in the Revolution and was captured.

He read law in Salisbury, N.C., moved to Nashville, Tenn., speculated in land, married, and practiced law. In 1796 he helped draft the constitution of Tennessee and for a year occupied its one seat in Congress. He was in the Senate in 1797, and again in 1823. He defeated the Creek Indians at Horseshoe Bend, Ala., 1814. With 6,000 backwoods fighters he defeated Packenham's 12,000 British troops at the Chalmette, outside New Orleans, Jan. 8, 1815. In 1818 he briefly invaded Spanish Florida to quell Seminoles and outlaws who harassed frontier settlements. In 1824 he ran for president against John Quincy Adams and had the most popular and electoral votes but not a majority; the election was decided by the House, which chose Adams. In 1828 he defeated Adams, carrying the West and South. He was a noisy debater and a duelist and introduced rotation in office called the "spoils system." Suspicious of privilege, he ruined the Bank of the United States by depositing federal funds with state banks. Though "Let the people rule" was his slogan, he at times supported strict constructionist policies against the expansionist West. He killed the Congressional caucus for nominating presidential candidates and substituted the national convention, 1832. When South Carolina refused to collect imports under his protective tariff he ordered army and naval forces to Charleston. Jackson recognized the Republic of Texas, 1836. He died at the Hermitage, June 8, 1845.

Martin Van Buren

Martin Van Buren, 8th president, Democrat, was born Dec. 5, 1782, at Kinderhook, N.Y., the son of Abraham Van Buren, a Dutch farmer, and Mary Hoes. He was surrogate of Columbia County, N.Y., state senator and attorney general. He was U.S. senator 1821, reelected, 1827, elected governor of New York, 1828. He helped swing eastern support to Jackson in 1828 and was his secretary of state 1829-31. In 1832 he was elected vice president. He was a consummate politician, known as "the little magician," and influenced Jackson's policies. In 1836 he defeated William Henry Harrison for president and took office as the Panic of 1837 initiated a 5-year nationwide depression. He inaugurated the independent treasury system. His refusal to spend land revenues led to his defeat by Harrison in 1840. He lost the Democratic nomination of 1844 to Polk. In 1848 he ran for president on the Free Soil ticket and lost. He died July 24, 1862, at Kinderhook.

William Henry Harrison

William Henry Harrison, 9th president, Whig, who served only 31 days, was born in Berkeley, Charles City Co., Va., Feb. 9, 1773, the 3d son of Benjamin Harrison, signer of the Declaration of Independence. He attended Hampden Sydney College. He was secretary of the Northwest Territory, 1798; its delegate in Congress, 1799; first governor of Indiana Territory, 1800; and superintendent of Indian affairs. With 900 men he routed Tecumseh's Indians at Tippecanoe, Nov. 7, 1811. A major general, he defeated British and Indians at Battle of the Thames, Oct. 5, 1813. He served in Congress, 1816-19; Senate, 1825-28. In 1840, when 68, he was elected president with a "log cabin and hard cider" slogan. He caught pneumonia during the inauguration and died Apr. 4, 1841.

John Tyler

John Tyler, 10th president, independent Whig, was born Mar. 29, 1790, in Greenway, Charles City Co., Va., son of John Tyler and Mary Armistead. His father was governor of Virginia, 1808-11. Tyler was graduated from William and Mary, 1807; member of the House of Delegates, 1811; in congress, 1816-21; in Virginia legislature, 1823-25; governor of Virginia, 1825-26; U.S. senator, 1827-36. In 1840 he was elected vice president and, on Harrison's death, succeeded him. He favored pre-emption, allowing settlers to get government land; rejected a national bank bill and thus alienated most Whig supporters; refused to honor the spoils system. He signed the resolution annexing Texas, Mar. 1, 1845. He accepted renomination, 1844, but withdrew before election. In 1861, he chaired an unsuccessful Washington conference called to avert civil war. After its failure he supported secession, sat in the provisional Confederate Congress, became a member of the Confederate House, but died, Jan. 18, 1862, before it met.

James Knox Polk

James Knox Polk, 11th president, Democrat, was born in Mecklenburg Co., N.C., Nov. 2, 1795, the son of Samuel Polk, farmer and surveyor of Scotch-Irish descent, and Jane Knox. He graduated from the Univ. of North Carolina, 1818; member of the Tennessee state legislature, 1823-25. He served in Congress 1825-39 and as speaker 1835-39. He was governor of Tennessee 1839-41, but was defeated 1841 and 1843. In 1844, when both Clay and Van Buren announced opposition to annexing Texas, the Democrats made Polk the first dark horse nominee because he demanded control of all Oregon and annexation of Texas. Polk reestablished the independent treasury system originated by Van Buren. His expansionist policy was opposed by Clay, Webster, Calhoun; he sent troops under Zachary Taylor to the Mexican border and, when Mexicans attacked, declared war existed. The Mexican war ended with the annexation of California and much of the Southwest as part of America's "manifest destiny." He compromised on the Oregon boundary ("54-40 or fight!") by accepting the 49th parallel and giving Vancouver to the British. Polk died in Nashville, June 15, 1849.

Zachary Taylor

Zachary Taylor, 12th president, Whig, who served only 16 months, was born Nov. 24, 1784, in Orange Co., Va., the son of Richard Taylor, later collector of the port of Louisville, Ky., and Sarah Strother. Taylor was commissioned first lieutenant, 1808; fought in the War of 1812; the Black

Hawk War, 1832; and the second Seminole War, 1837. He was called Old Rough and Ready. He settled on a plantation near Baton Rouge, La. In 1845 Polk sent him with an army to the Rio Grande. When the Mexicans attacked him, Polk declared war. Taylor was successful at Palo Alto and Resaca de la Palma, 1846; occupied Monterey. Polk made him major general but sent many of his troops to Gen. Winfield Scott. Outnumbered 4-1, he defeated Santa Anna at Buena Vista, 1847. A national hero, he received the Whig nomination in 1848, and was elected president. He resumed the spoils system and though once a slave-holder worked to have California admitted as a free state. He died in office July 9, 1850.

Millard Fillmore

Millard Fillmore, 13th president, Whig, was born Jan. 7, 1800, in Cayuga Co., N.Y., the son of Nathaniel Fillmore and Phoebe Miller. He taught school and studied law; admitted to the bar, 1823. He was a member of the state assembly, 1829-32; in Congress, 1833-35 and again 1837-43. He opposed the entrance of Texas as slave territory and voted for a protective tariff. In 1844 he was defeated for governor of New York. In 1848 he was elected vice president and succeeded as president July 10, 1850, after Taylor's death. Fillmore favored the Compromise of 1850 and signed the Fugitive Slave Law. His policies pleased neither expansionists nor slave-holders and he was not renominated in 1852. In 1856 he was nominated by the American (Know-Nothing) party and accepted by the Whigs, but defeated by Buchanan. He died in Buffalo, Mar. 8, 1874.

Franklin Pierce

Franklin Pierce, 14th president, Democrat, was born in Hillsboro, N. H., Nov. 23, 1804, the son of Benjamin Pierce, veteran of the Revolution and governor of New Hampshire, 1827. He graduated from Bowdoin, 1824. A lawyer, he served in the state legislature 1829-33; in Congress, supporting Jackson, 1833-37; U.S. senator, 1837-42. He enlisted in the Mexican War, became brigadier general under Gen. Winfield Scott. In 1852 Pierce was nominated on the 49th ballot over Lewis Cass, Stephen A. Douglas, and James Buchanan, and defeated Gen. Scott, Whig. Though against slavery, Pierce was influenced by Southern pro-slavery men. He ignored the Ostend Manifesto that the U.S. either buy or take Cuba. He approved the Kansas-Nebraska Act, leaving slavery to popular vote ("squatter sovereignty"), 1854. He signed a reciprocity treaty with Canada and approved the Gadsden Purchase from Mexico, 1853. Denied renomination by the Democrats, he spent most of his remaining years in Concord, N.H., where he died Oct. 8, 1869.

James Buchanan

James Buchanan, 15th president, Federalist, later Democrat, was born of Scottish descent near Mercersburg, Pa., Apr. 23, 1791. He graduated Dickinson, 1809; was a volunteer in the War of 1812; member, Pennsylvania legislature, 1814-16, Congress, 1820-31; Jackson's minister to Russia, 1831-33; U.S. senator 1834-45. As Polk's secretary of state, 1845-49, he ended the Oregon dispute with Britain, supported the Mexican War and annexation of Texas. As minister to Britain, 1853, he signed the Ostend Manifesto. Nominated by Democrats, he was elected, 1856, over John C. Fremont (Republican) and Millard Fillmore (American Know-Nothing and Whig tickets). On slavery he favored popular sovereignty and choice by state constitutions; he accepted the pro-slavery Dred Scott decision as binding. He denied the right of states to secede. A strict constructionist, he desired to keep peace and found no authority for using force. He died at Wheatland, near Lancaster, Pa., June 1, 1868.

Abraham Lincoln

Abraham Lincoln, 16th president, Republican, was born Feb. 12, 1809, in a log cabin on a farm then in Hardin Co., Ky., now in Larue. He was the son of Thomas Lincoln, a carpenter, and Nancy Hanks.

The Lincolns moved to Spencer Co., Ind., near Gentryville, when Abe was 7. Nancy died 1818, and his father married Mrs. Sarah Bush Johnston, 1819; she had a favorable influence on Abe. In 1830 the family moved to Macon Co., Ill. Lincoln lost election to the Illinois General Assembly, 1832, but later won 4 times, beginning in 1834. He enlisted in the militia for the Black Hawk War, 1832. In New Salem he ran a store, surveyed land, and was postmaster.

In 1837 Lincoln was admitted to the bar and became partner in a Springfield, Ill., law office. He was elected to Congress, 1847-49. He opposed the Mexican War. He supported Zachary Taylor, 1848. He opposed the Kansas-Nebraska Act and extension of slavery, 1854. He failed, in his bid for the Senate, 1855. He supported John C. Fremont, 1856.

In 1858 Lincoln had Republican support in the Illinois legislature for the Senate but was defeated by Stephen A. Douglas, Dem., who had sponsored the Kansas-Nebraska Act.

Lincoln was nominated for president by the Republican party on an anti-slavery platform, 1860. He ran against Douglas, a northern Democrat; John C. Breckinridge, southern pro-slavery Democrat; John Bell, Constitutional Union party. When he won the election, South Carolina seceded from the Union Dec. 20, 1860, followed in 1861 by 10 Southern states.

The Civil War erupted when Fort Sumter was attacked Apr. 12, 1861. On Sept. 22, 1862, 5 days after the battle of Antietam, he announced that slaves in territory then in rebellion would be free Jan. 1, 1863, date of the Emancipation Proclamation, His speeches, including his Gettysburg and Inaugural addresses, are remembered for their eloquence.

Lincoln was reelected, 1864, over Gen. George B. McClellan, Democrat. Lee surrendered Apr. 9, 1865. On Apr. 14, Lincoln was shot by actor John Wilkes Booth in Ford's Theatre, Washington. He died the next day.

Andrew Johnson

Andrew Johnson, 17th president, Democrat, was born in Raleigh, N.C., Dec. 29, 1808, the son of Jacob Johnson, porter at an inn and church sexton, and Mary McDonough. He was apprenticed to a tailor but ran away and eventually settled in Greenville, Tenn. He became an alderman, 1828; mayor, 1830; state representative and senator, 1835-43; member of Congress, 1843-53; governor of Tennessee, 1853-57; U.S. senator, 1857-62. He supported John C. Breckinridge against Lincoln in 1860. He had held slaves, but opposed secession and tried to prevent his home state, Tennessee, from seceding. In Mar. 1862, Lincoln appointed him military governor of occupied Tennessee. In 1864 he was nominated for vice president with Lincoln on the National Union ticket to win Democratic support. He succeeded Lincoln as president April 15, 1865. In a controversy with Congress over the president's power over the South, he proclaimed, May 26, 1865, an amnesty to all Confederates except certain leaders if they would ratify the 13th Amendment abolishing slavery. States doing so added anti-Negro provisions that enraged Congress, which restored military control over the South. When Johnson removed Edwin M. Stanton, secretary of war, without notifying the Senate, thus repudiating the Tenure of Office Act, the House impeached him for this and other reasons. He was tried by the Senate, and acquitted by only one vote, May 26, 1868. He returned to the Senate in 1875. Johnson died July 31, 1875.

Ulysses Simpson Grant

Ulysses S. Grant, 18th president, Republican, was born at Point Pleasant, Oh., Apr. 27, 1822, son of Jesse R. Grant, a tanner, and Hannah Simpson. The next year the family moved to Georgetown, Oh. Grant was named Hiram Ulysses, but on entering West Point, 1839, his name was entered as Ulysses Simpson and he adopted it. he was graduated in 1843; served under Gens. Taylor and Scott in the Mexican War; resigned, 1854; worked in St. Louis until 1860, then went to Galena, Ill. With the start of the Civil War, he was named colonel of the 21st Illinois Vols., 1861, then brigadier general; took Forts Henry and Donelson; fought at Shiloh, took Vicksburg. After his victory at Chattanooga, Lincoln placed him in command of the Union Armies. He accepted Lee's surrender at Appomattox, Apr., 1865. President Johnson appointed Grant secretary of war when he suspended Stanton, but Grant was not confirmed. He was nominated for president by the Republicans and elected over Horatio Seymour, Democrat. The 15th Amendment, amnesty bill, and civil service reform were events of his administration. The Liberal Republicans and Democrats opposed him with Horace Greeley, 1872, but he was reelected. An attempt by the Stalwarts (Old Guard) to nominate him in 1880 failed. In 1884 the collapse of Grant & Ward, investment house, left him penniless. He wrote his personal memoirs while ill with cancer and completed them 4 days before his death at Mt. McGregor, N.Y., July 23, 1885. The book realized over $450,000.

Rutherford Birchard Hayes

Rutherford B. Hayes, 19th president, Republican, was born in Delaware, Oh., Oct. 4, 1822, the posthumous son of Rutherford Hayes, a farmer, and Sophia Birchard. He was raised by his uncle Sardis Birchard. He graduated from Kenyon College, 1842, and Harvard Law School, 1845. He practiced law in Lower Sandusky, Oh., now Fremont; was city solicitor of Cincinnati, 1858-61. In the Civil War, he was major of the 23d Ohio Vols., was wounded several times, and rose to the rank of brevet major general, 1864. He served in Congress 1864-67, supporting Reconstruction and Johnson's impeachment. He was elected governor of Ohio, 1867 and 1869; beaten in the race for Congress, 1872; reelected governor, 1875. In 1876 he was nominated for president and believed he had lost the election to Samuel J. Tilden, Democrat. But a few Southern states submitted 2 different sets of electoral votes and the result was in dispute. An electoral commission, appointed by Congress, 8 Republicans and 7 Democrats, awarded all disputed votes to Hayes allowing him to become president by one electoral vote. Hayes, keeping a promise to southerners, withdrew troops from areas still occupied in the South, ending the era of Reconstruction. He proceeded to reform the civil service, alienating political spoilsmen. He advocated repeal of the Tenure of Office Act. He supported sound money and specie payments. Hayes died in Fremont, Oh., Jan. 17, 1893.

James Abram Garfield

James A. Garfield, 20th president, Republican, was born Nov. 19, 1831, in Orange, Cuyahoga Co., Oh., the son of Abram Garfield and Eliza Ballou. His father died in 1833. He worked as a canal bargeman, farmer, and carpenter; attended Western Reserve Eclectic, later Hiram College, and was graduated from Williams in 1856. He taught at Hiram, and later became principal. He was in the Ohio senate in 1859. Anti-slavery and anti-secession, he volunteered for the war, became colonel of the 42d Ohio Infantry and brigadier in 1862. He fought at Shiloh, was chief of staff for Rosecrans and was made major general for gallantry at Chickamauga. He entered Congress as a radical Republican in 1863; supported specie payment as against paper money (greenbacks). On the electoral commission in 1876 he voted for Hayes against Tilden on strict party lines. He was senator-elect in 1880 when he became the Republican nominee for president. He was chosen as a compromise over Gen. Grant, James G. Blaine, and John Sherman. This alienated the Grant following but Garfield was elected. On July 2, 1881, Garfield was shot by mentally disturbed office-seeker, Charles J. Guiteau, while entering a railroad station in Washington. He died Sept. 19, 1881, at Elberon, N.J.

Chester Alan Arthur

Chester A. Arthur, 21st president, Republican, was born at Fairfield, Vt., Oct. 5, 1829, the son of the Rev. William Arthur, from County Antrim, Ireland, and Malvina Stone. He graduated Union College, 1848, taught school at Pownall, Vt., studied law in New York. In 1853 he argued in a fugitive slave case that slaves transported through N.Y. State were thereby freed; in 1885 he obtained a ruling that Negroes were to be treated the same as whites on street cars. He was made collector of the Port of New York, 1871. President Hayes, reforming the civil service, forced Arthur to resign, 1879. This made the New York machine stalwarts enemies of Hayes. Arthur and the stalwarts tried to nominate Grant for a 3d term in 1880. When Garfield was nominated, Arthur received 2d place in the interests of harmony. When Garfield died, Arthur became president. He supported civil service reform and the tariff of 1883. He was defeated for renomination by James G. Blaine. He died in New York City Nov. 18, 1886.

Grover Cleveland

(According to a ruling of the State Dept., Grover Cleveland is both the 22d and the 24th president, because his 2 terms were not consecutive. By individuals, he is only the 22d.)

Grover Cleveland, 22d and 24th president, Democrat, was born in Caldwell, N.J. Mar. 18, 1837, the son of Richard F. Cleveland, a Presbyterian minister, and Ann Neale. He was named Stephen Grover, but dropped the Stephen. He clerked in Clinton and Buffalo, N.Y., taught at the N.Y. City Institution for the Blind; was admitted to the bar in Buffalo, 1859; became assistant district attorney, 1863; sheriff, 1871; mayor, 1881; governor of New York, 1882. He was an independent, honest administrator who hated corruption. He was nominated for president over Tammany Hall opposition, 1884, and defeated Republican James G. Blaine. He enlarged the civil service, vetoed many pension raids on the Treasury. In 1888 he was defeated by Benjamin Harrison, although his popular vote was larger. Reelected over Harrison in 1892, he faced a money crisis brought about by lowering of the gold reserve, circulation of paper and exorbitant silver purchases under the Sherman Act; obtained a repeal of the latter and a reduced tariff. A severe depression and labor troubles racked his administration but he refused to interfere in business matters and rejected Jacob Coxey's demand for unemployment relief. He broke the Pullman strike, 1894. In 1896, the Democrats repudiated his administration and chose silverite William Jennings Bryan as their candidate. Cleveland died in Princeton, N.J., June 24, 1908.

Benjamin Harrison

Benjamin Harrison, 23d president, Republican, was born at North Bend, Oh., Aug. 20, 1833. His great-grandfather, Benjamin Harrison, was a signer of the Declaration of Independence; his grandfather, William Henry Harrison, was 9th President; his father, John Scott Harrison, was a member of Congress. His mother was Elizabeth F. Irwin. He attended school on his father's farm; graduated from Miami Univ. at Oxford, Oh., 1852; admitted to the bar, 1853, and practiced in Indianapolis. In the Civil War, he rose to the rank of brevet brigadier general, fought at Kennesaw Mountain, Peachtree Creek, Nashville, and in the Atlanta campaign. He failed to be elected governor of Indiana, 1876; but became senator, 1881, and worked for the G. A. R. pensions vetoed by Cleveland. In 1888 he defeated Cleveland for president despite having fewer popular votes. He expanded the pension list; signed the McKinley high tariff bill and the Sherman Silver Purchase Act. During his administration, 6 states were admitted to the union. He was defeated for reelection, 1892. He represented Venezuela in a boundary arbitration with Great Britain in Paris, 1899. He died at Indianapolis, Mar. 13, 1901.

William McKinley

William McKinley, 25th president, Republican, was born in Niles, Oh., Jan. 29, 1843, the son of William McKinley, an ironmaker, and Nancy Allison. McKinley attended school in Poland, Oh., and Allegheny College, Meadville, Pa., and enlisted for the Civil War at 18 in the 23d Ohio, in which Rutherford B. Hayes was a major. He rose to captain and in 1865 was made brevet major. He studied law in the Albany, N.Y., law school; opened an office in Canton, Oh., in 1867, and campaigned for Grant and Hayes. He served in the House of Representatives, 1877-83, 1885-91, and led the fight for passage of the McKinley Tarriff, 1890. Defeated for reelection on the issue in 1890, he was governor of Ohio, 1892-96. He had support for president in the convention that nominated Benjamin Harrison in 1892. In 1896 he was elected president on a protective tariff, sound money (gold standard) platform over William Jennings Bryan, Democratic proponent of free silver. McKinley was reluctant to intervene in Cuba but the loss of the battleship Maine at Havana crystallized opinion. He demanded Spain's withdrawal from Cuba; Spain made some concessions but Congress announced state of war as of Apr. 21. He was reelected in the 1900 campaign, defeating Bryan's anti-imperialist arguments with the promise of a "full dinner pail." McKinley was respected for his conciliatory nature, but conservative on business issues. On Sept. 6, 1901, while welcoming citizens at the Pan-American Exposition, Buffalo, N.Y., he was shot by Leon Czolgosz, an anarchist. He died Sept. 14.

Theodore Roosevelt

Theodore Roosevelt, 26th president, Republican, was born in N.Y. City, Oct. 27, 1858, the son of Theodore Roosevelt, a glass importer, and Martha Bulloch. He was a 5th cousin of Franklin D. Roosevelt and an uncle of Mrs. Eleanor Roosevelt. Roosevelt graduated from Harvard, 1880; attended Columbia Law School briefly; sat in the N.Y. State Assembly, 1882-84; ranched in North Dakota, 1884-86; failed election as mayor of N.Y. City, 1886; member of U.S. Civil Service Commission, 1889; president, N.Y. Police Board, 1895, supporting the merit system; assistant secretary of the Navy under McKinley, 1897-98. In the war with Spain, he organized the 1st U.S. Volunteer Cavalry (Rough Riders) as lieutenant colonel; led the charge up Kettle Hill at San Juan. Elected New York governor, 1898-1900, he fought the spoils system and achieved taxation of corporation franchises. Nominated for vice president, 1900, he became nation's youngest president when McKinley died. As president he fought corruption of politics by big business; dissolved Northern Securities Co. and others for violating anti-trust laws; intervened in coal strike on behalf of the public, 1902; obtained Elkins Law forbidding rebates to favored corporations, 1903; Hepburn Law regulating railroad rates, 1906; Pure Food and Drugs Act, 1906, Reclamation Act and employers' liability laws. He organized conservation, mediated the peace between Japan and Russia, 1905; won the Nobel Peace Prize. He was the first to use the Hague Court of International Arbitration. By recognizing the new Republic of Panama he made Panama Canal possible. He was reelected in 1904.

In 1908 he obtained the nomination of William H. Taft, who was elected. Feeling that Taft had abandoned his policies, Roosevelt unsuccessfully sought the nomination in 1912. He bolted the party and ran on the Progressive "Bull Moose", ticket against Taft and Woodrow Wilson, splitting the Republicans and insuring Wilson's election. He was shot during the campaign but recovered. In 1916 he supported Charles E. Hughes, Republican. A strong friend of Britain, he fought American isolation in World War I. He wrote some 40 books on many topics; his *Winning of the West* is best known. He died Jan. 6, 1919, at Sagamore Hill, Oyster Bay, N.Y.

William Howard Taft

William Howard Taft, 27th president, Republican, was born in Cincinnati, Oh., Sept. 15, 1857, the son of Alphonso Taft and Louisa Maria Torrey. His father was secretary of war and attorney general in Grant's cabinet; minister to Austria and Russia under Arthur. Taft was graduated from Yale, 1878; Cincinnati Law School, 1880; became law reporter for Cincinnati newspapers; was assistant prosecuting attorney, 1881-83; assistant county solicitor, 1885; judge, superior court, 1887; U.S. solicitor-general, 1890; federal circuit judge, 1892. In 1900 he became head of the U.S. Philippines Commission and was first civil governor of the Philippines, 1901-04; secretary of war, 1904; provisional governor of Cuba, 1906. He was groomed for president by Roosevelt and elected over Bryan, 1908. His administration dissolved Standard Oil and tobacco trusts; instituted Dept. of Labor; drafted direct election of senators and income tax amendments. His tariff and conservation policies angered progressives; though renominated he was opposed by Roosevelt; the result was Democract Woodrow Wilson's election. Taft, with some reservations, supported the League of Nations. He was professor of constitutional law, Yale, 1913-21; chief justice of the U.S., 1921-30; illness forced him to resign. He died in Washington, Mar. 8, 1930.

Woodrow Wilson

Woodrow Wilson, 28th president, Democract, was born at Staunton, Va., Dec. 28, 1856, as Thomas Woodrow Wilson, son of a Presbyterian minister, the Rev. Joseph Ruggles Wilson and Janet (Jessie) Woodrow. In his youth Wilson lived in Augusta, Ga., Columbia, S.C., and Wilmington, N.C. He attended Davidson College, 1873-74; was graduated from Princeton, A.B., 1879; A.M., 1882; read law at the Univ. of Virginia, 1881; practiced law, Atlanta, 1882-83; Ph.D., Johns Hopkins, 1886. He taught at Bryn Mawr, 1885-88; at Wesleyan, 1888-90; was professor of jurisprudence and political economy at Princeton, 1890-1910; president of Princeton, 1902-1910; governor of New Jersey, 1911-13. In 1912 he was nominated for president with the aid of William Jennings Bryan, who sought to block James "Champ" Clark and Tammany Hall. Wilson won the election because the Republican vote for Taft was split by the Progressives under Roosevelt.

Wilson protected American interests in revolutionary Mexico and fought for American rights on the high seas. His sharp warnings to Germany led to the resignation of his secretary of state, Bryan, a pacifist. In 1916 he was reelected by a slim margin with the slogan, "He kept us out of war." Wilson's attempts to mediate in the war failed. After 4 American ships had been sunk by the Germans, he secured a declaration of war against Germany on Apr. 6, 1917.

Wilson proposed peace Jan. 8, 1918, on the basis of his "Fourteen Points," a state paper with worldwide influence. His doctrine of self-determination continues to play a major role in territorial disputes. The Germans accepted his terms and an armistice, Nov. 11.

Wilson went to Paris to help negotiate the peace treaty, the crux of which he considered the League of Nations. The Senate demanded reservations that would not make the U.S. subordinate to the votes of other nations in case of war. Wilson refused to consider any reservations and toured the country to get support. He suffered a stroke, Oct., 1919. An invalid for months, he clung to his executive powers while his wife and doctor sought to shield him from affairs which would tire him.

He was awarded the 1919 Nobel Peace Prize, but the treaty embodying the League of Nations was rejected by the Senate, 1920. He died Feb. 3, 1924.

Warren Gamaliel Harding

Warren Gamaliel Harding, 29th president, Republican, was born near Corsica, now Blooming Grove, Oh., Nov. 2, 1865, the son of Dr. George Tyron Harding, a physician, and Phoebe Elizabeth Dickerson. He attended Ohio Central College. He was state senator, 1900-04; lieutenant governor, 1904-06; defeated for governor, 1910; chosen U.S. senator, 1915. He supported Taft, opposed federal control of food and fuel; voted for anti-strike legislation, woman's suffrage, and the Volstead prohibition enforcement act over President Wilson's veto; and opposed the League of Nations. In 1920 he was nominated for president and defeated James M. Cox in the election. The Republicans capitalized on war weariness and fear that Wilson's League of Nations would curtail U.S. sovereignty. Harding stressed a return to "normalcy"; worked for tariff revision and repeal of excess profits law and high income taxes. Two Harding appointees, Albert B. Fall (interior) and Harry Daugherty (attorney general), became involved in the Teapot Dome scandal that embittered Harding's last days. He called the International Conference on Limitation of Armaments, 1921-22. Returning from a trip to Alaska he became ill and died in San Francisco, Aug. 2, 1923.

Calvin Coolidge

Calvin Coolidge, 30th president, Republican, was born in Plymouth, Vt., July 4, 1872, the son of John Calvin Coolidge, a storekeeper, and Victoria J. Moor, and named John Calvin Coolidge. Coolidge graduated from Amherst in 1895. He entered Republican state politics and served as mayor of Northampton, Mass., state senator, lieutenant governor, and, in 1919, governor. In Sept., 1919, Coolidge attained national prominence by calling out the state guard in the Boston police strike. He declared: "There is no right to strike against the public safety by anybody, anywhere, anytime." This brought his name before the Republican convention of 1920, where he was nominated for vice president. He succeeded to the presidency on Harding's death. He opposed the League of Nations; approved the World Court; vetoed the soldiers' bonus bill, which was passed over his veto. In 1924 he was reelected by a huge majority. He reduced the national debt by $2 billion in 3 years. He twice vetoed the McNary-Haugen farm bill, which would have provided relief to financially hard-pressed farmers. With Republicans eager to renominate him he announced, Aug. 2, 1927: "I do not choose to run for president in 1928." He died in Northampton, Jan. 5, 1933.

Herbert Hoover

Herbert C. Hoover, 31st president, Republican, was born at West Branch, Ia., Aug. 10, 1874, son of Jesse Clark Hoover, a blacksmith, and Hulda Randall Minthorn. Hoover grew up in Indian Territory (now Oklahoma) and Oregon; won his A.B. in engineering at Stanford, 1891. He worked briefly with U.S. Geological Survey and western mines; then was a mining engineer in Australia, Asia, Europe, Africa, America. While chief engineer, imperial mines, China, he directed food relief for victims of Boxer Rebellion, 1900. He directed American Relief Committee, London, 1914-15; U.S. Comm. for Relief in Belgium, 1915-1919; was U.S. Food Administrator, 1917-1919; American Relief Administrator, 1918-1923, feeding children in defeated nations; Russian Relief, 1918-1923. He was secy. of commerce, 1921-28. He was elected president over Alfred E. Smith, 1928. In 1929 the stock market crashed and the economy collapsed. During the depression, Hoover opposed federal aid to the unemployed. He was defeated in the 1932 election by Franklin D. Roosevelt. President Truman made him coordinator of European Food Program, 1947, chairman of the Commission for Reorganization of the Executive Branch, 1947-49. He founded the Hoover Institution on War, Revolution, and Peace at Stanford Univ. He died in N.Y. City, Oct. 20, 1964.

Franklin Delano Roosevelt

Franklin D. Roosevelt, 32d president, Democrat, was born near Hyde Park, N.Y., Jan. 30, 1882, the son of James Roosevelt and Sara Delano. He graduated Harvard, 1904; attended Columbia Law School; was admitted to the bar. He went to the N.Y. Senate, 1910 and 1913. In 1913 President Wilson made him assistant secretary of the navy.

Roosevelt ran for vice president, 1920, with James Cox and was defeated. From 1920 to 1928 he was a N.Y. lawyer and vice president of Fidelity & Deposit Co. In Aug., 1921, polio paralyzed his legs. He learned to walk with leg braces and a cane.

Roosevelt was elected governor of New York, 1928 and 1930. In 1932, W. G. McAdoo, pledged to John N. Garner, threw his votes to Roosevelt, who was nominated. The depression and the promise to repeal prohibition insured his election. He asked emergency powers, proclaimed the New Deal, and put into effect a vast number of administrative changes. Foremost was the use of public funds for relief and public works, resulting in deficit financing. He greatly expanded the controls of the central government over business, and by an excess profits tax and progressive income taxes produced a redistribution of earnings on an unprecedented scale. The Wagner Act gave labor many advantages in organizing and collective bargaining. He was the last president inaugurated on Mar. 4 (1933) and the first inaugurated on Jan. 20 (1937).

Roosevelt was the first president to use radio for "fireside chats." When the Supreme Court nullified some New Deal laws, he sought power to "pack" the court with additional justices, but Congress refused to give him the authority. He was the first president to break the "no 3d term" tradition (1940) and was elected to a 4th term, 1944, despite failing health. He was openly hostile to fascist governments before World War II and launched a lend-lease program on behalf of the Allies. He wrote the principles of fair dealing into the Atlantic Charter, Aug. 14, 1941 (with Winston Churchill), and urged the Four Freedoms (freedom of speech, of worship, from want, from fear) Jan. 6, 1941. When Japan attacked Pearl Harbor, Dec. 7, 1941, the U.S. entered the war. He conferred with allied heads of state at Casablanca, Jan., 1943; Quebec, Aug., 1943; Teheran, Nov.-Dec., 1943; Cairo, Dec., 1943; Yalta, Feb., 1945. He died at Warm Springs, Ga., Apr. 12, 1945.

Harry S. Truman

Harry S. Truman, 33d president, Democrat, was born at Lamar, Mo., May 8, 1884, the son of John Anderson Truman and Martha Ellen Young. A family disagreement on whether his middle name was Shippe or Solomon, after names of 2 grandfathers, resulted in his using only the middle initial S. He attended public schools in Independence, Mo., worked for the Kansas City Star, 1901, and as railroad timekeeper, and helper in Kansas City banks up to 1905. He ran his family's farm, 1906-17. He was commissioned a first lieutenant and took part in the Vosges, Meuse-Argonne, and St. Mihiel actions in World War I. After the war he ran a haberdashery, became judge of Jackson Co. Court, 1922-24; attended Kansas City School of Law, 1923-25.

Truman was elected U.S. senator in 1934; reelected 1940. In 1944 with Roosevelt's backing he was nominated for vice president and elected. On Roosevelt's death Truman became president. In 1948 he was elected president although polls had predicted his defeat.

Truman authorized the first uses of the atomic bomb (Hiroshima and Nagasaki, Aug. 6 and 9, 1945), bringing World War II to a rapid end. He was responsible for creating NATO, the Marshall Plan, and what came to be called the Truman Doctrine (to aid nations such as Greece and Turkey, threatened by Russian or other communist takeover). He broke a Russian blockade of West Berlin with a massive airlift, 1948-49. When communist North Korea invaded South Korea, June, 1950, he won UN approval for a "police action" and sent in forces under Gen. Douglas MacArthur. When MacArthur sought to pursue North Koreans into China, Truman removed him from command.

On the domestic front, Truman was responsible for higher minimum-wage, increased social-security, and aid-for-housing laws. Truman died Dec. 26, 1972, in Independence, Mo.

Dwight David Eisenhower

Dwight D. Eisenhower, 34th president, Republican, was born Oct. 14, 1890, at Denison, Tex., the son of David Jacob Eisenhower and Ida Elizabeth Stover. The next year, the family moved to Abilene, Kan. He graduated from West Point, 1915. He was a lieutenant colonel at Camp Colt, Gettysburg, Pa., 1918. He was on the American military mission to the Philippines, 1935-39 and during 4 of those years on the staff of Gen. Douglas MacArthur. He was made commander of Allied forces landing in North Africa, 1942, full general, 1943. He became supreme Allied commander in Europe, 1943, and as such led the Normandy invasion June 6, 1944. He was given the rank of general of the army Dec. 20, 1944, made permanent in 1946. On May 7, 1945, he received the surrender of the Germans at Rheims. He returned to the U.S. to serve as chief of staff, 1945-1948. In 1948, Eisenhower published *Crusade in Europe*, his war memoirs, which quickly became a best seller. From 1948 to 1953, he was president of Columbia Univ., but took leave of absence in 1950, to command NATO forces.

Eisenhower resigned from the army and was nominated for president by the Republicans, 1952. He defeated Adlai E. Stevenson in the election. He was renominated and again defeated Stevenson, 1956. He called himself a moderate, favored "free market system" vs. government price and wage controls; kept goverment out of labor disputes; reorganized defense establishment; promoted missile programs. With support of John Foster Dulles, his secretary of state, he continued foreign aid; sped end of Korean fighting; endorsed Taiwan and SE Asia defense treaties; backed UN in condemning Anglo-French raid on Egypt; advocated "open skies" policy of mutual inspection to USSR. He sent U.S. troops into Little Rock, Ark., Sept., 1957, during the segregation crisis and ordered Marines into Lebanon July-Aug., 1958.

During his retirement at his farm near Gettysburg, Pa., Eisenhower took up the role of elder statesman, counseling his 3 successors in the White House. He died Mar. 28, 1969, in Washington.

John Fitzgerald Kennedy

John F. Kennedy, 35th president, Democrat, was born May 29, 1917, in Brookline, Mass., the son of Joseph P. Kennedy, financier, who later became ambassador to Great Britain, and Rose Fitzgerald. He entered Harvard, attended the London School of Economics briefly in 1935, received a B.S., from Harvard, 1940. He served in the Navy, 1941-1945, commanded a PT boat in the Solomons and won the Navy and Marine Corps Medal. He wrote *Profiles in Courage*, which won a Pulitzer prize. He served as representative in Congress, 1947-1953; was elected to the Senate in 1952, reelected 1958. He nearly won the vice presidential nomination in 1956.

In 1960, Kennedy won the Democratic nomination for president and defeated Richard M. Nixon, Republican. He was the first Roman Catholic president.

Kennedy's most important act was his successful demand Oct. 22, 1962, that the Soviet Union dismantle its missile bases in Cuba. He established a quarantine of arms shipments to Cuba and continued surveillance by air. He defied Soviet attempts to force the Allies out of Berlin. He made the steel industry rescind a price rise. He backed civil rights, a mental health program, arbitration of railroad disputes, and expanded medical care for the aged. Astronaut flights and satellite orbiting were greatly developed during his administration.

On Nov. 22, 1963, Kennedy was assassinated in Dallas, Tex.

Lyndon Baines Johnson

Lyndon B. Johnson, 36th president, Democrat, was born near Stonewall, Tex., Aug. 27, 1908, son of Sam Ealy Johnson and Rebekah Baines. His family moved to Johnson City in 1913. He received a B.S. degree at Southwest Texas State Teachers College, 1930, attended Georgetown Univ. Law School, Washington, 1935. He taught public speaking in Houston High School, 1930-32; served as secretary to Rep. R. M. Kleberg, 1932-35. In 1937 Johnson won a contest to fill the vacancy caused by the death of a representative and in 1938 was elected to the full term, after which he returned for 4 terms. He was elected U.S. senator in 1948 and reelected in 1954. He became Democratic whip, 1951, and leader, 1953. Johnson was Texas' favorite son for the Democratic presidential nomination in 1956 and had strong support in the 1960 convention, where the nominee, John F. Kennedy, asked him to run for vice president. His campaigning helped overcome religious bias against Kennedy in the South.

Johnson became president on the death of Kennedy. Johnson worked hard for welfare legislation, signed civil rights, anti-proverty, and tax reduction laws, and averted strikes on railroads. He was elected to a full term, 1964. The war in Vietnam overshadowed other developments, 1965-68.

In face of increasing division in the nation and his own party over his handling of the war, Johnson announced that he would not seek another term, Mar. 31, 1968.

Retiring to his ranch near Johnson City, Tex., Johnson wrote his memoirs and oversaw the construction of the Lyndon Baines Johnson Library on the campus of the Univ. of Texas in Austin. He died Jan. 22, 1973.

Richard Milhous Nixon

Richard M. Nixon, 37th president, Republican, was the only president to resign without completing an elected term. He was born in Yorba Linda, Cal., Jan. 9, 1913, the son of Francis Anthony Nixon and Hannah Milhous. In 1922, the family moved to Whittier, Cal. Nixon graduated from Whittier College, 1934; Duke Univ. Law School, 1937. After practicing law in Whittier and serving briefly in the Office of Price Administration in 1942, he entered the navy, serving in the South Pacific, and was discharged as a lieutenant commander.

Nixon was elected to the House of Representatives in 1946 and 1948. He achieved prominence as the House Un-American Activities Committee member who forced the showdown that resulted in the Alger Hiss perjury conviction. In 1950 Nixon moved to the Senate.

He was elected vice president in the Eisenhower landslides of 1952 and 1956. With Eisenhower's endorsement, Nixon won the Republican nomination in 1960. He was defeated by Democract John F. Kennedy, returned to Cal. and was defeated in his race for governor, 1962.

In 1968, he won the presidential nomination and went on to defeat Democrat Hubert H. Humphrey.

Nixon became the first U.S. president to visit China and Russia (1972). He and his foreign affairs advisor, Henry A. Kissinger, achieved a detente with China and a partial strategic arms limitation agreement with the Soviet Union.

In 1971, faced with trade and balance of payments deficits and inflation, Nixon announced wage and price controls and devaluation of the dollar. Nixon appointed 4 new Supreme Court justices, including the chief justice, thus altering the court's balance in favor of a more conservative view.

Reelected 1972, Nixon secured a cease-fire agreement in Vietnam and completed the withdrawal of U.S. troops. Early in 1973, Nixon ended most wage and price controls and announced a further devaluation of the dollar.

Nixon's 2d term was cut short by a series of scandals beginning with the burglary of Democratic party national headquarters in the Watergate office complex on June 17, 1972. From the beginning, Nixon denied any White House involvement in the Watergate break-in. On July 16, 1973, a White House aide, under questioning by a Senate committee, revealed that most of Nixon's office conversations and phone calls had been recorded. Nixon claimed executive privilege to keep the tapes secret and the courts and Congress sought the tapes for criminal proceedings against former White House aides and for a House inquiry into possible impeachment.

On Oct. 10, 1973, Nixon fired the Watergate special prosecutor and the attorney general resigned in protest. The public outcry which followed caused Nixon to appoint a new special prosecutor and to turn over to the courts a number of subpoenaed tape recordings. Public reaction also brought the initiation of a formal inquiry into impeachment.

On July 24, 1974, the Supreme Court ruled that Nixon's claim of executive privilege must fall before the special prosecutor's subpoenas of tapes relevant to criminal trial proceedings. That same day, the House Judiciary Committee opened debate on impeachment. On July 30, the committee recommended House adoption of 3 articles of impeachment charging Nixon with obstruction of justice, abuse of power, and contempt of Congress.

On Aug. 5, Nixon released transcripts of conversations held 6 days after the Watergate break-in showing that Nixon had known of, approved, and directed Watergate cover-up activities. Nixon resigned from office Aug. 9.

Gerald Rudolph Ford

Gerald R. Ford, 38th president, Republican, was born July 14, 1913, in Omaha, Neb., son of Leslie King and Dorothy Gardner, and was named Leslie Jr. When he was 2, his parents were divorced and his mother moved with the boy to Grand Rapids, Mich. There she met and married Gerald R. Ford, who formally adopted the boy and gave him his own name.

He graduated from the Univ. of Michigan, 1935 and was most valuable player on the 1934 football team. He turned down a professional football bid, went to Yale Law School and graduated, 1941.

He began practicing law in Grand Rapids, but in 1942 joined the navy and served in the Pacific, leaving the service in 1946 as a lieutenant commander.

Back in Grand Rapids, he resumed his law practice. He entered congress in 1948 and continued to win elections, spending 25 years in the House, 8 of them as Republican leader.

As congressman and GOP leader, he was consistently conservative, opposing much social welfare legislation but giving support to final passage of civil rights bills.

On Oct. 12, 1973, after Vice President Spiro T. Agnew resigned, Ford was nominated by President Nixon to replace him. It was the first use of the procedures set out in the 25th Amendment.

When Nixon resigned Aug. 9, 1974, Ford became president, the first to serve without being chosen in a national election. On Sept. 8 he pardoned Nixon for any federal crimes he might have committed as president. Ford veoted 48 bills in his first 21 months in office, including aid bills for housing, schools, health, day care, and farms; strip mining curbs, jobs creation, and tax cuts extension, saying most would prove too costly. He visited China. In 1976, he was defeated in the election by Democrat Jimmy Carter.

Jimmy (James Earl) Carter

Jimmy (James Earl) Carter, 39th president, Democrat, was the first president from the Deep South since before the Civil War. He was born Oct. 1, 1924, at Plains, Ga., where his parents, James and Lillian Gordy Carter, had a farm and several businesses.

After studying at Georgia Tech, he entered the Naval Academy at Annapolis. On graduating, he entered the Navy's nuclear submarine program as an aide to Adm. Hyman Rickover, and also studied nuclear physics at Union College, Schenectady.

His father died in 1953 and Carter left the Navy to take over the family businesses — peanut-raising, warehousing, and cotton-ginning. He became a Baptist Church deacon, a Sunday school teacher, and public school board member, was elected to the Georgia state senate, was defeated for governor, 1966, but elected in 1970.

Carter won the Democratic nomination and defeated President Gerald R. Ford in the election of 1976.

As president, Carter launched a campaign on behalf of worldwide human rights, calling in his inaugural address, for people in all nations to join the U.S. in an effort to achieve human freedom and dignity.

In 1979, Carter played a major role in the peace negotiations between Israel and Egypt. He was criticized for his failure to control inflation and his inability to formulate a sound energy policy. In April, he announced decontrol of oil and natural gas prices in an effort to make the nation less dependent on foreign energy sources.

In Sept. an AP-NBC poll gave Carter the lowest job rating of any U.S. president in 3 decades. In Nov., Sen. Edward Kennedy (D., Mass.) announced that he would oppose Carter for the Democratic presidential nomination.

Wives and Children of the Presidents

Listed in order of presidential administrations.

Name	State	Born	Married	Died	Sons	Daughters
Martha Dandridge Custis Washington	Va.	1732	1759	1802	...	...
Abigail Smith Adams	Mass.	1744	1764	1818	3	2
Martha Wayles Skelton Jefferson	Va.	1748	1772	1782	1	5
Dorothea "Dolley" Payne Todd Madison	N.C.	1768	1794	1849	...	...
Elizabeth Kortright Monroe	N.Y.	1768	1786	1830	... (1)	2
Louise Catherine Johnson Adams	Md. (2)	1775	1797	1852	3	1
Rachel Donelson Robards Jackson	Va.	1767	1791	1828	...	...
Hannah Hoes Van Buren	N.Y.	1783	1807	1819	4	...
Anna Symmes Harrison	N.J.	1775	1795	1864	6	4
Letitia Christian Tyler	Va.	1790	1813	1842	3	4
Julia Gardiner Tyler	N.Y.	1820	1844	1889	5	2
Sarah Childress Polk	Tenn.	1803	1824	1891	...	...
Margaret Smith Taylor	Md.	1788	1810	1852	1	5
Abigail Powers Fillmore	N.Y.	1798	1826	1853	1	1
Caroline Carmichael McIntosh Fillmore	N.J.	1813	1858	1881	...	...
Jane Means Appleton Pierce	N.H.	1806	1834	1863	3	...
Mary Todd Lincoln	Ky.	1818	1842	1882	4	...
Eliza McCardle Johnson	Tenn.	1810	1827	1876	3	2
Julia Dent Grant	Mo.	1826	1848	1902	3	1
Lucy Ware Webb Hayes	Oh.	1831	1852	1889	7	1
Lucretia Rudolph Garfield	Oh.	1832	1858	1918	4	1
Ellen Lewis Herndon Arthur	Va.	1837	1859	1880	2	1
Frances Folsom Cleveland	N.Y.	1864	1886	1947	2	3
Caroline Lavinia Scott Harrison	Oh.	1832	1853	1892	1	1
Mary Scott Lord Dimmick Harrison	Pa.	1858	1896	1948	...	1
Ida Saxton McKinley	Oh.	1847	1871	1907	...	2
Alice Hathaway Lee Roosevelt	Mass.	1861	1880	1884	...	1
Edith Kermit Carow Roosevelt	Conn.	1861	1886	1948	4	1
Helen Herron Taft	Oh.	1861	1886	1943	2	1
Ellen Louise Axson Wilson	Ga.	1860	1885	1914	...	3
Edith Bolling Galt Wilson	Va.	1872	1915	1961	...	...
Florence Kling De Wolfe Harding	Oh.	1860	1891	1924	...	...
Grace Anna Goodhue Coolidge	Vt.	1879	1905	1957	2	...
Lou Henry Hoover	Ia.	1875	1899	1944	2	...
Anna Eleanor Roosevelt Roosevelt	N.Y.	1884	1905	1962	4 (1)	1
Bess Wallace Truman	Mo.	1885	1919	...	...	1
Mamie Geneva Doud Eisenhower	Ia.	1896	1916	...	1 (1)	...
Jacqueline Lee Bouvier Kennedy	N.Y.	1929	1953	...	1 (1)	1
Claudia "Lady Bird" Alta Taylor Johnson	Tex.	1912	1934	...	...	2
Thelma Catherine Patricia Ryan Nixon	Nev.	1912	1940	...	...	2
Elizabeth Bloomer Warren Ford	Ill.	1918	1948	...	3	1
Rosalynn Smith Carter	Ga.	1927	1946	...	3	1

James Buchanan, 15th president, was unmarried. (1) plus one infant, deceased. (2) Born London, father a Md. citizen.

Presidents Pro Tempore of the Senate

Until 1890, presidents "pro tem" were named "for the occasion only." Beginning with that year, they have served "until the Senate otherwise ordered." Sen. John J. Ingalls, chosen under the old rule in 1887, was again elected, under the new rule, in 1890. Party designations are D, Democrat; R, Republican.

Name	Party	State	Elected
John J. Ingalls	R	Kan.	Apr. 3, 1890
Charles F. Manderson	R	Neb.	Mar. 2, 1891
Isham G. Harris	D	Tenn.	Mar. 22, 1893
Matt W. Ransom	D	N.C.	Jan. 7, 1895
Isham G. Harris	D	Tenn.	Jan. 10, 1895
William P. Frye	R	Me.	Feb. 7, 1896
Charles Curtis	R	Kan.	Dec. 4, 1911
Augustus O. Bacon	D	Ga.	Jan. 15, 1912
Jacob H. Gallinger	R	N.H.	Feb. 12, 1912
Henry Cabot Lodge	R	Mass.	Mar. 25, 1912
Frank R. Brandegee	R	Conn.	May 25, 1912
James P. Clarke	D	Ark.	Mar. 23, 1915
Willard Saulsbury	D	Del.	Dec. 14, 1916
Albert B. Cummins	R	Ia.	May 19, 1919
George H. Moses	R	N.H.	Mar. 6, 1925
Key Pittman	D	Nev.	Mar. 9, 1933
William H. King	D	Ut.	Nov. 19, 1940
Pat Harrison	D	Miss.	Jan. 6, 1941
Carter Glass	D	Va.	July 10, 1941
Kenneth McKellar	D	Tenn.	Jan. 6, 1945
Arthur H. Vandenberg	R	Mich.	Jan. 4, 1947
Kenneth McKellar	D	Tenn.	Jan. 3, 1949
Styles Bridges	R	N.H.	Jan. 3, 1953
Walter F. George	D	Ga.	Jan. 5, 1955
Carl Hayden	D	Ariz.	Jan. 3, 1957
Richard B. Russell	D	Ga.	Jan. 3, 1969
Allen J. Ellender	D	La.	Jan. 22, 1971
James O. Eastland	D	Miss.	July 28, 1972
Warren G. Magnuson	D	Wash.	Jan. 23, 1979

Speakers of the House of Representatives

Party designations: A, American; D, Democratic; DR, Democratic Republican; F, Federalist; R, Republican; W, Whig. *Served only one day.

Name	Party	State	Tenure
Frederick Muhlenberg	F	Pa.	1789-1791
Jonathan Trumbull	F	Conn.	1791-1793
Frederick Muhlenberg	F	Pa.	1793-1795
Jonathan Dayton	F	N.J.	1795-1799
Theodore Sedgwick	F	Mass.	1799-1801
Nathaniel Macon	DR	N.C.	1801-1807
Joseph B. Varnum	DR	Mass.	1807-1811
Henry Clay	DR	Ky.	1811-1814
Langdon Cheves	DR	S.C.	1814-1815
Henry Clay	DR	Ky.	1815-1820
John W. Taylor	DR	N.Y.	1820-1821
Philip P. Barbour	DR	Va.	1821-1823
Henry Clay	DR	Ky.	1823-1825
John W. Taylor	D	N.Y.	1825-1827
Andrew Stevenson	D	Va.	1827-1834
John Bell	D	Tenn.	1834-1835
James K. Polk	D	Tenn.	1835-1839
Robert M. T. Hunter	D	Va.	1839-1841
John White	W	Ky.	1841-1843
John W. Jones	D	Va.	1843-1845
John W. Davis	D	Ind.	1845-1847
Robert C. Winthrop	W	Mass.	1847-1849
Howell Cobb	D	Ga.	1849-1851
Linn Boyd	D	Ky.	1851-1855
Nathaniel P. Banks	A	Mass.	1856-1857
James L. Orr	D	S.C.	1857-1859
William Pennington	R	N.J.	1860-1861
Galusha A. Grow	R	Pa.	1861-1863
Schuyler Colfax	R	Ind.	1863-1869
*Theodore M. Pomeroy	R	N.Y.	1869-1869
James G. Blaine	R	Me.	1869-1875
Michael C. Kerr	D	Ind.	1875-1876
Samuel J. Randall	D	Pa.	1876-1881
Joseph W. Keifer	R	Oh.	1881-1883
John G. Carlisle	D	Ky.	1883-1889
Thomas B. Reed	R	Me.	1889-1891
Charles F. Crisp	D	Ga.	1891-1895
Thomas B. Reed	R	Me.	1895-1899
David B. Henderson	R	Ia.	1899-1903
Joseph G. Cannon	R	Ill.	1903-1911
Champ Clark	D	Mo.	1911-1919
Frederick H. Gillett	R	Mass.	1919-1925
Nicholas Longworth	R	Oh.	1925-1931
John N. Garner	D	Tex.	1931-1933
Henry T. Rainey	D	Ill.	1933-1935
Joseph W. Byrns	D	Tenn.	1935-1936
William B. Bankhead	D	Ala.	1936-1940
Sam Rayburn	D	Tex.	1940-1947
Joseph W. Martin Jr.	R	Mass.	1947-1949
Sam Rayburn	D	Tex.	1949-1953
Joseph W. Martin Jr.	R	Mass.	1953-1955
Sam Rayburn	D	Tex.	1955-1961
John W. McCormack	D	Mass.	1962-1971
Carl Albert	D	Okla.	1971-1977
Thomas P. O'Neill Jr.	D	Mass.	1977-

National Political Parties

As of June, 1980

Republican Party

National Headquarters—310 First St., SE, Washington, DC 20003.

Chairman—Bill Brock.

Co-Chairman—Mary Crisp.

Vice Chairmen—Ray C. Bliss, Ranny Riecker, Mary H. Boatwright, Clarke Reed, Bernard M. Shanley, Paula F. Hawkins, David B. Kennedy, Jo Anne Gray.

Secretary—June N. Gibbs.

Treasurer—Wm. J. McManus.

General Counsel—James T. Lynn.

Finance Chairman—Joe M. Rodgers.

Democratic Party

National Headquarters—1625 Massachusetts Ave., NW, Washington, DC 20036.

Chairman—John White.

Vice Chairpersons—Coleman Young, Carmela G. Lacayo.

Secretary—Dorothy V. Bush.

Treasurer—Peter G. Kelly.

Finance Chairman—Charles Manatt.

Other Major Political Organizations

Americans For Democratic Action

(1411 K St. NW, Washington, DC 20005)

President—Patsy T. Mink.

National Director—Leon Shull.

Chairperson Exec. Comm.—Winn Newman.

Comm. on Political Education, AFL-CIO

(AFL-CIO Building, 815 16th St., Wash., DC 20006)

Chairman—Lane Kirkland.

Secretary-Treasurer—Thomas R. Donahue.

Conservative Party of the State of N.Y.

(15 E. 40th St., New York, NY 10016)

Chairman—J. Daniel Mahoney.
Executive Director—Serphin R. Maltese.
Secretary—Barbara A. Keating.
Treasurer—James E. O'Doherty.

Liberal Party of New York State

(1560 Broadway, New York, NY 10036)

Chairman—Donald S. Harrington.
First Vice Chairman—David Dubinsky.
Secretary—Ben Davidson.
Treasurer—Bernice Benedick.
Executive Director—James F. Notaro.

Libertarian National Committee

(2300 Wisconsin Ave. NW, Washington, DC 20007)

Chair—David P. Bergland.
Vice-Chair—Mary Louise Hanson.
Secretary—Sylvia Sanders.
Treasurer—Dallas Cooley.
National Director—William D. Burt.

National States' Rights Party

(P.O. Box 1211, Marietta, GA 30061)

Chairman—J.B. Stoner.
Secretary—Edward R. Fields.
Treasurer—Peter Xavier.

Prohibition National Committee

(P.O. Box 2635, Denver, CO 80201)

National Chairman—Earl F. Dodge.

Socialist Labor Party

In Minnesota: Industrial Gov't. Party
(914 Industrial Ave., Palo Alto, CA 94303)

National Secretary—Nathan Karp.

Socialist Workers Party

(14 Charles Lane, New York, NY 10014)

National Secretary—Jack Barnes.
Organization Secretary—Barry Sheppard.

America's Third Parties

Since 1860, there have been only 4 presidential elections in which all third parties together polled more than 10% of the vote: the Populists (James Baird Weaver) in 1892, the National Progressives (Theodore Roosevelt) in 1912, the La Follette Progressives in 1924, and George Wallace's American Party in 1968. In 1948, the combined third parties (Henry Wallace's Progessives, Strom Thurmond's States' Rights party or Dixiecrats, Prohibition, Socialists, and others) received only 5.75% of the vote. In most elections since 1860, fewer than one vote in 20 has been cast for a third party. The only successful third party in American history was the Republican Party in the election of Abraham Lincoln in 1860.

Major Third Parties

Party	Presidential nominee	Election	Issues	Strength in
Anti-Masonic	William Wirt	1832	Against secret societies and oaths	Pa., Vt.
Free Soil	Martin Van Buren	1848	Anti-slavery	New York, Ohio
American (Know Nothing)	Millard Fillmore	1856	Anti-immigrant	Northeast, South
Greenback	Peter Cooper	1876	For "cheap money,"	
Greenback	James B. Weaver	1880	labor rights	National
Prohibition	(numerous)	1872	Anti-liquor	National
Populist	James B. Weaver	1892	For "cheap money," end of national banks	South, West
Socialist	Eugene V. Debs	1900-20	For public ownership	National
Socialist	Norman Thomas	1928-48	Liberal reforms	National
Progressive (Bull Moose)	Theodore Roosevelt	1912	Against high tariffs	Midwest, West
Union	William Lemke	1936	Anti "New Deal"	National
Progressive	Robert M. LaFollette	1924	Farmer & labor rights	Midwest, West
States' Rights	Strom Thurmond	1948	For segregation	South
Progressive	Henry Wallace	1948	Anti-cold war	New York, California
American	George Wallace	1968	For states' rights	South
American	John G. Schmitz	1972	For "law and order"	Far West, Oh., La.

The Electoral College

The president and the vice president of the United States are the only elective federal officials not elected by direct vote of the people. They are elected by the members of the Electoral College, an institution that has survived since the founding of the nation despite repeated attempts in Congress to alter or abolish it. In the elections of 1824, 1876 and 1888 the presidential candidate receiving the largest popular vote failed to win a majority of the electoral votes.

On presidential election day, the first Tuesday after the first Monday in November of every 4th year, each state chooses as many electors as it has senators and representatives in Congress. In 1964, for the first time, as provided by the 23d Amendment to the Constitution, the District of Columbia voted for 3 electors. Thus, with 100 senators and 435 representatives, there are 538 members of the Electoral College, with a majority of 270 electoral votes needed to elect the president and vice president.

Political parties customarily nominate their lists of electors at their respective state conventions. An elector cannot be a member of Congress or any person holding federal office.

Some states print the names of the candidates for president and vice president at the top of the November ballot while others list only the names of the electors. In either case, the electors of the party receiving the highest vote are elected. The electors meet on the first Monday after the 2d Wednesday in December in their respective state capitals or in some other place prescribed by state legislatures. By long-established custom they vote for their party nominees, although the Constitution does not require them to do so. All of the state's electoral votes are then awarded to the winners. The only Constitutional requirement is that at least one of the persons each elector votes for shall not be an inhabitant of that elector's home state.

Certified and sealed lists of the votes of the electors in each state are mailed to the president of the U.S. Senate. He opens them in the presence of the members of the Senate and House of Representatives in a joint session held on Jan. 6 (the next day if that falls on a Sunday), and the electoral votes of all the states are then counted. If no candidate for president has a majority, the House of Representatives chooses a president from among the 3 highest candidates, with all representatives from each state combining to cast one vote for that state. If no candidate for vice president has a majority, the Senate chooses from the top 2, with the senators voting as individuals.

In 1977, Pres. Carter urged elimination of the electoral college system and substitution of a plurality of the national popular vote.

UNITED STATES GOVERNMENT

The Carter Administration

As of mid-1980

Terms of office of the president and vice president, from Jan. 20, 1977 to Jan. 20, 1981. No person may be elected president of the United States for more than two 4-year terms.

President — Jimmy (James Earl) Carter of Georgia receives salary of $200,000 a year taxable; in addition an expense allowance of $50,000 to assist in defraying expenses resulting from his official duties. Also there may be expended not exceeding $100,000, nontaxable, a year for travel expenses and $12,000 for official entertainment available for allocation within the Executive Office of the President. Congress has provided lifetime pensions of $69,630 a year, free mailing privileges, free office space, and up to $96,000 a year for office help for former Presidents except for the first 30 month period during which a former President is entitled to staff assistance for which an amount up to $150,000 a year may be paid, and $20,000 annually for their widows.

Vice President — Walter F. Mondale of Minnesota, salary $79,125 a year and $10,000 for expenses, all of which is taxable.

For succession to presidency, see Succession in Index.

The Cabinet

(Salary: $69,630 per annum)

Secretary of State — Edmund Muskie, Me.
Secretary of Treasury — G. William Miller, Cal.
Secretary of Defense — Harold Brown, Cal.
Attorney General — Benjamin R. Civiletti, Md.
Secretary of Interior — Cecil D. Andrus, Ida.
Secretary of Agriculture — Bob S. Bergland, Minn.
Secretary of Commerce — Philip M. Klutznick, Ill.
Secretary of Labor — F. Ray Marshall, Tex.
Secretary of Health and Human Services — Patricia Roberts Harris, Wash., D.C.
Secretary of Housing and Urban Development — Moon Landrieu, La.
Secretary of Transportation — Neil E. Goldschmidt, Ore.
Secretary of Energy — Charles W. Duncan Jr., Tex.
Secretary of Education — Shirley M. Hufstedler, Cal.

The White House Staff

1600 Pennsylvania Ave. NW 20500

Chief of Staff — Jack H. Watson Jr.
Press Secretary to the President — Jody Powell.
Counsel to the President — Lloyd N. Cutler
Personal Assistant to the President — Susan Clough.
Senior Advisor to the President — Hedley Donovan.
Advisor to the President on Inflation — Alfred E. Kahn.
Presidential Assistants — Eugene Eidenberg (Intergovernmental Affairs & Secy. to the Cabinet); Stuart E. Eizenstat (Domestic Affairs & Policy); Alonzo Lowry McDonald Jr. (Staff Director); Frank B. Moore (Congressional Liaison); Sarah C. Weddington; Anne Wexler; Stephen R. Aiello (Ethnic Affairs); Hugh A. Carter Jr. (Administration); Richard M. Harden (Information Management); C. Ray Jenkins; Louis E. Martin; Alfred H. Moses; Esther Peterson (Consumer Affairs); Esteban E. Torres (Hispanic Affairs).
Press Secretary to the First Lady — Mary Finch Hoyt.
Physician to the President. — R. Adm. William M. Lukash.
Chief Usher — Rex W. Scouten.

Executive Agencies

National Security Council — Assistant to the President for Natl. Security Affairs — Zbigniew Brzezinski.
Council of Economic Advisers — Charles Schultze, chmn.
Council on Environmental Quality — James Speth, chmn.
Central Intelligence Agency — Adm. Stansfield Turner, dir.
Office of Management and Budget — James McIntyre, dir.
U.S. Trade Representative — Reubin Askew.
Council on Wage and Price Stability — R. Robert Russell, Dir.
Office of Science and Technology Policy — Frank Press, Dir.

Department of State

2201 C St. NW 20520

Secretary of State — Edmund S. Muskie.
Deputy Secretary — Warren Christopher.
Under Sec. for Political Affairs — David D. Newsom.
Under Sec. for Security Assistance, Science and Technology — Matthew Nimetz.
Under Sec. for Economic Affairs — Richard N. Cooper.
Deputy Under Secretary — Ben H. Read (for management).
Ambassadors at Large — Elliot L. Richardson, Gerard C. Smith, Henry L. Owen, W. Beverly Carter, Victor H. Palmieri, Robert Krueger.
Director of Press Relations — John Trattner.
Counselor — Rozanne Ridgway.
Legal Advisor — Robert B. Owens.
Assistant Secretaries for:
- **Administration** — Thomas M. Tracy.
- **African Affairs** — Richard M. Moose Jr.
- **Congressional Relations** — J. Brian Atwood.
- **Economic Affairs** — Deane R. Hinton.
- **European Affairs** — George S. Vest.
- **Human Rights & Humanitarian Affairs** — Patt Derian.
- **Inter-American Affairs** — William G. Bowdler.
- **International Organization Affairs** — William McCall.
- **Near-Eastern & S. Asian Affairs** — Harold H. Saunders
- **Public Affairs** — William J. Dyess.
- **Oceans & International Environmental & Scientific Affairs** — Thomas R. Pickering.

Consular Affairs — Barbara M. Watson.
Chief of Protocol — Abelardo L. Valdez.
Dir. General, Foreign Service & Dir. of Personnel — Harry G. Barnes.
Dir. of Intelligence & Research — Ronald I. Spiers.
Dir. of Politico-Military Affairs — Reginald Bartholomew.
Office of Inspector General — Robert C. Brewster.
Foreign Service Inst. — George S. Springsteen.
Policy Planning Staff — Anthony Lake.
Agency for International Development — Douglas J. Bennet Jr.
ACTION — Sam Brown.
U.S. Rep. to the UN — Donald F. McHenry.

Treasury Department

1500 Pennsylvania Ave. NW 20220

Secretary of the Treasury — G. William Miller.
Deputy Sec. of the Treasury — Robert Carswell.
Under Sec. for Monetary Affairs — vacant.
Under Sec. — Bette Anderson.
General Counsel — Robert H. Mundheim.
Assistant Secretaries: — Roger C. Altman, Richard J. Davis, Gene E. Godley, Joseph Laitin, Walter J. McDonald, Paul H. Taylor, Donald C. Lubick, Curt A. Hessler.
Bureaus:
- **Alcohol, Tobacco, and Firearms** — G. R. Dickerson, dir.
- **Comptroller of the Currency** — John G. Heimann.
- **Customs** — Robert E. Chasen, comm.
- **Engraving & Printing** — Harry R. Clements, dir.
- **Government Financial Operations** — vacant.

Internal Revenue Service — Jerome Kurtz, comm.
Mint — Stella B. Hackel, dir.
Public Debt — H. J. Hintgen, comm.
Treasurer of the U.S. — Azie Taylor Morton.
U.S. Secret Service — H. Stuart Knight, dir.

Department of Defense

The Pentagon 20301

Secretary of Defense — Harold Brown.
Deputy Secretary — W. Graham Claytor Jr.
Special Asst. to the Secretary and Deputy Secretary of Defense — Peter B. Hamilton.
Under Secretaries of Defense:
Policy — Robert W. Komer.
Policy and International Security Affairs — David E. McGiffert.
Policy Planning — Walter Slocombe.
Policy Review — Daniel J. Murphy.
Research and Engineering — William J. Perry.
Research and Engineering and Communications, Command, Control and Intelligence — Gerald P. Dinneen.
Assistant Secretaries of Defense:
Atomic Energy — James P. Wade Jr.
Comptroller — Jack Borsting.
Health Affairs — John Moxley 3d.
Manpower, Reserve Affairs and Logistics — Robert B. Pirie Jr.
Program Analysis and Evaluation — Russell Murray 2d.
Public Affairs — Thomas B. Ross.
Legislative Affairs — Jack L. Stempler.
Inspector General for Defense Intelligence — Werner E. Michel.
Chairman, Joint Chiefs of Staff — Gen. David C. Jones, USAF.
NATO Affairs: — Gen. Richard H. Groves.
General Counsel — Togo D. West Jr.

Department of the Army

The Pentagon 20301

Secretary of the Army — Clifford L. Alexander Jr.
Under Secretary — Robert H. Spiro.
Assistant Secretaries for:
Civil Works — Michael Blumenfeld.
Installations, Logistics and Financial Management — Alan J. Gibbs.
Research, Development and Acquisition — Percy A. Pierre.
Manpower & Reserve Affairs — William E. Peacock.
Chief of Public Affairs — Maj. Gen. Robert A. Sullivan.
Chief of Staff — Gen. Edward C. Meyer.
General Counsel — Sara Lister.
Comptroller of the Army — Lt. Gen. Richard L. West.
Surgeon General — Lt. Gen. Charles C. Pixley.
Adjutant General — Maj. Gen. James C. Pennington.
Inspector General — Lt. Gen. Richard G. Trefry.
Judge Advocate General — Maj. Gen. Alton Harvey.
Deputy Chiefs of Staff:
Logistics — Lt. Gen. Arthur J. Gregg.
Operations & Plans — Lt. Gen. Glenn T. Otis.
Research, Development, Acquisition — Lt. Gen. Donald R. Keith.
Personnel — Lt. Gen. Robert G. Yerks.
Ass't. Chief of Staff, Intellingence — Maj. Gen. Edmund R. Thompson.
Commanders:
U.S. Army Material Development and Readiness Command — Gen. John R. Guthrie.
U.S. Army Forces Command — Gen. Robert M. Shoemaker.
U.S. Army Training and Doctrine Command — Gen. Donn A. Starry.
First U.S. Army — Lt. Gen. John C. Forrest.
Fifth U.S. Army — Lt. Gen. William B. Caldwell 3d.
Sixth U.S. Army — Lt. Gen. Charles M. Hall.
Military Dist. of Washington — Maj. Gen. Robert Arter.

Department of the Navy

The Pentagon 20350

Secretary of the Navy — Edward Hidalgo.
Under Secretary — Robert J. Murray.
Assistant Secretaries for:
Financial Management — George A. Peapples.
Manpower, Reserve Affairs, & Logistics — Joseph A. Doyle.
Research, Engineering, & Systems — Dr. David E. Mann.
Judge Advocate General — RADM C. E. McDowell.
Chief of Naval Operations — Adm. Thomas B. Hayward.
Chief of Naval Materiel — Adm. A. J. Whittle Jr.
Chief of Information — RADM David M. Cooney.
Surgeon General/Chief, Bureau of Medicine & Surgery — V. Adm. W. P. Arentzen.
Naval Military Personnel Command — RADM Robert F. Dunn.
Military Sealift Command — RADM Bruce Keener 3d.
U.S. Marine Corps: (zip code: 20380)
Commandant — Gen. Robert H. Barrow, USMC
Chief of Staff — Gen. Kenneth McLennan, USMC.
Commandants, Naval Districts:
4th, Philadelphia — RADM C. A. Brettschneider.
5th, Norfolk — RADM James H. Scott.
6th, Charleston — RADM Robert B. McClinton.
8th, New Orleans — RADM F. F. Palmer.
11th, San Diego — RADM J. E. Langille 3d.
13th, Seattle — RADM William A. Williams.
Naval District, Wash., D.C. — RADM K. J. Bernstein.

Department of the Air Force

The Pentagon 20330

Secretary of the Air Force — Hans M. Mark.
Under Secretary — Antonio Handler Chayes.
Assistant Secretaries for:
Financial Management — Willard Mitchell, Act.
Research, Development & Logistics — Robert J. Hermann.
Manpower, Reserve Affairs & Installations — Joseph C. Zengerle, 3d.
General Counsel — Stuart R. Reichart.
Director of Information — Brig. Gen. H. J. Dalton Jr.
Director of Space Systems — Jimmie D. Hill.
Chief of Staff — Gen. Lew Allen Jr.
Surgeon General — Lt. Gen. Paul W. Myers.
Judge Advocate — Maj. Gen. Walter D. Reed.
Inspector General — Lt. Gen. Howard M. Lane.
Deputy Chiefs of Staff:
Logistics & Engineering — Lt. Gen. Billy M. Minter.
Programs & Evaluation — Lt. Gen. Abbott C. Greenleaf.
Manpower & Personnel — Lt. Gen. Andrew P. Iosue.
Research, Development & Acquisition — Lt. Gen. Kelly H. Burke.
Operations, Plans & Readiness — Lt. Gen. Charles A. Gabriel.
Major Air Commands:
AF Logistics Command — Gen. Bryce Poe 2d.
AF Systems Command — Gen. Alton D. Slay.
Air Training Command — Gen. Bennie L. Davis.
Military Airlift Command — Gen. Robert E. Huyser.
Strategic Air Command — Gen. Richard H. Ellis.
Tactical Air Command — Gen. Wilbur L. Creech.
Alaskan Air Command — Lt. Gen. Winfield W. Scott Jr.
Pacific Air Forces — Lt. Gen. James D. Hughes.
USAF Europe — Gen. John W. Pauly.
Electronic Security Command — Maj. Gen. Doyle E. Larson.
AF Communications Command — Maj. Gen. Robert T. Herres.

Department of Justice

Constitution Ave. & 10th St. NW 20530

Attorney General — Benjamin R. Civiletti.
Deputy Attorney General — Charles R. Ruff.
Associate Attorney General — John H. Schenfield.
Solicitor General — Wade H. McCree.
Antitrust Division — Sanford Litvack.
Civil Division — Alice Daniel, act.
Civil Rights Division — Drew S. Days 3d.
Criminal Division — Philip B. Heymann.
Drug Enforcement Admin. — Peter B. Bensinger.
Land & Natural Resources Division — James W. Moorman.
Legal Counsel — John M. Harmon.
Office of Legislative Affairs — Alan Parker.
Office of Management & Finance — Kevin D. Rooney.
Tax Division — M. Carr Ferguson.
Fed. Bureau of Investigation — William H. Webster, dir.
Board of Immigration Appeals — David L. Milhollan, chmn.
Bureau of Prisons — Norman A. Carlson, dir.
Public Information — Robert M. Smith.
Immigration and Naturalization Service — David Crocland, comm.
Law Enforcement Assistance Admin. — Henry S. Dogin, adm.
Pardon Attorney — John R. Stanish.
U.S. Parole Commission — Cecil C. McCall, chmn.

Department of the Interior

C St. between 18th & 19th Sts. NW 20240

Secretary of the Interior — Cecil D. Andrus.
Under Secretary — James A. Joseph.
Assistant Secretaries for:
Fish, Wildlife and Parks — Robert Herbst.
Energy & Minerals — Joan M. Davenport.
Land and Water Resources — Guy Richard Martin.
Policy, Budget, and Administration — Larry E. Meierotto.
Indian Affairs — Sidney L. Mills, act. dir.
Bureau of Land Management — Frank Gregg, dir.
Bureau of Mines — Lindsay Norman, act. dir.
Bureau of Reclamation — Keith Higginson, comm.
Fish & Wildlife Service — Lynn Greenwalt.
Geological Survey — H. W. Menard Jr., dir.
National Park Service — Russell Dickenson.
Public Affairs — Harmon Kallman, act.
Office of Water Research and Technology — Gary D. Cobb, dir.
Solicitor — Clyde O. Martz.

Department of Agriculture

14th & Independence Ave. SW 20250

Secretary of Agriculture — Bob Bergland.
Deputy Secretary — Jim Williams.
Administration — Joan S. Wallace.
Conservation, Research, & Education — M. Rupert Cutler.
Internat. Affairs & Commodity Programs — Dale E. Hathaway.
Food & Consumer Services — Carol Tucker Foreman.
Marketing Services & Transportation — P. R. Smith.
Rural Development — Alex P. Mercure.
Economics, Policy Analysis and Budget — Howard W. Hjort, dir.
Governmental & Public Affairs — James C. Webster, dir.
Agricultural Marketing Service — Barbara L. Schlei, admin.
Agric. Stabilization & Conserv. Service — Ray Fitzgerald, admin.
Animal & Plant Health Inspection Ser. — F. J. Mulhern.
Economics, Statistics, and Cooperatives Service — Kenneth R. Farrell, admin.
Energy — Weldon Barton, dir.
Farmers Home Admin. — Gordon Cavanaugh, admin.
Fed. Crop Insurance Corp. — James Deal, mgr.
Federal Grain Inspection Service — Leland E. Bartelt, admin.
Food & Nutrition Serv. — Bob Greenstein, act. admin.
Food Safety and Quality Service — Donald Houston, act. admin.
Foreign Agric. Service — Thomas R. Hughes, admin.
Forest Service — R. Max Petersen, chief.
General Counsel — Dan Marcus.
Inspector General — Thomas McBride.
International Cooperation & Development — Quenton West, dir.
Rural Electrific. Admin. — Robert Faragen, admin.
Science & Education Admin. — Anson R. Bertrand, dir.
Soil Conservation Service — Norman A. Berg, admin.
Transportation — Ronald Schrader, act. admin.
Public Participation — Linley Jones.
General Sales Mgr. — Kelly Harrison.
World Food & Agricultural Outlook Situation Board — Dawson Ahalt, act.

Department of Commerce

14th St. between Constitution & E St. NW 20230

Secretary of Commerce — Philip M. Klutznick.
Under Secretary — Luther H. Hodges.
General Counsel — Homer Moyer.
Maritime Affairs — Samuel B. Nemirow.
Off. of Productivity, Technology & Innovation — Jordan Baruch.
Administration — Elsa A. Porter.
Bureau of the Census — Vincent P. Barabba.
Bureau of Economic Analysis — George Jaszi.
Bureau of Export Development — Peter Gould.
Bureau of East-West Trade — Kempton Jenkins.
Bureau of Domestic Business Development — Thomas Murphy, act.
International Trade Admin. — Robert E. Herzstein.
Chief Economist — Courtenay M. Slater.
Natl. Oceanic & Atmospheric Admin. — Richard A. Frank, admin.
Natl. Technical Info. Service — Melvin Day, dir.
Economic Develop. Admin. — Robert T. Hall.
Natl. Bureau of Standards — Ernest Ambler.
Minority Business Development Agency — Daniel P. Henson, dir.
Office of Product Standards — Howard I. Forman.
Natl. Telecomm & Information Admin. — Henry Geller, dir.
Tourism — Jean Westphal, act.
Bureau of Industrial Economics — Beatrice N. Vaccaro.

Department of Labor

200 Constitution Ave. NW 20210

Secretary of Labor — F. Ray Marshall.
Under Secretary — John N. Gentry.
Executive Assistant-Counselor — Paul Jensen.
Assistant Secretaries for:
Administration and Management — Alfred M. Zuck.
Employment Standards — Donald Elisburg.
Employment and Training — Ernest Green.
Mine Safety & Health — Robert Lagather.
Occupational Safety & Health — Eula Bingham.
Policy, Evaluation and Research — Arnold H. Packer.
Labor Management Relations — William Hobgood.
Solicitor of Labor — Carin A. Clauss.
Comm. of Labor Statistics — Janet Norwood.
Dep. Under Secy. for Internatl. Affairs — Dean Clowes.
Dep. Under Secy. for Legislation & Intergovernmental Relations — Nik B. Edes.
Office of Information, Publications & Reports — John W. Leslie.
Dir. of Women's Bureau — Alexis Herman.

Department of Health and Human Services

200 Independence Ave. SW 20201

Secretary of HEW — Patricia Roberts Harris.
Under Secretary — Nathan J. Stark.
Assistant Secretaries for:
Management and Budget — Frederick M. Bohen.
Public Affairs — Bill Wise.
Health — Dr. Julius B. Richmond.
Planning and Evaluation — John L. Palmer.
Education — Dr. Mary Berry.
Human Development — Cesar A. Perales.
Legislation — William B. Welsh.
Personnel Administration — Thomas McFee.
General Counsel — Joan Bernstein.
Civil Rights — Roma J. Stewart.
Health Care Financing Admin. — Howard N. Newman, adm.
Social Security — William J. Driver, comm.

Department of Housing and Urban Development

451 7th St. SW 20410

Secretary of Housing & Urban Development — Moon Landrieu.
Under Secretary — Victor Marrero.
Assistant Secretaries for:
Administration — William A. Medina.
Community Planning & Development — Robert C. Embry.
Fair Housing & Equal Opportunity — Sterling Tucker.
Housing & Federal Housing Commissioner — Lawrence B. Simons.
Legislation & Intergovernmental Relations — H. Dicken Cherry.
Neighborhoods, Voluntary Assns. & Consumer Protection — Geno Baroni.
Policy Development & Research — Donna E. Shalala.
President, Govt. Natl. Mortgage Assn. — Robert P. Laurent.
Public Affairs — Eugene Russell.
International Affairs — Tila M. de Hancock.
Labor Relations — Elizabeth Raymond.
General Counsel — Jane L. McGrew.
Inspector General — Charles L. Dempsey.

Department of Transportation

400 7th St. SW 20590

Secretary of Transportation — Neil E. Goldschmidt.
Deputy Secretary — William C. Beckham.
Assistant Secretaries — Edward W. Scott Jr., Mortimer L. Downey, William B. Johnston.
General Counsel — Thomas G. Allison.
National Highway Traffic Safety Admin. — Joan Claybrook.
U. S. Coast Guard Commandant — John B. Hayes.
Federal Aviation Admin. — Langhorne M. Bond.
Federal Highway Admin. — John S. Hassell, act.
Federal Railroad Admin. — John M. Sullivan.
Urban Mass Transportation Admin. — Theodore C. Lutz.
Research & Special Programs Admin. — Howard Duqoff.

Department of Energy

1000 Independence Ave. SW 20585

Secretary of Energy — Charles W. Duncan Jr.
Deputy Secy. — John Sawhill.
Federal Energy Regulatory Comm. — Charles B. Curtis, chmn.
Off. of Hearings & Appeals — Melvin Goldstein, dir.
Inspector General — J. K. Mansfield.
Off. of Economic Opportunity — Marion A. Bowden, dir.
Economic Regulatory Admin. — Hazel Rollins.
International Affairs — Leslie Goldman.
Conservation & Solar Applications — Omi Walden.
Energy Information Adm. — Thomas Nelson.
Resource Applications — Ruth Davis.

Department of Education

Wash., D.C. 20202

Secretary of Education — Shirley A. Hufstedler.
Under Secretary — Steven A. Minter.
Deputy Under Secretaries — Michael Bakalis, Margaret McKenna.
General Counsel — Betsy Levin.
Assistant Secretaries:
Management — John Gabusi.
Budget and Planning — C. William Fischer.
Public Affairs — Elizabeth Carpenter.
Elementary and Secondary Education — Thomas Minter.
Postsecondary Education — Albert H. Bowker.
Educational Research and Improvement — F. James Rutherford.
Non-Public Education — Edward D'Allessio.
Vocational & Adult Education — Daniel B. Taylor.
Special Education and Rehabilitative Services — Edwin Martin.
Civil Rights — Cynthia G. Brown.

Judiciary of the U.S.

Data as of June, 1980

Justices of the United States Supreme Court

The Supreme Court comprises the chief justice of the United States and 8 associate justices, all appointed by the president with advice and consent of the Senate. Salaries: chief justice $84,675 annually, associate justice $81,288.

Name; apptd from *Chief Justices in italics*	Service Term	Service Yrs.	Born	Died
John Jay, N. Y.	1789-1795	5	1745	1829
John Rutledge, S. C.	1789-1791	1	1739	1800
William Cushing, Mass.	1789-1810	20	1732	1810
James Wilson, Pa.	1789-1798	8	1742	1798
John Blair, Va.	1789-1796	6	1732	1800
James Iredell, N. C.	1790-1799	9	1751	1799
Thomas Johnson, Md.	1791-1793	1	1732	1819
William Paterson, N. J.	1793-1806	13	1745	1806
John Rutledge, S.C.	1795(a)	—	1739	1800
Samuel Chase, Md.	1796-1811	15	1741	1811
Oliver Ellsworth, Conn.	1796-1800	4	1745	1807
Bushrod Washington, Va.	1798-1829	31	1762	1829
Alfred Moore, N. C.	1799-1804	4	1755	1810
John Marshall, Va.	1801-1835	34	1755	1835
William Johnson, S. C.	1804-1834	30	1771	1834
Henry B. Livingston, N. Y.	1806-1823	16	1757	1823
Thomas Todd, Ky.	1807-1826	18	1765	1826
Joseph Story, Mass.	1811-1845	33	1779	1845
Gabriel Duval, Md.	1811-1835	22	1752	1844
Smith Thompson, N. Y.	1823-1843	20	1768	1843
Robert Trimble, Ky.	1826-1828	2	1777	1828
John McLean, Oh.	1829-1861	32	1785	1861
Henry Baldwin, Pa.	1830-1844	14	1780	1844
James M. Wayne, Ga.	1835-1867	32	1790	1867
Roger B. Taney, Md.	1836-1864	28	1777	1864
Philip P. Barbour, Va.	1836-1841	4	1783	1841
John Catron, Tenn.	1837-1865	28	1786	1865
John McKinley, Ala.	1837-1852	15	1780	1852

Name; apptd from	Service Term	Yrs.	Born	Died
Peter V. Daniel, Va.	1841-1860	19	1784	1860
Samuel Nelson, N. Y.	1845-1872	27	1792	1873
Levi Woodbury, N. H.	1845-1851	5	1789	1851
Robert C. Grier, Pa.	1846-1870	23	1794	1870
Benjamin R. Curtis, Mass.	1851-1857	6	1809	1874
John A. Campbell, Ala.	1853-1861	8	1811	1889
Nathan Clifford, Me.	1858-1881	23	1803	1881
Noah H. Swayne, Oh.	1862-1881	18	1804	1884
Samuel F. Miller, Ia.	1862-1890	28	1816	1890
David Davis, Ill.	1862-1877	14	1815	1886
Stephen J. Field, Cal.	1863-1897	34	1816	1899
Salmon P. Chase, Oh.	1864-1873	8	1808	1873
William Strong, Pa.	1870-1880	10	1808	1895
Joseph P. Bradley, N. J.	1870-1892	21	1813	1892
Ward Hunt, N. Y.	1872-1882	9	1810	1886
Morrison R. Waite, Oh.	1874-1888	14	1816	1888
John M. Harlan, Ky.	1877-1911	34	1833	1911
William B. Woods, Ga.	1880-1887	6	1824	1887
Stanley Matthews, Oh.	1881-1889	7	1824	1889
Horace Gray, Mass.	1881-1902	20	1828	1902
Samuel Blatchford, N. Y.	1882-1893	11	1820	1893
Lucius Q. C. Lamar, Miss.	1888-1893	5	1825	1893
Melville W. Fuller, Ill.	1888-1910	21	1833	1910
David J. Brewer, Kan.	1889-1910	20	1837	1910
Henry B. Brown, Mich.	1890-1906	15	1836	1913
George Shiras Jr., Pa.	1892-1903	10	1832	1924
Howell E. Jackson, Tenn.	1893-1895	2	1832	1895
Edward D. White, La.	1894-1910	16	1845	1921
Rufus W. Peckman, N. Y.	1895-1909	13	1838	1909
Joseph McKenna, Cal.	1898-1925	26	1843	1926
Oliver W. Holmes, Mass.	1902-1932	29	1841	1935
William R. Day, Oh.	1903-1922	19	1849	1923
William H. Moody, Mass.	1906-1910	3	1853	1917
Horace H. Lurton, Tenn.	1909-1914	4	1844	1914
Charles E. Hughes, N. Y.	1910-1916	5	1862	1948
Willis Van Devanter, Wy.	1910-1937	26	1859	1941
Joseph R. Lamar, Ga.	1910-1916	5	1857	1916
Edward D. White, La.	1910-1921	10	1845	1921
Mahlon Pitney, N. J.	1912-1922	10	1858	1924
James C. McReynolds, Tenn.	1914-1941	26	1862	1946
Louis D. Brandeis, Mass.	1916-1939	22	1856	1941
John H. Clarke, Oh.	1916-1922	5	1857	1945
William H. Taft, Conn.	1921-1930	8	1857	1930
George Sutherland, Ut.	1922-1938	15	1862	1942
Pierce Butler, Minn.	1922-1939	16	1866	1939
Edward T. Sanford, Tenn.	1923-1930	7	1865	1930
Harlan F. Stone, N. Y.	1925-1941	16	1872	1946
Charles E. Hughes, N. Y.	1930-1941	11	1862	1948
Owen J. Roberts, Pa.	1930-1945	15	1875	1955
Benjamin N. Cardozo, N.Y.	1932-1938	6	1870	1938
Hugo L. Black, Ala.	1937-1971	34	1886	1971
Stanley F. Reed, Ky.	1938-1957	19	1884	1980
Felix Frankfurter, Mass.	1939-1962	23	1882	1965
William O. Douglas, Conn.	1939-1975	36	1898	1980
Frank Murphy, Mich.	1940-1949	9	1890	1949
Harlan F. Stone, N. Y.	1941-1946	5	1872	1946
James F. Byrnes, S. C.	1941-1942	1	1879	1972
Robert H. Jackson, N. Y.	1941-1954	12	1892	1954
Wiley B. Rutledge, Ia.	1943-1949	6	1894	1949
Harold H. Burton, Oh.	1945-1958	13	1888	1964
Fred M. Vinson, Ky.	1946-1953	7	1890	1953
Tom C. Clark, Tex.	1949-1967	18	1899	1977
Sherman Minton, Ind.	1949-1956	7	1890	1965
Earl Warren, Cal.	1953-1969	16	1891	1974
John Marshall Harlan, N. Y.	1955-1971	16	1899	1971
William J. Brennan Jr., N. J.	1956 —	—	1906	—
Charles E. Whittaker, Mo.	1957-1962	5	1901	1973
Potter Stewart, Oh.	1958 —	—	1915	—
Byron R. White, Col.	1962 —	—	1917	—
Arthur J. Goldberg, Ill.	1962-1965	3	1908	—
Abe Fortas, Tenn.	1965-1969	4	1910	—
Thurgood Marshall, N.Y.	1967 —	—	1908	—
Warren E. Burger, Va.	1969 —	—	1907	—
Harry A. Blackmun, Minn.	1970 —	—	1908	—
Lewis F. Powell Jr., Va.	1972 —	—	1907	—
William H. Rehnquist, Ariz.	1972 —	—	1924	—
John Paul Stevens, Ill.	1975 —	—	1920	—

(a) Rejected Dec. 15, 1795.

U.S. Court of Customs and Patent Appeals

Washington, DC 20439 (Salaries, $65,000)

Chief Judge — Howard T. Markey.

Associate Judges — Giles S. Rich, Phillip B. Baldwin, Donald E. Lane, Jack R. Miller.

U.S. Customs Court

New York, NY 10007 (Salaries, $61,500)

Chief Judge — Edward D. Re.

Judges — Paul P. Rao, Morgan Ford, Scovel Richardson, Frederick Landis, James L. Watson, Herbert N. Maletz, Bernard Newman, Nils A. Boe.

U.S. Court of Claims

Washington, DC 20005 (Salaries, $65,000)

Chief Judge — Daniel M. Friedman

Associate Judges — Oscar H. Davis, Shiro Kashiwa, Robert L. Kunzig, Marion T. Bennett, Philip Nichols Jr., Edward S. Smith.

U.S. Tax Court

Washington DC 20217 (Salaries, $61,500)

Chief Judge — C. Moxley Featherston.

Judges — William M. Drennen, Irene F. Scott, William M. Fay, Howard A. Dawson Jr., Theodore Tannenwald Jr., Charles R. Simpson, Leo H. Irwin, Samuel B. Sterrett, William A. Goffe, Cynthia H. Hall, Darrell D. Wiles, Richard C. Wilbur, Herbert L. Chabot.

U.S. Courts of Appeals

(Salaries, $65,000. CJ means Chief Judge)

District of Columbia — J. Skelly Wright, CJ; Carl McGowan, Edward Allen Tamm, Spottswood W. Robinson III, Roger Robb, George E. MacKinnon, Malcolm Richard Wilkey, Patricia M. Wald, Abner J. Mikva; Clerk's Office, Washington, DC 20001.

First Circuit (Me., Mass., N.H., R.I., Puerto Rico) — Frank M. Coffin, CJ; Levin H. Campbell, Hugh H. Bownes; Clerk's Office, Boston, MA 02109.

Second Circuit (Conn., N.Y., Vt.) — Irving R. Kaufman, CJ Wilfred Feinberg, Walter R. Mansfield, William H. Mulligan James L. Oakes, William H. Timbers, Ellsworth Van Graafeiland Thomas J. Meskill, Jon O. Newman, Amalya Lyle Kearse; Clerk's Office, New York, NY 10007.

Third Circuit (Del., N.J., Pa., Virgin Is.) — Collins J. Seitz, CJ Ruggero J. Aldisert, Arlin M. Adams, John J. Gibbons, Max Rosenn, James Hunter 3d, Joseph F. Weis Jr., Leonard I. Garth, A Leon Higginbotham Jr., Dolores K. Sloviter; Clerk's Office, Philadelphia, PA 19106.

Fourth Circuit (Md., N.C., S.C., Va., W.Va.) — Clement F Haynsworth Jr., CJ; Harrison L. Winter, Kenneth K. Hall, John D. Butzner Jr., Donald Stuart Russell, H. Emory Widener Jr., James D. Phillips Jr., Francis D. Murnaghan Jr., James M. Sprouse; Clerk's Office, Richmond, VA 23219.

Fifth Circuit (Ala., Fla., Ga., La., Miss., Tex., Canal Zone) — James P. Coleman, CJ; John R. Brown, Irving L. Goldberg, Robert A. Ainsworth Jr., John C. Godbold, Charles Clark, Thomas G. Gee, Paul H. Roney, Gerald B. Tjoflat, James C. Hill, Peter T. Fay, Alvin B. Rubin, Robert S. Vance, Phyllis A. Kravitch, Frank M. Johnson, Reynaldo G. Garza, Albert J. Henderson Jr., Thomas M. Reavley, Joseph W. Hatchett, Henry A. Politz, R. Lanier Anderson, Carolyn D. Randall, Samuel D. Johnson, Albert Tate Jr. Thomas A. Clark; Clerk's Office, New Orleans, LA 70130.

Sixth Circuit (Ky., Mich., Ohio, Tenn.) — Anthony J. Celebrezze, CJ; Paul C. Weick, Albert J. Engel, Pierce Lively, Gilbert S. Merritt, Damon J. Keith, Bailey Brown, Cornelia G. Kennedy, Boyce F. Martin Jr., Nathaniel R. Jones; Clerk's Office, Cincinnati, OH 45202.

Seventh Circuit (Ill., Ind., Wis.) — Thomas E. Fairchild, CJ; Luther M. Swygert, Walter J. Cummings, Wilbur F. Pell Jr., Robert A. Sprecher, Philip W. Tone, Harlington Wood Jr., William J. Bauer, Richard D. Cudahy; Clerk's Office, Chicago, IL 60604.

Eighth Circuit (Ark., Ia., Minn., Mo., Neb., N.D., S.D.) — Floyd R. Gibson, CJ; Donald P. Lay, Gerald W. Heaney, Myron H. Bright, Donald R. Ross, Roy L. Stephenson, J. Smith Henley, Theodore McMillian; Clerk's Office, St. Louis, MO 63101.

Ninth Circuit (Ariz., Cal., Ida., Mont., Nev., Ore., Wash., Alaska, Ha., Guam) — James R. Browning, CJ; Eugene A.

right, Herbert Y. C. Choy, J. Clifford Wallace, Alfred T. Goodin, Anthony M. Kennedy, J. Blaine Anderson, Procter Hug Jr., omas Tang, Joseph T. Sneed, Jerome Farris, Betty B. Fletcher, ary M. Schroeder, Otto R. Skopil Jr., Harry Pregerson, Arthur Alarcon; Clerk's Office, San Francisco, CA 94101.

Tenth Circuit (Col., Kan., N.M., Okla., Ut., Wy.) — Oliver th, CJ; William J. Holloway Jr., Robert H. McWilliams, James Barrett, William E. Doyle, Monroe G. McKay, James K. Lon, Stephanie K. Seymour; Clerk's Office, Denver, CO 80294.

Temporary Emergency Court of Appeals — Edward Allen amm, CJ; Clerk's Office, Washington, DC 20001.

U.S. District Courts

(Salaries, $61,500. CJ means Chief Judge)

Alabama — Northern: Frank H. McFadden, CJ; Sam C. Pointer ., James Hughes Hancock, J. Foy Guin Jr.; Clerk's Office, Biringham 35203. **Middle:** Robert E. Varner, CJ; Jane P. Gordon; lerk's Office, Montgomery 36101. **Southern:** Virgil Pittman, CJ; illiam Brevard Hand; Clerk's Office, Mobile 36601.

Alaska — James A. von der Heydt, CJ; James M. Fitzgerald; lerk's Office, Anchorage 99513.

Arizona — C. A. Muecke, CJ; William P. Copple, Mary Ann ichey, Vlademar A. Cordova, Richard M. Bilby; Clerk's Office, hoenix 85025.

Arkansas — Eastern: Garnett Thomas Eisele, CJ; Elsijane Trimle Roy, Richard S. Arnold, William Ray Overton; Clerk's Office, ittle Rock 72203. **Western:** Paul X. Williams, CJ; Elsijane Trimle Roy, Richard S. Arnold; Clerk's Office, Fort Smith 72902.

California — Northern: Robert F. Peckham, CJ; Lloyd H. urke, Stanley A. Weigel, Robert H. Schnacke, Samuel Conti, pencer M. Williams, Charles B. Renfrew; William H. Orrick Jr., illiam H. Schwarzer, William A. Ingram, Cecil F. Poole; Clerk's ffice, San Francisco 94102. **Eastern:** Philip C. Wilkins, CJ; M. D. rocker, Lawrence K. Karlton, Milton L. Schwartz; Clerk's Office, acramento 95814. **Central:** Irving Hill, CJ; A. Andrew Hauk, Wilam P. Gray, Warren J. Ferguson, Manuel L. Real, David W. Wilams, Robert J. Kelleher, Wm. Matthew Byrne Jr., Lawrence T. ydick, Malcolm M. Lucas, Robert Firth, Robert M. Takasugi, aughlin E. Waters, Mariana R. Pfaelzer; Clerk's Office, Los Aneles 90012. **Southern:** Edward J. Schwartz, CJ; Howard B. Turentine, Gordon Thompson Jr., Leland C. Nielsen, William B. Enight; Clerk's Office, San Diego 92189.

Colorado — Fred M. Winner, CJ; Sherman G. Finesilver, Richrd P. Matsch, John L. Kane, Jim R. Carrigan, Zita L. Weinhienk; Clerk's Office, Denver 80294.

Connecticut — T. Emmet Clarie, CJ; T. F. Gilroy Daly, Ellen B. Burns, Warren W. Eginton; Clerk's Office, New Haven 06505.

Delaware — James L. Latchum, CJ; Walter K. Stapleton, Muray M. Schwartz; Clerk's Office, Wilmington 19801.

District of Columbia — William B. Bryant, CJ; Oliver Gasch, John Lewis Smith Jr., Aubrey E. Robinson Jr., Gerhard A. Gesell, John H. Pratt, June L. Green, Barrington D. Parker, Charles R. Richey, Thomas A. Flannery, Louis F. Oberdorfer, Harold H. Greene, John Garrett Penn, Joyce Hens Green; Clerk's Office, Washington DC 20001.

Florida — Northern: Winston E. Arnow, CJ; William H. Stafford Jr., Lyle C. Higby; Clerk's Office, Tallahassee 32302. **Middle:** George C. Young, CJ; Ben Krentzman, Howell W. Melton, William Terrell Hodges, John A. Reed Jr., George G. Carr, Susan H. Black, William J. Castagna; Clerk's Office, Jacksonville 32201. **Southern:** C. Clyde Atkins, CJ; Joe Eaton, James Lawrence King, Norman C. Roettger Jr.; Sidney M. Aronovitz, William H. Hoeveler, Jose A. Gonzalez, James W. Kehoe, Eugene P. Spellman, Edward B. Davis, James C. Paine, Alcee L. Hastings; Clerk's Office, Miami 33101.

Georgia — Northern: Charles A.Moye Jr., CJ; William C.O'Kelley, Richard C. Freeman, Newell Edenfield, Harold L. Murphy, Marvin H. Shoob, G. Ernest Tidwell, Orinda Dale Evans, Robert L. Vining Jr., Robert H. Hall; Clerk's Office, Atlanta 30303. **Middle:** J. Robert Elliott, CJ; Wilbur D. Owens Jr.; Clerk's Office, Macon 31202. **Southern:** Anthony A. Alaimo, CJ; B. Avant Edenfield, Dudley Bowen Jr.; Clerk's Office, Savannah 31402.

Hawaii — Samuel P. King, CJ; Martin Pence; Clerk's Office, Honolulu 96850.

Idaho — Ray McNichols, CJ; Marion J. Callister; Clerk's Office, Boise 83724.

Illinois — Northern: James B. Parsons, CJ; Bernard M. Decker, Frank J. McGarr, Thomas R. McMillen, Prentice H. Marshall, Joel M. Flaum, John F. Grady, George N. Leighton, John Powers Crowley, Nicholas J. Bua, Stanley J. Roszkowski, James B. Moran, Marvin E. Aspen; Clerk's Office, Chicago 60604. **Central:** Robert D. Morgan, CJ; J. Waldo Ackerman, Harold A. Baker; Clerk's Office, Peoria 61650. **Southern:** James L. Foreman, CJ; William L. Beatty; Clerk's Office, E. St. Louis 62202.

Indiana — Northern: Jesse E. Eschbach, CJ; Allen Sharp, Phil M. McNagny Jr.; Clerk's Office, South Bend 46601. **Southern:** William E. Steckler, CJ; Cale J. Holder, S. Hugh Dillin, James E. Noland, Gene E. Brooks; Clerk's Office, Indianapolis 46204.

Iowa — Northern: Edward J. McManus, CJ; Donald E. O'-Brien; Clerk's Office, Cedar Rapids 52407. **Southern:** William C. Stuart, CJ; Donald E. O'Brien, Harold D. Vietor; Clerk's Office, Des Moines 50309.

Kansas — Frank G. Theis, CJ; Earl E. O'Connor, Richard Dean Rogers, Dale E. Saffels; Clerk's Office, Wichita 67201.

Kentucky — Eastern: Bernard T. Moynahan Jr., CJ; Howard David Hermansdorfer, Eugene E. Siler Jr., Scott Reed; Clerk's Office, Lexington 40501. **Western:** Charles M. Allen, CJ; Eugene E. Siler Jr., Edward H. Johnstone, Thomas A. Ballantine; Clerk's Office, Louisville 40202.

Louisiana — Eastern: Frederick J. R. Heebe, CJ; Edward J. Boyle Sr., Lansing L. Mitchell, Fred J. Cassibry, Jack M. Gordon, Morey L. Sear, Charles Schwartz Jr., Adrian A. Duplantier, Robert F. Collins, George Arceneaux Jr., Veronica D. Wicker, Patrick E. Carr, Peter Hill Beer; Clerk's Office, New Orleans 70130. **Middle:** John V. Parker, CJ; E. Gordon West; Clerk's Office, Baton Rouge 70801. **Western:** Nauman S. Scott, CJ; Tom Stagg, W. Eugene Davis, Earl Ernest Veron, John M. Shaw; Clerk's Office, Shreveport 71161.

Maine — Edward Thaxter Gignoux, CJ; Clerk's Office, Portland 04101.

Maryland — Edward S. Northrop, CJ; Frank A. Kaufman, Alexander Harvey 2d, James R. Miller Jr., Joseph H. Young, Herbert F. Murray, C. Stanley Blair, Shirley B. Jones, Joseph C. Howard; Clerk's Office, Baltimore 21201.

Massachusetts — Andrew A. Caffrey, CJ; W. Arthur Garrity Jr., Frank H. Freedman, Joseph L. Tauro, Walter Jay Skinner, A. David Mazzone, Robert E. Keeton, John J. McNaught, Rya W. Zobel, David S. Nelson; Clerk's Office, Boston 02109.

Michigan — Eastern: John Feikens, CJ; Philip Pratt, Robert E. DeMascio, Charles W. Joiner, James Harvey, James P. Churchill, Ralph B. Guy Jr., Julian A. Cook, Patricia A. Boyle, Stewart A. Newblatt, Avern Cohn, Anna Diggs Taylor; Clerk's Office, Detroit 48226. **Western:** Wendell A. Miles, CJ; Douglas W. Hillman, Benjamin F. Gibson; Clerk's Office, Grand Rapids 49503.

Minnesota — Edward J. Devitt, CJ; Miles W. Lord, Donald D. Alsop, Harry H. MacLaughlin; Clerk's Office, St. Paul 55101.

Mississippi — Northern: William C. Keady, CJ; Clerk's Office, Oxford 38655. **Southern:** Dan M. Russell Jr., CJ; William Harold Cox, Walter L. Nixon Jr.; Clerk's Office, Jackson 39205.

Missouri — Eastern: H. Kenneth Wangelin, CJ; William R. Collinson, John F. Nangle, Edward D. Filippine, William L. Hungate; Clerk's Office, St. Louis 63101. **Western:** John W. Oliver, CJ; William R. Collinson, Elmo B. Hunter, H. Kenneth Wangelin, Russell G. Clark, Harold Sachs, Scott O. Wright; Clerk's Office, Kansas City 64106.

Montana — James F. Battin, CJ; Paul G. Hatfield; Clerk's Office, Billings 59101.

Nebraska — Warren K. Urbom, CJ; Robert V. Denney, Albert G. Schatz; Clerk's Office, Omaha 68101.

Nevada — Roger D. Foley, CJ; Harry E. Claiborne, Edward C. Reed; Clerk's Office, Las Vegas 89101.

New Hampshire — Shane Devine, CJ; Martin J. Loughlin; Clerk's Office, Concord 03301.

New Jersey — Clarkson S. Fisher, CJ; Frederick B. Lacey, Vincent P. Biunno, Herbert J. Stern, H. Curtis Meanor, John F. Gerry, Stanley S. Brotman, Anne E. Thompson, D. R. Debevoise, H. Lee Sarokin; Clerk's Office, Trenton 08605.

New Mexico — Howard C. Bratton, CJ; Edwin L. Mechem, Santiago E. Campos, Juan G. Burciaga; Clerk's Office, Albuquerque 87103.

New York — Northern: James T. Foley, CJ; Howard G. Munson, Neal P. McCurn; Clerk's Office, Albany 12201. **Eastern:** Jack B. Weinstein, CJ; Mark A. Costantino, Edward R. Neaher, Thomas C. Platt Jr., Henry Bramwell, George C. Pratt, Charles P. Sifton, Eugene H. Nickerson; Clerk's Office, Brooklyn 11201. **Southern:** David N. Edelstein, CJ; Edward Weinfeld, Lloyd F. MacMahon, Constance Baker Motley, Milton Pollack, Morris E. Lasker, Lawrence W. Pierce, Lee P. Gagliardi, Charles L. Brieant, Whitman Knapp, Charles E. Stewart Jr., Thomas P. Griesa, Robert L. Carter, Robert J. Ward, Kevin Thomas Duffy, William C. Conner, Richard Owen, Leonard B. Sand, Mary Johnson Lowe, Henry F. Werker, Gerard L. Goettel, Charles S. Haight Jr., Vincent L. Broderick, Pierre N. Laval, Robert W. Sweet, Abraham D. Sofaer; Clerk's Office N. Y. City 10007. **Western:** John T. Curtin, CJ; Harold P. Burke, John T. Elfvin; Clerk's Office, Buffalo 14202.

North Carolina — Eastern: Franklin T. Dupree Jr., CJ; Clerk's Office, Raleigh 27611. **Middle:** Eugene A. Gordon, CJ; Hiram H. Ward; Clerk's Office, Greensboro 27402. **Western:** Woodrow Wilson Jones, CJ; James B. McMillan; Clerk's Office, Asheville 28802.

North Dakota — Paul Benson, CJ; Bruce M. Van Sickle; Clerk's Office, Bismarck 58501.

Ohio — Northern: Frank J. Battisti, CJ; Don J. Young, William K. Thomas, Thomas D. Lambros, Robert B. Krupansky, Nicholas J. Walinski, Leroy J. Contie Jr., John M. Manos; Clerk's Office, Cleveland 44114. **Southern:** Carl B. Rubin, CJ; Joseph P. Kinneary, Robert M. Duncan; Clerk's Office, Columbus 43215.

Oklahoma — Northern: H. Dale Cook, CJ; Frederick A. Daugherty, James O. Ellison, Thomas R. Brett; Clerk's Office, Tulsa 74103. **Eastern:** Frederick A. Daugherty, CJ; H. Dale Cook, Frank H. Seay; Clerk's Office, Muskogee 74401. **Western:** Frederick A. Daugherty, CJ; Luther B. Eubanks, H. Dale Cook, Ralph G. Thompson, Lee R. West; Clerk's Office, Oklahoma City 73102.

Oregon — James M. Burns, CJ; Robert C. Belloni; Clerk's Office, Portland 97207.

Pennsylvania — Eastern: Joseph S. Lord 3d, CJ; Alfred L. Luongo, John P. Fullam, Charles R. Weiner, E. Mac Troutman, John B. Hannum, Daniel H. Huyett 3d, Donald W. VanArtsdalen, J. William Ditter Jr., Edward R. Becker, Raymond J. Broderick, Clarence C. Newcomer, Clifford Scott Green, Louis Charles Bechtle, Joseph L. McGlynn Jr., Edward N. Cahn, Louis H. Pollak, Norma L. Shapiro; Clerk's Office, Philadelphia 19106. **Middle:** William J. Nealon Jr., CJ; R. Dixon Herman, Malcolm Muir, Richard P. Conaboy, Sylvia H. Rambo; Clerk's Office, Scranton 18501. **Western:** Gerald J. Weber, CJ; William W. Knox, Hubert I. Teitelbaum, Barron P. McCune, Daniel J. Snyder Jr., Maurice B. Cohill Jr., Paul A. Simmons, Gustave Diamond, Donald E. Zeigler, Alan N. Bloch; Clerk's Office, Pittsburgh 15230.

Rhode Island — Raymond J. Pettine, CJ; Francis J. Boyle; Clerk's Office, Providence 02901.

South Carolina — J. Robert Martin Jr., CJ; Robert W. Hemphill, Charles E. Simons Jr., Solomon Blatt Jr., Robert F. Chapman, C. Weston Houck, Falcon B. Hawkins, Matthew J. Perry Jr.; Clerk's Office, Columbia 29202.

South Dakota — Fred J. Nichol, CJ; Andrew A. Bogue, Donald J. Porter; Clerk's Office, Sioux Falls 57102.

Tennessee — Eastern: Frank W. Wilson, CJ; Robert L. Taylor, C. G. Neese; Clerk's Office, Knoxville 37901. **Middle:** L. Clure Morton, CJ, Thomas A. Wiseman Jr.; Clerk's Office, Nashville 37203. **Western:** Robert M. McRae Jr., CJ; Harry W. Wellford; Clerk's Office, Memphis 38103.

Texas — Northern: Halbert O. Woodward, CJ; Eldon B. Mahon, Robert M. Hill, Robert W. Porter, Patrick E. Higginbotham, Mary Lou Robinson, Barefoot Sanders, David O. Belew Jr.; Clerks's Office, Dallas 75242. **Southern:** John V. Singleton Jr., CJ; Woodrow B. Seals, Carl O. Bue Jr., Owen D. Cox, Robert O'Conor Jr., Ross N. Sterling, Norman W. Black, James De And George E. Cire, Gabrielle K. McDonald, George P. Kazen, Hug Gibson; Clerk's Office, Houston 77208. **Eastern:** Joe J. Fisher, C William Wayne Justice, William M. Steger, Robert Parker; Clerk Office, Beaumont 77704. **Western:** Jack Roberts, CJ; William Sessions, Lucius D. Bunton 3d, Harry Lee Hudspeth; Clerk's Office, San Antonio 78206.

Utah — Aldon J. Anderson, CJ; Bruce S. Jenkins; Clerk's Offic Salt Lake City 84101.

Vermont — James S. Holden, CJ; Albert W. Coffrin; Clerk Office, Burlington 05402.

Virginia — Eastern: John A. MacKenzie, CJ; Robert R. Mehige Jr., Richard B. Kellam, Albert V. Bryan Jr., D. Dortch Warriner, J. Calvitt Clarke; Clerk's Office, Norfolk 23501. **Western:** James C. Turk, CJ; Glen M. Williams; Clerk's Office, Roanok 24006.

Washington — Eastern: Marshall A. Neill, CJ; Jack E. Tanne Clerk's Office, Spokane 99210. **Western:** Walter T. McGovern, C. Morell E. Sharp, Donald S. Voorhees, Jack E. Tanner; Clerk's Office, Seattle 98104.

West Virginia — Northern: Robert Earl Maxwell, CJ; Charle H. Haden 2d; Clerk's Office, Elkins 26241. **Southern:** Dennis Raymond Knapp, CJ; John T. Copenhaver Jr., Charles H. Haden 2c Robert Staker; Clerk's Office, Charleston 25329.

Wisconsin — Eastern: John W. Reynolds, CJ; Myron L. Gordon, Robert W. Warren; Clerk's Office, Milwaukee 53202. **Western:** James E. Doyle, CJ; Barbara B. Crabb; Clerk's Office, Madison 53701.

Wyoming — Clarence A. Brimmer; Clerk's Office, Cheyenn 82001.

U.S. Territorial District Courts

Canal Zone — Clerk's Office, Balboa Heights.

Guam — Cristobal C. Duenas; Clerk's Office, P.O. Box DC Agana 96910.

Puerto Rico — Jose V. Toledo, CJ; Hernan G. Pesquera, Jua R. Torruella; Clerk's Office, San Juan 00904.

Virgin Islands — Almeric L. Christian, CJ; Warren H. Young Clerk's Office, Charlotte Amalie, St. Thomas 00801.

State Officials, Salaries, Party Membership

Compiled from data supplied by state officials, mid-1980

Alabama

Governor — Forrest "Fob" James, D., $50,000.
Lt. Gov. — George McMillan Jr. D., $65 per legislative day, plus annual salary of $400 per month.
Sec. of State — Don Siegelman, D., $25,800.
Atty. Gen. — Charles Graddick, D., $25,800.
Treasurer — Mrs. Annie Laurie Gunter, D., $25,800.
Legislature: meets annually the first Tuesday in Apr. (first year of term of office, first Tuesday in Feb. (2d and 3d years), 2d Tuesday in Jan. (4th year) at Montgomery. Members receive $400 per month, plus $65 per day during legislative sessions, and mileage of 10c per mile.
Senate — Dem., 35; Rep., 0. Total, 35.
House — Dem., 101; Rep., 4. Total, 105.

Alaska

Governor — Jay S. Hammond, R., $70,000.
Lt. Gov. — Terry Miller, R., $65,300.
Atty. General — Wilson Condon, D., $63,100.
Legislature: meets annually in January at Juneau, for as long as may be necessary. First session in odd years. Members receive $17,280 per year plus $67 per day while in session (Juneau legislators receive $50 per day). Also $4,000 for postage, personal stationery, and other expenses.
Senate — Dem., 9; Rep., 11. Total, 20.
House — Dem., 25; Rep., 14; Libertarian 1. Total, 40.

Arizona

Governor — Bruce Babbitt, D., $50,000.
Sec. of State — Rose Mofford, D., $28,000.
Atty. Gen. — Bob Corbin, R., $45,000.
Treasurer — Clark Dierks, R., $30,000.
Legislature: meets annually in January at Phoenix. Each member receives an annual salary of $6,000.
Senate — Dem., 14; Rep., 16. Total, 30.
House — Dem., 18; Rep., 42. Total, 60.

Arkansas

Governor — Bill Clinton, D., $35,000.
Lt. Gov. — Joe Purcell, D., $14,000.
Sec. of State — Paul Riviere, D., $22,500.
Atty. Gen. — Steve Clark, D., $26,500.
Treasurer — Mrs. Nancy J. Hall, D., $22,500.
General Assembly: meets odd years in January at Little Rock. Members receive $7,500 per year, $45 a day while in regular session, plus 13c a mile travel expense.
Senate — Dem., 35; Rep., 0. Total, 35.
House — Dem., 94; Rep., 6. Total, 100.

California

Governor — Edmund G. Brown Jr., D., $49,100.
Lt. Gov. — Mike Curb, R., $42,500.
Sec. of State — March Fong Eu, D., $42,500.
Controller — Kenneth Cory, D., $42,500.
Atty. Gen. — George Deukmejian, R., $47,500.
Treasurer — Jesse M. Unruh, D., $42,500.
Legislature: meets at Sacramento; regular sessions commence on the first Monday in Dec. of every even-numbered year; each session lasts 2 years. Members receive $28,110 per year plus mileage and $46 per diem.
Senate — Dem., 23; Rep., 17. Total, 40.
Assembly — Dem., 50; Rep., 30. Total, 80.

Colorado

Governor — Dick Lamm, D., $50,000.
Lt. Gov. — Nancy Dick, D., $25,000.
Secy. of State — Mary Estill Buchanan, R., $27,500.
Atty. Gen. — J.D. MacFarlane, D., $35,000.
Treasurer — Roy Romer, D., $27,500.
General Assembly: meets annually in January at Denver. Members receive $12,000 annually, plus $50 per day for non-session meetings up to a maximum of $1,050 in any calendar year.
Senate — Dem., 13; Rep., 22. Total, 35.
House — Dem., 27; Rep., 38. Total, 65.

Connecticut

Governor — Ella T. Grasso. D., $42,000.
Lt. Gov. — William A. O'Neill, D., $25,000.
Sec. of State — Barbara B. Kennelly, D., $25,000.
Treasurer — Henry E. Parker, D., $25,000.
Comptroller — J. Edward Caldwell, D., $25,000.
Atty. Gen. — Carl R. Ajello, D., $38,500.
General Assembly: meets annually odd years in January and even years in February at Hartford. Salary $17,000 per 2-year term plus $2,000 per 2-year term for expenses, plus 15c per mile travel allowance.
Senate — Dem., 26; Rep., 10. Total, 36.
House — Dem., 103; Rep., 48. Total, 151.

Delaware

Governor — Pierre S. duPont 4th, R., $35,000.

Lt. Gov. — James D. McGinnis, D., $12,000.
Sec. of State — Glenn C. Kenton, R., $35,400.
Atty. Gen. — Richard S. Gebelein, R., $30,000.
Treasurer — Thomas R. Carper, D., $18,000.
General Assembly: meets annually at Dover from the 2d Tuesday in January to midnight June 30. Members receive $9,000 base salary.
Senate — Dem., 13; Rep., 8. Total, 21.
House — Dem., 20; Rep., 21. Total, 41.

Florida

Governor — Robert Graham, D., $56,017.
Lt. Gov. — Wayne Mixon, D., $44,814.
Sec. of State — George Firestone, D., $44,814.
Comptroller — Gerald Lewis, D., $44,814.
Atty. Gen. — Jim Smith, D., $44,814.
Treasurer — Bill Gunter, D., $44,814.
Legislature: meets annually in April at Tallahassee. Members receive $12,000 per year plus expense allowance while on official business.
Senate — Dem., 30; Rep., 10. Total, 40.
House — Dem., 89; Rep., 31. Total, 120.

Georgia

Governor — George Busbee, D., $50,000.
Lt. Gov. — Zell Miller, D., $28,846.
Sec. of State — David B. Poythress, D., $38,400.
Comptroller General — Johnnie L. Caldwell, D., $38,400.
Atty. Gen. — Arthur K. Bolton, D., $46,000.
General Assembly: meets annually at Atlanta. Members receive $7,200 per year. During session $36 per day for expenses.
Senate — Dem., 51; Rep., 5. Total, 56.
House — Dem., 161; Rep., 19. Total, 180.

Hawaii

Governor — George R. Ariyoshi, D., $50,000.
Lt. Gov. — Jean King, D., $45,000.
Dir., Budg. & Finance — Eileen Anderson, D., $42,500.
Atty. Gen. — Wayne Minami, D., $42,500.
Comptroller — Hideo Murakami, D., $42,500.
Dir., Finance & Budget — Jensen S. L. Hee, D., $42,500.
Legislature: meets annually on 3d Wednesday in January at Honolulu. Members receive $12,000 per year plus expenses.
Senate — Dem., 18. Rep., 7. Total, 25.
House — Dem., 42. Rep., 9. Total, 51.

Idaho

Governor — John V. Evans, D., $40,000.
Lt. Gov. — Philip E. Batt, R., $12,000.
Sec. of State — Pete T. Cenarrusa, R., $28,000.
Treasurer — Marjorie Ruth Moon, D., $28,000.
Atty. Gen. — David Leroy, R., $35,000.
Legislature: meets annually on the Monday after the first day in January at Boise. Members receive $4,200 per year, plus $25 per day when authorized, plus travel allowances.
Senate — Dem., 16; Rep., 19. Total, 35.
House — Dem., 20; Rep., 50. Total, 70.

Illinois

Governor — James R. Thompson, R., $58,000.
Lt. Gov. — David C. O'Neal, R., $45,500.
Sec. of State — Alan J. Dixon, D., $50,500.
Comptroller — Roland W. Burris, D., $48,000.
Atty. Gen. — William J. Scott, R., $50,500.
Treasurer — Jerome A. Cosentimo, D., $48,000.
General Assembly: meets annually in January at Springfield. Members receive $28,000 per annum.
Senate — Dem., 32; Rep., 27. Total, 59.
House — Dem., 89; Rep., 88. Total, 177.

Indiana

Governor — Otis R. Bowen, R., $36,000 plus discretionary expenses.
Lt. Gov. — Robert Orr, R., $23,500 plus legislative per diem.
Sec. of State — Edwin J. Simcox, R., $34,000.
Atty. Gen. — Theodore L. Sendak, R., $34,000.
Treasurer — Julian Ridlen, R., $34,000.
General Assembly: meets annually in January. Members receive $8,000 per year plus $44 per day while in session, $12.50 per day while not in session.
Senate — Dem., 21; Rep., 29. Total, 50.
House — Dem., 46; Rep., 54. Total, 100.

Iowa

Governor — Robert D. Ray, R., $55,000 plus $5,000 expenses.
Lt. Gov. — Terry Branstad, R., $18,000 plus personal expenses and travel allowances at same rate as for a senator.
Sec. of State — Melvin D. Synhorst, R., $30,000.
Atty. Gen. — Tom Miller, D., $40,000.
Treasurer — Maurice E. Baringer, R., $30,000.
General Assembly: meets annually in January at Des Moines. Members receive $12,000 annually plus maximum expense allowance of $30 per day for first 120 days of first session, and first 100 days of 2d session; mileage expenses at 15c a mile.
Senate — Dem., 22; Rep., 28. Total, 50.
House — Dem., 56; Rep., 44. Total, 100.

Kansas

Governor — John Carlin, D., $45,000.
Lt. Gov. — Paul V. Dugan, D., $13,500 plus expenses.
Sec. of State — Jack H. Brier, R., $27,500.
Atty. Gen. — Robert T. Stephan, R., $40,000.
Treasurer — Joan Finney, D., $27,500.
Legislature: meets annually in January at Topeka. Members receive $40 a day plus $50 a day expenses while in session, plus $400 per month while not in session.
Senate — Dem., 19; Rep., 21. Total, 40.
House — Dem., 56; Rep., 69. Total, 125.

Kentucky

Governor — John Y. Brown Jr., D., $45,000.
Lt. Gov. — Martha A. Collins, D., $38,640.
Sec. of State — Francis Jones Mills, D., $38,640.
Atty. Gen. — Steve Beshear, D., $38,640.
Treasurer — Drexel Davis, D., $38,640.
General Assembly: meets even years in January at Frankfort. Members receive $50 per day and $75 per day during session and $750 per month for expenses for interim.
Senate — Dem., 29; Rep., 9. Total, 38.
House — Dem., 75; Rep., 25. Total, 100.

Louisiana

Governor — David C. Treen, R., $52,400.
Lt. Gov. — Robert L. Freeman, D., $42,400.
Sec. of State — James H. Brown, D., $37,400.
Atty. Gen. — William J. Guste Jr., D., $37,400.
Treasurer — Mary Evelyn Parker, D., $37,400.
Legislature: meets annually for 60 legislative days commencing on 3d Monday in April. Members receive $50 per day and mileage at 19c a mile for 8 round trips, plus $1,000 per month expense allowance.
Senate — Dem., 39; Rep., 0. Total, 39.
House — Dem., 96; Rep., 9. Total, 105.

Maine

Governor — Joseph E. Brennan, D., $35,000.
Sec. of State — Rodney Quinn, D., $25,000.
Atty. Gen. — Richard S. Cohen, R., $36,637.
Treasurer — Jerrold B. Speers, R., $25,000.
Legislature: meets biennially in January at Augusta. Members receive $4,500 for regular sessions, $2,500 for special session plus expenses; presiding officers receive 50% more.
Senate — Dem., 13; Rep., 19; 1 Ind. Total, 33.
House — Dem., 77; Rep., 73; 1 Ind. Total, 151.

Maryland

Governor — Harry Hughes, D., $60,000.
Lt. Gov. — Samuel Bogley, D., $52,500.
Comptroller — Louis L. Goldstein, D., $50,000.
Atty. Gen. — Stephen H. Sachs, D., $50,000.
Sec. of State — Fred L. Winiland, D., $36,000.
Treasurer — William S. James, D., $50,000.
General Assembly: meets 90 days annually on the 2d Wednesday in January at Annapolis. Members receive $16,750 per year.
Senate — Dem., 40; Rep., 7. Total, 47.
House — Dem., 125; Rep., 16. Total, 141.

Massachusetts

Governor — Edward J. King, D., $60,000.
Lt. Gov. — Thomas P. O'Neill 3d, D., $40,000.
Sec. of the Commonwealth — Michael Joseph Connolly, D., $40,000.
Atty. Gen. — Francis X. Bellotti, D., $47,500.
Treasurer — Robert Q. Crane, D., $40,000.
General Court (Legislature): meets each January in Boston. Salaries $20,335 per annum.
Senate — Dem., 34; Rep., 6. Total, 40.
House — Dem., 130; Rep., 30. Total, 160.

Michigan

Governor — William G. Milliken, R., $61,500.
Lt. Gov. — James H. Brickley, R., $42,500.
Sec. of State — Richard H. Austin, D., $60,000.
Atty. Gen. — Frank J. Kelley, D., $60,000.
Treasurer — Allison Green, Non-Part., $47,950.
Legislature: meets annually in January at Lansing. Members receive $25,500 per year, plus $4,900 expense allowance.
Senate — Dem., 24; Rep., 14. Total, 38.
House — Dem., 68; Rep., 42. Total, 110.

Minnesota

Governor — Al Quie, IR, $58,000.

Lt. Gov. — Lou Wangberg, IR, $36,000.
Sec. of State — Joan Anderson Growe, DFL., $30,000.
Atty. Gen. — Warren Spannaus, DFL., $49,000.
Treasurer — Jim Lord, DFL., $30,000.
Legislature: meets for a total of 120 days within every 2 years at St. Paul. Members receive $18,500 per year, plus expense allowance during session.
Senate — DFL., 45; IR, 22. Total, 67.
House — DFL., 68; IR, 66. Total, 134.
(DFL means Democratic-Farmer-Labor. IR means Independent Republican.)

Mississippi

Governor — William Winter, D., $53,000.
Lt. Gov. — Brad Dye, D., $34,000 per regular legislative session, plus expense allowance.
Sec. of State — Edwin Lloyd Pittman, D., $34,000.
Atty. Gen. — William A. Allain, D., $41,000.
Treasurer — John L. Dale, D., $34,000.
Legislature: meets annually in January at Jackson. Members receive $8,100 per regular session plus travel allowance, and $210 per month while not in session.
Senate — Dem., 48; Rep., 4. Total, 52.
House — Dem., 116; Rep., 4; Ind., 2. Total, 122.

Missouri

Governor — Joseph P. Teasdale, D., $37,500.
Lt. Gov. — William C. Phelps, R., $16,000.
Sec. of State — James C. Kirkpatrick, D., $25,000.
Atty. Gen. — John Ashcroft, R., $25,000.
Treasurer — James I. Spainhower, D., $20,000.
General Assembly: meets annually in Jefferson City on the first Wednesday after first Monday in January; adjournment in odd-numbered years by June 30, in even-numbered years by May 15. Members receive $15,000 annually.
Senate — Dem., 22; Rep., 12. Total, 34.
House — Dem., 117; Rep., 46. Total, 163.

Montana

Governor — Thomas L. Judge, D., $37,500.
Lt. Gov. — Ted Schwinden, D., $26,800.
Sec. of State — Frank Murray, D., $24,500.
Atty. Gen. — Mike Greely, D., $34,500.
Legislative Assembly: meets odd years in January at Helena. Members receive $37.38 per legislative day plus $40 per day for expenses while in session.
Senate — Dem., 24; Rep., 26. Total, 50.
House — Dem., 55; Rep., 45. Total, 100.

Nebraska

Governor — Charles Thone, R., $40,000.
Lt. Gov. — Roland Luedtke, R., $32,000.
Sec. of State — Allen J. Beermann, R., $32,000.
Atty. Gen. — Paul Douglas, R., $39,500.
Treasurer — Frank Marsh, R., $32,000.
Legislature: meets annually in January at Lincoln. Members receive salary of $4,800 annually plus travelling expenses for one round trip to and from session.
Unicameral body composed of 49 members who are elected on a nonpartisan ballot and are classed as senators.

Nevada

Governor — Robert List, R., $50,000.
Lt. Gov. — Myron E. Leavitt, D., $8,000 plus $60 per day when acting as governor and president of the Senate during legislative sessions.
Sec. of State — William D. Swackhamer, D., $32,500.
Comptroller — Wilson McGowen, R., $31,500.
Atty. Gen. — Richard H. Bryan, D., $40,500.
Treasurer — Stanton B. Colton, D., $31,500.
Legislature: meets odd years in January at Carson City. Members receive $80 per day for 60 days (20 days for special sessions), plus per diem of $40 per day for entire length of session. Travel allowance of 17c per mile.
Senate — Dem., 15; Rep., 5. Total, 20.
Assembly — Dem., 26; Rep., 14. Total, 40.

New Hampshire

Governor — Hugh J. Gallen, D., $44,520.
Sec. of State — William M. Gardner, D., $31,270.
Atty. Gen. — Gregory H. Smith, $38,690.
Comptroller — Arthur H. Fowler.
Treasurer — Robert W. Flanders, R., $31,270.
General Court (Legislature): meets odd years in January at Concord. Members receive $200; presiding officers $250.
Senate — Dem., 12; Rep., 12. Total, 24.
House — Rep., 225; Dem., 173; 2 vacancies. Total, 400.

New Jersey

Governor — Brendan Byrne, D., $65,000.
Sec. of State — Donald Lan, $49,000.
Atty. Gen. — John J. Degnan, $49,000.
Treasurer — Clifford Goldman, $49,000.
Legislature: meets annually in January at Trenton. Members receive $10,000 per year, except president of Senate and speaker of Assembly who receive 1/3 more.
Senate — Dem., 27; Rep., 13. Total, 40.
Assembly — Dem., 43; Rep. 37. Total, 80.

New Mexico

Governor — Bruce King, D., $50,000.
Lt. Gov. — Roberto Mondragon, D., $35,000. $75 per day when presiding over Senate. Acting governor, $100 per day.
Sec. of State — Shirley Hooper, D., $35,000.
Atty. Gen. — Jeff Bingaman, D., $40,000.
Treasurer — Jan Alan Hartke, D., $35,000.
Legislature: meets in January at Sante Fe; odd years for 60 days, even years for 30 days. Members receive $40 per day while in session.
Senate — Dem., 32; Rep., 10. Total, 42.
House — Dem., 41; Rep., 29. Total, 70.

New York

Governor — Hugh L. Carey, D., $85,000.
Lt. Gov. — Mario M. Cuomo, D., $60,000.
Sec. of State — Basil A. Paterson, D., $54,000.
Comptroller — Edward V. Regan, R., $60,000.
Atty. Gen. — Robert Abrams, D., $60,000.
Legislature: meets annually in January at Albany. Members receive $23,500 per year.
Senate — Dem., 25; Rep., 35. Total, 60.
Assembly — Dem., 86; Rep., 64. Total, 150.

North Carolina

Governor — James B. Hunt, D., $50,085 plus $10,000 per year expenses.
Lt. Gov. — James C. Green, D., $41,484 per year, plus $10,000 per year expense allowance.
Sec. of State — Thad Eure, D., $41,484.
Atty. Gen. — Rufus L. Edmisten, D., $46,728.
Treasurer — Harlan E. Boyles, D., $41,484.
General Assembly: meets odd years in January at Raleigh. Members receive $6,000 annual salary and $1,800 annual expense allowance, plus $44 per diem subsistence and travel allowance while in session.
Senate — Dem., 44; Rep., 6. Total, 50.
House — Dem., 106; Rep., 14. Total, 120.

North Dakota

Governor — Arthur A. Link, D., $27,500.
Lt. Gov. — Wayne Sanstead, D., $5,000.
Sec. of State — Ben Meier, R., $22,500.
Atty. Gen. — Allen I. Olson, R., $25,000.
Treasurer — Walter Christensen, $22,500.
Legislative Assembly: meets odd years in January at Bismarck. Members receive $65 per day during session and $150 per month when not in session.
Senate — Dem., 15; Rep., 35. Total, 50.
House — Dem., 71; Rep., 29. Total, 100.

Ohio

Governor — James A. Rhodes, R., $50,000.
Lt. Gov. — George V. Voinovich, R., $30,000.
Sec. of State — Anthony J. Celebrezze Jr., D., $50,000.
Atty. Gen. — William J. Brown, D., $50,000.
Treasurer — Gertrude W. Donahey, D., $50,000.
General Assembly: meets odd years at Columbus on first Monday in January. Members receive $22,500 per annum.
Senate — Dem., 18; Rep., 15. Total, 33.
House — Dem., 62; Rep., 37. Total, 99.

Oklahoma

Governor — George Nigh, D., $48,000.
Lt. Gov. — Spencer T. Bernard, D., $27,500.
Sec. of State — Jeannette B. Edmondson, D., $24,000.
Atty. Gen. — Jan Cartwright, D., $35,000.
Treasurer — Leo Winters, D., $30,000.
Legislature: meets annually in January at Oklahoma City. Members receive $12,948.
Senate — Dem., 40; Rep., 8. Total, 48.
House — Dem., 75; Rep., 26. Total, 101.

Oregon

Governor — Victor Atiyeh, R., $50,372, plus $1,000 monthly expenses.
Sec. of State — Norma Paulus, R., $41,461.
Atty. Gen. — James A. Redden, R., $41,461.
Treasurer — Clay Myers, R., $41,461.
Legislative Assembly: meets odd years in January at Salem. Members receive $654 monthly and $44 expenses per day while in session; $225 per month while not in session.
Senate — Dem., 23; Rep., 7. Total, 30.
House — Dem., 34; Rep., 26. Total, 60.

Pennsylvania

Governor — Dick Thornburgh, R., $66,000.
Lt. Gov. — William W. Scranton 3d, R., $49,500.
Sec. of the Commonwealth — William R. Davis, R., $38,500.
Atty. Gen. — Harvey Bartle, 3d (act.), R., $44,000.
Treasurer — Robert E. Casey, D., $42,500.
General Assembly — convenes annually in January at Harrisburg. Members receive $25,000 per year plus $7,500 for expenses.
Senate — Dem., 28; Rep., 22. Total, 50.
House — Dem., 103; Rep., 99; 1 vacancy. Total, 203.

Rhode Island

Governor — J. Joseph Garrahy, D., $42,500.
Lt. Gov. — Thomas R. DiLuglio, D., $30,500.
Sec. of State — Robert F. Burns, D., $30,500.
Atty. Gen. — Dennis J. Roberts 2d, D., $36,875.
Treasurer — Anthony J. Solomon, D., $30,500.
General Assembly: meets annually in January at Providence. Members receive $5 per day for 60 days, and travel allowance of 8c per mile.
Senate — Dem., 45; Rep., 5. Total, 50.
House — Dem., 84; Rep., 16. Total, 100.

South Carolina

Governor — Richard W. Riley, D., $60,000.
Lt. Gov. — Nancy Stevenson, D., $30,000.
Sec. of State — John T. Campbell, D., $45,000.
Comptroller Gen. — Earle E. Morris Jr., D., $45,000.
Atty. Gen. — Daniel R. McLeod, D., $45,000.
Treasurer — G.L. Patterson Jr., D., $45,000.
General Assembly: meets annually in January at Columbia. Members receive $10,000 per year and expense allowance of $35 per day, plus travel and postage allowance.
Senate — Dem., 43; Rep., 3. Total, 46.
House — Dem. 108; Rep., 16. Total, 124.

South Dakota

Governor — William J. Janklow, R., $45,000.
Lt. Gov. — Lowell C. Hansen 2d, R., $8,000 odd years $5,000 even years, plus $40 per day during legislative session.
Sec. of State — Alice Kundert, R., $30,000.
Treasurer — David Volk, R., $30,000.
Atty. Gen. — Mark Meierhenry, R., $38,000.
Legislature: meets annually in January at Pierre. Members receive $3,600 for 45-day session in odd-numbered years, and $2,400 for 30-day session in even-numbered years, plus $50 per legislative day.
Senate — Dem., 11; Rep., 24. Total, 35.
House — Dem., 22; Rep., 48. Total, 70.

Tennessee

Governor — Lamar Alexander, R., $68,226.
Lt. Gov. — John S. Wilder, D., $8,308.
Sec. of State — Gentry Crowell, D., $46,524.
Comptroller — William Snodgrass, D., $51,504.
Atty. Gen. — William M. Leech, D., $57,799.
General Assembly: meets annually in January at Nashville. Members receive $8,308 yearly plus $66.47 expenses for each day in session, plus mileage and expense allowances.
Senate — Dem., 20; Rep., 12; Ind., 1. Total, 33.
House — Dem., 60; Rep., 38; Ind., 1. Total, 99.

Texas

Governor — William P. Clements Jr., R., $71,400.
Lt. Gov. — Bill Hobby, D., $7,200, plus living quarters. Governor's salary when acting as governor.
Sec. of State — George W. Strake Jr., R., $44,900.
Comptroller — Bob Bullock, D., $48,500.
Atty. Gen. — Mark White, D., $48,500.
Treasurer — Warren G. Harding, D., $48,500.
Legislature: meets odd years in January at Austin. Members receive annual salary not exceeding $7,200, per diem while in session, and travel allowance.
Senate — Dem., 27; Rep., 4. Total, 31.
House — Dem., 128; Rep., 21. Total, 149.

Utah

Governor — Scott M. Matheson, D., $48,000.
Sec. of State/Lt. Gov. — David S. Monson, R., $33,500.
Atty. Gen. — Robert B. Hansen, R., $36,500.
Treasurer — Linn C. Baker, D., $33,500.
Legislature: convenes for 60 days on 2d Monday in January in odd-numbered years; for 20 days in even-numbered years; members receive $25 per day, $15 daily expenses, and mileage.
Senate — Dem., 10; Rep., 19. Total, 29.
House — Dem., 24; Rep., 51. Total, 75.

Vermont

Governor — Richard A. Snelling, R., $41,340.
Lt. Gov. — Madeleine M. Kunin, D., $17,702.
Sec. of State — James A. Guest, D., $22,472.
Atty. Gen. — M. Jerome Diamond, D., $28,938.
Treasurer — Emory H. Hebard, R., $22,472.
General Assembly: meets odd years in January at Montpelier. Members receive $200 weekly while in session, with a limit of $6,750 for a regular session and $40 per day for special session, plus specified expenses.
Senate — Dem., 10; Rep., 20. Total, 30.
House — Dem., 68; Rep., 81; Ind., 1. Total, 150.

Virginia

Governor — John N. Dalton, R., $60,000.
Lt. Gov. — Charles S. Robb, D., $16,000.
Atty. Gen. — J. Marshall Coleman, R., $45,000.
Sec. of the Commonwealth — Frederick T. Gray Jr., R., $25,000.
Treasurer — Robert C. Watts Jr., R., $37,900.
General Assembly: meets annually in January at Richmond. Members receive $5,475 annually plus expense and mileage allowances.
Senate — Dem., 34; Rep., 6. Total, 40.
House — Dem., 76; Rep., 22; Ind., 2. Total, 100.

Washington

Governor — Dixy Lee Ray, D., $63,000.
Lt. Gov. — John A. Cherberg, D., $28,600.
Sec. of State — Bruce K. Chapman, R., $31,000.
Atty. Gen. — Slade Gorton, R., $47,100.
Treasurer — Robert S. O'Brien, D., $37,200.
Legislature: meets odd years in January at Olympia. Members receive $9,800 annually, plus $44 per day while in session and 10¢ per mile.
Senate — Dem., 30; Rep., 19. Total, 49.
House — Dem., 49; Rep., 49. Total, 98.

West Virginia

Governor — John D. Rockefeller 4th, D., $60,000.
Sec. of State — A. James Manchin, D., $36,000.
Atty. Gen. — Chauncey Browning Jr., D., $42,000.
Treasurer — Larrie Bailey, D., $42,000.
Comm. of Agric. — Gus R. Douglas, D., $39,000.
Legislature: meets annually in January at Charleston. Members receive compensation fixed by citizens' commission.
Senate — Dem., 26; Rep., 8. Total, 34.
House — Dem., 74; Rep., 26. Total, 100.

Wisconsin

Governor — Lee Sherman Dreyfus, R., $65,801.
Lt. Gov. — Russell A. Olson, R., $36,151.
Sec. of State — Vel R. Phillips, D., $32,608.
Treasurer — Charles P. Smith, D., $32,608.
Atty. Gen. — Bronson C. La Follette, D., $50,780.
Superintendent of Public Instruction — Barbara Thompson, $45,840.
Legislature: meets in January at Madison. Members receive $22,632 annually plus $30 per day expenses.
Senate — Dem., 21; Rep., 12. Total, 33.
Assembly — Dem., 59; Rep., 39; 1 vacancy. Total, 99.

Wyoming

Governor — Ed Herschler, D., $55,000.
Sec. of State — Thyra Thomson, R., $37,500.
Atty. Gen. — John D. Troughton.
Treasurer — Shirley Wittler, R., $37,500.
Legislature: meets odd years in January, even years in February, at Cheyenne. Members receive $30 per day while in session, plus $44 per day for expenses.
Senate — Dem., 11; Rep., 19. Total, 30.
House — Dem., 20; Rep. 42. Total, 62.

Puerto Rico

Governor — Carlos Romero-Barcelo.
Secretaries
Agric. — Heriberto J. Martinez Torres.
Commerce — Juan H. Cintron Garcia.
Consumer Affairs — Carmen Pesquera.
Drug Addiction — Sila Nazario De Ferrer.
Educ. — Carlos Chardon.
Health — Juan Rivera Dueno.
Housing — Jorge A. Pierluiso.
Justice — Miguel Gimenez Munoz.
Labor — Carlos S. Quirós.
Natural Resources — Fred Soltero Harrington.
Social Services — Genaro Collazo Collazo.
State — Pedro Vasquez.
Trans. & Public Works — Elmer Olivieri Cintron.
Treasury — Julio Cesar Perez.
All officials belong to the New Progressive party.
Legislative Assembly: composed of a Senate of 27 members and a House of Representatives of 51 members. Meets annually, in January at San Juan.

U.S. Government Independent Agencies

Source: General Services Administration
Address: Washington, DC. Location and ZIP codes of agencies in parentheses; as of July, 1980.

ACTION — Sam Brown, dir. (806 Connecticut Ave., NW, 20525).
Administrative Conference of the United States — vacancy, chmn. (2120 L St., NW, 20037).
American Battle Monuments Commission — Mark W. Clark, chmn. (5127 Pulaski Bldg., 20314).
Appalachian Regional Commission — Albert P. Smith Jr., federal co-chmn.; Gov. John D. Rockefeller, 4th, states co-chmn. (1666 Connecticut Ave. NW, 20235).
Arms Control & Disarmament Agency — Robert Earle 2d, dir. (Department of State Bldg. 20451).

Board for International Broadcasting — John A. Gronouski, chmn. (1130 15th St., 20005).

Central Intelligence Agency — Adm. Stansfield Turner, dir. (Wash., DC 20505).
Civil Aeronautics Board — Marvin S. Cohen, chmn. (1825 Connecticut Ave. NW, 20428).
Commission on Civil Rights — Arthur S. Flemming, chmn. (1121 Vermont Ave. NW, 20425).
Commission of Fine Arts — J. Carter Brown, chmn. (708 Jackson Pl. NW, 20006).
Commodity Futures Trading Commission — James M. Stone, chmn. (2033 K St. NW, 20581).
Community Services Administration — vacancy, dir. (1200 19th St. NW, 20506).
Consumer Product Safety Commission — Susan B. King, chmn. (1111 18th St. NW, 20036).

Environmental Protection Agency — Douglas M. Costle, adm. (401 M St., SW, 20460).
Equal Employment Opportunity Commission — Eleanor Holmes Norton, chmn. (2401 E St., NW, 20506).
Export-Import Bank of the United States — John L. Moore Jr., pres. and chmn. (811 Vermont Ave. NW, 20571).

Farm Credit Administration — Ralph N. Austin, chmn. (490 L'Enfant Plaza East SW, 20578).
Federal Communications Commission — Charles D. Ferris, chmn. (1919 M St. NW, 20554).
Federal Deposit Insurance Corporation — Irvine H. Sprague, chmn. (550 17th St. NW, 20429).
Federal Election Commission — Robert O. Tiernan, chmn. (1325 K St. NW, 20463).
Federal Emergency Management Agency — John W. Macy Jr., dir. (1725 I St., 20472).
Federal Home Loan Bank Board — John Janis, chmn. (1700 G St. NW, 20552).
Federal Labor Relations Authority — Ronald W. Haughton, chmn. (1900 E St. NW, 20424).
Federal Maritime Commission — Richard J. Daschbach, chmn. (1100 L St. NW, 20573).
Federal Mediation and Conciliation Service — Wayne L. Horvitz, dir. (2100 K St. NW, 20427).
Federal Reserve System — Chairman, board of governors: Paul A. Volcker. (20th St. & Constitution Ave. NW, 20551).
Federal Trade Commission — Commissioners: Michael Pertschuk, chmn., Paul Rand Dixon, Robert Pitofsky, David A. Clanton, Patricia P. Bailey (Pennsylvania Ave. at 6th St. NW, 20580).

General Accounting Office — Comptroller general of the U.S.; Elmer B. Staats. (441 G St. NW, 20548).
General Services Administration — Roland G. Freeman, 3d, adm. (18th & F Sts. NW, 20405).
Government Printing Office — Public printer: Samuel L. Saylor, act. (North Capitol and H Sts. NW, 20401).

Inter-American Foundation — Peter T. Jones, chmn. (1515 Wilson Blvd., Rosslyn, VA 22209).
International Communication Agency — John E. Reinhardt, Dir. (1750 Pennsylvania Ave. NW, 20547).
Interstate Commerce Commission — Darius W. Gaskins Jr., chmn. (12th St. and Constitution Ave. NW, 20423).

Library of Congress — Daniel J. Boorstin, Librarian (10 First St. SE, 20540).

Merit Systems Protection Board — Ruth T. Prokop, chmn. (1717 H St. NW, 20419).

National Aeronautics and Space Administration — Robert A. Frosch, admin. (400 Maryland Ave., SW 20546).
National Capital Planning Commission — David M. Childs, chmn. (1325 G St., 20576).
National Credit Union Administration — Lawrence Connell, adm. (1776 G St. NW, 20456).
National Foundation on the Arts and Humanities — Livingston L. Biddle Jr. chmn. (arts). Joseph D. Duffey, chmn. (arts: 2401 E St. NW, 20506; humanities: 806 15th St. NW, 20506).
National Labor Relations Board — John H. Fanning, chmn. (1717 Pennsylvania Ave. NW, 20570).
National Mediation Board — Robert O. Harris, chmn. (1425 K St. NW, 20572).
National Science Foundation — Norman Hackerman, chmn. (1800 G St. NW, 20550).
National Transportation Safety Board — James B. King, chmn. (800 Independence Ave. SW, 20594).
Nuclear Regulatory Commission — John F. Ahearne, chmn. (1717 H St. NW, 20555).

Occupational Safety and Health Review Commission — Timothy F. Cleary, chmn. (1825 K St. NW, 20006).
Office of Personnel Management — Alan K. Campbell, dir., (1900 E St. NW, 20415).
Overseas Private Investment Corporation — J. Bruce Llewellyn, pres. (1129 20th St. NW, 20527).

Panama Canal Commission — Dennis P. McAuliffe, adm. (in Panama); Thomas A. Constant, secy. (in Washington).
Pennsylvania Avenue Development Corporation — Thomas F. Murphy, chmn., Board of Directors (425 13th St. NW, 20004).
Pension Benefit Guaranty Corporation — Robert E. Nagle, exec. dir. (2020 K St. NW, 20006).
Postal Rate Commission — A. Lee Fritschler, chmn. (2000 L St. NW, 20268).

Railroad Retirement Board — William P. Adams, chmn. (Rm. 444, 425 13th St. NW, 20004), Main Office (844 Rush St., Chicago, IL 60611).

Securities and Exchange Commission — Commissioners: Harold M. Williams, chmn.; Irving M. Pollack, Philip Loomis Jr., John R. Evans, Stephen J. Friedman (500 N. Capitol St., 20549).
Selective Service System — Bernard D. Rostker, dir. (600 E St. NW, 20435).
Small Business Administration — A. Vernon Weaver Jr., admin. (1441 L St. NW, 20416).
Smithsonian Institution — S. Dillon Ripley, secy. (1000 Jefferson Dr. SW, 20560).

Tennessee Valley Authority — Chairman, board of directors: S. David Freeman. (400 Commerce Ave., Knoxville, TN 37902 and Woodward Bldg. 15th and H Sts. NW, Washington, D.C. 20444).

United States International Development Cooperation Agency — Thomas Ehrlich, dir. (320 21st St., 20523).
United States International Trade Commission — Bill Alberger, chmn. (701 E St. NW, 20436).
United States Metric Board — Louis F. Polk, chmn. (1815 N. Lynn St. Arlington, Va. 22209).
United States Postal Service — William F. Bolger, postmaster general (475 L'Enfant Plaza West SW, 20260).

Veterans Administration — Max Cleland, adm. (810 Vermont Ave. NW, 20420).

NATIONAL DEFENSE

Data as of July, 1980

Chairman, Joint Chiefs of Staff
David C. Jones (USAF)

The Joint Chiefs of Staff consists of the Chairman of the Joint Chiefs of Staff; the Chief of Staff, U.S. Army; the Chief of Naval Operations; the Chief of Staff, U.S. Air Force; and the Commandant of the Marine Corps.

Army

	Date of Rank
General of the Army	
Bradley, Omar N.	Sept. 20, 1950
Chief of Staff—Edward C. Meyer	
Generals	
Guthrie, John R.	May 1, 1977
Kroesen, Frederick J.	Oct. 1, 1976
Meyer, Edward C.	June 22, 1979
Rogers, Bernard W.	Nov. 7, 1974
Shoemaker, Robert M.	Aug. 22, 1978
Starry, Donn A.	Jul. 1, 1977
Vessey Jr., John W.	Nov. 1, 1976
Warner, Volney F.	Aug. 1, 1979
Wickham, John A.	July 10, 1979

Air Force

Chief of Staff—Lew Allen Jr.
Generals

Allen, James R.	Aug. 1, 1977
Allen Jr., Lew	July 1, 1978
Creech, Wilbur L.	May 1, 1978
Davis, Benny L.	Apr. 1, 1979
Ellis, Richard H.	Sept. 30, 1973
Hill, James A.	July 10, 1978
Hill, James E.	Dec. 21, 1977
Huyser, Robert E.	Sept. 1, 1975
Jones, David C.	June 21, 1978
Mathis, Robert C.	Mar. 1, 1980
Pauly, John W.	Aug. 1, 1978
Poe, Bryce, II	Feb. 2, 1978
Slay, Alton D.	Apr. 1, 1978
Smith, William Y.	July 1, 1979

Navy

Chief of Naval Operations
Admiral Thomas B. Hayward (aviator)

Admirals

Crow, William J., Jr. (submariner)	May 30, 1980
Davis, Donald C. (aviator)	May 9, 1978
Hayward, Thomas B. (aviator)	Aug. 12, 1976
Long, Robert L.J. (submariner)	July 5, 1977
Rickover, Hyman G. (retired, serving on active duty)	Nov. 16, 1973
Shear, Harold E. (submariner)	May 24, 1974
Train, Harry D. II (surface warfare)	Oct. 1, 1978
Watkins, James D. (submariner)	Sept. 18, 1979
Whittle, Afred J. Jr. (submariner)	Aug. 1, 1978

Marine Corps

Corps Commandant, with rank of General
Robert H. Barrow . . . . July 1, 1978

Asst. Commandant and Chief of Staff, with rank of General
Kenneth McLennan . . . . July 1, 1979

Coast Guard

Commandant, with rank of Admiral
John B. Hayes. . . . . May 31, 1978

Vice Commandant, with rank of Vice Admiral
Robert H. Scarborough. . . . . June 30, 1978

United States Unified and Specified Commands

Atlantic Command—Admiral Harry D. Train II, USN

HQ Aerospace Defense Command—Lt. Gen. James V. Hartinger, USAF

U.S. European Command—General Bernard W. Rogers, USA

Pacific Command—Admiral Robert L. Long, USN

U.S. Southern Command—Lt. Gen. Wallace H. Nutting, USA

Strategic Air Command—General Richard H. Ellis, USAF

U.S. Readiness Command—General Volney F. Warner, USA

Military Air Lift Command—General Robert E. Huyser, USAF

Military Sea Lift Command—Rear Admiral John D. Johnson Jr., USN

North Atlantic Treaty Organization International Commands

Supr. Allied Commander, Europe (SACEUR)—Gen. Bernard W. Rogers, USA

Deputy SACEUR—Gen. Sir Harry Tuzo (UK), Gen. Gerd Schmuckle (Germany)

C-in-C Allied Forces, Northern Europe—Gen. Peter Whitely (UK)

C-in-C Allied Forces, Central Europe—Gen. F.J. Schulze, (Germany)

C-In-C Allied Forces, Southern Europe—Adm. Harold E. Shear, USN

Supr. Allied Commander Atlantic (SACLANT)—Adm. Harry D. Train II, USN

Deputy SACLANT—Adm. David A. Loram (UK)

Commander Strike Force South—Adm. James D. Watkins, USN

Allied Commander in Chief, Channel—Adm. Sir Edward Ashmore (UK)

Principal U.S. Military Training Centers

Army

Name, P.O. address	Zip	Nearest city
Aberdeen Proving Ground, MD	21005	Aberdeen
Carlisle Barracks, PA	17013	Carlisle
Fort Belvoir, VA	22060	Alexandria
Fort Benning, GA	31905	Columbus
Fort Bliss, TX	79916	El Paso
Fort Bragg, NC	28307	Fayetteville
Fort Devens, MA	01433	Ayer
Fort Dix, NJ	08640	Trenton
Fort Eustis, VA	23604	Newport News
Fort Gordon, GA	30905	Augusta
Fort Benjamin Harrison, IN	46216	Indianapolis
Fort Sam Houston, TX	78234	San Antonio
Fort Huachuca, AZ	85613	Sierra Vista
Fort Jackson, SC	29207	Columbia
Fort Knox, KY	40121	Louisville

Name, P.O. address	Zip	Nearest city
Fort Leavenworth, KS	66027	Leavenworth
Fort Lee, VA	23801	Petersburg
Fort McClellan, AL	36205	Anniston
Fort Monmouth, NJ	07703	Red Bank
Fort Rucker, AL	36362	Dothan
Fort Sill, OK	73503	Lawton
Fort Leonard Wood, MO	65473	Rolla
Redstone Arsenal, AL	35809	Huntsville
The Judge Advocate General School, VA	22901	Charlottesville

Navy

Name, P.O. address	Zip	Nearest city
Great Lakes, IL	60088	North Chicago
San Diego, CA	92133	San Diego
Orlando, FL	32813	Orlando

Marine Corps

Name, P.O. address	Zip	Nearest city
MCB Camp Lejeune, NC	28542	Jacksonville
MCB Camp Pendleton, CA	92055	Oceanside
MCB Camp Butler, Okinawa	FPO Seattle 98773	Futenma, Okinawa
MCB Twentynine Palms, CA	92278	Palm Springs
MCDEC Quantico, VA	22134	Quantico
MCRD Parris Island, SC	29905	Beaufort
MCRD San Diego, CA	92140	San Diego
MCAS Cherry Point, NC	28533	Cherry Point
MCAS El Toro (Santa Ana), CA	92709	Santa Ana
MCAS (Helo) Santa Ana, CA	92709	Santa Ana
MCAS (Helo) New River, NC	28540	Jacksonville
MCAS Iwakuni, Japan	FPO Seattle 98764	Iwakuni
MCAS Kaneohe Bay, Oahu, HI	FPO San Francisco 96615	Kailua
MCAS (Helo) Futenma, Okinawa	FPO Seattle 98764	Futenma
MCAS Beaufort, SC	29902	Beaufort
MCAS Yuma, AZ	85364	Yuma

MCB = Marine Corps Base. MCDEC = Marine Corps Development & Education Command. MCAS = Marine Corps Air Station. Helo = Helicopter.

Air Force

Name, P.O. address	Zip	Nearest city
Chanute AFB, IL	61878	Rantoul
Columbus AFB, MS	36701	Columbus
Fairchild AFB, MS	99011	Spokane
Goodfellow AFB, TX	76903	San Angelo
Keesler AFB, MS	39534	Biloxi
Lackland AFB, TX	78236	San Antonio
Laughlin AFB, TX	78840	Del Rio
Lowry AFB, CO	80230	Denver
Mather AFB, CA	95655	Sacramento
Maxwell AFB, AL	36112	Montgomery
Randolph AFB, TX	78148	San Antonio
Reese AFB, TX	79401	Lubbock
Sheppard AFB, TX	76311	Wichita Falls
Vance AFB, OK	73701	Enid
Williams AFB, AZ	85224	Chandler
Wright Patterson AFB, OH	45433	Dayton

Personal Salutes and Honors

The United States national salute, 21 guns, is also the salute to a national flag. The independence of the United States is commemorated by the salute to the union — one gun for each state — fired at noon on July 4 at all military posts provided with suitable artillery.

A-21-gun salute on arrival and departure, with 4 ruffles and flourishes, is rendered to the President of the United States, to an ex-President and to a President-elect. The national anthem or *Hail to the Chief,* as appropriate, is played for the President, and the national anthem for the others. A 21-gun salute on arrival and departure with 4 ruffles and flourishes, also is rendered to the sovereign or chief of state of a foreign country or a member of a reigning royal family; the national anthem of his or her country is played. The music is considered an inseparable part of the salute and will immediately follow the ruffles and flourishes without pause.

Rank	Salute—guns Arrive	Salute—guns Leave	Ruffles, flourishes	Music
Vice President of United States	19		4	Hail Columbia
Speaker of the House	19		4	March
American or foreign ambassador	19		4	Nat. anthem of official
Premier or prime minister	19		4	Nat. anthem of official
Secretary of Defense, Army, Navy or Air Force	19	19	4	March
Other Cabinet members, Senate President pro tempore, Governor, or Chief Justice of U.S.	19		4	March
Chairman, Joint Chiefs of Staff	19	19	4	
Army Chief of Staff, Chief of Naval Operations, Air Force Chief of Staff, Marine Commandant	19	19	4	General's or Admiral's March
General of the Army, General of the Air Force, Fleet Admiral	19	19	4	
Generals, Admirals	17	17	4	
Assistant Secretaries of Defense, Army, Navy or Air Force	17	17	4	March
Chairman of a Committee of Congress	17		4	March

Other salutes (on arrival only) include 15 guns for American envoys or ministers and foreign envoys or ministers accredited to the United States; 15 guns for a lieutenant general or vice admiral; 13 guns for a major general or rear admiral (upper half); 13 guns for American ministers resident and ministers resident accredited to the U.S.; 11 guns for a brigadier general or rear admiral (lower half); 11 guns for American charges d'affaires and like officials accredited to U.S.; and 11 guns for consuls general accredited to U.S.

Military Units, U.S. Army and Air Force

Army units. Squad. In infantry usually ten men under a staff sergeant. **Platoon.** In infantry 4 squads under a lieutenant. **Company.** Headquarters section and 4 platoons under a captain. (Company in the artillery is a battery; in the cavalry, a troop.) **Battalion.** Hdqts. and 4 or more companies under a lieutenant colonel. (Battalion size unit in the cavalry is a squadron.) **Brigade.** Hdqts. and 3 or more battalions under a colonel. **Division.** Hdqts. and 3 brigades with artillery, combat support, and combat service support units under a major general. **Army Corps.** Two or more divisions with corps troops under a lieutenant general. **Field Army.** Hdqts. and two or more corps with field Army troops under a general.

Air Force Units. Flight. Numerically designated flights are the lowest level unit in the Air Force. They are used primarily where there is a need for small mission elements to be incorporated into an organized unit. **Squadron.** A squadron is the basic unit in the Air Force. It is used to designate the mission units in operational commands. **Group.** The group is a flexible unit composed of two or more squadrons whose functions may be either tactical, support or administrative in nature. **Wing.** An operational wing normally has two or more assigned mission squadrons in an area such as combat, flying training or airlift. **Air Division.** The organization of the air division may be similar to that of the numbered air force, though on a much smaller scale. Functions are usually limited to operations and logistics. **Numbered Air Forces.** Normally an operationally oriented agency, the numbered air force is designed for the control of two or more air divisions or units of comparable strength. It is a flexible organization and may be of any size. Its wings may be assigned to air divisions or directly under the numbered air force. **Major Command.** A major subdivision of the Air Force that is assigned a major segment of the USAF mission.

U.S. Army Insignia and Chevrons

Source: Department of the Army

Grade — **Insignia**

General of the Armies

General John J. Pershing, the only person to have held this rank, was authorized to prescribe his own insignia, but never wore in excess of four stars. The rank originally was established by Congress for George Washington in 1799, and he was promoted to the rank by joint resolution of Congress, approved by Pres. Ford Oct. 19, 1976.

General of Army. . . Five silver stars fastened together in a circle and the coat of arms of the United States in gold color metal with shield and crest enameled.

Grade	Insignia
General	Four silver stars
Lieutenant General	Three silver stars
Major General	Two silver stars
Brigadier General	One silver star
Colonel	Silver eagle
Lieutenant Colonel	Silver oak leaf
Major	Gold oak leaf
Captain	Two silver bars
First Lieutenant	One silver bar
Second Lieutenant	One gold bar

Warrant officers

Grade Four—Silver bar with 4 enamel black bands.
Grade Three—Silver bar with 3 enamel black bands.
Grade Two—Silver bar with 2 enamel black bands.
Grade One—Silver bar with 1 enamel black band.

Non-commissioned Officers

Sergeant Major of the Army (E-9). Same as Command Sergeant Major (below) but with 2 stars. Also wears distinctive red and white shield on lapel.

Command Sergeant Major (E-9). Three chevrons above three arcs with a 5-pointed star with a wreath around the star between the chevrons and arcs.

Sergeant Major (E-9). Three chevrons above three arcs with a five-pointed star between the chevrons and arcs.

First Sergeant (E-8). Three chevrons above three arcs with a lozenge between the chevrons and arcs.

Master Sergeant (E-8). Three chevrons above three arcs.

Platoon Sergeant or Sergeant First Class (E-7). Three chevrons above two acrs.

Staff Sergeant (E-6). Three chevrons above one arc.

Sergeant (E-5). Three chevrons.

Corporal (E-4). Two chevrons.

Specialists

Specialist Seven (E-7). Three arcs above the eagle device.
Specialist Six (E-6). Two arcs above the eagle device.
Specialist Five (E-5). One arc above the eagle device.
Specialist Four (E-4). Eagle device only.

Other enlisted

Private First Class (E-3). One chevron above one arc.
Private (E-2). One chevron.
Private (E-1). None.

U.S. Army

Source: Department of the Army

Army Military Personnel on Active Duty[1]

June 30[2]	Total strength	Commissioned officers			Warrant officers		Enlisted personnel		
		Total	Male	Female[3]	Male[4]	Female	Total	Male	Female
1940	267,767	17,563	16,624	939	763	—	249,441	249,441	—
1942	3,074,184	203,137	190,662	12,475	3,285	—	2,867,762	2,867,762	—
1943	6,993,102	557,657	521,435	36,222	21,919	0	6,413,526	6,358,200	55,325
1944	7,992,868	740,077	692,351	47,726	36,893	10	7,215,888	7,144,601	71,287
1945	8,266,373	835,403	772,511	62,892	56,216	44	7,374,710	7,283,930	90,780
1946	1,889,690	257,300	240,643	16,657	9,826	18	1,622,546	1,605,847	16,699
1950	591,487	67,784	63,375	4,409	4,760	22	518,921	512,370	6,551
1955	1,107,606	111,347	106,173	5,174	10,552	48	985,659	977,943	7,716
1960	871,348	91,056	86,832	4,224	10,141	39	770,112	761,833	8,279
1965	967,049	101,812	98,029	3,783	10,285	23	854,929	846,409	8,520
1968	1,567,900	145,988	140,919	5,069	20,158	27	1,401,727	1,391,016	10,711
1969	1,509,637	148,836	143,699	5,137	23,734	20	1,337,047	1,316,326	10,721
1970	1,319,735	143,704	138,469	5,235	23,005	13	1,153,013	1,141,537	11,476
1971	1,120,822	130,261	125,240	5,021	18,670	19	971,872	960,047	11,825
1972	807,985	105,364	100,961	4,403	15,907	19	686,695	674,346	12,349
1973	798,177	101,194	96,936	4,258	14,990	21	681,972	665,515	16,457
1974	780,464	91,873	87,504	4,369	14,106	19	674,466	648,138	26,328
1975	781,316	89,756	85,184	4,572	13,214	22	678,324	640,621	37,703
1976 (Apr. 30)	766,979	85,515	80,588	4,927	12,748	30	668,686	625,792	42,894
1977 (Mar. 31)	774,664	84,984	79,599	5,385	13,005	36	676,639	631,410	45,229
1978 (May 31)	772,202	96,553	90,749	5,804	13,160	57	662,432	614,961	47,471
1979 (May 31)	757,822	87,420	80,922	6,498	13,181	78	657,143	606,872	50,271
1980 (Mar. 31)	762,739	83,117	76,237	6,880	13,093	103	666,426	608,223	58,203

(1) Represents strength of the active Army, including Philippine Scouts, retired Regular Army personnel on extended active duty, and National Guard and Reserve personnel on extended active duty; excludes U.S. Military Academy cadets, contract surgeons, and National Guard and Reserve personnel not on extended active duty.
(2) Data for 1940 to 1947 include personnel in the Army Air Forces and its predecessors (Air Service and Air Corps).
(3) Includes: women doctors, dentists, and Medical Service Corps officers for 1946 and subsequent years, women in the Army Nurse Corps for all years, and the Women's Army Corps and Women's Medical Specialists Corps (dieticians, physical therapists, and occupational specialists) for 1943 and subsequent years.
(4) Act of Congress approved April 27, 1926, directed the appointment as warrant officers of field clerks still in active service. Includes flight officers as follows: 1943, 5,700; 1944, 13,615; 1945, 31,117; 1946, 2,580.

U.S. Navy Insignia

Source: Department of the Navy

Navy

Stripes and corps device are of gold embroidery.

	Stripes
Fleet Admiral	1 two inch with 4 one-half inch.
Admiral	1 two inch with 3 one-half inch.
Vice Admiral.	1 two inch with 2 one-half inch.
Rear Admiral	1 two inch with 1 one-half inch.
Commodore (War time only)	1 two inch.
Captain.	4 one-half inch.
Commander	3 one-half inch.
Lieut. Commander	2 one-half inch, with 1 one-quarter inch between.
Lieutenant	2 one-half inch.
Lieutenant (j.g.)	1 one-half inch with one-quarter inch above.
Ensign	1 one-half inch.

Warrant Officers—One 1/2" (1/2" for Warrant officer W-1) broken with 1/2" intervals of blue as follows:

Chief Warrant Officer W-4—1 break

Chief Warrant Officer W-3—2 breaks, 2" apart

Chief Warrant Officer W-2—3 breaks, 2" apart

The breaks are symmetrically centered on outer face of the sleeve.

Enlisted personnel (non-Commissioned petty officers). . .A rating badge worn on the upper left arm, consisting of a spread eagle, appropriate number of chevrons, and centered specialty mark.

Marine Corps

Marine Corps and Army officer insignia are similar. Marine Crops and Army enlisted insignia, although basically similar, differ in color, design, and fewer Marine Corps subdivisions. The Marine Corps' distinctive cap and collar ornament is a combination of the American eagle, globe, and anchor.

Coast Guard

Coast Guard insignia follow Navy custom, with certain minor changes such as the officer cap insignia. The Coast Guard shield is worn on both sleeves of officers and on the right sleeve of all enlisted men.

U.S. Naval Budget Appropriations

Fiscal year	Total amount expended	Shipbuilding conversion and modernizations	Aircraft and weapons procurement	Military construction	All other expenditures
1940	$885,769,794	$328,819,394	$24,011,998	$72,503,151	$460,435,251
1945	29,380,421,832	7,228,192,871	3,541,009,589	1,576,096,922	17,035,122,450
1950	4,065,484,778	281,328,056	452,723,233	86,054,932	3,245,378,557
1960	11,848,690,002	1,380,031,231	2,027,098,025	284,928,383	8,228,632,362
1970	2,501,628,282	2,065,660,211	3,183,464,921	333,271,852	16,919,231,298
1975	27,934,000,000	3,111,000,000	3,516,000,000	578,000,000	20,730,000,000
1978	39,639,000,000	5,780,000,000	5,820,000,000	558,000,000	27,481,000,000
1979	41,733,000,000	5,073,000,000	6,229,000,000	792,000,000	29,639,000,000
1980 (plan)	47,038,000,000	6,525,000,000	6,346,000,000	628,000,000	33,539,000,000

U.S. Navy Personnel on Active Duty

June 30	Officers[1]	Nurses	Enlisted[2]	Off. Cand.	Total
1940	13,162	442	144,824	2,569	160,997
1945	320,293	11,086	2,988,207	61,231	3,380,817
1950	42,687	1,964	331,860	5,037	381,538
1960	67,456	2,103	544,040	4,385	617,984
1970	78,488	2,273	605,899	6,000	692,660
1975	65,900	—	483,500	—	549,400
1979	62,400	—	459,500	—	521,900
1980	63,900	—	464,300	—	528,200

(1) Nurses are included after 1973. (2) Officer candidates are included after 1973.

Marine Corps Personnel On Active Duty

Yr.	Officers	Enl.	Total	Yr.	Officers	Enl.	Total	Yr.	Officers	Enl.	Total
1955	18,417	186,753	205,170	1965	17,258	172,955	190,213	1975	18,100	174,100	192,200
1960	16,203	154,408	170,621	1970	24,941	234,796	259,737	1980	17,900	167,300	185,200

The Medal of Honor

The Medal of Honor is the highest military award for bravery that can be given to any individual in the United States. The first Army Medals were awarded on March 25, 1863, and the first Navy Medals went to sailors and Marines on April 3, 1863.

The Medal of Honor, established by Joint Resolution of Congress, 12 July 1862 (amended by Act of 9 July 1918 and Act of 25 July 1963) is awarded in the name of Congress to a person who, while a member of the Armed Forces, distinguishes himself conspicuously by gallantry and intrepidity at the risk of his life above and beyond the call of duty while engaged in an action against any enemy of the United States; while engaged in military operations involving conflict with an opposing foreign force; or while serving with friendly foreign forces engaged in an armed conflict against an opposing armed force in which the United States is not a belligerent party. The deed performed must have been one of personal bravery or self-sacrifice so conspicuous as to clearly distinguish the individual above his comrades and must have involved risk of life. Incontestable proof of the performance of service is exacted and each recommendation for award of this decoration is considered on the standard of extraordinary merit.

Prior to World War I, the 2,625 Army Medal of Honor awards up to that time were reviewed to determine which past awards met new stringent criteria. The Army removed 911 names from the list, most of them former members of a volunteer infantry group during the Civil War who had been induced to extend their enlistments when they were promised the Medal.

Since that review Medals of Honor have been awarded in the following numbers:

World War I	124	Korean War	131
World War II	432	Vietnam (to date)	238

U.S. Air Force

Source: Department of the Air Force

The Army Air forces were started Aug. 1, 1907, as the Aeronautical Division of the Signal Corps, U.S. Army. The division consisted of one officer and two enlisted men, and it was more than a year before it carried out its first mission in an airplane of its own. When the U.S. entered World War I (April 6, 1917), the Aviation Service, as it was called then, had 55 planes and 65 officers, only 35 of whom were fliers. On the day the Japanese struck at Pearl Harbor (Dec. 7, 1941), the Army Air Forces, as they had been renamed 6 months previously, had 10,329 planes, of which only 2,846 were suited for combat service. But when the Army's air arm reached its peak during World War II (in July, 1944), it had 79,908 of all types of aircraft and (in May 1945) 43,248 combat aircraft and (in March, 1944) 2,411,294 officers and enlisted men. The Air Force was established under the Armed Services Unification Act of July 26, 1947.

USAF Personnel at Home and Overseas — Officers and Enlisted

June 30	Continental U.S.	Overseas	Total	June 30	Continental U.S.	Overseas	Total
1940	40,229	10,936	51,165	1965	635,430	189,232	824,662
1945	1,153,373	1,128,886	2,282,259	1970	531,386	255,819	787,205
1950	317,816	93,461	411,277	1975	457,484	150,853	608,337
1955	689,635	270,311	959,946	1978	439,762	130,454	570,216
1957[1]	651,674	268,161	919,835	1979	417,196	140,660	557,856
1960[2]	607,383	207,369	814,752	1980	434,646	118,604	553,250

(1) Since 1957 continental U.S. includes Air Force Academy Cadets as follows: (1957) 504; (1960) 1,949; (1963) 2,660; (1964) 2,838; (1965) 2,907; (1966) 3,152; (1967) 3,361; (1968) 3,652; (1969) 3,941; (1970) 4,144; (1971) 2,997; (1972) 2,885; (1973) 4,356; (1974) 4,412; (1975) 4,414; (1976) 4,415; (1977) 4,680; (1978) 4,524; (1979) 4,578; (1980) 4,618.
(2) Since 1960 Overseas includes Alaska and Hawaii. All figures include Mobilized Personnel.

USAF Military Personnel

June 30	Officers & airmen	Male commissioned officers: USAF (Reg.) & RA	USAFR & ORC	ANG & NG	AFUS & AUS	Total warrant officers
1955	959,946	23,463	105,587	984	2	3,961
1960	814,752	49,584	72,115	248	3	4,069
1965	824,662	62,076	62,537	280	54	2,532
1970	787,205	63,678	65,852	168	105	639
1975	603,317	57,854	42,131	128	28	39
1978	570,216	56,838	39,598	148	18	2
1979	557,856	55,815	39,688	142	15	2
1980	553,250	54,621	35,454	115	6	1

(1) Selected reserves only.

Female Commissioned Officers, and Enlisted Personnel

June 30	Female commissioned officers: Total	USAF	Nurses	WMSC	Female WO	Enlisted personnel: Total	Male	Female
1960	3,858	679	3,020	159	5	685,063	679,412	5,651
1965	4,099	708	3,185	206	1	690,177	685,436	4,741
1970	4,667	1,072	3,407	188	0	657,402	648,415	8,987
1975	4,981	1,542	3,236	203	0	503,176	477,944	25,232
1978	5,762	2,269	3,112	381	0	478,139	437,253	40,886
1979	6,698	3,061	3,128	509	0	466,774	421,016	45,758
1980	8,060	4,291	3,200	569	0	454,994	404,480	50,514

Veteran Population

Source: Veterans Administration

	April 1980
Veterans in civil life, end of month — Total	**30,076,000**
War Veterans — Total	**26,159,000**
Vietnam Era — Total (a)	8,965,000
And service in Korean Conflict	548,000
No service in Korean Conflict	8,417,000
Korean Conflict — Total (includes line 4)	5,841,000
And service in WW II	1,175,000
No service in WW II	4,666,000
World War II (includes line 7)	12,526,000
World War I	550,000
Spanish-American War	163
Post-Vietnam Era	863,000
Service between Korean Conflict (January 31, 1955) and Vietnam (August 5, 1964) only (b)	3,054,000

(a) Service after Aug. 4, 1964; (b) excludes men who served on active duty for training only.

Pension Cases and Compensation Payments

Fiscal year	Living veteran cases No.	Deceased veteran cases No.	Total cases No.	Total disbursement Dollars	Fiscal year	Living veteran cases No.	Deceased veteran cases No.	Total cases No.	Total disbursement Dollars
1890	415,654	122,290	537,944	106,093,850	1965	3,204,275	1,277,009	4,481,284	3,901,598,010
1900	752,510	241,019	993,529	138,462,130	1970	3,127,338	1,487,176	4,614,514	5,113,649,490
1910	602,622	318,461	921,083	159,974,056	1973	3,256,746	1,654,287	4,911,033	6,426,647,000
1920	419,627	349,916	769,543	316,418,029	1974	3,241,263	1,627,482	4,868,745	6,615,599,000
1930	542,610	298,223	840,833	418,432,808	1975	3,226,701	1,628,146	4,854,847	7,600,000,000
1940	610,122	239,176	849,298	429,138,465	1976	3,235,778	1,630,830	4,866,608	8,074,488,000
1950	2,368,238	658,123	3,026,361	2,009,462,298	1977	3,272,821	1,628,488	4,901,309	8,874,720,000
1955	2,668,786	808,303	3,477,089	2,634,292,537	1978	3,283,120	1,622,269	4,905,389	9,371,704,000
1960	3,008,935	950,802	3,959,737	3,314,761,383	1979	3,240,283	1,529,206	4,769,489	10,324,258,000

Monthly Pay Scale of

Fiscal

Commissioned Officers

Pay grade	Army rank (Rank or pay grade)	Navy rank	Under 2 (Cumulative years of service)	Over 2	Over 3	Over 4	Over 6	Over 8
0-10[1]	General*	Admiral	$3,529.80	$3,654.00	$3,654.00	$3,654.00	$3,654.00	$3,794.10
0-9	Lieutenant General	Vice Admiral	3,128.40	3,210.60	3,278.70	3,278.70	3,278.70	3,362.40
0-8	Major General	Rear Admiral (up. half)	2,833.50	2,918.40	2,987.70	2,987.70	2,987.70	3,210.60
0-7	Brigadier General	Rear Admiral (low half)	2,354.40	2,514.60	2,514.60	2,514.60	2,627.10	2,627.10
0-6	Colonel	Captain	1,745.10	1,917.60	2,042.70	2,042.70	2,042.70	2,042.70
0-5	Lieutenant Colonel	Commander	1,395.90	1,639.20	1,752.30	1,752.30	1,752.30	1,752.30
0-4	Major	Lieutenant Comdr.	1,176.60	1,432.20	1,528.20	1,528.20	1,556.10	1,625.40
0-3	Captain	Lieutenant	1,093.50	1,222.20	1,306.50	1,445.70	1,514.70	1,569.60
0-2	First Lieutenant	Lieutenant (J.G.)	953.10	1,041.30	1,250.70	1,293.00	1,319.70	1,319.70
0-1	Second Lieutenant	Ensign	827.40	861.30	1,041.30	1,041.30	1,041.30	1,041.30
Commissioned officers with over 4 years service as enlisted members								
0-3	Capitain	Lieutenant	0.00	0.00	0.00	1,445.70	1,514.70	1,569.60
0-2	First Lieutenant	Lieutenant (J.G.)	0.00	0.00	0.00	1,293.00	1,319.70	1,361.70
0-1	Second Lieutenant	Ensign	0.00	0.00	0.00	1,041.30	1,112.10	1,153.20

Warrant Officers

Pay grade	Army rank	Navy rank	Under 2	Over 2	Over 3	Over 4	Over 6	Over 8
W-4	Chief Warrant	Comm. Warrant	1,113.90	1,194.90	1,194.90	1,222.20	1,278.00	1,334.40
W-3	Chief Warrant	Comm. Warrant	1,012.50	1,098.30	1,098.30	1,112.10	1,125.30	1,207.50
W-2	Chief Warrant	Comm. Warrant	886.30	959.10	959.10	987.00	1,041.30	1,098.30
W-1	Warrant Officer	Warrant Officer	738.90	847.20	847.20	917.70	959.10	1,000.50

Enlisted Personnel[2]

Pay grade	Army rank	Navy rank	Under 2	Over 2	Over 3	Over 4	Over 6	Over 8
E-9[3]	Sergeant Major**	Master C.P.O.	0.00	0.00	0.00	0.00	0.00	0.00
E-8[3]	Master Sergeant	Senior C.P.O.	0.00	0.00	0.00	0.00	0.00	1,061.70
E-7	Sgt. 1st Class	Chief Petty Officer	741.30	800.10	829.80	858.60	888.30	916.20
E-6	Staff Sergeant	Petty Officer 1st Class	640.20	698.10	727.20	757.80	786.00	814.80
E-5	Sergeant	Petty Officer 2nd Cl.	562.20	611.70	641.40	669.30	713.10	742.20
E-4	Corporal	Petty Officer 3rd Cl.	540.30	570.60	603.90	651.00	676.80	676.80
E-3	Private 1st Class	Seaman	519.60	548.10	570.30	592.80	592.80	592.80
E-2	Private	Seaman Apprentice	500.10	500.10	500.10	500.10	500.10	500.10
E-1	Private	Seaman Recruit	448.80	448.80	448.80	448.80	448.80	448.80

The pay scale also applies to: Coast Guard and Marine Corps, National Oceanic and Atmospheric Administration, Public Health Service, National Guard, and the Organized Reserves.

*Basic pay is limited to $4,466.40 by Level V of the Executive Schedule and further limited by Sec. 101C, P.L. 96-86 to $4,176.00 max. Four star General or Admiral—personal money allowances of $2,200 per annum, or $4,000 if Chief of Staff of the Army, Chief of Staff of the Air Force, Chief of Naval Operations, Commandant of the Marine Corps, or Commandant of the Coast Guard. Three star General or Admiral—personal money allowance of $500 per annum.

**A new title of Chief Master Sergeant created in 1965 rates E-9 classification.

(1) While serving as Chairman of Joint Chiefs of Staff, Chief of Staff of the Army, Chief of Naval Operations, Chief of Staff of the Air Forces, or Commandant of the Marine Corps, basic pay for this grade is $5,114.70 regardless of years of service, limited by Executive Schedule to $3,958.20

(2) Air Force enlisted personnel pay grades, E-9, Chief Master Sergeant; E-8, Sr. Master Sergeant; E-7, Master Sergeant; E-6, Technical Sergeant; E-5, Staff Sergeant; E-4, Sergeant; E-3, Airman 1st Class; E-2, Airman; E-1, Basic Airman.

Marine Corps enlisted ranks are as follows: E-9, Sergeant Major and Master Gunnery Sergeant; E-8, First Sergeant and Master Sergeant: E-7, Gunnery Sergeant; E-6, Staff Sergeant; E-5, Sergeant; E-4, Corporal; E-3, Lance Corporal; E-2, Private, First Class Marine; E-1, Private.

Marine Corps and Air Force officer ranks are same as Army.

(3) While serving as Sergeant Major of the Army, Master Chief Petty Officer of the Navy, Chief Master Sergeant of the Air Force, or Sergeant Major of the Marine Corps, basic pay for this grade is $1,980.90 regardless of years of service.

American Military Actions, 1900-1973

1900—Occupation of Puerto Rico (ceded to U.S., 1899).

1900—500 Marines, 1,500 Army troops help relieve Peking in Boxer Rebellion.

1900-1902—Occupation of Cuba.

1900-1902—Guerrilla war in Philippines.

1903—Sailors and Marines from U.S.S. Nashville stop Colombian Army at Panama.

1904—Brief intervention in Dominican Republic.

1906-1909—Intervention in Cuba.

1909—Brief intervention in Honduras.

1910, 1912-1913—Intervention in Nicaragua.

1911—Intervention (to collect customs) in Honduras, Nicaragua, Dominican Republic.

1912-1917—Intervention in Cuba.

1914—Intervention in Dominican Republic.

1914—April 21 to Nov. 23. Marines in Vera Cruz.

1914—Navy and Marines enter Haiti, stay until 1934.

1916—Gen. John J. Pershing and 10,000 into Northern Mexico to stop raids by Pancho Villa, Mar. 15-Nov. 24.

1916-1924—Marines in Dominican Republic.

1917—Apr. 6 to Nov. 11, 1918. War with Germany, Austria-Hungary.

1918-1920—Expeditions into North Russia, Siberia.

1918-1923—Occupation of Germany.

1922-1924—Marines in Nicaragua.

1926-1933—Marines in Nicaragua.

1927—1,000 Marines in China.

1941-1945—War with Japan, Germany, Italy and allies.

1950-1953—U.S. and other UN countries aid the Republic of Korea to repel North Korean invaders; U.S. Navy protects Taiwan.

1956—U.S. Fleet evacuates U.S. nationals during Suez crisis.

1957—U.S. Fleet to Near East during Jordan crisis.

1958—Navy, Marines and Army units support Lebanon.

1960—Navy patrol in Caribbean to protect Guatemala and Nicaragua.

1961—Army units to Vietnam.

1962—Units of Navy on Cuban quarantine duty. Marines in Thailand.

the Uniformed Services

Year 1980

Commissioned Officers

Cumulative years of service								Basic allowances for quarters	
Over 10	Over 12	Over 14	Over 16	Over 18	Over 20	Over 22	Over 26	Without dependents	With dependents
$3,794.10	$4,084.80	$4,084.80	$4,377.00*	$4,377.00*	$4,669.80*	$4,669.80*	$4,961.10*	$383.10	$479.10
3,362.40	3,501.90	3,501.90	3,794.10	3,794.10	4,084.80	4,084.80	4,377.00*	383.10	479.10
3,210.60	3,362.40	3,302.40	3,501.90	3,654.00	3,794.10	3,946.20	3,946.20	383.10	479.10
2,779.80	2,779.80	2,918.40	3,210.60	3,431.10	3,431.10	3,431.10	3,431.10	383.10	479.10
2,042.70	2,042.70	2,112.00	2,446.50	2,571.60	2,627.10	2,779.80	3,014.70	343.80	419.40
1,805.70	1,902.30	2,029.50	2,181.60	2,307.00	2,376.60	2,459.70	2,459.70	316.80	381.60
1,736.10	1,833.90	1,917.60	2,001.30	2,057.10	2,057.10	2,057.10	2,057.10	282.30	340.50
1,653.90	1,736.10	1,778.70	1,778.70	1,778.70	1,778.70	1,778.70	1,778.70	248.10	306.30
1,319.70	1,319.70	1,319.70	1,319.70	1,319.70	1,319.70	1,319.70	1,319.70	215.40	272.70
1,041.30	1,041.30	1,041.30	1,041.30	1,041.30	1,041.30	1,041.30	1,041.30	168.00	219.00
1,653.90	1,736.10	1,805.70	1,805.70	1,805.70	1,805.70	1,805.70	1,805.70	248.10	306.30
1,432.20	1,487.40	1,528.20	1,528.20	1,528.20	1,528.20	1,528.20	1,528.20	215.40	272.70
1,194.90	1,236.60	1,293.00	1,293.00	1,293.00	1,293.00	1,293.00	1,293.00	168.00	219.00

Warrant Officers

1,390.20	1,487.40	1,556.10	1,611.30	1,653.90	1,707.90	1,765.20	1,902.30	271.80	328.20
1,278.00	1,319.70	1,361.70	1,402.50	1,445.70	1,501.50	1,556.10	1,611.30	242.40	298.80
1,139.70	1,181.40	1,222.20	1,265.10	1,306.50	1,347.90	1,402.50	1,402.50	210.90	268.20
1,041.30	1,084.20	1,125.30	1,166.70	1,207.50	1,250.70	1,250.70	1,250.70	190.50	246.60

Enlisted Personnel

1,265.40	1,294.20	1,323.60	1,354.20	1,384.20	1,411.20	1,485.60	1,629.60	205.20	288.60
1,091.40	1,120.50	1,149.90	1,179.90	1,207.20	1,236.90	1,309.50	1,455.60	189.00	266.70
945.60	975.00	1,019.10	1,047.90	1,077.60	1,091.40	1,164.90	1,309.50	160.80	248.10
844.80	888.30	916.30	945.60	960.00	960.00	960.00	960.00	146.10	228.30
771.90	800.10	814.80	814.80	814.80	814.80	814.80	814.80	140.40	209.70
676.80	676.80	676.80	676.80	676.80	676.80	676.80	676.80	123.90	184.50
592.80	592.80	592.80	592.80	592.80	592.80	592.80	592.80	110.70	160.80
500.10	500.10	500.10	500.10	500.10	500.10	500.10	500.10	97.80	160.80
448.80	448.80	448.80	448.80	448.80	448.80	448.80	448.80	92.40	160.80

*Limited under existing law to $4,176.00

Basic Allowance for Subsistence

This allowance, the quarters allowance, and any other allowance are not subject to income tax.

Officers — Subsistence (food) is paid to all officers regardless of rank. . . . . $67.21 per month

Enlisted members: When on leave or authorized to mess separately. . . . . $3.21 per day

When rations in kind are not available. . . . . $3.62 per day

When assigned to duty under emergency conditions where no government messing facilities are available . . . . $4.79 per day (maximum rate)

Family Separation Allowance

Under certain conditions of family separation of more than 30 days, a member in Pay Grades E-4 (with over 4 years' service) and above will be allowed $30 a month in addition to any other allowances to which he is entitled. When separated from family and required to maintain a home for his family and one for himself, the member is entitled to an additional monthly basic allowance for quarters at the "without dependents" rate for his grade.

1962-1965—U.S. Military Assistance Command, Vietnam; units of Army, Navy, Air Force, Marine Corps, Coast Guard.

1965—Navy, Marines, Army units to Dominican Republic.

1965—American commanders in Vietnam authorized to send U.S. Armed Force into combat.

1969—President Nixon announces, June 8, first phase of withdrawal of U.S. troops from Vietnam.

1970—Army units participate in Cambodian sanctuary operations, Apr. 29-June 30.

1973—Last U.S. troops leave Vietnam, U.S. Military Assistance Command deactivated, March 29.

1973—End of all U.S. bombing operations over Indochina, Aug. 15.

The Federal Service Academies

U.S. Military Academy, West Point, N.Y. Founded 1802. Awards B.S. degree and Army commission for a 5-year service obligation. For admissions information, write Admissions Office, USMA, West Point, NY 10996.

U.S. Naval Academy, Annapolis, Md. Founded 1845. Awards B.S. degree and Navy or Marine Corps commission for a 6-year service obligation. For admissions information, write Dean of Admissions, Naval Academy, Annapolis, MD 21402.

U.S. Air Force Academy, Colorado Springs, Colo. Founded 1954. Awards B.S. degree and Air Force commission for a 5-year service obligation. For admissions information, write Registrar, U.S. Air Force Academy, CO 80840.

U.S. Coast Guard Academy, New London, Conn. Founded 1876. Awards B.S. degree and Coast Guard commission for a 5-year service obligation. For admissions information, write Director of Admissions, Coast Guard Academy, New London, CT 06320.

U.S. Merchant Marine Academy, Kings Point, N.Y. Founded 1943. Awards B.S. degree, a license as a deck, engineer, or dual officer, and a U.S. Naval Reserve commission. Service obligations vary according to options taken by the graduate. For admissions information, write Admission Office, U.S. Merchant Marine Academy, Kings Point, NY 11024.

Strategic Nuclear Armaments: U.S. and USSR

Source: International Institute for Strategic Services, London

United States

		Range[2] (statute miles)	Estimated warhead yield[3]	Deployed (July 1977)
Land-based missiles[1]				
ICBM	Titan 2	7,000	5-10 MT	54
	Minuteman 2	7,000	1-2 MT	450
	Minuteman 3	7,500	3x170 KT	550
Sea-based missiles				
SLBM (nuclear subs)	Polaris A3	2,880	3x200 KT	160
	Poseidon C3	2,880	10x50 KT	496

		Range[8] (statute miles)	Weapons load (lb)	Deployed (July 1976)
Aircraft[7]				
Long-range	B-52D	11,500	60,000	373[8]
	B-52G-H	12,500	70,000	
Medium range	FB-111A	3,800	37,500	68
Strike aircraft; land-based	F-105D	2,100	16,500	(350)[9]
	F-4C-J	2,300	16,000	
	F-111A/E	3,800	25,000	
	A-7D	3,400	15,000	
Strike aircraft: carrier-based	A-4	2,055	10,000	(200)[9]
	A-6A	3,225	18,000	
	A-7A/B/E	3,400	15,000	
	F-4	2,000	16,000	

Soviet Union

		Range[2] (statute miles)	Estimated warhead yield[3]	Deployed (July 1977)
Land-based missiles[1]				
ICBM	SS-7 Saddler	6,900	5 MT	109
	SS-8 Sasin	6,900	5 MT	
	SS-9 Scarp	7,500	18-25 MT[4]	238
	SS-11 Sego	6,500	1-2 MT[5]	840
	SS-13 Savage	5,000	1 MT	60
	SS-17	6,500	4x KT	40
	SS-18	7,500	15-25 MT[6]	50
	SS-19	6,500	6x KT	140
Sea-based missiles				
SLBM (nuclear subs)	SS-N-6-Sawfly	1,750	MT	544
	SS-N-8	4,800	MT	284

	Range[8] (statute miles)	Weapons load (lb)	Deployed (July 1976)
Aircraft[7]			
Tu-95 Bear	8,000	40,000	100
Mya-4 Bison	6,000	20,000	35
Tu-16 Badger	4,000	20,000	740
Backfire B	5,500	20,000	65
Il-28 Beagle	2,500	4,850	(1,000)[9]
Su-7 Fitter A	900	4,500	
Tu-22 Blinder	1,400	12,000	
MiG-21 Fishbed J/K/L	1,150	2,000	
MiG-27 Flogger D	1,800	2,800	
Su-17/20 Fitter C	1,100	5,000	
Su-19A Fencer	1,800	8,000	

(1) ICBM = intercontinental ballistic missile. IRBM = intermediate-range ballistic missile. MRBM = medium-range missile. SLBM = submarine-launched ballistic missile. SLCM = sub-launched cruise missile. (2) Operation range depends upon the payload carried; use of maximum payload may reduce missile range by up to 25%. (3) MT = megaton range = 1,000,000 tons of TNT equivalent or over; KT = kiloton range = 1,000 tons of TNT equivalent or more, but less than 1 MT. (4) Some SS-9 missiles carry 3 warheads of 4-5 MT each. (5) Some SS-11 missiles may carry 3xKT warheads. (6) Some SS-18 may carry 8xMT warheads. (7) All aircraft listed are dual-capable and many, especially in the categories of strike aircraft, would be more likely to carry conventional than nuclear weapons. (8) Theoretical maximum range, with internal fuel only, at optimum altitude and speed. Ranges for strike aircraft assume no weapons load. Especially in the case of strike aircraft, therefore, range falls sharply for flights at lower altitude, at higher speed, or with full weapons load. (9) Figures in parentheses are estimates of Europe-based systems only.

Women in the Armed Forces

The Army, Navy, Air Force, Marines, and Coast Guard are all fully integrated. Expansion of military women's programs began in the Department of Defense in fiscal year 1973. The planned end strength for fiscal year 1983 is approximately 199,000 which is 11.1% of the planned strength of the active forces.

Although women are prohibited by law and directives based on law from serving in combat positions, policy changes in the department have resulted in making possible the assignment of women to almost all other career fields. Career progression for women is now comparable to that for male personnel. Women are routinely assigned to overseas locations formerly closed to female personnel. Test programs have been initiated to place women in pilot training and in command of activities and units which have missions other than administration of women.

Admission of women to the service academies began in the fall of 1976 and will further the goal of increased numbers of women officers. The academies will provide single track education, allowing only for minor variations in the cadet program based on physiological differences between men and women.

Army — Information: Chief, Office of Public Affairs, Dept. of Army, Wash., DC 20310; 6,791 women officers, including Army Nurse Corps, and 57,218 enlisted women; women excluded only from direct combat roles—8% of jobs.

Army Nurse Corps — Brig. Gen. Hazel Johnson, Chief, Army Nurse Corps, Office of the Surgeon General, Dept. of Army, Wash., DC 20310; includes 30% men.

Navy — Information: Chief of Information (Code 2252), Dept. of Navy, Wash., DC 20350; 4,562 women officers; 27,372 enlisted women.

Navy Nurse Corps — Rear Adm. Frances T. Shea, Director, Navy Nurse Corps, Bureau of Medicine and Surgery, Dept. of Navy, Wash., DC 20372; 1,988 women officers; includes 30% men.

Air Force — Information: USAF Recruiting Service, Randolph Air Force Base, TX 78148; 7,787 women officers; 49,425 enlisted women.

Air Force Nurse Corps — Brig. Gen. Sarah P. Wells, Chief, Air Force Nurse Corps, Office of the Surgeon Gen., USAF, Bolling AFB, Wash., DC 20332; 4,041 officers; includes men.

Marines — Information: Commandant of the Marine Corps (Code M), Headquarters, Marine Corps, Wash., DC 20380; 468 women officers; 5,972 enlisted women.

Coast Guard — Information: Commandant (G-APA), U.S. Coast Guard, Wash., DC 20593; 80 women officers; 1,400 enlisted women.

Casualties in Principal Wars of the U.S.

Data on Revolutionary War casualties is from **The Toll of Independence,** Howard H. Peckham, ed., U. of Chicago Press, 1974.

Data prior to World War I are based on incomplete records in many cases. Casualty data are confined to dead and wounded personnel and therefore exclude personnel captured or missing in action who were subsequently returned to military control. Dash (—) indicates information is not available.

			Casualties			
Wars	Branch of service	Number serving	Battle deaths	Other deaths	Wounds not mortal[8]	Total
Revolutionary War	**Total**	—	**6,824**	**18,500**	**8,445**	**33,769**
1775-1783	Army	184,000	5,992	—	7,988	13,980
	Navy &	to	—	—	—	—
	Marines	250,000	832	—	457	1,289
War of 1812	**Total**	**[9]286,730**	**2,260**	—	**4,505**	**6,765**
1812-1815	Army	—	1,950	—	4,000	5,950
	Navy	—	265	—	439	704
	Marines	—	45	—	66	111
Mexican War	**Total**	**[9]78,718**	**1,733**	**11,550**	**4,152**	**17,435**
1846-1848	Army	—	1,721	11,500	4,102	17,373
	Navy	—	1	—	3	4
	Marines	—	11	—	47	58
Civil War	**Total**	**[9]2,213,363**	**140,414**	**224,097**	**281,881**	**646,392**
(Union forces only)	Army	2,128,948	138,154	221,374	280,040	639,568
1861-1865	Navy	—	2,112	2,411	1,710	6,233
	Marines	84,415	148	312	131	591
Confederate forces	**Total**	—	**74,524**	**59,297**	—	**133,821**
(estimate)[1]	Army	600,000	—	—	—	—
1863-1866	Navy	to	—	—	—	—
	Marines	1,500,000	—	—	—	—
Spanish-American War	**Total**	**306,760**	**385**	**2,061**	**1,662**	**4,108**
1898	Army[4]	280,564	369	2,061	1,594	4,024
	Navy	22,875	10	0	47	57
	Marines	3,321	6	0	21	27
World War I	**Total**	**4,743,826**	**53,513**	**63,195**	**204,002**	**320,710**
April 6, 1917-	Army[5]	4,057,101	50,510	55,868	193,663	300,041
Nov. 11, 1918	Navy	599,051	431	6,856	819	8,106
	Marines	78,839	2,461	390	9,520	12,371
	Coast Gd.	8,835	111	81	—	192
World War II	**Total**	**16,353,659**	**292,131**	**115,185**	**670,846**	**1,078,162**
Dec. 7, 1941-	Army[6]	11,260,000	234,874	83,400	565,861	884,135
Dec. 31, 1946[2]	Navy[7]	4,183,466	36,950	25,664	37,778	100,392
	Marines	669,100	19,733	4,778	67,207	91,718
	Coast Gd.	241,093	574	1,343	—	1,917
Korean War	**Total**	**5,764,143**	**33,629**	**20,617**	**103,284**	**157,530**
June 25, 1950-	Army	2,834,000	27,704	9,429	77,596	114,729
July 27, 1953[3]	Navy	1,177,000	458	4,043	1,576	6,077
	Marines	424,000	4,267	1,261	23,744	29,272
	Air Force	1,285,000	1,200	5,884	368	7,452
	Coast Gd.	44,143	—	—	—	—
Vietnam (preliminary)[10]	**Total**	**8,744,000**	**47,192**	**10,903**	**155,419**	**213,514**
Aug. 4, 1964-	Army	4,368,000	30,839	7,242	96,811	134,892
Jan. 27, 1973	Navy	1,842,000	1,592	907	4,180	6,679
	Marines	794,000	13,053	1,682	51,399	66,134
	Air Force	1,740,000	1,708	1,072	3,029	5,809

(1) Authoritative statistics for the Confederate Forces are not available. An estimated 26,000-31,000 Confederate personnel died in Union prisons.

(2) Data are for the period Dec. 1, 1941 through Dec. 31, 1946 when hostilities were officially terminated by Presidential Proclamation, but few battle deaths or wounds not mortal were incurred after the Japanese acceptance of Allied peace terms on Aug. 14, 1945. Numbers serving from Dec. 1, 1941-Aug. 31, 1945 were: Total—14,903,213; Army—10,420,000; Navy—3,883,520; and Marine Corps—599,693.

(3) Tentative final data based upon information available as of Sept. 30, 1954, at which time 24 persons were still carried as missing in action.

(4) Number serving covers the period April 21-Aug. 13, 1898, while dead and wounded data are for the period May 1-Aug. 31, 1898. Active hostilities ceased on Aug. 13, 1898, but ratifications of the treaty of peace were not exchanged between the United States and Spain until April 11, 1899.

(5) Includes Air Service Battle deaths and wounds not mortal include casualties suffered by American forces in Northern Russia to Aug. 25, 1919 and in Siberia to April 1, 1920. Other deaths covered the period April 1, 1917-Dec. 31, 1918.

(6) Includes Army Air Forces.

(7) Battle deaths and wounds not mortal include casualties incurred in Oct. 1941 due to hostile action.

(8) Marine Corps data for World War II, the Spanish-American War and prior wars represent the number of individuals wounded, whereas all other data in this column represent the total number (incidence) of wounds.

(9) As reported by the Commissioner of Pensions in his Annual Report for Fiscal Year 1903.

(10) Number serving covers the period Aug. 4 1964-Jan. 27, 1973 (date of ceasefire). Number of casualties incurred in connection with the conflict in Vietnam from Jan. 1, 1961-Sept. 30, 1977. Includes casualties incurred in Mayaguez Incident. **Wounds not mortal exclude 150,375 persons not requiring hospital care.**

American Military Cemeteries and Memorials on Foreign Soil

Administered by the American Battle Monuments Commission, Washington, DC 20314
(Numbers of graves and numbers of commemorated missing in parentheses)
All of the cemeteries are closed to further interments.

World War I Cemeteries

Aisne-Marne, Belleau (Aisne) France (2,288-1,060)
Brookwood (Surrey) England (468-563)
Flanders Field, Waregem, Belgium (368-43)
Meuse-Argonne, Romagne (Meuse), France (14,246-954)
Oise-Aisne, Seringes (Aisne), near Fere-en-Tardenois (Aisne), France (6,012-241)
St. Mihiel, Thiaucourt (M. et M.), France (4,153-284)
Somme, Bony (Aisne), France (1,844-333)
Suresnes (Seine), France (1,541-974). In this cemetery rest also 24 of our unknown dead of World War II. The World War I chapel was, by the addition of two loggias, converted into a shrine to commemorate our dead of both wars. Senior representatives of the American and French governments assemble here on ceremonial occasions to pay homage to our military dead of these wars.

World War I Monuments

Audenarde, Belgium.
Bellicourt (Aisne), France.
Brest (Finistere), France.
Cantigny (Somme), France.
Chateau-Thierry (Aisne), Fr.
Gibraltar.
Kemmel, Ypres, Belgium.
Montfaucon (Meuse), France.
Montsec (Meuse), France.
Sommepy (Marne), France.
Tours (Indre et Loire), France.

World War II Monument

Pointe du Hoc (Calvados), France.

World War II Cemetery Memorials

Ardennes, Neupre (Neuville-en-Condroz), Belgium (5,325-462)
Brittany, St. James (Manche), France (4,410-497)
Cambridge, Cambridge, England (3,811-5,126)
Epinal, Epinal (Vosges), France (5,255-424)
Florence, Florence (Tuscany), Italy (4,402-1,409)
Henri-Chapelle, Henri-Chapelle, Belgium (7,989-450)
Lorraine, St. Avold (Moselle), France (10,489-444)
Luxembourg, Hamm, Luxembourg (5,076-370)
Manila, Manila, Rep. of the Philippines (17,206-36,279)
Netherlands, Margraten, Holland (8,301-1,722)
Normandy, St. Laurent (Calvados), Fr. (9,386-1,557)
North Africa, Carthage, Tunisia (2,841-3,724)
Rhone, Draguignan (Var), France (861-293)
Sicily-Rome, Nettuno, Italy (7,862-3,094)

World War II Memorials

To commemorate those who met their deaths in the American coastal waters of the Atlantic and Pacific Oceans the commission has erected a memorial in Battery Park, NYC, on which are inscribed 4,596 names, and at the Presidio of San Francisco, Cal., which carries 412 names. At the Honolulu Cemetery a memorial was erected which records the names of 18,094 missing of World War II, 8,194 missing from the Korean War and 2,489 missing from the Vietnam War.

In addition to the above, the Commission maintains the Mexico City National Cemetery in Mexico and the Corozal American Cemetery in the Republic of Panama. Interred in a mass grave at the Mexico City National Cemetery are the remains of 750 unknown American soldiers who gave their lives in the Mexican War (1846-48); additionally, 813 Americans and others are interred in the wall crypts of the cemetery. Interred in the Corozal American Cemetery are 3,818 Americans, 331 of whom are veterans.

World War II Merchant Marine Casualties

Source: U.S. Coast Guard

Died from direct causes while serving on American flag ships, 845; died in prisoner-of-war camps, 37; listed as missing, 4,807; most lost at sea and presumed dead.

There were 572 released prisoners of war, and one prisoner unaccounted for. Another 500 men died while serving on foreign flag ships under U.S. control.

The number of U.S. flag ships lost was 605 of 6,000,000 deadweight tons.

Debts Owed U.S. Arising from World War I

Source: U.S. Treasury Department (Dec. 31, 1979)

Country	[1]Original indebtedness	Interest thru Dec. 31, 1979	Total	Cumulative payments Principal	Cumulative payments Interest	Total outstanding
Armenia	$11,959,917	$36,064,585	$48,024,503	$32	—	$48,024,470
Austria[2]	26,843,149	12,057,583	38,900,732	862,668	—	38,038,064
Belgium	423,587,630	432,503,932	856,091,563	19,157,630	$33,033,643	803,900,290
Cuba	10,000,000	2,286,752	12,286,752	10,000,000	2,286,752	—
Czechoslovakia	185,071,023	218,715,475	403,786,498	19,829,914	304,178	383,652,406
Estonia	16,958,373	29,546,429	46,504,802	11	1,248,432	45,256,360
Finland	9,000,000	12,661,578	21,661,578	[3]9,000,000	[3]12,661,578	—
France	4,128,326,088	4,972,527,828	9,100,853,916	226,039,588	260,036,303	8,614,778,025
Great Britain	4,933,701,642	9,016,164,069	13,949,865,711	434,181,642	1,590,672,656	11,925,011,413
Greece	[4]34,319,844	6,891,681	41,211,525	1,949,589	6,453,141	[5]32,808,795
Hungary[6]	2,051,898	3,612,532	5,664,431	1,624,923	3,611,879	427,628
Italy	2,044,870,444	596,555,688	2,641,426,133	37,464,319	63,365,561	2,540,596,252
Latvia	7,094,654	12,457,293	19,551,947	9,200	752,349	18,790,398
Liberia	26,000	10,472	36,472	26,000	10,472	—
Lithuania	6,618,395	11,499,529	18,117,924	234,783	1,003,174	16,879,968
Nicaragua[7]	141,950	26,625	168,576	141,950	26,625	—
Poland	[8]213,506,132	375,477,878	588,984,010	1,287,297	21,359,000	566,337,713
Romania	68,359,192	91,244,069	159,603,261	[9]4,498,632	292,375	154,812,254
Russia	192,601,297	596,505,030	789,106,327	—	[10]8,750,312	780,356,015
Yugoslavia	63,577,713	52,888,142	116,465,854	1,952,713	636,059	113,877,083
Total	**12,378,615,343**	**16,479,697,172**	**28,858,312,515**	**768,260,892**	**2,006,504,489**	**26,083,547,133**

(1) Includes capitalized interest. (2) The Federal Republic of Germany has recognized liability for securities falling due between March 12, 1938, and May 8, 1945. (3) $8,480,090 has been made available for educational exchange programs with Finland pursuant to 22 U.S.C. 2455(e). (4) Includes $13,155,921 refunded by the agreement of May 28, 1964 which was ratified by Congress Nov. 5, 1966. (5) Includes $12,190,255 on agreement of May 28, 1964. (6) Interest payment from December 15, 1932, to June 15, 1937 were paid in pengo equivalent. (7) The indebtedness of Nicaragua was canceled pursuant to the agreement of April 14, 1938. (8) Excludes claim allowance of $1,813,429 dated December 15, 1969. (9) Excludes payment of $100,000 on June 14, 1940, as a token of good faith. (10) Principally proceeds from liquidation of Russian assets in the United States.

Major New U.S. Weapons Systems

Source: DMS, Inc., U.S. Defense Department

(As of April 1, 1980)

Item	Description	Estimated total cost (millions)	Estimated unit cost (thousands)	Estimated production	Major contractors	Comment
F-14 Tomcat	Swing-wing jet fighter.	$12,208.8	$23,800	521	Grumman	In production
F-15 Eagle	Tactical jet fighter. Air Force.	14,218.7	14,400	929	McDonnell Douglas	In production; 40 for Israel, 100 for Japan, 60 for S. Arabia
F-16 Condor	Supersonic, day-time fighter, defense. Air Force.	18,463.5	10,100	1,811	General Dynamics	In production; 348 for NATO, 75 for Israel
F-18 Hornet	All-weather fighter and attack plane. Fleet escort, Marine Corps ground support.	29,128.9	19,100	800 for U.S.	McDonnell Douglas; Northrop	Advanced development; several hundred more may be sold abroad
YAH-64	Attack helicopter: anti-tank, air cavalry, escort. Army.	5,774.4	7,800	536	Hughes	Advanced development
Trident	Nuclear-powered submarine carries 24 missiles with 4,000-mile range	28,251.0	Boat = 1,200,000 missile = 10,500	20? boats; 690 missiles	General Dynamics; Lockheed	Boats in production, missiles in development
CG-47 Aegis	Cruise missile	17,134.9	820.2	21	Litton Ind.	In production
SSN-688 Los Angeles	Nuclear-powered attack submarines to destroy enemy shipping, subs.	16,082	473,000	34	Newport News; General Dynamics	In production
FFG-7	Guided-missile frigate; anti-sub, anti-aircraft, attack and defense.	12,300	196,600	59 thru '84	Bath; Todd	In production
PHM	Patrol Combatant Missile (hydrofoil boat)	399.9	66,650	6	Boeing	In production
XM-1 Abrams	Main battle tank. Army.	12,869.1	1,550	7,058	Chrysler	In production
IFV/CFV	Infantry or Cavalry fighting vehicle	7,682.0	1,200	6,882	FMC Corp., Chrysler	Advanced development
Copperhead	Cannon-launched, laser-guided projectile; 10-12 mile range. Army.	1,147.9	25	80,000 (max.)	Martin Marietta	In production
Hellfire	Missile for AH-64; may be laser-guided.	1,003.8	10	28,000	Rockwell	In development
Patriot (SAM-D)	Surface-to-air missile for field air defense.	6,172.2	45,200	51 batteries[1]	Martin Marietta; Raytheon	In engineering development
MX	Advanced ICBM to replace Minuteman.	33,800	(Unknown)	200	Martin Marietta	In development
GLCM	Ground-launched, surface-to-surface cruise missile.	2,069.1	1,370	696	General Dynamics	In development
ALCM	Air-launched, air-to-ground	5,232.7	1,130.4	3,000?	Boeing	In development
Tomahawk SLCM	Sea-launched; strategic potential	2,244.9	689	1,160?	Gen. Dynam.	Near production

(1) Batteries consist of 5 launch vehicles and 2 fire control centers.

Some comparable costs: Total moon program, $30 billion, Bay Area Rapid Transit system, $1.6 billion; World Trade Center, land acquisition and construction, $1 billion; one manned moon shot, $400 million; December 1977 welfare payments to families with dependent children, $855 million; fiscal 1977 Ohio state budget outlays, $8.2 billion. 1977 Philadelphia public library operations costs, $17.3 million.

Armed Services Senior Enlisted Adviser

The U.S. Army, Navy and Air Force in 1966-67 each created a new position of senior enlisted adviser whose primary job is to represent the point of view of his services' enlisted men and women on matters of welfare, morale, and any problems concerning enlisted personnel. The senior adviser will have direct access to the military chief of his branch of service and policy-making bodies.

The senior enlisted adviser for each Dept. is:

Army-Sgt. Major of the Army William A. Connelly.

Navy-Master Chief Petty Officer of the Navy Thomas S. Crow.

Air Force-Chief Master Sgt. of the AF James M. McCoy.

Marines-Sgt. Major of the Marine Corps Leland D. Crawford.

ASSOCIATIONS AND SOCIETIES

Source: World Almanac questionnaire

Arranged according to **key words** in titles. Founding year of organization in parentheses; last figure after ZIP code indicates membership.

Aaron Burr Assn. (1946), 213 Leach St., Front Royal, VA 22630; 500.

Abortion Federation, Natl. (1977), 110 E. 59th St., Suite 1011, N.Y., NY 10022; 350.

Abortion Rights Action League, Natl. (1969), 825 15th St. NW, Wash., DC 20005; 60,000.

Accountants, Amer. Institute of Certified Public (1887), 1211 Ave. of the Americas, N.Y., NY 10036; 154,998.

Accountants, Natl. Assn. of (1919), 919 Third Ave., N.Y., NY 10022; 93,270.

Accountants, Natl. Society of Public (1945), 1717 Pennsylvania Ave., NW, Wash., DC 20006; 17,000.

Acoustical Society of America (1929), 335 E. 45 St., N.Y., NY 10017; 5,500.

Actors' Equity Assn. (1913), 165 W. 46 St., N.Y., NY 10036; 28,000.

Actors' Fund of America (1882), 1501 Broadway, N.Y., NY 10036; 4,000.

Actuaries, Society of (1949), 208 S. La Salle St., Chicago, Il. 60604; 6,700.

Adirondack Mountain Club (1922), 172 Ridge St., Glens Falls, NY 12801; 8,000.

Adult Education Assn. of the U.S.A. (1951), 810 18th St. NW, Wash., DC 20006; 4,000.

Advertisers, Assn. of Natl. (1910), 155 E. 44th St., N.Y., NY 10017; 400 cos.

Advertising Agencies, Amer. Assn. of (1917), 200 Park Ave., N.Y., NY 10017; 450 agencies.

Aeronautic Assn., Natl. (1905), 821 15th St. NW, Wash., DC 20005; 170,000.

Aeronautics and Astronautics, Amer. Institute of (1932), 1290 Ave. of the Americas, N.Y., NY 10019; 29,000.

Aerospace Industries Assn. of America (1919), 1725 De Sales St. NW, Wash., DC 20036; 58 cos.

Aerospace Medical Assn. (1929), Washington Natl. Airport, Wash., DC 20001; 3,500.

Afro-American Life and History, Assn. for the Study of (1915), 1401 14th St. NW, Wash., DC 20005; 16,289.

Aging Assn., Amer. (1970), Univ. of Nebraska Medical Center, 42d & Dewey Ave., Omaha, NE 68105; 500.

Agricultural Chemicals Assn., Natl. (1933), 1155 15th St. NW, Wash., DC 20005; 125 cos.

Agricultural Economics Assn., Amer. (1910), Univ. of Kentucky, Lexington, KY 40506; 4,500.

Agricultural Engineers, Amer. Society of (1907), 2950 Niles Rd., St. Joseph, MI 49085; 8,700.

Agricultural History Society (1919) ESCS, U.S. Dept. of Agriculture, Wash., DC 20250; 800.

Air, Citizens for Clean (1965), 32 Broad St., N.Y., NY 10004; 2,000.

Aircraft Assn., Experimental (1953), 11311 W. Forest Home Ave., Franklin, WI 53132; 70,000.

Aircraft Owners and Pilots Assn. (1939), 7315 Wisconsin Ave., Bethesda, MD 20014; 245,000.

Air Force Aid Society (1942), 1117 N. 19th St., Arlington, VA 22209; 24,000.

Air Force Assn. (1946), 1750 Pennsylvania Ave. NW, Wash., DC 20006; 150,000.

Air Force Sergeants Assn. (1961), 4235 28th Ave., Marlow Heights, MD 20031; 128,000.

Air Line Employees Assn. (1952), 5600 S. Central Ave., Chicago, IL 60638; 12,000.

Air Line Pilots Assn. (1931), 1625 Massachusetts Ave. NW, Wash., DC 20036; 32,000.

Air Pollution Control Assn. (1907), 211 S. Dithridge St., Pittsburgh, PA 15213; 7,192.

Airport Operators Council Intl. (1946), 1700 K St. NW, Wash., DC 20006; 178.

Air Transport Assn., Intl. (1945), P.O. Box 550, Intl. Aviation Sq., Montreal, Quebec, Canada H3A 2R4; 105 airlines.

Air Transport Assn. of America (1936), 1709 New York Ave. NW, Wash., DC 20006; 31 airlines.

Albert Schweitzer Fellowship (1939), 866 UN Plaza, N.Y., NY 10017.

Albert Schweitzer Friendship House (1966), R.D. 1; Box 7, Hurlburt Rd., Great Barrington, MA 01230.

Alcohol Problems, Amer. Council on (1895), 119 Constitution Ave. NE, Wash., DC 20002; 10,000.

Alcoholics Anonymous (1935), P.O. Box 459, Grand Central Station, N.Y., NY 10017, over 1,000,000.

Alcoholism, Natl. Council on (1944), 733 Third Ave., N.Y., NY 10017; 207 affiliates.

Allergy, Amer. Academy of (1943), 611 E. Wells St., Milwaukee, WI 53202; 2,906.

Alpine Club, Amer. (1902), 113 E. 90th St., N.Y., NY 10028; 1,450.

Altrusa Intl. (1917), 332 S. Michigan Ave., Chicago, IL 60604; 19,800.

American Federation of Labor & Congress of Industrial Organizations (AFL-CIO) (1955, by merging **American Federation of Labor** estab. 1881 and **Congress of Industrial Organizations** estab. 1935), 815 16th St. NW, Wash., DC 20006; 13,600,000.

Amer. Field Service (1947), 313 E. 43d St., N.Y., NY 10017; 164,000.

Amer. Indian Affairs, Assn. on (1923), 432 Park Ave. So., N.Y., NY, 10016; 50,000.

American Legion, The (1919), 700 N. Pennsylvania St., Indianapolis, IN 46206; 2,600,000. **American Legion Auxiliary** (1920), 777 N. Meridian St., Indianapolis, IN 46204; 1,000,000.

Amer. States, Organization of (1948), General Secretariat, Wash., DC 20006; 28 countries.

Amer. Veterans of World War II, Korea & Vietnam (AMVETS), (1947), 1710 Rhode Island Ave. NW, Wash., DC 20036; 125,000. **AMVETS Auxiliary** (1947), Saco Rd., Old Orchard Beach, ME 04064; 25,000.

Amnesty Intl. (1965), 304 W. 58th St., N.Y., NY 10019; 100,000.

Amputation Foundation, Natl. (1919), 12-45 150th St., Whitestone, NY 11357; 2,500.

Animal Ecologist Society (1978), P.O. Box 160371, Sacramento, CA 95816; 29.

Animal Protection Institute of America (1968), 5894 S. Land Park Dr., Sacramento, CA 95822; 100,000.

Animal Welfare Institute (1951), P.O. Box 3650, Wash., DC 20007; 5,000.

Animals, Amer. Society for Prevention of Cruelty to (ASPCA) (1866), 441 E. 92d St., N.Y., NY 10028; 3,000.

Animals, Friends of (1957), 11 W. 60th St., N.Y., NY 10023; 123,000.

Animals, The Fund for (1967), 140 W. 57th St., N.Y., NY 10019; 128,000.

Anthropological Assn., Amer. (1902), 1703 New Hampshire Ave. NW, Wash., DC 20009; 10,000.

Antiquarian Society, Amer. (1812), 185 Salisbury St., Worcester, MA 01609; 357.

Anti-Vivisection Society, Amer. (1883), Suite 204, Noble Plaza, 801 Old York Rd., Jenkintown, PA 19046; 10,500.

Appalachian Mountain Club (1876), 5 Joy St., Boston, MA 02108; 24,000.

Appalachian Trail Conference (1925), Box 236, Harpers Ferry, WV 25425; 12,500.

Appraisers, Amer. Society of (1936), 11800 Sunrise Valley Dr., Intl. Center, Reston, VA 22091; 5,220.

Arab Americans, Natl. Assn. of (1972), Suite 211, 1825 Connecticut Ave. NW, Wash., DC 20009; 3,000.

Arbitration Assn., Amer. (1926), 140 W. 51st St., N.Y., NY 10020; 5,000.

Arboriculture, Intl. Society of (1924), P.O. Box 71, 5 Lincoln Sq., Urbana, IL 61801; 3,500.

Archaeological Institute of America (1879), 53 Park Place, N.Y., NY 10007; 7,500.

Archaeology, Institute of Nautical (1973), Drawer AU, College Station, TX 77840; 429.

Archery Assn. of the U.S., Natl. (1879), 1951 Geraldson Dr., Lancaster, PA 17601; 5,000.

Architects, Amer. Institute of (1857), 1735 New York Ave. NW, Wash., DC 20006; 28,500.

Architectural Historians, Society of (1940), 1700 Walnut St., Phila., PA 19103; 5,000.

Archivists, Society of Amer. (1938), 330 S. Wells St., Suite 810, Chicago, IL 60680; 4,000.

Armed Forces Communications and Electronics Assn. (1946), 5205 Leesburg Pike, Falls Church, VA 22041; 14,800.

Army, Assn. of the United States (1950), 2425 Wilson Blvd., Arlington, VA 22201; 115,789.

Art, Natl. Assn. of Schools of (1944), 11250 Roger Bacon Dr. 5, Reston, VA 22090; 99 institutions.

Arts, Amer. Federation of (1909), 41 E. 65th St., N.Y., NY 10021; 1,500.

Arts, Associated Councils of the (1969), 570 Seventh Ave., N.Y., NY 10018; 2,000.

Arts, Natl. Endowment for the (1965), 2401 E. St. NW, Wash., DC 20506.

Arts and Letters, Amer. Academy and Institute of (1898), 633 W. 155th St., N.Y., NY 10032; 242.

Arts and Letters, Natl. Society of (1944), 9915 Litzsinger Rd., St. Louis, MO 63124; 1,800.

Arts & Psychology, Assn. for the (1976), P.O. Box 160371, Sacramento, CA 95816.

Arts & Sciences, Amer. Academy of (1780), 165 Allandale St., Jamaica Plain Sta., Boston, MA 02130; 2,500.

Assistance League, Natl. (1935), 5627 Fernwood Ave., Hollywood, CA 90028; 14,000.

Astrologers, Amer. Federation of (1938), P.O. Box 22040, Tempe, AZ 85282; 4,200.

Astronautical Society, Amer. (1953), 6060 Duke St., Alexandria, VA 22304; 1,000.

Astronomical Society, Amer. (1899), 1816 Jefferson Pl. NW, Wash., DC 20036; 3,700.

Atheist Assn. (1925), 3024 5th Ave., San Diego, CA 92103; 500.

Atheists, Amer. (1963), 2210 Hancock Dr., Austin, TX 78756; 100,000 families.

Athletic Assn., Natl. Jr. College (1937), 12 E. 2d, Hutchinson, KS 67501; 1,052.

Athletic Associations, Natl. Federation of State High School (1920), 11724 Plaza Circle, Box 20626, Kansas City, MO 64195; 51.

Athletic Union of the U.S., Amateur (1888), 3400 W. 86th St., Indianapolis, IN 46268; 380,000.

Audubon Society, Natl. (1905), 950 Third Ave., N.Y., NY 10022; 400,000.

Authors and Composers, Amer. Guild of (1931), 40 W. 57th St., N.Y., NY 10019; 3,500.

Authors League of America (1912), 234 W. 44th St., N.Y., NY 10036; 8,100.

Autistic Children, Natl. Society for, 1234 Massachusetts Ave. NW, Wash., DC 20005; 4,500.

Automobile Assn., Amer. (1902), 8111 Gatehouse Rd., Falls Church, VA 22042; 21 million.

Automobile Club, Natl. (1924), One Market Plaza, San Francisco, CA 94105; 465,000.

Automobile Club of America, Antique (1935), 501 W. Governor Rd., Hershey, PA 17033; 44,000.

Automobile Dealers Assn., Natl. (1917), 8400 Westpark Dr., McLean, VA 22102; 21,000.

Automobile License Plate Collectors' Assn. (1954), P.O. Box 712, Weston, W. VA 26452; 1,500.

Automotive Booster Clubs Intl. (1921), 5105 Tollview Dr., Rolling Meadows, IL 60008; 3,008.

Automotive Organization Team (1939), P.O. Box 1742, Midland, MI 48640; 3,000.

Aviation Historical Society, Amer. (1956), P.O. Box 99, Garden Grove, CA 92642; 4,000.

Backpackers' Assn., Intl. (1973), P.O. Box 85, Lincoln Center, ME 04458; 22,861.

Badminton Assn., U.S. (1938), P.O. Box 237, Swartz Creek, MI 48473; 1,200.

Ballplayers of Amer., Assn. of Professional (1924), 12062 Valley View St., #211, Garden Grove, CA 92645; 6,000.

Bankers Assn., Amer. (1875), 1120 Connecticut Ave. NW, Wash., DC 20036; 13,100 banks.

Bankers Assn. of America, Independent (1930), 1168 S. Main St., Sauk Centre, MN 56378; 7,300 banks.

Banks, Natl. Assn. of Mutual Savings (1920), 200 Park Ave., N.Y., NY 10017.

Bar Assn., Amer. (1878), 1155 E. 60th St., Chicago, IL 60637; 250,000.

Bar Assn., Federal (1920), 1815 H St. NW, Wash., DC 20006; 15,000.

Barbershop Quartet Singing in America, Society for the Preservation & Encouragement of (1938), 6315 Third Ave., Kenosha, WI 53141; 36,000.

Baseball Congress, Amer. Amateur (1935), 212 Plaza Bldg., 2855 W. Market St., P.O. Box 5332, Akron, OH 44313; 6,511 teams.

Baseball Congress of America, Natl. (1930), 338 S. Sycamore, Wichita, KS 67213; 6,750.

Baseball Players of America, Assn. of Professional (1924), 12062 Valley View St., Suite 211, Garden Grove, CA 92645; 10,200.

Basketball Assn., Natl. (1946), 645 5th Ave., N.Y., NY 10022; 22 teams.

Baton Twirling Assn. of America & Abroad, Intl. (1967), Box 234, Waldwick, NJ 07463; 1,800.

Battleship Assn., Amer. (1963), P.O. Box 11247, San Diego, CA 92111; 2,000.

Beer Can Collectors of America (1970), 747 Merus Ct., Fenton, MO 63026; 11,000.

Beta Gamma Sigma, 11500 Olive Blvd., Suite 142, St. Louis, MO 63141; 120,000.

Beta Sigma Phi (1931), 1800 W. 91st Pl., Kansas City, MO 64114; 250,000.

Bible Society, Amer. (1816), 1865 Broadway, N.Y., NY 10023; 450,000.

Biblical Literature, Society of (1880), Union Theological Seminary, 3401 Brook Rd., Richmond, VA 23227; 4,800.

Bibliographical Society of America (1904), P.O. Box 397, Grand Central Sta., N.Y., NY 10017; 1,500.

Bide-A-Wee Home Assn. (1903), 410 E. 38th St., N.Y., NY 10016; 8,600.

Big Brothers/Big Sisters of America (1977), 117 S. 17th St., Suite 1200, Phila., PA 19103; 370 affiliates.

Biological Chemists, Amer. Society of (1906), 9650 Rockville Pike, Bethesda, MD 20014; 5,000.

Biological Sciences, Amer. Institute of (1947), 1401 Wilson Blvd., Arlington, VA 22209; 8,000.

Blind, Amer. Foundation for the (1921), 15 W. 16th St., N.Y., NY 10011.

Blind, Natl. Federation of the (1940), 1346 Connecticut Ave. NW, Suite 212, DuPont Circle Bldg., Wash., DC 20036; 50,000.

Blind & Visually Handicapped, Natl. Accreditation Council for Agencies Serving the (1967), 79 Madison Ave., N.Y., NY 10016; 106 agencies and schools.

Blindness, Natl. Society to Prevent (1908), 79 Madison Ave., N.Y., NY 10016.

Blindness, Research to Prevent (1960), 598 Madison Ave., N.Y., NY 10022; 1,161.

Blizzard Club, January 12th, 1888, (1940), c/o Historian, 4827 Hillside Ave., Lincoln, NE 68506; 72.

Blood Banks, Amer. Assn. of (1947), 1828 L St. NW, Wash., DC 20036; 8,199.

Blue Cross Assn. (1948), 840 N. Lake Shore Dr., Chicago, IL 60611; 74 plans.

Blue Shield Plans, Natl. Assn. of (1946), 211 E. Chicago Ave., Chicago, IL 60611; 70 plans.

Blueberry Council, No. Amer. (1968), P.O. Box 166, Marmora, NJ 08223; 30 organizations.

B'nai B'rith Intl. (1843), 1640 Rhode Island Ave. NW, Wash., DC 20036; 550,000.

Boat Owners Assn. of the U.S. (1966), 880 S. Pickett St., Alexandria, VA 22304; 55,000.

Booksellers Assn., Amer. (1900), 122 E. 42d St., N.Y., NY 10017; 5,000.

Botanical Gardens & Arboreta, Amer. Assn. of (1940), Dept. of Biology, 124 Botany Bldg., Univ. of Cal., Los Angeles, CA 90024; 900.

Bottle Clubs, Federation of Historical (1969), 5001 Queen Ave. N., Minneapolis, MN 55430; 125 clubs.

Bowling Congress, Amer. (1895), 5301 S. 76th St., Greendale, WI 53129; 4.7 million.

Boys' Brigades of America, United (1893), P.O. Box 8406, Baltimore, MD 21234; 150.

Boys' Clubs of America (1906), 771 First Ave., N.Y., NY 10017; 1,000,000+.

Boy Scouts of America (1910), P.O. Box 61030, Dallas/Ft. Worth Airport, TX; 4,200,000.

Brand Names Foundation (1943), 477 Madison Ave., N.Y., NY 10022; 400.

Bread for the World (1974), 32 Union Sq. E., N.Y., NY 10003; 31,000.

Brick Institute of America (1934), 1750 Old Meadow Rd., McLean, VA 22101; 100 cos.

Bridge, Tunnel and Turnpike Assn., Intl. (1932), 1225 Connecticut Ave. NW, Suite 307, Wash., DC 20036; 200.

Brith Sholom (1905), 1235 Chestnut St., Phila., PA 19107; 20,000.

Broadcasters, Natl. Assn. of (1927), 1771 N St. NW, Wash., DC 20036; 5,500.

Burroughs Bibliophiles, The (1960), 454 Elaine Dr., Pittsburgh, PA 15236; 375.

Bus Assn., Amer. (1926), 1025 Connecticut Ave. NW, Wash., DC 20036; 700.

Business Bureaus, Council of Better (1970), 1150 17th St. NW, Wash., DC 20036; 146.

Business Clubs, Natl. Assn. of Amer. (1922), 3315 No. Main St., High Point, NC 27262; 5,641.

Business Communication Assn., Amer. (1935), 911 S. Sixth St., Champaign, IL 61820; 1,500.

Business Communicators, Intl. Assn. of (1970), 870 Market St., Suite 928, San Francisco, CA 94102; 7,000+.

Business Education Assn., Natl. (1946), 1906 Association Dr., Reston, VA 22091; 18,000.

Business Law Assn., Amer. (1924), Georgia State Univ.,

University Plaza, Atlanta, GA 30303; 800.

Business-Professional Advertising Assn. (1922), 205 E. 42d St., N.Y., NY 10017; 3,445.

Button Society, Natl. (1938), 353 Stockton St., Hightstown, NJ 08520; 1,765.

Byron Society, The (1971 England, 1973 in U.S.), 259 New Jersey Ave., Collingswood, NJ 08108; 275.

CARE (Cooperative For American Relief Everywhere) (1945), 660 First Ave., N.Y., NY 10016; 26 agencies.

CORE (Congress of Racial Equality) (1942), 1916-38 Park Ave., N.Y., NY 10037.

Cable Television Assn., Natl. (1952), 918 16th St. NW, Wash., DC 20006; 1,450.

Campers & Hikers Assn., Natl. (1949), 7172 Transit Rd., Buffalo, NY 14221; 42,500 families.

Camp Fire Girls (1910), 4601 Madison Ave., Kansas City, MO 64112; 500,000.

Camping Assn., Amer. (1910), Bradford Woods, Martinsville, IN 46151; 6,000.

Cancer Council, United (1963), 1803 N. Meridian St., Indianapolis, IN 46202.

Cancer Society, Amer. (1913), 777 Third Ave., N.Y., NY 10017; 242.

Candy Brokers Assn. of America (1956), Box 512, Bryan, TX 77801; 300.

Canners Assn., Natl. (1907), 1133 20th St. NW, Wash., DC 20036; 600 companies.

Canoe Assn., U.S. (1968), 606 Ross St., Middletown, OH 45042; 2,000.

Captive European Nations, Assembly of (1954), 29 W. 57th St., N.Y., NY 10019; 9 national committees.

Carillonneurs in North America, Guild of (1936), 3718 Settle Rd., Cincinnati, OH 45227; 491.

Carnegie Hero Fund Commission (1904), 606 Oliver Bldg., Pittsburgh, PA 15222.

Cartoonists Society, Natl. (1946), 9 Ebony Ct., Brooklyn, NY 11229; 500.

Cat Fanciers' Assn. (1919), P.O. Box 430, 11 Globe Ct., Red Bank, NJ 07701; 550 clubs.

Catch Society of America, The (1968), Dept. of English, SUNY—Fredonia; Fredonia, NY 14063; 300.

Catholic Bishops, Natl. Conference of/U.S. Catholic Conference (1966), 1312 Massachusetts Ave. NW, Wash., DC 20005; 285.

Catholic Charities, Natl. Conference of (1910), 1346 Connecticut Ave. NW, Wash., DC 20036; 3,000.

Catholic Church Extension Society of the U.S.A. (1905), 35 E. Wacker Dr., Chicago, IL 60601; 20,000.

Catholic Daughters of America (1903), 10 W. 71st St., N.Y., NY 10023; 170,000.

Catholic Educational Assn., Natl. (1904), One Dupont Circle NW, Wash., DC 20036; 14,000.

Catholic Press Assn. (1912), 119 N. Park Ave., Rockville Centre, NY 11570; 568.

Catholic Rural Life Conference, Natl. (1923), 4625 NW Beaver Dr., Des Moines, IA 50322; 3,000.

Catholic War Veterans of the U.S.A. (1935), 2 Massachusetts Ave. NW, Wash., DC 20001; 35,000.

Cemetery Assn., Amer. (1887), 250 E. Broad St., Columbus, OH 43215; 1,100.

Ceramic Society, Amer. (1899), 65 Ceramic Dr., Columbus, OH 43214; 7,500.

Cerebral Palsy Assns., United (1949), 66 E. 34th St., N.Y., NY 10016.

Chamber of Commerce of the U.S.A. (1912), 1615 H St. NW, Wash., DC 20062; 95,304.

Chamber Music Players, Amateur (1948), P.O. Box 547, Vienna, VA 22180; 5,000.

Chaplain's Assn., Natl. (1900), Gatlinburg, TN 37738; 2,500.

Chaplains Assn. of the U.S.A., Military (1925), 7758 Wisconsin Ave. NW, Wash., DC 20014; 1,938.

Chartered Life Underwriters, Amer. Society of (1928), 270 Bryn Mawr Ave., Bryn Mawr, PA 19010; 27,000.

Chartered Property & Casualty Underwriters, Society of (1944), Providence & Sugartown Rds., Malvern, PA 19355; 8,800.

Chemical Engineers, Amer. Institute of (1908), 345 E. 47th St., N.Y., NY 10017; 45,000.

Chemical Manufacturers Assn. (1872), 1825 Connecticut Ave. NW, Wash., DC 20009; 202 cos.

Chemical Society, Amer. (1876), 1155 16th St. NW, Wash., DC 20036; 116,000.

Chemistry, Amer. Assn. for Clinical (1948), 1725 K St. NW, Wash., DC 20006; 5,100.

Chemists, Amer. Institute of (1923), 7315 Wisconsin Ave., Wash., DC 20014; 5,387.

Chemists and Chemical Engineers, Assn. of Consulting (1928), 50 E. 41st St., N.Y. NY 10017; 110.

Chemists Assn., Manufacturing (1872), 1825 Connecticut Ave. NW, Wash., DC 20009; 200 cos.

Chess Federation, U.S. (1939), 186 Rte. 9W, New Windsor, NY 12550; 51,000.

Chess League of Amer., Correspondence (1909), Box 124, Algonquin, IL 60102; 1,200.

Child Welfare League of America (1920), 67 Irving Pl., N.Y., NY 10003; 387 agencies.

Childbirth Without Pain Education Assn. (1964), P.O. Box 233, Dana Point, CA 92629; 200.

Childhood Education Intl., Assn. for (1892), 3615 Wisconsin Ave. NW, Wash., DC 20016; 20,000.

Children of the Amer. Revolution, Natl. Society (1895), 1776 D St. NW, Wash., DC 20006; 12,500.

Children's Aid Society (1853), 105 E. 22d St., N.Y., NY 10010.

Children's Book Council (1945), 67 Irving Pl., N.Y., NY 10003; 70 publishing houses.

Chiropractic Assn., Amer. (1963), 2200 Grand Ave., Des Moines, IA 50312; 15,250.

Chiropractors Assn., Intl. (1926), 1901 L St. NW, Wash., DC 20036; 6,000.

Christian Culture Society (1974), P.O. Box 325, Kokomo, IN 46901; 14,105.

Christian Endeavor, Intl. Society of (1881), 1221 E. Broad St., P.O. Box 1110, Columbus, OH 43216; 1,000,000.

Christian Laity Counseling Board (1970), 5901 Plainfield Dr., Charlotte, NC 28215; 38,000,000.

Christians and Jews, Natl. Conference of (1928), 43 W. 57th St., N.Y., NY 10019; 200,000.

Churches, U.S. Conference for the World Council of (1948), 475 Riverside Dr., Room 1062, N.Y., NY 10027; 28 churches.

Church Women United in the U.S.A. (1941), 475 Riverside Dr., N.Y., NY 10027; 2,000 units.

Cincinnati, Society of the (1783), 2118 Massachusetts Ave. NW, Wash., DC 20008; 2,800.

Circulation Managers Assn., Intl. (1898), 11600 Sunrise Valley Dr., Reston, VA 22070; 1,350.

Circus Fans Assn. of America (1926), P.O. Box 69, 4 Center Dr., Camp Hill, PA 17011; 2,400.

Cities, Natl. League of (1924), 1620 Eye St. NW, Wash., DC 20006; 15,000 municipalities.

Citizens Band Radio Patrol (1972), 1100 NE 125th St., N. Miami, FL 33161; 60,000.

Citizens Band Radio Patrol, Amer. Law Enforcement Officers (1975), 1100 NE 125th St., N. Miami, FL 33161; 30,000.

City Management Assn., Intl. (1914), 1140 Connecticut Ave. NW, Wash., DC 20036; 7,000.

Civil Engineers, Amer. Society of (1852), 345 E. 47th St., N.Y., NY 10017; 76,000.

Civil Liberties Union, Amer. (1920), 132 W. 43 St., N.Y., NY 10016; 200,000.

Civitan Internatl. (1920), P.O. Box 2102, Birmingham, AL 35201; 31,000.

Classical League, Amer. (1918), Miami Univ., Oxford, OH 45056; 3,000.

Clergy, Academy of Parish (1968), P.O. Box 86, Princeton, NJ 08540; 1,000.

Clinical Pastoral Education, Assn. for (1976), 475 Riverside Dr., N.Y., NY 10027; 3,000.

Clinical Pathologists, Amer. Society of (1922), 2100 W. Harrison St., Chicago, IL 60612; 20,000.

Clowns of America (1968), P.O. Box 3906, Balto, MD 21222; 4,000.

Coal Assn., Natl. (1917), 1130 17th St. NW, Wash., DC 20036; 200 companies.

Cocoa Exchange, New York (1925), 127 John St., N.Y., NY 10038; 183.

Collectors Assn., Amer. (1939), 4040 W. 70th St., Minneapolis, MN 55435; 2,778.

College Athletic Assn., Natl. Junior (1938), 12 E. 2d, Box 1586, Hutchinson, KS 67501; 995.

College Athletic Conference, Eastern (1938), 1311 Craigville Beach Rd., P.O. Box 3, Centerville, MA 02632; 229.

College Board, The (1900), 888 Seventh Ave., N.Y., NY 10019; 2,500 institutions.

College Physical Education Assn. for Men, Natl. (1897), 108 Cooke Hall, Univ. of Minnesota, Minneapolis, MN 55455; 1,200.

College Placement Council (1956), 65 E. Elizabeth Ave., Bethlehem, PA 18018; 2,300.

Colleges, Assn. of Amer. (1915), 1818 R St. NW, Wash., DC 20009; 653 institutions.

Collegiate Athletic Assn., Natl. (1906), 653 Nall Ave. at 63d

St., Shawnee Mission, KS 66222; 860.

Collegiate Schools of Business, Amer. Assembly of (1916), 760 Office Parkway, St. Louis, MO 63141; 650 schools.

Colonial Dames of America (1890), 421 E. 61 St., N.Y., NY 10021; 2,000.

Colonial Dames XVII Century, Natl. Society (1915), 1300 New Hampshire Ave. NW, Wash., DC 20036; 15,000.

Colonial Wars, General Society of (1891), 840 Woodbine Ave., Glendale, OH 45246; 4,200.

Colored Women's Clubs, Natl. Assn. of (1896), 5808 16th St. NW, Wash., DC 20011; 50,000.

Commercial Law League of America (1895), 222 W. Adams St., Chicago, IL 60606; 6,500.

Commercial Travelers of America, Order of United (1888), 632 N. Park St., Columbus, OH 43215; 219,354.

Common Cause (1970), 2030 M St. NW, Wash., DC 20036; 229,000.

Community Cultural Center Assoc., Amer. (1979), 19 Foothills Dr., Pompton Plains, NJ 07444; 20.

Composers/USA, Natl. Assn. of (1975), P.O. Box 49652, Barrington Sta., Los Angeles, CA 90049; 350.

Composers, Authors & Publishers, Amer. Society of (ASCAP) (1914), One Lincoln Plaza, N.Y., NY 10023; 24,000.

Computing Machinery, Assn. for (1947), 1133 Ave. of the Americas, N.Y., NY 10036; 45,000.

Concrete Institute, Amer. (1905), 22400 W. Seven Mile Rd., Detroit, MI 48219; 13,000.

Conference Board, The (1916), 845 Third Ave., N.Y., NY 10022; 4,000.

Consairway (1942), P.O. Box 1642, La Mesa, CA 92041; 500.

Conscientious Objectors, Central Committee for (1948), 2016 Walnut St., Phila., PA 19103.

Conservation Engineers, Assn. of (1961), Missouri Dept. of Conservation, P.O. Box 180, Jefferson City, MO 65101; 161.

Conservation Foundation (1948), 1717 Massachusetts Ave. NW, Wash., DC 20036.

Construction Industry Manufacturers Assn. (1903), 111 E. Wisconsin Ave., Milwaukee, WI 53202; 200 companies.

Construction Specifications Institute (1948), 1150 17th St. NW, Wash., DC 20036; 11,500.

Consumer Credit Assn., Intl. (1912), 375 Jackson Ave., St. Louis, MO 63130; 45,025.

Consumer Federation of America (1968), 1012 14th St. NW, Wash., DC 20005; 220 organizations.

Consumer Interests, Amer. Council on (1953), 162 Stanley Hall, Univ. of Missouri, Columbia, MO 65211; 3,000.

Consumers League, Natl. (1899), 1522 K St. NW, Suite 406, Wash., DC 20005; 650.

Consumers Union of the U.S. (1936), 256 Washington St., Mount Vernon, NY 10550; 250,000.

Consumers Unions, Intl. Organization of (1960), 9 Emmastraat, The Hague, Netherlands; 111 organizations.

Contract Bridge League, Amer. (1927), 2200 Democrat Rd., Memphis, TN 38116; 200,000.

Contractors of Amer., General (1918), 1957 E St. NW, Wash., DC 20036; 30,000.

Cooperative League of the U.S.A. (1916), 1828 L St. NW, Wash., DC 20036; 176 co-ops.

Correctional Assn., Amer. (1870), 4321 Hartwick Rd., Suite L-208, College Park, MD 20740; 10,000.

Correctional Officers, Amer. Assn. of (1978), Northern Michigan Univ., 111 Pierce Hall, Marquette, MI 49855; 2,400.

Cosmopolitan Intl. (1914), 7341 W. 108 Pl., Overland Park, KS 66204; 4,000.

Cotton Council of America, Natl. (1938), 1918 North Parkway, Memphis, TN 38112.

Country Music Assn. (1958), 7 Music Circle No., Nashville, TN 37202; 5,500.

Creative Children and Adults, Natl. Assn. for (1974), 8080 Springvalley Dr., Cincinnati, OH 45236; 1,000.

Credit Management, Nat. Assn. of (1896), 475 Park Ave. So., N.Y., NY 10016; 43,200.

Credit Union Natl. Assn. (1934), 5710 Mineral Point Rd., Madison, WI 53701; 22,069 credit unions.

Crime and Delinquency, Natl. Council on (1907), 411 Hackensack Ave., Hackensack, NJ 07601; 60,000.

Crime Prevention Rehabilitative Services, Amer. (1975), 320 N. Magnolia Ave., Orlando, FL 32801; 1,300.

Criminology, Amer. Assn. of (1953), P.O. Box 1115, North Marshfield, MA 02059; 2,500.

Crop Science Society of America (1955), 677 S. Segoe Rd., Madison, WI 53711; 4,035.

Cross-Examination Debate Assn. (1971), Speech Dept., Cal. State Univ., Long Beach, CA 90840; 33 institutions.

Cryptogram Assn., Amer. (1932) 9504 Forest Rd., Bethesda, MD 20014; 1,000.

Cyprus, Sovereign Order of (1192, 1964 in U.S.), 853 Seventh Ave., N.Y., NY 10019; 446.

Dairy Council, Natl. (1915), 6300 N. River Rd., Rosemont, IL 60018; 700.

Dairy and Food Industries Supply Assn. (1919), 5530 Wisconsin Ave., Wash., DC 20015; 435 organizations.

Dairylea Cooperative (1919), One Blue Hill Plaza, Pearl River, NY 10965; 5,850.

Daughters of the American Revolution, Natl. Society, (1890), 1776 D St. NW, Wash., DC 20006; 209,000.

Daughters of the Confederacy, United (1894), 328 N. Blvd., Richmond, VA 23220; 35,000.

Daughters of 1812, Natl. Society, U.S. (1892), 1461 Rhode Island Ave. NW, Wash., DC 20005; 5000+.

Daughters of Union Veterans of the Civil War (1885), 503 S. Walnut St., Springfield, IL 62704; 7,000.

Deaf, Alexander Graham Bell Assn. for the (1890), 3417 Volta Pl. NW, Wash., DC 20007; 6,250.

Deaf, Natl. Assn. of the (1880), 814 Thayer Ave., Silver Spring, MD 20910; 18,000.

Defense Preparedness Assn., Amer. (1919), 1700 N. Moore St., Arlington, VA 22209; 31,000.

Delta Kappa Gamma Society Intl. (1929), P.O. Box 1589, Austin, TX 78767; 147,000.

Deltiologists of America (1960), 3709 Gradyville Rd., Newton Square, PA 19073; 1,675.

Democratic Natl. Committee (1848), 1625 Massachusetts Ave. NW, Wash., DC 20036; 365.

DeMolay, Intl. Council, Order of (1919), 201 E. Armour Blvd., Kansas City, MO 64111; 110,000.

Dental Assn., Amer. (1859), 211 E. Chicago Ave., Chicago, IL 60611; 136,000.

Dental Assn., Natl. (1913), P.O. Box 197, Charlottesville, VA 22902; 1,500.

Descendants of the Colonial Clergy, Society of the (1933), 30 Leewood Rd., Wellesley, MA 02181; 1,400.

Descendants of the Signers of the Declaration of Independence (1907), 1300 Locust St., Phila., PA 19107; 1,050.

Descendants of Washington's Army at Valley Forge, Society of (1976), P.O. Box 608, Manhasset, NY 11030; 286.

Desert Protective Council (1959), Box 4294, Palm Springs, CA 92263; 400.

Diabetes Assn., Amer. (1940), 600 Fifth Ave., N.Y., NY 10020; 3,400.

Dialect Society, Amer. (1889), c/o Dept. of English, Univ. of Western Ontario, London, Canada N6A 3K7; 760.

Dietetic Assn., Amer. (1917), 430 N. Michigan Ave., Chicago, IL 60611; 39,276.

Ding-A-Ling Club, Natl. (1971), Box 2188, Glen Ellyn, IL 60137; 1,965.

Direct Mail/Marketing Assn. (1916), 6 E. 43d St., N.Y., NY 10017; 3,500 companies.

Directors Guild of America (1936), 7950 Sunset Blvd., Los Angeles, CA 90046; 5,877.

Disabled Amer. Veterans (1921), P.O. Box 14301, Cincinnati, OH 45214; 656,000.

Disabled Officers Assn. (1919), 927 S. Walter Reed Dr. #6, Arlington, VA 22204; 5,000.

Divorce Reform, U.S. (1961), P.O. Box 243, Kenwood, CA 95452; 6,000.

Dowsers, Amer. Society of (1961), P.O. Box 24, Danville, VT 05328; 1,875.

Dracula Society, Count (1962), 334 W. 54th St., Los Angeles, CA 90037; 500.

Dragon, Imperial Order of the (1900), P.O. Box 1707, San Francisco, CA 94101.

Drug, Chemical and Allied Trades Assn. (1890), 42-40 Bell Blvd., Suite 204, Bayside, NY 11361; 500 cos.

Drum Corps Internatl. (1971), 719 S. Main St., Lombard, IL 60148; 26.

Ducks Unlimited (1937), P.O. Box 66300, Chicago, IL 60666; 350,000.

Dulcimer Assn., Southern Appalachian (1974), Rte. 1, Box 473, Helena, AL 35080; 114.

Dutch Settlers Soc. of Albany (1924), 1088 Cortland St., Albany, NY 12203; 325.

Dwelling Sculpture Institute (1978), 431 Crestvale Dr., Sierra Madre, CA 91024; 25.

Earth, Friends of the (1969), 124 Spear St., San Francisco, CA 94105; 23,000.

Easter Seal Society for Crippled Children and Adults, Natl. (1919), 2023 W. Ogden Ave., Chicago, IL 60612.

Eastern Star, Order of the (1876), 1618 New Hampshire Ave. NW, Wash., DC 20009; 3,000,000.

Ecological Society of America (1915), c/o Dr. E. J. Kormondy, Evergreen State College, Olympia, WA 98505; 5,700.

Economic Assn., Amer. (1885), 1313 21st Ave. So., Nashville, TN 37212; 19,450.

Economic Development, Committee for (1942), 477 Madison Ave., N.Y., NY 10022.

Edison Electric Institute (1933), 1111 19th St. NW, Wash., DC 20036; 193 cos.

Educational Exchange, Council on Intl. (1947), 205 E. 42d St., N.Y., NY 10017; 174 organizations.

Education, Amer. Council on (1918), One Dupont Circle NW, Wash., DC 20036; 1,400 schools.

Education, Council for Advancement & Support of (1974), 11 Dupont Circle NW, Wash., DC 20036; 9,000 schools.

Education, Council for Basic (1956), 725 15th St. NW, Wash., DC 20005; 8,000.

Education, Natl. Committee for Citizens in (1973), 410 Wilde Lake Village Green, Columbia, MD 21044; 312.

Education, Natl. Society for the Study of (1902), 5835 Kimbark Ave., Chicago, IL 60637; 4,500.

Education, Society for the Advancement of (1939), 1860 Broadway, N.Y., NY 10023; 3,000.

Education, Institute of Intl. (1919), 809 United Nations Plaza, N.Y., NY 10017.

Education Assn., Natl. (1857), 1201 16th St. NW, Wash., DC 20036; 1,600,000.

Education Society, Comparative and Intl. (1956), 302 WPH, Univ. Park, Univ. of S. California, Los Angeles, CA 90007; 2,500.

Education of Young Children, Natl. Assn. for the (1926), 1834 Connecticut Ave. NW, Wash., DC 20009; 32,000.

Educational Broadcasters, Natl. Assn. of (1925), 1346 Connecticut Ave. NW, Wash., DC 20036; 2,500.

Educational Research Assn., Amer. (1916), 1230 17th St. NW, Wash., DC 20036; 13,500.

Educators for World Peace, Intl. Assn. of (1969), P.O. Box 3282, Blue Springs Sta., Huntsville, AL 35810; 12,500.

Electric Railroaders Assn. (1934), Grand Central Terminal, 89 E. 42d St., N.Y., NY 10017; 1,800.

Electrical and Electronics Engineers, Institute of (1884), 345 E. 47th St., N.Y., NY 10017; 202,000.

Electrical Manufacturers Assn., Natl. (1926), 2101 L St. NW, Wash., DC 20037; 560 companies.

Electrochemical Society (1902), P.O. Box 2071, Princeton, NJ 08540; 4,741.

Electronic Industries Assn. (1924), 2001 Eye St. NW, Wash., DC 20006; 280 firms.

Electronic Service Dealers Assn., Natl. (1963), 2708 W. Berry, Ft. Worth, TX 76109; 1,920.

Electronics Technicians, Intl. Society of Certified (1970), 2708 W. Berry, Ft. Worth, TX 76109; 1,100.

Electroplaters' Society, Amer. (1909), 1201 Louisiana Ave., Winter Park, FL 32789; 7,400.

Elks of the U.S.A., Benevolent and Protective Order of (1869), 2750 N. Lake View Ave., Chicago, IL 60614; 1,644,496.

Energy, Intl. Assn. for Hydrogen (1974), P.O. Box 24866, Coral Gables, FL 33124; 1,500.

Engine and Boat Manufacturers, Natl. Assn. of (1904), 666 Third Ave., N.Y., NY 10017; 435 firms.

Engineering, Natl. Academy of (1964), 2101 Constitution Ave. NW, Wash., DC 20418; 854.

Engineering Education, Amer. Society for (1893), One Dupont Circle, Wash., DC 20036; 12,000.

Engineering Societies, Amer. Assn. of (1979), 345 E. 47th St., N.Y., NY 10017; 38 societies.

Engineering Society of N. America, Illuminating (1906), 345 E. 47th St., N.Y., NY 10017; 9,000.

Engineering Technicians, Amer. Society of Certified (1964), 4550 W. 109th, Suite 220, Overland Park, KS 66211; 6,500.

Engineering Trustees, United (1904), 345 E. 47th St., N.Y., NY 10017.

Engineers, Amer. Society of Lubrication (1944), 838 Busse Hwy., Park Ridge, IL 60068; 3,200.

Engineers, Assn. of Energy (1977), 4025 Pleasantdale Rd., Suite 340, Atlanta, GA 30340; 3,000.

Engineers, Natl. Society of Professional (1934), 2029 K St. NW, Wash., DC 20006; 80,000.

Engineers, Institute of Transportation (1930), 525 School St. SW, Suite 410, Wash., DC 20024; 6,500.

Engineers, Soc. of American Military (1920), Suite 905, 740 15th St., NW, Wash., DC 20005; 22,000.

Engineers, Soc. of Manufacturing (1932), P.O. Box 930, Dearborn, MI 48128; 50,000.

English Assn., College (1939), Kean College of N.J., Union, NJ 07083; 2,000.

English-Speaking Union of the U.S. (1920), 16 E. 69th St., N.Y., NY 10021; 33,500.

Entomological Society of America (1889), 4603 Calvert Rd., P.O. Box AJ, College Park, MD 20740; 7,500.

Epigraphic Society, Inc., The (1974), 6 Woodland St., Arlington, MA 02174; 800.

Esperanto League for North America (1952), P.O. Box 1129, El Cerrito, CA 94530; 700.

Euthanasia Foundation, Amer. (1972), 95 N. Birch Rd., Ft. Lauderdale, FL 33304; 30,000.

Evangelicals, Natl. Assn. of (1942), Box 28, Wheaton, IL 60187.

Evangelism Crusades, Intl. (1959), 7970 Woodman Ave., Van Nuys, CA 91402; 50,000.

Exchange Club, Natl. (1911), 3050 Central Ave., Toledo, OH 43606; 50,000.

Experiment in Internatl. Living (1932), Kipling Rd., Brattleboro, VT 05301; 64,000.

Fairs & Expositions, Intl. Assn. of (1885), P.O. Box 985, Springfield, MO 65801; 1,000.

Family Life, Natl. Alliance for, Inc., Suite 220, 1801 K St. NW, Wash., DC 20006; 5,000.

Family Service Assn. of America (1911), 44 E. 23d St., N.Y., NY 10010, 300 agencies.

Farm Bureau Federation, Amer. (1919), 225 Touhy Ave., Park Ridge, IL 60068; 3,198,631 families.

Farmer Cooperatives, Natl. Council of (1929), 1800 Massachusetts Ave. NW, Wash., DC 20036; 140 co-ops.

Farmers of America, Future (1928), Box 15160, Alexandria, VA 22309; 507,108.

Farmers Educational and Co-Operative Union of America (1902), 12025 E. 45th Ave., Denver, CO 80251; 300,000 families.

Fat Americans, Natl. Assn. to Aid (NAAFA) (1969), P.O. Box 43, Bellerose, NY 11426; 2,000.

Federal Employees, Natl. Federation of (1917), 1016 16th St. NW, Wash., DC 20036; 150,000.

Federal Employees Veterans Assn. (1954), P.O. Box 183, Merion Sta., PA 19066; 643.

Feline Society, Amer. (1938), 41 Union Sq. W., N.Y., NY 10003; 450.

Feminists for Life of America (1972), 1503 N. 47, Milwaukee, WI 53208; 1,000.

Fencers League of America, Amateur (1891), 601 Curtis St., Albany, CA 94706; 6,000.

Fiddlers Assn., Amer. Old Time (1965), 6141 Morrill Ave., Lincoln, NE 68507; 5,000.

Film Library Assn., Educational (1943), 17 W. 60 St., N.Y., NY 10023; 1,800.

Financial Analysts Federation (1947), 1633 Broadway, N.Y., NY 10019; 14,500.

Financial Executives Institute (1931), 633 Third Ave., N.Y., NY 10017; 10,600.

Fire Chiefs, Intl. Assn. of (1872), 1329 18th St. NW, Wash., DC 20036; 7,921.

Fire Fighters, Intl. Assn. of (1918), 1750 New York Ave. NW, Wash., DC 20006; 175,000.

Fire Marshals Assn. of No. America (1906), Suite 570-S., 1800 M St. NW, Wash., DC 20036; 1,000.

Fire Protection Assn., Natl. (1896), 470 Atlantic Ave., Boston MA 02210; 32,500.

Fire Protection Engineers, Society of (1950), 60 Batterymarch St., Boston, MA 02110; 2,750.

Fish Assn., Intl. Game (1939), 3000 E. Las Olas Blvd., Ft. Lauderdale, FL 33316; 15,000.

Fishing Institute, Sport (1949), 608 13th St. NW, Wash., DC 20005; 24,500.

Fishing Tackle Manufacturers Assn., Amer. (1933), 2625 Clearbrook Dr., Arlington Heights, IL 60005; 400 companies.

Flag Assn., Amer. (1888), P.O. Box 1121, Denver, CO 80201.

Flag Institute, The Amer. (1976), 205 E. 78th St., N.Y., NY 10021; 611.

Fluid Power Society (1957), 909 N. Mayfair Rd., Milwaukee, WI 53226; 2,600.

Food Processing Machinery and Supplies Assn. (1885), 1828 L St. NW, Wash., DC 20036; 465 organizations.
Food Processors Assn., Natl. (1907), 1133 20th St. NW, Wash., DC 20036; 700.
Football Assn., U.S. Touch and Flag (1976), 2705 Normandy Dr., Youngstown, OH 44511; 20,000.
Footwear Industries Assn., Amer. (1869), 1611 N. Kent St., Arlington, VA 22209; 400.
Foreign Policy Assn. (1918), 205 Lexington Ave., N.Y., NY 10016.
Foreign Relations, Council on (1921), 58 E. 68th St., N.Y., NY 10021; 1,948.
Foreign Student Affairs, Natl. Assn. for (1948), 1860 19th St. NW, Wash., DC 20009; 3,400.
Foreign Study, Amer. Institute for (1964), 102 Greenwich Ave., Greenwich, CT 06830; 110,000.
Foreign Trade Council, Inc., Natl. (1914), 10 Rockefeller Center, N.Y., NY 10020; 600 companies.
Forensic Sciences, Amer. Academy of (1948), 11400 Rockville Pike, Rockville, MD 20852.
Forest Institute, Amer. (1932), 1619 Massachusetts Ave. NW, Wash., DC 20036; 60 companies.
Forest Products Assn., Natl. (1902), 1619 Massachusetts Ave. NW, Wash., DC 20036; 41.
Forest Products Research Society (1947), 2801 Marshall Ct., Madison, WI 53705; 5,000.
Foresters, Society of Amer. (1900), 5400 Grosvenor La., Wash., DC 20014; 21,752.
Forestry Assn., Amer. (1875), 1319 18th St. NW, Wash., DC 20036; 80,000.
Fortean Organization, Intl. (1965), 7317 Baltimore Ave., College Park, MD 20740; 1,000.
Foundrymen's Society, Amer. (1896), Golf & Wolf Rds., Des Plaines, IL 60016; 17,000.
4-H Clubs (1901-1905), Extension Service, U.S. Dept of Agriculture, Wash., DC 20250; 5.8 million.
Franklin D. Roosevelt Philatelic Society (1963), P.O. Box 150, Clinton Corners, NY 12514; 340.
Freedom, Young Americans for (1960), Woodland Rd., Sterling, VA 22170; 80,000.
Freidreich's Ataxia Group in Amer. (1970), P.O. Box 11116, Oakland, CA 94611; 2,500.
French Institute (1911), 22 E. 60th St., N.Y., NY 10022; 24,000.
Friends Service Committee, Amer. (1917), 1501 Cherry St., Phila., PA 19102; 120,000.
Frisbee Assn. (1958), P.O. Box 970, San Gabriel, CA 91776; 110,000.
Funeral and Memorial Services, Continental Assn. of (1963), 1828 L St. NW, Wash., DC 20036; 900,000.

GASP (Group Against Smokers' Pollution) (1971), P.O. Box 632, College Park, MD 20740; 25,000.
Gamblers Anonymous (1957), 2703A W. 8th St., Los Angeles, CA 90005; 6,000.
Garden Club of America (1913), 598 Madison Ave., N.Y., NY 10022; 14,000.
Garden Clubs, Natl. Council of State (1929), 4401 Magnolia Ave., St. Louis, MO 63110; 350,524.
Garden Clubs of America, Men's (1932), 5560 Merle Hay Rd., Des Moines, IA 50323; 10,000.
Gas Appliance Manufacturers Assn. (1935), 1901 N. Ft. Myer Dr., Arlington, VA 22209; 246 companies.
Gas Assn., Amer. (1918), 1515 Wilson Blvd., Arlington, VA 22209; 300.
Gay Academic Union (1974), P.O. Box 927, Los Angeles, CA 90028; 650.
Gay Task Force, Natl. (1973), 80 Fifth Ave., Suite 1601, N.Y., NY 10011; 10,000.
Genealogical Society, Natl. (1903), 1921 Sunderland Pl. NW, Wash., DC 20036; 5,000.
Genetic Assn., Amer. (1903), 818 18th St. NW, Wash., DC 20006; 1,600.
Geographers, Assn. of Amer. (1904), 1710 16th St. NW, Wash., DC 20009; 5,000.
Geographic Education, Natl. Council for (1914), 115 N. Marion St., Oak Park, IL 60301; 5,000.
Geographic Society, Natl. (1888), 17th & M Sts. NW, Wash., DC 20036, 10,700,000.
Geographical Society, Amer. (1851), Broadway at 156th St., N.Y., NY 10032; 3,000.
Geolinguistics, Amer. Society of (1965), Bronx Community College, 120 E. 181st St., Bronx, NY 10453; 100.
Geological Institute, Amer. (1948), One Skyline Pl., 5205 Leesburg Pike, Falls Church, VA 22041; 18 societies.
Geological Society of America (1888), 3300 Penrose Pl., Boulder, CO 80301; 12,500.
Geologists, Assn. of Engineering (1957), 8310 San Fernando Way, Dallas, TX 75218; 2,745.
Geophysicists, Society of Exploration (1930), P.O. Box 3098, Tulsa, OK 74135; 12,000.
George Smith Patton, Jr. Historical Society (1970), 11307 Vela Dr., San Diego, CA 92126.
Geriatrics Society, Amer. (1942), 10 Columbus Circle, N.Y., NY 10019; 9,000.
Gideons Intl. (1899), 2900 Lebanon Rd., Nashville, TN 37214; 66,000.
Gifted Children, Amer. Assn. for (1946), 15 Gramercy Park, N.Y., NY 10003.
Gifted Children, Natl. Assn. for (1953), 217 Gregory Dr., Hot Springs, AR 71901; 5,000.
Girls Clubs of America (1945), 205 Lexington Ave., N.Y., NY 10016; 220,000.
Girl Scouts of the U.S.A. (1912), 830 Third Ave., N.Y., NY 10022; 2,971,000.
Gladiolus Council, No. Amer. (1945), 6425 Adams St., Lincoln, Nebraska 68507; 1,550.
Goat Assn., American Dairy (1904), P.O. Box 865, Spindale, NC 28160; 8,500.
Gold Star Mothers, Amer. (1929), 2128 Leroy Pl. NW, Wash., DC 20008; 8,000.
Golf Association, U.S. (1894), Golf House, Far Hills, NJ 07931; 5,000 clubs.
Golf Assn., Natl. Amputee (1949), 24 Lakeview Terr., Watchung, NJ 07060; 500.
Goose Island Bird & Girl Watching Society (1960), 301 Arthur Ave., Park Ridge, IL 60068; 923.
Gospel Music Assn. (1964), 38 Music Sq. W., P.O. Box 23201, Nashville, TN 37203; 1,963.
Governmental Research Assn. (1914), 901 Ocean Gate Dr., Ocean Gate, NJ 08740; 400.
Graduate Schools in the U.S., Council of (1961), One Dupont Circle NW, Wash., DC 20036; 365 institutions.
Grandmother Clubs of America, Natl. Federation of (1938), 203 N. Wabash Ave., Chicago, IL 60601; 20,000.
Grange, Natl. (1867), 1616 H St. NW, Wash., DC 20006; 475,000.
Graphic Artists, Society of Amer. (1915), 32 Union Sq., 1214, N.Y., NY 10003; 240.
Graphic Arts, Amer. Institute of (1914), 1059 Third Ave., N.Y., NY 10021; 1,700.
Gray Panthers (1970), 3635 Chestnut, Phila., PA 19104; 50,000.
Greek-Amer. War Veterans in America, Natl. Legion (1938), 739 W. 186th St., N.Y., NY 10033; 48.
Grocers, Natl. Assn. of Retail (1893), 11800 Sunrise Valley Dr., Reston, VA 22091; 38,000.
Grocery Manufacturers of America (1908), Dodge Center, Georgetown, Wash., DC 20003; 140 firms.
Guide Dog Foundation for the Blind (1946), 109-19 72d Ave., Forest Hills, NY 11375; 35,000.
Gyro Intl. (1912), 1096 Mentor Ave., Painesville, OH 44077; 5,600.

HIAS (Hebrew Immigrant Aid Society) (1884), 200 Park Ave. S, N.Y., NY 10003; 14,000.
Hadassah, the Women's Zionist Organization of America (1912), 50 W. 58th St., N.Y., NY 10019; 370,000.
Hairdressers and Cosmetologists Assn., Natl. (1921), 3510 Olive St., St. Louis, MO 63103; 70,000.
Handball Assn., U.S. (1950), 4101 Dempster St., Skokie, IL 60076; 15,000.
Handicapped, Federation of the (1935), 211 W. 14th St., N.Y., NY 10011; 650.
Handicapped, Natl. Assn. of the Physically (1958), 76 Elm St., London, OH 43140; 1,100.
Hang Gliding Assn., U.S. (1971), 11312 1/2 Venice Blvd., Los Angeles, CA 90066; 8,000.
Health Council, Natl. (1920), 1740 Broadway, N.Y., NY 10019; 83 agencies.
Health Insurance Assn. of America (1956), 1750 K St. NW, Wash., DC 20006; 306 companies.
Health Insurance Institute (1956), 1850 K St. NW, Wash., DC; 325 companies.
Health, Physical Education, Recreation and Dance, Amer.

Alliance for (1885), 1900 Association Dr., Reston, VA 22091; 45,000.
Hearing Aid Society, Natl. (1951), 20361 Middlebelt Rd., Livonia, MI 48152; 3,600.
Hearing and Speech Action, Natl. Assn. for (1919), 814 Thayer Ave., Silver Spring, MD 20910; 12,000.
Heart Assn., Amer. (1924), 7320 Greenville Ave., Dallas TX 75231; 110,000.
Hearts, Mended (1955), 721 Huntington Ave., Boston, MA 02115; 9,000.
Heating, Refrigerating & Air Conditioning Engineers, Amer. Society of (1895), 345 E. 47th St., N.Y., NY 10017; 36,000.
Helicopter Assn. of America (1948), 1156 15th St. NW, Wash., DC 20005; 700 companies.
Helicopter Society, Amer. (1943), 1325 18th St. NW, Wash., DC 20036; 3,500.
Hemispheric Affairs, Council on (1975), 1201 16th St. NW, Wash., DC 20036.
High School Assns., Natl. Federation of State (1920), 11724 Plaza Circle, Box 20626, Kansas City, MO 64195; 51.
High Twelve Internatl. (1921), 3681 Lindell Blvd., St. Louis, MO 63108; 20,000.
Historians, Organization of Amer. (1907), 112 N. Bryan St., Bloomington, IN 47401; 8,500.
Historical Assn., Amer. (1884), 400 A St. SE, Wash., DC 20003; 15,000.
Historic Preservation, Natl. Trust for (1949), 1785 Massachusetts Ave. NW, Wash., DC 20036; 160,000.
Hockey Assn. of the U.S., Amateur (1937), 2997 Broadmoor Valley Rd., Colorado Springs, CO 80906; 10,805.
Holiday Institute of Yonkers (1969), Box 414, Yonkers, NY 10710.
Holy Cross of Jerusalem, Order of (1965), 853 Seventh Ave., N.Y., NY 10019; 2,003.
Home Builders, Natl. Assn. of (1942), 15th & M Sts. NW, Wash., DC 20005; 85,000 firms.
Home Economics Assn., Amer. (1909), 2010 Massachusetts Ave. NW, Wash., DC 20036; 40,000.
Home Improvement Council, Natl. (1956), 11 E. 44th St., N.Y., NY 10017; 3,200.
Homemakers of America, Future (1945), 2010 Massachusetts Ave. NW, Wash., DC 20036; 450,000.
Homemakers Council, Natl. Extension (1936), 1139 19th Ave., Longview, WA 98632; 487,488.
Horatio Alger Society (1961), 4907 Allison Dr., Lansing, MI 48910; 250.
Horse Protection Assn., Amer. (1966), 1312 18th St. NW, Wash., DC 20036; 15,000.
Horse Show Assn. of America Ltd., Natl. (1883), 527 Madison Ave., N.Y., NY 10022.
Horse Shows Assn., Amer. (1917), 598 Madison Ave., N.Y., NY 10022; 25,000.
Hospital Assn., Amer. (1898), 840 N. Lake Shore Dr., Chicago, IL 60611; 31,242.
Hospital Public Relations, Amer. Society for (1965), 840 N. Lake Shore Dr., Chicago, IL 60611; 1,069.
Hotel & Motel Assn., Amer. (1910), 888 Seventh Ave., N.Y., NY 10019; 7,447 hotels & motels.
Hot Rod Assn., Natl. (1951), 10639 Riverside Dr., N. Hollywood, CA 91602; 40,000.
Humane Legislation, Committee for (1967), 11 W. 60th St., N.Y., NY 10023; 60,000.
Humane Society of the U.S. (1954), 2100 L St. NW, Wash., DC 20037; 75,000.
Humanics Foundation, Amer. (1948), 912 Baltimore Ave., Kansas City, MO 64111; 1,400.
Humanities, Natl. Endowment for the (1965), 806 15th St. NW, Wash., DC 20506.
Human Rights and Social Justice, Americans for (1977), 109 Bentbridge Rd., Greenville, SC 29611; 1,400.

Iceland Veterans (1948), 2101 Walnut St., Phila., PA 19103; 1,600+.
Identification, Intl. Assn. for (1915), P.O. Box 139, Utica, NY 13503; 2,500.
Illustrators, Society of (1901), 128 E. 63d St., N.Y., NY 10021; 700.
Indian Rights Assn. (1882), 1505 Race St., Phila., PA 19102; 2,500.
Industrial Democracy, League for (1905), 275 Seventh Ave., N.Y., NY 10001; 1,500.
Industrial Designers Society of America, 1717 N St. NW, Wash., DC 20036; 1,700.
Industrial Engineers, Amer. Institute of (1948), 25 Technology Park, Norcross, GA 30092; 31,000.
Industrial Health Foundation (1935), 5231 Centre Ave. Pittsburgh, PA 15232; 150 companies.
Industrial Management Society (1937), 570 Northwes Hwy., Des Plaines, IL 60016; 1,000.
Infant Death Syndrome (SIDS) Foundation, Natl. Sudden (1962), 310 S. Michigan Ave., Chicago, IL 60604.
Information, Freedom of, Center (1958), P.O. Box 858, Columbia, MO 65205; 2,000.
Information Managers, Associated (1978), 316 Pennsylvania Ave. SE, Suite 502, Wash., DC 20003; 850.
Information Industry Assn. (1968), 316 Pennsylvania Ave S.E., Suite 502, Wash., DC 20003; 130 corporations.
Insurance Assn., Amer. (1866), 85 John St., N.Y., NY 10038 147 companies.
Intelligence Officers, Assn. of Former (1975), 6723 Whittier Ave., Suite 303A, McLean, VA 22101; 2,800.
Intercollegiate Athletics, Natl. Assn. of (1940), 122* Baltimore Ave., Kansas City, MO 64105; 514 schools.
Interior Designers, Amer. Society of (1975), 730 Fifth Ave. N.Y., NY 10019; 17,000.
Inventors, Amer. Assn. of (1975), 6562 E. Curtis Rd. Bridgeport, MI 48722; 5,000.
Investment Clubs, Natl. Assn. of (1951), 1515 E. Eleven Mile Rd., Royal Oak, MI 48067; 3,884 clubs.
Iron Castings Society (1975), 20611 Center Ridge Rd. Rocky River, OH 44116; 250 firms.
Iron and Steel Engineers, Assn. of (1907), Three Gateway Center, Suite 2350, Pittsburgh, PA 15222; 13,447.
Iron and Steel Institute, Amer. (1908), 1000 16th St. NW Wash., DC 20036; 2,500.
Italian Historical Society of America (1949), 111 Columbia Heights, Bklyn., NY 11201; 2,300.
Italy-America Chamber of Commerce (1887), 350 Fifth Ave., N.Y., NY 10001; 850.
Izaak Walton League of America, The (1922), 1800 N. Kent St., Arlington, VA 22209; 52,000.

Jamestowne Society (1936), P.O. Box 7389, Richmond, VA 23221; 2,000.
Japanese Amer. Citizens League (1929), 1765 Sutter St., San Francisco, CA 94115; 30,000.
Jaycees, U.S. (1920), 4 W. 21st St., Tulsa, OK 74121; 380,000.
Jewish Appeal, United (1939), 1290 Ave. of the Americas, N.Y., NY 10019.
Jewish Center Workers, Assn. of (1918), 15 E. 26th St., N.Y., NY 10010; 1,050.
Jewish Committee, Amer. (1906), 165 E. 56th St., N.Y., NY 10022; 40,000.
Jewish Congress, Amer. (1918), 15 E. 84th St., N.Y., NY 10028; 50,000.
Jewish Federations, Council of (1932), 575 Lexington Ave., N.Y., NY 10022; 200 agencies.
Jewish Historical Society, Amer. (1892), 2 Thornton Rd., Waltham, MA 02154; 3,450.
Jewish War Veterans of the U.S.A. (1896), 1712 New Hampshire Ave. NW, Wash., DC 20009; 73,000.
Jewish Welfare Board, Natl. (1917), 15 E. 26th St., N.Y., NY 10010; serves 1,000,000.
Jewish Women, Natl. Council of (1893), 15 E. 26th St., N.Y., NY 10010; 100,000.
Job's Daughters, Internatl. Order of (1921), 1820 Douglas, Masonic Temple, Omaha, NE 68102; 78,000.
Jockey Club (1894), 380 Madison Ave., N.Y., NY 10017; 88.
Jogging Assn., Natl. (1968), 2420 K St. NW, Wash., DC 20037; 35,000.
John Birch Society (1958), 395 Concord Ave., Belmont, MA 02178; 60,000 to 100,000.
Journalists, Society of Professional; (Sigma Delta Chi) (1909), 35 E. Wacker Dr., Chicago, IL 60601; 80,000.
Journalists and Authors, Amer. Society of (1948), 1501 Broadway, Suite 1907, N.Y., NY 10036; 550.
Judaism, Amer. Council for (1943), 307 Fifth Ave., N.Y., NY 10016.
Judicature Society, Amer. (1913), 200 W. Monroe, Suite 1606, Chicago, IL 60606; 36,000.
Juggler's Assn., Intl. (1947), 40 E. Village Green, Budd Lake, NJ 07828; 1,000.
Junior Achievement (1919), 550 Summer St., Stamford, CT 06901; 300,000.
Junior Colleges, Amer. Assn. of Community and (1921), One Dupont Circle NW, Wash., DC 20036; 900.
Junior Leagues, Assn. of (1921), 825 Third Ave., N.Y., NY 10022; 130,000.

Kennel Club, Amer. (1884), 51 Madison Ave., N.Y., NY 0010; 406 clubs.
Key Club Intl. (1925), 101 E. Erie St., Chicago, IL 60611; 2,000.
Kitefliers Assn., Intl. (1955), 321 E. 48th St., N.Y., NY 10017; 0,000.
Kiwanis Intl. (1915), 101 E. Erie St., Chicago, IL 60611; 00,000.
Knights of Columbus (1882), One Columbus Plaza, New aven, CT 06507; 1,316,207.
Knights Templar U.S.A., Grand Encampment (1816), 14 E. ackson Blvd., Suite 1700, Chicago, IL 60604; 360,000.

Lacrosse Foundation (1959), Newton H. White Athletic Ctr., omewood, Baltimore, MD 21218; 5,500.
La Leche League Intl. (1956), 9616 Minneapolis, Franklin ark, IL 60131; 50,000.
Lambs, The (1874), 131 W. 56th St., N.Y., NY 10019; 400.
Landscape Architects, Amer. Society of (1899), 1900 M t. NW, Wash., DC 20036; 4,700.
Law, Amer. Society of Intl. (1906), 2223 Massachusetts ve. NW, Wash., DC 20008; 5,500.
Law Enforcement Officers Assn., Amer. (1972), 2000 P St. W, Rm 615, Wash., DC 20036; 90,000.
Law Libraries, Amer. Assn. of (1906), 53 W. Jackson Blvd., hicago, IL 60604; 3,019.
Law and Social Policy, Center for (1969), 1751 N St. NW, Vash., DC 20036.
Learned Societies, Amer. Council of (1919), 800 Third ve., N.Y., NY 10022; 43 Societies.
Lefthanders, League of (1975), P.O. Box 89, New Milford, J 07646; 400.
Lefthanders Intl. (1975), 3601 SW 29th St., Topeka, KS 6614; 5,000.
Legal Secretaries, Natl. Assn. of (1949), 3005 E. Skelly Dr., ulsa, OK 74105; 25,000.
Legion of Valor of the U.S.A. (1890), 621 S. Taylor St., Arington, VA 22204; 750.
Leprosy Missions, Amer. (1906), 1262 Broad St., Bloomield, NJ 07003; 45,000 donor members.
Leukemia Society of America (1949), 800 Second Ave., .Y., NY 10017; 1,400 trustees.
Lewis Carroll Society of N. America (1974), 617 Rockford d., Silver Spring, MD 20902; 350.
Liberty Lobby (1955), 300 Independence Ave. SE, Wash., C 20003; 27,000.
Libraries Assn., Special (1909), 235 Park Ave. So., N.Y., NY 0003; 11,500.
Library Assn., Amer. (1876), 50 E. Huron St., Chicago, IL 0611; 35,524.
Library Assn., Medical (1898), 919 N. Michigan Ave., Chiago, IL 60611; 5,300.
Life Insurance, Amer. Council of (1976), 1850 K St. NW, Vash., DC 20006; 444 companies.
Life Office Management Assn. (1924), 100 Colony Sq., Atanta, GA 30361; 600 companies.
Life Underwriters, Natl. Assn. of (1890), 1922 F St. NW, Vash., DC 20006; 135,000.
Lighter-Than-Air Society (1952), 1800 Triplett Blvd., Akron, OH 44306; 1,000.
Lions Clubs, Intl. Assn. of (1917), 300 22d St., Oak Brook, L 60570; 1,260,000.
Literacy Volunteers of America (1962), 623 Midtown Plaza, 700 E. Water St., Syracuse, NY 13210; 22,000.
Little League Baseball (1939), P.O. Box 3485, Williamsport, PA 17701; 13,000 leagues.
Little People of America (1960), Box 126, Owatonna, MN 55060; 5,000.
Log Rolling Assn., Intl. (1926), 1407 1st Ave. S., Escanaba, MI 49829; 225.
London Club (1975), P.O. Box 4527, Topeka, KS 66604; 1,000+.
Lung Assn., Amer. (1904), 1740 Broadway, N.Y., NY 10019.
Lutheran Education Assn. (1942), 7400 Augusta St., River Forest, IL 60305; 2,745.
Lutheran World Ministries, 360 Park Ave. S., N.Y., NY 10010.

Macaroni Manufacturers Assn., Natl. (1904), 19 S. Bothwell, Box 336, Palatine, IL 60067; 91 firms.
Magazine Publishers Assn. (1919), 575 Lexington Ave., N.Y., NY 10022; 156 companies.
Magicians, Intl. Brotherhood of (1926), 28 N. Main St., Kenton, OH 43326; 11,000.
Magicians, Society of Amer. (1902), 66 Marked Tree Rd., Needham, MA 02192; 5,500.
Magicians Guild of America (1943), 20 W. 40th St., N.Y., NY 10018; 167.
Male Nurse Assn., Natl. (1975), 2309 State St. W., Saginaw, MI 48602; 14,729.
Management Assns., Amer. (1923), 135 W. 50th St., N.Y., NY 10020; 75,000.
Management Consultants, Institute of (1968), 347 Madison Ave., N.Y., NY 10017; 825.
Management Engineers, Assn. of Consulting (1929), 230 Park Ave., N.Y., NY 10017; 52 firms.
Manufacturers, Natl. Assn. of (1895), 1776 F St. NW, Wash., DC 20006; 13,000 companies.
Manufacturers' Agents Natl. Assn. (1947), 2021 Business Center Dr., Irvine, CA 92713; 6,000.
Manuscript Society, 1206 N. Stoneman Ave., 15, Alhambra, CA 91801; 1,500.
Man Watchers (1974), 2865 State St., San Diego, CA 92103; 4,000.
March of Dimes, Natl. Foundation of the (1938), 1275 Mamaroneck Ave., White Plains, NY 10605; 1,100 chapters.
Marijuana Laws, Natl. Organization for the Reform of (NORML) (1970), 2317 M St. NW, Wash., DC 20037; 25,000.
Marine Corps League (1937), 933 N. Kenmore St., Arlington, VA 22201; 25,000.
Marine Manufacturers Assn., Natl. (1979), 666 Third Ave., N.Y., NY 10017; 960.
Marine Surveyors, Natl. Assn. of (1948), 86 Windsor Gate Dr., N. Hills, NY 11040; 350.
Marine Technology Society (1963), 1730 M St. NW, Wash., DC 20036; 4,000.
Marketing Assn., Amer. (1937), 222 S. Riverside Plaza, Chicago, IL 60606; 26,000.
Masonic Relief Assn. of U.S. and Canada (1885), 32613 Seidel Dr., Burlington, WS 53105; 14,700.
Masonic Service Assn. of the U.S. (1919), 8120 Fenton St., Silver Spring, MD 20910; 43 Grand Lodges.
Masons, Ancient and Accepted Scottish Rite, Southern Jurisdiction, Supreme Council (1801), 1733 16th St. NW, Wash., DC 20009; 661,000.
Masons, Supreme Council 33°, Ancient and Accepted Scottish Rite, Northern Masonic Jurisdiction (1813), 33 Marret Rd., Lexington, MA 02173; 508,117.
Masons, Royal Arch, General Grand Chapter (1797), P.O. Box 5320, Lexington, KY 40505; 455,000.
Mathematical Assn. of America (1915), 1225 Connecticut Ave. NW, Wash., DC 20036; 18,500.
Mathematical Society, Amer. (1894), Box 6248, Providence, RI 02904; 19,324.
Mathematical Statistics, Institute of (1935), 3401 Investment Blvd., 6, Hayward, CA 94545; 3,200.
Mathematics, Society for Industrial and Applied (1952), 33 S. 17th St., Phila., PA 19103; 4,615.
Mayflower Descendants, General Society of (1897), P.O. Box 297, Plymouth, MA 02360; 18,075.
Mayors, U.S. Conference of (1932), 1620 Eye St. NW, Wash., DC 20006; 500 cities.
Mechanical Engineers, Amer. Society of (1880), 345 E. 47th St., N.Y., NY 10017; 75,000.
Mechanics, Amer. Academy of (1969), Engineering Science and Mechanics Dept., Virginia Polytechnic Institute and State Univ., Blacksburg, VA 24061; 975.
Mechanics, Assn. of Chairmen of Departments of (1969), Dept. of Theoretical and Applied Mechanics, Univ. of Ill. at Urbana-Champaign, Urbana, IL 61801; 96.
Mechanics, Junior Order of United Amer. (1853), 170 Railway Rd., Crafton, VA 23692; 3,000.
Mediaeval Academy of America (1925), 1430 Massachusetts Ave., Cambridge, MA 02138; 4,100.
Medical Assn., Amer. (1847), 535 N. Dearborn St., Chicago, IL 60610; 223,000.
Medical Assn., Natl. (1895), 1720 Massachusetts Ave. NW, Wash., DC 20036; 6,400.
Medical Record Assn., Amer. (1928), 875 N. Michigan Ave., Chicago, IL 60611; 20,500.
Medical Technologists, Amer. College of (1942), 5608 Lane, Raytown, MO 64133; 368.
Memorabilia Americana (1973), 1211 Ave. Eye, Brooklyn, NY 11230; 720.
Mensa, Amer. (1960), 1701 W. 3d St., Brooklyn, NY 11223; 40,000.
Mental Health, Natl. Assn. for (1909), 1800 N. Kent St., Arlington, VA 22209; 1,000,000.
Mental Health Program Directors, Natl. Assn. of State (1963), 1001 3d St. SW, Wash., DC 20024, 54.
Merchant Marine Library Assn., Amer. (1921), One World Trade Center, Suite 2601, N.Y., NY 10048.
Merchants Assn., Natl. Retail (1911), 100 W. 31st St., N.Y., NY 10001; 35,000 stores.

Metal Finishers, Natl. Assn. of (1951), 111 E. Wacker Dr., Chicago, IL 60601; 960.

Metallurgy Institute, Amer. Powder (1959), P.O. Box 2054, Princeton, NJ 08540; 2,000.

Metal Powder Industries Federation, (1946), P.O. Box 2054, Princeton, NJ 08540; 225 cos.

Metals, Amer. Society for (1913), Metals Park, OH 44073; 43,000.

Meteorological Society, Amer. (1919), 45 Beacon St., Boston, MA 02108; 9,700.

Metric Assn., U.S. (1916), Sugarloaf Star Rte., Boulder, CO 80302; 2,600.

Microbiology, Amer. Society for (1899), 1913 Eye St. NW, Wash. DC 20006; 30,000.

Micrographics Assn., Natl. (1943), 8719 Colesville Rd., Silver Spring, MD 20910; 9,000.

Mideast Educational and Training Services, America-, formerly **Amer. Friends of the Middle East** (1951), 1717 Massachusetts Ave. NW, Wash., DC 20036; 390.

Military Order of the Loyal Legion of the U.S.A. (1865), 1805 Pine St., Phila., PA 19103; 1,200.

Military Order of the Purple Heart (1782, by Gen. George Washington; reactivated Feb. 22, 1932, by President Herbert Hoover and Chief of Staff Douglas MacArthur), 1022 Wilson Blvd., Arlington, VA 22209; 10,000.

Military Order of the World Wars (1920), 1100 17th St. NW, Wash., DC 20036; 14,500.

Mining, Metallurgical and Petroleum Engineers, Amer. Institute of (1871), 345 E. 47th St., N.Y., NY 10017; 63,754.

Mining and Metallurgical Society of America (1908), 230 Park Ave., N.Y., NY 10017; 310.

Ministerial Assn., Amer. (1929), 446 Salem Ave., P.O. Box 1252, York, PA 17405; 18,179.

Model Railroad Assn., Natl. (1935), 7061 Twin Oaks Dr., Indianapolis, IN 46226; 29,500.

Modern Language Assn. of America (1883), 62 Fifth Ave., N.Y., NY 10011; 28,000.

Modern Language Teachers Assns., Natl. Federation of (1916), Dept. of Foreign Languages, Gannon Coll., Erie, PA 16541; 7,800.

Monopoly Assn., U.S. (1963), 1646 City National Bank Bldg., Detroit, MI 48226; 625.

Moose, Loyal Order of (1913), Mooseheart, IL 60539; 1,700,522.

Mothers Committee, Amer. (1933), Waldorf Astoria Hotel, 301 Park Ave., N.Y., NY 10022; 5,000.

Mothers-in-Law Club Intl. (1970), 420 Adelberg Ln., Cedarhurst, NY 11516; 5,000.

Mothers of Twins Clubs, Natl. Organization of (1960), 5402 Amberwood Ln., Rockville, MD 20853; 7,986.

Motion Picture Arts & Sciences, Academy of (1929), 8949 Wilshire Blvd., Beverly Hills, CA 90211; 4,225.

Motion Pictures, Natl. Board of Review of (1909), P.O. Box 589, N.Y., NY 10021; 200.

Motion Picture & Television Engineers, Society of (1916), 862 Scarsdale Ave., Scarsdale, NY 10583; 9,000.

Motor Car Club of America, Veteran (1938), 15 Newton St., Brookline, MA 02146; 6,850.

Motor Vehicle Administrators, Amer. Assn. of (1933), 1201 Connecticut Ave. NW, Wash., DC 20036.

Motor Vehicle Manufacturers Assn. (1913), 300 New Center Building, Detroit, MI 48202; 12 companies.

Motorcyclist Assn., Amer. (1924), 33 Collegeview Ave., Westerville, OH 43081; 130,000.

Multiple Sclerosis Society, Natl. (1946), 205 E. 42d St., N.Y., NY 10017; 450,000.

Municipal Finance Officers Assn. of the U.S. & Canada (1906), 180 N. Michigan Ave., Suite 800, Chicago, IL 60601; 7,200.

Municipal League, Natl. (1894), 47 E. 68th St., N.Y., NY 10021; 6,500.

Mural Painters, Natl. Society of (1895), 41 E. 65th St., N.Y., NY 10021; 150.

Muscular Dystrophy Assn. (1950), 810 Seventh Ave., N.Y., NY 10019, 28,000.

Museums, Amer. Assn. of (1906), 1055 Thomas Jefferson St. NW, Wash., DC 20007; 6,166.

Music, Natl. Assn. of Schools of (1924), 11250 Roger Bacon Dr. #5, Reston, VA 22090; 500 institutions.

Music Center, Amer. (1940), 250 W. 57th St., N.Y., NY 10019; 1,000+.

Music Clubs, Natl. Federation of (1898), 310 S. Michigan Ave., Chicago, IL 60604; 500,000.

Music Conference, Amer. (1947), 1000 Skokie Blvd., Wilmette, IL 60091; 400.

Music Council, Natl. (1940), 250 W. 54th St., N.Y., NY 10019; 65.

Music Educators Natl. Conference (1907), 1902 Association Dr., Reston, VA 22091; 60,000.

Musicians, Amer. Federation of (1896), 1500 Broadway, N.Y., NY 10036; 330,000.

Musicological Society, Amer. (1934), 201 S. 34th St., Phila PA 19104, 4,700.

Music Publishers' Assn., Natl. (1917), 110 E. 59th St., N.Y NY 10022; 203.

Music Scholarship Assn., Amer. (1956), 1826 Carew Tower Cincinnati, OH 45202; 1,500.

Music Teachers Natl. Assn. (1876), 2113 Carew Tower, Cincinnati, OH 45202; 19,740.

Muzzle Loading Rifle Assn., Natl. (1933), P.O. Box 67 Friendship, IN 47021; 24,000.

Mystic Seaport (1929), 30 Greenmanville Ave., Mystic, CT 06355; 17,000.

NAACP (Natl. Assn. for the Advancement of Colored People (1909), 1790 Broadway, N.Y., NY 10019, 500,000.

Name Society, Amer. (1951). N. Country Community College, Saranac Lake, NY 12983; 930.

Narcolepsy and Cataplexy Foundation of Amer. (1975) 1410 York Ave., Suite 2D, N.Y. NY 10021; 3,200.

Narcolepsy Assoc., Amer. (1975), P.O. Box 5846, Stanford CA 94305; 3,400.

National Guard Assn. of the U.S. (1878), One Massachusetts Ave. NW, Wash., DC 20001; 48,000.

Nationalities Service, Amer. Council for (1918), 20 W. 40th St., N.Y., NY 10018; 31 agencies.

Naturalists, Assn. of Interpretive (1961), 6700 Needwood Rd., Derwood, MD 20855; 1,000.

Natural Science for Youth Foundation (1942), 763 Silvermine Rd., New Canaan, CT 06840; 375.

Nature Conservancy (1950), 1800 N. Kent St., Arlington, VA 22209; 70,000.

Nature & Natural Resources, Intl. Union for Conservation of (1948), Avenue du Mont Blanc, 1196 Gland, Switzerland; 449 organizations.

Nature Study Society, Amer. (1908), 790 Ewing Ave., Franklin Lakes, NJ 07417; 1,000.

Navajo Code Talkers Assn. (1971), Red Rock State Park, P.O. Box 328, Church Rock, NM 87311; 90.

Naval Architects & Marine Engineers, Society of (1893), One World Trade Center, Suite 1369, N.Y., NY 10048; 12,500.

Naval Engineers, Amer. Society of (1888), 1012 14th St. NW, Wash., DC 20005; 5,000.

Naval Institute, U.S. (1873), U.S. Naval Academy, Annapolis, MD 21402; 70,000.

Naval Reserve Assn. (1954), 910 17th St. NW, Wash., DC 20006; 19,500.

Navigation, Institute of (1945), 815 15th St. NW, Suite 832, Wash., DC 20005; 2,500.

Navy Club of the U.S.A. Auxiliary (1940), 216 W. Suttenfield, Fort Wayne, IN 46807; 1,000.

Navy League of the U.S. (1902); 818 18th St. NW, Wash., DC 20006; 40,000.

Needlework Guild of America (1885), 1342 E. Lincoln Hwy., Langhorne, PA 19047; 5,000.

Negro College Fund, United (1944), 600 E. 62d St., N.Y., NY 10021; 41 institutions.

Newspaper Editors, Amer. Society of (1922), 1350 Sullivan Trail, Easton, PA 18042; 860.

Newspaper Promotion Assn., Intl. (1930), 11600 Sunrise Valley Dr., Reston, VA 22091; 1,300.

Newspaper Publishers Assn., Amer. (1887), 11600 Sunrise Valley Dr., Reston, VA 22091; 1,300 newspapers.

Ninety-Nines (Internatl. Organization of Women Pilots) (1929), P.O. Box 59965; Will Rogers World Airport, Oklahoma City, OK 73159, 5,500.

Non-Commissioned Officers Assn. (1960), 10635 IH 35 No., San Antonio, TX 78233; 200,000.

Non-Parents, Natl. Organization for (1972), 3 N. Liberty, Baltimore, MD 21201; 1,500.

Notaries, Amer. Society of (1965), 810 18th St. NW, Wash., DC 20006; 11,102.

Nuclear Society, Amer. (1954), 555 N. Kensington Ave., La Grange Park, IL 60525; 12,825.

Numismatic Assn., Amer. (1891), 818 N. Cascade Ave., Colorado Springs, CO 80903; 34,000.

Numismatic Society, Amer. (1858), Broadway at 155th St., N.Y., NY 10032; 1,995.

Nurse Education and Service, Natl. Assn. for Practical (1941), 122 E. 42d St., N.Y., NY 10017; 33,000.

Nurses, Natl. Federation of Licensed Practical (1949), 888 7th Ave., N.Y., NY 10019; 18,000.

Nurses' Assn., Amer. (1896), 2420 Pershing Rd., Kansas City, MO 64108; 200,000.

Nursing, Natl. League for (1952), 10 Columbus Circle, N.Y., NY 10019; 17,000.

Nutrition, Amer. Institute of (1928), 9650 Rockville Pike, Bethesda, MD 20014; 2,000.

ORT Federation, Amer. (Org. for Rehabilitation through Training) (1922), 817 Broadway, N.Y., NY 10013, 150,000.
Odd Fellows, Soverign Grand Lodge Independent Order of (1819), 16 W. Chase St., Baltimore, MD 21201; 739,826.
Old Crows, Assn. of (1964), 2300 9th St. S., Arlington, VA 22204; 10,000.
Olympic Committee, U.S. (1921), 1750 E. Boulder St., Colorado Springs, CO 80909.
Optical Society of America (1916), 1816 Jefferson Pl. NW, Wash., DC 20036; 8,652.
Optimist Intl. (1919), 4494 Lindell Blvd., St. Louis, MO 63108; 125,000.
Optometric Assn., Amer. (1898), 243 N. Lindbergh Blvd., St. Louis, MO 63141; 20,025.
Oral and Maxillofacial Surgeons, Amer. Assn. of (1918), 211 E. Chicago Ave., Chicago, IL 60611; 3,730.
Organists, Amer. Guild of (1896), 815 Second Ave., Suite 318, N.Y., NY 10017; 16,900.
Oriental Society, Amer. (1842), 329 Sterling Memorial Library, Yale Sta., New Haven, CT 06520, 1,500.
Ornithologists' Union, Amer. (1883), c/o National Museum of Natural History, Smithsonian Institution, Wash., DC 20560; 4,000.
Osteopathic Assn., Amer. (1901), 212 E. Ohio St., Chicago, IL 60611; 14,000.
Ostomy Assn., United (1962), 2001 W. Beverly Blvd., Los Angeles, CA 90057; 40,000.
Outlaw and Lawman History, Natl. Assn. and Center for (1974), Utah State Univ., Merrill Library 104, UMC 30, Logan, Utah 84321; 400.
Overeaters Anonymous (1960), 2190 190th St., Torrance, CA 90504; 100,000.
Over-the-Counter Cos., Natl. Assn. of (1973), Box 110, Jenkintown, PA 19046; 225 cos.

PTA (Parents Teachers Assn.), Natl. (1897), 700 N. Rush St., Chicago, IL 60611; 6.5 million.
Paleontological Research Institution (1932), 1259 Trumansburg Rd., Ithaca, NY 14850, 600.
Paper Converters Assn. (1934), 1619 Massachusetts Ave. NW, Wash., DC 20036; 25 companies.
Paper Institute, Amer. (1964), 260 Madison Ave., N.Y., NY 10016; 200 companies.
Parasitologists, Amer. Society of (1925), 1041 New Hampshire St., Box 368, Lawrence, KS 66044; 1,800.
Parenthood, Natl. Alliance for Optional (1972), 2010 Massachusetts Ave. NW, Wash., DC 20036; 2,000.
Parents Without Partners (1958), 7910 Woodmont Ave. NW, Wash., DC 20014; 182,559.
Parking Assn., Natl. (1951), 1101 17th St. NW, Wash., DC 20036; 700 companies.
Parkinson's Disease Foundation (1957), Wm. Black Research Bldg., 640 W. 168th St., N.Y., NY 10032.
Pathologists, Amer. Assn. of (1976), 9650 Rockville Pike, Bethesda, MD 20014; 2,100.
Patriotism, Natl. Committee for Responsible (1967), P.O. Box 5336, Grand Central Sta., N.Y., NY 10017; 150.
Patriotism, Natl. Council for the Encouragement of (1968), 1502 Janice Ln., Munster, IN 46321; 2,000.
Pearl Harbor Survivors Assn. (1958). Drawer 00, McLean, VA 22101; 7,900.
P.E.N. Amer. Center (1921), 47 Fifth Ave., N.Y., NY 10003; 1,800.
Pen Women, Natl. League of Amer. (1897), 1300 17th St. NW, Wash., DC 20036; 6,200.
Pennsylvania Society (1899), Suite 594, Waldorf Astoria Hotel, 301 Park Ave., N.Y., NY 10022; 2,100.
P.E.O (Philanthropic Educational Organization) Sisterhood (1869), 3700 Grand Ave., Des Moines, IA 50312; 212,000.
Personnel Administration, Amer. Society for (1948), 30 Park Dr., Berea, OH 44017; 27,000.
Personnel & Guidance Assn., Amer. (1952), 1607 New Hampshire Ave. NW, Wash., DC 20009; 40,000.
Petroleum Geologists, Amer. Assn. of (1917), Box 979, 1444 S. Boulder, Tulsa, OK 74101; 18,734.
Petroleum Institute, Amer. (1919), 2101 L St. NW, Wash., DC 20037; 7,500.
Petroleum Landmen, Amer. Assn. of (1955), 2408 Continental Life Bldg., Fort Worth, TX 76102; 6,200.
Pharmaceutical Assn., Amer. (1852), 2215 Constitution Ave. NW, Wash., DC 20037; 56,000.
Philatelic Americans, Society of (1894), 58 W. Salisbury Dr., Wilmington, DE 19809; 8,500.
Philatelic Society, Amer. (1886), P.O. Box 800, 336 S. Fraser St., State College, PA 16801; 50,170.
Philatelists of Amer., Jr. (1976), P.O. Box 116, Ashton, RI 02864; 800.
Philaticians, Society of (1972), P.O. Box 150, Salt Point Tpke., Clinton Corners, NY 12514; 285.
Philological Assn., Amer. (1869), 617 Hamilton Hall, Columbia Univ., N.Y., NY 10027; 2,800.
Philosophical Assn., Amer. (1900), Univ. of Delaware, Newark, DE 19711; 6,200.
Philosophical Enquiry, Intl. Society for (1974), 12 N. Church Rd., Saddle River, NJ 07458; 192.
Philosophical Society, Amer. (1743), 104 S. 5th St., Phila., PA 19106; 628.
Photographers of America, Professional (1880), 1090 Executive Way, Des Plaines, IL 60018; 15,000.
Photographic Society of Amer. (1934), 2005 Walnut St., Phila. PA 19103; 17,000.
Physical Therapy Assn., Amer. (1921), 1156 15th St. NW. Wash., DC 20005; 32,161.
Physicians, Amer. Academy of Family (1947), 1740 W. 92nd St., Kansas City, MO 64114; 43,000.
Physics, Amer. Institute of (1931), 335 E. 45th St., N.Y., NY 10017; 60,000.
Physiological Society, Amer. (1887), 9650 Rockville Pike, Bethesda, MD 20014; 5,200.
Pilgrim Society (1820), 75 Court St., Plymouth, MA 02360; 1,000.
Pilgrims of the U.S. (1903), 74 Trinity Pl., N.Y., NY 10006; 1,000.
Pilot Club Intl. (1921), 244 College St., Box 4844 Macon, GA 31208; 20,000.
Pioneer Women, The Women's Labor Zionist Organization of America (1925), 200 Madison Ave., N.Y., NY 10016; 50,000.
Planned Parenthood Federation of America (1916), 810 Seventh Ave., N.Y., NY 10019; 189 affiliates.
Planners, Amer. Institute of (1917), 1776 Massachusetts Ave., NW, Wash., DC 20036; 11,838.
Plastic Modelers Society, Intl. (1964), P.O. Box 7704, Long Beach, CA 90807; 6,000.
Plastics Engineers, Society of (1942), 14 Fairfield Dr., Brookfield Cntr., CT 06805; 22,200.
Plastics Industry, Society of (1937), 355 Lexington Ave., N.Y., NY 10017; 1,400 companies.
Platform Assn., Intl. (1831), 2564 Berkshire Rd., Cleveland Heights, OH 44106; 5,700.
Podiatry Assn., Amer. (1912), 20 Chevy Chase Circle NW, Wash., DC 20015; 7,000.
Poetry Day Committee, Natl. (1947), 1110 N. Venetian Dr., Miami, FL 33139; 17,000.
Poetry Society of America (1910), 15 Gramercy Park, N.Y., NY 10003; 1,000.
Poets, Academy of Amer. (1934), 1078 Madison Ave., N.Y., NY 10028.
Polar Society, Amer. (1934), c/o Secretary, 98-20 62d Dr., Apt. 7H, Rego Park, NY 11374; 2,391.
Police, Internatl. Assn. of Chiefs of (1893), 11 Firstfield Rd., Gaithersburg, MD 20760; 12,000.
Police Reserve Officers Assn., Natl. (1967), 609 W. Main St., Louisville, KY 40202; 11,000.
Polish Army Veterans Assn. of America (1921), 19 Irving Pl., N.Y., NY 10003; 9,762.
Polish Cultural Society of America (1940), 43 John St., N.Y., NY 10038; 66,305.
Polish Legion of American Veterans (1920), 3024 N. Laramie Ave., Chicago, IL 60641; 150,000.
Political Items Collectors, Amer. (1945), 1054 Sharpsburg Dr., Huntsville, AL 35803; 2,100.
Political Science, Academy of (1880), 619 W. 114th St., Suite 500, N.Y., NY 10025; 10,000.
Political Science Assn., Amer. (1903), 1527 New Hampshire Ave. NW, Wash., DC 20036; 13,075.
Political & Social Science, Amer. Academy of (1889), 3937 Chestnut St., Phila., PA 19104; 10,715.
Pollution Control, Internatl. Assn. for (1970), 1625 Eye St. NW, Wash. DC 20006; 500.
Polo Assn., U.S. (1890), 1301 W. 22d St., Oak Brook, IL 60521; 1,500.
Population Assn. of America (1931), 806 15th St. NW, Wash., DC 20005; 2,600.
Portuguese Continental Union of the U.S.A. (1925), 899 Boylston St., Boston, MA 02115; 9,341.
Postmasters of the U.S., Natl. Assn. of (1935), 1616 N. Ft. Myer Dr., Arlington, VA 22209; 28,000.
Postmasters of the U.S., Natl. League of (1904), 1745 Jefferson Davis Hwy., Arlington, VA 20010; 19,500.
Poultry Science Assn. (1908), 309 W. Clark, Champaign, IL 61820; 1,700.
Power Boat Assn., Amer. (1903), 17640 E. Nine Mile Rd., E. Detroit, MI 48021; 6,000.
Precancel Collectors, Natl. Assn. of (1950), 5121 Park Blvd., Wildwood, NJ 08260; 6,000.

Press, Associated (1848), 50 Rockefeller Plaza, N.Y., NY 10020; 1,365 newspapers & 3,600 broadcast stations.
Press Club, Natl. (1908), 529 14th St. NW, Wash., DC 20045; 4,500.
Press Intl., United (1907), 220 E. 42d St., N.Y., NY 10017.
Press and Radio Club (1948), P.O. Box 7023, Montgomery, AL 36107; 699.
Press Women, Natl. Federation of (1937), 1105 Main St., Blue Springs, MD 64015; 5,000.
Procrastinators' Club of America (1956), 1111 Broad–Locust Bldg., Phila., PA 19102; 3,600.
Propeller Club of the U.S. (1927), 1730 M St. NW, Suite 413, Wash., DC 20036; 14,000.
Psychiatric Assn., Amer. (1894), 1700 18th St. NW, Wash., DC 20009; 25,440.
Psychical Research, Amer. Society for (1907), 5 W. 73d St., N.Y., NY 10023; 2,500.
Psychoanalytic Assn., Amer. (1911), One E. 57th St., N.Y., NY 10022; 2,620.
Psychological Assn., Amer. (1892), 1200 17th St. NW, Wash., DC 20036; 50,000.
Psychological Assn. for Psychoanalysis, Natl. (1948), 150 W. 13th St., N.Y., NY 10011; 218.
Psychological Minorities, Society for the Aid of (1953), 42-25 Hampton St., Elmhurst, NY 11373; 635.
Psychotheatrics, Assn. for (1976), P.O. Box 160371, Sacramento, CA 95816; 121.
Psychotherapy Assn., Amer. Group (1942), 1995 Broadway, N.Y., NY 10023; 3,000.
Public Health Assn., Amer. (1872), 1015 15th St. NW, Wash., DC 20005; 30,000.
Public Relations Society of America (1948), 845 Third Ave., N.Y., NY 10022; 9,217.
Publishers, Assn. of Amer. (1970), One Park Ave., N.Y., NY 10016; 450 publishing houses.
Puppeteers of Amer. (1936), 2311 Connecticut Ave. NW #501, Wash., DC 20008; 2,700.

Quality Control, Amer. Society for (1946), 161 W. Wisconsin Ave., Milwaukee, WI 53203; 26,000.

Rabbinical Alliance of America (1945), 156 5th Ave., N.Y., NY 10010; 500.
Rabbinical Assembly (1900), 3080 Broadway, N.Y., NY 10027; 1,100.
Rabbis, Central Conference of Amer. (1889), 790 Madison Ave., N.Y., NY 10021; 1,300.
Racquetball Assn., U.S. (1973), 4101 Dempster St., Skokie, IL 60076; 45,000.
Radio Union, Internatl. Amateur (1925), P.O. Box AAA, Newington, CT 06111; 104 societies.
Radio and Television Society, Intl. (1940), 420 Lexington Ave., N.Y., NY 10017; 1,300+.
Radio Relay League, Amer. (1914), 225 Main St., Newington, CT 06111; 160,000.
Railroad Passengers, Natl. Assn. of (1967), 417 New Jersey Ave. SE, Wash., DC 20003; 9,000.
Railroads, Assn. of Amer. (1934), 1920 L St. NW, Wash., DC 20036; 78.
Railway Historical Society, Natl. (1935), P.O. Box 2051, Phila., PA 19103; 10,602.
Railway Progress Institute (1908), 801 N. Fairfax St., Alexandria, VA 22314; 145 companies.
Range Management, Society for (1947), 2760 W. 5th Ave., Denver, CO 80204; 5,700.
Rape, Feminist Alliance Against (1974), 2000 P St. NW, Wash., DC 20036.
Real Estate Appraisers, Natl. Assn. of (1967), 853 Broadway, N.Y., NY 10003; 1,000.
Real Estate Investment Trusts, Natl. Assn. of (1960), 1101 17th St. NW, Wash., DC 20036; 141 trusts, 223 associates.
Reconciliation, Fellowship of (1915), 523 N. Broadway, Nyack, NY 10960; 25,000.
Recording Industry Assn. of America (1951), 1633 Broadway, N.Y., NY 10019; 68.
Records Managers & Administrators, Assn. of (1975), 4200 Somerset Dr., Suite 215, Prairie Village, KS 66208.
Recreation and Park Assn., Natl. (1965), 1601 N. Kent St., Arlington, VA 22209; 16,000.
Red Cross, Amer. Natl. (1881), 17th & D Sts. NW, Wash., DC 20006; 3,108 chapters.
Red Men, Improved Order Of (1765), 1525 West Ave., P.O. Box 683, Waco, TX 76707; 50,000.
Redwoods League, Save-the- (1918), 114 Sansome St., San Francisco, CA 94104; 55,000.
Regional Plan Assn. (1929), 235 E. 45th St., N.Y., NY 10017; 2,700.
Rehabilitation Assn., Natl. (1925), 1522 K St. NW, Wash DC 20005; 25,000.
Religion, Amer. Academy of (1909), Dept. of Religious Stu ies, Cal. State Univ., Chico, CA 95929; 4,200.
Renaissance Society of America (1954), 1161 Amsterda Ave., N.Y., NY 10027; 2,900.
Reserve Officers Assn. of the U.S. (1922), One Constitutio Ave., NE, Wash., DC 20002; 117,000.
Restaurant Assn., Natl. (1919), 311 First St. NW, Wash., D 20001; 10,000 businesses.
Retarded Citizens, Natl. Assn. for (1950), P.O. Box 610 2709 Ave. E East, Arlington, TX 76011; 250,000.
Retired Federal Employees, Natl. Assn. of (1921), 153 New Hampshire Ave. NW, Wash., DC 20036; 300,000.
Retired Officers Assn. (1929), 201 N. Washington St., Ale andria, VA 22314; 275,000.
Retired Persons, Amer. Assn. of (1958), 1909 K St. N Wash., DC 20049; 11,500,000.
Retired Teachers Assn., Natl. (1947), 1909 K St. N Wash., DC 20049; 540,000.
Retreads (of World War I & II) (1947), 40-07 154th S Flushing, NY 11354; 1,400.
Revolver Assn., U.S. (1900), 59 Alvin St., Springfield, M 01104; 1,350.
Reye's Syndrome Foundation, Natl. (1974), 509 Rosemon Bryan, OH 43506; 4,000.
Richard III Society (1924), P.O. Box 217, Sea Cliff, N 11579; 2,600.
Rifle Assn., Natl. (1871), 1600 Rhode Island Ave. NW, Wash DC 20036; 1,600,000.
Road & Transportation Builders' Assn., Amer. (1902), 52 School St. SW, Wash., DC 20024; 5,800.
Rodeo Cowboys Assn., Professional (1936), 101 Pro Ro deo Dr., Colorado Springs, CO 80919; 5,000.
Roller Skating, U.S. Amateur Confederation of (1974 7700 A St., Lincoln, NE 68501; 29,989.
Roller Skating Rink Operators Assn. (1937), 7700 A St Lincoln, NE 68510; 1,912.
Rose Society, Amer. (1891), Jefferson Paige Rd., Shreve port, LA 71109; 16,500.
Rosicrucian Fraternity (1614, Germany, 1861 in U.S.), R.D No. 3, Box 220, Quakertown, PA 18951.
Rosicrucian Order, AMORC (1915), Rosicrucian Park, Sa Jose, CA 95191; 250,000.
Rosicrucians, Society of (1909), 321 W. 101st St., N.Y., N 10025.
Rotary Intl. (1905), 1600 Ridge Ave., Evanston, IL 6020 853,000.
Ruritan Natl. (1928), Ruritan Natl. Rd., Dublin, VA 2408 38,790.
Russian Orthodox Clubs, Federated (1927), 10 Downs Dr (Plains), Wilkes-Barre, PA 18705; 5,000.

Safety Council, Natl. (1913), 444 N. Michigan Ave., Chicago IL 60611; 17,000.
Safety Engineers, Amer. Society of (1911), 850 Buss Hwy., Park Ridge, IL 60090; 15,000.
St. Dennis of Zante, Sovereign Greek Order of (109 1953 in U.S.), 739 W. 186th St., N.Y., NY 10033; 901.
St. Paul, Natl. Guild of (1937), 601 Hill 'n Dale, Lexington, K 40503; 13,652.
Salesmen, Natl. Assn. of Professional (1970), 266 Tra Rd., Columbia, SC 29210; 20,000.
Salt Institute (1914), 206 N. Washington St., Alexandria, V 22314; 29 cos.
Samuel Butler Society (1978), 4100 Cathedral Ave. NW Wash., DC 20016; 100.
Sane World, A Citizen's Organization for a (1957), 514 C St. NE, Wash., DC 20002; 19,000.
Savings & Loan League, Natl. (1943), 1101 15th St. NW Wash., DC 20005; 300.
School Administrators, Amer. Assn. of (1865), 1801 N Moore St., Arlington, VA 22209; 19,500.
School Boards Assn., Natl. (1940), 1055 Thomas Jefferso St. NW, Wash., DC 20007; 16,000 boards.
School Counselor Assn., Amer. (1953), 2 Skyline Pl., Suit 400, 5203 Leesburg Pk., Falls Church, VA 22041; 11,000.
Schools & Colleges, Amer. Council on (1927), 446 Salen Ave., P.O. Box 1252, York, PA 17405; 121 institutions.
Science, Amer. Assn. for the Advancement of (1848 1515 Massachusetts Ave. NW, Wash., DC 20005; 128,308.
Science Club of Amer., Jr. (1978), 2505 Prestwick, Rich mond, VA 23229; 116.
Science Fiction, Fantasy and Horror Films, Academy o (1972), 334 W. 54th St., Los Angeles, CA 90037; 3,000.
Sciences, Natl. Academy of (1863), 2101 Constitution Ave

NW, Wash., DC 20418; 1,215.
Science Service (1921), 1719 N St. NW, Wash., DC 20036.
Science Teachers Assn., Natl. (1944), 1742 Connecticut Ave. NW, Wash., DC 20009; 40,000.
Science Writers, Natl. Assn. of (1943), P.O. Box 294, Greenlawn, NY 11740; 995.
Scientists, Federation of Amer. (1946), 307 Massachusetts Ave. NE, Wash., DC 20002; 7,000.
Screen Actors Guild (1933), 7750 Sunset Blvd., Hollywood, CA 90046; 42,000.
Sculpture Society, Natl. (1893), 15 E. 26th St., N.Y., NY 10010; 310.
Seamen's Service, United (1942), One World Trade Ctr., Suite 2601, N.Y., NY 10048.
2d Air Division Assn. (1947), 1 Jeffrey's Neck Rd., Ipswich, MA 01938; 4,186.
Secondary School Principals, Natl. Assn. of (1916), 1904 Association Dr., Reston, VA 22091; 35,000.
Secretaries, Natl. Assn. of Legal (1950), 3005 E. Skelly Dr., Tulsa, OK 74105; 23,000.
Secularists of America, United (1947), 377 Vernon St., Oakland, CA 94610.
Securities Industry Assn. (1972), 20 Broad St., N.Y., NY 10005; 490 firms.
Security Industrial Assn., Natl. (1944), 740 15th St. NW, Wash., DC 20005; 260 corporations.
Seeing Eye, The (1929), Washington Valley Rd., Morristown, NJ 07960.
Semantics, Institute of General (1938), R.R. 1; Box 215, Lakeville, CT 06039; 464.
Separation of Church & State, Americans United for (1948), 8120 Fenton St., Silver Spring, MD 20910; 150,000.
Sertoma Internatl. (1912), 1912 E. Meyer Blvd., Kansas City, MO 64132; 35,000.
Sex Information & Education Council of the U.S. (SIECUS) (1964), 84 5th Ave., N.Y., NY 10011; 1,000.
Shakespeare Assn. of America (1972), Box 6328, Sta. B, Nashville, TN 37205; 650.
Sheriff's Assn., Natl. (1940), 1250 Connecticut Ave. NW, Wash., DC 20036; 60,000.
Shipbuilders Council of America (1921), 600 New Hampshire Ave. NW, Wash., DC 20037; 36 companies.
Ship Society, World (1946), 3319 Sweet Dr., Lafayette, CA 94549; 3,900.
Shoe Retailers Assn., Natl. (1912), 200 Madison Ave., N.Y., NY 10016; 4,000.
Shore & Beach Preservation Assn., Amer. (1926), 412 O'-Brien Hall, Univ. of California, Berkeley, CA 94720; 1,200.
Shrine, Ancient Arabic Order of the Nobles of the Mystic (1872), 2900 Rocky Pt. Dr., Tampa, FL 33607; 1,000,000.
Shut-In Day Society, Natl. (1970), 237 Franklin St., Reading, PA 19602; 1,300.
Sierra Club (1892), 530 Bush St., San Francisco, CA 94108; 180,000.
Silurians, Society of the (1924), 45 John St., N.Y., NY 10010; 740.
Skating Union of the U.S., Amateur (1928), 4423 W. Deming Pl., Chicago, IL 60639; 2,000.
Skeet Shooting Assn., Natl. (1946), P.O. Box 28188, San Antonio, TX 78238; 18,000.
Ski Assn., U.S. (1904), 1726 Champa St., Denver, CO 80202; 110,000.
Small Business, Amer. Federation of (1963), 407 S. Dearborn St., Chicago, IL 60605; 5,000.
Small Business Assn., Natl. (1937), 1604 K St. NW, Wash., DC 20006; 50,000.
Smoking & Health, Natl. Clearinghouse for (1965), Center for Disease Control, 1600 Clifton Road NE, Atlanta, GA 30333.
Soaring Society of America (1932), 3200 Airport Ave., Rm. 25, Santa Monica, CA 90066; 15,700.
Soccer Federation, U.S. (1913), 350 Fifth Ave., N.Y., NY 10001; 44 assns.
Social Biology, Society for the Study of (1926), Medical Dept., Brookhaven Natl. Laboratory, Upton, NY 11973; 415.
Social Science Research Council (1924), 605 Third Ave., N.Y., NY 10016.
Social Sciences, Natl. Institute of (1899), 150 Amsterdam Ave., N.Y., NY 10023; 680.
Social Service, Intl., Amer. Branch (1925), 291 Broadway, N.Y., NY 10007.
Social Welfare, Intl. Council on (1928), 345 E. 46th St., N.Y., NY 10017; 70 natl. committees.
Social Welfare, Natl. Conference on (1873), 22 W. Gay St., Columbus, OH 43215; 5,000.
Social Work Education, Council on (1952), 345 E. 46th St., N.Y., NY 10017; 4,500.
Social Workers, Natl. Assn. of (1955), 1425 H St. NW, Wash., DC 20005; 80,000.
Sociological Assn., Amer. (1905), 1722 N St. NW, Wash., DC 20036; 14,000.
Softball Assn. of America, Amateur (1933), 2801 N.E. 50th St., Oklahoma City, OK 73111; 1,575,000.
Softball League, Cinderella (1956), P.O. Box 1411, Corning, NY 14830; 5,000.
Soft Drink Assn., Natl. (1919), 1101 16th St. NW, Wash., DC 20036; 1,500.
Soil Conservation Society of America (1945), 7515 N.E. Ankeny Rd., Ankeny, IA 50021; 15,000.
Soil Science Society of America (1936), 677 S. Segoe Rd., Madison, WI 53711; 4,595.
Sojourners, Natl. (1921), 8301 E. Boulevard Dr., Alexandria, VA 22308; 9,000.
Soldier's, Sailor's and Airmen's Club (1919), 283 Lexington Ave., N.Y., NY 10016.
Sons of the Amer. Legion (1935), 700 N. Pennsylvania, Indianapolis, IN 46206; 40,000.
Sons of the American Revolution, Natl. Society of (1889), 1000 S. 4th, Louisville, KY 40203; 22,500.
Sons of Confederate Veterans (1896), Southern Sta., P.O. Box 5164, Hattiesburg, MS 39401; 5,000.
Sons of the Desert (1964), P.O. Box 8341, Universal City, CA 91608; 5,000+.
Sons of Italy in America, Order (1905), 1520 Locust St., Phila., PA 19102; 400,000.
Sons of Norway (1895), 1455 W. Lake St., Minneapolis, MN 55408; 105,429.
Sons of Poland, Assn. of the (1903), 665 Newark Ave., Jersey City, NJ 07306; 10,700.
Sons of St. Patrick, Society of the Friendly (1784), 80 Wall St., N.Y., NY 10005; 1,300.
Sons of Sherman's March to the Sea (1966), 1725 Farmers Ave., Tempe, AZ 85281; 370.
Sons of Union Veterans of the Civil War (1881), P.O. Box 24, Gettysburg, PA 17325; 3,500.
Soroptimist Intl. of the Americas (1921), 1616 Walnut St., Phila., PA 19103; 32,000.
Southern Christian Leadership Conference (1957), 334 Auburn Ave. NE, Atlanta, GA 30303; 1,000,000.
Southern Regional Council (1944), 75 Marietta St. NW, Atlanta, GA 30303.
Space Education Assoc., U.S. (1973), 746 Turnpike Rd., Elizabethtown, PA 17022; 8 countries.
Space Exploration Establishment (1977), 3775 Hambletonian Dr., Florissant, MO 63033; 50.
Spanish War Veterans, United (1904), P.O. Box 1915, Wash., DC 20013; 70.
Speech Communication Assn. (1914), 5105 Backlick Rd., Annandale, VA 22003; 5,500.
Speech-Language-Hearing Assn., Amer. (1925), 10801 Rockville Pike, Rockville, MD 20852; 32,000.
Speleological Society, Natl. (1941), Cave Ave., Huntsville, AL 35810; 4,800.
Sports Car Club of America (1947), 1602 S. Parker Rd., Denver, CO 80231; 20,000.
Sports Club, Indoor (1930), 1145 Highland St., Napoleon, OH 43545.
Standards Institute, Amer. Natl. (1918), 1430 Broadway, N.Y., NY 10018; 1,000.
State Communities Aid Assn. (1872), 105 E. 22d St., N.Y., NY 10010; 220.
State Governments, Council of (1933), P.O. Box 11910, Iron Works Pike, Lexington, KY 40578; 50 states.
State & Local History, Amer. Assn. for (1940), 1400 8th Ave. So., Nashville, TN 37203; 5,800.
Statistical Assn., Amer. (1839), 806 15th St. NW, Wash., DC 20005; 13,700.
Steamship Historical Society of America (1935), 414 Pelton Ave., Staten Island, NY 10310; 3,023.
Steel Construction, Amer. Institute of (1921), 400 N. Michigan Ave., Chicago, IL 60611; 350.
Sterilization, Assn. for Voluntary (1937), 708 Third Ave., N.Y., NY 10016; 6,000.
Stock Car Auto Racing, Natl. Assn. for (NASCAR) (1948), 1801 Speedway Blvd., Daytona Beach, FL 32015; 17,000.
Stock Exchange, Amer. (1911), 86 Trinity Pl., N.Y., NY 10006; 653.
Stock Exchange, New York (1792), 11 Wall St., N.Y., NY 10005; 1,366.
Stock Exchange, Philadelphia (1790), 17th St., Stock Exchange Pl., Phila., PA 19103; 381.
Structural Stability Research Council (1944), Fritz Engineering Laboratory No. 13, Lehigh Univ., Bethlehem, PA 18015; 200.
Student Assn., U.S. (1947), 1220 G St. SE, Wash., DC 20003; 3,500,000.
Student Councils, Natl. Assn. of (1940), 1904 Association Dr., Reston, VA 22090; 7,000 secondary schools.
Students Consumer Protection Council, Natl. (1972), Villanova Univ., Villanova, PA 19085; 50.

Stuttering Project, Natl. (1977), 4438 Park Blvd., Oakland, CA 94602; 602.

Sugar Brokers Assn., Natl. (1903), 1 World Trade Center N.Y., NY 10047; 250.

Sunbathing Assn., Amer. (1931), 810 N. Mills Ave., Orlando, FL 32803; 25,000.

Sunday League (1933), 279 Highland Ave., Newark, NJ 07104; 25,000.

Surfing Assn., Amer. (1966), 2131 Kalakaua Ave., Honolulu, HI 96815; 2,000 teams.

Surgeons, Amer. College of (1913), 55 E. Erie St., Chicago IL 60611; 42,000.

Surgeons, Intl. College of (1935), 1516 N. Lake Shore Dr., Chicago IL 60610; 12,000.

Surgeons of the U.S., Assn. of Military (1891), 10605 Concord St., Kensington, MD 20795; 11,519.

Surveying & Mapping, Amer. Congress on (1941), 210 Little Falls, Falls Church, VA 22046; 10,000.

Symphony Orchestra League, Amer. (1942), P.O. Box 669, Vienna, VA 22180; 4,000.

Systems Management, Assn. for (1947), 24587 Bagley Rd., Cleveland, OH 44138; 9,500.

Table Tennis Assn., U.S. (1933), 3466 Bridgeland Dr. Suite 209, St. Louis, MO 63044; 5,400.

Tall Buildings and Urban Habitat, Council on (1969), Fritz Engineering Laboratory No. 13, Lehigh Univ., Bethlehem, PA 18015; 2,000.

Tattoo Club of America (1970), 112 W. First St., Mt. Vernon, NY 10550; 10,000.

Tax Accountants, Natl. Assn. of Enrolled Federal (1960), 6108 N. Harding Ave., Chicago, IL 60659; 500.

Tax Administrators, Federation of (1937), 444 N. Capitol St. NW, Wash., DC 20001; 50 revenue departments.

Tax Assn.-Natl. Tax Institute of America (1907), 21 E. State St., Columbus, OH 43215; 2,100.

Tax Foundation (1937), 1875 Connecticut Ave. NW, Wash., DC 20009; 1,900.

Tea Assn. of the U.S.A. (1899), 230 Park Ave., N.Y., NY 10017; 350.

Teachers of English, Natl. Council of (1911), 1111 Kenyon Rd., Urbana, IL 61801; 85,000.

Teachers of French, Amer. Assn. of (1927), 57 E. Armory Ave., Champaign, IL 61820; 10,000.

Teachers of German, Amer. Assn. of (1928), 523 Bldg., Suite 201, Route 38, Cherry Hill, NJ 08034; 7,738.

Teachers of Singing, Natl. Assn. of (1944), 250 W. 57th St., N.Y., NY 10019; 3,500.

Teachers of Spanish & Portuguese, Amer. Assn. of (1917), Holy Cross Coll., Worcester, MA 01610; 12,561.

Technical Communication, Society for (1958), 1010 Vermont Ave. NW, Wash., DC 20005; 5,000.

Telephone Pioneers of Amer. (1911), 195 Broadway, N.Y., NY 10007; 525,926.

Television Arts & Sciences, Natl. Academy of (1947), 291 S. La Cienega Blvd., Beverly Hills, CA 90211; 11,000.

Television Bureau of Advertising (1954), 1345 Ave. of the Americas, N.Y., NY 10019; 560 stations.

Television & Radio Artists, Amer. Federation of (1937), 1350 Ave. of the Americas; N.Y., NY 10019; 40,000.

Telluride Assn. (1911), 217 West Ave., Ithaca, NY 14850; 76.

Tennis Assn., U.S. (1881), 51 E. 42d St., N.Y., NY 10017; 150,000.

Terrain Vehicle Owners Assn., Natl. All (1971), P.O. Box 574, Feasterville, PA 19047; 1,179.

Testing & Materials, Amer. Society for (1898), 1916 Race St., Phila., PA 19103; 28,500.

Textile Assn., Northern (1854), 211 Congress St., Boston, MA 02110; 150.

Textile Manufacturers Institute, Amer. (1949), 2124 Wachovia Ctr., Charlotte, NC 28285; 250 companies.

Theatre & Academy, Amer. Natl. (1935), 245 W. 52d St., N.Y., NY 10019; 1,000.

Theatre Assn., Amer. (1936), 1000 Vermont Ave. NW, Wash., DC 20005; 5,300.

Theatre Organ Society, Amer. (1955), P.O. Box 1002, Middleburg, VA 22117; 6,000 families.

Theodore Roosevelt Assn. (1919), P.O. Box 720, Oyster Bay, NY 11771; 650.

Theological Library Assn., Amer. (1947), Lutheran Theological Seminary, 7301 Germantown Ave., Phila., PA 19119; 450.

Theological Schools in the U.S. and Canada, Assn. of (1918), 42 E. Natl. Rd., P.O. Box 130, Vandalia, OH 45377; 197 schools.

Theosophical Society (1875), P.O. Box 270, 1926 N. Main St., Wheaton, IL 60187; 5,000.

Thoreau Society (1941), SUNY-Geneseo, Geneseo, NY 14454; 1,200.

Thoroughbred Racing Assn. of North America (1942), 8000 Marcus Ave., Lake Success, NY 11040; 53 racetracks.

Titanic Historical Society (1963), P.O. Box 53, Indian Orchard, MA 01151; 1,735.

Toastmasters Intl. (1924), 2200 N. Grand Ave., Santa Ana,, CA 92711; 75,000.

Toastmistress Clubs, Intl. (1938), 9068 E. Firestone Blvd., Downey CA 90241; 25,000.

Topical Assn., Amer. (1949), 3306 N. 50th St., Milwaukee, WI 53216; 10,000.

Torch Clubs, Internatl. Assn. of (1924), P.O. Box 30578, Lincoln, NE 68503; 4,300.

Toy Manufacturers of America (1916), 200 Fifth Ave., N.Y., NY 10010; 250.

Trade Relations Council of the U.S. (1885), 1001 Connecticut Ave. NW, Wash., DC 20036; 50 companies.

Traffic and Transportation, Amer. Society of (1946), P.O. Box 33095, Louisville, KY 40232; 2,598.

Training Corps, Amer. (1960), 107-12 Jamaica Ave., Richmond Hill, NY 11418; 125.

Training & Development, Amer. Society for (1944), P.O. Box 5307, Madison, WI 53705; 15,000.

Transit Assn., Amer. Public (1974), 1100 17th St. NW, Wash., DC 20036; 620.

Translators Assn., Amer. (1959), P.O. Box 129, Croton-on-Hudson, NY 10520; 1,500+.

Transportation Assn. of America (1935), 1100 17th St. NW, Wash., DC 20036; 500 companies.

Trapshooting Assn., Amateur (1924), 601 W. National Rd. Vandalia, OH 45377; 90,000.

Travel Agents, Amer. Society of (1931), 711 Fifth Ave., N.Y., NY 10022; 16,500.

Travel Organizations, Discover America (1939), 1899 L St NW, Wash., DC 20036; 1,200.

Travelers Aid-Intl. Social Service of America (1972), 345 E. 46th St., N.Y., NY 10017; 1,010 U.S. & foreign agencies.

Trucking Assn., Amer. (1933), 1616 P St. NW, Wash., DC 20036; 51 assns.

True Sisters, United Order (1846), 150 W. 85th St., N.Y., NY 10024; 15,000.

Turners, Amer. (1848), 415 E. Michigan St., Indianapolis, IN 46204; 16,000.

UFOs (Unidentified Flying Objects), Natl. Investigations Commitee on (1967), 7970 Woodman Ave., Van Nuys, CA 91402; 300.

UNICEF, U.S. Committee for (1947), 331 E. 38th St., N.Y., NY 10016.

Uniformed Services, Natl. Assn. for (1968), 903 S. Highland St., Arlington, VA 22204; 26,000.

UNIMA (l'Union Internationale de la Marionnette)–USA (1966), 117 E. 69th St., N.Y., NY 10021; 600.

United Nations Assn. of the U.S.A. (1923, as League of Nations Assn.) 300 E. 42d St., N.Y., NY 10017; 24,500.

United Service Organizations (USO) (1941), 237 E. 52d St., N.Y., NY 10022.

U.S., Amer. Assn. for Study of in World Affairs (1948), 3813 Annandale Rd., Annandale, VA 22003; 1,000.

United Way of America (1918), 801 N. Fairfax St., Alexandria, VA 22314; 1,139.

Universities, Assn. of Amer. (1900), One Dupont Circle NW, Wash., DC 20036; 50 institutions.

Universities & Colleges, Assn. of Governing Boards of (1921), One Dupont Circle NW, Wash., DC 20036; 21,000.

University Extension Assn., Natl. (1915), One Dupont Circle, Suite 360, NW, Wash., DC 20036; 1,200.

University Foundation, Intl. (1973), 501 E. Armour Blvd., Kansas City, MO 64109; 425.

University Professors, Amer. Assn. of (1915), One Dupont Circle, Suite 500, NW, Wash., DC 20036; 70,000.

University Professors for Academic Order (1970), 635 SW 4th St., Corvallis, OR 97330; 525.

University Women, Amer. Assn. of (1881), 2401 Virginia Ave. NW, Wash., DC 20037; 190,000.

Urban Coalition, Natl. (1968), 1201 Connecticut Ave. NW, Wash., DC 20024.

Urban League, Natl. (1910), 500 E. 62d St., N.Y., NY 10021.

Utility Commissioners, Natl. Assn. of Regulatory (1889), 1102 ICC Bldg., P.O. Box 684, Wash., DC 20044; 334.

Valley Forge, Society of the Descendants of Washington's Army at (1976), P.O. Box 608, Manhasset, NY 11030; 251.
Variety Clubs Intl. (1928), 58 W. 58th St., N.Y., NY 10019; 11,000.
VASA Order of America (1896), 3720 Daryl Dr., Landisville, PA 17538; 38,000.
Veterans Assn., Blinded (1945), 1735 DeSales St. NW, Wash., DC 20036; 3,000.
Veterans Assn., China-Burma-India (1947), 750 N. Lincoln Memorial Dr., Milwaukee, WI 53201; 3,221+.
Veterans Committee, Amer. (1944), 1346 Connecticut Ave. NW, Wash., DC 20036; 25,000.
Veterans of Foreign Wars of the U.S. (1898) **& Ladies Auxiliary** (1914), 406 W. 34th St., Kansas City, MO 64111; 1,873,474 & 620,000.
Veterans of World War I U.S.A. (1953), 916 Prince St., Alexandria, VA 22314; 99,000.
Veterinary Medical Assn., Amer. (1863), 930 N. Meacham Rd., Schaumburg, IL 60196; 31,686.
Victorian Society in America (1966), The Athenaeum, East Washington Sq., Phila., PA 19106; 7,000.
Vocational Assn., Amer. (1925), 2020 N. 14th St., Arlington, VA 22201; 56,000.
Volleyball Assn., U.S. (1928), 1750 E. Boulder, Colorado Springs, CO 80909; 20,000.

Walking Assn. (1976), 4113 Lee Hwy., Arlington, VA 22207; 130.
War of 1812, General Society of the (1814), 1307 New Hampshire Ave. NW, Wash., DC 20036; 1,432.
War Mothers, Amer. (1917), 2615 Woodley Pl. NW, Wash., DC 20008; 11,000.
Warrant and Warrant Officers' Assn., Chief, U.S. Coast Guard (1929), 492 L'Enfant Plaza E., SW, Wash., DC 20024; 3,284.
Watch & Clock Collectors, Natl. Assn. of (1943), 514 Poplar St., Columbia, PA 17512; 34,000.
Watercolor Society, Amer. (1866), 1083 Fifth Ave., N.Y., NY 10028; 500.
Water Pollution Control Federation (1928), 2626 Pennsylvania Ave. NW, Wash., DC 20037; 29,000.
Water Resources Assn., Amer. (1964), St. Anthony Falls Hydraulic Lab, Mississippi River at 3d Ave. SE, Minneapolis, MN 55414; 2,382.
Water Ski Assn., Amer. (1939), State Rte. 550 at Carl Floyd Rd., Winter Haven, FL 33880; 16,000.
Water Well Assn., Natl. (1948), 500 W. Wilson Bridge Rd., Worthington, OH 43085; 8,200.
Water Works Assn., Amer. (1881), 6666 W. Quincy Ave., Denver, CO 80235; 31,000.
Watts Family Assn. (1974), 12401 Burton St., N. Hollywood, CA 91605; 20,000.
Weather Modification Assn. (1969), P.O. Box 8116, Fresno, CA 93727; 250.
Welding Society, Amer. (1919), 2501 NW 7th St., Miami, FL 33125; 30,000+.
Wheelchair Athletic Assn., Natl. (1958), 40-24 62d St., Woodside, NY 11377; 2,000.
Wilderness Society (1935), 1901 Pennsylvania Ave. NW, Wash., DC 20006; 50,000.
Wild Horse Organized Assistance (WHOA!) (1971), 140 Greenstone Dr., Reno, NV 89512; 10,000.
Wildlife, Defenders of (1925), 1244 19th St. NW, Wash., DC 20036; 35,000.
Wildlife Federation, Natl. (1936), 1412 16th St. NW, Wash., DC 20036; 4,600,000.
Wildlife Foundation, No. Amer. (1935), 1000 Vermont Ave. NW, Wash., DC 20005.
Wildlife Fund, World (1961), 1601 Connecticut Ave. NW, Wash., DC 20009.
Wildlife Management Institute (1911), 1000 Vermont Ave. NW, Wash., DC 20005.
William Penn Assn. (1886), 429 Forbes Ave., Pittsburgh, PA 15219; 65,520.
Wireless Pioneers, Society of (1968), P.O. Box 530, 3366—15 Mendocino Ave., Santa Rosa, CA 95401; 4,340.
Wizard of Oz Club, Internatl. (1957), Box 95, Kinderhook, IL 62345; 1,750.
Woman's Assn., Amer. (1914), 1271 Ave. of the Americas, N.Y., NY 10020; 250.
Woman's Christian Temperance Union, Natl. (1874), 1730 Chicago Ave., Evanston, IL 60201; 250,000.
Women, Natl. Assn. of Bank (1921), 111 E. Wacker Dr., Chicago, IL 60601; 24,057.
Women, Natl. Organization for (NOW) (1966), 425 13th St. NW, Wash., DC 20004; 125,000.
Women Artists, Natl. Assn. (1889), 41 Union Sq., N.Y., NY 10003; 700.
Women, Rural American (1977), 1522 K St. NW, Wash., DC 20005; 22,000.
Women Engineers, Society of (1950), 345 E. 47th St., N.Y., NY 10017; 9,000.
Women in Communications (1909), P.O. Box 9561, Austin, TX 78766; 9,000.
Women Geographers, Society of (1925), 1619 New Hampshire Ave. NW, Wash., DC 20009; 500.
Women Marines Assn. (1960), P.O. Box 19827, Irvine, CA 92714; 2,408.
Women Strike for Peace (1961), 145 S. 13th St., Phila., PA 19107.
Women's Army Corps Veterans Assn. (1946), 6709 Hildegarde Dr. NE, Albuquerque, NM 87109; 2,300.
Women's Clubs, General Federation of (1889), 1734 N St. NW, Wash., DC 20036; 10,000,000.
Women's Clubs, Natl. Federation of Business & Professional (1919), 2012 Massachusetts Ave. NW, Wash., DC 20036; 160,000.
Women's Educational & Industrial Union (1877), 356 Boylston St., Boston, MA 02116; 3,200.
Women's Intl. League for Peace & Freedom (1915), 1213 Race St., Phila., PA 19107; 9,000.
Women's Overseas Service League (1921), P.O. Box 39058, Friendship Sta., Wash., DC 20016; 1,400.
Women of the U.S., Natl. Council of (1888), 777 U.N. Plaza, N.Y., NY 10017; 28 organizations.
Women Voters of the U.S., League of (1920), 1730 M St. NW, Wash., DC 20036; 122,000.
Women World War Veterans (1919), 237 Madison Ave., N.Y., NY 10016; 75,000.
Woodmen of America, Modern (1883), 1701 First Ave., Rock Island, IL 61201; 500,000.
Woodmen of the World (1890), 1450 Speer Blvd., Denver, CO 80204; 28,954.
Wool Growers Assn., Natl. (1865), 1776 F St. NW, Wash., DC 20005; 24 state assns.
Workmen's Circle (1900), 45 E. 33d St., N.Y., NY 10016; 56,305.
World Future Society (1966), 4916 St. Elmo Ave., Wash., DC 20014; 50,000.
World Health, U.S. Committee for (1951), 777 United Nations Plaza, N.Y., NY 10017; 2,017.
Writers of America, Western (1953), 1505 W. D St., N. Platte, NE 69101; 381.
Writers Assn. of America, Outdoor (1927), 4141 W. Bradley Rd., Milwaukee, WI 53209; 1,500.
Writers Guild of America, West (1931), 8955 Beverly Blvd., Los Angeles, CA 90048; 5,500.

Yeoman F. Natl. (1936), 223 El Camino Real, Vallejo, CA 94590; 800.
Young Americans for Freedom (1960), Woodland Rd., Sterling, VA 22170; 55,000.
Young Men's Christian Assns. of the U.S.A., Natl. Council of (1851), 291 Broadway, N.Y., NY 10007; 10,000,000.
YM-YWHAs of Greater New York, Associated (1957), 130 E. 59th St., N.Y., NY 10022; 65,000.
Young Women's Christian Assn. of the U.S.A. (1855), 600 Lexington Ave., N.Y., NY 10022; 2,500,000.
Young Scientists of Amer. Foundation (1959), P.O. Box 9006, Phoenix, AZ 85068; 260 school chapters.
Youth, Allied (1936), 1556 Wisconsin Ave., Wash., DC 20007; 10,000.
Youth Hostels, Amer. (1934), Natl. Campus, Delaplane, VA 22025; 80,000.

Zero Population Growth (1968), 1346 Connecticut Ave. NW, Wash., DC 20036; 8,000.
Ziegfeld Club (1936), 55 W. 42d St., N.Y., NY 10036; 376.
Zionist Organization of America (1897), 4 E. 34th St., N.Y., NY 10016; 130,000.
Zonta Intl. (1919), 35 E. Wacker Dr., Rm. 2040, Chicago, IL 60605; 30,000.
Zoological Parks & Aquariums, Amer. Assn. of (1924), Oglebay Park, Wheeling, WV 26003; 3,000.
Zoologists, Amer. Society of (1913), Box 2739, California Lutheran College, Thousand Oaks, CA 91360; 4,500.

Census of Religious Groups in the U.S.

Source: World Almanac questionnaire and 1980 Yearbook of American and Canadian Churches

Membership figures in the following table are the latest available. Some denominations submitted carefully compiled data while others approached the task more casually. The number of churches is given in parentheses. Asterisk (*) indicates church declines to publish membership figures.

Group	Members
Adventist churches:	
Advent Christian Ch. (381)	31,324
Primitive Advent Christian Ch. (10)	550
Seventh-day Adventists (3,667)	556,567
American Rescue Workers (15)	**2,140**
Anglican Orthodox Church (37)	**2,630**
Baha'i Faith (7,000)	*
Baptist churches:	
Amer. Baptist Chs. in U.S.A. (5,897)	1,231,646
Baptist General Conference (701)	131,000
Baptist Missionary Assn. of America (1,487)	130,360
Conservative Baptist Assn. of America (1,125)	219,697
Duck River (and Kindred) Assn. of Baptists (85)	8,632
Free Will Baptists (2,437)	231,169
Gen. Assn. of General Baptists (894)	73,046
Gen. Assn. of Regular Baptist Chs. (1,544)	243,141
Natl. Baptist Convention of America (11,398)	2,668,799
Natl. Baptist Convention, U.S.A. (30,000)	6,300,000
Natl. Primitive Baptist Convention (606)	250,000
No. Amer. Baptist Conference (253)	42,499
Seventh Day Baptist General Conference (60)	5,181
Southern Baptist Convention (35,357)	13,191,394
Brethren (German Baptists):	
Brethren Ch. (Ashland, Ohio) (120)	15,056
Christian Congregation (La Follette, IN) (1,161)	83,259
Ch. of the Brethren (1,045)	175,335
Fellowship of Grace Brethren Chs. (262)	39,605
Old German Baptist Brethren (50)	4,898
Brethren, River:	
Brethren in Christ Ch. (156)	11,384
Buddhist Churches of America (60)	**60,000**
Calvary Grace Christian Churches of Faith (350)	*
Calvary Grace Church of Faith, Inc. (150)	**15,000**
Christadelphians (100)	*
The Christian and Missionary Alliance (1,319)	**161,435**
Christian Catholic Church (6)	**2,500**
Christian Church (Disciples of Christ) (4,347)	**1,231,817**
Christian Churches and Churches of Christ (5,535)	**1,054,266**
Christian Nation Church U.S.A. (18)	**2,000**
Christian Union (104)	**4,590**
Churches of Christ (17,000)	**2,500,000**
Churches of Christ in Christian Union (250)	**10,500**
Churches of God:	
Chs. of God, General Conference (347)	35,314
Church of God (2,035)	75,890
Ch. of God (Anderson, Ind.) (2,259)	175,113
Ch. of God (Seventh Day), Denver, Col. (104)	8,000
Church of Christ, Scientist (3,000)	*
The Church of God by Faith (105)	**4,500**
Church of the Nazarene (4,727)	**469,449**
Church of Revelation (8)	**750**
National Council of Community Churches (200)	**190,000**
Natl. Assn. of Congregational Christian Churches (392)	**100,000**
Conservative Congregational Christian Conference (130)	**22,750**
Eastern Orthodox churches:	
Albanian Orth. Diocese of America (16)	40,000
American Carpatho-Russian Orth. Greek Catholic Ch. (70)	100,000
Antiochian Orth. Christian Archdiocese of No. Amer. (110)	152,000
Diocese of the Armenian Ch. of America (50)	600,000
Bulgarian Eastern Orth. Ch. (13)	86,000
Coptic Orthodox Ch. (14)	40,000
Greek Orth. Archdiocese of N. and S. America (535)	1,950,000
Orthodox Ch. in America (440)	1,000,000
Romanian Orth. Episcopate of America (34)	35,000
Patriarchal Parishes of the Russian Orth. Ch. in the U.S.A. (41)	51,500
Serbian Eastern Orth. Ch. (52)	65,000
Syrian Orth. Ch. of Antioch (Archdiocese of the U.S.A. and Canada) (14)	35,000
Ukrainian Orth. Ch. of America (Ecumenical Patriarchate) (28)	25,000
The Episcopal Church in the U.S.A. (7,152)	**2,825,254**
American Ethical Union (Ethical Culture Movement) (21)	**5,000**
Evangelical Christian Churches (131)	**25,080**
Evangelical Christian Churches, California Synod (154)	**66,075**
Evangelical Church of North America (138)	**12,210**
Evangelical Congregational Church (161)	**28,459**
The Evangelical Covenant Church of America (552)	**76,239**
Evangelical Free Church of America (621)	**100,000**
Evangelical associations:	
Apostolic Christian Chs. of America (80)	17,888
Apostolic Christian Ch. (Nazarean) (42)	4,804
Christian Congregation (1,133)	81,604
Friends:	
Evangelical Friends Alliance (257)	25,531
Friends General Conference (233)	26,184
Friends United Meeting (522)	62,080
Religious Society of Friends (Conservative) (27)	1,728
Religious Society of Friends (Unaffiliated Meetings) (87)	5,696
Independent Fundamental Churches of America (614)	**125,563**
Grace Gospel Fellowship (48)	**3,500**
Jehovah's Witnesses (7,464)	**533,781**
Jewish congregations:	
Agudath Israel of America (Orthodox) (40)	100,000
Union of Amer. Hebrew Congregations (Reformed) (750)	1,200,000
Natl. Council of Young Israel (Orthodox) (163)	185,000
Union of Orthodox Jewish Congregations of America (1,700)	1,000,000
United Synagogue of America (Conservative) (835)	1,500,000
Latter-day Saints:	
Ch. of Jesus Christ (Bickertonites) (60)	2,551
Ch. of Jesus Christ of Latter-day Saints (Mormon) (6,714)	3,176,000
Reorganized Ch. of Jesus Christ of Latter Day Saints (1,064)	190,685
Lutheran churches:	
American Lutheran Ch. (4,849)	2,363,762
Ch. of the Lutheran Brethren (129)	9,704
Ch. of the Lutheran Confession (72)	9,316
Assn. of Evangelical Lutheran Chs. (175)	113,000
Evangelical Lutheran Synod (108)	19,705
Assn. of Free Lutheran Congregations (133)	15,500
Latvian Evangelical Lutheran Church in America (56)	12,308
Lutheran Ch. in America (5,737)	2,941,597
Lutheran Ch.-Missouri Synod (5,576)	2,639,408
Protestant Conference (Lutheran) (9)	2,660
Wisconsin Evangelical Lutheran Synod (1,135)	405,512
Mennonite churches:	
Beachy Amish Mennonite Chs. (74)	4,762
Evangelical Mennonite Ch. (21)	3,634
General Conference of Mennonite Brethren Chs. (120)	16,042
The General Conference Mennonite Ch. (200)	36,775

Group	Members
Hutterian Brethren (35)	3,500
Mennonite Ch. (1,107)	97,808
Old Order Amish Ch. (513)	33,000
Old Order (Wisler) Mennonite Ch. (60)	8,400
Methodist churches:	
African Methodist Episcopal Ch. (3,050)	1,970,000
African Methodist Episcopal Zion Ch. (6,020)	1,093,001
Evangelical Methodist Ch. (133)	10,778
Free Methodist Ch. of North America (1,023)	70,000
Fundamental Methodist Ch. (15)	745
Primitive Methodist Ch., U.S.A. (88)	10,222
Reformed Methodist Union Episcopal Ch. (20)	45,000
Southern Methodist Ch. (169)	11,000
United Methodist Ch. (36,682)	9,731,779
Moravian churches:	
Moravian Ch. (Unitas Fratrum), Northern Province (95)	32,519
Moravian Ch. in America (Unitas Fratrum), Southern Province (52)	21,002
Unity of the Brethren (26)	*
Muslims	**2,000,000**
New Apostolic Church of North America (367)	**26,384**
North American Old Roman Catholic Church (121)	**67,314**
Old Catholic churches:	
American Catholic Ch. (Syro-Antiochean) (3)	501
Christ Catholic Ch. (7)	1,365
Mariavite Old Cath. Ch. Province of North America (159)	350,536
No. Amer. Old Roman Cath. Ch. (Schweikert) (121)	60,124
Pentecostal churches:	
Apostolic Faith (45)	4,100
Assemblies of God (9,410)	1,293,394
Bible Church of Christ (5)	2,300
Bible Way Church of Our Lord Jesus Christ World Wide (350)	30,000
Church of God (Cleveland, Tenn.) (5,018)	411,385
Church of God of Prophecy (1,791)	65,801
Congregational Holiness Ch. (175)	5,925
Gen. Conference, Christian Ch. of No. Amer. (102)	10,000
Intl. Ch. of the Foursquare Gospel (915)	131,879
Open Bible Standard Chs. (265)	30,000
Pentecostal Assemblies of the World (150)	15,000
Pentecostal Church of Christ (50)	1,659
Pentecostal Church of God (1,189)	110,870
United Pentecostal Ch. (2,792)	462,000
Pentecostal Free-Will Baptist Ch. (125)	3,500
Plymouth Brethren (800)	**74,000**
Polish Natl. Catholic Church (162)	**282,411**
Presbyterian churches:	
Associate Reformed Presbyterian Ch. (Gen. Synod) (158)	32,139
Cumberland Presbyterian Ch. (850)	93,268
Orthodox Presbyterian Ch. (136)	15,806
Presbyterian Ch. in America (460)	87,553
Presbyterian Ch. in the U.S. (4,007)	866,500
Reformed Presbyterian Ch., Evangelical Synod (193)	27,500
Reformed Presbyterian Ch. of No. Amer. (68)	4,878
United Presbyterian Ch. in the U.S.A. (8,567)	2,520,367
Reformed churches:	
Christian Reformed Ch. (651)	212,642
Hungarian Reformed Ch. in America (29)	10,500
Protestant Reformed Chs. in America (21)	4,040
Reformed Ch. in America (915)	215,384
Reformed Ch. in the U.S. (26)	3,790
The Roman Catholic Church (18,695)	**49,602,035**
The Salvation Army (1,134)	**414,035**
The Schwenkfelder Church (5)	**2,748**
Social Brethren (30)	**1,784**
Natl. Spiritualist Assn. of Churches (164)	**5,168**
Gen. Convention, The Swedenborgian Church (47)	**2,640**
Unitarian Universalist Assn. (946)	**170,352**
United Brethren:	
Ch. of the United Brethren in Christ (275)	27,957
United Christian Ch. (11)	430
United Church of Christ (6,491)	**1,769,104**
Universal Fellowship of Metropolitan Community Chs. (120)	**35,000**
Vendanta Society (12)	**1,000**
Volunteers of America (602)	**36,380**
The Wesleyan Church (1,812)	**106,250**
Worldwide Church of God (330)	**52,023**

Religious Population of the World

Source: The 1980 Encyclopaedia Britannica Book of the Year

Religion	N. America[1]	S. America	Europe[2]	Asia[3]	Africa	Oceania[4]	Totals
Total Christian	235,109,500	177,266,000	342,630,400	95,987,240	129,717,000	18,063,500	998,773,640
Roman Catholic	132,489,000	165,640,000	176,087,300	55,077,000	47,224,500	4,395,500	580,913,300
Eastern Orthodox	4,763,000	517,000	57,035,600	2,428,000	14,306,000	414,000	79,463,600
Protestant[5]	97,857,500	11,109,000	109,507,500	38,482,240	68,186,500	13,254,000	338,396,740
Jewish	6,155,340	635,800	4,061,620	3,212,860	176,400	76,000	14,318,020
Muslim	371,200	251,500	14,145,000	427,266,000	145,214,700	87,000	587,335,400
Zoroastrian	250	2,100	7,000	254,000	650	—	264,000
Shinto	60,000	92,000	—	57,003,000	200	—	57,155,200
Taoist	16,000	10,000	—	31,261,000	—	—	31,287,000
Confucian	97,100	70,150	—	157,887,500	1,500	80,300	158,136,550
Buddhist	171,250	192,300	192,000	254,241,000	14,000	30,000	254,840,550
Hindu	88,500	849,300	350,000	473,073,000	1,079,800	499,000	475,939,600
Totals	242,069,140	179,369,150	361,386,020	1,500,185,600	276,204,250	18,835,800	2,578,049,960
Population[6]	365,314,000	242,560,000	749,373,000	2,460,380,000	447,905,000	23,035,000	4,288,567,000

(1) Includes Central America and West Indies. (2) Includes communist countries where it is difficult to determine religious affiliation. (3) Includes areas in which persons have traditionally enrolled in several religions, as well as China, with an official communist establishment. (4) Includes Australia, New Zealand, and islands of the South Pacific. (5) Protestant figures outside Europe usually include "full members" (adults) rather than all baptized persons and are not comparable to those of ethnic religions or churches counting all adherents. (6) United Nations data, midyear 1979.

National Council of Churches

The National Council of the Churches of Christ in the U.S.A. is a cooperative federation of 32 Protestant and Orthodox churches which seeks to advance programs and policies of mutual interest to its members. The NCC was formed in 1950 by the merger of 12 inter-denominational agencies. The Council's member churches now have an aggregate membership totaling approximately 40 million. The NCC is not a governing body and has no control over the policies or operations of any church belonging to it. The work of the Council is divided into 3 divisions — Church and Society; Education and Ministry; Overseas Ministries — and 5 commissions — Faith and Order; Regional and Local Ecumenism; Communication; Stewardship; and Justice, Liberation, and Human Fulfillment. The chief administrative officer of the NCC is Dr. Claire Randall, 475 Riverside Drive, N.Y., NY 10027.

Headquarters, Leaders of U.S. Religious Groups

See Associations and Societies section for religious organizations. (year organized in parentheses)

Adventist churches:

Advent Christian Church (1854) — Pres., Joe Tom Tate; exec. v.p., Rev. Adrian B. Shepard, Box 23152, Charlotte, NC 28212.

Seventh-day Adventists (1863) — Pres., Neal C. Wilson; sec., C.O. Franz, 6840 Eastern Ave. NW, Wash., DC 20012.

Baha'i Faith — Chpsn., Judge James E. Nelson; sec., Glenford E. Mitchell, 536 Sheridan Rd., Wilmette, IL 60091.

Baptist churches:

American Baptist Assn. (1905) — Pres., Dr. Vernon L. Barr; rec. clk., W E. Norris, 4605 N. State Line, Texarkana, TX 75501.

American Baptist Churches in the U.S.A. (1907) — Pres., Rev. Dr. William F. Keucher; gen. sec., Rev. Dr. Robert C. Campbell, Valley Forge, PA 19481.

Baptist General Conference (1879) — Gen. sec., Dr. Warren Magnuson, 1233 Central St., Evanston, IL 60201.

Baptist Missionary Assn. of America (formerly **North American Baptist Assn.**) (1950) — Pres., Rev. Jack R. Courtney; rec. sec., Rev. Ralph Cottrell, Box 2866, Texarkana, AR 75501.

Conservative Baptist Assn. of America (1947) — Pres., Rev. Robert C. Becker, Box 66, Wheaton, IL 60187.

Free Will Baptists (1727) — Mod., Rev. Bobby Jackson; exec. sec., Dr. Melvin Worthington, Box 1088, Nashville, TN 37202.

General Assn. of General Baptists (1823) — Exec. sec., Rev. Glen Spence, 100 Stinson Dr., Poplar Bluff, MO 63901.

General Assn. of Regular Baptist Churches (1932) — Chpsn., Dr. John Balyo; natl. rep., Dr. Paul N. Tassell, 1300 N. Meacham Rd., Schaumburg, IL 60195.

Natl. Baptist Convention, U.S.A. (1880) — Pres., Dr. J.H. Jackson, 405 E. 31st St., Chicago, IL 60616.

North American Baptist Conference (1865) — Mod., Dr. Peter Fehr; exec. sec., Dr. John Binder, 1 S. 210 Summit Ave., Oakbrook Terrace, IL 60181.

Southern Baptist Convention (1945) — Pres., Rev. Adrian Rogers; exec. sec., Dr. Harold C. Bennett, 460 James Robertson Pkwy., Nashville, TN 37219.

United Free Will Baptist Church (1870) — Vice-mod., Rev. O.L. Williams; gen. rec. sec., Rev. J.H. O'Neal, Kinston College, 1000 University St., Kinston, NC 28501.

Brethren in Christ Church (1798) — Chpsn., Bishop Alvin J. Book; sec., Dr. Arthur M. Climenhaga, 1093 Twp. Rd. 1704, RD 4, Ashland, OH 44805.

Brethren (German Baptists):

Brethren Church (Ashland, Oh.) (1708) — Mod., William Kerner, 524 College Ave., Ashland, OH 44805.

Church of the Brethren (1719) — Mod., William R. Eberly; gen. sec., Robert Neff, 1451 Dundee Ave., Elgin, IL 60120.

Buddhist Churches of America (1899) — Bishop, Rt. Rev. Kenryu Tsuji, 1710 Octavia St., San Francisco, CA 94109.

Calvary Grace Christian Church of Faith (1898) — Intl. gen. supt., Col. Herman Keck Jr., P.O. Box 6005, March Air Force Base, CA 92518.

Calvary Grace Church of Faith (1874) — Intl. gen. supt., Rev. A.C. Spern, Box 333, Rillton, PA 15678.

The Christian and Missionary Alliance (1887) — Pres., Dr. Louis L. King; sec., Dr. R.W. Battles, 350 N. Highland Ave., Nyack, NY 10960.

Christian Church (Disciples of Christ) (1809) — Gen. minister and pres., Dr. Kenneth L. Teegarden, 222 S. Downey Ave., Box 1986, Indianapolis, IN 46206.

The Christian Congregation (1887) — Gen. supt., Rev. Ora Wilbert Eads, 804 W. Hemlock St., LaFollette, TN 37766.

Churches of Christ in Christian Union (1909) — Gen. supt., Rev. Robert Kline; gen. sec., Rev. Paul Dorsey, Box 30, Circleville, OH 43113.

Churches of God:

Churches of God, General Conference (1825) — Admin., Dr. Richard E. Wilken, Box 926, Findlay, OH 45840.

Church of God (Anderson, Ind.) (1880) — Chpsn., Paul L. Hart; exec. sec., Paul A. Tanner, Box 2420, Anderson, IN 46011.

Church of Christ, Scientist (1879) — Pres., Saville R. Davis; clerk, Robert H. Mitchell, Christian Science Center, Boston, MA 02115.

Church of the Nazarene (1908) — Gen. sec., B. Edgar Johnson, 6401 The Paseo, Kansas City, MO 64131.

National Association of Congregational Christian Churches (1955) — Mod., Helen J. Berkaw; exec. sec., Rev. Erwin A. Britton, D.D., Box 1620, Oak Creek, WI 53154.

Eastern Orthodox churches:

Antiochian Orthodox Christian Archdiocese of North America (formerly **Syrian Antiochian Orthodox Church**) (1894) — Primate, Metropolitan Archbishop Philip (Saleba); aux., Archbishop Michael Shaheen, 358 Mountain Rd., Englewood, NJ 07631.

Diocese of the Armenian Church of America (1889) — Primate, His Eminence Archbishop Torkom Manoogian; sec., V. Rev. Arshen Aivazian, 630 2d Ave., N.Y., NY 10016.

Coptic Orthodox Ch. — Correspnt., Archpriest Fr. Gabriel Abdelsayed, 427 West Side Ave., Jersey City, NJ 07304.

Greek Orthodox Archdiocese of North and South America (1864) — Primate, Archbishop Iakovos; chan., V. Rev. George Bacopulos, 8-10 E. 79th St., N.Y., NY 10021.

Orthodox Church in America (formerly **Russian Orthodox Greek Catholic Church of North America**) (1794) — Primate, Metropolitan Theodosius; chan., V. Rev. Daniel Hubiak, Rt. 25A, Box 675, Syosset, NY 11791.

Romanian Orthodox Episcopate of America (1929) — Bishop, Archbishop Valerian (D. Trifa); sec., Rev. Laurence C. Lazar, 2522 Grey Tower Rd., Jackson, MI 49201.

Serbian Eastern Orthodox Church for the U.S.A. and Canada — Bishops, Rt. Rev. Bishop Firmilian, Dionisije and Iriney; Rt. Rev. Bishop Gregory; Bishop Christopher; St. Sava Monastery, Libertyville, IL 60048.

Syrian Orthodox Church of Antioch, Archdiocese of the U.S.A. and Canada (1957) — Primate, Archbishop Marathanasius Y. Samuel; gen. sec., Rev. Fr. John Meno, 293 Hamilton Pl., Hackensack, NJ 07601.

Ukrainian Orthodox Church in America (Ecumenical Patriarchate) (1928) — Primate, Most. Rev. Bishop Andrei Kuschak, 90-34 139th St., Jamaica, NY 11435.

Ukrainian Orthodox Church in the U.S.A. (1919) — Metropolitan, Most Rev. Mstyslav S. Skrypnyk, Box 495, South Bound Brook, NJ 08880.

The Episcopal Church (1789) — Presiding bishop, Rt. Rev. John M. Allin; exec. off., Rev. James R. Gundrum, 815 2d Ave., N.Y., NY 10017.

Evangelical Christian Churches (1966) — Pres., Rev. John Wahnert, 2075-AN, John Russell Circle, Elkins Park, PA 19117.

Evangelical Christian Churches, California Synod (1966) — Pres.-Treas., Dr. Richard W. Hart Sr., 2450 First Ave., San Bernardino, CA 92405.

The Evangelical Covenant Church of America (1885) — Pres., Dr. Milton B. Engebretson; sec., Rev. Clifford Bjorklund, 5101 N. Francisco Ave., Chicago, IL 60625.

Friends:

Evangelical Friends Alliance (1965) — Pres., Stanley Perisho, 4595 Eliot St., Denver, CO 80211.

Friends General Conference (1900) — Clk., Dorothea C. Morse, 1520B Race St., Phila., PA 19102.

Friends United Meeting (formerly **Five Years Meeting of Friends**) (1902) — Presiding clerk, Walter E. Schutt, 101 Quaker Hill Dr., Richmond, IN 47374.

Independent Fundamental Churches of America (1930) — Pres., Rev. Robert L. Gray, 2105 Sunnyside, Westchester, IL 60153.

Islamic Center of Washington — 2551 Massachusetts Ave. NW, Washington, DC 20008.

Jehovah's Witnesses (1884) — Watch Tower Pres., Frederick W. Franz, 124 Columbia Heights, Brooklyn, NY 11201.

Jewish congregations:

Union of American Hebrew Congregations (Reform) — Pres., Rabbi Alexander M. Schindler, 838 5th Ave., N.Y., NY 10021.

National Council of Young Israel (Orthodox) (1912) — Pres., Nathaniel Saperstein; exec. v.p., Rabbi Ephraim H. Sturm, 3 W. 16th St., N.Y., NY 10011.
Union of Orthodox Jewish Congregations of America — Pres., Julius Berman, 116 E. 27th St., N.Y., NY 10016.
United Synagogue of America (Conservative) — Pres., Simon Schwartz, exec. v.p., Rabbi Benjamin Z. Kreitman, 155 5th Ave., N.Y., NY 10010.

Latter-day Saints:
The Church of Jesus Christ of Latter-day Saints (Mormon) (1830) — Pres., Spencer W. Kimball, 47 E. South Temple St., Salt Lake City, UT 84111.
Reorganized Church of Jesus Christ of Latter Day Saints (1830) — Pres., Wallace B. Smith, The Auditorium, Independence, MO 64051.

Lutheran churches:
The American Lutheran Church (1961) — Pres., Dr. David W. Preus; gen. sec., Dr. A.R. Mickelson, 422 S. 5th St., Minneapolis, MN 55415.
Church of the Lutheran Brethren (1900) — Pres., Rev. Everald H. Strom; sec., Rev. George Aase, 1007 Westside Dr., Box 655, Fergus Falls, MN 56537.
Church of the Lutheran Confession (1961) — Pres., Rev. Egbert Albrecht; sec., Rev. Paul Nolting, Rt. 2, Markesan, WI 53946.
Assn. of Evangelical Lutheran Churches (1976) — Pres., Dr. William H. Kohn; exec. sec., Elwyn Ewald, 12015 Manchester Rd., St. Louis, MO 63131.
Evangelical Lutheran Synod (1853) — Pres., Rev. W.W. Petersen; sec., Rev. Alf Merseth, 106 13th St. S., Northwood, IA 50459.
Assn. of Free Lutheran Congregations (1962) — Pres., Rev. Richard Snipstead; sec. Rev. Einar Unseth, 3110 E. Medicine Lake Blvd., Minneapolis, MN 55441.
Lutheran Church in America (1962) — Pres., Rev. Dr. James R. Crumley; sec., Rev. Dr. Reuben T. Swanson, 231 Madison Ave., N.Y. NY 10016.
Lutheran Church — Missouri Synod (1847) — Pres., Dr. J.A.O. Preus; sec., Rev. Herbert A. Mueller, 500 N. Broadway, St. Louis, MO 63102.
Wisconsin Evangelical Lutheran Synod (1850) — Pres., Rev. Carl H. Mischke; 3512 W. North Ave., Milwaukee, WI 53208; sec., Heinrich J. Vogel, 11757 N. Seminary Dr., 65W, Mequon, WI 53092.

Mennonite churches:
The General Conference Mennonite Church (1860) — Pres. Elmer Neufeld; gen. sec., Vern Preheim, 722 Main, Box 347, Newton, KS 67114.
Mennonite Church (1690) — Mod., Glendon L. Blosser; sec., Ivan J. Kauffmann, 528 E. Madison St., Lombard, IL 60148.

Methodist churches:
African Methodist Episcopal Zion Church (1796) — Sr. Bishop, Herbert Shaw; gen. sec.-aud., Rev. Herman L. Anderson, Box 32843, Charlotte, NC 28232.
Evangelical Methodist Church (1946) — Gen. supt., John F. Kunkle; gen. sec., Rev. R.D. Driggers, 3000 W. Kellogg Dr., Wichita, KS 67213.
Free Methodist Church of North America (1860) — Bishops B. Andrews, D. Bastian, W. Cryderman, E. Parsons, C. Van Valin, gen. conf. sec., C.T. Denbo, 901 College Ave., Winona Lake, IN 46590.
The United Methodist Church (1968) — Pres., Bishop Ralph T. Alton; sec., Bishop James K. Mathews, 100 Maryland Ave. NE, Wash., DC 20002.

Universal Fellowship of Metropolitan Community Churches —Mod., Rev. Troy Perry; 5300 Santa Monica Blvd., Suite 304, Los Angeles, CA 90029.

Moravian Church (Unitas Fratum) (1740) **Northern Province** — Pres., Dr. J.S. Groenfeldt, 69 W. Church St., Box 1245, Bethlehem, PA 18018. **Southern Province** — Pres., Dr. Richard F. Amos, 459 S. Church St., Winston-Salem, NC 27101.

Old Catholic churches:
Mariavite Old Catholic Church-Province of North America (1932) — Prime bishop, Most Rev. Robert R.J.M. Zaborowski O.M., D.D., 2803 10th St., Wyandotte, MI 48192.
North American Old Roman Catholic Church (1915) — Archbishop, Most Rev. J.E. Schweikert, 4200 N. Kedvale Ave., Chicago, IL 60641.

Pentecostal churches:
Assemblies of God (1914) — Gen. supt., Thomas F. Zimmerman; gen. sec., Joseph R. Flower, 1445 Boonville Ave., Springfield, MO 65802.
Bible Way Church of Our Lord Jesus Christ World Wide (1927) — Presiding bishop, Dr. Smallwood E. Williams, 1100 New Jersey Ave. NW, Wash., DC 20001.
Gen. Council, Christian Church of No. America (1948) — Gen. overseer; Rev. Dr. Carmine Saginario; gen. sec., Rev. Richard Tedesco, Box 801, 1818 State St., Sharon, PA 16146.
The Church of God (1903) — Gen. overseer, Bishop Voy M. Bullen, 2504 Arrow Wood Dr. SE, Huntsville, AL 35803.
Church of God (Cleveland, Tenn.) (1886) — Gen. overseer, Dr. Ray H. Hughes; gen. sec.-treas., E. C. Thomas, Keith at 25th St. NW, Cleveland, TN 37311.
International Church of the Foursquare Gospel (1927) — Pres., Dr. Rolf K. McPherson; sec., Dr. Leland E. Edwards, 1100 Glendale Blvd., Los Angeles, CA 90026.
Open Bible Standard Churches (1919) — Gen. supt., Ray E. Smith; sec.-treas., O. Ralph Isbill, 2020 Bell Ave., Des Moines, IA 50315.
Pentecostal Church of God (1919) — Gen. supt., Rev. Roy M. Chappell; sec.-treas., Rev. Ronald R. Minor, P.O. Box 850, Joplin, MO 64801.
United Pentecostal Church International (1945) — Gen. supt., Nathaniel A. Urshan; gen. sec., Robert L. McFarland, 8855 Dunn Rd., Hazelwood, MO 63042.
Pentecostal Free Will Baptist Church (1959) — Gen. supt., Rev. Herbert Carter; gen. sec., Rev. Don Sauls, Box 1081, Dunn, NC 28334.

Presbyterian churches:
Cumberland Presbyterian Church (1810) — Mod., James E. Gilbert; stated clerk, T.V. Warnick, Box 4149, Memphis, TN 38104.
The Orthodox Presbyterian Church (1936) — Mod. George E. Haney, stated clerk, Richard A. Barker, 7401 Old York Rd., Phila., PA 19126.
Presbyterian Church in America (1973) — Ruling Elder, William F. Joseph, Jr.; stated clerk, Rev. Morton H. Smith, Box 312, Brevard, NC 28712.
Presbyterian Church in the U.S. (1865) — Mod., Albert C. Winn; stated clerk, James E. Andrews, 341 Ponce de Leon Ave. NE, Atlanta, GA 30308.
Reformed Presbyterian Church, Evangelical Synod (1965) — Stated clerk, Dr. Paul R. Gilchrist, 107 Hardy Rd., Lookout Mountain, TN 37350.
United Presbyterian Church in the U.S.A. (1958) — Mod., Rev. Howard L. Rice; stated clerk, William P. Thompson, 475 Riverside Dr., N.Y., NY 10027.

Reformed Episcopal Church (1873) — Pres., Rev. Theophilos J. Herter; sec., Rev. D. Ellsworth Raudenbush, 560 Fountain St., Havre de Grace, MD 21078.

Reformed churches:
Christian Reformed Church in North America (1857) — Stated clerk, Rev. William P. Brink, 2850 Kalamazoo Ave., SE, Grand Rapids, MI 49560.
Reformed Church in America (1628) — Pres., Rev. Dr. Edwin G. Mulder; gen. sec., Rev. Dr. Arie R. Brouwer, 475 Riverside Dr., N.Y., NY 10027.

Roman Catholic Church — National Conference of Catholic Bishops. Pres., Archbishop John R. Quinn; sec., Bishop Thomas C. Kelly, O.P., 1312 Massachusetts Ave. NW, Wash., DC 20005.

The Salvation Army (1880) — Natl. cmdr., Ernest W. Holz; natl. chief sec., Col. G. Ernest Murray, 120-130 W. 14th St., N.Y., NY 10011.

Sikh (1972) — Chief adm., Siri Singh Sahib, Harbhajan Singh Khalsa Yogiji; sec. gen., Mukhia Sardarni Sahiba, Sardarni Premka Kaur Khalsa, 1649 S. Robertson Blvd., Los Angeles, CA 90035.

Unitarian Universalist Assn. (1961) — Pres., Rev. Dr. Eugene Pickett; sec., Lori Pederson, 25 Beacon St., Boston, MA 02108.

United Brethren in Christ (1789) — Chpsn., Bishop C. Ray Miller; 302 Lake St., Box 650, Huntington, IN 46750.

United Church of Christ (1957) — Pres., Rev. Avery D. Post; sec., Rev. Joseph H. Evans, 105 Madison Ave., N.Y., NY 10016.

Volunteers of America (1896) — Cmdr.-in-chief, Gen. John F. McMahon; natl. field sec., Lt. Col. Belle Leach, 340 W. 85th St., N.Y., NY 10024.

The Wesleyan Church (1968) — Gen. supts., Drs. J. Abbott, R. McIntyre, V. Mitchell, M. Snyder; sec., D. Wayne Brown, Box 2000, Marion, IN 46952.

Worldwide Church of God (1934) — Pastor gen., Herbert W. Armstrong; 300 W. Green St., Pasadena, CA 91123.

Headquarters of Religious Groups in Canada

(year organized in parentheses)

Anglican Church of Canada (creation of General Synod 1893) - Primate, Most Rev. E.W. Scott; 600 Jarvis St., Toronto, Ont. M4Y 2J6.

Antiochian Orthodox Christian Church (Syrian) - Rev. Anthony Gabriel, 555-575 Jean Talon E., Montreal, Que., H2R 1T8.

Apostolic Church in Canada - H.O. 27 Castlefield Ave., Toronto, Ont. M4R 1G3; Pres., Rev. D.S. Morris, 388 Gerald St., La Salle, Que.

Baha'is of Canada, The National Spiritual Assembly of the (1949) - Gen. Sec. J.D. Martin, 7200 Leslie St., Thornhill, Ont. L3T 2A1.

Baptist Federation of Canada - Pres., Jerry Zeman; Gen. Sec.-Treasurer, Rev. R. Fred Bullen, 91 Queen St., Brantford, Ont. N3T 5T6.

Bible Holiness Movement, The (1949) - Pres., Evangelist Wesley H. Wakefield, Box 223, Stn. A, Vancouver, B.C. V6C 2M3.

Buddhist Churches of Canada (1945) - Administrative H.O., 220 Jackson Ave., Vancouver, B.C. V6A 3B3.

Canadian Council of Churches, The (1938) - Gen. Sec., Rev. Donald W. Anderson, 40 St. Clair Ave. E., Toronto, Ont. M4T 1M9.

Christian and Missionary Alliance in Canada, The (1889) - Pres., Rev. M.P. Sylvester, Box 4048, Regina, Sask. S4P 3R9.

Christian Church (Disciples of Christ) (All Canada Committee formed 1922) - Exec. Min. Robert K. Leland, 39 Arkell Rd., R.R. 2, Guelph, Ont. N1H 6H8.

Christian Science in Canada - Mr. J.D. Fulton, 339 Bloor St. W., Ste. 214, Toronto, Ont. M5S 1W7.

Church of Jesus Christ of Latter Day Saints (Mormons) (1830) - Pres. Calgary Stake, R.H. Walker, 930 Prospect Ave. S.W., Calgary Alta. T2T 0W5; Pres. Edmonton Stake, Warren Wilde, 5108-112 St., Edmonton, Alta. T6H 3J2; Pres. Toronto Stake, C.L. Merkley, 2 The Outlook, Islington, Ont. M9B 2X6; Pres. Vancouver Stake, R.W. Komm, 1348 Chartwell Dr., West Vancouver, B.C. V7S 2R5.

Church of the Nazarene (1902) - Dist. Superintendent of Canada Central District, Rev. Lorne MacMillan, 38 Riverhead Dr., Rexdale, Ont. M9W 4G6; Chairman of Exec. Board, Rev. Alexander Ardrey, 2236 Capitol Hill Cres. N.W., Calgary, Alta. T2M 4B9.

Fellowship of Evangelical Baptist Churches in Canada (1953) - Gen. Sec. Dr. Roy W. Lawson, 74 Sheppard Ave. W., Willowdale, Ont. M2N 1M3.

Free Methodist Church in Canada (1880) - Pres., Bishop D.N. Bastian, 3 Harrowby Ct., Islington, Ont. M9B 3H3; Exec. Sec., Rev. C.A. Horton, 833-D Upper James St., Hamilton, Ont. L9C 3A3.

Greek Orthodox Church in Canada - His Grace Bishop Sotirios, 27 Teddington Park Ave., Toronto, Ont. M4N 2C4.

Jehovah's Witnesses (Branch Office estab. in Winnipeg 1918) - Branch Coordinator, Mr. Kenneth A. Little, 150 Bridgeland Ave., Toronto, Ont. M6A 1Z5.

Jewish Congress, Canadian (1919) - Exec. Vice-Pres., Alan Rose, 1590 Avenue Docteur Penfield, Montreal, Que. H3G 1C5.

Lutheran Council in Canada (a joint body of **The Evangelical Lutheran Church of Canada, Lutheran Church-Canada,** and **Lutheran Church in America - Canada Section**) - Pres., Rev. Val Hennig; Exec. Dir. W.A. Schultz, 500-365 Hargrave St., Winnipeg, Man. R3B 2K3.

Mennonite Brethren Churches of North America, Canadian Conference (inc. 1945) - Mod., Rev. Peter R. Toews, 145 Henderson Highway, Winnipeg, Man.

Mennonites in Canada, Conference of (1903) - Chairman, David P. Neufeld, 600 Shaftesbury Blvd., Winnipeg, Man. R3P 0M4.

Pentecostal Assemblies of Canada, The (inc. 1919) - Gen. Supt., Rev. Robert W. Taitinger, 10 Overlea Blvd., Toronto, Ont. M4H 1A5.

Presbyterian Church in Canada, The (1875) - Mod., Dr. K.G. McMillan, 50 Wynford Dr., Don Mills, Ont. M3C 1J7.

Religious Society of Friends (Quakers), (Canadian Yearly Meeting of the Religious Society of Friends formed 1955) - Presiding Clerk, C. Leroy Jones, 60 Lowther Ave., Toronto, Ont. M5R 1C7.

Reorganized Church of Jesus Christ of Latter-Day Saints (Canada) (1830) - Ont. Regional Pres., D. Frank Silverthorn; Bishop of Canada and Ont. Region, Kenneth G. Fisher, 390 Speedvale Ave. E., Guelph, Ont. N1E 1N5.

Roman Catholic Church in Canada - Apostolic Pro Nuncio, His Excellency the Most Reverend Angelo Palmas; counsellor, Mons. Dante Pasquinelli; attache, Rev. George Panikulam; Sec., Gerard Yelle, s.s., 724 Manor Ave., Ottawa, Ont. K1M 0E3.

Salvation Army, The (1882) - Commissioner John D. Waldron, 20 Albert St., Toronto, Ont. M5G 1A6.

Seventh-day Adventist Church in Canada - Pres., L.L. Reile; Sec., A.N. How; 1148 King St. E., Oshawa, Ont. L1H 1H8.

Ukrainian Greek Orthodox Church in Canada - Primate, Metropolitan of Winnipeg and of all Canada, His Beatitude Metropolitan Andrew (Metiuk), 9 St. Johns Ave., Winnipeg, Man. R2W 0T9.

Union of Spiritual Communities of Christ (Orthodox Doukhobors in Canada) (1938) - Honorary Chmn. of the Exec. Comm., John J. Verigin, Box 760, Grand Forks, B.C. V0H 1B0.

Unitarian Council, Canadian (1961) - Pres., Brian Reid; Admin. Sec. Mrs. Thelma Peters, 175 St. Clair Ave. W., Toronto, Ont. M4V 1P7.

United Church of Canada, The (1925) - Mod. Rt. Rev. George Tuttle; Sec. of General Council, Rev. Donald Ray, 85 St. Clair Ave. E., Toronto, Ont. M4T 1M8.

Protestant Episcopal Calendar and Altar Colors

White—from Christmas Day through the Epiphany; First Sunday after Epiphany; Maundy Thursday (at the Eucharist); from the Vigil of Easter to Whitsunday; Trinity Sunday; Feasts of the Lord (except Holy Cross Day); St. Joseph; St. Mary Magdalene, St. Mary the Virgin, and St. Michael and All Angels. **Red**—Pentecost (Whitsunday); Holy Cross Day; all feasts of apostles, evangelists, and martyrs. **Violet**—Advent, Lent, Ember days, and Holy Innocents' Day. Optional color scheme for Lent: **Lenten White** from Ash Wednesday to Palm Sunday; **Crimson** during Holy Week. **Green**—Epiphany season and season after Pentecost. **Black**—optional for Good Friday and funerals.

Days, etc.	1980	1981	1982	1983	1984	1985
Golden Number	5	6	7	8	9	10
Sunday Letter	FE	D	C	B	AG	F
Sundays after Epiphany*	3(6)	5(8)	4(7)	3(6)	9	6
Septuagesima**						
Ash Wednesday	Feb. 20	Mar. 4	Feb. 24	Feb. 16	Mar. 7	Feb. 24
First Sunday in Lent	Feb. 24	Mar. 8	Feb. 28	Feb. 20	Mar. 11	Feb. 24
Passion Sunday**						
Palm Sunday	Mar. 30	Apr. 12	Apr. 4	Mar. 27	Apr. 15	Mar. 31
Good Friday	Apr. 4	Apr. 17	Apr. 9	Apr. 1	Apr. 20	Apr. 5
Easter Day	Apr. 6	Apr. 19	Apr. 11	Apr. 3	Apr. 22	Apr. 7
Rogation Sunday**						
Ascension Day	May 15	May 28	May 20	May 12	May 31	May 16
Whitsunday	May 25	June 7	May 30	May 22	June 10	May 26
Trinity Sunday	June 1	June 14	June 6	May 29	June 17	June 2
Sundays after Trinity***	26	24	25	26	24	26
First Sunday in Advent	Nov. 30	Nov. 29	Nov. 28	Nov. 27	Dec. 2	Dec. 1

In the Protestant Episcopal Church the days of fasting are Ash Wednesday and Good Friday. Other days of abstinence are the 40 days of Lent, the Ember Days, and all Fridays of the year except those in the Christmas and Easter seasons. Ember Days (optional) are days of abstinence and prayer for ordinands and the increase of the ministry. They fall on the Wednesday, Friday, and Saturday after the first Sunday in Lent, the Feast of Pentecost (Whitsunday), Sept. 14, and Dec. 13. Rogation Days (also optional) are the three days before Ascension Day, and are days of solemn supplication for God's blessing upon the fields and harvests of the world.

The Episcopal Church having adopted a revised calendar in 1979, the following changes in the foregoing table now obtain: *The three Sundays before Lent having been suppressed, the number of Sundays after Epiphany are increased by three. **These Sundays are no longer observed. ***The Sundays "after Trinity" are now counted as "Sundays after Pentecost," and are one more in number than formerly.

Ash Wednesday and Easter Sunday

Year	Ash Wed.	Easter Sunday	Year	Ash Wed.	Easter Sunday	Year	Ash Wed.	Easter Sunday	Year	Ash Wed.	Easter Sunday
1901	Feb. 20	Apr. 7	1951	Feb. 7	Mar. 25	2001	Feb. 28	Apr. 15	2051	Feb. 15	Apr. 2
1902	Feb. 12	Mar. 30	1952	Feb. 27	Apr. 13	2002	Feb. 13	Mar. 31	2052	Mar. 6	Apr. 21
1903	Feb. 25	Apr. 12	1953	Feb. 18	Apr. 5	2003	Mar. 5	Apr. 20	2053	Feb. 19	Apr. 6
1904	Feb. 17	Apr. 3	1954	Mar. 3	Apr. 18	2004	Feb. 25	Apr. 11	2054	Feb. 11	Mar. 29
1905	Mar. 8	Apr. 23	1955	Feb. 23	Apr. 10	2005	Feb. 9	Mar. 27	2055	Mar. 3	Apr. 18
1906	Feb. 28	Apr. 15	1956	Feb. 15	Apr. 1	2006	Mar. 1	Apr. 16	2056	Feb. 16	Apr. 2
1907	Feb. 13	Mar. 31	1957	Mar. 6	Apr. 21	2007	Feb. 21	Apr. 8	2057	Mar. 7	Apr. 22
1908	Mar. 4	Apr. 19	1958	Feb. 19	Apr. 6	2008	Feb. 6	Mar. 23	2058	Feb. 27	Apr. 14
1909	Feb. 24	Apr. 11	1959	Feb. 11	Mar. 29	2009	Feb. 25	Apr. 12	2059	Feb. 12	Mar. 30
1910	Feb. 9	Mar. 27	1960	Mar. 2	Apr. 17	2010	Feb. 17	Apr. 4	2060	Mar. 3	Apr. 18
1911	Mar. 1	Apr. 16	1961	Feb. 15	Apr. 2	2011	Mar. 9	Apr. 24	2061	Feb. 23	Apr. 10
1912	Feb. 21	Apr. 7	1962	Mar. 7	Apr. 22	2012	Feb. 22	Apr. 8	2062	Feb. 8	Mar. 26
1913	Feb. 5	Mar. 23	1963	Feb. 27	Apr. 14	2013	Feb. 13	Mar. 31	2063	Feb. 28	Apr. 15
1914	Feb. 25	Apr. 12	1964	Feb. 12	Mar. 29	2014	Mar. 5	Apr. 20	2064	Feb. 20	Apr. 6
1915	Feb. 17	Apr. 4	1965	Mar. 3	Apr. 18	2015	Feb. 18	Apr. 5	2065	Feb. 11	Mar. 29
1916	Mar. 8	Apr. 23	1966	Feb. 23	Apr. 10	2016	Feb. 10	Mar. 27	2066	Feb. 24	Apr. 11
1917	Feb. 21	Apr. 8	1967	Feb. 8	Mar. 26	2017	Mar. 1	Apr. 16	2067	Feb. 16	Apr. 3
1918	Feb. 13	Mar. 31	1968	Feb. 28	Apr. 14	2018	Feb. 14	Apr. 1	2068	Mar. 7	Apr. 22
1919	Mar. 5	Apr. 20	1969	Feb. 19	Apr. 6	2019	Mar. 6	Apr. 21	2069	Feb. 27	Apr. 14
1920	Feb. 18	Apr. 4	1970	Feb. 11	Mar. 29	2020	Feb. 26	Apr. 12	2070	Feb. 12	Mar. 30
1921	Feb. 9	Mar. 27	1971	Feb. 24	Apr. 11	2021	Feb. 17	Apr. 4	2071	Mar. 4	Apr. 19
1922	Mar. 1	Apr. 16	1972	Feb. 16	Apr. 2	2022	Mar. 2	Apr. 17	2072	Feb. 24	Apr. 10
1923	Feb. 14	Apr. 1	1973	Mar. 7	Apr. 22	2023	Feb. 22	Apr. 9	2073	Feb. 8	Mar. 26
1924	Mar. 5	Apr. 20	1974	Feb. 27	Apr. 14	2024	Feb. 14	Mar. 31	2074	Feb. 28	Apr. 15
1925	Feb. 25	Apr. 12	1975	Feb. 12	Mar. 30	2025	Mar. 5	Apr. 20	2075	Feb. 20	Apr. 7
1926	Feb. 17	Apr. 4	1976	Mar. 3	Apr. 18	2026	Feb. 18	Apr. 5	2076	Mar. 4	Apr. 19
1927	Mar. 2	Apr. 17	1977	Feb. 23	Apr. 10	2027	Feb. 10	Mar. 28	2077	Feb. 24	Apr. 11
1928	Feb. 22	Apr. 8	1978	Feb. 8	Mar. 26	2028	Mar. 1	Apr. 16	2078	Feb. 16	Apr. 3
1929	Feb. 13	Mar. 31	1979	Feb. 28	Apr. 15	2029	Feb. 14	Apr. 1	2079	Mar. 8	Apr. 23
1930	Mar. 5	Apr. 20	1980	Feb. 20	Apr. 6	2030	Mar. 6	Apr. 21	2080	Feb. 21	Apr. 7
1931	Feb. 18	Apr. 5	1981	Mar. 4	Apr. 19	2031	Feb. 26	Apr. 13	2081	Feb. 12	Mar. 30
1932	Feb. 10	Mar. 27	1982	Feb. 24	Apr. 11	2032	Feb. 11	Mar. 28	2082	Mar. 4	Apr. 19
1933	Mar. 1	Apr. 16	1983	Feb. 16	Apr. 3	2033	Mar. 2	Apr. 17	2083	Feb. 17	Apr. 4
1934	Feb. 14	Apr. 1	1984	Mar. 7	Apr. 22	2034	Feb. 22	Apr. 9	2084	Feb. 9	Mar. 26
1935	Mar. 6	Apr. 21	1985	Feb. 20	Apr. 7	2035	Feb. 7	Mar. 25	2085	Feb. 28	Apr. 15
1936	Feb. 26	Apr. 12	1986	Feb. 12	Mar. 30	2036	Feb. 27	Apr. 13	2086	Feb. 13	Mar. 31
1937	Feb. 10	Mar. 28	1987	Mar. 4	Apr. 19	2037	Feb. 18	Apr. 5	2087	Mar. 5	Apr. 20
1938	Mar. 2	Apr. 17	1988	Feb. 17	Apr. 3	2038	Mar. 10	Apr. 25	2088	Feb. 25	Apr. 11
1939	Feb. 22	Apr. 9	1989	Feb. 8	Mar. 26	2039	Feb. 23	Apr. 10	2089	Feb. 16	Apr. 3
1940	Feb. 7	Mar. 24	1990	Feb. 28	Apr. 15	2040	Feb. 15	Apr. 1	2090	Mar. 1	Apr. 16
1941	Feb. 26	Apr. 13	1991	Feb. 13	Mar. 31	2041	Mar. 6	Apr. 21	2091	Feb. 21	Apr. 8
1942	Feb. 18	Apr. 5	1992	Mar. 4	Apr. 19	2042	Feb. 19	Apr. 6	2092	Feb. 13	Mar. 30
1943	Mar. 10	Apr. 25	1993	Feb. 24	Apr. 11	2043	Feb. 11	Mar. 29	2093	Feb. 25	Apr. 12
1944	Feb. 23	Apr. 9	1994	Feb. 16	Apr. 3	2044	Mar. 2	Apr. 17	2094	Feb. 17	Apr. 4
1945	Feb. 14	Apr. 1	1995	Mar. 1	Apr. 16	2045	Feb. 22	Apr. 9	2095	Mar. 9	Apr. 24
1946	Mar. 6	Apr. 21	1996	Feb. 21	Apr. 7	2046	Feb. 7	Mar. 25	2096	Feb. 29	Apr. 15
1947	Feb. 19	Apr. 6	1997	Feb. 12	Mar. 30	2047	Feb. 27	Apr. 14	2097	Feb. 13	Mar. 31
1948	Feb. 11	Mar. 28	1998	Feb. 25	Apr. 12	2048	Feb. 19	Apr. 5	2098	Mar. 5	Apr. 20
1949	Mar. 2	Apr. 17	1999	Feb. 17	Apr. 4	2049	Mar. 3	Apr. 18	2099	Feb. 25	Apr. 12
1950	Feb. 22	Apr. 9	2000	Mar. 8	Apr. 23	2050	Feb. 23	Apr. 10	2100	Feb. 10	Mar. 28

A lengthy dispute over the date for the celebration of Easter was settled by the first Council of the Christian Churches at Nicaea, in Asia Minor, in 325 A.D. The Council ruled that Easter would be observed on the first Sunday following the 14th day of the Paschal Moon, referred to as the Paschal Full Moon. The Paschal Moon is the first moon whose 14th day comes on or after March 21. Dates of the Paschal Full Moon, which are not necessarily the same as those of the real or astronomical full moon, are listed in the table below with an explanation of how to compute the date of Easter.

If the Paschal Full Moon falls on a Sunday, then Easter is the following Sunday. The earliest date on which Easter can fall is March 22; it fell on that date in 1761 and 1818 but will not do so in the 20th or 21st century. The latest possible date for Easter is April 25; it fell on that date in 1943 and will again in 2038.

For western churches Lent begins on Ash Wednesday, which comes 40 days before Easter Sunday, not counting Sundays. Originally it was a period of but 40 hours. Later it comprised 30 days of fasting, omitting all the Sundays and also all the Saturdays except one. Pope Gregory (590-604) added Ash Wednesday to the fast, together with the remainder of that week.

The last seven days of Lent constitute Holy Week, beginning with Palm Sunday. The last Thursday — Maundy Thursday — commemorates the institution of the Eucharist. The following day, Good Friday, commemorates the day of the Crucifixion.

Easter is the chief festival of the Christian year, commemorating the Resurrection of Christ. It occurs about the same time as the ancient Roman celebration of the Vernal Equinox, the arrival of spring. In the second century, A.D., Easter Day among Christians in Asia Minor was the 14th Nisan, the seventh month of the Jewish calendar. The Christians in Europe observed the nearest Sunday.

Date of Paschal Full Moon, 1900-2199

The Golden Number, used in determining the date of Easter, is greater by unity (one) than the remainder obtained upon dividing the given year by 19. For example, when dividing 1981 by 19, one obtains a remainder of 5. Adding 1 gives 6 as the Golden Number for the year 1981. From the table then the date of the Paschal Full Moon is Apr. 18, 1981. Since this is a Saturday, Easter is celebrated on the next day, Apr. 19.

Golden Number	Date	Golden Number	Date	Golden Number	Date	Golden Number	Date
1	Apr. 14	6	Apr. 18	11	Mar. 25	16	Mar. 30
2	Apr. 3	7	Apr. 8	12	Apr. 13	17	Apr. 17
3	Mar. 23	8	Mar. 28	13	Apr. 2	18	Apr. 7
4	Apr. 11	9	Apr. 16	14	Mar. 22	19	Mar. 27
5	Mar. 31	10	Apr. 5	15	Apr. 10		

Jewish Holy Days, Festivals, and Fasts

Source: Synagogue Council of America

Festivals and fasts	Hebrew date		5741 (1980-1981)	5742 (1981-1982)	5743 (1982-1983)	5744 (1983-1984)
Rosh Hashana (New Year)[1]	Tishri	1	Sept. 11 Th	Sept. 29 Tu	Sept. 18 Sa	Sept. 8 Th
Fast of Gedalia	Tishri	3	....	Oct. 1 Th	Sept. 20 Mo	....
Fast of Gedalia	Tishri	4	Sept. 14 Su	....	....	Sept. 11 Su
Yom Kippur (Day of Atonement)	Tishri	10	Sept. 20 Sa	Oct. 8 Th	Sept. 27 Mo	Sept. 17 Sa
Sukkoth (Feast of Tabernacles), 1st Day[1]	Tishri	15	Sept. 25 Th	Oct. 13 Tu	Oct. 2 Sa	Sept. 22 Th
Sukkoth, 8th Day of Assembly (Shemini Atzereth)	Tishri	22	Oct. 2 Th	Oct. 20 Tu	Oct. 9 Sa	Sept. 29 Th
Simchat Torah (Rejoicing of the Law)	Tishri	23	Oct. 3 Fr	Oct. 21 We	Oct. 10 Su	Sept. 30 Fr
Chanukah (Feast of Lights)	Kislev	25	Dec. 3 We	Dec. 21 Mo	Dec. 11 Sa	Dec. 1 Th
Fast of Tebet[2]	Tebet	10	Dec. 17 We	Jan. 5 Tu	Dec. 26 Su	Dec. 16 Fr
Fast of Esther[2]	Adar	13	....	Mar. 8 Mo	Feb. 24 Th	....
Fast of Esther[2]	Adar II	13	Mar. 19 Th	....	....	Mar. 15 Th
Purim (Feast of Lots)	Adar	14	....	Mar. 9 Tu	Feb. 27 Su	....
Purim	Adar II	14	Mar. 20 Fr	....	....	Mar. 18 Su
Pesach (Passover), 1st Day[1]	Nisan	15	Apr. 19 Su	Apr. 8 Th	Mar. 29 Tu	Apr. 17 Tu
Pesach, 7th Day[1]	Nisan	21	Apr. 25 Sa	Apr. 14 We	Apr. 4 Mo	Apr. 23 Mo
Lag B'Omer	Iyar	18	May 22 Fr	May 11 Tu	May 1 Su	May 20 Su
Shavuoth (Feast of Weeks)[1]	Sivan	6	June 8 Mo	May 28 Fr	May 18 We	June 6 We
Fast of Tammuz[2]	Tammuz	17	July 19 Su	July 8	June 28 Tu	July 17 Tu
Tisha B'Av (Fast of Av)[2]	Av	9	Aug. 9 Su	July 29 Th	July 19 Tu	Aug. 7 Tu

The months of the Jewish year are: 1) Tishri; 2) Cheshvan (also Marcheshvan); 3) Kislev; 4) Tebet (also Tebeth); 5) Shebat (also Shebhat); 6) Adar; 6a) Adar Sheni (II) added in leap years; 7) Nisan; 8) Iyar; 9) Sivan; 10) Tammuz; 11) Av (also Abh); 12) Elul. All Jewish holy days, etc., begin at sunset on the day previous. (1) Also observed the following day. (2) Hebrew date varies to avoid conflict with Sabbath.

Greek Orthodox Church Calendar, 1981

Date		Holy Days
Jan.	1	Circumcision of Jesus Christ; feast day of St. Basil
Jan.	6	Epiphany: Baptism of Jesus Christ - Sanctification of the Waters
Jan.	7	Feast day of St. John the Baptist
Jan.	30	Feast day of the Three Hierarchs: St. Basil the Great, St. Gregory the Theologian, and St. John Chrysostom
Feb.	2	Presentation of Jesus Christ in the Temple
*Mar.	9	Easter Lent begins
*Mar.	15	Sunday of Orthodoxy (1st Sun. of Lent)
Mar.	25	Annunciation of the Virgin Mary
*Apr.	19	Palm Sunday
*Apr.	19-25	Holy Week
*Apr.	24	Holy (Good) Friday: Burial of Jesus Christ
*Apr.	26	Easter Sunday: Resurrection of Jesus Christ
*Apr.	23	Feast day of St. George
May	21	Feast day of Sts. Constantine and Helen
*June	4	Ascension of Jesus Christ
*June	14	Sunday of Pentecost
June	29	Feast day of Sts. Peter and Paul
June	30	Feast day of the Twelve Apostles of Jesus Christ
Aug.	6	Transfiguration of Jesus Christ
Aug.	15	Dormition of the Virgin Mary
Aug.	29	Beheading of St. John the Baptist
Sept.	1	Beginning of the Church Year
Sept.	14	Adoration of the Holy Cross
Oct.	23	Feast day of St. James
Oct.	26	Feast day of St. Demetrios the Martyr
Nov.	15	Christmas Lent begins
Nov.	21	Presentation of the Virgin Mary
Nov.	30	Feast day of St. Andrew the Apostle
Dec.	6	Feast day of St. Nicholas, Bishop of Myra
Dec.	25	Christmas Day: Nativity of Jesus Christ

*Movable holy days dependent upon the date of Easter. (The feast day of St. George is normally celebrated Apr. 23. If this day arrives during Lent, it is then celebrated the day after Easter.) The Greek Orthodox Church celebrates holy days in accordance with the Gregorian Calendar. Some Eastern Orthodox Churches still adhere to the Julian Calendar and observe the holy days (with the exception of the Easter cycle) 13 days later.

Islamic (Moslem) Calendar 1980-1981

The Islamic Calendar, often referred to as Mohammedan, is a lunar reckoning from the year of the *hegira*, 622 A.D., when Muhammed moved to Medina from Mecca. It runs in cycles of 30 years, of which the 2d, 5th, 7th, 10th, 13th, 16th, 18th, 21st, 24th, 26th, and 29th are leap years; 1401 and 1402 are the 21st and 22nd years, respectively, of the cycle. Common years have 354 days, leap years 355, the extra day being added to the last month, Zu'lhijjah. Except for this case, the 12 months beginning with Muharram have alternately 30 and 29 days.[1]

Year	Name of month	Month begins
1401	Muharram (New Year)	Nov. 9, 1980
1401	Safar	Dec. 9, 1980
1401	Rabia I.	Jan. 7, 1981
1401	Rabia II	Feb. 6, 1981
1401	Jumada I	Mar. 7, 1981
1401	Jumada II	Apr. 6, 1981
1401	Rajab	May 5, 1981
1401	Shaban	June 4, 1981
1401	Ramadan	July 3, 1981
1401	Shawwai	Aug. 2, 1981
1401	Zu'lkadah	Aug. 31, 1981
1401	Zu'lhijjah	Oct. 1, 1981

Year	Name of Month	Month begins
1402	Muharram (New Year)	Oct. 30, 1981
1402	Safar	Nov. 30, 1981
1402	Rabia I	Dec. 29, 1981
1402	Rabia II	Jan. 28, 1982
1402	Jumada I	Feb. 26, 1982
1402	Jumada II	Mar. 28, 1982
1402	Rajab	Apr. 26, 1982
1402	Shaban	May 26, 1982
1402	Ramadan	June 24, 1982
1402	Shawwai	July 24, 1982
1402	Zu'lkadah	Aug. 22, 1982
1402	Zu'lhijjah	Sept. 21, 1982

(1) The date on which Ramadan begins may vary from the calendar date. It actually starts only after the new moon is sighted from the Naval Observatory in Cairo.

The Major World Religions

Buddhism

Founded: About 525 BC, reportedly near Benares, India.
Founder: Gautama Siddhartha (ca. 563-480), the Buddha, who achieved enlightenment through intense meditation.
Sacred Texts: The *Tripitaka*, a collection of the Buddha's teachings, rules of monastic life, and philosophical commentaries on the teachings; also a vast body of Buddhist teachings and commentaries, many of which are called *sutras*.
Organization: The basic institution is the *sangha* or monastic order through which the traditions are passed to each generation. Monastic life tends to be democratic and anti-authoritarian. Large lay organizations have developed in some sects.
Practice: Varies widely according to the sect and ranges from austere meditation to magical chanting and elaborate temple rites. Many practices, such as exorcism of devils, reflect pre-Buddhist beliefs.
Divisions: A wide variety of sects grouped into 3 primary branches: Therevada (sole survivor of the ancient Hinayana schools) which emphasizes the importance of pure thought and deed; Mahayana, which includes Zen and Soka-gakkai, ranges from philosophical schools to belief in the saving grace of higher beings or ritual practices, and to practical meditative disciplines; and Tantrism, an unusual combination of belief in ritual magic and sophisticated philosophy.
Location: Throughout Asia, from Ceylon to Japan. Zen and Soka-gakkai have several thousand adherents in the U.S.
Beliefs: Life is misery and decay, and there is no ultimate reality in it or behind it. The cycle of endless birth and rebirth continues because of desire and attachment to the unreal "self". Right meditation and deeds will end the cycle and achieve Nirvana, the Void, nothingness.

Hinduism

Founded: Ca. 1500 BC by Aryan invaders of India where their Vedic religion intermixed with the practices and beliefs of the natives.
Sacred texts: The *Veda*, including the *Upanishads*, a collection of rituals and mythological and philosophical commentaries; a vast number of epic stories about gods, heroes and saints, including the *Bhagavadgita*, a part of the *Mahabharata*, and the *Ramayana;* and a great variety of other literature.
Organization: None, strictly speaking. Generally, rituals should be performed or assisted by Brahmins, the priestly caste, but in practice simpler rituals can be performed by anyone. Brahmins are the final judges of ritual purity, the vital element in Hindu life. Temples and religious organizations are usually presided over by Brahmins.
Practice: A variety of private rituals, primarily passage rites (eg. initiation, marriage, death, etc.) and daily devotions, and a similar variety of public rites in temples. Of the latter, the *puja*, a ceremonial dinner for a god, is the most common.
Divisions: There is no concept of orthodoxy in Hinduism, which presents a bewildering variety of sects, most of them devoted to the worship of one of the many gods. The 3 major living traditions are those devoted to the gods Vishnu and Shiva and to the goddess Shakti; each of them divided into further sub-sects. Numerous folk beliefs and practices, often in amalgamation with the above groups, exist side-by-side with sophisticated philosophical schools and exotic cults.
Location: Confined to India, except for the missionary work of Vedanta, the Krishna Consciousness society, and individual *gurus* (teachers) in the West.
Beliefs: There is only one divine principle; the many gods are only aspects of that unity. Life in all its forms is an aspect of the divine, but it appears as a separation from the divine, a meaningless cycle of birth and rebirth (*samsara*) determined by the purity or impurity of past deeds (*karma*). To improve one's *karma* or escape *samsara* by pure acts, thought, and/or devotion is the aim of every Hindu.

Islam (submission)

Founded: 622 AD in Medina, Arabian peninsula.
Founder: Mohammed (ca. 570-632), the Prophet, as a result of visions.
Sacred texts: *Koran*, the words of God, delivered to Mohammed by the angel Gabriel; *Hadith*, collections of the sayings of the Prophet.
Organization: Theoretically the state and religious community are one, administered by a caliph. In practice, Islam is a loose collection of congregations united by a very conservative tradition. Islam is basically egalitarian and non-authoritarian.
Practice: Every Moslem is supposed to make the profession of faith ("There is no god but Allah . . ."), pray 5 times a day, give a regular portion of his goods to charity, fast during the day in the month of Ramadan, and make at least one pilgrimage to Mecca if possible. Additionally saints' days are celebrated and pilgrimages made to shrines.
Divisions: The 2 major sects of Islam are the Sunni (orthodox) and the Shi'ah. The Shi'ah believe in 12 *imams*, perfect teachers, who still guide the faithful from Paradise. Shi'ah practice tends toward the ecstatic, while the Sunni is staid and simple. The Shi'ah sect affirms man's free will; the Sunni is deterministic. The mystic tradition in Islam is Sufism. A Sufi adept believes he has acquired a special inner knowledge direct from Allah.
Location: From the west coast of Africa to the Philipines across a broad band that includes Tanzania, southern USSR and western China, India, Malaysia and Indonesia. Islam has perhaps 100,000 adherents among American blacks.
Beliefs: Strictly monotheistic. God is creator of the universe, omnipotent, just, and merciful. Man is God's highest creation, but limited and sinful. He is misled by Satan, a prideful angel. God gave the *Koran* to Mohammed to guide men to the truth. Those who repent and sincerely submit to God return to a state of sinlessness. In the end, the sinless go to Paradise, a place of physical and spiritual pleasure, and the wicked burn in Hell.

Judaism

Founded: About 1300 BC, reportedly at Mt. Sinai.
Founder: Moses, probably an historical person.
Sacred Texts: Torah, or divine teaching, found particularly in the first 5 books of the Bible; Talmud and Midrash, commentaries on Torah.
Organization: Originally theocratic, Judaism has evolved a congregational polity. The basic institution is the local synagogue, operated by the congregation and led by a rabbi of their choice. Chief Rabbis in France and Great Britain have authority only over those who accept it; in Israel, the 2 Chief Rabbis have civil authority in family law.
Practice: Among the very conservative, prayers accompany almost every action of daily life. Synagogue services center around the Torah reading. The chief annual observances are Passover, celebrating the liberation of the Israelites from Egypt and marked by the ritual Seder meal in the home, and the 10 days from Rosh Hashana (New Year) to Yom Kippur (Day of Atonement), a period of fasting and penitence.
Divisions: Judaism is an unbroken spectrum from ultra-conservative to ultra-liberal. Distinctions depend primarily on the care taken to observe the many prescribed duties and prohibitions in daily life, particularly the dietary and Sabbath regulations, and whether these are seen as binding or optional. The amount of Hebrew used in services distinguishes groups on the liberal end of the spectrum. Hasidism is a pietistic movement which emphasizes joyful devotion and the charismatic power of individual Hasidic leaders.
Location: Almost world-wide, with concentrations in Israel and the U.S.
Beliefs: Strictly monotheistic. God is the creator and absolute ruler of the universe. Men are free to choose to rebel against God's rule. God established a particular relationship with the Hebrew people: by obeying the divine law God gave them they would be a special witness to God's mercy and justice. The emphasis in Judaism is on ethical behavior (and, among the conservative, careful ritual obedience) as the true worship of God.

Major Christian Denominations:

Italics indicate that area which, generally speaking, most

Denomination	Origins	Organization	Authority	Special rites
Baptists	In radical Reformation objections to infant baptism, demands for church-state separation; John Smyth, English Separatist in 1609; Roger Williams, 1638, Providence, R.I.	Congregational, *i.e.*, each local church is autonomous.	Scripture; some Baptists, particularly in the South, interpret the Bible literally.	Baptism, after about age 12, by total immersion; Lord's Supper.
Church of Christ (Disciples)	Among evangelical Presbyterians in Ky. (1804) and Penn. (1809), in distress over Protestant factionalism and decline of fervor. Organized 1832.	Congregational.	*"Where the Scriptures speak, we speak; where the Scriptures are silent, we are silent."*	Adult baptism, Lord's Supper (weekly).
Episcopalians	Henry VIII separated English Catholic Church from Rome, 1534, for political reasons. Protestant Episcopal Church in U.S. founded 1789.	*Bishops, in apostolic succession, are elected by diocesan representatives; part of Anglican Communion, symbolically headed by Archbishop of Canterbury.*	Scripture as interpreted by tradition, esp. *39 Articles* (1563); not dogmatic. Tri-annual convention of bishops, priests, and laymen.	Infant baptism, Holy Communion, others. Sacrament is symbolic, but has real spiritual effect.
Lutherans	Martin Luther in Wittenberg, Germany, 1517, objected to Catholic doctrine of salvation by merit and sale of indulgences; break complete by 1519.	Varies from congregational to episcopal; in U.S. a combination of regional synods and congregational polities is most common.	*Scripture, and tradition as spelled out in Augsburg Confession (1530) and other creeds. These confessions of faith are binding although interpretations vary.*	Infant baptism, Lord's Supper. Bread and wine in Supper is less than the actual body and blood of Christ, but more than simply symbolic.
Methodists	Rev. John Wesley began movement, 1738, to infuse pietist enthusiasm into Church of England formalism. First U.S. conference, 1773.	*Bishops (not a priestly order, only an office) are elected for life, appoint district superintendants and local ministers.*	Scripture as interpreted by tradition, reason, and personal insight.	Infant baptism, Lord's Supper.
Mormons	In visions of the Angel Moroni by Joseph Smith, 1827, in New York, in which he received a new revelation on golden tablets: *The Book of Mormon.*	Theocratic; all male adults are in priesthood which culminates in Council of 12 Apostles and 1st Presidency (1st President, 2 counselors).	*The Bible, Book of Mormon and other revelations to Smith, and certain pronouncements of the 1st Presidency.*	Adult baptism, laying on of hands (which grants gifts of the Spirit), Lord's Supper. Temple rites: baptism for the dead, marriage for eternity, others.
Orthodox	Original Christian proselytizing in 1st century; broke with Rome, 1054, after centuries of doctrinal disputes and diverging traditions.	Synods of bishops in autonomous, usually national, churches elect a patriarch, archbishop or metropolitan. These men, as a group, are the heads of the church.	Scripture, tradition, and the first 7 church councils up to Nicaea II in 787. Bishops in council have authority in doctrine and policy.	Seven sacraments: infant baptism and anointing, Eucharist (both bread and wine), ordination, penance, anointing of the sick, marriage.
Pentecostal	In Topeka, Kansas (1901), and Los Angeles (1906) in reaction fo loss of evangelical fervor among Methodists and other denominations.	Originally a movement, not a formal organization, Pentecostalism now has a variety of organized forms and continues also as a movement.	Scripture, individual charismatic leaders, the teachings of the Holy Spirit.	*Spirit baptism, esp. as shown in "speaking in tongues"; healing and sometimes exorcism; adult baptism, Lord's Supper.*
Presbyterians	In Calvinist Reformation in 1500s; differed with Lutherans over sacraments, church government. John Knox founded Scotch Presbyterian church about 1560.	*Highly structured representational system of ministers and laypersons (presbyters) in local, regional and national bodies. (synods).*	Scripture.	Infant baptism, Lord's Supper; bread and wine symbolize Christ's spiritual presence.
Roman Catholics	Traditionally, by Jesus who named St. Peter the 1st Vicar; historically, in early Christian proselytizing and the conversion of imperial Rome in the 4th century.	Hierarchy with supreme power vested in Pope elected by cardinals. Councils of Bishops advise on matters of doctrine and policy.	*The Pope, when speaking for the whole church in matters of faith and morals, and tradition, which is partly recorded in scripture and expressed in church councils.*	Seven sacraments: baptism, contrition and penance, confirmation, Eucharist, marriage, ordination, and anointing of the sick (unction).
United Church of Christ	*By ecumenical union, 1957, of Congregationalists and Evangelical & Reformed, representing both Calvinist and Lutheran traditions.*	Congregational; a General Synod, representative of all congregations, sets general policy.	Scripture.	Infant baptism, Lord's Supper.

How Do They Differ?

distinguishes that denomination from any other.

Practice	Ethics	Doctrine	Other	Denomination
Worship style varies from staid to evangelistic. Extensive missionary activity.	Usually opposed to alcohol and tobacco; sometimes tends toward a perfectionist ethical standard.	*No creed; true church is of believers only, who are all equal.*	Since no authority can stand between the believer and God, the Baptists are strong supporters of church-state separation.	**Baptists**
Tries to avoid any rite or doctrine not explicitly part of the 1st century church. Some congregations may reject instrumental music.	Some tendency toward perfectionism; increasing interest in social action programs.	Simple New Testament faith; avoids any elaboration not firmly based on Scripture.	Highly tolerant in doctrinal and religious matters; strongly supportive of scholarly education.	**Church of Christ (Disciples)**
Formal, based on *Book of Common Prayer* (1549); services range from austerely simple to highly elaborate.	Tolerant; sometimes permissive; some social action programs.	*Apostles' Creed* is basic; otherwise, considerable variation ranges from rationalist and liberal to acceptance of most Roman Catholic dogma.	Strongly ecumenical, holding talks with all other branches of Christendom.	**Episcopalians**
Relatively simple formal liturgy with emphasis on the sermon.	Generally, conservative in personal and social ethics; doctrine of "2 kingdoms" (worldly and holy) supports conservatism in secular affairs.	Salvation by faith alone through grace. Lutheranism has made major contributions to Protestant theology.	Though still somewhat divided along ethnic lines (German, Swede, etc.), main divisions are between funamentalists and liberals.	**Lutherans**
Worship style varies; usually staid, sometimes evangelistic.	Originally pietist and perfectionist with a tendency to withdraw from secular affairs; now with strong social activist elements.	No distinctive theological development; *25 Articles*, abridged from Church of England's 39, not binding.	In 1968, the United Methodist Church was formed by the union of the major Methodist church and the 1946 union of Evangelical and United Brethren churches.	**Methodists**
Staid service with hymns, sermon. Secret temple ceremonies may be more elaborate. Strong missionary activity.	Temperance; strict tithing. Combine a strong work ethic with communal self-reliance.	God is a material being; he created the universe out of pre-existing matter; all persons can be saved and many will become divine. Most other beliefs are traditionally Christian.	Mormons regard mainline churches as apostate, corrupt. Reorganized Church (founded 1852) rejects most Mormon doctrine and practice except Book of Mormon.	**Mormons**
Elaborate liturgy, usually in the vernacular, though extremely traditional. The liturgy is the essence of Orthodoxy. Veneration of icons.	Tolerant; very little social action; divorce, remarriage permitted in some cases. Priests need not be celibate; bishops are.	Emphasis on Christ's resurrection, rather than crucifixion; the Holy Spirit proceeds from God the Father only.	Orthodox Church in America, orginally under Patriarch of Moscow, was granted autonomy in 1970. Greek Orthodox do not recognize this autonomy.	**Orthodox**
Loosely structured service with rousing hymns and sermons, culminating in spirit baptism.	Usually, emphasis on perfectionism with varying degrees of tolerance.	Simple traditional beliefs, usually Protestant, with emphasis on the immediate presence of God in the Holy Spirit	Once confined to lower-class "holy rollers," Pentecostalism now appears in mainline churches and has established middle-class congregations.	**Pentecostal**
A simple, sober service in which the sermon is central.	Traditionally, a tendency toward strictness with firm church- and self-discipline; otherwise tolerant.	Emphasizes the sovereignty and justice of God; no longer doctrinaire.	While traces of belief in predestination (that God has foreordinated salvation for the "elect") remain, this idea is no longer a central element in Presbyterianism.	**Presbyterians**
Relatively elaborate ritual; wide variety of public and private rites, eg., rosary recitation, processions, novenas.	Theoretically very strict; tolerant in practice on most issues. Divorce and remarriage not accepted. Celibate clergy, except in Eastern rite.	Highly elaborated. Salvation by merit gained through faith. Unusual development of doctrines surrounding Mary. Dogmatic.	Roman Catholicism is presently in a period of relatively rapid change as a result of Vatican Councils I and II.	**Roman Catholics**
Usually simple services with emphasis on the sermon.	Tolerant; some social action emphasis.	Standard Protestant; *Statement of Faith* (1959) is not binding.	The 2 main churches in the 1957 union represented earlier unions with small groups of almost every Protestant denomination.	**United Church of Christ**

Roman Catholic Hierarchy

Source: Apostolic Delegation, Washington, D.C.

Supreme Pontiff

At the head of the Roman Catholic Church is the Supreme Pontiff, Pope John Paul II, Karol Wojtyla, born at Wadowice (Krakow), Poland, May 18, 1920; ordained priest Nov. 1, 1946; promoted to Archbishop of Krakow Jan. 13, 1964; proclaimed Cardinal June 26, 1967; elected pope as successor of Pope John Paul I Oct. 16, 1978; solemn commencement as pope Oct. 22, 1978.

Cardinals

Name	Office	Nationality	Born	Named
Alfrink, Bernard		Dutch	1900	1960
Antonelli, Ferdinando		Italian	1896	1973
Aponte Martinez, Luis	Archbishop of San Juan in Puerto Rico	American	1922	1973
Aramburu, Juan	Archbishop of Buenos Aires	Argentinian	1912	1976
Arns, Paulo	Archbishop of Sao Paulo	Brazilian	1921	1973
Bafile, Corrado	Prefect of the Sacred Congregation for the Causes of Saints	Italian	1903	1976
Baggio, Sebastiano	Prefect of the Sacred Congregation for the Bishops	Italian	1913	1969
Ballestrero, Anastasio A.	Archbishop of Turin	Italian	1913	1979
Baum, William	Prefect of the Sacred Congregation for Catholic Education	American	1926	1976
Benelli, Giovanni	Archbishop of Florence	Italian	1921	1977
Beras Rojas, Octavio	Archbishop of Santo Domingo	San Domingan	1906	1976
Bertoli, Paolo	Chamberlain of the Holy Roman Church	Italian	1908	1969
Brandao Vilela, Avelar	Archbishop of Sao Salvador da Bahia	Brazilian	1912	1973
Bueno y Monreal, Jose M.	Archbishop of Seville	Spanish	1904	1958
Caprio, Giuseppe	President of Administration of Patrimony of the Holy See	Italian	1914	1979
Carberry, John		American	1904	1969
Carpino, Francesco		Italian	1905	1967
Carter, Gerald E.	Archbishop of Toronto	Canadian	1912	1979
Casariego, Mario	Archbishop of Guatemala	Guatemalan	1909	1969
Casaroli, Agostino	Secretary of State of His Holiness	Italian	1914	1979
Cè, Marco	Patriarch of Venice	Italian	1925	1979
Ciappi, O.P., Mario Luigi	Pro-Theologian of Pontifical Household	Italian	1909	1977
Civardi, Ernesto		Italian	1906	1979
Cody, John P.	Archbishop of Chicago	American	1907	1967
Colombo, Giovanni	Archbishop of Milan	Italian	1902	1965
Confalonieri, Carlo	Dean of the Sacred College	Italian	1893	1958
Cooke, Terence	Archbishop of New York	American	1921	1969
Cooray, Thomas B.		Ceylonese	1901	1965
Cordeiro, Joseph	Archbishop of Karachi	Pakistanian	1918	1973
Corripio Ahumada, Ernesto	Archbishop of Mexico City	Mexican	1919	1979
Darmojuwono, Justin	Archbishop of Semarang	Indonesian	1914	1967
de Araujo Sales, Eugenio	Archbishop of St. Sebastian of Rio de Janeiro	Brazilian	1920	1969
Dearden, John	Archbishop of Detroit	American	1907	1969
de Furstenberg, Maximilian		Belgian	1904	1967
Duval, Leon-Etienne	Archbishop of Algiers	Algerian	1903	1965
Ekandem, Dominic	Bishop of Ikot Ekpene	Nigerian	1917	1976
Enrique y Tarancon, Vicente	Archbishop of Madrid	Spanish	1907	1969
Etchegaray, Roger	Archbishop of Marseilles	French	1922	1979
Felici, Pericle	President of Pontifical Commission for the Revision of Code of Canon Law, Prefect of Supreme Tribunal of Apostolic Signatura	Italian	1911	1967
Flahiff, George	Archbishop of Winnipeg	Canadian	1905	1969
Florit, Ermenegildo		Italian	1901	1965
Freeman, James	Archbishop of Sydney	Australian	1907	1973
Gantin, Bernardin	President, Pontifical Commission "Justitia et Pax"	Benin	1922	1977
Garrone, Gabriel-Marie		French	1901	1967
Gonzalez Martin, Marcelo	Archbishop of Toledo	Spanish	1918	1973
Gouyon, Paul	Archbishop of Rennes	French	1910	1969
Gray, Gordon	Archbishop of St. Andrews and Edinburgh	Scottish	1910	1969
Guerri, Sergio	Pro-President of the Pontifical Comm. for Vatican City State	Italian	1905	1969
Guyot, Jean		French	1905	1973
Hoffner, Joseph	Archbishop of Cologne	German	1906	1969
Hume, George Basil	Archbishop of Westminster	English	1923	1976
Jubany Arnau, Narciso	Archbishop of Barcelona	Spanish	1913	1973
Kim, Stephan Sou Hwan	Archbishop of Seoul	Korean	1922	1969
Knox, James	Prefect of the Sacred Congregations of the Sacraments and of Divine Worship	Australian	1914	1973
König, Franz	Archbishop of Vienna	Austrian	1905	1958
Krol, John	Archbishop of Philadelphia	American	1910	1967
Landazuri, Ricketts Juan	Archbishop of Lima	Peruvian	1913	1962
Léger, Paul		Canadian	1904	1953
Lékai, Laszlo	Archbishop of Esztergom	Hungarian	1910	1976
Lorscheider, Aloisio	Archbishop of Fortaleza	Brazilian	1924	1976

Name	Office	Nationality	Born	Named
Macharski, Franciszek	Archbishop of Cracow	Polish	1927	1979
Malula, Joseph	Archbishop of Kinshasa	Congolese	1917	1969
Manning, Timothy	Archbishop of Los Angeles	American	1909	1973
Marella, Paolo		Italian	1895	1959
Marty, Francois	Archbishop of Paris	French	1904	1969
Maurer, Jose	Archbishop of Sucre	Bolivian	1900	1967
McCann, Owen	Archbishop of Cape Town	S. African	1907	1965
Medeiros, Humberto	Archbishop of Boston	American	1915	1973
Miranda y Gomez, Miguel		Mexican	1895	1969
Motta, Carlos Carmelo de Vasconcellos	Archbishop of Aparecida	Brazilian	1890	1946
Mozzoni, Umberto		Italian	1904	1973
Munoz Duque, Anibal	Archbishop of Bogota	Colombian	1908	1973
Munoz Vega, Paolo	Archbishop of Quito	Ecuadorian	1903	1969
Nasalli Rocca di Corneliano, Mario		Italian	1903	1969
Nsubuga, Emmanuel	Archbishop of Kampala	Ugandan	1914	1976
O'Boyle, Patrick		American	1896	1967
Oddi, Silvio	Prefect of Sacred Congregation for the Clergy	Italian	1910	1969
O'Fiaich, Tomás	Archbishop of Armagh, Primate of all Ireland	Irish	1923	1979
Otunga, Maurice	Archbishop of Nairobi	Kenyan	1923	1973
Palazzini, Pietro		Italian	1912	1973
Pappalardo, Salvatore	Archbishop of Palermo	Italian	1918	1973
Parecattil, Joseph	Archbishop of Ernakulam	Indian	1912	1969
Parente, Pietro		Italian	1891	1967
Paupini, Giuseppe	Grand Penitentiary	Italian	1907	1969
Pellegrino, Michele		Italian	1903	1967
Philippe, Paul	Prefect of the Sacred Congregation for the Oriental Churches	French	1905	1973
Picachy, Lawrence	Archbishop of Calcutta	Indian	1916	1976
Pignedoli, Sergio	President of the Secretariat for Non-Christians	Italian	1910	1973
Pironio, Eduardo	Prefect of the Sacred Congregation for Religious and for Secular Institutes	Argentinian	1920	1976
Poletti, Ugo	Vicar General of His Holiness for the City of Rome	Italian	1914	1973
Poma, Antonio	Archbishop of Bologna	Italian	1910	1969
Primatesta, Raul Francisco	Archbishop of Cordoba	Argentinian	1919	1973
Quintero, Jose	Archbishop of Caracas	Venezuelan	1902	1961
Ratzinger, Joseph	Archbishop of Munich	German	1927	1977
Razafimahatratra, Victor	Archbishop of Tananarive	Madagascan	1921	1976
Renard, Alexandre	Archbishop of Lyon	French	1906	1967
Ribeiro, Antonio	Patriarch of Lisbon	Portuguese	1928	1973
Righi-Lambertini, Egano	Papal Nuncio to France	Italian	1906	1979
Rosales, Julio	Archbishop of Cebu	Filipino	1906	1969
Rossi, Agnelo	Prefect of the Sacred Congregation for the Evangelization of Peoples	Brazilian	1913	1965
Rossi, Opilio	President of the Council for the Laity and the Committee for the Family	Italian	1910	1976
Roy, Maurice	Archbishop of Quebec	Canadian	1905	1965
Rubin, Wladyslaw		Polish	1917	1979
Rugambwa, Laurean	Archbishop of Dar-es-Salaam	Tanzanian	1912	1960
Salazar Lopez, Jose	Archbishop of Guadalajara	Mexican	1910	1973
Samore, Antonio	Librarian and Archivist of the Holy Roman Church	Italian	1905	1967
Satowaki, Joseph A.	Archbishop of Nagasaki	Japanese	1904	1979
Scherer, Alfred	Archbishop of Porto Alegre	Brazilian	1903	1969
Schroeffer, Joseph		German	1903	1976
Sensi, Giuseppe		Italian	1907	1976
Seper, Franjo	Prefect of Sacred Congregation for the Doctrine of the Faith	Yugoslav	1905	1965
Shehan, Lawrence		American	1898	1965
Sidarouss, Stephanos	Coptic Patriarch of Alexandria	Egyptian	1904	1965
Silva Henriquez, Raul	Archbishop of Santiago	Chilean	1907	1962
Sin, Jaime	Archbishop of Manila	Filipino	1928	1976
Siri, Giuseppe	Archbishop of Genoa	Italian	1906	1953
Slipyj, Josyf	Ukrainian Archbishop of Lwow	Ukrainian	1892	1965
Suenens, Leo	Archbishop of Malines-Brussels	Belgian	1904	1962
Taofinu'u, Pio	Bishop of Samoa and Tokelau	Samoan	1923	1973
Thiandoum, Hyacinthe	Archbishop of Dakar	Senegalese	1921	1976
Tomasek, Frantisek	Archbishop of Prague	Czechoslovakian	1899	1977
Trinh Van Can, Joseph-Marie	Archbishop of Hanoi	Vietnamese	1921	1979
Ursi, Corrado	Archbishop of Naples	Italian	1908	1967
Vagnozzi, Edigio	Pres. of the Prefecture of the Holy See's Economic Affairs	Italian	1906	1967
Volk, Hermann	Bishop of Mainz	German	1903	1973
Willebrands, John	President of Secretariat for the Union of Christians Archbishop of Utrecht	Dutch	1909	1969
Wyszynski, Stefan	Archbishop of Gniezno-Warsaw	Polish	1901	1953
Zoungrana, Paul	Archbishop of Ouagadougou	Upper Voltan	1917	1965

NOTED PERSONALITIES

Widely Known Americans of the Present

Statesmen, authors, military men, and other prominent persons not listed in other categories.

Name (Birthplace)	Birthdate
Abel, I. W. (Magnolia, Oh.)	8/11/08
Abernathy, Ralph (Linden, Ala.)	3/11/26
Abzug, Bella (New York, N.Y.)	7/24/20
Adams, Brockman (Atlanta, Ga.)	1/13/27
Agnew, Spiro (Baltimore, Md.)	11/9/18
Albert, Carl (McAlester, Okla.)	5/10/08
Aldrin, Edwin E. Jr. "Buzz" (Glen Ridge, N.J.)	1/20/30
Alsop, Joseph W. Jr. (Avon, Conn.)	10/11/10
Anderson, Jack (Long Beach, Cal.)	10/19/22
Anderson, John B. (Rockford, Ill.)	2/15/22
Andrus, Cecil (Hood River, Ore.)	8/25/31
Armstrong, Neil (Wapakoneta, Oh.)	8/5/30
Askew, Reubin (Muskogee, Okla.)	9/11/28
Bailey, F. Lee (Waltham, Mass.)	6/10/33
Baker, Howard (Huntsville, Tenn.)	11/15/25
Baker, Russell (Loudoun Co., Va.)	8/14/25
Ball, George (Des Moines, Ia.)	12/21/09
Bayh, Birch (Terre Haute, Ind.)	1/22/28
Bell, Griffin (Americus, Ga.)	10/31/18
Belli, Melvin (Sonora, Cal.)	7/29/07
Bentsen, Lloyd (Mission, Tex.)	2/11/21
Bergland, Bob (Roseau, Minn.)	7/22/28
Blackmun, Harry (Nashville, Ill.)	11/12/08
Blumenthal, W. Michael (Berlin, Germany)	1/3/26
Bok, Derek (Ardmore, Pa.)	3/22/30
Bond, Julian (Nashville, Tenn.)	1/14/40
Borman, Frank (Gary, Ind.)	3/14/28
Bowles, Chester (Springfield, Mass.)	4/5/01
Bradley, Omar N. (Clark, Mo.)	2/12/93
Bradley, Thomas (Calvert, Tex.)	12/29/17
Brennan, William J. (Newark, N.J.)	4/25/06
Breslin, Jimmy (Jamaica, N.Y.)	10/17/30
Brewster, Kingman (Longmeadow, Mass.)	6/17/19
Brinkley, David (Wilmington, N.C.)	7/10/20
Brokaw, Tom (Webster, S. Dak.)	2/6/40
Brooke, Edward (Washington, D.C.)	10/26/19
Brown, Edmund G. Jr. (San Francisco, Cal.)	4/7/38
Brown, Harold (New York, N.Y.)	9/19/27
Brown, Helen Gurley (Green Forest, Ark.)	2/18/22
Brzezinski, Zbigniew (Warsaw, Poland)	3/28/28
Buchwald, Art (Mt. Vernon, N.Y.)	10/20/25
Buckley, William F. (New York, N.Y.)	11/24/25
Bundy, McGeorge (Boston, Mass.)	3/30/19
Bunker, Ellsworth (Yonkers, N.Y.)	5/11/94
Burger, Warren (St. Paul, Minn.)	9/17/07
Burns, Arthur F. (Stanislau, Aust.)	4/27/04
Burton, Phillip (Cincinnati, Oh.)	6/1/26
Bush, George (Milton, Mass.)	6/12/24
Byrd, Robert (N. Wilkesboro, N.C.)	1/15/18
Byrne, Jane M. (Chicago, Ill.)	5/24/34
Califano, Joseph A. Jr. (Brooklyn, N.Y.)	3/15/21
Carey, Hugh (Brooklyn, N.Y.)	4/11/19
Carter, Amy (Plains, Ga.)	10/19/67
Carter, Billy (Plains, Ga.)	3/29/37
Carter, Donnel Jeffrey "Jeff" (New London, Conn.)	8/18/52
Carter, James Earl III "Chip" (Honolulu, Ha.)	4/12/50
Carter, Jimmy (Plains, Ga.)	10/1/24
Carter, John William "Jack" (Portsmouth, Va.)	7/3/47
Carter, Lillian (Richland, Ga.)	8/15/98
Carter, Rosalynn (Plains, Ga.)	8/18/27
Case, Clifford (Franklin Park, N.J.)	4/16/04
Chancellor, John (Chicago, Ill.)	7/14/27
Chandler, Otis (Los Angles, Cal.)	11/23/27
Chavez, Cesar (Yuma, Ariz.)	3/31/27
Chisholm, Shirley (Brooklyn, N.Y.)	11/30/24
Church, Frank (Boise, Ida.)	7/25/24
Civiletti, Benjamin R. (Peekskill, N.Y.)	7/17/35
Cleland, J. Maxwell (Atlanta, Ga.)	8/24/42
Commager, Henry Steele (Pittsburgh, Pa.)	10/25/02
Commoner, Barry (Brooklyn, N.Y.)	5/28/17
Connally, John B. (Floresville, Tex.)	2/28/17
Cooke, Terence Cardinal (New York, N.Y.)	3/1/21
Cooney, Joan Ganz (Phoenix, Ariz.)	10/30/29
Cosell, Howard (Winston-Salem, N.C.)	1920
Cousins, Norman (Union Hill, N.J.)	6/24/12
Cox, Archibald (Plainfield, N.J.)	5/17/12
Crane, Philip (Chicago, Ill.)	11/3/30
Cranston, Alan (Palo Alto, Cal.)	6/19/14
Cronkite, Walter (St. Joseph, Mo.)	11/4/16
Curtis, Charlotte (Chicago, Ill.)	1929
Davis, Angela (Birmingham, Ala.)	1/26/44
Denenberg, Herbert (Omaha, Neb.)	10/20/29
Dole, Robert (Russell, Kan.)	7/22/23
Doolittle, James H. (Alameda, Cal.)	12/14/96
Dubinsky, David (Brest-Litovsk, Poland)	2/22/92
Eagleton, Thomas (St. Louis, Mo.)	9/4/29
Eastland, James O. (Doddsville, Miss.)	11/28/04
Ehrlichman, John (Tacoma, Wash.)	3/20/25
Eisenhower, Milton S. (Abilene, Kan.)	9/15/99
Eizenstat, Stuart E. (Chicago, Ill.)	1943
Ervin, Sam (Morganton, N.C.)	9/27/96
Farmer, James (Marshall, Tex.)	1/12/20
Fischer, Bobby (Chicago, Ill.)	3/9/43
Fitzsimmons, Frank (Jeannette, Pa.)	4/7/08
Flynt, Larry (Salyersville, Ky.)	11/1/42
Fong, Hiram (Honolulu, Ha.)	10/1/07
Ford, Elizabeth (Mrs. Gerald) (Chicago, Ill.)	4/8/18
Ford, Gerald R. (Omaha, Neb.)	7/14/13
Fraser, Douglas A. (Glasgow, Scotland)	12/18/16
Friedan, Betty (Peoria, Ill.)	2/4/21
Friedman, Milton (Brooklyn, N.Y.)	7/31/12
Fulbright, J. William (Sumner, Mo.)	4/9/05
Galbraith, John Kenneth (Ontario, Can.)	10/15/08
Gardner, John (Los Angeles, Cal.)	10/8/12
Ginsberg, Allen (Paterson, N.J.)	6/3/21
Glenn, John (Cambridge, Oh.)	7/18/21
Goheen, Robert F. (Vengurla, India)	8/15/19
Goldberg, Arthur J. (Chicago, Ill.)	8/8/08
Goldwater, Barry M. (Phoenix, Ariz.)	1/1/09
Graham, Billy (Charlotte, N.C.)	11/7/18
Graham, Katharine (New York, N.Y.)	6/16/17
Grasso, Ella (Windsor Locks, Conn.)	5/10/19
Greenspan, Alan (New York, N.Y.)	3/6/26
Griffin, Robert P. (Traverse City, Mich.)	11/6/23
Haig, Alexander (Philadelphia, Pa.)	12/2/24
Hanks, Nancy (Miami Beach, Fla.)	12/31/27
Harriman, W. Averell (New York, N.Y.)	11/15/91
Harris, Patricia Roberts (Mattoon, Ill.)	5/31/24
Hartman, David (Pawtucket, R.I.)	5/19/35
Hatfield, Mark O. (Dallas, Ore.)	7/12/22
Hayakawa, S.I. (Vancouver, British Columbia)	7/18/06
Hefner, Hugh (Chicago, Ill.)	4/9/26
Heller, Walter (Buffalo, N.Y.)	8/27/15
Helms, Richard (St. Davids, Pa.)	3/30/13
Hershey, Lenore (New York, N.Y.)	3/20/20
Hesburgh, Theodore (Syracuse, N.Y.)	5/25/17
Hills, Carla (Los Angeles, Cal.)	1/3/34
Hiss, Alger (Baltimore, Md.)	11/11/04
Hollings, Ernest (Charleston, S.C.)	1/1/22
Hughes, Harold (Ida Grove, Ia.)	2/10/22
Inouye, Daniel (Honolulu, Ha.)	9/7/24
Jackson, Henry (Everett, Wash.)	5/31/12
Jackson, Jesse (Greenville, N.C.)	10/8/41
Jackson, Maynard (Dallas, Tex.)	3/23/38
Javits, Jacob K. (New York, N.Y.)	5/18/04
Johnson, Lady Bird (Mrs. Lyndon) (Karnack, Tex.)	12/22/12
Jones, David C. (Aberdeen, S.D.)	7/9/21
Jordan, Barbara (Houston, Tex.)	2/21/36
Jordan, Hamilton (Charlotte, N.C.)	9/21/44,
Jordan, Vernon (Atlanta, Ga.)	8/15/35
Kahn, Alfred E. (Paterson, N.J.)	10/17/17
Kennedy, Edward M. (Brookline, Mass.)	2/22/32
Kennedy, Rose (Mrs. Joseph P.) (Boston, Mass.)	7/22/90
Kerr, Walter (Evanston, Ill.)	7/8/13
King, Coretta (Mrs. Martin L.) (Marion, Ala.)	4/27/27
Kirbo, Charles (Bainbridge, Ga.)	3/15/17
Kirkland, Lane (Camden, S.C.)	3/12/22
Kissinger, Henry (Fuerth, Germany)	5/27/23
Koch, Edward I. (New York, N.Y.)	12/12/24
Kreps, Juanita M. (Lynch, Ky.)	1/11/21

Name (Birthplace)	Birthdate
Laird, Melvin (Omaha, Neb.)	9/1/22
Lance, Thomas B. "Bert" (Young Harris, Ga.)	6/3/31
Landers, Ann (Sioux City, Ia.)	7/4/18
Landon, Alfred (West Middlesex, Pa.)	9/9/87
Landrieu, Moon (New Orleans, La.)	7/23/30
LeMay, Curtis (Ohio)	11/15/06
Lemnitzer, Lyman L. (Honesdale, Pa.)	8/29/99
Levi, Edward (Chicago, Ill.)	6/26/11
Lindbergh, Anne Morrow (Englewood, N.J.)	1906
Lipshutz, Robert J. (Atlanta, Ga.)	12/27/21
Lodge, Henry Cabot (Nahant, Mass.)	7/5/02
Long, Russell B. Shreveport, La.)	11/3/18
Luce, Clare Boothe (New York, N.Y.)	4/10/03
Maddox, Lester (Atlanta, Ga.)	9/30/15
Mansfield, Mike (New York, N.Y.)	3/16/03
Marshall, Freddie Ray (Oak Grove, La.)	8/22/28
Marshall, Thurgood (Baltimore, Md.)	7/2/08
Mayer, Martin (New York, N.Y.)	1/14/28
McCarthy, Eugene (Watkins, Minn.)	3/29/16
McCormack, John W. (Boston, Mass.)	12/21/91
McCloskey, Paul (San Bernardino, Cal.)	9/29/27
McCree, Wade H. Jr. (Des Moines, Ia.)	7/3/20
McGovern, George (Avon, S.D.)	7/19/22
McNamara, Robert S. (San Francisco, Cal.)	6/9/16
Miller, Arnold (Leewood, W. Va.)	4/25/23
Miller, G. William (Sapulpa, Okla.)	3/9/25
Millett, Kate (St. Paul, Minn.)	9/14/34
Milliken, William (Traverse City, Mich.)	3/26/22
Mitchell, John (Detroit, Mich.)	9/15/13
Mondale, Joan (Eugene, Ore.)	8/8/30
Mondale, Walter (Ceylon, Minn.)	1/5/28
Morgan, Marabel (Crestline, Oh.)	6/25/37
Moses, Robert (New Haven, Conn.)	12/18/88
Moynihan, Daniel P. (Tulsa, Okla.)	3/16/27
Mudd, Roger (Washington, D.C.)	2/9/28
Muskie, Edmund (Rumford, Me.)	3/28/14
Nader, Ralph (Winsted, Conn.)	2/27/34
Nixon, Julie (Mrs. David Eisenhower) (Wash., D.C.)	7/5/48
Nixon, Pat (Mrs. Richard) (Ely, Nev.)	3/16/12
Nixon, Richard (Yorba Linda, Cal.)	1/9/13
Nixon, Tricia (Mrs. Edward Cox) (Cal.)	2/21/46
Nizer, Louis (London, England)	2/6/02
Norton, Eleanor Holmes (Washington, D.C.)	6/13/37
Nunn, Sam (Perry, Ga.)	9/8/38
O'Brien, Lawrence F. (Springfield, Mass.)	7/7/17
Onassis, Jacqueline (Southampton, N.Y.)	7/28/29
O'Neill, Thomas P. (Cambridge, Mass.)	12/9/12
Paley, William S. (Chicago, Ill.)	9/28/01
Pauley, Jane (Indianapolis, Ind.)	10/31/50
Pauling, Linus (Portland, Ore.)	2/28/01
Peale, Norman Vincent (Bowersville, Oh.)	5/31/98
Percy, Charles H. (Pensacola, Fla.)	9/27/19
Powell, Jody (Cordele, Ga.)	9/30/43
Powell, Lewis F. (Suffolk, Va.)	9/19/07
Proxmire, William (Lake Forest, Ill.)	1/11/15
Rather, Dan (Wharton, Tex.)	10/31/31
Ray, Dixy Lee (Tacoma, Wash.)	9/3/14
Reagan, Ronald (Tampico, Ill.)	2/6/11
Reasoner, Harry (Dakota City, Ia.)	4/17/23
Rehnquist, William (Milwaukee, Wis.)	10/1/24
Reston, James (Clydebank, Scotland)	11/3/09
Rhodes, John (Council Grove, Kan.)	9/18/16
Ribicoff, Abe (New Britain, Conn.)	4/9/10
Richardson, Elliot L. (Boston, Mass.)	7/20/21
Rickover, Hyman (Makowa, Poland)	1/27/00
Rockefeller, David (New York, N.Y.)	6/12/15
Rockefeller, John D. 4th "Jay" (New York, N.Y.)	6/18/37
Rockefeller, Laurance S. (New York, N.Y.)	5/26/10
Rodino, Peter (Newark, N.J.)	6/7/09
Romney, George W. (Chihuahua, Mexico)	7/8/07
Roosevelt, Elliot (New York, N.Y.)	9/23/10
Roosevelt, Franklin D. Jr. (Canada)	8/17/14
Ruckelshaus, William (Indianapolis, Ind.)	7/24/32
Rumsfeld, Donald (Chicago, Ill.)	7/9/32
Rusk, Dean (Cherokee Co., Ga.)	2/9/09

Name (Birthplace)	Birthdate
Safer, Morley (Toronto, Ontario)	11/8/31
Safire, William (New York, N.Y.)	12/17/29
Sagan, Carl (New York, N.Y.)	11/9/34
Salk, Jonas (New York, N.Y.)	10/28/14
Samuelson, Paul A. (Gary, Ind.)	5/15/15
Schlafly, Phyllis (St. Louis, Mo.)	8/15/24
Schlesinger, Arthur Jr. (Columbus, Oh.)	10/15/17
Schlesinger, James R. (New York, N.Y.)	2/15/29
Schultze, Charles (Alexandria, Va.)	12/22/24
Scott, Hugh (Fredericksburg, Va.)	11/11/00
Scranton, William W. (Madison, Conn.)	7/19/17
Seaborg, Glenn T. (Ishpeming, Mich.)	4/19/12
Sevareid, Eric (Velva, N.D.)	11/26/12
Shanker, Albert (New York, N.Y.)	9/14/28
Shirer, William L. (Chicago, Ill.)	2/23/04
Shriver, R. Sargent (Westminster, Md.)	11/9/15
Shultz, George (New York, N.Y.)	12/13/20
Simon, William (Paterson, N.J.)	1927
Sirica, John J. (Waterbury, Conn.)	3/19/04
Smeal, Eleanor (Ashtabula, Oh.)	7/30/39
Smith, Howard K. (Ferriday, La.)	5/12/14
Smith, Margaret Chase (Skowhegan, Me.)	12/14/97
Snyder, Tom (Milwaukee, Wisc.)	5/12/36
Spock, Benjamin (New Haven, Conn.)	5/2/03
Stassen, Harold (West St. Paul, Minn.)	4/13/07
Steinem, Gloria (Toledo, Oh.)	3/25/34
Stennis, John (Kamper City, Miss.)	8/3/01
Stevens, John Paul (Chicago, Ill.)	4/20/20
Stevenson 3d, Adlai (Chicago, Ill.)	10/10/30
Stewart, Potter (Jackson, Mich.)	1/23/15
Stokes, Carl (Cleveland, Oh.)	6/21/27
Strauss, Robert S. (Lockhart, Tex.)	10/19/18
Sulzberger, Arthur Ochs (New York, N.Y.)	2/5/26
Symington, Stuart (Amherst, Mass.)	6/26/01
Taft, Robert Jr. (Cincinnati, Oh.)	2/26/17
Talmadge, Herman (Lovejoy, Ga.)	8/9/13
Taylor, Maxwell D. (Keytesville, Mo.)	8/26/01
Thomas, Helen (Winchester, Ky.)	8/4/20
Thomas, Lowell (Woodington, Oh.)	4/6/92
Thompson, James R. (Chicago, Ill.)	5/8/36
Thurmond, J. Strom (Edgefield, S.C.)	12/5/02
Tower, John (Houston, Tex.)	9/29/25
Truman, Mrs. Harry (Independence, Mo.)	2/13/85
Truman, Margaret (Mrs. Clifton Daniel) (Independence, Mo.)	2/17/24
Tuchman, Barbara (New York, N.Y.)	1/30/12
Turner, Stansfield (Chicago, Ill.)	2/1/33
Udall, Morris K. (St. Johns, Ariz.)	6/15/22
Ullman, Al (Great Falls, Mont.)	3/9/14
Van Buren, Abigail (Sioux City, Ia.)	7/4/18
Vance, Cyrus R. (Clarksburg, W. Va.)	3/27/17
Vanderbilt, Alfred G. (London, England)	9/22/12
Veeck, Bill (Chicago, Ill.)	2/9/14
Volcker, Paul A. (Cape May, N.J.)	9/5/27
Wallace, George (Clio, Ala.)	8/25/19
Wallace, Mike (Brookline, Mass.)	5/9/18
Walters, Barbara (Boston, Mass.)	9/25/31
Warnke, Paul (Webster, Mass.)	1/31/20
Washington, Walter E. (Dawson, Ga.)	4/15/15
Webster, William H. (St. Louis, Mo.)	3/6/24
Weicker, Lowell (Paris, France)	5/16/31
Westmoreland, William (Spartanburg, S.C.)	3/26/14
White, Byron R. (Ft. Collins, Col.)	6/8/17
White, E.B. (Mt. Vernon, N.Y.)	7/11/99
White, Theodore (Boston, Mass.)	5/6/15
Wicker, Tom (Hamlet, N.C.)	6/18/26
Wilkins, Roy (St. Louis, Mo.)	8/30/01
Williams, Edward Bennett (Hartford, Conn.)	5/31/20
Wolfe, Tom (Richmond, Va.)	3/2/31
Woodcock, Leonard (Providence, R.I.)	2/15/11
Wright, James C. Jr. (Ft. Worth, Tex.)	12/22/22
Wriston, Walter B. (Middletown, Conn.)	8/3/19
Wurf, Jerry (New York, N.Y.)	5/18/19
Young, Andrew (New Orleans, La.)	3/12/22
Zumwalt, Elmo (San Francisco, Cal.)	11/29/20

Noted Black Americans

Names of black athletes and entertainers are not included here as they are listed elsewhere in The World Almanac.

The Rev. Dr. Ralph David Abernathy, b. 1926, organizer, 1957, and president, 1968, of the Southern Christian Leadership Conference.

Crispus Attucks, c. 1723-1770, agitator led group which precipitated the "Boston Massacre," Mar. 5, 1770.

James Baldwin, b. 1924, author, playwright; *Another Country, The Fire Next Time, Blues for Mister Charlie, Just Above My Head.*

Benjamin Banneker, 1731-1806, inventor, astronomer, mathematician, and gazeteer; served on commission which surveyed and laid out Washington, D. C.
Imamu Amiri Baraka, b. LeRoi Jones, 1934, poet, playwright.
James P. Beckwourth, 1798-c. 1867, western fur-trader, scout, after whom Beckwourth Pass in northern California is named.
Dr. Mary McCleod Bethune, 1875-1955, adviser to presidents F. D. Roosevelt and Truman; division administrator, National Youth Administration, 1935; founder, president of Bethune-Cookman College.
Henry Blair, 19th century, obtained patents (believed the first issued to a black) for a corn-planter, 1834, and for a cotton-planter, 1836.
Julian Bond, b. 1940, civil rights leader first elected to the Georgia state legislature, 1965; helped found Student Nonviolent Coordinating Committee.
Edward Bouchet, 1852-1918, first black to earn a Ph.D., Yale, 1876, at a U. S. university; first black to be elected to Phi Beta Kappa.
Thomas Bradley, b. 1917, elected mayor of Los Angeles, 1973.
Andrew F. Brimmer, b. 1926, first black member, 1966, Federal Reserve Board.
Edward W. Brooke, b. 1919, attorney general, 1962, of Massachusetts; first black elected to U. S. Senate, 1967, since 19th century Reconstruction.
Gwendolyn Brooks, b. 1917, poet, novelist; first black to win a Pulitzer Prize, 1950, for *Annie Allen.*
William Wells Brown, 1815-1884, novelist, dramatist; first American black to publish a novel.
Dr. Ralph Bunche, 1904-1971, first black to win the Nobel Peace Prize, 1950; undersecretary of the UN, 1950.
George E. Carruthers, b. 1940, physicist developed the Apollo 16 lunar surface ultraviolet camera/spectograph.
George Washington Carver, 1861-1943, botanist, chemurgist, and educator; his extensive experiments in soil building and plant diseases revolutionized the economy of the South.
Charles Waddell Chestnutt, 1858-1932, author known primarily for his short stories, including *The Conjure Woman.*
Shirley Chisholm, b. 1924, first black woman elected to House of Representatives, Brooklyn, N. Y., 1968.
Countee Cullen, 1903-1946, poet; won many literary prizes.
Lt. Gen. Benjamin O. Davis Jr. b. 1912, West Point, 1936, first black Air Force general, 1954.
Brig. Gen. Benjamin O. Davis Sr., 1877-1970, first black general, 1940, in U. S. Army.
William L. Dawson, 1886-1970, Illinois congressman, first black chairman of a major House of Representatives committee.
Isaiah Dorman, 19th century, U. S. Army interpreter, killed with Custer, 1876, at Battle of the Little Big Horn.
Aaron Douglas, 1900-1979, painter; called father of black American art.
Frederick Douglass, 1817-1895, author, editor, orator, diplomat; edited the abolitionist weekly, The North Star, in Rochester, N. Y.; U.S. minister and counsul general to Haiti.
Dr. Charles Richard Drew, 1904-1950, pioneer in development of blood banks; director of American Red Cross blood donor project in World War II.
William Edward Burghardt Du Bois, 1868-1963, historian, sociologist; a founder of the National Association for the Advancement of Colored People (NAACP), 1909, and founder of its magazine The Crisis; author, *The Souls of Black Folk.*
Paul Laurence Dunbar, 1872-1906, poet, novelist; won fame with *Lyrics of Lowly Life,* 1896.
Jean Baptiste Point du Sable, c. 1750-1818, pioneer trader and first settler of Chicago, 1779.
Ralph Ellison, b. 1914, novelist, winner of 1952 National Book Award, for *Invisible Man.*
Estevanico, explorer led Spanish expedition of 1538 into the American Southwest.
James Farmer, b. 1920, a founder of the Congress of Racial Equality, 1942; asst. secretary, Dept. of HEW, 1969.
Henry O. Flipper, 1856-1940, first black to graduate, 1877, from West Point.
Marcus Garvey, 1887-1940, founded Universal Negro Improvement Assn., 1911.
Kenneth Gibson, b. 1932, elected mayor of Newark, N.J., 1970.
Charles Gordone, b. 1925, won 1970 Pulitzer Prize in Drama, with *No Place to Be Somebody.*
Vice Adm. Samuel L. Gravely Jr. b. 1922, first black admiral, 1971, served in World War II, Korea, and Vietnam; commander, Third Fleet.
Alex Haley, b. 1921, Pulitzer Prize-winning author; *Roots, The Autobiography of Malcolm X.*
Jupiter Hammon, c. 1720-1800, poet; the first black American to have his works published, 1761.
Lorraine Hansberry, 1930-1965, playwright; won N. Y. Drama Critics Circle Award, 1959, with *Raisin in the Sun.*
Patricia Roberts Harris, b. 1924, U. S. ambassador to Luxembourg, 1965-67, secretary; Dept. of HUD, 1977-1979, Dept. of H.H.S., 1979-.
William H. Hastie, 1904-1976 first black federal judge, appointed 1937; governor of Virgin Islands, 1946-49; judge, U.S. Circuit Court of Appeals, 1949.
Matthew A. Henson, 1866-1955, member of Peary's 1909 expedition to the North Pole; placed U.S. flag at the Pole.
Dr. William A. Hinton, 1883-1959, developed the Hinton and Davies-Hinton tests for detection of syphilis; first black professor, 1949, at Harvard Medical School.
Benjamin L. Hooks, b. 1925, first black member, 1972-1979, Federal Communications Comm.; exec. dir., 1977, NAACP.
Langston Hughes, 1902-1967, poet; story, song lyric author.
The Rev. Jesse Jackson, b. 1941, national director, Operation Bread Basket, and major community leader in Chicago.
Maynard Jackson, b. 1938, elected mayor of Atlanta, 1973.
Gen. Daniel James Jr. 1920-1978, first black 4-star general, 1975; Commander, North American Air Defense Command.
Pvt. Henry Johnson, 1897-1929, the first American decorated by France in World War I with the Croix de Guerre.
James Weldon Johnson, 1871-1938, poet, lyricist, novelist; first black admitted to Florida bar; U.S. consul in Venezuela and Nicaragua.
Barbara Jordan, b. 1936, former congresswoman from Texas; member, House Judiciary Committee.
Vernon E. Jordan, b. 1935, exec. dir. Natl. Urban League, 1972.
Ernest E. Just, 1883-1941, marine biologist, studied egg development; author, Biology of Cell Surfaces, 1941.
The Rev. Dr. Martin Luther King Jr., 1929-1968, led 382-day, Montgomery, Ala., boycott which brought 1956 U.S. Supreme Court decision holding segregation on buses unconstitutional; founder, president of the Southern Christian Leadership Conference, 1957; won Nobel Peace Prize, 1964.
Lewis H. Latimer, 1848-1928, associate of Edison; supervised installation of first electric street lighting in N.Y.C.
Malcom X, 1925-1965, leading spokesman for black pride, founded, 1963, Organization of Afro-American Unity.
Thurgood Marshall, b. 1908, first black U.S. solicitor general 1965; first black justice of the U. S. Supreme Court, 1967; as a lawyer led the legal battery which won the historic decision from the Supreme Court declaring racial segregation of public schools unconstitutional, 1954.
Jan Matzeliger, 1852-1889, invented lasting machine, patented 1883, which revolutionized the shoe industry.
Wade H. McCree Jr., b. 1920, solicitor general of the U.S.
Donald E. McHenry, b. 1936, U.S. ambassador to the United Nations, 1979-.
Dorie Miller, 1919-1943, Navy hero of Pearl Harbor attack; awarded the Navy Cross.
Ernest N. Morial, b. 1929, elected first black mayor of New Orleans, 1977.
Willard Motley, 1912-1965, novelist; *Knock on Any Door.*
Elijah Muhammad, 1897-1975, founded the Black Muslims, 1931.
Pedro Alonzo Nino, navigator of the Nina, one of Columbus' 3 ships on his first voyage of discovery to the New World, 1492.
Adam Clayton Powell, 1908-1972, early civil rights leader, congressman, 1945-1969; chairman, House Committee on Education and Labor, 1960-1967.
Joseph H. Rainey, 1832-1887, first black elected to House of Representatives, 1869, from South Carolina.
A. Philip Randolph, 1889-1979, organized the Brotherhood of Sleeping Car Porters, 1925; organizer of 1941 and 1963 March on Washington movements; vice president, AFL-CIO.
Charles Rangel, b. 1930, congressman from N.Y.C., 1970; chairman, Congressional Black Caucus.
Hiram R. Revels, 1822-1901, first black U.S. senator, elected in Mississippi, served 1870-1871.
Wilson C. Riles, b. 1917, elected, 1970, California State Superintendent of Public Instruction.
Norbert Rillieux, 1806-1894; invented a vacuum pan evaporator, 1846, revolutionizing the sugar-refining industry.
Carl T. Rowan, b. 1925, prize-winning journalist; director of the U.S. Information Agency, 1964, the first black to sit on the National Security Council; U. S. ambassador to Finland, 1963.
John B. Russwurm, 1799-1851, with **Samuel E. Cornish,** 1793-1858, founded, 1827, the nation's first black newspaper, Freedom's Journal, in N.Y.C.
Bayard Rustin, b. 1910, organizer of the 1963 March on Washington; executive director, A. Philip Randolph Institute.
Peter Salem, at the Battle of Bunker Hill, June 17, 1775, shot and killed British commander Maj. John Pitcairn.
Ntozake Shange, b. Paulette Williams, 1948, playwright, *For Colored Girls Who Have Considered Suicide/When the Rainbow is Enuf.*
Bishop Stephen Spottswood, 1897-1974, board chairman of NAACP from 1966.
Willard Townsend, 1895-1957, organized the United Transport Service Employees, 1935 (redcaps, etc.); vice pres. AFL-CIO.
Sojourner Truth, 1797-1883, born Isabella Baumfree; preacher,

abolitonist; raised funds for Union in Civil War; worked for black educational opportunities.
Harriet Tubman, 1823-1913, Underground Railroad conductor served as nurse and spy for Union Army in the Civil War.
Nat Turner, 1800-1831, leader of the most significant of over 200 slave revolts in U.S. history, in Southampton, Va.; he and 16 others were hanged.
Booker T. Washington, 1856-1915, founder, 1881, and first president of Tuskegee Institute; author, *Up From Slavery.*
Dr. Robert C. Weaver, b. 1907, first black member of the U.S. Cabinet, secretary, Dept. of HUD, 1966.
Phillis Wheatley, c. 1753-1784, poet; 2d American woman and first black woman to have her works published, 1770.
Walter White, 1893-1955, exec. secretary, NAACP, 1931-1955.
Roy Wilkins, b. 1901, executive director, NAACP, 1955-1977.
Dr. Daniel Hale Williams, 1858-1931, performed one of first 2 open-heart operations, 1893; founded Provident, Chicago's first Negro hospital; first black elected a fellow of the American College of Surgeons.
Granville T. Woods, 1856-1910, invented the third-rail system now used in subways, a complex railway telegraph device that helped reduce train accidents, and an automatic air brake.
Dr. Carter G. Woodson, 1875-1950, historian; founded Assn. for the Study of Negro Life and History, 1915, and Journal of Negro History, 1916.
Richard Wright, 1908-1960, novelist; Native Son, Black Boy.
Frank Yerby, b. 1916, most successful of American black novelists; *The Foxes of Harrow, Vixen.*
Andrew Young, b. 1932, civil rights leader, congressman from Georgia, U.S. ambassador to the United Nations, 1977-79.
Whitney M. Young Jr., 1921-1971, exec. director, 1961, National Urban League; author, lecturer, newspaper columnist.

About 5,000 blacks served in the Continental Army during the **American Revolution,** mostly in integrated units, some in all-black combat units. Some 200,000 blacks served in the Union Army during the **Civil War;** 38,000 gave their lives; 22 won the Medal of Honor, the nation's highest award. Of 367,000 blacks in the armed forces during **World War I,** 100,000 served in France. More than 1,000,000 blacks served in the armed forces during **World War II;** all-black fighter and bomber AAF units and infantry divisions gave distinguished service. In 1954 the policy of all-black units was finally abolished. Of 274,937 blacks who served in the armed forces during the **Vietnam War** (1965-1974), 5,681 were killed in combat.

As of July, 1979, there were 191 black mayors, 2,235 members of municipal governing bodies, 402 county officers, 307 state legislators, and 17 U.S. representatives. There are now 4,607 blacks holding elected office in the U.S. and Virgin Islands, an increase of 2% over the previous year, according to a survey by the Joint Center for Political Studies, Washington, D.C.

Notable American Fiction Writers and Playwrights

Name (Birthplace)	Birthdate
Abbott, George (Forestville, N.Y.)	6/25/87
Albee, Edward (Washington, D.C.)	3/12/28
Algren, Nelson (Detroit, Mich.)	3/28/09
Anderson, Robert (New York, N.Y.)	4/28/17
Asimov, Isaac (Petrovichi, Russia)	1/2/20
Auchincloss, Louis (Lawrence, N.Y.)	9/27/17
Baldwin, James (New York, N.Y.)	8/2/24
Barth, John (Cambridge, Md.)	5/27/30
Barthelme, Donald (Philadelphia, Pa.)	1931
Bellow, Saul (Quebec, Canada)	7/10/15
Benchley, Nathaniel (Newton, Mass.)	11/13/15
Benchley, Peter (New York, N.Y.)	5/8/40
Bishop, Jim (Jersey City, N.J.)	11/21/07
Blume, Judy (Elizabeth, N.J.)	2/12/38
Bradbury, Ray (Waukegan, Ill.)	8/22/20
Brooks, Gwendolyn (Topeka, Kan.)	6/7/17
Burrows, Abe (New York, N.Y.)	12/18/10
Caldwell, Erskine (Coweta Co., Ga.)	12/17/03
Caldwell, Taylor (London, England)	1900
Calisher, Hortense (New York, N.Y.)	12/20/11
Capote, Truman (New Orleans, La.)	9/30/24
Chase, Mary (Denver, Col.)	2/25/07
Chayefsky, Paddy (New York, N.Y.)	1/29/23
Cheever, John (Quincy, Mass.)	5/27/12
Clavell, James (England)	10/10/24
Connelly, Marc (McKeesport, Pa.)	12/13/90
Crews, Harry (Alma, Ga.)	6/6/35
Crichton, Michael (Chicago, Ill.)	10/23/42
De Vries, Peter (Chicago, Ill.)	2/27/10
Dickey, James (Atlanta, Ga.)	2/2/23
Didion, Joan (Sacramento, Cal.)	12/5/34
Doctorow, E. L. (New York, N.Y.)	1/6/31
Drury, Allen (Houston, Tex.)	9/2/18
Elkin, Stanley (New York, N.Y.)	5/11/30
Ellison, Ralph (Oklahoma City, Okla.)	3/1/14
Fast, Howard (New York, N.Y.)	11/11/14
Geisel, Theodore ("Dr. Seuss," Springfield, Mass.)	3/2/04
Gibson, William (New York, N.Y.)	11/13/14
Gilroy, Frank (New York, N.Y.)	10/13/25
Goldman, William (Chicago, Ill.)	8/12/31
Grau, Shirley Ann (New Orleans, La.)	7/8/29
Hailey, Arthur (Luton, England)	4/5/20
Haley, Alex (Ithaca, N.Y.)	8/11/21
Hawkes, John (Stamford, Conn.)	8/17/25
Heinlein, Robert (Butler, Mon.)	7/7/07
Heller, Joseph (Brooklyn, N.Y.)	5/1/23
Hellman, Lillian (New Orleans, La.)	6/20/07
Hersey, John (Tientsin, China)	6/17/14
Himes, Chester (Jefferson City, Mo.)	7/29/09
Irving, John (Exeter, N.H.)	3/2/42
Jong, Erica (New York, N.Y.)	4/26/42
Kazan, Elia (Constantinople, Turkey)	9/7/09
Kerr, Jean (Scranton, Pa.)	7/?/23
Kesey, Ken (La Hunta, Col.)	9/17/35
Kingsley, Sidney (New York, N.Y.)	10/22/06
Knowles, John (Fairmont, W. Va.)	9/16/26
Kosinski, Jerzy (Lódz, Poland)	6/14/33
L'Amour, Louis (Jamestown, N.D.)	———
Lee, Harper (Alabama)	1926
LeGuin, Ursula (Berkeley, Cal.)	10/21/29
Levin, Ira (New York, N.Y.)	8/27/29
Loos, Anita (Sisson, Cal.)	4/26/93
Ludlum, Robert (New York, N.Y.)	5/25/27
MacDonald, John D. (Sharon, Pa.)	7/24/16
MacDonald, Ross (Los Gatos, Cal.)	12/13/15
MacInnes, Helen (Glasgow, Scotland)	10/7/07
Mailer, Norman (Long Branch, N.J.)	1/31/23
Malamud, Bernard (Brooklyn, N.Y.)	4/26/14
Mamet, David (Chicago, Ill.)	11/30/47
McCarthy, Mary (Seattle, Wash.)	6/21/12
McMurtry, Larry (Wichita Falls, Tex.)	6/3/36
Michener, James A. (New York, N.Y.)	2/3/07
Miller, Arthur (New York, N.Y.)	10/17/15
Oates, Joyce Carol (Lockport, N.Y.)	6/16/38
Percy, Walker (Birmingham, Ala.)	5/28/16
Porter, Katherine Ann (Indian Creek, Tex.)	5/15/90
Potok, Chaim (New York, N.Y.)	2/17/29
Puzo, Mario (New York, N.Y.)	10/15/20
Pynchon, Thomas (Glen Cove, N.Y.)	5/8/37
Rand, Ayn (St. Petersburg, Russia)	1905
Reed, Ishmael (Chattanooga, Tenn.)	2/22/38
Robbins, Harold (New York, N.Y.)	5/21/12
Rossner, Judith (New York, N.Y.)	3/31/35
Roth, Henry (Austria-Hungary)	2/8/06
Roth, Philip (Newark, N.J.)	3/19/33
Salinger, J. D. (New York, N.Y.)	1/1/19
Saroyan, William (Fresno, Cal.)	8/31/08
Schary, Dore (Newark, N.J.)	8/31/05
Schisgal, Murray (New York, N.Y.)	11/25/26
Schulberg, Budd (New York, N.Y.)	3/27/14
Segal, Erich (Brooklyn, N.Y.)	6/16/37
Sendak, Maurice (New York, N.Y.)	6/10/28
Shaw, Irwin (New York, N.Y.)	2/27/13
Simon, Neil (New York, N.Y.)	7/4/27
Singer, Isaac Bashevis (Radzymin, Poland)	7/14/04
Slaughter, Frank (Washington, D.C.)	2/25/08
Spillane, Mickey (Brooklyn, N.Y.)	3/9/18
Stegner, Wallace (Lake Mills, Ia.)	2/18/09

Name, (Birthplace)	Birthdate
Stone, Irving (San Francisco, Cal.)	7/14/03
Styron, William (Newport News, Va.)	6/11/25
Theroux, Paul (Medford, Mass.)	4/10/41
Tryon, Thomas (Hartford, Conn.)	1/14/26
Updike, John (Shillington, Pa.)	3/18/32
Uris, Leon (Baltimore, Md.)	8/3/24
Vidal, Gore (West Point, N.Y.)	10/3/25
Vonnegut, Kurt Jr. (Indianapolis, Ind.)	11/11/22

Name (Birthplace)	Birthdate
Wallace, Irving (Chicago, Ill.)	3/18/16
Wambaugh, Joseph (East Pittsburgh, Pa.)	1/22/37
Warren, Robert Penn (Guthrie, Ky.)	4/24/05
Welty, Eudora (Jackson, Miss.)	4/13/09
Williams, Tennessee (Columbus, Miss.)	3/26/11
Willingham, Calder (Atlanta, Ga.)	12/23/22
Wouk, Herman (New York, N.Y.)	5/27/15
Yerby, Frank (Augusta, Ga.)	9/5/16
Zindel, Paul (New York, N.Y.)	5/15/36

American Architects and Some of Their Achievements

Max Abramovitz, b. 1908, Avery Fisher Hall, Lincoln Center, N.Y.C.

Henry Bacon, 1866-1924, Lincoln Memorial.

Pietro Belluschi, b. 1899, Juilliard School of Music, Lincoln Center, N.Y.C.

Marcel Breuer, b. 1902, Whitney Museum of American Art, N.Y.C. (with Hamilton Smith).

Charles Bulfinch, 1763-1844, State House, Boston; Capitol, Wash. D.C., (part).

Daniel H. Burnham, 1846-1912, Union Station, Wash. D.C.; Flatiron, N.Y.C.

Ralph Adams Cram, 1863-1942, Cathedral of St. John the Divine, N.Y.C.; U.S. Military Academy (part).

R. Buckminster Fuller, b. 1895, U.S. Pavilion, Expo 67, Montreal (geodesic domes).

Cass Gilbert, 1859-1934, Custom House, Woolworth Bldg., N.Y.C.; Supreme Court bldg., Wash., D.C.

Bertram G. Goodhue, 1869-1924, Capitol, Lincoln, Neb.; St. Thomas, St. Bartholomew, N.Y.C.

Walter Gropius, 1883-1969, Pan Am Building, N.Y.C. (with Pietro Belluschi).

Peter Harrison, 1716-1775, Touro Synagogue, Redwood Library, Newport, R.I.

Wallace K. Harrison, b. 1895, Metropolitan Opera House, Lincoln Center, N.Y.C.

Thomas Hastings, 1860-1929, Public Library, Frick Mansion, N.Y.C.

James Hoban, 1762-1831, The White House.

William Holabird, 1854-1923, Crerar Library, City Hall, Chicago.

Raymond Hood, 1881-1934, Rockefeller Center, N.Y.C. (part); Daily News, N.Y.C.; Tribune, Chicago.

Richard M. Hunt, 1827-1895, Metropolitan Museum, N.Y.C. (part); Natl. Observatory, Wash., D.C.

William Le Baron Jenney, 1832-1907, Home Insurance, Chicago (demolished 1931).

Philip C. Johnson, b. 1906, N.Y. State Theater, Lincoln Center, N.Y.C.

Albert Kahn, 1869-1942, Athletic Club Bldg., General Motors Bldg., Detroit.

Louis Kahn, 1901-1974, Salk Laboratory, La Jolla, Cal.; Yale Art Gallery.

Christopher Grant LaFarge, 1862-1938, Roman Catholic Chapel, West Point.

Benjamin H. Latrobe, 1764-1820, U.S. Capitol (part).

William Lescaze, 1896-1969, Philadelphia Savings Fund Society; Borg-Warner Bldg., Chicago.

Charles F. McKim, 1847-1909, Public Library, Boston, Columbia Univ., N.Y.C. (part).

Charles M. McKim, b. 1920, KUHT-TV Transmitter Building, Houston; Lutheran Church of the Redeemer, Houston.

Ludwig Mies van der Rohe, 1886-1969, Seagram Building, N.Y.C. (with Philip C. Johnson); National Gallery, Berlin.

Robert Mills, 1781-1855, Washington Monument.

Richard J. Neutra, 1892-1970, Mathematics Park, Princeton; Orange Co. Courthouse, Santa Ana, Cal.

Gyo Obata, b. 1923, Natl. Air & Space Mus., Smithsonian Institution; Dallas-Ft. Worth Airport.

Frederick L. Olmsted, 1822-1903, Central Park, N.Y.C.; Fairmount Park, Philadelphia.

Ieoh Ming Pei, b. 1917, National Center for Atmospheric Research, Boulder, Col.

William Pereira, b. 1909, Cape Canaveral; Transamerica Bldg., San Francisco.

John Russell Pope, 1874-1937, National Gallery.

John Portman, b. 1924, Peachtree Center, Atlanta.

James Renwick Jr., 1818-1895, Grace Church, St. Patrick's Cathedral, N.Y.C.; Smithsonian, Corcoran Galleries, Wash., D.C.

Henry H. Richardson, 1838-1886, Trinity Church, Boston.

Kevin Roche, b. 1922, Oakland Cal. Museum; Fine Arts Center, U. of Mass.

James Gamble Rogers, 1867-1947, Columbia-Presbyterian Medical Center, N.Y.C.; Northwestern Univ., Chicago.

John Weldon Root, b. 1887, Palmolive Building, Chicago; Hotel Statler, Washington; Hotel Tamanaco, Caracas.

Paul Rudolph, b. 1918, Jewitt Art Center, Wellesley College; Art & Architecture Bldg., Yale.

Eero Saarinen, 1910-1961, Gateway to the West Arch, St. Louis; Trans World Flight Center, N.Y.C.

Louis Skidmore, 1897-1962, AEC town site, Oak Ridge, Tenn.; Terrace Plaza Hotel, Cincinnati.

Clarence S. Stein, b. 1882, Temple Emanu-El, N.Y.C.

Edward Durell Stone, 1902-1978, U.S. Embassy, New Delhi, India; (H. Hartford) Gallery of Modern Art, N.Y.C.

Louis H. Sullivan, 1856-1924, Auditorium, Chicago.

Richard Upjohn, 1802-1878, Trinity Church, N.Y.C.

Ralph T. Walker, 1889-1973, N.Y. Telephone Hdqrs., N.Y.C.; IBM Research Lab., Poughkeepsie, N.Y.

Roland A. Wank, 1898-1970, Cincinnati Union Terminal; head architect TVA, 1933-44.

Stanford White, 1853-1906, Washington Arch; first Madison Square Garden, N.Y.C.

Frank Lloyd Wright, 1867 or 1869-1959, Imperial Hotel, Tokyo; Guggenheim Museum, N.Y.C.

William Wurster, b. 1895, Ghirardelli Sq., San Francisco; Cowell College, U. Cal., Berkeley.

Minoru Yamasaki, b. 1912, World Trade Center, N.Y.C.

Noted American Cartoonists

Charles Addams, b. 1912, noted for macabre cartoons.

Peter Arno, 1904-1968, noted for urban characterizations.

George Baker, 1915-1975, The Sad Sack.

C. C. Beck, b. 1910, Captain Marvel.

Herb Block (Herblock), b. 1909, leading political cartoonist.

Clare Briggs, 1875-1930, Mr. & Mrs.

Ernie Bushmiller, b. 1905, Nancy.

Milton Caniff, b. 1907, Terry & the Pirates; Steve Canyon.

Al Capp, 1909-1979, Li'l Abner.

Roy Crane, 1901-1977, Captain Easy; Buz Sawyer.

Jay N. Darling (Ding), 1876-1962, political cartoonist.

Billy DeBeck, 1890-1942, Barney Google.

Rudolph Dirks, 1877-1968, The Katzenjammer Kids.

Walt Disney, 1901-1966, producer of animated cartoons created Mickey Mouse & Donald Duck.

Jules Feiffer, b. 1929, satirical *Village Voice* cartoonist.

Bud Fisher, 1884-1954, Mutt & Jeff.

Ham Fisher, 1900-1955, Joe Palooka.

James Montgomery Flagg, 1877-1960, illustrator created the famous Uncle Sam recruiting poster during WWI.

Hal Foster, b. 1892, Tarzan; Prince Valiant.

Fontaine Fox, 1884-1964, Toonerville Folks.

Rube Goldberg, 1883-1970, Boob McNutt.

Chester Gould, b. 1900, Dick Tracy.

Harold Gray, 1894-1968, Little Orphan Annie.

Jimmy Hatlo, 1898-1963, They'll Do It Everytime, Little Iodine.

John Held Jr., 1889-1958, "Jazz Age" cartoonist.

George Herriman, 1881-1944, Krazy Kat.

Harry Hershfield, 1885-1974, Abie the Agent.

Burne Hogarth, b. 1911, Tarzan.

Helen Hokinson, 1900-1949, known for satirical drawings of plump, bewildered suburban matrons and clubwomen.

Walt Kelly, 1913-1973, Pogo.

Hank Ketcham, b. 1920, Dennis the Menace.

Ted Key, b. 1912 Hazel.

Frank King, 1883-1969, Gasoline Alley.

Jack Kirby, b. 1917, Captain America.

Rollin Kirby, 1875-1952, political cartoonist.

Bill Mauldin, b. 1921, depicted squalid life of the G.I. in WWII.

Winsor McCay, 1872-1934, Little Nemo.

John T. McCutcheon, 1870-1949, noted for cartoons of midwestern rural life.
George McManus, 1884-1954, Bringing Up Father (Maggie & Jiggs).
Dale Messick, b. 1906, Brenda Starr.
Bob Montana, 1920-1975, Archie.
Willard Mullin, 1902-1978, sports cartoonist created the Dodgers "Bum" and the Mets "Kid".
Thomas Nast, 1840-1902, political cartoonist instrumental in breaking the corrupt Boss Tweed ring in N.Y. Created the Democratic donkey and Republican elephant.
Frederick Burr Opper, 1857-1937, Happy Hooligan.
Richard Outcault, 1863-1928, Yellow Kid; Buster Brown.
Alex Raymond, 1909-1956, Flash Gordon; Jungle Jim.
Charles Schulz, b. 1922, Peanuts.
Elzie C. Segar, 1894-1938, Popeye.
Sydney Smith, 1887-1935, The Gumps.
Otto Soglow, 1900-1975, Little King; Canyon Kiddies.
James Swinnerton, 1875-1974, Little Jimmy.
James Thurber, 1894-1961, *New Yorker* cartoonist of the smugly childish line coupled with the sophisticated caption.
Mort Walker, b. 1923, Beetle Bailey.
Russ Westover, 1887-1966, Tillie the Toiler.
Frank Willard, 1893-1958, Moon Mullins.
J. R. Williams, 1888-1957, The Willets Family; Out Our Way.
Gahan Wilson, b. 1930, cartoonist of the macabre.
Art Young, 1866-1943, political radical and satirist.
Chic Young, 1901-1973, Blondie.

Business Hall of Fame

Established and supported by Junior Achievement Inc. Laureates selected by *Fortune* board of editors.

William M. Allen
William Milfred Batten
Stephen D. Bechtel Sr.
William Blackie
Andrew Carnegie
Frederick Coolidge Crawford
Harry B. Cunningham
Arthur Vining Davis
Walter E. Disney
Georges Frederic Doriot
Donald W. Douglas
George Eastman
Thomas A. Edison
Henry Ford
Benjamin Franklin
Roswell Garst
Amadeo P. Giannini
Florence Nightingale Graham
Walter Abraham Haas
Joyce Clyde Hall
H.J. Heinz
James J. Hill
Conrad N. Hilton
J. Erik Jonsson
Henry John Kaiser
Robert Justus Kleberg Sr.
Albert D. Lasker
Royal Little
Francis Cabot Lowell
Henry R. Luce
Ian Kinloch MacGregor
Charles E. Merrill
John J. McCloy
Cyrus H. McCormick
J. Irwin Miller
George S. Moore
J. Pierpont Morgan
David MacKenzie Ogilvy
John Henry Patterson
William Allan Patterson
James Cash Penney
William C. Procter
M.J. Rathbone
John D. Rockefeller
David Sarnoff
Alfred P. Sloan Jr.
Cyrus R. Smith
Charles Clinton Spaulding
Alexander T. Stewart
J. Edgar Thomson
Theodore N. Vail
Cornelius Vanderbilt
De Witt Wallace
Lila Acheson Wallace
George Washington
Thomas J. Watson Jr.
George Westinghouse
Frederick W. Weyerhaeuser
Eli Whitney
Joseph C. Wilson
Robert Elkington Wood
Robert W. Woodruff

Noted Political Leaders of the Past

(Excluding U.S. presidents and most U.S. vice presidents, Supreme Court justices and signers of the Declaration of Independence; listed elsewhere.)

Abu Bakr, 573-634, Mohammedan leader, first caliph, chosen successor to Mohammed.
Dean Acheson, 1893-1971, (U.S.) secretary of state, chief architect of cold war foreign policy.
Samuel Adams, 1722-1803, (U.S.) patriot, Boston Tea Party firebrand.
Konrad Adenauer, 1876-1967, (G.) West German chancellor.
Emilio Aguinaldo, 1869-1964, (Philip.) revolutionary, fought against Spain and the U.S.
Akbar, 1542-1605, greatest Mogul emperor of India.
Salvador Allende Gossens, 1908-1973, (Chil.) president, advocate of democratic socialism.
Herbert H. Asquith, 1852-1928, (Br.) Liberal prime minister, instituted an advanced program of social reform.
Atahualpa, ?-1533, Inca (ruling chief) of Peru, executed by Pizarro.
Kemal Atatürk, 1881-1938, (Turk.) founded modern Turkey.
Clement Attlee, 1883-1967, (Br.) Labour party leader, prime minister, enacted national health, nationalized gas, electric, coal, iron, steel industries.
Stephen F. Austin, 1793-1836, (U.S.) led Texas colonization.
Mikhail Bakunin, 1814-1876, (R.) revolutionary, leading exponent of anarchism.
Arthur J. Balfour, 1848-1930, (Br.) as foreign secretary under Lloyd George issued Balfour Declaration expressing official British approval of Zionism.
Bernard M. Baruch, 1870-1965, (U.S.) financier, gvt. adviser.
Fulgencio Batista y Zaldívar, 1901-1973, (Cub.) dictator overthrown by Castro.
Lord Beaverbrook, 1879-1964, (Br.) financier, statesman, newspaper owner (Daily and Sunday Express, Evening Standard).
Eduard Benes, 1884-1948, (Czech.) president during interwar and post-WW II eras.
David Ben-Gurion, 1886-1973, (Isr.) first premier of Israel.
Thomas Hart Benton, 1782-1858, (U.S.) Missouri senator, championed agrarian interests and westward expansion.
Lavrenti Beria, 1899-1953, (USSR) Communist leader prominent in political purges under Stalin.
Aneurin Bevan, 1897-1960, (Br.) Labour party leader, developed socialized medicine system.
Ernest Bevin, 1881-1951, (Br.) Labour party leader, foreign minister, helped lay foundation for NATO.
Otto von Bismarck, 1815-1898, (G.) statesman known as the Iron Chancellor, uniter of Germany, 1870.
James G. Blaine, 1830-1893, (U.S.) Republican politician, diplomat, influential in launching Pan-American movement.
Léon Blum, 1872-1950, (F.) socialist leader, writer, headed first Popular Front government.
Simón Bolívar, 1783-1830, (Venez.) South American revolutionary who liberated much of the continent from Spanish rule.
William E. Borah, 1865-1940, (U.S.) isolationist senator, instrumental in blocking U.S. membership in League of Nations and the World Court.
Cesare Borgia, 1476-1507, (It.) soldier, politician, an outstanding figure of the Italian Renaissance.
Aristide Briand, 1862-1932, (F.) foreign minister, chief architect of Locarno Pact and anti-war Kellogg-Briand Pact.
William Jennings Bryan, 1860-1925, (U.S.) Democratic, populist leader, orator, 3 times lost race for presidency.
Nikolai Bukharin, 1888-1938, (USSR) communist leader.
William C. Bullitt, 1891-1967, (U.S.) diplomat, first ambassador to USSR, ambassador to France.
Ralph Bunche, 1904-1971, (U.S.) a founder and key diplomat of United Nations for more than 20 years.
John C. Calhoun, 1782-1850, (U.S.) political leader, champion of states' rights and a symbol of the Old South.
Robert Castlereagh, 1769-1822, (Br.) foreign secretary, guided Grand Alliance against Napoleon, major figure at the Congress of Vienna, 1814-15.
Camillo Benso Cavour, 1810-1861, (It.) statesman, largely responsible for uniting Italy under the House of Savoy.
Austen Chamberlain, 1863-1937, (Br.) Conservative party leader, largely responsible for Locarno Pact of 1925.
Neville Chamberlain, 1869-1940, (Br.) Conservative prime minister whose appeasement of Hitler led to Munich Pact.
Salmon P. Chase, 1808-1873, (U.S.) public official, abolitionist, jurist, 6th Supreme Court chief justice.
Chiang Kai-shek, 1887-1975, (Chin.) Nationalist Chinese president whose govt. was driven from mainland to Taiwan.
Chou En-lai, 1898-1976, (Chin.) diplomat, prime minister, a leading figure of the Chinese Communist party.
Winston Churchill, 1874-1965, (Br.) prime minister, soldier, author, guided Britain through WW II.
Galeazzo Ciano, 1903-1944, (It.) fascist foreign minister, helped create Rome-Berlin Axis, executed by Mussolini.
Henry Clay, 1777-1852, (U.S.) "The Great Compromiser," one of most influential pre-Civil War political leaders.
Georges Clemenceau, 1841-1929, (F.) twice premier, Wilson's chief antagonist at Paris Peace Conference after WW I.
DeWitt Clinton, 1769-1828, (U.S.) political leader, responsible for promoting idea of the Erie Canal.
Robert Clive, 1725-1774, (Br.) first administrator of Bengal, laid foundation for British Empire in India.
Jean Baptiste Colbert, 1619-1683, (F.) statesman, influential under Louis XIV, created the French navy.

James M. Cox, 1870-1957, (U.S.) newspaper publisher and reformist Ohio governor.

Oliver Cromwell, 1599-1658, (Br.) Lord Protector of England, led parliamentary forces during Civil War.

Curzon of Kedleston, 1859-1925, (Br.) viceroy of India, foreign secretary, major force in dealing with post-WW I problems in Europe and Far East.

Édouard Daladier, 1884-1970, (F.) radical socialist politician, arrested by Vichy, interned by Germans until liberation in 1945.

Georges Danton, 1759-1794, (F.) a leading figure in the French Revolution.

Jefferson Davis, 1808-1889, (U.S.) president of the Confederate States of America.

Charles G. Dawes, 1865-1951, (U.S.) statesman, banker, advanced Dawes Plan to stabilize post-WW I German finances.

Alcide De Gasperi, 1881-1954, (It.) premier, founder of the Christian Democratic party.

Charles DeGaulle, 1890-1970, (F.) general, statesman, and first president of the Fifth Republic.

Thomas E. Dewey, 1902-1971, (U.S.) New York governor, twice loser in try for presidency.

Ngo Dinh Diem, 1901-1963, (Viet.) South Vietnamese president, assassinated in government take-over.

Everett M. Dirksen, 1896-1969, (U.S.) Senate Republican minority leader, orator.

Benjamin Disraeli, 1804-1881, (Br.) prime minister, considered founder of modern Conservative party.

Engelbert Dollfuss, 1892-1934, (Aus.) chancellor, assassinated by Austrian Nazis.

Andrea Doria, 1466-1560, (It.) Genoese admiral, statesman, called "Father of Peace" and "Liberator of Genoa."

Stephen A. Douglas, 1813-1861, (U.S.) Democratic leader, orator, opposed Lincoln for the presidency.

John Foster Dulles, 1888-1959, (U.S.) secretary of state under Eisenhower, cold war policy maker.

Friedrich Ebert, 1871-1925, (G.) Social Democratic movement leader, instrumental in bringing about Weimar constitution.

Sir Anthony Eden, 1897-1977, (Br.) foreign secretary, prime minister during Suez invasion of 1956.

Ludwig Erhard, 1897-1977, (G.) economist, West German chancellor, led nation's economic rise after WW II.

Hamilton Fish, 1808-1893, (U.S.) secretary of state, successfully mediated disputes with Great Britain, Latin America.

James V. Forrestal, 1892-1949, (U.S.) secretary of navy, first secretary of defense.

Francisco Franco, 1892-1975, (Sp.) leader of rebel forces during Spanish Civil War and dictator of Spain.

Benjamin Franklin, 1706-1790, (U.S.) printer, publisher, author, inventor, scientist, diplomat.

Louis de Frontenac, 1620-1698, (F.) governor of New France (Canada) where he encouraged explorations and fought Iroquois.

Hugh Gaitskell, 1906-1963, (Br.) Labour party leader, major force in reversing its stand for unilateral disarmament.

Albert Gallatin, 1761-1849, (U.S.) second secretary of treasury, instrumental in negotiating end of War of 1812.

Léon Gambetta, 1838-1882, (F.) statesman, politician, one of the founders of the Third Republic.

Mohandas K. Gandhi, 1869-1948, (Ind.) political leader, ascetic, led nationalist movement against British rule.

Giuseppe Garibaldi, 1807-1882, (It.) patriot, soldier, a leading figure in the Risorgimento, the Italian unification movement.

Genghis Khan, c. 1167-1227, brilliant Mongol conqueror, ruler of vast Asian empire.

William E. Gladstone, 1809-1898, (Br.) prime minister 4 times, dominant force of Liberal party from 1868 to 1894.

Paul Joseph Goebbels, 1897-1945, (G.) Nazi propagandist, master of mass psychology.

Hermann Goering, 1893-1946, (G.) Nazi leader, founded and headed Gestapo.

Klement Gottwald, 1896-1953, (Czech.) communist leader ushered communism into his country.

Che (Ernesto) Guevara, 1928-1967, (Arg.) guerilla leader, prominent in Cuban revolution, killed in Bolivia.

Haile Selassie, 1891-1975, (Eth.) emperor, maintained traditional monarchy in face of foreign invasion, occupation, and internal resistance.

Alexander Hamilton, 1755-1804, (U.S.) first treasury secretary, champion of strong central government.

Dag Hammarskjold, 1905-1961, (Swed.) statesman, UN secretary general.

John Hancock, 1737-1793, (U.S.) revolutionary leader, first signer of Declaration of Independence.

John Hay, 1838-1905, (U.S.) secretary of state, primarily associated with Open Door Policy toward China.

Patrick Henry, 1736-1799, (U.S.) major revolutionary figure, remarkable orator.

Édouard Herriot, 1872-1957, (F.) Radical Socialist leader, twice premier, president of National Assembly.

Theodor Herzl, 1860-1904, (Aus.) founder of modern Zionism.

Heinrich Himmler, 1900-1945, (G.) chief of Nazi SS and Gestapo, primarily responsible for the Holocaust.

Paul von Hindenburg, 1847-1934, (G.) field marshal, president.

Adolf Hitler, 1889-1945, (G.) dictator, founder of National Socialism.

Ho Chi Minh, 1890-1969, (Viet.) North Vietnamese president, Vietnamese Communist leader, national hero.

Harry L. Hopkins, 1890-1946, (U.S.) New Deal administrator, closest adviser to FDR during WW II.

Edward M. House, 1858-1938, (U.S.) diplomat, confidential adviser to Woodrow Wilson.

Samuel Houston, 1793-1863, (U.S.) leader of struggle to win control of Texas from Mexico.

Cordell Hull, 1871-1955, (U.S.) secretary of state, initiated reciprocal trade to lower tariffs, helped organize UN.

Hubert H. Humphrey, 1911-1978, (U.S.) Minnesota Democrat, senator, vice president, spent 32 years in public service.

Ibn Saud, c. 1888-1953, (S. Arab.) founder of Saudi Arabia and its first king.

Benito Juarez, 1806-1872, (Mex.) national hero, rallied countrymen against foreign threats, sought to create democratic, federal republic.

Frank B. Kellogg, 1856-1937, (U.S.) secretary of state, negotiated Kellogg-Briand Pact to outlaw war.

Robert F. Kennedy, 1925-1968, (U.S.) attorney general, senator, assassinated while seeking presidential nomination.

Aleksandr Kerensky, 1881-1970, (R.) revolutionary, served as premier after Feb. 1917 revolution until Bolshevik overthrow.

Nikita Khrushchev, 1894-1971, (USSR) communist leader, premier, first secretary of Communist party, initiated de-Stalinization.

Pyotr Kropotkin, 1842-1921, (R.) anarchist, championed the peasants but opposed Bolshevism.

Kublai Khan, c. 1215-1294, Mongol emperor, founder of Yüan dynasty in China.

Béla Kun, 1886-c.1939, (Hung.) communist dictator, member of 3d International, tried to foment worldwide revolution.

Robert M. LaFollette, 1855-1925, (U.S.) Wisconsin public official, leader of progressive movement.

Pierre Laval, 1883-1945, (F.) politician, Vichy foreign minister, executed for treason.

Andrew Bonar Law, 1858-1923, (Br.) Conservative party politician, led opposition to Irish home rule.

Vladimir Ilyich Lenin (Ulyanov), 1870-1924, (USSR) revolutionary, founder of Bolshevism, Soviet leader 1917-1924.

Ferdinand de Lesseps, 1805-1894, (F.) diplomat, engineer, conceived idea of Suez Canal.

Liu Shao-ch'i, c.1898-1974, (Chin.) communist leader, fell from grace during "cultural revolution."

Maxim Litvinov, 1876-1951, (USSR), revolutionary, commissar of foreign affairs, proponent of cooperation with western powers.

David Lloyd George, 1863-1945, (Br.) Liberal party prime minister, laid foundations for the modern welfare state.

Henry Cabot Lodge, 1850-1924, (U.S.) conservative Republican senator, led opposition to participation in League of Nations.

Huey P. Long, 1893-1935, (U.S.) Louisiana political demagogue, governor, assassinated.

Rosa Luxemburg, 1871-1919, (G.) revolutionary, leader of the German Social Democratic party and Spartacus party.

J. Ramsay MacDonald, 1866-1937, (Br.) first Labour party prime minister of Great Britain.

Joseph R. McCarthy, 1908-1957, (U.S.) senator notorious for his witch hunt for communists in the government.

Makarios III, 1913-1977, (Cypr.) Greek Orthodox archbishop, first president of Cyprus.

Malcolm X (Malcolm Little), 1925-1965, (U.S.) black separatist leader, assassinated.

Mao Tse-tung, 1893-1976, (Chin.) chief Chinese Marxist theorist, soldier, lead Chinese revolution establishing his nation as an important communist state.

Jean Paul Marat, 1743-1793, (F.) revolutionary politician, identified with radical Jacobins, assassinated by Charlotte Corday.

José Marti, 1853-1895, (Cub.) patriot, poet, leader of Cuban struggle for independence.

Jan Masaryk, 1886-1948, (Czech.) foreign minister, died by mysterious suicide following communist coup.

Thomas G. Masaryk, 1850-1937, (Czech.) statesman, philosopher, first president of Czechoslovak Republic.

Jules Mazarin, 1602-1661, (F.) cardinal, statesman, prime minister under Louis XIII and queen regent Anne of Austria.

Tom Mboya, 1930-1969, (Kenyan) political leader, instrumental in securing independence for his country.

Cosimo I de' Medici, 1519-1574 (It.) Duke of Florence, grand duke of Tuscany.

Lorenzo de' Medici, the Magnificent, 1449-1492, (It.) merchant prince, a towering figure in Italian Renaissance.

Catherine de Medicis, 1519-1589, (F.) queen consort of Henry II, regent of France, influential in Catholic-Huguenot wars.

Golda Meir, 1898-1978, (Isr.) prime minister, 1969-74.

Klemens W.N.L. Metternich, 1773-1859, (Aus.) statesman, arbiter of post-Napoleonic Europe.

Anastas Mikoyan, 1895-1978, (USSR) prominent Soviet leader from 1917; president, 1964-65.

Guy Mollet, 1905-1975, (F.) socialist politician, resistance leader.

Henry Morgenthau Jr., 1891-1967, (U.S.) secretary of treasury, raised funds to finance New Deal and U.S. WW II activities.

Gouverneur Morris, 1752-1816, (U.S.) statesman, diplomat, financial expert who helped plan decimal coinage system.

Wayne Morse, 1900-1974, (U.S.) senator, long-time critic of Vietnam War.

Muhammad Ali, 1769?-1849, (Egypt), pasha, founder of dynasty that encouraged emergence of modern Egyptian state.

Benito Mussolini, 1883-1945, (It.) dictator and leader of the Italian fascist movement.

Imre Nagy, c. 1895-1958, (Hung.) communist premier, assassinated after Soviets crushed 1956 uprising.

Gamel Abdel Nasser, 1918-1970, (Egypt.) leader of Arab unification, second Egyptian president.

Jawaharlal Nehru, 1889-1964, (Ind.) prime minister, guided India through its early years of independence.

Kwame Nkrumah, 1909-1972, (Ghan.) dictatorial prime minister, deposed in 1966.

Frederick North, 1732-1792, (Br.) prime minister, his inept policies led to loss of American colonies.

Daniel O'Connell, 1775-1847, (Ir.) political leader, known as The Liberator.

Omar, c.581-644, Mohammedan leader, 2d caliph, led Islam to become an imperial power.

Ignace Paderewski, 1860-1941, (Pol.) statesman, pianist, composer, briefly prime minister, an ardent patriot.

Viscount Palmerston, 1784-1865, (Br.) Whig-Liberal prime minister, foreign minister, embodied British nationalism.

George Papandreou, 1888-1968, (Gk.) Republican politician, served three times as prime minister.

Franz von Papen, 1879-1969, (G.) politician, played major role in overthrow of Weimar Republic and rise of Hitler.

Charles Stewart Parnell, 1846-1891, (Ir.) nationalist leader, "uncrowned king of Ireland."

Lester Pearson, 1897-1972, (Can.) diplomat, Liberal party leader, prime minister.

Robert Peel, 1788-1850, (Br.) reformist prime minister, founder of the Conservative party.

Juan Perón, 1895-1974, (Arg.) president, dictator.

Joseph Pilsudski, 1867-1935, (Pol.) statesman, instrumental in re-establishing Polish state in the 20th century.

Charles Pinckney, 1757-1824, (U.S.) founding father, his Pinckney plan was largely incorporated into constitution.

William Pitt, the Elder, 1708-1778, (Br.) statesman, called the "Great Commoner," transformed Britain into imperial power.

William Pitt, the Younger, 1759-1806, (Br.) prime minister during the French Revolutionary wars.

Georgi Plekhanov, 1857-1918, (R.) revolutionary, social philosopher, called "father of Russian Marxism."

Raymond Poincaré, 1860-1934, (F.) 9th president of the Republic, advocated harsh punishment of Germany after WW I.

Georges Pompidou, 1911-1974, (F.) Gaullist political leader, president from 1969 to 1974.

Grigori Potemkin, 1739-1791, (R.) field marshal, favorite of Catherine II.

Edmund Randolph, 1753-1813, (U.S.) attorney, prominent in drafting, ratification of constitution.

John Randolph, 1773-1833, (U.S.) southern planter, strong advocate of states' rights.

Jeanette Rankin, 1880-1973, (U.S.) pacifist, first woman member of U.S. Congress.

Walter Rathenau, 1867-1922, (G.) industrialist, social theorist, statesman.

Sam Rayburn, 1882-1961, (U.S.) Democratic leader, representative for 47 years, House speaker for 17.

Paul Reynaud, 1878-1966, (F.) statesman, premier in 1940 at the time of France's defeat by Germany.

Syngman Rhee, 1875-1965, (Kor.) first president of the Republic of Korea.

Cecil Rhodes, 1853-1902, (Br.) imperialist, industrial magnate, established Rhodes scholarships in his will.

Cardinal de Richelieu, 1585-1642, (F.) statesman, known as "red eminence," chief minister to Louis XIII.

Maximilien Robespierre, 1758-1794, (F.) leading figure of French Revolution, responsible for much of Reign of Terror.

Nelson Rockefeller, 1908-1979, (U.S.) Republican whose career spanned 40 years; gov. of N.Y., 1958-73; U.S. vice president, 1974-77.

Eleanor Roosevelt, 1884-1962, (U.S.) humanitarian, United Nations diplomat.

Elihu Root, 1845-1937, (U.S.) lawyer, statesman, diplomat, leading Republican supporter of the League of Nations.

John Russell, 1792-1878, (Br.) Liberal prime minister during the Irish potato famine.

António de O. Salazar, 1899-1970, (Port.) statesman, long-time dictator.

José de San Martin, 1778-1850, South American revolutionary, protector of Peru.

Eisaku Sato, 1901-1975, (Jap.) prime minister, presided over Japan's post-WW II emergence as major world power.

Philipp Scheidemann, 1865-1939, (G.) Social Democratic leader, first chancellor of the German republic.

Robert Schuman, 1886-1963, (F.) statesman, founded European Coal and Steel Community.

Carl Schurz, 1829-1906, (U.S.) German-American political leader, journalist, orator, dedicated reformer.

Kurt Schuschnigg, 1897-1977, (Aus.) chancellor, unsuccessful in stopping his country's annexation by Germany.

William H. Seward, 1801-1872, (U.S.) anti-slavery activist, as Lincoln's secretary of state purchased Alaska.

Carlo Sforza, 1872-1952, (It.) foreign minister, prominent Italian anti-fascist.

Alfred E. Smith, 1873-1944, (U.S.) New York Democratic governor, first Roman Catholic to run for presidency.

Jan C. Smuts, 1870-1950, (S.Af.) statesman, philosopher, soldier, prime minister.

Paul Henri Spaak, 1899-1972, (Belg.) statesman, socialist leader.

Joseph Stalin, 1879-1953, (USSR) Soviet dictator from 1924 to 1953.

Edwin M. Stanton, 1814-1869, (U.S.) Lincoln's secretary of war during the Civil War.

Edward R. Stettinius Jr., 1900-1949, (U.S.) industrialist, secretary of state who coordinated aid to WW II allies.

Adlai E. Stevenson, 1900-1965, (U.S.) Democratic leader, diplomat, Illinois governor, presidential candidate.

Henry L. Stimson, 1867-1950, (U.S.) statesman, served in 5 administrations, influenced foreign policy in 1930s and 1940s.

Gustav Stresemann, 1878-1929, (G.) chancellor, foreign minister, dedicated to regaining friendship for post-WW I Germany.

Sukarno, 1901-1970, (Indon.) dictatorial first president of the Indonesian republic.

Sun Yat-sen, 1866-1925, (Chin.) revolutionary, leader of Kuomintang, regarded as the father of modern China.

Robert A. Taft, 1889-1953, (U.S.) conservative Senate leader, called "Mr. Republican."

Charles de Talleyrand, 1754-1838, (F.) statesman, diplomat, the major force of the Congress of Vienna of 1814-15.

U Thant, 1909-1974, (Bur.) statesman, UN secretary-general.

Norman M. Thomas, 1884-1968, (U.S.) social reformer, 6 times unsuccessful Socialist party presidential candidate.

Josip Broz Tito, 1892-1980, (Yug.) president of Yugoslavia from 1953, World War II guerrilla chief, postwar rival of Stalin, leader of 3d world movement.

Palmiro Togliatti, 1893-1964, (It.) major leader of Italian Communist party.

Hideki Tojo, 1885-1948, (Jap.) statesman, soldier, prime minister during most of WW II.

François Toussaint L'Ouverture, c. 1744-1803, (Hait.) patriot, martyr, thwarted French colonial aims.

Leon Trotsky, 1879-1940, (USSR) revolutionary, communist leader, founded Red Army, expelled from party in conflict with Stalin.

Rafael L. Trujillo Molina, 1891-1961, (Dom.) absolute dictator, assassinated.

Moise K. Tshombe, 1919-1969, (Cong.) politician, president of secessionist Katanga, premier of Repubic of Congo (Zaire).

William M. Tweed, 1823-1878, (U.S.) politician, absolute leader of Tammany Hall, NYC's Democratic political machine.

Walter Ulbricht, 1893-1973, (G.) communist leader of German Democratic Republic.

Arthur H. Vandenberg, 1884-1951, (U.S.) senator, proponent of anti-communist bipartisan foreign policy after WW II.

Eleutherios Venizelos, 1864-1936, (Gk.) most prominent Greek statesman in early 20th century, considerably expanded Greek territory through his diplomacy.

Hendrik F. Verwoerd, 1901-1966, (S.Af.) prime minister, rigorously applied apartheid policy despite protest.

Robert Walpole, 1676-1745, (Br.) statesman, generally considered Britain's first prime minister.

Daniel Webster, 1782-1852, (U.S.) orator, politician, enthusiastic nationalist, advocate of business interests during Jacksonian agrarianism.

Chaim Weizmann, 1874-1952, Zionist leader, scientist, first Israeli president.

Wendell L. Willkie, 1892-1944, (U.S.) Republican who tried to unseat FDR when he ran for his 3d term.

Emiliano Zapata, c. 1879-1919, (Mex.) revolutionary, major influence on modern Mexico.

Notable Military and Naval Leaders of the Past

Creighton Abrams, 1914-1974, (U.S.) commanded forces in Vietnam, 1968-72.

Harold Alexander, 1891-1969, (Br.) led Allied invasion of Italy, 1943.

Ethan Allen, 1738-1789, (U.S.) headed Green Mountain Boys; captured Ft. Ticonderoga, 1775.

Edmund Allenby, 1861-1936, (Br.) in Boer War, WW1; led Egyptian expeditionary force, 1917-18.

Benedict Arnold, 1741-1801, (U.S.) victorious at Saratoga; tried to betray West Point to British.

Henry "Hap" Arnold, 1886-1950, (U.S.) commanded Army Air Force in WW2.

Petr Bagration, 1765-1812, (R.) hero of Napoleonic wars.

John Barry, 1745-1803, (U.S.) won numerous sea battles during revolution.

Pierre Beauregard, 1818-1893, (U.S.) Confederate general ordered bombardment of Ft. Sumter that began the Civil War.

Gebhard v. Blücher, 1742-1819, (G.) helped defeat Napoleon at Waterloo.

Napoleon Bonaparte, 1769-1821, (F.) defeated Russia and Austria at Austerlitz, 1805; invaded Russia, 1812; defeated at Waterloo, 1815.

Edward Braddock, 1695-1755, (Br.) commanded forces in French and Indian War.

John Burgoyne, 1722-1792, (Br.) defeated at Saratoga.

Claire Chennault, 1890-1958, (U.S.) headed Flying Tigers in WW2.

Karl v. Clausewitz, 1780-1831, (G.) wrote books on military theory.

Henry Clinton, 1738-1795, (Br.) commander of forces in America, 1778-81.

Lucius D. Clay, 1897-1978, (U.S.) led Berlin airlift, 1948-49.

Charles Cornwallis, 1738-1805, (Br.) victorious at Brandywine, 1777; surrendered at Yorktown.

Crazy Horse, 1849-1877, (U.S.) Sioux war chief victorious at Little Big Horn.

George A. Custer, 1839-1876, (U.S.) defeated and killed at Little Big Horn.

Stephen Decatur, 1779-1820, (U.S.) naval hero of Barbary wars, War of 1812.

Anton Denikin, 1872-1947, (R.) led White forces in Russian civil war.

George Dewey, 1837-1917, (U.S.) destroyed Spanish fleet at Manila, 1898.

Hugh C. Dowding, 1883-1970, (Br.) headed RAF, 1936-40.

Jubal Early, 1816-1894, (U.S.) Confederate general led raid on Washington, 1864.

Dwight D. Eisenhower, 1890-1969, (U.S.) commanded Allied forces in Europe, WW2.

David Farragut, 1801-1870, (U.S.) Union admiral captured New Orleans, Mobile Bay.

Ferdinand Foch, 1851-1929, (F.) headed victorious Allied armies, 1918.

Nathan Bedford Forrest, 1821-1877, (U.S.) Confederate general led cavalry raids against Union supply lines.

Frederick the Great, 1712-1786, (G.) led Prussia in The Seven Years War.

Charles G. Gordon, 1833-1885, (Br.) led forces in China; killed at Khartoum.

Horatio Gates, 1728-1806, (U.S.) commanded army at Saratoga.

Ulysses S. Grant, 1822-1885, (U.S.) headed Union army, 1864-65; forced Lee's surrender, 1865.

Heinz Guderian, 1888-1953, (G.) tank theorist led panzer forces in Poland, France, Russia.

Douglas Haig, 1861-1928, (Br.) led British armies in France, 1915-18.

William F. Halsey, 1882-1959, (U.S.) defeated Japanese fleet at Leyte Gulf, 1944.

Richard Howe, 1726-1799, (Br.) commanded navy in America, 1776-78; first of June victory against French, 1794.

William Howe, 1729-1814, (Br.) commanded forces in America, 1776-78.

Isaac Hull, 1773-1843, (U.S.) sunk British frigate Guerriere, 1812.

Thomas (Stonewall) Jackson, 1824-1863, (U.S.) Confederate general led forces in the Shenandoah Valley campaign; killed at Chancellorsville.

Joseph Joffre, 1852-1931, (F.) headed Allied armies, won Battle of the Marne, 1914.

John Paul Jones, 1747-1792, (U.S.) raided British coast; commanded Bonhomme Richard in victory over Serapis, 1779.

Stephen Kearny, 1794-1848, (U.S.) headed Army of the West in Mexican War.

Ernest J. King, 1878-1956, (U.S.) chief naval strategist in WW2.

Horatio H. Kitchener, 1850-1916, (Br.) led forces in Boer War; victorious at Khartoum; organized army in WW1.

Lavrenti Kornilov, 1870-1918, (R.) Commander-in-Chief, 1917; led counter-revolutionary march on Petrograd.

Thaddeus Kosciusko, 1746-1817, (P.) aided American cause in revolution.

Mikhail Kutuzov, 1745-1813, (R.) fought French at Borodino, 1812; abandoned Moscow; forced French retreat.

Marquis de Lafayette, 1757-1834, (F.) aided American cause in the revolution.

Thomas E. Lawrence (of Arabia), 1888-1935, (Br.) organized revolt of Arabs against Turks in WW1.

Henry (Light-Horse Harry) Lee, 1756-1818, (U.S.) cavalry officer in revolution.

Robert E. Lee, 1807-1870, (U.S.) Confederate general defeated at Gettysburg; surrendered to Grant, 1865.

James Longstreet, 1821-1904, (U.S.) aided Lee at Gettysburg.

William D. Leahy, 1875-1959, (U.S.) personal chief of staff to Roosevelt during WW2.

Douglas MacArthur, 1880-1964, (U.S.) commanded forces in SW Pacific in WW2; headed occupation forces in Japan, 1945-50; UN commander in Korean War.

Francis Marion, 1733-1795, (U.S.) led guerrilla actions in S.C. during revolution.

Duke of Marlborough, 1650-1722, (Br.) led forces against Louis XIV in War of the Spanish Sucession.

George C. Marshall, 1880-1959, (U.S.) chief of staff in WW2; authored Marshall Plan.

George B. McClellan, 1826-1885, (U.S.) Union general commanded Army of the Potomac, 1861-62.

George Meade, 1815-1872; (U.S.) commanded Union forces at Gettysburg.

Billy Mitchell, 1879-1936, (U.S.) air-power advocate; court-martialed for insubordination, later vindicated.

Helmuth v. Moltke, 1800-1891; (G.) victorious in Austro-Prussian, Franco-Prussian wars.

Louis de Montcalm, 1712-1759, (F.) headed troops in Canada; defeated at Quebec, 1759.

Bernard Law Montgomery, 1887-1976, (Br.) stopped German offensive at Alamein, 1942; helped plan Normandy invasion.

Daniel Morgan, 1736-1802, (U.S.) victorious at Cowpens, 1781.

Louis Mountbatten, 1900-1979, (Br.) Supreme Allied Commander of SE Asia, 1943-46.

Joachim Murat, 1767-1815, (F.) leader of cavalry at Marengo, 1800; Austerlitz, 1805; and Jena, 1806.

Horatio Nelson, 1758-1805, (Br.) naval commander destroyed French fleet at Trafalgar.

Michel Ney, 1769-1815, (F.) commanded forces in Switzerland, Austria, Russia; defeated at Waterloo.

Chester Nimitz, 1885-1966, (U.S.) commander of naval forces in Pacific in WW2.

George S. Patton, 1885-1945, (U.S.) led assault on Sicily, 1943; headed 3d Army invasion of German-occupied Europe.

Oliver Perry, 1785-1819, (U.S.) won Battle of Lake Erie in War of 1812.

John Pershing, 1860-1948, (U.S.) commanded Mexican border campaign, 1916; American expeditionary forces in WW1.

Henri Philippe Pétain, 1856-1951, (F.) defended Verdun, 1916; headed Vichy government in WW2.

George E. Pickett, 1825-1875, (U.S.) Confederate general famed for "charge" at Gettysburg.

Erwin Rommel, 1891-1944, (G.) headed Afrika Korps in WW2.

Karl v. Rundstedt, 1875-1953, (G.) supreme commander in West, 1943-45.

Aleksandr Samsonov, 1859-1914, (R.) led invasion of E. Prussia, defeated at Tannenberg, 1914.

Winfield Scott, 1786-1866, (U.S.) hero of War of 1812; headed forces in Mexican war, took Mexico City.

Philip Sheridan, 1831-1888, (U.S.) Union cavalry officer headed Army of the Shenandoah, 1864-65.

William T. Sherman, 1820-1891, (U.S.) Union general sacked Atlanta during "march to the sea," 1864.

Carl Spaatz, 1891-1974, (U.S.) directed strategic bombing against Germany, later Japan, in WW2.

Raymond Spruance, 1886-1969, (U.S.) victorious at Midway Island, 1942.

Joseph W. Stilwell, 1883-1946, (U.S.) headed forces in the China, Burma, India theater in WW2.

J.E.B. Stuart, 1833-1864, (U.S.) Confederate cavalry commander.

George H. Thomas, 1816-1870, (U.S.) saved Union army at Chattanooga, 1863; victorious at Nashville, 1864.

Semyon Timoshenko, 1895-1970, (USSR) defended Moscow, Stalingrad; led winter offensive, 1942-43.

Alfred v. Tirpitz, 1849-1930, (G.) responsible for submarine blockade in WW1.

Jonathan M. Wainwright, 1883-1953, (U.S.) forced to surrender on Corregidor, 1942.

George Washington, 1732-1799, (U.S.) led Continental army, 1775-83.

Archibald Wavell, 1883-1950, (Br.) commanded forces in N. and E. Africa, and SE Asia in WW2.

Anthony Wayne, 1745-1796, (U.S.) captured Stony Point, 1779; defeated Indians at Fallen Timbers, 1794.

Duke of Wellington, 1769-1852, (Br.) defeated Napoleon at Waterloo.

James Wolfe, 1727-1759, (Br.) captured Quebec from French, 1758.

Georgi Zhukov, 1895-1974, (USSR) defended Moscow, 1941; led assault on Berlin.

Noted Writers of the Past

Henry Adams, 1838-1918, (U.S.) historian, philosopher. *The Education of Henry Adams.*

George Ade, 1866-1944, (U.S.) humorist. *Fables in Slang.*

Conrad Aiken, 1889-1973, (U.S.) poet, critic. *Collected Poems.*

Louisa May Alcott, 1832-1888, (U.S.) novelist. *Little Women.*

Sholom Aleichem, 1859-1916. (R.) Yiddish writer. *Tevye's Daughter, The Great Fair.*

Horatio Alger, 1832-1899, (U.S.) author of "rags-to-riches" boys' books.

Maxwell Anderson, 1888-1959, (U.S.) playwright. *What Price Glory?, High Tor, Winterset, Key Largo.*

Sherwood Anderson, 1876-1941, (U.S.) author. *Winesburg, Ohio.*

Matthew Arnold, 1822-1888, (Br.) poet, critic. "Thrysis," "Dover Beach."

Jane Austen, 1775-1817, (Br.) novelist. *Pride and Prejudice, Sense and Sensibility, Emma, Mansfield Park.*

Isaac Babel, 1894-1941, (R.) short-story writer, playwright. *Odessa Tales, Red Cavalry.*

James M. Barrie, 1860-1937, (Br.) playwright, novelist. *Peter Pan, Dear Brutus, What Every Woman Knows.*

Honoré de Balzac, 1799-1850, (Fr.) novelist. *Le Père Goriot, Cousine Bette, Eugénie Grandet, The Human Comedy.*

Charles Baudelaire, 1821-1867, (Fr.) symbolist poet. *Les Fleurs du Mal.*

L. Frank Baum, 1856-1919, (U.S.) children's author. Wizard of Oz series.

Brendan Behan, 1923-1964, (Ir.) playwright. *The Quare Fellow, The Hostage, Borstal Boy.*

Robert Benchley, 1889-1945, (U.S.) humorist. *From Bed to Worse, My Ten Years in a Quandary.*

Stephen Vincent Benét, 1898-1943, (U.S.) poet, novelist. *John Brown's Body.*

John Berryman, 1914-1972, (U.S.) poet. *Homage to Mistress Bradstreet.*

Ambrose Bierce, 1842-1914, (U.S.) short-story writer, journalist. *In the Midst of Life, The Devil's Dictionary.*

William Blake, 1757-1827, (Br.) poet, mystic, artist. *Songs of Innocence, Songs of Experience.*

Giovanni Boccaccio, 1313-1375, (It.) poet, storyteller. *Decameron, Filostrato.*

James Boswell, 1740-1795, (Sc.) author. *The Life of Samuel Johnson.*

Anne Bradstreet, c. 1612-1672, (U.S.) poet. *The Tenth Muse Lately Sprung Up in America.*

Bertolt Brecht, 1898-1956, (G.) dramatist, poet. *The Threepenny Opera, Mother Courage and Her Children.*

Charlotte Brontë, 1816-1855, (Br.) novelist. *Jane Eyre.*

Emily Brontë, 1818-1848, (Br.) novelist. *Wuthering Heights.*

Elizabeth Barrett Browning, 1806-1861, (Br.) poet. *Sonnets from the Portuguese.*

Robert Browning, 1812-1889, (Br.) poet. "My Last Duchess," "Soliloquy of the Spanish Cloister."

Pearl Buck, 1892-1973, (U.S.) novelist. *The Good Earth.*

Mikhail Bulgakov, 1891-1940, (R.) novelist, playwright. *The Heart of a Dog, The Master and Margarita.*

John Bunyan, 1628-1688, (Br.) writer. *Pilgrim's Progress.*

Robert Burns, 1759-1796, (Sc.) poet. "Flow Gently, Sweet Afton," "My Heart's in the Highlands," "Auld Lang Syne."

Edgar Rice Burroughs, 1875-1950, (U.S.) novelist. *Tarzan of the Apes.*

George Gordon Lord Byron, 1788-1824, (Br.) poet. *Don Juan, Childe Harold.*

Albert Camus, 1913-1960, (F.) novelist. *The Plague, The Stranger, Caligula, The Fall.*

Lewis Carroll, 1832-1898, (Br.) writer, mathematician. *Alice's Adventures in Wonderland, Through the Looking Glass.*

Karel Capek, 1890-1938, (Czech.) playwright, novelist, essayist. *R.U.R. (Rossum's Univeral Robots).*

Giacomo Casanova, 1725-1798, (It.) Venetian adventurer, author, world famous for his memoirs.

Willa Cather, 1876-1947, (U.S.) novelist, essayist. *O Pioneers!, My Ántonia.*

Miguel de Cervantes Saavedra, 1547-1616, (Sp.) novelist, dramatist, poet. *Don Quixote de la Mancha.*

Raymond Chandler, 1888-1959, (U.S.) writer of detective fiction. Philip Marlowe series.

Geoffrey Chaucer, c. 1340-1400, (Br.) poet. *The Canterbury Tales.*

Anton Chekhov, 1860-1904, (R.) short-story writer, dramatist. *Uncle Vanya, The Cherry Orchard, The Three Sisters.*

G.K. Chesterton, 1874-1936, (Br.) author, Fr. Brown series.

Agatha Christie, 1891-1976, (Br.) mystery writer. *And Then There Were None, Murder on the Orient Express.*

Jean Cocteau, 1889-1963, (F.) writer, visual artist, filmmaker. *The Beauty and the Beast, Enfants Terribles.*

Samuel Taylor Coleridge, 1772-1834, (Br.) poet, man of letters. "Kubla Khan," "The Rime of the Ancient Mariner."

Sidonie Colette, 1873-1954, (F.) novelist. *Claudine, Gigi.*

Joseph Conrad, 1857-1924, (Br.) novelist. *Lord Jim, Heart of Darkness, The Nigger of the Narcissus.*

James Fenimore Cooper, 1789-1851, (U.S.) novelist. *Leather-Stocking Tales.*

Pierre Corneille, 1606-1684, (F.) Dramatist. *Medeé, Le Cid, Horace, Cinna, Polyeucte.*

Hart Crane, 1899-1932, (U.S.) poet. "The Bridge."

Stephen Crane, 1871-1900, (U.S.) novelist. *The Red Badge of Courage.*

e.e. cummings, 1894-1962, (U.S.) poet. *Tulips and Chimneys, Is 5, 95 Poems, The Enormous Room.*

Gabriele D'Annunzio, 1863-1938, (It.) poet, novelist, dramatist. *The Child of Pleasure, The Intruder, The Victim.*

Dante Alighieri, 1265-1321, (It.) poet. *The Divine Comedy.*

Daniel Defoe, 1660-1731, (Br.) writer. *Robinson Crusoe, Moll Flanders, Journal of the Plague Year.*

Charles Dickens, 1812-1870, (Br.) novelist. *David Copperfield, Oliver Twist, Great Expectations, The Pickwick Papers.*

Emily Dickinson, 1830-1886, (U.S.) poet.

Isak Dinesen (Karen Blixen), 1885-1962, (Dan.) author. *Out of Africa, Seven Gothic Tales, Winter's Tales.*

John Donne, 1573-1631, (Br.) poet. *Songs and Sonnets, Holy Sonnets,* "Death Be Not Proud."

John Dos Passos, 1896-1970, (U.S.) author. *U.S.A., Midcentury.*

Fyodor Dostoyevsky, 1821-1881, (R.) author. *Crime and Punishment, The Brothers Karamazov, The Possessed, The Idiot.*

Arthur Conan Doyle, 1859-1930, (Br.) author, created Sherlock Holmes.

Theodore Dreiser, 1871-1945, (U.S.) novelist. *An American Tragedy, Sister Carrie.*

John Dryden, 1631-1700, (Br.) poet, dramatist, critic. *Fables, Ancient and Modern.*

Alexandre Dumas, 1802-1870, (F.) novelist, dramatist. *The Three Musketeers, The Count of Monte Cristo.*

Alexandre Dumas (fils), 1824-1895, (F.) dramatist, novelist. *La Dame aux camélias, Le Demi-Monde.*

Ilya G. Ehrenburg, 1891-1967, (R.) novelist, journalist. *The Thaw.*

George Eliot, 1819-1880, (Br.) novelist. *Adam Bede, Silas Marner, The Mill on the Floss.*

T.S. Eliot, 1888-1965, (Br.) poet, critic. *The Wasteland,* "The Love Song of J. Alfred Prufrock," *Murder in the Cathedral.*

Ralph Waldo Emerson, 1803-1882, (U.S.) poet, essayist. "The Concord Hymn," "Brahma," "The Rhodora."

James T. Farrell, 1904-1979, (U.S.) novelist. Studs Lonigan trilogy.

William Faulkner, 1897-1962, (U.S.) novelist. *Sanctuary, Light in August, The Sound and the Fury, Absalom, Absalom!*

Edna Ferber, 1885-1968, (U.S.) novelist, dramatist. *Show Boat, Saratoga Trunk, Giant, Dinner at Eight.*

Henry Fielding, 1707-1754, (Br.) novelist. *Tom Jones.*

F. Scott Fitzgerald, 1896-1940, (U.S.) short-story writer, novelist. *The Great Gatsby, Tender is the Night.*

Gustave Flaubert, 1821-1880, (F.) novelist. *Madame Bovary.*

C.S. Forester, 1899-1966, (Br.) novelist. Horatio Hornblower series.

E.M. Forster, 1879-1970, (Br.) novelist. *A Passage to India, Where Angels Fear to Tread, Maurice.*

Anatole France, 1844-1924. (F.) writer. *Penguin Island, My Friend's Book, Le Crime de Sylvestre Bonnard.*

Robert Frost, 1874-1963, (U.S.) poet. *A Boy's Will,* "Birches," "Fire and Ice," "Stopping by Woods on a Snowy Evening."

John Galsworthy, 1867-1923, (Br.) novelist, dramatist. *The Forsythe Saga, A Modern Comedy.*

Erle Stanley Gardner, 1889-1970, (U.S.) author, lawyer.

Perry Mason series.

André Gide, 1869-1951, (F.) writer, *The Immoralist, The Pastoral Symphony, Strait is the Gate.*

Jean Giraudoux, 1882-1944, (F.) novelist, dramatist. *Electra, The Madwoman of Chaillot, Ondine, Tiger at the Gate.*

Johann W. von Goethe, 1749-1832, (G.) poet, dramatist, novelist. *Faust.*

Nikolai Gogol, 1809-1852, (R.) short-story writer, dramatist, novelist. *Dead Souls, The Inspector General.*

Oliver Goldsmith, 1730?-1774, (Br.-Ir.) writer. *The Vicar of Wakefield, She Stoops to Conquer.*

Maxim Gorky, 1868-1936, (R.) writer, founder of Soviet realism. *Mother, The Lower Depths.*

Thomas Gray, 1716-1771, (Br.) poet. "Elegy Written in a Country Churchyard."

Zane Grey, 1875-1939, (U.S.) writer of western stories.

Jakob Grimm, 1785-1863, (G.) philologist, folklorist. *German Methodology, Grimm's Fairy Tales.*

Wilhelm Grimm, 1786-1859, (G.) philologist, folklorist. *Grimm's Fairy Tales.*

Edgar A. Guest, 1881-1959, (U.S.) poet. *A Heap of Livin!*

Dashiell Hammett, 1894-1961, (U.S.) writer of detective fiction, created Sam Spade.

Thomas Hardy, 1840-1928, (Br.) novelist, poet. *The Return of the Native, Tess of the D'Urbervilles, Jude the Obscure.*

Joel Chandler Harris, 1848-1908, (U.S.) short-story writer. Uncle Remus series.

Moss Hart, 1904-1961, (U.S.) playwright. *Once in a Lifetime, You Can't Take It With You.*

Bret Harte, 1836-1902, (U.S.) short-story writer, poet. *The Luck of Roaring Camp.*

Jaroslav Hasek, 1883-1923, (Czech.) writer. *The Good Soldier Schweik.*

Nathaniel Hawthorne, 1804-1864, (U.S.) novelist, short story writer. *The Scarlet Letter, The House of the Seven Gables.*

Heinrich Heine, 1797-1856, (G.) poet. *Book of Songs.*

Ernest Hemingway, 1899-1961, (U.S.) novelist, short-story writer. *A Farewell to Arms, For Whom the Bell Tolls.*

O. Henry (W.S. Porter), 1862-1910, (U.S.) short-story writer. "The Gift of the Magi."

Hermann Hesse, 1877-1962, (G.) novelist, poet. *Death and the Lover, Steppenwolf, Siddhartha.*

Oliver Wendell Holmes, 1809-1894, (U.S.) poet, novelist. *The Autocrat of the Breakfast-Table.*

Alfred E. Housman, 1859-1936, (Br.) poet. *A Shropshire Lad.*

Langston Hughes, 1902-1967, (U.S.) poet, playwright. *The Weary Blues, One-Way Ticket, Shakespeare in Harlem.*

Victor Hugo, 1802-1885, (F.) poet, dramatist, novelist. *Notre Dame de Paris, Les Misérables.*

Aldous Huxley 1894-1963, (Br.) author. *Point Counter Point, Brave New World.*

Henrik Ibsen, 1828-1906, (Nor.) dramatist, poet. *A Doll's House, Ghosts, The Wild Duck, Hedda Gabler.*

William Inge, 1913-1973, (U.S.) playwright. *Come Back Little Sheba, Bus Stop, The Dark at the Top of the Stairs, Picnic.*

Washington Irving, 1783-1859, (U.S.) essayist, author. "Rip Van Winkle," "The Legend of Sleepy Hollow."

Shirley Jackson, 1919-1965, (U.S.) writer. *The Lottery.*

Henry James, 1843-1916, (U.S.) novelist, critic. *Washington Square, Portrait of a Lady, The American.*

Robinson Jeffers, 1887-1962, (U.S.) poet, dramatist. *Tamar and Other Poems, Medea.*

Samuel Johnson, 1709-1784, (Br.) author, scholar, critic. *Dictionary of the English Language.*

Ben Jonson, 1572-1637, (Br.) dramatist, poet. *The Alchemist, Volpone.*

James Joyce, 1882-1941, (Ir.) novelist. *Ulysses, A Portrait of the Artist as a Young Man, Finnegans Wake.*

Franz Kafka, 1883-1924, (G.) novelist, short-story writer. *The Trial, Amerika, The Castle.*

George S. Kaufman, 1889-1961, (U.S.) playwright. *The Man Who Came to Dinner, You Can't Take It With You, Stage Door.*

Nikos Kazantzakis, 1883?-1957, (Gk.) novelist. *Zorba the Greek, A Greek Passion.*

Joyce Kilmer, 1886-1918, (U.S.) poet, "Trees."

Rudyard Kipling, 1865-1936, (Br.) author, poet. "The White Man's Burden," "Gunga Din," *The Jungle Book.*

Jean de la Fontaine, 1621-1695, (F.) poet. *Fables choisies.*

Pär Lagerkvist, 1891-1974, (Swed.) poet, dramatist, novelist. *Barabbas, The Sybil.*

Selma Lagerlöf, 1858-1940, (Swed.) novelist. *Jerusalem, The Ring of the Lowenskolds.*

Alphonse de Lamartine, 1790-1869, (F.) poet, novelist, statesman. *Méditations poétiques.*

Charles Lamb, 1775-1834, (Br.) essayist. *Specimens of English Dramatic Poets, Essays of Elia.*

Giuseppe di Lampedusa, 1896-1957, (It.) novelist. *The Leopard.*

Ring Lardner, 1885-1933, (U.S.) short story writer, humorist. *You Know Me, Al.*

D. H. Lawrence, 1885-1930, (Br.) novelist. *Women in Love, Lady Chatterley's Lover, Sons and Lovers.*

Mikhail Lermontov, 1814-1841, (R.) novelist, poet. "Demon," *Hero of Our Time.*

Alain-René Lesage, 1668-1747, (F.) novelist. *Gil Blas de Santillane.*

Gotthold Lessing, 1729-1781, (G.) dramatist, philosopher, critic. *Miss Sara Sampson, Minna von Barnhelm.*

Sinclair Lewis, 1885-1951, (U.S.) novelist, playwright. *Babbitt, Arrowsmith, Dodsworth, Main Street.*

Vachel Lindsay, 1879-1931, (U.S.) poet. *General William Booth Enters into Heaven, The Congo.*

Hugh Lofting, 1886-1947, (Br.) children's author. Dr. Doolittle series.

Jack London, 1876-1916, (U.S.) novelist, journalist. *Call of the Wild, The Sea-Wolf.*

Henry Wadsworth Longfellow, 1807-1882, (U.S.) poet. "The Wreck of the Hesperus," *Evangeline, The Song of Hiawatha.*

Amy Lowell, 1874-1925, (U.S.) poet, critic. *A Dome of Many-Colored Glass,* "Patterns," "Lilacs."

James Russell Lowell, 1819-1891, (U.S.) poet, editor. *Poems, The Bigelow Papers.*

Robert Lowell, 1917-1977, (U.S.) poet. "Lord Weary's Castle."

Emil Ludwig, 1881-1948, (G.) biographer. *Goethe, Beethoven, Napoleon, Bismarck.*

Niccolò Machiavelli, 1469-1527, (It.) author, statesman. *The Prince, Discourses on Livy.*

Stéphane Mallarmé, 1842-1898, (F.) poet. *The Afternoon of a Faun.*

Thomas Malory, ?-1471, (Br.) writer. *Morte d'Arthur.*

Andre Malraux, 1901-1976, (F.) novelist. *Man's Fate, The Voices of Silence.*

Osip Mandelstam, 1891-1938, (R.) Acmeist poet.

Thomas Mann, 1875-1955, (G.) novelist, essayist. *Buddenbrooks, Death in Venice, The Magic Mountain.*

Katherine Mansfield, 1888-1923, (Br.) short story writer. *Bliss, The Garden Party.*

Christopher Marlowe, 1564-1593, (Br.) dramatist, poet. *Tamburlaine the Great, Dr. Faustus, The Jew of Malta.*

John Masefield, 1878-1967, (Br.) poet. "Sea Fever," "Cargoes," *Salt Water Ballads.*

Edgar Lee Masters, 1869-1950, (U.S.) poet, biographer. *Spoon River Anthology.*

W. Somerset Maugham, 1874-1965, (Br.) author. *Of Human Bondage, The Razor's Edge, The Moon and Sixpence.*

Guy de Maupassant, 1850-1893, (F.) novelist, short-story writer. *A Life, Bel-Ami,* "The Necklace."

Vladimir Mayakovsky, 1893-1930, (R.) poet, dramatist. *The Cloud in Trousers.*

Carson McCullers, 1917-1967, (U.S.) novelist. *The Heart is a Lonely Hunter, Member of the Wedding.*

Herman Melville, 1819-1891, (U.S.) novelist, poet. *Moby Dick, Typee, Billy Budd, Omoo.*

H.L. Mencken, 1880-1956, (U.S.) author, critic, editor. *Prejudices, The American Language.*

George Meredith, 1828-1909, (Br.) novelist, poet. *The Ordeal of Richard Feverel, The Egoist.*

Prosper Mérimée, 1803-1870, (F.) author. *Carmen, Colomba.*

Edna St. Vincent Millay, 1892-1950, (U.S.) poet. *The Harp Weaver and Other Poems, A Few Figs from Thistles.*

A.A. Milne, 1882-1956, (Br.) author. *When We Were Very Young, Winnie-the-Pooh, The House at Pooh Corner.*

John Milton, 1608-1674, (Br.) poet. *Paradise Lost, Samson Agonistes.*

Gabriela Mistral, 1889-1957, (Chil.) poet. *Sonnets of Death, Desolación, Tala, Lagar.*

Margaret Mitchell, 1900-1949, (U.S.) novelist. *Gone With the Wind.*

Jean Baptiste Molière, 1622-1673, (F.) dramatist. *Le Tartuffe, Le Misanthrope, Le Bourgeois Gentilhomme.*

Ferenc Molnár, 1878-1952, (Hung.) dramatist, novelist. *Liliom, The Guardsman, The Swan.*

Michel de Montaigne, 1533-1592, (F.) essayist. *Essais.*

Clement C. Moore, 1779-1863, (U.S.) poet, educator. "A Visit from Saint Nicholas."

Marianne Moore, 1887-1972, (U.S.) poet. *Observations, O to Be a Dragon.*

Thomas More, 1478-1535, (Br.) author. *Utopia.*

H.H. Munro (Saki), 1870-1916, (Br.) author. *Reginald, The Chronicles of Clovis, Beasts and Super-Beasts.*

Alfred de Musset, 1810-1857, (F.) poet, dramatist. *Confession d'un enfant du siècle.*

Vladimir Nabokov, 1899-1977, (U.S.) author. *Lolita, Ada.*

Ogden Nash, 1902-1971, (U.S.) poet. *Hard Lines, I'm a Stranger Here Myself, The Private Dining Room.*

Pablo Neruda, 1904-1973, (Chil.) poet. *Twenty Love Poems and One Song of Despair, Toward the Splendid City.*

Sean O'Casey, 1884-1964, (Ir.) dramatist. *Juno and the Paycock, The Plough and the Stars.*

Flannery O'Connor, 1925-1964, (U.S.) novelist, short story writer. *Wise Blood,* "A Good Man Is Hard to Find," "Everything That Rises Must Converge."

Clifford Odets, 1906-1963, (U.S.) playwright. *Waiting for Lefty, Awake and Sing, Golden Boy, The Country Girl.*

John O'Hara, 1905-1970, (U.S.) novelist. *Butterfield 8, From the Terrace, Appointment in Samarra.*

Omar Khayyam, c. 1028-1122, (Per.) poet, mathematician. *Rubaiyat.*

Eugene O'Neill, 1888-1953, (U.S.) playwright. *Emperor Jones, Anna Christie, Long Day's Journey into Night, Desire Under the Elms, Mourning Becomes Electra.*

George Orwell, 1903-1950, (Br.) novelist, essayist. *Animal Farm, Nineteen Eighty-Four.*

Thomas (Tom) Paine, 1737-1809, (U.S.) author, political theorist. *Common Sense.*

Dorothy Parker, 1893-1967, (U.S.) poet, short-story writer. *Enough Rope, Laments for the Living.*

Boris Pasternak, 1890-1960, (R.) poet, novelist. *Doctor Zhivago, My Sister, Life.*

Samuel Pepys, 1633-1703, (Br.) public official, author of the greatest diary in the English language.

S. J. Perelman, 1904-1979, (U.S.) humorist. *The Road to Milltown, Under the Spreading Atrophy.*

Francesco Petrarca, 1304-1374, (It.) poet, humanist. *Africa; Trionfi, Canzoniere, On Solitude.*

Luigi Pirandello, 1867-1936, (It.) novelist, dramatist. *Six Characters in Search of an Author.*

Edgar Allan Poe, 1809-1849, (U.S.) poet, short-story writer, critic. "Annabel Lee," "The Raven," "The Purloined Letter."

Alexander Pope, 1688-1744, (Br.) poet. *The Rape of the Lock, An Essay on Man.*

Ezra Pound, 1885-1972, (U.S.) poet. *Cantos.*

Marcel Proust, 1871-1922, (F.) novelist. *A la recherche du temps perdu (Remembrance of Things Past).*

Aleksandr Pushkin, 1799-1837, (R.) poet, prose writer. *Boris Godunov, Eugene Onegin, The Bronze Horseman.*

François Rabelais, 1495-1553, (F.) writer, physician. Gargantua, Pantagruel.

Jean Racine, 1639-1699, (F.) dramatist. *Andromaque, Phèdre, Bérénice, Britannicus.*

Erich Maria Remarque, 1898-1970, (Ger.-U.S.) novelist. *All Quiet on the Western Front.*

Samuel Richardson, 1689-1761, (Br.) novelist. *Clarissa Harlowe, Pamela; or, Virtue Rewarded.*

James Whitcomb Riley, 1849-1916, (U.S.) poet. "When the Frost is on the Pumpkin," "Little Orphant Annie."

Rainer Maria Rilke, 1875-1926, (G.) poet. *Life and Songs, Divine Elegies, Sonnets to Orpheus.*

Arthur Rimbaud, 1854-1891, (F.) *A Season in Hell,* "Le Bateau ivre."

Edwin Arlington Robinson, 1869-1935, (U.S.) poet. "Richard Cory," "Miniver Cheevy."

Theodore Roethke, 1908-1963, (U.S.) poet. *Open House, The Waking, The Far Field.*

Romain Rolland, 1866-1944, (F.) novelist, biographer. *Jean-Christophe.*

Pierre de Ronsard, 1524-1585, (F.) poet. *Sonnets pour Hélène.*

Edmond Rostand, 1868-1918, (F.) poet, dramatist. *Cyrano de Bergerac.*

Damon Runyon, 1884-1946, (U.S.) short-story writer, journalist. *Guys and Dolls, Blue Plate Special.*

John Ruskin, 1819-1900, (Br.) critic, social theorist. *Modern Painters, The Seven Lamps of Architecture.*

Antoine de Saint-Exupery, 1900-1944, (F.) writer, aviator. *Wind, Sand and Stars, Le Petit Prince.*

George Sand, 1804-1876, (F.) novelist. *Consuelo, The Haunted Pool, Les Maitres sonneurs.*

Carl Sandburg, 1878-1967, (U.S.) poet. *Chicago Poems, Smoke and Steel, Harvest Poems.*

George Santayana, 1863-1952, (U.S.) poet, essayist, philosopher. *The Sense of Beauty, The Realms of Being.*

Friedrich von Schiller, 1759-1805, (G.) dramatist, poet, historian. *Don Carlos, Maria Stuart, Wilhelm Tell.*

Sir Walter Scott, 1771-1832, (Sc.) novelist, poet. Ivanhoe, Rob Roy, The Bride of Lammermoor.

William Shakespeare, 1564-1616, (Br.) dramatist, poet. *Romeo and Juliet, Hamlet, King Lear, The Merchant of Venice.*

George Bernard Shaw, 1856-1950, (Ir.) playwright, critic. *St. Joan, Pygmalion, Major Barbara, Man and Superman.*

Mary Wollstonecraft Shelley, 1797-1851, (Br.) author. *Frankenstein.*

Percy Bysshe Shelley, 1792-1822, (Br.) poet. *Prometheus Unbound, Adonais,* "Ode to the West Wind," "To a Skylark."

Richard B. Sheridan, 1751-1816, (Br.) dramatist. *The Rivals, School for Scandal.*

Robert Sherwood, 1896-1955, (U.S.) playwright. *The Petrified Forest, Abe Lincoln in Illinois, Reunion in Vienna.*

Upton Sinclair, 1878-1968, (U.S.) novelist. *The Jungle.*

Edmund Spenser, 1552-1599, (Br.) poet. *The Faerie Queen.*

Richard Steele, 1672-1729, (Br.) essayist, playwright, began the Tatler and Spectator. *The Conscious Lovers.*

Lincoln Steffens, 1866-1936, (U.S.) editor, author. *The Shame of the Cities.*

Gertrude Stein, 1874-1946, (U.S.) author. *Three Lives.*

John Steinbeck, 1902-1968, (U.S.) novelist. *Grapes of Wrath, Of Mice and Men, Winter of Our Discontent.*

Stendhal (Marie Henri Beyle), 1783-1842, poet. novelist. *The Red and the Black, The Charterhouse of Parma.*

Laurence Sterne, 1713-1768, (Br.) novelist. *Tristram Shandy.*

Wallace Stevens, 1879-1955, (U.S.) poet. *Harmonium, The Man With the Blue Guitar, Transport to Summer.*

Robert Louis Stevenson, 1850-1894, (Br.) novelist, poet, essayist. *Treasure Island, A Child's Garden of Verses.*

Rex Stout, 1886-1975, (U.S.) mystery novelist, created Nero Wolfe.

Harriet Beecher Stowe, 1811-1896, (U.S.) novelist. *Uncle Tom's Cabin.*

Lytton Strachey, 1880-1932, (Br.) biographer, critic. *Eminent Victorians, Queen Victoria, Elizabeth and Essex.*

August Strindberg, 1849-1912, (Swed.) dramatist, novelist. *The Father, Miss Julie, The Creditors.*

Jonathan Swift, 1667-1745, (Br.) author. *Gulliver's Travels.*

Algernon C. Swinburne, 1837-1909, (Br.) poet, critic. *Songs Before Sunrise.*

John M. Synge, 1871-1909, (Ir.) poet, dramatist. *Riders to the Sea, The Playboy of the Western World.*

Rabindranath Tagore, 1861-1941, (Ind.), author, poet. *Sadhana, The Realization of Life, Gitanjali.*

Booth Tarkington, 1869-1946, (U.S.) novelist. *Seventeen, Alice Adams, Penrod.*

Sara Teasdale, 1884-1933, (U.S.) poet. *Helen of Troy and Other Poems, Rivers to the Sea, Flame and Shadow.*

Alfred Lord Tennyson, 1809-1892, (Br.) poet. *Idylls of the King, In Memoriam,* "The Charge of the Light Brigade."

William Makepeace Thackeray, 1811-1863, (Br.) novelist. *Vanity Fair.*

Dylan Thomas, 1914-1953, (Welsh) poet. *Under Milk Wood, A Child's Christmas in Wales.*

James Thurber, 1894-1961, (U.S.) humorist, artist. *The New Yorker, The Owl in the Attic, Thurber Carnival.*

J.R.R. Tolkien, 1892-1973, (Br.) author. *The Hobbit, Lord of the Rings.*

Lev Tolstoy, 1828-1910, (R.) novelist. *War and Peace, Anna Karenina.*

Anthony Trollope, 1815-1882, (Br.) novelist. *The Warden, Barchester Towers,* The Palliser novels.

Ivan Turgenev, 1818-1883, (R.) novelist, short-story writer. *Fathers and Sons, First Love, A Month in the Country.*

Mark Twain (Samuel Clemens), 1835-1910, (U.S.) novelist, humorist. *The Adventures of Huckleberry Finn, Tom Sawyer.*

Sigrid Undset, 1881-1949, (Nor.) novelist. poet. *Kristin Lavransdatter.*

Paul Valéry, 1871-1945, (F.) poet, critic. *La Jeune Parque, The Graveyard by the Sea.*

Jules Verne, 1828-1905, (F.) novelist, originator of modern science fiction. *Twenty Thousand Leagues Under the Sea.*

François Villon, 1431-1463?, (F.) poet. *Le petit et le Grand, Testament.*

Evelyn Waugh, 1903-1966, (Br.) satirist. *The Loved One.*

H.G. Wells, 1866-1946, (Br.) author. *The Time Machine, The Invisible Man, The War of the Worlds.*

Edith Wharton, 1862-1937, (U.S.) novelist. *The Age of Innocence, The House of Mirth.*

T.H. White, 1906-1964, (Br.) author. *The Once and Future King.*

Walt Whitman, 1819-1892, (U.S.) poet. *Leaves of Grass.*

John Greenleaf Whittier, 1807-1892, (U.S.) poet, journalist. *Snow-bound.*

Oscar Wilde, 1854-1900, (Ir.) author, wit. *The Picture of Dorian Gray, The Importance of Being Earnest.*

Thornton Wilder, 1897-1975, (U.S.) playwright. *Our Town, The Skin of Our Teeth, The Matchmaker.*

William Carlos Williams, 1883-1963, (U.S.) poet, physician. *Tempers, Al Que Quiere!, Paterson.*

Edmund Wilson, 1895-1972, (U.S.) author, literary and social critic. *Axel's Castle, To the Finland Station.*

P.G. Wodehouse, 1881-1975, (U.S.) poet, dramatist. The "Jeeves" novels, *Anything Goes.*

Thomas Wolfe, 1900-1938, (U.S.) novelist. *Look Homeward, Angel, You Can't Go Home Again, Of Time and the River.*

Virginia Woolf, 1882-1941, (Br.) novelist, essayist. *Mrs. Dalloway, To the Lighthouse, The Waves.*

William Wordsworth, 1770-1850, (Br.) poet. "Tintern Abbey," "Ode: Intimations of Immortality."

William Butler Yeats, 1865-1939, (Ir.) poet, playwright. *The Wild Swans at Coole, The Tower, Last Poems.*

Émile Zola, 1840-1902, (F.) novelist. *Nana, The Dram Shop.*

Poets Laureate of England

There is no authentic record of the origin of the office of Poet Laureate of England. According to Warton, there was a Versificator Regis, or King's Poet, in the reign of Henry III (1216-1272), and he was paid 100 shillings a year. Geoffrey Chaucer (1340-1400) assumed the title of Poet Laureate, and in 1389 got a royal grant of a yearly allowance of wine. In the reign of Edward IV (1461-1483), John Kay held the post. Under Henry VII (1485-1509), Andrew Bernard was the Poet Laureate, and was succeeded under Henry VIII (1509-1547) by John Skelton. Next came Edmund Spenser, who died in 1599; then Samuel Daniel, appointed 1599, and then Ben Jonson, 1619. Sir William D'Avenant was appointed in 1637. He was a godson of William Shakespeare.

Others were John Dryden, 1670; Thomas Shadwell, 1688; Nahum Tate, 1692; Nicholas Rowe, 1715; the Rev. Laurence Eusden, 1718; Colley Cibber, 1730; William Whitehead, 1757, on the refusal of Gray; Rev. Thomas Warton, 1785, on the refusal of Mason; Henry J. Pye, 1790; Robert Southey, 1813, on the refusal of Sir Walter Scott; William Wordsworth, 1843; Alfred, Lord Tennyson, 1850; Alfred Austin, 1896; Robert Bridges, 1913; John Masefield, 1930; Cecil Day Lewis, 1967; Sir John Betjeman, 1972.

Noted Artists and Sculptors of the Past

Artists are painters unless otherwise indicated.

Washington Allston, 1779-1842, landscapist. The Deluge.

Albrecht Altdorfer, 1480-1538, landscapist. Birth of the Virgin.

Andrea del Sarto, 1486-1530, frescoes. Madonna of the Harpies.

Fra Angelico, 1387-1455, Renaissance muralist. Madonna of the Linen Drapers' Guild.

Aleksandr Archipenko, 1887-1967, Boxing Match, Medranos.

John James Audubon, 1785-1851, Birds of America.

Hans Baldun-Grien, 1484-1545, Todentanz.

Ernst Barlach, 1870-1938, Expressionist sculptor. Man Drawing a Sword.

Frederic-Auguste Bartholdi, 1834-1904, Liberty Enlightening the World, Lion of Belfort.

Fra Bartolommeo, 1472-1517, Vision of St. Bernard.

Aubrey Beardsley, 1872-1898, illustrator. Salome, Lysistrata.

Max Beckmann, 1884-1950, Expressionist. The Descent from the Cross.

Gentile Bellini, 1426-1507, Renaissance. Procession in St. Mark's Square.

Giovanni Bellini, 1428-1516, St. Francis in Ecstasy.

Jacopo Bellini, 1400-1470, Crucifixion.

George W. Bellows, 1882-1925, sports artist. Stag at Sharkey's.

Thomas Hart Benton, 1889-1975, American regionalist. Threshing Wheat, Arts of the West.

Gian Lorenzo Bernini, 1598-1680, Baroque reliefs. The Assumption.

Albert Bierstadt, 1830-1902, landscapist. The Rocky Mountains, Mount Corcoran.

George Caleb Bingham, 1811-1879, Fur Traders Descending the Missouri.

William Blake, 1752-1827, engraver. Book of Job, Songs of Innocence, Songs of Experience.

Rosa Bonheur, 1822-1899, The Horse Fair.

Pierre Bonnard, 1867-1947, Intimist. The Breakfast Room.

Paul-Emile Borduas, 1905-1960, Abstractionist. Leeward of the Island, Enchanted Shields.

Gutzon Borglum, 1871-1941, Mt. Rushmore Memorial.

Hieronymus Bosch, 1450-1516, religious allegories. The Crowning with Thorns.

Sandro Botticelli, 1444-1510, Renaissance. Birth of Venus.

Constantin Brancusi, 1876-1957, Abstract sculptor. Flying Turtle, The Kiss.

Georges Braque, 1882-1963, Cubist. Violin and Palette.

Pieter Bruegel the Elder, 1525-1569, Flemish landscapist. The Peasant Dance.

Pieter Bruegel the Younger, 1564-1638, Village Fair, The Crucifixon.

Edward Burne-Jones, 1833-1898, Pre-Raphaelite artist-craftsman. The Mirror of Venus.

Alexander Calder, 1898-1976, sculptor. Lobster Trap and Fish Tail.

Caravaggio, 1573-1610, Baroque. The Supper at Emmaus.

Emily Carr, 1871-1945, landscapist. Blunden Harbour, Big Raven.

Carlo Carra, 1881-1966, Metaphysical school. Lot's Daughters.

Mary Cassatt, 1845-1926, Impressionist. Woman Bathing.

George Catlin, 1796-1872, American Indian life. Gallery of Indians.

Benvenuto Cellini, 1500-1571, Mannerist sculptor, goldsmith. Perseus.

Paul Cezanne, 1839-1906, early Cubist. Card Players, Mont-Sainte-Victoire with Large Pine Trees.

Jean-Baptiste-Simeon-Chardin, 1699-1779, still lifes. The Kiss, The Grace.

Frederic Church, 1826-1900, Hudson River school. Niagara, Andes of Ecuador.

Cimabue, 1240-1302, Byzantine mosaicist. Madonna Enthroned with St. Francis.

Claude Lorrain, 1600-1682, ideal-landscapist. The Enchanted Castle.

Thomas Cole, 1801-1848, Hudson River school. The Oxbow.

John Constable, 1776-1837, landscapist. Salisbury Cathedral from the Bishop's Grounds.

John Singleton Copley, 1738-1815, portraitist. Samuel Adams, Watson and the Shark.

Lovis Corinth, 1858-1925, Expressionist. Apocalypse.

Jean-Baptiste-Camille Corot, 1796-1875, landscapist. Souvenir de Mortefontaine, Pastorale.

Correggio, 1494-1534, Renaissance muralist. Mystic Marriage of St. Catherine.

Gustave Courbet, 1819-1877, Realist. The Artist's Studio.

Lucas Cranach the Elder, 1472-1553, Protestant Reformation portraitist. Luther.

Nathaniel Currier, 1813-1888, and **James M. Ives,** 1824-1895, lithographers. A Midnight Race on the Mississippi.

Honore Daumier, 1808-1879, caricaturist. The Third-Class Carriage.

Jacques-Louis David, 1748-1825, Neoclassicist. The Oath of the Horatii.

Arthur Davies, 1862-1928, Romantic landscapist. Unicorns.

Edgar Degas, 1834-1917, The Ballet Class.

Eugene Delacroix, 1798-1863, Romantic. Massacre at Chios.

Paul Delaroche, 1797-1859, historical themes. Children of Edward.

Luca Della Robbia, 1400-1482, Renaissance terracotta artist. Cantoria (singing gallery), Florence cathedral.

Donato Donatello, 1386-1466, Renaissance sculptor. David, Gattamelata.

Raoul Dufy, 1877-1953, Fauvist. Chateau and Horses.

Asher Brown Durand, 1796-1886, Hudson River school. Kindred Spirits.

Albrecht Durer, 1471-1528, Renaissance engraver, woodcuts. St. Jerome in His Study, Melancholia I, Apocalypse.

Thomas Eakins, 1844-1916, Realist. The Gross Clinic.

Jacob Epstein, 1880-1959, religious and allegorical sculptor. Genesis, Ecce Homo.

Jan Van Eyck, 1366-1440, naturalistic panels. Adoration of the Lamb.

Anselm Feuerbach, 1829-1880, Romantic Classicism. Judgement of Paris, Iphigeneia.

John Bernard Flannagan, 1895-1942, primitive animal sculptor. Triumph of the Egg.

Jean-Honore Fragonard, 1732-1806, Rococo. The Swing.

Daniel C. French, 1850-1931, The Minute Man of Concord; seated Lincoln, Lincoln Memorial, Washington, D.C.

Caspar Daniel Friedrich, 1774-1840, Romantic landscapes. Man and Woman Gazing at the Moon.

Thomas Gainsborough, 1727-1788, portraitist. The Blue Boy.

Paul Gauguin, 1848-1903, Post-impressionist. The Tahitians.

Lorenzo Ghiberti, 1378-1455, Renaissance sculptor. Gates of Paradise baptistry doors, Florence.

Alberto Giacometti, 1901-1966, attenuated sculptures of solitary figures. Man Pointing.

Giorgione, 1477-1510, Renaissance. The Tempest.

Giotto, 1276-1337, Renaissance. Presentation of Christ in the Temple.

Francois Girardon, 1628-1715, Baroque sculptor of classical themes. Apollo Tended by the Nymphs.

Vincent van Gogh, 1853-1890, The Starry Night, L'Arlesienne.
Arshile Gorky, 1905-1948, Surrealist. The Liver Is the Cock's Comb.
Francisco de Goya y Lucientes, 1746-1828, The Naked Maya, The Disasters of War (etchings).
El Greco, 1541-1614, View of Toledo, Burial of the Count of Orgaz.
Horatio Greenough, 1805-1852, Neo-classical sculptor. George Washington.
Matthias Grünewald, 1480-1528, mystical religious themes. The Resurrection.
Franz Hals, 1580-1666, portraitist. Laughing Cavalier, Gypsy Girl.
Childe Hassam, 1859-1935, Impressionist. Southwest Wind.
Edward Hicks, 1780-1849, primitive folk painter. The Peaceable Kingdom.
Hans Hofmann, 1880-1966, early Abstract Expressionist. Spring. The Gate.
William Hogarth, 1697-1764, caricaturist. The Rake's Progress.
Katsushika Hokusai, 1760-1849, printmaker. Crabs.
Hans Holbein the Elder, 1460-1524, late Gothic. Presentation of Christ in the Temple.
Hans Holbein the Younger, 1497-1543, portraitist. Henry VIII.
Winslow Homer, 1836-1910, marine themes. Marine Coast, High Cliff.
Edward Hopper, 1882-1967, realistic urban scenes. Sunlight in a Cafeteria.
Jean-Auguste-Dominique Ingres, 1780-1867, Classicist. Valpincon Bather.
George Innes, 1825-1894, luminous landscapist. Delaware Water Gap.
Vasily Kandinsky, 1866-1944, Abstractionist. Capricious Forms.
Paul Klee, 1879-1940, Abstractionist. Twittering Machine.
Kathe Kollwitz, 1867-1945, printmaker, social justice themes. The Peasant War.
Gaston Lachaise, 1882-1935, figurative sculptor. Standing Woman.
John La Farge, 1835-1910, muralist. Red and White Peonies.
Fernand Leger, 1881-1955, machine art. The Cyclists, Adam and Eve.
Leonardo da Vinci, 1452-1519, Mona Lisa, Last Supper, The Annunciation.
Emanuel Leutz, 1816-1868, historical themes. Washington Crossing the Delaware.
Jacques Lipchitz, 1891-1973, Cubist sculptor. Harpist.
Filippino Lippi, 1457-1504, Renaissance. The Vision of St. Bernard.
Fra Filippo Lippi, 1406-1469, Renaissance. Coronation of the Virgin.
Aristide Maillol, 1861-1944, sculptor. Night, The Mediterranean.
Edouard Manet, 1832-1883, forerunner of Impressionism. Luncheon on the Grass, Olympia.
Andrea Mantegna, 1431-1506, Renaissance frescoes. Triumph of Caesar.
Franz Marc, 1880-1916, Expressionist. Blue Horses.
John Marin, 1870-1953, expressionist seascapes. Maine Island.
Reginald Marsh, 1898-1954, satirical artist. Tattoo and Haircut.
Tommaso Masaccio, 1401-1428, Renaissance. The Tribute Money.
Henri Matisse, 1869-1954, Fauvist. Woman with the Hat.
Michelangelo Buonarroti, 1475-1564, Pieta, David, Moses, Battle of Cascina, The Last Judgment.
Carl Milles, 1875-1955, expressive rhythmic sculptor. Playing Bears.
Jean-Francois Millet, 1814-1875, painter of peasant subjects. The Gleaners, The Man with a Hoe.
David Milne, 1882-1953, landscapist. Boston Corner, Berkshire Hills.
Amadeo Modigliani, 1884-1920, Reclining Nude.
Piet Mondrian, 1872-1944, Abstractionist. Composition.
Claude Monet, 1840-1926, Impressionist. The Bridge at Argenteuil, Haystacks.
Gustave Moreau, 1826-1898, Symbolist. The Apparition, Dance of Salome.
James Wilson Morrice, 1865-1924, landscapist. The Ferry, Quebec, Venice, Looking Over the Lagoon.
Grandma Moses, 1860-1961, primitive folk painter. Out for the Christmas Trees.
Edvard Munch, 1863-1944, Expressionist death themes. The Cry.
Bartolome Murillo, 1618-1682, Baroque religious artist. Vision of St. Anthony. The Two Trinities.
Barnett Newman, 1905-1970, Abstract Expressionist. Stations of the Cross.
Jose Clemente Orozco, 1883-1949, frescoes. House of Tears.
Charles Willson Peale, 1741-1827, American Revolutionary portraitist. Washington, Franklin, Jefferson, John Adams.
Rembrandt Peale, 1778-1860, post-Revolutionary portraitist. Thomas Jefferson.
Pietro Perugino, 1446-1523, Renaissance. Delivery of the Keys to St. Peter.
Pablo Picasso, 1881-1973, Guernica, Dove, Head of a Woman.
Piero della Francesca, 1420-1492, Renaissance. Duke of Urbino, Flagellation of Christ.
Camille Pissarro, 1830-1903, Impressionist. Morning Sunlight.
Jackson Pollock, 1912-1956, Abstract Expressionist. Autumn Rhythm.
Nicholas Poussin, 1594-1665, Baroque pictorial classicism. St. John on Patmos.
Maurice B. Prendergast, 1861-1924, Post-impressionist water colorist. Umbrellas in the Rain.
Pierre-Paul Prud'hon, 1758-1823, Romanticist. Crime pursued by Vengenance and Justice.
Puvis de Chavannes, 1824-1898, muralist. The Poor Fisherman.
Raphael, 1483-1520, Renaissance. Disputa, School of Athens.
Man Ray, 1890-1976, Dadaist. Observing Time, The Lovers.
Odilon Redon, 1840-1916, Symbolist lithographer. In the Dream.
Rembrandt van Rijn, 1606-1669, The Bridal Couple, The Night Watch.
Frederic Remington, 1861-1909, portrayal of the American West. Bronco Buster, Cavalry Charge on the Southern Plains.
Pierre-Auguste Renoir, 1841-1919, Impressionist. The Luncheon of the Boating Party.
Ilya Repin, 1844-1918, historical canvases. Zaporozhye Cossacks.
Joshua Reynolds, 1723-1792, portraitist. Mrs. Siddons as the Tragic Muse.
Diego Rivera, 1886-1957, frescoes. The Fecund Earth.
Auguste Rodin, 1840-1917, The Thinker, The Burghers of Calais.
Mark Rothko, 1903-1970, Abstract Expressionist. Light, Earth and Blue.
Georges Rouault, 1871-1958, Expressionist. The Old King.
Henri Rousseau, 1844-1910, primitive exotic themes. The Snake Charmer.
Theodore Rousseau, 1812-1867, landscapist. Under the Birches, Evening.
Peter Paul Rubens, 1577-1640, Baroque. Mystic Marriage of St. Catherine.
Andrey Rublyov, 1370-1430, iconographer. Old Testament Trinity.
Albert Pinkham Ryder, 1847-1917, seascapes and allegories. Toilers of the Sea.
Augustus Saint-Gaudens, 1848-1901, memorial statues. Farragut, Mrs. Henry Adams (Grief).
Andrea Sansovino, 1460-1529, Renaissance sculptor. Baptism of Christ.
Jacopo Sansovino, 1486-1570, Renaissance sculptor. St. John the Baptist.
John Singer Sargent, 1856-1925, Edwardian society portraitist. The Wyndham Sisters, Madam X.
Johann Gottfried Schadow, 1764-1850, monumental sculptor. Quadriga, Bradenburg Gate.
Georges Seurat, 1859-1891, Pointillist. Sunday Afternoon on the Island of Grande Jatte.
Gino Severini, 1883-1891, Futurist and Cubist. Dynamic Hieroglyph of the Bal Tabarin.
Ben Shahn, 1898-1969, social and political themes. Sacco and Vanzetti series, Seurat's Lunch, Handball.
Charles Sheeler, 1883-1965, Abstractionist. Upper Deck, Rolling Power.
David Alfaro Siqueiros, 1896-1974, political muralist. March of Humanity.
John F. Sloan, 1871-1951, depictions of New York City. Wake of the Ferry.
David Smith, 1906-1965, welded metal sculpture. Hudson River Landscape, Zig, Cubi series.
Gilbert Stuart, 1755-1828, portraitist. George Washington.
Thomas Sully, 1783-1872, portraitist. Col. Thomas Handasyd Perkins, The Passage of the Delaware.
Yves Tanguy, 1900-1955, Surrealist. Rose of the Four Winds.
Thomas J. Thomson, 1877-1918, landscapist. Spring Ice.
Giovanni Battista Tiepolo, 1696-1770, Rococo frescoes. The Crucifixion.
Tintoretto, 1518-1594, Mannerist. The Last Supper.
Titian, 1477-1576, Renaissance. Venus and the Lute Player,

The Bacchanal.

Henri de Toulouse-Lautrec, 1864-1901, At the Moulin Rouge.

John Trumbull, 1756-1843, historical themes. The Declaration of Independence.

J.M.W. Turner, 1755-1851, Romantic landscapist. Snow Storm.

Paolo Uccello, 1397-1475, Gothic-Renaissance. The Rout of San Romano.

Maurice Utrillo, 1883-1955, Impressionist. Sacre-Coeur de Montmartre.

John Vanderlyn, 1775-1852, Neo-classicist. Ariadne Asleep on the Island of Naxos.

Anthony Van Dyck, 1599-1641, Baroque portraitist. Portrait of Charles I Hunting.

Diego Velazquez, 1599-1660, Baroque. Las Meninas, Portrait of Juan de Pareja.

Jan Vermeer, 1632-1675, interior genre subjects. Young Woman with a Water Jug.

Paolo Veronese, 1528-1588, devotional themes, vastly peopled canvases. The Temptation of St. Anthony.

Andrea del Verrocchio, 1435-1488, Florentine sculptor. Colleoni.

Maurice de Vlaminck, 1876-1958, Fauvist landscapist. The Storm.

Antoine Watteau, 1684-1721, Rococo painter of "scenes of gallantry". The Embarkation for Cythera.

George Frederic Watts, 1817-1904, painter and sculptor of grandiose allegorical themes. Hope, Physical Energy.

Benjamin West, 1738-1820, realistic historical themes. Death of General Wolfe.

James Abbott McNeill Whistler, 1834-1903, Arrangement in Grey and Black, No. 1: The Artist's Mother.

Archibald M. Willard, 1836-1918, The Spirit of '76.

Grant Wood, 1891-1942, Midwestern regionalist. American Gothic, Daughters of Revolution.

Osip Zadkine, 1890-1967, School of Paris sculptor. The Destroyed City, Musicians, Christ.

Noted Philosophers and Religionists of the Past

Lyman Abbott, 1835-1922, (U.S.) clergyman, reformer; advocate of Christian Socialism.

Pierre Abelard, 1079-1142, (F.) philosopher, theologian, and teacher, used dialectic method to support Christian dogma.

Felix Adler, 1851-1933, (U.S.) German-born founder of the Ethical Culture Society.

St. Augustine, 354-430, Latin bishop considered the founder of formalized Christian theology.

Averroes, 1126-1198, (Sp.) Islamic philosopher.

Roger Bacon, c.1214-1294, (Br.) philosopher and scientist.

Karl Barth, 1886-1968, (Sw.) theologian, a leading force in 20th-century Protestantism.

St. Benedict, c.480-547, (It.) founded the Benedictines.

Jeremy Bentham, 1748-1832, (Br.) philosopher, reformer, founder of Utilitarianism.

Henri Bergson, 1859-1941, (F.) philosopher of evolution.

George Berkeley, 1685-1753, (Ir.) philosopher, churchman.

John Biddle, 1615-1662, (Br.) founder of English Unitarianism.

Jakob Boehme, 1575-1624, (G.) theosophist and mystic.

William Brewster, 1567-1644, (Br.) headed Pilgrims, signed Mayflower Compact.

Emil Brunner, 1889-1966, (Sw.) theologian.

Giordano Bruno, 1548-1600, (It.) philosopher.

Martin Buber, 1878-1965, (G.) Jewish philosopher, theologian, wrote *I and Thou.*

Buddha (Siddhartha Gautama), c.563-c.483 BC, (Ind.) philosopher, founded Buddhism.

John Calvin, 1509-1564, (F.) theologian, a key figure in the Protestant Reformation.

Rudolph Carnap, 1891-1970, (U.S.) German-born philosopher, a founder of logical positivism.

William Ellery Channing, 1780-1842, (U.S.) clergyman, early spokesman for Unitarianism.

Auguste Comte, 1798-1857, (F.) philosopher, the founder of positivism.

Confucius, 551-479 BC, (Chin.) founder of Confucianism.

John Cotton, 1584-1652, (Br.) Puritan theologian.

Thomas Cranmer, 1489-1556, (Br.) churchman, wrote much of the first *Book of Common Prayer;* promoter of the English Reformation.

René Descartes, 1596-1650, (F.) philosopher, mathematician.

John Dewey, 1859-1952, (U.S.) philosopher, educator; helped inaugurate the progressive education movement.

Denis Diderot, 1713-1784, (F.) philosopher, creator of first modern encyclopedia.

Mary Baker Eddy, 1821-1910, (U.S.) founder of Christian Science.

Jonathan Edwards, 1703-1758, (U.S.) preacher, theologian.

(Desiderius) Erasmus, c.1466-1536, (Du.) Renaissance humanist.

Johann Fichte, 1762-1814, (G.) philosopher, the first of the Transcendental Idealists.

George Fox, 1624-1691, (Br.) founder of the Quakers.

St. Francis of Assisi, 1182-1226, (It.) founded the Franciscans.

al Ghazali, 1058-1111, Islamic philosopher.

Georg W. Hegel, 1770-1831, (G.) Idealist philosopher.

Martin Heidegger, 1889-1976, (G.) existentialist philosopher, affected fields ranging from physics to literary criticism.

Johann G. Herder, 1744-1803, (G.) philosopher, cultural historian; a founder of German Romanticism.

David Hume, 1711-1776, (Sc.) philosopher, historian.

Jan Hus, 1369-1415, (Czech.) religious reformer.

Edmund Husserl, 1859-1938, (G.) philosopher, founded the Phenomenological movement.

Thomas Huxley, 1825-1895, (Br.) agnostic philosopher, educator.

Ignatius of Loyola, 1491-1556, (Sp.) founder of the Jesuits.

William Inge, 1860-1954, (Br.) theologian, explored the mystic aspects of Christianity.

William James, 1842-1910, (U.S.) philosopher, psychologist; advanced theory of the pragmatic nature of truth.

Karl Jaspers, 1883-1969, (G.) existentialist philosopher.

Immanuel Kant, 1724-1804, (G.) metaphysician, preeminent founder of modern critical philosophy.

Soren Kierkegaard, 1813-1855, (Du.) philosopher, considered the father of Existentialism.

John Knox, 1505-1572, (Sc.) leader of the Protestant Reformation in Scotland.

Lao-Tzu, 604-531 BC, (Chin.) philosopher, considered the founder of the Taoist religion.

Gottfried von Leibniz, 1646-1716, (G.) philosopher, mathematician.

Martin Luther, 1483-1546, (G.) leader of the Protestant Reformation, founded Lutheran church.

Maimonides, 1135-1204, (Sp.) Jewish physician and philosopher.

Jacques Maritain, 1882-1973, (F.) Neo-Thomist philosopher.

Cotton Mather, 1663-1728, (U.S.) defender of orthodox Puritanism; founded Yale, 1703.

Aimee Semple McPherson, 1890-1944, (U.S.) evangelist.

Philipp Melanchthon, 1497-1560, (G.) theologian, humanist; an important voice in the Reformation.

Mohammed, c.570-632, Arab prophet of the religion of Islam.

Dwight Moody, 1837-1899, (U.S.) evangelist.

George E. Moore, 1873-1958, (Br.) ethical theorist.

Elijah Muhammad, 1897-1975, (U.S.) leader of the Black Muslim sect.

Heinrich Muhlenberg, 1711-1787, (G.) organized the Lutheran Church in America.

John H. Newman, 1801-1890, (Br.) Roman Catholic cardinal, led Oxford Movement.

Reinhold Niebuhr, 1892-1971, (U.S.) Protestant theologian, social and political critic.

Friedrich Nietzsche, 1844-1900, (G.) moral philosopher.

Blaise Pascal, 1623-1662, (F.) philosopher and mathematican.

St. Patrick, c.389-c.461, brought Christianity to Ireland.

St. Paul, ?-c.67, a founder of the Christian religion.

Charles S. Peirce, 1839-1914, (U.S.) philosopher, logician; originated concept of Pragmatism, 1878.

Josiah Royce 1855-1916, (U.S.) Idealist philosopher.

Charles T. Russell, 1852-1916, (U.S.) founder of Jehovah's Witnesses.

Fredrich von Schelling, 1775-1854, (G.) philosopher.

Friedrich Schleiermacher, 1768-1834, (G.) theologian, a founder of modern Protestant theology.

Arthur Schopenhauer, 1788-1860, (G.) philosopher.

Joseph Smith, 1805-1844, (U.S.) founded Latter Day Saints (Mormon) movement, 1830.

Herbert Spencer, 1820-1903, (Br.) philosopher of evolution.

Baruch Spinoza, 1632-1677, (Du.) rationalist philosopher.

Billy Sunday, 1862-1935, (U.S.) evangelist.

Daisetz Teitaro Suzuki, 1870-1966, (Jap.) Buddhist scholar.

Emanuel Swedenborg, 1688-1722, (Swed.) philosopher, mystic.

Thomas a Becket, 1118-1170, (Br.) archbishop of Canterbury, opposed Henry II.

Thomas a Kempis, c.1380-1471, (G.) theologian probably

wrote *Imitation of Christ.*

Thomas Aquinas, 1225-1274, (It.) theologian and philosopher.

Paul Tillich, 1886-1965, (U.S.) German-born philosopher and theologian.

John Wesley, 1703-1791, (Br.) theologian, evangelist; founded Methodism.

Alfred North Whitehead, 1861-1947, (Br.) philosopher, mathematician.

William of Occam, c.1285-c.1349 (Br.) philosopher.

Roger Williams, c.1603-1683, (U.S.) clergyman, championed religious freedom and separation of church and state.

Ludwig Wittgenstein, 1889-1951, (Aus.) philosopher.

John Wycliffe, 1320-1384, (Br.) theologian, reformer.

Brigham Young, 1801-1877, (U.S.) Mormon leader, colonized Utah.

Huldrych Zwingli, 1484-1531, (Sw.) theologian, led Swiss Protestant Reformation.

Noted Social Reformers and Educators of the Past

Jane Addams, 1860-1935, (U.S.) co-founder of Hull House; won Nobel Peace Prize, 1931.

Susan B. Anthony, 1820-1906, (U.S.) a leader in temperance, anti-slavery, and women's suffrage movements.

Henry Barnard, 1811-1900, (U.S.) public school reformer.

Thomas Barnardo, 1845-1905, (Br.) social reformer, pioneered in the care of destitute children.

Clara Barton, 1821-1912, (U.S.) organizer of the American Red Cross.

Henry Ward Beecher, 1813-1887, (U.S.) clergyman, abolitionist.

Amelia Bloomer, 1818-1894, (U.S.) social reformer, women's rights advocate.

William Booth, 1829-1912, (Br.) founded the Salvation Army.

Nicholas Murray Butler, 1862-1947, (U.S.) educator headed Columbia Univ., 1902-45; won Nobel Peace Prize, 1931.

Francis X. (Mother) Cabrini, 1850-1917, (U.S.) Italian-born nun founded numerous charitable institutions; first American to be canonized.

Carrie Chapman Catt, 1859-1947, (U.S.) suffragette, helped win passage of the 19th amendment.

Eugene V. Debs, 1855-1926, (U.S.) labor leader, led Pullman strike, 1894; 4-time Socialist presidential candidate.

Melvil Dewey, 1851-1931, (U.S.) devised decimal system of library-book classification.

Dorothea Dix, 1802-1887, (U.S.) crusader for humane care of mentally ill.

Frederick Douglass, 1817-1895, (U.S.) abolitionist.

W.E.B. DuBois, 1868-1963, (U.S.) Negro-rights leader, educator, and writer.

William Lloyd Garrison, 1805-1879, (U.S.) abolitionist, reformer.

Giovanni Gentile, 1875-1944, (It.) philosopher, educator; reformed Italian educational system.

Samuel Gompers, 1850-1924, (U.S.) labor leader; a founder and president of AFL.

William Green, 1873-1952, (U.S.) president of AFL, 1924-52.

Sidney Hillman, 1887-1946, (U.S.) labor leader, helped organize CIO.

Samuel G. Howe, 1801-1876, (U.S.) social reformer, changed public attitudes toward the handicapped.

Helen Keller, 1880-1968, (U.S.) crusader for better treatment for the handicapped.

Martin Luther King Jr., 1929-1968, (U.S.) civil rights leader; won Nobel Peace Prize, 1964.

John L. Lewis, 1880-1969, (U.S.) labor leader, headed United Mine Workers, 1920-60.

Horace Mann, 1796-1859, (U.S.) pioneered modern public school system.

William H. McGuffey, 1800-1873, (U.S.) author of *Reader* the mainstay of 19th century U.S. public education.

Alexander Meiklejohn, 1872-1964, (U.S.) British-born educator, championed academic freedom and experimental curricula.

Lucretia Mott, 1793-1880, (U.S.) reformer, pioneer feminist.

Philip Murray, 1886-1952, (U.S.) Scotch-born labor leader.

Florence Nightingale, 1820-1910, (Br.) founder of modern nursing.

Emmeline Pankhurst, 1858-1928, (Br.) woman suffragist.

Elizabeth P. Peabody, 1804-1894, (U.S.) education pioneer, founded 1st kindergarten in U.S., 1860.

Walter Reuther, 1907-1970, (U.S.) labor leader, headed UAW.

Jacob Riis, 1849-1914, (U.S.) crusader for urban reforms.

Margaret Sanger, 1883-1966, (U.S.) social reformer, pioneered the birth control movement.

Elizabeth Seton, 1774-1821, (U.S.) established parochial school education in U.S.

Earl of Shaftesbury (A.A. Cooper), 1801-1885, (Br.) social reformer.

Elizabeth Cady Stanton, 1815-1902, (U.S.) women's suffrage pioneer.

Lucy Stone, 1818-1893, (U.S.) feminist, abolitionist.

Harriet Tubman, c.1820-1913, (U.S.) abolitionist, ran Underground Railroad.

Booker T. Washington, 1856-1915, (U.S.) educator, reformer; championed vocational training for blacks.

Walter F. White, 1893-1955, (U.S.) headed NAACP, 1931-55.

William Wilberforce, 1759-1833, (Br.) social reformer, prominent in struggle to abolish the slave trade.

Emma Hart Willard, 1787-1870, (U.S.) pioneered higher education for women.

Frances E. Willard, 1839-1898, (U.S.) temperance, woman's rights leader.

Whitney M. Young Jr., 1921-1971, (U.S.) civil rights leader, headed National Urban League, 1961-71.

Noted Historians, Economists, and Social Scientists of the Past

Brooks Adams, 1848-1927, (U.S.) historian, political theoretician.

Francis Bacon, 1561-1626, (Br.) philosopher, essayist, and statesman.

George Bancroft, 1800-1891, (U.S.) historian, wrote 10-volume *History of the United States.*

Charles A. Beard, 1874-1948, (U.S.) historian, attacked motives of the Founding Fathers.

Bede (the Venerable), c.673-735, (Br.) scholar, historian.

Ruth Benedict, 1887-1948, (U.S.) anthropologist, studied Indian tribes of the Southwest.

Louis Blanc, 1811-1882, (F.) Socialist leader and historian whose ideas were a link between utopian and Marxist socialism.

Franz Boas, 1858-1942, (U.S.) German-born anthropologist, studied American Indians.

Van Wyck Brooks, 1886-1963, (U.S.) cultural historian, critic.

Edmund Burke, 1729-1797, (Ir.) British parliamentarian and political philosopher; influenced many Federalists.

Thomas Carlyle, 1795-1881, (Sc.) philospher, historian, and critic.

Edward Channing, 1856-1931, (U.S.) historian wrote 6-volume *A History of the United States.*

John R. Commons, 1862-1945, (U.S.) economist, labor historian.

Benedetto Croce, 1866-1952, (It.) philosopher, statesman, and historian.

Bernard A. De Voto, 1897-1955, (U.S.) historian, won Pulitzer prize in 1948 for *Across the Wide Missouri.*

Emile Durkheim, 1858-1917, (F.) a founder of modern sociology.

Friedrich Engels, 1820-1895, (G.) political writer, with Marx wrote the *Communist Manifesto.*

Irving Fisher, 1867-1947, (U.S.) economist, contributed to the development of modern monetary theory.

John Fiske, 1842-1901, (U.S.) historian and lecturer, popularized Darwinian theory of evolution.

Charles Fourier, 1772-1837, (F.) utopian socialist.

Henry George, 1839-1897, (U.S.) economist, reformer, led single-tax movement.

Edward Gibbon, 1737-1794, (Br.) historian, wrote *The History of the Decline and Fall of the Roman Empire.*

Francesco Guicciardini, 1483-1540, (It.) historian, wrote *Storia d'Italia,* principal historical work of the 16th-century.

Alvin Hansen, 1887-1975, (U.S.) economist.

Thomas Hobbes, 1588-1679, (Br.) social philosopher.

Richard Hofstadter, 1916-1970, (U.S.) historian, wrote *The Age of Reform.*

John Maynard Keynes, 1883-1946, (Br.) economist, principal advocate of deficit spending.

Alfred L. Kroeber, 1876-1960, (U.S.) cultural anthropologist, studied Indians of North and South America.

James L. Laughlin, 1850-1933, (U.S.) economist, helped establish Federal Reserve System.

Lucien Lévy-Bruhl, 1857-1939, (F.) philosopher, studied the psychology of primitive societies.

Kurt Lewin, 1890-1947, (U.S.) German-born psychologist, studied human motivaion and group dynamics.

John Locke, 1632-1704, (Br.) political philosopher.

Thomas B. Macauley, 1800-1859, (Br.) historian, statesman.

Bronislaw Malinowski, 1884-1942, (Pol.) anthropologist, considered the father of social anthropology.

Thomas R. Malthus, 1766-1834, (Br.) economist, famed for *Essay on the Principal of Population.*

Karl Mannheim, 1893-1947, (Hung.) sociologist, historian.

Karl Marx, 1818-1883, (G.) political philosopher, proponent of modern communism.

Giuseppe Mazzini, 1805-1872, (It.) political philosopher.

George H. Mead, 1863-1931, (U.S.) philosopher and social psychologist.

James Mill, 1773-1836, (Sc.) philosopher, historian, and economist; a proponent of Utilitarianism.

John Stuart Mill, 1806-1873, (Br.) philosopher, political economist.

Perry G. Miller, 1905-1963, (U.S.) historian, interpreted 17th-century New England.

Theodor Mommsen, 1817-1903, (G.) historian, wrote *The History of Rome.*

Charles-Louis Montesquieu, 1689-1755, (F.) social philosopher.

Samuel Eliot Morison, 1887-1976, (U.S.) historian, chronicled voyages of early explorers.

Allen Nevins, 1890-1971, (U.S.) historian, biographer; twice won Pulitzer prize.

Jose Ortega y Gasset, 1883-1955, (Sp.) philosopher and humanist; advocated control by an elite.

Robert Owen, 1771-1858, (Br.) political philosopher, reformer.

Vilfredo Pareto, 1848-1923, (It.) economist, sociologist.

Francis Parkman, 1823-1893, (U.S.) historian, wrote 8-volume *France and England in North America, 1851-92.*

Marco Polo, c.1254-1324, (It.) narrated an account of his travels to China.

William Prescott, 1796-1859, (U.S.) early American historian.

Pierre Joseph Proudhon, 1809-1865, (F.) social theorist, regarded as the father of anarchism.

Francois Quesnay, 1694-1774, (F.) economic theorist, demonstrated the circular flow of economic activity throughout society.

David Ricardo, 1772-1823, (Br.) economic theorist, advocated free international trade.

James H. Robinson, 1863-1936, (U.S.) historian, educator.

Jean-Jacques Rousseau, 1712-1778, (F.) social philosopher, author.

Bertrand Russell, 1872-1970, (Br.) political philosopher, mathematician; wrote *Principia Mathematica.*

Hjalmar Schacht, 1877-1970, (G.) economist.

Joseph Schumpeter, 1883-1950, (U.S.) Czech.-born economist, championed big business, capitalism.

Albert Schweitzer, 1875-1965, (Alsatian) social philosopher, theologian, and humanitarian.

George Simmel, 1858-1918, (G.) sociologist, philosopher.

Adam Smith, 1723-1790, (Br.) economist, advocated laissez-faire economy and free trade.

Jared Sparks, 1789-1866, (U.S.) historian, among first to do research from original documents.

Oswald Spengler, 1880-1936, (G.) philosopher and historian, wrote *The Decline of the West.*

William G. Sumner, 1840-1910, (U.S.) social scientist, economist; championed laissez-faire economy, Social Darwinism.

Hippolyte Taine, 1828-1893, (F.) historian.

Frank W. Taussig, 1859-1940, (U.S.) economist, educator.

Alexis de Tocqueville, 1805-1859, (F.) political scientist, historian.

Francis E. Townsend, 1897-1960, (U.S.) author of old-age pension plan.

Arnold Toynbee, 1889-1975, (Br.) historian, wrote 10-volume *A Study of History.*

Heinrich von Treitschke, 1834-1896, (G.) historian, political writer.

George Trevelyan, 1838-1928, (Br.) historian, statesman.

Frederick J. Turner, 1861-1932, (U.S.) historian, educator.

Thorstein B. Veblen, 1857-1929, (U.S.) economist, social philosopher.

Giovanni Vico, 1668-1744, (It.) historian, philosopher.

Voltaire (F.A. Arouet), 1694-1778, (F.) philosopher, historian, and poet.

Izaak Walton, 1593-1683, (Br.) author, wrote first biographical works in English literature.

Sidney J., 1859-1947, and wife **Beatrice,** 1858-1943, **Webb** (Br.) leading figures in Fabian Society and British Labour Party.

Walter P. Webb, 1888-1963, (U.S.) historian of the West.

Max Weber, 1864-1920, (G.) sociologist.

Noted Scientists of the Past

Howard H. Aiken, 1900-1973, (U.S.) mathematician, designed world's first large-scale digital computer (Mark I) for IBM.

Albertus Magnus, 1193-1280, (G.) theologian, philosopher, scientist, established medieval Christian study of natural science.

Andre-Marie Ampère, 1775-1836, (F.) scientist known for contributions to electrodynamics.

Amedeo Avogadro, 1776-1856, (It.) chemist, physicist, advanced important theories on properties of gases.

A.C. Becquerel, 1788-1878, (F.) physicist, pioneer in electrochemical science.

A.H. Becquerel, 1852-1908, (F.) physicist, discovered radioactivity in uranium.

Daniel Bernoulli, 1700-1782, (Swiss) mathematician, advanced kinetic theory of gases and fluids.

Jöns Jakob Berzelius, 1779-1848, (Swed.) chemist, developed modern chemical symbols and formulas.

Henry Bessemer, 1813-1898, (Br.) engineer, invented Bessemer steel-making process.

Louis Blériot, 1872-1936, (F.) engineer, pioneer aviator, invented and constructed monoplanes.

Niels Bohr, 1885-1962, (Dan.) physicist, leading figure in the development of quantum theory.

Max Born, 1882-1970, (G.) physicist known for research in quantum mechanics.

Robert Bunsen, 1811-1899, (G.) chemist, invented Bunsen burner.

Luther Burbank, 1849-1926, (U.S.) plant breeder whose work developed plant breeding into a modern science.

Vannevar Bush, 1890-1974, (U.S.) electrical engineer, developed differential analyzer, first electronic analogue computer.

Alexis Carrel, 1873-1944, (F.) surgeon, biologist, developed methods of suturing blood vessels and transplanting organs.

George Washington Carver, 1860?-1943, (U.S.) agricultural chemist, experimenter, benefactor of South, a black hero.

Henry Cavendish, 1731-1810, (Br.) chemist, physicist, discovered hydrogen.

James Chadwick, 1891-1974, (Br.) physicist, discovered the neutron.

Jean M. Charcot, 1825-1893, (F.) neurologist known for work on hysteria, hypnotism, sclerosis.

John D. Cockcroft, 1897-1967, (Br.) nuclear physicist, constructed first atomic particle accelerator with E.T.S. Walton.

William Crookes, 1832-1919, (Br.) physicist, chemist, discovered thallium, invented a cathode-ray tube, radiometer.

Marie Curie, 1867-1934, (Pol.-F.) physical chemist known for work on radium and its compounds.

Pierre Curie, 1859-1906, (F.) physical chemist known for work with his wife on radioactivity.

Gottlieb Daimler, 1834-1900, (G.) engineer, inventor, pioneer automobile manufacturer.

John Dalton, 1766-1844, (Br.) chemist, physicist, formulated atomic theory, made first table of atomic weights.

Charles Darwin, 1809-1882, (Br.) naturalist, established theory of organic evolution.

Humphry Davy, 1778-1829, (Br.) chemist, research in electrochemistry led to isolation of potassium, sodium, calcium, barium, boron, magnesium, and strontium.

Lee De Forest, 1873-1961, (U.S.) inventor, pioneer in development of wireless telegraphy, sound pictures, television.

Rudolf Diesel, 1858-1913, (G.) mechanical engineer, patented Diesel engine.

Thomas Dooley, 1927-1961, (U.S.) "jungle doctor," noted for efforts to supply medical aid to underdeveloped countries.

Christian Doppler, 1803-1853, (Aus.) physicist, demonstrated Doppler effect (change in energy wavelengths caused by motion).

Thomas A. Edison, 1847-1931, (U.S.) inventor, held over 1,000 patents, including incandescent electric lamp, phonograph.

Paul Ehrlich, 1854-1915, (G.) bacteriologist, pioneer in modern immunology and bacteriology.

Albert Einstein, 1879-1955, (U.S.) theoretical physicist, known for formulation of relativity theory.

Gabriel Fahrenheit, 1686-1736, (G.) physicist, introduced Fahrenheit scale for thermometers.

Michael Faraday, 1791-1867, (Br.) chemist, physicist, known for work in field of electricity.

Pierre de Fermat, 1601-1665, (F.) mathematician, discovered analytic geometry, founded modern theory of numbers and calculus of probabilities.

Enrico Fermi, 1901-1954, (It.) physicist, one of chief architects of the nuclear age.

Galileo Ferraris, 1847-1897, (It.) physicist, electrical engineer, discovered principle of rotary magnetic field.

Camille Flammarion, 1842-1925, (F.) astronomer, popularized study of astronomy.

Alexander Fleming, 1881-1955, (Br.) bacteriologist, discovered penicillin.

Jean B.J. Fourier, 1768-1830, (F.) mathematician, discovered theorem governing periodic oscillation.

James Franck, 1882-1964, (G.) physicist, proved value of quantum theory.

Sigmund Freud, 1856-1939, (Aus.) psychiatrist, founder of psychoanalysis.

Galileo Galilei, 1564-1642, (It.) astronomer, physicist, a founder of the experimental method.

Luigi Galvani, 1737-1798, (It.) physician, physicist, known as founder of galvanism.

Joseph Gay-Lussac, 1778-1850, (F.) chemist, physicist, investigated behavior of gases, discovered law of combining volumes.

Josiah W. Gibbs, 1839-1903, (U.S.) theoretical physicist, chemist, founded chemical thermodynamics.

George W. Goethals, 1858-1928, (U.S.) army engineer, built the Panama Canal.

William C. Gorgas, 1854-1920, (U.S.) sanitarian, U.S. army surgeon-general, his work to prevent yellow fever, malaria helped insure construction of Panama Canal.

Ernest Haeckel, 1834-1919, (G.) zoologist, evolutionist, a strong proponent of Darwin.

Otto Hahn, 1879-1968, (G.) chemist, worked on atomic fission.

J.B.S. Haldane, 1892-1964, (Sc.) scientist, known for work as geneticist and application of mathematics to science.

James Hall, 1761-1832, (Br.) geologist, chemist, founded experimental geology, geochemistry.

Edmund Halley, 1656-1742, (Br.) astronomer, calculated the orbits of many planets.

William Harvey, 1578-1657, (Br.) physician, anatomist, discovered circulation of the blood.

Hermann v. Helmholtz, 1821-1894, (G.) physicist, anatomist, physiologist, made fundamental contributions to physiology, optics, electrodynamics, mathematics, meteorology.

William Herschel, 1738-1822, (Br.) astronomer, discovered Uranus.

Heinrich Hertz, 1857-1894, (G.) physicist, his discoveries led to wireless telegraphy.

David Hilbert, 1862-1943, (G.) mathematician, formulated first satisfactory set of axioms for modern Euclidean geometry.

Edwin P. Hubble, 1889-1953, (U.S.) astronomer, produced first observational evidence of expanding universe.

Alexander v. Humboldt, 1769-1859, (G.) explorer, naturalist, propagator of earth sciences, originated ecology, geophysics.

Julian Huxley, 1887-1975, (Br.) biologist, a gifted exponent and philosopher of science.

Edward Jenner, 1749-1823, (Br.) physician, discovered vaccination.

William Jenner, 1815-1898, (Br.) physician, pathological anatomist.

Frederic Joliot-Curie, 1900-1958, (F.) physicist, with his wife continued work of Curies on radioactivity.

Irene Joliot-Curie, 1897-1956, (F.) physicist, continued work of Curies in radioactivity.

James P. Joule, 1818-1889, (Br.) physicist, determined relationship between heat and mechanical energy (conservation of energy).

Carl Jung, 1875-1961, (Sw.) psychiatrist, founder of analytical psychology.

Wm. Thomas Kelvin, 1824-1907, (Br.) mathematician, physicist, known for work on heat and electricity.

Sister Elizabeth Kenny, 1886-1952, (Austral.) nurse, developed method of treatment for polio.

Johannes Kepler, 1571-1630, (G.) astronomer, discovered important laws of planetary motion.

Joseph Lagrange, 1736-1813, (F.) geometer, astronomer, worked in all fields of analysis, and number theory, and analytical and celestial mechanics.

Jean B. Lamarck, 1744-1829, (F.) naturalist, forerunner of Darwin in evolutionary theory.

Irving Langmuir, 1881-1957, (U.S.) physical chemist, his studies of molecular films on solid and liquid surfaces opened new fields in colloid research and biochemistry.

Pierre S. Laplace, 1749-1827, (F.) astronomer, physicist, put forth nebular hypothesis of orgin of solar system.

Antoine Lavoisier, 1743-1794, (F.) chemist, founder of modern chemistry.

Ernest O. Lawrence, 1901-1958, (U.S.) physicist, invented the cyclotron.

Louis Leakey, 1903-1972, (Br.) anthropologist, discovered important fossils, remains of early hominids.

Anton van Leeuwenhoek, 1632-1723, (Du.) microscopist, father of microbiology.

Gottfried Wilhelm Leibniz, 1646-1716, (G.) mathematician, developed theories of differential and integral calculus.

Justus von Liebig, 1803-1873, (G.) chemist, established quantitative organic chemical analysis.

Percival Lowell, 1855-1961, (U.S.) astronomer, predicted the existence of Pluto.

Guglielmo Marconi, 1874-1937, (It.) physicist, known for his development of wireless telegraphy.

James Clerk Maxwell, 1831-1879, (Sc.) physicist, known especially for his work in electricity and magnetism.

Maria Goeppert Mayer, 1906-1972, (G.-U.S.) physicist, independently developed theory of structure of atomic nuclei.

Margaret Mead, 1901-1978, (U.S.) cultural anthropologist, popularized field.

Lise Meitner, 1878-1968, (Aus.) physicist whose work contributed to the development of the atomic bomb.

Gregor J. Mendel, 1822-1884, (Aus.) botanist, known for his experimental work on heredity.

Franz Mesmer, 1734-1815, (G.) physician, developed theory of animal magnetism.

Albert A. Michelson, 1852-1931, (U.S.) physicist, established speed of light as a fundamental constant.

Robert A. Millikan, 1868-1953, (U.S.) physicist, noted for study of elementary electronic charge and photoelectric effect.

Thomas Hunt Morgan, 1866-1945, (U.S.) geneticist, embryologist, established chromosome theory of heredity.

Isaac Newton, 1642-1727, (Br.) natural philosopher, mathematician, discovered law of gravitation, laws of motion.

J. Robert Oppenheimer, 1904-1967, (U.S.) physicist, director of Los Alamos during development of the atomic bomb.

Wilhelm Ostwald, 1853-1932, (G.) physical chemist, philosopher, chief founder of physical chemistry.

Louis Pasteur, 1822-1895, (F.) chemist, originated process of pasteurization.

Max Planck, 1858-1947, (G.) physicist, originated and developed quantum theory.

Henri Poincaré, 1854-1912, (F.) mathematician, physicist, influenced cosmology, relativity, and topology.

Joseph Priestley, 1733-1804, (Br.) chemist, one of the discoverers of oxygen.

Walter S. Reed, 1851-1902, (U.S.) army pathologist, bacteriologist, proved mosquitos transmit yellow fever.

Wilhelm Roentgen, 1845-1923, (G.) physicist, discovered X-rays.

Ernest Rutherford, 1871-1937, (Br.) physicist, discovered the atomic nucleus.

Giovanni Schiaparelli, 1835-1910, (It.) astronomer, hypothesized canals on the surface of Mars.

Angelo Secchi, 1818-1878, (It.) astronomer, pioneer in classifying stars by their spectra.

Harlow Shapley, 1885-1972, (U.S.) astronomer, noted for his studies of the galaxy.

Charles P. Steinmetz, 1865-1923, (U.S.) electrical engineer, developed fundamental ideas on alternating current systems.

Leo Szilard, 1898-1964, (U.S.) physicist, helped create first sustained nuclear reaction.

Rudolf Virchow, 1821-1902, (G.) pathologist, a founder of cellular pathology.

Alessandro Volta, 1745-1827, (It.) physicist, pioneer in electricity.

Alfred Russell Wallace, 1823-1913, (Br.) naturalist, proposed concept of evolution similar to Darwin.

August v. Wasserman, 1866-1925, (G.) bacteriologist, discovered reaction used as test for syphilis.

James E. Watt, 1736-1819, (Sc.) mechanical engineer, inventor, invented modern steam condensing engine.

Alfred L. Wegener, 1880-1930, (G.) meteorologist, geophysicist, postulated theory of continental drift.

Norbert Wiener, 1894-1964, (U.S.) mathematician, founder of the science of cybernetics.

Ferdinand v. Zeppelin, 1838-1917 (G.) soldier, aeronaut, airship designer.

Noted Business Leaders, Industrialists, and Philanthropists of the Past

Elizabeth Arden (F.N. Graham), 1884-1966, (U.S.) Canadian-born businesswoman founded and headed cosmetics empire.

Philip D. Armour, 1832-1901, (U.S.) industrialist, streamlined meat packing.

John Jacob Astor, 1763-1848, (U.S.) German-born fur trader, banker, real estate magnate; at death, richest in U.S.

Francis W. Ayer, 1848-1923, (U.S.) ad industry pioneer.

August Belmont, 1816-1890, (U.S.) German-born financier.

James B. (Diamond Jim) Brady, 1856-1917, (U.S.) financier, philanthropist, legendary bon vivant.

Adolphus Busch, 1839-1913, (U.S.) German-born businessman, established brewery empire.

Asa Candler, 1851-1929, (U.S.) founded Coca-Cola Co.

Andrew Carnegie, 1835-1919, (U.S.) Scots-born industrialist, founded U.S. Steel; financed over 2,800 libraries.

William Colgate, 1783-1857, (U.S.) British-born businessman,

philanthropist; founded soap-making empire.
Jay Cooke, 1821-1905, (U.S.) financier, sold $1 billion in Union bonds during Civil War.
Peter Cooper, 1791-1883, (U.S.) industrialist, inventor, philanthropist.
Ezra Cornell, 1807-1874, (U.S.) businessman, philanthropist; headed Western Union, established univ.
Erastus Corning, 1794-1872, (U.S.) financier, headed N.Y. Central.
Charles Crocker, 1822-1888, (U.S.) railroad builder, financier.
Samuel Cunard, 1787-1865, (Can.) pioneered trans-Atlantic steam navigation.
Marcus Daly, 1841-1900, (U.S.) Irish-born copper magnate.
Walt Disney, 1901-1966, (U.S.) pioneer in cinema animation, built entertainment empire.
Herbert H. Dow, 1866-1930, (U.S.) Canadian-born founder of chemical co.
James Duke, 1856-1925, (U.S.) founded American Tobacco, Duke Univ.
Eleuthere I. du Pont, 1771-1834, (U.S.) French-born gunpowder manufacturer; founded one of world's largest business empires.
Thomas C. Durant, 1820-1885, (U.S.) railroad official, financier.
William C. Durant, 1861-1947, (U.S.) industrialist, formed General Motors.
George Eastman, 1854-1932, (U.S.) inventor, manufacturer of photographic equipment.
Marshall Field, 1834-1906, (U.S.) merchant, founded Chicago's largest department store.
Harvey Firestone, 1868-1938, (U.S.) industrialist, founded tire co.
Henry M. Flagler, 1830-1913, (U.S.) financier, helped form Standard Oil; developed Florida as resort state.
Henry Ford, 1863-1947, (U.S.) auto maker, developed first popular low-priced car.
Henry C. Frick, 1849-1919, (U.S.) industrialist, helped organize U.S. Steel.
Jakob Fugger (Jakob the Rich), 1459-1525, (G.) headed leading banking house, trading concern, in 16th-century Europe.
Alfred C. Fuller, 1885-1973, (U.S.) Canadian-born businessman, founded brush co.
Elbert H. Gary, 1846-1927, (U.S.) U.S. Steel head, 1903-27.
Amadeo P. Giannini, 1870-1949, (U.S.) founded Bank of America.
Stephen Girard, 1750-1831, (U.S.) French-born financier, philanthropist; richest man in U.S. at his death.
Jean Paul Getty, 1892-1976, (U.S.) founded oil empire.
Jay Gould, 1836-1892, (U.S.) railroad magnate, financier, speculator.
Hetty Green, 1834-1916, (U.S.) financier, the "witch of Wall St."; richest woman in U.S in her day.
William Gregg, 1800-1867, (U.S.) launched textile industry in the South.
Meyer Guggenheim, 1828-1905, (U.S.) Swiss-born merchant, philanthropist; built merchandising, mining empires.
Edward H. Harriman, 1848-1909, (U.S.) railroad financier, administrator; headed Union Pacific.
Henry J. Heinz, 1844-1919, (U.S.) founded food empire.
James J. Hill, 1838-1916, (U.S.) Canadian-born railroad magnate, financier; founded Great Northern Railway.
Conrad N. Hilton, 1888-1979, (U.S.) intl. hotel chain founder.
Howard Hughes, 1905-1976, (U.S.) industrialist, financier, movie maker.
H.L. Hunt, 1889-1974, (U.S.) oil magnate.
Collis P. Huntington, 1821-1900, (U.S.) railroad magnate.
Henry E. Huntington, 1850-1927, (U.S.) railroad builder, philanthropist.
Howard Johnson, 1896-1972, (U.S.) founded restaurant chain.
Henry J. Kaiser, 1882-1967, (U.S.) industrialist, built empire in steel, aluminum.
Minor C. Keith, 1848-1929, (U.S.) railroad magnate; founded United Fruit Co.
Will K. Kellogg, 1860-1951, (U.S.) businessman, philanthropist, founded breakfast food co.
Richard King, 1825-1885, (U.S.) cattleman, founded half-million acre King Ranch in Texas.
William S. Knudsen, 1879-1948, (U.S.) Danish-born auto industry executive.
Samuel H. Kress, 1863-1955, (U.S.) businessman, art collector, philanthropist; founded "dime store" chain.
Alfred Krupp, 1812-1887, (G.) armaments magnate.
Albert Lasker, 1880-1952, (U.S.) businessman, philanthropist.
Thomas Lipton, 1850-1931, (Ir.) merchant, built tea empire.
James McGill, 1744-1813, (Can.) Scots-born fur trader, founded univ.
Andrew W. Mellon, 1855-1937, (U.S.) financier, industrialist; benefactor of National Gallery of Art.
Charles E. Merrill, 1885-1956, (U.S.) financier, developed firm of Merrill Lynch.
John Pierpont Morgan, 1837-1913, (U.S.) most powerful figure in finance and industry at the turn-of-the-century.
Malcolm Muir, 1885-1979, (U.S.) created *Business Week* magazine; headed *Newsweek,* 1937-61.
Samuel Newhouse, 1895-1979, (U.S.) publishing and broadcasting magnate, built communications empire.
Aristotle Onassis, 1900-1975, (Gr.) shipping magnate.
George Peabody, 1795-1869, (U.S.) merchant, financier, philanthropist.
James C. Penney, 1875-1971, (U.S.) businessman, developed department store chain.
William C. Procter, 1862-1934, (U.S.) headed soap co.
John D. Rockefeller, 1839-1937, (U.S.) industrialist, established Standard Oil; became world's wealthiest person.
John D. Rockefeller Jr., 1874-1960, (U.S.) philanthropist, established foundation; provided land for United Nations.
Meyer A. Rothschild, 1743-1812, (G.) founded international banking house.
Thomas Fortune Ryan, 1851-1928, (U.S.) financier, dominated N.Y. City public transportation; helped found American Tobacco.
Russell Sage, 1816-1906, (U.S.) financier.
David Sarnoff, 1891-1971, (U.S.) broadcasting pioneer, established first radio network, NBC.
Richard W. Sears, 1863-1914, (U.S.) founded mail-order co.
(Ernst) Werner von Siemens, 1816-1892, (G.) industrialist, inventor.
Alfred P. Sloan, 1875-1966, (U.S.) industrialist, philanthropist; headed General Motors.
A. Leland Stanford, 1824-1893, (U.S.) railroad official, philanthropist; founded univ.
Nathan Strauss, 1848-1931, (U.S.) German-born merchant, philanthropist; headed Macy's.
Levi Strauss, c.1829-1902, (U.S.) pants manufacturer.
Clement Studebaker, 1831-1901, (U.S.) wagon, carriage manufacturer.
Gustavus Swift, 1839-1903, (U.S.) pioneer meat-packer; promoted refrigerated railroad cars.
Gerard Swope, 1872-1957, (U.S.) industrialist, economist; headed General Electric.
James Walter Thompson, 1847-1928, (U.S.) ad executive.
Theodore N. Vail, 1845-1920, (U.S.) organized Bell Telephone system, headed ATT.
Cornelius Vanderbilt, 1794-1877, (U.S.) financier, established steamship, railroad empires.
Henry Villard, 1835-1900, (U.S.) German-born railroad executive, financier.
Charles R. Walgreen, 1873-1939, (U.S.) founded drugstore chain.
John Wanamaker, 1838-1922, (U.S.) pioneered department-store merchandising.
Aaron Montgomery Ward, 1843-1913, (U.S.) established first mail-order firm.
Thomas J. Watson, 1874-1956, (U.S.) headed IBM, 1924-49.
Charles E. Wilson, 1890-1961, (U.S.) auto industry executive; public official.
Frank W. Woolworth, 1852-1919, (U.S.) created 5 & 10 chain.
William Wrigley Jr., 1861-1932, (U.S.) founded chewing gum co.

Composers of the Western World

Carl Philipp Emanuel Bach, 1714-1788, (G.) Prussian and Wurtembergian Sonatas.
Johann Christian Bach, 1735-1782, (G.) Concertos; sonatas.
Johann Sebastian Bach, 1685-1750, (G.) St. Matthew Passion, The Well-Tempered Clavichord.
Samuel Barber, b. 1910, (U.S.) Adagio for Strings, Vanessa.
Bela Bartok, 1881-1945, (Hung.) Concerto for Orchestra, The Miraculous Mandarin.
Ludwig Van Beethoven, 1770-1827, (G.) Concertos (Emperor); sonatas (Moonlight, Pastorale, Pathetique); symphonies (Eroica).
Vincenzo Bellini, 1801-1835, (It.) La Sonnambula, Norma, I Puritani.
Alban Berg, 1885-1935, (Aus.) Wozzeck, Lulu.
Hector Berlioz, 1803-1869, (F.) Damnation of Faust, Symphonie Fantastique, Requiem.
Leonard Bernstein, b. 1918, (U.S.) Jeremiah, West Side Story.
Georges Bizet, 1838-1875, (F.) Carmen, Pearl Fishers.
Ernest Bloch, 1880-1959, (Swiss) Schelomo, Voice in the

Wilderness, Sacred Service.
Luigi Boccherini, 1743-1805, (It.) Cello Concerto in B Flat, Symphony in C.
Alexander Borodin, 1834-1887, (R.) Prince Igor, In the Steppes of Central Asia.
Johannes Brahms, 1833-1897, (G.) Liebeslieder Waltzes, Rhapsody in E Flat Major, Opus 119 for Piano, Academic Festival Overture; symphonies; quartets.
Benjamin Britten, 1913-1976, (Br.) Peter Grimes, Turn of the Screw, Ceremony of Carols.
Anton Bruckner, 1824-1896, (Aus.) Symphonies (Romantic), Intermezzo for String Quintet.
Ferruccio Busoni, 1866-1924, (It.) Doctor Faust, Comedy Overture.
Dietrich Buxtehude, 1637-1707, (D.) Cantatas, trio sonatas.
William Byrd, 1543-1623, (Br.) Masses, sacred songs.
Alexis Emmanuel Chabrier, 1841-1894, (Fr.) Le Roi Malgre Lui, Espana.
Gustave Charpentier, 1860-1956, (F.) Louise.
Frederic Chopin, 1810-1849, (P.) Concertos, Polonaise No. 6 in A Flat Major (Heroic); sonatas.
Aaron Copland, b. 1900, (U.S.) Appalachian Spring.
Claude Achille Debussy, 1862-1918, (F.) Pelleas et Melisande, La Mer, Prelude to the Afternoon of a Faun.
C.P. Leo Delibes, 1836-1891, (F.) Lakme, Coppelia, Sylvia.
Norman Dello Joio, b. 1913, (U.S.), Triumph of St. Joan, Psalm of David.
Gaetano Donizetti, 1797-1848, (It.) Elixir of Love, Lucia Di Lammermoor, Daughter of the Regiment.
Paul Dukas, 1865-1935, (Fr.) Sorcerer's Apprentice.
Antonin Dvorak, 1841-1904, (C.) Symphony in E Minor (From the New World).
Edward Elgar, 1857-1934, (Br.) Pomp and Circumstance.
Manuel de Falla, 1876-1946, (Sp.) La Vide Breve, El Amor Brujo.
Gabriel Faure, 1845-1924, (Fr.) Requiem, Ballade.
Friedrich von Flotow, 1812-1883, (G.) Martha.
Cesar Franck, 1822-1890, (Belg.) D Minor Symphony.
George Gershwin, 1898-1937, (U.S.) Rhapsody in Blue, American in Paris, Porgy and Bess.
Umberto Giordano, 1867-1948, (It.) Andrea Chenier.
Alex K. Glazunoff, 1865-1936, (R.) Symphonies, Stenka Razin.
Mikhail Glinka, 1804-1857, (R.) Ruslan & Ludmilla.
Christoph W. Gluck, 1714-1787, (G.) Alceste, Iphigenie en Tauride.
Charles Gounod, 1818-1893, (F.) Faust, Romeo and Juliet.
Edvard Grieg, 1843-1907, (Nor.) Peer Gynt Suite, Concerto in A Minor.
George Frederick Handel, 1685-1759, (G., Br.) Messiah, Xerxes, Berenice.
Howard Hanson, b. 1896, (U.S.) Symphonies No. 1 (Nordic) and 2 (Romantic).
Roy Harris, b. 1898, (U.S.) Symphonies, Amer. Portraits.
Joseph Haydn, 1732-1809, (Aus.) Symphonies (Clock); oratorios; chamber music.
Paul Hindemith, 1895-1963, (U.S.) Mathis Der Maler.
Gustav Holst, 1874-1934, (Br.) The Planets.
Arthur Honegger, 1892-1955, (Swiss) Judith, Le Roi David, Pacific 231.
Alan Hovhaness, b. 1911, (U.S.) Symphonies, Magnificat.
Engelbert Humperdinck, 1854-1921, (G.) Hansel and Gretel.
Charles Ives, 1874-1954, (U.S.) Third Symphony.
Aram Khachaturian, 1903-1978, (R.) Gayane (ballet), symphonies.
Zoltan Kodaly, 1882-1967, (Hung.) Hary Janos, Psalmus Hungaricus.
Fritz Kreisler, 1875-1962, (Aus.) Caprice Viennois, Tambourin Chinois.
Rodolphe Kreutzer, 1766-1831, (F.) 40 etudes for violin.
Edouard V.A. Lalo, 1823-1892, (F.) Symphonie Espagnole.
Ruggiero Leoncavallo, 1858-1919, (It.) I Pagliacci.
Franz Liszt, 1811-1886, (Hung.) 20 Hungarian rhapsodies; symphonic poems.
Edward MacDowell, 1861-1908, (U.S.) To a Wild Rose.
Gustav Mahler, 1860-1911, (Aus.) Lied von der Erde.
Pietro Mascagni, 1863-1945, (It.) Cavalleria Rusticana.
Jules Massenet, 1842-1912, (F.) Manon, Le Cid, Thais.
Mendelssohn-Bartholdy, 1809-1847, (G.) Midsummer Night's Dream, Songs Without Words.
Gian-Carlo Menotti, b. 1911, (It.-U.S.) The Medium, The Consul, Amahl and the Night Visitors.
Claudio Monteverdi, 1567-1643, (It.) Opera; masses; madrigals.
Wolfgang Amadeus Mozart, 1756-1791, (Aus.) Magic Flute, Marriage of Figaro; concertos; symphonies, etc.
Modest Moussorgsky, 1835-1881, (R.) Boris Godunov, Pictures at an Exhibition.
Jacques Offenbach, 1819-1880, (F.) Tales of Hoffman.
Karl Orff, b. 1895, (G.) Carmina Burana.
Ignace Paderewski, 1860-1941, (P.) Minuet in G.
Giovanni P. da Palestrina, 1524-1594, (It.) Masses; madrigals.
Amilcare Ponchielli, 1834-1886, (It.) La Gioconda.
Francis Poulenc, 1899-1963, (F.) Dialogues des Carmelites.
Serge Prokofiev, 1891-1953, (R.) Love for Three Oranges, Lt. Kije, Peter and the Wolf.
Giacomo Puccini, 1858-1924, (It.) La Boheme, Manon Lescaut, Tosca, Madame Butterfly.
Sergei Rachmaninov, 1873-1943, (R.) Prelude in C Sharp Minor.
Maurice Ravel, 1875-1937, (Fr.) Bolero, Daphnis et Chloe, Rapsodie Espagnole.
Nikolai Rimsky-Korsakov, 1844-1908, (R.) Golden Cockerel, Capriccio Espagnol, Scheherazade, Russian Easter Overture.
Gioacchino Rossini, 1792-1868, (It.) Barber of Seville, Semiramide, William Tell.
Chas. Camille Saint-Saens, 1835-1921, (F.) Samson and Delilah, Danse Macabre.
Alessandro Scarlatti, 1659-1725, (It.) Cantatas; concertos.
Arnold Schoenberg, 1874-1951, (Aus.) Pelleas and Melisande, Transfigured Night, De Profundis.
Franz Schubert, 1797-1828, (A.) Lieder; symphonies (Unfinished); overtures (Rosamunde).
William Schuman, b. 1910, (U.S.) Credendum, New England Triptych.
Robert Schumann, 1810-1856, (G.) Symphonies, songs.
Aleksandr Scriabin, 1872-1915, (R.) Prometheus.
Dimitri Shostakovich, 1906-1975, (R.) Symphonies, Lady Macbeth of Minsk, The Nose.
Jean Sibelius, 1865-1957, (Finn.) Finlandia, Karelia.
Bedrich Smetana, 1824-1884, (Cz.). The Bartered Bride.
Karlheinz Stockhausen, b. 1928, (G.) Kontrapunkte, Kontakte.
Richard Strauss, 1864-1949, (G.) Salome, Elektra, Der Rosenkavalier, Thus Spake Zarathustra.
Igor F. Stravinsky, 1882-1971, (R.-U.S.) Oedipus Rex, Le Sacre du Printemps, Petrushka.
Peter I. Tchaikovsky, 1840-1893, (R.) Nutcracker Suite, Swan Lake, Eugene Onegin.
Ambroise Thomas, 1811-1896, (F.) Mignon.
Virgil Thomson, b. 1896, (U.S.) Opera, ballet; Four Saints in Three Acts.
Ralph Vaughan Williams, 1872-1958, (Br.) Job, London Symphony, Symphony No. 7 (Antarctica).
Giuseppe Verdi, 1813-1901, (It.) Aida, Rigoletto, Don Carlo, Il Trovatore, La Traviata, Falstaff, Macbeth.
Hector Villa-Lobos, 1887-1959, (Brazil) Choros.
Antonio Vivaldi, 1678-1741, (It.) Concerti, The Four Seasons.
Richard Wagner, 1813-1883, (G.) Rienzi, Tannhauser, Lohengrin, Tristan und Isolde.
Karl Maria von Weber, 1786-1826, (G.) Der Freischutz.

Composers of Operettas, Musicals, and Popular Music

Richard Adler, b. 1921, (U.S.) *Pajama Game; Damn Yankees.*
Milton Ager, 1893-1979, (U.S.) I Wonder What's Become of Sally; Hard Hearted Hannah; Ain't She Sweet?
Leroy Anderson, 1908-1975, (U.S.) Syncopated Clock; Blue Tango; Sleigh Ride.
Harold Arlen, b. 1905, (U.S.) Stormy Weather; Over the Rainbow; Blues in the Night; That Old Black Magic.
Burt Bacharach, b. 1928, (U.S.) Raindrops Keep Fallin' on My Head; Walk on By; What the World Needs Now is Love.
Ernest Ball, 1878-1927, (U.S.) Mother Machree; When Irish Eyes Are Smiling.
Irving Berlin, b. 1888, (U.S.) *This is the Army; Annie Get Your Gun; Call Me Madam;* God Bless America; White Christmas.
Eubie Blake, b. 1883, (U.S.) *Shuffle Along;* I'm Just Wild about Harry.
Jerry Bock, b. 1928, (U.S.) *Mr. Wonderful; Fiorello; Fiddler on the Roof; The Rothschilds.*
Carrie Jacobs Bond, 1862-1946, (U.S.) I Love You Truly.
Nacio Herb Brown, 1896-1964, (U.S.) Singing in the Rain; You Were Meant for Me; All I Do Is Dream of You.
Hoagy Carmichael, b. 1899, (U.S.) Stardust; Georgia on My Mind; Old Buttermilk Sky.
George M. Cohan, 1878-1942, (U.S.) Give My Regards to Broadway; You're A Grand Old Flag; Over There.
Noel Coward, 1899-1973 (Br.) *Bitter Sweet;* Mad Dogs and Englishmen; Mad About the Boy.
Walter Donaldson, 1893-1947, (U.S.) My Buddy; Carolina in the Morning; You're Driving Me Crazy; Makin' Whoopee.
Vernon Duke, 1903-1969, (U.S.) April in Paris.
Gus Edwards, 1879-1945, (U.S.) School Days; By the Light of the Silvery Moon; In My Merry Oldsmobile.

Sherman Edwards, b. 1919, (U.S.) See You in September; Wonderful! Wonderful!

Sammy Fain, b. 1902, Wedding Bells Are Breaking Up That Old Gang of Mine; Let a Smile Be Your Umbrella.

Fred Fisher, 1875-1942, (U.S.) Peg O' My Heart; Chicago; Dardanella.

Stephen Collins Foster, 1826-1864, (U.S.) My Old Kentucky Home; Old Folks At Home.

Rudolf Friml, 1879-1972, (naturalized U.S.) *The Firefly; Rose Marie; Vagabond King; Bird of Paradise.*

John Gay, 1685-1732, (Br.) *The Beggar's Opera.*

Edwin F. Goldman, 1878-1956, (U.S.) marches.

Percy Grainger, 1882-1961, (Br.) Country Gardens.

John Green, b. 1908, (U.S.) Body and Soul; Out of Nowhere; I Cover the Waterfront.

Ferde Grofe, 1892-1972, (U.S.) Grand Canyon Suite.

W. C. Handy, 1873-1958, (U.S.) St. Louis Blues.

Ray Henderson, 1896-1970, (U.S.) *George White's Scandals;* That Old Gang of Mine; Five Foot Two, Eyes of Blue.

Victor Herbert, 1859-1924, (Ir.-U.S.) *Mlle. Modiste; Babes in Toyland; The Red Mill; Naughty Marietta; Sweethearts.*

Jerry Herman, b. 1932, (U.S.) *Milk and Honey; Hello Dolly; Mame; Dear World.*

Al Hoffman, 1902-1960, (U.S.) Heartaches, Mairzy Doats.

Scott Joplin, 1868-1917, (U.S.) *Treemonisha.*

John Kander, b. 1927, (U.S.) *Cabaret; Chicago; Funny Lady.*

Jerome Kern, 1885-1945, (U.S.) *Sally; Sunny; Show Boat; Cat and the Fiddle; Music in the Air; Roberta.*

Burton Lane, b. 1912, (U.S.) *Three's a Crowd; Finian's Rainbow; On A Clear Day You Can See Forever.*

Franz Lehar, 1870-1948, (Hung.) *Merry Widow.*

Mitch Leigh, b. 1928, (U.S.) *Man of La Mancha.*

Frank Loesser, 1910-1969, (U.S.) *Guys and Dolls; Where's Charley?; The Most Happy Fella; How to Succeed . . .*

Frederick Loewe, b. 1901, (Aust.-U.S.) *The Day Before Spring; Brigadoon; Paint Your Wagon; My Fair Lady; Camelot.*

Henry Mancini, b. 1924, (U.S.) Moon River; Days of Wine and Roses; Pink Panther Theme.

Jimmy McHugh, 1894-1969, (U.S.) I Can't Give You Anything But Love; I Feel a Song Coming On.

Joseph Meyer, b. 1894, (U.S.) If You Knew Susie; California, Here I Come; Crazy Rhythm.

Chauncey Olcott, 1858-1932, (U.S.) Mother Machree; My Wild Irish Rose.

Cole Porter, 1893-1964, (U.S.) *Anything Goes; Jubilee; DuBarry Was a Lady; Panama Hattie; Mexican Hayride; Kiss Me Kate; Can Can; Silk Stockings.*

Andre Previn, b. 1929, (U.S.) *Coco.*

Richard Rodgers, 1902-1979, (U.S.) *Garrick Gaieties; Connecticut Yankee; America's Sweetheart; On Your Toes; Babes in Arms; The Boys from Syracuse; Oklahoma!; Carousel; South Pacific; The King and I; Flower Drum Song; The Sound of Music.*

Sigmund Romberg, 1887-1951, (Hung.) *Maytime; The Student Prince; Desert Song; Blossom Time.*

Harold Rome, b. 1908, (U.S.) *Pins and Needles; Call Me Mister; Wish You Were Here; Fanny; Destry Rides Again.*

Vincent Rose, b. 1880-1944, (U.S.) Avalon; Whispering; Blueberry Hill.

Harry Ruby, 1895-1974, (U.S.) Three Little Words; Who's Sorry Now?

Arthur Schwartz, b. 1900, (U.S.) *The Band Wagon; Inside U.S.A.; A Tree Grows in Brooklyn.*

Stephen Sondheim, b. 1930, (U.S.) *A Little Night Music; Company.*

John Philip Sousa. 1854-1932, (U.S.) *El Capitan;* Stars and Stripes Forever.

Oskar Straus, 1870-1954, (Aus.) *Chocolate Soldier.*

Johann Strauss, 1825-1899, (Aus.) *Gypsy Baron; Die Fledermaus;* waltzes: Blue Danube, Artist's Life.

Charles Strouse, b. 1928, (U.S.) *Bye Bye, Birdie; All American; Golden Boy; Applause; Annie.*

Jule Styne, b. 1905, (b. London-U.S.) *Gentlemen Prefer Blondes; Bells Are Ringing; Gypsy; Funny Girl.*

Arthur S. Sullivan, 1842-1900, (Br.) *H.M.S. Pinafore, Pirates of Penzance; The Mikado.*

Deems Taylor, 1885-1966, (U.S.) *Peter Ibbetson.*

Egbert van Alstyne, 1882-1951, (U.S.) In the Shade of the Old Apple Tree; Memories; Pretty Baby.

James Van Heusen, b. 1913, (U.S.) Moonlight Becomes You Swinging on a Star.

Albert von Tilzer, 1878-1956, (U.S.) I'll Be With You in Apple Blossom Time; Take Me Out to the Ball Game.

Harry von Tilzer, 1872-1946, (U.S.) Only a Bird in a Gilded Cage; On a Sunday Afternoon.

Harry Warren, b. 1893, (U.S.) You're My Everything; We're in the Money; I Only Have Eyes for You; September in the Rain.

Kurt Weill, 1900-1950, (G.-U.S.) *Threepenny Opera; Lady in the Dark; Knickerbocker Holiday; One Touch of Venus.*

Percy Wenrich, 1887-1952, (U.S.) When You Wore a Tulip Moonlight Bay; Put On Your Old Gray Bonnet.

Richard A. Whiting, 1891-1938, (U.S.) Till We Meet Again Sleepytime Gal; Beyond the Blue Horizon.

Meredith Willson, b. 1902, (U.S.) *The Music Man.*

Vincent Youmans, 1898-1946, (U.S.) *Two Little Girls in Blue Wildflower; No, No, Nanette; Hit the Deck; Rainbow; Smiles.*

Lyricists

Sammy Cahn, b. 1913, (U.S.) High Hopes; Love and Marriage; The Second Time Around.

Betty Comden, b. 1919 (U.S.) and **Adolph Green,** b. 1915 (U.S.) The Party's Over; Just in Time; New York, New York.

Buddy De Sylva, 1895-1950, (U.S.) When Day is Done; Look for the Silver Lining; April Showers.

Hal David, b. 1921 (U.S.) What the World Needs Now Is Love.

Howard Dietz, b. 1896, (U.S.) Dancing in the Dark; You and the Night and the Music.

Al Dubin, 1891-1945, (U.S.) Tiptoe Through the Tulips; Anniversary Waltz; Lullaby of Broadway.

Dorothy Fields, 1905-1974, (U.S.) On the Sunny Side of the Street; Don't Blame Me; The Way You Look Tonight.

Ira Gershwin, b. 1896, (U.S.) The Man I Love; Fascinating Rhythm; S'Wonderful; Embraceable You.

Wm. S. Gilbert, 1836-1911, (Br.) *The Mikado; H.M.S. Pinafore.*

Oscar Hammerstein II, 1895-1960, (U.S.) Ol' Man River; *Oklahoma; Carousel.*

E. Y. (Yip) Harburg, b. 1898, (U.S.) Brother, Can You Spare a Dime; April in Paris; Over the Rainbow.

Lorenz Hart, 1895-1943, (U.S.) Isn't It Romantic; Blue Moon; Lover; Manhattan; My Funny Valentine.

DuBose Heyward, 1885-1940, (U.S.) Summertime; A Woman Is A Sometime Thing.

Gus Kahn, 1886-1941, (U.S.) Memories; Ain't We Got Fun.

Johnny Mercer, 1909-1976, (U.S.) Blues in the Night; Come Rain or Come Shine; Laura; That Old Black Magic.

Jack Norworth, 1879-1959, (U.S.) Take Me Out to the Ball Game; Shine On Harvest Moon.

Jack Yellen, b. 1892, (U.S.) Down by the O-Hi-O; Ain't She Sweet; Happy Days Are Here Again.

Noted Jazz Artists

Jazz has been called America's only completely unique contribution to Western culture. The following individuals have made major contributions in this field:

Julian "Cannonball" Adderley, 1928-1975: alto sax.

Henry "Red" Allen, 1908-1967: trumpet.

Albert Ammons, 1907-1949: boogie-woogie pianist.

Louis "Satchmo" Armstrong, 1900-1971: trumpet, singer; originated the "scat" vocal.

Mildred Bailey, 1907-1951: blues singer.

Count Basie, b. 1904: orchestra leader, piano.

Sidney Bechet, 1897-1950: early innovator, soprano sax.

Bix Beiderbecke, 1903-1931: cornet, piano, composer.

Bunny Berrigan, 1909-1942: trumpet, singer.

Barney Bigard, b. 1906: clarinet.

Art Blakey, b. 1919: drums, leader.

Jimmy Blanton, 1921-1942: bass.

Charles "Buddy" Bolden, 1868-1931: cornet; formed the first jazz band in the 1890s.

Big Bill Broonzy, 1893-1958: blues singer, guitar.

Dave Brubeck, b. 1920: piano, combo leader.

Harry Carney, 1910-1975: baritone sax.

Benny Carter, b. 1907: alto sax, trumpet, clarinet.

Sidney Catlett, 1910-1951: drums.

Charlie Christian, 1919-1942: guitar; often given credit for the term "bebop".

Kenny Clarke, b. 1914: pioneer of modern drums; founder-member Modern Jazz Quartet, 1952.

Buck Clayton, b. 1911: trumpet, arranger.

Al Cohn, b. 1925: tenor sax, composer.

Cozy Cole, b. 1909: drums.

Ornette Coleman, b. 1930: saxophone; unorthodox style.

John Coltrane, 1926-1967: tenor sax innovator.

Eddie Condon, 1904-1973: guitar, band leader; promoter of Dixieland.

Chick Corea, b. 1941: pianist, composer.

Miles Davis, b. 1926: trumpet; pioneer of cool jazz.

Wild Bill Davison, b. 1906: cornet, leader; prominent in early Chicago jazz.

Buddy De Franco, b. 1933: clarinet.

Paul Desmond, 1924-1977: alto sax.
Vic Dickenson, b. 1906: trombone, composer.
Warren "Baby" Dodds, 1898-1959: Dixieland drummer.
Johnny Dodds, 1892-1940: clarinet.
Jimmy Dorsey, 1904-1957: clarinet, alto sax; band leader.
Tommy Dorsey, 1905-1956: trombone; band leader.
Roy Eldridge, b. 1911: trumpet, drums, singer.
Duke Ellington, 1899-1974: piano, orchestra leader, composer.
Bill Evans, b. 1929: piano.
Gil Evans, b. 1912: composer, piano.
Ella Fitzgerald, b. 1918: singer.
Erroll Garner, 1921-1977: piano, composer, "Misty".
Stan Getz, b. 1927: tenor sax.
Dizzy Gillespie, b. 1917: trumpet, composer; a developer of bop.
Benny Goodman, b. 1909: clarinet, band and combo leader.
Dexter Gordon, b. 1923: tenor sax; bop-derived style.
Stephane Grappelli, b. 1908: violin.
Bobby Hackett, 1915-1976: trumpet, cornet.
Lionel Hampton, b. 1913: vibes, drums, piano, combo leader.
W. C. Handy, 1873-1958: composer, "St. Louis Blues."
Coleman Hawkins, 1904-1969: tenor sax; 1939 recording of "Body and Soul", a classic.
Roy Haynes, b. 1926: drums.
Fletcher Henderson, 1898-1952: orchestra leader, arranger; pioneered jazz and dance bands of the 30s.
Woody Herman, b. 1913: clarinet, alto sax, band leader.
Jay C. Higginbotham, 1906-1973: trombone.
Earl "Fatha" Hines, b. 1905: piano, songwriter.
Johnny Hodges, b. 1906: alto sax.
Billie Holiday, 1915-1959: blues singer, "Strange Fruit."
Sam "Lightnin' " Hopkins, b. 1912: blues singer, guitar.
Mahalia Jackson, 1911-1972: gospel singer; and example of the link between the religious and secular roots of jazz.
Milt Jackson, b. 1923: vibes, piano, guitar.
Illinois Jacquet, b. 1922: tenor sax.
Keith Jarrett, b. 1945: technically phenomenal pianist.
Blind Lemon Jefferson, 1897-1930: blues singer, guitar.
Bunk Johnson, 1879-1949: cornet, trumpet.
James P. Johnson, 1891-1955: piano, composer.
J. J. Johnson, b. 1924: trombone, composer.
Jo Jones, b. 1911: drums.
Quincy Jones, b. 1933: arranger.
Thad Jones, b. 1923: trumpet, cornet.
Scott Joplin, 1868-1917: composer; "Maple Leaf Rag."
Stan Kenton, 1912-1979: orchestra leader, composer, piano.
John Kirby, 1908-1952: major combo leader of the 30s.
Lee Konitz, b. 1927: alto sax.
Gene Krupa, 1909-1973: drums, band and combo leader.
Tommy Ladnier, 1900-1939: trumpet.
Eddie Lang, 1904-1933: guitar.
Huddie Ledbetter (Leadbelly), 1888-1949: blues singer, guitar.
John Lewis, b. 1920: composer, piano, combo leader.
Jimmie Lunceford, 1902-1947: band leader, sax.
Jimmy McPartland, b. 1907: trumpet.
Glenn Miller, 1904-1944: trombone, dance band leader.
Charles Mingus, 1922-1979: bass, composer, combo leader.
Thelonious Monk, b. 1920: piano, composer, combo leader; a developer of bop.
Wes Montgomery, 1925-1971: guitar.
"Jelly Roll" Morton, 1885-1941: composer, piano, singer.
Bennie Moten, 1894-1935: piano; an early organizer of large jazz orchestras.
Gerry Mulligan, b. 1927: baritone sax, arranger, leader.
Turk Murphy, b. 1915: trombone, band leader.
Theodore "Fats" Navarro, 1923-1950: trumpet.
Red Nichols, 1905-1965: cornet, combo leader.
Jimmie Noone, 1895-1944: clarinet, leader.
Red Norvo, b. 1908: vibes, band leader.
Anita O'Day, b. 1919: singer.
King Oliver, 1885-1938: cornet, band leader; teacher of Louis Armstrong.
Kid Ory, 1886-1973: trombone, composer, "Muskrat Ramble".
Charlie "Bird" Parker, 1920-1955: alto sax, composer; rated by many as the greatest jazz improviser.
Oscar Peterson, b. 1925: piano, composer, combo leader.
Oscar Pettiford, 1922-1960: a leading bassist in the bop era.
Bud Powell, 1924-1966: piano, composer; modern jazz pioneer.
Gertrude "Ma" Rainey, 1886-1939: first of the great blues singers.
Don Redman, 1900-1964: composer, arranger; pioneer in the evolution of the large orchestra.
Django Reinhardt, 1910-1953: guitar; Belgian gypsy, first European to influence American jazz.
Buddy Rich, b. 1917: drums, band leader.
Max Roach, b. 1925: drums.
Shorty Rogers, b. 1924: composer, trumpet, band leader.
Sonny Rollins, b. 1929: tenor sax.
Pete Rugolo, b. 1915: composer, orchestra leader.
Jimmy Rushing, 1903-1972: blues singer.
Pee Wee Russell, 1906-1969: clarinet.
Artie Shaw, b. 1910: clarinet, combo leader.
George Shearing, b. 1919: piano, composer, "Lullaby of Birdland".
Horace Silver, b. 1928: piano, combo leader.
Zoot Sims, b 1925: tenor, alto sax; clarinet.
Zutty Singleton, 1898-1975: Dixieland drummer.
Bessie Smith, 1894-1937: blues singer.
Clarence "Pinetop" Smith, 1904-1929: piano, singer; pioneer of boogie woogie.
Joe Smith, 1902-1937: trumpet.
Willie "The Lion" Smith, 1897-1973: stride style pianist.
Muggsy Spanier, 1906-1967: cornet, band leader.
Billy Strayhorn, 1915-67: composer, piano; with Duke Ellington from 1939.
Sonny Stitt, b. 1924: alto, tenor sax.
Art Tatum, 1910-1956: piano; technical virtuoso.
Cecil Taylor, b. 1933: avant-garde pianist, composer.
Jack Teagarden, 1905-1964: trombone, singer.
Dave Tough, 1908-1948: drums.
Lennie Tristano, b. 1919: piano, composer.
Joe Turner, b. 1911: blues singer.
Joe Turner, b. 1907: stride piano.
McCoy Tyner, b. 1938: piano, composer.
Sarah Vaughan, b. 1924: singer.
Joe Venuti, 1904-1978: first great jazz violinist.
Thomas "Fats" Waller, 1904-1943: piano, singer, composer, "Ain't Misbehavin' ".
Dinah Washington, 1924-1963: singer.
Chick Webb, 1902-1939: band leader, drums; generally credited with laying the foundations for jazz percussion.
Paul Whiteman, 1890-1967: orchestra leader; a major figure in the introduction of jazz to a large audience.
Charles "Cootie" Williams, b. 1908: trumpet, band leader.
Mary Lou Williams, b. 1914: pianist, composer.
Teddy Wilson, b. 1912: piano, composer.
Kai Winding, b. 1922: trombone, composer.
Jimmy Yancey, 1894-1951: piano.
Lester "Pres" Young, 1909-1959: tenor sax, composer: a bop pioneer.

Popular American Songs

(m-music; w-words)

After You've Gone: Turner Layton(m); Henry Creamer(w); 1918; popularized by Al Jolson, Sophie Tucker.
Ain't She Sweet: Milton Ager(m); Jack Yellen(w); 1927; introduced by Paul Ash orch., Oriental Theater, Chicago.
Alexander's Ragtime Band: Irving Berlin(m,w); 1911.
Always (I'll Be Loving You): Irving Berlin(m,w); 1925.
April In Paris: Vernon Duke(m); E. Y. Harburg(w); 1932.
April Showers: Louis Silvers(m); Buddy De Sylva(w); 1921; introduced by Al Jolson in musical *Bombo*.
As Time Goes By: Herman Hupfeld(m,w); 1931, in musical *Everbody's Welcome*, also movie *Casablanca*, in 1942.
Baby Face: Harry Akst(m); Benny Davis(w); 1926; introduced by Jan Garber on RCA Victor record.
The Band Played On: C. B. Ward(m); J. E. Palmer(w); 1895; song owned and promoted by newspaper, New York *World*.
Beer Barrel Polka: J. Vejvoda and Lew Brown(w); 1934; music was a Czech popular song.
The Best Things in Life Are Free: Ray Henderson(m); Buddy De Sylva and Lew Brown(w); 1927; in musical *Good News*.
Beyond the Blue Horizon: R. A. Whiting(m); Leo Robin(w); 1930; introduced by Jeanette MacDonald in movie *Monte Carlo*.
Blowin' in the Wind: Bob Dylan(m,w); 1963.
Blue Skies: Irving Berlin(m,w); 1926.
Body and Soul: John Green(m); E. Heyton, R. Sour, F. Eyton(w); 1930; introduced by Gertrude Lawrence on BBC.
Bye, Bye Blackbird: R. Henderson(m); Mort Dixon(w); 1926; popularized by Eddie Cantor.
By the Beautiful Sea: Harry Carroll(m); Harold Atteridge(w); 1914; vaudeville.
By the Light of the Silvery Moon: Gus Edwards(m); Edward Madden(w); 1909; in revue *School Boys and Girls*.
Chicago: Fred Fisher(m,w); 1922; vaudeville.
California, Here I Come: Joseph Meyer(m); Al Jolson, Buddy De Sylva(w); 1923; by Al Jolson in road tour of *Bombo*.
Daisy Bell (Bicycle Built for Two): Harry Dacre(m,w); circa

1892; London tune popularized in U.S. by Tony Pastor.

Dancing in the Dark: Arthur Schwartz(m); Howard Dietz(w); 1931; in revue *The Band Wagon.*

Down by the Old Mill Stream: Tell Taylor(m,w); 1910.

Easter Parade: Irving Berlin(m,w); 1933; introduced by Clifton Webb and Marilyn Miller in musical *As Thousands Cheer.*

Feelings: Paul Evans(m); Paul Parnes(w); 1969.

For Me and My Gal: G. W. Meyer(m); Edgar Leslie, E. R. Goetz(w); 1917; sung by Jolson, Cantor, Sophie Tucker, others.

Give My Regards to Broadway: George M. Cohan(m,w); 1904; in musical *Little Johnny Jones.*

Good Night Irene: Huddie Ledbetter(m,w); 1936; found by John Lomax in Louisiana State Prison, Angola, La.

Hail, Hail, the Gang's All Here: Arthur S. Sullivan(m); T. A. Morse(w), under pseudonym. D. A. Esrom; 1917.

Happy Days Are Here Again: Milton Ager(m); Jack Yellen(w); 1929; introduced on Black Thursday (10-24-29).

Heartaches: Al Hoffman(m); John Klenner(w); 1931; popularized by Ted Weems.

Hello, Dolly: Jerry Herman(m,w); 1964; by Carol Channing in musical of same name.

Home on the Range: Daniel E. Kelly?(m); Brewster (Bruce) Higley (w,m); 1904, called Arizona Home(w) 1873; composer and author uncertain.

Hot Time in the Old Town Tonight: T. M. Metz(m); Joe Hayden(w); 1896; minstrel show.

I Can't Give You Anything But Love: Jimmy McHugh(m); Dorothy Fields(w); 1928; in revue *Delmar's Revels.*

I Could Have Danced All Night: F. Loewe(m); A. J. Lerner(w); 1956; by Julie Andrews in *My Fair Lady.*

I Don't Know Why I Love You Like I Do: F. E. Ahlert(m); Roy Turk(w); 1931.

If You Knew Susie: Bud De Sylva and Joseph Meyer(w,m); 1925; by Al Jolson in *Big Boy.*

I Got Plenty o'Nothin': G. Gershwin(m); I. Gershwin, DuBose Heyward(w); 1935; in *Porgy and Bess.*

I'll Be Seeing You: Sammy Fain(m); Irving Kahal(w); 1938; popularized by Sinatra, Hildegarde, in 1943.

I'll See You in My Dreams: Isham Jones(m); Gus Kahn(w); 1924.

I Love You Truly: Carrie Jacobs Bond(m,w); 1901; originally an art song, later picked up by vaudeville.

I'm in the Mood for Love: J. McHugh(m); Dorothy Fields(w); 1935; by Alice Faye in movie *Every Night at Eight.*

The Impossible Dream: Mitch Leigh(m); Joe Darion(w); 1966; in musical *Man of La Mancha.*

I'm Sitting on Top of the World: Ray Henderson(m); Sam M. Lewis, Joe Young(w); 1925; popularized by Jolson in 1929 movie *The Singing Fool.*

In the Good Old Summertime: George Evans(m); Ren Shields(w); 1902.

I Only Have Eyes for You: Harry Warren(m); Al Dubin(w); 1934; by Dick Powell in movie *Dames.*

It Had To Be You: Isham Jones(m); Gus Kahn(w); 1924.

It's Been a Long, Long Time: Julie Styne(m); Sammy Cahn(w); 1945.

It Was a Very Good Year: Ervin Drake(m,w); 1965; introduced by Kingston Trio on record; popularized by Sinatra.

I've Got You Under My Skin: Cole Porter(m,w); 1936.

I Want a Girl Just Like the Girl: Harry von Tilzer(m); William Dilion(w); 1911.

I Wish You Love: J.W. Stole, Del Roma(m); Arthur Altman, Norman Gimbel(w); 1963.

I Wonder Who's Kissing Her Now: J. E. Howard, H. Orlob(m); Wm. M. Hough, F. R. Adams(w); 1909.

Jeannie With the Light Brown Hair: Stephen Foster(m,w); 1854.

June is Busting Out All Over: R. Rodgers(m); O. Hammerstein II(w); 1945; in *Carousel.*

Lazy River: S. Arodin, Hoagy Carmichael(m,w); 1931; on record by Carmichael with band including both Dorseys, Teagarden, Krupa, Goodman, Venuti, and Beiderbecke.

Let Me Call You Sweetheart: Leo Friedman(m); Beth Slater Whitson(w); 1910.

Lover: R. Rodgers(m); Lorenz Hart(w); 1933; by Jeanette MacDonald in movie *Love Me Tonight.*

Lullaby of Broadway: Harry Warren(m); Al Dubin(w); 1935; in movie *Gold Diggers of Broadway.*

Memories: Egbert van Alstyne(m); Gus Kahn(w); 1915.

Misty: Erroll Garner(m); Johnny Burke(w); 1955.

Moon River: Henry Mancini(m); Johnny Mercer(w); 1961; by Andy Williams under title for movie *Breakfast at Tiffany's.*

Moonlight Bay: Percy Wenrich(m); Edward Madden(w); 1912; vaudeville.

My Blue Heaven: Walter Donaldson(m); George Whiting(w); 1927; Tommy Lyman radio theme song.

Melancholy Baby; Ernie Burnett(m); George A. Norton(w); 1912; vaudeville.

My Wild Irish Rose: Chauncey Olcott(m,w); 1899; in musical *A Romance of Athlone.*

Night and Day: Cole Porter(m,w); 1932; by Fred Astaire and Claire Luce in musical *Gay Divorce;* title of Porter film biography.

Oh, What a Beautiful Mornin': R. Rodgers(m); O. Hammerstein II(w); 1943; by Alfred Drake in *Oklahoma!*

Oh! You Beautiful Doll: Nat D. Ayer(m); A. Seymour Brown(w); 1911; vaudeville.

Old Folks at Home (Swanee River): Stephen Foster(m,w); 1851; minstrel show.

Ol' Man River: Jerome Kern(m); O. Hammerstein II(w); 1927; by Jules Bledsoe in *Show Boat.*

On the Sunny Side of the Street: J. McHugh(m); Dorothy Fields(w); 1930; in *International Revue* with Gertrude Lawrence.

Over The Rainbow: Harold Arlen(m); E. Y. Harburg(w); 1939; by seventeen-year-old Judy Garland in *Wizard of Oz.*

Peg O'My Heart: Fred Fisher(m); Alfred Bryan(w); in *Ziegfeld Follies of 1913.*

Pennies From Heaven: Arthur Johnston(m); Johnny Burke(w); 1936; by Bing Crosby in movie of same name.

People: Jule Styne(m); Bob Merrill(w); 1964; by Barbra Streisand in musical *Funny Girl.*

Pretty Baby: E. van Alstyne, Tony Jackson(m); Gus Kahn(w); 1916; by Dolly Hackett in musical *The Passing Show.*

A Pretty Girl Is Like a Melody: Irving Berlin(m,w); in *Ziegfeld Follies of 1919;* became Follies theme song.

Put On Your Old Gray Bonnet: Percy Wenrich(m); Stanley Murphy(w); 1909.

Put Your Arms Around Me, Honey: Albert von Tilzer(m); Junie McCree(w); 1910; vaudeville.

Raindrops Keep Falling on My Head: Burt Bacharach(m); Hal David(w); 1969, in film *Butch Cassidy and the Sundance Kid.*

Rudolph, the Red-Nosed Reindeer: Johnny Marks(m,w); 1949; by Gene Autry on Columbia record.

School Days: Gus Edwards(m); Will D. Cobb(w); 1907; vaudeville.

September Song: Kurt Weill(m); Maxwell Anderson(w); 1938; by Walter Huston in play *Knickerbocker Holiday.*

The Shadow of Your Smile: Johnny Mandel(m); Paul Francis Webster(w); 1965; in film *The Sandpiper.*

Shine On Harvest Moon: Nora Bayes, Jack Norworth(m); Norworth(w); introduced by Nora Bayes in *Ziegfeld Follies of 1908.*

Sidewalks of New York: J. W. Blake, C. B. Lawlor(m,w); 1894; by Lottie Gilson at Old London Theatre on the Bowery.

Singing in the Rain: Nacio Herb Brown(m); Arthur Freed(w); 1929; by Cliff Edwards in movie *Hollywood Revue of 1929.*

Smoke Gets in Your Eyes: Jerome Kern(m); Otto Harbach(w); 1933; by Tamara in musical *Roberta.*

Somebody Loves Me: G. Gershwin(m); B. DeSylva, B. MacDonald(w); 1924; *George White's Scandals of 1924.*

Some Enchanted Evening: R. Rodgers(m); O. Hammerstein II(w); 1949; by Ezio Pinza in *South Pacific.*

Stardust: Hoagy Carmichael(m); Mitchell Parish(w); 1929.

Stormy Weather: Harold Arlen(m); Ted Koehler(w); 1933; popularized by Ethel Waters.

Strike Up the Band: George Gershwin(m); Ira Gershwin(w); 1930; in musical of the same name.

Summertime: George Gershwin(m); DuBose Heyward(w); 1935; by Abbie Mitchell opening *Porgy and Bess.*

Sweet Georgia Brown: Ben Bernie, M. Pinkard, K. Casey(m,w); 1925.

Sweethearts: Victor Herbert(m); R. B. Smith(w); 1913; in musical of the same name.

Take Me Out to the Ball Game: Albert von Tilzer(m); Jack Norworth(w); 1908; vaudeville.

Tea for Two: Vincent Youmans(m); Irving Caesar(w); 1920; by Louise Groody, John Barker, in *No, No, Nanette.*

Tennessee Waltz: Redd Stewart, Pee Wee King(m,w); 1948; popularized by Patti Page.

That Old Black Magic: Harold Arlen(m); Johnny Mercer(w); 1942; in movie *Star Spangled Rhythm.*

Three Little Words: Harry Ruby(m); Bert Kalmar(w); 1930; by Bing Crosby in Amos & Andy movie *Check and Double Check.*

Toot, Toot, Tootsie, Goodbye: Dan Russo(m); Gus Kahn, Ernie Erdman(w); 1922; by Jolson in *Bombo;* later in first talkie *The Jazz Singer.*

When Irish Eyes Are Smiling: Ernest R. Ball(m); C. Olcott, G. Graft(w); 1912; by Olcott in musical *Isle of Dreams.*

When Johnny Comes Marching Home: Louis Lambert(m,w); 1863; Lambert thought pen-name for Patrick S. Gilmore.

When You're Smiling: M. Fisher, J. Goodwin, L. Shay(m,w); 1928.

When You Wish Upon A Star: Leigh Harline(m); Ned Washington(w); 1940; by Cliff Edwards in animated *Pinocchio.*

When You Wore a Tulip: Percy Wenrich(m); Jack Mahoney(w); 1914; vaudeville.

Whispering: John Schonberger, Vincent Rose(m); Richard Coburn(w); 1920; introduced by Paul Whiteman.

White Christmas: Irving Berlin(m,w); 1942; by Bing Crosby in movie *Holiday Inn.*

With a Song in My Heart: R. Rodgers(m); Lorenz Hart(w); 1929; in musical *Spring Is Here.*

Without a Song: Vincent Youmans(m); Billy Rose, E. Eliscu(w); 1929; in musical *Great Day.*

Yellow Rose of Texas: nothing is known of the songwriter but initials "J. K."; 1853; minstrel show.

Yes, Sir, That's My Baby: Walter Donaldson(m); Gus Kahn(w); 1925; popularized by Eddie Cantor.

You and the Night and the Music: Arthur Schwartz(m); Howard Dietz(w); 1934; in musical play *Revenge With Music.*

You Are My Sunshine: Jimmie Davis(m); C. Mitchell(w); 1940; in Tex Ritter movie *Take Me Back to Oklahoma.* Davis governor of Louisiana, 1944-48.

You Made Me Love You: J. V. Monaco(m); Joe McCarthy(w); 1913; by Al Jolson in musical *Honeymoon Express.*

Entertainment Personalities — Where and When Born

Actors, Actresses, Dancers, Musicians, Producers, Radio-TV Performers, Singers

Name	Birthplace	Born
Abbott, George	Forestville, N.Y.	6/25/87
Abel, Walter	St. Paul, Minn.	6/6/98
Ackermann, Bettye	Cottageville, S.C.	2/28/28
Acuff, Roy	Maynardsville, Tenn.	9/15/03
Adams, Don	New York, N.Y.	4/19/27
Adams, Edie	Kingston, Pa.	4/16/29
Adams, Joey	New York, N.Y.	1/6/11
Adams, Julie	Waterloo, Ia.	10/17/28
Addams, Dawn	Suffolk, England	9/21/30
Adler, Larry	Baltimore, Md.	2/10/14
Adler, Luther	New York, N.Y.	5/4/03
Agar, John	Chicago, Ill.	1/31/21
Aherne, Brian	Worcestershire, England.	5/2/02
Ailey, Alvin	Rogers, Tex.	1/5/31
Aimee, Anouk	Paris, France	4/27/32
Akins, Claude	Nelson, Ga.	5/25/18
Albanese, Licia	Bari, Italy	7/22/13
Alberghetti, Anna Maria.	Pesaro, Italy	5/15/36
Albert, Eddie	Rock Island, Ill.	4/22/08
Albert, Edward	Los Angeles, Cal.	2/20/51
Albertson, Jack	Malden, Mass.	6/16/10
Albright, Lola	Akron, Oh.	7/20/25
Alda, Alan	New York, N.Y.	1/28/36
Alda, Robert	New York, N.Y.	2/26/14
Alexander, Jane	Boston, Mass.	10/28/39
Allan, Elizabeth	England	1910
Allen, Mel	Birmingham, Ala.	2/14/13
Allen, Steve	New York, N.Y.	12/26/21
Allen, Woody	Brooklyn, N.Y.	12/1/35
Allison, Fran	LaPorte City, Ia.	—
Allyson, June	Lucerne, N.Y.	10/7/23
Alpert, Herb	Los Angeles, Cal.	3/31/35
Altman, Robert	Kansas City, Mo.	2/20/25
Ameche, Don	Kenosha, Wis.	5/31/08
Ames, Ed	Boston, Mass.	1929
Ames, Leon	Portland, Ind.	1/20/03
Amos, John	Newark, N.J.	—
Amsterdam, Morey	Chicago, Ill.	12/14/14
Anderson, Ian	Blackpool, England	8/10/47
Anderson, Judith	Adelaide, Australia	2/10/98
Anderson, Loni	St. Paul, Minn.	8/5/-
Anderson, Lynn	Grand Forks, N.D.	9/26/47
Anderson, Marian	Philadelphia, Pa.	2/17/02
Anderson, Mary	Birmingham, Ala.	1922
Anderson, Melissa Sue	Berkeley, Cal.	9/26/62
Anderson, Michael Jr.	London, England	1943
Anderson, Richard	Long Branch, N.J.	8/8/26
Andersson, Bibi	Stockholm, Sweden	11/11/35
Andress, Ursula	Switzerland	1936
Andrews, Dana	Collins, Miss.	1/1/12
Andrews, Edward	Griffin, Ga.	10/9/15
Andrews, Julie	Walton, England	10/1/35
Andrews, Maxene	Minneapolis, Minn.	1918
Andrews, Patty	Minneapolis, Minn.	1920
Angel, Heather	Oxford, England	2/9/09
Anka, Paul	Ottawa, Ont.	7/30/41
Ann-Margret	Stockholm, Sweden	4/28/41
Annabella	Paris, France	1912
Ansara, Michael	Lowell, Mass.	4/15/27
Arden, Eve	Mill Valley, Cal.	4/30/12
Arkin, Alan	New York, N.Y.	3/26/34
Arnaz, Desi	Santiago, Cuba	3/2/17
Arnaz, Desi Jr.	Los Angeles, Cal.	1/19/53
Arnaz, Lucie	Hollywood, Cal.	7/17/51
Arness, James	Minneapolis, Minn.	5/26/23
Arnold, Eddy	Henderson, Tenn.	5/15/18
Arrau, Claudio	Chillau, Chile	2/6/03
Arroyo, Martina	New York, N.Y.	1937
Arthur, Beatrice	New York, N.Y.	5/13/26
Arthur, Jean	New York, N.Y.	10/17/08
Ashley, Elizabeth	Ocala, Fla.	8/30/41
Asner, Edward	Kansas City, Kan.	11/15/29
Astaire, Fred	Omaha, Neb.	5/10/99
Astin, John	Baltimore, Md.	3/30/30
Astor, Mary	Quincy, Ill.	5/3/06
Atkins, Chet	Luttrell, Tenn.	6/20/24
Attenborough, Richard	Cambridge, England	8/29/23
Aumont, Jean-Pierre	Paris, France	1/5/09
Autry, Gene	Tioga, Tex.	9/29/07
Avalon, Frankie	Philadelphia, Pa.	9/8/40
Aykroyd, Dan	Ottowa, Ont.	7/1/52
Ayres, Lew	Minneapolis, Minn.	12/28/08
Aznavour, Charles	Paris, France	5/22/24
Bacall, Lauren	New York, N.Y.	9/16/24
Backus, Jim	Cleveland, Oh.	2/25/13
Baddeley, Hermione	Shropshire, England	11/13/06
Baer, Max Jr.	Oakland, Cal.	12/4/37
Baez, Joan	Staten Island, N.Y.	1/9/41
Bailey, Pearl	Newport News, Va.	3/29/18
Bailey, Raymond	San Francisco, Cal.	1904
Bain, Barbara	Chicago, Ill.	1934
Bain, Conrad	Lethbridge, Alta.	2/4/23
Baio, Scott	Brooklyn, N.Y.	9/22/61
Baird, Bil	Grand Island, Neb.	8/15/04
Baker, Carroll	Johnstown, Pa.	5/28/31
Baker, Diane	Hollywood, Cal.	1938
Baker, Joe Don	Groesbeck, Tex.	2/12/36
Baker, Kenny	Monrovia, Cal.	9/30/12
Bakewell, William	Hollywood, Cal.	1908
Balanchine, George	St. Petersburg, Russia	1/9/04
Ball, Lucille	Jamestown, N.Y.	8/6/11
Ballard, Kaye	Cleveland, Oh.	11/20/26
Balsam, Martin	New York, N.Y.	11/4/19
Bancroft, Anne	New York, N.Y.	9/17/31
Barber, Red	Columbus, Miss.	2/17/08
Bardot, Brigitte	Paris, France	1934
Bari, Lynn	Roanoke, Va.	1917
Barrault, Jean-Louis	Le Vesinet, France	1919
Barrie, Mona	London, England	12/18/09
Barris, Chuck	Philadelphia, Pa.	6/2/29
Barry, Gene	New York, N.Y.	6/4/22
Barry, Jack	Lindenhurst, N.Y.	3/20/18
Bartholomew, Freddie	London, England	3/28/24
Bartok, Eva	Budapest, Hungary	1929
Baryshnikov, Mikhail	Riga, Latvia	1/28/48
Basehart, Richard	Zanesville, Oh.	8/31/19
Basie, Count (Wm.)	Red Bank, N.J.	8/21/04
Bassey, Shirley	Cardiff, Wales	1937
Bates, Alan	Allestree, England	2/17/34
Baum, Kurt	Cologne, Germany	1908
Bavier, Frances	New York, N.Y.	1905
Baxter, Anne	Michigan City, Ind.	5/7/23
Baxter-Birney, Meredith	Los Angeles, Cal.	6/21/-
Beal, John	Joplin, Mo.	8/13/09
Bean, Orson	Burlington, Vt.	7/22/28
Beatty, Robert	Hamilton, Ont.	10/19/09
Beatty, Warren	Richmond, Va.	3/30/38
Becker, Sandy	New York, N.Y.	1922
Bedelia, Bonnie	New York, N.Y.	3/25/48
Bee Gees		
Gibb, Barry	Manchester, England	9/1/46
Gibb, Robin	" "	12/22/49
Gibb, Maurice	" "	12/22/49
Beery, Noah Jr.	New York, N.Y.	8/10/16
Belafonte, Harry	New York, N.Y.	3/1/27
Bel Geddes, Barbara	New York, N.Y.	10/31/22
Bellamy, Ralph	Chicago, Ill.	6/17/04

Name	Birthplace	Born
Belmondo, Jean-Paul	Neuilly-sur-Seine, France	4/9/33
Belushi, John	Chicago, Ill.	1/24/49
Benjamin, Richard	New York, N.Y.	5/22/38
Bennett, Joan	Palisades, N.J.	2/27/10
Bennett, Michael	Buffalo, N.Y.	4/8/43
Bennett, Tony	Astoria, N.Y.	8/3/26
Benson, Robby	Dallas, Tex.	1957
Bentley, John	Warwickshire, England	12/2/16
Bergen, Candice	Beverly Hills, Cal.	5/9/46
Bergen, Polly	Knoxville, Tenn.	7/14/30
Bergerac, Jacques	Biarritz, France	5/26/27
Bergman, Ingmar	Uppsala, Sweden	7/14/18
Bergman, Ingrid	Stockholm, Sweden	8/29/15
Bergner, Elisabeth	Vienna, Austria	8/22/00
Berle, Milton	New York, N.Y.	7/12/08
Berlinger, Warren	Brooklyn, N.Y.	8/31/37
Berman, Shelley	Chicago, Ill.	2/3/26
Bernardi, Herschel	New York, N.Y.	1923
Bernstein, Elmer	New York, N.Y.	4/4/22
Bernstein, Leonard	Lawrence, Mass.	8/25/18
Berry, Chuck	San Jose, Cal.	1/5/26
Berry, Ken	Moline, Ill.	—
Bertinelli, Valerie	Wilmington, Del.	4/23/60
Bessell, Ted	Flushing, N.Y.	1936
Bikel, Theodore	Vienna, Austria	5/2/24
Birney, David	Washington, D.C.	4/23/40
Bishop, Joey	Bronx, N.Y.	2/3/18
Bisoglio, Val	New York, N.Y.	5/7/26
Bisset, Jacqueline	Weybridge, England	9/13/46
Bixby, Bill	San Francisco, Cal.	1/22/34
Black, Karen	Park Ridge, Ill.	7/1/42
Blaine, Vivian	Newark, N.J.	11/21/23
Blair, Janet	Altoona, Pa.	4/23/21
Blair, Linda	St. Louis, Mo.	1/22/59
Blake, Amanda	Buffalo, N.Y.	2/20/31
Blake, Robert	Nutley, N.J.	9/18/38
Blakeley, Ronee	Idaho	1946
Blakely, Susan	Germany	—
Blanc, Mel	San Francisco, Cal.	5/30/08
Bloch, Ray	Alsace-Lorraine	1902
Bloom, Claire	London, England	2/15/31
Blyth, Ann	Mt. Kisco, N.Y.	8/16/28
Bohm, Karl	Graz, Austria	8/28/94
Bogarde, Dirk	London, England	3/28/21
Bogdanovich, Peter	Kingston, N.Y.	7/30/39
Bolger, Ray	Dorchester, Mass.	11/10/04
Bondi, Beulah	Chicago, Ill.	5/3/92
Bono, Sonny	Detroit, Mich.	2/16/40
Boone, Debby	Hackensack, N.J.	9/22/56
Boone, Pat	Jacksonville, Fla.	6/1/34
Boone, Richard	Los Angeles, Cal.	6/18/17
Booth, Shirley	New York, N.Y.	8/30/07
Borge, Victor	Copenhagen, Denmark	1/30/09
Borgnine, Ernest	Hamden, Conn.	1/24/17
Bosley, Tom	Chicago, Ill.	10/1/27
Bottoms, Timothy	Santa Barbara, Cal.	8/30/51
Bowie, David	London, England	1/8/47
Boyle, Peter	Philadelphia, Pa.	1933
Bracken, Eddie	Astoria, N.Y.	2/7/20
Brand, Neville	Kewanee, Ill.	8/13/21
Brando, Marlon	Omaha, Neb.	4/3/24
Brasselle, Keefe	Elyria, Oh.	2/7/23
Brazzi, Rossano	Bologna, Italy	9/18/16
Brennan, Eileen	Los Angeles, Cal.	9/3/37
Brenner, David	Philadelphia, Pa.	1945
Brewer, Teresa	Toledo, Oh.	5/7/31
Brian, David	New York, N.Y.	8/5/14
Bridges, Beau	Hollywood, Cal.	12/9/41
Bridges, Jeff	Los Angeles, Cal.	1950
Bridges, Lloyd	San Leandro, Cal.	1/15/13
Bridges, Todd	San Francisco, Cal.	5/27/65
Broderick, James	Charlestown, N.H.	3/7/27
Brolin, James	Los Angeles, Cal.	7/10/42
Bronson, Charles	Scooptown, Pa.	11/13/22
Brooks, Louise	Cherryvale, Kan.	1906
Brooks, Mel	New York, N.Y.	1926
Brooks, Stephen	Columbus, Oh.	1942
Brown, James	Pulaski, Tenn.	6/17/28
Brown, Jimmy	St. Simons Island, Ga.	2/17/36
Brown, Les	Reinerton, Pa.	3/14/12
Brown, Ray	Pittsburgh, Pa.	10/13/26
Brown, Tom	New York, N.Y.	1/6/13
Browne, Roscoe Lee	Woodbury, N.J.	1925
Bruce, Carol	Great Neck, N.Y.	11/15/19
Bruce, Virginia	Minneapolis, Minn.	1910
Bryant, Anita	Barnsdale, Okla.	3/25/40
Brynner, Yul	Sakhalin, Japan	7/11/20
Buchholz, Horst	Berlin, Germany	12/4/33
Bujold, Genevieve	Montreal, Que.	7/1/42
Bumbry, Grace	St. Louis, Mo.	1/4/37
Buono, Victor	Los Angeles, Cal.	1938
Burghoff, Gary	Bristol, Conn.	5/24/-
Burke, Paul	New Orleans, La.	7/21/26
Burnett, Carol	San Antonio, Tex.	4/26/36
Burns, George	New York, N.Y.	1/20/96
Burr, Raymond	New Westminster, B.C.	5/21/17
Burstyn, Ellen	Detroit, Mich.	12/7/32
Burton, Richard	South Wales	11/10/25
Bushell, Anthony	Kent, England	1904
Buttons, Red	New York, N.Y.	2/5/19
Buzzi, Ruth	Westerly, R.I.	7/24/36
Caan, James	New York, N.Y.	3/26/39
Caballe, Montserrat	Barcelona, Spain	4/12/33
Caesar, Sid	Yonkers, N.Y.	9/8/22
Cagney, James	New York, N.Y.	7/17/99
Caine, Michael	London, England	3/14/33
Caldwell, Sarah	Maryville, Mo.	1929
Caldwell, Zoe	Melbourne, Australia	9/14/33
Calhoun, Rory	Los Angeles, Cal.	8/8/22
Callan, Michael	Philadelphia, Pa.	1935
Callas, Charlie	Brooklyn, N.Y.	12/20/-
Calloway, Cab	Rochester, N.Y.	12/25/07
Calvert, Phyllis	London, England	2/18/15
Calvet, Corinne	Paris, France	4/30/26
Cameron, Rod	Calgary, Canada	12/7/12
Campbell, Glen	Billstown, Ark.	4/22/36
Cannon, Dyan	Tacoma, Wash.	1/4/37
Canova, Judy	Starke, Fla.	11/20/16
Cantinflas	Mexico City, Mex.	1917
Cantrell, Lana	Sydney, Australia	8/7/43
Capra, Frank	Palermo, Italy	5/18/97
Cardinale, Claudia	Tunisia	1939
Carey, Macdonald	Sioux City, Ia.	3/15/13
Carey, Phil	Hackensack, N.J.	7/15/25
Carle, Frankie	Providence, R.I.	1903
Carlisle, Kitty	New Orleans, La	9/3/15
Carman, Eric	Cleveland, Oh.	8/11/49
Carmichael, Hoagy	Bloomington, Ind	11/22/99
Carmichael, Ian	Hull, England	6/18/20
Carne, Judy	Northampton, England	1939
Carney, Art	Mt. Vernon, N.Y.	11/4/18
Carnovsky, Morris	St. Louis, Mo.	9/5/97
Caron, Leslie	Boulogne, France	7/1/31
Carpenter, Karen	New Haven, Conn.	3/2/50
Carpenter, Richard	New Haven, Conn.	10/15/46
Carr, Vikki	El Paso, Tex.	7/19/42
Carradine, David	Hollywood, Cal.	12/8/36
Carradine, John	New York, N.Y.	2/5/06
Carradine, Keith	San Mateo, Cal.	8/8/50
Carreras, Jose	Barcelona, Spain	1946
Carroll, Diahann	Bronx, N.Y.	7/17/35
Carroll, Madeleine	W. Bromwich, England	2/26/06
Carroll, Pat	Shreveport, La.	5/5/27
Carson, Johnny	Corning, Ia.	10/23/25
Carter, Jack	New York, N.Y.	6/24/23
Carter, June	Maces Spring, Va.	6/23/29
Carter, Lynda	Phoenix, Ariz.	7/24/-
Casadesus, Gaby	Marseilles, France	1902
Cash, Johnny	Kingsland, Ark.	2/26/32
Cass, Peggy	Boston, Mass.	5/21/24
Cassavetes, John	New York, N.Y.	12/9/29
Cassidy, David	New York, N.Y.	4/12/50
Cassidy, Shaun	Los Angeles, Cal.	9/27/58
Castellano, Richard	New York, N.Y.	9/4/33
Caulfield, Joan	West Orange, N.J.	6/1/22
Cavallaro, Carmen	New York, N.Y.	1913
Cavett, Dick	Gibbon, Neb.	11/19/36
Chamberlain, Richard	Beverly Hills, Cal.	3/31/35
Champion, Gower	Geneva, Ill.	6/22/21
Champion, Marge	Los Angeles, Cal.	9/2/23
Channing, Carol	Seattle, Wash.	1/31/23
Channing, Stockard	New York, N.Y.	—
Chaplin, Geraldine	Santa Monica, Cal.	1944
Chaplin, Sydney	Beverly Hills, Cal.	3/31/26
Charisse, Cyd	Amarillo, Tex.	3/8/23
Charles, Ray	Albany, Ga.	9/23/30
Chase, Chevy	New York, N.Y.	10/8/43
Checker, Chubby	Philadelphia, Pa.	10/3/41
Cher	El Centro, Cal.	5/20/46
Christian, Linda	Tampico, Mexico	11/13/24
Christie, Julie	Chukur, India	4/14/41
Christopher, Jordon	Youngstown, Oh.	1941
Christy, June	Springfield, Ill.	1925
Cilento, Diane	Queensland, Australia	1933
Claire, Ina	Washington, D.C.	1892
Clapton, Eric	Surrey, England	3/30/45
Clark, Dane	New York, N.Y.	2/18/15

Name	Birthplace	Born
Clark, Dick	Mt. Vernon, N.Y.	11/30/29
Clark, Petula	Ewell, Surrey, England	11/15/34
Clark, Roy	Meherrin, Va.	4/15/33
Clark, Susan	Sarnia, Ont.	3/4/44
Clayburgh, Jill	New York, N.Y.	4/30/44
Clayton, Jan	Tularosa, N.M.	—
Cliburn, Van	Shreveport, La.	7/12/34
Clooney, Rosemary	Maysville, Ky.	5/23/28
Coburn, James	Laurel, Neb.	8/31/28
Coca, Imogene	Philadelphia, Pa.	11/18/08
Coco, James	New York, N.Y.	3/21/30
Cohen, Myron	Grodno, Poland	1902
Colbert, Claudette	Paris, France	9/18/05
Cole, Michael	Madison, Wis.	1945
Cole, Natalie	Los Angeles, Cal.	2/6/50
Coleman, Gary	Zion, Ill.	2/8/68
Collins, Dorothy	Windsor, Ont.	11/18/26
Collins, Joan	London, England	5/23/33
Collins, Judy	Seattle, Wash.	5/1/39
Colonna, Jerry	Boston, Mass.	1903
Comden Betty	Brooklyn, N.Y.	5/3/19
Como, Perry	Canonsburg, Pa.	5/18/12
Conner, Nadine	Compton, Cal.	1913
Connery, Sean	Edinburgh, Scotland	8/25/30
Conniff, Ray	Attleboro, Mass.	11/6/16
Connors, Chuck	Brooklyn, N.Y.	4/10/21
Connors, Michael	Fresno, Cal.	8/15/25
Conrad, Robert	Chicago, Ill.	3/1/35
Conrad, William	Louisville, Ky.	9/27/20
Conried, Hans	Baltimore, Md.	4/1/15
Constantine, Michael	Reading, Pa.	5/22/27
Convy, Bert	St. Louis, Mo.	7/23/34
Conway, Gary	Boston, Mass.	1938
Conway, Tim	Willoughby, Oh.	12/15/33
Coogan, Jackie	Los Angeles, Cal.	10/26/14
Cook, Barbara	Atlanta, Ga.	10/25/27
Cooke, Alistair	England	11/20/08
Coolidge, Rita	Nashville, Tenn.	1944
Cooper, Alice	Detroit, Mich.	2/4/48
Cooper, Jackie	Los Angeles, Cal.	9/15/22
Coppola, Francis Ford	Detroit, Mich.	4/7/39
Corby, Ellen	Racine, Wis.	1913
Corelli, Franco	Ancona, Italy	4/8/23
Corey, Jeff	New York, N.Y.	8/10/14
Cosby, Bill	Philadelphia, Pa.	7/12/37
Cotten, Joseph	Petersburg, Va.	5/15/05
Courtenay, Tom	Hull, England	2/25/37
Crabbe, Buster	Oakland, Cal.	2/07/08
Crain, Jeanne	Barstow, Cal.	5/25/25
Crawford, Broderick	Philadelphia, Pa.	12/9/11
Crawford, Michael	Salisbury, England	1942
Crenna, Richard	Los Angeles, Cal.	11/30/27
Cronyn, Hume	London, Ont.	7/18/11
Crosby, Bob	Spokane, Wash.	8/23/13
Crosby, David	Los Angeles, Cal.	8/14/41
Crowley, Pat	Scranton, Pa.	1929
Crystal, Billy	Long Beach, N.Y.	3/14/47
Cugat, Xavier	Barcelona, Spain	1/1/00
Cullen, Bill	Pittsburgh, Pa.	2/18/20
Cullum, John	Knoxville, Tenn.	3/2/30
Culp, Robert	Oakland, Cal.	8/16/30
Cummings, Constance	Seattle, Wash.	5/15/10
Cummings, Robert	Joplin, Mo.	6/9/10
Curtin, Phyllis	Clarksburg, W.Va.	12/3/30
Curtis, Keene	Salt Lake City, Ut.	2/15/23
Curtis, Ken	Lamar, Col.	7/2/16
Curtis, Tony	New York, N.Y.	6/3/25
Cusack, Cyril	Durban, S. Africa	11/26/10
Cushing, Peter	Surrey, England	5/26/13
Dagmar (Egnor)	Huntington, W.Va.	1926
Dahl, Arlene	Minneapolis, Minn.	8/11/28
Dalrymple, Jean	Morristown, N.J.	9/2/10
Dalton, Abby	Las Vegas, Nev.	1935
Daly, John	Johannesburg, S. Africa	2/20/14
Damone, Vic	Brooklyn, N.Y.	6/12/28
Dana, Bill	Quincy, Mass.	1924
Dangerfield, Rodney	Babylon, N.Y.	1921
Daniels, William	Brooklyn, N.Y.	3/31/27
Danilova, Alexandra	Peterhof, Russia	1907
Danner, Blythe	Philadelphia, Pa.	—
Danton, Ray	New York, N.Y.	9/19/31
Darby, Kim	Hollywood, Cal.	7/8/48
Darcel, Denise	Paris, France	9/8/25
Darren, James	Philadelphia, Pa.	6/8/36
Darrieux, Danielle	Bordeaux, France	5/1/17
Darrow, Henry	New York, N.Y.	1933
Da Silva, Howard	Cleveland, Oh.	5/4/09
Dassin, Jules	Middletown, Conn.	12/18/11
Davidson, John	Pittsburgh, Pa.	1943
Davis, Ann B.	Schenectady, N.Y.	5/5/26
Davis, Bette	Lowell, Mass.	4/5/08
Davis, Clifton	Chicago, Ill.	1945
Davis, Jim	Edgerton, Mo.	8/26/-
Davis, Mac	Lubbock, Tex.	1/21/42
Davis, Ossie	Cogdell, Ga.	12/18/17
Davis, Sammy Jr.	New York, N.Y.	12/8/25
Dawber, Pam	Detroit, Mich.	10/18/-
Dawn, Hazel	Ogden, Ut.	1898
Dawson, Richard	Hampshire, England	11/20/-
Day, Dennis	New York, N.Y.	1917
Day, Doris	Cincinnati, Oh.	4/3/24
Day, Laraine	Roosevelt, Ut.	10/13/20
Dean, Jimmy	Plainview, Tex.	8/10/28
De Camp, Rosemary	Prescott, Ariz.	1913
DeCarlo, Yvonne	Vancouver, B.C.	9/1/24
Dee, Frances	Los Angeles, Cal.	1907
Dee, Joey	Passaic, N.J.	1940
Dee, Ruby	Cleveland, Oh.	10/27/23
Dee, Sandra	Bayonne, N.J.	4/23/42
Defore, Don	Cedar Rapids, Ia.	8/25/17
DeHaven, Gloria	Los Angeles, Cal.	1925
de Havilland, Olivia	Tokyo, Japan	7/1/16
De Niro, Robert	New York, N.Y.	1945
Del Rio, Dolores	Durango, Mexico	8/3/08
Dell, Gabriel	Brooklyn, N.Y.	1921
Della Chiesa, Vivienne	Chicago, Ill.	1920
Delon, Alain	Sceaux, France	11/8/35
DeLuise, Dom	Brooklyn, N.Y.	8/1/33
Demarest, William	St. Paul, Minn.	2/27/92
De Mille, Agnes	New York, N.Y.	1905
Dempster, Carol	Duluth, Minn.	1901
Deneuve, Catherine	Paris, France	10/22/43
Denning, Richard	Poughkeepsie, N.Y.	1914
Dennis, Sandy	Hastings, Neb.	4/27/37
Denver, Bob	New Rochelle, N.Y.	1935
Denver, John	Roswell, N.M.	12/31/43
Derek, John	Hollywood, Cal.	1926
Dern, Bruce	Chicago, Ill.	6/4/36
Desmond, Johnny	Detroit, Mich.	11/14/21
Devane, William	Albany, N.Y.	9/5/37
DeVito, Danny	Neptune, N.J.	11/17/-
Dewhurst, Colleen	Montreal, Que.	6/3/26
DeWitt, Joyce	Wheeling, W.Va.	4/23/49
Dey, Susan	Pekin, Ill.	12/10/52
Diamond, Neil	Brooklyn, N.Y.	1/24/41
Dickinson, Angie	Kulm, N.D.	9/30/31
Dierkop, Charles	La Crosse, Wis.	9/11/36
Dietrich, Marlene	Berlin, Germany	1901
Diller, Phyllis	Lima, Oh.	7/17/17
Dillman, Bradford	San Francisco, Cal.	4/14/30
Dixon, Ivan	New York, N.Y.	4/6/31
Domingo, Placido	Madrid, Spain	1/21/41
Domino, Fats	New Orleans, La.	2/26/28
Donahue, Phil	Cleveland, Oh.	12/21/35
Donahue, Troy	New York, N.Y.	1/27/36
Donald, James	Aberdeen, Scotland	5/18/17
Donnelly, Ruth	Trenton, N.J.	1896
Donovan	Glasgow, Scotland	5/10/46
Dors, Diana	Swindon, England	10/23/31
d'Orsay, Fifi	Montreal, Que.	1908
Douglas, Donna	Baywood, La.	9/26/39
Douglas, Kirk	Amsterdam, N.Y.	12/9/18
Douglas, Melvyn	Macon, Ga.	4/5/01
Douglas, Michael	New Brunswick, N.J.	9/25/45
Douglas, Mike	Chicago, Ill.	8/11/25
Downey, Morton	Wallingford, Conn.	11/14/01
Downs, Hugh	Akron, Oh.	2/14/21
Doyle, David	Lincoln, Neb.	12/1/29
Dragon, Daryl	Los Angeles Cal.	8/27/42
Drake, Alfred	Bronx, N.Y.	10/7/14
Drake, Betsy	Paris, France	1923
Drew, Ellen	Kansas City, Mo.	11/23/15
Dreyfuss, Richard	Brooklyn, N.Y.	10/29/47
Dru, Joanne	Logan, W.Va.	1/31/23
Drury, James	New York, N.Y.	1934
Duchin, Peter	New York, N.Y.	7/28/37
Duff, Howard	Bremerton, Wash.	11/24/17
Duffy, Patrick	Townsend, Mont.	3/17/49
Dufour, Val	New Orleans, La.	2/5/27
Duke, Patty	New York, N.Y.	12/14/46
Dullea, Keir	Cleveland, Oh.	5/30/36
Dunaway, Faye	Bascom, Fla.	1/14/41
Duncan, Sandy	Henderson, Tex.	2/20/46
Duncan, Todd	Danville, Ky.	1900
Duncan, Vivian	Los Angeles, Cal.	1902

Name	Birthplace	Born
Dunham, Katherine	Chicago, Ill.	6/22/10
Dunne, Irene	Louisville, Ky.	12/20/04
Dunnock, Mildred	Baltimore, Md.	1/25/06
Durbin, Deanna	Winnipeg, Man.	12/4/22
Duvall, Robert	San Diego, Cal.	1931
Duvall, Shelley	Houston, Tex.	1949
Dylan, Bob	Duluth, Minn.	5/24/41
Eastwood, Clint	San Francisco, Cal.	5/31/30
Ebsen, Buddy	Belleville, Ill.	4/2/08
Eckstine, Billy	Pittsburgh, Pa.	7/8/14
Edelman, Herb	Brooklyn, N.Y.	11/5/33
Eden, Barbara	Tucson, Ariz.	1934
Edwards, Ralph	Merino, Col.	1913
Edwards, Vincent	Brooklyn, N.Y.	7/7/28
Egan, Richard	San Francisco, Cal.	7/29/23
Eggar, Samantha	London, England	3/5/39
Ekberg, Anita	Malmo, Sweden	9/29/31
Ekland, Britt	Stockholm, Sweden	1942
Elam, Jack	Miami, Ariz.	11/13/16
Eldridge, Florence	Brooklyn, N.Y.	1901
Elgart, Larry	New London, Conn.	3/20/22
Elgart, Les	New Haven, Conn.	1918
Elliott, Bob	Boston, Mass.	1923
Emerson, Faye	Elizabeth, La.	7/8/17
Erickson, Leif	Alameda, Cal.	10/27/11
Esmond, Jill	London, England	1908
Estrada, Erik	New York, N.Y.	3/16/49
Evans, Dale	Uvalde, Tex.	10/31/12
Evans, Gene	Holbrook, Ariz.	7/11/24
Evans, Maurice	Dorchester, England	6/3/01
Evans, Robert	New York, N.Y.	6/29/30
Everett, Chad	South Bend, Ind.	6/11/37
Everly, Don	Brownie, Ky.	2/1/37
Everly, Phil	Brownie, Ky.	1/19/38
Evers, Jason	New York, N.Y.	1/2/27
Ewell, Tom	Owensboro, Ky.	4/29/09
Fabares, Shelley	Santa Monica, Cal.	1944
Fabian (Forte)	Philadelphia, Pa.	2/6/43
Fabray, Nanette	San Diego, Cal.	10/27/20
Fadiman, Clifton	Brooklyn, N.Y.	5/15/04
Fairbanks, Douglas Jr.	New York, N.Y.	12/9/09
Falk, Peter	New York, N.Y.	9/16/27
Farber, Barry	Baltimore, Md.	1930
Farentino, James	Brooklyn, N.Y.	2/24/38
Fargo, Donna	Mt. Airy, N.C.	11/10/49
Farr, Jamie	Toledo, Oh.	7/1/36
Farrell, Charles	Onset Bay, Mass.	8/9/01
Farrell, Eileen	Willimantic, Conn.	2/13/20
Farrell, Mike	St. Paul, Minn.	2/6/42
Farrow, Mia	Los Angeles, Cal.	2/9/45
Fawcett, Farrah	Corpus Christi, Tex.	2/2/47
Faye, Alice	New York, N.Y.	5/5/15
Feld, Fritz	Berlin, Germany	10/15/00
Feldman, Marty	England	1933
Feldon, Barbara	Pittsburgh, Pa.	3/12/41
Feliciano, Jose	Puerto Rico	9/10/45
Fell, Norman	Philadelphia, Pa.	3/24/25
Fellini, Federico	Rimini, Italy	1/20/20
Fellows, Edith	Boston, Mass.	1923
Ferrer, Jose	Santurce, P.R.	1/8/12
Ferrer, Mel	Elberon, N.J.	8/25/17
Ferrigno, Lou	Brooklyn, N.Y.	11/9/52
Ferris, Barbara	London, England	1942
Fetchit, Stepin	Key West, Fla.	1902
Field, Sally	Pasadena, Cal.	11/6/46
Finney, Albert	Salford, England	5/9/36
Firkusny, Rudolf	Napajedla, Czechoslovakia	2/11/12
Fischer-Dieskau, Dietrich	Berlin, Germany	5/28/25
Fisher, Carrie	Beverly Hills, Cal.	10/21/56
Fisher, Eddie	Philadelphia, Pa.	8/10/28
Fitzgerald, Ella	Newport News, Va.	4/25/18
Fitzgerald, Geraldine	Dublin, Ireland	11/24/13
Fitzgerald, Pegeen	Norcatur, Kan.	1910
Fix, Paul	Dobbs Ferry, N.Y.	3/13/02
Flack, Roberta	Black Mountain, N.C.	2/10/40
Fleming, Rhonda	Hollywood, Cal.	8/10/23
Flanders, Ed	Minneapolis, Minn.	12/29/34
Fletcher, Louise	Birmingham, Ala.	1936
Foch, Nina	Leyden, Netherlands	4/20/24
Fonda, Henry	Grand Island, Neb.	5/16/05
Fonda, Jane	New York, N.Y.	12/21/37
Fonda, Peter	New York, N.Y.	2/23/39
Fontaine, Joan	Tokyo, Japan	10/22/17
Fontanne, Lynn	London, England	12/6/87
Fonteyn, Margot	Reigate, England	5/18/19
Forbes, Bryan	London, England	7/22/26
Ford (Tenn.), Ernie	Bristol, Tenn.	2/13/19
Ford, Glenn	Quebec, Canada	5/1/16
Ford, Harrison	Chicago, Ill.	1942
Ford, Ruth	Hazelhurst, Miss.	1920
Forrest, Steve	Huntsville, Tex.	9/29/25
Forsythe, John	Penns Grove, N.J.	1/29/18
Fosse, Bob	Chicago, Ill.	6/23/27
Foster, Jodie	Los Angeles, Cal.	1962
Foster, Phil	Brooklyn, N.Y.	3/29/14
Fox, James	London, England	1939
Foxx, Redd	St. Louis, Mo.	12/9/22
Foy, Eddie Jr.	New Rochelle, N.Y.	2/4/05
Frampton, Peter	Kent, England	4/22/50
Francescatti, Zino	Marseilles, France	8/9/05
Franciosa, Anthony	New York, N.Y.	10/25/28
Francis, Anne	Ossining, N.Y.	9/16/32
Francis, Arlene	Boston, Mass.	10/20/08
Francis, Connie	Newark, N.J.	12/12/38
Franciscus, James	Clayton, Mo.	1/31/34
Frankenheimer, John	Malba, N.Y.	2/19/30
Franklin, Aretha	Memphis, Tenn.	3/25/42
Franklin, Bonnie	Santa Monica, Cal.	1/6/44
Franklin, Joe	New York, N.Y.	1929
Franz, Arthur	Perth Amboy, N.J.	2/29/20
Freberg, Stan	Pasadena, Cal.	8/7/26
Freed, Bert	New York, N.Y.	11/3/19
Freeman, Mona	Baltimore, Md.	1926
Frost, David	Tenterden, England	4/7/39
Frye, David	Brooklyn, N.Y.	1934
Funicello, Annette	Utica, N.Y.	1942
Funt, Allen	New York, N.Y.	9/16/14
Furness, Betty	New York, N.Y.	1/3/16
Gabel, Martin	Philadelphia, Pa.	6/19/12
Gabor, Eva	Hungary	1921
Gabor, Zsa Zsa	Hungary	1919
Gail, Max	Detroit, Mich.	4/5/43
Galloway, Don	Brooksville, Ky.	7/27/37
Galway, James	Galway, Ireland	12/8/39
Gam, Rita	Pittsburgh, Pa.	1929
Gambling, John	New York, N.Y.	1930
Garagiola, Joe	St. Louis, Mo.	2/12/26
Garbo, Greta	Stockholm, Sweden	9/18/05
Gardenia, Vincent	Naples, Italy	1/7/22
Gardner, Ava	Smithfield, N.C.	12/24/22
Garfunkel, Art	New York, N.Y.	10/13/42
Garland, Beverly	Santa Cruz, Cal.	10/17/29
Garner, James	Norman, Okla.	4/7/28
Garner, Peggy Ann	Canton, Oh.	2/3/32
Garrett, Betty	St. Joseph, Mo.	5/23/19
Garroway, Dave	Schenectady, N.Y.	7/13/13
Garson, Greer	Co. Down, N. Ireland	9/29/08
Gary, John	Watertown, N.Y.	11/29/32
Gavin, John	Los Angeles, Cal.	4/8/32
Gaye, Marvin	Washington, D.C.	4/2/39
Gayle, Crystal	Paintsville, Ky.	1951
Gaynor, Janet	Philadelphia, Pa.	10/6/06
Gaynor, Mitzi	Chicago, Ill.	9/4/31
Gazzara, Ben	New York, N.Y.	8/28/30
Gedda, Nicolai	Sweden	1925
Geeson, Judy	Sussex, England	9/10/48
Gennaro, Peter	Metairie, La.	1924
Gentry, Bobbie	Chickasaw Co., Miss.	7/27/44
Gere, Richard	Philadelphia, Pa.	1950
Ghostley, Alice	Eve, Mo.	8/14/26
Giannini, Giancarlo	Spezia, Italy	8/1/42
Gibb, Andy	Manchester, England	3/5/58
Gibson, Henry	Germantown, Pa.	9/21/35
Gielgud, John	London, England	4/14/04
Gilbert, Melissa	Los Angeles, Cal.	5/8/64
Gilford, Jack	New York, N.Y.	7/25/07
Gillette, Anita	Baltimore, Md.	8/16/36
Gingold, Hermione	London, England	12/9/97
Ginty, Robert	New York, N.Y.	11/14/48
Gish, Lillian	Springfield, Oh.	10/14/96
Givot, George	Omaha, Neb.	1903
Glaser, Paul Michael	Cambridge, Mass.	3/25/-
Glass, Ron	Evansville, Ind.	7/1/-
Gleason, Jackie	Brooklyn, N.Y.	2/26/16
Gobel, George	Chicago, Ill.	5/20/19
Godard, Jean Luc	Paris, France	12/3/30
Goddard, Paulette	Great Neck, N.Y.	6/3/15
Godfrey, Arthur	New York, N.Y.	8/31/03
Goldsboro, Bobby	Marianne, Fla.	1/18/41
Goodman, Benny	Chicago, Ill.	5/30/09
Goodman, Dody	Columbus, Oh.	10/28/29
Gordon, Gale	New York, N.Y.	2/2/06

Name	Birthplace	Born
Gordon, Ruth	Wollaston, Mass.	10/30/96
Gorin, Igor	Ukraine, Russia	1909
Gorme, Eydie	Bronx, N.Y.	8/16/32
Gorshin, Frank	Pittsburgh, Pa.	4/5/34
Gortner, Marjoe	Long Beach, Cal.	1/14/44
Gosden, Freeman (Amos)	Richmond, Va.	5/5/99
Gossett, Louis	Brooklyn, N.Y.	5/27/36
Gould, Elliott	Brooklyn, N.Y.	8/29/38
Gould, Morton	Richmond Hill, N.Y.	12/10/13
Goulding, Ray	Lowell, Mass.	3/20/22
Goulet, Robert	Lawrence, Mass.	11/26/33
Gowdy, Curt	Green River, Wyo.	1919
Grady, Don	San Diego, Cal.	1944
Graham, Martha	Pittsburgh, Pa.	5/11/94
Graham, Virginia	Chicago, Ill.	7/4/12
Grahame, Gloria	Los Angeles, Cal.	11/28/29
Grahame, Margot	Canterbury, England	1911
Granger, Farley	San Jose, Cal.	7/1/25
Granger, Stewart	London, England	5/6/13
Granville, Bonita	New York, N.Y.	1923
Grant, Cary	Bristol, England	1/18/04
Grant, Kathryn	Houston, Tex.	1933
Grant, Lee	New York, N.Y.	10/31/31
Graves, Peter	Minneapolis, Minn.	3/18/26
Gray, Coleen	Staplehurst, Neb.	10/23/22
Gray, Dolores	Chicago, Ill.	6/7/24
Grayson, Kathryn	Winston-Salem, N.C.	2/9/23
Graziano, Rocky	New York, N.Y.	6/7/22
Greco, Buddy	Philadelphia, Pa.	8/14/26
Greco, Jose	Abruzzi, Italy	12/23/18
Green, Adolph	New York, N.Y.	12/2/15
Green, Al	Forest City, Ark.	4/13/46
Greene, Lorne	Ottawa, Ont.	2/12/15
Greene, Richard	England	1918
Greenwood, Joan	London, England	3/4/21
Greer, Jane	Washington, D.C.	9/9/24
Gregory, Dick	St. Louis, Mo.	10/12/32
Gregory, James	Bronx, N.Y.	12/23/11
Grey, Joel	Cleveland, Oh.	4/11/32
Griffin, Merv	San Mateo, Cal.	7/6/25
Griffith, Andy	Mount Airy, N.C.	6/1/26
Grimes, Gary	San Francisco, Cal.	1955
Grimes, Tammy	Lynn, Mass.	1/30/36
Grizzard, George	Roanoke Rapids, N.C.	4/1/28
Grodin, Charles	Pittsburgh, Pa.	4/21/35
Guardino, Harry	New York, N.Y.	12/23/25
Guillaume, Robert	St. Louis, Mo.	11/30/-
Guinness, Alec	London, England	4/2/14
Gunn, Moses	St. Louis, Mo.	10/2/29
Guthrie, Arlo	New York, N.Y.	7/10/47
Hackett, Buddy	Brooklyn, N.Y.	8/31/24
Hackett, Joan	New York, N.Y.	3/1/-
Hackman, Gene	San Bernardino, Cal.	1/30/31
Hagen, Uta	Gottingen, Germany	6/12/19
Haggard, Merle	Bakersfield, Cal.	4/6/37
Hagman, Larry	Ft. Worth, Tex.	9/21/31
Hale, Barbara	DeKalb, Ill.	1922
Haley, Bill	Detroit, Mich.	1927
Hall, Huntz	New York, N.Y.	1920
Hall, Monty	Winnipeg, Man.	1925
Hall, Tom T.	Olive Hill, Ky.	5/25/36
Hamilton, George	Memphis, Tenn.	8/12/39
Hamilton, Margaret	Cleveland, Oh.	9/12/02
Hamilton, Neil	Lynn, Mass	1899
Hampshire, Susan	London, England	5/12/42
Hampton, Lionel	Birmingham, Ala.	4/20/14
Harding, Ann	Ft. Sam Houston, Tex.	8/7/02
Harmon, Mark	Burbank, Cal.	9/2/-
Harper, David W.	Abilene, Tex.	10/4/61
Harper, Valerie	Suffern, N.Y.	8/22/40
Harrington, Pat Jr.	New York, N.Y.	8/13/29
Harris, Barbara	Evanston, Ill.	1935
Harris, Emmy Lou	Birmingham, Ala.	1949
Harris, Julie	Grosse Pte. Park, Mich.	12/2/25
Harris, Phil	Linton, Ind.	6/24/06
Harris, Richard	Co. Limerick, Ireland	10/1/33
Harris, Rosemary	Ashby, England	9/19/30
Harrison, George	Liverpool, England	2/25/43
Harrison, Rex	Huyton, England	3/5/08
Hartman, David	Pawtucket, R.I.	5/19/35
Hasso, Signe	Stockholm, Sweden	8/15/18
Haver, June	Rock Island, Ill.	6/10/26
Havoc, June	Vancouver, B.C.	11/8/16
Hawn, Goldie	Washington, D.C.	11/21/45
Haworth, Jill	Sussex, England	1945

Name	Birthplace	Born
Hayden, Melissa	Toronto, Ont.	4/25/23
Hayden, Russell	Chico, Cal.	6/12/12
Hayden, Sterling	Montclair, N.Y.	3/26/16
Hayes, Helen	Washington, D.C.	10/10/00
Hayes, Isaac	Covington, Tenn.	8/20/42
Hayes, Peter Lind	San Francisco, Cal.	6/25/15
Haynes, Lloyd	South Bend, Ind.	1934
Hayward, Louis	Johannesburg, S. Africa	1909
Hayworth, Rita	New York, N.Y.	10/17/18
Healy, Mary	New Orleans, La.	4/14/18
Heatherton, Joey	Rockville Centre, N.Y.	9/14/44
Heckart, Eileen	Columbus, Oh.	3/29/19
Hefner, Hugh	Chicago, Ill.	4/9/26
Heifetz, Jascha	Vilna, Russia	2/2/01
Helmond, Katherine	Galveston, Tex.	7/5/-
Helpmann, Robert	Mt. Gambier, Australia	4/9/09
Hemmings, David	Guilford, England	11/2/41
Hemsley, Sherman	Philadelphia, Pa.	2/1/-
Henderson, Florence	Dale, Ind.	2/14/34
Henderson, Skitch	Halstad, Minn.	1/27/18
Henner, Marilu	Chicago, Ill.	4/6/-
Henning, Doug	Ft. Garry, Man., Canada	1947
Henreid, Paul	Trieste, Italy	1/10/08
Henson, Jim	Greenville, Miss.	9/24/36
Hepburn, Audrey	Brussels, Belgium	5/4/29
Hepburn, Katharine	Hartford, Conn.	11/8/09
Herbert, Evelyn	Philadelphia, Pa.	1898
Hesseman, Howard	Lebanon, Ore.	2/27/40
Heston, Charlton	Evanston, Ill.	10/4/24
Heywood, Anne	Birmingham, England	1937
Hickman, Darryl	Los Angeles, Cal.	1931
Hickman, Dwayne	Los Angeles, Cal.	1934
Hildegarde	Adell, Wis.	2/1/06
Hill, Arthur	Melfort, Sask.	8/1/22
Hiller, Wendy	Stockport, England	8/15/12
Hines, Earl (Fatha)	Duquesne, Pa.	12/28/05
Hines, Jerome	Hollywood, Cal.	11/8/21
Hines, Mimi	Vancouver, B.C.	1933
Hingle, Pat	Denver, Col.	7/19/23
Hirsch, Judd	Bronx, N.Y.	3/15/35
Hirt, Al	New Orleans, La.	11/7/22
Ho, Don	Kakaako, Oahu, Ha.	1930
Hoffman, Dustin	Los Angeles, Cal.	8/8/37
Holbrook, Hal	Cleveland, Oh.	2/17/25
Holden, William	O'Fallon, Ill.	4/17/18
Holder, Geoffrey	Trinidad	8/1/30
Holliday, Peggy	Jaspar, Ala.	7/2/37
Holliman, Earl	Delhi, La.	9/11/28
Holloway, Stanley	London, England	10/1/90
Holloway, Sterling	Cedartown, Ga.	1905
Holm, Celeste	New York, N.Y.	4/29/19
Holtz, Lou	San Francisco, Cal.	1893
Homeier, Skip	Chicago, Ill.	10/5/30
Hooks, Robert	Washington, D.C.	4/18/37
Hope, Bob	London, England	5/29/03
Hopkins, Anthony	Wales	12/31/37
Hopper, Dennis	Dodge City, Kan.	5/17/36
Horne, Lena	Brooklyn, N.Y.	6/30/17
Horne, Marilyn	Bradford, Pa.	1/16/34
Horowitz, Vladimir	Kiev, Russia	10/1/04
Horton, Robert	Los Angeles, Cal.	7/29/24
Houseman, John	Bucharest, Romania	9/22/02
Howard, Clint	Burbank, Cal.	1959
Howard, Ken	El Centro, Cal.	3/28/44
Howard, Ron	Duncan, Okla.	3/1/54
Howard, Trevor	Kent, England	9/29/16
Howes, Sally Ann	London, England	7/20/34
Hudson, Rock	Winnetka, Ill.	11/17/25
Humperdinck, Engelbert	Madras, India	5/2/36
Hunt, Lois	York, Pa.	11/26/25
Hunt, Marsha	Chicago, Ill.	10/17/17
Hunter, Kim	Detroit, Mich.	11/12/22
Hunter, Ross	Cleveland, Oh.	5/6/26
Hunter, Tab	New York, N.Y.	7/11/31
Hussey, Olivia	Buenos Aires, Argentina	1952
Hussey, Ruth	Providence, R.I.	10/30/17
Huston, John	Nevada, Mo.	8/5/06
Hutchinson, Josephine	Seattle, Wash.	1916
Hutton, Betty	Battle Creek, Mich.	2/26/21
Hutton, Ina Ray	Chicago, Ill.	1918
Hutton, Lauren	Charleston, S.C.	1944
Hyde-White, Wilfrid	Gloucester, England	5/12/03
Ian, Janis	New York, N.Y.	5/7/51
Ingels, Marty	Brooklyn, N.Y.	3/9/36
Ireland, Jill	London, England	4/24/36
Ireland, John	Vancouver, B.C.	1/30/15

Name	Birthplace	Born
Ives, Burl	Hunt, Ill.	6/14/09
Jackson, Anne	Allegheny, Pa.	9/3/26
Jackson, Glenda	Cheshire, England	5/9/36
Jackson, Kate	Birmingham, Ala.	10/29/49
Jackson, Michael	Gary, Ind.	8/29/58
Jaeckel, Richard	Long Beach, Cal.	10/10/26
Jaffe, Sam	New York, N.Y.	3/8/91
Jagger, Dean	Columbus Grove, Oh.	11/7/05
Jagger, Mick	Dartford, England	7/26/44
James, Dennis	Jersey City, N.J.	8/24/17
James, Harry	Albany, Ga.	3/15/16
Janis, Conrad	New York, N.Y.	2/11/28
Jason, Rick	New York, N.Y.	5/21/26
Jeanmaire, Renee	Paris, France	4/29/24
Jeffreys, Anne	Goldsboro, N.C.	1/26/23
Jeffries, Fran	San Jose, Cal.	1939
Jeffries, Lionel	England	1926
Jennings, Waylon	Littlefield, Tex.	6/15/37
Jens, Salome	Milwaukee, Wis.	5/8/35
Jepson, Helen	Titusville, Pa.	1907
Jessel, George	New York, N.Y.	4/3/98
Joel, Billy	Bronx, N.Y.	5/9/49
John, Elton	Middlesex, England	3/25/47
Johns, Glynis	Durban, S. Africa	10/5/23
Johnson, Arte	Benton Harbor, Mich.	1/20/34
Johnson, Ben	Foraker, Okla.	1918
Johnson, Van	Newport, R.I.	8/20/16
Jones, Allan	Scranton, Pa.	1907
Jones, Carolyn	Amarillo, Tex.	4/28/33
Jones, Chris	Jackson, Tenn.	1941
Jones, Dean	Morgan Co., Ala.	1/25/35
Jones, Grandpa	Niagara, Ky.	10/20/13
Jones, Henry	Philadelphia, Pa.	8/1/12
Jones, Jack	Hollywood, Cal.	1938
Jones, James Earl	Tate Co., Miss.	1/17/31
Jones, Jennifer	Tulsa, Okla.	3/2/19
Jones, Shirley	Smithton, Pa.	3/31/34
Jones, Tom	Pontypridd, Wales	6/7/40
Jory, Victor	Dawson, Yukon, Canada	11/23/02
Joslyn, Allyn	Milford, Pa.	7/21/05
Jourdan, Louis	Marseilles, France	6/19/21
Jurado, Katy	Guadalajara, Mexico	1927
Kahn, Madeline	Boston, Mass.	9/29/42
Kaplan, Gabe	Brooklyn, N.Y.	3/31/45
Kaufman, Andy	New York, N.Y.	1/17/49
Kaye, Danny	Brooklyn, N.Y.	1/18/13
Kaye, Sammy	Lakewood, Oh.	3/13/13
Kazan, Elia	Constantinople, Turkey	9/7/09
Kazan, Lainie	New York, N.Y.	5/16/40
Keach, Stacy	Savannah, Ga.	6/2/41
Keaton, Diane	Santa Ana, Cal.	1949
Keel, Howard	Gillespie, Ill.	4/13/19
Keeler, Ruby	Halifax, N.S.	8/25/10
Keeshan, Bob	Lynbrook, N.Y.	6/27/27
Keitel, Harvey	Brooklyn, N.Y.	1947
Keith, Brian	Bayonne, N.J.	11/14/21
Keller, Marthe	Basel, Switzerland	1945
Kellerman, Sally	Long Beach, Cal.	6/2/37
Kelley, DeForrest	Atlanta, Ga.	1920
Kelly, Gene	Pittsburgh, Pa.	8/23/12
Kelly, Grace	Philadelphia, Pa.	11/12/29
Kelly, Jack	Astoria, N.Y.	1927
Kelly, Nancy	Lowell, Mass.	3/25/21
Kelly, Patsy	Brooklyn, N.Y.	1/12/10
Kennedy, Arthur	Worcester, Mass.	2/17/14
Kennedy, George	New York, N.Y.	2/18/26
Kent, Allegra	Los Angeles, Cal.	8/11/38
Kerr, Deborah	Helensburgh, Scotland	9/30/21
Kerr, John	New York, N.Y.	11/15/31
Kert, Larry	Los Angeles, Cal.	12/5/30
Keyes, Evelyn	Port Arthur, Tex.	1925
Kiley, Richard	Chicago, Ill.	3/21/22
King, Alan	Brooklyn, N.Y.	12/26/27
King, B. B.	Itta Bena, Miss.	9/16/25
King, Carole	Brooklyn, N.Y.	2/9/41
King, Walter Woolf	San Francisco, Cal.	1899
King, Wayne	Savannah, Ill.	1901
Kirby, Durward	Covington, Ky.	8/24/12
Kirk, Lisa	Brownsville, Pa.	1925
Kirk, Phyllis	Plainfield, N.J.	9/18/30
Kirsten, Dorothy	Montclair, N.J.	7/6/19
Kitt, Eartha	North, S.C.	1/26/28
Klemperer, Werner	Cologne, Germany	3/22/20
Klein, Robert	New York, N.Y.	2/8/42
Klugman, Jack	Philadelphia, Pa.	4/27/22
Knight, Gladys	Atlanta, Ga.	5/28/44

Name	Birthplace	Born
Knight, Ted	Terryville, Conn.	1923
Knotts, Don	Morgantown, W. Va.	7/21/24
Knowles, Patric	Horsforth, England	11/11/11
Knox, Alexander	Strathroy, Canada	1/16/07
Korjus, Miliza	Warsaw, Poland	1912
Korman, Harvey	Chicago, Ill.	2/15/27
Kramer, Stanley	New York, N.Y.	9/29/13
Kristofferson, Kris	Brownsville, Tex.	6/22/36
Kruger, Hardy	Berlin, Germany	4/12/28
Kubelik, Rafael	Bychori, Czechoslovakia	6/29/14
Kubrick, Stanley	Bronx, N.Y.	7/26/28
Kulp, Nancy	Harrisburg, Pa.	8/28/21
Kwan, Nancy	Hong Kong	1939
Kyser, Kay	Rocky Mount, N.C.	1905
Ladd, Cheryl	Huron, S.D.	7/12/51
Laine, Frankie	Chicago, Ill.	3/30/13
Lamarr, Hedy	Vienna, Austria	1915
Lamas, Fernando	Buenos Aires, Argentina	1/9/15
Lamb, Gil	Minneapolis, Minn.	6/14/06
Lamour, Dorothy	New Orleans, La.	12/10/14
Lancaster, Burt	New York, N.Y.	11/2/13
Lanchester, Elsa	London, England	10/28/02
Landau, Martin	Brooklyn, N.Y.	1934
Landon, Michael	Forest Hills, N.Y.	—
Lane, Abbe	Brooklyn, N.Y.	1932
Lane, Lola	Macy, Ind.	1909
Lane, Priscilla	Indianola, Ia.	1917
Lange, Hope	Redding Ridge, Conn.	11/28/33
Langella, Frank	Bayonne, N.J.	1/1/46
Langford, Frances	Lakeland, Fla.	4/4/13
Lansbury, Angela	London, England	10/16/25
Lansing, Robert	San Diego, Cal.	6/5/29
Lanson, Snooky (Roy)	Memphis, Tenn.	1919
La Rosa, Julius	Brooklyn, N.Y.	1930
La Rue, Jack	New York, N.Y.	—
Lasser, Louise	New York N.Y.	1941
Laughlin, Tom	Minneapolis, Minn.	1938
Laurie, Piper	Detroit, Mich.	1/22/32
Lavin, Linda	Portland, Me.	10/15/37
Lawford, Peter	London, England	9/7/23
Lawrence, Carol	Melrose Park, Ill.	9/5/34
Lawrence, Steve	Brooklyn, N.Y.	7/8/35
Lawrence, Vicki	Inglewood, Cal.	3/26/49
Leachman, Cloris	Des Moines, Ia.	1926
Lean, David	Croydon, England	3/25/08
Lear, Norman	New Haven, Conn.	7/27/22
Learned, Michael	Washington, D.C.	4/9/39
Lederer, Francis	Prague, Czechoslovakia	11/6/06
Lee, Brenda	Atlanta, Ga.	12/11/44
Lee, Christopher	London, England	5/27/22
Lee, Michele	Los Angeles, Cal.	1942
Lee, Peggy	Jamestown, N.D.	5/26/20
Lee, Pinky	St. Paul, Minn.	—
Le Gallienne, Eva	London, England	1/11/99
Legrand, Michel	Paris, France	1932
Leibman, Ron	New York, N.Y.	10/11/37
Leigh, Janet	Merced, Cal.	7/6/27
Leinsdorf, Erich	Vienna, Austria	2/4/12
Lembeck, Harvey	New York, N.Y.	1923
Lemmon, Jack	Boston, Mass.	2/8/25
Lennon, Dianne	Los Angeles, Cal.	1939
Lennon, Janet	Culver City, Cal.	1946
Lennon, John	Liverpool, England	10/9/40
Lennon, Kathy	Santa Monica, Cal.	1944
Lennon, Peggy	Los Angeles, Cal.	1941
Lenya, Lotte	Vienna, Austria	10/18/00
Leonard, Sheldon	New York, N.Y.	2/22/07
Leontovich, Eugenie	Moscow, Russia	3/21/00
LeRoy, Mervyn	San Francisco, Cal.	10/15/00
Leslie, Joan	Detroit, Mich.	1/26/25
Lester, Jerry	Chicago, Ill.	1911
Levene, Sam	Russia	8/28/05
Levenson, Sam	New York, N.Y.	12/28/11
Levine, James	Cincinnati, Oh.	6/23/43
Lewis, Jerry	Newark, N.J.	3/16/26
Lewis, Jerry Lee	Ferriday, La.	9/29/35
Lewis, Monica	Chicago, Ill.	5/5/25
Lewis, Robert Q.	New York, N.Y.	1924
Lewis, Shari	New York, N.Y.	1/17/34
Liberace	West Allis, Wis.	5/16/19
Lightfoot, Gordon	Orillia, Ont.	11/17/38
Lillie, Beatrice	Toronto, Ont.	5/29/94
Linden, Hal	New York, N.Y.	3/20/31
Lindfors, Viveca	Uppsala, Sweden	12/29/20
Lindsay, Margaret	Dubuque, Ia.	1910
Lindsey, Mort	Newark, N.J.	1923
Linkletter, Art	Saskatchewan, Canada	7/17/12

Name	Birthplace	Born
Linkletter, Jack	San Francisco, Cal.	11/20/37
Lipton, Peggy	Lawrence, N.Y.	1948
Lisi, Virna	Italy	1937
Little, Cleavon	Chickasha, Okla.	6/1/39
Little, Rich	Ottawa, Ont.	11/26/38
Little Richard	Macon, Ga.	1935
Livingston, Barry	Los Angeles, Cal.	1953
Livingston, Stanley	Los Angeles, Cal.	1950
Livingstone, Mary	Seattle, Wash.	1909
Lockhart, June	New York, N.Y.	6/25/25
Lockwood, Margaret	Karachi, India	9/15/16
Loden, Barbara	Marion, N.C.	1937
Loder, John	London, England	1898
Logan, Joshua	Texarkana, Tex.	10/5/08
Loggins, Kenny	Everett, Wash.	1/7/48
Lollobrigida, Gina	Subiaco, Italy	7/4/28
Lom, Herbert	Prague, Czechoslovakia	1917
London, Julie	Santa Rosa, Cal.	9/26/26
Longet, Claudine	France	1/29/42
Lopez, Trini	Dallas, Tex.	5/15/37
Lord, Jack	New York, N.Y.	—
Loren, Sophia	Rome, Italy	9/20/34
Loudon, Dorothy	Boston, Mass.	9/17/33
Louise, Tina	New York, N.Y.	1934
Love, Bessie	Midland, Tex.	9/10/98
Loy, Myrna	Helena, Mon.	8/2/05
Luckinbill, Laurence	Ft. Smith, Ark.	11/21/34
Ludwig, Christa	Berlin, Germany	1928
Luke, Keye	Canton, China	1904
Lulu	Glasgow, Scotland	1948
Lumet, Sidney	Philadelphia, Pa.	6/25/24
Lund, John	Rochester, N.Y.	1913
Lupino, Ida	London, England	2/4/18
Lynde, Paul	Mt. Vernon, Oh.	6/13/26
Lynley, Carol	New York, N.Y.	2/13/42
Lynn, Jeffrey	Auburn, Mass.	1909
Lynn, Loretta	Butcher Hollow, Ky.	4/14/35
Lyon, Sue	Davenport, Ia.	7/10/46
Maazel, Lorin	Paris, France	3/6/30
MacArthur, James	Los Angeles, Cal.	12/8/37
MacGraw, Ali	Pound Ridge, N.Y.	4/1/39
MacKay, Jim	Philadelphia, Pa.	1921
MacKenzie, Gisele	Winnipeg, Man.	1/10/27
MacLaine, Shirley	Richmond, Va.	4/24/34
MacMurray, Fred	Kankakee, Ill.	8/30/08
MacNeil, Cornell	Minneapolis, Minn.	9/24/22
MacRae, Gordon	East Orange, N.J.	3/12/21
MacRae, Meredith	Houston, Tex.	1945
MacRae, Sheila	London, England	9/24/24
Macy, Bill	Revere, Mass.	5/18/22
Madison, Guy	Bakersfield, Cal.	1/19/22
Majors, Lee	Wyandotte, Mich.	4/23/40
Makarova, Natalia	Leningrad, USSR	11/21/40
Malbin, Elaine	New York, N.Y.	1932
Malden, Karl	Chicago, Ill.	3/22/13
Malone, Dorothy	Chicago, Ill.	1/30/25
Manchester, Melissa	Bronx, N.Y.	2/15/51
Mancini, Henry	Cleveland, Oh.	4/16/24
Mandrell, Barbara	Houston, Tex.	12/25/48
Manilow, Barry	New York, N.Y.	6/17/46
Mann, Herbie	New York, N.Y.	4/16/30
Manning, Irene	Cincinnati, Oh.	1918
Marceau, Marcel	France	3/22/23
Margo	Mexico City, Mexico	5/10/18
Margolin, Janet	New York, N.Y.	1943
Markova, Alicia	London, England	12/1/10
Marlowe, Hugh	Philadelphia, Pa.	1/20/11
Marsh, Jean	London, England	7/1/34
Marshall, E. G.	Awatonna, Minn.	6/18/10
Marshall, Penny	New York, N.Y.	10/15/43
Marshall, Peter	Huntington, W.Va.	3/30/-
Marshall, William	Chicago, Ill.	10/12/17
Martin, Dean	Steubenville, Oh.	6/17/17
Martin, Dick	Detroit, Mich.	1/30/22
Martin, Mary	Weatherford, Tex.	12/1/13
Martin, Ross	Poland	3/22/20
Martin, Steve	Waco, Tex.	1945
Martin, Strother	Kokomo, Ind.	1920
Martin, Tony	San Francisco, Cal.	12/25/13
Martino, Al	Philadelphia, Pa.	1927
Marvin, Lee	New York, N.Y.	2/19/24
Mason, Jackie	Sheboygan, Wis.	1931
Mason, James	Huddersfield, England	5/15/09
Mason, Marsha	St. Louis, Mo.	4/3/42
Mason, Pamela	London, England	3/10/22
Massey, Curt	Midland, Tex.	—
Massey, Raymond	Toronto, Ont.	8/30/96

Name	Birthplace	Born
Mastroianni, Marcello	Rome, Italy	9/28/24
Matheson, Tim	Glendale, Cal.	12/31/47
Mathieu, Mireille	Avignon, France	1946
Mathis, Johnny	San Francisco, Cal.	9/30/35
Matthau, Walter	New York, N.Y.	10/1/20
Mature, Victor	Louisville, Ky.	1/19/16
May, Billy	Pittsburgh, Pa.	1916
May, Elaine	Philadelphia, Pa.	4/21/32
Mayehoff, Eddie	Baltimore, Md.	7/7/14
Mayo, Virginia	St. Louis, Mo.	1920
Mazurki, Mike	Austria	12/25/09
Mazursky, Paul	Brooklyn, N.Y.	4/25/30
McArdle, Andrea	Philadelphia, Pa.	11/4/63
McBride, Patricia	Teaneck, N.J.	8/23/42
McCallum, David	Glasgow, Scotland	9/19/33
McCambridge, Mercedes	Joliet, Ill.	3/17/18
McCarthy, Kevin	Seattle, Wash.	2/15/15
McCartney, Paul	Liverpool, England	6/18/42
McClure, Doug	Glendale, Cal.	5/11/38
McCord, Kent	Los Angeles, Cal.	1942
McCrary, Tex (John)	Calvert, Tex.	1910
McCrea, Joel	Los Angeles, Cal.	11/5/05
McDonough, Mary	Los Angeles, Cal.	5/4/61
McDowall, Roddy	London, England	9/17/28
McDowell, Malcolm	Leeds, England	6/19/43
McEachin, James	Pennert, N.C.	1930
McFarland, George (Spanky)	Dallas, Tex.	1928
McGavin, Darren	San Joaquin, Cal.	5/7/22
McGee, Fibber	Peoria, Ill.	1896
McGoohan, Patrick	New York, N.Y.	3/19/28
McGuire, Dorothy	Omaha, Neb.	6/14/19
McGuire Sisters:		
Christine	Middletown, Oh.	1928
Dorothy	Middletown, Oh.	1930
Phyllis	Middletown, Oh.	1931
McHugh, Frank	Homestead, Pa.	5/23/99
McIntire, John	Spokane, Wash.	6/27/07
McKechnie, Donna	Pontiac, Mich.	11/16/42
McKenna, Siobhan	Belfast, Ireland	5/24/23
McLean, Don	New Rochelle, N.Y.	10/2/45
McLerie, Allyn	Grand Mere, Que.	12/1/26
McLeod, Gavin	Mt. Kisco, N.Y.	2/28/-
McMahon, Ed	Detroit, Mich.	3/6/23
McNair, Barbara	Chicago, Ill.	1939
McNichol, Jimmy	Los Angeles, Cal.	7/2/61
McNichol, Kristy	Los Angeles, Cal.	9/11/62
McQueen, Butterfly	Tampa, Fla.	1/7/11
McQueen, Steve	Indianapolis, Ind.	3/24/30
Meadows, Audrey	Wu Chang, China	1924
Meadows, Jayne	Wu Chang, China	9/27/26
Meara, Anne	New York, N.Y.	1929
Meeker, Ralph	Minneapolis, Minn.	11/21/20
Mehta, Zubin	Bombay, India	4/29/36
Melanie	New York, N.Y.	1/3/47
Menuhin, Yehudi	New York, N.Y.	4/22/16
Mercouri, Melina	Athens, Greece	10/18/25
Meredith, Burgess	Cleveland, Oh.	11/16/08
Merkel, Una	Covington, Ky.	12/10/03
Merman, Ethel	Astoria, N.Y.	1/16/09
Merrick, David	Hong Kong	11/27/12
Merrill, Dina	New York, N.Y.	12/9/25
Merrill, Gary	Hartford, Conn.	8/2/15
Merrill, Robert	Brooklyn, N.Y.	6/4/19
Messina, Jim	Maywood, Cal.	12/5/47
Middleton, Ray	Chicago, Ill.	2/8/07
Midler, Bette	Paterson, N.J.	12/1/45
Milanov, Zinka	Zagreb, Yugoslavia	5/17/08
Miles, Sarah	Ingatestone, England	12/31/43
Miles, Vera	near Boise City, Okla.	11/23/30
Milland, Ray	Neath, Wales	1/3/08
Miller, Ann	Houston, Tex.	4/12/23
Miller, Cheryl	Sherman Oaks, Cal.	2/4/43
Miller, Jason	Scranton, Pa.	4/22/40
Miller, Mitch	Rochester, N.Y.	7/4/11
Miller, Roger	Ft. Worth, Tex.	1/2/36
Mills, Hayley	London, England	4/18/46
Mills, John	Suffolk, England	2/22/08
Mills, Juliet	London, England	11/21/41
Milner, Martin	Detroit, Mich.	12/28/31
Milnes, Sherrill	Downers Grove, Ill.	1/10/35
Milsap, Ronnie	Robinsville, N.C.	1/16/-
Milstein, Nathan	Odessa, Russia	12/31/04
Mimieux, Yvette	Hollywood, Cal.	1/8/42
Minnelli, Liza	Los Angeles, Cal.	3/12/46
Mitchell, Cameron	Dallastown, Pa.	11/4/18
Mitchell, Guy	Detroit, Mich.	2/22/25

Name	Birthplace	Born
Mitchell, Joni	McLeod, Alta.	11/7/43
Mitchum, Robert	Bridgeport, Conn.	8/6/17
Moffo, Anna	Wayne, Pa.	6/27/34
Molinaro, Al.	Kenosha, Wis.	6/24/-
Montalban, Ricardo	Mexico City, Mexico	11/25/20
Montand, Yves.	Monsummano, Italy	10/31/21
Montgomery, Elizabeth	Hollywood, Cal.	4/15/33
Montgomery, George	Brady, Mon.	8/29/16
Montgomery, Robert	Beacon, N.Y.	5/21/04
Moore, Clayton	Chicago, Ill.	9/14/14
Moore, Constance	Sioux City, Ia.	1/18/22
Moore, Dudley	London, England	4/19/35
Moore, Garry	Baltimore, Md.	1/31/15
Moore, Mary Tyler	Brooklyn, N.Y.	12/29/37
Moore, Melba	New York, N.Y.	10/29/45
Moore, Roger	London, England	10/14/27
Moore, Terry	Los Angeles, Cal.	1/1/32
Moreau, Jeanne	Paris, France	1/23/28
Moreno, Rita	Humacao, P.R.	12/11/31
Morgan, Dennis	Prentice, Wis.	1910
Morgan, Harry	Detroit, Mich.	4/10/15
Morgan, Henry	New York, N.Y.	3/31/15
Morgan, Jane	Boston, Mass.	1920
Morgana, Nina	Buffalo, N.Y.	1895
Moriarty, Michael	Detroit, Mich.	4/5/41
Morini, Erika	Vienna, Austria	1/5/10
Morley, Robert	Wiltshire, England	5/26/08
Morris, Greg	Cleveland, Oh.	1934
Morris, Howard	New York, N.Y.	9/4/25
Morrow, Vic	Bronx, N.Y.	2/14/32
Morse, Robert	Newton, Mass.	5/18/31
Moss, Arnold	Brooklyn, N.Y.	1/28/10
Mulhare, Edward	Ireland	1923
Munsel, Patrice	Spokane, Wash.	5/14/25
Murphy, George	New Haven, Conn.	7/4/02
Murray, Anne	Springhill, Nova Scotia	6/20/-
Murray, Arthur	New York, N.Y.	4/4/95
Murray, Don	Hollywood, Cal.	7/31/29
Murray, Jan	New York, N.Y.	1917
Murray, Kathryn	Jersey City, N.J.	9/15/06
Murray, Ken	New York, N.Y.	7/14/03
Musante, Tony	Bridgeport, Conn.	6/30/-
Musburger, Brent	Portland, Ore.	5/26/39
Nabors, Jim	Sylacauga, Ala.	6/12/33
Natwick, Mildred	Baltimore, Md.	6/19/08
Neal, Patricia	Packard, Ky.	1/20/26
Neff, Hildegarde	Ulm, Germany	12/28/25
Negri, Pola	Lipno, Poland	1899
Nelson, Barry	San Francisco, Cal.	1920
Nelson, David	New York, N.Y.	10/24/36
Nelson, Ed	New Orleans, La.	1928
Nelson, Gene	Seattle, Wash.	3/24/20
Nelson, Harriet (Hilliard)	Des Moines, Ia.	7/18/14
Nelson, Ricky	Teaneck, N.J.	5/8/40
Nelson, Willie	Waco, Tex.	4/30/33
Nero, Peter	New York, N.Y.	5/22/34
Nesbit, Cathleen	Cheshire, England	11/24/89
Newhart, Bob	Oak Park, Ill.	9/5/29
Newley, Anthony	Hackney, England	9/24/31
Newman, Barry	Boston, Mass.	11/7/38
Newman, Paul	Cleveland, Oh.	1/26/25
Newman, Phyllis	Jersey City, N.J.	3/19/35
Newman, Randy	Los Angeles, Cal.	11/28/43
Newmar, Julie	Los Angeles, Cal.	1935
Newton, Wayne	Roanoke, Va.	4/3/42
Newton-John, Olivia	Cambridge, England	9/26/48
Nichols, Mike	Berlin, Germany	11/6/31
Nicholson, Jack	Neptune, N.J.	4/28/37
Nielsen, Leslie	Regina, Sask	2/11/26
Nilsson, Birgit	Karop, Sweden	1918
Nimoy, Leonard	Boston, Mass.	3/26/31
Niven, David	Kirriemuir, Scotland	3/1/10
Nolan, Doris	New York, N.Y.	1916
Nolan, Jeannette	Los Angeles, Cal.	1911
Nolan, Kathy	St. Louis, Mo.	9/27/33
Nolan, Lloyd	San Francisco, Cal.	8/11/02
Nolte, Nick	Omaha, Neb.	1940
North, Jay	Hollywood, Cal.	1953
North, John Ringling	Baraboo, Wis.	8/14/03
North, Sheree	Los Angeles, Cal.	1/17/33
Norton-Taylor, Judy	Santa Monica, Cal.	1/29/58
Novak, Kim	Chicago, Ill.	2/18/33
Nugent, Elliott	Dover, Oh.	9/20/99
Nureyev, Rudolf	Russia	3/17/38
Nuyen, France	Marseilles, France	7/31/39
Oakland, Simon	New York, N.Y.	1922
O'Brian, Hugh	Rochester, N.Y.	4/19/30
O'Brien, Edmond	New York, N.Y.	9/10/15
O'Brien, Margaret	San Diego, Cal.	1/15/37
O'Brien, Pat	Milwaukee, Wis.	11/11/99
O'Connell, Arthur	New York, N.Y.	3/29/08
O'Connell, Helen	Lima, Oh.	1920
O'Connor, Carroll	New York, N.Y.	8/2/24
O'Connor, Donald	Chicago, Ill.	8/28/25
Odetta	Birmingham, Ala.	12/31/30
O'Driscoll, Martha	Tulsa, Okla.	1922
O'Hara, Jill	Warren, Pa.	1947
O'Hara, Maureen	Dublin, Ireland	8/17/21
O'Herlihy, Dan	Wexford, Ireland	5/1/19
O'Keefe, Walter	Hartford, Conn.	1907
Olivier, Laurence	Dorking, England	5/22/07
O'Malley, J. Pat	Burnley, England	1901
O'Neal, Patrick	Ocala, Fla.	9/26/27
O'Neal, Ryan	Los Angeles, Cal.	4/20/41
O'Neal, Tatum	Los Angeles, Cal.	11/5/63
O'Neill, Jennifer	Brazil	2/20/49
Opatoshu, David	New York, N.Y.	1/30/18
Orbach, Jerry	New York, N.Y.	10/20/35
Orlando, Tony	New York, N.Y.	4/3/44
Ormandy, Eugene	Budapest, Hungary	11/18/99
Osmond, Donny	Ogden, Ut.	12/9/57
Osmond, Marie	Ogden, Ut.	10/13/59
O'Sullivan, Maureen	Boyle, Ireland	5/17/11
O'Toole, Peter	Connemara, Ireland	8/2/34
Owens, Buck	Sherman, Tex.	8/12/29
Owens, Gary	Mitchell, S.D.	5/10/36
Paar, Jack	Canton, Oh.	5/1/18
Pacino, Al	New York, N.Y.	4/25/40
Page, Geraldine	Kirksville, Mo.	11/22/24
Page, LaWanda	Cleveland, Oh.	10/19/20
Page, Patti	Claremore, Okla.	11/8/27
Paige, Janis	Tacoma, Wash.	9/16/22
Palance, Jack	Lattimer, Pa.	2/18/20
Palillo, Ron	New Haven, Conn.	4/2/-
Palmer, Betsy	East Chicago, Ind.	11/1/29
Palmer, Lilli	Posen, Germany	5/24/14
Papas, Irene	Greece	1926
Papp, Joseph	Brooklyn, N.Y.	6/22/21
Parker, Eleanor	Cedarville, Oh.	6/26/22
Parker, Fess	Ft. Worth, Tex.	8/16/25
Parker, Frank	New York, N.Y.	1906
Parker, Jean	Deer Lodge, Mon.	1916
Parker, Suzy	San Antonio, Tex.	10/28/33
Parkins, Barbara	Vancouver, B.C.	1942
Parks, Bert	Atlanta, Ga.	12/30/14
Parsons, Estelle	Lynn, Mass.	11/20/27
Parton, Dolly	Sevierville, Tenn.	1/19/46
Pasternak, Joseph	Hungary	9/19/01
Patterson, Neva	Nevada, Ia.	1922
Paulsen, Pat	South Bend, Wash.	—
Pavan, Marisa	Cagliari, Sardinia	6/19/32
Pavarotti, Luciano	Modena, Italy	10/12/35
Payne, John	Roanoke, Va.	1912
Pearl, Minnie	Centerville, Tenn.	10/25/12
Peck, Gregory	La Jolla, Cal.	4/5/16
Peckinpah, Sam	Fresno, Cal.	2/21/25
Peerce, Jan	New York, N.Y.	1904
Penn, Arthur	Philadelphia, Pa.	9/27/22
Peppard, George	Detroit, Mich.	10/1/28
Perkins, Anthony	New York, N.Y.	4/4/32
Perlman, Itzhak	Tel Aviv, Israel	10/31/45
Perrine, Valerie	Galveston, Tex.	9/3/43
Persoff, Nehemiah	Jerusalem, Palestine	8/14/20
Peters, Bernadette	Queens, N.Y.	2/28/48
Peters, Brock	New York, N.Y.	7/2/27
Peters, Jean	Canton, Oh.	10/15/26
Peters, Roberta	New York, N.Y.	5/4/30
Petit, Pascale	France	1937
Pettet, Joanna	London, England	1944
Piazza, Marguerite	New Orleans, La.	5/6/26
Phillips, MacKenzie	Alexandria, Va.	11/10/59
Phillips, Michelle	Long Beach, Cal.	4/6/44
Pickens, Slim	Kingsberg, Cal.	6/29/19
Picon, Molly	New York, N.Y.	6/1/98
Pidgeon, Walter	E. St. John, N.B.	9/23/97
Pleasance, Donald	Worksop, England	10/5/21
Pleshette, Suzanne	New York, N.Y.	1/31/37
Plowright, Joan	Brigg, England	10/28/29
Plummer, Christopher	Toronto, Ont.	12/13/29
Poitier, Sidney	Miami, Fla.	2/20/27
Polanski, Roman	Paris, France	8/18/33
Pollard, Michael	Passaic, N.J.	5/30/39
Ponselle, Rosa	Meriden, Conn.	1/22/97
Ponti, Carlo	Milan, Italy	12/11/13
Poston, Tom	Columbus, Oh.	10/17/21

Name	Birthplace	Born
Powell, Eleanor	Springfield, Mass.	11/21/12
Powell, Jane	Portland, Ore.	4/1/29
Powell, William.	Pittsburgh, Pa.	7/29/92
Powers, Mala	San Francisco, Cal.	1931
Powers, Stefanie	Hollywood, Cal.	11/12/42
Preminger, Otto	Vienna, Austria	12/5/06
Prentiss, Paula.	San Antonio, Tex.	3/4/39
Preston, Robert	Newton, Mass.	6/8/18
Previn, Andre	Berlin, Germany	4/6/29
Price, Leontyne	Laurel, Miss.	2/10/27
Price, Ray	Perryville, Tex.	1/12/26
Price, Roger	Charleston, W.Va.	3/6/20
Price, Vincent	St. Louis, Mo.	5/27/11
Pride, Charlie	Sledge, Miss.	3/18/38
Prince, William	Nichols, N.Y.	1/26/13
Provine, Dorothy	Deadwood, S.D.	1/20/37
Prowse, Juliet	Bombay, India.	9/25/36
Pryor, Richard	Peoria, Ill.	12/1/40
Pyle, Denver	Bethune, Col.	5/11/20
Qualen, John.	Vancouver, B.C.	1899
Quayle, Anthony.	Lancashire, England	9/7/13
Quillan, Eddie	Philadelphia, Pa.	3/31/07
Quinn, Anthony	Chihuahua, Mexico	4/21/15
Rabb, Ellis	Memphis, Tenn.	6/20/30
Radnor, Gilda	Detroit, Mich.	6/28/-
Rae, Charlotte	Milwaukee, Wis.	4/22/26
Raffin, Deborah	Los Angeles, Cal.	1953
Raft, George	New York, N.Y.	1895
Rainer, Luise	Vienna, Austria	1912
Raines, Ella	Snoqualmie Falls, Wash.	8/6/21
Raitt, John	Santa Ana, Cal.	1/19/17
Ralston, Esther	Bar Harbor, Me.	9/19/02
Ralston, Vera	Prague, Czechoslovakia	1921
Randall, Tony	Tulsa, Okla.	2/26/20
Rawls, Lou	Chicago, Ill.	12/1/35
Ray, Aldo.	Pen Argyl, Pa.	9/25/26
Ray, Johnnie	Dallas, Ore.	1927
Rayburn, Gene	Christopher, Ill.	12/17/17
Raye, Martha	Butte, Mon.	8/27/16
Raymond, Gene	New York, N.Y.	8/13/08
Reddy, Helen	Melbourne, Australia	10/25/41
Redford, Robert	Santa Monica, Cal.	8/18/37
Redgrave, Lynn	London, England	3/8/43
Redgrave, Michael	Bristol, England	3/20/08
Redgrave, Vanessa	London, England	1/30/37
Reed, Donna.	Denison, Ia.	1/27/21
Reed, Jerry	Atlanta, Ga.	3/20/37
Reed, Rex	Ft. Worth, Tex.	10/2/38
Reed, Robert	Highland Park, Ill.	1932
Reese, Della	Detroit, Mich.	7/6/32
Regan, Phil.	Brooklyn, N.Y.	5/28/06
Reid, Kate	London, England	11/4/30
Reilly, Charles Nelson	New York, N.Y.	1/13/31
Reiner, Carl	Bronx, N.Y.	3/20/22
Reiner, Rob	Bronx, N.Y.	3/6/45
Remick, Lee	Boston, Mass.	12/14/35
Renaldo, Duncan	Camden, N.J.	4/23/04
Resnik, Regina.	New York, N.Y.	8/30/24
Rey, Alejandro.	Buenos Aires, Argentina	2/8/30
Reynolds, Burt	Waycross, Ga.	2/11/36
Reynolds, Debbie	El Paso, Tex.	4/1/32
Reynolds, Marjorie	Buhl, Ida.	8/12/21
Rhodes, Hari	Cincinnati, Oh.	1932
Rich, Charlie	Forest City, Ark.	12/14/32
Rich, Irene	Buffalo, N.Y.	10/13/97
Richardson, Ralph.	Cheltenham, England	12/19/02
Richardson, Tony	Shipley, England	6/5/28
Rickles, Don	New York, N.Y.	9/8/26
Riddle, Nelson	Hackensack, N.J.	6/1/21
Rigg, Diana.	Doncaster, England	7/20/38
Ritter, John.	Burbank, Cal.	9/17/48
Ritz, Harry	Newark, N.J.	1908
Ritz, Jimmy.	Newark, N.J.	1905
Rivera, Chita	Washington, D.C.	1/23/33
Rivers, Joan	Brooklyn, N.Y.	1937
Robards, Jason Jr.	Chicago, Ill.	7/26/22
Robbins, Jerome	New York, N.Y.	10/11/18
Robbins, Marty	Glendale, Ariz.	9/26/25
Roberts, Pernell	Waycross, Ga.	5/18/-
Robertson, Cliff	La Jolla, Cal.	9/9/25
Robertson, Dale	Oklahoma City, Okla.	7/14/23
Robson, Flora	South Shields, England	3/28/02
Rodgers, Jimmie	Camas, Wash.	1933
Rodriquez, Johnny	Sabinal, Tex.	12/10/51
Rogers, Chas. (Buddy)	Olathe, Kan.	8/13/04
Rogers, Ginger	Independence, Mo.	7/16/11
Rogers, Kenny.	Houston, Tex.	1941
Rogers, Roy	Cincinnati, Oh.	11/5/12
Roland, Gilbert.	Juarez, Mexico	12/11/05
Rolle, Esther	Pompano Beach, Fla.	11/8/-
Roman, Ruth.	Boston, Mass.	12/23/24
Romero, Cesar	New York, N.Y.	2/15/07
Ronstadt, Linda	Tucson, Ariz.	7/15/46
Rooney, Mickey	Brooklyn, N.Y.	9/23/20
Rose, George	Bicester, England	2/19/20
Rose Marie.	New York, N.Y.	—
Ross, Diana	Detroit, Mich.	3/26/44
Ross, Katharine	Hollywood, Cal.	1/29/43
Ross, Lanny	Seattle, Wash.	1/19/06
Roundtree, Richard	New Rochelle, N.Y.	7/9/42
Rowan, Dan	Beggs, Okla.	7/2/22
Rowlands, Gena.	Cambria, Wis.	6/19/36
Rubin, Benny.	Boston, Mass.	1899
Rubinoff, David	Grodno, Russia	1897
Rubinstein, Arthur	Lodz, Poland	1/28/89
Rudolf, Max	Frankfurt, Germany	6/15/02
Rule, Janice	Norwood, Oh.	8/15/31
Rush, Barbara	Denver, Col.	1/4/30
Russell, Jane	Bemidji, Minn.	6/21/21
Russell, Ken	Southampton, England.	7/3/27
Russell, Kurt	Springfield, Mass.	3/17/51
Russell, Nipsey	Atlanta, Ga.	1924
Rutherford, Ann	Toronto, Ont.	1924
Ryan, Peggy	Long Beach, Cal.	8/28/24
Rydell, Bobby	Philadelphia, Pa.	1942
Sahl, Mort	Montreal, Que.	5/11/27
Saint, Eva Marie	Newark, N.J.	7/4/24
St. James, Susan	Los Angeles, Cal.	8/14/46
St. John, Jill	Los Angeles, Cal.	8/19/40
Sainte-Marie, Buffy	Maine	2/20/41
Saks, Gene	New York, N.Y.	11/8/21
Sales, Soupy.	Franklinton, N.C.	1926
Sand, Paul	Los Angeles, Cal.	3/5/35
Sands, Tommy	Chicago, Ill.	8/27/37
Sanford, Isabel.	New York, N.Y.	8/29/-
Santana, Carlos	Mexico	7/20/47
Sarnoff, Dorothy.	New York, N.Y.	1919
Sarrazin, Michael	Quebec City, Que.	5/22/40
Savalas, Telly	Garden City, N.Y.	1/21/27
Saxon, John	Brooklyn, N.Y.	8/5/35
Sayao, Bidu	Rio de Janeiro, Brazil	5/11/08
Sayer, Leo	Sussex, England	5/21/48
Schallert, William	Los Angeles, Cal.	7/6/22
Scheider, Roy	Orange, N.J.	11/10/35
Schell, Maria.	Vienna, Austria	1/15/26
Schell, Maximilian	Vienna, Austria	12/8/30
Schenkel, Chris	Bippus, Ind.	1924
Schnabel, Stefan	Berlin, Germany	2/2/12
Schneider, Alexander	Vilna, Poland	10/21/08
Schneider, Romy	Austria	9/23/38
Schreiber, Avery.	Chicago, Ill.	1935
Schwarzkopf, Elisabeth.	Jarotschin, Poland	12/9/15
Scofield, Paul	Hurst, Pierpont, England	1/21/22
Scorsese, Martin	New York, N.Y.	11/17/42
Scott, George C.	Wise, Va.	10/18/27
Scott, Hazel	Trinidad	1920
Scott, Lizabeth.	Scranton, Pa.	1923
Scott, Martha	Jamesport, Mo.	9/22/14
Scott, Randolph	Orange Co., Va.	1/23/03
Scotto, Renata.	Savona, Italy	2/24/34
Scourby, Alexander	New York, N.Y.	11/13/13
Sebastian, John	New York N.Y.	3/17/44
Sedaka, Neil	New York, N.Y.	3/13/39
Seeger, Pete.	New York, N.Y.	5/3/19
Segal, George	Great Neck, N.Y.	2/13/34
Segal, Vivienne	Philadelphia, Pa.	4/19/97
Segovia, Andres	Linares, Spain.	2/21/93
Serkin, Rudolf	Eger, Austria	3/28/03
Severinsen, Doc	Arlington, Ore.	7/7/27
Shankar, Ravi	India	4/7/20
Sharif, Omar	Alexandria, Egypt.	4/10/32
Shatner, William	Montreal, Que.	3/22/31
Shaw, Robert	Red Bluff, Cal.	4/30/16
Shawn, Dick	Buffalo, N.Y.	12/1/29
Shearer, Moira.	Scotland	1/17/26
Shearer, Norma	Montreal Que.	1904
Sheen, Martin	Dayton, Oh.	8/3/40
Sheldon, Jack	Jacksonville, Fla.	1931
Shepherd, Cybill	Memphis, Tenn.	2/18/50
Shepherd, Jean	Chicago, Ill.	7/26/29
Shera, Mark	Bayonne, N.J.	7/10/49
Sherwood, Roberta	St. Louis, Mo.	1913
Shields, Brooke	New York, N.Y.	5/31/65
Shire, Talia.	New York, N.Y.	4/25/46
Shirley, Ann	New York, N.Y.	1918

Name	Birthplace	Born
Shore, Dinah	Winchester, Tenn.	3/1/18
Sidney, Sylvia	New York, N.Y.	8/8/10
Siepi, Cesare	Milan, Italy	2/10/23
Signoret, Simone	Wiesbaden, Germany	3/25/21
Sills, Beverly	Brooklyn, N.Y..	5/25/29
Silvers, Phil	Brooklyn, N.Y..	5/11/12
Simmons, Jean	London, England	1/31/29
Simon, Carly	New York, N.Y.	6/25/45
Simon, Paul	Newark, N.J.	11/13/42
Simon, Simone	Marseilles, France	4/23/14
Simone, Nina	Tyron, N.C.	2/21/33
Sinatra, Frank	Hoboken, N.J.	12/12/15
Sinatra, Frank Jr.	Jersey City, N.J.	1944
Sinatra, Nancy	Jersey City, N.J.	6/8/40
Skelton, Red (Richard)	Vincennes, Ind.	7/18/13
Slezak, Walter	Vienna, Austria	5/3/02
Slick, Grace	Chicago, Ill.	10/30/39
Smith, Alexis	Penticton, B.C.	6/8/21
Smith, Bob	Buffalo, N.Y..	1917
Smith, Connie	Elkhart, Ind.	1941
Smith, Ethel	Pittsburgh, Pa.	1921
Smith, Jaclyn	Houston, Tex.	10/26/48
Smith, Kate	Greenville, Va.	5/1/09
Smith, Keeley	Norfolk, Va.	3/9/35
Smith, Maggie	Ilford, England	12/28/34
Smith, Patti	Chicago, Ill.	1946
Smith, Roger	South Gate, Cal.	12/18/32
Smothers, Dick	New York, N.Y.	11/20/39
Smothers, Tom	New York, N.Y.	2/2/37
Snodgress, Carrie	Park Ridge, Ill.	10/27/45
Snow, Hank	Nova Scotia, Canada	5/9/14
Solti, Georg	Budapest, Hungary	10/21/12
Somes, Michael	nr. Stroud, England	1917
Somers, Suzanne	San Bruno, Cal.	10/16/46
Sommer, Elke	Berlin, Germany	11/5/41
Sorvino, Paul	Brooklyn, N.Y..	1939
Sothern, Ann	Valley City, N.D.	1/22/12
Soul, David	Chicago, Ill.	8/28/-
Spacek, Sissy	Quitman, Tex.	12/25/49
Spencer, Danielle	Bronx, N.Y.	6/24/65
Spewack, Bella	Hungary	1899
Spivak, Lawrence	Brooklyn, N.Y..	6/11/00
Springsteen, Bruce	Freehold, N.J.	9/23/49
Stack, Robert	Los Angeles, Cal.	1/13/19
Stafford, Jo	Coalinga, Cal.	1918
Stallone, Sylvester	New York, N.Y.	7/6/46
Stamp, Terence	London, England	1940
Stang, Arnold	Chelsea, Mass.	1925
Stanley, Kim	Tularosa, N.M.	2/11/25
Stanwyck, Barbara	Brooklyn, N.Y..	7/16/07
Stapleton, Jean	New York, N.Y.	1/19/23
Stapleton, Maureen	Troy, N.Y.	6/21/25
Starr, Kay	Dougherty, Okla.	7/21/22
Starr, Ringo	Liverpool, England	7/7/40
Steber, Eleanor	Wheeling, W. Va.	7/17/16
Steele, Tommy	London, England	12/17/36
Steiger, Rod	W. Hampton, N.Y.	4/14/25
Steinberg, David	Winnipeg, Man.	8/9/42
Stephens, James	Mt. Kisco, N.Y..	5/18/51
Sterling, Jan	New York, N.Y.	4/3/23
Sterling, Robert	New Castle, Pa.	11/13/17
Stern, Isaac	Kreminiecz, Russia	7/21/20
Stevens, Cat	London, England	1947
Stevens, Connie	Brooklyn, N.Y..	8/8/38
Stevens, Kaye	Pittsburgh, Pa.	1935
Stevens, Mark	Cleveland, Oh.	12/13/22
Stevens, Rise	New York, N.Y.	6/11/13
Stevens, Stella	Yazoo City, Miss.	10/1/36
Stevens, Warren	Clark's Summit, Pa.	11/2/19
Stevenson, McLean	Normal, Ill..	11/14/-
Stevenson, Parker	Philadelphia, Pa.	6/4/53
Stewart, James	Indiana, Pa.	5/20/08
Stewart, Rod	London, England	1/10/45
Stickney, Dorothy	Dickinson, N.D.	6/21/00
Stiers, David Ogden	Peoria, Ill.	10/31/42
Stills, Stephen	Dallas, Tex.	1/3/45
Stockwell, Dean	Hollywood, Cal.	3/5/36
Stone, Ezra	New Bedford, Mass.	12/2/17
Storch, Larry	New York, N.Y.	1/8/25
Storm, Gale	Bloomington, Tex.	4/5/22
Storrs, Suzanne	Salt Lake City, Ut.	1934
Straight, Beatrice	Old Westbury, N.Y..	8/2/18
Strasberg, Susan	New York, N.Y.	5/22/38
Stratas, Teresa	Toronto, Ont.	5/26/39
Strauss, Peter	New York, N.Y.	1947
Streep, Meryl	Summit, N.J.	—
Streisand, Barbra	Brooklyn, N.Y..	4/24/42
Stritch, Elaine	Detroit, Mich.	2/2/26
Strode, Woody	Los Angeles, Cal.	1914
Struthers, Sally	Portland, Ore.	7/28/48
Sullivan, Barry	New York, N.Y.	8/29/12
Sumac, Yma	Ichocan, Peru	9/10/27
Summer, Donna	Boston, Mass.	12/31/49
Susskind, David	New York, N.Y.	12/19/20
Sutherland, Donald	St. John, New Brunswick	7/17/34
Sutherland, Joan	Sydney, Australia	11/7/26
Suzuki, Pat	Cressey, Cal	1931
Swanson, Gloria	Chicago, Ill.	3/27/99
Sweet, Blanche	Chicago, Ill.	6/18/95
Swit, Loretta	Passaic, N.J.	11/4/-
Talbot, Lyle	Pittsburgh, Pa.	1902
Talbot, Nita	New York, N.Y.	1930
Tallchief, Maria	Fairfax, Okla.	1/24/25
Tamblyn, Russ	Los Angeles, Cal.	12/30/35
Tandy, Jessica	London, England	6/7/09
Taylor, Elizabeth	London, England	2/27/32
Taylor, James	Boston, Mass.	3/12/48
Taylor, Kent	Nashua, Ia.	5/11/07
Taylor, Rod	Sydney, Australia	1/11/30
Tebaldi, Renata	Pesaro, Italy	2/1/22
Temple, Shirley	Santa Monica, Cal.	4/23/28
Tennille, Toni	Montgomery, Ala.	5/8/43
Terris, Norma	Columbus, Kan.	1904
Terry-Thomas	London, England	7/14/11
Thaxter, Phyllis	Portland, Me.	11/20/21
Thebom, Blanche	Monessen, Pa.	9/19/19
Thibault, Conrad	Northbridge, Mass.	11/13/08
Thinnes, Roy	Chicago, Ill.	1938
Thomas, B.J.	Houston, Tex.	8/7/42
Thomas, Danny	Deerfield, Mich.	1/6/14
Thomas, Lowell	Woodrington, Oh.	4/6/92
Thomas, Marlo	Detroit, Mich.	11/21/43
Thomas, Richard	New York, N.Y.	6/13/51
Thompson, Marshall	Peoria, Ill.	11/27/26
Thompson, Sada	Des Moines, Ia.	9/27/29
Thulin, Ingrid	Sweden	1/27/29
Tiegs, Cheryl	California	—
Tierney, Gene	Brooklyn, N.Y..	11/20/20
Tierney, Lawrence	Brooklyn, N.Y..	3/15/19
Tiffin, Pamela	Oklahoma City, Okla.	10/13/42
Tillis, Mel	Tampa, Fla.	8/8/32
Tillstrom, Burr	Chicago, Ill.	10/13/17
Tiny Tim	New York, N.Y.	—
Tobias, George	New York, N.Y.	1901
Todd, Richard	Dublin, Ireland	6/11/19
Tomlin, Lily	Detroit, Mich.	1939
Tomlinson, David	Scotland	5/7/17
Toomey, Regis	Pittsburgh, Pa.	8/13/02
Torme, Mel	Chicago, Ill.	9/13/25
Torn, Rip	Temple, Tex.	2/6/31
Totter, Audrey	Joliet, Ill.	12/20/23
Tracy, Arthur	Kamenetz, Podolsk, Russia	6/25/03
Travers, Mary	Louisville, Ky.	11/9/36
Travolta, John	Englewood, N.J.	2/18/54
Trevor, Claire	New York, N.Y.	3/8/09
Truffaut, Francois	Paris, France	2/6/32
Tucker, Forrest	Plainfield, Ind.	2/12/19
Tucker, Orrin	St. Louis, Mo.	1911
Tucker, Tanya	Seminole, Tex.	10/10/58
Tucker, Tommy	Souris, N.D.	1907
Turner, Ike	Clarksdale, Miss.	11/5/31
Turner, Lana	Wallace, Ida.	2/8/20
Turner, Tina	Brownsville, Tex.	11/25/41
Tushingham, Rita	Liverpool, England	3/14/42
Twiggy (Leslie Hornby)	London, England	9/19/49
Twitty, Conway	Friar's Point, Miss.	9/1/33
Tyrell, Susan	New Canaan, Conn.	1946
Tyson, Cicely	New York, N.Y.	12/19/33
Uggams, Leslie	New York, N.Y.	5/25/43
Ullmann, Liv	Tokyo, Japan	12/16/39
Umeki, Miyoshi	Hokkaido, Japan	1929
Ustinov, Peter	London, England	4/16/21
Vaccaro, Brenda	Brooklyn, N.Y..	11/18/39
Vale, Jerry	New York, N.Y.	1931
Valente, Caterina	Paris, France	1/14/32
Valentine, Karen	Santa Rosa, Cal.	1947
Vallee, Rudy	Island Pond, Vt.	7/28/01
Valli, Alida	Pola, Italy	5/31/21
Valli, Frankie	Newark, N.J.	5/3/37
Van Cleef, Lee	Somerville, N.J.	1/9/25
Van Devere, Trish	Tenafly, N.J.	1945
Van Doren, Mamie	Rowena, S.D.	2/6/33

Name	Birthplace	Born
Van Dyke, Dick	West Plains, Mo.	12/13/25
Van Dyke, Jerry	Danville, Ill.	1932
Van Fleet, Jo	Oakland, Cal.	1922
Van Patten, Dick	New York, N.Y.	12/9/28
Van Vooren, Monique	Brussels, Belgium	4/17/33
Varnay, Astrid	Stockholm, Sweden	4/25/18
Varsi, Diane	San Francisco, Cal.	1938
Vaughan, Sarah	Newark, N.J.	3/27/24
Vaughn, Robert	New York, N.Y.	11/22/32
Venuta, Benay	San Francisco, Cal.	1/27/11
Vera-Ellen	Cincinnati, Oh.	1926
Verdon, Gwen	Los Angeles, Cal.	1/13/25
Vereen, Ben	Miami, Fla.	10/10/46
Vernon, Jackie	New York, N.Y.	1929
Vickers, Jon	Prince Albert, Sask.	10/26/26
Vidor, King Wallis	Galveston, Tex.	2/8/95
Vigoda, Abe	New York, N.Y.	2/24/21
Villella, Edward	Long Island, N.Y.	10/1/36
Vincent, Jan-Michael	Ventura, Cal.	7/15/44
Vinson, Helen	Beaumont, Tex.	1907
Vinton, Bobby	Canonsburg, Pa.	4/16/35
Vogel, Mitch	Alhambra, Cal.	1956
Voight, Jon	Yonkers, N.Y.	12/29/38
Von Furstenberg, Betsy.	Neihem Heusen, Germany	8/16/31
Von Sydow, Max	Lund, Sweden	4/10/29
Von Zell, Harry	Indianapolis, Ind.	7/11/06
Voorhees, Donald	Allentown, Pa.	7/26/03
Waggoner, Lyle	Kansas City, Kan.	4/13/35
Wagner, Lindsay	Los Angeles, Cal.	6/22/49
Wagner, Robert	Detroit, Mich.	2/10/30
Wagoner, Porter	West Plains, Mo.	8/12/27
Wain, Bea	Bronx, N.Y.	1917
Waite, Ralph	White Plains, N.Y.	6/22/28
Walker, Clint	Hartford, Ill.	5/30/27
Walker, Jimmy	New York, N.Y.	—
Walker, Nancy	Philadelphia, Pa.	5/10/21
Wallach, Eli	Brooklyn, N.Y.	12/7/15
Wallenstein, Alfred	Chicago, Ill.	10/7/98
Wallis, Hal	Chicago, Ill.	9/14/99
Ward, Simon	London, England	10/19/41
Warden, Jack	Newark, N.J.	9/18/20
Warfield, William	W. Helena, Ark.	1/22/20
Warhol, Andy	Pittsburgh, Pa.	8/6/27
Waring, Fred	Tyrone, Pa.	6/9/00
Warwick, Dionne	E. Orange, N.J.	12/12/41
Watts, Andre	Nuremberg, Germany	6/20/46
Wayne, David	Traverse City, Mich.	1/30/14
Weaver, Dennis	Joplin, Mo.	6/4/25
Weaver, Fritz	Pittsburgh, Pa.	1/19/26
Webb, Jack	Santa Monica, Cal.	4/2/20
Weissmuller, Johnny	Windber, Pa.	6/2/04
Welch, Raquel	Chicago, Ill.	9/5/42
Weld, Tuesday	New York, N.Y.	8/27/43
Welk, Lawrence	nr. Strasburg, N.D.	3/11/03
Welles, Orson	Kenosha, Wis.	5/6/15
Wells, Kitty	Nashville, Tenn.	8/30/19
Werner, Oskar	Vienna, Austria	11/13/22
West, Mae	Brooklyn, N.Y.	8/17/92
White, Barry	Galveston, Tex.	9/12/44
White, Betty	Oak Park, Ill.	1/17/-
White, Jesse	Buffalo, N.Y.	1/8/19
Whiting, Margaret	Detroit, Mich.	7/22/24
Whitman, Stuart	San Francisco, Cal.	2/1/26

Name	Birthplace	Born
Whitmore, James	White Plains, N.Y.	10/1/21
Widmark, Richard	Sunrise, Minn.	12/26/14
Wilcoxon, Henry	British West Indies	1905
Wilde, Cornel	New York, N.Y.	10/13/18
Wilder, Billy	Vienna, Austria	6/22/06
Wilder, Gene	Milwaukee, Wis.	6/11/35
Williams, Andy	Wall Lake, Ia.	12/3/30
Williams, Cindy	Van Nuys, Cal.	8/22/48
Williams, Clarence	New York, N.Y.	8/21/39
Williams, Emlyn	Mostyn, Wales	11/26/05
Williams, Esther	Los Angeles, Cal.	8/8/23
Williams Jr., Hank	Shreveport, La.	5/26/49
Williams, Joe	Cordele, Ga.	1918
Williams, Mason	Abilene, Tex.	1938
Williams, Paul	Omaha, Neb.	9/19/40
Williams, Robin	Edinburgh, Scotland	7/21/55
Williams, Roger	Omaha, Neb.	1926
Williamson, Nicol	Hamilton, Scotland	9/14/38
Wilson, Demond	Valdosta, Ga.	—
Wilson, Dolores	Philadelphia, Pa.	1929
Wilson, Don	Lincoln, Neb.	1900
Wilson, Flip	Jersey City, N.J.	12/8/33
Wilson, Nancy	Chillicothe, Oh.	2/20/37
Winchell, Paul	New York, N.Y.	12/21/22
Windom, William	New York, N.Y.	9/28/23
Winkler, Henry	New York, N.Y.	10/30/45
Winters, Jonathan	Dayton, Oh.	11/11/25
Winters, Shelley	St. Louis, Mo.	8/18/22
Winwood, Estelle	Lee, England	1884
Wiseman, Joseph	Montreal, Que.	5/15/18
Withers, Jane	Atlanta, Ga.	1927
Wonder, Stevie	Saginaw, Mich.	5/13/50
Wood, Helen	Clarksville, Tenn.	1937
Wood, Natalie	San Francisco, Cal.	7/20/38
Woodward, Joanne	Thomasville, Ga.	2/27/30
Worley, Jo Anne	Lowell, Ind.	9/6/37
Worth, Irene	Nebraska	6/23/16
Wray, Fay	Alberta, Canada	9/10/07
Wright, Martha	Seattle, Wash.	1926
Wright, Teresa	New York, N.Y.	10/27/18
Wrightson, Earl	Baltimore, Md.	1916
Wyatt, Jane	Campgaw, N.J.	8/12/12
Wyler, William	Mulhouse, France	7/1/02
Wyman, Jane	St. Joseph, Mo.	1/4/14
Wynette, Tammy	Red Bay, Ala.	5/5/42
Wynn, Keenan	New York, N.Y.	7/27/16
Wynter, Dana	London, England	6/8/30
Yarborough, Glenn	Milwaukee, Wis.	1930
Yarrow, Peter	New York, N.Y.	5/31/38
York, Dick	Ft. Wayne, Ind.	9/4/28
York, Michael	Fulmer, England	3/27/42
York, Susannah	London, England	1/9/41
Young, Alan	Northumberland, England	11/19/19
Young, Loretta	Salt Lake City, Ut.	1/6/13
Young, Neil	Toronto, Ont.	11/12/45
Young, Robert	Chicago, Ill.	2/22/07
Youngman, Henny	Liverpool, England	1906
Zeffirelli, Franco	Florence, Italy	2/12/23
Zimbalist, Efrem	Rostov, Russia	4/9/89
Zimbalist, Efrem Jr.	New York, N.Y.	11/30/23
Zimmer, Norma	Larsen, Ida	—
Zorina, Vera	Berlin, Germany	1/2/17
Zukerman, Pinchas	Tel Aviv, Israel	7/16/48

Entertainment Personalities of the Past

Born	Died	Name
1896	**1974**	Abbott, Bud
1872	**1953**	Adams, Maude
1931	**1968**	Adams, Nick
1855	**1926**	Adler, Jacob P.
1898	**1933**	Adoree, Renee
1909	**1964**	Albertson, Frank
1885	**1952**	Alda, Frances
1894	**1956**	Allen, Fred
1906	**1964**	Allen, Gracie
1883	**1950**	Allgood, Sara
1882	**1971**	Anderson, Gilbert (Bronco Billy)
1886	**1954**	Anderson, John Murray
1915	**1967**	Andrews, Laverne
1933	**1971**	Angeli, Pier
1876	**1958**	Anglin, Margaret
1887	**1933**	Arbuckle, Fatty (Roscoe)
1900	**1976**	Arlen, Richard
1868	**1946**	Arliss, George
1900	**1971**	Armstrong, Louis
1890	**1956**	Arnold, Edward
1905	**1974**	Arquette, Cliff (Charlie Weaver)
1885	**1946**	Atwill, Lionel
1845	**1930**	Auer, Leopold
1905	**1967**	Auer, Mischa
1900	**1972**	Austin, Gene
1898	**1940**	Ayres, Agnes
1864	**1922**	Bacon, Frank
1903	**1951**	Bailey, Mildred
1891	**1968**	Bainter, Fay
1895	**1957**	Baker, Belle
1906	**1975**	Baker, Josephine
1898	**1963**	Baker, Phil
1882	**1956**	Bancroft, George
1903	**1968**	Bankhead, Tallulah
1890	**1952**	Banks, Leslie
1897	**1950**	Banks, Monty

Born	Died	Name
1890	1955	Bara, Theda
1810	1891	Barnum, Phineas T.
1912	1978	Barrie, Wendy
1879	1959	Barrymore, Ethel
1882	1942	Barrymore, John
1878	1954	Barrymore, Lionel
1848	1905	Barrymore, Maurice
1897	1963	Barthelmess, Richard
1890	1962	Barton, James
1873	1951	Bauer, Harold
1893	1951	Baxter, Warner
1880	1928	Bayes, Nora
1904	1965	Beatty, Clyde
1904	1962	Beavers, Louise
1887	1955	Beecher, Janet
1884	1946	Beery, Noah
1889	1949	Beery, Wallace
1901	1970	Begley, Ed
1854	1931	Belasco, David
1906	1968	Benaderet, Bea
1906	1964	Bendix, William
1904	1965	Bennett, Constance
1873	1944	Bennett, Richard
1894	1974	Benny, Jack
1924	1970	Benzell, Mimi
1899	1966	Berg, Gertrude
1903	1978	Bergen, Edgar
1895	1976	Berkeley, Busby
1863	1927	Bernard, Sam
1844	1923	Bernhardt, Sarah
1893	1943	Bernie, Ben
1889	1967	Bickford, Charles
1911	1960	Bjoerling, Jussi
1898	1973	Blackmer, Sidney
1882	1951	Blaney, Charles E.
1900	1943	Bledsoe, Jules
1928	1972	Blocker, Dan
1909	1979	Blondell, Joan
1888	1959	Blore, Eric
1901	1975	Blue, Ben
1899	1957	Bogart, Humphrey
1885	1965	Boland, Mary
1897	1969	Boles, John
1903	1960	Bond, Ward
1833	1893	Booth, Edwin
1796	1852	Booth, Junius Brutus
1894	1953	Bordoni, Irene
1888	1960	Bori, Lucrezia
1867	1943	Bosworth, Hobart
1905	1965	Bow, Clara
1874	1946	Bowes, Maj. Edward
1895	1972	Boyd, William
1899	1978	Boyer, Charles
1893	1939	Brady, Alice
1871	1936	Breese, Edmund
1898	1964	Brendel, El
1901	1948	Breneman, Tom
1894	1974	Brennan, Walter
1875	1948	Brian, Donald
1891	1951	Brice, Fanny
1891	1959	Broderick, Helen
1904	1951	Bromberg, J. Edward
1892	1973	Brown, Joe E.
1926	1966	Bruce, Lenny
1895	1953	Bruce, Nigel
1903	1979	Buchanan, Edgar
1891	1957	Buchanan, Jack
1885	1957	Buck, Gene
1885	1970	Burke, Billie
1912	1967	Burnette, Smiley
1896	1956	Burns, Bob
1902	1971	Burns, David
1882	1941	Burr, Henry
1883	1966	Bushman, Francis X.
1896	1946	Butterworth, Charles
1893	1971	Byington, Spring
1905	1972	Cabot, Bruce
1918	1977	Cabot, Sebastian
1895	1956	Calhern, Louis
1923	1977	Callas, Maria
1853	1942	Calve, Emma
1933	1976	Cambridge, Godfrey
1865	1940	Campbell, Mrs. Patrick
1892	1964	Cantor, Eddie
1878	1947	Carey, Harry
1876	1941	Carle, Richard
1880	1961	Carrillo, Leo
1892	1972	Carroll, Leo G.
1905	1965	Carroll, Nancy
1910	1963	Carson, Jack
1862	1937	Carter, Mrs. Leslie
1873	1921	Caruso, Enrico
1876	1973	Casals, Pablo
1893	1969	Castle, Irene
1887	1918	Castle, Vernon
1889	1960	Catlett, Walter
1874	1944	Cavalieri, Lina
1887	1950	Cavanaugh, Hobart
1873	1938	Chaliapin, Feodor
1919	1961	Chandler, Jeff
1883	1930	Chaney, Lon
1906	1973	Chaney Jr., Lon
1889	1977	Chaplin, Charles
1893	1940	Chase, Charlie
1893	1961	Chatterton, Ruth
1888	1971	Chevalier, Maurice
1888	1960	Clark, Bobby
1914	1968	Clark, Fred
1887	1950	Clayton, Lou
1920	1966	Clift, Montgomery
1932	1963	Cline, Patsy
1900	1937	Clive, Colin
1892	1967	Clyde, Andy
1911	1976	Cobb, Lee J.
1877	1961	Coburn, Charles
1887	1934	Cody, Lew
1878	1942	Cohan, George M.
1876	1916	Cohan, Josephine
1919	1965	Cole, Nat (King)
1878	1955	Collier, Constance
1866	1944	Collier, William Sr.
1890	1965	Collins, Ray
1891	1958	Colman, Ronald
1908	1934	Columbo, Russ
1907	1944	Compton, Betty
1887	1940	Connolly, Walter
1855	1909	Conried, Henrich
1918	1975	Conte, Richard
1904	1967	Conway, Tom
1901	1961	Cook, Donald
1890	1959	Cook, Joe
1893	1958	Cook, Phil
1901	1961	Cooper, Gary
1891	1971	Cooper, Gladys
1896	1973	Cooper, Melville
1914	1968	Corey, Wendell
1893	1974	Cornell, Katherine
1890	1972	Correll, Charles (Andy)
1876	1951	Cossart, Ernest
1904	1957	Costello, Helene
1906	1959	Costello, Lou
1877	1950	Costello, Maurice
1899	1973	Coward, Noel
1890	1950	Cowl, Jane
1924	1973	Cox, Wally
1847	1924	Crabtree, Lotta
1875	1945	Craven, Frank
1903	1977	Crawford, Joan
1916	1944	Cregar, Laird
1880	1942	Crews, Laura Hope
1880	1974	Crisp, Donald
1942	1973	Croce, Jim
1910	1960	Cromwell, Richard
1903	1977	Crosby, Bing
1897	1975	Cross, Milton
1893	1966	Crouse, Russell
1878	1968	Currie, Finlay
1816	1876	Cushman, Charlotte
1917	1978	Dailey, Dan
1923	1965	Dandridge, Dorothy
1869	1941	Danforth, William
1894	1963	Daniell, Henry
1901	1971	Daniels, Bebe
1860	1935	Daniels, Frank
1936	1973	Darin, Bobby
1921	1965	Darnell, Linda
1879	1967	Darwell, Jane
1866	1949	Davenport, Harry
1900	1961	Davies, Marion
1908	1961	Davis, Joan
1931	1955	Dean, James
1881	1950	DeCordoba, Pedro
1905	1968	Dekker, Albert
1898	1965	Demarco, Tony
1881	1959	DeMille, Cecil B.
1891	1967	Denny, Reginald
1901	1974	DeSica, Vittorio
1878	1949	Desmond, William
1905	1977	Devine, Andy
1942	1972	De Wilde, Brandon
1907	1974	De Wolfe, Billy
1865	1950	De Wolfe, Elsie
1879	1947	Digges, Dudley
1890	1944	Dinehart, Alan
1901	1966	Disney, Walt
1895	1949	Dix, Richard
1856	1924	Dockstader, Lew
1892	1941	Dolly, Jennie
1892	1970	Dolly, Rosie
1905	1958	Donat, Robert
1903	1972	Donlevy, Brian
1907	1959	Douglas, Paul
1889	1956	Draper, Ruth
1881	1965	Dresser, Louise
1869	1934	Dressler, Marie
1820	1897	Drew, Mrs. John
1853	1927	Drew, John (son)
1879	1920	Drew, Sydney
1909	1951	Duchin, Eddy
1890	1965	Dumont, Margaret
1878	1927	Duncan, Isadora
1905	1967	Dunn, James
1873	1947	Dupree, Minnie
1893	1980	Durante, Jimmy
1907	1968	Duryea, Dan
1858	1924	Duse, Eleanora
1894	1929	Eagels, Jeanne
1896	1930	Eames, Clare
1865	1952	Eames, Emma
1901	1967	Eddy, Nelson
1897	1971	Edwards, Cliff
1879	1945	Edwards, Gus
1899	1974	Ellington, Duke
1941	1974	Elliot, Cass
1871	1940	Elliott, Maxine
1891	1967	Elman, Mischa
1881	1951	Errol, Leon
1903	1967	Erwin, Stuart
1888	1976	Evans, Edith
1913	1967	Evelyn, Judith
1883	1939	Fairbanks, Douglas
1915	1970	Farmer, Frances
1870	1929	Farnum, Dustin
1876	1953	Farnum, William
1882	1967	Farrar, Geraldine
1904	1971	Farrell, Glenda
1868	1940	Faversham, William
1861	1939	Fawcett, George
1897	1960	Fay, Frank
1895	1962	Fazenda, Louise
1894	1979	Fiedler, Arthur
1918	1973	Field, Betty
1898	1979	Fields, Gracie
1867	1941	Fields, Lew
1880	1946	Fields, W.C.
1931	1978	Fields, Totie
1916	1977	Finch, Peter
1902	1975	Fine, Larry
1865	1932	Fiske, Minnie Maddern
1888	1961	Fitzgerald, Barry
1895	1962	Flagstad, Kirsten
1900	1971	Flippen, Jay C.
1909	1959	Flynn, Errol
1925	1974	Flynn, Joe
1880	1942	Fokine, Michel
1910	1968	Foley, Red
1905	1951	Forbes, Ralph
1853	1937	Forbes-Robertson, J.
1887	1970	Ford, Ed (Senator)
1895	1973	Ford, John
1901	1976	Ford, Paul
1899	1966	Ford, Wallace
1806	1872	Forrest, Edwin
1904	1970	Foster, Preston
1857	1928	Foy, Eddie
1905	1968	Francis, Kay
1893	1966	Frawley, William
1885	1938	Frederick, Pauline
1870	1955	Friganza, Trixie
1890	1958	Frisco, Joe
1860	1915	Frohman, Charles

Born	Died	Name
1851	1940	Frohman, Daniel
1885	1947	Fyffe, Will
1901	1960	Gable, Clark
1889	1963	Galli-Curci, Amelita
1877	1967	Garden, Mary
1913	1952	Garfield, John
1922	1969	Garland, Judy
1893	1963	Gaxton, William
1902	1978	Geer, Will
1904	1954	George, Gladys
1879	1961	George, Grace
1892	1962	Gibson, Hoot
1890	1957	Gigli, Beniamino
1894	1971	Gilbert, Billy
1897	1936	Gilbert, John
1855	1937	Gillette, William
1867	1943	Gillmore, Frank
1879	1939	Gilpin, Charles
1898	1968	Gish, Dorothy
1886	1959	Gleason, James
1884	1938	Gluck, Alma
1874	1955	Golden, John
1884	1974	Goldwyn, Samuel
1917	1969	Gorcey, Leo
1884	1940	Gordon, C. Henry
1887	1948	Gordon, Vera
1869	1944	Gottschalk, Ferdinand
1829	1869	Gottschalk, Louis
1916	1973	Grable, Betty
1901	1959	Gray, Gilda
1879	1954	Greenstreet, Sydney
1875	1948	Griffith, David Wark
1885	1957	Guitry, Sacha
1912	1967	Guthrie, Woody
1875	1959	Gwenn, Edmund
1888	1942	Hackett, Charles
1902	1958	Hackett, Raymond
1870	1943	Haines, Robert T.
1892	1950	Hale, Alan
1899	1979	Haley, Jack
1847	1919	Hammerstein, Oscar
1895	1960	Hammerstein, Oscar 2d
1879	1955	Hampden, Walter
1924	1964	Haney, Carol
1893	1964	Hardwicke, Sir Cedric
1892	1957	Hardy, Oliver
1883	1939	Hare, T.E. (Ernie)
1911	1937	Harlow, Jean
1872	1946	Harned, Virginia
1844	1911	Harrigan, Edward
1895	1943	Hart, Lorenz
1870	1946	Hart, William S.
1907	1955	Hartman, Grace
1928	1973	Harvey, Laurence
1876	1945	Harwood, John
1910	1973	Hawkins, Jack
1890	1973	Hayakawa, Sessue
1885	1969	Hayes, Gabby
1918	1980	Haymes, Dick
1902	1971	Hayward, Leland
1919	1975	Hayward, Susan
1896	1937	Healy, Ted
1910	1971	Heflin, Van
1879	1936	Heggie, O.P.
1873	1918	Held, Anna
1903	1947	Hellinger, Mark
1942	1970	Hendrix, Jimi
1913	1969	Henie, Sonja
1879	1942	Herbert, Henry
1887	1951	Herbert, Hugh
1886	1956	Hersholt, Jean
1895	1942	Hibbard, Edna
1899	1980	Hitchcock, Alfred
1865	1929	Hitchcock, Raymond
1914	1955	Hodiak, John
1894	1973	Holden, Fay
1923	1965	Holliday, Judy
1936	1959	Holly, Buddy
1898	1978	Homolka, Oscar
1888	1951	Holt, Jack
1871	1947	Homer, Louise
1902	1973	Hopkins, Miriam
1858	1935	Hopper, DeWolf
1874	1959	Hopper, Edna Wallace
1890	1966	Hopper, Hedda
1888	1970	Horton, Edward Everett
1874	1926	Houdini, Harry
1881	1965	Howard, Eugene
1867	1961	Howard, Joe
1893	1943	Howard, Leslie
1897	1975	Howard, Moe
1885	1955	Howard, Tom
1885	1949	Howard, Willie
1914	1972	Hudson, Rochelle
1890	1977	Hull, Henry
1886	1957	Hull, Josephine
1907	1967	Hume, Benita
1895	1958	Humphrey, Doris
1895	1945	Hunter, Glenn
1925	1969	Hunter, Jeffrey
1901	1962	Husing, Ted
1884	1950	Huston, Walter
1892	1950	Ingram, Rex
1895	1969	Ingram, Rex
1895	1980	Iturbi, Jose
1838	1905	Irving, Henry
1871	1944	Irving, Isabel
1872	1914	Irving, Laurence
1862	1938	Irvin, May
1875	1942	Jackson, Joe
1911	1972	Jackson, Mahalia
1889	1956	Janis, Elsie
1886	1950	Jannings, Emil
1930	1980	Janssen, David
1829	1905	Jefferson, Joseph
1859	1923	Jefferson, Thomas
1900	1974	Jenkins, Allen
1862	1930	Jewett, Henry
1892	1962	Johnson, Chic
1878	1952	Johnson, Edward
1886	1950	Jolson, Al
1899	1940	Jones, Billy
1889	1942	Jones, Buck
1911	1965	Jones, Spike
1943	1970	Joplin, Janis
1897	1961	Jordan, Marian (Molly McGee)
1890	1955	Joyce, Alice
1910	1966	Kane, Helen
1887	1969	Karloff, Boris
1893	1970	Karns, Roscoe
1811	1868	Kean, Charles
1806	1880	Kean, Mrs. Charles
1787	1833	Kean, Edmund
1895	1966	Keaton, Buster
1858	1929	Keenan, Frank
1830	1873	Keene, Laura
1841	1893	Keene, Thomas W.
1899	1960	Keith, Ian
1894	1973	Kellaway, Cecil
1898	1979	Kelly, Emmett
1899	1956	Kelly, Paul
1873	1939	Kelly, Walter C.
1909	1968	Kelton, Pert
1823	1895	Kemble, Agnes
1775	1854	Kemble, Charles
1809	1893	Kemble, Fannie
1848	1935	Kendal, Dame Madge
1843	1917	Kendal, William H.
1926	1959	Kendall, Kay
1890	1948	Kennedy, Edgar
1885	1965	Kennedy, Tom
1886	1945	Kent, William
1880	1947	Kerrigan, J. Warren
1886	1956	Kibbee, Guy
1902	1966	Kiepura, Jan
1888	1964	Kilbride, Percy
1863	1933	Kilgour, Joseph
1894	1944	King, Charles
1897	1971	King, Dennis
1889	1938	Kohler, Fred
1897	1957	Korngold, Erich W.
1901	1980	Kostelanetz, Andre
1919	1962	Kovacs, Ernie
1885	1974	Kruger, Otto
1909	1973	Krupa, Gene
1913	1964	Ladd, Alan
1895	1967	Lahr, Bert
1919	1973	Lake, Veronica
1904	1948	Landi, Elissa
1919	1948	Landis, Carole
1904	1972	Landis, Jessie Royce
1884	1944	Langdon, Harry
1853	1929	Langtry, Lillie
1921	1959	Lanza, Mario
1881	1958	Lasky, Jesse L.
1870	1950	Lauder, Harry
1899	1962	Laughton, Charles
1890	1965	Laurel, Stan
1892	1954	Laurie Jr., Joe
1898	1952	Lawrence, Gertrude
1890	1929	Lawrence, Margaret
1907	1952	Lee, Canada
1914	1970	Lee, Gypsy Rose
1848	1929	Lehmann, Lilli
1888	1976	Lehmann, Lotte
1896	1950	Lehr, Lew
1913	1967	Leigh, Vivien
1852	1908	Leighton, Margaret
1922	1976	Leighton, Margaret
1894	1931	Leitzel, Lillian
1831	1905	Lemoyne, W. J.
1870	1941	Leonard, Eddie
1911	1973	Leonard, Jack E.
1906	1972	Levant, Oscar
1881	1955	Levy, Ethel
1902	1971	Lewis, Joe E.
1892	1971	Lewis, Ted
1874	1944	Lhevinne, Josef
1889	1952	Lincoln, Elmo
1820	1887	Lind, Jenny
1889	1968	Lindsay, Howard
1869	1952	Lipman, Clara
1893	1971	Lloyd, Harold
1870	1922	Lloyd, Marie
1891	1957	Lockhart, Gene
1876	1943	Loftus, Cissie (Marie)
1913	1969	Logan, Ella
1909	1942	Lombard, Carole
1902	1977	Lombardo, Guy
1927	1974	Long, Richard
1895	1975	Lopez, Vincent
1890	1950	Lord, Pauline
1888	1968	Lorne, Marion
1904	1964	Lorre, Peter
1917	1970	Louise, Anita
1914	1962	Lovejoy, Frank
1892	1971	Lowe, Edmund
1892	1947	Lubitsch, Ernst
1884	1956	Lugosi, Bela
1891	1971	Lukas, Paul
1892	1977	Lunt, Alfred
1853	1932	Lupino, George
1893	1942	Lupino, Stanley
1897	1957	Lyman, Abe
1926	1971	Lynn, Diana
1885	1954	Lytell, Bert
1867	1936	Lytton, Henry
1907	1965	MacDonald, Jeanette
1902	1969	MacLane, Barton
1909	1973	Macready, George
1861	1946	Macy, George Carleton
1908	1973	Magnani, Anna
1896	1967	Mahoney, Will
1890	1975	Main, Marjorie
1933	1967	Mansfield, Jayne
1854	1907	Mansfield, Richard
1905	1980	Mantovani, Annunzio
1897	1975	March, Fredric
1920	1970	March, Hal
1865	1950	Marlowe, Julia
1890	1966	Marshall, Herbert
1864	1943	Marshall, Tully
1885	1969	Martinelli, Giovanni
1888	1964	Marx, Arthur (Harpo)
1890	1977	Marx, Julius (Groucho)
1887	1961	Marx, Leonard (Chico)
1862	1951	Maude, Cyril
1922	1972	Maxwell, Marilyn
1879	1948	May, Edna
1885	1957	Mayer, Louis B.
1895	1973	Maynard, Ken
1884	1945	McCormack, John
1907	1962	McCormick, Myron
1888	1931	McCoy, Bessie
1883	1936	McCullough, Paul
1895	1952	McDaniel, Hattie
1924	1965	McDonald, Marie

Born	Died	Name
1913	1975	McGiver, John
1879	1949	McIntyre, Frank J.
1857	1937	McIntyre, James
1879	1937	McKinley, Mabel
1883	1959	McLaglen, Victor
1907	1971	McMahon, Horace
1920	1980	Medford, Kay
1880	1946	Meek, Donald
1879	1936	Meighan, Thomas
1861	1931	Melba, Nellie
1890	1973	Melchior, Lauritz
1904	1961	Melton, James
1890	1963	Menjou, Adolphe
1902	1966	Menken, Helen
1882	1939	Mercer, Beryl
1880	1946	Merivale, Phillip
1904	1944	Miller, Glenn
1860	1926	Miller, Henry
1898	1936	Miller, Marilyn
1895	1927	Mills, Florence
1939	1976	Mineo, Sal
1903	1955	Minnevitch, Borrah
1913	1955	Miranda, Carmen
1875	1957	Mitchell, Grant
1892	1962	Mitchell, Thomas
1880	1940	Mix, Tom
1845	1909	Modjeska, Helena
1926	1962	Monroe, Marilyn
1911	1973	Monroe, Vaughn
1875	1964	Monteux, Pierre
1818	1861	Montez, Lola
1919	1951	Montez, Maria
1901	1947	Moore, Grace
1885	1955	Moore, Tom
1876	1962	Moore, Victor
1906	1974	Moorehead, Agnes
1882	1949	Moran, George
1884	1952	Moran, Polly
1890	1949	Morgan, Frank
1900	1941	Morgan, Helen
1888	1956	Morgan, Ralph
1901	1970	Morris, Chester
1849	1925	Morris, Clara
1914	1959	Morris, Wayne
1943	1971	Morrison, Jim
1915	1977	Mostel, Zero
1897	1969	Mowbray, Alan
1895	1967	Muni, Paul
1894	1953	Munn, Frank
1906	1955	Munson, Ona
1924	1971	Murphy, Audie
1885	1965	Murray, Mae
1896	1970	Nagel, Conrad
1900	1973	Naish, J. Carroll
1898	1961	Naldi, Nita
1888	1950	Nash, Florence
1865	1945	Nash, George
1879	1945	Nazimova, Alla
1846	1905	Neilson, Ada
1848	1880	Neilson, Adelaide
1868	1957	Neilson-Terry, Julia
1907	1975	Nelson, Ozzie
1885	1967	Nesbit, Evelyn
1870	1951	Nethersole, Olga
1905	1956	Newton, Robert
1874	1948	Niblo, Fred
1890	1950	Nijinsky, Vaslav
1893	1974	Nilsson, Anna Q.
1898	1930	Normand, Mabel
1879	1959	Norworth, Jack
1905	1968	Novarro, Ramon
1893	1951	Novello, Ivor
1903	1978	Oakie, Jack
1860	1926	Oakley, Annie
1911	1979	Oberon, Merle
1898	1943	O'Connell, Hugh
1883	1959	O'Connor, Una
1878	1945	O'Hara, Fiske
1908	1968	O'Keefe, Dennis
1880	1938	Oland, Warner
1860	1932	Olcott, Chauncey
1883	1942	Oliver, Edna May
1892	1963	Olsen, Ole
1849	1920	O'Neill, James
1876	1949	Ouspenskaya, Maria
1887	1972	Owen, Reginald

Born	Died	Name
1860	1941	Paderewski, Ignace
1889	1954	Pallette, Eugene
1894	1958	Pangborn, Franklin
1914	1975	Parks, Larry
1881	1972	Parsons, Louella
1881	1940	Pasternack, Josef A.
1837	1908	Pastor, Tony
1843	1919	Patti, Adelina
1840	1889	Patti, Carlotta
1885	1931	Pavlova, Anna
1900	1973	Paxinou, Katina
1917	1966	Pearce, Alice
1885	1950	Pemberton, Brock
1899	1967	Pendleton, Nat
1905	1941	Penner, Joe
1892	1937	Perkins, Osgood
1893	1956	Peters, Brandon
1915	1963	Piaf, Edith
1893	1979	Pickford, Mary
1892	1957	Pinza, Ezio
1900	1963	Pitts, Zasu
1904	1976	Pons, Lili
1903	1969	Portman, Eric
1904	1963	Powell, Dick
1869	1931	Power, F. Tyrone
1913	1958	Power, Tyrone E.
1872	1935	Powers, Eugene
1935	1977	Presley, Elvis
1900	1964	Price, George E.
1856	1919	Primrose, George
1954	1977	Prinze, Freddie
1879	1956	Prouty, Jed
1871	1942	Pryor, Arthur
1925	1970	Pyne, Joe
1905	1946	Ragland, John (Rags)
1890	1967	Rains, Claude
1889	1970	Rambeau, Marjorie
1900	1947	Rankin, Arthur
1892	1967	Rathbone, Basil
1897	1960	Ratoff, Gregory
1883	1953	Rawlinson, Herbert
1891	1943	Ray, Charles
1941	1967	Redding, Otis
1860	1916	Rehan, Ada
1893	1923	Reid, Wallace
1873	1943	Reinhardt, Max
1909	1971	Rennie, Michael
1870	1940	Richman, Charles
1895	1972	Richman, Harry
1872	1961	Ring, Blanche
1888	1958	Risdon, Elizabeth
1897	1977	Ritchard, Cyril
1907	1974	Ritter, Tex
1905	1969	Ritter, Thelma
1903	1966	Ritz, Al
1898	1976	Robeson, Paul
1878	1949	Robinson, Bill
1893	1973	Robinson, Edward G.
1865	1942	Robson, May
1905	1977	Rochester (E. Anderson)
1897	1933	Rodgers, Jimmy
1894	1958	Rodzinsky, Artur
1879	1935	Rogers, Will
1897	1937	Roland, Ruth
1880	1962	Rooney, Pat
1899	1966	Rose, Billy
1910	1980	Roth, Lillian
1882	1936	Rothafel, S. L. (Roxy)
1878	1953	Ruffo, Titta
1892	1970	Ruggles, Charles
1864	1936	Russell, Annie
1924	1961	Russell, Gail
1861	1922	Russell, Lillian
1911	1976	Russell, Rosalind
1892	1972	Rutherford, Margaret
1902	1973	Ryan, Irene
1909	1973	Ryan, Robert
1877	1968	St. Denis, Ruth
1884	1955	Sakall, S.Z.
1885	1936	Sale (Chic), Charles
1906	1972	Sanders, George
1934	1973	Sands, Diana
1896	1960	Savo, Jimmy
1879	1954	Scheff, Fritzi
1892	1930	Schenck, Joe
1895	1964	Schildkraut, Joseph

Born	Died	Name
1865	1930	Schildkraut, Rudolph
1889	1965	Schipa, Tito
1882	1951	Schnabel, Artur
1910	1949	Schumann, Henrietta
1861	1936	Schumann-Heink, E.
1866	1945	Scott, Cyril
1914	1965	Scott, Zachary
1843	1896	Scott-Siddons, Mrs.
1938	1979	Seberg, Jean
1892	1974	Seeley, Blossom
1902	1965	Selznick, David O.
1858	1935	Sembrich, Marcella
1880	1960	Sennett, Mack
1881	1951	Shattuck, Arthur
1860	1929	Shaw, Mary
1927	1978	Shaw, Robert
1891	1972	Shawn, Ted
1868	1949	Shean, Al
1915	1967	Sheridan, Ann
1924	1973	Sherman, Allan
1885	1934	Sherman, Lowell
1918	1970	Shriner, Herb
1875	1953	Shubert, Lee
1755	1831	Siddons, Mrs. Sarah
1882	1930	Sills, Milton
1914	1970	Silvera, Frank
1900	1976	Sim, Alastair
1878	1946	Sis Hopkins (Melville)
1891	1934	Skelly, Hal
1858	1942	Skinner, Otis
1870	1952	Skipworth, Alison
1892	1970	Skulnik, Menasha
1863	1948	Smith, C. Aubrey
1917	1979	Soo, Jack
1826	1881	Sothern, Edward A.
1859	1933	Sothern, Edward H.
1884	1957	Sothern, Harry
1854	1932	Sousa, John Philip
1884	1957	Sparks, Ned
1876	1948	Speaks, Oley
1890	1970	Spitalny, Phil
1873	1937	Standing, Guy
1871	1956	Stephenson, Henry
1900	1941	Stephenson, James
1883	1939	Sterling, Ford
1882	1928	Stevens, Emily A.
1934	1970	Stevens, Inger
1896	1961	Stewart, Anita
1882	1977	Stokowski, Leopold
1873	1959	Stone, Fred
1879	1953	Stone, Lewis
1904	1980	Stone, Milburn
1871	1954	Straus, Oskar
1911	1960	Sullavan, Margaret
1902	1974	Sullivan, Ed
1903	1956	Sullivan, Francis L.
1892	1946	Summerville, Slim
1904	1969	Swarthout, Gladys
1893	1957	Talmadge, Norma
1900	1972	Tamiroff, Akim
1878	1947	Tanguay, Eva
1899	1934	Tashman, Lilyan
1885	1966	Taylor, Deems
1899	1958	Taylor, Estelle
1887	1946	Taylor, Laurette
1911	1969	Taylor, Robert
1878	1938	Tearle, Conway
1884	1953	Tearle, Godfrey
1892	1937	Tell, Alma
1881	1934	Tellegen, Lou
1864	1942	Tempest, Marie
1910	1963	Templeton, Alec
1847	1928	Terry, Ellen
1871	1940	Tetrazzini, Luisa
1899	1936	Thalberg, Irving
1857	1914	Thomas, Brandon
1892	1960	Thomas, John Charles
1882	1976	Thorndike, Sybil
1869	1936	Thurston, Howard
1896	1960	Tibbett, Lawrence
1887	1940	Tinney, Frank
1909	1958	Todd, Michael
1906	1935	Todd, Thelma
1874	1947	Toler, Sidney
1906	1968	Tone, Franchot
1878	1933	Torrence, Ernest
1867	1957	Toscanini, Arturo

Born	Died	Name
1898	1968	Tracy, Lee
1900	1967	Tracy, Spencer
1903	1972	Traubel, Helen
1894	1975	Treacher, Arthur
1853	1917	Tree, Herbert Beerbohm
1889	1973	Truex, Ernest
1915	1975	Tucker, Richard
1884	1966	Tucker, Sophie
1911	1970	Tufts, Sonny
1869	1940	Turpin, Ben
1908	1959	Twelvetrees, Helen
1894	1970	Ulric, Lenore
1933	1975	Ure, Mary
1895	1926	Valentino, Rudolph
1870	1950	Van, Billy B.
1912	1979	Vance, Vivian
1893	1943	Veidt, Conrad
1885	1957	Von Stroheim, Erich
1887	1969	Walburn, Raymond
1874	1946	Waldron, Charles D.
1904	1966	Walker, June
1914	1951	Walker, Robert
1876	1962	Walter, Bruno
1878	1936	Walthall, Henry B.
1872	1952	Ward, Fannie
1866	1951	Warfield, David
1876	1958	Warner, H. B.
1878	1964	Warwick, Robert
1924	1963	Washington, Dinah
1900	1977	Waters, Ethel
1867	1945	Watson, Billy
1879	1962	Watson, Lucille
1890	1965	Watson, Minor
1907	1979	Wayne, John
1896	1966	Webb, Clifton
1867	1942	Weber, Joe
1905	1973	Webster, Margaret
1876	1926	Welch, Ben
1873	1918	Welch, Joe
1896	1975	Wellman, William
1883	1953	Werrenrath, Reinald
1879	1942	Westley, Helen
1895	1968	Wheeler, Bert
1889	1938	White, Pearl
1891	1967	Whiteman, Paul
1865	1948	Whitty, Dame May
1906	1966	Whorf, Richard
1912	1979	Wilding, Michael
1895	1948	William, Warren
1877	1922	Williams, Bert
1867	1918	Williams, Evan
1923	1953	Williams, Hank
1902	1978	Wills, Chill
1917	1972	Wilson, Marie
1884	1969	Winninger, Charles
1904	1959	Withers, Grant
1881	1931	Wolheim, Louis
1907	1961	Wong, Anna May
1892	1978	Wood, Peggy
1888	1963	Woolley, Monty
1889	1938	Woolsey, Robert
1881	1956	Wycherty, Margaret
1886	1966	Wynn, Ed
1906	1964	Wynyard, Diana
1890	1960	Young, Clara Kimball
1917	1978	Young, Gig
1887	1953	Young, Roland
1902	1979	Zanuck, Darryl F.
1869	1932	Ziegfeld, Florenz
1873	1976	Zukor, Adolph

Ancient Greeks and Latins

Greeks

Aeschines, orator, 389-314BC.
Aeschylus, dramatist, 525-456BC.
Aesop, fableist, c620-c560BC.
Anacreon, poet, c582-c485BC.
Anaxagoras, philosopher, c500-428BC.
Archimedes, math. c287-212BC.
Aristophanes, dramatist, c448-380BC.
Aristotle, philosopher, 384-322BC.
Athenaeus, scholar, fl.c200.
Callicrates, architect, fl.5th cent.BC.
Callimachus, poet, c305-240BC.
Democritus, philosopher, c460-370BC.
Demosthenes, orator, 384-322BC.
Diodorus, historian, fl.20BC.
Diogenes, philosopher, c372-c287BC.
Dionysius, historian, d.c7BC.
Empedocles, philosopher, c490-430BC.
Epictetus, philosopher, c55-c135.
Epicurus, philosopher, 341-270BC.
Euclid, mathematician, fl.c300BC.
Euripedes, dramatist, c484-406BC.
Heraclitus, philosopher, c535-c475BC.
Herodotus, historian, c484-420BC.
Hesiod, poet, 8th cent. BC.
Hippocrates, physician, c460-377BC.
Homer, poet, believed lived c850BC.
Menander, dramatist, 342-292BC.
Pindar, poet, c518-c438BC.
Plato, philosopher, c428-c347BC.
Plutarch, biographer, c46-120.
Polybius, historian, c200-c118BC.
Pythagoras, phil., math., c580-c500BC.
Sappho, poet, c610-c580BC.
Simonides, poet, 556-c468BC.
Socrates, philosopher, c470-399BC.
Sophocles, dramatist, C496-406BC.
Strabo, geographer, c63BC-AD24.
Thales, philosopher, c634-c546BC.
Themistocles, politician, c524-c460BC.
Theocritus, poet, c310-250BC.
Theophrastus, phil. c372-c287BC.
Thucydides, historian, fl.5th cent.BC.
Timon, philosopher, c320-c230BC.
Xenophon, historian, c434-c355BC.
Zeno, philospher, c495-c430BC.

Latins

Ammianus, historian, c330-395.
Apuleius, satirist, c124-c170.
Boethius, scholar, c480-524
Caesar, Julius, general, 100-44BC.
Cato (Elder), statesman, 234-149BC.
Catullus, poet, c84-54BC.
Cicero, orator, 106-43BC.
Claudian, poet, c370-c404.
Gellius, author, c130-c165.
Horace, poet, 65-8BC.
Juvenal, satirist, c60-c127.
Livy, historian, 59BC-AD17.
Lucan, poet, 39-65.
Lucilius, poet, c180-c102BC.
Lucretius, poet, c99-c55BC.
Martial, epigrammatist, c38-c103.
Nepos, historian, c100-c25BC.
Ovid, poet, 43BC-AD17.
Persius, satirist, 34-62.
Plautus, dramatist, c254-c184BC.
Pliny, scholar, 23-79.
Pliny (Younger), author, 62-113.
Quintilian, rhetorician, c35-c97.
Sallust, historian, 86-34BC.
Seneca, philosopher, 4BC-AD65.
Silius, poet, c25-101.
Statius, poet, c45-c96.
Suetonius, biographer, c69-c122.
Tacitus, historian, c56-c120.
Terence, dramatist, 185-c159BC.
Tibullus, poet, c55-c19BC.
Virgil, poet, 70-19BC.
Vitruvius, architect, fl.1st cent.BC.

Rulers of England and Great Britain

England

Name		Began	Died	Age	Rgd
	Saxons and Danes				
Egbert	King of Wessex, won allegiance of all English	829	839	—	10
Ethelwulf	Son, King of Wessex, Sussex, Kent, Essex	839	858	—	19
Ethelbald	Son of Ethelwulf, displaced father in Wessex	858	860	—	2
Ethelbert	2d son of Ethelwulf, united Kent and Wessex	860	866	—	6
Ethelred I	3d son, King of Wessex, fought Danes	866	871	—	5
Alfred	The Great, 4th son, defeated Danes, fortified London	871	899	52	28
Edward	The Elder, Alfred's son, united English, claimed Scotland	899	924	55	25
Athelstan	The Glorious, Edward's son, King of Mercia, Wessex	924	940	45	16
Edmund I	3d son of Edward, King of Wessex, Mercia	940	946	25	6
Edred	4th son of Edward	946	955	32	9
Edwy	The Fair, eldest son of Edmund, King of Wessex	955	959	18	3
Edgar	The Peaceful, 2d son of Edmund, ruled all English	959	975	32	17
Edward	The Martyr, eldest son of Edgar, murdered by stepmother	975	978	17	4
Ethelred II	The Unready, 2d son of Edgar, married Emma of Normandy	978	1016	48	37
Edmund II	Ironside, son of Ethelred II, King of London	1016	1016	27	0
Canute	The Dane, gave Wessex to Edmund, married Emma	1016	1035	40	19
Harold I	Harefoot, natural son of Canute	1035	1040	—	5
Hardecanute	Son of Canute by Emma, Danish King	1040	1042	24	2
Edward	The Confessor, son of Ethelred II (Canonized 1161)	1042	1066	62	24
Harold II	Edward's brother-in-law, last Saxon King	1066	1066	44	0
	House of Normandy				
William I	The Conqueror, defeated Harold at Hastings	1066	1087	60	21
William II	Rufus, 3d son of William I, killed by arrow	1087	1100	43	13
Henry I	Beauclerc, youngest son of William I	1100	1135	67	35

	House of Blois				
Stephen	Son of Adela, daughter of William I, and Count of Blois	**1135**	**1154**	50	19
	House of Plantagenet				
Henry II	Son of Geoffrey Plantagenet (Angevin) by Matilda, dau. of Henry I	**1154**	**1189**	56	35
Richard I	Coeur de Lion, son of Henry II, crusader	**1189**	**1199**	42	10
John	Lackland, son of Henry II, signed Magna Carta, 1215	**1199**	**1216**	50	17
Henry III	Son of John, acceded at 9, under regency until 1227	**1216**	**1272**	65	56
Edward I	Longshanks, son of Henry III	**1272**	**1307**	68	35
Edward II	Son of Edward I, deposed by Parliament, 1327	**1307**	**1327**	43	20
Edward III	Of Windsor, son of Edward II	**1327**	**1377**	65	50
Richard II	Grandson of Edw. III, minor until 1389, deposed 1399	**1377**	**1400**	34	22
	House of Lancaster				
Henry IV	Son of John of Gaunt, Duke of Lancaster, son of Edw. III	**1399**	**1413**	47	13
Henry V	Son of Henry IV, victor of Agincourt	**1413**	**1422**	34	9
Henry VI	Son of Henry V, deposed 1461, died in Tower	**1422**	**1471**	49	39
	House of York				
Edward IV	Great-great-grandson of Edward III, son of Duke of York	**1461**	**1483**	41	22
Edward V	Son of Edward IV, murdered in Tower of London	**1483**	**1483**	13	0
Richard III	Crookback, bro. of Edward IV, fell at Bosworth Field	**1483**	**1485**	35	2
	House of Tudor				
Henry VII	Son of Edmund Tudor, Earl of Richmond, whose father had married the widow of Henry V; descended from Edward III through his mother, Margaret Beaufort via John of Gaunt. By marriage with dau. of Edward IV he united Lancaster and York	**1485**	**1509**	53	24
Henry VIII	Son of Henry VII by Elizabeth, dau. of Edward IV.	**1509**	**1547**	56	38
Edward VI	Son of Henry VIII, by Jane Seymour, his 3d queen. Ruled under regents. Was forced to name Lady Jane Grey his successor. Council of State proclaimed her queen July 10, 1553. Mary Tudor won Council, was proclaimed queen July 19, 1553. Mary had Lady Jane Grey beheaded for treason, Feb., 1554	**1547**	**1553**	16	6
Mary I	Daughter of Henry VIII, by Catherine of Aragon	**1553**	**1558**	43	5
Elizabeth I	Daughter of Henry VIII, by Anne Boleyn	**1558**	**1603**	69	44
	Great Britain				
	House of Stuart				
James I	James VI of Scotland, son of Mary, Queen of Scots. *First to call himself King of Great Britain. This became official with the Act of Union, 1707*	**1603**	**1625**	59	22
Charles I	Only surviving son of James I; beheaded Jan. 30, 1649	**1625**	**1649**	48	24
	Commonwealth, 1649-1660				
	Council of State, 1649; Protectorate, 1653				
The Cromwells	Oliver Cromwell, Lord Protector	**1653**	**1658**	59	—
	Richard Cromwell, son, Lord Protector, resigned May 25, 1659	**1658**	**1712**	86	—
	House of Stuart (Restored)				
Charles II	Eldest son of Charles I, died without issue	**1660**	**1685**	55	25
James II	2d son of Charles I. Deposed 1688. Interregnum Dec. 11, 1688, to Feb. 13, 1689	**1685**	**1701**	68	3
William III	Son of William, Prince of Orange, by Mary, dau. of Charles I	**1689**	**1702**	51	13
and Mary II	Eldest daughter of James II and wife of William III		**1694**	33	6
Anne	2d daughter of James II	**1702**	**1714**	49	12
	House of Hanover				
George I	Son of Elector of Hanover, by Sophia, grand-dau. of James I	**1714**	**1727**	67	13
George II	Only son of George I, married Caroline of Brandenburg	**1727**	**1760**	77	33
George III	Grandson of George II, married Charlotte of Mecklenburg	**1760**	**1820**	81	59
George IV	Eldest son of George III, Prince Regent, from Feb., 1811	**1820**	**1830**	67	10
William IV	3d son of George III, married Adelaide of Saxe-Meiningen	**1830**	**1837**	71	7
Victoria	Dau. of Edward, 4th son of George III; married (1840) Prince Albert of Saxe-Coburg and Gotha, who became Prince Consort	**1837**	**1901**	81	63
	House of Saxe-Coburg and Gotha				
Edward VII	Eldest son of Victoria, married Alexandra, Princess of Denmark	**1901**	**1910**	68	9
	House of Windsor				
	Name Adopted July 17, 1917				
George V	2d son of Edward VII, married Princess Mary of Teck	**1910**	**1936**	70	25
Edward VIII	Eldest son of George V; acceded Jan. 20, 1936, abdicated Dec. 11	**1936**	**1972**	77	1
George VI	2d son of George V; married Lady Elizabeth Bowes-Lyon	**1936**	**1952**	56	15
Elizabeth II	Elder daughter of George VI, acceded Feb. 6, 1952	**1952**	—	—	—

Rulers of Scotland

Kenneth I MacAlpin was the first Scot to rule both Scots and Picts, 846 AD.

Duncan I was the first general ruler, 1034. Macbeth seized the kingdom 1040, was slain by Duncan's son, Malcolm III MacDuncan (Canmore), 1057.

Malcolm married Margaret, Saxon princess who had fled from the Normans. Queen Margaret introduced English language and English monastic customs. She was canonized, 1250. Her son Edgar, 1097, moved the court to Edinburgh. His brothers Alexander I and David I succeeded. Malcolm IV, the Maiden, 1153, grandson of David I, was followed by his brother, William the Lion, 1165, whose son was Alexander II, 1214. The latter's son, Alexander III, 1249, defeated the Norse and regained the Hebrides. When he died, 1286, his granddaughter, Margaret, child of Eric of Norway and grandniece of Edward I of England, known as the Maid of Norway, was chosen ruler, but died 1290, aged 8.

John Baliol, 1292-1296. (Interregnum, 10 years).

Robert Bruce (The Bruce), 1306-1329, victor at Bannockburn, 1314.

David II, only son of Robert Bruce, ruled 1329-1371.

Robert II, 1371-1390, grandson of Robert Bruce, son of Walter, the Steward of Scotland, was called The Steward, first of the so-called Stuart line.

Robert III, son of Robert II, 1390-1406.

James I, son of Robert III, 1406-1437.

James II, son of James I, 1437-1460.
James III, eldest son of James II, 1460-1488.
James IV, eldest son of James III, 1488-1513.
James V, eldest son of James IV, 1513-1542.

Mary, daughter of James V, born 1542, became queen when one week old; was crowned 1543. Married, 1558, Francis, son of Henry II of France, who became king 1559, died 1560. Mary ruled Scots 1561 until abdication, 1567. She also married (2) Henry Stewart, Lord Darnley, and (3) James, Earl of Bothwell. Imprisoned by Elizabeth I, Mary was beheaded 1587.

James VI, 1567-1625, son of Mary and Lord Darnley, became King of England on death of Elizabeth in 1603. Although the thrones were thus united, the legislative union of Scotland and England was not effected until the Act of Union, May 1, 1707.

Rulers of France: Kings, Queens, Presidents

Caesar to Charlemagne

Julius Caesar subdued the Gauls, native tribes of Gaul (France) 57 to 52 BC. The Romans ruled 500 years. The Franks, a Teutonic tribe, reached the Somme from the East ca. 250 AD. By the 5th century the Merovingian Franks ousted the Romans. In 451 AD, with the help of Visigoths, Burgundians and others, they defeated Attila and the Huns at Chalons-sur-Marne.

Childeric I became leader of the Merovingians 458 AD. His son Clovis I (Chlodwig, Ludwig, Louis), crowned 481, founded the dynasty. After defeating the Alemanni (Germans) 496, he was baptized a Christian and made Paris his capital. His line ruled until Childeric III was deposed, 751.

The West Merovingians were called Neustrians, the eastern Austrasians. Pepin of Herstal (687-714) major domus, or head of the palace, of Austrasia, took over Neustria as dux (leader) of the Franks. Pepin's son, Charles, called Martel (the Hammer) defeated the Saracens at Tours-Poitiers, 732; was succeeded by his son, Pepin the Short, 741, who deposed Childeric III and ruled as king until 768.

His son, Charlemagne, or Charles the Great (742-814) became king of the Franks, 768, with his brother Carloman, who died 771. He ruled France, Germany, parts of Italy, Spain, Austria, and enforced Christianity. Crowned Emperor of the Romans by Pope Leo III in St. Peter's, Rome, Dec. 25, 800 AD. Succeeded by son, Louis I the Pious, 814. At death, 840, Louis left empire to sons, Lothair (Roman emperor); Pepin I (king of Aquitaine); Louis II (of Germany); Charles the Bald (France). They quarreled and by the peace of Verdun, 843, divided the empire.

AD Name, year of accession

The Carolingians

843 Charles I (the Bald), Roman Emperor, 875
877 Louis II (the Stammerer), son
879 Louis III (died 882) and Carloman, brothers
885 Charles II (the Fat), Roman Emperor, 881
888 Eudes (Odo) elected by nobles
898 Charles III (the Simple), son of Louis II, defeated by
922 Robert, brother of Eudes, killed in war
923 Rudolph (Raoul) Duke of Burgundy
936 Louis IV, son of Charles III
954 Lothair, son, aged 13, defeated by Capet
986 Louis V (the Sluggard), left no heirs

The Capets

987 Hugh Capet, son of Hugh the Great
996 Robert II (the Wise), his son
1031 Henry I, his son, last Norman
1060 Philip I (the Fair), son
1108 Louis VI (the Fat), son
1137 Louis VII (the Younger), son
1180 Philip II (Augustus), son, crowned at Reims
1223 Louis VIII (the Lion), son
1226 Louis IX, son, crusader; Louis IX (1214-1270) reigned 44 years, arbitrated disputes with English King Henry III; led crusades, 1248 (captured in Egypt 1250) and 1270, when he died of plague in Tunis. Canonized 1297 as St. Louis.
1270 Philip III (the Hardy), son
1285 Philip IV (the Fair), son, king at 17
1314 Louis X (the Headstrong), son. His posthumous son, John I, lived only 7 days
1316 Philip V (the Tall), brother of Louis X
1322 Charles IV (the Fair), brother of Louis X

House of Valois

1328 Philip VI (of Valois), grandson of Philip III
1350 John II (the Good), his son, retired to England
1364 Charles V (the Wise), son
1380 Charles VI (the Beloved), son
1422 Charles VII (the Victorious), son. In 1429 Joan of Arc (Jeanne d'Arc) promised Charles to oust the English, who occupied northern France. Joan won at Orleans and Patay and had Charles crowned at Reims July 17, 1429. Joan was captured May 24, 1430, and executed May 30, 1431, at Rouen for heresy. Charles ordered her rehabilitation, effected 1455.
1461 Louis XI (the Cruel), son, civil reformer
1483 Charles VIII (the Affable), son
1498 Louis XII, great-grandson of Charles V
1515 Francis I, of Angouleme, nephew, son-in-law. Francis I (1494-1547) reigned 32 years, fought 4 big wars, was patron of the arts, aided Cellini, del Sarto, Leonardo da Vinci, Rabelais, embellished Fontainebleau.
1547 Henry II, son, killed at a joust in a tournament. He was the husband of Catherine de Medicis (1519-1589) and the lover of Diane de Poitiers (1499-1566). Catherine was born in Florence, daughter of Lorenzo de Medicis. By her marriage to Henry II she became the mother of Francis II, Charles IX, Henry III and Queen Margaret (Reine Margot) wife of Henry IV. She persuaded Charles IX to order the massacre of Huguenots on the Feast of St. Bartholomew, Aug. 24, 1572, the day her daughter was married to Henry of Navarre.
1559 Francis II, son. In 1548, Mary, Queen of Scots since infancy, was betrothed when 6 to Francis, aged 4. They were married 1558. Francis died 1560, aged 16; Mary ruled Scotland, abdicated 1567.
1560 Charles IX, brother
1574 Henry III, brother, assassinated

House of Bourbon

1589 Henry IV, of Navarre, assassinated. Henry IV made enemies when he gave tolerance to Protestants by Edict of Nantes, 1598. He was grandson of Queen Margaret of Navarre, literary patron. He married Margaret of Valois, daughter of Henry II and Catherine de Medicis; was divorced; in 1600 married Marie de Medicis, who became Regent of France, 1610-17 for her son, Louis XIII, but was exiled by Richelieu, 1631.
1610 Louis XIII (the Just), son. Louis XIII (1601-1643) married Anne of Austria. His ministers were Cardinals Richelieu and Mazarin.
1643 Louis XIV (The Grand Monarch), son. Louis XIV was king 72 years. He exhausted a prosperous country in wars for thrones and territory. By revoking the Edict of Nantes (1685) he caused the emigration of the Huguenots. He said: "I am the state."
1715 Louis XV, great-grandson. Louis XV married a Polish princess; lost Canada to the English. His favorites, Mme. Pompadour and Mme. Du Barry, influenced policies. Noted for saying "After me, the deluge"
1774 Louis XVI, grandson; married Marie Antoinette, daughter of Empress Maria Therese of Austria. King and queen beheaded by Revolution, 1793. Their son, called Louis XVII, died in prison, never ruled.

First Republic

1792 National Convention of the French Revolution
1795 Directory, under Barras and others
1799 Consulate, Napoleon Bonaparte, first consul. Elected consul for life, 1802.

First Empire

1804 Napoleon I, emperor. Josephine (de Beauharnais) empress, 1804-09; Marie Louise, empress, 1810-1814. Her son, Francois (1811-1832), titular King of Rome, later Duke de Reichstadt and "Napoleon II," never ruled. Napoleon abdicated 1814, died 1821.

Bourbons Restored

1814 Louis XVIII king; brother of Louis XVI.
1824 Charles X, brother; reactionary; deposed by the July Revolution, 1830.

House of Orleans

1830 Louis-Philippe, the "citizen king."

Second Republic

1848 Louis Napoleon Bonaparte, president, nephew of Napoleon I. He became:

Second Empire

1852 Napoleon III, emperor; Eugenie (de Montijo) empress. Lost Franco-Prussian war, deposed 1870. Son, Prince

Imperial (1856-79), died in Zulu War. Eugenie died 1920.

Third Republic—Presidents

1871 Thiers, Louis Adolphe (1797-1877)
1873 MacMahon, Marshal Patrice M. de (1808-1893)
1879 Grevy, Paul J. (1807-1891)
1887 Sadi-Carnot, M. (1837-1894), assassinated
1894 Casimir-Perier, Jean P. P. (1847-1907)
1895 Faure, Francois Felix (1841-1899)
1899 Loubet, Emile (1838-1929)
1906 Fallieres, C. Armand (1841-1931)
1913 Poincare, Raymond (1860-1934)
1920 Deschanel, Paul (1856-1922)
1920 Millerand, Alexandre (1859-1943)
1924 Doumergue, Gaston (1863-1937)
1931 Doumer, Paul (1857-1932), assassinated
1932 Lebrun, Albert (1871-1950), resigned 1940
1940 **Vichy govt.** under German armistice: Henri Philippe Petain (1856-1951) Chief of State, 1940-1944.
Provisional govt. after liberation: Charles de Gaulle (1890-1970) Oct. 1944-Jan. 21, 1946; Felix Gouin (1884-1977) Jan. 23, 1946; Georges Bidault (1899-) June 24, 1946.

Fourth Republic—Presidents

1947 Auriol, Vincent (1884-1966)
1954 Coty, Rene (1882-1962)

Fifth Republic—Presidents

1959 de Gaulle, Charles Andre J. M. (1890-1970)
1969 Pompidou, Georges (1911-1974)
1974 Giscard d'Estaing, Valery (1926-)

Rulers of Middle Europe; Rise and Fall of Dynasties

Carolingian Dynasty

Charles the Great, or Charlemagne, ruled France, Italy, and Middle Europe; established Ostmark (later Austria); crowned Roman emperor by pope in Rome, 800 AD; died 814.

Louis I (Ludwig) the Pious, son; crowned by Charlemagne 814, d. 840.

Louis II, the German, son; succeeded to East Francia (Germany) 843-876.

Charles the Fat, son; inherited East Francia and West Francia (France) 876, reunited empire, crowned emperor by pope, 881, deposed 887.

Arnulf, nephew, 887-899. Partition of empire.

Louis the Child, 899-911, last direct descendant of Charlemagne.

Conrad I, duke of Franconia, first elected German king, 911-918, founded House of Franconia.

Saxon Dynasty; First Reich

Henry I, the Fowler, duke of Saxony, 919-936.

Otto I, the Great, 936-973, son; crowned Holy Roman Emperor by pope, 962.

Otto II, 973-983, son; failed to oust Greeks and Arabs from Sicily.

Otto III, 983-1002, son; crowned emperor at 16.

Henry II, the Saint, duke of Bavaria, 1002-1024, great-grandson of Otto the Great.

House of Franconia

Conrad II, 1024-1039, elected king of Germany.

Henry III, the Black, 1039-1056, son; deposed 3 popes; annexed Burgundy.

Henry IV, 1056-1106, son; regency by his mother, Agnes of Poitou. Banned by Pope Gregory VII, he did penance at Canossa.

Henry V, 1106-1125, son; last of Salic House.

Lothair, duke of Saxony, 1125-1137. Crowned emperor in Rome, 1134.

House of Hohenstaufen

Conrad III, duke of Swabia, 1138-1152. In 2d Crusade.

Frederick I, Barbarossa, 1152-1190; Conrad's nephew.

Henry VI, 1190-1196, took lower Italy from Normans. Son became king of Sicily.

Philip of Swabia, 1197-1208, brother.

Otto IV, of House of Welf, 1198-1215; deposed.

Frederick II, 1215-1250, son of Henry VI; king of Sicily; crowned king of Jerusalem; in 5th Crusade.

Conrad IV, 1250-1254, son; lost lower Italy to Charles of Anjou.

Conradin (1252-1268) son, king of Jerusalem and Sicily, beheaded. Last Hohenstaufen.

Interregnum, 1254-1273, Rise of the Electors.

Transition

Rudolph I of Hapsburg, 1273-1291, defeated King Ottocar II of Bohemia. Bequeathed duchy of Austria to eldest son, Albert.

Adolph of Nassau, 1292-1298, killed in war with Albert of Austria.

Albert I, king of Germany, 1298-1308, son of Rudolph.

Henry VII, of Luxemburg, 1308-1313, crowned emperior in Rome. Seized Bohemia, 1310.

Louis IV of Bavaria (Wittelsbach), 1314-1347. Also elected was Frederick of Austria, 1314-1330 (Hapsburg). Abolition of papal sanction for election of Holy Roman Emperor.

Charles IV, of Luxemburg, 1347-1378, grandson of Henry VII, German emperor and king of Bohemia, Lombardy, Burgundy; took Mark of Brandenburg.

Wenceslaus, 1378-1400, deposed.

Rupert, Duke of Palatine, 1400-1410.

Hungary

Stephen I, house of Arpad, 997-1038. Crowned king 1000; converted Magyars; canonized 1083. After several centuries of feuds Charles Robert of Anjou became Charles I, 1308-1342.

Louis I, the Great, son, 1342-1382; joint ruler of Poland with Casimir III, 1370. Defeated Turks.

Mary, daughter, 1382-1395, ruled with husband. Sigismund of Luxemburg, 1387-1437, also king of Bohemia. As bro. of Wenceslaus he succeeded Rupert as Holy Roman Emperor, 1410.

Albert II, 1438-1439, son-in-law of Sigismund; also Roman emperor. *(see under Hapsburg.)*

Ulaszlo I of Poland, 1440-1444.

Ladislaus V, posthumous son of Albert II, 1444-1457. John Hunyadi (Hunyadi Janos) governor (1446-1452), fought Turks, Czechs; died 1456.

Matthias I (Corvinus) son of Hunyadi, 1458-1490. Shared rule of Bohemia, captured Vienna, 1485, annexed Austria, Styria, Carinthia.

Ladislas II (king of Bohemia), 1490-1516.

Louis II, son, aged 10, 1516-1526. Wars with Suleiman, Turk. In 1527 Hungary was split between Ferdinand I, Archduke of Austria, bro.-in-law of Louis II, and John Zapolya of Transylvania. After Turkish invasion, 1547, Hungary was split between Ferdinand, Prince John Sigismund (Transylvania) and the Turks.

House of Hapsburg

Albert V of Austria, Hapsburg, crowned king of Hungary, Jan. 1438, Roman emperor, March, 1438, as Albert II; died 1439.

Frederick III, cousin, 1440-1493. Fought Turks.

Maximilian I, son, 1493-1519. Assumed title of Holy Roman Emperor (German), 1493.

Charles V, grandson, 1519-1556. King of Spain with mother co-regent; crowned Roman emperor at Aix, 1520. Confronted Luther at Worms; attempted church reform and religious conciliation; abdicated 1556.

Ferdinand I, king of Bohemia, 1526, of Hungary, 1527; disputed. German king, 1531. Crowned Roman emperor on abdication of brother Charles V, 1556.

Maximilian II, son, 1564-1576.

Rudolph II, son, 1576-1612.

Matthias, brother, 1612-1619, king of Bohemia and Hungary.

Ferdinand II of Styria, king of Bohemia, 1617, of Hungary, 1618, Roman emperor, 1619. Bohemian Protestants deposed him, elected Frederick V of Palatine, starting Thirty Years War.

Ferdinand III, son, king of Hungary, 1625, Bohemia, 1627, Roman emperor, 1637. Peace of Westphalia, 1648, ended war. Leopold I, 1658-1705; Joseph I, 1705-1711; Charles VI, 1711-1740.

Maria Theresa, daughter, 1740-1780, Archduchess of Austria, queen of Hungary; ousted pretender, Charles VII, crowned 1742; in 1745 obtained election of her husband Francis I as Roman emperor and co-regent (d. 1765). Fought Seven Years' War with Frederick II (the Great) of Prussia. Mother of Marie Antoinette, Queen of France.

Joseph II, son 1765-1790, Roman emperor, reformer; powers restricted by Empress Maria Theresa until her death, 1780. First partition of Poland. Leopold II, 1790-1792.

Francis II, son, 1792-1835. Fought Napoleon. Proclaimed first hereditary emperor of Austria, 1804. Forced to abdicate as Roman emperor, 1806; last use of title. Ferdinand I, son, 1835-1848, abdicated during revolution.

Austro-Hungarian Monarchy

Francis Joseph I, nephew, 1848-1916, emperor of Austria, king of Hungary. Dual monarchy of Austria-Hungary formed, 1867. After assassination of heir, Archduke Francis Ferdinand, June 28, 1914, Austrian diplomacy precipitated World War I.

Charles I, grand-nephew, 1916-1918, last emperor of Austria and king of Hungary. Abdicated Nov. 11-13, 1918, died 1922.

Rulers of Prussia

Nucleus of Prussia was the Mark of Brandenburg. First mar-ave was Albert the Bear (Albrecht), 1134-1170. First Hohen-ollern margrave was Frederick, burgrave of Nuremberg, 417-1440.

Frederick William, 1640-1688, the Great Elector. Son, Frederck III, 1688-1713, was crowned King Frederick of Prussia, 1701.

Frederick William I, son, 1713-1740.

Frederick II, the Great, son, 1740-1786, annexed Silesia part f Austria.

Frederick William II, nephew, 1786-1797.

Frederick William III, son, 1797-1840. Napoleonic wars.

Frederick William IV, son, 1840-1861. Uprising of 1848 and irst parliament and constitution.

Second and Third Reich

William I, 1861-1888, brother. Annexation of Schleswig and Hanover; Franco-Prussian war, 1870-71, proclamation of German Reich, Jan. 18, 1871, at Versailles; William, German emperor (Deutscher Kaiser), Bismarck, chancellor.

Frederick III, son, 1888.

William II, son, 1888-1918. Led Germany in World War I, abdicated as German emperor and king of Prussia, Nov. 9, 1918. Died in exile in Netherlands June 4, 1941. Minor rulers of Bavaria, Saxony, Wurttemberg also abdicated.

Germany proclaimed a republic at Weimar, July 1, 1919. Presidents: Frederick Ebert, 1919-1925, Paul von Hindenburg-Beneckendorff, 1925, reelected 1932, d. Aug. 2, 1934. Adolf Hitler, chancellor, chosen successor as Leader-Chancellor (Fuehrer & Reichskanzler) of Third Reich. Annexed Austria, March, 1938. Precipitated World War II, 1939-1945. Committed suicide April 30, 1945.

Rulers of Denmark, Sweden, Norway

Denmark

Earliest rulers invaded Britain; King Canute, who ruled in London 1016-1035, was most famous. The Valdemars furnished kings until the 15th century. In 1282 the Danes won the first national assembly, Danehof, from King Erik V.

Most redoubtable medieval character was Margaret, daughter of Valdemar IV, born 1353, married at 10 to King Haakon VI of Norway. In 1376 she had her first infant son Olaf made king of Denmark. After his death, 1387, she was regent of Denmark and Norway. In 1388 Sweden accepted her as sovereign. In 1389 she made her grand-nephew, Duke Erik of Pomerania, titular king of Denmark, Sweden, and Norway, with herself as regent. In 1397 she effected the Union of Kalmar of the three kingdoms and had Erik VII crowned. In 1439 the three kingdoms deposed him and elected, 1440, Christopher of Bavaria king (Christopher III). On his death, 1448, the union broke up.

Succeeding rulers were unable to enforce their claims as rulers of Sweden until 1520, when Christian II conquered Sweden. He was thrown out 1522, and in 1523 Gustavus Vasa united Sweden. Denmark continued to dominate Norway until the Napoleonic wars, when Frederick VI, 1808-1839, joined the Napoleonic cause after Britain had destroyed the Danish fleet, 1807. In 1814 he was forced to cede Norway to Sweden and Helgoland to Britain, receiving Lauenburg. Successors Christian VIII, 1839; Frederick VII, 1848; Christian IX, 1863; Frederick VIII, 1906; Christian X, 1912; Frederick IX, 1947; Margrethe II, 1972.

Sweden

Early kings ruled at Uppsala, but did not dominate the country. Sverker, c1130-c1156, united the Swedes and Goths. In 1435 Sweden obtained the Riksdag, or parliament. After the Union of Kalmar, 1397, the Danes either ruled or harried the country until Christian II of Denmark conquered it anew, 1520. This led to a rising under Gustavus Vasa, who ruled Sweden 1523-1560, and established an independent kingdom. Charles IX, 1599-1611, crowned 1604, conquered Moscow. Gustavus II Adolphus, 1611-1632, was called the Lion of the North. Later rulers: Christina, 1632; Charles X, Gustavus 1654; Charles XI, 1660; Charles XII (invader of Russia and Poland, defeated at Poltava, June 28, 1709), 1697; Ulrika Eleanora, sister, elected queen 1718; Frederick I (of Hesse), her husband, 1720; Adolphus Frederick, 1751; Gustavus III, 1771; Gustavus IV Adolphus, 1792; Charles XIII, 1809. (Union with Norway began 1814.) Charles XIV John, 1818. He was Jean Bernadotte, Napoleon's Prince of Ponte Corvo, elected 1810 to succeed Charles XIII. He founded the present dynasty: Oscar I, 1844, Charles XV, 1859; Oscar II, 1872; Gustavus V, 1907; Gustav VI Adolf, 1950; Carl XVI Gustaf, 1973.

Norway

Overcoming many rivals, Harald Haarfager, 872-930, conquered Norway, Orkneys, and Shetlands; Olaf I, great-grandson, 995-1000, brought Christianity into Norway, Iceland, and Greenland. In 1035 Magnus the Good also became king of Denmark. Haakon V, 1299-1319, had married his daughter to Erik of Sweden. Their son, Magnus became ruler of Norway and Sweden at 6. His son, Haakon VI, married Margaret of Denmark; their son Olaf IV became king of Norway and Denmark, followed by Margaret's regency and the Union of Kalmar, 1397.

In 1450 Norway became subservient to Denmark. Christian IV, 1588-1648, founded Christiania, now Oslo. After Napoleonic wars, when Denmark ceded Norway to Sweden, a strong nationalist movement forced recognition of Norway as an independent kingdom united with Sweden under the Swedish kings, 1814-1905. In 1905 the union was dissolved and Prince Carl of Denmark became Haakon VII. He died Sept. 21, 1957, aged 85; succeeded by son, Olav V, b. July 2, 1903.

Rulers of the Netherlands and Belgium

The Netherlands (Holland)

William Frederick, Prince of Orange, led a revolt against French rule, 1813, and was crowned King of the Netherlands, 1815. Belgium seceded Oct. 4, 1830, after a revolt, and formed a separate government. The change was ratified by the two kingdoms by treaty Apr. 19, 1839.

Succession: William II, son, 1840; William III, son, 1849; Wilhelmina, daughter of William III and his 2d wife Princess Emma of Waldeck, 1890; Wilhelmina abdicated, Sept. 4, 1948, in favor of daughter, Juliana. Juliana abdicated Apr. 30, 1980, in favor of daughter, Beatrix.

Belgium

A national congress elected Prince Leopold of Saxe-Coburg King; he took the throne July 21, 1831, as Leopold I. Succession: Leopold II, son 1865; Albert I, nephew of Leopold II, 1909; Leopold III, son of Albert, 1934; Prince Charles, Regent 1944; Leopold returned 1950, yielded powers to son Baudouin, Prince Royal, Aug. 6, 1950, abdicated July 16, 1951. Baudouin I took throne July 17, 1951.

For political history prior to 1830 see articles on the Netherlands and Belgium.

Roman Rulers

From Romulus to the end of the Empire in the West. Rulers of the Roman Empire in the East sat in Constantinople and for a brief period in Nicaea, until the capture of Constantinople by the Turks in 1453, when Byzantium was succeeded by the Ottoman Empire.

BC	Name
	The Kingdom
753	Romulus (Quirinus)
716	Numa Pompilius
673	Tullus Hostilius
640	Ancus Marcius
616	L. Tarquinius Priscus
578	Servius Tullius
534	L. Tarquinius Superbus
	The Republic
509	Consulate established
509	Quaestorship instituted
498	Dictatorship introduced
494	Plebeian Tribunate created
494	Plebeian Aedileship created
444	Consular Tribunate organized
435	Censorship instituted

BC	Name
366	Praetorship established
366	Curule Aedileship created
362	Military Tribunate elected
326	Proconsulate introduced
311	Naval Duumvirate elected
217	Dictatorship of Fabius Maximus
133	Tribunate of Tiberius Gracchus
123	Tribunate of Gaius Gracchus
82	Dictatorship of Sulla
60	First Triumvirate formed (Caesar, Pompeius, Crassus)
46	Dictatorship of Caesar
43	Second Triumvirate formed (Octavianus, Antonius, Lepidus)
	The Empire
27	Augustus (Gaius Julius

AD	Name
	Caesar Octavianus)
14	Tiberius I
37	Gaius Caesar (Caligula)
41	Claudius I
54	Nero
68	Galba
69	Galba; Otho, Vitellius
69	Vespasianus
79	Titus
81	Domitianus
96	Nerva
98	Trajanus
117	Hadrianus
138	Antoninus Pius
161	Marcus Aurelius and Lucius Verus
169	Marcus Aurelius (alone)

180 Commodus
193 Pertinax; Julianus I
193 Septimius Severus
211 Caracalla and Geta
212 Caracalla (alone)
217 Macrinus
218 Elagabalus (Heliogabalus)
222 Alexander Severus
235 Maximinus I (the Thracian)
238 Gordianus I and Gordianus II; Pupienus and Balbinus
238 Gordianus III
244 Philippus (the Arabian)
249 Decius
251 Gallus and Volusianus
253 Aemilianus
253 Valerianus and Gallienus
258 Gallienus (alone)
268 Claudius II (the Goth)
270 Quintillus
270 Aurelianus
275 Tacitus
276 Florianus
276 Probus
282 Carus
283 Carinus and Numerianus
284 Diocletianus
286 Diocletianus and Maximianus
305 Galerius and Constantius I
306 Galerius, Maximinus II, Severus I
307 Galerius, Maximinus II, Constantinus I, Licinius, Maxentius
311 Maximinus II, Constantinus I, Licinius, Maxentius
314 Maximinus II, Constantinus I, Licinius
314 Constantinus I and Licinius
324 Constantinus I (the Great)
337 Constantinus II, Constans I, Constantius II
340 Constantius II and Constans I
350 Constantius II
361 Julianus II (the Apostate)
363 Jovianus

West (Rome) and East (Constantinople)

364 Valentinianus I (West) and Valens (East)
367 Valentinianus I with Gratianus (West) and Valens (East)
375 Gratianus with Valentinianus II (West) and Valens (East)
378 Gratianus with Valentinianus II (West) Theodosius I (East)
383 Valentinianus II (West) and Theodosius I (East)
394 Theodosius I (the Great)
395 Honorius (West) and Arcadius (East)
408 Honorius (West) and Theodosius II (East)
423 Valentinianus III (West) and Theodosius II (East)
450 Valentinianus III (West) and Marcianus (East)
455 Maximus (West), Avitus (West); Marcianus (East)
456 Avitus (West), Marcianus (East)
457 Majorianus (West), Leo I (East)
461 Severus II (West), Leo I (East)
467 Anthemius (West), Leo I (East)
472 Olybrius (West), Leo I (East)
473 Glycerius (West), Leo I (East)
474 Julius Nepos (West), Leo II (East)
475 Romulus Augustulus (West) and Zeno (East)
476 End of Empire in West; Odovacar, King, drops title of Emperor; murdered by King Theodoric of Ostrogoths 493 AD

Rulers of Modern Italy

After the fall of Napoleon in 1814, the Congress of Vienna, 1815, restored Italy as a political patchwork, comprising the Kingdom of Naples and Sicily, the Papal States, and smaller units. Piedmont and Genoa were awarded to Sardinia, ruled by King Victor Emmanuel I of Savoy.

United Italy emerged under the leadership of Camillo, Count di Cavour (1810-1861), Sardinian prime minister. Agitation was led by Giuseppe Mazzini (1805-1872) and Giuseppe Garibaldi (1807-1882), soldier, Victor Emmanuel I abdicated 1821. After a brief regency for a brother, Charles Albert was King 1831-1849, abdicating when defeated by the Austrians at Novara. Succeeded by Victor Emmanuel II, 1849-1861.

In 1859 France forced Austria to cede Lombardy to Sardinia, which gave rights to Savoy and Nice to France. In 1860 Garibaldi led 1,000 volunteers in a spectacular campaign, took Sicily and expelled the King of Naples. In 1860 the House of Savoy annexed Tuscany, Parma, Modera, Romagna, the Two Sicilies, the Marches, and Umbria. Victor Emmanuel assumed the title of King of Italy at Turin Mar. 17, 1861. In 1866 he allied with Prussia in the Austro-Prussian War, with Prussia's victory received Venetia. On Sept. 20, 1870, his troops under Gen. Raffaele Cardorna entered Rome and took over the Papal States, ending the temporal power of the Roman Catholic Church.

Succession: Umberto I; 1878, assassinated 1900; Victor Emmanuel III, 1900, abdicated 1946, died 1947; Umberto II, 1946, ruled a month. In 1921 Benito Mussolini (1883-1945) formed the Fascist party and became prime minister Oct. 31, 1922. He made the King Emperor of Ethiopia, 1937; entered World War II as ally of Hitler. He was deposed July 25, 1943.

At a plebiscite June 2, 1946, Italy voted for a republic; Premier Alcide de Gasperi became chief of state June 13, 1946. On June 28, 1946, the Constituent Assembly elected Enrico de Nicola, Liberal, provisional president. Successive presidents: Luigi Einaudi, elected May 11, 1948, Giovanni Gronchi, Apr. 29, 1955; Antonio Segni, May 6, 1962; Giuseppe Saragat, Dec. 28, 1964; Giovanni Leone, Dec. 29, 1971; Alessandro Pertini, July 9, 1978.

Rulers of Spain

From 8th to 11th centuries Spain was dominated by the Moors (Arabs and Berbers). The Christian reconquest established small competing kingdoms of the Asturias, Aragon, Castile, Catalonia, Leon, Navarre, and Valencia. In 1474 Isabella (Isabel), b. 1451, became Queen of Castile & Leon. Her husband, Ferdinand, b. 1452, inherited Aragon 1479, with Catalonia, Valencia, and the Balearic Islands, became Ferdinand V of Castile. By Isabella's request Pope Sixtus IV established the Inquisition, 1478. Last Moorish kingdom, Granada, fell 1492. Columbus opened New World of colonies, 1492. Isabella died 1504, succeeded by her daughter, Juana "the Mad," but Ferdinand ruled until his death 1516.

Charles I, b. 1500, son of Juana and grandson of Ferdinand and Isabella, and of Maximilian I of Hapsburg; succeeded later as Holy Roman Emperor, Charles V, 1520; abdicated 1556. Philip II, son, 1556-1598, inherited only Spanish throne; conquered Portugal, fought Turks, persecuted non-Catholics, sent Armada against England. Was briefly married to Mary I of England, 1554-1558. Succession: Philip III, 1598-1621; Philip IV, 1621-1665; Charles II, 1665-1700, left Spain to Philip of Anjou, grandson of Louis XIV, who as Philip V, 1700-1746, founded Bourbon dynasty. Ferdinand VI, 1746-1759; Charles III, 1759-1788; Charles IV, 1788-1808, abdicated.

Napoleon now dominated politics and made his brother Joseph King of Spain 1808, but the Spanish ousted him finally in 1813. Ferdinand VII, 1808, 1814-1833, lost American colonies; succeeded by daughter Isabella II, aged 3, with wife Maria Christina of Naples regent until 1843. Isabella deposed by revolution 1868. Elected king by the Cortes, Amadeo of Savoy, 1870; abdicated 1873. First republic, 1873-1874. Alphonso XII, son of Isabella, 1875-1885. His posthumous son was Alphonso XIII, with his mother, Queen Maria Christina regent; Spanish-American war, Spain lost Cuba, gave up Puerto Rico, Philippines, Sulu Is., Marianas. Alphonso took throne 1902, aged 16, married British Princess Victoria Eugenia of Battenberg. The dictatorship of Primo de Rivera, 1923-30, precipitated the revolution of 1931. Alphonso agreed to leave without formal abdication. The monarchy was abolished and the second republic established, with strong socialist backing. Presidents were Niceto Alcala Zamora, to 1936, when Manuel Azaña was chosen.

In July, 1936, the army in Morocco revolted against the government and General Francisco Franco led the troops into Spain. The revolution succeeded by Feb., 1939, when Anzana resigned. Franco became chief of state, with provisions that if he was incapacitated the Regency Council by two-thirds vote may propose a king to the Cortes, which must have a two-thirds majority to elect him.

Alphonso XIII died in Rome Feb. 28, 1941, aged 54. His property and citizenship had been restored.

A succession law restoring the monarchy was approved in a 1947 referendum. Prince Juan Carlos, son of the pretender to the throne, was designated by Franco and the Cortes in 1969 as the future king and chief of state. Upon Franco's death, Nov. 20, 1975, Juan Carlos was proclaimed king, Nov. 22, 1975.

Leaders in the South American Wars of Liberation

Simon Bolivar (1783-1830), Jose Francisco de San Martin (1783-1850), and Francisco Antonio Gabriel Miranda (1750-1816), are among the heroes of the early 19th century struggles of South American nations to free themselves from Spain. All three, and their contemporaries, operated in periods of intense factional strife, during which soldiers and civilians suffered.

Miranda, a Venezuelan, who had served with the French in the American Revolution and commanded parts of the French Revolutionary armies in the Netherlands, attempted to start a revolt in Venezuela in 1806 and failed. In 1810, with British and American backing, he returned and was briefly a dictator, until the British withdrew their support. In 1812 he was overcome by the royalists in Venezuela and taken prisoner, dying in a Spanish prison in 1816.

San Martin was born in Argentina and during 1789-1811 served in campaigns of the Spanish armies in Europe and Africa. He first joined the independence movement in Argentina in 1812 and then in 1817 invaded Chile with 4,000 men over the high mountain passes. Here he and General Bernardo O'Higgins (1778-1842) defeated the Spaniards at Chacabuco, 1817, and O'Higgins was named Liberator and became first director of Chile, 1817-1823. In 1821 San Martin occupied Lima and Callao, Peru, and became protector of Peru.

Bolivar, the greatest leader of South American liberation from Spain, was born in Venezuela, the son of an aristocratic family. His organizing and administrative abilities were superior and he foresaw many of the political difficulties of the future. He first served under Miranda in 1812 and in 1813 captured Caracas, where he was named Liberator. Forced out next year by civil strife, he led a campaign that captured Bogota in 1814. In 1817 he was again in control of Venezuela and was named dictator. He organized Nueva Granada with the help of General Francisco de Paula Santander (1792-1840). By joining Nueva Granada, Venezuela, and the present terrain of Panama and Ecuador, the republic of Colombia was formed with Bolivar president. After numerous setbacks he decisively defeated the Spaniards in the second battle of Carabobo, Venezuela, June 24, 1821.

In May, 1822, Gen. Antonio Jose de Sucre, Bolivar's trusted lieutenant, took Quito. Bolivar went to Guayaquil to confer with San Martin, who resigned as protector of Peru and withdrew from politics. With a new army of Colombians and Peruvians Bolivar defeated the Spaniards in a saber battle at Junín in 1824 and cleared Peru.

De Sucre organized Charcas (Upper Peru) as Republica Bolivar (now Bolivia) and acted as president in place of Bolivar, who wrote its constitution. De Sucre defeated the Spanish faction of Peru at Ayacucho, Dec. 19, 1824.

Continued civil strife finally caused the Colombian federation to break apart. Santander turned against Bolivar, but the latter defeated him and banished him. In 1828 Bolivar gave up the presidency he had held precariously for 14 years. He became ill from tuberculosis and died Dec. 17, 1830. He was honored as the great liberator and is buried in the national pantheon in Caracas.

Rulers of Russia; Premiers of the USSR

First ruler to consolidate Slavic tribes was Rurik, leader of the Russians who established himself at Novgorod, 862 A.D. He and his immediate successors had Scandinavian affiliations. They moved to Kiev after 972 AD and ruled as Dukes of Kiev. In 988 Vladimir was converted and adopted the Byzantine Greek Orthodox service, later modified by Slav influences. Important as organizer and lawgiver was Yaroslav, 1019-1054, whose daughters married kings of Norway, Hungary, and France. His grandson, Vladimir II (Monomakh), 1113-1125, was progenitor of several rulers, but in 1169 Andrew Bogolubski overthrew Kiev and began the line known as Grand Dukes of Vladimir.

Of the Grand Dukes of Vladimir, Alexander Nevsky, 1246-1263, had a son, Daniel, first to be called Duke of Muscovy (Moscow) who ruled 1294-1303. His successors became Grand Dukes of Muscovy. After Dmitri III Donskoi defeated the Tartars in 1380, they also became Grand Dukes of all Russia. Independence of the Tartars and considerable territorial expansion were achieved under Ivan III, 1462-1505.

Tsars of Muscovy—Ivan III was referred to in church ritual as Tsar. He married Sofia, niece of the last Byzantine emperor. His successor, Basil III, died in 1533 when Basil's son Ivan was only 3. He became Ivan IV, "the Terrible"; crowned 1547 as Tsar of all the Russias, ruled till 1584. Under the weak rule of his son, Feodor I, 1584-1598, Boris Godunov had control. The dynasty died, and after years of tribal strife and intervention by Polish and Swedish armies, the Russians united under 17-year-old Michael Romanov, distantly related to the first wife of Ivan IV. He ruled 1613-1645 and established the Romanov line. Fourth ruler after Michael was Peter I.

Tsars, or Emperors of Russia (Romanovs)—Peter I, 1682-1725, known as Peter the Great, took title of Emperor in 1721. His successors and dates of accession were: Catherine, his widow, 1725, Peter II, his grandson, 1727-1730; Anne, Duchess of Courland, 1730, daughter of Peter the Great's brother, Tsar Ivan V; Ivan VI, 1740-1741, great-grandson of Ivan V, child, kept in prison and murdered 1764; Elizabeth, daughter of Peter I, 1741; Peter III, grandson of Peter I, 1761, deposed 1762 for his consort, Catherine II, former princess of Anhalt Zerbst (Germany) who is known as Catherine the Great, 1762-1796; Paul I, her son, 1796, killed 1801; Alexander I, son of Paul, 1801-1825, defeated Napoleon; Nicholas I, his brother, 1825; Alexander II, son of Nicholas, 1855, assassinated 1881 by terrorists; Alexander III, son, 1881-1894.

Nicholas II, son, 1894-1917, last Tsar of Russia, was forced to abdicate by the Revolution that followed losses to Germany in WWI. The Tsar, the Empress, the Tsesarevich (Crown Prince) and the Tsar's 4 daughters were murdered by the Bolsheviks in Ekaterinburg, July 16, 1918.

Provisional Government—Prince Georgi Lvov and Alexander Kerensky, premiers, 1917.

Union of Soviet Socialist Republics

Bolshevik Revolution, Nov. 7, 1917, displaced Kerensky; council of People's Commissars formed, Lenin (Vladimir Ilyich Ulyanov), premier. Lenin died Jan. 21, 1924. Aleksei Rykov (executed 1938) and V. M. Molotov held the office, but actual ruler was Joseph Stalin (Joseph Vissarionovich Djugashvili), general secretary of the Central Committee of the Communist Party. Stalin became president of the Council of Ministers (premier) May 7, 1941, died Mar. 5, 1953. Succeeded by Georgi M. Malenkov, as head of the Council and premier and Nikita S. Khrushchev, first secretary of the Central Committee. Malenkov resigned Feb. 8, 1955, became deputy premier, was dropped July 3, 1957. Marshal Nikolai A. Bulganin became premier Feb. 8, 1955; was demoted and Khrushchev became premier Mar. 27 1958. Khrushchev was ousted Oct. 14-15, 1964, replaced by Leonid I. Brezhnev as first secretary of the party and by Aleksei N. Kosygin as premier. On June 16, 1977, Brezhnev took office as president.

Governments of China

(Until 221 BC and frequently thereafter, China was not a unified state. Where dynastic dates overlap, the rulers or events referred to appeared in different areas of China.)

Hsia	c1994BC	-	c1523BC
Shang	c1523	-	c1028
Western Chou	c1027	-	770
Eastern Chou	770	-	256
Warring States	403	-	222
Ch'in (first unified empire)	221	-	206
Han	202BC	-	220AD
Western Han (expanded Chinese state beyond the Yellow and Yangtze River valleys)	202BC	-	9AD
Hsin (Wang Mang, usurper)	9AD	-	23AD
Eastern Han (expanded Chinese state into Indo-China and Turkestan)	25	-	220
Three Kingdoms (Wei, Shu, Wu)	220	-	265
Chin (western)	265	-	317
(eastern)	317	-	420
Northern Dynasties (followed several short-lived governments by Turks, Mongols, etc.)	386	-	581
Southern Dynasties (capital: Nanking)	420	-	589
Sui (reunified China)	581	-	618
Tang (a golden age of Chinese culture; capital: Sian)	618	-	906
Five Dynasties (Yellow River basin)	902	-	960
Ten Kingdoms (southern China)	907	-	979
Liao (Khitan Mongols; capital: Peking)	947	-	1125
Sung	960	-	1279
Northern Sung (reunified central and southern China)	960	-	1126
Western Hsai (non-Chinese rulers in northwest)	990	-	1227
Chin (Tartars; drove Sung out of central China)	1115	-	1234
Yuan (Mongols; Kublai Khan made Peking his capital in 1267)	1271	-	1368
Ming (China reunified under Chinese rule; capital: Nanking, then Peking in 1420)	1368	-	1644
Ch'ing (Manchus, descendents of Tartars)	1644	-	1911
Republic (disunity; provincial rulers, warlords)	1912	-	1949
People's Republic of China (Nationalist China established on Taiwan)	1949	-	—

Chronological List of Popes

Source: Annuario Pontificio Table lists year of accession of each Pope.

The Roman Catholic Church names the Apostle Peter as founder of the Church in Rome. He arrived there c. 42, was martyred there c. 67, and raised to sainthood.

The Pope's temporal title is: Sovereign of the State of Vatican City.

The Pope's spiritual titles are: Bishop of Rome, Vicar of Jesus Christ, Successor of St. Peter, Prince of the Apostles, Supreme Pontiff of the Universal Church, Patriarch of the West, Primate of Italy, Archbishop and Metropolitan of the Roman Province.

Anti-Popes are in *Italics.* Anti-Popes were illegitimate claimants of or pretenders to the papal throne.

Year	Name of Pope
See above.	St. Peter
67	St. Linus
76	St. Anacletus or Cletus
88	St. Clement I
97	St. Evaristus
105	St. Alexander I
115	St. Sixtus I
125	St. Telesphorus
136	St. Hyginus
140	St. Pius I
155	St. Anicetus
166	St. Soter
175	St. Eleutherius
189	St. Victor I
199	St. Zephyrinus
217	St. Callistus I
217	*St. Hippolytus*
222	St. Urban I
230	St. Pontian
235	St. Anterus
236	St. Fabian
251	St. Cornelius
251	*Novatian*
253	St. Lucius I
254	St. Stephen I
257	St. Sixtus II
259	St. Dionysius
269	St. Felix I
275	St. Eutychian
283	St. Caius
296	St. Marcellinus
308	St. Marcellus I
309	St. Eusebius
311	St. Melchiades
314	St. Sylvester I
336	St. Marcus
337	St. Julius I
352	Liberius
355	*Felix II*
366	St. Damasus I
366	*Ursinus*
384	St. Siricius
399	St. Anastasius I
401	St. Innocent I
417	St. Zosimus
418	St. Boniface I
418	*Eulalius*
422	St. Celestine I
432	St. Sixtus III
440	St. Leo I
461	St. Hilary
468	St. Simplicius
483	St. Felix III (II)
492	St. Gelasius I
496	Anastasius II
498	St. Symmachus
498	*Lawrence (501-505)*
514	St. Hormisdas
523	St. John I, Martyr
526	St. Felix IV (III)
530	Boniface II
530	*Dioscorus*
533	John II
535	St. Agapitus I
536	St. Silverius, Martyr
537	Vigilius
556	Pelagius I
561	John III
575	Benedict I
579	Pelagius II
590	St. Gregory I
604	Sabinian
607	Boniface III
608	St. Boniface IV
615	St. Deusdedit or Adeodatus
619	Boniface V
625	Honorius I
640	Severinus
640	John IV
642	Theodore I
649	St. Martin I, Martyr
654	St. Eugene I
657	St. Vitalian
672	Adeodatus II
676	Donus
678	St. Agatho
682	St. Leo II
684	St. Benedict II
685	John V
686	Conon
687	*Theodore*
687	*Paschal*
687	St. Sergius I
701	John VI
705	John VII
708	Sisinnius
708	Constantine
715	St. Gregory II
731	St. Gregory III
741	St. Zachary
752	Stephen II (III)
757	St. Paul I
767	*Constantine*
768	*Philip*
768	Stephen III (IV)
772	Adrian I
795	St. Leo III
816	Stephen IV (V)
817	St. Paschal I
824	Eugene II
827	Valentine
827	Gregory IV
844	*John*
844	Sergius II
847	St. Leo IV
855	Benedict III
855	*Anastasius*
858	St. Nicholas I
867	Adrian II
872	John VIII
882	Marinus I
884	St. Adrian III
885	Stephen V (VI)
891	Formosus
896	Boniface VI
896	Stephen VI (VII)
897	Romanus
897	Theodore II
898	John IX
900	Benedict IV
903	Leo V
903	*Christopher*
904	Sergius III
911	Anastasius III
913	Landus
914	John X
928	Leo VI
928	Stephen VII (VIII)
931	John XI
936	Leo VII
939	Stephen VIII (IX)
942	Marinus II
946	Agapitus II
955	John XII
963	Leo VIII
964	Benedict V
965	John XIII
973	Benedict VI
974	*Boniface VII*
974	Benedict VII
983	John XIV
985	John XV
996	Gregory V
997	*John XVI*
999	Sylvester II
1003	John XVII
1004	John XVIII
1009	Sergius IV
1012	Benedict VIII
1012	*Gregory*
1024	John XIX
1032	Benedict IX
1045	Sylvester III
1045	Benedict IX
1045	Gregory VI
1046	Clement II
1047	Benedict IX
1048	Damasus II
1049	St. Leo IX
1055	Victor II
1057	Stephen IX (X)
1058	*Benedict X*
1059	Nicholas II
1061	Alexander II
1061	*Honorius II*
1073	St. Gregory VII
1080	*Clement III*
1086	Bl. Victor III
1088	Bl. Urban II
1099	Paschal II
1100	*Theodoric*
1102	*Albert*
1105	*Sylvester IV*
1118	Gelasius II
1118	*Gregory VIII*
1119	Callistus II
1124	Honorius II
1124	*Celestine II*
1130	Innocent II
1130	*Anacletus II*
1138	*Victor IV*
1143	Celestine II
1144	Lucius II
1145	Bl. Eugene III
1153	Anastasius IV
1154	Adrian IV
1159	Alexander III
1159	*Victor IV*
1164	*Paschal III*
1168	*Callistus III*
1179	*Innocent III*
1181	Lucius III
1185	Urban III
1187	Gregory VIII
1187	Clement III
1191	Celestine III
1198	Innocent III
1216	Honorius III
1227	Gregory IX
1241	Celestine IV
1243	Innocent IV
1254	Alexander IV
1261	Urban IV
1265	Clement IV
1271	Bl. Gregory X
1276	Bl. Innocent V
1276	Adrian V
1276	John XXI
1277	Nicholas III
1281	Martin IV
1285	Honorius IV
1288	Nicholas IV
1294	St. Celestine V
1294	Boniface VIII
1303	Bl. Benedict XI
1305	Clement V
1316	John XXII
1328	*Nicholas V*
1334	Benedict XII
1342	Clement VI
1352	Innocent VI
1362	Bl. Urban V
1370	Gregory XI
1378	Urban VI
1378	*Clement VII*
1389	Boniface IX
1394	*Benedict XIII*
1404	Innocent VII
1406	Gregory XII
1409	*Alexander V*
1410	*John XXIII*
1417	Martin V
1431	Eugene IV
1439	*Felix V*
1447	Nicholas V
1455	Callistus III
1458	Pius II
1464	Paul II
1471	Sixtus IV
1484	Innocent VIII
1492	Alexander VI
1503	Pius III
1503	Julius II
1513	Leo X
1522	Adrian VI
1523	Clement VII
1534	Paul III
1550	Julius III
1555	Marcellus II
1555	Paul IV
1559	Pius IV
1566	St. Pius V
1572	Gregory XIII
1585	Sixtus V
1590	Urban VII
1590	Gregory XIV
1591	Innocent IX
1592	Clement VIII
1605	Leo XI
1605	Paul V
1621	Gregory XV
1623	Urban VIII
1644	Innocent X
1655	Alexander VII
1667	Clement IX
1670	Clement X
1676	Bl. Innocent XI
1689	Alexander VIII
1691	Innocent XII
1700	Clement XI
1721	Innocent XIII
1724	Benedict XIII
1730	Clement XII
1740	Benedict XIV
1758	Clement XIII
1769	Clement XIV
1775	Pius VI
1800	Pius VII
1823	Leo XII
1829	Pius VIII
1831	Gregory XVI
1846	Pius IX
1878	Leo XIII
1903	St. Pius X
1914	Benedict XV
1922	Pius XI
1939	Pius XII
1958	John XXIII
1963	Paul VI
1978	John Paul I
1978	John Paul II

AWARDS — MEDALS — PRIZES

The Alfred B. Nobel Prize Winners

Alfred B. Nobel, inventor of dynamite, bequeathed $9,000,000, the interest to be distributed yearly to those who had most benefited mankind in physics, chemistry, medicine-physiology, literature, and peace. The first Nobel Memorial Prize in Economics was awarded in 1969. No awards given for years omitted. In 1979, each prize was worth approximately $190,000.

Physics

1979 Steven Weinberg, Sheldon L. Glashow, both U.S.; Abdus Salam, Pakistani
1978 Pyotr Kapitsa, USSR; Arno Penzias, Robert Wilson, both U.S.
1977 John H. Van Vleck, Philip W. Anderson, both U.S.; Nevill F. Mott, British
1976 Burton Richter, U.S.
Samuel C.C. Ting, U.S.
1975 James Rainwater, U.S.
Ben Mottelson, U.S.-Danish,
Aage Bohr, Danish
1974 Martin Ryle, British
Antony Hewish, British
1973 Ivar Giaever, U.S.
Leo Esaki, Japan
Brian D. Josephson, British
1972 John Bardeen, U.S.
Leon N. Cooper, U.S.
John R. Schrieffer, U.S.
1971 Dennis Gabor, British
1970 Louis Neel, French
Hannes Alfven, Swedish
1969 Murray Gell-Mann, U.S.
1968 Luis W. Alvarez, U.S.
1967 Hans A. Bethe, U.S.
1966 Alfred Kastler, French
1965 Richard P. Feynman, U.S.
Julian S. Schwinger, U.S.
Shinichiro Tomnaga, Japanese
1964 Nikolai G. Basov, USSR
Aleksander M. Prochorov, USSR
Charles H. Townes, U.S.
1963 Maria Goeppert-Mayer, U.S.
J. Hans D. Jensen, German
Eugene P. Wigner, U.S.
1962 Lev. D. Landau, USSR
1961 Robert Hofstadter, U.S.
Rudolf L. Mossbauer, German
1960 Donald A. Glaser, U.S.
1959 Owen Chamberlain, U.S.
Emilio G. Segre, U.S.
1958 Pavel Cherenkov, Ilya Frank, Igor Y. Tamm, all USSR
1957 Tsung-dao Lee,
Chen Ning Yang, both U.S.
1956 John Bardeen, U.S.
Walter H. Brattain, U.S.
William Shockley, U.S.
1955 Polykarp Kusch, U.S.
Willis E. Lamb, U.S.
1954 Max Born, British
Walter Bothe, German
1953 Frits Zernike, Dutch
1952 Felix Bloch, U.S.
Edward M. Purcell, U.S.
1951 Sir John D. Cockroft, British
Ernest T. S. Walton, Irish
1950 Cecil F. Powell, British
1949 Hideki Yukawa, Japanese
1948 Patrick M. S. Blackett, British
1947 Sir Edward V. Appleton, British
1946 Percy Williams Bridgman, U.S.
1945 Wolfgang Pauli, U.S.
1944 Isidor Isaac Rabi, U.S.
1943 Otto Stern, U.S.
1939 Ernest O. Lawrence, U.S.
1938 Enrico Fermi, U.S.
1937 Clinton J. Davisson, U.S.
Sir George P. Thomson, British
1936 Carl D. Anderson, U.S.
Victor F. Hess, Austrian
1935 Sir James Chadwick, British
1933 Paul A. M. Dirac, British
Erwin Schrodinger, Austrian
1932 Werner Heisenberg, German
1930 Sir Chandrasekhara V. Raman, Indian
1929 Prince Louis-Victor de Broglie, French
1928 Owen W. Richardson, British
1927 Arthur H. Compton, U.S.
Charles T. R. Wilson, British
1926 Jean B. Perrin, French
1925 James Franck,
Gustav Hertz, both German
1924 Karl M. G. Siegbahn, Swedish
1923 Robert A. Millikan, U.S.
1922 Niels Bohr, Danish
1921 Albert Einstein, Ger.-U.S.
1920 Charles E. Guillaume, French
1919 Johannes Stark, German
1918 Max K. E. L. Planck, German
1917 Charles G. Barkla, British
1915 Sir William H. Bragg, British
Sir William L. Bragg, British
1914 Max von Laue, German
1913 Heike Kamerlingh-Onnes, Dutch
1912 Nils G. Dalen, Swedish
1911 Wilhelm Wien, German
1910 Johannes D. van der Waals, Dutch
1909 Carl F. Braun, German
Guglielmo Marconi, Italian
1908 Gabriel Lippmann, French
1907 Albert A. Michelson, U.S.
1906 Sir Joseph J. Thomson, British
1905 Philipp E. A. von Lenard, Ger.
1904 John W. Strutt, Lord Rayleigh, British
1903 Antoine Henri Becquerel,
Marie and Pierre Curie, all French
1902 Hendrik A. Lorentz,
Pieter Zeeman, both Dutch
1901 Wilhelm C. Roentgen, German

Chemistry

1979 Herbert C. Brown, U.S.
George Wittig, German
1978 Peter Mitchell, British
1977 Ilya Prigogine, Belgian
1976 William L. Lipscomb, U.S.
1975 John Cornforth, Austral.-Brit.,
Vladimir Prelog, Yugo.-Switz.
1974 Paul J. Flory, U.S.
1973 Ernst Otto Fischer, W. German
Geoffrey Wilkinson, British
1972 Christian B. Anfinsen, U.S.
Stanford Moore, U.S.
William H. Stein, U.S.
1971 Gerhard Herzberg, Canadian
1970 Luis F. Leloir, Arg.
1969 Derek H. R. Barton, British
Odd Hassel, Norwegian
1968 Lars Onsager, U.S.
1967 Manfred Eigen, German
Ronald G. W. Norrish, British
George Porter, British
1966 Robert S. Mulliken, U.S.
1965 Robert B. Woodward, U.S.
1964 Dorothy C. Hodgkin, British
1963 Giulio Natta, Italian
Karl Ziegler, German
1962 John C. Kendrew, British
Max F. Perutz, British
1961 Melvin Calvin, U.S.
1960 Willard F. Libby, U.S.
1959 Jaroslav Heyrovsky, Czech
1958 Frederick Sanger, British
1957 Sir Alexander R. Todd, British
1956 Sir Cyril N. Hinshelwood, British
Nikolai N. Semenov, USSR
1955 Vincent du Vigneaud, U.S.
1954 Linus C. Pauling, U.S.
1953 Hermann Staudinger, German
1952 Archer J. P. Martin, British
Richard L. M. Synge, British
1951 Edwin M. McMillan, U.S.
Glenn T. Seaborg, U.S.
1950 Kurt Alder, German
Otto P. H. Diels, German
1949 William F. Giauque, U.S.
1948 Arne W. K. Tiselius, Swedish
1947 Sir Robert Robinson, British
1946 James B. Sumner, John H. Northrop, Wendell M. Stanley, all U.S.
1945 Artturi I. Virtanen, Finnish
1944 Otto Hahn, German
1943 Georg de Hevesy, Hungarian
1939 Adolf F. J. Butenandt, German
Leopold Ruzicka, Swiss
1938 Richard Kuhn, German
1937 Walter N. Haworth, British
Paul Karrer, Swiss
1936 Peter J. W. Debye, Dutch
1935 Frederic Joliot-Curie, French
Irene Joliot-Curie, French
1934 Harold C. Urey, U.S.
1932 Irving Langmuir, U.S.
1931 Friedrich Bergius, German
Karl Bosch, German
1930 Hans Fischer, German
1929 Sir Arthur Harden, British
Hans von Euler-Chelpin, Swed.
1928 Adolf O. R. Windaus, German
1927 Heinrich O. Wieland, German
1926 Theodor Svedberg, Swedish
1925 Richard A. Zsigmondy, German
1923 Fritz Pregl, Austrian
1922 Francis W. Aston, British
1921 Frederick Soddy, British
1920 Walther H. Nernst, German
1918 Fritz Haber, German
1915 Richard M. Willstatter, German
1914 Theodore W. Richards, U.S.
1913 Alfred Werner, Swiss
1912 Victor Grignard, French
Paul Sabatier, French
1911 Marie Curie, French
1910 Otto Wallach, German
1909 Wilhelm Ostwald, German
1908 Ernest Rutherford, British
1907 Eduard Buchner, German
1906 Henri Moissan, French
1905 Adolf von Baeyer, German
1904 Sir William Ramsay, British
1903 Svante A. Arrhenius, Swedish
1902 Emil Fischer, German
1901 Jacobus H. van't Hoff, Dutch

Physiology or Medicine

1979 Allan M. Cormack, U.S.
Geoffrey N. Hounsfield, British
1978 Daniel Nathans, Hamilton O. Smith, both U.S.; Werner Arber, Swiss
1977 Rosalyn S. Yalow, Roger C.L. Guillemin, Andrew V. Schally, all

U.S.
1976 Baruch S. Blumberg, U.S.
Daniel Carleton Gajdusek, U.S.
1975 David Baltimore, Howard Temin, both U.S.; Renato Dulbecco, Ital.-U.S.
1974 Albert Claude, Lux.-U.S.; George Emil Palade, Rom.-U.S.; Christian Rene de Duve, Belg.
1973 Karl von Frisch, Ger.; Konrad Lorenz, Ger.-Austrian; Nikolaas Tinbergen, Brit.
1972 Gerald M. Edelman, U.S.
Rodney R. Porter, British
1971 Earl W. Sutherland Jr., U.S.
1970 Julius Axelrod, U.S.
Sir Bernard Katz, British
Ulf von Euler, Swedish
1969 Max Delbruck,
Alfred D. Hershey,
Salvador Luria, all U.S.
1968 Robert W. Holley,
H. Gobind Khorana,
Marshall W. Nirenberg, all U.S.
1967 Ragnar Granit, Swedish
Haldan Keffer Hartline, U.S.
George Wald, U.S.
1966 Charles B. Huggins,
Francis Peyton Rous, both U.S.
1965 Francois Jacob, Andre Lwoff,
Jacques Monod, all French
1964 Konrad E. Bloch, U.S.
Feodor Lynen, German
1963 Sir John C. Eccles, Australian
Alan L. Hodgkin, British
Andrew F. Huxley, British
1962 Francis H. C. Crick, British
James D. Watson, U.S.
Maurice H. F. Wilkins, British
1961 Georg von Bekesy, U.S.
1960 Sir F. MacFarlane Burnet, Australian
Peter B. Medawar, British
1959 Arthur Kornberg, U.S.
Severo Ochoa, U.S.
1958 George W. Beadle, U.S.
Edward L. Tatum, U.S.
Joshua Lederberg, U.S.
1957 Daniel Bovet, Italian
1956 Andre F. Cournand, U.S.
Werner Forssmann, German
Dickinson W. Richards, Jr., U.S.
1955 Alex H. T. Theorell, Swedish
1954 John F. Enders,
Frederick C. Robbins,
Thomas H. Weller, all U.S.
1953 Hans A. Krebs, British
Fritz A. Lipmann, U.S.
1952 Selman A. Waksman, U.S.
1951 Max Theiler, U.S.
1950 Philip S. Hench,
Edward C. Kendall, both U.S.
Tadeus Reichstein, Swiss
1949 Walter R. Hess, Swiss
Antonio Moniz, Portuguese
1948 Paul H. Müller, Swiss
1947 Carl F. Cori,
Gerty T. Cori, both U.S.
Bernardo A. Houssay, Arg.
1946 Hermann J. Muller, U.S.
1945 Ernst B. Chain, British
Sir Alexander Fleming, British
Sir Howard W. Florey, British
1944 Joseph Erlanger, U.S.
Herbert S. Gasser, U.S.
1943 Henrik C. P. Dam, Danish
Edward A. Doisy, U.S.
1939 Gerhard Domagk, German
1938 Corneille J. F. Heymans, Belg.
1937 Albert Szent-Gyorgyi, U.S.
1936 Sir Henry H. Dale, British
Otto Loewi, U.S.
1935 Hans Spemann, German
1934 George R. Minot, Wm. P. Murphy, G. H. Whipple, all U.S.
1933 Thomas H. Morgan, U.S.
1932 Edgar D. Adrian, British
Sir Charles S. Sherrington, Brit.
1931 Otto H. Warburg, German
1930 Karl Landsteiner, U.S.
1929 Christiaan Eijkman, Dutch
Sir Frederick G. Hopkins, British
1928 Charles J. H. Nicolle, French
1927 Julius Wagner-Jauregg, Aus.
1926 Johannes A. G. Fibiger, Danish
1924 Willem Einthoven, Dutch
1923 Frederick G. Banting, Canadian
John J. R. Macleod, Scottish
1922 Archibald V. Hill, British
Otto F. Meyerhof, German
1920 Schack A. S. Krogh, Danish
1919 Jules Bordet, Belgian
1914 Robert Barany, Austrian
1913 Charles R. Richet, French
1912 Alexis Carrel, French
1911 Allvar Gullstrand, Swedish
1910 Albrecht Kossel, German
1909 Emil T. Kocher, Swiss
1908 Paul Ehrlich, German
Elie Metchnikoff, French
1907 Charles L. A. Laveran, French
1906 Camillo Golgi, Italian
Santiago Roman y Cajal, Sp.
1905 Robert Koch, German
1904 Ivan P. Pavlov, Russian
1903 Niels R. Finsen, Danish
1902 Sir Ronald Ross, British
1901 Emil A. von Behring, German

Literature

1979 Odysseus Elytis, Greek
1978 Isaac Bashevis Singer, U.S. (Yiddish)
1977 Vicente Aleixandre, Spanish
1976 Saul Bellow, U.S.
1975 Eugenio Montale, Ital.
1974 Eyyvind Johnson, Harry Edmund Martinson, both Swedish
1973 Patrick White, Australian
1972 Heinrich Boll, W. German
1971 Pablo Neruda, Chilean
1970 Aleksandr I. Solzhenitsyn, Russ.
1969 Samuel Beckett, Irish
1968 Yasunari Kawabata, Japanese
1967 Miguel Angel Asturias, Guate.
1966 Samuel Joseph Agnon, Israeli
Nelly Sachs, Swedish
1965 Mikhail Sholokhov, Russian
1964 Jean Paul Sartre, French (Prize declined)
1963 Giorgos Seferis, Greek
1962 John Steinbeck, U.S.
1961 Ivo Andric, Yugoslavian
1960 Saint-John Perse, French
1959 Salvatore Quasimodo, Italian
1958 Boris L. Pasternak, Russian (Prize declined)
1957 Albert Camus, French
1956 Juan Ramon Jimenez, Puerto Rican-Span.
1955 Halldor K. Laxness, Icelandic
1954 Ernest Hemingway, U.S.
1953 Sir Winston Churchill, British
1952 Francois Mauriac, French
1951 Par F. Lagerkvist, Swedish
1950 Bertrand Russell, British
1949 William Faulkner, U.S.
1948 T.S. Eliot, British
1947 Andre Gide, French
1946 Hermann Hesse, Swiss
1945 Gabriela Mistral, Chilean
1944 Johannes V. Jensen, Danish
1939 Frans E. Sillanpaa, Finnish
1938 Pearl S. Buck, U.S.
1937 Roger Martin du Gard, French
1936 Eugene O'Neill, U.S.
1934 Luigi Pirandello, Italian
1933 Ivan A. Bunin, French
1932 John Galsworthy, British
1931 Erik A. Karlfeldt, Swedish
1930 Sinclair Lewis, U.S.
1929 Thomas Mann, German
1928 Sigrid Undset, Norwegian
1927 Henri Bergson, French
1926 Grazia Deledda, Italian
1925 George Bernard Shaw, British
1924 Wladyslaw S. Reymont, Polish
1923 William Butler Yeats, Irish
1922 Jacinto Benavente, Spanish
1921 Anatole France, French
1920 Knut Hamsun, Norwegian
1919 Carl F. G. Spitteler, Swiss
1917 Karl A. Gjellerup, Danish
Henrik Pontoppidan, Danish
1916 Verner von Heidenstam, Swed.
1915 Romain Rolland, French
1913 Rabindranath Tagore, Indian
1912 Gerhart Hauptmann, German
1911 Maurice Maeterlinck, Belgian
1910 Paul J. L. Heyse, German
1909 Selma Lagerlof, Swedish
1908 Rudolf C. Eucken, German
1907 Rudyard Kipling, British
1906 Giosue Carducci, Italian
1905 Henryk Sienkiewicz, Polish
1904 Frederic Mistral, French
Jose Echegaray, Spanish
1903 Bjornsterne Bjornson, Norw.
1902 Theodor Mommsen, German
1901 Rene F. A Sully Prudhomme, French

Peace

1979 Mother Theresa of Calcutta, Yugoslavian-Indian
1978 Anwar Sadat, Egyptian
Menachem Begin, Israeli
1977 Amnesty International
1976 Mairead Corrigan, Betty Williams, N. Irish
1975 Andrei Sakharov, USSR
1974 Eisaku Sato, Japanese, Sean MacBride, Irish
1973 Henry Kissinger, U.S.
Le Duc Tho, N. Vietnamese (Tho declined)
1971 Willy Brandt, W. German
1970 Norman E. Borlaug, U.S.
1969 Intl. Labor Organization
1968 Rene Cassin, French
1965 U.N. Children's Fund (UNICEF)
1964 Martin Luther King Jr., U.S.
1963 International Red Cross, League of Red Cross Societies
1962 Linus C. Pauling, U.S.
1961 Dag Hammarskjold, Swedish
1960 Albert J. Luthuli, South African
1959 Philip J. Noel-Baker, British
1958 Georges Pire, Belgian
1957 Lester B. Pearson, Canadian
1954 Office of the UN High Commissioner for Refugees
1953 George C. Marshall, U.S.
1952 Albert Schweitzer, French
1951 Leon Jouhaux, French
1950 Ralph J. Bunche, U.S.
1949 Lord John Boyd Orr of Brechin Mearns, British
1947 Friends Service Council, Brit.
Amer. Friends Service Com.
1946 Emily G. Balch,
John R. Mott, both U.S.
1945 Cordell Hull, U.S.
1944 International Red Cross
1938 Nansen International Office for Refugees
1937 Viscount Cecil of Chelwood, Brit.
1936 Carlos de Saavedra Lamas, Arg.
1935 Carl von Ossietzky, German
1934 Arthur Henderson, British
1933 Sir Norman Angell, British

1931 Jane Addams, U.S.
Nicholas Murray Butler, U.S.
1930 Nathan Soderblom, Swedish
1929 Frank B. Kellogg, U.S.
1927 Ferdinand E. Buisson, French
Ludwig Quidde, German
1926 Aristide Briand, French
Gustav Stresemann, German
1925 Sir J. Austen Chamberlain, Brit.
Charles G. Dawes, U.S.
1922 Fridtjof Nansen, Norwegian
1921 Karl H. Branting, Swedish
Christian L. Lange, Norwegian
1920 Leon V.A. Bourgeois, French
1919 Woodrow Wilson, U.S.
1917 International Red Cross
1913 Henri La Fontaine, Belgian
1912 Elihu Root, U.S.
1911 Tobias M.C. Asser, Dutch
Alfred H. Fried, Austrian
1910 Permanent International Peace Bureau
1909 Auguste M. F. Beernaert, Belg.
Paul H. B. B. d'Estournelles de Constant, French
1908 Klas P. Arnoldson, Swedish
Fredrik Bajer, Danish
1907 Ernesto T. Moneta, Italian
Louis Renault, French
1906 Theodore Roosevelt, U.S.
1905 Baroness Bertha von Suttner, Austrian
1904 Institute of International Law
1903 Sir William R. Cremer, British
1902 Elie Ducommun,
Charles A. Gobat, both Swiss
1901 Jean H. Dunant, Swiss
Frederic Passy, French

Nobel Memorial Prize in Economics

1979 Theodore W. Schultz, U.S.,
Sir Arthur Lewis, British
1978 Herbert A. Simon, U.S.
1977 Bertil Ohlin, Swedish
James E. Meade, British
1976 Milton Friedman, U.S.
1975 Tjalling Koopmans, Dutch-U.S.,
Leonid Kantorovich, USSR
1974 Gunnar Myrdal, Swed.,
Friedrich A. von Hayek, Austrian
1973 Wassily Leontief, U.S.
1972 Kenneth J. Arrow, U.S.
John R. Hicks, British
1971 Simon Kuznets, U.S.
1970 Paul A. Samuelson, U.S.
1969 Ragnar Frisch, Norwegian
Jan Tinbergen, Dutch

Pulitzer Prizes in Journalism, Letters, and Music

The Pulitzer Prizes were endowed by Joseph Pulitzer (1847-1911), publisher of The World, New York, N.Y., in a bequest to Columbia University, New York, N.Y., and are awarded annually by the president of the university on recommendation of the Pulitzer Prize Board for work done during the preceding year. The administrator is Prof. Richard T. Baker of Columbia Univ. All prizes are $1,000 (originally $500) in each category, except Meritorious Public Service for which a gold medal is given.

Journalism

Meritorious Public Service

For distinguished and meritorious public service by a United States newspaper.

1918—New York Times. Also special award to Minna Lewinson and Henry Beetle Hough.
1919—Milwaukee Journal.
1921—Boston Post.
1922—New York World.
1923—Memphis (Tenn.) Commercial Appeal.
1924—New York World.
1926—Enquirer-Sun, Columbus, Ga.
1927—Canton (Oh.) Daily News.
1928—Indianapolis Times.
1929—Evening World, New York.
1931—Atlanta (Ga.) Constitution
1932—Indianapolis (Ind.) News.
1933—New York World-Telegram.
1934—Medford (Ore.) Mail-Tribune.
1935—Sacramento (Cal.) Bee.
1936—Cedar Rapids (Ia.) Gazette.
1937—St. Louis Post-Dispatch.
1938—Bismarck (N.D.) Tribune.
1939—Miami (Fla.) Daily News.
1940—Waterbury (Conn.) Republican and American.
1941—St. Louis Post-Dispatch.
1942—Los Angeles Times.
1943—Omaha World Herald.
1944—New York Times.
1945—Detroit Free Press.
1946—Scranton (Pa.) Times.
1947—Baltimore Sun.
1948—St. Louis Post-Dispatch.
1949—Nebraska State Journal.
1950—Chicago Daily News; St. Louis Post-Dispatch.
1951—Miami (Fla.) Herald and Brooklyn Eagle.
1952—St. Louis Post-Dispatch.
1953—Whiteville (N.C.) News Reporter; Tabor City (N.C.) Tribune.
1954—Newsday (Long Island, N.Y.)
1955—Columbus (Ga.) Ledger and Sunday Ledger-Enquirer.
1956—Watsonville (Cal.) Register-Pajaronian.
1957—Chicago Daily News.
1958—Arkansas Gazette, Little Rock.
1959—Utica (N.Y.) Observer-Dispatch and Utica Daily Press.
1960—Los Angeles Times.
1961—Amarillo (Tex.) Globe-Times.
1962—Panama City (Fla.) News-Herald.
1963—Chicago Daily News.
1964—St. Petersburg (Fla.) Times.
1965—Hutchinson (Kan.) News.
1966—Boston Globe.
1967—The Louisville Courier-Journal; The Milwaukee Journal.
1968—Riverside (Cal.) Press-Enterprise.
1969—Los Angeles Times.
1970—Newsday (Long Island, N.Y.).
1971—Winston Salem (N.C.) Journal & Sentinel.
1972—New York Times.
1973—Washington Post.
1974—Newsday (Long Island, N.Y.).
1975—Boston Globe.
1976—Anchorage Daily News.
1977—Lufkin (Tex.) News.
1978—Philadelphia Inquirer.
1979—Point Reyes (Cal.) Light.
1980—Gannett News Service

Reporting

This category originally embraced all fields, local, national, and international. Later separate categories were created for the different fields of reporting.

1917—Herbert Bayard Swope, New York World.
1918—Harold A. Littledale, New York Evening Post.
1920—John J. Leary, Jr., New York World.
1921—Louis Seibold, New York World.
1922—Kirke L. Simpson, Associated Press.
1923—Alva Johnston, New York Times.
1924—Magner White, San Diego Sun.
1925—James W. Mulroy and Alvin H. Goldstein, Chicago Daily News.
1926—William Burke Miller, Louisville Courier-Journal.
1927—John T. Rogers, St. Louis Post-Dispatch.
1929—Paul Y. Anderson, St. Louis Post-Dispatch.
1930—Russell D. Owens, New York Times. Also $500 to W.O. Dapping, Auburn (N.Y.) Citizen.
1931—A.B. MacDonald, Kansas City (Mo.) Star.
1932—W.C. Richards, D.D. Martin, J.S. Pooler, F.D. Webb, J.N.W. Sloan, Detroit Free Press.
1933—Francis A. Jamieson, Associated Press.
1934—Royce Brier, San Francisco Chronicle.
1935—William H. Taylor, New York Herald Tribune.
1936—Lauren D. Lyman, New York Times.
1937—John J. O'Neill, N. Y. Herald Tribune; William L. Laurence, N.Y Times; Howard W. Blakeslee, A. P.; Gobind Behan Lal, University Service; and David Dietz, Scripps-Howard Newspapers.
1938—Raymond Sprigle, Pittsburgh Post-Gazette.
1939—Thomas L. Stokes, Scripps-Howard Newspaper Alliance.
1940—S. Burton Heath, New York World-Telegram.
1941—Westbrook Pegler, New York World-Telegram.
1942—Stanton Delaplane, San Francisco Chronicle.
1943—George Weller, Chicago Daily News.
1944—Paul Schoenstein, N.Y. Journal-American.
1945—Jack S. McDowell, San Francisco Call-Bulletin.
1946—William L. Laurence, New York Times.
1947—Frederick Woltman, N.Y. World-Telegram.
1948—George E. Goodwin, Atlanta Journal.
1949—Malcolm Johnson, New York Sun.
1950—Meyer Berger, New York Times.
1951—Edward S. Montgomery, San Francisco Examiner.
1952—Geo. de Carvalho, San Francisco Chronicle.

(1) General or Spot; (2) Special or Investigative

1953—(1) Providence (R.I.) Journal and Evening Bulletin; (2) Edward J. Mowery, N.Y. World-Telegram & Sun.
1954—(1) Vicksburg (Miss.) Sunday Post-Herald; (2) Alvin Scott McCoy, Kansas City (Mo.) Star.
1955—(1) Mrs. Caro Brown, Alice (Tex.) Daily Echo; (2) Roland K. Towery, Cuero (Tex.) Record.
1956—(1) Lee Hills, Detroit Free Press; (2) Arthur Daley, New York Times.
1957—(1) Salt Lake Tribune, Salt Lake City, Ut.; (2) Wallace Turner and William Lambert, Portland Oregonian.
1958—(1) Fargo, (N.D.) Forum; (2) George Beveridge, Evening Star, Washington, D.C.
1959—(1) Mary Lou Werner, Washington Evening Star; (2) John Harold Brislin, Scranton (Pa.) Tribune, and The Scrantonian.
1960—(1) Jack Nelson, Atlanta Constitution; (2) Miriam Ottenberg, Washington Evening Star.
1961—(1) Sanche de Gramont, N.Y. Herald Tribune; (2) Edgar May, Buffalo Evening News.
1962—(1) Robert D. Mullins, Deseret News, Salt Lake City; (2) George Bliss, Chicago Tribune.

1963—(1) Shared by Sylvan Fox, William Longgood, and Anthony Shannon, N.Y. World-Telegram & Sun; (2) Oscar Griffin, Jr., Pecos (Tex.) Independent and Enterprise.

(1) General Reporting; (2) Special Reporting.

1964—(1) Norman C. Miller, Wall Street Journal; (2) Shared by James V. Magee, Albert V. Gaudiosi, and Frederick A. Meyer, Philadelphia Bulletin.

1965—(1) Melvin H. Ruder, Hungry Horse News (Columbia Falls, Mon.); (2) Gene Goltz, Houston Post.

1966—(1) Los Angeles Times Staff; (2) John A. Frasca, Tampa (Fla.) Tribune.

1967—(1) Robert V. Cox, Chambersburg (Pa.) Public Opinion; (2) Gene Miller, Miami Herald.

1968—Detroit Free Press Staff; (2) J. Anthony Lukas, N.Y. Times.

1969—(1) John Fetterman, Louisville Courier-Journal and Times; (2) Albert L. Delugach, St. Louis Globe Democrat, and Denny Walsh, Life.

1970—(1) Thomas Fitzpatrick, Chicago Sun-Times; (2) Harold Eugene Martin, Montgomery Advertiser & Alabama Journal.

1971—(1) Akron Beacon Journal Staff, (2) William Hugh Jones, Chicago Tribune.

1972—(1) Richard Cooper and John Machacek, Rochester Times-Union; (2) Timothy Leland, Gerard M. O'Neill, Stephen Kurkjian and Anne De Santis, Boston Globe.

1973—(1) Chicago Tribune; (2) Sun Newspapers of Omaha.

1974—(1) Hugh F. Hough, Arthur M. Petacque, Chicago Sun-Times; (2) William Sherman, N.Y. Daily News.

1975—(1) Xenia (Oh.) Daily Gazette; (2) Indianapolis Star.

1976—(1) Gene Miller, Miami Herald; (2) Chicago Tribune.

1977—(1) Margo Huston, Milwaukee Journal; (2) Acel Moore, Wendell Rawls Jr., Philadelphia Inquirer.

1978—(1) Richard Whitt, Louisville Courier-Journal; (2) Anthony R. Dolan, Stamford (Conn.) Advocate.

1979—(1) San Diego (Cal.) Evening Tribune; (2) Gilbert M. Gaul, Elliot G. Jaspin, Pottsville (Pa.) Republican.

1980—(1) Philadelphia Inquirer; (2) Stephen A. Korkjian, Alexander B. Hawes Jr., Nils Bruzelius, Joan Vennochi, Boston Globe.

Criticism or Commentary

(1) Criticism; (2) Commentary

1970—(1) Ada Louise Huxtable, N.Y. Times; (2) Marquis W. Childs, St. Louis Post-Dispatch.

1971—(1) Harold C. Schonberg, N.Y. Times; (2) William A. Caldwell, The Record, Hackensack, N.J.

1972—(1) Frank Peters Jr., St. Louis Post-Dispatch; (2) Mike Royko, Chicago Daily News.

1973—(1) Ronald Powers, Chicago Sun-Times; (2) David S. Broder, Washington Post.

1974—(1) Emily Genauer, Newsday, (N.Y.); (2) Edwin A. Roberts, Jr., National Observer.

1975—(1) Roger Ebert, Chicago Sun Times; (2) Mary McGrory, Washington Star.

1976—(1) Alan M. Kriegsman, Washington Post; (2) Walter W. (Red) Smith, N.Y. Times.

1977—(1) William McPherson, Washington Post; (2) George F. Will, Wash. Post Writers Group.

1978—(1) Walter Kerr, New York Times; (2) William Safire, New York Times.

1979—(1) Paul Gapp, Chicago Tribune; (2) Russell Baker, New York Times.

1980—(1) William A. Henry III, Boston Globe; (2) Ellen Goodman, Boston Globe.

National Reporting

1942—Louis Stark, New York Times.

1944—Dewey L. Fleming, Baltimore Sun.

1945—James B. Reston, New York Times.

1946—Edward A. Harris, St. Louis Post-Dispatch.

1947—Edward T. Folliard, Washington Post.

1948—Bert Andrews, New York Herald Tribune; Nat S. Finney, Minneapolis Tribune.

1949—Charles P. Trussell, New York Times.

1950—Edwin O. Guthman, Seattle Times.

1952—Anthony Leviero, New York Times.

1953—Don Whitehead, Associated Press.

1954—Richard Wilson, Cowles Newspapers.

1955—Anthony Lewis, Washington Daily News.

1956—Charles L. Bartlett, Chattanooga Times.

1957—James Reston, New York Times.

1958—Relman Morin, AP; Clark Mollenhoff, Des Moines Register & Tribune.

1959—Howard Van Smith, Miami (Fla.) News.

1960—Vance Trimble, Scripps-Howard, Washington, D.C.

1961—Edward R. Cony, Wall Street Journal.

1962—Nathan G. Caldwell and Gene S. Graham, Nashville Tennessean.

1963—Anthony Lewis, New York Times.

1964—Merriman Smith, UPI.

1965—Louis M. Kohlmeier, Wall Street Journal.

1966—Haynes Johnson, Washington Evening Star.

1967—Monroe Karmin and Stanley Penn, Wall Street Journal.

1968—Howard James, Christian Science Monitor; Nathan K. Kotz, Des Moines Register.

1969—Robert Cahn, Christian Science Monitor.

1970—William J. Eaton, Chicago Daily News.

1971—Lucinda Franks & Thomas Powers, UPI.

1972—Jack Anderson, United Features.

1973—Robert Boyd and Clark Hoyt, Knight Newspapers.

1974—James R. Polk, Washington Star-News; Jack White, Providence Journal-Bulletin.

1975—Donald L. Barlett and James B. Steele, Philadelphia Inquirer.

1976—James Risser, Des Moines Register.

1977—Walter Mears, Associated Press.

1978—Gaylord D. Shaw, Los Angeles Times.

1979—James Risser, Des Moines Register.

1980—Charles Stafford, Bette Swenson Orsini, St. Petersburg (Fla.) Times.

International Reporting

1942—Laurence Edmund Allen, Associated Press.

1943—Ira Wolfert, No. Am. Newspaper Alliance.

1944—Daniel DeLuce, Associated Press.

1945—Mark S. Watson, Baltimore Sun.

1946—Homer W. Bigart, New York Herald Tribune.

1947—Eddy Gilmore, Associated Press.

1948—Paul W. Ward, Baltimore Sun.

1949—Price Day, Baltimore Sun.

1950—Edmund Stevens, Christian Science Monitor.

1951—Keyes Beech and Fred Sparks, Chicago Daily News; Homer Bigart and Marguerite Higgins, New York Herald Tribune; Relman Morin and Don Whitehead, AP.

1952—John M. Hightower, Associated Press.

1953—Austin C. Wehrwein, Milwaukee Journal.

1954—Jim G. Lucas, Scripps-Howard Newspapers.

1955—Harrison Salisbury, New York Times.

1956—William Randolph Hearst, Jr., Frank Conniff, Hearst Newspapers; Kingsbury Smith, INS.

1957—Russell Jones, United Press.

1958—New York Times.

1959—Joseph Martin and Philip Santora, N.Y. News.

1960—A.M. Rosenthal, New York Times.

1961—Lynn Heinzerling, Associated Press.

1962—Walter Lippmann, N.Y. Herald Tribune Synd.

1963—Hal Hendrix, Miami (Fla.) News.

1964—Malcolm W. Browne, AP; David Halberstam, N.Y. Times.

1965—J.A. Livingston, Philadelphia Bulletin.

1966—Peter Arnett, AP.

1967—R. John Hughes, Christian Science Monitor.

1968—Alfred Friendly, Washington Post.

1969—William Tuohy, L.A. Times.

1970—Seymour M. Hersh, Dispatch News Service.

1971—Jimmie Lee Hoagland, Washington Post.

1972—Peter R. Kann, Wall Street Journal.

1973—Max Frankel, N.Y. Times.

1974—Hedrick Smith, N.Y. Times.

1975—William Mullen and Ovie Carter, Chicago Tribune.

1976—Sydney H. Schanberg, N.Y. Times.

1978—Henry Kamm, N.Y. Times.

1979—Richard Ben Cramer, Philadelphia Inquirer.

1980—Joel Brinkley, Jay Mather, Louisville (Ky.) Courier-Journal.

Correspondence

For Washington or foreign correspondence. Category was merged with those in national and international reporting in 1948.

1929—Paul Scott Mowrer, Chicago Daily News.

1930—Leland Stowe, New York Herald Tribune.

1931—H.R. Knickerbocker, Philadelphia Public Ledger and New York Evening Post.

1932—Walter Duranty, New York Times, and Charles G. Ross, St. Louis Post-Dispatch.

1933—Edgar Ansel Mowrer, Chicago Daily News.

1934—Frederick T. Birchall, New York Times.

1935—Arthur Krock, New York Times.

1936—Wilfred C. Barber, Chicago Tribune.

1937—Anne O'Hare McCormick, New York Times.

1938—Arthur Krock, New York Times.

1939—Louis P. Lochner, Associated Press.

1940—Otto D. Tolischus, New York Times.

1941—Bronze plaque to commemorate work of American correspondents on war fronts.

1942—Carlos P. Romulo, Philippines Herald.

1943—Hanson W. Baldwin, New York Times.

1944—Ernest Taylor Pyle, Scripps-Howard Newspaper Alliance.

1945—Harold V. (Hal) Boyle, Associated Press.

1946—Arnaldo Cortesi, New York Times.

1947—Brooks Atkinson, New York Times.

Editorial Writing

1917—New York Tribune.

1918—Louisville (Ky.) Courier-Journal.

1920—Harvey E. Newbranch, Omaha Evening World-Herald.

1922—Frank M. O'Brien, New York Herald.

1923—William Allen White, Emporia Gazette.

1924—Frank Buxton, Boston Herald, Special Prize. Frank I. Cobb, New York World.

1925—Robert Lathan, Charleston (S.C.) News and Courier.

1926—Edward M. Kingsbury, N. Y. Times.

1927—F. Lauriston Bullard, Boston Herald.

1928—Grover C. Hall, Montgomery Advertiser.

1929—Louis Isaac Jaffe, Norfolk Virginian-Pilot.

1931—Chas. Ryckman, Fremont (Neb.) Tribune.

1933—Kansas City (Mo.) Star

1934—E. P. Chase, Atlantic (Ia.) News Telegraph.

1936—Felix Morley, Washington Post. George B. Parker, Scripps-Howard Newspapers.

1937—John W. Owens, Baltimore Sun.

1938—W.W. Waymack. Des Moines (Ia.) Register and Tribune.

1939—Ronald G. Callvert, Portland Oregonian.

1940—Bart Howard, St. Louis Post-Dispatch.

1941—Reuben Maury, Daily News, N.Y.

1942—Geoffrey Parsons, New York Herald Tribune.

1943—Forrest W. Seymour, Des Moines (Ia.) Register and Tribune.

1944—Henry J. Haskell, Kansas City (Mo.) Star.

1945—George W. Potter, Providence (R.I.) Journal-Bulletin.

1946—Hodding Carter, Greenville (Miss.) Delta Democrat-Times.
1947—William H. Grimes, Wall Street Journal.
1948—Virginius Dabney, Richmond (Va.) Times-Dispatch.
1949—John H. Crider, Boston (Mass.) Herald, Herbert Elliston, Washington Post.
1950—Carl M. Saunders, Jackson (Mich.) Citizen-Patriot.
1951—William H. Fitzpatrick, New Orleans States.
1952—Louis LaCoss, St. Louis Globe Democrat.
1953—Vermont C. Royster, Wall Street Journal.
1954—Don Murray, Boston Herald.
1955—Royce Howes, Detroit Free Press.
1956—Lauren K. Soth, Des Moines (la.) Register and Tribune.
1957—Buford Boone, Tuscaloosa (Ala.) News.
1958—Harry S. Ashmore, Arkansas Gazette.
1959—Ralph McGill, Atlanta Constitution.
1960—Lenoir Chambers, Norfolk Virginian-Pilot.
1961—William J. Dorvillier, San Juan (Puerto Rico) Star.
1962—Thomas M. Storke, Santa Barbara (Cal.) News-Press.
1963—Ira B. Harkey, Jr., Pascagoula (Miss.) Chronicle.
1964—Hazel Brannon Smith, Lexington (Miss.) Advertiser.
1965—John R. Harrison, The Gainesville (Fla.) Sun.
1966—Robert Lasch, St. Louis Post-Dispatch.
1967—Eugene C. Patterson, Atlanta Constitution.
1968—John S. Knight, Knight Newspapers.
1969—Paul Greenberg, Pine Bluff (Ark.) Commercial.
1970—Philip L. Geyelin, Washington Post.
1971—Horance G. Davis, Jr., Gainesville (Fla.) Sun.
1972—John Strohmeyer, Bethlehem (Pa.) Globe-Times.
1973—Roger B. Linscott, Berkshire Eagle, Pittsfield, Mass.
1974—F. Gilman Spencer, Trenton (N.J.) Trentonian.
1975—John D. Maurice, Charleston (W. Va.) Daily Mail.
1976—Philip Kerby, Los Angeles Times.
1977—Warren L. Lerude, Foster Church, and Norman F. Cardoza, Reno (Nev.) Evening Gazette and Nevada State Journal.
1978—Meg Greenfield, Washington Post.
1979—Edwin M. Yoder, Washington Star.
1980—Robert L. Bartley, Wall Street Journal.

Editorial Cartooning

1922—Rollin Kirby, New York World.
1924—Jay N. Darling, New York Herald Tribune.
1925—Rollin Kirby, New York World.
1926—D. R. Fitzpatrick, St. Louis Post-Dispatch.
1927—Nelson Harding, Brooklyn Eagle.
1928—Nelson Harding, Brooklyn Eagle.
1929—Rollin Kirby, New York World.
1930—Charles Macauley, Brooklyn Eagle.
1931—Edmund Duffy, Baltimore Sun.
1932—John T. McCutcheon, Chicago Tribune.
1933—H. M. Talburt, Washington Daily News.
1934—Edmund Duffy, Baltimore Sun.
1935—Ross A. Lewis, Milwaukee Journal.
1937—C. D. Batchelor, New York Daily News.
1938—Vaughn Shoemaker, Chicago Daily News.
1939—Charles G. Werner, Daily Oklahoman.
1940—Edmund Duffy, Baltimore Sun.
1941—Jacob Burck, Chicago Times.
1942—Herbert L. Block, Newspaper Enterprise Assn.
1943—Jay N. Darling, New York Herald Tribune.
1944—Clifford K. Berryman, Washington Star.
1945—Bill Mauldin, United Feature Syndicate.
1946—Bruce Alexander Russell, Los Angeles Times.
1947—Vaughn Shoemaker, Chicago Daily News.
1948—Reuben L. (Rube) Goldberg, N. Y. Sun.
1949—Lute Pease, Newark (N.J.) Evening News.
1950—James T. Berryman, Washington Star.
1951—Reginald W. Manning, Arizona Republic.
1952—Fred L. Packer, New York Mirror.
1953—Edward D. Kuekes, Cleveland Plain Dealer.
1954—Herbert L. Block, Washington Post & Times-Herald.
1955—Daniel R. Fitzpatrick, St. Louis Post-Dispatch.
1956—Robert York, Louisville (Ky.) Times.
1957—Tom Little, Nashville Tennessean.
1958—Bruce M. Shanks, Buffalo Evening News.
1959—Bill Mauldin, St. Louis Post-Dispatch.
1961—Carey Orr, Chicago Tribune.
1962—Edmund S. Valtman, Hartford Times.
1963—Frank Miller, Des Moines Register.
1964—Paul Conrad, Denver Post.
1966—Don Wright, Miami News.
1967—Patrick B. Oliphant, Denver Post.
1968—Eugene Gray Payne, Charlotte Observer.
1969—John Fischetti, Chicago Daily News.
1970—Thomas F. Darcy, Newsday.
1971—Paul Conrad, L. A. Times.
1972—Jeffrey K. MacNelly, Richmond News-Leader.
1974—Paul Szep, Boston Globe.
1975—Garry Trudeau, Universal Press Syndicate.
1976—Tony Auth, Philadelphia Inquirer.
1977—Paul Szep, Boston Globe.
1978—Jeffrey K. MacNelly, Richmond News Leader.
1979—Herbert L. Block, Washington Post.
1980—Don Wright, Miami (Fla.) News.

Spot News Photography

1942—Milton Brooks, Detroit News.
1943—Frank Noel, Associated Press.
1944—Frank Filan, AP; Earl L. Bunker, Omaha World-Herald.
1945—Joe Rosenthal, Associated Press, for photograph of planting American flag on Iwo Jima.
1947—Arnold Hardy, amateur, Atlanta, Ga.
1948—Frank Cushing, Boston Traveler.
1949—Nathaniel Fein, New York Herald Tribune.
1950—Bill Crouch, Oakland (Cal.) Tribune.
1951—Max Desfor, Associated Press.
1952—John Robinson and Don Ultang, Des Moines Register and Tribune.
1953—William M. Gallagher, Flint (Mich.) Journal.
1954—Mrs. Walter M. Schau, amateur.
1955—John L. Gaunt, Jr., Los Angeles Times.
1956—New York Daily News.
1957—Harry A. Trask, Boston Traveler.
1958—William C. Beall, Washington Daily News.
1959—William Seaman, Minneapolis Star.
1960—Andrew Lopez, UPI.
1961—Yasushi Nagao, Mainichi Newspapers, Tokyo.
1962—Paul Vathis, Associated Press.
1963—Hector Rondon, La Republica, Caracas, Venezuela.
1964—Robert H. Jackson, Dallas Times-Herald.
1965—Horst Faas, Associated Press.
1966—Kyoichi Sawada, UPI.
1967—Jack R. Thornell, Associated Press.
1968—Rocco Morabito, Jacksonville Journal.
1969—Edward Adams, AP.
1970—Steve Starr, AP.
1971—John Paul Filo, Valley Daily News & Daily Dispatch of Tarentum & New Kensington, Pa.
1972—Horst Faas and Michel Laurent, AP.
1973—Huynh Cong Ut, AP.
1974—Anthony K. Roberts, AP.
1975—Gerald H. Gay, Seattle Times.
1976—Stanley Forman, Boston Herald American.
1977—Neal Ulevich, Associated Press; Stanley Forman, Boston Herald American.
1978—Jim Schweiker, UPI.
1979—Thomas J. Kelly III, Pottstown (Pa.) Mercury.
1980—UPI.

Feature Photography

1968—Toshio Sakai, UPI.
1969—Moneta Sleet Jr., Ebony.
1970—Dallas Kinney, Palm Beach Post.
1971—Jack Dykinga, Chicago Sun-Times.
1972—Dave Kennerly, UPI.
1973—Brian Lanker, Topeka Capitol-Journal.
1974—Slava Veder, AP.
1975—Matthew Lewis, Washington Post.
1976—Louisville Courier-Journal and Louisville Times.
1977—Robin Hood, Chattanooga News-Free Press.
1978—J. Ross Baughman, AP.
1979—Staff Photographers, Boston Herald American.
1980—Erwin H. Hagler, Dallas Times-Herald.

Special Citation

1938—Edmonton (Alberta) Journal, bronze plaque.
1941—New York Times.
1944—Byron Price and Mrs. William Allen White. Also to Richard Rodgers and Oscar Hammerstein 2d, for musical, Oklahoma!
1945—Press cartographers for war maps.
1947—(Pulitzer centennial year.) Columbia Univ. and the Graduate School of Journalism, and St. Louis Post-Dispatch.
1948—Dr. Frank Diehl Fackenthal.
1951—Cyrus L. Sulzberger, New York Times.
1952—Max Kase, New York Journal-American.
1953—The New York Times; Lester Markel.
1957—Kenneth Roberts, for his historical novels.
1958—Walter Lippmann, New York Herald Tribune.
1960—Garrett Mattingly, for The Armada.
1961—American Heritage Picture History of the Civil War.
1964—The Gannett Newspapers.
1973—James T. Flexner, for "George Washington," a four-volume biography.
1976—John Hohenberg, for services to American journalism.
1977—Alex Haley, for Roots, $1,000.
1978—Richard Lee Strout, Christian Science Monitor and New Republic.
—E.B. White, for his work.

Feature Writing

Category was inaugurated in 1979.
1979—Jon D. Franklin, Baltimore Evening Sun.
1980—Madeleine Blais, Miami Herald Tropic Magazine.

Letters

Fiction

For fiction in book form by an American author, preferably dealing with American life.
1918—Ernest Poole, His Family.
1919—Booth Tarkington, The Magnificent Ambersons.
1921—Edith Wharton, The Age of Innocence.
1922—Booth Tarkington, Alice Adams.
1923—Willa Cather, One of Ours.
1924—Margaret Wilson, The Able McLaughlins.
1925—Edna Ferber, So Big.
1926—Sinclair Lewis, Arrowsmith. (Refused prize.)
1927—Louis Bromfield, Early Autumn.
1928—Thornton Wilder, Bridge of San Luis Rey.
1929—Julia M. Peterkin, Scarlet Sister Mary.
1930—Oliver LaFarge, Laughing Boy.

1931—Margaret Ayer Barnes, Years of Grace.
1932—Pearl S. Buck, The Good Earth.
1933—T. S. Stribling, The Store.
1934—Caroline Miller, Lamb in His Bosom.
1935—Josephine W. Johnson, Now in November.
1936—Harold L. Davis, Honey in the Horn.
1937—Margaret Mitchell, Gone with the Wind.
1938—John P. Marquand, The Late George Apley.
1939—Marjorie Kinnan Rawlings, The Yearling.
1940—John Steinbeck, The Grapes of Wrath.
1942—Ellen Glasgow, In This Our Life.
1943—Upton Sinclair, Dragon's Teeth.
1944—Martin Flavin, Journey in the Dark.
1945—John Hersey, A Bell for Adano.
1947—Robert Penn Warren, All the King's Men.
1948—James A Michener, Tales of the South Pacific.
1949—James Gould Cozzens, Guard of Honor.
1950—A. B. Guthrie Jr., The Way West.
1951—Conrad Richter, The Town.
1952—Herman Wouk, The Caine Mutiny.
1953—Ernest Hemingway, The Old Man and the Sea.
1955—William Faulkner, A Fable.
1956—MacKinlay Kantor, Andersonville.
1958—James Agee, A Death in the Family.
1959—Robert Lewis Taylor, The Travels of Jaimie McPheeters.
1960—Allen Drury, Advise and Consent.
1961—Harper Lee, To Kill a Mockingbird.
1962—Edwin O'Connor, The Edge of Sadness.
1963—William Faulkner, The Reivers.
1965—Shirley Ann Grau, The Keepers of the House.
1966—Katherine Anne Porter, Collected Stories of Katherine Anne Porter.
1967—Bernard Malamud, The Fixer.
1968—William Styron, The Confessions of Nat Turner.
1969—N. Scott Momaday, House Made of Dawn.
1970—Jean Stafford, Collected Stories.
1972—Wallace Stegner, Angle of Repose.
1973—Eudora Welty, The Optimist's Daughter.
1975—Michael Shaara, The Killer Angels.
1976—Saul Bellow, Humboldt's Gift.
1978—James Alan McPherson, Elbow Room.
1979—John Cheever, The Stories of John Cheever.
1980—Norman Mailer, The Executioner's Song.

Drama

For an American play, preferably original and dealing with American life.

1918—Jesse Lynch Williams, Why Marry?
1920—Eugene O'Neill, Beyond the Horizon.
1921—Zona Gale, Miss Lulu Bett.
1922—Eugene O'Neill, Anna Christie.
1923—Owen Davis, Icebound.
1924—Hatcher Hughes, Hell-Bent for Heaven.
1925—Sidney Howard, They Knew What They Wanted.
1926—George Kelly, Craig's Wife.
1927—Paul Green, In Abraham's Bosom.
1928—Eugene O'Neill, Strange Interlude.
1929—Elmer Rice, Street Scene.
1930—Marc Connelly, The Green Pastures.
1931—Susan Glaspell, Alison's House.
1932—George S. Kaufman, Morrie Ryskind and Ira Gershwin, Of Thee I Sing.
1933—Maxwell Anderson, Both Your Houses.
1934—Sidney Kingsley, Men in White.
1935—Zoe Akins, The Old Maid.
1936—Robert E. Sherwood, Idiot's Delight.
1937—George S. Kaufman and Moss Hart, You Can't Take It With You.
1938—Thornton Wilder, Our Town.
1939—Robert E. Sherwood, Abe Lincoln in Illinois.
1940—William Saroyan, The Time of Your Life.
1941—Robert E. Sherwood, There Shall Be No Night.
1943—Thornton Wilder, The Skin of Our Teeth.
1945—Mary Chase, Harvey.
1946—Russel Crouse and Howard Lindsay, State of the Union.
1948—Tennessee Williams, A Streetcar Named Desire.
1949—Arthur Miller, Death of a Salesman.
1950—Richard Rodgers, Oscar Hammerstein 2d, and Joshua Logan, South Pacific.
1952—Joseph Kramm, The Shrike.
1953—William Inge, Picnic.
1954—John Patrick, Teahouse of the August Moon.
1955—Tennessee Williams, Cat on a Hot Tin Roof.
1956—Frances Goodrich and Albert Hackett, The Diary of Anne Frank.
1957—Eugene O'Neill, Long Day's Journey Into Night.
1958—Ketti Frings, Look Homeward, Angel.
1959—Archibald MacLeish, J. B.
1960—George Abbott, Jerome Weidman, Sheldon Harnick and Jerry Bock, Fiorello.
1961—Tad Mosel, All the Way Home.
1962—Frank Loesser and Abe Burrows, How To Succeed In Business Without Really Trying.
1965—Frank D. Gilroy, The Subject Was Roses.
1967—Edward Albee, A Delicate Balance.
1969—Howard Sackler, The Great White Hope.
1970—Charles Gordone, No Place to Be Somebody.
1971—Paul Zindel, The Effect of Gamma Rays on Man-in-the-Moon Marigolds.
1973—Jason Miller, That Championship Season.
1975—Edward Albee, Seascape.
1976—Michael Bennett, James Kirkwood, Nicholas Dante, Marvin Hamlisch, Edward Kleban, A Chorus Line.
1977—Michael Cristofer, The Shadow Box.
1978—Donald L. Coburn, The Gin Game.
1979—Sam Shepard, Buried Child.
1980—Lanford Wilson, Talley's Folly.

History

For a book on the history of the United States.

1917—J. J. Jusserand, With Americans of Past and Present Days.
1918—James Ford Rhodes, History of the Civil War.
1920—Justin H. Smith, The War with Mexico.
1921—William Sowden Sims, The Victory at Sea.
1922—James Truslow Adams, The Founding of New England.
1923—Charles Warren, The Supreme Court in United States History.
1924—Charles Howard McIlwain, The American Revolution: A Constitutional Interpretation.
1925—Frederick L. Paxton, A History of the American Frontier.
1926—Edward Channing, A History of the U.S.
1927—Samuel Flagg Bemis, Pinckney's Treaty.
1928—Vernon Louis Parrington, Main Currents in American Thought.
1929—Fred A. Shannon, The Organization and Administration of the Union Army, 1861-65.
1930—Claude H. Van Tyne, The War of Independence.
1931—Bernadotte E. Schmitt, The Coming of the War, 1914.
1932—Gen. John J. Pershing, My Experiences in the World War.
1933—Frederick J. Turner, The Significance of Sections in American History.
1934—Herbert Agar, The People's Choice.
1935—Charles McLean Andrews, The Colonial Period of American History.
1936—Andrew C. McLaughlin, The Constitutional History of the United States.
1937—Van Wyck Brooks, The Flowering of New England.
1938—Paul Herman Buck, The Road to Reunion, 1865-1900.
1939—Frank Luther Mott, A History of American Magazines.
1940—Carl Sandburg, Abraham Lincoln: The War Years.
1941—Marcus Lee Hansen, The Atlantic Migration, 1607-1860.
1942—Margaret Leech, Reveille in Washington.
1943—Esther Forbes, Paul Revere and the World He Lived In.
1944—Merle Curti, The Growth of American Thought.
1945—Stephen Bonsal, Unfinished Business.
1946—Arthur M. Schlesinger Jr., The Age of Jackson.
1947—James Phinney Baxter 3d, Scientists Against Time.
1948—Bernard De Voto, Across the Wide Missouri.
1949—Roy F. Nichols, The Disruption of American Democracy.
1950—O. W. Larkin, Art and Life in America.
1951—R. Carlyle Buley, The Old Northwest: Pioneer Period 1815-1840.
1952—Oscar Handlin, The Uprooted.
1953—George Dangerfield, The Era of Good Feelings.
1954—Bruce Catton, A Stillness at Appomattox.
1955—Paul Horgan, Great River: The Rio Grande in North American History.
1956—Richard Hofstadter, The Age of Reform.
1957—George F. Kennan, Russia Leaves the War.
1958—Bray Hammond, Banks and Politics in America—From the Revolution to the Civil War.
1959—Leonard D. White and Jean Schneider, The Republican Era; 1869-1901.
1960—Margaret Leech, In the Days of McKinley.
1961—Herbert Feis, Between War and Peace: The Potsdam Conference.
1962—Lawrence H. Gibson, The Triumphant Empire: Thunderclouds Gather in the West.
1963—Constance McLaughlin Green, Washington: Village and Capital, 1800-1878.
1964—Sumner Chilton Powell, Puritan Village: The Formation of A New England Town.
1965—Irwin Unger, The Greenback Era.
1966—Perry Miller, Life of the Mind in America.
1967—William H. Goetzmann, Exploration and Empire: the Explorer and Scientist in the Winning of the American West.
1968—Bernard Bailyn, The Ideological Origins of the American Revolution.
1969—Leonard W. Levy, Origin of the Fifth Amendment.
1970—Dean Acheson, Present at the Creation: My Years in the State Department.
1971—James McGregor Burns, Roosevelt: The Soldier of Freedom.
1972—Carl N. Degler, Neither Black Nor White.
1973—Michael Kammen, People of Paradox: An Inquiry Concerning the Origins of American Civilization.
1974—Daniel J. Boorstin, The Americans: The Democratic Experience.
1975—Dumas Malone, Jefferson and His Time.
1976—Paul Horgan, Lamy of Santa Fe.
1977—David M. Potter, The Impending Crisis.
1978—Alfred D. Chandler, Jr., The Visible Hand: The Managerial Revolution in American Business.
1979—Don E. Fehrenbacher, The Dred Scott Case: Its Significance in American Law and Politics.
1980—Leon F. Litwack, Been in the Storm So Long.

Biography or Autobiography

For a distinguished biography or autobiography by an American author, preferably on an American subject.

1917—Laura E. Richards and Maude Howe Elliott, assisted by Florence Howe Hall, Julia Ward Howe.
1918—William Cabell Bruce, Benjamin Franklin, Self-Revealed.
1919—Henry Adams, The Education of Henry Adams.
1920—Albert J. Beveridge, The Life of John Marshall.
1921—Edward Bok, The Americanization of Edward Bok.
1922—Hamlin Garland, A Daughter of the Middle Border.
1923—Burton J. Hendrick, The Life and Letters of Walter H. Page.
1924—Michael Pupin, From Immigrant to Inventor.

1925—M. A. DeWolfe Howe, Barrett Wendell and His Letters.
1926—Harvey Cushing, Life of Sir William Osler.
1927—Emory Holloway, Whitman: An Interpretation in Narrative.
1928—Charles Edward Russell, The American Orchestra and Theodore Thomas.
1929—Burton J. Hendrick, The Training of an American: The Earlier Life and Letters of Walter H. Page.
1930—Marquis James, The Raven (Sam Houston).
1931—Henry James, Charles W. Eliot.
1932—Henry F. Pringle, Theodore Roosevelt.
1933—Allan Nevins, Grover Cleveland.
1934—Tyler Dennett, John Hay.
1935—Douglas Southall Freeman, R. E. Lee
1936—Ralph Barton Perry, The Thought and Character of William James.
1937—Allan Nevins, Hamilton Fish: The Inner History of the Grant Administration.
1938—Divided between Odell Shepard, Pedlar's Progress; Marquis James, Andrew Jackson.
1939—Carl Van Doren, Benjamin Franklin.
1940—Ray Stannard Baker, Woodrow Wilson, Life and Letters.
1941—Ola Elizabeth Winslow, Jonathan Edwards.
1942—Forrest Wilson, Crusader in Crinoline.
1943—Samuel Eliot Morison, Admiral of the Ocean Sea (Columbus).
1944—Carleton Mabee, The American Leonardo: The Life of Samuel F. B. Morse.
1945—Russell Blaine Nye, George Bancroft; Brahmin Rebel.
1946—Linny Marsh Wolfe, Son of the Wilderness.
1947—William Allen White, The Autobiography of William Allen White.
1948—Margaret Clapp, Forgotten First Citizen: John Bigelow.
1949—Robert E. Sherwood, Roosevelt and Hopkins.
1950—Samuel Flag Bemis, John Quincy Adams and the Foundations of American Foreign Policy.
1951—Margaret Louise Colt, John C. Calhoun: American Portrait.
1952—Merlo J. Pusey, Charles Evans Hughes.
1953—David J. Mays, Edmund Pendleton, 1721-1803.
1954—Charles A. Lindbergh, The Spirit of St. Louis.
1955—William S. White, The Taft Story.
1956—Talbot F. Hamlin, Benjamin Henry Latrobe.
1957—John F. Kennedy, Profiles in Courage.
1958—Douglas Southall Freeman (decd. 1953), George Washington, Vols. I-VI: John Alexander Carroll and Mary Wells Ashworth, Vol. VII.
1959—Arthur Walworth, Woodrow Wilson: American Prophet.
1960—Samuel Eliot Morison, John Paul Jones.
1961—David Donald, Charles Sumner and The Coming of the Civil War.
1963—Leon Edel, Henry James: Vol. II. The Conquest of London, 1870-1881; Vol. III, The Middle Years, 1881-1895.
1964—Walter Jackson Bate, John Keats.
1965—Ernest Samuels, Henry Adams.
1966—Arthur M. Schlesinger Jr., A Thousand Days.
1967—Justin Kaplan, Mr. Clemens and Mark Twain.
1968—George F. Kennan, Memoirs (1925-1950).
1969—B. L. Reid, The Man from New York: John Quinn and his Friends.
1970—T. Harry Williams, Huey Long.
1971—Lawrence Thompson, Robert Frost: The Years of Triumph, 1915-1938.
1972—Joseph P. Lash, Eleanor and Franklin.
1973—W. A. Swanberg, Luce and His Empire.
1974—Louis Sheaffer, O'Neill, Son and Artist.
1975—Robert A. Caro, The Power Broker: Robert Moses and the Fall of New York.
1976—R.W.B. Lewis, Edith Wharton: A Biography.
1977—John E. Mack, A Prince of Our Disorder, The Life of T.E. Lawrence.
1978—Walter Jackson Bate, Samuel Johnson.
1979—Leonard Baker, Days of Sorrow and Pain: Leo Baeck and the Berlin Jews.
1980—Edmund Morris, The Rise of Theodore Roosevelt.

American Poetry

Before this prize was established in 1922, awards were made from gifts provided by the Poetry Society: **1918**—Love Songs, by Sara Teasdale. **1919**—Old Road to Paradise, by Margaret Widemer; Corn Huskers, by Carl Sandburg.
1922—Edwin Arlington Robinson, Collected Poems.
1923—Edna St. Vincent Millay, The Ballad of the Harp-Weaver; A Few Figs from Thistles; Eight Sonnets in American Poetry, 1922; A Miscellany.
1924—Robert Frost, New Hampshire: A Poem with Notes and Grace Notes.
1925—Edwin Arlington Robinson, The Man Who Died Twice.
1926—Amy Lowell, What's O'Clock.
1927—Leonora Speyer, Fiddler's Farewell.
1928—Edwin Arlington Robinson, Tristram.
1929—Stephen Vincent Benet, John Brown's Body.
1930—Conrad Aiken, Selected Poems.
1931—Robert Frost, Collected Poems.
1932—George Dillon, The Flowering Stone.
1933—Archibald MacLeish, Conquistador.
1934—Robert Hillyer, Collected Verse.
1935—Audrey Wurdemann, Bright Ambush.
1936—Robert P. Tristram Coffin, Strange Holiness.
1937—Robert Frost, A Further Range.
1938—Marya Zaturenska, Cold Morning Sky.
1939—John Gould Fletcher, Selected Poems.
1940—Mark Van Doren, Collected Poems.
1941—Leonard Bacon, Sunderland Capture.
1942—William Rose Benet, The Dust Which Is God.
1943—Robert Frost, A Witness Tree.
1944—Stephen Vincent Benet, Western Star.
1945—Karl Shapiro, V-Letter and Other Poems.
1947—Robert Lowell, Lord Weary's Castle.
1948—W. H. Auden, The Age of Anxiety.
1949—Peter Viereck, Terror and Decorum.
1950—Gwendolyn Brooks, Annie Allen.
1951—Carl Sandburg, Complete Poems.
1952—Marianne Moore, Collected Poems.
1953—Archibald MacLeish, Collected Poems.
1954—Theodore Roethke, The Waking.
1955—Wallace Stevens, Collected Poems.
1956—Elizabeth Bishop, Poems, North and South.
1957—Richard Wilbur, Things of This World.
1958—Robert Penn Warren, Promises: Poems 1954-1956.
1959—Stanley Kunitz, Selected Poems 1928-1958.
1960—W. D. Snodgrass, Heart's Needle.
1961—Phyllis McGinley, Times Three: Selected Verse from Three Decades.
1962—Alan Dugan, Poems.
1963—William Carlos Williams, Pictures From Breughel.
1964—Louis Simpson, At the End of the Open Road.
1965—John Berryman, 77 Dream Songs.
1966—Richard Eberhart, Selected Poems.
1967—Anne Sexton, Live or Die.
1968—Anthony Hecht, The Hard Hours.
1969—George Oppen, Of Being Numerous.
1970—Richard Howard, Untitled Subjects.
1971—William S. Merwin, The Carrier of Ladders.
1972—James Wright, Collected Poems.
1973—Maxine Winokur Kumin, Up Country.
1975—Gary Snyder, Turtle Island.
1976—John Ashbery, Self-Portrait in a Convex Mirror.
1977—James Merrill, Divine Comedies.
1978—Howard Nemerov, Collected Poems.
1979—Robert Penn Warren, Now and Then: Poems 1976-1978.
1980—Donald Justice, Selected Poems.

General Non-Fiction

For best book by an American, not eligible in any other category.
1962—Theodore H. White, The Making of the President 1960.
1963—Barbara W. Tuchman, The Guns of August.
1964—Richard Hofstadter, Anti-Intellectualism in American Life.
1965—Howard Mumford Jones, O Strange New World.
1966—Edwin Way Teale, Wandering Through Winter.
1967—David Brion Davis, The Problem of Slavery in Western Culture.
1968—Will and Ariel Durant, Rousseau and Revolution.
1969—Norman Mailer, The Armies of the Night; and Rene Jules Dubos, So Human an Animal: How We Are Shaped by Surroundings and Events.
1970—Eric H. Erikson, Gandhi's Truth.
1971—John Toland, The Rising Sun.
1972—Barbara W. Tuchman, Stilwell and the American Experience in China, 1911-1945.
1973—Frances FitzGerald, Fire in the Lake: The Vietnamese and the Americans in Vietnam; and Robert Coles, Children of Crisis, Volumes II and III.
1974—Ernest Becker, The Denial of Death.
1975—Annie Dillard, Pilgrim at Tinker Creek.
1976—Robert N. Butler, Why Survive? Being Old in America.
1977—William W. Warner, Beautiful Swimmers.
1978—Carl Sagan, The Dragons of Eden.
1979—Edward O. Wilson, On Human Nature.
1980—Douglas R. Hofstadter, Gödel, Escher, Bach: An Eternal Golden Braid.

Music

For composition by an American (before 1977, by a composer resident in the U.S.), in the larger forms of chamber, orchestra or choral music or for an operatic work including ballet. A special posthumous award was granted in 1976 to Scott Joplin.
1943—William Schuman, Secular Cantata No. 2, A Free Song.
1944—Howard Hanson, Symphony No. 4, Op. 34.
1945—Aaron Copland, Appalachian Spring.
1946—Leo Sowerby, The Canticle of the Sun.
1947—Charles E. Ives, Symphony No. 3.
1948—Walter Piston, Symphony No. 3.
1949—Virgil Thomson, Louisiana Story.
1950—Gian-Carlo Menotti, The Consul.
1951—Douglas Moore, Giants in the Earth.
1952—Gail Kubil, Symphony Concertante.
1954—Quincy Porter, Concerto for Two Pianos and Orchestra.
1955—Gian-Carlo Menotti, The Saint of Bleecker Street.
1956—Ernest Toch, Symphony No. 3.
1957—Norman Dello Joio, Meditations on Ecclesiastes.
1958—Samuel Barber, Vanessa.
1959—John La Montaine, Concerto for Piano and Orchestra.
1960—Elliott Carter, Second String Quartet.
1961—Walter Piston, Symphony No. 7.
1962—Robert Ward, The Crucible.
1963—Samuel Barber, Piano Concerto No. 1.
1966—Leslie Bassett, Variations for Orchestra.
1967—Leon Kirchner, Quartet No. 3.
1968—George Crumb, Echoes of Time and The River.
1969—Karel Husa, String Quartet No. 3.
1970—Charles W. Wuorinen, Time's Encomium.
1971—Mario Davidovsky, Synchronisms No. 6.
1972—Jacob Druckman, Windows.
1973—Elliott Carter, String Quartet No. 3.
1974—Donald Martino, Notturno. (Special citation) Roger Sessions.
1975—Dominick Argento, From the Diary of Virginia Woolf.

1976—Ned Rorem, Air Music.
1977—Richard Wernick, Visions of Terror and Wonder.
1978—Michael Colgrass, Deja Vu for Percussion and Orchestra.
1979—Joseph Schwantner, Aftertones of Infinity.
1980—David Del Tredici, In Memory of a Summer Day.

Special Awards

Awarded in 1980 unless otherwise designated

Books, Allied Arts

Academy of American Poets Fellowship, for distinguished achievement, $10,000: Mark Strand.

American Academy and Institute of Arts and Letters Awards, $4,000 each: Ann Beattie, William Dickey, Paul Fussell, Maxine Kumin, George Open, Robert Pinsky, Lewis Thomas, Larry Woiwode; William Dean Howells Medal for Fiction: William Maxwell, *So Long, See You Tomorrow;* Richard and Hinda Rosenthal Award, $3,000: Stanley Elkin, *The Living End;* Morton Dauwen Zabel Award, $2,500: Donald Finkel; Witter Bynner Prize for Poetry, $1,350: Pamela White Hadas; Award of Merit Medal for Poetry, $1,000: Richard Howard; Rome Fellowship in Creative Writing, $2,000: Mary Morris; Sue Kaufman Prize for First Fiction, $1,000: Jayne Anne Phillips; Harold D. Vursell Memorial Award, $5,000: Tom Wolfe.

American Book Awards: National Medal for Literature, $15,000: Eudora Welty; fiction: William Styron, *Sophie's Choice;* paperback: John Irving, *The World According to Garp;* first novel: William Wharton, *Birdy;* general nonfiction: Tom Wolfe, *The Right Stuff;* paperback: Peter Matthiessen, *The Snow Leopard;* history: Henry Kissinger, *White House Years;* paperback: Barbara W. Tuchman, *A Distant Mirror;* biography: Edmund Morris, *The Rise of Theodore Roosevelt;* paperback: Scott Berg, *Max Perkins;* poetry: Philip Levine, *Ashes;* autobiography: Lauren Bacall, *By Myself;* paperback: Malcolm Cowley, *And I Worked at the Writer's Trade;* children's: Joan W. Blos, *A Gathering of Days;* paperback: Madeline L'Engle, *A Swiftly Tilting Planet.*

American Historical Association Awards: Herbert Baxter Adams Prize: Kendall E. Bailes, *Technology and Society Under Lenin and Stalin: Origins of the Soviet Technical Intelligentsia, 1917-1941;* George Louis Beer Prize: Edward W. Bennett, *German Rearmament and the West, 1932-33;* Albert J. Beveridge Award, $1,000: Calvin Martin, *Keepers of the Game: Indian-Animal Relationships and the Fur Trade;* John K. Fairbank Prize: Guy S. Alitto, *The Last Confucian: Liang Shu-Ming and the Chinese Dilemma of Modernity;* Leo Gershoy Award: Robert Darnton, *The Business of Enlightenment: A Publishing History of the Encyclopédie, 1775-1800;* Howard R. Marraro Prize: John W. O'Malley, *Praise and Blame in Renaissance Rome: Rhetoric, Doctrine, and Reform in the Sacred Orators of the Papal Court.*

Bancroft Prizes, by Columbia Univ., for American history: Robert Dallek, *Franklin D. Roosevelt and American Foreign Policy, 1932-45;* Thomas Dublin, *Women at Work: the Transformation of Work and Community in Lowell, Massachusetts, 1826-1860;* Donald Worster, *Dust Bowl: The Southern Plains in the 1930s.*

Bennet Award, by *The Hudson Review,* $12,500: V.S. Naipaul.

Best Illustrated Children's Books, by *New York Times Book Review* (1979): *Garden of Abdul Gasazi,* Chris Van Allsburg; *Ox-Cart Man,* Barbara Cooney; *Tilly's House,* Faith Jaques; *The Treasure,* Uri Shulevitz; *The Long Dive,* Mr. and Mrs. Smith; *The Tale of Fancy Nancy,* Marion Koenig; *By Camel or by Car,* Guy Billout; *King Krakus and the Dragon,* Janina Domanska; *Natural History,* M.B. Goffstein; *Happy Birthday Oliver!,* Pierre Le-Tan.

Boston Globe-Horn Children's Book Awards: fiction: Sid Fleischman, *Humbug Mountain;* David Kheridian: *The Road from Home: The Story of an Armenian Girl;* illustration: Raymond Briggs, *The Snowman.*

Burroughs Medal, by John Burroughs Memorial Association, for natural history book (1979): Barry Lopez, *Wolves and Men.*

Randolph Caldecott Medal, by American Library Association, for children's book illustration: Barbara Cooney, *Ox-Cart Man.*

Canada Council Children's Literature Prizes (1979): $2,500 each: Barbara Claassen Smucker, *Days of Terror;* Laszlo Gal, *The Twelve Dancing Princesses;* Gabrielle Roy, *Courte-Queue;* Roger Paré, *Une fenêtre dans ma tête.*

Canadian Governor General's Literary Awards (1979): fiction: Jack Hodgins, *The Resurrection of Joseph Bourne;* Marie-Claire Blais, *Le sourd dans la ville;* non fiction; Maria Tippett, *Emily Carr: A Biography;* Dominique Clift, Sheila McLeod Arnopolous, *Le fait anglais au Québec;* poetry and drama: Michael Ondaatje, *There's a Trick with a Knife I'm Learning to Do;* Robert Mélancon: *Peinture aveugle.*

Dorothy Canfield Fisher Children's Book Award, by Vermont State PTA and Vermont Dept. of Libraries (1979): Susan Beth Pfeffer, *Kid Power.*

Carey-Thomas Awards, by *Publishers Weekly,* for distinguished book publishing project: George Braziller, for art books and innovative fiction.

Lewis Carroll Shelf Awards (1979), by School of Education, Univ. of Wisconsin at Madison: David Kherdian, *The Road from Home;* Nancy Willard, David McPhail (illus.), *The Island of the Grass King;* Laurence Yep, *Dragonwings;* Bernard Waber, *Lyle, Lyle Crocodile;* Robert Cormier, *The Chocolate War;* Ursula K. Le Guin, Ruth Robbins (illus.), *A Wizard of Earthsea;* Raymond Briggs, *The Snowman.*

Child Study Children's Book Committee Award, by Bank Street College, Columbia Univ.: Doris Orgel, *The Devil in Vienna.*

Christopher Awards, by the Christophers, for affirmation of human spirit: *The Habit of Being: Letters of Flannery O'-Connor,* ed. Sally Fitzgerald; *Lest Innocent Blood Be Shed,* Philip Hallie; *The Medusa and the Snail,* Lewis Thomas; *The Rise of Theodore Roosevelt,* Edmund Morris; *The Sinking Ark,* Norman Myers; *Blessings,* Mary Craig; *The Dancing Wu Li Masters,* Gary Zukov; *A Distant Grief,* Kefa Sempangi with Barbara Thompson; *All Together Now,* Sue Ellen Bridgers; *Federick's Alligator,* Esther Allen Peterson; *The New York Kid's Book,* ed. Catherine Edmonds, Joan Gross, Olga Litowinsky, Stephen Mooser, Pamela Morton, Barbara Beasley Murphy, Barbara Seuling, Bebe Willoughby; *What Happened in Hamelin,* Gloria Skurzynski.

George Freedley Memorial Award, by Theater Library Association, for book on theater: George Winchester Stone Jr., George M. Kahri, *David Garrick: A Critical Biography.*

Friends of American Writers Juvenile Awards: Gloria Whelan, *A Clearing in the Forest;* Jamie Gilson, *Harvey, the Beer Can King;* special artistic award: Carol Lerner, *On the Forest Edge.*

Golden Kite Awards, by Society of Children's Book Writers: fiction: Carole S. Adler, *The Magic of the Glits;* nonfiction: Arnold Madison, *Runaway Teens.*

Association of Jewish Libraries Book Awards: Doris Orgel, *The Devil in Vienna;* body of work award: Sydney Taylor, All of a Kind Family books.

Harold Morton Landon Award, by Academy of American Poets, for translation: Saralyn R. Daly, *The Book of True Love,* by Juan Ruiz; Edmund Keeley, *Ritsos in Parentheses,* by Yannis Ritsos.

Frederich C. Melcher Book Award, by Unitarian Universalist Association, for contribution to religious liberalism $1,000: Frank E. Manuel, Fritzie P. Manuel, *Utopian Thought in the Western World.*

National Magazine Awards, by Columbia Univ. School of Journalism: service to the individual: *Saturday Review,* Susan Schiefelbein; photojouralism: *GEO;* specialized journalism: *IEEE Spectrum;* single-topic issue: *Scientific American;* public service: *Texas Monthly,* Gene Lyons; fiction: *Anateus,* Joy Williams; essays and criticism: *Natural History,* Stephen Jay Gould; reporting: *Mother Jones,* Mark Dowie.

New Writers Awards, by Great Lakes Colleges Association (1979): poetry: Leslie Ullman, *Natural Histories;* Caroline Richards, *Sweet Country.*

John Newbery Medal, by American Library Association, for children's book: Joan W. Bos, *A Gathering of Days, A New England Girl's Journal, 1830-32.*

Phi Beta Kappa Book Awards: Ralph Waldo Emerson Award: Elizabeth Lewisohn Eisenstein: *The Printing Press as an Agent of Change, Vols. I and II;* Christian Gauss Award: Robert Bechtold Heilman, *The Ways of the World: Comedy and Society;* Science Award: John Imbrie, Katherine Palmer Imbrie: *Ice Ages: Solving the Mystery.*

Poetry Society of America Awards (1979): Emily Dickinson Award: Virginia Linton; Cecil Hemley Memorial Award: L.L. Zeiger; W.C. Williams Award: David Ray, *The Tramp's Cup;* Witter Bynner Poetry Translation Prize, $1,000: John and Bogdana Carpenter, *Selected Poems of Zbigniew Herbert;* Witter Bynner Grant-in-Aid, $1,000: Charles Guenther, *Anselm Hollo.*

George Polk Book Award: William Shawcross, *Sideshow: Kissinger, Nixon and the Destruction of Cambodia.*

Regina Medal, by Catholic Library Association, for continued contribution to children's literature (1980): Beverly Cleary.

Walt Whitman Award, by Academy of American Poets, $1,000: Jared Carter, *Work, for the Night is Coming.*

Western Writers of America Spur Awards: novel: Norman Zollinger, *Riders to Cibola;* nonfiction: Janet Lecompte: *Pueblo, Hardscrabble, Greenhorn.*

Laura Ingalls Wilder Award, by American Library Association, for lasting contribution to children's literature: Theodore Geisel (Dr. Seuss).

Journalism Awards

American Penal Press Awards, by School of Journalism, Southern Illinois Univ. at Carbondale (1979): continued excellence: *FYSK Magazine,* Virginia State Penitentiary, Richmond Va., editors Henry L. Clere, James E. Pittman, Robert A. Bailey; printed magazine: *The Messenger,* So. Dakota State Penitentiary, Sioux Falls, S.D., editor Roger Flittie; mimeographed publication: *La Roca,* Arizona State Prison, Florence, Ariz., editor Bill Farni; printed newspaper: *The Menard Time,* Menard Correctional Center, Menard, Ill., editor Robert Russo.

American Legion Fourth Estate Award, for media activities that help preserve the American way of life (1979), $1,000: Frank Mankiewicz, National Public Radio.

Claude Bernard Science Journalism Awards, $3,000: Bruce DeSilva, *Providence* (R.I.) *Journal;* Joan Arehart-Treichel, *New York Magazine.*

Business Journalism Awards, by Univ. of Missouri School of Journalism (1979), $1,000: William Dougherty, *Alaska Advocate;* Stuart Diamond, *Newsday;* Peter Meyer, *Harper's;* Chris Welles, *Institutional Investor.*

Catholic Press Association Awards: general excellence, magazines: general interest: *U.S. Catholic;* mission: *Maryknoll:* religious order: *National Jesuit News;* professional: *Columbia, Catholic Lawyer;* clergy and religious: *Pastoral Life;* scholarly: *Theological Studies, Communio;* devotional/inspirational: *God's Word Today;* newsletters: *Word One,* Claretian Publications; general excellence, newspapers: national: *National Catholic Reporter,* Kansas City, Mo.; diocesan: *Prairie Messenger,* Muenster, Saskatchewan; *Green Bay Catholic Compass,* Green Bay, Wis.; *Record,* Louisville, Ky.

Eugene Cervi Award, for continuing public service through journalism, by International Society of Weekly Newspaper editors (1979): Houstoun Waring, Independent Newspapers of Littleton, Col.

Raymond Clapper Memorial Award, for reporting on government affairs, by Washington Standing Committee of Correspondents (1979), $1,500: Gordon E. White, *Deseret News,* Salt Lake City, Ut.; John Wallach, Hearst newspapers.

Clarion Awards, by Women in Communications (1979): magazines: Peter Goldman, Dennis Williams, *Newsweek;* Eileen Lynch, *Philadelphia;* Elizabeth Rodgers Dobell, *Redbook;* newspapers: Patricia Fanning, *Wall Street Journal;* Bruce Olds, *Bucks County* (Pa.) *Courier Times;* Caryn Eve Wiener, *Times Herald-Record,* Middletown, N.Y.

Golden Quill Award, for editorial writing, by International Society of Weekly Newspaper Editors (1979): R.W. van de Velde, *Valley Voice,* Middlebury, Vt.

Jester Award, by Newspaper Comics Council, for contribution to comics (1979): Mort Walker.

Kappa Tau Alpha Research Award, for best book in journalism, by National Journalism Scholarship Society (1979), $250: David Halberstam, *The Powers That Be.*

Robert F. Kennedy Journalism Awards, for coverage of problems of disadvantaged (1979): grand prize and print first prize, $3,000: Paul Lieberman, Chester Goolrick, Charlene P. Smith-Williams, Lee May, Steve Johnson, *Atlanta Constitution;* photojournalism: photographic staff, *Philadelphia Daily News.*

National Press Club Awards: consumer journalism, $1,000: David Hess, *Akron* (Oh.) *Beacon Journal* and Moira Johnston, *New West magazine;* newspaper: David Hess; James A. Haught, *Charleston* (W. Virginia) *Gazette;* wire service and print syndicate: Jeffrey Mills, Associated Press; periodicals: Peter J. Ognibene, *Saturday Review;* Moira Johnston; Fourth Estate Award: Clayton Kirkpatrick, Chicago Tribune Company.

Penney-Missouri Newspaper Awards, $1,000 each: single-story: Dan D. Morain, *Daily News,* Longview, Wash.; series: Kathy Satterfield, Carol Viescas, *E. Paso* (Texas) *Times,* consumer affairs: Diane Clark, Dan Carson, *San Diego* (Calif.) *Union;* fashion and clothing: Nancy Webb Hatton, *Miami* (Fla.) *News.*

Penney-Missouri Magazine Awards, $6,000: contemporary living: Bil Gilbert, *Sports Illustrated;* consumerism: Susan Quinn, *Boston Magazine;* health: Janet Malcolm, *The New Yorker;* personal lifestyle: Malcolm Cowley, *Life;* expanding opportunities: Elizabeth Pope Frank, *Good Housekeeping;* smaller magazine excellence: Michael Ryan, *Boston Magazine.*

George Polk Awards: foreign reporting: John Kifner, *New York Times;* national reporting: Brian Donovan, Bob Wyrick, Stuart Diamong, *Newsday;* regional reporting: Jim Adams, Jim Detjen, *Louisville Courier-Journal;* metropolitan reporting: Walt Bogdanich, Walter Johns Jr., *Cleveland Press;* local reporting: Ed Petykiewicz, *Saginaw* (Mich.) *News;* political reporting: Jack Newfield, *Village Voice;* commentary: "Notes and Comment," *The New Yorker;* news photography: UPI, for "Firing Squad"; special interest reporting: Wilbert Rideau, Billy Sinclair, *The Agolite;* special award: Alden Whitman, *New York Times.*

Science in Society Awards, by National Association of Science Writers (1979), $1,000: Michael Harwood, *Harper's;* R. Jeffrey Smith, *Science.*

Science Writing Awards, by American Association for the Advancement of Science-Westinghouse (1979), $1,000: Karen Freiberg, Martha Mangelsdorf, *Wichita* (Kan.) *Eagle & Beacon;* Joseph Donohue, *Press* and *Sunday Press,* Atlantic City, N.J.; Thomas V. Canby, *National Geographic.*

Scripps-Howard Foundation Awards: Walker Stone Editorial Award, $1,000: Barbara Standon, *Detroit Free Press;* Ernie Pyle Award, $1,000: Bob Morris, *Fort Myers* (Fla.) *News-Press;* Edward J. Meeman Conservation Award: grand prize, $2,500: Rod Nordland, Josh Friedman, *Philadelphia Inquirer;* first place, $1,000: Jim Adams, Jim Detjen, *Louisville Courier-Journal;* Chris Conway, John Schneller, Nick Kelsch, *Columbia* (Mo.) *Daily Tribune;* Edward Willis Scripps First Amendment Award, $2,500: David Chandler, *Norfolk* (Va.) *Ledger-Star;* Roy W. Howard Public Service Award, $2,500: Gordon Eliot White, Monroe News Bureau.

Sigma Delta Chi Awards, by the Society of Professional Journalists (1979): general reporting: Gene Miller, Carl Hiaasen, Patrick Malone, William D. Montalbano, *Miami* (Fla.) *Herald;* editorial writing: Rick Sinding, *Hackensack* (N.J.) *Record;* Washington correspondence: Gordon Eliot White, *Deseret News,* Salt Lake City, Ut.; foreign correspondence: Karen DeYoung, *Washington Post;* news photography: Eddie Adams, Associated Press; editorial cartoon: John P. Trever, Albuquerque Journal; public service in newspaper journalism: *Miami* (Fla.) *Herald;* public service in magazine journalism: *National Geographic;* magazine reporting: Michael W. Vargo, *Pennsylvania Illustrated;* research about journalism: Lloyd Wendt, Sarasota, Fla.

Merriman Smith Award, for Presidential print news coverage, by Merriman Smith Memorial Fund (1979), $750: Edward J. Walsh, *Washington Post;* Carl Leubsdorf, *Baltimore Sun.*

Edward Weintal Prizes, for U.S. foreign policy reporting and analysis (1979), $5,000: Richard Dudman, *St. Louis Post-Dispatch;* Joseph Hirsch, *Christian Science Monitor.*

William Allen White Citation, fo service to the community and the profession of journalism, by University of Kansas (1979): Eugene Patterson, *St. Petersburg* (Fla.) *Times.*

John Peter Zenger Award, for service in behalf of freedom of the press (1979), $500: Robert H. Estabrook, *Lakeville* (Conn.) *Journal.*

Broadcasting and Theater Awards

American Academy and Institute of Arts and Letters Gold Medal for Drama: Edward Albee.

Susan Smith Blackburn Playwriting Prize, $2,000: Barbara Schneider, *Details Without a Map.*

Clarion Awards, by Women in Communication (1979): radio documentary: Amy Sabrin, Patti Berman, Associated Press Network, Wash., D.C., "Minus Three and Counting"; Jack Miller, Marc J. Weiner, WCBS/FM "CBS/FM Remembers Elvis"; Beryl Pfizer, Hank Miles, NBC, New York, "Killer Cargo"; John Merrow, Barbara Reinhardt, National Public Radio, Wash., D.C., "Colleges Today: Women's Colleges"; radio series: David Ross, KIRO Newsradio 71, Seattle, "Northwest Journal: Police Shootings"; Irene Cornell, WCBS Newsradio 88, New York, "Running on Borrowed Time"; Robert Hyland, KMOX Radio, St. Louis, "At Your Service Goes to Washington"; television documentary: CBS, New York, "The Defection of Simas Kudirka"; CBS, New York, "The Body Human: The Red River"; Office of Telecommunications, Smithsonian Institution, Wash., D.C., "The Smithsonian Institution with S. Dillon Ripley, Secretary"; television series: Herbert Brodkin, Robert Berger, NBC, New York, "Holocaust"; Paula Woodward, Sam Allen, KBTV, Denver, "The Scarlet R"; Dan Sitarski, Erna Akuginow, WCAU-TV, Philadelphia, "Eye On. . .The Lessons of the Holocaust"; Darrell Barton, Ron Turner, KTVY, Oklahoma City, "Essays"; Patricia Lynch, NBC, New York, NBC Nightly News, "Synanon."

Clarence Derwent Awards, by Actors Equity, for most promising actors $1,000 each: Dianne Wiest, *The Art of Dining;* Eric Peterson, *Billy Bishop Goes to War.*

Alfred E. duPont-Columbia Univ. Awards in Broadcast Journalism: KCTS-TV, Seattle, "Do I Look Like I Want to Die"; KDFW-TV, Dallas, for reporting on aliens and children; KUTV, Salt Lake City, for "Clouds of Doubt"; KXL Radio, Portland, Ore., "The Air Space—How Safe?"; WGBH-TV, Boston, "World/Inside Europe: F-16 Sale of the Century"; WHA-TV, Madison, Wis., Catalyst Films and Wisconsin Educational TV Network, "An American Ism: Joe McCarthy"; ABC News, "Closeup—Arson: Fire for Hire!"; ABC News, "World News Tonight—Second to None"; CBS News, "CBS Reports—the Boat People"; CBS News, "60 Minutes"; Bill D. Moyers, CBS-TV, WNET-TV, reporting.

Gavel Awards, by American Bar Association, for coverage of justice system (1979): television: CBS News, "The Politics of Abortion"; WBBM-TV, Chicago, "The public Guardian"; KTLA/Golden West Broadcasters, Los Angeles, "Scared Straight"; WDBO-TV/Channel 6, Orlando, Fla., "Cameras in the Courtroom"; WPBT, No. Miami, Fla., "TV on Trial"; radio: KMOX, St. Louis, Mo., "In the Common Good"; WRFM, New York, "What Eric Learned in Jail Today"; WNCI, Columbus, Oh., "What Are They Doing to Our Children?"; WGIR, Boston, "A Night with the Manchester Police Department"; KHVH, Honolulu, "The Law Report"; National Public Radio, "The Supreme Court Reporting/Nina Totenberg"; Pacifica KPFA-FM, Los Angeles, documentary series on civil liberties.

Roy W. Howard Public Service Award, by Scripps-Howard Foundation, $2,500: Jack Bowen, KOCO-TV, Oklahoma City, "Wednesday's Child."

Robert F. Kennedy Journalism Awards, for coverage of problems of disadvantaged (1979), $1,000: radio: Greg Barron, David Carlton Felland, KSJN, Minnesota Public Radio; television: Howard Husock, WGBH, Boston.

George Jean Nathan Award, for dramatic criticism, $7,500: Jack Kroll, *Newsweek.*

New York Drama Critics Circle Awards: play: Lanford Wilson, *Talley's Folly;* musical: Andrew Lloyd Weber, Tim Rice, *Evita;* foreign play: Harold Pinter, *Betrayal;* special citation: Peter Brook's Le Centre International de Creations Theatrales.

New York Film Critics Awards: best actor: Dustin Hoffman, *Kramer vs. Kramer;* best actress: Sally Field, *Norma Rae;* supporting actor: Melvyn Douglas, *Being There;* supporting actress: Meryl Streep, *Kramer vs. Kramer;* director: Woody Allen, *Manhattan.*

Obie Awards, for Off-Broadway and Off-Off-Broadway theater: playwrights: Lee Breuer, *A Prelude to Death in Venice;* Christopher Durang, *Sister Mary Ignatius Explains It All For You;* Romulus Linney, *Tennessee;* Roland Muldoon, *Full Confessions of a Socialist;* Jeff Weiss, *That's How the Rent Gets Paid* (Part III); performers: Michael Burrell, *Hess;* Michael Cristofer, *Chinchilla;* Lindsay Crouse, *Reunion;* Elizabeth Franz, *Sister Mary Ignatius Explains It All for You;* Morgan Freeman, *Mother Courage* and *Coriolanus;* John Heard, *Othello* and *Split;* Michael Higgins, *Reunion;* Madeleine Le Roux, *La Justice;* Jon Polito, performances with Dodger Theater and BAM Theater Companies; Bill Raymond, *A Prelude to Death in Venice;* Dianne Wiest, *The Art of Dining;* Hattie Winston, *Mother Courage* and *The Michigan;* directors: A.J. Antoon, *The Art of Dining;* Edward Cornell, *Johnny on a Spot;* Elizabeth LaCompte, *Point Judith;* designers: Ruth Maleczech, Julie Archer, *Vanishing Pictures;* Sally Jacobs, *Conference of the Birds;* Beverly Emmons, lighting design; Laura Crow, costumes, *Mary Stuart.*

Antoinette Perry Awards (Tonys): play: Mark Medoff, *Children of a Lesser God;* musical: *Evita;* book of a musical: Tim Rice, *Evita;* score of a musical: Andrew Lloyd Weber, Tim Rice, *Evita;* actor, play: John Rubenstein, *Children of a Lesser God;* actress, play: Phyllis Frelich, *Children of a Lesser God;* actor, musical: Jim Dale, *Barnum;* actress, musical: Patti LuPone, *Evita;* featured actor, play: David Rounds, *Morning's at Seven;* featured actress, play: Priscilla Lopez, *A Day in Hollywood/A Night in the Ukraine;* director, play: Vivian Matalon, *Morning's at Seven;* director, musical: Harold Prince, *Evita;* scenic designer: John Lee Beatty, *Talley's Folly,* tied with David Mitchell, *Barnum;* costume designer: Theoni V. Aldredge, *Barnum;* lighting designer: David Hersey, *Evita;* choreographer: Tommy Tune, Thommie Walsh, *A Day in Hollywood/A Night in the Ukraine;* revival: *Morning's At Seven;* special awards: Actors Theater, Louisville; Goodspeed Opera House; Mary Tyler Moore; Lawrence Langner Award for Distinguished Achievement: Helen Hayes; Theater Award '80: Hobe Morrison, *Variety;* Richard Fitzgerald, Sound Associates.

Theater Hall of Fame: Harold Arlen, Boris Aronson, Leonard Bernstein, Ray Bolger, Abe Burrows, Morris Carnovsky, Harold Clurman, Cheryl Crawford, Maurice Evans, Bob Fosse, Julie Harris, Rex Harrison, Lotte Lenya, Alan Jay Lerner, Frederick Loewe, David Merrick, Arthur Miller, Geraldine Page, Jose Quintero, Sir Ralph Richardson, Jason Robards, Jessica Tandy, Tennessee Williams, Irene Worth, Ira Aldridge, Ned Harrigan, Tony Hart, William Inge, Lawrence Langner, Frank Loesser, Zero Mostel, Margaret Webster.

Miscellaneous Awards

Achievement in Life Award, by Encyclopaedia Britannica: exploration/business: Col. Frank Borman; journalism: Norman Cousins; science and medicine: Dr. Michael E. DeBakey; television: Hugh Downs; performing arts: Ella Fitzgerald; music: Benny Goodman; sports: Red Kelly; literature: James Michener; education: Dr. Edmund D. Pellegrino.

American Academy and Institute of Arts and Letters Awards in Art, $4,000 each: Richard Anuszkiewicz, Edward Dugmore, Marion Lerner Levine, Charmion von Wiegand,

Howard Newman; Richard and Hinda Rosenthal Foundation Award, $3,000: Dolores Milmoe; Marjorie Peabody Award, $1,500: Sidney Laufman; Gold Medal: Peggy Bacon.

American Academy and Institute of Arts and Letters Awards in Music, $4,000 each: Donald Grantham, Eugene O'Brien, Malcolm C. Peyton, Lawrence L. Widdoes; Charles Ives Scholarships, $4,000 each: Thomas E. Barber, Laura Clayton, Lowell Lieberman, William Maiben, Mario H. Pelusi, George Tsontakis; Goddard Lieberson Fellowships, $10,000 each: David Chaitkin, Robert Xavier Rodriguez.

American College Theatre Festival Awards: national playwriting: Lee Blessing, Univ. of Iowa, Iowa City; Norman Lear Comedy Playwrighting: Peter Baloff, Univ. of Florida, Gainesville; Lorraine Hansberry Award: Richard Russell, San Jose (Cal.) State Univ.; Daniel Du Plantis, Nicholls State Univ., Thibodaux, La.; David Library of American Revolution Award: Peter Baloff, Univ. of Florida; Irene Ryan Scholarships: Sharon Rolf, Univ. of Evansville (Ind.); Larry LoVerde, Rhode Island College, Providence, R.I.; ACTF-Critics Institute Scholarship: Gerard W. Pauwells, Indiana Univ., Bloomington; ACTF Awards for Theatrical Design: set: William Buckingham, Univ. of Minnesota; costume: Jeffrey Ross Struckman, Webster College, St. Louis, Mo.

American Institute for Public Service Awards: Jefferson Awards, $5,000 each: Cyrus R. Vance; U.S. Olympic hockey team; by private citizen: Dr. Norman Borlaugh, International Maize and Wheat Improvement Center; benefit to disadvantaged: Allard K. Lowenstein; benefit to communities, $1,000 each: John Carpenter, Heaven on Earth Ranch, Cal.; Elaine Griebenow, Minneapolis; Tilda Kemplen, Mountain Communities Child Care Development Centers, Tenn.; Lee Klein, Deed Club Children's Cancer Clinic, Univ. of Miami, Fla.; Dr. Louis Matucci, The Bridge at Fox Chase, Phila., Pa.

America's Next Great Designer Award, by Intl. Ladies Garment Workers Union: Ernest Harris.

Association for Retarded Citizens Achievement Awards: media: ABC-TV; national TV: "One Day at a Time"; national print: *Patient Care;* community media: *Detroit News;* community TV: KETV, Omaha, Neb.; community print: *General News,* General Telephone Co., Everett, Wash.; teacher: Nancy Fischer, Warren School, Warren, Ore.; educator: Dr. Claudine Sherrill, Texas Women's Univ., Denton; Boggs Award in recreation: Mankato, Minn. Assoc. for Retarded Citizens; Mitchell Award in recreation: Arlington, Mass.

Capezio Dance Award by Capezio Foundation, $1,000: Walter Terry.

Dance Magazine Awards (1979): Erick Hawkins; Aaron Copland; Jorge Donn.

Albert Einstein Peace Prize, $50,000: Alva Myrdal.

Avery Fisher Prize, for American instrumentalist, $5,000: Richard Goode.

Jefferson Lecturer, National Endowment for the Humanities, $10,000 : Barbara Tuchman.

Kennedy Center Honors Awards, for lifetime achievement in performing arts: Aaron Copland, Henry Fonda, Martha Graham, Tennessee Williams, Ella Fitzgerald.

John F. Kennedy Center/Rockefeller Foundation International Competition Winner: Bradford Gowen, pianist.

National Black Music Colloquium and Competition, $2,000 each: piano: Alison Deane; string-instrument: John Clayton, Marcus Thompson.

National Society of Film Critics Awards (1979): film: *Breaking Away;* actor: Dustin Hoffman, *Kramer vs. Kramer* and *Agatha;* actress: Sally Field, *Norma Rae;* director: Woody Allen, *Manhattan* and Robert Benton, *Kramer vs. Kramer;* supporting actor: Frederic Forrest, *Apocalypse Now* and *The Rose;* supporting actress: Meryl Streep, *Manhattan, Kramer vs. Kramer,* and *The Seduction of Joe Tynan;* cinematography: Caleb Deschanel, *The Black Stallion* and *Being There;* screenplay: Steve Tesich, *Breaking Away.*

National Spelling Bee Champion, by Scripps-Howard Newspapers: Jacques Bailly, *Rocky Mountain News.*

Record of the Year Award, by *Stereo Review:* Award of Merit: Earl "Fatha" Hines.

Rhode Island School of Design President's Fellows Awards: Diana Vreeland, Ellsworth Kelly, Roy Hamilton, Warren Platner, Container Corp. of America.

Society of Publication Designers Gold Medals: cover design: Jerelle Kraus, *New York Times; Art Direction;* overall design: *Family in Distress;* single-issue: *Metropolitan Museum of Art Bulletin; National Lampoon;* story presentation: *Audubon;* illustration, single spread: *Playboy;* illustration, story presentation: *The Lamp;* photography, single spread: *Rolling Stone;* photography, story presentation: *New York.*

Templeton Prize for Progress in Religion, by John M. Templeton Foundation, $206,000: Ralph Wendell Burhoe.

Westinghouse Science Talent Search, $12,000 each: Lisa J. Randall, Queens, New York, and John M. Andersland, East Lansing, Mich.

Motion Picture Academy Awards (Oscars)

1927-28
Actor: Emil Jannings, *The Way of All Flesh.*
Actress: Janet Gaynor, *Seventh Heaven.*
Picture: *Wings,* Paramount.

1928-29
Actor: Warner Baxter, *In Old Arizona.*
Actress: Mary Pickford, *Coquette.*
Picture: *Broadway Melody,* MGM.

1929-30
Actor: George Arliss, *Disraeli.*
Actress: Norma Shearer, *The Divorcee.*
Picture: *All Quiet on the Western Front,* Univ.

1930-31
Actor: Lionel Barrymore, *Free Soul.*
Actress: Marie Dressler, *Min and Bill.*
Picture: *Cimarron,* RKO.

1931-32
Actor: Fredric March, *Dr. Jekyll and Mr. Hyde;* Wallace Beery, *The Champ* (tie).
Actress: Helen Hayes, *Sin of Madelon Claudet.*
Picture: *Grand Hotel,* MGM.
Special: Walt Disney, *Mickey Mouse.*

1932-33
Actor: Charles Laughton, *Private Life of Henry VIII.*
Actress: Katharine Hepburn, *Morning Glory.*
Picture: *Cavalcade,* Fox.

1934
Actor: Clark Gable, *It Happened One Night.*
Actress: Claudette Colbert, same.
Picture: *It Happened One Night,* Columbia.

1935
Actor: Victor McLaglen, *The Informer.*
Actress: Bette Davis, *Dangerous.*
Picture: *Mutiny on the Bounty,* MGM.

1936
Actor: Paul Muni, *Story of Louis Pasteur.*
Actress: Luise Rainer, *The Great Ziegfeld.*
Picture: *The Great Ziegfeld,* MGM.

1937
Actor: Spencer Tracy, *Captains Courageous.*
Actress: Luise Rainer, *The Good Earth.*
Picture: *Life of Emile Zola,* Warner.

1938
Actor: Spencer Tracy, *Boys Town.*
Actress: Bette Davis, *Jezebel.*
Picture: *You Can't Take It With You,* Columbia.

1939
Actor: Robert Donat, *Goodbye Mr. Chips.*
Actress: Vivien Leigh, *Gone With the Wind.*
Picture: *Gone With the Wind,* Selznick International.

1940
Actor: James Stewart, *The Philadelphia Story.*
Actress: Ginger Rogers, *Kitty Foyle.*
Picture: *Rebecca,* Selznick International.

1941
Actor: Gary Cooper, *Sergeant York.*
Actress: Joan Fontaine, *Suspicion.*
Picture: *How Green Was My Valley,* 20th Cent.-Fox.

1942
Actor: James Cagney, *Yankee Doodle Dandy.*

Actress: Greer Garson, *Mrs. Miniver.*
Picture: *Mrs. Miniver,* MGM.

1943

Actor: Paul Lukas, *Watch on the Rhine.*
Actress: Jennifer Jones, *The Song of Bernadette.*
Picture: *Casablanca,* Warner.

1944

Actor: Bing Crosby, *Going My Way.*
Actress: Ingrid Bergman, *Gaslight.*
Picture: *Going My Way,* Paramount.

1945

Actor: Ray Milland, *The Lost Weekend.*
Actress: Joan Crawford, *Mildred Pierce.*
Picture: *The Lost Weekend,* Paramount.

1946

Actor: Fredric March, *Best Years of Our Lives.*
Actress: Olivia de Havilland, *To Each His Own.*
Picture: *The Best Years of Our Lives,* Goldwyn, RKO.

1947

Actor: Ronald Colman, *A Double Life.*
Actress: Loretta Young, *The Farmer's Daughter.*
Picture: *Gentleman's Agreement,* 20th Cent.-Fox.

1948

Actor: Laurence Olivier, *Hamlet.*
Actress: Jane Wyman, *Johnny Belinda.*
Picture: *Hamlet,* Two Cities Film, Universal International.

1949

Actor: Broderick Crawford. *All the King's Men.*
Actress: Olivia de Havilland, *The Heiress.*
Picture: *All the King's Men,* Columbia.

1950

Actor: Jose Ferrer, *Cyrano de Bergerac.*
Actress: Judy Holliday, *Born Yesterday.*
Picture: *All About Eve,* 20th Century-Fox.

1951

Actor: Humphrey Bogart, *The African Queen.*
Actress: Vivien Leigh, *A Streetcar Named Desire.*
Picture: *An American in Paris,* MGM.

1952

Actor: Gary Cooper, *High Noon.*
Actress: Shirley Booth, *Come Back, Little Sheba.*
Picture: *Greatest Show on Earth,* C.B. DeMille, Paramount.

1953

Actor: William Holden, *Stalag 17.*
Actress: Audrey Hepburn, *Roman Holiday.*
Picture: *From Here to Eternity,* Columbia.

1954

Actor: Marlon Brando, *On the Waterfront.*
Actress: Grace Kelly, *The Country Girl.*
Picture: *On the Waterfront,* Horizon-American, Colum.

1955

Actor: Ernest Borgnine, *Marty.*
Actress: Anna Magnani, *The Rose Tattoo.*
Picture: *Marty,* Hecht and Lancaster's Steven Prods., U.A.

1956

Actor: Yul Brynner, *The King and I.*
Actress: Ingrid Bergman, *Anastasia.*
Picture: *Around the World in 80 Days,* Michael Todd, U.A.

1957

Actor: Alec Guinness, *The Bridge on the River Kwai.*
Actress: Joanne Woodward, *The Three Faces of Eve.*
Picture: *The Bridge on the River Kwai,* Columbia.

1958

Actor: David Niven, *Separate Tables.*
Actress: Susan Hayward, *I Want to Live.*
Picture: *Gigi,* Arthur Freed Production, MGM.

1959

Actor: Charlton Heston, *Ben-Hur.*
Actress: Simone Signoret, *Room at the Top.*
Picture: *Ben-Hur,* MGM.

1960

Actor: Burt Lancaster, *Elmer Gantry.*
Actress: Elizabeth Taylor, *Butterfield 8.*
Picture: *The Apartment,* Mirisch Co., U.A.

1961

Actor: Maximilian Schell, *Judgment at Nuremberg.*
Actress: Sophia Loren, *Two Women.*
Picture: *West Side Story,* United Artists.

1962

Actor: Gregory Peck, *To Kill a Mockingbird.*
Actress: Anne Bancroft, *The Miracle Worker.*
Picture: *Lawrence of Arabia,* Columbia.

1963

Actor: Sidney Poitier, *Lilies of the Field.*
Actress: Patricia Neal, *Hud.*
Picture: *Tom Jones,* Woodfall Prod., UA-Lopert Pictures.

1964

Actor: Rex Harrison, *My Fair Lady.*
Actress: Julie Andrews, *Mary Poppins.*
Picture: *My Fair Lady,* Warner Bros.

1965

Actor: Lee Marvin, *Cat Ballou.*
Actress: Julie Christie, *Darling.*
Picture: *The Sound of Music,* 20th Century-Fox.

1966

Actor: Paul Scofield, *A Man for All Seasons.*
Actress: Elizabeth Taylor, *Who's Afraid of Virginia Woolf?*
Picture: *A Man for All Seasons,* Columbia.

1967

Actor: Rod Steiger, *In the Heat of the Night.*
Actress: Katharine Hepburn, *Guess Who's Coming to Dinner.*
Picture: *In the Heat of the Night.*

1968

Actor: Cliff Robertson, *Charly.*
Actress: Katharine Hepburn, *The Lion in Winter;* Barbra Streisand, *Funny Girl* (tie).
Picture: *Oliver.*

1969

Actor: John Wayne, *True Grit.*
Actress: Maggie Smith, *The Prime of Miss Jean Brodie.*
Picture: *Midnight Cowboy.*

1970

Actor: George C. Scott, *Patton* (refused).
Actress: Glenda Jackson, *Women in Love.*
Picture: *Patton.*

1971

Actor: Gene Hackman, *The French Connection.*
Actress: Jane Fonda, *Klute.*
Picture: *The French Connection.*

1972

Actor: Marlon Brando, *The Godfather* (refused).
Actress: Liza Minnelli, *Cabaret.*
Picture: *The Godfather.*

1973

Actor: Jack Lemmon, *Save the Tiger.*
Actress: Glenda Jackson, *A Touch of Class.*
Picture: *The Sting.*

1974

Actor: Art Carney, *Harry and Tonto.*
Actress: Ellen Burstyn, *Alice Doesn't Live Here Anymore.*
Picture: *The Godfather, Part II.*

1975

Actor: Jack Nicholson, *One Flew Over the Cuckoo's Nest.*
Actress: Louise Fletcher, same.
Picture: *One Flew Over the Cuckoo's Nest.*

1976

Actor: Peter Finch, *Network.*
Actress: Faye Dunaway, same.
Picture: *Rocky.*

1977

Actor: Richard Dreyfuss, *The Goodbye Girl.*
Actress: Diane Keaton, *Annie Hall.*
Picture: *Annie Hall.*

1978

Actor: Jon Voight, *Coming Home.*
Actress: Jane Fonda, *Coming Home.*
Picture: *The Deer Hunter.*

1979

Actor: Dustin Hoffman, *Kramer vs. Kramer.*
Actress: Sally Field, *Norma Rae.*
Picture: *Kramer vs. Kramer.*
Foreign Film: *The Tin Drum.*
Director: Robert Benton, *Kramer vs. Kramer.*
Supporting Actor: Melvyn Douglas, *Being There.*
Supporting Actress: Meryl Streep, *Kramer vs. Kramer.*
Screenplay: (original) Steven Tesich, *Breaking Away;* (adapted) Robert Benton, *Kramer vs. Kramer.*
Cinematography: Vittorio Storaro, *Apocalypse Now.*
Score: (original) George Delerue, *A Little Romance.* (adapted) Ralph Burns, *All That Jazz.*
Song: It Goes Like It Goes, *Norma Rae.*
Art Direction: Philip Rosenberg, Tony Walton, Edward Stewart, Gary Brink, *All That Jazz.*
Costumes: Albert Wolsky, *All That Jazz.*
Sound: Walter Murch, Mark Berger, Richard Beggs, Nat Boxer, *Apocalypse Now.*
Visual effects: H.R. Giger, Carlo Rambaldi, Brian Johnson, Nich Allder, Denys Ayling, *Alien.*

Canadian Film Awards

Source: Canadian Film Institute

1969

Actor: Chris Wiggins, The Best Damn Fiddler From Calabogie to Kaladar
Actress: Jackie Burroughs, Dulcima
Picture: The Best Damn Fiddler from Calabogie to Kaladar

1970

Actor: Doug McGrath and Paul Bradley (tied), Goin' Down the Road
Actress: Genevieve Bujold, Act of the Heart
Picture: Psychocratie

1971

Actor: Jean Duceppe, Mon oncle Antoine
Actress: Ann Knox, The Only Thing You Know
Picture: Mon oncle Antoine

1972

Actor: Gordon Pinsent, The Rowdyman
Actress: Micheline Lanctot, Vrai nature de Bernadette
Picture: Wedding in White

1973

Actor: Jacques Godin, O.K. Laliberte
Actress: Genevieve Bujold, Kamouraska
Picture: Slipstream

1974

No awards

1975

Actor: Stuart Gillard, Why Rock the Boat?
Actress: Margot Kidder, Black Christmas and A Quiet Day in Belfast
Picture: Les Ordres
Film of the Year: The Apprenticeship of Duddy Kravitz

1976

Actor: Andre Melancon, Partis pur la gloire
Actress: Marilyn Lightstone, Lies My Father Told Me
Picture: Lies My Father Told Me

1977

Actor: Len Cariou, One Man
Actress: Monique Mercure, J.A. Martin: Photographe
Picture: J.A. Martin: Photographe

1978

Actor: Richard Gabourie, Three Card Monte
Actress: Helen Shaver, In Praise of Older Women
Picture: The Silent Partner

1979

Actor: Christopher Plummer, Murder By Decree
Actress: Kate Lynch, Meatballs
Picture: The Changeling

The Spingarn Medal

The Spingarn Medal has been awarded annually since 1914 by the National Association for the Advancement of Colored People for the highest achievement by a black American.

1946 Dr. Percy L. Julian
1947 Channing H. Tobias
1948 Ralph J. Bunche
1949 Charles Hamilton Houston
1950 Mabel Keaton Staupers
1951 Harry T. Moore
1952 Paul R. Williams
1953 Theodore K. Lawless
1954 Carl Murphy
1955 Jack Roosevelt Robinson
1956 Martin Luther King Jr.
1957 Mrs. Daisy Bates and the Little Rock Nine
1958 Edward Kennedy (Duke) Ellington
1959 Langston Hughes
1960 Kenneth B. Clark
1961 Robert C. Weaver
1962 Medgar Wiley Evers
1963 Roy Wilkins
1964 Leontyne Price
1965 John H. Johnson
1966 Edward W. Brooke
1967 Sammy Davis Jr.
1968 Clarence M. Mitchell Jr.
1969 Jacob Lawrence
1970 Leon Howard Sullivan
1971 Gordon Parks
1972 Wilson C. Riles
1973 Damon Keith
1974 Henry (Hank) Aaron
1975 Alvin Ailey
1976 Alex Haley
1977 Andrew Young
1978 Mrs. Rosa L. Parks
1979 Dr. Rayford W. Logan

National Teacher of the Year Award

Awarded by the Council of Chief State School Officers, Encyclopaedia Britannica, and the Ladies' Home Journal for service in elementary and secondary schools until 1980, when awarded by Council, Britannica, and Good Housekeeping magazine.

1966 Mona Dayton, first grade, Walter Douglas Elementary, Tucson, Ariz.
1967 Roger Tenney, music, Owatonna Junior-Senior H.S., Owatonna, Minn.
1968 David E. Graf, vocational education & industrial arts, Sandwich Comm. H.S., Sandwich, Ill.
1969 Barbara Goleman, language arts, Miami Jackson H.S., Miami, Fla.
1970 Johnnie T. Dennis, physics, math analysis, Walla Walla H.S., Walla Walla, Wash.
1971 Martha Marion Stringfellow, first grade, Lewisville Elementary, Chester Co., S.C.
1972 James Marshall Rogers, American history & Black studies, Durham H.S., Raleigh, N.C.
1973 John A. Ensworth, sixth grade, Kenwood School, Bend, Ore.
1974 Vivian Tom, social studies, Lincoln H.S. Yonkers, N.Y.
1975 Robert G. Heyer, science, Johanna Junior H.S., St. Paul, Minn.
1976 Ruby S. Murchison, social studies, Washington Drive J.H.S., Fayetteville, N.C.
1977 Myrra Leonore Lee, social studies, Helix H.S., La Mesa, Cal.
1978 Elaine Barbour, Coal Creek Elementary, Montrose, Col.
1979 Marilyn Williams Black, art, Bernice A. Ray Elementary, Hanover, N.H.
1980 Beverly Bimes, Hazelwood East H.S., St. Louis, Mo.

The Molson Prize

The Molson Prizes are given annually for outstanding contributions in the arts, humanities or social sciences. The prizes, worth $20,000 each, are financed from an endowment established by the Molson Foundation.

1966 Rev. Georges-Henri Levesque; H. McLennan
1967 Arthur Erickson; Anne Hebert; Marshall McLuhan
1968 Glenn Gould; Jean Le Moyne
1969 Jean-Paul Audet; Morley Callaghan; Arnold Spohr
1970 Northrop Frye; Duncan Macpherson; Yves Pheriault
1971 Maureen Forrester; Rina Lasnier; Norman McLaren
1972 John Deutsch; Alfred Pellan; George Woodcock
1973 W.A.C.H. Dobson; Celia Franca; Jean-Paul Lemieux
1974 Alex Colville, Margaret Laurence; Pierre Dansereau
1975 Jon Vickers; Denise Pelletier; the Orford String Quartet: Andrew Dawes; Terrence Helmer; Kenneth Perkins and Marcel St-Cyr
1976 John Hirsch; Bill Reid; Jean-Louis Roux
1977 Gabrielle Roy; Jack Shadbolt; George Story
1978 Jean Duceppe; Betty Oliphant; Michael Snow
1979 Michel Brault, Lois Marshall, Robert Weaver

ARTS AND MEDIA

Notable New York Theater Openings, 1979-80 Season

A Day in Hollywood/A Night in the Ukraine, musical-comedy by Dick Vosburgh and Frank Lazarus; with Priscilla Lopez, Frank Lazarus, and David Garrison.

Barnum, musical by Cy Coleman and Michael Stewart based on the life of the 19th-century showman; with Jim Dale.

Bent, drama by Martin Sherman about 2 homosexual German refugees in a Nazi concentration camp; with Richard Gere and David Dukes.

Betrayal, play by Harold Pinter about an affair; with Blythe Danner, Roy Scheider, and Raul Julia.

Billy Bishop Goes to War, musical by Joan Gray and Eric Peterson about Canada's World War 1 flying ace; with Eric Peterson.

Camelot, revival of the Lerner and Loewe musical; with Richard Burton.

Children of a Lesser God, play by Mark Medoff about a speech therapist who falls in love with one of his deaf patients; with John Rubinstein and Phyllis Frelich.

Clothes For a Summer Hotel, drama by Tennessee Williams based on the later years of F. Scott and Zelda Fitzgerald; with Geraldine Page and Kenneth Haigh.

Devour the Snow, play by Abe Polsky; with Kevin O'-Connor, Stephen Joyce, and Jon DeVries.

Every Good Boy Deserves Favour, comedy by Tom Stoppard; with Eli Wallach and Rene Auberjonois.

Evita, musical by Andrew Lloyd Webber and Tim Rice about the life of Eva Peron; with Patti LuPone.

Fearless Frank, musical by Andrew Davies and Dave Brown based on the life of Frank Harris; with Niall Toibin.

Goodbye Fidel, drama by Howard Sackler about wealthy Cuban exiles; with Jane Alexander.

Happy New Year, musical based on "Holiday" by Philip Barry, with selected songs of Cole Porter.

Harold and Maude, play by Colin Higgins; with Janet Gaynor, Keith McDermott, and Ruth Ford.

Hide and Seek, thriller by Lezley Havard; with Elizabeth Ashley and David Ackroyd.

Home, play by Samm-Art Williams about a young black man who leaves the South to live in a northern city; with Charles Brown and L. Scott Caldwell.

Horowitz and Mrs. Washington, comedy by Henry Denker about an elderly widower and his black nurse; with Sam Levene and Esther Rolle.

I Ought to Be in Pictures, comedy by Neil Simon about a screenwriter's reunion with the daughter he deserted 16 years earlier; with Ron Leibman, Dinah Manoff, and Joyce Van Patten.

Last Licks, play by Frank D. Gilroy; with Ed Flanders and Susan Kellerman.

Morning's at Seven, revival of the Paul Osborn play about 4 elderly sisters; with Teresa Wright, Maureen O'Sullivan, Nancy Marchand, Elizabeth Wilson, and Gary Merrill.

Night and Day, comedy-drama by Tom Stoppard set in an African nation of the brink of civil war; with Maggie Smith.

Oklahoma!, revival of the Rodgers and Hammerstein musical; with Laurence Guittard and Christine Andreas.

Once a Catholic, comedy by Mary O'Malley about students at a Roman Catholic school; with Rachel Roberts, Peggy Cass, and Mia Dillon.

Othello, Shakespeare's tragedy; with Richard Dreyfuss and Raul Julia.

Peter Pan, revival of the James M. Barrie classic; with Sandy Duncan.

Romantic Comedy, play by Bernard Slade about a dramatist and his attraction for his female theatrical collaborator; with Anthony Perkins and Mia Farrow.

Sugar Babies, burlesque musical which takes place from 1900 to 1930; with Mickey Rooney and Ann Miller.

Talley's Folly, play by Lanford Wilson about a wartime romance between a Jewish man and a Missouri woman; with Judd Hirsch, Trish Hawkins.

The Lady from Dubuque, play by Edward Albee about 3 couples visited by an older woman; with Irene Worth.

The Most Happy Fella, revival of the Frank Loesser musical; with Giorgio Tozzi.

The Music Man, revival of the Meredith Willson musical; with Dick Van Dyke.

Watch on the Rhine, revival of the Lillian Hellman play; with Joyce Ebert and George Hearn.

West Side Story, revival of the Leonard Bernstein, Stephen Sondheim musical; with Ken Marshall and Jossie de Guzman.

Record Long Run Broadway Plays *Still Running July 26, 1980

Grease	3,388
Fiddler on the Roof	3,242
Life With Father	3,224
Tobacco Road	3,182
Hello Dolly	2,844
My Fair Lady	2,717
Man of La Mancha	2,329
Abie's Irish Rose	2,327
Oklahoma!	2,212
*Chorus Line	2,059
Pippin	1,900
Magic Show	1,859
Harvey	1,775
Hair	1,742
South Pacific	1,694
The Wiz	1,666
Born Yesterday	1,643
*Oh! Calcutta! (Revival)	1,614
Mary, Mary	1,572
Voice of the Turtle	1,557
Barefoot in the Park	1,532
Mame	1,508
Arsenic and Old Lace	1,444
Same Time, Next Year	1,444
The Sound of Music	1,443
How To Succeed in Business Without Really Trying	1,417
Hellzapoppin	1,404
The Music Man	1,375
*Annie	1,365
Funny Girl	1,348
*Gemini	1,333
Oh! Calcutta!	1,316
Angel Street	1,295
Lightnin'	1,291
Promises, Promises	1,281
The King and I	1,246
Cactus Flower	1,234
Sleuth	1,222
"1776"	1,217
Equus	1,207
Guys and Dolls	1,200
Cabaret	1,166
Mister Roberts	1,157
Annie Get Your Gun	1,147
Butterflies Are Free	1,128
Pins and Needles	1,108
Plaza Suite	1,097
Kiss Me Kate	1,070

Plays in London *Still running June 28, 1980

*The Mousetrap	11,474
Black and White Minstrels	4,354
Oh! Calcutta!	3,863
*No Sex Please, We're British	3,788
*Jesus Christ Superstar	3,293
Oliver	2,618
There's a Girl in my Soup	2,547
Pyjama Tops	2,498
Sound of Music	2,386
Sleuth	2,359
Salad Days	2,283
My Fair Lady	2,281
Chu Chin Chow	2,238
Charley Girl	2,202
The Boy Friend	2,084
Canterbury Tales	2,082
Boeing Boeing	2,035

Symphony Orchestras of the U.S. and Canada

Source: American Symphony Orchestra League
(as of March 1980)

Classifications are based on annual incomes or budgets of orchestras.

Major Symphony Orchestras

Orchestra	Address	Conductor
Atlanta Symphony	1280 Peachtree St., NE, Atlanta, GA 30309	Robert Shaw
Baltimore Symphony	1313 St. Paul St., Baltimore, MD 21210	Sergiu Comissiona
Boston Symphony	Symphony Hall, Boston, MA 02115	Seiji Ozawa
Buffalo Philharmonic	26 Richmond Ave., Buffalo, NY 14222	Julius Rudel
Chicago Symphony	220 S. Michigan Ave., Chicago, IL 60604	Sir Georg Solti
Cincinnati Symphony	1241 Elm St., Cincinnati, OH 45210	Michael Gielen
Cleveland Orchestra	11001 Euclid Ave., Cleveland, OH 44106	Lorin Maazel
Dallas Symphony	P.O. Box 26207, Dallas, TX 75226	Eduardo Mata
Denver Symphony	1245 Champa St., Denver, CO 80204	Gaetano Delogu
Detroit Symphony	20 Auditorium Dr., Detroit, MI 48226	Antal Dorati
Honolulu Symphony	1000 Bishop St., Honolulu, HI 96813	Donald Johanas
Houston Symphony	615 Louisiana, Houston, TX 77002	Michael Palmer
Indianapolis Symphony	P.O. Box 88207, Indianapolis, IN 46208	John Nelson
Kansas City Philharmonic	200 W. 14th Street, Kansas City, MO 64105	Maurice Peress
Los Angeles Philharmonic	135 North Grand, Los Angeles, CA 90012	Carlo Giulini
Milwaukee Symphony	929 N. Water St., Milwaukee, WI 53202	Vacant
Minnesota Orchestra	1111 Nicollet Mall, Minneapolis, MN 55403	Neville Marriner
Montreal Symphony	200 de Maisonneuve W., Montreal, Que. H2X 1Y9	Charles Dutoit
National Symphony	JFK Center for the Performing Arts, Wash., DC 20566	Mstislav Rostropovich
New Jersey Symphony	213 Washington St., Newark, NJ 07101	Thomas Michalak
New Orleans Philharmonic	203 Carondelet St., New Orleans, LA 70130	Philippe Entremont
New York Philharmonic	Avery Fisher Hall, New York, NY 10023	Zubin Mehta
North Carolina Symphony	P.O. Box 28026, Raleigh, NC 28026	Lawrence Smith
Philadelphia Orchestra	1420 Locust St., Philadelphia, PA 19102	Eugene Ormandy
Pittsburgh Symphony	600 Penn Ave., Pittsburgh, PA 15222	Andre Previn
Rochester Philharmonic	20 Grove Pl., Rochester, NY 14605	David Zinman
St. Louis Symphony	718 N. Grand Blvd., St. Louis, MO 63103	Leonard Slatkin
San Antonio Symphony	109 Lexington Ave., San Antonio, TX 78205	Lawrence Smith
San Francisco Symphony	107 War Memorial Veterans' Bldg., San Fran., CA 94102	Edo de Waart
Seattle Symphony	305 Harrison St., Seattle, WA 98108	Rainer Miedel
Syracuse Symphony	411 Montgomery St., Syracuse, NY 13202	Christopher Keene
Toronto Symphony	215 Victoria St., Toronto, Ont. M5B 1V1	Andrew Davis
Utah Symphony	123 W. South Temple, Salt Lake City, UT 84101	Varujan Kojian
Vancouver Symphony	873 Beatty St., Vancouver, B.C. V6B 2M6	Kazuyoshi Akiyama

Regional Orchestras

Orchestra	Address	Conductor
Alabama Symphony	2114 First Ave., N., Birmingham, AL 35201	Amerigo Marino
American Symphony	119 W. 57th St., New York, NY 10019	Sergiu Comissiona
Calgary Philharmonic	300-330 9th Ave. SW, Calgary, Alta. T2P 1K7	Arpad Joo
Charlotte Symphony	110 E. 7th Street, Charlotte, NC 28202	Leo Driehuys
Columbus Symphony	101 E. Town St., Columbus, OH 43215	Evan Whallon
Edmonton Symphony Society	11712 87 Avenue, Edmonton, Alta. T6G 0Y3	Yuval Zaliouk
Flint Symphony	1025 E. Kearsley St., Flint, MI 48503	John Covelli
Florida Philharmonic	150 S.E. 2d Ave., Miami, FL 33131	Ranier Meidel
Florida Symphony	P.O. Box 782, Orlando, FL 32802	Pavle Despalj
Fort Worth Symphony	4401 Trail Lake Dr., Fort Worth, TX 76109	John Giordano
Grand Rapids Symphony	Exhibitors Bldg., Grand Rapids, MI 49503	Semyon Bychkov
Hartford Symphony	470 Capitol Ave., Hartford, CT 06106	Arthur Winograd
Hudson Valley Philharmonic	Box 191, Poughkeepsie, NY 12602	Imre Pallo
Jacksonville Symphony	333 Laura St., Jacksonville, FL 32202	Willis Page
Long Beach Symphony	121 Linden Ave., Long Beach, CA 90802	Murry Sidlin
Louisville Orchestra	333 W. Broadway, Louisville, KY 40202	Akira Endo
Memphis Symphony	3100 Walnut Grove Rd., Memphis, TN 38111	Vincent de Frank
Nashville Symphony	1805 West End Ave., Nashville, TN 37203	Michael Charry
Oakland Symphony	P.O. Box 1619, Oakland, CA 94604	Calvin Simmons
Oklahoma Symphony	512 Civic Center Music Hall, Oklahoma City, OK 73102	Luis Herrera dela Fuente
Omaha Symphony	478 Aquila Ct., Omaha, NE 68102	Thomas Briccetti
Oregon Symphony	1119 SW Park Ave., Portland, OR 97205	Lawrence Smith
Phoenix Symphony	6328 N. 7th St., Phoenix, AZ 85014	Theo Alcantara
Puerto Rico Symphony	P.O. Box 2350, San Juan, PR 00936	John Barnett
Quebec Symphony	116, Cote de la Montagne, Quebec G1K 4E5	James De Priest
Richmond Symphony	15 S. Fifth St., Richmond, VA 23219	Jacques Houtmann
San Diego Symphony	P.O. Box 3175, San Diego, CA 92103	Peter Eros
San Jose Symphony	170 Park Center Plaza, San Jose, CA 95112	George Cleve
St. Paul Chamber Orchestra	75 W. Fifth St., St. Paul, MN 55102	Pinchas Zukerman
Toledo Symphony	1 Stranahan Sq., Toledo, OH 43604	Joseph Silverstein
Tulsa Philharmonic	2210 South Main, Tulsa, OK 74114	Joel Lazar
Victoria Symphony	631 Superior St., Victoria, B.C. V8V 1V1	Paul Freeman
Wichita Symphony	225 W. Douglas, Wichita, KS 67202	Michael Palmer
Winnipeg Symphony	555 Main St., Winnipeg, Man. R3B 1C3	Piero Gamba

Metropolitan Orchestras

Orchestra	Address	Conductor
Akron Symphony	Thomas Hall, Hill & Center Sts., Akron, OH 44325	Louis Lane
Alameda County CETA Symphony	680 W. Tennyson Rd., Hayward, CA 94544	Edgar Braun
Albany Symphony	19 Clinton Ave., Albany, NY 12207	Julius Hegyi
Amarillo Symphony	P.O. Box 2552, Amarillo, TX 79105	Thomas Conlin
Arkansas Symphony	604 E. 6th St., Little Rock, AR 72202	Kurt Klippstatter
Austin Symphony	1101 Red River St., Austin, TX 78701	Akira Endo

B.C. Pops Orchestra	233 Main St., Vestal City, NY 13850	David L. Agard
Baton Rouge Symphony	P.O. Box 103, Baton Rouge, LA 70821	James Yestadt
Battle Creek Symphony	P.O. Box 1319, Battle Creek, MI 49016	William Stein
Boise Philharmonic	P.O. Box 2205, Boise, IA 83701	Daniel Stern
(Greater) Bridgeport Symphony	Univ. of Bridgeport, Bridgeport, CT 06602	Gustav Meier
Brooklyn Philharmonia	30 Lafayette Ave., Brooklyn, NY 11217	Lukas Foss
California Chamber Orchestra	6380 Wilshire Blvd., Los Angeles, CA 90048	Henri Temianka
Canton Symphony	1001 Market Ave. N., Canton, OH 44702	Gerhardt Zimmerman
Cedar Rapids Symphony	223 Dows Bldg., Cedar Rapids, IA 52401	Richard D. Williams
Charleston Symphony	1210 Virginia St. E., Charleston, WV 25328	William McNeil
Chattanooga Symphony	730 Cherry St., Chattanooga, TN 37402	Richard Cormier
Chautauqua Symphony	Chautauqua Institute, Chautauqua, NY 14722	Sergiu Comissiona
Chicago Pops Orchestra	100 N. LaSalle St., Chicago, IL 60602	Stanley M. Ackerman
Clarion Music Society	1860 Broadway, New York, NY 10023	Newell Jenkins
Colorado Music Festival	Chautauqua Park, Boulder, CO 80302	Giora Bernstein
Colorado Springs Symphony	P.O. Box 1692, Colorado Springs, CO 80901	Charles Ansbacher
Concerto Soloists of Philadelphia	1732 Spruce St., Philadelphia, PA 19103	Marc Mostovoy
Corpus Christi Symphony	P.O. Box 495, Corpus Christi, TX 78403	Cornelius Eberhardt
County Symphony of Westchester	Box 333, Scarsdale, NY 10583	Stephen Simon
Dayton Philharmonic	210 N. Main St., Dayton, OH 45402	C. Wendelken-Wilson
Delaware Symphony	P.O. Box 1870, Wilmington, DE 19899	Stephen Gunzenhauser
Des Moines Symphony	602 Employers Mutual Bldg., Des Moines, IA 50309	Yuri Krasnapolsky
Duluth-Superior Symphony	506 W. Michigan St., Duluth, MN 55802	Taavo Virkhaus
Eastern Philharmonic	200 N. Davie St., Greensboro, NC 27401	Sheldon Morgenstern
Elkhart Symphony	P.O. Box 144, Elkhart, IN 46514	Michael J. Esselstrom
El Paso Symphony	P.O. Box 180, El Paso, TX 79942	Abraham Chavez Jr.
Erie Philharmonic	409 G. Daniel Baldwin Bldg., Erie, PA 16501	Walter Hendl
Evansville Philharmonic	14 1/2 SE Second St., Evansville, IN 47708	George Trautwein
Florida Gulf Coast Symphony	P.O. Box 569, St. Petersburg, FL 33731	Irwin Hoffman
Florida West Coast Symphony	709 N. Tamiami Trail, Sarasota, FL 33577	Paul C. Wolfe
Fort Lauderdale Symphony	1430 N. Federal Hwy., Fort Lauderdale, FL 33304	Emerson Buckley
Fort Wayne Philharmonic	227 E. Washington Blvd., Fort Wayne, IN 46802	Ronald Ondrejka
Fresno Philharmonic	1382 N. Fresno St., Fresno, CA 93703	Guy Taylor
Glendale Symphony	401 N. Brand Blvd., Glendale, CA 91203	Carmen Dragon
Greensboro Symphony	200 N. Davie St., Greensboro, NC 27401	Peter Paul Fuchs
Hamilton Philharmonic	Sta. A., P.O. 2080, Hamilton, Ont. L8N 3Y7	Boris Brott
Harrisburg Symphony	22 S. Third St., Harrisburg, PA 17101	Larry Newland
Hartford Chamber Orchestra	179 Allyn St., Hartford, CT 06103	Daniel Parker
Jackson Symphony	P.O. Box 39216, Jackson, MS 39216	Lewis Dalvit
Johnstown Symphony	230 Walnut St., Johnstown, PA 15901	Donald Barra
Kalamazoo Symphony	426 S. Park St., Kalamazoo, MI 49007	Yoshimi Takeda
Kern Philharmonic	400 Trustun Ave., Bakersfield, CA 93301	John Farrer
Kitchener-Waterloo Symphony	Box 2, Waterloo, Ont., N2J 3Z6	Raffi Armenian
Knoxville Symphony	618 Gay St., Knoxville, TN 37902	Zoltan Rozsnyai
Lansing Symphony	230 N. Washington Sq., Lansing, MI 48933	Gustav Meier
Lexington Philharmonic	P.O. Box 838, Lexington, KY 40587	George Zack
Lincoln Symphony	1315 Sharp Bldg., Lincoln, NE 68508	Robert Emile
London Symphony	520 Wellington St., London, Ont. N6A 3R2	Victor Feldbrill
Long Island Philharmonic	P.O. Box 199, Huntington, NY 11743	Christopher Keene
Los Angeles Chamber Orchestra	285 W. Green St., Pasadena, CA 91105	Gerard Schwarz
Lubbock Symphony	1721 Broadway, Lubbock, TX 79401	William A. Harrod
Madison Symphony	211 N. Carroll St., Madison, WI 53703	Roland Johnson
Marin Symphony	P.O. Box 127, San Rafael, CA 94902	Sandor Salgo
Miami Beach Symphony	420 Lincoln Rd. Mall, Miami Beach, FL 33139	Barnett Breeskin
Midland-Odessa Symphony	P.O. Box 6266, Midland, TX 79701	Thomas Hohstadt
Monterey County Symphony	P.O. Box 3965, Carmel, CA 93921	Haymo Taeuber
Municipal Concerts	50 E. 42d St., New York, NY 10017	Julius Grossman
Music for Westchester Symphony	Box 35, Gedney Station, White Plains, NY 10605	Siegfried Landau
Nevada Symphonic	P.O. Box 3098, Reno, NV 89505	Vacant
New Haven Symphony	33 Whitney Ave., New Haven, CT 06511	Murry Sidlin
New Mexico Symphony	P.O. Box 769, Albuquerque, NM 87103	Yoshima Takeda
Northwest Chamber Orchestra	119 S. Main St., Seattle, WA 98104	Barbara Zimmer
Northeastern Pennsylvania Philharmonic	P.O. Box 71, Avoca, PA 18641	Thomas Michalak
Opera Orchestra of N.Y.	10 E. 53d St., N.Y., NY 10022	John Broome
Orchestra da Camera	5 Jardin Pl., N. Babylon, NY 11703	James Conlon
(Greater) Palm Beach Symphony	P.O. Box 996, Palm Beach, FL 33480	John Iuele
Pasadena Symphony	300 E. Green St., Pasadena, CA 91101	Daniel Lewis
Peoria Symphony	416 Hamilton, Peoria, IL 61602	William Wilsen
Portland Symphony	30 Myrtle St., Portland, ME 04111	Bruce Hangen
Queens Symphony	99-11 Queens Blvd., Rego Park, NY 11374	David Katz
Regina Symphony	200 Lakeshore Dr., Regina, Sask. S4S 0B3	Gregory Millar
Rhode Island Philharmonic	334 Westminster Mall, Providence, RI 02903	George Kent
Rockford Symphony	415 N. Church St., Rockford, IL 61103	Crawford Gates

Sacramento Symphony	451 Parkfair Dr., Sacramento, CA 95825	Carter Nice
Saginaw Symphony	P.O. Box 415, Saginaw, MI 48606	Paul D. Freeman
Santa Barbara Symphony	3 W. Carrillo, Santa Barbara, CA 93101	Frank Collura
Santa Rosa Symphony	P.O. Box 1081, Santa Rosa, CA 95402	Corrick L. Brown
Saskatoon Symphony	P.O. Box 1361, Saskatoon, Sask. S7K 3N9	Ruben Gurevich
Savannah Symphony	P.O. Box 9505, Savannah, GA 31412	Christian Badea
Shreveport Symphony	P.O. Box 4057, Shreveport, LA 71104	John Shenaut
Sioux City Symphony	P.O. Box 754, Sioux City, IA 51102	Tom Lewis
South Bend Symphony	215 W. North Shore Drive, South Bend, IN 46617	Herbert Butler
South Dakota Symphony	101 W. 37th St., Sioux Falls, SD 57105	Emanuel Vardi
Spokane Symphony	W. 621 Mallon, Spokane, WA 99201	Donald Thulean
Springfield (Mass.) Symphony	284 State St., Springfield, MA 01105	Robert Gutter
Springfield (Ohio) Symphony	Box 1374, Springfield, OH 45501	John E. Ferritto
Stockton Symphony	Box 4273, Stockton, CA 95204	Kyung-Soo Won
Tacoma Symphony	P.O. Box 19, Tacoma, WA 98401	Edward Sefarian
Thunder Bay Symphony	P.O. Box 2004, Station P, Thunder Bay, Ont. P7B 5E7	Dwight Bennett
Tri-City Symphony	P.O. Box 67, Davenport, IA 52805	James Dixon
Tucson Symphony	443 So. Stone Ave., Tucson, AZ 85701	George Trautwein
Vermont Symphony	77 College St., Burlington VT 05401	Efrain Guigui
Virginia Orchestra Group	P.O. Box 26, Norfolk, VA 23501	Russell Stanger
Warren Symphony	4504 E. Nine Mile Rd., Warren, MI 48091	David Daniels
Wheeling Symphony	51 16th St., Wheeling, WV 26003	Jeff Holland Cook
Windsor Symphony	586 Ouellette Ave., Windsor, Ont. N9A 1B7	Laszlo Gati
Winston-Salem Symphony	610 Coliseum Dr., Winston-Salem, NC 27106	Peter Perret
Youngstown Symphony	260 Federal Plaza West, Youngstown, OH 44503	Franz Bibo

Major U.S. and Canadian Opera Companies

Source: Central Opera Service, New York, N.Y.

Arizona Opera Company (Tucson); Jim Sullivan, gen. dir.
Artists Internationale (Providence, R.I.); Ken Russell Slade, bus. mgr.
Asolo Opera Company (Sarasota); Philip Hall, exec. dir.
Baltimore Opera Company; Robert J. Collinge, gen. mgr.
Canadian Opera Company (Toronto); Lotfi Mansouri, gen. dir.
Central City Opera (Colo.); Robert Darling, art. dir.
Charlotte Opera Assn.; Richard Marshall, gen. dir.
Chautauqua Opera (N.Y.); Leonard Treash, dir.
Chicago Opera Theatre; Alan Stoner, art. dir.
Cincinnati Opera Assn.; James DeBlasis, gen. mgr.
Civic Opera of the Palm Beaches (Fla.); Paul Csonka, art. dir.
Cleveland Opera; David Bamberger, art. dir.
Colorado Opera Festival (Colorado Springs); Donald Jenkins, art. dir.
Columbus Opera Symphony (O.); Evan Whallon, mus. dir.
Connecticut Opera Assn. (Hartford); George Osborne, gen. mgr.
Dallas Civic Opera; Plato Karayanis, gen. dir.
Dayton Opera Assn.; Lester Freedman, gen. dir.
Edmonton Opera Assn.; Lorin J. Moore, gen. mgr.
Florentine Opera Company (Milwaukee, Wis.); Robert L. Caulfield, gen. mgr.
Fort Worth Opera Assn.; Rudolf Kruger, gen. mgr.
Goldovsky Opera Institute and Theatre (N.Y., N.Y.); Boris Goldovsky, art. dir.
Greater Miami Opera Assn.; Robert Herman, gen. mgr.
Hawaii Opera Theatre (Honolulu); Robert C. Bickley, gen. mgr.
Hidden Valley Music Seminar (Carmel Valley, Cal.); Peter Meckel, dir.
Houston Grand Opera; David Gockley, gen. dir.
Kentucky Opera Assn. (Louisville); Moritz Bomhard, dir.
Lake George Opera Company (Glens Falls, N.Y.); David Lloyd, gen. dir.
Lyric Opera of Chicago; Carol Fox, gen. mgr.
Lyric Opera of Kansas City (Mo.); Russell Patterson, gen. mgr.
Manitoba Opera Assn. (Winnipeg); Irving Guttman, art. dir.
Metropolitan Opera Assn. (N.Y., N.Y.); Anthony A. Bliss, exec. dir.
Michigan Opera Theatre (Detroit); David DiChiera, gen. dir.
Minnesota Opera Company (St. Paul); Charles Fullmer, mgr.
Music Theatre of Wichita; James Miller, dir.
National Opera Assn. (Raleigh, N.C.); David Witherspoon, gen. mgr.
Nevada Opera Guild (Reno); Ted Puffer, dir.
New Jersey State Opera (Newark); Alfredo Silipigni, art. dir.
New Orleans Opera Assn.; Arthur Cosenza, gen. dir.
New York City Opera Company; Beverly Sills, gen. dir.
Opera Company of Boston; Sarah Caldwell, art. dir.
Opera Company of Philadelphia; Margaret Everitt, act. gen. dir.
Opera Memphis; Kenneth Caswell, gen. dir.
Opera/Omaha; Martha Elsberry, gen. dir.
Opera Orchestra of New York (NYC); Eve Queler, dir.
Opera/South (Jackson, Miss.); Dolores Ardoyno, gen. mgr.
Opera Theatre of St. Louis; Richard Gaddes, gen. mgr.
Opera Theatre of Syracuse; Robert Driver, gen. mgr.
Ottawa Festival Opera; Donald MacSween, gen. dir.
Pittsburgh Opera; Vincent Artz, mgr.
Portland Opera Assn. (Ore.) Stefan Minde, gen. dir.
San Antonio Opera and Symphony; Nat Greenberg, mgr.
San Diego Opera; Tito Capobianco, gen. dir.
San Francisco Opera Assn.; Kurt Herbert Adler, gen. dir.
Santa Fe Opera/Opera Assn. of New Mexico; John Crosby, gen. dir.
Seattle Opera Assn.; Glynn Ross, gen. dir.
Skylight Opera (Milwaukee, Wis.); Colin Cabot, mng. dir.
Southern Alberta Opera Assn. (Calgary); Brian Hanson, gen. mgr.
Spoleto Festival USA (Charleston, S.C.); James Kearny, gen. mgr.
Spring Opera Theater of San Francisco; Kurt Herbert Adler, gen. dir.
Texas Opera Theatre (Houston); Jane Weaver, mgr.
Toledo Opera Assn.; Lester Freedman, gen. dir.
Tri-Cities Opera Company (Binghampton, N.Y.); Peyton Hibbitt and Carmen Savoca, dirs.
Tulsa Opera; Edward Purrington, gen. mgr.
Virginia Opera Assn. (Norfolk); Peter Mark, art. dir.
Vancouver Opera Assn.; Hamilton McClymont, gen. mgr.
The Washington Opera (D.C.); Martin Feinstein, exec. dir.
Western Opera Theater (San Francisco); Earl Jay Schub, mgr.
Wilmington Opera Society; I. Duncan, pres.
Wolf Trap Company (Vienna, Va.); E. Craig Hankenson, exec. dir.

Recordings

Record and Tape Shipments Down

Manufacturers' shipments of phonograph records and pre-recorded tapes declined by 6% in 1979 from record 1978 levels. Dollar volume was calculated at $3.7 billion suggested retail list price, according to the Recording Industry of America. Shipments of all records, both LPs and singles, were down 5% at 502.2 million units, with suggested retail list price off 12% to $2.4 billion; LP shipments of 290.2 million units represented a 15% decline, with suggested retail list price off 17% to $2.1 billion; shipments of singles were 212 million units, a 12% gain, at suggested retail list price of $353.6 million, a 36% increase reflecting the higher-priced 12-inch disco format; total tape shipments of 180.8 million units represented a 7% decline, with suggested retail list price off 10% to $1.3 billion; total 8-track shipments of 102.3 million units were down 23%, dollar volume at suggested retail list price down 28% to $684.3 million. The RIAA confers Gold Record Awards on single records that sell one million units, Platinum Awards to those selling 2 million, Gold Awards to LP albums and their tape equivalents that sell 500,000 units, Platinum Awards to those selling one million. Awards in 1979-80 follow (most Platinum Award winners also won Gold Awards):

Artists and Recording Titles

A-album, S-single, G-gold, P-platinum

Aug. 1979

The Cars; *Candy-O;* A,P.
Charlie Daniels Band; *Million Mile Reflection;* A,P.
Rickie Lee Jones; *Rickie Lee Jones;* A,P.
Knack; *Get the Knack;* A,P.
Amii Stewart; *Knock on Wood;* S,P.
Donna Summer; *Hot Stuff;* S,P.
Chuck Brown & The Soul Searchers; *Bustin' Loose;* A,G.
Cheap Trick; *In Color;* A,G.
Crusaders; *Street Life;* A,G.
Con Funk Shun; *Candy;* A,G.
McFadden & Whitehead; *McFadden & Whitehead;* A,G.
Stephanie Mills; *What Cha Gonna Do with My Lovin?;* A,G.
Willie Nelson & Leon Russell; *One for the Road;* A,G.
Raydio; *Rock-On;* A,G.
Various artists; *A Night at Studio 54;* A,G.
Robin Williams; *Reality. . . What a Concept;* A,G.
Neil Young; *Decade;* A,G.
Neil Young; *Rust Never Sleeps;* A,G.
Cheap Trick; *I Want You to Want Me;* S,G.
Charlie Daniels; *The Devil Went Down to Georgia;* S,G.
Dr. Hook; *When You're in Love with a Beautiful Woman;* S,G.
The Jones Girls; *You're Gonna Make Me Love Somebody Else;* S,G.
Elton John; *Mama Can't Buy You Love;* S,G.
The Knack; *My Sharona;* S,G.
Kiss; *I Was Made for Lovin' You;* S,G.
Barbra Streisand; *The Main Event;* S,G.

Sept. 1979

Waylon Jennings; *Greatest Hits;* A,P.
Donna Summer; *Bad Girl;* S,P.
Dr. Hook; *Pleasure & Pain;* A,G.
Joe Jackson; *Look Sharp;* A,G.
Original Soundtrack; *The Main Event;* A,G.
The Outlaws; *Bring It Back Alive;* A,G.
Spyro Gyra; *Morning Dance;* A,G.
Dionne Warwick; *Dionne;* A,G.
Herb Alpert; *Rise;* S,G.
Robert John; *Sad Eyes;* S,G.
Maxine Nightingale; *Lead Me On;* S,G.

Oct. 1979

G.Q.; *Disco Nights;* A,P.
Journey; *Evolution;* A,P.
The Who; *The Kids Are Alright;* A,P.
LTD; *Devotion;* A,G.
Mormon Tabernacle Choir; *Joy of Christmas;* A,G.
Ronnie Milsap; *Ronnie Milsap Live;* A,G.
Dionne Warwick; *I'll Never Love This Way Again;* S,G.

Nov. 1979

Little River Band; *First Under the Wire;* A,P.
Eddie Money; *Eddie Money;* A,P.
Abba; *Voulez-Vouz;* A,G.
New Riders of the Purple Sage; *Adventures of Panama Red;* A,G.
Dolly Parton; *Great Balls of Fire;* A,G.
Electric Light Orchestra; *Don't Bring Me Down;* S,G.
Patrick Hernandez; *Born to be Alive;* S,G.
Michael Jackson; *Don't Stop Till You Get Enough;* S,G.

Dec. 1979

Chic; *Risque;* A,P.
Dan Fogelberg; *Nether Lands;* A,P.
Michael Jackson; *Off the Wall;* A,P.
O'Jays; *Identify Yourself;* A,P.
AC/DC; *Highway to Hell;* A,G.
Ashford and Simpson; *Stay Free;* A,G.
Jimmy Buffet; *Volcano;* A,G.
Cameo; *Secret Omen;* A,G.
Chicago; *Chicago XIII;* A,G.
Bob Dylan; *Slow Train Coming;* A,G.
Dan Fogelberg; *Home Free;* A,G.
Johnny Mathis; *Give Me Your Love for Christmas;* A,G.
Original Soundtrack; *The Muppet Movie;* A,G.
R.E.O. Speedwagon; *Nine Lives;* A,G.
McFadden & Whitehead; *Pop Muzik;* S,G.
Donna Summer; *Dim All the Lights;* S,G.

Jan. 1980

Led Zeppelin; *In Through the Out Door;* A,P.
Foreigner; *Head Games;* A,P.
Kenny Rogers; *Kenny;* A,P.
Kool & the Gang; *Ladies Night;* A,P.
Barry Manilow; *One Voice;* A,P.
Kinks; *Low Budget;* A,G.
Molly Hatchet; *Flirtin' with Disaster;* A,G.
Crystal Gayle; *Miss the Mississippi;* A,G.
Isaac Hayes; *Don't Let Go;* A,G.
Funkadelic; *Uncle Jam Wants You;* A,G.
Steve Martin; *Comedy Is Not Pretty;* A,G.
Blackfoot; *Strikes;* A,G.
Village People; *Live & Sleazy;* A,G.
Rupert Holmes; *Escape;* G,S.
Styx; *Babe;* S,G.

Feb. 1980

John Denver & The Muppets; *A Christmas Together;* A,P.
The Eagles; *A Long Run;* A,P.
Styx; *Cornerstone;* A,P.
Herb Alpert; *Rise;* A,P.
Cheap Trick; *Dream Police;* A,P.
Neil Young; *Rust Never Sleeps;* A,P.
Gordon Lightfoot; *Summertime Dream;* A,P.
Fleetwood Mac; *Tusk;* A,P.
Donna Summer; *On the Radio—Greatest Hits Vol. I & II;* A,P.
Molly Hatchet; *Flirtin' with Disaster;* A,P.
Barbra Streisand; *Wet;* A,P.
The Bee Gees; *Bee Gees Greatest;* A,P.
Prince; *Prince;* A,P.
Tom Petty & the Heartbreakers; *Damn the Torpedoes;* A,P.
Kenny Loggins; *Keep the Fire;* A,G.
Black Sabbath; *We Sold Our Soul for Rock n' Roll;* A,G.
Peaches & Herb; *Twice the Fire;* A,G.

Jethro Tull; *Stormwatch;* A,G.
Anne Murray; *I'll Always Love You;* A,G.
The Alan Parsons Project; *Eve;* A,G.
The Bar-Kays; *Injoy;* A,G.
Rod Stewart; *Rod Stewart's Greatest Hits;* A,G.

March, 1980

Dionne Warwick; *Dionne;* A,P.
Pink Floyd; *The Wall;* A,P.
Dan Fogelberg; *Phoenix;* A,P.
AC/DC; *Highway to Hell;* A,P.
The Whispers; *The Whispers;* A,P.
Waylon Jennings; *What Goes Around;* A,P.
ZZ Top; *Deguello;* A,G.
Toto; *Hydra;* A,G.
Willie Nelson; *Willie Nelson Sings Kristofferson;* A,G.
Crystal Gayle; *Classic Crystal;* A,G.
Jefferson Starship; *Freedom at Point Zero;* A,G.
Rufus & Chaka; *Masterjam;* A,G.
Neil Young & Crazy Horse; *Live Rust;* A,G.
Parliament; *Gloryhallastoopid;* A,G.
Teddy Pendergrass; *Teddy Live!;* A,G.
Pink Floyd; *The Wall;* A,G.
Electric Light Orchestra; *ELO Greatest Hits;* A,G.
Arrowsmith; *Night in the Ruts;* A,G.
Neil Diamond; *September Morn;* A,G.
Richard Pryor; *Richard Pryor's Greatest Hits;* A,G.
The Grateful Dead; *The Best of Skeletons from the Closet;* A,G.
Rush; *Permanent Waves;* A,G.
The Oakridge Boys; *Y'All Come Back Saloon;* A,G.
Lynyrd Skynyrd; *Gold & Platinum;* A,G.
Pat Benatar; *In the Heat of the Night;* A,G.
Kenny Rogers; *Coward of the Country;* S,G.
Donna Summer; *On the Radio;* S,G.
The Whispers; *And the Beat Goes On;* S,G.
Prince; *I Wanna Be Your Lover;* S,G.
Teri DeSario & K.C.; *Yes, I'm Ready;* S,G.
Pink Floyd; *Another Brick in the Wall (Part II);* S,G.

April, 1980

Lynyrd Skynyrd Band; *Gold and Platinum;* A,P.
Pablo Cruise; *A Place in the Sun;* A,P.
Bob Seger & the Silver Bullet Band; *Against the Wind;* A,P.
Ray, Goodman, & Brown; *Ray, Goodman, & Brown;* A,G.
Shalamar; *Big Fun;* A,G.
Original Soundtrack; *American Gigolo;* A,G.
Bette Midler; *The Rose;* A,G.
The Knack; *But the Little Girls Understand;* A,G.
Gap Band; *Gap Band II;* A,G.
J. Geils Band; *Love Stinks;* A,G.
Abba; *Greatest Hits, Vol. 2;* A,G.
Chuck Mangione; *Fun and Games;* A,G.
Brothers Johnson; *Light up the Night;* A,G.
Blondie; *Call Me;* S,G.
The Spinners; *Workin' My Way Back to You;* S,G.

May, 1980

Billy Joel; *Glass Houses;* A,P.
Bob Dylan; *Slow Train Coming;* A,P.
Neil Diamond; *September Morn;* A,P.
Linda Ronstadt; *Mad Love;* A,P.
Kenny Rogers; *Gideon;* A,P.
Mickey Mouse; *Mickey Mouse Disco;* A,P.
Journey; *Departure;* A,G.
Heart; *Bebe Le Strange;* A,G.
Roberta Flack; *Chapter Two;* A,G.
Andy Gibb; *After Dark;* A,G.
Christopher Cross; *Christopher Cross;* A,G.
Frank Sinatra; *The Sinatra Christmas Album;* A,G.
Rupert Holmes; *Partners in Crime;* A,G.
Lipps, Inc.; *Mouth to Mouth;* A,G.
Reo Speedwagon; *Riding Out the Storm;* A,G.
Billy Joel; *Turnstiles;* A,G.
Van Halen; *Women and Children First;* A,G.
Queen; *Crazy Little Thing Called Love;* S,G.
Ray, Goodman & Brown; *Special Lady;* S,G.

June, 1980

Van Halen; *Women and Children First;* A,P.
The Isley Brothers; *Go All the Way;* A,P.
Bette Midler; *The Rose;* A,P.
Pretenders; *Pretenders;* A,G.
Boz Scaggs; *Middle Man;* A,G.
Roberta Flack, Donny Hathaway; *Roberta Flack Featuring Donny Hathaway;* A,G.
Larry Gatlin; *Straight Ahead;* A,G.
Stephanie Mills; *Sweet Sensation;* A,G.
Kansas; *Song for America;* A,G.
Original Soundtrack; *The Empire Strikes Back;* A,G.
Eric Clapton; *Just One Night;* A,G.
Con Funk Shun; *Spirit of Love;* A,G.
S.O.S. Band; *Take Your Time;* S,G.
Bette Midler; *The Rose;* S,G.

July, 1980

Journey; *Departure;* A,P.
Blondie; *Eat to the Beat;* A,P.
Original Soundtrack; *Urban Cowboy;* A,P.
Lipps, Inc.; *Funky Town;* S,P.

Miss America Winners

1921	Margaret Gorman, Washington, D.C.
1922-23	Mary Campbell, Columbus, Ohio
1924	Ruth Malcolmson, Philadelphia, Pennsylvania
1925	Fay Lamphier, Oakland, California
1926	Norma Smallwood, Tulsa, Oklahoma
1927	Lois Delaner, Joliet, Illinois
1933	Marion Bergeron, West Haven, Connecticut
1935	Henrietta Leaver, Pittsburgh, Pennsylvania
1936	Rose Coyle, Philadelphia, Pennsylvania
1937	Bette Cooper, Bertrand Island, New Jersey
1938	Marilyn Meseke, Marion, Ohio
1939	Patricia Donnelly, Detroit, Michigan
1940	Frances Marie Burke, Philadelphia, Pennsylvania
1941	Rosemary LaPlanche, Los Angeles, California
1942	Jo-Caroll Dennison, Tyler, Texas
1943	Jean Bartel, Los Angeles, California
1944	Venus Ramey, Washington, D.C.
1945	Bess Myerson, New York City, N.Y.
1946	Marilyn Buferd, Los Angeles, California
1947	Barbara Walker, Memphis, Tennessee
1948	BeBe Shopp, Hopkins, Minnesota
1949	Jacque Mercer, Litchfield, Arizona
1951	Yolande Betbeze, Mobile, Alabama
1952	Coleen Kay Hutchins, Salt Lake City, Utah
1953	Neva Jane Langley, Macon, Georgia
1954	Evelyn Margaret Ay, Ephrata, Pennsylvania
1955	Lee Meriwether, San Francisco, California
1956	Sharon Ritchie, Denver, Colorado
1957	Marian McKnight, Manning, South Carolina
1958	Marilyn Van Derbur, Denver, Colorado
1959	Mary Ann Mobley, Brandon, Mississippi
1960	Lynda Lee Mead, Natchez, Mississippi
1961	Nancy Fleming, Montague, Michigan
1962	Maria Fletcher, Asheville, North Carolina
1963	Jacquelyn Mayer, Sandusky, Ohio
1964	Donna Axum, El Dorado, Arkansas
1965	Vonda Kay Van Dyke, Phoenix, Arizona
1966	Deborah Irene Bryant, Overland Park, Kansas
1967	Jane Anne Jayroe, Laverne, Oklahoma
1968	Debra Dene Barnes, Moran, Kansas
1969	Judith Anne Ford, Belvidere, Illinois
1970	Pamela Anne Eldred, Birmingham, Michigan
1971	Phyllis Ann George, Denton, Texas
1972	Laurie Lea Schaefer, Columbus, Ohio
1973	Terry Anne Meeuwsen, DePere, Wisconsin
1974	Rebecca Ann King, Denver, Colorado
1975	Shirley Cothran, Fort Worth, Texas
1976	Tawney Elaine Godin, Yonkers, N.Y.
1977	Dorothy Kathleen Benham, Edina, Minnesota
1978	Susan Perkins, Columbus, Ohio
1979	Kylene Baker, Galax, Virginia
1980	Cheryl Prewitt, Ackerman, Mississippi

Best-Selling Books of 1979-80

Listed according to frequency of citation on best seller reports from Aug. 1979 through July 1980.
Numbers in parentheses show rank on top ten list for calendar year 1979, according to *Publishers Weekly.*

Hardcover Fiction

1. Jailbird, Kurt Vonnegut (5)
2. Triple, Ken Follett (11)
3. Princess Daisy, Judith Krantz
4. The Bourne Identity, Robert Ludlum
5. Sophie's Choice, William Styron (2)
6. The Devil's Alternative, Frederick Forsyth
7. Smiley's People, John le Carré (10)
8. The Last Enchantment, Mary Stewart (7)
9. The Establishment, Howard Fast (8)
10. The Dead Zone, Stephen King (6)
11. Portraits, Cynthia Freeman
12. The Matarese Circle, Robert Ludlum (1)
13. Memories of Another Day, Harold Robbins (4)
14. Random Winds, Belva Plain
15. The Executioner's Song, Norman Mailer
16. No Love Lost, Helen Van Slyke
17. The Third World War: Aug. 1985, Gen. Sir John Hackett, et al.
18. Shibumi, Trevanian
19. The Bleeding Heart, Marilyn French
20. Shadow of the Moon, M.M. Kaye
21. Who's on First, William F. Buckley, Jr.
22. Class Reunion, Rona Jaffe
23. The Green Ripper, John D. MacDonald
   (tie) Kane & Abel, Jeffrey Archer
24. Innocent Blood, P.D. James
   (tie) The Top of the Hill, Irwin Shaw
25. The Ninja, Eric Van Lustbader

Hardcover Nonfiction

1. Aunt Erma's Cope Book, Erma Bombeck (1)
2. The Complete Scarsdale Medical Diet, Herman Tarnower, M.D. & Samm Sinclair Baker (2)
3. The Brethren, Bob Woodward & Scott Armstrong (8)
4. Free to Choose, Milton & Rose Friedman
5. The Pritikin Program for Diet and Exercise, Nathan Pritikin & Patrick McGrady, Jr. (5)
6. Cruel Shoes, Steve Martin (4)
7. How to Prosper During the Coming Bad Years, Howard J. Ruff (3)
8. Donahue, Phil Donahue
9. Anatomy of an Illness, Norman Cousins
10. White House Years, Henry Kissinger
11. James Herriot's Yorkshire, James Herriot
   (tie) The Third Wave, Alvin Toffler
12. The Right Stuff, Tom Wolfe
13. Thy Neighbor's Wife, Gay Talese
14. Restoring the American Dream, Robert J. Ringer (3)
15. Men in Love, Nancy Friday
16. All You Need to Know about the IRS, Paul N. Strassels with Robert Wool
17. Broca's Brain, Carl Sagan
18. Will, Gordon Liddy
19. How You Can Become Financially Independent by Investing in Real Estate, Albert J. Lowry
20. The Medusa and the Snail, Lewis Thomas
21. Jim Fixx's Second Book of Running, Jim Fixx
22. The Powers That Be, David Halberstam
23. The Real War, Richard Nixon
24. The Bronx Zoo, Sparky Lyle and Peter Golenbock
25. The Americans, Alistair Cooke

Mass Market Paperback

1. The Complete Scarsdale Medical Diet, Herman Tarnower, M.D. & Samm Sinclair Baker
2. Chesapeake, James Michener
3. Fools Die, Mario Puzo
4. Mommie Dearest, Christina Crawford
5. Evergreen, Belva Plain
6. The Matarese Circle, Robert Ludlum
   (tie) The Americans, John Jakes
   (tie) Nurse, Peggy Anderson
7. The Far Pavilions, M.M. Kaye
8. Second Generation, Howard Fast
9. How to Prosper During the Coming Bad Years, Howard J. Ruff
10. The Stand, Stephen King
11. Wifey, Judy Blume
12. Lauren Bacall by Myself, Lauren Bacall
13. Bright Flows the River, Taylor Caldwell
14. A Necessary Woman, Helen van Slyke
15. Ghost Story, Peter Straub
16. The Amityville Horror, Jay Anson
17. Star Trek, Gene Roddenberry
18. Eye of the Needle, Ken Follett
19. Overload, Arthur Hailey
20. War and Remembrance, Herman Wouk
21. The Empire Strikes Back, Donald F. Glut
22. Pulling Your Own Strings, Wayne W. Dyer
23. Petals on the Wind, V.C. Andrews
24. Scruples, Judith Krantz
25. Oregon!, Dana Fuller Ross

Hardcover Fiction
Best Sellers, Calendar Year 1979

1. The Matarese Circle, Robert Ludlum
2. Sophie's Choice, William Styron
3. Overload, Arthur Hailey
4. Memories of Another Day, Harold Robbins
5. Jailbird, Kurt Vonnegut
6. The Dead Zone, Stephen King
7. The Last Enchantment, Mary Stewart
8. The Establishment, Howard Fast
9. The Third World War, Gen. Sir John Hackett, et al.
10. Smiley's People, John le Carre

Hardcover Nonfiction

1. Aunt Erma's Cope Book, Erma Bombeck
2. The Complete Scarsdale Medical Diet, Herman Tarnower, M.D. & Samm Sinclair Baker
3. How to Prosper During the Coming Bad Years, Howard J. Ruff
4. Cruel Shoes, Steve Martin
5. The Pritikin Program for Diet and Exercise, Nathan Pritikin & Patrick McGrady Jr.
6. White House Years, Henry Kissinger
7. Lauren Bacall By Myself, Lauren Bacall
8. The Brethren, Bob Woodward and Scott Armstrong
9. Restoring the American Dream, Robert J. Ringer
10. The Winner's Circle, Charles Paul Conn

Selected U.S. Daily Newspaper Circulation

Source: Audit Bureau of Circulations' FAS-FAX Report. Average paid circulation for 6 months to Mar. 31, 1980. †3 months. For the 6 months up to Sept. 30, 1979, 1,769 English language dailies in the U.S. (361 morning, 1,386 evening, 22 all day) had an average audited circulation of 62,088,960. Sunday papers included 694 with audited average circulation of 53,545,394. (m) morning; (e) evening; *Mon.-Fri.

average. Includes all ABC newspapers with daily circulation over 100,000.

Newspaper	Daily	Sunday
Albany, N.Y. Times-Union (m)	82,207	149,516
Albany, N.Y. Knickerbocker News (e)	*51,780	
Akron Beacon Journal (e)	161,835	218,969
Allentown Call (m)	*103,258	154,805
Asbury Park Press (e)	105,368	139,787
Atlanta Constitution (m)	218,807	
Atlanta Journal (e)	211,081	501,867
Baltimore News-American (e)	*150,502	229,777
Baltimore Sun (m&e)	*350,848	374,989
Bergen Co. (N.J.) Record (e)	†150,378	†213,799
Birmingham News (e)	*178,074	217,352
Birmingham Post-Herald (m)	*68,349	
Boston Globe (m&e)	491,682	710,731
Boston Herald American (m)	*241,021	306,484
Buffalo Courier-Express (m)	126,197	254,482
Buffalo News (e)	*269,474	170,410
Camden (N.J.) Courier-Post (e)	†126,498	
Charlotte News (e)	51,809	
Charlotte Observer (m)	169,400	241,194
Chicago Sun-Times (m)	*657,275	700,315
Chicago Tribune (m&e)	*789,767	1,146,474
Christian Science Monitor (m)	*172,470	
Cincinnati Enquirer (m)	186,732	293,826
Cincinnati Post (e)	168,227	
Cleveland Plain Dealer (m)	392,688	454,922
Cleveland Press (e)	300,889	
Columbia, S.C. State (m)	106,180	126,300
Columbia, S.C. Record (e)	32,882	
Columbus, Ga. Enquirer (m)	*34,590	70,841
Columbus, Ga. Ledger (e)	*30,904	
Columbus, O. Citizen-Journal (m)	112,195	
Columbus, O. Dispatch (e)	202,949	341,568
Dallas News (m)	286,955	353,677
Dallas Time Herald (e)	*249,890	345,736
Dayton Journal-Herald (m)	100,886	
Dayton News (e)	140,674	217,220
Denver Post (e)	*260,331	351,149
Denver: Rocky Mountain News (m)	271,153	293,004
Des Moines Register (m)	210,577	390,537
Des Moines Tribune (e)	82,201	
Detroit Free Press (m)	*601,721	710,018
Detroit News (e)	*630,573	827,168
Flint Journal (e)	†106,777	†106,045
Fort Lauderdale News (e)	*102,065	201,543
Ft. Worth Star-Telegram (m&e)	240,579	256,664
Fresno Bee (m)	130,279	151,766
Grand Rapids Press (e)	†125,222	†147,360
Hartford Courant (m)	212,244	289,124
Honolulu Advertiser (m)	85,640	
Honolulu Star-Bulletin (e)	118,952	203,938
Houston Chronicle (e)	*348,601	436,940
Houston Post (m)	*330,203	394,853
Indianapolis News (e)	†143,449	
Indianapolis Star (m)	†215,858	†357,694
Jacksonville Journal (e)	*47,177	
Jacksonville: Fla. Times Union (m)	153,508	199,315
Kansas City Star (e)	*273,758	406,467
Kansas City Times (m)	314,007	
Knoxville News-Sentinel (e)	102,488	158,987
Little Rock: Ark. Democrat (e)	*66,275	119,052
Little Rock: Ark. Gazette (m)	*129,274	154,569
Long Beach Independent (m)	*64,709	135,811
Long Beach Press-Telegram (e)	*70,704	
Long Island, N.Y.: Newsday (e)	492,580	557,933
Los Angeles Herald-Examiner (e)	*283,710	302,525
Los Angeles Times (m)	*1,024,322	1,276,195
Louisville Courier-Journal (m)	190,942	331,103
Louisville Times (e)	151,977	
Madison, Wis. State Journal	76,348	127,830
Memphis Commercial Appeal (m)	203,847	282,484
Memphis Press Scimitar (e)	94,731	
Miami Herald (m)	444,058	576,261
Miami News (e)	61,910	
Milwaukee Journal (e)	323,932	515,108
Milwaukee Sentinel (m)	163,224	
Minneapolis Star (e)	*206,700	
Minneapolis Tribune (m)	*230,815	597,180
Nashville Banner (e)	84,134	
Newark Star-Ledger (m)	*†407,844	†574,966
New Haven Register (e)	100,093	140,979
New Haven Journal-Courier (m)	*37,264	
New Orleans Times-Picayune (m)	†213,283	†323,302
New Orleans States-Item (e)	*†111,043	
New York News (m)	*1,554,604	2,202,601
New York Post (e)	*654,314	
New York Times (m)	*914,938	1,477,499
Norfolk Ledger-Star (e)	†94,332	
Norfolk Virginia-Pilot (m)	†125,787	†200,680
Oakland Tribune (m&e)	*190,189	180,628
Oklahoma City Oklahoman (m)	*181,994	287,371
Oklahoma City Times (e)	*84,657	
Omaha World-Herald (m&e)	*235,313	278,520
Orange Co. (Cal.) Register (m&e)	*230,533	259,783
Orlando Sentinel-Star (m&e)	*201,383	243,704
Palm Beach Post (m)	*93,117	141,097
Palm Beach Times (e)	*31,019	
Peoria Journal Star (m&e)	102,556	120,003
Philadelphia Bulletin (e)	*458,849	529,706
Philadelphia Inquirer (m)	*425,075	837,209
Philadelphia News (e)	*231,310	
Phoenix Gazette (e)	†112,781	
Phoenix Republic (m)	†260,090	†399,819
Pittsburgh Post Gazette (m)	*185,215	
Pittsburgh Press (e)	*271,502	659,998
Portland, Me. Press-Herald (m)	53,616	
Portland, Me. Express (e) & Maine Sunday Telegram	29,813	115,519
Portland Oregonian (m)	248,229	420,938
Portland: Oregon Journal (e)	*105,485	
Providence Bulletin (e)	*141,759	
Providence Journal (m)	*75,435	228,306
Raleigh News & Observer (m)	†131,921	†165,289
Raleigh Times (e)	†35,194	
Richmond News Leader (e)	114,295	
Richmond Times Dispatch (m)	135,360	216,047
Rochester Democrat-Chronicle (m)	125,316	232,367
Rochester Times-Union (e)	121,897	
Sacramento Bee (m)	203,779	233,034
Sacramento Union (m)	103,859	105,303
St. Louis Globe-Democrat (m)	*264,609	264,603
St. Louis Post-Dispatch (e)	*247,237	241,904
St. Paul Dispatch (e)	*114,858	
St. Paul Pioneer Press (m)	*100,672	241,904
St. Petersburg Independent (e)	43,593	
St. Petersburg Times (m)	230,143	288,775
Salt Lake City Tribune (m)	113,956	189,310
Salt Lake City Deseret News (e)	75,865	
San Antonio Express (m)	*82,371	185,413
San Antonio News (e)	*76,594	
San Antonio Light (e)	*122,600	187,857
San Diego Union (m)	†201,798	†321,792
San Diego Tribune (e)	†125,756	
San Francisco Examiner (e)	*159,325	
San Francisco Chronicle (m)	*506,600	669,665
San Jose Mercury (m)	*154,983	269,821
San Jose News (e)	*68,000	
Seattle Post-Intelligencer (m)	*197,123	222,998
Seattle Times (e)	*260,762	348,678
Shreveport Times (m)	†87,822	†126,255
South Bend Tribune (e)	106,370	125,754
Spokane Chronicle (e)	61,580	
Spokane Spokesman-Review (m)	76,648	124,185
Springfield, Ill. State Journal-Register (m&e)	71,171	71,788
Springfield, Mass. Union (m)	72,195	
Springfield, Mass. News (e) & Sunday Republican	75,729	142,380
Syracuse Herald-Journal (e)	113,678	231,470
Syracuse Post-Standard (m)	82,181	
Tacoma News Tribune (e)	107,860	111,071
Toledo Blade (e)	167,590	209,154
Tucson Daily Star (m)	†74,284	†138,266
Tulsa Tribune (e)	†76,314	
Tulsa World (m)	†122,385	†211,152
Wall St. Journal (m) (total)	*1,798,416	
Washington, D.C. Post (m)	*601,417	827,938
Washington, D.C. Star (e)	*345,641	326,512
Wichita Eagle (m)	120,043	174,832
Wichita Beacon (e)	37,221	
Winston-Salem Journal (m)	71,696	95,143
Winston-Salem Sentinel (e)	37,731	
Youngstown Vindicator (e)	†103,298	†153,036

Circulation of Leading U.S. Magazines

Source: Audit Bureau of Circulations' FAS-FAX Report

General magazines, exclusive of groups and comics. Based on total average paid circulation during the 6 months prior to June 30, 1980.

Magazine	Circulation
TV Guide	18,870,730
Reader's Digest	18,193,255
National Geographic Magazine	10,560,885
Better Homes & Gar.	8,057,386
Woman's Day	7,574,478
Family Circle	7,366,482
McCall's	6,256,183
Playboy	5,746,536
Ladies' Home Journal	5,403,015
Good Housekeeping	5,138,948
National Enquirer	5,013,475
Time	4,451,816
Redbook	4,234,141
The Star	3,380,779
Newsweek	2,952,515
Cosmopolitan	2,812,507
Sr. Scholastic	2,613,340
American Legion	2,591,644
Sports Illustrated	2,343,380
People Weekly	2,308,635
Consumer Reports	2,300,000*
U.S. News-World Report	2,085,229
Field & Stream	2,019,102
Popular Science	1,913,879
Smithsonian	1,890,466
Glamour	1,846,691
Southern Living	1,812,834
Outdoor Life	1,714,138
Popular Mechanics	1,695,733
V.F.W. Magazine	1,686,754
Today's Education	1,674,413
Mechanix Illustrated	1,669,808
The Elks Magazine	1,648,809
Globe	1,572,476
The Workbasket	1,561,727
Boys' Life	1,537,601
Parents	1,489,507
Changing Times	1,482,863
Seventeen	1,455,561
Life	1,410,273
Sunset	1,405,685
True Story	1,369,634
Nation's Business	1,272,173
Ebony	1,270,143
New Woman	1,253,868
Sport	1,204,086
Psychology Today	1,171,362
Bon Appetit	1,155,303
1001 Decorating Ideas	1,104,698
'Teen	1,054,920
Vogue	1,053,181
House & Garden	1,050,733
Family Handyman	1,038,783
Discovery	1,013,765
US	1,006,188
Golf Digest	1,005,812
Travel & Leisure	944,222
Mother Earth News	939,056
House Beautiful	929,532
Mademoiselle	922,049
Hot Rod	921,049
Scouting	900,030
Grit	879,908
Popular Photography	868,980
Decorating and Craft Ideas	859,947
Oui	851,960
Yankee	850,371
Money	837,436
Weight Watchers Magazine	826,205
Apartment Life	818,980
Business Week	816,366
Self	809,937
Family Health	809,469
Junior Scholastic	804,648
Co-ed	801,453
Cuisine	800,981
Playgirl	784,935
Motor Trend	756,644
Soap Opera Digest	741,739
Golf	737,714
Car and Driver	724,636
Scientific American	705,124
Forbes	690,258
Rolling Stone	690,198
Eagle	685,971
Fortune	677,642
Workbench	673,950
Gourmet	671,178
Esquire Magazine	651,596
National Lampoon	647,653
Harper's Bazaar	634,997
Modern Photography	631,962
Signature	629,109
Gallery	623,380
Games	600,828
Essence	600,041
Road & Track	590,507
The Lutheran	576,062
Sports Afield	571,514
The Saturday Evening Post	552,941
Club	551,698
Stereo Review	543,726
Colonial Homes	538,484
Flower & Garden	511,425
The New Yorker	501,629
Girl Scout Leader	488,230
Easyriders	482,702
Architectural Digest	482,552
Guns & Ammo	480,121
Cycle	474,821
Tennis	469,509
The Rotarian	465,693
Natural History	460,896
Westways	449,195
New York Magazine	426,069
Skiing Magazine	420,973
Ski	420,873
Car Craft	420,357
Capper's Weekly	416,610
The Sporting News	416,076
GQ-Gentlemen's Quarterly	414,983
Cheri	410,000
Vogue Patterns	400,085

* Circulation figure provided by publisher.

Sunday Magazines Weekly Circulation

Family Weekly (356 papers)	12,300,000
Parade (130 papers)	21,622,793

Selected Canadian Daily Newspaper Circulation

Source: Audit Bureau of Circulations' FAS-FAX Report of average paid circulation for 6 months ending Mar. 31, 1980.

For the 6 months up to Sept. 30, 1979. 121 daily newspapers in Canada (24 morning: 96 evening, 1 all day) had an average audited circulation of 5,159,841; 13 Sunday newspapers had an average circulation of 1,536,471.

Newspaper	Daily	Saturday
Calgary Albertan (m)	44,679	
Calgary Herald (e)	*133,217	165,740
Edmonton Journal (e)[2]	*172,908	215,301
Halifax Chronicle-Herald (m)	71,967	
Halifax Mail-Star (e)	57,347	
Hamilton Spectator (e)	†147,996	
Kingston Whig-Standard (e)	†36,411	
Kitchener-Waterloo Record (e)	†71,851	
London Free Press (m & e)[2]	131,482	136,782
Montreal Gazette (m)	*208,749	275,849
Montreal: La Presse (e)	*174,945	264,765
Montreal: Le Devoir (m)	*42,404	42,872
Montreal: Le Journal de Montreal (m)	*322,301	**283,987
Montreal Star (e)[1]	*166,056	232,702
Ottawa Citizen (e)	*126,760	162,858
Ottawa Journal (e)[2]	*67,785	79,602
Ottawa: Le Droit (e)	*48,366	53,575
Quebec: Le Journal de Quebec (m)	*103,238	94,142
Quebec: Le Soleil (e)[1]	*130,148	
Regina Leader Post (e)	68,283	
St. Catharines Standard (e)	†130,736	
St. John's Telegram (e)	*31,486	44,732
Saint John Telegraph-Journal (m)	*32,088	67,340
Saint John Times Globe (e)	*31,754	
Saskatoon Star-Phoenix (e)	54,840	
Sherbrooke: La Tribune (m)	*42,156	44,790
Sudbury Star (e)	30,538	
Sydney: Cape Breton Post (e)	31,052	
Toronto Globe and Mail (m)	290,715	
Toronto Star (e)	*484,764	780,677
Toronto Sun (m)	*222,784	*379,260
Trois Rivieres Nouvelliste (e)	*52,915	
Vancouver Province (m)	119,427	
Vancouver Sun (e)	227,034	
Victoria Colonist (m)	46,348	**51,681
Victoria Times (e)	35,531	
Windsor Star (e)	92,237	
Winnipeg Free Press (e)	*140,055	170,901
Winnipeg Tribune (e)	106,207	

(m) Morning; (e) Evening; * Based on Monday to Friday average; **Sunday. (†) Indicates 3 month circulation average. (1) Data for Apr. 1 to June 15, 1979. (2) Data for 6 months ending Mar. 31, 1979.

Circulation of Leading Canadian Magazines

Source: Audit Bureau of Circulations' FAS-FAX Report.

General magazines, exclusive of groups and comics. Statistics based on average paid circulation during the 6 months prior to June 30, 1980.

Magazine	Circulation	Magazine	Circulation	Magazine	Circulation
Reader's Digest (Eng.-Fr.)	1,630,699	Legion Magazine	478,135	MacLean's Magazine	638,188
Chatelaine (English-French)	1,319,238	Time Canada	338,305	L'Actualite	239,200
Reader's Digest (English)	1,300,307	Selection du Reader's Digest	330,392	Flare	180,129
Chatelaine (English)	1,034,566	Chatelaine (French)	284,672	Le Lundi	123,106
TV Guide (English-French)	1,002,791	T.V. Hebdo	280,287	Saturday Night	117,188

America's Favorite Television Programs

Source: A.C. Nielsen
(Percent of TV households and persons in TV households)

Network Programs (Oct. to Dec. 1979)

(Nielsen average audience estimates)

	TV Households	Women	Men	Teens	Children
60 Minutes	28.8	22.3	24.1	—	—
3's Company	27.5	21.0	16.5	20.8	19.0
Alice	27.1	22.9	17.6	—	—
M A S H	25.7	19.5	15.7	19.3	—
Jeffersons	25.5	21.7	16.4	—	—
One Day at a Time	25.1	20.9	17.1	—	—
Dallas	24.6	21.3	15.0	—	—
8 is Enough	23.9	18.7	—	18.5	20.8
Taxi	23.9	18.5	15.0	16.9	—
Archie Bunker's Place	23.8	19.4	17.7	—	—
WKRP in Cin.	23.3	17.8	—	17.9	—
Little House...	23.3	20.4	—	—	18.2
Happy Days	22.3	—	—	16.7	20.6
Angie	22.3	16.9	—	14.8	17.1
Dukes of Hazzard	22.1	—	15.2	—	26.0
Trapper John MD		—	18.2	—	—
Mork & Mindy	—	—	15.2	22.1	27.1
NFL Mon. Night Football	—	—	19.3	—	—
ABC Sun. Night Movies	—	—	17.9	18.8	—
White Shadow	—	—	—	17.3	—
Buck Rogers	—	—	—	16.7	19.0
Chips	—	—	—	15.1	18.6
Wonder' World of Disney	—	—	—	—	22.8
Incred. Hulk	—	—	—	—	19.3
Soap	—	—	—	15.5	—

Syndicated Programs (Nov. 1979)

(Average ratings for total U.S.)

	TV households	Women	Men	Teens	Children
Muppets	13.0	8.8	7.7	8.8	19.1
Hee Haw	11.6	8.7	8.6	5.4	7.4
Lawrence Welk	11.1	9.7	6.7	—	—
Family Feud-PM	10.9	8.8	6.8	5.1	6.4
M A S H	10.1	6.9	6.7	7.4	5.7
Happy Days	9.8	5.5	4.8	12.0	12.7
Tic Tac Dough	8.8	7.1	5.2	3.8	—
Newlywed Game	8.4	6.5	5.3	4.5	—
Dance Fever	7.5	5.8	4.6	6.9	7.3
Donahue Show	7.3	5.8	—	—	—
Sha Na Na	7.1	5.0	4.2	5.3	7.7
Name That Tune	6.4	5.2	3.8	—	—
Jokers Wild	6.1	4.8	—	—	—
Hollywood Sqs.	6.0	4.6	3.7	—	—
Sanford & Son	6.0	—	3.6	6.0	5.9
Tom & Jerry	—	—	—	4.1	9.6
Brady Bunch	—	—	—	6.2	9.0
Bugs Bunny	—	—	—	3.5	7.7
Gilligan's Isl.	—	—	—	5.2	7.5
PM Magazine	—	4.0	—	—	—
Wild Kingdom	—	—	4.1	—	—
In Search Of	—	—	3.7	—	—
Carol Burnett	—	—	—	3.9	—
I Love Lucy	—	—	—	3.5	—
Flintstones	—	—	—	—	7.1
Popeye	—	—	—	—	5.9
Woody Woodpecker	—	—	—	—	5.9

Total TV households — 76.3 million; in TV households: 18+ women — 80.65 million, 18+ men — 72.38 million, teens 12-17 — 22.75 million, children 2-11 — 31.02 million.

Average Television Viewing Time

Source: A.C. Nielsen estimates, Nov. 1979 (hours: minutes, per week)

		Total	Mon.-Fri. 10am-4:30pm	Mon.-Fri. 4:30pm-7:30pm	Mon.-Sun. 8-11pm	Sat. 8am-1pm	Mon.-Fri. 11:30pm-1am
Avg. all persons		29:04	4:04	4:32	9:08	:46	1:05
Women	Total 18+	33:14	6:20	4:55	10:08	:28	1:23
	18-24	27:15	5:24	3:40	8:13	:41	1:05
	55+	37:01	7:17	6:23	10:59	:21	1:11
Men	Total 18+	27:24	2:17	3:57	9:14	:26	1:17
	18-24	20:32	1:24	2:22	6:33	:31	1:11
	55+	34:16	3:54	5:58	10:52	:25	1:13
Teens	Female	23:58	3:43	4:08	7:54	:47	:37
	Male	23:50	2:05	3:57	8:02	1:00	:43
Children	2-5	26:47	5:04	5:22	5:26	2:23	:04
	6-11	25:29	2:19	5:04	8:08	2:05	:13

All-time Top Television Programs

Source: A.C. Nielsen estimates

Program	Date	Network	Households
Roots	1/30/77	ABC	36,380,000
Super Bowl XIV	1/20/80	CBS	35,330,000
Super Bowl XIII	1/21/79	NBC	35,090,000
Super Bowl XII	1/15/78	CBS	34,410,000
Gone With The Wind, Pt. 1	11/7/76	NBC	33,960,000
Gone With The Wind, Pt. 2	11/8/76	NBC	33,750,000
Roots	1/28/77	ABC	32,680,000
Roots	1/27/77	ABC	32,540,000
Roots	1/25/77	ABC	31,900,000
Super Bowl XI	1/9/77	NBC	31,610,000
Roots	1/24/77	ABC	31,400,000
Roots	1/26/77	ABC	31,190,000
Roots	1/29/77	ABC	30,120,000
Jaws (movie)	11/4/79	ABC	29,830,000
Super Bowl X	1/18/76	CBS	29,440,000
Super Bowl IX	1/12/75	NBC	29,040,000
Roots	1/23/77	ABC	28,840,000
Three's Company	3/13/79	ABC	28,610,000
World Series Game 7	10/17/79	ABC	28,150,000
Airport (movie)	11/11/73	ABC	28,000,000
WBA World Heavyw't Championship	9/15/78	ABC	27,790,000
Super Bowl VII	1/14/73	NBC	27,670,000
Rocky (movie)	2/4/79	CBS	27,640,000
World Series Game 7	10/22/75	NBC	27,560,000
Super Bowl VIII	1/13/74	CBS	27,540,000
Super Bowl VI	1/16/72	CBS	27,450,000

U.S. Television Sets and Stations Received

Set Ownership
(Nielsen est. as of Sept. 1979)

Total TV homes	76,300,000	100%
(98% of U.S. homes own at least one TV set)		
Homes with:		
Color TV sets	63,329,000	83%
B&W only	12,971,000	17
2 or more sets	38,150,000	50
One set	38,150,000	50
CATV (Feb. 1980)	15,147,000	20

Number of Stations
(FCC, June, 1979)

Commercial	**746**
Educational	**267**
Total	**1,013**

Stations Receivable
(Nielsen, Jan. 1980)

% of TV homes receiving:

1-3 stations	3%
4	7
5	10
6	13
7	10
8	8
9	11
10+	38

Estimated Advertising Expenditures in the U.S.

Source: Advertising Age; prepared by Robert J. Coen of McCann-Erickson, Inc.

Medium	1976		1977		1978		1979[1]		
	Dollars (millions)	Per cent of total	Dollars (millions)	Per cent of total	Dollars (millions)	Percent of total	Dollars (millions)	Percent of total	% change '79 vs. '78
Newspapers									
Total	$ 9,910	29.4	$11,132	29.4	$12,707	28.9	$14,493	29.2	+14.1
National	1,502	4.5	1,677	4.4	1,787	4.1	2,085	4.2	+16.6
Local	8,408	4.9	9,455	24.9	10,920	24.8	12,408	25.0	+13.6
Magazines									
Total	1,789	5.3	2,162	5.7	2,597	5.9	2,930	5.9	+12.8
Weeklies	748	2.2	903	2.4	1,158	2.6	1,315	2.6	+13.4
Women's	457	1.4	565	1.5	672	1.5	735	1.5	+ 9.4
Monthlies	584	1.7	694	1.8	767	1.8	880	1.8	+14.5
Farm publications	86	0.3	90	0.1	104	0.2	120	0.2	+14.0
Television									
Total	6,721	19.9	7,612	20.1	8,979	20.4	10,195	20.5	+13.5
Network	2,857	8.5	3,460	9.1	3,975	9.0	4,540	9.1	+14.2
Spot	2,154	6.4	2,204	5.8	2,581	5.9	2,890	5.8	+12.0
Local	1,710	5.0	1,948	5.1	2,423	5.5	2,765	5.6	+14.0
Radio									
Total	2,330	6.9	2,634	6.9	3,052	6.9	3,385	6.8	+11.0
Network	105	0.3	137	0.4	147	0.3	170	0.3	+15.0
Spot	518	1.5	546	1.4	620	1.4	680	1.4	+ 9.8
Local	1,707	5.1	1,951	5.1	2,285	5.2	2,535	5.1	+11.0
Direct Mail	4,813	14.3	5,164	13.6	5,987	13.6	6,650	13.4	+11.1
Business publications	1,035	3.1	1,221	3.2	1,400	3.2	1,595	3.2	+14.0
Outdoor									
Total	383	1.1	418	1.1	466	1.1	535	1.1	+14.8
National	252	0.7	290	0.8	307	0.7	350	0.7	+14.0
Local	131	0.4	128	0.3	159	0.4	185	0.4	+16.4
Miscellaneous									
Total	6,653	19.7	7,487	19.7	8,678	19.8	9,817	19.7	+13.1
National	3,474	10.3	3,899	10.3	4,485	10.2	5,060	10.2	+12.8
Local	3,179	9.4	3,588	9.5	4,193	9.6	4,757	9.5	+13.5
Total									
National	18,585	55.1	20,850	55.0	23,980	54.6	27,070	54.4	+12.8
Local	15,135	44.9	17,070	44.0	19,990	45.4	22,650	45.6	+13.4
Grand total	**33,720**	**100.0**	**37,920**	**100.0**	**43,970**	**100.0**	**49,720**	**100.0**	**+13.1**

(1) Preliminary figures, subject to adjustment when final 1979 FCC broadcast data are released.

Network TV Program Ratings

Source: A. C. Nielson, November, 1979

Program or type	TV Households Rating %	TV Households No. (000)	Audience Composition (thousands) Men (18+)	Women (18+)	Teens 12-17	Children 2-11
Today (7:30-8:00)	4.4	3,360	1,520	2,780	100	350
Morning (7:15-8:00)	2.5	1,910	880	1,180	70	290
Good Morning Amer. (7:30-8:00)	3.9	2,980	1,270	2,330	210	300
Daytime						
Drama (Soaps)	7.6	5,830	1,100	5,280	500	400
Quiz & Aud. Participation	4.7	3,570	1,120	2,960	260	460
All 10am-4:30pm	6.6	5,010	1,110	4,380	440	450
Evening						
Informational News Mon.-Fri.	8.2	2,470	7,120	8,630	970	1,300
General Drama	21.0	16,020	9,340	14,060	2,440	3,770
Susp. & Mystery	17.7	13,540	8,790	11,070	2,370	2,470
Sit. Comedy	21.6	16,470	9,660	13,290	3,340	4,670
Feature Film	19.6	14,990	10,130	12,360	3,000	2,520
All 7-11pm regular	19.8	15,130	10,050	12,030	2,840	3,460

Television Network Addresses

American Broadcasting Company (ABC)
1330 Avenue of Americas
New York, NY 10019

Columbia Broadcasting System (CBS)
51 W. 52nd St.
New York, NY 10019

National Broadcasting Company (NBC)
30 Rockefeller Plaza
New York, NY 10020

Westinghouse Broadcasting (Group W)
90 Park Ave.
New York, NY 10016

Metromedia
485 Lexington Ave.
New York, NY 10017

Public Broadcasting Service (PBS)
609 Fifth Ave.
New York, NY 10017

Canadian Broadcasting Corp. (CBC)
1500 Bronson Ave.
Ottawa, Ontario, Canada K1G 3J5

50 Leading U.S. Advertisers, 1979

Source: Advertising Age, Sept. 11, 1980; copyright © Crain Communications Inc. 1980.

Rank	Company	Ad Costs (000)	Sales (000)	Ads as % sales
	Appliances, TV, radio			
24	RCA Corp.	$158,600	$ 7,454,600	2.1
31	General Electric	139,408	22,460,600	0.6
	Automobiles			
4	General Motors Corp.	323,395	66,311,200	0.5
10	Ford Motor Corp.	215,000	1,409,003	0.5
40	Chrysler Corp.	118,000	12,000,000	1.0
	Chemicals			
34	American Cyanamid Co.	127,000	3,186,998	4.0
	Communications			
29	CBS Inc.	146,118	3,729,701	3.9
46	Time Inc.	102,360	2,504,060	4.1
48	Transamerica Corp.	95,048	4,044,647	2.3
	Drugs			
36	Richardson-Merrell	123,800	1,090,546	11.4
43	SmithKline Corp.	107,737	1,351,145	8.0
49	Sterling Drug Co.	92,000	81,180	11.2
	Food			
2	General Foods Corp.	393,000	5,959,600	6.5
14	McDonald's Corp.	202,807	5,385,000	3.8
16	General Mills	190,746	4,170,287	4.6
17	Esmark Inc.	170,547	6,771,883	2.5
21	Norton Simon Inc.	163,188	2,755,934	5.9
27	Beatrice Foods Co.	150,000	8,290,509	1.8
33	Pillsbury Co.	131,549	3,032,000	4.3
39	Kraft Inc.	119,654	6,432,935	1.9
42	Ralston Purina Co.	108,028	4,600,000	2.3
45	Consolidated Foods Corp.	105,000	5,000,000	2.1
50	Kellogg Co.	91,646	1,850,000	5.0
	Oil			
20	Mobil Corp.	165,841	48,241,000	2.9
	Retail Chains			
3	Sears, Roebuck & Co.	379,313	17,514,000	2.1
6	Kmart	287,095	12,731,145	2.3
38	J.C. Penney Co.	122,000	11,274,000	1.1
	Soaps, cleansers			
1	Procter & Gamble	614,900	10,772,186	5.7
23	Unilever U.S. Inc.	160,000	2,124,000	7.5
37	Colgate-Palmolive Co.	122,500	4,949,000	2.7
	Soft drinks			
11	PepsiCo Inc.	212,000	5,050,566	4.2
18	Coca-Cola Co.	169,271	4,961,400	3.4
	Telephones			
9	American T & T	219,756	45,408,078	0.4
32	International T & T	132,400	17,197,423	0.8
	Tobacco			
5	Philip Morris	291,201	8,302,892	3.5
7	R.J. Reynolds Industries	258,115	8,935,200	2.9
41	B.A.T. Industries	116,396	1,440,000	8.1
	Toiletries, cosmetics			
8	Warner-Lambert Co.	220,242	3,217,208	6.8
12	Bristol-Meyers Co.	210,600	2,752,777	7.7
13	American Home Products	206,000	3,649,476	5.6
35	Gillette Co.	126,960	1,984,722	6.4
44	Chesebrough-Pond's	107,342	1,174,274	9.1
	Wine, beer, liquor			
19	Seagram Co.	168,000	2,553,096	6.6
22	Anheuser-Busch	160,524	3,263,744	4.9
26	Heublein Inc.	155,000	1,769,074	8.8
	Miscellaneous			
15	Gulf & Western Industries	191,500	6,507,000	2.9
25	Johnson & Johnson	157,700	2,372,128	6.6
28	U.S. Government	146,121	----	---
30	Loews Corp.	144,468	4,065,475	3.6

Major Movies of the Year (Sept. 1, 1979 to Aug. 31, 1980)

Listed below, alphabetically, are some of the major films rated by the New York Daily News star system: ★★★★ is for excellent, ★★★½ very good, ★★★ good, ★★½ fair, ★★ mediocre, ★½ poor, ★very poor, 0★ not worth rating.

Kathleen Carroll, N. Y. Daily News Movie Editor and Critic

Movie	Rating	Stars	Director
Airplane	★★	Robert Hays, Julie Hagerty	Jim Abrahams
All That Jazz	★★★	Roy Scheider, Jessica Lange	Bob Fosse
American Gigolo	★★	Richard Gere, Lauren Hutton	Paul Schrader
And Justice For All	★★½	Al Pacino, Jack Warden	Norman Jewison
Arabian Adventure	★★★	Christopher Lee, Milo O'Shea	Kevin Connor
Being There	★★★★	Peter Sellers, Shirley MacLaine	Hal Ashby
The Big Red One	★★★	Lee Marvin, Mark Hamill	Samuel Fuller
The Black Hole	★★½	Maximilian Schell, Anthony Perkins	Gary Nelson
The Black Stallion	★★★	Kelly Reno, Teri Garr	Carroll Ballard
The Blues Brothers	★★	John Belushi, Dan Aykroyd	John Landis
The Blue Lagoon	★★½	Brooke Shields, Christopher Atkins	Randal Kleiser
Brubaker	★★★	Robert Redford, Jane Alexander	Stuart Rosenberg
Caddyshack	★★	Chevy Chase, Rodney Dangerfield	Harold Ramis
Can't Stop The Music	★★	Bruce Jenner, Valerie Perrine	Nancy Walker
The Changeling	★★	George C. Scott, Trish Van Devere	Peter Medak
Coal Miner's Daughter	★★★½	Sissy Spacek, Tommy Lee Jones	Michael Apted
Cuba	★★½	Sean Connery, Brooke Adams	Richard Lester
Death Ship	★★	George Kennedy, Sally Ann Howes	Alvin Rakoff
Dressed To Kill	★★½	Michael Caine, Angie Dickinson	Brian De Palma
The Empire Strikes Back	★★★½	Mark Hamill, Harrison Ford	Irvin Kershner
Electric Horseman	★★★½	Robert Redford, Jane Fonda	Sidney Pollack
Fame	★★★	Irene Cara, Lee Curreri	Alan Parker
Fatso	★★	Dom DeLuise, Anne Bancroft	Anne Bancroft
Ffolkes	★★½	Roger Moore, James Mason	Andrew McLaglen
The Fiendish Plot Of Dr. Fu Manchu	★★★½	Peter Sellers, Sid Caesar	Piers Haggard
The Fish That Saved Pittsburgh	★★	Julius Erving, Jonathan Winters	Gilbert Moses
The Fog	★★	Hal Holbrook, Janet Leigh	John Carpenter
Foxes	★★	Scott Baio, Jodie Foster	Adrian Lyne
Gilda Live	★★½	Gilda Radner	Mike Nichols
The Great Santini	★★★½	Robert Duvall, Blythe Danner	Lewis John Carlino
Happy Birthday, Gemini	★★½	Madeline Kahn, Rita Moreno	Richard Benner
Head Over Heels	★★★	John Heard, Mary Beth Hurt	John M. Silver
Heart Beat	★★½	Nick Nolte, Sissy Spacek, John Heard	John Byrum
Hero At Large	★★	John Ritter, Anne Archer	Martin Davidson
Home Movies	★★	Nancy Allen, Mary Davenport	Brian De Palma
Honeysuckle Rose	★★	Willie Nelson, Dyan Cannon	Jerry Schatzberg
The Human Factor	★★	John Gielgud, Nicol Williamson	Otto Preminger
How To Beat The High Cost Of Living	★★½	Susan Saint James, Jane Curtin	Robert Scheerer
The Jerk	★★	Steve Martin, Bernadette Peters	Carl Reiner
Just Tell Me What You Want	★★½	Ali MacGraw, Alan King	Sidney Lumet
The Kidnapping Of The President	★★½	William Shatner, Hal Holbrook	George Mendeluk
Kramer vs. Kramer	★★★★	Dustin Hoffman, Meryl Streep	Robert Benton
The Last Married Couple In America	★★	George Segal, Natalie Wood	Gilbert Cates
Little Darlings	★★	Tatum O'Neal, Kristy McNichol	Ronald Maxwell
The Long Riders	★★★	David Carradine, Stacy Keach	Walter Hill
The Marriage Of Maria Braun	★★★	Hanna Schygulla, Klaus Loewitach	R. W. Fassbinder
My Brilliant Career	★★★½	Judy Davis, San Neill	Gillian Armstrong
Nijinsky	★★★	Alan Bates, Leslie Browne	Herbert Ross
1941	★★	John Belushi, Dan Aykroyd	Stephen Spielberg
On The Nickel	★★	Donald Moffat, Ralph Waite	Ralph Waite
The Onion Field	★★★½	John Savage, James Woods	Harold Becker
The Outsider	★★★	Craig Wasson, Sterling Hayden	Tony Luraschi
The Private Files Of J. Edgar Hoover	★★½	Broderick Crawford, Rip Torn	Larry Cohen
Promises In The Dark	★★★½	Marsha Mason	Jerome Hellman
Raise The Titanic	★★½	Richard Jordan, Jason Robards	Jerry Jameson
The Rose	★★★½	Bette Midler, Alan Bates	Mark Rydell
Rough Cut	★★½	Burt Reynolds, Lesley-Anne Down	Don Siegel
The Runner Stumbles	★★½	Dick Van Dyke, Kathleen Quinlan	Stanley Kramer
Saturn 3	★★½	Farrah Fawcett, Kirk Douglas	Stanley Donen
The Serial	★★½	Martin Mull, Tuesday Weld	Bill Persky
The Shining	★★	Jack Nicholson, Shelley Duvall	Stanley Kubrick
The Shout	★★★½	Alan Bates, Susannah York	Jerry Skolimowski
Simon	★★	Alan Arkin, Madeline Kahn	Marshall Brickman
Sitting Ducks	★★★	Michael Emil, Zack Norman	Henry Jaglom
Smokey And The Bandit II	★★	Burt Reynolds, Dom DeLuise	Hal Needham
Something Short Of Paradise	★★½	Susan Sarandon, David Steinberg	David Helpern Jr.
Star Trek-The Motion Picture	★★½	William Shatner, Leonard Nimoy	Robert Wise
Starting Over	★★★	Jill Clayburgh, Burt Reynolds	Alan Pakula
10	★★★	Dudley Moore, Bo Derek	Blake Edwards
Time After Time	★★★½	Malcolm McDowell, David Warner	Nicholas Meyer
The Tin Drum	★★★½	David Bennent, Mario Adorf	Volker Schondorff
The 39 Steps	★★	Robert Powell, David Warner	Don Sharp
Tom Horn	★★	Steve McQueen, Linda Evans	William Wiard
Twinkle, Twinkle 'Killer' Kane	★★½	Stacy Keach, Scott Wilson	William Peter Blatty
Up The Academy	★★½	Ron Liebman, Wendell Brown	Robert Downey
Urban Cowboy	★★★	John Travolta, Debra Winger	James Bridges
When A Stranger Calls	★★	Charles Durning, Carol Kane	Fred Walton
Willie And Phil	★★★	Michael Ontkean, Margot Kidder	Paul Mazursky
Wise Blood	★★★½	Ned Beatty, Amy Wright	John Huston
Xanadu	★★★	Olivia Newton-John, Gene Kelly	Robert Greenwald
Yanks	★★★½	Richard Gere, Vanessa Redgrave	John Schlesinger

Tides and Their Causes

Source: National Oceanic and Atmospheric Administration, U.S. Commerce Department

The tides are a natural phenomenon involving the alternating rise and fall in the large fluid bodies of the earth caused by the combined gravitational attraction of the sun and moon. The combination of these two variable force influences produce the complex recurrent cycle of the tides. Tides may occur in both oceans and seas, to a limited extent in large lakes, the atmosphere, and, to a very minute degree, in the earth itself. The period between succeeding tides varies as the result of many factors and force influences.

The tide-generating force represents the difference between (1) the centrifugal force produced by the revolution of the earth around the common center-of-gravity of the earth-moon system and (2) the gravitational attraction of the moon acting upon the earth's overlying waters. Since, on the average, the moon is only 238,857 miles from the earth compared with the sun's much greater distance of 93,000,000 miles, this closer distance outranks the much smaller mass of the moon compared with that of the sun, and the moon's tide-raising force is, accordingly, 2¹/₅ times that of the sun.

The effect of the tide-generating forces of the moon and sun acting tangentially to the earth's surface (the so-called "tractive force") tends to cause a maximum accumulation of the waters of the oceans at two diametrically opposite positions on the surface of the earth and to withdraw compensating amounts of water from all points 90° removed from the positions of these tidal bulges. As the earth rotates beneath the maxima and minima of these tide-generating forces, a sequence of two high tides, separated by two low tides, ideally is produced each day.

Twice in each lunar month, when the sun, moon, and earth are directly aligned, with the moon between the earth and the sun (at new moon) or on the opposite side of the earth from the sun (at full moon), the sun and the moon exert their gravitational force in a mutual or additive fashion. Higher high tides and lower low tides are produced. These are called *spring* tides. At two positions 90° in between, the gravitational forces of the moon and sun — imposed at right angles—tend to counteract each other to the greatest extent, and the range between high and low tides is reduced. These are called *neap* tides. This semi-monthly variation between the spring and neap tides is called the *phase inequality.*

The inclination of the moon's orbit to the equator also produces a difference in the height of succeeding high tides and in the extent of depression of succeeding low tides which is known as the *diurnal inequality.* In extreme cases, this phenomenon can result in only one high tide and one low tide each day.

The actual amount of the uplift of the waters in the deep ocean may amount to only one or two feet. However, as this tide approaches shoal waters and its effects are augmented the tidal range may be greatly increased. In Nova Scotia along the narrow channel of the Bay of Fundy, the range of tides or difference between high and low waters, may reach 43 1/2 feet or more (under spring tide conditions) due to resonant amplification.

At New Orleans, the periodic rise and fall of the tide varies with the state of the Mississippi, being about 10 inches at low stage and zero at high. The Canadian Tide Tables for 1972 gave a maximum range of nearly 50 feet at Leaf Basin, Ungava Bay.

In every case, actual high or low tide can vary considerably from the average due to weather conditions such as strong winds, abrupt barometric pressure changes, or prolonged periods of extreme high or low pressure.

The Average Rise and Fall of Tides

Places	Ft.	In.	Places	Ft.	In.	Places	Ft.	In.
Baltimore, Md.	1	1	Mobile, Ala.	1	6	San Diego, Cal.	4	1
Boston, Mass.	9	6	New London, Conn.	2	7	Sandy Hook, N.J.	4	7
Charleston, S.C.	5	2	Newport, R.I.	3	6	San Francisco, Cal.	4	0
Colon, Panama	1	1	New York, N.Y.	4	6	Savannah, Ga.	7	5
Eastport, Me.	18	2	Old Pt. Comfort, Va.	2	6	Seattle, Wash.	7	7
Galveston, Tex.	1	5	Philadelphia, Pa.	5	11	Tampa, Fla.	2	10
Halifax, N.S.	4	5	Portland, Me.	9	0	Vancouver, B.C.	10	6
Key West, Fla.	1	4	St. John's, Nfld.	2	7	Washington, D.C.	2	11

Speed of Winds in the U.S.

Source: National Oceanic and Atmospheric Administration, U.S. Commerce Department

Miles per hour — average through 1979. High through 1979. Wind velocities in true values.

Station	Avg.	High	Station	Avg.	High	Station	Avg.	High
Albuquerque, N.M.	9.0	90	Helena, Mont.	7.9	73	New York, N.Y.(c)	9.4	70
Anchorage, Alas.	6.7	61	Honolulu, Ha.	11.8	67	Omaha, Neb.	10.8	109
Atlanta, Ga.	9.1	70	Jacksonville, Fla.	11.3	84	Pensacola, Fla.	8.4	53
Bismarck, N.D.	10.4	72	Key West, Fla.	11.2	122	Philadelphia, Pa.	9.6	73
Boston, Mass.	12.6	61	Knoxville, Tenn.	7.2	73	Pittsburgh, Pa.	9.3	58
Buffalo, N.Y.	12.3	91	Little Rock, Ark.	8.1	65	Portland, Ore.	7.9	88
Cape Hatteras, N.C.	11.4	(b)110	Louisville, Ky.	8.4	61	Rochester, N.Y.	9.8	73
Chattanooga, Tenn.	6.3	82	Memphis, Tenn.	9.1	46	St. Louis, Mo.	9.5	(b)60
Chicago, Ill.	10.4	60	Miami, Fla.	9.2	(a)74	Salt Lake City, Ut.	8.8	71
Cincinnati, Oh.	7.1	49	Minneapolis, Minn.	10.5	92	San Diego, Cal.	6.7	51
Cleveland, Oh.	10.8	74	Mobile, Ala.	9.1	(b)63	San Francisco, Cal.	10.5	58
Denver, Col.	9.0	56	Montgomery, Ala.	6.7	72	Savannah, Ga.	8.0	66
Detroit, Mich.	10.2	46	Mt. Washington, N.H.	35.0	231	Spokane, Wash.	8.7	59
Fort Smith, Ark.	7.6	58	Nashville, Tenn.	7.9	73	Toledo, Oh.	9.5	72
Galveston, Tex.	11.0	(d)100	New Orleans, La.	8.3	(b)98	Washington, D.C.	9.3	78

(a) Highest velocity ever recorded in Miami area was 132 mph, at former station in Miami Beach in September, 1926.
(b) Previous location. (c) Data for Central Park, Battery Place data through 1960, avg. 14.5, high 113. (d) Recorded before anemometer blew away. Estimated high 120.

Men's Names Added to Hurricane List

U.S. government agencies responsible for weather and related communications have used girls' names to identify major tropical storms since 1953. A U.S. proposal that both male and female names be adopted for hurricanes, starting in 1979, was accepted by a committee of the World Meteorological Organization.

Names assigned to Atlantic hurricanes, 1981 — Arlene, Bret, Cindy, Dennis, Emily, Floyd, Gert, Harvey, Irene, Jose, Katrina, Lenny, Maria, Nate, Ophelia, Philippe, Rita, Stan, Tammy, Vince, Wilma.

Names assigned to Eastern Pacific hurricanes, 1981 — Adrian, Beatriz, Calvin, Dora, Eugene, Fernanda, Greg, Hilary, Irwin, Jova, Knut, Lidia, Max, Norma, Otis, Pilar, Ramon, Selma, Todd, Veronica, Wiley.

National Weather Service Watches and Warnings

Source: National Weather Service, NOAA, U.S. Commerce Department

National Weather Service forecasters issue a Tornado Watch for a specific area where it is reasonably possible that tornadoes may occur during the valid time of the watch. A Watch is to alert people to watch for tornado activity and listen for a Tornado Warning. A Tornado Warning means that a tornado has been sighted or indicated by radar, and that safety precautions should be taken at once. A Hurricane Watch means that an existing hurricane poses a threat to coastal and inland communities in the area specified by the Watch. A Hurricane Warning means hurricane force winds and/or dangerously high water and exceptionally high waves are expected in a specified coastal area within 24 hours.

Tornado—A violent rotating column of air pendant from a thundercloud, usually recognized as a funnel-shaped vortex accompanied by a loud roar. With rotating winds est. up to 300 mph., it is the most destructive storm. Tornado paths have varied in length from a few feet to nearly 300 miles (avg. 5 mi.); diameter from a few feet to over a mile (average 220 yards); average forward speed, 25-40 mph.

Cyclone—An atmospheric circulation of winds rotating counterclockwise in the northern hemisphere and clockwise in the southern hemisphere. Tornadoes, hurricanes, and the lows shown on weather maps are all examples of cyclones having various sizes and intensities. Cyclones are usually accompanied by precipitation or stormy weather.

Hurricane—A severe cyclone originating over tropical ocean waters and having winds 74 miles an hour or higher. (In the western Pacific, such storms are known as typhoons.) The area of strong winds takes the form of a circle or an oval, sometimes as much as 500 miles in diameter. In the lower latitudes hurricanes usually move toward the west or northwest at 10 to 15 mph. When the center approaches 25° to 30° North Latitude, direction of motion often changes to northeast, with increased forward speed.

Blizzard—A severe weather condition characterized by low temperatures and by strong winds bearing a great amount of snow (mostly fine, dry snow picked up from the ground). The National Weather Service specifies, for blizzard, a wind of 35 miles an hour or higher, temperatures 20°F. or lower, and sufficient falling and/or blowing snow to reduce visibility to less than 1/4 of a mile. For "severe blizzard" wind speeds of 45 mph or more, temperature near or below 10°F., and visibility reduced by snow to near zero.

Monsoon—A name for seasonal winds (derived from Arabic "mausim," a season). It was first applied to the winds over the Arabian Sea, which blow for six months from northeast and six months from southwest, but it has been extended to similar winds in other parts of the world. The monsoons are strongest on the southern and eastern sides of Asia.

Flood—The condition that occurs when water overflows the natural or artificial confines of a stream or other body of water, or accumulates by drainage over low-lying areas.

National Weather Service Marine Warnings and Advisories

Small Craft Advisory: A Small Craft Advisory alerts mariners to sustained (exceeding two hours) weather and/or sea conditions either present or forecast, potentially hazardous to small boats. Hazardous conditions may include winds of 18 to 33 knots and/or dangerous wave or inlet conditions. It is the responsibility of the mariner, based on his experience and size or type of boat, to determine if the conditions are hazardous. When a mariner becomes aware of a Small Craft Advisory, he should immediately obtain the latest marine forecast to determine the reason for the Advisory.

Gale Warning indicates that winds within the range 34 to 47 knots are forecast for the area.

Storm Warning indicates that winds 48 knots and above, no matter how high the speed, are forecast for the area. However, if the winds are associated with a tropical cyclone (hurricane), the storm warning indicates that winds within the range 48 to 63 knots are forecast.

Hurricane Warning indicates that winds 64 knots and above are forecast for the area.

Primary sources of dissemination are commercial radio, TV, U.S. Coast Guard Radio stations, and NOAA VHF-FM broadcasts. These broadcasts on 162.40 and 162.55 MHz can usually be received 20-40 miles from the transmitting antenna site, depending on terrain and quality of the receiver used. Where transmitting antennas are on high ground, the range is somewhat greater, reaching 60 miles or more.

Wind Chill Table

Source: National Oceanic and Atmospheric Administration, U.S. Commerce Department

Both temperature and wind cause heat loss from body surfaces. A combination of cold and wind makes a body feel colder than the actual temperature. The table shows, for example, that a temperature of 20 degrees Fahrenheit, plus a wind of 20 miles per hour, causes a body heat loss equal to that in minus 10 degrees with no wind. In other words, the wind makes 20 degrees feel like minus 10.

Top line of figures shows actual temperatures in degrees Fahrenheit. Column at left shows wind speeds.

MPH	35	30	25	20	15	10	5	0	−5	−10	−15	−20	−25	−30	−35	−40	−45
5	33	27	21	19	12	7	0	−5	−10	−15	−21	−26	−31	−36	−42	−47	−52
10	22	16	10	3	−3	−9	−15	−22	−27	−34	−40	−46	−52	−58	−64	−71	−77
15	16	9	2	−5	−11	−18	−25	−31	−38	−45	−51	−58	−65	−72	−78	−85	−92
20	12	4	−3	−10	−17	−24	−31	−39	−46	−53	−60	−67	−74	−81	−88	−95	−103
25	8	1	−7	−15	−22	−29	−36	−44	−51	−59	−66	−74	−81	−88	−96	−103	−110
30	6	−2	−10	−18	−25	−33	−41	−49	−56	−64	−71	−79	−86	−93	−101	−109	−116
35	4	−4	−12	−20	−27	−35	−43	−52	−58	−67	−74	−82	−89	−97	−105	−113	−120
40	3	−5	−13	−21	−29	−37	−45	−53	−60	−69	−76	−84	−92	−100	−107	−115	−123
45	2	−6	−14	−22	−30	−38	−46	−54	−62	−70	−78	−85	−93	−102	−109	−117	−125

(Wind speeds greater than 45 mph have little additional chilling effect.)

Explanation of Normal Temperatures

Normal temperatures listed in the tables on pages 419 and 421 are based on records of the National Weather Service for the 30-year period from 1941-1970 inclusive. To obtain the average maximum or minimum temperature for any month, the daily temperatures are added; the total is then divided by the number of days in that month.

The normal maximum temperature for January, for example, is obtained by adding the average maximums for Jan., 1941, Jan., 1942, etc., through Jan., 1970. The total is then divided by 30. The normal minimum temperature is obtained in a similar manner by adding the average minimums for each January in the 30-year period and dividing by 30. The normal temperature for January is one half of the sum for the normal maximum and minimum temperatures for that month. The mean temperature for any one day is one-half the total of the maximum and minimum temperatures for that day.

Monthly Normal Temperature and Precipitation

Source: National Oceanic and Atmospheric Administration, U.S. Commerce Department

These normals are based on records for the 30-year period 1941 to 1970 inclusive. See explanation on page 418. For stations that did not have continuous records from the same instrument site for the entire 30 years, the means have been adjusted to the record at the present site.

Airport station; *city office stations. T, temperature in Fahrenheit; P, precipitation in inches; L, less than .05 inch.

	Jan.		Feb.		Mar.		Apr.		May		June		July		Aug.		Sept.		Oct.		Nov.		Dec.	
Station	T.	P.	T.	P.	T.	P.	T.	P.	T.	P.	T.	P.	T.	P.	T.	P.	T.	P.	T.	P.	T.	P.	T.	P.
Albany, N.Y.	22	2.2	24	2.1	33	2.6	47	2.7	58	3.3	68	3.0	72	3.1	70	2.9	62	3.1	51	2.6	40	2.8	26	2.9
Albuquerque, N.M.	35	0.3	40	0.4	46	0.5	56	0.5	65	0.5	75	0.5	79	1.4	77	1.3	70	0.8	58	0.8	45	0.3	36	0.5
Anchorage, Alas.	12	0.8	18	0.8	24	0.6	35	0.6	46	0.6	55	1.1	58	2.1	56	2.3	48	2.4	35	1.4	21	1.0	13	1.1
Asheville, N.C.	38	3.4	39	3.6	46	4.7	56	3.5	64	3.3	71	4.0	74	4.9	73	4.5	67	3.6	57	3.3	46	2.9	39	3.6
Atlanta, Ga.	42	4.3	45	4.4	51	5.8	61	4.6	69	3.7	76	3.7	78	4.9	78	3.5	72	3.2	62	2.5	51	3.4	44	4.2
Baltimore, Md.	33	2.9	35	2.8	43	3.7	54	3.1	64	3.6	72	3.8	77	4.1	75	4.2	69	3.1	57	2.8	46	3.1	35	3.3
Barrow, Alas.	-15	0.2	-19	0.2	-15	0.2	-1	0.2	19	0.2	33	0.4	39	0.9	38	1.0	30	0.6	15	0.6	-1	0.3	-12	0.2
Birmingham, Ala.	44	4.8	47	5.3	53	6.2	63	4.6	71	3.6	77	4.0	80	5.2	79	4.3	74	3.6	63	2.6	52	3.7	45	5.2
Bismarck, N.D.	8	0.5	14	0.4	25	0.7	43	1.4	54	2.2	64	3.6	71	2.2	69	2.0	58	1.3	47	0.8	29	0.6	16	0.5
Boise, Ida.	29	1.5	36	1.2	41	1.0	49	1.1	57	1.3	65	1.1	75	0.2	72	0.3	63	0.4	52	0.8	40	1.3	32	1.4
Boston, Mass.	29	3.7	30	3.5	38	4.0	49	3.5	59	3.5	68	3.2	73	2.7	71	3.5	65	3.2	55	3.0	45	4.5	33	4.2
Buffalo, N.Y.	24	2.9	24	2.6	32	2.9	45	3.2	55	3.0	66	2.2	70	2.9	68	3.5	62	3.3	52	3.0	40	3.7	28	3.0
Burlington, Vt.	17	1.7	19	1.7	29	1.9	43	2.6	55	3.0	65	3.5	70	3.5	67	3.7	59	3.1	49	2.7	37	2.9	23	2.2
Caribou, Me.	11	2.0	13	2.1	24	2.2	37	2.4	50	3.0	60	3.4	65	4.0	62	3.8	54	3.5	44	3.3	31	3.5	16	2.6
Charleston, S.C.	49	2.9	51	3.3	57	4.8	65	3.0	72	3.8	78	6.3	80	8.2	80	6.4	75	5.2	66	3.1	56	2.1	49	3.1
Chicago, Ill.	24	1.9	27	1.6	37	2.7	50	3.8	60	3.4	71	4.0	75	4.1	74	3.1	66	3.0	55	2.6	40	2.2	29	2.1
Cincinnati, Oh.*	32	3.4	34	3.0	43	4.1	55	3.9	64	4.0	73	3.9	76	4.0	75	3.0	68	2.7	58	2.2	45	3.1	34	2.9
Cleveland, Oh.	27	2.6	28	2.2	36	3.1	48	3.5	58	3.5	68	3.3	71	3.5	70	3.0	64	2.8	54	2.6	42	2.8	30	2.4
Columbus, Oh.	28	2.9	30	2.3	39	3.4	51	3.7	61	4.1	70	4.1	74	4.2	72	2.9	65	2.4	54	1.9	42	2.7	31	2.4
Dallas-Ft. Worth, Tex.	45	1.8	49	2.4	55	2.5	65	4.3	73	4.5	81	3.1	85	1.8	85	2.3	78	3.2	68	2.7	56	2.0	48	1.8
Denver, Col.	30	0.6	33	0.7	37	1.2	48	1.9	57	2.6	66	1.9	73	1.8	72	1.3	63	1.1	52	1.1	39	0.8	33	0.4
Des Moines, Ia.	19	1.1	24	1.1	34	2.3	50	2.9	61	4.2	71	4.9	75	3.3	73	3.3	64	3.1	54	2.1	38	1.4	25	1.1
Detroit, Mich.	26	1.9	27	1.8	35	2.3	48	3.1	58	3.4	69	3.0	73	3.0	72	3.0	65	2.3	54	2.5	41	2.3	30	2.2
Dodge City, Kan.	31	0.5	35	0.6	41	1.1	54	1.7	64	3.1	74	3.3	79	3.1	78	2.6	69	1.7	58	1.7	43	0.6	33	0.5
Duluth, Minn.	9	1.2	12	0.9	24	1.8	39	2.6	49	3.4	59	4.4	66	3.7	64	3.8	54	3.1	45	2.3	28	1.7	14	1.4
Eureka, Cal.*	47	7.4	48	5.2	48	4.8	50	3.0	53	2.1	55	0.7	56	0.1	57	0.3	57	0.7	54	3.2	52	5.8	49	6.6
Fairbanks, Alas.	-12	0.6	-3	0.5	10	0.5	29	0.3	47	0.7	59	1.4	61	1.9	55	2.2	44	1.1	25	0.7	3	0.7	-10	0.7
Fresno, Cal.	45	1.8	50	1.7	54	1.6	60	1.2	67	0.3	74	0.1	81	L	78	L	74	0.1	64	0.4	54	1.2	46	1.7
Galveston, Tex.*	54	3.0	56	2.7	61	2.6	69	2.6	76	3.2	81	4.1	83	4.4	83	4.4	80	5.6	73	2.8	64	3.2	57	3.7
Grand Junction, Col.	27	0.6	34	0.6	41	0.8	52	0.8	62	0.6	71	0.6	79	0.5	75	1.1	67	0.8	55	0.9	40	0.6	30	0.6
Gr. Rapids, Mich.	23	1.9	25	1.5	33	2.5	47	3.4	57	3.2	67	3.4	72	3.1	70	2.5	62	3.3	52	2.6	39	2.8	27	2.2
Hartford, Conn.	25	3.3	27	3.2	36	3.8	48	3.8	58	3.5	68	3.5	73	3.4	70	3.9	63	3.6	53	3.0	41	4.3	28	4.1
Helena, Mon.	18	0.6	25	0.4	31	0.7	43	0.9	52	1.8	59	2.4	68	1.0	66	1.0	56	1.0	45	0.6	32	0.6	23	0.6
Honolulu, Ha.	72	4.4	72	2.5	73	3.2	75	1.4	77	1.0	79	0.3	80	0.6	81	0.8	80	0.7	79	1.5	77	3.0	74	3.7
Houston, Tex.	52	3.6	55	3.5	61	2.7	69	3.5	76	5.1	81	4.5	83	4.1	83	4.4	79	4.7	71	4.1	61	4.0	55	4.0
Huron, S.D.	13	0.4	18	0.8	29	1.1	46	2.0	57	2.8	67	3.8	74	2.2	72	2.0	61	1.8	50	1.5	32	0.7	19	0.5
Indianapolis, Ind.	28	2.9	31	2.4	40	3.8	52	3.9	62	4.1	72	4.2	75	3.7	73	2.8	66	2.9	56	2.5	42	3.1	31	2.7
Jackson, Miss.	47	4.5	50	4.6	56	5.6	66	4.7	73	4.4	79	3.4	82	4.3	81	3.6	76	3.0	66	2.2	55	3.9	49	5.0
Jacksonville, Fla.	55	2.8	56	3.6	61	3.6	68	3.1	74	3.2	79	6.3	81	7.4	81	7.9	78	7.8	71	4.5	61	1.8	55	2.6
Juneau, Alas.	24	3.9	28	3.4	32	3.6	39	3.0	47	3.3	53	2.9	56	4.7	54	5.0	49	6.9	42	7.9	33	5.5	27	4.5
Kansas City, Mo.	27	1.3	32	1.3	41	2.6	54	3.5	64	4.3	73	5.6	78	4.4	77	3.8	68	4.2	58	3.2	42	1.5	31	1.5
Knoxville, Tenn.	41	4.7	43	4.7	50	4.9	60	3.6	68	3.3	76	3.6	78	4.7	77	3.2	72	2.8	61	2.7	49	3.6	42	4.5
Lander, Wyo.	20	0.5	26	0.7	31	1.2	43	2.4	53	2.6	61	1.9	71	0.6	69	0.4	58	1.1	47	1.2	32	0.9	23	0.5
Little Rock, Ark.	40	4.2	43	4.4	50	4.9	62	5.3	70	5.3	78	3.5	81	3.4	81	3.0	73	3.6	62	3.0	50	3.9	42	4.1
Los Angeles, Cal.*	57	3.0	58	2.8	59	2.2	62	1.3	65	0.1	68	L	73	L	74	L	73	0.2	68	0.3	63	2.0	58	2.2
Louisville, Ky.	33	3.5	36	3.5	44	5.1	56	4.1	65	4.2	73	4.1	77	3.8	76	3.0	69	2.9	58	2.4	45	3.3	36	3.3
Marquette, Mich.*	18	1.5	20	1.5	27	1.9	40	2.6	50	2.9	60	3.4	66	3.1	66	3.0	57	3.5	49	2.4	34	3.0	24	2.0
Memphis, Tenn.	41	4.9	44	4.7	51	5.1	63	5.4	71	4.4	79	3.5	82	3.5	80	3.3	74	3.0	63	2.6	51	3.9	43	4.7
Miami, Fla.	67	2.2	68	2.0	71	2.1	75	3.6	78	6.1	81	9.0	82	6.9	83	6.7	82	8.7	78	8.2	72	2.7	68	1.6
Milwaukee, Wis.	19	1.6	23	1.1	31	2.2	45	2.8	54	2.9	65	3.6	70	3.4	69	2.7	61	3.0	51	2.0	37	2.0	24	1.8
Minneapolis, Minn.	12	0.7	17	0.8	28	1.7	45	2.0	57	3.4	67	3.9	72	3.7	70	3.1	60	2.7	50	1.8	32	1.2	19	0.9
Mobile, Ala.	51	4.7	54	4.8	59	7.1	68	5.6	75	4.5	80	6.1	82	8.9	82	6.9	78	6.6	69	2.6	59	3.4	53	5.9
Moline, Ill.	22	1.7	26	1.3	36	2.6	51	3.8	61	3.9	71	4.4	75	4.6	73	3.4	65	3.8	54	2.7	39	1.9	27	1.8
Nashville, Tenn.	38	4.8	41	4.4	49	5.0	60	4.1	69	4.1	77	3.4	80	3.8	79	3.2	72	3.1	61	2.2	48	3.5	40	4.5
Newark, N.J.	31	2.9	33	3.0	41	3.9	52	3.4	62	3.6	71	3.0	76	4.0	75	4.3	68	3.4	58	2.8	46	3.6	35	3.5
New Orleans, La.	53	4.5	56	4.8	61	5.5	69	4.2	75	4.2	80	4.7	82	6.7	82	5.3	78	5.6	70	2.3	60	3.9	55	5.1
New York, N.Y.*	32	2.7	33	2.9	41	3.7	52	3.3	62	3.5	72	3.0	77	3.7	75	4.0	68	3.3	59	2.9	47	3.8	36	3.5
Nome, Alas.	6	0.9	5	0.8	7	0.8	19	0.7	35	0.7	46	1.0	50	2.4	49	3.6	42	2.4	29	1.4	16	1.0	4	0.7
Norfolk, Va.	41	3.4	41	3.3	48	3.4	58	2.7	67	3.3	75	3.6	78	5.7	77	5.9	72	4.2	62	3.1	52	2.9	42	3.1
Okla. City, Okla.	37	1.1	41	1.3	48	2.1	60	3.5	68	5.2	77	4.2	82	2.7	81	2.6	73	3.6	62	2.6	49	1.4	40	1.3
Omaha, Neb.	23	0.8	28	1.0	37	1.6	52	3.0	63	4.1	72	4.9	77	3.7	76	4.0	66	3.3	56	1.9	40	1.1	28	0.8
Parkersburg, W.Va.*	33	3.1	35	2.8	43	3.8	55	3.5	64	3.6	72	4.0	75	4.3	74	3.3	67	2.8	57	2.1	45	2.5	35	2.8
Philadelphia, Pa.	32	2.8	34	2.6	42	3.7	53	3.3	63	3.4	72	3.7	77	4.1	75	4.1	68	3.0	57	2.5	46	3.4	35	3.3
Phoenix, Ariz.	51	0.7	55	0.6	60	0.8	68	0.3	76	0.1	85	0.1	91	0.8	89	1.2	84	0.7	72	0.5	60	0.5	53	0.8
Pittsburgh, Pa.	28	2.8	29	2.4	38	3.6	50	3.4	60	3.6	69	3.5	72	3.8	70	3.2	64	2.5	53	2.5	41	2.5	31	2.5
Portland, Me.	22	3.4	23	3.5	32	3.6	43	3.3	53	3.3	62	3.1	68	2.6	66	2.6	59	3.1	49	3.3	39	4.9	26	4.1
Portland, Ore.	38	5.9	43	4.1	46	3.6	51	2.2	57	2.1	62	1.6	67	0.5	67	0.8	62	1.6	54	3.6	45	5.6	41	6.0
Providence, R.I.	28	3.5	29	3.5	37	4.0	47	3.7	57	3.5	66	2.7	72	2.9	70	3.9	63	3.3	54	3.3	43	4.5	32	4.1
Raleigh, N.C.	41	3.2	42	3.3	49	3.4	60	3.1	67	3.3	74	3.7	78	5.1	77	4.9	71	3.8	60	2.8	50	2.8	41	3.1
Rapid City, S.D.	22	0.5	26	0.6	31	1.0	45	2.1	55	2.8	64	3.7	73	2.1	72	1.5	61	1.2	50	0.9	35	0.5	27	0.4
Reno, Nev.	32	1.2	37	0.9	40	0.7	47	0.5	55	0.7	62	0.4	69	0.3	67	0.2	60	0.2	50	0.4	40	0.7	33	1.1
Richmond, Va.	38	2.9	39	3.0	47	3.4	58	2.8	67	3.4	74	3.5	78	5.6	76	5.1	70	3.6	59	2.9	49	3.2	39	3.2
St. Louis, Mo.	31	1.9	35	2.1	43	3.0	57	3.9	66	3.9	75	4.4	79	3.7	77	2.9	70	2.9	59	2.8	45	2.5	35	2.0
Salt Lake City, Ut.	28	1.3	33	1.2	40	1.6	49	2.1	58	1.5	66	1.3	77	0.7	75	0.9	65	0.7	52	1.2	39	1.3	30	1.4
San Antonio, Tex.	51	1.7	55	2.1	61	1.5	70	2.5	76	3.1	82	2.8	85	1.7	85	2.4	79	3.7	71	2.8	60	1.8	53	1.5
San Diego, Cal.	55	1.9	57	1.5	58	1.6	61	0.8	63	0.2	66	0.1	70	L	71	0.1	70	0.1	66	0.3	61	1.3	57	1.7
San Francisco, Cal.	48	4.4	51	3.0	53	2.5	55	1.6	58	0.4	62	0.1	63	L	63	L	64	0.2	61	1.0	55	2.3	50	4.0
San Juan, P.R.	75	3.7	75	2.5	76	2.0	78	3.4	79	6.5	81	5.6	81	6.4	81	7.0	81	6.1	81	5.6	79	5.5	77	4.7
Sault Ste. Marie, Mich.*	14	1.9	15	1.5	24	1.7	38	2.2	49	3.0	59	3.3	64	2.6	63	3.1	55	3.9	46	2.9	33	3.3	20	2.4
Savannah, Ga.	50	2.9	52	2.9	58	4.4	66	2.9	73	4.2	79	5.9	81	7.9	81	6.5	76	5.6	67	2.8	57	1.9	50	3.3
Seattle, Wash.	38	5.8	42	4.2	44	3.6	49	2.5	55	1.7	60	1.5	65	0.7	64	1.1	60	2.0	52	3.9	45	5.9	41	5.9
Spokane, Wash.	25	2.5	32	1.7	38	1.5	46	1.1	55	1.5	62	1.4	70	0.4	68	0.6	60	0.8	48	1.4	36	2.2	29	2.4
Springfield, Mo.	33	1.7	37	2.2	44	3.0	57	4.3	65	4.9	74	4.7	78	3.6	77	2.9	69	4.1	59	3.4	46	2.3	36	2.5
Syracuse, N.Y.	24	2.7	25	2.8	33	3.0	47	3.1	57	3.0	67	3.1	72	3.1	70	3.5	63	2.7	53	3.1	41	3.3	28	3.1
Tampa, Fla.	60	2.3	62	2.9	66	3.9	72	2.1	77	2.4	81	6.5	82	8.4	82	8.0	81	6.4	75	2.5	67	1.8	62	2.2
Trenton, N.J.*	32	2.8	33	2.7	41	3.8	52	3.2	62	3.4	71	3.2	76	4.7	74	4.2	67	3.2	57	2.5	46	3.3	35	3.3
Washington, D.C.	36	2.6	37	2.5	45	3.3	56	2.9	66	3.7	75	3.5	79	4.1	77	4.7	71	3.1	60	2.7	48	2.9	37	3.0
Wilmington, Del.	32	2.9	34	2.8	42	3.7	52	3.2	62	3.4	71	3.2	76	4.3	74	4.0	68	3.4	57	2.6	46	3.5	35	3.3

Annual Climatological Data

Source: National Oceanic and Atmospheric Administration, U.S. Commerce Department

1979		Temperature °F				Precipitation[1]						Fastest Wind		No. of days			
									Sleet or snow								
Station	Elev. ft.	Highest	Date	Lowest	Date	Total (in.)	Greatest in 24 hrs.	Date	Total (in.)	Greatest in 24 hrs.	Date	MPH	Date	Clear*	Cloudy*	Prec. .01 in. or more	Snow, sleet 1 in. or more
Albany, N.Y.	275	95	7/14	−19	2/18	37.14	2.18	7/26	46.0	6.5	1/7-8	44	9/14	68	195	129	13
Albuquerque, N.M.	5311	105	7/14	8	1/30	10.35	0.85	5/20	14.5	3.0	2/16	47	8/19	172	92	59	5
Anchorage, Alas.	114	79	7/3	−16	12/31	21.15	0.96	7/24-25	77.6	13.3	3/17-18	52	2/14	76	231	139	26
Asheville, N.C.	2140	92	8/9	4	1/3	57.44	3.31	11/1-2	23.0	8.6	2/18	37	12/17	103	165	128	6
Atlanta, Ga.	1010	97	8/7	10	1/3	54.71	5.58	4/12-13	4.6	4.2	2/17-18	35	7/18	95	180	115	1
Baltimore, Md.	148	94	8/10	−3	2/10	58.98	4.41	9/5-6	39.2	20.0	2/18-19	44	1/18	104	168	127	7
Barrow, Alas.	31	70	8/24	−42	2/6	3.01	0.30	7/4	15.3	1.1	10/6	37	4/22	71	167	83	2
Birmingham, Ala.	620	99	7/5	12	1/9	69.70	—	—	T	—	—	—	—	—	—	113	0
Bismarck, N.D.	1647	95	7/8	−30	2/1	11.81	0.84	8/20-21	59.0	8.9	2/22	47	5/19	87	174	89	18
Boise, Ida.	2838	102	7/17	−13	1/30	12.07	1.61	8/13	25.2	4.0	11/25-26	40	10/19	112	164	98	8
Boston, Mass.	15	95	6/16	−3	2/11	44.17	2.72	1/20-21	19.7	4.2	1/17	45	1/25	103	163	131	7
Buffalo, N.Y.	705	90	7/20	−18	2/18	43.74	4.94	9/13-14	116.5	20.1	12/30-31	49	12/7	58	227	177	31
Burlington, Vt.	332	93	7/25	−30	2/12	31.56	1.64	9/6-7	62.4	10.4	1/7-8	40	12/15	58	213	154	18
Charleston, S.C.	40	98	8/7	20	2/10	57.98	6.40	9/4-5	1.8	1.7	2/17-18	38	9/4	110	157	117	1
Charleston, W. Va.	1016	91	8/9	1	2/11	48.87	1.97	9/20-21	54.4	7.2	2/18-19	35	1/14	67	204	183	17
Chicago, Ill.	607	92	8/7	−19	1/15	38.04	2.84	8/17-18	56.9	16.5	1/13	58	4/5	70	191	127	15
Cincinnati, Oh.	869	92	8/8	−9	2/5	52.76	4.54	9/13-14	31.9	5.4	1/27-28	35	6/20	83	197	141	11
Cleveland, Oh.	777	91	8/7	−9	2/11	39.84	2.49	5/24-25	38.6	6.9	2/26	40	4/6	59	237	159	11
Columbus, Oh.	812	90	8/7	−7	2/17	49.17	4.86	9/13-14	35.1	6.6	2/12	48	3/13	64	214	146	10
Concord, N.H.	342	94	7/14	−16	2/13	41.27	2.38	5/24-25	55.5	10.6	1/13-14	41	12/8	82	184	135	15
Dallas, Tex.	551	103	6/30	13	1/2	32.42	1.99	5/3	2.5	1.3	1/29	53	1/19	133	142	85	1
Denver, Col.	5283	99	8/6	−11	1/1	20.36	1.68	8/9-10	90.9	14.0	11/19-20	40	12/5	132	130	94	27
Des Moines, Ia.	938	97	8/7	−19	2/9	31.84	2.25	6/27	38.0	7.7	1/12-13	56	8/19	102	163	102	12
Detroit, Mich.	633	92	8/7	−11	1/15	33.04	3.08	7/11	28.4	4.8	1/13-14	56	4/5	80	192	135	11
Dodge City, Kan.	2582	101	7/8	−12	1/14	23.62	2.82	7/22-23	23.8	3.8	1/12-13	55	1/22	150	112	88	9
Duluth, Minn.	1428	88	7/11	−32	1/11	30.92	3.25	5/9-10	66.6	7.7	2/22-23	41	6/3	58	206	147	22
Fairbanks, Alas.	436	82	7/24	−51	2/7	10.33	0.76	7/5-6	42.9	6.2	1/30-31	30	12/4	81	203	119	16
Fresno, Cal.	328	111	8/1	26	12/28	9.95	0.92	1/14-15	T	T	3/13	29	5/5	182	105	52	0
Galveston, Tex.	7	92	8/6	23	1/2	59.35	13.01	7/25-26	0.0	0.0	—	49	1/20	—	—	114	0
Grand Rapids, Mich.	784	90	8/7	−21	1/11	32.64	1.80	12/24-25	71.8	10.9	1/13-14	49	4/5	68	226	141	22
Helena, Mont.	3828	98	8/5	−25	1/30	10.39	1.78	6/18-19	47.9	6.0	4/23	45	4/6	91	167	84	11
Honolulu, Ha.	7	93	10/11	57	1/3	16.93	2.73	2/3-4	0.0	0.0	—	34	12/31	76	99	89	0
Houston, Tex.	96	97	6/30	17	1/2	58.97	7.09	9/19-20	T	T	11/23	37	5/22	111	152	111	0
Huron, S.D.	1281	106	6/14	−25	1/5	15.95	1.51	4/11	42.4	6.3	1/26	42	3/13	102	160	92	16
Indianapolis, Ind.	792	92	8/8	−16	2/5	44.60	4.35	7/12-13	38.7	8.3	2/25-26	42	3/30	84	196	151	10
Jackson, Miss.	291	98	7/5	13	1/9	92.75	8.42	4/11-12	T	T	2/17	40	7/6	129	150	112	0
Jacksonville, Fla.	26	96	7/4	19	1/3	61.76	3.81	9/9-10	0.0	0.0	—	34	8/5	93	149	128	0
Juneau, Alas.	12	80	8/23	−10	2/13	49.29	2.59	11/19-20	101.0	9.4	12/17	—	—	—	—	195	29
Kansas City, Mo.	973	94	8/7	−12	2/5	31.75	1.79	6/7-8	21.5	5.6	1/12-13	36	10/20	114	151	103	8
Lander, Wyo.	5563	101	8/5	−31	1/31	11.51	1.75	5/1-2	123.5	20.2	4/10-11	61	12/4	112	134	64	24
Little Rock, Ark.	257	98	7/4	10	2/9	64.49	—	—	11.2	—	—	—	—	—	—	103	5
Los Angeles, Cal.	97	103	6/10	34	1/29	13.52	1.70	3/26-27	0.0	0.0	—	45	10/28	143	99	39	0
Louisville, Ky.	477	95	8/8	0	1/15	59.80	5.46	7/25-26	20.4	4.7	2/18	38	2/22	87	186	134	5
Marquette, Mich.	1415	89	7/12	−34	2/17	40.92	—	—	180.7	—	—	42	4/6	—	—	184	47
Memphis, Tenn.	258	97	7/4	9	2/9	70.89	3.64	4/1-2	10.4	3.3	2/6-7	46	4/11	123	157	119	5
Miami, Fla.	7	94	6/4	40	1/3	60.11	16.21	4/24-25	0.0	0.0	—	37	9/25	72	135	123	0
Milford, Ut.	5028	101	8/4	−24	1/30	7.55	0.77	3/27-28	46.1	5.1	1/5-6	45	5/5	163	105	64	17
Milwaukee, Wis.	672	94	8/7	−16	1/15	30.87	2.03	4/25-26	52.4	12.6	1/12-13	52	12/24	80	184	131	11
Minneapolis, Minn.	834	96	8/6	−28	1/11	31.07	2.29	8/20-21	46.2	5.0	2/20-21	38	4/5	82	183	116	15
Mobile, Ala.	211	97	7/5	18	2/10	79.25	8.55	9/12-13	T	T	1/29	63	9/12	101	157	116	0
Moline, Ill.	582	94	8/7	−27	1/2	34.50	2.49	8/19-20	37.9	15.1	1/12-13	49	4/11	90	164	122	12
Nashville, Tenn.	590	95	8/20	−3	2/10	70.12	6.68	9/13-14	27.5	8.3	2/6-7	32	9/13	100	178	133	7
New Orleans, La.	4	97	7/5	23	1/3	60.24	5.25	2/5-6	T	T	1/29	44	7/11	103	163	111	0
New York, N.Y.	132	95	8/10	0	2/18	52.13	3.91	1/20-21	30.2	12.7	2/19	52	9/6	—	—	129	7
Nome, Alas.	13	73	6/4	−31	12/29	22.06	1.05	7/22-23	65.0	8.7	11/14-15	46	1/14	105	202	152	20
Norfolk, Va.	24	98	8/10	14	2/18	64.96	4.36	9/5-6	13.7	6.7	2/18	46	8/8	93	160	111	3
Oklahoma City, Okla.	1285	97	8/14	−3	2/9	41.12	4.76	7/5-6	10.1	6.1	2/6	45	1/23	148	126	86	2
Omaha, Neb.	1309	98	6/14	−17	2/16	28.30	2.57	10/30	32.5	6.1	3/3	37	12/7	119	139	99	12
Philadelphia, Pa.	5	94	7/13	−2	2/11	52.79	2.70	1/20-21	44.7	14.3	2/18-19	50	11/26	87	187	143	10
Phoenix, Ariz.	1110	117	6/28	29	1/30	6.80	1.08	1/16-17	0.0	0.0	—	53	8/11	201	79	36	0
Pittsburgh, Pa.	1137	88	8/8	−12	2/11	40.56	2.09	8/10-11	37.5	6.1	2/18-19	41	4/6	62	209	166	13
Portland, Me.	43	92	5/9	−13	2/18	61.15	3.59	4/27	73.3	27.1	1/17-18	35	4/6	89	186	145	14
Portland, Ore.	21	104	7/16	14	1/1	35.75	1.67	12/1-2	3.0	1.1	2/3	44	4/12	73	220	148	1
Providence, R.I.	51	92	7/13	−7	2/14	58.19	6.71	8/3-4	15.1	4.5	2/7-8	38	12/8	95	175	130	6
Raleigh, N.C.	434	98	8/8	8	2/10	45.37	2.57	9/4-5	17.6	10.4	2/18-19	29	1/21	113	146	107	4
Rapid City, S.D.	3162	103	6/13	−23	1/14	13.99	1.24	7/3-4	19.8	3.6	1/11-12	57	8/30	108	149	91	7
Reno, Nev.	4404	102	7/18	1	1/1	6.03	1.02	12/23-24	14.3	2.6	1/15	49	10/25	139	115	53	6
Richmond, Va.	164	97	8/10	−8	2/10	57.12	3.25	9/21-22	20.2	10.9	2/18-19	43	8/8	102	173	119	4
Rochester, N.Y.	547	95	7/23	−19	2/18	34.90	3.54	9/13-14	117.9	11.3	2/1	60	4/6	55	225	186	33
St. Louis, Mo.	535	98	7/14	−10	2/9	29.48	4.91	4/10-11	25.5	4.7	1/26-27	40	3/14	96	173	119	9
Salt Lake City, Ut.	4221	104	8/4	−8	1/31	8.70	1.08	10/19-20	50.6	7.3	12/21-22	40	2/14	135	160	80	17
San Antonio, Tex.	788	98	10/3	15	1/2	36.64	3.87	6/1	T	T	11/22	48	7/10	99	151	99	0
San Diego, Cal.	13	101	6/10	40	1/29	11.62	2.64	1/30-31	0.0	0.0	—	28	10/29	140	121	46	0
San Francisco, Cal.	8	100	9/12	31	1/29	24.57	2.86	12/23-24	T	T	1/15	35	8/27	153	123	67	0
Sault Ste. Marie, Mich.	721	90	7/12	−35	2/17	43.35	2.69	8/7	138.7	11.5	4/5-6	47	4/6	72	212	170	40
Savannah, Ga.	46	99	7/4	20	1/3	61.92	6.80	9/4-5	T	T	2/18	58	9/4	100	177	127	0
Seattle, Wash.	400	98	7/16	20	1/1	32.26	2.61	12/14-15	2.1	1.2	12/15	38	2/13	63	205	129	1
Sioux City, Ia.	1095	99	6/14	−24	2/1	32.49	4.55	10/29-30	29.8	5.9	3/3-4	54	7/30	106	156	102	11
Spokane, Wash.	2357	102	7/20	−22	1/1	14.35	0.92	10/18-19	44.8	6.1	1/9-10	45	2/6	101	185	104	18
Springfield, Mo.	1268	94	8/8	−17	2/9	48.94	4.01	6/23	25.7	4.4	1/27	45	10/30	123	160	107	10
Syracuse, N.Y.	410	93	7/15	−26	2/18	38.53	2.33	9/6	89.1	9.4	3/11-12	48	4/6	56	222	173	30
Tampa, Fla.	19	94	7/3	28	1/3	66.46	11.84	5/7-8	0.0	0.0	—	39	5/8	104	117	104	0
Trenton, N.J.	56	93	7/13	−1	2/18	53.68	3.16	1/20-21	33.2	8.5	2/18-19	54	9/6	92	190	133	9
Washington, D.C.	10	97	8/10	6	2/18	47.33	3.69	9/5-6	34.9	18.7	2/18-19	49	1/18	88	181	126	5
Williston, N.D.	1899	103	6/13	−30	7/16	11.25	1.17	6/27-28	38.9	7.2	4/12	44	3/12	86	156	74	13
Wilmington, Del.	74	94	8/10	−6	2/18	53.31	2.51	8/2-3	43.6	16.5	2/18-19	35	8/2	87	184	136	11

*To get partly cloudy days deduct the total of clear and cloudy days from 365 (1 yr.). T—trace. (1) Date shown is the starting date of the storm (in some cases it lasted more than one day).

Normal Temperatures, Highs, Lows, Precipitation

Source: National Oceanic and Atmospheric Administration, U.S. Commerce Department

These normals are based on records for the thirty-year period 1941-1970. (See explanation on page 418.) The extreme temperatures (through 1979) are listed for the stations shown and may not agree with the states records shown on page 422.

Airport stations; * designates city office stations. The minus (−) sign indicates temperatures below zero. Fahrenheit thermometer registration.

State	Station	Normal temperature — January Max.	January Min.	July Max.	July Min.	Extreme temperature Highest	Lowest	Normal annual precipitation (inches)
Alabama	Mobile	61	41	91	73	104	7	66.98
Alabama	Montgomery	58	37	91	72	105	5	49.86
Alaska	Juneau	29	18	64	48	90	−22	54.67
Arizona	Phoenix	65	38	105	78	118	17	7.05
Arkansas	Little Rock	50	29	93	70	108	−5	48.52
California	Los Angeles*	67	47	83	64	110	28	14.05
California	San Francisco	55	41	71	54	106	20	19.53
Colorado	Denver	44	16	87	59	104	−30	15.51
Connecticut	Hartford	33	16	84	61	102	−26	43.37
Delaware	Wilmington	40	24	86	66	102	−6	40.25
Dist. of Col.	Washington	44	28	88	69	103	1	38.89
Florida	Jacksonville	65	45	90	72	105	12	54.47
Florida	Key West	76	66	89	80	95	46	39.99
Florida	Miami	76	59	89	76	98	31	59.80
Georgia	Atlanta	51	33	87	69	103	−3	48.34
Hawaii	Honolulu	79	65	87	73	93	53	22.90
Idaho	Boise	37	21	91	59	111	−23	11.50
Illinois	Chicago-Midway	32	17	84	65	104	−19	34.44
Indiana	Indianapolis	36	20	85	65	104	−20	38.74
Iowa	Des Moines	28	11	85	65	105	−24	30.85
Iowa	Dubuque	26	9	82	61	99	−28	40.27
Kansas	Wichita	41	21	92	70	113	−12	30.58
Kentucky	Louisville	42	25	87	66	105	−20	43.11
Louisiana	New Orleans	62	44	90	73	100	14	56.77
Maine	Portland	31	12	79	57	103	−39	40.80
Maryland	Baltimore	42	25	87	67	102	−7	40.46
Massachusetts	Boston	36	23	81	65	102	−12	42.52
Michigan	Detroit-City	32	19	83	63	105	−16	30.96
Michigan	Sault Ste. Marie*	22	6	75	53	98	−35	31.70
Minnesota	Minn.-St. Paul	21	3	82	61	104	−34	25.94
Mississippi	Jackson	58	36	93	71	103	6	49.19
Missouri	St. Louis	40	23	88	69	106	−14	35.89
Montana	Helena	28	8	84	52	105	−42	11.38
Nebraska	Omaha	33	12	89	66	114	−22	30.18
Nevada	Winnemucca	41	16	91	51	106	−34	8.47
New Hampshire	Concord	31	10	83	57	102	−37	36.17
New Jersey	Atlantic City	41	24	85	65	106	−11	45.46
New Mexico	Albuquerque	47	24	92	65	105	−17	7.77
New Mexico	Roswell	55	21	95	64	107	−9	10.61
New York	Albany	30	13	84	60	100	−28	33.36
New York	New York-La Guardia	38	26	84	69	107	−2	41.61
No. Carolina	Charlotte	52	32	88	69	104	−3	42.72
No. Carolina	Raleigh	51	30	88	67	105	−1	42.54
No. Dakota	Bismarck	19	−3	84	57	109	−44	16.16
Ohio	Cincinnati-Abbe	40	24	87	66	109	−17	40.03
Ohio	Cleveland	33	20	82	61	103	−19	34.99
Oklahoma	Oklahoma City	48	26	93	70	108	−4	31.37
Oregon	Portland	44	33	79	55	107	−3	37.61
Pennsylvania	Harrisburg	38	23	87	65	107	−8	36.47
Pennsylvania	Philadelphia	40	24	87	67	104	−5	39.93
Rhode Island	Block Island	37	25	76	63	92	−4	40.51
So. Carolina	Charleston	60	37	89	71	103	8	52.12
So. Dakota	Huron	23	2	87	61	112	−39	19.44
So. Dakota	Rapid City	34	10	86	59	110	−27	17.12
Tennessee	Nashville	48	29	90	69	107	−15	46.00
Texas	Amarillo	49	23	91	66	108	−14	20.28
Texas	Galveston*	59	48	87	79	101	8	42.20
Texas	Houston	63	42	94	73	102	17	48.19
Utah	Salt Lake City	37	19	93	61	107	−30	15.17
Vermont	Burlington	26	8	81	59	101	−30	32.54
Virginia	Norfolk	49	32	87	70	103	5	44.68
Washington	Seattle-Tacoma	43	33	75	54	99	0	38.79
Washington	Spokane	31	20	84	55	108	−25	17.42
West Virginia	Parkersburg*	41	24	86	65	106	−27	38.44
Wisconsin	Madison	25	8	81	59	104	−37	30.25
Wisconsin	Milwaukee	27	11	80	59	101	−24	29.07
Wyoming	Cheyenne	38	15	84	55	100	−34	14.65
Puerto Rico	San Juan	82	69	87	75	96	60	59.15

Mean Annual Snowfall (inches) based on record through 1979: Boston, Mass. 43; Sault Ste. Marie, Mich., 112; Albany, N.Y. 65.8; Rochester, N.Y. 89.1; Burlington, Vt., 79.1; Cheyenne, Wyo., 52.6; Juneau, Alas. 106.1.

Wettest Spot: Mount Waialeale, Ha., on the island of Kauai, is the rainiest place in the world, according to the National Geographic Society, with an average annual rainfall of 460 inches.

Highest Temperature: A temperature of 136° F. observed at Azizia, Tripolitania in Northern Africa on Sept. 13, 1922, is generally accepted as the world's highest temperature recorded under standard conditions.

The record high in the United States was 134° in Death Valley, Cal., July 10, 1913.

Lowest Temperature: A record low temperature of −126.9° F. (−88.3° C.) was recorded at the Soviet Antarctic station Vostok on Aug. 24, 1960.

The record low in the United States was −80° at Prospect Creek, Alas., Jan. 23, 1971.

The lowest official temperature on the North American continent was recorded at 81 degrees below zero in February, 1947, at a lonely airport in the Yukon called Snag.

These are the meteorological champions—the official temperature extremes—but there are plenty of other claimants to thermometer fame. However, sun readings are unofficial records, since meteorological data to qualify officially must be taken on instruments in a sheltered and ventilated location.

Record Temperatures by States Through 1979

Source: National Oceanic and Atmospheric Administration, U.S. Commerce Department

State	Lowest °F	Highest	Latest date	Station	Approximate elevation in feet
Alabama	−27		Jan. 30, 1966	New Market	725
		112	Sept. 5, 1925	Centerville	345
Alaska	−79.8		Jan. 23, 1971	Prospect Creek Camp	1,100
		100	June 27, 1915	Fort Yukon	*419
Arizona	−40		Jan. 7, 1971	Hawley Lake	8,180
		127	July 7, 1905	Parker	345
Arkansas	−29		Feb. 13, 1905	Pond	1,250
		120	Aug. 10, 1936	Ozark	396
California	−45		Jan. 20, 1937	Boca	5,532
		134	July 10, 1913	Greenland Ranch	−178
Colorado	−60		Feb. 1, 1951	Taylor Park	9,206
		118	July 11, 1888	Bennett	5,484
Connecticut	−32		Feb. 16, 1943	Falls Village	585
		105	July 22, 1926	Waterbury	409
Delaware	−17		Jan. 17, 1893	Millsboro	20
		110	July 21, 1930	Millsboro	20
Dist. of Col.	−15		Feb. 11, 1899	Washington	112
		106	July 20, 1930	Washington	112
Florida	−2		Feb. 13, 1899	Tallahassee	193
		109	June 29, 1931	Monticello	207
Georgia	−17		Jan. 27, 1940	CCC Camp F-16	1,000
		113	May 27, 1978	Greenville	860
Hawaii	14		Jan. 2, 1961	Haleakala, Maui	9,750
		100	Apr. 27, 1931	Pahala	850
Idaho	−60		Jan. 16, 1943	Island Park Dam	6,285
		118	July 28, 1934	Orofino	1,027
Illinois	−35		Jan. 22, 1930	Mount Carroll	817
		117	July 14, 1954	E. St. Louis	410
Indiana	−35		Feb. 2, 1951	Greensburg	954
		116	July 14, 1936	Collegeville	672
Iowa	−47		Jan. 12, 1912	Washta	1,157
		118	July 20, 1934	Keokuk	614
Kansas	−40		Feb. 13, 1905	Lebanon	1,812
		121	July 24, 1936	Alton (near)	1,651
Kentucky	−34		Jan. 28, 1963	Cynthiana	719
		114	July 28, 1930	Greensburg	581
Louisiana	−16		Feb. 13, 1899	Minden	194
		114	Aug. 10, 1936	Plain Dealing	268
Maine	−48		Jan. 19, 1925	Van Buren	510
		105	July 10, 1911	North Bridgton	450
Maryland	−40		Jan. 13, 1912	Oakland	2,461
		109	July 10, 1936	Cumberland and Frederick	623-325
Massachusetts	−34		Jan. 18, 1957	Birch Hill Dam	840
		107	Aug. 2, 1975	Chester and New Bedford	120-640
Michigan	−51		Feb. 9, 1934	Vanderbilt	785
		112	July 13, 1936	Mio	963
Minnesota	−59		Feb. 16, 1903	Pokegama Dam	1,280
		114	July 6, 1936	Moorhead	904
Mississippi	−19		Jan. 30, 1966	Corinth	420
		115	July 29, 1930	Holly Springs	600
Missouri	−40		Feb. 13, 1905	Warsaw	700
		118	July 14, 1954	Warsaw and Union	687-560
Montana	−70		Jan. 20, 1954	Rogers Pass	5,470
		117	July 5, 1937	Medicine Lake	1,950
Nebraska	−47		Feb. 12, 1899	Camp Clarke	3,700
		118	July 24, 1936	Minden	2,169
Nevada	−50		Jan. 8, 1937	San Jacinto	5,200
		122	June 23, 1954	Overton	1,240
New Hampshire	−47		Jan. 1934	Mt. Washington	6,262
		106	July 4, 1911	Nashua	125
New Jersey	−34		Jan. 5, 1904	River Vale	70
		110	July 10, 1936	Runyon	18
New Mexico	−50		Feb. 1, 1951	Gavilan	7,350
		116	July 14, 1934	Orogrande	4,171
New York	−52		Feb. 9, 1934	Stillwater Reservoir	1,670
		108	July 22, 1926	Troy	35
North Carolina	−29		Jan. 30, 1966	Mt. Mitchell	6,525
		109	Sept. 7, 1954	Weldon	81
North Dakota	−60		Feb. 15, 1936	Parshall	1,929
		121	July 6, 1936	Steele	1,857
Ohio	−39		Feb. 10, 1899	Milligan	800
		113	July 21, 1934	Gallipolis (near)	673
Oklahoma	−27		Jan. 18, 1930	Watts	958
		120	July 26, 1943	Tishmoningo	670
Oregon	−54		Feb. 10, 1933	Seneca	4,700
		119	Aug. 10, 1938	Pendleton	1,074
Pennsylvania	−42		Jan. 5, 1904	Smethport	1,469
		111	July 10, 1936	Phoenixville	100
Rhode Island	−23		Jan. 11, 1942	Kingston	100
		104	Aug. 2, 1975	Providence	51
South Carolina	−20		Jan. 18, 1977	Caesar's Head	3,100
		111	June 28, 1954	Camden	170
South Dakota	−58		Feb. 17, 1936	McIntosh	2,277
		120	July 5, 1936	Gannvalley	1,750

State	Lowest °F	Highest	Latest date	Station	Approximate elevation in feet
Tennessee	−32		Dec. 30, 1917	Mountain City	2,471
		113	*Aug. 9, 1930*	*Perryville*	*377*
Texas	−23		Feb. 8, 1933	Seminole	3,275
		120	*Aug. 12, 1936*	*Seymour*	*1,291*
Utah	−50		Jan. 5, 1913	Strawberry Tunnel	7,650
		116	*June 28, 1892*	*Saint George*	*2,880*
Vermont	−50		Dec. 30, 1933	Bloomfield	915
		105	*July 4, 1911*	*Vernon*	*310*
Virginia	−29		Feb. 10, 1899	Monterey	3,008
		110	*July 15, 1954*	*Balcony Falls*	*725*
Washington	−48		Dec. 30, 1968	Mazama	2,120
	−48		Dec. 30, 1968	Winthrop	1,755
		118	*Aug. 5, 1961*	*Ice Harbor Dam*	*475*
West Virginia	−37		Dec. 30, 1917	Lewisburg	2,200
		112	*July 10, 1936*	*Martinsburg*	*435*
Wisconsin	−54		Jan. 24, 1922	Danbury	908
		114	*July 13, 1936*	*Wisconsin Dells*	*900*
Wyoming	−63		Feb. 9, 1933	Moran	6,770
		114	*July 12, 1900*	*Basin*	*3,500*

Canadian Normal Temperatures, Highs, Lows, Precipitation

Source: Atmospheric Environment Service, Environment Canada

These normals are based on varying periods of record over the thirty-year period 1941 to 1970 inclusive. Extreme temperatures are based on varying periods of record for each station through 1979. Airport station; * designates city office stations. The minus (−) sign indicates temperatures below zero. Celsius thermometer registration.

Province	Station	Temperature — Normal — January Max.	January Min.	July Max.	July Min.	Extreme — Highest	Extreme — Lowest	Precipitation normal annual (millimeters)
Alberta	Calgary	−5	−17	24	10	36	−45	437
Alberta	Edmonton (Industrial Airport)	−10	−19	23	12	34	−48	446
British Columbia	Prince George	−7	−16	22	8	34	−50	621
British Columbia	Victoria	6	2	20	11	35	−16	657
British Columbia	Vancouver	5	0	22	13	33	−18	1068
Manitoba	Churchill	−24	−31	17	7	33	−45	397
Manitoba	Winnipeg	−13	−23	26	14	41	−45	535
Newfoundland	Gander	−2	−10	22	11	36	−27	1078
Newfoundland	St. John's	−1	−7	20	10	31	−23	1511
New Brunswick	Fredericton	−4	−14	26	13	37	−37	1060
New Brunswick	Moncton	−3	−13	25	13	37	−32	1099
New Brunswick	Saint John	−2	−13	22	11	34	−37	1400
Nova Scotia	Halifax	−2	−10	23	13	34	−26	1396
Nova Scotia	Sydney	−1	−8	23	13	35	−25	1341
Ontario	Ottawa	−6	−16	26	15	38	−36	851
Ontario	Sudbury	−8	−18	25	13	36	−38	835
Ontario	Toronto	−1	−8	27	17	41	−33	790
Ontario	Windsor	−1	−8	28	17	38	−26	836
Prince Edward Island	Charlottetown	−3	−11	23	14	34	−28	1128
Quebec	Montreal	−5	−14	26	16	36	−38	941
Quebec	Quebec City	−7	−16	25	13	36	−36	1089
Quebec	Val-d'Or	−11	−23	23	11	34	−44	902
Saskatchewan	Prince Albert	−15	−27	25	11	38	−50	389
Saskatchewan	Regina	−12	−23	26	12	43	−50	398
Northwest Territories	Alert*	−28	−36	7	1	20	−49	156
Northwest Territories	Yellowknife	−24	−33	21	11	32	−51	250
Yukon Territory	Dawson*	−25	−32	22	9	35	−58	325
Yukon Territory	Whitehorse*	−15	−23	20	8	34	−52	260

Low and High Temperature Records Through 1979

Source: Atmospheric Environment Service, Environment Canada

Province	Lowest °C	Highest	Latest date	Station	Approximate elevation in meters
Alberta	−61		Jan. 11, 1911	Fort Vermillion	278
		42	*July 12, 1886*	*Medicine Hat*	721
British Columbia	−59		Jan. 31, 1947	Smith River	673
		44	*July 17, 1941*	*Chinock Cove*	404
		44	*July 17, 1941*	*Lillooet*	290
		44	*July 17, 1941*	*Lytton*	183
Manitoba	−53		Jan. 9, 1899	Norway House	219
		44	*July 12, 1936*	*Emerson*	241
Newfoundland	−49		Mar. 7, 1968	Twin Falls	457
		42	*Aug. 11, 1914*	*Northwest River*	61
New Brunswick	−47		Feb. 1, 1955	Sisson Dam	278
		39	*Aug. 19, 1935*	*Rexton*	6
Nova Scotia	−41		Jan. 31, 1920	Upper Stewiacke	23
		38	*Aug. 19, 1935*	*Collegeville*	76
Ontario	−58		Jan. 23, 1935	Iroquois Falls	244
		42	*July 13, 1936*	*Fort Frances*	354
Prince Edward Island	−37		Jan. 26, 1884	Kilmahumaig	6
		37	*Aug. 19, 1935*	*Charlottetown*	22
Quebec	−54		Feb. 5, 1923	Doucet	376
		40	*Aug. 15 1928*	*Bark Lake*	365
Saskatchewan	−57		Feb. 1, 1893	Prince Albert	436
		45	*July 5, 1937*	*Midale*	582
		45	*July 5, 1937*	*Yellow Grass*	579
North West Territories	−57		Dec. 26, 1917	Fort Smith	202
		39	*July 18, 1941*	*Fort Smith*	207
Yukon Territory	−63		Feb. 3, 1947	Snag	586
		35	*June 18, 1950*	*Mayo*	495

Canadian Normal Temperature and Precipitation

Source: Atmospheric Environment Service, Environment Canada

Normal refers to the mean daily temperature and total monthly precipitation based on varying periods of record over the thirty-year period 1941 to 1970 inclusive. In most cases no adjustment factor was used.

Airport station; *designates city office stations. T, temperature in Celsius; P, precipitation in millimeters.

	Jan.		Feb.		Mar.		Apr.		May		June		July		Aug.		Sept.		Oct.		Nov.		Dec.	
Station	T.	P.	T.	P.	T.	P.	T.	P.	T.	P.	T.	P.	T.	P.	T.	P.	T.	P.	T.	P.	T.	P.	T.	P.
Calgary, Alta.	−11	17	−7	20	−4	20	3	30	9	50	13	92	17	68	15	56	11	35	6	19	−3	16	−8	15
Charlottetown, P.E.I.	−7	111	−7	95	−3	85	2	82	9	82	14	83	18	73	18	93	14	86	9	97	3	126	−4	116
Churchill, Man.	−28	14	−27	13	−20	18	−11	24	−2	28	6	40	12	49	12	58	6	52	−1	40	−12	40	−22	20
Dawson, Yukon*	−29	19	−23	16	−14	13	−2	9	8	22	14	37	16	53	13	51	6	28	−3	27	−17	25	−25	26
Edmonton, Alta.	−15	25	−11	20	−5	17	4	23	11	37	15	75	18	83	16	72	11	36	5	19	−4	19	−11	21
Fredericton, N.B.	−9	95	−8	93	−2	69	4	74	11	81	16	79	19	88	18	88	13	82	8	88	2	109	−6	114
Frobisher Bay, N.W.T.	−26	24	−25	28	−22	21	−14	22	−3	23	4	38	8	53	7	58	2	43	−5	42	−12	37	−20	26
Halifax, N.S.	−6	137	−7	128	−2	104	3	108	9	99	15	79	18	80	18	108	14	95	9	118	4	163	−3	179
Hamilton, Ont.*	−5	66	−4	60	0	66	7	78	13	72	19	71	22	72	21	77	17	71	11	69	5	67	−2	67
Kitchener, Ont.*	−7	61	−6	56	−1	71	7	71	13	83	18	81	21	89	20	79	16	73	10	71	3	78	−4	74
London, Ont.	−6	76	−6	65	−1	72	7	78	12	75	18	81	21	81	20	73	16	79	10	74	3	83	−4	87
Moncton, N.B.	−8	107	−8	100	−3	93	3	84	10	80	15	91	19	80	18	80	14	73	8	91	2	113	−5	109
Montreal, Que.	−10	76	−9	71	−2	71	6	74	13	67	19	83	21	85	20	87	15	80	9	75	2	87	−7	86
Ottawa, Ont.	−11	60	−10	57	−3	61	6	68	12	70	18	73	21	81	19	82	15	79	9	66	1	79	−8	77
Quebec City, Que.	−12	86	−11	77	−4	69	3	75	11	81	16	102	19	108	18	103	13	106	7	82	0	100	−9	101
Regina, Sask.	−17	18	−14	17	−8	18	3	23	11	41	15	83	19	58	18	50	12	36	5	19	−5	18	−13	16
Saint John, N.B.	−7	145	−8	131	−3	105	3	112	9	102	14	95	17	89	16	99	13	103	8	110	3	154	−5	157
St. John's, Nfld.	−4	145	−4	156	−2	133	1	114	6	99	10	89	15	83	15	113	12	112	7	139	4	161	−1	167
Saskatoon, Sask.	−19	18	−15	18	−9	17	3	21	11	34	15	57	19	53	17	45	11	33	5	19	−6	19	−14	18
Sault Ste. Marie, Ont.	−11	81	−11	55	−5	57	3	56	9	85	15	88	18	72	18	67	13	95	8	79	1	106	−6	94
Toronto, Ont.	−4	63	−4	57	1	66	8	67	13	73	19	63	22	81	21	67	17	61	11	62	5	67	−2	64
Vancouver, B.C.	2	147	4	117	6	94	9	61	12	48	15	45	17	30	17	37	14	61	10	122	6	141	4	165
Victoria, B.C.	4	107	6	76	7	49	9	34	12	21	14	21	16	12	16	20	14	33	11	74	7	95	5	115
Whitehorse, Yukon.	−19	19	−13	14	−8	15	0	11	7	14	12	29	14	33	12	36	8	29	1	20	−9	22	−16	20
Windsor, Ont.	−4	55	−3	52	1	66	8	81	14	83	20	84	22	83	21	82	17	61	12	63	4	62	−2	64
Winnipeg, Man.	−18	24	−16	19	−8	26	3	37	11	57	17	80	20	80	19	74	13	53	7	35	−4	27	−14	23
Yellowknife, N.W.T.	−29	14	−26	12	−19	12	−8	10	4	14	12	17	16	33	14	36	7	28	−1	31	−14	24	−24	19

Canadian Annual Climatological Data

Source: Atmospheric Environment Service, Environment Canada

Station		Temperature (Celsius)				Precipitation			Snowfall			Fastest wind		No. of days	
1978	Elev. meters	Highest	Date D/Mo.	Lowest	Date D/Mo.	Total (mm)	Greatest in 24 hrs.	Date D/Mo.	Total (cm)	Greatest in 24 hrs.	Date D./Mo.	Km/h	Date D/Mo.	Precip., measurable	Snow, sleet
Calgary, Alta.	1084	34.3	21/7	−33.8	15/2	284.6	26.0	20/6	129.9	9.4	14/12	96	sev.	108	61
Charlottetown, P.E.I.	55	29.8	16/6	−23.9	12,13/2	1513.5	70.0	17/7	194.9	15.0	14/1	96	8/12	180	63
Churchill, Manitoba	29	33.8	7/7	−45.4	13/2	340.9	20.2	1/8	175.1	17.0	5/3	85	16/10	156	101
Dawson, Yukon	369	29.5	25/7	−55.8	11/2	365.0	23.5	18/7	125.0	12.0	19/3	52	29/11	n.a.	n.a.
Edmonton, Alberta	671	33.3	19/7	−32.1	15/2	484.7	48.4	11/7	136.4	25.8	9/12	98	6/12	111	56
Fredericton, N.B.	20	33.9	10/7	−26.7	17/1	1520.6	58.0	13/8	188.0	16.4	26/2	87	6/5	176	60
Frobisher, N.W.T.	34	18.0	12/7	−44.7	17.2	636.7	40.4	1/9	102.9	24.9	10/11	130	12/3	170	78
Halifax, N.S.	145	30.4	16/6	−22.4	18/2	1746.4	75.8	5/8	80.8	75.8	18/1	83	sev.	181	40
Hamilton, Ont.	237	31.0	15/7	−25.5	17/2	918.1	38.8	14/9	143.4	29.2	9/4	119	6/4	166	44
London, Ont.	278	30.5	14/8	−25.9	17/2	1020.7	50.7	1/8	1623	12.8	14/3	100	26/11	n.a.	n.a.
Moncton, N.B.	71	30.9	16/6	−25.3	18.2	1583.7	73.6	17/7	238.5	19.4	26/2	82	19/3	193	68
Montreal, Que.	36	32.3	14/7	−28.5	18/2	922.5	81.9	14/9	151.5	32.8	21/1	117	6/10	216	50
Ottawa, Ont.	114	32.8	14/7	−29.3	11/2	1111.3	63.0	14/9	205.7	30.0	21/1	89	16/6	164	55
Quebec, Que.	73	32.0	25/7	−30.1	17/2	1340.9	81.2	14/9	303.3	26.4	21/1	96	sev.	174	51
Regina, Sask.	577	36.2	13/6	−36.6	13/1	286.1	20.6	sev.	115.3	23.2	12/4	126	17/4	111	62
St. John, N.B.	109	30.2	16/6	−23.8	18.2	1974.6	78.0	8/1	176.0	14.8	26/2	93	14/5	193	54
St. John's, Nfld.	140	29.6	4/8	−18.6	21/2	1491.7	47.6	27/12	243.2	35.5	9/1	120	11/12	280	76
Saskatoon, Sask.	501	34.3	19/7	−39.7	15/2	336.5	28.3	21/5	128.2	13.6	13/2	98	1/8	123	69
Sault Ste. Marie, Ont.	192	31.4	4/7	−38.7	17/2	1097.0	59.1	7/8	300.1	27.0	6/4	89	6/4	188	83
Thunder Bay, Ont.	199	33.8	21/7	−39.0	16/1	670.0	34.4	10/5	253.0	18.0	22/3	82	5/9	141	61
Toronto, Ont.	111	30.4	16/6	−24.7	17/2	873.6	41.8	24/1	177.5	27.0	1/12	108	6/4	149	36
Vancouver, B.C.	2	28.7	17/7	−11.2	1/1	986.1	87.5	17/12	10.1	4.0	26/1	85	9/12	153	8
Victoria, B.C.	69	32.1	16/7	−10.8	1/1	780.7	70.2	17/12	16.7	7.3	2/2	59	14/12	115	4
Waterloo-Wellington, Ont.	314	31.1	14/7	−29.2	18/2	928.4	36.2	23/8	82.4	11.9	4/4	83	sev.	176	57
Whitehorse, Yukon	703	27.5	sev.	−45.2	sev.	256.6	17.4	7/7	96.0	8.2	2/3	74	sev.	122	60
Windsor, Ont.	190	33.9	7/8	−21.6	15.1	888.7	61.2	9/7	84.3	8.4	15/1	100	5/4	146	42
Winnipeg, Man.	239	34.0	13/6	−38.8	16/2	471.5	40.8	1/8	127.8	8.8	13/3	93	8/1	140	76
Yellowknife, N.W.T.	205	30.2	17/8	−46.8	13/2	279.7	14.2	20/8	143.3	11/2	28/5	67	sev.	109	85

sev. - several

Speed of Winds in Canada

Source: Atmospheric Environment Service, Environment Canada

Kilometers-per-hour average in most cases is for the period of record 1955 to 1972. High is based on varying periods of record dependent on the origin of the station through 1979.

Station	Avg.	High	Station	Avg.	High	Station	Avg.	High
Calgary, Alta.	21.4	105	London, Ont.	16.4	101	Sault Ste. Marie, Ont.	15.3	89
Charlottetown, P.E.I.	19.3	103	Moncton, N.B.	18.7	100	Thunder Bay, Ont.	14.2	81
Churchill, Man.	25.2	126	Montreal, Que.	15.8	82	Toronto, Ont.	17.2	90
Dawson, Yukon.	6.7	52	Ottawa, Ont.	15.1	87	Vancouver, B.C.	12.1	89
Edmonton, Alta.	14.9	71	Quebec City, Que.	16.7	109	Victoria, B.C.	17.7	109
Fredericton, N.B.	14.2	81	Regina, Sask.	21.5	97	Whitehorse, Yukon	15.1	81
Frobisher Bay, N.W.T.	16.6	129	Saint John, N.B.	19.0	97	Windsor, Ont.	17.1	92
Halifax, N.S.	18.3	97	Saint John's, Nfld.	24.3	137	Winnipeg, Man.	19.3	90
Hamilton, Ont.	12.8	66	Saskatoon, Sask.	17.9	105	Yellowknife, N.W.T.	16.1	72

WEIGHTS AND MEASURES

Source: National Bureau of Standards, U.S. Commerce Department

U.S. Moving, Inch by 25.4 mm, to Metric System

On July 2, 1971, following the report of a metric conversion study committee, Commerce Secy. Maurice H. Stans recommended a gradual U.S. changeover during a 10-year period at the end of which the U.S. would be predominantly, but not exclusively, on the metric system. The Metric Conversion Act of 1975, signed Dec. 23, 1975, declared a national policy of coordinating voluntary increasing use of the Metric System and established a U. S. Metric Board to coordinate the change over.

Currently conversion to metric is confined to the following industries: automotive, construction and farm equipment, computer, and bottling. In addition, with encouragement of the U.S. Education Department, our school systems are emphasizing teaching of the metric system.

The International System of Units

Two systems of weights and measures exist side by side in the United States today, with roughly equal but separate legislative sanction: the U.S. Customary System and the International (Metric) System. Throughout U.S. history, the Customary System (inherited from, but now different from, the British Imperial System) has been, as its name implies, customarily used; a plethora of federal and state legislation has given it, through implication, standing as our primary weights and measures system. However, the Metric System (incorporated in the scientists' new SI or Systeme International d'Unites) is the only system that has ever received specific legislative sanction by Congress. The "Law of 1866" reads:

It shall be lawful throughout the United States of America to employ the weights and measures of the metric system; and no contract or dealing, or pleading in any court, shall be deemed invalid or liable to objection because the weights or measures expressed or referred to therein are weights or measures of the metric system.

Over the last 100 years, the Metric System has seen slow, steadily increasing use in the United States and, today, is of importance nearly equal to the Customary System.

On Feb. 10, 1964, the National Bureau of Standards issued the following bulletin:

Henceforth it shall be the policy of the National Bureau of Standards to use the units of the International System (SI), as adopted by the 11th General Conference on Weights and Measures (October 1960), except when the use of these units would obviously impair communication or reduce the usefulness of a report.

What had been the Metric System became the International System (SI), a more complete scientific system.

Seven units have been adopted to serve as the base for the International System as follows: **length**—meter; **mass**—kilogram; **time**—second; **electric current**—ampere; **thermodynamic temperature**—kelvin; **amount of substance**—mole; and **luminous intensity**—candela.

Prefixes

The following prefixes, in combination with the basic unit names, provide the multiples and submultiples in the International System. For example, the unit name "meter," with the prefix "kilo" added, produces "kilometer," meaning "1,000 meters."

Prefix	Symbol	Multiples and submultiples	Equivalent	Prefix	Symbol	Multiples and submultiples	Equivalent
exa	E	10^{18}	quintillionfold	deci	d	10^{-1}	tenth part
peta	P	10^{15}	quadrillionfold	centi	c	10^{-2}	hundredth part
tera	T	10^{12}	trillionfold	milli	m	10^{-3}	thousandth part
giga	G	10^{9}	billionfold	micro	mu	10^{-6}	millionth part
mega	M	10^{6}	millionfold	nano	n	10^{-9}	billionth part
kilo	k	10^{3}	thousandfold	pico	p	10^{-12}	trillionth part
hecto	h	10^{2}	hundredfold	femto	f	10^{-15}	quadrillionth part
deka	da	10	tenfold	atto	a	10^{-18}	quintillionth part

Tables of Metric Weights and Measures

Linear Measure

10 millimeters (mm)	= 1 centimeter (cm)
10 centimeters	= 1 decimeter (dm) = 100 millimeters
10 decimeters	= 1 meter (m) = 1,000 millimeters
10 meters	= 1 dekameter (dam)
10 dekameters	= 1 hectometer (hm) = 100 meters
10 hectometers	= 1 kilometer (km) = 1,000 meters

Area Measure

100 square millimeters (mm^2)	= 1 square centimeter (cm^2)
10,000 square centimeters	= 1 square meter (m^2) = 1,000,000 square millimeters
100 square meters	= 1 are (a)
100 ares	= 1 hectare (ha) = 10,000 square meters
100 hectares	= 1 square kilometer (km^2) = 1,000,000 square meters

Fluid Volume Measure

10 milliliters (mL)	= 1 centiliter (cL)
10 centiliters	= 1 deciliter (dL) = 100 milliliters
10 deciliters	= 1 liter (L) = 1,000 milliliters
10 liters	= 1 dekaliter (daL)
10 dekaliters	= 1 hectoliter (hL) = 100 liters
10 hectoliters	= 1 kiloliter (kL) = 1,000 liters

Cubic Measure

1,000 cubic millimeters (mm^3)	= 1 cubic centimeter (cm^3)
1,000 cubic centimeters	= 1 cubic decimeter (dm^3) = 1,000,000 cubic millimeters
1,000 cubic decimeters	= 1 cubic meter (m^3) = 1 stere = 1,000,000 cubic centimeters = 1,000,000,000 cubic millimeters

Weight

10 milligrams (mg)	= 1 centigram (cg)
10 centigrams	= 1 decigram (dg) = 100 milligrams
10 decigrams	= 1 gram (g) = 1,000 milligrams
10 grams	= 1 dekagram (dag)
10 dekagrams	= 1 hectogram (hg) = 100 grams
10 hectograms	= 1 kilogram (kg) = 1,000 grams
1,000 kilograms	= 1 metric ton (t)

Table of U.S. Customary Weights and Measures

Linear Measure

12 inches (in)	= 1 foot (ft)
3 feet	= 1 yard (yd)
5 1/2 yards	= 1 rod (rd), pole, or perch (16 1/2 feet)
40 rods	= 1 furlong (fur) = 220 yards = 660 feet
8 furlongs	= 1 survey mile (mi) = 1,760 yards = 5,280 feet
3 miles	= 1 league = 5,280 yards = 15,840 feet
6076.11549 feet	= 1 International Nautical Mile

Liquid Measure

When necessary to distinguish the liquid pint or quart from the dry pint or quart, the word "liquid" or the abbreviation "liq" should be used in combination with the name or abbreviation of the liquid unit.

4 gills	= 1 pint (pt) = 28.875 cubic inches
2 pints	= 1 quart (qt) = 57.75 cubic inches
4 quarts	= 1 gallon (gal) = 231 cubic inches = 8 pints = 32 gills

Area Measure

Squares and cubes of units are sometimes abbreviated by using "superior" figures. For example. ft^2 means square foot, and ft^3 means cubic foot.

144 square inches	= 1 square foot (ft^2)
9 square feet	= 1 square yard (yd^2) = 1,296 square inches
30 ¼ square yards	= 1 square rod (rd^2) = 272 ¼ square feet
160 square rods	= 1 acre = 4,840 square yards = 43,560 square feet
640 acres	= 1 square mile (mi^2)
1 mile square	= 1 section (of land)
6 miles square	= 1 township = 36 sections = 36 square miles

Cubic Measure

1 cubic foot (ft^3)	= 1,728 cubic inches (in^3)
27 cubic feet	= 1 cubic yard (yd^3)

Gunter's or Surveyors' Chain Measure

7.92 inches (in)	= 1 link
100 links	= 1 chain (ch) = 4 rods = 66 feet
80 chains	= 1 survey mile (mi) = 320 rods = 5,280 feet

Troy Weight

24 grains	= 1 pennyweight (dwt)
20 pennyweights	= 1 ounce troy (oz t) = 480 grains
12 ounces troy	= 1 pound troy (lb t) = 240 pennyweights = 5,760 grains

Dry Measure

When necessary to distinguish the dry pint or quart from the liquid pint or quart, the word "dry" should be used in combination with the name or abbreviation of the dry unit.

2 pints (pt)	= 1 quart (qt) = 67.2006 cubic inches
8 quarts	= 1 peck (pk) = 537.605 cubic inches = 16 pints
4 pecks	= 1 bushel (bu) = 2,150.42 cubic inches = 32 quarts

Avoirdupois Weight

When necessary to distinguish the avoirdupois ounce or pound from the troy ounce or pound, the word "avoirdupois" or the abbreviation "avdp" should be used in combination with the name or abbreviation of the avoirdupois unit.

(The "grain" is the same in avoirdupois and troy weight.)

27 11/32 grains	= 1 dram (dr)
16 drams	= 1 ounce (oz) = 437 ½ grains
16 ounces	= 1 pound (lb) = 256 drams = 7,000 grains
100 pounds	= 1 hundredweight (cwt)°
20 hundredweights	= 1 ton = 2,000 pounds°

In "gross" or "long" measure, the following values are recognized.

112 pounds	= 1 gross or long hundredweight°
20 gross or long hundredweights	= 1 gross or long ton = 2,240 pounds°

°When the terms "hundredweight" and "ton" are used unmodified, they are commonly understood to mean the 100-pound hundredweight and the 2,000-pound ton, respectively: these units may be designated "net" or "short" when necessary to distinguish them from the corresponding units in gross or long measure.

Tables of Equivalents

In this table it is necessary to distinguish between the "international" and the "survey" foot. The international foot, defined in 1959 as exactly equal to 0.3048 meter, is shorter than the old survey foot by approximately 6 parts in 10 million. The survey foot is still used in data expressed in feet in geodetic surveys within the U.S. In this table the survey foot is italicized.

When the name of a unit is enclosed in brackets thus, [1 hand], this indicates (1) that the unit is not in general current use in the United States, or (2) that the unit is believed to be based on "custom and usage" rather than on formal definition.

Equivalents involving decimals are, in most instances, rounded off to the third decimal place except where they are exact, in which cases these exact equivalents are so designated.

Lengths

1 angstrom (A)	0.1 nanometer (exactly) 0.000 1 micron (exactly) 0.000 000 1 millimeter (exactly) 0.000 000 004 inch
1 cable's length	120 fathoms (exactly) 720 *feet* (exactly) 219 meters
1 centimeter (cm)	0.3937 inch
1 chain (ch) (Gunter's or surveyors)	66 *feet* (exactly) 20.1168 meters
1 chain (engineers)	100 feet 30.48 meters (exactly)
1 decimeter (dm)	3.937 inches
1 degree (geographical)	364,566.929 feet 69.047 miles (avg.) 111.123 kilometers (avg.)
-of latitude	68.078 miles at equator 69.043 miles at poles
-of longitude	69.171 miles
1 dekameter (dam)	32.808 feet
1 fathom	6 *feet* (exactly) 1.8288 meters (exactly)
1 foot (ft)	0.3048 meters (exactly)
1 furlong (fur)	10 chains (surveyors) (exactly) 660 *feet* (exactly) ⅛ survey mile (exactly) 201.168 meters
[1 hand] (height measure for horses from ground to top of shoulders)	4 inches
1 inch (in)	2.54 centimeters (exactly)
1 kilometer (km)	0.621 mile 3,281.5 feet
1 league (land)	3 survey miles (exactly) 4.828 kilometers
1 link (Gunter's or surveyors)	7.92 inches (exactly) 0.201 meter
1 link engineers	1 foot 0.305 meter
1 meter (m)	39.37 inches 1.094 yards
1 micron (u) [the Greek letter mu]	0.001 millimeter (exactly) 0.000 039 37 inch
1 mil	0.001 inch (exactly) 0.025 4 millimeter (exactly)
1 mile (mi) (survey or land)	5,280 *feet* (exactly) 1.609 kilometers
1 international nautical mile (INM)	1.852 kilometers (exactly) 1.150779 survey miles 6,076.11549 feet
1 millimeter (mm)	0.039 37 inch
1 nanometer (nm)	0.001 micron (exactly) 0.000 000 039 37 inch
1 pica (typography)	12 points
1 point (typography)	0.013 837 inch (exactly) 0.351 millimeter
1 rod (rd), pole, or perch	16 ½ *feet* (exactly) 5.029 meters
1 yard (yd)	0.9144 meter (exactly)

Areas or Surfaces

1 acre	43,560 square *feet* (exactly) 4,840 square yards 0.405 hectare
1 are (a)	119.599 square yards 0.025 acre

(continued)

1 bolt (cloth measure):	
length	100 yards (on modern looms)
width	42 inches (usually, for cotton) 60 inches (usually, for wool)
1 hectare (ha)	2.471 acres
[1 square (building)]	100 square feet
1 square centimeter (cm^2)	0.155 square inch
1 square decimeter (dm^2)	15.500 square inches
1 square foot (ft^2)	929.030 square centimeters
1 square inch (in^2)	6.4516 square centimeters (exactly)
1 square kilometer (km^2)	247.105 acres 0.386 square mile
1 square meter (m^2)	1.196 square yards 10.764 square feet
1 square mile (mi^2)	258.999 hectares
1 square millimeter (mm^2)	0.002 square inch
1 square rod (rd^2) sq. pole, or sq. perch	25.293 square meters
1 square yard (yd^2)	0.836 square meter

Capacities or Volumes

1 barrel (bbl) liquid	31 to 42 gallons°

°There are a variety of "barrels," established by law or usage. For example: federal taxes on fermented liquors are based on a barrel of 31 gallons: many state laws fix the "barrel for liquids" as 31 ½ gallons; one state fixes a 36-gallon barrel for cistern measurement; federal law recognizes a 40-gallon barrel for "proof spirits"; by custom, 42 gallons comprise a barrel of crude oil or petroleum products for statistical purposes, and this equivalent is recognized "for liquids" by 4 states.

1 barrel (bbl), standard, for fruits, vegetables, and other dry commodities except dry cranberries	7,056 cubic inches 105 dry quarts 3.281 bushels, struck measure
1 barrel (bbl), standard, cranberry	5,826 cubic inches 86 45/64 dry quarts 2.709 bushels, struck measure
1 board foot (lumber measure)	a foot-square board 1 inch thick
1 bushel (bu) (U.S.) (struck measure)	2,150.42 cubic inches (exactly) 35.238 liters
[1 bushel, heaped (U.S.)]	2,747.715 cubic inches 1.278 bushels, struck measure°

°Frequently recognized as 1¼ bushels, struck measure.

[1 bushel (bu) (British Imperial) (struck measure)]	1.032 U.S. bushels struck measure 2,219.36 cubic inches
1 cord (cd) firewood	128 cubic feet (exactly)
1 cubic centimeter (cm^3)	0.061 cubic inch
1 cubic decimeter (dm^3)	61.024 cubic inches
1 cubic inch (in^3)	0.554 fluid ounce 4.433 fluid drams 16.387 cubic centimeters
1 cubic foot (ft^3)	7.481 gallons 28.317 cubic decimeters
1 cubic meter (m^3)	1.308 cubic yards
1 cubic yard (yd^3)	0.765 cubic meter
1 cup, measuring	8 fluid ounces (exactly) ½ liquid pint (exactly)
[1 dram, fluid (fl dr) (British)]	0.961 U.S. fluid dram 0.217 cubic inch 3.552 milliliters
1 dekaliter (dal)	2.642 gallons 1.135 pecks
1 gallon (gal) (U.S.)	231 cubic inches (exactly) 3.785 liters 0.833 British gallon 128 U.S. fluid ounces (exactly)
[1 gallon (gal) British Imperial]	277.42 cubic inches 1.201 U.S. gallons 4.546 liters 160 British fluid ounces (exactly)
1 gill (gi)	7.219 cubic inches 4 fluid ounces (exactly) 0.118 liter
1 hectoliter (hl)	26.418 gallons 2.838 bushels
1 liter (l) (1 cubic decimeter exactly)	1.057 liquid quarts 0.908 dry quart 61.025 cubic inches
1 milliliter (ml) (1 cu cm exactly)	0.271 fluid dram 16.231 minims 0.061 cubic inch
1 ounce, liquid (U.S.)	1.805 cubic inches 29.573 milliliters 1.041 British fluid ounces
[1 ounce, fluid (fl oz) (British)]	0.961 U.S. fluid ounce 1.734 cubic inches 28.412 milliliters
1 peck (pk)	8.810 liters
1 pint (pt), dry	33.600 cubic inches 0.551 liter
1 pint (pt), liquid	28.875 cubic inches (exactly) 0.473 liter
1 quart (qt) dry (U.S.)	67.201 cubic inches 1.101 liters 0.969 British quart
1 quart (qt) liquid (U.S.)	57.75 cubic in (exactly) 0.946 liter 0.833 British quart
[1 quart (qt) (British)]	69.354 cubic inches 1.032 U.S. dry quarts 1.201 U.S. liquid quarts
1 tablespoon	3 teaspoons°(exactly) 4 fluid drams ½ fluid ounce (exactly)
1 teaspoon	⅓ tablespoon°(exactly) 1⅓ fluid drams°

°The equivalent "1 teaspoon—1⅓ fluid drams" has been found by the bureau to correspond more closely with the actual capacities of "measuring" and silver teaspoons than the equivalent "1 teaspoon—1 fluid dram" which is given by many dictionaries.

Weights or Masses

1 assay ton°° (AT)	29.167 grams

°°Used in assaying. The assay ton bears the same relation to the milligram that a ton of 2,000 pounds avoirdupois bears to the ounce troy; hence the weight in milligrams of precious metal obtained from one assay ton of ore gives directly the number of troy ounces to the net ton.

1 bale (cotton measure)	500 pounds in U.S. 750 pounds in Egypt
1 carat (c)	200 milligrams (exactly) 3.086 grains
1 dram avoirdupois (dr avdp)	27 11/32 (=27.344) grains 1.772 grams
gamma, see microgram	
1 grain	64.799 milligrams
1 gram	15.432 grains 0.035 ounce, avoirdupois
1 hundredweight, gross or long°°° (gross cwt)	112 pounds (exactly) 50.802 kilograms
1 hundredweight, net or short (cwt. or net cwt.)	100 pounds (exactly) 45.359 kilograms
1 kilogram (kg)	2.205 pounds
1 microgram (μg [The Greek letter mu in combination with the letter g])	0.000001 gram (exactly)
1 milligram (mg)	0.015 grain
1 ounce, avoirdupois (oz avdp)	437.5 grains (exactly) 0.911 troy ounce 28.350 grams
1 ounce, troy (oz t)	480 grains (exactly) 1.097 avoirdupois ounces 31.103 grams
1 pennyweight (dwt)	1.555 grams
1 pound, avoirdupois (lb avdp)	7,000 grains (exactly) 1.215 troy pounds 453.592 37 grams (exactly)
1 pound, troy (lb t)	5,760 grains (exactly) 0.823 avoirdupois pound 373.242 grams
1 ton, gross or long°°° (gross ton)	2,240 pounds (exactly) 1.12 net tons (exactly) 1.016 metric tons

°°°The gross or long ton and hundredweight are used commercially in the United States to only a limited extent, usually in restricted industrial fields. These units are the same as British "ton" and "hundredweight."

1 ton, metric (t)	2,204.623 pounds 0.984 gross ton 1.102 net tons
1 ton, net or short (sh ton)	2,000 pounds (exactly) 0.893 gross ton 0.907 metric ton

Tables of Interrelation of Units of Measurement

Units of length and area of the international and survey measures are included in the following tables. Units unique to the survey measure are italicized. See pg 426, Tables of Equivalents, 1st para.

1 international foot = 0.999 998 survey foot (exactly)
1 survey foot = 1200/3937 meter (exactly)
1 international foot = 12 × 0.0254 meter (exactly)

Bold face type indicates exact values

Units of Length

Units	Inches	*Links*	Feet	Yards	*Rods*	*Chains*	Miles	cm	Meters
1 inch=	**1**	0.126 263	0.083 333	0.027 778	0.005 051	0.001 263	0.000 016	**2.54**	**0.025 4**
1 *link*=	**7.92**	**1**	**0.66**	**0.22**	**0.04**	**0.01**	**0.000 125**	20.117	0.201 168
1 foot=	**12**	1.515 152	**1**	0.333 333	0.060 606	0.015 152	0.000 189	**30.48**	**0.304 8**
1 yard=	**36**	4.545 45	**3**	**1**	0.181 818	0.045 455	0.000 568	**91.44**	**0.914 4**
1 *rod*=	**198**	**25**	**16.5**	**5.5**	**1**	**0.25**	**0.003 125**	502.92	5.029 2
1 *chain*=	**792**	**100**	**66**	**22**	**4**	**1**	**0.012 5**	2011.68	20.116 8
1 mile=	**63 360**	**8000**	**5280**	**1760**	**320**	**80**	**1**	**160 934.4**	**1609.344**
1 cm=	0.3937	0.049 710	0.032 808	0.010 936	0.001 988	0.000 497	0.000 006	**1**	**0.01**
1 meter=	39.37	4.970 960	3.280 840	1.093 613	0.198 838	0.049 710	0.000 621	**100**	**1**

Units of Area

Units	Sq. inches	*Sq. links*	Sq. feet	Sq. yards	*Sq. rods*	*Sq. chains*
1 sq. inch=	**1**	.015 942 3	0.006 944	0.000 771 605	0.000 025 5	0.000 001 594
1 sq. *link*=	62.726 4	**1**	**0.435 6**	**0.0484**	**0.0016**	**0.000 1**
1 sq. foot=	**144**	2.295 684	**1**	0.111 111 1	0.003 673 09	0.000 229 568
1 sq. yard=	**1296**	20.661 16	**9**	**1**	0.033 057 85	0.002 066 12
1 sq. *rod*=	**39 204**	**625**	**272.25**	**30.25**	**1**	**0.062 5**
1 sq. *chain*=	**627 264**	**10 000**	**4 356**	**484**	**16**	**1**
1 *acre*=	**6 272 640**	**100 000**	**43 560**	**4 840**	**160**	**10**
1 sq. mile=	**4 014 489 600**	**64 000 000**	**27 878 400**	**3 097 600**	**102 400**	**6400**
1 sq. cm=	0.155 000 3	0.002 471 05	0.001 076	0.000 119 599	0.000 003 954	0.000 000 247
1 sq. meter=	1550.003	24.710 44	10.763 91	1.195 990	0.039 536 70	0.002 471 044
1 *hectare*=	15 500 031	247 104	107 639.1	11 959.90	395.367 0	24.710 44

Units	*Acres*	Sq. miles	Sq. cm	Sq. meters	*Hectares*
1 sq. inch=	0.000 000 159 423	0.000 000 000 249 10	**6.451 6**	**0.000 645 16**	0.000 000 065
1 sq. *link*=	**0.000 01**	**0.000 000 015 625**	404.685 642 24	0.040 468 56	0.000 004 047
1 sq. foot=	0.000 022 956 84	0.000 000 035 870 06	929.034 1	0.092 903 41	0.000 009 290
1 sq. yard=	0.000 206 611 6	0.000 000 322 830 6	**8 361.273 6**	**0.836 127 36**	0.000 083 613
1 sq. *rod*=	**0.006 25**	**0.000 009 765 625**	252 929.5	25.292 95	0.002 529 295
1 sq. *chain*=	**0.1**	**0.000 156 25**	4 046 873	404.687 3	0.040 468 73
1 *acre*=	**1**	**0.001 562 5**	40 468 73	4 046.873	0.404 687 3
1 sq. mile=	**640**	**1**	25 899 881 103	2 589 988.11	258.998 811 034
1 sq. cm=	0.000 000 024 711	0.000 000 000 038 610	**1**	**0.000 1**	**0.000 000 01**
1 sq. meter=	0.000 247 104 4	0.000 000 386 102 2	**10 000**	**1**	**0.0001**
1 *hectare*=	2.471 044	0.003 861 006	**100 000 000**	**10 000**	**1**

Units of Mass Not Greater than Pounds and Kilograms

Units	Grains	Pennyweights	Avdp drams	Avdp ounces
1 grain=	**1**	0.041 666 67	0.036 571 43	0.002 285 71
1 pennyweight=	**24**	**1**	0.877 714 3	0.054 857 14
1 dram avdp=	**27.343 75**	1.139 323	**1**	**0.062 5**
1 ounce avdp=	**437.5**	18.229 17	**16**	**1**
1 ounce troy=	**480**	**20**	17.554 29	1.097 143
1 pound troy=	**5760**	**240**	210.651 4	13.165 71
1 pound avdp=	**7000**	291.666 7	**256**	**16**
1 milligram=	0.015 432	0.000 643 015	0.000 564 383	0.000 035 274
1 gram=	15.432 36	0.643 014 9	0.564 383 4	0.035 273 96
1 kilogram=	15 432.36	643.014 9	564.383 4	35.273 96

Units	Troy ounces	Troy pounds	Avdp pounds	Milligrams	Grams	Kilograms
1 grain=	0.002 083 33	0.000 173 611	0.000 142 857	**64.798 91**	**0.064 798 91**	0.000 064 799
1 pennyw't.=	**0.05**	0.004 166 667	0.003 428 571	**1555.173 84**	**1.555 173 84**	0.001 555 174
1 dram avdp=	0.056 966 15	0.004 747 179	0.003 906 25	1771.845 195	1.771 845 195	0.001 771 845
1 oz avdp=	0.911 458 3	0.075 954 86	**0.062 5**	**28 349.523 125**	**28.349 523 125**	0.028 349 52
1 oz troy=	**1**	0.083 333 333	0.068 571 43	**31 103.476 8**	**31.103 476 8**	0.031 103 48
1 lb troy=	**12**	**1**	0.822 857 1	**373 241.721 6**	**373.241 721 6**	0.373 241 722
1 lb avdp=	14.583 33	1.215 278	**1**	**453 592.37**	**453.592 37**	**0.453 592 37**
1 milligram=	0.000 032 151	0.000 002 679	0.000 002 205	**1**	**0.001**	**0.000 001**
1 gram=	0.032 150 75	0.002 679 229	0.002 204 623	**1000**	**1**	**0.001**
1 kilogram=	32.150 75	2.679 229	2.204 623	**1 000 000**	**1000**	**1**

Units of Mass Not Less than Avoirdupois Ounces

Units	Avdp oz	Avdp lb	Short cwt	Short tons	Long tons	Kilograms	Metric tons
1 oz av=	**1**	**0.0625**	**0.000 625**	**0.000 031 25**	0.000 027 902	0.028 349 523	0.000 028 350
1 lb av=	**16**	**1**	**0.01**	**0.000 5**	0.000 446 429	**0.453 592 37**	0.000 453 592
1 sh cwt=	**1 600**	**100**	**1**	**0.05**	0.044 642 86	**45.359 237**	**0.045 359 237**
1 sh ton=	**32 000**	**2000**	**20**	**1**	0.892 857 1	**907.184 74**	**0.907 184 74**
1 long ton=	**35 840**	**2240**	**22.4**	**1.12**	**1**	**1016.046 908 8**	1.016 046 909
1 kg=	35.273 96	2.204 623	0.022 046 23	0.001 102 311	0.000 984 207	**1**	**0.001**
1 metric ton=	35 273.96	2 204.623	22.046 23	1.102 311	0.984 206 5	**1000**	**1**

(continued)

Units of Volume

Units	Cubic inches	Cubic feet	Cubic yards	Cubic cm	Cubic dm	Cubic meters
1 cubic inch=	**1**	0.000 578 704	0.000 021 433	**16.387 064**	0.016 387	0.000 016 387
1 cubic foot=	**1728**	**1**	0.037 037 04	**28 316.846 592**	28.316 847	0.028 316 847
1 cubic yard=	**46 656**	**27**	**1**	**764 554.857 984**	764.554 858	0.764 554 858
1 cubic cm=	0.061 023 74	0.000 035 315	0.000 001 308	**1**	**0.001**	**0.000 001**
1 cubic dm=	61.023 74	0.035 314 67	0.001 307 951	**1 000**	**1**	**0.001**
1 cubic meter	61 023.74	35.314 67	1.307 951	**1 000 000**	**1000**	**1**

Units of Capacity (Liquid Measure)

Units	Minims	Fluid drams	Fluid ounces	Gills	Liquid pt
1 minim=	**1**	0.016 666 7	0.002 083 33	0.000 520 833	0.000 130 208
1 fluid dram=	**60**	**1**	**0.125**	**0.031 25**	**0.007 812 5**
1 fluid ounce=	**480**	**8**	**1**	**0.25**	**0.062 5**
1 gill=	**1920**	**32**	**4**	**1**	**0.25**
1 liquid pint=	**7680**	**128**	**16**	**4**	**1**
1 liquid quart=	**15 360**	**256**	**32**	**8**	**2**
1 gallon=	**61 440**	**1024**	**128**	**32**	**8**
1 cubic inch=	265.974	4.432 900	0.554 112 6	0.138 528 1	0.034 632 03
1 cubic foot=	459 603.1	7 660.052	957.506 5	239.376 6	59.844 16
1 milliliter=	16.230 73	0.270 512 18	0.033 814 02	0.008 453 506	.002 113 376
1 liter=	16 230.73	270.512 18	33.814 02	8.453 506	2.113 376

Units	Liquid quarts	Gallons	Cubic inches	Cubic feet	Liters
1 minim=	0.000 065 104 17	0.000 016 276 04	0.003 759 766	0.000 002 175 790	0.000 061 611 52
1 flu. dram=	**0.003 906 25**	**0.000 976 562 5**	0.225 585 9	0.000 130 547 4	0.003 696 691
1 fluid oz=	**0.031 25**	**0.007 812 5**	**1.804 687 5**	0.001 044 379	0.029 573 53
1 gill=	**0.125**	**0.031 25**	**7.218 75**	0.004 177 517	0.118 294 118
1 liquid pt=	**0.5**	**0.125**	**28.875**	0.016 710 07	0.473 176 473
1 liquid qt=	**1**	**0.25**	**57.75**	0.033 420 14	0.946 352 946
1 gallon=	**4**	**1**	**231**	0.133 680 6	3.785 411 784
1 cubic in.=	0.017 316 02	0.004 329 004	**1**	0.000 578 703 7	0.016 387 064
1 cubic foot=	29.922 08	7.480 519	**1728**	**1**	**28.316 846 592**
1 liter=	1.056 688	0.264 172 05	61.023 74	0.035 314 67	**1**

Units of Capacity (Dry Measure)

Units	Dry pints	Dry quarts	Pecks	Bushels	Cubic in.	Liters
1 dry pint=	**1**	**0.5**	**0.062 5**	**0.015 625**	**33.600 312 5**	0.550 610 47
1 dry quart=	**2**	**1**	**0.125**	**0.031 25**	**67.200 625**	1.101 220 9
1 peck=	**16**	**8**	**1**	**0.25**	**537.605**	8.809 767 5
1 bushel=	**64**	**32**	**4**	**1**	**2150.42**	35.239 07
1 cubic inch=	0.029 761 6	0.014 880 8	0.001 860 10	0.000 465 025	**1**	0.016 387 06
1 liter=	1.816 166	0.908 083	0.113 510 37	0.028 377 59	61.023 74	**1**

Measures of Force and Pressure

Dyne = force necessary to accelerate a 1-gram mass 1 centimeter per second per second = 0.000072 poundals

Poundal = force necessary to accelerate a 1-pound mass 1 foot per second per second = 13,825.5 dynes = 0.138255 newtons

Newton = force which, applied for 1 second, will give a velocity of 1 meter per second to a 1-kilogram mass = 100 dynes per square centimeter = 100 microbars = 7.233 poundals

Pascal (pressure) = 1 newton per square meter = 0.020885 pound per square foot

Atmosphere (air pressure at sea level) = 2,116.102 pounds per square foot = 14.6952 pounds per square inch = 1.0332 kilograms per square centimeter = 101,323 newtons

Miscellaneous Measures

Caliber—the diameter of a gun bore. In the U.S., caliber is traditionally expressed in hundredths of inches, eg. .22 or .30. In Britain, caliber is often expressed in thousandths of inches, eg. .270 or .465. Now, it is commonly expressed in millimeters, eg. the 7.62 mm. M14 rifle and the 5.56 mm. M16 rifle. Heavier weapons' caliber has long been expressed in millimeters, eg. the 81 mm. mortar, the 105 mm. howitzer (light), the 155 mm. howitzer (medium or heavy).

Naval guns' caliber refers to the barrel length as a multiple of the bore diameter. A 5-inch, 50-caliber naval gun has a 5-inch bore and a barrel length of 250 inches.

Carat, karat—a measure of the amount of alloy per 24 parts in gold. Thus 24-carat gold is pure; 18-carat gold is one-fourth alloy.

Decibel (db)—a measure of the relative loudness or intensity of sound. A 20-decibel sound is 10 times louder than a 10-decibel sound; 30 decibels is 100 times louder; 40 decibels is 1,000 times louder, etc. One decibel is the smallest difference between sounds detectable by the human ear. A 140-decibel sound is painful.

10 decibels	– a light whisper
20	– quiet conversation
30	– normal conversation
40	– light traffic
50	– typewriter, loud conversation
60	– noisy office
70	– normal traffic, quiet train
80	– rock music, subway
90	– heavy traffic, thunder
100	– jet plane at takeoff

Em—a printer's measure designating the square width of any given type size. Thus, an em of 10-point type is 10 points. An en is half an em.

Gauge—a measure of shotgun bore diameter. Gauge numbers originally referred to the number of lead balls of the gun barrel diameter in a pound. Thus, a 16 gauge shotgun's bore was smaller than a 12-gauge shotgun's. Today, an international agreement assigns millimeter measures to each gauge, eg:

Gauge	Bore diameter in mm.
6	23.34
10	19.67
12	18.52
14	17.60
16	16.81
20	15.90

Horsepower—the energy needed to lift 550 pounds one foot in one second, or to lift 33,000 pounds one foot in one minute. Equivalent to 746 watts or 2,546.0756 btu.

Quire—25 sheets of paper

Ream—500 sheets of paper

Spirits Measures

Pony	0.5 jigger
Shot	0.666 jigger; 1.0 ounce
Jigger	1.5 shot
Pint	16 shots; 0.625 fifth
Fifth	25.6 shots; 1.6 pints; 0.8 quart; 0.75706 liter
Quart	32 shots; 1.25 fifth
Magnum	2 quarts; 2.49797 bottles (wine)

For champagne and brandy only:

Jeroboam	6.4 pints; 1.6 magnum; 0.8 gallon

For champagne only:

Rehoboam	3 magnums
Methuselah	4 magnums
Salmanazar	6 magnums
Balthazar	8 magnums
Nebuchadnezzar	10 magnums

Wine bottle (standard): 0.800633 quart; 0.7576778 liter

Ancient Measures

Biblical

Cubit = 21.8 inches
Omer = 0.45 peck
3.964 liters
Ephah = 10 omers
Shekel = 0.497 ounce
14.1 grams

Greek

Cubit = 18.3 inches
Stadion = 607.2 or 622 feet
Obolos = 715.38 milligrams
Drachma = 4.2923 grams
Mina = 0.9463 pounds
Talent = 60 mina

Roman

Cubit = 17.5 inches
Stadium = 202 yards
As, libra, pondus = 325.971 grams, .71864 pounds

Electrical Units

The **watt** is the unit of power (electrical, mechanical, thermal, etc.). Electrical power is given by the product of the voltage and the current.

Energy is sold by the **joule,** but in common practice the billing of electrical energy is expressed in terms of the **kilowatt-hour,** which is 3,600,000 joules or 3.6 megajoules.

The **horsepower** is a non-metric unit sometimes used in mechanics. It is equal to 746 watts.

The **ohm** is the unit of electrical resistance and represents the physical property of a conductor which offers a resistance to the flow of electricity, permitting just 1 ampere to flow at 1 volt of pressure.

Weight of Water

1	cubic inch	.0360	pound
12	cubic inches	.433	pound
1	cubic foot	62.4	pounds
1	cubic foot	7.48052	U.S. gal
1.8	cubic feet	112.0	pounds
35.96	cubic feet	2240.0	pounds
1	imperial gallon	10.0	pounds
11.2	imperial gallons	112.0	pounds
224	imperial gallons	2240.0	pounds
1	U.S. gallon	8.33	pounds
13.45	U.S. gallons	112.0	pounds
269.0	U.S. gallons	2240.0	pounds

Density of Gases and Vapors

Source: National Bureau of Standards (kilograms per cubic meter)

Gas	Wgt.	Gas	Wgt.	Gas	Wgt.
Acetylene	1.171	Ethylene	1.260	Methyl fluoride	1.545
Air	1.293	Fluorine	1.696	Mono methylamine	1.38
Ammonia	.759	Helium	.178	Neon	.900
Argon	1.784	Hydrogen	.090	Nitric oxide	1.341
Arsene	3.48	Hydrogen bromide	3.50	Nitrogen	1.250
Butane-iso	2.60	Hydrogen chloride	1.639	Nitrosyl chloride	2.99
Butane-n	2.519	Hydrogen iodide	5.724	Nitrous oxide	1.997
Carbon dioxide	1.977	Hydrogen selenide	3.66	Oxygen	1.429
Carbon monoxide	1.250	Hydrogen sulfide	1.539	Phosphine	1.48
Carbon oxysulfide	2.72	Krypton	3.745	Propane	2.020
Chlorine	3.214	Methane	.717	Silicon tetrafluoride	4.67
Chlorine monoxide	3.89	Methyl chloride	2.25	Sulfur dioxide	2.927
Ethane	1.356	Methyl ether	2.091	Xenon	5.897

Temperature Conversion Table

The numbers in **bold face type** refer to the temperature either in degrees Celsius or Fahrenheit which are to be converted. If converting from degrees Fahrenheit to Celsius, the equivalent will be found in the column on the left, while if converting from degrees Celsius to Fahrenheit the answer will be found in the column on the right.

For temperatures not shown. To convert Fahrenheit to Celsius subtract 32 degrees and multiply by 5, divide by 9; to convert Celsius to Fahrenheit, multiply by 9, divide by 5 and add 32 degrees.

Celsius		Fahrenheit	Celsius		Fahrenheit	Celsius		Fahrenheit
− 273.2	**− 459.7**	....	− 17.8	**0**	32	35.0	**95**	203
− 184	**− 300**	....	− 12.2	**10**	50	36.7	**98**	208.4
− 169	**− 273**	− 459.4	− 6.67	**20**	68	37.8	**100**	212
− 157	**− 250**	− 418	− 1.11	**30**	86	43	**110**	230
− 129	**− 200**	− 328	4.44	**40**	104	49	**120**	248
− 101	**− 150**	− 238	10.0	**50**	122	54	**130**	266
− 73.3	**− 100**	− 148	15.6	**60**	140	60	**140**	284
− 45.6	**− 50**	− 58	21.1	**70**	158	66	**150**	302
− 40.0	**− 40**	− 40	23.9	**75**	167	93	**200**	392
− 34.4	**− 30**	− 22	26.7	**80**	176	121	**250**	482
− 28.9	**− 20**	− 4	29.4	**85**	185	149	**300**	572
− 23.3	**− 10**	14	32.2	**90**	194			

Water boils at 212° Fahrenheit at sea level. For every 550 feet above sea level, boiling point of water is lower by about 1° Fahrenheit. Methyl alcohol boils at 148° Fahrenheit. Average human oral temperature, 98.6° Fahrenheit. Water freezes at 32° Fahrenheit. Although "Centigrade" is still frequently used, the International Committee on Weights and Measures and the National Bureau of Standards have recommended since 1948 that this scale be called "Celsius."

Breaking the Sound Barrier; Speed of Sound

The prefix Mach is used to describe supersonic speed. It derives from Ernst Mach, a Czech-born German physicist, who contributed to the study of sound. When a plane moves at the speed of sound it is Mach 1. When twice the speed of sound it is Mach 2. When it is near but below the speed of sound its speed can be designated at less than Mach 1, for example, Mach .90. Mach is defined as "in jet propulsion, the ratio of the velocity of a rocket or a jet to the velocity of sound in the medium being considered."

When a plane passes the sound barrier—flying faster than sound travels—listeners in the area hear thunderclaps, but pilots do not hear them.

Sound is produced by vibrations of an object and is transmitted by alternate increase and decrease in pressures that radiate outward through a material media of molecules —somewhat like waves spreading out on a pond after a rock has been tossed into it.

The frequency of sound is determined by the number of times the vibrating waves undulate per second, and is measured in cycles per second. The slower the cycle of waves, the lower the sound. As frequencies increase, the sound is higher.

Sound is audible to human beings only if the frequency falls within a certain range. The human ear is usually not sensitive to frequencies of less than 20 vibrations per second, or more than about 20,000 vibrations per second—although this range varies among individuals. Anything at a pitch higher than the human ear can hear is termed ultrasonic.

Intensity or loudness is the strength of the pressure of these radiating waves, and is measured in decibels. The human ear responds to intensity in a range from zero to 120 decibels. Any sound with pressure over 120 decibels is painful.

The speed of sound is generally placed at 1,088 ft. per second at sea level at 32°F. It varies in other temperatures and in different media. Sound travels faster in water than in air, and even faster in iron and steel. If in air it travels a mile in 5 seconds, it does a mile under water in 1 second, and through iron in 1/3 of a second. It travels through ice cold vapor at approximately 4,708 ft. per sec., ice-cold water, 4,938; granite, 12,960; hardwood, 12,620; brick, 11,960; glass, 16,410 to 19,690; silver, 8,658; gold, 5,717.

Colors of the Spectrum

Color, an electromagnetic wave phenomenon, is a sensation produced through the excitation of the retina of the eye by rays of light. The colors of the spectrum may be produced by viewing a light beam refracted by passage through a prism, which breaks the light into its wave lenghts.

Customarily, the primary colors of the spectrum are thought of as those 6 monochromatic colors which occupy relatively large areas of the spectrum: red, orange, yellow, green, blue, and violet. However, Sir Isaac Newton named a 7th, indigo, situated between blue and violet on the spectrum. Aubert estimated (1865) the solar spectrum to contain approximately 1,000 distinguishable hues of which according to Rood (1881) 2 million tints and shades can be distinguished; Luckiesh stated (1915) that 55 distinctly different hues have been seen in a single spectrum.

By many physicists only 3 primary colors are recognized: red, yellow, and blue (Mayer, 1775); red, green, and violet (Thomas Young, 1801); red, green, and blue (Clerk Maxwell, 1860).

The color sensation of black is due to complete lack of stimulation of the retina, that of white to complete stimulation. The infra-red and ultra-violet rays, below the red (long) end of the spectrum and above the violet (short) end respectively, are invisible to the naked eye. Heat is the principal effect of the infra-red rays and chemical action that of the ultra-violet rays.

Common Fractions Reduced to Decimals

8ths	16ths	32ds	64ths	
			1	.015625
		1	2	.03125
			3	.046875
	1	2	4	.0625
			5	.078125
		3	6	.09375
			7	.109375
1	2	4	8	.125
			9	.140625
		5	10	.15625
			11	.171875
	3	6	12	.1875
			13	.203125
		7	14	.21875
			15	.234375
2	4	8	16	.25
			17	.265625
		9	18	.28125
			19	.296875
	5	10	20	.3125
			21	.328125
		11	22	.34375

8ths	16ths	32ds	64ths	
			23	.359375
3	6	12	24	.375
			25	.390625
		13	26	.40625
			27	.421875
	7	14	28	.4375
			29	.453125
		15	30	.46875
			31	.484375
4	8	16	32	.5
			33	.515625
		17	34	.53125
			35	.546875
	9	18	36	.5625
			37	.578125
		19	38	.59375
			39	.609375
5	10	20	40	.625
			41	.640625
		21	42	.65625
			43	.671875
	11	22	44	.6875

8ths	16ths	32ds	64ths	
			45	.703125
		23	46	.71875
			47	.734375
6	12	24	48	.75
			49	.765625
		25	50	.78125
			51	.796875
	13	26	52	.8125
			53	.828125
		27	54	.84375
			55	.859375
7	14	28	56	.875
			57	.890625
		29	58	.90625
			59	.921875
	15	30	60	.9375
			61	.953125
		31	62	.96875
			63	.984375
8	16	32	64	1.

Simple Interest Table

	Time	4%	5%	6%	7%	8%
$1.00	1 month.	$.003	$.004	$.005	$.005	$.006
..	2 months	.007	.008	.010	.011	.013
..	3.	.010	.013	.015	.017	.020
..	6.	.020	.025	.030	.035	.040
..	12.	.040	.050	.060	.070	.080
$100.00	1 day	.011	.013	.016	.019	.022
..	2 days.	.022	.027	.032	.038	.044
..	3.	.033	.041	.050	.058	.067

	Time	4%	5%	6%	7%	8%
$100.00	4 days.	$.045	$.053	$.066	$.077	$.089
..	5.	.056	.069	.082	.097	.111
..	6.	.067	.083	.100	.116	.133
..	1 month	.334	.416	.500	.583	.667
..	2 months . . .	.667	.832	1.000	1.166	1.333
..	3.	1.000	1.250	1.500	1.750	2.000
..	6.	2.000	2.500	3.000	3.500	4.000
..	12.	4.000	5.000	6.000	7.000	8.000

Mathematical Formulas

To find the CIRCUMFERENCE of a:

Circle — Multiply the diameter by 3.14159265 (usually 3.1416).

To find the AREA of a:

Circle — Multiply the square of the diameter by .785398 (usually .7854).

Rectangle — Multiply the length of the base by the height.

Sphere (surface) — Multiply the square of the radius by 3.1416 and multiply by 4.

Square — Square the length of one side.

Trapezoid — Add the two parallel sides, multiply by the height and divide by 2.

Triangle — Multiply the base by the height and divide by 2.

To find the VOLUME of a:

Cone — Multiply the square of the radius of the base by 3.1416, multiply by the height, and divide by 3.

Cube — Cube the length of one edge.

Cylinder — Multiply the square of the radius of the base by 3.1416 and multiply by the height.

Pyramid — Multiply the area of the base by the height and divide by 3.

Rectangular Prism — Multiply the length by the width by the height.

Sphere — Multiply the cube of the radius by 3.1416, multiply by 4 and divide by 3.

Playing Cards and Dice Chances

Poker Hands

Hand	Number possible	Odds against
Royal flush	4	649,739 to 1
Other straight flush	36	72,192 to 1
Four of a kind	624	4,164 to 1
Full house	3,744	693 to 1
Flush	5,108	508 to 1
Straight	10,200	254 to 1
Three of a kind	54,912	46 to 1
Two pairs	123,552	20 to 1
One pair	1,098,240	4 to 3 (1.37 to 1)
Nothing	1,302,540	1 to 1
Total	**2,598,960**	

Dice
(probabilities on 2 dice)

Total	Odds against (Single toss)	Total	Odds against (Single toss)
2	35 to 1	8	31 to 5
3	17 to 1	9	8 to 1
4	11 to 1	10	11 to 1
5	8 to 1	11	17 to 1
6	31 to 5	12	35 to 1
7	5 to 1		

Dice
(Probabilities of consecutive winning plays)

No. consecutive wins	By 7, 11, or point	No. consecutive wins	By 7, 11 or point
1	244 in 495	6	1 in 70
2	6 in 25	7	1 in 141
3	3 in 25	8	1 in 287
4	1 in 17	9	1 in 582
5	1 in 34		

Pinochle Auction

(Odds against finding in "widow" of 3 cards)

Open places	Odds against	Open places	Odds against
1	5 to 1	4	3 to 2 for
2	2 to 1	5	2 to 1 for
3	Even		

Bridge

The odds—against suit distribution in a hand of 4-4-3-2 are about 4 to 1, against 5-4-2-2 about 8 to 1, against 6-4-2-1 about 20 to 1, against 7-4-1-1 about 254 to 1, against 8-4-1-0 about 2,211 to 1, and against 13-0-0-0 about 158,753,389,899 to 1.

Medical Signs and Abbreviations

Source: American Medical Association

℞ (Lat. Recipe)	take
ʒ	drachm
f ʒ	fluid drachm
℥	ounce
f ℥	fluid ounce
℥ ss	half an ounce
℥ i	one ounce
℥ iss	one ounce and a half
℥ ii	2 ounces
m.	minim, or drop
o	pint
aa	of each
a.c.	before meals
ad	to, up to
ad libitum	at pleasure
agit	shake
aqua	water
b.i.d.	twice daily
cap	capsule
cum, or c.	with
e.m.p.	as directed
fiant(ft)	make
gargarisma	a gargle
Gm	gram
gr.	grain
gtt	drops
h.s.	at bedtime
inject	injection
lb.	pound
m.	mix
mg.	milligram
ml	milliliter
non. rep. or n.r.	do not repeat
p.c.	after meals
p.r.n.	as circumstances may require
pulvis	powder
q. 3 h.	every 3 hours
q.i.d.	4 times daily
q.s.	as much as is sufficient
sig.	sign, write
solutio.	a solution
ss	one-half
stat	at once
tab	tablet
t.i.d.	3 times daily
ung	ointment
ut dict	as directed

Large Numbers

U.S.	Number of zeros	French British, German	U.S.	Number of zeros	French British, German
million	6	million	sextillion	21	1,000 trillion
billion	9	milliard	septillion	24	quadrillion
trillion	12	billion	octillion	27	1,000 quadrillion
quadrillion	15	1,000 billion	nonillion	30	quintillion
quintillion	18	trillion	decillion	33	1,000 quintillion

Squares, Square Roots, Cubes and Cube Roots of Nos. 1 to 100

Square and cube roots are approximate

No.	Sq.	Cube	Sq. root	Cube root	No.	Sq.	Cube	Sq. root	Cube root	No.	Sq.	Cube	Sq. root	Cube root
1	1.000	1.000	1.000	1.000	35	1225	42875	5.916	3.271	68	4624	314432	8.246	4.081
2	4	8	1.414	1.259	36	1296	46656	6.000	3.301	69	4761	328509	8.306	4.101
3	9	27	1.732	1.442	37	1369	50653	6.082	3.332	70	4900	343000	8.366	4.121
4	16	64	2.000	1.587	38	1444	54872	6.164	3.362	71	5041	357911	8.426	4.140
5	25	125	2.236	1.710	39	1521	59319	6.245	3.391	72	5184	373248	8.485	4.160
6	36	216	2.449	1.817	40	1600	64000	6.324	3.420	73	5329	389017	8.544	4.179
7	49	343	2.645	1.913	41	1681	68921	6.403	3.448	74	5476	405224	8.602	4.198
8	64	512	2.828	2.000	42	1764	74088	6.480	3.476	75	5625	421875	8.660	4.217
9	81	729	3.000	2.080	43	1849	79507	6.557	3.503	76	5776	438976	8.717	4.235
10	100	1000	3.162	2.154	44	1936	85184	6.633	3.530	77	5929	456533	8.775	4.254
11	121	1331	3.316	2.224	45	2025	91125	6.708	3.556	78	6084	474552	8.831	4.272
12	144	1728	3.464	2.289	46	2116	97336	6.782	3.583	79	6241	493039	8.888	4.290
13	169	2197	3.605	2.351	47	2209	103823	6.855	3.608	80	6400	512000	8.944	4.308
14	196	2744	3.741	2.410	48	2304	110592	6.928	3.634	81	6561	531441	9.000	4.326
15	225	3375	3.873	2.466	49	2401	117649	7.000	3.659	82	6724	551368	9.055	4.344
16	256	4096	4.000	2.519	50	2500	125000	7.071	3.684	83	6889	571787	9.110	4.362
17	289	4913	4.123	2.571	51	2601	132651	7.141	3.708	84	7056	592704	9.165	4.379
18	324	5832	4.242	2.620	52	2704	140608	7.211	3.732	85	7225	614125	9.219	4.396
19	361	6859	4.358	2.668	53	2809	148877	7.280	3.756	86	7396	636056	9.273	4.414
20	400	8000	4.472	2.714	54	2916	157464	7.348	3.779	87	7569	658503	9.327	4.431
21	441	9261	4.582	2.758	55	3025	166375	7.416	3.803	88	7744	681472	9.380	4.448
22	484	10648	4.690	2.802	56	3136	175616	7.483	3.825	89	7921	704969	9.434	4.464
23	529	12167	4.795	2.843	57	3249	185193	7.549	3.848	90	8100	729000	9.486	4.481
24	576	13824	4.899	2.884	58	3364	195112	7.615	3.870	91	8281	753571	9.539	4.497
25	625	15625	5.000	2.924	59	3481	205379	7.681	3.893	92	8464	778688	9.591	4.514
26	676	17576	5.099	2.962	60	3600	216000	7.746	3.914	93	8649	804357	9.643	4.530
27	729	19683	5.196	3.000	61	3721	226981	7.810	3.936	94	8836	830584	9.695	4.546
28	784	21952	5.291	3.036	62	3844	238328	7.874	3.957	95	9025	857375	9.746	4.562
29	841	24389	5.385	3.072	63	3969	250047	7.937	3.979	96	9216	884736	9.798	4.578
30	900	27000	5.477	3.107	64	4096	262144	8.000	4.000	97	9409	912673	9.848	4.594
31	961	29791	5.567	3.141	65	4225	274625	8.062	4.020	98	9604	941192	9.899	4.610
32	1024	32768	5.656	3.174	66	4356	287496	8.124	4.041	99	9801	970299	9.949	4.626
33	1089	35937	5.744	3.207	67	4489	300763	8.185	4.061	100	10000	1000000	10.000	4.641
34	1156	39304	5.831	3.239										

Square Roots and Cube Roots, 1000 to 2000

No.	Square root	Cube root	No.	Square root	Cube root	No.	Square root	Cube root	No.	Square root	Cube root
1000	31.62	10.00	1255	35.43	10.79	1510	38.86	11.47	1765	42.01	12.09
1005	31.70	10.02	1260	35.50	10.80	1515	38.92	11.49	1770	42.07	12.10
1010	31.78	10.03	1265	35.57	10.82	1520	38.99	11.50	1775	42.13	12.11
1020	31.94	10.07	1275	35.71	10.84	1530	39.12	11.52	1785	42.25	12.13
1025	32.02	10.08	1280	35.78	10.86	1535	39.18	11.54	1790	42.31	12.14
1030	32.09	10.10	1285	35.85	10.87	1540	39.24	11.55	1795	42.37	12.15
1035	32.17	10.12	1290	35.92	10.89	1545	39.31	11.56	1800	42.43	12.16
1045	32.33	10.15	1300	36.06	10.91	1555	39.43	11.59	1810	42.54	12.19
1050	32.40	10.16	1305	36.12	10.93	1560	39.50	11.60	1815	42.60	12.20
1060	32.56	10.20	1315	36.26	10.96	1570	39.62	11.62	1825	42.72	12.22
1065	32.63	10.21	1320	36.33	10.97	1575	39.69	11.63	1830	42.78	12.23
1075	32.79	10.24	1330	36.47	11.00	1585	39.81	11.66	1840	42.90	12.25
1080	32.86	10.26	1335	36.54	11.01	1590	39.87	11.67	1845	42.95	12.26
1085	32.94	10.28	1340	36.61	11.02	1595	39.94	11.68	1850	43.01	12.28
1090	33.02	10.29	1345	36.67	11.04	1600	40.00	11.70	1855	43.07	12.29
1095	33.09	10.31	1350	36.74	11.05	1605	40.06	11.71	1860	43.13	12.30
1100	33.17	10.32	1355	36.81	11.07	1610	40.12	11.72	1865	43.19	12.31
1105	33.24	10.34	1360	36.88	11.08	1615	40.19	11.73	1870	43.24	12.32
1110	33.32	10.35	1365	36.95	11.09	1620	40.25	11.74	1875	43.30	12.33
1115	33.39	10.37	1370	37.01	11.11	1625	40.31	11.76	1880	43.36	12.34
1120	33.47	10.38	1375	37.08	11.12	1630	40.37	11.77	1885	43.42	12.35
1125	33.54	10.40	1380	37.15	11.13	1635	40.44	11.78	1890	43.47	12.36
1130	33.62	10.42	1385	37.22	11.15	1640	40.50	11.79	1895	43.53	12.37
1135	33.69	10.43	1390	37.28	11.16	1645	40.56	11.80	1900	43.59	12.39
1140	33.76	10.45	1395	37.35	11.17	1650	40.62	11.82	1905	43.65	12.40
1145	33.84	10.46	1400	37.42	11.19	1655	40.68	11.83	1910	43.70	12.41
1150	33.91	10.48	1405	37.48	11.20	1660	40.74	11.84	1915	43.76	12.42
1155	33.99	10.49	1410	37.55	11.21	1665	40.80	11.85	1920	43.82	12.43
1160	34.06	10.51	1415	37.62	11.23	1670	40.87	11.86	1925	43.87	12.44
1165	34.13	10.52	1420	37.68	11.24	1675	40.93	11.88	1930	43.93	12.45
1170	34.21	10.54	1425	37.75	11.25	1680	40.99	11.89	1935	43.99	12.46
1175	34.28	10.55	1430	37.82	11.27	1685	41.05	11.90	1940	44.05	12.47
1180	34.35	10.57	1435	37.88	11.28	1690	41.11	11.91	1945	44.10	12.48
1185	34.42	10.58	1440	37.95	11.29	1695	41.17	11.92	1950	44.16	12.49
1190	34.50	10.60	1445	38.01	11.31	1700	41.23	11.93	1955	44.22	12.50
1195	34.57	10.61	1450	38.08	11.32	1705	41.29	11.95	1960	44.27	12.51
1200	34.64	10.63	1455	38.14	11.33	1710	41.35	11.96	1965	44.33	12.53
1205	34.71	10.64	1460	38.21	11.34	1715	41.41	11.97	1970	44.38	12.54
1210	34.79	10.66	1465	38.28	11.36	1720	41.47	11.98	1975	44.44	12.55
1215	34.86	10.67	1470	38.34	11.37	1725	41.53	11.99	1980	44.50	12.56
1220	34.93	10.69	1475	38.41	11.38	1730	41.59	12.00	1985	44.55	12.57
1225	35.00	10.70	1480	38.47	11.40	1735	41.65	12.02	1990	44.61	12.58
1235	35.14	10.73	1490	38.60	11.42	1745	41.77	12.04	1995	44.67	12.59
1245	35.28	10.76	1500	38.73	11.45	1755	41.89	12.06	2000	44.72	12.60

Roman Numerals

I	–	1	VI	–	6	XI	–	11	L	–	50	CD	–	400	$\overline{X}$	–	10,000
II	–	2	VII	–	7	XIX	–	19	LX	–	60	D	–	500	$\overline{L}$	–	50,000
III	–	3	VIII	–	8	XX	–	20	XC	–	90	CM	–	900	$\overline{C}$	–	100,000
IV	–	4	IX	–	9	XXX	–	30	C	–	100	M	–	1,000	$\overline{D}$	–	500,000
V	–	5	X	–	10	XL	–	40	CC	–	200	$\overline{V}$	–	5,000	$\overline{M}$	–	1,000,000

WORLD FACTS

Early Explorers of the Western Hemisphere

The first men to discover the New World or Western Hemisphere are believed to have walked across a "land bridge" from Siberia to Alaska, an isthmus since broken by the Bering Strait. From Alaska, these ancestors of the Indians spread through North, Central, and South America. Anthropologists have placed these crossings at between 18,000 and 14,000 B.C.; but evidence found in 1967 near Puebla, Mex., indicates mankind reached there as early as 35,000-40,000 years ago.

At first, these people were hunters using flint weapons and tools. In Mexico, about 7000-6000 B.C., they founded farming cultures, developing corn, squash, etc. Eventually, they created complex civilizations — Olmec, Toltec, Aztec, and Maya and, in South America, Inca. Carbon-14 tests show men lived about 8000 B.C. near what are now Front Royal, Va., Kanawha, W. Va., and Dutchess Quarry, N.Y. The Hopewell Culture, based on farming, flourished about 1000 B.C.; remains of it are seen today in large mounds in Ohio and other states.

Norsemen (Norwegian Vikings sailing out of Iceland and Greenland) are credited by most scholars with being the first Europeans to discover America, with at least 5 voyages around 1000 A.D. to areas they called Helluland, Markland, Vinland—possibly Labrador, Nova Scotia or Newfoundland, and New England.

Christopher Columbus, most famous of the explorers, was born at Genoa, Italy, but made his discoveries sailing for the Spanish rulers Ferdinand and Isabella. Dates of his voyages, places he discovered, and other information follow:

1492—First voyage. Left Palos, Spain, Aug. 3 with 88 men (est.). Discovered San Salvador (Guanahani or Watling Is., Bahamas) Oct. 12. Also Cuba, Hispaniola (Haiti-Dominican Republic); built Fort La Navidad on latter.

1493—Second voyage, first part, Sept. 25, with 17 ships, 1,500 men. Dominica (Lesser Antilles) Nov. 3; Guadeloupe, Montserrat, Antigua, San Martin, Santa Cruz, Puerto Rico, Virgin Islands. Settled Isabela on Hispaniola. **Second part** (Columbus having remained in Western Hemisphere), Jamaica, Isle of Pines, La Mona Is.

1498—Third voyage. Left Spain May 30, 1498, 6 ships. Discovered Trinidad. Saw South American continent Aug. 1, 1498, but called it Isla Sancta (Holy Island). Entered Gulf of Paria and landed, first time on continental soil. At mouth of Orinoco Aug. 14 he decided this was the mainland.

1502—Fourth voyage, 4 caravels, 150 men. St. Lucia, Guanaja off Honduras; Cape Gracias a Dios, Honduras; San Juan River, Costa Rica; Almirante, Portobelo, and Laguna de Chiriqui, Panama.

Year	Explorer	Nationality and employer	Discovery or exploration
1497	John Cabot	Italian-English	Newfoundland or Nova Scotia
1498	John and Sebastian Cabot	Italian-English	Labrador to Hatteras
1499	Alonso de Ojeda	Spanish	South American coast, Venezuela
1500, Feb.	Vicente y Pinzon	Spanish	South American coast, Amazon River
1500, Apr.	Pedro Alvarez Cabral	Portuguese	Brazil (for Portugal)
1500-02	Gaspar Corte-Real	Portuguese	Labrador
1501	Rodrigo de Bastidas	Spanish	Central America
1513	Vasco Nunez de Balboa	Spanish	Pacific Ocean
1513	Juan Ponce de Leon	Spanish	Florida
1515	Juan de Solis	Spanish	Rio de la Plata
1519	Alonso de Pineda	Spanish	Mouth of Mississippi River
1519	Hernando Cortes	Spanish	Mexico
1520	Ferdinand Magellan	Portuguese-Spanish	Straits of Magellan, Tierra del Fuego
1524	Giovanni da Verrazano	Italian-French	Atlantic Coast-New York harbor
1532	Francisco Pizarro	Spanish	Peru
1534	Jacques Cartier	French	Canada, Gulf of St. Lawrence
1536	Pedro de Mendoza	Spanish	Buenos Aires
1536	A.N. Cabeza de Vaca	Spanish	Texas coast and interior
1539	Francisco de Ulloa	Spanish	California coast
1539-41	Hernando de Soto	Spanish	Mississippi River near Memphis
1539	Marcos de Niza	Italian-Spanish	Southwest (now U.S.)
1540	Francisco V. de Coronado	Spanish	Southwest (now U.S.)
1540	Hernando Alarcon	Spanish	Colorado River
1540	Garcia de L. Cardenas	Spanish	Grand Canyon of the Colorado
1541	Francisco de Orellana	Spanish	Amazon River
1542	Juan Rodriquez Cabrillo	Portuguese-Spanish	San Diego harbor
1565	Pedro Menendez	Spanish	St. Augustine
1576	Martin Frobisher	Engish	Frobisher's Bay, Canada
1577-80	Francis Drake	English	California Coast
1582	Antonio de Espejo	Spanish	Southwest (named New Mexico)
1584	Amadas & Barlow (for Raleigh)	English	Virginia
1585-87	Sir Walter Raleigh's men	English	Roanoke Is., N.C.
1595	Sir Walter Raleigh	English	Orinoco River
1603-09	Samuel de Champlain	French	Canadian interior, Lake Champlain
1607	Capt. John Smith	English	Atlantic coast
1609-10	Henry Hudson	English-Dutch	Hudson River, Hudson Bay
1634	Jean Nicolet	French	Lake Michigan; Wisconsin
1673	Jacques Marquette, Louis Jolliet	French	Mississippi S to Arkansas
1682	Sieur de La Salle	French	Mississippi S to Gulf of Mexico
1789	Alexander Mackenzie	Canadian	Canadian Northwest

Arctic Exploration

Early Explorers

1587 — John Davis (England). Davis Strait to Sanderson's Hope, 72° 12′ N.

1596 — Willem Barents and Jacob van Heemskerck (Holland). Discovered Bear Island, touched northwest tip of Spitsbergen, 79° 49′ N, rounded Novaya Zemlya, wintered at Ice Haven.

1607 — Henry Hudson (England). North along Greenland's east coast to Cape Hold-with-Hope, 73° 30′, then north of Spitsbergen to 80° 23′. Returning he discovered Hudson's Touches (Jan Mayen).

1616 — William Baffin and Robert Bylot (England). Baffin Bay to Smith Sound.

1728 — Vitus Bering (Russia). Proved Asia and America were separated by sailing through strait.

1733-40 — Great Northern Expedition (Russia). Surveyed Siberian Arctic coast.

1741 — Vitus Bering (Russia). Sighted Alaska from sea, named Mount St. Elias. His lieutenant, Chirikof, discovered coast.

1771 — Samuel Hearne (Hudson's Bay Co.). Overland from Prince of Wales Fort (Churchill) on Hudson Bay to mouth of Coppermine River.

1778 — James Cook (Britain). Through Bering Strait to Icy Cape, Alaska, and North Cape, Siberia.

1789 — Alexander Mackenzie (North West Co., Britain). Montreal to mouth of Mackenzie River.

1806 — William Scoresby (Britain). North of Spitsbergen to 81° 30'.

1820-3 — Ferdinand von Wrangel (Russia). Completed a survey of Siberian Arctic coast. His exploration joined that of James Cook at North Cape, confirming separation of the continents.

1845 — Sir John Franklin (Britain) was one of many to seek the Northwest Passage—an ocean route connecting the Atlantic and Pacific via the Arctic. His 2 ships (the Erebus and Terror) were last seen entering Lancaster Sound July 26.

1888 — Fridtjof Nansen (Norway) crossed Greenland's icecap, 1893-96 — Nansen in Fram drifted from New Siberian Is. to Spitsbergen; tried polar dash in 1895, reached Franz Josef Land.

1896 — Salomon A. Andree (Sweden) and companion, in June, made first attempt to reach North Pole by balloon; failed and returned in August. On July 11, 1897, Andree and 2 others started in balloon from Danes, Is., Spitsbergen, to drift across pole to America, and disappeared. Over 33 years later, Aug. 6, 1930, Dr. Gunnar Horn (Norway) found their frozen bodies on White Is., 82° 57' N 29° 52' E.

1903-06 — Roald Amundsen (Norway) first sailed Northwest Passage.

Discovery of North Pole

Robert E. Peary began exploring in 1886 on Greenland, when he was 30. With his hq. at McCormick Bay he explored Greenland's coast 1891-92, tried for North Pole 1893, returned with large meteorites. In 1900 he reached northern limit of Greenland and 83° 50' N; in 1902 he reached 84° 06' N; in 1906 he went from Ellesmere Is. to 87° 06' N. He sailed in the Roosevelt, July, 1908, to winter off Cape Sheridan, Grant Land. The dash for the North Pole began Mar. 1 from Cape Columbia, Ellesmere Land. Peary reached the pole, 90° N, Apr. 6, 1909.

Peary had several supporting groups carrying supplies until the last group, under Capt. Robt. A. Bartlett, turned back at 87° 47' N. Peary, Matthew Henson, and 4 eskimos proceeded with dog teams and sleds. They crossed the pole several times, finally built an igloo at 90°, remained 36 hours. Started south Apr. 7 at 4 p.m. for Cape Columbia. Eskimos were Coqueeh, Ootah, Eginwah, and Seegloo. Adm. Peary died Feb. 20, 1920. Henson, a Negro, born Aug. 8, 1866, died in New York, N.Y., Mar. 9, 1955, aged 88. Ootah, the last survivor, died near Thule, Greenland, May, 1955, aged 80.

1914 — Donald Macmillan (U.S.). Northwest, 200 miles, from Axel Hieberg Island to seek Peary's Crocker Land.

1915-17 — Vihjalmur Stefansson (Canada) discovered Borden, Brock, Meighen, and Lougheed Islands.

1918-20 — Amundsen sailed Northeast Passage.

1925 — Roald Amundsen and Lincoln Ellsworth (U.S.) reached 87° 44' N in attempt to fly to North Pole from Spitsbergen.

1926 — Richard E. Byrd and Floyd Bennett (U.S.) first over North Pole by air, May 9.

1926 — Amundsen, Ellsworth, and Umberto Nobile (Italy) flew from Spitsbergen over North Pole May 12, to Teller, Alaska, in dirigible Norge.

1928 — Nobile crossed North Pole in airship Italia May 24, crashed May 25. Amundsen lost while trying to effect rescue by plane.

1928 — Sir Hubert Wilkins and Eielson flew from Point Barrow to Spitsbergen, 84° N.

North Pole Exploration Records

On Aug. 3, 1958, the Nautilus, under Comdr. William R. Anderson, became the first ship to cross the North Pole beneath the Arctic ice.

On Aug. 12, 1958, the nuclear submarine Skate, Comdr. James F. Calvert, became the 2d ship to make an underwater crossing of the North Pole.

In March, 1959, the Skate returned to the Arctic and on its 3d attempt, broke through at the North Pole, the first time any ship had been on the surface at 90° N.

The nuclear-powered U.S. submarine Seadragon, Comdr. George P. Steele 2d, made the first east-west underwater transit through the Northwest Passage during August, 1960. It sailed from Portsmouth N.H., headed between Greenland and Labrador through Baffin Bay, then west through Lancaster Sound and McClure Strait to the Beaufort Sea. Traveling submerged for the most part, the submarine made 850 miles from Baffin Bay to the Beaufort Sea in 6 days.

On Aug. 16, 1977, according to press dispatches from Moscow, the Soviet nuclear icebreaker Arktika reached the North Pole and became the first surface ship to break through the Arctic ice pack to the top of the world.

On April 30, 1978, Naomi Uemura, a Japanese explorer, became the first man to reach the North Pole alone by dog sled. During the 54-day, 600-mile trek over the frozen Arctic, Uemura survived attacks by a marauding polar bear.

Antarctic Exploration

Early History

Antarctica has been approached since 1773-75, when Capt. Jas. Cook (Britain) reached 71° 10' S. Many sea and landmarks bear names of early explorers. Bellingshausen (Russia) discovered Peter I and Alexander I Islands, 1819-21. Nathaniel Palmer (U.S.) discovered Palmer Peninsula, 60° W, 1820, without realizing that this was a continent. Jas. Weddell (Britain) found Weddell Sea, 74° 15' S, 1823.

First to announce existence of the continent of Antarctica was Charles Wilkes (U.S.), who followed the coast for 1,500 mi., 1840. Adelie Coast, 140° E, was found by Dumont d'Urville (France), 1840. Ross Ice Shelf was found by Jas. Clark Ross (Britain), 1841-42.

1895 — Leonard Kristensen, Norwegian whaling captain, landed a party on the coast of Victoria Land in Jan. 1895. They were the first ashore on the main continental mass. C.E. Borchgrevink, a member of that party, returned in 1899 with a British expedition, first to winter on Antarctica.

1902-04 — Robert F. Scott (Britain) discovered Edward VII Peninsula. In 1902 he reached 82° 17' S, 146° 33' E from McMurdo Sound.

1908-09 — Ernest Shackleton, in 1908, introduced the use of Manchurian ponies in Antarctic sledging. In 1909 he reached 88° 23' S, discovering a route on to the plateau by way of the Beardmore Glacier and pioneering the way to the pole.

Discovery of South Pole

1911 — Roald Amundsen (Norway) with 4 men and dog teams reached the pole Dec. 14, 1911.

1912 — Capt. Scott reached the pole from Ross Island Jan. 18, 1912, with 4 companions, where they found Amundsen's tent. None of Scott's party survived. They were found Nov. 12, 1912.

1928 — First man to use an airplane over Antarctica was Hubert Wilkins (Britain).

1929 — Richard E. Byrd (U.S.) established Little America on Bay of Whales. On 1600-mi. airplane flight begun Nov. 28 he crossed South Pole Nov. 29 with his pilot, a radio operator, and a photographer. Dropped U.S. flag over pole, temp. 16° below zero.

1934-35 — Richard E. Byrd (U.S.) led 2d expedition to Little America, which explored 450,000 sq. mi. Byrd wintered alone at an advance weather station in 80° 08' S.

1934-37 — John Rymill led British Graham Land expedition of 1934-37; discovered that Palmer Peninsula is part of Antarctic mainland.

1935 — Lincoln Ellsworth (U.S.) flew south along Palmer Peninsula's east coast, then crossed continent to Little America, making 4 landings on unprepared terrain in bad weather, a new feat.

1939-41 — U.S. Antarctic Service built West Base on Ross Ice Shelf under Paul Siple, and East Base on Palmer Peninsula under Richard Black. U.S. Navy plane flights discovered about 150,000 sq. miles of new land.

1940 — Richard E. Byrd (U.S.) charted most of coast between Ross Sea and Palmer Peninsula.

1946-47 — U.S. Navy undertook Operation High-jump under Rear Admiral Byrd. Expedition included 13 ships and 4,000 men. Twenty-nine land-based flights from Little America and 35 by seaplanes from tenders photomapped coastline and penetrated beyond pole.

1946-48 — Ronne Antarctic Research Expedition, Comdr. Finn Ronne, USNR, determined the Antarctic to be only one continent with no strait between Weddell Sea and Ross Sea; discovered 250,000 sq. miles of land by flights to 79° S Lat., and made 14,000 aerial photographs over 450,000 sq. miles of land. Mrs. Ronne and Mrs. H. Darlington, who accompanied their husbands, were the first women to winter on Antarctica.

1955-57 — U.S. Navy's Operation Deep Freeze led by Adm. Richard E. Byrd. Supporting U.S. scientific efforts for the International Geophysical Year, the operation was commanded by Rear Adm. George Dufek. It established 5 coastal stations fronting the Indian, Pacific, and Atlantic Oceans and also 3 interior stations; explored more than 1,000,000 sq. miles in Wilkes Land. Seven Navy men under Adm. Dufek landed by plane at the Pole Oct. 31, 1956, and landed radar reflectors.

1957-58 — During the International Geophysical year, July, 1957, through Dec. 1958, scientists from 12 countries conducted ambitious programs of Antarctic research. A network of some 60 stations on the continent and sub-Arctic islands studied oceanography, glaciology, meteorology, seismology, geomagnetism, the ionosphere, cosmic rays, aurora, and airglow. A party from Ellsworth IGY station (U.S.) south of Weddell Sea under the direction of Captain Finn Ronne explored beyond 1947 flight and delineated Berkner Island imbedded in the Filchner Ice Shelf.

Dr. V.E. Fuchs led a 12-man Trans-Antarctic Expedition on the first land crossing of Antarctica. Starting from the Weddell Sea, they reached Scott Station Mar. 2, 1958, after traveling 2,158 miles in 98 days.

1958 — A group of 5 U.S. scientists led by Edward C. Thiel, seismologist, moving by tractor from Ellsworth Station on Weddell Sea, identified a huge mountain range, 5,000 ft. above the ice sheet and 9,000 ft. above sea level. The range, originally seen by a Navy plane, was named the Dufek Massif, for Rear Adm. George Dufek.

1959 — Twelve nations — Argentina, Australia, Belgium, Chile, France, Japan, New Zealand, Norway, South Africa, the Soviet Union, the United Kingdom, and the U.S. — signed a treaty suspending any territorial claims for 30 years and reserving the continent for research.

1961-62 — Scientists discovered a trough, the Bentley Trench, running from Ross Ice Shelf, Pacific, into Marie Byrd Land, around the end of the Ellsworth Mtns., toward the Weddell Sea, which may be the long-suspected link between the Atlantic and Pacific Oceans.

1962 — First nuclear power plant began operation at McMurdo Sound.

1963 — On Feb. 22 a U.S. plane made the longest nonstop flight ever made in the S. Pole area, covering 3,600 miles in 10 hours. The flight was from McMurdo Station south past the geographical S. Pole to Shackleton Mtns., southeast to the "Area of Inaccessibility" and back to McMurdo Station.

1963 — Three turbine-powered helicopters made the first copter landings on the S. Pole.

1964 — A British survey team was landed by helicopter on Cook Island, the first recorded visit since its discovery in 1775.

1964 — New Zealanders completed one of the last and most important surveys when they mapped the mountain area from Cape Adare west some 400 miles to Pennell Glacier.

1966-67 — Fifteen Antarctic areas set aside as Specially Protected Areas for the conservation of flora and fauna.

Volcanoes of the World

Year of last eruption in parentheses.

More than 75 per cent of the world's 850 active volcanoes lie within the "Ring of Fire," a zone running along the west coast of the Americas from Chile to Alaska and down the east coast of Asia from Siberia to New Zealand. Twenty per cent of these volcanoes are located in Indonesia. Other prominent groupings are located in Japan, the Aleutian Islands, and Central America. Almost all active regions are found at the boundaries of the large moving plates which comprise the earth's surface. The "Ring of Fire" marks the boundary between the plates underlying the Pacific Ocean and those underlying the surrounding continents. Other active regions, such as the Mediterranean Sea and Iceland, are located on plate boundaries.

Major Historical Eruptions

Approximately 7,000 years ago, Mazama, a 3,000-meter-high volcano in southern Oregon, erupted violently, ejecting about 40 cubic kilometers of ash and lava. The ash spread over the entire northwestern United States and as far away as Saskatchewan, Canada. During the eruption, the top of the mountain collapsed, leaving a caldera 10 kilometers across and about one kilometer deep, which filled with rain water to form what is now called Crater Lake.

In 79 A.D., Vesuvio, or Vesuvius, a 1281-meter volcano overlooking Naples Bay became active after several centuries of quiescence. On Aug. 24 of that year, a heated mud and ash flow swept down the mountain engulfing the cities of Pompeii, Herculaneum, and Stabiae with debris up to 20 meters deep. About 10 percent of the population of the 3 towns were killed.

The largest eruptions in recent centuries have been in Indonesia. In 1883, an eruption similar to the Mazama eruption occurred on the island of Krakatau. On August 27, the 800-meter-high peak of the volcano collapsed to 300 meters below sea level, leaving only a small portion of the island standing above the sea. Ash from the eruption covered nearly 1,000,000 square kilometers and colored sunsets around the world for 2 years. A tsunami ("tidal wave") generated by the collapse killed 36,000 people in nearby Java and Sumatra and eventually reached England. A similar, but even more powerful, eruption had taken place 68 years earlier at Tambora volcano on the Indonesian island of Sumbawa.

Events in 1979-80

Mt. St. Helens in the Cascade Range of southwest Washington exploded May 18, 1980 with a thud felt 100 miles away. At least 6 persons were killed with 29 others missing. A rain of volcanic ash spread across large areas of the Pacific Northwest endangering crops and water supplies, disrupting business, education, and government activities, and creating an extreme health hazard.

On Mar. 27, the volcano, which had been dormant for 123 years, spewed forth clouds of steam and puffs of ash. The last volcano to erupt in the continental United States was California's Mt. Lassen, which did so periodically from 1914 to 1917.

Mt. Etna erupted Aug. 4 and Aug. 6, 1979 and spewed black ash over a broad area of eastern Sicily. Europe's largest and most active volcano erupted Sept. 12, 1979 in its strongest activity in 20 years. Nine persons were killed and 23 injured.

The On-Take volcano in central Honshu, Japan had its first eruption in historic time Oct. 27, 1979. Muddy acidic water flowed from vents for several months. Activity at the Sakurazima volcano in Kyushu, Japan continued in 1979 with 149 recorded eruptions. Tephra cracked airplane windshields twice during December.

In 1980, the Suwanosezima volcano in Ryukyu Islands, Japan, continued to be active. Explosions and ejections of ash have continued almost monthly since Nov. 1956.

Name	Location	Meters
Africa		
Kilimanjaro	Tanzania	5,895
Cameroon	Cameroons	4,070
Teide (Tenerife) (1909)	Canary Is.	3,713
Nyirangongo (1977)	Zaire	3,465
Nyamuragira (1980)	Zaire	3,056
Ol Doinyo Lengai (1960)	Tanzania	2,886
Fogo (1951)	Cape Verde Is.	2,829
Piton de la Fournaise (1979)	Reunion Is.	2,631
Palma (1971)	Canary Is.	2,423
Karthala (1977)	Comoro Is.	2,361
Erta-Ale (1973)	Ethiopia	615
Antarctica		
Erebus (1979)	Ross Island	3,743
Big Ben (1960)	Heard Island	2,745
Melbourne	Victoria Land	2,590
Darnley (1956)	South Sandwich Islands	1,100
Deception Island (1970)	South Shetland Islands	602
Asia-Oceania		
Klyuchevskaya (1974)	USSR	4,850
Kerintji (1968)	Sumatra	3,805
Fuji	Japan	3,776
Rindjani (1966)	Indonesia	3,726
Semeru (1976)	Java	3,676
Ichinskaya	USSR	3,631
Kronotskaya (1923)	USSR	3,528
Koryakskaya (1957)	USSR	3,456
Slamet (1967)	Java	3,432
Shiveluch (1964)	USSR	3,395
Ardjuno-Welirang	Java	3,339
Raung (1945)	Java	3,332
Dempo (1940)	Sumatra	3,173
Sundoro (1906)	Java	3,150
Agung (1964)	Bali	3,142
Piosky Tolbachik (1976)	USSR	3,085
Tjiremai (1938)	Java	3,078
On-Take (1979)	Japan	3,063
Mayon (1978)	Philippines	2,990
Gede (1949)	Java	2,958
Zhupanovsky (1959)	USSR	2,958
Apo	Philippines	2,953
Merapi (1976)	Java	2,911
Marapi (1979)	Sumatra	2,891
Tambora (1913)	Indonesia	2,851
Bezymianny (1979)	USSR	2,800
Ruapehu (1975)	New Zealand	2,796
Peuetsagoe (1921)	Sumatra	2,780
Avachinskaya (1945)	USSR	2,751
Papandajan (1925)	Java	2,665
Balbi	Solomon Is.	2,593
Geureudong	Sumatra	2,590
Asama (1973)	Japan	2,542
Sumbing (1921)	Sumatra	2,508
Canlaon (1969)	Philippines	2,465
Sinabung	Sumatra	2,460
Yake Dake (1963)	Japan	2,455
Tandikat (1914)	Sumatra	2,438
Niigata Yakeyama (1974)	Japan	2,400

Name	Location	Meters
Idjen (1936)	Java	2,386
Alaid (1972)	Kuril Is.	2,339
Bromo (1950)	Java	2,329
Ulawun (1973)	New Britain	2,300
Ngauruhoe (1975)	New Zealand	2,291
Guntur	Java	2,249
Bamus	New Britain	2,248
Chokai (1974)	Japan	2,230
Butak Petarangan (1939)	Java	2,222
Sibajak	Sumatra	2,212
Galunggung (1918)	Java	2,168
Sorikmerapi (1917)	Sumatra	2,145
Amburombu (1969)	Indonesia	2,124
Tangkuban Prahu (1967)	Java	2,084
Tokachi (1962)	Japan	2,077
Azuma (1978)	Japan	2,024
Tongariro	New Zealand	1,978
Zheltovskaya (1923)	USSR	1,953
Kaba (1941)	Sumatra	1,952
Sangeang Api (1966)	Indonesia	1,949
Nasu (1977)	Japan	1,917
Manam (1980)	Papua New Guinea	1,830
Tiatia (1973)	Kuril Islands	1,822
Siau (1976)	Indonesia	1,784
Soputan (1968)	Celebes	1,784
Lamington (1952)	Papua New Guinea	1,780
Kelud (1967)	Java	1,731
Batur (1968)	Bali	1,717
Ternate (1963)	Indonesia	1,715
Lewotobi (1935)	Indonesia	1,703
Bagana (1960)	Solomon Islands	1,702
Kirisima (1979)	Japan	1,700
Ili Boleng (1950)	Indonesia	1,659
Malinao	Philippines	1,657
Lamongan	Java	1,651
Keli Mutu (1968)	Indonesia	1,640
Akita Komaga take (1970)	Japan	1,637
Gamkunoro (1949)	Indonesia	1,635
Aso (1979)	Japan	1,592
Lewotobi Laki-Laki (1968)	Indonesia	1,584
Lokon-Empung (1970)	Celebes	1,579
Bulusan (1980)	Philippines	1,559
Me-akan (1966)	Japan	1,503
Karkar (1980)	Papua New Guinea	1,500
Sarycheva (1976)	Kuril Islands	1,497
Karymskaya (1976)	USSR	1,486
Lopevi (1960)	New Hebrides	1,447
Ibu (1911)	Indonesia	1,340
Ambrym (1979)	New Hebrides	1,334
Catarman (1952)	Philippines	1,332
Mahawu	Celebes	1,331
Awu (1968)	Indonesia	1,320
Ili Lewotolo (1920)	Indonesia	1,319
Langila (1980)	New Britain	1,189
Tongkoko	Celebes	1,149
Komaga take (1942)	Japan	1,140
Sakurazima (1979)	Japan	1,118
Dukono (1971)	Indonesia	1,087
Bangum	New Britain	1,052
Ili Werung (1948)	Indonesia	1,018
Lolobau (1905)	New Britain	932
Suwanosezima (1979)	Japan	799
O-Sima (1977)	Japan	758
Usu (1978)	Japan	725
White Island (1980)	New Zealand	321
Taal (1977)	Philippines	300
Central America—Caribbean		
Tajumulco	Guatemala	4,220
Tacana	Guatemala	4,092
Acatenango (1972)	Guatemala	3,976
Santiaguito (Santa Maria) (1980)	Guatemala	3,772
Fuego (1980)	Guatemala	3,736
Atitlan	Guatemala	3,537
Irazu (1967)	Costa Rica	3,432
Poas (1979)	Costa Rica	2,704
Pacaya (1980)	Guatemala	2,552
San Miguel (1976)	El Salvador	2,130
Izalco (1966)	El Salvador	1,965
Rincon de la Vieja (1968)	Costa Rica	1,806
El Viejo (San Cristobal) (1980)	Nicaragua	1,745
Ometepe (Concepcion) (1978)	Nicaragua	1,610
Arenal (1979)	Costa Rica	1,552
La Soufriére	Guadeloupe	1,467
Pelée (1932)	Martinique	1,397
Conchagua (1947)	El Salvador	1,250
Momotombo (1905)	Nicaragua	1,191
Soufriere (1979)	St. Vincent	1,178
Telica (1980)	Nicaragua	1,010
Masaya (1980)	Nicaragua	635
South America		
Guallatiri (1960)	Chile	6,060
Cotopaxi (1975)	Ecuador	5,897
El Misti	Peru	5,825
Ubinas (1969)	Peru	5,672
Lascar (1968)	Chile	5,641
Tupungatito (1980)	Chile	5,640
Tolima (1943)	Colombia	5,525
Sangay (1976)	Ecuador	5,230
Tungurahua (1944)	Ecuador	5,016
Pichincha	Ecuador	4,787
Purace (1977)	Colombia	4,600
Reventador (1976)	Ecuador	3,485
Lautaro (1960)	Chile	3,380
Llaima (1979)	Chile	3,124
Villarrica (1979)	Chile	2,840
Hudson (1973)	Chile	2,600
Rinihue	Chile	2,430
Puyehue (1960)	Chile	2,240
Calbuco (1961)	Chile	2,015
Fernandina (1977)	Galapagos Is.	1,546
Alcedo (1954)	Galapagos Is.	1,127
Mid-Pacific		
Mauna Kea	Hawaii	4,206
Mauna Loa (1978)	Hawaii	4,170
Haleakala	Hawaii	3,055
Kilauea (1979)	Hawaii	1,222
Mid-Atlantic Ridge		
Beerenberg (1970)	Jan Mayen Is.	2,277
Tristan da Cunha (1962)	Tristan da Cunha Is.	2,060
Askja (1961)	Iceland	1,510
Hekla (1970)	Iceland	1,491
Faial (1968)	Azores	1,043
Katla (1918)	Iceland	900
Leirhnukur (1975)	Iceland	650
Krafla (1980)	Iceland	650
Helgatell (1973)	Iceland	226
Surtsey (1967)	Iceland	174
Europe		
Etna (1979)	Italy	3,290
Vesuvio (1944)	Italy	1,281
Stromboli (1975)	Italy	926
Vulcano	Italy	500
Santorini (1950)	Greece	130
North America		
Citlaltepec	Mexico	5,676
Popocatepetl (1920)	Mexico	5,452
Rainier	Washington	4,395
Wrangell	Alaska	4,320
Colima (1975)	Mexico	3,960
Spurr (1953)	Alaska	3,375
Baker	Washington	3,316
Lassen (1915)	California	3,186
Paricutin (1952)	Mexico	3,170
Redoubt (1966)	Alaska	3,110
Iliamna (1978)	Alaska	3,073
Shishaldin (1979)	Aleutian Is.	2,858
Pavlof (1977)	Aleutian Is.	2,715
Veniaminof	Alaska	2,560
Chiginagak	Alaska	2,420
Douglas	Alaska	2,328
Pogromni	Alaska	2,286
Katmai (1931)	Alaska	2,285
Mageik (1912)	Alaska	2,210
Tanaga	Aleutian Is.	2,125
Trident (1963)	Alaska	2,070
Kukak	Alaska	2,046
Makushin	Aleutian Is.	2,036
Martin (1912)	Alaska	1,830
Great Sitkin (1974)	Aleutian Is.	1,750
Cleveland (1951)	Aleutian Is.	1,730
Gareloi	Aleutian Is.	1,627
Westdahl (1978)	Aleutian Is.	1,532
Korovin	Aleutian Is.	1,480
Kanaga	Aleutian Is.	1,348
Aniakchak	Alaska	1,348
Akutan (1977)	Aleutian Is.	1,293
Kiska (1969)	Aleutian Is.	1,220
Augustine (1976)	Alaska	1,210
Little Sitkin	Aleutian Is.	1,195
Okmok (1945)	Aleutian Is.	1,072
Seguam (1977)	Alaska	1,050

Continental Drift: Lithospheric

(Illustrations adapted from U.S.

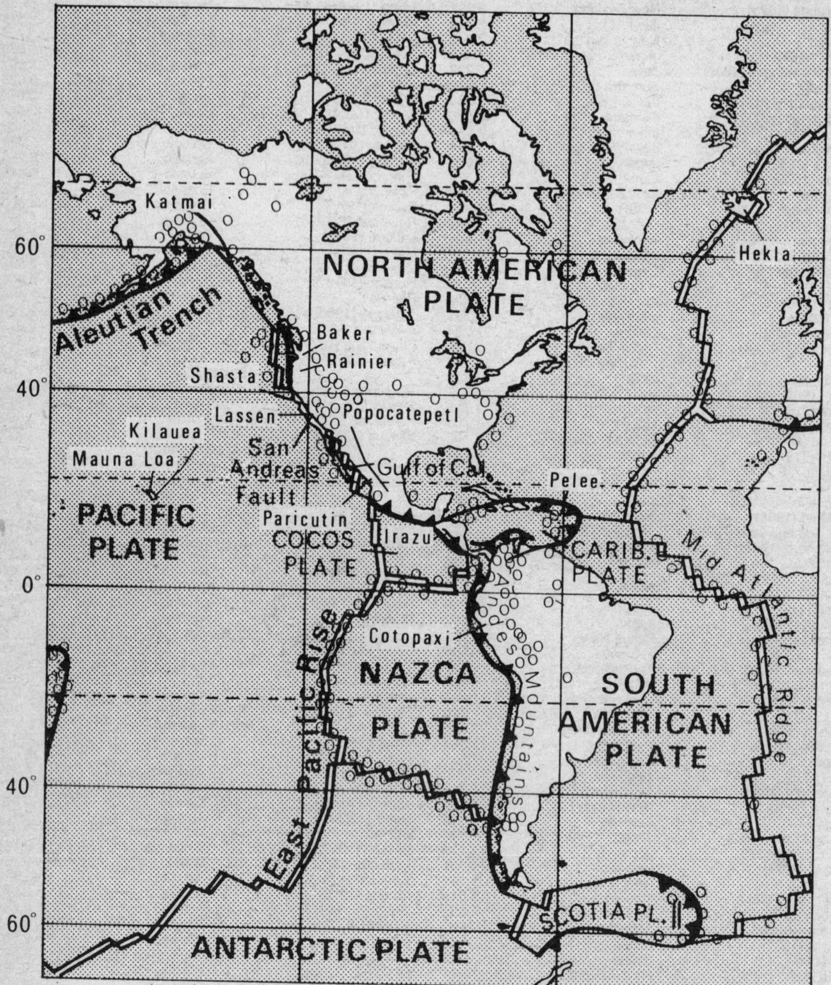

The earth's crust is broken into moving plates of "lithosphere" (litho=rock). There are 7 major plates and at least 12 minor ones (not all of which are shown above). Each plate is more than 50 miles thick and has at least 2 levels. On top, a relatively shallow part can be deformed by brittle breaking or by bending. The deeper bottom part yields to pressure like firm clay. The plates rest on and slide over a layer of viscous material.

Map Symbols

The plate boundaries shown above are those that are presently active. The *double line* indicates a zone of spreading where plates are moving away from each other. A *single line* represents a slip-strike fault, along which plates are sliding by each other (the San Andreas fault in California and the long line stretching from the western Himalayas toward Africa). A *barbed line* marks a subduction zone, an area where one plate is being pushed down under another; the barbs show the direction of motion of the overriding plate.

Volcanoes and earthquakes tend to occur along plate boundaries, although there are notable exceptions such as the volcanoes of Hawaii. The *white circles* in the maps indicate areas of strong earthquakes, while 20 volcanoes are indicated by name.

Earthquakes are caused by the grinding of the lithospheric plates against each other and by the extensive deformations of the earth's surface that can occur thousands of miles away from a zone where one plate is riding over another. Volcanoes are caused by the upwelling of material from deep within the lithosphere which breaks through the thinner plate material of the ocean floor or

Plates, Earthquakes and Volcanoes

Geological Survey Annual Report 1976).

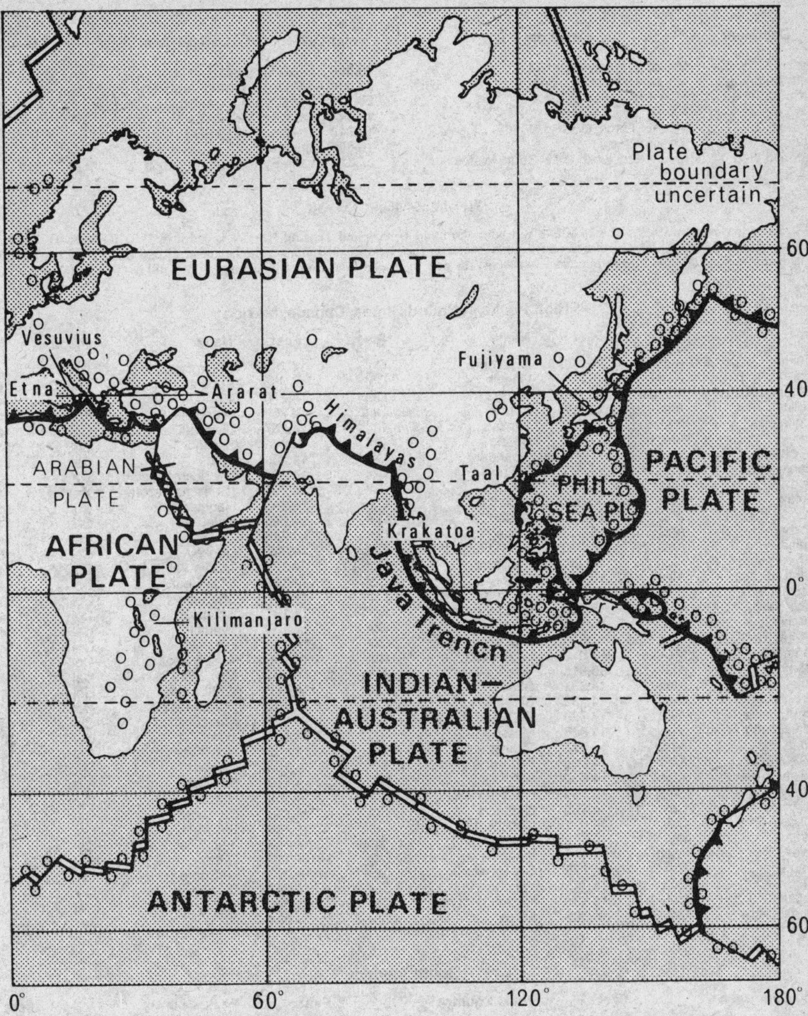

through weakened plates along the overriding edge of subduction zones.

Undersea volcanic activity along the Mid-Atlantic Ridge and East Pacific Rise has broken the once solid lithosphere into plates and is pushing the plates apart at rates estimated at one-half inch to as much as 8 inches a year. In Hawaii, volcanic activity has not been strong enough or widespread enough to break the lithosphere into separate plates.

Wegener's Hypothesis

The theory of continental drift was first systematically proposed early in the 20th century, although laymen and scientists, noting the close fit between the bulge of South America and the bight of west Africa, had suggested the idea as early as 1620. In 1912, a German meteorologist and astronomer, Alfred Wegener, postulated that all the earth's continents had once formed a single large land mass that began to break up about 40 million years ago (the breakup is now dated to 190 million years ago).

Wegener's hypothesis was roundly attacked from all sides, particularly because no force was known to be strong enough to break up the original continent and set its pieces adrift. After some 15 years of bitter controversy, Wegener's idea was disregarded by most scientists. Then in the 1960s new data, particularly oceanographic studies that confirmed sea-floor spreading along the Mid-Atlantic Ridge, brought strong support to the theory. Today the idea of continental drift is widely accepted because of a variety of convincing evidence, even though the nature of the powerful forces that cause the drift has yet to be understood.

Highest and Lowest Continental Altitudes

Source: National Geographic Society, Washington, D.C.

Continent	Highest point	Feet elevation	Lowest point	Feet below sea level
Asia	Mount Everest, Nepal-Tibet	29,028	Dead Sea, Israel-Jordan	1,312
South America	Mount Aconcagua, Argentina	22,834	Valdes Peninsula, Argentina	131
North America	Mount McKinley, Alaska	20,320	Death Valley, California	282
Africa	Kilimanjaro, Tanzania	19,340	Lake Assal, Djibouti	512
Europe	Mount El'brus, USSR	18,510	Caspian Sea, USSR	92
Antarctica	Vinson Massif	16,860	Unknown	...
Australia	Mount Kosciusko, New South Wales	7,310	Lake Eyre, South Australia	52

Height of Mount Everest

Mt. Everest was considered to be 29,002 ft. tall when Edmund Hillary and Tenzing Norgay scaled it in 1953. This triangulation figure had been accepted since 1850. In 1954 the Surveyor General of the Republic of India set the height at 29,028 ft., plus or minus 10 ft. because of snow. The National Geographic Society accepts the new figure, but many mountaineering groups still use 29,002 ft.

High Peaks in United States, Canada, Mexico

Name	Place	Feet
McKinley	Alas	20,320
Logan	Can	19,850
Citlaltepec (Orizaba)	Mexico	18,700
St. Elias	Alas-Can	18,008
Popocatepetl	Mexico	17,887
Foraker	Alas	17,400
Iztaccihuatl	Mexico	17,343
Lucania	Can	17,147
King	Can	16,971
Steele	Can	16,644
Bona	Alas	16,550
Blackburn	Alas	16,390
Kennedy	Alas	16,286
Sanford	Alas	16,237
South Buttress	Alas	15,885
Wood	Can	15,885
Vancouver	Alas-Can	15,700
Churchill	Alas	15,638
Fairweather	Alas-Can	15,300
Zinantecatl (Toluca)	Mexico	15,016
Hubbard	Alas-Can	15,015
Bear	Alas	14,831
Walsh	Can	14,780
East Buttress	Alas	14,730
Matlalcueyetl	Mexico	14,636
Hunter	Alas	14,573
Alverstone	Alas-Can	14,565
Browne Tower	Alas	14,530
Whitney	Cal	14,494
Elbert	Col	14,433
Massive	Col	14,421
Harvard	Col	14,420
Rainier	Wash	14,410
Williamson	Cal	14,375
Blanca	Col	14,345
La Plata	Col	14,336
Uncompahgre	Col	14,309
Crestone	Col	14,294
Lincoln	Col	14,286
Grays	Col	14,270
Antero	Col	14,269
Torreys	Col	14,267
Castle	Col	14,265
Quandary	Col	14,265
Evans	Col	14,264
Longs	Col	14,256
McArthur	Can	14,253
Wilson	Col	14,246
White	Cal	14,246
North Palisade	Cal	14,242
Shavano	Col	14,229
Belford	Col	14,197
Princeton	Col	14,197
Crestone Needle	Col	14,197
Yale	Col	14,196
Bross	Col	14,172
Kit Carson	Col	14,165
Wrangell	Alas	14,163
Shasta	Cal	14,162
Sill	Cal	14,162
El Diente	Col	14,159
Maroon	Col	14,156
Tabeguache	Col	14,155
Oxford	Col	14,153
Sneffels	Col	14,150
Point Success	Wash	14,150
Democrat	Col	14,148
Capitol	Col	14,130
Liberty Cap	Wash	14,112
Pikes Peak	Col	14,110
Snowmass	Col	14,092
Windom	Col	14,087
Russell	Cal	14,086
Eolus	Col	14,084
Columbia	Col	14,073
Augusta	Alas-Can	14,070
Missouri	Col	14,067
Humboldt	Col	14,064
Bierstadt	Col	14,060
Sunlight	Col	14,059
Split	Cal	14,058
Nauhcampatepetl (Cofre de Perote)	Mexico	14,049
Handies	Col	14,048
Culebra	Col	14,047
Langley	Cal	14,042
Lindsey	Col	14,042
Middle Palisade	Cal	14,040
Little Bear	Col	14,037
Sherman	Col	14,036
Redcloud	Col	14,034
Tyndall	Cal	14,018
Pyramid	Col	14,018
Wilson Peak	Col	14,017
Muir	Cal	14,015
Wetterhorn	Col	14,015
North Maroon	Col	14,014
San Luis	Col	14,014
Huron	Col	14,005
Holy Cross	Col	14,005
Colima	Mexico	14,003
Sunshine	Col	14,001
Grizzly	Col	14,000
Barnard	Cal	13,990
Stewart	Col	13,980
Keith	Cal	13,977
Ouray	Col	13,971
Le Conte	Cal	13,960
Meeker	Col	13,911
Kennedy	Can	13,905

South America

Peak, Country	Feet
Aconcagua, Argentina	22,834
Ojos del Salado, Arg.-Chile	22,572
Bonete, Argentina	22,546
Tupungato, Argentina-Chile	22,310
Pissis, Argentina	22,241
Mercedario, Argentina	22,211
Huascaran, Peru	22,205
Llullaillaco, Argentina-Chile	22,057
El Libertador, Argentina	22,047
Cachi, Argentina	22,047
Yerupaja, Peru	21,709
Galan, Argentina	21,654
El Muerto, Argentina-Chile	21,457
Sajama, Bolivia	21,391
Nacimiento, Argentina	21,302
Illimani, Bolivia	21,201
Coropuna, Peru	21,083
Laudo, Argentina	20,997
Ancohuma, Bolivia	20,958
Ausangate, Peru	20,945
Toro, Argentina-Chile	20,932
Illampu, Bolivia	20,873
Tres Cruces, Argentina-Chile	20,853
Huandoy, Peru	20,852
Parinacota, Bolivia-Chile	20,768
Tortolas, Argentina-Chile	20,745
Ampato, Peru	20,702
Condor, Argentina	20,669
Salcantay, Peru	20,574
Chimborazo, Ecuador	20,561
Huancarhuas, Peru	20,531
Famatina, Argentina	20,505
Pumasillo, Peru	20,492
Solo, Argentina	20,492
Polleras, Argentina	20,456
Pular, Chile	20,423
Chani, Argentina	20,341
Aucanquilcha, Chile	20,295
Juncal, Argentina-Chile	20,276
Negro, Argentina	20,184
Quela, Argentina	20,128
Condoriri, Bolivia	20,095
Palermo, Argentina	20,079
Solimana, Peru	20,068
San Juan, Argentina-Chile	20,049
Sierra Nevada, Arg.-Chile	20,023
Antofalla, Argentina	20,013
Marmolejo, Argentina-Chile	20,013
Chachani, Peru	19,931
Licancabur, Argentina-Chile	19,425

The highest point in the West Indies is in the Dominican Republic, Pico Duarte (10,417 ft.)

Africa, Australia, and Oceania

Peak, country	Feet
Kilimanjaro, Tanzania	19,340
Kenya, Kenya	17,058
Margherita Pk., Uganda-Zaire	16,763
Jaja, New Guinea	16,500
Trikora, New Guinea	15,585
Mandala, New Guinea	15,420
Ras Dashan, Ethiopia	15,158
Meru, Tanzania	14,979
Wilhelm, New Guinea	14,793
Karisimbi, Zaire-Rwanda	14,787
Elgon, Kenya-Uganda	14,178
Batu, Ethiopia	14,131
Guna, Ethiopia	13,881
Gughe, Ethiopia	13,780
Toubkal, Morocco	13,665
Kinabalu, Malaysia	13,455
Kerinci, Sumatra	12,467
Cook, New Zealand	12,349
Teide, Canary Islands	12,198
Semeru, Java	12,060
Kosciusko, Australia	7,310

Europe

Peak, country	Feet
Alps	
Mont Blanc, Fr. It.	15,771
Monte Rosa (highest peak of group), Switz.	15,203
Dom, Switz.	14,911
Liskamm, It., Switz.	14,852
Weisshom, Switz.	14,780
Taschhorn, Switz.	14,733
Matterhorn, It., Switz.	14,690
Dent Blanche, Switz.	14,293
Nadelhorn, Switz.	14,196
Grand Combin, Switz.	14,154
Lenzpitze, Switz.	14,088
Finsteraarhorn, Switz.	14,022
Castor, Switz.	13,865
Zinalrothorn, Switz.	13,849
Hohberghom, Switz.	13,842
Alphubel, Switz.	13,799
Rimpfischhom, Switz.	13,776
Aletschorn, Switz.	13,763
Strahlhorn, Switz.	13,747
Dent D'Herens, Switz.	13,686
Breithorn, It., Switz.	13,665
Bishorn, Switz.	13,645
Jungfrau, Switz.	13,642
Ecrins, Fr.	13,461
Monch, Switz.	13,448
Pollux, Switz.	13,422
Schreckhorn, Switz.	13,379
Ober Gabelhorn, Switz.	13,330
Gran Paradiso, It.	13,323
Bernina, It., Switz.	13,284
Fiescherhorn, Switz.	13,283
Grunhorn, Switz.	13,266
Lauteraarhorn, Switz.	13,261
Durrenhorn, Switz.	13,238
Allalinhorn, Switz.	13,213
Weissmies, Switz.	13,199
Lagginhorn, Switz.	13,156
Zupo, Switz.	13,120
Fletschhorn, Switz.	13,110
Adlerhorn, Switz.	13,081
Gletscherhorn, Switz.	13,068
Schalihorn, Switz.	13,040
Scerscen, Switz.	13,028
Eiger, Switz.	13,025
Jagerhorn, Switz.	13,024
Rottalhorn, Switz.	13,022
Pyrenees	
Aneto, Sp.	11,168
Posets, Sp.	11,073
Perdido, Sp.	11,007
Vignemale, Fr., Sp.	10,820
Long, Sp.	10,479
Estats, Sp.	10,304
Montcalm, Sp.	10,105
Caucasus (Europe-Asia)	
El'brus, USSR	18,510
Shkara, USSR	17,064
Dykh Tau, USSR	17,054
Kashtan Tau, USSR	16,877
Dzhangi Tau, USSR	16,565
Kazbek, USSR	16,558

Asia

Peak	Country	Feet
Everest	Nepal-Tibet	29,028
K2 (Godwin Austen)	Kashmir	28,250
Kanchenjunga	India-Nepal	28,208
Lhotse I (Everest)	Nepal-Tibet	27,923
Makalu I	Nepal-Tibet	27,824
Lhotse II (Everest)	Nepal-Tibet	27,560
Dhaulagiri	Nepal	26,810
Manaslu I	Nepal	26,760
Cho Oyu	Nepal-Tibet	26,750
Nanga Parbat	Kashmir	26,660
Annapurna I	Nepal	26,504
Gasherbrum	Kashmir	26,470
Broad	Kashmir	26,400
Gosainthan	Tibet	26,287
Annapurna II	Nepal	26,041
Gyachung Kang	Nepal-Tibet	25,910
Disteghil Sar	Kashmir	25,868
Himalchuli	Nepal	25,801
Nuptse (Everest)	Nepal-Tibet	25,726
Masherbrum	Kashmir	25,660
Nanda Devi	India	25,645
Rakaposhi	Kashmir	25,550
Kamet	India-Tibet	25,447
Namcha Barwa	Tibet	25,445
Gurla Mandhata	Tibet	25,355
Ulugh Muz Tagh	Sinkiang-Tibet	25,340
Kungur	Sinkiang	25,325
Tirich Mir	Pakistan	25,230
Makalu II	Nepal-Tibet	25,120
Minya Konka	China	24,900
Kula Gangri	Bhutan-Tibet	24,784
Changtzu (Everest)	Nepal-Tibet	24,780
Muz Tagh Ata	Sinkiang	24,757
Skyang Kangri	Kashmir	24,750
Communism Peak	USSR	24,590
Jongsang Peak	India-Nepal	24,472
Pobedy Peak	Sinkiang-USSR	24,406
Sia Kangri	Kashmir	24,350
Haramosh Peak	Pakistan	24,270
Istoro Nal	Pakistan	24,240
Tent Peak	India-Nepal	24,165
Chomo Lhari	Bhutan-Tibet	24,040
Chamlang	Nepal	24,012
Kabru	India-Nepal	24,002
Alung Gangri	Tibet	24,000
Baltoro Kangri	Kashmir	23,990
Mussu Shan	Sinkiang	23,890
Mana	India	23,860
Baruntse	Nepal	23,688
Nepal Peak	India-Nepal	23,500
Amne Machin	China	23,490
Gauri Sankar	Nepal-Tibet	23,440
Badrinath	India	23,420
Nunkun	Kashmir	23,410
Lenina Peak	USSR	23,405
Pyramid	India-Nepal	23,400
Api	Nepal	23,399
Pauhunri	India-Tibet	23,385
Trisul	India	23,360
Kangto	India-Tibet	23,260
Nyenchhen Thanglha	Tibet	23,255
Trisuli	India	23,210
Pumori	Nepal-Tibet	23,190
Dunagiri	India	23,184
Lombo Kangra	Tibet	23,165
Saipal	Nepal	23,100
Macha Pucchare	Nepal	22,958
Numbar	Nepal	22,817
Kanjiroba	Nepal	22,580
Ama Dablam	Nepal	22,350
Cho Polu	Nepal	22,093
Lingtren	Nepal-Tibet	21,972
Khumbutse	Nepal-Tibet	21,785
Hlako Gangri	Tibet	21,266
Mt. Grosvenor	China	21,190
Thagchhab Gangri	Tibet	20,970
Damavand	Iran	18,606
Ararat	Turkey	16,946

Antarctica

Peak	Feet
Vinson Massif	16,860
Tyree	16,290
Shinn	15,750
Gardner	15,375
Epperly	15,100
Kirkpatrick	14,855
Elizabeth	14,698
Markham	14,290
Bell	14,117
Mackellar	14,098
Anderson	13,957
Bentley	13,934
Kaplan	13,878
Andrew Jackson	13,750
Sidley	13,720
Ostenso	13,710
Minto	13,668
Miller	13,650
Long Gables	13,620
Dickerson	13,517
Giovinetto	13,412
Wade	13,400
Fisher	13,386
Fridtjof Nansen	13,350
Wexler	13,202
Lister	13,200
Shear	13,100
Odishaw	13,008
Donaldson	12,894
Ray	12,808
Sellery	12,779
Waterman	12,730
Anne	12,703
Press	12,566
Falla	12,549
Rucker	12,520
Goldthwait	12,510
Morris	12,500
Erebus	12,450
Campbell	12,434
Don Pedro Christophersen	12,355
Lysaght	12,326
Huggins	12,247
Sabine	12,200
Astor	12,175
Mohl	12,172
Frankes	12,064
Jones	12,040
Gjelsvik	12,008
Coman	12,000

How Deep Is the Ocean?

Principal ocean depths. **Source:** Defense Mapping Agency Hydrographic/Topographic Center

Name of area	Location		Depth Meters	Depth Fathoms	Feet	Ship and/or country	Year
Pacific Ocean							
Mariana Trench	11°21′N,	142°12′E	11,034	6,033	36,198	Vityaz (USSR)	1957
Tonga Trench	23°15.3′S,	174°44.7′W	10,882	5,950	35,702	Vityaz (USSR)	1957
Kuril Trench	44°15.2′N,	150°34.2′E	10,542	5,764	34,587	Vityaz (USSR)	1954
Philippine Trench	10°24′N.	126°40′E	10,539	5,763	34,578	Galathea (Danish)	1951
Izu Trench	30°32′N,	142°31′E	10,374	5,673	34,033	USS Ramapo	1932
Kermadec Trench	31°52.8′S,	177°20.6′W	10,047	5,494	32,964	Vityaz (USSR)	1957
Bonin Trench	24°30′N,	143°24′E	9,156	5,005	30,032	Vityaz (USSR)	1964
New Britain Trench	06°34′S,	153°55′E	9,140	4,998	29,988	Planet (German)	1910
Yap Trench	08°33′N,	138°02′E	8,527	4,662	27,976	Vityaz (USSR)	1958
Japan Trench	36°08′N,	142°43′E	8,412	4,597	27,591	Bathymetric Map (USSR)	1964
Palau Trench	07°40′N,	135°04′E	8,138	4,449	26,693	Stefan (Germany)	1905
Aleutian Trench	50°53′N,	176°23′E	8,100	4,429	26,574	USCGC Bering Strait	1953
Peru Chile Trench	23°18′S,	71°41′W	8,064	4,409	26,454	R/V Spencer F. Baird	1957
(Atacama Trench)	23°27′S,	71°21′W	8,064	4,409	26,454	IGY	
New Hebrides Trench	20°36′S,	168°37′E	7,570	4,138	24,830	Planet (Germany)	1910
Ryukyu Trench	25°15′N,	128°32′E	7,507	4,105	24,629	Mansyu (Japan)	1925
Mid. America Trench	14°02′N,	93°39′W	6,669	3,642	21,852	USS Epce	1965
Atlantic Ocean							
Puerto Rico Trench	19°35′N,	68°17′W	8,648	4,729	28,374	SS Archerfish	1961
Cayman Trench	19°12′N,	80°00′W	7,535	4,120	24,720	R/V Vema (U.S.)	1960
So. Sandwich Trench	55°14′S,	26°29′W	8,252	4,512	27,072	USS Eltanin	1963
Romanche Gap	00°16′S,	18°35′W	7,864	4,300	25,800	R/V Vema	1957
Brazil Basin	09°10′S,	23°02′W	6,119	3,346	20,076	R/V Vema (U.S.)	1956
Indian Ocean							
Java Trench	10°15′S,	109°E(approx.)	7,725	4,224	25,344	Natl Geographic	1967
Ob Trench	(no position)		6,874	3,759	22,553	Nat'l Geographic	1967
Vema Trench	(no position		6,402	3,501	21,004	Nat'l Geographic	1967
Agulhas Basin	(no position)		6,195	3,388	20,325	Nat'l Geographic	1967
Diamantina Trench	35°00′S,	105°35′E	6,062	3,315	19,800	Nat'l Geographic	1967
Arctic Ocean							
Eurasia Basin	82°23′N,	19°31′E	5,450	2,980	17,880	Fidor Lithke (USSR)	1955
Mediterranean Sea							
Ionian Basin	36°32′N,	21°06′E	5,150	2,816	16,896	USS Tanner,	1955

Ocean Areas and Average Depths

Four major bodies of water are recognized by geographers and mapmakers. They are: the Pacific, Atlantic, Indian, and Arctic oceans. The Atlantic and Pacific oceans are considered divided at the equator into the No. and So. Atlantic; the No. and So. Pacific. The Arctic Ocean is the name for waters north of the continental land masses in the region of the Arctic Circle.

	Sq. miles	Avg. depth in feet
Pacific Ocean	64,186,300	13,739
Atlantic Ocean	33,420,000	12,257
Indian Ocean	28,350,500	12,704
Arctic Ocean	5,105,700	4,362
South China Sea	1,148,500	4,802
Caribbean Sea	971,400	8,448
Mediterranean Sea	969,100	4,926
Bering Sea	873,000	4,893
Gulf of Mexico	582,100	5,297
Sea of Okhotsk	537,500	3,192
Sea of Japan	391,100	5,468

	Sq. miles	Avg. depth in feet
Hudson Bay	281,900	305
East China Sea	256,600	620
Andaman Sea	218,100	3,667
Black Sea	196,100	3,906
Red Sea	174,900	1,764
North Sea	164,900	308
Baltic Sea	147,500	180
Yellow Sea	113,500	121
Persian Gulf	88,800	328
Gulf of California	59,100	2,375

The Malayan Sea is not considered a geographical entity but a term used for convenience for waters between the South Pacific and the Indian Ocean.

Continental Statistics

Source: National Geographic Society, Washington, D.C.

Continents	Area (sq. mi.)	% of Earth	Population (est.)	% World total	Highest point (in feet)	Lowest point
Asia	16,998,000	29.7	2,628,500,000	59.5	Everest, 29,028	Dead Sea, −1,312
Africa	11,682,000	20.4	472,000,000	10.7	Kilimanjaro, 19,340	Lake Assal, −512
North America	9,366,000	16.3	368,000,000	8.3	McKinley, 20,320	Death Valley, −282
South America	6,881,000	12.0	239,000,000	5.4	Aconcagua, 22,834	Valdes Penin., −131
Europe	4,017,000	7.0	684,500,000	15.5	El'brus, 18,510	Caspian Sea, −92
Australia	2,966,000	5.2	14,600,000	0.3	Kosciusko, 7,310	Lake Eyre, −52
Antarctica	5,100,000	8.9	—	—	Vinson Massif, 16,860	Not Known
Est. World Population			4,414,000,000			

Important Islands and Their Areas

Source: National Geographic Society, Washington, D.C.

Figure in parentheses shows rank among the world's 10 largest islands; some islands have not been surveyed accurately; in such cases estimated areas are shown.

Location-Ownership

Area in square miles

Arctic Ocean

Canadian

Axel Heiberg	16,671
Baffin (5)	195,928
Banks	27,038
Bathurst	6,194
Devon	21,331
Ellesmere (10)	75,767
Melville	16,274
Prince of Wales	12,872
Somerset	9,570
Southampton	15,913
Victoria (9)	83,896

USSR

Franz Josef Land	8,000
Novaya Zemlya (two is.)	35,000
Wrangel	2,800

Norwegian

Svalbard	23,940
Nordaustlandet	5,410
Spitsbergen	15,060

Atlantic Ocean

Anticosti, Canada	3,066
Ascension, UK	34
Azores, Portugal	902
Faial	67
Sao Miguel	291
Bahamas	5,380
Bermuda Is., UK	20
Block, Rhode Island	10
Canary Is., Spain	2,808
Fuerteventura	668
Gran Canaria	592
Tenerife	795
Cape Breton, Canada	3,981
Cape Verde Is.	1,557
Faeroe Is., Denmark	540
Falkland Is., UK	4,700
Fernando de Noronha Archipelago, Brazil	7
Greenland, Denmark (1)	840,000
Iceland	39,769
Long Island, N. Y.	1,396
Bioko Is. Equatorial Guinea	785
Madeira Is., Portugal	307
Marajo, Brazil	15,528
Martha's Vineyard, Mass.	91
Mount Desert, Me.	108
Nantucket, Mass.	46
Newfoundland, Canada	43,359
Prince Edward, Canada	2,184
St. Helena, UK	47
South Georgia, UK	1,450
Tierra del Fuego, Chile and Argentina	18,800
Tristan da Cunha, UK	40

British Isles

Great Britain, mainland (8)	84,200
Channel Islands	75
Guernsey	24
Jersey	45
Sark	2
Hebrides	2,744
Ireland	32,599
Irish Republic	27,136
Northern Ireland	5,463
Man	227
Orkney Is.	390
Scilly Is.	6
Shetland Is.	567
Skye	670
Wight	147

Baltic Sea

Aland Is., Finland	581
Bornholm, Denmark	227
Gotland, Sweden	1,164

Caribbean Sea

Antigua	108
Aruba, Netherlands	75
Barbados	166
Cuba	44,218
Isle of Pines	1,182
Curacao, Netherlands	171
Dominica	290
Guadeloupe, France	687
Hispaniola, Haiti and Dominican Republic	29,530
Jamaica	4,244
Martinique, France	425
Puerto Rico, U.S.	3,435
Tobago	116
Trinidad	1,864
Virgin Is., UK	59
Virgin Is., U.S.	133

Indian Ocean

Andaman Is., India	2,500
Madagascar (4)	226,658
Mauritius	720
Pemba, Tanzania	380
Reunion, France	969
Seychelles	171
Sri Lanka	25,332
Zanzibar, Tanzania	640

Persian Gulf

Bahrain	240

Mediterranean Sea

Balearic Is., Spain	1,936
Corfu, Greece	229
Corsica, France	3,365
Crete, Greece	3,186
Cyprus	3,572
Elba, Italy	86
Euboea, Greece	1,409
Malta	122
Rhodes, Greece	542
Sardinia, Italy	9,262
Sicily, Italy	9,822

Pacific Ocean

Aleutian Is., U.S.	6,821
Adak	289
Amchitka	121
Attu	388
Kanaga	135
Kiska	110
Tanaga	209
Umnak	675
Unalaska	1,064
Unimak	1,600
Canton, Kiribati*	4
Caroline Is., U.S. trust terr.	472
Christmas, Kiribati*	94
Diomede, Big, USSR	11
Diomede, Little, U.S.	2
Easter, Chile	69
Fiji	7,056
Vanua Levi	2,242
Viti Levu	4,109
Funafuti, Tuvalu*	2
Galapagos Is., Ecuador	3,043
Guadalcanal, UK	2,500
Hainan, China	13,000
Hawaiian Is., U.S.	6,450
Hawaii	4,037
Oahu	593
Hong Kong, UK	29
Japan	143,809
Hokkaido	30,144
Honshu (7)	87,805
Iwo Jima	8
Kyushu	14,114
Okinawa	459
Shikoku	7,049
Kodiak, U.S.	3,670
Mariana Is., U.S. trust terr. excluding Guam	185
Guam, U.S.	212
Marquesas Is., France	492
Marshall Is., U.S. trust terr.	70
Bikini*	2
Nauru	8
New Caledonia, France	6,530
New Guinea (2)	306,000
New Hebrides	5,700
New Zealand	103,883
Chatham	372
North	44,204
South	58,304
Stewart	674
Philippines	115,831
Leyte	2,787
Luzon	40,880
Mindanao	36,775
Mindoro	3,790
Negros	4,907
Palawan	4,554
Panay	4,446
Samar	5,050
Quemoy	56
Sakhalin, USSR	29,500
Samoa Is.	1,177
American Samoa	76
Tutuila	52
Samoa (Western)	1,101
Savaii	670
Upolu	429
Santa Catalina, U.S.	72
Tahiti, France	402
Taiwan	13,812
Tasmania, Australia	26,178
Tonga Is.	270
Vancouver, Canada	12,079

East Indies

Bali, Indonesia	2,147
Borneo, Indonesia-Malaysia, UK (3)	280,100
Celebes, Indonesia	69,255
Java, Indonesia	48,763
Madura, Indonesia	2,113
Moluccas, Indonesia	28,766
New Britain, Papua New Guinea	14,050
New Ireland, Papua New Guinea	2,700
Sumatra, Indonesia (6)	165,000
Timor	11,570

***Atolls:** Bikini (lagoon area, 230 sq. mi., land area 2 sq. mi.), U.S. Trust Territory of the Pacific Islands; Canton (lagoon 20 sq. mi., land 4 sq. mi.), Kiribati; Christmas (lagoon 140 sq. mi., land 94 sq. mi.), Kiribati; Funafuti (lagoon 84 sq. mi., land 2 sq. mi.), Tuvalu.

Australia, often called an island, is a continent. Its mainland area is 2,939,975 sq. mi.

Islands in minor waters; Manhattan (23 sq mi.) Staten (58 sq. mi.) and Governors (173 acres), all in New York Harbor, U.S.; Isle Royale (209 sq. mi.), Lake Superior, U.S.; Manitoulin (1,068 sq. mi.), Lake Huron, Canada; Pinang (110 sq. mi.), Strait of Malacca, Malaysia; Singapore (224 sq. mi.), Singapore Strait, Singapore.

Major Rivers in North America

Source: U.S. Geological Survey

River	Source or Upper Limit of Length	Outflow	Miles
Alabama	Gilmer County, Ga.	Mobile River	735
Albany	Lake St. Joseph, Ont., Can.	James Bay	610
Allegheny	Potter County, Pa.	Ohio River	325
Altamaha-Ocmulgee	Junction of Yellow and South Rivers, Newton County, Ga.	Atlantic Ocean	392
Apalachicola-Chattahoochee	Towns County, Ga.	Gulf of Mexico, Fla.	524
Arkansas	Lake County, Col.	Mississippi River, Ark.	1,459
Assiniboine	Eastern Saskatchewan	Red River	450
Attawapiskat	Attawapiskat, Ont., Can.	James Bay	465
Big Black (Miss.)	Webster County, Miss.	Mississippi River	330
Big Horn	Junction of Wind and Popo Agie Rivers, Fremont County, Wyo.	Yellowstone River, Mon.	336
Black (N.W.T.)	Contwoyto Lake	Chantrey Inlet	600
Brazos	Junction of Salt and Double Mountain Forks, Stonewall County, Tex.	Gulf of Mexico	870
Canadian	Las Animas County, Col.	Arkansas River, Okla.	906
Cedar (Iowa)	Dodge County, Minn.	Iowa River, Ia.	329
Cheyenne	Junction of Antelope Creek and Dry Fork, Converse County, Wyo.	Missouri River	290
Churchill	Methy Lake	Hudson Bay	1,000
Cimarron	Colfax County, N.M.	Arkansas River, Okla.	600
Clark Fork-Pend Oreille	Silver Bow County, Mon.	Columbia River, B.C.	505
Colorado (Ariz.)	Rocky Mountain National Park, Col. (90 miles in Mexico)	Gulf of Cal., Mexico	1,450
Colorado (Texas)	West Texas	Matagorda Bay	840
Columbia	Columbia Lake, British Columbia	Pacific Ocean, bet. Ore. and Wash.	1,243
Columbia, Upper	Columbia Lake, British Columbia	To mouth of Snake River	890
Connecticut	Third Connecticut Lake, N.H.	L.I. Sound, Conn.	407
Coppermine (N.W.T.)	Lac de Gras	Coronation Gulf (Atlantic Ocean)	525
Cumberland	Letcher County, Ky.	Ohio River	720
Delaware	Schoharie County, N.Y.	Liston Point, Delaware Bay	390
Fraser	Near Mount Robson (on Continental Divide)	Strait of Georgia	850
Gila	Catron County, N.M.	Colorado River, Ariz.	630
Green (Ut.-Wyo.)	Junction of Wells and Trail Creeks, Sublette County, Wyo.	Colorado River, Ut.	730
Hamilton (Lab.)	Lake Ashuanipi	Atlantic Ocean	600
Hudson	Henderson Lake, Essex County, N.Y.	Upper N.Y. Bay, N.Y.,-N.J.	306
Illinois	St. Joseph County, Ind.	Mississippi River	420
James (N.D.-S.D.)	Wells County, N.D.	Missouri River, S.D.	710
James (Va.)	Junction of Jackson and Cowpasture Rivers, Botetourt County, Va.	Hampton Roads	340
Kanawha-New	Junction of North and South Forks of New River, N.C.	Ohio River	352
Kentucky	Junction of North and Middle Forks, Lee County, Ky.	Ohio River	259
Klamath	Lake Ewauna, Klamath Falls, Ore.	Pacific Ocean	250
Koyukuk	Endicott Mountains, Alaska	Yukon River	470
Kuskokwim	Alaska Range	Kuskokwim Bay	680
Liard	Southern Yukon, Alaska	Mackenzie River	693
Little Missouri	Crook County, Wyo.	Missouri River	560
Mackenzie	Great Slave Lake	Arctic Ocean	900
Milk	Junction of North and South Forks, Alberta Province	Missouri River, Mon.	625
Minnesota	Big Stone Lake, Minn.	Mississippi River, St. Paul, Minn.	332
Mississippi	Lake Itasca, Minn.	Mouth of Southwest Pass	2,348
Mississippi, Upper	Lake Itasca, Minn.	To mouth of Missouri R.	1,171
Mississippi-Missouri-Red Rock	Source of Red Rock, Beaverhead Co., Mon.	Mouth of Southwest Pass	3,710
Missouri	Junction of Jefferson, Madison, and Gallatin Rivers, Madison County, Mon.	Mississippi River	2,315
Missouri-Red Rock	Source of Red Rock, Beaverhead Co., Mon.	Mississippi River	2,533
Mobile-Alabama-Coosa	Gilmer County, Ga.	Mobile Bay	780
Nelson (Manitoba)	Lake Winnipeg	Hudson Bay	410
Neosho	Morris County, Kan.	Arkansas River, Okla.	460
Niobrara	Niobrara County, Wyo.	Missouri River, Neb.	431
North Canadian	Union County, N.M.	Canadian River, Okla.	760
North Platte	Junction of Grizzly and Little Grizzly Creeks, Jackson County, Col.	Platte River, Neb.	618
Ohio	Junction of Allegheny and Monongahela Rivers, Pittsburgh, Pa.	Mississippi River, Ill.-Ky.	981
Ohio-Allegheny	Potter County, Pa.	Mississippi River	1,306
Osage	East-central Kansas	Missouri River, Mo.	500
Ottawa	Lake Capimitchigama	St. Lawrence	790
Ouachita	Polk County, Ark.	Red River, La.	605
Peace	Stikine Mountains, B.C.	Slave River	1,195
Pearl	Neshoba County, Miss.	Gulf of Mexico, Miss.-La.	411
Pecos	Mora County, N.M.	Rio Grande, Tex.	735
Pee Dee-Yadkin	Watauga County, N.C.	Winyah Bay, S.C.	435
Pend Oreille	Near Butte, Mon.	Columbia River	490
Platte	Junction of North and South Platte Rivers, Neb.	Missouri River, Neb.	310
Porcupine	Ogilvie Mountains, Alaska	Yukon River, Alaska	460
Potomac	Garrett County, Md.	Chesapeake Bay	383
Powder	Junction of South and Middle Forks, Wyo.	Yellowstone River, Mon.	375

River	Source or Upper Limit of Length	Outflow	Miles
Red (Okla.-Tex.-La.)	Curry County, N.M.	Mississippi River	1,270
Red River of the North	Junction of Otter Tail and Bois de Sioux Rivers, Wilkin County, Minn.	Lake Winnipeg, Manitoba	545
Republican	Junction of North Fork and Arikaree River, Neb.	Kansas River, Kan.	445
Rio Grande	San Juan County, Col.	Gulf of Mexico	1,885
Roanoke	Junction of North and South Forks, Montgomery County, Va.	Albemarle Sound, N.C.	380
Rock (Ill.-Wis.)	Dodge County, Wis.	Mississippi River, Ill.	300
Sabine	Junction of South and Caddo Forks, Hunt County, Tex.	Sabine Lake, Tex.-La.	380
Sacramento	Siskiyou County, Cal.	Suisun Bay	377
St. Francis	Iron County, Mo.	Mississippi River, Ark.	425
St. Lawrence	Lake Ontario	Gulf of St. Lawrence (Atlantic Ocean)	800
Salmon (Idaho)	Custer County, Ida.	Snake River, Ida.	420
San Joaquin	Junction of South and Middle Forks, Madera County, Cal.	Suisun Bay	350
San Juan	Silver Lake, Archuleta County, Col.	Colorado River, Ut.	360
Santee-Wateree-Catawba	McDowell County, N.C.	Atlantic Ocean, S.C.	538
Saskatchewan, North	Rocky Mountains	Lake Winnipeg	1,100
Saskatchewan, South	Rocky Mountains	Lake Winnipeg	1,205
Savannah	Junction of Seneca and Tugaloo Rivers, Anderson County, S.C.	Atlantic Ocean, Ga.-S.C.	314
Severn (Ontario)	Sandy Lake	Hudson Bay	610
Smoky Hill	Cheyenne County, Col.	Kansas River, Kan.	540
Snake	Teton County, Wyo.	Columbia River, Wash.	1,038
South Platte	Junction of South and Middle Forks, Park County, Col.	Platte River, Neb.	424
Susitna	Alaska Range	Cook Inlet	300
Susquehanna	Otsego Lake, Otsego County, N.Y.	Chesapeake Bay, Md.	444
Tallahatchie	Tippah County, Miss.	Yazoo River, Miss.	301
Tanana	Wrangell Mountains	Yukon River, Alaska	620
Tennessee	Junction of French Broad and Holston Rivers	Ohio River, Ky.	652
Tennessee-French Broad	Bland County, Va.	Ohio River	900
Tombigbee	Prentiss County, Miss.	Mobile River, Ala.	525
Trinity	North of Dallas, Tex.	Galveston Bay, Tex.	360
Wabash	Darke County, Oh.	Ohio River, Ill.-Ind.	529
Washita	Hemphill County, Tex.	Red River, Okla.	500
White (Ark.-Mo.)	Madison County, Ark.	Mississippi River	720
Willamette	Douglas County, Ore.	Columbia River	270
Wisconsin	LeVieux Desert, Vilas County, Wis.	Mississippi River	430
Yellowstone	Park County, Wyo.	Missouri River, N.D.	671
Yukon	Junction of Lewes and Pelly Rivers, Yukon	Bering Sea, Alaska	1,770

Flows of Largest U.S. Rivers

Source: U.S. Geological Survey (average discharges for the period 1941-70). Ranked according to average discharge in cubic feet per second (cfs) at mouth.

Rank	River	Average discharge	Length[a] (miles)	Drainage area	Most distant source	Maximum discharge at gauging station farthest downstream	Date
1	Mississippi	[b]640,000	[c]3,710	[d]1,247,300	Beaverhead Co., Mont.	2,080,000	2-17-37
2	Columbia	262,000	1,243	258,000	Columbia Lake, B.C.	1,240,000	June 1894
3	Ohio	258,000	1,306	203,900	Potter Co., Pa.	1,850,000	2-1-37
4	St. Lawrence	[e]243,000	—	[e]302,000	—	[f]350,000	July 1973
5	Yukon	[g]240,000	1,770	327,600	Coast Mountains, B.C.	1,030,000	6-22-64
6	[h]Atchafalaya	183,000	135	95,105	Curry Co., N. Mex.	—	—
7	Missouri	76,300	2,533	529,400	Beaverhead Co., Mont.	892,000	June 1844
8	Tennessee	[m]64,000	900	40,910	Bland Co., Va.	500,000	2-17-48
9	Red	[i]62,300	1,270	93,244	Curry Co., N. Mex.	233,000	4-17-45
10	Kuskokwim	62,000	680	49,000	Alaska Range, Alas.	392,000	6-5-64
11	Mobile	61,400	780	43,800	Gilmer, Co., Ga.	—	—
12	Snake	50,000	1,038	109,000	Teton Co., Wyo.	409,000	June 1894
13	Arkansas	45,100	1,459	160,600	Lake Co., Col.	536,000	5-27-43
14	Copper	[j]43,000	280	24,000	Alaska Range, Alas.	265,000	7-15-71
15	Tanana	[k]41,000	620	44,000	Wrangell Mtn., Alas.	186,000	8-18-67
16	Susitna	[l]40,000	300	20,000	Alaska Range, Alas.	197,000	6-16-77
17	Susquehanna	37,190	444	27,570	Otsego Co., N.Y.	1,080,000	6-23-72
18	Willamette	35,660	270	11,200	Douglas Co., Ore.	500,000	12-4-1861
19	Alabama	32,400	735	22,600	Gilmer Co., Ga.	267,000	3-7-61
20	White	32,100	720	28,000	Madison Co., Ark.	343,000	4-17-45
21	Wabash	30,400	529	33,150	Darke Co., Oh.	428,000	3-30-13
22	Pend Oreille	29,900	490	25,820	Near Butte, Mont.	171,300	6-13-48
23	Tombigbee	27,300	525	20,100	Prentiss Co., Miss.	286,000	4-22-79
24	Cumberland	[m]26,900	720	18,080	Letcher Co., Ky.	209,000	3-16-75
25	Stikine	[n]26,000	310	20,000	Stikine Range, B.C.	219,000	8-12-76
26	Sacramento	—	377	27,100	Siskiyou Co., Cal.	[o]322,000	12-25-64
27	Apalachicola	24,700	524	19,600	Towns Co., Ga.	293,000	3-20-29
28	Illinois	22,800	420	27,900	St. Joseph Co., Ind.	123,000	May 1943
29	Koyukuk	[p]22,000	470	32,400	Endicott Mtns., Alas.	266,000	6-6-64
30	Porcupine	[q]20,000	460	45,000	Ogilvie Mtns., Alas.	299,000	5-24-73
31	Hudson	19,500	306	13,370	Essex Co., N.Y.	215,000	3-19-36
32	Allegheny	19,290	325	11,700	Potter Co., Pa.	365,000	3-18-36
33	Delaware	[r]17,200	390	11,440	Schoharie Co., N.Y.	329,000	8-20-55

(a) Because river lengths and methods of measurement may change from time to time, the length figures given are subject to revision; (b) about 25 percent of flow occurs in the Atchafalaya River; (c) the length from mouth to source of the Mississippi River in Minnesota is 2,348 miles; (d) at Baptiste Collete Bayou, Louisiana; (e) at international boundary lat. 45°; (f) maximum monthly discharge; (g) period

1957-70; (h) continuation of Red River; (i) flow of Ouachita River added; (j) period 1956-69; (k) period 1962-69; (l) based on records o Chulitna, Talkeetna, and Yetna rivers; (m) period 1931-60; (n) period 1954-63; summer records only; (o) discharge of American River no included (p) period 1960-69; (q) period 1964-69; (r) at Liston Point on Delaware Bay.

Large Rivers in Canada

Source: "Inland Waters Directorate," Department of Fisheries and the Environment.

(Ranked according to average discharge in cubic feet per second (cfs). Figures indicate discharge and drainage to river mouths.

Rank	River	Average discharge	Length (miles	Drainage area (sq. mi.)
1	St. Lawrence (to Nicolet)	355,000	1,900	396,000[1]
2	Mackenzie	350,000	2,635	690,000
3	Fraser	128,000	850	89,900[2]
4	Columbia (International Boundary)	102,000	498	59,700[3]
5	Nelson	100,000	1,600	437,000[4]
6	Kokosak	85,500	543	51,500
7	Yukon (International Boundary)	83,000	714	115,000[5]
8	Ottawa	70,500	790	56,500
9	Saguenay (to head of Peribonea)	62,200	434	34,000
10	Skeena	62,100	300	21,200

(1) Including 195,000 sq. mi. in U.S. (2) Including diversion. (3) Including 20,000 sq. mi. in U.S. (4) Including 69,500 sq. mi. in U.S. (5) Including 9,000 sq. mi. in U.S.

Principal World Rivers

Source: National Geographic Society, Washington, D.C. (length in miles)

River	Outflow	Lgth	River	Outflow	Lgth	River	Outflow	Lgth
Albany	James Bay	610	Indus	Arabian Sea	1,800	Red River of N.	Lake Winnipeg	545
Amazon	Atlantic Ocean	4,000	Irrawaddy	Bay of Bengal	1,300	Rhine	North Sea	820
Amu	Aral Sea	1,578	Japura	Amazon River	1,750	Rhone	Gulf of Lions	505
Amur	Tatar Strait	2,744	Jordan	Dead Sea	200	Rio de la Plata	Atlantic Ocean	150
Angara	Yenisey River	1,151	Kootenay	Columbia River	485	Rio Grande	Gulf of Mexico	1,885
Arkansas	Mississippi	1,459	Lena	Laptev Sea	2,734	Rio Roosevelt	Aripuana	400
Back	Arctic Ocean	605	Loire	Bay of Biscay	634	Saguenay	St. Lawrence R.	434
Brahmaputra	Bay of Bengal	1,800	Mackenzie	Arctic Ocean	2,635	St. John	Bay of Fundy	418
Bug, Southern	Dnieper River	532	Madeira	Amazon River	2,013	St. Lawrence	Gulf of St. Law.	800
Bug, Western	Wisla River	481	Magdalena	Caribbean Sea	956	Salween	Andaman Sea	1,500
Canadian	Arkansas River	906	Marne	Seine River	326	Sao Francisco	Atlantic Ocean	1,988
Chang	E. China Sea	3,964	Mekong	S. China Sea	2,600	Saskatchewan	Lake Winnipeg	1,205
Churchill, Man.	Hudson Bay	1,000	Meuse	North Sea	580	Seine	English Chan.	482
Churchill, Que.	Atlantic Ocean	532	Mississippi	Gulf of Mexico	2,348	Shannon	Atlantic Ocean	230
Colorado	Gulf of Calif.	1,450	Missouri	Mississippi	2,533	Snake	Columbia River	1,038
Columbia	Pacific Ocean	1,243	Murray-Darling	Indian Ocean	2,310	Sungari	Amur River	1,150
Congo	Atlantic Ocean	2,900	Negro	Amazon	1,400	Syr	Aral Sea	1,370
Danube	Black Sea	1,776	Nelson	Hudson Bay	1,600	Tajo, Tagus	Atlantic Ocean	626
Dnieper	Black Sea	1,420	Niger	Gulf of Guinea	2,590	Tennessee	Ohio River	652
Dniester	Black Sea	877	Nile	Mediterranean	4,145	Thames	North Sea	215
Don	Sea of Azov	1,224	Ob-Irtysh	Gulf of Ob	3,362	Tiber	Tyrrhenian Sea	252
Drava	Danube River	447	Oder	Baltic Sea	567	Tigris	Shatt al-Arab	1,180
Dvina, North	White Sea	824	Ohio	Mississippi	975	Tisza	Danube River	600
Dvina, West	Gulf of Riga	634	Orange	Atlantic Ocean	1,300	Tocantins	Para River	1,677
Ebro	Mediterranean	565	Orinoco	Atantic Ocean	1,600	Ural	Caspian Sea	1,575
Elbe	North Sea	724	Ottawa	St. Lawrence R.	790	Uruguay	Rio de la Plata	1,000
Euphrates	Shatt al-Arab	1,700	Paraguay	Parana River	1,584	Volga	Caspian Sea	2,194
Fraser	Str. of Georgia	850	Parana	Rio de la Plata	2,485	Weser	North Sea	454
Gambia	Atlantic Ocean	700	Peace	Slave River	1,195	Wisla	Bay of Danzig	675
Ganges	Bay of Bengal	1,560	Pilcomayo	Paraguay River	1,000	Yellow (See Huang)		
Garonne	Bay of Biscay	357	Po	Adriatic Sea	405	Yenisey	Kara Sea	2,543
Hsi	S. China Sea	1,200	Purus	Amazon River	2,100	Yukon	Bering Sea	1,979
Huang	Yellow Sea	2,903	Red	Mississippi	1,270	Zambezi	Indian Ocean	1,700

Famous Waterfalls

Source: National Geographic Society, Washington, D.C.

The earth has thousands of waterfalls, some of considerable magnitude. Their importance is determined not only by height but volume of flow, steadiness of flow, crest width, whether the water drops sheerly or over a sloping surface, and in one leap or a succession of leaps. A series of low falls flowing over a considerable distance is known as a cascade.

Sete Quedas or Guaira is the world's greatest waterfall when its mean annual flow (estimated at 470,000 cusecs, cubic feet per second) is combined with height. A greater volume of water passes over Boyoma Falls (Stanley Falls), though not one of its seven cataracts, spread over nearly 60 miles of the Congo River, exceeds 10 feet.

Estimated mean annual flow, in cusecs, of other major waterfalls are: Niagara, 212,200; Paulo Afonso, 100,000; Urubupunga, 97,000; Iguazu, 61,000; Patos-Maribondo, 53,000; Victoria, 38,400; and Kaieteur, 23,400.

Height = total drop in feet in one or more leaps. † = falls of more than one leap; * = falls that diminish greatly seasonally; ** = falls that reduce to a trickle or are dry for part of each year. If river names not shown, they are same as the falls. R. = river; L. = lake; (C) = cascade type.

Name and location	Ht.
Africa	
Angola	
Duque de Braganca, Lucala R.	344
Ruacana, Cuene R.	406
Ethiopia	
Dal Verme, Dorya R.	98
Fincha	508
Tesissat, Blue Nile R.	140
Lesotho	
*Maletsunyane	630
Zimbabwe-Zambia	
*Victoria, Zambezi R.	343
South Africa	
*Augrabies, Orange R.	480
Howick, Umgeni R.	364
† Tugela	2,014
Highest fall	597
Tanzania-Zambia	
*Kalambo	726
Uganda	
Kabalega (Murchison) Victoria Nile R.	130
Asia	
India—*Cauvery	330
*Gokak, Ghataprabha R.	170
*Jog (Gersoppa), Sharavathi R.	830

Name and location	Ht.
Japan	
*Kegon, Daiya R.	330
Laos	
Khon Cataracts, Mekong R. (C)	70
Australasia	
Australia	
New South Wales	
† Wentworth	614
Highest fall	360
Wollomombi	1,100
Queensland	
Coomera	210
Tully	885
† Wallaman, Stony Cr.	1,137
Highest fall	937
New Zealand	
Bowen	540
Helena	890
Stirling	505
† Sutherland, Arthur R.	1,904
Highest fall	815
Europe	
Austria—† Gastein	492
Highest fall	280
† *Golling, Schwarzbach R.	250
† Krimml	1,312
France—*Gavarnie	1,385
Great Britain—Scotland	
Glomach	370
Wales	
Cain	150
Rhaiadr	240
Iceland—Detti	144
† Gull, Hvita R.	105
Italy—Frua, Toce R. (C)	470
Norway	
Mardalsfossen (Northern)	1,535
† Mardalsfossen (Southern)	2,149
† **Skjeggedal, Nybuai R.	1,378
**Skykje	984
Vetti, Morka-Koldedola R.	900
Voring, Bjoreio R.	597
Sweden	
† Handol	427
† Tannforsen, Are R.	120
Switzerland	
† Diesbach	394
Giessbach (C)	984
Handegg, Aare R.	150
Iffigen	120
Pissevache, Salanfe R.	213
† Reichenbach	656
Rhine	79
† Simmen	459
Staubbach	984
† Trummelbach	1,312
North America	
Canada	
Alberta	
Panther, Nigel Cr.	600
British Columbia	
† Della	1,443
† Takakkaw, Daly Glacier	1,200
Northwest Territories	
Virginia, S. Nahanni R.	294
Quebec	
Montmorency	274
Canada—United States	
Niagara: American	182
Horseshoe	173
United States	
California	
*Feather, Fall R.	640
Yosemite National Park	
*Bridalveil	620
*Illilouette	370
*Nevada, Merced R.	594
**Ribbon	1,612
**Silver Strand, Meadow Br.	1,170
*Vernal, Merced R.	317
† **Yosemite	2,425
Yosemite (upper)	1,430
Yosemite (lower)	320
Yosemite (middle) (C)	675
Colorado	
† Seven, South Cheyenne Cr.	300
Hawaii	
Akaka, Kolekole Str.	442
Idaho	
**Shoshone, Snake R.	212
Twin, Snake R.	120
Kentucky	
Cumberland	68
Maryland	
*Great, Potomac R. (C)	71
Minnesota	
**Minnehaha	53
New Jersey	
Passaic	70
New York	
*Taughannock	215
Oregon	
† Multnomah	620
Highest fall	542
Tennessee	
Fall Creek	256
Washington	
Mt. Rainier Natl. Park	
Narada, Paradise R.	168
Sluiskin, Paradise R.	300
Palouse	197
**Snoqualmie	268
Wisconsin	
*Big Manitou, Black R. (C)	165
Wyoming	
Yellowstone Natl. Pk. Tower	132
*Yellowstone (upper)	109
*Yellowstone (lower)	308
Mexico	
El Salto	218
**Juanacatlan, Santiago R.	72
South America	
Argentina-Brazil	
Iguazu	230
Brazil	
Glass	1,325
Patos-Maribondo, Grande R.	115
Paulo Afonso, Sao Francisco R.	275
Urubupunga, Parana R.	40
Brazil-Paraguay	
Sete Qeudas	
Parana R.	130
Colombia	
Catarata de Candelas, Cusiana R.	984
*Tequendama, Bogota R.	427
Ecuador	
*Agoyan, Pastaza R.	200
Guyana	
Kaieteur, Potaro R.	741
Great, Kamarang R.	1,600
† Marina, Ipobe R.	500
Highest fall	300
Venezuela—	
† *Angel	3,212
Highest fall	2,648
Cuquenan	2,000

Notable Deserts of the World

Arabian (Eastern), 70,000 sq. mi. in Egypt between the Nile river and Red Sea, extending southward into Sudan.

Atacama, 600 mi. long area rich in nitrate and copper deposits in N. Chile.

Black Rock, 1,000 sq. mi. barren plain in NW Nev.

Death Valley, 2,936 sq. mi. in E. Cal. and SW Nev. Contains lowest point below sea level (282 ft.) in western hemisphere.

Gibson, 250,000 sq. mi. in the interior of W. Australia.

Gobi, 500,000 sq. mi. in Mongolia and China.

Great Sandy, 150,000 sq. mi. in W. Australia.

Great Victoria, 250,000 sq. mi. in W. and S. Australia.

Kalahari, 225,000 sq. mi. in southern Africa.

Kara-Kum, 110,000 sq. mi. in Turkmen, SSR.

Kavir (Dasht-e-Kavir), great salt waste in central Iran some 400 mi. long.

Kyzyl-Kum, 100,000 sq. mi. in Kazakh and Uzbek; SSRs.

Libyan, 600,000 sq. mi. in the Sahara extending from Lybia through SW Egypt into Sudan.

Lut (Dasht-e-Lut), 20,000 sq. mi. in E. Iran.

Mojave, 15,000 sq. mi. in S. Cal.

Nafud (An Nafud), 50,000 sq. mi. near Jawf in Saudi Arabia.

Namib, long narrow area extending 800 miles along SW coast of Africa.

Nubian, 120,000 sq. mi. in the Sahara in NE Sudan.

Painted Desert, section of high plateau in N. Ariz. extending 150 mi.

Rub al-Khali (Empty Quarter), 250,000 sq. mi. in the south Arabian Peninsula. World's largest continuous sand area.

Sahara, 3,320,000 sq. mi. in N. Africa extending westward to the Atlantic. Largest tropical and climatic desert in the world.

Simpson, 120,000 sq. mi. in central Australia.

Sonoran, 120,000 sq. mi. in SW Ariz. and SE Cal. extending into Mexico.

Syrian, 100,000 sq. mi. arid wasteland extending over much of N. Saudi Arabia, E. Jordan, S. Syria, and W. Iraq.

Taklamakan, 125,000 sq. mi. in Sinkiang Province, China.

Thar (Great Indian), 100,000 sq. mi. arid area extending 400 mi. along India-Pakistan border.

The Great Lakes

Source: National Ocean Survey, U.S. Commerce Department

The Great Lakes form the largest body of fresh water in the world and with their connecting waterways are the largest inland water transportation unit. Draining the great North Central basin of the U.S., they enable shipping to reach the Atlantic via their outlet, the St. Lawrence R., and also the Gulf of Mexico via the Illinois Waterway, from Lake Michigan to the Mississippi R. A third outlet connects with the Hudson R. and thence the Atlantic via the N. Y. State Barge Canal System.

Only one of the lakes, Lake Michigan, is wholly in the United States; the others are shared with Canada. Ships carrying grain, lumber and iron ore move from the shores of Lake Superior to Whitefish Bay at the east end of the lake, thence through the Soo (Sault Ste. Marie) locks, through the St. Mary's River and into Lake Huron. To reach the steel mills at Gary, and Port of Indiana and South Chicago, Ill., ore ships move west from Lake Huron to Lake Michigan through the Straits of Mackinac.

Lake Huron discharges its waters into Lake Erie through a narrow waterway, the St. Clair R., Lake St. Clair (both included in the drainage basin figures) and the Detroit R. Lake St. Clair, a marshy basin, is 26 miles long and 24 miles wide at its maximum. A ship channel has been dredged through the lake.

Lake Superior is 600 feet above mean water level at Point-au-Pere, Quebec, on the International Great Lakes Datum (1955). From Duluth, Minn., to the eastern end of Lake Ontario is 1,156 mi.

	Superior	Michigan	Huron	Erie	Ontario
Length in miles	350	307	206	241	193
Breadth in miles	160	118	183	57	53
Deepest soundings in feet	1,330	923	750	210	802
Volume of water in cubic miles	2,900	1,180	850	116	393
Area (sq. miles) water surface—U.S.	20,600	22,300	9,100	4,980	3,460
Canada	11,100	.....	13,900	4,930	3,880
Area (sq. miles) entire drainage basin—U.S.	16,900	45,600	16,000	18,000	12,500
Canada	32,400	.....	34,700	4,720	10,900
Total Area (sq. miles) U.S. and Canada	**81,000**	**67,900**	**73,700**	**32,630**	**30,740**
Mean surface above mean water level at Point-au-Pere, Quebec, aver. level in feet (1900-1979)	600.58	578.21	578.21	570.35	244.70
Latitude, North	46° 25′	41° 37′	43° 00′	41° 23′	43° 11′
	49° 00′	46° 06′	46° 17′	42° 52′	44° 15′
Longitude, West	84° 22′	84° 45′	79° 43′	78° 51′	76° 03′
	92° 06′	88° 02′	84° 45′	83° 29′	79° 53′
National boundary line in miles	282.8	None	260.8	251.5	174.6
United States shore line (mainland only) miles	863	1,400	580	431	300

Largest Lake in Each Province of Canada

Source: "Inland Waters Directorate" and others.

Province	Largest within:	Largest partly in:	Shared with:	Origin	Area (sq. miles)	Ft. above sea level
Alberta	Claire			Natural	555	700
		Athabasca	Saskatchewan	Natural	3,066	700
British Columbia	Williston			Manmade	640	2,180
Manitoba	Winnipeg			Natural	9,417	713
Newfoundland	Smallwood Reservoir			Manmade	2,520	S.L.
New Brunswick	Grand			Natural	70	4
Northwest Territories	Great Bear			Natural	12,096	512
Nova Scotia	Bras d'Or			Natural	424	Tidal
Ontario	Nipigon			Natural	1,872	1,050
		Huron	U.S.	Natural	15,241	580
Prince Edward Island	Forest Hill Pond			Manmade	.7	50
Quebec	Mistassinl			Natural	902	1,230
Saskatchewan	Wollaston			Natural	1,035	1,306
		Athabasca	Alberta	Natural	3,066	700

Lakes of the World

Source: National Geographic Society, Washington, D.C.

A lake is a body of water surrounded by land. Although some lakes are called seas, they are lakes by definition. The Caspian Sea is bounded by the Soviet Union and Iran and is fed by eight rivers.

Name	Continent	Area sq. mi.	Length mi.	Depth feet	Elev. feet
Caspian Sea	Asia-Europe	143,244	760	3,363	−92
Superior	North America	31,700	350	1,330	600
Victoria	Africa	26,828	250	270	3,720
Aral Sea	Asia	24,904	280	220	174
Huron	North America	23,000	206	750	579
Michigan	North America	22,300	307	923	579
Tanganyika	Africa	12,700	420	4,708	2,534
Baykal	Asia	12,162	395	5,315	1,493
Great Bear	North America	12,028	192	1,356	512
Malawi	Africa	11,150	360	2,280	1,550
Great Slave	North America	11,031	298	2,015	513
Erie	North America	9,910	241	210	570
Winnipeg	North America	9,417	266	60	713
Ontario	North America	7,550	193	802	245
Ladoga	Europe	6,835	124	738	13
Balkhash	Asia	7,115	376	85	1,115
Chad	Africa	6,300	175	24	787
Maracaibo	South America	5,217	133	115	Sea level
Onega	Europe	3,710	145	328	108
Volta	Africa	3,276	250	....	....
Titicaca	South America	3,200	122	922	12,500
Athabasca	North America	3,064	208	407	700
Nicaragua	North America	3,100	102	230	102
Eyre	Australia	3,600	90	4	−52
Rudolf	Africa	2,473	154	240	1,230
Reindeer	North America	2,568	143	720	1,106
Issyk Kul	Asia	2,355	115	2,303	5,279
Torrens	Australia	2,230	130	....	92
Vanern	Europe	2,156	91	328	144
Winnipegosis	North America	2,075	141	38	830
Albert	Africa	2,075	100	168	2,030
Kariba	Africa	2,050	175	390	1,590
Nettilling	North America	2,140	67	Sea level	95
Nipigon	North America	1,872	72	540	1,050
Gairdner	Australia	1,840	90	....	112
Manitoba	North America	1,799	140	12	813
Urmia	Asia	1,815	90	49	4,180

Largest Lake in Each State of the U.S.

Source: National Geographic Society, Washington, D.C.
*indicates reservoir

State	Largest entirely within state	Largest partly in another state	Shared with	Origin	Total area (square miles)	Feet above sea level	Maximum depth (feet)	Shoreline length (miles)
Ala.	Guntersville			Man-made	108	595	94	962
		Walter F. George	Ga.	Man-made	71	190	90	640
Alas.	Iliamna			Natural	1,150	150	1,289	230
Ariz.	Theodore Roosevelt			Man-made	27	2,136	280	88
		Powell	Ut.	Man-made	252	3,700	580	1,800
Ark.	Ouachita			Man-made	63	578	179	690
		Bull Shoals	Mo.	Man-made	71	654	175	740
Cal.	Salton Sea			Natural	360	-235	48	—
		Tahoe	Nev.	Natural	192	6,229	1,644	71
Col.	Blue Mesa*			Man-made	14	7,519	325	95
		Navajo*	N.M.	Man-made	24	6,085	382	150
Conn.	Candlewood			Man-made	8	429	85	75
Del.	Lum's Pond			Man-made	.34	44	22	5
Fla.	Okeechobee			Natural	700	14	15	96
Ga.	Sidney Lanier			Man-made	59	1,070	156	540
		Clark Hill	S.C.	Man-made	109	330	150	1,200
Ha.	Waita*			Man-made	.66	242	—	4
Ida.	Pend Oreille			Natural	136	2,063	1,200	127
Ill.	Carlyle*			Man-made	41	445	40	83
		Michigan	Wis., Ind., Mich	Natural	22,300	579	923	1,660
Ind.	Monroe*			Man-made	29	556	75	100
		Michigan	Wis., Ill., Mich.	Natural	22,300	579	923	1,660
Ia.	Rathbun*			Man-made	18	904	55	180
Kan.	Tuttle Creek*			Man-made	25	1,079	90	112
Ky.	Cumberland			Man-made	79	760	183	1,255
		Kentucky	Tenn.	Man-made	250	359	90	2,380
La.	Pontchartrain			Natural	621	sea lev.	18	112
Me.	Moosehead			Natural	117	1,042	246	190
Md.	Deep Creek			Man-made	6	2,462	72	62
		Conowingo*	Pa.	Man-made	13	109	110	38
Mass.	Quabbin*			Man-made	39	524	150	104
Mich.	Houghton			Natural	31	1,138	20	30
		Superior	Wis., Minn., Ont.	Natural	31,700	600	1,330	2,980
Minn.	Red			Natural	452	1,172	—	—
		Superior	Wis., Mich., Ont.	Natural	31,700	600	1,330	2,980
Miss.	Grenada			Man-made	100	231	102	282
Mo.	Lake of the Ozarks			Man-made	93	659	148	1,300
Mon.	Fort Peck*			Man-made	375	2,246	220	1,540
Neb.	McConaughy			Man-made	50	3,260	130	105
Nev.	Pyramid			Natural	169	3,789	330	66
		Mead	Ariz.	Man-made	247	1,221	432	550
N.H.	Winnipesaukee			Natural	70	504	169	240
N.J.	Hopatcong			Natural	4	924	58	32
N.M.	Elephant Butte*			Man-made	57	4,450	176	201
N.Y.	Oneida			Natural	80	369	55	63
		Erie	Mich., Pa., Ont., Oh.	Natural	9,910	570	210	856
N.C.	Mattamuskeet			Natural	67	3	5	—
		John H. Kerr*	Va.	Man-made	76	300	99	800
N.D.	Sakakawea			Man-made	575	1,850	180	1,600
		Oahe*	S.D.	Man-made	556	1,617	200	2,250
Oh.	Grand			Man-made	17	869	10	60
		Erie	Mich., Pa., N.Y., Ont.	Natural	9,910	570	210	856
Okla.	Eufaula			Man-made	160	585	87	600
Ore.	Upper Klamath			Natural	143	4,143	50	165
		Goose Lake	Cal.	Natural	194	4,716	24	90
Pa.	Raystown*			Man-made	13	786	185	110
		Erie	Mich., N.Y., Oh., Ont.	Natural	9,910	570	210	856
R.I.	Scituate			Man-made	5	284	94	38
S.C.	Marion			Man-made	173	75	55	300
S.D.	Francis Case			Man-made	159	1,375	140	540
		Oahe*	N.D.	Man-made	556	1,617	200	2,250
Tenn.	Watts Bar			Man-made	61	741	75	783
		Kentucky	Ky.	Man-made	250	359	90	2,380
Tex.	Sam Rayburn*			Man-made	179	164	74	—
		Toledo Bend*	La.	Man-made	284	172	92	—
Ut.	Great Salt Lake			Natural	1,438	4,200	36	334
Vt.	Bomoseen			Natural	4	413	—	—
		Champlain	N.Y., Que.	Natural	437	95	400	379
Va.	Smith Mountain			Man-made	31	795	200	500
		John H. Kerr*	N.C.	Man-made	76	300	99	800
Wash.	F.D. Roosevelt			Man-made	123	1,288	375	325
W. Va.	Summersville			Man-made	4	1,652	267	65
Wis.	Winnebago			Natural	215	747	21	78
		Superior	Minn., Mich., Ont.	Natural	31,700	600	1,330	2,980
Wyo.	Yellowstone			Natural	137	7,733	309	110
		Flaming Gorge*	Utah	Man-made	—	6,040	437	—

Notable Bridges in North America

Source: State Highway Engineers: Canadian Civil Engineering — ASCE

Asterisk (*) designates railroad bridge. Span of a bridge is distance (in feet) between its supports.

Suspension

Year	Bridge	Location	Longest span
1964	Verrazano-Narrows	New York, N.Y.	4,260
1937	Golden Gate	San Fran. Bay, Cal.	4,200
1957	Mackinac	Sts. of Mackinac	3,800
1931	Geo. Washington	Hudson River	3,500
1952	Tacoma	Washington	2,800
1936	[1]Transbay	San Fran. Bay, Cal.	2,310
1939	Bronx-Whitestone	East R., N.Y.C.	2,300
1970	Pierre Laporte	Quebec	2,190
1951	Del. Memorial	Wilmington, Del.	2,150
1968	Del. Mem. (new)	Wilmington, Del.	2,150
1957	Walt Whitman	Phila., Pa.	2,000
1929	Ambassador	Detroit-Canada	1,850
1961	Throgs Neck	Long Is. Sound	1,800
1926	Benjamin Franklin	Philadelphia	1,750
1924	Bear Mt., N.Y.	Hudson River	1,632
1952	[2]Wm. Preston Lane Mem.	Sandy Point, Md.	1,600
1903	Williamsburg	East R., N.Y.C.	1,600
1969	Newport	Narragansett Bay, R.I.	1,600
1883	Brooklyn	East R., N.Y.C.	1,595
1939	Lions Gate	Burrard Inlet, B.C.	1,550
1930	Mid-Hudson, N.Y.	Poughkeepsie	1,500
1964	Vincent Thomas	Los Angeles Harbor	1,500
1909	Manhattan	East R., N.Y.C.	1,470
1936	Triborough	East R., N.Y.C.	1,380
1931	St. Johns	Portland, Ore.	1,207
1929	Mount Hope	Rhode Island	1,200
1939	Deer Isle	Maine	1,080
1931	Maysville (Ky.)	Ohio River	1,060
1867	Cincinnati	Ohio River	1,057
1971	Dent	Clearwater Co., Ida.	1,050
1900	Miampimi	Mexico	1,030
1849	Wheeling, W. Va.	Ohio River	1,010

Cantilever

Year	Bridge	Location	Longest span
1917	Quebec	Quebec	1,800
1970	Commodore Barry	Chester, Pa.	1,644
1958	New Orleans, La.	Mississippi R.	1,575
1936	Transbay	San Fran. Bay	1,400
1968	Baton Rouge, La.	Mississippi R.	1,235
1955	Nyack-Tarrytown	Hudson River	1,212
1930	Longview, Wash.	Columbia River	1,200
1909	Queensboro	East R., N.Y.C.	1,182
1927	Carquinez Strait	California	1,100
1958	Parallel Span	"	1,100
1930	Jacques Cartier	Montreal, P.Q.	1,097
1968	Isaiah D. Hart	Jacksonville, Fla.	1,088
1957	[3]Richmond	San Fran. Bay, Cal.	1,070
1929	Grace Memorial	Charleston, S.C.	1,050
1963	Newburgh-Beacon	Hudson, R., N.Y.	1,000
1975	Caruthersville, Mo.	Mississippi R.	920
1977	Saint Marys	Saint Marys, W. Va.	900
1969	Silver Memorial	Pt. Pleasant, W. Va.	900
1940	Natchez	Mississippi R.	875
1938	Blue Water	Pt. Huron, Mich.	871
1972	Vicksburg	Mississippi River	870
1954	Sunshine Skyway	St. Petersburg, Fla.	864
1940	*Baton Rouge	Mississippi R.	848
1899	*Cornwall	St. Lawrence R.	843
1940	Greenville	Mississippi R.	840
1961	Helena, Ark.	Mississippi R.	840
1963	Brent Spence	Covington, Ky.	831
1963	Cincinnati, Oh.	Ohio River	830
1956	Earl C. Clements	Ohio R., Ill-Ky.	825[6]
1930	*Vicksburg	Mississippi R.	825
1929	Louisville	Ohio River	820
1961	Campbellton-Cross Point	New Brunswick-Quebec	815
1943	Jeff'rson Barr'ks., Mo.	Mississippi R.	804
1950	Maurice J. Tobin	Boston, Mass.	800
1935	Rip Van Winkle	Catskill, N.Y.	800
1938	Cairo	Ohio River, Ill.-Ky.	800
1940	Ludlow Ferry	Potomac R.	800
1932	Washington Mem.	Seattle, Wash.	800
1936	McCullough	Coos Bay, Ore.	793
1935	[4]Huey P Long	New Orleans	790
1916	*Memphis (Harahan)	Mississippi R.	790
1892	*Memphis	Mississippi R.	790
1949	Memphis-Arkansas	Mississippi R.	790
1904	*Mingo Jct., W. Va.	Ohio River	769
1910	*Beaver, Pa.	Ohio River	767
1966	[5]S.N. Pearman	Charleston, S.C.	760
1940	Owensboro	Ohio River	750
1911	Sewickley, Pa.	Ohio River	750
1928	Outerbridge, N.Y.-N.J.	Arthur Kill	750
1964	Sunshine, Don'ville	Mississippi, La.	750

Simple Truss

Year	Bridge	Location	Longest span
1977	Chester	Chester, W. Va.	746
1917	*Metropolis	Ohio River	720
1929	Irvin S. Cobb	Ohio River-Ill.-Ky.	716
1922	*Tanana River	Nenana, Alaska	700
1933	*Henderson	Ohio River-Ind.-Ky.	665
1967	I-77, Ohio River	Marietta, Oh.	650
1917	MacArthur, Ill.-Mo.	St. Louis	647
1919	Louisville	Ohio River	644
1933	Atchafalaya	Morgan City, La.	608
1924	*Castleton	Hudson River	598
1889	*Cincinnati	Ohio River	542
1951	Allegheny River	Allegheny Co., Pa.	533
1914	Pittsburgh	Allegheny R.	531
1930	*Martinez	California	528
1967	Tanana River	Alaska	500
1974	Fort Hill, I-64	Charleston, W. Va.	465

Steel Truss

Year	Bridge	Location	Longest span
1940	Gov. Nice Mem.	Potomac River, Md.	800
1975	I-24	Tenn R., Ky.	720
1938	US-62, Ky.	Green River	700
1952	US-62, Ky.	Cumberland River	700
1940	Jamestown	Jamestown, R.I.	640
1940	Greenville	Mississippi R., Ark.	640
1949	Memphis	Mississippi R., Ark.	621
1938	US-22	Delaware River, N.J.	540
1972	Mississippi River	Muscatine, Ia.	512
1896	Newport	Ohio River, Ky.	511
1931	US-60	Cumberland R., Ky.	500
1958	Lake Oahe	Mobridge, S.D.	500
1958	Lake Oahe	Gettysburg, S.D.	500
1910	McKinley, St. Louis	Mississippi River	500
1963	Millard E. Tydings	Susquehanna R., Md.	490
1955	Four Bears	Missouri R., N.D.	475
1930	Lake Champlain	Lake Champlain, N.Y.	434
1947	Mayo	Suwanee R., Fla.	420
1929	Clarendon	White River, Ark.	400
1931	US-60	Tennessee R., Ky.	400

Continuous Truss

Year	Bridge	Location	Longest span
1966	Astoria, Ore.	Columbia R.	1,232
1966	Marquam	Willamette R., Ore.	1,044
1969	Miss. R.	Dyersburg, Tenn.	900
1969	Irondequoit Bay	Rochester, N.Y.	891
1943	Dubuque, Ia.	Mississippi R.	845
1953	John E. Mathews	Jacksonville, Fla.	810
1957	Kingston-Rhinecliff	Hudson R., N.Y.	800
1918	*Sciotoville	Ohio River	775
1974	Betsy Ross	Philadelphia, Pa.	729
1929	Madison-Milton	Ohio River	727
1966	Matthew E. Welsh	Mauckport	707[6]
1962	Champlain	Montreal, P.Q.	707
1975	Girard Point	Philadelphia, Pa.	700
1929	Chain of Rocks	Mississippi R.	699
1966	Braga	Taunton R., Mass.	682
1938	Port Arthur-Orange	Texas	680
1929	*Cincinnati	Ohio River	675
1928	Cape Girardeau, Mo.	Mississippi R.	672
1946	Chester, Ill.	Mississippi R.	670
1930	Quincy, Ill.	Mississippi R.	628
1959	US 181, over harbor	Corpus Christi, Tex.	620
1934	Bourne	Cape Cod Canal	616
1935	Sagamore	Cape Cod Canal	616
1965	Clarion River	Clarion Co., Pa.	612
1957	Blatnik	Duluth, Minn.	600
1965	Rio Grande Gorge	Taos, N.M.	600
1941	Columbia River	Kettle Falls, Wash.	600
1954	Columbia River	Umatilla, Ore.	600
1954	Columbia River	The Dalles, Ore.	576
1962	W. Br. Feather River	Oroville, Cal.	576
1936	Meredosia	Illinois River	567
1936	Mark Twain Mem.	Hannibal, Mo.	562
1957	Mackinac	Mackinac Straits, Mich.	560
1937	Homestead	Pittsburgh	553
1961	Ship Canal	Seattle, Wash.	552

Year	Bridge	Location	Longest span
1932	Pulaski Skyway	Passaic R., N.J.	550
1973	I-95, Thames River	New London, Conn.	540
1927	Ross Island	Portland, Ore.	535
1958	Interstate	Portland, Ore.	531
1936	South Omaha	Missouri R, Neb.-Ia.	525
1932	Savanna, Ill.-Sabula	Mississippi R.	520
1962	Columbia River	Beebe, Wash.	520
1970	Snake River	Central Ferry, Wash.	520

Continuous Box and Plate Girder

Year	Bridge	Location	Longest span
1967	San Mateo-Hayward No. 2	San Fran. Bay, Cal.	750
1963	Gunnison River	Gunnison, Col.	720
1969	San Diego-Coronado	San Diego Bay, Cal.	660[7]
1973	Ship Channel	Houston, Tex.	630
1967	Poplar St.	St. Louis, Mo.	600
1977	US-64, Tennessee R.	Savannah, Tenn.	525
1965	McDonald-Cartier	Ottawa, Ont.	520
1971	Lake Koocanusa	Lincoln Co., Mon.	500
1972	Sitka Harbor	Sitka, Alaska	450
1974	I-430	Arkansas R.	430
1972	I-635, Kansas City	Missouri R., Kan.-Mo.	425
1967	Chattanooga	Tennessee R., Tenn.	420
1978	Snake River	Clarkston, Wash.	420
1975	Yukon River	North Slope Road, Alas.	410
1972	I-75, Tennessee River	Loudon, Co., Tenn	400
1941	Susquehanna	Susquehanna R., Md.	400
1963	Lake Charles B'Pass	Louisiana	399
1957	Conn. Turnpike	Quinnipiac R.	387
1960	Route 34	New Haven, Conn.	379
1971	S.H. No. 1	Pendleton, Ark.	377
1960	Tennessee River	Chattanooga, Tenn.	375
1966	I-80, LeClaire, Ia.	Mississippi	370
1971	Sacramento R.	Bryte, Cal.	370
1963	I-40, Tennessee River	Benton Co., Tenn.	365
1967	San Mateo Creek	Hillsborough, Cal.	360
1950	US-62, Kentucky Dam	Tennessee R., Ky.	350
1961	Whiskey Creek	Trinity Co., Cal.	350
1972	Franklin Falls	Snoq'lmie Pass, Wash.	350
1971	Don Pedro Reserv	Tuolumne Co., Cal.	350

Continuous Plate

Year	Bridge	Location	Longest span
1965	New Chain of Rocks	Mississippi R., Ill.	5,411[9]
1973	Great Congress Gty.	Schenectady, N.Y.	1,870
1971	Congress St.	Troy, N.Y.	1,420
1967	Mississippi River	LaCrescent, Minn.	450
1966	I-480	Missouri R., Ia.-Neb.	425
1970	I-435	Missouri R., Mo.	425
1972	I-80	Missouri R., Ia.-Neb.	425
1971	St. Croix River	Hudson, Minn.	390
1968	Lafayette St.	St. Paul, Minn.	362
1970	Green River	Hendersonville, N.C.	350
1974	Mississippi R.	Praire du Chien, Wisc.	350
1969	Fort Smith	Arkansas River	340
1964	Lexington Ave.	St. Paul, Minn.	340

I-Beam Girder

Year	Bridge	Location	Longest span
1941	US-31E	Rolling Fork R., Ky.	340
1948	US-27	Licking River, Ky.	316
1947	US-31E	Green River, Ky.	316
1941	US-62	Rolling Fork, Ky.	240
1942	Licking River	Owingsville, Ky.	240
1954	Fuller Warren	Jacksonville, Fla.	224

Steel Arch

Year	Bridge	Location	Longest span
1977	New River Gorge	Fayetteville, W. Va.	1,700
1931	Bayonne, N.J.	Kill Van Kull	1,652
1972	Fremont	Portland, Ore.	1,255
1964	Port Mann	British Columbia	1,200
1967	Trois-Rivieres	St. Lawrence R., P.Q.	1,100
1959	Glen Canyon	Colorado River	1,028
1962	Lewiston-Queenston	Niagara River, Ont.	1,000
1976	Perrine	Twin Falls, Ida.	993
1917	*Hell Gate	East R., N.Y.C.	977
1941	Rainbow	Niagara Falls	950
1972	I-40, Mississippi R.	Memphis, Tenn.	900[10]
1970	Lake Quinsigamond	Worcester, Mass.	849
1966	Charles Braga	Somerset, Mass.	840
1967	Lincoln Trail	Ohio R., Ind.-Ky.	825
1961	Sherman Minton	Louisville, Ky.	800
1936	Henry Hudson	Harlem River	800
1936	French King	Conn. R. (Rt. 2, Mass.)	782
1931	West End	Pittsburgh	778
1972	Piscataqua R.	I-95, N.H.-Me.	756
1979	SR 156, Tennessee R.	So. Pittsburgh, Tenn.	750
1963	Cold Spring Canyon	Santa Barbara, Cal.	700
1973	I-24, Paducah, Ky.	Ohio River	700

Concrete Arch

Year	Bridge	Location	Longest span
1971	Selah Creek (twin)	Selah, Wash.	549
1968	Cowlitz River	Mossyrock, Wash.	520
1931	Westinghouse	Pittsburgh	425
1923	Cappelen	Minneapolis	400
1930	Jack's Run	Pittsburgh	400
1973	Elwha River	Port Angeles, Wash.	380
1931	Bixby Creek	Monterey Coast, Cal.	330
1953	Arroyo Seco	Pasadena, Cal.	320
1927	Mendota	Ft. Snelling, Minn.	304

Twin Concrete Trestle

Year	Bridge	Location	Longest span
1963	Slidell, La.	L. Pontchartrain	28,547[9]

Concrete Slab Dam

Year	Bridge	Location	Longest span
1927	Conowingo Dam	Maryland	4,611
1952	John H. Kerr Dam	Roanoke River, Va.	2,785
1936	Hoover Dam	Boulder City, Nev.	1,324

Drawbridges

Vertical Lift

Year	Bridge	Location	Longest span
1959	*Arthur Kill	N.Y.-N.J.	558
1935	*Cape Cod Canal	Massachusetts	544
1960	*Delair, N.J.	Delaware River	542
1937	Marine Parkway	New York City	540
1931	Burlington, N.J.	Delaware R.	534
1912	*A-S-B Fratt	Kansas City	428
1945	*Harry S. Truman	Kansas City	427
1932	*M-K-T R.R.	Missouri R.	414
1969	Wilm'gtn Mem.	Wilmington, N.C.	408
1930	Aerial	Duluth, Minn.	386
1941	Main St.	Jacksonville, Fla.	386
1962	Burlington	Ontario	370
1922	*Cincinnati	Ohio River	365
1967	Benj. Harrison Mem.	James River, Va.	363
1961	Corpus Christi Harbor	Corpus Christi, Tex.	344[4]
1962	Sand Island Access	Oahu, Hawaii	340
1941	U.S. 1&9, Passaic R.	Newark, N.J.	332
1929	Carlton	Bath-Woolwich, Me.	328
1930	*Martinez	California	328
1960	St. Andrews Bay	Panama City, Fla.	327
1929	*Penn-Lehigh	Newark Bay	322
1920	*Chattanooga	Tennessee R.	310
1936	Triboro, N.Y.C.	Harlem River	310
1936	Hardin	Illinois River	309
1960	Sacramento River	Rio Vista, Cal.	306
1957	Claiborne Ave.	New Orleans	305
1927	Cochrane	Mobile, Ala.	300
1928	James River	Newport News	300
1929	San Mateo	California	300
1926	*Missouri Pacific	Kragen, Ark.	300

Bascule

Year	Bridge	Location	Longest span
1926	Fort Madison	Mississippi R.	525[4]
1969	Pearl River	Slidell, La.	482
1916	Keokui Municipal	Mississippi R., Ia.	377
1917	SR-8, Tennessee River	Chattanooga, Tenn.	306
1940	Lorain, Ohio	Black River	300
1958	Morrison	Portland, Ore.	285
1969	Elizabeth River	Chesapeake, Va.	281
1957	Craig Memorial	I-280, Toledo, Oh.	245
1952	Downtown	Norfolk, Va.	230

Swing Bridges

Year	Bridge	Location	Longest span
1950	Douglass Memorial	Anac'tia R., Wash. D.C.	386
1945	Lord Delaware	Mattaponi River, Va.	252
1957	Eltham	Pamunkey River, Va.	237
1939	Chickahominy River	Route 5, Va.	222
1930	Nansemond River	Route 125, Va.	200

Swing Span

Year	Bridge	Location	Longest span
1908	*Willamette R.	Portland, Ore.	521
1903	*East Omaha	Missouri R.	519
1952	Yorktown	York River, Va.	500
1897	*Duluth, Minn.	St. Louis Bay	486
1899	*C.M.&N.R.R.	Chicago	474
1897	Sioux City, Ia.	Missouri R. (Nebr.-Ia.)	470
1914	*Coos Bay	Oregon	458

Floating Pontoon

Year	Bridge	Location	Longest span
1963	Evergreen Pt.	Seattle, Wash.	7,518
1940	Lacey V. Murrow	Seattle	6,561
1961	Hood Canal	Pt. Gamble, Wash.	6,471

(1) The Transbay Bridge has 2 spans of 2,310 ft. each. (2) A second bridge in parallel will be completed. (3) The Richmond Bridge has twin spans 1,070 ft. each. (4) Railroad and vehicular bridge. (5) Two spans each 760 ft. (6) Two spans each 707 ft. (7) Two spans each 660 ft. (8) Two spans each 825 ft. (9) Total length of bridge. (10) Two spans each 900 ft.

Construction Details of Large and Unusual Bridges

Verrazano-Narrows Bridge, between Staten Island and Brooklyn, N.Y., has a suspension span of 4,260 ft., exceeding the Golden Gate Bridge, San Francisco, by 60 ft. One level in use Nov., 1964, second opened Jun. 28, 1969. The name is a compromise; it spans the Narrows and commemorates a visit to New York Harbor in Apr., 1524, deduced from certain notes left by Giovanni da Verrazano, Italian navigator sailing for Francis I of France.

Allegheny River Bridge (Interstate 80) near Emlenton, Pa., 270 ft. above the water, tallest in eastern U.S., a continuous truss, 688 ft. long, 1968.

Angostura, suspension type, span 2,336 feet, 1967 at Ciudad Bolivar, Venezuela. Total length, 5,507.

Charles Braga Bridge over Taunton River between Fall River and Somerset, Mass. It is 5,780 feet long.

Bendorf Bridge on the Rhine River, 5 mi. n. of Coblenz, completed 1965, is a 3-span cement girder bridge, 3,378 ft. overall length, 101 ft. wide, with the main span 682 ft.

Burro Creek Bridge with 4 spans over Burro Creek on highway 93 near Kingman, Ariz. Main span steel truss 680 ft. Others plate girder, 110 and 2 of 85 ft. 1966.

Champlain Bridge at Montreal crossing the St. Lawrence River was opened 1962. It is 4 miles long.

Chesapeake Bay Bridge-Tunnel, opened Apr. 15, 1964 on US-13, connects Virginia Beach-Norfolk with the Eastern Shore of Virginia. Shore to shore, 17.6 miles. Twelve miles of trestles, 4 man-made islands, 2 mile-long tunnels, and 2 bridges.

Cross Bay Parkway Bridge (N.Y.), 3,000 feet long with 6 traffic lanes, 11 eight foot wide precast, prestressed concrete T girders to support spans 130 feet long each with main span 275 feet.

Delaware Memorial Bridge over Delaware River near Wilmington. A twin suspension bridge paralleling the original 250 ft. upstream has a 2,150-ft. main span suspended from 440-ft. towers.

Eads Bridge across the Mississippi R. between St. Louis and E. St. Louis, built in 1874 has 4 main spans 1,520 ft., 2,502 ft., and 1,118 ft. crossing Miss. R., a railroad and a road.

Evergreen Point Bridge, Wash. consists of 33 floating concrete pontoons weighing 4,700 tons each, held in place by 77 ton crete anchors. Pontoon structure is 6,561 ft. long; with approaches bridge is 12,596 ft. long.

Fremont Bridge. Part of Stadium Freeway, Portland, Ore., crossing Willamette R. 1,255 ft. steel arch span with two 452 ft. flanking steel arch spans. 1971.

Frontenac Bridge, Quebec, suspension, span 2,190 ft., open 1970.

Gladesville Bridge at Sydney, Australia, has the longest concrete arch in the world (1,000 ft. span).

George Washington Bridge, New York City, 4th longest suspension bridge in the world, spans the Hudson River between W. 178th St., Manhattan, and Ft. Lee, N.J.; 4,760 ft. between anchorages, two levels, 14 traffic lanes. Triborough Bridge connects Manhattan, the Bronx, and Queens; project comprises a suspension bridge, a vertical lift bridge, and a fixed bridge, all connected by long viaducts. The famous Brooklyn Bridge over the East River, connecting Manhattan and Brooklyn, was completed in 1883, breaking all previous records by spanning 1,595 ft.

Golden Gate Bridge, crossing San Francisco Bay, has the second longest single span, 4,200 ft.

Hampton Roads Bridge-Tunnel, Va. A crossing completed in 1957 consisting of 2 man-made islands, 2 concrete trestle bridges, and one tunnel, under Hampton Roads with a length of 7,479 ft. A parallel facility with a 7,315 ft. tunnel is now open to traffic.

Hood Canal Floating Bridge, Wash., 23 floating concrete pontoons 4,980 tons each. Roadway is supported on crete T-beam sections mounted on pontoons 20 feet above canal. Floating section is 6,471 ft. long, overall 7,866 ft. Closed Feb. 13, 1979; severe storm damage.

Humber Bridge, with a suspension span of 4,626 ft., the longest in the world, crosses the Humber estuary 5 miles west of the city of Kingston upon Hull, England. Unique in a large suspension bridge are the towers of reinforced concrete instead of steel.

International Bridge, a series of 8 arch and truss bridges crossing St. Mary's and the Soo Locks between Mich. and Ontario. Two-mile toll completed 1962.

Lacy V. Murrow Floating Bridge, Wash., 25 floating pontoons of 4,558 tons each. Bridge with approaches is 8,583 ft.

Lake Pontchartrain Twin Causeway, a twin-span crete trestle bridge and 24-mile link within metropolitan New Orleans that connects the north and south shore. First span opened 1956, second 1969.

Lavaca Bay Causeway, Tex., 2.2 miles long, consisting of one 260 ft. continuous plate girder unit and 194 precast, prestressed concrete spans of 60 ft. length. 1961.

Newport Bridge between Newport and Jamestown, R.I. Total length 11,248 ft., a main suspension span of 1,600 feet, 2 side spans each 688 feet long. It has U.S.A.'s first prefabricated wire strands.

New York City bridges, *see Verrazano-Narrows Bridge and George Washington Bridge above.*

Ogdensburg-Prescott Internat'l Bridge across the St. Lawrence River from Ogdensburg, N.Y., to Johnston, Ont., opened 1970, is 13,510 ft. long with approaches and 7,260 ft. between abutments.

Oland Island Bridge in Sweden was completed in 1972. It is 19,882 feet long, Europe's longest.

Oosterscheldebrug, opened Dec. 15, 1965, is a 3.125-mile causeway for automobiles over a sea arm in Zeeland, the Netherlands. It completes a direct connection between Flushing and Rotterdam.

Poplar St. Bridge over the Mississippi at St. Louis, a 5-span continuous orthotropic deck plate girder bridge, longest span 600 ft. Eight lanes, 2,165 ft. long.

Quebec Road, suspension, span 2,190 feet, 1969, Quebec, Canada.

Rio-Niteroi, Guanabara Bay, Brazil, under construction, will be world's longest continuous box and plate girder bridge, 8 miles, 3,363 feet long, with a center span of 984 feet and a span on each side of 656 feet.

Robert Opie Norris Bridge, Rappahannock R. between Greys Pt. and White Stone, Va. 9,989 ft. long. Main spans are two 144 foot cantilever truss spans with a 360 foot truss span suspended between them.

Rockville Bridge, world's longest 4-track stone arch bridge, 3,810 ft., with 48 arches. Part of the Consolidated Rail Corp. system west of Harrisburg, Pa. It contains 440 million lbs. of stone, 100,000 cubic yds. of masonry and crosses the Susquehanna Riv. to Rockville, Pa.

Royal Gorge Bridge, 1,053 ft. above the Arkansas River in Colorado, is the highest bridge above water. Opened Dec. 8, 1929, it is 1,260 ft. long with a main span of 880 ft., width 18 ft.

San Mateo-Hayward Bridge across San Francisco Bay is first major orthotropic bridge in U.S. It is 6.7 miles long, 4.9 mile low-level concrete trestle and 1.8 miles high-level steel bridge.

Seven Mile Bridge is the longest of an expanse of bridges connecting the Florida Keys. It was built by the Florida East Coast Railway between 1904 and 1916, now a state highway.

Shenandoah River Bridges, one spans the south fork, 1,924 ft. long, the other the north fork, 1,090 ft. long. Warren County, Va.

Straits of Mackinac Bridge, completed in 1957, is the longest suspension bridge between anchorages and with approaches extends nearly 5 mi. between Mackinaw City and St. Ignace, Mich.

Sunshine Skyway, a 15-mile-long bridge-causeway with twin roadbeds that crosses Tampa Bay at St. Petersburg, Fla., a system of twin bridges 864 feet long and 4 smaller bridges with 6 causeways. The main span of the south bound bridge was torn away May 9, 1980, when support tower was hit by a cargo ship.

Tagus River Bridge near Lisbon, Portugal, longest suspension bridge outside the United States, has a 3,323-ft. main span. Opened Aug. 6, 1966, it was named Salazar Bridge for the former premier.

Thomas A. Edison Memorial Bridge (causeway) across Sandusky Bay between Martin Point and Danbury, Oh., is 2.67 miles long. The main bridge is 2,044 feet long.

Thousand Island Bridge, St. Lawrence River. American span 800 ft.; Canadian 750 ft.

Union St. Bridge in Woodstock, Vt., a timber lattice truss with a span of 122 feet built in 1969 using old time procedure of hand drilled holes and wooden pegs.

Vancouver Bridge, Canada's longest railway lift span connecting Vancouver and North Vancouver over Burrard Inlet. It is in 3 sections, the longest 493 ft. Spans are part of a project that includes a 2-mile tunnel under Vancouver Hts.

Woodrow Wilson Memorial Bridge across the Potomac River at Alexandria, Va., is over a mile long.

Zoo Bridge across the Rhine at Cologne, with steel box girders, has a main span of 850 ft.

The Interstate Highway 610 crossing of the Houston Ship Channel in Texas is 6,300 feet in length and consists of various lengths of prestressed concrete beam and slab approach spans and a 1,233 foot main unit of two 471'6" plate girder units and one 290 ft. simple span.

Underwater Vehicular Tunnels in North America

(3,000 feet in length or more)

Name	Location	Waterway	Lgth. Ft.
Bart Trans-Bay Tubes (Rapid Transit)	San Francisco, Cal.	S.F. Bay	3.6 miles
Brooklyn-Battery	New York, N.Y.	East River	9,117
Holland Tunnel	New York, N.Y.	Hudson River	8,557
Lincoln Tunnel	New York, N.Y.	Hudson River	8,216
Baltimore Harbor Tunnel	Baltimore, Md.	Patapsco River	7,650
Hampton Roads	Norfolk, Va.	Hampton Roads	7,479
Queens Midtown	New York, N.Y.	East River	6,414
Thimble Shoal Channel	Cape Henry, Va.	Chesapeake Bay	5,738
Sumner Tunnel	Boston, Mass.	Boston Harbor	5,650
Chesapeake Channel	Cape Charles, Va.	Chesapeake Bay	5,450
Louis-Hippolyte Lafontaine Tunnel	Montreal, Que.	St. Lawrence River	5,280
Detroit-Windsor	Detroit, Mich.	Detroit River	5,135
Callahan Tunnel	Boston, Mass.	Boston Harbor	5,046
Midtown Tunnel	Norfolk, Va.	Elizabeth River	4,194
Baytown Tunnel	Baytown, Tex.	Houston Ship Channel	4,111
Posey Tube	Oakland, Cal.	Oakland Estuary	3,500
Downtown Tunnel	Norfolk, Va.	Elizabeth River	3,350
Webster St.	Alameda, Cal.	Oakland Estuary	3,350
Bankhead Tunnel	Mobile, Ala.	Mobile River	3,109
I-10 Twin Tunnel	Mobile, Ala.	Mobile River	3,000

Land Vehicular Tunnels in U.S.

(over 1,200 feet in length.)

Name	Location	Lgth. Ft.	Name	Location	Lgth. Ft.
Eisenhower Memorial	Route 70, Col.	8,941	F.D. Roosevelt Dr.	81-89 Sts. N.Y.C.	2,400
Copperfield	Copperfield, Ut.	6,989	Dewey Sq.	Boston, Mass.	2,400
Allegheny (twin)	Penna. Turnpike	6,070	Battery Park	N.Y.C.	2,300
Liberty Tubes	Pittsburgh, Pa.	5,920	Battery St.	Seattle, Wash.	2,140
Zion Natl. Park	Rte. 9, Utah	5,766	Big Oak Flat	Yosemite Natl. Park	2,083
East River Mt. (twin)	Interstate 77, W. Va.-Va.	5,661	Carlin	I-80, Nev.	1,993
Tuscarora (twin)	Penna. Turnpike	5,326	Prudential	Boston, Mass.	1,980
Kittatinny (twin)	Penna. Turnpike	4,727	Internatl. Underpass	Los Angeles, Cal.	1,910
Lehigh	Penna. Turnpike	4,379	Street-Car	Providence, R.I.	1,793
Blue Mountain (twin)	Penna. Turnpike	4,339	Broadway	San Francisco, Cal.	1,616
Wawona	Yosemite Natl. Park	4,233	9th Street Expy.	Washington, D.C.	1,610
Squirrel Hill	Pittsburgh, Pa.	4,225	F.D. Roosevelt Dr.	42-48 Sts. N.Y.C.	1,600
Big Walker Mt.	Route I-77, Va.	4,200	Lowry Hill	Minneapolis	1,496
Fort Pitt	Pittsburgh, Pa.	3,560	Wheeling	Interstate 70, W. Va.	1,490
Mall Tunnel	Dist. of Columbia	3,400	Mt. Baker Ridge (3)	Seattle, Wash.	1,466
Caldecott	Oakland, Cal.	3,371	Knowls Creek	Lane County, Ore.	1,430
Cody No. 1	U.S. 14, 16, 20, Wyo.	3,224	Mule Pass	Near Bisbee, Ariz.	1,400
Kalihi	Honolulu, Ha.	2,780	Arch Cape	Oregon Coast Hwy. 9	1,228
Memorial	W. Va. Tpke. (I-77)	2,669	Queen Creek	Superior, Ariz.	1,200
Cross-Town	178 St. N.Y.C.	2,414	West Rock	New Haven, Conn.	1,200

World's Longest Railway Tunnels

Source: Railway Directory & Year Book 1980. Tunnels over 4.9 miles in length.

Tunnel	Date	Miles	Yds	Operating railway	Country
Dai-shimizu	1979	13	1,384	Japanese National	Japan
Simplon No. 1 and 2	1906, 1922	12	546	Swiss Fed. & Italian St.	Switz.-Italy
Kanmon	1975	11	1,093	Japanese National	Japan
Apennine	1934	11	881	Italian State	Italy
Rokko	1972	10	158	Japanese National	Japan
Gotthard	1882	9	552	Swiss Federal	Switzerland
Lotschberg	1913	9	130	Bern-Lotschberg-Simplon	Switzerland
Hokuriku	1962	8	1,079	Japanese National	Japan
Mont Cenis (Frejus)	1871	8	847	Italian State	France-Italy
Shin-Shimizu	1961	8	675	Japanese National	Japan
Aki	1975	8	161	Japanese National	Japan
Cascade	1929	7	1,388	Burlington Northern	U.S.
Flathead	1970	7	1,319	Great Northern	U.S.
Keijo	1970	7	88	Japanese National	Japan
Lierasen	1973	6	1,135	Norwegian State	Norway
Santa Lucia	1977	6	656	Italian State	Italy
Arlberg	1884	6	643	Austrian Federal	Austria
Moffat	1928	6	366	Denver & Rio Grande Western	U.S.
Shimizu	1931	6	44	Japanese National	Japan
Kvineshei	1943	5	1,107	Norwegian State	Norway
Bigo	1975	5	927	Japanese National	Japan
Rimutaka	1955	5	816	New Zealand Gov.	New Zealand
Ricken	1910	5	603	Swiss Federal	Switzerland
Kaimai	1978	5	873	New Zealand Gov.	New Zealand
Grenchenberg	1915	5	575	Swiss Federal	Switzerland
Otira	1923	5	559	New Zealand Gov.	New Zealand
Tauern	1909	5	546	Austrian Federal	Austria
Haegebostad	1943	5	462	Norwegian State	Norway
Ronco	1889	5	272	Italian State	Italy
Hauenstein (Lower)	1916	5	90	Swiss Federal	Switzerland
Connaught	1916	5	34	Canadian Pacific	Canada
Karawanken	1906	4	1,677	Austrian Federal	Austria-Yugo.
Kobe	1972	4	1,671	Japanese National	Japan
New Tanna	1964	4	1,658	Japanese National	Japan

Major World Dams

Source: Water and Power Resources Service, U.S. Interior Department. *Replaces existing dam.
Volume in cubic yards. **Capacity** (gross) in acre feet. Year of completion. **U.C.** under construction.
Type: A—Arch. B—Buttress. E—Earthfill. G—Gravity. R—Rockfill. MA—Multi-arch.

Name of dam	Type	Year	River and basin	Country	Height Feet	Crest Length Feet	Vol.-ume (1,000 C.Y.)	Res. cap. (1,000 A.F.)
Afsluitdijk	E	1932	Zuider Zee	Netherlands	62	105,000	82,927	4,864
Akosombo-Main	R	1965	Volta	Ghana	463	2,100	10,400	120,000
Almendra	A	1970	Turmes-Douro	Spain	662	1,860	2,188	2,148
Alpe Gera	G	1965	Comor-Adda-Po	Italy	584	1,710	2,252	53
Bagdad Tailings	E	1973	Maroney Gulch	U.S.	121	2,601	37,304	40
Beas	G	1975	Beas-Indus	India	435	6,400	45,800	6,600
W.A.C. Bennett*	E	1967	Peace-Mackenzie	Canada	600	6,700	57,203	57,006
Bhakra	G	1963	Sutlend-Indus	India	742	1,700	5,400	8,000
Bratsk	GE	1964	Angara	USSR	410	16,864	18,283	137,220
Brouwershavense Gat	E	1972		Netherlands	118	20,341	35,316	466
Castaic	E	1973	Castaic Cr.	U.S.	340	5,200	44,000	432
Charvak	E	1970	Chirchik-Sir Darya	USSR	551	2,483	24,983	1,620
Chirkey	A	1975	Sulak-Caspian Sea	USSR	764	1,109	1,602	2,252
Chivor	R	1975	Bata	Colombia	778	919	14,126	661
Cochiti	E	1975	Rio Grande	U.S.	253	26,891	64,631	513
Copper Cities Tailing 2	E	1973	Tinhorn Wash	U.S.	325	7,598	30,003	4
Cougar	R	1964	S.F. McKenzie	U.S.	519	1,600	13,000	219
Dartmouth	R	1978	Mitta-Mitta	Australia	591	2,200	18,312	5,232
Dneprodzerzhinsk	GE	1964	Dnieper	USSR	112	118,090	28,503	1,994
Don Pedro*	R	1971	Tuolume-San Joaquin	U.S.	585	1,900	16,760	2,030
Dworshak	G	1974	N. Fork Clearwater	U.S.	717	3,287	6,500	3,453
El Chocon	E	1974	Limay	Argentina	282	7,546	17,004	17,025
Emosson	A	1974	Barberine	Switz.	590	1,818	1,426	184
Esperanza Tailings	E	1973	Santa Cruz	U.S.	121	10,600	39,704	5
Fort Peck	E	1940	Missouri	U.S.	250	21,026	125,612	19,133
Fort Randall	E	1956	Missouri	U.S.	165	10,700	50,205	5,701
Gardiner*	E	1968	South Saskatchewan	Canada	223	16,700	85,743	8,000
Garrison	E	1956	Missouri	U.S.	203	11,300	66,506	24,321
Gepatsch	R	1965	Faggenbach-Inn	Austria	500	1,908	9,810	113
Glen Canyon	A	1964	Colorado	U.S.	710	1,560	4,901	27,000
Goscheneralp	E	1960	Goschener	Switz.	508	1,771	12,230	62
Grand Coulee	G	1942	Columbia	U.S.	550	4,173	10,585	9,724
Grande Dixence	G	1962	Dixence-Rhone	Switz.	935	2,280	7,792	325
Guri	GE	1968	Caroni-Orinoco	Venezuela	348	2,264	4,917	14,349
Haringvliet	E	1970	Haringvliet	Netherlands	79	18,044	26,160	527
High Aswan (Sadd-El-Aali)	ER	1970	Nile	Egypt	364	12,565	57,203	137,000
Hirakud	GE	1956	Mahandi	India	202	15,748	25,100	6,600
Hoover	AG	1936	Colorado	U.S.	726	1,244	4,400	29,755
Hungry Horse	AG	1953	S. Fork Flathead	U.S.	564	2,115	3,086	3,468
Ilha Solteira	EG	1973	Parana Rio de la Plata	Brazil	295	20,308	29,454	27,730
Irkutsk	GE	1956	Angara	USSR	144	8,989	16,219	37,290
Ivankova	EG	1937	Volga-Caspian S.	USSR	98	31,398	20,207	908
Jari	E	1967	Jari	Pakistan	234	5,700	42,400	400
Daniel Johnson*	MA	1968	Manicougan-St. Lawrence	Canada	703	4,311	2,950	115,000
Kakhovka	EG	1955	Dnieper	USSR	121	5,380	46,617	14,755
Kanev	E	1974	Dnieper	USSR	82	52,950	49,520	2,125
Kapchagay	E	1970	Ili	USSR	164	1,542	5,078	22,813
Kariba	A	1959	Zambesi	Rhodesia-Zambia	420	2,025	1,350	130,000
Keban	ERG	1974	First (Euphrates)	Turkey	679	3,881	20,900	25,110
Kiev	E	1964	Dnieper	USSR	72	177,448	57,552	3,021
King Paul (Kremasta)	ER	1965	Acheloos	Greece	541	1,510	10,686	3,850
Kremenchug	EG	1961	Dnieper	USSR	108	39,844	41,192	10,945
Kurobegawa No. 4	A	1964	Kurobe	Japan	610	1,603	1,782	162
Lauwerszee	E	1969	Lauwerszee	Netherlands	75	42,650	46,532	40
Ludington	E	1973	Lake Michigan	U.S.	170	29,301	37,703	83
Luzzone	A	1963	Brenno di Luzzone	Switz.	682	1,738	1,739	71
Mangla	E	1967	Jhelum	Pakistan	380	11,000	85,872	5,150
Marimbondo	E	1975	Grande	Brazil	315	12,297	24,328	5,184
Mauvoisin	A	1957	Drance de Bagnes	Switz.	777	1,706	2,655	148
Mica	R	1974	Columbia	Canada	794	2,600	42,000	20,000
Mingechaur	E	1953	Kura	USSR	262	5,085	20,400	12,970
Navajo	E	1963	San Juan	U.S.	407	3,648	26,841	1,709
New Bullards Bar	A	1970	North Yuba-Sacramento	U.S.	637	2,200	2,700	960
New Cornelia Tailings	E	1973	Ten Mile Wash, Ariz.	U.S.	98	35,600	274,026	20
New Melones	R	1975	Stanislaus-San Joaquin	U.S.	625	1,600	15,970	2,400
Oahe	E	1963	Missouri	U.S.	245	9,300	92,008	23,591
Okutadami	G	1961	Tadami	Japan	515	1,575	2,145	487
Oroville	E	1968	Feather-Sacramento	U.S.	770	6,920	78,008	3,538
Owen Falls	G	1954	Lake Victoria-Nile	Uganda	100	2,725		166,000
Place Moulin	AG	1965	Buthier-Dora Baltea	Italy	502	2,181	1,962	81
Reza Shah Kabir	A	1975	Karoun	Iran	656	1,247	1,570	2,351
Rybinsk	GE	1941	Volga-Caspian S.	USSR	98	2,060	3,329	20,590
Sakuma	G	1956	Tenryu	Japan	510	963	1,465	265
San Luis	E	1967	San Luis-San Joaquin	U.S.	382	18,600	77,666	2,039
Saratov	E	1967	Volga-Caspian S.	USSR	131	37,204	52,843	10,458
Shasta	AG	1945	Sacramento	U.S.	602	3,460	8,711	4,552
Swift	E	1958	Lewis-Columbia	U.S.	610	2,100	15,800	756
Tabka	E	1975	Euphrates	Syria	197	14,764	60,168	11,350
Talbingo	R	1971	Tamut	Australia	530	2,300	18,950	747
Tarbela	ER	1975	Indus	Pakistan	486	9,000	158,268	11,100
Trinity	E	1962	Trinity-Klamath	U.S.	537	2,600	29,252	2,448
Tsimlyansk	EG	1952	Don	USSR	128	43,411	44,323	17,715
Tuttle Creek	E	1962	Big Blue-Missouri	U.S.	154	7,500	22,937	413
Twin Buttes	E	1963	Concho-Colorado, Texas	U.S.	134	42,463	21,442	641
Twin Buttes Tailings	E	1973	Santa Cruz	U.S.	239	11,299	38,604	209
Vilyui	ER	1967	Vilyui	USSR	246	2,297	3,793	29,104
Volga-22d congress USSR	ERG	1958	Volga-Caspian S.	USSR	144	13,108	33,020	27,160
Volga-V. I. Lenin	EG	1955	Volga-Caspian S.	USSR	148	12,405	44,298	47,020
Yellowtail	A	1966	Bighorn-Missouri	U.S.	525	1,480	1,456	1,375
Zeya	G	1975	Zeya	USSR	369	2,343	3,139	55,452

Major U.S. Public and Private Dams and Reservoirs

Source: Corps of Engineers, U.S. Army
Heights over 350 feet.

Height—Difference in elevation in feet, between lowest point in foundation and top of dam, exclusive of parapet or other projec-ns. **Length**—Overall length of barrier in feet, main dam and its integral features as located between natural abutments. **Volume**—otal volume in cubic yards of all material in main dam and its appurtenant works. **Year**—Date structure was originally completed for se. (UC) Under construction subject to revision. **River**—Mainstream. **Purpose**—I-Irrigation; C-Flood Control; H-Hydroelectric; N-avigation; S-Water Supply; R-Recreation; D-Debris Control; O-Other. **Parentheses** after name indicate type of dam as follows: E)-Earth; (PG)-Gravity; (ER)-Rockfill; (CB)-Buttress; (VA)-Arch; (MV)-Multi-arch; (OT)-Other. †Replacing existing dam.

Name of dam	State	River	Ht.	Lgth.	Vol. (1,000)	Purpose	Year
roville (RE)	Cal.	Feather River	770	6800	78000	IR	1968
oover (VA)	Nev.	Colorado River	726	1242	4400	IHCO	1936
allisaw Creek Site 8 (RE)	Okla.	Sallisaw Creek	721	800	186	CR	1964
worshak (PG)	Ida.	North Fork of Clearwater	717	3287	6450	HCR	1973
len Canyon (VA)	Ariz.	Colorado River	710	1560	4901	HCSR	1964
ew Bullards Bar (VA)	Cal.	North Yuba River	635	2200	2600	SD	1970
ew Melones (ER)	Cal.	Stanislaus River	625	1560	16000	IH	1979
wift Dam (RE)	Wash.	North Fork Lewis River	610	2100	15400	HR	1958
lossyrock Dam (VA)	Wash.	Cowlitz River	606	1648	1270	HCR	1968
hasta (PG)	Cal.	Sacramento River	602	3460	8711	ISHN	1945
ankee Doodle Tailings (ER)	Mon.	Yankee Doodle and Silver Bow Cr.	570	13200	200000	O	1972
on Pedro (RE)	Cal.	Tuolumne River	568	1800	16000	HI	1971
ungry Horse (VA)	Mon.	South Fork of Flathead River	564	2115	3086	IHCN	1953
rand Coulee (PG)	Wash.	Columbia River	550	4173	10585	IHCN	1942
Vaverly Lower Reservoir (RE)	N.Y.	Dry Brook	540	310	91	S	1880
oss Dam (VA)	Wash.	Skagit River	540	1300	919	HR	1949
rinity (RE)	Cal.	Trinity River	537	2600	29410	IHCR	1962
ohn's Branch No. 2 (OT)	W.Va.	John's Branch of Toney Fork	534	2250	8218	O	1963
ellowtail (VA)	Mon.	Bighorn River	525	1360	146	ICHR	1966
ougar (ER)	Ore.	South Fork McKenzie River	519	1600	13000	HCIR	1964
laming Gorge (VA)	Ut.	Green River	502	1285	987	HCSR	1964
hawville Dam (PG)	N.Y.	Oswegatchie	500	230	11	H	1909
tirrat No. 15 Waste Embank. (OT)	W.Va.	Rockhouse Br. of Island Cr.	500	1800	11000	O	1977
ontana Dam (PG)	N.C.	Little Tennessee River	480	2365	3576	H	1944
lew Exchequer (ER)	Cal.	Merced River	479	1240	5169	HI	1926
Vyco No. 2 Refuse Embank. (OT)	W.Va.	Guyandot River	469	1500	6453	O	1978
lorrow Point (VA)	Col.	Gunnison River	468	741	365	HCRO	1968
ry Fork Slurry Impound (OT)	W.Va.	Trib. Dry Fork of Tug Fork	465	2100	14406	O	1960
Aill Branch Coal Refuse Dam (OT)	W.Va.	Crane Fork of Clear Fork	465	1584	4000	O	1963
arters Main Dam (ER,RE)	Ga.	Coosawattee River	464	1950	15000	CHR	1974
etroit (PG)	Ore.	North Santiam River	463	1580	1500	HCRI	1953
nderson Ranch (RE)	Ida.	South Fork Boise River	456	1350	9653	IHCR	1950
Jnion Valley (RE)	Cal.	Silver Creek	453	1800	10000	SH	1963
Round Butte Dam (RE,ER)	Ore.	Deschutes River	440	1450	9600	HR	1964
ine Flat Lake (PG)	Cal.	Kings River	440	1840	2400	CIRH	1954
ocassee (ER)	S.C.	Keowee River	435	1800	11600	H	1973
'Shaughnessy (PG)	Cal.	Moccasin Creek	430	900	663	H	1923
Aud Mountain Dam (ER)	Wash.	White River	425	700	2300	C	1948
ibby Dam (PG)	Mon.	Kootenai River	422	2890	375	HC	1973
Disposal Area No. 21 (RE)	Md.	Offstream	420	4500		O	1968
Pacoima (VA)	Cal.	Pacoima Creek	420	640	226	C	1929
Owyhee Dam (VA)	Ore.	Owyhee River	417	833	538	ICR	1932
ower Hell Hole (ER)	Cal.	Rubicon River	410	1550	8315	SD	1966
Castaic (RE)	Cal.	Castaic Creek	410	5200	4400	IR	1973
Mammoth Pool (RE)	Cal.	San Joaquin River	406	820	5355	HS	1960
Navajo (RE)	N.M.	San Juan River	402	3648	26840	IR	1963
ittle Blue Run Dam (RE)	Pa.	Little Blue Run of Ohio River	400	2100	13000	O	1977
Toxaway Lake (RE)	S.C.	Jocassee River	400	1000		H	1972
Pyramid (ER)	Cal.	Piru Creek	400	1080	6952	IR	1973
Brownlee Dam (ER)	Ida.	Snake River	395	1380	6000	H	1958
Summersville Dam (ER)	W.Va.	Gauley River	390	2280	13565	CRSO	1965
Blue Mesa (RE)	Col.	Gunnison River	390	785	3093	HCRO	1966
Diablo Dam (VA)	Wash.	Skagit River	386	1180	350	HR	1929
San Luis (RE)	Cal.	San Luis Creek	382	18600	77664	ISHR	1967
Green Peter (PG)	Ore.	Middle Santiam River	378	1517	1142	CHRI	1967
Merriman Dam (RE)	N.Y.	Roundout Creek	375	2400	5800	S	1945
Turkey Gap Mine Refuse (OT)	W.Va.	Rt. Hand Fork of Widemouth	368	1300	1200	O	1979
Jenkins Refuse Dam (OT)	Ky.	Elkhorn Creek	363	1700	12229	D	1974
San Gabriel No. 1 (ER)	Cal.	San Gabriel River	360	1520	10600	C	1938
Spruce Lick Fork Refuse Disp. (OT)	W.Va.	Spruce Lick Fk. of West Pond	360	400	17736	O	1977
Steel Trap Br. Refuse Dam (OT)	Ky.	Steel Trap Br. of Phillips Fk.	358	650	4250	O	1979
Abiquiu Dam (RE)	N.M.	Rio Chama	354	1540	11793	CD	1963

World's Largest Dams

Source: Water and Power Resources Service, U.S. Interior Department

Based on total volume of structure. All dams listed are predominantly earthfill or rockfill and may contain concrete section.

Name of dam	Cubic yards	Completed
New Cornelia Tailings, U.S.	274,026,000	1973
Tarbela, Pakistan	158,268,000	1975
Fort Peck, U.S.	125,612,000	1940
Oahe, U.S.	92,008,000	1963
Mangla, Pakistan	85,872,000	1967
Gardiner, Canada	85,743,000	1968
Afsluitdijk, Netherlands	82,927,000	1932
Oroville, U.S.	78,008,000	1968
San Luis, U.S.	77,666,000	1967
Garrison, U.S.	66,506,000	1956
Cochiti, U.S.	64,631,000	1975
Tabka, Syria	60,168,000	1975
Kiev, USSR	57,552,000	1964
W.A.C. Bennett, Canada	57,203,000	1967
High Aswan Sadd-El-Aili, Egypt	57,203,000	1970
Dantiwada Left Earthenbank, India	53,680,000	1965
Saratov, U.S.S.R.	52,843,000	1967
Mission Tailings, No. 2, U.S.	52,435,000	1973
Fort Randall, U.S.	50,205,000	1956
Kanev, USSR	49,520,000	1974
Kakhovka, USSR	46,617,000	1955
Lauwerszee, Netherlands	46,532,000	1969
Beas, India	45,800,000	1975
Volga, V.I. Lenin, USSR	44,298,000	1955
Castaic, U.S.	44,000,000	1971
Jari, Pakistan	42,400,000	1967

Superlative U.S. Statistics

Source: National Geographic Society, Washington, D.C.

Area for 50 states	Total	3,618,467 sq. mi
	Land 3,540,023 sq. mi.—Water 78,444 sq. mi.	
Largest state	Alaska	589,757 sq. mi
Smallest state	Rhode Island	1,214 sq. mi
Largest county	San Bernardino County, California	20,119 sq. mi
Smallest county	New York, New York	23 sq. mi
Northernmost city	Barrow, Alaska	71°17′N
Northernmost point	Point Barrow, Alaska	71°23′N
Southernmost city	Hilo, Island of Hawaii	19°43′N
Southernmost town	Naalehu, Island of Hawaii	19°03′N
Southernmost point	Ka Lae (South Cape), Island of Hawaii	18°56′N. (155°41′W.)
Easternmost city	Eastport, Maine	66°59′02″W
Easternmost town	Lubec, Maine	66°58′49″W
Easternmost point	West Quoddy Head, Maine	66°57′W
Westernmost city	Lihue, Island of Kauai, Hawaii	159°22′W
Westernmost town	Adak, Aleutians, Alaska	176°45′W
Westernmost point	Cape Wrangell, Attu Island, Aleutians, Alaska	172°27′E
Highest city	Leadville, Colorado	10,200 ft.
Lowest town	Calipatria, California	−184 ft.
Highest point on Atlantic coast	Cadillac Mountain, Mount Desert Is., Maine	1,530 ft.
Largest and oldest national park	Yellowstone National Park (1872), Wyoming, Montana, Idaho	3,468 sq. mi.
Largest national monument	Wrangell-St. Elias, Alaska	18,630 sq. mi.
Highest waterfall	Yosemite Falls—Total in three sections	2,425 ft.
	Upper Yosemite Fall	1,430 ft.
	Cascades in middle section	675 ft.
	Lower Yosemite Fall	320 ft.
Longest river	Mississippi-Missouri	3,710 mi.
Highest mountain	Mount McKinley, Alaska	20,320 ft.
Lowest point	Death Valley, California	−282 ft.
Deepest lake	Crater Lake, Oregon	1,932 ft.
Rainiest spot	Mt. Waialeale, Hawaii	Annual aver. rainfall 460 inches
Largest gorge	Grand Canyon, Colorado River, Arizona	277 miles long, 1 to 20 miles wide, 1 mile deep
Deepest gorge	Hell's Canyon, Snake River, Idaho	7,900 ft.
Strongest surface wind	Mount Washington, New Hampshire recorded 1934	231 mph
Biggest dam	New Cornelia Tailings, Ten Mile Wash, Arizona	274,026,000 cu. yds. material used
Tallest building	Sears Tower, Chicago, Illinois	1,454 ft.
Largest building	Boeing 747 Manufacturing Plant, Everett, Washington	205,600,000 cu. ft.; covers 47 acres.
Tallest structure	TV tower, Blanchard, North Dakota	2,063 ft.
Longest bridge span	Verrazano-Narrows, New York	4,260 ft.
Highest bridge	Royal Gorge, Colorado	1,053 ft. above water
Deepest well	Gas well, Washita County, Oklahoma	31,441 ft.

The 49 States, Including Alaska

Area for 49 states	Total	3,612,017 sq. mi.
	Land 3,533,598 sq. mi.—Water 78,419 sq. mi.	

The 48 Contiguous States

Area for 48 states	Total	3,022,260 sq. mi.
	Land 2,963,998 sq. mi.—Water 58,262 sq. mi.	
Largest state	Texas	267,338 sq. mi
Northernmost town	Angle Inlet, Minnesota	49°22′N.
Northernmost point	Northwest Angle, Minnesota	49°23′N.
Southernmost city	Key West, Florida	24°33′N.
Southernmost mainland city	Florida City, Florida	25°27′N.
Southernmost point	Key West, Florida	24°33′N.
Westernmost town	La Push, Washington	124°38′W.
Westernmost point	Cape Alava, Washington	124°44′W.
Highest mountain	Mount Whitney, California	14,494 ft.

Note to users: The distinction between cities and towns varies from state to state. In this table the U.S. Bureau of the Census usage was followed.

Geodetic Datum Point of North America

The geodetic datum point of the U.S. is the National Ocean Survey's triangulation station Meades Ranch in Osborne County, Kansas, at latitude 39° 13′26″. 686 N and longitude 98° 32′30″. 506 W. This geodetic datum point is a fundamental point from which all latitude and longitude computations originate for North America and Central America.

Statistical Information about the U.S.

In the *Statistical Abstract of the United States* the Bureau of the Census, U.S. Dept. of Commerce, annually publishes a summary of social, political, and economic information. A book of more than 1,000 pages, it presents in 34 sections comprehensive data on population, housing, health, education, employment, income, prices, business, banking, energy, science, defense, trade, government finance, foreign country comparison, and other subjects. Special features include an appendix on statistical methodology and reliability and a summary of recent trends. The book is prepared under the direction of William Lerner, Data User Services Division, Bureau of the Census. Supplements to the *Statistical Abstract* are *Pocket Data Book USA, 1976* (1979 edition in preparation); *County and City Data Book, 1977; Congressional District Data Book, 93rd Congress with supplements for the 3 states that redistricted for the 94th Congress; Historical Statistics of the United States, Colonial Times to 1970;* and *State and Metropolitan Area Data Book, 1979* (in preparation). Information concerning these and other publications may be obtained from the Supt. of Documents, Government Printing Office, Wash., D.C. 20402, or from the U.S. Bureau of the Census, Data User Services Division, Wash., D.C. 20233.

Highest and Lowest Altitudes in the U.S. and Territories

Source: Geological Survey, U.S. Interior Department. (Minus sign means below sea level; elevations are in feet.)

	Highest Point			Lowest Point		
State	Name	County	Elev.	Name	County	Elev.
Alabama	Cheaha Mountain	Cleburne	2,407	Gulf of Mexico		Sea level
Alaska	Mount McKinley		20,320	Pacific Ocean		Sea level
Arizona	Humphreys Peak	Coconino	12,633	Colorado R.	Yuma	70
Arkansas	Magazine Mountain	Logan	2,753	Ouachita R.	Ashley Union	55
California	Mount Whitney	Inyo-Tulare	14,494	Death Valley	Inyo	−282
Colorado	Mount Elbert	Lake	14,433	Arkansas R.	Prowers	3,350
Connecticut	Mount Frissell	Litchfield	2,380	L.I. Sound		Sea level
Delaware	On Ebright Road	New Castle	442	Atlantic Ocean		Sea level
Dist. of Col.	Tenleytown	N. W. part	410	Potomac R.		1
Florida	SE of Paxton	Walton	345	Atlantic Ocean		Sea level
Georgia	Brasstown Bald	Towns-Union	4,784	Atlantic Ocean		Sea level
Guam	Mount Lamlam	Agat District	1,329	Pacific Ocean		Sea level
Hawaii	Mauna Kea	Hawaii	13,796	Pacific Ocean		Sea level
Idaho	Borah Peak	Custer	12,662	Snake R.	Nez Perce	710
Illinois	Charles Mound	Jo Daviess	1,235	Mississippi R.	Alexander	279
Indiana	Franklin Township	Wayne	1,257	Ohio R.	Posey	320
Iowa	NE of Sibley	Osceola	1,670	Mississippi R.	Lee	480
Kansas	Mount Sunflower	Wallaae	4,039	Verdigris R.	Montgomery	680
Kentucky	Black Mountain	Harlan	4,145	Mississippi R.	Fulton	257
Louisiana	Driskill Mountain	Bienville	535	New Orleans	Orleans	−5
Maine	Mount Katahdin	Piscataquis	5,268	Atlantic Ocean		Sea level
Maryland	Backbone Mountain	Garrett	3,360	Atlantic Ocean		Sea level
Massachusetts	Mount Greylock	Berkshire	3,491	Atlantic Ocean		Sea level
Michigan	Mount Curwood	Baraga	1,980	Lake Erie		572
Minnesota	Eagle Mountain	Cook	2,301	Lake Superior		602
Mississippi	Woodall Mountain	Tishomingo	806	Gulf of Mexico		Sea level
Missouri	Taum Sauk Mt.	Iron	1,772	St. Francis R.	Dunklin	230
Montana	Granite Peak	Park	12,799	Kootenai R.	Lincoln	1,800
Nebraska	Johnson Township	Kimball	5,426	S.E. cor. State	Richardson	840
Nevada	Boundary Peak	Esmeralda	13,143	Colorado R.	Clark	470
New Hamp.	Mt. Washington	Coos	6,288	Atlantic Ocean		Sea level
New Jersey	High Point	Sussex	1,803	Atlantic Ocean		Sea level
New Mexico	Wheeler Peak	Taos	13,161	Red Bluff Res.	Eddy	2,817
New York	Mount Marcy	Essex	5,344	Atlantia Ocean		Sea level
North Carolina	Mount Mitchell	Yancey	6,684	Atlantic Ocean		Sea level
North Dakota	White Butte	Slope	3,506	Red R.	Pembina	750
Ohio	Campbell Hill	Logan	1,550	Ohio R.	Hamilton	433
Oklahoma	Black Mesa	Cimarron	4,973	Little R.	McCurtain	287
Oregon	Mount Hood	Clackamas-Hood R.	11,239	Pacific Ocean		Sea level
Pennsylvania	Mt. Davis	Somerset	3,213	Delaware R.	Delaware	Sea level
Puerto Rico	Cerro de Punta	Ponce	4,389	Atlantic Ocean		Sea level
Rhode Island	Jerimoth Hill	Providence	812	Atlantic Ocean		Sea level
Samoa	Lata Mountain	Tau Island	3,160	Pacific Ocean		Sea level
South Carolina	Sassafras Mountain	Pickens	3,560	Atlantic Ocean		Sea level
South Dakota	Harney Peak	Pennington	7,242	Big Stone Lake	Roberts	962
Tennessee	Clingmans Dome	Sevier	6,643	Mississippi R.	Shelby	182
Texas	Guadalupe Peak	Culberson	8,749	Gulf of Mexico		Sea level
Utah	Kings Peak	Duchesne	13,528	Beaverdam Cr.	Washington	2,000
Vermont	Mount Mansfield	Lamoille	4,393	Lake Champlain	Franklin	95
Virginia	Mount Rogers	Grayson-Smyth	5,729	Atlantic Ocean		Sea level
Virgin Islands	Crown Mountain	Is. St. Thomas	1,556	Atlantic Ocean		Sea level
Washington	Mount Rainier	Pierce	14,410	Pacific Ocean		Sea level
West Virginia	Spruce Knob	Pendleton	4,863	Potomac R.	Jefferson	240
Wisconsin	Timms Hill	Price	1,952	Lake Michigan		581
Wyoming	Gannett Peak	Fremont	13,804	B. Fourche R.	Crook	3,100

U.S. Coastline by States

Source: NOAA, U.S. Commerce Department
(statute miles)

State	Coastline[1]	Shoreline[2]	State	Coastline[1]	Shoreline[2]
Atlantic coast	**2,069**	**28,673**	Virginia	112	3,315
Connecticut	0	618	**Gulf coast**	**1,631**	**17,141**
Delaware	28	381	Alabama	53	607
Florida	580	3,331	Florida	770	5,095
Georgia	100	2,344	Louisiana	397	7,721
Maine	228	3,478	Mississippi	44	359
Maryland	31	3,190	Texas	367	3,359
Massachusetts	192	1,519	**Pacific coast**	**7,623**	**40,298**
New Hampshire	13	131	Alaska	5,580	31,383
New Jersey	130	1,792	California	840	3,427
New York	127	1,850	Hawaii	750	1,052
North Carolina	301	3,375	Oregon	296	1,410
Pennsylvania	0	89	Washington	157	3,026
Rhode Island	40	384	**Arctic coast, Alaska**	**1,060**	**2,521**
South Carolina	187	2,876	**United States**	**12,383**	**88,633**

(1) Figures are lengths of general outline of seacoast. Measurements were made with a unit measure of 30 minutes of latitude on charts as near the scale of 1:1,200,000 as possible. Coastline of sounds and bays is included to a point where they narrow to width of unit measure, and includes the distance across at such point. (2) Figures obtained in 1939-40 with a recording instrument on the largest-scale charts and maps then available. Shoreline of outer coast, offshore islands, sounds, bays, rivers, and creeks is included to the head of tidewater or to a point where tidal waters narrow to a width of 100 feet.

States: Settled, Capitals, Entry into Union, Area, Rank

The original 13 states—The 13 colonies that seceded from Great Britain and fought the War of Independence (American Revolution) became the 13 original states. They were: Delaware, Pennsylvania, New Jersey, Georgia, Connecticut, Massachusetts, Maryland, South Carolina, New Hampshire, Virginia, New York, North Carolina, and Rhode Island. The order for the original 13 states is the order in which they ratified the Constitution.

State	Settled*	Capital	Entered Union		Extent in miles (approx. mean)		Area in square miles			Rank in area
			Date	Order	Long	Wide	Land	Inland water	Total	
Ala.	1702	Montgomery	Dec. 14, 1819	22	330	190	50,708	901	51,609	29
Alas.	1784	Juneau	Jan. 3, 1959	49	(a)1,480	810	569,600	20,157	589,757	1
Ariz.	1776	Phoenix	Feb. 14, 1912	48	400	310	113,417	492	113,909	6
Ark.	1686	Little Rock	June 15, 1836	25	260	240	51,945	1,159	53,104	27
Cal.	1769	Sacramento	Sept. 9, 1850	31	770	250	156,361	2,332	158,693	3
Col.	1858	Denver	Aug. 1, 1876	38	380	280	103,766	481	104,247	8
Conn.	1634	Hartford	Jan. 9, 1788	5	110	70	4,862	147	5,009	48
Del.	1638	Dover	Dec. 7, 1787	1	100	30	1,982	75	2,057	49
D.C.		Washington			...	...	61	6	67	51
Fla.	1565	Tallahassee	Mar. 3, 1845	27	500	160	54,090	4,470	58,560	22
Ga.	1733	Atlanta	Jan. 2, 1788	4	300	230	58,073	803	58,876	21
Ha.	1820	Honolulu	Aug. 21, 1959	50	...	...	6,425	25	6,450	47
Ida.	1842	Boise	July 3, 1890	43	570	300	82,677	880	83,557	13
Ill.	1720	Springfield	Dec. 3, 1818	21	390	210	55,748	652	56,400	24
Ind.	1733	Indianapolis	Dec. 11, 1816	19	270	140	36,097	194	36,291	38
Ia.	1788	Des Moines	Dec. 28, 1846	29	310	200	55,941	349	56,290	25
Kan.	1727	Topeka	Jan. 29, 1861	34	400	210	81,787	477	82,264	14
Ky.	1774	Frankfort	June 1, 1792	15	380	140	39,650	745	40,395	37
La.	1699	Baton Rouge	Apr. 30, 1812	18	380	130	44,930	3,593	48,523	31
Me.	1624	Augusta	Mar. 15, 1820	23	320	190	30,920	2,295	33,215	39
Md.	1634	Annapolis	Apr. 28, 1788	7	250	90	9,891	686	10,577	42
Mass.	1620	Boston	Feb. 6, 1788	6	190	50	7,826	431	8,257	45
Mich.	1668	Lansing	Jan. 26, 1837	26	490	240	56,817	1,399	58,216	23
Minn.	1805	St. Paul	May 11, 1858	32	400	250	79,289	4,779	84,068	12
Miss.	1699	Jackson	Dec. 10, 1817	20	340	170	47,296	420	47,716	32
Mo.	1735	Jefferson City	Aug. 10, 1821	24	300	240	68,995	691	69,686	19
Mon.	1809	Helena	Nov. 8, 1889	41	630	280	145,587	1,551	147,138	4
Neb.	1823	Lincoln	Mar. 1, 1867	37	430	210	76,483	744	77,227	15
Nev.	1849	Carson City	Oct. 31, 1864	36	490	320	109,889	651	110,540	7
N.H.	1623	Concord	June 21, 1788	9	190	70	9,027	277	9,304	44
N.J.	1664	Trenton	Dec. 18, 1787	3	150	70	7,521	315	7,836	46
N.M.	1610	Santa Fe	Jan. 6, 1912	47	370	343	121,412	254	121,666	5
N.Y.	1614	Albany	July 26, 1788	11	330	283	47,831	1,745	49,576	30
N.C.	1660	Raleigh	Nov. 21, 1789	12	500	150	48,798	3,788	52,586	28
N.D.	1812	Bismarck	Nov. 2, 1889	39	340	211	69,273	1,392	70,665	17
Oh.	1788	Columbus	Mar. 1, 1803	17	220	220	40,975	247	41,222	35
Okla.	1889	Oklahoma City	Nov. 16, 1907	46	400	220	68,782	1,137	69,919	18
Ore.	1811	Salem	Feb. 14, 1859	33	360	261	96,184	797	96,981	10
Pa.	1682	Harrisburg	Dec. 12, 1787	2	283	160	44,966	367	45,333	33
R.I.	1636	Providence	May 29, 1790	13	40	30	1,049	165	1,214	50
S.C.	1670	Columbia	May 23, 1788	8	260	200	30,225	830	31,055	40
S.D.	1859	Pierre	Nov. 2, 1889	40	380	210	75,955	1,092	77,047	16
Tenn.	1769	Nashville	June 1, 1796	16	440	120	41,328	916	42,244	34
Tex.	1692	Austin	Dec. 29, 1845	28	790	660	262,134	5,204	267,338	2
Ut.	1847	Salt Lake City	Jan. 4, 1896	45	350	270	82,096	2,820	84,916	11
Vt.	1724	Montpelier	Mar. 4, 1791	14	160	80	9,267	342	9,609	43
Va.	1607	Richmond	June 25, 1788	10	430	200	39,780	1,037	40,817	36
Wash.	1811	Olympia	Nov. 11, 1889	42	360	240	66,570	1,622	68,192	20
W.Va.	1727	Charleston	June 20, 1863	35	240	130	24,070	111	24,181	41
Wis.	1766	Madison	May 29, 1848	30	310	260	54,464	1,690	56,154	26
Wy.	1834	Cheyenne	July 10, 1890	44	360	280	97,203	711	97,914	9

*First European permanent settlement. (a) Aleutian Islands and Alexander Archipelago are not considered in these lengths.

The Continental Divide

Source: Geological Survey, U.S. Interior Department

The Continental Divide: watershed, created by mountain ranges or table-lands of the Rocky Mountains, from which the drainage is easterly or westerly; the easterly flowing waters reaching the Atlantic Ocean chiefly through the Gulf of Mexico, and the westerly flowing waters reaching the Pacific Ocean through the Columbia River, or through the Colorado River, which flows into the Gulf of California.

The location and route of the Continental Divide across the United States may briefly be described as follows:

Beginning at point of crossing the United States-Mexican boundary, near long. 108°45'W., the Divide, in a northerly direction, crosses New Mexico along the western edge of the Rio Grande drainage basin, entering Colorado near long. 106°41'W.

Thence by a very irregular route northerly across Colorado along the western summits of the Rio Grande and of the Arkansas, the South Platte, and the North Platte River basins, and across Rocky Mountain National Park, entering Wyoming near long. 106°52'W.

Thence in a northwesterly direction, forming the western rims of the North Platte, Big Horn, and Yellowstone River basins, crossing the southwestern portion of Yellowstone National Park.

Thence in a westerly and then a northerly direction forming the common boundary of Idaho and Montana, to a point on said boundary near long. 114°00'W.

Thence northeasterly and northwesterly through Montana and the Glacier National Park, entering Canada near long. 114°04'W.

Chronological List of Territories

Source: National Archives and Records Service

Name of territory	Date of Organic Act	Organic Act effective	Admission as state	Yrs. terr.
Northwest Territory(a)	July 13, 1787	No fixed date	Mar. 1, 1803(b)	16
Territory southwest of River Ohio	May 26, 1790	No fixed date	June 1, 1796(c)	6
Mississippi	Apr. 7, 1798	When president acted	Dec. 10, 1817	19
Indiana	May 7, 1800	July 4, 1800	Dec. 11, 1816	16
Orleans	Mar. 26, 1804	Oct. 1, 1804	Apr. 30, 1812(d)	7
Michigan	Jan. 11, 1805	June 30, 1805	Jan. 26, 1837	31
Louisiana-Missouri(e)	Mar. 3, 1805	July 4, 1805	Aug. 10, 1821	16
Illinois	Feb. 3, 1809	Mar. 1, 1809	Dec. 3, 1818	9
Alabama	Mar. 3, 1817	When Miss. became a state	Dec. 14, 1819	2
Arkansas	Mar. 2, 1819	July 4, 1819	June 15, 1836	17
Florida	Mar. 30, 1822	No fixed date	Mar. 3, 1845	23
Wisconsin	Apr. 20, 1836	July 3, 1836	May 29, 1848	12
Iowa	June 12, 1838	July 3, 1838	Dec. 28, 1846	7
Oregon	Aug. 14, 1848	Date of act	Feb. 14, 1859	10
Minnesota	Mar. 3, 1849	Date of act	May 11, 1858	9
New Mexico	Sept. 9, 1850	On president's proclamation	Jan. 6, 1912	61
Utah	Sept. 9, 1850	Date of act	Jan. 4, 1896	44
Washington	Mar. 2, 1853	Date of act	Nov. 11, 1889	36
Nebraska	May 30, 1854	Date of act	Mar. 1, 1867	12
Kansas	May 30, 1854	Date of act	Jan. 29, 1861	6
Colorado	Feb. 28, 1861	Date of act	Aug. 1, 1876	15
Nevada	Mar. 2, 1861	Date of act	Oct. 31, 1864	3
Dakota	Mar. 2, 1861	Date of act	Nov. 2, 1889	28
Arizona	Feb. 24, 1863	Date of act	Feb. 14, 1912	49
Idaho	Mar. 3, 1863	Date of act	July 3, 1890	27
Montana	May 26, 1864	Date of act	Nov. 8, 1889	25
Wyoming	July 25, 1868	When officers were qualified	July 10, 1890	22
Alaska	May 17, 1884	No fixed date	Jan. 3, 1959	75
Oklahoma	May 2, 1890	Date of act	Nov. 16, 1907	17
Hawaii	Apr. 30, 1900	June 14, 1900	Aug. 21, 1959	59

(a) Included Ohio, Indiana, Illinois, Michigan, Wisconsin, eastern Minnesota; (b) as the state of Ohio; (c) as the state of Tennessee; (d) as the state of Louisiana; (e) organic act for Missouri Territory of June 4, 1812, became effective Dec. 7, 1812.

Geographic Centers, U.S. and Each State

Source: Geological Survey, U.S. Interior Department

United States, including Alaska and Hawaii — South Dakota; Butte County, 17 miles W of Castle Rock, 14 miles E of junction of borders of South Dakota, Montana, and Wyoming. Approx. lat. 44°58'N. long. 103°46'W.

Contiguous U. S. (48 states) — Near Lebanon, Smith Co., Kansas, lat. 39°50'N. long. 98°35'W.

North American continent — The geographic center is in Pierce County, North Dakota, 6 miles W of Balta, latitude 48°10', longitude 100°10'W.

State—county, locality

Alabama—Chilton, 12 miles SW of Clanton.
Alaska—lat. 63°50'N. long. 152°W. Approx. 60 mi. NW of Mt. McKinley.
Arizona—Yavapai, 55 miles ESE of Prescott.
Arkansas—Pulaski, 12 miles NW of Little Rock.
California—Madera, 38 miles E of Madera.
Colorado—Park, 30 miles NW of Pikes Peak.
Connecticut—Hartford, at East Berlin.
Delaware—Kent, 11 miles S of Dover.
District of Columbia—Near Fourth and "L" Streets, NW.
Florida—Hernando, 12 miles NNW of Brooksville.
Georgia—Twiggs, 18 miles SE of Macon.
Hawaii—Hawaii, 20°15'N, 156°20'W, off Maui Island.
Idaho—Custer, at Custer, SW of Challis.
Illinois—Logan, 28 miles NE of Springfield.
Indiana—Boone, 14 miles NNW of Indianapolis.
Iowa—Story, 5 miles NE of Ames.
Kansas—Barton, 15 miles NE of Great Bend.
Kentucky—Marion, 3 miles NNW of Lebanon.
Louisiana—Avoyelles, 3 miles SE of Marksville.
Maine—Piscataquis, 18 miles north of Dover.
Maryland—Prince Georges, 4.5 miles NW of Davidsonville.
Massachusetts—Worcester, north part of city.
Michigan—Wexford, 5 miles NNW of Cadillac.
Minnesota—Crow Wing, 10 miles SW of Brainerd.
Mississippi—Leake, 9 miles WNW of Carthage.
Missouri—Miller, 20 miles SW of Jefferson City.
Montana—Fergus, 12 miles west of Lewistown.
Nebraska—Custer, 10 miles NW of Broken Bow.
Nevada—Lander, 26 miles SE of Austin.
New Hampshire—Belknap, 3 miles E of Ashland.
New Jersey—Mercer, 5 miles SE of Trenton.
New Mexico—Torrance, 12 miles SSW of Willard.
New York—Madison, 12 miles S of Oneida and 26 miles SW of Utica.
North Carolina—Chatham, 10 miles NW of Sanford.
North Dakota—Sheridan, 5 miles SW of McClusky.
Ohio—Delaware, 25 miles NNE of Columbus.
Oklahoma—Oklahoma, 8 miles N of Oklahoma City.
Oregon—Crook, 25 miles SSE of Prineville.
Pennsylvania—Centre, 2.5 miles SW of Bellefonte.
Rhode Island—Kent, 1 mile SSW of Crompton.
South Carolina—Richland, 13 miles SE of Columbia.
South Dakota—Hughes, 8 miles NE of Pierre.
Tennessee—Rutherford, 5 mi. NE of Murfreesboro.
Texas—McCulloch, 15 miles NE of Brady.
Utah—Sanpete, 3 miles N of Manti.
Vermont—Washington, 3 miles E of Roxbury.
Virginia—Buckingham, 5 miles SW of Buckingham.
Washington—Chelan, 10 mi. WSW of Wenatchee.
West Virginia—Braxton, 4 miles E of Sutton.
Wisconsin—Wood, 9 miles SE of Marshfield.
Wyoming—Fremont, 58 miles ENE of Lander.

There is no generally accepted definition of geographic center, and no satisfactory method for determining it. The geographic center of an area may be defined as the center of gravity of the surface, or that point on which the surface of the area would balance if it were a plane of uniform thickness.

No marked or monumented point has been established by any government agency as the geographic center of either the 50 states, the contiguous United States, or the North American continent. A monument was erected in Lebanon, Kan., contiguous U.S. center, by a group of citizens.

International Boundary Lines of the U.S.

The length of the northern boundary of the contiguous U.S. — the U.S.-Canadian border, excluding Alaska — is 3,987 miles according to the U.S. Geological Survey, Dept. of the Interior. The length of the Alaskan-Canadian border is 1,538 miles. The length of the U.S.-Mexican border, from the Gulf of Mexico to the Pacific Ocean, is approximately 1,933 miles (1963 boundary agreement).

Origin of the Names of U.S. States

Source: State officials, the Smithsonian Institution, and the Topographic Division, U.S. Geological Survey.

Alabama—Indian for tribal town, later a tribe (Alabamas or Alibamons) of the Creek confederacy.

Alaska—Russian version of Aleutian (Eskimo) word, alakshak, for "peninsula" or "great lands."

Arizona—Spanish version of Pima Indian word for "little spring place," or Aztec arizuma, meaning "silver-bearing."

Arkansas—French variant of Kansas, a Sioux Indian name for "south wind people."

California—Bestowed by the Spanish conquistadors (possibly by Cortez). It was the name of an imaginary island, an earthly paradise, in "Las Serges de Esplandian," a Spanish romance written by Montalvo in 1510. Baja California (Lower California, in Mexico) was first visited by Spanish in 1533. The present U.S. state was called Alta (Upper) California.

Colorado—Spanish, red, first applied to Colorado River.

Connecticut—From Mohican and other Algonquin words meaning "long river place."

Delaware—Named for Lord De La Warr, early governor of Virginia; first applied to river, then to Indian tribe (Lenni-Lenape), and the state.

District of Columbia—For Columbus, 1791.

Florida—Named by Ponce de Leon on Pascua Florida, "Flowery Easter," on Easter Sunday, 1513.

Georgia—For King George II of England by James Oglethorpe, colonial administrator, 1732.

Hawaii—Possibly derived from native world for homeland, Hawaiki or Owhyhee.

Idaho—A coined name with an invented Indian meaning: "gem of the mountains;" originally suggested for the Pike's Peak mining territory (Colorado), then applied to the new mining territory of the Pacific Northwest.

Illinois—French for Illini or land of Illini, Algonquin word meaning men or warriors.

Indiana—Means "land of the Indians."

Iowa—Indian word variously translated as "one who puts to sleep" or "beautiful land."

Kansas—Sioux word for "south wind people."

Kentucky—Indian word variously translated as "dark and bloody ground," "meadow land" and "land of tomorrow."

Louisiana—Part of territory called Louisiana by Sieur de La Salle for French King Louis XIV.

Maine—From Maine, ancient French province.

Maryland—For Queen Henrietta Maria, wife of Charles I of England.

Massachusetts—From Indian tribe named after "large hill place" identified by Capt. John Smith as near Milton, Mass.

Michigan—From Chippewa words mici gama meaning "great water," after the lake of the same name.

Minnesota—From Dakota Sioux word meaning "cloudy water" or "sky-tinted water" of the Minnesota River.

Mississippi—Probably Chippewa; mici zibi, "great river" or "gathering-in of all the waters."

Missouri—Indian tribe named after Missouri River, meaning "muddy water."

Montana—Latin or Spanish for "mountainous."

Nebraska—From Omaha or Otos Indian word meaning "broad water" or "flat river," describing the Platte River.

Nevada—Spanish, meaning snow-clad.

New Hampshire—Named 1629 by Capt. John Mason of Plymouth Council for county in England.

New Jersey—The Duke of York, 1664, gave a patent to John Berkeley and Sir George Carteret to be called Nova Caesaria, or New Jersey, after England's Isle of Jersey.

New Mexico—Spaniards in Mexico applied term to land north and west of Rio Grande in the 16th century.

New York—For Duke of York and Albany who received patent to New Netherland from his brother Charles II and sent an expedition to capture it, 1664.

North Carolina—In 1619 Charles I gave a large patent to Sir Robert Heath to be called Province of Carolana, from Carolus, Latin name for Charles. A new patent was granted by Charles II to Earl of Clarendon and others. Divided into North and South Carolina, 1710.

North Dakota—Dakota is Sioux for friend or ally.

Ohio—Iroquois word for "fine or good river."

Oklahoma—Choctaw coined word meaning red man, proposed by Rev. Allen Wright, Choctaw-speaking Indian.

Oregon—Origin unknown.

Pennsylvania—William Penn, the Quaker, who was made full proprietor by King Charles II in 1681, suggested Sylvania, or woodland, for his tract. The king's government owed Penn's father, Admiral William Penn, £16,000, and the land being granted in part settlement, the king added the Penn to Sylvania, against the desires of the modest proprietor, in honor of the admiral.

Puerto Rico—Spanish for Rich Port.

Rhode Island—Named Roode Eylandt by Adriaen Block, Dutch explorer, because of its red clay. Name of Roger Williams' settlement was added to give the small state its long, official title: State of Rhode Island and Providence Plantations.

South Carolina—See North Carolina.

South Dakota—See North Dakota.

Tennessee—Tanasi was the name of Cherokee villages on the Little Tennessee River. From 1784 to 1788 this was the State of Franklin, or Frankland.

Texas—Variant of word used by Caddo and other Indians meaning friends or allies, and applied to them by the Spanish in eastern Texas. Also written texias, tejas, teysas.

Utah—From a Navajo word meaning upper, or higher up, as applied to a Shoshone tribe called Ute. Spanish form is Yutta, English Uta or Utah. Proposed name Deseret, "land of honeybees," from Book of Mormon, was rejected by Congress.

Vermont—From French words vert, green, and mont, mountain. The Green Mountains were said to have been named by Samuel de Champlain. The Green Mountain Boys were Gen. Stark's men in the Revolution. When the state was formed, 1777, Dr. Thomas Young suggested combining vert and mont into Vermont.

Virginia—Named by Sir Walter Raleigh, who fitted out the expedition of 1584, in honor of Queen Elizabeth, the Virgin Queen of England.

Washington—Named after George Washington. When the bill creating the Territory of Columbia was introduced in the 32d Congress, the name was changed to Washington because of the existence of the District of Columbia.

West Virginia—So named when western counties of Virginia refused to secede from the United States, 1863.

Wisconsin—An Indian name, spelled Ouisconsin and Misconsing by early chroniclers. Believed to mean "grassy place" in Chippewa. Congress made it Wisconsin.

Wyoming—The word was taken from Wyoming Valley, Pa., which was the site of an Indian massacre and became widely known by Campbell's poem, "Gertrude of Wyoming." In Algonquin it means "large prairie place."

Accession of Territory by the U.S.

Source: Statistical Abstract of the United States

Division	Year	Sq. mi.[1]	Division	Year	Sq. mi.[1]	Division	Year	Sq. mi.[1]
Total U.S.	**1970**	**3,630,857**	Oregon	**1846**	285,580	American Samoa	**1900**	76
50 states & D.C.		3,618,467	Mexican Cession	**1848**	529,017	Corn Islands[4]	**1914**	4
Territory in 1790[2]		888,685	Gadsden Purchase	**1853**	29,640	Virgin Islands, U.S.	**1917**	133
Louisiana Purchase	**1803**	827,192	Alaska	**1867**	589,757	Trust Territory of the Pacific Is.	**1947**	8,489
By treaty with Spain:			Hawaii	**1898**	6,450	All other[5]		42
Florida	**1819**	58,560	The Philippines[3]	**1898**	115,600			
Other areas	**1819**	13,443	Puerto Rico	**1899**	3,435			
Texas	**1845**	390,143	Guam	**1899**	212			

(1) Gross area (land and water). (2) Includes drainage basin of Red River on the north, south of 49th parallel, sometimes considered a part of the Louisiana Purchase. (3) Area not included in total; became Republic of the Philippines July 4, 1946. (4) Leased from Nicaragua for 99 years but returned Apr. 25, 1971; area not included in total. (5) See index for Outlying Areas, U.S.

Public Lands of the U. S.

Source: Bureau of Land Management, U.S. Interior Department

Acquisition of the Public Domain 1781-1867

Acquisition	Area* (acres) Land	Water	Total	Cost[1]
State Cessions (1781-1802)	233,415,680	3,409,920	236,825,600	[2]$6,200,000
Louisiana Purchase (1803)[3]	523,446,400	6,465,280	529,911,680	23,213,568
Red River Basin[4]	29,066,880	535,040	29,601,920	
Cession from Spain (1819)	43,342,720	2,801,920	46,144,640	6,674,057
Oregon Compromise (1846)	180,644,480	2,741,760	183,386,240	
Mexican Cession (1848)	334,479,360	4,201,600	338,680,960	16,295,149
Purchase from Texas (1850)	78,842,880	83,840	78,926,720	15,496,448
Gadsden Purchase (1853)	18,961,920	26,880	18,988,800	10,000,000
Alaska Purchase (1867)	362,516,480	12,787,200	375,303,680	7,200,000
Total	**1,804,716,800**	**33,053,440**	**1,837,770,240**	**$85,079,222**

*All areas except Alaska were computed in 1912, and have not been adjusted for the recomputation of the area of the United States which was made for the 1950 Decennial Census. (1) Cost data for all except "State Cessions" obtained from U.S. Geological Survey. (2) Paid by federal government for Georgia cession, 1802 (56,689,920 acres). (3) Excludes areas eliminated by Treaty of 1819 with Spain. (4) Basin of the Red River of the North, south of the 49th parallel.

Disposition of Public Lands 1781 to 1970

Disposition by methods not elsewhere classified[1]	Acres
Disposition by methods not elsewhere classified[1]	303,500,000
Granted or sold to homesteaders	287,500,000
Granted to railroad corporations	94,300,000
Granted to veterans as military bounties	61,100,000
Confirmed as private land claims[2]	34,000,000
Sold under timber and stone law[3]	13,900,000
Granted or sold under timber culture law[4]	10,900,000
Sold under desert land law[5]	10,700,000

Granted to states for:	Acres
Support of common schools	77,600,000
Reclamation of swampland	64,900,000
Construction of railroads	37,100,000
Support of misc. institutions[6]	21,700,000
Purposes not elsewhere classified[7]	117,500,000
Canals and rivers	6,100,000
Construction of wagon roads	3,400,000
Total granted to states	**328,300,000**
Grand Total	**1,144,200,000**

(1) Chiefly public, private, and preemption sales, but includes mineral entries, script locations, sales of townsites and townlots. (2) The Government has confirmed title to lands claimed under valid grants made by foreign governments prior to the acquisition of the public domain by the United States. (3) The law provided for the sale of lands valuable for timber or stone and unfit for cultivation. (4) The law provided for the granting of public lands to settlers on condition that they plant and cultivate trees on the lands granted. (5) The law provided for the sale of arid agricultural public lands to settlers who irrigate them and bring them under cultivation. (6) Universities, hospitals, asylums, etc. (7) For construction of various public improvements (individual items not specified in the granting act) reclamation of desert lands, construction of water reservoirs, etc.

Public Lands Administered by Federal Agencies

Agency (Acres, Sept. 30, 1978)	Public domain	Acquired	Total
Bureau of Land Management	478,082,433	2,368,000	480,450,433
Forest Service	160,299,670	28,608,064	188,907,734
Fish and Wildlife Service	26,893,001	4,256,719	31,149,720
National Park Service	20,177,356	6,353,878	26,531,234
U.S. Army	6,545,265	3,927,852	10,473,117
U.S. Air Force	6,923,865	1,361,075	8,284,940
Corps of Engineers	659,293	7,478,129	8,137,422
U.S. Navy	2,498,315	4,396,350	6,894,665
Water and Power Resources Services	4,741,482	1,940,843	6,682,325
Bureau of Indian Affairs	2,945,506	433,531	3,379,037
Energy Research and Development Admin.	1,438,510	668,377	2,106,887
Others	756,328	1,495,341	2,251,669
Total	**711,961,024**	**63,288,159**	**775,249,183**

The Homestead Act; Sale of Public Land

On October 21, 1976 Congress repealed the Homestead Act of 1862 for all states except Alaska. At the present time the exception for Alaska has little meaning since homesteading along with all disposal laws had been suspended from operation by the Alaska Native Claims Settlement Act. The suspension which was first imposed by Secretarial order in 1969, will remain in effect until all claims for Federal land by Alaska's native Eskimos, Indians and Aleuts have been satisfied. The Homestead Act is scheduled to expire in Alaska in 1986.

The Homestead Act was repealed because there was no longer any land in the public domain suitable for cultivation. The law had been in effect for 114 years. During that time it had exerted a profound influence on the settlement of the west. Under the authority of the Homestead Act more than 1.6 million settlers claimed more than 270 million acres of public lands. The influx of settlers into the west in pursuit of homestead land made such states as Oklahoma, Kansas, Nebraska, and North and South Dakota a reality and brought substantial numbers of settlers into many other western states.

Public Land Sale

From time to time the Bureau of Land Management sells public land to private individuals. Public land is always sold for its fair market value as determined by public auction. The Federal Govt. offers no free land. Persons wishing to purchase public land should contact the Bureau of Land Management, Wash., DC 20240, or one of the Bureau's Land Offices in the public land states.

The Bureau stresses that it is the only authoritative source of information on the sale of land under its jurisdiction.

National Recreation Areas Administered by Forest Service

Name	State	Year	Acreage
Arapaho	Col.	1978	36,235
Flaming Gorge	Ut.-Wyo.	1968	204,114
Hell's Canyon	Ida.-Ore.	1975	514,400
Mount Rogers	Va.	1966	154,000
Oregon Dunes	Ore.	1972	28,289
Sawtooth	Ida.	1972	754,999
Shasta-Trinity	Cal.	1965	153,200
Spruce Knob-Seneca Rocks	W. Va.	1965	100,000

National Parks, Other Areas Administered by Nat'l Park Service

Figures given are date area was set aside by Congress or proclaimed by president, and gross area in acres Dec. 31, 1979.

National Parks

Acadia, Me. (1916) 38,632. Includes Mount Desert Island, half of Isle au Haut, Schoodic Point on mainland. Highest elevation on Eastern seaboard.

Arches, Ut. (1929) 73,379. Contains giant red sandstone arches and other products of erosion.

Badlands, S.D. (1929) 243,302; eroded prairie, bison, bighorn and antelope. Renamed national park in 1978.

Big Bend, Tex. (1935) 708,118. Rio Grande, Chisos Mts.

Bryce Canyon, Ut. (1923) 35,835. Spectacularly colorful and unusual display of erosion effects.

Canyonlands, Ut. (1964) 337,570. At junction of Colorado and Green rivers, extensive evidence of prehistoric Indians.

Capitol Reef, Ut. (1937) 241,904. A 70-mile uplift of sandstone cliffs dissected by high-walled gorges.

Carlsbad Caverns, N.M. (1923) 46,755. Largest known underground caverns, not yet fully explored.

Channel Islands, Cal. (1938) 124,740. Park absorbed national monument in 1980 park act.

Crater Lake, Ore. (1902) 160,290. Extraordinary blue lake in crater of extinct volcano encircled by lava walls 500 to 2,000 feet high.

Everglades, Fla. (1934) 1,398,800. Largest remaining subtropical wilderness in Continental U.S.

Glacier, Mon. (1910) 1,013,595. Superb Rocky Mountain scenery, numerous glaciers and glacial lakes. Part of Waterton-Glacier International Peace Park established by U.S. and Canada in 1932.

Grand Canyon, Ariz. (1908) 1,218,375. Most spectacular part of Colorado River's greatest canyon.

Grand Teton, Wy. (1929) 310,516. Most impressive part of the Teton Mountains, winter feeding ground of largest American elk herd.

Great Smoky Mountains, N.C.-Tenn. (1926) 517,379. Largest eastern mountain range, magnificent forests.

Guadalupe Mountains, Tex. (1966) 76,293. Extensive Permian limestone fossil reef; tremendous earth fault.

Haleakala, Ha. (1960) 28,655. 10,023 foot dormant volcano on Maui.

Hawaii Volcanoes, Ha. (1916) 229,177. Contains Kilauea and Mauna Loa, active volcanoes.

Hot Springs, Ark. (1832) 5,826. Government supervised bath houses use waters of 45 of the 47 natural hot springs.

Isle Royale, Mich. (1931) 571,796. Largest island in Lake Superior, noted for its wilderness area and wildlife.

Kings Canyon, Cal. (1890) 460,136. Mountain wilderness, dominated by Kings River Canyons and High Sierra; contains giant sequoias.

Lassen Volcanic, Cal. (1907) 106,372. Contains Lassen Peak, recently active volcano, and other volcanic phenomena.

Mammoth Cave, Ky. (1926) 52,452. 144 miles of surveyed underground passages, beautiful natural formations, river 360 feet below surface.

Mesa Verde, Col. (1906) 52,085. Most notable and best preserved prehistoric cliff dwellings in the United States.

Mount McKinley, Alas. (1917) 1,939,493. Highest mountain in North America, large glaciers, and unusual wildlife.

Mount Rainier, Wash. (1899) 235,404. Greatest single-peak glacial system in the U.S. radiates from this dormant volcano.

North Cascades, Wash. (1968) 504,780. Spectacular mountainous region with many glaciers, lakes.

Olympic, Wash. (1909) 908,781. Mountain wilderness containing finest remnant of Pacific Northwest rain forest, active glaciers, Pacific shoreline, rare elk.

Petrified Forest, Ariz. (1906) 93,493. Extensive petrified wood and Indian artifacts. Contains part of Painted Desert.

Redwood, Cal. (1968) 109,027. Forty miles of Pacific coastline, groves of ancient redwoods.

Rocky Mountain, Col. (1915) 263,809. On the continental divide, includes 107 named peaks over 11,000 feet.

Sequoia, Cal. (1890) 403,023. Groves of giant sequoias, highest mountain in contiguous United States — Mount Whitney (14,494 feet).

Shenandoah, Va. (1926) 194,826. Portion of the Blue Ridge Mountains; overlooks Shenandoah Valley.

Theodore Roosevelt, N.D. (1947) 70,416; contains part of T.R.'s ranch and scenic badlands. National park in 1978.

Virgin Islands, V.I. (1956) 14,695. Covers 75% of St. John Island, lush growth, lovely beaches, Indian relics, evidence of colonial Danes.

Voyageurs, Minn. (1971) 219,128. Abundant lakes, forests, wildlife, canoeing, boating.

Wind Cave, S.D. (1903) 28,292. Limestone Caverns in Black Hills. Extensive wildlife includes a herd of bison.

Yellowstone, Ida., Mon., Wy., (1872) 2,219,823. Oldest and largest national park. World's greatest geyser area has about 3,000 geysers and hot springs; spectacular falls and impressive canyons of the Yellowstone River, grizzly bear, moose, bison, other wildlife are major attractions.

Yosemite, Cal. (1890) 760,917. Yosemite Valley, the nation's highest waterfall, 3 groves of sequoias, and mountainous.

Zion, Ut. (1909) 146,551. Unusual shapes and landscapes have resulted from erosion and faulting; Zion Canyon, with sheer walls ranging up to 2,500 feet, is readily accessible.

National Historical Parks

Appomattox Court House, Va. (1930) 1,319. Where Lee surrendered to Grant.

Boston, Mass. (1974) 40. Includes Faneuil Hall, Old North Church, Bunker Hill, Paul Revere House.

Chesapeake and Ohio Canal, Md.-W.Va.-D.C. (1961) 20,781. 185 mile historic canal; D.C. to Cumberland, Md.

Colonial, Va. (1930) 9,462. Includes most of Jamestown Island, site of first successful English colony; Yorktown, site of Cornwallis' surrender to George Washington; Cape Henry Memorial, approximate site of the first landing of the Jamestown colonists; and the Colonial Parkway.

Cumberland Gap, Ky.-Tenn.-Va. (1940) 20,351. Mountain pass of the Wilderness Road which carried the first great migration of pioneers into America's interior.

George Rogers Clark, Vincennes, Ind. (1966) 24. Commemorates American defeat of British in west during Revolution.

Harpers Ferry, Md., W. Va. (1944) 1,909. At the confluence of the Shenandoah and Potomac rivers, the site of John Brown's 1859 raid on the Army arsenal. Scene of several Civil War maneuvers.

Independence, Pa. (1948) 37. Contains several properties in Philadelphia associated with the Revolutionary War and the founding of the U.S.

Jean Laffite (and preserve), La. (1978) 20,000. Includes Chalmette, site of 1814 Battle of New Orleans; French Quarter.

Kaloko-Honokohau, Ha. (1978) 1,250. Culture center has 234 historic features and grave of first king, Kamehameha.

Klondike Gold Rush, Alas.-Wash. (1976) 13,270. Skagway, Alaskan Trails in 1898 Gold Rush. Museum in Seattle.

Lowell, Mass. (1978) 134. Seven mills, canal, 19th C. structures, park to show planned city of Industrial Revolution.

Minute Man, Mass. (1959) 752. Where the colonial Minute Men battled the British, April 19, 1775. Also contains Nathaniel Hawthorne's home.

Morristown, N.J. (1933) 1,677. Sites of important military encampments during the Revolutionary War; Washington's headquarters 1777, 1779-80.

Nez Perce, Ida. (1965) 2,109. Illustrates the history and culture of the Nez Perce Indian country. 22 separate sites.

Pu'uhonua o Honaunau, Ha. (1955) 182. Until 1819, a sanctuary for Hawaiians vanquished in battle, and those guilty of crimes or breaking taboos.

San Antonio Missions, Tex. (1978) 2,500. Four of finest Spanish missions in U.S., 18th C. irrigation system.

San Juan Island, Wash. (1966) 1,752. Commemorates peaceful relations of the U.S., Canada and Great Britain since the 1872 boundary disputes.

Saratoga, N.Y. (1938) 2,455. Scene of a major battle which became a turning point in the War of Independence.

Sitka, Alas. (1910) 108. Scene of last major resistance of the Tlingit Indians to the Russians, 1804.

Valley Forge, Pa. (1976) 2,551. Continental Army campsite in 1777-78 winter.

War in the Pacific, Guam (1978) 1,920. Scenic park memorial for WWII combatants in Pacific.

National Battlefields

Antietam, Md. (1890) 3,250. Battle ended first Confederate invasion of North, Sept. 17, 1862.

Big Hole, Mon. (1910) 656. Site of major battle with Nez Perce Indians.

Cowpens, S.C. (1929) 841. Revolutionary War battlefield.

Fort Necessity, Pa. (1931) 901. First battle of French and Indian War.

Monocacy, Md. (1976) 1,220. Civil War battle in defense of Wash., D.C., July 9, 1864.

Petersburg, Va. (1926) 1,536. Scene of 10-month Union campaign 1864-65.

Stones River, Tenn. (1927) 331. Civil War battle leading to Sherman's "March to the Sea."

Tupelo, Miss. (1929) 1. Crucial battle over Sherman's supply line.

Wilson's Creek, Mo. (1960) 1,750. Civil War battle for control of Missouri.

National Battlefield Parks

Kennesaw Mountain, Ga. (1917) 2,884. Two major battles of Atlanta campaign in Civil War.

Manassas, Va. (1940) 3,032. Two early Civil War battles.

Richmond, Va. (1936) 769. Site of battles defending Confederate capital.

National Battlefield Site

Brices Cross Roads, Miss. (1929) 1. Civil War battlefield.

National Military Parks

Chickamauga and Chattanooga, Ga.-Tenn. (1890) 8,098. Four Civil War battlefields.

Fort Donelson, Tenn. (1928) 536. Site of first major Union victory.

Fredericksburg and Spotsylvania County, Va. (1927) 5,889. Sites of several major Civil War battles and campaigns.

Gettysburg, Pa. (1895) 3,862. Site of decisive Confederate defeat in North. Gettysburg Address.

Guilford Courthouse, N.C. (1917) 220. Revolutionary War battle site.

Horseshoe Bend, Ala. (1956) 2,040. On Tallapoosa River, where Gen. Andrew Jackson broke the power of the Creek Indian Confederacy.

Kings Mountain, S.C. (1931) 3,945. Revolutionary War battle.

Moores Creek, N.C. (1926) 87. Pre-Revolutionary War battle.

Pea Ridge, Ark. (1956) 4,300. Civil War battle.

Shiloh, Tenn. (1894) 3,838. Major Civil War battle; site includes some well-preserved Indian burial mounds.

Vicksburg, Miss. (1899) 1,741. Union victory gave North control of the Mississippi and split the Confederacy in two.

National Memorials

Arkansas Post, Ark. (1960) 389. First permanent French settlement in the lower Mississippi River valley.

Chamizal, El Paso, Tex. (1966) 55. Commemorates 1963 settlement of 99-year border dispute with Mexico.

Coronado, Ariz. (1952) 4,977. Commemorates first European exploration of the Southwest.

DeSoto, Fla. (1948) 30. Commemorates 16th-century Spanish explorations.

Federal Hall, N.Y. (1939) 0.45. First seat of U.S. government under the Constitution.

Fort Caroline, Fla. (1950) 139. On St. Johns River, overlooks site of second attempt by French Huguenots to colonize North America.

Fort Clatsop, Ore. (1958) 130. Lewis and Clark encampment 1805-06.

General Grant, N.Y. (1958) 0.76. Tombs of Pres. and wife.

Hamilton Grange, N.Y. (1962) 0.71. Home of Alexander Hamilton.

John F. Kennedy Center for the Performing Arts, D.C. (1972) 18.

Johnstown Flood, Pa. (1964) 176. Commemorates tragic flood of 1889.

Lincoln Boyhood, Ind. (1962) 198. Lincoln grew up here.

Lincoln Memorial, D.C. (1911) 164.

Lyndon B. Johnson Grove on the Potomac, D.C. (1973) 17.

Mount Rushmore, S.D. (1925) 1,278. World famous sculpture of 4 presidents.

Perry's Victory and International Peace Memorial, Oh. (1936) 26. American naval victory, War of 1812.

Roger Williams, R.I. (1965) 5. Memorial to founder of Rhode Island.

Thaddeus Kosciuszko, Pa. (1972) 0.02. Memorial to Polish hero of American Revolution.

Theodore Roosevelt Island, D.C. (1947) 89.

Thomas Jefferson Memorial, D.C. (1943) 18.

Washington Monument, D.C. (1848) 106.

Wright Brothers, N.C. (1927) 431. Site of first powered flight.

National Historic Sites

Abraham Lincoln Birthplace, Hodgenville, Ky. (1916) 117.

Adams, Quincy, Mass. (1946) 9. Home of Presidents John Adams, John Quincy Adams, and celebrated descendants.

Allegheny Portage Railroad, Pa. (1964) 1,476. Part of the Pennsylvania Canal system.

Andersonville, Andersonville, Ga. (1970) 476. Noted Civil War prison.

Andrew Johnson, Greeneville, Tenn. (1935) 17. Home of the President.

Bent's Old Fort, Col. (1960) 800. Old West fur-trading post.

Carl Sandburg Home, N.C. (1968) 247. Poet's farm home.

Christiansted, St. Croix; V.I. (1952) 27. Commemorates Danish colony.

Clara Barton, Md. (1974) 9. Home of founder of American Red Cross.

Edgar Allan Poe, Pa. (1978) 0.51. Poet's home.

Edison, West Orange, N.J. (1955) 21. Home and laboratory.

Eisenhower, Gettysburg, Pa. (1967) 690. Home of 34th president.

Eleanor Roosevelt, Hyde Park, N.Y. (1977) 180.

Ford's Theatre, Washington, D.C. (1866) 0.29. Includes theater, now restored, where Lincoln was assassinated, house where he died, and Lincoln Museum.

Fort Bowie, Ariz. (1964) 1,000. Focal point of operations against Geronimo and the Apaches.

Fort Davis, Tex. (1961) 460. Frontier outpost battled Comanches and Apaches.

Fort Laramie, Wy. (1938) 841. Military post on Oregon Trail.

Fort Larned, Kan. (1964) 718. Military post on Sante Fe Trail.

Fort Point, San Francisco, Cal. (1970) 29. Largest West Coast fortification.

Fort Raleigh, N.C. (1941) 157. First English settlement.

Fort Scott, Kan. (1978) 17. Commemorates events of Civil War period.

Fort Smith, Ark. (1961) 63. Active post from 1817 to 1890.

Fort Union Trading Post, Mon., N.D. (1966) 436. Principal fur-trading post on upper Missouri, 1828-1867.

Fort Vancouver, Wash. (1948) 209. Hdqts. for Hudson's Bay Company in 1825. Early military and political seat.

Frederick Law Olmsted, Mass. (1979) 1.75. Home of famous park planner (1822-1903).

Friendship Hill, Pa. (1978) 675. Home of Alfred Gallatin, Jefferson's Sec'y of Treasury.

Golden Spike, Utah (1957) 2,203. Commemorates completion of first transcontinental railroad in 1869.

Grant-Kohrs Ranch, Mon. (1972) 1,528. Ranch house and part of 19th century ranch.

Hampton, Md. (1948) 59. 18th-century Georgian mansion.

Herbert Hoover, West Branch, Ia. (1965) 187. Birthplace and boyhood home of 31st president.

Home of Franklin D. Roosevelt, Hyde Park, N.Y. (1944) 264. Birthplace, home and "Summer White House".

Hopewell Village, Pa. (1938) 848. 19th-century iron making village.

Hubbell Trading Post, Ariz. (1965) 160. Indian trading post.

Jefferson National Expansion Memorial, St. Louis, Mo. (1935) 91. Commemorates westward expansion with park and memorial arch.

John Fitzgerald Kennedy, Brookline, Mass. (1967) .09. Birthplace and childhood home of the President.

John Muir, Martinez, Cal. (1964) 9. Home of early conservationist and writer.

Knife River Indian Villages, N.D. (1974) 1,293. Remnants of 5 Hidatsa villages.

Lincoln Home, Springfield, Ill. (1971) 12. Lincoln's residence when he was elected President, 1860.

Longfellow, Cambridge, Mass. (1972) 2. Longfellow's home, 1837-82, and Washington's hq. during Boston Siege, 1775-76. **No federal facilities.**

Lyndon B. Johnson, Johnson City, Tex. (1969) 256. Birthplace and boyhood home of the 36th president.

Maggie L. Walker, Va. (1978) 1.29. Richmond home of black leader and 1903 founder of bank.

Mar-A-Largo, Fla. (1969) 17. Mansion expresses the affluent Palm Beach life of the 1920s. Not open to public.

Martin Van Buren, N.Y. (1974) 40. Lindenwald, home of 8th president, near Kinderhook.

Ninety Six, S.C. (1976) 1,115. Colonial trading village.

Palo Alto Battlefield, Tex. (1978) 50. One of 2 Mexican War battles fought in U.S.

Puukohola Heiau, Ha. (1972) 77. Ruins of temple built by King Kamehameha.

Sagamore Hill, Oyster Bay, N.Y. (1962) 78. Home of President Theodore Roosevelt from 1885 until his death in 1919.

Saint-Gaudens, Cornish, N.H. (1964) 149. Home, studio and gardens of American sculptor Augustus Saint-Gaudens.

Salem Maritime, Mass. (1938) 9. Only port never seized from the patriots by the British. Major fishing and whaling port.

San Juan, P.R. (1949) 53. 16th-century Spanish fortifications.

Saugus Iron Works, Mass. (1968) 9. Reconstructed 17th-century colonial ironworks.

Sewall-Belmont House, D.C. (1974) 0.35. National Women's Party headquarters 1929-74.

Springfield Armory, Mass. (1974) 55. Small arms manufacturing center for nearly 200 years.

Theodore Roosevelt Birthplace, N.Y., N.Y. (1962) 0.11.

Theodore Roosevelt Inaugural, Buffalo, N.Y. (1966) 1. Wilcox House where he took oath of office, 1901.

Thomas Stone, Md. (1978) 328. Home of signer of Declaration, built in 1771.

Tuskegee Institute, Ala. (1974) 74. College founded by Booker T. Washington in 1881 for blacks, includes student-made brick buildings.

Vanderbilt Mansion, Hyde Park, N.Y. (1940) 212. Mansion of 19th-century financier.

Whitman Mission, Wash. (1936) 98. Site where Dr. and Mrs. Marcus Whitman ministered to the Indians until slain by them in 1847.

William Howard Taft, Cincinnati, Oh. (1969) 4. Birthplace and early home of the 27th president.

National Capital Parks

District of Columbia — Maryland — Virginia (1790) 6,468.

Comprises 346 units.

White House

Washington, D.C. (1792) 18. Presidential residence since November 1800.

National Monuments

Name	State	Year	Acreage
Agate Fossil Beds	Neb.	1965	3,055
Alibates Flint Quarries	N.M.-Tex.	1965	1,333
Aniakchak	Alas.	1978	364,000
Aztec Ruins	N.M.	1923	27
Bandelier	N.M.	1916	36,971
Bering Land Bridge	Alas.	1978	2,848,000
Biscayne	Fla.	1968	103,643
Black Canyon of the Gunnison	Col.	1933	13,672
Booker T. Washington	Va.	1956	224
Buck Island Reef	V.I.	1961	880
Cabrillo	Cal.	1913	144
Canyon de Chelly	Ariz.	1931	83,840
Cape Krusenstern	Alas.	1978	677,000
Capulin Mountain	N.M.	1916	775
Casa Grande Ruins	Ariz.	1892	473
Castillo de San Marcos	Fla.	1924	20
Castle Clinton	N.Y.	1946	1
Cedar Breaks	Ut.	1933	6,155
Chaco Canyon	N.M.	1907	21,509
Chiricahua	Ariz.	1924	11,088
Colorado	Col.	1911	20,457
Congaree Swamp	S.C.	1976	15,200
Craters of the Moon	Ida.	1924	53,545
Custer Battlefield	Mon.	1879	765
Death Valley	Cal.-Nev.	1933	2,067,795
Denali	Alas.	1978	3,993,000
Devils Postpile	Cal.	1911	798
Devils Tower	Wy.	1906	1,347
Dinosaur	Col.-Ut.	1915	211,058
Effigy Mounds	Ia.	1949	1,475
El Morro	N.M.	1906	1,279
Florissant Fossil Beds**	Col.	1969	5,998
Fort Frederica	Ga.	1936	214
Fort Jefferson	Fla.	1935	47,125
Fort Matanzas	Fla.	1924	299
Fort McHenry National Monument and Historic Shrine	Md.	1925	43
Fort Pulaski	Ga.	1924	5,616
Fort Stanwix	N.Y.	1935	16
Fort Sumter	S.C.	1948	64
Fort Union	N.M.	1954	721
Fossil Butte	Wy.	1972	8,198
Gates of the Arctic	Alas.	1978	9,432,000
G. Washington Birthplace	Va.	1930	538
George Washington Carver	Mo.	1943	210
Gila Cliff Dwellings	N.M.	1907	533
Glacier Bay	Alas.	1925	3,355,269
Grand Portage	Minn.	1951	710
Gran Quivira	N.M.	1909	611
Great Sand Dunes	Col.	1932	38,952
Hohokam Pima*	Ariz.	1972	1,690
Homestead Nat'l. Monument of America	Neb.	1936	195
Hovenweep	Col.-Ut.	1923	785
Jewel Cave	S.D.	1908	1,275
John Day Fossil Beds	Ore.	1974	14,044
Joshua Tree	Cal.	1936	559,960
Katmai	Alas.	1918	4,293,126
Kenai Fjords	Alas.	1978	672,000
Kobuk Valley	Alas.	1978	1,764,000
Lake Clark	Alas.	1978	2,930,000
Lava Beds	Cal.	1925	46,821
Lehman Caves	Nev.	1922	640
Montezuma Castle	Ariz.	1906	858
Mound City Group	Oh.	1923	68
Muir Woods	Cal.	1908	554
Natural Bridges	Ut.	1908	7,779
Navajo	Ariz.	1909	360
Noatak	Alas.	1978	5,800,000
Ocmulgee	Ga.	1934	683
Oregon Caves	Ore.	1909	474
Organ Pipe Cactus	Ariz.	1937	330,689
Pecos	N.M.	1965	365
Pinnacles	Cal.	1908	16,222
Pipe Spring	Ariz.	1923	40
Pipestone	Minn.	1937	282
Rainbow Bridge	Ut.	1910	160
Russell Cave	Ala.	1961	310
Saguaro	Ariz.	1933	83,576
Saint Croix Island**	Me.	1949	35
Scotts Bluff	Neb.	1919	2,988
Statue of Liberty	N.J.-N.Y.	1924	58
Sunset Crater	Ariz.	1930	3,040
Timpanogos Cave	Ut.	1922	250
Tonto	Ariz.	1907	1,120
Tumacacori	Ariz.	1908	17
Tuzigoot	Ariz.	1939	849
Walnut Canyon	Ariz.	1915	2,249
White Sands	N.M.	1933	144,458
Wrangell-St. Elias	Alas.	1978	11,923,000
Wupatki	Ariz.	1924	35,253
Yucca House*	Col.	1919	10
Yukon-Charley	Alas.	1978	2,520,000

National Preserves

Name	State	Year	Acreage
Big Cypress	Fla.	1974	570,000
Big Thicket	Tex.	1974	84,550

National Seashores

Name	State	Year	Acreage
Assateague Island	Md.-Va.	1965	39,631
Canaveral	Fla.	1975	57,627
Cape Cod	Mass.	1961	44,596
Cape Hatteras	N.C.	1937	30,319
Cape Lookout**	N.C.	1966	28,400
Cumberland Island	Ga.	1972	36,978
Fire Island	N.Y.	1964	19,579
Gulf Islands	Fla.-Miss.	1971	139,775
Padre Island	Tex.	1962	133,919
Point Reyes	Cal.	1962	67,265

National Parkways

Name	State	Year	Acreage
Blue Ridge	Va.-N.C.-Ga.	1936	81,562
George Washington Memorial	Va.-Md.	1930	7,142
John D. Rockefeller Jr. Mem.	Wy.	1972	23,777
Natchez Trace	Ala.-Miss.-Tenn.	1938	48,374

National Lakeshores

Name	State	Year	Acreage
Apostle Islands	Wis.	1970	42,009
Indiana Dunes	Ind.	1966	12,535
Pictured Rocks	Mich.	1966	70,757
Sleeping Bear Dunes	Mich.	1970	71,105

National Rivers

Name	State	Year	Acreage
Big South Fork	Ky.-Tenn.	1976	122,960
Buffalo	Ark.	1972	94,146
New River Gorge	W.Va.	1978	62,024

National Scenic Rivers and Riverways

Name	State	Year	Acreage
Delaware	N.Y.-N.J.-Pa.	1978	2,750
Lower Saint Croix	Minn.-Wis.	1972	8,716
Obed Wild	Tenn.	1976	5,250
Ozark	Mo.	1964	82,301
Rio Grande	Tex.	1978	9,600
Saint Croix	Minn.-Wis.	1968	62,696
Upper Delaware	N.Y.-N.J.	1978	75,000

Parks (no other classification)

Name	State	Year	Acreage
Arlington House, The Robert E. Lee Memorial	Va.	1925	28
Catoctin Mountain	Md.	1954	5,769
Fort Benton	Mon.	1976	...
Fort Washington	Md.	1930	341
Frederick Douglass Home	D.C.	1962	8
Greenbelt	Md.	1933	1,167
Piscataway	Md.	1961	4,251
Prince William Forest	Va.	1948	18,572
Rock Creek	D.C.	1890	1,754
Wolf Trap Farm Park for the Performing Arts	Va.	1966	130

National Recreation Areas

Name	State	Year	Acreage
Amistad	Tex.	1965	62,452
Bighorn Canyon	Mon.-Wy.	1964	120,280
Chattahoochee R.	Ga.	1978	8,515
Chickasaw	Okla.	1976	9,500
Coulee Dam	Wash.	1946	100,059
Curecanti	Col.	1965	42,114
Cuyahoga Valley	Oh.	1974	32,460
Delaware Water Gap	N.J.-Pa.	1965	71,000
Gateway	N.Y.-N.J.	1972	26,172
Glen Canyon	Ariz.-Ut.	1958	1,236,880
Golden Gate	Cal.	1972	38,677
Lake Chelan	Wash.	1968	61,890
Lake Mead	Ariz.-Nev.	1936	1,496,601
Lake Meredith	Tex.	1965	44,994
Ross Lake	Wash.	1968	117,574
Santa Monica Mts.	Cal.	1978	150,000
Whiskeytown	Cal.	1962	42,497

Name	State	Year	Acreage
National Mall	D.C.	1933	146
National Visitor Center	D.C.	1968	...

National Scenic Trail

Name	State	Year	Acreage
Appalachian	Me. to Ga.	1968	52,034

*Not open to the public **No federal facilities

Federal and State Indian Reservations

Source: U.S. Commerce Department (data as of circa Dec., 1972)

State	No. of reservations	Tribally-owned acreage[1]	Allotted acreage[1]	No. of tribes[3]	No. of persons[4]	Avg. unemp. rate%[5]	Major tribes
Alaska	13[2]	(2)	(2)	6	35,817	NA	Eskimo, Tlingit, Haida, Aleut, Athapascan[6]
Arizona	17	23,467,727	892,917	13	173,412	41	Navaho, Apache, Papago, Hopi, Pima
California	76	386,954	67,390	(7)	6,905	45	Quechan, Hoopa, Paiute, mission bands[7]
Colorado	2	888,155	14,425	1	2,144	37	Ute
Connecticut	4	795	—	3	25	NA	Pequot, Mohegan[8]
Florida	5	183,319	—	2	1,511	31	Seminole, Miccosukee[9]
Idaho	4	274,428	36,723	5	4,849	36	Shoshone, Bannock, Nez Perce
Iowa	1	3,476	—	1	561	35	Sac and Fox[10]
Kansas	4	2,436	24,030	5	3,009	10	Potawatomi, Kickapoo, Iowa
Louisiana	1	262	—	1	268	NA	Chitimacha
Maine	3	27,546	—	2	1,077	45	Passamaquoddy, Penobscot
Massachusetts	1	12	—	1	1	0	Hassanamisco-Nipmuk[11]
Michigan	5	4,425	12,210	2	2,069	38	Chippewa, Potawatomi
Minnesota	11	682,534	50,935	2	10,739	40	Chippewa, Sioux
Mississippi	1	17,381	209	1	3,294	10	Choctaw
Montana	7	1,792,383	3,279,926	10	24,137	38	Blackfeet, Sioux, Crow, Assiniboine, Cheyenne
Nebraska	3	27,193	45,467	3	2,601	62	Omaha, Winnebago, Santee Sioux
Nevada	23	1,133,529	32,691	3	4,784	46	Paiute, Shoshone, Washoe
New Mexico	24	3,329,270	119,877	7	30,125	43	Keresan, Zuni, Apache, Tanoan, Navajo[12]
New York	9	88,158	—	7	11,616	27	Seneca, Mohawk, Onondaga, Oneida[13]
North Carolina	1	56,573	—	1	4,880	21	Cherokee
North Dakota	4	375,936	996,744	5	16,735	41	Chippewa, Sioux, Mandan, Arikara, Hidatsa
Oklahoma[14]	—	56,741	991,715	27	80,994	24	Cherokee, Creek, Choctaw, Chicasaw, Cheyenne, Arapaho[14]
Oregon	4	495,842	165,778	8	2,718	41	Warm Springs, Wasco, Paiute, Umatilla
South Dakota	8	1,807,623	2,371,427	1	29,119	37	Sioux
Texas	2	4,400	—	3	1,000	30	Tigua (Pueblo), Alabama, Coushatta
Utah	4	1,095,531	48,095	3	1,961	36	Ute, Southern Paiute, Goshute
Virginia	2	925	—	1	110	NA	Algonquian
Washington	22	1,920,850	537,876	20	18,138	45	Yakima, Confederated, Lummi, Quinault
Wisconsin	10	61,911	82,977	6	7,497	38	Chippewa, Oneida, Winnebago
Wyoming	1	1,776,136	109,344	2	4,435	47	Shoshone, Arapaho

(1) Approximations. Ownership of reservation land is very complex. Most tribally-owned land listed here is owned by tribal organizations, but some of it is held in trust by the government and some is leased to or occupied by non-Indians. Government-owned land, even that held for the exclusive use of Indians, and non-Indian land formally included in reservations is not counted here.

Allotted land was land held by Indian individuals or families. The Department of Commerce data is not clear on whether all land listed as allotted is still securely held by Indians.

(2) Alaskan Indian affairs are handled under the Native Claims Settlement Act (Dec. 18, 1971). The act provides for the establishment of regional and village corporations to conduct business for profit. There are 12 regional corporations. Within each regional corporation, village corporations must be organized. These village corporations then receive title to lands previously held in reservations. There were approximately 2.5 million acres in reservations subject to the Settlement Act. Another 86,471 acres remain outside the Act in the Annette Island Reserve. Latest figures show that 5,687 acres have been assigned to village corporations, while an additional 13,490 acres have been surveyed but not yet assigned.

(3) The concept of "tribe" is, in many cases, a white man's invention and, at first, was used to define loosely associated Indians with cultural similarities. Today, "tribe" is a formal status of Indians organized by law. Some present day "tribes" such as the Blackfeet are really confederacies of smaller groups. The Alaskan natives are organized, on paper, into general linguistic groups.

(4) Number of Indians living on or adjacent to reservations. When these figures are compared to 1970 census figures, it appears that nearly 64% of Indians are living on or near reservations.

(5) Unemployment rate of Indian labor force living on or adjacent to reservations.

(6) Aleuts and Eskimos are racially and linguistically related. Athapascans are related to the Navaho and Apache Indians.

(7) Many California Indians are historically associated with groups which settled near Spanish missions where much of the traditional culture was destroyed. Many of these bands, however, still retain some of their Indian language and customs. Excluding the bands, there are 22 tribes represented on California reservations.

(8) The Mohegan or Mohican are a branch of the Pequot.

(9) "Seminole" means "runaways" and these Indians from various tribes were originally refugees from whites in the Carolinas and Georgia. Later joined by runaway slaves, the Seminole were united by their hostility to the United States. Formal peace with the Seminoles in Florida was not achieved until 1934. The Miccosukee are a branch of the Seminole; they retain their Indian religion and have not made formal peace with the U.S.

(10) Once two tribes, the Sac and Fox formed a political alliance in 1734.

(11) Reservation prior to 1728 consisted of 8,000 acres. The land was sold to whites who put the Indians' money in a bank. Over the years the money was "lost" or "borrowed." In 1848, the state granted 11.9 acres to one Indian family of which there are about 20 direct descendants today.

(12) Tanoan, Keresan, and Zuni are all pueblo-dwelling Indians.

(13) These 4 tribes along with the Cayuga and Tuscarora made up the Iroquois League, which ruled large portions of New York, New England, and Pennsylvania and ranged into the Mid-West and South. The Onondaga, who traditionally provide the president of the League, maintain that they are a foreign nation within New York and the U.S.

(14) Indian land status in Oklahoma is unique and there are no reservations in the sense that the term is used elsewhere in the U.S. Likewise, many of the Oklahoma tribes are unique in their high degree of assimilation to the white culture.

Declaration of Independence

The Declaration of Independence was adopted by the Continental Congress in Philadelphia, on July 4, 1776. John Hancock was president of the Congress and Charles Thomson was secretary. A copy of the Declaration, engrossed on parchment, was signed by members of Congress on and after Aug. 2, 1776. On Jan. 18, 1777, Congress ordered that "an authenticated copy, with the names of the members of Congress subscribing the same, be sent to each of the United States, and that they be desired to have the same put upon record." Authenticated copies were printed in broadside form in Baltimore, where the Continental Congress was then in session. The following text is that of the original printed by John Dunlap at Philadelphia for the Continental Congress.

IN CONGRESS, July 4, 1776.

A DECLARATION

By the REPRESENTATIVES of the

UNITED STATES OF AMERICA,

In GENERAL CONGRESS assembled

When in the Course of human Events, it becomes necessary for one People to dissolve the Political Bands which have connected them with another, and to assume among the Powers of the Earth, the separate and equal Station to which the Laws of Nature and of Nature's God entitle them, a decent Respect to the Opinions of Mankind requires that they should declare the causes which impel them to the Separation.

We hold these Truths to be self-evident, that all Men are created equal, that they are endowed by their Creator with certain unalienable Rights, that among these are Life, Liberty, and the Pursuit of Happiness—That to secure these Rights, Governments are instituted among Men, deriving their just Powers from the Consent of the Governed, that whenever any Form of Government becomes destructive of these Ends, it is the Right of the People to alter or to abolish it, and to institute new Government, laying its Foundation on such Principles, and organizing its Powers in such Form, as to them shall seem most likely to effect their Safety and Happiness. Prudence, indeed, will dictate that Governments long established should not be changed for light and transient Causes; and accordingly all Experience hath shewn, that Mankind are more disposed to suffer, while Evils are sufferable, than to right themselves by abolishing the Forms to which they are accustomed. But when a long Train of Abuses and Usurpations, pursuing invariably the same Object, evinces a Design to reduce them under absolute Despotism, it is their Right, it is their Duty, to throw off such Government, and to provide new Guards for their future Security. Such has been the patient Sufferance of these Colonies; and such is now the Necessity which constrains them to alter their former Systems of Government. The History of the present King of Great-Britain is a History of repeated Injuries and Usurpations, all having in direct Object the Establishment of an absolute Tyranny over these States. To prove this, let Facts be submitted to a candid World.

He has refused his Assent to Laws, the most wholesome and necessary for the public Good.

He has forbidden his Governors to pass Laws of immediate and pressing Importance, unless suspended in their Operation till his Assent should be obtained; and when so suspended, he has utterly neglected to attend to them.

He has refused to pass other Laws for the Accommodation of large Districts of People, unless those People would relinquish the Right of Representation in the Legislature, a Right inestimable to them, and formidable to Tyrants only.

He has called together Legislative Bodies at Places unusual, uncomfortable, and distant from the Depository of their Public Records, for the sole Purpose of fatiguing them into Compliance with his Measures.

He has dissolved Representative Houses repeatedly, for opposing with manly Firmness his Invasions on the Rights of the People.

He has refused for a long Time, after such Dissolutions, to cause others to be elected; whereby the Legislative Powers, incapable of Annihilation, have returned to the People at large for their exercise; the State remaining in the mean time exposed to all the Dangers of Invasion from without, and Convulsions within.

He has endeavoured to prevent the Population of these States; for that Purpose obstructing the Laws for Naturalization of Foreigners; refusing to pass others to encourage their Migrations hither, and raising the Conditions of new Appropriations of Lands.

He has obstructed the Administration of Justice, by refusing his Assent to Laws for establishing Judiciary Powers.

He has made Judges dependent on his Will alone, for the Tenure of their Offices, and the Amount and payment of their Salaries.

He has erected a Multitude of new Offices, and sent hither Swarms of Officers to harrass our People, and eat out their Substance.

He has kept among us, in Times of Peace, Standing Armies, without the consent of our Legislatures.

He has affected to render the Military independent of, and superior to the Civil Power.

He has combined with others to subject us to a Jurisdiction foreign to our Constitution, and unacknowledged by our Laws; giving his Assent to their Acts of pretended Legislation:

For quartering large Bodies of Armed Troops among us:

For protecting them, by a mock Trial, from Punishment for any Murders which they should commit on the Inhabitants of these States:

For cutting off our Trade with all Parts of the World:

For imposing Taxes on us without our Consent:

For depriving us, in many Cases, of the Benefits of Trial by Jury:

For transporting us beyond Seas to be tried for pretended Offences:

For abolishing the free System of English Laws in a neighbouring Province, establishing therein an arbitrary Government, and enlarging its Boundaries, so as to render it at once an Example and fit Instrument for introducing the same absolute Rule into these Colonies:

For taking away our Charters, abolishing our most valuable Laws, and altering fundamentally the Forms of our Governments:

For suspending our own Legislatures, and declaring themselves invested with Power to legislate for us in all Cases whatsoever.

He has abdicated Government here, by declaring us out of his Protection and waging War against us.

He has plundered our Seas, ravaged our Coasts, burnt our towns, and destroyed the Lives of our People.

He is, at this Time, transporting large Armies of foreign Mercenaries to compleat the works of Death, Desolation, and Tyranny, already begun with circumstances of Cruelty and Perfidy, scarcely paralleled in the most barbarous Ages, and totally unworthy the Head of a civilized Nation.

He has constrained our fellow Citizens taken Captive on the high Seas to bear Arms against their Country, to become the Executioners of their Friends and Brethren, or to fall themselves by their Hands.

He has excited domestic Insurrections amongst us, and has endeavoured to bring on the Inhabitants of our Frontiers, the merciless Indian Savages, whose known Rule of Warfare, is an undistinguished Destruction, of all Ages, Sexes and Conditions.

In every stage of these Oppressions we have Petitioned for Redress in the most humble Terms: Our repeated Petitions have been answered only by repeated Injury. A Prince, whose Character is thus marked by every act which may define a Tyrant, is unfit to be the Ruler of a free People.

Nor have we been wanting in Attentions to our British Brethren. We have warned them from Time to Time of Attempts by their Legislature to extend an unwarrantable Jurisdiction over us. We have reminded them of the Circumstances of our Emigration and Settlement here. We have appealed to their native Justice and Magnanimity, and we have conjured them by the Ties of our common Kindred to disavow these Usurpations, which, would inevitably interrupt our Connections and Correspondence. They too have been deaf to the Voice of Justice and of Consanguinity. We must, therefore, acquiesce in the Necessity, which denounces our Separation, and hold them, as we hold the rest of Mankind, Enemies in War, in Peace, Friends.

We, therefore, the Representatives of the UNITED STATES OF AMERICA, in General Congress, Assembled, appealing to the Supreme Judge of the World for the Rectitude of our Intentions, do, in the Name, and by Authority of the good People of these Colonies, solemnly Publish and Declare, That these United Colonies are, and of Right ought to be, Free and Independent States; that they are absolved from all Allegiance to the British Crown, and that all political Connection between them and the State of Great-Britain, is and ought to be totally dissolved; and that as Free and Independent States, they have full Power to levy War, conclude Peace, contract Alliances, establish Commerce, and to do all other Acts and Things which Independent States may of right do. And for the support of this declaration, with a firm Reliance on the Protection of divine Providence, we mutually pledge to each other our lives, our Fortunes, and our sacred Honor.

JOHN HANCOCK, President

Attest.
CHARLES THOMSON, Secretary.

Signers of the Declaration of Independence

Delegate and state	Vocation	Birthplace	Born	Died
Adams, John (Mass.)	Lawyer	Braintree (Quincy), Mass.	Oct. 30, 1735	July 4, 1826
Adams, Samuel (Mass.)	Political leader	Boston, Mass.	Sept. 27, 1722	Oct. 2, 1803
Bartlett, Josiah (N.H.)	Physician, judge	Amesbury, Mass.	Nov. 21, 1729	May 19, 1795
Braxton, Carter (Va.)	Farmer	Newington Plantation, Va.	Sept. 10, 1736	Oct. 10, 1797
Carroll, Chas. of Carrollton (Md.)	Lawyer	Annapolis, Md.	Sept. 19, 1737	Nov. 14, 1832
Chase, Samuel (Md.)	Judge	Princess Anne, Md.	Apr. 17, 1741	June 19, 1811
Clark, Abraham (N.J.)	Surveyor	Roselle, N.J.	Feb. 15, 1726	Sept. 15, 1794
Clymer, George (Pa.)	Merchant	Philadelphia, Pa.	Mar. 16, 1739	Jan. 23, 1813
Ellery, William (R.I.)	Lawyer	Newport, R.I.	Dec. 22, 1727	Feb. 15, 1820
Floyd, William (N.Y.)	Soldier	Brookhaven, N.Y.	Dec. 17, 1734	Aug. 4, 1821
Franklin, Benjamin (Pa.)	Printer, publisher.	Boston, Mass.	Jan. 17, 1706	Apr. 17, 1790
Gerry, Elbridge (Mass.)	Merchant	Marblehead, Mass.	July 17, 1744	Nov. 23, 1814
Gwinnett, Button (Ga.)	Merchant	Down Hatherly, England	c. 1735	May 19, 1777
Hall, Lyman (Ga.)	Physician	Wallingford, Conn.	Apr. 12, 1724	Oct. 19, 1790
Hancock, John (Mass.)	Merchant	Braintree (Quincy), Mass.	Jan. 12, 1737	Oct. 8, 1793
Harrison, Benjamin (Va.)	Farmer	Berkeley, Va.	Apr. 5, 1726	Apr. 24, 1791
Hart, John (N.J.)	Farmer	Stonington, Conn.	c. 1711	May 11, 1779
Hewes, Joseph (N.C.)	Merchant	Princeton, N.J.	Jan. 23, 1730	Nov. 10, 1779
Heyward, Thos. Jr. (S.C.)	Lawyer, farmer	St. Luke's Parish, S.C.	July 28, 1746	Mar. 6, 1809
Hooper, William (N.C.)	Lawyer	Boston, Mass.	June 28, 1742	Oct. 14, 1790
Hopkins, Stephen (R.I.)	Judge, educator	Providence, R.I.	Mar. 7, 1707	July 13, 1785
Hopkinson, Francis (N.J.)	Judge, author	Philadelphia, Pa.	Sept. 21, 1737	May 9, 1791
Huntington, Samuel (Conn.)	Judge	Windham County, Conn.	July 3, 1731	Jan. 5, 1796
Jefferson, Thomas (Va.)	Lawyer	Shadwell, Va.	Apr. 13, 1743	July 4, 1826
Lee, Francis Lightfoot (Va.)	Farmer	Westmoreland County, Va.	Oct. 14, 1734	Jan. 11, 1797
Lee, Richard Henry (Va.)	Farmer	Westmoreland County, Va.	Jan. 20, 1732	June 19, 1794
Lewis, Francis (N.Y.)	Merchant	Llandaff, Wales	Mar., 1713	Dec. 31, 1802
Livingston, Philip (N.Y.)	Merchant	Albany, N.Y.	Jan. 15, 1716	June 12, 1778
Lynch, Thomas Jr. (S.C.)	Farmer	Winyah, S.C.	Aug. 5, 1749	(at sea) 1779
McKean, Thomas (Del.)	Lawyer	New London, Pa.	Mar. 19, 1734	June 24, 1817
Middleton, Arthur (S.C.)	Farmer	Charleston, S.C.	June 26, 1742	Jan. 1, 1787
Morris, Lewis (N.Y.)	Farmer	Morrisania (Bronx County), N.Y.	Apr. 8, 1726	Jan. 22, 1798
Morris, Robert (Pa.)	Merchant	Liverpool, England	Jan. 20, 1734	May 9, 1806
Morton, John (Pa.)	Judge	Ridley, Pa.	1724	Apr., 1777
Nelson, Thos. Jr. (Va.)	Farmer	Yorktown, Va.	Dec. 26, 1738	Jan. 4, 1789
Paca, William (Md.)	Judge	Abingdon, Md.	Oct. 31, 1740	Oct. 23, 1799
Paine, Robert Treat (Mass.)	Judge	Boston, Mass.	Mar. 11, 1731	May 12, 1814
Penn, John (N.C.)	Lawyer	Near Port Royal, Va.	May 17, 1741	Sept. 14, 1788
Read, George (Del.)	Judge	Near North East, Md.	Sept. 18, 1733	Sept. 21, 1798
Rodney, Caesar (Del.)	Judge	Dover, Del.	Oct. 7, 1728	June 29, 1784
Ross, George (Pa.)	Judge	New Castle, Del.	May 10, 1730	July 14, 1779
Rush, Benjamin (Pa.)	Physician	Byberry, Pa. (Philadelphia)	Dec. 24, 1745	Apr. 19, 1813
Rutledge, Edward (S.C.)	Lawyer	Charleston, S.C.	Nov. 23, 1749	Jan. 23, 1800
Sherman, Roger (Conn.)	Lawyer	Newton, Mass.	Apr. 19, 1721	July 23, 1793
Smith, James (Pa.)	Lawyer	Dublin, Ireland	c. 1719	July 11, 1806
Stockton, Richard (N.J.)	Lawyer	Near Princeton, N.J.	Oct. 1, 1730	Feb. 28, 1781
Stone, Thomas (Md.)	Lawyer	Charles County, Md.	1743	Oct. 5, 1787
Taylor, George (Pa.)	Ironmaster	Ireland	1716	Feb. 23, 1781
Thornton, Matthew (N.H.)	Physician	Ireland	1714	June 24, 1803
Walton, George (Ga.)	Judge	Prince Edward County, Va.	1741	Feb. 2, 1804
Whipple, William (N.H.)	Merchant, judge	Kittery, Me.	Jan. 14, 1730	Nov. 28, 1785
Williams, William (Conn.)	Merchant	Lebanon, Conn.	Apr. 23, 1731	Aug. 2, 1811
Wilson, James (Pa.)	Judge	Carskerdo, Scotland	Sept. 14, 1742	Aug. 28, 1798
Witherspoon, John (N.J.)	Educator	Gifford, Scotland	Feb. 5, 1723	Nov. 15, 1794
Wolcott, Oliver (Conn.)	Judge	Windsor, Conn.	Dec. 1, 1726	Dec. 1, 1797
Wythe, George (Va.)	Lawyer	Elizabeth City Co. (Hampton), Va.	1726	June 8, 1806

Constitution of the United States

The Original 7 Articles

PREAMBLE

We, the people of the United States, in order to form a more perfect Union, establish justice, insure domestic tranquility, provide for the common defense, promote the general welfare, and secure the blessings of liberty to ourselves and our posterity do ordain and establish this Constitution for the United States of America.

ARTICLE I.

Section 1—Legislative powers; in whom vested:

All legislative powers herein granted shall be vested in a Congress of the United States, which shall consist of a Senate and House of Representatives.

Section 2—House of Representatives, how and by whom chosen. Qualifications of a Representative. Representatives and direct taxes, how apportioned. Enumeration. Vacancies to be filled. Power of choosing officers, and of impeachment.

1. The House of Representatives shall be composed of members chosen every second year by the people of the several States, and the electors in each State shall have the qualifications requisite for electors of the most numerous branch of the State Legislature.

2. No person shall be a Representative who shall not have attained to the age of twenty-five years, and been seven years a citizen of the United States, and who shall not, when elected, be an inhabitant of that State in which he shall be chosen.

3. *(Representatives and direct taxes shall be apportioned among the several States which may be included within this Union, according to their respective numbers, which shall be determined by adding to the whole number of free persons, including those bound to service for a term of years, and excluding Indians not taxed, three-fifths of all other persons.) (The previous sentence was superseded by Amendment XIV, section 2.)* The actual enumeration shall be made within three years after the first meeting of the Congress of the United States, and within every subsequent term of ten years, in such manner as they shall by law direct. The number of Representatives shall not exceed one for every thirty thousand, but each State shall have at least one Representative; and until such enumeration shall be made, the State of New Hampshire shall be entitled to choose three, Massachusetts eight, Rhode Island and Providence Plantations one, Connecticut five, New York six, New Jersey four, Pennsylvania eight, Delaware one, Maryland six, Virginia ten, North Carolina five, South Carolina five, and Georgia three.

4. When vacancies happen in the representation from any State, the Executive Authority thereof shall issue writs of election to fill such vacancies.

5. The House of Representatives shall choose their Speaker and other officers; and shall have the sole power of impeachment.

Section 3—Senators, how and by whom chosen. How classified. Qualifications of a Senator. President of the Senate, his right to vote. President pro tem., and other officers of the Senate, how chosen. Power to try impeachments. When President is tried, Chief Justice to preside. Sentence.

1. The Senate of the United States shall be composed of two Senators from each State, *(chosen by the Legislature thereof), (The preceding five words were superseded by Amendment XVII, section 1.)* for six years; and each Senator shall have one vote.

2. Immediately after they shall be assembled in consequence of the first election, they shall be divided as equally as may be into three classes. The seats of the Senators of the first class shall be vacated at the expiration of the second year, of the second class at the expiration of the fourth year, and of the third class at the expiration of the sixth year, so that one-third may be chosen every second year; *(and if vacancies happen by resignation, or otherwise, during the recess of the Legislature of any State, the Executive thereof may make temporary appointments until the next meeting of the Legislature, which shall then fill such vacancies.) (The words in parentheses were superseded by Amendment XVII, section 2.)*

3. No person shall be a Senator who shall not have attained to the age of thirty years, and been nine years a citizen of the United States, and who shall not, when elected, be an inhabitant of that State for which he shall be chosen.

4. The Vice President of the United States shall be President of the Senate, but shall have no vote, unless they be equally divided.

5. The Senate shall choose their other officers, and also a President pro tempore, in the absence of the Vice President, or when he shall exercise the office of President of the United States.

6. The Senate shall have the sole power to try all impeachments. When sitting for that purpose, they shall be on oath or affirmation. When the President of the United States is tried, the Chief Justice shall preside: and no person shall be convicted without the concurrence of two-thirds of the members present.

7. Judgment in cases of impeachment shall not extend further than to removal from office, and disqualification to hold and enjoy any office of honor, trust or profit under the United States: but the party convicted shall nevertheless be liable and subject to indictment, trial, judgment and punishment, according to law.

Section 4—Times, etc., of holding elections, how prescribed. One session each year.

1. The times, places and manner of holding elections for Senators and Representatives, shall be prescribed in each State by the Legislature thereof; but the Congress may at any time by law make or alter such regulations, except as to the places of choosing Senators.

2. The Congress shall assemble at least once in every year, and such meeting shall *(be on the first Monday in December,) (The words in parentheses were superseded by Amendment XX, section 2).* unless they shall by law appoint a different day.

Section 5—Membership, quorum, adjournments, rules. Power to punish or expel. Journal. Time of adjournments, how limited, etc.

1. Each House shall be the judge of the elections, returns and qualifications of its own members, and a majority of each shall constitute a quorum to do business; but a smaller number may adjourn from day to day, and may be authorized to compel the attendance of absent members, in such manner, and under such penalties as each House may provide.

2. Each House may determine the rules of its proceedings, punish its members for disorderly behavior, and, with the concurrence of two-thirds, expel a member.

3. Each House shall keep a journal of its proceedings, and from time to time publish the same, excepting such parts as may in their judgment require secrecy; and the yeas and nays of the members of either House on any question shall, at the desire of one-fifth of those present, be entered on the journal.

4. Neither House, during the session of Congress, shall, without the consent of the other, adjourn for more than three days, nor to any other place than that in which the two Houses shall be sitting.

Section 6—Compensation, privileges, disqualifications in certain cases.

1. The Senators and Representatives shall receive a compensation for their services, to be ascertained by law, and paid out of the Treasury of the United States. They shall in all cases, except treason, felony and breach of the peace, be privileged from arrest during their attendance at the session of their respective Houses, and in going to and returning from the same; and for any speech or debate in either House, they shall not be questioned in any other place.

2. No Senator or Representative shall, during the time for which he was elected, be appointed to any civil office under the authority of the United States, which shall have been created, or the emoluments whereof shall have been increased during such time; and no person holding any office under the United States, shall be a member of either House

during his continuance in office.

Section 7—House to originate all revenue bills. Veto. Bill may be passed by two-thirds of each House, notwithstanding, etc. Bill, not returned in ten days, to become a law. Provisions as to orders, concurrent resolutions, etc.

1. All bills for raising revenue shall originate in the House of Representatives; but the Senate may propose or concur with amendments as on other bills.

2. Every bill which shall have passed the House of Representatives and the Senate, shall, before it becomes a law, be presented to the President of the United States; if he approves he shall sign it, but if not he shall return it, with his objections to that House in which it shall have originated, who shall enter the objections at large on their journal, and proceed to reconsider it. If after such reconsideration two-thirds of that House shall agree to pass the bill, it shall be sent, together with the objections, to the other House, by which it shall likewise be reconsidered, and if approved by two-thirds of that House, it shall become a law. But in all such cases the votes of both Houses shall be determined by yeas and nays, and the names of the persons voting for and against the bill shall be entered on the journal of each House respectively. If any bill shall not be returned by the President within ten days (Sundays excepted) after it shall have been presented to him, the same shall be a law, in like manner as if he had signed it, unless the Congress by their adjournment prevent its return, in which case it shall not be a law.

3. Every order, resolution, or vote to which the concurrence of the Senate and House of Representatives may be necessary (except on a question of adjournment) shall be presented to the President of the United States; and before the same shall take effect, shall be approved by him, or being disapproved by him, shall be repassed by two-thirds of the Senate and House of Representatives, according to the rules and limitations prescribed in the case of a bill.

Section 8—Powers of Congress.

The Congress shall have power

1. To lay and collect taxes, duties, imposts and excises, to pay the debts and provide for the common defense and general welfare of the United States; but all duties, imposts and excises shall be uniform throughout the United States;

2. To borrow money on the credit of the United States;

3. To regulate commerce with foreign nations, and among the several States, and with the Indian tribes;

4. To establish a uniform rule of naturalization, and uniform laws on the subject of bankruptcies throughout the United States;

5. To coin money, regulate the value thereof, and of foreign coin, and fix the standard of weights and measures;

6. To provide for the punishment of counterfeiting the securities and current coin of the United States;

7. To establish post-offices and post-roads;

8. To promote the progress of science and useful arts, by securing for limited times to authors and inventors the exclusive right to their respective writings and discoveries;

9. To constitute tribunals inferior to the Supreme Court;

10. To define and punish piracies and felonies committed on the high seas, and offenses against the law of nations;

11. To declare war, grant letters of marque and reprisal, and make rules concerning captures on land and water;

12. To raise and support armies, but no appropriation of money to that use shall be for a longer term than two years;

13. To provide and maintain a navy;

14. To make rules for the government and regulation of the land and naval forces;

15. To provide for calling forth the militia to execute the laws of the Union, suppress insurrections and repel invasions;

16. To provide for organizing, arming, and disciplining the militia, and for governing such part of them as may be employed in the service of the United States, reserving to the States respectively, the appointment of the officers, and the authority of training and militia according to the discipline prescribed by Congress;

17. To exercise exclusive legislation in all cases whatsoever, over such district (not exceeding ten miles square) as may, by cession of particular States, and the acceptance of Congress, become the seat of the Government of the United States, and to exercise like authority over all places purchased by the consent of the Legislature of the State in which the same shall be, for the erection of forts, magazines, arsenals, dockyards, and other needful buildings;—And

18. To make all laws which shall be necessary and proper for carrying into execution the foregoing powers, and all other powers vested by this Constitution in the Government of the United States, or in any department or officer thereof.

Section 9—Provision as to migration or importation of certain persons. Habeas corpus, bills of attainder, etc. Taxes, how apportioned. No export duty. No commercial preference. Money, how drawn from Treasury, etc. No titular nobility. Officers not to receive presents, etc.

1. The migration or importation of such persons as any of the States now existing shall think proper to admit, shall not be prohibited by the Congress prior to the year one thousand eight hundred and eight, but a tax or duty may be imposed on such importation, not exceeding ten dollars for each person.

2. The privilege of the writ of habeas corpus shall not be suspended, unless when in cases of rebellion or invasion the public safety may require it.

3. No bill of attainder or ex post facto law shall be passed.

4. No capitation, or other direct, tax shall be laid, unless in proportion to the census or enumeration herein before directed to be taken. *(Modified by Amendment XVI.)*

5. No tax or duty shall be laid on articles exported from any State.

6. No preference shall be given by any regulation of commerce or revenue to the ports of one State over those of another: nor shall vessels bound to, or from, one State, be obliged to enter, clear, or pay duties in another.

7. No money shall be drawn from the Treasury, but in consequence of appropriations made by law; and a regular statement and account of the receipts and expenditures of all public money shall be published from time to time.

8. No title of nobility shall be granted by the United States: and no person holding any office of profit or trust under them, shall, without the consent of the Congress, accept of any present, emolument, office, or title, of any kind whatever, from any king, prince, or foreign state.

Section 10—States prohibited from the exercise of certain powers.

1. No State shall enter into any treaty, alliance, or confederation; grant letters of marque and reprisal; coin money; emit bills of credit; make anything but gold and silver coin a tender in payment of debts; pass any bill of attainder, ex post facto law, or law impairing the obligation of contracts, or grant any title of nobility.

2. No State shall, without the consent of the Congress, lay any imposts or duties on imports or exports, except what may be absolutely necessary for executing its inspection laws: and the net produce of all duties and imposts, laid by any State on imports or exports, shall be for the use of the Treasury of the United States; and all such laws shall be subject to the revision and control of the Congress.

3. No State shall, without the consent of Congress, lay any duty of tonnage, keep troops, or ships of war in time of peace, enter into any agreement or compact with another State, or with a foreign power, or engage in war, unless actually invaded, or in such imminent danger as will not admit of delay.

ARTICLE II.

Section 1—President: his term of office. Electors of President; number and how appointed. Electors to vote on same day. Qualification of President. On whom his duties devolve in case of his removal, death, etc. President's compensation. His oath of office.

1. The Executive power shall be vested in a President of the United States of America. He shall hold his office during the term of four years, and together with the Vice President, chosen for the same term, be elected as follows

2. Each State shall appoint, in such manner as the Legis-

lature thereof may direct, a number of electors, equal to the whole number of Senators and Representatives to which the State may be entitled in the Congress: but no Senator or Representative, or person holding an office of trust or profit under the United States, shall be appointed an elector.

(The electors shall meet in their respective States, and vote by ballot for two persons, of whom one at least shall not be an inhabitant of the same State with themselves. And they shall make a list of all the persons voted for, and of the number of votes for each; which list they shall sign and certify, and transmit sealed to the seat of the Government of the United States, directed to the President of the Senate. The President of the Senate shall, in the presence of the Senate and House of Representatives, open all the certificates, and the votes shall then be counted. The person having the greatest number of votes shall be the President, if such number be a majority of the whole number of electors appointed; and if there be more than one who have such majority, and have an equal number of votes, then the House of Representatives shall immediately choose by ballot one of them for President; and if no person have a majority, then from the five highest on the list the said House shall in like manner choose the President. But in choosing the President, the votes shall be taken by States, the representation from each State having one vote; a quorum for this purpose shall consist of a member or members from two-thirds of the States, and a majority of all the States shall be necessary to a choice. In every case, after the choice of the President, the person having the greatest number of votes of the electors shall be the Vice President. But if there should remain two or more who have equal votes, the Senate shall choose from them by ballot the Vice President.)

(This clause was superseded by Amendment XII.)

3. The Congress may determine the time of choosing the electors, and the day on which they shall give their votes; which day shall be the same throughout the United States.

4. No person except a natural born citizen, or a citizen of the United States, at the time of the adoption of this Constitution, shall be eligible to the office of President; neither shall any person be eligible to that office who shall not have attained to the age of thirty-five years, and been fourteen years a resident within the United States.

(For qualification of the Vice President, see Amendment XII.)

5. In case of the removal of the President from office, or of his death, resignation, or inability to discharge the powers and duties of the said office, the same shall devolve on the Vice President, and the Congress may by law provide for the case of removal, death, resignation or inability, both of the President and Vice President, declaring what officer shall then act as President, and such officer shall act accordingly, until the disability be removed, or a President shall be elected.

(This clause has been modified by Amendments XX and XXV.)

6. The President shall, at stated times, receive for his services, a compensation, which shall neither be increased nor diminished during the period for which he shall have been elected, and he shall not receive within that period any other emolument from the United States, or any of them.

7. Before he enter on the execution of his office, he shall take the following oath or affirmation:

"I do solemnly swear (or affirm) that I will faithfully execute the office of President of the United States, and will to the best of my ability, preserve, protect and defend the Constitution of the United States."

Section 2—President to be Commander-in-Chief. He may require opinions of cabinet officers, etc., may pardon. Treaty-making power. Nomination of certain officers. When President may fill vacancies.

1. The President shall be Commander-in-Chief of the Army and Navy of the United States, and of the militia of the several States, when called into the actual service of the United States; he may require the opinion, in writing, of the principal officer in each of the executive departments, upon any subject relating to the duties of their respective offices, and he shall have power to grant reprieves and pardons for offenses against the United States, except in cases of impeachment.

2. He shall have power, by and with the advice and consent of the Senate, to make treaties, provided two-thirds of the Senators present concur; and he shall nominate, and by and with the advice and consent of the Senate, shall appoint ambassadors, other public ministers and consuls, judges of the Supreme Court, and all other officers of the United States, whose appointments are not herein otherwise provided for, and which shall be established by law: but the Congress may by law vest the appointment of such inferior officers, as they think proper, in the President alone, in the courts of law, or in the heads of departments.

3. The President shall have power to fill up all vacancies that may happen during the recess of the Senate, by granting commissions, which shall expire at the end of their next session.

Section 3—President shall communicate to Congress. He may convene and adjourn Congress, in case of disagreement, etc. Shall receive ambassadors, execute laws, and commission officers.

He shall from time to time give to the Congress information of the state of the Union, and recommend to their consideration such measures as he shall judge necessary and expedient; he may, on extraordinary occasions, convene both Houses, or either of them, and in case of disagreement between them, with respect to the time of adjournment, he may adjourn them to such time as he shall think proper; he shall receive ambassadors and other public ministers; he shall take care that the laws be faithfully executed, and shall commission all the officers of the United States.

Section 4—All civil offices forfeited for certain crimes.

The President, Vice President, and all civil officers of the United States, shall be removed from office on impeachment for, and conviction of, treason, bribery, or other high crimes and misdemeanors.

ARTICLE III.

Section 1—Judicial powers, Tenure. Compensation.

The judicial power of the United States, shall be vested in one Supreme Court, and in such inferior courts as the Congress may from time to time ordain and establish. The judges, both of the Supreme and inferior courts, shall hold their offices during good behavior, and shall at stated times, receive for their services, a compensation, which shall not be diminished during their continuance in office.

Section 2—Judicial power; to what cases it extends. Original jurisdiction of Supreme Court; appellate jurisdiction. Trial by jury, etc. Trial, where.

1. The judicial power shall extend to all cases, in law and equity, arising under this Constitution, the laws of the United States, and treaties made, or which shall be made, under their authority; to all cases affecting ambassadors, other public ministers and consuls; to all cases of admiralty and maritime jurisdiction; to controversies to which the United States shall be a party; to controversies between two or more States; between a State and citizens of another State; between citizens of different States, between citizens of the same State claiming lands under grants of different States, and between a State, or the citizens thereof, and foreign states, citizens or subjects.

(This section is modified by Amendment XI.)

2. In all cases affecting ambassadors, other public ministers and consuls, and those in which a State shall be party, the Supreme Court shall have original jurisdiction. In all the other cases before mentioned, the Supreme Court shall have appellate jurisdiction, both as to law and fact, with such exceptions, and under such regulations as the Congress shall make.

3. The trial of all crimes, except in cases of impeachment, shall be by jury; and such trial shall be held in the State where the said crimes shall have been committed; but when not committed within any State, the trial shall be at such place or places as the Congress may by law have directed.

Section 3—Treason Defined, Proof of, Punishment of.

1. Treason against the United States, shall consist only in levying war against them, or in adhering to their enemies,

giving them aid and comfort. No person shall be convicted of treason unless on the testimony of two witnesses to the same overt act, or on confession in open court.

2. The Congress shall have power to declare the punishment of treason, but no attainder of treason shall work corruption of blood, or forfeiture except during the life of the person attainted.

ARTICLE IV.

Section 1—Each State to give credit to the public acts, etc., of every other State.

Full faith and credit shall be given in each State to the public acts, records, and judicial proceedings of every other State. And the Congress may by general laws prescribe the manner in which such acts, records and proceedings shall be proved, and the effect thereof.

Section 2—Privileges of citizens of each State. Fugitives from justice to be delivered up. Persons held to service having escaped, to be delivered up.

1. The citizens of each State shall be entitled to all privileges and immunities of citizens in the several States.

2. A person charged in any State with treason, felony, or other crime, who shall flee from justice, and be found in another State, shall on demand of the Executive authority of the State from which he fled, be delivered up, to be removed to the State having jurisdiction of the crime.

(3. No person held to service or labor in one State, under the laws thereof, escaping into another, shall in consequence of any law or regulation therein, be discharged from such service or labor, but shall be delivered up on claim of the party to whom such service or labor may be due.) (This clause was superseded by Amendment XIII.)

Section 3—Admission of new States. Power of Congress over territory and other property.

1. New States may be admitted by the Congress into this Union; but no new State shall be formed or erected within the jurisdiction of any other State; nor any State be formed by the junction of two or more States, or parts of States, without the consent of the Legislatures of the States concerned as well as of the Congress.

2. The Congress shall have power to dispose of and make all needful rules and regulations respecting the territory or other property belonging to the United States; and nothing in this Constitution shall be so construed as to prejudice any claims of the United States, or of any particular State.

Section 4—Republican form of government guaranteed. Each state to be protected.

The United States shall guarantee to every State in this Union a Republican form of government, and shall protect each of them against invasion; and on application of the Legislature, or of the Executive (when the Legislature cannot be convened) against domestic violence.

ARTICLE V.

Constitution: how amended; proviso.

The Congress, whenever two-thirds of both Houses shall deem it necessary, shall propose amendments to this Constitution, or, on the application of the Legislatures of two-thirds of the several States, shall call a convention for proposing amendments, which, in either case, shall be valid to all intents and purposes, as part of this Constitution, when ratified by the Legislatures of three-fourths of the several States, or by conventions in three-fourths thereof, as the one or the other mode of ratification may be proposed by the Congress; provided that no amendment which may be made prior to the year one thousand eight hundred and eight shall in any manner affect the first and fourth clauses in the Ninth Section of the First Article; and that no State, without its consent, shall be deprived of its equal suffrage in the Senate.

ARTICLE VI.

Certain debts, etc., declared valid. Supremacy of Constitution, treaties, and laws of the United States. Oath to support Constitution, by whom taken. No religious test.

1. All debts contracted and engagements entered into, before the adoption of this Constitution, shall be as valid against the United States under this Constitution, as under the Confederation.

2. This Constitution, and the laws of the United States which shall be made in pursuance thereof; and all treaties made, or which shall be made, under the authority of the United States, shall be the supreme law of the land; and the judges in every State shall be bound thereby, any thing in the Constitution or laws of any State to the contrary notwithstanding.

3. The Senators and Representatives before mentioned, and the members of the several State Legislatures, and all executive and judicial officers, both of the United States and of the several States, shall be bound by oath or affirmation, to support this Constitution; but no religious test shall ever be required as a qualification to any office or public trust under the United States.

ARTICLE VII.

What ratification shall establish Constitution.

The ratification of the Conventions of nine States, shall be sufficient for the establishment of this Constitution between the States so ratifying the same.

Done in convention by the unanimous consent of the States present the Seventeenth day of September in the year of our Lord one thousand seven hundred and eighty seven, and of the independence of the United States of America the Twelfth. In witness whereof we have hereunto subscribed our names.

George Washington, President and deputy from Virginia.

New Hampshire—John Langdon, Nicholas Gilman.

Massachusetts—Nathaniel Gorham, Rufus King.

Connecticut—Wm. Saml. Johnson, Roger Sherman.

New York—Alexander Hamilton.

New Jersey—Wil: Livingston, David Brearley, Wm. Paterson, Jona: Dayton.

Pennsylvania—B. Franklin, Thomas Mifflin, Robt. Morris, Geo. Clymer, Thos. FitzSimons, Jared Ingersoll, James Wilson, Gouv. Morris.

Delaware—Geo: Read, Gunning Bedford Jun., John Dickinson, Richard Bassett, Jaco: Broom.

Maryland—James McHenry, Daniel of Saint Thomas' Jenifer, Danl. Carroll.

Virginia—John Blair, James Madison Jr.

North Carolina—Wm. Blount, Rich'd. Dobbs Spaight, Hugh Williamson.

South Carolina—J. Rutledge, Charles Cotesworth Pinckney, Charles Pinckney, Pierce Butler.

Georgia—William Few, Abr. Baldwin.

Attest: William Jackson, Secretary.

Ten Original Amendments: The Bill of Rights

In force Dec. 15, 1791

(The First Congress, at its first session in the City of New York, Sept. 25, 1789, submitted to the states 12 amendments to clarify certain individual and state rights not named in the Constitution. They are generally called the Bill of Rights.

(Influential in framing these amendments was the Declaration of Rights of Virginia, written by George Mason (1725-1792) in 1776. Mason, a Virginia delegate to the Constitutional Convention, did not sign the Constitution and opposed its ratification on the ground that it did not sufficiently oppose slavery or safeguard individual rights.

(In the preamble to the resolution offering the proposed amendments, Congress said: "The conventions of a number of the States having at the time of their adopting the Constitution, expressed a desire, in order to prevent misconstruction or abuse of its powers, that further declaratory and restrictive clauses should be added, and as extending the ground of public confidence in the government will best insure the beneficent ends of its institution, be it resolved," etc.

(Ten of these amendments now commonly known as one to 10 inclusive, but originally 3 to 12 inclusive, were ratified by the states as follows: New Jersey, Nov. 20, 1789; Maryland, Dec. 19, 1789; North Carolina, Dec. 22, 1789; South Carolina, Jan. 19, 1790; New Hampshire, Jan 25, 1790; Delaware, Jan 28, 1790; New York, Feb. 24, 1790; Pennsylvania, Mar. 10, 1790; Rhode

Island, June 7, 1790; Vermont, Nov 3, 1791; Virginia, Dec. 15, 1791; Massachusetts, Mar. 2, 1939; Georgia, Mar. 18, 1939; Connecticut, Apr. 19, 1939. These original 10 ratified amendments follow as Amendments I to X inclusive.

(Of the two original proposed amendments which were not ratified by the necessary number of states, the first related to apportionment of Representatives; the second, to compensation of members.)

AMENDMENT I.

Religious establishment prohibited. Freedom of speech, of the press, and right to petition.

Congress shall make no law respecting an establishment of religion, or prohibiting the free exercise thereof; or abridging the freedom of speech, or of the press; or the right of the people peaceably to assemble, and to petition the Government for a redress of grievances.

AMENDMENT II.

Right to keep and bear arms.

A well-regulated militia, being necessary to the security of a free State, the right of the people to keep and bear arms, shall not be infringed.

AMENDMENT III.

Conditions for quarters for soldiers.

No soldier shall, in time of peace be quartered in any house, without the consent of the owner, nor in time of war, but in a manner to be prescribed by law.

AMENDMENT IV.

Right of search and seizure regulated.

The right of the people to be secure in their persons, houses, papers, and effects, against unreasonable searches and seizures, shall not be violated, and no warrants shall issue, but upon probable cause, supported by oath or affirmation, and particularly describing the place to be searched, and the persons or things to be seized.

AMENDMENT V.

Provisions concerning prosecution. Trial and punishment—private property not to be taken for public use without compensation.

No person shall be held to answer for a capital, or otherwise infamous crime, unless on a presentment or indictment of a Grand Jury, except in cases arising in the land or naval forces, or in the militia, when in actual service in time of war or public danger; nor shall any person be subject for the same offense to be twice put in jeopardy of life or limb; nor shall be compelled in any criminal case to be a witness against himself, nor be deprived of life, liberty, or property, without due process of law; nor shall private property be taken for public use without just compensation.

AMENDMENT VI.

Right to speedy trial, witnesses, etc.

In all criminal prosecutions, the accused shall enjoy the right to a speedy and public trial, by an impartial jury of the State and district wherein the crime shall have been committed, which district shall have been previously ascertained by law, and to be informed of the nature and cause of the accusation; to be confronted with the witnesses against him; to have compulsory process for obtaining witnesses in his favor, and to have the assistance of counsel for his defense.

AMENDMENT VII.

Right of trial by jury.

In suits at common law, where the value in controversy shall exceed twenty dollars, the right of trial by jury shall be preserved, and no fact tried by a jury shall be otherwise reexamined in any court of the United States, than according to the rules of the common law.

AMENDMENT VIII.

Excessive bail or fines and cruel punishment prohibited.

Excessive bail shall not be required, nor excessive fines imposed, nor cruel and unusual punishments inflicted.

AMENDMENT IX.

Rule of construction of Constitution.

The enumeration in the Constitution, of certain rights, shall not be construed to deny or disparage others retained by the people.

AMENDMENT X.

Rights of States under Constitution.

The powers not delegated to the United States by the Constitution, nor prohibited by it to the States, are reserved to the States respectively, or to the people.

Amendments Since the Bill of Rights

AMENDMENT XI.

Judicial powers construed.

The judicial power of the United States shall not be construed to extend to any suit in law or equity, commenced or prosecuted against one of the United States by citizens of another State, or by citizens or subjects of any foreign state.

(This amendment was proposed to the Legislatures of the several States by the Third Congress on March 4, 1794, and was declared to have been ratified in a message from the President to Congress, dated Jan. 8, 1798.

(It was on Jan 5, 1798, that Secretary of State Pickering received from 12 of the States authenticated ratifications, and informed President John Adams of that fact.

(As a result of later research in the Department of State, it is now established that Amendment XI became part of the Constitution on Feb. 7, 1795, for on that date it had been ratified by 12 States as follows:

(1. New York, Mar. 27, 1794. 2. Rhode Island, Mar. 31, 1794. 3. Connecticut, May 8, 1794. 4. New Hampshire, June 16, 1794. 5. Massachusetts, June 26, 1794. 6. Vermont, between Oct 9, 1794, and Nov. 9, 1794. 7. Virginia, Nov. 18, 1794. 8. Georgia, Nov. 29, 1794. 9. Kentucky, Dec. 7, 1794. 10. Maryland, Dec. 26, 1794. 11. Delaware, Jan 23, 1795. 12. North Carolina, Feb. 7, 1795.

(On June 1, 1796, more than a year after Amendment XI had become a part of the Constitution (but before anyone was officially aware of this), Tennessee had been admitted as a State; but not until Oct. 16, 1797, was a certified copy of the resolution of Congress proposing the amendment sent to the Governor of Tennessee (John Sevier) by Secretary of State Pickering, whose office was then at Trenton, New Jersey, because of the epidemic of yellow fever at Philadelphia; it seems, however, that the Legislature of Tennessee took no action on Amendment XI, owing doubtless to the fact that public announcement of its adoption was made soon thereafter.

(Besides the necessary 12 States, one other, South Carolina, ratified Amendment XI, but this action was not taken until Dec. 4, 1797; the two remaining States, New Jersey and Pennsylvania, failed to ratify.)

AMENDMENT XII.

Manner of choosing President and Vice-President.

(Proposed by Congress Dec. 9, 1803; ratification completed June 15, 1804.)

The Electors shall meet in their respective States and vote by ballot for President and Vice-President, one of whom, at least, shall not be an inhabitant of the same State with themselves; they shall name in their ballots the person voted for as President, and in distinct ballots the person voted for as Vice-President, and they shall make distinct lists of all persons voted for as President, and of all persons voted for as Vice-President, and of the number of votes for each, which lists they shall sign and certify, and transmit sealed to the seat of the Government of the United States, directed to the President of the Senate; the President of the Senate shall, in the presence of the Senate and House of Representatives, open all the certificates and the votes shall then be counted;—The person having the greatest number of votes for President, shall be the President, if such number be a majority of the whole number of Electors appointed; and if no person have such majority, then from the persons having the highest numbers not exceeding three on the list of those voted for as President, the House of Representatives shall choose immediately, by ballot, the President. But in choosing the President, the votes shall be taken by States, the representation from each State having one vote; a quorum for this purpose shall consist of a member or members from two-thirds of the States, and a majority of all the States shall be necessary to a choice. *(And if the House of Representatives shall not choose a President whenever the right of choice shall devolve upon them, before the fourth day of March next following, then the Vice-President shall act as President, as in the case of the death or other constitutional disability of the President.) (The words in parentheses were superseded by Amendment XX, section 3.)* The person having the greatest number of votes as Vice-President, shall be the Vice-President, if such number be a majority of the whole number of Electors appointed, and if no person have a majority, then from the two highest numbers on the list, the Senate shall choose the Vice-President; a quorum for the purpose shall consist of two-thirds of the whole number of Senators, and a majority of the whole number shall be necessary to a choice. But no person constitutionally ineligible to the office of President shall be eligible to that of Vice-President of the United States.

THE RECONSTRUCTION AMENDMENTS

(Amendments XIII, XIV, and XV are commonly known as the Reconstruction Amendments, inasmuch as they followed the Civil War, and were drafted by Republicans who were bent on imposing their own policy of reconstruction on the South. Post-bellum legislatures there—Mississippi, South Carolina, Georgia, for example—had set up laws which, it was charged, were contrived to perpetuate Negro slavery under other names.)

AMENDMENT XIII.

Slavery abolished.

(Proposed by Congress Jan. 31, 1865; ratification completed Dec. 18, 1865. The amendment, when first proposed by a resolution in Congress, was passed by the Senate, 38 to 6, on Apr. 8, 1864, but was defeated in the House, 95 to 66 on June 15, 1864. On reconsideration by the House, on Jan. 31, 1865, the resolution passed, 119 to 56. It was approved by President Lincoln on Feb. 1, 1865, although the Supreme Court had decided in 1798 that the President has nothing to do with the proposing of amendments to the Constitution, or their adoption.)

1. Neither slavery nor involuntary servitude, except as a punishment for crime whereof the party shall have been duly convicted, shall exist within the United States or any place subject to their jurisdiction.

2. Congress shall have power to enforce this article by appropriate legislation.

AMENDMENT XIV.

Citizenship rights not to be abridged.

(The following amendment was proposed to the Legislatures of the several states by the 39th Congress, June 13, 1866, and was declared to have been ratified in a proclamation by the Secretary of State, July 28, 1868.

(The 14th amendment was adopted only by virtue of ratification subsequent to earlier rejections. Newly constituted legislatures in both North Carolina and South Carolina (respectively July 4 and 9, 1868), ratified the proposed amendment, although earlier legislatures had rejected the proposal. The Secretary of State issued a proclamation, which, though doubtful as to the effect of attempted withdrawals by Ohio and New Jersey, entertained no doubt as to the validity of the ratification by North and South Carolina. The following day (July 21, 1868), Congress passed a resolution which declared the 14th Amendment to be a part of the Constitution and directed the Secretary of State so to promulgate it. The Secretary waited, however, until the newly constituted Legislature of Georgia had ratified the amendment, subsequent to an earlier rejection, before the promulgation of the ratification of the new amendment.)

1. All persons born or naturalized in the United States, and subject to the jurisdiction thereof, are citizens of the United States and of the State wherein they reside. No State shall make or enforce any law which shall abridge the privileges or immunities of citizens of the United States; nor shall any State deprive any person of life, liberty, or property, without due process of law; nor deny to any person within its jurisdiction the equal protection of the laws.

2. Representatives shall be apportioned among the several States according to their respective numbers, counting the whole number of persons in each State, excluding Indians not taxed. But when the right to vote at any election for the choice of Electors for President and Vice-President of the United States, Representatives in Congress, the executive and judicial officers of a State, or the members of the Legislature thereof, is denied to any of the male inhabitants of such State, being twenty-one years of age, and, citizens of the United States, or in any way abridged, except for participation in rebellion, or other crime, the basis of representation therein shall be reduced in the proportion which the number of such male citizens shall bear to the whole number of male citizens twenty-one years of age in such State.

3. No person shall be a Senator or Representative in Congress, or Elector of President and Vice-President, or hold any office, civil or military, under the United States, or under any State, who, having previously taken an oath, as a member of Congress, or as an officer of the United States, or as a member of any State Legislature, or as an executive or judicial officer of any State, to support the Constitution of the United States, shall have engaged in insurrection or rebellion against the same, or given aid or comfort to the enemies thereof. But Congress may by a vote of two-thirds of each House, remove such disability.

4. The validity of the public debt of the United States, authorized by law, including debts incurred for payment of pensions and bounties for services in suppressing insurrection or rebellion, shall not be questioned. But neither the United States nor any State shall assume or pay any debt or obligation incurred in aid of insurrection or rebellion against the United States, or any claim for the loss or emancipation of any slave; but all such debts, obligations and claims, shall be held illegal and void.

5. The Congress shall have power to enforce, by appropriate legislation, the provisions of this article.

AMENDMENT XV.

Race no bar to voting rights.

(The following amendment was proposed to the legislatures of the several States by the 40th Congress, Feb. 26, 1869, and was declared to have been ratified in a proclamation by the Secretary of State, Mar. 30, 1870.)

1. The right of citizens of the United States to vote shall not be denied or abridged by the United States or by any State on account of race, color, or previous condition of servitude.

2. The Congress shall have power to enforce this article by appropriate legislation.

AMENDMENT XVI.

Income taxes authorized.

(Proposed by Congress July 12, 1909; ratification declared by the Secretary of State Feb. 25, 1913.)

The Congress shall have power to lay and collect taxes on incomes, from whatever source derived, without apportionment among the several States, and without regard to any census or enumeration.

AMENDMENT XVII.

United States Senators to be elected by direct popular vote.

(Proposed by Congress May 13, 1912; ratification declared by the Secretary of State May 31, 1913.)

1. The Senate of the United States shall be composed of two Senators from each State, elected by the people thereof, for six years; and each Senator shall have one vote. The electors in each State shall have the qualifications requisite for electors of the most numerous branch of the State Legislatures.

2. When vacancies happen in the representation of any State in the Senate, the executive authority of such State shall issue writs of election to fill such vacancies: Provided, That the Legislature of any State may empower the Executive thereof to make temporary appointments until the peo-

ple fill the vacancies by election as the Legislature may direct.

3. This amendment shall not be so construed as to affect the election or term of any Senator chosen before it becomes valid as part of the Constitution.

AMENDMENT XVIII.

Liquor prohibition amendment.

(Proposed by Congress Dec. 18, 1917; ratification completed Jan. 16, 1919. Repealed by Amendment XXI, effective Dec. 5, 1933.)

(1. After one year from the ratification of this article the manufacture, sale, or transportation of intoxicating liquors within, the importation thereof into, or the exportation thereof from the United States and all territory subject to the jurisdiction thereof for beverage purposes is hereby prohibited.

(2. The Congress and the several States shall have concurrent power to enforce this article by appropriate legislation.

(3. This article shall be inoperative unless it shall have been ratified as an amendment to the Constitution by the Legislatures of the several States, as provided in the Constitution, within seven years from the date of the submission hereof to the States by the Congress.)

(The total vote in the Senates of the various States was 1,310 for, 237 against—84.6% dry. In the lower houses of the States the vote was 3,782 for, 1,035 against—78.5% dry.

(The amendment ultimately was adopted by all the States except Connecticut and Rhode Island.)

AMENDMENT XIX.

Giving nationwide suffrage to women.

(Proposed by Congress June 4, 1919; ratification certified by Secretary of State Aug. 26, 1920.)

1. The right of citizens of the United States to vote shall not be denied or abridged by the United States or by any State on account of sex.

2. Congress shall have power to enforce this Article by appropriate legislation.

AMENDMENT XX.

Terms of President and Vice President to begin on Jan. 20; those of Senators, Representatives, Jan. 3.

(Proposed by Congress Mar. 2, 1932; ratification completed Jan. 23, 1933.)

1. The terms of the President and Vice President shall end at noon on the 20th day of January, and the terms of Senators and Representatives at noon on the 3rd day of January, of the years in which such terms would have ended if this article had not been ratified; and the terms of their successors shall then begin.

2. The Congress shall assemble at least once in every year, and such meeting shall begin at noon on the 3rd day of January, unless they shall by law appoint a different day.

3. If, at the time fixed for the beginning of the term of the President, the President elect shall have died, the Vice President elect shall become President. If a President shall not have been chosen before the time fixed for the beginning of his term, or if the President elect shall have failed to qualify, then the Vice President elect shall act as President until a President shall have qualified; and the Congress may by law provide for the case wherein neither a President elect nor a Vice President elect shall have qualified, declaring who shall then act as President, or the manner in which one who is to act shall be selected, and such person shall act accordingly until a President or Vice President shall have qualified.

4. The Congress may by law provide for the case of the death of any of the persons from whom the House of Representatives may choose a President whenever the right of choice shall have devolved upon them, and for the case of the death of any of the persons from whom the Senate may choose a Vice President whenever the right of choice shall have devolved upon them.

5. Sections 1 and 2 shall take effect on the 15th day of October following the ratification of this article (Oct., 1933).

6. This article shall be inoperative unless it shall have been ratified as an amendment to the Constitution by the Legislatures of three-fourths of the several States within seven years from the date of its submission.

AMENDMENT XXI.

Repeal of Amendment XVIII.

(Proposed by Congress Feb. 20, 1933; ratification completed Dec. 5, 1933.)

1. The eighteenth article of amendment to the Constitution of the United States is hereby repealed.

2. The transportation or importation into any State, Territory, or Possession of the United States for delivery or use therein of intoxicating liquors, in violation of the laws thereof, is hereby prohibited.

3. This article shall be inoperative unless it shall have been ratified as an amendment to the Constitution by conventions in the several States, as provided in the Constitution, within seven years from the date of the submission hereof to the States by the Congress.

AMENDMENT XXII.

Limiting Presidential terms of office.

(Proposed by Congress Mar. 24, 1947; ratification completed Feb. 27, 1951.)

1. No person shall be elected to the office of the President more than twice, and no person who has held the office of President, or acted as President, for more than two years of a term to which some other person was elected President shall be elected to the office of the President more than once. But this Article shall not apply to any person holding the office of President when this Article was proposed by the Congress, and shall not prevent any person who may be holding the office of President, or acting as President, during the term within which this Article becomes operative from holding the office of President or acting as President during the remainder of such term.

2. This article shall be inoperative unless it shall have been ratified as an amendment to the Constitution by the Legislatures of three-fourths of the several States within seven years from the date of its submission to the States by the Congress.

AMENDMENT XXIII.

Presidential vote for District of Columbia.

(Proposed by Congress June 16, 1960; ratification completed Mar. 29, 1961.)

1. The District constituting the seat of Government of the United States shall appoint in such manner as the Congress may direct:

A number of electors of President and Vice President equal to the whole number of Senators and Representatives in Congress to which the District would be entitled if it were a State, but in no event more than the least populous State; they shall be in addition to those appointed by the States, but they shall be considered, for the purposes of the election of President and Vice President, to be electors appointed by a State; and they shall meet in the District and perform such duties as provided by the twelfth article of amendment.

2. The Congress shall have power to enforce this article by appropriate legislation.

AMENDMENT XXIV.

Barring poll tax in federal elections.

(Proposed by Congress Aug. 27, 1962; ratification completed Jan. 23, 1964.)

1. The right of citizens of the United States to vote in any primary or other election for President or Vice President, for electors for President or Vice President, or for Senator or Representative in Congress, shall not be denied or abridged by the United States or any State by reason of failure to pay any poll tax or other tax.

2. The Congress shall have power to enforce this article by appropriate legislation.

AMENDMENT XXV.

Presidential disability and succession.

(Proposed by Congress July 6, 1965; ratification completed Feb. 10, 1967.)

1. In case of the removal of the President from office or of

his death or resignation, the Vice President shall become President.

2. Whenever there is a vacancy in the office of the Vice President, the President shall nominate a Vice President who shall take office upon confirmation by a majority vote of both houses of Congress.

3. Whenever the President transmits to the President pro tempore of the Senate and the Speaker of the House of Representatives his written declaration that he is unable to discharge the powers and duties of his office, and until he transmits to them a written declaration to the contrary, such powers and duties shall be discharged by the Vice President as Acting President.

4. Whenever the Vice President and a majority of either the principal officers of the executive departments or of such other body as Congress may by law provide, transmit to the President pro tempore of the Senate and the Speaker of the House of Representatives their written declaration that the President is unable to discharge the powers and duties of his office, the Vice President shall immediately assume the powers and duties of the office as Acting President.

Thereafter, when the President transmits to the President pro tempore of the Senate and the Speaker of the House of Representatives his written declaration that no inability exists, he shall resume the powers and duties of his office unless the Vice President and a majority of either the principal officers of the executive department or of such other body as Congress may by law provide, transmit within four days to the President pro tempore of the Senate and the Speaker of the House of Representatives their written declaration that the President is unable to discharge the powers and duties of his office. Thereupon Congress shall decide the issue, assembling within forty-eight hours for that purpose if not in session. If the Congress, within twenty-one days after receipt of the latter written declaration, or, if Congress is not in session, within twenty-one days after Congress is required to assemble, determines by two-thirds vote of both houses that the President is unable to discharge the powers and duties of his office, the Vice President shall continue to discharge the same as Acting President; otherwise, the President shall resume the powers and duties of his office.

AMENDMENT XXVI.

Lowering voting age to 18 years.

(Proposed by Congress Mar. 8, 1971; ratification completed July 1, 1971.)

1. The right of citizens of the United States, who are 18 years of age or older, to vote shall not be denied or abridged by the United States or any state on account of age.

2. The Congress shall have the power to enforce this article by appropriate legislation.

PROPOSED EQUAL RIGHTS AMENDMENT

(Proposed by Congress Mar. 22, 1972; ratified, as of mid-1980, by 35 states: 5 voted later to rescind their approval. Total of 38 needed for approval before deadline, originally Mar. 22, 1979; extended to June 30, 1982, by Senate action Oct. 6, 1978.)

1. Equality of rights under the law shall not be denied or abridged by the United States or by any State on account of sex.

2. The Congress shall have the power to enforce, by appropriate legislation, the provisions of this article.

3. This amendment shall take effect two years after the date of ratification.

PROPOSED D.C. REPRESENTATION AMENDMENT

(Proposed by Congress Aug. 22, 1978; ratified, as of mid-1980, by 8 states.)

1. For purposes of representation in the Congress, election of the President and Vice President, and article V of this Constitution, the District constituting the seat of government of the United States shall be treated as though it were a State.

2. The exercise of the rights and powers conferred under this article shall be by the people of the District constituting the seat of government, and as shall be provided by the Congress.

3. The twenty-third article of amendment to the Constitution of the United States is hereby repealed.

4. This article shall be inoperative, unless it shall have been ratified as an amendment to the Constitution by the legislatures of three-fourths of the several States within seven years from the date of its submission.

Origin of the Constitution

The War of Independence was conducted by delegates from the original 13 states, called the Congress of the United States of America and generally known as the Continental Congress. In 1777 the Congress submitted to the legislatures of the states the Articles of Confederation and Perpetual Union, which were ratified by New Hampshire, Massachusetts, Rhode Island, Connecticut, New York, New Jersey, Pennsylvania, Delaware, Virginia, North Carolina, South Carolina, and Georgia, and finally, in 1781, by Maryland.

The first article of the instrument read: "The stile of this confederacy shall be the United States of America." This did not signify a sovereign nation, because the states delegated only those powers they could not handle individually, such as power to wage war, establish a uniform currency, make treaties with foreign nations and contract debts for general expenses (such as paying the army). Taxes for the payment of such debts were levied by the individual states. The president under the Articles signed himself "President of the United States in Congress assembled," but here the United States were considered in the plural, a cooperating group. Canada was invited to join the union on equal terms but did not act.

When the war was won it became evident that a stronger federal union was needed to protect the mutual interests of the states. The Congress left the initiative to the legislatures. Virginia in Jan. 1786 appointed commissioners to meet with representatives of other states, with the result that delegates from Virginia, Delaware, New York, New Jersey, and Pennsylvania met at Annapolis. Alexander Hamilton prepared for their call by asking delegates from all states to meet in Philadelphia in May 1787 "to render the Constitution of the Federal government adequate to the exigencies of the union." Congress endorsed the plan Feb. 21, 1787. Delegates were appointed by all states except Rhode Island.

The convention met May 14, 1787. George Washington was chosen president (presiding officer). The states certified 65 delegates, but 10 did not attend. The work was done by 55, not all of whom were present at all sessions. Of the 55 attending delegates, 16 failed to sign, and 39 actually signed Sept. 17, 1787, some with reservations. Some historians have said 74 delegates (9 more than the 65 actually certified) were named and 19 failed to attend. These 9 additional persons refused the appointment, were never delegates and never counted as absentees. Washington sent the Constitution to Congress with a covering letter and that body, Sept. 28, 1787, ordered it sent to the legislatures, "in order to be submitted to a convention of delegates chosen in each state by the people thereof."

The Constitution was ratified by votes of state conventions as follows: Delaware, Dec. 7, 1787, unanimous; Pennsylvania, Dec. 12, 1787, 43 to 23; New Jersey, Dec. 18, 1787, unanimous; Georgia, Jan 2, 1788, unanimous; Connecticut, Jan. 9, 1788, 128 to 40; Massachusetts, Feb. 6, 1788, 187 to 168; Maryland, Apr. 28, 1788, 63 to 11; South Carolina, May 23, 1788, 149 to 73; New Hampshire, June 21, 1788, 57 to 46; Virginia, June 26, 1788, 89 to 79; New York, July 26, 1788, 30 to 27. Nine states were needed to establish the operation of the Constitution "between the states so ratifying the same" and New Hampshire was the 9th state. The government did not declare the Constitution in effect until the first Wednesday in Mar. 1789 which was Mar. 4. After that North Carolina ratified it Nov. 21, 1789, 194 to 77; and Rhode Island, May 29, 1790, 34 to 32. Vermont in convention ratified it Jan. 10, 1791, and by act of Congress approved Feb. 18, 1791, was admitted into the Union as the 14th state, Mar. 4, 1791.

How the Declaration of Independence Was Adopted

On June 7, 1776, Richard Henry Lee, who had issued the first call for a congress of the colonies, introduced in the Continental Congress at Philadelphia a resolution declaring "that these United Colonies are, and of right ought to be, free and independent states, that they are absolved from all allegiance to the British Crown, and that all political connection between them and the state of Great Britain is, and ought to be, totally dissolved."

The resolution, seconded by John Adams on behalf of the Massachusetts delegation, came up again June 10 when a committee of 5, headed by Thomas Jefferson, was appointed to express the purpose of the resolution in a declaration of independence. The others on the committee were John Adams, Benjamin Franklin, Robert R. Livingston, and Roger Sherman.

Drafting the Declaration was assigned to Jefferson, who worked on a portable desk of his own construction in a room at Market and 7th Sts. The committee reported the result June 28, 1776. The members of the Congress suggested a number of changes, which Jefferson called "deplorable." They didn't approve Jefferson's arraignment of the British people and King George III for encouraging and fostering the slave trade, which Jefferson called "an execrable commerce." They made 86 changes, eliminating 480 words and leaving 1,337. In the final form capitalization was erratic. Jefferson had written that men were endowed with "inalienable" rights; in the final copy it came out as "unalienable" and has been thus ever since.

The Lee-Adams resolution of independence was adopted by 12 yeas July 2 — the actual date of the act of independence. The Declaration, which explains the act, was adopted July 4, in the evening.

After the Declaration was adopted, July 4, 1776, it was turned over to John Dunlap, printer, to be printed on broadsides. The original copy was lost and one of his broadsides was attached to a page in the journal of the Congress. It was read aloud July 8 in Philadelphia, Easton, Pa., and Trenton, N.J. On July 9 at 6 p.m. it was read by order of Gen. George Washington to the troops assembled on the Common in New York City (City Hall Park).

The Continental Congress of July 19, 1776, adopted the following resolution:

"Resolved, That the Declaration passed on the 4th, be fairly engrossed on parchment with the title and stile of 'The Unanimous Declaration of the thirteen United States of America' and that the same, when engrossed, be signed by every member of Congress."

Not all delegates who signed the engrossed Declaration were present on July 4. Robert Morris (Pa.), William Williams (Conn.) and Samuel Chase (Md.) signed on Aug. 2, Oliver Wolcott (Conn.), George Wythe (Va.), Richard Henry Lee (Va.) and Elbridge Gerry (Mass.) signed in August and September, Matthew Thornton (N. H.) joined the Congress Nov. 4 and signed later. Thomas McKean (Del.) rejoined Washington's Army before signing and said later that he signed in 1781.

Charles Carroll of Carrollton was appointed a delegate by Maryland on July 4, 1776, presented his credentials July 18, and signed the engrossed Declaration Aug. 2. Born Sept. 19, 1737, he was 95 years old and the last surviving signer when he died Nov. 14, 1832.

Two Pennsylvania delegates who did not support the Declaration on July 4 were replaced.

The 4 New York delegates did not have authority from their state to vote on July 4. On July 9 the New York state convention authorized its delegates to approve the Declaration and the Congress was so notified on July 15, 1776. The 4 signed the Declaration on Aug. 2.

The original engrossed Declaration is preserved in the National Archives Building in Washington.

The Liberty Bell: Its History and Significance

The Liberty Bell, in Independence Hall, Philadelphia, is an object of great reverence to Americans because of its association with the historic events of the War of Independence.

The original Province bell, ordered to commemorate the 50th anniversary of the Commonwealth of Pennsylvania, was cast by Thomas Lister, Whitechapel, London, and reached Philadelphia in Aug. 1752. It bore an inscription from Leviticus XXV, 10: "Proclaim liberty throughout all the land unto all the inhabitants thereof."

The bell was cracked by a stroke of its clapper in Sept. 1752 while it hung on a truss in the State House yard for testing. Pass & Stow, Philadelphia founders, recast the bell, adding 1 1/2 ounces of copper to a pound of the original metal to reduce brittleness. It was found that the bell contained too much copper, injuring its tone, so Pass & Stow recast it again, this time successfully.

In June 1753 the bell was hung in the wooden steeple of the State House, erected on top of the brick tower. In use while the Continental Congress was in session in the State House, it rang out in defiance of British tax and trade restrictions, and proclaimed the Boston Tea Party and the first public reading of the Declaration of Independence.

On Sept. 18, 1777, when the British Army was about to occupy Philadelphia, the bell was moved in a baggage train of the American Army to Allentown, Pa. where it was hidden in the Zion Reformed Church until June 27, 1778. It was moved back to Philadelphia after the British left.

In July 1781 the wooden steeple became insecure and had to be taken down. The bell was lowered into the brick section of the tower. Here it was hanging in July, 1835, when it cracked while tolling for the funeral of John Marshall, chief justice of the United States. Because of its association with the War of Independence it was not recast but remained mute in this location until 1846, the year of the Mexican War, when it was placed on exhibition in the Declaration Chamber of Independence Hall.

In 1876, when many thousands of Americans visited Philadelphia for the Centennial Exposition, it was placed in its old walnut frame in the tower hallway. In 1877 it was hung from the ceiling of the tower by a chain of 13 links. It was returned again to the Declaration Chamber and in 1896 taken back to the tower hall, where it occupied a glass case. In 1915 the case was removed so that the public might touch it. On Jan. 1, 1976, just after midnight to mark the opening of the Bicentennial Year, the bell was moved to a new glass and steel pavilion behind Independence Hall for easier viewing by the larger number of visitors expected during the year.

The measurements of the bell follow: circumference around the lip, 12 ft.; circumference around the crown, 7 ft. 6 in.; lip to the crown, 3 ft.; height over the crown, 2 ft. 3 in.; thickness at lip, 3 in.; thickness at crown, 1 1/4 in.; weight, 2080 lbs.; length of clapper, 3 ft. 2 in.; cost, £60 14s 5d.

Confederate States and Secession

The American Civil War, 1861-65, grew out of sectional disputes over the continued existence of slavery in the South and the contention of Southern legislators that the states retained many sovereign rights, including the right to secede from the Union.

The war was not fought by state against state but by one federal regime against another, the Confederate government in Richmond assuming control over the economic, political, and military life of the South, under protest from Georgia and South Carolina.

South Carolina voted an ordinance of secession from the Union, repealing its 1788 ratification of the U.S. Constitution on Dec. 20, 1860, to take effect Dec. 24. Other states seceded in 1861. Their votes in conventions were:

Mississippi, Jan. 9, 84-15; Florida, Jan. 10, 62-7; Alabama, Jan. 11, 61-39; Georgia, Jan. 19, 208-89; Louisiana, Jan. 26, 113-17; Texas, Feb. 1, 166-7, ratified by popular vote Feb. 23 (for 34,794, against 11,325); Virginia, Apr. 17, 88-55, ratified by popular vote May 23 (for 128,884; against 32,134); Arkansas, May 6, 69-1; Tennessee, May 7, ratified by popular vote June 8 (for 104,019, against 47,238); North Carolina, May 21.

Missouri Unionists stopped secession in conventions Feb. 28 and Mar. 9. The legislature condemned secession Mar. 7. Under the protection of Confederate troops, secessionist members of the legislature adopted a resolution of secession at Neosho, Oct. 31. The Confederate Congress seated the secessionists' representatives.

Kentucky did not secede and its government remained Unionist. In a part occupied by Confederate troops, Kentuckians approved secession and the Confederate Congress admitted their representatives.

The Maryland legislature voted against secession Apr. 27, 53-13. Delaware did not secede. Western Virginia held conventions at Wheeling, named a pro-Union governor June 11, 1861; admitted to Union as West Virginia June 30, 1863; its constitution provided for gradual abolition of slavery.

Confederate Government

Forty-two delegates from South Carolina, Georgia, Alabama, Mississippi, Louisiana, and Florida met in convention at Montgomery, Ala., Feb. 4, 1861. They adopted a provisional constitution of the Confederate States of America, and elected Jefferson Davis (Miss.) provisional president, and Alexander H. Stephens (Ga.) provisional vice president.

A permanent constitution was adopted Mar. 11; it abolished the African slave trade. The Congress moved to Richmond, Va. July 20. Davis was elected president in October, and was inaugurated Feb. 22, 1862.

The Congress adopted a flag, consisting of a red field with a white stripe, and a blue jack with a circle of white stars. Later the more popular flag was the red field with blue diagonal cross bars that held 13 white stars. The stars represented the 11 states actually in the Confederacy plus Kentucky and Missouri.

(*See also Civil War, U.S., in Index*)

Lincoln's Address at Gettysburg, 1863

Fourscore and seven years ago our fathers brought forth on this continent a new nation, conceived in liberty and dedicated to the proposition that all men are created equal.

Now we are engaged in a great civil war, testing whether that nation or any nation so conceived and so dedicated can long endure. We are met on a great battle field of that war. We have come to dedicate a portion of that field, as a final resting-place for those who here gave their lives that that nation might live. It is altogether fitting and proper that we should do this.

But, in a larger sense, we can not dedicate — we can not consecrate — we can not hallow — this ground. The brave men, living and dead, who struggled here, have consecrated it, far above our poor power to add or detract. The world will little note, nor long remember, what we say here, but it can never forget what they did here. It is for us the living, rather, to be dedicated here to the unfinished work which they who fought here have thus far so nobly advanced. It is rather for us to be here dedicated to the great task remaining before us — that from these honored dead we take increased devotion to that cause for which they gave the last full measure of devotion — that we here highly resolve that these dead shall not have died in vain — that this nation, under God, shall have a new birth of freedom — and that government of the people, by the people, for the people, shall not perish from the earth.

History of the Address

President Lincoln delivered his address at the dedication of the military cemetery at Gettysburg, Pa., Nov. 19, 1863. The battle had been fought July 1-3, 1863. He was preceded by Edward Everett, former president of Harvard, secretary of state and senator from Massachusetts, then 69 and one of the nation's great orators. Everett gave a full resume of the battle, Lincoln's speech was so short that the photographer did not get his camera adjusted in time. The report that newspapers ignored Lincoln's address is not entirely accurate; Everett's address swamped their columns, but the greatness of Lincoln's speech was immediately recognized. Everett wrote him: "I should be glad if I could flatter myself that I came as near the central idea of the occasion in 2 hours as you did in 2 minutes."

Five copies of the Gettysburg address in Lincoln's hand are extant. The first and 2d drafts, prepared in Washington and Gettysburg just before delivery, are in the Library of Congress. The 3d draft, written at the request of Everett to be sold at a fair in New York for the benefit of soldiers, was given the Illinois State Historical Library by popular subscription.

The 4th copy was written out by Lincoln for George Bancroft, the historian, and remained in custody of the Bancroft family until 1929, when it was acquired by Mrs. Nicholas H. Noyes, of Indianapolis, Ind. In 1949 Mrs. Noyes presented this copy to the Cornell University Library, Ithaca, N.Y. The 5th copy, usually described as the clearest and best, was also written by Lincoln for George Bancroft. It is in the Lincoln Room of the White House, where it was placed in Mar. 1959. Lincoln's spelling of battle field and can not as separated words in that version is reproduced above.

The National Anthem — The Star-Spangled Banner

The Star-Spangled Banner was ordered played by the military and naval services by President Woodrow Wilson in 1916. It was designated the National Anthem by Act of Congress, Mar. 3, 1931. It was written by Francis Scott Key, of Georgetown, D. C., during the bombardment of Fort McHenry, Baltimore, Md., Sept. 13-14, 1814. Key was a lawyer, a graduate of St. John's College, Annapolis, and a volunteer in a light artillery company. When a friend, Dr. Beanes, a physician of Upper Marlborough, Md., was taken aboard Admiral Cockburn's British squadron for interfering with ground troops, Key and J. S. Skinner, carrying a note from President Madison, went to the fleet under a flag of truce on a cartel ship to ask Beanes' release. Admiral Cockburn consented, but as the fleet was about to sail up the Patapsco to bombard Fort McHenry he detained them, first on H. M. S. Surprise, and then on a supply ship.

Key witnessed the bombardment from his own vessel. It began at 7 a.m., Sept. 13, 1814, and lasted, with intermissions, for 25 hours. The British fired over 1,500 shells, each weighing as much as 220 lbs. They were unable to approach closely because the Americans had sunk 22 vessels in the channel. Only four Americans were killed and 24 wounded. A British bomb-ship was disabled.

During the bombardment Key wrote a stanza on the back of an envelope. Next day at Indian Queen Inn, Baltimore, he wrote out the poem and gave it to his brother-in-law, Judge J. H. Nicholson. Nicholson suggested the tune, Anacreon in Heaven, and had the poem printed on broadsides, of which two survive. On Sept. 20 it appeared in the "Baltimore American." Later Key made 3 copies; one is in the Library of Congress and one in the Pennsylvania Historical Society.

The copy that Key wrote in his hotel Sept. 14, 1814, remained in the Nicholson family for 93 years. In 1907 it was sold to Henry Walters of Baltimore. In 1934 it was bought at auction in New York from the Walters estate by the Walters Art Gallery, Baltimore, for $26,400. The Walters Gallery in 1953 sold the manuscript to the Maryland Historical Society for the same price.

The flag that Key saw during the bombardment is preserved in the Smithsonian Institution, Washington. It is 30 by 42 ft., and has 15 alternate red and white stripes and 15 stars, for the original 13 states plus Kentucky and Vermont.

It was made by Mary Young Pickersgill. The Baltimore Flag House, a museum, occupies her premises, which were restored in 1953.

The Star-Spangled Banner

I

Oh, say can you see by the dawn's early light
What so proudly we hailed at the twilight's last gleaming?
Whose broad stripes and bright stars thru the perilous fight,
O'er the ramparts we watched were so gallantly streaming?
And the rocket's red glare, the bomb bursting in air,
Gave proof through the night that our flag was still there.
Oh, say does that star-spangled banner yet wave
O'er the land of the free and the home of the brave?

II

On the shore, dimly seen through the mists of the deep,
Where the foe's haughty host in dread silence reposes,
What is that which the breeze, o'er the towering steep,
As it fitfully blows, half conceals, half discloses?
Now it catches the gleam of the morning's first beam,
In full glory reflected now shines in the stream:
'Tis the star-spangled banner! Oh long may it wave
O'er the land of the free and the home of the brave!

III

And where is that band who so vauntingly swore
That the havoc of war and the battle's confusion,
A home and a country should leave us no more!
Their blood has washed out their foul footsteps' pollution.
No refuge could save the hireling and slave
From the terror of flight, or the gloom of the grave:
And the star-spangled banner in triumph doth wave
O'er the land of the free and the home of the brave!

IV

Oh! thus be it ever, when freemen shall stand
Between their loved home and the war's desolation!
Blest with victory and peace, may the heav'n rescued land
Praise the Power that hath made and preserved us a nation.
Then conquer we must, when our cause it is just,
And this be our motto: "In God is our trust."
And the star-spangled banner in triumph shall wave
O'er the land of the free and the home of the brave!

Statue of Liberty National Monument

Since 1886, the Statue of Liberty Enlightening the World has stood as a symbol of freedom in New York harbor. It also commemorates French-American friendship for it was given by the people of France, designed by Frederic Auguste Bartholdi (1834-1904). A $2.5 million building housing the American Museum of Immigration was opened by Pres. Nixon Sept. 26, 1972, at the base of the statue. It houses a permanent exhibition of photos, posters, and artifacts tracing the history of American immigration. In addition, there is a small immigration library. The Monument is administered by the National Park Service.

Nearby Ellis Island, gateway to America for more than 12 million immigrants between 1892 and 1954, was proclaimed part of the National Monument in 1965 by Pres. Johnson. It can be visited between May and October.

Edouard de Laboulaye, French historian and admirer of American political institutions, suggested that the French present a monument to the United States, the latter to provide pedestal and site. Bartholdi visualized a colossal statue at the entrance of New York harbor, welcoming the peoples of the world with the torch of liberty.

The French approved the idea and formed the Franco-American Union to raise funds, which eventually reached $250,000. Bartholdi began work about 1874 in Paris.

On Washington's birthday, Feb. 22, 1877, Congress approved the use of a site on Bedloe's Island suggested by Bartholdi. This island of 12 acres had been owned in the 17th century by a Walloon named Isaac Bedloe. It was called Bedloe's until Aug. 3, 1956, when Pres. Eisenhower approved a resolution of Congress changing the name to Liberty Island.

The statue was finished May 21, 1884, and formally presented to U.S. Minister Morton July 4, 1884, by Ferdinand de Lesseps, head of the Franco-American Union, promoter of the Panama Canal, and builder of the Suez Canal.

On Aug. 5, 1884, the Americans laid the cornerstone for the pedestal. This was to be built on the foundations of Fort Wood, which had been erected by the Government in 1811. The American committee had raised $125,000, but this was found to be inadequate. Joseph Pulitzer, owner of the New York World, appealed on Mar. 16, 1885, for general donations. By Aug. 11, 1885, he had raised $100,000.

The statue arrived dismantled, in 214 packing cases, from Rouen, France, in June, 1885: The last rivet of the statue was driven Oct. 28, 1886, when Pres. Grover Cleveland dedicated the monument.

The statue weighs 450,000 lbs. or 225 tons. The copper sheeting weighs 200,000 lbs. There are 167 steps from the land level to the top of the pedestal, 168 steps inside the statue to the head, and 54 rungs on the ladder leading to the arm that holds the torch.

Dimensions of the Statue	Ft.	In.
Height from base to torch (45.3 meters)	151	1
Foundation of pedestal to torch (91.5 meters)	305	1
Heel to top of head	111	1
Length of hand	16	5
Index finger	8	0
Circumference at second joint	3	6
Size of finger nail	13x10 in.	
Head from chin to cranium	17	3
Head thickness from ear to ear	10	0
Distance across the eye	2	6
Length of nose	4	6
Right arm, length	42	0
Right arm, greatest thickness	12	0
Thickness of waist	35	0
Width of mouth	3	0
Tablet, length	23	7
Tablet, width	13	7
Tablet, thickness	2	0

Emma Lazarus' Famous Poem

A poem by Emma Lazarus is graven on a tablet within the pedestal on which the statue stands.

The New Colossus

Not like the brazen giant of Greek fame,
With conquering limbs astride from land to land;
Here at our sea-washed, sunset gates shall stand
A mighty woman with a torch, whose flame
Is the imprisoned lightning, and her name
Mother of Exiles. From her beacon-hand
Glows world-wide welcome; her mild eyes command
The air-bridged harbor that twin cities frame.
"Keep ancient lands, your storied pomp!" cries she
With silent lips. "Give me your tired, your poor,
Your huddled masses yearning to breathe free,
The wretched refuse of your teeming shore.
Send these, the homeless, tempest-tost to me,
I lift my lamp beside the golden door!"

Forms of Address for Persons of Rank and Public Office

In these examples John Smith is used as a representative American name. The salutation Dear Sir or Dear Madam is always permissible when addressing a person not known to the writer.

President of the United States

Address: The President, The White House, Washington, DC 20500. Also, The President and Mrs. ___.

Salutation: Dear Sir or Mr. President or Dear Mr. President. More intimately: My dear Mr. President. Also: Dear Mr. President and Mrs. ___

The vice president takes the same forms.

Cabinet Officers

Address: Mr. John Smith, Secretary of State, Washington, D.C. or The Hon. John Smith. Similar addresses for other members of the cabinet. Also: Secretary and Mrs. John Smith.

Salutation: Dear Sir, or Dear Mr. Secretary. Also: Dear Mr. and Mrs. Smith.

The Bench

Address: The Hon. John Smith, Chief Justice of the United States. The Hon. John Smith, Associate Justice of the Supreme Court of the United States. The Hon. John Smith, Associate Judge, U.S. District Court.

Salutation: Dear Sir, or Dear Mr. Chief Justice. Dear Mr. Justice. Dear Judge Smith.

Members of Congress

Address: The Hon. John Smith, United States Senate, Washington, DC 20510, or Sen. John Smith, etc. Also The Hon. John Smith, House of Representatives, Washington, DC 20515, or Rep. John Smith, etc.

Salutation: Dear Mr. Senator or Dear Mr. Smith; for Representative, Dear Mr. Smith.

Officers of Armed Forces

Address: Careful attention should be given to the precise rank, thus: General of the Army John Smith, Fleet Admiral John Smith. The rules for Air Force are same as Army.

Salutation: Dear Sir, or Dear General. All general officers, whatever rank, are entitled to be addressed as generals. Likewise a lieutenant colonel is addressed as colonel and first and second lieutenants are addressed as lieutenant.

Warrant officers and flight officers are addressed as Mister. Chaplains are addressed as Chaplain. A Catholic chaplain may be addressed as Father. Cadets of the United States Military Academy and Air Force Academy are addressed as Cadet. Noncommissioned officers are addressed by their titles. In the U. S. Navy all men from midshipman at Annapolis up to and including lieutenant commander are addressed as Mister.

Ambassador, Governor, Mayor

Address: The Hon. John Smith, followed by his or her title. They can be addressed either at their embassy, or at the Department of State, Washington, D.C. An ambassador from a foreign nation may be addressed as His or Her Excellency. An American is not to be so addressed.

Salutation: Dear Mr. or Madam Ambassador. An ambassador from a foreign nation may be called Your Excellency.

Governors and mayors are often addressed as The Hon. Jane Smith, Governor of ______, or The Hon. John Smith, Mayor of ______; also Governor John Smith, State House, Albany, N.Y., or Mayor Jane Smith, City Hall, Erie, Pa.

The Clergy

Address: His Holiness, the Pope, or His Holiness Pope (name), State of Vatican City, Italy.

Salutation: Your Holiness or Most Holy Father.

Also: His Eminence, John, Cardinal Smith; salutation: Your Eminence. An archbishop or a bishop is addressed The Most Reverend, and the salutation is Your Excellency. A monsignor who is a papal chamberlain is The Very Reverend Monsignor and the salutation is Dear Sir or Very Reverend Monsignor; a monsignor who is a domestic prelate is The Right Reverend Monsignor and salutation is Right Reverend Monsignor. A priest is addressed Reverend John Smith. A brother of an order is addressed Brother —. A sister takes the same form.

A bishop of the Protestant Episcopal Church is The Right Reverend John Smith; salutation is Right Reverend Sir, or Dear Bishop Smith. If a clergyman is a doctor of divinity, he is addressed: The Reverend John Smith, D.D., and the salutation is Reverend Sir, or Dear Dr. Smith. When a clergyman does not have the degree the salutation is Dear Mr. Smith.

A bishop of the Methodist Church is addressed Bishop John Smith with titles following.

Royalty and Nobility

An emperor is to be addressed in a letter as Sir, or Your Imperial Majesty.

A king or queen is addressed as His Majesty (Name), King of (Name), or Her Majesty (Name), Queen of (Name). Salutation: Sir, or Madam, or May it please Your Majesty.

Princes and princesses and other persons of royal blood are addressed as His (or Her) Royal Highness, and saluted with May it please Your Royal Highness.

A duke or marquis is My Lord Duke (or Marquis), a duke is His (or Your) Grace.

Code of Etiquette for Display and Use of the U.S. Flag

Although the Stars and Stripes originated in 1777, it was not until 146 years later that there was a serious attempt to establish a uniform code of etiquette for the U.S. flag. The War Department issued Feb. 15, 1923, a circular on the rules of flag usage. These were adopted almost in their entirety June 14, 1923, by a conference of 68 patriotic organizations in Washington. Finally, on June 22, 1942, a joint resolution of Congress, amended by Public Law 94-344 July 7, 1976, codified "existing rules and customs pertaining to the display and use of the flag. . ."

When to Display the Flag—The flag should be displayed on all days, especially on legal holidays and other special occasions, on official buildings when in use, in or near polling places on election days, and in or near schools when in session. A citizen may fly the flag at any time he wishes. It is customary to display the flag only from sunrise to sunset on buildings and on stationary flagstaffs in the open. However, it may be displayed at night on special occasions, preferably lighted. In Washington, the flag now flies over the White House both day and night. It flies over the Senate wing of the Capitol when the Senate is in session and over the House wing when that body is in session. It flies day and night over the east and west fronts of the Capitol, without floodlights at night but receiving light from the illuminated Capitol Dome. It flies 24 hours a day at several other places, including the Fort McHenry Nat'l Monument in Baltimore, where it inspired Francis Scott Key to write The Star Spangled Banner.

How to Fly the Flag—The flag should be hoisted briskly and lowered ceremoniously, and should never be allowed to touch the ground or the floor. When hung over a sidewalk from a rope extending from a building to a pole, the union should be away from the building. When hung over the center of a street it should have the union to the north in an east-west street and to the east in a north-south street. No other flag may be flown above or, if on the same level, to the right of the U.S. flag, except that at the United Nations Headquarters the UN flag may be placed above flags of all member nations and other national flags may be flown with equal prominence or honor with the flag of the U.S. At services by Navy chaplains at sea, the church pennant may be flown above the flag.

When two flags are placed against a wall with crossed staffs, the U.S. flag should be at right—its own right, and its staff should be in front of the staff of the other flag; when a number of flags are grouped and displayed from staffs, it should be at the center and highest point of the group.

Church and Platform Use—In an auditorium, the flag may be displayed flat, above and behind the speaker. When displayed from a staff in a church or public auditorium, the flag should hold the position of superior prominence, in advance of the audience, and in the position of honor at the clergyman's or speaker's right as he faces the audience. Any other flag so displayed should be placed on the left of the clergyman or speaker or to the right of the audience.

When the flag is displayed horizontally or vertically against a wall, the stars should be uppermost and at the observer's left.

When to Salute the Flag—All persons present should face the flag, stand at attention and salute on the following occasions: (1) When the flag is passing in a parade or in a review, (2) During the ceremony of hoisting or lowering, (3) When the National Anthem is played, and (4) During the Pledge of Allegiance. Those present in uniform should render the military salute. When not in uniform, men should remove the hat with the right hand holding it at the left shoulder, the hand being over the heart. Men without hats should salute in the same manner. Aliens should stand at attention. Women should salute by placing the right hand over the heart.

On Memorial Day, the flag should fly at half-staff until noon, then be raised to the peak.

As provided by Presidential proclamation the flag should fly at half-staff for 30 days from the day of death of a president or former president; for 10 days from the day of death of a vice president, chief justice or retired chief justice of the U.S., or speaker of the House of Representatives; from day of death until burial of an associate justice of the Supreme Court, cabinet member, former vice president, or Senate president pro tempore, majority or minority Senate leader, or majority or minority House leader; for a U.S. senator, representative, territorial delegate, or the resident commissioner of Puerto Rico, on day of death and the following day within the metropolitan area of the District of Columbia and from day of death until burial within the decedent's state, congressional district, territory or commonwealth; and for the death of the governor of a state, territory, or possession of the U.S., from day of death until burial within that state, territory, or possession.

When used to cover a casket, the flag should be placed so that the union is at the head and over the left shoulder. It should not be lowered into the grave nor touch the ground.

Prohibited Uses of the Flag—The flag should not be dipped to any person or thing. It should never be displayed with the union down save as a distress signal. It should never be carried flat or horizontally, but always aloft and free.

It should not be displayed on a float, motor car or boat except from a staff.

It should never be used as a covering for a ceiling, nor have placed upon it any word, design, or drawing. It should never be used as a receptacle for carrying anything. It should not be used to cover a statue or a monument.

The flag should never be used for advertising purposes, nor be embroidered on such articles as cushions or hankerchiefs, printed or otherwise impressed on boxes or used as a costume or athletic uniform. Advertising signs should not be fastened to its staff or halyard.

The flag should never be used as drapery of any sort, never festooned, drawn back, nor up, in folds, but always allowed to fall free. Bunting of blue, white and red always arranged with the blue above and the white in the middle, should be used for covering a speaker's desk, draping the front of a platform, and for decoration in general.

An Act of Congress approved Feb. 8, 1917, provided certain penalties for the desecration, mutilation or improper use of the flag within the District of Columbia. A 1968 federal law provided penalties of up to a year's imprisonment or a $1,000 fine or both, for publicly burning or otherwise desecrating any flag of the United States. In addition, many states have laws against flag desecration.

How to Dispose of Worn Flags—The flag, when it is in such condition that it is no longer a fitting emblem for display, should be destroyed in a dignified way, preferably by burning in private.

Pledge of Allegiance to the Flag

I pledge allegiance to the flag of the United States of America and to the republic for which it stands, one nation under God, indivisible, with liberty and justice for all.

This, the current official version of the Pledge of Allegiance, has developed from the original pledge, which was first published in the Sept. 8, 1892, issue of the Youth's Companion, a weekly magazine then published in Boston. The original pledge contained the phrase "my flag," which was changed more than 30 years later to "flag of the United States of America." An act of Congress in 1954 added the words "under God."

The authorship of the pledge has been in dispute for many years. The Youth's Companion stated in 1917 that the original draft was written by James B. Upham, an executive of the magazine who died in 1910. A leaflet circulated by the magazine later named Upham as the originator of the draft "afterwards condensed and perfected by him and his associates of the Companion force."

Francis Bellamy, a former member of the Youth's Companion editorial staff, publicly claimed authorship of the pledge in 1923. The United States Flag Assn., acting on the advice of a committee named to study the controversy, upheld in 1939 the claim of Bellamy, who had died 8 years earlier. The Library of Congress issued in 1957 a report attributing the authorship to Bellamy.

The Flag of the U.S.—The Stars and Stripes

The 50-star flag of the United States was raised for the first time officially at 12:01 a.m. on July 4, 1960, at Fort McHenry National Monument in Baltimore, Md. The 50th star had been added for Hawaii; a year earlier the 49th, for Alaska. Before that, no star had been added since 1912, when N.M. and Ariz. were admitted to the Union.

History of the Flag

The true history of the Stars and Stripes has become so cluttered by a volume of myth and tradition that the facts are difficult, and in some cases impossible, to establish. For example, it is not certain who designed the Stars and Stripes, who made the first such flag, or even whether it ever flew in any sea fight or land battle of the American Revolution.

One thing all agree on is that the Stars and Stripes originated as the result of a resolution offered by the Marine Committee of the Second Continental Congress at Philadelphia and adopted June 14, 1777. It read:

Resolved: that the flag of the United States be thirteen stripes, alternate red and white; that the union be thirteen stars, white in a blue field, representing a new constellation.

Congress gave no hint as to the designer of the flag, no instructions as to the arrangement of the stars, and no information on its appropriate uses. Historians have been unable to find the original flag law.

The resolution establishing the flag was not even published until Sept. 2, 1777. Despite repeated requests, Washington did not get the flags until 1783, after the Revolutionary War was over. And there is no certainty that they were the Stars and Stripes.

Early Flags

Although it was never officially adopted by the Continental Congress, many historians consider the first flag of the United States to have been the Grand Union (sometimes called Great Union) flag. This was a modification of the British Meteor flag, which had the red cross of St. George and the white cross of St. Andrew combined in the blue canton. For the Grand Union flag, 6 horizontal stripes were imposed on the red field, dividing it into 13 alternate red and white stripes. On Jan. 1, 1776, when the Continental Army came into formal existence, this flag was unfurled on Prospect Hill, Somerville, Mass. Washington wrote that "we hoisted the Union Flag in compliment to the United Colonies."

One of several flags about which controversy has raged for years is at Easton, Pa. Containing the devices of the national flag in reversed order, this has been in the public library at Easton for over 150 years. Some contend that this flag was actually the first Stars and Stripes, first displayed on July 8, 1776. This flag has 13 red and white stripes in the canton, 13 white stars centered in a blue field.

A flag was hastily improvised from garments by the defenders of Fort Schuyler at Rome, N.Y., Aug. 3-22, 1777. Historians believe it was the Grand Union Flag.

The Sons of Liberty had a flag of 9 red and white stripes, to signify 9 colonies, when they met in New York in 1765 to oppose the Stamp Tax. By 1775, the flag had grown to 13 red and white stripes, with a rattlesnake on it.

At Concord, Apr. 19, 1775, the minute men from Bedford, Mass., are said to have carried a flag having a silver arm with sword on a red field.

At Cambridge, Mass., the Sons of Liberty used a plain red flag with a green pine tree on it.

In June 1775, Washington went from Philadelphia to Boston to take command of the army, escorted to New York by the Philadelphia Light Horse Troop. It carried a yellow flag which had an elaborate coat of arms — the shield charged with 13 knots, the motto "For These We Strive" — and a canton of 13 blue and silver stripes.

In Feb., 1776, Col. Christopher Gadsden, member of the Continental Congress, gave the South Carolina Provincial Congress a flag "such as is to be used by the commander-in-chief of the American Navy." It had a yellow field, with a rattlesnake about to strike and the words "Don't Tread on Me."

At the battle of Bennington, Aug. 16, 1777, patriots used a flag of 7 white and 6 red stripes with a blue canton extending down 9 stripes and showing an arch of 11 white stars over the figure 76 and a star in each of the upper corners. The stars are seven-pointed. This flag is preserved in the Historical Museum at Bennington, Vt.

At the Battle of Cowpens, Jan. 17, 1781, the 3d Maryland Regt. is said to have carried a flag of 13 red and white stripes, with a blue canton containing 12 stars in a circle around one star.

Legends about the Flag

Who Designed the Flag? No one knows for a certainty. Francis Hopkinson, designer of a naval flag, declared he also had designed the flag and in 1781 asked Congress to reimburse him for his services. Congress did not do so. Dumas Malone of Columbia Univ. wrote: "This talented man . . . designed the American flag."

Who Called the Flag Old Glory? — The flag is said to have been named Old Glory by William Driver, a sea captain of Salem, Mass. One legend has it that when he raised the flag on his brig, the Charles Doggett, in 1824, he said: "I name thee Old Glory." But his daughter, who presented the flag to the Smithsonian Institution, said he named it at his 21st birthday celebration Mar. 17, 1824, when his mother presented the homemade flag to him.

The Betsy Ross Legend — The widely publicized legend that Mrs. Betsy Ross made the first Stars and Stripes in June 1776, at the request of a committee composed of George Washington, Robert Morris, and George Ross, an uncle, was first made public in 1870, by a grandson of Mrs. Ross. Historians have been unable to find a historical record of such a meeting or committee.

Adding New Stars

The flag of 1777 was used until 1795. Then, on the admission of Vermont and Kentucky to the Union, Congress passed and Pres. Washington signed an act that after May 1, 1795, the flag should have 15 stripes, alternate red and white, and 15 white stars on a blue field in the union.

When new states were admitted it became evident that the flag would become burdened with stripes. Congress thereupon ordered that after July 4, 1818, the flag should have 13 stripes, symbolizing the 13 original states; that the union have 20 stars, and that whenever a new state was admitted a new star should be added on the July 4 following admission. No law designates the permanent arrangement of the stars. However, since 1912 when a new state has been admitted, the new design has been announced by executive order. No star is specifically identified with any state.

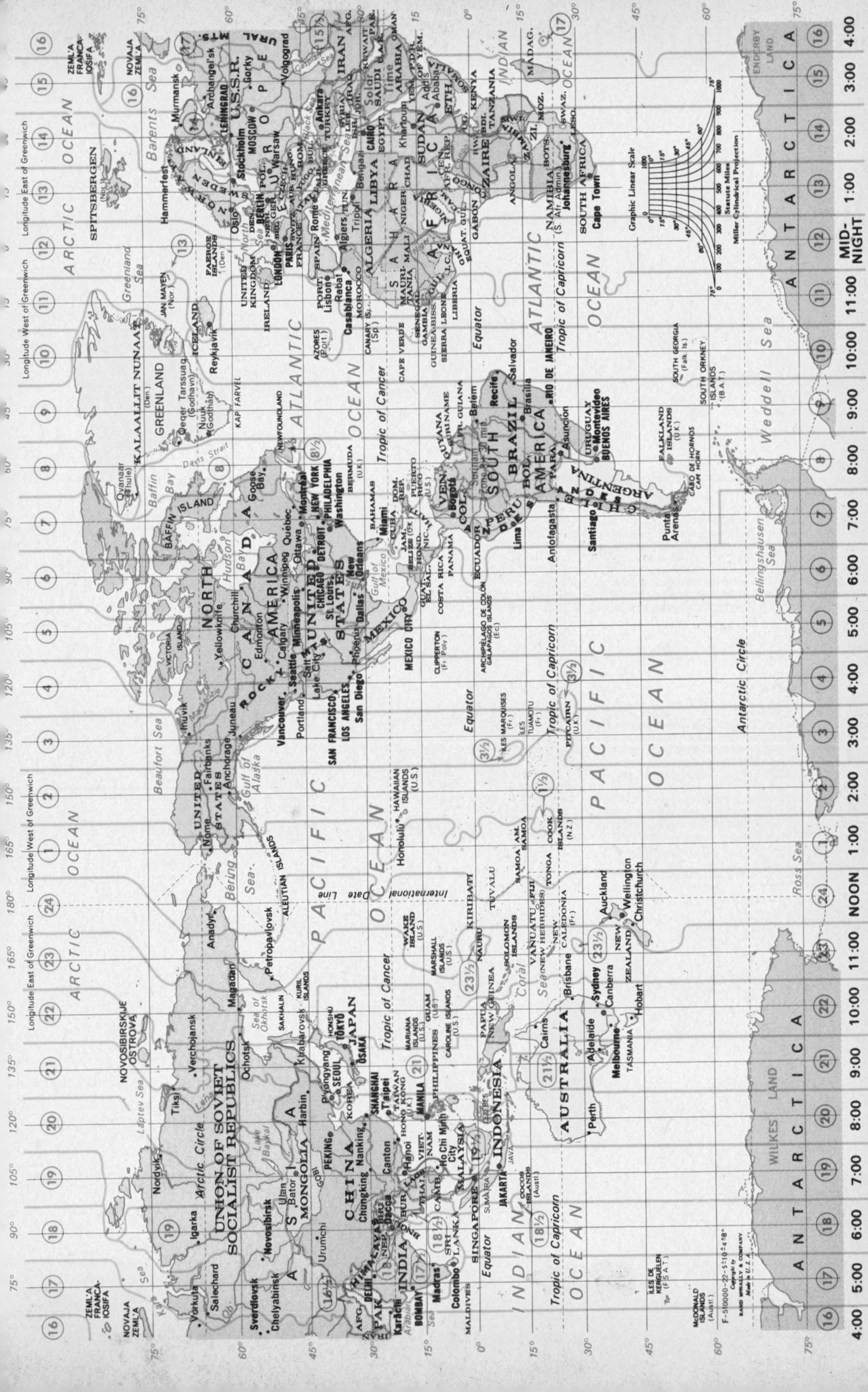
4:00
5:00
6:00
7:00
8:00
9:00
10:00
11:00
NOON
1:00
2:00
3:00
4:00
5:00
6:00
7:00
8:00
9:00
10:00
11:00
MID-NIGHT
1:00
2:00
3:00
4:00
Longitude East of Greenwich
Longitude West of Greenwich
ARCTIC OCEAN
PACIFIC OCEAN
ATLANTIC OCEAN
INDIAN OCEAN
NORTH AMERICA
SOUTH AMERICA
AFRICA
EUROPE
ASIA
AUSTRALIA
ANTARCTICA
UNION OF SOVIET SOCIALIST REPUBLICS
CHINA
INDIA
JAPAN
INDONESIA
CANADA
UNITED STATES
MEXICO
BRAZIL
ARGENTINA
GREENLAND
KALAALLIT NUNAAT
ICELAND
SPITSBERGEN
Arctic Circle
Tropic of Cancer
Equator
Tropic of Capricorn
Antarctic Circle
International Date Line
Graphic Linear Scale
Statute Miles
Miller Cylindrical Projection
WILKES LAND
ENDERBY LAND
Weddell Sea
Ross Sea
Bellingshausen Sea

INDEX

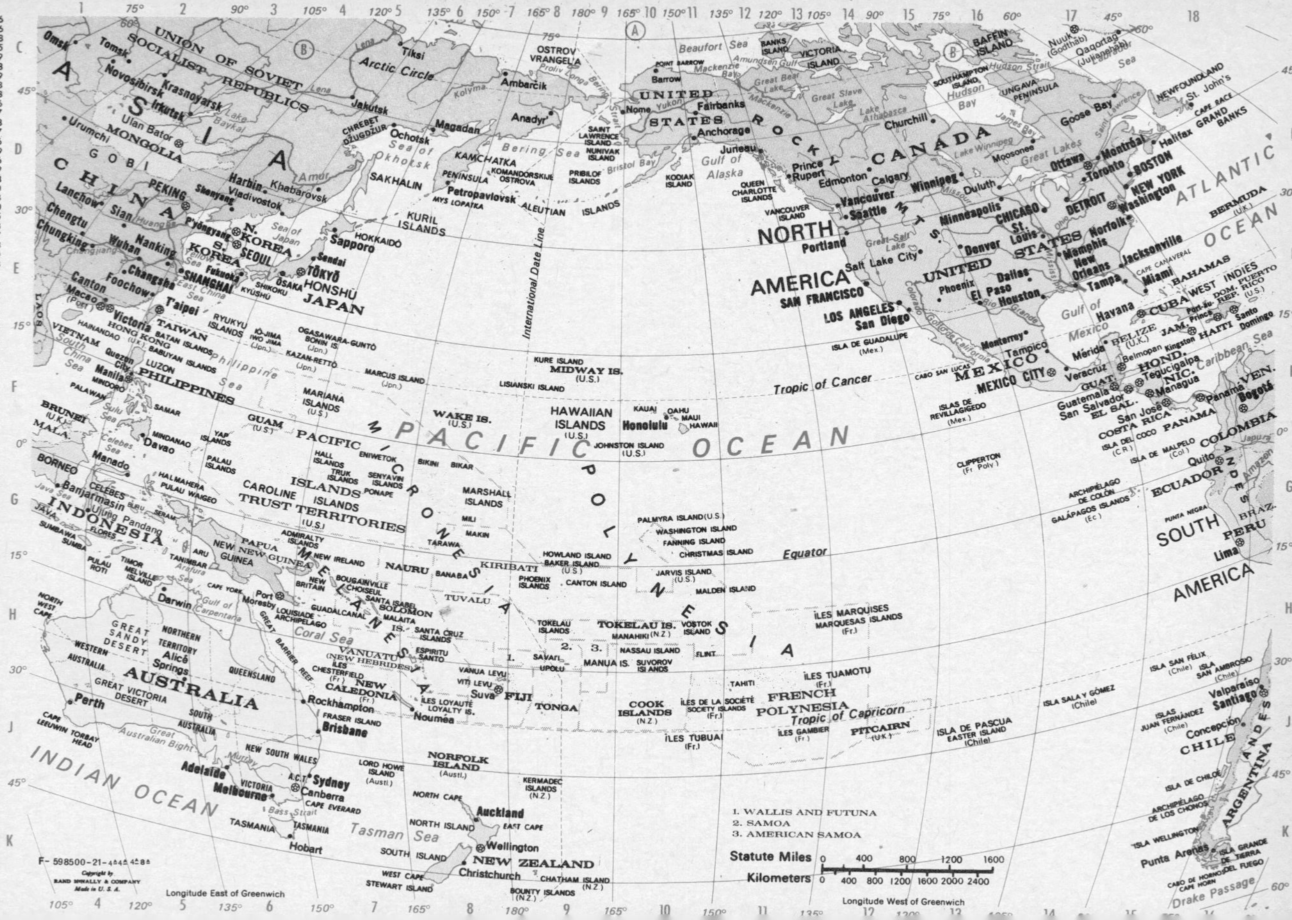
PACIFIC OCEAN
ATLANTIC OCEAN
INDIAN OCEAN
ASIA
UNION OF SOVIET SOCIALIST REPUBLICS
CHINA
MONGOLIA
JAPAN
N. KOREA
S. KOREA
PHILIPPINES
INDONESIA
AUSTRALIA
NEW ZEALAND
NORTH AMERICA
CANADA
UNITED STATES
MEXICO
SOUTH AMERICA
MICRONESIA
MELANESIA
POLYNESIA
International Date Line
Tropic of Cancer
Equator
Tropic of Capricorn
Arctic Circle
HAWAIIAN ISLANDS
Honolulu
MIDWAY IS. (U.S.)
WAKE IS. (U.S.)
GUAM (U.S.)
CAROLINE ISLANDS
PACIFIC ISLANDS TRUST TERRITORIES (U.S.)
MARSHALL ISLANDS
KIRIBATI
TUVALU
NAURU
FIJI
TONGA
COOK ISLANDS (N.Z.)
FRENCH POLYNESIA
PITCAIRN (U.K.)
ISLA DE PASCUA EASTER ISLAND (Chile)
NORFOLK ISLAND (Austl.)
Tasman Sea
Coral Sea
Bering Sea
Sea of Okhotsk
Gulf of Alaska
1. WALLIS AND FUTUNA
2. SAMOA
3. AMERICAN SAMOA
Statute Miles 0 400 800 1200 1600
Kilometers 0 400 800 1200 1600 2000 2400
Longitude East of Greenwich
Longitude West of Greenwich
F-598500-21-4445 4585
Copyright by RAND McNALLY & COMPANY Made in U. S. A.

INDEX

PROVINCES OF CHINA

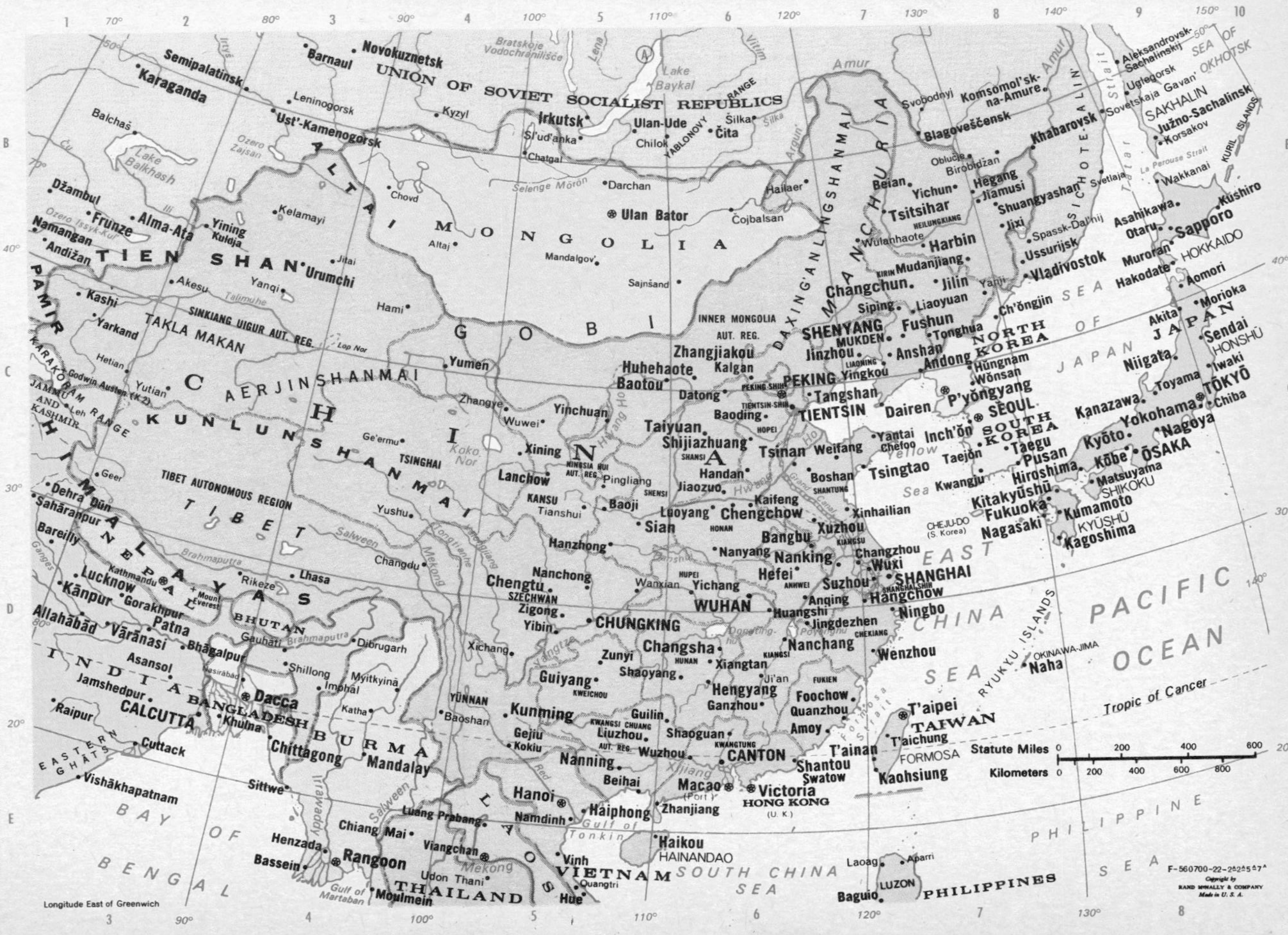

INDEX

MISCELLANEOUS

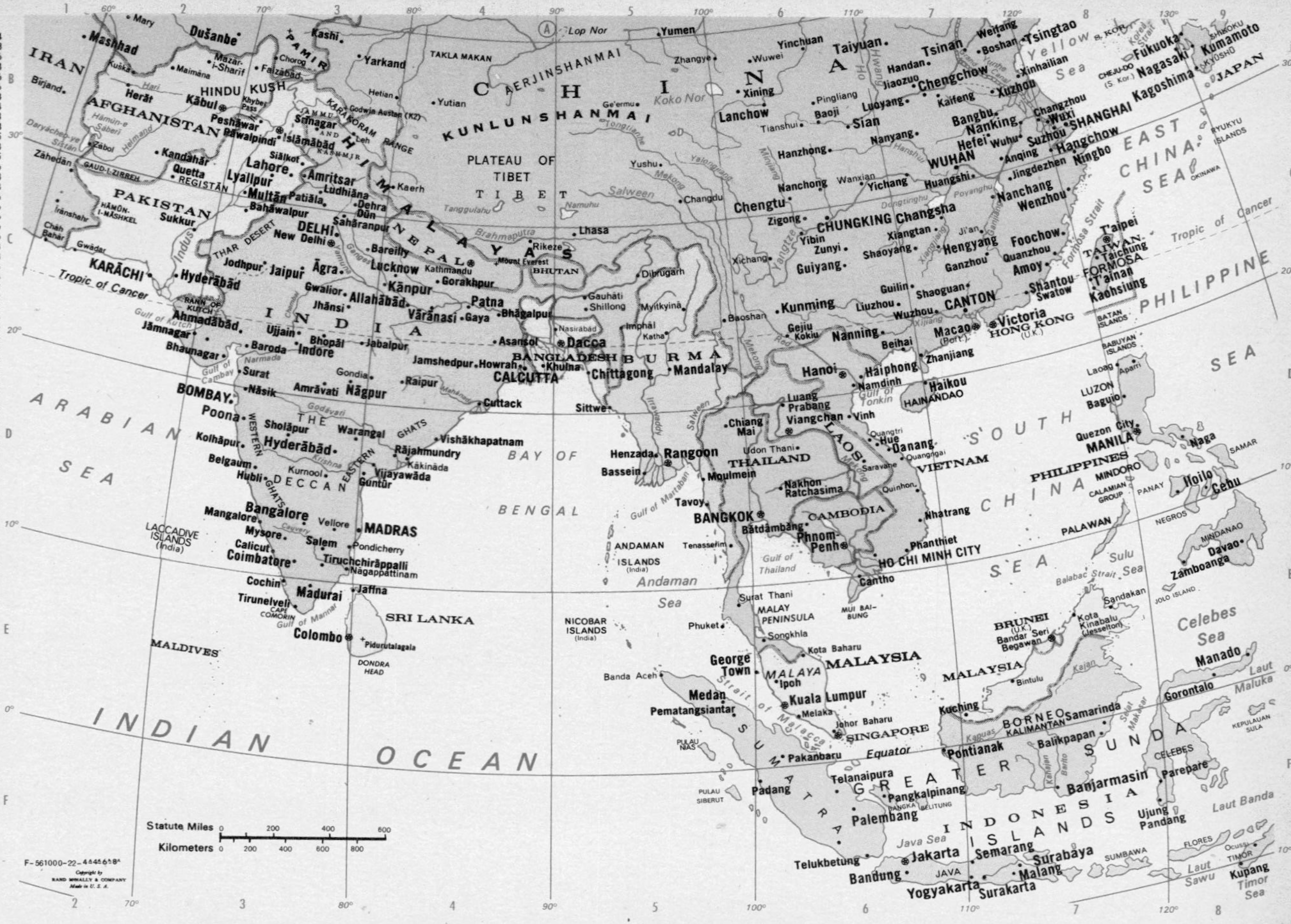

INDEX

ARCTIC OCEAN
UNION OF SOVIET SOCIALIST REPUBLICS
EUROPE
ASIA
AFRICA
CHINA
MONGOLIA
INDIA
INDIAN OCEAN
PACIFIC OCEAN
ARABIAN SEA
Bay of Bengal
SOUTH CHINA SEA
INDONESIA
PHILIPPINES
JAPAN
Longitude West of Greenwich
Longitude East of Greenwich
CONVENTIONAL LIMITS OF THE CONTINENT OF ASIA
Statute Miles 0 300 600 900 1200
Kilometers 0 300 600 900 1200 1500 1800
F-560000-22-4-4-5-8
Copyright by RAND McNALLY & COMPANY
Made in U. S. A.

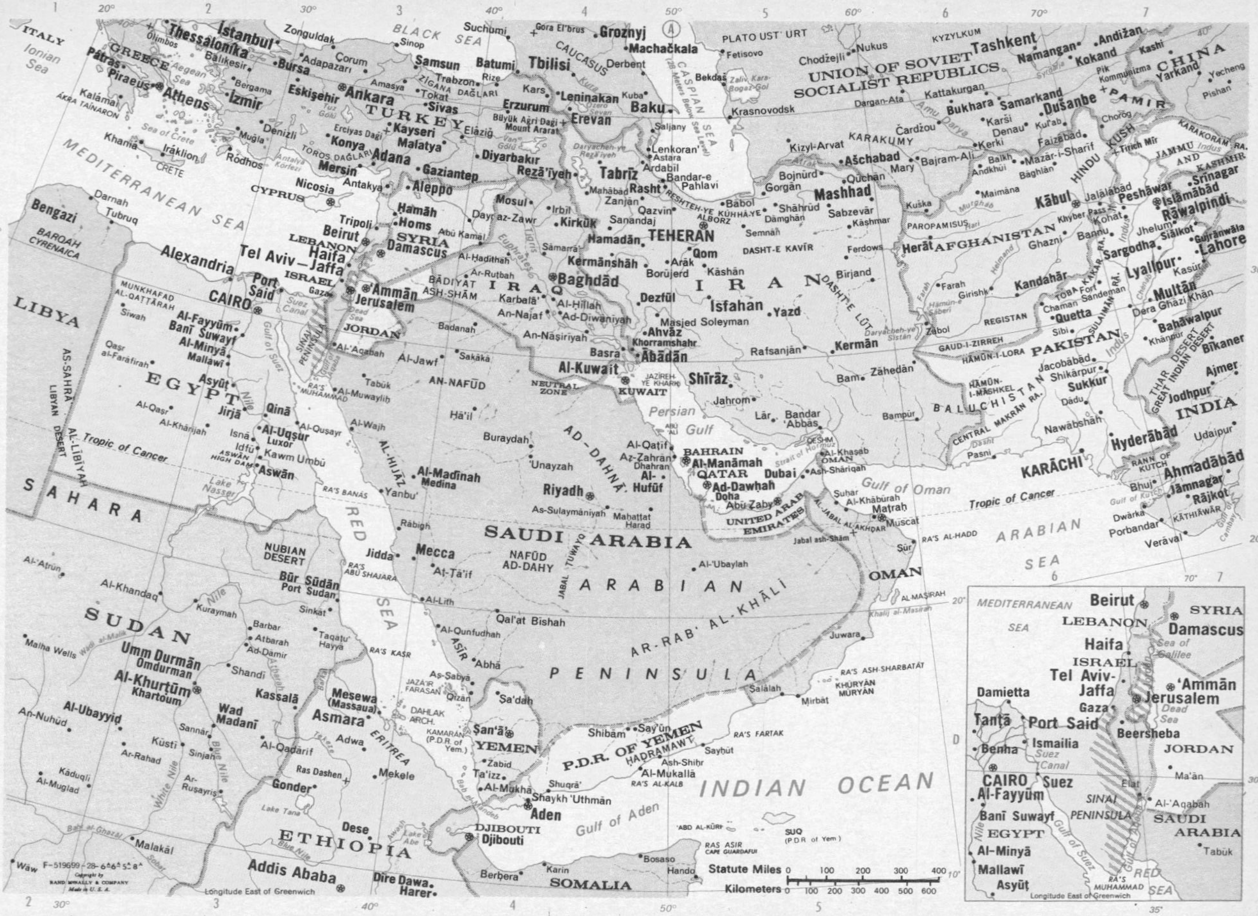

UNION OF SOVIET SOCIALIST REPUBLICS
TURKEY
SYRIA
LEBANON
ISRAEL
JORDAN
IRAQ
IRAN
AFGHANISTAN
PAKISTAN
INDIA
CHINA
KUWAIT
SAUDI ARABIA
QATAR
BAHRAIN
UNITED ARAB EMIRATES
OMAN
P.D.R. OF YEMEN
YEMEN
EGYPT
LIBYA
SUDAN
ETHIOPIA
DJIBOUTI
SOMALIA
CYPRUS
GREECE
ITALY
MEDITERRANEAN SEA
BLACK SEA
CASPIAN SEA
RED SEA
ARABIAN SEA
INDIAN OCEAN
Persian Gulf
Gulf of Oman
Gulf of Aden
ARABIAN PENINSULA
SAHARA
Tropic of Cancer
Statute Miles 0 100 200 300 400
Kilometers 0 100 200 300 400 500 600
Longitude East of Greenwich
F-519699-28-6^6-5^2-8^A
Copyright by RAND McNALLY & COMPANY Made in U.S.A.

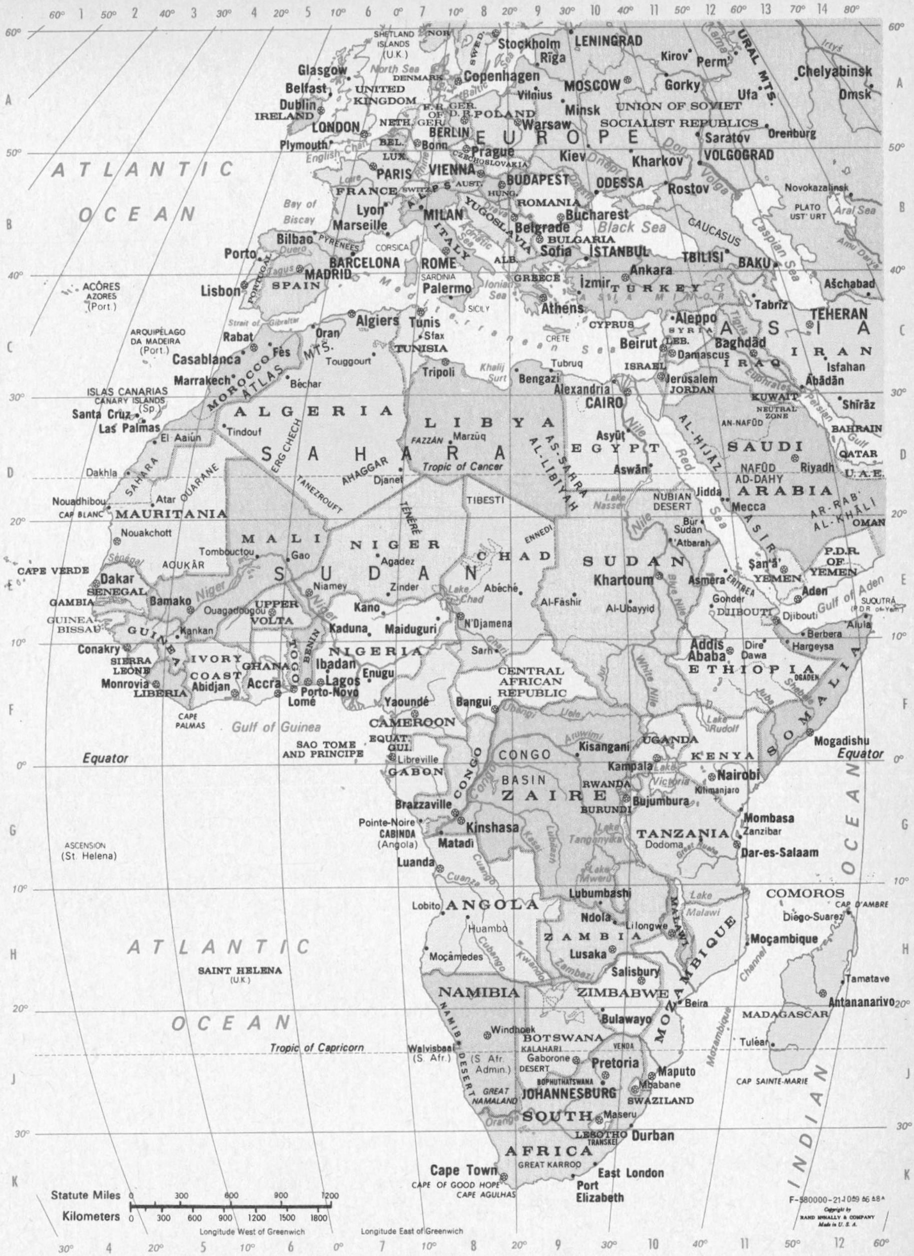

INDEX

COUNTRIES

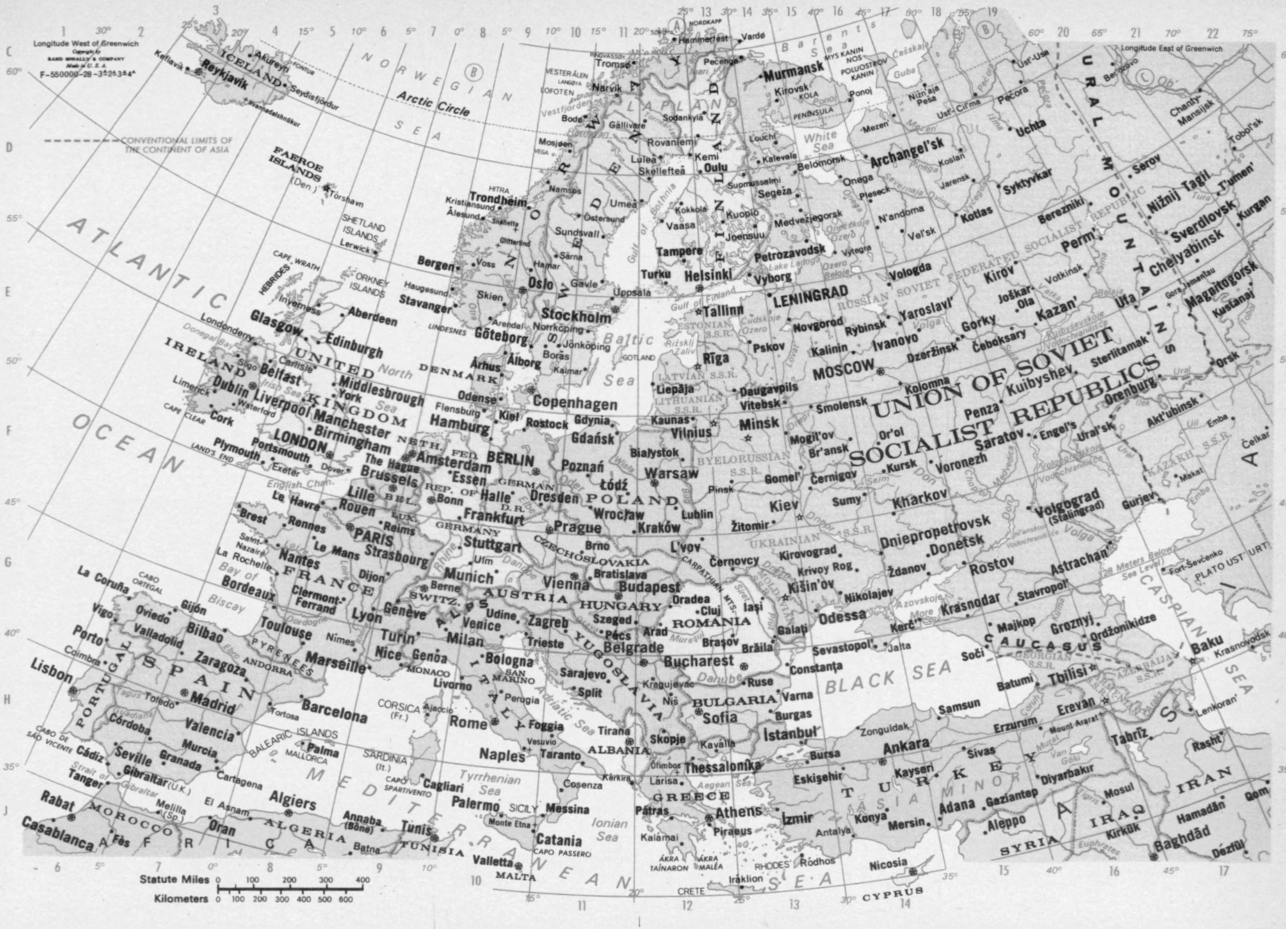
Longitude West of Greenwich
Copyright by RAND McNALLY & COMPANY
Made in U. S. A.
F-550000-28-3-2-3-4-
Longitude East of Greenwich
CONVENTIONAL LIMITS OF THE CONTINENT OF ASIA
NORWEGIAN SEA
Arctic Circle
ATLANTIC OCEAN
Barents Sea
White Sea
Baltic Sea
North Sea
BLACK SEA
CASPIAN SEA
MEDITERRANEAN SEA
Adriatic Sea
Tyrrhenian Sea
Ionian Sea
Aegean Sea
Bay of Biscay
English Chan.
Irish Sea
ICELAND
FAEROE ISLANDS (Den.)
SHETLAND ISLANDS
ORKNEY ISLANDS
HEBRIDES
IRELAND
UNITED KINGDOM
NORWAY
SWEDEN
FINLAND
LAPLAND
DENMARK
NETH.
BEL.
LUX.
FED. REP. OF GERMANY
GERMAN D.R.
POLAND
CZECHOSLOVAKIA
AUSTRIA
SWITZ.
HUNGARY
ROMANIA
YUGOSLAVIA
BULGARIA
ALBANIA
GREECE
ITALY
FRANCE
SPAIN
PORTUGAL
ANDORRA
MONACO
SAN MARINO
CORSICA (Fr.)
SARDINIA (It.)
SICILY
MALTA
CRETE
RHODES
CYPRUS
BALEARIC ISLANDS
MOROCCO
ALGERIA
TUNISIA
AFRICA
TURKEY
ASIA MINOR
SYRIA
IRAQ
IRAN
UNION OF SOVIET SOCIALIST REPUBLICS
RUSSIAN SOVIET FEDERATED SOCIALIST REPUBLIC
ESTONIAN S.S.R.
LATVIAN S.S.R.
LITHUANIAN S.S.R.
BYELORUSSIAN S.S.R.
UKRAINIAN S.S.R.
MOLDAVIAN S.S.R.
GEORGIAN S.S.R.
ARMENIAN S.S.R.
AZERBAIJAN S.S.R.
KAZAKH S.S.R.
URAL MOUNTAINS
CAUCASUS
ALPS
PYRENEES
CARPATHIAN MTS.
KOLA PENINSULA
PLATO UST' URT
Reykjavík
London
Paris
Madrid
Lisbon
Rome
BERLIN
Warsaw
Prague
Vienna
Budapest
Bucharest
Sofia
Athens
Belgrade
Oslo
Stockholm
Helsinki
Copenhagen
Dublin
Amsterdam
Brussels
MOSCOW
LENINGRAD
Kiev
Minsk
Riga
Tallinn
Vilnius
Murmansk
Archangel'sk
Volgograd (Stalingrad)
Odessa
Istanbul
Ankara
Baku
Tbilisi
Erevan
Statute Miles
Kilometers

INDEX

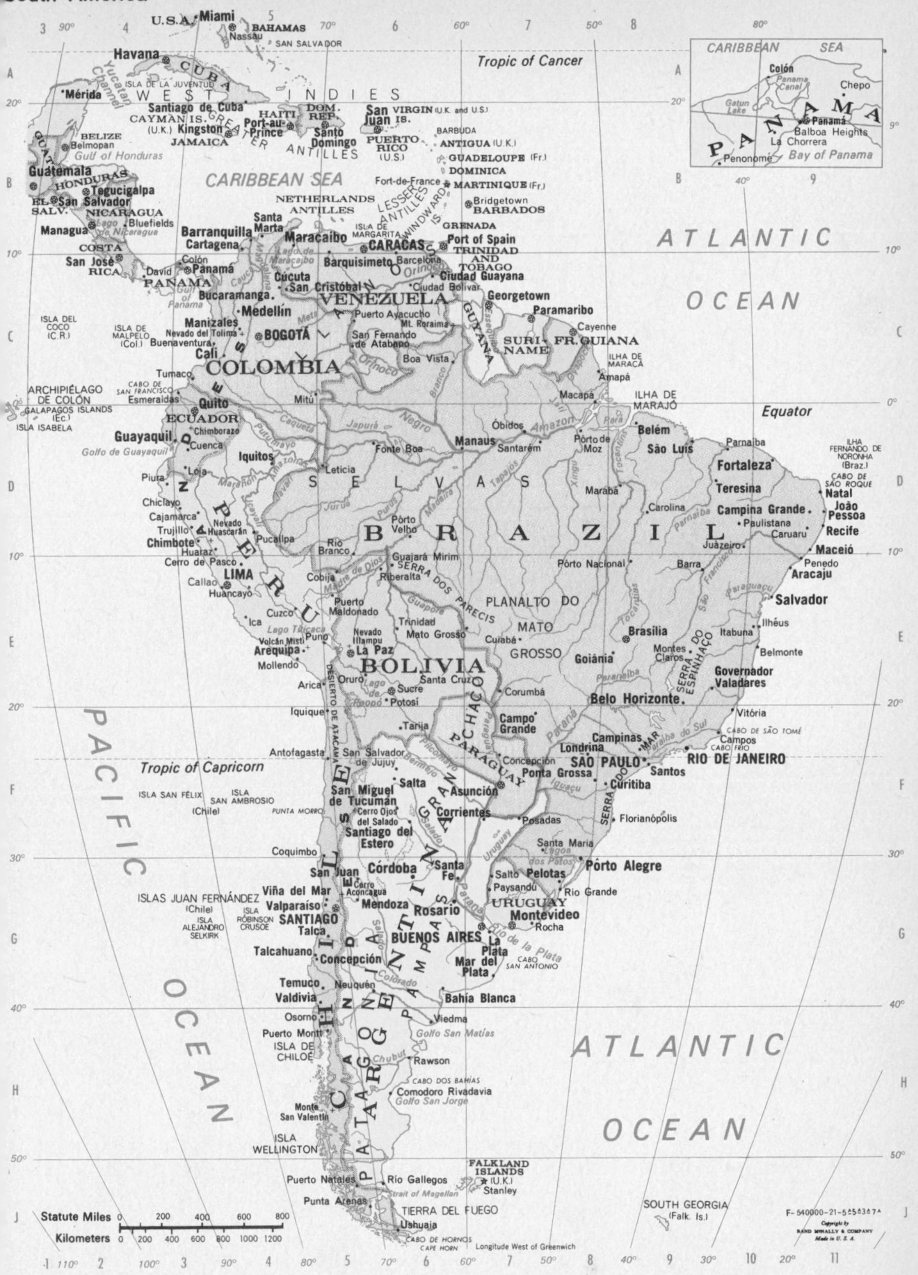

INDEX

ISLANDS

INDEX

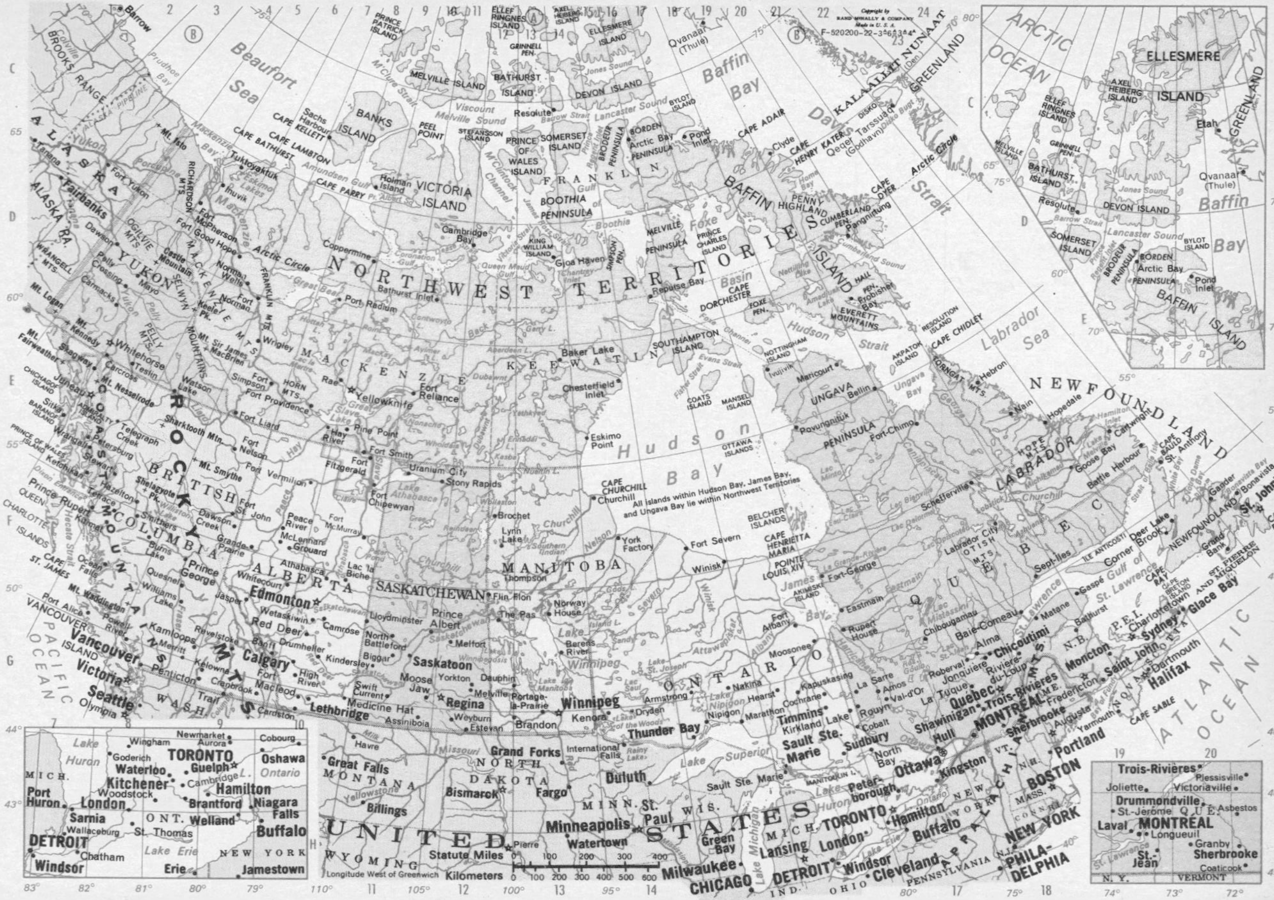

Copyright by RAND McNALLY & COMPANY Made in U.S.A.
F-520200-22-3-6-3-4-4
NORTHWEST TERRITORIES
FRANKLIN
KEEWATIN
MACKENZIE
YUKON
BRITISH COLUMBIA
ALBERTA
SASKATCHEWAN
MANITOBA
ONTARIO
QUEBEC
NEWFOUNDLAND
LABRADOR
ALASKA
UNITED STATES
KALAALLIT NUNAAT GREENLAND (Den.)
Beaufort Sea
Baffin Bay
Davis Strait
Labrador Sea
Hudson Bay
Hudson Strait
James Bay
Ungava Bay
ATLANTIC OCEAN
PACIFIC OCEAN
ARCTIC OCEAN
All islands within Hudson Bay, James Bay, and Ungava Bay lie within Northwest Territories
ROCKY MTS
Arctic Circle
BAFFIN ISLAND
VICTORIA ISLAND
BANKS ISLAND
ELLESMERE ISLAND
DEVON ISLAND
SOUTHAMPTON ISLAND
BOOTHIA PENINSULA
UNGAVA PENINSULA
Statute Miles 0 100 200 300 400
Kilometers 0 100 200 300 400 500 600
Longitude West of Greenwich
Trois-Rivières
MONTREAL
Sherbrooke
TORONTO
Hamilton
Buffalo
DETROIT
Windsor

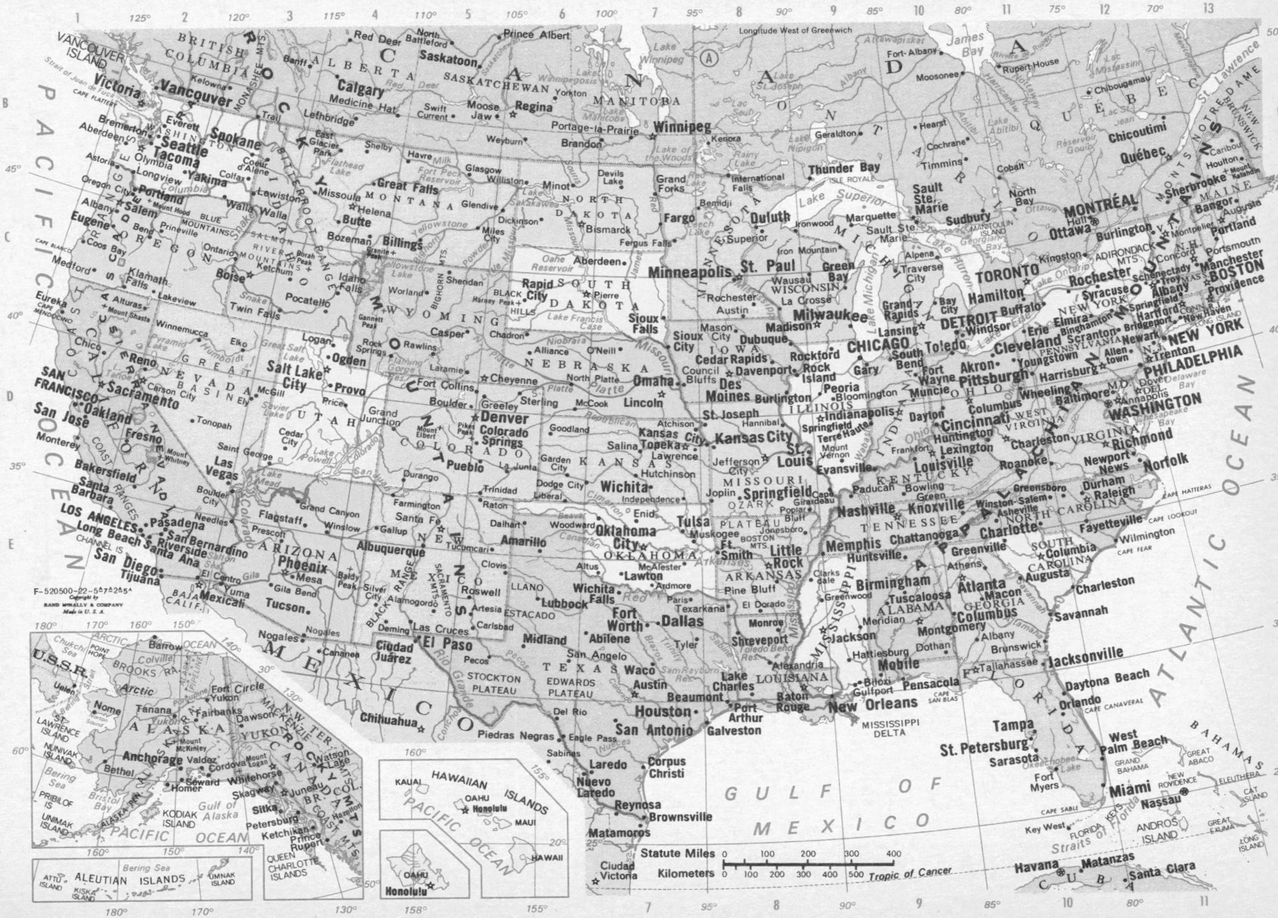
Longitude West of Greenwich
CANADA
BRITISH COLUMBIA
ALBERTA
SASKATCHEWAN
MANITOBA
ONTARIO
QUÉBEC
Vancouver
Victoria
Calgary
Saskatoon
Regina
Winnipeg
Thunder Bay
Toronto
Ottawa
Montréal
Québec
Seattle
Portland
San Francisco
Los Angeles
San Diego
Denver
Minneapolis
St. Paul
Chicago
Detroit
Cleveland
Philadelphia
New York
Boston
Washington
Atlanta
Miami
New Orleans
Houston
Dallas
Kansas City
St. Louis
MEXICO
PACIFIC OCEAN
ATLANTIC OCEAN
GULF OF MEXICO
Statute Miles 0 100 200 300 400
Kilometers 0 100 200 300 400 500
Tropic of Cancer
HAWAIIAN ISLANDS
ALASKA
ALEUTIAN ISLANDS
F-520500-22-5-7-2-5-A
Copyright by RAND McNALLY & COMPANY
Made in U.S.A.

INDEX

WORLD FLAGS AND MAPS

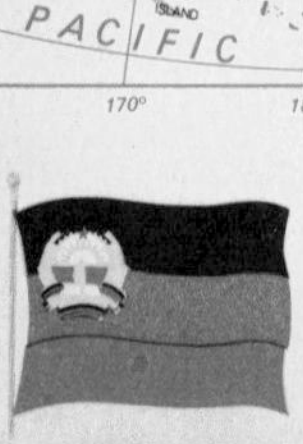
AFGHANISTAN

ALBANIA

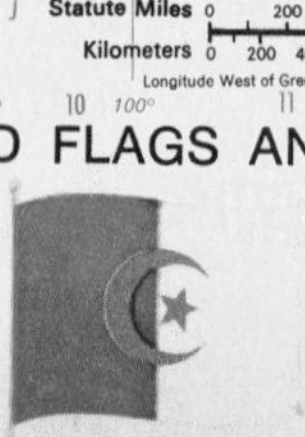
ALGERIA

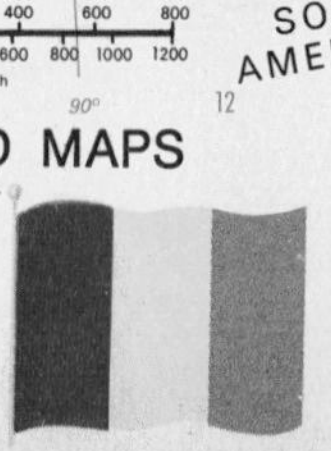
ANDORRA

ANGOLA

Flags shown are *national* flags in common use and vary slightly from official *state* flags, most particularly by omitting coats of arms in some cases.

ARGENTINA

AUSTRALIA

AUSTRIA

BAHAMAS

BAHRAIN

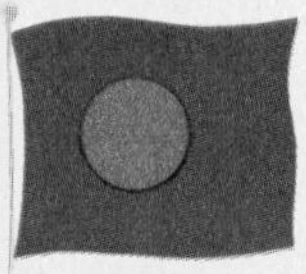
BANGLADESH

BARBADOS

BELGIUM

BENIN

BHUTAN

BOLIVIA

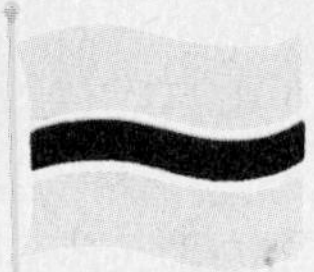
BOTSWANA

BRAZIL

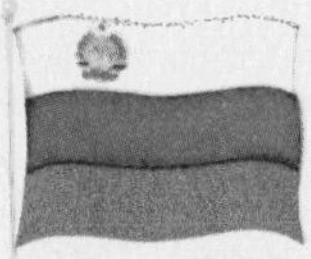
BULGARIA

BURMA

BURUNDI

CAMBODIA (KAMPUCHEA)

CAMEROON

CANADA

CAPE VERDE

CENTRAL AFRICAN REPUBLIC

CHAD

CHILE

CHINA (MAINLAND)

CHINA (TAIWAN)

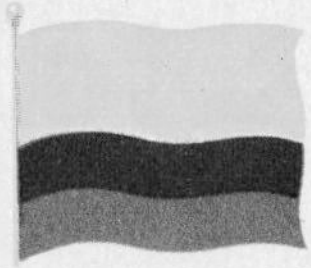
COLOMBIA

COMOROS

CONGO

COSTA RICA

CUBA

CYPRUS

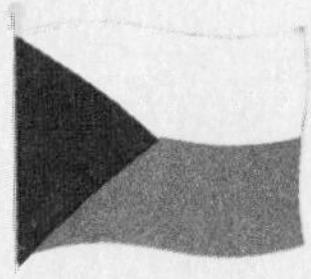
CZECHOSLOVAKIA

DENMARK

DJIBOUTI

DOMINICA

DOMINICAN REPUBLIC

ECUADOR

EGYPT

EL SALVADOR

EQUATORIAL GUINEA

ETHIOPIA

FIJI

FINLAND

FRANCE

GABON

GAMBIA

GERMAN DEM. REP.

GERMANY, FED. REP. OF

GHANA

GREECE

GRENADA

GUATEMALA

GUINEA

GUINEA-BISSAU

GUYANA

HAITI

HONDURAS

HUNGARY

ICELAND

INDIA

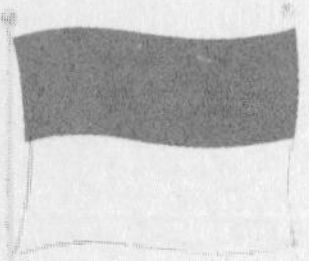
INDONESIA

IRAN

IRAQ

IRELAND

ISRAEL

ITALY

IVORY COAST

JAMAICA

JAPAN

JORDAN

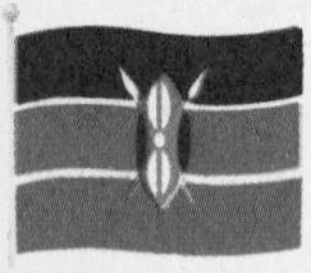
KENYA

KIRIBATI

KOREA, NORTH

KOREA, SOUTH

KUWAIT

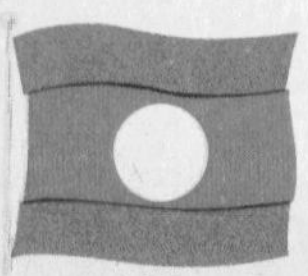
LAOS

LEBANON

LESOTHO

LIBERIA

LIBYA

LIECHTENSTEIN

LUXEMBOURG

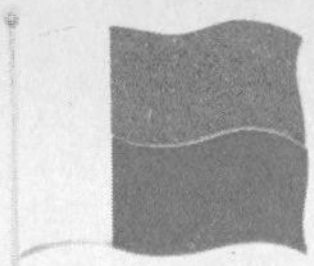
MADAGASCAR

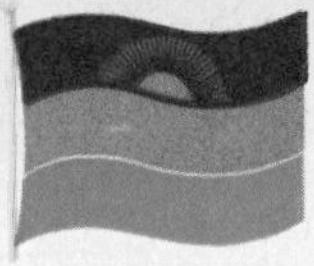
MALAWI

MALAYSIA

MALDIVES

MALI

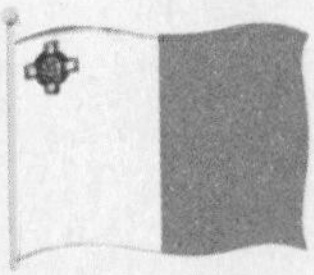
MALTA

MAURITANIA

MAURITIUS

MEXICO

MONACO

MONGOLIA

MOROCCO

MOZAMBIQUE

NAURU

NEPAL

NETHERLANDS

NEW ZEALAND

NICARAGUA

NIGER

NIGERIA

NORWAY

OMAN

PAKISTAN

PANAMA

PAPUA NEW GUINEA

PARAGUAY

PERU

PHILIPPINES

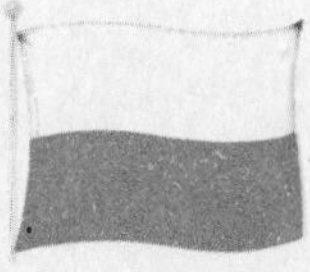
POLAND

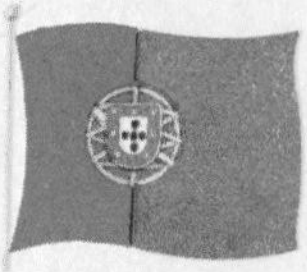
PORTUGAL

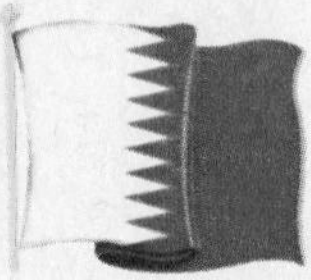
QATAR

ROMANIA

RWANDA

SAINT LUCIA

ST. VINCENT/ GRENADINES

SAMOA

SAN MARINO

SAO TOME & PRINCIPE

SAUDI ARABIA

SENEGAL

SEYCHELLES

SIERRA LEONE

SINGAPORE

SOLOMON ISLANDS

SOMALIA

SOUTH AFRICA

SPAIN

SRI LANKA

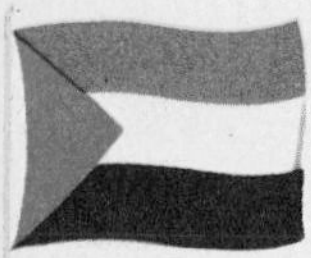
SUDAN

SURINAME

SWAZILAND

SWEDEN

SWITZERLAND

SYRIA

TANZANIA

THAILAND

TOGO

TONGA

TRINIDAD & TOBAGO

TUNISIA

TURKEY

TUVALU

UGANDA

U.S.S.R.

UNITED ARAB EMIRATES

UNITED KINGDOM

UNITED STATES

UPPER VOLTA

URUGUAY

VATICAN CITY

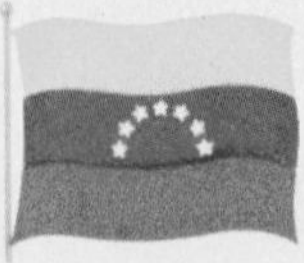
VENEZUELA

VIETNAM

YEMEN

YEMEN, P.D.R. OF

YUGOSLAVIA

ZAIRE

ZAMBIA

ZIMBABWE

CANADA

See Index for Calgary, Edmonton, Halifax, Hamilton, Kitchener-Waterloo, Lethbridge, Montreal, Ottawa, Quebec, Regina, Saskatoon, Toronto, Vancouver, Windsor, Winnipeg.

Capital: Ottawa. Area: 3,831,033 sq. mi. Population (Govt. est., Jan. 1980): 23,809,800. Monetary unit: Canadian dollar.

The Land

The world's second largest country in land size, Canada stretches 3,223 miles from east to west and extends southward from the North Pole to the U.S. border. Its seacoast includes 36,356 miles of mainland and 115,133 miles of islands, including the Arctic islands almost from Greenland to near the Alaskan border.

Canada's continental climate, while generally temperate, varies from freezing winter cold to blistering summer heat - a range beyond 100 degrees Fahrenheit.

Major cities, industrial centres, agricultural regions, and the vast majority of the population are situated along a thin, southern fringe bordering the United States. To the north lie vast expanses of varied, virgin land. The remote north, due to extreme cold, is virtually uninhabitable.

Fragmented by history, geography, and economic factors, the country is as diverse as it is large. Regionally, Canada's 10 provinces can be put into 5 groups: the industrially-poor Atlantic Provinces of New Brunswick, Newfoundland, Nova Scotia, and Prince Edward Island; predominantly French-speaking Quebec; Ontario, financial and governmental heartland of the nation; the Prairies, including Manitoba, Saskatchewan, and oil-rich Alberta; and British Columbia, separated from the rest of the country by the Rocky Mountains.

Despite continuing problems of regional disparity in political, economic, and cultural outlook, Canada has survived as a nation by accepting the need to recognize and tolerate differences. Unlike the U.S., Canada has never been a melting pot, nor has it strived to become one.

History

French explorer Jacques Cartier, who discovered the Gulf of St. Lawrence in 1534, is generally regarded as the founder of Canada. But English seaman John Cabot sighted Newfoundland 37 years earlier, in 1547, and Vikings are believed to have reached the Atlantic coast centuries before either explorer.

Canadian settlement was pioneered by the French who established Quebec City (1608) and Montreal (1642) and declared New France a colony in 1663.

Britain, as part of its American expansion, acquired Acadia (later Nova Scotia) in 1717 and, through military victory over French forces in Canada (an extension of a European conflict between the 2 powers), captured Quebec (1759) and obtained control of the rest of New France in 1763. The French, through the Quebec Act of 1774, retained the rights to their own language, religion, and civil law.

The British presence in Canada increased during the American Revolution when many colonials, proudly calling themselves United Empire Loyalists, moved north to Canada.

Fur traders and explorers led Canadians westward across the continent. Sir Alexander Mackenzie reached the Pacific in 1793 and scrawled on a rock by the ocean, "from Canada by land."

In Upper and Lower Canada (later called Ontario and Quebec) and in the Maritimes, legislative assemblies appeared in the 18th century and reformers called for responsible government. But the War of 1812 intervened. The war, a conflict between Great Britain and the United States fought mainly in Upper Canada, ended in a stalemate in 1814.

In 1837 political agitation for more democratic government culminated in rebellions in Upper and Lower Canada. Britain sent Lord Durham to investigate and, in a famous report (1839), he recommended union of the 2 parts into one colony called Canada. The union lasted until Confederation, July 1, 1867, when proclamation of the British North America (BNA) Act launched the Dominion of Canada, consisting of Ontario, Quebec, and the former colonies of Nova Scotia and New Brunswick.

Since 1840 the Canadian colonies had held the right to internal self-government. The BNA act, which became the country's written constitution, established a federal system of government on the model of a British parliament and cabinet structure under the crown. Canada was proclaimed a self-governing Dominion within the British Empire in 1931. Empire has given way to Commonwealth, of which Canada is an independent member.

The Government

Canada is a constitutional monarchy with a parliamentary system of government. It is also a federal state. Official head of state remains England's Queen Elizabeth, represented by a resident governor-general. But in practice the nation is governed by the Prime Minister, leader of the party able to command the support of a majority of members of the House of Commons, dominant chamber of Canada's bicameral Parliament.

The Commons' 282 members are elected at least every 5 years - sooner if the Prime Minister so chooses or if the government is defeated in Parliament. This can occur either through passage of a motion of nonconfidence in the government or by defeat of a major piece of government legislation.

The upper house of Canada's Parliament is the Senate, comprised of 104 members traditionally appointed by party patronage and serving to age 75.

Legislation becomes law by receiving 3 "readings" in the Commons, passing in the Senate and obtaining assent from the governor-general. The latter 2 steps are, in practice, mere formality.

The Prime Minister heads the executive branch of government composed of the cabinet and governor-general. The cabinet is chosen by the Prime Minister, almost always from among members of his party holding seats in the House of Commons.

Provincial governments follow a modified version of the Ottawa pattern, with a unicameral legislature and an executive head usually referred to as the Premier.

Several federal-provincial conferences have been held in recent years to resolve disagreement between the two levels of government on such matters as control of resources, restructure of the Senate to provide regional representation, and the "patriation" (bringing home from Britain) of Canada's constitution - the outmoded British North America Act. Conferences in the fall of 1978, spring of 1979, and spring of 1980 failed to resolve any major areas of contention.

Politics

The Liberal government of Prime Minister Pierre Trudeau returned to power in February 1980, after only 9 months out of office. The Liberals gained a majority of seats in the House of Commons in a surprise election called after the Conservative government led by Joe Clark received a parliamentary vote of no-confidence on a proposed budget presented in December 1979. The budget was opposed by both the Liberal and New Democratic parties which, combined, had more members in the House than the Conservatives.

As with the 1979 election, voting was split along linguistic and regional lines, increasing fears of polarization in an already-fragmented nation. The Liberals captured 74 out of 75 seats in predominantly French-speaking Quebec but only 2 out of 80 seats west of Ontario. The Conservatives won only one seat in Quebec but 51 in western Canada, an area of increasing political importance because of the westward shift of economic power - especially to Alberta, rich in natural resources. The election results and voting pattern increased the alienation that some western Canadians feel toward the central Government.

The separatist movement in Quebec, a far greater immediate threat to national unity, received a severe setback in May 1980, with the defeat of a provincial referendum proposing "sovereignty association" - a watered-down form of independence in which Quebec would have retained economic links with Canada. The referendum question, put forward by the separatist Parti Quebecois which has formed the government in Quebec since 1976, was rejected by 59.4% of Quebec voters despite a strong campaign by popular PQ leader Rene Levesque. The likelihood of Quebec independence would be further reduced if the PQ fails to retain power in the provincial election which must be held before the end of 1981. Provincial Liberal leader Claude Ryan wants more autonomy for Quebec but would stay within Canada. During the referendum campaign, Prime Minister Trudeau promised Quebecers his support for a "renewed federalism" with altered provincial rights enshrined in a new constitution.

If Quebec did separate, the economic and political effect on Canada could be staggering. The province is the country's largest in size, 2d in population (26% of the nation's total), 2d in manufacturing output and shipments, and 3d both in energy and mineral production. Further, Quebec separation would create an enormous geographical barrier between the rest of Canada and the already-isolated Atlantic provinces. The continued feasibility of Confederation might be questioned as rumblings of discontent from other provinces would likely grow louder and stronger. The loss of Quebec could also greatly alter the federal political makeup by depriving the Liberal party of its main base of support.

The Economy

The Canadian economy, influenced strongly by economic trends in the U.S., continued to perform sluggishly during 1979 and the first quarter of 1980. Real growth in the Gross Domestic Product (a measure of all goods and services produced in the country and considered the best barometer of economic activity) declined by .5% during the first 3 months of 1980. It grew by only 2.9% in 1979 - down from a 3.4% growth in 1978.

The inflation rate, as measured by the Consumer Price Index, was 9.4% in May, 1980. The unemployment rate for 1979 was 7.5% - an improvement over the 1978 rate of 8.4%.

The value of the Canadian dollar rose slightly during the first half of 1980 (it was near .87 U.S. in July), encouraged by Arctic and east coast energy discoveries and healthy merchandise trade figures. Up to the end of May 1980, Canada showed a merchandise trade surplus of $2.28 billion. The nation relies on this excess of merchandise exports over imports to offset a chronic deficit in payments to investors abroad and for foreign travel by Canadians.

Principal Canadian industries are motor vehicle manufacturing, petroleum refining, pulp and paper production, slaughtering and meat processing, iron and steel production, the manufacture of miscellaneous machinery and equipment, saw and planing mill industries, and smelting and refining.

In Canada, an historical tradition of state aid necessitated by a harsh climate and sparse population has fostered development of a mixed economic system in which publicly-owned corporations exist alongside - and sometimes compete with - private enterprise. Most hydroelectric and many transportation and communication facilities are owned by either federal, provincial, or municipal governments. Air Canada and the Canadian National Railways, both large federal crown corporations, compete with the privately-owned Canadian Pacific, Ltd., whose 1979 assets were the 3rd largest of any company in Canada. The Canadian Broadcasting Corp., publicly owned though independently managed, shares airwaves with a string of private radio chains and television networks.

Social Security

Income security and social service programs are provided by the federal, provincial and local governments. Federal responsibilities include: Unemployment Insurance; Family Allowances; Veterans' Benefits; the Canada Pension Plan; the Old Age Security pension; a Guaranteed Income Supplement; Canada Assistance Plan whereby the federal government shares in the cost of social assistance and welfare services provided under provincial and municipal programs.

The provinces are responsible for social assistance, social welfare and institutional care. Quebec operates the Quebec Pension Plan. Some provinces provide supplementary old age benefits, family allowances and work income supplements.

Hospital insurance programs have operated in all provinces since 1961. Provincial medical care insurance programs, partially funded by the federal government, have existed in all provinces since 1972. Financial arrangements between the federal and provincial governments were altered in 1977 to allow greater provincial flexibility in the operation of these programs.

Foreign Policy

Canada's major foreign ally and trading partner remains the United States with whom she shares a broad range of mutually beneficial ties. Canada supported the U.S.-led boycott of the Olympic Games in Moscow to protest the Soviet invasion of Afghanistan, and agreed to support the U.S. embargo on grain sales to the Soviet Union for the 1980 crop year. In Feb., 1980, the friendship between the 2 nations was highlighted by the Canadian rescue of 6 U.S. embassy personnel in Iran. In May, 1980, Canada announced a full embargo on exports to Iran.

At the same time, Canada-U.S. relations have been chilled by disagreements over east coast maritime boundaries and fish catch quotas. Tentative agreements signed in March of 1979 had not yet been ratified by the U.S. Senate a year and a half later. In a June, 1980, speech, External Affairs Minister Mark MacGuigan criticized the U.S. for delaying the treaty and described amendments proposed by some U.S. senators as "wholly unacceptable." In 1978, the dispute led both Canada and the U.S. to temporarily suspend cross-boundary commercial fishing.

As part of a "Third Option" policy adopted in 1972 with the aim of reducing vulnerability to U.S. interests, Canada has expanded relations with the European Economic Community and Japan. Visits by Prime Minister Pierre Trudeau to both these areas in 1976 culminated in the signing of separate framework agreements for economic co-operation. Canada seeks a balanced economic exchange with Europe and Japan through easier access to their markets for more Canadian processed and manufactured goods.

Canada also hopes to broaden political and economic ties with Mexico, Venezuela and Brazil. In 1979, Venezuela was Canada's chief foreign source of oil—providing 40% of imports—and was a major exporter of Canadian goods and services. Following a series of high-level meetings in 1980, Mexico agreed to export to Canada 50,000 barrels of oil daily. Canada had sought a more formal commitment providing 100,000 barrels daily.

Canada continues to support efforts to promote disarmament despite increased East-West tensions. As an important exporter of uranium and nuclear reactors, Canada has adopted strict safeguards designed to allow it to provide nuclear technology while minimizing the risk of proliferating nuclear weapons. Shipments are restricted to nations that ratify the Non-Proliferation Treaty or otherwise accept international safeguards on their entire nuclear program.

Canada's Native Peoples

Canada's native population consists of 2 groups, the Indian and Inuit (Eskimo). Both are thought to have crossed from Asia via the Bering Sea several thousand years before the arrival of Europeans in North America.

Most populous are the Indians, of whom more than 300,000 are registered under the Indian Act. The number of non-registered Indians is unknown. Of those registered, 71% live on federal reserves or on other government land; 82% of the total live in Ontario and the 4 western provinces. Only Newfoundland has no registered Indians. There are 575 Indian bands for which 2,240 reserves have been set aside.

Registered Indians or those entitled to be registered receive a broad range of government benefits administered through the federal Department of Indian Affairs and Northern Development. Those living on reserves are eligible for direct federal assistance in such areas as education, housing, social services and community development.

More than 75% of Canada's approximately 23,000 Inuit (meaning "the people" in their language, Inuktitut; Eskimo is an Indian word adopted by European settlers) live in the Northwest Territories, the remainder in Arctic Quebec and northern Labrador.

Due to the remoteness of their settlements close to the northern coasts where sea mammals provided the chief source of food, fuel and clothing, the Inuit lifestyle was affected later and less directly than that of the Indian by the encroachment of western civilization. Many Inuit still live by their traditional skills of hunting, trapping and fishing as well as through the production and sale of artwork. But increasing numbers now find work outside their communities, particularly since the search for oil, gas and minerals has brought more jobs to the north. Through the Indian and Inuit Affairs Program the federal government aims to provide equality of opportunity for all native peoples whether they choose a traditional or contemporary lifestyle. In either case communities and individuals are encouraged to strive for self-reliance.

The Inuit are eligible for a range of benefits similar to those available to registered Indians. These are provided through the provincial and territorial governments as well as the federal Department of Indian Affairs and Northern Development.

To represent Inuit cultural and legal interests in Ottawa, the Inuit Tapirisat (Eskimo Brotherhood) was founded in 1971 with financial aid from the Department of the Secretary of State. A major Tapirisat task is the presentation of native land claims. The National Indian Brotherhood performs a similar role for Indians.

Approximately half the registered Indians in Canada (mainly those living in Ontario and the 3 Prairie provinces) are entitled to payments as a result of treaties between their ancestors and the Crown. In remote northern areas, however, no such legal settlements were made, and recently Indian and Inuit groups have pressed claims to aboriginal rights to vast areas of land in northern British Columbia, the Yukon and Northwest Territories, and northern Quebec and Labrador.

In 1973 the federal government agreed to consider native claims. Thus far 2 settlements have been reached: In 1975 the Inuit, Cree and Naskapis in the James Bay area surrendered claim to 400,000 sq. mi. in return for $225 million and a range of rights and privileges. In October, 1978, the government reached a tentative settlement with the 2,500 Inuvialuit of the western Arctic providing payment of $118 million over 14 years. The agreement also gives the Inuvialuit a clear grant to 37,000 sq. mi. of land.

Provinces of Canada

Alberta

People. Population (Jan. 1980): 2,053,100; **rank:** 4. **Pop. density:** 8.3 per sq. mi. **Urban** (1976) 75%. **Ethnic distrib.** (1976): English 80.7%; German 4.3%; Ukrainian 3.5%; French 2.4%. **Net migration** (1978-79) +30,369.

Geography: Total area: 255,285 sq. mi.; **rank:** 4. **Land area:** 248,800 sq. mi. **Acres forested land:** 68,341,000. **Location:** Canada's 2d most westerly province, bounded to the W by British Columbia, to the E by Saskatchewan, to the N by the Northwest Territories, and to the S by Montana. **Climate:** great variance in temperatures between regions and seasons; summer highs can range between 16°C and 32°C; winter temperatures can drop as low as −45°C; mean Jan. temperature in Edmonton is −14°C. **Topography:** ranges from the Rocky Mountains in the SW to flat prairie in the SE; the far north is a wilderness of forest and muskeg.

Economy. Principal industries: mining, oil production, agriculture, manufacturing, construction. **Principal manufactured goods:** foods and beverages, wood products, fabricated metal, transportation equipment, refined petroleum. **Value added by manufacture** (1977): $2 billion. **Gross Domestic Product** (1978): $28.1 billion. **Agriculture: Chief crops:** wheat, barley, rapeseed, sugar beets, flaxseed. **Livestock** (1978): 3,857,000 cattle; 990,000 pigs; 106,000 sheep; 9,998,000 poultry. **Forestry production** (1977): $26.5 million. **Mineral production** (1978): total value, $10 billion; fuels, $9.8 billion (97% of national production of petroleum, 92% of natural gas); elemental sulphur, $1 billion (98% of national total); metals, $247 million; structural materials, $177 million. **Commercial fishing:** (1977) $1.2 million. **Value of construction** (1978): $6.53 billion. **Employment distribution** (1979): 28% services; 18% trade; 11% construction; 9% manufacturing; 8.2% agriculture; 6% public administration. **Per capita income** (1978): $8,407. **Unemployment** (1979): 3.9%

Finance: No. banks: 720; **No. credit unions, caisses populaires:** 177.

International airports: Edmonton, Calgary.

Federal government: No. federal employees (1979): 30,673; **Federal payroll** (1979): $456.3 million.

Energy. Electricity production, by mwh, (1979): mineral, 20,187,627; hydroelectric, 1,415,187.

Education. No schools: 1,350 elementary; 177 secondary; 25 higher education. **Avg. salary, public school teachers** (1978-79): $19,121.

Provincial data. Motto: none. **Flower:** The Wild Rose. **Bird:** Great horned owl. **Date entered Confederation:** 1905. **Capital:** Edmonton.

Politics. Premier: Peter Lougheed (Progressive Conservative). **Leaders, opposition parties:** Robert Clark (Social Credit), Grant Notley (New Democratic), Nick Taylor (Liberal). **Composition of legislature** (June, 1980): PC 74; SC 4; NDP 1; Independent 1. **Date of last election:** Mar. 14, 1979.

Tourist attractions: Banff, Jasper, and Waterton Lakes national parks; resorts at Banff, Jasper and Lake Louise; spectacular skiing, hiking, trail riding and camping in the Canadian Rockies; the Badlands near Drumheller; Elk Island National Park.

British Columbia

People. Population (Jan. 1980): 2,611,700; **rank:** 3. **Pop. density:** 7.3 per sq. mi. **Urban** (1976) 76.9%. **Ethnic distrib.** (1976): English 82.6%; German 3.3%; Chinese 1.9%; French 1.6%; Italian 1.1%. **Net migration** (1978-79): +20,111.

Geography. Total area: 366,255 sq. mi.; **rank:** 3. **Land area:** 359,279 sq. mi. **Acres forested land:** 134,652,000. **Location:** bounded to the N by the Yukon and Northwest

Territories, to the NW by the Alaskan panhandle, to the W by the Pacific Ocean, to the E by Alberta, and to the S by Washington, Idaho and Montana. **Climate:** maritime with mild termperatures and abundant rainfall in the coastal areas; continental climate with temperature extremes in the interior and northeast. **Topography:** mostly mountainous except for the NE corner which is an extension of the Great Plains.

Economy. Principal industries: forestry, mining, tourism, fuels, fishing, manufacturing. **Principal manufactured goods:** paper and allied products, wood products, mineral products and associated machinery, food and beverages, transportation equipment, chemicals. **Value added by manufacture** (1977): $4.6 billion. **Gross Domestic Product** (1978): $27.9 billion (including GDP for Yukon and NWT). **Agriculture: Chief crops:** fruits and vegetables, barley, oats. **Livestock** (1978): 593,000 cattle; 67,000 pigs; 30,500 sheep; 12,019,000 poultry. **Forestry production** (1977): $729.8 million. **Mineral production** (1978): total value, $1.9 billion; metals, $868 million; fuel, $810 million; structural materials, $143 million. **Commercial fishing:** (1977) $167.9 million. **Value of construction** (1978): $5.35 billion. **Employment distribution** (1979): 30% services; 18% trade; 16% manufacturing; 7% construction; 6% public administration; 2% agriculture. **Per capita income** (1978): $8,784. **Unemployment** (1979): 7.7%.

Finance: No. banks: 871; **No. credit unions, caisses populaires:** 163.

International airports: Vancouver, Victoria.

Federal government: No. federal employees (1979): 41,848. **Federal payroll** (1979): $636.8 million.

Energy. Electricity production, by mwh, (1979): mineral, 2,244,884, hydroelectric, 40,928,251.

Education. No schools: 1,545 elementary; 335 secondary; 26 higher education. **Avg. salary, public school teachers** (1978-79): $19,894.

Provincial data. Motto: Splendor Sine Occasu (Spendor Without Diminishment). **Flower:** Dogwood. **Bird:** None. **Date entered Confederation:** 1871. **Capital:** Victoria.

Politics. Premier: William R. Bennett (Social Credit). **Leaders, opposition parties:** Dave Barrett (New Democratic), Jev Tothill (Liberal), Joan Gillanders (Progressive Conservative). **Composition of legislature** (June 1980): SC 31; NDP 26. **Date of last election:** May 10, 1979.

Tourist attractions. Victoria: Butchart Gardens, Crystal Garden, Provincial Museum; Vancouver: Stanley Park Zoo, Capilano Canyon, Gastown, Public Aquarium, Grouse Mountain, Planetarium; also Pacific Rim National Park, the Gulf Islands, Okanagan Valley, Yellowhead Highway, Totem Triangle Tour.

Manitoba

People. Population (Jan. 1980): 1,026,200; **rank:** 5. **Pop. density:** 4.8 per sq. mi. **Urban** (1976) 69.9%. **Ethnic distrib.** (1976): English 71.2%; German 7.2%; Ukrainian 5.9%; French 5.4%; Native Indians 2.4%. **Net migration** (1978-79): −10,934.

Geography. Total area: 251,000 sq. mi.; **rank:** 6. **Land area:** 211,755 sq. mi. **Acres forested land:** 33,476,000. **Location:** bounded to the N by the Northwest Territories, to the S by Minnesota and North Dakota, to the E by Ontario and Hudson Bay, to the W by Saskatchewan. **Climate:** continental, with seasonal extremes: Winnipeg avg. Jan. low −23°C, avg. July high 26°C. **Topography:** the land rises gradually S and W from Hudson Bay; most of the province is between 500 and 1,000 feet above sea level.

Economy. Principal industries: manufacturing, agriculture, slaughtering and meat processing, mining. **Principal manufactured goods:** agricultural implements, processed food, machinery, transportation equipment, clothing. **Value added by manufacture** (1977): $1.2 billion. **Gross Domestic Product** (1978): $9.3 billion. **Agriculture: Chief crops:** cereal grains, sunflower seeds, rape, flax, sugarbeets. **Livestock** (1978): 1,201,000 cattle; 680,000 pigs; 14,800 sheep; 6,817,000 poultry. **Forestry production** (1977): $11.4 million. **Mineral production** (1978): total value, $459.6 million; metals, $330 million; structural materials, $76 million; fuels, $46 million. **Commercial fishing:** (1977) $10 million. **Value of construction** (1978): $1.39 billion. **Employment distribution** (1979): 28% services; 18% trade; 14% manufacturing; 9.6% agriculture; 7% public administration; 6% construction. **Per capita income** (1978): $7,456. **Unemployment** (1979): 5.4%

Finance: No. banks: 363; **No. credit unions, caisses populaires:** 166.

International airports: Winnipeg.

Federal Government: No. federal employees (1979): 19,791. **Federal payroll** (1979): $304.3 million.

Energy. Electricity production, by mwh, (1979): mineral, 170,811; hydroelectric, 20,443,217.

Education. No. schools: 706 elementary; 116 secondary; 15 higher education. **Avg. salary, public school teachers** (1978-79): $18,472.

Provincial data. Motto: None. **Flower:** Prairie crocus. **Bird:** none. **Date entered Confederation:** July 15, 1870. **Capital:** Winnipeg.

Politics. Premier: Sterling Lyon (Progressive Conservative). **Leaders, opposition parties:** Howard Pawley (New Democratic). **Composition of legislature:** (June 1980): PC 33; NDP 22; Lib. 1; 1 independent. **Date of last election:** Sept. 11, 1977.

Tourist attractions. Museum of Man and Nature (Winnipeg), Lower Fort Garry (near Lockport), Red River cruises, Riding Mountain National Park, canoeing, fishing and camping on northern lakes.

New Brunswick

People. Population (Jan. 1980): 704,800; **rank:** 8. **Pop. density:** 25.7 per sq. mi. **Urban** (1976) 52.3%. **Ethnic distrib.** (1976): English 64.4%; French 33%. **Net migration** (1978-79): +1,133.

Geography. Total area: 28,345 sq. mi.; **rank:** 8. **Land area:** 27,385 sq. mi. **Acres forested land:** 15,594,000. **Location:** bounded by Quebec to the N, Nova Scotia and the Bay of Fundy to the S, the Gulf of St. Lawrence and Northumberland Strait to the E, and Maine to the W. **Climate:** humid continental climate except along the shores where there is a marked maritime effect; avg. Jan. low in Fredericton is −14°C, avg. July high 22°C. **Topography:** upland, lowland and plateau regions throughout the province.

Economy. Principal industries: manufacturing, mining, forestry, pulp and paper. **Principal manufactured goods:** paper and allied products, wood products, fish products, semi-processed mineral products. **Value added by manufacture** (1977): $677.7 million. **Gross Domestic Product** (1978): $4.4 billion. **Agriculture: Chief crops:** potatoes, apples, blueberries, oats. **Livestock** (1978): 102,000 cattle; 41,000 pigs; 7,000 sheep; 2,632,000 poultry. **Forestry production** (1977): $73 million. **Mineral production** (1978): total value, $339.6 million; metals, $281.8 million; structural materials, $37.7 million; fuels, $8.8 million. **Commercial fishing:** (1977) $34.4 million. **Value of construction** (1978): $936.6 million. **Employment distribution** (1979): 27% services; 18% trade; 15% manufacturing; 9% construction; 8% public administration; 2.5% agriculture. **Per capita income** (1978): $5,984. **Unemployment** (1979): 11.1%.

Finance: No. banks: 178; **No. credit unions, caisses populaires:** 133.

International airports: none.

Federal Government: No. federal employees (1979): 14,514. **Federal payroll** (1979): $217.9 million.

Energy. Electricity production, by mwh, (1979): mineral, 6,052,493; hydroelectric, 3,113,015.

Education. No. schools: 419 elementary; 65 secondary; 13 higher education. **Avg. salary, public school teachers** (1978-79): $16,972.

Provincial Data. Motto: Spem Reduxit (Hope Restored). **Flower:** Purple violet. **Bird:** none. **Date entered Confederation:** 1867. **Capital:** Fredericton.

Politics. Premier: Richard Hatfield (Progressive Conservative). **Leaders, opposition parties:** Joseph Daigle (Liberal). **Composition of legislature** (June, 1980): P.C.

30; Lib. 28. **Date of last election:** Oct. 23, 1978.

Tourist attractions: Roosevelt-Campobello International Memorial Park; the tidal bore at Chignacto Bay (Moncton); Magnetic Hill (Moncton); sport salmon fishing in the Miramichi River; 108 covered bridges including the world's longest at Hartland.

Newfoundland

People. Population (Jan. 1980): 577,400; **rank:** 9. **Pop. density:** 4 per sq. mi. **Urban** (1976) 58.9%. **Ethnic distrib.** (1976): English 98%. **Net migration** (1978-79): −1,872.

Geography. Total area: 156,185 sq. mi.; **rank:** 7. **Land area:** 143,045 sq. mi. **Acres forested land:** 31,504,000. **Location:** 2 parts: a 43,359 sq. mi. Atlantic island and 112,826 sq. mi. mainland Labrador, bordered to the E by northern Quebec and to the W by the Atlantic Ocean. **Climate:** ranges from subarctic in Labrador and northern tip of island to humid continental with cool summers and heavy precipitation. **Topography:** highlands of the Long Range (max. elev. 2,673 ft.) along the western coast; central plateau contains uplands descending to lowlands towards the northeast; interior barren and rocky with many lakes and bogs; Labrador is part of the Canadian Shield.

Economy. Principal industries: mining, manufacturing, fishing, pulp and paper, electricity production. **Principal manufactured goods:** fish products, paper products. **Value added by manufacture** (1977): $351.2 million. **Gross Domestic Product** (1978): $3 billion. **Agriculture: Livestock** (1978): 952,000 poultry. **Forestry production** (1977): $40 million. **Mineral production** (1978): total value, $675 million; metals, $634 million; asbestos, $18 million; structural materials, $16 million. **Commercial fishing:** (1977) $85.5 million. **Value of construction** (1978): $668.9 million. **Employment distribution** (1979): 26% services; 18% trade; 14% manufacturing; 9.7% construction; 8.7% public administration. **Per capita income** (1978): $5,313. **Unemployment** (1979): 15.4%.

Finance: No. banks: 143; **no. credit unions, caisses populaires:** 15.

International airports: Gander.

Federal Government: No. federal employees (1979): 8,799. **Federal payroll** (1979): $126.1 million.

Energy. Electricity production, by mwh, (1979): mineral, 1,303,777; hydroelectric, 42,212,087.

Education. No. schools: 543 elementary; 144 secondary; 7 higher education. **Avg. salary, public school teachers** (1978-79): $17,500.

Provincial data. Motto: Quaerite prime regnum Dei (Seek ye first the kingdom of God). **Flower:** Pitcher plant. **Bird:** none. **Date entered Confederation:** 1949. **Capital:** St. John's.

Politics. Premier: Brian Peckford (Progressive Conservative). **Leaders, opposition parties:** Don Jamieson (Liberal) John Greene, (New Democratic). **Composition of legislature** (June, 1980): PC 34; Lib. 18; **Date of last election:** June 18, 1979.

Tourist attractions: numerous picturesque "outport" fishing villages; Signal Hill National Historical Park (St. John's); the Aviation Museum at Gander International Airport; Witless Bay Island Seabird Sanctuary.

Nova Scotia

People. Population (Jan. 1980): 851,000; **rank:** 7. **Pop. density:** 41.7 per sq. mi. **Urban** (1976) 55.8%. **Ethnic distrib.** (1976): English 92.7%; French 4.4%. **Net migration** (1978-79): +1,384.

Geography. Total area: 21,425 sq. mi.; **rank:** 9. **Land area:** 20,402 sq. mi. **Acres forested land:** 10,762,000. **Location:** connected to New Brunswick by a 17-mi. isthmus, otherwise surrounded by water - the Gulf of St. Lawrence, Atlantic Ocean and Bay of Fundy. **Climate:** humid continental, with some moderating effects due to the province's maritime location; avg. July temperature high in Halifax is 23°C, avg. Jan. low −10°C. **Topography:** the Atlantic Uplands in the southern half of the province descend to lowlands in the northern portion; 6,479 mi. of coastline, 3,000 lakes, hundreds of rivers.

Economy. Principal industries: manufacturing, fishing, mining, tourism, agriculture, petroleum refining. **Principal manufactured goods:** paper and allied products, fish products, dairy products, ships. **Value added by manufacture** (1977): $776.2 million. **Gross Domestic Product** (1978); $5.6 billion. **Agriculture: Chief crops:** apples, blueberrries, strawberries, oats, potatoes. **Livestock** (1978): 125,000 cattle; 80,000 pigs; 23,000 sheep; 3,118,000 poultry. **Forestry production** (1977): $24.4 million. **Mineral production** (1978): total value, $210.7 million; fuels, $120.7 million (all from coal); structural materials, $43 million; gypsum, $25 million. **Commercial fishing:** (1977) $133.1 million. **Value of construction** (1978): $983.7 million. **Employment distribution** (1979): 28% services; 18% trade; 15% manufacturing; 9% public administration; 8% construction; 2.3% agriculture. **Per capita income** (1978); $6,447. **Unemployment** (1979): 10.2%.

Finance: No. banks: 245; **No. credit unions, caisses populaires:** 116.

International airports: Halifax.

Federal Government: No. federal employees (1979): 35,906. **Federal payroll** (1979): $541.7 million.

Energy. Electricity production, by mwh, (1979): mineral, 4,989,343; hydroelectric, 1,176,267.

Education. No. schools: 537 elementary; 78 secondary; 24 higher education. **Avg. salary, public school teachers** (1978-79): $18,306.

Provincial Data. Motto: Munit Haec et Altera Vincit (One Defends and the Other Conquers). **Flower:** Trailing arbutus. **Bird:** None. **Date entered Confederation:** 1867. **Capital:** Halifax.

Politics. Premier: John M. Buchanan (Progressive conservative). **Leaders, opposition parties:** A.M. "Sandy" Cameron (Liberal); vacant (New Democratic). **Composition of legislature** (June, 1980): P.C. 33; Lib 15; NDP 4. **Date of last election:** Sept. 18, 1978.

Tourist attractions: Cabot Trail around Cape Breton Island; Fortress Louisbourg; Peggy's Cove; Alexander Graham Bell Museum (Baddeck); the Miners' Museum (Glace Bay; Nova Scotia Museum (Halifax); Citadel Hill (Halifax).

Ontario

People. Population (Jan. 1980); 8,543,300; **rank:** 1. **Pop. density:** 24.8 per sq. mi. **Urban** (1976) 81.2% **Ethnic distrib.** (1976): English 78.1%; French 5.6%; German 1.9%; Portuguese 1%. **Net migration** (1978-79) −8,069.

Geography. Total area: 412,582 sq. mi.; **rank:** 2. **Land area:** 344,092 sq. mi. **Acres forested land:** 106,806,000. **Location:** Canada's most centrally-situated province, with Quebec on the E and Manitoba to the W; extends N to shores of James and Hudson Bays; southern boundary with New York, Michigan, Minnesota, and 4 great Lakes. **Climate:** ranges from humid continental in southern regions to subarctic in the far north, westerly winds bring winter storms; the Great lakes moderate winter temperatures. **Topography:** 2/3 of province is Precambrian rock of the Canadian Shield; lowland areas lie along the shores of Hudson Bay, the St. Lawrence River and the southern Great Lakes region.

Economy. Principal industries: manufacturing, construction, tourism, agriculture, mining, forestry, fisheries and wildlife. **Principal manufactured goods:** motor vehicles, iron and steel, motor vehicle parts and accessories, foods and beverages, paper and allied products. **Value added by manufacture** (1977): $24.3 billion. **Gross Domestic Product** (1978): $90 billion. **Agriculture: Chief crops:** corn, wheat, oats, barley, rye, tobacco, tree fruits. **Livestock** (1978): 3,005,000 cattle; 2,210,000 pigs; 114,000 sheep; 36,533,000 poultry. **Forestry production** (1977): $231.1 million. **Mineral production** (1978): total value, $2.7 billion; metals, $2 billion; structural materials, $528 million; fuels, $27 million. **Commercial fishing:** (1977) $14.3 million. **Value of construction** (1978): $11.06 billion. **Employment distribution** (1979): 27% services; 25% manufacturing; 17% trade; 6% public administration; 6% construction; 3.6% agriculture. **Per capita income** (1978): $8,735. **Unemployment** (1979): 6.5%

Finance: No. banks: 2,875; **No credit unions, caisses populaires:** 1,100

International airports: Toronto, Ottawa.

Federal Government: No. federal employees (1979): 169,393. **Federal payroll** (1979): $2.8 billion.

Energy. Electricity production, by mwh, (1979): mineral, 33,581,913; hydroelectric, 42,223,647; nuclear, 33,275,392.

Education. No. schools: 4,379 elementary; 803 secondary; 52 higher education. **Avg. salary, public school teachers** (1978-79): $20,029.

Provincial data. Motto: Ut Incepit Fidelis Sic Permanet (Loyal she began, loyal she remains). **Flower:** White trillium. **Bird:** none. **Date entered Confederation:** 1867. **Capital:** Toronto.

Politics. Premier: William (Bill) Davis (Progressive Conservative), **Leaders, opposition parties:** Dr. Stuart Smith (Liberal) Michael Cassidy (New Democratic). **Composition of legislature** (June 1980): PC 58; Lib. 34; NDP 33. **Date of last election:** June 9, 1977.

Tourist attractions. Toronto C.N. Tower, Ontario Science Centre, Ontario Place, Metro Toronto Zoo, McLaughlin Planetarium, Black Creek Pioneer Village, Canadian Nation Exhibition (mid Aug. to Labor Day); Ottawa's Parliament buildings; Niagara Falls; Polar Bear Express and Agawa Canyon train rides into northern Ontario.

Prince Edward Island

People. Population (Jan. 1980): 123,900; **rank:** 10. **Pop. density:** 56.7 per sq. mi. **Urban** (1976) 37.1% **Ethnic distrib.** (1976): English 92.7%; French 5.5%. **Net migration** (1978-79): −116.

Geography. Total area: 2,184 sq. mi.; **rank:** 10. **Land area:** 2,184 sq. mi. **Acres forested land:** 619,000. **Location:** an island 140 mi. long, between 40 and 140 mi. wide, situated in the Gulf of St. Lawrence approx. 10 mi. from the coasts of Nova Scotia and New Brunswick. **Climate:** humid continental with temperatures moderated by maritime location; avg. Jan. low in Charlottetown is −11°C, avg. July high 23°C. **Topography:** gently rolling hills; sharply indented coastline; many streams but only small rivers and lakes.

Economy. Principal industries: agriculture, tourism, fisheries, light manufacturing. **Principal manufactured goods:** paint, farm vehicles, metal products, electronic equipment. **Value added by manufacture** (1977): $45 million. **Gross Domestic Product** (1978): $633.7 million. **Agriculture: Chief crops:** potatoes, mixed grains, oats, barley. **Livestock** (1978): 94,000 cattle; 80,800 pigs; 4,100 sheep; 277,000 poultry. **Mineral production** (1978): total value, $2.068 million, all from sand and gravel. **Commercial fishing:** (1977) $15.2 million. **Value of construction** (1978): $139.6 million. **Employment distribution** (1979): 28% services; 17% trade; 11% agriculture; 9% manufacturing; 9% construction; 7% public administration. **Per capita income** (1978): $5,574. **Unemployment** (1979): 11.3%.

Finance: No. banks: 34; **No. credit unions, caisses populaires:** 13.

International airports: none.

Federal Government: No. federal employees (1979): 2,920. **Federal payroll:** (1979): $45 million.

Energy. Electricity production, by mwh, (1979): mineral, 151,126.

Education. No. schools: 60 elementary; 15 secondary; 3 higher education. **Avg. salary, public school teachers** (1978-79): $17,913.

Provincial Data. Motto: Parva Sub Ingenti (The small under the protection of the large). **Flower:** Lady's slipper. **Bird:** Blue jay. **Date entered Confederation:** 1873. **Capital:** Charlottetown.

Politics. Premier: Angus MacLean (Progressive Conservative). **Leaders, opposition parties:** W. Bennett Campbell (Liberal), Doreen Sark (New Democratic). **Composition of legislature** (June, 1980): P.C. 21; Lib. 10; 1 vacant. **Date of last election:** Apr. 23, 1979.

Tourist attractions: P.E.I. National Park; beaches all along the coastline; 9 golf courses; 70 campgrounds; Summerside Lobster Carnival, 3d wk. in July; Charlottetown Old Home Week, 3d wk. in Aug.; Charlottetown Confederation Centre; Woodleigh Replicas (Burlington).

Quebec

People. Population (Jan. 1980): 6,288,300; **rank:** 2. **Pop. density:** 12 per sq. mi. **Urban** (1976) 79.1%. **Ethnic distrib.** (1976): French 80%; English 12.8%; Italian 2%. **Net migration** (1978-79): −32,110.

Geography. Total area: 594,860 sq. mi.; **rank:** 1. **Land area:** 523,860 sq. mi. **Acres forested land:** 171,998,000. **Location:** borders Ontario on the W and Labrador and New Brunswick on the E; extends N to Hudson Strait and NW to James and Hudson Bays; the southern border touches New York, Vermont, New Hampshire and Maine. **Climate:** varies from subarctic in the northern half of the province to continental in the southern populated regions; avg. Jan. low in Montreal is −14°C, avg. Jan. High 26°C. **Topography:** half a million sq. mi. of Quebec consists of the Laurentian Uplands, part of the Canadian Shield; Appalachian Highlands are in southeastern Quebec; lowlands form a small area along the shore of the St. Lawrence River.

Economy. Principal industries: manufacturing, agriculture, electrical production, mining, meat processing, petroleum refining. **Principal manufactured goods:** foods and beverages, clothing, textiles, paper and paper products, furniture. **Value added by manufacture** (1977): $12.3 billion. **Gross Domestic Product** (1978): $56.2 billion. **Agriculture: Chief crops:** oats, corn grains, potatoes, mixed grains, tame hay, apples. **Livestock** (1978): 1,560,000 cattle; 1,989,000 pigs; 37,000 sheep; 25,279,000 poultry. **Forestry production** (1977): $285 million. **Mineral production** (1978): total value, $1.8 billion; metals, $799 million; asbestos, $440 million; structural materials, $440 million. **Commercial fishing:** (1977) $21.2 million. **Value of construction** (1978): $9.06 billion. **Employment distribution** (1979): 29% services; 23% manufacturing; 16% trade; 7% public administration; 5% construction; 2.6% agriculture. **Per capita income** (1978): $7,628. **Unemployment** (1979): 9.6%.

Finance: No. banks: 1,617; **no. credit unions, caisses populaires:** 1,575.

International airports: Dorval, Mirabel (both near Montreal).

Federal Government: No. federal employees (1979): 79,080. **Federal payroll** (1979): $1.2 billion.

Energy. Electricity production, by mwh, (1979): mineral, 481,443; hydroelectric, 88,506,367.

Education. No. schools: 2,990 elementary-secondary; 80 higher education. **Avg. salary, public school teachers** (1978-79): $n.a.

Provincial Data. Motto Je me souviens (I remember). **Flower:** Fleur de Lys. **Birds:** Alouette (lark). **Date entered Confederation:** 1867. **Capital:** Quebec City.

Politics. Premier: Rene Levesque (Parti Quebecois). **Leaders, opposition parties:** Claude Ryan (Liberal); vacant (Union Nationale); Camil Samson (Creditiste Democrate). **Composition of legislature** (June, 1980): PQ 68; Lib. 29; UN 5; CD 1; 3 independent; 1 vacant. **Date of last election:** Nov. 15, 1976.

Tourist attractions: Quebec City, often described as North America's "most European city", and sophisticated Montreal each offer numerous attractions; the north shore of the St. Lawrence River and the Gaspé Peninsula are picturesque.

Saskatchewan

People. Population (Jan. 1980): 965,300; **rank:** 6. **Pop. density:** 4.4 per sq. mi. **Urban** (1976) 55.5% **Ethnic distrib.** (1976): English 77.7%; German 6.6%; Ukrainian 5%; French 2.9%; Native Indian 2.3% **Net migration** (1978-79): +1,711.

Geography. Total area: 251,700 sq. mi.; **rank:** 5. **Land area:** 220,182 sq. mi. **Acres forested land:** 31,678,000. **Location:** borders on the Northwest Territories to the N, Manitoba to the E, Alberta to the W, and Montana and North Dakota to the S. **Climate:** continental, with cold winters (Jan. avg. low in Regina is −23°C) and hot summers (July avg. high in Regina is 26°C). **Topography:** southern 2/3ds of province are plains and grassland; northern 3d is Canadian Shield.

Economy. Principal industries: agriculture, mining of potash, meat processing, electricity production, petroleum refining. **Principal manufactured goods:** foods and beverages, agricultural implements, fabricated metals, nonmetallic mineral products. **Value added by manufacture** (1977): $489.2 million. **Gross Domestic product** 1978): $9.7 billion. **Agriculture: Chief crops:** wheat (60% of national total), barley, oats, mustard seed, rye, flax. **Livestock** (1978): 2,332,500 cattle; 515,000 pigs; 52,500 sheep; 5,140,000 poultry. **Forestry production** 1977): $18.3 million. **Mineral production** 1978): total value, $1.6 billion; fuels, $733 million; potash, $504 million; metals, $273 million; structural materials, $44 million. **Commercial fishing:** (1977) $3.3 million. **Value of construction** (1978): $1.67 billion. **Employment distribution** (1979): 25% services; 23% agriculture; 16% trade; 7% public administration; 7% construction; 6% manufacturing. **Per capita income** (1978): $7,432. **Unemployment** (1979): 4.2%.

Finance: No. banks: 378; **No. credit unions, caisses populaires:** 235.

International airports: none.

Federal Government: No. Federal employees (1979): 13,403. **Federal payroll** (1979): $204.9 million.

Energy. Electricity production, by mwh, (1979): mineral, 6,690,221; hydroelectric, 2,415,690.

Education. No. schools: 913 elementary; 149 secondary; 6 higher education. **Avg. salary, public school teachers** (1977-78); $15,920.

Provincial Data. Motto: none. **Flower:** Red prairie lily. **Bird:** Prairie sharp-tailed grouse. **Date entered Confederation:** 1905. **Capital:** Regina.

Politics. Premier: Allan Blakeney (New Democratic). **Leaders, opposition parties:** Grant Devine (Progressive Conservative); Dick Colver (Unionest). **Composition of legislature** (June, 1980): NDP 44; PC 15; Unst. 2. **Date of last election:** Oct. 18, 1978.

Tourist attractions. Regina: RCMP Museum, Museum of Natural History, Wascana Centre; Western Development Museums located at Saskatoon, Yorkton, North Battleford, Moose Jaw.

Territories of Canada

In addition to its 10 provinces, Canada contains the Yukon and Northwest Territories making up more than a third of the nation's land area but less than .3% of its population. Each territory is administered by a resident commissioner appointed by the federal government which retains control over natural resources excluding wildlife. An elected legislative assembly in each territory exercises jurisdiction over such matters as education, housing, social services and renewable resources. The Commissioner of the Northwest Territories serves as chairman of and acts on the advice of an executive committee of up to 9 members, 7 of them appointed from a 22-member elected assembly. The Yukon commissioner acts on the advice of a 5-member executive council, all of whom are appointed on the recommendation of the leader of the majority party in the assembly.

The NWT elects 2 members to the federal parliament, the Yukon one member. Each territory has one Senate representative. There is substantial support in both territories for increased autonomy or provincial status.

The Yukon

*Data applies to both Territories.

People. Population (Jan. 1980): 21,800; **Pop. density:** 0.1 per sq. mi. **Urban** (1976) 61%. **Ethnic distrib. by mother tongue** (1976): English 86.7%; French 2.4%; Native Indian 2.3%; German 1.9%. (Using other criteria Native Indians make up 19% of the population). **Net migration** (1978-79): −350*.

Geography. Total area: 186,299 sq. mi. **Land area:** 184,569 sq. mi. **Acres forested land:** 57,417,000. **Location:** extreme northwestern area of mainland Canada; bounded on the N by the Beaufort Sea, on the S by British Columbia, on the E by the Mackenzie District of the Northwest Territories, and on the W by Alaska. **Climate:** great variance in temperatures; warm summers, very cold winters; low precipitation. **Topography:** main feature is the Yukon plateau with 21 peaks exceeding 10,000 ft.; open tundra in the far north.

Economy. Principal industries: mining, tourism. **Principal manufactured goods:** small amounts of cement, explosives, forest products, and outdoor recreation equipment. **Value added by manufacture** (1977) $7 million*. **Gross domestic product** (1978): $705 million*. **Agriculture:** hay, oats, vegetable gardens for local use. **Mineral production** (1978): total value, $219 million; metals, $192 million; asbestos, $27 million. **Commercial fishing:** (1977) $2.4 million*. **Per capita income** (1978): $7,554.* **No. of banks:** 14.

Federal Government: No. federal employees (1979): 1,583. **Federal payroll** (1979): $22.1 million.

Energy. Electricity production, by mwh, (1979): minerals, 36,129; hydroelectric, 317,305.

Education. No. schools: 20 elementary; 2 secondary; 0 higher education. **Avg. salary, public school teachers** (1978-79): $21,914.

Territorial Data. Flower: Fireweed. **Date established:** June 13, 1898. **Capital:** Whitehorse. **Commissioner:** vacant. **Party leaders:** Chris Pearson (Progressive Conservative), Iain MacKay (Liberal), Tony Penikett (New Democratic). **Composition of assembly** (June 1980): P.C. 11; Lib. 2; NDP 1; 2 Independent. **Date of last election:** Nov. 20, 1978.

Tourist attractions: Whitehorse, Dawson City, the Klondike area, Miles Canyon.

The Northwest Territories

People. Population (Jan. 1980): 43,100; **Pop. density:** 0.03 per sq. mi. **Urban** (1976) 49.7% **Ethnic distrib. by mother tongue** (1976): English 54.2%; Inuit 26.7%; Native Indian 9.7%; French 2.6%. (Using other criteria the Inuit make up 35% of the population, Native Indians 17%.) **Net migration** (1978-79): −1,257.

Geography. Total area: 1,304,903 sq. mi. **Land area:** 1,253,438 sq. mi. **Acres forested land:** 135,194,000 **Location:** all land north of the 60th parallel between the Yukon Territory and Hudson Bay and all northern islands east to Greenland; land area bounded by the Yukon Territory to the W, Hudson Bay to the E, the Beaufort Sea to the N and B.C, Alta., Sask. and Man. to S. **Climate:** extreme temperatures and low precipitation; Arctic and sub-Arctic. **Topography:** mostly tundra plains formed on the rocks of the Canadian Shield; the Mackenzie Lowland is a continuation of the Great Plains; the Mackenzie River Valley is forested.

Economy. Principal industries: mining, mineral and hydrocarbon exploration; oil refining. **Value added by manufacture** (1977): see Yukon. **Gross domestic product** (1978): see Yukon. **Agriculture:** scattered market gardening in the southern Mackenzie district only. **Mineral production** (1978): total value, $310 million; metals, $271 million; fuels, $39 million. **Commercial fishing:** (1977): see Yukon. **Per capita income** (1978): see Yukon. **No. of banks** 17.

Federal Government: No. federal employees (1979): 2,970. **Federal payroll** (1979); $41.2 million.

Energy. Electricity production, by mwh, (1979): mineral, 98,317; hydroelectric, 289,573.

Education. No. schools: 65 elementary; 5 secondary; 0 higher education. **Avg. salary, public school teachers** (1978-79): $23,675.

Territorial Data. Flower: Mountain avens. **Date Established:** June 22, 1869. **Capital:** Yellowknife. **Commissioner:** John H. Parker. **Council:** 22 independent elected representatives.

Tourist attractions: Wood Buffalo, Auyuittuq, and Nahanni National Parks; Mackenzie River and Delta; annual Midnight Golf Tournament in Yellowknife July 21.

Head of State and Cabinet

Canada's official head of state, Queen Elizabeth of England, who succeeded to the throne in 1952, is represented by Governor-General Rt. Hon. Edward Schreyer, appointed in 1979. Titles: Minister unless otherwise stated or *Minister of State.

(listed according to precedence) (March 3, 1980)

Prime Minister — Pierre Elliott Trudeau
Deputy Prime Minister and Minister of Finance — Allan J. MacEachen
Government House Leader and President of the Privy Council — Yvon Pinard
***Department of Finance** — Pierre Bussieres
Secretary of State for External Affairs — Mark R. MacGuigan
Energy, Mines and Resources — Marc Lalonde
Leader of the Government in the Senate — Senator Ray Perrault
President of the Treasury Board — Donald Johnston
National Health and Welfare — Monique Begin
Industry, Trade and Commerce — Herb Gray
***Trade** — Ed Lumley
***Economic Development, Senate House Leader** — Senator H.A. (Bud) Olson
Employment and Immigration, *Status of Women — Lloyd Axworthy
Justice, Attorney-General, *Social Development — Jean Chretien
Transport — Jean-Luc Pepin
Communications, Secretary of State — Francis Fox
National Defence — Gilles Lamontagne
National Revenue — William Rompkey
Labor, *Sports — Gerald Regan
Indian Affairs and Northern Development — John Munro
Agriculture — Eugene Whelan
Supply and Services — Jean-Jacques Blais
Solicitor-General — Robert Kaplan
Consumer and Corporate Affairs, Postmaster-General — Andre Oullet
Regional Economic Expansion — Pierre De Bane
Fisheries and Oceans — Romeo LeBlanc
Veterans Affairs — Daniel MacDonald
Public Works with Responsibility for the Canada Mortgage and Housing Corp. — Paul Cosgrove
***Multiculturalism** — Jim Fleming
***Small Business** — Charles Lapointe
Environment, *Science and Technology — John Roberts
***Canadian Wheat Board** — Senator Hazen Argue
***Mines** — Judy Erola

Governors-General of Canada Since Confederation, 1867

Name	Term
The Viscount Monck of Ballytrammon	1867-1868
The Baron Lisgar of Lisgar and Bailieborough	1869-1872
The Earl of Dufferin	1872-1878
The Marquis of Lorne	1878-1883
The Marquis of Lansdowne	1883-1888
The Baron Stanley of Preston	1888-1893
The Earl of Aberdeen	1893-1898
The Earl of Minto	1898-1904
The Earl Grey	1904-1911
Field Marshall H.R.H. The Duke of Connaught	1911-1916
The Duke of Devonshire	1916-1921
General The Baron Byng of Vimy	1921-1926
The Viscount Willingdon of Ratton	1926-1931
The Earl of Bessborough	1931-1935
The Baron Tweedsmuir of Elsfield	1935-1940
Major General The Earl of Athlone	1940-1946
Field Marshall The Viscount Alexander of Tunis	1946-1952
The Right Hon. Vincent Massey	1952-1959
General The Right Hon. Georges P. Vanier	1959-1967
The Right Hon. Roland Michener	1967-1974
The Right Hon. Jules Leger	1974-1979
The Right Hon. Edward Schreyer	1979-

Fathers of Confederation

Union of the British North American colonies into the Dominion of Canada was discussed and its terms negotiated at 3 confederation conferences held at Charlottetown (C), Sept. 1, 1864; Quebec (Q), Oct. 10, 1864; and London (L), Dec. 4, 1866. The names of delegates are followed by the provinces they represented. Canada refers to what are now the provinces of Ontario and Quebec.

Adams G. Archibald, N.S.	(C,Q,L)
George Brown, Canada	(C,Q)
Alexander Campbell, Canada	(C,Q)
Frederick B.T. Carter, Nfld.	(Q)
George-Etienne Cartier, Canada	(C,Q,L)
Edward B. Chandler, N.B.	(C,Q)
Jean-Charles Chapais, Canada	(Q)
James Cockburn, Canada	(Q)
George H. Coles, P.E.I.	(C,Q)
Robert B. Dickey, N.S.	(Q)
Charles Fisher, N.B.	(Q,L)
Alexander T. Galt, Canada	(C,Q,L)
John Hamilton Gray, N.B.	(C,Q)
John Hamilton Gray, P.E.I.	(C,Q)
Thomas Heath Haviland, P.E.I.	(Q)
William A. Henry, N.S.	(C,Q,L)
William P. Howland, Canada	(L)
John M. Johnson, N.B.	(C,Q,L)
Hector L. Langevin, Canada	(C,Q,L)
Jonathan McCully, N.S.	(C,Q,L)
A.A. Macdonald, P.E.I.	(C,Q)
John A. Macdonald, Canada	(C,Q,L)
William McDougall, Canada	(C,Q,L)
Thomas D'Arcy McGee, Canada	(C,Q)
Peter Mitchell, N.B.	(Q,L)
Oliver Mowat, Canada	(Q)
Edward Palmer, P.E.I.	(C,Q)
William H. Pope, P.E.I.	(C,Q)
John W. Ritchie, N.S.	(L)
J. Ambrose Shea, Nfld.	(Q)
William H. Steeves, N.B.	(C,Q)
Sir Etienne-Paschal Tache, Canada	(Q)
Samuel Leonard Tilley, N.B.	(C,Q,L)
Charles Tupper, N.S.	(C,Q,L)
Edward Whelan, P.E.I.	(Q)
R.D. Wilmot, N.B.	(L)

The Political Parties

Canadian parties, from whatever point in the political spectrum they begin, gravitate towards the middle of the road where most of the votes lie. Despite variations in outlook and policy, all 3 official parties tend to adopt a practical rather than dogmatic line on most issues.

Progressive Conservatives — Canada's oldest party and theoretically the furthest to the right, the Conservatives have nevertheless endorsed an extension of social welfare. Though their support is based in western Canada, the Conservatives were the only party to elect at least one representative from each province in the 1980 election. The party has held office only briefly since 1962, and then only with minority governments, mainly due to a failure to gain support in Quebec. **Leader:** Joe Clark.

Liberals — Though politically situated between the Conservatives to the right and the New Democrats on the left, the Liberals are flexible enough to lean in either direction depending on specific issues and political situations. In 1975 they belatedly adopted a Conservative proposal for wage and price controls; in 1979 they sided with the NDP to oppose Conservative plans to return some government-owned corporations to the private sector. Most of their traditional electoral support comes from middle and upper class urban residents, from ethnic voters, and among French-speaking Canadians. **Leader:** Pierre Trudeau.

New Democratic Party — Successor to the Cooperative Commonwealth Federation, which combined the agrarian protest movement in western Canada with a democratic socialism of the British Labor Party variety, the NDP was founded in 1961. It now attempts to attract the vote of middle-class Canadians and fuse it with the party's labor support. **Leader:** Ed Broadbent.

Political power in Canada has been dominated by the Conservative and Liberal parties. Of 32 federal elections since Confederation, the Conservatives have won 13, holding power for 47 years; the Liberals have gained office 19 times, governing for 66 years. As a measure of Liberal strength, all of the party's 20th century leaders have been elected Prime Minister—though not always on the first attempt.

Despite the dominance of the Liberals and Conservatives, third parties have played an important role under Canada's parliamentary system in which a governing party holding less than half the seats in the House of Commons can remain in office and pass legislation only with the support of a minor party. A minority Conservative Government lost power in 1979 when none of the opposition parties supported its proposed budget.

The NDP has been the most influential of the third parties, consistently winning between 15% and 20% of the popular vote—though its proportion of elected members is always less. NDP pressure from the left has influenced policy decisions by both major parties. The Social Credit Party, once a strong political force with federal support in Quebec and the western provinces, has declined in stature over the past 2 decades and in 1980 failed to elect any members to Parliament.

Prime Ministers of Canada

Name	Party	Term	Name	Party	Term
Sir John A. MacDonald	Conservative	1867-1873 1878-1891	W.L.M. King.	Liberal	1921-1926 1926-1930 1935-1948
Alexander Mackenzie	Liberal	1873-1878			
Sir John J. C. Abbott	Conservative	1891-1892	R. B. Bennett.	Conservative	1930-1935
Sir John S. D. Thompson . . .	Conservative	1892-1894	Louis St. Laurent	Liberal	1948-1957
Sir Mackenzie Bowell	Conservative	1894-1896	John G. Diefenbaker.	Prog. Cons.	1957-1963
Sir Charles Tupper.	Conservative	1896	Lester B. Pearson	Liberal	1963-1968
Sir Wilfrid Laurier	Liberal	1896-1911	Pierre Elliott Trudeau	Liberal	1968-1979
Sir Robert L. Borden	Conservative Unionist	1911-1920	Joe Clark	Prog. Cons.	1979-1980
			Pierre Elliott Trudeau	Liberal	1980-
Arthur Meighen	Cons. Union.	1920-1921			

Election Results[1] by Province and Party, May 22, 1980

Province	Total Valid Votes	Liberal	Conservative	New Dem.	Soc. Cred.	Other
Alberta.	794,946	176,565	515,639	81,732	8,162	12,848
British Columbia.	1,209,453	268,069	501,921	426,857	1,709	10,897
Manitoba.	476,001	133,353	179,607	159,432	—	3,609
New Brunswick	335,702	168,316	109,053	54,481	—	3,852
Newfoundland.	203,045	95,354	72,999	33,943	—	749
Nova Scotia	422,281	168,303	163,436	88,115	—	2,427
Ontario.	4,000,162	1,675,164	1,420,263	874,092	804	29,839
Prince Edward Island.	66,174	31,055	30,576	4,335	—	208
Quebec	2,957,120	2,017,067	373,233	268,677	174,282	123,861
Saskatchewan	455,709	110,501	177,338	165,294	178	2,398
N.W. Territories	16,195	5,801	4,000	6,214	—	180
Yukon	9,669	3,825	3,926	1,918	—	—
TOTAL.	**10,946,457**	**4,853,373**	**3,551,991**	**2,165,090**	**185,135**	**190,868**
Percent.	100	44.34	32.45	19.78	1.69	1.71
Seats.	282	147	103	32	0	0

(1) Preliminary.

Party Representation by Regions, 1949-1980

Canada	1949	1953	1957	1958	1962	1963	1965	1968	1972	1974	1979	1980
Liberal.	193	171	105	48	100	129	131	155	109	141	114	147
Conservative	41	51	112	208	116	95	97	72	107	95	136	103
New Democratic[1]	13	23	25	8	19	17	21	22	31	16	26	32
Social Credit	10	15	19	—	30	24	14	14	15	11	6	0
Other	5	5	4	1	—	—	2	1	2	1	0	0
Ontario												
Liberal.	56	51	21	14	44	52	51	64	36	55	32	52
Conservative	25	33	61	67	35	27	25	17	40	25	57	38
New Democratic[1]	1	1	3	3	6	6	9	6	11	8	6	5
Quebec												
Liberal.	68	66	62	25	35	47	56	56	56	60	67	74
Conservative	2	4	9	50	14	8	8	4	2	3	2	1
Social Credit	—	—	—	—	26	20	9	14	15	11	6	—
Atlantic												
Liberal.	26	27	12	8	14	20	15	7	10	13	12	19
Conservative	7	5	21	25	18	13	18	25	22	17	18	13
New Democratic[1]	1	1	—	—	1	—	—	—	—	1	2	—
Western[2]												
Liberal.	43	27	10	1	7	10	9	28	7	13	3	2
Conservative	7	9	21	66	49	47	46	26	43	50	59	51
New Democratic[1]	11	21	22	5	12	11	12	16	20	7	18	27
Social Credit	10	15	19	—	4	4	5	—	—	—	—	—

(1) Prior to 1962 election was known as the Cooperative Commonwealth Federation.
(2) Includes the Yukon and Northwest Territories.

Canadian Armed Forces

In Feb., 1968, Canada carried out the unification of its traditionally separate services: the Royal Canadian Navy, the Canadian Army, and the Royal Canadian Air Force. The first step towards a unified force was taken in 1964 when the 3 services were brought together under one control with common logistics and supply and training systems, but retaining their separate legal entities. The positions of Chairman of the Chiefs of Staff and Chiefs of the Navy, Army, and Air Force were abolished and replaced by the Chief of the Defense Staff. On Feb. 1, 1968, the 3 services ceased to exist. They were unified into the Canadian Armed Forces in which all officers, men, and women are managed within a single body, with a common uniform.

Chief of the Defense Staff: Gen. R.M. Withers
Vice Chief of the Defense Staff: Lieut. Gen. G.C.E. Theriault

Maritime Command — Vice Admiral J.A. Fulton
Mobile Command — Lieut. Gen. J. J. Paradis
Air Command — Lieut. Gen. K.E. Lewis
Communications Command — Brig. Gen. D. P. Harrison
Canadian Forces Europe — Maj. Gen. J.E. Hannah

Regular Forces Strength

(as of March 31)

Year	Navy	Army	Air Force	Total	Year	Total	Year	Total	Year	Total
1945	92,529	494,258	174,254	761,041	1970	91,433	1975	78,448	1978	79,656
1955	19,207	49,409	49,461	118,077	1973	81,443	1976	78,394	1979	78,974
1965	19,756	46,264	48,144	114,164	1974	80,639	1977	78,091	1980	79,909

Canadian Military Participation in Major Conflicts

Northwest Rebellion (1885)(1)
Participants—3,323
Killed—38
Last veteran died at the age of 104 in 1971.
South African War (1899-1902)
Participants—7,368(2)
Killed—89
Living Veterans—less than 30
First World War (1914-1918)
Participants—626,636(3)
Killed—61,332(4)
Living Veterans—42,222(5)
Second World War (1939-1945)
Participants—1,086,343 (inc. 45,423 women)
Killed—32,714 (inc. 8 women)
Living Veterans—747,365(5)(6)
Korean War (1950-1953)
Participants—25,583
Killed—314

(1) First battle in history to be fought entirely by Canadian troops. (2) Includes Canadians in the South African constabulary and 8 nursing sisters. (3) Includes 2,854 nursing sisters. (4) Includes 21 nursing sisters and 1,563 airmen serving with the British air forces. (5) 1980 est. based on mortality rates applied to 1971 census data. (6) Includes Korean War veterans.

Canadian World War II Winners of the Victoria Cross

The Victoria Cross is Britain's highest military honor. It has been accorded to 94 Canadians since its inception in 1856. The cross was originally cast from metal of a Russian cannon captured during the Crimean War.

Name	Unit	Theater of war, date
Sgt. J. R. Osborn	Winnipeg Grenadiers	Hong Kong, Dec. 19, 1941
Lt. Col. C. E. Merritt	S. Sask. Regiment	Dieppe, Aug. 19, 1942
Capt. J. W. Foote	Royal Hamilton Light Infantry	Dieppe, Aug. 19, 1942
Capt. F. T. Peters	Royal Navy	Oran, North Africa, Nov. 8, 1942
Capt. Paul Triquet	Royal 22d Regiment	Casa Berardi, Dec. 14, 1943
Maj. C. F. Hoey	Lincolnshire Regiment	Burma, Feb. 16, 1944
Maj. John K. Mahoney	Westminster Regiment	Melfa River, May 24, 1944
P.O.A.C. Mynarksi	RCAF	Camria, France, June 12, 1944
Flt. Lieut. D. E. Hornell	RCAF	"Northern waters", June 25, 1944
Sqd. Ldr. Ian Bazalgette	RAF	Trossy St. Maximin, Aug. 4, 1944
Maj. D. V. Currie	South Alberta Regiment	Normandy, Aug. 20, 1944
Pvt. E. A. Smith	Seaforth Highlanders	Savio River, Italy, Oct. 22, 1944
Sgt. Aubrey Cosens	Queen's Own Rifles	Holland, Feb. 26, 1945
Maj. F. A. Tilston	Essex Scottish	Hochwald Forest, Mar. 1, 1945
Cpl. F. G. Topham	1st Canadian Parachute Battalion	Germany, Mar. 24, 1945
Lt. R. H. Gray	Royal Canadian Navy	Pacific, Aug. 9, 1945

Canadian Peacekeeping Operations

Canada has played a major role in the United Nations' efforts to preserve peace and promote international security, participating in almost all UN peacekeeping operations to date - in Egypt, Israel, Syria, Lebanon, Cyprus, Korea, India, Pakistan, West New Guinea, the Congo, Yemen and Nigeria.

Nearly 900 Canadian soldiers served in the Gaza Strip following the Israeli-Egyptian crisis of 1956 until the peacekeeping force there was disbanded in 1967. Another 850 Canadians served with the United Nations Emergency Force in the Middle East from 1973 until it was disbanded in Nov., 1979.

In the Congo, a 300-man signals unit provided communications for the UN force from 1960 to 1964.

Canadian participation in the International Commission for Control and Supervision in Vietnam and Laos began in 1954, and, at its height following U.S. military withdrawal from Vietnam in 1973, involved 245 Canadian Forces personnel. The Canadian Vietnam supervisory contingent was withdrawn in July 1973, the Laos mission in 1974.

Canadian peacekeeping operations in 1980 were as follows:

—some 515 Canadians in the UN Peacekeeping Force in Cyprus where Canadian participation began in 1964 and was augmented in 1974.

—250 Canadians, mostly logistics troops, with the UN Disengagement Observer Force in the Middle East.

—20 Canadian combat arms officers with the UN Truce Supervisory Organization, Israel.

Superlative Canadian Statistics

Source: Statistics Canada; Dept. of Energy, Mines and Resources

Area	Total: Land 3,539,462 sq. mi.; Water 291,571 sq. mi.	3,831,033 sq. mi.
Largest city in area	Timmins, Ont.	1,230 sq. mi.
Smallest city in area (east)	Vanier, Ont.	1.1 sq. mi.
Smallest city in area (west)	Chilliwack, B.C.	1.6 sq. mi.
Northernmost point	Cape Columbia, Ellesmere Island, N.W.T.	83°07'30"N.
Northernmost settlement	Alert, Ellesmere Island, N.W.T.	82°30'N.
Southernmost point	Middle Island (Lake Erie), Ont.	41°41'N.
Southernmost settlement	Pelee Island South, Essex Co., Ont.	41°45'N.
Easternmost point	Cape Spear, Nfld.	52°37'28"W.
Easternmost settlement	Blackhead, St. John's, Nfld.	52°39'W.
Westernmost point	Mount St. Elias, Yukon (at Alaskan border)	141°W.
Westernmost settlement	Beaver Creek, Yukon	140°52'W.
Highest city	Rossland, B.C. at R.R. Stn. (49°05'N,117°47'W)	3,465 ft.
Highest town	Lake Louise, Alta.	5,051 ft.
Highest waterfall	Takakkaw Falls (Daly Glacier), B.C. (51°30'N,116°29'W)	1,650 ft.
Longest river	Mackenzie (from head of Finlay R.)	2,635 mi.
Highest mountain	Mt. Logan (Yukon)	19,524 ft.
Rainiest spot	Henderson Lake, Vancouver Is. yrly. avg. rainfall	262 inches
Highest lake	Chilco Lake (51°20'N,124°05'W) 75.1 sq. mi.	3,842 ft.

Population and Area of Canada by Provinces

Source: Statistics Canada

		Area in square miles			Population		
Province, territory	Capital	Land	Fresh water	Total	1966 census	1976 census	Jan. 1980 estimate
Newfoundland	St. John's	143,045	13,140	156,185	493,396	557,725	577,400
Prince Edward Island	Charlottetown	2,184	...	2,184	108,645	118,229	123,900
Nova Scotia	Halifax	20,402	1,023	21,425	756,039	828,571	851,000
New Brunswick	Fredericton	27,385	519	28,345	616,788	677,250	704,800
Quebec	Quebec	523,860	71,000	594,860	5,780,845	6,234,445	6,288,300
Ontario	Toronto	344,092	68,490	412,582	6,960,870	8,264,465	8,543,300
Manitoba	Winnipeg	211,775	39,225	251,000	963,066	1,021,506	1,026,200
Saskatchewan	Regina	220,182	31,518	251,700	955,344	921,323	965,300
Alberta	Edmonton	248,800	6,485	255,285	1,463,203	1,838,037	2,053,100
British Columbia	Victoria	359,279	6,976	366,255	1,873,674	2,466,608	2,611,600
Northwest Territories	Yellowknife	1,253,438	51,465	1,304,903	28,738	42,609	43,100
Yukon Territory	Whitehorse	184,569	1,730	186,299	14,382	21,836	21,800
Total		**3,539,462**	**291,571**	**3,831,033**	**20,014,880**	**22,992,604**	**23,809,800**

Canadian Cities with Metropolitan Populations Over 100,000

Source: Statistics Canada

Census Metropolitan Areas. All figures shown are for the 1976 Census.

	Metro Area	City
Toronto, Ontario	2,803,101(1)	633,318
Montreal, Quebec	2,802,485	1,080,546
Vancouver, British Columbia	1,166,348	410,188
Ottawa-Hull, Ontario, Quebec	693,288	304,462
Winnipeg, Manitoba	578,217	560,874
Edmonton, Alberta	554,228	461,361
Quebec, Quebec	542,158	177,082
Hamilton, Ontario	529,371	312,003
Calgary, Alberta	469,917	469,917
St. Catharines-Niagara, Ontario	301,921	123,351
Kitchener, Ontario	272,158	131,870
London, Ontario	270,383	240,392
Halifax, Nova Scotia	267,991	117,882
Windsor, Ontario	247,582	196,526
Victoria, British Columbia	218,250	62,551
Sudbury, Ontario	157,030	97,604
Regina, Saskatchewan	151,191	149,593
St. John's, Newfoundland	143,390	86,576
Oshawa, Ontario	135,196	107,023
Saskatoon, Saskatchewan	133,750	133,750
Chicoutimi-Jonquiere, Quebec	128,643	57,737
Thunder Bay, Ontario	119,253	111,476
Saint John, New Brunswick	112,974	85,956

(1) Includes North York, pop. 563,000, given city status within metro Feb., 1979, and the city of Mississauga, 1976 pop. 230,073.

Immigration to Canada by Country of Last Permanent Residence

Source: Canadian Statistical Review, April 1980

Year	Total	UK and Ireland	France	Germany	Nether-lands	Greece	Italy
1976	149,429	22,187	3,251	2,672	1,359	2,487	4,530
1977	114,914	18,568	2,757	2,254	1,247	1,960	3,411
1978	86,313	12,270	1,754	1,471	1,237	1,474	2,976
1979	111,889	13,382	1,894	1,320	1,477	1,245	1,993

Year	Portugal	Other Europe	Asia	Austral-asia	United States	West Indies	All Other
1976	5,344	8,078	44,328	1,886	17,315	14,723	21,269
1977	3,579	6,972	31,368	1,545	12,888	12,022	16,343
1978	1,898	6,995	24,007	1,233	9,945	8,231	12,822
1979	2,175	9,296	50,412	1,394	9,588	6,238	11,475

Immigration to Canada, by Province of Intended Destination

Source: Canadian Statistical Review, April 1980

Year	Canada	Nfld.	P.E.I.	N.S.	N.B.	Que.	Ont.	Man.	Sask.	Alta.	B.C.	N.W.T. Yukon
1973	184,200	984	273	2,548	1,729	26,871	103,187	6,621	1,866	11,904	27,949	268
1974	218,465	1,036	311	2,601	2,207	33,458	120,115	7,423	2,244	14,289	34,481	300
1975	187,881	1,106	235	2,124	2,093	28,042	98,471	7,134	2,837	16,277	29,272	290
1976	149,429	725	235	1,942	1,752	29,282	72,031	5,509	2,323	14,896	20,484	250
1977	114,914	583	192	1,587	1,158	19,248	56,594	5,058	2,231	12,694	15,395	174
1978	86,313	374	145	980	661	14,290	42,397	3,574	1,564	9,826	12,331	171
1979	111,889	552	289	1,334	1,140	19,524	51,863	4,900	2,761	12,756	16,561	209

Canadian Population by Mother Tongue, 1976

Source: Statistics Canada

Province	English	French	Italian	German	Ukrainian	Indian, Eskimo	Chinese	Portuguese	Other
Newfoundland	545,340	2,760	170	450	40	1,555	535	210	6,665
Prince Edward Island	109,745	6,545	30	145	30	70	55	—	1,610
Nova Scotia	768,070	36,870	1,135	1,555	570	2,340	800	185	17,045
New Brunswick	435,975	223,780	550	1,020	170	1,695	495	110	13,455
Quebec	800,680	4,989,245	124,575	22,630	10,975	18,375	10,680	19,150	238,135
Ontario	6,457,645	462,070	309,810	154,625	76,035	21,285	51,660	88,495	642,840
Manitoba	727,240	54,745	5,875	73,375	60,250	24,855	3,705	5,455	66,010
Saskatchewan	715,685	26,710	1,260	61,250	45,920	20,860	3,390	220	46,030
Alberta	1,482,725	44,440	13,745	79,925	64,960	17,690	14,430	3,445	116,680
British Columbia	2,037,645	38,430	26,715	80,970	22,775	8,245	46,655	9,245	195,930
Yukon	18,940	525	45	405	140	510	45	—	1,230
Northwest Territories	23,085	1,095	135	365	195	15,525	120	25	2,066
Total	**14,122,770**	**5,887,205**	**484,050**	**476,715**	**282,060**	**133,005**	**132,560**	**126,535**	**1,347,696**

Population by Religious Denomination

Source: Statistics Canada

Denomination	1961	1971	Denomination	1961	1971
Adventist	25,999	28,590	Lutheran	662,744	715,740
Anglican	2,409,068	2,543,180	Mennonite(2)	152,452	168,150
Baptist	593,553	667,245	Mormon	50,016	66,635
Buddhist	11,611	16,175	Orthodox(3)	239,766	316,605
Chr. & Miss'nary Alliance	18,006	23,630	Pentecostal	143,877	220,390
Christian Reformed	62,257	83,390	Presbyterian	818,588	872,335
Ch. of Christ, Disciples	19,512	16,405	Roman Catholic	8,342,826	9,974,895
Confucian	5,089	2,165	Salvation Army	92,054	119,665
Doukhobor	13,234	9,107	Ukrainian Catholic(4)	189,653	227,730
Free Methodist	14,245	19,125	Unitarian	15,062	20,995
Hutterite	(1)	13,650	United Church	3,664,008	3,768,800
Jehovah's Witnesses	68,018	174,810	Other	277,508	293,240
Jewish	254,368	276,025	No religion	94,763	929,575

(1) Included with Mennonite. (2) Includes Hutterites in 1961. (3) Those churches which observe the Eastern Orthodox rite, including Greek, Russian, Ukrainian, and Syrian Orthodox. (4) Includes other "Greek Catholic."

Births and Deaths in Canada by Province

Source: Statistics Canada

Province	Births 1978	Births 1979[1]	Deaths 1978	Deaths 1979[1]	Province	Births 1978	Births 1979[1]	Deaths 1978	Deaths 1979[1]
Newfoundland	10,480	10,650	3,115	3,170	Saskatchewan	16,550	16,130	7,749	7,290
Prince Edward Island	1,985	1,930	994	1,020	Alberta	35,396	34,860	11,944	12,020
Nova Scotia	12,548	12,250	6,877	6,800	British Columbia	37,231	37,100	19,058	20,090
New Brunswick	10,790	10,680	5,183	5,420	Yukon	447	470	89	110
Quebec	94,860	93,510	43,552	43,360	Northwest Territories	1,204	1,200	205	190
Ontario	120,964	123,070	61,116	62,550	**Total**	**358,852**	**357,590**	**168,179**	**170,580**
Manitoba	16,397	15,740	8,297	8,560					

(1) estimates.

Marriages, Divorces in Canada

Source: Statistics Canada
(Rates per 1,000 population)

Year	Marriages No.	Marriages Rate	Divorces No.	Divorces Rate	Year	Marriages No.	Marriages Rate	Divorces No.	Divorces Rate
1940	125,709	10.8	2,416	0.21	1975	197,585	8.7	50,611	2.22
1950	125,083	9.1	5,386	0.39	1976	198,020	8.6	54,207	2.36
1960	130,338	7.3	6,980	0.39	1977	187,344	8.0	55,370	2.38
1970	188,428	8.8	29,775	1.39	1978	185,523	7.9	57,155	2.43

Canadian Legal or Public Holidays, 1981

Legal public holidays in all provinces are: New Year's Day, Good Friday, Easter Monday, Victoria Day, Dominion Day, Labor Day, Remembrance Day and Christmas Day. Additional holidays may be proclaimed provincially by the Lieutenant-Governor or in the municipalities by an order of the local council. For some holidays, government and business closing practices vary. In most provinces the provincial Ministry or Department of Labor can provide details of holiday closings.

Chief Legal or Public Holidays

Jan. 1 (Thursday) - New Year's Day. All provinces.

Apr. 17 - Good Friday. All provinces.

Apr. 20 - Easter Monday. Que. (businesses remain open in other provinces)

May 18 (the Monday preceding May 25) - Victoria Day. All provinces.

July 1 (Wednesday) - Dominion Day. All provinces.

Aug. 3 (1st Monday in Aug.) - Civic Holiday. Alb. B.C. Man. N.B. NWT Ont. Sask.

Sept. 7 (1st Monday in Sept.) - Labor Day. All provinces.

Oct. 12 (2d Monday in Oct.) - Thanksgiving. All provinces.

Nov. 11 (Wednesday) - Remembrance Day. Observed in all provinces but most businesses remain open.

Dec. 25 (Friday) - Christmas Day. All provinces.

Dec. 26 (Saturday) - Boxing Day. All provinces except Que.

Other Legal or Public Holidays

Jan. 11 (Sunday) - Sir John A. MacDonald's Birthday. Schools closed in some provinces.

March 16 (Monday) - St. Patrick's Day. Nfld.

April 20 (Monday) - St. George's Day. Nfld.

June 22 (Monday) - Discovery Day. Nfld.

June 24 (Wednesday) - St. John the Baptist's Day. Que.

July 6 (Monday) - Orangemen's Day. Nfld.

Aug. 17 (3d Monday in Aug.) - Discovery Day. Yukon.

Widely Known Canadians of the Present

Statesmen, authors, performers, artists, industrialists, and other prominent persons. (Canadians widely known in the North American entertainment industry are found on pages 369–383; some sports personalities can be found on pages 815–817).

Name (Birthplace)	Birthdate
Amiel, Barbara (Watford, England)	12/4/40
Anderson, Doris (Calgary, Alta.)	11/10/25
Atwood, Margaret (Ottawa, Ont.)	11/18/39
Augustyn, Frank (Hamilton, Ont.)	1/27/53
Axworthy, Lloyd (Winnipeg, Man.)	12/21/39
Ballard, Harold (Toronto, Ont.)	7/30/03
Bennett, William (Kelowna, B.C.)	4/14/32
Berton, Pierre (Whitehorse, Yukon)	7/12/20
Birney, Earle (Calgary, Alta.)	5/13/04
Black, Conrad (Montreal, Que.)	8/25/44
Blakeney, Allan (Bridgewater, N.S.)	9/7/25
Bouey, Gerald (Axford, Sask.)	4/2/20
Broadbent, Ed (Oshawa, Ont.)	3/21/36
Bronfman, Charles (Montreal, Que.)	9/20/29
Buchanan, John M. (Sydney, N.S.)	4/22/31
Bulloch, John (Toronto, Ont.)	8/24/33
Callaghan, Morley (Toronto, Ont.)	2/22/03
Camp, Dalton (Woodstock, N.B.)	9/11/20
Carrier, Roch (Ste.-Justine-de-Dorchester, Que.)	5/13/37
Charlebois, Robert (Montreal, Que.)	6/25/44
Chretien, Jean (Shawinigan, Que.)	1/11/34
Clark, Joe (High River, Alta.)	6/5/39
Cohen, Leonard (Montreal, Que.)	9/21/34
Colville, Alex (Toronto, Ont.)	8/24/20
Connors, Stompin' Tom (Skinner's Pond, P.E.I.)	2/9/36
Cranston, Toller (Kirkland Lake, Ont.)	4/20/49
Crombie, David (Toronto, Ont.)	4/24/36
Crosbie, John (St. John's, Nfld.)	1/30/31
Cummings, Burton (Winnipeg, Man.)	12/31/47
Danby, Ken (Sault Ste. Marie, Ont.)	3/16/40
Davies, Robertson (Thamesville, Ont.)	8/28/13
Davey, Keith (Toronto, Ont.)	4/21/26
Davis, William (Brampton, Ont.)	7/30/29
de Cotret, Bob (Ottawa, Ont.)	2/20/44
Deschamps, Yvon (Montreal, Que.)	7/31/35
Desmarais, Paul (Sudbury, Ont.)	1/4/27
Douglas, Tommy (Falkirk, Scotland)	10/20/04
Drapeau, Jean (Montreal, Que.)	2/18/16
Eagleson, Alan (St. Catharines, Ont.)	4/24/33
Forrester, Maureen (Montreal, Que.)	7/25/30
Fotheringham, Allan (Hearne, Sask.)	8/31/32
Fox, Francis (Montreal, Que.)	12/2/39
Frum, Barbara (Niagara Falls, Ont.)	9/8/38
Frye, Northrop (Sherbrooke, Que.)	7/14/12
Fulford, Robert (Ottawa, Ont.)	2/13/32
Gagnon, Andre (St.-Pacome, Que.)	8/2/37
Gordon, Walter (Toronto, Ont.)	1/27/06
Gould, Glenn (Toronto, Ont.)	9/25/32
Gray, Herb (Windsor, Ont.)	5/25/31
Gzowski, Peter (Toronto, Ont.)	7/13/34
Harron, Don (Toronto, Ont.)	9/19/24
Hatfield, Richard (Hartland, N.B.)	4/9/31
Herzberg, Gerhard (Hamburg, Germany)	12/25/04
Hewitt, Foster (Toronto, Ont.)	11/21/03
Hill, Dan (Toronto, Ont.)	6/3/54
Horner, Jack (Blain Lake, Sask.)	7/20/27
Irving, K.C. (Buctouche, N.B.)	1899
Kain, Karen (Hamilton, Ont.)	3/28/51
Karsh, Yousuf (Armenia-in-Turkey)	12/23/08
Lalonde, Marc (Ile Perrot, Que.)	7/26/29
Lapierre, Laurier (Lac Megantic, Que.)	11/21/29
Laskin, Bora (Fort William, Ont.)	10/5/12
Laurence, Margaret (Neepawa, Man.)	7/18/26
Layton, Irving (Neamtz, Romania)	3/12/12
Leger, Jules (St. Anicet, Que.)	4/4/13
Levesque, Rene (New Carlisle, Que.)	8/24/22
Lewis, David (Swislocz, Poland)	6/23/09
Lightfoot, Gordon (Orillia, Ont.)	11/17/38
Lougheed, Peter (Calgary, Alta.)	7/26/28
Lyon, Sterling (Windsor, Ont.)	1/30/27
MacDonald, Donald (Ottawa, Ont.)	3/1/32
Macdonald, Flora (North Sydney, N.S.)	6/3/26
MacEachen, Allan (Inverness, N.S.)	7/6/21
MacGuigan, Mark (Charlottetown, P.E.I.)	2/17/31
Mackassey, Bryce (Quebec City, Que.)	8/25/27
MacLean, J. Angus (Lewis, Belle River, P.E.I.)	5/15/14
Maloney, Arthur (Eganville, Ont.)	11/26/19
McDermott, Dennis (England)	11/3/22
McLauchlan, Murray (Paisley, Scotland)	6/30/48
McLuhan, Marshall (Edmonton, Alta.)	7/21/11
McTeer, Maureen (Ottawa, Ont.)	2/27/52
Mitchell, W.O. (Weyburn, Sask.)	3/13/14
Morin, Claude (Montmorency, Que.)	1929
Mowat, Farley (Belleville, Ont.)	5/12/21
Mulroney, Brian (Baie Comeau, Que.)	3/20/39
Munro, Alice (Wingham, Ont.)	11/10/31
Newman, Peter C. (Vienna, Austria)	5/10/29
Parizeau, Jacques (Montreal, Que.)	8/9/30
Peckford, Brian (Whitbourne, Nfld.)	8/27/42
Pepin, Jean-Luc (Drummondville, Que.)	11/1/24
Pratt, Christopher (St. John's, Nfld.)	12/9/35
Regan, Gerald (Windsor, N.S.)	2/13/28
Richardson, James (Winnipeg, Man.)	3/28/22
Richler, Mordecai (Montreal, Que.)	1/27/31
Robarts, John (Banff, Alta.)	1/11/17
Rohmer, Richard (Hamilton, Ont.)	1/24/24

Name (Birthplace)	Birthdate
Roman, Stephen (Slovakia)	4/17/21
Roy, Gabrielle (St. Boniface, Man.)	3/22/09
Ryan, Claude (Montreal, Que.)	1/26/25
Rubes, Jan (Volyne, Czechoslovakia)	6/6/20
Russell, Craig (Toronto, Ont.)	1/10/48
Sauve, Jeanne (Prud'Homme, Sask.)	4/26/22
Schreyer, Edward (Beausejour, Man.)	12/21/35
Selye, Hans (Vienna, Austria)	1/26/07
Shulman, Morton (Toronto, Ont.)	4/2/25
Simard, Rene (Chicoutimi, Que.)	2/28/61
Simmonds, Robert H. (Hafford, Sask.)	4/6/26
Sinclair, Gordon (Toronto, Ont.)	6/3/00
Smallwood, Joey (Gambo, Nfld.)	11/24/00
Smythe, Conn (Toronto, Ont.)	2/1/95
Stanfield, Robert (Truro, N.S.)	4/11/14
Stevens, Sinclair (Esquesing Twp., Ont.)	2/11/27
Suzuki, David (Vancouver, B.C.)	3/24/36
Taylor, E.P. (Ottawa, Ont.)	1/29/01
Taylor, Ken (Calgary, Alta.)	10/5/34
Templeton, Charles (Toronto, Ont.)	10/7/15
Thomson, Ken (Toronto, Ont.)	9/1/23
Trudeau, Margaret (Vancouver, B.C.)	9/10/48
Trudeau, Pierre (Montreal, Que.)	10/18/19
Turner, John (Richmond, England)	6/7/29
Vannelli, Gino (Montreal, Que.)	6/16/52
Vigneault, Gilles (Natashquan, Que.)	11/27/28
Weston, Galen (England)	10/26/40
Whelan, Eugene (Amherstburg, Ont.)	7/11/24

Noted Canadian Personalities of the Past

Statesmen

Name	Born	Died
Aberhart, William	**1878**	**1943**
Baldwin, Robert	**1804**	**1858**
Bennett, Richard B.	**1870**	**1957**
Blake, Edward	**1833**	**1912**
Borden, Robert	**1854**	**1937**
Bowell, Mackenzie	**1823**	**1917**
Brown, George	**1818**	**1880**
Cartier, Georges	**1814**	**1873**
Diefenbaker, John	**1895**	**1979**
Howe, Joseph	**1804**	**1873**
King, W. Mackenzie	**1874**	**1950**
Laurier, Wilfrid	**1841**	**1919**
Macdonald, John A.	**1815**	**1891**
Mackenzie, Alexander	**1822**	**1892**
Mackenzie, Wm. Lyon	**1795**	**1861**
Massey, Vincent	**1887**	**1967**
McGee, Thomas D'Arcy	**1825**	**1868**
Meighen, Arthur	**1874**	**1960**
Mowat, Oliver	**1820**	**1903**
Papineau, Louis-Joseph	**1786**	**1871**
Pearson, Lester B.	**1897**	**1972**
Riel, Louis	**1844**	**1885**
Tilley, Samuel Leonard	**1818**	**1896**
Tupper, Charles H.	**1855**	**1927**
Woodsworth, James S.	**1874**	**1942**

Scientists, Industrialists

Name	Born	Died
Aitken, William M. (Lord Beaverbrook)	**1879**	**1964**
Allan, Hugh	**1810**	**1882**
Banting, Fredk. G.	**1891**	**1941**
Beatty, Edward W.	**1877**	**1943**
Best, Charles H.	**1910**	**1978**
Bethune, Norman	**1890**	**1939**
Bronfman, Samuel	**1891**	**1971**
Eaton, Timothy	**1834**	**1907**
Eddy, Ezra Butler	**1827**	**1906**
Fleming, Sandford	**1827**	**1915**
Hilton, Hugh G.	**1889**	**1966**
Macleod, John J.R.	**1876**	**1935**
McDougald, John (Bud)	**1908**	**1978**
McLaughlin, R. Sam	**1871**	**1972**
Osler, William	**1849**	**1919**
Penfield, Wilder	**1891**	**1976**
Thompson, Roy (Lord Thomson of Fleet)	**1894**	**1976**
Van Horne, William	**1843**	**1915**
Weston, Garfield	**1898**	**1978**

Authors

Name	Born	Died
Belaney, George S. (Grey Owl)	**1888**	**1938**
Bourassa, Henri	**1868**	**1952**
Buchan, John (Baron Tweedsmuir)	**1875**	**1940**
Campbell, W. Wilfred	**1861**	**1918**
Carman, W. Bliss	**1861**	**1929**
Clark, Gregory	**1892**	**1977**
Cremazie, Octave	**1827**	**1879**
Creighton, Donald	**1902**	**1979**
Dafoe, John Wesley	**1866**	**1944**
Dawson, R. MacGregor	**1895**	**1958**
De Mille, James	**1836**	**1880**
Doughty, Arthur G.	**1860**	**1936**
Duncan, Sara J.	**1862**	**1932**
Edwards, Robert (Bob)	**1864**	**1922**
Frechette, Louis H.	**1839**	**1908**
Gordon, Chas. W. (Ralph Connor)	**1860**	**1937**
Grove, Frederick	**1871**	**1948**
Haliburton, Thos. C.	**1796**	**1865**
Innis, H.A.	**1894**	**1952**
Kirby, William	**1817**	**1906**
Johnson, Pauline	**1862**	**1913**
Lampman, Archibald	**1861**	**1899**
Leacock, Stephen	**1869**	**1944**
Lowry, Malcolm	**1909**	**1957**
McClung, Nellie	**1873**	**1951**
McCrae, John	**1872**	**1918**
Montgomery, Lucy M.	**1874**	**1942**
Moodie, Susanna	**1803**	**1885**
Morin, Paul	**1889**	**1963**
Nelligan, Emile	**1879**	**1941**
Parker, Gilbert	**1862**	**1932**
Pickthall, Marjorie	**1883**	**1922**
Pratt, Edwin J.	**1883**	**1964**
Roberts, Chas. G.D.	**1860**	**1943**
Roche, Mazo de la	**1885**	**1961**
Routhier, Adolphe B.	**1839**	**1920**
Sangster, Charles	**1822**	**1893**
Scott, Duncan C.	**1862**	**1947**
Service, Robert W.	**1874**	**1958**

Anthropologists, Geologists, and Naturalists

Name	Born	Died
Adams, Frank D.	**1859**	**1942**
Anderson, Rudolph M.	**1876**	**1961**
Billings, Elkanah	**1820**	**1876**
Dionne, Charles Eusibe	**1846**	**1925**
Hale, Horatio	**1817**	**1896**
Hill-Tout, Charles	**1859**	**1944**
Hunt, Thomas Sterry	**1826**	**1892**
Jenness, Diamond	**1886**	**1969**
Logan, William E.	**1798**	**1875**
Macoun, John	**1831**	**1920**
Miner, John T. (Jack)	**1865**	**1944**
Provancher, Leon, abbe	**1820**	**1892**
Rowan, William	**1891**	**1957**
Saunders, Charles E.	**1867**	**1937**
Saunders, William	**1836**	**1914**
Taverner, Percy A.	**1875**	**1947**
Traill, Catharine Parr	**1802**	**1899**
Tyrrell, Joseph Burr	**1858**	**1957**

Canadian Government Budget

Source: Canadian Statistical Review (April 1980)
(millions of Canadian dollars)

Expenditures

Fiscal Year	National defense	Health and welfare	Agriculture	Post Office	Public works	Transport	Veterans affairs	Payments to provinces	Total expenditures
1973-74. .	2,232	3,775	426	591	470	827	538	1,874	20,056
1974-75. .	2,509	5,199	664	732	524	1,303	619	2,639	26,055
1975-76. .	2,973	9,731	651	913	624	1,185	684	2,460	33,977
1976-77. .	3,365	10,952	631	1,104	684	1,314	754	3,356	38,951
1977-78. .	3,771	11,635	959	1,237	1,431	1,478	841	3,003	42,902
1978-79. .	4,108	13,056	768	1,275	1,657	1,628	890	3,028	46,923

Revenues[1]

Fiscal year	Personal income tax	Corporation income tax	Sales tax	Other excise tax[2]	Excise duties	Customs duties	Estate taxes	Post Office	Total budgetary revenues
1973-74. .	7,925	3,411	2,693	695	686	1,385	15	480	19,383
1974-75. .	10,069	4,285	2,900	2,083	748	1,809	7	485	24,909
1975-76. .	12,708	5,748	3,939	1,501	817	1,887	12	443	29,956
1976-77. .	14,620	5,377	4,529	1,146	865	2,097	70	615	32,650
1977-78. .	13,439	5,828	5,026	904	882	2,312	66	773	32,866
1978-79. .	14,048	6,262	5,245	827	878	2,747	77	903	35,216

(1) This statement includes only receipts relating to revenue. Excluded are non-budgetary revenues such as Old Age Security Fund taxes, Prairie Farm Assistance Act levies, employer and employee contributions to government-held funds. (2) Beginning in Dec. 1973, this category includes oil export tax.

Canada's Largest Corporations

Source: The Financial Post 500; Toronto, Canada; June, 1980

Industrials Company (Home office)	Sales or operating revenue C$000	Assets	Foreign owner-ship %	Foreign owner(s)
General Motors of Canada Ltd. (Oshawa, Ont.)	9,409,838[1]	2,223,124	100	General Motors Corp., Detroit
Canadian Pacific Ltd. (Montreal, Que.)	8,150,000[2]	11,002,393	35	U.S. 22%; Britain 6%; other 7%
Ford Motor Co. of Canada (Oakville, Ont.)	7,149,200[1]	2,338,200	89	Ford Motor Co., Dearborn, Mich.
Imperial Oil Ltd. (Toronto, Ont.)	6,623,000[3]	4,655,000	71	Exxon Corp., New York 70%
George Weston Ltd. (Toronto, Ont.)	5,867,102	1,507,338	—	
Bell Canada (Montreal, Que.)	5,264,739	10,376,513	4	Wide distribution
Alcan Aluminium Ltd. (Montreal, Que.)	5,132,163[4]	5,238,282	61	U.S. 53%; other 8%
Massey-Ferguson Ltd. (Toronto, Ont.)	3,483,424[4]	3,256,097	37	Wide distribution
Shell Canada Ltd. (Toronto, Ont.)	3,436,000[3]	2,963,000	71	Royal Dutch/Shell Group
Hudson's Bay Co. (Winnipeg, Man.)	3,435,209[5]	2,651,593	—	
Canadian National Railways (Montreal, Que.)	3,294,335	5,143,131	—	
Gulf Canada Ltd. (Toronto, Ont.)	3,007,000[3]	3,288,000	60	Gulf Oil Corp., Pittsburgh
Inco Ltd. (Toronto, Ont.)	2,915,079[4]	5,057,665	38	U.S. 24%; other 12%
Canada Packers Inc. (Toronto, Ont.)	2,711,214	481,498	2	
Dominion Stores Ltd. (Toronto, Ont.)	2,663,857	454,101	—	
Texaco Canada Inc. (Toronto, Ont.)	2,642,626[3]	2,299,735	91	Texaco Inc., New York
Simpsons-Sears Ltd. (Toronto, Ont.)	2,618,213	1,577,885	50	Sears Roebuck, Chicago
TransCanada Pipelines Ltd. (Calgary, Alta.)	2,580,972	2,538,771	—	
Chrysler Canada Ltd. (Windsor, Ont.)	2,570,160[1]	821,230	100	Chrysler Corp., Detroit
Ontario Hydro (Toronto, Ont.)	2,568,120	14,514,000	—	

(1) Figures include sales to parent and affiliated companies: General Motors $4,014 million; Chrysler unstated; Ford $4,300 million (plus $1,829 million overseas subsidiaries). (2) After eliminating inter-company transactions. (3) Excise taxes deducted. (4) Converted from $U.S. or British pounds at average rate during fiscal year; assets converted at fiscal year end rate.

Assets and Deposits of Chartered Banks in Canada

Source: Supplement to the Canada Gazette, May 20, 1980
(as of March 31, 1980 - thousands of Canadian dollars)

Bank	Assets	Deposits	Bank	Assets	Deposits
Royal Bank of Canada	57,407,220	49,967,411	Banque Nationale du Canada	15,748,379	14,685,947
Canadian Imperial Bank of Commerce	50,752,721	45,979,846	Mercantile Bank of Canada	3,470,275	3,197,359
Bank of Montreal	41,031,441	35,544,567	Bank of British Columbia	2,141,392	1,978,796
Bank of Nova Scotia	39,092,506	35,630,178	Continental Bank of Canada	1,566,798	1,384,511
Toronto-Dominion Bank	30,520,521	26,975,985	Commercial and Industrial Bank	603,472	518,380
			Northland Bank	179,221	120,451

Personal Expenditure on Consumer Goods and Services in Current Dollars

Source: Statistics Canada (millions of dollars)

	1971	1972	1973	1974	1975	1976	1977	1978
Food, beverages and tobacco	12,148	13,437	15,395	17,762	20,757	22,695	24,859	27,833
Clothing and footwear	4,143	4,550	5,120	6,412	7,155	8,116	8,784	9,537
Gross rent, fuel and power	10,581	11,412	12,506	14,271	16,445	19,173	22,058	24,638
Furniture, furnishings household equipment and operation	5,295	6,135	7,304	8,652	9,884	11,115	12,006	13,078
Medical care and health services	1,618	1,804	2,054	2,466	2,896	3,325	3,596	3,971
Transportation and communication	8,014	9,030	10,551	12,161	14,292	16,380	17,988	19,652
Recreation, entertainment, education and cultural services	5,364	6,288	7,265	8,655	9,972	11,595	12,721	13,844
Personal goods and services	8,357	9,423	10,912	12,870	15,062	17,316	19,063	21,277
Total	**55,616**	**62,208**	**71,278**	**83,388**	**96,995**	**110,655**	**122,425**	**135,220**
Durable goods	7,883	9,440	11,481	13,139	15,320	17,033	18,459	20,102
Semi-durable goods	7,133	7,962	9,059	11,184	12,428	14,134	15,359	16,756
Non-durable goods	17,521	19,432	22,302	26,218	30,422	33,987	37,563	42,034
Services	23,079	25,374	28,436	32,847	38,825	45,501	51,044	56,328

Canadian Consumer Price Index

Source: Statistics Canada
(All items: 1971 = 100)

Year	Avg.	Year	Avg.	Year	Avg.	Year	Avg.
1965	80.5	1969	94.1	1973	112.7	1977	160.8
1966	83.5	1970	97.2	1974	125.0	1978	175.2
1967	86.5	1971	100.0	1975	138.5	1979	191.2
1968	90.0	1972	104.8	1976	148.9	1980(Feb.)	201.8

Price Indexes By Item

Source: Canadian Statistical Review, April 1980 (1971 = 100)

Year and month	All items	Food	Shelter	Clothing	Trans-portation	Health, personal	Recreation, education	Tobacco, alcohol	Total services
1975	138.5	161.9	130.9	125.1	129.4	133.0	128.5	125.3	133.4
1976	148.9	166.2	145.7	132.0	143.3	144.3	136.2	134.3	149.6
1977	160.8	180.1	159.3	141.0	153.3	155.0	142.7	143.8	163.2
1978	175.2	208.0	170.8	146.4	162.2	166.2	148.2	155.5	174.3
1979	191.2	235.4	180.5	159.9	178.0	181.2	158.4	166.7	186.5
1980 (Feb.)	201.8	248.4	187.0	171.1	190.9	191.2	167.0	175.9	195.2

Canadian Foreign Trade

Source: Canadian Statistical Review (April 1980)
(millions of Canadian dollars)

Year	Exports[1] All countries	Exports[1] U.S.	Exports[1] Japan	Exports[1] UK	Exports[1] All other countries	Imports All countries	Imports U.S.	Imports Japan	Imports UK	Imports All other countries
1973	25,419.5	17,129	1,813.7	1,604.3	4,872.5	23,393.6	16,502	1,010.8	1,005.3	4,353
1974	32,176.7	21,325.1	2,229	1,902.9	6,719.7	31,639.3	21,305.9	1,428.1	1,126.5	6,488
1975	33,245.5	21,697.1	2,133.4	1,800.4	7,614.6	34,690.7	23,616.3	1,205.3	1,221.9	7,540.4
1976	38,396.6	25,893.9	2,396.5	1,877.9	8,228.3	37,444.4	25,751.7	1,523.9	1,149.7	9,019.1
1977	44,553.5	31,111.5	2,518.6	1,946.1	8,977.3	42,332.3	29,814.9	1,792.9	1,278.8	9,445.7
1978	52,842.3	37,175.3	3,062.2	2,006.5	10,598.3	49,937.7	35,246.3	2,268.5	1,599.9	10,823.0
1979(p)	65,518.2	44,454.1	4,097.1	2,622.4	14,344.6	62,677.6	45,391.9	2,157.0	1,928.2	13,200.5

(1) including re-exports, p-preliminary

Canadian Shipping Traffic

Source: Statistics Canada (thousand short tons)
Total cargo handled includes cargo loaded and unloaded in foreign and coastwise shipping.

Year	Halifax	Saint John	Quebec	Montreal	Toronto	Vancouver	All Ports	Coastwise
1973	13,703	12,181	15,946	21,177	4,170	39,126	320,498	122,436
1974	13,290	9,998	12,943	19,654	4,605	36,761	302,138	118,241
1975	11,743	10,851	12,496	18,633	4,891	35,521	303,098	119,871
1976	11,547	11,121	13,405	17,159	3,098	29,244	307,605	118,790
1977	12,213	11,251	15,334	18,529	2,982	32,767	325,477	128,548
1978	12,143	13,824	15,081	17,899	2,824	43,929	330,307	133,749

Canadian Sea Fish Catch and Exports

Source: Canadian Statistical Review, Sept. 1979

Year	Total Value	Landings of Sea Fish (in metric tons) Total	Nfld.	P.E.I.	N.S.	N.B.	Que.	B.C.	Exports to[1] (in millions of pounds) Total	U.S.	Other	Exports[1] Salmon	Lobster
1972	$219,829,000	1,004,763	294,520	27,170	296,652	178,944	82,600	152,726	642.0	443.6	169.3	77.6	19.8
1973	296,288,000	993,559	306,586	28,531	279,144	129,774	73,165	176,359	752.6	491.6	211.1	93.1	20.1
1974	259,108,000	834,165	234,510	16,329	283,045	160,120	53,524	132,904	551.4	394.6	155.0	78.5	18.2
1975	225,423,000	688,591	86,637	13,608	263,993	121,564	48,988	114,306	558.9	397.8	191.1	51.3	19.5
1976	364,754,000	1,063,071	340,241	17,123	368,456	117,937	41,948	177,366	652.9	427.2	225.7	30.6	19.3
1977	456,130,000	1,211,408	394,148	19,801	407,368	131,937	54,292	203,862	830.6	450.7	379.9	66.6	20.0
1978	497,964,000	1,053,100	329,142	22,001	380,862	121,461	62,601	137,033	931.2	494.0	436.9	78.2	21.9

(1) Exports include sea and freshwater fish and shellfish products but exclude bait, meal, oils, offal, livers, fish roe, and fishery foods and feeds.

Marketed Value of Canadian Fish Catches

Source: Fisheries and Oceans Canada (thousands of Canadian dollars)

Province	1977[1]	1978[1]	Province	1977	1978
Newfoundland	252,726	325,004	Manitoba	19,334	15,242
Prince Edward Island	28,128	42,614	Saskatchewan	6,936	4,521
Nova Scotia	315,037	441,305	Alberta	1,384	1,154
New Brunswick	139,627	166,225	British Columbia	364,801	517,557
Quebec	43,883	53,264	Yukon & NWT	2,059	2,333
Ontario	29,110	34,322	**Total**[2]	**1,174,981**	**1,549,521**

(1) Value after processing; both sea and freshwater fisheries; includes marine plants, aquatic mammals etc. (2) The sum of the provincial totals differs from the Canada total due to removal of inter-provincial shipments.

Canadian Grain Deliveries at Western Grain Centers

Source: Canadian Grain Commission
(thousands of tons)

Crop year 1978-79

Province or area	Wheat	Oats	Barley	Rye	Flaxseed	Rapeseed	Total
Western Canada	14,473	363	5,364	247	425	2,945	23,816
Manitoba	1,914	116	1,039	42	234	473	3,818
Saskatchewan	9,646	108	1,838	110	152	1,130	12,984
Alberta & B.C.	2,913	139	2,487	94	39	1,342	7,014

Crop year 1977-78

Province or area	Wheat	Oats	Barley	Rye	Flaxseed	Rapeseed	Total
Western Canada	19,110	764	5,237	256	494	1,759	27,620
Manitoba	2,518	283	1,165	63	263	257	4,548
Saskatchewan	13,016	203	1,728	112	184	678	15,921
Alberta & B.C.	3,576	278	2,344	82	47	824	7,151

NATIONS OF THE WORLD

The nations of the world are listed in alphabetical order. Initials in the following articles include UN (United Nations), OAS (Org. of American States), NATO (North Atlantic Treaty Org.), EC (European Communities or Common Market), OAU (Org. of African Unity). **Sources:** Population figures: International Demographic Data Center, U.S. Bureau of the Census; areas: U.S. State Department; crude steel production statistics: International Iron and Steel Institute, Brussels. Health and education statistics as reported in *World Military and Social Expenditures 1980,* Ruth Leger Sivard; copyright © 1980 by World Priorities Inc., Box 1003, Leesburg, VA 22075.

PQLI - Physical Quality of Life Index: a composite index of infant mortality, life expectancy at age one, and literacy (each indexed on a scale from 0 to 100), calculated by averaging the 3 indexes, giving equal weight to each. **Source:** *The United States and World Development: Agenda 1980,* by Martin M. McLaughlin and the Staff of the Overseas Development Council (New York: Praeger Publishers, 1980). © Overseas Development Council.

See special color section for maps and flags of all nations.

Afghanistan

Democratic Republic of Afghanistan

People: Population (1979 est.): 14,699,000. **Pop. density:** 58.12 per sq. mi. **Ethnic groups:** Pushtuns (Pathans) nearly 60%; Tajiks nearly 30%; Uzbek over 5%; Hazara, others. **Languages:** Pushtu (Iranian), Dari Persian (spoken by Tajiks, Hazaras), Uzbek (Turkic). **Religions:** Moslem, mostly Sunni.

Geography: Area: 260,000 sq. mi., slightly smaller than Texas. **Location:** Between Soviet Central Asia and the Indian subcontinent. **Neighbors:** Pakistan on E, S, Iran on W, USSR on N; the NE tip touches China. **Topography:** The country is landlocked and mountainous, much of it over 4,000 ft. above sea level. The Hindu Kush Mts. tower 16,000 ft. above Kabul and reach a height of 25,000 ft. to the E. Trade with Pakistan flows through the 35-mile long Khyber Pass. The climate is dry, with extreme temperatures, and large desert regions, though mountain rivers produce intermittent fertile valleys. **Capital:** Kabul. **Cities** (1978 est.): Kabul 318,094; Kandahar 209,000; Herat 157,000; Baghlan 110,874; Kundus 108,000.

Government: Head of state, head of government, and secy. gen., People's Democratic Party: Pres. Babrak Karmal; in office: Dec. 27, 1979. **Local divisions:** 24 provinces, each under a governor. **Armed forces:** regulars 90,000; reserves 150,000.

Economy: Industries: Textiles, carpets, cement, sheepskin coats. **Chief crops:** Cotton, oilseeds, fruits. **Minerals:** Copper, lead, gas, coal, zinc, iron, silver, asbestos. **Crude oil reserves** (1978): 284 mln. bbls. **Other resources:** Wool, hides, karacul pelts. **Per capita arable land:** 1.3 acres. **Meat prod.** (1978): beef: 66,000 metric tons; lamb: 122,000 metric tons. **Electricity prod.** (1977): 700.00 mln. kwh. **Labor force:** 80% agric.

Finance: Currency: Afghani (Jan. 1980: 42.95 = $1 US). **Gross domestic product** (1976 est.): $2.2 bln. **Per capita income** (1975): $125. **Imports** (1978): $395 mln.; partners (1976): USSR 24%, Jap. 19%, W.Ger. 12%, Ind. 12%. **Exports** (1979): $419 mln.; partners (1976): USSR 39%, Ind. 12%, Pak. 12%, W.Ger. 10%. **Tourists** (1977): 117,100; receipts: $38 mln. **International reserves less gold** (Mar. 1980): $409.11 mln. **Gold:** 964,00 oz t. **Consumer prices** (change in 1976): 0.04%

Transport: Motor vehicles: in use (1971): 38,400 passenger cars, 26,100 comm. vehicles **Civil aviation:** 290 mln. passenger-km (1977); 13.9 mln. freight ton-km.

Communications: Radios: 115,000 in use (1976). **Telephones in use** (1978): 31,200. **Daily newspaper circ.** (1977): 77,000; 4 per 1,000 pop.

Health: Life expectancy at birth (1975): 39.9 male; 40.7 female. **Births** (per 1,000 pop. 1978): 45.2. **Deaths** (per 1,000 pop. 1978): 21.1 **Natural increase** (1978): 2.4%. **Hospital beds** (per 100,000 pop. 1977): 21. **Physicians** (per 100,000 pop. 1977): 5.

Education (1977): **Literacy:** 12% **Pop. 5-19:** in school: 13%, teachers per 1,000: 4. **PQLI:** 14.

Afghanistan, occupying a favored invasion route since antiquity, has been variously known as Ariana or Bactria (in ancient times) and Khorasan (in the Middle Ages). Foreign empires alternated rule with local emirs and kings until the 18th century, when a unified kingdom was established. In 1973, a military coup ushered in a republic.

Afghanistan has received aid from the U.S., USSR, and China. Largest trade partner is the USSR, natural gas the chief export. Pro-Soviet leftists took power in a bloody 1978 coup, and concluded a 20-year economic and military treaty with the USSR. The U.S. cut off aid, 1979, following the Feb. 14 death of its ambassador in a shootout between government and rebel forces.

Late in Dec. 1979, the USSR began a massive military airlift into Kabul. The three-month old regime of Hafizullah Amin ended with a Soviet backed coup, Dec. 27th. He was replaced by Babrak Karmal, considered a more pro-Soviet leader. Soviet troops, estimated at between 60,000-100,000, fanned out over Afghanistan, fighting rebels. *(For later developments and the U.S. boycott of the Moscow Olympics, see Index.)*

Albania

People's Socialist Republic of Albania

People: Population (1979 est.): 2,626,000. **Pop. density:** 235.14 per sq. mi. **Urban** (1977): 38%. **Ethnic groups:** Albanians (Gegs in N, Tosks in S) 95%, Greeks 2.5%. **Languages:** Albanian (Tosk is official dialect), Greek. **Religions:** (historically) Moslems 70%, Orthodox 20%, Roman Catholic 10%. All public worship and religious institutions were outlawed in 1967.

Geography: Area: 11,100 sq. mi., slightly larger than Maryland. **Location:** On SE coast of Adriatic Sea. **Neighbors:** Greece on S, Yugoslavia on N, E. **Topography:** Apart from a narrow coastal plain, Albania consists of hills and mountains covered with scrub forest, cut by small E-W rivers. **Capital:** Tirana. **Cities** (1978 est.): Tirana 169,300; Shkoder 62,500; Durres 61,000; Vlone 58,400.

Government: Head of state: Pres. Haxhi Lleshi; b. 1913; in office: Aug. 1, 1953. **Head of government:** Chmn. Mehmet Shehu; b. Jan. 10, 1913; in office: July 20, 1954. **Head of Communist Party:** Enver Hoxha; b. Oct. 16, 1908; in office: Nov. 8, 1941. **Local divisions:** 29 administrative districts and one independent city. **Armed forces:** regulars 43,000; reserves 60,000.

Economy: Industries: Chem. fertilizers, textiles, electric cables. **Chief crops:** Grain, corn, sugar beets, cotton, tobacco, fruits. **Minerals:** Chromium, coal, copper, bitumen, iron, oil. **Other resources:** Forests. **Per capita arable land:** 0.5 acres. **Meat prod.** (1978): beef: 20,000 metric tons; pork: 12,000 metric tons; lamb: 23,000 metric tons. **Electricity prod.** (1977): 2.15 bln. kwh. **Labor force:** 61% agric.

Finance: Currency: Lek (Mar. 1980: 7.00 = $1 US). **Gross domestic product** (1976 est.) $1.3 bln. **Per capita income** (1976): $490. **Imports** (1976): $250 mln.; partners (1975): China, E. Eur., It. **Exports** (1976): $200 mln.; partners (1975): China, E. Eur.

Transport: Motor vehicles: in use (1971): 38,400 passenger cars, 26,100 comm. vehicles. **Chief ports:** Durres, Vlone.

Communications: Television sets: 4,500 in use (1976). **Radios:** 180,000 in use (1976). **Daily newspaper circ.** (1976): 115,000; 45 per 1,000 pop.

Health: Life expectancy at birth (1966): 64.9 male; 67.0 female. **Births** (per 1,000 pop. 1971): 33.3. **Deaths** (per 1,000 pop. 1971): 8.1 **Natural increase** (1971): 2.5%. **Hospital beds** (per 100,000 pop. 1977): 649. **Physicians** (per 100,000 pop. 1977): 104. **Infant mortality** (per 1,000 live births 1971): 86.8.

Education (1977): **Literacy:** 75%. **Pop. 5-19:** in school: 64%, teachers per 1,000: 29. **PQLI:** 76.

Ancient Illyria was conquered by Romans, Slavs, and Turks (15th century); the latter Islamized the population. Independent Albania was proclaimed in 1912, republic was formed in 1920. Self-styled King Zog I ruled 1925-39, until Italy invaded.

Communist partisans took over in 1944, allied Albania with USSR, then broke with USSR in 1960 over de-Stalinization. Strong political alliance with China followed, leading to several billion dollars in aid, which was curtailed after 1974. China cut off aid in 1978 when Albania attacked its policies after the 1977 death of Chinese ruler Mao Tse-tung.

In 1971, after years of mistrust, Albania resumed relations with Greece and Yugoslavia, but ties with U.S. and USSR are still rejected.

Industrialization, pressed in 1960s, slowed in 1970s. Large-scale purges of officials occurred 1973-76.

Algeria

Democratic and Popular Republic of Algeria

People: Population (1979 est.); 18,145,000. **Age distrib.** (%): 0–14: 47.2; 15–59: 46.2; 60+: 6.6. **Pop. density:** 20.12 per sq. mi. **Urban** (1974): 52.0%. **Ethnic groups:** Arabs 75%, Berbers 25%. **Languages:** Arab, Berber (indigenous language), French. **Religions:** Sunni Moslem (state religion).

Geography: Area: 919,951 sq. mi., more than 3 times the size of Texas. **Location:** In NW Africa, from Mediterranean Sea into Sahara Desert. **Neighbors:** Morocco on W, Mauritania, Mali, Niger on S, Libya, Tunisia on E. **Topography:** The Tell, located on the coast, comprises fertile plains 50-100 miles wide, with a moderate climate and adequate rain. Two major chains of the Atlas Mts., running roughly E-W, and reaching 7,000 ft., enclose a dry plateau region. Below lies the Sahara, mostly desert with major mineral resources. **Capital:** Algiers. **Cities** (1966 cen.): Algiers 9,903,530; Oran 327,493; Constantine 243,558; Annaba 152,006.

Government: Head of state: Pres. Chadli Bendjedid; b. Apr. 14, 1929; in office: Feb. 9, 1979. **Head of government:** Mohammed Behahmed Abdelghani; in office: Mar. 8, 1979. **Local divisions:** 31 wilayas (states); governors are responsible to the center. **Armed forces:** regulars 88,800; reserves 100,000.

Economy: Industries: Wine, cigarettes, oil products, iron, steel, textiles, fertilizer, plastics. **Chief crops:** Grains, corn, winegrapes, potatoes, artichokes, flax, olives, tobacco, dates, figs, pomegranates. **Minerals:** Mercury, oil, iron, zinc, lead, coal, copper, natural gas, phosphates. **Crude oil reserves** (1980): 8.44 bln. bbls. **Other resources:** Cork trees. **Per capital arable land:** .9 acres. **Meat prod.** (1978): beef: 29,000 metric tons; lamb: 58,000 metric tons. **Fish catch** (1977): 43,500 metric tons. **Electricity prod.** (1978): 4.70 bln. kwh. **Crude steel prod.** (1979): 600,000 metric tons. **Labor force:** 60% agric.; 11% manuf.

Finance: Currency: Dinar (Mar. 1980: 3.96 = $1 US). **Gross domestic product** (1977): $19.75 bln. **Per capita income** (1975): $780. **Imports** (1979): $8.10 bln.; partners (1977); France 24%, W. Ger. 15%, It. 10%, U.S. 9%. **Exports** (1979): $8.2 bln.; partners (1977): U.S. 52%, W. Ger. 15%, France 13%, It. 5%. **Tourists** (1977): 241,700; receipts: $56 mln. **National budget** (1974): $5.68 bln. revenues; $2.99 bln. expenditures. **International reserves less gold** (Mar. 1980): $3.04 bln. **Gold:** 5.56 mln. oz t. **Consumer prices** (change in 1978): 17.1%.

Transport: Railway traffic (1977): 1.51 bln. passenger-km; 1.94 bln. net ton-km. **Motor vehicles:** in use (1975): 286,100 passenger cars, 154,700 comm. vehicles; assembled (1977): 6,360 comm. vehicles. **Chief ports:** Algiers, Oran.

Communications: Television sets: 525,000 in use (1976), 54,000 manuf. (1976). **Radios:** 3.00 mln. in use (1976), 21,000 manuf. (1976). **Telephones in use** (1978): 297,689. **Daily newspaper circ.** (1977): 236,000; 13 per 1,000 pop.

Health: Life expectancy at birth (1975): 52.9 male; 55.0 female. **Births** (per 1,000 pop. 1975): 48.8. **Deaths** (per 1,000 pop. 1975): 15.4. **Natural increase** (1975); 3.3%. **Hospital beds,** (per 100,000 pop. 1977): 263. **Physicians** (per 100,000 pop. 1977): 19. **Infant mortality** (per 1,000 live births 1975): 86.3.

Education (1977): **Literacy:** 36%. **Pop. 5-19:** in school: 55%, teachers per 1,000: 16. **PQLI:** 45.

Earliest known inhabitants were ancestors of Berbers, followed by Phoenicians, Romans, Vandals, and, finally, Arabs; but 25% still speak Berber dialects. Turkey ruled 1518 to 1830, when France took control.

Large-scale European immigration and French cultural inroads did not prevent an Arab nationalist movement from launching guerilla war. Peace, and French withdrawal, was negotiated with French Pres. Charles de Gaulle. One million Europeans left.

Ahmed Ben Bella was the victor of infighting, and ruled 1962-65, when an army coup installed Col. Houari Boumedienne as leader. Ben Bella remained under house arrest until 1979.

In 1967, Algeria declared war with Israel, broke with U.S., and moved toward eventual military and political ties with the USSR. French oil interests were partly seized in 1971, but relations with the West have since improved, based on oil and gas exports; U.S. ties were resumed 1974.

Algeria, strongly backing Saharan guerillas' demands for a cease fire and self-determination, encouraged Mauritania to come to terms with the Polisario Front, 1979.

The one-party Socialist regime faces endemic mass unemployment and poverty, despite land reform and industrialization attempts.

Andorra

Valleys of Andorra

People: Population (1979 est.): 34,000. **Age distrib.** (%): 0–14: 29.2; 14–59: 61.7; 60+: 9.1. **Pop. density:** 166.67 per sq. mi. **Ethnic groups:** Spanish over 60%, Andorran 30% French 6%. **Languages:** Catalan (official), Spanish, French. **Religions:** Roman Catholic.

Geography: Area: 180 sq. mi., half the size of New York City. **Location:** In Pyrenees Mtns. **Neighbors:** Spain on S, France on N. **Topography:** High mountains and narrow valleys over the country. **Capital:** Andorra la Vella.

Government: Head of state: Co-princes are the president of France (Valery Giscard d'Estaing, b. Feb. 2, 1926, in office: May 27, 1974) and the Roman Catholic bishop of Urgel in Spain (Joan Marti y Alanis, in office: Jan. 31, 1971). **Head of govt.:** Syndic Estanislao Sangra Font, in office: Jan 1, 1979. **Local divisions:** 7 parishes. **Economy: Industries:** Tourism, sheep raising.

Finance: Currency: Franc, Peseta.

Communications: Television sets: 3,000 in use (1976). **Radios:** 6,600 in use (1976). **Telephones in use** (1978): 10,361.

Health: Births (per 1,000 pop. 1976): 16.5. **Deaths** (per 1,000 pop. 1976): 5.0. **Natural increase** (1976): 1.2%.

The present political status, with joint sovereignty by France and the bishop of Urgel, dates from 1278.

Tourism, especially skiing, is the economic mainstay. A free port, allowing for an active trading center, draws more than 7 million tourists annually. The ensuing economic prosperity accompanied by Andorra's virtual law-free status, has given rise to calls for reform.

Angola

People's Republic of Angola

People: Population (1979 est.): 6,543,000. **Pop. density:** 13.98 per sq. mi. **Ethnic groups:** Ovimbundu 38%, Kimbundu 23%; Bacongo 13%, European 1%; Mesticos 2%. **Languages:** Portuguese (official), various Bantu languages. **Religions:** Roman Catholic 30%, Protestant 12%, others.

Geography: Area: 481,351 sq. mi., larger than Texas and California combined. **Location:** In SW Africa on Atlantic coast. **Neighbors:** Namibia (SW Africa) on S, Zambia on E, Zaire on N; Cabinda, an enclave separated from rest of country by short Atlantic coast of Zaire, borders Congo Republic. **Topography:** Most of Angola consists of a plateau elevated 3,000 to 5,000 feet above sea level, rising from a narrow coastal strip. There is also a temperate highland area in the west-central region, a desert in the S, and a tropical rain forest covering Cabinda. **Capital:** Luanda. **Cities** (1970 cen.): Luanda (met.) 475,328.

Government: Head of state: Pres. Jose Eduardo dos Santos b. Aug. 28, 1942; in office: Sept. 20, 1979. **Local divisions:** 17 provinces. **Armed forces:** regulars 40,000.

Economy: Industries: Alcohol, cotton goods, fishmeal, paper, palm oil, footwear. **Chief crops:** Coffee (5% of world crop), corn, sugar, palm oil, cotton, wheat, tobacco, caeao, sisal, wax. **Minerals:** Iron, diamonds (over 2 mln. carats a year), copper, manganese, sulphur, phosphates, oil. **Crude oil reserves** (1980): 1.2 bln. bbls. **Per capita arable land:** 0.5 acres. **Meat prod.** (1978): beef: 52,000 metric tons; pork: 12,000 metric tons. **Fish catch** (1977): 113,400 metric tons. **Electricity prod.** (1977): 1.36 bln. kwh. **Labor force:** 80% agric.

Finance: Currency: Kwanza (Sept. 1979: 31.50 = $1 US). **Per capita income** (1976): $500. **Imports** (1974): $541 mln.; partners: Port. 22%, W. Ger. 13%, U.S. 10%, S. Afr. 10%. **Exports** (1974): $541 mln.; partners: U.S. 38%, Port. 27%, Can. 8%, Jap. 6%. **Tourists** (1974): 995,100; receipts: bb $109 bln.

Transport: Railway traffic (1974): 418 mln. passenger-km; 5.46 bln. net ton-km. **Motor vehicles:** in use (1973): 127,300 passenger cars, 35,700 comm. vehicles. **Chief ports:** Lobito,

Luanda.

Communications: Radios: 116,000 in use (1976), 38,000 manuf. (1974). **Telephones in use** (1978): 29,796. **Daily newspaper circ.** (1976): 119,000; 19 per 1,000 pop.

Health: Life expectancy at birth (1975): 37.0 male; 40.1 female. **Births** (per 1,000 pop. 1975): 48.0. **Deaths** (per 1,000 pop. 1975): 25.3. **Natural increase** (1975): 2.3%. **Hospital beds** (per 100,000 pop. 1977): 306. **Physicians** (per 100,000 pop 1977): 6. **Infant mortality** (per 1,000 live births 1975): 24.1.

Education (1977): **Literacy:** 12%. **Pop. 5-19:** in school: 28%, teachers per 1,000: 9. **PQLI:** 14.

From the early centuries AD to 1500, Bantu tribes penetrated most of the region. Portuguese came in 1583, allied with the Bakongo kingdom in the north, and developed the slave trade. Large-scale colonization did not begin until the 20th century, when 400,000 Portuguese immigrated.

A guerrilla war begun in 1961 lasted until 1974, when Portugal offered independence. Violence between the National Front, based in Zaire, the Soviet-backed Popular Movement, and the National Union, aided by the U.S. and S. Africa, killed thousands of blacks, drove most whites to emigrate, and completed economic ruin. Some 15,000 Cuban troops and massive Soviet aid helped the Popular Movement win most of the country after independence Nov. 11, 1975. Some units of the National Union continued to resist in 1978.

In the first such large-scale action since 1978, 3,000 S. African troops crossed the southern Angolan border June 7, killing more than 300 civilians and occupying several towns.

Russian influence, backed by 25,000 Cubans, East Germans, and Portuguese Communists, is strong in the Marxist regime.

Argentina

Argentine Republic

People: Population (1979 est.): 27,210,000. **Age distrib.** (%): 0–14: 28.5; 15–59: 59.6; 60+: 11.9. **Pop. density:** 24.62 per sq. mi. **Urban** (1977): 72%. **Ethnic groups:** Europeans 97% (Spanish, Italian), Indians, Mestizos, Arabs. **Languages:** Spanish. **Religions:** Roman Catholic 94%, Protestant 2%, Jewish 2%.

Geography: Area: 1,072,067 sq. mi., 4 times the size of Texas, second largest in S. America. **Location:** Occupies most of southern S. America. **Neighbors:** Chile on W, Bolivia, Paraguay on N, Brazil, Uruguay on NE. **Topography:** The mountains in W: the Andean, Central, Misiones, and Southern. Aconcagua is the highest peak in the Western hemisphere, alt. 22,834 ft. E of the Andes are heavily wooded plains, called the Gran Chaco in the N, and the fertile, treeless Pampas in the central region. Patagonia, in the S, is bleak and arid. Rio de la Plata, 170 by 140 mi., is mostly fresh water, from 2,500-mi. Paranak and 1,000-mi. Uruguay rivers. **Capital:** Buenos Aires. **Cities** (1978 est.): Buenos Aires 2,982,000; Cordoba 781,565; Rosario 750,455; La Plata 391,247; San Miguel de Tucuman 321,567.

Government: Head of state: Pres. Jorge Rafael Videla; b. Aug. 2, 1925; in office: Mar. 29, 1976. **Local divisions:** 22 provinces, 1 natl. terr. and 1 federal dist., under military governors. **Armed forces:** regulars 132,900; reserves 250,000.

Economy: Industries: Meat processing, flour milling, chemicals, textiles, machinery, autos. **Chief crops:** Cotton, grains, corn, grapes, linseed, sugar, fruit, tobacco, peanuts. Grains are exported. **Minerals:** Oil, coal, lead, zinc, iron, sulphur, silver, copper, gold. **Crude oil reserves** (1980): 2.40 bln. bbls. **Per capita arable land:** 2.3 acres. **Meat prod.** (1978): beef: 3.19 mln. metric tons; pork: 211,000 metric tons; lamb: 137,000 metric tons. **Fish catch** (1977): 392,800 metric tons. **Electricity prod.** (1978): 29.05 bln. kwh. **Crude steel prod.** (1979): 3.2 mln. metric tons. **Labor force:** 19% agric.; 25% manuf.

Finance: Currency: Peso (Mar. 1980: 1,745.5 = $1 US). **Gross domestic product** (1975): $36.75 bln. **Per capita income** (1975): $1,388. **Imports** (1978): $3.83 bln.; partners (1977): U.S. 19%, W. Ger. 10%, Braz. 9%, Jap. 9%. **Exports** (1978): $6.4 bln.; partners (1977): Neth. 10%, Braz. 8%, It. 8%, U.S. 7%. **Tourists** (1977): 1,350,000; receipts: $213 mln. **National budget** (1978): $4.28 bln. revenues; $6.64 bln. expenditures. **International reserves less gold** (Jan. 1980): $9.67 bln. **Gold:** 4.37 mln. oz t. **Consumer prices** (change in 1979): 169.0%.

Transport: Railway traffic (1978): 11.24 bln. passenger-km; 10.37 bln. net ton-km. **Motor vehicles:** in use (1974): 2.03 mln. passenger cars, 879,800 comm. vehicles; manuf. (1978): 135,600 passenger cars, 45,480 comm. vehicles. **Civil aviation:** 5,292 mln. passenger-km (1978); 128,568 mln. freight ton-km (1978). **Chief ports:** Buenos Aires, Bahia Blanca, La Plata.

Communications: Television sets: 4.5 mln. in use (1975), 254,000 manuf. (1977). **Radios:** 21 mln. in use (1975). **Telephones in use** (1978): 2,584,801. **Daily newspaper circ.** (1976): 2,682,000.

Health: Life expectancy at birth (1975): 65.16 male; 71.38 female. **Births** (per 1,000 pop. 1970): 22.9. **Deaths** (per 1,000 pop. 1970): 9.4. **Natural increase** (1970): 1.4%. **Hospital beds** (per 100,000 pop. 1977): 524. **Physicians** (per 100,000 pop. 1977): 192. **Infant mortality** (per 1,000 live births 1970): 59.0.

Education (1977): **Literacy:** 93%. **Pop. 5-19:** in school: 59%, teachers per 1,000: 37. **PQLI:** 85.

Nomadic Indians roamed the Pampas when Spaniards arrived, 1515-1516, led by Juan Diaz de Solis. Nearly all the Indians were killed by the late 19th century. The colonists won independence, 1810-1819, and a long period of disorders ended in a strong centralized government.

Large-scale Italian, German, and Spanish immigration in the decades after 1880 spurred modernization, making Argentina the most prosperous, educated, and industrialized of the major Latin American nations. Social reforms were enacted in the 1920s, but military coups prevailed 1930-46, until the election of Gen. Juan Peron as president.

Peron, with his wife Eva Duarte effected labor reforms, but also suppressed speech and press freedoms, closed religious schools, and ran the country into debt. A 1955 coup exiled Peron, who was followed by a series of military and civilian regimes. Peron returned in 1973, and was once more elected president. He died 10 months later, succeeded by his wife, Isabel, who had been elected vice president, and who became the first woman head of state in the Western hemisphere.

A military junta ousted Mrs. Peron in 1976 amid charges of corruption. Under a continuing state of siege, the army battled guerrillas and leftists, killed 5,000 people, and jailed and tortured others. The government rejected a report of the Inter-American Human Rights Commission, 1980, which charged widespread killing, torture, and arbitrary detention.

Argentina has contracted with W. Germany for its 3d nuclear reactor. The USSR made heavy Argentine grain and oilseed purchases, as a result of the Jan. 1980 U.S. boycott.

Australia

Commonwealth of Australia

People: Population (1979 est): 14,417,000. **Age distrib.** (%): 0–14: 26.6; 15–59: 60.2; 60+: 13.2. **Pop. density:** 4.81 per sq. mi. **Urban** (1976): 86%. **Ethnic groups:** British 95%, other European 3%, aborigines (including mixed) 1.5%. **Languages:** English. **Religions:** Anglican 36%, other Protestant 20%, Roman Catholic 25%.

Geography: Area: 2,965,368 sq. mi., almost as large as the 48 contiguous U.S. states. **Location:** SE of Asia, Indian O. is W and S, Pacific O. (Coral, Tasman seas) is E; they meet N of Australia in Timor and Arafura seas: Tasmania lies 150 mi. S of Victoria state, across Bass Strait. **Neighbors:** Nearest are Indonesia, Papua New Guinea on N, Solomons, Fiji, and New Zealand on E. **Topography:** An island continent. The Great Dividing Range along the E coast has Mt. Kosciusko, 7,310 ft. The W plateau rises to 2,000 ft., with arid areas in the Great Sandy and Great Victoria deserts. The NW part of Western Australia and Northern Terr. are arid and hot. The NE has heavy rainfall and Cape York Peninsula has jungles. The Murray R. rises in New South Wales and flows 1,600 mi. to the Indian O. **Capital:** Canberra. **Cities** (1976 census): Sidney 2,765,040; Melbourne 2,479,225; Brisbane 892,987; Adelaide 857,196; Perth 731,275.

Government: Head of state: Queen Elizabeth II, represented by Gov.-Gen. Zelman Cowen; b. Oct. 7, 1919; in office: Dec. 8, 1977. **Head of government:** Prime Min. John Malcolm Fraser; b. May 21, 1930; in office: Nov. 11, 1975. **Local divisions:** 6 states, with elected governments and substantial powers; 2 territories. **Armed forces:** regulars 70,261; reserves 25,049.

Economy: Industries: Iron, steel, textiles, electrical equip., chemicals, autos, aircraft, ships, machinery. **Chief crops:** Wheat (a leading export), sugar, wine, fruit, vegetables. **Minerals:** Bauxite, antimony, coal, cobalt, copper, gold, iron, lead, manganese, nickel, silver, tin, tungsten, uranium, zinc. **Crude oil reserves** (1980): 2.13 bln. bbls. **Other resources:** Wool (30% of world output). **Per capita arable land:** 7.8 acres. **Meat prod.** (1978): beef: 2.13 mln. metric tons; pork: 197,000 metric; lamb: 516,000 metric tons. **Fish catch** (1977): 127,800 metric tons.

Electricity prod. (1978): 88.52 bln. kwh. **Crude steel prod.** (1979): 8.1 mln. metric tons. **Labor force:** 6.1% agric.; 22% manuf.

Finance: Currency: Dollar (Mar. 1980: 1 = $1.08 US). **Gross domestic product** (1978): $109.08 bln. **Per capita income** (1978): $7,515. **Imports** (1979): $18.23 bln; partners (1978): U.S. 22%, Jap. 19%, UK 11%, W. Ger. 7%. **Exports** (1979): $18.67 bln.; partners (1978): Jap. 30%, U.S. 11%, NZ 5%. **Tourists** (1977): 548,900; receipts: $343 mln. **National budget** (1979): $30.42 bln. revenues; $33.40 bln. expenditures. **International reserves less gold** (Mar. 1980): $1.70 bln. **Gold:** 7.93 mln. oz t. **Consumer prices** (change in 1979): 9.1%.

Transport: Railway traffic (1977): 32.03 bln. net ton-km. **Motor vehicles:** in use (1977): 5.55 mln. passenger cars, 1.33 mln. comm. vehicles; manuf. (1978): 315,600 passenger cars; 69,600 comm. vehicles. **Civil aviation:** 11,946 mln. passenger-miles (1977); 256,587 mln. freight ton-miles (1977). **Chief ports:** Sydney, Melbourne, Newcastle, Port Kemble, Fremantle, Geelong.

Communications: Television sets: 4.8 mln. licensed (1976), 525,000 manuf. (1977). **Radios:** 10.5 mln. licensed (1976), 68,000 manuf. (1977). **Telephones in use** (1978): 5,583,330. **Daily newspaper circ.** (1977): 4,365,000; 310 per 1,000 pop.

Health: Life expectancy at birth (1967): 67.63 male; 74.15 female. **Births** (per 1,000 pop. 1978): 15.8. **Deaths** (per 1,000 pop. 1978): 7.6. **Natural increase** (1978): .8%. **Hospital beds** (per 100,000 pop. 1977): 1,244. **Physicians** (per 100,000 pop. 1977): 154. **Infant mortality** (per 1,000 live births 1978): 12.5.

Education (1977): **Literacy:** 98%. **Pop. 5-19:** in school: 73%, teachers per 1,000: 44. **PQLI:** 95.

Capt. James Cook explored the E coast in 1770, when the continent was inhabited by a variety of different tribes. Within decades, Britain had claimed the entire continent, which became a penal colony until immigration increased in the 1850s. The commonwealth was proclaimed Jan. 1, 1901. Northern Terr. was granted limited self-rule July 1, 1978. Their capitals and 1979 pop.:

	Area (sq. mi.)	**Population**
New South Wales, Sydney	309,418	5,011,600
Victoria, Melbourne	87,854	3,818,700
Queensland, Brisbane	666,699	2,166,700
South Aust., Adelaide	379,824	1,287,600
Western Aust., Perth	974,843	1,222,100
Tasmania, Hobart	26,178	413,700
Aust. Capital Terr., Canberra	926	215,900
Northern Terr., Darwin	519,633	112,300

Australia's racially discriminatory immigration policies were abandoned in 1973, after 3 million Europeans (half British) had entered since 1945. The 50,000 aborigines and 150,000 part-aborigines are mostly detribalized, but there are several preserves in the Northern Territory. They remain economically disadvantaged.

Australia's agricultural success makes it among the top exporters of beef, lamb, wool, and wheat. Major mineral deposits have been developed as well, largely for exports. Industrialization has been completed since 1945.

Australia harbors many plant and animal species not found elsewhere, including the kangaroo, koala bear, platypus, dingo (wild dog), Tasmanian devil (racoon-like marsupial), wombat (bear-like marsupial), and barking and frilled lizards.

Australian External Territories

Norfolk Is., area 13½ sq. mi., pop. (1978) 1,900, was taken over, 1914. The soil is very fertile, suitable for citrus fruits, bananas, and coffee. Many of the inhabitants are descendants of the Bounty mutineers, moved to Norfolk 1856 from Pitcairn Is. Australia offered the island limited home rule, 1978.

Coral Sea Is. Territory, 1 sq. mi., is administered from Norfolk Is.

Territory of Ashmore and Cartier Is., area 2 sq. mi., in the Indian O. came under Australian authority 1934 and are administered as part of Northern Territory. **Heard** and **McDonald Is.** are administered by the Dept. of Science.

Cocos (Keeling) Is., 27 small coral islands in the Indian O. 1,750 mi. NW of Australia. Pop. (1978) 435, area: 5½ sq. mi.

Christmas Is., 52 sq. mi., pop. 3,094 (1978), 230 mi. S of Java, was transferred by Britain in 1958. It has phosphate deposits.

Australian Antarctic Territory was claimed by Australia in 1933, including 2,472,000 sq. mi. of territory S of 60th parallel S Lat. and between 160th-45th meridians E Long.

Austria

Republic of Austria

People: Population (1979 est.): 7,506,000. **Age distrib.** (%): 0–14: 22.8; 15–59: 57.0; 60+: 20.2. **Pop. density:** 231.98 per sq. mi. **Urban** (1971): 51.9%. **Ethnic groups:** German 98%, Slovene, Croatian, Hungarian, Italian. **Languages:** German, Slovene. **Religions:** Roman Catholic 88%, Protestant 6%, none 4.5%.

Geography: Area: 32,374 sq. mi., slightly smaller than Maine. **Location:** In S Central Europe. **Neighbors:** Switzerland, Liechtenstein on W, W. Germany, Czechoslovakia on N, Hungary on E, Yugoslavia, Italy on S. **Topography:** Austria is primarily mountainous, with the Alps and foothills covering the western and southern provinces. The eastern provinces and Vienna are located in the Danube River Basin. **Capital:** Vienna. **Cities** (1978 est.): Vienna 1,592,800; Graz 250,893; Linz 208,000.

Government: Head of state: Pres. Rudolf Kirchschlaeger; b. Mar. 20, 1915; in office: July 8, 1974. **Head of government:** Chancellor Bruno Kreisky; b. Jan. 22, 1911; in office: Apr. 21, 1970. **Local divisions:** 9 lander (states), each with a legislature. **Armed forces:** regulars 38,000; reserves 117,700.

Economy: Industries: Steel, machinery, autos, electrical and optical equip., glassware, sport goods, paper, textiles, chemicals, cement. **Chief crops:** Grains, corn, potatoes, beets, grapes. **Minerals:** Iron ore, oil, magnesite, aluminum, coal, lignite, copper, graphite. **Crude oil reserves** (1980): 140 mln. bbls. **Other resources:** Forests, hydro power. **Per capita arable land:** 0.5 acres. **Meat prod.** (1978): beef: 185,000 metric tons; pork: 317,000 metric tons. **Electricity prod.** (1978): 38.09 bln. kwh. **Crude steel prod.** (1979): 4.9 mln. metric tons. **Labor force:** 13.8% agric.; 60% manuf.

Finance: Currency: Schilling (Mar. 1980: 13.91 = $1 US). **Gross domestic product** (1978): $58.05 bln. **Per capita income** (1978): $6,739. **Imports** (1979): $20.26 bln.; partners (1978): W. Ger. 43%, It. 9%, Switz. 6%. **Exports** (1979): $15.48 bln.; partners (1978): W. Ger. 29%, It. 9%, Switz. 8%. **Tourists** (1977): 11,747,800; receipts: $3.32 bln. **National budget** (1978): $11.77 bln. revenues; $14.14 bln. expenditures. **International reserves less gold** (Mar. 1980): $3.77 bln. **Gold:** 21.11 mln. oz t. **Consumer prices** (change in 1979): 3.7%.

Transport: Railway traffic (1978): 7.31 bln. passenger-km; 9.62 bln. net ton-km. **Motor vehicles:** in use (1977): 1.87 mln. passenger cars, 472,100 comm. vehicles; manuf. (1978): 360 passenger cars; 6,240 comm. vehicles. **Civil aviation:** 1,034 mln. passenger-km (1978); 12.492 mln. freight ton-km (1978).

Communications: Television sets: 1.77 mln. licensed (1976), 429,000 manuf. (1977). **Radios:** 2.19 mln. licensed (1976), 82,000 manuf. (1972). **Telephones in use** (1978): 2,443,412. **Daily newspaper circ.** (1977): 2,529,000; 336 per 1,000 pop.

Health: Life expectancy at birth (1976): 68.07 male; 75.05 female. **Births** (per 1,000 pop. 1978): 11.3. **Deaths** (per 1,000 pop. 1978): 12.5. **Natural increase** (1978): −.1%. **Hospital beds** (per 100,000 pop. 1977): 1,128. **Physicians** (per 100,000 pop. 1977): 233. **Infant mortality** (per 1,000 live births 1978): 14.9.

Education (1977): **Literacy:** 99%. **Pop. 5-19:** in school: 65%, teachers per 1,000: 38. **PQLI:** 94.

Rome conquered Austrian lands from Celtic tribes around 15 BC. In 788 the territory was incorporated into Charlemagne's empire. By 1300, the House of Hapsburg had gained control; they added vast territories in all parts of Europe to their realm in the next few hundred years.

Austrian dominance of Germany was undermined in the 18th century and ended by Prussia by 1866. But the Congress of Vienna, 1815, confirmed Austrian control of a large empire in southeast Europe consisting of Germans, Hungarians, Slavs, Italians, and others.

The dual Austro-Hungarian monarchy was established in 1867, giving autonomy to Hungary and 50 years of peace.

World War I, started after the June 28, 1914 assassination of Archduke Ferdinand, the Hapsburg heir, by a Serbian nationalist, destroyed the empire. By 1918 Austria was reduced to a small republic, with the borders it has today.

Nazi Germany invaded Austria Mar. 13, 1938, after four years of control by right-wing dictators Dollfuss and Schuschnigg. The republic was reestablished in 1945, under Allied occupation. Full independence and neutrality were guaranteed by a 1955 treaty with the major powers.

Austria produces 85% of its food, as well as an array of industrial products. A large part of Austria's economy is controlled by state enterprises. Socialists have shared or alternated power with the conservative People's Party.

Economic agreements with the Common Market give Austria access to a free-trade area encompassing most of West Europe.

Bahamas

Commonwealth of the Bahamas

People: Population (1979 est.): 236,000. **Age distrib.** (%): 0–14: 43.6; 15–59: 50.9; 60+: 5.5. **Pop. density:** 52.23 per sq. mi. **Urban** (1970): 57.9%. **Ethnic groups:** Negro 85%, Caucasian (British, Canadian, U.S.). **Languages:** English. **Religions:** Baptist 29%, Anglican 23%, Roman Catholic 22%.

Geography: Area: 4,404 sq. mi., slightly smaller than Connecticut. **Location:** In Atlantic O., E of Florida. **Neighbors:** Nearest are U.S. on W, Cuba on S. **Topography:** Nearly 700 islands (30 inhabited) and over 2,000 islets in the western Atlantic extend 760 mi. NW to SE. **Capital:** Nassau. **Cities** (1970 cen.): Nassau 3,233.

Government: Head of state: Queen Elizabeth II, represented by Gov.-Gen. Gerald C. Cash; b. May 28, 1917, in office: Sept. 29, 1979. **Head of government:** Prime Min. Lynden Oscar Pindling; b. Mar. 22, 1930; in office: Jan. 16, 1967. **Local divisions:** 18 districts.

Economy: Industries: Tourism, intl. banking, rum, drugs. **Chief crops:** Fruits, vegetables. **Minerals:** Salt. **Other resources:** Lobsters. **Per capita arable land:** 0.02 acres. **Electricity prod.** (1977): 650.00 mln. kwh. **Labor force:** 9% agric.

Finance: Currency: Dollar (Mar. 1980: 1 = $1 US). **Gross domestic product** (1975 est.): $500 mln. **Imports** (1978): $2.45 bln.; partners (1977): U.S. 35%, S. Arab. 24%, Iran 10%, Nigeria 9%. **Exports** (1978): $2.11 bln.; partners (1977): U.S. 81%, S. Arab. 10%. **Tourists** (1977): 942,600; receipts: $372 mln. **National budget** (1978): $166 mln. revenues; $186 mln. expenditures. **International reserves less gold** (Mar. 1980): $90.6 mln. **Gold** (Jan. 1980): 17,000 oz t. **Consumer prices** (change in 1979): 9.1%.

Transport: Motor vehicles: in use (1976): 36,500 passenger cars, 5,300 comm. vehicles. **Chief ports:** Nassau, Freeport.

Communications: Radios: 96,000 in use (1976). **Telephones in use** (1978): 61,756. **Daily newspaper circ.** (1976): 25,000; 118 per 1,000 pop.

Health: Life expectancy at birth (1971): 64.0 male; 67.3 female. **Births** (per 1,000 pop. 1976): 24.8. **Deaths** (per 1,000 pop. 1976): 4.6. **Natural increase** (1976): 2.0%. **Infant mortality** (per 1,000 live births 1976): 24.7. **PQLI:** 88.

Christopher Columbus first set foot in the New World on San Salvador (Watling I.) in 1492, when Arawak Indians inhabited the islands. British settlement began in 1647; the islands became a British colony in 1783. Internal self-government was granted in 1964; full independence within the Commonwealth was attained July 10, 1973.

International banking and investment management has become a major industry alongside tourism, despite controversy over financial irregularities.

Bahrain

State of Bahrain

People: Population (1979 est.): 370,000. **Age distrib.** (%): 0–14: 44.3; 15–59: 51.1; 60+: 4.6. **Pop. density:** 1,471.86 per sq. mi. **Urban** (1971): 78.1%. **Ethnic groups:** Arabs 88%, Iranians 4%, Indians, Pakistanis 5%. **Languages:** Arabic, Persian. **Religions:** Sunni Moslem 50%, Shiite Moslem 50%.

Geography: Area: 231 sq. mi., smaller than New York City. **Location:** In Persian Gulf. **Neighbors:** Nearest are Saudi Arabia on W. Qatar on E. **Topography:** Bahrain Island, and several adjacent, smaller islands, are flat, hot and humid, with little rain. **Capital:** Manama. **Cities** (1971 cen.): Manama 88,785.

Government: Head of state: Amir Isa bin Salman Al-Khalifa; b. July 3, 1933; in office: Nov. 2, 1961. **Head of government:** Prime Min. Khalifa bin Salman Al–Khalifa; b. 1935; in office: Jan. 19, 1970. **Local divisions:** 6 towns and cities. **Armed forces:** regulars 2,300.

Economy: Industries: Oil products, aluminum smelting, shipping. **Chief crops:** Fruits, vegetables. **Minerals:** Oil, gas. **Crude oil reserves** (1980): 240 mln. bbls. **Per capita arable land:** 0.007 acres. **Electricity prod.** (1977): 896.00 mln. kwh. **Labor force:** 5% agric.; 14% manuf.

Finance: Currency: Dinar (Mar. 1980: 1 = $2.65 US). **Gross domestic product** (1974 est.): $1.1 bln. **Per capita income** (1976): $2,060. **Imports** (1978): $2.05 bln.; partners (1977): Sau. Ar. 43%, UK 11%, Jap. 8%, U.S. 7%. **Exports** (1979): $2.41 bln.; partners (1977): Jap. 14%, Sau. Ar. 14%, UAE 9%, U.S. 8%. **National Budget** (1977): $575 mln. revenues; $613 mln. expenditures. **International reserves less gold** (Mar. 1980): $620.0 mln. **Gold:** 150,000 oz t. **Consumer prices** (change in 1979): 2.3%.

Transport: Motor vehicles: in use (1977): 35,500 passenger cars, 13,200 comm. vehicles. **Chief ports:** Sitra.

Communications: Television sets: 31,000 in use (1976). **Radios:** 100,000 in use (1975). **Telephones in use** (1978): 38,284.

Health: Births (per 1,000 pop. 1975): 30.0. **Hospital beds** (per 100,000 pop. 1977): 303. **Physicians** (per 100,000 pop. 1977): 62.

Education (1977): **Literacy:** 40%. **Pop. 5–19:** in school: 60%, teachers per 1,000: 36. **PQLI:** 61.

Long ruled by the Khalifa family, Bahrain was a British protectorate from 1861 to 1971, when it regained independence.

Pearls, shrimp, fruits, and vegetables were the mainstays of the economy until oil was discovered in 1932. By the 1970s, oil reserves were depleted; international banking thrived.

Bahrain took part in the 1973-74 Arab oil embargo against the U.S. and other nations. The government bought controlling interest in the oil industry in 1975.

Saudi Arabia announced, Dec., 1979, that it will build a 15-mile, $1 billion causeway linking Bahrain with the Arab mainland.

Bangladesh

People's Republic of Bangladesh

People: Population (1979 est.): 88,092,000. **Age distrib.** (%): 0-14: 43.2; 15-59: 52.4; 60+: 4.4. **Pop. density:** 1,535.75 per sq. mi. **Urban** (1974): 8.8%. **Ethnic groups:** Bengali 98%, Bihari, tribesmen. **Languages:** Bangla (official), English. **Religions:** Moslems 85%, Hindus 14%.

Geography: Area: 55,126 sq. mi. slightly smaller than Wisconsin. **Location:** In S Asia, on N bend of Bay of Bengal. **Neighbors:** India nearly surrounds country on W, N, E; Burma on SE. **Topography:** The country is mostly a low plain cut by the Ganges and Brahmaputra rivers and their delta. The land is alluvial and marshy along the coast, with hills only in the extreme SE and NE. A tropical monsoon climate prevails, among the rainiest in the world. **Capital:** Dacca. **Cities** (1974 cen.): Dacca (met.) 1,730,253; Chittagong (met.) 889,760; Khulna (met.) 437,304.

Government: Head of state: Pres. Ziaur Rahman; b. Jan. 19, 1936; in office: Nov. 7, 1975. **Head of government:** Prime Minister Shah Mohammad Azizur Rahman, b. 1925, in office: Mar. 16, 1979. **Local divisions:** 19 districts. **Armed forces:** regulars 76,500; para-military 66,000.

Economy: Industries: Cement, textiles, jute, fertilizers. **Chief crops:** Jute (most of world output), rice. **Minerals:** Natural gas, offshore oil. **Other resources:** Water. **Per capita arable land:** 0.3 acres. **Meat prod.** (1978): beef: 159,000 metric tons; lamb: 30,000 metric tons. **Fish catch** (1977): 835,000 metric tons. **Electricity prod.** (1978): 2.00 bln. kwh. **Labor force:** 70% agric.

Finance: Currency: Taka (Mar. 1980: 16.03 = $1 US). **Gross domestic product** (1979): $9.52 bln. **Per capita income** (1976): $85. **Imports** (1978): $1.56 bln.; partners: U.S. 14%, Jap. 12%, UK 9%, Can. 6%. **Exports** (1979): $641 mln.; partners: U.S. 15%, UK 9%, Pak. 8%, Jap. 6%. **Tourists** (1977): 45,300; receipts: $3 mln. **International reserves less gold** (Mar. 1980): $360.9 mln. **Gold:** 54,000 oz t. **Consumer prices** (change in 1979): 12.7%.

Transport: Railway traffic (1973): 3.33 bln. passenger-miles; 639 mln. net ton-miles. **Motor vehicles:** in use (1972): 31,700 passenger cars, 24,800 comm. vehicles. **Chief ports:** Chittagong, Chalna.

Communications: Telephones in use (1978): 89,211. **Daily newspaper circ.** (1976) 350,000.

Health: Life expectancy at birth (1974): 45.8 male; 46.6 female. **Births** (per 1,000 pop. 1975): 47.4. **Deaths** (per 1,000 pop. 1975): 20.5. **Natural increase** (1975): 2.7%. **Hospital beds** (per 100,000 pop. 1977): 22. **Physicians** (per 100,000 pop. 1977): 8.

Education (1977): **Literacy:** 29%. **Pop. 5–19:** in school: 35%, teachers per 1,000: 9. **PQLI:** 32.

Moslem invaders conquered the formerly Hindu area in the 12th century. British rule lasted from the 18th century to 1947, when East Bengal became part of Pakistan.

Charging West Pakistani domination, the Awami League, based in the East, won National Assembly control in 1971. Assembly sessions were postponed; riots broke out. Pakistani troops attacked Mar. 25; Bangladesh independence was proclaimed the next day. In the ensuing civil war, one million died amid charges of Pakistani atrocities. Ten million fled to India.

War between India and Pakistan broke out Dec. 3, 1971. Pakistan surrendered in the East Dec. 15. Sheik Mujibur Rahman became prime minister. The country moved into the Indian and Soviet orbits, in response to U.S. support of Pakistan, and much of the economy was nationalized.

In 1974, the government took emergency powers to curb widespread violence; Mujibur was assassinated and a series of coups followed.

Chronic destitution among the densely crowded population has been worsened by the decline of jute as a major world commodity.

A Ganges waterpact with India, signed 1977, was recommitted by the 2 nations, 1979. Martial law, in force since 1975, was lifted on Apr. 6, 1979, prior to the opening of the new parliament.

Barbados

People: Population (1979) est.): 279,000. **Age distrib.** (%): 0–14: 31.5; 15–59: 54.9; 60+: 13.6. **Pop. density:** 1,506.02 per sq. mi. **Urban** (1970): 3.7%. **Ethnic groups:** Negro 90%, mixed 5%, Caucasian 5%. **Languages:** English. **Religions:** Anglican 70%, Methodist, Pentecostal, Roman Catholic.

Geography: Area: 166 sq. mi. **Location:** In Atlantic, farthest E of W. Indies. **Neighbors:** Nearest are Trinidad, Grenada on SW. **Topography:** The island lies alone in the Atlantic almost completely surrounded by coral reefs. Highest point is Mt. Hillaby, 1,115 ft. **Capital:** Bridgetown. **Cities** (1970 cen.): Bridgetown 8,789.

Government: Head of state: Queen Elizabeth II, represented by Gov.-Gen. Deighton L. Ward; b. May 16, 1909; in office: Nov. 17, 1976. **Head of government:** Prime Min. John M.G. Adams; b. Sept. 24, 1931; in office: Sept. 2, 1976. **Local divisions:** 11 parishes, one city.

Economy: Industries: Rum, molasses, tourism. **Chief crops:** Sugar, cotton. **Minerals:** Lime. **Crude oil reserves** (1980): 1.5 mln. bbls. **Other resources:** Fish. **Per capita arable land:** 0.3 acres. **Electricity prod.** (1978): 264.00 mln. kwh. **Labor force:** 18% agric.

Finance: Currency: Dollar (Mar. 1980: 2.01 = $1 US). **Gross domestic product** (1978): $508.13 mln. **Per capita income** (1976): $1,450. **Imports** (1978): $312 mln.; partners (1977): U.S. 24%, UK 19%, Trin./Tob. 10%, Can. 7%. **Exports** (1978): $129 mln.; partners (1977): U.S. 32%, Trin./Tob. 11%, Ire. 11%, UK 8%. **Tourists** (1977): 235,000; receipts: $83 million. **National budget** (1977): $133 mln. revenues; $164 mln. expenditures. **International reserves less gold** (Feb. 1980): $66.63 mln. **Consumer prices** (change in 1979): 13.2%.

Transport: Motor vehicles: in use (1976): 24,700 passenger cars; 4,000 comm. vehicles. **Chief ports:** Bridgetown.

Communications: Television sets: 48,000 in use (1976). **Radios:** 130,000 in use (1976). **Telephones in use** (1978): 47,266. **Daily newspaper circ.** (1976): 29,000; 115 per 1,000 pop.

Health: Life expectancy at birth (1961): 62.74 male; 67.43 female. **Births** (per 1,000 pop. 1976): 18.6. **Deaths** (per 1,000 pop. 1976): 9.2. **Natural increase** (1976): .9%. **Hospitals beds** (per 100,000 pop. 1977): 833. **Physicians** (per 100,000 pop. 1977): 76. **Infant mortality** (per 1,000 live births 1976): 28.3.

Education (1977): **Literacy:** 97%. **Pop. 5-19:** in school: 75%, teachers per 1,000: 36. **PQLI:** 91.

Barbados was probably named by Portuguese sailors in reference to bearded fig trees. An English ship visited in 1605, and British settlers arrived on the uninhabited island in 1627. Slaves worked the sugar plantations, but were freed in 1834.

Self-rule came gradually, with full independence proclaimed Nov. 30, 1966. British traditions have remained.

Belgium

Kingdom of Belgium

People: Population (1979 est.): 9,849,000. **Age distrib.** (%): 0–14: 21.8; 15–59: 59.3; 60+: 18.9 **Pop. density:** 835.39 per sq. mi. **Urban** (1976): 94.6%. **Ethnic groups:** Flemings 58%, Walloons 41%. **Languages:** Flemish (Dutch), French. **Religions:** Roman Catholic 90%, Protestant.

Geography: Area: 11,779 sq. mi., slightly larger than Maryland. **Location:** In NW Europe, on N. Sea. **Neighbors:** France on W, S, Luxembourg on SE, W. Germany on E, Netherlands on N. **Topography:** Mostly flat, the country is trisected by the Scheldt and Meuse, major commercial rivers. The land becomes hilly and forested in the SE (Ardennes) region. **Capital:** Brussels. **Cities** (1978 est.): Antwerp 222,775; Ghent 148,166; Liege 144,875; Brugge 118,023; Brussels 103,712.

Government: Head of state: King Baudouin; b. Sept. 7, 1930; in office: July 17, 1951. **Head of government:** Prime Min. Wilfried Martens; b. Apr. 19, 1936; in office: Apr. 3, 1979. **Local divisions:** 9 provinces. **Armed forces:** regulars 86,800; reserves 54,400.

Economy: Industries: Steel, glassware, diamond cutting, textiles, chemicals. **Chief crops:** Grains, potatoes, sugar beets. **Minerals:** Coal. **Other resources:** Forests. **Per capita arable land** (incl. Lux.): 0.2 acres. **Meat prod.** (1978): beef: 289,000 metric tons; pork: 628,000 metric tons. **Fish catch** (1977): 44,400 metric tons. **Electricity prod.** (1978): 50.84 bln. kwh. **Crude steel prod.** (1979): 13.4 mln. metric tons. **Labor force:** 3.4% agric.; 37% manuf.

Finance: Currency: Franc (Mar. 1980: 31.17 = $1 US). **Gross domestic product** (1978): $96.91 bln. **Per capita income** (1978): $9,025. *Note:* the following trade and tourist data includes Luxembourg. **Imports** (1979): $60.39 bln.; partners (1978): W. Ger. 23%, Neth. 16%, France 16%, UK 8%. **Exports** (1979): $56.25 bln.; partners (1978): W. Ger. 23%, France 19%, Neth. 16%, UK 7%. **Tourists** (1977): 7,623,300; receipts: $993 mln. **National budget** (1979): $32.56 bln. revenues; $39.79 bln. expenditures. **International reserves less gold** (Mar. 1980): $4.12 bln. **Gold:** 34.18 mln. oz t. **Consumer prices** (change in 1979): 4.4%.

Transport: Railway traffic (1978): 7.14 bln. passenger-km; 7.10 bln. net ton-km. **Motor vehicles:** in use (1977): 2.81 mln. passenger cars, 297,100 comm. vehicles; assembled (1978): 1.01 mln. passenger cars; 37,090 comm. vehicles. **Civil aviation:** 4,500 mln. passenger-km (1978); 386 mln. freight ton-km (1978). **Chief ports:** Antwerp, Zeebrugge, Ghent.

Communications: Television sets: 2.6 mln. licensed (1976), 588,000 manuf. (1977). **Radios:** 4.04 mln. licensed (1976), 1.89 mln. manuf. (1977). **Telephones in use** (1978): 3,100,109. **Daily newspaper circ.** (1977): 2,369,000; 241 per 1,000 pop.

Health: Life expectancy at birth (1972): 67.79 male; 74.21 female. **Births** (per 1,000 pop. 1978): 12.4. **Deaths** (per 1,000 pop. 1978): 11.7. **Natural increase** (1978) .07%. **Hospital beds** (per 100,000 pop. 1977): 894. **Physicians** (per 100,000 pop. 1977): 211. **Infant mortality** (per 1,000 live births 1978): 11.9.

Education (1977): **Literacy:** 99%. **Pop. 5-19:** in school: 58%, teachers per 1,000: 40. **PQLI:** 94.

Belgium derives its name from the Belgae, the first recorded inhabitants, probably Celts. The land was conquered by Julius Caesar, and was ruled for 1800 years by conquerors, including Rome, the Franks, Burgundy, Spain, Austria, and France. After 1815, Belgium was made a part of the Netherlands, but it became an independent constitutional monarchy in 1830.

Belgian neutrality was violated by Germany in both world wars. King Leopold III surrendered to Germany, May 28, 1940. After the war, he was forced by political pressure to abdicate in favor of his son, King Baudouin.

The Flemings of northern Belgium speak Dutch while French is the language of the Walloons in the south. The language difference has been a perennial source of controversy. Disagreement between the 2 groups has caused government crises twice in 2 years.

Belgium lives by its foreign trade; about 50% of its entire production is sold abroad. The poor economy, with a 7.6% unemployment rate, deteriorated public finances, and weakened balance of payments, is the prime concern of the second Martens government.

Benin

People's Republic of Benin

People: Population (1979 est.): 3,379,000. **Age distrib.** (%): 0–14: 46.1; 15–59: 48.3; 60+: 5.6. **Pop. density:** 77.73 per sq. mi. **Urban** (1978): 13.8%. **Ethnic groups:** Fons, Adjas, Baribas, Yorubas. **Languages:** French is only common language. **Religions:** Christian 15% (south), Moslem 13% (north), others.

Geography: Area: 43,483 sq. mi., slightly smaller than Pennsylvania. **Location:** In W Africa on Gulf of Guinea. **Neighbors:** Togo on W, Upper Volta, Niger on N, Nigeria on E. **Topography:** most of Benin is flat and covered with dense vegetation. The coast is hot, humid, and rainy. **Capitals:** Porto–Novo, Cotonou. **Cities** (1978 est.): Cotonou 178,000; Porto-Novo 104,000.

Government: Head of state: Pres. Mathieu Kerekou; b. Sept. 2, 1933; in office: Oct. 27, 1972. **Local divisions:** 6 departments. **Armed forces:** regulars 2,200; para-military 1,000.

Economy: Chief crops: Palm products, peanuts, cotton, kapok, coffee, tobacco. **Minerals:** Oil. **Per capita arable land:** 2.1 acres. **Fish catch** (1977): 24,900 metric tons. **Electricity prod.** (1977): 5.00 mln. kwh. **Labor force:** 90% agric.

Finance: Currency: CFA franc (Mar. 1980: 223.92 = $1 US). **Gross domestic product** (1977): $604 mln. **Per capita income** (1975): $162. **Imports** (1978): $288 mln.; partners (1977): Fr. 23%, UK 13%, W. Ger. 8%, Neth. 6%. **Exports** (1978): $27 mln.; partners (1977): Fr. 25%, Jap. 20%, Neth. 13%, W. Ger. 8%. **Tourists** (1977): 23,000; receipts b.b. $3 mln. **International reserves less gold** (Jan. 1980): $15.7 mln. **Gold:** 11,000 oz t.

Transport: Railway traffic (1978): 133.2 mln. passenger-km; 152 mln. net ton-km. **Motor vehicles:** in use (1976): 17,000 passenger cars, 9,500 comm. vehicles. **Chief ports:** Cotonou.

Communications: Radios: 150,000 in use (1976). **Daily newspaper circ.** (1976): 1,000; 0.3 per 1,000 pop.

Health: Life expectancy at birth (1975): 44.8 male; 45.0 female. **Births** (per 1,000 pop. 1975): 49.0. **Deaths** (per 1,000 pop. 1975): 21.1. **Natural increase** (1975): 2.8%. **Hospital beds** (per 100,000 pop. 1977): 137. **Physicians** (per 100,000 pop. 1977): 3. **Infant mortality** (per 1,000 live births 1975): 109.6.

Education (1977): **Literacy:** 20%. **Pop. 5-19:** in school: 29%, teachers per 1,000: 7. **PQLI:** 26.

The Kingdom of Abomey, rising to power in wars with neighboring kingdoms in the 17th century, came under French domination in the late 19th century, and was incorporated into French West Africa by 1904.

Under the name Dahomey, the country became independent Aug. 1, 1960. The name was changed to Benin in 1975. In the fifth coup since independence Maj. Mathieu Kerekou took power in 1972; two years later he declared a socialist state with a "Marxist-Leninist" philosophy. A 3-yr. economic plan started in 1977 relies on the development of agriculturally-based industries.

Bhutan

Kingdom of Bhutan

People: Population (1979 est.): 1,273,000. **Pop. density:** 64.23 per sq. mi. **Ethnic groups:** Bhotia (Tibetan) 60%. Nepalese, Lepcha (indigenous), Indians. **Languages:** Dzongkha Tibetan (official), Nepali. **Religions:** Buddhist 75%, Hindu 25%.

Geography: Area: 19,305 sq. mi., the size of Vermont and New Hampshire combined. **Location:** In eastern Himalayan Mts. **Neighbors:** India on W (Sikkim) and S, China on N. **Topography:** Bhutan is comprised of very high mountains in the N, fertile valleys in the center, and thick forests in the Duar Plain in the S. **Capital:** Thimphu. **City** (1978 est.): Thimphu 8,992.

Government: Head of state: King Jigme Singye Wangchuk; b. Nov. 11, 1955; in office: July 21, 1972. **Local divisions:** 4 regions comprised of 15 districts.

Economy: Industries: Cloth. **Chief crops:** Rice, corn, wheat, oranges, cardamon, yak butter, lac, wax. **Other resources:** Elephants, timber. **Per capita arable land:** 0.5 acres.

Finance: Currency: Ngultrum (Oct. 1979: 1 = $0.12 US) (Indian Rupee also used). **Gross domestic product** (1976 est.): $90 mln. **Per capita income** (1976): $70. **Imports** (1976): $1.4 mln.; partners India 99%. **Exports** (1976): $1 mln.; partners India 99%.

Communications: Radios: 10,000 licensed (1976). **Telephones in use** (1978): 1,355.

Health: Life expectancy at birth (1975): 42.0 male; 40.5 female. **Births** (per 1,000 pop. 1975): 43.7. **Deaths** (per 1,000 pop. 1975): 22.3. **Natural increase** (1975): 2.5%. **Pop. per hospital bed** (1975): 1,616. **Pop. per physician** (1975): 4,264.

The region came under Tibetan rule in the 16th century. British influence grew in the 19th century. A monarchy, set up in 1907, became a British protectorate by a 1910 treaty. The country became independent in 1949, with India guiding foreign relations and supplying aid.

Links to India have been strengthened by airline service and a road network. Most of the population engages in subsistence agriculture.

Bolivia

Republic of Bolivia

People: Population (1979 est.): 5,213,000. **Age distrib.** (%): 0–14: 41.9; 15–59: 52.0; 60+: 6.4. **Pop. density:** 12.12 per sq. mi. **Ethnic groups:** Quechua 30%, Aymara 25%, Mestizo (cholo) 25-30%, European 5-15%. **Languages:** Spanish (official) 55%, Quechua, Aymara. **Religions:** Roman Catholic 95%.

Geography: Area: 424,162 sq. mi., the size of Texas and California combined. **Location:** In central Andes Mtns. **Neighbors:** Peru, Chile on W, Argentina, Paraguay on S, Brazil on E and N. **Topography:** The great central plateau, at an altitude of 12,000 ft., over 500 mi. long, lies between two great cordilleras having 3 of the highest peaks in S. America. Lake Titicaca, on Peruvian border, is highest lake in world on which steamboats ply (12,506 ft.). The E central region has semitropical forests; the llanos, or Amazon-Chaco lowlands are in E. **Capitals:** Sucre, La Paz. **Cities** (1976 cen.): La Paz 654,713; Santa Cruz 237,128; Cochabamba 194,156.

Government: Head of state: Pres. Luis Garcia Meza; in office: July 17, 1980. **Local divisions:** 9 departments headed by prefects, 94 provinces. **Armed forces:** regulars 22,500.

Economy: Chief crops: Potatoes, sugar, coffee, barley, cocoa, rice, corn, bananas, citrus. **Minerals:** Antimony, tin, tungsten, silver, copper, lead, zinc, oil, gas, bismuth, wolfram, gold, iron, cadmium, borate of lime. **Crude oil reserves** (1980): 150 mln. bbls. **Other resources:** rubber, cinchona bark. **Per capita arable land:** 1.5 acres. **Meat prod.** (1978): beef: 78,000 metric tons; pork: 29,000 metric tons; lamb: 25,000 metric tons. **Electricity prod.** (1977): 1.15 bln. kwh. **Labor force:** 67% agric.

Finance: Currency: Peso (Mar. 1980: 24.51 = $1 US). **Gross domestic product** (1978): $4.18 bln. **Per capita income** (1975): $477. **Imports** (1978): $848 mln.; partners (1977): U.S. 27%, Arg. 12%, Jap. 12%, Braz. 10%. **Exports** (1978): $627 mln.; partners (1977): U.S. 34%, Arg. 20%, UK 12%, Neth. 5%. **Tourist receipts** (1977): $29 mln. **National budget** (1978): $437 mln. revenues; $590 mln. expenditures. **International reserves less gold** (Mar. 1980): $107.5 mln. **Gold:** 712,000 oz t. **Consumer prices** (change in 1978): 10.4%.

Transport: Railway traffic (1977): 395 mln. passenger-km; 579 mln. net ton-miles. **Motor vehicles:** in use (1977): 35,300 passenger cars, 25,400 comm. vehicles. **Civil aviation:** 347 mln. passenger-miles (1977); 17,244 freight ton-miles (1977).

Communications: Radios: 430,000 in use (1976). **Telephones in use** (1978): 101,500. **Daily newspaper circ.** (1976): 150,000; 26 per 1,000 pop.

Health: Life expectancy at birth (1975): 46.5 male; 51.1 female. **Births** (per 1,000 pop. 1975): 46.6. **Deaths** (per 1,000 pop. 1975): 18.0. **Natural increase** (1975): 2.9%. **Hospital beds** (per 100,000 pop. 1977): 228. **Physicians** (per 100,000 pop. 1977): 38. **Infant mortality** (per 1,000 live births 1975): 77.3.

Education (1977): **Literacy:** 50%. **Pop. 5-19:** in school: 58%, teachers per 1,000: 25. **PQLI:** 47.

The Incas conquered the region from earlier Indian inhabitants in the 13th century. Spanish rule began in the 1530s, and lasted until Aug. 6, 1825. The country is named after Simon Bolivar, independence fighter.

In a series of wars, Bolivia lost its Pacific coast to Chile, the oilbearing Chaco to Paraguay, and rubber-growing areas to Brazil, 1879-1935.

Economic unrest, especially among the militant mine workers, has contributed to continuing political instability. A reformist government under Victor Paz Estenssoro, 1951-64, nationalized tin mines and attempted to improve conditions for the Indian majority, but was overthrown by a military junta. A series of coups and countercoups continued through 1980, when military forces took control to head off the expected congressional choice of a leftist as the nation's democratically elected president.

Botswana

Republic of Botswana

People: Population (1979 est.): 764,000. **Age distrib.** (%): 0–14: 46.1; 15–59: 43.1; 60+: 7.4. **Pop. density:** 3.32 per sq. mi. **Urban** (1974): 12.3%. **Ethnic groups:** Bantus (8 main tribes), Bushmen. **Languages:** English (official), Setswana. **Religions:** Christian 15%, others.

Geography: Area: 220,000 sq. mi., slightly smaller than Texas. **Location:** In southern Africa. **Neighbors:** Namibia (S.W. Africa) on N and W, S. Africa on S, Zimbabwe on NE; Botswana claims border with Zambia on N. **Topography:** The Kalahari Desert, supporting nomadic Bushmen and wildlife, spreads over SW; there are swamplands and farming areas in N, and rolling plains in E where livestock are grazed. **Capital:** Gaborone. **Cities** (1971 cen.): Gaborone 18,799.

Government: Head of state: Acting Pres. Quett Masire; in office: July 13, 1980. **Local divisions:** 9 districts and 4 independent towns, all with local councils. **Armed forces:** regulars 1,000; para-military 1,260.

Economy: Industries: Tourism. **Chief crops:** Corn, sorghum, beans, peanuts. **Minerals:** Copper, coal, nickel, diamonds. **Other resources:** Big game. **Per capita arable land:** 4.6 acres. **Meat prod.** (1978): beef: 40,000 metric tons; lamb: 5,000 metric tons. **Electricity prod.** (1977): 348.00 mln. kwh. **Labor force:** 75% agric.

Finance: Currency: Pula (Feb. 1980: 1 = $1.27 US). **Gross domestic product** (1978): $401 mln. **Per capita income** (1976): $483. **Imports** (1978): $354 mln.; partners (1976): S. Africa 80%. **Exports** (1978): $222 mln.; partners (1976): UK 47%, S. Africa 24%, U.S. 22%. **National budget** (1978): $157 mln. revenues; $176 mln. expenditures. **International reserves less gold** (Feb. 1980): $277.9 mln. **Consumer prices** (change in 1978): 9.4%.

Transport: Railway traffic (1978): 1.04 bln. net ton km. **Motor vehicles:** in use (1977): 3,400 passenger cars, 10,800 comm. vehicles.

Communications: Radios: 60,000 in use (1976). **Daily newspaper circ.** (1977): 17,000; 24 per 1,000 pop.

Health: Life expectancy at birth (1975): 44.3 male; 47.5 female. **Births** (annual per 1,000 pop. 1975): 50.7 **Deaths** (per 1,000 pop. 1975): 19.4. **Natural increase** (1975): 3.1%. **Hospital beds** (per 100,000 pop. 1977): 303. **Physicians** (per 100,000 pop. 1977): 14.

Education (1977): **Literacy:** 27%. **Pop. 5-19:** in school: 49%; teachers per 1,000: 16. **PQLI:** 51.

First inhabited by bushmen, then by Bantus, the region became the British protectorate of Bechuanaland in 1886, halting encroachment by Boers and Germans from the south and southwest. The country became fully independent Sept. 30, 1966, changing its name to Botswana.

Cattle-raising and mining (diamonds, copper, nickel) have contributed to the country's rapid economic growth. Many workers are migrants in S. Africa, and much of Botswana's exports go to that country.

Brazil

Federative Republic of Brazil

People: Population (1979 est.): 119,175,000. **Age distrib.** (%): 0–14: 41.1; 15–59: 53.7; 60+: 5.2. **Pop. density:** 35.11 per sq. mi. **Urban** (1977): 61.2%. **Ethnic groups:** Portuguese, Africans, and mulattoes make up the vast majority; Italians, Germans, Japanese, Indians, Jews, Arabs. **Languages:** Portuguese. **Religions:** Roman Catholic 89%, Protestant 10%.

Geography: Area: 3,286,470 sq. mi., larger than contiguous 48 U.S. states; largest country in S. America. **Location:** Occupies eastern half of S. America. **Neighbors:** French Guiana, Suriname, Guyana, Venezuela on N, Colombia, Peru, Bolivia, Paraguay, Argentina on W, Uruguay on S. **Topography:** Brazil's Atlantic coastline stretches 4,603 miles. In N is the heavily-wooded Amazon basin covering half the country. Its network of rivers navigable for 15,814 mi. The Amazon itself flows 2,093 miles in Brazil, all navigable. The NE region is semiarid scrubland, heavily settled and poor. The S central region, favored by climate and resources, has 45% of the population, produces 75% of farm goods and 80% of industrial output. The narrow coastal belt includes most of the major cities. Almost the entire country has a tropical or semitropical climate. **Capital:** Brasilia. **Cities** (1978 est.): Sao Paulo 7,198,608; Rio de Janeiro 4,857,716; Belo Horizonte 1,557,464; Recife 1,249,821; Salvador 1,237,393; Fortaleza 1,109,839; Porto Alegre 1,043,964; Nova Iguacu 931,954; Belem 771,665; Curitiba 765,716; Brasilia 763,254.

Government: Head of state: Pres. Joao Baptista Figueiredo; b. Jan. 15, 1918; in office: Mar. 15, 1979. **Local divisions:** 22 states, with individual constitutions and elected governments; 4 territories, 1 federal district. **Armed forces:** regulars 281,000; para-military 200,000.

Economy: Industries: Textiles, steel, autos, aluminum, chemicals, drugs, plastics, ships, appliances, shoes, paper, glass, machinery. **Chief crops:** Coffee (largest grower), cotton, soybeans, sugar, cocoa, rice, corn, fruits. **Minerals:** Chromium, iron, manganese, tin, quartz crystals, beryl, sheet mica, columbium, titanium, diamonds, thorium, gold, nickel, gem stones, coal, tin, tungsten, bauxite, oil. **Crude oil reserves** (1980): 1.22 bln. bbls. **Per capita arable land:** 0.7 acres. **Meat prod.** (1978): beef: 2.25 mln. metric tons; pork: 850,000 metric tons; lamb: 48,000 metric tons. **Fish catch** (1977): 790,100 metric tons. **Electricity prod.** (1977): 99.87 bln. kwh. **Crude steel prod.** (1979): 13.9 mln. metric tons. **Labor force:** 38% agric.; 20% manuf.

Finance: Currency: Cruzeiro (Mar. 1980: 46.8 = $1 US). **Gross domestic product** (1978): $188.71 bln. **Per capita income** (1978): $1,523. **Imports** (1979): $19.68 bln.; partners (1977): U.S. 20%, Sau. Ar. 11%, Iraq 9%, W. Ger. 9%, Jap. 7%. **Exports** (1979): $15.24 bln.; partners (1977): U.S. 18%, W. Ger. 9%, Neth. 8%, Japan 6%. **Tourists** (1977): 634,600; receipts: $55 mln. **National budget** (1979): $18.91 bln. revenues; $18.83 bln. expenditures. **International reserves less gold** (Jan. 1980): $7.84 bln. **Gold:** 1.7 mln. oz t. **Consumer prices** (change in 1979): 52.7%.

Transport: Railway traffic (1977): 11.70 bln. passenger-km; 60.72 bln. net ton-km. **Motor vehicles:** in use (1976): 5.92 mln. passenger cars, 1.4 mln. comm. vehicles; manuf. (1978): 537,600 passenger cars; 525,600 comm. vehicles. **Civil aviation:** 8,724 mln. passenger-km (1978); 478 mln. freight ton-km (1978). **Chief ports:** Santos, Rio de Janeiro, Vitoria, Salvador, Rio Grande, Recife.

Communications: Television sets: 10.53 mln. in use (1976), 1.64 mln. manuf. (1976). **Radios:** 16.98 mln. in use (1975), 759,000 manuf. (1976). **Telephones in use** (1978): 4,708,000. **Daily newspaper circ.** (1976): 4,895,000; 45 per 1,000 pop.

Health: Life expectancy at birth (1970): 57.61 male; 61.10 female. **Births** (per 1,000 pop. 1975): 37.1. **Deaths** (per 1,000 pop. 1975): 8.8. **Natural increase** (1975): 2.8%. **Hospital beds** (per 100,000 pop. 1977): 327. **Physicians** (per 100,000 pop. 1977): 59.

Education (1977): **Literacy:** 70%. **Pop. 5-19:** in school: 51%, teachers per 1,000: 25. **PQLI:** 69.

Pedro Alvares Cabral, a Portuguese navigator, is generally credited as the first European to reach Brazil, in 1500. The country was thinly settled by various Indian tribes. Only a few have survived to the present, mostly in the Amazon basin.

In the next centuries, Portuguese colonists gradually pushed inland, bringing along large numbers of African slaves. Slavery was not abolished until 1888.

The King of Portugal, fleeing before Napoleon's army, moved the seat of government to Brazil in 1808. Brazil thereupon became a kingdom under Dom Joao VI. After his return to Portugal, his son Pedro proclaimed the independence of Brazil, Sept. 7, 1822, and was acclaimed emperor. The second emperor, Dom Pedro II, was deposed in 1889, and a republic proclaimed, called the United States of Brazil. In 1967 the country was renamed the Federative Republic of Brazil.

A military junta took control in 1930; dictatorial power was assumed by Getulio Vargas, who alternated with military coups until finally forced out by the military in 1954. A democratic regime prevailed 1956-64, during which time the capital was moved from Rio de Janeiro to Brasilia in the interior.

The next 5 presidents were all military leaders. Censorship was imposed, and much of the opposition was suppressed amid charges of torture. In 1974 elections, the official opposition party made gains in the chamber of deputies; some relaxation of censorship occurred, though church liberals, labor leaders, and intellectuals continued to report cases of arrest and torture.

Close ties with the U.S. were damaged in 1977, when the U.S. criticized the human rights situation in Brazil, and opposed construction of a nuclear fuel reprocessing plant. West Germany had agreed in 1975 to supply Brazil with the technology for a complete nuclear energy industry. The ambitious program was lagging far behind schedule, 1979.

Since 1930, successive governments have pursued industrial and agricultural growth and the development of interior areas. Exploiting vast mineral resources, fertile soil in several regions, and a huge labor force, Brazil became the leading industrial power of Latin America by the 1970s, while agricultural output soared. The 1979 government declared an amnesty and enacted democratic reforms.

However, income maldistribution, a return of inflation (83% in 1980), a long autoworkers strike, and government land policies have all come under attack. A huge oil import bill increased the $53 bln. foreign debt.

Bulgaria

People's Republic of Bulgaria

People: Population (1979 est.): 8,827,000. **Age distrib.** (%): 0–14: 22.3; 15–59: 61.7; 60+: 16.0. **Pop. density:** 205.7 per sq. mi. **Urban** (1978): 60.5%. **Ethnic groups:** Bulgarians 85%, Turks 9%, Gypsies 2%. **Languages:** Bulgarian, Turkish, Greek. **Religions:** Orthodox 70%, Moslem 9%.

Geography: Area: 42,829 sq. mi., slightly larger than Tennessee. **Location:** In eastern Balkan Peninsula on Black Sea. **Neighbors:** Romania on N, Yugoslavia on W, Greece, Turkey on S. **Topography:** The Stara Planina (Balkan) Mts. stretch E-W across the center of the country, with the Danubian plain on N, the Rhodope Mts. on SW, and Thracian Plain on SE. **Capital:** Sofia. **Cities** (1978 est.): Sofia 976,015; Plovdiv 307,414; Varna 257,731.

Government: Head of state: Pres. Todor Zhivkov; b. Sept. 7, 1911; in office: July 7, 1971. **Head of government:** Prime Min. Stanko Todorov; b. Dec. 10, 1920; in office: July 7, 1971. **Head of Communist Party:** First Sec. Todor Zhivkov; in office: Jan. 1954. **Local divisions:** 27 provinces, one city. **Armed forces:** regulars 150,000; reserves 240,000.

Economy: Industries: Chemicals, machinery, metals, textiles, fur, leather goods, vehicles, wine, processed food. **Chief crops:** Grains, fruit, corn, potatoes, tobacco. **Minerals:** Lead, molybdenum, coal, oil, zinc. **Per capita arable land:** 1.1 acres. **Meat prod.** (1978): beef: 118,000 metric tons; pork: 281,000 metric tons; lamb: 67,000 metric tons. **Fish catch** (1977): 138,100 metric tons. **Electricity prod.** (1978): 31.79 bln. kwh. **Crude steel prod.** (1979): 2.4 mln. metric tons. **Labor force:** 24% agric.; 32% manuf.

Finance: Currency: Lev (Mar. 1980: .85 = $1 US). **Net material product** (1978): $14.4 bln. **Per capita income** (1976): $2,100. **Imports** (1979): $8.45 bln.; partners: USSR 57%, E. Ger. 7%, W. Ger. 5%. **Exports** (1979): $8.88 bln.; partners: USSR 55%, E. Ger. 8%, Pol. 5%. **Tourists** (1977): 4,569,700; receipts (1975): $230 mln.

Transport: Railway traffic (1978): 7.14 bln. passenger-km; 17.15 bln. net ton-km. **Motor vehicles:** manuf. (1977): 15,000 passenger cars, 6,900 comm. vehicles. **Chief ports:** Burgas, Varna.

Communications: Television sets: 1.55 mln. licensed (1976), 65,000 manuf. (1977). **Radios:** 2.75 mln. licensed (1974), 147,000 manuf. (1977). **Telephones in use** (1978): 946,023. **Daily newspaper circ.** (1977): 2,083,000; 237 per 1,000 pop.

Health: Life expectancy at birth (1976): 68.68 male; 73.91 female. **Births** (per 1,000 pop. 1978): 15.5. **Deaths** (per 1,000 pop. 1978): 10.5. **Natural increase** (1977): .5%. **Hospital beds** (per 100,000 pop. 1977): 872. **Physicians** (per 100,000 pop. 1977): 226. **Infant mortality** (per 1,000 live births 1978): 21.8

Education (1977): **Literacy:** 95%. **Pop. 5-19:** in school: 57%, teachers per 1,000: 30. **PQLI:** 90.

Bulgaria was settled by Slavs in the 6th century. Turkic Bulgars arrived in the 7th century, merged with the Slavs, became Christians by the 9th century, and set up powerful empires in the 10th and 12th centuries. The Ottomans prevailed in 1396 and remained for 500 years.

A revolt in 1876 led to an independent kingdom in 1908. Bulgaria expanded after the first Balkan War but lost its Aegean coastline in World War I, when it sided with Germany. Bulgaria joined the Axis in World War II, but withdrew in 1944. Communists took power with Soviet aid; the monarchy was abolished Sept. 8, 1946.

Industrialization has advanced. Bulgaria is Moscow's most loyal supporter in international questions.

Burma

Socialist Republic of the Union of Burma

People: Population (1979 est.): 33,590,000. **Age distrib.** (%): 0–14: 40.5; 15–59: 53.5; 60+: 6.0. **Pop. density:** 123.04 per sq. mi. **Ethnic groups:** Burmans (related to Tibetans) 72%; Karen 7%, Shan 6%, Kachin 2%, Chinese 2%, Indians 3%, others. **Languages:** Burmese (official) 80%, English, others. **Religions:** Buddhist 85%; Hinduism, Islam, Christianity, others.

Geography: Area: 261,789 sq. mi., nearly as large as Texas. **Location:** Between S. and S.E. Asia, on Bay of Bengal. **Neighbors:** Bangladesh, India on W, China, Laos, Thailand on E. **Topography:** Mountains surround Burma on W, N, and E, and dense forests cover much of the nation. N-S rivers provide habitable valleys and communications, especially the Irrawaddy, navigable for 900 miles. The country has a tropical monsoon climate. **Capital:** Rangoon. **Cities** (1978 est.): Rangoon 2,276,000; Mandalay 458,000; Karbe ('73 cen.): 253,600; Moulmein 188,000.

Government: Head of state: Pres. Ne Win; b. May 24, 1911; in office: Mar. 2, 1962. **Head of government:** Prime Min. Maung Maung Kha; b. Nov. 2, 1917; in office: Mar. 29, 1977. **Local divisions:** 7 states and 7 divisions. **Armed forces:** regulars 169,500; para-military 73,000.

Economy: Chief crops: Rice, cotton, maize, tobacco. **Minerals:** Oil, lead, silver, tin, tungsten, zinc, rubies, sapphires, jade. **Crude oil reserves** (1980): 25 mln. bbls. **Other resources:** Rubber, teakwood. **Per capita arable land:** 0.7 acres. **Meat prod.** (1978): beef: 94,000 metric tons; pork: 74,000 metric tons; lamb: 4,000 metric tons. **Fish catch** (1977): 518,700 metric tons. **Electricity prod.** (1978): 960.00 mln. kwh. **Labor force:** 65% agric.

Finance: Currency: Kyat (Mar. 1980: 6.84 = $1 US). **Gross domestic product** (1976): $3.95 bln. **Per capita income** (1977): $113. **Imports** (1979): $324 mln.; partners (1978): Jap. 25%, Sing. 12%, UK 8%, W. Ger. 7%. **Exports** (1979): $370 mln.; partners (1978): Sing. 15%, Indon. 14%, Bang. 14%, Sri Lanka 10%. **Tourists** (1976): 18,280; receipts (1975): $3 mln. **National budget** (1976): $484 mln. revenues; $524 mln. expenditures. **International reserves less gold** (Mar. 1980): $224.0 mln. **Gold:** 251,000 oz t. **Consumer prices** (change in 1979): 5.4%.

Transport: Railway traffic (1978): 3.07 bln. passenger-km; 468 mln. net ton-km. **Motor vehicles:** in use (1977): 38,600 passenger cars, 41,300 comm. vehicles. **Civil aviation:** 101 mln. passenger-miles (1975); 745 mln. freight ton-miles (1975). **Chief ports:** Rangoon, Sittwe, Bassein, Moulmein, Tavoy.

Communications: Radios: 665,000 licensed (1976), 12,000 manuf. (1977). **Telephones in use** (1978): 32,616. **Daily newspaper circ.** (1977): 329,000; 11 per 1,000 pop.

Health: Life expectancy at birth (1975): 48.6 male; 51.5 female. **Births** (per 1,000 pop. 1975): 39.4. **Deaths** (per 1,000 pop. 1975): 15.8. **Natural increase** (1975): 2.4%. **Hospital beds** (per 100,000 pop. 1977): 89. **Physicians** (per 100,000 pop. 1977): 19. **Infant mortality** (per 1,000 live births 1975): 195-300.

Education (1977): **Literacy:** 70%. **Pop. 5-19:** in school: 40%, teachers per 1,000: 8. **PQLI:** 53.

The Burmese arrived from Tibet before the 9th century, displacing earlier cultures, and a Buddhist monarchy was established by the 11th. Burma was conquered by the Mongol dynasty of China in 1272, then ruled by Shans as a Chinese tributary, until the 16th century.

Britain subjugated Burma in 3 wars, 1824-84, and ruled the country as part of India until 1937, when it became self-governing. Independence outside the Commonwealth was achieved Jan. 4, 1948.

Gen. Ne Win has dominated politics since 1958. He led a Revolutionary Council set up in 1962, which drove Indians from the civil service and Chinese from commerce. Socialization of the economy was advanced, isolation from foreign countries enforced. Lagging production and export have begun to turn around, due to government incentives in the agriculture and petroleum sectors and receptivity to foreign investment in the economy.

Phased repatriation to Burma of Moslem refugees in Bangladesh was begun, 1979.

Burundi

Republic of Burundi

People: Population (1979 est.): 4,192,000. **Age distrib.** (%): 0–14: 44.1; 15–59: 51.9; 60+: 4.1. **Pop. density:** 396.68 per sq. mi. **Urban** (1970): 2.2%. **Ethnic groups:** Hutu 85%, Tutsi 14%, Twa (pygmy) 1%. **Languages:** French, Kirundi (official), Swahili. **Religions:** Roman Catholic 50%, Protestant 4%, others.

Geography: Area: 10,739 sq. mi., the size of Maryland. **Location:** In central Africa. **Neighbors:** Rwanda on N, Zaire on W, Tanzania on E. **Topography:** Much of the country is grassy highland, with mountains reaching 8,900 ft. The southernmost source of the White Nile is located in Burundi. Lake Tanganyika is the second deepest lake in the world. **Capital:** Bujumbura. **Cities** (1978 est.): Bujumbura (met.) 78,810.

Government: Head of state and head of government: Pres. Jean Baptiste Bagaza; b. Aug. 29, 1946; in office: Nov. 9, 1976 (govt: Oct. 1978). **Local divisions:** 8 provinces and capital city. **Armed forces:** regulars 5,000; para-military 1,500.

Economy: Chief crops: Coffee (chief export), cotton, tea. **Minerals:** Nickel. **Per capita arable land:** 0.6 acres. **Fish catch** (1977): 18,900 metric tons. **Electricity prod.** (1977): 27.00 mln. kwh. **Labor force:** 92% agric.

Finance: Currency: Franc (Mar. 1980: 90 = $1 US). **Gross domestic product** (1974 est.): $340 mln. **Per capita income** (1979): $70. **Imports** (1979): $152 mln.; partners (1978): Benelux 23%, W. Ger. 10%, France 9%, Jap. 7%. **Exports** (1979): $105 mln.; partners (1978): U.S. 47%, China 6%. **Tourists** (1977): 32,000; receipts (1975): $1 mln. **National budget** (1978): $108 mln. revenues; $108 mln. expenditures. **International reserves less gold** (Mar. 1980): $100.2 mln. **Gold:** 17,000 oz t. **Consumer prices** (change in 1979): 36.2%.

Transport: Motor vehicles: in use (1976): 5,100 passenger cars, 2,200 comm. vehicles.

Communications: Radios: 105,000 in use (1976). **Telephones in use** (1978): 4,995. **Daily newspaper circ.** (1970): 300; 0.1 per 1,000 pop.

Health: Life expectancy at birth (1971): 40 male; 43 female. **Births** (per 1,000 pop. 1971): 42.0. **Deaths** (per 1,000 pop. 1971): 20.4. **Natural increase** (1971): 2.2%. **Hospital beds** (per 100,000 pop. 1977): 118. **Physicians** (per 100,000 pop. 1977): 3. **Infant mortality** (per 1,000 live births 1971): 150.

Education (1977): **Literacy:** 18%. **Pop. 5-19:** in school: 10%, teachers per 1,000: 3. **PQLI:** 30.

The pygmy Twa were the first inhabitants, followed by Bantu Hutus, who were conquered in the 16th century by the tall Tutsi (Watusi), probably from Ethiopia. Under German control in 1899, the area fell to Belgium in 1916, which exercised successively a League of Nations mandate and UN trusteeship over Ruanda-Urundi (now 2 countries).

Independence came in 1962, and the monarchy was overthrown in 1966. An unsuccessful Hutu rebellion in 1972-73 left 10,000 Tutsi and 150,000 Hutu dead. Over 100,000 Hutu fled to Tanzania and Zaire. The present regime is pledged to ethnic reconciliation.

Burundi is one of the poorest and most densely populated countries in Africa.

Cambodia

Cambodian People's Republic

People: Population (1979 est.): 5,767,000. **Pop. density:** 122.6 per sq. mi. **Ethnic groups:** Khmers 90%, Vietnamese 4%, Chinese 3%. **Languages:** Khmer, French. **Religions:** Buddhism prevails.

Geography: Area: 69,900 sq. mi., the size of Missouri. **Location:** In Indochina Peninsula. **Neighbors:** Thailand on W, N, Laos on NE, Vietnam on E. **Topography:** The central area, formed by the Mekong R. basin and Tonle Sap lake, is level. Hills and mountains are in SE, a long escarpment separates the country from Thailand on NW. 75% of the area is forested. **Capital:** Phnom Penh. **Cities** (1979 est.): Phnom Penh 300,000.

Government: Head of government: Pres., People's Revolutionary Council Heng Samrin; in office: Jan. 7, 1979. **Local divisions:** 5 regions and a special capital region.

Economy: Industries: Textiles, paper, plywood, oil products. **Chief crops:** Rice, corn, pepper, tobacco, cotton, oil seeds, beans, palm sugar. **Minerals:** Iron, copper, manganese, gold. **Other resources:** Forests, rubber, kapok. **Per capita arable land:** 0.8 acres. **Meat prod.** (1978): beef: 22,000 metric tons; pork: 32,000 metric tons. **Fish catch** (1977): 84,700 metric tons. **Electricity prod.** (1977): 150.00 mln. kwh.

Finance: Currency: Riel (Sept. 1979: 1,200 = $1 US). **Per capita income** (1976): $90. **Imports** (1977): $185 mln. **Exports** (1973): $13 mln. **Tourists** (1973): 16,500.

Transport: Railway traffic (1973): 33.53 mln. passenger-miles; 6.21 mln. net ton-miles. **Motor vehicles:** in use (1972): 27,200 passenger cars, (1973) 10,100 comm. vehicles. **Chief ports:** Kompong Som.

Communications: Television sets: 35,000 in use (1976). **Radios:** 110,000 in use (1975). **Telephones in use** (1977): 71,000.

Health: Life expectancy at birth (1975): 44.0 male; 46.9 female. **Births** (per 1,000 pop. 1975): 45.9. **Deaths** (per 1,000 pop. 1975): 16.9. **Natural increase** (1975): 2.9%. **Hospital beds** (per 100,000 pop. 1977): 106. **Physicians** (per 100,000 pop. 1977): 7.

Education (1977): **Literacy:** 48%. **Pop. 5-19:** (1975): in school: 40%, per teacher: 124. **PQLI:** 36.

Early kingdoms dating from that of Funan in the 1st century AD culminated in the great Khmer empire which flourished from the 9th century to the 13th, encompassing present-day Thailand, Cambodia, Laos, and southern Vietnam. The peripheral areas were lost to invading Siamese and Vietnamese, and France established a protectorate in 1863. Independence came in 1953.

Prince Norodom Sihanouk, king 1941-1955 and head of state from 1960, tried to maintain neutrality. Relations with the U.S. were broken in 1965, after South Vietnam planes attacked Vietcong forces within Cambodia. Relations were restored in 1969, after Sihanouk charged Viet communists with arming Cambodian insurgents.

In 1970, pro-U.S. premier Lon Nol seized power, demanding removal of 40,000 North Viet troops; the monarchy was abolished. Sihanouk formed a government-in-exile in Peking, and open war began between the government and Khmer Rouge. The U.S. provided heavy military and economic aid. U.S. troops fought Vietcong forces within Cambodia for 2 months in 1970.

Khmer Rouge forces captured Phnom Penh April 17, 1975. Over 100,000 people had died in 5 years of fighting. The new government evacuated all cities and towns, and shuffled the rural population, sending virtually the entire population to clear jungle, forest, and scrub, which covered half the country.

The government guarded its international isolation, but repeated reports from refugees in Thailand and Vietnam indicated that over one million people were killed in executions and enforced hardships that continued unabated through 1978.

Severe border fighting broke out with Vietnam in 1978; developed into a full-fledged Vietnamese invasion. The Vietnamese-backed Kampuchean National United Front for National Salvation, a Cambodian rebel movement, announced, Jan. 8, 1979, the formation of a government one day after the Vietnamese capture of Phnom Pehn. Civil war continued into 1980; thousands of refugees flowed into Thailand. Widespread starvation was reported; by Sept., when the UN confirmed diplomatic recognition to the ousted Pol Pot government, international food assistance was allowed to aid the famine-stricken country.

Cameroon

United Republic of Cameroon

People: Population (1979 est.): 8,323,000. **Age distrib.** (%): 0–14: 43.4; 15–59: 50.8; 60+: 5.8. **Pop. density:** 43.91 per sq. mi. **Urban** (1970): 20.3%. **Ethnic groups:** Some 200 tribes; largest are Bamileke 30%, Fulani 7%. **Languages:** English, French (both official), 24 others. **Religions:** Roman Catholic 20%, Protestant 15%, Islam (mostly in N) 12%, others.

Geography: Area: 183,568 sq. mi., somewhat larger than California. **Location:** Between W and central Africa. **Neighbors:** Nigeria on NW, Chad, Central African Republic on E, Congo, Gabon, Equatorial Guinea on S. **Topography:** A low coastal plain with rain forests is in S; plateaus in center lead to forested mountains in W, including Mt. Cameroon, 13,000 ft.; grasslands in N lead to marshes around Lake Chad. **Capital:** Yaounde. **Cities** (1975 est.): Douala 485,797; Yaounde 274,399.

Government: Head of state: Pres. Ahmadou Ahidjo; b. Aug. 5, 1924; in office: Jan. 1, 1960. **Head of government:** Paul Biya; b. Feb. 13, 1933; in office: June 30, 1975. **Local divisions:** 7 provinces with appointed governors. **Armed forces:** regulars 8,500; para-military 5,700.

Economy: Industries: Aluminum processing, palm products. **Chief crops:** Cocoa, coffee, peanuts, tea, bananas, cotton, tobacco. **Crude oil reserves** (1980): 140 mln. bbls. **Other resources:** Timber, rubber. **Per capita arable land:** 2.1 acres. **Meat prod.** (1978): beef: 47,000 metric tons; pork: 19,000 metric tons; lamb: 17,000 metric tons. **Fish catch** (1977): 71,600 metric tons. **Electricity prod.** (1978): 1.31 bln. kwh. **Labor force:** 82% agric.

Finance: Currency: CFA franc (Mar. 1980: 223.92 = $1 US). **Gross domestic product** (1977): $3.22 bln. **Per capita income** (1975): $366. **Imports** (1978): $1.06 bln.; partners (1977): Fr. 43%, W. Ger. 7%, U.S. 7%, Jap. 6%. **Exports** (1978): $802 mln.; partners (1977): Fr. 27%, Neth. 26%, W. Ger. 10%, It. 8%. **Tourists** (1974): 96,100; receipts (1977): $21 mln. **National budget** (1978): $707 mln. revenues; $685 mln. expenditures. **International reserves less gold** (Dec. 1979): $125.67 mln. **Gold:** 30,000 oz t. **Consumer prices** (change in 1978): 12.5%.

Transport: Railway traffic (1978): 230.4 mln. passenger-km; 513.6 mln. net ton-km. **Motor vehicles:** in use (1976): 59,500 passenger cars, 51,200 comm. vehicles. **Chief ports:** Douala.

Communications: Radios: 603,000 in use (1975), 80,000 manuf. (1977). **Telephones in use** (1978): 14,321. **Daily newspaper circ.** (1976): 30,000; 5 per 1,000 pop.

Health: Life expectancy at birth (1975): 41.9 male; 45.1 female. **Births** (per 1,000 pop. 1975): 42.1. **Deaths** (per 1,000 pop. 1975): 21.2. **Natural increase** (1975): 2.1%. **Hospital beds** (per 100,000 pop. 1977): 269. **Physicians** (per 100,000 pop. 1977): 6.

Education (1977): **Literacy:** 20%. **Pop. 5-19:** in school: 49%, teachers per 1,000: 10. **PQLI:** 30.

Portuguese sailors were the first Europeans to reach Cameroon, in the 15th century. The European and American slave trade was very active in the area. German control lasted from 1884 to 1916, when France and Britain divided the territory, later receiving League of Nations mandates and UN trusteeships. French Cameroon became independent Jan. 1, 1960; one part of British Cameroon joined Nigeria in 1961, the other part joined Cameroon. Stability has allowed for development of roads, railways, and agriculture.

Canada

See also Canada in Index.

People: Population (1979 est.): 23,688,000. **Age distrib.** (%): 0–14: 24.9; 15–59: 62.2; 60+: 12.8. **Pop. density:** 6.10 per sq. mi. **Urban** (1976): 75.5%. **Cities** (met. 1978 est.): Montreal 2,798,000; Toronto 2,741,000; Vancouver 1,137,000; Ottawa 626,000; Winnipeg 570,000; Edmonton 529,000.

Government: Head of state: Queen Elizabeth II, represented by Gov.-Gen. Edward R. Schreyer; b. Dec. 21, 1935; in office: Jan. 22, 1979. **Head of government:** Prime Min. Pierre Elliott Trudeau; b. Oct. 18, 1919; in office: Mar. 3, 1980. **Local divisions:** 10 provinces, 2 territories. **Armed forces:** regulars 80,000; reserves 19,100.

Economy: Minerals: Nickel, zinc, antimony, cobalt, copper, gold, iron, lead, molybdenum, potash, silver, tungsten, uranium. **Crude oil reserves** (1980): 6.8 bln. bbls. **Per capita arable land:** 4.6 acres. **Meat prod.** (1978): beef: 1.06 mln. metric tons; pork 570,000 metric tons. **Fish catch** (1977): 1.3 mln. metric tons. **Electricity prod.** (1978): 335.71 bln. kwh. **Crude steel prod.** (1979): 16.1 mln. metric tons. **Labor force:** 5% agric.; 30% manuf.

Finance: Currency: Dollar (Mar. 1980: 1.19 = $1 US). **Gross domestic product** (1979): $228.56 bln. **Per capita income** (1978): $7,572. **Imports** (1979): $56.78 bln.; partners (1978): U.S. 71%, Jap. 5%. **Exports** (1979): $58.19 bln.; partners (1978): U.S. 70%, Jap. 6%. **Tourists** (1977): 12,702,800; receipts: $1.62 bln. **National budget** (1978): 38.18 bln. revenues; $44.75 bln. expenditures. **International reserves less gold** (Mar. 1980): $2.72 bln. **Gold:** 21.78 mln. oz t. **Consumer prices** (change in 1979): 9.2%.

Transport: Railway traffic (1978): 3.07 bln. passenger-km; 215.35 bln. net ton-km. **Motor vehicles:** in use (1977): 9.02 mln. passenger cars, 2.32 mln. comm. vehicles; manuf. (1978): 1.14 mln. passenger cars; 610,800 comm. vehicles. **Civil aviation:** 26,964 mln. passenger-km (1978); 676 mln. freight ton-km (1978).

Communications: Television sets: 9.9 mln. in use (1976), 606,000 manuf. (1977). **Radios:** 23.4 mln. in use (1976), 837,000 manuf. (1976). **Telephones in use** (1978): 14,505,728. **Daily newspaper circ.** (1977): 5,150,000; 221 per 1,000 pop.

Health: Life expectancy at birth (1972): 69.34 male; 76.36 female. **Births** (per 1,000 pop. 1977): 15.5. **Deaths** (per 1,000 pop. 1977): 7.2. **Natural increase** (1977): .8%. **Hospital beds** (per 100,000 pop. 1977): 875. **Physicians** (per 100,000 pop. 1977): 178. **Infant mortality** (per 1,000 live births 1977): 12.4.

Education (1977): **Literacy:** 98%. **Pop. 5-19:** in school: 76%, teachers per 1,000: 40. **PQLI:** 95.

Cape Verde

Republic of Cape Verde

People: Population (1979 est.): 328,000. **Age distrib.** (%): 0–14: 46.9; 15–59: 44.9; 60+: 7.9. **Pop. density:** 199.10 per sq. mi. **Urban** (1970): 19.7%. **Ethnic groups:** Creole (mulatto) 70%, African 28%, European 1%. **Languages:** Portuguese (official), Crioulo. **Religions:** Roman Catholicism prevails.

Geography: Area: 1,557 sq. mi., a bit larger than Rhode Island. **Location:** In Atlantic O., off western tip of Africa. **Neighbors:** Nearest are Mauritania, Senegal. **Topography:** Cape Verde Islands are 15 in number, volcanic in origin (active crater on Fogo). The landscape is eroded and stark, with vegetation mostly in interior valleys. **Capital:** Praia. **Cities** (1970 cen.): Mindelo 28,797; Praia 21,494.

Government: Head of state: Pres. Aristides Pereira; b. Nov. 17, 1923; in office: July 5, 1975. **Head of government:** Prime Min. Pedro Pires, b. Apr. 29, 1934; in office: July 5, 1975. **Local divisions:** 24 electoral districts.

Economy: Chief crops: Bananas, coffee, sugarcane, grain. **Minerals:** Salt. **Other resources:** Fish. **Per capita arable land:** 0.3 acres. **Electricity prod.** (1977): 7.00 mln. kwh.

Finance: Currency: Escudo (Jan. 1979: 47.22 = $1 US). **Gross domestic product** (1976 est.): $130 mln. **Per capita income** (1978): $170. **Imports** (1976): $26.8 mln.; partners: Port. 58%, Neth. 5%. **Exports** (1976): $14.1 mln.; partners: Port. 63%, Ang. 14%, UK 5%, Zaire 5%. **Consumer prices** (change in 1977): 4.8%.

Transport: Motor vehicles: in use (1977): 3,100 passenger cars, 900 comm. vehicles. **Chief ports:** Mindelo, Praia.

Communications: Radios: 36,000 licensed (1976). **Telephones in use** (1978): 1,717.

Health: Life expectancy at birth (1975): 56.3 male; 60.0 female. **Births** (per 1,000 pop. 1975): 27.6. **Deaths** (per 1,000 pop. 1975): 9.4. **Natural increase** (1975): 1.8%. **Pop. per hospital bed** (1977): 516. **Pop. per physician** (1977): 7,750. **Infant mortality** (per 1,000 live births 1975): 104.9. **PQLI:** 53.

The uninhabited Cape Verdes were discovered by the Portuguese in 1456 or 1460. The first Portuguese colonists landed in 1462; African slaves were brought soon after, and most Cape Verdeans descend from both groups. Cape Verde independence came July 5, 1975. The government backs eventual union with Guinea-Bissau.

The islands have suffered from repeated extreme droughts and famines, especially 1978; the banana crop, the sole export, has declined.

Central African Republic

People: Population (1979 est.): 2,284,000. **Pop. density:** 10.82 per sq. mi. **Ethnic groups:** Banda 47%, Baya 27%, 80 other groups. **Languages:** French (official), Sangho (national). **Religions:** Protestant, Roman Catholic 35-65%, Moslem 8%, others.

Geography: Area: 241,313 sq. mi., slightly smaller than Texas. **Location:** In central Africa. **Neighbors:** Chad on N, Cameroon on W, Congo, Zaire on S, Sudan on E. **Topography:** Mostly rolling plateau, average altitude 2,000 ft., with rivers draining S to the Congo and N to Lake Chad. Open, well-watered savanna covers most of the area, with an arid area in NE, and tropical rainforest in SW. **Capital:** Bangui. **Cities** (1978 est.): Bangui (met.) 187,000.

Government: Head of state: Pres. David Dacko, b. Mar. 24, 1930; in office: Sept. 20, 1979. **Head of government:** Prime Min. Bernard Ayandho; in office: Sept. 26, 1979. **Local divisions:** 14 prefectures. **Armed forces:** regulars 1,200; paramilitary 1,400.

Economy: Industries: Textiles, radios. **Chief crops:** Cotton, coffee, peanuts, corn, sorghum. **Minerals:** Diamonds (chief export), uranium, iron, copper. **Other resources:** Timber. **Per capita arable land:** 5.5 acres. **Meat prod.** (1978): beef: 21,000 metric tons. **Fish catch** (1977): 13,000 metric tons. **Electricity prod.** (1977): 58.00 mln. kwh. **Labor force:** 87% agric.

Finance: Currency: CFA franc (Mar. 1980: 223.92 = $1 US). **Gross domestic product** (1974 est.): $310 mln. **Per capita income** (1976): $150. **Imports** (1978): $61 mln.; partners (1977): Fr. 55%, W. Ger. 7%, Jap. 5%. **Exports** (1978): $77 mln.; partners (1977): Fr. 63%, Bel.-Lux. 16%. **Tourists** (1974): 4,100; receipts (1977): $3 mln. **International reserves less gold** (Dec. 1979): $44.11 mln. **Gold:** 11,000 oz t. **Consumer prices** (change in 1978): 11.9%.

Transport: Motor vehicles: in use (1974): 9,100 passenger cars, 3,900 comm. vehicles.

Communications: Radios: 75,000 in use (1976), 11,000 manuf. (1977).

Health: Life expectancy at birth (1960): 33 male; 36 female. **Births** (per 1,000 pop. 1975): 41.0. **Deaths** (per 1,000 pop. 1975): 20.7%. **Natural increase** (1975): 2.0%. **Hospital beds** (per 100,000 pop. 1977): 138. **Physicians** (per 100,000 pop. 1977): 5. **Infant mortality** (per 1,000 live births 1975): 190.

Education (1977): **Literacy:** 16%. **Pop. 5-19:** in school: 37%, teachers per 1,000: 7. **PQLI:** 21.

Various Bantu tribes migrated through the region for centuries before French control was asserted in the late 19th century, when the region was named Ubangi-Shari. Complete independence was attained Aug. 13, 1960.

All political parties were dissolved in 1960, and the country became a center for Chinese political influence in Africa. Relations with China were severed after 1965. Elizabeth Domitien, premier 1975-76, was the first woman to hold that post in an African country. Pres. Jean-Bedel Bokassa, who seized power in a 1965 military coup, proclaimed himself constitutional emperor of the renamed Central African Empire Dec. 1976.

Emp. Bokassa's rule was characterized by virtually unchecked ruthless and cruel authority, and human rights violations. Bokassa was ousted in a bloodless coup aided by the French government, Sept. 20, 1979, and replaced by his cousin David Dacko, former president from 1960 to 1965.

The landlocked nation has been unable to develop its large mineral resources.

Chad

Republic of Chad

People: Population (1979 est.): 4,528,000. **Age distrib.** (%): 0–14: 40.7; 15–59: 54.9; 60+: 4.4. **Pop. density:** 8.69 per sq. mi. **Urban** (1978): 18.4%. **Ethnic groups:** Sudanese Arab 30%, Sudanic tribes 25%, Nilotic, Saharan tribes. **Languages:** French (official), Arabic, others. **Religions:** Moslems 40%, Christians 30%, others.

Geography: Area: 495,752 sq. mi., four-fifths the size of Alaska. **Location:** In central N. Africa. **Neighbors:** Libya on N, Niger, Nigeria, Cameroon on W, Central African Republic on S, Sudan on E. **Topography:** Southern wooded savanna, steppe, and desert, part of the Sahara, in the N. Southern rivers flow N to Lake Chad, surrounded by marshland. **Capital:** N'Djamena. **Cities** (1978 est.): N'Djamena (met.) 179,000.

Government: Head of state: Pres. Goukouni Oueddei; in office: Aug. 21, 1979. **Local divisions:** 14 prefectures with appointed governors. **Armed forces:** regulars 5,200; para-military 6,000.

Economy: Chief crops: Cotton. **Minerals:** Uranium. **Per capita arable land:** 4.0 acres. **Meat prod.** (1978): beef: 28,000 metric tons; lamb: 16,000 metric tons. **Fish catch** (1977): 115,000 metric tons. **Electricity prod.** (1978): 62.40 mln. kwh. **Labor force:** 90% agric.

Finance: Currency: CFA franc (Mar. 1980: 223.92 = $1 US). **Gross domestic product** (1976 est.): $540 mln. **Per capita income** (1976): $73. **Imports** (1976): $113 mln.; partners (1975): Fr. 37%, Nigeria 10%, Neth. 7%, U.S. 6%. **Exports** (1976): $59 mln.; partners (1975): Nigeria 20%, Fr. 7%, Congo 5%. **Tourist receipts** (1977): $7 mln. **National budget** (1976): $63 mln. revenues; $97 mln. expenditures. **International reserves less gold** (Dec. 1979): $11.25 mln. **Gold:** 11,000 oz t. **Consumer prices** (change in 1977): 9.3%.

Transport: Motor vehicles: in use (1973): 5,800 passenger cars, 6,300 comm. vehicles.

Communications: Radios: 76,000 in use (1976). **Telephones in use** (1978): 3,850.

Health: Life expectancy at birth (1964): 29 male; 35 female. **Births** (per 1,000 pop. 1975): 43.8. **Deaths** (per 1,000 pop. 1975): 22.7. **Natural increase** (1975): 2.1%. **Hospital beds** (per 100,000 pop. 1977): 82. **Physicians** (per 100,000 pop. 1977): 2. **Infant mortality** (per 1,000 live births 1975): 160.

Education (1977): **Literacy:** 15%. **Pop. 5-19:** in school: 16%, teachers per 1,000: 2. **PQLI:** 23.

Chad was the site of paleolithic and neolithic cultures before the Sahara Desert formed. A succession of kingdoms and Arab slave traders dominated Chad until France took control around 1900. Independence came Aug. 11, 1960.

Northern Moslem rebels, reportedly aided by Libya, have fought animist and Christian southern government and French troops from 1966, despite numerous cease-fires and peace pacts.

A Libyan offensive on the uranium and iron-rich Aouzou strip in the north failed, Apr., 1979.

Chile

Republic of Chile

People: Population (1979 est.): 10,848,000. **Age distrib.** (%): 0–14: 34.4; 15–59: 57.7; 60+: 7.9. **Pop. density:** 37.92 per sq. mi. **Urban** (1978): 79.8%. **Ethnic groups:** Mestizo 66%, Spanish 25%, Indian 5%. **Languages:** Spanish. **Religions:** Roman Catholic 90%, Protestants 6%.

Geography: Area: 286,396 sq. mi., larger than Texas. **Location:** Occupies western coast of southern S. America. **Neighbors:** Peru on N, Bolivia on NE, Argentina on E. **Topography:** Andes Mtns. are on E border including some of the world's highest peaks; on W is 2,650-mile Pacific Coast. Width varies between 100 and 250 miles. In N is Atacama Desert, in center are agricultural regions, in S are forests and grazing lands. **Capital:** Santiago. **Cities** (1978 est.) Santiago 3,448,700; Vina del Mar 262,100; Valparaiso 248,200.

Government: Head of state: Pres. Augusto Pinochet Ugarte; b. Nov. 25, 1915; in office: Sept. 11, 1973. **Local divisions:** 12 regions and Santiago region, comprised of 25 provinces. **Armed forces:** regulars 85,000; reserves 160,000.

Economy: Industries: Steel, textiles, wood products. **Chief crops:** Grain, rice, beans, potatoes, peas, fruits, grapes. **Minerals:** Copper (10% world output), molybdenum, silver, nitrates, iodine (half world output), iron, coal, oil, gas, gold, cobalt, zinc, manganese, borate, mica, mercury, salt, sulphur, marble, onyx. **Crude oil reserves** (1980): 400 mln. bbls. **Other resources:** Water, forests. **Per capita arable land:** 1.3 acres. **Meat prod.** (1978): beef: 184,000 metric tons; pork: 38,000 metric tons; lamb: 26,000 metric tons. **Fish catch** (1977): 1.3 mln. metric tons. **Electricity prod.** (1978): 10.16 bln. kwh. **Crude steel prod.** (1979): 642,000 metric tons. **Labor force:** 19% agric.; 25% manuf.

Finance: Currency: Peso (Mar. 1980: 39 = $1 US). **Gross domestic product** (1977): $14.92 bln. **Per capita income** (1976): $712. **Imports** (1979): $4.22 bln.; partners (1978): U.S. 23%, Braz. 8%, Jap. 7%, Arg. 7%. **Exports** (1979): $3.76 bln.; partners (1978): W. Ger. 14%, Braz. 13%, Jap. 12%, U.S. 12%. **Tourists** (1977): 296,900; receipts: $97 mln. **National budget** (1975): $1.57 bln. revenues; $1.48 bln. expenditures. **International reserves less gold** (Mar. 1980): $2.32 bln. **Gold:** 1.58 mln. oz t. **Consumer prices** (change in 1979): 33.4%.

Transport: Railway traffic (1978): 2.12 bln. passenger-km; 2.04 bln. net ton-km. **Motor vehicles:** in use (1977): 297,100 passenger cars, 182,000 comm. vehicles; assembled (1977): 9,000 passenger cars; 3,200 comm. vehicles. **Civil aviation:** 1,433 mln. passenger-km (1977); 108 mln. freight ton-km (1977). **Chief ports:** Valparaiso, Arica, Antofagasta.

Communications: Television sets: 710,000 in use (1976), 139,000 manuf. (1977). **Radios:** 1.8 mln. in use (1976), 68,000 manuf. (1977). **Telephones in use** (1978): 483,225.

Health: Life expectancy at birth (1970): 60.48 male; 66.01 female. **Births** (per 1,000 pop. 1976): 23.9. **Deaths** (per 1,000 pop. 1976): 7.7. **Natural increase** (1976): 1.6%. **Hospital beds** (per 100,000 pop. 1977): 359. **Physicians** (per 100,000 pop. 1977): 62. **Infant mortality** (per 1,000 live births 1975): 54.7.

Education (1977): **Literacy:** 90%. **Pop. 5–19:** in school: 72%, teachers per 1,000: 25. **PQLI:** 79.

Northern Chile was under Inca rule before the Spanish conquest, 1536-40. The southern Araucanian Indians resisted until the late 19th century. Independence was gained 1810-18, under Jose de San Martin and Bernardo O'Higgins; the latter, as supreme director 1817-23, sought social and economic reforms until deposed. Chile defeated Peru and Bolivia in 1836-39 and 1879-84, gaining mineral-rich northern land.

Eduardo Frei Montalva came into office in 1964, instituting social programs and gradual nationalization of foreign-owned mining companies. In 1970, Salvador Allende Gossens, a Marxist, became president with a third of the national vote, despite reported attempts by the U.S. Central Intelligence Agency and the International Telephone & Telegraph Corp. to foment a military coup.

The Allende government furthered nationalizations, and improved conditions for the poor. But illegal and violent actions by extremist supporters of the government, the regime's failure to attain majority support, and poorly planned socialist economic programs led to political and financial chaos.

A military junta seized power Sept. 11, 1973, and said Allende killed himself. The junta named a mostly-military cabinet, and announced plans to "exterminate Marxism."

According to a 1977 statement of the Conference of Chilean Bishops, about 900 Chilean political prisoners had disappeared since the coup.

The economy continued to deteriorate under the new regime, though inflation had been reduced to 30% by 1980. Soaring increased world copper prices, which provide more than half of Chile's foreign income, were expected to cover the higher cost of petroleum imports in 1980.

Tierra del Fuego is the largest (17,800 sq. mi.) island in the archipelago of the same name at the southern tip of South America, an area of majestic mountains, tortuous channels, and high winds. It was discovered 1520 by Magellan and named the Land of Fire because of its many Indian bonfires. Part of the island is in Chile, part in Argentina. Punta Arenas, on a mainland peninsula, is a center of sheep-raising and the world's southernmost city (pop. 67,600); Puerto Williams, pop. 949, is the southernmost settlement.

China

People's Republic of China

People: Population (1979 est.): 1,012,197,000. **Pop. density:** 259.58 per sq. mi. **Ethnic groups:** Han Chinese 94%, Mongol, Korean, Turkic groups, Manchu, others. **Languages:** Mandarin Chinese (official), Shanghai, Canton, Fukien, Hakka dialects; Tibetan, Vigus (Turkic). **Religions:** Confucianism, Buddhism, Taoism, are traditional; Moslems 5%.

Geography: Area: 3,691,502 sq. mi., slightly larger than the U.S. **Location:** Occupies most of the habitable mainland of E. Asia. **Neighbors:** Mongolia on N, USSR on NE and NW, Afghanistan, Pakistan on W, India, Nepal, Bhutan, Burma, Laos, Vietnam on S, N. Korea on NW. **Topography:** Two-thirds of the vast territory is mountainous or desert, and only one-tenth is cultivated. Rolling topography rises to high elevations in the N in the Daxinganlingshanmai separating Manchuria and Mongolia; the Tienshan in Xinjiang; the Himalayan and Kunlunshanmai in the SW and in Tibet. Length is 1,860 mi. from N to S, width E to W is more than 2,000 mi. The eastern half of China is one of the best-watered lands in the world. Three great river systems, the Changjiang, the Huanghe, and the Xijiang provide water for vast farmlands. **Capital:** Peking. **Cities** (1970 est.): Shanghai 10,820,000; Peking 7,570,000; Tianjin 4,280,000; Canton 3,000,000; Shenyang 3,000,000; Wuhan 2,700,000; (1957 est.): Chongqing 2,121,000; Harbin 1,552,000; Lushun 1,508,000; Nanjing 1,419,000; Xian 1,310,000; Qingdao 1,121,000; Chengdu 1,107,000; Taiyuan 1,020,000.

Government: Head of state: Chmn. Natl. People's Congress Ye Jianying; b. 1899; in office: Mar. 5, 1978. **Head of government:** Prime Min. Hua Guofeng; b. 1920; in office: Feb. 7, 1976. **Effective head of government:** First Dep. Prime Min. Deng Xiaoping; b. Aug. 22, 1904; in office: July 22, 1977. **Communist Party Chmn.:** Hua Guofeng; in office: Oct. 7, 1976. **Local divisions:** 21 provinces, 5 ethnic autonomous regions, and 3 cities. **Armed forces:** regulars 4,360,000.

Economy: Industries: Textiles, steel, chemicals, cement, plastics, agriculture implements, trucks. **Chief crops:** Grain, corn, peas, soybeans in N; rice, sugar in S, abutilon, hemp, jute, ramie, flax, cotton, tea. **Minerals:** Tungsten, antimony, coal, iron, lead, manganese, mercury, molybdenum, phosphates, potash, tin. **Crude oil reserves** (1980): 20 bln. bbls. **Other resources:** Silk. **Per capita arable land:** 0.3 acres. **Meat prod.** (1978): beef: 2.24 mln. metric tons; pork: 14.06 mln. metric tons; lamb: 716,000 metric tons. **Fish catch** (1977): 6.9 mln. metric tons. **Electricity prod.** (1978): 256 bln. kwh. **Crude steel prod.** (1979 est). 34.4 mln. metric tons. **Labor force:** 63% agric.

Finance: Currency: Yuan (Mar. 1980): 1.51 = $1 US). **Gross domestic product** (1976 est.): $340 bln. **Per capita income** (1979): $232. **Imports** (1976): $6.1 bln.; partners (1978): Jap. 30%, W. Ger. 10%, U.S. 8%, Austral. 5%. **Exports** (1976): $7.2 bln.; partners (1978): Hong Kong 20%, Jap. 19%, N. Kor. 6%. **Foreign currency reserves** (1978): $3 bln.

Transport: Railway traffic (1971): 301 bln. net ton-km. **Motor vehicles:** in use (1973): 30,000 passenger cars, 650,000 comm. vehicles. **Chief ports:** Shanghai, Tianjin, Luda.

Communications: Television sets: over 1 mln. in use (1978). **Radios:** 12 mln. in use (1970).

Health: Life expectancy at birth (1975): 60.7 male; 64.4 female. **Births** (per 1,000 pop. 1975): 26.0. **Deaths** (per 1,000 pop. 1975): 9.4. **Natural increase** (1975): 1.7%. **Hospital beds** (per 100,000 pop. 1977): 185. **Physicians** (per 100,000 pop. 1977): 33.

Education (1977): **Literacy:** 70%. **Pop. 5-19:** in school: 65%, teachers per 1,000: 18. **PQLI:** 71.

History. Remains of various man-like creatures who lived as early as several hundred thousand years ago have been found in many parts of China. Neolithic agricultural settlements dotted the Huanghe basin from about 5,000 BC. Their language, religion, and art were the sources of later Chinese civilization.

Bronze metallurgy reached a peak and Chinese pictographic writing, similar to today's, was in use in the more developed culture of the Shang Dynasty (c. 1500 BC-c. 1000 BC) which ruled much of North China.

A succession of dynasties and interdynastic warring kingdoms ruled China for the next 3,000 years. They expanded Chinese political and cultural domination to the south and west, and developed a brilliant technologically and culturally advanced society. Rule by foreigners (Mongols in the Yuan Dynasty, 1271-1368, and Manchus in the Ch'ing Dynasty, 1644-1911) did not alter the underlying culture.

A period of relative stagnation left China vulnerable to internal and external pressures in the 19th century. Rebellions left tens of millions dead, and Russia, Japan, Britain, and other powers exercised political and economic control in large parts of the country. China became a republic Jan. 1, 1912, following the Wuchang Uprising inspired by Dr. Sun Yat-sen.

For a period of 50 years, 1894-1945, China was involved in conflicts with Japan. In 1895, China ceded Korea, Taiwan, and other areas. On Sept. 18, 1931, Japan seized the Northeastern Provinces (Manchuria) and set up a puppet state called Manchukuo. The border province of Jehol was cut off as a buffer state in 1933. Japan invaded China proper July 7, 1937. After its defeat in World War II, Japan gave up all seized land.

After the war with Japan ended, Aug. 15, 1945, internal disturbances arose involving the Kuomintang, communists, and other factions. China proper came under domination of communist armies, 1949-1950. The Kuomintang government moved to Taiwan (Formosa), 90 mi. off the mainland, Dec. 8, 1949.

The People's Republic of China was proclaimed in Peking Sept. 21, 1949, by the Chinese People's Political Consultative Conference under Mao Tse-tung, communist leader.

The communist regime and the USSR signed a 30-year treaty of "friendship, alliance and mutual assistance," Feb. 15, 1950, repudiating the 1945 treaty between the Soviet Union and the Kuomintang government authorized by the Yalta Agreement. Great Britain recognized the People's Republic in 1950 and France did so in 1964. By 1975, over 100 nations had recognized the regime.

The U.S. refused recognition, and after its consular officers met with abuse, withdrew them. On Nov. 26, 1950, the People's Republic sent armies into Korea against U.S. troops and forced a stalemate.

By the 1960s, relations with the USSR deteriorated, with disagreements on borders, idealogy and leadership of world communism. The USSR cancelled aid accords, and China, with Albania, launched anti-Soviet propaganda drives.

China sought to promote revolutionary movements in Africa, Asia and South America.

On Oct. 25, 1971, the UN General Assembly ousted the Taiwan government from the UN and seated Communist China in its place. The U.S. had supported the mainland's admission but opposed Taiwan's expulsion.

In April 1971, after the U.S. relaxed restrictions on visits by its citizens, a U.S. table tennis team toured the People's Republic.

U.S. Pres. Nixon visited China Feb. 21-28, 1972, on invitation from Premier Chou En-lai, ending years of antipathy between the 2 nations. China and the U.S. opened liaison offices in each other's capitals, May-June 1973. The U.S., Dec. 15, 1978, formally recognized the People's Republic of China as the sole legal government of China; diplomatic relations between the 2 nations were established, Jan. 1, 1979. Trade between the two countries neared $1 billion in 1974, largely U.S. grain exports, declined in subsequent years, but was revitalized with U.S. recognition, 1979.

Internal developments. After an initial period of consolidation, 1949-52, industry, agriculture, and social and economic institutions were forcibly molded according to Maoist ideals. However, frequent drastic changes in policy and violent factionalism have interfered with economic development.

In 1957, Mao Tse-tung admitted an estimated 800,000 people had been executed 1949-54; opponents claimed much higher figures. Some 110,000 political prisoners seized in 1957 were released in 1978.

The Great Leap Forward, 1958-60, tried to force the pace of economic development through intensive labor on huge new rural communes, and through emphasis on ideological purity and enthusiasm. The program caused resistance and was largely abandoned. Serious food shortages developed, and the government was forced to buy grain from the West.

The Great Proletarian Cultural Revolution, 1965, was an attempt to oppose pragmatism and bureaucratic power and instruct a new generation in revolutionary principles. Massive purges took place. A program of forcibly relocating millions of urban teenagers into the countryside was launched.

By 1968 the movement had run its course; many purged officials returned to office in subsequent years, and reforms in education and industry that had placed ideology above expertise were gradually weakened.

In the mid-1970s, factional and ideological fighting increased, and emerged into the open after the 1976 deaths of Mao and Premier Chou En-lai. Chiang Ching, Mao's widow and 3 other leading leftists were purged and placed under arrest, after reportedly trying to seize power. Their opponents said the "gang of four" had used severe repression and mass torture, had sparked local fighting and had disrupted production. The new ruling group modified Maoist policies in education, culture, and industry, and sought better ties with non-communist countries.

Relations with Vietnam deteriorated in 1978 as China charged persecution of ethnic Chinese. In retaliation for Vietnam's invasion of Cambodia, China attacked 4 Vietnamese border provinces Feb. 17, 1979; heavy border fighting ensued. Peace talks between the 2 countries continued through the year.

About 800,000 people were killed in 1976 when an earthquake leveled the northern industrial city of Tangshan. Drought and transport disruptions reportedly caused food shortages.

Increased army influence was reflected by a series of nuclear test explosions in 1976. The first Chinese atomic bomb was exploded in 1964; the first hydrogen bomb in 1967. There is a growing stockpile of nuclear weapons and intermediate range missiles. Long range missiles have been tested. The Chinese navy has been built into the world's third largest. The first orbiting space satellite was launched in 1970.

Manchuria. Home of the Manchus, rulers of China 1644-1911, Manchuria has accommodated millions of Chinese settlers in the 20th century. Under Japanese rule 1931-45, the area became industrialized. China no longer uses the name Manchuria for the region, which is divided into the 3 NE provinces of Heilongjiang, Jilin, and Liaoning.

Guandong is the southernmost part of Manchuria. Russia in 1898 forced China to lease it Guandong, and built Port Arthur (Lushun) and the port of Dairen (Luda). Japan seized Port Arthur in 1905. It was turned over to the USSR by the 1945 Yalta agreement, but finally returned to China in 1950.

Inner Mongolia was organized by the People's Republic in 1947. Its boundaries have undergone frequent changes, reaching its greatest extent (and restored in 1979) in 1956, with an area of 460,000 sq. mi., allegedly in order to dilute the minority Mongol population. Chinese settlers outnumber the Mongols more than 10 to 1. Total pop., 8.5 million. Capital: Hohhot.

Xinjiang Uygur Autonomous Region, in Central Asia, is 633,802 sq. mi., pop. 11 million (75% Uygurs, a Turkic Moslem group, with a heavy Chinese increase in recent years). Capital: Urumqi. It is China's richest region in strategic minerals. Some Uygurs have fled to the USSR, claiming national oppression.

Tibet, 470,000 sq. mi., is a thinly populated region of high plateaus and massive mountains, the Himalayas on the S, the Kunluns on the N. High passes connect with India and Nepal; roads lead into China proper. Capital: Lhasa. Average altitude is 15,000 ft. Jiachan, 15,870 ft., is believed to be the highest inhabited town on earth. Agriculture is primitive. Pop. 1.7 million (of whom 500,000 are Chinese). Another 4 million Tibetans form the majority of the population of vast adjacent areas that have long been incorporated into China.

China ruled all of Tibet from the 18th century, but independence came in 1911. China reasserted control in 1951, and a communist government was installed in 1953, revising the theocratic Lamaist Buddhist rule. Serfdom was abolished, but all land remained collectivized.

A Tibetan uprising within China in 1956 spread to Tibet in 1959. The rebellion was crushed with Chinese troops, and Buddhism was almost totally suppressed. The Dalai Lama and 100,000 Tibetans fled to India. Chinese have taken nearly all major posts in the Tibet Autonomous Region set up in 1965. Revolts continued in 1965-66, and fighting was reported as late as 1976. The International Commission of Jurists charged the Chinese regime with genocide in Tibet in 1961.

China (Taiwan)

Republic of China

People: Population (1979 est.): 17,456,000. **Pop. density:** 1,181 per sq. mi. **Ethnic groups:** Han Chinese 98% (18% from mainland), aborigines (of Indonesian origin) 2%. **Languages:** Mandarin Chinese (official), Taiwan, Hakka dialects, Japanese, English. **Religions:** Buddhism, Taoism, Confucianism prevail, Christians 2.5%.

Geography: Area: 13,892 sq. mi., the size of Maryland and Delaware combined. **Location:** Off SE coast of China, between E. and S. China Seas. **Neighbors:** Nearest is China. **Topography:** A mountain range forms the backbone of the island; the eastern half is very steep and craggy, the western slope is flat, fertile, and well-cultivated. **Capital:** Taipei. **Cities** (1979 est.): Taipei (met.) 2,183,500; (1978) Kaohsiung 1,062,999; Taichung 578,935; Tainan 557,075.

Government: Head of state: Chiang Ching-kuo; b. Mar. 18, 1910; in office: May 20, 1978. **Head of government:** Prime Min. Sun Yun-suan; b. Nov. 11, 1913; in office: May 30, 1978. **Local divisions:** Taiwan province, Taipei Municipality. **Armed forces:** regulars 539,000; reserves 1,170,000.

Economy: Industries: Textiles, clothing, electrical and electronic equip., processed foods, chemicals, glass, machinery. **Chief crops:** Rice, bananas, pineapples, sugar cane, sweet potatoes, wheat, soybeans, peanuts. **Minerals:** Coal, gold, copper, sulphur, oil. **Crude oil reserves** (1980): 10.2 mln. bbls. **Per capita arable land:** 0.2 acres. **Meat prod.** (1977): beef: 15,798 metric tons; pork: 574,656 metric tons. **Fish catch** (1977): 854,900 metric tons. **Crude steel prod.** (1979): 4.3 mln. metric tons. **Labor force:** 27.1% agric.; 37.8% manuf.

Finance: Currency: New Taiwan dollar (Mar. 1980: 36.10 = $1 US). **Gross domestic product** (1978): $24.13 bln. **Per capita income** (1978): $1,300. **Imports** (1979): $14.78 bln.; partners (1978): Jap. 33%, U.S. 22%, Kuw. 7%, Saudi Ar. 6%. **Exports** (1979): $16.07 bln.; partners (1978): U.S. 40%, Jap. 12%, Hong Kong 7%. **Tourists** (1978): 1,270,977; receipts (1978): $608 mln. **National budget** (1978): $4.03 bln. revenues; $3.10 bln. expenditures. **International reserves less gold** (Mar. 1980): $1.51 bln. **Gold:** 2.49 mln. oz t. **Consumer prices** (change in 1979): 9.7%.

Transport: Motor vehicles: in use (1978): 256,000 passenger cars, 171,000 comm. vehicles; assembled (1975): 23,000 passenger cars, 6,500 comm. vehicles. **Chief ports:** Kaohsiung, Keelung, Hualien, Taichung.

Communications: Television sets: 3 mln. in use (1978). **Radios:** 3.5 mln. in use (1974). **Telephones in use** (1978): 1,685,132. **Daily newspaper circ.** (1974): 1,300,000; 83 per 1,000 pop.

Health: Life expectancy at birth (1972): 66.8 male; 72.0 female. **Births** (per 1,000 pop. 1978): 24.1. **Deaths** (per 1,000 pop. 1978): 4.7. **Natural increase** (1978): 1.90%. **Hospital beds** (per 100,000 pop. 1977): 143. **Physicians** (per 100,000 pop. 1977): 33. **Infant mortality** (per 1,000 live births 1973): 18.

Education (1977): **Literacy:** 85%. **Pop. 5-19:** in school: 65%, teachers per 1,000: 17. **PQLI:** 87.

Large-scale Chinese immigration began in the 17th century. The island came under mainland control after an interval of Dutch rule, 1620-62. Taiwan (also called Formosa) was ruled by Japan 1895-1945. Two million Kuomintang supporters fled to Taiwan in 1949. Both the Taipei and Peking governments consider Taiwan an integral part of China.

The U.S. upon its recognition of the People's Republic of China, Dec. 15, 1978, severed diplomatic ties with Taiwan. It maintains the unofficial American Institute in Taiwan, while Taiwan has established the Coordination Council for North American Affairs in Washington, D.C.

Land reform, government planning, U.S. aid and investment, and free universal education have brought huge advances in industry, agriculture, and mass living standards.

The Penghu (Pescadores), 50 sq. mi., pop. 120,000, lie between Taiwan and the mainland. **Quemoy** and **Matsu,** pop. 75,000, lie just off the mainland.

Colombia

Republic of Colombia

People: Population (1979 est.): 26,205,000. **Age distrib.** (%): 0–14: 44.6; 15–59: 50.7; 60+: 4.7. **Pop. density:** 56.31 per sq. mi. **Urban** (1973): 59.5%. **Ethnic groups:** Mestizo 58%, Caucasian 20%, Mulatto 14%, Negro 4%, Indian 1%. **Languages:** Spanish. **Religions:** Roman Catholic 95%, Protestant under 1%.

Geography: Area: 455,355 sq. mi., larger than Texas and California combined. **Location:** At the NW corner of S. America. **Neighbors:** Panama on NW, Ecuador, Peru on S, Brazil, Venezuela on E. **Topography:** Three ranges of Andes, the Western, Central, and Eastern Cordilleras, run through the country from N to S. The eastern range consists mostly of high table lands, densely populated. The Magdalena R. rises in Andes, flows N to Carribean, through a rich alluvial plain. Sparsely-settled plains in E are drained by Orinoco and Amazon systems. **Capital:** Bogota. **Cities** (1973 cen.): Bogota 2,836,361; Medellin 1,112,390; Cali 967,908; Barranquilla 690,471.

Government: Head of state: Pres. Julio Cesar Turbay Ayala; b. June 8, 1916; in office: Aug. 7, 1978. **Local divisions:** 22 departments, 9 national territories, and federal district of Bogota. **Armed forces:** regulars 67,500; reserves 500,000.

Economy: Industries: Textiles, rubber goods, hides, steel, paper, cement, chemicals. **Chief crops:** Coffee (2d in exports), rice, tobacco, cotton, cocoa, maize, potatoes, sugar, bananas. **Minerals:** Oil, gas, emeralds (95% world output), gold, silver, copper, lead, mercury, cinnabar, manganese, platinum, coal, iron, nickel, salt. **Crude oil reserves** (1980): 710 mln. bbls. **Other resources:** Rubber, balsam, dye-woods, copaiba, hydro power. **Per capita arable land:** 0.4 acres. **Meat prod.** (1978): beef: 431,000 metric tons; pork: 110,000 metric tons; lamb 7,000 metric tons. **Fish catch** (1977): 75,100 metric tons. **Electricity prod.** (1977): 15.22 bln. kwh. **Crude steel prod.** (1979): 361,000 metric tons. **Labor force:** 45% agric.

Finance: Currency: Peso (Mar. 1980: 45.6 = $1 US). **Gross domestic product** (1978): $22.82 bln. **Per capita income** (1978): $803. **Imports** (1979): $4.44 bln.; partners (1977): U.S. 42%, W. Ger. 10%, Jap. 12%, Venez. 7%. **Exports** (1979): $3.38 bln.; partners (1977): U.S. 32%, W. Ger. 19%, Venez. 6%, Jap. 5%. **Tourists** (1977): 622,900; receipts: $201 mln. **National budget** (1978): $2.14 bln. revenues; $1.99 bln. expenditures. **International reserves less gold** (Mar. 1980): $4.02 bln. **Gold** 2.43 mln. oz t. **Consumer prices** (change in 1979): 24.4%.

Transport: Railway traffic (1977): 3.91 bln. passenger-km; 1.22 bln. net ton-km. **Motor vehicles:** in use (1977): 453,600 passenger cars, 104,500 comm. vehicles; assembled (1976): 26,900 passenger cars; 9,500 comm. vehicles. **Civil aviation:** 2,072 mln. passenger-miles (1977); 109.381 mln. freight ton-miles (1977). **Chief ports:** Buena Ventura, Santa Marta, Barranquilla, Cartagena.

Communications: Television sets: 1.7 in use (1976), 76,000 manuf. (1974). **Radios:** 2.9 in use (1976). **Telephones in use** (1978): 1,396,591. **Daily newspaper circ.** (1976): 1,330,000.

Health: Life expectancy at birth (1975): 58.5 male; 61.2 female. **Births** (per 1,000 pop. 1975): 34.1. **Deaths** (per 1,000 pop. 1975): 9.0. **Natural increase** (1975): 2.5%. **Hospital beds** (per 100,000 pop. 1977): 161. **Physicians** (per 100,000 pop. 1977): 51. **Infant mortality** (per 1,000 live births 1975): 46.6%.

Education (1977): **Literacy:** 80%. **Pop. 5-19:** in school: 54%, teachers per 1,000: 19. **PQLI:** 69.

Spain subdued the local Indian kingdoms (Funza, Tunja) by the 1530s, and ruled Colombia and neighboring areas as New Granada for 300 years. Independence was won by 1819. Venezuela and Ecuador broke away in 1829-30, and Panama withdrew in 1903.

One of the few functioning Latin American democracies, Colombia is nevertheless plagued by rural and urban violence, though scaled down from "La Violencia" of 1948-58, which claimed 200,000 lives. Attempts at land and social reform, and progress in industrialization have not yet succeeded in reducing massive social problems aggravated by a very high birth rate.

Comoros

Federal and Islamic Republic of the Comoros

People: Population (1979 est.): 359,000. **Age distrib.** (%): 0–14: 43.0; 15–59: 47.0; 60+: 8.0. **Pop. density:** 461.76 per sq. mi. **Ethnic groups:** Arabs, Africans, East Indians. **Languages:** Arabic, French, Swahili. **Religions:** Islam prevails.

Geography: Area: 693 sq. mi., half the size of Rhode Island. **Location:** 3 islands (Grande Comore, Anjouan, and Moheli) in the Mozambique Channel between NW Madagascar and SE Africa. **Neighbors:** Nearest are Mozambique on W, Madagascar on E. **Topography:** The islands are of volcanic origin, with an active volcano on Grand Comoro. **Capital:** Moroni. **Cities** (1978 est.): Moroni (met.) 12,000.

Government: Head of state: Pres. Ahmed Abdallah; in office: May 23, 1978. **Head of govt.:** Prime Min. Salim Ben Ali; in office: Dec. 22, 1978. **Local divisions:** each of the 3 main islands is a prefecture.

Economy: Industries: Perfume. **Chief crops:** Vanilla, copra, perfume plants, fruits. **Per capita arable land:** 0.6 acres. **Electricity prod.** (1977): 3.0 mln. kwh. **Labor force:** 87% agric.

Finance: Currency: CFA franc (Mar. 1980: 223.92 = $1 US). **Gross domestic product** (1975 est.): $70 mln. **Per capita income** (1976): $153. **Imports** (1976): $13 mln.; partners: Fr. 30%, Madag. 23%, Ken. 13%. **Exports** (1976): $9 mln.; partners: Fr. 59%, U.S. 15%, W. Ger. 10%.

Transport: Chief ports: Dzaoudzi.

Communications: Radios: 36,000 in use (1976). **Telephones in use** (1977): 1,035.

Health: Life expectancy at birth (1975): 43.4 male; 46.6 female. **Births** (per 1,000 pop. 1975): 44.4 **Deaths** (per 1,000 pop. 1975): 19.3. **Natural increase** (1975): 2.5%. **Infant mortality** (per 1,000 live births 1975): 51.7. **PQLI:** 44.

The islands were controlled by Moslem sultans until the French acquired them 1841-1909. A 1974 referendum favored independence, with only the Christian island of Mayotte preferring association with France. The French National Assembly decided to allow each of the islands to decide its own fate. The Comoro Chamber of Deputies declared independence July 6, 1975. In a referendum in 1976, Mayotte voted to remain French. A leftist regime that seized power in 1975 was deposed in a pro-French 1978 coup.

Congo

People's Republic of the Congo

People: Population (1979 est.): 1,508,000. **Pop. density:** 11.06 per sq. mi. **Ethnic groups:** Bakongo 45%, Bateke 20%, others. **Languages:** French (official), others. **Religions:** Christians 50% (two-thirds Roman Catholic), others.

Geography: Area: 132,046 sq. mi., slightly smaller than Montana. **Location:** In western central Africa. **Neighbors:** Gabon, Cameroon on W, Central African Republic on N, Zaire on E, Angola (Cabinda) on SW. **Topography:** Much of the Congo is covered by thick forests. A coastal plain leads to the fertile Niari Valley. The center is a plateau; the Congo R. basin consists of flood plains in the lower and savanna in the upper portion. **Capital:** Brazzaville. **Cities** (1974 cen.): Brazzaville (met.) 289,700; Pointe-Noire 141,700.

Government: Head of state: Pres. Denis Sassou-Nguesso; b. 1943; in office: Feb. 8, 1979. **Head of government:** Prime Min. Louis Sylvain Ngoma; in office: Dec. 18, 1975. **Local divisions:** 9 regions and capital district. **Armed forces:** regulars 7,000; para-military 3,900.

Economy: Chief crops: Palm oil and kernels, cocoa, coffee, bananas, peanuts. **Minerals:** Oil, potash, lead, zinc. **Crude oil reserves** (1980): 400 mln. bbls. **Per capita arable land:** 1.1 acres. **Fish catch** (1977): 16,400 metric tons. **Electricity prod.** (1978): 97.20 mln. kwh. **Labor force:** 37% agric.

Finance: Currency: CFA franc (Mar. 1980; 223.92 = $1 US). **Gross domestic product** (1976 est.): $670 mln. **Per capita income** (1976): $430. **Imports** (1978): $282 mln.; partners (1977): Fr. 49%, W. Ger. 6%, U.S. 5%. **Exports** (1978): $149 mln.; partners (1977): Ital. 30%, Fr. 12%, U.S. 7%, Sp. 7%. **Tourist receipts** (1977): $4 mln. **International reserves less gold** (Dec. 1979): $42.23 mln. **Gold:** 11,000 oz t. **Consumer prices** (change in 1978): 10.1%.

Transport: Railway traffic (1978): 294 mln. passenger-km; 478.8 mln. net ton-km. **Motor vehicles:** in use (1976): 20,000 passenger cars, 13,000 comm. vehicles. **Chief ports:** Pointe-Noire, Brazzaville.

Communications: Television sets: 3,300 in use (1976). **Radios:** 83,000 in use (1976). **Telephones in use** (1978): 13,376.

Health: Life expectancy at birth (1975): 41.9 male; 45.1 female. **Births** (per 1,000 pop. 1975): 45.0. **Deaths** (per 1,000 pop. 1975): 20.9. **Natural increase** (1975): 2.4%. **Hospital beds** (per 100,000 pop. 1977): 499. **Physicians** (per 100,000 pop. 1977): 14. **Infant mortality** (per 1,000 live births 1975): 180.

Education (1977): **Literacy:** 40%. **Pop. 5-19:** in school: 75%, teachers per 1,000: 20. **PQLI:** 37.

The Loango Kingdom flourished in the 15th century, as did the Anzico Kingdom of the Batekes; by the late 17th century they had become weakened. France established control by 1885. Independence came Aug. 15, 1960.

After a 1963 coup sparked by trade unions, the country adopted a Marxist-Leninist stance, with the USSR and China vying for influence. Tribal divisions remain strong. France remains a dominant trade partner and source of technical assistance, and French-owned private enterprise retained a major economic role. However, the government of Pres. Sassou-Nguesso favored a strengthening of relations with the USSR; a socialist constitution was adopted, 1979.

Costa Rica

Republic of Costa Rica

People: Population (1979 est.): 2,184,000. **Age distrib.** (%): 0–14: 44.0; 15–59: 50.4; 60+: 5.6. **Pop. density:** 107.36 per sq. mi. **Urban** (1973): 40.6%. **Ethnic groups:** Spanish (with Mestizo minority); Indians 0.4%, Jamaican Negroes 2%. **Languages:** Spanish (official), English. **Religions:** Roman Catholicism prevails.

Geography: Area: 19,653 sq. mi., smaller than W. Virginia. **Location:** In central America. **Neighbors:** Nicaragua on N, Panama on S. **Topography:** Lowlands by the Caribbean are tropical. The interior plateau, with an altitude of about 4,000 ft., is temperate. **Capital:** San Jose. **Cities** (1978 est.): San Jose 236,747.

Government: Head of state: Pres. Rodrigo Carazo Odio; b. Dec. 27, 1926; in office May 8, 1978. **Local divisions:** 7 provinces and 80 cantons. **Armed forces:** para-military 5,000.

Economy: Industries: Fiberglass, aluminum, textiles, fertilizers, roofing, cement. **Chief crops:** Coffee (chief export), bananas, sugar, cocoa, cotton, hemp. **Minerals:** Gold, salt, sulphur, iron. **Other resources:** Fish, forests. **Per capita arable land:** 0.3 acres. **Meat prod.** (1978): beef: 63,000 metric tons; pork: 9,000 metric tons. **Fish catch** (1977): 13,000 metric tons. **Electricity prod.** (1978): 1.80 bln. kwh. **Labor force:** 35% agric.; 15% manuf.

Finance: Currency: Colone (Mar. 1980: 8.57 = $1 US). **Gross domestic product** (1978): $3.47 bln. **Per capita income** (1978): $1,512. **Imports** (1979): $1.41 bln.; partners (1977): U.S. 34%, Jap. 13%, Guat. 6%, W. Ger. 5%. **Exports** (1979): $923 mln.; partners (1977): U.S. 29%, W. Ger. 12%, Nic. 7%, Neth. 7%. **Tourists** (1977): 327,500; receipts: $54 mln. **National budget** (1978): $480 mln. revenues; $633 mln. expenditures. **International reserves less gold** (Feb. 1980): $89.51 mln. **Gold:** 87,000 oz t. **Consumer prices** (change in 1979): 9.2%.

Transport: Railway traffic (1974): 81 mln. passenger-km; 14 mln. net ton-km. **Motor vehicles:** in use (1976): 64,900 passenger cars, 42,400 comm. vehicles. **Civil aviation:** 360 mln. passenger-km (1978); 19 mln. freight ton-km (1978). **Chief ports:** Limon, Puntarenas.

Communications: Television sets: 155,000 in use (1976). **Radios:** 150,000 in use (1976). **Telephones in use** (1978): 145,069. **Daily newspaper circ.** (1976): 210,000; 104 per 1,000 pop.

Health: Life expectancy at birth (1974): 66.26 male; 70.49 female. **Births** (per 1,000 pop. 1977): 31.1. **Deaths** (per 1,000 pop. 1977): 4.3. **Natural increase** (1977): 2.7%. **Hospital beds** (per 100,000 pop 1977): 345. **Physicians** (per 100,000 pop. 1977): 72. **Infant mortality** (per 1,000 live births 1977): 27.8.

Education (1977): **Literacy:** 90%. **Pop. 5-19:** in school: 58%, teachers per 1,000: 21. **PQLI:** 86.

Guaymi Indians inhabited the area when Spaniards arrived, 1502. Independence came in 1821. Costa Rica seceded from the Central American Federation in 1838. Since the civil war of 1948-49, there has been no violent social conflict, and free political institutions have been preserved.

Costa Rica, though still a largely agricultural country, has achieved a relatively high standard of living and social services, and land ownership is widespread.

The country has generally followed a pro-U.S. foreign policy.

Cuba

Republic of Cuba

People: Population (1979 est.): 9,824,000. **Age distrib.** (%): 0–14: 36.9; 15–59: 53.5; 60+: 9.6. **Pop. density:** 220.05 per sq. mi. **Urban** (1970): 60.3%. **Ethnic groups:** Spanish, Negro, and mixtures. **Languages:** Spanish. **Religions:** Roman Catholicism prevailed in past.

Geography: Area: 44,218 sq. mi., nearly as large as Pennsylvania. **Location:** Westernmost of West Indies. **Neighbors:** Bahamas, U.S., on N, Mexico on W, Jamaica on S, Haiti on E. **Topography:** The coastline is about 2,500 miles. The N coast is steep and rocky, the S coast low and marshy. Low hills and fertile valleys cover more than half the country. Sierra Maestra, in the E is the highest of 3 mountain ranges. **Capital:** Havana. **Cities** (1978 est.): Havana 1,008,500; Santiago de Cuba 315,801; Camaguey 221,826.

Government: Head of state: Pres. Fidel Castro Ruz; b. Aug. 13, 1926; in office: Dec. 3, 1976 (formerly Prime Min. since Feb. 16, 1959). **Local divisions:** 14 provinces, 169 municipal assemblies. **Armed forces:** regulars 189,000; reserves 90,000.

Economy: Industries: Texiles, wood products, cement, chemicals, cigars. **Chief crops:** Sugar cane (80% of exports), tobacco, coffee, pineapples, bananas, citrus fruit, coconuts. **Minerals:** Cobalt, nickel, iron, copper, manganese, salt. **Other resources:** Forests. **Per capita arable land:** 0.6 acres. **Meat prod.** (1978): beef: 143,000 metric tons; pork: 63,000 metric tons. **Fish catch** (1977): 185,200 metric tons. **Electricity prod.** (1977): 7.70 bln. kwh. **Crude steel prod.** (1979 est.): 300,000 metric tons. **Labor force:** 34% agric.

Finance: Currency: Peso (Mar. 1980: .72 = $1 US). **Net material product** (1974): $6.1 bln. **Per capita income** (1977): $840. **Imports** (1976): $1.5 bln.; partners (1975): USSR 40%, Jap. 12%, Sp. 5%, W. Ger. 5%. **Exports** (1976): $3.2 bln.; partners (1975): USSR 56%, Spain 8%, Jap. 8%.

Transport: Railway traffic (1976): 767 mln. passenger-km; 1.85 bln. net ton-km. **Motor vehicles:** in use (1976): 80,000 passenger cars, 40,000 comm. vehicles. **Chief ports:** Havana, Matanzas, Cienfuegos, Santiago de Cuba.

Communications: Television sets: 650,000 in use (1976). **Radios:** 2.1 mln. in use (1976), 120,000 manuf. (1977). **Telephones in use** (1978): 321,054.

Health: Life expectancy at birth: (1970): 68.5 male; 71.8 female. **Births** (per 1,000 pop. 1977): 17.6 **Deaths** (per 1,000 pop. 1977): 5.8 **Natural increase** (1977): 1.2%. **Hospital beds** (per 100,000 pop. 1977): 413. **Physicians** (per 100,000 pop. 1977): 94. **Infant mortality** (per 1,000 live births 1977): 24.8.

Education (1977): **Literacy:** 94%. **Pop. 5-19:** in school: 75% teachers per 1,000: 43. **PQLI:** 92.

Some 50,000 Indians lived in Cuba when it was discovered by Columbus in 1492. Its name derives from the Indian Cubanacan. Except for British occupation of Havana, 1762-63, Cuba remained Spanish until 1898. A slave-based sugar plantation economy developed from the 18th century, aided by early mechanization of milling. Sugar remains the chief product and chief export despite government attempts to diversify.

A ten-year uprising ended in 1878 with guarantees of rights by Spain, which Spain failed to carry out. A full-scale movement under Jose Marti began Feb. 24, 1895.

The U.S. declared war on Spain in April, 1898, after the sinking of the U.S.S. Maine in Havana harbor, and defeated it in the short Spanish-American War. Spain gave up all claims to Cuba. U.S. troops withdrew in 1902, but under 1903 and 1934 agreements, the U.S. leases a site at Guantanamo Bay in the SE as a naval base. U.S. and other foreign investments acquired a dominant role in the economy.

In 1952, former president Fulgencio Batista seized control and established a dictatorship, which grew increasingly harsh and corrupt. Former student leader Fidel Castro assembled a rebel band in 1956; guerrilla fighting intensified in 1958. Batista fled Jan. 1, 1959, and in the resulting political vacuum Castro took power, becoming premier Feb. 16.

The government, quickly dominated by extreme leftists, began a program of sweeping economic and social changes, without restoring promised liberties. Opponents were imprisoned and some were executed. Some 700,000 Cubans emigrated in the years after the Castro takeover, mostly to the U.S.

Cattle and tobacco lands were nationalized, while a system of cooperatives was instituted. By the end of 1960 all banks and industrial companies had been nationalized, including over $1 billion worth of U.S.-owned properties, mostly without compensation.

Soviet, Chinese, and Eastern European economic penetration was extended by trade and credit agreements. Cuba is a member of Comecon, the Soviet economic union.

Poor sugar crops resulted in collectivization of farms, stringent labor controls, and rationing, despite continued aid from the USSR and other Communist countries.

The U.S. cut back Cuba's sugar quota in 1960, and imposed a partial export embargo, which became total in 1962, severely damaging the economy. In 1961, some 1,400 Cubans, trained and backed by the U.S. Central Intelligence Agency, unsuccessfully tried to invade and overthrow the regime. It was revealed in 1975 that CIA agents had plotted to kill Castro in 1959 or 1960.

In the fall of 1962, the U.S. learned that the USSR had brought nuclear missiles to Cuba. After an Oct. 22 warning from Pres. Kennedy, the missiles were removed.

The Organization of American States voted 15-4 in 1964 for mandatory sanctions against Cuba and for cooperation against Cuban revolutionary activities in Latin America. The sanctions were lifted in 1975, with the tacit concurrence of the U.S.

In 1973, Cuba and the U.S. signed an agreement providing for extradition or punishment of hijackers of planes or vessels, and for each nation to bar activity from its territory against the other. In 1977, the 2 countries signed agreements to exchange diplomats, without restoring full ties, and to regulate offshore fishing. In 1978, and again in 1980, the U.S. agreed to accept political prisoners released by Cuba.

But relations were strained by continued Cuban military involvement abroad. In 1975-78, Cuba sent over 20,000 troops to aid one faction in the Angola Civil War. Some 20,000 other Cuban troops or advisers were reported in the Congo, Ethiopia (where they fought Somali and Eritrean insurgents), Equatorial Guinea, Guinea, Guinea-Bissau, Somalia, and Mozambique.

Cyprus

Republic of Cyprus

People: Population (1979 est.): 620,000. **Age distrib.** (%): 0–14: 25.0; 15–59: 61.0; 60+: 14.0. **Pop. density:** 173.57 per sq. mi. **Urban** (1974): 42.2%. **Ethnic groups:** Greeks 75%, Turks 20%, Armenians, Maronites. **Languages:** Greek, Turkish. **Religions:** Orthodox 76%, Moslems 20%.

Geography: Area: 3,572 sq. mi., smaller than Connecticut. **Location:** In eastern Mediterranean Sea, off Turkish coast. **Neighbors:** Nearest are Turkey on N, Syria, Lebanon on E. **Topography:** Two mountain ranges run E-W, separated by a wide, fertile plain. **Capital:** Nicosia. **Cities** (1973 cen.): Nicosia (met. 115,700.

Government: Head of state: Pres. Spyros Kyprianou; b. Oct. 28, 1932; in office: Aug. 3, 1977. **Local divisions:** 6 districts. **Armed forces:** Greek: regulars 10,000; reserves 20,000; Turkish: 5,000.

Economy: Industries: Wine, clothing, shoes, tourism. **Chief crops:** Grains, grapes, carobs, citrus fruits, potatoes, olives. **Minerals:** Copper, iron, asbetos, gypsum, chrome, umber. **Per capita arable land:** 1.5 acres. **Meat prod.** (1978): pork: 16,000 metric tons; lamb: 10,000 metric tons. **Electricity prod.** (1978): 924.00 mln. kwh. **Labor force:** 36% agric.; 47% manuf.

Finance: Currency: Pound (Mar. 1980: 1 = $2.70 US). **Gross domestic product** (1978): $1.39 bln. **Per capita income** (1978): $2,200. **Imports** (1979): $1.03 bln.; partners (1978): UK 22%, It. 12%, W. Ger. 7%, Gr. 6%. **Exports** (1979): $465 mln.; partners (1978): UK 23%, Leb. 9%, Sau. Ar. 9%, Syria 5%. **Tourists** (1977): 178,200; receipts: $60 mln. **National budget** (1974): $136 mln. revenues; $203 mln. expenditures. **International reserves less gold** (Dec. 1979): $353.1 mln. **Gold** (Jan. 1980): 453,000 oz t. **Consumer prices** (change in 1979): 9.4%.

Transport: Motor vehicles: in use (1977): 74,500 passenger cars, 18,600 comm. vehicles. **Civil aviation:** 524 mln. passenger-km (1978); 21 mln. freight ton-km (1978). **Chief ports:** Famagusta, Limassol.

Communications: Television sets: 57,000 licensed (1976). **Radios:** 200,000 licensed (1976). **Telephones in use** (1978): 82,800. **Daily newspaper circ.** (1976): 72,000; (1975) 107 per 1,000 pop.

Health: Life expectancy at birth (1973): 70.0 male; 72.9 female. **Births** (per 1,000 pop. 1975): 18.4. **Deaths** (per 1,000 pop. 1975): 9.8. **Natural increase** (1975): .9%. **Hospital beds** (per 100,000 pop. 1977): 538. **Physicians** (per 100,000 pop. 1977): 82. **Infant mortality** (per 1,000 live births 1975): 17.5.

Education (1977): **Literacy:** 86%. **Pop. 5-19:** in school: 54%, teachers per 1,000: 22. **PQLI:** 85.

Agitation for enosis (union) with Greece increased after World War II, with the Turkish minority opposed, and broke into violence in 1955-56. In 1959, Britain, Greece, Turkey, and Cypriot leaders approved a plan for an independent republic, with constitutional guarantees for the Turkish minority and permanent division of offices on an ethnic basis. Greek and Turkish Communal Chambers dealt with religion, education, and other matters.

Archbishop Makarios, formerly the leader of the enosis movement, was elected president, and full independence became final Aug. 16, 1960. Makarios was re-elected in 1968 and 1973.

Further communal strife led the United Nations to send a peace-keeping force in 1964; its mandate has been repeatedly renewed.

The Cypriot National Guard, led by officers from the army of Greece, seized the government July 15, 1974, and named Nikos Sampson, and advocate of union with Greece, president. Makarios fled the country. On July 20, Turkey invaded the island; Greece mobilized its forces but did not intervene. A cease-fire was arranged July 22. On the 23d, Sampson turned over the presidency to Glafkos Clerides (on the same day, Greece's military junta resigned). A peace conference collapsed Aug. 14; fighting resumed. By Aug. 16 Turkish forces had occupied the NE 40% of the island, despite the presence of UN peace forces. Makarios resumed the presidency in Dec., until his death, 1977.

Turkish Cypriots voted overwhelmingly, June 8, 1975, to form a separate Turkish Cypriot federated state. A president and assembly were elected in 1976. Some 200,000 Greeks had left the Turkish-controlled area, replaced by thousands of Turks, some from the mainland.

Czechoslovakia

Czechoslovak Socialist Republic

People: Population (1979 est.): 15,239,000. **Age distrib.** (%): 0–14: 23.4; 15–59: 52.5; 60+: 17.4. **Pop. density:** 306.66 per sq. mi. **Urban** (1974): 66.7%. **Ethnic groups:** Czechs 65%, Slovaks 30%, Hungarians 4%, Germans, Poles, Ukrainians. **Languages:** Czech, Slovak, Hungarian. **Religions:** Roman Catholics were majority, Lutherans, Orthodox.

Geography: Area: 49,371 sq. mi., the size of New York. **Location:** In E central Europe. **Neighbors:** Poland, E. Germany on N, W. Germany on W. Austria, Hungary on S, USSR on E. **Topography:** Bohemia, in W, is a plateau surrounded by mountains; Moravia is hilly, Slovakia, in E, has mountains (Carpathians) in N, fertile Danube plain in S. Vltava (Moldau) and Labe (Elbe) rivers flow N from Bohemia to G. **Capital:** Prague. **Cities** (1978 est.): Prague 1,173,031; Brno 361,561; Bratislava 345,515; Ostrava 302,111.

Government: Head of state: Pres. Gustav Husak; b. Jan 10, 1913; in office: May 29, 1975; **Head of government:** Prime Min. Lubomir Strougal; b. Oct. 19, 1924; in office: Jan. 28, 1970. **Head of Communist Party:** First Sec. Gustav Husak; in office: Apr. 17, 1969. **Local divisions:** Czech and Slovak republics each have an assembly. **Armed forces:** regulars 194,000; reserves 350,000.

Economy: Industries: Machinery, oil products, weapons, steel, glass, chemicals, aircraft, textiles, shoes. **Chief crops:** Wheat, sugar beets, potatoes, rye, hops. **Minerals:** Mercury, coal, iron. Jachymor has Europe's greatest pitchblende (for uranium and radium) deposits. **Per capita arable land:** 0.8 acres. **Meat prod.** (1978): beef: 393,000 metric tons; pork: 815,000 metric tons; lamb 6,000 metric tons. **Fish catch** (1977): 18,300 metric tons. **Electricity prod.** (1978): 69.06 bln. kwh. **Crude**

steel prod. (1979): 14.8 mln. metric tons. **Labor force:** 14% agric.; manuf. 39%.

Finance: Currency: Koruna (Mar. 1980: 10.44 = $1 US). **Net material product** (1978): $40.6 bln. **Per capita income** (1976): $3,985. **Imports** (1979): $14.3 bln.; partners (1977): USSR 34%, E. Ger. 11%, Pol. 8%, W. Ger. 6%. **Exports** (1979): $13.2 bln.; partners (1977): USSR 33%, E. Ger. 12%, Pol. 9%, Hung. 6%. **Tourists** (1977): 6,982,700; receipts $184 mln. **Consumer prices** (change in 1979): 3.7%.

Transport: Railway traffic (1978): 18.64 bln. passenger-km; 72.34 bln. net ton-km. **Motor vehicles:** in use (1977): 1.83 mln. passenger cars, 289,800 comm. vehicles; manuf. (1978): 175,200 passenger cars; (1977): 80,400 comm. vehicles. **Civil aviation:** 1,584 mln. passenger-km (1978); 18 mln. freight ton-km (1978).

Communications: Television sets: 3.8 mln. licensed (1976), 461,000 manuf. (1977). **Radios:** 3.93 mln. licensed (1976), 235,000 manuf. (1977). **Telephones in use** (1978): 2,863,307. **Daily newspaper circ.** (1977): 4,453,000; 296 per 1,000 pop.

Health: Life expectancy at birth (1976): 66.99 male; 74.05 female. **Births** (per 1,000 pop. 1978): 18.4 **Deaths** (per 1,000 pop. 1978): 11.5. **Natural increase** (1978): .7%. **Hospital beds** (per 100,000 pop. 1977): 1,229. **Physicians** (per 100,000 pop. 1977): 254. **Infant mortality** (per 1,000 live births 1978): 18.7.

Education (1977): **Literacy:** 99%. **Pop. 5–19:** in school: 60%, teachers per 1,000: 30. **PQLI:** 92.

Bohemia, Moravia and Slovakia were part of the Great Moravian Empire in the 9th century. Later, Slovakia was overrun by Magyars, while Bohemia and Moravia became part of the Holy Roman Empire. Under the kings of Bohemia, Prague in the 14th century was the cultural center of Central Europe. Bohemia and Hungary became part of Austria-Hungary.

In 1914-1918 Thomas G. Masaryk and Eduard Benes formed a provisional government with the support of Slovak leaders including Milan Stefanik. They proclaimed the Republic of Czechoslovakia Oct. 30, 1918.

By 1938 Nazi Germany had worked up disaffection among German-speaking citizens in Sudetenland and demanded its cession. Prime Min. Neville Chamberlain of Britain, with the acquiescense of France, signed with Hitler at Munich, Sept. 30, 1938, an agreement to the cession, with a guarantee of peace by Hitler and Mussolini. Germany occupied Sudetenland Oct. 1-2.

Hitler on Mar. 15, 1939, dissolved Czechoslovakia, made protectorates of Bohemia and Moravia, and supported the autonomy of Slovakia, which was proclaimed independent Mar. 14, 1939, with Josef Tiso president.

Soviet troops with some Czechoslovak contingents entered eastern Czechoslovakia in 1944 and reached Prague in May 1945; Benes returned as president. In May 1946 elections, the Communist Party won 38% of the votes, and Benes accepted Klement Gottwald, a Communist, as prime minister. Tiso was executed in 1947.

In February, 1948, the Communists seized power in advance of scheduled elections. In May 1948 a new constitution was approved. Benes refused to sign it. On May 30 the voters were offered a one-slate ballot and the Communists won full control. Benes resigned June 7. Gottwald became president and Benes died Sept. 3. A harsh Stalinist period followed, with complete and violent suppression of all opposition.

In Jan. 1968 a liberalization movement spread explosively through Czechoslovakia. Antonin Novotny, long the Stalinist boss of the nation, was deposed as party leader and succeeded by Alexander Dubcek, a Slovak, who declared he intended to make communism democratic. On Mar. 22 Novotny resigned as president and was succeeded by Gen. Ludvik Svoboda. On Apr. 6, Premier Joseph Lenart resigned and was succeeded by Oldrich Cernik, whose new cabinet was pledged to carry out democratization and economic reforms.

In July 1968 the USSR and 4 hard-core Warsaw Pact nations demanded an end to liberalization. On Aug. 20, the Russian, Polish, East German, Hungarian, and Bulgarian armies invaded Czechoslovakia.

Despite demonstrations and riots by students and workers, press censorship was imposed, liberal leaders were ousted from office and promises of loyalty to Soviet policies were made by some old-line Communist Party leaders.

On Apr. 17, 1969, Dubcek resigned as leader of the Communist Party and was succeeded by Gustav Husak. In Jan. 1970, Premier Cernik was ousted. Censorship was tightened and the Communist Party expelled a third of its members. In 1972, more than 40 liberals were jailed on subversion charges. In 1973, amnesty was offered to some of the 40,000 who fled the country after the 1968 invasion, but repressive policies remained in force through 1976.

More than 700 leading Czechoslovak intellectuals and former party leaders signed a human rights manifesto in 1977, called Charter 77, prompting a renewed crackdown by the regime.

Czechoslovakia has long been an industrial and technological leader of the eastern European countries, though its relative standing has declined in recent years.

Denmark

Kingdom of Denmark

People: Population (1979 est.): 5,118,000. **Age distrib.** (%): 0–14: 22.4 15–59: 58.7; 60+: 18.9. **Pop. density:** 299.5 per sq. mi. **Urban** (1970): 66.9%. **Ethnic groups:** Almost all Scandinavian. **Languages:** Danish. **Religions:** Lutherans 97%.

Geography: Area: 17,028 sq. mi., the size of Massachusetts and New Hampshire combined. **Location:** In northern Europe, separating the North and Baltic seas. **Neighbors:** W. Germany on S., Norway on NW, Sweden on NE. **Topography:** Denmark consists of the Jutland Peninsula and about 500 islands, 100 inhabited. The land is flat or gently rolling, and is almost all in productive use. **Capital:** Copenhagen. **Cities** (1978 est.): Copenhagen 699,300; Arhus 246,111.

Government: Head of state: Queen Margrethe II; b. Apr. 16, 1940; in office: Jan. 14, 1972. **Head of government:** Prime Min. Anker Joergensen; b. July 13, 1922; in office: Feb. 13, 1975. **Local divisions:** 14 counties and one city (Copenhagen). **Armed forces:** regulars 34,650; reserves 154,260.

Economy: Industries: Machinery, ships, textiles, furniture, steel. **Chief crops:** Dairy products, grains, potatoes. **Crude oil reserves** (1980): 375 mln. bbls. **Per capita arable land:** 1.2 acres. **Meat prod.** (1978): beef: 240,000 metric tons; pork: 790,000 metric tons. **Fish catch** (1977): 1.81 mln. metric tons. **Electricity prod.** (1978): 20.52 bln. kwh. **Crude steel prod.** (1979): 804,000 metric tons. **Labor force:** 8.5% agric.; 44% manuf.

Finance: Currency: Krone (Mar. 1980: 6.03 = $1 US). **Gross domestic product** (1978): $55.89 bln. **Per capita income** (1978): $9,869. **Imports** (1979): $18.45 bln.; partners (1978): W. Ger. 21% Swed. 13%, UK 11%, Neth. 6%. **Exports** (1979): $14.61 bln.; partners (1978): W. Ger. 17%, UK 14%, Swed. 13%, Nor. 7%. **Tourists** (1976): 16,231,900; receipts: $805 mln. **National budget** (1975): $11.87 bln. revenues; $13.79 bln. expenditures. **International reserves less gold** (Mar. 1980): $1.84 bln. **Gold:** 1.63 mln. oz t. **Consumer prices** (change in 1979): 9.6%.

Transport: Railway traffic (1978): 3.08 bln. passenger-km; 1.76 bln. net ton-km. **Motor vehicles:** in use (1977): 1.38 mln. passenger cars, 274,900 comm. vehicles; assembled (1975): 1,000 passenger cars; (1977): 900 comm. vehicles. **Civil aviation:** 2,832 mln. passenger-km (1978); 136 mln. freight ton-km (1978). **Chief ports:** Copenhagen, Alborg, Arhus, Odense.

Communications: Television sets: 1.64 mln. licensed (1976), 77,000 manuf. (1977). **Radios:** 1.85 mln. licensed (1976), 161,000 manuf. (1977). **Telephones in use** (1978): 2,743,758. **Daily newspaper circ.** (1977): 1,840,000; 362 per 1,000 pop.

Health: Life expectancy at birth (1976): 71.1 male; 76.8 female. **Births** (per 1,000 pop. 1978): 12.2. **Deaths** (per 1,000 pop. 1978): 10.4. **Natural increase** (1978): .2%. **Hospital beds** (per 100,000 pop. 1977): 853. **Physicians** (per 100,000 pop. 1977): 204. **Infant mortality** (per 1,000 live births 1978): 8.9.

Education (1977): **Literacy:** 99%. **Pop. 5–19:** in school: 70%, teachers per 1,000; 51. **PQLI:** 97.

The origin of Copenhagen dates back to ancient times, when the fishing and trading place named Havn (port) grew up on a cluster of islets, but Bishop Absalon (1128-1201) is regarded as the actual founder of the city.

Danes formed a large component of the Viking raiders in the early Middle Ages. The Danish kingdom was a major north European power until the 17th century, when it lost its land in southern Sweden. Norway was separated in 1815, and Schleswig-Holstein in 1864. Northern Schleswig was returned in 1920.

The **Faeroe Islands** in the N. Atlantic, about 300 mi. NE of the Shetlands, and 850 mi. from Denmark proper, 18 inhabited, have an area of 540 sq. mi. and pop. (1979) of 43,000. They are self-governing in most matters.

Greenland

Greenland, a huge island between the N. Atlantic and the Polar Sea, is separated from the North American continent by Davis Strait and Baffin Bay. Its total area is 840,000 sq. mi., 705,234 of which are ice-capped. Most of the island is a lofty plateau 9,000 to 10,000 ft. in altitude. The average thickness of the cap is 1,000 ft. The population (1979) is 49,000. Under the 1953 Danish constitution the colony became an integral part of the realm with representatives in the Folketing. The Danish parliament, 1978, approved home rule for Greenland, effective May 1, 1979. Accepting home rule the islanders elected a socialist-dominated legislature, Apr. 4th. With home rule, Greenlandic place names came into official use. The technically-correct name for Greenland is now Kalaallit Nunaat; its capital is Nuuk, rather than Gothab. Fish and fur are exported.

Djibouti

Republic of Djibouti

People: Population (1979 est.): 386,000. **Pop. density:** 12.23 per sq. mi. **Ethnic groups:** Issa (Somali) 47%; Afar 37%; European 8%; Arab 6%. **Languages:** Somali, Afar, French, Arabic. **Religions:** Most are Moslems; Europeans are Roman Catholic.

Geography: Area: 8,996 sq. mi., about the size of Massachusetts. **Location:** On E coast of Africa, separated from Arabian Peninsula by the strategically vital strait of Bab el-Mandeb. **Neighbors:** Ethiopia on N (Eritera) and W, Somalia on S. **Topography:** The territory, divided into a low coastal plain, mountains behind, and an interior plateau, is arid, sandy, and desolate. The climate is generally hot and dry. **Capital:** Djibouti. **Cities** (1978 est): Djibouti (met.) 62,000.

Government: Head of state: Pres. Hassan Gouled Aptidon b. 1916; in office: June 24, 1977; **Head of government:** Prem. Barkat Gourad Hamadou; in office: Sept. 30, 1978. **Local divisions:** 5 cercles (districts). **Armed forces:** regulars 3,000; para-military 10,000.

Economy: Minerals: Salt. **Electricity prod.** (1977): 62 mln. kwh.

Finance: Currency: Franc (1976: 166=$1 US). **Per capita income** (1976): $1,000. **Imports** (1974): $117 mln.; partners (1973): Fr. 49%, Eth. 12%, Jap. 6%, UK 6%. **Exports** (1974): $20 mln.; partners (1973): Fr. 84%.

Transport: Motor vehicles: in use (1977): 11,800 passenger cars, 3,300 commercial vehicles. **Chief ports:** Djibouti.

Communications: Television sets: 3,500 in use (1976). **Radios:** 15,000 in use (1976). **Telephones in use** (1978): 3,675.

Health: Births (per 1,000 pop. 1970): 42.0. **Deaths** (per 1,000 pop. 1970): 7.6. **Natural increase** (1970): 3.4%.

France gained control of the territory in stages between 1862 and 1900.

Ethiopia and Somalia have renounced their claims to the area, but each has accused the other of trying to gain control. There were clashes between Afars (ethnically related to Ethiopians) and Issas (related to Somalis) in 1976. Immigrants from both countries continued to enter the country up to independence, which came June 27, 1977.

Unemployment is about 80%. There are few natural resources; trade is the main contributor to domestic product. French aid is the mainstay of the economy and 7,000 French troops are present.

Dominica

Commonwealth of Dominica

People: Population (1979 est.): 78,000. **Pop. density:** 275.86 per sq. mi. **Ethnic groups:** nearly all African or mulatto, Caribs. **Languages:** English, French patois. **Religions:** mainly Roman Catholic.

Geography: Area: 290 sq. mi., about one-fourth the size of Rhode Island. **Location:** In Eastern Caribbean, most northerly Windward Is. **Neighbors:** Guadeloupe to N, Martinique to S. **Topography:** Mountainous, a central ridge running from N to S, terminating in cliffs; volcanic in origin, with numerous thermal springs; rich deep topsoil on leeward side, red tropical clay on windward coast. **Capital** (1976 est.) Roseau 16,800.

Government: Head of state: Pres. Aurelius Marie; in office: 1980. **Head of government:** Prime Min. Mary Eugenia Charles; elected to office: July 21, 1980. **Local divisions:** 25 village councils and 2 town councils.

Economy: Industries: Agriculture, tourism. **Chief crops:** Bananas, citrus fruits, coconuts. **Minerals:** Pumice. **Other resources:** Forests. **Per capita arable land:** 0.2 acres. **Electricity prod.** (1977): 16 mln. kwh.

Finance: Currency: East Caribbean dollar (Mar. 1980: 2.70 = $1 US). **Gross domestic product** (1977): $33.48 mln. **Per capita income** (1976): $460. **Imports** (1975): $16.70 mln.; partners (1975): UK 30%, U.S. 10%, Can. 10%. **Exports** (1975): $8.81 mln.; partners (1975): UK 78%. **Tourists** (1977): 31,000; receipts: $3 mln. **National budget** (1976): $6.29 mln. revenues; $7.51 mln. expenditures. **Consumer prices** (change in 1978): 7.7%.

Transport: Chief ports: Roseau.

Communications: Telephones in use (1978): 4,036.

Health: Life expectancy at birth (1962): 56.97 male; 59.18 female. **Births** (per 1,000 pop. 1978): 21.4. **Deaths** (per 1,000 pop. 1978): 5.3. **Natural increase** (1978): 1.6%. **Pop. per hospital bed** (1973): 234. **Pop. per physician** (1971): 5,385. **Infant mortality** (per 1,000 live births 1978): 19.6.

Education: Pop. 5–19: in school (1975): 24,113. **PQLI:** 68.

A British colony since 1805, Dominica was granted self government in 1967. Independence was achieved Nov. 3, 1978. Tourism is a small sector of the economy. France was expected to increase aid to the island.

Hurricane David struck, Aug. 30, 1979, devastating the island and destroying the banana plantations, Dominica's economic mainstay.

Dominican Republic

People: Population (1979 est.): 5,551,000. **Age distrib.** (%): 0–14: 47.5; 15–59: 47.5; 60+: 4.9. **Pop. density:** 273.74 per sq. mi. **Urban** (1978): 49.1%. **Ethnic groups:** Caucasian 16%, mulatto 73%, Negro 11%. **Languages:** Spanish. **Religions:** Roman Catholic 95%, Protestant 2%.

Geography: Area: 18,704 sq. mi., the size of Vermont and New Hampshire combined. **Location:** In West Indies, sharing I. of Hispaniola with Haiti. **Neighbors:** Haiti on W. **Topography:** The Cordillera Central range crosses the center of the country, rising to over 10,000 ft., highest in the Caribbean. The Cibao valley to the N is major agricultural area. **Capital:** Santo Domingo. **Cities** (1970 cen.): Santo Domingo 673,470; Santiago de Los Caballeros 155,000.

Government: Head of state: Pres. Antonio Guzman Fernandez; b. Feb. 12, 1911; in office Aug. 16, 1978. **Local divisions:** 26 provinces and a national district. **Armed forces:** regulars 18,500; para-military 10,000.

Economy: Industries: Molasses, rum, alcohol, cement, textiles, furniture, apparel. **Chief crops:** sugar, cocoa, coffee, tobacco, corn, peanuts, bananas. **Minerals:** Nickel, gold, copper, iron, salt, chalk, bauxite, marble, amber, kaolin. **Other resources:** Timber. **Per capita arable land:** 0.4 acres. **Meat prod.** (1978): beef: 39,000 metric tons; pork: 23,000 metric tons. **Electricity prod.** (1977): 2.67 bln. kwh. **Labor force:** 44% agric.; 8% manuf.

Finance: Currency: Peso (Mar. 1980: 1 = $1 US). **Gross domestic product** (1977): $4.47 bln. **Per capita income** (1978): $841. **Imports** (1979): $1.24 bln.; partners (1978): U.S. 43%, Venez. 15%, Jap. 9%. **Exports** (1979): $866 mln.; partners (1978): U.S. 55% Swit. 9%, Venez. 8%, Neth. 6%. **Tourists** (1977): 265,000; receipts: $93 mln. **National budget** (1978): $596 mln. revenues; $664 mln. expenditures. **International reserves less gold** (Mar. 1980): $143.5 mln. **Gold:** 123,000 oz t. **Consumer prices** (change in 1979): 9.1%.

Transport: Motor vehicles: in use (1976): 77,300 passenger cars, 39,400 comm. vehicles. **Chief ports:** Santo Domingo, San Pedro de Macoris, Puerto Plata.

Communications: Television sets: 160,000 in use (1976). **Radios:** 120,000 in use (1976). **Telephones in use** (1978): 139,412. **Daily newspaper circ.** (1976): 208,000; 28 per 1,000 pop.

Health: Life expectancy at birth (1961): 57.15 male; 58.59 female. **Births** (per 1,000 pop. 1975): 42.0. **Deaths** (per 1,000 pop. 1975): 10.7. **Natural increase** (1975): 3.1%. **Hospital beds** (per 100,000 pop. 1977): 233. **Physicians** (per 100,000 pop. 1977): 53. **Infant mortality** (per 1,000 live births 1975): 37.2.

Education (1977): **Literacy:** 68%. **Pop. 5–19:** in school: 51%, teachers per 1,000: 12. **PQLI:** 64.

Carib and Arawak Indians inhabited the island of Hispaniola

when Columbus landed in 1492. The city of Santo Domingo, founded 1496, is the oldest settlement by Europeans in the hemisphere and has the supposed ashes of Columbus in an elaborate tomb in its ancient cathedral.

The western third of the island was ceded to France in 1697. Santo Domingo itself was ceded to France in 1795. Haitian leader Toussaint L'Ouverture seized it, 1801. Spain returned intermittently 1803-21, as several native republics came and went. Haiti ruled again, 1822-44, and Spanish occupation occurred 1861-63.

The country was occupied by U.S. Marines from 1916 to 1924, when a constitutionally elected government was installed.

In 1930, Gen. Rafael Leonidas Trujillo Molina was elected president. Trujillo ruled brutally until his assassination in 1961. Pres. Joaquin Balaguer, appointed by Trujillo in 1960, resigned under pressure in 1962. Juan Bosch, elected president in the first free elections in 38 years, was overthrown in 1963.

On April 24, 1965, a revolt was launched by followers of Bosch and others, including a few communists. Four days later 405 U.S. Marines intervened against the pro-Bosch forces; their numbers grew to 21,000. Token units were later sent by 5 So. American countries as a peace-keeping force.

A provisional government supervised a June 1966 election, in which Balaguer defeated Bosch by a 3-2 margin; there were some charges of election fraud.

The Inter-American Peace Force completed its departure Sept. 20, 1966. Balaguer was reelected, 1970 and 1974, the latter time without real opposition.

In 1971, scores of leftists were reported killed by terrorists. Renewed violence occurred in 1975.

Continued depressed world prices affected the main export commodity, sugar. Hurricane David devastated the island, killing over 600, Aug. 1979.

Ecuador

Republic of Ecuador

People: Population (1979 est.): 7,763,000 **Age distrib.** (%): 0–14: 44.5; 15–59: 49.6; 60+: 6.0. **Pop. density:** 73.9 per sq. mi. **Urban** (1978): 42.8% **Ethnic groups:** Indians 40%, Mestizos 40%, Caucasians 10%, Negroes 10%. **Languages:** Spanish 93%, Quechua dialects 7%. **Religions:** Roman Catholics 94%, Protestants 6%.

Geography: Area: 105,685 sq. mi., the size of Colorado. **Location:** In NW S. America, on Pacific coast, astride Equator. **Neighbors:** Colombia to N, Peru to E and S. **Topography:** Two ranges of Andes run N and S, splitting the country into 3 zones: hot, humid lowlands on the coast; temperate highlands between the ranges, and rainy, tropical lowlands to the E. **Capital:** Quito. **Cities** (1978 est.): Guayaquil 1,022,010; Quito 742,858.

Government: Head of state: Pres. Jaime Roldos Aguilera; b. Nov. 5, 1940; in office: Aug. 10, 1979. **Local divisions:** 20 provinces. **Armed forces:** regulars 32,800; para-military 5,800.

Economy: Industries: Cement, edible oils, textiles, sugar, chemicals, oil products, paper. **Chief crops:** Bananas (largest exporter), rice, grains, potatoes, fruits, cocoa, kapok. **Minerals:** Oil, copper, iron, lead, coal, sulphur. **Crude oil reserves** (1980): 1.1 bln. bbls. **Other resources:** Rubber, bark. **Per capita arable land:** 1.3 acres. **Meat prod.** (1978): beef: 70,000 metric tons; pork: 36,000 metric tons; lamb: 13,000 metric tons. **Fish catch** (1977): 476,000 metric tons. **Electricity prod.** (1977): 2.15 bln. kwh. **Labor force:** 54% agric.

Finance: Currency: Sucre (Mar. 1980: 25.00 = $1 US). **Gross domestic product** (1978): $7.48 bln. **Per capita income** (1977): $741. **Imports** (1978): $1.58 bln.; partners (1977): U.S. 38%, Jap. 16%, W. Ger. 8%. **Exports** (1978): $1.52 bln.; partners (1977): U.S. 36%, Pan. 10%, Peru 9%, Chile 7%. **Tourists** (1977): 201,900; receipts: $36 mln. **National budget** (1978): $762 mln. revenues; $913 mln. expenditures. **International reserves less gold** (Mar. 1980): $903.3 mln. **Gold:** 414,000 oz t. **Consumer prices** (change in 1979): 10.2%.

Transport: Railway traffic (1978) 65.3 mln. passenger-km; 34.2 mln. net ton-km. **Motor vehicles:** in use (1975): 51,300 passenger cars, 77,200 comm. vehicles. **Chief ports:** Guayaquil, Manta, Esmeraldas.

Communications: Television sets: 300,000 in use (1976), 5,000 manuf. (1975). **Radios:** 1.7 mln. in use (1970). **Telephones in use** (1978): 221,578. **Daily newspaper circ.** (1977): 350,000 46 per 1,000 pop.

Health: Life expectancy at birth (1974): 54.89 male; 58.07 female. **Births** (per 1,000 pop. 1975): 42.2. **Deaths** (per 1,000 pop. 1975): 12.1. **Natural increase** (1975): 3.0%. **Hospital beds** (per 100,000 pop.1977): 204. **Physicians** (per 100,000 pop. 1977): 64. **Infant mortality** (per 1,000 live births 1975): 65.8.

Education (1977): Literacy: 74%. **Pop. 5–19:** in school: 60%, teachers per 1,000: 20. **PQLI:** 70.

Spain conquered the region, which was the northern Inca empire, in 1633. Liberation forces defeated the Spanish May 24, 1822, near Quito. Ecuador became part of the Great Colombia Republic but seceded, May 13, 1830.

Liberals became a dominant force in political life in 1895, but had been unable to end instability and a succession of military coups.

Ecuador had been ruled by civilian and military dictatorships since 1968. A peaceful transfer of power from the military junta to the democratic civilian government took place, 1979.

Since 1972, the economy has revolved around its petroleum exports. Despite this, Ecuador remains an underdeveloped country.

Ecuador and Peru have long disputed their Amazon Valley boundary.

The **Galapagos Islands,** 600 mi. to the W, are the home of huge tortoises and other unusual animals.

Egypt

Arab Republic of Egypt

People: Population (1979 est.): 40,993,000. **Pop. density:** 109.13 per sq. mi. **Urban** (1977): 44.1%. **Ethnic groups:** Egyptians, Bedouins, Nubians. **Languages:** Arabic. **Religions:** Sunni Moslems (state religion) 92%, Christians 7% (mostly Copts).

Geography: Area: 363,250 sq. mi (excluding Sinai Peninsula, 23,622 sq. mi.) the size of Texas and Oregon combined. **Location:** NE corner of Africa. **Neighbors:** Libya on W, Sudan on S, Israel on E. **Topography:** Almost entirely desolate and barren, with hills and mountains in E and along Nile. The Nile Valley, where most of the people live, stretches 550 miles. **Capital:** Cairo. **Cities** (1976 cen.): Cairo 5,084,463; Alexandria 2,318,655; Giza 1,246,713; Subra-El Khema 393,700; El-Mahalla El-Kubra 292,853.

Government: Head of state and head of gov't.: Pres. Mohamed Anwar El-Sadat; b. Dec. 25, 1918; in office: Sept. 28, 1970 (P.M.: May 14, 1980). **Local divisions:** 25 governorates. **Armed forces:** regulars 395,000; reserves 500,000.

Economy: Industries: Textiles, chemicals, steel, cement, fertilizers, motion pictures. **Chief crops:** Cotton (one of largest producers), grains, vegetables, sugar cane, fruits. **Minerals:** Oil, phosphates, salt, iron, manganese, cement, gold, gypsum, kaolin, titanium. **Crude oil reserves** (1980): 3.1 bln. bbls. **Per capita arable land:** 0.2 acres. **Meat prod.** (1978): beef: 241,000 metric tons; lamb: 49,000 metric tons. **Fish catch** (1977): 104,500 metric tons. **Electricity prod.** (1977): 13.00 bln. kwh. **Crude steel prod.** (1979 est.): 800,000 metric tons. **Labor force:** 50% agric.

Finance: Currency: Pound (Mar. 1980: 1 = $1.43 US). **Gross domestic product** (1977): $18.76 bln. **Per capita income** (1977): $448. **Imports** (1979): $3.84 bln.; partners (1978): U.S. 16%, W. Ger. 11%, It. 8%, UK 8%. **Exports** (1979): $1.84 bln.; partners (1978): USSR 17%, It. 12%, U.S. 12%, Neth. 5%. **Tourists** (1977): 1,003,900; receipts: $658 mln. **International reserves less gold** (Dec. 1979): $529 mln. **Gold:** 2.47 mln. oz t. **Consumer prices** (change in 1979): 9.9%

Transport: Railway traffic (1976): 8.75 bln. passenger-km; 2.20 bln. net ton-km. **Motor vehicles:** in use (1977): 283,200 passenger cars, 64,000 comm. vehicles; assembled (1978): 15,024 passenger cars; 4,080 comm. vehicles. **Civil aviation:** 2,040 mln. passenger-km (1977); 25 mln. freight ton-km (1977). **Chief ports:** Alexandria, Port Said, Suez.

Communications: Television sets: 620,000 in use (1975), 138,000 manuf. (1977). **Radios:** 5.25 mln. in use (1976), 265,000 manuf. (1977). **Telephones in use** (1977): 503,947. **Daily newspaper circ.** (1976): 3,012,000; 79 per 1,000 pop.

Health: Life expectancy at birth (1960): 51.6 male; 53.8 female. **Births** (per 1,000 pop. 1978): 37.6. **Deaths** (per 1,000 pop. 1978): 10.5. **Natural increase** (1978): 2.7%. **Hospital beds** (per 100,000 pop. 1977): 209. **Physicians** (per 100,000 pop. 1977): 92. **Infant mortality** (per 1,000 live births 1978): 89.2.

Education (1977): **Literacy:** 44%. **Pop. 5-19:** in school: 44%, teachers per 1,000: 13. **PQLI:** 52.

Archeological records of ancient Egyptian civilization date back to 4000 BC. A unified kingdom arose around 3200 BC, and extended its way south into Nubia and north as far as Syria. A high culture of rulers and priests was built on an economic base of serfdom, fertile soil, and annual flooding of the Nile banks.

Imperial decline facilitated conquest by Asian invaders (Hyksos, Assyrians). The last native dynasty fell in 341 BC to the Persians, who were in turn replaced by Greeks (Alexander and the Ptolemies), Romans, Byzantines, and Arabs, who introduced Islam and the Arabic language. The ancient Egyptian language is preserved only in the liturgy of the Coptic Christians.

Egypt was ruled as part of larger Islamic empires for several centuries. The Mamluks, a military caste of Caucasian origin, ruled Egypt from 1250 until defeat by the Ottoman Turks in 1517. Under Turkish sultans the khedive as hereditary viceroy had wide authority. Britain intervened in 1882 and took control of administration, though nominal allegiance to the Ottoman Empire continued until 1914.

The country was a British protectorate from 1914 to 1922. A 1936 treaty strengthened Egyptian autonomy, but Britain retained bases in Egypt and a condominium over the Sudan. Britain fought German and Italian armies from Egypt, 1940-42, but Egypt did not declare war against Germany until 1945. In 1951 Egypt abrogated the 1936 treaty. The Sudan became independent in 1956.

The uprising of July 23, 1952, led by the Society of Free Officers, named Maj. Gen. Mohammed Naguib commander in chief and forced King Farouk to abdicate. When the republic was proclaimed June 18, 1953, Naguib became its first president and premier. Lt. Col. Gamal Abdel Nasser removed Naguib and became premier in 1954. In 1956, he was voted president. Nasser died in 1970 and was replaced by Vice Pres. Anwar Sadat.

Egypt adopted the name Arab Republic of Egypt, 1971, dropping the name United Arab Republic which it had used since its brief union with Syria, 1958-1961.

A series of decrees in July, 1961, nationalized about 90% of industry. Economic liberalization was begun, 1974, with more emphasis on private domestic and foreign investment.

In July, 1956, the U. S. and UK withdrew support for loans to start the Aswan High Dam. Nasser obtained credits and technicians from the USSR to build the dam. The billion-dollar Aswan High Dam project, begun 1960, completed 1971, provided irrigation for more than a million acres of land and a potential of 10 billion kwh of electricity per year. Artesian wells, drilled in the Western Desert, reclaimed 43,000 acres, 1960-66.

When the state of Israel was proclaimed in 1948, Egypt joined other Arab nations invading Israel and was defeated; no peace treaties were made.

After terrorist raids across its border, Israel invaded Egypt's Sinai Peninsula, Oct. 29, 1956. Egypt rejected a cease-fire demand by Britain and France; on Oct. 31 the 2 nations dropped bombs and on Nov. 5-6 landed forces. Egypt and Israel accepted a UN cease-fire; fighting ended Nov. 7.

A UN Emergency Force guarded the 117-mile long border between Egypt and Israel until May 19, 1967, when it was withdrawn at Nasser's demand. Egyptian troops entered the Gaza Strip and the heights of Sharm el Sheikh and 3 days later closed the Strait of Tiran to all Israeli shipping. Full-scale war broke out June 5 and before it ended under a UN cease-fire June 10, Israel had captured Gaza and the Sinai Peninsula, controlled the east bank of the Suez Canal and reopened the gulf.

Sporadic fighting with Israel broke out late in 1968 and continued almost daily, 1969-70. Military and economic aid was received from the USSR; it was est. in 1971 there were 19,000 or more Soviet military personnel in Egypt. Israel and Egypt agreed, Aug. 7, 1970, to a cease-fire and peace negotiations proposed by the U.S. Negotiations failed to achieve results, but the cease-fire continued into 1973.

In July 1972 Sadat ordered most of the 20,000 Soviet military advisers and personnel to leave Egypt; they complied. Some Soviet military shipments have continued, despite an Egyptian debt of several billion dollars.

In a surprise attack Oct. 6, 1973, Egyptian forces crossed the Suez Canal into the Sinai. (At the same time, Syrian forces attacked Israelis on the Golan Heights.) Egypt was supplied by a USSR military airlift; the U.S. responded with an airlift to Israel. Israel counter-attacked, crossed the canal, surrounded Suez City. A UN cease-fire took effect Oct. 24.

A disengagement agreement was signed Jan. 18, 1974. Under it, Israeli forces withdrew from the canal's W bank; limited numbers of Egyptian forces occupied a strip along the E bank. A second accord was signed in 1975, with Israel yielding Sinai oil fields. Pres. Sadat's suprise visit to Jerusalem, Nov. 1977, opened the prospect of peace with Israel, but worsened relations with Libya (border clashes, July 1977). On Mar. 26, 1979, Egypt and Israel signed a formal peace treaty, ending 30 years of war, and establishing diplomatic relations. Negotiations concerning the West Bank and Gaza Strip elections opened, amid Arab World reprisals against Egypt.

The U.S. and Egypt resumed, in Feb. 1974, diplomatic relations severed by Egypt after the 1967 war.

The **Suez Canal,** 103 mi. long, links the Mediterranean and Red seas. It was built by a French corporation 1859-69, but Britain obtained controlling interest in 1875. The last British troops were removed June 13, 1956. On July 26, Egypt nationalized the canal. French and British stockholders eventually received some compensation.

Egypt had barred Israeli ships and cargoes destined for Israel since 1948, and closed the canal to all shipping after the 1967 Arab-Israeli War. The canal was reopened in 1975; Egypt agreed to allow passage to Israeli cargo in third party ships. By 1979, annual tolls, at $700 million, had once more become a major source of government revenue. A $1.3 billion expansion project will enable the canal to accomodate larger tankers.

El Salvador

Republic of El Salvador

People: Population (1979 est.): 4,662,000. **Age distrib.** (%): 0–14; 46.2; 15–59: 48.4; 60+: 5.4. **Pop. density:** 526.63 per sq. mi. **Urban** (1974): 38.8%. **Ethnic groups:** Mestizos 89%, Indians 10%, Caucasians 1%. **Languages:** Spanish, Nahuatl (among some Indians). **Religions:** Roman Catholicism prevails.

Geography: Area: 8,260 sq. mi., the size of Massachusetts. **Location:** In Central America. **Neighbors:** Guatemala on W, Honduras on N. **Topography:** A hot Pacific coastal plain in the south rises to a cooler plateau and valley region, densely populated. The N is mountainous, including many volcanoes. **Capital:** San Salvador. **Cities** (1971 cen.): San Salvador 335,930.

Government: Military-civilian junta headed by Jaime Abdul Gutierrez; in office: Oct. 15, 1979. **Local divisions:** 14 departments; pres. appoints governors. **Armed forces:** regulars 6,930; para-military 3,000.

Economy: Industries: Cement, textiles, refined sugar. **Chief crops:** Coffee, cotton, rice, maize, cacao, tobacco, indigo, sugar. **Other resources:** Rubber, forests. **Per capita arable land:** 0.3 acres. **Meat prod.** (1978): beef: 34,000 metric tons; pork: 14,000 metric tons. **Electricity prod.** (1978): 1.45 bln. kwh. **Labor force:** 47% agric.

Finance: Currency: Colon (Mar. 1980: 2.50 = $1 US). **Gross domestic product** (1978): $3.07 bln. **Per capita income** (1978): $639. **Imports** (1978): $1.03 bln.; partners (1977): U.S. 29%, Guat. 13%, Jap. 11%, Venez. 9%. **Exports** (1979): $1.12 bln.; partners (1977): U.S. 33%, W. Ger. 19%, Guat. 13%, Neth. 9%. **Tourists** (1976): 277,900; receipts (1977): $23 mln. **National budget** (1978): $419 mln. revenues; $474 mln. expenditures. **International reserves less gold** (Mar. 1980): $88.7 mln. **Gold:** 516,000 oz t. **Consumer prices** (change in 1978): 13.2%.

Transport: Motor vehicles: in use (1974): 41,000 passenger cars, 19,100 comm. vehicles. **Chief ports:** La Union, Acajutla.

Communications: Television sets: 136,000 in use (1976), 109,000 (includes radios) manuf. (1977). **Radios:** 1.4 mln. in use (1976). **Telephones in use** (1978): 70,400. **Daily newspaper circ.** (1976): 331,000.

Health: Life expectancy at birth (1961): 56.56 male; 60.42 female. **Births** (per 1,000 pop. 1977): 41.7. **Deaths** (per 1,000 pop. 1977): 7.8. **Natural increase** (1977): 3.4%. **Hospital beds** (per 100,000 pop. 1977): 161. **Physicians** (per 100,000 pop. 1977): 27. **Infant mortality** (per 1,000 live births 1977): 59.5.

Education (1977): **Literacy:** 63%. **Pop. 5–19:** in school: 50%, teachers per 1,000: 11. **PQLI:** 66.

El Salvador became independent of Spain in 1821, and of the Central American Federation in 1839.

A fight with Honduras in 1969 over the presence of 300,000 Salvadorean workers left 2,000 dead. Clashes were renewed 1970 and 1974.

A military coup overthrew the Romero government, 1979, but the ruling military-civilian junta has failed to quell the extremist violence and unrest that contines to undermine the economy.

Equatorial Guinea

Republic of Equatorial Guinea

People: Population (1979 est.): 244,000. **Age distrib.** (%): 0–14: 35.2; 15–59: 57.1; 60+: 7.7. **Pop. density:** 32.31 per sq. mi. **Ethnic groups:** Fangs 75%, several other groups. **Languages:** Spanish (official), Fang, English. **Religions:** Roman Catholics 60%, Protestants, others.

Geography: Area: 10,832 sq. mi., the size of Maryland. **Location:** Bioko Is. off W. Africa coast in Gulf of Guinea, and Rio Muni, mainland enclave. **Neighbors:** Gabon on S, Cameroon on E, N. **Topography:** Bioko Is. consists of 2 volcanic mountains and a connecting valley. Rio Muni, with over 90% of the area, has a coastal plain and low hills beyond. **Capital:** Malabo. **Cities** (1973 est.): Bata 50,000; Malabo 23,000.

Government: Head of state: Pres., Supreme Military Council Teodoro Obiang Nguema Mbasogo; b. June 5, 1942; in office: Oct. 10, 1979. **Local divisions:** 2 provinces.

Economy: Chief crops: Cocoa, coffee, bananas, palm oil. **Other resources:** Timber. **Per capita arable land:** 0.9 acres. **Electricity prod.** (1977): 23 mln. kwh. **Labor force:** 95% agric.

Finance: Currency: Ekuele (Sept. 1979: 69 = $1 US). **Gross domestic product** (1976 est.): $112 mln. **Per capita income** (1975): $342. **Imports** (1976): $13.5 mln.; partner (1970): Spain 80%. **Exports** (1976): $42 mln.; partner (1970): Spain 91%.

Transport: Chief ports: Malabo, Bata.

Communications: Radios: 80,000 in use (1976).

Health: Life expectancy at birth (1975): 41.9 male; 45.1 female. **Births** (per 1,000 pop. 1975): 42.1. **Deaths** (per 1,000 pop. 1975): 21.2. **Natural increase** (1975): 2.1% **Hospital beds** (per 100,000 pop. 1977): 704. **Physicians** (per 100,000 pop. 1977): 2. **Infant mortality** (per 1,000 live births 1975): 53.2.

Education (1977): **Literacy:** 20%. **Pop. 5–19:** in school: 45%, teachers per 1,000: 9.

Fernando Po (now Bioko) Island was discovered by Portugal in the late 15th century and ceded to Spain in 1778. Independence came Oct. 12, 1968. Riots occurred in 1969 over disputes between the island and the more backward Rio Muni province on the mainland. Masie Nguema Biyogo, himself from the mainland, became president for life in 1972.

Masie's 11-year reign was described as one of the most brutal in Africa, resulting in a bankrupted nation. Most of the nation's 7,000 Europeans emigrated. In 1976, 45,000 Nigerian workers were evacuated amid charges of a reign of terror. According to reports, slavery had been revived and as many as 50,000 people were murdered by government forces. Masie was ousted in a military coup, Aug., 1979.

The U.S. suspended relations in 1976.

Ethiopia

People: Population (1979 est.): 31,780,000. **Age distrib.** (%): 0–14: 43.1; 15–59: 52.5; 60+: 4.4. **Pop. density:** 64.99 per sq. mi. **Urban** (1978): 12.9%. **Ethnic groups:** Galla 33%, Amhara 25%, Tigre 12%, Somali, Afar, Sidama. **Languages:** Amharic, Tigre (Semitic languages); Galla (Hamitic), Arabic, others. **Religions:** Orthodox Christian 40%, Moslem 40%.

Geography: Area: 457,142 sq. mi., four-fifths the size of Alaska. **Location:** In E. Africa. **Neighbors:** Sudan on W, Kenya on S. Somalia, Djibouti on E. **Topography:** A high central plateau, between 6,000 and 10,000 ft. high, rises to higher mountains near the Great Rift Valley, cutting in from the SW. The Blue Nile and other rivers cross the plateau, which descends to plains on both W and SE. **Capital:** Addis Ababa. **Cities** (1978 est.): Addis Ababa 1,196,300; Asmara 393,800.

Government: Head of state and head of gov't.: Chmn. of Provisional Military Administrative Council Mengistu Haile Mariam; b. 1937; in office: Feb. 11, 1977. **Local divisions:** 14 provinces. **Armed forces:** regulars 221,600; reserves: 20,000; paramilitary 169,000.

Economy: Industries: Food processing, cement, shoes, textiles. **Chief crops:** Coffee (50% export earnings), grains, tobacco, sugar. **Minerals:** Coal, iron, platinum, gold, silver, manganese, tin, copper, asbestos, potash, sulphur, mica, cement, salt. **Other resources:** Hydro power potential. **Per capita arable land:** 1.1 acres. **Meat prod.** (1978): beef: 212,000 metric tons; lamb: 131,000 metric tons. **Fish catch** (1977): 26,800 metric tons. **Electricity prod.** (1978): 696 mln. kwh. **Labor force:** 86% agric.

Finance: Currency: Birr (Mar. 1980: 2.07 = $1 US). **Gross domestic product** (1976): $2.90 bln. **Per capita income** (1975): $91. **Imports** (1979): $555 mln.; partners (1977): Jap. 16%, Saud. Ar. 10%, Ital. 10%, U.S. 9%. **Exports** (1979): $424 mln.; partners (1977): U.S. 26%, E. Ger. 15%, W. Ger. 9%, Saud. Ar. 8%. **Tourists** (1976): 36,900; receipts (1977): $3 mln. **National budget** (1976): $376 mln. revenues; $553 mln. expenditures. **International reserves less gold** (Mar. 1980): $147.5 mln. **Gold:** 309,000 oz t. **Consumer prices** (change in 1979): 16.0%.

Transport: Railway traffic (1976): 132 mln. passenger-km; 260 mln. net ton-km. **Motor vehicles:** in use (1976): 52,500 passenger cars, 13,100 comm. vehicles. **Civil aviation:** 512 mln. passenger-km (1978); 26 mln. freight ton-km (1978). **Chief ports:** Masewa, Aseb.

Communications: Television sets: 21,000 in use (1976), **Radios:** 210,000 in use (1976). **Telephones in use** (1978): 73,691. **Daily newspaper circ.** (1977): 35,000; 1 per 1,000 pop.

Health: Life expectancy at birth (1975): 37.0 male; 40.1 female. **Births** (per 1,000 pop. 1975): 49.9. **Deaths** (per 1,000 pop. 1975): 25.4. **Natural increase** (1975): .3%. **Hospital beds** (per 100,000 pop. 1977): 29. **Physicians** (per 100,000 pop. 1977): 1. **Infant mortality** (per 1,000 live births 1975): 84.2.

Education (1977): **Literacy:** 7%. **Pop 5-19:** in school: 12%, teachers per 1,000: 3. **PQLI:** 21.

Ethiopian culture was influenced by Egypt and Greece. The ancient monarchy was invaded by Italy in 1880, but maintained its independence until another Italian invasion in 1936. British forces freed the country in 1941.

The last emperor, Haile Selassie I, established a parliament and judiciary system in 1931, but barred all political parties.

A series of droughts since 1972 have killed hundreds of thousands. An army mutiny, strikes, and student demonstrations led to the dethronement of Selassie in 1974. The ruling junta pledged to form a one-party socialist state, and instituted a successful land reform; opposition was violently suppressed. The influence of the Coptic Church, embraced in 330 AD, was curbed, and the monarchy was abolished in 1975. A new famine and a locust plague threatened 1.5 million people in 1978.

The regime, torn by bloody coups, faced uprisings by tribal and political groups in part aided by Sudan and Somalia. Ties with the U.S., once a major arms and aid source, deteriorated, while cooperation accords were signed with the USSR in 1977. In 1978, Soviet advisors and 20,000 Cuban troops helped defeat Somali rebels & Somalia forces.

Eritrea, an Italian colony since 1890, reverted to Ethiopia in 1952 in accordance with a UN General Assembly vote. Since 1970 secessionist guerrillas, aided by Arab states, have seized most of the area.

Fiji

Dominion of Fiji

People: Population (1979 est.): 618,000. **Age distrib.** (%): 0–14: 41.1; 15–59: 54.7; 60+: 4.0. **Pop. density:** 86.45 per sq. mi. **Urban** (1976): 37.2%. **Ethnic groups:** Indian 50%, Fijians (Melanesian-Polynesian) 42%, Europeans 2%. **Languages:** English (official), Fijian, Hindi. **Religions:** Most Fijians are Methodist, most Indians are Hindu.

Geography: Area: 7,056 sq. mi., the size of New Jersey. **Location:** In western S. Pacific O. **Neighbors:** Nearest are Solomons on NW, Tonga on E. **Topography:** 840 islands (106 inhabited), many mountainous, with tropical forests and large fertile areas. Viti Levu, the largest island, has over half the total land area. **Capital:** Suva. **Cities** (1976 cen.): Suva 63,628.

Government: Head of state: Queen Elizabeth II, represented by Gov. Gen. George Cakobau; b. Nov. 6, 1912; in office: Jan. 13, 1973. **Head of government:** Prime Min. Kamisese Mara; b. May 13, 1920; in office: Oct. 10, 1970. **Local divisions:** 4 administrative divisions. **Armed forces:** regulars 870; para-military: 900.

Economy: Industries: Cement, shipyards, light industry, molasses, tourism. **Chief crops:** Sugar, coconut products, ginger. **Minerals:** Gold. **Other resources:** Timber. **Per capita arable land:** 0.6 acres. **Electricity prod.** (1977): 290.00 mln. kwh. **Labor force:** 44% agric.

Finance: Currency: Dollar (Mar. 1980: 1 = $1.16 US). **Gross domestic product** (1978): $937 mln. **Per capita income** (1977): $1,230. **Imports** (1979): $467 mln.; partners (1978): Austral. 30%, Jap. 16%, N.Z. 15%, UK 9%, **Exports**

(1979): $256 mln.; partners (1978): UK 40%, Austral. 11%, U.S. 10%, N.Z. 9%. **Tourists** (1977): 173,000; receipts $87 mln. **National budget** (1977): $144 mln. revenues; $183 mln. expenditures. **International reserves less gold** (Mar. 1980): $149.88 mln. **Gold:** 11,000 oz t. **Consumer prices** (change in 1979): 8.7%.

Transport: Motor vehicles: in use (1977): 19,300 passenger cars, 11,000 comm. vehicles. **Chief ports:** Suva, Lautoka.

Communications: Radios: 300,000 in use (1976). **Telephones in use** (1978): 32,721. **Daily newspaper circ.** (1976): 38,000; 66 per 1,000 pop.

Health: Life expectancy at birth (1975): 68.5 male; 71.7 female. **Births** (per 1,000 pop. 1975): 29.1. **Deaths** (per 1,000 pop. 1975): 4.4. **Natural increase** (1975): 2.5%. **Hospital beds** (per 100,000 pop. 1977): 264. **Physicians** (per 100,000 pop. 1977): 50. **Infant mortality** (per 1,000 live births 1975): 14.5.

Education (1977): **Literacy:** 75%. **Pop. 5-19:** in school: 74%, teachers per 1,000 27. **PQLI:** 79.

A British colony since 1874, Fiji became an independent parliamentary democracy Oct. 10, 1970.

Cultural differences between the majority Indian community, descendants of contract laborers brought to the islands in the 19th century, and the less modernized native Fijians, who by law own 83% of the land in communal villages, have led to political polarization.

The discovery of copper on Viti Levu, and favorable off-shore oil prospects, along with an expected all-time high in sugar production bode well for the economy.

Finland

Republic of Finland

People: Population (1979 est.): 4,764,000. **Age distrib.** (%): 0–14: 21.7; 15–59: 62.6; 60+: 15.7. **Pop. density:** 36.51 per sq. mi. **Urban** (1976): 59.0%. **Ethnic groups:** Finns, Swedes. **Languages:** Finnish 93.5%, Swedish 6.5% (both official). **Religions:** Lutheran 92%, Russian Orthodox 1.3%.

Geography: Area: 130,119 sq. mi., slightly smaller than Montana. **Location:** In northern Baltic region of Europe. **Neighbors:** Norway on N, Sweden on W, USSR on E. **Topography:** South and central Finland are mostly flat areas with low hills and many lakes. The N has mountainous areas, 3,000-4,000 ft. **Capital:** Helsinki. **Cities** (1978 est.): Helsinki 496,263; Tampere 166,177; Turku 164,344.

Government: Head of state: Pres. Urho K. Kekkonen; b. Sept. 3, 1900; in office: March 1, 1956. **Head of government:** Prime Min. Mauno Koivisto, b. Nov. 25, 1923; in office: May 26, 1979. **Local divisions:** 12 laanit (provinces). **Armed forces:** regulars 39,900; reserves 700,000.

Economy: Industries: Machinery, metal, shipbuilding, textiles, leather, chemicals, tourism. **Chief crops:** Grains, potatoes. **Minerals:** Chromium, cobalt, mercury, copper, iron, zinc, lead. **Other resources:** Forests (55% of exports). **Per capita arable land:** 1.3 acres. **Meat prod.** (1978): beef: 105,000 metric tons; pork: 148,000 metric tons. **Fish catch** (1977): 117,000 metric tons. **Electricity prod.** (1978): 34.20 bln. kwh. **Crude steel prod.** (1979): 2.5 mln. metric tons. **Labor force:** 6% agric.; 38% manuf.

Finance: Currency: Mark (Mar. 1980: 3.89 = $1 US). **Gross domestic product** (1979): $41.28 bln. **Per capita income** (1978): $6,090. **Imports** (1979): $11.35 bln.; partners (1978): USSR 19%, Swed. 14%, W. Ger. 13%, UK 9%. **Exports** (1979): $11.17 bln.; partners (1978): USSR 18%, Swed. 15%, UK 13%, W. Ger. 10%. **Tourists** (1977): 259,000. **National budget** (1978): $8.25 bln. revenues; $8.12 bln. expenditures. **International reserves less gold** (Mar. 1980): $1.67 bln. **Gold** 986,000 oz t. **Consumer prices** (change in 1979): 7.5%.

Transport: Railway traffic (1978): 2.99 bln. passenger-km; 6.32 bln. net ton-km. **Motor vehicles:** in use (1977): 1.08 mln. passenger cars, 145,000 comm. vehicles; manuf. (1976): 27,300 passenger cars. **Civil aviation:** 1,644 mln. passenger-km (1978); 42 mln. freight ton-km (1978). **Chief ports:** Helsinki, Turku.

Communications: Television sets: 1.71 mln. licensed (1976), 275,000 manuf. (1976). **Radios:** 2.18 licensed (1976), 185,000 manuf. (1976). **Telephones in use** (1978): 2,032,280. **Daily newspaper circ.** (1977): 2,235,000; 472 per 1,000 pop.

Health: Life expectancy at birth (1975): 67.38 male; 75.93 female. **Births** (per 1,000 pop. 1978): 13.5. **Deaths** (per 1,000 pop. 1978): 9.2. **Natural increase** (1978): .4%. **Hospital beds** (per 100,000 pop. 1977): 1,531. **Physicians** (per 100,000 pop. 1977): 160. **Infant mortality** (per 1,000 live births 1978): 12.0.

Education (1977): **Literacy:** 99%. **Pop. 5–19:** in school: 71%, teachers per 1,000: 41. **PQLI:** 95.

The early Finns probably migrated from the Ural area at about the beginning of the Christian era. Swedish settlers brought the country into Sweden, 1154 to 1809, when Finland became an autonomous grand duchy of the Russian Empire. Russian exactions created a strong national spirit; on Dec. 6, 1917, Finland declared its independence and in 1919 became a republic. On Nov. 30, 1939, the Soviet Union invaded, and the Finns were forced to cede 16,173 sq. mi., including the Karelian Isthmus, Viipuri, and an area on Lake Ladoga. After World War II, in which Finland tried to recover its lost territory, further cessions were exacted. In 1948, Finland signed a treaty of mutual assistance with the USSR. In 1956 Russia returned Porkkala, which had been ceded as a military base.

Finland is oriented toward the West in trade and culture, but Soviet infuence is strong. The governing coalition usually includes the Communist Party.

Aland, constituting an autonomous department, is a group of small islands, 572 sq. mi., in the Gulf of Bothnia, 25 mi. from Sweden, 15 mi. from Finland. Mariehamn is the principal port.

France

French Republic

People: Population (1979 est.): 53,478,000. **Age distrib.** (%): 0–14: 23.1; 15–59: 59.4; 60+: 17.5. **Pop. density:** 250.17 per sq. mi. **Urban** (1975): 73.0%. **Ethnic groups:** A mixture of various European and Mediterranean groups. **Languages:** French; minorities speak Breton, Alsatian German, Flemish, Italian, Basque, Catalan. **Religions:** Roman Catholic 90%, Protestant 1%, Jewish 1%, Moslems 1%.

Geography: Area: 212,973 sq. mi., four-fifths the size of Texas. **Location:** In western Europe, between Atlantic O. and Mediterranean Sea. **Neighbors:** Spain on S, Italy, Switzerland, W. Germany on E, Luxembourg, Belgium on N. **Topography:** A wide plain covers more than half of the country, in N and W, drained to W by Seine, Loire, Garonne rivers. The Massif Central is a mountainous plateau in center. In E are Alps (Mt. Blanc is tallest in W. Europe, 15,771 ft.), the lower Jura range, and the forested Vosges. The Rhone flows from Lake Geneva to Mediterranean. Pyrenees are in SW, on border with Spain. **Capital:** Paris. **Cities** (1975 cen.): Paris 2,296,945; Marseille 912,130; Lyon 457,410; Toulouse 371,835; Nice 344,040; Nantes 255,700; Strasbourg 253,355; Bordeaux 223,845.

Government: Head of state: Pres. Valery Giscard d'Estaing; b. Feb. 2, 1926; in office: May 27, 1974. **Head of government:** Prime Min. Raymond Barre; b. Apr. 12, 1924; in office: Aug. 25, 1976. **Local divisions:** 96 departments. **Armed forces:** regulars 509,300; reserves 350,000.

Economy: Industries: Steel, chemicals, autos, textiles, wine, perfume, aircraft, ships, instruments, plastics, electronic equipment. **Chief crops:** Grains, corn, rice, fruits, vegetables. France is largest food producer, exporter, in W. Eur. **Minerals:** Bauxite, iron, potash, silver, uranium, cobalt, nickel, coal, asphalt, rock salt. **Crude oil reserves** (1980): 50 mln. bbls. **Other resources:** Forests. **Per capita arable land:** 0.8 acres. **Meat prod.** (1978): beef: 1.68 mln. metric tons; pork: 1.67 mln. metric tons; lamb: 160,000 metric tons. **Fish catch** (1977): 760,300 metric tons. **Electricity prod.** (1978): 222.55 bln. kwh. **Crude steel prod.** (1979): 23.4 mln. metric tons. **Labor force:** 11.5% agric.; 37.5 manuf.

Finance: Currency: Franc (Mar. 1980: 4.48 = $1 US). **Gross domestic product** (1978): $471.59 bln. **Per capita income** (1978): $7,908. **Imports** (1979): $107 bln.; partners (1978): W. Ger. 19%, It. 10%, Belg. 9%, U.S. 7%. **Exports** (1979): $100.7 bln.; partners (1978): W. Ger. 17%, It. 11%, Belg. 10%, UK 7%. **Tourists** (1977) 26,265,000; receipts: $4.38 bln. **National budget** (1978): $97.80 bln. revenues; $101.59 bln. expenditures. **International reserves less gold** (Mar. 1980): $21.07 bln. **Gold:** 81.86 mln. oz t. **Consumer prices** (change in 1979): 10.7%.

Transport: Railway traffic (1978): 53.51 bln. passenger-km; 68.69 bln. net ton-km. **Motor vehicles:** in use (1977): 16.7 mln. passenger cars, 2.6 mln. comm. vehicles; manuf. (1978): 3.62 mln. passenger cars; 456,000 comm. vehicles. **Civil aviation:** 30,216 mln. passenger-km (1978); 1,810 mln. freight ton-km

(1978). **Chief ports:** Marseille, LeHavre, Nantes, Bordeaux, Rouen.

Communications: Television sets: 14.5 mln. licensed (1976), 1.91 mln. manuf. (1977). **Radios:** 17.4 mln. licensed (1976), 3.57 mln. manuf. (1977). **Telephones in use** (1978): 17,518,813. **Daily newspaper circ.** (1977): 10,863,000; 205 per 1,000 pop.

Health: Life expectancy at birth (1976): 69.2 male; 77.2 female. **Births** (per 1,000 pop. 1977): 14.0. **Deaths** (per 1,000 pop. 1977): 10.1. **Natural increase** (1977): .4%. **Hospital beds** (per 100,000 pop. 1977): 1,125. **Physicians** (per 100,000 pop. 1977): 164. **Infant mortality** (per 1,000 live births 1977): 11.4.

Education (1977): **Literacy:** 99%. **Pop. 5-19:** in school: 68%, teachers per 1,000: 41. **PQLI:** 96.

Celtic Gaul was conquered by Julius Caesar 58-51 BC; Romans ruled for 500 years. Under Charlemagne, Frankish rule extended over much of Europe. After his death France emerged as one of the successor kingdoms.

The monarchy was overthrown by the French Revolution (1789-93) and succeeded by the First Republic; followed by the First Empire under Napoleon (1804-15), a monarchy (1814-48), the Second Republic (1848-52), the Second Empire (1852-70), the Third Republic (1871-1946), the Fourth Republic (1946-58), and the Fifth Republic (1958 to present).

France suffered severe losses in manpower and wealth in the first World War, 1914-18, when it was invaded by Germany. By the Treaty of Versailles, France exacted return of Alsace and Lorraine, French provinces seized by Germany in 1871. Germany invaded France again in May, 1940, and signed an armistice with a government based in Vichy. After France was liberated by the Allies Sept. 1944, Gen. Charles de Gaulle became head of the provisional government, serving until 1946.

De Gaulle again became premier in 1958, during a crisis over Algeria, and obtained voter approval for a new constitution, ushering in the Fifth Republic. Using strong executive powers, he promoted French economic and technological advances in the context of the European Economic Community, and guarded French foreign policy independence.

France had withdrawn from Indochina in 1954, and from Morocco and Tunisia in 1956. Most of its remaining African territories were freed 1958-62, but France retained strong economic and political ties.

France tested atomic bombs in the Sahara beginning in 1960. Land-based and submarine launched strategic missiles were also developed. In 1966, France withdrew all its troops from the integrated military command of NATO, though 60,000 remained stationed in Germany. France continued to attend political meetings of NATO.

In May 1968 rebellious students in Paris and other centers rioted, battled police, and were joined by workers who launched nationwide strikes. The government awarded pay increases to the strikers May 26. In elections to the Assembly in June, de Gaulle's backers won a landslide victory. Nevertheless, he resigned from office in April, 1969, after losing a nationwide referendum on constitutional reform. De Gaulle's policies were largely continued after his death in 1970.

The island of **Corsica,** in the Mediterranean W of Italy and N of Sardinia, is an official region of France comprising 2 departments. Area: 3,369 sq. mi.; pop. (1975 cen.): 289,842. The capital is Ajaccio, birthplace of Napoleon. A militant separatist movement led to violence after 1975.

Overseas Departments

French Guiana is on the NE coast of South America with Suriname on the W and Brazil on the E and S. Its area is 35,135 sq. mi.; pop. (1979 est.): 63,000. Guiana sends one senator and one deputy to the French Parliament. Guiana is administered by a prefect and has a Council General of 16 elected members; capital is Cayenne.

The famous penal colony, Devil's Island, was phased out between 1938 and 1951.

Immense forests of rich timber cover 90% of the land. Placer gold mining is the most important industry. Exports are cocoa, bananas, wood, gold, fish glue, rum and brandy, rosewood essence, shrimp, and hides.

Guadeloupe, in the West Indies' Leeward Islands, consists of 2 large islands, Basse-Terre and Grande-Terre, separated by the Salt River, plus Marie Galante and the Saintes group to the S and, to the N, Desirade, St. Barthelemy, and over half of St. Martin (the Netherlands portion is St. Maarten). A French possession since 1635, the department is represented in the French Parliament by 2 senators and 3 deputies; administration consists of a prefect (governor) and an elected General Council.

Area of the islands is 686 sq. mi.; pop. (1979 est.) 312,000, mainly descendants of slaves; capital is Basse-Terre on Basse-Terre Is. The land is fertile; sugar, rum, and bananas are exported; tourism is an important industry.

Martinique, one of the Windward Islands, in the West Indies, has been a possession since 1635, and a department since March, 1946. It is represented in the French Parliament by 2 senators and 3 deputies. The island was the birthplace of Napoleon's Empress Josephine.

It has an area of 431 sq. mi.; pop. (1979 est.) 310,000, mostly descendants of slaves. The capital is Fort-de-France. It is a popular tourist stop. The chief exports are sugar, rum, bananas, pineapples, and cocoa.

Mayotte, formerly part of Comoros, voted in 1976 to become an overseas department of France. An island NW of Madagascar, area is 144 sq. mi., pop. (1978 est.) 51,800.

Reunion is a volcanic island in the Indian O. about 420 mi. E of Madagascar, and has belonged to France since 1665. Area, 970 sq. mi.; pop. (1979 est.) 503,000, 30% of French extraction. Capital: Saint-Denis. The chief products are sugar, rum, corn, perfume essences, vanilla, and spices. It elects 3 deputies, 2 senators to the French Parliament.

St. Pierre and Miquelon, formerly an Overseas Territory, made the transition to department status in 1976. It consists of 2 groups of rocky islands near the SW coast of Newfoundland, inhabited by fishermen. The exports are chiefly fish products. The St. Pierre group has an area of 10 sq. mi.; Miquelon, 83 sq. mi. Total pop. (1979 est.), 6,000. The capital is St. Pierre. A deputy and a senator are elected to the French Parliament.

Overseas Territories

French Polynesia Overseas Territory, comprises 130 islands widely scattered among 5 archipelagos in the South Pacific; administered by a governor. Territorial Assembly and a Council with headquarters at Papeete, Tahiti, one of the **Society Islands** (which include the **Windward** and **Leeward** islands). A deputy and a senator are elected to the French Parliament.

Other groups are the **Marquesas Islands,** the **Tuamotu Archipelago,** including the **Gambier Islands,** and the **Austral Islands.**

Total area of the islands administered from Tahiti is 1,544 sq. mi.; pop. (1979 est.), 144,000, more than half on Tahiti. Tahiti is picturesque and mountainous with a productive coastline bearing coconut, banana and orange trees, sugar cane and vanilla.

Tahiti was visited by Capt. James Cook in 1769 and by Capt. Bligh in the Bounty, 1788-89. Its beauty impressed Herman Melville, Paul Gauguin, and Charles Darwin; Robert Louis Stevenson, buried there, called Tahitians "God's sweetest works."

French Southern and Antarctic Lands Overseas Territory, comprises **Adelie Land,** on Antarctica, and 4 island groups in the Indian O. Adelie, discovered 1840, has a research station, a coastline of 185 mi. and tapers 1,240 mi. inland to the South Pole. The U.S. does not recognize national claims in Antarctica. There are 2 huge glaciers, Ninnis, 22 mi. wide, 99 mi. long, and Mentz, 11 mi. wide, 140 mi. long. The Indian O. groups are:

Kerguelen Archipelago, discovered 1772, one large and 300 small islands. The chief is 87 mi. long, 74 mi. wide, and has Mt. Ross, 6,429 ft. tall. Principal research station is Port-aux-Francais. Seals often weigh 2 tons; there are blue whales, coal, peat, semi-precious stones. **Crozet Archipelago,** discovered 1772, covers 195 sq. mi. Eastern Island rises to 6,560 ft. **Saint Paul,** in southern Indian O., has warm springs with earth at places heating to 120° to 390° F. **Amsterdam** is nearby; both produce cod and rock lobster.

New Caledonia and its dependencies, an overseas territory, are a group of islands in the Pacific O. about 1,115 mi. E of Australia and approx. the same distance NW of New Zealand. Dependencies are the **Loyalty Islands,** the **Isle of Pines, Huon Islands** and the **Chesterfield Islands.**

New Caledonia, the largest, has 6,530 sq. mi. Total area of the territory is 8,548 sq. mi.; population (1979 est.) 136,000. The group was acquired by France in 1853.

The territory is administered by a governor and government council. There is a popularly elected Territorial Assembly. A deputy and a senator are elected to the French Parliament. Capital: Noumea.

Mining is the chief industry. New Caledonia is the world's 3d largest nickel producer. Other minerals found are chrome, iron, cobalt, manganese, silver, gold, lead, and copper. Agricultural products include coffee, copra, cotton, manioc (cassava), corn, tobacco, bananas and pineapples.

Wallis and Futuna Islands, 2 archipelagos raised to status of overseas territory July 29, 1961, are in the SW Pacific S of the Equator between Fiji and Samoa. The islands have a total area of 106 sq. mi. and population (1979 est.) of 10,000. **Alofi,** attached to Futuna, is uninhabited. Capital: Mata-Utu. Chief products are copra, yams, taro roots, bananas. A senator and a deputy are elected to the French Parliament.

New Hebrides

New Hebrides, a condominium administered since 1906 by France and Great Britain. It gained independence as Vanuatu, July 29, 1980. A group of 11 main islands and about 69 islets 250 mi. NE of New Caledonia and 500 mi. W of Fiji, area 5,700 sq. mi., pop. (1979 est.) of 114,000, mostly Melanesian. Capital is Port-Vila. Chief products are copra, frozen fish, cocoa, and coffee.

Gabon

Gabonese Republic

People: Population (1979 est.): 637,000. **Pop. density:** 5.28 per sq. mi. **Urban** (1970): 32.0%. **Ethnic groups:** Fangs 25%, Bapounon 10%, others. **Languages:** French (official), Fang, Bantu languages. **Religions:** Roman Catholics 25%, Protestants 10%, others.

Geography: Area: 102,317 sq. mi., the size of Colorado. **Location:** On Atlantic coast of central Africa. **Neighbors:** Equatorial Guinea, Cameroon on N, Congo on E, S. **Topography:** Heavily forested, the country consists of coastal lowlands plateaus in N, E, and S, mountains in N, SE, and center. The Ogooue R. system covers most of Gabon. **Capital:** Libreville. **Cities** (1974 est.): Libreville 251,400; Port-Gentil 77,111.

Government: Head of state: Pres. El Hadj Omar Bongo; b. Dec. 30, 1935; in office: Dec. 2, 1967. **Head of government:** Prime Min. Leon Mebiame, b. Sept. 1, 1934; in office: Apr. 16, 1975. **Local divisions:** 9 provinces. **Armed forces:** regulars 1,300; para-military 1,600.

Economy: Industries: Oil products. **Chief crops:** Cocoa, coffee, rice, peanuts, palm products, cassava, bananas. **Minerals:** Manganese, uranium, oil, iron, gas. **Crude oil reserves** (1980): 500 mln. bbls. **Other resources:** Timber. **Per capita arable land:** 1.2 acres. **Electricity prod.** (1978): 324.00 mln. kwh. **Labor force:** 70% agric.

Finance: Currency: CFA franc (Mar. 1980: 223.92 = $1 US). **Gross domestic product** (1978) $2.66 bln. **Per capita income** (1978): $3,725. **Imports** (1979): $569 mln.; partners (1976): Fr. 69%, U.S. 6%. **Exports** (1979): $1.73 bln.; partners (1976): Fr. 42%, U.S. 17%, UK 10%, Bah. 10%. **Tourists receipts** (1977): $17 mln. **National budget** (1976): $791 mln. revenues; $1.42 bln. expenditures. **International reserves less gold** (Dec. 1979): $20.14 mln. **Gold:** 13,000 oz t. **Consumer prices** (change in 1978): 10.7%.

Transport: Motor vehicles: in use (1974): 10,100 passenger cars, 7,300 comm. vehicles. **Chief ports:** Libreville, Port-Gentil.

Communications: Television sets: 8,500 licensed (1976). **Radios:** 93,000 licensed (1976).

Health: Life expectancy at birth (1961): 25 male; 45 female. **Births** (per 1,000 pop. 1975): 31.4. **Deaths** (per 1,000 pop. 1975): 23.2 **Natural increase** (1975): .8%. **Hospital beds** (per 100,000 pop. 1977): 736. **Physicians** (per 100,000 pop. 1977): 32. **Infant mortality** (per 1,000 live births 1975): 229.

Education (1977): **Literacy:** 40%. **Pop. 5-19:** in school: 74%, teachers per 1,000: 26. **PQLI:** 21.

France established control over the region in the second half of the 19th century. Gabon became independent Aug. 17, 1960. It is one of the most prosperous black African countries, thanks to abundant natural resources, foreign private investment, and government development programs.

Gambia

Republic of The Gambia

People: Population (1979 est.): 585,000. **Age distrib.** (%): 0–14: 45.9; 15–59: 54.4; 60+: 3.8. **Pop. density:** 142.39 per sq. mi. **Urban** (1973): 15.9%. **Ethnic groups:** Mandingo 40%, Fula 13%, Wolof 12%, others. **Languages:** English (official), others. **Religions:** Moslems 85%, Christian 4%, others.

Geography: Area: 4,003 sq. mi., smaller than Connecticut. **Location:** On Atlantic coast near western tip of Africa. **Neighbors:** Surrounded on 3 sides by Senegal. **Topography:** A narrow strip of land on each side of the lower Gambia. **Capital:** Banjul. **Cities** (1978 est.): Banjul 45,604.

Government: Head of state: Pres. Dawda Kairaba Jawara; b. May 16, 1924; in office: Apr. 24, 1970 (prime min. from June 12, 1962). **Local divisions:** 5 divisions and Banjul.

Economy: Industries: Tourism. **Chief crops:** Peanuts (main export), rice. **Per capita arable land:** 1.1 acres. **Fish catch** (1977): 10,800 metric tons. **Electricity prod.** (1978): 31.40 mln. kwh. **Labor force:** 84% agric.

Finance: Currency: Dalasi (Mar. 1980: 1 = $.54 US). **Gross domestic product** (1978): $103.95 mln. **Per capita income** (1976): $190. **Imports** (1979): $148 mln.; partners (1978): UK 33%, China 10%, Fr. 7%, W. Ger. 7%. **Exports** (1979): $61 mln.; partners (1978): Fr. 27%, UK 25%, Swit. 18%, Ghana 7%. **Tourist receipts** (1977): $8 mln. **National budget** (1978): $34 mln. revenues; $48 mln. expenditures. **International reserves less gold** (Mar. 1980): $11.84 mln. **Consumer prices** (change in 1979): 6.1%.

Transport: Motor vehicles: in use (1973): 3,000 passenger cars, (1972): 2,500 comm. vehicles. **Chief ports:** Banjul.

Communications: Radios: 61,000 in use (1976). **Telephones in use** (1978): 2,779.

Health: Life expectancy at birth (1975): 39.4 male; 42.5 female. **Births** (per 1,000 pop. 1975): 46.7. **Deaths** (per 1,000 pop. 1975): 23.1. **Natural increase** (1975): 2.4%. **Hospital beds** (per 100,000 pop. 1977): 123. **Physicians** (per 100,000 pop. 1977): 8.

Education (1977): **Literacy:** 12%. **Pop. 5-19:** in school: 17%, teachers per 1,000: 10. **PQLI:** 22.

The tribes of Gambia were at one time associated with the West African empires of Ghana, Mali, and Songhay. The area became Britain's first African possession in 1588.

Independence came Feb. 18, 1965; republic status within the Commonwealth was achieved in 1970. Gambia is one of the only functioning democracies in Africa. The country suffered from severe famine in 1977-78.

Germany

Now comprises 2 nations: Federal Republic of Germany (West Germany), German Democratic Republic (East Germany).

Germany, prior to World War II, was a central European nation composed of numerous states which had a common language and traditions and which had been united in one country since 1871; since World War II it has been split in 2 parts.

History and government. Germanic tribes were defeated by Julius Caesar, 55 and 53 BC, but Roman expansion N of the Rhine was stopped in 9 AD. Charlemagne, ruler of the Franks, consolidated Saxon, Bavarian, Rhenish, Frankish, and other lands; after him the eastern part became the German Empire. The Thirty Years' War, 1618-1648, split Germany into small principalities and kingdoms. After Napoleon, Austria contended with Prussia for dominance, but lost the Seven Weeks' War to Prussia, 1866. Otto von Bismarck, Prussian chancellor, formed the North German Confederation, 1867.

In 1870 Bismarck maneuvered Napoleon III into declaring war. After the quick defeat of France, Bismarck formed the **German Empire** and on Jan. 18, 1871, in Versailles, proclaimed King Wilhelm I of Prussia German emperor (Deutscher kaiser).

The German Empire reached its peak before World War I in 1914, with 208,780 sq. mi., plus a colonial empire. After that war Germany ceded Alsace-Lorraine to France; West Prussia and Posen (Poznan) province to Poland; part of Schleswig to Denmark; lost all of its colonies and the ports of Memel and Danzig.

Republic of Germany, 1919-1933, adopted the Weimar constitution; met reparation payments and elected Friedrich Ebert and Gen. Paul von Hindenburg presidents.

Third Reich, 1933-1945, Adolf Hitler led the National Socialist German Workers' (Nazi) party after World War I. In 1923 he attempted to unseat the Bavarian government and was imprisoned. Pres. von Hindenburg named Hitler chancellor Jan. 30, 1933; on Aug. 3, 1934, the day after Hindenburg's death, the cabinet joined the offices of president and chancellor and made Hitler fuehrer (leader). Hitler abolished freedom of speech and assembly, and began a long series of persecutions climaxed by the murder of millions of Jews and opponents.

Hitler repudiated the Versailles treaty and reparations agreements. He remilitarized the Rhineland 1936 and annexed Austria (Anschluss, 1938). At Munich he made an agreement with Neville Chamberlain, British prime minister, which permitted Hitler to annex part of Czechoslovakia. He signed a non-aggression treaty with the USSR, 1939. He declared war on Poland Sept. 1, 1939, precipitating World War II.

With total defeat near, Hitler committed suicide in Berlin Apr. 1945. The victorious Allies voided all acts and annexations of Hitler's Reich.

Postwar changes. The zones of occupation administered by the Allied Powers and later relinquished gave the USSR Saxony, Saxony-Anhalt, Thuringia, and Mecklenburg, and the former Prussian provinces of Saxony and Brandenburg.

The territory E of the Oder-Neisse line within 1937 boundaries comprising the provinces of Silesia, Pomerania, and the southern part of East Prussia, totaling about 41,220 sq. mi., was taken by Poland. Northern East Prussia was taken by the USSR.

The Western Allies ended the state of war with Germany in 1951. The USSR did so in 1955.

There was also created the area of Greater Berlin, within but not part of the Soviet zone, administered by the 4 occupying powers under the Allied Command. In 1948 the USSR withdrew, established its single command in East Berlin, and cut off supplies. The Allies utilized a gigantic airlift to bring food to West Berlin, 1948-1949. In Aug. 1961 the East Germans built a wall dividing Berlin, after over 3 million E. Germans had emigrated.

East Germany

German Democratic Republic

People: Population (1979 est.): 16,758,000. **Age distrib.** (%): 0–14: 20.6; 15–59: 58.7; 60+: 20.7. **Pop. density:** 412.34 per sq. mi. **Urban** (1976): 75.5%. **Ethnic groups:** Germans, Wends (0.7%). **Languages:** German. **Religions:** Protestant 80%, Roman Catholic 11%.

Geography: Area: 40,646 sq. mi., the size of Virginia. **Location:** In E. Central Europe. **Neighbors:** W. Germany on W, Czechoslovakia on S, Poland on E. **Topography:** E. Germany lies mostly on the North German plains, with lakes in N, Harz Mtns., Elbe Valley, and sandy soil of Bradenburg in center, and highlands in S. **Capital:** East Berlin. **Cities** (1978 est.): Berlin 1,111,398; Leipzig 565,178; Dresden 511,223.

Government: Head of state: Chmn. Erich Honecker; b. Aug. 25, 1912; in office: Oct. 29, 1976. **Head of government:** Prime Min. Willi Stoph; b. July 9, 1914; in office: Oct. 29, 1976. **Head of Communist Party:** Sec.-Gen. Erich Honecker; in office: May 3, 1971. **Local divisions:** 15 administrative districts. **Armed forces:** regulars 159,000; reserves 305,000.

Economy: Industries: Steel, chemicals, cement, textiles, shoes, oil products, machinery. **Chief crops:** Grains, potatoes, sugar beets. **Minerals:** Potash, lignite, uranium, cobalt, bismuth, arsenic, antimony. **Per capita arable land:** 0.7 acres. **Meat prod.** (1978): beef: 427,000 metric tons; pork: 1.17 mln. metric tons; lamb: 15,000 metric tons. **Fish catch** (1977): 209,400 metric tons. **Electricity prod.** (1978): 95.95 bln. kwh. **Crude steel prod.** (1979): 7.0 mln metric tons. **Labor force:** 10.9% agric.; 42.5% manuf.

Finance: Currency: Mark (Mar. 1980: 1.76 = $1 US). **Net material product** (1978): $113.4 bln. **Per capita income** (1976): $4,000. **Imports:** (1978): $14.57 bln.; partners (1977): USSR 35%, Czech. 8%, Pol. 8%, W. Ger. 7%. **Exports** (1978): $13.27 bln.; partners (1977): USSR 32%, Czech. 9%, W. Ger. 9%, Pol. 8%. **Tourists** (1977): 1,100,000.

Transport: Railway traffic (1978): 22.32 bln. passenger-km; 58.92 bln. net ton-km. **Motor vehicles:** in use (1977): 2.24 mln. passenger cars, 570,000 comm. vehicles; manuf. (1978): 170,400 passenger cars; 37,200 comm. vehicles. **Chief ports:** Rostock, Wismar, Stralsund.

Communications: Television sets: 5.18 mln. licensed (1976), 525,000 manuf. (1977). **Radios:** 6.17 mln. licensed (1976), 1.13 mln. manuf. (1977). **Telephones in use** (1978): 2,860,069. **Daily newspaper circ.** (1977): 8,317,000; 496 per 1,000 pop.

Health: Life expectancy at birth (1976): 68.82 male; 74.42 female. **Births** (per 1,000 pop. 1978): 13.9. **Deaths** (per 1,000 pop. 1978): 13.9. **Natural increase** (1978): 0.0%. **Hospital beds** (per 100,000 pop. 1977): 1,065. **Physicians** (per 100,000 pop. 1977): 190. **Infant mortality** (per 1,000 live births 1978): 13.2.

Education (1977): **Literacy:** 99%. **Pop. 5-19:** in school: 66%, teachers per 1,000: 43. **PQLI:** 94.

The German Democratic Republic was proclaimed in the Soviet sector of Berlin Oct. 7, 1949. It was proclaimed fully sovereign in 1954, but 400,000 Soviet troops remain on grounds of security and the 4-power Potsdam agreement.

Coincident with the entrance of W. Germany into the European Defense community in 1952, the East German government decreed a prohibited zone 3 miles deep along its 600-mile border with W. Germany and cut Berlin's telephone system in two. Berlin was further divided by erection of a fortified wall in 1961, but the exodus of refugees to the West continued, though on a smaller scale. By 1979, nearly 150,000 had fled to the West. Some 20,000 others held in East German jails were released upon West German payments totalling $250 million.

The government signed a 20-year friendship treaty with the USSR in 1964. The economy has been integrated with other communist nations.

E. Germany suffered severe economic problems until the mid-1960s. A "new economic system" was introduced, easing the former central planning controls and allowing factories to make profits provided they were reinvested in operations or redistributed to workers as bonuses. By the early 1970s, the economy was highly industrialized. In May 1972 the few remaining private firms were ordered sold to the government. The nation was credited with the highest standard of living among communist countries. But growth slowed in the late 1970s, due to shortages of natural resources and labor, and a huge debt to lenders in the West.

Travel restrictions between the 2 Germanies were eased in their first formal treaty, in 1972, and millions of West Germans have since visited the GDR.

The GDR gained admission to the UN in 1973. The U.S. and East Germany established diplomatic relations in 1974.

West Germany

Federal Republic of Germany

People: Population (1979 est.): 61,302,000. **Age distrib.** (%): 0–14: 20.3; 15–59: 58.4; 60+: 19.7. **Pop. density:** 639.88 per sq. mi. **Ethnic groups:** Germans, immigrant workers from Spain, Italy, Yugoslavia, Turkey. **Languages:** German. **Religions:** Protestant 49%, Roman Catholic 45%.

Geography: Area: 95,815 sq. mi., the size of Oregon. **Location:** In central Europe. **Neighbors:** Denmark on N, Netherlands, Belgium, Luxembourg, France on W, Switzerland, Austria on S, Czechoslovakia, E. Germany on E. **Topography:** West Germany is flat in N, hilly in center and W, and mountainous in Bavaria. Chief rivers are Elbe, Weser, Ems, Rhine, and Main, all flowing toward North Sea, and Danube, flowing toward Black Sea. **Capital:** Bonn. **Cities** (1978 est.): Berlin 1,926,826; Hamburg 1,680,340; Munich 1,313,939; Cologne 976,761; Essen 664,408; Frankfurt 632,565; Dortmund 617,590; Dusseldorf 607,560; Stuttgart 584,554.

Government: Head of state: Pres. Karl Carstens; b. Dec. 14, 1914; in office: July 1, 1979. **Head of government:** Chan. Helmut Schmidt; b. Dec. 23, 1918; in office: May 16, 1974. **Local divisions:** West Berlin and 10 laender (states) with substantial powers: Schleswig-Holstein, Hamburg, Lower Saxony, Bremen, North Rhine-Westphalia, Hessen, Rhineland-Palatinate, Baden-Wurttemberg, Bavaria, Saarland. **Armed forces:** regulars 495,000; reserves 1,250,000.

Economy: Industries: Steel, ships, oil products, autos, machinery, textiles, electrical and electronic equip., wine. **Chief crops:** Grains, potatoes, sugar beets, fruits, tobacco, nuts. **Minerals:** Coal, mercury, potash, lignite, iron, zinc, lead, copper, salt, oil. **Crude oil reserves** (1980): 480 mln. bbls. **Per capita arable land:** 0.3 acres. **Meat prod.** (1978): beef: 1.38 mln. metric tons; pork: 2.6 mln. metric tons; lamb: 23,000 metric tons. **Fish catch** (1977): 432,100 metric tons. **Electricity prod.** (1978): 353.41 bln. kwh. **Crude steel prod.** (1979): 46.0 mln. metric tons. **Labor force:** 8.4% agric.; 36.3% manuf.

Finance: Currency: Mark (Mar. 1980: 1.94 = $1 US). **Gross domestic product** (1979): $758.96 bln. **Per capita income** (1978): 9,278. **Imports** (1979): $159.71 bln.; partners (1978): Neth. 13%, Fr. 12%, It. 10%, Belg. 8%. **Exports** (1979): $171.89 bln.; partners (1978): Fr. 12%, Neth. 10%, Belg. 8%, It. 7%. **Tourists** (1977): 7,832,300; receipts $3.83 bln. **National budget** (1979): $101.9 bln. revenues; $116.13 bln. expenditures. **International reserves less gold** (Mar. 1980): $46.22 bln.

Gold: 95.18 mln. oz t. **Consumer prices** (change in 1979): 4.1%.

Transport: Railway traffic (1978): 36.79 bln. passenger-km; 57.32 bln. net ton-km. **Motor vehicles:** in use (1977): 20.02 mln. passenger cars, 1.39 mln. comm. vehicles; manuf. (1978): 3.9 mln. passenger cars; 300,000 comm. vehicles. **Civil aviation:** 17,568 mln. passenger-km (1978); 1,411 mln. freight ton-km (1978). **Chief ports:** Hamburg, Bremen, Lubeck.

Communications: Television sets: 19.23 mln. licensed (1975), 4.08 mln. manuf. (1977). **Radios:** 20.2 mln. licensed (1976) 5.59 mln. manuf. (1977). **Telephones in use** (1978): 22,931,683. **Daily newspaper circ.** (1977): 25,968,000; 423 per 1,000 pop.

Health: Life expectancy at birth (1977): 68.61 male; 75.21 female. **Births** (per 1,000 pop. 1978): 9.3. **Deaths** (per 1,000 pop. 1978): 11.8. **Natural increase** (1978): −.3%. **Hospital beds** (per 100,000 pop. 1977): 1,178. **Physicians** (per 100,000 pop. 1977): 204. **Infant mortality** (per 1,000 live births 1978): 15.5.

Education (1977): **Literacy:** 99%. **Pop. 5-19:** in school: 69%, teachers per 1,000: 35. **PQLI:** 94.

The Federal Republic of Germany was proclaimed May 23, 1949, in Bonn, after a constitution had been drawn up by a consultative assembly formed by representatives of the 11 laender (states) in the French, British, and American zones. Later reorganized into 9 units, the laender numbered 10 with the addition of the Saar, 1957. Berlin also was granted land (state) status, but the 1945 occupation agreements placed restrictions on it.

The occupying powers, the U.S., Britain, and France, restored the civil status, Sept. 21, 1949. The U. S. resumed diplomatic relations July 2, 1951. The powers lifted controls and the republic became fully independent May 5, 1955.

Dr. Konrad Adenauer, Christian Democrat, was made chancellor Sept. 15, 1949, re-elected 1953, 1957, 1961. Willy Brandt, heading a coalition of Social Democrats and Free Democrats, became chancellor Oct. 21, 1969.

In 1970 Brandt signed friendship treaties with the USSR and Poland. In 1971, the U.S., Britain, France, and the USSR signed an agreement on Western access to West Berlin. In 1972 the Bundestag approved the USSR and Polish treaties and East and West Germany signed their first formal treaty, implementing the agreement easing access to West Berlin. In 1973 a West Germany-Czechoslovakia pact normalized relations and nullified the 1938 "Munich Agreement." In 1974 Bonn agreed to extend $350 million yearly in long-term credits to East Germany until 1981. Other credits spurred trade with the East European countries.

In May 1974 Brandt resigned, saying he took full responsibility for "negligence" for allowing an East German spy to become a member of his staff. Helmut Schmidt, Brandt's finance minister, succeeded him.

West Germany has experienced tremendous economic growth since the 1950s. It is the world's 4th greatest economic power. The country leads Europe in provisions for worker participation in the management of industry.

About 240,000 U.S., 64,000 British, and 60,000 French troops are stationed in West Germany.

Helgoland, an island of 130 acres in the North Sea, was taken from Denmark by a British Naval Force in 1807 and later ceded to Germany to become a part of Schleswig-Holstein province in return for rights in East Africa. The heavily fortified island was surrendered to UK, May 23, 1945, demilitarized in 1947, and returned to W. Germany, Mar 1, 1952. It is a free port.

Ghana

Republic of Ghana

People: Population (1979 est.): 11,742,000. **Age distrib.** (%): 0–14: 46.9; 15-59: 47.7; 60+: 5.3. **Pop. density:** 119.11 per sq. mi. **Urban** (1974): 31.4%. **Ethnic groups:** Akan 44%, Moshi-Dagomba 16%, Ewe 13%, Ga 8%, others. **Languages:** English (official), others. **Religions:** Protestant 29%, Roman Catholic 14%, Moslem 12%, others.

Geography: Area: 92,100 sq. mi., slightly smaller than Oregon. **Location:** On southern coast of W. Africa. **Neighbors:** Ivory Coast on W, Upper Volta on N, Togo on E. **Topography:** Most of Ghana consists of low fertile plains and scrubland, cut by rivers and by the artificial Lake Volta. **Capital:** Accra. **Cities** (1970 cen.): Accra 564,194; Kumasi 260,286.

Government: Head of government: Pres. Hilla Limmann; b. 1934; in office: Sept. 24, 1979. **Local divisions:** 9 regions. **Armed forces:** regulars 20,000; para-military 3,000.

Economy: Industries: Aluminum, light industry. **Chief crops:** Cocoa (largest producer), coffee, palm products, corn, rice, cassava, plantain, peanuts, yams, tobacco. **Minerals:** Gold, manganese, industrial diamonds, bauxite. **Crude oil reserves:** (1980): 7 mln. bbls. **Other resources:** Timber, rare woods, rubber. **Per capita arable land:** 0.2 acres. **Meat prod.** (1978): beef: 12,000 metric tons; pork: 7,000 metric tons; lamb: 10,000 metric tons. **Fish catch** (1977): 383,000 metric tons. **Electricity prod.** (1977): 4.30 bln. kwh. **Labor force:** 60% agric.

Finance: Currency: Cedi (Mar. 1980: 1 = $.36 US). **Gross domestic product** (1976): $5.68 bln. **Per capita income** (1976): $514. **Imports** (1977): $1.02 bln.; partners (1975): U.S. 16%, UK 15%, W. Ger. 11%, Nigeria 7%. **Exports** (1977): $962 mln.; partners (1975): UK 15%, U.S. 11%, Neth. 10%, Swit. 8%. **Tourists** (1977): 58,900; receipts $6 mln. **National budget** (1976): $773 mln. revenues; $1.30 bln. expenditures. **International reserves less gold** (Jan. 1980): $266.6 mln. **Gold:** 237,000 oz t. **Consumer prices** (change in 1979): 54.4%.

Transport: Railway traffic (1972): 431 mln. passenger-km; 305 mln. net ton-km. **Motor vehicles:** in use (1977): 72,400 passenger cars, 49,300 comm. vehicles. **Civil aviation:** 234 mln. passenger-km (1977); 3.6 mln. freight ton-km (1977). **Chief ports:** Tema, Sekondi-Takoradi.

Communications: Television sets: 35,000 in use (1976), 2,000 manuf. (1975). **Radios:** 1.08 mln. in use (1976), 90,000 manuf. (1975). **Telephones in use** (1978): 66,405. **Daily newspaper circ.** (1976): 435,000; 42 per 1,000 pop.

Health: Life expectancy at birth (1975): 41.9 male; 45.1 female. **Births** (per 1,000 pop. 1975): 48.6. **Deaths** (per 1,000 pop. 1975): 19.1. **Natural increase** (1975): 3.0%. **Hospital beds** (per 100,000 pop. 1977): 146. **Physicians** (per 100,000 pop. 1977): 10. **Infant mortality** (per 1,000 live births 1975): 156.

Education (1977): **Literacy:** 30%. **Pop. 5–19:** in school: 45%, teachers per 1,000: 18. **PQLI:** 41.

Named for an African empire along the Niger River, 400-1240 AD, Ghana was ruled by Britain for 113 years as the Gold Coast. The UN in 1956 approved merger with the British Togoland trust territory. Independence came March 6, 1957. Republic status within the Commonwealth was attained in 1960.

Pres. Kwame Nkrumah built hospitals and schools, promoted development projects like the Volta R. hydroelectric and aluminum plants, but ran the country into debt, jailed opponents, and was accused of corruption. A 1964 referendum gave Nkrumah dictatorial powers and set up a one-party socialist state.

Nkrumah was overthrown in 1966 by a police-army coup, which expelled Chinese and East German teachers and technicians. Elections were held in 1969, but 3 further coups occurred in 1972, 1978, and 1979. The June 1979 coup, led by Flight Lieut. Jerry Rawlings, returned the government to civilian rule, Sept. The stagnant economy has further deteriorated.

Greece

Hellenic Republic

People: Population (1979 est.): 9,444,000. **Age distrib.** (%): 0–14: 23.7; 15-59: 58.9; 60+: 17.5. **Pop. density:** 185.17 per sq. mi. **Urban** (1971): 64.8%. **Ethnic groups:** Greeks 98.5%, Turks 0.9%, Pomaks 0.3%, Armenians 0.2%. **Languages:** Greek, others. **Religions:** Greek Orthodox 97%, Moslem 1.2%.

Geography: Area: 50,547 sq. mi., the size of New York State. **Location:** Occupies southern end of Balkan Peninsula in SE Europe. **Neighbors:** Albania, Yugoslavia, Bulgaria on N, Turkey on E. **Topography:** About 75% of Greece is non-arable, with mountains in all areas. Pindus Mts. run through the country N to S. The heavily indented coastline is 9,385 mi. long. Of over 2,000 islands, only 169 are inhabited, among them Crete, Rhodes, Milos, Kerkira (Corfu), Chios, Lesbos, Samos, Euboea, Delos, Mykonos. **Capital:** Athens. **Cities** (1971 cen.): Athens 867,023; Thessaloniki 345,799; Piraeus 187,362.

Government: Head of state: Pres. Constantine Karamanlis; b. Feb. 23, 1907; in office: May 15, 1980. **Head of government:** Prime Min. George Rallis; b. Dec. 26, 1918; in office: May 10, 1980. **Local divisions:** 51 prefectures. **Armed forces:** regulars 184,600; reserves 290,000.

Economy: Industries: Textiles, chemicals, aluminum, wine, food processng, cement. **Chief crops:** Grains, corn, rice, cotton, tobacco, olives, citrus fruits, raisins, figs. **Minerals:** Bauxite, iron, emery, lignite, oil, silver, manganese, chromite, nickel, baryte. **Crude oil reserves** (1980): 150 mln. bbls. **Per capita arable**

land: 0.8 acres. **Meat prod.** (1978): beef: 104,000 metric tons; pork: 118,000 metric tons; lamb: 119,000 metric tons. **Fish catch** (1977): 105,600 metric tons. **Electricity prod.** (1978): 19.46 bln. kwh. **Crude steel prod.** (1979): 1 mln. metric tons. **Labor force:** 34% agric.; 26% manuf.

Finance: Currency: Drachma (Mar. 1980: 41.89 = $1 US). **Gross domestic product** (1978): $31.59 bln. **Per capita income** (1978): $3,209. **Imports** (1979): $9.70 bln.; partners (1978): W. Ger. 16%, Jap. 13%, It. 10%, Fr. 6%. **Exports** (1979): $3.88 bln.; partners (1978): W. Ger. 21%, It. 11%, Fr. 7%, Saudi Ar. 6%. **Tourists** (1977): 3,961,000; receipts $980 mln. **National budget** (1978): $6.60 bln. revenues; $7.78 bln. expenditures. **International reserves less gold** (Dec. 1979): $951 mln. **Gold:** 3.81 mln. oz t. **Consumer prices** (change in 1979): 19.0%.

Transport: Railway traffic (1978): 1.57 bln. passenger-km; 854.4 mln. net ton-km. **Motor vehicles:** in use (1977): 618,800 passenger cars, 276,100 comm. vehicles. **Civil aviation:** 4,356 mln. passenger-km (1977); 58 mln. freight ton-km (1977). **Chief ports:** Piraeus, Thessaloniki, Patrai.

Communications: Television sets: 1.17 mln. in use (1976), 187,000 manuf. (1976). **Radios:** 2.8 mln. in use (1976). **Telephones in use** (1978): 2,319,797. **Daily newspaper circ.** (1970): 705,000; 80 per 1,000 pop.

Health: Life expectancy at birth (1970): 70.13 male; 73.64 female. **Births** (per 1,000 pop. 1977): 15.4. **Deaths** (per 1,000 pop. 1977): 8.9. **Natural increase** (1977): .7%. **Hospital beds** (per 100,000 pop. 1977): 638. **Physicians** (per 100,000 pop. 1977): 221. **Infant mortality** (per 1,000 live births 1977): 20.3.

Education (1977): **Literacy:** 84%. **Pop. 5–19:** in school: 69%, teachers per 1,000: 25. **PQLI:** 90.

The achievements of ancient Greece in art, architecture, science, mathematics, philosophy, drama, literature, and democracy became legacies for succeeding ages. Greece reached the height of its glory and power, particularly in the Athenian city-state, in the 5th century BC.

Greece fell under Roman rule in the 2d and 1st centuries BC. In the 4th century AD it became part of the Byzantine Empire and, after the fall of Constantinople to the Turks in 1453, part of the Ottoman Empire.

Greece won its war of independence from Turkey 1821-1829, and became a kingdom. A republic was established 1925; the monarchy was restored, 1935, and George II, King of the Hellenes, resumed the throne. In Oct., 1940, Greece rejected an ultimatum from Italy. Nazi support resulted in its defeat and occupation by Germans, Italians, and Bulgarians. By the end of 1944 the invaders withdrew. Communist resistance forces were defeated by Royalist and British troops. A plebiscite recalled King George II. He died Apr. 1, 1947, was succeeded by his brother, Paul I.

Communists waged guerrilla war 1947-49 against the government but were defeated with the aid of the U.S. (acting under the Truman Doctrine).

A period of reconstruction and rapid development followed, mainly with conservative governments under Premier Constantine Karamanlis. The Center Union led by George Papandreou won elections in 1963 and 1964. King Constantine, who acceded in 1964, forced Papandreou to resign. A period of political maneuvers ended in the military takeover of April 21, 1967, by Col. George Papadopoulos. King Constantine tried to reverse the consolidation of the harsh dictatorship Dec. 13, 1967, but failed and fled to Italy. Papadopoulos was ousted Nov. 25, 1973, in a coup led by rightist Brig. Demetrius Ioannides.

Greek army officers serving in the National Guard of Cyprus staged a coup on the island July 15, 1974. Turkey invaded Cyprus a week later, precipitating the collapse of the Greek junta, which was implicated in the Cyprus coup.

The military turned the government over to Karamanlis, who named a civilian cabinet, freed political prisoners, and sought to solve the Cyprus crisis. In Nov. 1974 elections his party won a large parliamentary majority, reduced by socialist gains in 1977. A Dec. 1974 referendum resulted in the proclamation of a republic.

The new government promoted educational and agricultural reforms, and sought to advance from associate to full membership in the EC.

Stalled talks on Greece's military reintegration into NATO led to a deterioration in relations with the U.S. A six-year dispute concerning civilian air traffic over the Aegean Sea was ended by Turkey, Feb. 1980. Stringent government economic measures incited labor unrest, but did not halt inflation.

Grenada

State of Grenada

People: Population (1979 est.): 105,000. **Pop. density:** 751.88 per sq. mi. **Ethnic groups:** Negroes over 52%, whites 1%, mulattoes 43% (including some E. Indians), Carib. Indians. **Languages:** English, French-African patois. **Religions:** Roman Catholics, Anglicans.

Geography: Area: 133 sq. mi., twice the size of Washington, D.C. **Location:** Southernmost of West Indies, 90 mi. N. of Venezuela. **Topography:** Main island is mountainous; country includes Carriacon and Petit Martinique islands. **Capital:** St. George's. **Cities** (1975 est.): St. George's 30,000.

Government: Head of state: Queen Elizabeth II, represented by Gov.-Gen. Paul Scoon, b. July 4, 1935; in office: Sept. 30, 1978. **Head of government:** Prime Min. Maurice Bishop, b. May 29, 1944; in office: Mar. 13, 1979. **Local divisions:** 6 parishes and one dependency.

Economy: Industries: Rum. **Chief crops:** Nutmegs, bananas, cocoa, sugar, mace. **Per capita arable land:** 0.05 acres. **Electricity prod.** (1977): 28.00 mln. kwh. **Labor force:** 40% agric.

Finance: Currency: East Caribbean dollar (Mar. 1980: 2.70 = $1 US). **Gross domestic product** (1974 est.): $44 mln. **Per capita income** (1976): $340. **Imports** (1979): $45 mln.; partners (1973): UK 27%, Trin./Tob. 20%, U.S. 9%, Can. 8%. **Exports** (1979): $22 mln.; partners (1973): UK 33%, W. Ger. 19%, Neth. 14%, U.S. 8%. **Tourists** (1977): 28,500; receipts (1976): $8 mln. **National budget** (1977): $12.46 mln. revenues; $12.88 mln. expenditures. **International reserves less gold** (Nov. 1979): $16.54 mln.

Transport: Motor vehicles: in use (1971): 3,800 passenger cars, 100 comm. vehicles. **Chief ports:** Saint George's.

Communications: Radios: 22,000 in use (1976). **Telephones in use** (1978): 5,217. **Daily newspaper circ.** (1970): 2,600.

Health: Life expectancy at birth (1961): 60.14 male; 65.60 female. **Births** (per 1,000 pop. 1975): 27.4. **Deaths** (per 1,000 pop. 1975): 5.9. **Natural increase** (1975): 2.2%. **Infant mortality** (per 1,000 live births 1975): 23.5. **PQLI:** 78.

Columbus sighted the island 1498. First European settlers were French, 1650. The island was held alternately by France and England until final British occupation, 1784. Grenada became fully independent Feb. 7, 1974 during a general strike. It is the smallest independent nation in the Western Hemisphere.

Guatemala

Republic of Guatemala

People: Population (1979 est.): 6,849,000. **Age distrib.** (%): 0–14: 45.1; 15–59: 50.6; 60+: 4.4. **Pop. density:** 157.46 per sq. mi. **Urban** (1975): 35.6%. **Ethnic groups:** Indians 54%, Mestizos 42%, whites 4%. **Languages:** Spanish, 18 Maya-Quiche dialects. **Religions:** Roman Catholics over 90%; Mayan religion practiced.

Geography: Area: 42,042 sq. mi., the size of Tennessee. **Location:** In Central America. **Neighbors:** Mexico N, W; El Salvador on S, Honduras, Belize on E. **Topography:** The central highland and mountain areas are bordered by the narrow Pacific coast and the lowlands and fertile river valleys on the Caribbean. There are numerous volcanoes in S, more than half a dozen over 11,000 ft. **Capital:** Guatemala City. **Cities** (1973 cen.): Guatemala City 700,504.

Government: Head of state: Pres. Romeo Lucas Garcia; b. July 4, 1924; in office: July 1, 1978. **Local divisions:** Guatemala City and 22 departments. **Armed forces:** regulars 17,960; paramilitary 3,000.

Economy: Industries: Shoes, textiles. **Chief crops:** Coffee (one third of exports), sugar, bananas, cotton. **Minerals:** Zinc, lead, antimony, tungsten, cadmium, silver, copper, nickel, gas. **Crude oil reserves** (1980): 16 mln. bbls. **Other resources:** Rare woods, fish, chicle. **Per capita arable land:** 0.5 acres. **Meat prod.** (1978): beef: 78,000 metric tons; pork: 12,000 metric tons. **Electricity prod.** (1977): 1.29 bln. kwh. **Labor force:** 57% agric.; 14% manuf.

Finance: Currency: Quetzal (Mar. 1980: 1.00 = $1 US). **Gross domestic product** (1977): $5.59 bln. **Per capita income** (1977): $749. **Imports** (1977): $1.05 bln.; partners: U.S. 39%, Jap. 11%, W. Ger. 7%, Venez. 6%. **Exports** (1977): $1.18 bln.; partners: U.S. 32%, W. Ger. 13%, El Salv. 9%, Jap. 8%. **Tourists** (1977): 444,800; receipts: $105 mln. **National budget**

(1978): $735 mln. revenues; $728 mln. expenditures. **International reserves less gold** (Mar. 1980): $670.6 mln. **Gold:** 522,000 oz t. **Consumer prices** (change in 1979): 11.5%.

Transport: Railway traffic (1976): 117 mln. net ton-km. **Motor vehicles:** in use (1976): 82,700 passenger cars, 50,100 comm. vehicles. **Civil aviation:** 153 mln. passenger-km (1978); 7 mln. freight ton-km (1978). **Chief ports:** Puerto Barrios, San Jose.

Communications: Television sets: 120,000 in use (1976). **Radios:** 265,000 in use (1976). **Telephones in use** (1978): 70,614. **Daily newspaper circ.** (1976): 214,000.

Health: Life expectancy at birth (1965): 48.29 male; 49.74 female. **Births** (per 1,000 pop. 1976): 42.6. **Deaths** (per 1,000 pop. 1976): 13.1. **Natural increase** (1976): 3.0% **Hospital beds** (per 100,000 pop. 1977): 187. **Physicians** (per 100,000 pop. 1977): 40. **Infant mortality** (per 1,000 live births 1976): 76.5.

Education (1977): **Literacy:** 47%. **Pop. 5-19:** in school: 31%, teachers per 1,000: 11. **PQLI:** 59.

The old Mayan Indian empire flourished in what is today Guatemala for over 1,000 years before the Spanish.

Guatemala was a Spanish colony 1524-1821; briefly a part of Mexico and then of the U.S. of Central America, the republic was established in 1839.

Since 1945 when a liberal government was elected to replace the long-term dictatorship of Jorge Ubico, the country has seen a swing toward socialism, an armed revolt, renewed attempts at social reform and a military coup. Assassinations and political violence from left and right plagued the country. The Guerrilla Army of the Poor, an insurgent group founded 1975, has stepped up their military offensive by attacking army posts and has succeeded in incorporating segments of the large Indian population in its struggle against the government.

Guatemala has a long-standing claim to Belize.

Guinea

People's Revolutionary Republic of Guinea

People: Population (1979 est.): 5,275,000. **Pop. density:** 50.14 per sq. mi. **Ethnic groups:** Fula 40%, Mandingo 25%, Soussous 10%, 15 other tribes. **Languages:** French (official), tribal languages. **Religions:** Moslems 70%, Christians 1%, others.

Geography: Area: 94,925 sq. mi., slightly smaller than Oregon. **Location:** On Atlantic coast of W. Africa. **Neighbors:** Guinea-Bissau, Senegal, Mali on N, Ivory Coast on E, Liberia on S. **Topography:** A narrow coastal belt leads to the mountainous middle region, the source of the Gambia, Senegal, and Niger rivers. Upper Guinea, farther inland, is a cooler upland. The SE is forested. **Capital:** Conakry. **Cities** (1972 est.): Conakry (met.) 525,671.

Government: Head of state: Pres. Ahmed Sekou Toure; b. Jan. 9, 1922; in office: Oct. 2, 1958. **Head of government:** Prime Min. Lansana Beavogui; b. 1923; in office: Apr. 26, 1972. **Local divisions:** 33 districts. **Armed forces:** regulars 8,650; para-military 8,000.

Economy: Chief crops: Bananas, pineapples, rice, corn, palm nuts, coffee, honey. **Minerals:** Bauxite, iron, diamonds. **Per capita arable land:** 2.2 acres. **Meat prod.** (1978): beef 11,000 metric tons. **Electricity prod.** (1977) 500.00 mln. kwh. **Labor force:** 84% agric.

Finance: Currency: Syli (Mar. 1979: 19.2 = $1 US). **Gross domestic product** (1976 est.): $750 mln. **Per capita income** (1976): $150. **Imports** (1975): $180 mln.; partners (1977): Fr. 20% USSR 11%, U.S. 6% It. 6%. **Exports** (1975): $160 mln.; partners (1977): U.S. 18%, Fr. 13%, W. Ger. 12%, USSR 12%.

Transport: Motor vehicles: in use (1972): 10,200 passenger cars, 10,800 comm. vehicles. **Chief ports:** Conakry.

Communications: Radios: 120,000 in use (1976). **Daily newspaper circ.** (1976): 10,000; 2 per 1,000 pop.

Health: Life expectancy at birth (1975): 39.4 male; 42.6 female. **Births** (per 1,000 pop. 1975): 46.6. **Deaths** (per 1,000 pop. 1975): 22.9. **Natural increase** (1975): 2.4%. **Hospital beds** (per 100,000 pop. 1977): 158. **Physicians** (per 100,000 pop. 1977): 6. **Infant mortality** (per 1,000 live births 1975): 216.

Education (1977): **Literacy:** 15%. **Pop. 5-19:** in school: 18%, teachers per 1,000: 8. **PQLI:** 20.

Part of the ancient West African empires, Guinea fell under French control 1849-98. Under Sekou Toure, it opted for full independence in 1958, and France withdrew all aid.

Toure turned to communist nations for support, and set up a militant one-party state. France and Guinea restored ties in 1975, after a 10-year break. Western firms, as well as the Soviet government, have invested in Guinea's vast bauxite mines.

According to reports, thousands of opponents were jailed in the 1970s, in the aftermath of an unsuccessful Portuguese invasion. Many were tortured and killed.

Guinea-Bissau

Republic of Guinea-Bissau

People: Population (1979 est.): 638,000. **Pop. density:** 39.43 per sq. mi. **Ethnic groups:** Balanta 30%, Fula 20%, Mandyako 14%, other tribes. **Languages:** Portuguese (official), Crioulo, tribal languages. **Religions:** Moslems 30%, Christians 1%, others.

Geography: Area: 13,948 sq. mi. **Location:** On Atlantic coast of W. Africa. **Neighbors:** Senegal on N, Guinea on E, S. **Topography:** A swampy coastal plain covers most of the country; to the east is a low savanna region. **Capital:** Bissau. **Cities** (1971 est.): Bissau 65,000.

Government: Head of state: Pres. Luis de Almeida Cabral; b. 1931; in office: July 22, 1973. **Head of government:** Principal Comm. Joao Bernardo Vieira; in office: Sept. 28, 1978. **Local divisions:** 8 regions. **Armed forces:** regulars 6,100; para-military 2,000.

Economy: Chief crops: Peanuts, palm oil. **Minerals:** Bauxite, oil. **Per capita arable land:** 1.1 acres. **Electricity prod.** (1977): 24.00 mln. kwh. **Labor force:** 86% agric.

Finance: Currency: Peso (Mar. 1979: 34.19 = $1 US). **Gross domestic product** (1976 est.): $200 mln. **Per capita income** (1976): $330. **Imports** (1977): $35.9 mln.; partners: Port. 40%, Swed. 8%, USSR 8%, Fr. 7%. **Exports** (1977): $12.4 mln.; partners: Port. 59%, Egypt 18% Sen. 11%.

Communications: Radios: 11,000 licensed (1976). **Daily newspaper circ.** (1976): 6,000; 11 per 1,000 pop.

Health: Life expectancy at birth (1975): 37.0 male; 40.1 female. **Births** (per 1,000 pop. 1975): 40.1. **Deaths** (per 1,000 pop. 1975): 25.1. **Natural increase** (1975): 1.5%. **Infant mortality** (per 1,000 live births 1969): 47.1. **PQLI:** 14.

Portuguese mariners explored the area in the mid-15th century; the slave trade flourished in the 17th and 18th centuries, and colonization began in the 19th.

Beginning in the 1960s, an independence movement waged a guerrilla war and formed a government in the interior that achieved international support. Full independence came Sept. 10, 1974, after the Portuguese regime was overthrown.

Union with Cape Verde was foreseen in a number of cooperation accords signed in 1976.

Guyana

Cooperative Republic of Guyana

People: Population (1979 est.): 832,000. **Age distrib.** (%): 0–14: 43.7; 5–59: 50.7; 60+: 5.6. **Pop. density:** 9.88 per sq. mi. **Urban** (1971): 29.6%. **Ethnic groups:** East Indians 55%, Negroes 36%, others (Amerindians, Chinese, Europeans) 10%. **Languages:** English (official), Hindi, Portuguese, Chinese, Negro patois. **Religions:** Christians 57%, Hindus 33%, Moslems 9%, others.

Geography: Area: 83,000 sq. mi., the size of Idaho. **Location:** On N coast of S. America. **Neighbors:** Venezuela on W, Brazil on S, Suriname on E. **Topography:** Dense tropical forests cover much of the land, although a flat coastal area up to 40 mi. wide, where 90% of the population lives, provides rich alluvial soil for agriculture. A grassy savanna divides the 2 zones. **Capital:** Georgetown. **Cities** (1978 est.): Georgetown 72,049.

Government: Head of state: Pres. Arthur Chung; b. Jan. 10, 1918; in office: Mar. 17, 1970. **Head of government:** Prime Min. Linden Forbes Burnham; b. Feb. 20, 1923; in office: Dec. 14, 1964. **Local divisions:** 6 regions. **Armed forces:** regulars 5,000; para-military 10,000.

Economy: Industries: Cigarettes, rum, clothing, furniture, drugs. **Chief crops:** Sugar, rice, coconuts, coffee, cocoa, citrus and other fruits. **Minerals:** Bauxite (5th largest producer), gold, diamonds. **Other resources:** Timber, shrimp. **Per capita arable land:** 1.1 acres. **Fish catch** (1977): 21,800 metric tons. **Electricity prod.** (1977): 416.00 mln. kwh. **Labor force:** 30% agric.

Finance: Currency: Dollar (Mar. 1980: 2.55 = $1 US). **Gross domestic product** (1977): $437 mln. **Per capita in-**

come (1976): $499. **Imports** (1978): $278 mln.; partners (1977): U.S. 27%, Trin-Tob. 23%, UK 21%. **Exports** (1978): $296 mln.; partners (1977): UK 33%, U.S. 18%, Trin-Tob. 6%. **Tourist receipts** (1977): $3 mln. **National budget** (1973): $74 mln. revenues; $141 mln. expenditures. **International reserves less gold** (Nov. 1979): $14.57 mln. **Consumer prices** (change in 1978): 15.3%.

Transport: Railway traffic (1974): 6 mln. passenger-km. **Motor vehicles:** in use (1977): 28,400 passenger cars, 14,700 comm. vehicles. **Chief ports:** Georgetown.

Communications: Radios: 275,000 in use (1976). **Telephones in use** (1978): 27,064. **Daily newspaper circ.** (1976): 50,000; 63 per 1,000 pop.

Health: Life expectancy at birth (1961): 59.03 male; 63.01 female. **Births** (per 1,000 pop. 1978): 28.3. **Deaths** (per 1,000 pop. 1978): 7.3. **Natural increase** (1978): 2.1% **Hospital beds** (per 100,000 pop. 1977): 485. **Physicians** (per 100,000 pop. 1977): 25. **Infant mortality** (per 1,000 live births 1972): 50.5.

Education (1977): **Literacy:** 85%. **Pop. 5-19:** in school: 62%, teachers per 1,000: 24. **PQLI:** 84.

Guyana became a Dutch possession in the 17th century, but sovereignty passed to Britain in 1815. Indentured servants from India soon outnumbered African slaves. Ethnic tension has affected political life.

Guyana became independent May 26, 1966. A Venezuelan claim to the western half of Guyana was suspended in 1970 for 12 years. The Suriname border is also disputed. The government has nationalized most of the economy in recent years.

The Port Kaituma ambush of U.S. Rep. Leo J. Ryan and others investigating mistreatment of American followers of the Rev. Jim Jones' People's Temple cult, triggered a mass suicide-execution of 911 cultists in the Guyana jungle, Nov. 18, 1979.

Haiti

Republic of Haiti

People: Population (1979 est.): 5,670,000. **Age distrib.** (%): 4–14: 41.2; 15–59: 52.9; 60+: 5.9. **Pop. density:** 450.81 per sq. mi. **Urban** (1978): 24.3%. **Ethnic groups:** Negroes 95%, mulattoes 5%. **Languages:** French (official), Creole. **Religions:** Roman Catholics 80%, Protestants 10%; Voodoo widely practiced.

Geography: Area: 10,714 sq. mi., the size of Maryland. **Location:** In West Indies, occupies western third of I. of Hispaniola. **Neighbors:** Dominican Republic on E, Cuba on W. **Topography:** About two-thirds of Haiti is mountainous. Much of the rest is semiarid. Coastal areas are warm and moist. **Capital:** Port-au-Prince. **Cities** (1978 est.): Port-au-Prince 745,700.

Government: Head of state: Pres. Jean-Claude Duvalier; b. July 3, 1951; in office: Apr. 22, 1971. **Local divisions:** 9 departments. **Armed forces:** regulars 6,550; para-military 14,900.

Economy: Industries: Rum, molasses, tourism. **Chief crops:** Coffee, sisal, cotton, sugar, bananas, cocoa, tobacco, rice. **Minerals:** Bauxite, copper, gold, silver, cement. **Other resources:** Timber. **Per capita arable land:** 0.3 acres. **Meat prod.** (1978): beef: 18,000 metric tons; pork: 25,000 metric tons; lamb: 5,000 metric tons. **Electricity prod.** (1977): 215 mln. kwh. **Labor force:** 77% agric.

Finance: Currency: Gourde (Mar. 1980: 5.00 = $1 US). **Gross domestic product** (1978): $1.34 bln. **Per capita income** (1976): $248. **Imports** (1977): $225 mln.; partners: U.S. 56%, Neth. Ant. 7%, Jap. 6%. Can. 6%. **Exports** (1978): $152 mln.; partners (1977): U.S. 61%, Fr. 10%, It. 6%, Belg. 5%. **Tourists** (1977): 96,000; receipts $37 mln. **National budget** (1978): $269 mln. revenues; $195 mln. expenditures. **International reserves less gold** (Feb. 1980): $46.2 mln. **Gold:** 18,000 oz t. **Consumer prices** (change in 1979): 13.0%.

Transport: Motor vehicles: in use (1976): 18,700 passenger cars, 2,400 comm. vehicles. **Chief ports:** Port-au-Prince, Les Cayes.

Communications: Television sets: 14,000 in use (1976). **Radios:** 95,000 in use (1976). **Telephones in use** (1977): 17,800. **Daily newspaper circ.** (1976): 92,000; 20 per 1,000 pop.

Health: Life expectancy at birth (1975): 47.1 male; 50.0 female. **Births** (per 1,000 pop. 1975): 42.7. **Deaths** (per 1,000 pop. 1975): 17.4. **Natural increase** (1975): 2.5%. **Hospital beds** (per 100,000 pop. 1977): 72. **Physicians** (per 100,000 pop. 1977): 7.

Education (1977): **Literacy:** 22%. **Pop. 5-19:** in school: 32%, teachers per 1,000: 9. **PQLI:** 37.

Haiti, visited by Columbus, 1492, and a French colony from 1677, attained its independence, 1804, following the rebellion led by former slave Toussaint L'Ouverture. Following a period of political violence, the U.S. occupied the country 1915-34.

Dr. Francois Duvalier was voted president in 1957; in 1964 he was named president for life. Upon his death in 1971, he was succeeded by his son, Jean-Claude. Under the latter's less violent rule, foreign investment and tourism revived. But drought in 1975-77 brought famine, aggravated by erosion caused by the destruction of most trees for charcoal.

Honduras

Republic of Honduras

People: Population (1979 est.): 3,645,000. **Age distrib.** (%): 0–14: 48.1; 15–59: 47.5; 60+: 4.5. **Pop. density:** 79.49 per sq. mi. **Urban** (1974): 31.4%. **Ethnic groups:** Mestizo 90%, Caucasian, Negroes, Indians. **Languages:** Spanish, English (on N coast). **Religions:** Roman Catholics

Geography: Area: 43,277 sq. mi., slightly larger than Tennessee. **Location:** In Central America. **Neighbors:** Guatemala on W, El Salvador, Nicaragua on S. **Topography:** The Caribbean coast is 500 mi. long. Pacific coast, on Gulf of Fonseca, is 40 mi. long. Honduras is mountainous, with wide fertile valleys and rich forests. **Capital:** Tegucigalpa. **Cities** (1974 cen.) Tegucigalpa 273,894; San Pedro Sula 150,991.

Government: President of military junta: Gen. Policarpo Paz Garcia; in office: Aug. 8, 1978. **Local divisions:** 18 departments. **Armed forces:** regulars 11,300; para-military 3,000.

Economy: Industries: Clothing, textiles, cement, chemicals. **Chief crops:** Bananas (chief export), coffee, cotton, sugar, timber, tobacco. **Minerals:** Gold, silver, copper, lead, zinc, iron, antimony, coal. **Other resources:** Timber. **Per capita arable land:** 0.5 acres. **Meat prod.** (1978): beef: 51,000 metric tons; pork: 10,000 metric tons. **Electricity prod.** (1977): 701.00 mln. kwh. **Labor force:** 67% agric.

Finance: Currency: Lempira (Mar. 1980): 2.00 = $1 US). **Gross domestic product** (1978): $1.82 bln. **Per capita income** (1977): $403. **Imports** (1978): $700 mln.; partners (1977): U.S. 43%, Jap. 11%, Guat. 6%, Venez. 5%. **Exports** (1978): $597 mln.; partners (1977): U.S. 49%, W. Ger. 18%, Jap. 6%, Neth. 5%. **Tourist receipts** (1977): $14 mln. **National budget** (1978): $275 mln. revenues; $290 mln. expenditures. **International reserves less gold** (Jan. 1980): $207.47 mln. **Gold:** (Feb. 1980): 14,000 oz t. **Consumer prices** (change in 1978): 6.2%.

Transport: Motor vehicles: in use (1976) 20,500 passenger cars, 30,200 comm. vehicles. **Civil aviation:** 256 mln. passenger-km (1976); 5 mln. freight ton-km (1976). **Chief ports:** Puerto Cortes, La Ceiba.

Communications: Television sets: 48,000 in use (1976). **Radios:** 161,000 in use (1976). **Telephones in use** (1977): 19,227. **Daily newspaper circ.** (1976): 140,000.

Health: Life expectancy at birth (1975): 52.4 male; 55.9 female. **Births** (per 1,000 pop. 1975): 48.6. **Deaths** (per 1,000 pop. 1975): 13.7. **Natural increase** (1975): 3.5%. **Hospital beds** (per 100,000 pop. 1977): 32. **Physicians** (per 100,000 pop. 1977): 137. **Infant mortality** (per 1,000 live births 1975): 31.4.

Education (1977): **Literacy:** 57%. **Pop. 5-19:** in school: 42%, teachers per 1,000: 14. **PQLI:** 57.

Mayan civilization flourished in Honduras in the 1st millenium AD. Columbus arrived in 1502. Honduras became independent after freeing itself from Spain, 1821 and from the Fed. of Central America, 1838.

Gen. Oswaldo Lopez Arellano, president for most of the period 1963-75 by virtue of 1 election and 2 coups, was ousted by the Army in 1975 over charges of pervasive bribery by United Brands Co. of the U.S.

A constitutional assembly was elected, 1980; direct elections for president were scheduled for early 1981, with only civilian candidates expected to run. The government has resumed land distribution, raised minimum wages, and started a literacy campaign.

Hungary

Hungarian People's Republic

People: Population (1979 est.): 10,710,000. **Age distrib.** (%): 0–14: 21.0; 15–59: 61.5; 60+: 17.5. **Pop. density:** 297.61

per sq. mi. **Urban** (1977): 51.8%. **Ethnic groups:** Magyar 98%, German 0.5%, Slovak 0.3%, Gypsy 0.3%, Croatian 0.3%. **Languages:** Hungarian (Magyar). **Religions:** Roman Catholics 55%, Calvinist 20%, Lutherans 5%, Jews 1%.

Geography: Area: 35,919 sq. mi., slightly smaller than Indiana. **Location:** In East Central Europe. **Neighbors:** Czechoslovakia on N, Austria on W, Yugoslavia on S, Romania, USSR on E. **Topography:** The Danube R. forms the Czech border in the NW, then swings S to bisect the country. The eastern half of Hungary is mainly a great fertile plain, the Alfold; the W and N are hilly. **Capital:** Budapest. **Cities** (1978 est.): Budapest 2,085,615; Miskolc 205,610; Debrecen 193,958.

Government: Head of state: Pres. Pal Losonczi; b. Sept. 18, 1919; in office: Apr. 14, 1967. **Head of government:** Chmn. Gyorgy Lazar; b. Sept. 15, 1924; in office: May 15, 1975. **Head of Communist Party:** Janos Kadar; b. May 26, 1912; in office: Oct. 25, 1956. **Local divisions:** 19 counties, 5 cities with county status. **Armed forces:** regulars 104,000; reserves 143,000.

Economy: Industries: Iron and steel, machinery, chemicals, vehicles, communications equip., milling, distilling. **Chief crops:** Grains, vegetables, fruits, grapes. **Minerals:** Bauxite, natural gas. **Per capita arable land:** 1.2 acres. **Meat prod.** (1978): beef: 145,000 metric tons; pork: 880,000 metric tons. **Fish catch** (1977): 34,700 metric tons. **Electricity prod.** (1978): 25.42 bln. kwh. **Crude steel prod.** (1979): 3.9 mln. metric tons. **Labor force:** 23% agric.; 36% manuf.

Finance: Currency: Forint (Mar. 1980: 20.31 = $1 US). **Net material product** (1978): $29.1 bln. **Per capita income** (1976): $2,100. **Imports** (1979): $8.67 bln.; partners (1978): USSR 28%, W. Ger. 12%, E. Ger. 8%, Czech. 5%. **Exports** (1979): $7.94 bln.; partners (1978): USSR 30%, E. Ger. 8%, W. Ger. 8%, Czech. 7%. **Tourists** (1977): 7,194,000; receipts $320 mln. **Consumer prices** (change in 1979): 8.8%.

Transport: Railway traffic (1978): 12.6 bln. passenger-km; 23.9 bln. net ton-km. **Motor vehicles:** in use (1977): 744,700 passenger cars, 228,900 comm. vehicles; manuf. (1978): 14,880 comm. vehicles.

Communications: Television sets: 2.5 mln. licensed (1976), 423,000 manuf. (1977). **Radios:** 2.54 mln. licensed (1975), 259,000 manuf. (1977). **Telephones in use** (1978): 1,103,843. **Daily newspaper circ.** (1977): 2,585,000; 243 per 1,000 pop.

Health: Life expectancy at birth (1974): 66.54 male; 72.42 female. **Births** (per 1,000 pop. 1978): 15.7. **Deaths** (per 1,000 pop. 1978): 13.1. **Natural increase** (1978): .3%. **Hospital beds** (per 100,000 pop. 1977): 690. **Physicians** (per 100,000 pop. 1977): 230. **Infant mortality** (per 1,000 live births 1978): 24.3.

Education (1977): **Literacy:** 98%. **Pop. 5-19:** in school: 55%, teachers per 1,000: 27. **PQLI:** 91.

Earliest settlers, chiefly Slav and Germanic, were overrun by Huns and Magyars from the east. Stephen I (997-1038) was made king by Pope Sylvester II in 1000 AD. The country suffered repeated Turkish invasions in the 15th-17th centuries. After the defeats of the Turks, 1686-1697, Austria dominated, but Hungary obtained concessions until it regained internal independence in 1867, with the emperor of Austria as king of Hungary in a dual monarchy with a single diplomatic service. Defeated with the Central Powers in 1918, Hungary lost Transylvania to Romania, Croatia and Bacska to Yugoslavia, Slovakia and Carpatho-Ruthenia to Czechoslovakia, all of which had large Hungarian minorities. A republic under Michael Karolyi and a bolshevist revolt under Bela Kun were followed by a vote for a monarchy in 1920 with Admiral Nicholas Horthy as regent.

Hungary joined Germany in World War II, and was allowed to annex most of its lost territories. Russian troops captured the country, 1944-1945. By terms of an armistice with the Allied powers Hungary agreed to give up territory acquired by the 1938 dismemberment of Czechoslovakia and to return to its borders of 1937.

A republic was declared Feb. 1, 1946; Zoltan Tildy was elected president. In 1947 the communists forced Tildy out. Premier Imre Nagy, in office since mid-1953, was ousted for his moderate policy of favoring agriculture and consumer production, April 18, 1955.

In 1956, popular demands for the ousting of Erno Gero, Communist party secretary, and for formation of a government by Nagy, resulted in the latter's appointment Oct. 23; demonstrations against communist rule developed into open revolt. Gero called in Soviet forces. On Nov. 4 Soviet forces launched a massive attack against Budapest with 200,000 troops, 2,500 tanks and armored cars.

Estimates varied from 6,500 to 32,000 dead, and thousands deported. About 200,000 persons fled the country. The U.S. received 38,248 under a refugee emergency program. In the spring of 1963 the regime freed many anti-communists and captives from the revolution in a sweeping amnesty. Nagy was executed by the Russians.

Some 40,000 Soviet troops are stationed in Hungary. Hungarian troops participated in the 1968 Warsaw Pact invasion of Czechoslovakia.

Major economic reforms were launched early in 1968, switching from a central planning system to one in which market forces and profit control much of production. Productivity and living standards have improved. By the 1970s, Hungary led the communist states in comparative tolerance for cultural freedoms and small private enterprise. Some 60,000 of the 1956 emigres have returned.

In 1973 Hungary agreed to pay the U.S. $18,900,000 for nationalized U.S. properties in Hungary, and trade ties improved.

Iceland

Republic of Iceland

People: Population (1979 est.): 226,000. **Age distrib.** (%): 0–14: 29.0; 15–59: 58.0; 60+: 13.1. **Pop. density:** 5.54 per sq. mi. **Urban** (1977): 87.4% **Ethnic groups:** Homogeneous, descendants of Norwegians, Celts. **Language:** Icelandic. **Religon:** Lutherans 98%.

Geography: Area: 39,702 sq. mi., the size of Virginia. **Location:** At N end of Atlantic O. **Neighbors:** Nearest is Greenland. **Topography:** Iceland is of recent volcanic origin. Three-quarters of the surface is wasteland: glaciers, lakes, a lava desert. There are geysers and hot springs, and the climate is moderated by the Gulf Stream. **Capital:** Reykjavik. **Cities** (1978 est.): Reykjavik 83,887.

Government: Head of state: Pres. Vigdis Finnbogadottir; b. Apr. 15, 1930; in office: Aug. 1, 1980. **Head of government:** Prime Min. Gunnar Thoroddsen, b. Dec. 29, 1910; in office: Feb. 8, 1980. **Local divisions:** 18 syslur (counties); 25–30 kaupstaudr (urban municipalities.)

Economy: Industries: Fish products, aluminum, cement, chemicals. **Chief crops:** Potatoes, turnips, hay. **Per capita arable land:** 0.09 acres. **Meat prod.** (1978): lamb: 15,000 metric tons. **Fish catch** (1977): 1.4 mln. metric tons. **Electricity prod.** (1978): 2.66 bln. kwh. **Labor force:** 10% agric.; 26% manuf.

Finance: Currency: Krona (Mar. 1980: 429.15 = $1 US). **Gross domestic product** (1978): $2.18 bln. **Per capita income** (1978): $6,392. **Imports** (1979): $738 mln.; partners (1978): W. Ger. 11%, UK 11%, Den. 10%, Swed. 9%. **Exports** (1979): $705 mln.; partners (1978): U.S. 29%, UK 17%, W. Ger. 8%. **Tourists** (1977): 72,700; receipts: $15 mln. **National budget** (1977): $538 mln. revenues; $546 mln. expenditures. **International reserves less gold** (Mar. 1980): $143.1 mln. **Gold:** 49,000 oz t. **Consumer prices** (change in 1979): 44.0%.

Transport: Motor vehicles: in use (1977): 70,100 passenger cars, 7,900 comm. vehicles. **Civil aviation:** 2,118 mln. passenger-km (1978); 37 mln. freight ton-km (1978). **Chief ports:** Reykjavik.

Communications: Television sets: 53,000 in use (1976). **Radios:** 64,000 licensed (1976). **Telephones in use** (1978): 95,515. **Daily newspaper circ.** (1977): 123,000; 554 per 1,000 pop.

Health: Life expectancy at birth (1976): 73.0 male; 79.2 female. **Births** (per 1,000 pop. 1978): 18.6. **Deaths** (per 1,000 pop. 1978): 6.5. **Natural increase** (1978): 1.2%. **Hospital beds** (per 100,000 pop. 1977): 1,700. **Physicians** (per 100,000 pop. 1977): 180. **Infant mortality** per (1,000 live births 1978): 10.8.

Education (1977): **Literacy:** 99%. **Pop. 5-19:** in school: 70%, teachers per 1,000: 46. **PQLI:** 98.

Iceland was an independent republic from 930 to 1262, when it joined with Norway. Its language has maintained its purity for 1,000 years. Danish rule lasted from 1380-1918; the last ties with the Danish crown were severed in 1941. The Althing, or assembly, is the world's oldest surviving parliament.

A four-year dispute with Britain ended in 1976 when the latter accepted Iceland's 200-mile territorial waters claim.

A conservative coalition won power in 1974 and stopped plans to oust U.S. NATO air and naval personnel, which totalled 2,859 in 1979.

India

Republic of India

People: Population (1979 est.): 667,326,000. **Age distrib.** (%): 0–14: 40.8; 15–59: 53.9; 60+: 5.3. **Pop. density:** 519.13 per sq. mi. **Urban** (1977): 21.2%. **Ethnic groups:** Indo-Aryan groups 72%, Dravidians 25%, Mongoloids 3%. **Languages:** 15 languages, including Hindi (official) and English (associate official). **Religions:** Hindus 84%, Moslems 10%, Christians 2.6%, Sikhs 1.9%, Buddhists 0.7%, Jains 0.5%, others.

Geography: Area: 1,229,737 sq. mi., one third the size of the U.S. **Location:** Occupies most of the Indian subcontinent in S. Asia. **Neighbors:** Pakistan on W, China, Nepal, Bhutan on N, Burma, Bangladesh on E. **Topography:** The Himalaya Mts., highest in world, stretch across India's northern borders. Below, the Ganges Plain is wide, fertile, and among the most densely populated regions of the world. The area below includes the Deccan Peninsula. Close to one quarter the area is forested. The climate varies from tropical heat in S to near-Arctic cold in N. Rajasthan Desert is in NW; NE Assam Hills get 400 in. of rain a year. **Capital:** New Delhi. **Cities** (1971 cen.): Bombay 5,970,575; Calcutta 3,148,746; Delhi 3,287,883; Madras 2,469,449; Hyderabad 1,607,396; Ahmedabad 1,585,544; Bangalore 1,540,741; Kanpur 1,154,388.

Government: Head of state: Pres. Neelam Sanjiva Reddy; b. May 19, 1913; in office: July 25, 1977. **Head of government:** Prime Min. Indira Gandhi, b. Nov. 19, 1917; in office: Jan. 14, 1980. **Local divisions:** 22 states, 9 union territories. **Armed forces:** regulars 1,096,000; reserves 200,000.

Economy: Industries: Textiles, steel, processed foods, cement, machinery, chemicals, fertilizers, consumer appliances, autos. **Chief crops:** Rice, grains, coffee, sugar cane, spices, tea, cashews, cotton, copra, coir, juta, linseed. **Minerals:** Chromium, coal, iron, manganese, mica salt, bauxite, gypsum, oil. **Crude oil reserves** (1980): 2.60 bln. bbls. **Other resources:** Rubber, timber. **Per capita arable land:** 0.6 acres. **Meat prod.** (1978): beef: 188,000 metric tons; pork: 65,000 metric tons; lamb: 393,000 metric tons. **Fish catch** (1977): 2.5 mln. metric tons. **Electricity prod.** (1978): 101.00 bln. kwh. **Crude steel prod.** (1979): 10.1 mln. metric tons. **Labor force:** 74% agric.

Finance: Currency: Rupee (Mar. 1980: 8.19 = $1 US). **Gross domestic product** (1977): $99.69 bln. **Per capita income** (1977): $150. **Imports** (1979): $8.8 bln.; partners (1978): U.S. 13%, Iran 9%, W. Ger. 9%, UK 8%. **Exports** (1979): $6.94 bln.; partners (1978): U.S. 13%, USSR 12%, UK 10%, Jap. 9%. **Tourists** (1977): 640,400; receipts: $350 mln. **National budget** (1977): $10.54 bln. revenues; $13.07 bln. expenditures. **International reserves less gold** (Jan. 1980): $7.64 bln. **Gold:** 8.56 mln. oz t. **Consumer prices** (change in 1979): 6.3%.

Transport: Railway traffic (1977): 176.7 bln. passenger-km; (1978) 152.52 bln. net ton-km. **Motor vehicles:** in use (1977): 805,400 passenger cars, 690,400 comm. vehicles; manuf. (1978): 45,600 passenger cars, 48,720 comm. vehicles. **Civil aviation:** 8,316 mln. passenger-km (1977); 304 mln. freight ton-km (1977). **Chief ports:** Calcutta, Bombay, Madras, Cochin, Vishakhapatnam.

Communications: Television sets: 280,000 licensed (1976). **Radios:** 14.85 mln. licensed (1976), 1.81 mln. manuf. (1977). **Telephones in use** (1978): 2,247,187. **Daily newspaper circ.** (1977): 10,672,000.

Health: Life expectancy at birth (1960): 41.89 male; 40.55 female. **Births** (per 1,000 pop. 1976): 34.4. **Deaths** (per 1,000 pop. 1976): 15.0. **Natural increase** (1976): 1.9%. **Hospital beds** (per 100,000 pop. 1977): 75. **Physicians** (per 100,000 pop. 1977): 26. **Infant mortality** (per 1,000 live births 1976): 122.

Education (1977): **Literacy:** 36%. **Pop. 5-19:** in school: 42%, teachers per 1,000: 13. **PQLI:** 43.

India has one of the oldest civilizations in the world. Excavations trace the Indus Valley civilization back for at least 5,000 years. Paintings in the mountain caves of Ajanta, richly carved temples, the Taj Mahal in Agra, and the Kutab Minar in Delhi are among relics of the past.

Aryan tribes, speaking Sanskrit, invaded from the NW around 1500 BC, and merged with the earlier inhabitants to create classical Indian civilization.

Asoka ruled most of the Indian subcontinent in the 3d century BC, and established Buddhism. But Hinduism revived and eventually predominated. During the Gupta kingdom, 4th-6th century AD, science, literature, and the arts enjoyed a "golden age."

Arab invaders established a Moslem foothold in the W in the 8th century, and Turkish Moslems gained control of North India by 1200. The Mogul emperors ruled 1526-1707.

Vasco de Gama established Portuguese trading posts 1498-1503. The Dutch followed. The British East India Co. sent Capt. William Hawkins, 1609, to get concessions from the Mogul emperor for spices and textiles. Operating as the East India Co. the British gained control of most of India. The British parliament assumed political direction; under Lord Bentinck, 1828-35, rule by rajahs was curbed. After the Sepoy troops mutinied, 1857-58, the British supported the native rulers.

Nationalism grew rapidly after World War I. The Indian National Congress and the Moslem League demanded constitutional reform. A leader emerged in Mohandas K. Gandhi (called Mahatma, or Great Soul), born Oct. 2, 1869, assassinated Jan. 30, 1948. He began advocating self-rule, non-violence, removal of untouchability in 1919. In 1930 he launched "civil disobedience," including boycott of British goods and rejection of taxes without representation.

In 1935 Britain gave India a constitution providing a bicameral federal congress. Mohammed Ali Jinnah, head of the Moslem League, sought creation of a Moslem nation, Pakistan.

The British government partitioned British India into the dominions of India and Pakistan. Aug. 15, 1947, was designated Indian Independence Day. India became a self-governing member of the Commonwealth and a member of the UN. It became a democratic republic, Jan. 26, 1950.

More than 12 million Hindu & Moslem refugees crossed the India-Pakistan borders in a mass transferral of some of the 2 peoples during 1947; about 200,000 were killed in communal fighting.

After Pakistan troops began attacks on Bengali separatists in East Pakistan, Mar. 25, 1971, some 10 million refugees fled into India. On Aug. 9, India and the USSR signed a 20-year friendship pact while U.S.-India relations soured. India and Pakistan went to war Dec. 3, 1971, on both the East and West fronts. Pakistan troops in the East surrendered Dec. 16; Pakistan agreed to a cease-fire in the West Dec. 17.

India and Pakistan signed a pact agreeing to withdraw troops from their borders and seek peaceful solutions, July 3, 1972. In Aug. 1973 India agreed to release 93,000 Pakistanis held prisoner since 1971; the return was completed in Apr. 1974. The 2 countries resumed full relations in 1976.

In 2 days of carnage, the Bengali population of the village of Mandai, Tripura State, 700 people, were massacred in a raid by indigenous tribal residents of the area, June 8-9, 1980. A similar year-long campaign against Bengali immigrants had been going on in Assam State.

Prime Min. Mrs. Indira Gandhi, named Jan. 19, 1966, was the 2d successor to Jawaharlal Nehru, India's prime minister from 1947 to his death, May 27, 1964.

Long the dominant power in India's politics, the Congress party lost some of its near monopoly by 1967. The party split into New and Old Congress parties in 1969. Mrs. Gandhi's New Congress party won control of the House.

Threatened with adverse court rulings in a voting law case, an opposition protest campaign and strikes, Gandhi invoked emergency provisions of the constitution June, 1975. Thousands of opponents were arrested and press censorship imposed. Measures to control prices, protect small farmers, and improve productivity were adopted.

The emergency, especially enforcement of coercive birth control measures in some areas, and the prominent extra-constitutional role of Indira Gandhi's son Sanjay, was widely resented. Opposition parties, united in the Janata coalition, scored massive victories in federal and state parliamentary elections in 1977, turning the New Congress Party from power.

Amid growing political tensions within the majority Janata party, and facing a censure vote in Parliament, Prime Min. Morarji R. Desai resigned, July 15, 1979. He was succeeded by the coalition government of Charan Singh, which only lasted 24 days before the prime minister's resignation in the face of opposition from Indira Gandhi's New Congress Party.

With 350 candidates of her party winning seats to Parliament, Indira Gandhi became prime minister for the second time, Jan. 14, 1980.

Indian agriculture has made progress with high-yield seeds, fertilizers, irrigation and limited mechanization.

For many years India has had large textile industries with a wide variety of cotton, woolen, and silk products.

Himalayan lowland villages in Uttar Pradesh have been buried by erosion-related avalanches, due to stripping of the forests.

India's 1st nuclear power plant, built with U.S. help, was dedicated in 1970 near Bombay; Canada helped India build 2 reactors. In May, 1974, India exploded a nuclear device underground, assertedly for peaceful development. Canada halted shipments of nuclear equipment and material to India. Restricted shipments from both the U.S. & Canada resumed in 1976. An Indian space satellite was launched by the USSR April 19, 1975.

Sikkim, bordered by Tibet, Bhutan, Nepal and India, formerly British protected, became a protectorate of India in 1950. Area, 2,818 sq. mi.; pop. 1977 est. 250,000; capital, Gangtok. In Sept. 1974 India's Parliament voted to make Sikkim an associate Indian state, absorbing it into India. The monarchy was abolished in an April, 1975, referendum.

Kashmir, a predominantly Moslem region in the northwest, has been in dispute between India and Pakistan since 1947. A cease-fire was negotiated by the UN Jan. 1, 1949; it gave Pakistan control of one-third of the area, in the west and northwest, and India the remaining two-thirds, the Indian state of Jammu and Kashmir, which enjoys internal autonomy. Repeated clashes broke out along the line.

There were also clashes in April 1965 along the Assam-East Pakistan border and in the **Rann** (swamp) **of Kutch** area along the West Pakistan-Gujarat border near the Arabian Sea. An international arbitration commission on Feb. 19, 1968, awarded 90% of the Rann to India, 10% to Pakistan.

France, 1952-54, peacefully yielded to India its 5 colonies, former French India, comprising Pondicherry, Karikal, Mahe, Yanaon (which became Pondicherry Union Territory, area 185 sq. mi., pop. 1971 471,707) and Chandernagor (which was incorporated into the state of West Bengal).

Goa, 1,429 sq. mi., pop., 1971, 795,120, which had been ruled by Portugal since 1505 AD, was taken by India by military action Dec. 18, 1961, together with 2 other Portuguese enclaves, Daman and Diu, located near Bombay.

Indonesia

Republic of Indonesia

People: Population (1979 est.): 148,085,000. **Age distrib.** (%): 0–14: 44.0; 15–59: 51.5; 60+: 4.5. **Pop. density:** 197.34 per sq. mi. **Urban** (1974): 18.2%. **Ethnic groups:** Javanese 45%, Sundanese 13.6%, Chinese 2.3%, others. **Languages:** Bahasa Indonesian (Malay) (official), Javanese, other Austronesian languages. **Religions:** Moslems 90%, Christians 5%, Hindus 3%.

Geography: Area: 735,268 sq. mi. **Location:** Archipelago SE of Asia along the Equator. **Neighbors:** Malaysia on N, Papua New Guinea on E. **Topography:** Indonesia comprises 13,000 islands, including Java (one of the most densely populated areas in the world with 1,500 persons to the sq. mi.), Sumatra, Kalimantan (most of Borneo), Sulawesi (Celebes), and West Irian (Irian Jaya, the W. half of New Guinea). Also: Bangka, Billiton, Madura, Bali, Timor. The mountains and plateaus on the major islands have a cooler climate than the tropical lowlands. **Capital:** Jakarta. **Cities** (1971 cen.): Jakarta 4,576,009; Surabaja 1,556,255; Bandung 1,201,730; Semarang 646,590; Medan 635,562.

Government: Head of state: Pres. Suharto; b. June 8, 1921; in office: Mar. 6, 1967. **Local divisions:** 27 provinces with elected legislatures, appointed governors. **Armed forces:** regulars 239,000; para-military 112,000.

Economy: Industries: Food processing, textiles, light industry. **Chief crops:** Rice, maize, cassava, peanuts, soybeans, tobacco, coffee, pepper, kapok, coconuts, palm oil, tea, sugar, indigo. **Minerals:** Nickel, tin, oil, coal, bauxite, manganese, copper, gold, silver. **Crude oil reserves** (1980): 9.6 bln. bbls. **Other resources:** Rubber, cinchona. **Per capita arable land:** 0.3 acres. **Meat prod.** (1978): beef: 182,000 metric tons; pork: 108,000 metric tons, lamb: 38,000 metric tons. **Fish catch** (1977): 1.55 mln. metric tons. **Electricity prod.** (1977): 4.38 bln. kwh. **Crude steel prod.** (1979): 518,000 metric tons. **Labor force:** 61% agric.; 6% manuf.

Finance: Currency: Rupiah (Mar. 1980: 629 = $1 US). **Gross domestic product** (1978): $49.29 bln. **Per capita income** (1978): $304. **Imports** (1979): $7.23 bln.; partners (1978): Jap. 30%, U.S. 12%, W. Ger. 9%, Sing. 7%. **Exports** (1979): $15.58 bln.; partners (1978): Jap. 39%, U.S. 25%, Sing. 11%, Trin./Tob. 5%. **Tourists** (1977): 457,000; receipts: $39 mln. **National budget** (1978): $9.82 bln. revenues; $10.09 bln. expenditures. **International reserves less gold** (Mar. 1980): $4.18 bln. **Gold:** 1.03 mln. oz t. **Consumer prices** (change in 1979): 24.4%.

Transport: Railway traffic (1978): 4.46 bln. passenger-km; 980.4 mln. net ton-km. **Motor vehicles:** in use (1977): 479,300 passenger cars, 327,100 comm. vehicles; assembled (1977): 20,000 passenger cars, 69,400 comm. vehicles. **Civil aviation:** 3,912 mln. passenger-km (1977); 57 mln. freight ton-km (1977). **Chief ports:** Jakarta, Surabaja, Medan, Palembang, Semarang.

Communications: Television sets: 325,000 in use (1976), 482,000 manuf. (1977). **Radios:** 5.1 mln. licensed (1976), 1.0 mln. manuf. (1977). **Telephones in use** (1978): 324,546. **Daily newspaper circ.** (1976): 2,358,000.

Health: Life expectancy at birth (1960): 47.5 male; 47.5 female. **Births** (per 1,000 pop. 1975): 41.5. **Deaths** (per 1,000 pop. 1975): 16.7. **Natural increase** (1975): 2.5%. **Hospital beds** (per 100,000 pop. 1977): 60. **Physicians** (per 100,000 pop. 1977): 7. **Infant mortality** (per 1,000 live births 1975): 125.

Education (1977): **Literacy:** 62%. **Pop. 5-19:** in school: 39%, teachers per 1,000: 14. **PQLI:** 55.

Hindu and Buddhist civilization from India reached the peoples of Indonesia nearly 2,000 years ago, taking root especially in Java. Islam spread along the maritime trade routes in the 15th century, and became predominant by the 16th century. The Dutch replaced the Portuguese as the most important European trade power in the area in the 17th century. They secured territorial control over Java by 1750. The outer islands were not finally subdued until the early 20th century, when the full area of present-day Indonesia was united under one rule for the first time in history.

Following Japanese occupation, 1942-45, nationalists led by Sukarno and Hatta proclaimed a republic. The Netherlands ceded sovereignty Dec. 27, 1949, after 4 years of fighting. West Irian, on New Guinea, remained under Dutch control.

After the Dutch in 1957 rejected proposals for new negotiations over West Irian, Indonesia stepped up the seizure of Dutch property. A U.S. mediator's plan was adopted in 1962. In 1963 the UN turned the area over to Indonesia, which promised a plebiscite. In 1969, voting by tribal chiefs favored staying with Indonesia, despite an uprising and widespread opposition.

Sukarno suspended Parliament in 1960, and was named president for life in 1963. Russian-armed Indonesian troops staged raids in 1964 and 1965 into Malaysia, whose formation Sukarno had opposed. Indonesia withdrew from the UN in 1965; anti-American demonstrations were staged.

Indonesia's popular, pro-Peking Communist party tried to seize control in 1965; the army smashed the coup, later intimated that Sukarno had played a role in it. In parts of Java, Communists seized several districts before being defeated; over 300,000 Communists were executed.

Gen. Suharto, head of the army, was named president for 5 years in 1968, reelected 1973 and 1978. A coalition of his supporters won a strong majority in House elections in 1971, the first national vote in 16 years. Moslem opposition parties made gains in 1977 elections. The military retains a predominant political role.

In 1966 Indonesia and Malaysia signed an agreement ending hostility, and Indonesia reentered the UN. After ties with Peking were cut in 1967, there were riots against the economically important ethnic Chinese minority. Riots against Chinese and Japanese also occurred in 1974.

The former Portuguese Timor became Indonesia's 27th province in 1976 during a local civil war. Thousands of civilians were reportedly killed by the Indonesians.

Oil export earnings, and a decline in the high birth rate, have given hope for future improvements in very low living conditions.

Iran

Islamic Republic of Iran

People: Population (1979 est.): 37,430,000. **Age distrib.** (%): 0–14: 44.4; 15–59: 50.3; 60+: 5.2. **Pop. density:** 55.33 per sq. mi. **Urban** (1976): 46.8%. **Ethnic groups:** Iranian groups 66%, Turkish groups 25%, Kurds 5%, Arabs 4%. **Languages:** Persian, Turk, Kurdish, Arabic. **Religions:** Moslems 98% (Shiite [official] 93%, Sunni 5%), Christians, Jews, Zoroastrians.

Geography: Area: 636,363 sq. mi. **Location:** Between the Middle East and S. Asia. **Neighbors:** Turkey, Iraq on W, USSR of N (Armenia, Azerbaijan, Turkmenistan), Afghanistan, Pakistan on E. **Topography:** Interior highlands and plains are surrounded by high mountains, up to 18,000 ft. Large salt deserts cover much of the area, but there are many oases and forest areas. Most of the population inhabits the N and NW. **Capital:** Teheran. **Cities** (1976 cen.): Teheran 4,496,159; Isfahan 671,825; Mashhad 670,180; Tabriz 598,576.

Government: Religious head (Faghi): Ayatollah Ruhollah Khomeini, b. 1901. **Head of state:** Pres. Abolhassan Bani-Sadr, b. 1933; in office: Feb. 4, 1980. **Local divisions:** 21 provinces, 2 governorates. **Armed forces:** regulars 415,000; reserves 300,000.

Economy: Industries: Steel, petrochemicals, cement, auto assembly, sugar refining, carpets. **Chief crops:** Grains, rice, fruits, sugar beets, cotton, grapes. **Minerals:** Chromium, oil, gas, copper, iron, lead, manganese, zinc, barite, sulphur, coal, emeralds, turquoise. **Crude oil reserves** (1980): 58.00 bln. bbls. **Other resources:** Gums, wool, silk, caviar. **Per capita arable land:** 1.1 acres. **Meat prod.** (1978): beef: 118,000 metric tons; lamb: 243,000 metric tons. **Electricity prod.** (1977): 18.00 bln. kwh. **Crude steel prod.** (1979 est.) 1.4 mln. metric tons. **Labor force:** 37% agric.; 27% manuf.

Finance: Currency: Rial (Mar. 1980: 70.48 = $1 US). **Gross domestic product** (1977): $76.37 bln. **Per capita income** (1976): $1,986. **Imports** (1979): $7.62 bln.; partners (1978 est.): U.S. 20%, W. Ger. 19%, Jap. 15%, UK 8%. **Exports** (1979): $19.43 bln.; partners (1978 est.): Jap. 17%, U.S. 13%, W. Ger. 9%, U.S. Vir. Is. 7%. **Tourists** (1977): 690,500; receipts: $153 mln. **National budget** (1978): $22.87 bln. revenues; $29.61 bln. expenditures. **International reserves less gold** (Dec. 1979): $15.21 bln. **Gold:** 3.90 mln. oz t. **Consumer prices** (change in 1978): 11.6%.

Transport: Railway traffic (1976): 3.51 bln. passenger-km; 4.63 bln. net ton-km. **Motor vehicles:** in use (1977): 932,700 passenger cars, 204,000 comm. vehicles; assembled (1977): 103,000 passenger cars; 65,000 comm. vehicles. **Chief ports:** Khorramshahr, Bushehr, Bandar-e Shahpur, Bendar Abbas.

Communications: Television sets: 1.7 mln. in use (1976), 293,000 manuf. (1976). **Radios:** 2.1 mln. in use (1976), 151,000 manuf. (1976). **Telephones in use** (1978): 828,576. **Daily newspaper circ.** (1976): 473,000.

Health: Life expectancy at birth (1976): 57.63 male; 57.44 female. **Births** (per 1,000 pop. 1975): 42.5. **Deaths** (per 1,000 pop. 1975): 11.5. **Natural increase** (1975): 3.1%. **Hospital beds** (per 100,000 pop. 1977): 148. **Physicians** (per 100,000 pop. 1977): 39. **Infant mortality** (per 1,000 live births 1975): 108.1.

Education (1977): **Literacy:** 50% **Pop. 5-19:** in school: 51%, teachers per 100,000: 20. **PQLI:** 52.

Iran is the official name of the country long known as Persia. The Iranians, who supplanted an earlier agricultural civilization, came from the E during the 2d millenium BC; they were an Indo-European group related to the Aryans of India.

In 549 BC Cyrus the Great united the Medes and Persians in the Persian Empire, conquered Babylonia in 538 BC, restored Jerusalem to the Jews. Alexander the Great conquered Persia in 333 BC, but Persians regained their independence in the next century under the Parthians, themselves succeeded by Sassanian Persians in 226 AD. Arabs brought Islam to Persia in the 7th century, replacing the indigenous Zoroastrian faith. After Persian political and cultural autonomy was reasserted in the 9th century, the arts and sciences flourished for several centuries.

Turks and Mongols ruled Persia in turn from the 11th century to 1502, when a native dynasty reasserted full independence. The British and Russian empires vied for influence in the 19th century, and Afghanistan was severed from Iran by Britain in 1857.

The previous dynasty was founded by Reza Khan, a military leader, in 1925. He abdicated as shah in 1941, and was succeeded by his son, Mohammad Reza Pahlavi.

British and Russian forces entered Iran Aug. 25, 1941, withdrawing later. Britain and the USSR signed an agreement Jan. 29, 1942, to respect Iranian integrity and give economic aid. In 1946 a Soviet attempt to take over the Azerbaijan region in the NW was defeated when a puppet regime was ousted by force.

Parliament, under Premier Mohammed Mossadegh, nationalized the oil industry in 1951, leading to a British blockade. Mossadegh was overthrown in 1953; the shah assumed control. Under his rule, Iran underwent economic and social change. However, political opposition was not tolerated. Thousands were arrested in the 1970s, while hundreds of purported terrorists were executed.

Conservative Moslem protests led to 1978 violence. Martial law in 12 cities was declared Sept. 8. A military government was appointed Nov. 6 to deal with striking oil workers. Continued clashes with demonstrators led to greater violence; oil production fell to a 27-year low, Dec. 27. In a 3d change of government in 5 months, Prime Min. Shahpur Bakhtiar was designated by the shah to head a regency council in his absence. The shah left Iran Jan. 16, 1979.

Violence continued throughout January. Exiled religious leader Ayatollah Ruhollah Khomeini named a provisional government council in preparation for his return to Iran, Jan. 31. Clashes between Khomeini's supporters and government troops culminated in a rout of Iran's elite Imperial Guard Feb. 11, leading to the fall of Bakhtiar's government. Ayatollah Khomeini's choice for prime minister, Mehdi Bazargan, headed an interim government pledged to establish an Islamic republic, but resigned Nov. 6, 1979, conceding power to the Islamic authority of Ayatollah Khomeini.

Iranian militants seized the U.S. embassy, Nov. 4, 1979, and took 90 hostages including some 65 Americans. The students vowed to stay in the embassy until the deposed shah was returned to Iran to stand trial. Despite international condemnations and U.S. efforts, including an abortive Apr., 1980, rescue attempt, the crisis continued. The U.S. broke diplomatic relations with Iran, Apr. 7th. The shah died in Egypt, July 27th.

The Iranian revolution was marked by revolts among the ethnic minorities and by a continuing struggle between the clerical forces and westernized intellectuals and liberals. The Islamic Constitution, drafted under the domination of the clergy, established final authority to be vested in a Faghi, the Ayatollah Khomeini. (*See Index for Chronology.*)

Iraq

Republic of Iraq

People: Population (1979 est.): 12,906,000. **Age distrib.** (%): 0–14: 48.3; 15–59: 46.5; 60+: 5.3. **Pop. density:** 71.69 per sq. mi. **Urban** (1977): 65.9%. **Ethnic groups:** Arabs 78%, Kurds 18%, Persians 1.2%, Turks 1.2%, Assyrians 0.5%. **Languages:** Arabic (official), Kurdish, others. **Religions:** Moslems 95% (Shiites two-thirds, Sunnis one-third), Christians 3%.

Geography: Area: 172,000 sq. mi., larger than California. **Location:** In the Middle East, occupying most of historic Mesopotamia. **Neighbors:** Jordan, Syria on W, Turkey on N, Iran on E, Kuwait, Saudi Arabia on S. **Topography:** Mostly an alluvial plain, including the Tigris and Euphrates rivers, descending from mountains in N to desert in SW. Persian Gulf region is marshland. **Capital:** Baghdad. **Cities** (1975 est.): Baghdad (met.) 3,205,645.

Government: Head of state: Pres. Saddam Hussein, b. 1935 in office: July 16, 1979. **Local divisions:** 18 governorates. **Armed forces:** regulars 222,000; reserves 250,000.

Economy: Industries: Textiles, food processing, cigarettes, oil refining, cement. **Chief crops:** Grains, rice, dates, cotton, tobacco. **Minerals:** Oil, gas. **Crude oil reserves** (1980): 31.00 bln. bbls. **Other resources:** Wool, hides. **Per capita arable land:** 1.0 acres. **Meat prod.** (1978): beef: 50,000 metric tons; lamb: 50,000 metric tons. **Fish catch** (1977): 26,100 metric tons. **Electricity prod.** (1977): 5.00 bln. kwh. **Labor force:** 50% agric.

Finance: Currency: Dinar (Mar. 1980: 1 = $3.39 US). **Gross domestic product** (1976): $16.45 bln. **Per capita income** (1978): $1,561. **Imports** (1978): $4.21 bln.; partners (1977): W. Ger. 18%, Jap. 18%, UK 7%, Fr. 6%. **Exports** (1979): $21.45 bln.; partners (1977): Fr. 17%, It. 16%, Braz. 9%, UK 8%. **Tourists** (1977): 721,600; receipts (1975): $84 mln. **International reserves less gold** (Dec. 1977): $6.82 bln. **Gold:** 4.14 mln. oz t. **Consumer prices** (change in 1978): 4.5%.

Transport: Railway traffic (1976): 797 mln. passenger-km; 2.25 bln. net ton-km. **Motor vehicles:** in use (1977): 150,400 passenger cars, 74,500 comm. vehicles. **Civil aviation:** 1,334 mln. passenger-km (1978); 41 mln. freight ton-km (1978). **Chief ports:** Basra.

Communications: Television sets: 425,000 in use (1976), 25,000 manuf. (1975). **Radios:** 1.25 mln. in use (1975). **Telephones in use** (1978): 319,591. **Daily newspaper circ.** (1976): 202,000.

Health: Life expectancy at birth (1975): 51.2 male; 54.3 female. **Births** (per 1,000 pop. 1975): 47.4. **Deaths** (per 1,000 pop. 1975): 14.6. **Natural increase** (1975): 3.3%. **Hospital beds** (per 100,000 pop. 1977): 199. **Physicians** (per 100,000 pop. 1977): 44. **Infant mortality** (per 1,000 live births 1975): 33.1.

Education (1977): **Literacy:** 30%. **Pop. 5-19:** in school: 60%, teachers per 1,000: 22. **PQLI:** 45.

The Tigris-Euphrates valley, formerly called Mesopotamia, was the site of one of the earliest civilizations in the world. The Sumerian city-states of 3,000 BC originated the culture later developed by the Semitic Akkadians, Babylonians, and Assyrians.

Mesopotamia ceased to be a separate entity after the conquests of the Persians, Greeks, and Arabs. The latter founded Baghdad, from where the caliph ruled a vast empire in the 8th and 9th centuries. Mongol and Turkish conquests led to a decline in population, the economy, cultural life, and the irrigation system.

Britain secured a League of Nations mandate over Iraq after World War I. Independence under a king came in 1932. A leftist, pan-Arab revolution established a republic in 1958, which oriented foreign policy toward the USSR. Most industry has been nationalized, and large land holdings broken up.

A local faction of the international Baath Arab Socialist party has ruled by decree since 1968. Russia and Iraq signed an aid pact in 1972, and arms were sent along with several thousand advisers. The 1978 execution of 21 Communists and a shift of trade to the West signalled a more neutral policy, straining relations with the USSR. In the 1973 Arab-Israeli war Iraq sent forces to aid Syria. Relations with Syria were improving steadily to negotiations of uniting the 2 nations as a single political entity, but were halted by the Hussein government, July, 1979. Within a month of assuming power, Saddam Hussein instituted a bloody purge in the wake of a reported coup attempt against the new regime.

Iraq played a leading role in uniting Arab opponents to the U.S.-backed Egyptian-Israeli peace treaty.

U.S. trade and diplomatic contracts increased in the 1970s, despite suspension of diplomatic relations in 1967. The first parliamentary elections in 22 years were held June 1980, under government restrictions.

Years of battling with the Kurdish minority resulted in total defeat for the Kurds in 1975, when Iran withdrew support. Kurdish rebels continued their war, 1979; fighting led to Iraqi bombing of Kurdish villages in Iran, causing relations with Iran to deteriorate.

Ireland

Irish Republic

People: Population (1979 est.): 3,365,000. **Age distrib. (%):** 0–14: 31.2; 15–59: 53.5; 60+:15.3. **Pop. density:** 121.8 per sq. mi. **Urban** (1971): 52.2%. **Ethnic groups:** Irish, Anglo-Irish minority. **Languages:** English predominates, Irish (Gaelic) spoken by minority. **Religions:** Roman Catholics 94%, Episcopalians 5%.

Geography: Area: 26,600 sq. mi. **Location:** In the Atlantic O. just W of Great Britain. **Neighbors:** United Kingdom (Northern Ireland). **Topography:** Ireland consists of a central plateau surrounded by isolated groups of hills and mountains. The coastline is heavily indented by the Atlantic O. **Capital:** Dublin. **Cities** (1971 cen.): Dublin 566,034; Cork (met.) 128,235.

Government: Head of State: Pres. Patrick J. Hillery; b. May 2, 1923; in office: Dec. 3, 1976. **Head of government:** Prime Min. Charles J. Haughey; b. Sept. 26, 1925; in office: Dec. 11, 1979. **Local divisions:** 26 counties. **Armed forces:** regulars 14,581; reserves 18,661.

Economy: Industries: Tobacco, food processing, auto assembly, metals, textiles, chemicals, brewing, electrical and non-electrical machinery, tourism. **Chief crops:** Potatoes, grain, sugar beets, fruits, vegetables. **Minerals:** Zinc, lead, silver, gas. **Per capita arable land:** 0.8 acres. **Meat prod.** (1978): beef: 384,000 metric tons; pork: 132,000 metric tons; lamb: 40,000 metric tons. **Fish catch** (1977): 95,500 metric tons. **Electricity prod.** (1978): 9.97 bln. kwh. **Crude steel prod.** (1979): 72,000 metric tons. **Labor force:** 23% agric.; 30% manuf.

Finance: Currency: Pound (Mar. 1980: 1 = $1.94 US). **Gross domestic product** (1978): 12.04 bln. **Per capita income** (1977): $2,711. **Imports** (1979): $9.86 bln.; partners (1978): UK 49% U.S. 8%, W. Ger. 7%, Fr. 5%. **Exports** (1979): $7.17 bln.; partners (1978): UK 47%, Fr. 9%, W. Ger. 8%, U.S. 6%. **Tourists** (1977): 566,000; receipts: $308 mln. **National budget** (1979): $5.09 bln. revenues; $7.25 bln. expenditures. **International reserves less gold** (Mar. 1980): $2.04 bln. **Gold:** 352,000 oz t. **Consumer prices** (change in 1979): 13.2%.

Transport: Railway traffic (1978): 964.8 mln. passenger-km; 630 mln. net ton-km. **Motor vehicles:** in use (1977): 577,600 passenger cars, 58,300 comm. vehicles; assembled (1978): 45,492 passenger cars; 2,376 comm. vehicles. **Civil aviation:** 1,836 mln. passenger-km (1978); 86 mln. freight ton-km. (1978). **Chief ports:** Dublin, Cork.

Communications: Television sets: 655,000 licensed (1976), 112,000 manuf. (1977). **Radios:** 949,000 licensed (1975), 72,000 manuf. (1973). **Telephones in use** (1978): 519,000. **Daily newspaper circ.** (1977): 702,000; 220 per 1,000 pop.

Health: Life expectancy at birth (1972): 68.77 male; 73.52 female. **Births** (per 1,000 pop. 1977): 21.4. **Deaths** (per 1,000 pop. 1977): 10.5. **Natural increase** (1977): 1.1%. **Hospital beds** (per 100,000 pop. 1977): 1,051. **Physicians** (per 100,000 pop. 1977): 116. **Infant mortality** (per 1,000 live births 1977): 15.7.

Education (1977): **Literacy:** 99%. **Pop. 5-19:** in school: 72%, teachers per 1,000: 30. **PQLI:** 93.

Celtic tribes invaded the islands about the 4th century BC; their Gaelic culture and literature flourished and spread to Scotland and elsewhere in the 5th century AD, the same century in which St. Patrick converted the Irish to Christianity. Invasions by Norsemen began in the 8th century, ended with defeat of the Danes by the Irish King Brian Boru in 1014. English invasions started in the 12th century; for over 700 years the Anglo-Irish struggle continued with bitter rebellions and savage repressions.

The Easter Monday Rebellion (1916) failed but was followed by guerrilla warfare and harsh reprisals by British troops, the "Black and Tans." The Dail Eireann, or Irish parliament, reaffirmed independence in Jan. 1919. The British offered dominion status to Ulster (6 counties) and southern Ireland (26 counties) Dec. 1921. The constitution of the Irish Free State, a British dominion, was adopted Dec. 11, 1922. Northern Ireland remained part of the United Kingdom.

A new constitution adopted by plebiscite came into operation Dec. 29, 1937. It declared the name of the state Eire in the Irish language (Ireland in the English) and declared it a sovereign democratic state.

On Dec. 21, 1948, an Irish law declared the country a republic rather than a dominion and withdrew it from the Commonwealth. The British Parliament recognized both actions, 1949, but reasserted its claim to incorporate the 6 northeastern counties in the United Kingdom. This claim has not been recognized by Ireland. *(See United Kingdom — Northern Ireland.)*

First president was William T. Cosgrave, 1922-32. Eamon de Valera, hero of the rebellion, was president 1932-37, 1959-66, 1966-73; prime minister 1937-48, 1951-54, 1957-59.

Irish governments have favored peaceful unification of all Ireland. Ireland cooperated with England against terrorist groups.

Industralization increased after 1962, with over 750 new factories, many with foreign participation. Common Market membership has aided the economy since 1973. A mining boom has followed the discovery of zinc, lead, and silver deposits. Ireland's growth economy was severely affected by the oil shortage that followed Iran's revolution. The major energy crisis of 1979 coincided with one of the worst recorded winters in meteorological history.

Israel

State of Israel

People: Population (1979 est.): 3,783,000. **Age distrib.** (%): 0–14: 33.2; 15–59: 63.0; 60+: 11.7. **Pop. density:** 448.96 per sq. mi. **Urban** (1977): 87.2%. **Ethnic groups:** Jews (half Ashkenazi, half Sephardi), Arabs, Druzes. **Languages:** Hebrew and Arabic (official), Yiddish, various European and West Asian languages. **Religions:** Jews 85%, Moslems 11%, Christians 2.5%, Druzes 1.2%.

Geography: Area: 8,219 sq. mi. (the size of Massachusetts), the "Green Line" border before the 1967 war; 2,986 sq. mi. occupied territory, excluding Sinai Peninsula, 23,622 sq. mi. **Location:** On eastern end of Mediterranean Sea. **Neighbors:** Lebanon on N, Syria, Jordan on E, Egypt on W. **Topography:** The Mediterranean coastal plain is fertile and well-watered. In the center is the Judean Plateau. A triangular-shaped semi-desert region, the Negev, extends from south of Beersheba to an apex at the head of the Gulf of Aqaba. The eastern border drops sharply into the Jordan Rift Valley, including Lake Tiberias (Sea of Galilee) and the Dead Sea, which is 1,296 ft. below sea level, lowest point on the earth's surface. **Capital:** Jerusalem. **Cities** (1978 est.): Jerusalem 376,000; Tel Aviv-Yafo 343,300; Haifa 227,800.

Government: Head of state: Pres. Yitzhak Navon; b. Apr. 19, 1921; in office: May 29, 1978. **Head of government:** Prime Min. Menachem Begin; b. Aug. 16, 1913; in office: June 21, 1977. **Local divisions:** 6 administrative districts. **Armed forces:** regulars 165,600; reserves 460,000.

Economy: Industries: Diamond cutting, textiles, electronics, machinery, plastics, tires, drugs, aircraft, munitions, wine. **Chief crops:** Citrus fruit, grains, olives, fruits, grapes, figs, cotton, vegetables. **Minerals:** Potash, limestone, gypsum, copper, iron, phosphates, magnesium, manganese, salt, sulphur. **Crude oil reserves** (1980): 1.0 mln. bbls. **Per capita arable land:** 0.2 acres. **Meat prod.** (1978): beef: 26,000 metric tons; pork: 10,000 metric tons. **Fish catch** (1977): 24,400 metric tons. **Electricity prod.** (1978): 11.89 bln. kwh. **Crude steel prod.** (1979): 107,000 metric tons. **Labor force:** 6.5% agric.; 25.3% manuf.

Finance: Currency: Shekel (Mar. 1980: 4.15 =$1 US). **Gross domestic product** (1979): $16.99 bln. **Per capita income** (1978): $3,332. **Imports** (1978): $7.4 bln.; partners: U.S. 19%, Switz. 11%, W. Ger. 10%, UK 9%. **Exports** (1978): $4.55 bln.; partners: U.S. 17%, W. Ger. 9%, HK 8%, UK 7%. **Tourists** (1977): 893,900; receipts $461 mln. **National budget** (1977): $7.71 bln. revenues; $10.52 bln. expenditures. **International reserves less gold** (Feb. 1980): $3.04 bln. **Gold:** 1.23 mln. oz t. **Consumer prices** (change in 1979): 78.3%.

Transport: Railway traffic (1978): 220.8 mln. passenger-km; 636 mln. net ton-km. **Motor vehicles:** in use (1977): 312,700 passenger cars, 107,600 comm. vehicles; assembled (1978): 2,604 passenger cars, 4,140 comm. vehicles. **Civil aviation:** 4,692 mln. passenger-km (1977); 179 mln. freight ton-km (1977). **Chief ports:** Haifa, Ashdod, Eilat.

Communications: Television sets: 475,000 in use (1976), 48,000 manuf. (1977). **Radios:** 655,000 in use (1976), 10,000 manuf. (1976). **Telephones in use** (1978): 929,837. **Daily newspaper circ.** (1976): 801,000; 231 per 1,000 pop.

Health: Life expectancy at birth (1977): 71.32 male; 74.68 female. **Births** (per 1,000 pop. 1977): 26.4. **Deaths** (per 1,000 pop. 1977): 6.9%. **Natural increase** (1977): 2.0%. **Hospital beds** (per 100,000 pop. 1977): 556. **Physicians** (per 100,000 pop. 1977): 277. **Infant mortality** (per 1,000 live births 1977): 17.8.

Education (1977): **Literacy:** 88%. **Pop. 5-19:** in school: 62%, teachers per 1,000: 50. **PQLI:** 91.

Occupying the SW corner of the ancient Fertile Crescent, Israel contains some of the oldest known evidence of agriculture and of primitive town life. A more advanced civilization emerged in the 3d millenium BC. The Hebrews, a people speaking a language similar to that of the earlier inhabitants, probably arrived early in the 2d millenium BC. Under King David and his successors (c.1000 BC-597 BC), Judaism was developed and secured. After conquest by Babylonians, Persians, and Greeks, an independent Jewish kingdom was revived, 168 BC, but Rome took effective control in the next century, suppressed Jewish revolts in 70 AD and 135 AD, and renamed Judea Palestine, after the earlier coastal inhabitants, the Philistines.

Arab invaders conquered Palestine in 636. The Arabic language and Islam prevailed within a few centuries, but a Jewish minority always remained. The land was ruled from the 11th century as a part of larger non-Arab empires by the Seljuks, the Mamluks, and the Ottomans (with a crusader interval, 1098-1291).

After 4 centuries of Ottoman rule, during which the population declined to a low of 350,000 (1785), the land was taken in 1917 by Britain, which in the Balfour Declaration that year pledged to support a Jewish national homeland there, as foreseen by the Zionists. In 1920 a British Palestine Mandate was recognized; in 1922 the land east of the Jordan was detached.

Jewish immigration, begun in the late 19th century, swelled in the 1930s with refugees from the Nazis; heavy Arab immigration from Syria and Lebanon also occurred. Arab opposition to Jewish immigration turned violent in 1920, 1921, 1929, and 1936. The UN General Assembly voted in 1947 to partition Palestine into an Arab and a Jewish state. Britain withdrew in May 1948.

Israel was declared an independent state May 14, 1948; the Arabs rejected partition. Egypt, Jordan, Syria, Lebanon, Iraq, and Saudi Arabia invaded, but failed to destroy the Jewish state, which gained territory. Separate armistices with the Arab nations were signed in 1949; Jordan occupied the West Bank, Egypt occupied Gaza, but neither granted Palestinian autonomy. No peace settlement was obtained, and the Arab nations continued policies of economic boycott, blockade in the Suez Canal, and support of guerrillas. Several hundred thousand Arabs left the area of Jewish control; an equal number of Jews left the Arab countries for Israel 1949-53.

After persistent terrorist raids, Israel invaded Egypt's Sinai, Oct. 29, 1956, aided briefly by British and French forces. A UN cease-fire was arranged Nov. 6.

An uneasy truce between Israel and the Arab countries, supervised by a UN Emergency Force, prevailed until May 19, 1967, when the UN force withdrew at the demand of Egypt's Pres. Nasser. Egyptian forces reoccupied the Gaza Strip and closed the Gulf of Aqaba to Israeli shipping. In a 6-day war that started June 5, the Israelis took the Gaza Strip, occupied the Sinai Peninsula to the Suez Canal, and captured Old Jerusalem, Syria's Golan Heights, and Jordan's West Bank. The fighting was halted June 10 by UN-arranged cease-fire agreements.

In 1969-70 there were almost daily Egyptian-Israeli engagements. Palestinian guerrilla raids and Israeli reprisals continued across the Jordanian, Syrian, and Lebanese frontiers; there were also encounters with Syrian and Jordanian forces.

Egypt and Syria attacked Israel, Oct. 6, 1973 (Yom Kippur, most solemn day on the Jewish calendar). Egypt and Syria were supplied by massive USSR military airlifts; the U.S. responded with an airlift to Israel. Israel counter-attacked, driving the Syrians back, and crossed the Suez Canal.

A cease fire took effect Oct. 24; a UN peace-keeping force went to the area. A disengagement agreement was signed Jan. 18, 1974, following negotiations by U.S. Secretary of State Henry Kissinger. Israel withdrew from the canal's W bank. A second withdrawal was completed in 1976; Israel yielded additional territory including an oil field. Some 200 unarmed American technicians were stationed to monitor the cease-fire. The U.S. agreed to provide substantial arms aid to Israel.

Israel and Syria agreed to disengage June 1; Israel completed withdrawing from its salient (and a small part of the land taken in the 1967 war) June 25. Nearly all black African nations broke relations with Israel in 1972-74, reportedly at the urging of Libya, despite Israel's technical aid programs.

In the wake of the war, Golda Meir, long Israel's premier, resigned; severe inflation gripped the nation. Palestinian guerrillas staged massacres, killing scores of civilians 1974-75. Israel conducted preventive attacks in Lebanon through 1975. Israel aided Christian forces in the 1975-76 Lebanese civil war.

Israeli forces raided Entebbe, Uganda, July 3, 1976, and rescued 103 hostages seized by Arab and German terrorists.

In 1977, the conservative opposition, led by Menachem Begin, was voted into office for the first time. Egypt Pres. Sadat's visit to Jerusalem Nov. 1977 raised peace hopes, but the issue of Arab Palestinian autonomy or independence complicated negotiations. On Mar. 26, 1979, Egypt and Israel signed a formal peace treaty, ending 30 years of war, and establishing diplomatic relations.

A massive Israeli invasion of S. Lebanon, March 1978, following a Lebanon-based terrorist attack in Israel, left over 1,000 Lebanese and Palestinians dead. Israel withdrew in favor of a 6,000-man UN force, but continued to aid Christian militiamen.

A 5-day occupation of Israeli forces in southern Lebanon took place April 1980, in retaliation to the Palestinian raid on a kibbutz earlier that month. Violence on the Israeli-occupied West Bank rose in 1980. (*See Index for Chronology.*)

Israel's economy has grown rapidly, aided by German reparations payments, U.S. aid (mostly since 1970), international loans, and contributions. In 1975, Israel signed agreements with the U.S. to facilitate investments in Israel, and with the Common Market allowing free trade.

Israel's first atomic reactor began operations in 1960. The nation launched its first successful solid-fuel rocket in 1961, Israel has denied reports that it has assembled 10-20 atom bombs.

Israel affirmed the entire city of Jerusalem as its capital, July, 1980, encompassing the annexed Arab East Jerusalem.

Italy

Italian Republic

People: Population (1979 est.): 56,877,000. **Age distrib.** (%): 0–14: 23.7; 15–59: 58.8; 60+: 17.5. **Pop. density:** 487.52 per sq. mi. **Ethnic groups:** Italians, small minorities of Germans, Slovenes, Albanians, French, Ladins, Greeks. **Languages:** Italian. **Religions:** Roman Catholics 99%.

Geography: Area: 116,303 sq. mi., slightly larger than Arizona. **Location:** In S Europe, jutting into Mediterranean S. **Neighbors:** France on W, Switzerland, Austria on N, Yugoslavia on E. **Topography:** Occupies a long boot-shaped peninsula, extending SE from the Alps into the Mediterranean, with the islands of Sicily and Sardinia offshore. The alluvial Po Valley drains most of N. The rest of the country is rugged and mountainous, except for intermittent coastal plains, like the Campajna, S of Rome. Appenine Mts. run down through center of peninsula. **Capital:** Rome. **Cities** (1978 est.): Rome 2,897,505; Milan 1,706,268; Naples 1,225,227; Turin 1,181,567; Genoa 795,027.

Government: Head of state: Pres. Alessandro Pertini; b. Sept. 25, 1896; in office: July 9, 1978; **Head of government:** Prime Min. Francesco Cossiga; b. July 26, 1928; in office: Aug. 5, 1979. **Local divisions:** 20 regions with some autonomy, 93 provinces. **Armed forces:** regulars 365,000; reserves 738,000.

Economy: Industries: Steel, machinery, autos, textiles, shoes, machine tools, chemicals, oil products, typewriters. **Chief crops:** Grapes, olives, citrus fruits, vegetables, wheat, rice. **Minerals:** Mercury, potash, gas, marble, sulphur, coal. **Crude oil reserves** (1980): 645 mln. bbls. **Per capita arable land:** 0.4 acres. **Meat prod.** (1978): beef: 1.10 mln. metric tons; pork: 920,000 metric tons; lamb: 53,000 metric tons. **Fish catch** (1977): 427,000 metric tons. **Electricity prod.** (1978): 174.77 bln. kwh. **Crude steel prod.** (1979): 24.3 mln. metric tons. **Labor force:** 15% agric.; 43% manuf.

Finance: Currency: Lira (Mar. 1980: 898.25 = $1 US). **Gross domestic product** (1978): $260.11 bln. **Per capita income** (1977): $3,076 **Imports** (1979): $77.96 bln.; partners (1978): W. Ger. 17%, Fr. 15%, U.S. 7%. **Exports** (1979): $72.24 bln.; partners (1978): W. Ger. 19%, Fr. 14%, U.S. 7%, UK 6%. **Tourists** (1977): 14,836,100; receipts $4.76 bln. **National budget** (1978): $63.45 bln. revenues; $95.32 bln. expenditures. **International reserves less gold** (Mar. 1980): $19.17 bln. **Gold:** 66.67 mln. oz t. **Consumer prices** (change in 1979): 14.7%.

Transport: Railway traffic (1978): 39.2 bln. passenger-km; 16.6 bln. net ton-km. **Motor vehicles:** in use (1977): 16.4 mln. passenger cars, (1976) 1.7 comm. vehicles; manuf. (1978): 1.51 mln. passenger cars, 146,400 comm. vehicles. **Civil aviation:** 12,816 mln. passenger-km (1977); 528 mln. freight ton-km (1977). **Chief ports:** Genoa, Venice, Trieste, Taranto, Naples, La Spezia.

Communications: Television sets: 12.38 mln. licensed (1976), 1.8 mln. manuf. (1976). **Radios:** 13.02 mln. licensed (1976), 1.54 mln. manuf. (1976). **Telephones in use** (1978): 16,118,928. **Daily newspaper circ.** (1977): 5,491,000; 97 per 1,000 pop.

Health: Life expectancy at birth (1972): 68.97 male; 74.88 female. **Births** (per 1,000 pop. 1977): 13.2. **Deaths** (per 1,000 pop. 1977): 9.6. **Natural increase** (1977): .4%. **Hospital beds** (per 100,000 pop. 1977): 1,036. **Physicians** (per 100,000 pop. 1977): 208. **Infant mortality** (per 1,000 live births 1977): 17.6.

Education (1977): **Literacy:** 94%. **Pop. 5-19:** in school: 62%, teachers per 1,000: 42. **PQLI:** 94.

Rome emerged as the major power in Italy after 500 BC, dominating the more civilized Etruscans to the N and Greeks to the S. Under the Empire, which lasted until the 5th century AD, Rome ruled most of Western Europe, the Balkans, the Near East, and North Africa.

After the Germanic invasions, lasting several centuries, a high civilization arose in the city-states of the N, culminating in the Renaissance. But German, French, Spanish, and Austrian intervention prevented the unification of the country. In 1859 Lombardy came under the crown of King Victor Emmanuel II of Sardinia. By plebiscite in 1860, Parma, Modena, Romagna, and Tuscany joined, followed by Sicily and Naples, and by the Marches and Umbria. The first Italian parliament declared Victor Emmanuel king of Italy Mar. 17, 1861. Mantua and Venetia were added in 1866 as an outcome of the Austro-Prussian war. The Papal States were taken by Italian troops Sept. 20, 1870, on the withdrawal of the French garrison. The states were annexed to the kingdom by plebiscite. Italy recognized the State of Vatican City as independent Feb. 11, 1929.

Fascism appeared in Italy Mar. 23, 1919, led by Benito Mussolini, who took over the government at the invitation of the king Oct. 28, 1922. Mussolini acquired dictatorial powers. He made war on Ethiopia and proclaimed Victor Emmanuel III emperor, defied the sanctions of the League of Nations, joined the Berlin-Tokyo axis, sent troops to fight for Franco against the Republic of Spain and joined Germany in World War II.

After Fascism was overthrown in 1943, Italy declared war on Germany and Japan and contributed to the Allied victory. It surrendered conquered lands and lost its colonies. Mussolini was killed by partisans Apr. 28, 1945.

Victor Emmanuel III abdicated May 9, 1946; his son Humbert II was king until June 10, when Italy became a republic after a referendum, June 2-3.

Reorganization of the Fascist party is forbidden. The cabinet normally represents a coalition of the Christian Democrats, largest of Italy's many parties, and one or 2 other parties. The 39th government since World War II was formed Apr. 1980, a center-left coalition that included socialists for the first time in 6 years.

The Vatican agreed in 1976 to revise its 1929 concordat with the state, depriving Roman Catholicism of its status as state religion. In 1974 Italians voted by a 3-to-2 margin to retain a 3-year-old law permitting divorce, which was opposed by the church.

Italy has enjoyed an extraordinary growth in industry and living standards since World War II, in part due to membership in the Common Market. Italy joined the European Monetary System, 1980. But in 1973-74, a fourfold increase in international oil prices helped disrupt the economy. Taxes were boosted in 1974. Western aid helped ease the crisis in 1975, but inflation and decline in confidence continued through 1980. A wave of left-wing political violence worsened in 1977 with kidnappings and assassinations and continued through 1979. Christian Dem. leader and former Prime Min. Moro was murdered May 1978 by Red Brigade terrorists.

Sicily, 9,822 sq. mi., pop. (1980) 5,000,000, is an island 180 by 120 mi., seat of a region that embraces the island of **Pantelleria,** 32 sq. mi., and the **Lipari** group, 44 sq. mi., 63 14,000, including 2 active volcanoes: **Vulcano,** 1,637 ft. and **Stromboli,** 3,038 ft. From prehistoric times Sicily has been settled by various peoples; a Greek state had its capital at Syracuse. Rome took Sicily from Carthage 215 BC. **Mt. Etna,** 10,705 ft. active volcano, is tallest peak.

Sardinia, 9,262 sq. mi., pop. (1976) 1,600,000, lies in the Mediterranean, 115 mi. W of Italy and 7-½ mi. S of Corsica. It is 160 mi. long, 68 mi. wide, and mountainous, with mining of coal, zinc, lead, copper. In 1720 Sardinia was added to the possessions of the Dukes of Savoy in Piedmont and Savoy to form the Kingdom of Sardinia. Giuseppe Garibaldi is buried on the nearby isle of Caprera. **Elba,** 86 sq. mi., lies 6 mi. W of Tuscany. Napoleon I lived in exile on Elba 1814-1815.

Trieste. An agreement, signed Oct. 5, 1954, by Italy and Yugoslavia, confirmed, Nov. 10, 1975, gave Italy provisional administration over the northern section and the seaport of Trieste, and Yugoslavia the part of Istrian peninsula it has occupied.

Ivory Coast

Republic of Ivory Coast

People: Population (1979 est.): 7,761,000. **Age distrib.** (%): 0–14: 44.6; 15–59: 52.0; 60+: 3.4. **Pop. density:** 61.12 per sq. mi. **Urban** (1975): 32.4%. **Ethnic groups:** Baule 23%, Bete 18%, Senufo 15%, Malinke 11%, others. **Languages:** French (official), tribal languages. **Religions:** Moslems 25%, Christians 12%.

Geography: Area: 124,503 sq. mi., slightly larger than New Mexico. **Location:** On S. coast of W. Africa. **Neighbors:** Liberia, Guinea on W, Mali, Upper Volta on N, Ghana on E. **Topography:** Forests cover the W half of the country, and range from a coastal strip to halfway to the N on the E. A sparse inland plain leads to low mountains in NW. **Capital:** Abidjan. **Cities** (1976 est.): Abidjan 1,388,320; Bouaké (1977 cen.) 805,356.

Government: Head of state: Pres. Felix Houphouet-Boigny; b. Oct. 18, 1905; in office: Aug. 7, 1960. **Local divisions:** 25 departments. **Armed forces:** regulars 4,950; para-military 3,000.

Economy: Chief crops: Coffee, cocoa, bananas, cotton, pineapples, rice, oil palms. **Minerals:** Diamonds, manganese. **Other resources:** Tropical woods, rubber. **Per capita arable**

land: 2.6 acres. **Meat prod.** (1978): beef: 39,000 metric tons; pork: 6,000 metric tons; lamb: 12,000 metric tons. **Fish catch** (1977): 83,400 metric tons. **Electricity prod.** (1978): 1.42 bln. kwh. **Labor force:** 75% agric.

Finance: Currency: CFA franc (Mar. 1980: 223.92 = $1 US). **Gross domestic product** (1978): $7.71 bln. **Per capita income** (1978): $906. **Imports** (1978): $2.33 bln.; partners: Fr. 39%, W. Ger. 7%, Jap. 7%, U.S. 5%. **Exports** (1978): $2.32 bln.; partners: Fr. 23%, Neth. 19%, U.S. 15%, It. 6%. **Tourists** (1976): 122,200; receipts: $26 mln. **International reserves less gold** (Jan. 1980): $51.6 mln. **Gold:** 45,000 oz t. **Consumer prices** (changed in 1979): 16.5%.

Transport: Railway traffic (1978): 1.27 bln. passenger-km; 532.8 mln. net ton-km. **Motor vehicles:** in use (1976): 84,900 passenger cars, 43,500 comm. vehicles; assembled (1976): 7,000 passenger cars. **Chief ports:** Abidjan, Sassandra.

Communications: Television sets: 257,000 in use (1976). **Radios:** 600,000 in use (1976), 80,000 manuf. (1975). **Telephones in use** (1978): 58,558. **Daily newspaper circ.** (1976): 63,000; 13 per 1,000 pop.

Health: Life expectancy at birth (1975): 41.9 male; 45.1 female. **Births** (per 1,000 pop. 1975): 49.0. **Deaths** (per 1,000 pop. 1975): 20.4. **Natural increase** (1975): 2.9%. **Hospital beds** (per 100,000 pop. 1977): 124. **Physicians** (per 100,000 pop. 1977): 4. **Infant mortality** (per 1,000 live births 1975): 138.

Education (1977): **Literacy:** 22%. **Pop. 5-19:** in school: 37%, teachers per 1,000: 9. **PQLI:** 31.

A French protectorate from 1842, Ivory Coast became independent in 1960. It is the most prosperous of tropical African nations, due to diversification of agriculture for export, close ties to France, and encouragement of foreign investment. About 20% of the population are workers from neighboring countries. Ivory Coast is a leader of the pro-Western bloc in Africa.

Jamaica

People: Population (1979 est.): 2,215,000. **Age distrib.** (%): 0–14: 45.9; 15–59: 45.7; 60+: 8.5. **Pop. density:** 501.89 per sq. mi. **Urban** (1970): 37.1%. **Ethnic groups:** Negroes 85%, mixed 10%, Chinese, Caucasians, East Indians. **Languages:** English, Jamaican Creole. **Religions:** Protestants 75%, Roman Catholics, 5%.

Geography: Area: 4,244 sq. mi., slightly smaller than Connecticut. **Location:** In West Indies. **Neighbors:** Nearest are Cuba on N, Haiti on E. **Topography:** The country is four-fifths covered by mountains. **Capital:** Kingston. **Cities** (1970 cen.): Kingston 111,879.

Government: Head of state: Queen Elizabeth II, represented by Gov.-Gen. Florizel A. Glasspole; b. Sept. 25, 1909; in office: Mar. 2, 1973. **Head of government:** Prime Min. Michael Manley; b. Dec. 10, 1924; in office: Mar. 2, 1972. **Local divisions:** 12 parishes; Kingston and St. Andrew corporate area. **Armed forces:** regulars 4,000; para-military 8,200.

Economy: Industries: Aluminum, rum, molasses, cigars, oil products, tourism. **Chief crops:** Sugar cane, coffee, bananas, coconuts, ginger, cocoa, pimento, fruits. **Minerals:** Bauxite, marble, silica, gypsum. **Per capita arable land:** 0.2 acres. **Meat prod.** (1978): beef: 12,000 metric tons; pork: 9,000 metric tons. **Fish catch** (1977): 10,100 metric tons. **Electricity prod.** (1978): 1.42 bln. kwh. **Labor force:** 28.1% agric.

Finance: Currency: Dollar (Mar. 1980: 1 = $.56 US). **Gross domestic product** (1978): $2.70 bln. **Per capita income** (1977): $1,349. **Imports** (1978): $777 mln.; partners (1977): U.S. 36%, Venez. 16%, Neth. Ant. 11%, UK 10%. **Exports** (1978): $701 mln.; partners (1977): U.S. 44%, UK 20%, Nor. 11%, Can. 9%. **Tourists** (1977): 264,900; receipts: $106 mln. **National budget** (1978): $621 mln. revenues; $1.04 bln. expenditures. **International reserves less gold** (Feb. 1980): $99.1 mln. **Consumer prices** (change in 1979): 29.0%.

Transport: Railway traffic (1977): 83 mln. passenger-km; 186 mln. net ton-km. **Chief ports:** Kingston, Montego Bay.

Communications: Television sets: 111,000 in use (1976), 5,000 manuf. (1977). **Radios:** 555,000 in use (1976), 7,000 manuf. (1975). **Telephones in use** (1978): 111,192. **Daily newspaper circ.** (1977): 101,000; 49 per 1,000 pop.

Health: Life expectancy at birth (1961): 62.65 male; 66.63 female. **Births** (per 1,000 pop. 1976): 29.8. **Deaths** (per 1,000 pop. 1976): 7.1 **Natural increase** (1976): 2.3%. **Hospital beds** (per 100,000 pop. 1977): 369. **Physicians** (per 100,000 pop. 1977): 28. **Infant mortality** (per 1,000 live births 1976): 20.4.

Education (1977): **Literacy:** 86%. **Pop. 5-19:** in school: 63%, teachers per 1,000: 23. **PQLI:** 87.

Jamaica was visited by Columbus, 1494, and ruled by Spain (under whom Arawak Indians died out) until seized by Britain, 1655. Jamaica won independence Aug. 6, 1962.

In 1974 Jamaica sought an increase in taxes paid by U.S. and Canadian companies which mine bauxite on the island. The socialist government acquired 50% ownership of the companies' Jamaican interests in 1976, and was reelected that year. Rudimentary welfare state measures have been passed, but unemployment has increased. Relations with the U.S. and UK became strained, as those with Cuba and the USSR improved.

Japan

People: Population (1979 est.): 115,880,000. **Age distrib.** (%): 0–14: 24.2; 15–59: 63.6; 60+: 12.2. **Pop. density:** 800.28 per sq. mi. **Urban** (1975): 75.9%. **Ethnic groups:** Japanese 99.4%, Korean 0.5%. **Religions:** Buddhism, Shintoism shared by large majority, Christians 0.8%.

Geography: Area: 143,574 sq. mi., slightly smaller than Montana. **Location:** Archipelago off E. coast of Asia. **Neighbors:** USSR on N, S. Korea on W. **Topography:** Japan consists of 4 main islands: Honshu ("mainland"), 87,805 sq. mi.; Hokkaido, 30,144 sq. mi.; Kyushu, 14,114 sq. mi.; and Shikoku, 7,049 sq. mi. The coast, deeply indented, measures 16,654 mi. The northern islands are a continuation of the Sakhalin Mts. The Kunlun range of China continues into southern islands, the ranges meeting in the Japanese Alps. In a vast transverse fissure crossing Honshu E-W rises a group of volcanoes, mostly extinct or inactive, including 12,388 ft. Fuji-San (Fujiyama) near Tokyo. **Capital:** Tokyo. **Cities** (1978 est.): Tokyo 8,543,775; Osaka 2,723,752; Yokohama 2,694,569; Nagoya 2,083,616; Kyoto 1,464,964; Kobe 1,366,397; Sapporo 1,307,686; Kitakyushu 1,067,915; Fukuoka 1,039,286; Kawasaki 1,032,852.

Government: Head of state: Emp. Hirohito; b. Apr. 29, 1901; in office: Dec. 25, 1926. **Head of government:** Prime Min. Zenko Suzuki; b. Jan. 11, 1911; in office: July 17, 1980. **Local divisions:** 43 prefectures and 4 major municipal units. **Armed forces:** regulars 241,000; reserves 39,600.

Economy: Industries: Steel, vehicles, machinery, ships, electronics, precision instruments, chemicals, textiles, ceramics, wood products. **Chief crops:** Rice, grains, potatoes, tobacco, tea, beans, fruits. **Minerals:** Gold, molybdenum, silver, zinc, copper, lead, chromite, coal, sulphur, salt, oil. **Crude oil reserves** (1980): 55 mln. bbls. **Per capita arable land:** 0.09 acres. **Meat prod.** (1978): beef: 364,000 metric tons; pork: 1.23 mln. metric tons. **Fish catch** (1977): 10.7 mln. metric tons. **Electricity prod.** (1978): 495.18 bln. kwh. **Crude steel prod.** (1979): 111.8 mln. metric tons. **Labor force:** 12% agric.; 25% manuf.

Finance: Currency: Yen (Mar. 1980: 249.7 = $1 US). **Gross domestic product** (1978): $973.90 bln. **Per capita income** (1978): $7,153. **Imports** (1979): $109.82 bln.; partners (1978): U.S. 19%, Saudi Ar. 11%, Austral. 7%, Indon. 7%. **Exports** (1979): $102.28 bln.; partners (1978): U.S. 26%, S. Kor. 6%. **Tourists** (1977): 890,700; receipts: $425 mln. **National budget** (1979): $86.33 bln. revenues; $140.04 bln. expenditures. **International reserves less gold** (Mar. 1980): $17.8 bln. **Gold:** 24.23 mln. **Consumer prices** (change in 1979): 3.6%.

Transport: Railway traffic (1978): 311.2 bln. passenger-km; 40.3 bln. net ton-km. **Motor vehicles:** in use (1977): 19.83 mln. passenger cars, 11.55 mln. comm. vehicles; manuf. (1978): 5.98 mln. passenger cars; 3.26 mln. comm. vehicles. **Civil aviation:** 25,656 mln. passenger-km (1978); 1,316 mln. freight ton-km (1978). **Chief ports:** Yokohama, Tokyo, Kobe, Osaka, Nagoya, Chiba, Kawasaki, Hakodate.

Communications: Television sets: 26.55 mln. in use (1975), 15.21 mln. manuf. (1977). **Radios:** 59.65 mln. in use (1976), 19.93 mln. manuf. (1977). **Telephones in use** (1978): 50,625,589. **Daily newspaper circ.** (1977): 62,221,000; 546 per 1,000 pop.

Health: Life expectancy at birth (1976): 72.15 male; 77.35 female. **Births** (per 1,000 pop. 1977): 15.5. **Deaths** (per 1,000 pop. 1977): 6.0. **Natural increase** (1977): 1.0%. **Hospital beds** (per 100,000 pop. 1977): 1,060. **Physicians** (per. 100,000 pop. 1977): 119. **Infant mortality** (per 1,000 live births 1977): 8.9.

Education (1977): **Literacy:** 99%. **Pop. 5–19:** in school: 71%, teachers per 1,000: 25. **PQLI:** 97.

According to Japanese legend, the empire was founded by Emperor Jimmu, 660 BC, but earliest records of a unified Japan date from 1,000 years later. Chinese influence was strong in the formation of Japanese civilization. Buddhism was introduced before the 6th century.

A feudal system, with locally powerful noble families and their samurai warrior retainers, dominated from 1192. Central power was held by successive families of shoguns (military dictators), 1192-1867, until recovered by the Emperor Meiji, 1868. The Portuguese and Dutch had minor trade with Japan in the 16th and 17th centuries; U.S. Commodore Matthew C. Perry opened it to U.S. trade in a treaty ratified 1854. Japan fought China, 1894-95, gaining Taiwan. After war with Russia, 1904-05, Russia ceded S half of Sakhalin and gave concessions in China. Japan annexed Korea 1910. In World War I Japan ousted Germany from Shantung, took over German Pacific islands. Japan took Manchuria 1931, started war with China 1932. Japan launched war against the U.S. by attack on Pearl Harbor Dec. 7, 1941. Japan surrendered Aug. 14, 1945.

In a new constitution adopted May 3, 1947, Japan renounced the right to wage war; the emperor gave up claims to divinity; the Diet became the sole law-making authority.

The U.S. and 48 other non-communist nations signed a peace treaty and the U.S. a bilateral defense agreement with Japan, in San Francisco Sept. 8, 1951, restoring Japan's sovereignty as of April 28, 1952. Japan signed separate treaties with Nationalist China, 1952; India, 1952; a declaration with USSR ending a technical state of war, 1956. In Dec. 1965 Japan and South Korea agreed to resume diplomatic relations.

On June 26, 1968, the U.S. returned to Japanese control the Bonin Is., the Volcano Is. (including Iwo Jima) and Marcus Is. On May 15, 1972, Okinawa, the other Ryukyu Is. and the Daito Is. were returned to Japan by the U.S.; it was agreed the U.S. would continue to maintain military bases on Okinawa. Japan and the USSR have failed to resolve disputed claims of sovereignty over 4 of the Kurile Is. and over offshore fishing rights.

On Sept. 29, 1972, Japan and mainland China agreed to resume diplomatic relations; Japan and Taiwan severed diplomatic relations. A Japan-China friendship treaty was signed 1978.

Industrialization was begun in the late 19th century. After World War II, Japan emerged as the 3d most powerful economy in the world, and as a leader in technology. Huge trade surpluses caused the yen to soar in value in the late 1970s.

The Liberal Democratic (conservative) party controlled almost every post-war government, but by declining margins.

During 1969 the U.S. began turning over 50 military installation sites, a third of its facilities in Japan, to the Japanese. By 1980, U.S. forces had been reduced to 46,000 men and women.

The government announced a further commitment to energy conservation, 1979, in light of the considerable deterioration of world oil following the Iranian revolution.

Jordan

Hashemite Kingdom of Jordan

People: Population (1979 est.): 3,189,000. **Age distrib.** (%): 0–14: 51.6; 15–59: 44.4; 60+: 4.0. **Pop. density:** 79.9 per sq. mi. **Urban** (1974): 42.0%. **Ethnic groups:** Arabs, small minorities of Circassians, Armenians, Kurds. **Languages:** Arabic is universal. **Religions:** Sunni Moslems 93.6%, Christians 6.4%.

Geography: Area: 37,297 sq. mi., slightly larger than Indiana. **Location:** In W Asia. **Neighbors:** Israel on W, Saudi Arabia on S, Iraq on E, Syria on N. **Topography:** About 88% of Jordan is arid. Fertile areas are in W. Only port is on short Aqaba Gulf coast. Country shares Dead Sea (1,296 ft. below sea level) with Israel. **Capital:** Amman. **Cities** (1978 est.): Amman 711,850; Zarka 263,400; Irbid 136,770.

Government: Head of state: King Hussein I; b. Nov. 14, 1935; in office: Aug. 11, 1952. **Head of government:** Prime Min. Sharif Abdul Hamid Sharaf, b. July 8, 1939; in office: Dec. 19, 1979. **Local divisions:** 8 governorates. **Armed forces:** regulars 67,200; reserves 30,000.

Economy: Industries: Textiles, plastics, cement, food processing. **Chief crops:** Grains, olives, vegetables, fruits. **Minerals:** Phosphates, potash. **Per capita arable land:** 1.0 acres. **Electricity prod.** (1977): 601 mln. kwh. **Labor force:** 23% agric.

Finance: Currency: Dinar (Mar. 1980: 1 = $3.24 US). **Gross domestic product** (1979): $2.11 bln. **Per capita income** (1976): $552. **Imports** (1978): $1.5 bln.; partners (1977): U.S. 15%, W. Ger. 14%, Saudi Ar. 9%, UK 7%. **Exports** (1978): $297 mln.; partners (1977): Saudi Ar. 30%, Syria 11%, Iran 9%, Iraq. 6%. **Tourists** (1977): 937,100; receipts: $180 mln. **National budget** (1978): $530.73 mln. revenues; $1.16 bln. expenditures. **International reserves less gold** (Mar. 1980): $1.09 bln. **Gold:** 816,000 oz t. **Consumer prices** (change in 1979): 14.3%.

Transport: Motor vehicles: in use (1977): 57,000 passenger cars, 21,000 comm. vehicles. **Civil aviation:** 1,254 mln. passenger-km (1978); 52 mln. freight ton-km (1978). **Chief ports:** Aqaba.

Communications: Television sets: 125,000 licensed (1976). **Radios:** 531,000 in use (1976). **Telephones in use** (1978): 53,107. **Daily newspaper circ.** (1977): 85,000; 29 per 1,000 pop.

Health: Life expectancy at birth (1963): 52.6 male; 52.0 female. **Births** (per 1,000 pop. 1975): 47.2. **Deaths** (per 1,000 pop. 1975): 14.7. **Natural increase** (1975): 3.3%. **Hospital beds** (per 100,000 pop. 1977): 86. **Physicians** (per 100,000 pop. 1977): 37. **Infant mortality** (per 1,000 live births 1975): 14.9.

Education (1977): **Literacy:** 54%. **Pop. 5-19:** in school: 56%, teachers per 1,000: 20. **PQLI:** 56.

From ancient times to 1922 the lands to the E of the Jordan were culturally and politically united with the lands to the W. Arabs conquered the area in the 7th century; the Ottomans took control in the 16th. Britain's 1920 Palestine Mandate covered both sides of the Jordan. In 1921, Abdullah, son of the ruler of Hejaz in Arabia, was installed by Britain as emir of an autonomous Transjordan, covering two-thirds of Palestine. An independent kingdom was proclaimed, 1946.

During the 1948 Arab-Israeli war the West Bank and old city of Jerusalem were added to the kingdom, which changed its name to Jordan. All these territories were lost to Israel in the 1967 war, which swelled the number of Arab refugees on the East Bank. A 1974 Arab summit conference designated the Palestine Liberation Organization as the sole representative of Arabs on the West Bank. Jordan accepted the move, and was granted an annual subsidy by Arab oil states. The U.S. has also provided substantial economic and military support.

In 1970 and 1971, Jordan dispersed all PLO commandos who threatened to seize power in Jordan, which they considered part of Palestine. Relations with the PLO improved, 1979.

King Hussein actively promoted rejection of the Egyptian-Israeli peace treaty; Jordan was the first Arab country to sever diplomatic relations with Egypt, Mar. 1979. Jordan abandoned its traditionally pro-Western orientation in favor of non-alignment, 1979.

Kampuchea

See Cambodia

Kenya

Republic of Kenya

People: Population (1979 est.): 15,778,000. **Age distrib.** (%): 0–14: 48.4; 15–59: 46.3; 60+: 5.4. **Pop. density:** 66.06 per sq. mi. **Urban** (1969): 9.9%. **Ethnic groups:** Kikuyu 20%, Tuo 15%, Balhya 13%, Kamba 11%, others, including 280,000 Asians, Arabs, Europeans. **Languages:** Swahili, English both official. **Religions:** Protestants 37%, Roman Catholics 22%, Moslems 3%, others.

Geography: Area: 224,960 sq. mi., slightly smaller than Texas. **Location:** On Indian O. coast of E. Africa. **Neighbors:** Uganda on W, Tanzania on S, Somalia on E, Ethopia, Sudan on N. **Topography:** The northern three-fifths of Kenya is arid. To the S, a low coastal area and a plateau varying from 3,000 to 10,000 ft. The Great Rift Valley enters the country N-S, flanked by high mountains. **Capital:** Nairobi. **Cities** (1978 est.): Nairobi (met.) 818,000; Mombasa (met.) 391,000.

Government: Head of state: Pres. Daniel Arap Moi, b. Sept., 1924; in office: Aug. 22, 1978. **Local divisions:** Nairobi and 7 provinces. **Armed forces:** regulars 12,400; para-military 2,000.

Economy: Industries: Tourism, light industry. **Chief crops:** Coffee, tea, cereals, cotton, sisal. **Minerals:** Gold, limestone, diatomite, salt, barytes, magnesite, felspar, sapphires, fluospar, garnets. **Other resources:** Timber, hides. **Per capita arable land:** 0.3 acres. **Meat prod.** (1978): beef: 145,000 metric tons; pork: 5,000 metric tons; lamb: 31,000 metric tons. **Fish catch** (1977): 39,000 metric tons. **Electricity prod.** (1978): 1.12 bln. kwh. **Labor force:** 76% agric.

Finance: Currency: Shilling (Mar. 1980: 7.72 = $1 US). **Gross domestic product** (1978): $5.5 bln. **Per capita income** (1977): $207. **Imports** (1978): $1.71 bln.; partners: UK 22%, W. Ger. 13%, Jap. 10%, Iran 7%. **Exports** (1978): $1.02 bln.; partners: W. Ger. 14%, UK 14%, Ugan. 10%, Neth. 6%. **Tourists** (1977): 346,500; receipts: $121 mln. **National budget** (1979): $1.39 bln. revenues; $1.73 bln. expenditures. **International reserves less gold** (Mar. 1980): $572.8 mln. **Gold:** 80,000 oz t. **Consumer prices** (change in 1978): 16.9%.

Transport: Motor vehicles: in use (1977): 114,100 passenger cars, 83,900 comm. vehicles. **Chief ports:** Mombasa.

Communications: Television sets: 50,000 in use (1976). **Radios:** 514,000 in use (1976). **Telephones in use** (1978): 143,768. **Daily newspaper circ.** (1976): 154,000; 11 per 1,000 pop.

Health: Life expectancy at birth (1969): 46.9 male; 51.2 female. **Births** (per 1,000 pop. 1975): 50.5. **Deaths** (per 1,000 pop. 1975): 14.0. **Natural increase** (1975): 3.7%. **Hospital beds** (per 100,000 pop. 1977): 128. **Physicians** (per 100,000 pop. 1977): 8. **Infant mortality** (per 1,000 live births 1975): 51.4.

Education (1977): **Literacy:** 40%. **Pop. 5-19:** in school: 57%, teachers per 1,000: 18. **PQLI:** 48.

Arab colonies exported spices and slaves from the Kenya coast as early as the 8th century. Britain obtained control in the 19th century. Kenya won independence Dec. 12, 1963, 4 years after the end of the violent Mau Mau uprising.

Kenya has shown steady growth in industry and agriculture under a modified private enterprise system, and has had a relatively free political life. But stability was shaken in 1974-5, with opposition charges of corruption and oppression.

In 1968 ties with Somalia were restored after 4 years of skirmishes. In 1976-77, relations with Uganda deteriorated. Tanzania closed its Kenya border in 1977 in a dispute over the collapse of the East African Community. Kenya welcomed the overthrow of Idi Amin.

The U.S. agreed in 1976 to sell several jet fighters to Kenya. A military and economic aid accord giving the U.S. access to air and naval bases was concluded, Apr. 1980.

Kiribati

Republic of Kiribati

People: Population (1979 est.): 57,000. **Pop. density:** 212.12 per sq. mi. **Ethnic groups:** nearly all Micronesian, some Polynesians, Europeans. **Languages:** Gilbertese and English. **Religions:** mainly Christian, evenly divided between Protestant and Roman Catholic.

Geography: Area: 264 sq. mi., slightly smaller than New York City. **Location:** 33 Micronesian islands (the Gilbert, Line, and Phoenix groups) in the mid-Pacific scattered in a 2-mln. sq. mi. chain around the point where the International Date Line cuts the Equator. **Neighbors:** Nearest are Nauru to SW, Tuvalu and Tokelau Is. to S. **Topography:** except Banaba (Ocean) I., all are low-lying; with soil of coral sand and rock fragments, subject to erratic rainfall. **Capital** (1979 est.): Tarawa 17,000.

Government: Head of state and of government: Pres. Ieremia T. Tabai, b. Dec. 16, 1950; in office: July 12, 1979.

Economy: Industries: Copra. **Chief crops:** Coconuts, breadfruit, pandanus, bananas, paw paw. **Other resources:** Fish. **Electricity prod.** (1977): 36.00 mln. kwh.

Finance: Currency: Australian dollar. **Imports** (1977): $14.87 mln.; partners (1976): Austral. 51%, NZ 11%, UK 9%, Jap. 6%. **Exports** (1977): $20.20 mln.; partners (1976): Austral. 63%, NZ 31%, UK 5%. **National budget** (1977): $16.37 mln. revenues; $14.87 mln. expenditures.

Transport: Chief port: Tarawa.

Communications: Radios: 8,200 in use (1976). **Telephones in use** (1978): 1,386.

Health: Pop. per hospital bed (1977): 200.

Education: Pop. 5–19: in school (1977): 13,679.

A British protectorate since 1892, the Gilbert and Ellice Islands colony was completed with the inclusion of the Phoenix Islands, 1937. Self-rule was granted 1971; the Ellice Islands separated from the colony 1975 and became independent Tuvalu, 1978 *(see Index)*. Kiribati (pronounced *Kiribass)* independence was attained July 12, 1979. Under a Treaty of Friendship, pending ratification by the U.S. Senate, the U.S. relinquishes its claims to several of the Line and Phoenix islands, including Christmas, Canton, and Enderbury.

Tarawa Atoll was the scene of some of the bloodiest fighting in the Pacific during WW II. Banaba (Ocean) I. has been desecrated by strip mining of phosphate, now virtually exhausted.

North Korea

Democratic People's Republic of Korea

People: Population (1979 est.): 18,717,000. **Pop. density:** 364.99 per sq. mi. **Ethnic groups:** Korean. **Languages:** Korean. **Religions:** Buddhism, Confucianism, Shamanism, Chondolsyo prevailed before 1945, repressed since.

Geography: Area: 46,768 sq. mi., slightly smaller than Mississippi. **Location:** In northern E. Asia. **Neighbors:** China, USSR on N, S. Korea on S. **Topography:** Mountains and hills cover nearly all the country, with narrow valleys and small plains in between. The N and the E coast are the most rugged areas. **Capital:** Pyongyang. **Cities** (1973 est.): Pyongyang 957,000; Hamhung 484,000; Chongjin 306,000.

Government: Head of state: Pres. Kim Il-song; b. Apr. 15, 1912; in office: Dec. 28, 1972. **Head of government:** Prime Min. Yi Chong-ok; in office: Dec. 15, 1977. **Head of Communist Party:** Gen. Sec. Kim Il-song; in office: 1945. **Local divisions:** 9 provinces, 4 municipalities, one urban district. **Armed forces:** regulars 632,000-672,000; reserves 260,000.

Economy: Industries: Textiles, fertilizers, cement. **Chief crops:** Grain, rice. **Minerals:** Coal, lead tungsten, zinc, graphite, magnesite, iron, copper, gold, phosphate, salt, fluorspar. **Per capita arable land:** 0.3 acres. **Meat prod.** (1978): beef: 27,000 metric tons; pork: 84,000 metric tons. **Fish catch** (1977): 1.6 mln. metric tons. **Crude steel prod.** (1979 est.) 5.3 mln. metric tons. **Labor force:** 50% agric.

Finance: Currency: Won (Sept. 1979): .91 = $1 US). **Gross domestic product** (1976 est.): $7.6 bln. **Per capita income** (1976): $450. **Imports** (1978): $1.59 bln.; partners: China 50%, USSR 18%, Jap. 13%. **Exports** (1978): $1.36 bln.; partners: USSR 25% China 40%, Jap. 9%, W.Ger. 5%.

Transport: Chief ports: Chonglin, Hamhung, Nampo.

Health: Life expectancy at birth (1975): 58.8 male; 62.5 female. **Births** (per 1,000 pop. 1975): 35.7. **Deaths** (per 1,000 pop. 1975): 9.4. **Natural increase** (1975): 2.6%. **Hospital beds** (per 100,000 pop. 1977): 59. **Physicians** (per 100,000 pop. 1977): 40.

Education (1977): Literacy: 85%. **Pop. 5-19:** in school: 61%, teachers per 1,000: 13. **PQLI:** 75.

The Democratic People's Republic of Korea was founded May 1, 1948, in the zone occupied by Russian troops after World War II. Its armies tried to conquer the south, 1950. After 3 years of fighting with Chinese and U.S. intervention, a cease-fire was proclaimed. N. Korea has maintained ties with both China and Russia. The U.S. has no diplomatic ties.

N. Korea's attempts to purchase western technology in the 1970s foundered over $1 billion in defaulted loans. Industry, begun by the Japanese during their 1910-45 occupation, and nationalized in the 1940s, had grown substantially, using N. Korea's abundant mineral and hydroelectric resources. Political life is dominated by a cult of personality around Pres. Kim Il-song.

South Korea

Republic of Korea

People: Population (1979 est.): 39,140,000. **Age distrib.** (%): 0–14: 38.1; 15–59: 56.3; 60+: 5.6. **Pop. density:** 973.42 per sq. mi. **Urban** (1975): 48.4%. **Ethnic groups:** Korean. **Languages:** Korean. **Religions:** Buddhism, Confucianism, Shamanism, Chondokyo widespread; Protestants 13%, Roman Catholics 3%.

Geography: Area: 38,031 sq. mi., slightly larger than Indiana. **Location:** In Northern E. Asia. **Neighbors:** N. Korea on N. **Topography:** The country is mountainous, with a rugged east coast. The western and southern coasts are deeply indented, with many islands and harbors. **Capital:** Seoul. **Cities** (1975 cen.): Seoul 6,879,464; Pusan 2,450,125; Taegu 1,309,131; Inchon 797,143; Kwangchu 606,468.

Government: Head of state: Pres. Choi Kyu Hah; b. July 16,

1919; in office: Oct. 27, 1979. **Head of government:** Prime Min. Park Choong Hoon; in office: May 21, 1980. **Local divisions:** 9 provinces, 2 special cities. **Armed forces:** regulars 619,000; reserves 1,215,000.

Economy: Industries: Electronics, ships, rubber, glass, chemicals, oil products, steel. **Chief crops:** Rice, grain, tobacco, beans. **Minerals:** Molybdenum, tungsten, coal, iron, bismuth, fluorspar, graphite. **Per capita arable land:** 0.1 acres. **Meat prod.** (1978): beef: 81,000 metric tons; pork: 187,000 metric tons. **Fish catch:** (1977): 2.4 mln. metric tons. **Electricity prod.** (1978): 31.51 bln. kwh. **Crude steel prod.** (1979): 7.6 mln. metric tons. **Labor force:** 43% agric.; 21% manuf.

Finance: Currency: Won (Mar. 1980: 586.1 = $1 US). **Gross domestic product** (1979): $61.5 bln. **Per capita income** (1978): $1,187. **Imports** (1979): $20.34 bln.; partners (1977): Jap. 36%, U.S. 23%, Saudi Ar. 10%, Kuw. 5%. **Exports** (1979): $15.06 bln.; partners (1977): U.S. 31%, Jap. 21%, Saudi Ar. 7%, W. Ger. 5%. **Tourists** (1977): 949,700; receipts: $370 mln. **National budget** (1979): $12.90 bln. revenues; $12.26 bln. expenditures. **International reserves less gold** (Feb. 1980): $2.74 bln. **Gold:** (Mar. 1980): 296,000 oz t. **Consumer prices** (change in 1979): 18.3%.

Transport: Railway traffic (1978): 20.1 bln. passenger-km; 10.7 bln. net ton-km. **Motor vehicles:** in use (1977): 125,600 passenger cars, 144,900 comm. vehicles; assembled (1978): 92,328 passenger cars; 65,616 comm. vehicles. **Chief ports:** Pusan, Inchon.

Communications: Television sets: 2.3 mln. licensed (1976), 2.99 mln. manuf. (1977). **Radios:** 5 mln. in use (1976), 6.4 mln. manuf. (1977). **Telephones in use** (1978): 1,978,366. **Daily newspaper circ.** (1977): 7,169,000; 197 per 1,000 pop.

Health: Life expectancy at birth (1970): 63 male; 67 female. **Births** (per 1,000 pop. 1975): 28.8. Deaths (per 1,000 pop. 1975): 8.9. **Natural increase** (1975): 2.0%. **Hospital beds** (per 100,000 pop. 1977): 68. **Physicians** (per 100,000 pop. 1977): 49.

Education (1977): **Literacy:** 91%. **Pop. 5-19:** in school: 65%, teachers per 1,000: 14. **PQLI:** 83.

Korea, once called the Hermit Kingdom, has a recorded history since the 1st century BC. It was united in a kingdom under the Silla Dynasty, 668 AD. It was at times associated with the Chinese empire; the treaty that concluded the Sino-Japanese war of 1894-95 recognized Korea's complete independence. In 1910 Japan forcibly annexed Korea as Chosun.

At the Potsdam conference, July, 1945, the 38th parallel was designated as the line dividing the Soviet and the American occupation. Russian troops entered Korea Aug. 10, 1945, U.S. troops entered Sept. 8, 1945. The Soviet military organized socialists and communists and blocked efforts to let the Koreans unite their country. *(See Index for Korean War.)*

The South Koreans formed the Republic of Korea in May 1948 with Seoul as the capital. Dr. Syngman Rhee was chosen president July 20 but a movement spearheaded by college students forced his resignation Apr. 26, 1960.

In an army coup May 16, 1961, Gen. Park Chung Hee became chairman of the ruling junta. He was formally elected president, 1963; a 1972 referendum provided more presidential powers and allowed him to be reelected for 6 year terms unlimited times. Park was assassinated by the chief of the Korean CIA, Oct. 26, 1979. The initial calm of the new government was halted abruptly by the rise of Gen. Chon Too Hwan, head of the military intelligence, who reinstated martial law, and reverted South Korea to being the police state it was under Park. *(See Index for Chronology.)*

North Korean raids across the border tapered off in 1971, but incidents occurred in 1973 and 1974. In July 1972 South and North Korea agreed on a common goal of reunifying the 2 nations by peaceful means. Red Cross delegates from both nations met to find ways to aid divided families.

The U.S. announced in 1977 that it would withdraw 39,000 ground troops by 1982. Some 12,000 Air Force and logistics troops would remain. Alleged Korean agents were charged in 1976-77 with giving questionable gifts to U.S. congresspersons to promote foreign aid.

Kuwait

State of Kuwait

People: Population (1979 est.): 1,277,000. **Age distrib.** (%): 0–14: 44.4; 15–59: 53.1; 60+: 2.6. **Pop. density:** 154.24 per sq. mi. **Ethnic groups:** Arabs 85%, Iranians, Indians, Pakistanis 13%. **Languages:** Arabic, others. **Religions:** Moslems (most Sunni) predominate.

Geography: Area: 7,780 sq. mi., the size of Massachusetts. **Location:** In Middle East, at N end of Persian Gulf. **Neighbors:** Iraq on N, Saudi Arabia on S. **Topography:** The country is flat, very dry, and extremely hot. **Capital:** Kuwait. **Cities** (1970 cen.): Hawalli 106,542; Kuwait City 80,405.

Government: Head of state: Amir Shaikh Jaber Al-Ahmad Al-Sabah; b. 1928; in office: Jan. 1, 1978. **Head of government:** Prime Min. Shaikh Sa'ad Abdulla Al-Sabah; in office: Feb. 8, 1978. **Local divisions:** 3 governorates. **Armed forces:** regulars 11,100; para-military 15,000.

Economy: Industries: Oil products. **Minerals:** Oil, gas. **Crude oil reserves** (1980): 65.4 bln. bbls. **Per capita arable land:** 0.002 acres. **Electricity prod.** (1978): 7.00 bln. kwh. **Labor force:** 2% agric.; 8%. manuf.

Finance: Currency: Dinar (Mar. 1980: 1 = $3.62 US). **Gross domestic product** (1977): $1.1 bln. **Per capita income** (1975): $11,431. **Imports** (1978): $4.6 bln.; partners (1977): Jap. 20%, U.S. 14%, UK 10%, W. Ger. 9%. **Exports** (1979): $17.56 bln.; partners (1977): Jap. 25%, UK 9%, Neth. 7%, It. 7%. **National budget** (1978): $11.2 bln. revenues; $6.26 bln. expenditures. **International reserves less gold** (Mar. 1980): $2.66 bln. **Gold:** 2.54 mln. oz t. **Consumer prices** (change in 1978): 9.0%.

Transport: Motor vehicles: in use (1977): 285,800 passenger cars, 95,100 comm. vehicles. **Chief ports:** Mina al-Ahmadi.

Communications: Television sets: 182,000 in use (1975). **Radios:** 506,000 in use (1976). **Telephones in use** (1978): 152,517. **Daily newspaper circ.** (1977): 180,000; 159 per 1,000 pop.

Health: Life expectancy at birth (1970): 66.4 male; 71.5 female. **Births** (per 1,000 pop. 1977): 41.5. **Deaths** (per 1,000 pop. 1977): 4.8. **Natural increase** (1977): 3.7%. **Hospital beds** (per 100,000 pop. 1977): 388. **Physicians** (per. 100,000 pop. 1977): 124. **Infant mortality** (per 1,000 live births 1977): 39.1.

Education (1977): **Literacy:** 60%. **Pop. 5-19:** in school: 68%, teachers per 1,000: 49. **PQLI:** 77.

Kuwait is ruled by the Al-Sabah dynasty, founded 1759. Britain ran foreign relations and defense from 1899 until independence in 1961. The majority of the population is non-Kuwaiti, with many Palestinians, and cannot vote.

Iraqi troops crossed the Kuwait border in 1973 but soon withdrew. Kuwait has ordered advanced weapons from France and the U.S.

Oil, first exported in 1946, is the fiscal mainstay. Reserves are 15% of the world total. Oil pays for free medical care, education, and social security. There are no taxes, except customs duties.

Laos

Lao People's Democratic Republic

People: Population (1979 est.): 3,440,000. **Pop. density:** 38.83 per sq. mi. **Urban** (1973): 14.7%. **Ethnic groups:** Lao 50%, Thai 20%, Meo and Yao 15%, others. **Languages:** Lao (official), others. **Religions:** Buddhists 90%, animists, Christians 1.5%.

Geography: Area: 91,428 sq. mi., slightly larger than Utah. **Location:** In Indochina Peninsula in SE Asia. **Neighbors:** Burma, China on N, Vietnam on E, Cambodia on S, Thailand on W. **Topography:** Landlocked, dominated by jungle. High mountains along the eastern border are the source of the E-W rivers slicing across the country to the Mekong R., which defines most of the western border. **Capital:** Vientiane. **Cities** (1973 cen.): Vientiane 176,637.

Government: Head of state: Pres. Souphanouvong; b. July 13, 1909; in office: Dec. 2, 1975. **Head of government:** Prime Min. Kaysone Phomvihan; b. Dec. 13, 1920; in office: Dec. 2, 1975. **Head of Communist Party:** Gen. Sec. Kaysone Phomvihan; in office: 1955. **Local divisions:** 13 provinces. **Armed forces:** regulars 48,550.

Economy: Industries: Wood products. **Chief crops:** Rice, corn, tobacco, cotton, opium, citrus fruits, coffee. **Minerals:** Tin. **Other resources:** Forests. **Per capita arable land:** 0.7 acres. **Meat prod.** (1978): beef: 19,000 metric tons; pork: 26,000 metric tons. **Fish catch** (1977): 20,000 metric tons. **Electricity prod.** (1977): 250 mln. kwh. **Labor force:** 76% agric.

Finance: Currency: New kip (Nov. 1979: 16 = $1 US).

Gross domestic product (1976 est.): $300 mln. **Per capita income** (1976 est.): $85. **Imports** (1974): $65 mln.; partners (1974): Thai. 49%, Jap. 19%, Fr. 7%, W. Ger. 7%. **Exports** (1974): $11 mln.; partners (1974): Thai. 73%, Malaysia 11%, HK 10%. **Tourists** (1973): 23,100; receipts: $3 mln. **Consumer prices** (change in 1975): 84.3%.

Transport: Motor vehicles: in use (1974): 14,100 passenger cars, 2,500 comm. vehicles.

Communications: Radios: 200,000 licensed (1976).

Health: Life expectancy at birth (1975): 39.1 male; 41.8 female. **Births** (per 1,000 pop. 1975): 44.6. **Deaths** (per 1,000 pop. 1975): 22.8. **Natural increase** (1975): 2.2%. **Hospital beds** (per 100,000 pop. 1977): 98. **Physicians** (per 100,000 pop. 1977): 6.

Education: (1977): **Literacy:** 28%. **Pop. 5-19:** in school: 35%, teachers per 1,000: 14. **PQLI:** 26.

Laos became a French protectorate in 1893, but regained independence as a constitutional monarchy July 19, 1949.

Conflicts among neutralist, communist and conservative factions created a chaotic political situation. Armed conflict increased after 1960.

The 3 factions formed a coalition government in June 1962, with neutralist Prince Souvanna Phouma as premier. A 14-nation conference in Geneva signed agreements, 1962, guaranteeing neutrality and independence. By 1964 the Pathet Lao had withdrawn from the coalition, and, with aid from N. Vietnamese troops, renewed sporadic attacks. U.S. planes bombed the Ho Chi Minh trail, supply line from N. Vietnam to communist forces in Laos and S. Vietnam. An estimated 2.75 million tons of bombs were dropped on Laos during the fighting.

In 1970 the U.S. stepped up air support and military aid. There were an est. 67,000 N. North Vietnamese troops in Laos, and some 15,000 Thais financed by the U.S.

After Pathet Lao military gains, Souvanna Phouma in May 1975 ordered government troops to cease fighting; the Pathet Lao took effective control. A Lao People's Democratic Republic was proclaimed Dec. 3, 1975; it is strongly influenced by Vietnam.

While signing alliances with Cambodia and Thailand, Laos moved further away from China, 1979.

Lebanon

Republic of Lebanon

People: Population (1979 est.): 2,943,000. **Age distrib.** (%): 0–14: 42.6; 15–59: 49.6; 60+: 7.7. **Pop. density:** 749.69 per sq. mi. **Urban** (1970): 60.1%. **Ethnic groups:** Arabs 93%, Armenians 6%. **Languages:** Arabic, French, Armenian. **Religions:** Moslems (Sunni and Shiite) 57%, Christians (Maronite, Orthodox) 40%, Druze 3%.

Geography: Area: 4,015 sq. mi., smaller than Connecticut. **Location:** On Eastern end of Mediterranean Sea. **Neighbors:** Syria on E. Israel on S. **Topography:** There is a narrow coastal strip, and 2 mountain ranges running N-S enclosing the fertile Beqaa Valley. The Litani R. runs S through the valley, turning W to empty into the Mediterranean. **Capital:** Beirut. **Cities** (1978 est.): Beirut 702,000; Tripoli 175,000.

Government: Head of state: Pres. Elias Sarkis; b. July 20, 1924; in office: Sept. 23, 1976; **Head of government:** Prime Min. Salim Ahmad al-Huss; b. Dec. 20, 1929; in office: Dec. 9, 1976. **Local divisions:** 5 provinces. **Armed forces:** regulars 8,750; para-military 5,000.

Economy: Industries: Trade, food products, textiles, cement, oil products. **Chief crops:** Fruits, olives, tobacco, grapes, vegetables, grains. **Minerals:** Iron. **Per capita arable land:** 0.2 acres. **Meat prod.** (1978): beef: 10,000 metric tons; lamb: 11,000 metric tons. **Electricity prod.** (1977): 1.60 bln. kwh. **Labor force:** 18% agric.; 17% manuf.

Finance: Currency: Pound (Mar. 1980: 3.42 = $1 US). **Gross domestic product** (1972): $2.09 bln. **Per capita income** (1975): $1,142. **Imports** (1979): $2.41 bln.; partners (1978): It. 12%, Fr. 9%, U.S. 7%, Saudi Ar. 7%. **Exports** (1979): $705 mln.; partners (1978): Saudi Ar. 41%, Syria 8%, Jor. 7%, Kuw. 6%. **Tourists** (1975): 1,554,900; receipts (1977): $65 mln. **International reserves less gold** (Mar. 1980): $1.42 bln. **Gold:** 9.22 mln. oz t. **Consumer prices** (change in 1975): 3.9%.

Transport: Railway traffic (1974): 2 mln. passenger-km; 42 mln. net ton-km. **Motor vehicles:** in use (1974): 220,200 passenger cars, 23,400 comm. vehicles. **Civil aviation:** 1,548 mln. passenger-km (1977); 543 mln. freight ton-km (1977). **Chief ports:** Beirut, Tripoli, Sidon.

Communications: Television sets: 425,000 in use (1976). **Radios:** 1.6 mln. in use (1976). **Daily newspaper circ.** (1976): 281,000.

Health: Life expectancy at birth (1975): 61.4 male; 65.1 female. **Births** (per 1,000 pop. 1975): 34.5. **Deaths** (per 1,000 pop. 1975): 9.5. **Natural increase** (1975): 2.5%. **Hospital beds** (per 100,000 pop. 1977): 384. **Physicians** (per 100,000 pop. 1977): 75. **Infant mortality** (per 1,000 live births 1975): 13.6.

Education: (1977): **Literacy:** 76%. **Pop. 5-19:** in school: 69%, teachers per 1,000: 40. **PQLI:** 72.

Formed from 5 former Turkish Empire districts, Lebanon became an independent state Sept. 1, 1920, administered under French mandate 1920-41. French troops withdrew in 1946.

Under the 1943 National Covenant, all public positions were divided among the various religious communities, with Christians in the majority. By the 1970s, Moslems became the majority, and demanded a larger political and economic role.

U.S. Marines intervened, May-Oct. 1958, during a Syrian-aided revolt. Lebanon's efforts to restrain Palestinian commandos caused armed clashes in 1969. Continued raids against Israeli civilians, 1970-75, brought Israeli attacks against guerrilla camps and villages. Israeli troops occupied S. Lebanon, March 1978, but were replaced by a UN force, and again in Apr. 1980.

An estimated 60,000 were killed and billions of dollars in damage inflicted in a 1975-76 civil war. Palestinian units and leftist Moslems fought against the Maronite militia, the Phalange, and other Christians. Several Arab countries provided political and arms support to the various factions, while Israel aided Christian forces. Up to 15,000 Syrian troops intervened in 1976, and fought Palestinian groups. Arab League troops from several nations tried to impose a cease-fire. But sporadic fighting, among Palestinian factions, among Christian factions, and between Palestinians and Christians near Israel continued in 1979.

Lebanon has a free enterprise economy. Literacy and life expectancy are higher than in most Arab lands.

Lesotho

Kingdom of Lesotho

People: Population (1979 est.): 1,305,000. **Age distrib.** (%): 0–14: 39.5; 15–59: 53.9; 60+: 6.6. **Pop. density:** 109.25 per sq. mi. **Ethnic groups:** Sotho 85%, Nguni 15%. **Languages:** English, Lesotho both official. **Religions:** Christians 70%, others.

Geography: Area: 11,716 sq. mi., slightly larger than Maryland. **Location:** In Southern Africa. **Neighbors:** Completely surrounded by Republic of South Africa. **Topography:** Landlocked and mountainous, with altitudes ranging from 5,000 to 11,000 ft. **Capital:** Maseru. **Cities** (1976 est.): Maseru 45,000.

Government: Head of state: King Moshoeshoe II, b. May 2, 1938; in office: Mar. 12, 1960. **Head of government:** Prime Min. Leabua Jonathan; b. Oct. 31, 1914; in office: Oct. 4, 1966. **Local divisions:** 9 districts.

Economy: Industries: Diamond polishing. **Chief crops:** Corn, grains, peas, beans. **Other resources:** Wool, mohair. **Per capita arable land:** 0.7 acres. **Electricity prod.** (1967): 5.00 mln. kwh. **Labor force:** 95% agric.

Finance: Currency: Maloti (Sept. 1979: .83 = $1 US). **Gross domestic product** (1976 est.): $200 mln. **Per capita income** (1976): $240. **Imports** (1976): $206 mln.; partners: Mostly So. Afr. **Exports** (1977): $14 mln.; partners: Mostly So. Afr. **National budget** (1978): $56.2 mln. revenues; $104.4 mln. expenditures. **Consumer prices** (change in 1978): 13%.

Transport: Motor vehicles: in use (1975): 4,600 passenger cars, 3,200 comm. vehicles.

Communications: Radios: 23,000 licensed (1976). **Daily newspaper circ.** (1976): 1,300; 1 per 1,000 pop.

Health: Life expectancy at birth (1975): 46.7 male; 48.9 female. **Births** (per 1,000 pop. 1971): 36.7. **Deaths** (per 1,000 pop. 1971): 14.5. **Natural increase** (1971): 2.2%. **Hospital beds** (per 100,000 pop. 1977): 205. **Physicians** (per 100,000 pop. 1977): 8. **Infant mortality** (per 1,000 live births 1971): 114.4.

Education (1977): **Literacy:** 50%. **Pop. 5-19:** in school: 58%, teachers per 1,000: 12. **PQLI:** 52.

Lesotho (once called Basutoland) became a British protectorate in 1868 when Chief Moshesh sought protection against the Boers. Independence came Oct. 4, 1966. Elections were suspended in 1970. Over 50% of males work abroad in So. Africa. Livestock raising is the chief industry; wool and mohair are the chief exports.

Liberia

Republic of Liberia

People: Population (1979 est.): 1,788,000. **Age distrib.** (%): 0–14: 40.9; 15–59: 53.1; 60+: 5.9. **Pop. density:** 40.47 per sq. mi. **Urban** (1971): 27.6%. **Ethnic groups:** Americo-Liberians 2.5%, 16 tribes 97.5%. **Languages:** English (official), 28 tribal languages. **Religions:** Moslems 10-20%, Christians 10%, others.

Geography: Area: 43,000 sq. mi., slightly smaller than Pennsylvania. **Location:** On SW coast of W. Africa. **Neighbors:** Sierra Leone on W, Guinea on N, Ivory Coast on E. **Topography:** Marshy Atlantic coastline rises to low mountains and plateaus in the forested interior; 6 major rivers flow in parallel courses to the ocean. **Capital:** Monrovia. **Cities** (1974 cen.): Monrovia 171,680.

Government: Head of state: Pres. Samuel K. Doe; in office: Apr. 12, 1980. **Local divisions:** 9 counties. **Armed forces:** regulars 5,250; para-military 7,600.

Economy: Industries: Food processing and other light industry. **Chief crops:** Fibers, palm kernels, rice, cassava, coffee, cocoa, sugar. **Minerals:** Iron, diamonds, gold. **Other resources:** Rubber, timber. **Per capita arable land:** 0.2 acres. **Fish catch** (1977): 16,500 metric tons. **Electricity prod.** (1977): 887.00 mln. kwh. **Labor force:** 74% agric.

Finance: Currency: Dollar (Mar. 1980: 1 = $1 US). **Gross domestic product** (1978): $744 mln. **Per capita income** (1976): $453. **Imports** (1978): $481 mln.; partners (1977): U.S. 26%, W. Ger. 9%, Jap. 9%, Neth. 9%. **Exports** (1978): $486 mln.; partners (1977): W. Ger. 24%, U.S. 21%, It. 13%, Fr. 8%. **National budget** (1976): $157.3 mln. revenues; (1975) $121.80 mln. expenditures. **International reserves less gold** (Mar. 1980): $35.48 mln. **Consumer prices** (change in 1978): 7.1%.

Transport: Motor vehicles: in use (1974): 12,100 passenger cars, 10,000 comm. vehicles. **Chief ports:** Monrovia, Buchanan.

Communications: Television sets: 8,900 in use (1976). **Radios:** 265,000 in use (1976). **Telephones in use** (1978): 8,420. **Daily newspaper circ.** (1976): 8,000.

Health: Life expectancy at birth (1971): 45.8 male; 44.0 female. **Births** (per 1,000 pop. 1971): 49.8. **Deaths** (per 1,000 pop. 1971): 20.9. **Natural increase** (1971): 2.9%. **Hospital beds** (per 100,000 pop. 1977): 161. **Physicians** (per 100,000 pop. 1977): 12. **Infant mortality** (per 1,000 live births 1971): 159.2

Education (1977): **Literacy:** 18%. **Pop. 5-19:** in school: 33%, teachers per 1,000: 9. **PQLI:** 51.

Liberia was founded in 1822 by U.S. black freedmen who settled at Monrovia with the aid of colonization societies. It became a republic July 26, 1847, with a constitution modeled on that of the U.S. Descendants of freedmen dominated politics.

Charging rampant corruption, an Army Redemption Council of enlisted men staged a bloody predawn coup, April 12, 1980, in which Pres. Tolbert was killed and replaced as head of state by Sgt. Samuel Doe. The new regime was rebuffed by the Organization of African Unity.

Libya

Socialist People's Libyan Arab Jamahiriya

People: Population: (1979 est.): 2,920,000. **Age distrib.** (%): 0–14: 51.4; 15–59: 42.6; 60+: 5.9. **Pop. density:** 4.05 per sq. mi. **Urban** (1974): 29.8%. **Ethnic groups:** Arab-Berber 97%, Italian 1.4%, others. **Languages:** Arabic. **Religions:** Sunni Moslems 97%, Christians 2.5%.

Geography: Area: 679,536 sq. mi., larger than Alaska. **Location:** On Mediterranean coast of N. Africa. **Neighbors:** Tunisia, Algeria on W, Niger, Chad on S, Sudan, Egypt on E. **Topography:** Desert and semidesert regions cover 92% of the land, with low mountains in N, higher mountains in S, and a narrow coastal zone. **Capital:** Tripoli. **Cities** (1973 cen.): Tripoli 551,477; Benghazi 282,192.

Government: Head of state: Sec.-Gen. Abdul Ali al-Obeidi; b. 1933; in office: Mar. 1, 1979. **Head of government:** Chmn. Jadallah Azzuz al Talhi; in office: Mar. 1, 1979. **Local divisions:** 10 regions. **Armed forces:** regulars 42,000.

Economy: Industries: Carpets, textiles, shoes. **Chief crops:** Dates, olives, citrus and other fruits, grapes, tobacco. **Minerals:** Oil, gas. **Crude oil reserves** (1980): 23.5 bln. bbls. **Per capita arable land:** 2.2 acres. **Meat prod.** (1978): beef: 11,000 metric tons; lamb: 40,000 metric tons. **Electricity prod.** (1978): 1.55 bln. kwh. **Labor force:** 20% agric.

Finance: Currency: Dinar (Mar. 1980): 1 = $3.38 US). **Gross domestic product** (1977): $19.36 bln. **Per capita income** (1978): $6,335. **Imports** (1979): $7.9 bln.; partners (1977): It. 27%, W. Ger. 13%, Fr. 8%, Jap. 7%. **Exports** (1979): $15.24 bln.; partners (1977): U.S. 40%, It. 17%, W. Ger. 17%, Sp. 5%. **Tourists** (1977): 125,700; receipts: $8 mln. **International reserves less gold** (Mar. 1980): $7.96 bln. **Gold:** 2.67 mln. oz t. **Consumer prices** (change in 1977): 6.4%.

Transport: Motor vehicles: in use (1975): 263,100 passenger cars, 131,300 comm. vehicles. **Chief ports:** Tripoli, Benghazi.

Communications: Television sets: 10,000 licensed (1975). **Radios:** 110,000 licensed (1976). **Daily newspaper circ.** (1976): 64,000; 26 per 1,000 pop.

Health: Life expectancy at birth (1975): 51.4 male; 54.5 female. **Births** (per 1,000 pop. 1975): 49.0 **Deaths** (per 1,000 pop. 1975): 14.8. **Natural increase** (1975): 3.4%. **Hospital beds** (per 100,000 pop. 1977): 476. **Physicians** (per 100,000 pop. 1977): 106.

Education (1977): **Literacy:** 40%. **Pop. 5-19:** in school: 79%, teachers per 1,000: 40. **PQLI:** 49.

First settled by Berbers, Libya was ruled by Carthage, Rome, and Vandals, the Ottomans, Italy from 1912, and Britain and France after WW II. It became an independent constitutional monarchy Jan. 2, 1952. In 1969 a junta lead by Col. Muammar al-Qadhafi seized power, instituting socialist policies.

In the mid-1970s, it was widely reported that Libya had armed violent revolutionary groups in Egypt and Sudan, and had aided terrorists of various nationalities including Moslem rebels in the Philippines. The USSR sold several billion dollars worth of advanced arms after 1975, and established close political ties.

Libya and Egypt fought several air and land battles along their border in July, 1977. Chad charged Libya with military occupation of its uranium-rich northern region in 1977. Libya's 1979 offensive into the Aouzou Strip was repulsed by Chadian forces.

Despite a new system of government of elected people's congresses, Qaddafi remained the nation's leader. Widespread nationalization, arrests, imposition of currency regulations and wholesale conscription of civil servants into the army, from Jan. 1980, paralysed the economy. Over half the one million Libyan work force are foreigners.

Liechtenstein

Principality of Liechtenstein

People: Population (1979 est.): 26,000. **Age distrib.** (%): 0–14: 27.9; 15–59: 60.2; 60+: 11.9. **Pop. density:** 491.8 per sq. mi. **Ethnic groups:** Germanic. **Languages:** German. **Religions:** Roman Catholics 90%, Protestants 10%.

Geography: Area: 61 sq. mi., the size of Washington, D.C. **Location:** In the Alps. **Neighbors:** Switzerland on W, Austria on E. **Topography:** The Rhine Valley occupies one-third of the country, the Alps cover the rest. **Capital:** Vaduz. **Cities** (1977 cen.): Vaduz 4,704.

Government: Head of state: Prince Franz Josef II; b. Aug. 16, 1906; in office: Mar. 30, 1938. **Head of government:** Hans Brunhart; b. Mar. 28, 1945; in office: Apr. 26, 1978. **Local divisions:** 11 communes.

Economy: Industries: Machines, textiles, precision instruments, false teeth, drugs, ceramics. **Per capita arable land:** 0.3 acres.

Finance: Currency: Swiss Franc. **Tourists** (1977): 80,425.

Communications: Radios: 8,000 licensed (1976). **Telephones in use** (1978): 17,163. **Daily newspaper circ.** (1976): 12,000; 527 per 1,000 pop.

Health: Births (per 1,000 pop. 1977): 12.5. **Deaths** (per 1,000 pop. 1977): 6.0. **Natural increase** (1977): .7%. **Infant mortality**

(per 1,000 live births 1977): 6.5.

Liechtenstein became sovereign in 1866. Austria administered Liechtenstein's ports up to 1920; Switzerland has administered its postal services since 1921. Liechtenstein is united with Switzerland by a customs and monetary union. Taxes are low; many international corporations have headquarters there. Foreign workers comprise a third of the population.

Luxembourg

Grand Duchy of Luxembourg

People: Population: (1979 est.): 358,000. **Age distrib.** (%): 0–14: 20.2; 15–59: 61.4; 60+: 18.2. **Pop. density:** 360.36 per sq. mi. **Urban** (1974): 67.9%. **Ethnic groups:** Mixture of French and Germans predominate, Italians 7%. **Languages:** French, German, Luxembourgish. **Religions:** Roman Catholics 94%, Protestants 1%.

Geography: Area: 999 sq. mi., smaller than Rhode Island. **Location:** In W. Europe. **Neighbors:** Belgium on W, France on S, W. Germany on E. **Topography:** Heavy forests (Ardennes) cover N, S is a low, open plateau. **Capital:** Luxembourg. **Cities** (1978 est.): Luxembourg 78,400.

Government: Head of state: Grand Duke Jean; b. Jan. 5, 1921; in office: Nov. 12, 1964. **Head of government:** Prime Min. Pierre Werner, b. Dec. 29, 1913; in office: July 16, 1979. **Local divisions:** 3 districts, 12 cantons. **Armed forces:** regulars 660; para-military 430.

Economy: Industries: Steel (90% of exports), chemicals, beer, tires, tobacco, metal products, cement. **Chief crops:** Grain, potatoes, roses. **Minerals:** Iron. **Per capita arable land:** (see Belgium). **Electricity prod.** (1978): 1.39 bln. kwh. **Crude steel prod.** (1979): 5.0 mln. metric tons. **Labor force:** 6% agric.; 46% manuf.

Finance: Currency: Franc (Mar. 1980: 31.17 = $1 US). **Gross domestic product** (1978): $3.39 bln. **Per capita income** (1978): $10,040. **Note:** trade and tourist data included in Belgian statistics. **Consumer prices** (change in 1979): 4.2%.

Transport: Railway traffic (1978): 295.2 mln. passenger-km; 649.2 mln. net ton-km. **Motor vehicles:** in use (1977): 141,400 passenger cars, 10,800 comm. vehicles. **Civil aviation:** 84 mln. passenger-miles (1974); 142,000 freight ton-miles (1974).

Communications: Television sets: 105,000 in use (1976). **Radios:** 205,000 in use (1976). **Telephones in use** (1978): 185,549. **Daily newspaper circ.** (1976): 150,000.

Health: Life expectancy at birth (1973): 67.0 male; 73.9 female. **Births** (per 1,000 pop. 1978): 11.4. **Deaths** (per 1,000 pop. 1978): 11.8. **Natural increase** (1978): –.04%. **Hospital beds** (per 100,000 pop. 1977): 978. **Physicians** (per 100,000 pop. 1977): 112. **Infant mortality** (per 1,000 live births 1978): 10.6.

Education (1977): **Literacy:** 98%. **Pop. 5–19:** in school: 59%, teachers per 1,000: 40. **PQLI:** 93.

Luxembourg, founded about 963, was ruled by Burgundy, Spain, Austria, and France from 1448 to 1815. It left the Germanic Confederation in 1866. Overrun by Germany in 2 world wars, Luxembourg ended its neutrality in 1948, when a customs union with Belgium and Netherlands was adopted.

Madagascar

Democratic Republic of Madagascar

People: Population (1979 est.): 8,349,000. **Pop. density:** 36.57 per sq. mi. **Urban** (1970): 14.1%. **Ethnic groups:** 18 Malayan-Indonesian tribes (Merina 26%), with Arab and African presence. **Languages:** Malagasy spoken in various dialects by all tribes, Merina dialect official. **Religions:** Roman Catholics 20%, Protestants 18%, Moslems 9%, others.

Geography: Area: 226,658 sq. mi., slightly smaller than Texas. **Location:** In the Indian O., off the SE coast of Africa. **Neighbors:** Comoro Is., Mozambique (across Mozambique Channel). **Topography:** Humid coastal strip in the E, fertile valleys in the mountainous center plateau region, and a wider coastal strip on the W. **Capital:** Tananarive. **Cities** (1978 est.): Antananarivo 400,000; Toamasina 59,100; Majunga 57,500.

Government: Head of state: Pres. Didier Ratsiraka; b. Nov. 4, 1936; in office: June 15, 1975. **Head of government:** Prime Min. Desire Rakotoarijaona, b. June 19, 1934; in office: Aug. 4, 1977. **Local divisions:** 6 provinces. **Armed forces:** regulars 10,500; para-military 7,000.

Economy: Industries: Light industry. **Chief crops:** Coffee, cloves, vanilla (80% world supply), rice, sugar, sisal, tobacco, peanuts. **Minerals:** Chromium, graphite. **Per capita arable land:** 0.7 acres. **Meat prod.** (1978): beef: 106,000 metric tons; pork: 21,000 metric tons; lamb: 6,000 metric tons. **Fish catch** (1977): 56,000 metric tons. **Electricity prod.** (1978): 300.00 mln. kwh. **Labor force:** 90% agric.

Finance: Currency: Franc (Mar. 1980: 223.92 = $1 US). **Gross domestic product** (1978): $2.1 bln. **Per capita income** (1975): $227. **Imports** (1978): $443 mln.; partners (1976): Fr. 37%, Qatar 9%, W. Ger. 9%. **Exports** (1978): $387 mln.; partners (1976): Fr. 29%, U.S. 16% Jap. 7%, W. Ger. 7%. **Tourists** (1977): 9,000; receipts: $3 mln. **National budget** (1974): $242 mln. revenues; $263 mln. expenditures. **International reserves less gold** (Aug. 1979): $63.1 mln. **Consumer prices** (change in 1979): 14.1%.

Transport: Railway traffic (1978): 296.4 mln. passenger-km; 211.2 mln. net ton-km. **Motor vehicles:** in use (1977): 57,400 passenger cars, 52,300 comm. vehicles. **Civil aviation:** 280 mln. passenger-km (1977); 8 mln. freight ton-km (1977). **Chief ports:** Tamatave, Diego-Suarez, Majunga, Tulear.

Communications: Television sets: 8,000 in use (1976). **Radios:** 609,000 in use (1976). **Telephones in use** (1978): 28,686.

Health: Life expectancy at birth (1966): 37.5 male; 38.3 female. **Births** (per 1,000 pop. 1966): 46.0. **Deaths** (per 1,000 pop. 1966): 25.0. **Natural increase** (1966): 2.1%. **Hospital beds** (per 100,000 pop. 1977): 245. **Physicians** (per 100,000 pop. 1977): 10. **Infant mortality** (per 1,000 live births 1966): 102.

Education (1977): **Literacy:** 45%. **Pop. 5-19:** in school: 48%, teachers per 1,000: 9. **PQLI:** 46.

Madagascar was settled 2,000 years ago by Malayan-Indonesian people, whose descendants still predominate. A unified kingdom ruled the 18th and 19th centuries. The island became a French protectorate, 1885, and a colony 1896. Independence came June 26, 1960.

Discontent with inflation and French domination led to a coup in 1972. The new regime nationalized French-owned financial interests, closed French bases and a U.S. space tracking station, and obtained Chinese aid. The government conducted a program of arrests, expulsion of foreigners, and repression of strikes, 1979.

Malawi

Republic of Malawi

People: Population (1979 est.): 5,862,000. **Age distrib.** (%): 0–14: 43.9; 15–59: 50.4; 60+: 5.6. **Pop. density:** 123.94 per sq. mi. **Urban** (1972): 10.1%. **Ethnic groups:** Chewa, Nyanja, Lonwe, other Bantu tribes. **Languages:** English (official), Chichewa, other Bantu languages. **Religions:** Christians 50% (half Roman Catholic, half Protestant), Moslems 30%.

Geography: Area: 45,747 sq. mi., the size of Pennsylvania. **Location:** In SE Africa. **Neighbors:** Zambia on W, Mozambique on SE, Tanzania on N. **Topography:** Malawi stretches 560 mi. N-S along Lake Malawi (Lake Nyasa), most of which belongs to Malawi. High plateaus and mountains line the Rift Valley the length of the nation. **Capital:** Lilongwe. **Cities** (1978 est.): Blantyre-Limbe (met.) 219,000; Lilongwe (met.) 75,000.

Government: Head of state: Pres. Hastings Kamuzu Banda, b. May 14, 1906; in office: July 6, 1966. **Local divisions:** 3 regions, 24 districts, 3 subdistricts. **Armed forces:** regulars 5,000; para-military 460.

Economy: Industries: Textiles, sugar, farm implements. **Chief crops:** Tea, tobacco, peanuts, cotton, sugar, soybeans, coffee. **Other resources:** Rubber. **Per capita arable land:** 1.0 acres. **Fish catch** (1977): 68,200 metric tons. **Electricity prod.** (1978): 276.00 mln. kwh. **Labor force:** 90% agric.

Finance: Currency: Kwacha (Mar. 1980: .84 = $1 US). **Gross domestic product** (1979): $1.3 bln. **Per capita income** (1975): $119. **Imports** (1979): $412 mln.; partners (1977): So. Afr. 37%, UK 19%, Jap. 9%, U.S. 5%. **Exports** (1979): $237 mln.; partners (1977): UK 42%, U.S. 10%, Neth. 7%, So. Afr. 7%. **Tourists** (1975): 40,500; receipts (1976): $3 mln. **National**

budget (1979): $192 mln. revenues; $301 mln. expenditures. **International reserves less gold** (Mar. 1980): $33.98 mln. **Gold:** 13,000 oz t. **Consumer prices** (change in 1979): 11.1%.

Transport: Railway traffic (1978): 67.2 mln. passenger-km; 200.4 mln. net ton-km. **Motor vehicles:** in use (1976): 10,200 passenger cars, 10,600 comm. vehicles. **Civil aviation:** 138 mln. passenger-km (1978); 7 mln. freight ton-km (1978).

Communications: Radios: 130,000 in use (1976). **Telephones in use** (1978): 22,582. **Daily newspaper circ.** (1977): 18,000; 3 per 1,000 pop.

Health: Life expectancy at birth (1972): 40.9 male; 44.2 female. **Births** (per 1,000 pop. 1972): 50.5. **Deaths** (per 1,000 pop. 1972): 26.5. **Natural increase** (1972): 2.4%. **Hospital beds** (per 100,000 pop. 1977): 174. **Physicians** (per 100,000 pop. 1977): 2. **Infant mortality** (per 1,000 live births 1972): 142.1.

Education (1977): **Literacy:** 25%. **Pop. 5-19:** in school: 32%, teachers per 1,000: 6. **PQLI:** 31.

Bantus came in the 16th century, Arab slavers in the 19th. The area became the British protectorate Nyasaland, in 1891. It became independent July 6, 1964, and a republic in 1966. It has a pro-West foreign policy and cooperates economically with Zimbabwe and S. Africa.

Malaysia

People: Population (1979 est.): 13,674,000. **Age distrib.** (%): 0–14: 41.5; 15–59: 53.0; 60+: 5.4. **Pop. density:** 100.99 per sq. mi. **Urban** (1970): 20.6%. **Ethnic groups:** Malays 44%, Chinese 36%, Indians 10%, others. **Languages:** Malay (official), English, Chinese, Indian languages. **Religions:** Malays, some Indians are Moslem; Chinese, Indian, and local religions.

Geography: Area: 128,328 sq. mi., slightly larger than New Mexico. **Location:** On the SE tip of Asia, plus the N. coast of the island of Borneo. **Neighbors:** Thailand on N, Indonesia on S. **Topography:** Most of W. Malaysia is covered by tropical jungle, including the central mountain range that runs N-S through the peninsula. The western coast is marshy, the eastern, sandy. E. Malaysia has a wide, swampy coastal plain, with interior jungles and mountains. **Capital:** Kuala Lumpur. **Cities** (1970 cen.): Kuala Lumpur 451,977; George Town 269,603; Ipoh 247,953.

Government: Head of state: Paramount Ruler Ahmad Shah ibni Sultan Abu Bakar; b. Oct. 24, 1930; in office: Mar. 29, 1979. **Head of government:** Prime Min. Datuk Hussein bin Onn; b. Feb. 12, 1922; in office: Jan. 15, 1976. **Local divisions:** 13 states, each with legislature, chief minister, and titular ruler. **Armed forces:** regulars 64,500; reserves 27,000.

Economy: Industries: Rubber goods, pottery, fertilizers. **Chief crops:** Palm oil, copra, rice, tapioca, sugar, pepper. **Minerals:** Tin (35% world output), iron. **Crude oil reserves** (1980): 2.80 bln. bbls. **Other resources:** Rubber (35% world output). **Per capita arable land:** 0.6 acres. **Meat prod.** (1978): beef: 13,000 metric tons; pork: 48,000 metric tons. **Fish catch** (1977): 619,000 metric tons. **Electricity prod.** (1978): 8.20 bln. kwh. **Crude steel prod.** (1979): 233,000 metric tons. **Labor force:** 51% agric.

Finance: Currency: Ringgit (Mar. 1980: 2.27 = $1 US). **Gross domestic product** (1978): $15.47 bln. **Per capita income** (1975): $714. **Imports** (1978): $5.93 bln.; partners: Jap. 23%, U.S. 14%, Sing. 9%, UK 7%. **Exports** (1978): $7.41 bln.; partners: Jap. 22%, U.S. 19% Sing. 16%, Neth. 6%. **Tourists** (1977): 1,289,000; receipts: $38 mln. **National budget** (1978): $3.81 bln. revenues; $4.57 bln. expenditures. **International reserves less gold** (Jan. 1980): $4.01 bln. **Gold:** 2.13 mln. oz t. **Consumer prices** (change in 1979): 3.6%.

Transport: Railway traffic (incl. Singapore) (1978): 1.27 bln. passenger-km; 1.29 bln. net ton-km. **Motor vehicles:** in use (1977): 572,100 passenger cars, 196,200 comm. vehicles; assembled (1978): 61,200 passenger cars; 11,724 comm. vehicles. **Civil aviation:** 2,532 mln. passenger-km (1978); 87 mln. freight ton-km (1978). **Chief ports:** George Town, Kelang, Melaka, Kuching.

Communications: Television sets: 555,000 in use (1976), 142,000 manuf. (1977). **Radios:** 1.45 mln. in use (1976). **Telephones in use** (1978): 374,676. **Daily newspaper circ.** (1976): 1,834,000; 75 per 1,000 pop.

Health: Life expectancy at birth (1976): 66.2 male; 71.4 female. **Births** (per 1,000 pop. 1977): 30.7. **Deaths** (per 1,000 pop. 1977): 6.3. **Natural increase** (1977): 2.4%. **Hospital beds** (per 100,000 pop. 1977): 308. **Physicians** (per 100,000 pop. 1977): 12. **Infant mortality** (per 1,000 live births 1977): 31.8.

Education (1977): **Literacy:** 60%. **Pop. 5-19:** in school: 60%, teachers per 1,000: 20. **PQLI:** 73.

European traders appeared in the 16th century; Britain established control in 1867. Malaysia was created Sept. 16, 1963. It included Malaya (which had become independent in 1957 after the suppression of Communist rebels), plus the formerly-British Singapore, Sabah (N Borneo), and Sarawak (NW Borneo). Singapore was separated in 1965, in order to end tensions between Chinese, the majority in Singapore, and Malays in control of the Malaysian government. Chinese have charged economical and political discrimination.

A monarch is elected by a council of hereditary rulers of the Malayan states every 5 years.

Abundant natural resources have assured prosperity, and foreign investment has aided industrialization.

The influx of thousands of Vietnamese refugees reached crisis proportions, June 1979.

Maldives

Republic of Maldives

People: Population (1979 est.): 150,000. **Age distrib.** (%): 0–14: 44.9; 15–59: 51.3; 60+: 3.8. **Pop. density:** 1,217.39 per sq. mi. **Urban** (1967): 11.3%. **Ethnic groups:** Sinhalese, Dravidian, Arab mixture. **Languages:** Divehi (Sinhalese dialect). **Religions:** Sunni Moslems.

Geography: Area: 115 sq. mi., twice the size of Washington, D.C. **Location:** In the Indian O. SW of India. **Neighbors:** Nearest is India on N. **Topography:** 19 atolls with 1,087 islands, 203 inhabited. None of the islands are over 5 sq. mi. in area, and all are nearly flat. **Capital:** Male. **Cities** (1978 cen.): Male 29,555.

Government: Head of state: Pres. Maumoon Abdul Gayoom; b. Dec. 29, 1937; in office: Nov. 11, 1978. **Local divisions:** 19 atolls, each with an elected committee and a government-appointed chief.

Economy: Industries: Fish processing, tourism. **Chief crops:** Coconuts, fruit, millet. **Other resources:** Shells. **Fish catch** (1977): 26,700 metric tons. **Electricity prod.** (1977): 2.00 mln. kwh.

Finance: Currency: Rupee (Dec. 1977: 8.93 = $1 US). **Gross domestic product** (1976 est.): $20 mln. **Per capita income** (1976): $100. **Imports** (1975): $10 mln.; partners: Jap., UK, Thai., Sri Lan. **Exports** (1975): $4.2 mln.; partners: Jap., Sri Lan., Thai. **Tourists** (1976): 15,000.

Transport: Chief ports: Male Atoll.

Communications: Radios: 3,500 licensed (1976). **Telephones in use** (1978): 556.

Health: Births (per 1,000 pop. 1977): 40.5. **Deaths** (per 1,000 pop. 1977): 11.8. **Natural increase** (1977): 2.9%. **Pop. per hospital bed** (1977): 3,500. **Pop. per physician** (1977): 15,555. **Infant morality** (per 1,000 live births 1977): 118.8.

Education (1975): **Literacy:** 36%. **Pop. 5-19:** in school: 40%, per teacher: 80.

The islands had been a British protectorate since 1887. The country became independent July 26, 1965. Long a sultanate, the Maldives became a republic in 1968. Natural resources and tourism are being developed.

A cultural and scientific agreement was signed with the USSR, 1980.

Mali

Republic of Mali

People: Population (1979 est.): 6,464,000. **Age distrib.** (%): 0–14: 47.9; 15–59: 49.1; 60+: 3.0. **Pop. density:** 13.53 per sq. mi. **Urban** (1976): 16.6%. **Ethnic groups:** Mande (Bambara, Malinke, Sarakolle) 50%, Peul 17%, Voltaic 12%, Songhai, Tuareg, Moors. **Languages:** French (official), Bambara, others. **Religions:** Moslems 90%, Christians 1%, others.

Geography: Area: 464,873 sq. mi., larger than Texas and California combined. **Location:** In the interior of W. Africa. **Neighbors:** Mauritania, Senegal on W, Guinea, Ivory Coast, Upper Volta on S, Niger on E, Algeria on N. **Topography:** A landlocked grassy plain in the upper basins of the Senegal and Niger rivers, extending N into the Sahara. **Capital:** Bamako. **Cities** (1976 cen.): Bamako (met.) 404,022.

Government: Head of state and head of govt.: Pres. Moussa Traore; b. Sept. 25, 1936; in office: Dec. 6, 1968 (state); Sept. 19, 1969 (govt.) **Local divisions:** 6 regions. **Armed forces:** regulars 4,450; para-military 5,700.

Economy: Chief crops: Millet, rice, peanuts, cotton. **Other resources:** Rubber. **Per capita arable land:** 3.8 acres. **Meat prod.** (1978): beef: 34,000 metric tons; lamb: 41,000 metric tons. **Fish catch** (1977): 100,000 metric tons. **Electricity prod.** (1977): 98 mln. kwh. **Labor force:** 80% agric.

Finance: Currency: Franc (Mar. 1980: 447.85 = $1 US). **Gross domestic product** (1974): $423 mln. **Per capita income** (1976): $90. **Imports** (1978): $218 mln.; partners (1976): Fr. 40% Ivory Coast 14%, Sen. 10%, China 7%. **Exports** (1978): $102 mln.; partners (1976): Fr. 31%, Ivory Coast 13%, W. Ger. 11%, China 10%. **Tourists** (1977): 19,500; receipts: $8 mln. **International reserves less gold** (Mar. 1980): $8.9 mln. **Gold:** 18,000 oz t. **Consumer prices** (change in 1976): 8%.

Transport: Railway traffic (1977): 129 mln. passenger-km; 148 mln. net ton-km. **Motor vehicles:** in use (1974): 11,900 passenger cars, 7,600 comm. vehicles. **Civil aviation:** 97 mln. passenger-km (1977); 612,000 freight ton-km (1977).

Communications: Radios: 82,000 in use (1976).

Health: Life expectancy at birth (1975): 39.4 male; 42.5 female. **Births** (per 1,000 pop. 1975): 49.0. **Deaths** (per 1,000 pop. 1975): 23.2. **Natural increase** (1975): 2.6%. **Hospital beds** (per 100,000 pop. 1977): 56. **Physicians** (per 100,000 pop. 1977): 5. **Infant mortality** (per 1,000 live births 1975): 120.

Education (1977): Literacy: 10%. **Pop. 5-19:** in school: 14%, teachers per 1,000: 4. **PQLI:** 18.

Until the 15th century the area was part of the great Mali Empire. Timbuktu was a center of Islamic study. French rule was secured, 1898. The Sudanese Rep. and Senegal became independent as the Mali Federation June 20, 1960, but Senegal withdrew, and the Sudanese Rep. was renamed Mali.

Mali signed economic agreements with France and, in 1963, with Senegal. In 1968, a coup ended the socialist regime. Famine struck in 1973-74, killing as many as 100,000 people. Drought conditions returned 1977-78. Loss of livestock and dislocation of Tuareg nomads remained problems.

Malta

People: Population (1979 est.): 347,000. **Age distrib.** (%): 0–14: 24.6; 15–59: 63.2; 60+: 12.2. **Pop. density:** 2,786.89 per sq. mi. **Ethnic groups:** Italian, Arab, English, and Phoenician mixture. **Languages:** Maltese, English both official. **Religions:** Roman Catholics 98%.

Geography: Area: 122 sq. mi., twice the size of Washington, D.C. **Location:** In center of Mediterranean Sea. **Neighbors:** Nearest is Italy on N. **Topography:** Island of Malta is 95 sq. mi.; other islands in the group: Gozo, 26 sq. mi., Comino, 1 sq. mi. The coastline is heavily indented. Low hills cover the interior. **Capital:** Valletta. **Cities** (1977 est.): Valletta 14,096.

Government: Head of state: Pres. Anton Buttigieg; b. Feb. 19, 1912; in office: Dec. 27, 1976. **Head of government:** Prime Min. Dom Mintoff; b. Aug. 6, 1916; in office: June 17, 1971. **Armed forces:** regulars 1,000; para-military 1,400.

Economy: Industries: Ship repair, textiles, tourism. **Chief crops:** Wheat, potatoes, onions, beans. **Per capita arable land:** 0.1 acres. **Electricity prod.** (1978): 456.00 mln. kwh. **Labor force:** 23% manuf.

Finance: Currency: Pound (Mar. 1980: 1 = $2.75 US). **Gross domestic product** (1978): $721 mln. **Per capita income** (1978): $2,036. **Imports** (1978): $609 mln.; partners: UK 26%, It. 20%, W. Ger. 13%, U.S. 6%. **Exports** (1978): $363 mln.; partners: W. Ger. 33%, UK 21%, Libya 8%, China 5%. **Tourists** (1977): 361,900; receipts: $81 mln. **National budget** (1977): $249 mln. revenues; $228 mln. expenditures. **International reserves less gold** (Feb. 1980): $976.6 mln. **Gold:** 366,000 oz t. **Consumer prices** (change in 1979): 7.1%.

Transport: Motor vehicles: in use (1977): 60,700 passenger cars, 12,500 comm. vehicles. **Civil aviation:** 532 mln. passenger-km (1978); 4 mln. freight ton-km (1978). **Chief ports:** Valletta.

Communications: Television sets: 63,000 licensed (1976). **Radios:** 63,000 licensed (1976). **Telephones in use** (1978): 67,250.

Health: Life expectancy at birth (1976): 68.27 male; 73.10 female. **Births** (per 1,000 pop. 1978): 17.4. **Deaths** (per 1,000 pop. 1978): 10.0. **Natural increase** (1978): .7%. **Hospital beds** (per 100,000 pop. 1977): 1,040. **Physicians** (per 100,000 pop. 1977): 127. **Infant mortality** (per 1,000 live births 1978): 14.4.

Education (1977): **Literacy:** 85%. **Pop. 5–19:** in school: 69% teachers per 1,000: 36. **PQLI:** 90.

Malta was ruled by Phoenicians, Romans, Arabs, Normans, the Knights of Malta, France, and Britain (since 1814). It became independent Sept. 21, 1964, with Britain retaining a naval base. Malta became a republic in 1974. The withdrawal of the last of its sailors, Apr. 1, 1979, ended 179 years of British military presence on the island.

Maltese is a Semitic language, with Italian influences, written in the Latin alphabet. Malta is democratic but nonaligned, and receives aid from Libya and China.

Mauritania

Islamic Republic of Mauritania

People: Population (1979 est.): 1,474,000. **Age distrib.** (%): 0–14: 42.2; 15–59: 49.8; 60+: 13.4. **Pop. density:** 3.67 per sq. mi. **Urban** (1977): 22.8%. **Ethnic groups:** Arab-Berber 80%, Negroes 20%. **Languages:** French, Hassaniya Arabic, Niger-Congo languages. **Religions:** Moslems 95%, others.

Geography: Area: 419,229 sq. mi., the size of Texas and California combined. **Location:** In W. Africa. **Neighbors:** Morocco on N, Algeria, Mali on E, Senegal on S. **Topography:** The fertile Senegal R. valley in the S gives way to a wide central region of sandy plains and scrub trees. The N is arid and extends into the Sahara. **Capital:** Nouakchott. **Cities** (1976 cen.): Nouakchott (met.) 134,986.

Government: Head of state and head of govt.: Pres. Mohamed Khouna Ould Haidala, b. 1940: in office: May 31, 1979 (govt.); Jan. 4, 1980 (state). **Local divisions:** 8 regions, one district. **Armed forces:** regulars 9,450; para-military 6,000.

Economy: Chief crops: Dates, grain. **Minerals:** Iron, copper. **Per capita arable land:** 0.3 acres. **Meat prod.** (1978): beef: 16,000 metric tons; lamb: 12,000 metric tons. **Fish catch** (1977): 34,200 metric tons. **Electricity prod.** (1978): 96.00 mln. kwh. **Labor force:** 85% agric.

Finance: Currency: Ouguiya (Feb. 1980: 45.87 = $1 US). **Gross domestic product** (1977): $533 mln. **Per capita income** (1975): $264. **Imports** (1979): $259 mln.; partners (1978): Fr. 28%, Bel. 12%, W. Ger. 9%, Sp. 9%. **Exports** (1979): $142 mln.; partners (1978): Fr. 26%, It. 17%, Jap. 13%, UK 10%. **Tourists** (1975): 20,700; receipts (1976): $7 mln. **International reseves less gold** (Feb. 1980): $126.3 mln. **Gold:** 11,000 oz t. **Consumer prices** (change in 1979): 10.4%

Transport: Railway traffic (1974): 7.81 bln. net ton-km. **Motor vehicles:** in use (1972): 4,400 passenger cars, 5,000 comm. vehicles. **Chief ports:** Nouakchott, Nouadhibou.

Communications: Radios: 95,000 in use (1976).

Health: Life expectancy at birth (1975): 39.4 male; 42.5 female. **Births** (per 1,000 pop. 1975): 49.9. **Deaths** (per 1,000 pop. 1975): 23.3. **Natural increase** (1975): 2.7%. **Hospital beds** (per 100,000 pop. 1977): 38. **Physicians** (per 100,000 pop. 1977): 7. **Infant mortality** (per 1,000 live births 1975): 187.

Education (1977): **Literacy:** 10%. **Pop. 5-19:** in school: 15%, teachers per 1,000: 4. **PQLI:** 21.

Mauritania became independent Nov. 28, 1960. It annexed the south of former Spanish Sahara in 1976. Saharan guerrillas stepped up attacks in 1977; 8,000 Moroccan troops and French bomber raids aided the government. Mauritania signed a peace treaty with the Polsario Front, 1980, resumed diplomatic relations with Algeria while breaking a defense treaty with Morocco, and renounced sovereignty over its share of former Spanish Sahara. Morocco annexed the territory.

Famine struck in 1973-74 and again in 1977-78. France, China, and the U.S. have sent aid.

Mauritius

People: Population (1979 est.): 941,000. **Age distrib.** (%): 0–14: 36.3; 15–59: 57.2; 60+: 6.4. **Pop. density:** 1,169 per sq. mi. **Urban** (1976): 43.6%. **Ethnic groups:** Indians 69%, mulattoes, whites 28%, Chinese 3%. **Languages:** English (official), French, Creole, Hindi, Urdu, Chinese. **Religions:** Hindu 49%, Roman Catholic 32%, Moslems 16%, Protestants 1%.

Geography: Area: 787 sq. mi., smaller than Rhode Island. **Location:** In the Indian O., 500 mi. E of Madagascar. **Neighbors:** Nearest is Madagascar on W. **Topography:** A volcanic island nearly surrounded by coral reefs. A central plateau is encircled by mountain peaks. **Capital:** Port Louis. **Cities** (1978 est.): Port Louis 141,022.

Government: Head of state: Queen Elizabeth II, represented by Gov.-Gen. Dayendranath Burrenchobay; b. Mar. 24, 1919; in office: Mar. 23, 1978. **Head of government:** Prime Min. Seewoosagur Ramgoolam, b. 1900; in office: 1961. **Local divisions:** 9 administrative divisions.

Economy: Industries: Tourism. **Chief crops:** Sugar cane, tea. **Per capita arable land:** 0.3 acres. **Electricity prod.** (1978): 336.00 mln. kwh. **Labor force:** 30% agric.

Finance: Currency: Rupee (Mar. 1980: 7.96 = $1 US). **Gross domestic product** (1977): $737 mln. **Per capita income** (1977): $832. **Imports** (1978): $501 mln.; partners (1977): UK 18%, Fr. 11%, So. Afr. 11%, Jap. 8%. **Exports** (1978): $325 mln.; partners (1977): UK 67%, Fr. 8%, U.S. 6%. **Tourists** (1975): 74,600; receipts (1977): $32 mln. **National budget** (1978): $201 mln. revenues; $291 mln. expenditures. **International reserves less gold** (Mar. 1980): $42.8 mln. **Gold:** 38,000 oz t. **Consumer prices** (change in 1979): 14.4%.

Transport: Motor vehicles: in use (1977): 24,300 passenger cars, 13,000 comm. vehicles. **Chief ports:** Port Louis.

Communications: Television sets: 41,000 licensed (1976). **Radios:** 200,000 licensed (1976). **Telephones in use** (1978): 29,145. **Daily newspaper circ.** (1977): 85,000; 94 per 1,000 pop.

Health: Life expectancy at birth (1973): 60.68 male; 65.31 female. **Births** (per 1,000 pop. 1978): 27.0. **Deaths** (per 1,000 pop. 1978): 7.1. **Natural increase** (1978): 2.0%. **Hospital beds** (per 100,000 pop. 1977): 354. **Physicians** (per 100,000 pop. 1977): 44. **Infant mortality** (per 1,000 live births 1978): 33.8.

Education (1977): **Literacy:** 80%. **Pop. 5-19:** in school: 63%, teachers per 1,000: 24. **PQLI:** 77.

Mauritius was uninhabited when settled in 1638 by the Dutch, who introduced sugar cane. France took over in 1721, bringing African slaves. Britain ruled from 1810 to Mar. 12, 1968, bringing Indian workers for the sugar plantations. Mauritius has a free political life and high literacy and life expectancy. The 1970s brought declining birth rates and some economic growth.

Mexico

United Mexican States

People: Population (1979 est.): 65,770,000. **Age distrib.** (%): 0–14: 46.2; 15–59: 50.0; 60+: 4.8. **Pop. density:** 87.89 per sq. mi. **Urban** (1978): 65.2%. **Ethnic groups:** Mestizo 60%, Indian 30%, Caucasian 10%. **Languages:** Spanish, Indian languages 1.5%, bilingual 6.5%. **Religions:** Roman Catholics 96%, Protestants 2%.

Geography: Area: 761,601 sq. mi., three times the size of Texas. **Location:** In southern N. America. **Neighbors:** U.S. on N, Guatemala, Belize on S. **Topography:** The Sierra Madre Occidental Mts. run NW-SE near the west coast; the Sierra Madre Oriental Mts., run near the Gulf of Mexico. They join S of Mexico City. Between the 2 ranges lies the dry central plateau, 5,000 to 8,000 ft. alt., rising toward the S, with temperate vegetation. Coastal lowlands are tropical. About 45% of land is arid. **Capital:** Mexico City. **Cities** (1978 est.): Mexico City 8,988,230; Netzahualcoyotl 2,067,992; Guadalajara 1,813,131; Monterrey 1,054,029; Puebla de Zaragoza 677,959.

Government: Head of state: Pres. Jose Lopez Portillo; b. June 16, 1920; in office: Dec. 1, 1976. **Local divisions:** Federal district and 31 states. **Armed forces:** regulars 100,000; reserves 250,000.

Economy: Industries: Steel, chemicals, electric goods, textiles, rubber, paper, cement, shoes, glass, handicrafts, tourism. **Chief crops:** Cotton, coffee, sugar cane, tomatoes, wheat, corn, rice, tobacco, beans, cocoa, sisal (50% world supply) bananas. **Minerals:** Silver, antimony, lead, manganese, mercury, molybdenum, zinc, gold, arsenic, graphite, sulphur, coal, opal, oil, gas. **Crude oil reserves** (1980): 31.25 bln. bbls. **Per capita arable land:** 0.8 acres. **Meat prod.** (1978): beef: 562,000 metric tons; pork: 440,000 metric tons; lamb: 31,000 metric tons. **Fish catch** (1977): 670,100 metric tons. **Electricity prod.** (1978): 56.05 bln. kwh. **Crude steel prod.** (1979): 7.0 mln. metric tons. **Labor force:** 41% agric.; 18% manuf.

Finance: Currency: Peso (Mar. 1980: 22.85 = $1 US). **Gross domestic product** (1978): $92.44 bln. **Per capita income** (1978): $1,244. **Imports** (1979): $11.92 bln.; partners (1978): U.S. 60%, Jap. 8%, W. Ger. 7%. **Exports** (1979): $8.58 bln.; partners (1978): U.S. 63%. **Tourists** (1977): 3,338,000; receipts: $781 mln. **National budget** (1976): $10.46 bln. revenues; $13.17 bln. expenditures. **International reserves less gold** (Dec. 1979): $2.03 bln. **Gold:** 1.98 mln. oz t. **Consumer prices** (change in 1979): 18.2%.

Transport: Railway traffic (1977): 5.4 bln. passenger-km; 36.2 bln. net ton-km. **Motor vehicles:** in use (1977): 2.68 mln. passenger cars, 1.08 mln. comm. vehicles; manuf. (1978): 253,200 passenger cars, 105,600 comm. vehicles. **Civil aviation:** 8,532 mln. passenger-km (1977); 96 mln. freight ton-km (1977). **Chief ports:** Veracruz, Tampico, Mazatlan, Coatzacoalcos.

Communications: Television sets: 4.88 mln. in use (1975), 699,000 manuf. (1977). **Radios:** 17.15 mln. in use (1975), 976,000 manuf. (1977). **Telephones in use** (1978): 3,712,407. **Daily newspaper circ.** (1976): 3,994,000.

Health: Life expectancy at birth (1975): 62.76 male; 66.57 female. **Births** (per 1,000 pop. 1975): 42.0. **Deaths** (per 1,000 pop. 1975): 8.6. **Natural increase** (1975): 3.3%. **Hospital beds** (per 100,000 pop. 1977): 115. **Physicians** (per 100,000 pop. 1977): 57. **Infant mortality** (per 1,000 live births 1975): 54.7.

Education (1977): **Literacy:** 80%. **Pop. 5-19:** in school: 64%, teachers per 1,000: 19. **PQLI:** 76.

Mexico was the site of advanced Indian civilizations. The Mayas, an agricultural people, moved up from Yucatan, built immense stone pyramids, invented a calendar. The Toltecs were overcome by the Aztecs, who founded Tenochtitlan 1325 AD, now Mexico City. Hernando Cortes, Spanish conquistador, destroyed the Aztec empire, 1519-1521.

After 3 centuries of Spanish rule the people rose, under Fr. Miguel Hidalgo y Costilla, 1810, Fr. Morelos y Payon, 1812, and Gen. Agustin Iturbide, who made independence effective Sept. 27, 1821, but made himself emperor as Agustin I. A republic was declared in 1823.

Mexican territory extended into the present American Southwest and California until Texas revolted and established a republic in 1836; the Mexican legislature refused recognition but was unable to enforce its authority there. After numerous clashes, the U.S.-Mexican War, 1846-48, resulted in the loss by Mexico of the lands north of the Rio Grande.

French arms supported an Austrian archduke on the throne of Mexico as Maximilian I, 1864-67, but pressure from the U.S. forced France to withdraw. A dictatorial rule by Porfirio Diaz, president 1877-80, 1884-1911, led to fighting by rival forces until the new constitution of Feb. 5, 1917 provided social reform. Since then Mexico has developed large-scale programs of social security, labor protection, and school improvement. A constitutional provision requires management to share profits with labor.

The Institutional Revolutionary Party has been dominant in politics since 1929. Radical opposition, including some guerrilla activity, has been contained by strong measures.

The presidency of Luis Echeverria, 1970-76, was marked by a more leftist foreign policy and domestic rhetoric. Some land redistribution begun in 1976 was reversed under the succeeding administration.

Gains in agriculture, industry, and social services have been achieved since 1940. The land is rich, but the rugged topography and lack of sufficient rainfall are major obstacles. Crops and farm prices are controlled, as are export and import. Large estates have been expropriated; since 1915 the government has distributed about 160 million acres to small farmers through landholding communities (ejidos), yet 4 million peasants are still without land, and 5 million others hold minimal plots. Economic prospects brightened with the discovery of vast oil reserves, perhaps the world's greatest. But half the work force is jobless or underemployed.

Monaco

Principality of Monaco

People: Population (1979 est.): 26,000. **Age distrib.** (%): 0–14: 12.7; 15–59: 56.3 60+: 30.7. **Ethnic groups:** French

58%, Italian 17%, Monegasque 15%. **Languages:** French (official), Monegasque, Italian, English. **Religions:** Roman Catholics 95%.

Geography: Area: 600 acres. **Location:** On the NW Mediterranean coast. **Neighbors:** France to W, N, E. **Topography:** Monaco-Ville sits atop a high promontory, the rest of the principality rises from the port up the hillside. **Capital:** Monaco.

Government: Head of state: Prince Rainier III; b. May 31, 1923; in office: May 9, 1949. **Head of government:** Min. of State Andre Saint-Mleux; b. Sept. 25, 1920; in office: May 24, 1972.

Economy: Industries: Tourism, gambling.

Finance: Currency: French franc or Monégasque franc. **Tourists** (1976): 181,000.

Transport: Chief ports: La Condamine.

Communications: Television sets: 16,000 in use (1976). **Radios:** 7,500 in use (1976). **Telephones in use** (1978): 32,000. **Daily newspaper circ.** (1977): 11,000; 420 per 1,000 pop.

Health: Births (per 1,000 pop. 1977): 7.5. **Deaths** (per 1,000 pop. 1977): 10.6. **Natural increase** (1977): –.3%. **Infant mortality** (per 1,000 live births 1970): 9.3.

An independent principality for over 300 years, Monaco has belonged to the House of Grimaldi since 1297 except during the French Revolution. It was placed under the protectorate of Sardinia in 1815, and under that of France, 1861. The Prince of Monaco was an absolute ruler until a 1911 constitution.

Monaco's fame as a tourist resort is widespread. It is noted for its mild climate and magnificent scenery. The area has been extended by land reclamation.

Mongolia

Mongolian People's Republic

People: Population (1979 est.): 1,616,000. **Pop. density:** 2.61 per sq. mi. **Urban** (1973): 46.4%. **Ethnic groups:** Khalkha Mongols 76%, other Mongols 8%, Kazakhs 5%, other Turks, Russians, Chinese. **Languages:** Khalkha Mongolian (official, written in Cyrillic letters since 1941), Turkic 7%. **Religions:** Lama Buddhism prevailed, has been curbed.

Geography: Area: 604,247 sq. mi., more than twice the size of Texas. **Location:** In E Central Asia. **Neighbors:** USSR on N, China on S. **Topography:** Mostly a high plateau with mountains, salt lakes, and vast grasslands. Arid lands in the S are part of the Gobi Desert. **Capital:** Ulan Bator. **Cities** (1978 est.): Ulan Bator 400,000.

Government: Head of state: Chmn. Yumjaagiyn Tsedenbal; b. Sept. 17, 1916; in office: June 11, 1974. **Head of government:** Chmn. Jambyn Batmounkh; b. Mar. 10, 1926; in office: June 11, 1974. **Head of Communist Party:** First Sec. Yumjaagiyn Tsedenbal; in office: Nov. 22, 1958. **Local divisions:** 18 provinces, 2 autonomous municipalities. **Armed forces:** regulars 30,000; reserves 30,000.

Economy: Industries: Food processing, textiles, chemicals, cement. **Chief crops:** Grain. **Minerals:** Coal, tungsten, copper, molybdenum, gold, tin. **Per capita arable land:** 1.7 acres. **Meat prod.** (1978): beef: 57,000 metric tons; lamb: 96,000 metric tons. **Electricity prod.** (1977): 990 mln. kwh. **Labor force:** 52% agric.; 10% manuf.

Finance: Currency: Tugrik (Mar. 1980: 2.85 = $1 US). **Gross domestic product** (1976 est.): $1.20 bln. **Per capita income** (1976 est.): $750. **Imports** (1975): $550 mln.; partners (1976): USSR 93%. **Exports** (1975): $220 mln.; partners (1976): USSR 81%, Czech. 6%.

Transport: Railway traffic (1977): 227 mln. passenger-km; 2.54 bln. net ton-km.

Communications: Television sets: 3,600 in use (1976). **Radios:** 115,000 in use (1976). **Telephones in use** (1977): 37,792. **Daily newspaper circ.** (1976): 112,000; 75 per 1,000 pop.

Health: Life expectancy at birth (1975): 59.1 male; 62.3 female. **Births** (per 1,000 pop. 1975): 38.8. **Deaths** (per 1,000 pop. 1975): 9.6. **Natural increase** (1975): 2.9%. **Hospital beds** (per 100,000 pop. 1977): 1,067. **Physicians** (per 100,000 pop. 1977): 209.

Education (1977): **Literacy:** 95%. **Pop. 5-19:** in school: 56%, teachers per 1,000: 21. **PQLI:** 78.

One of the world's oldest countries, Mongolia reached the zenith of its power in the 13th century when Genghis Khan and his successors conquered all of China and extended their influence as far W as Hungary and Poland. In later centuries, the empire dissolved and Mongolia came under the suzerainty of China.

With the advent of the 1911 Chinese revolution, Mongolia, with Russian backing, declared its independence. A Mongolian Communist regime was established July 11, 1921.

In the early 1970s Mongolia was changing from a nomadic culture to one of settled agriculture and growing industries with aid from the USSR and East European nations.

Mongolia has sided with the Russians in the Sino-Soviet dispute. A Mongolian-Soviet mutual assistance pact was signed Jan. 15, 1966, and thousands of Soviet troops are based in the country. Ties were expanded in a 1976 pact.

Morocco

Kingdom of Morocco

People: Population (1979 est.): 20,368,000. **Age distrib.** (%): 0–14: 46.4; 15–59: 49.2; 60+: 4.2. **Pop. density:** 109.97 per sq. mi. **Urban** (1974): 37.9%. **Ethnic groups:** Arabs 65%, Berbers 33%, Europeans 1%. **Languages:** Arabic, Berber, French. **Religions:** Sunni Moslems 99%.

Geography: Area: 171,953 sq. mi., larger than California. **Location:** on NW coast of Africa. **Neighbors:** Mauritania on S, Algeria on E. **Topography:** Consists of 5 natural regions: mountain ranges (Riff in the N, Middle Atlas, Upper Atlas, and Anti-Atlas); rich plains in the W; alluvial plains in SW; well-cultivated plateaus in the center; a pre-Sahara arid zone extending from SE. **Capital:** Rabat. **Cities** (1978 est.): Casablanca 1,371,330; Rabat-Sale 435,510; Marrakech 330,400.

Government: Head of state: King Hassan II; b. July 9, 1929; in office: Mar. 3, 1961. **Head of government:** Prime Min. Maati Bouabid; b. Nov. 11, 1927; in office: Mar. 23, 1979. **Local divisions:** 2 urban prefectures, 33 provinces. **Armed forces:** regulars 98,000; para-military 30,000.

Economy: Industries: Carpets, clothing, leather goods, tourism. **Chief crops:** Grain, fruits, dates, grapes. **Minerals:** Antimony, cobalt, manganese, phosphate, zinc, lead, oil, coal. **Crude oil reserves** (1980): 100 mln. bbls. **Per capita arable land:** 1.0 acres. **Meat prod.** (1978): beef: 76,000 metric tons; lamb: 59,000 metric tons. **Fish catch** (1977): 260,600 metric tons. **Electricity prod.** (1978): 3.59 bln. kwh. **Labor force:** 50% agric.

Finance: Currency: Dirham (Mar. 1980: 4.09 = $1 US). **Gross domestic product** (1978): $12.43 bln. **Per capita income** (1977): $555. **Imports** (1979): $2.97 bln.; partners (1978): Fr. 26%, Sp. 10 %, U.S. 8%, W. Ger. 7%. **Exports** (1978): $1.51 bln.; partners (1978): Fr. 27%, W. Ger. 11%, Sp. 7%, It. 6%. **Tourists** (1977): 1,427,500; receipts $375 mln. **National budget** (1974): $1.68 bln. revenues; $2.00 bln. expenditures. **International reserves less gold** (Feb. 1980): $407 mln. **Gold:** 704,000 oz t. **Consumer prices** (change in 1978): 9.7%.

Transport: Railway traffic (1978): 871.2 mln. passenger-km; 3.78 bln. net ton-km. **Motor vehicles:** in use (1976): 347,400 passenger cars, 145,700 comm. vehicles; assembled (1976): 25,000 passenger cars; 6,000 comm. vehicles. **Civil aviation:** 1,227 mln. passenger-km (1976); 18 mln. freight ton-km (1976). **Chief ports:** Tangier, Casablanca, Kenitra.

Communications: Television sets: 522,000 licensed (1976). **Radios:** 1.5 mln. licensed (1976), 157,000 manuf. (1975). **Telephones in use** (1978): 210,000. **Daily newspaper circ.** (1976): 190,000.

Health: Life expectancy at birth (1975): 51.4 male; 54.5 female. **Births** (per 1,000 pop. 1975): 46.8. **Deaths** (per 1,000 pop. 1975): 15.7. **Natural increase** (1975): 3.1%. **Hospital beds** (per 100,000 pop. 1977): 123. **Physicians** (per 100,000 pop. 1977): 9. **Infant mortality** (per 1,000 live births 1975): 149.

Education (1977): **Literacy:** 24%. **Pop. 5-19:** in school: 29%, teachers per 1,000: 9. **PQLI:** 43.

Berbers were the original inhabitants, followed by Carthaginians and Romans. Arabs conquered in 683. In the 11th and 12th centuries, a Berber empire ruled all NW Africa and most of Spain from Morocco.

Part of Morocco came under Spanish rule in the 19th century; France controlled the rest in the early 20th. Tribal uprisings lasted from 1911 to 1933. The country became independent Mar. 2, 1956. Tangier, an internationalized seaport, was turned over to Morocco, 1956. Ifni, a Spanish enclave, was ceded in 1969.

Morocco annexed over 70,000 sq. mi. of phosphate-rich land Apr. 14, 1976, two-thirds of former Spanish Sahara, with the remainder annexed by Mauritania. Spain had withdrawn in February. Polisario, a guerrilla movement, proclaimed the region independent Feb. 27, and launched attacks with Algerian support. Morocco accepted U.S. military and economic aid. When Mauritania signed a treaty with the Polisario Front, and gave up its portion of the former Spanish Sahara, Morocco occupied the area, 1980. Morocco accused Algeria of instigating Polisario attacks.

Mozambique

People's Republic of Mozambique

People: Population (1979 est.): 10,030,000. **Age distrib.** (%): 0–14: 45.3; 15–59: 50.6; 60+: 4.1. **Pop. density:** 32.8 per sq. mi. **Ethnic groups:** Bantu tribes. **Languages:** Portuguese (official), others. **Religions:** Christians 15%, Moslems 12.5%, others.

Geography: Area: 303,073 sq. mi., larger than Texas. **Location:** On SE coast of Africa. **Neighbors:** Tanzania on N, Malawi, Zambia, Zimbabwe on W, South Africa, Swaziland on S. **Topography:** Coastal lowlands comprise nearly half the country with plateaus rising in steps to the mountains along the western border. **Capital:** Maputo. **Cities:** (1970 cen.): Maputo 383,775.

Government: Head of state: Pres. Samora Machel; b. Sept. 29, 1933; in office: June 25, 1975. **Local divisions:** 10 provinces. **Armed forces:** regulars 24,000.

Economy: Industries: Cement, alcohol, textiles. **Chief crops:** Cashews, cotton, sugar, copra, sisal, tea. **Minerals:** Coal, tantalite, copper, iron, bauxite, gold. **Per capita arable land:** 0.7 acres. **Meat prod.** (1978): beef: 37,000 metric tons; pork: 7,000 metric tons. **Fish catch** (1977): 14,000 metric tons. **Electricity prod.** (1978): 7.68 bln. kwh. **Labor force:** 74% agric.

Finance: Currency: Escudo (Sept. 1979: 33 = $1 US). **Gross domestic product** (1974 est.): $3 bln. **Per capita income** (1976 est.): $260. **Imports** (1977): $311 mln.; partners: So. Afr. 20%, W. Ger. 15%, Zimb. 13%, Port. 10%. **Exports** (1977): $143 mln.; partners: U.S. 27%, Port. 16%, UK 7%, So. Afr. 6%. **National budget** (1977): $190 mln. revenues; $292 mln. expenditures. **Consumer prices** (change in 1976): 4.5%.

Transport: Railway traffic (1973): 396 mln. passenger-km; 3.4 bln. net ton-km. **Motor vehicles:** in use (1972): 89,300 passenger cars, 21,500 comm. vehicles. **Chief ports:** Maputo, Beira, Nacala.

Communications: Radios: 225,000 licensed (1976), 24,000 manuf. (1974). **Telephones in use** (1977): 52,270. **Daily newspaper circ.** (1976): 42,000; 4 per 1,000 pop.

Health: Life expectancy at birth (1975): 41.9 male; 45.1 female. **Births** (per 1,000 pop. 1975): 45.5. **Deaths** (per 1,000 pop. 1975): 21.0. **Natural increase** (1975): 2.5%. **Hospital beds** (per 100,000 pop. 1977): 129. **Physicians** (per 100,000 pop. 1977): 6. **Infant mortality** (per 1,000 live births 1975): 19.1

Education (1977): **Literacy:** 10%. **Pop. 5-19:** in school: 20%, teachers per 1,000: 4. **PQLI:** 27.

The first Portuguese post on the Mozambique coast was established in 1505, on the trade route to the East. Mozambique became independent June 25, 1975, after a ten-year war against Portuguese colonial domination. The 1974 revolution in Portugal paved the way for the orderly transfer of power to Frelimo (Front for the Liberation of Mozambique). Frelimo took over local administration Sept. 20, 1974, over the opposition, in part violent, of some blacks and whites. The new government, led by Maoist Pres. Samora Machel, promised a gradual transition to a communist system, beginning with indoctrination to combat "individualism" and capitalist or traditionalist values. All private schools were closed. Rural collective farms were called for in a July 27, 1975, directive. All private homes were nationalized in 1976. Economic problems included the emigration of most of the country's 160,000 whites, a politically untenable economic dependence on white-ruled South Africa, and a large external debt.

Mozambique closed its border with Rhodesia in March 1976. Border clashes intensified, with Rhodesian troops attacking black Rhodesian guerrillas within Mozambique. Soviet arms were sent following a 1977 friendship treaty. But most aid comes from the West, with which most trade is conducted.

Early in 1979 the government announced that the country was in a state of war as a result of increased guerrilla activities. Incidents and reprisals continued.

Nauru

Republic of Nauru

People: Population (1979): 8,000. **Pop density:** 906.75 per sq. mi. **Ethnic groups:** Polynesians, Chinese 15%, European 7%. **Languages:** Nauruan, English. **Religions:** Christianity nearly universal.

Geography: Area: 8 sq. mi. **Location:** In Western Pacific O. just S of Equator. **Neighbors:** Nearest are Solomon Is. **Topography:** Mostly a plateau bearing high grade phosphate deposits, surrounded by a coral cliff and a sandy shore in concentric rings. **Capital:** Yaren.

Government: Head of state: Pres. Hammer De Robурт, b. Sept. 25, 1922; in office: May 11, 1978. **Local divisions:** 14 districts.

Economy: Electricity prod. (1977): 26.00 mln. kwh.

Finance: Currency: Australian dollar. **Gross domestic product** (1976 est.): $100 mln. **Per capita income** (1976): $12,000. **Imports** (1976): $15 mln.; partners (1974): Austral. 58%, Neth. 30%. **Exports** (1976): $41 mln.; partners (1974): Austral. 51%, NZ 41%, Jap. 5%. **National budget** (1979): $46 mln. revenues; $38 mln. expenditures.

Communications: Radios: 3,600 in use (1976). **Telephones in use** (1978): 1,500.

Health: Births (per 1,000 pop. 1976): 19.8. **Deaths** (per 1,000 pop. 1976): 4.5. **Natural increase** (1976): 1.5%. **Infant mortality** (per 1,000 live births 1976): 19.0.

The island was discovered in 1798 by the British but was formally annexed to the German Empire in 1886. After World War I, Nauru became a League of Nations mandate administered by Australia. During World War II the Japanese occupied the island and shipped 1,200 Nauruans to the fortress island of Truk as slave laborers.

In 1947 Nauru was made a UN trust territory, administered by Australia. Nauru became an independent republic Jan. 31, 1968.

Phosphate exports provide one of the world's highest per capita revenues for the 4,032 native Nauruans (some 3,975 Chinese, Europeans, and Pacific Islanders also live in Nauru, many working in the phosphate industry). The deposits are expected to be nearly exhausted by 1990.

Nepal

Kingdom of Nepal

People: Population (1979 est.): 14,608,000. **Age distrib.** (%): 0–14: 40.5; 15–59: 53.9; 60+: 5.6. **Pop. density:** 246.86 per sq. mi. **Urban** (1971): 4.0%. **Ethnic groups:** The many tribes are descendants of Indian, Tibetan, and Central Asian migrants. **Languages:** Nepali (official) (an Indic language), Newari, 11 others. **Religions:** Hindus 90%, Buddhists 9%.

Geography: Area: 54,362 sq. mi., the size of North Carolina. **Location:** Astride the Himalaya Mts. **Neighbors:** China on N, India on S. **Topography:** The Himalayas stretch across the N, the hill country with its fertile valleys extends across the center, while the southern border region is part of the flat, subtropical Ganges Plain. **Capital:** Kathmandu. **Cities** (1971 cen.): Kathmandu 150,402.

Government: Head of state: King Birendra Bir Bikram Shah Dev; b. Dec. 28, 1945; in office: Jan. 31, 1972. **Head of government:** Prime Min. Surya Bahadur Thapa; in office: June 1, 1979. **Local divisions:** 14 zones; 75 districts. **Armed forces:** regulars 20,000; para-military 12,000.

Economy: Industries: Hides, drugs, tourism. **Chief crops:** Jute, rice, grain. **Minerals:** Quartz. **Other resources:** Forests. **Per capita arable land:** 0.4 acres. **Meat prod.** (1978): beef: 22,000 metric tons; pork: 5,000 metric tons; lamb: 18,000 metric tons. **Electricity prod.** (1977): 180 mln. kwh. **Labor force:** 94% agric.; 1% manuf.

Finance: Currency: Rupee (Mar. 1980: 12.00 = $1 US). **Gross domestic product** (1977): $1.39 bln. **Per capita in-**

come (1975): $114. **Imports** (1979): $254 mln.; partners (1978): India 31%, Jap. 16%. **Exports** (1979): $109 mln.; partners (1978): India 48%, Jap. 8%, U.S. 5%, W. Ger. 5%. **Tourists** (1977): 129,300; receipts: $2 mln. **National budget** (1979): $141 mln. revenues; $260 mln. expenditures. **International reserves less gold** (Mar. 1980): $179.6 mln. **Gold:** 151,000 oz t. **Consumer prices** (change in 1979): 6.0%.

Communications: Radios: 150,000 in use (1976). **Telephones in use** (1978): 9,425. **Daily newspaper circ.** (1976): 96,000.

Health: Life expectancy at birth (1975): 42.2 male; 45.0 female. **Births** (per 1,000 pop. 1975): 44.4. **Deaths** (per 1,000 pop. 1975): 22.5. **Natural increase** (1975): 2.2%. **Hospital beds** (per 100,000 pop. 1977): 15. **Physicians** (per 100,000 pop. 1977): 3.

Education (1977): **Literacy:** 19%. **Pop. 5-19:** in school: 22%, teachers per 1,000: 7. **PQLI:** 29.

Nepal was originally a group of petty principalities, the inhabitants of one of which, the Gurkhas, became dominant about 1769. In 1951 King Tribhubana Bir Bikram, member of the Shah family, ended the system of rule by hereditary premiers of the Ranas family, who had kept the kings virtual prisoners, and established a cabinet system of government.

Virtually closed to the outside world for centuries, Nepal is now linked to India and Pakistan by roads and air service and to Tibet by road. Polygamy, child marriage, and the caste system were officially abolished in 1963.

India, the largest aid donor, is the chief trade partner, but Nepal has cultivated good relations with China as well.

Students and political opponents were arrested in 1974 following violent protests. A new wave of protests, 1979, led to more arrests and executions, but a change in premiers.

The promised referendum on Nepalese government was held May 2, 1980, backing the retention of the partyless form of government. Political reforms were promised by the king.

Netherlands

Kingdom of the Netherlands

People: Population (1979 est.) 14,029,000. **Age distrib.** (%): 0–14: 24.2; 15–59: 60.5; 60+: 15.4. **Pop. density:** 988.44 per sq. mi. **Urban** (1976): 88.4%. **Ethnic groups:** Dutch. **Languages:** Dutch. **Religions:** Roman Catholics 40%, Protestants 40%.

Geography: Area: 14,103 sq. mi., the size of Mass., Conn., and R.I. combined. **Location:** In NW Europe on North Sea. **Topography:** The land is flat, an average alt. of 37 ft. above sea level, with much land below sea level reclaimed and protected by 1,500 miles of dikes. Since 1927 the government has been draining the IJsselmeer, formerly the Zuider Zee. By 1972, 410,000 of a planned 550,000 acres had been drained and reclaimed. **Capital:** Amsterdam. **Cities** (1978 est.): Amsterdam 733,593; Rotterdam 595,662; Hague 467,997; Utrecht 243,001.

Government: Head of state: Queen Beatrix; b. Jan. 31, 1938; in office: Apr. 30, 1980. **Head of government:** Prime Min. Andries A.M. van Agt, b. Feb. 2, 1931; in office: Dec. 19, 1977. **Seat of govt.:** The Hague. **Local divisions:** 11 provinces. **Armed forces:** regulars 114,820; reserves 171,000.

Economy: Industries: Metals, machinery, food products, chemicals, textiles, oil refinery, diamond cutting, pottery, electronics, tourism. **Chief crops:** Grains, potatoes, sugar beets, vegetables, fruits, flowers. **Minerals:** Natural gas, oil. **Crude oil reserves** (1980): 60 mln. bbls. **Per capita arable land:** 0.1 acres. **Meat prod.** (1978): beef: 374,000 metric tons; pork: 1.05 mln. metric tons; lamb: 16,000 metric tons. **Fish catch** (1977): 313,000 metric tons. **Electricity prod.** (1978): 61.70 bln. kwh. **Crude steel prod.** (1979): 5.8 mln. metric tons. **Labor force:** 6% agric.; 23% manuf.

Finance: Currency: Guilder (Mar. 1980: 2.13 = $1 US). **Gross domestic product** (1978): $130.78 bln. **Per capita income** (1978): $8,509. **Imports** (1979): $68.21 bln.; partners (1978): W. Ger. 25%, Belg. 13%, U.S. 9%, Fr. 8%. **Exports** (1979): $63.67 bln.; partners (1978): W. Ger. 31%, Belg. 15%, Fr. 11%, UK 7%. **Tourists** (1977): 2,939,400; receipts: $1.11 bln. **National budget** (1979): $52.76 bln. revenues; $57.00 bln. expenditures. **International reserves less gold** (Mar. 1980): $8.48 bln. **Gold:** 43.94 mln. oz t. **Consumer prices** (change in 1979): 4.2%.

Transport: Railway traffic (1978): 8.1 bln. passenger-km; 2.9 bln. net ton-km. **Motor vehicles:** in use (1977): 3.85 mln. passenger cars, 355,000 comm. vehicles; manuf. (1978): 62,400 passenger cars; 11,520 comm. vehicles. **Civil aviation:** 12,384 mln. passenger-km (1978); 82.3 mln. freight ton-km (1978). **Chief ports:** Rotterdam, Amsterdam, IJmuiden.

Communications: Television sets: 3.77 mln. licensed (1976). **Radios:** 4 mln. licensed (1976). **Telephones in use** (1978): 5,845,894. **Daily newspaper circ.** (1976): 4,371,000.

Health: Life expectancy at birth (1977): 72.0 male; 78.4 female. **Births** (per 1,000 pop. 1978): 12.6. **Deaths** (per 1,000 pop. 1978): 8.2. **Natural increase** (1978): .4%. **Hospital beds** (per 100,000 pop. 1977): 1,009. **Physicians** (per 100,000 pop. 1977): 172. **Infant mortality** (per 1,000 live births 1978): 9.5.

Education (1977): **Literacy:** 99%. **Pop. 5-19:** school: 63%, teachers per 1,000: 29. **PQLI:** 97.

Julius Caesar conquered the region in 55 BC, when it was inhabited by Celtic and Germanic tribes.

After the empire of Charlemagne fell apart, the Netherlands (Holland, Belgium, Flanders) split among counts, dukes and bishops, passed to Burgundy and thence to Charles V of Spain. His son, Philip II, tried to check the Dutch drive toward political freedom and Protestantism (1568-1573). William the Silent, prince of Orange, led a confederation of the northern provinces, called Estates, in the Union of Utrecht, 1579. The Estates retained individual sovereignty, but were represented jointly in the States-General, a body that had control of foreign affairs and defense. In 1581 they repudiated allegiance to Spain. The rise of the Dutch republic to naval, economic, and artistic eminence came in the 17th century.

The United Dutch Republic ended 1795 when the French formed the Batavian Republic. Napoleon made his brother Louis king of Holland, 1806; Louis abdicated 1810 when Napoleon annexed Holland. In 1813 the French were expelled. In 1815 the Congress of Vienna formed a kingdom of the Netherlands, including Belgium, under William I. In 1830, the Belgians seceded and formed a separate kingdom.

The constitution, promulgated 1814, and subsequently revised, assures a hereditary constitutional monarchy.

The Netherlands maintained its neutrality in World War I, but was invaded and brutally occupied by Germany from 1940 to 1945. After the war, neutrality was abandoned, and the country joined NATO, the Western European Union, the Benelux Union, and, in 1957, became a charter member of the Common Market.

In 1949, after several years of fighting, the Netherlands granted independence to Indonesia, where it had ruled since the 17th century. In 1963, West New Guinea was turned over to Indonesia, after five years of controversy and seizure of Dutch property in Indonesia.

Some 200,000 Indonesians emigrated to the Netherlands. Of them, 35,000 were from the South Moluccan islands. Terrorists demanding independence for South Molucca from Indonesia staged train hijackings and other incidents in the Netherlands in 1975 and 1977.

The independence of Suriname, 1975, instigated mass emigrations to the Netherlands, adding to problems of unemployment.

Though the Netherlands has been heavily industrialized, its productive small farms export large quantitites of pork and dairy foods.

Rotterdam, located along the principal mouth of the Rhine, handles the most cargo of any ocean port in the world. Canals, of which there are 3,478 miles, are important in transportation.

Citing age, Queen Juliana abdicated, Apr. 30, 1980, in favor of her eldest daughter, Princess Beatrix.

Netherlands Antilles

The **Netherlands Antilles,** constitutionally on a level of equality with the Netherlands homeland within the kingdom, consist of 2 groups of islands in the West Indies. **Curacao, Aruba,** and **Bonaire** are near the South American coast; **St. Eustatius, Saba,** and the southern part of **St. Maarten** are SE of Puerto Rico. Northern two-thirds of St. Maarten belong to French Guadeloupe; the French call the island St. Martin. Total area of the 2 groups is 385 sq. mi., including: Aruba 74, Bonaire 111, Curacao 171, St. Eustatius 11, Saba 5, St. Maarten (Dutch part) 13.

Total pop. (est. 1979) was 240,000. Willemstad, on Curacao, is the capital. Chief products are corn, pulse, salt and phosphate; principal industry is the refining of crude oil from Venezuela. Tourism is an important industry, as are electronics and shipbuilding.

New Zealand

People: Population: (1979 est.): 3,107,000. **Age distrib.** (%): 0–14: 29.0; 15–59: 57.9; 60+: 13.1. **Pop. density:** 29.94 per sq. mi. **Urban** (1976): 83.0%. **Ethnic groups:** European (mostly British) 90%, Polynesian (mostly Maori) 9%. **Languages:** English, Maori. **Religions:** Protestants 70%, Roman Catholics 16%.

Geography: Area: 103,883 sq. mi., the size of Colorado. **Location:** In SW Pacific O. **Neighbors:** Nearest are Australia on W, Fiji, Tonga on N. **Topography:** Each of the 2 main islands (North and South Is.) is mainly hilly and mountainous. The east coasts consist of fertile plains, especially the broad Canterbury Plains on South Is. A volcanic plateau is in center of North Is. South Is. has glaciers and 15 peaks over 10,000 ft. **Capital:** Wellington. **Cities** (1978 est.): Christchurch 172,400; Auckland 149,000; Manukau 142,200; Wellington 139,200.

Government: Head of state: Queen Elizabeth II, represented by Gov.-Gen. Keith Jacka Holyoake; b. Feb. 11, 1904; in office: Oct. 26, 1977. **Head of government:** Prime Min. Robert David Muldoon; b. Sept. 21, 1921; in office: Dec. 12, 1975. **Local divisions:** 96 counties, 132 boroughs, 3 towns, 4 districts. **Armed forces:** regulars 12,739; reserves 4,541.

Economy: Industries: Food processing, paper, steel, aluminum, oil products. **Chief crops:** Grain. **Minerals:** Oil, gas, gold, iron, limestone, diatomite, coal, pumice. **Crude oil reserves** (1980): 110 mln. bbls. **Other resources:** Wool, timber. **Per capita arable land:** 0.3 acres. **Meat prod.** (1978): beef: 529,000 metric tons; pork: 41,000 metric tons; lamb: 519,000 metric tons. **Fish catch** (1977): 110,500 metric tons. **Electricity prod.** (1978): 21.35 bln. kwh. **Crude steel prod.** (1979): 229,000 metric tons. **Labor force:** 10% agric.; 24% manuf.

Finance: Currency: Dollar (Mar. 1980: 1 = $.94 US). **Gross domestic product** (1978): $18.41 bln. **Per capita income** (1977): $4,303. **Imports** (1979): $4.55 bln.; partners (1978): Austral. 22%, UK 16%, U.S. 14%, Jap. 13%. **Exports** (1979): $4.71 bln.; partners (1978): UK 18%, U.S. 15%, Jap. 14%, Austral. 12%. **Tourists** (1977): 389,500; receipts $155 mln. **National budget** (1978): $6.02 bln. revenues; $6.64 bln. expenditures. **International reserves less gold** (Mar. 1980): $545 mln. **Gold:** 22,000 oz t. **Consumer prices** (change in 1979): 13.8%.

Transport: Railway traffic (1978): 500 mln. passenger-km; 3.4 bln. net ton-km. **Motor vehicles:** in use (1977): 1.21 mln. passenger cars; (1976): 221,700 comm. vehicles; assembled (1978): 51,828 passenger cars; 11,088 comm. vehicles. **Civil aviation:** 4,116 mln. passenger-km (1978); 146 mln. freight ton-km (1978). **Chief ports:** Auckland, Wellington, Lyttleton, Tauranga.

Communications: Television sets: 813,000 mln. licensed (1976), 119,000 manuf. (1977). **Radios:** 2.7 mln. in use (1976), 169,000 manuf. (1977). **Telephones in use** (1978): 1,715,343. **Daily newspaper circ.** (1976): 848,000.

Health: Life expectancy at birth (1972): 68.55 male; 74.60 female. **Births** (per 1,000 pop. 1977): 17.4. **Deaths** (per 1,000 pop. 1977): 8.4. **Natural increase** (1977): .9%. **Hospital beds** (per 100,000 pop. 1977): 1,022. **Physicians** (per 100,000 pop. 1977): 135. **Infant mortality** (per 1,000 live births 1977): 14.2

Education (1977): **Literacy:** 98%. **Pop. 5-19:** in school: 81%, teachers per 1,000: 35. **PQLI:** 94.

The Maoris, a Polynesian group from the eastern Pacific, reached New Zealand before and during the 14th century. The first European to sight New Zealand was Dutch navigator Abel Janszoon Tasman, but Maoris refused to allow him to land. British Capt. James Cook explored the coasts, 1769-1770.

British sovereignty was proclaimed in 1840, with organized settlement beginning in the same year. Representative institutions were granted in 1853. Maori Wars ended in 1870 with British victory. The colony became a dominion in 1907, and is an independent member of the Commonwealth.

New Zealand fought on the side of the Allies in both world wars, and signed the ANZUS Treaty of Mutual Security with the U.S. and Australia in 1951. New Zealand joined with Australia and Britain in a pact to defend Singapore and Malaysia; New Zealand units are stationed in those 2 countries.

A labor tradition in politics dates back to the 19th century. Private ownership is basic to the economy, but state ownership or regulation affects many industries. Transportation, broadcasting, mining, and forestry are largely state-owned.

The native Maoris numbered an estimated 200,000 in the early 19th century; violence and European diseases cut them to 40,000 by the end of the century. Recently they have increased at 3% annually and totaled over 250,000 in 1976. Four of 92 members of the House of Representatives are elected directly by the Maori people.

New Zealand comprises **North Island,** 44,204 sq. mi.; **South Island,** 58,304 sq. mi.; **Stewart Island,** 674 sq. mi.; **Chatham Islands,** 372 sq. mi.

In 1965, the **Cook Islands** (pop. 1976 cen., 18,112; area 93 sq. mi.) became self-governing although New Zealand retains responsibility for defense and foreign affairs. **Niue** attained the same status in 1974; it lies 400 mi. to W (pop. 1977 est., 6,000; area 100 sq. mi.). **Tokelau Is.,** (pop. 1976 cen., 1,575; area 4 sq. mi.) are 300 mi. N of Samoa.

Ross Dependency, administered by New Zealand since 1923, comprises 160,000 sq. mi. of Antarctic territory.

Nicaragua

Republic of Nicaragua

People: Population (1979 est.): 2,365,000. **Age distrib.** (%): 0–14: 48.1; 15–59: 47.2; 60+: 4.7. **Pop. density:** 42.0 per sq. mi. **Urban** (1972): 48.6%. **Ethnic groups:** Mestizo 70%, Caucasian 17%, Negro 9%, Indian 4%. **Languages:** Spanish, English (on Caribbean coast). **Religions:** Roman Catholics 95%.

Geography: Area: 57,143 sq. mi., slightly larger than Wisconsin. **Location:** In Central America. **Neighbors:** Honduras on N, Costa Rica on S. **Topography:** Both Atlantic and Pacific coasts are over 200 mi. long. The Cordillera Mtns., with many volcanic peaks, runs NW-SE through the middle of the country. Between this and a volcanic range to the E lie Lakes Managua and Nicaragua. **Capital:** Managua. **Cities** (1971 cen.): Managua 398,514.

Government: 5-member junta, effective head: Sergio Ramirez Mercado, b. Aug 5, 1942; took power: July 20, 1979. **Local divisions:** 16 departments; one national district. **Armed forces:** regulars 8,300; para-military 4,000.

Economy: Industries: Oil refining, chemicals, textiles. **Chief crops:** Bananas, cotton, fruit, yucca, coffee, sugar, corn, beans, cocoa, rice, sesame, tobacco, wheat. **Minerals:** Gold, silver, copper, tungsten. **Other resources:** Forests, shrimp. **Per capita arable land:** 1.4 acres. **Meat prod.** (1978): beef: 85,000 metric tons; pork: 20,000 metric tons. **Fish catch:** (1977): 22,400 metric tons. **Electricity prod.** (1977): 1.18 bln. kwh. **Labor force:** 53% agric.

Finance: Currency: Cordoba (Mar. 1980: 10.00 = $1 US). **Gross domestic product** (1978): $2.17 bln. **Per capita income** (1978): $825. **Imports** (1978): $596 mln.; partners (1977): U.S. 30%, Venez. 12%, Jap. 9%, Costa Rica 8%. **Exports** (1978): $646 mln.; partners (1977): U.S. 22%, W. Ger. 13%, Jap. 11%, Costa Rica 8%. **Tourists** (1976): 207,000; receipts: $28 mln. **National budget** (1978): $228 mln. revenues; $393 mln. expenditures. **International reserves less gold** (Nov. 1979): $85.36 mln. **Gold:** 18,000 oz t. **Consumer prices** (change in 1979): 47.9%.

Transport: Railway traffic (1977): 19 mln. passenger-miles; 11 mln. net ton-miles. **Motor vehicles:** in use (1973): 32,000 passenger cars, 20,000 comm. vehicles. **Chief ports:** Corinto, Puerto Somoza, San Juan del Sur.

Communications: Television sets: 90,000 in use (1976). **Radios:** 126,000 in use (1975). **Telephones in use** (1978): 55,803. **Daily newspaper circ.** (1976): 113,000; 51 per 1,000 pop.

Health: Life expectancy at birth (1975): 51.2 male; 54.6 female. **Births** (per 1,000 pop. 1975): 48.3. **Deaths** (per 1,000 pop. 1975): 13.8. **Natural increase** (1975): 3.5%. **Hospital beds** (per 100,000 pop. 1977): 207. **Physicians** (per 100,000 pop. 1977): 60. **Infant mortality** (per 1,000 live births 1975): 37.0.

Education (1977): **Literacy:** 58%. **Pop. 5-19:** in school: 43%, teachers per 1,000: 13. **PQLI:** 54.

Nicaragua, inhabited by various Indian tribes, was conquered by Spain in 1552. After gaining independence from Spain, 1821, Nicaragua was united for a short period with Mexico, then with the United Provinces of Central America, finally becoming an independent republic, 1838.

U.S. Marines occupied the country at times in the early 20th century, the last time from 1926 to 1933.

Gen. Anastasio Somoza-Debayle was elected president 1967. He resigned 1972, but was elected president again Sept. 1, 1974. The Somozas, richest Nicaraguan family, have dominated politics for 4 decades. Martial law was imposed in Dec. 1974, after officials were kidnapped by the Marxist Sandinista guerrillas. The country's Roman Catholic bishops charged in 1977 that the government had tortured, raped, and executed civilians in its anti-guerrilla campaign. The Inter-American Commission on Human Rights made a similar report to the OAS, 1978. Violent opposition spread to nearly all classes, 1978; a nationwide strike called against the government Aug. 25 touched off a state of civil war at Matagalpa. Nicaragua rejected a U.S.-supported mediation offer to end the strife; the U.S. cut off military ties and aid.

Months of simmering civil war erupted when Sandinist guerrillas invaded Nicaragua May 29, 1979, touching off a 7-week-offensive that culminated in the resignation and exile of Somoza, July 17. A 5-member provisional junta governs, modeling their own form of socialism, which includes a private sector and independent political opinion.

Niger

Republic of Niger

People: Population (1979 est.): 5,346,000. **Age distrib.** (%): 0–14: 43.0; 15–59: 52.2; 60+: 4.8. **Pop. density:** 10.2 per sq. mi. **Ethnic groups:** Hausas 50%, Djermas 23%, Fulanis 15%, Tuaregs 12%. **Languages:** French (official), Hausa, Djerma, others. **Religions:** Moslems 85%, others.

Geography: Area: 489,206 sq. mi., almost twice the size of Texas. **Location:** In the interior of N. Africa. **Neighbors:** Libya, Algeria on N, Mali, Upper Volta on W, Benin, Nigeria on S, Chad on E. **Topography:** Mostly arid desert and mountains. A narrow savanna in the S and the Niger R. basin in the SW contain most of the population. **Capital:** Niamey. **Cities** (1978 est.): Niamey 130,299.

Government: Head of state: Pres. Seyni Kountche; b. 1931; in office: Apr. 15, 1974. **Local divisions:** 7 departments. **Armed forces:** regulars 2,150; para-military 1,800.

Economy: Chief crops: Peanuts, cotton. **Minerals:** Uranium (5th largest reserves in the world). **Per capita arable land:** 7.4 acres. **Meat prod.** (1978): beef: 24,000 metric tons; lamb: 24,000 metric tons. **Electricity prod.** (1977): 70.00 mln. kwh. **Labor force:** 90% agric.

Finance: Currency: CFA franc (Mar. 1980: 223.92 = $1 US). **Gross domestic product** (1976 est.): $650 mln. **Per capita income** (1976 est.): $125. **Imports** (1976): $122 mln.; partners (1978): Fr. 41%, U.K. 8%, Jap. 8%, U.S. 7%, **Exports** (1976): $129 mln.; partners (1978): Fr. 75%, Nigeria 11%, W. Ger. 6%. **International reserves less gold** (Jan. 1980): $137 mln. **Gold:** 11,000 oz t. **Consumer prices** (change in 1979): 7.3%.

Transport: Motor vehicles: in use (1976): 9,900 passenger cars, 11,800 comm. vehicles.

Communications: Radios: 145,000 in use (1970). **Telephones in use** (1977): 8,147. **Daily newspaper circ.** (1977): 3,000; 1 per 1,000 pop.

Health: Life expectancy at birth (1975): 39.4 male; 42.5 female. **Births** (per 1,000 pop. 1975): 50.8. **Deaths** (per 1,000 pop. 1975): 23.4. **Natural increase** (1975): 2.7%. **Hospital beds** (per 100,000 pop 1977): 69. **Physicians** (per 100,000 pop. 1977): 2. **Infant mortality** (per 1,000 live births 1975): 200.

Education (1977): **Literacy:** 5%. **Pop. 5-19:** in school: 11%, Teachers per 1,000: 3. **PQLI:** 16.

Niger was part of ancient and medieval African empires. European explorers reached the area in the late 18th century. The French colony of Niger was established 1900-22, after the defeat of Tuareg fighters, who had invaded the area from the N a century before. The country became independent Aug. 3, 1960. The next year it signed a bilateral agreement with France retaining close economic and cultural ties, which have continued. Hamani Diori, Niger's first president, was ousted in a 1974 coup. Drought and famine struck in 1973-74, and again in 1975, and half the country's livestock died.

Nigeria

Federal Republic of Nigeria

People: Population (1979 est.): 74,595,000. **Pop. density:** 202.47 per sq. mi. **Ethnic groups:** Yoruba 18%, Ibo 18%, Hausa-Fulani 32%, 250 others. **Languages:** English (official), Hausa, Yoruba, Ibo, others. **Religions:** Moslems 47% (in N), Christians 34% (in S), others.

Geography: Area: 356,699 sq. mi., more than twice the size of California. **Location:** On the S coast of W. Africa. **Neighbors:** Benin on W, Niger on N, Chad, Cameroon on E. **Topography:** 4 E-W regions divide Nigeria: a coastal mangrove swamp 10-60 mi. wide, a tropical rain forest 50-100 mi. wide, a plateau of savanna and open woodland, and semidesert in the N. **Capital:** Lagos. **Cities:** (1978 est.): Lagos 1,060,848; Ibadan 847,000; Ogbomosho 432,000; Kano 399,000.

Government: Head of state: Pres. Alhaji Shehu Shagari; b. Apr. 25, 1925; in office: Oct. 1, 1979. **Local divisions:** 19 states, Federal Capital Territory. **Armed forces:** regulars 173,000; reserves 2,000.

Economy: Industries: Food processing, assembly of vehicles and other equipment. **Chief crops:** Cocoa (main export crop), tobacco, palm products, peanuts, cotton, soybeans. **Minerals:** Oil, gas, coal, iron, limestone, columbium, tin. **Crude oil reserves** (1980): 17.4 bln. bbls. **Other resources:** Timber, rubber, hides. **Per capita arable land:** 0.8 acres. **Meat prod.** (1978): beef: 197,000 metric tons; pork: 36,000 metric tons; lamb: 106,000 metric tons. **Fish catch** (1977): 506,000 metric tons. **Electricity prod.** (1978): 3.50 bln. kwh. **Labor force:** 70% agric.

Finance: Currency: Naira (Mar. 1980: 1 = $1.76 US). **Gross domestic product** (1977): $32.26 bln. **Per capita income** (1977): $682. **Imports** (1979): $9.69 bln.; partners (1977): UK 22%, W. Ger. 16%, U.S. 11%, Jap. 11%. **Exports** (1979): $17.8 bln.; partners (1977): U.S. 40%, Neth. Ant. 15%, Neth. 11%, UK 8%. **Tourist receipts** (1977): $60 mln. **National budget** (1977): $9.7 bln. revenues; $13.80 bln. expenditures. **International reserves less gold** (Mar. 1980): $6.52 mln. **Gold:** 629,000 oz t. **Consumer prices** (change in 1978): 24.4%.

Transport: Railway traffic (1974): 785 mln. passenger-km; 972 mln. net ton-km. **Motor vehicles:** in use (1973): 150,000 passenger cars, 82,000 comm. vehicles. **Civil aviation:** 852 mln. passenger-km (1977); 6 mln. freight ton-km (1977). **Chief ports:** Port Harcourt, Bonny, Lagos.

Communications: Television sets: 105,000 licensed (1976), 14,000 manuf. (1976). **Radios:** 5.1 mln. licensed (1976), 112,000 manuf. (1976). **Telephones in use** (1978): 128,352. **Daily newspaper circ.** (1976): 527,000.

Health: Life expectancy at birth (1966): 37.2 male; 36.7 female. **Births** (per 1,000 pop. 1975): 50.3. **Deaths** (per 1,000 pop. 1975): 19.7. **Natural increase** (1975): 3.1%. **Hospital beds** (per 100,000 pop. 1977): 80. **Physicians** (per 100,000 pop. 1977): 7.

Education (1977): **Literacy:** 25%. **Pop. 5-19:** in school: 22%, teachers per 1,000: 7. **PQLI:** 28.

Early cultures in Nigeria date back to at least 700 BC. From the 12th to the 14th centuries, more advanced cultures developed in the Yoruba area, at Ife, and in the north, where Moslem influence prevailed.

Portuguese and British slavers appeared from the 15th-16th centuries. Britain seized Lagos, 1861, during an anti-slave trade campaign, and gradually extended control inland until 1900. Nigeria became independent Oct. 1, 1960, and a republic Oct. 1, 1963.

On May 30, 1967, the Eastern Region seceded, proclaiming itself the Republic of Biafra, plunging the country into civil war. Casualties in the war were est. at over 1 million, including many "Biafrans" (mostly Ibos) who died of starvation despite international efforts to provide relief. The secessionists, after steadily losing ground, capitulated Jan. 12, 1970. Within a few years, the Ibos were reintegrated into national life, but mistrust among the regions persists.

Under "indigenization" programs, various industries were to be run by majority Nigerian control by 1979. Oil revenues have made possible a massive economic development program, largely using private enterprise, but agriculture has lagged. Nigeria nationalized British Petroleum's facilities, July, 1979.

Nigeria led in the formation of the Economic Community of

West African States, 1975, linking 15 countries.

After 13 years of military rule, the nation experienced a peaceful return to civilian government, Oct., 1979.

Norway

Kingdom of Norway

People: Population (1979 est.): 4,074,000. **Age distrib.** (%): 0–14: 23.5; 15–59: 57.2; 60+: 19.6. **Pop. density:** 32.43 per sq. mi. **Urban** (1977): 44.2%. **Ethnic groups:** Only minority are Lapps 0.5%. **Languages:** Norwegian, Lapp. **Religions:** Lutherans 95%.

Geography: Area: 125,181 sq. mi., slightly larger than New Mexico. **Location:** Occupies the W part of Scandinavian peninsula in NW Europe (extends farther north than any European land). **Neighbors:** Sweden, Finland, USSR on E. **Topography:** A highly indented coast is lined with tens of thousands of islands. Mountains and plateaus cover most of the country, which is only 25% forested. **Capital:** Oslo. **Cities** (1978 est.): Oslo 461,437; Bergen 212,308.

Government: Head of state: King Olav V, b. July 2, 1903; in office: Sept. 21, 1957. **Head of government:** Prime Min. Odvar Nordli, b. Nov. 3, 1927; in office: Jan. 12, 1976. **Local divisions:** Oslo and 19 fylker (counties). **Armed forces:** regulars 39,000; reserves 160,000.

Economy: Industries: Paper, shipbuilding, engineering, metals, chemicals, food processing shipping. **Chief crops:** Grains, potatoes, fruits. **Minerals:** Oil, copper, pyrites, nickel, iron, zinc, lead. **Crude oil reserves** (1980): 5.75 bln. bbls. **Other resources:** Forests. **Per capita arable land:** 0.5 acres. **Meat prod.** (1978): beef: 72,000 metric tons; pork: 80,000 metric tons; lamb: 19,000 metric tons. **Fish catch** (1977): 3.6 mln. metric tons. **Electricity prod.** (1978): 81.11 bln. kwh. **Crude steel prod.** (1979): 891,000 metric tons. **Labor force:** 17% agric.; 24% manuf.

Finance: Currency: Krone (Mar. 1980: 5.17 = $1 US). **Gross domestic product** (1978): $39.98 bln. **Per capita income** (1978): $7,949. **Imports** (1979): $13.74 bln.; partners (1978): Swed. 18%, W. Ger. 14%, UK 12%, U.S. 7%. **Exports** (1979): $13.47 bln.; partners (1978): UK 37%, Swed. 11%, W. Ger. 8%, Den. 6%. **Tourists** (1977): 447,800; receipts: $478 mln. **National budget** (1976): $7.59 bln. revenues; $7.99 bln. expenditures. **International reserves less gold** (Mar. 1980): $4.46 bln. **Gold:** 1.18 mln. oz t. **Consumer prices** (change in 1979): 4.8%.

Transport: Railway traffic (1978): 2.71 bln. passenger-km; 2.06 bln. net ton-km. **Motor vehicles:** in use (1977): 1.11 mln. passenger cars, 161,900 comm. vehicles. **Civil aviation:** 3,792 mln. passenger-km (1978); 145 mln. freight ton-km (1978). **Chief ports:** Bergen, Stavanger, Oslo, Tonsberg.

Communications: Television sets: 1.09 mln. licensed (1976), 108,000 manuf. (1975). **Radios:** 1.29 mln. licensed (1976), 111,000 manuf. (1973). **Telephones in use** (1978): 1,562,500. **Daily newspaper circ.** (1977): 1,740,000; 430 per 1,000 pop.

Health: Life expectancy at birth (1977): 72.12 male; 78.42 female. **Births** (per 1,000 pop. 1978): 12.7. **Deaths** (per 1,000 pop. 1978): 9.9. **Natural increase** (1978): .3%. **Hospital beds** (per 100,000 pop. 1977): 1,481. **Physicians** (per 100,000 pop. 1977): 186. **Infant mortality** (per 1,000 live births 1977): 9.2.

Education (1977): **Literacy:** 99%. **Pop. 5-19:** in school: 69%, teachers per 1,000: 46. **PQLI:** 97.

The first supreme ruler of Norway was Harald the Fairhaired who came to power in 872 AD. Between 800 and 1000, Norway's Vikings raided and occupied widely dispersed parts of Europe.

The country was united with Denmark 1381-1814, and with Sweden, 1814-1905. In 1905, the country became independent with Prince Charles of Denmark as king.

Norway remained neutral during World War I. Germany attacked Norway Apr. 9, 1940, and held it until liberation May 8, 1945. The country abandoned its neutrality after the war, and joined the NATO alliance. Norway, a member of the European Free Trade Assoc., rejected membership in the Common Market in a 1972 referendum.

Abundant hydroelectric resources provided the base for Norway's industrialization, producing one of the highest living standards in the world.

Despite an almost total lack of unemployment and an increasing labor shortage, Norway has refused to admit more than a small number of foreign workers.

Norway's merchant marine is the world's fourth largest.

Norway and the Soviet Union have disputed their territorial waters boundary in the Barents Sea, north of the 2 countries' common border.

Petroleum output from oil and mineral deposits under the continental shelf raised state revenues; new refinery facilities opened in 1979, and new offshore fields were discovered.

Svalbard is a group of mountainous islands in the Arctic O., c. 23,957 sq. mi., pop. varying seasonally from 1,500 to 3,500. The largest, Spitsbergen (formerly called West Spitsbergen), 15,060 sq. mi., seat of governor, is about 370 mi. N of Norway. By a treaty signed in Paris, 1920, major European powers recognized the sovereignty of Norway, which incorporated it in 1925. Both Norway and the USSR mine rich coal deposits. Mt. Newton (Spitsbergen) is 5,633 ft. tall.

Oman

Sultanate of Oman

People: Population (1979 est.): 864,000. **Pop. density:** 10.24 per sq. mi. **Ethnic groups:** Arab 88%, Baluchi 4%, Persian 3%, Indian 2%, African 2%. **Languages:** Arabic, Persian, Urdu, others. **Religions:** Ibadi Moslems 50%, Sunni Moslems 25%, some Hindus.

Geography: Area: 82,000 sq. mi., the size of Kansas. **Location:** On SE coast of Arabian peninsula. **Neighbors:** United Arab Emirates, Saudi Arabia, South Yemen on W. **Topography:** Oman has a narrow coastal plain up to 10 mi. wide, a range of barren mountains reaching 9,900 ft., and a wide, stony, mostly waterless plateau, avg. alt. 1,000 ft. Also the tip of the Ruus-al-Jebal peninsula controls access to the Persian Gulf. **Capital:** Muscat. **Cities** (1975 est.): Matrah 20,000; Muscat 7,000.

Government: Head of state: Sultan Qaboos bin Said; b. Nov. 18, 1942; in office: July 23, 1970. **Local divisions:** 1 province, 9 regions, and districts. **Armed forces:** regulars 19,200; para-military 3,300.

Economy: Chief crops: Dates, fruits vegetables, wheat, frankincense. **Minerals:** Oil. **Crude oil reserves** (1980): 2.40 bln. bbls. **Per capita arable land:** 0.05 acres. **Fish catch** (1977): 198,000 metric tons. **Electricity prod.** (1977): 550.00 mln. kwh. **Labor force:** 83% agric.

Finance: Currency: Rial (Mar. 1980; .35 = $1 US). **Gross domestic product** (1979): $3.39 bln. **Per capita income** (1976): $2,400. **Imports** (1978): $947 mln.; partners: UK 21%, UAE 16%, Jap. 16%, W. Ger. 6%. **Exports** (1979): $2.16 bln.; partners: Jap. 57%, U.S. 15%, Nor. 7%, Neth. 6%. **National budget** (1978): $1.45 bln. revenues; $1.57 bln. expenditures. **International reserves less gold** (Feb. 1980): $645.2 mln. **Gold:** 187,000 oz t.

Transport: Chief ports: Matrah, Muscat.

Communications: Telephones in use (1978): 13,068.

Health: Hospital beds (per 100,000 pop. 1977): 173. **Physicians** (per 100,000 pop. 1977): 49.

Education (1977): **Literacy:** 50%. **Pop. 5-19:** in school: 25%, teachers per 1,000: 13. **PQLI:** 33.

A long history of rule by other lands, including Portugal in the 16th century, ended with the ouster of the Persians in 1744. By the early 19th century, Muscat and Oman was one of the most important countries in the region, controlling much of the Persian and Pakistan coasts, and ruling far-away Zanzibar, which was separated in 1861 under British mediation.

British influence was confirmed in a 1951 treaty, and Britain helped supress an uprising by traditionally rebellious interior tribes against control by Muscat in the 1950s. Enclaves on the Pakistan coast were sold to that country in 1958.

On July 23, 1970, Sultan Said bin Taimur was overthrown by his son. The new sultan changed the nation's name to Sultanate of Oman. He launched a domestic development program, and battled leftist rebels in the southern Dhofar area to their defeat, Dec. 1975. Warfare was resumed, 1979.

Oil, discovered in 1964, has been the major source of income for the sultanate.

Economic and military aid accords with the U.S. gave U.S. forces access to air and naval bases around the Indian O., 1980.

Pakistan

Islamic Republic of Pakistan

People: Population (1979 est.): 84,075,000. **Pop. density:** 223.98 per sq. mi. **Urban** (1972): 25.5%. **Ethnic groups:** Punjabi 66%, Sindhi 13%, Pushtun (Iranian) 8.5%, Urdu 7.6%, Baluchi 2.5%, others. **Languages:** Urdu, English are both official. **Religions:** Moslems 96%, Christians 1.4%, Hindus 1.5%.

Geography: Area: 342,750 sq. mi., larger than Texas. **Location:** In W part of South Asia. **Neighbors:** Iran on W, Afghanistan, China on N, India on E. **Topography:** The Indus R. rises in the Hindu Kush and Himalaya mtns. in the N (highest is K2, or Godwin Austen, 28,250 ft., 2d highest in world), then flows over 1,000 mi. through fertile valley and empties into Arabian Sea. Thar Desert, Eastern Plains flank Indus Valley. **Capital:** Islamabad. **Cities** (1972 cen.): Karachi 3,498,634; Lahore 2,165,372; Lyallpur 822,263; Hyderabad 628,310; Rawalpindi 615,392.

Government: Head of state and head of government: Pres. Mohammad Zia ul-Haq; b. 1924; in office: Sept. 16, 1978 (state), July 5, 1977 (govt.). **Local divisions:** Federal capital and 4 provinces with elected legislatures. **Armed forces:** regulars 429,000; reserves 513,000.

Economy: Industries: Textiles, cement, paper, sugar, chemicals, fertilizers, surgical instruments. **Chief crops:** Rice, wheat, cotton, oilseeds, tobacco, sugar. **Minerals:** Sulphur, gypsum, salt, chromite, cement, oil, gas, asbestos, antimony, magnesite, silica. **Crude oil reserves** (1980): 200 mln. bbls. **Other resources:** Wool. **Per capita arable land:** 0.6 acres. **Meat prod.** (1978): beef: 331,000 metric tons; lamb: 239,000 metric tons. **Fish catch** (1977): 248,500 metric tons. **Electricity prod.** (1977): 11.05 bln. kwh. **Labor force:** 57% agric.; 12% manuf.

Finance: Currency: Rupee (Mar. 1980: 9.90 = $1 US). **Gross domestic product** (1979): $19.73 bln. **Per capita income** (1975): $183. **Imports** (1979): $3.96 bln.; partners (1978): Jap. 13%, U.S. 11%, UK 9%, W. Ger. 8%. **Exports** (1979): $2.06 bln.; partners (1978): Jap. 9%, Iran 8%, UK 7%, HK 6%. **Tourists** (1977): 220,400; receipts: $61 mln. **National budget** (1978): $2.54 bln. revenues; $3.11 bln. expenditures. **International reserves less gold** (Mar. 1980): $757 mln. **Gold:** 1.82 mln. oz t. **Consumer prices** (change in 1979): 9.5%.

Transport: Railway traffic (1978): 13.98 bln. passenger-km; 7.8 bln. net ton-km. **Motor vehicles:** in use (1975): 196,100 passenger cars, 91,700 comm. vehicles. **Civil aviation:** 4,644 mln. passenger-km (1978); 200 mln. freight ton-km (1978). **Chief ports:** Karachi.

Communications: Television sets: 350,000 in use (1976). **Radios:** 1.20 mln. licensed (1976). **Telephones in use** (1975): 240,000. **Daily newspaper circ.** (1976): 965,000.

Health: Life expectancy at birth (1962): 53.72 male; 48.80 female. **Births** (per 1,000 pop. 1968): 36. **Deaths** (per 1,000 pop. 1968): 12. **Natural increase** (1968): 2.4%. **Hospital beds** (per 100,000 pop. 1977): 50. **Physicians** (per 100,000 pop. 1977): 25. **Infant mortality** (per 1,000 live births 1968): 124.

Education (1977): **Literacy:** 23%. **Pop. 5-19:** in school: 27%, teachers per 1,000: 9. **PQLI:** 38.

Present-day Pakistan shares the 5,000-year history of the India-Pakistan sub-continent. At present day Harappa and Mohenjo Daro, the Indus Valley Civilization, with large cities and elaborate irrigation systems, flourished c. 4,000-2,500 BC.

Aryan invaders from the NW conquered the region around 1,500 BC, forging a Hindu civilization that dominated Pakistan as well as India for 2,000 years.

Beginning with the Persians in the 6th century BC, and continuing with Alexander the Great and with the Sassanians, successive nations to the west ruled or influenced Pakistan, eventually separating the area from the Indian cultural sphere.

The first Arab invasion, 712 AD, introduced Islam. Under the Mogul empire (1526-1867), Moslems ruled most of India, yielding to British encroachment and resurgent Hindus.

After World War I the Moslems of British India began agitation for minority rights in elections. Mohammad Ali Jinnah (1876-1948) was the principal architect of Pakistan. A leader of the Moslem League from 1916, he worked for dominion status for India; from 1940 he advocated a separate Moslem state.

When the British withdrew Aug. 14, 1947, the Islamic majority areas of India acquired self-government as Pakistan, with dominion status in the Commonwealth. Pakistan was divided into 2 sections, West Pakistan and East Pakistan. The 2 areas were nearly 1,000 mi. apart on opposite sides of India.

Pakistan became a republic in 1956. Pakistan had a National Assembly (legislature) with equal membership from East and West Pakistan, and 2 Provincial Assemblies. In Oct. 1958, Gen. Mohammad Ayub Khan took power in a coup. He was elected president in 1960, reelected in 1965.

As a member of the Central Treaty Organization, Pakistan had been aligned with the West. Following clashes between India and China in 1962, Pakistan made commercial and aid agreements with Communist China. U.S. aid to both Pakistan and India was suspended during the 1966 war over Kashmir but both economic aid and "nonlethal" military aid were resumed in 1966. The embargo was modified in 1973, lifted in 1975.

Ayub resigned Mar. 25, 1969, after several months of violent rioting and unrest, most of it in East Pakistan, which demanded autonomy. The government was turned over to Gen. Agha Mohammad Yahya Khan and martial law was declared; Yahya assumed the presidency.

The Awami League, which sought regional autonomy for East Pakistan, won a majority in Dec. 1970 elections to a National Assembly which was to write a new constitution. In March, 1971 Yahya postponed the Assembly. Rioting and strikes broke out in the East.

On Mar. 25, 1971, government troops launched attacks in the East. The Easterners, aided by India, proclaimed the independent nation of Bangladesh. In months of widespread fighting, countless thousands were killed. Some 10 million Easterners fled into India.

Full scale war between India and Pakistan had spread to both the East and West fronts by December 3. Pakistan troops in the East surrendered Dec. 16; Pakistan agreed to a cease-fire in the West Dec. 17. On July 3, 1972, Pakistan and India signed a pact agreeing to withdraw troops from their borders and seek peaceful solutions to all problems.

In Aug. 1973 India agreed to release 93,000 Pakistani prisoners held since 1971. The return was completed in April, 1974. Pakistan agreed to repatriate 200,000 Bengali nationals stranded in Pakistan, and agreed to accept some Biharis (non-Bengalis) unwanted in Bangladesh. India and Pakistan agreed in 1976 to resume full diplomatic relations.

Zulfikar Ali Bhutto, leader of the Pakistan People's party, which had won the most West Pakistan votes in the Dec. 1970 elections, became president Dec. 20. In 1972 he announced new land reforms and said the government would control management of major industries.

A new constitution adopted Apr. 10, 1973, made Pakistan a federal Islamic republic. Bhutto became prime minister Aug. 14.

Bhutto was overthrown in a military coup July, 1977. Some 300 people had been killed in protests over alleged rigging of parliamentary elections earlier in the year. Convicted of complicity in a 1974 political murder, Bhutto was executed Apr.4, 1979. The new military rulers made concessions to Moslem conservatives.

Relations with the U.S. were strained, 1979, when the U.S. embassy in Islamabad was stormed and burned and 2 Americans were killed, Nov. 21st, along with attacks on other U.S. installations.

Panama

Republic of Panama

People: Population (1979 est.): 1,876,000. **Age distrib.** (%): 0–14: 43.4; 15–59: 51.0; 60+: 5.7. **Pop. density:** 64.15 per sq. mi. **Urban** (1978): 56.6%. **Ethnic groups:** Mestizo 70%, Negro 13%, Caucasian 10%, Indian 6%. **Languages:** Spanish (official), English. **Religions:** Roman Catholics 93%, Protestants 6%.

Geography: Area: 29,306 sq. mi., slightly larger than West Virginia. **Location:** In Central America. **Neighbors:** Costa Rica on W., Colombia on E. **Topography:** 2 mountain ranges run the length of the isthmus. Tropical rain forests cover the Caribbean coast and eastern Panama. **Capital:** Panama. **Cities** (1978 est.): Panama 439,310; San Miguelito 146,310.

Government: Head of state and head of government: Pres. Aristides Royo; b. Aug. 14, 1940; in office: Oct. 11, 1978. **Local divisions:** 9 provinces, 1 territory. **Armed forces:** paramilitary 11,000.

Economy: Industries: Oil refining, shipping, international banking. **Chief crops:** Bananas, pineapples, cocoa, coconuts, sugar. **Minerals:** Cement, clay, salt, copper. **Other resources:** Forests (mahogany), shrimp. **Per capita arable land:** 0.6 acres.

Meat prod. (1978): beef: 52,000 metric tons; pork: 6,000 metric tons. **Fish catch** (1977): 228,000 metric tons. **Electricity prod.** (1978): 1.26 bln. kwh. **Labor force:** 40% agric.

Finance: Currency: Balboa (Mar. 1980: 1.00 = $1 US). **Gross domestic product** (1978): $2.31 bln. **Per capita income** (1978): $1,116. **Imports** (1978): $941 mln.; partners (1977): U.S. 31%, Ecuador 15%, Venez. 8%, Saudi Ar. 7%. **Exports** (1979): $288 mln.; partners (1977): U.S. 45%, Canal Zone 10%, W. Ger. 8%, Neth. 5%. **Tourists** (1977): 361,900; receipts: $145 mln. **National budget** (1978): $436 mln. revenues; $511 mln. expenditures. **International reserves less gold** (Feb. 1980): $94.7 mln. **Consumer prices** (change in 1979): 7.9%.

Transport: Motor vehicles: in use (1975): 66,200 passenger cars, 19,600 comm. vehicles. **Chief ports:** Balboa, Cristobal, Puerto Armuelles.

Communications: Television sets: 186,000 in use (1976). **Radios:** 270,000 in use (1976). **Telephones in use** (1978): 156,668. **Daily newspaper circ.** (1976): 136,000; 79 per 1,000 pop.

Health: Life expectancy at birth (1970): 64.26 male; 67.50 female. **Births** (per 1,000 pop. 1975): 35.1. **Deaths** (per 1,000 pop. 1975): 6.9. **Natural increase** (1975): 2.8%. **Hospital beds** (per 100,000 pop. 1977): 386. **Physicians** (per 100,000 pop. 1977): 78. **Infant mortality** (per 1,000 live births 1975): 22.7.

Education (1977): **Literacy:** 82%. **Pop. 5-19:** in school: 68%, teachers per 1,000: 24. **PQLI:** 81.

The coast of Panama was sighted by Rodrigo de Bastidas, sailing with Columbus for Spain in 1501, and was visited by Columbus in 1502. Vasco Nunez de Balboa crossed the isthmus and "discovered" the Pacific O. Sept. 13, 1513. Spanish colonies were ravaged by Francis Drake, 1572-95, and Henry Morgan, 1668-71. Morgan destroyed the old city of Panama which had been founded in 1519. Freed from Spain, Panama joined Colombia in 1821.

Panama declared its independence from Colombia Nov. 3, 1903, with U.S. recognition. U.S. naval forces deterred action by Colombia. On Nov. 18, 1903, Panama granted use, occupation and control of the Canal Zone to the U.S. by treaty, ratified Feb. 26, 1904. *(See also Panama Canal.)*

Rioting began Jan. 9, 1964, in a dispute over the flying of the U.S. and Panamanian flags and terms of the 1903 treaty. At least 21 Panamanians and 3 U.S. soldiers died in the rioting.

In 1967 new treaties were proposed, but Panama rejected them in 1970. In Feb. 1974 the U.S. and Panama agreed to negotiate a new treaty which would give the U.S. the right to operate and protect the canal for a certain period, with Panama sharing in the revenues, and would also set a date for final transfer of jurisdiction to Panama. Opposition by U.S. senators stalled the talks.

The U.S. and Panama initialed two treaties in 1977 that would provide for a gradual takeover by Panama of the canal, and withdrawal of U.S. troops, to be completed by 1999. U.S. payments would be substantially increased in the interim. The permanent neutrality of the canal would also be guaranteed. The treaties were ratified by the U.S. Senate in 1978.

After ruling single-handedly for a decade, Gen. Omar Torrijos Herrera abruptly handed over the government to former Education Minister Aristides Royo, Oct. 1978.

Due to easy Panama ship regulations and strictures in the U.S., merchant tonnage registered in Panama since World War II ranks high in size. Similarly easy financial regulations have made Panama a center for international banking.

Inflation, unemployment, and uncertainty over the canal have recently marred a record of economic growth and social improvement from 1950 to 1973.

Japan and Panama agreed, Mar. 1980, on a feasibility study for a second Panama Canal, large enough to accomodate fully-loaded 300,000-ton tankers.

Papua New Guinea

People: Population (1979 est.): 3,076,000. **Age distrib.** (%): 0–14: 43.8; 15–59: 50.3; 60+: 11.4. **Pop. density:** 16.83 per sq. mi. **Urban** (1976): 12.9%. **Ethnic groups:** Papuans (in S and interior), Melanesian (N,E), pygmies, minorities of Chinese, Australians, Polynesians. **Languages:** Melanesian Pidgin, Police Motu, English, 750 local languages. **Religions:** Protestants 33%, Roman Catholic 18%, local religions.

Geography: Area: 178,260 sq. mi., slightly larger than California. **Location:** Occupies eastern half of island of New Guinea. **Neighbors:** Indonesia (West Irian) on W, Australia on S. **Topography:** Thickly forested mtns. cover much of the center of the country, with lowlands along the coasts. Included are some of the nearby islands of Bismarck and Solomon groups, including Admiralty Is., New Ireland, New Britain, and Bougainville. **Capital:** Port Moresby. **Cities** (1976 cen.): Port Moresby (met.) 113,449.

Government: Head of state: Queen Elizabeth II, represented by Gov. Gen. Tore Lokoloko, b. Sept. 21, 1930; in office: Mar. 1, 1977. **Head of government:** Prime Min. Julius Chan; b. Aug. 29, 1939; in office: Mar. 13, 1980. **Local divisions:** National capital and 19 provinces with elected legislatures. **Armed forces:** regulars 3,500.

Economy: Chief crops: Coffee, coconuts, cocoa. **Minerals:** Gold, copper, silver, gas. **Per capita arable land:** 0.01 acres. **Meat prod.** (1978): pork: 22,000 metric tons. **Fish catch** (1977): 39,900 metric tons. **Electricity prod.** (1977): 1.12 bln. kwh. **Labor force:** 84% agric.

Finance: Currency: Kina (Mar. 1980: 1 = $1.41 US). **Gross domestic product** (1978): $1.88 bln. **Per capita income** (1976): $453. **Imports** (1978): $826 mln.; partners (1977): Austral. 43%, Jap. 17%, Sing. 10%. **Exports** (1978): $816 mln.; partners (1977): Jap. 25%, W. Ger. 19%, Austral. 12%, U.S. 10%. **International reserves less gold** (Mar. 1980): $494.33 mln. **Gold:** 58,000 oz t. **Consumer prices** (change in 1979): 5.8%.

Transport: Motor vehicles: in use (1976): 17,700 passenger cars, 19,200 comm. vehicles. **Chief ports:** Port Moresby, Lae.

Communications: Telephones in use (1978): 37,848. **Daily newspaper circ.** (1977) 25,000; 9 per 1,000 pop.

Health: Life expectancy at birth (1975): 47.5 male; 47.0 female. **Births** (per 1,000 pop. 1975): 42.0. **Deaths** (per 1,000 pop. 1975): 17.5. **Natural increase** (1975): 2.5%. **Hospital beds** (per 100,000 pop. 1977): 469. **Physicians** (per 100,000 pop. 1977): 7.

Education (1977): **Literacy:** 32%. **Pop. 5-19:** in school: 28%, teachers per 1,000: 10. **PQLI:** 43.

Human remains have been found in the interior of New Guinea dating back at least 10,000 years and possibly much earlier. Successive waves of peoples probably entered the country from Asia through Indonesia. Europeans visited in the 15th century, but land claims did not begin until the 19th century, when the Dutch took control of the western half of the island.

The southern half of eastern New Guinea was first claimed by Britain in 1884, and transferred to Australia in 1905. The northern half was claimed by Germany in 1884, but captured in World War I by Australia, which was granted a League of Nations mandate and then a UN trusteeship over the area. The 2 territories were administered jointly after 1949, given self-government Dec. 1, 1973, and became independent Sept. 16, 1975. Australia promised $1 billion in aid for the 5 years starting 1976-77, and pledged assistance in defense and foreign affairs.

The indigenous population consists of a huge number of tribes, many living in almost complete isolation with mutually unintelligible languages.

A secession movement in copper-rich Bougainville led to violence in 1973 and 1976. Indonesian border incursions were reported in 1978.

A series of strikes besieged the country, 1979. Tribal warfare in the western highlands took an est. 400 lives; a state of emergency was proclaimed.

Paraguay

Republic of Paraguay

People: Population (1979 est.): 3,117,000. **Age distrib.** (%): 0–14: 45.1; 15–59: 49.7; 60+: 5.2. **Pop. density:** 18.4 per sq. mi. **Urban** (1975): 39.6%. **Ethnic groups:** Mestizos 95%, small Caucasian, Indian, Negro minorities. **Languages:** Spanish, 75%, Guarani 90%. **Religions:** Roman Catholics 95%, Mennonites.

Geography: Area: 157,047 sq. mi., the size of California. **Location:** One of the 2 landlocked countries of S. America. **Neighbors:** Bolivia on N, Argentina on S, Brazil on E. **Topography:** Paraguay R. bisects the country. To E are fertile plains, wooded slopes, grasslands. To W is the Chaco plain, with marshes and scrub trees. Extreme W is arid. **Capital:** Asuncion. **Cities** (1978 est.): Asuncion 434,928.

Government: Head of state: Pres. Alfredo Stroessner; b. Nov. 3, 1912; in office: Aug. 15, 1954. **Local divisions:** 16 departments. **Armed forces:** regulars 15,500; para-military 4,000.

Economy: Industries: Food processing, wood products. **Chief crops:** Corn, wheat, cotton, beans, peanuts, tobacco, citrus fruits, yerba mate. **Minerals:** Iron, manganese, limestone. **Other resources:** Forests. **Per capita arable land:** 0.8 acres. **Meat prod.** (1978): beef: 134,000 metric tons; pork: 61,000 metric tons. **Electricity prod.** (1977): 626.00 mln. kwh. **Labor force:** 53% agric.

Finance: Currency: Guarani (Mar. 1980 126.00 = $1 US). **Gross domestic product** (1977): $2.09 bln. **Per capita income** (1978): $776. **Imports** (1979): $521 mln.; partners (1978): Braz. 20%, Arg. 15%, Algeria 11%, UK 10%. **Exports** (1979): $299 mln.; partners (1978): W. Ger. 15%, Jap. 13%, Neth. 10%, Arg. 9%. **Tourist receipts** (1977): $35 mln. **National budget** (1977): $249 mln. revenues; $232 mln. expenditures. **International reserves less gold** (Mar. 1980): $620.49 mln. **Gold:** 35,000 oz t. **Consumer prices** (change in 1979): 28.1%.

Transport: Railway traffic (1977): 23 mln. passenger-km; 17 mln. net ton-km. **Motor vehicles:** in use (1971): 16,000 passenger cars, 14,000 comm. vehicles. **Chief ports:** Asuncion.

Communications: Television sets: 55,000 in use (1976). **Radios:** 180,000 in use (1976). **Telephones in use** (1977): 41,644. **Daily newspaper circ.** (1976): 106,000; 39 per 100,000 pop.

Health: Life expectancy at birth (1975): 60.3 male; 63.6 female. **Births** (per 1,000 pop. 1975): 39.8. **Deaths** (per 1,000 pop. 1975): 8.9. **Natural increase** (1975): 3.1%. **Hospital beds** (per 100,000 pop. 1977): 135. **Physicians** (per 100,000 pop. 1977): 77. **Infant mortality** (per 1,000 live births 1971): 38.6.

Education (1977): **Literacy:** 82%. **Pop. 5-19:** in school: 52%, teachers per 1,000: 24. **PQLI:** 75.

The Guarani Indians were settled farmers speaking a common language before the arrival of Europeans.

Visited by Sebastian Cabot in 1527 and settled as a Spanish possession in 1535, Paraguay gained its independence from Spain in 1811. It lost much of its territory to Brazil, Uruguay, and Argentina in the War of the Triple Alliance, 1865-1870. Large areas were won from Bolivia in the Chaco War, 1932-35.

Gen. Alfredo Stroessner has ruled since 1954. Suppression of the opposition and decimation of small Indian groups has been charged by international rights groups.

The first stages of a large hydroelectric project were completed in 1968-70. In 1973 Brazil and Paraguay agreed to build a 10-million kilowatt hydroelectric plant, largest in the world, at Itaipu of the Parana R. Income from the project fueled an economic boom in 1977-78. Other major hydroelectric power generator projects are in beginning stages.

Peru

Republic of Peru

People: Population (1979 est.): 17,164,000. **Age distrib.** (%): 0–14: 44.2; 15–59: 50.6; 60+: 5.2. **Pop. density:** 33.9 per sq. mi. **Urban** (1975): 62.5%. **Ethnic groups:** Indians 46%, Mestizos 43%, Caucasians 11%. **Languages:** Spanish, Quechua both official, Aymara; 30% speak no Spanish. **Religions:** Roman Catholics over 90%.

Geography: Area: 496,222 sq. mi., five-sixths the size of Alaska. **Location:** On the Pacific coast of S. America. **Neighbors:** Ecuador, Colombia on N, Brazil, Bolivia on E, Chile on S. **Topography:** An arid coastal strip, 10 to 100 mi. wide, supports much of the population thanks to widespread irrigation. The Andes cover 27% of land area. The uplands are well-watered, as are the eastern slopes reaching the Amazon basin, which covers half the country with its forests and jungles. **Capital:** Lima. **Cities** (1972 cen.): Lima 2,833,609; Arequipa 302,316.

Government: Head of state: Pres. Fernando Belaunde Terry; b. Oct. 7, 1912; in office: July 28, 1980. **Head of government:** Prime Min. Manuel Ulloa; in office: July 28, 1980. **Local divisions:** 23 departments, 1 province. **Armed forces:** regulars 92,000; para-military 25,000.

Economy: Industries: Fish meal, steel. **Chief crops:** Cotton, sugar, coffee, rice, potatoes, beans, corn, barley, tobacco. **Minerals:** Copper, lead, molybdenum, silver, zinc, iron, oil. **Crude oil reserves** (1980): 655 mln. bbls. **Other resources:** Wool, sardines. **Per capita arable land:** 0.5 acres. **Meat prod.** (1978): beef: 82,000 metric tons; pork: 70,000 metric tons; lamb: 33,000 metric tons. **Fish catch** (1977): 2.5 mln. metric tons. **Electricity prod.** (1977): 8.56 bln. kwh. **Crude steel prod.** (1979): 436,000 metric tons. **Labor force:** 4% agric.; 15% manuf.

Finance: Currency: Sol (Mar. 1980: 266.37 = $1 US). **Gross domestic product** (1979): $13.59 bln. **Per capita income** (1977): $586. **Imports** (1978): $1.96 bln.; partners (1977): U.S. 29%, Ecu. 10%, Venez. 9%, W. Ger. 7%. **Exports** (1978): $1.95 bln.; partners (1977): U.S. 30%, Jap. 12%, It. 5%. **Tourists** (1976): 264,000; receipts (1977): $113 mln. **National budget** (1978): $1.69 bln. revenues; $2.22 bln. expenditures. **International reserves less gold** (Feb. 1980): $1.39 bln. **Gold:** 1.23 mln. oz t. **Consumer prices** (change in 1979): 66.7%.

Transport: Railway traffic (1976): 528 mln. passenger-km; (1977) 612 mln. net ton-km. **Motor vehicles:** in use (1977): 300,400 passenger cars, 166,200 comm. vehicles; assembled (1975): 21,200 passenger cars; 12,900 comm. vehicles. **Chief ports:** Callao, Chimbate, Mollendo.

Communications: Television sets: 600,000 in use (1976), 100,000 manuf. (1975). **Radios:** 2.07 mln. in use (1976). **Telephones in use** (1978): 402,459. **Daily newspaper circ.** (1977): 828,000; 51 per 1,000 pop.

Health: Life expectancy at birth (1965): 52.59 male; 55.48 female. **Births** (per 1,000 pop. 1975): 41.0. **Deaths** (per 1,000 pop. 1975): 13.6. **Natural increase** (1975): 2.7%. **Hospital beds** (per 100,000 pop. 1977): 184. **Physicians** (per 100,000 pop. 1977): 64. **Infant mortality** (per 1,000 live births 1972): 70.3.

Education (1977): **Literacy:** 72%. **Pop. 5-19:** in school: 62%, teachers per 1,000: 17. **PQLI:** 65.

The powerful Inca empire had its seat at Cuzco in the Andes covering most of Peru, Bolivia, and Ecuador, as well as parts of Colombia, Chile, and Argentina. Building on the achievements of 800 years of Andean civilization, the Incas had a high level of skill in architecture, engineering, textiles, and social organization.

A civil war had weakened the empire when Francisco Pizarro, Spanish conquistador, began raiding Peru for its wealth, 1532. In 1533 he had the seized ruling Inca, Atahualpa, fill a room with gold as a ransom, then executed him and enslaved the natives.

Lima was the seat of Spanish viceroys until the Argentine liberator, Jose de San Martin, captured it in 1821; Spain was defeated by Simon Bolivar and Antonio J. de Sucre; recognized Peruvian independence, 1824. Chile defeated Peru and Bolivia, 1879-84, and took Tarapaca, Tacna, and Arica; returned Tacna, 1929.

On Oct. 3, 1968, a military coup ousted Pres. Fernando Belaunde Terry. In 1968-74, the military government put through sweeping agrarian changes, and nationalized oil, mining, fishmeal, and banking industries.

Food shortages, escalating foreign debt, and strikes led to another coup, Aug. 29, 1976, and to a slowdown of socialist programs. Labor protests culminated in a general strike in July, 1977. Moderate leftists led in free 1978 voting for a constituent assembly.

After 12 years of military rule, Peru returned to democratic leadership under former Pres. Fernando Belaunde Terry, July 1980. The new government planned to encourage the return of private enterprise to stimulate the inflation-ridden economy.

Peru is normally the world's top fishing nation; it takes about a sixth of total world tonnage, mostly anchovies from the plankton-rich waters of the coastal Peru current. The industry was crippled, 1972, by a disappearance of anchovies from off-shore waters. The government nationalized the industry, 1973. A shift in the ocean currents, 1974, brought at least some of the anchovies back.

Philippines

Republic of the Philippines

People: Population (1979 est.): 47,678,000. **Age distrib.** (%): 0–14: 42.9; 15–59: 52.5; 60+: 4.6. **Pop. density:** 400.15 per sq. mi. **Urban** (1970): 31.8%. **Ethnic groups:** Malays the large majority, Chinese, Americans, Spanish are minorities. **Languages:** Filipino (based on Tagalog), Spanish, English all official; 90 others spoken. **Religions:** Roman Catholics 85%, Moslems 5%, Philippine Independents 4%, Protestants 3%.

Geography: Area: 115,831 sq. mi., slightly larger than Nevada. **Location:** An archipelago off the SE coast of Asia. **Neighbors:** Nearest are Malaysia, Indonesia on S, Taiwan on N. **Topography:** The country consists of some 7,100 islands stretching 1,100 mi. N-S. About 95% of area and population are on 11 largest islands, which are mountainous, except for the heavily indented coastlines and for the central plain on Luzon. **Capital:** Quezon City (Manila is de facto capital). **Cities** (1978 est.): Manila 1,438,252; Quezon City 994,679; Davao 515,520.

Government: Head of state and head of govt.: Pres. Ferdinand E. Marcos; b. Sept. 11, 1917; in office: Dec. 30, 1965 (pres.), Jan. 17, 1973 (premier). **Local divisions:** 12 regions, 72 provinces, 60 chartered cities. **Armed forces:** regulars 103,000; reserves 124,000.

Economy: Industries: Food processing, clothing, drugs, paper, appliances. **Chief crops:** Hemp, copra, sugar, rice, corn, pineapple, tobacco. **Minerals:** Chromium, cobalt, copper, gold, nickel, silver, gypsum, sulphur, mercury, phosphates, zinc, iron, coal, manganese. **Crude oil reserves** (1980): 25 mln. bbls. **Other resources:** Forests (42% of area). **Per capita arable land:** 0.3 acres. **Meat prod.** (1978): beef: 142,000 metric tons; pork: 387,000 metric tons; lamb: 6,000 metric tons. **Fish catch** (1977): 1.5 mln. metric tons. **Electricity prod.** (1977): 15.80 bln. kwh. **Crude steel prod.** (1979): 397,000 metric tons. **Labor force:** 57% agric.

Finance: Currency: Peso (Mar. 1980: 7.44 = $1 US). **Gross domestic product** (1979): $29.8 bln. **Per capita income** (1978): $457. **Imports** (1979): $6.56 bln.; partners (1978): Jap. 27%, U.S. 21%, Saudi Ar. 6%. **Exports** (1979): $4.53 bln.; partners (1978): U.S. 33%, Jap. 24%, Neth. 8%. **Tourists** (1977): 730,100; receipts: $311 mln. **National budget** (1979): $4.77 bln. revenues; $4.84 bln. expenditures. **International reserves less gold** (Mar. 1980): $2.33 bln. **Gold:** 1.75 mln. oz t. **Consumer prices** (change in 1979): 18.8%.

Transport: Railway traffic (1978): 621.6 mln. passenger-km; 38.4 mln. net ton-km. **Motor vehicles:** in use (1976): 386,200 passenger cars, 281,000 comm. vehicles; assembled (1977): 34,300 passenger cars; 24,400 comm. vehicles. **Civil aviation:** 3,600 mln. passenger-km (1977); 134 mln. freight ton-km (1977). **Chief ports:** Cebu, Manila, Iloilo, Davao.

Communications: Television sets: 800,000 in use (1976), 107,000 manuf. (1976). **Radios:** 1.88 mln. in use (1976), 124,000 manuf. (1976). **Telephones in use** (1978): 567,321. **Daily newspaper circ.** (1976): 919,000.

Health: Life expectancy at birth (1975): 56.9 male; 60.0 female. **Births** (per 1,000 pop. 1975): 41.0. **Deaths** (per 1,000 pop. 1975): 10.3. **Natural increase** (1975): 3.1%. **Hospital beds** (per 100,000 pop. 1977): 146. **Physicians** (per 100,000 pop. 1977): 36. **Infant mortality** (per 1,000 live births 1975): 47.6.

Education (1977): **Literacy:** 85%. **Pop. 5-19:** in school: 55%, teachers per 1,000: 17. **PQLI:** 72.

The Malay peoples of the Philippine islands, whose ancestors probably migrated from Southeast Asia, were mostly hunters, fishers, and unsettled cultivators when first visited by Europeans.

The archipelago was visited by Magellan, 1521. The Spanish founded Manila, 1571. The islands, named for King Philip II of Spain, were ceded by Spain to the U.S. for $20 million, 1898, following the Spanish-American War. U.S. troops suppressed a guerrilla uprising in a brutal 6-year war, 1899-1905.

Japan attacked the Philippines Dec. 8, 1941 (Far Eastern time). Japan conquered the islands in May, 1942. It was ousted by Sept. 1945.

On July 4, 1946, independence was proclaimed in accordance with an act passed by the U.S. Congress in 1934. A republic was established.

A rebellion by Communist-led Huk guerrillas was put down by 1954. But urban and rural political violence periodically reappears.

The Philippines and the U.S. have treaties for U.S. military and naval bases and a 1951 Mutual Defense Treaty. President Ferdinand E. Marcos in 1966 concluded a pact reducing U.S. base leases from 99 to 25 years. Riots by radical youth groups and terrorism by leftist guerrillas and outlaws, increased from 1970. On Sept. 21, 1972, Marcos declared martial law. Ruling by decree, he ordered some land reform and stabilized prices. But opposition was suppressed, and a high population growth rate aggravated poverty and unemployment. Political corruption was believed to be widespread. On Jan. 17, 1973, Marcos proclaimed a new constitution with himself as president. His wife received wide powers in 1978 to supervise planning and development. Diplomatic and trade ties were set with China in 1975 and with the USSR in 1976.

Government troops battled Moslem (Moro) secessionists, 1973-76, in southern Mindanao. Fighting resumed, 1977, after a Libyan-mediated agreement on autonomy was rejected by the region's mainly Christian voters. Casualties have been est. at 50,000, half civilians (10,000 civilians dead). Clashes continued through 1980 when 4 days of arson and bombing caused 19 deaths and 174 injuries.

The archipelago has a coastline of 10,850 mi. Manila Bay, with an area of 770 sq. mi., and a circumference of 120 mi., is the finest harbor in the Far East.

In 1972 and 1974 severe floods destroyed crops in central Luzon. In 1974 the first in a series of flood-control dams, built with U.S. aid, was dedicated. Manufacturing has shown steady gains.

All natural resources of the Philippines belong to the state; their exploitation is limited to citizens of the Philippines or corporations of which 60% of the capital is owned by citizens. In 1946 the right to develop natural resources and to own and operate public utilities until 1974 was extended to U.S. citizens.

Poland

Polish People's Republic

People: Population (1979 est.): 35,227,000. **Age distrib.** (%): 0–14: 23.9; 15–59: 62.7; 60+: 13.5. **Pop. density:** 290.88 per sq. mi. **Urban** (1977): 57.0%. **Ethnic groups:** Polish 98%, Germans, Ukrainians, Byelorussians. **Language:** Polish. **Religions:** Roman Catholics 90%, Protestants 1.5%.

Geography: Area: 120,359 sq. mi. **Location:** On the Baltic Sea in E Central Europe. **Neighbors:** E. Germany on W, Czechoslovakia on S, USSR (Lithuania, Byelorussia, Ukraine) on E. **Topography:** Mostly lowlands forming part of the Northern European Plain. The Carpathian Mts. along the southern border rise to 8,200 ft. **Capital:** Warsaw. **Cities** (1978 est.): Warsaw 1,474,200, Lodz 814,800; Cracow 707,000; Wroclaw 588,700, Poznan 531,600.

Government: Head of state: Pres. Henryk Jablonski; b. Dec. 27, 1909; in office: Mar. 28, 1972. **Head of government:** Prime Min. Edward Babiuch; b. 1927; in office: Feb. 18, 1980. **Head of Communist Party:** First Sec. Edward Gierek; b. Jan. 6, 1913; in office: Dec. 20, 1970. **Local divisions:** 49 provinces. **Armed forces:** regulars 317,500; reserves 605,000.

Economy: Industries: Shipbuilding, textiles, chemicals, wood products, metals, autos, aircraft, machinery, cement, aluminum, oil products. **Chief crops:** Grains, potatoes, sugar beets, tobacco, flax. **Minerals:** Coal, copper, silver, zinc, sulphur, salt, cadmium, iron. **Per capita arable land:** 1.0 acres. **Meat prod.** (1978): beef: 750,000 metric tons; pork: 1.83 mln. metric tons; lamb: 18,000 metric tons. **Fish catch** (1977): 665,000 metric tons. **Electricity prod.** (1978): 115.56 bln. kwh. **Crude steel prod.** (1979): 19.2 mln. metric tons. **Labor force:** 28% agric.; 24% manuf.

Finance: Currency: Zloty (Mar. 1980: 33.20 = $1 US). **Net material product** (1978): $57.3 bln. **Per capita income** (1976 est.): $2,500. **Imports** (1979): $17.49 bln.; partners (1978): USSR 30%, E. Ger. 8% W. Ger. 7% Czech. 6%. **Exports** (1979): $16.23 bln.; partners (1978): USSR 34%, E. Ger. 8%, Czech. 7%, W. Ger. 7%. **Tourists** (1977): 10,544,500; receipts (1976): $157 mln. **Consumer prices** (change in 1978): 68%.

Transport: Railway traffic (1978): 46.7 bln. passenger-km; 138.1 bln. net ton-km. **Motor vehicles:** in use (1977): 1.55 mln. passenger cars, 569,000 comm. vehicles; manuf. (1978): 325,200 passenger cars; 69,600 comm. vehicles. **Civil aviation:** 2,088 mln. passenger-km (1978); 18 mln. freight ton-km (1978). **Chief ports:** Gdansk, Gdynia, Szczecin.

Communications: Television sets: 6.8 mln. licensed (1976), 920,000 manuf. (1977). **Radios:** 8.3 mln. licensed (1976), 2.29 mln. manuf. (1977). **Telephones in use** (1978): 2,925,450. **Daily newspaper circ.** (1977): 8,331,000; 240 per 1,000 pop.

Health: Life expectancy at birth (1976): 66.92 male; 74.55 female. **Births** (per 1,000 pop. 1978): 19.0. **Deaths** (per 1,000 pop. 1978): 9.3. **Natural increase** (1978): 1.0%. **Hospital beds** (per 100,000 pop. 1977): 767. **Physicians** (per 100,000 pop.

1977): 166. **Infant mortality** (per 1,000 live births 1978): 22.4.

Education (1977): **Literacy:** 98%. **Pop. 5-19:** in school: 54%, teachers per 1,000: 27. **PQLI:** 92.

Slavic tribes in the area were converted to Latin Christianity in the 10th century. Poland was a great power from the 14th to the 17th centuries. In 3 partitions (1772, 1793, 1795) it was apportioned among Prussia, Russia, and Austria. Overrun by the Austro-German armies in World War I, its independence, self-declared on Nov.11, 1918, was recognized by the Treaty of Versailles, June 28, 1919. Large territories to the east were taken in a war with Russia, 1921.

Nazi Germany and the USSR invaded Poland Sept. 1-27, 1939, and divided the country. During the war, some 6 million Polish citizens were killed by the Nazis, half of them Jews. With Germany's defeat, a Polish government-in-exile in London was recognized by the U.S., but the USSR pressed the claims of a rival group. The election of 1947 was completely dominated by the Communists.

In compensation for 69,860 sq. mi. ceded to the USSR, 1945, Poland received approx. 40,000 sq. mi. of German territory E of the Oder-Neisse line comprising Silesia, Pomerania, West Prussia, and part of East Prussia.

In 12 years of rule by Stalinists, large estates were abolished, industries nationalized, schools secularized, and Roman Catholic prelates jailed. Farm production fell off. Harsh working conditions caused a riot in Poznan June 28-29, 1956.

A new Politburo, committed to development of a more independent Polish Communism, was named Oct. 1956, with Wladyslaw Gomulka as first secretary of the Communist Party. Collectivization of farms was ended and many collectives were abolished.

In 1968, Poland joined other Soviet bloc nations in invading Czechoslovakia.

In Dec. 1970 workers in port cities rioted because of price rises and new incentive wage rules. On Dec. 20 Gomulka resigned as party leader; he was succeeded by Edward Gierek; the incentive rules were dropped, price rises were revoked. In June 1971 a new 5-year plan was announced, placing more stress on housing and consumer goods production.

Poland was the first Communist state to get most-favored nation trade terms from the U.S. A 10-year W. Germany cooperation pact was signed in 1974.

A law promulgated Feb. 13, 1953, required government consent to high Roman Catholic church appointments. In 1956 Gomulka agreed to permit religious liberty and religious publications, provided the church kept out of politics. In 1961 religious studies in public schools were halted. Government relations with the Church improved in the 1970s. The number of priests and churches was greater in 1971 than in 1939, and 24 seminaries continued to function. Pope John Paul II, born Karol Wojtyla, was elected the first Polish Pope of Rome, Oct. 16, 1978.

Key industries are state owned and operate under a planned economy. But about 85% of the farms and close to 200,000 small businesses are privately owned. Poland has become an important industrial power. Heavy indebtedness to Western lenders and rising import prices pose economic problems. The lagging economy caused the ouster of Prime Min. Piotr Jaroszewicz, Feb. 1980.

Portugal

Republic of Portugal

People: Population (1979 est.): 9,843,000. **Age distrib.** (%): 0–14: 27.9; 15–59: 57.9; 60+: 14.3. **Pop. density:** 277.31 per sq. mi. **Ethnic groups:** Homogeneous, with small African minority. **Languages:** Portuguese. **Religions:** Roman Catholics 98%.

Geography: Area: 35,340 sq. mi., slightly smaller than Indiana. **Location:** At SW extreme of Europe. **Neighbors:** Spain on N, E. **Topography:** Portugal N of Tajus R, which bisects the country NE-SW, is mountainous, cool and rainy. To the S there are drier, rolling plains, and a warm climate. **Capital:** Lisbon. **Cities** (1978 est.): Lisbon 829,900; Porto 335,700.

Government: Head of state: Pres. Antonio dos Santos Ramalho Eanes; b. Jan. 25, 1935; in office: July 14, 1976. **Head of government:** Prime Min. Francisco de Sa Carneiro, b. Nov. 14, 1932; in office: Jan. 3, 1980. **Local divisions:** 18 provinces, 2 autonomous districts. **Armed forces:** regulars 60,500; paramilitary 31,850.

Economy: Industries: Textiles, pottery, shipbuilding, oil products, paper, glassware, tourism. **Chief crops:** Grains, corn, rice, grapes, olives, fruits. **Minerals:** Tungsten, uranium, coal, copper, tin, kaolin, gold, iron, manganese. **Other resources:** Forests (world leader in cork production). **Per capita arable land:** 0.8 acres. **Meat prod.** (1978): beef: 81,000 metric tons; pork: 144,000 metric tons; lamb: 26,000 metric tons. **Fish catch** (1977): 310,300 metric tons. **Electricity prod.** (1978): 13.50 bln. kwh. **Crude steel prod.** (1979): 670,000 metric tons. **Labor force:** 28% agric.; 24% manuf.

Finance: Currency: Escudo (Mar. 1980: 49.78 = $1 US). **Gross domestic product** (1978): $17.79 bln. **Per capita income** (1976): $1,509. **Imports** (1978): $5.24 bln.; partners: W. Ger. 14%, U.S. 12%, UK 10%, Fr. 9%. **Exports** (1978): $2.41 bln.; partners: UK 18%, W. Ger. 13%, Fr. 9%, U.S. 7%. **Tourists** (1977): 1,409,600; receipts: $404 mln. **National budget** (1976): $2.40 bln. revenues; $3.60 bln. expenditures. **International reserves less gold** (Feb. 1980): $814 mln. **Gold:** 22.15 mln. oz t. **Consumer prices** (change in 1979): 23.8%.

Transport: Railway traffic (1978): 5.51 bln. passenger-km; 932.4 mln. net ton-km. **Motor vehicles:** in use (1976): 1.03 mln. passenger cars, 288,000 comm. vehicles; assembled (1978): 20,172 passenger cars; 57,324 comm. vehicles. **Civil aviation:** 3,012 mln. passenger-km (1977); 92 mln. freight ton-km (1977). **Chief ports:** Lisbon, Setubal, Leixoes.

Communications: Television sets: 723,000 licensed (1976), 404,000 manuf. (1977). **Radios:** 1.53 licensed (1976), 717,000 manuf. (1977). **Telephones in use** (1978): 1,174,853. **Daily newspaper circ.** (1977): 527,000; 54 per 1,000 pop.

Health: Life expectancy at birth (1974): 65.29 male; 72.03 female. **Births** (per 1,000 pop. 1977): 18.4. **Deaths** (per 1,000 pop. 1977): 9.6. **Natural increase** (1977): .9%. **Hospital beds** (per 100,000 pop. 1977): 528. **Physicians** (per 100,000 pop. 1977): 142. **Infant mortality** (per 1,000 live births 1977): 38.9.

Education (1977): **Literacy:** 72%, **Pop. 5-19:** in school: 62%, teachers per 1,000: 30. **PQLI:** 80.

Portugal, an independent state since the 12th century, was a kingdom until a revolution in 1910 drove out King Manoel II and a republic was proclaimed.

From 1932 a strong, repressive government was headed by Premier Antonio de Oliveira Salazar. Illness forced his retirement in Sept. 1968; he was succeeded by Marcello Caetano.

On Apr. 25, 1974, the government was seized by a military junta led by Gen. Antonio de Spinola, who was named president.

The new government reached agreements providing independence for Guinea-Bissau, Mozambique, Cape Verde Islands, Angola, and Sao Tome and Principe. Spinola resigned Sept. 30, 1974, in face of increasing pressure from leftist officers. Despite a 64% victory for democratic parties in April 1975, the Soviet-supported Communist party increased its influence. Banks, insurance companies, and other industries were nationalized. A countercoup in November halted this trend. Free elections under the new constitution were held, 1976, with the Socialist party gaining a parliamentary plurality. After 3 years of turmoil the economy and political life were in disarray, despite aid from the U.S. and West European countries.

Azores Islands, in the Atlantic, 740 mi. W. of Portugal, have an area of 904 sq. mi. and a pop. (1975) of 292,000. A 1951 agreement gave the U.S. rights to use defense facilities in the Azores. The **Madeira Islands,** 360 mi. off the NW coast of Africa, have an area of 307 sq. mi. and a pop. (1976) of 270,000. Both groups were offered partial autonomy in 1976.

Macao, area of 6 sq. mi., is an enclave, a peninsula and 2 small islands, at the mouth of the Canton R. in China. Portugal granted broad autonomy in 1976. Pop. (1979 est.): 282,000.

Qatar

State of Qatar

People: Population (1979 est.): 210,000. **Pop. density:** 50.0 per sq. mi. **Ethnic groups:** Arabs 56%, Iranians 23%, Pakistani 7%, others. **Languages:** Arabic (official), Farsi (Persian). **Religions:** Moslems 98%.

Geography: Area: 4,000 sq. mi., smaller than Connecticut. **Location:** Occupies peninsula on W coast of Persian Gulf. **Neighbors:** Saudi Arabia on W, United Arab Emirates on S. **Topography:** Mostly a flat desert, with some limestone ridges, vegetation of any kind is scarce. **Capital:** Doha. **Cities** (1978 est.): Doha 130,000.

Government: Head of state and head of government: Amir Khalifa bin Hamad Al-Thani; b. 1932; in office: Feb. 22, 1972 (amir), 1970 (prime min.) **Armed forces:** regulars 4,700.

Economy: Crude oil reserves (1980): 3.76 bln. bbls. **Per capita arable land:** 0.02 acres. **Electricity prod.** (1977): 900 mln. kwh. **Crude steel prod.** (1979): 396,000 metric tons.

Finance: Currency: Riyal (Mar. 1980: 1 = $.27 US). **Gross domestic product** (1976 est.): $2.3 bln. **Per capita income** (1974): $12,500. **Imports** (1978): $1.07 bln.; partners: Jap. 20%, W. Ger. 19%, UK 16%, U.S. 10%. **Exports** (1979): $3.65 bln.; partners (1978): Jap. 22%, Fr. 19%, U.S. 13%, Thai. 9%. **National budget** (1977): $2.06 bln. revenues; $1.85 bln. expenditures. **International reserves less gold** (Dec. 1978): $210.7 mln. **Gold:** 251,000 oz t.

Transport: Chief ports: Doha, Musayid.

Communications: Radios: 40,000 in use (1976). **Telephones in use** (1978): 29,703.

Health: Hospital beds (per 100,000 pop. 1977): 389. **Physicians** (per 100,000 pop. 1977): 105.

Education (1977): **Literacy:** 20%. **Pop. 5-19:** in school: 60%, teachers per 1,000: 48. **PQLI:** 32.

Qatar was under Bahrain's control until the Ottoman Turks took power, 1872 to 1915. In a treaty signed 1916, Qatar gave Great Britain responsibility for its defense and foreign relations. After Britain announced it would remove its military forces from the Persian Gulf area by the end of 1971, Qatar sought a federation with other British protected States in the area; this failed and Qatar declared itself independent, Sept. 1 1971.

Qatar's first ruler under independence, Amir Ahmed bin Ali Al-Thani, was replaced by his cousin, Khalifa bin Hamad Al-Thani, Feb. 22, 1972, in a bloodless coup.

Oil revenues give Qatar a per capita income among the highest in the world, but lack of skilled labor hampers development plans.

Romania

Socialist Republic of Romania

People: Population (1979 est.): 22,057,000. **Age distrib.** (%): 0–14: 25.4; 15–59; 60.5; 60+: 14.2. **Pop. density:** 238.28 per sq. mi. **Urban** (1977): 47.5%. **Ethnic groups:** Romanians 85%, Hungarians 9%, Germans 2%, Serbo-Croats, Ukrainians, Greeks, Turks. **Languages:** Romanian, Hungarian. **Religions:** Orthodox 80%, Roman Catholics 9%, Calvinists, Jews, Lutherans.

Geography: Area: 91,699 sq. mi., slightly smaller than Oregon. **Location:** In SE Europe on the Black Sea. **Neighbors:** USSR on E (Moldavia) and N (Ukraine), Hungary, Yugoslavia on W, Bulgaria on S. **Topography:** The Carpathian Mts. encase the north-central Transylvanian plateau. There are wide plains S and E of the mountains, through which flow the lower reaches of the rivers of the Danube system. **Capital:** Bucharest. **Cities** (1978 cen.): Bucharest 1,807,044; Timisoara 268,785.

Government: Head of state: Pres. Nicolae Ceausescu; b. Jan. 26, 1918; in office; Dec. 9, 1967. **Head of government:** Prime Min. Ilie Verdet; b. 1925; in office; Mar. 30, 1979. **Head of Communist Party:** Pres. Nicolae Ceausescu; in office: Mar. 23, 1965. **Local divisions:** Bucharest and 39 districts. **Armed forces:** regulars 180,500; reserves 502,000.

Economy: Industries: Steel, metals, machinery, oil products, chemicals, textiles, shoes, tourism. **Chief crops:** Corn, wheat, sugar beets, grapes, fruits. **Minerals:** Oil, gas, coal, salt, bauxite, manganese, lead, zinc, gold, silver. **Other resources:** Timber. **Per capita arable land:** 1.1 acres. **Meat prod.** (1978): beef: 287,000 metric tons; pork: 750,000 metric tons; lamb: 72,000 metric tons. **Fish catch** (1977): 150,700 metric tons. **Electricity prod.** (1978): 64.26 bln. kwh. **Crude steel prod. (1979):** 12.9 mln. metric tons. **Labor force:** 36% agric.; 40% manuf.

Finance: Currency: Leu (Apr. 1980: 4.47 = $1 US). **Gross domestic product** (1976 est.): $40 bln. **Per capita income** (1976): $1,600. **Imports** (1978): $9.09 bln.; partners (1977): USSR 19%, W. Ger. 8% E. Ger. 7%, Czech. 5%. **Exports** (1978): $8.24 bln.; partners (1977): USSR 19%, W. Ger. 7%, E. Ger. 7%, Czech. 5%. **Tourists** (1977): 3,684,800; receipts (1976): $112 mln. **National budget** (1979): $76 mln. revenues; $75 mln. expenditures. **International reserves less gold** (Apr. 1980): $400 mln.

Transport: Railway traffic (1977): 23.2 bln. passenger-km; 70 bln. net ton-km. **Motor vehicles:** in use (1975): 138,000 passenger cars; (1972): 50,000 comm. vehicles; manuf. (1978): 81,360 passenger cars; 50,520 comm. vehicles. **Civil aviation:** 1,109 mln. passenger-km (1978); 13 mln. freight ton-km (1978). **Chief ports:** Constanta, Galati, Braila.

Communications: Television sets: 2.96 mln. licensed (1976), 476,000 manuf. (1977). **Radios:** 3.10 mln. licensed (1976), 730,000 manuf. (1977). **Telephones in use** (1975): 1,196,000. **Daily newspaper circ.** (1977): 3,711,000; 171 per 1,000 pop.

Health: Life expectancy at birth (1976): 67.37 male; 71.97 female. **Births** (per 1,000 pop. 1977): 19.6. **Deaths** (per 1,000 pop. 1977): 9.6. **Natural increase** (1977): 1.0%. **Hospital beds** (per 100,000 pop. 1977): 919. **Physicians** (per 100,000 pop. 1977): 135. **Infant mortality** (per 1,000 live births 1977): 31.2.

Education (1977): **Literacy:** 98%. **Pop. 5-19:** in school: 64%, teachers per 1,000: 30. **PQLI:** 91.

Romania's earliest known people merged with invading Proto-Thracians, preceding by centuries the Dacians. The Dacian kingdom was occupied by Rome, 106 AD-271 AD; people and language were Romanized. The principalities of Wallachia and Moldavia, dominated by Turkey, were united in 1859, became Romania in 1861. In 1877 Romania proclaimed independence from Turkey, became an independent state by the Treaty of Berlin, 1878, a kingdom, 1881, under Carol I. In 1886 Romania became a constitutional monarchy with a bicameral legislature.

Romania helped Russia in its war with Turkey, 1877-78. After World War I it acquired Bessarabia, Bukovina, Transylvania, and Banat. In 1940 it ceded Bessarabia and Northern Bukovina to the USSR and part of Southern Dobrudja to Bulgaria.

Marshal Ion Antonescu, leader of a militarist movement, forced Romania to join Germany against the USSR in World War II in 1941. In 1944 Antonescu was overthrown by King Michael with Soviet help and Romania joined the Allies.

With occupation by Soviet troops the Communist-headed National Democratic Front displaced the National Peasant party. A People's Republic was proclaimed, Dec. 30, 1947; Michael was forced to abdicate. Land owners were dispossessed; most banks, factories and transportation units were nationalized.

On Aug. 22, 1965, a new constitution proclaimed Romania a Socialist, rather than a People's Republic. Since 1966, Romania has adopted an independent attitude toward the USSR, witnessed by the visit of U.S. Pres. Nixon in Aug. 1969 and Chinese Communist party chief Hua Guofeng in 1978. Romanian Pres. Nicolae Ceausescu visited the U.S. in 1970 and 1973. The U.S. granted most-favored-nation tariff treatment in 1975, and a 10-year U.S. trade pact was signed in 1976. Since 1959, USSR troops have not been permitted to enter Romania. Romania has maintained friendly relations with China, and has refused to sever diplomatic and trade ties with Israel.

Internal policies remain oppressive. Ethnic Hungarians have protested cultural and job discrimination.

Romania has become industrialized, but lags in consumer goods and in personal freedoms. All industry is state owned, and state farms and cooperatives own over 90% of arable land. Romania is one of the few countries in Europe self-sufficient in oil, though reserves have been depleted.

A major earthquake struck Bucharest in March, 1977, killing over 1,300 people and causing extensive damage to housing and industry.

Rwanda

Republic of Rwanda

People: Population (1979 est.): 4,955,000. **Age distrib.** (%): 0–14: 50.8; 15–59: 46.2; 60+: 3.0. **Pop. density:** 443.5 per sq. mi. **Urban** (1974): 3.5%. **Ethnic groups:** Hutu 89%, Tutsi 10%, Twa (pygmies) 1%. **Languages:** French, Kinyarwandu (both official), Swahili. **Religions:** Roman Catholics 45%, Protestants 9%, Moslems 1%.

Geography: Area: 10,169 sq. mi., the size of Maryland. **Location:** In E central Africa. **Neighbors:** Uganda on N, Zaire on W, Burundi on S, Tanzania on E. **Topography:** Grassy uplands and hills cover most of the country, with a chain of volcanoes in the NW. The source of the Nile R. has been located in the headwaters of the Kagera (Akagera) R., SW of Kigali. **Capital:** Kigali.

Cities (1977 est.): Kigali 89,950.

Government: Head of state: Pres. Juvenal Habyarimana; b. Mar. 8, 1937; in office: July 5, 1973. **Local divisions:** 10 prefectures. **Armed forces:** regulars 3,750; para-military 1,200.

Economy: Chief crops: Coffee, cotton, tea, pyrethrum, tobacco. **Minerals:** Tin, gold, wolframite. **Per capita arable land:** 0.4 acres. **Electricity prod.** (1977): 149 mln. kwh. **Labor force:** 95% agric.

Finance: Currency: Franc (Mar. 1980: 92.84 = $1 US). **Gross domestic product** (1977): $771 mln. **Per capita income** (1977): $172. **Imports** (1978): $179 mln.; partners (1977): Belg. 21%, Jap. 12%, Kenya 11%, W. Ger. 8%. **Exports** (1978): $90 mln.; partners (1977): Kenya 81%, Belg. 6%. **National budget** (1977): $93.87 mln. revenues; $103.64 mln. expenditures. **International reserves less gold** (Mar. 1980): $161.49 mln. **Gold:** 4,000 oz t. **Consumer prices** (change in 1979): 15.7%.

Transport: Motor vehicles: in use (1975): 6,500 passenger cars, 4,800 comm. vehicles.

Communications: Radios: 70,000 in use (1976), 17,000 manuf. (1976). **Telephones in use** (1978): 4,543. **Daily newspaper circ.** (1977): 200; 0.1 per 1,000 pop.

Health: Life expectancy at birth (1975): 41.8 male; 45.0 female. **Births** (per 1,000 pop. 1970): 51.0. **Deaths** (per 1,000 pop. 1970): 22.0. **Natural increase** (1970): 2.9%. **Hospital beds** (per 100,000 pop. 1977): 154. **Physicians** (per 100,000 pop. 1977): 13. **Infant mortality** (per 1,000 live births 1970): 127.

Education (1977): **Literacy:** 25%. **Pop. 5-19:** in school: 27%, teachers per 1,000: 6. **PQLI:** 32.

For centuries, the Tutsi (an extremely tall people) dominated the Hutus (90% of the population). A civil war broke out in 1959 and Tutsi power was ended. A referendum in 1961 abolished the monarchic system.

Rwanda, which had been part of the Belgian UN trusteeship of Rwanda-Urundi, became independent July 1, 1962. The government was overthrown in a 1973 military coup. Rwanda is one of the most densely populated countries in Africa. All available arable land is being used, and is being subject to erosion. The government has carried out economic and social improvement programs, using foreign aid and volunteer labor on public works projects.

Saint Lucia

People: Population (1979 est.): 121,000. **Age distrib.** (%): 0–20: 49.6; 21–64: 42.7; 65+: 7.7. **Pop. density:** 462.18 per sq. mi. **Ethnic groups:** African or mulatto 97%, white 3%. **Languages:** English (official), French patois. **Religions:** Mainly Roman Catholic.

Geography: Area: 238 sq. mi., about one-fifth the size of Rhode Island. **Location:** In Eastern Caribbean, 2d largest of the Windward Is. **Neighbors:** Martinique to N, St. Vincent to SW. **Topography:** Mountainous, volcanic in origin; Soufriere, a volcanic crater, in the S. Wooded mountains run N-S to Mt. Gimie, 3,145 ft., with streams through fertile valleys. **Capital:** Castries. **City:** Castries (1979 est.): 45,000.

Government: Head of state: Queen Elizabeth II, represented by Gov.-Gen. Boswell Williams; in office: June 19, 1980. **Head of government:** Prime Min. Allan Louisy, b. 1916; in office: July 4, 1979. **Local divisions:** Rural community councils.

Economy: Industries: Agriculture, tourism, construction, manufacturing. **Chief crops:** Bananas, coconuts, cocoa, citrus fruits, spices. **Other resources:** Forests. **Per capita arable land:** 0.1 acres. **Electricity prod.** (1977): 50.00 mln. kwh. **Labor force:** 40% agric.

Finance: Currency: East Caribbean dollar (Mar. 1980: 2.70 = $1 US). **Gross domestic product** (1978): $73.67 mln. **Per capita income** (1978): $698. **Imports** (1976): $46.6 mln.; partners: UK 25%, U.S. 20%, Trin./Tob. 15%, Can. 12%. **Exports** (1976): $18.5 mln.; partners: UK 45%, Lee-Wind-Is. 17%, Trin.-/Tob. 12%, Barb. 8%. **Tourists** (1977): 137,100; receipts (1975): $3.9 mln. **National budget** (1977-78 est.): $18.4 mln. revenues; $17.2 mln. expenditures. **Consumer prices** (change in 1978): 11%.

Transport: Motor vehicles: in use (1976): 3,700 passenger cars, 1,800 comm. vehicles. **Chief ports:** Castries, Vieux Fort.

Communications: Television sets: 1,700 in use (1975). **Radios:** 82,000 in use (1976). **Telephones in use** (1978): 7,157. **Daily newspaper circ.** (1976): 4,000; 36 per 1,000 pop.

Health: Life expectancy at birth (1961): 55.13 male; 58.47 female. **Births** (per 1,000 pop. 1975): 35.0. **Deaths** (per 1,000 pop. 1975): 7.3. **Natural increase** (1975): 2.8%. **Pop. per hospital bed** (1975): 202. **Pop. per physician** (1975): 4,231. **Infant mortality** (per 1,000 live births 1975): 36.5.

Education: Pop. 5–19: in school (1975): 34,178. **PQLI:** 63.

St. Lucia was ceded to Britain by France at the Treaty of Paris, 1814. Self government was granted with the West Indies Act, 1967. Independence was attained Feb. 22, 1979.

Primarily an agricultural economy, St. Lucia is undertaking an ambitious development program, including an oil transshipment terminal and free-port zone being built by U.S. oil company Amerada Hess. Aid has come from the Caribbean Community and Venezuela.

Saint Vincent and the Grenadines

People: Population (1979 est.): 111,000. **Pop. density:** 740 per sq. mi. **Ethnic groups:** Mainly of African or mixed origin; also, some Asians, Europeans, and Caribs. **Languages:** English. **Religions:** Methodists, Anglicans, Roman Catholics.

Geography: Area: 150 sq. mi., about twice the size of Washington, D.C. **Location:** In the eastern Caribbean, St. Vincent (133 sq. mi.) and the northern islets of the Grenadines form a part of the Windward chain. **Neighbors:** St. Lucia to N, Barbados to E, Grenada to S. **Topography:** St. Vincent is volcanic, with a ridge of thickly-wooded mountains running its length; Soufriere, rising in the N, erupted in Apr. 1979. **Capital:** Kingstown. **Cities** (1978): Kingstown 25,000.

Government: Head of state: Queen Elizabeth II, represented by Gov.-Gen. Sir Sydney Douglas Gun-Munro; b. Nov. 29, 1916; in office: Jan. 1, 1977. **Head of government:** Robert Milton Cato; b. June 3, 1915; in office: Dec. 11, 1974.

Economy: Industries: Agriculture, tourism. **Chief crops:** Bananas, arrowroot, coconuts. **Per capita arable land:** 0.3 acres. **Electricity prod.** (1977): 20 mln. kwh. **Labor force:** 30% agric.

Finance: Currency: East Caribbean dollar (May 1980: 2.70 = $1 US). **Per capita income** (1979): $250. **Imports** (1977): $30.3 mln.; partners (1974): UK 30%, Trin./Tob. 15%, Can. 13%, U.S. 9%. **Exports** (1977): $9.89 mln.; partners (1974): UK 66%, Barb. 15%, Trin./Tob. 9%. **Tourists** (1977): 42,000; receipts (1977): $5.44 mln. **National budget** (1979): $12 mln. revenues; $11.6 mln. expenditures.

Transport: Motor vehicles: in use (1976): 3,500 passenger cars, 800 comm. vehicles. **Chief ports:** Kingstown.

Communications: Telephones in use (1978): 5,302.

Health: Life expectancy at birth (1961): 58.46 male; 59.67 female. **Births** (per 1,000 pop. 1977): 31. **Deaths** (per 1,000 pop. 1973): 10.0. **Natural increase** (1973): 2.2%. **Pop. per hospital bed** (1972): 170. **Infant mortality** (per 1,000 pop. under 1 yr. 1977): 55.

Education (1979): **Literacy:** 95%. **Pop. 5–19:** in school (1975): 26,938; per teacher: 18.5. **PQLI:** 67.

Columbus landed on St. Vincent on Jan. 22, 1498 (St. Vincent's Day). Britain and France both laid claim to the island in the 17th and 18th centuries; the Treaty of Versailles, 1783, finally ceded it to Britain. Associated State status was granted 1969; independence was attained Oct. 27, 1979.

The entire economic life of St. Vincent, dependent upon few crops and tourism, was devastated by the eruption of Mt. Soufriere, Apr. 13, 1979.

Samoa

People: Population (1979 est.): 155,000. **Age distrib.** (%): 0–14: 50.4; 15–59: 45.4; 60+: 4.3. **Pop. density:** 132.39 per sq. mi. **Urban** (1978): 21.3%. **Ethnic groups:** Samoans (Polynesians) 88%, Euronesians (mixed) 10%, Europeans, other Pacific Islanders. **Languages:** Samoan, English both official. **Religions:** Protestants 75%, Roman Catholics 20%.

Geography: Area: 1,133 sq. mi., the size of Rhode Island. **Location:** In the S. Pacific O. **Neighbors:** Nearest are Fiji on W, Tonga on S. **Topography:** Main islands, Savai'i (660 sq. mi.) and Upolu (430 sq. mi.), both ruggedly mountainous, and small islands Manono and Apolima. **Capital:** Apia. **Cities** (1978 est.): Apia (met.) 32,616.

Government: Head of state: King Malietoa Tanumafili II; b. Jan. 4, 1913; in office: Jan. 1, 1962. **Head of government:** Prime Min. Taisi Tufuga Tupuola Efi; b. Mar. 1, 1938; in office: Mar. 24, 1976. **Local divisions:** 24 districts.

Economy: Chief crops: Cocoa, coconuts, bananas, taro, coffee, bark cloth. **Other resources:** Hardwoods, fish. **Per capita arable land:** 0.9 acres. **Electricity prod.** (1977): 25.00 mln. kwh. **Labor force:** 67% agric.

Finance: Currency: Tala (Feb. 1980: 1 = $1.08 US). **Gross domestic product** (1976 est.): $50 mln. **Per capita income** (1976): $320. **Imports** (1978): $65 mln.; partners (1977): NZ 29% Austral. 17%, Jap. 15%, U.S. 9%. **Exports** (1978): $14 mln.; partners (1977): NZ 16%, W. Ger. 46%, U.S. 10%, Neth. 10%. **Tourists** (1977): 22,000; receipts (1976): $3 mln. **International reserves less gold** (Feb. 1980): $3.06 mln. **Consumer prices** (change in 1979): 10.8%.

Transport: Motor vehicles: in use (1976): 1,300 passenger cars, 1,900 comm. vehicles. **Chief ports:** Apia, Asau.

Communications: Radios: 50,000 in use (1975). **Telephones in use** (1978): 3,810.

Health: Life expectancy at birth (1966): 60.8 male; 65.2 female. **Births** (per 1,000 pop. 1978): 20.0. **Deaths** (per 1,000 pop. 1978): 2.8. **Natural increase** (1978): 1.7%. **Pop. per hospital bed** (1977): 214. **Pop. per physician** (1977): 2,884. **Infant mortality** (per 1,000 live births 1978): 10.4. **PQLI:** 84.

Western Samoa was a German colony, 1899 to 1914, when New Zealand landed troops and took over. It became a New Zealand mandate under the League of Nations and, in 1945, a New Zealand UN Trusteeship.

An elected local government took office in Oct. 1959 and the country became fully independent Jan. 1, 1962. New Zealand has continued economic aid and educational assistance.

The country's name was changed to Samoa in 1977.

San Marino

Most Serene Republic of San Marino

People: Population (1979 est.): 21,000. **Age distrib.** (%): 0–14: 23.9; 15–59: 61.3; 60+: 14.8. **Pop. density:** 833.33 per sq. mi. **Urban** (1970): 92.4%. **Ethnic groups:** Italian. **Languages:** Italian. **Religions:** Roman Catholics predominate.

Geography: Area: 24 sq. mi. **Location:** In N central Italy near Adriatic coast. **Neighbors:** Completely surrounded by Italy. **Topography:** The country lies on the slopes of Mt. Titano. **Capital:** San Marino. **City** (1978 est.): San Marino 4,628.

Government: Head of state: Captains Regent: Primo Marani, Pietro Chiaruzzi; in office: Apr. 1, 1980 (6 mo. term). **Local divisions:** 9 sectors. **Armed forces:** 180-man ceremonial army.

Economy: Industries: Postage stamps, tourism, woolen goods, paper, cement, ceramics. **Per capita arable land:** 0.1 acres.

Finance: Currency: Lira. **Tourists** (1977): 2,564,500.

Communications: Television sets: 4,000 licensed (1976). **Radios:** 6,000 licensed (1976). **Telephones in use** (1978): 6,276. **Daily newspaper circ.** (1976): 1,300; 65 per 1,000 pop.

Births (per 1,000 pop. 1977): 14.2. **Deaths** (per 1,000 pop. 1977): 6.9. **Natural increase** (1977): .8%. **Infant mortality** (per 1,000 live births 1977): 24.1.

San Marino claims to be the oldest state in Europe and to have been founded in the 4th century. A communist-led coalition ruled 1947-57; a similar coalition took power in 1978. It has had a treaty of friendship with Italy since 1862.

Sao Tome and Principe

Democratic Republic of Sao Tome and Principe

People: Population (1979 est.): 82,000. **Pop. density:** 215.05 per sq. mi. **Ethnic groups:** Portuguese-African mixture, African minority (Angola, Mozambique immigrants). **Languages:** Portuguese. **Religions:** Christians 80%.

Geography: Area: 372 sq. mi., slightly larger than New York City. **Location:** In the Gulf of Guinea about 125 miles off W Central Africa. **Neighbors:** Gabon, Equatorial Guinea on E. **Topography:** Sao Tome and Principe islands, part of an extinct volcano chain, are both covered by lush forests and croplands. **Capital:** Sao Tome. **Cities** (1976 est.): Sao Tome 20,000.

Government: Head of state and head of government: Pres. Manuel Pinto da Costa, b. 1910; in office: July 12, 1975. **Local divisions:** 2 provinces, 12 counties.

Economy: Chief crops: Coffee, cocoa, coconut products, cinchona. **Per capita arable land:** 0.03 acres. **Electricity prod.** (1977): 8.00 mln. kwh.

Finance: Currency: Dobra (Sept. 1979): 34.70 = $1 US). **Gross domestic product** (1976 est.): $40 mln. **Per capita income** (1976): $270. **Imports** (1976): 6.9 mln.; partners (1975): Port. 61%, Angola 13%. **Exports** (1976): $6.5 mln.; partners (1975): Neth. 52%, Port. 33%, W. Ger. 8%.

Transport: Motor vehicles: in use (1973): 1,600 passenger cars, 400 comm. vehicles. **Chief ports:** Sao Tome, Santo Antonio.

Communications: Radios: 20,000 in use (1976).

Health: Births (per 1,000 pop. 1972): 45.0. **Deaths** (per 1,000 pop. 1972): 11.2. **Natural increase** (1972): 3.4%. **Pop. per hospital bed** (1976): 160. **Pop. per physician** (1973): 6,666. **Infant mortality** (per 1,000 live births 1972): 64.3.

The islands were uninhabited when discovered in 1471 by the Portuguese, who brought the first settlers — convicts and exiled Jews. Sugar planting was replaced by the slave trade as the chief economic activity until coffee and cocoa were introduced in the 19th century.

Portugal agreed, 1974, to turn the colony over to the Gabon-based Movement for the Liberation of Sao Tome and Principe, which proclaimed as first president its East German-trained leader Manuel Pinto da Costa. Independence came July 12, 1975.

Low cocoa prices, the emigration of most of the 1,000 whites, and the repatriation of Cape Verdean plantation foremen stymied the economy.

Saudi Arabia

Kingdom of Saudi Arabia

People: Population (1979 est.): 9,292,000. **Pop. density:** 9.01 per sq. mi. **Ethnic groups:** Arab tribes, immigrants from other Arab and Moslem countries. **Languages:** Arabic. **Religions:** Moslems 99%.

Geography: Area: 873,000 sq. mi., one-fourth the size of the U.S. **Location:** Occupies most of Arabian Peninsula in Middle East. **Neighbors:** Kuwait, Iraq, Jordan on N, Yemen, South Yemen, Oman on S, United Arab Emirates, Qatar on E. **Topography:** The highlands on W, up to 9,000 ft., slope as an arid, barren desert to the Persian Gulf. **Capital:** Riyadh. **Cities** (1974 cen.): Riyadh 666,840; Jidda 561,104; Mecca 366,801.

Government: Head of state and head of government: King Khalid ibn Abdul Aziz Al Saud; b. 1913; in office: Mar. 28, 1975. **Effective head of government:** Dep. Prime Min. Fahd ibn Abdul Aziz Al Saud, b. 1922; in office: Mar. 28, 1975. **Local divisions:** 6 major and 12 minor provinces. **Armed forces:** regulars 44,500; para-military 26,500.

Economy: Industries: Oil products. **Chief crops:** Dates, wheat, barley, fruit. **Minerals:** Oil, gas, gold, silver, iron. **Crude oil reserves** (1980): 163.35 bln. bbls. **Per capita arable land:** 0.3 acres. **Meat prod.** (1978): beef: 12,000 metric tons, lamb: 35,000 metric tons. **Fish catch** (1977): 18,400 metric tons. **Electricity prod.** (1977): 2.50 bln. kwh. **Labor force:** 75% agric.; 10% manuf.

Finance: Currency: Riyal (Mar. 1980: 3.33 = $1 US). **Gross domestic product** (1978): $65.82 bln. **Per capita income** (1975): $6,089. **Imports** (1979): $27.74 bln.; partners (1977): U.S. 19%, Jap. 12%, W. Ger. 8%, UK 6%. **Exports** (1979): $59.33 bln.; partners (1977): Jap. 19%, U.S. 10%, Fr. 10%, It. 7%. **Tourist receipts** (1977): $823 mln. **International reserves less gold** (Mar. 1980): $18.11 bln. **Gold:** 4.57 mln. oz t. **Consumer prices** (change in 1979): 1.9%.

Transport: Railway traffic (1974): 72 mln. passenger-km; 66 mln. net ton-km. **Motor vehicles:** in use (1974): 59,400 passenger cars, 52,600 comm. vehicles. **Chief ports:** Jidda, Ad-Dammam, Ras Tannurah.

Communications: Television sets: 130,000 in use (1976).

Radios: 260,000 in use (1976). **Telephones in use** (1978): 185,000. **Daily newspaper circ.** (1976): 143,000.

Health: Life expectancy at birth (1975): 44.2 male; 46.5 female. **Births** (per 1,000 pop. 1975): 49.5. **Deaths** (per 1,000 pop. 1975): 20.2. **Natural increase** (1975): 2.9%. **Hospital beds** (per 100,000 pop. 1977): 155. **Physicians** (per 100,000 pop. 1977): 60.

Education (1977): **Literacy:** 15%. **Pop. 5-19:** in school: 36%, teachers per 1,000: 22. **PQLI:** 29.

Arabia was united for the first time by Mohammed, in the early 7th century. His successors conquered the entire Near East and North Africa, bringing Islam and the Arabic language. But Arabia itself soon returned to its former status as political and cultural backwater.

Nejd, long an independent state and center of the Wahhabi sect, fell under Turkish rule in the 18th century, but in 1913 Ibn Saud, founder of the Saudi dynasty, overthrew the Turks and captured the Turkish province of Hasa; took the Hejaz in 1925 and by 1926, most of Asir. The discovery of oil by an American oil company in the 1930s transformed the new country.

Crown Prince Khalid was proclaimed king on Mar. 25, 1975, after the assassination of King Faisal. There is no constitution and no parliament. The king exercises authority together with a Council of Ministers. The Islamic religious code is the law of the land. Alcohol and public entertainments are restricted, and women have an inferior legal status.

Saudi units fought against Israel in the 1948 and 1973 Arab-Israeli wars. Many billions of dollars of advanced arms have been purchased from Britain, France, and the U.S., including jet fighters and missiles. Beginning with the 1967 Arab-Israeli war, Saudi Arabia provided large annual financial gifts to Egypt; aid was later extended to Syria, Jordan, and Palestinian guerrilla groups, as well as to other Moslem countries. The country has aided anti-radical forces in Yemen and Oman.

Faisal played a leading role in the 1973-74 Arab oil embargo against the U.S. and other nations in an attempt to force them to adopt an anti-Israel policy. Saudi Arabia joined most other Arab states, 1979, in condemning Egypt's peace treaty with Israel.

Between 1973 and 1976, Saudi Arabia acquired full ownership of Aramco (Arabian American Oil Co.). Saudi Arabia announced, 1979, it will build a $1 billion causeway linking the island state Bahrain to the Arab mainland. A third 5-year $250 billion development plan was approved in 1980.

The Hejaz contains the holy cities of Islam — Medina where the Mosque of the Prophet enshrines the tomb of Mohammed, who died in the city June 7, 632, and Mecca, his birthplace. More than 600,000 Moslems from 60 nations pilgrimage to Mecca annually. The regime faced its first serious opposition when young Moslem fundamentalists seized the Grand Mosque in Mecca, Nov. 20, 1979. (See Index for Chronology.)

Senegal

Republic of Senegal

People: Population (1979 est.): 5,532,000. **Age distrib.** (%): 0–14: 44.2; 15–59: 50.5; 60+: 5.3. **Pop. density:** 70.67 per sq. mi. **Urban** (1971): 31.7%. **Ethnic groups:** Wolof 36%, Peuhl 17.5%, Serere 16.5%, Toucouleur 9%, others. **Languages:** French (official), tribal languages. **Religions:** Moslems 90%, Christians 6%.

Geography: Area: 76,124 sq. mi., the size of South Dakota. **Location:** At western extreme of Africa. **Neighbors:** Mauritania on N, Mali on E, Guinea, Guinea-Bissau on S, Gambia surrounded on three sides. **Topography:** Low rolling plains cover most of Senegal, rising somewhat in the SE. Swamp and jungles are in SW. **Capital:** Dakar. **Cities** (1976 cen.): Dakar 798,792; Thies 117,333; Kaolack 106,899.

Government: Head of state: Pres. Leopold Senghor; b. Oct. 9, 1906; in office: Sept. 5, 1960. **Head of government:** Prime Min. Abdou Diouf; b. Sept. 7, 1935; in office: Feb. 26, 1970. **Local divisions:** 8 regions. **Armed forces:** regulars 8,350; paramilitary 1,600.

Economy: Industries: Food processing, chemicals, cement. **Chief crops:** Peanuts are chief export; millet, corn, rice. **Minerals:** Phosphates. **Per capita arable land:** 1.1 acres. **Meat prod.** (1978): beef: 36,000 metric tons; pork: 7,000 metric tons; lamb: 10,000 metric tons. **Fish catch** (1977): 288,800 metric tons. **Electricity prod.** (1978): 456.00 mln. kwh. **Labor force:** 70% agric.

Finance: Currency: CFA franc (Mar. 1980: 223.92 = $1 US). **Gross domestic product** (1978): $2.19 bln. **Per capita income** (1975): $342. **Imports** (1977): $797 mln.; partners Fr. 45%, Neth. 7%, It. 6%, U.S. 5%. **Exports** (1977): $650 mln.; partners Fr. 49%, UK 10%, It. 6%, Nigeria 5%. **Tourists** (1977): 168,300; receipts $11 mln. **International reserves less gold** (Jan. 1980): $26 mln. **Gold:** 29,000 oz t. **Consumer prices** (change in 1979): 9.4%.

Transport: Railway traffic (1976): 180 mln. passenger-km; 164 mln. net ton-km. **Motor vehicles:** in use (1974): 44,800 passenger cars, 25,000 comm. vehicles. **Chief ports:** Dakar, Saint-Louis.

Communications: Television sets: 2,000 in use (1976). **Radios:** 290,000 in use (1976). **Telephones in use** (1978): 42,105. **Daily newspaper circ.** (1976): 25,000; 5 per 1,000 pop.

Health: Life expectancy at birth (1975): 39.4 male; 42.5 female. **Births** (per 1,000 pop. 1975): 47.0. **Deaths** (per 1,000 pop. 1975): 23.1. **Natural increase** (1975): 2.4%. **Hospital beds** (per 100,000 pop. 1977): 111. **Physicians** (per 100,000 pop. 1977): 2. **Infant mortality** (per 1,000 live births 1960-61): 92.9.

Education (1977): **Literacy:** 10%. **Pop. 5-19:** in school: 21%, teachers per 1,000: 4. **PQLI:** 23.

Portuguese settlers arrived in the 15th century, but French control grew from the 17th century. The last independent Moslem state was subdued in 1893. Dakar became the capital of French West Africa.

Independence as part, along with the Sudanese Rep., of the Mali Federation, came June 20, 1960. Senegal withdrew Aug. 20 that year. French political and economic influence is strong.

A long drought brought famine, 1972-73, and again in 1978.

Senegal is recognized as the most democratic of the French-speaking West African nations. Opposition parties were allowed to form in 1976 and 1979, and free elections were held, 1978.

Seychelles

People: Population (1979 est.): 64,000. **Age distrib.** (%): 0–14: 41.5; 15–59: 49.7; 60+: 8.8. **Pop. density:** 350.88 per sq. mi. **Urban** (1971): 26.1% **Ethnic groups:** Creoles (mixture of Asians, Africans, and French) predominate. **Languages:** English (official), Creole 94%, French 5%, others. **Religions:** Roman Catholics 90%, Protestants 8%, Hindus, Moslems.

Geography: Area: 171 sq. mi. **Location:** In the Indian O. 700 miles NE of Madagascar. **Neighbors:** Nearest are Madagascar on SW, Somalia on NW. **Topography:** A group of 86 islands, about half of them composed of coral, the other half granite, the latter predominantly mountainous. **Capital:** Victoria. **Cities** (1971 cen.): Port Victoria (met.) 13,736.

Government: Head of state: Pres. France Albert Rene, b. Nov. 16, 1935; in office: June 5, 1977.

Economy: Industries: Food processing. **Chief crops:** Coconut products, cinnamon, vanilla, patchouli. **Other resources:** Guano, shark fins, tortoise shells, fish. **Electricity prod.** (1977): 36.00 mln. kwh. **Labor force:** 27% agric.; 55% manuf.

Finance: Currency: Rupee (Sept. 1979: 6.20 = $1 US). **Gross domestic product** (1976 est.): $27 mln. **Per capita income** (1976): $430. **Imports** (1977): $45 mln.; partners UK 27%, Kenya 12%, So. Afr. 9%, Jap. 7%. **Exports** (1977): $10 mln.; partners: Pak. 18%. **Tourists** (1977): 50,000; receipts: $22 mln. **Consumer prices** (change in 1976): 14.9%.

Transport: Motor vehicles: in use (1977): 3,000 passenger cars, 900 comm. vehicles. **Port:** Victoria.

Communications: Radios: 17,000 in use (1976). **Telephones in use** (1978): 4,560. **Daily newspaper circ.** (1977): 4,000; 65 per 1,000 pop.

Health: Life expectancy at birth (1972): 61.9 male; 68.0 female. **Births** (per 1,000 pop. 1977): 25.9. **Deaths** (per 1,000 pop. 1977): 7.7. **Natural increase** (1977): 1.8%. **Pop. per hospital bed** (1975): 200. **Pop. per physician** (1975): 2,857. **Infant mortality** (per 1,000 live births 1977): 43.2. **PQLI:** 72.

The islands were occupied by France in 1768, and seized by Britain in 1794. Ruled as part of Mauritius from 1814, the Seychelles became a separate colony in 1903. The ruling party had opposed independence as impractical, but pressure from the OAU and the UN became irresistible, and independence was declared June 29, 1976. The first president was ousted in a coup a year later by a socialist leader.

A new Constitution announced Mar. 1979, turned the country into a one-party state. The Seychelles, strategically located in the Indian O., have been courted by the Soviet Union.

Sierra Leone

Republic of Sierra Leone

People: Population (1979 est.): 3,309,000. **Age distrib.** (%): 0–14: 40.6; 15–59: 51.5; 60+: 7.8. **Pop. density:** 117.82 per sq. mi. **Ethnic groups:** Temne 30%, Mende 30%, other tribes. **Languages:** English (official), Krio (pidgin), tribal languages. **Religions:** Moslems 25%, Christians 5%, others.

Geography: Area: 27,925 sq. mi., slightly smaller than North Carolina. **Location:** On W coast of W. Africa. **Neighbors:** Guinea on N, E, Liberia on S. **Topography:** The heavily-indented, 210-mi. coastline has mangrove swamps. Behind are wooded hills, rising to a plateau and mountains in the E. **Capital:** Freetown. **Cities** (1978 est.): Freetown 214,443.

Government: Head of state and head of government: Pres. Siaka P. Stevens; b. Aug. 24, 1905; in office: Apr. 21, 1971 (state), June 14, 1978 (gov't.). **Local divisions:** 3 provinces and one region including Freetown. **Armed forces:** regulars 3,000; para-military 800.

Economy: Industries: Wood products. **Chief crops:** Cocoa, coffee, palm kernels, kola nuts, ginger. **Minerals:** Diamonds, iron ore, bauxite. **Per capita arable land:** 3.0 acres. **Fish catch** (1977): 80,100 metric tons. **Electricity prod.** (1977): 200 mln. kwh. **Labor force:** 75% agric.

Finance: Currency: Leone (Mar. 1980: 1 = $.92 US). **Gross domestic product** (1978): $776 mln. **Per capita income** (1977): $199. **Imports** (1978): $277 mln.; partners (1977): UK 18%, China 13%, Nigeria 10%, U.S. 7%. **Exports** (1979): $149 mln.; partners (1977): UK 40%, U.S. 36%, Neth. 7%, W. Ger. 7%. **Tourists** (1977): 24,100; receipts: $4 mln. **National budget** (1977): $104 mln. revenues; $150 mln. expenditures. **International reserves less gold** (Mar. 1980): $39.9 mln. **Consumer prices** (change in 1979): 21.2%.

Transport: Motor vehicles: in use (1976): 18,900 passenger cars, 6,300 comm. vehicles. **Chief ports:** Freetown, Bonthe.

Communications: Television sets: 8,500 in use (1976). **Radios:** 62,000 in use (1975). **Telephones in use** (1977): 15,060. **Daily newspaper circ.** (1970): 45,000; 18 per 1,000 pop.

Health: Life expectancy at birth (1975): 41.8 male; 45.0 female. **Births** (per 1,000 pop. 1975): 45.6. **Deaths** (per 1,000 pop. 1975): 21.1. **Natural increase** (1975): 2.5%. **Hospital beds** (per 100,000 pop. 1977): 99. **Physicians** (per 100,000 pop. 1977): 6.

Education (1977): **Literacy:** 15%. **Pop. 5-19:** in school: 24%, teachers per 1,000: 9. **PQLI:** 31.

Freetown was founded in 1787 by the British government as a haven for freed slaves. Their descendants, known as Creoles, number more than 60,000.

Successive steps toward independence followed the 1951 constitution. Full independence arrived Apr. 27, 1961. Sierra Leone became a republic Apr. 19, 1971. A one-party state approved by referendum 1978, brought political stability, but the ailing economy in 1979 was characterized by inflation, corruption, and heavy dependence upon the International Monetary Fund and other creditors.

Singapore

Republic of Singapore

People: Population (1979 est.): 2,363,000. **Age distrib.** (%): 0–14: 29.6; 15–59: 63.4; 60+: 7.0. **Pop. density:** 10,309.734 per sq. mi. **Ethnic groups:** Chinese 74%, Malays 14%, Indians, Pakistanis 8%. **Languages:** Chinese, Malay, Tamil, English all official. **Religions:** Buddhism, Taoism, Islam, Hinduism, Christianity.

Geography: Area: 226 sq. mi., smaller than New York City. **Location:** Off tip of Malayan Peninsula in S.E. Asia. **Neighbors:** Nearest are Malaysia on N, Indonesia on S. **Topography:** Singapore is a flat, formerly swampy island. The nation includes 40 nearby islets. **Capital:** Singapore. **Cities** (1978 est.): Singapore 2,334,400.

Government: Head of state: Pres. Benjamin H. Sheares; b. Aug. 12, 1907; in office: Jan. 2, 1971. **Head of government:** Prime Min. Lee Kuan Yew; b. Sept. 16, 1923; in office: June 5, 1959. **Armed forces:** regulars 36,000; reserves 45,000.

Economy: Industries: Shipbuilding, oil refining, electronics, banking, textiles, food, rubber, lumber processing, tourism. **Per capita arable land:** 0.002 acres. **Meat prod.** (1978): pork: 41,000 metric tons. **Fish catch** (1977): 15,100 metric tons. **Electricity prod.** (1978): 5.89 bln. kwh. **Crude steel prod.** (1979): 297,000 metric tons. **Labor force:** 2% agric.; 27% manuf.

Finance: Currency: Dollar (Mar. 1980: 2.27 = $1 US). **Gross domestic product** (1979): $9.01 bln. **Per capita income** (1975): $2,279. **Imports** (1979): $17.64 bln.; partners (1978): Jap. 19%, Saudi Ar. 13%, Malay. 13%, U.S. 13%. **Exports** (1979): $14.23 bln., partners (1978): U.S. 16%, Malay. 14%, Jap. 10%, HK 7%. **Tourists** (1977): 1,506,700; receipts $300 mln. **National budget** (1979): $2.17 bln. revenues; $1.80 bln. expenditures. **International reserves** (Dec. 1979): $5.82 bln. **Consumer prices** (change in 1979): 4.1%.

Transport: Motor vehicles: in use (1977): 142,100 passenger cars, 54,900 comm. vehicles. **Civil aviation:** 9,756 mln. passenger-km (1978); 420 mln. freight ton-km (1978).

Communications: Television sets: 294,000 licensed (1976). **Radios:** 356,000 licensed (1976). **Telephones in use** (1978): 455,120. **Daily newspaper circ.** (1977): 497,000; 215 per 1,000 pop.

Health: Life expectancy at birth (1970): 65.1 male; 70.0 female. **Births** (per 1,000 pop. (1978): 17.0. **Deaths** (per 1,000 pop. 1978): 5.2. **Natural increase** (1978): 1.2%. **Hospital beds** (per 100,000 pop. 1977): 371. **Physicians** (per 100,000 pop. 1977): 78. **Infant mortality** (per 1,000 live births 1978): 12.5.

Education (1977): **Literacy:** 76%. **Pop. 5–19:** in school: 59%, teachers per 1,000: 21. **PQLI:** 86.

Founded in 1819 by Sir Thomas Stamford Raffles, Singapore was a British colony until 1959 when it became autonomous within the Commonwealth. On Sept. 16, 1963, it joined with Malaya, Sarawak and Sabah to form the Federation of Malaysia.

Tensions between Malayans, dominant in the federation, and ethnic Chinese, dominant in Singapore, led to an agreement under which Singapore became a separate nation, Aug. 9, 1965.

Singapore is the world's 4th largest port. Manufacturing has surpassed shipping, pushing per capita income to second place in Asia, following Japan. Standards in health, education, and housing are high. International banking has grown.

Formerly democratic, the government has suppressed opposition in recent years.

Solomon Islands

People: Population (1979 est.): 222,000. **Age distrib.** (%): 0–14: 48.4; 15–59: 46.5; 60+: 5.1. **Pop. density:** 18.26 per sq. mi. **Urban** (1976): 9.1%. **Ethnic groups:** A variety of Melanesian groups and mixtures, some Polynesians. **Languages:** Pidgin English, Melanesian, and Papuan languages. **Religions:** Christianity, traditional religions.

Geography: Area: 11,500 sq. mi., slightly larger than Maryland. **Location:** Melanesian archipelago in the western Pacific O. **Neighbors:** Nearest is Papua New Guinea on W. **Topography:** 10 large volcanic and rugged islands and 4 groups of smaller ones. **Capital:** Honiara. **Cities:** (1976 cen.): Honiara 14,942.

Government: Head of state: Queen Elizabeth II, represented by Gov.-Gen. Baddeley Devesi; b. Oct. 16, 1941; in office: July 7, 1978. **Head of government:** Prime Min. Peter Kenilorea; b. May 23, 1943; in office: July 14, 1976. **Local divisions:** 4 districts.

Economy: Industries: Fish canning. **Chief crops:** Coconuts, cocoa, rice, oil palm. **Other resources:** Forests, marine shell. **Per capita arable land:** 0.6 acres. **Fish catch** (1977): 15,800 metric tons. **Electricity prod.** (1977): 18.00 mln. kwh.

Finance: Currency: Dollar (Mar. 1979: .89 = $1 US). **Gross domestic product** (1976): $64.1 mln. **Per capita income** (1976): $300. **Imports** (1976): $24 mln.; partners (1976): Austral. 36%, Sing. 14%, Jap. 12%, UK 10%. **Exports** (1976): $26.1 mln.; partners (1976): Jap. 34%, U.S. 26%, UK 13%, Neth. 8%. **Consumer prices** (change in 1976): 4.3%.

Communications: Radios: 11,000 in use (1976). **Tele-**

phones in use (1978): 1,984.

Health: Births (per 1,000 pop. 1969): 36.1. **Deaths** (per 1,000 pop. 1969): 13.0. **Natural increase** (1969): 2.3%. **Infant mortality** (per 1,000 live births 1969): 52.4.

The Solomon Islands were sighted in 1568 by an expedition from Peru. Britain established a protectorate in the 1890s over most of the group, inhabited by Melanesians. The islands saw major World War II battles. Self-government came Jan. 2, 1976, and independence was formally attained July 7, 1978.

Somalia

Somali Democratic Republic

People: Population (1979 est.): 3,474,000. **Pop. density:** 13.97 per sq. mi. **Ethnic groups:** Somalis, related tribes 95%, Bantus 3.6%, Arabs 1.1%. **Languages:** Somali (official), Arabic, Italian, English. **Religions:** Sunni Moslems 99%.

Geography: Area: 246,155 sq. mi., slightly smaller than Texas. **Location:** Occupies the eastern horn of Africa. **Neighbors:** Djibouti, Ethiopia, Kenya on W. **Topography:** The coastline extends for 1,700 mi. Hills cover the N; the center and S are flat. **Capital:** Mogadishu. **Cities** (1978 est.): Mogadishu 230,000.

Government: Head of state: Pres. Mohammed Siyad Barre; b. 1919; in office: Oct. 21, 1969. **Local divisions:** 15 regions. **Armed forces:** regulars 46,500; para-military 29,500.

Economy: Chief crops: Incense, sugar, bananas, sorghum, corn, kapole, gum. **Minerals:** Iron, tin, gypsum, sandstone, bauxite, meerschaum, titanium, uranium. **Per capita arable land:** 0.8 acres. **Meat prod.** (1978): beef: 47,000 metric tons; lamb: 65,000 metric tons. **Fish catch** (1977): 32,600 metric tons. **Electricity prod.** (1977): 45.00 mln. kwh. **Labor force:** 60% agric.

Finance: Currency: Shilling (Mar. 1980: 6.30 = $1 US). **Gross domestic product** (1976 est.): $350 mln. **Per capita income** (1976): $105. **Imports** (1978): $241 mln.; partners: It. 29%, UK 10%, India 9%, W. Ger. 5%. **Exports** (1978): $107 mln.; partners: Saudi Ar. 35%, It. 19%, USSR 9%, Jap. 6%. **Tourist receipts** (1977): $4 mln. **International reserves less gold** (Jan. 1980): $46.1 mln. **Gold:** 19,000 oz t. **Consumer prices** (change in 1978): 9.9%.

Transport: Motor vehicles: in use (1972): 8,000 passenger cars, 8,000 comm. vehicles. **Chief ports:** Mogadishu, Berbera.

Communications: Radios: 69,000 in use (1976). **Daily newspaper circ.** (1970): 4,500; 2 per 1,000 pop.

Health: Life expectancy at birth (1975): 39.4 male; 42.6 female. **Births** (per 1,000 pop. 1975): 47.2. **Deaths** (per 1,000 pop. 1975): 21.6. **Natural increase** (1975): 2.6%. **Hospital beds** (per 100,000 pop. 1977): 179. **Physicians** (per 100,000 pop. 1977): 3.

Education (1977): **Literacy:** 5%. **Pop. 5-19:** in school: 19%, teachers per 1,000: 7. **PQLI:** 34.

Arab trading posts developed into sultanates. The Italian Protectorate of Somalia, acquired from 1885 to 1927, extended along the Indian O. from the Gulf of Aden to the Juba R. The UN in 1949 approved eventual creation of Somalia as a sovereign state and in 1950 Italy took over the trusteeship held by Great Britain since World War II.

British Somaliland was formed in the 19th century in the NW. Britain gave it independence June 26, 1960; on July 1 it joined with the former Italian part to create the independent Somali Republic.

On Oct. 21, 1969, a Supreme Revolutionary Council seized power in a bloodless army and police coup, named a Council of Secretaries of State, to aid it, and abolished the Assembly. In May, 1970, several foreign companies were nationalized.

A severe drought in 1975 killed tens of thousands, and spurred efforts to resettle nomads on collective farms. The U.S. charged in 1975 that Soviet naval facilities at Berbera included a missile storage site.

Somalia has laid claim to Ogaden, the huge eastern region of Ethiopia, peopled mostly by Somalis. Ethiopia battled Somali rebels and accused Somalia of sending troops and heavy arms in 1977. Russian forces were expelled in 1977 in retaliation for Soviet support of Ethiopia. Some 11,000 Cuban troops with Soviet arms defeated Somali army troops and ethnic Somali rebels in Ethiopia, 1978. As many as 1.3 mln. refugees entered Somalia.

U.S. negotiations for military facilities along Somalia's coast were bogged down by the Ogaden conflict.

South Africa

Republic of South Africa

People: Population (1979 est.): 27,799,000. **Age distrib.** (%): 0–14: 41.5; 15–59: 54.5; 60+: 3.8. **Pop. density:** 58.71 per sq. mi. **Urban** (1972): 47.9%. **Ethnic groups:** Bantus 70% (of which Zulu 19%, Xhosa 18%, Tswana 8%), whites 17.5%, Colored 9.4%, Asiatic 2.9% **Religions:** Bantu Christian 14.5%, Dutch Reformed 14.3%, Methodist 10.7%, Anglican 8.8%, Roman Catholic 6.7%, other Christian 18.4%, Moslems, Hindus, and Jews 4%. **Languages:** Afrikaans, English, Bantu and Indian languages.

Geography: Area: 471,819 sq. mi., four-fifths the size of Alaska. **Location:** At the southern extreme of Africa. **Neighbors:** Namibia (SW Africa), Botswana, Zimbabwe on N, Mozambique, Swaziland on E; surrounds Lesotho. **Topography:** The large interior plateau reaches close to the country's 2,700-mi. coastline. There are few major rivers or lakes; rainfall is sparse in W, more plentiful in E. **Capitals:** Cape Town (legislative). Pretoria (administrative), and Bloemfontein (judicial). **Cities** (1970 cen.): Durban 729,857; Cape Town 691,296; Johannesburg 654,682; Pretoria 543,950; Port Elizabeth 386,577.

Government: Head of state: Pres. Marais Viljoen, b. Dec. 2, 1915, in office: June 19, 1979. **Head of government:** Prime Min. Pieter Willem Botha; b. Jan. 12, 1916; in office: Sept. 28, 1978. **Local divisions:** 4 provinces. **Armed forces:** regulars 63,250; reserves 135,000.

Economy: Industries: Steel, tires, motors, textiles, plastics. **Chief crops:** Corn, grain, tobacco, sugar, fruit, peanuts, grapes. **Minerals:** Largest world production of gold, chromium, antimony, coal, iron, manganese, nickel, phosphates, tin, uranium, gem diamonds, platinum, copper, vanadium. **Other resources:** Wool. **Per capita arable land:** 1.3 acres. **Meat prod.** (1978): beef: 500,000 metric tons; pork: 90,000 metric tons; lamb: 154,000 metric tons. **Fish catch** (1977): 1.0 mln. metric tons. **Electricity prod.** (1978): 84.77 bln. kwh. **Crude steel prod.** (1979): 8.9 mln. metric tons. **Labor force:** 28% agric.; 13% manuf.

Finance: Currency: Rand (Mar. 1980: 1 = $1.24 US). **Gross domestic product** (1978): $45.86 bln. **Per capita income** (1978): $1,296. **Imports** (1979): $8.99 bln.; partners (1978): W. Ger. 20%, UK 17%, U.S. 16%, Jap. 13%. **Exports** (1979): $18.4 bln.; partners (1978): U.S. 19%, UK 17%, Jap. 10%, W. Ger. 9%. **Tourist receipts** (1977): $321 mln. **National budget** (1979): $11.56 bln. revenues; $14.06 bln. expenditures. **International reserves less gold** (Mar. 1980): $649 mln. **Gold:** 11.43 mln. oz t. **Consumer prices** (change in 1979): 13.2%.

Transport: Railway traffic (1978): 80.96 bln. net ton-km. **Motor vehicles:** in use (1977): 2.16 mln. passenger cars, 821,200 comm. vehicles; assembled (1977): 131,800 passenger cars; 57,900 comm. vehicles. **Civil aviation:** 7,248 mln. passenger-km (1978): 240 mln. freight ton-km (1978). **Chief ports:** Durban, Cape Town, East London, Port Elizabeth.

Communications: Radios: 2.5 mln. in use (1976), 385,000 manuf. (1977). **Telephones in use** (1978): 2,319,558. **Daily newspaper circ.** (1976): 1,728,000; 66 per 1,000 pop.

Health: Life expectancy at birth (1975): 56.6 male; 59.4 female. **Births** (per 1,000 pop. 1975): 37.7. **Deaths** (per 1,000 pop. 1975): 11.5. **Natural increase** (1975): 2.6%. **Hospital beds** (per 100,000 pop. 1977): 614. **Physicians** (per 100,000 pop. 1977): 6.

Education (1977): **Literacy:** 50%. **Pop. 5-19:** in school: 61%, teachers per 1,000: 13. **PQLI:** 60.

Bushmen and Hottentots were the original inhabitants. Bantus, including Zulu, Xhosa, Swazi, and Sotho, had occupied the area from Transvaal to south of Transkei before the 17th century.

The Cape of Good Hope area was settled by Dutch, beginning in the 17th century. Britain seized the Cape in 1806. Many Dutch trekked north and founded 2 republics, the Transvaal and the Orange Free State. Diamonds were discovered, 1867, and gold, 1886. The Dutch (Boers) resented encroachments by the British and others; the Anglo-Boer War followed, 1899-1902. Britain won and, effective May 31, 1910, created the Union of South Africa, incorporating the British colonies of the Cape and Natal, the Transvaal and the Orange Free State. After a referendum, the Union became the Republic of South Africa, May 31, 1961, and withdrew from the Commonwealth.

With the election victory of Daniel Malan's National party in

1948, the policy of separate development of the races, or apartheid, already existing unofficially, became official. This called for separate development, separate residential areas, and ultimate political independence for the whites, Bantus, Asians, and Coloreds. In 1959 the government passed acts providing the eventual creation of several Bantu nations or Bantustans on 13% of the country's land area, though most black leaders have opposed the plan.

Under apartheid, blacks are severely restricted to certain occupations, and are paid far lower wages than are whites for similar work. Only whites may vote or run for public office, and militant white opposition has been curbed. There is an advisory Indian Council, partly elected, partly appointed. In 1969, a Colored People's Representative Council was created. Minor liberalization measures were allowed in the 1970s.

At least 600 persons, mostly Bantus, were killed in 1976 riots protesting apartheid. Black protests continued through 1980 partly fueled by rising unemployment.

In 1963, the Transkei, an area in the SE, became the first of these partially self-governing territories or "Homelands." Transkei became independent on Oct. 26, 1976, Bophuthatswana on Dec. 6, 1977, and Venda on Sept. 13, 1979; none received international recognition.

Bophuthatswana: Population (1976 est.): 2,500,000. **Area:** 15,571 sq. mi., 6 discontinuous geographic units. **Capital:** Mmabatho. **Cities:** (1977 est.): Ga-Rankawa, Mabopane (comb. metro area): 153,000. **Head of state:** Pres. Kgosi Lucas Manyane Mangope, b. Dec. 27, 1923; in office: Dec. 6, 1977.

Transkei: Population (1979 est.): 2,200,000. **Area:** 15,831 sq. mi., 3 discontinuous geographic units. **Capital:** Umtata (1978 est.): 30,000. **Head of state:** Pres. Kaiser Matanzima; in office: Feb. 20, 1979. **Head of government:** Prime Min. George Matanzima; in office: Feb. 20, 1979.

Venda: Population (1978 est.): 357,000. **Area:** 2,448 sq. mi., 2 discontinuous geographic units. **Capital:** Thohoyandou. **City:** Makearela (1976 est.): 1,972. **Head of state:** Patrick Mphephu; in office: Sept. 13, 1979.

John Vorster, who dominated South African politics as prime minister for 11 years before becoming president in 1979, resigned his post upon accusations of covering up government misappropriations.

Namibia (South-West Africa)

South-West Africa is a sparsely populated land twice the size of California. Made a German protectorate in 1884, it was surrendered to South Africa in 1915 and was administered by that country under a League of Nations mandate. S. Africa refused to accept UN authority under the trusteeship system.

Other African nations charged S. Africa imposed apartheid, built military bases, and exploited S-W Africa. The UN General Assembly, May 1968, created an 11-nation council to take over administration of S-W Africa and lead it to independence. The council charged that S. Africa had blocked its efforts to visit S-W Africa.

In 1968 the UN General Assembly gave the area the name Namibia. In Jan. 1970 the UN Security Council condemned S. Africa for "illegal" control of the area. In an advisory opinion, June 1971, the International Court of Justice declared S. Africa was occupying the area illegally.

In a 1977 referendum, white voters backed a plan for a multiracial interim government to lead to independence. The Marxist South-West Africa People's Organization rejected the plan, and launched a guerrilla war. Both S. Africa and Namibian rebels agreed to a UN plan for independence by the end of 1978. S. Africa rejected the plan, Sept. 20, 1978, and held elections, without UN supervision, for Namibia's constituent assembly, Dec., that were ignored by the major black opposition parties.

The UN peace plan, proposed 1980, called for a cease-fire and a demilitarized zone 31 miles deep on each side of S-W Africa's borders with Angola and Zambia that would be patrolled by UN peacekeeping forces against guerrilla actions. Impartial elections would follow.

Most of Namibia is a plateau, 3,600 ft. high, with plains in the N, Kalahari Desert to the E, Orange R. on the S, Atlantic O. on the W. Area is 318,261 sq. mi.; pop. (1979 est.) 994,000 including about 100,000 whites; capital, Windhoek.

Products include cattle, sheep, diamonds, copper, lead, zinc, fish. People include Namas (Hottentots), Ovambos (Bantus), Bushmen, and others.

Walvis Bay, the only deepwater port in the country, was turned over to South African administration in 1922. S. Africa said in 1978 it would discuss sovereignty only after Namibian independence.

Spain

Spanish State

People: Population (1979 est.): 37,077,000. **Age distrib.** (%): 0–14: 27.6; 15–59: 58.0; 60+: 14.4. **Pop. density:** 188.73 per sq. mi. **Ethnic groups:** Spanish (Castilian, Valencian, Andalusian, Asturian) 72.8%, Catalan 16.4%, Galician 8.2%, Basque 2.3%. **Languages:** Spanish (official), Catalan, Galician, Valencian, Basque all legally recognized. **Religions:** Roman Catholicism nearly universal.

Geography: Area: 194,883 sq. mi., the size of Colorado and Wyoming combined. **Location:** In SW Europe. **Neighbors:** Portugal on W. France on N. **Topography:** The interior is a high, arid plateau broken by mountain ranges and river valleys. The NW is heavily watered, the south has lowlands and a Mediterranean climate. **Capital:** Madrid. **Cities** (1978 est.): Madrid 3,520,320; Barcelona 1,809,722; Valencia 713,026; Seville 588,784; Zaragoza 547,317; Bilbao 457,655; Malaga 402,978.

Government: Head of state: King Juan Carlos I de Borbon y Borbon, b. Jan. 5, 1938; in office: Nov. 22, 1975. **Head of government:** Prime Min. Adolfo Suarez; b. Sept. 25, 1932; in office: July 3, 1976. **Local divisions:** 50 provinces with appointed governors. **Armed forces:** regulars 321,000; reserves 1,085,000.

Economy: Industries: Machinery, textiles, shoes, paper, autos, ships, cement, tourism. **Chief crops:** Grains, olives, grapes, citrus fruits, onions, almonds, esparto, flax, hemp, pulse, tobacco, cotton, rice. **Minerals:** Mercury, potash, uranium, lead, iron, copper, zinc, coal, cobalt, silver, sulphur, phosphates, oil. **Crude oil reserves** (1980): 150 mln. bbls. **Other resources:** Forests (cork). **Per capita arable land:** 1.1 acres. **Meat prod.** (1978): beef: 445,000 metric tons; pork: 760,000 metric tons; lamb: 153,000 metric tons. **Fish catch** (1977): 1.5 mln. metric tons. **Electricity prod.** (1978): 99.26 bln. kwh. **Crude steel prod.** (1979): 12.3 mln. metric tons. **Labor force:** 23% agric.; 37% manuf.

Finance: Currency: Peseta (Mar. 1980: 72.3 = $1 US). **Gross domestic product** (1978): $147.24 bln. **Per capita income** (1978): $3,625. **Imports** (1979): $25.44 bln.; partners (1978): U.S. 13%, W. Ger. 10%, Saudi Ar. 9%, Fr. 9%. **Exports** (1979): $18.21 bln.; partners (1978): Fr. 17%, W. Ger. 11%, U.S. 9%, UK 6%. **Tourists** (1977): 34,266,700; receipts: $4.00 bln. **National budget** (1978): $19.05 bln. revenues; $20.74 bln. expenditures. **International reserves less gold** (Jan. 1980): $13.42 bln. **Gold** (Feb. 1980): 14.61 mln. oz t. **Consumer prices** (change in 1979): 15.6%.

Transport: Railway traffic (1978): 16.76 bln. passenger-km; 9.72 bln. net ton-km. **Motor vehicles:** in use (1977): 5.94 mln. passenger cars, 1.56 mln. comm. vehicles; manuf. (1978): 988,800 passenger cars; 150,000 comm. vehicles. **Civil aviation:** 14,604 mln. passenger-km (1978): 386 mln. freight ton-km (1978). **Chief ports:** Barcelona, Bilbao, Valencia, Cartagena, Gijon.

Communications: Television sets: 6.64 mln. in use (1976), 631,000 manuf. (1976). **Radios:** 9.3 mln. in use (1976), 363,000 manuf. (1976). **Telephones in use** (1978): 9,527,781. **Daily newspaper circ.** (1977): 4,710,000; 128 per 1,000 pop.

Health: Life expectancy at birth (1970): 69.69 male; 74.96 female. **Births** (per 1,000 pop. 1977): 18.0. **Deaths** (per 1,000 pop. 1977): 7.7. **Natural increase** (1977): 1.0%. **Hospital beds** (per 100,000 pop. 1977): 543. **Physicians** (per 100,000 pop. 1977): 176. **Infant mortality** (per 1,000 live births 1977): 15.6.

Education (1977): **Literacy:** 93%. **Pop. 5-19:** in school: 66%, teachers per 1,000: 28. **PQLI:** 93.

Spain was settled by Iberians, Basques, and Celts, partly overrun by Carthaginians, conquered by Rome c.200 BC. The Visigoths, in power by the 5th century AD, adopted Christianity but by 711 AD lost to the Islamic invasion from Africa. Christian reconquest from the N led to a Spanish nationalism. In 1469 the kingdoms of Aragon and Castile were united by the marriage of Ferdinand II and Isabella I, and the last Moorish power was broken by the fall of the kingdom of Granada, 1492. Spain became a bulwark of Roman Catholicism.

Spain obtained a colonial empire with the discovery of America by Columbus, 1492, the conquest of Mexico by Cortes, and Peru by Pizarro. It also controlled the Netherlands and parts of Italy and Germany. Spain lost its American colonies in the early 19th century. It lost Cuba, the Philippines, and Puerto Rico during the Spanish-American War, 1898.

Primo de Rivera became dictator in 1923. King Alfonso XIII revoked the dictatorship, 1930, but was forced to leave the country 1931. A republic was proclaimed which disestablished the church, curtailed its privileges, and secularized education. A conservative reaction occurred 1933 but was followed by a Popular Front (1936-1939) composed of socialists, communists, republicans, and anarchists.

Army officers under Francisco Franco revolted against the government, 1936. In a destructive 3-yr. war, in which one million were said to have died, Franco received massive help and troops from Italy and Germany, while the USSR, France, and Mexico supported the republic. War ended Mar. 28, 1939. Franco was named caudillo, leader of the nation. Spain was neutral in World War II but its relations with fascist countries caused its exclusion from the UN in 1946. It was admitted in 1955.

In July 1969, Franco and the Cortes designated Prince Juan Carlos as the future king and chief of state. After Franco's death, Nov. 20, 1975, Juan Carlos was sworn in as king. He presided over the formal dissolution of the institutions of the Franco regime. In free elections June 1976, moderates and democratic socialists emerged as the largest parties.

Catalonia and the Basque country were granted autonomy, Jan. 1980, following overwhelming approval in home-rule referendums. Basque extremists, however, continued their violent campaign for independence.

Between 1960 and 1975 Spain changed from an agricultural nation to one of the world's important industrial powers.

The **Balearic Islands** in the western Mediterranean, 1,935 sq. mi., are a province of Spain; they include **Majorca** (Mallorca), with the capital, Palma; **Minorca, Cabrera, Ibiza** and **Formentera.** The **Canary Islands,** 2,807 sq. mi., in the Atlantic W of Morocco, form 2 provinces, including the islands of **Tenerife, Palma, Gomera, Hierro, Grand Canary, Fuerteventura,** and **Lanzarote** with Las Palmas and Santa Cruz thriving ports. **Ceuta** and **Melilla,** small enclaves on Morocco's Mediterranean coast, are part of Metropolitan Spain.

Spain has sought the return of Gibraltar, in British hands since 1704. (*See Index.*)

Sri Lanka

Democratic Socialist Republic of Sri Lanka

People: Population (1979 est.): 14,594,000. **Age distrib.** (%): 0–14: 39.0; 15–59: 54.7; 60+: 6.4. **Pop. density:** 566.48 per sq. mi. **Urban** (1971): 22.4%. **Ethnic groups:** Sinhalese 72%, Ceylon Tamil 11%, Indian Tamil 9.4%, Moor 6.7%. **Languages:** Sinhala (official), Tamil, English. **Religions:** Buddhists 67%, Hindus 18%, Christians 7.7%, Moslems 7.2%.

Geography: Area: 25,332 sq. mi. **Location:** In Indian O. off SE coast of India. **Neighbors:** India on NW. **Topography:** The coastal area and the northern half are flat; the S-central area is hilly and mountainous. **Capital:** Colombo. **Cities** (1978 est.): Colombo 592,000; Dahiwala-Mount Lavina 162,000.

Government: Head of state: Pres. Junius Richard Jayewardene; b. Sept. 17, 1906; in office: Feb. 4, 1978. **Head of government:** Ranasinghe Premadasa, b. June 23, 1924, in office: Feb. 6, 1978. **Local divisions:** 22 districts. **Armed forces:** regulars 13,700; reserves 10,700.

Economy: Industries: Plywood, paper, glassware, ceramics, cement, chemicals, textiles. **Chief crops:** Tea, coconuts, rice, cacao, cinnamon, citronella, tobacco. **Minerals:** Graphite, limestone, iron, ilmenite, monazite, zircon, quartz, precious and semiprecious stones. **Other resources:** Forests, rubber. **Per capita arable land:** 0.2 acres. **Meat prod.** (1978): beef: 19,000 metric tons. **Fish catch** (1977): 138,700 metric tons. **Electricity prod.** (1978): 1.38 bln. kwh. **Labor force:** 45% agric.

Finance: Currency: Rupee (Mar. 1980: 16.27 = $1 US). **Gross domestic product** (1978): $2.69 bln. **Per capita income** (1978): $168. **Imports** (1978): $967 mln.; partners: Jap. 11%, Saudi Ar. 10%, UK 10%, India 9%. **Exports** (1978): $845 mln.; partners: UK 7%, U.S. 7%, Jap. 6%, Pak. 5%. **Tourists** (1977): 153,700; receipts: $40 mln. **National budget** (1978): $745 mln. revenues; $1.13 bln. expenditures. **International reserves less gold** (Feb. 1980): $472 mln. **Gold:** 63,000 oz t. **Consumer prices** (change in 1978): 12.1%

Transport: Railway traffic (1978): 3.7 bln. passenger-km; 246 mln. net ton-km. **Motor vehicles:** in use (1976): 93,800 passenger cars, 49,200 comm. vehicles. **Civil aviation:** 413 mln. passenger-km (1977); 2.5 mln. freight ton-km (1977). **Chief ports:** Colombo, Trincomalee, Galle.

Communications: Radios: 800,000 in use (1976), 55,000 manuf. (1976). **Telephones in use** (1978): 74,166.

Health: Life expectancy at birth (1967): 64.8 male; 66.9 female. **Births** (per 1,000 pop. 1972): 29.5. **Deaths** (per 1,000 pop. 1972): 7.7. **Natural increase** (1972): 2.2%. **Hospital beds** (per 100,000 pop. 1977): 296. **Physicians** (per 100,000 pop. 1977): 16. **Infant mortality** (per 1,000 live births 1972): 45.1.

Education (1977): **Literacy:** 81%. **Pop. 5-19:** in school: 47%, teachers per 1,000: 22. **PQLI:** 81.

The island was known to the ancient world as Taprobane (Greek for copper-colored) and later as Serendip (from Arabic). Colonists from northern India subdued the indigenous Veddahs about 543 BC; their descendants, the Buddhist Sinhalese, still form most of the population. Hindu descendants of Tamil immigrants from southern India account for one-fifth of the population; separatism has grown. Parts were occupied by the Portuguese in 1505 and by the Dutch in 1658. The British seized the island in 1796. As Ceylon it became an independent member of the Commonwealth in 1948. On May 22, 1972, Ceylon became the Republic of Sri Lanka.

Prime Min. W. R. D. Bandaranaike was assassinated Sept. 25, 1959. In new elections, the Freedom Party was victorious under Mrs. Sirimavo Bandaranaike, widow of the former prime minister. In Apr., 1962, the government expropriated British and U.S. oil companies. In Mar. 1965 elections, the conservative United National Party won; the new government agreed to pay compensation for the seized oil companies. The U.S., July 1965, resumed economic aid.

After May 1970 elections, Mrs. Bandaranaike became prime minister again. In 1971 the nation suffered economic problems and terrorist activities by ultra-leftists, thousands of whom were executed. Unemployment and food shortages plagued the nation from 1973 to 1976. Massive land reform and nationalization of foreign-owned plantations was undertaken in the mid-1970s. Mrs. Bandaranaike was ousted in 1977 elections by the United Nationals. A presidential form of government was installed in 1978 to restore stability. The economy made significant gains in 1979 due to liberalization of trade and a concentration of major development projects.

Sudan

Democratic Republic of the Sudan

People: Population (1979 est.): 18,167,000. **Pop. density:** 17.96 per sq. mi. **Urban** (1976): 20.4%. **Ethnic groups:** North: Arabs, Nubians; South; Nilotic; Sudanic, Negro tribes. **Languages:** Arabic 51%, 32 other languages. **Religions:** Moslems 72%, Christians 5%, traditional 20%.

Geography: Area: 967,491 sq. mi., the largest country in Africa, over one-fourth the size of the U.S. **Location:** At the E end of Sahara desert zone. **Neighbors:** Egypt on N, Libya, Chad, Central African Republic on W, Zaire, Uganda, Kenya on S, Ethiopia on E. **Topography:** The N consists of the Libyan Desert in the W, and the mountainous Nubia desert in E, with narrow Nile valley between. The center contains large, fertile, rainy areas with fields, pasture, and forest. The S has rich soil, heavy rain. **Capital:** Khartoum. **Cities** (1973 cen.): Khartoum 333,921; Omdurman 299,401; North Khartoum 150,991; Port Sudan 132,631.

Government: Head of state and head of government: Pres., Prime Min. Gaafar Mohammed Nimeiri; b. Jan. 1, 1930; in office: May 25, 1969 (P.M.: Sept. 10, 1977). **Local divisions:** 15 provinces; the southern 3 have a regional government. **Armed forces:** regulars 62,900; para-military 3,500.

Economy: Industries: Textiles, food processing. **Chief crops:** Gum arabic (principal world source), durra (sorghum), cotton (main export), sesame, peanuts, rice, coffee, sugar cane, tobacco, wheat, dates. **Minerals:** Chrome, gold, copper, white mica, vermiculite, asbestos. **Other resources:** Mahogany. **Per**

capita arable land: 1.1 acres. **Meat prod.** (1978): beef: 170,000 metric tons; lamb: 123,000 metric tons; **Fish catch** (1977): 24,700 metric tons. **Electricity prod.** (1977): 810 mln. kwh. **Labor force:** 86% agric.

Finance: Currency: Pound (Mar. 1980: 1 = $2.00 US). **Gross domestic product** (1976): $5.1 bln. **Per capita income** (1975): $304. **Imports** (1978): $1.19 bln.; partners (1977): UK 14%, W. Ger. 12%, Jap. 11%, Iraq 10%. **Exports** (1978): $536 mln.; partners (1977): It. 12%, India 9%, China 9%, Jap. 8%. **Tourists** (1977): 36,700; receipts: $11 mln. **National Budget** (1978): $1.13 bln. revenues; $1.48 bln. expenditures. **International reserves less gold** (Mar. 1980): $72.4 mln. **Consumer prices** (change in 1978): 19.9%.

Transport: Railway traffic (1973): 2.3 bln. net ton-km. **Motor vehicles:** in use (1972): 29,200 passenger cars, 21,200 comm. vehicles. **Civil aviation:** 556 mln. passenger-km (1977); 10 mln. freight ton-km (1977). **Chief ports:** Port Sudan.

Communications: Television sets: 100,000 in use (1975). **Radios:** 1.3 mln. licensed (1975). **Telephones in use** (1978): 62,297. **Daily newspaper circ.** (1976): 26,000.

Health: Life expectancy at birth (1975): 43.0 male; 45.0 female. **Births** (per 1,000 pop. 1975): 45.8. **Deaths** (per 1,000 pop. 1975): 20.2 **Natural increase** (1975): 2.6%. **Hospital beds** (per 100,000 pop. 1977): 100. **Physicians** (per 100,000 pop. 1977): 50. **Infant mortality** (per 1,000 live births 1975): 93.6.

Education (1977): **Literacy:** 20%. **Pop. 5-19:** in school: 26%, teachers per 1,000: 8. **PQLI:** 32.

Northern Sudan, ancient Nubia, was settled by Egyptians in antiquity, and was converted to Coptic Christianity in the 6th century. Arab conquests brought Islam in the 15th century.

In the 1820s Egypt took over the Sudan, defeating the last of earlier empires, including the Fung. In the 1880s a revolution was led by Mohammed Ahmed who called himself the Mahdi (leader of the faithful) and his followers, the dervishes.

In 1898 an Anglo-Egyptian force crushed the Mahdi's successors. In 1951 the Egyptian Parliament abrogated its 1899 and 1936 treaties with Great Britain, and amended its constitution, Oct. 16, to provide for a separate Sudanese constitution.

Sudan voted for complete independence as a parliamentary government effective Jan. 1, 1956. Gen. Ibrahim Abboud took power 1958, but resigned under pressure, 1964.

In 1969, in a second military coup, a Revolutionary Council took power, but a civilian premier and cabinet were appointed; the government announced it would create a socialist state. The northern 12 provinces are predominantly Arab-Moslem and have been dominant in the central government. The 3 southern provinces are Negro and predominantly pagan. A 1972 peace agreement gave the South regional autonomy.

The government nationalized a number of businesses in May 1970. An attempted communist coup in July 1971 failed, leading to a temporary diplomatic break with the USSR. Soviet arms shipments were announced in 1975, but relations later deteriorated and U.S. ties improved.

Diplomatic relations with the U.S., broken by Sudan during the 1967 Arab-Israeli war, were restored in 1972.

On Mar. 2, 1973, the U.S. ambassador and the charge d'affaires and a Belgian diplomat were slain in Khartoum by 8 Palestinian terrorists. The 8 were freed and turned over to a Palestinian liberation group in Egypt.

Sudan charged Libya with aiding an unsuccessful coup in Sudan in 1976. Sudan has backed the Eritrean separatist movement in neighboring Ethiopia.

Economic problems plagued the nation, 1979, and were aggravated by the influx of an est. 500,000 Ethiopian and Ugandan refugees.

Suriname

People: Population (1979 est.): 404,000. **Pop. density:** 5.85 per sq. mi. **Ethnic groups** (before independence): East Indians 35%, Creoles (racially mixed descendants of freed slaves) 30%, Javanese 15%, Bush Negroes (descendants of runaway slaves) 10%, Europeans, Chinese, Amerindians. **Languages:** Dutch (official), Sranan Tongo (Creole) universal, English, others. **Religions:** Hindus, Christians, Moslems.

Geography: Area: 63,251 sq. mi., slightly larger than Georgia. **Location:** On N shore of S. America. **Neighbors:** Guyana on W, Brazil on S, French Guiana on E. **Topography:** A flat Atlantic coast, where dikes permit agriculture. Inland is a forest belt; to the S, largely unexplored hills cover 75% of the country. **Capital:** Paramaribo. **Cities** (1974 cen.): Paramaribo 110,867.

Government: Head of state: Pres. Johann H.E. Ferrier; b. May 12, 1910; in office: Nov. 25, 1975. **Head of government:** Prime Min. Henck R. Chin A Sen; in office: Mar. 1980. **Local divisions:** 9 districts.

Economy: Industries: Aluminum. **Chief crops:** Rice, sugar, fruits. **Minerals:** Bauxite. **Other resources:** Forests, shrimp. **Per capita arable land:** 0.2 acres. **Electricity prod.** (1977): 1.42 bln. kwh. **Labor force:** 29% agric.

Finance: Currency: Guilder (Mar. 1980: 1.79 = $1 US). **Gross domestic product** (1975): $501.28 mln. **Per capita income** (1975): $1,217. **Imports** (1977): $396 mln.; partners: U.S. 31%, Neth. 21%, Trin./Tob. 14%, Jap. 7%. **Exports** (1977): $309 mln.; partners: U.S. 40%, Nor. 14%, Neth. 11%, UK 8%. **Tourists** (1976): 54,700; receipts: $10 mln. **National budget** (1976): $160 mln. revenues; $238 mln. expenditures. **International reserves less gold** (Mar. 1980): $169.9 mln. **Gold:** 54,000 oz t. **Consumer prices** (change in 1979): 14.9%.

Transport: Motor vehicles: in use (1976): 28,800 passenger cars, 10,200 comm. vehicles. **Chief ports:** Paramaribo, Nieuw-Nickerie.

Communications: Television sets: 38,000 in use (1976). **Radios:** 112,000 in use (1976). **Telephones in use** (1978): 20,787. **Daily newspaper circ.** (1977): 33,000; 74 per 1,000 pop.

Health: Life expectancy at birth (1963): 62.5 male; 66.7 female. **Births** (per 1,000 pop. 1966): 36.9. **Deaths** (per 1,000 pop. 1966): 7.2. **Natural increase** (1966): 3.0%. **Pop. per hospital bed** (1975): 184. **Pop. per physician** (1974): 2,030. **Infant mortality** (per 1,000 live births 1966): 30.4. **PQLI:** 83.

The Netherlands acquired Suriname in 1667 from Britain, in exchange for New Netherlands (New York). The 1954 Dutch constitution raised the colony to a level of equality with the Netherlands and the Netherlands Antilles. In the 1970s the Dutch government pressured for Suriname independence, which came Nov. 25, 1975, despite objections from East Indians and some Bush Negroes. Some 40% of the population (mostly East Indians) emigrated to the Netherlands in the months before independence. The Netherlands promised $1.5 billion in aid for the first decade of independence.

A military coup staged by non-commissioned officers, Feb. 1980, installed civilians to its ruling National Military Council.

Swaziland

Kingdom of Swaziland

People: Population (1979 est.): 541,000. **Age distrib.** (%): 0–14: 48.3; 15–59: 47.4; 60+: 4.3. **Pop. density:** 80.54 per sq. mi. **Urban** (1973): 7.9%. **Ethnic groups:** Swazi 90%, Zulu 2.3%, European 2.1%, other African, non-African groups. **Languages:** siSwati, English, (both official). **Religions:** Christians 60%, others.

Geography: Area: 6,705 sq. mi., slightly smaller than New Jersey. **Location:** In southern Africa, near Indian O. coast. **Neighbors:** South Africa on N, W, S; Mozambique on E. **Topography:** The country descends from W-E in broad belts, becoming more arid in the lowveld region, then rising to a plateau in the E. **Capital:** Mbabane. **Cities** (1976 cen.): Mbabane 22,262; Manzini 16,000.

Government: Head of state: King Sobhuza II; b. July 22, 1899; in office: 1921. **Head of government:** Prime Min. Maphevu Dlamini; in office: Mar. 31, 1976. **Local divisions:** 4 districts, 2 municipalities.

Economy: Industries: Wood pulp. **Chief crops:** Corn, cotton, rice, pineapples, sugar, citrus fruits. **Minerals:** Asbestos, iron, coal. **Other resources:** Forests. **Per capita arable land:** 0.7 acres. **Meat prod.** (1978): beef: 15,000 metric tons. **Electricity prod.** (1977): 173.00 mln. kwh. **Labor force:** 85% agric.

Finance: Currency: Lilangeni (Apr. 1980: 1 = $1.2504 US). **Gross domestic product** (1977): $313 mln. **Per capita income** (1975): $664. **Imports** (1978): $316 mln.; partners (1975): So. Afr., UK. **Exports** (1978): $195 mln.; partners (1975): UK,

U.S., So. Afr., Jap. **International reserves less gold** (Mar. 1980): $122 mln. **Consumer prices** (change in 1978): 8.5%.

Transport: Motor vehicles: in use (1976): 7,900 passenger cars, 7,100 comm. vehicles.

Communications: Radios: 60,000 in use (1976). **Telephones in use** (1978): 9,190. **Daily newspaper circ.** (1976): 5,000; 10 per 1,000 pop.

Health: Life expectancy at birth (1975): 41.8 male; 45 female. **Births** (per 1,000 pop. 1975): 48.3. **Deaths** (per 1,000 pop. 1975): 21.2. **Natural increase** (1975): 2.7%. **Hospital beds** (per 100,000 pop. 1977): 345. **Physicians** (per 100,000 pop. 1977): 11.

Education (1977): **Literacy:** 36%. **Pop. 5-19:** in school: 72%, teachers per 1,000: 21. **PQLI:** 43.

The royal house of Swaziland traces back 400 years, and is one of Africa's last ruling dynasties. The Swazis, a Bantu people, were driven to Swaziland from lands to the N by the Zulus in 1820. Their autonomy was later guaranteed by Britain and Transvaal, with Britain assuming control after 1903. Independence came Sept. 6, 1968. In 1973 the king repealed the constitution and assumed full powers.

A new Parliament was opened, 1979. Under the new constitution political parties were forbidden; Parliament's role in government was limited to debate and advice.

Fertile lands and mineral resources have aided development. About 8,000 Swazis hold jobs in South Africa, which has a customs union with Swaziland. The population is homogeneous, except for 6,000 whites who dominate the economy.

Sweden

Kingdom of Sweden

People: Population (1979 est.): 8,296,000. **Age distrib.** (%): 0–14: 20.6; 15–59: 58.2; 60+: 21.2. **Pop. density:** 47.68 per sq. mi. **Urban** (1975): 82.7%. **Ethnic groups:** Swedish 93%, Finnish 3%, Lapps, European immigrants. **Languages:** Swedish, Finnish. **Religions:** Lutherans (official) 95%, other Protestants 5%.

Geography: Area: 173,665 sq. mi., larger than California. **Location:** On Scandinavian Peninsula in N. Europe. **Neighbors:** Norway on W, Denmark on S (across Kattegat), Finland on E. **Topography:** Mountains along NW border cover 25% of Sweden, flat or rolling terrain covers the central and southern areas, which includes several large lakes. **Capital:** Stockholm. **Cities** (1978 est.): Stockholm 661,258; Goteborg 442,410; Malmo 240,220.

Government: Head of state: King Carl XVI Gustaf; b. Apr. 30, 1946; in office: Sept. 19, 1973. **Head of government:** Prime Min. Thorbjorn Falldin; b. Apr. 24, 1926; in office: Oct. 11, 1979. **Local divisions:** 24 lan (counties). **Armed forces:** regulars 65,900; reserves 500,000.

Economy: Industries: Steel, machinery, instruments, autos, shipbuilding, shipping, paper. **Chief crops:** Grains, potatoes, sugar beets. **Minerals:** Zinc, iron, lead, copper, gold, silver. **Other resources:** Forests (half the country); yield one fourth exports. **Per capita arable land:** 0.9 acres. **Meat prod.** (1978): beef: 148,000 metric tons; pork: 306,000 metric tons; lamb: 5,000 metric tons. **Fish catch** (1977): 192,100 metric tons. **Electricity prod.** (1978): 90.18 bln. kwh. **Crude steel prod.** (1979): 4.7 mln. metric tons. **Labor force:** 5% agric.; 45% manuf.

Finance: Currency: Krona (Mar. 1980: 4.46 = $1 US). **Gross domestic product** (1978): $87.33 bln. **Per capita income** (1978): $9,274. **Imports** (1979): $28.6 bln.; partners (1978): W. Ger. 18%, UK 11%, U.S. 7%, Den. 7%. **Exports** (1979): $28.56 bln.; partners (1978): UK 11%, W. Ger. 11%, Nor. 10%, Den. 9%. **National budget** (1978): $24.32 bln. revenues; $27.44 bln. expenditures. **International reserves less gold** (Mar. 1980): $3.38 bln. **Gold:** 6.07 mln. oz t. **Consumer prices** (change in 1979): 7.3%.

Transport: Railway traffic (1978): 5.56 bln. passenger-km; 14.76 bln. net ton-km. **Motor vehicles:** in use (1976): 2.88 mln. passenger cars, 162,400 comm. vehicles; manuf. (1978): 258,000 passenger cars; (1975): 49,200 comm. vehicles. **Civil aviation:** 4,068 mln. passenger-km (1978): 203 mln. freight ton-km (1978). **Chief ports:** Goteborg, Stockholm, Malmo.

Communications: Television sets: 2.98 mln. licensed (1976), 367,000 manuf. (1976). **Radios:** 3.2 mln. licensed (1976), 159,000 manuf. (1976). **Telephones in use** (1978): 5,930,276. **Daily newspaper circ.** (1977): 4,358,000; 528 per 1,000 pop.

Health: Life expectancy at birth (1976): 72.10 male; 77.75 female. **Births** (per 1,000 pop. 1978): 11.2. **Deaths** (per 1,000 pop. 1978): 10.8. **Natural increase** (1978): 0.4%. **Hospital beds** (per 100,000 pop. 1977): 1,496. **Physicians** (per 100,000 pop. 1977): 178. **Infant mortality** (per 1,000 live births (1978): 7.7.

Education (1977): **Literacy:** 99%. **Pop. 5-19:** in school: 72%, teachers per 1,000: 46. **PQLI:** 98.

The Swedes have lived in present-day Sweden for at least 5,000 years, longer than nearly any other European people. Gothic tribes from Sweden played a major role in the disintegration of the Roman Empire. Other Swedes helped create the first Russian state in the 9th century.

The Swedes were Christianized from the 11th century, and a strong centralized monarchy developed. A parliament, the Riksdag, was first called in 1435, the earliest parliament on the European continent, with all classes of society represented.

Swedish independence from rule by Danish kings (dating from 1397) was secured by Gustavus I in a revolt, 1521-23; he built up the government and military and established the Lutheran Church. In the 17th century Sweden was a major European power, gaining most of the Baltic seacoast, but its international position subsequently declined.

The Napoleonic wars, in which Sweden acquired Norway (it became independent 1905), were the last in which Sweden participated. Armed neutrality was maintained in both world wars.

Over 4 decades of Social Democratic rule was ended in 1976 parliamentary elections. Although 90% of the economy is in private hands, the government holds a large interest in water power production and the railroads are operated by a public agency.

Consumer cooperatives are in extensive operation and also are important in agriculture and housing. Per capita GNP, 1977, was among the highest in the world.

The U.S. and Sweden in 1974 ended a 15-month diplomatic "freeze" and exchanged ambassadors.

Swedish voters in a national referendum, Mar. 1980, voted to support limited expansion of nuclear energy.

A labor crisis of strikes locking out more than 800,000 workers, May 1980, brought the country to an industrial standstill and shattered its image of labor tranquillity.

Switzerland

Swiss Confederation

People: Population (1979 est.): 6,343,000. **Age distrib.** (%): 0–14: 21.0; 15–59: 61.1; 60+: 17.9. **Pop. density:** 397.72 per sq. mi. **Urban** (1970): 54.6%. **Ethnic groups:** Defined by mother tongue. **Languages:** German, French, Italian, Romansch (all official). **Religions:** Protestant 48%, Roman Catholic 49%, Jews.

Geography: Area: 15,941 sq. mi., as large as Mass., Conn., and R.I., combined. **Location:** In the Alps Mts. in Central Europe. **Neighbors:** France on W, Italy on S, Austria on E, W. Germany on N. **Topography:** The Alps cover 60% of the land area, the Jura, near France, 10%. Running between, from NE to SW, are midlands, 30%. **Capital:** Bern. **Cities** (1978 est.): Zurich 379,600; Basel 185,300; Geneva 150,100; Bern 145,500.

Government: Head of government: Pres. Georges-Andre Chevallaz; b. Feb. 7, 1915; in office: Jan. 1-Dec. 31, 1980. **Local divisions:** 20 full cantons, 6 half cantons. **Armed forces:** regulars 18,500; reserves 621,500.

Economy: Industries: Machinery, machine tools, steel, instruments, watches, textiles, foodstuffs (cheese, chocolate), chemicals, drugs, banking, tourism. **Chief crops:** Grains, potatoes, sugar beets, vegetables, tobacco. **Minerals:** Salt. **Other resources:** Hydro power potential. **Per capita arable land:** 0.1 acres. **Meat prod.** (1978): beef: 150,000 metric tons; pork: 263,000 metric tons. **Electricity prod.** (1978): 42.10 bln. kwh. **Crude steel prod.** (1979): 886,000 metric tons. **Labor force:** 8% agric.; 38% manuf.

Finance: Currency: Franc (Mar. 1980: 1.83 = $1 US). **Gross domestic product** (1979): $93.58 bln. **Per capita income**

(1978): $12,408. **Imports** (1979): $29.36 bln.; partners (1978): W. Ger. 29%, Fr. 12%, It. 10%, U.S. 8%. **Exports** (1979): $26.54 bln.; partners (1978): W. Ger. 18%, Fr. 9%, It. 7%, U.S. 7%. **Tourists** (1977): 8,341,400; receipts: $1.94 bln. **National budget** (1978): $8.43 bln. revenues; $8.63 bln. expenditures. **International reserves less gold** (Mar. 1980): $13.48 bln. **Gold:** 83.28 mln. oz t. **Consumer prices** (change in 1979): 3.6%.

Transport: Railway traffic (1978): 9.3 bln. passenger-km; 9.3 bln. net ton-km. **Motor vehicles:** in use (1977): 1.93 mln. passenger cars, 154,000 comm. vehicles. **Civil aviation:** 10,152 mln. passenger-km (1978); 431 mln. freight ton-km (1978).

Communications: Television sets: 1.81 mln. licensed (1976). **Radios:** 2.11 mln. licensed (1976). **Telephones in use** (1978): 4,145,169. **Daily newspaper circ.** (1977): 2,622,000; 414 per 1,000 pop.

Health: Life expectancy at birth (1973): 70.29 male; 76.22 female. **Births** (per 1,000 pop. 1978): 11.3. **Deaths** (per 1,000 pop. 1978): 9.0. **Natural increase** (1978): .2%. **Hospital beds** (per 100,000 pop. 1977): 1,141. **Physicians** (per 100,000 pop. 1977): 201. **Infant mortality** (per 1,000 live births 1977): 9.8.

Education (1977): **Literacy:** 99%. **Pop. 5–19:** in school: 62%, teachers per 1,000: 45. **PQLI:** 96.

Switzerland, the Roman province of Helvetia, is a federation of 23 cantons (20 full cantons and 6 half cantons), 3 of which in 1291 created a defensive league and later were joined by other districts. Voters in the French-speaking part of Canton Bern voted for self-government, 1978; Canton Jura was created Jan. 1, 1979.

In 1648 the Swiss Confederation obtained its independence from the Holy Roman Empire. The cantons were joined under a federal constitution in 1848, with large powers of local control retained by each canton.

Switzerland has maintained an armed neutrality since 1815, and has not been involved in a foreign war since 1515. It is not a member of NATO or the UN. However, the Cabinet took steps, Mar. 28, 1979, to recommend Swiss membership in the UN. Switzerland is a member of several UN agencies and of the European Free Trade Assoc. and has ties with the EC. It is also the seat of many UN and other international agencies.

Switzerland is a leading world banking center; stability of the currency brings funds from many quarters. Some 20% of all workers are foreign residents.

Syria

Syrian Arab Republic

People: Population (1979 est.): 8,506,000. **Age distrib.** (%): 0–14: 48.9; 15–59: 44.9; 60+: 6.2. **Pop. density:** 113.15 per sq. mi. **Urban** (1978): 48.8%. **Ethnic groups:** Arabs 88%, Kurds 6.3%, Armenians 2.8%, Turks, Circassians, Assyrians. **Languages:** Arabic (official), French, Kurdish, Armenian. **Religions:** Moslems (Sunni, Alawi, Druze) 88%, Christians 12%.

Geography: Area: 71,498 sq. mi., the size of North Dakota. **Location:** At eastern end of Mediterranean Sea. **Neighbors:** Lebanon, Israel on W, Jordan on S, Iraq on E, Turkey on N. **Topography:** Syria has a short Mediterranean coastline, then stretches E and S with fertile lowlands and plains, alternating with mountains and large desert areas. **Capital:** Damascus. **Cities** (1978 est.): Damascus 1,142,000; Aleppo 878,000; Homs 306,000.

Government: Head of state: Pres. Hafez al-Assad; b. Mar. 1930; in office: Feb. 22, 1971. **Head of government:** Prime Min. Abdul Rauf Qasim; in office: Jan. 16, 1980. **Local divisions:** Damascus and 13 provinces. **Armed forces:** regulars 227,500; reserves 102,500.

Economy: Industries: Oil products, textiles, cement, tobacco, glassware, sugar, brassware. **Chief crops:** Cotton, grain, olives, fruits, vegetables. **Minerals:** Oil, phosphate, gypsum. **Crude oil reserves** (1980): 2.00 bln. bbls. **Other resources:** Wool. **Per capita arable land:** 1.6 acres. **Meat prod.** (1978): beef: 14,000 metric tons; lamb: 60,000 metric tons. **Electricity prod.** (1977): 2.04 bln. kwh. **Labor force:** 51% agric.; 15% manuf.

Finance: Currency: Pound (Mar. 1980: 3.95 = $1 US). **Gross domestic product** (1978): $7.77 bln. **Per capita income** (1975): $702. **Imports** (1978): $2.44 bln.; partners: W. Ger. 11%, Fr. 8%, It. 8%, Iraq 7%. **Exports** (1978): $1.05 bln.; partners: Fr. 10%, W. Ger. 10%, USSR 9%, Neth. 9%. **Tourists** (1977): 681,100; receipts: $110 mln. **International reserves less gold** (July 1979): $527 mln. **Gold** (Dec. 1979): 833,000 oz t. **Consumer prices** (change in 1979): 4.6%.

Transport: Railway traffic (1978): 321.6 mln. passenger-km; 270 mln. net ton-km. **Motor vehicles:** in use (1976): 62,800 passenger cars, 55,900 comm. vehicles. **Chief ports:** Latakia, Tartus.

Communications: Television sets: 230,000 in use (1976), 55,000 manuf. (1977). **Radios:** 1.37 mln. in use (1970). **Telephones in use** (1978): 193,044. **Daily newspaper circ.** (1976): 65,000.

Health: Life expectancy at birth (1970): 54.49 male; 58.73 female. **Births** (per 1,000 pop. 1975): 46.5. **Deaths** (per 1,000 1975): 13.6. **Natural increase** (1975): 3.3%. **Hospital beds** (per 100,000 pop. 1977): 104. **Physicians** (per 100,000 pop. 1977): 39. **Infant mortality** (per 1,000 live births 1976): 15.3.

Education (1977): **Literacy:** 45%. **Pop. 5-19:** in school: 59%, teachers per 1,000: 20. **PQLI:** 57.

Syria contains some of the most ancient remains of civilization. It was the center of the Seleucid empire, but later became absorbed in the Roman and Arab empires. Ottoman rule prevailed for 4 centuries, until the end of World War I.

The state of Syria was formed from former Turkish districts, made a separate entity by the Treaty of Sevres 1920 and divided into the states of Syria and Greater Lebanon. Both were administered under a French League of Nations mandate 1920-1941.

Syria was proclaimed a republic by the occupying French Sept. 16, 1941, and exercised full independence effective Jan. 1, 1944. French troops left in 1946. Syria joined in the Arab invasion of Israel in 1948.

Syria joined with Egypt in Feb. 1958 in the United Arab Republic but seceded Sept. 30, 1961. The Socialist Baath party and military leaders seized power in Mar. 1963. The Baath, a pan-Arab organization, became the only legal party. The government has been dominated by members of the minority Alawite sect, many of whom were assassinated in 1977-78.

In the Arab-Israeli war of June 1967, Israel seized and occupied the Golan Heights area inside Syria, from which Israeli settlements had for years been shelled by Syria.

Syria aided Palestinian guerrillas fighting Jordanian forces in Sept. 1970 and, after a renewal of that fighting in July 1971, broke off relations with Jordan. But by 1975 the 2 countries had entered a military coordination pact.

Syria received large shipments of arms from the USSR in 1972-73 and on Oct. 6, 1973, Syria joined Egypt in an attack on Israel. Arab oil states agreed in 1974 to give Syria $1 billion a year to aid anti-Israel moves. Military supplies used or lost in the 1973 war were replaced by the USSR in 1974 and increased shipments of planes, tanks, and missiles were reported in 1978. U.S. economic aid has been extended. Some 30,000 Syrian troops entered Lebanon in 1976 to mediate in a civil war, and fought Palestinian guerrillas and, later, fought Christian militiamen.

Tanzania

United Republic of Tanzania

People: Population (1979 est.) 17,364,000. **Pop. density:** 45.61 per sq. mi. **Urban** (1973): 7.3%. **Ethnic groups:** Sukuma 12.6%, Maleonde 4%, 130 other tribes (most Bantu); Europeans, Arabs, Asians. **Languages:** Swahili, English are official. **Religions:** Moslems 30%, Christians 30%, Traditional 40%.

Geography: Area: 362,820 sq. mi., more than twice the size of California. **Location:** On coast of E. Africa. **Neighbors:** Kenya, Uganda on N, Rwanda, Burundi, Zaire on W, Zambia, Malawi, Mozambique on S. **Topography:** Hot, arid central plateau, surrounded by the lake region in the W, temperate highlands in N and S, the coastal plains. Mt. Kilimanjaro, 19,340 ft., is highest in Africa. **Capital:** Dar-es-Salaam. **Cities** (1978 cen.): Dar-es-Salaam 870,020.

Government: Head of state: Pres. Julius Kambarage Nyerere; b. Mar. 1922; in office: Apr. 26, 1964. **Head of government:** Edward M. Sokoine, b. 1938; in office: Feb. 13, 1977. **Local divisions:** 21 regions (4 on Zanzibar), Dar-es-Salaam.

Armed forces: regulars 51,700; para-military 36,400.

Economy: Industries: Food processing, clothing. **Chief crops:** Sisal, cotton, coffee, tea, tobacco. **Minerals:** Diamonds, gold, salt, tin, mica. **Other resources:** Hides. **Per capita arable land:** 0.6 acres. **Meat prod.** (1978): beef: 131,000 metric tons; lamb: 30,000 metric tons. **Fish catch** (1977): 250,000 metric tons. **Electricity prod.** (1978): 696.00 mln. kwh. **Labor force:** 90% agric.

Finance: Currency: Shilling (Dec. 1979: 8.22 = $1 US). **Gross domestic product** (1978): $4.35 bln. **Per capita income** (1978): $253. **Imports** (1978): $1.16 bln.; partners (1976): UK 12%, Kenya 11%, Iran 9%, W. Ger. 8%. **Exports** (1978): $473 mln.; partners (1976): W. Ger. 14%, UK 13%, U.S. 9%, Sing. 7%. **Tourists** (1977): 93,000; receipts: $9 mln. **National budget** (1976): $485 mln. revenues; $755 mln. expenditures. **International reserves less gold** (Nov. 1979): $77.80 mln. **Consumer prices** (change in 1978): 11.6%.

Transport: Motor vehicles: in use (1977): 43,600 passenger cars, 46,400 comm. vehicles. **Chief ports:** Dar-es-Salaam, Tanga.

Communications: Radios: 300,000 in use (1976), 177,000 manuf. (1975). **Telephones in use** (1978): 74,264. **Daily newspaper circ.** (1977): 133,000; 8 per 1,000 pop.

Health: Life expectancy at birth (1967): 40 male; 41 female. **Births** (per 1,000 pop. 1967): 47.0. **Deaths** (per 1,000 pop. 1967): 22.0. **Natural increase** (1967): 2.5%. **Hospital beds** (per 100,000 pop. 1977): 206. **Physicians** (per 100,000 pop. 1977): 20. **Infant mortality** (per 1,000 live births 1967): 160-165.

Education (1977): **Literacy:** 37%. **Pop. 5–19:** in school: 36%, teachers per 1,000: 7. **PQLI:** 50.

The Republic of Tanganyika in E. Africa and the island Republic of Zanzibar, off the coast of Tanganyika, joined into a single nation, the United Republic of Tanzania, Apr. 26, 1964. Zanzibar retains internal self-government. In 1973 Dodoma, in the country's center, was named the future capital.

Tanganyika. Arab colonization and slaving began in the 8th century AD; Portuguese sailors explored the coast by about 1500. Other Europeans followed.

In 1885 Germany established German East Africa of which Tanganyika formed the bulk. It became a League of Nations mandate and, after 1946, a UN trust territory, both under Britain. It became independent Dec. 9, 1961, and a republic within the Commonwealth a year later.

In 1967 the government set on a socialist course; it nationalized all banks and many industries. The government also ordered that Swahili, not English, be used in all official business. Nine million people have been moved into cooperative villages.

Tanzania exchanged invasion attacks with Uganda, 1978-79. Tanzanian forces drove Idi Amin from Uganda, Mar., 1979.

Zanzibar, the Isle of Cloves, lies 23 mi. off the coast of Tanganyika; its area is 640 sq. mi. The island of **Pemba,** 25 mi. to the NE, area 380 sq. mi., is included in the administration. The total population (1978 cen.) is 475,655.

Chief industry is the production of cloves and clove oil of which Zanzibar and Pemba produce the bulk of the world's supply.

Zanzibar was for centuries the center for Arab slave-traders. Portugal ruled for 2 centuries until ousted by Arabs around 1700. Zanzibar became a British Protectorate in 1890; independence came Dec. 10, 1963. Revolutionary forces overthrew the Sultan Jan. 12, 1964. The new government ousted American and British diplomats and newsmen, slaughtered thousands of Arabs, and nationalized farms. Union with Tanganyika followed, 1964. The ruling parties of Tanganyika and Zanzibar were united in 1977, as political tension eased; but a movement for greater autonomy began, 1979.

Thailand

Kingdom of Thailand

People: Population (1979 est.): 46,687,000. **Age distrib.** (%): 0–14: 42.8; 15–59: 52.3; 60+: 4.9. **Pop. density:** 227.26 per sq. mi. **Urban** (1970): 13.2%. **Ethnic groups:** Thais 75%, Chinese 14%, Malays 3%, Khmers, Soais, Karens, Indians. **Languages:** Thai, Chinese. **Religions:** Buddhists 94%, Moslems 4%, Christians 0.6%.

Geography: Area: 198,455 sq. mi., three-fourths the size of Texas. **Location:** On Indochinese and Malayan Peninsulas in S.E. Asia. **Neighbors:** Burma on W. Laos on N, Cambodia on E, Malaysia on S. **Topography:** A plateau dominates the NE third of Thailand, dropping to the fertile alluvial valley of the Chao Phraya R. in the center. Forested mountains are in N, with narrow fertile valleys. The southern peninsula region is covered by rain forests. **Capital:** Bangkok. **Cities** (1977 cen.): Bangkok (met.): 4,178,000; Thonburi 627,989.

Government: Head of state: King Bhumibol Adulyadej; b. Dec. 5, 1927; in office: June 9, 1946. **Head of government:** Prime Min. Prem Tinsulanonda; in office: Mar. 3, 1980. **Local divisions:** 72 provinces. **Armed forces:** regulars 216,000; reserves 500,000.

Economy: Industries: Auto assembly, drugs, textiles, electrical goods. **Chief crops:** Rice (a major export), corn tapioca, jute, sugar, coconuts, tobacco, pepper, peanuts, beans, cotton. **Minerals:** Antimony, tin (5th largest producer), tungsten, iron, manganese, gas. **Crude oil reserves** (1979): 200 bbls. **Other resources:** Forests (teak is exported), rubber. **Per capita arable land:** 0.9 acres. **Meat prod.** (1978): beef: 211,000 metric tons; pork: 152,000 metric tons. **Fish catch** (1977): 2.2 mln. metric tons. **Electricity prod.** (1977): 11.69 bln. kwh. **Crude steel prod.** (1979 est.): 400,000 metric tons. **Labor force:** 76% agric.; 7% manuf.

Finance: Currency: Baht (Mar. 1980: 20.43 = $1 US). **Gross domestic product** (1978): $21.84 bln. **Per capita income** (1978): $444. **Imports** (1978): $5.36 bln.; partners : Jap. 31%, U.S. 14%, Saudi Ar. 6%, W. Ger. 6%. **Exports** (1978): $4.09 bln.; partners : Jap. 20%, Neth. 15%, U.S. 11%, Sing. 8%. **Tourists** (1977): 1,220,700; receipts: $211 mln. **National budget** (1978): $3.20 bln. revenues; $3.85 bln. expenditures. **International reserves less gold** (Mar. 1980): $1.70 bln. **Gold:** 2.46 mln. oz t. **Consumer prices** (change in 1979): 9.9%.

Transport: Railway traffic (1977): 5.63 bln. passenger-km; 2.51 bln. net ton-km. **Motor vehicles:** in use (1975): 266,100 passenger cars, 266,700 comm. vehicles; assembled (1976): 15,000 passenger cars; (1974): 8,600 comm. vehicles. **Civil aviation:** 4,200 mln. passenger-km (1978); 140 mln. freight ton-km (1978). **Chief ports:** Bangkok, Sattahip.

Communication: Television sets: 761,000 in use (1976), 90,000 manuf. (1976). **Radios:** 5.5 mln. in use (1975). **Telephones in use** (1978): 366,862. **Daily newspaper circ.** (1970): 749,000; 21 per 1,000 pop.

Health: Life expectancy at birth (1960): 53.6 male; 58.7 female. **Births** (per 1,000 pop. 1975): 39.6. **Deaths** (per 1,000 pop. 1975): 10.5. **Natural increase** (1975): 2.9%. **Hospital beds** (per 100,000 pop. 1977): 121. **Physicians** (per 100,000 pop. 1977): 12. **Infant mortality** (per 1,000 live births 1976): 25.5.

Education (1977): **Literacy:** 82%. **Pop. 5-19:** in school: 47%, teachers per 1,000: 16. **PQLI:** 75.

Thais began migrating from southern China in the 11th century. Thailand is the only country in SE Asia never taken over by a European power, thanks to King Mongkut and his son King Chulalongkorn who ruled from 1851 to 1910, modernized the country, and signed trade treaties with both Britain and France. A bloodless revolution in 1932 limited the monarchy.

Japan occupied the country in 1941. After the war, Thailand followed a pro-West foreign policy. Some 11,000 Thai troops fought in S. Vietnam, but were withdrawn by 1972.

Clashes with Laos and especially with Cambodia have continued to 1980. Tribal and political rebels have conducted guerrilla fighting in the NE and extreme S, 1965-80. Vietnamese infantry were at the Thai-Cambodia border, June 1980.

The military took over the government in a bloody 1976 coup. Kriangsak Chomanan, prime minister since a 1977 military coup, resigned, Feb. 1980, under opposition over soaring inflation, oil price increases, labor unrest and growing crime.

The fertile land yields a rice surplus. Foreign investment has been encouraged.

Togo

Republic of Togo

People: Population (1979 est.): 2,544,000. **Age distrib.** (%): 0-14: 49.8; 15-59: 44.6; 60+:5.6.**Pop. density:** 110.28 per sq. mi. **Urban** (1974): 15.2%. **Ethnic groups:** Ewe 20%, Mina 6%,

Kabye 14%. **Languages:** French (official), others. **Religions:** Roman Catholics 18%, Protestants 6.5%, Moslems 9%, others.

Geography: Area: 21,853 sq. mi., slightly smaller than West Virginia. **Location:** On S coast of W. Africa. **Neighbors:** Ghana on W, Upper Volta on N, Benin on E. **Topography:** A range of hills running SW-NE splits Togo into 2 savanna plains regions. **Capital:** Lome. **Cities** (1976 est.): Lome 214,200.

Government: Head of state: Pres. Gnassingbe Eyadema; b. Dec. 26, 1937; in office: Apr. 14, 1967. **Local divisions:** 19 circumscriptions. **Armed forces:** regulars 3,250; para-military 1,400.

Economy: Industries: Textiles, shoes. **Chief crops:** Coffee, cocoa, palm kernels, copra, cotton, kapok, peanuts. **Minerals:** Phosphates. **Per capita arable land:** 2.3 acres. **Electricity prod.** (1978): 67.20 mln. kwh. **Labor force:** 78% agric.

Finance: Currency: CFA franc (Mar. 1980: 223.92 = $1 US). **Gross domestic product** (1976): $560 mln. **Per capita income** (1977): $266. **Imports** (1978): $483 mln.; partners (1977): Fr. 34%, U.K 10%, W. Ger. 9%, U.S. 8%. **Exports** (1978): $260 mln.; partners (1977): Neth. 32%, Fr. 21%, W. Ger. 12%, Pol. 8%. **International reserves less gold** (Jan. 1980): $6.5 mln. **Gold:** 13,000 oz t. **Consumer prices** (change in 1978): .44%.

Transport: Railway traffic (1976): 91.2 mln. passenger-km; 37.7 mln. net ton-km. **Motor vehicles:** in use (1974): 13,000 passenger cars, 7,000 comm. vehicles. **Chief ports:** Lome.

Communications: Radios: 52,000 in use (1976). **Telephones in use** (1978): 4,749. **Daily newspaper circ.** (1976): 7,000; 3 per 1,000 pop.

Health: Life expectancy at birth (1961): 31.6 male; 38.5 female. **Births** (per 1,000 pop. 1975): 49.1 **Deaths** (per 1,000 pop. 1975): 21.0. **Natural increase** (1975): 2.8%. **Hospital beds** (per 100,000 pop. 1977): 143. **Physicians** (per 100,000 pop. 1977): 6. **Infant mortality** (per 1,000 live births 1975): 127.

Education (1977): **Literacy:** 18%. **Pop. 5-19:** in school: 55%, teachers per 1,000: 10. **PQLI:** 27.

The Ewe arrived in southern Togo several centuries ago. The country later became a major source of slaves. Germany took control from 1884 on. France and Britain administered Togoland as UN trusteeships. The French sector became the republic of Togo Apr. 27, 1960.

The population is divided between Bantus in the S and Hamitic tribes in the N. Togo has actively promoted regional integration, as a means of stimulating the backward economy.

Tonga

Kingdom of Tonga

People: Population (1979 est.): 96,000. **Age distrib.** (%): 0–14: 44.4;-15–59; 50.5; 60+:5.1. **Pop. density:** 333.33 per sq. mi. **Ethnic groups:** Tongans (Polynesians). **Languages:** Tongan, English. **Religions:** Methodism.

Geography: Area: 270 sq. mi., smaller than New York City. **Location:** In western S. Pacific O. **Neighbors:** Nearest is Fiji, on W, New Zealand, on S. **Topography:** Tonga comprises 150 volcanic and coral islands, 45 inhabited. **Capital:** Nuku'alofa. **Cities** (1976 cen.): Nuku'alofa (met.) 18,312.

Government: Head of state: King Taufa'ahau Tupou IV; b. July 4, 1918; in office: Dec. 16, 1965. **Head of government:** Prime Min. Fatafehi Tu'ipelehake; b. Jan. 7, 1922; in office: Dec. 16, 1965. **Local divisions:** 3 island districts.

Economy: Industries: Tourism. **Chief crops:** Coconut products, bananas are exported. **Other resources:** Fish. **Per capita arable land:** 0.4 acres. **Electricity prod.** (1977): 7.00 mln. kwh. **Labor force:** 75% agric.

Finance: Currency: Pa'anga (Sept. 1979: .89 = $1 US). **Gross domestic product** (1976 est.): $40 mln. **Per capita income** (1976): $430. **Imports** (1978): $32 mln.; partners: N Z 37%, Austral. 28%, Jap. 7%, UK 6%. **Exports** (1978): $7.1 mln.; partners (1978): Neth. 29%, N Z 22%, UK 21%, W. Ger. 11%. **Tourists** (1975): 70,000; receipts: $3 mln. **Consumer prices** (change in 1976): 7.1%.

Transport: Motor vehicles: in use (1974): 1,000 passenger cars, 400 comm. vehicles. **Chief ports:** Nuku'alofa.

Communications: Radios: 15,000 in use (1976). **Telephones in use** (1978): 1,285.

Health: Births (per 1,000 pop. 1976): 13.0. **Deaths** (per 1,000 pop. 1976): 1.9. **Natural increase** (1976): 1.1%. **Pop. per hospital bed** (1976): 300. **Pop. per physician** (1976): 3,000. **Infant mortality** (per 1,000 live births 1976): 20.5.

The islands were first visited by the Dutch in the early 17th century. A series of civil wars ended in 1845 with establishment of the Tupou dynasty. In 1900 Tonga became a British protectorate. On June 4, 1970, Tonga became completely independent and a member of the Commonwealth. Tonga suffered from a severe balance of payments problem, 1979.

Trinidad and Tobago

People: Population (1979 est.): 1,150,000. **Age distrib.** (%): 0–14: 38.0; 15–59: 55.4; 60+: 6.6. **Pop. density:** 570.71 per sq. mi. **Urban** (1970): 49.4%. **Ethnic groups:** Negroes 43%, East Indians 36%, white 2%, Chinese 1%, mixed 16%. **Languages:** English, Hindi. **Religions:** Roman Catholics 36%, Protestants 30%, Hindus 23%, Moslems 6%.

Geography: Area: 1,980 sq. mi., the size of Delaware. **Location:** Off eastern coast of Venezuela. **Neighbors:** Nearest is Venezuela on SW. **Topography:** Three low mountain ranges cross Trinidad E-W, with a well-watered plain between N and Central Ranges. Parts of E and W coasts are swamps. Tobago, 116 sq. mi., lies 20 mi. NE. **Capital:** Port-of-Spain. **Cities** (1975 est.): Port-of-Spain (met.) 250,000; San Fernando 50,000.

Government: Head of state: Pres. Ellis E. I. Clarke; b. Dec. 28, 1917; in office: July 31, 1976. **Head of government:** Prime Min. Eric E. Williams; b. Sept. 25, 1911; in office: Sept. 24, 1956. **Local divisions:** 8 counties, Ward of Tobago, 3 municipalities.

Economy: Industries: Oil products, rum, cement, tourism. **Chief crops:** Sugar, cocoa, coffee, citrus fruits, bananas. **Minerals:** Asphalt, oil, **Crude oil reserves** (1980): 700 mln. bbls. **Per capita arable land:** 0.1 acres. **Electricity prod.** (1978): 1.62 bln. kwh. **Labor force:** 13% agric., 50% manuf.

Finance: Currency: Dollar (Mar. 1980: 2.41 = $1 US). **Gross domestic product** (1978): $3.93 bln. **Per capita income** (1976): $2,090. **Imports** (1979): $1.95 bln.; partners (1977): Saudi Ar. 22%, U.S. 21%, Indo. 14%, UK 13%. **Exports** (1979): $2.48 bln.; partners (1977): U.S. 69%. **Tourists** (1976): 158,700; receipts: $87 mln. **National budget** (1972): $275.47 mln. revenues; $295.89 mln. expenditures. **International reserves less gold** (Mar. 1980): $1.98 bln. **Gold:** 54,000 oz t. **Consumer prices** (change in 1979): 14.7%.

Transport: Motor vehicles: in use (1977): 117,700 passenger cars, 32,000 comm. vehicles; assembled (1978): 13,752 passenger cars; 2,412 comm. vehicles. **Civil aviation:** 678 mln. passenger-km (1978); 13 mln. freight ton-km (1978). **Chief ports:** Port-of-Spain.

Communications: Television sets: 110,000 in use (1976), 13,000 manuf. (1977). **Radios:** 270,000 licensed (1976), 15,000 manuf. (1977). **Telephones in use** (1978): 74,908. **Daily newspaper circ.** (1976): 144,000.

Health: Life expectancy at birth (1970): 64.08 male; 68.11 female. **Births** (per 1,000 pop. 1978): 25.3. **Deaths** (per 1,000 pop. 1978): 6.6. **Natural increase** (1978): 1.9%. **Hospital beds** (per 100,000 pop. 1977): 445. **Physicians** (per 100,000 pop 1977): 54. **Infant mortality** (per 1,000 pop. 1978): 28.6.

Education (1977): **Literacy:** 92%. **Pop. 5-19:** in school: 48%, teachers per 1,000: 22. **PQLI:** 87.

Columbus sighted Trinidad in 1498. A British possession since 1802, Trinidad and Tobago won independence Aug. 31, 1962. It became a republic in 1976. The People's National Movement party has held control of the government since 1956.

The nation is one of the most prosperous in the Caribbean, but unemployment usually averages 13%. Oil production has increased with offshore finds. Middle Eastern oil is refined and exported, mostly to the U.S.

Tunisia

Republic of Tunisia

People: Population (1979 est.): 6,312,000. **Age distrib.** (%) 0–14: 43.3 15–59: 50.9; 60+: 5.8. **Pop. density:** 95.93 per sq. mi. **Ethnic groups:** Arabs, small Berber minority; Europeans 1%. **Languages:** Arabic, French. **Religions:** Islam nearly universal.

Geography: Area: 63,378 sq. mi., slightly larger than Florida. **Location:** On N coast of Africa. **Neighbors:** Algeria on W, Libya on E. **Topography:** The N is wooded and fertile. The central coastal plains are given to grazing and orchards. The S is arid, approaching Sahara Desert. **Capital:** Tunis. **Cities** (1976 est.): Tunis 944,000; Sfax 475,000.

Government: Head of state: Pres. Habib Bourguiba; b. Aug. 3, 1903; in office: July 25, 1957. **Head of government:** Prime Min. Mohamed Mzali; b. Dec. 23, 1925; in office: Apr. 23, 1980. **Local divisions:** 13 governorates. **Armed forces:** regulars 22,300; para-military 2,500.

Economy: Industries: Food processing, textiles, clothing, leather, oil products, construction materials, tourism. **Chief crops:** Grains, dates, olives, citrus fruits, figs, vegetables, grapes. **Minerals:** Phosphates, iron, oil, lead, zinc. **Crude oil reserves** (1980): 2.25 bln. bbls. **Per capita arable land:** 1.3 acres. **Meat prod.** (1978): beef: 35,000 metric tons; lamb: 43,000 metric tons. **Fish catch** (1977): 38,400 metric tons. **Electricity prod.** (1978): 1.79 bln. kwh. **Crude steel prod.** (1979 est.): 150,000 metric tons. **Labor force:** 45% agric.

Finance: Currency: Dinar (Mar. 1980: .42 = $1 US). **Gross domestic product** (1978): $5.89 bln. **Per capita income** (1978) $934. **Imports** (1979): $2.56 bln.; partners (1978): Fr. 34%, W. Ger. 12%, It. 10%. **Exports** (1979): $1.58 bln.; partners (1978): It. 16%, Fr. 16%, W. Ger. 16%, Gr. 9%. **Tourists** (1977): 1,016,000; receipts: $323 mln. **National budget** (1978): $1.92 bln. revenues; $2.08 bln. expenditures. **International reserves less gold** (Mar. 1980): $539.7 mln. **Gold:** 170,000 oz t. **Consumer prices** (change in 1979): 7.8%.

Transport: Railway traffic (1978): 705.6 mln. passenger-km; 1.37 bln. net ton-km. **Motor vehicles:** in use (1975): 102,600 passenger cars, 67,000 comm. vehicles; assembled (1978): 2,124 passenger cars; 4,848 comm. vehicles. **Civil aviation:** 1,182 mln. passenger-km (1978); 11 mln. freight ton-km (1978). **Chief ports:** Tunis, Sfax, Bizerte.

Communications: Television sets: 208,000 in use (1976), 53,000 manuf. (1977). Radios: 810,000 in use (1976), 71,000 manuf. (1977). **Telephones in use** (1978): 144,116. **Daily newspaper circ.** (1976): 232,000.

Health: Life expectancy at birth (1975): 54.0 male; 56.0 female. **Births** (per 1,000 pop. 1975): 36.5. **Deaths** (per 1,000 pop. 1975): 12.5. **Natural increase** (1975): 2.4%. **Hospital beds** (per 100,000 pop. 1977): 229. **Physicians** (per 100,000 pop. 1977): 4. **Infant mortality** (per 1,000 pop. under 1 yr. 1975): 125.

Education (1977): **Literacy:** 40%. **Pop. 5-19:** in school: 50%, teachers per 1,000: 16. **PQLI:** 49.

Site of ancient Carthage, and a former Barbary state under the suzerainty of Turkey, Tunisia became a protectorate of France under a treaty signed May 12, 1881. The nation became independent Mar. 20, 1956, and ended the monarchy the following year. Habib Bourguiba has headed the country since independence.

Although Tunisia is a member of the Arab League, Bourguiba in the 1960s urged negotiations to end Arab-Israeli disputes and was denounced by other members. In 1966 he broke relations with Egypt but resumed them after the 1967 Arab-Israeli war. He again urged negotiations with Israel in June 1973.

Dozens were killed in rioting and labor violence in 1978, protesting wage curbs.

Tunisia survived a Libyan-engineered raid against the southern mining center of Gafsa, Jan. 1980. A liberal-minded government undertook steps to ease the blocked political situation.

Turkey

Republic of Turkey

People: Population (1979 est.): 44,561,000. **Age distrib.** (%): 0–14: 40.0; 15–59: 52.6; 60+: 7.2. **Pop. density:** 143.37 per sq. mi. **Urban** (1977): 44.6%. **Ethnic groups:** Turks 90%, Kurds 7%, Arabs 1.2%, Circassians, Greeks, Armenians, Georgians, Jews. **Languages:** Turkish, Kurdish. **Religions:** Moslems over 99%.

Geography: Area: 301,380 sq. mi., twice the size of California. **Location:** Occupies Asia Minor, between Mediterranean and Black Seas. **Neighbors:** Bulgaria, Greece on W, USSR (Georgia, Armenia) on N, Iran on E, Iraq, Syria on W. **Topography:** Central Turkey has wide plateaus, with hot, dry summers and cold winters. High mountains ring the interior on all but W, with more than 20 peaks over 10,000 ft. Rolling plains are in W; mild, fertile coastal plains are in S, W. **Capital:** Ankara. **Cities** (1978 est.): Istanbul 2,534,839; Ankara 1,698,542; Izmir 636,078; Adana 467,122.

Government: Head of state: Acting Pres. Ihsan Sabri Caglayangil; b. 1908; in office: Apr. 7, 1980. **Head of government:** Prime Min. Suleyman Demirel; b. 1924; in office: Nov. 12, 1979. **Local divisions:** 67 provinces, with appointed governors. **Armed forces:** regulars 566,000; reserves 425,000.

Economy: Industries: Silk, textiles, steel, shoes, furniture, cement, paper, glassware, appliances. **Chief crops:** Tobacco (6th largest producer), cereals, cotton, olives, figs, nuts, sugar, opium gums. **Minerals:** Antimony, chromium, mercury, borate, copper, molybdenum, magnesite, asbestos. **Crude oil reserves** (1980): 125 mln. bbls. **Other resources:** Wool, silk, forests. **Per capita arable land:** 1.4 acres. **Meat prod.** (1978): beef: 240,000 metric tons; lamb: 384,000 metric tons. **Fish catch** (1977): 155,300 metric tons. **Electricity prod.** (1978): 21.60 bln. kwh. **Crude steel prod.** (1979): 2.4 mln. metric tons. **Labor force:** 68% agric.; 16% manuf.

Finance: Currency: Lira (Mar. 1980: 70.7 = $1 US). **Gross domestic product** (1978): $52.47 bln. **Per capita income** (1975): $873. **Imports** (1979): $10.6 bln.; partners (1978): W. Ger. 16%, Fr. 8%, It. 6%, U.S. 6%, **Exports** (1979): $2.26 bln.; partners (1978): W. Ger. 22%, It. 8%, U.S. 7%, Fr. 6%. **Tourists** (1977): 1,661,400; receipts: $205 mln. **National budget** (1975): $7.36 bln. revenues; $8.19 bln. expenditures. **International reserves less gold** (Feb. 1980): $825 mln. **Gold:** 3.77 mln. oz t. **Consumer prices** (change in 1979): 58.7%.

Transport: Railway traffic (1978): 5.6 bln. passenger-km; 5.7 bln. net ton-km. **Motor vehicles:** in use (1976): 471,500 passenger cars, 230,800 comm. vehicles; assembled (1978): 54,120 passenger cars; 35,784 comm. vehicles. **Civil aviation:** 2,220 mln. passenger-km (1977); 19 mln. freight ton-km (1977). **Chief ports:** Istanbul, Izmir, Mersin, Samsun.

Communications: Television sets: 1.7 mln. in use (1976), 684,000 manuf. (1977). **Radios:** 4.2 mln. licensed (1976), 324,000 manuf. (1977). **Telephones in use** (1978): 1,378,620.

Health: Life expectancy at birth (1966): 53.7 male; 53.7 female. **Births** (per 1,000 pop. 1967): 39.6. **Deaths** (per 1,000 pop. 1967): 14.6. **Natural increase** (1967): 2.5%. **Hospital beds** (per 100,000 pop.1977): 195. **Physicians** (per 100,000 pop. 1977): 56. **Infant mortality** (per 1,000 pop. under 1 yr. 1967): 153.

Education (1977): **Literacy:** 60%. **Pop. 5-19:** in school: 49%, teachers per 1,000: 15. **PQLI:** 60.

Ancient inhabitants of Turkey were among the worlds first agriculturalists. Such civilizations as the Hittite, Phrygian, and Lydian flourished in Asiatic Turkey (Asia Minor), as did much of Greek civilization. After the fall of Rome in the 5th century, Constantinople was the capital of the Byzantine Empire for 1,000 years. It fell in 1453 to Ottoman Turks, who ruled a vast empire for over 400 years.

Just before World War I, Turkey, or the Ottoman Empire, ruled what is now Syria, Lebanon, Iraq, Jordan, Israel, Arabia, Yemen, and islands in the Aegean Sea.

Turkey joined Germany and Austria in World War I and its defeat resulted in loss of much territory and fall of the sultanate. A republic was declared Oct. 29, 1923. The Caliphate (spiritual leadership of Islam) was renounced 1924. Martial law, imposed in 1971, was ended in 1973 and political life is active and free.

Long embroiled with Greece over Cyprus, off Turkey's south coast, Turkey invaded the island July 20, 1974, after Greek officers seized the Cypriot government as a step toward unification with Greece. Turkey sought a new government for Cyprus, with Greek Cypriot and Turkish Cypriot zones. In reaction to Turkey's moves, the U.S. Congress cut off military aid in 1975. Turkey, in turn, suspended the use of most U.S. bases. A new base accord was tentatively reached in March, 1976 and aid was restored in 1978. Turkey and the USSR signed a nonaggression pact in 1978.

In June, 1971, Turkey agreed to stop all opium poppy production, in return for $37.5 million in economic aid from the U.S. In 1974 it announced it would resume opium production, with U.S. and U.N. controls, for medical use only.

Religious and ethnic tensions and active left and right extremists have caused endemic violence. Martial law was in effect from 1979, in approx. one-third of the nation's provinces.

Tuvalu

People: Population (1979 est.): 7,000. **Pop. density:** 700 per sq. mi. **Ethnic group:** Polynesian. **Languages:** Tuvaluan, English. **Religions:** mainly Protestant.

Geography: Area: 10 sq. mi., less than one-half the size of Manhattan. **Location:** 9 islands forming a NW-SE chain 360 mi. long in the SW Pacific O. **Neighbors:** Nearest are Samoa on SE, Fiji on S. **Topography:** The islands are all low-lying atolls, nowhere rising more than 15 ft. above sea level, composed of coral reefs. **Capital:** Funafuti.

Government: Head of state: Queen Elizabeth II, represented by Gov.-Gen. Fiatau Penitala Teo, b. July 23, 1911; in office: Oct. 1, 1978. **Head of government:** Prime Min. Toarlipi Lauti, b. Nov. 20, 1928; in office: Sept. 9, 1977. **Local divisions:** 8 island councils on the permanently inhabited islands.

Economy: Industries: Copra. **Chief crops:** Coconuts. **Labor force:** Approx. 1,500 Tuvaluans work overseas in the Gilberts' phosphate industry, or as overseas seamen.

Finance: Currency: Australian dollar. **Exports** (1976): $5,781; partners: UK.

Transport: Chief port: Funafuti.

Health: (including former Gilbert Is.) **Life expectancy at birth** (1962): 56.9 male; 59.0 female. **Births** (per 1,000 pop. 1971): 22.3. **Deaths** (per 1,000 pop. 1971): 6.5. **Natural increase** (1971): 1.6%. **Infant mortality** (per 1,000 pop. under 1 yr. 1971) : 48.9.

Education: Pop. 5–19: in school (1976): 1,794.

The Ellice Islands separated from the British Gilbert and Ellice Islands colony, 1975, and became independent Tuvalu Oct. 1, 1978. Under a Treaty of Friendship, pending ratification by the U.S. Senate, the U.S. relinquishes its claims to Funafuti, Nukufetau, Nukulailai (Nukulaelae), and Nurakita (Niulakita).

The only cash crop, copra, was devastated by hurricane damage, 1972. Britain is committed to providing extensive economic aid. Australian funding has provided for a marine training school and a deep-sea wharf.

Uganda

Republic of Uganda

People: Population (1979 est.): 13,225,000. **Age distrib.** (%): 0–14: 46.1; 15–59: 47.9; 60+: 5.8. **Pop. density:** 140.23 per sq. mi. **Urban** (1972): 7.1%. **Ethnic groups:** Bantu, Nilotic, Nilo-Hamitic, Sudanic tribes. **Languages:** English (official), Swahili (national), Luganda, others. **Religions:** Christians 50%, Moslems 6%, others.

Geography: Area: 91,134 sq. mi., slightly smaller than Oregon. **Location:** In E. Central Africa. **Neighbors:** Sudan on N, Zaire on W, Rwanda, Tanzania on S, Kenya on E. **Topography:** Most of Uganda is a high plateau 3,000-6,000 ft. high, with high Ruwenzori range in W (Mt. Margherita 16,750 ft.), volcanoes in SW, NE is arid, W and SW rainy. Lakes Victoria, Edward, Albert form much of borders. **Capital:** Kampala. **Cities** (1969 cen.): Kampala (met.) 330,700.

Government: Head of state: Presidential commission. **Head of government:** Chmn. military commission Paulo Muwenga; in office: May 12, 1980. **Local divisions:** 10 provinces. **Armed forces:** regulars 21,000 (pre-invasion).

Economy: Chief Crops: Coffee (68% of 1973 earnings), cotton, tea, corn, peanuts, sisal, oil seeds, tobacco, sugar. **Minerals:** Copper, tin. **Per capita arable land:** 0.7 acres. **Meat prod.** (1978): beef: 72,000 metric tons; lamb: 13,000 metric tons. **Fish catch** (1977): 178,600 metric tons. **Electricity prod.** (1978): 720.00 mln. kwh. **Labor force:** 90% agric.

Finance: Currency: Shilling (Mar. 1980: 7.33 = $1 US). **Gross domestic product** (1978): $8.36 bln. **Per capita income** (1975): $208. **Imports** (1978): $265 mln.; partners: Kenya 57%, UK 9%, W. Ger. 9%, It. 6%. **Exports** (1979): $434 mln.; partners: U.S. 38%, UK 17%, Neth. 6%, Fr. 5%. **Tourists** (1974): 10,300; receipts (1977): $1 mln. **National budget** (1972): $214.45 mln. revenues; $341.69 mln. expenditures. **International reserves less gold** (Aug. 1979): $134.8 mln. **Consumer prices** (change in 1978): 36.5%.

Transport: Motor vehicles: in use (1974): 27,000 passenger cars, 8,900 comm. vehicles.

Communications: Television sets: 71,000 in use (1976). **Radios:** 250,000 in use (1976). **Telephones in use** (1978): 48,884. **Daily newspaper circ.** (1976): 35,000; 3 per 1,000 pop.

Health: Life expectancy at birth (1975): 48.3 male; 51.7 female. **Births** (per 1,000 pop. 1975): 44.9. **Deaths** (per 1,000 pop. 1975): 16.0. **Natural increase** (1975): 2.9%. **Hospital beds** (per 100,000 pop. 1977): 157. **Physicians** (per 100,000 pop. 1977): 20. **Infant mortality** (per 1,000 live births 1975): 160.

Education (1977): **Literacy:** 25%. **Pop. 5-19:** in school: 27%, teachers per 1,000: 8. **PQLI:** 42.

Britain obtained a protectorate over Uganda in 1894. The country became independent Oct. 9, 1962, and a republic within the Commonwealth a year later. In 1967, the traditional kingdoms, including the powerful Buganda state, were abolished and the central government strengthened.

Gen. Idi Amin seized power from Prime Min. Milton Obote in 1971. As many as 300,000 of his opponents were reported killed in subsequent years. Amin was named president for life in 1976.

In 1972 Amin expelled nearly all of Uganda's 45,000 Asians. In 1973 the U.S., Canada, and Norway ended economic aid programs; the U.S. withdrew all diplomatic personnel.

A June 1977 Commonwealth conference condemned the Amin government for its "disregard for the sanctity of human life."

Amid worsening economic and domestic crises, Uganda's troops exchanged invasion attacks with long-standing foe Tanzania, 1978 to 1979. Tanzanian forces, coupled with Ugandan exiles and rebels, ended the dictatorial rule of Amin, Apr. 11, 1979. Two coups followed the provisional government of Yusufu Lule.

The U.S. reopened its embassy, reinstated economic aid, and ended its trade embargo in 1979.

Tanzanian troops still occupy the country, completely devastated by war.

Union of Soviet Socialist Republics

People: Population (1979 cen.): 262,436,000. **Age distrib.** (%): 0–19: 36.7; 20-59: 50.5; 60+: 12.7. **Pop. density:** 30.24 per sq. mi. **Urban** (1979): 62%. **Ethnic groups:** Russians 53%, Ukrainians 17%, Uzbeks 4%, Byelorussians 4%, 150 others. **Languages:** Slavic (Russian, Ukrainian, Byelorussian, Polish), Altaic (Turkish, etc.), other Indo-European, Uralian, Caucasian. **Religions:** Russian Orthodox 18%, Moslems 9%, other Orthodox, Protestants, Jews, Buddhists.

Geography: Area: 8,649,490 sq. mi., the largest country in the world, nearly 2½ times the size of the U.S. **Location:** Stretches from E. Europe across N Asia to the Pacific O. **Neighbors:** Finland, Poland, Czechoslovakia, Hungary, Romania on W, Turkey, Iran, Afghanistan, China, Mongolia, N. Korea on S. **Topography:** Covering one-sixth of the earth's land area, the USSR contains every type of climate except the distinctly tropical, and has a varied topography.

The European portion is a low plain, grassy in S, wooded in N with Ural Mtns. on the E. Caucasus Mts. on the S. Urals stretch N-S for 2,500 mi. The Asiatic portion is also a vast plain, with mountains on the S and in the E; tundra covers extreme N, with forest belt below; plains, marshes are in W, desert in SW. **Capital:** Moscow. **Cities** (1979 cen.): Moscow 7,831,000; Leningrad 4,073,000; Kiev 2,144,000; Tashkent 1,779,000; Kharkov 1,444,000; Gorky 1,344,000; Novosibirsk 1,312,000; Minsk 1,262,000; Kuibyshev 1,216,000; Sverdlovsk 1,211,000; Dnepropetrovsk 1,066,000; Tbilisi 1,066,000; Odessa 1,046,000; Chelyabinsk 1,031,000; Baku 1,022,000; Donetsk 1,021,000; Yerevan 1,019,000; Omsk, 1,014,000.

Government: Head of state: Pres. Leonid I. Brezhnev; b. Dec. 19, 1906; in office: June 16, 1977. **Head of government:** Chmn. Alexei N. Kosygin; b. Feb. 20, 1904; in office: Oct. 15, 1964. **Head of Communist Party:** Gen. Sec. Leonid Brezhnev; in office: Oct. 14, 1964. **Local divisions:** 15 union republics, within which are 20 autonomous republics, 6 krays (territories), 120 oblasts (regions), 8 autonomous oblasts, 10 national areas. **Armed forces:** regulars 3,658,000; reserves 5,000,000; paramilitary 460,000.

Economy: Industries: Steel, machinery, machine tools, vehicles, chemicals, cement, textiles, appliances, paper. **Chief crops:** Grain, cotton, sugar beets, potatoes, vegetables, sunflowers. **Minerals:** Iron (41% of world reserves), manganese (88%), mercury, potash, antimony, bauxite, cobalt, chromium, copper, coal (58%), gold, lead, molybdenum, nickel, phosphates (30%), silver, tin, tungsten, zinc, oil (59%), potassium salts (54%). **Crude oil reserves** (1980): 67.00 bln. bbls. **Other resources:** Forests (25% of world reserves). **Per capita arable land:** 2.1 acres. **Meat prod.** (1978): beef: 7.1 mln. metric tons; pork: 5.1 mln. metric tons; lamb: 885,000 metric tons. **Fish catch** (1977): 9.4 mln. metric tons. **Electricity prod.** (1978): 1,200 bln. kwh. **Crude steel prod.** (1979): 149.0 mln. metric tons. **Labor force:** 23% agric.; 38% manuf. & constr.

Finance: Currency: Ruble (Mar. 1980: .64 = $1 US). **Net material product** (1978): $278.9 bln. **Per capita income** (1976): $2,600. **Imports** (1979): $57.77 bln.; partners (1978): E. Ger. 11%, Pol. 10%, Czech. 9%, Bulg. 9%. **Exports** (1979): $54.76 bln.; partners (1978): E. Ger. 11%, Pol. 10%, Bulg. 9%, Czech. 8%. **Tourists** (1977): 4,399,800. **Consumer prices** (change in 1979): 0.7%.

Transport: Railway traffic (1978): 332.4 bln. passenger-km; 3,426 bln. net ton-km. **Motor vehicles:** in use (1975): 4.7 mln. passenger cars, 5.1 mln. comm. vehicles; manuf. (1977): 1.28 mln. passenger cars; 781,200 comm. vehicles. **Civil aviation** (international only): 8.4 bln. passenger-km (1978); 270 mln. freight ton-km (1978). **Chief ports:** Leningrad, Odessa, Murmansk, Kaliningrad, Archangelsk, Riga, Vladivostock.

Communications: Television sets: 55.2 mln. in use (1975), 7.07 mln. manuf. (1977). **Radios:** 122.5 mln. in use (1975), 8.65 mln. manuf. (1977). **Telephones in use** (1978): 19,600,000. **Daily newspaper circ.** (1977): 102,462,000; 396 per 1,000 pop.

Health: Life expectancy at birth (1972): 64 male; 74 female. **Births** (per 1,000 pop. 1977): 18.1. **Deaths** (per 1,000 pop. 1976): 9.6. **Natural increase** (1976): .9%. **Hospital beds** (per 100,000 pop. 1977): 1,213. **Physicians** (per 100,000 pop. 1977): 346. **Infant mortality** (per 1,000 live births 1974): 27.7.

Education (1977): **Literacy:** 99%. **Pop. 5-19:** in school: 58%, teachers per 1,000: 37. **PQLI:** 92.

The USSR is nominally a federation consisting of 15 union republics, the largest being the Russian Soviet Federated Socialist Republic. Important positions in the republics are filled by centrally chosen appointees, often ethnic Russians.

Beginning in 1939 the USSR by means of military action and negotiation overran contiguous territory and independent republics, including all or part of Lithuania, Latvia, Estonia, Poland, Czechoslovakia, Romania, Germany, Tannu Tuva, and Japan. The union republics are:

Republic	**Area** sq. mi.	**Pop.** (cen. 1979)
Russian SFSR	6,593,391	137,552,000
Ukrainian SSR	232,046	49,757,000
Uzbek SSR	158,069	15,391,000
Kazakh SSR	1,064,092	14,685,000
Byelorussian SSR	80,154	9,559,000
Azerbaijan SSR	33,436	6,028,000
Georgian SSR	26,911	5,016,000
Moldavian SSR	13,012	3,948,000
Tadzhik SSR	54,019	3,801,000
Kirghiz SSR	76,642	3,529,000
Lithuanian SSR	26,173	3,399,000
Armenian SSR	11,306	3,031,000
Turkmen SSR	188,417	2,759,000
Latvian SSR	24,695	2,521,000
Estonian SSR	17,413	1,466,000

The **Russian Soviet Federated Socialist Republic** contains over 50% of the population of the USSR and includes 76% of its territory. It extends from the old Estonian, Latvian, and Finnish borders and the Byelorussian and Ukrainian lines on the W, to the shores of the Pacific, and from the Arctic on the N to the Black and Caspian seas and the borders of Kazakh SSR, Mongolia, and Manchuria on the S. Siberia encompasses a large part of the RSFSR area. Capital: Moscow.

Parts of eastern and western Siberia have been transformed by steel mills, huge dams, oil and gas industries, electric railroads, and highways.

The **Ukraine,** the most densely populated of the republics, borders on the Black Sea, with Poland, Czechoslovakia, Hungary, and Romania on the W and SW. Capital: Kiev.

The Ukraine contains the arable black soil belt, the chief wheat-producing section of the Soviet Union. Sugar beets, potatoes, and livestock are important.

The Donets Basin has large deposits of coal, iron and other metals. There are chemical and machine industries and salt mines.

Byelorussia (White Russia). Capital: Minsk. Chief industries include machinery, tools, appliances, tractors, clocks, cameras, steel, cement, textiles, paper, leather, glass. Main crops are grain, flax, potatoes, sugar beets.

Azerbaijan boasts near Baku, the capital, important oil fields. Its natural wealth includes deposits of iron ore, cobalt, etc. A high-yield winter wheat is grown, as are fruits. It produces iron, steel, cement, fertilizers, synthetic rubber, electrical and chemical equipment. It borders on Iran and Turkey.

Georgia, in the western part of Transcaucasia, contains the largest manganese mines in the world. There are rich timber resources and coal mines. Basic industries are food, textiles, iron, steel. Grain, tea, tobacco, fruits, grapes are grown. Capital: Tbilisi (Tiflis). Despite massive party and government purges since 1972, illegal private enterprise and Georgian nationalist feelings persist; attempts to repress them have led to violence.

Armenia is mountainous, sub-tropical, extensively irrigated. Copper, zinc, aluminum, molybdenum, and marble are mined. Instrument making is important. Capital: Erevan.

Uzbekistan, most important economically of the Central Asia republics, produces 67% of USSR cotton, 50% of rice, 33% of silk, 34% of astrakhan, 85% of hemp. Industries include iron, steel, cars, tractors, TV and radio sets, textiles, food. Mineral wealth includes coal, sulphur, copper, and oil. Capital: Tashkent.

Turkmenistan in Central Asia, produces cotton, maize, carpets, chemicals. Minerals: oil, coal, sulphur, barite, lime, salt, gypsum. The Kara Kum desert occupies 80% of the area. Capital: Ashkhabad.

Tadzhikistan borders on China and Afghanistan. Over half the population are Tadzhiks, mostly Moslems, speaking an Iranian dialect. Chief occupations are farming and cattle breeding. Cotton, grain, rice, and a variety of fruits are grown. Heavy industry, based on rich mineral deposits, coal and hydroelectric power, has replaced handicrafts. Capital: Dushanbe.

Kazakhstan extends from the lower reaches of the Volga in Europe to the Altai Mtns. on the Chinese border. It has vast deposits of coal, oil, iron, tin, copper, lead, zinc, etc. Fish for its canning industry are caught in Lake Balkhash and the Caspian and Aral seas. The capital is Alma-Ata. About 50% of the population is Russian or Ukrainian, working in the virgin-grain lands opened up after 1954, and in the growing industries.

Kirghizia is the eastern part of Soviet Central Asia, on the frontier of Xinjiang, China. The people breed cattle and horses and grow tobacco, cotton, rice, sugar beets. Industries include machine and instrument making, chemicals. Capital: Frunze.

Moldavia, in the SW part of the USSR, is a fertile black earth plain bordering Romania and includes Bessarabia. It is an agricultural region that grows grains, fruits, vegetables, and tobacco. Textiles, wine, food and electrical equipment industries have been developed. Capital: Kishinev. The region was taken from Romania in 1940; the people speak Romanian.

Lithuania, on the Baltic, produces cattle, hogs, electric motors, and appliances. The capital is Vilnius (Vilna). **Latvia** on the Baltic and the Gulf of Riga, has timber and peat resources est. at 3 bln. tons. In addition to agricultural products it produces rubber goods, dyes, fertilizers, glassware, telephone apparatus, TV and radio sets, railroad cars. Capital: Riga.

Estonia, also on the Baltic, has textiles, shipbuilding, timber, roadmaking and mining equipment industries and a shale oil refining industry. Capital: Tallinn. The 3 Baltic states were provinces of imperial Russia before World War I, were independent nations between World Wars I and II, but were conquered by Russia in 1940. The U.S. has never formally recognized the takeover.

Economy. Almost all legal economic enterprises are state-owned. There were 29,600 collective farms in 1976, along with 18,064 larger state farms. A huge illegal black market plays an important role in distribution; illegal private production and service firms are periodically exposed.

The USSR is incalculably rich in natural resources; distant Siberian reserves are being exploited with Japanese assistance. Its heavy industry is 2d only to the U.S. It leads the world in oil and steel production. Consumer industries have lagged comparatively. Agricultural output has expanded, but in poor crop years the USSR has been forced to make huge grain purchases from the West. Shortages and rationing of basic food products periodically occur.

Exports include petroleum and its products, iron and steel, rolled non-ferrous metals, industrial plant equipment, arms, lumber, cotton, asbestos, gold, manganese, and others. 55% of its trade is with Communist nations, 33% with the West, which supplies advanced technology. The USSR had a $4 billion trade deficit with the West in 1976, financed by gold sales, long-term loans, and a trade surplus with East Europe and underdeveloped countries. Debt to the West reached $14.4 billion by 1977.

Industrial growth in 1979 dropped, due to short falls in oil, coal, and steel industries, as well as the worst grain harvest since 1975.

History. Slavic tribes began migrating into Russia from the W in the 5th century AD. The first Russian state, founded by Scandinavian chieftains, was established in the 9th century, centering in Novgorod and Kiev.

In the 13th century the Mongols overran the country. It recovered under the grand dukes and princes of Muscovy, or Moscow, and by 1480 freed itself from the Mongols. Ivan the Terrible was the first to be formally proclaimed Tsar (1547). Peter the Great (1682-1725), extended the domain and in 1721, founded the Russian Empire.

Western ideas and the beginnings of modernization spread through the huge Russian empire in the 19th and early 20th centuries. But political evolution failed to keep pace.

Military reverses in the 1905 war with Japan and in World War I led to the breakdown of the Tsarist regime. The 1917 Revolution began in March with a series of sporadic strikes for higher wages by factory workers. A provisional democratic government under Prince Georgi Lvov was established but was quickly followed in May by the second provisional government, led by Alexander Kerensky. The Kerensky government and the freely-elected Constituent Assembly were overthrown in a Communist coup led by Vladimir Ilyich Lenin Nov. 7.

Lenin's death Jan. 21, 1924, resulted in an internal power struggle from which Joseph Stalin eventually emerged the absolute ruler of Russia. Stalin secured his position at first by exiling opponents, but from the 1930s to 1953, he resorted to a series of "purge" trials, mass executions, and mass exiles in work camps. These measures resulted in millions of deaths, according to most estimates.

Germany and the USSR signed a non-aggression pact Aug. 1939; Nazi forces launched a massive invasion of the Soviet Union, June 1941. Notable heroic episode was the "900 days" siege of Leningrad, lasting to Jan. 1944, and causing 1,000,000 deaths; the city was never taken. Russian winter counterthrusts, 1941 to '42 and 1942 to '43, stopped the German advance. Turning point was the failure of German troops to take and hold Stalingrad, Sept. 1942 to Feb. 1943. With British and U.S. Lend-Lease aid and sustaining great casualties, the Russians drove the Axis from eastern Europe and the Balkans in the next 2 years.

After Stalin died, Mar. 5, 1953, Nikita Khrushchev was elected first secretary of the Central Committee. In 1956 he condemned Stalin. "De-Stalinization" of the country on all levels was effected after Stalin's body was removed from the Lenin-Stalin tomb in Moscow.

Under Khrushchev the open antagonism of Poles and Hungarians toward domination by Moscow was brutally suppressed in 1956. He advocated peaceful co-existence with the capitalist countries, but continued arming the USSR with nuclear weapons. He aided the Cuban revolution under Fidel Castro but withdrew Soviet missiles from Cuba during confrontation by U.S. Pres. Kennedy, Sept.-Oct. 1962.

The USSR, the U.S., and Great Britain initialed a joint treaty July 25, 1963, banning above-ground nuclear tests.

Khrushchev was suddenly deposed, Oct. 1964, and replaced as party first secretary by Leonid I. Brezhnev, and as premier by Aleksei N. Kosygin.

In 1968, the U.S. and USSR joined 59 other nations in signing a treaty to bar spread of nuclear weapons.

In Aug. 1968 Russian, Polish, East German, Hungarian, and Bulgarian military forces invaded Czechoslovakia to put a curb on liberalization policies of the Czech government. The USSR declared it had a duty to intervene in nations where socialism was "imperiled" according to the "Brezhnev Doctrine."

The USSR in 1971 continued heavy arms shipments to Egypt. In July 1972 Egypt ordered most of the 20,000 Soviet military personnel in that country to leave. When Egypt and Syria attacked Israel in Oct. 1973, the USSR launched huge arms airlifts to the 2 Arab nations. In 1974, the Soviet replenished the arms used or lost by the Syrians in the 1973 war, and continued some shipments to Egypt.

Massive Soviet military aid to North Vietnam in the late 1960s and early 1970s helped assure Communist victories throughout Indo-China. Soviet arms aid and advisers were sent to several African countries in the 1970s, including Algeria, Angola, Somalia, and Ethiopia.

In 1972, the U.S. and USSR reached temporary agreements to freeze intercontinental missiles at their current levels, to limit defensive missiles to 200 each and to cooperate on health, environment, space, trade, and science. The U.S. and USSR, June 18, 1979, signed a strategic arms treaty limiting both nations to the same maximum number of long-range bombers and missiles.

Meanwhile, under Brezhnev, dissident intellectuals were repressed and purge-type trials resumed.

On Aug. 1, 1975, 35 countries of Europe and North America signed a European security pact tacitly approving current boundaries and urging freer movement of people and ideas. Most members of Russian groups set up to monitor the pact were jailed in a 1978 crackdown.

More than 130,000 Jews and over 40,000 ethnic Germans were allowed to emigrate from the USSR in the 1970s, following pressure from the West. Many leading figures in the arts also left the country.

Government. The Communist Party leadership dominates all areas of national life. A Politburo of 14 full members and 8 candidate members makes all major political, economic, and foreign policy decisions. Party membership in 1978 was reported to be over 16,000,000.

United Arab Emirates

People: Population (1979 est.): 871,000. **Pop. density:** 22.19 per sq. mi. **Ethnic groups:** Arabs 72%, Iranians, Pakistanis and Indians 26%. **Languages:** Arabic (official), Persian, Hindi, Urdu. **Religions:** Moslems 96.7%, Christians 1.3%.

Geography: Area: 32,000 sq. mi., the size of Maine. **Location:** On the S shore of the Persian Gulf. **Neighbors:** Qatar on N, Saudi Ar. on W, S, Oman on E. **Topography:** A barren, flat coastal plain gives way to uninhabited sand dunes on the S. Hajar Mtns. are on E. **Capital:** Abu Dhabi. **Cities** (1975 est.): Dubai 66,000; Abu Dhabi 55,000.

Government: Head of state: Pres. Zayed bin Sultan Al Nahyan, b. 1923; in office: Dec. 2, 1971. **Head of government:** Prime Min. Rashid bin Saeed Al Maktoum; in office: June 25, 1979. **Local divisions:** 7 autonomous emirates: Abu Dhabi, Ajman, Dubai, Fujaira, Ras al-Khaimah, Sharjah, Umm al-Qaiwain.

Armed forces: regulars 25,150.

Economy: Chief crops: Vegetables. **Minerals:** Oil. **Crude oil reserves** (1980): 29.4 bln. bbls. **Per capita arable land:** 0.02 acres. **Fish catch** (1977): 64,400 metric tons. **Electricity prod.** (1977): 700.00 mln. kwh.

Finance: Currency: Dirham (Mar. 1980: 3.74 = $1 US). **Gross domestic product** (1978): $13.79 bln. **Per capita income** (1976): $11,000. **Imports** (1978): $5.36 bln.; partners (1977): Jap. 19%, UK 18%, U.S. 11%, W. Ger. 9%. **Exports** (1979): $13.39 bln.; partners (1977): Jap. 26%, U.S. 16%, Fr. 12%, Neth. 7%. **International reserves less gold** (Mar. 1980): $1.09 bln. **Gold:** 577,000 oz t.

Transport: Chief ports: Dubai, Abu Dhabi.

Communications: Radios: 55,000 in use (1975). **Telephones in use** (1978): 96,847. **Daily newspaper circ.,** (1977): 2,000, 8 per 1,000 pop.

Health: Hospital beds (per 100,000 pop. 1977): 228. **Physicians** (per 100,000 pop. 1977): 130.

Education (1977): **Literacy:** 21%. **Pop. 5-19:** in school: 35%, teachers per 1,000: 24. **PQLI:** 35.

The 7 "Trucial Sheikdoms" gave Britain control of defense and foreign relations in the 19th century. They merged to become an independent state Dec. 2, 1971.

The Abu Dhabi Petroleum Co. was fully nationalized in 1975. Oil revenues have given the UAE one of the highest per capita GNPs in the world. International banking has grown in recent years.

United Kingdom of Great Britain and Northern Ireland

People: Population (1979 est.): 55,901,000. **Age distrib.** (%): 0–4: 22.9; 15–59: 57.4; 60+: 19.7. **Pop. density:** 592.48 per sq. mi. **Urban** (1973): Eng. & Wales: 77.7%, N. Ire.: 54.7%, Scot. (1974): 70.0%. **Ethnic groups:** English 81.5%, Scottish 9.6%, Irish 2.4, Welsh 1.9%, Ulster 1.8%; West Indian, Indian, Pakistani over 2%; others. **Languages:** English nearly universal; Welsh spoken in western Wales. **Religions:** Church of England 55%, Roman Catholics 10%, Presbyterians 3%, Methodists 1%, Jews 1%, other Protestants, Hindus, Moslems.

Geography: Area: 94,214 sq. mi., slightly smaller than Oregon. **Location:** Off the NW coast of Europe, across English Channel, Strait of Dover, and North Sea. **Neighbors:** Ireland to W, France to SE. **Topography:** England is mostly rolling land, rising to Uplands of southern Scotland; Lowlands are in center of Scotland, granite Highlands are in N. Coast is heavily indented, especially on W. British Isles have milder climate than N Europe, due to the Gulf Stream, and ample rainfall. Severn, 220 mi., and Thames, 215 mi., are longest rivers. **Capital:** London. **Cities** (1978 est.): London 7,028,200; Birmingham 1,058,800; Glasgow 832,097; Leeds 744,500; Sheffield 588,000; Liverpool 539,700; Manchester 490,000; Edinburgh 463,923; Bradford 458,900; Bristol 416,300; Belfast 357,600.

Government: Head of state: Queen Elizabeth II; b. Apr. 21, 1926; in office: Feb. 6, 1952. **Head of government:** Prime Min. Margaret Thatcher; b. Oct. 13, 1925; in office: May 4, 1979. **Local divisions:** England and Wales: 47 non-metro counties, 6 metro counties, Greater London; Scotland: 9 regions, 3 island areas; N. Ireland: 26 districts. **Armed forces:** regulars 322,891; reserves 257,640.

Economy: Industries: Steel, metals, vehicles, shipbuilding, shipping, banking, insurance, appliances, textiles, chemicals, electronics, aircraft, machinery, scientific instruments, distilling. **Chief crops:** Grains, sugar beets, fruits, vegetables. **Minerals:** Coal, tin, oil, gas, limestone, iron, salt, clay, chalk, gypsum, lead, silica. **Crude oil reserves** (1980): 15.4 bln. bbls. **Per capita arable land:** 0.3 acres. **Meat prod.** (1978): beef: 970,000 metric tons; pork: 800,000 metric tons; lamb: 235,000 metric tons. **Fish catch** (1977): 1 mln. metric tons. **Electricity prod.** (1978): 287.74 bln. kwh. **Crude steel prod.** (1979): 21.6 mln. metric tons. **Labor force:** 3% agric.; 33% manuf.

Finance: Currency: Pound (Mar. 1980: 1 = $2.17 US). **Gross domestic product** (1978): $309.65 bln. **Per capita income** (1978): $4,955. **Imports** (1979): $102.95 bln.; partners (1978): W. Ger. 11%, U.S. 10%, Fr. 8%, Neth. 6%. **Exports** (1979): $91.02 bln.; partners (1978): U.S. 9%, W. Ger. 8%, Fr. 7%, Neth. 6%. **Tourists** (1977): 11,490,000; receipts $3.81 bln. **National budget** (1978): $103.86 bln. revenues; $115.95 bln. expenditures. **International reserves less gold** (Mar. 1980): $19.99 bln. **Gold:** 18.25 mln. oz t. **Consumer prices** (change in 1979): 13.4%.

Transport: Railway traffic (1978): 30.7 bln. passenger-km; 19.98 bln. net ton-km. **Motor vehicles:** in use (1976): 14.56 mln. passenger cars, 1.90 mln. comm. vehicles; manuf. (1978): 1.22 mln. passenger cars; 384,000 comm. vehicles. **Civil aviation:** 40,416 mln. passenger-km (1978); 1,160 mln. freight ton-km (1978). **Chief ports:** London, Liverpool, Glasgow, Southampton, Cardiff, Belfast.

Communications: Television sets: 17.7 mln. licensed (1976), 2.18 mln. manuf. (1977). **Radios:** 39.5 mln. licensed (1976), 891,000 manuf. (1977). **Telephones in use** (1978): 23,182,239. **Daily newspaper circ.** (1977): 22,900,000; 410 per 1,000 pop.

Health: Life expectancy at birth: (1970): 67.8 male; 73.8 female. **Births:** (per 1,000 pop. 1977): 11.8. **Deaths:** (per 1,000 pop. 1977): 11.7. **Natural increase:** (1977): .01%. **Hospital beds** (per 100,000 pop. 1977): 894. **Physicians** (per 100,000 pop. 1977): 153. **Infant mortality:** (per 1,000 live births 1977): 14.0.

Education (1977): **Literacy:** 99%. **Pop. 5-19:** in school: 83%, teachers per 1,000: 45. **PQLI:** 94.

The United Kingdom of Great Britain and Northern Ireland comprises England, Wales, Scotland, and Northern Ireland.

Queen and Royal Family. The ruling sovereign is Elizabeth II of the House of Windsor, born Apr. 21, 1926, elder daughter of King George VI. She succeeded to the throne Feb. 6, 1952, and was crowned June 2, 1953. She was married Nov. 20, 1947, to Lt. Philip Mountbatten, born June 10, 1921, former Prince of Greece. He was created Duke of Edinburgh, Earl of Merioneth, and Baron Greenwich, and given the style H.R.H., Nov. 19, 1947; he was given the title Prince of the United Kingdom and Northern Ireland Feb. 22, 1957. Prince Charles Philip Arthur George, born Nov. 14, 1948, is the Prince of Wales and heir apparent.

Parliament is the legislative governing body for the United Kingdom, with certain powers over dependent units. It consists of 2 houses: The **House of Lords** includes 763 hereditary and 314 life peers and peeresses, certain judges, 2 archbishops and 24 bishops of the Church of England. Total membership is over 1,000. The **House of Commons** has 635 members, who are elected by direct ballot and divided as follows: England 516; Wales 36; Scotland 71; Northern Ireland 12.

Resources and Industries. Great Britain's major occupations are manufacturing and trade. Metals and metal-using industries contribute more than 50% of the exports. Of about 60 million acres of land in England, Wales and Scotland, 46 million are farmed, of which 17 million are arable, the rest pastures.

Large oil and gas fields have been found in the North Sea. Commercial oil production began in 1975; self-sufficiency is expected by the early 1980s with projected output of 2 million barrels a day. There are large deposits of coal; 1977-78 output was 119 million tons.

The railroads, nationalized since 1948, have been reduced in total length, with a basic network, Dec. 1978, of 11,123 mi. The merchant marine totaled 49,700,000 gross registered tons in July 1978, comprising nearly 7.5% of active world shipping.

The world's first power station using atomic energy to create electricity for civilian use began operation Oct. 17, 1956, at Calder Hall in Cumbria.

The Labor government raised taxes, 1966-69; devalued the pound to $2.40 in 1967 and took various measures to improve exports and cut imports. The Conservative government put a freeze on prices, wages and rents in 1972 to combat inflation. In 1973 it substituted "restraints." A Labor government elected in 1974, obtained trade union approval of wage curbs, confirmed in 1977. Yet inflation continued, and the pound dropped to record lows in 1976. Unemployment rose to a postwar high in 1977. Inflation eased by 1978 but unemployment remained a problem. The 1979 Conservative government set goals to restrain trade unions, cut personal income taxes, and bolster the armed forces.

Britain imports all of its cotton, rubber, sulphur, 80% of its wool, half of its food and iron ore, also certain amounts of paper, tobacco, chemicals. Manufactured goods made from these basic materials have been exported since the industrial age began. Main exports are machinery, chemicals, woolen and synthetic textiles, clothing, autos and trucks, iron and steel, locomotives, ships, jet aircraft, farm machinery, drugs, radio, TV, radar and navigation equipment, scientific instruments, arms, whisky.

Religion and Education. The Church of England is Protestant Episcopal. The queen is its temporal head, with rights of appointments to archbishoprics, bishoprics, and other offices. There are 2 provinces, Canterbury and York, each headed by an archbishop. About 48% of the population is baptized into the Church, less than 10% is confirmed. Most famous church is Westminster Abbey (1050-1760), site of coronations, tombs of Elizabeth I, Mary of Scots, kings, poets, and of the Unknown Warrior.

Other major religious affiliations represented in the UK: Roman Catholics, Methodists, Jews, Baptists, United Reformed Church (Congregational and Presbyterian), Calvinistic Methodist (Presbyterian) Church of Wales, Unitarians, Society of Friends, Mormons, Church of Christ Scientist, The Presbyterian Church in Ireland, The Church of Scotland (Presbyterian), Hindus, Moslems.

Education is free and compulsory from 5 to 16. The most celebrated British universities are Oxford and Cambridge, each dating to the 13th century. There are 40 other universities.

History. Britain was part of the continent of Europe until about 6,000 BC, but migration of peoples across the English Channel continued long afterward. Celts arrived 2,500 to 3,000 years ago. Their language survives in Welsh, Cornish, and Gaelic enclaves.

England was added to the Roman Empire in 43 AD. After the withdrawal of Roman legions in 410, waves of Jutes, Angles, and Saxons arrived from German lands. They contended with Danish raiders for control from the 8th through 11th centuries.

The last successful invasion was by French-speaking Normans in 1066, who united the country with their dominions in France.

Opposition by nobles to royal authority forced King John to sign the Magna Carta in 1215, a guarantee of rights and the rule of law. In the ensuing decades, the foundations of the parliamentary system were laid.

English dynastic claims to large parts of France led to the Hundred Years War, 1338-1453, and the defeat of England. A long civil war, the War of the Roses, lasted 1455-85, and ended with the establishment of the powerful Tudor monarchy. A distinct English civilization flourished. The economy prospered over long periods of domestic peace unmatched in continental Europe. Religious independence was secured when the Church of England was separated from the authority of the Pope in 1534.

Under Queen Elizabeth I, Britain became a major naval power, leading to the founding of colonies in the new world and the expansion of trade with Europe and the Orient. Scotland was united with England when James VI of Scotland was crowned James I of England in 1603.

A struggle between Parliament and the Stuart kings led to a bloody civil war, 1642-49, and the establishment of a republic under the Puritan Oliver Cromwell. The monarchy was restored in 1660, but the "Glorious Revolution" of 1688 confirmed the sovereignty of Parliament: a Bill of Rights was granted 1689.

In the 18th century, parliamentary rule was strengthened. Technological and entrepreneurial innovations led to the Industrial Revolution. The 13 North American colonies were lost, but replaced by growing empires in Canada and India. Britain's role in the defeat of Napoleon, 1815, strengthened its position as the leading world power.

The extension of the franchise in 1832 and 1867, the formation of trade unions, and the development of universal public education were among the drastic social changes which accompanied the spread of industrialization and urbanization in the 19th century. Large parts of Africa and Asia were added to the empire during the reign of Queen Victoria, 1837-1901.

Though victorious in World War I, Britain suffered huge casualties and economic dislocation. Ireland became independent in 1921, and independence movements became active in India and other colonies.

The country suffered major bombing damage in World War II, but held out against Germany singlehandedly for a year after the fall of France in 1940.

Industrial growth continued in the postwar period, but Britain lost its leadership position to other powers. Labor governments passed socialist programs nationalizing some basic industries and expanding social security. Nearly all of the empire was given independence. Britain joined the NATO alliance and, in 1973, the European Communities (Common Market).

Wales

The Principality of Wales in western Britain has an area of 8,016 sq. mi. and a population (est. 1977) of 2,768,200. Cardiff is the capital, pop. (1977 est.) 278,900.

England and Wales are administered as a unit. Less than 20% of the population of Wales speak both English and Welsh; about 32,000 speak Welsh solely. Welsh nationalism is advocated by a segment. A 1979 referendum rejected, 4-1, the creation of an elected Welsh Assembly.

Early Anglo-Saxon invaders drove Celtic peoples into the mountains of Wales, terming them Waelise (Welsh, or foreign). There they developed a distinct nationality. Members of the ruling house of Gwynedd in the 13th century fought England but were crushed, 1283. Edward of Caernarvon, son of Edward I of England, was created Prince of Wales, 1301.

Scotland

Scotland, a kingdom now united with England and Wales in Great Britain, occupies the northern 37% of the main British island, and the Hebrides, Orkney, Shetland and smaller islands. Length, 275 mi., breadth approx. 150 mi., area, 30,405 sq. mi., population (est. 1977) 5,195,600.

The Lowlands, a belt of land approximately 60 mi. wide from the Firth of Clyde to the Firth of Forth, divide the farming region of the Southern Uplands from the granite Highlands of the North, contain 75% of the population and most of the industry. The Highlands, famous for hunting and fishing, have been opened to industry by many hydroelectric power stations.

Edinburgh, pop. (1978 est.) 463,929, is the capital. Glasgow, pop. (1978 est.) 832,097, is Britain's greatest industrial center. It is a shipbuilding complex on the Clyde and an ocean port. Aberdeen, pop. (1978 est.) 208,340, NE of Edinburgh, is a major port, center of granite industry, fish processing, and North Sea oil exploitation. Dundee, pop. (1978 est.) 192,765, NE of Edinburgh, is an industrial and fish processing center. About 90,000 persons speak Gaelic as well as English.

History. Scotland was called Caledonia by the Romans who battled early Pict and Celtic tribes and occupied southern areas from the 1st to the 4th centuries. Missionaries from Britain introduced Christianity in the 4th century; St. Columba, an Irish monk, converted most of Scotland in the 6th century.

The Kingdom of Scotland was founded in 1018. William Wallace and Robert Bruce both defeated English armies 1297 and 1314, respectively.

In 1603 James VI of Scotland, son of Mary, Queen of Scots, succeeded to the throne of England as James I, and effected the Union of the Crowns. In 1707 Scotland received representation in the British Parliament, resulting from the union of former separate Parliaments. Its executive in the British cabinet is the Secretary of State for Scotland. The growing Scottish National Party urges independence. A 1979 referendum on the creation of an elected Scotland Assembly was defeated.

There are 8 universities. Memorials of Robert Burns, Sir Walter Scott, John Knox, Mary, Queen of Scots draw many tourists, as do the beauties of the Trossachs, Loch Katrine, Loch Lomond and abbey ruins.

Industries. Engineering products are the most important industry, with growing emphasis on office machinery, autos, electronics and other consumer goods. Oil has been discovered offshore in the North Sea, stimulating on-shore support industries.

Scotland produces fine woolens, worsteds, tweeds, silks, fine linens and jute. It is known for its special breeds of cattle and sheep. Fisheries have large hauls of herring, cod, whiting. Whisky is the biggest export.

The Hebrides are a group of c. 500 islands, 100 inhabited, off the W coast. The Inner Hebrides include **Skye, Mull,** and **Iona,** the last famous for the arrival of St. Columba, 563 AD. The Outer Hebrides include **Lewis** and **Harris.** Industries include sheep raising and weaving. The **Orkney Islands,** c. 90, are to the NE. The capital is Kirkwall, on Pomona Is. Fish curing, sheep raising and weaving are occupations. NE of the Orkneys are the 200 **Shetland Islands,** 24 inhabited, home of Shetland pony. The Orkneys and Shetlands have become centers for the North Sea oil industry.

Northern Ireland

Six of the 9 counties of Ulster, the NE corner of Ireland, constitute Northern Ireland, with the parliamentary boroughs of Belfast and Londonderry. Area 5,463 sq. mi., 1978 est. pop. 1,540,000, capital and chief industrial center, Belfast, (1978 est.) 357,600.

Industries. Shipbuilding, including large tankers, has long been an important industry, centered in Belfast, the largest port. Linen manufacture is also important, along with apparel, rope, and twine. Growing diversification has added engineering products, synthetic fibers, and electronics. They are large numbers of cattle, hogs, and sheep, potatoes, poultry, and dairy foods are also produced.

Government. An act of the British Parliament, 1920, divided Northern from Southern Ireland, each with a parliament and government. When Ireland became a dominion, 1921, and later a republic, Northern Ireland chose to remain a part of the United Kingdom. It elects 12 members to the British House of Commons.

During 1968-69, large demonstrations were conducted by Roman Catholics who charged they were discriminated against in voting rights, housing, and employment. The Catholics, a minority comprising about a third of the population, demanded abolition of property qualifications for voting in local elections. Violence and terrorism intensified, involving branches of the Irish Republican Army (outlawed in the Irish Republic), Protestant groups, police, and up to 15,000 British troops.

A succession of Northern Ireland prime ministers pressed reform programs but failed to satisfy extremists on both sides. Over 2,000 were killed in over 10 years of bombings and shootings through Mar. 1980, some in England itself. Britain suspended the Northern Ireland parliament Mar. 30, 1972, and imposed direct British rule. A coalition government was formed in 1973 when moderates won election to a new one-house Assembly. But a Protestant general strike overthrew the government in 1974. Direct rule continued in 1978, after the failure of a constitutional convention to achieve a settlement.

Education and Religion. Northern Ireland is 2/3 Protestant, 1/3 Roman Catholic. Elementary education is compulsory through age 15. There are 2 universities and 24 technical colleges.

Channel Islands

The Channel Islands, area 75 sq. mi., cen. pop. 1977 131,027, off the NW coast of France, the only parts of the one-time Dukedom of Normandy belonging to England, are **Jersey, Guernsey** and the dependencies of Guernsey — **Alderney, Brechou, Great Sark, Little Sark, Herm, Jethou and Lihou.** Jersey and Guernsey have separate legal existences and lieutenant governors named by the Crown. The islands were the only British soil occupied by German troops in World War II.

Isle of Man

The Isle of Man, area 227 sq. mi., 1979 est. pop. 64,000, is in the Irish Sea, 20 mi. from Scotland, 30 mi. from Cumberland. It is rich in lead and iron. The island has its own laws and a lieutenant governor appointed by the Crown. The Tynwald (legislature) consists of the Legislative Council, partly elected, and House of Keys, elected. Capital: Douglas. Farming, tourism, fishing (kippers, scallops) are chief occupations. Man is famous for the Manx tailless cat.

Gibraltar

Gibraltar, a dependency on the southern coast of Spain, guards the entrance to the Mediterranean. The Rock has been in British possession since 1704. The Rock is 2.75 mi. long, 3/4 of a mi. wide and 1,396 ft. in height; a narrow isthmus connects it with the mainland. Est. pop. 1979, 29,000.

In 1966 Spain called on Britain to give "substantial sovereignty" of Gibraltar to Spain and imposed a partial blockade. In 1967, residents voted 12,138 for remaining under Britain, 44 for returning to Spain. A new constitution, May 30, 1969, gave an elected House of Assembly more control in domestic affairs. A UN General Assembly resolution requested Britain to end Gibraltar's colonial status by Oct. 1, 1969. No settlement has been reached.

British West Indies

Swinging in a vast arc from the coast of Venezuela NE, then N and NW toward Puerto Rico are the Windward and Leeward Islands, forming a coral and volcanic barrier sheltering the Caribbean from the open Atlantic. Many of the islands are self-governing British possessions. Universal suffrage was instituted 1951-54; ministerial systems were set up 1956-1960.

Moving northward from the southern end of the arc lie the former British **Windward Islands. St. Vincent and the Grenadines** gained full independence from UK in 1979; **St. Lucia** became independent earlier that year; and **Dominica** gained independence in 1978 *(See Index).*

Further north, in the **Leeward Islands,** are **Montserrat** (1977 pop. 12,160, area 32 sq. mi., capital Plymouth), **Antigua** (1979 pop. 74,000, area 171 sq. mi., capital St. John's), and **St. Kitts (St. Christopher)-Nevis-Anguilla,** 3 islands (1979 pop. 57,000, area 136 sq. mi., capital Basseterre on St. Kitts). Nearby are the small **British Virgin Islands.**

Britain granted self-government to 5 of these islands (exception, Montserrat) and island groups in 1967-1969; each became an Associated State, with Britain controlling foreign affairs and defense.

Anguilla declared its independence from St. Kitts June 16, 1967. A 1976 constitution provides for an autonomous elected government. Area 35 sq. mi., pop. 6,500.

Sugar is the major crop of Antigua and St. Kitts; all the islands have Sea Island cotton. Tourism is growing.

The three **Cayman Islands,** a dependency, lie S of Cuba, NW of Jamaica. Pop. is 16,000 (1979), most of it on Grand Cayman. It is a free port; in the 1970s Grand Cayman became a tax-free refuge for foreign funds and branches of many Western banks were opened there. Total area 93 sq. mi., capital Georgetown.

The **Turks and Caicos Islands,** at the SE end of the Bahama Islands, are a separate possession. There are about 30 islands, only 6 inhabited, 1979 pop. est. 7,000, area 166 sq. mi., capital Grand Turk. Salt, crayfish and conch shells are the main exports.

Bermuda

Bermuda is a British dependency governed by a royal governor and an Assembly, dating from 1620, the oldest legislative body among British dependencies. Capital is Hamilton.

It is a group of 360 small islands of coral formation, 20 inhabited, comprising 21 sq. mi. in the western Atlantic, 580 mi. E of North Carolina. Pop., 1979 est., was 63,000 (about 60% of African descent). Density is high.

The police commissioner was shot to death in 1972. Gov. Richard Sharples and an aide were slain by gunmen in 1973. Racial hostility increased with the 1977 execution of two blacks convicted of the killings.

The U.S. has air and naval bases under long-term lease, and a NASA tracking station.

Bermuda boasts many resort hotels, serving over 500,000 visitors a year. The government raises most revenue from import duties. Exports: lilies, drugs, cosmetics.

Belize

Belize (formerly called British Honduras) is in Central America facing the Caribbean to the E, with Mexico on the N and Guatemala on the W. Pop. (1979 est.) 152,000, area 8,866 sq. mi., capital Belmopan.

Internal self-government was granted by Britain in 1964.

The area has long been claimed by Guatemala, but also was promised independence by Britain. In Apr. 1968, a mediator proposed that British Honduras be made independent but have close association with Guatemala. The proposal was rejected by Belize. Britain moved several hundred troops to Belize in 1977 to counter Guatemalan "bellicosity."

Main export is sugar, along with citrus fruits, mahogany and other hardwoods, chicle, seafood.

South Atlantic

Falkland Islands and Dependencies, a British dependency, lies 300 mi. E of the Strait of Magellan at the southern end of South America.

The Falklands or Islas Malvinas include about 200 islands, area 4,700 sq. mi., pop. (1977 est.) 2,000. Sheep-grazing is the main industry; wool is the principal export. There are indications of large oil and gas deposits. The islands are also claimed by Argentina though 97% of inhabitants are of British origin. **South Georgia,** area 1,450 sq. mi., and the uninhabited **South Sandwich Is.** are dependencies of the Falklands.

British Antarctic Territory, south of 60° S lat., was made a separate colony in 1962 and comprises mainly the **South Shetland Islands,** the **South Orkneys** and **Graham's Land.** A chain of meteorological stations is maintained.

St. Helena, an island 1,200 mi. off the W coast of Africa and 1,800 E of South America, has 47 sq. mi. and est. pop., 1979 of 6,000. Flax, lace and rope making are the chief industries. After Napoleon Bonaparte was defeated at Waterloo the Allies exiled him to St. Helena, where he lived from Oct. 16, 1815, to his death, May 5, 1821. Capital is Jamestown.

Tristan da Cunha is the principal of a group of islands of volcanic origin, total area 40 sq. mi., half way between the Cape of Good Hope and South America. A volcanic peak 6,760 ft. high erupted in 1961. The 262 inhabitants were removed to England, but most returned in 1963. The islands are dependencies of St.

Helena.

Ascension is an island of volcanic origin, 34 sq. mi. in area, 700 mi. NW of St. Helena, through which it is administered. It is a communications relay center for Britain, and has a U.S. satellite tracking center. Est. pop., 1976, was 1,179, half of them communications workers. The island is noted for sea turtles.

Asia and Indian Ocean

Brunei was between 1888 and 1971 a protected sultanate. It is on the N side of the Island of Borneo, between the Malaysian states of Sarawak and Sabah. Its area is 2,226 sq. mi., the size of Delaware, with population (1979 est.) 213,000, two-thirds Malay and indigenous races, one-third of Chinese descent.

A 1959 constitution was amended, 1965, to provide for general elections to the Legislative Council. There is a sultan and a British high commissioner. A 1971 agreement gave Brunei full self-government, with Britain responsible for foreign affairs. Independence was set for 1983.

Brunei's rich Seria oifield provides tax revenues well in excess of expenditures. Rubber is also exported.

Hong Kong is a Crown Colony at the mouth of the Canton R. in China, 90 mi. S of Canton. Its nucleus is Hong Kong Is., 35½ sq. mi., acquired from China 1841, on which is located Victoria, the capital. Opposite is Kowloon Peninsula, 3 sq. mi. and Stonecutters Is., ¼ sq. mi., added, 1860. An additional 355 sq. mi. known as the New Territories, a mainland area and islands, were leased from China, 1898, for 99 years. Total area of the colony is 398 sq. mi., with a population, 1979 est., of 4,900,000 including fewer than 20,000 British. From 1949 to 1962 Hong Kong absorbed more than a million refugees from the mainland. The flow of refugees continued into the 1970s.

Hong Kong harbor was long an important British naval station and one of the world's great trans-shipment ports. Britain announced in 1975 a reduction of its garrison to 6,400 men.

Principal industries are textiles and apparel (39% of exports); also tourism, shipbuilding, iron and steel, fishing, cement, and small manufactures. Total exports exceeded $11 billion in 1978.

Spinning mills, among the best in the world, and low wages compete with textiles elsewhere and have resulted in the protective measures in some countries. Hong Kong also has a booming electronics industry.

British Indian Ocean Territory was formed Nov. 1965, embracing islands formerly dependencies of Mauritius or Seychelles: the Chagos Archipelago (including Diego Garcia), Aldabra, Farquhar and Des Roches. The latter 3 were transferred to Seychelles, which became independent in 1976. Area 22 sq mi.; pop. 1977 est. 2,000. In 1973 the U. S. Navy established a communications station on Diego Garcia and in 1975 began constructing a naval base.

Pacific Ocean

Pitcairn Island is in the Pacific, halfway between South America and Australia. The island was discovered in 1767 by Carteret but was not inhabited until 23 years later when the mutineers of the Bounty landed there. The area is 18 sq. mi. and pop. 1978, was 68. It is a British colony and is administered by a British Representative in New Zealand and a local Council. The uninhabited islands of **Henderson, Ducie** and **Oeno** are in the Pitcairn group.

The **Gilbert Islands** became independent in 1979 (*see Index for Kiribati*).

Tuvalu, formerly called the Ellice Islands, became independent in 1978 (*see Index*).

New Hebrides, a condominium jointly administered since 1906 by Great Britain and France, gained independence as *Vanuatu,* July 29, 1980. The group of 11 main islands and about 69 islets lying 500 mi. W of Fiji, has an aggregate area of 5,700 sq. mi. Capital is Port-Vila. Pop. 1979 est., 114,000, mostly Melanesian. Chief products are copra, cotton, cocoa, fish and coffee.

United States of America

People: Population (1980 est.): 222,020,000. **Age distrib.**(%): 0–14: 23.9; 15–59: 61.0; 60+: 15.2. **Pop. density:** 61.19 per sq. mi. **Urban** (1970): 73.5%. **Cities** (1975 est.): New York 7,481,613; Chicago 3,099,391; Los Angeles 2,727,399; Philadelphia 1,815,808; Houston 1,397,562; Detroit 1,335,085.

Armed forces: regulars 2,022,000; reserves 797,000.

Economy: Minerals: Coal, copper, lead, molybdenum, phosphates, uranium, bauxite, gold, iron, mercury, nickel, potash, silver, tungsten, zinc. **Crude oil reserves** (1980): 26.50 bln. bbls. **Per capita arable land:** 2.1 acres. **Meat prod.** (1978): beef: 11.33 mln. metric tons; pork: 6.13 mln. metric tons; lamb: 155,000 metric tons. **Fish catch** (1977): 3.1 mln. metric tons. **Electricity prod.** (1978): 2,211 bln. kwh. **Crude steel prod.** (1979): 123.3 mln. metric tons.

Finance: Gross domestic product (1979): $2,343.5 bln. **Per capita income** (1978): $8,612. **Imports** (1979): $218.93 bln.; partners (1978); Can. 19%, Jap. 14%, W. Ger. 6%. **Exports** (1979): $186.8 bln.; partners (1978): Can. 20%, Jap. 9%, W. Ger. 5%, UK 5%. **Tourists** (1977): 18,609,800; receipts $6.16 bln. **National budget** (1979): $480.53 bln. revenues; $508.66 bln. expenditures and lending. **International reserves less gold** (Mar. 1980): $10.28 bln. **Gold:** 264.6 mln. oz t. **Consumer prices** (change in 1979): 11.3%.

Transport: Railway traffic (1978): 16.5 bln. passenger-km; 1,252.8 bln. net ton-km. **Motor vehicles:** in use (1976): 109.0 mln. passenger cars, 26.15 mln. comm. vehicles; manuf. (1978): 9.17 mln. passenger cars; 3.71 mln. comm. vehicles. **Civil aviation:** 359,628 mln. passenger-km (1978); 10,080 mln. freight ton-km (1978).

Communications: Television sets: 121.1 mln. in use (1975), 7.86 mln. manuf. (1977). **Radios:** 402 mln. in use (1975), 12.49 mln. manuf. (1977). **Telephones in use** (1978): 162,076,000. **Daily newspaper circ.** (1977): 62,159,000; 287 per 1,000 pop.

Health: Life expectancy at birth (1975): 68.7 male; 76.5 female. **Births** (per 1,000 pop. 1977): 15.3. **Deaths** (per 1,000 pop. 1977): 8.8. **Natural increase** (1977): .7%. **Hospital beds** (per 100,000 pop. 1977): 630. **Physicians** (per 100,000 pop. 1977): 176. **Infant mortality** (per 1,000 live births 1977): 14.0.

Education (1977): **Literacy:** 99%. **Pop. 5-19:** in school: 85%, teachers per 1,000: 43. **PQLI:** 95.

Upper Volta

Republic of Upper Volta

People: Population (1979 est.): 6,661,000. **Pop. density:** 61.87 per sq. mi. **Ethnic groups:** Voltaic groups (Mossi, Bobo), Mande. **Languages:** French (official), More, Sudanic tribal languages. **Religions:** Moslems 20%, Roman Catholics 5%, others.

Geography: Area: 105,869 sq. mi., the size of Colorado. **Location:** In W. Africa, S of the Sahara. **Neighbors:** Mali on NW, Niger on NE, Benin, Togo, Ghana, Ivory Coast on S. **Topography:** Landlocked Upper Volta is in the savannah region of W. Africa. The N is arid, hot, and thinly populated. **Capital:** Ouagadougou. **Cities** (1975 cen.): Ouagadougou 168,607; Bobo-Dioulasso 112,572.

Government: Head of state: Pres. Aboubacar Sangoule Lamizana; b. 1916; in office: Jan. 3, 1966. **Head of government:** Prime Min. Joseph Conombo; in office: July 16, 1978. **Local divisions:** 10 departments. **Armed forces:** regulars 4,070; para-military 1,850.

Economy: Chief crops: Cotton, rice, peanuts, karite, grain, corn. **Minerals:** Manganese, gold, diamonds. **Per capita arable land:** 2.1 acres. **Meat prod.** (1978): beef: 22,000 metric tons; lamb: 12,000 metric tons. **Electricity prod.** (1977): 70.00 mln. kwh. **Labor force:** 95% agric.

Finance: Currency: CFA franc (Mar. 1980: 223.92 = $1 US). **Gross domestic product** (1976 est.): $500 mln. **Per capita income** (1976): $75. **Imports** (1977): $218 mln.; partners (1977): Fr. 45%, Ivory Coast 13%, U.S. 9%, W. Ger. 6%. **Exports** (1977): $134 mln.; partners (1977): Ivory Coast 32%, Den. 22%, Neth. 11%, Fr. 7%. **Tourists** (1977): 23,000; receipts: (1975): $2 mln. **International reserves less gold** (Jan. 1980): $60.6 mln. **Gold:** 11,000 oz t. **Consumer prices** (change in 1979): −6.3%.

Transport: Motor vehicles: in use (1975): 9,500 passenger cars, 10,100 comm. vehicles.

Communications: Television sets: 6,000 in use (1975). **Radios:** 105,000 in use (1976). **Telephones in use** (1978): 3,564. **Daily newspaper circ.** (1976): 1,500; 0.2 per 1,000 pop.

Health: Life expectancy at birth (1961): 32.1 male; 31.1 female. **Births** (per 1,000 pop. 1975): 47.9. **Deaths** (per 1,000 pop. 1975): 23.2. **Natural increase** (1975): 2.5%. **Hospital beds** (per 100,000 pop. 1977): 57. **Physicians** (per 100,000 pop. 1977): 3. **Infant mortality** (per 1,000 live births 1975): 182.

Education (1977): **Literacy:** 7%. **Pop. 5-19:** in school: 7%, teachers per 1,000: 2. **PQLI:** 17.

The Mossi tribe entered the area in the 11th to 13th centuries. Their kingdoms ruled until defeated by the Mali and Songhai empires.

French control came by 1896, but Upper Volta was not finally established as a separate territory until 1947. Full independence came Aug. 5, 1960, and a pro-French government was elected. A 1966 coup established the current regime. Free multi-party presidential and parliamentary elections were held in 1978.

Several hundred thousand farm workers migrate each year to Ivory Coast and Ghana. A long drought brought famine in 1973-74; renewed drought occurred in 1977-78.

Uruguay

Oriental Republic of Uruguay

People: Population (1979 est.): 2,910,000. **Age distrib.** (%): 0–14: 27.0; 15–59: 58.7; 60+: 14.3. **Pop. density:** 41.72 per sq. mi. **Urban** (1975): 83.0%. **Ethnic groups:** Caucasians (Iberians, Italians) 90%, mestizos 5-10%, mulatto and Negro 3-5%. **Languages:** Spanish. **Religions:** Roman Catholics 66%, Jews 2%, Protestants 2%.

Geography: Area: 68,548 sq. mi., the size of Washington State. **Location:** In southern S. America, on the Atlantic O. **Neighbors:** Argentina on W, Brazil on N. **Topography:** Uruguay is composed of rolling, grassy plains and hills, well-watered by rivers flowing W to Uruguay R. **Capital:** Montevideo. **Cities** (1975 cen.): Montevideo 1,173,254.

Government: Head of state: Pres. Aparicio Mendez Manfredini; b. Aug. 24, 1904; in office: Sept. 1, 1976. **Local divisions:** 19 departments. **Armed forces:** regulars 27,500; paramilitary 2,200.

Economy: Industries: Meat-packing, metals, textiles, wine, cement, oil products. **Chief crops:** Corn, wheat, citrus fruits, rice, oats, linseed. **Per capita arable land:** 1.6 acres. **Meat prod.** (1978): beef: 354,000 metric tons; pork: 16,000 metric tons; lamb: 35,000 metric tons. **Fish catch** (1977): 48,400 metric tons. **Electricity prod.** (1977): 3.04 bln. kwh. **Crude steel prod.** (1979): 14,000 metric tons. **Labor force** 11% agric.

Finance: Currency: New Peso (Mar. 1980: 8.66 = $1 US). **Gross domestic product** (1978): $4.95 bln. **Per capita income** (1978): $1,612. **Imports** (1978): $774 mln.; partners (1977): Braz. 13%, Arg. 12%, U.S. 10%, Iraq 9%. **Exports** (1978): $688 mln.; partners (1977): Braz. 19%, U.S. 17%, W. Ger. 12%, Neth. 7%. **Tourists** (1976): 491,700; receipts (1977): $180 mln. **National budget** (1978): $1.13 bln. revenues; $1.15 bln. expeditures. **International reserves less gold** (Jan. 1980): $413 mln. **Gold:** 3.81 mln. oz t. **Consumer prices** (change in 1978): 44.5%.

Transport: Railway traffic (1977): 389 mln. passenger-km; 307 mln. net ton-km. **Motor vehicles:** in use (1976): 127,100 passenger cars, 104,200 comm. vehicles. **Civil aviation:** 74 mln. passenger-km (1977); 288,000 freight ton-km (1977). **Chief ports:** Montevideo.

Communications: Television sets: 355,000 in use (1976). **Radios:** 1.6 mln. in use (1976). **Telephones in use** (1978): 268,026.

Health: Life expectancy at birth (1964): 65.51 male; 71.56 female. **Births** (per 1,000 pop. 1976): 20.9. **Deaths** (per 1,000 pop. 1976): 10.2. **Natural increase** (1976): 1.1%. **Hospital beds** (per 100,000 pop. 1977): 418. **Physicians:** (per 100,000 pop. 1977): 139. **Infant mortality** (per 1,000 live births 1976): 45.9.

Education (1977): **Literacy:** 94%. **Pop. 5-19:** in school: 60%, teachers per 1,000: 34. **PQLI:** 87.

Spanish settlers did not begin replacing the indigenous Charrua Indians until 1624. Portuguese from Brazil arrived later, but Uruguay was attached to the Spanish Viceroyalty of Rio de la Plata in the 18th century. Rebels fought against Spain beginning in 1810. An independent republic was declared Aug. 25, 1825.

Liberal governments adopted socialist measures as far back as 1911. More than a third of the workers are employed by the state, which owns the power, telephone, railroad, cement, oil-refining and other industries. Social welfare programs are among the most advanced in the world.

Uruguay's standard of living was one of the highest in South America, and political and labor conditions among the freest. Economic stagnation, inflation, plus floods, drought in 1967 and a general strike in 1968 brought attempts by the government to strengthen the economy through a series of devaluations of the peso and wage and price controls. But inflation continued. The cost of living rose 1,200% between 1968 and 1976.

Tupamaros, leftist guerrillas drawn from the upper classes, increased terrorist actions in 1970; a U.S. police adviser was slain in Aug. In 1971 the guerrillas kidnaped and, after 8 months, freed the British ambassador. Violence continued and in Feb. 1973 Pres. Juan Maria Bordaberry agreed to military control of his administration. In June he abolished Congress and set up a Council of State in its place. By 1974 the military had apparently defeated the Tupamaros, using severe repressive measures. The economic decline continued. Bordaberry was removed by the military in a 1976 coup. Elections were promised for 1981.

Vatican

State of Vatican City

People: Population (1978 est.): 729. **Ethnic groups:** Italians, Swiss. **Languages:** Italian, Latin. **Religion:** Roman Catholicism.

Geography: Area: 108.7 acres. **Location:** In Rome, Italy. **Neighbors:** Completely surrounded by Italy.

Currency: Lira.

The popes for many centuries, with brief interruptions, held temporal sovereignty over mid-Italy (the so-called Papal States), comprising an area of some 16,000 sq. mi., with a population in the 19th century of more than 3 million. This territory was incorporated in the new Kingdom of Italy, the sovereignty of the pope being confined to the palaces of the Vatican and the Lateran in Rome and the villa of Castel Gandolfo, by an Italian law, May 13, 1871. This law also guaranteed to the pope and his successors a yearly indemnity of over $620,000. The allowance, however, remained unclaimed.

A Treaty of Conciliation, a concordat and a financial convention were signed Feb. 11, 1929, by Cardinal Gasparri and Premier Mussolini. The documents established the independent state of Vatican City, and gave the Catholic religion special status in Italy. The treaty (Lateran Agreement) was made part of the Constitution of Italy (Article 7) in 1947. Italy and the Vatican reached preliminary agreement in 1976 on revisions of the concordat, that would eliminate Roman Catholicism as the state religion and end required religious education in Italian schools.

Vatican City includes St. Peter's, the Vatican Palace and Museum covering over 13 acres, the Vatican gardens, and neighboring buildings between Viale Vaticano and the Church. Thirteen buildings in Rome, outside the boundaries, enjoy extraterritorial rights; these buildings house congregations or officers necessary for the administration of the Holy See.

The legal system is based on the code of canon law, the apostolic constitutions and the laws especially promulgated for the Vatican City by the pope. The Secretariat of State represents the Holy See in its diplomatic relations. By the Treaty of Conciliation the pope is pledged to a perpetual neutrality unless his mediation is specifically requested. This, however, does not prevent the defense of the Church whenever it is persecuted. A total of 84 nations maintain diplomatic representatives in Vatican City. The U.S. does not have an official ambassador.

The present sovereign of the State of Vatican City is the Supreme Pontiff John Paul II, Karol Wojtyla, born in Wadowice, Poland, May 18, 1920, elected Oct. 16, 1978 (the first non-Italian to be elected pope in 456 years), in succession to John Paul I, Albino Luciani, who died Sept. 28, 1978, after serving as pope only 34 days.

Venezuela

Republic of Venezuela

People: Population (1979 est.): 14,529,000. **Age distrib.** (%): 0–14: 42.8; 15–59: 52.4; 60+: 4.8. **Pop. density:** 37.26 per sq. mi. **Urban** (1977): 75.1%. **Ethnic groups:** Mestizo 70%, white (Spanish, Portuguese, Italian) 20%, Negro 8%, Indian 2%. **Languages:** Spanish, Indian languages 2%. **Religions:** Roman Catholics 96%, Protestants 2%.

Geography: Area: 352,143 sq. mi., more than twice the size of California. **Location:** On the Caribbean coast of S. America.

Neighbors: Colombia on W, Brazil on S, Guyana on E. **Topography:** Flat coastal plain and Orinoco Delta are bordered by Andes Mtns. and hills. Plains, called llanos, extend between mountains and Orinoco. Guyana Highlands and plains are S of Orinoco, which stretches 1,700 mi. and drains 80% of Venezuela. **Capital:** Caracas. **Cities** (1978 est.): Caracas 1,662,627; Maracaibo 792,000; Valencia 439,000; Barquisimeto 430,000.

Government: Head of state: Pres. Luis Herrera Campins; b. May 4, 1925; in office: Mar. 12, 1979. **Local divisions:** 20 states, 2 federal territories, federal district. **Armed forces:** regulars 41,500; para-military 10,000.

Economy: Industries: Steel, oil products, textiles, containers, tobacco, paper, tires, shoes. **Chief crops:** Coffee, cocoa, fruits, sugar. **Minerals:** Oil (5th largest producer), iron (extensive reserves and production), gold, copper, salt, coal, nickel, manganese, asbestos, diamonds, mica. **Crude oil reserves** (1980): 17.87 bln. bbls. **Per capita arable land:** 0.9 acres. **Meat prod.** (1978): beef: 282,000 metric tons; pork: 91,000 metric tons; lamb: 10,000 metric tons. **Fish catch** (1977): 152,200 metric tons. **Electricity prod.** (1977): 23.05 bln. kwh. **Crude steel prod.** (1979): 1.5 mln. metric tons. **Labor force:** 20% agric.; 19% manuf.

Finance: Currency: Bolivar (Mar. 1980: 4.29 = $1 US). **Gross domestic product** (1978): $39.68 bln. **Per capita income** (1978): $2,772. **Imports** (1979): $10.6 bln.; partners (1977): U.S. 39%, W. Ger. 12%, Jap. 11%, It. 6%. **Exports** (1979): $13.13 bln.; partners (1977): U.S. 36%, Neth. Ant. 18%, Can. 12%. **Tourists** (1977): 652,400; receipts: $261 mln. **National budget** (1979): $11.65 bln. revenues; $10.73 bln. expenditures. **International reserves less gold** (Feb. 1980): $6.61 bln. **Gold:** 11.46 mln. oz t. **Consumer prices** (change in 1979): 12.3%.

Transport: Railway traffic (1971): 42 mln. passenger-km; 15 mln. net ton-km. **Motor vehicles:** in use (1975): 955,200 passenger cars, 369,400 comm. vehicles; assembled (1976): 97,000 passenger cars; 66,000 comm. vehicles. **Civil aviation:** 3,012 mln. passenger-km (1977); 118 mln. freight ton-km (1977). **Chief ports:** Maracaibo, La Guaira, Puerto Cabello.

Communications: Television sets: 1.43 mln. in use (1976), 86,000 manuf. (1972). **Radios:** 5.03 mln. in use (1976), 74,000 manuf. (1972). **Telephones in use** (1978): 847,318. **Daily newspaper circ.** (1977): 2,263,000; 178 per 1,000 pop.

Health: Life expectancy at birth (1961): 66.41 male; 66.41 female. **Births** (per 1,000 pop. 1975): 36.2. **Deaths** (per 1,000 pop. 1975): 7.1. **Natural increase** (1975): 2.9%. **Hospital beds** (per 100,000 pop. 1977): 292. **Physicians** (per 100,000 pop. 1977): 107. **Infant mortality** (per 1,000 live births 1977): 40.4.

Education (1977): **Literacy:** 82%. **Pop. 5-19:** in school: 58%, teachers per 1,000: 19. **PQLI:** 79.

Columbus first set foot on the South American continent on the peninsula of Paria, Aug. 1498. Alonso de Ojeda, 1499, found Lake Maracaibo, called the land Venezuela, or Little Venice, because natives had houses on stilts. Venezuela was under Spanish domination until 1821. The republic was formed after secession from the Colombian Federation in 1830.

Military strongmen ruled Venezuela for most of the 20th century. They promoted the oil industry; some social reforms were implemented. Since 1959, the country has enjoyed progressive, democratically-elected governments.

Venezuela helped found the Organization of Petroleum Exporting States (OPEC). The government, Jan. 1, 1976, nationalized the oil industry with compensation. Development has begun of the Orinoco tar belt, believed to contain the world's largest oil reserves. Oil production rose 11% in 1979, as a result of the decline in Iranian oil exports.

Construction is booming, including a new $3.8 billion city, Ciudad Guyana, 300 mi. SE of Caracas. Oil profits help finance the extensive industrial development. Government efforts at income redistribution were thwarted by inflation in 1974-5, but public works and welfare programs in slum areas have improved.

Foreign investment is being encouraged.

Vietnam

Socialist Republic of Vietnam

People: Population (1979 est.): 52,127,000 **Pop. density:** 394.59 per sq. mi. **Ethnic groups:** Vietnamese 80%, Khmer, Tais, Montagnards, Tays, Muong, Nung. **Languages:** Vietnamese, others. **Religions:** Buddhism and Taoism most numerous, Roman Catholics 5%, Cao Dai, Hoa Hao.

Geography: Area: 126,436 sq. mi., the size of New Mexico. **Location:** On the E coast of the Indochinese Peninsula in SE Asia. **Neighbors:** China on N, Laos, Cambodia on W. **Topography:** Vietnam is long and narrow, with a 1,400-mi. coast. About 24% of country is readily arable, including the densely settled Red R. valley in the N, narrow coastal plains in center, and the wide, often marshy Mekong R. Delta in the S. The rest consists of semi-arid plateaus and barren mountains, with some stretches of tropical rain forest. **Capital:** Hanoi. **Cities** (1976 cen.): Ho Chi Minh City 1,845,000; Haiphong 1,515,000; Hanoi 597,000.

Government: Head of state: Acting Pres. Nguyen Hau Tho; in office: Mar. 30, 1980. **Head of government:** Prime Min. Pham Van Dong; b. 1906; in office: Sept. 20, 1955. **Head of Communist Party:** First Sec. Le Duan; b. 1907; in office: Sept. 10, 1960. **Local divisions:** 36 provinces. **Armed forces:** regulars 1,023,000; para-military 1,570,000.

Economy: Industries: Food processing, textiles, paper. **Chief crops:** Rice, corn, sugar cane, sweet potatoes, coffee, tea, cotton, manioc, tobacco. **Minerals:** Phosphates, coal, iron, manganese, bauxite, apatite, chromate. **Other resources:** Forests. **Per capita arable land:** 0.2 acres. **Meat prod.** (1978): beef: 93,000 metric tons; pork: 457,000 metric tons. **Fish catch** (1977): 1 mln. metric tons. **Electricity prod.** (1975): 1.32 bln. kwh. **Labor force:** 80% agric.

Finance: Currency: Dong (Sept. 1979: 2.18 = $1 US). **Per capita income** (1976): $160. **Imports** (1978 est.): $1.5 bln.; partners: USSR 30%, Jap. 16%, Fr. 7%, It. 5%. Exports (1978 est.): $416 mln.; partners: USSR 54%, Jap. 11%.

Transport: Railway traffic (1973): 170 mln. passenger-km; 1.00 mln. net ton-km. **Motor vehicles:** in use (S. Vietnam only) (1974): 70,000 passenger cars, 100,000 comm. vehicles. **Chief ports:** Ho Chi Minh City, Haiphong, Da Nang, Cam Ranh.

Communications: Radios: 2.6 in use (1974), 87,000 manuf. (South only) (1973). **Daily newspaper circ.** (1977): 250,000; 5 per 1,000 pop.

Health: Life expectancy at birth (1975): 43.2 male; 46.0 female. **Births** (per 1,000 pop. 1975): 41.0. **Deaths** (per 1,000 pop. 1975): 19.8. **Natural increase** 1975): 2.12%. **Hospital beds** (per 100,000 pop. 1977): 343. **Physicians** (per 100,000 pop. 1977): 18.

Education (1977): **Literacy:** 75%. **Pop. 5-19:** in school: 62%, teachers per 1,000: 24. **PQLI:** 59.

Vietnam's recorded history began in Tonkin before the Christian era. Settled by Viets from central China, Vietnam was held by China, 111 BC-939 AD, and was a vassal state during subsequent periods. Vietnam defeated the armies of Kublai Khan, 1288. Conquest by France began in 1858 and ended in 1884 with the protectorates of Tonkin and Annam in the N. and the colony of Cochin-China in the S.

In 1940 Vietnam was occupied by Japan; nationalist aims gathered force. A number of groups formed the Vietminh (Independence) League, headed by Ho Chi Minh, communist guerrilla leader. In Aug. 1945 the Vietminh forced out Bao Dai, former emperor of Annam, head of a Japan-sponsored regime. France, seeking to reestablish colonial control, battled communist and nationalist forces, 1946-1954, and was finally defeated at Dienbienphu, May 8, 1954. Meanwhile, on July 1, 1949, Bao Dai had formed a State of Vietnam, with himself as chief of state, with French approval. Communist China backed Ho Chi Minh.

A cease-fire accord signed in Geneva July 21, 1954, divided Vietnam along the Ben Hai R. It provided for a buffer zone, withdrawal of French troops from the North and elections to determine the country's future. Under the agreement the communists gained control of territory north of the 17th parallel, 22 provinces with area of 62,000 sq. mi. and 13 million pop., with its capital at Hanoi and Ho Chi Minh as president. South Vietnam came to comprise the 39 southern provinces with approx. area of 65,000 sq. mi. and pop. of 12 million. Some 900,000 North Vietnamese fled to South Vietnam. Neither South Vietnam nor the U.S. signed the agreement.

On Oct. 26, 1955, Ngo Dinh Diem, premier of the interim government of South Vietnam, proclaimed the Republic of Vietnam and became its first president.

The Democratic Republic of Vietnam, established in the North, adopted a constitution Dec. 31, 1959, based on communist principles and calling for reunification of all Vietnam. Pres. Ho Chi Minh, re-elected July 15, 1960, by unanimous vote of the National Assembly, had held office since 1945. He died Sept. 3, 1969.

North Vietnam sought to take over South Vietnam beginning in 1954. Fighting persisted from 1956, with the communist Vietcong, aided by North Vietnam, pressing war in the South and South Vietnam receiving U.S. aid. Northern aid to Vietcong guerrillas was intensified in 1959, and large-scale troop infiltration began in 1964 with Russian and Chinese arms assistance. Large Northern forces were stationed in border areas of Laos and Cambodia.

A serious political conflict arose in the South in 1963 when Buddhists denounced authoritarianism and brutality. This paved the way for a military coup Nov. 1-2, 1963, which overthrew Diem. Several military coups followed. In elections Sept. 3, 1967, Chief of State Nguyen Van Thieu was chosen president.

In 1964, the U.S. began air strikes against North Vietnam. Beginning in 1965, the raids were stepped up and U.S. troops became combatants. U.S. troop strength in Vietnam, which reached a high of 543,400 in Apr. 1969, was ordered reduced by U.S. President Nixon in a series of withdrawals, beginning in June 1969. U.S. bombings were resumed in 1972-73.

A ceasefire agreement was signed in Paris Jan. 27, 1973 (EST), by the U.S., North and South Vietnam, and the Vietcong. It was never implemented. U.S. aid was curbed in 1974 by the U.S. Congress. Heavy fighting continued for two years throughout Indochina.

Massive numbers of North Vietnamese troops, aided by tanks, launched attacks against remaining government outposts in the Central Highlands in the first months of 1975. Government retreats turned into a rout, and the Saigon regime surrendered April 30. Conquest of the country was effectively completed within days.

A Provisional Revolutionary Government assumed control, aided by officials and technicians from Hanoi, and first steps were taken to transform society along communist lines. All businesses and farms were to be collectivized by 1979.

The U.S. accepted over 165,000 Vietnamese fleeing the new regime, while scores of thousands more sought refuge in other countries.

The war's toll included — Combat deaths: U.S. 46,079; South Vietnam over 200,000; other allied forces 5,225. Civilian casualties were over a million. Displaced war refugees in South Vietnam totaled over 6.5 million.

After the fighting ended, 8 Northern divisions remained stationed in the South, while Southern forces of over 900,000 were demobilized, adding to severe economic problems. Over 1 million urban residents and 260,000 Montagnards were resettled in the countryside by 1978, the first of 10 million scheduled for forced resettlement. An unknown number were sent to long-term re-education camps, including thousands of adherents of the Hoa Hao sect. A 1977 crop failure caused food shortages; the south remained more prosperous than the north.

The first National Assembly of both parts of the country met June 24, 1976. The country was officially reunited July 2, 1976. The Northern capital, flag, anthem, emblem, and currency were applied to the new state. Nearly all major government posts went to officials of the former Northern government, and thousands of Northern officials were sent south.

The U.S. agreed in 1977 not to bar Vietnam's membership in the UN.

Heavy fighting with Cambodia took place, 1977-80, amid mutual charges of aggression and atrocities against civilians. Increasing numbers of Vietnamese civilians, ethnic Chinese, escaped the country, via the sea, or the overland route across Cambodia.

Relations with China soured as 140,000 ethnic Chinese left Vietnam charging discrimination; China cut off economic aid. Reacting to Vietnam's invasion of Cambodia, China attacked 4 Vietnamese border provinces, Feb., 1979, instigating heavy fighting. Soviet ties remained strong: Vietnam joined Comecon (Soviet trade bloc) in 1978. China said a Soviet guided missile base had been built in Vietnam.

Yemen

Yemen Arab Republic

People: Population (1978 est.): 5,126,000. **Pop. density:** 75.04 per sq. mi. **Ethnic groups:** Arabs, some Negroids. **Languages:** Arabic. **Religions:** Sunni Moslems 50%, Shiite Moslems 50%.

Geography: Area: 75,290 sq. mi., slightly smaller than South Dakota. **Location:** On the southern Red Sea coast of the Arabian Peninsula. **Neighbors:** Saudi Arabia on NE, South Yemen on S. **Topography:** A sandy coastal strip leads to well-watered fertile mountains in interior. **Capital:** Sana. **Cities** (1975 cen.): Sana 134,588.

Government: Head of state: Pres. Ali Abdullah Saleh, b. 1942; in office: July 17, 1978. **Head of government:** Prime Min. Abdul Aziz Abdul-Ghani; in office: Jan. 16, 1975. **Local divisions:** 11 governorates. **Armed forces:** regulars 36,600; paramilitary 20,000.

Economy: Industries: Textiles, cement. **Chief crops:** Coffee, cotton, gat, grain, dates, cotton, sesame, herbs, fruits. **Minerals:** Salt. **Crude oil reserves** (1978): 370 mln. bbls. **Per capita arable land:** 0.7 acres. **Meat prod.** (1978): beef: 14,000 metric tons; lamb: 50,000 metric tons. **Fish catch** (1977): 17,500 metric tons. **Electricity prod.** (1977): 65.00 mln. kwh. **Labor force:** 73% agric.

Finance: Currency: Rial (Mar. 1980: 4.56 = $1 US). **Gross domestic product** (1976): $1.65 bln. **Per capita income** (1976): $310. **Imports** (1977): $1.04 bln.; partners (1976): Saudi Ar. 12%, Jap. 10%, India 7%, Austral. 7%. **Exports** (1977): $11 mln.; partners (1976): China 33%, S. Yemen 25%, It. 19%, Saudi Ar. 15%. **International reserves less gold** (Mar. 1980): $1.4 bln. **Gold:** 7,000 oz t. **Consumer prices** (change in 1977): 24.8%.

Transport: Chief ports: Al-Hudaydah, Al-Mukha.

Communications: Radios: 90,000 in use (1976). **Daily newspaper circ.** (1970): 56,000; 10 per 1,000 pop.

Health: Life expectancy at birth (1975): 37.3 male; 38.7 female. **Births** (per 1,000 pop. 1975): 48.7. **Deaths** (per 1,000 pop. 1975): 26.3. **Natural increase** (1975): 2.2%. **Hospital beds** (per 100,000 pop. 1977): 58. **Physicians** (per 100,000 pop. 1977): 8.

Education (1977): **Literacy:** 12%. **Pop. 5-19:** in school: 15%, teachers per 1,000: 4. **PQLI:** 27.

Yemen's territory once was part of the ancient kindgom of Sheba, or Saba, a prosperous link in trade between Africa and India. A Biblical reference speaks of its gold, spices and precious stones as gifts borne by the Queen of Sheba to King Solomon.

Yemen became independent in 1918, after years of Ottoman Turkish rule, but remained politically and economically backward. Imam Ahmed ruled 1948-1962. The king was reported assassinated Sept. 26, 1962, and a revolutionary group headed by Brig. Gen. Abdullah al-Salal declared the country to be the Yemen Arab Republic.

The Imam Ahmed's heir, the Imam Mohamad al-Badr, fled to the mountains where tribesmen joined royalist forces; internal warfare between them and the republican forces continued. Egypt sent 70,000 troops to aid the republicans; Saudi Arabia supported the royalists with military aid. About 150,000 people were killed in the fighting.

After its defeat in the June 1967 Arab-Israeli war, Egypt announced it would withdraw its troops from Yemen; the last of them left Nov. 29, 1967; Saudi Arabia said it would stop aiding the royalists.

This was accompanied by a bloodless coup Nov. 5, 1967. Fighting continued between the republican and royalist forces. Saudi Arabia announced in Feb. 1968 it was renewing its aid to the royalists.

In April 1970 hostilities ended with an agreement between Yemen and Saudi Arabia and appointment of several royalists to the Yemen government.

There were border skirmishes with forces of the People's Democratic Republic of Yemen in 1972-73. The U.S. and Yemen in 1972 resumed diplomatic relations, broken by Yemen after the 1967 Arab-Israeli war.

On June 13, 1974, an Army group, led by Col. Ibrahim al-Hamidi, seized the government. Hamidi pursued close Saudi and U.S. ties; he was killed in 1977 by unknown assassins. His successor was murdered, reportedly by pro-South Yemen forces or by the S. Yemen government.

The People's Democratic Republic of Yemen went to war with Yemen on Feb. 24, 1979. Swift Arab mediation led to a ceasefire and a mutual withdrawal of forces, Mar. 19th. An Arab League-sponsored agreement between North and South Yemen on unification of the 2 countries was signed Mar. 29th.

There are periodic droughts. Per capita GNP is among the

lowest in the world. A prolonged drought has forced imports of food. The remittances from 400,000 Yemenis living in Arab oil countries provide most of foreign earnings.

South Yemen

People's Democratic Republic of Yemen

People: Population (1979 est.): 1,863,000. **Age distrib.** (%): 0–14: 49.4; 15–59: 45.5; 60+: 5.5. **Pop. density:** 16.67 per sq. mi. **Urban** (1973): 33.3%. **Ethnic groups:** Arabs, 75%, Indians 11%, Somalis 8%, others. **Languages:** Arabic. **Religions:** Moslems (Sunni) 91%, Christians 4%, Hindus 3.5%.

Geography: Area: 111,000 sq. mi., the size of Nevada. **Location:** On the southern coast of the Arabian Peninsula. **Neighbors:** Yemen on W, Saudi Arabia on N, Oman on E. **Topography:** The entire country is very hot and very dry. A sandy coast rises to mountains which give way to desert sands. **Capital:** Aden. **Cities** (1978 est.): Aden 271,590.

Government: Head of state: Pres. Ali Nasir Muhammad al-Hasani; in office: Apr. 21, 1980. **Head of Communist Party:** Sec. Gen. Ali Nasir Muhammad Al-Hasani; in office: April 21, 1980. **Local divisions:** 6 governorates. **Armed forces:** regulars 20,800; para-military 15,000.

Economy: Industries: Transshipment. **Chief crops:** Cotton (main export), grains. **Per capita arable land:** 0.3 acres. **Meat prod.** (1978) lamb: 11,000 metric tons. **Fish catch** (1977): 161,700 metric tons. **Electricity prod.** (1977) 180.00 mln. kwh. **Labor force:** 70% agric.

Finance: Currency: Dinar (Mar. 1980: 1 = $2.86 US). **Gross domestic product** (1976 est.): $430 mln. **Per capita income** (1976): $230. **Imports** (1977) $544 mln.; partners (1976): Kuw. 17%, Jap. 13%, Qatar 9%, UK 7%. **Exports** (1978): $221 mln.; partners (1976): Can. 75%, Jap. 7%. **Tourists** (1976): 18,000; receipts (1974): $4 mln. **National budget** (1977): $101 mln. revenues; $137 mln. expenditures. **International reserves less gold** (Nov. 1979): $210.33 mln. **Gold:** 35,000 oz t. **Consumer prices** (change in 1977): 5.2%.

Transport: Motor vehicles: in use (1976): 11,900 passenger cars, 10,500 comm. vehicles. **Chief ports:** Aden.

Communications: Television sets: 32,000 in use (1976). **Radios:** 100,000 in use (1976). **Daily newspaper circ.** (1976): 4,000; 12 per 1,000 pop.

Health: Life expectancy at birth (1975): 40.6 male; 42.4 female. **Births** (per 1,000 pop. 1975): 48.2 **Deaths** (per 1,000 pop. 1975): 23.1. **Natural increase** (1975): 2.5%. **Hospital beds** (per 100,000 pop. 1977): 154. **Physicians** (per 100,000 pop. 1977): 11.

Education (1977): **Literacy:** 20%. **Pop. 5-19:** in school: 41%, teachers per 1,000: 16. **PQLI:** 32.

Aden, mentioned in the Bible, has been a port for trade in incense, spice and silk between the East and West for 2,000 years. British rule began in 1839. Aden provided Britain with a controlling position at the southern entrance to the Red Sea.

A war for independence began in 1963. The National Liberation Front (NLF) and the Egypt-supported Front for the Liberation of Occupied South Yemen, waged a guerrilla war against the British and local dynastic rulers. The 2 groups vied with each other for control. The NLF won out. Independence came Nov. 30, 1967. In 1969, the left wing of the NLF seized power and inaugurated a thorough nationalization of the economy and regimentation of daily life.

The new government broke off relations with the U.S. and nationalized some foreign firms. Aid has been furnished by the USSR and China, with the USSR supplying most military aid.

In 1972-73 there were border skirmishes with forces of the Yemen Arab Republic. South Yemen aided leftist guerrillas in neighboring Oman. Relations with Saudi Arabia later improved. S. Yemen troops fought in Ethiopia against Eritrean rebels in 1978; 500 Cuban troops and some Soviet facilities were reported in Yemen.

Pres. Salem Robaye Ali, who had tried to improve relations with Yemen, Saudi Arabia, Oman, and the U.S., was executed after a bloody coup June 1978. The new ruling faction was accused by N. Yemen of the murder of N. Yemen's president 2 days earlier. N. Yemen, Egypt, and Saudi Arabia froze ties with S. Yemen in July.

The People's Democratic Republic of Yemen went to war with Yemen on Feb. 24, 1979. Swift Arab mediation led to a cease-fire and a mutual withdrawal of forces, Mar. 19th. An Arab League-sponsored agreement between North and South Yemen on unification of the 2 countries was signed Mar. 29th.

The Port of Aden is the country's most valuable resource, but with the closing of the Suez Canal after the Arab-Israeli War in June 1967, the port lost much of its business. The canal was reopened in 1975.

Socotra, the largest island in the Arabian Sea, Kamaran, an island in the Red Sea near the coast of North Yemen, and Perim, an island in the strait between the Gulf of Aden and the Red Sea, are controlled by South Yemen.

Yugoslavia

Socialist Federal Republic of Yugoslavia

People: Population (1979 est.): 22,174,000. **Age distrib.** (%): 0–14: 25.6; 15-59: 61.6; 60+: 12.7. **Pop. density:** 221.84 per sq. mi. **Urban** (1971): 38.6%. **Ethnic groups:** Serbs 40%, Croats 23%, Slovenes 8.6%, Macedonians 5.6%, Bosnian Moslems 5%, Albanians 5%, Montenegrin Serbs 2%, Hungarians 2%, Turks 1%. **Languages:** Serbo-Croatian, Macedonian, Slovene all official. **Religions:** Orthodox 50%, Roman Catholics 30%, Moslems 10%, Protestants 1%.

Geography: Area: 98,766 sq. mi., the size of Wyoming. **Location:** On the Adriatic coast of the Balkan Peninsula in SE Europe. **Neighbors:** Italy on W, Austria, Hungary on N, Romania, Bulgaria on E, Greece, Albania on S. **Topography:** The Dinaric Alps run parallel to the Adriatic coast, which is lined by offshore islands. Plains stretch across N and E river basins. S and NW are mountainous. **Capital:** Belgrade. **Cities** (1971 cen.): Belgrade 746,105; Zagreb 566,224; Skoplje 312,980.

Government: Head of state: Pres. H. E. Cvijetin Mijatovic; b. 1913; in office: May 15, 1980. **Head of government:** Prime Min. Veselin Djuranovic; b. May 17, 1925; in office: Feb. 4, 1977; **Head of Communist Party:** H. E. Cvijetin Mijatovic; in office: May 15, 1980. **Local divisions:** 6 republics: Serbia, Croatia, Slovenia, Bosnia-Herzegovina, Macedonia, Montenegro; 2 autonomous provinces: Vojvodina, Kosovo. **Armed forces:** regulars 259,000; reserves, para-military 500,000.

Economy: Industries: Steel, chemicals, wood products, cement, textiles, tourism. **Chief crops:** Corn, grains, tobacco, hops, fruits, sugar beets, sunflowers. **Minerals:** Antimony, bauxite, lead, mercury, coal, iron, copper, chrome, manganese, zinc, salt. **Crude oil reserves** (1980): 275 mln. bbls. **Per capita arable land:** 0.8 acres. **Meat prod.** (1978): beef: 340,000 metric tons; pork: 656,000 metric tons; lamb: 61,000 metric tons. **Fish catch:** (1977): 60,900 metric tons. **Electricity prod.** (1978): 51.35 bln. kwh. **Crude steel prod.** (1979): 3.5 mln. metric tons. **Labor force:** 45% agric.; 18% manuf.

Finance: Currency: Dinar (Mar. 1980: 20.31 = $1 US). **Gross domestic product** (1977): $40.3 bln. **Imports** (1979): $12.86 bln.; partners (1978): W. Ger. 18%, USSR 14%, It. 8%, U.S. 6%. **Exports** (1979): $6.49 bln.; partners (1978): USSR 25%, It. 9%, W. Ger. 8%, U.S. 7%. **Tourists** (1977): 5,625,100; receipts: $841 mln. **National budget** (1977): $9.45 bln. revenues; $10.11 bln. expenditures. **International reserves less gold** (Mar. 1980): $836 mln. **Gold:** 1.79 mln. oz t. **Consumer prices** change in 1979): 21.4%.

Transport: Railway traffic (1978): 10.4 bln. passenger-km; 23.38 bln. net ton-km. **Motor vehicles:** in use (1977): 1.92 mln. passenger cars, 199,200 comm. vehicles; manuf. (1978): 193,200 passenger cars; 62,400 comm. vehicles. **Civil aviation:** 2,724 mln. passenger-km (1978); 29 mln. freight ton-km (1978). **Chief ports:** Rijeka, Split, Dubrovnik.

Communications: Television sets: 3.5 mln. licensed (1976), 427,000 manuf. (1977). **Radios:** 4.5 mln. licensed (1976), 187,000 manuf. (1977). **Telephones in use** (1978): 1,555,663. **Daily newspaper circ.** (1977): 2,085,000; 96 per 1,000 pop.

Health: Life expectancy at birth (1972): 65.42 male; 70.22 female. **Births** (per 1,000 pop. 1978): 17.4. **Deaths** (per 1,000 pop. 1978): 8.7. **Natural increase** (1978): .9%. **Hospital beds** (per 100,000 pop. 1977): 603. **Physicians** (per 100,000 pop. 1977): 131. **Infant mortality** (per 1,000 live births 1978): 33.6

Education (1977): **Literacy:** 85%. **Pop. 5–19:** in school: 60%, teachers per 1,000: 26. **PQLI:** 84.

Serbia, which had since 1389 been a vassal principality of Turkey, was established as an independent kingdom by the Treaty of Berlin, 1878. Montenegro, independent since 1389, also obtained international recognition in 1878. After the Balkan wars Serbia's boundaries were enlarged by the annexation of Old Serbia and Macedonia, 1913.

When the Austro-Hungarian empire collapsed after World War I, the Kingdom of the Serbs, Croats, and Slovenes was formed from the former provinces of Croatia, Dalmatia, Bosnia, Herzegovina, Slovenia, Voyvodina and the independent state of Montenegro. The name was later changed to Yugoslavia.

Nazi Germany invaded in 1941. Many Yugoslav partisan troops continued to operate. Among these were the Chetniks led by Draja Mikhailovich, who fought other partisans led by Josip Broz, known as Marshal Tito. Tito, backed by the USSR and Britain from 1943, was in control by the time the Germans had been driven from Yugoslavia in 1945. Mikhailovich was executed July 17, 1946, by the Tito regime.

A constituent assembly proclaimed Yugoslavia a republic Nov. 29, 1945. It became a federated republic Jan. 31, 1946, and Marshal Tito, a communist, became head of the government.

The Stalin policy of dictating to all communist nations was rejected by Tito. He accepted economic aid and military equipment from the U.S. and received aid in foreign trade also from France and Great Britain. Tito also supported the liberal government of Czechoslovakia in 1968 before the Russian invasion, but he paid a friendship visit to Moscow in 1972.

A separatist movement among Croatians, 2d to the Serbs in numbers, brought arrests and a change of leaders in the Croatian Republic in Jan. 1972. Violence by extreme Croatian nationalists and fears of Soviet political intervention have led to restrictions on political and intellectual dissent, which had previously been freer than in other East European countries. Serbians, Montenegrins, and Macedonians use Cyrillic, Croatians and Slovenians use Latin letters. Croatia and Slovenia have been the most prosperous republics.

Most industry is socialized and private enterprise is restricted to small-scale production. Since 1952 workers are guaranteed a basic wage and a share in cooperative profits. Management of industrial enterprises is handled by workers' councils. Farmland is 85% privately owned but farms are restricted to 25 acres.

Beginning in 1965, reforms designed to decentralize the administration of economic development and to force industries to produce more efficiently in competition with foreign producers were introduced.

Yugoslavia has developed considerable trade with Western Europe as well as with Eastern Europe. Money earned by Yugoslavs working temporarily in Western Europe helps pay for imports. Unemployment and inflation became serious in 1975. The U.S. agreed in 1977 to expand arms sales.

Pres. Tito died May 4, 1980; with his death, the post as head of the Collective Presidency and also that as head of the League of Communists became a rotating system of succession among the members representing each republic and autonomous province.

Zaire

Republic of Zaire

People: Population (1979 est.): 28,090,000. **Pop. density:** 30.66 per sq. mi. **Urban** (1977): 30.3%. **Ethnic groups:** Mostly Bantus: Luba 18%, Mongo 17%, Kongo 12%, Ruanda 10%, others. **Languages:** French (official), others. **Religions:** Roman Catholics, Protestants, syncretic sects 60%, Moslems 1%, others.

Geography: Area: 905,063 sq. mi., one-fourth the size of the U.S. **Location:** In central Africa. **Neighbors:** Congo on W, Central African Republic, Sudan on N, Uganda, Rwanda, Burundi, Tanzania on E, Zambia, Angola on S. **Topography:** Zaire includes the bulk of the Zaire (Congo) R. Basin. The vast central region is a low-lying plateau covered by rain forest. Mountainous terraces in the W, savannas in the S and SE, grasslands toward the N, and the high Ruwenzori Mtns. on the E surround the central region. A short strip of territory borders the Atlantic O. The Zaire R. is 2,718 mi. long. **Capital:** Kinshasa. **Cities** (1978 est.): Kinshasa 2,008,352; Kananga 601,239; Luluabourg 506,033.

Government: Head of state: Pres. Mobutu Sese Seko; b. Oct. 14, 1930; in office: Nov. 25, 1965. **Head of government:** First State Comm. Bo-Boliko Lokonga, in office: Mar. 6, 1979. **Local divisions:** 8 regions, capital district. **Armed forces:** regulars 20,500; para-military 35,000.

Economy: Chief crops: Coffee, cotton, rice, sugar cane, bananas, plantains, coconuts, manioc, mangoes, tea, cacao, palm oil. **Minerals:** Cobalt (two-thirds of world output), copper, cadmium, gold, silver, tin, germanium, zinc, iron, tungsten, manganese, uranium, radium. **Crude oil reserves** (1980): 135 mln. bbls. **Other resources:** Forests, rubber, ivory. **Per capita arable land:** 0.5 acres. Meat prod. (1978): beef: 22,000 metric tons; pork: 29,000 metric tons; lamb: 9,000 metric tons. **Fish catch** (1977): 107,000 metric tons. **Electricity prod.** (1977): 4.10 bln. kwh. **Labor force:** 78% agric.

Finance: Currency: Zaire (Feb. 1980: 2.92 = $1 US). **Gross domestic product** (1977): $4.5 bln. **Per capita income** (1975): $127. **Imports** (1978): $589 mln.; partners (1977): Belg. 20%, U.S. 12%, W. Ger. 11%, Fr. 9%. **Exports** (1978): $925 mln.; partners (1977): Belg. 22%, UK 19%, It. 11%, Gr. 9%. **Tourists** (1977): 24,500; receipts (1976): $11 mln. **National budget** (1975): $864 mln. revenues; $1.42 bln. expenditures. **International reserves less gold** (Jan. 1980): $216.19 mln. **Gold:** 259,000 oz t. **Consumer prices** (change in 1979): 97.7%.

Transport: Railway traffic (1976): 467 mln. passenger-km; 2.20 bln. net ton-km. **Motor vehicles:** in use (1974): 84,800 passenger cars, 76,400 comm. vehicles; assembled (1975): 2.11 mln. comm. vehicles. **Civil aviation:** 662 mln. passenger-km (1977); 41 mln. freight ton-km (1977). **Chief ports:** Matadi, Boma.

Communications: Television sets: 7,000 in use (1976). **Radios:** 2.45 mln. in use (1974). **Telephones in use** (1977): 48,000. **Daily newspaper circ.** (1976): 45,000; 9 per 1,000 pop.

Health: Life expectancy at birth (1975): 41.9 male; 45.1 female. **Births** (per 1,000 pop. 1975): 46.8. **Deaths** (per 1,000 pop. 1975): 20.7. **Natural increase** (1975): 2.6%. **Hospital beds** (per 100,000 pop. 1977): 291. **Physicians** (per 100,000 pop. 1977): 2. **Infant mortality** (per 1,000 live births 1975): 104.

Education (1977): **Literacy:** 30%. **Pop. 5-19:** in school: 45%, teachers per 1,000: 11. **PQLI:** 32.

The earliest inhabitants of Zaire may have been the pygmies, followed by Bantus from the E and Nilotic tribes from the N. The large Bantu Bakongo kingdom ruled much of Zaire and Angola when Portuguese explorers visited in the 15th century.

Leopold II, king of the Belgians, formed an international group to exploit the Congo in 1876. In 1877 Henry M. Stanley explored the Congo and in 1878 the king's group sent him back to organize the region and win over the native chiefs. The Conference of Berlin, 1884-85, organized the Congo Free State with Leopold as king and chief owner. Exploitation of native laborers on the rubber plantations caused international criticism and led to granting of a colonial charter, 1908.

Belgian and Congolese leaders agreed Jan. 27, 1960, that the Congo would become independent June 30. In the first general elections, May 31, the National Congolese movement of Patrice Lumumba won 35 of 137 seats in the National Assembly. He was appointed premier June 21, and formed a coalition cabinet.

Widespread violence caused Europeans and others to flee. Katanga, rich in minerals, seceded from the republic July 11, but ended the secession in 1963. The UN Security Council Aug. 9, 1960, called on Belgium to withdraw its troops and sent a UN contingent. President Kasavubu removed Lumumba as premier. Lumumba fought for control backed by Ghana, Guinea and India; he was murdered in 1961.

The last UN troops left the Congo June 30, 1964, and Moise Tshombe became president.

On Sept. 7, 1964, leftist rebels set up a "People's Republic" in Stanleyville. Tshombe hired foreign mercenaries and sought to rebuild the Congolese Army. In Nov. and Dec. 1964 rebels slew scores of white hostages and thousands of Congolese; Belgian paratroops, dropped from U.S. transport planes, rescued hundreds. By July 1965 the rebels had lost their effectiveness.

In 1965 Gen. Joseph D. Mobutu was named president. He later changed his name to Mobutu Sese Seko. On July 1 he renamed Leopoldville, Kinshasa; Stanleyville, Kisangani; and Elisabethville, Lubumbashi.

The country changed its name to Republic of Zaire on Oct. 27, 1971; in 1972 Zairians with Christian names were ordered to change them to African names.

In 1969-74, political stability under Mobutu was reflected in improved economic conditions. In 1974 most foreign-owned businesses were ordered sold to Zaire citizens, but in 1977 the government asked the original owners to return. A fall in copper prices in 1975 brought a surge in foreign debt and economic difficulties, causing political unrest, which continued through 1980.

In 1977, a force of Zairians, apparently trained by Cubans, invaded Shaba province (Katanga) from Angola. Zaire repelled the attack, with the aid of Egyptian pilots and 1,500 Moroccan troops flown in by France. The U.S. sent "nonlethal" supplies. But many Belgian and other European mining experts failed to return after a second unsuccessful invasion from Angola in May 1978, suppressed by French, Belgian, and Moroccan troops.

Zambia

Republic of Zambia

People: Population (1979 est.): 5,649,000. **Age distrib.** (%): 0–14: 46.5; 15–59: 49.3; 60+: 4.1. **Pop. density:** 18.82 per sq. mi. **Urban** (1978): 39.3%. **Ethnic groups:** Africans 99%, mostly Bantu tribes, Europeans and Asians 1%. **Languages:** English (official), 70 others. **Religions:** Christians 15%, traditional religions.

Geography: Area: 290,724 sq. mi., larger than Texas. **Location:** In southern central Africa. **Neighbors:** Zaire on N, Tanzania, Malawi, Mozambique on E, Zimbabwe, Namibia on S, Angola on W. **Topography:** Zambia is mostly high plateau country covered with thick forests, and drained by several important rivers, including the Zambezi. **Capital:** Lusaka. **Cities** (1978 est.): Lusaka 559,000; Kitwe 310,000; Ndola 291,000.

Government: Head of state: Pres. Kenneth David Kaunda; b. Apr. 28, 1924; in office: Oct. 24, 1964. **Head of government:** Prime Min. Daniel Lisulo; in office: June 16, 1978. **Local divisions:** 9 provinces. **Armed forces:** regulars 14,300; paramilitary 1,200.

Economy: Chief crops: Corn, tobacco, peanuts, cotton, sugar. **Minerals:** Cobalt, copper, zinc, gold, lead, vanadium, manganese, coal. **Other resources:** Rubber, ivory. **Per capita arable land:** 2.3 acres. **Meat prod.** (1978): beef: 28,000 metric tons; pork: 11,000 metric tons. **Fish catch** (1977): 53,700 metric tons. **Electricity prod.** (1978): 7.88 bln. kwh. **Labor force:** 85% agric.

Finance: Currency: Kwacha (Mar. 1980: 1 = $1.22 US). **Gross domestic product** (1978): $2.82 bln. **Per capita income** (1978): $414. **Imports** (1978): $748 mln.; partners (1977): UK 23%, Saudi Ar. 12%, W. Ger. 12%, U.S. 11%. **Exports** (1978): $817 mln.; partners (1977): Jap. 17%, UK 16%, W. Ger. 14%, It. 10%. **Tourists** (1976): 56,200; receipts (1977): $12 mln. **National budget** (1978): $679 mln. revenues; $784 mln. expenditures. **International reserves less gold** (Feb. 1980): $77.5 mln. **Gold:** 217,000 oz t. **Consumer prices** (change in 1978): 16.2%.

Transport: Motor vehicles: in use (1976): 93,500 passenger cars, 78,400 comm. vehicles. **Civil aviation:** 499 mln. pasenger-km (1977); 33 mln. freight ton-km (1977).

Communications: Television sets: 25,000 in use (1976). **Radios:** 110,000 in use (1976), 28,000 manuf. (1977). **Telephones in use** (1978): 54,475. **Daily newspaper circ.** (1976): 101,000; 20 per 1,000 pop.

Health: Life expectancy at birth (1975): 44.3 male; 47.5 female. **Births** (per 1,000 pop. 1975): 49.6. **Deaths** (per 1,000 pop. 1975): 19.1. **Natural increase** (1975): 3.1%. **Hospital beds** (per 100,000 pop. 1977): 366. **Physicians** (per 100,000 pop. 1977): 5. **Infant mortality** (per 1,000 live births 1975): 259.

Education (1977): **Literacy:** 49%. **Pop. 5-19:** in school: 52%, teachers per 1,000: 12. **PQLI:** 41.

As Northern Rhodesia, the country was under the administration of the South Africa Company, 1889 until 1924, when the office of governor was established, and, subsequently, a legislature. The country became an independent republic within the Commonwealth Oct. 24, 1964.

After the white government of Rhodesia declared its independence from Britain Nov. 11, 1965, relations between Zambia and Rhodesia became strained and use of their jointly owned railroad was disputed.

Britain gave Zambia an extra $12 million aid in 1966 after imposing an oil embargo on Rhodesia, and Zambia set up a temporary airlift to carry copper out from its mines and gasoline in. In Aug. 1968 a 1,058-mi. pipeline was completed, bringing oil from Tanzania. In 1973 a truck road to carry copper to Tanzania's port of Dar es Salaam was completed with U.S. aid. A railroad, built with Chinese aid across Tanzania, reached the Zambian border in 1974.

As part of a program of government participation in major industries, a government corporation in 1970 took over 51% of the ownership of 2 foreign-owned copper mining companies, paying with bonds. Privately-held land and other enterprises were nationalized in 1975, as were all newspapers. Decline in copper prices hurt the economy in the late 1970s, but was partly offset by increased Western aid.

Drought in 1979 caused further shortage of food supplies; the economy further deteriorated.

Zimbabwe

People: Population (1979 est.): 7,254,000. **Age distrib.** (%): 0–14: 49.2; 15–59: 47.8; 60+: 3.0. **Pop. density:** 46.1 per sq. mi. **Urban** (1978): 19.6%. **Ethnic groups:** Bantu tribes 96%, Caucasians 3%, Coloreds, Asians 1%. **Languages:** English (official), Shona, Ndebele. **Religions:** Christians and part Christians 75%, Moslems.

Geography: Area: 150,333 sq. mi., nearly as large as California. **Location:** In southern Africa. **Neighbors:** Zambia on N, Botswana on W, S. Africa on S, Mozambique on E. **Topography:** Rhodesia is high plateau country, rising to mountains on eastern border, sloping down on the other borders. **Capital:** Salisbury. **Cities** (1977 est.): Salisbury (met.) 610,000; Bulawayo (met.) 358,000.

Government: Head of state: Pres. Cannan Banana, b. Mar. 5, 1936; in office: Apr. 18, 1980. **Head of government:** Prime Min. Robert G. Mugabe; b. Apr. 14, 1928; in office: Apr. 18, 1980. **Local divisions:** 7 provinces. **Armed forces:** regulars 21,500; para-military 52,500.

Economy: Industries: Clothing, chemicals, light industries. **Chief crops:** Tobacco, sugar, cotton, corn, tea. **Minerals:** Chromium, gold, nickel, asbestos, copper, iron, coal. **Per capita arable land:** 0.9 acres. **Meat prod.** (1978): beef: 150,000 metric tons; pork: 11,000 metric tons; lamb: 10,000 metric tons. **Electricity prod.** (1978): 4.51 bln. kwh. **Crude steel prod.** (1979): 740,000 metric tons. **Labor force:** 63% agric.

Finance: Currency: Dollar (1976: 1 = $1.54 US). **Gross domestic product** (1976 est.): $3.25 bln. **Per capita income** (1976): $501. **Imports** (1973): $553 mln.; partners (1965): UK 30%, So. Afr. 23%, U.S. 7%, Jap. 6%. **Exports** (1973): $664 mln.; partners (1965): Zamb. 25%, UK 22%, So. Afr. 10%, W. Ger. 9%. **Consumer prices** (change in 1977): 11.9%.

Transport: Railway traffic (1978): 4.87 bln. net ton-km. **Motor vehicles:** in use (1974): 180,000 passenger cars, 70,000 comm. vehicles.

Communications: Television sets: 72,000 in use (1976). **Radios:** 255,000 in use (1976). **Telephones in use** (1978): 196,750. **Daily newspaper circ.** (1976): 78,000; 12 per 1,000 pop.

Health: Life expectancy at birth (1975): 49.8 male; 53.3 female. **Births** (per 1,000 pop. 1975): 47.5. **Deaths** (per 1,000 pop. 1975): 14.9. **Natural increase** (1975): 3.3%. **Hospital beds** (per 100,000 pop. 1977): 258. **Physicians** (per 100,000 pop. 1977): 9. **Infant mortality** (per 1,000 live births 1975): 122.

Education (1977): **Literacy:** 30%. **Pop. 5-19:** in school: 39%, teachers per 1,000: 11. **PQLI:** 46.

Britain took over the area as Southern Rhodesia in 1923 from the British South Africa Co. (which, under Cecil Rhodes, had conquered the area by 1897) and granted internal self-government. Under a 1961 constitution, voting was restricted to maintain whites in power. On Nov. 11, 1965, Prime Min. Ian D. Smith announced his country's unilateral declaration of independence. Britain termed the act illegal, and demanded Rhodesia broaden voting rights to provide for eventual rule by the majority Africans.

Urged by Britain, the UN imposed sanctions, including embargoes on oil shipments to Rhodesia. Some oil and gasoline reached Rhodesia, however, from South Africa and Mozambique, before the latter became independent in 1975. In May 1968, the UN Security Council ordered a trade embargo.

A new constitution came into effect, Mar. 2, 1970, providing for a republic with a president and prime minister. The election law effectively prevented full black representation through income tax requirements.

A proposed British-Rhodesian settlement was dropped in May 1972 when a British commission reported most Rhodesian blacks opposed it. Intermittent negotiations between the government and various black nationalist groups failed to prevent increasing skirmishes. By mid-1978, over 6,000 soldiers and civilians had been killed. Rhodesian troops battled guerrillas within Mozambique and Zambia. An "internal settlement" signed Mar. 1978 in which Smith and 3 popular black leaders share control until transfer of power to the black majority was rejected by guerrilla leaders.

In the country's first universal-franchise election, Apr. 21, 1979, Bishop Abel Muzorewa's United African National Council gained a bare majority control of the black-dominated parliament. Britain's Thatcher government, 1979, began efforts to normalize its relationship with Zimbabwe. A British cease-fire was accepted by all parties, Dec. 5th; elections were held in 1980. Independence was finally achieved Apr. 18, 1980.

United Nations

The 35th regular session of the United Nations General Assembly was scheduled to open in September, 1980. *See Chronology for developments at UN sessions during 1980.*

UN headquarters are in New York, N.Y., between First Ave. and Roosevelt Drive and E. 42d St. and E. 48th St. The General Assembly Bldg., Secretariat, Conference and Library bldgs. are interconnected. A new UN office building-hotel was opened in New York in 1976.

A European office at Geneva includes Secretariat and agency staff members. Other offices of UN bodies and related organizations are scattered throughout the world.

The UN has a post office originating its own stamps. *See Index for Postal Information.*

Proposals to establish an organization of nations for maintenance of world peace led to the United Nations Conference on International Organization at San Francisco, Apr. 25-June 26, 1945, where the charter of the United Nations was drawn up. It was signed June 26 by 50 nations, and by Poland, one of the original 51, on Oct. 15, 1945. The charter came into effect Oct. 24, 1945, upon ratification by the permanent members of the Security Council and a majority of other signatories.

Roster of the United Nations

(As of July 1980)

The 152 members of the United Nations, with the years in which they became members.

Member	Year	Member	Year	Member	Year	Member	Year
Afghanistan	1946	Dominica	1978	Laos	1955	Samoa (Western)	1976
Albania	1955	Dominican Rep.	1945	Lebanon	1945	Sao Tome e Principe	1975
Algeria	1962	Ecuador	1945	Lesotho	1966	Saudi Arabia	1945
Angola	1976	Egypt[2]	1945	Liberia	1945	Senegal	1960
Argentina	1945	El Salvador	1945	Libya	1955	Seychelles	1976
Australia	1945	Equatorial Guinea	1968	Luxembourg	1945	Sierra Leone	1961
Austria	1955	Ethiopia	1945	Madagascar (Malagasy)	1960	Singapore[1]	1965
Bahamas	1973	Fiji	1970	Malawi	1964	Solomon Islands	1978
Bahrain	1971	Finland	1955	Malaysia[1]	1957	Somalia	1960
Bangladesh	1974	France	1945	Maldives	1965	South Africa[5]	1945
Barbados	1966	Gabon	1960	Mali	1960	Spain	1955
Belgium	1945	Gambia	1965	Malta	1964	Sri Lanka	1955
Benin	1960	Germany, East	1973	Mauritania	1961	Sudan	1956
Bhutan	1971	Germany, West	1973	Mauritius	1968	Suriname	1975
Bolivia	1945	Ghana	1957	Mexico	1945	Swaziland	1968
Botswana	1966	Greece	1945	Mongolia	1961	Sweden	1946
Brazil	1945	Grenada	1974	Morocco	1956	Syria[2]	1945
Bulgaria	1955	Guatemala	1945	Mozambique	1975	Tanzania[3]	1961
Burma	1948	Guinea	1958	Nepal	1955	Thailand	1946
Burundi	1962	Guinea-Bissau	1974	Netherlands	1945	Togo	1960
Byelorussia	1945	Guyana	1966	New Zealand	1945	Trinidad & Tobago	1962
Cambodia (Kampuchea)	1955	Haiti	1945	Nicaragua	1945	Tunisia	1956
Cameroon	1960	Honduras	1945	Niger	1960	Turkey	1945
Canada	1945	Hungary	1955	Nigeria	1960	Uganda	1962
Cape Verde	1975	Iceland	1946	Norway	1945	Ukraine	1945
Central Afr. Rep.	1960	India	1945	Oman	1971	USSR	1945
Chad	1960	Indonesia[6]	1950	Pakistan	1947	United Arab Emirates	1971
Chile	1945	Iran	1945	Panama	1945	United Kingdom	1945
China[4]	1945	Iraq	1945	Papua New Guinea	1975	United States	1945
Colombia	1945	Ireland	1955	Paraguay	1945	Upper Volta	1960
Comoros	1975	Israel	1949	Peru	1945	Uruguay	1945
Congo	1960	Italy	1955	Philippines	1945	Venezuela	1945
Costa Rica	1945	Ivory Coast	1960	Poland	1945	Vietnam	1977
Cuba	1945	Jamaica	1962	Portugal	1955	Yemen	1947
Cyprus	1960	Japan	1956	Qatar	1971	Yemen, South	1967
Czechoslovakia	1945	Jordan	1955	Romania	1955	Yugoslavia	1945
Denmark	1945	Kenya	1963	Rwanda	1962	Zaire	1960
Djibouti	1977	Kuwait	1963	Saint Lucia	1979	Zambia	1964

(1) Malaya joined the UN in 1957. In 1963, its name was changed to Malaysia following the accession of Singapore, Sabah, and Sarawak. Singapore became an independent UN member in 1965. (2) Egypt and Syria were original members of the UN. In 1958, the United Arab Republic was established by a union of Egypt and Syria and continued as a single member of the UN. In 1961, Syria resumed its separate membership. (3) Tanganyika was a member of the United Nations from 1961 and Zanzibar was a member from 1963. Following the ratification in 1964 of Articles of Union between Tanganyika and Zanzibar, the United Republic of Tanganyika and Zanzibar continued as a single member of the United Nations, later changing its name to United Republic of Tanzania. (4) The General Assembly voted in 1971 to expel the Chinese government on Taiwan and admit the Peking government in its place. (5) The General Assembly rejected the credentials of the South African delegates in 1974, and suspended the country from the Assembly. (6) Indonesia withdrew from the UN in 1965 and rejoined in 1966.

Organization

The text of the UN Charter, and further information, may be obtained from the Office of Public Information, United Nations, N.Y.

General Assembly. The General Assembly is composed of representatives of all the member nations. Each nation is entitled to one vote.

The General Assembly meets in regular annual sessions

and in special session when necessary. Special sessions are convoked by the Secretary General at the request of the Security Council or of a majority of the members of the UN.

On important questions a two-thirds majority of members present and voting is required; on other questions a simple majority is sufficient.

The General Assembly must approve the budget and apportion expenses among members. A member in arrears will have no vote if the amount of arrears equals or exceeds the amount of the contributions due for the preceeding two full years.

Security Council. The Security Council consists of 15 members, 5 with permanent seats. The remaining 10 are elected for 2-year terms by the General Assembly; they are not eligible for immediate reelection.

Permanent members of the Council: China, France, USSR, United Kingdom, United States.

Non-permanent members were Bangladesh, Jamaica, Norway, Portugal, and Zambia (until Dec. 31, 1980); East Germany, Mexico, Niger, Philippines, and Tunisia (until Dec. 31, 1981).

The Security Council has the primary responsiblity within the UN for maintaining international peace and security. The Council may investigate any dispute that threatens international peace and security.

Any member of the UN at UN headquarters may participate in its discussions and a nation not a member of UN may appear if it is a party to a dispute.

Decisions on procedural questions are made by an affirmative vote of 9 members. On all other matters the affirmative vote of 9 members must include the concurring votes of all permanent members; it is this clause which gives rise to the so-called "veto." A party to a dispute must refrain from voting.

The Security Council directs the various truce supervisory forces deployed in the Middle East, India-Pakistan, and Cyprus.

Economic and Social Council. The Economic and Social Council consists of 54 members elected by the General Assembly for 3-year terms of office. The council is responsible under the General Assembly for carrying out the functions of the United Nations with regard to international economic, social, cultural, educational, health and related matters. The council meets usually twice a year.

Trusteeship Council. The administration of trust territories is under UN supervision. The only remaining trust territory is the Pacific Islands, administered by the U.S.

Secretariat. The Secretary General is the chief administrative officer of the UN. He may bring to the attention of the Security Council any matter that threatens international peace. He reports to the General Assembly.

Kurt Waldheim (Austria), secretary general, was reelected to a 2d 5-year term beginning Jan. 1, 1977.

The 1980-81 program budget was $1.25 billion, exclusive of trust funds, special contributions, and expenses for the Specialized or the Related Organizations.

The US contributes 25% of the regular budget, the Soviet Union 11.33%, Japan 8.66%, W. Germany 7.74%, and France, China, and Britain about 5% each.

International Court of Justice. The International Court of Justice is the principal judicial organ of the United Nations. All members are *ipso facto* parties to the statute of the Court, as are three nonmembers — Liechtenstein, San Marino, and Switzerland. Other states may become parties to the Court's statute.

The jurisdiction of the Court comprises cases which the parties submit to it and matters especially provided for in the charter or in treaties. The Court gives advisory opinions and renders judgments. Its decisions are only binding between the parties concerned and in respect to a particular dispute. If any party to a case fails to heed a judgment, the other party may have recourse to the Security Council.

The 15 judges are elected for 9-year terms by the General Assembly and the Security Council. Retiring judges are eligible for re-election. The Court remains permanently in session, except during vacations. All questions are decided by majority. The Court sits in The Hague, Netherlands.

Judges: 9-year term in office ending 1988: Robert Ago, Italy. Richard Baxter, U.S. Abdullah Ali, Egypt. Platon D. Morozov, USSR. Jose Sette Camara, Brazil. **9-year term in office ending 1985:** Taslim Olawala Elias, Nigeria, Hermann Mosier, W. Germany. Shigeru Oda, Japan. Salah El Dine Tarazi, Syria. Manfred Lachs, Poland. **9-year term in office ending 1982:** Isaac Forster, Senegal. Andre Gros, France. Jose Maria Ruda, Argentina. Nagendra Singh, India. Sir Humphrey Waldock, Britain.

The president until 1982 is Sir Humphrey Waldock, the vice president is Nagendra Singh.

Specialized and Related Agencies

These agencies are autonomous, with their own memberships and organs which have a functional relationship or working agreements with the UN. (Headquarters, number of member nations.)

International Labor Org. (ILO) aims to promote social justice, employment, and sound industrial relations; improve labor conditions and living standards. (Geneva, 142)

Food & Agriculture Org. (FAO) aims to increase production from farms, forests, and fisheries; improve distribution, marketing, and nutrition; better conditions for rural people. (Rome, 147)

United Nations Educational, Scientific, & Cultural Org. (UNESCO) aims to promote collaboration among nations in the fields of education, science, and culture and communication. (Paris, 150; one associate)

World Health Org. (WHO) aims to aid the attainment of the highest possible level of health. (Geneva, 155)

International Monetary Fund (IMF) aims to promote international monetary co-operation and currency stabilization. (Washington, D.C., 140)

International Civil Aviation Org. (ICAO) promotes international civil aviation standards and regulations. (Montreal, 146)

Universal Postal Union (UPU) aims to perfect postal services and promote international collaboration. (Berne, 162)

International Telecommunication Union (ITU) sets up international regulations of radio, telegraph, telephone and space radio-communications. Allocates radio frequencies. (Geneva, 154)

World Meteorological Org. (WMO) aims to co-ordinate and improve world meteorological work, and promotes operational hydrology. (Geneva, 152)

Intergovernmental Maritime Consultative Org. (IMCO) aims to promote co-operation on technical matters affecting international shipping. (London, 117)

World Intellectual Property Organization (WIPO) seeks to protect, through international cooperation, literary, industrial, scientific, and artistic works, i.e. "intellectual property." (Geneva, 114)

International Atomic Energy Agency (IAEA) aims to promote the safe, peaceful uses of atomic energy. (Vienna, 110)

General Agreement on Tariffs and Trade (GATT) is the only treaty setting rules for world trade. Provides a forum for settling trade disputes and negotiating trade liberalization. (Geneva, 85; 2 provisional, 30 de facto)

International Bank for Reconstruction and Development (World Bank) provides loans and technical assistance for economic development projects in developing member countries; encourages cofinancing for projects from other public and private sources, both bilateral and multilateral (Washington, D.C., 134). **International Development Association (IDA),** an affiliate of the Bank, provides funds for development projects on concessionary terms to the poorer developing member countries. (Washington, D.C., 121)

International Finance Corporation (IFC) promotes the growth of the private sector in developing member countries; encourages the development of local capital markets; stimulates the international flow of private capital. (Washington, D.C., 112)

Ambassadors and Envoys

As of June 1980.

The address of foreign embassies to the United States is Washington, D.C. The address of U.S. embassies abroad is simply the appropriate foreign capital. The following countries are not listed due to suspension of diplomatic relations with the U.S.: Albania[1], Angola[2], Cambodia[3], Republic of China (Taiwan)[4], Cuba[5], Iran[6], Iraq,[7], Vietnam[3], South Yemen[3].

Countries	Envoys from United States	Envoys to United States
Afghanistan	*Vacant*	A. Ghafar Farahi, Chargé
Algeria	Ulric St. Clair Haynes Jr., Amb.	Redha Malek, Amb.
Argentina	Raul H. Castro, Amb.	Jorge A. Aja Espil, Amb.
Australia	Philip H. Alston Jr., Amb.	Nicholas F. Parkinson, Amb.
Austria	Philip Mayer Kaiser, Amb.	Karl Herbert Schober, Amb.
Bahamas	William B. Schwartz Jr., Amb.	Reginald L. Wood, Amb.
Bahrain	Peter A. Sutherland, Amb.[9]	Abdulaziz Abdulrahman Buali, Amb.
Bangladesh	David T. Schneider, Amb.	Tabarak Husain, Amb.
Barbados	Sally A. Shelton, Amb.	Oliver H. Jackman, Amb.
Belgium	Anne Cox Chambers, Amb.	J. Raoul Schoumaker, Amb.
Benin	*Vacant*	Thomas S. Boya, Amb.
Bolivia	Marvin Weissman, Amb.	Roberto Arce A., Amb.
Botswana	Horace G. Dawson Jr., Amb.	Bias Mookodi, Amb.
Brazil	Robert Marion Sayre, Amb.	Antonio F.A. da Silveira, Amb.
Bulgaria	Jack Richard Perry, Amb.	Konstantin N. Grigorov, Amb.
Burma	Patricia M. Byrne, Amb.	U Hla Shwe, Amb.
Burundi	Frances D. Cook, Amb.[9]	Simon Sabimbona, Amb.
Cameroon	Hume A. Horan, Amb.[9]	Benoit Bindzi, Amb.
Canada	Kenneth M. Curtis, Amb.	Peter M. Towe, Amb.
Cape Verde	Edward Marks, Amb.	Viriato de Barros, Chargé
Centr. African Rep.	Goodwin Cooke, Amb.	Jacques Topandi-Makombo, Amb.
Chad	Donald R. Norland, Amb.	Mahamat Ali Adoum, Chargé
Chile	George W. Landau, Amb.	Jose Miguel Barros, Amb.
China, People's Rep.	Leonard Woodcock, Amb.	Chai Zemin, Amb.
Colombia	Diego C. Asencio, Amb.	Virgilio Barco, Amb.
Comoros	*Vacant*	*Vacant*
Congo	William L. Swing, Amb.	Nicolas Mondjo, Amb.
Costa Rica	Francis J. McNeil, Amb.[9]	Jose Rafael Echeverria, Amb.
Cyprus	Galen L. Stone, Amb.	Andrew J. Jacovides, Amb.
Czechoslovakia	Francis J. Meehan, Amb.	Jaromir Johanes, Amb.
Denmark	Warren Demian Manshel, Amb.	Otto R. Borch, Amb.
Djibouti	Jerrold M. North, Amb.[9]	*Vacant*
Dominica	Sally A. Shelton, Amb.	*Vacant*
Dominican Republic	Robert L. Yost, Amb.	Enriquillo A. del Rosario C., Amb.
Ecuador	Raymond E. González, Amb.	Ricardo Crespo-Zaldumbide, Amb.
Egypt	Alfred L. Atherton Jr., Amb.	Ashraf A. Ghorbal, Amb.
El Salvador	Robert E. White, Amb.	Francisco Aquino, Amb.
Equatorial Guinea	Hume A. Horan	Don Carmelo Nvono-Nca M. Oluy, Amb.
Estonia[8]		Ernst Jaakson, Consul General
Ethiopia	Frederic L. Chapin, Amb.	Tibabu Bekele, Chargé
Fiji	William Badde Jr., Amb.[9]	Berenado Vuniboro, Amb.
Finland	James E. Goodby, Amb.	Jaakko Iloniemi, Amb.
France	Arthur A. Hartman, Amb.	Francois de Laboulaye, Amb.
Gabon	Arthur T. Tienken, Amb.	Etienne Me Zui Me Ndo, Chargé
Gambia	Larry G. Piper, Amb.[9]	Ousman A. Sallah, Amb.
Germany, East	Herbert S. Okun, Amb.[9]	Horst Grunert, Amb.
Germany, West	Walter J. Stoessel Jr., Amb.	Peter Hermes, Amb.
Ghana	Thomas W.M. Smith, Amb.	Alex Quaison-Sackey, Amb.
Greece	Robert J. McCloskey, Amb.	John A. Tzounis, Amb.
Grenada	Sally A. Shelton, Amb.	Bernard K. Radix, Amb.
Guatemala	Frank V. Ortiz Jr., Amb.	Felipe D. Monterroso, Amb.
Guinea	Allen C. Davis, Amb.[9]	Mamady Lamine Conde, Amb.
Guinea-Bissau	Edward Marks, Amb.	Gil Vicente Vaz Fernandes, Amb.
Guyana	George B. Roberts Jr., Amb.	Laurence E. Mann, Amb.
Haiti	William Bowdoin Jones, Amb.	Serge Elie Charles, Amb.
Honduras	Mari-Luci Jaramillo, Amb.	Ricardo A. Midence, Amb.
Hungary	Harry E. Bergold Jr., Amb.	Ferenc Esztergalyos, Amb.
Iceland	Richard A. Ericson Jr., Amb.	Hans G. Andersen, Amb.
India	Robert F. Goheen, Amb.	Ashok B. Gokhale, Amb.
Indonesia	Edward E. Masters, Amb.	D. Ashari, Amb.
Ireland	William V. Shannon, Amb.	Sean Donlon, Amb.
Israel	Samuel W. Lewis, Amb.	Ephraim Evron, Amb.
Italy	Richard N. Gardner, Amb.	Paolo Pansa Cedronio, Amb.
Ivory Coast	Nancy V. Rawls, Amb.	Timothee N'Guetta Ahoua, Amb.
Jamaica	Loren E. Lawrence, Amb.	Alfred A. Rattray, Amb.
Japan	Michael J. Mansfield, Amb.	Yoshio Okawara, Amb.
Jordan	Nicholas A. Veliotes, Amb.	Al-Sharif Fawaz Sharaf, Amb.
Kenya	William C. Herrop, Amb.	John P. Mbogua, Amb.
Kiribati	William Badde Jr., Amb.[10]	*Vacant*
Korea, South	William H. Gleysteen Jr., Amb.	Yong Shik Kim, Amb.
Kuwait	Francois M. Dickman, Amb.	Khalid M. Jaffar, Amb.
Laos	*Vacant*	Khamtan Ratanavong, Chargé
Latvia[8]		Anatol Dinbergs, Chargé
Lebanon	John G. Dean, Amb.	Khalil Itani, Amb.
Lesotho	John R. Clingerman, Amb.	'M'alineo N. Tau, Amb.
Liberia	Robert P. Smith, Amb.	Herbert R.W. Brewer, Amb.
Libya	*Vacant*	*Vacant*
Lithuania[8]		Stasys A. Backis, Chargé
Luxembourg	James G. Lowenstein, Amb.	Adrien Meisch, Amb.

Countries	Envoys from United States	Envoys to United States
Madagascar	*Vacant*	Henri Jux Ratsimbazafy, Chargé
Malawi	Harold E. Horan, Amb.	Jacob T. X. Muwamba, Amb.
Malaysia	*Vacant*	Zain Azraai, Amb.
Maldives	Donald R. Toussaint, Amb.	*Vacant*
Mali	Anne F. Holloway, Amb.	Maki K. A. Tall, Amb.
Malta	Joan M. Clark, Amb.	Leslie N. Agius, Chargé
Mauritania	E. Gregory Kryza, Amb.	Sidi Bouna Ould Sidi, Amb.
Mauritius	Robert C.F. Gordon, Amb.	Chitmansing Jesseramsing, Chargé
Mexico	Julian Nava, Amb.	Hugo B. Margain, Amb.
Morocco	Angier B. Duke, Amb.	Ali Bengelloun, Amb.
Mozambique	Willard A. De Pree, Amb.	*Vacant*
Nauru	Philip H. Alston Jr., Amb.	T.W. Star, Amb.
Nepal	Phillip R. Trimble, Amb.	Keder Shrestha, Chargé
Netherlands	Geri M. Joseph, Amb.	Age R. Tammenoms Bakker, Amb.
New Zealand	Anne C. Martindell, Amb.	Hugo Judd, Chargé
Nicaragua	Lawrence A. Pezzullo, Amb.	Rafael Solis, Amb.
Niger	James K. Bishop, Amb.	Andre Wright, Amb.
Nigeria	Stephen Low, Amb.	Olujimi Jolaoso, Amb.
Norway	Sidney A. Rand, Amb.	Knut Hedemann, Amb.
Oman	Marshall W. Wiley, Amb.	Sadek J. Sulaiman, Amb.
Pakistan	Arthur W. Hummel Jr., Amb.	Muhammad Khan, Amb.
Panama	Ambler H. Moss Jr., Amb.	Juan Jose Amado, Amb.
Papua New Guinea	Harvey J. Feldman, Amb.	Paulias Nguna Matane, Amb.
Paraguay	*Vacant*	Mario Lopez Escobar, Amb.
Peru	Harry W. Shlaudeman, Amb.	Alfonso Arias-Schreiber, Amb.
Philippines	Richard W. Murphy, Amb.	Eduardo Z. Romualdez, Amb.
Poland	William E. Schaufele Jr., Amb.	Romuald Spasowski, Amb.
Portugal	Richard J. Bloomfield, Amb.	Joao Hall Themido, Amb.
Qatar	Charles E. Marthinsen, Amb.	Abdel Q.B. Al-Amari, Amb.
Romania	O. Rudolph Aggrey, Amb.	Nicolae Ionescu, Amb.
Rwanda	Harry R. Melone	Bonaventure Ubalijoro, Amb.
St. Lucia	Sally A. Shelton, Min.	Barry B.L. Auguste
Samoa	Anne C. Martindell, Amb.	Maiava Iulai Toma, Amb.
Sao Tome and Principe	Arthur T. Tienken, Amb.	*Vacant*
Saudi Arabia	John C. West, Amb.	Faisal Alhegelan, Amb.
Senegal	Walter C. Carrington, Amb.[9]	Andre Coulbary, Amb.
Seychelles	William C. Herrop, Amb.	*Vacant*
Sierra Leone	Theresa Ann Healy, Amb.[9]	Mohamed Morlai Turay, Amb.
Singapore	Richard F. Kneip, Amb.	Punch Coomaraswamy, Amb.
Solomon Islands	Harvey J. Feldman, Amb.	Francis Bugotu, Amb.
Somalia	Donald K. Petterson, Amb.	Abdullahi Ahmed Addou, Amb.
South Africa	William B. Edmondson, Amb.	Donald B. Sole, Amb.
Spain	Terence A. Todman, Amb.	Jose Llado, Amb.
Sri Lanka	Donald R. Toussaint, Amb.	W.S. Karunaratne, Amb.
Sudan	C. William Contos, Amb.	Omer Salih Eissa, Amb.
Suriname	John J. Crowley Jr., Amb.[9]	Roel F. Karamat, Amb.
Swaziland	Richard C. Matherson, Amb.	Norman M. Vilakati, Chargé
Sweden	Rodney O. Kennedy-Minott, Amb.	Wilhelm Wachtmeister, Amb.
Switzerland	Richard D. Vine, Amb.	Raymond Probst, Amb.
Syria	Talcott W. Seelye, Amb.	Sabah Kabbani, Amb.
Tanzania	Richard N. Viets, Amb.	Paul Bomani, Amb.
Thailand	Morton I. Abramowitz, Amb.	Prok Amaranand, Amb.
Togo	Marilyn P. Johnson, Amb.	Yao Grunitzky, Amb.
Tonga	William Badde Jr., Amb.	'Inoke F. Faletau, Amb.
Trinidad and Tobago	Irving G. Cheslaw, Amb.	Victor C. McIntyre, Amb.
Tunisia	Stephen W. Bosworth, Amb.	Ali Hedda, Amb.
Turkey	James W. Spain, Amb.	Sukru Elekdag, Amb.
Tuvalu	William Badde Jr., Amb.	Ionatana Ionatana, Amb.
Uganda	Gordon R. Beyer, Amb.	Joshua L. Zake, Amb.
USSR	Thomas J. Watson Jr., Amb.	Anatoliy F. Dobrynin, Amb.
United Arab Emirates	William D. Wolle, Amb.	Saeed Al-Shamsi
United Kingdom	Kingman Brewster Jr., Amb.	Nicholas Henderson, Amb.
Upper Volta	Thomas D. Boyatt, Amb.	Telesphore Yaguibou, Amb.
Uruguay	Lyle F. Lane	Jorge Pacheco Areco, Amb.
Venezuela	William H. Luers, Amb.	Marcial Perez-Chiriboga, Amb.
Yemen Arab Rep.	George M. Lane, Amb.	Yahya M. Al-Mutawakel, Amb.
Yugoslavia	Lawrence S. Eagleburger, Amb.	Budimir Loncar, Amb.
Zaire	Robert B. Oakley	Kasongo Mutuale, Amb.
Zambia	Frank G. Wisner II, Amb.	Putteho M. Ngonda, Amb.
Zimbabwe	Robert V. Keeley, Amb.	*Vacant*

Ambassadors at Large: W. Beverly Carter Jr., Victor H. Palmieri, Robert Krueger, Henry David Owen, Elliot L. Richardson, Gerard C. Smith.

Special Missions Headed by Ambassadors

U.S. Mission to North Atlantic Treaty Organization, Brussels—W. Tapley Bennett Jr.
U.S. Mission to the European Communities, Brussels—Thomas O. Enders
U.S. Mission to the International Atomic Energy Agency, Vienna—Gerard C. Smith
U.S. Mission to the United Nations, New York—Donald F. McHenry
U.S. Mission to the European Office of the UN, Geneva—Gerald B. Helman
U.S. Mission to the Organization for Economic Cooperation and Development, Paris—Herbert Salzman
U.S. Mission to the Organization of American States, Washington—Gale McGee.
United Nations Educational, Scientific, and Cultural Organization, Paris—Barbara W. Newell
Council of the International Civic Aviation Organization, Montreal—John E. Downs

(1) Relations severed in 1939. (2) Post temporarily closed in 1975. (3) U.S. embassy closed in 1975. (4) U.S. severed relations in 1978. (5) Relations severed in 1961; limited ties restored in 1977. (6) U.S. severed relations on Apr. 7, 1980. (7) Relations severed in 1967, limited staff returned in 1972; Belgium protects U.S. interests. (8) U.S. does not officially recognize 1940 annexation by USSR. (9) Nominated.

Major International Organizations

Association of Southeast Asian Nations (ASEAN), was formed in 1967 to promote political and economic cooperation among the non-communist states of the region. Members are Indonesia, Malaysia, Philippines, Singapore, Thailand. Annual ministerial meetings set policy; a central Secretariat in Jakarta and 11 permanent committees work in trade, transportation, communications, agriculture, science, finance, and culture.

The Commonwealth, originally called the British Commonwealth of Nations, is an association of nations and dependencies loosely joined by a common interest based on having been parts of the old British Empire. The British monarch is the symbolic head of the Commonwealth.

There are 43 self-governing independent nations in the Commonwealth, plus various colonies and protectorates. As of June 1980, the members were the United Kingdom of Great Britain and Northern Ireland and 14 other nations recognizing the British monarch, represented by a governor-general, as their head of state: Australia, Bahamas, Barbados, Canada, Fiji, Grenada, Jamaica, Mauritius, New Zealand, Papua New Guinea, St. Lucia, St. Vincent and the Grenadines, Solomon Islands, and Tuvalu (a special member); and 28 countries with their own heads of state: Bangladesh, Botswana, Cyprus, Dominica, The Gambia, Ghana, Guyana, India, Kenya, Kiribati, Lesotho, Malawi, Malaysia, Malta, Nauru (a special member), Nigeria, Samoa, Seychelles, Sierra Leone, Singapore, Sri Lanka, Swaziland, Tanzania, Tonga, Trinidad and Tobago, Uganda, Zambia, and Zimbabwe. In addition various Caribbean dependencies take part in certain Commonwealth activities.

The Commonwealth facilitates consultation among member states through meetings of prime ministers and finance ministers, and through a permanent Secretariat. Members consult on economic, scientific, educational, financial, legal, and military matters, and try to coordinate policies.

European Communities (EC) is the collective designation of three organizations with common membership: the European Economic Community (Common Market), the European Coal and Steel Community, and the European Atomic Energy Community. The 9 full members are: Belgium, Denmark, France, West Germany, Ireland, Italy, Luxembourg, Netherlands, United Kingdom. Greece signed a treaty, 1979, formally gaining full membership. Actual entry was set for Jan. 1, 1981. Portugual and Spain applied in 1977 for membership. Another 57 nations in Africa, the Caribbean, and the Pacific are affiliated under the Lomé Convention.

A merger of the 3 communities executives went into effect July 1, 1967, though the component organizations date back to 1951 and 1958. A Council of Ministers, a Commission, a European Parliament, and a Court of Justice comprise the permanent structure. The communities aim to integrate their economies, coordinate social developments, and ultimately, bring about political union of the democratic states of Europe.

European Free Trade Association (EFTA), consisting of Austria, Iceland, Norway, Portugal, Sweden, Switzerland and associated member Finland, was created Jan. 4, 1960, to gradually reduce customs duties and quantitative restrictions between members on industrial products. By Dec. 31, 1966, tariffs and restrictions had been eliminated. The United Kingdom and Denmark withdrew to become members of EC Jan. 1, 1973. Other EFTA members joined in an industrial tariff elimination pact with EC in 1972. All industrial customs barriers between the two blocs were removed July 1, 1976.

League of Arab States (The Arab League) was created Mar. 22, 1945, by Egypt, Iraq, Jordan, Lebanon, Saudi Arabia, Syria, and Yemen. Joining later were Algeria, Bahrain, Djibouti, Kuwait, Libya, Mauritania, Morocco, Oman, Qatar, Somalia, Sudan, Tunisia, United Arab Emirates and South Yemen. The Palestine Liberation Org. has been admitted as a full member. The League fosters cultural, economic, and communication ties and mediates disputes among the Arab states; it represents Arab states in certain international negotiations, and coordinates a military, economic, and diplomatic offensive against Israel. In retaliation to Egypt's signing a peace treaty with Israel, the League, Mar. 1979, suspended Egypt's membership and transferred the League's headquarters from Cairo to Tunis.

North Atlantic Treaty Org. (NATO) was created by treaty (signed Apr. 4, 1949; in effect Aug. 24, 1949) among Belgium, Canada, Denmark, France, Iceland, Italy, Luxembourg, the Netherlands, Norway, Portugal, the United Kingdom, and the U.S. Greece, Turkey, and West Germany have joined since. The members agreed to settle disputes by peaceful means; to develop their individual and collective capacity to resist armed attack; to regard an attack on one as an attack on all, and to take necessary action to repel an attack under Article 51 of the United Nations Charter.

The NATO structure consists of a Council and a Military Committee of 3 commands (Allied Command Europe, Allied Command Atlantic, Allied Command Channel) and the Canada-U.S. Regional Planning Group.

Following announcement in 1966 of nearly total French withdrawal from the military affairs of NATO, organization hq. moved, 1967, from Paris to Brussels. In August, 1974, Greece announced a total withdrawal of armed forces from NATO, in response to Turkish intervention in Cyprus. Nevertheless, Greece has continued to participate in NATO military planning activities.

Organization of African Unity (OAU), formed May 25, 1963, by 30 African countries (50 by 1980) to coordinate cultural, political, scientific and economic policies; to end colonialism in Africa; to promote a common defense of members' independence. It holds annual conferences of heads of state, has a council of foreign ministers meeting at least twice a year, a secretary-general and a mediation-arbitration commission. Hq. is in Addis Ababa, Ethiopia.

Organization of American States (OAS) was formed in Bogota, Colombia, in 1948. Hq. is in Washington, D.C. It has a Permanent Council, Inter-American Economic and Social Council, and Inter-American Council for Education, Science and Culture, a Juridical Committee and a Commission on Human Rights. The Permanent Council can call meetings of foreign ministers to deal with urgent security matters. A General Assembly meets annually. A secretary general and assistant are elected for 5-year terms. There are 28 members, each with one vote in the various organizations: Argentina, Barbados, Bolivia, Brazil, Chile, Colombia, Costa Rica, Cuba, Dominica, Dominican Republic, Ecuador, El Salvador, Grenada, Guatemala, Haiti, Honduras, Jamaica, Mexico, Nicaragua, Panama, Paraguay, Peru, St. Lucia, Suriname, Trinidad & Tobago, U.S., Uruguay, Venezuela. In 1962, the OAS excluded Cuba from OAS activities but not from membership.

Organization for Economic Cooperation and Development (OECD) was established in 1960 to promote stable economic growth in member countries and the world at large, and to help expand free trade. Nearly all the industrialized "free market" countries belong, with Yugoslavia as an associate member. OECD collects and disseminates economic and environmental information, and channels resources to developing countries. Members in 1980 were: Australia, Austria, Belgium, Canada, Denmark, Finland, France, West Germany, Greece, Iceland, Ireland, Italy, Japan, Luxembourg, Netherlands, New Zealand, Norway, Portugal, Spain, Sweden, Switzerland, Turkey, United Kingdom, United States. Hq. is in Paris.

Organization of Petroleum Exporting Countries (OPEC) was created Nov. 14, 1960 at Venezuelan initiative. The group has successfully maintained high oil prices, and has tried to advance members' interests in trade and development dealings with industrialized oil-consuming nations. Members in 1980 were Algeria, Ecuador, Gabon, Indonesia, Iran, Iraq, Kuwait, Libya, Nigeria, Qatar, Saudi Arabia, United Arab Emirates, Venezuela.

Warsaw Treaty Organization (Warsaw Pact) was created May 14, 1955, as a mutual defense alliance by Albania, Bulgaria, Czechoslovakia, East Germany, Hungary, Poland, Romania, and the USSR. Hq. is in Moscow. It provides for a unified military command; if one member is attacked, the others will aid it with all necessary steps including armed force; joint maneuvers are held; there is a Political Consultative Committee and a Committee of Defense Ministers. Albania was barred from meetings in 1962, withdrew in 1968.

U.S. Aid to Foreign Nations

Source: Bureau of Economic Analysis, U.S. Commerce Department

Figures are for calendar year 1979, and are in millions of dollars. (*Less than $500,000.) Data shown by country exclude the military supplies and services furnished under the Foreign Assistance Act and direct Defense Department appropriations. Data shown include credits which have been extended to private entities in the country specified.

Grants are largely outright gifts for which no payment is expected or which at most involve an obligation on the part of the receiver to extend aid to the U.S. or other countries to achieve a common objective. Net grants and credits take into account all known returns to the U.S. government, including reverse grants, returns of grants, and payments of principal. A minus sign (–) indicates that the total of these returns to the U.S. is greater than the total of grants or credits.

Other assistance represents the transfer of U.S. farm products in exchange for foreign currencies, less the government's disbursements of the currencies as grants, credits, or for purchases.

Amounts do not include investments in international financial institutions in 1979 as follows: Asian Development Bank, $29 million; Inter-American Development Bank, $239 million; International Development Assn., $241 million; International Bank for Reconstruction and Development, $16 million; International Finance Corp., $26 million.

	Total	Net grants	Net credits	Net other
TOTAL	**7,172**	**3,916**	**3,326**	**–70**
Military grants	**910**	**910**	**—**	**—**
Other grants, credits, ass't.	**6,262**	**3,006**	**3,326**	**–70**
Western Europe	**–110**	**39**	**–147**	**–2**
Austria	–5	—	–5	—
Belgium-Luxembourg	–7	—	–7	—
Denmark	–3	—	–3	—
Finland	–3	—	–3	*
France	–48	—	–48	—
Germany, West	–14	—	–14	*
Iceland	–5	—	–5	*
Ireland	–5	—	–5	—
Italy	–17	12	–29	—
Netherlands	–19	—	–19	—
Norway	–44	—	–44	—
Portugal	93	22	71	*
Spain	134	5	130	*
Sweden	–3	—	–3	—
Switzerland	–6	—	–6	—
United Kingdom	–125	—	–125	—
Yugoslavia	–25	—	–23	–1
Atomic EC	–5	—	–5	—
Coal-Steel EC	–7	—	–7	—
Other & unspecified	3	*	2	—
Eastern Europe	**206**	**—**	**230**	**–24**
Hungary	8	—	8	—
Poland	129	—	153	–24
Romania	76	—	76	—
Soviet Union	–7	—	–7	—
Near East & South Asia	**3,248**	**1,273**	**2,020**	**–44**
Afghanistan	38	19	19	*
Bangladesh	161	73	88	*
Cyprus	14	12	2	—
Egypt	890	112	806	–29
Greece	24	*	24	*
India	94	209	–118	3
Iran	–158	—	–158	*
Israel	1,539	659	880	*
Jordan	85	21	64	*
Lebanon	10	11	–1	*
Nepal	8	11	*	–3
Pakistan	17	14	17	–14
Saudi Arabia	–2	—	–2	—
Sri Lanka (Ceylon)	39	6	33	*
Syria	80	9	73	–2
Turkey	334	40	294	*
Yemen (Sana)	9	9	*	—
Other & unspecified	65	66	–1	—
East Asia & Pacific	**954**	**189**	**763**	**2**
Australia	–29	—	–29	—
Burma	*	*	–1	1
Cambodia	5	5	*	—
China-Taiwan	171	*	171	*
Fiji	1	1	—	—
Hong Kong	–5	*	–5	—
Indonesia	213	24	187	1
Japan	–69	—	–69	*
Korea (So.)	228	1	227	*
Laos	2	2	—	—
Malaysia	–16	1	–18	—
New Zealand	–3	—	–3	—
Philippines	140	30	110	*
Singapore	93	*	93	—
Thailand	107	7	100	—
Trust Terr. Pacific	111	111	—	—
Other & unspecified	6	6	*	—
Africa	**743**	**361**	**387**	**–5**
Algeria	150	1	149	—
Angola	1	2	–1	—
Benin	4	1	3	—
Botswana	11	10	1	—
Burundi	3	3	—	—
Cameroon	14	7	7	—
Cape Verde	4	4	—	—
Cen. African Rep.	1	1	—	—
Chad	12	12	—	—
Congo	1	1	—	—
Djibouti	1	1	—	—
Ethiopia	13	16	–3	*
Gambia	2	2	—	—
Ghana	20	13	7	1
Guinea	4	1	4	–1
Guinea-Bissau	1	1	—	—
Ivory Coast	1	2	–1	*
Kenya	26	10	17	—
Lesotho	11	11	—	—
Liberia	8	9	–1	—
Madagascar	2	3	*	—
Malawi	4	2	2	—
Mali	15	15	*	—
Mauritania	6	6	*	—
Mauritius	3	*	3	—
Morocco	35	18	18	–1
Mozambique	25	15	10	—
Niger	16	11	5	—
Nigeria	–3	1	–4	—
Rwanda	5	5	—	—
Senegal	29	28	2	*
Sierra Leone	5	5	*	*
Somalia	21	13	9	*
Sudan	25	6	19	—
Swaziland	3	3	*	—
Tanzania	24	13	11	—
Togo	6	5	1	—
Tunisia	10	12	1	–3
Upper Volta	24	24	—	—
Zaire	100	11	89	*
Zambia	40	3	37	—
Other & unspecified	58	55	3	—
Western Hemisphere	**351**	**270**	**78**	**2**
Argentina	–29	*	–29	—
Bahamas	–3	—	–3	—
Bermuda	–1	—	–1	—
Bolivia	36	24	12	*
Brazil	–17	2	–19	*
Canada	–9	—	–9	—
Cayman Islands	–2	—	–2	—
Chile	–184	13	–198	2
Colombia	–4	7	–12	*
Costa Rica	8	2	6	—
Dominica	1	1	—	—
Dominican Republic	59	10	49	—
Ecuador	8	5	3	—
El Salvador	10	6	4	—
Guatemala	17	10	7	—
Guyana	3	1	2	*
Haiti	29	20	10	—
Honduras	28	8	21	—
Jamaica	18	4	15	—
Mexico	103	17	87	—
Nicaragua	29	17	12	—
Panama	4	8	–4	—
Paraguay	2	3	–1	*
Peru	96	27	69	*
Suriname	–1	—	–1	—
Trinidad-Tobago	29	—	29	—
Uruguay	–3	*	–4	—
Venezuela	4	*	4	—
Other & unspecified	118	85	33	—
Intl. orgs. & unspecified	**869**	**873**	**–4**	**—**

Military Expenditures and Social Conditions

Source: World Military and Social Expenditures 1980 by Ruth Leger Sivard; copyright © 1980 by World Priorities Inc., Box 1003, Leesburg, VA 22075.

1977	Military public expenditures				Economic-social standing[2]
	per capita		per soldier[1]		
Country	Rank	U.S. $	Rank	U.S. $	Avg. Rank[3]
Afghanistan	116	4	134	527	133
Albania	47	55	102	2,915	55
Algeria	63	28	69	5,962	75
Angola	—	—	—	—	112
Argentina	52	46	44	9,254	33
Australia	20	184	10	36,914	11
Austria	39	73	32	14,892	11
Bahrain	29	112	29	18,000	38
Bangladesh	132	1	123	1,606	133
Barbados	116	4	126	1,000	36
Belgium	14	255	16	29,128	17
Benin	124	3	84	4,500	119
Bolivia	82	12	106	2,652	78
Botswana	—	—	—	—	86
Brazil	76	16	64	6,752	54
Bulgaria	42	68	89	4,020	26
Burma	111	5	131	900	115
Burundi	124	3	119	1,857	129
Cambodia	—	—	—	—	116
Cameroon	106	6	49	8,333	104
Canada	22	167	6	48,513	7
Central African Rep.	116	4	45	9,000	127
Chad	106	6	81	4,800	137
Chile	53	45	72	5,577	47
China	71	22	73	5,570	82
China, Taiwan	33	90	97	3,270	62
Colombia	103	7	103	2,877	69
Congo	67	25	78	5,143	90
Costa Rica	92	9	95	3,600	50
Cuba	53	45	112	2,275	42
Cyprus	58	41	108	2,500	51
Czechoslovakia	25	126	41	10,470	20
Denmark	17	207	14	30,086	4
Dominican Rep.	80	14	90	4,000	67
Ecuador	66	26	51	8,042	63
Egypt	28	119	33	13,409	85
El Salvador	85	11	59	7,143	79
Equatorial Guinea	71	22	126	1,000	105
Ethiopia	111	5	121	1,824	140
Fiji	103	7	90	4,000	48
Finland	32	92	40	10,950	9
France	11	281	15	29,705	10
Gabon	61	29	29	18,000	57
Gambia	—	—	—	—	121
East Germany	19	190	26	20,248	14
West Germany	10	282	11	35,417	6
Ghana	57	42	110	2,333	95
Greece	23	164	52	7,615	32
Guatemala	85	11	80	4,857	77
Guinea	116	4	96	3,500	125
Guyana	88	10	90	4,000	60
Haiti	127	2	119	1,857	117
Honduras	92	9	111	2,288	88
Hungary	40	69	58	7,165	29
Iceland	—	—	—	—	8
India	111	5	105	2,739	114
Indonesia	96	8	82	4,753	107
Iran	15	222	23	22,965	64
Iraq	24	138	46	8,862	66
Ireland	50	52	39	11,400	21
Israel	2	1,045	22	23,031	22
Italy	34	88	31	15,109	24
Ivory Coast	96	8	36	12,000	97
Jamaica	85	11	68	6,000	46
Japan	44	60	18	28,824	11
Jordan	40	69	101	2,985	81
Kenya	88	10	28	18,500	100
No. Korea	45	59	115	2,080	82
So. Korea	49	53	98	3,175	69
Kuwait	6	659	7	74,700	23
Laos	92	9	133	612	132
Lebanon	67	25	63	8,900	53
Lesotho	—	—	—	—	99
Liberia	116	4	124	1,400	102
Libya	27	125	37	11,724	33
Luxembourg	35	81	17	29,000	18
Madagascar	111	5	87	4,300	101
Malawi	124	3	53	7,500	128
Malaysia	51	49	42	9,953	58
Mali	116	4	65	6,500	138
Malta	75	21	60	7,000	33
Mauritania	60	30	67	6,143	125
Mauritius	132	1	126	1,000	58
Mexico	92	9	71	5,615	60
Mongolia	38	78	90	4,000	52
Morocco	59	38	47	8,600	98
Mozambique	111	5	107	2,579	130
Nepal	132	1	132	750	136
Netherlands	13	273	13	34,346	15
New Zealand	37	79	27	18,923	18
Nicaragua	71	22	54	7,429	68
Niger	127	2	90	4,000	135
Nigeria	63	28	48	8,502	103
Norway	12	276	19	28,615	3
Oman	4	844	5	52,846	74
Pakistan	82	12	113	2,152	119
Panama	96	8	118	1,875	42
Papua New Guinea	96	8	55	7,333	91
Paraguay	88	10	122	1,706	71
Peru	70	23	76	5,386	65
Philippines	82	12	74	5,556	92
Poland	30	108	35	12,202	27
Portugal	45	59	43	9,729	42
Qatar	1	1,257	4	60,000	30
Romania	53	45	75	5,400	31
Rwanda	116	4	88	4,250	124
Saudi Arabia	3	939	1	115,436	56
Senegal	96	8	55	7,333	118
Sierra Leone	127	2	100	3,000	122
Singapore	21	179	38	11,472	37
Somalia	88	10	126	1,000	131
South Africa	36	80	8	38,891	72
Spain	48	54	66	6,359	28
Sri Lanka	127	2	116	2,000	84
Sudan	80	14	85	4,385	109
Swaziland	127	2	126	1,000	87
Sweden	9	325	9	38,826	1
Switzerland	18	206	3	68,421	2
Syria	25	126	86	4,347	80
Tanzania	96	8	60	7,000	108
Thailand	79	15	99	3,133	89
Togo	103	7	77	5,333	110
Trinidad & Tobago	106	6	60	7,000	42
Tunisia	65	27	57	7,273	76
Turkey	43	63	70	5,807	73
Uganda	96	8	83	4,619	110
USSR	8	348	20	24,490	24
United Arab Emirates	5	822	21	24,346	49
UK	16	213	12	35,074	16
U.S.	7	465	7	48,337	5
Upper Volta	116	4	104	2,750	139
Uruguay	71	22	109	2,370	38
Venezuela	56	43	34	13,386	40
Vietnam	76	16	125	1,301	93
Yemen	76	16	116	2,000	123
So. Yemen	67	25	114	2,095	106
Yugoslavia	31	96	50	8,065	40
Zaire	106	6	79	5,000	112
Zambia	106	6	24	21,429	95
Zimbabwe	61	29	25	20,300	93

(1) "Soldier" represents all members of the armed forces. (2) Represents average ranks for Gross National Product per capita, education (encompassing public expenditures per capita, school-age population per teacher, percent school-age population in school, percent women in total university enrollment, literacy rate), and health (encompassing public expenditures per capita, population per physician, population per hospital bed, infant mortality rate, life expectancy). (3) Rank shows the standing of the country among those in the table. The rank order is repeated if more than one country has the same figure.

Population of World's Largest Urban Areas

City populations often cannot be used to compare urban areas because city limits may fall short of or exceed the built-up or urban area. The problem of comparison is compounded by the difficulty in obtaining reliable population data for a common year. The ranking of urban areas below represents one attempt at comparing the world's largest urban areas, taking into account, where necessary and within the limits of available data, urban development extending outward from the principal city named in the table.

New York, N.Y. (est. 1977)	16,962,000	Boston, Mass. (est. 1977)	3,898,000
Mexico City, Mexico (est. 1978)	13,993,866	Istanbul, Turkey (est. 1975)	3,864,493
Tokyo, Japan (est. 1977)	11,695,150	Santiago, Chile (est. 1978)	3,691,548
Los Angeles-Long Beach, Cal. (est. 1977)	10,605,000	Delhi-New Delhi, India (census, 1971)	3,647,023
Shanghai, China (est. 1978)	10,000,000	Madrid, Spain (est. 1974)	3,520,320
Buenos Aires, Argentina (est. 1978)	9,749,000	Wuhan, China (est. 1977)	3,500,000
Paris, France (census, 1975)	8,547,625	Karachi, Pakistan (census, 1972)	3,498,634
Peking, China (est. 1978)	8,000,000	Lima, Peru (census, 1972)	3,302,523
Moscow, USSR (est. 1978)	7,909,000	Madras, India (census, 1971)	3,169,930
Chicago, Ill. (est. 1977)	7,662,000	Berlin, E. and W. (both est. 1977)	3,038,224
Sao Paulo, Brazil (est. 1975)	7,198,608	Washington, D.C.-Md.-Va. (est. 1977)	3,033,000
Calcutta, India (census, 1971)	7,031,382	Sydney, Australia (census, 1976)	3,021,982
Tianjin, China (est. 1978)	7,000,000	Nanking, China (est. 1977)	3,000,000
London, England (est. 1977)	6,970,100	Rome, Italy (est. 1977)	2,897,505
Seoul, S. Korea (census, 1975)	6,879,464	Cleveland, Oh. (est. 1977)	2,874,000
Chongqing, China (est. 1977)	6,000,000	Bogota, Colombia (census, 1973)	2,855,065
Bombay, India (census, 1971)	5,970,575	Toronto, Ontario, Canada (census, 1976)	2,803,101
Philadelphia, Pa. (est. 1977)	5,627,000	Montreal, Quebec, Canada (census, 1976)	2,802,485
Cairo, Egypt (census, 1976)	5,084,463	Osaka, Japan (est. 1977)	2,723,752
Canton, China (est. 1977)	5,000,000	Houston, Tex. (est. 1977)	2,708,000
Rio de Janeiro, Brazil (est. 1975)	4,857,716	Yokohama, Japan (est. 1977)	2,694,569
San Francisco-Oakland, Cal. (est. 1977)	4,693,000	Manchester, England (est. 1977)	2,674,800
Detroit, Mich. (est. 1977)	4,620,000	Dallas-Ft. Worth, Tex. (est. 1977)	2,673,000
Hong Kong (est. 1978)	4,610,000	Melbourne, Australia (census, 1976)	2,604,035
Jakarta, Indonesia (census, 1971)	4,576,009	Caracas, Venezuela (est. 1976)	2,576,000
Manila, Philippines (est. 1975)	4,500,000	Ankara, Turkey (est. 1975)	2,572,562
Teheran, Iran (census, 1966)	4,496,159	Pusan, S. Korea (census, 1975)	2,450,125
Leningrad, USSR (est. 1978)	4,480,000	St. Louis, Mo. (est. 1977)	2,380,000
Shenyang, China (est. 1977)	4,400,000	Guadalajara, Mexico (est. 1976)	2,343,034
Luta, China (est. 1977)	4,200,000	Singapore (est. 1978)	2,334,400
Bangkok, Thailand (est. 1975)	4,178,000	Alexandria, Egypt (census, 1976)	2,318,655

U.S. Passport, Visa, and Health Requirements

Source: Passport Services, U.S. State Department and U.S. Public Health Service

Passports are issued by the United States Department of State to citizens and nationals of the United States for the purpose of documenting them for foreign travel and identifying them as Americans.

How to Obtain a Passport

An applicant for a passport who has never been previously issued a passport in his own name, must execute an application in person before (1) a passport agent; (2) a clerk of any federal court or state court of record or a judge or clerk of any probate court, accepting applications; (3) a postal employee designated by the postmaster at a Post Office which has been selected to accept passport applications; or (4) a diplomatic or consular officer of the U.S. abroad. Any children or brothers or sisters under age 13 may be included in the passport.

A passport previously issued to the applicant, or one in which he was included, will be accepted as proof of citizenship in lieu of the following documents. A person born in the United States shall present his birth certificate. To be acceptable, the certificate must show the given name and surname, the date and place of birth and that the birth record was filed shortly after birth. A delayed birth certificate (a record filed more than one year after the date of birth) is acceptable provided that it shows that the report of birth was supported by acceptable secondary evidence of birth.

If such primary evidence is not obtainable, a notice from the registrar shall be submitted stating that no birth record exists. The notice shall be accompanied by the best obtainable secondary evidence such as a baptismal certificate, a certificate of circumcision, or a hospital birth record.

A person in the U.S. who has been issued a passport in his own name within the last eight years may obtain a new passport by filling out, signing and mailing a passport by mail application together with his previous passport, two identical signed photographs and the established fee to the nearest Passport Agency or to the Passport Services in Wash., D.C. If, however, an applicant is applying for a passport for the first time, if his prior passport was issued before his 18th birthday, if he wishes to include a person other than himself in the passport, or if he is applying for an official, diplomatic, or other no-fee passport, he must execute a passport application in person.

A naturalized citizen should present his naturalization certificate. A person born abroad claiming citizenship through either a native-born or naturalized citizen must submit a certificate of citizenship issued by the Immigration and Naturalization Service; or a Consular Report of Birth or Certification of Birth issued by the Dept. of State. If one of the above documents has not been obtained, he must submit evidence of citizenship of the parent(s) through whom citizenship is claimed and evidence which would establish the parent/child relationship. Additionally, if through birth to American parent(s), parents' marriage certificate plus an affidavit from parent(s) showing periods and places of residence or physical presence in the U.S. and abroad, specifying periods spent abroad in the employment of the U.S. government, including the armed forces, or with certain international organizations; if through naturalization of parents, evidence of admission to the U.S. for permanent residence.

Under certain conditions, married women must present evidence of marriage. Special laws govern women married prior to Mar. 3, 1931 and should be investigated.

A person included in the passport of another may not use the passport for travel unless he is accompanied by the bearer.

Aliens — An alien leaving the U.S. must request passport facilities from his home government. He must have a permit from his local Collector of Internal Revenue, and if he wishes to return he should request a re-entry permit from the Immigration and Naturalization Service if it is required.

Contract Employees — Persons traveling because of a contract with the Government must submit with their applications letters from their employer stating position, destination and purpose of travel, armed forces contract number, and expiration date of contract when pertinent.

Photographs and Fees

Photographs — Identical photographs, sufficiently recent (normally taken within the past six months) to be a good likeness, both signed by the applicant, must accompany the passport application. An individual photograph of the passport bearer is required at all times. An additional photograph must be submitted showing other persons to be included in the passport.

Fees — The passport fee is $10. A fee of $4 shall be charged for execution of the application. No execution fee is payable where a passport is applied for by mail. All applicants must pay the passport fee and, where applicable, the execution fee unless specifically exempted by law.

The loss or theft of a valid passport is a serious matter and should be reported in writing immediately to the Passport Services, Dept. of State, Wash., D.C. 20524, or to the nearest passport agency, or to the nearest consular office of the U.S. when abroad.

Foreign Regulations

A visa, usually rubber stamped in a passport by a representative of the country to be visited, certifies that the bearer of the passport is permitted to enter that country for a certain purpose and length of time. Visa information can be obtained by writing directly to foreign consular officials.

Health Information

Smallpox — Some countries require an International Certificate of Vaccination against smallpox. Vaccination is not required for direct travel from the U.S. to most other countries.

Yellow Fever — A few African countries require vaccination of all travelers. A number of countries require vaccination if travelers arrive from infected or endemic areas. Vaccination is recommended for travel to infected areas and for travel outside the urban areas of countries in the endemic zones.

Cholera — A few countries require vaccination if travelers arrive from infected areas. Mozambique and Niger require vaccination of all travelers.

Plague — Vaccination is not indicated for most travelers to countries reporting cases of plague, particularly if their travel is limited to urban areas with modern hotels.

Malaria — There is a risk in the Caribbean, Central and South America, Africa, the Middle and Far East, and the Indian subcontinent. Travelers are strongly advised to seek information from their health department or private physician.

Return to the United States — No vaccinations are required to return to the United States from any country.

Vaccination Information — Yellow fever vaccine must be obtained at an officially designated Center, and the Certificate, valid for 10 years, must be stamped by the Center. The location of Centers is available from local health departments. Other vaccinations may be obtained from licensed physicians.

Travelers are advised to contact their local health department, physician, or agency that advises international travelers 2 weeks prior to departure to obtain the most current information.

Passports Issued and Renewed

Source: Bureau of Consular Affairs, U.S. State Department

Passports are actual count; other data based on sample.

Item	1960	1970[5]	1974	1975	1976	1977	1978	1979
New and renewed passports	853,087	2,219,159	2,415,003	2,334,359	2,816,683	3,107,122	3,234,471	3,169,999
Object of Travel[1]								
Government	115,910	146,169	149,523	131,739	134,883	153,992	142,901	146,879
Nongovernment	737,177	2,072,990	2,208,660	2,123,960	2,529,290	2,388,540	2,641,690	2,404,090
Personal reasons[2]	321,590	1,791,330	384,930	376,400	602,980	1,005,630	1,567,880	1,540,690
Pleasure[3]	350,897	216,700	1,382,100	1,315,600	1,511,060	1,102,250	821,070	552,580
Business[4]	24,540	39,940	267,980	273,110	272,600	190,890	163,770	202,450
Education	31,240	20,230	153,210	132,490	125,590	78,550	75,440	92,980
Religion	6,780	3,350	16,510	22,450	13,690	9,160	11,090	13,590
Health	1,460	640	1,860	1,510	1,500	1,090	980	610
Other	670	800	2,070	2,400	1,870	970	1,460	1,190
Not stated	NA	NA	56,820	78,660	152,510	564,590	449,880	619,030
First area designation:								
Africa	8,440	18,790	32,110	32,930	35,390	33,980	24,020	22,430
Australia and Oceania	35,220	51,210	101,250	96,300	106,540	108,280	95,670	107,180
Europe	669,662	1,910,169	1,714,613	1,611,410	1,990,993	2,291,942	2,535,381	2,392,029
Far East	55,960	116,730	162,130	154,660	180,090	187,130	170,010	187,820
North, Central, and South America	58,935	72,410	287,260	317,980	347,020	316,590	263,240	317,610
Middle-East	24,670	48,890	117,110	121,010	156,530	169,060	145,870	142,830
World Tour	200	960	530	60	120	140	280	100
Sex of passport recipients:								
Male	419,615	1,123,620	1,154,940	1,128,050	1,353,610	1,496,250	1,555,200	1,543,490
Female	433,472	1,095,539	1,260,063	1,206,309	1,463,073	1,610,872	1,679,271	1,626,509
Citizenship of passport recipients:								
Native	710,172	2,072,560	2,154,920	2,039,690	2,458,050	2,853,290	2,916,840	2,799,810
Naturalized	142,915	146,599	260,083	294,669	358,633	253,832	317,631	370,189

(1) Data not entirely comparable because of changes in classifications in 1961. (2) Includes "Personal business," "Join husband," "Accompany husband," "Business and pleasure," "Visit family." (3) Includes "Sightsee," "Vacation," "Visit," and "Tourist." (4) Includes applications formerly listed under "Employment" and "Commercial business." (5) Legislation effective Aug. 26, 1968 eliminated passport renewals.

Customs Exemptions and Advice to Travelers

United States residents returning after a stay abroad of at least 48 hours are, generally speaking, granted customs exemptions of $300 each. The duty-free articles must accompany the traveler at the time of his return, must be for his personal or household use, must have been acquired as an incident of his trip, and must be properly declared to Customs. Not more than one liter of alcoholic beverages may be included in the $300 exemption.

If a U.S. resident arrives directly or indirectly from American Samoa, Guam, or the Virgin Islands of the United States, his purchase may be valued up to $600 fair retail value, but not more than $300 of the exemption may be applied to the value of articles acquired elsewhere than in such insular possessions, and 4 liters of alcoholic beverages may be included in his exemption, but not more than 1 liter of such beverages may have been acquired elsewhere than in the designated islands.

In either case, the exemption for alcoholic beverages is accorded only when the returning resident has attained 21 years of age at the time of his arrival. One hundred cigars and 200 cigarettes may be included (except Cuban products) in either exemption. Cuban cigars may be included if obtained in Cuba and all articles acquired there do not exceed $100 in retail value.

The $300 or $600 exemption may be granted only if the exemption, or any part of it, has not been used within the preceding 30-day period and your stay abroad was for at least 48 hours. The 48-hour absence requirement does not apply if you return from Mexico or the Virgin Islands of the United States.

Bona fide gifts costing no more than $25 fair retail value or $40 from American Samoa, Guam, or Virgin Islands, may be mailed to friends at home duty-free; addressee cannot receive in a single day gifts exceeding the $25 limit.

U.S. Immigration Law

Source: Immigration and Naturalization Service, U.S. Justice Department

The Immigration and Nationality Act as amended by the Act of October 3, 1965, and the Immigration and Nationality Amendments of 1976 (P.L. 94-571) "marked the final end of an immigration quota system based on nationality." The latter amendments eliminated inequities in the existing law regarding the admission of immigrants from countries in the Western Hemisphere. The seven-category preference system, the 20,000 per-country limit, and the provisions for adjustment of status, all of which were in effect for Eastern Hemisphere countries, were extended to the Western Hemisphere.

The Immigration and Nationality Act, as amended, provides for the numerical limitation of most immigration. Not subject to any numerical limitations are immigrants classified as immediate relatives who are spouses or children of U.S. citizens, or parents of citizens who are 21 years of age or older; returning residents; certain former U.S. citizens; ministers of religion; and certain long-term U.S. government employees.

Numerical Limitation of Immigrants

Immigration to the U.S. is numerically limited to 290,000 per year. Within this quota there is an annual limitation of 20,000 for each country. The colonies and dependencies of foreign states are limited to 600 per year, chargeable to the country limitation of the mother country.

Visa Categories

Applicants for immigration are classified as either preference or nonpreference. The preference visa categories are based on certain relationships to persons in the U.S., i.e., unmarried sons and daughters over 21 of U.S. citizens, spouses and unmarried sons and daughters of resident aliens, married sons and daughters of U.S. citizens, brothers and sisters of U.S. citizens 21 or over (first, 2d, 4th, and 5th preference, respectively); members of the professions or persons of exceptional ability in the sciences and arts whose services are sought by U.S. employers (3d preference); and skilled and unskilled workers in short supply (6th preference); refugees (7th preference). Spouses and children of preference applicants are entitled to the same preference if accompanying or following to join such persons.

Except for refugee status, preference status is based upon approved petitions, filed with the Immigration and Naturalization Service, by the appropriate relative or employer (or in the 3d preference by the alien himself).

Other immigrants not within one of the above-mentioned preference groups may qualify as nonpreference applicants and receive only those visa numbers not needed by preference applicants.

Labor Certification

The Act of October 3, 1965, established new controls to protect the American labor market from an influx of skilled and unskilled foreign labor. Prior to the issuance of a visa, the would-be 3d, 6th, and nonpreference immigrant must obtain the Secretary of Labor's certification, establishing that there are not sufficient workers in the U.S. at the alien's destination who are able, willing, and qualified to perform the job; and that the employment of the alien will not adversely affect the wages and working conditions of workers in the U.S. similarly employed; or that there is satisfactory evidence that the provisions of that section do not apply to the alien's case.

Extension of Adjustment of Status

The Act of October 3, 1965, excluded Western Hemisphere natives from adjusting their status to permanent residence under Section 245 of the Immigration and Nationality Act which allows a nonimmigrant alien to adjust to permanent resident without leaving the U.S. to secure a visa. The 1976 Amendments restored the adjustment of status provision to Western Hemisphere natives, and declared ineligible for adjustment of status aliens who are not defined as immediate relatives and who accept unauthorized employment prior to filing their adjustment application.

Immigrants Admitted from All Countries

Fiscal Year Ends June 30 through 1976, Sept. 30 thereafter

Year	Number	Year	Number	Year	Number	Year	Number
1820	8,385	1881-1890	5,246,613	1941-1950	1,035,039	1974	394,861
1821-1830	143,439	1891-1900	3,687,564	1951-1960	2,515,479	1975	386,194
1831-1840	599,125	1901-1910	8,795,386	1961-1970	3,321,777	1976	398,613
1841-1850	1,713,251	1911-1920	5,735,811	1971	370,478	1976 July-Sept.	103,676
1851-1860	2,598,214	1921-1930	4,107,209	1972	384,685	1977	462,315
1861-1870	2,314,824	1931-1940	528,431	1973	400,063	1978	601,442
1871-1880	2,812,191					**1820-1977**	**42,664,965**

Naturalization: How to Become an American Citizen

Source: The Federal Statutes

A person who desires to be naturalized as a citizen of the United States may obtain the necessary application form as well as detailed information from the nearest office of the Immigration and Naturalization Service or from the clerk of a court handling naturalization cases.

An applicant must be at least 18 years old. He must have been a lawful resident of the United States continuously for 5 years. For husbands and wives of U.S. citizens the period is 3 years in most instances. Special provisions apply to certain veterans of the Armed Forces.

An applicant must have been physically present in this country for at least half of the required 5 years' residence.

Every applicant for naturalization must:

(1) demonstrate an understanding of the English language, including an ability to read, write, and speak words in ordinary usage in the English language (persons physically unable to do so, and persons who, on the date of their examinations, are over 50 years of age and have been lawful permanent residents of the United States for 20 years or more are exempt).

(2) have been a person of good moral character, attached to the principles of the Constitution, and well disposed to the good order and happiness of the United States for five years just before filing the petition or for whatever other period of residence is required in his case and continue to be such a person until admitted to citizenship; and

(3) demonstrate a knowledge and understanding of the fundamentals of the history, and the principles and form of government, of the U.S.

The petitioner also is obliged to have two credible citizen witnesses. These witnesses must have personal knowledge of the applicant.

When the applicant files his petition he pays the court clerk $25. At the preliminary hearing he may be represented by a lawyer or social service agency. There is a 30-day wait. If action is favorable, there is a final hearing before a judge, who administers the following oath of allegiance:

I hereby declare, on oath, that I absolutely and entirely renounce and abjure all allegiance and fidelity to any foreign prince, potentate, state or sovereignty, to whom or which I have heretofore been a subject or citizen; that I will support and defend the Constitution and laws of the United States of America against all enemies, foreign and domestic; that I will bear true faith and allegiance to the same; that I will bear arms on behalf of the United States when required by the law; that I will perform noncombatant service in the armed forces of the United States when required by the law; that I will perform work of national importance under civilian direction when required by the law; and that I take this obligation freely without any mental reservation or purpose of evasion; so help me God.

NORTH AMERICAN CITIES

Their History, Business and Industry, Educational Facilities, Cultural Advantages, Tourist Attractions and Transportation

Akron, Ohio

The World Almanac is sponsored in the Akron area by the Akron Beacon Journal, 44 E. Exchange Street, Akron, OH 44328; (216) 375-8111; a Knight-Ridder newspaper; founded 1839; circulation 161,835 daily, 218,969 Sunday; John S. Knight, editor emeritus; Paul Poorman, editor and vice president.

Population: 249,815 (city), 669,850 (metro) 5th in state; total employed (Jan., 1980) 285,100; 1979 average metro median family income $19,500.
Area: 56 sq. mi. (city), 413 sq. mi. (metro) on Ohio Canal, 30 mi. south of Lake Erie; founded 1825; Summit County seat.
Industry: home plants of Firestone, Goodyear, Goodrich, General and Goodyear Aerospace employ 29,304, use 40% of entire world rubber supply; other products mfd. in area include auto bodies, salt, clay, matches, rubber toys, road building equipment, missile components.
Transportation: Akron-Canton Airport served by 2 major carriers; Akron Muni Airport; Conrail covers 9 former private rail and trunk lines; birthplace of trucking industry, served by 79 motor common carriers; metro transit system; Greyhound and Continental Trailways; 3 taxicab firms; city bisected east-west and north-south by interstate highway systems.
Communications: 5 TV, one cablevision, and 5 radio stations; 2 public broadcast TV outlets.
New construction: record high $186 million in private investments in 1979 including Goodyear, General, Goodrich, Coca-Cola Bottling Co., Packard Electric, PPG Industries, Rockwell International, National Machine Co., Cummins Diesel.
Federal facilities: downtown federal office bldg.; Army Reserve Center; Navy-Marine Reserve Center.
Medical facilities: 7 major hospitals including specialized children's treatment center; State of Ohio Fallsview Psychiatric Hospital; Northeast Ohio Univ. College of Medicine.
Education: University of Akron and School of Law; Kent State University; Firestone Conservatory of Music.
Sports: NBA Cleveland Cavaliers play in nearby Richfield Township Coliseum; Firestone Country Club, home of the World Series of Golf, American Golf Classic; 35,000-seat Akron Rubber Bowl; Derby Downs, home of the All-American Soap Box Derby; home of the annual PBA $100,000 Firestone Tournament of Champions.
Cultural attractions: E. J. Thomas Performing Arts Center; Blossom Music Center, summer home of the Cleveland Orchestra; Stan Hywet mansion; Akron Art Institute; Akron Symphony Orchestra.
Other attractions: Children's Zoo; John Brown Home; Simon Perkins Mansion; Railway Museum.
Accommodations: nearly 2,500 Class A hotel and motel rooms in the metro area.
Further information: Akron Regional Development Board, Delaware Bldg., or Akron Convention Bureau, both 1 Cascade Plaza, Akron, OH 44308.

Albuquerque, New Mexico

The World Almanac is sponsored in the Albuquerque area by The Albuquerque Tribune, 717 Silver Avenue S.W., Albuquerque, NM 87102; (505) 842-2300; founded June 22, 1922 by Carl Magee; a Scripps-Howard Newspaper since Sept. 24, 1923; circulation 43,750; editor Ralph Looney; sponsors Tribune Annual Spelling Bee.

Population: 300,600 (city), 384,200 (county), 408,800 (metro area); first in state; total employed 187,100 (1980).
Area: 87.1 sq. mi. on Rio Grande and interstates 40, 25, and U.S. 66; Bernalillo County seat.
Industry: electronics with GTE-Lenkurt, Gulton, Sparton, Sandia Laboratories, General Electric, Digital Equipment Corp., Pertec, Honeywell, Intel; medical with Ethicon; clothing with Levi Strauss, Pioneer Wear.
Commerce: retail sales $1.917 billion; per capita income $7,546; financial assets $2.108 billion in 12 banks, $1.078 billion in 6 savings and loan assns.
Transportation: Santa Fe Railway, Amtrak; Continental Trailways and Greyhound bus lines; Albuquerque Int'l Airport, hub for 11 airlines, average 693 air movements daily.
Communications: 5 TV, 21 radio stations, 3 TV cable systems.
New construction: value of building permits $304 million in 1979, up from $285 million in 1978.
Medical facilities: 9 major hospitals.
Cultural facilities: symphony orchestra, light opera, 55 art galleries, 5 museums, 8 library branches, 16 legitimate theaters.
Educational facilities: Univ. of New Mexico, Univ. of Albuquerque, Technical-Vocational Institute; 107 public schools.
Recreational facilities: Sandia Peak ski area with longest tramway in North America; Rio Grande Zoo, Cibola National Forest, 12 golf courses, 21 swimming pools, 115 free city tennis courts, 16 other courts, 165 city parks.
Convention facilities: downtown convention center with underground parking facility and 300-room hotel; 111 motels and hotels.
Sports: Dukes baseball, pro volleyball, Univ. of New Mexico athletic activities.
History: founded Feb. 7, 1706; named for Duke of Albuquerque, viceroy of New Spain.
Further information: Chamber of Commerce, 401 2d NW, Albuquerque, NM 87102.

Allentown, Pennsylvania

The World Almanac is sponsored in the Allentown-Bethlehem-Easton area by Call-Chronicle Newspapers, 101 North 6th Street, Allentown, PA 18105; phone (215) 820-6500; Call founded 1883, daily circulation 117,000, Saturday Weekender 114,000, Sunday 157,000; editor & publisher Edward D. Miller; sponsors Park & Shop, housing development, newspaper-in-the-classroom; newsprint recycling, mini-marathon.

Population: Allentown 103,749, Bethlehem 72,396, Easton 28,282; metro area 637,000, 3d in state; total employed 275,200.
Area: 1,490 sq. mi. (metro) in eastern Pa. at Lehigh and Delaware rivers; Lehigh County seat.
Industry: Bethlehem Steel Corp., 2d largest in U.S.; home offices for Mack Truck Inc., Air Products & Chemicals, Martin Guitar, Rodale Press, New Jersey Zinc Co., Allen Products (ALPO); area leads in textile production; transistor developed in Western Electric here. Other industries include Kraft Foods, F.&M. Schaefer Brewing Co., American Can Co. (Dixie), Durkee Foods.
Commerce: 3d largest Pa. market; metro retail sales $2.6 billion; average family buying power $19,928.

Transportation: 3 major rail lines, 5 bus lines; 9 federal and state highways intersect area; jet airport serves 635,000 passengers annually on 5 airlines.
Communications: 4 TV and 12 radio stations.
Medical facilities: 6 major hospitals.
Cultural facilities: Allentown Art Museum (including Kress Renaissance and Baroque collection), Bethlehem Bach Choir, Allentown Symphony, 8 theater groups (plus 4 summer); Allentown Band is oldest continuing concert band in U.S.; 10 colleges including Lehigh Univ., Muhlenberg, Cedar Crest, and Lafayette serve 12,000 students.
Other attractions: center of "Pennsylvania Dutch" area, covered bridges; 1,400-acre park system; 1,170-acre game preserve, pre-Cambrian mountain range, access to Appalachian Trail, many historic houses, Allentown Fair, Kutztown Folk Festival, Liberty Bell Shrine, Bavarian Festival at Barnesville. Drum Corps Int'l Eastern Championship.
Sports: fishing, small game hunting, auto racing at Pocono Raceway, Allentown Jets basketball, Olympic bicycle velodrome at Trexlertown, Pennsylvania Stoners soccer.
History: settled in 1600s by Germans seeking religious freedom; Allentown founded 1762; hiding place for Liberty Bell during Revolutionary War; GAR founded Flag Day here 1906; Allentown one of 5 First Defender Companies in Civil War.
Further information: Chambers of Commerce in Allentown: 462 Walnut Street, 18105; Bethlehem: 11 W. Market Street, 18018; Easton: 157 S. 4th Street, 18042.

Amarillo, Texas

The World Almanac is sponsored in the Amarillo area by the Amarillo Globe-News, 900 S. Harrison, Amarillo, TX 79166; phone (806) 376-4488; a division of the Southwestern Newspapers Corp., and publisher of Daily News, Globe-Times and Sunday News-Globe; James L. Whyte, vice president and general manager; Jerry Huff, executive editor.

Population: 156,308 city; 178,033 metro area; total employed 86,060; 3.7% unemployed.
Area: 76.23 sq. mi. in central panhandle of Texas at junction of Interstate 40 and 27 in Potter and Randall counties; Potter County seat.
Industry: 3-state hub of $8.5 billion agribusiness market including wheat, beef, and produce, value $1.27 billion; ASARCO, Inc. copper refinery, Santa Fe Rail welding plant; Bell Helicopter, Levi Strauss, Iowa Beef Processors, Amarillo Gear, oil and gas, coal burning electricity plant, and Owens-Corning Fiberglas plant.
Commerce: wholesale-retail center for 5-state area; retail sales $737.9 million; bank resources $1.067 billion, 5 savings and loan assns.
Transportation: served by 6 airlines; 3 railroads, 4 bus lines, 18 truck lines; 2 interstate, 4 federal, and one state highway intersect Amarillo.
Communications: 4 TV, 12 radio stations.
Medical facilities: 9 hospitals including VA facilities in metro area; mental health centers, speech and hearing center.
Culture, recreation: Amarillo Symphony, fine arts complex, civic center complex and convention center, 2 dinner theaters, Amarillo Little Theatre (54th year of operation), Alibates National Monument, Lake Meredith, Wonderland Amusement Park and Storyland Zoo, Palo Duro Canyon State Park, Cal Farley's Boys Ranch, summer musical drama "Texas;" regional history museum, Discovery Center Planetarium, 46 parks, central library and 3 branches, 2 colleges, state vocational-technical school, National Helium Monument.
Sports: drag racing, stock car racing, college and high school football, basketball, baseball, wrestling, tennis, and track; Gold Sox baseball; rodeo, motorcycle racing.
History: settled 1887 as railroad crew camp, incorporated 1892; named for yellow lake clay.
Further information: Amarillo Chamber of Commerce, 1000 S. Polk, Amarillo, TX 79101.

Anchorage, Alaska

The World Almanac is sponsored in the Anchorage area by The Anchorage Times, 820 W. 4th Avenue, Anchorage, AK 99501, or P.O. Box 40, Anchorage, AK 99510; phone (907) 279-5622; founded 1915; circulation 48,000(E), 55,000(S); editor-publisher Robert B. Atwood; sponsors Alaska State Spelling Bee, Kodak Photo Contest.

Population: city, borough unified in 1975; total population of new municipality is 200,000 (1980 est.), almost half of state's population.
Area: 927 sq. mi. (census district), at head of Cook Inlet on south central coast.
Industry and commerce: business center for most of Alaska; aviation, oil companies, railroading, shipping, wholesaling, retailing, and national defense activities are largest elements in area's economy.
Transportation: Anchorage International Airport is major refueling stop on transpolar flights; thousands of small planes make city one of country's busiest air traffic centers with 5 airports and 25% of world's seaplanes in area; headquarters of Alaska Railroad; $12 million port.
Communications: 4 TV and 11 radio stations; 2 daily newspapers.
Medical facilities: 4 hospitals.
Federal facilities: Elmendorf AFB, Ft. Richardson.
Cultural facilities: annual Festival of Music; 4 theater groups; fine arts museum; community concert organization, opera company, civic symphony.
Educational facilities: 57 elementary and secondary schools enroll 37,000; Univ. of Alaska, Alaska Pacific Univ.
Recreation: 2 major alpine ski areas; cross-country skiing and bicycling; annual Fur Rendezvous with dogsled races; Iditarod dogsled race to Nome; Chugach National Forest.
Convention facilities: 7 major hotels and motels offer more than 2,000 rooms.
History: founded 1915 as headquarters for Alaska Railroad; twice winner of All America city award, for coping with rapid growth, and for swift recovery from catastrophic 1964 earthquake.
Further information: Chamber of Commerce, 612 F Street; or Convention and Visitors Bureau, 201 E 3d Avenue, both Anchorage, AK 99501.

Atlanta, Georgia

Population: 456,200 (city), 1,906,700 (metro), first in state, 19th in nation; total employed 900,800 (metro, 1979).
Area: 136 sq. mi. in north central Georgia, on Piedmont plateau of Blue Ridge foothills, 1,050 ft above sea level; 4,326 sq. mi. in 15-county metro area; state capital and Fulton County seat.
Industry: 2,200 manufacturers produce more than 3,500 commodities; 439 of Fortune 500 firms operate in Atlanta; Ford assembly plant, 2 GM assembly plants, Lockheed-Ga. Co.; home base for Coca-Cola, Fuqua, Ind., Delta Air Lines, Equifax, Scripto, Genuine Parts, Simmons Co., Gold Kist, Oxford Ind., Rollins, Inc., Georgia Pacific Corp., National Service Industries.
Commerce: financial, retail, wholesale center of Southeast; massive Merchandise Mart has 2d largest wholesale showroom in U.S. under one roof; 6th Federal Reserve District hdqtrs.; 75 banks, over 400 branches with resources of $9 billion (15-county metro); 21 savings and loan associations with 183 branches in metro area with deposits of $4 billion (1979).

Transportation: founded as railroad center; now served by 7 lines of 2 systems; Greyhound and Trailways bus terminal used by 3 companies with 167 buses in and out daily; 15 domestic and international passenger airlines, 3 commuter carriers, 2 freight only carriers; more than 1,600 scheduled flights daily; nonstop passenger service to 135 cities from Hartsfield International Airport, direct flights to 7 international cities including Brussels, London, Amsterdam, and Frankfurt; 2d busiest airport in world, 41 million passengers (1979) and No. one commuting point in nation's domestic air route pattern. Metropolitan Atlanta Rapid Transit Authority at $2.1 billion, most massive publicly financed project in Southeast since TVA; under construction is 52.9 mi. rapid rail, 8 mi. of rapid busways coordinated with street bus operations; Southeastern hub of 41,000 mi. interstate system with 6 legs of 3 interstate hwys. intersecting 100-acre downtown interchange; 63 mi. hwy. encircles city.
Communications: 8 TV stations, 39 radio stations, 8 cable TV companies; Protestant Radio and TV Center; largest Bell System toll-free dialing area; one of nation's 5 TV and radio network control centers; 10 daily newspapers.
New construction: $400 million expansion Hartsfield Int. Airport, $70 million federal office bldg., $14 million downtown library, $2.1 billion MARTA rapid transit system, $100 million Georgia Pacific office bldg., $37.7 million Georgia Power office bldg., $41.7 million Atlanta Apparel Mart, $100 million Southern Bell office bldg, total value city building permits (1979) $384 million.
Medical facilities: 56 hospitals with over 12,000 beds (metro), VA hospital; national Center for Disease Control of U.S. Pub. Health Dept., National Cancer Center at Emory Univ. Med. School.
Federal facilities: 31,500 federal, non-military employees (1979); Ft. McPherson, hdqtrs. U.S. Army Forces Command; Ft. Gillem; Dobbins AFB; NAS Atlanta.
Cultural facilities: Memorial Arts Center with museum, symphony orchestra, ballet, School of Art; Civic Center with auditorium-theater-exhibition hall; Callanwolde, multiuse arts center; 30 degree-granting colleges, including Ga. Tech, Ga. State Univ., Emory Univ.
Sports: NBA Hawks; NFL Falcons; NL Braves; stadium seats 52,000; Omni arena 16,500; World Championship Tennis, college football's Peach Bowl, PGA Atlanta Classic, the Atlanta Journal-Constitution Peachtree Road Race, The Atlanta Journal-Constitution Open International Tennis Championships, Chattahoochee River Festival; road, sports car racing, motocross.
Convention facilities: 860,000 convention delegates in 1979; Ga. World Congress Center has largest single display room in U.S. equal to 8 football fields; simultaneous translation facilities; 28,000 hotel/motel rooms, most downtown or near.
History: named 1845; chartered 1847; burned by Union Gen. Sherman 1864.
Further information: Chamber of Commerce, 1300 N. Omni International, Atlanta, GA 30302.

Augusta, Georgia

The World Almanac is sponsored in the Augusta area by the Chronicle-Herald, 725 Broad Street, Augusta, GA 30903; phone (404) 724-0851; Chronicle established in 1785, circulation 56,806, Herald 18,773, Sunday, 82,196; William S. Morris III publisher, E.B. Skinner general manager, David L. Playford managing editor, Herald; W.H. Eanes managing editor, Chronicle.

Population: 55,600 (city), 348,000 (metro area); total employed, 112,000 (metro).
Area: 1,695 sq. mi. (metro: Richmond, Columbia counties, Ga.; Aiken County, S.C.) straddling Savannah River; Augusta County seat.
Industry: diversified; Continental Can, Du Pont, Procter & Gamble, Lily-Tulip, Olin, Dymo, Monsanto, Columbia Nitrogen, A.E.C., TRW Corp., Owens-Corning, Kendall, Textron, Kimberly-Clark, Hall Printing, G.D. Searle, Emery Air Freight.
Commerce: wholesale, retail center of 17 counties in 2 states; 1979 retail sales $1.5 billion; per capita income $4,863, per family income $15,469; effective buying income $2.5 billion; 7 banks, 5 savings-loan assns.; distribution center.
Transportation: 5 railroads, 26 truck lines, 3 airlines at modern airport and in-city field for executive planes; Interstate 20, other federal highways; river shipping.
Communications: 3 TV and 13 radio stations.
Medical facilities: 9 major hospitals, including Eisenhower Memorial at Ft. Gordon, Medical College of Georgia.
Federal facilities: Ft. Gordon and Savannah River (AEC) Plant.
Cultural facilities: Augusta College, Medical College of Ga., Paine College, Univ. of S.C. at Aiken; museum, art gallery, arts council with 25 affiliates; Augusta Symphony, Augusta Opera Assn., Augusta Ballet Co.
Recreational facilities: hunting, fishing, boating, camping; 7 golf courses; home of Masters Golf Tournament.
Convention facilities: convention and civic center opened in 1979.
History founded as fort 1717; named for wife of Prince of Wales 1735; capital of Georgia 1778.
Further information: Chamber of Commerce of Greater Augusta, 600 Broad Street Plaza, Augusta, GA 30902.

Baltimore, Maryland

The World Almanac is sponsored in the Baltimore area by The Baltimore Sun, 501 N. Calvert Street, Baltimore, MD 21202; phone (301) 332-6000; founded in 1837; publishes The Sun, The Evening Sun and The Sunday Sun; daily circulation 350,848, Sunday 374,989. President and publisher, Donald H. Patterson Sr.; managing editor The Sun, Paul A. Banker; managing editor The Evening Sun, John M. Lemmon; The Sun has 8 foreign bureaus, in addition to the Washington Bureau and a west coast correspondent. News & feature stories from all 3 papers are syndicated nationally by The Field News Service.

Population: 820,700 (city), 2,164,200 (metro); city first in state, 8th in U.S.; 978,000 metro employed.
Area: 91 sq. mi. (city), 2,225 sq. mi. (metro) in central Maryland on Patapsco River, a tributary of Chesapeake Bay.
Industry: highly diversified; most important: steel production, electronic equipment, food processing, transportation equipment, chemical products.
Commerce: $12.7 billion effective buying income in city and 5 surrounding counties; average household EBI $17,294; retail sales over $6.1 billion in 1978; area supports 12 regional shopping malls, over 250 shopping centers, 8 traditional department stores.
Transportation: Baltimore-Washington International Airport 9 mi. from downtown; passenger terminal can handle 11 million passengers a year. Harbor Tunnel, Francis Scott Key Bridge carry traffic across harbor; Amtrak; state authorized buses; subway system under construction. Major interstate highways allow overnight trucking service to 67 million people.
Port facilities: nation's 4th largest port; furthest inland port on Atlantic Coast; responsible for 170,000 jobs and $3 billion in annual economic impact on market; World Trade Center focal point of port commerce. Leading cargoes: ores, petroleum products, grains.
New construction: Central business district rebuilt in last 18 years featuring Charles Center, Hopkins Plaza, Inner Harbor; new Inner Harbor construction includes: Hyatt Hotel, Baltimore Aquarium, Harborplace (2 pavilions of shops and eateries), reclamation of former fish market, rail yards, power plant, garment district to become restaurants, shops, offices, apartments. Mt. Royal District: new Md. Concert Center, renovation of Lyric Theatre, Md. Institute College of Art; major new shopping malls in Annapolis, Carroll-

ne, White Marsh; Coldspring, new 375-acre city neighhood.

nvention facilities: $45-million Baltimore Convention ter with 115,000 sq. ft. exhibition space, 26 meeting ms. Civic Center: 35 meeting rooms, 111,000 sq. ft. ext space; 3 downtown hotels, approx. 1,000 rooms.

tural facilities: Baltimore Symphony Orchestra, Md. let Co., Baltimore Opera Co., Baltimore Museum of Art, lters Art Gallery, Md. Science Center, Morris Mechanic eatre (pre-Broadway and touring shows), Center Stage pertory co.), Md. Historical Society.

cational facilities: 18 metro colleges, universities, 8 2-r colleges; Johns Hopkins Univ. and School of Medicine; iv. of Md. Professional Schools, Towson State Univ., rgan State Univ., Peabody Conservatory of Music, U.S. val Academy.

rts & Recreation: Orioles (baseball), Colts (NFL foot-); horse racing at Timonium, Pimlico (home of Preaks); steeplechase racing features Md. Hunt Cup; Chesake Bay offers fishing, boating, yachting, waterfowl nting; ocean and ski resorts within 3-hour drive.

mmunications: 3 daily newspapers (one morning, 2 eveg), 2 Sunday in city, 2 more dailies in metro area; 5 TV stations (4 commercial, 1 PBS), 31 radio stations.

Other attractions: City Fair, Timonium State Fair in Sept.; Preakness Festival Week in May; ethnic, craft, music festivals through summer; Ft. McHenry Historic Shrine where Francis Scott Key wrote "Star Spangled Banner;" Constellation, first ship in U.S. Navy; Baltimore & Ohio Transportation Museum; Edgar Allen Poe home and grave; Babe Ruth house; Washington Monument in Mt. Vernon Square; Baltimore Streetcar Museum; 142-acre zoo in Druid Hill Park; restored early-19th century rowhouses in Fells Point, Bolton Hill, Seton Hill, Otterbein.

History: founded in 1729 by members of Calvert family, the Lords of Baltimore; one of the 13 original colonies; nation's first railroad (Baltimore & Ohio) built to counter competition from new Erie Canal. Baltimore "firsts" include: first umbrella in U.S., first investment banking house in U.S., first commercial ice cream factory, first dental college in the world.

Further information: Baltimore Economic Development Corp., 22 Light Street; Baltimore Promotion Council, 1102 St. Paul Street both 21202; Baltimore Convention Bureau, One W. Pratt Street 21201.

Baton Rouge, Louisiana

The World Almanac is sponsored in the Baton Rouge area by the Morning Advocate and State-Times, 525 afayette Street, Baton Rouge, LA 70821; phone (504) 383-1111; founded 1842; combined daily circulation 9,876, Sunday 116,782; president, Charles P. Manship Jr.; publisher, Douglas L. Manship; vice president of ws and production, Richard Palmer; vice president of business and advertising, Charles Garvey; executive ditor, all newspapers, Jim Hughes; managing editor, Mike Walker (Morning Advocate).

opulation: 224,000 (city), 462,488 (metro); total 1979 MSA employment 207,500.

ea: city, 42.83 sq. mi.; parish, 407.01 sq. mi.; on east bank Mississippi River, 80 mi. northeast of New Orleans; state pital, East Baton Rouge Parish seat.

dustry: northern anchor of 100-mi. long petrochemical mplex along Mississippi River.

ommerce: marketing center for major trade area of 0,000; bank resources $2.5 billion; 6 banks, 7 savings and an associations.

ansportation: major transfer point on southern federal terstate system; 2 airports with 3 airlines; 2 bus lines; 4 ilroad trunk lines; Port of Baton Rouge, 4th largest in .S., handled over 77 million tons in 1979.

ommunications: 4 TV and 9 radio stations; 2 daily newspars, 2 weeklies.

ultural facilities: 6 museums, 4 theaters, symphony, planerium, 5 art galleries; "Riverside Centroplex" civic center.

Educational facilities: Louisiana State Univ., founded 1860, center of 8-campus system; Southern Univ., largest Negro land-grant college in U.S., center of 3-college system.

Sports: LSU Tigers and Southern Jaguars home stadia, football, basketball, track.

Other attractions: state capitol; city-parish zoo and arboretum; 67 parks; major recreational lakes.

History: first noted by French explorer Iberville in 1699, Baton Rouge (French: red stick) was already occupied by the Istrouma (also translates red stick) Indians; Louisiana's capital since 1882; government structure is a city-parish combination with a mayor-president and city-parish council.

Further information: Chamber of Commerce, P.O. Box 1868, Baton Rouge, 70821; Louisiana Tourist Commission, P.O. Box 44291, Capitol Station, Baton Rouge, 70804; Baton Rouge Area Convention and Visitors Bureau, P.O. Box 3202, Baton Rouge, 70821.

Billings, Montana

The World Almanac is sponsored in the Billings area by the Billings Gazette, 401 N. Broadway, Billings, MT 9101; phone (406) 657-1200; founded 1885; member of Lee Enterprises, Inc. since 1960; circulation daily 8,900, Sunday 61,140; publisher George D. Remington, editor William N. Roesgen.

opulation: 105,000 (metro area), first in state; total emloyed 49,300.

rea: south central Montana on Yellowstone River, 125 mi. om Yellowstone Park; Yellowstone County seat.

ndustry: 3 oil refineries, beet sugar refinery, 2 packing lants, 3d largest livestock auction yards in U.S., center for orthern Great Plains coal industry; district headquarters urlington Northern Railroad.

ommerce: wholesale-retail center for eastern Montana, orthern Wyoming; retail sales (1979) $430 million; 9 banks, savings and loan assns., average spendable family income 16,166.

ransportation: 4 airlines, one railroad, 2 bus lines, 98 mor carriers, interstates 90 and 94; Metro city bus transit.

ommunications: 2 TV, 9 radio stations, one weekly, one aily newspaper.

lew Construction: total permits, commercial $26 million, esidential $27 million, church/school $6 million.

ledical facilities: 2 hospitals, 478 beds, 75 dentists, 200 doctors, 5 nursing homes, Northern Rockies Regional Cancer Treatment Ctr., Regional Mental Health Ctr.

Cultural facilities: 5 art galleries, symphony orchestra, 2 western museums, studio theater, theater of performing arts, liberal arts college, private (church related) college, Metra Civic Center sports and concerts; 5 golf courses, 90 churches, vo-tech program, sheltered workshop, 37 public schools, 10 parochial schools, Center for Handicapped Children, Migrant Children's Program.

Other attractions: big game hunting, fishing, boating, skiing within one hour's drive; snowmobiling, bicycling, saddle clubs; auto & motorcycle, and horse racing; 23 city parks; 2,800 hotel/motel rooms, Metra civic center.

History: founded 1882 with arrival of Northern Pacific Railroad; named after Frederic Billings, then NP president; now largest city in 500-mile radius.

Further information: Tourist Information Bureau, Billings Chamber of Commerce, P.O. Box 2519, Billings, MT 59103.

Binghamton, New York

The World Almanac is sponsored in the Binghamton area by The Evening Press and The Sun-Bulletin, Vestal Parkway East, Binghamton, NY 13902; phone (607) 798-1234; circulation: evening 67,834, Sunday 82,9 morning 27,638, Saturday morning and holidays 73,472; president and publisher Fred G. Eaton, associ publisher and executive editor Sal DeVivo, Sun-Bulletin managing editor Soren W. Nielsen, Evening Pre managing editor Michael G. Doll.

Population: 57,900 (city), 303,400 (metro area), 8th among state metro areas; total employed 124,888.
Area: 10.98 sq. mi. at junction of Chenango and Susquehanna rivers; 715 sq. mi. in county; Broome County seat.
Industry: IBM, computers; Singer Co., transportation equipment products and simulators; Endicott Johnson Corp., shoes; Universal Instruments, production assembly equipment; General Electric, aircraft electronic equipment; Crowley Food, dairy food processing; GAF, graphic arts; Frito Lay, snack foods; Vail Ballou Press; Grosset & Dunlap, printing and publication.
Commerce: national headquarters of Security Mutual Life Insurance Co. and Columbian Mutual Life Insurance Co.; 12 banks.
Transportation: 7 airlines, major being USAir out of Broome County Airport; intersection Interstates 81 & 88 and Route 17; Conrail and Delaware & Hudson freight rail carriers.
Communications: 4 TV stations, 4 AM, 3 FM radio stations.
Medical facilities: 4 major hospitals.
Cultural facilities: Roberson Center for the Arts and S ences, Binghamton Museum of Fine Arts, Kopernik Obs vatory; Tri-Cities Opera, Binghamton Symphony & Cho Society, BC Pops; SUNY-Binghamton—Cider Mill Pl house, Harpur Jazz & Wind Ensemble, University Orches & Chorus, University Art Gallery; Broome Community C lege.
Other attractions: Veterans Memorial Arena, Oakdale M municipal parks zoo, 2 major state parks on outskirts, county parks.
Sports: Binghamton Whalers hockey; BC Open golf tour ment; Pro Bowlers Assn. eastern champion invitational.
History: settled 1800; became rail center by 1848, wi roads replacing old Chenango Canal that fed Erie Can named for Philadelphia patriot and multi-millionaire W liam Bingham.
Further information: Broome County Chamber of Co merce Tourist Information, 84 Court Street, Binghamtc NY 13902.

Birmingham, Alabama

The World Almanac is sponsored in the Birmingham area by The Birmingham Post-Herald, 2200 Fourth A enue N., Birmingham, AL 35202; phone (205) 325-2222; Post founded 1921 by Scripps-Howard Newspape Herald founded 1887; circulation, 75,630; editor Angus McEachran, vice president W. H. Metz, managing e tor George Cook; major public service projects include Goodfellow Christmas Fund, Alabama Favori Teacher selection.

Population: 280,544 (city, 1976 est.), 657,200 (county, 1978 est.), 818,200 (metro, 1978 est.); employment 358,100 (metro, 1979).
Area: 89 sq. mi. in north central Alabama; state's largest city; Jefferson County seat.
Industry: heavy manufacturing in metals; U.S. Steel is area's largest employer; U.S. Pipe and Foundry and American Cast Iron Pipe Co. are in top 10 employers; South Central Bell's 5-state headquarters located in city.
Commerce: wholesale-retail center for Alabama; retail sales (1979) $5.4 billion; bank debits (1978) $96.8 billion; 14 banks (county), 6 bank holding companies, 7 savings and loan assns.
Transportation: 5 major rail freight lines, Amtrak; Greyhound and Continental Trailways bus lines; Eastern, Delta, United, Republic and USAir air lines with modern airport terminal; 75 truck line terminals; 3 interstate highways, I-59 complete, I-65 and I-20 under construction.
Communications: 2 daily newspapers, 3 commercial TV stations, 16 commercial radio stations, one PBS TV and one PBS radio outlet.
Medical facilities: Univ. of Alabama in Birmingham Medical Center covers 60 sq. blocks; heart surgery team brings patients from all over the world; Veterans Administration hospital, in same complex, is the base of organ transplant program; Baptist Medical Centers have 2 major hospitals; 13 other hospitals.
Cultural facilities: symphony orchestra; Oscar Wells M seum of Art with more than $4 million in assets; Ci Opera; 4 resident civic theaters; 2 resident ballet companie
Education: Samford Univ., Birmingham-Southern, Mil and Daniel Payne colleges; Jefferson State and Lawson Sta junior colleges.
Convention facilities: civic center with exhibition hall, the ter, music hall, and coliseum; several new convention hot and motels in civic center area.
Sports: nicknamed "Football Capital of the South" f Univ. of Alabama and Auburn Univ. games played at m nicipal stadium, Legion Field.
Other attractions: world's 2d largest cast iron statue, Vu can, mythical god of the forge, overlooks Birmingham fro Red Mountain as a symbol of the steel industry; Arlingtc Shrine, antebellum home that housed federal troops duri Civil War; Botanical Gardens complex with Japanese Ga den; Jimmie Morgan Zoo; extensive city park system.
History: chartered 1871; soon became known as the "Mag City" because of its rapid growth brought on by the pre ence of the 3 ingredients in steelmaking — coal, iron or and lime; mining died out in recent years and most iron o is now imported by ship and barge to Birmingport on Wa rior River from South America; coal mining, in decline sinc the 1940s, is on the upswing.
Further information: Chamber of Commerce, 2027 First A enue N., Birmingham, AL 35202.

Bismarck, North Dakota

The World Almanac is sponsored in western North Dakota by the Bismarck Tribune, 707 Front Street, Bi marck, ND 58501; phone (701) 223-2500; founded 1873 as weekly, became daily 1881; circ. 29,750; pu lisher A.G. Sorlie, editor Charles W. Walk, general manager Sanders Hook, advertising manager James Hewitson; major awards include Pulitzer Prize Gold Medal, 1937.

Population: 44,300 (est. 1980), 3d in state; total employed 24,010.
Area: 18.5 sq. mi on Missouri River; state capital and Burleigh County seat.
Industry: agriculture, printing, trucking, farm machinery, state government, electric power, manufacturing, concrete products, railroad, insurance, livestock sales rings, lignite coal.
Commerce: retail trade area radius 100 miles, serving 160,000 people; retail sales (1978) $230 million; bank depos its (1979) $703 million; 6 banks, 5 building and loan assns.
Transportation: 2 rail lines; airport, hub for 5 airlines; truck lines, 4 bus lines, U.S. Highways 18 and 83, I-94.
Communications: one daily newspaper; 3 AM, 3 FM radi stations, 3 TV stations.
New construction: 1979 building permits, $71.3 million (77 housing units).
Medical facilities: 2 hospitals, 453 bed capacity, served b

10 MDs.
Federal facilities: federal buildings house 20 offices; 14th Radar Bomb Scoring Detachment.
Cultural facilities: Bismarck Junior College, Mary College; 2,000-volume public library, state library, state museum, Klan Gallery.
Recreation: 30 parks with over 1,450 acres, indoor artificial ice arena, 3 golf courses, 5 swimming pools, playgrounds, tennis courts, YMCA, duck and game hunting, fishing, nearby Fort Lincoln State Park.
Convention facilities: 8,000 seat Civic Center; 1,480 rooms in 18 motels, 5 banquet and meeting facilities for groups 200-1,200.
Other attractions: Dakota Zoo, Garrison Dam, United Tribes of North Dakota Educational Technical Center, state capitol.
History: founded 1872 as Edwinton, a rail town; name changed to Bismarck in 1873 to encourage German investment capital.
Further information: Chamber of Commerce, 412 Sixth Street, Bismarck, ND 58501.

Bloomington, Illinois

The World Almanac is sponsored in Bloomington-Normal and central Illinois by The Daily Pantagraph, 301 W. Washington Street, Bloomington, IL 61701; phone (309) 829-9411; founded 1837 by Jesse W. Fell; circulation 52,005; president Davis U. Merwin; publisher Peter E. Thieriot; editor Harold Liston; general manager William Diesel; managing editor Gene F. Smedley.

Population: 89,500 Bloomington-Normal, 126,000 (metro area) McLean County; mid-way between Chicago and St. Louis in central Illinois.
Industry: over 50 industries in county, ranks 9th in insurance cities in U.S., home offices of State Farm, Country Companies, Union Auto; uniform diversity of non-agricultural employment in all major work force areas; leads nation in corn and soybean production with 2,316 farms in county.
Commerce: 1978 metro retail sales $486.4 million; per household income $20,591; per household retail sales, $10,546.
Transportation: new terminal at B-N Airport, 4 bus lines, 6 federal and state highways, 4 railroads, Amtrak, 35 interstate and 23 intrastate motor carriers, Ozark Airlines and Britt Airways.
Communications: 6 radio stations.
Medical facilities: 3 hospitals; Watson-Gailey Foundation Eye Bank.
Cultural facilities: Illinois Wesleyan Univ., 1,550, in Bloomington; Illinois State Univ., 19,250; in Normal; 81 churches; home of American Passion Play; B-N Symphony, community players, amateur musical.
History: incorporated 1850; site of A. Lincoln's "Lost Speech" and David Davis mansion; state historical shrine; city's Stevenson family has produced 3 generations of leadership; vice president Adlai E.; governor, presidential candidate and UN Ambassador, Adlai E. II; and U.S. Senator Adlai E. III.
Further information: Association of Commerce and Industry of McLean County, 210 S. East Street, Bloomington, IL 61701.

Boise, Idaho

The World Almanac is sponsored in the Boise area by the Idaho Statesman, 1200 N. Curtis Road, Boise, ID 83704; phone (208) 377-6200; founded 1864 as Tri-Weekly; daily circulation 55,773, Sunday 70,502; publisher Eugene C. Dorsey, managing editor Rod Sandeen; a Gannett newspaper.

Population: 115,000 (city) (Dec., 1977), 145,000 (metro area), first in state; total employed 75,350.
Area: 1,054 sq. mi. on Boise River at foot of Salmon River Mountains; state capital and Ada County seat.
Industry: mobile home and recreational trailers produced $240 million in 1976; world headquarters Boise Cascade Corp., Morrison-Knudsen Co., and Albertson Food Stores.
Commerce: wholesale and retail center for southwest Idaho; retail sales $433.9 million (1976); bank resources $706.6 million in 6 banks with 27 branches; 4 savings and loan associations, and 7 insurance company offices.
Transportation: 3 major airlines, 2 feeder airlines, one rail freight line, 4 bus lines, 17 common carrier truck lines; Amtrak.
Communications: 4 TV and 9 radio stations.
Medical facilities: 3 major hospital complexes including a Veteran's Administration facility.
Cultural facilities: Boise Philharmonic Orchestra, art gallery, state museum, Boise Little Theatre, $1.4 million public library, Boise State Univ.
Other attractions: 33 parks, Southwestern Idaho Fairgrounds, 2 major recreational lakes, scenic mountain areas; Bogus Basin ski resort offers one of the world's longest illuminated ski runs.
History: founded 1863; named derived from "les bois" (the trees), a description for area used by French fur trappers in 1811.
Further information: Boise Chamber of Commerce, P. O. Box 2368, or Department of Commerce and Development, Idaho Statehouse, both Boise, ID 83701.

Boston, Massachusetts

The World Almanac is sponsored in the Boston area by the Boston Herald American, 300 Harrison Avenue, Boston, MA 02106; phone (617) 426-3000. The Herald American was established June 19, 1972; daily circulation 241,021, Sunday 306,484; publisher James T. Dorris, general manager Dennis Mulligan, editor Donald H. Forst; recent winner of 3 Pulitzers in photography (1976, '77 & '79); Sigma Delta Chi distinguished service awards, AP & UPI first place awards.

Population: 636,960 (city), 2,899,000 (metro area of 92 cities and towns around Boston.
Area: 46 sq. mi. on Massachusetts Bay; state capital and Suffolk County seat.
Commerce: northeast center for finance and insurance; home office for 50 insurance companies; banking center for New England with total commercial banking deposits of $16.422 billion (1978); accounts for 35% of the nation's mutual fund holdings; retail center for northern New England; major electronics industry and publishing center.
Transportation: terminating point for 2 railroads, Amtrak and Boston & Maine; MBTA (Massachusetts Bay Transportation Authority) provides surface and subway transportation for metropolitan Boston; Massachusetts Port Authority (operates Logan International Airport and the Port of Boston (shipping); 5 interstate highways.
Communications: 5 newspapers (3 daily, 2 weekly), 8 TV and 31 radio stations.
New construction: Quincy Market area, West End residential-office complex, the Waterfront building rehabilitation project, and the Ritz Carlton hotel/condominium complex.
Medical facilities: health care is Boston's largest industry in terms of dollars invested; major institutions: Mass. General, Children's, and New England medical centers; Boston City, Beth Israel, Deaconess hospitals; Harvard, Boston Univ., and Tufts medical schools; Lahey Clinic.
Federal facilities: 50 federal agencies employ 45,700 (military facilities not included).
Cultural facilities: the "Athens of America;" Boston Public Library includes capacity for 500,000 books on open shelf,

plus large lecture hall; Boston Symphony Orchestra; Boston Pops; Opera Company; Boston Ballet; Museum of Fine Art; Museum of Science and Hayden Planetarium; New England Aquarium; Isabella Stewart Gardner Museum; Museum of Transportation; Children's Museum.

Educational facilities: 16 degree-granting institutions in the city and 47 in the metro area, including Harvard, Boston College, Boston Univ., Tufts, M.I.T., Brandeis, Univ. of Mass., Suffolk, Emmanuel, Simmons, and Wentworth Inst.

Recreation: 2,327 acres of city recreation area, includes historic Boston Common and Public Garden; Metropolitan District Commission provides extensive facilities, including beaches and harbor islands.

Convention facilities: 49 hotels equipped to handle conventions; exhibition halls include Commonwealth Pier Exhibition Hall with 168,000 sq. ft. and John B. Hynes Veterans Auditorium in Prudential Center with 154,000 sq. ft. and auditorium seating 5,800.

Sports: professional teams include Red Sox (baseball), Celtics (basketball), New England Patriots (football), Bruins (hockey), Tea Men (soccer).

Other attractions: Quincy Market (a reconstruction of the historic Boston marketplace), Faneuil Hall, the "Freedom Trail", a 1½ mile walk through historic Boston; Beacon Hill and Back Bay historical districts; U.S.S. Constitution - "Old Ironsides" - the oldest commissioned ship in the U.S. Navy.

Nicknames: The Hub (of the Universe), Bean Town.

History: capital city of commonwealth, founded 1630; from 1770, Boston was scene of many events leading to American Revolution, including Boston Tea Party on Dec. 16, 1773; incorporated Feb. 23, 1822.

Further information: Boston Chamber of Commerce, 12 High Street, Boston, MA 02110.

Bridgeport, Connecticut

The World Almanac is sponsored in the Bridgeport area by The Bridgeport Post (eve.), The Telegram (morn.), and The Sunday Post; published by The Post Publishing Co., 410 State Street, Bridgeport, CT 06602; phone (203) 333-0161; circulation Post 75,848, Telegram 17,738, Sunday Post 94,976; John E. Pfriem president and general manager, Leonard E. Gilbert managing editor.

Population: 148,400 (State Dept. of Health) largest in state; planning region 309,200; 9-town district labor force 162,910.

Area: 17.5 sq. mi. on north shore of Long Island Sound at mouth of the Pequonnock R.; Fairfield County Seat.

Industry: "Industrial Capital of Connecticut;" products include machine tools, ammunition, wiring devices, brass goods, valves, electrical apparatus and appliances; nearby are Sikorsky Aircraft and Avco Lycoming; corporate headquarters: Warnaco, General Electric in Fairfield; Raybestos-Manhattan, and American Chain & Cable in Trumbull.

Commerce: retail sales $1.9 billion (1979); downtown renewal includes 64-store enclosed shopping complex with Gimbels and Sears stores, 2,000-car parking garage, U.S. Courthouse, 100-unit apartment building for senior citizens and handicapped; $24 million civic center in planning stages.

Transportation: railroad station served by Amtrak, adjacent to multi-transportation center and 500-car parking garage; city served by Conn. Turnpike (Interstate 95); historic U.S. 1 (Boston Post Road); municipal Sikorsky Memorial Airport; Conrail; 2 national bus lines; summer ferry to Port Jefferson, N.Y.

Medical facilities: 3 general hospitals, state mental health center; municipal convalescent hospital; major Easter Seal rehabilitation center.

Cultural facilities: Univ. of Bridgeport, Fairfield Univ., Sacred Heart Univ., Housatonic Comm. College; Museum of Art, Science, Industry; P. T. Barnum museum; symphony orchestra; city-supported downtown cabaret theater; American Shakespeare theater in adjoining town of Stratford.

Recreational facilities: "The Park City" has 1,200 acres of parks, including Seaside with 2-mile shoreline; zoo, municipal indoor ice-skating rink, 9,000-capacity Jai Alai fronton, summertime community-wide Barnum Festival.

Further information: Bridgeport Area Chamber of Commerce, 180 Fairfield Avenue, Bridgeport, CT 06604.

Buffalo, New York

The World Almanac is sponsored in the Buffalo area by the Courier-Express, 785 Main Street, Buffalo, NY 14240; phone (716) 855-6300; founded 1926 as merger of Courier and Express by William J. Conners Sr.; circulation mornings 125,994, Sunday 255,637; readership mornings 365,400, Sunday 613,500; publisher Roger B. Parkinson, senior vice president and associate publisher James B. Shaffer, vice president for public affairs Richard C. Lyons, operations director Donald Maul; sponsors miss the headpin tournament, learn to swim program, ski school, Goodfellow, tennis tournament.

Population: 1,294,100 (metro area, 1978), 389,500 (city, 1978), 3d in state; hub of broad 8 county area with population of 1,714,400.

Area: 49.6 sq. mi. city, 1,567 sq. mi. metro, at western end of N.Y. State on Lake Erie, Niagara River, and U.S.-Can. boundary; Erie County seat; metro area includes cities of Niagara Falls, Lockport, Tonawanda, N. Tonawanda, Lackawanna.

Industry: 1,584 manufacturing establishments, highly diversified; headquarters for Rich Products, Buffalo Forge, Trico Products, Fisher-Price Toys; large plants for Republic Steel, Bethlehem Steel, Chevrolet, Ford, Westinghouse, Union Carbide.

Commerce: wholesale and financial center for western N.Y.; retail sales $4.2 billion (metro); average income per household after taxes (metro) $15,947; distribution center for northeastern U.S. and Canada; $6.5 billion in trade between U.S. and Canada handled each year; 13 commercial banks, 8 savings banks, 4 savings and loans.

Transportation: Greater Buffalo Int. Airport served by 5 scheduled airlines with 3.5 million passengers, 164,717 scheduled and non-scheduled flights (1979); 6 major railroads, 22 freight terminals; about 350 motor carriers; highway system includes New York State Thruway and Kensington Expressway. Direct highway and rail service to all parts of Canada; direct water service to entire Great Lakes-St. Lawrence Seaways system, overseas, and Atlantic seaboard.

Communications: 2 major Buffalo newspapers, 3 additional dailies and one Sunday in surrounding cities; 5 TV, 20 AM and FM radio stations; 3 cable systems.

Cultural facilities: Buffalo Philharmonic in Kleinhans Music Hall; Albright-Knox Art Gallery; Studio Arena theater; Museum of Science; Historical Museum; Zoological Gardens (23 acres); Shaw Festival at Niagara-on-the-Lake, Ontario; performing arts center (Artpark) in Lewiston.

Educational facilities: State Univ. at Buffalo (now building $650 million new campus); State College at Buffalo, Niagara Univ., Canisius College; 5 other colleges; several 2-year institutions.

Convention facilities: Memorial Auditorium seats up to 17,000, new Buffalo convention center; Niagara Falls Convention Center seats up to 12,000; additional facilities available at several hotels and motels.

Sports: Bills football (NFL), Sabres hockey (NHL), Rich Stadium; Bisons pro women's softball, Bison baseball. Stallions Soccer [MISL].

Recreation: abundant facilities for all year around sports and activities; near both U.S. and Canada vacationlands.

Other attractions: Niagara Falls and river areas from Buffalo to Lake Ontario; Robert Moses and Adam Beck hydro stations; St. Lawrence Seaway, Welland Canal locks, aquarium (Niagara Falls), Our Lady of Victory Basilica (Lackawanna); Old Fort Niagara; Letchworth and Allegany parks.

Further information: Chamber of Commerce, 107 Delaware, Buffalo, NY 14202.

Calgary, Alberta, Canada

The World Almanac is sponsored in Calgary and southern Alberta by the Calgary Sun, 830 - 10th Avenue W., Calgary, Alberta, T2R 0B1; phone (1-403) 263-7730; known as the Calgary Albertan for 78 years up to ıg. 1, 1980; daily circulation 55,000, Sunday circulation 60,000; publisher Douglas Creighton, managing edi- Les Pyette, general manager Paul Whitlock.

pulation: 560,618.
ea: 235 sq. mi.; elevation 3,440 feet in the foothills of the ockies, 150 miles north of the Alberta-Montana border.
dustry: 526 oil and gas companies, 519 service and supply mpanies, 358 energy industry consultant firms, 400 data ocessing firms, and over 1,000 industrial plants in city; eatpacking, transportation, and fertilizer industries also ay a prominent part; manufacturing payroll (1979) $442 illion; trading area population over one million; more in- strial info. available from Bruce McDonald, director, siness Development, P.O. Box 2100, Calgary, Alberta.
ommerce: retail sales (1979) $3.25 billion; gross income of arket area (1979) $7.71 billion; per capita spending in mar- t area (1979) $3,200; no sales or gasoline tax.
ransportation: 2 railways; Greyhound Canadian headquar- rs; International Airport served by 9 airlines.
ommunications: 3 TV stations, 2 cable companies; 5 FM, 5 M radio stations; 2 daily and 4 weekly newspapers.
edical facilities: 7 major hospitals, 5 auxiliary hospitals, d one tuberculosis center.
ew construction: $1.1 billion in building permits (1977); .5 billion in construction expected in 1980 as oil and gas oom continues.
ultural facilities: 2,700 seat auditorium; Glenbow Mu- um; QR Arts Centre; Centennial Planterium; symphony orchestra; performing arts center under construction; live theater groups; ballet troupe; opera company, synchronized swimming group.
Education: 254 schools from elementary through senior high school; Univ. of Calgary, Alberta Vocational Centre, Mount Royal College, Southern Alberta Institute of Technology.
Recreation: One hour drive to 4 major ski resorts in Rocky Mountains; 22 ice arenas, 223 athletic parks, 2 ski areas within city, 14 golf courses.
Sports: home of the Calgary Flames starting first NHL season in 1980; Calgary Stampede in July attracts one million people over 10 days; Stampeders, Canadian Football League; Calgary Canucks, Alberta Junior Hockey League; Calgary Wranglers, Western Hockey League; Calgary Expos, baseball; Calgary Outlaws, semi-pro soccer.
Other attractions: Heritage Park reconstructs pioneer life on a lake; Calgary Zoo; Dinosaur Park with life-size models; Calgary Tower; more than 1,500 restaurants.
History: began as R.C.M.P. outpost in 1875; railroad arrived in 1883 as population reached 1,800; discovery of oil during 1914 in Turner Valley started Calgary on road to become Canada's oil capital.
Further information: Chamber of Commerce, 517 Centre Street; Calgary Tourist and Convention Association 1300 - 6th Avenue S.W., Calgary, Alberta.

Charleston, West Virginia

The World Almanac is sponsored in the Charleston area by The Charleston Gazette, 1001 Virginia Street, ast, Charleston, WV 25330; (304) 348-5140; circulation (morn) 56,311, (Sun.) 106,822; founded 1873 as the anawha Chronicle, became The Charleston Gazette 1898; W. E. Chilton III publisher; Don Marsh editor; Dal- as C. Higbee executive editor.

opulation: 66,965 (city), 227,300 (Kanawha County), most opulous county in state; county labor force, 122,200.
rea: 29.3 sq. mi. at meeting place of the Elk and Kanawha ivers; state capital.
ndustry: manufacturing including chemicals and fabricated etals; coal, glass, petroleum products, alloys.
ommerce: wholesale, retail center for West Virginia, So. hio, E. Kentucky; county retail sales, $903.4 million; aver- ge family income $19,742.
ransportation: 2 rail freight lines, Amtrak, bus lines, state's usiest airport; barge lines, 3 interstate highways.
ommunications: 4 TV and 7 radio stations.
Medical facilities: 6 hospitals, 2 of them major complexes.
Cultural facilities: modern civic center and auditorium, Sunrise Cultural and Art Center, symphony orchestra, Community Music Assn., Light Opera Guild, Kanawha Players, State Museum, Univ. of Charleston, W. Va. Univ.
Other attractions: Coonskin Park, Kanawha State Forest, 6 golf courses, public tennis, International League baseball.
History: first settlement, Fort Lee, 1788; Virginia Assembly established Charles Town 1794; named Charleston 1818.
Further information: Charleston Regional Chamber of Commerce and Development, 818 Virginia Street, East, Charleston, WV 25301.

Charlotte, North Carolina

The World Almanac is sponsored in the Charlotte area by The Charlotte Observer, 600 S. Tryon Street, Charlotte, NC 28233; phone (704) 379-6300; founded 1886 as Charlotte Chronicle; changed to Charlotte Daily Observer, March 1892; sold to Knight Newspapers Inc. 1955; circulation 171,769 daily, 238,470 Sunday; president and publisher Rolfe Neill; editor Rich Oppel.

Population: 333,405 (city), 408,848 (Mecklenburg County), 1.3 million (12-county metro area); labor force 341,400.
Area: 123.4 sq. mi. in Piedmont section of N.C., a plateau extending from the Appalachians to the Coastal Plains.
Industry: over 670 manufacturing companies, industrial chemicals, textiles, food products, machinery, printing and publishing.
Commerce: major trucking center, photographic and data processing center, 1,400 wholesale firms with $11.1 billion sales; retail sales $4.3 billion (Mecklenburg County); average household income $21,571; 15 banks, 11 mortgage banks, 6 building and loan associations.
Transportation: 115 trucking firms; 2 major railway lines; 4 bus lines; 5 airlines with 184 air movements per day.
Communications: 5 TV and 14 radio stations.
Medical facilities: an outstanding center in Southeast, 7 hospitals including 3 large general.
Cultural facilities: Opera Assn.; Charlotte Symphony Orchestra; Oratorio Society; Mint Museum (art); Nature Museum; Spirit Square (facility for all art activities under one roof); over 400 churches; Discovery Place (museum).
Education: Univ. of N.C.-Charlotte; Davidson College; Johnson C. Smith Univ.; Queens College; Central Piedmont Community College; Kings College; Hamilton College.
Convention facilities: Charlotte Coliseum-Auditorium, Civic Center, Trade Mart, Merchandise Mart.
Sports: Charlotte Motor Speedway (NASCAR) with World 600 and National 500 races; Charlotte Observer Marathon; Charlotte Chargers (pro football); Charlotte Orioles (pro baseball).
Other attractions: 2 major recreational lakes; Carowinds (family theme park); climate — four distinct seasons, avg. daily max. temp. 71.2, yearly avg. temp. 60.5; Festival in the Park; Southern Living Show.
History: incorporated 1768, named for Queen Charlotte of England; played major role in American Revolution; was gold mining capital of country before 1849; U.S. Mint built in 1836 to serve gold mining industry.
Further information: Chamber of Commerce, P.O. Box 32785, Charlotte, NC 28232; phone (704) 377-6911.

Chattanooga, Tennessee

The World Almanac is sponsored in the Chattanooga area by the Chattanooga News-Free Press, 400 11th Street, Chattanooga, TN 37401; phone (615) 756-6900; circulation 67,000 daily, 130,000 Sunday; pul lisher Roy McDonald, president Frank McDonald, senior vice president Everett Allen, vice president and edit Lee Anderson, secretary J. W. Hoback, treasurer Clifford Welch.

Population: 170,046 (city), 391,300 (metro area); 4th in state; 174,100 employed in labor force.
Area: 2,109.8 sq. mi. metropolitan shopping area at juncture of Tennessee River and north Georgia boundary line; Hamilton County seat.
Industry: about 600 manufacturers employ 57,300, producing more than 1,500 classified products including principal products of textile, fabricated metals, chemicals, primary metals, food products, machinery, apparel, paper products, and leather goods; receipts added by manufacture approximately $1 billion.
Commerce: wholesale and retail center; wholesale sales (1975) $752 million; bank assets (1976) $1.2 billion; 9 banks, 2 mortgage banks, 4 savings and loan assns., 3 major life insurance companies.
Transportation: 2 major freight lines, 2 bus lines, 13 federal and state highways; modern municipal airport.
New construction: multi-million-dollar TVA office complex and related downtown redevelopment; arena at Univ. of Tenn. at Chattanooga.
Communications: one cable TV, 5 TV, 20 radio stations; newspapers.
Medical facilities: speech and hearing rehabilitation cent children and adults rehabilitation and education center; Wi lie D. Miller Eye Center; 11 major hospital complexes i cluding psychiatric facility.
Cultural facilities: Univ. of Tenn. at Chattanooga; 3 liber arts colleges; state tech community college; state vocationa tech school; symphony orchestra; opera assn., civic choru community concert assn., Boys Choir, conservatory of m sic, Little Theatre, programs and performances at the Tivo Theater, Memorial Auditorium and Miller Park.
Other attractions: multi-million dollar vacation comple Chattanooga Choo-Choo, in one of the world's largest re taurants, in restored railroad terminal; recreational lake mountains, and museums.
History: explored by DeSoto 1540, settled 1828 at Ross Landing, incorporated 1839.
Further information: Chattanooga Convention and Visito Bureau, Civic Forum, Chattanooga, TN.

Chicago, Illinois

The World Almanac is sponsored in the Chicago area by the Chicago Tribune, 435 N. Michigan Avenue Chicago, IL 60611; (312) 222-3232; founded 1847; circulation daily 789,767, Sunday 1,146,474; publishe Stanton R. Cook, editor Maxwell McCrohon; major awards include 9 Pulitzer prizes won by staff members.

Population: est. 2.9 million (city), 2d largest in nation; est. 5.2 million (Cook County); est. 7.049 million (SMSA); est. resident labor force 3,456,000; est. 3.8 million suburban residents; est. 19% of U.S. pop dwells within a 300 mile radius.
Area: 228.124 sq. miles; 4,657 sq. miles (metro area).
Industry: est. 53 million tons of manufactures transported out of Chicago yearly; metro area is a leader in production of steel, metal products, sausages, cookies, candy, metal furniture, mattresses, envelopes, boxes, inorganic chemicals, soap, paint, gaskets, cans, saws, screws, bolts, barrels, machine tools, blowers, switchgear, radios, TV's, communications equipment, railroad equipment, and surgical appliances; Chicago produces a gross metro product of $97 billion, 4.6% of GNP.
Commerce: 14,400 manufacturers in Chicago with sales over $76 billion; 57,000 retailers in metro area with sales over $28 billion in 1977; 13,000 wholesalers in metro area with sales over $43 billion; 56,000 service establishments in the area do a $6.4 billion business; total personal income per household $28,700. Midwest Stock Exchange markets stocks and bonds; 7th Federal Reserve District Bank; world's leading grain futures market; Chicago Board of Trade; Mercantile Exchange.
Transportation: 3 major airports with 29 commercial airlines handle over 43 million passengers, 642,000 aircraft a year; 231 destinations are served by direct flights from Chicago; O'Hare is world's busiest and largest airport handling 404,000 tons of freight and mail and processing 41% of all U.S. International passengers; 314,000 trucks registered in Chicago; 38 million tons of manufactured goods shipped yearly; Chicago trucks service more than 54,000 communities; over 12 major highways, expressways, tollways; 3d largest Interstate Highway system in nation. Railways ship 23 million tons; 37,000 freight cars, 137,000 passengers handled daily; Amtrak headquarters. Ships carry 72 million tons of cargo in and out of metro area; barges carry 23 million tons; 318 overseas ships handled yearly; 14 overseas steamship lines carry freight to 47 ports in 24 countries.
Construction: $7.1 billion in industrial construction since 1965; $17 billion in residential construction; $8 billion in commercial construction; site of 3 of the tallest buildings in the U.S. — the John Hancock, the Standard Oil, and Sears Tower buildings.
Convention facilities: (1978) 1,089 conventions, 174 trade shows, 15,692 corporate meetings, est. 2.3 million total attendance; est. $525 million income generated.
Educational facilities: 95 institutions of higher learning, including Univ. of Chicago, Illinois Institute of Technology, Loyola Univ., Univ. of Illinois - Circle Campus.
Recreation: 131 forest preserves, 79 city parks, 147 golf courses, 15 athletic parks and race tracks; 35 museums, zoos, and permanent exhibitions; 73 swimming pools; athletic clubs, tennis courts.
Cultural facilities: Art Institute, Museum of Contemporary Art, Museum of Science and Industry; Shedd Aquarium is largest in world; Adler Planetarium; Lincoln Park and Brookfield zoos; museums of Academy of Science and Historical Society.
Sports: NFL Bears, AL White Sox, NL Cubs, NHL Black Hawks, NBA Bulls, NASL Sting.
History: Indians named the area Checagou after area's strong-smelling wild onions; incorporated 1837 with population of 4,170.
Further information: Visitors Bureau and Information Center, Association of Commerce and Industry, 130 S. Michigan Avenue, Chicago, IL 60603.

Cincinnati, Ohio

The World Almanac is sponsored in the Cincinnati area by The Cincinnati Post, a Scripps-Howard Newspaper, 800 Broadway, Cincinnati, OH 45202; phone (513) 352-2000; founded in 1881 by Alfred and Walter Wellman; evening circulation 172,061; editor William R. Burleigh, business manager John L. Feldmann.

Population: 396,900 (city), 1,377,000 (metro area), 2d in state, total employment 605,300.
Area: 2,154 sq. mi. (metro) in SW Ohio, SE Ind., and 3 N. Central counties in Ky.; Hamilton County seat.
Industry: home of Procter & Gamble, Federated, Kroger, Kenner, Armco Steel, U.S. Shoe, Western Southern, Union Central & Ohio National Life Insurances, Baldwin Piano and Organ, Cincinnati Milacron, Dubois Chemical, Senco Products, Stearns & Foster, Totes, Gibson Cards, GM, Ford, and GE plants; production of jet engines, playing

cards, chemicals, cosmetics, machine tools, belts, clothing, printing and publishing.

Communications: 6 TV stations; subscription TV and cable systems under construction; 12 AM and 25 FM radio stations; 28 weekly and 2 daily newspapers.

New constructions: Fountain Square South redevelopment scheduled for completion in 1981; expanding elevated walkways; Public Library construction underway; Riverfront Motel in planning stages; 220 units of Riverfront housing under construction.

Medical facilities: 30 hospitals with 9,652 beds; 187 physicians per 100,000 population; Children's Hospital Medical Center; UC Medical Center where Sabin oral polio vaccine was discovered; Shriners Burn Institute, VA Hospital.

Cultural facilities: Art Museum, Historical Society, Symphony Orchestra, Krohn Conservatory, Lloyd Library, May Festival, Taft Museum, Cincinnati Opera, Arts Consortium, Cincinnati Ballet, Museum of Natural History, Contemporary Arts Center, Playhouse in the Park, UC Observatory and Northern Kentucky Arts Council.

Educational facilities: Cincinnati, Xavier, Northern Kentucky universities; Cincinnati Bible, Mount St. Joseph, Edgecliff, Hebrew Union, St. Gregory, Thomas More colleges; 8 technical and 2-year colleges; 47 vocational schools.

Convention facilities: numerous hotels, motels, and restaurants; Convention and Exposition Center; Music Hall; Cincinnati Gardens; Emery and Taft auditoriums; Riverfront Stadium and Riverfront Coliseum.

Other attractions: Cincinnati Zoo, Cincinnati Reds baseball, Cincinnati Bengals football, Cincinnati Suds softball; Fountain Square Plaza, River Downs and Latonia race tracks, Kings Island Amusement Park, College Football Hall of Fame; Delta Queen and New Mississippi Queen excursion boats.

Further information: Chamber of Commerce, 120 West 5th Street, Cincinnati, OH 45202; phone (513) 579-3100.

Cleveland, Ohio

The World Almanac is sponsored in the Cleveland area by The Cleveland Press, 901 Lakeside Avenue, Cleveland, OH 44114; phone (216) 623-1111; founded 1878 by E.W. Scripps; circulation 305,000; editor Herbert Kamm, managing editor William Tanner, business manager William Holcombe; major awards include Pulitzer Prize, Lasker Award, Penney-Missouri Award.

Population: 609,200 (city), 1,938,900 (metro area), first in state; total employed 885,456 (non-agricultural).

Area: 1,519 sq. mi., SMSA 4 county area; along southern shore of Lake Erie, east and west of Cuyahoga River; Cuyahoga County seat.

Industry: city has been described as "an industrial powerhouse," bills itself "The Best Location in the Nation;" within 600 miles are 12 of the top 20 U.S. markets, 55% of U.S. population, 54% of U.S. households, 56% of U.S. effective buying income, 65% of U.S. manufacturing shipments, 64% of U.S. manufacturing plants, 74% of top 1,000 U.S. industrial corporate headquarters. No single industry dominates economy—metal and steel products are mainstays; manufacturing complex occupied essentially with machinery and tools, fabricated metal products, primary metals, automotive products; important industries include making of electric motors, products of petroleum, rubber, plastic, stone clay and glass, chemicals, paints, wearing apparel, measuring instruments, electronic components, food products; retail sales are more than $7.7 billion; median income of families is $16,211.

Transportation: Hopkins Airport with more than 7 million passengers each year; Burke Lakefront Airport, 5 minutes from Public Square and capable of handling intermediate jets; Port of Cleveland visited by more than 23 overseas steamship lines and Great Lakes fleet; largest city on Lake Erie and 3d largest on Great Lakes. Cleveland is only U.S. city with airport-to-downtown rail service; ride takes 20 minutes and costs about $11 less than a cab ride; Amtrak train service.

Communications: Cleveland Press, evening daily; Cleveland Plain Dealer, morning daily plus Sunday; numerous foreign language newspapers; 5 TV stations; 16 AM and 20 FM radio stations.

New construction: $50 million Medical Mutual Bldg., $60 million office complex, $26 million State of Ohio Bldg.

Cultural facilities: Cleveland Orchestra; Play House, nation's oldest and largest resident professional theater; Museum of Art, Karamu House for interracial arts, Western Reserve Historical Society, Health Museum, Natural Science Museum, Cultural Gardens, zoo; Blossom Music Center, Garden Center, Sea World, aquarium; only Salvador Dali Museum.

Educational facilities: Case Western Reserve Univ., John Carroll Univ., Cleveland State Univ.; Cuyahoga Community, Notre Dame, Ursuline, and Dyke colleges.

Sports: NFL Browns, American League Indians, NBA Cavaliers; golf, horse and car racing, boating, polo, and hunter trials.

Other attractions: downtown Convention Center is largest city-owned convention facility in U.S., public library is 5th in size of book collection in U.S.; Public Square, hub of city, marked by 52-story Terminal Tower. "The Forest City" is encircled by "Emerald Necklace," 18,500 acres of metropolitan parks; Cleveland Clinic, known for medical research, attracts patients throughout the world; University Hospitals of Cleveland has largest research and care center for cystic fibrosis in U.S.; center of a regional renal transplant program; Metropolitan General Hospital is noted for its neurological and burn clinic; many nationality restaurants, due to large ethnic population (close to 6,000 immigrants each year).

History: settlement established in summer, 1796 by Gen. Moses Cleaveland, was capital of the Western Reserve, became a city in 1836.

Further information: Greater Cleveland Growth Assn., 690 Union Commerce Building, Cleveland, OH 44115; Convention Visitor's Bureau of Greater Cleveland, 1301 E. 6th Street, Cleveland, OH 44114; phone (216) 621-4110.

Columbia, South Carolina

The World Almanac is sponsored in the Columbia area by Columbia Newspapers, Inc., P.O. Box 1333, Columbia, SC 29202; phone (803) 771-6161; circulation, The State (am) 103,471; The Columbia Record (pm) 33,244; The State (Sun.) 121,307 (ABC 3/31/79); Ben R. Morris, publisher and president; Cyril A. Washer, general manager and exec. vice president; James W. Holton Jr., assistant general manager and advertising director; William E. Rone, editorial page editor (The State); Thomas N. McLean, executive editor, The State and The Columbia Record.

Population: 115,000 (1970 census), city corporate limits; 2-county metro area (Richland and Lexington) estimated 406,000.

Area: 106.2 sq. mi. (Richland County); 1,525 sq. mi. (metro); center of South Carolina, at confluence of Broad and Saluda rivers (at Columbia).

Government: state capital with about 100 state agencies, 19 federal agencies; government employees total more than 33,000; Fort Jackson Military Post numbers over 20,000 personnel.

Industry: more than 50 national firms such as General Electric, Allied Chemical, Continental Can, Burlington, Litton, Bendix, M. Lowenstein, Rockwell Int., Square D, Westinghouse, Colite Ind., Tamper, Shakespeare, Allis-Chalmers; fibres, heavy equipment, electronics, textiles, fertilizer, and cement products. Columbia (SMSA) industrial wages for 1979 exceeded $267 million; industrial capital invested is estimated to exceed $475 million.

Commerce: retail sales (metro) over $1.3 billion ('79); consumer spendable income $2 billion; median household income (metro) $18,000; 11 commercial (main) banking institutions.
Transportation: Metropolitan Airport with 2 major airlines and freight service; 3 rail freight lines, Amtrak; 46 major freight companies; 3 interstate, 6 federal, and 6 state highways.
Communications: 4 TV and 12 radio stations.
Medical facilities: 6 general hospitals, including modern Richland Memorial; William S. Hall Psychiatric Institute; 2 state mental hospitals.
Cultural facilities: Town Theatre, the oldest continuous community theater in nation; 3 other theaters; Museum of Art and Sciences; Gibbes Planetarium; Township Auditorium, home of Artist Series; Dreher Auditorium with Philharmonic Orchestra, City Ballet, Lyric Theatre and Choral Society; Fraser Hall.
Recreation facilities: 13 golf courses; city park system; 2 municipal pools; wide range of hunting activities; Riverbanks Zoological Park, part of 135-acre complex; Lake Murray, water sports.
Sports: Williams-Brice Stadium, home of Univ. of South Carolina Fighting Gamecock football team; Carolina Coliseum for basketball, conventions.
Educational facilities: 29,000-student Univ. of South Carolina; 4 private colleges; Technical Education Center; Lutheran Seminary.
History: established 1786 as state capital; burned in 1865 by Union General Sherman.
Further information: Chamber of Commerce, 1308 Laurel Street, Columbia, SC 29202.

Columbus, Georgia — Phenix City, Alabama

The World Almanac is sponsored in the Columbus, Ga. - Phenix City, Ala., area by the Columbus Enquirer and the Columbus Ledger, 17 W. 12th Street, Columbus, GA 31994; phone (404) 324-5526; combined daily circulation 65,494, Sunday 70,841; Enquirer founded 1828, awarded Pulitzer Prize 1926; Ledger founded 1886, awarded Pulitzer Prize 1955. Published by the R. W. Page Corporation; Glenn Vaughn, president and publisher; Bill Brown, vice-president and executive editor; Rick Kaspar, vice-president and general manager. Owned by Knight-Ridder Newspapers, Inc.

Population: 171,200 (Columbus); 32,500 (Phenix City); 253,700 (metro); 81,700 employed (metro).
Area: 1,100 sq. miles (metro: Muscogee and Chattahoochee counties, Ga.; Russell County, Ala.) straddling the Chattahoochee River.
Industry: major textile production center: Fieldcrest Mills, Inc., Bibb Company, Swift Textiles, Westpoint Pepperell, Columbus Mills; Lummus Industries, Columbus Foundries, Interstate Brands, Union Carbide, TRW, Inc.; Internat'l. hqs. Tom's Foods, Ltd. and Burnham Van Service; lumber products, beverages, concrete, bakery goods, and paper.
Commerce: center of west Georgia—east Alabama finance, agriculture, textiles, hydroelectric power; metro retail sales $818.9 million; avg. household buying income $16,379; 9 banks, 6 savings and loan associations.
Federal facilities: Ft. Benning, world's largest infantry school, $353.6 million annual disbursements.
Transportation: 2 rail lines, 2 bus lines; Delta, Eastern, Southern airlines; 33 truck lines; Chattahoochee is navigable river.
Communications: 3 TV and 10 radio stations.
New construction: 234-room Hilton Hotel to accompany new convention and trade center; Ft. Benning expansion for One Station Unit Training; 417-bed hospital to replace Medical Center; North By-pass; expansions for Swift Textiles, Southeast Canners, SCM Corp.
Medical facilities: 5 hospitals.
Cultural facilities: Museum of Arts and Sciences, Springer Theater (state theater of Georgia), Three Arts Theater, Bradley Memorial Library; Columbus College, Chattahoochee Valley Community College.
Sports: Astros, Southern baseball league.
History: Columbus founded 1828; gained early prominence as shipping center for cotton, fish; birthplace of Coca-Cola formula. Phenix City founded 1883, growing from a Creek Indian trading post.
Further information: Columbus Chamber of Commerce, P.O. Box 1200, Columbus, GA 31902, or Phenix City-Russell County Chamber of Commerce, P.O. Box 1326, Phenix City, AL 36867.

Columbus, Ohio

The World Almanac is sponsored in the Columbus area by the Columbus Citizen-Journal, 34 S. Third Street, Columbus, OH 43216; phone (614) 461-5000; Citizen founded 1899, Journal 1811; circ. 111,000 a.m. daily except Sun.; owned by E. W. Scripps Co.; editor Richard R. Campbell, business manager Gregory A. Dembski, managing editor Seymour Raiz.

Population: 585,123 (city), 1,111,901 (metro area), 1979 ests.; 2d in state; total employed in SMSA 504,580.
Area: 180.49 sq. mi. city, 537.8 sq. mi. county, in central Ohio; state capital and Franklin County seat.
Industry: 1,013 manufacturers in county (1977) including General Motors, Rockwell International, Western Electric, Columbus Products Co., Borden (natl. hqs.); planes, missiles, refrigerators, mining machinery, telephones, auto parts; home office of Battelle Memorial Institute with worldwide research laboratories.
Commerce: wholesale, retail center for central, southern Ohio, parts of W. Va., Ky. Retail sales, $4.5 billion; financial assets of 8 banks, 20 savings and loan assns. $22.7 billion; 56 insurance co. home offices, assets $7.3 billion; per capita income (city) $7,602.
Transportation: 125 truck lines, 3 intercity bus lines, 3 railroads, 10 airlines using Port Columbus International with 679 air movements daily; 8 major highways.
Communications: 5 TV stations, 13 radio stations and 3 cable TV companies incl. QUBE, the first 2-way system.
Medical facilities: 18 hospitals, medical centers; Children's Hospital leads nation in children admitted; Ohio State Univ. School of Medicine.
Cultural facilities: Ohio Theatre, symphony orchestra, Cultural Arts Center, Bicentennial Park; art museums, open-air sculpture garden about Columbus Museum of Art; Players Theatre, 3 professional and 11 community theaters, 4 ballet cos.; public library, 22 branches; Center for Science and Industry, Ohio Historical Society, 19th century village.
Other attractions: Ohio Expositions Center with its coliseum and Ohio State Fair; German Village (restored South Side, urban); Lynn Street Mall, Park of Roses, world's largest; Ohio Railway Museum, 252 parks, zoo, boating, floating amphitheater.
Educational facilities: Ohio State, Capital, Franklin univs., Ohio Dominican College, Columbus College of Art & Design, Columbus Technical Inst., Ohio Inst. of Technology, Otterbein College.
New construction: Ohio Center (for conventions); Capitol South redevelopment, high rises; Municipal Courts high-rise; Port Columbus expansion and renovation; 2 existing hospitals to be replaced; 10 Arlington Place (condominiums).
Federal facilities: Defense Construction Supply Center.
Sports: Ohio Stadium and Franklin County Stadium; Clippers (baseball), Metros (Midwestern Football League), Pacesetters (women's football), Magic (soccer), Beulah Park (thoroughbreds), Scioto Downs (harness); Muirfield Memorial golf tournament.
History: founded 1812 as state capital, named for Christopher Columbus.
Further information: Chamber of Commerce, P. O. Box 1527, Columbus, OH 43216.

Corpus Christi, Texas

The World Almanac is sponsored in the Corpus Christi area by The Caller and The Times, P.O. Box 9136, Corpus Christi, TX 78408; Caller (a.m.) founded 1883; Times (p.m.) founded 1911; merged 1929; Caller circ. 62,142, Times 25,118, Sunday 86,104; publisher Edward H. Harte; president Richard T. Schlosberg 3d; executive editor Robert E. Rhodes; Caller managing editor John B. Anderson; Times managing editor Bill Duncan.

Population: 230,500 (est.); labor force 110,900.
Area: 328 sq. mi. (226 water), 210 miles SW of Houston on Corpus Christi Bay; Nueces County seat.
Industry: oil refineries; offshore oil rig fabrication; chemical, petrochemical, synthetics, aluminum, and zinc plants.
Commerce: Port of Corpus Christi handled 60.8 million tons in 1979; economic hub of south Texas; farming, ranching, oil and gas production, commercial fishing, tourist trade; 19 banks have deposits in excess of $1.1 billion.
Transportation: 5 airlines, 2 bus lines, 3 railroads but no rail passenger service.
Communications: 2 daily newspapers, 5 TV stations (one public service, one Spanish), 12 radio stations.
New construction: permits issued for $162 million in new construction in 1979.
Medical facilities: 9 hospitals, including a children's center, with 1,537 beds.
Federal facilities: Corpus Christi Naval Air Station is headquarters for Naval Air Training Command; Corpus Christi Army Depot is army's only complete helicopter overhaul plant; combined payroll more than $104 million.
Cultural facilities: Corpus Christi Museum, Art Museum of South Texas, Japanese Art Museum; symphony, little theater, Del Mar College, Corpus Christi State Univ.
Recreation: public beaches and fishing piers on the bay and along Gulf of Mexico on Mustang Island and in 88-mile-long Padre Island National Seashore; surf and charter boat fishing; sailing, city marina with launching ramps; large tennis center, 3 private tennis clubs, 5 golf courses.
History: Spanish explorer Alonzo de Pineda discovered Corpus Christi Bay in 1519; Blas Maria de la Garza Falcon established San Petronilla Ranch on Petronilla Creek about 1765; city grew from a frontier trading post est. in 1839; city incorporated Feb. 16, 1852.
Further information: Corpus Christi Chamber of Commerce, P.O. Box 640, Corpus Christi, TX 78403.

Dallas, Texas

The World Almanac is sponsored in Dallas by The Dallas Morning News, Communications Center, Dallas, TX 75265; phone (214) 745-8222; published by the oldest business in Texas, the News was founded in 1842 by Samuel Bangs; circulation, 353,677 Sunday, 286,955 daily; publisher Joe M. Dealey, president James M. Moroney Jr., managing editor Terence G. Walsh. Winner of numerous national awards including Freedoms Foundation and National Headliner. Sponsors Teen-age Citizenship Tribute, Fly-the-Flag program, Spelling Bee, Science Fair, Sports Show, Involved Citizen Award, etc.

Population: city, 914,000 (7th in nation); county 1,524,500; Dallas-Fort Worth metro area, 2.79 million (9th in nation); total employed 1,467,000 with 3.4% unemployment.
Area: 900 sq. mi. astride Trinity River in north Texas about 75 miles south of Oklahoma border; elevation from 450 to 750 feet; Dallas County seat.
Industry: banking and insurance capital of the Southwest, Dallas ranks 3d among U.S. cities in the number of million-dollar-net-worth companies with 1,119 such firms; 1,925 manufacturing plants shipped $16.2 billion worth of goods during 1979—principally oil field machinery, electronics, food, apparel, soaps and detergents.
Commerce: a $5.2 billion wholesale market; Dallas ranks first nationally in giftware, home furnishing and floor covering wholesaling, 2d in apparel and toys. Metro retail sales totaled $13.7 billion in 1979, while estimated buying income reached $24 billion and bank deposits $25 billion.
Transportation: Dallas-Fort Worth Airport is the nation's largest. In 1979, it was 3d in the world in air carrier operations with 445,163; 11.3 million passengers enplaned there. City is served by 12 major and 6 commuter air lines, 8 railroads, 2 trans-continental bus lines, 45 motor freight lines, 4 taxi companies with 543 cabs. Dallas Transit System serves 131,000 people daily on 108 lines, 543 route miles.
Communications: 2 metropolitan daily newspapers, numerous suburban dailies, 4 commercial VHF TV stations, public television, 1 UHF station, 16 AM and 21 FM radio stations, 2 city magazines.
New construction: $1.75 billion in building permits in 1979 ($918.5 million nonresidential); projects include $100 million Placid Oil Bldg., 72-acre $250 million mixed use development Quorum, $150 million Lincoln Centre.
Medical facilities: 41 hospitals with 9,000 beds, 403 bassinets. Baylor University Medical Center consistently ranks in the top 10 among the country's "super hospitals."
Culture: symphony orchestra, civic opera, summer musicals, civic ballet, Sunday concert series — among others — offer varied programs; drama at Dallas Theater Center, Theater Three, National Children's Theater, Repertory Theater, and 4 dinner theaters; 7 museums; SMU's Owens Fine Arts Center with a collection of paintings and sculpture; numerous art galleries.
Education: 206,968 students attend 23 colleges and universities within 50 miles of Dallas; Southern Methodist Univ., the Univ. of Texas at Dallas, Univ. of Dallas, North Texas State, Univ. of Texas at Arlington, Baylor Univ. College of Dentistry, Southwestern Medical School; the Dallas Community College system with 57,555 students on 7 campuses.
Convention facilities: 3 major convention centers, including expanded Dallas Convention Center with more combined meeting-exhibit space (611,000 sq. ft.) than any other in U.S.; 23,310 air-conditioned hotel rooms. Dallas always among nation's top 3 convention cities. In 1979, 1.67 million people attended 1,398 conventions.
Sports: professional sports include football, baseball, basketball, tennis, golf, hockey, soccer, and rodeo. Cotton Bowl is site of annual New Year's Day football game.
Other attractions: Six Flags Over Texas, Dallas Zoo, Reunion Arena, International Wildlife Park; Fair Park is home of State Fair of Texas 16 days each October; museums of fine arts, health and science, natural history; Hall of State; Garden Center and Music Hall; excellent lakes, golf courses, parks, luxury hotels, and restaurants.
History: first settler was Tennessee frontiersman John Neely Bryan who established a trading post and plotted the townsite in 1844; incorporated 1856; named for Vice-President George Mifflin Dallas. Since 1931, the city has had council-manager form of government. Spectacular population growth began after World War II, when aircraft manufacturing augmented an economy that had been built first on cotton, then on oil, banking, and insurance. Diversified economic expansion fed the growth of the 1970s.
Further information: Dallas Chamber of Commerce, Fidelity Union Tower, Dallas, TX 75201.

Dayton, Ohio

The World Almanac is sponsored in the Dayton area by The Journal Herald, 37 S. Ludlow Street, Dayton, OH 45402; phone 225-2421; founded as Dayton Repertory; circulation 100,589; editor Dennis Shere, managing editor William Worth; editorial page editor William Wild, "Day" section editor Mickey Davis.

Population: 197,744 (city), 838,000 (metro), 4th in state; total employed 364,900.
Area: 48.71 sq. mi. at junction Mad, Miami, and Stillwater rivers; Montgomery County seat.

Industry: NCR Corp., Dayton Press, Inc., General Motors Corp. (Delco Moraine, Delco Products, Delco Air, and Inland Mfg.); world headquarters for Frigidaire Co. (subsidiary of White Consolidated Ind.), Standard Register, Monarch Marking Systems, Mead Corp., Dayton Tire and Rubber Co., Diriron Co., Inc., Monsanto Research Corp., Ohio Bell, Dayton Newspapers, Inc., Dayton Power and Light; more than 800 other manufacturing facilities.
Commerce: retail sales $3.5 billion, average effective buying household income, $23,533.
Transportation: 2 airports, 6 airlines, 3 trunk rail systems, 4 bus lines, Dayton Regional Transit Auth.
Communications: 6 TV stations, 8 radio stations.
Medical facilities: 10 hospitals, including Wright Patterson AFB Hosp. and a VA facility.
Federal facilities: Wright Patterson AFB, headquarters for Air Force Logistics Command and Aeronautical Systems Div.; Defense Electronics Supply Center, Federal Bldg.
Convention facilities: modern downtown convention and exhibition center.
New or recent construction: downtown arcade, Gem City Savings Assn. headquarters, Great Miami River Low Dam (part of the Miami River Corridor Project), Dayton Career Academy, Courthouse Square Plaza, (includes dept. store, bank bldg., utilities bldg., Mead world headquarters, and 2 restaurants); Univ. of Dayton Law School, Wright State Med. School, expansion of Sinclair Community College.
Educational facilities: Univ. of Dayton, Wright State Univ. (new med. school); 2 jr. colleges: Sinclair (downtown campus), Miami Jacobs (business); United Theological sem., Central State Univ., Wilberforce Univ., Antioch College.
Cultural facilities: Dayton Art Institute, Philharmonic Orchestra, opera, ballet, 4 amateur theatrical groups, 2 professional companies; Diehl band shell, Deed's Carillon, dinner theater.
Sports: Amateur Trapshoot National Headquarters, college sports, Bogie Busters Pro/Am Golf Tourn. for Muscular Sclerosis, Dayton Hydroglobe, 5 amateur soccer teams.
Other attractions: Air Force Museum, Carillon Park, Aviation Hall of Fame, Dayton Air Fair, Old Courthouse Museum, A World A'Fair, Dayton River Corridor Festival, Paul Lawrence Dunbar Home, Wright Bros. Memorial, Oregon Historic District, Cox Arboretum, Aulwood Audubon Center and Farm.
History: "Birthplace of Aviation."
Further information: Dayton Area Chamber of Commerce, Suite 1980, Winters Bank Tower, 40 S. Main Street, Dayton, OH 45402.

Denver, Colorado

The World Almanac is sponsored in the Denver area by the Rocky Mountain News, 400 W. Colfax Avenue, Denver, CO 80201; phone (303) 892-5000; founded 1859 by William N. Byers; circulation daily 271,153, Sunday 293,004; editor Michael Balfe Howard, business manager William W. Fletcher; sponsors Colorado-Wyoming spelling bee, Golden Wedding party, Huck Finn Day, Showagon.

Population: 521,300 (city), 1.69 million (metro area), first in state, total employed 798,800.
Area: 116.4 sq. mi. on S. Platte River at edge of Great Plains near Rocky Mountains. State capital and Denver County seat.
Industry: Gates Rubber Co. is world's largest maker of v-belts and hose, 6th largest U.S. rubber company; Samsonite Corp. is world's largest luggage manufacturer, also makes furniture; Adolph Coors Co. is nation's 5th largest brewer of beer; center for smokeless industry with 1,650 mfg. firms.
Commerce: largest distribution center in region embracing one-third of U.S. geographical area; bank deposits $6.9 billion, 94 banks, 16 savings and loan associations, and 45 insurance company home offices; per capita income $6,589.
Transportation: 6 major rail freight lines, Amtrak; Continental and Greyhound bus lines; 3 interstate highways intersect city; Stapleton International Airport has 800 daily flights, hub for 8 trunk airlines; Frontier Air Lines; United Air Lines Flight Training Center.
Communications: 6 TV and 34 radio stations.
Medical facilities: largest medical center between Kansas City and San Francisco; one of 17 regional comprehensive cancer centers; Univ. of Colorado Medical Center. National Jewish Hospital, Children's Asthma Research Institute and Hospital (CARIH); 22 major hospitals.
Federal facilities: largest complex of federal offices outside Washington, D.C., with 38,000 federal employes; site of Energy Research and Development Administration's Rocky Flats plant, U.S. Mint, Lowry AFB, Air Force Accounting and Finance Center, Fitzsimons Army Medical Center, Army's Rocky Mountain Arsenal.
Cultural facilities: symphony orchestra, 3 nonprofessional orchestras, 3 choral groups, Denver Art Museum, 18 theater companies; 3-sq.-block convention center; 12,000-seat Red Rocks outdoor theater; Performing Arts Center.
Educational facilities: Univ. of Colorado, Univ. of Denver, Colorado School of Mines; Colorado Women's, Metropolitan State, Loretto Heights, and Regis colleges; Univ. of Colorado School of Medicine, Iliff School of Theology.
Recreational facilities: 150 parks, 8,030 acres of mountain parks, 40 golf courses in metro area. City Park Zoo, 2 amusement parks; many ski areas.
Sports: pro teams include Broncos, NFL; Bears, baseball, American Assn.; Nuggets, NBA; Rockies, NHL.
Other attractions: Museum of Natural History, Botanic Gardens, State Historical Museum.
History: founded 1858 with discovery of gold, fast became supply center for mountain mining camps; named for territorial governor.
Further information: Denver Chamber of Commerce, 1301 Welton Street, Denver, CO 80204; Hospitality Center, 280 14th Street, Denver, CO 80202.

Des Moines, Iowa

The World Almanac is sponsored in Iowa by the Des Moines Register and Tribune, 715 Locust Street, Des Moines, IA 50304; phone (515) 284-8000; founded 1849; circulation evening Tribune 89,084, morning Register 222,429, Sunday Register 421,631; board chairman and publisher David Kruidenier; president and editor Michael Gartner; executive vice president Gary Gerlach; executive editor James Gannon; major awards include 12 Pulitzer prizes.

Population: 201,404 (city, 1970), 337,600 (1979 est. metro area).
Area: 66 sq. mi., at juncture of Raccoon and Des Moines rivers, south central Iowa. State capital and Polk County seat.
Industry: considered to be 2d largest insurance center in nation (56 home companies) and 2d largest tire center with Firestone, Armstrong plants; publishing center — Meredith Co., Better Homes and Gardens, Wallace-Homestead, others; farm implements — North American headquarters and plant of Massey-Ferguson, John Deere; lawn and garden equipment, sporting goods, food products, cosmetics, dental equipment, automotive accessories, concrete forms, nozzles, tools; 700 wholesale and jobbing firms; Standard Oil credit card center, bulk mail center.
Commerce: retail sales in metro area $1.714 billion (1979); per capita income $8,208 (1979); average household income, $23,014.
Transportation: enlarged in-city airport, 5 major airlines; 4 bus lines, 4 railroads, 69 truck lines; Interstate Highways 80 and 35.
New construction: 30-story downtown hotel, 2 major hospital additions, botanical center, 2 large parking ramps with shops, several major downtown office bldgs., Osteopathic

College addition.
Communications: 13 radio, 4 TV stations, cablevision.
Medical facilities: 11 hospitals with 2,700 beds.
Cultural facilities: art center, Center of Science and Industry, community playhouse, drama workshop, Drake Univ., symphony orchestra, Grand View Junior, Area Community, and 2 bible colleges; College of Osteopathic Medicine and Surgery, Civic Center Theater.
Recreation: 1,400 acres of parks, 9 public golf courses, 10 public pools, tennis, YWCA, YMCA; 5,000-acre reservoir.
Other attractions: AAA baseball, Drake Relays, Missouri Valley and Big Eight (Iowa State U.) conferences; 15,000-seat auditorium; boys and girls state basketball tournaments, State Fair, Living History Farm, Children's Zoo, 36-story Ruan Center, tallest in Iowa, Terrace Hill (Governor's Mansion), state capitol and state historical bldg.
History: founded 1843 as a fort to protect rights of Indians; incorporated 1853, became Iowa capital 1857.
Further information: Chamber of Commerce, 8th and High Streets, Des Moines, IA 50309.

Detroit, Michigan

The World Almanac is sponsored in the Detroit area by The Detroit News, 615 Lafayette, Detroit, MI 48231; phone (313) 222-2000; founded 1873 by James E. Scripps; circulation (D) 630,573 (S) 827,168; president and publisher Peter B. Clark, sr. v.p. R. M. Spitzley, v.p. and general manager R.C. Nelson, v.p. and editor W. E. Giles; major awards won include Pulitzer Prize, Nat'l Headliners; over 50 community projects include NCAA Indoor Track Championships, Science Fair, Scholastic Writing Awards, Spelling Bee.

Population: 1,257,879 (city, 1978) first in state, 6th in U.S.; 4,386,400 (metro area).
Area: 139.6 sq. mi. on the Detroit River, a Great Lakes connecting link and the world's busiest inland waterway; Wayne County seat.
Industry: "The Motor City"; area plants produce 25% of the nation's cars and trucks, employing more than 195,100. Nonautomotive manufacturing and nonmanufacturing firms employ more than 1.2 million; other products are machine tools, iron products, metal stampings, hardware, industrial chemicals, drugs, paint, wire products.
Commerce: metro median income per household $19,710 (1978); area retail sales $18.8 billion (1979).
Transportation: served by 10 railroads, over 220 intercity truck lines, 19 airlines, and 25 steamship lines serving more than 40 countries.
Communications: 8 TV and 50 radio stations.
New construction: 2.4 acre, Phase II of Renaissance Center, $65 million twin office towers; 3.4 acre, $48 million West Clinical Service Bldg. of Henry Ford Hospital; 3.7 acre, $53 million New Center office-retail bldg.; 21 acre, $42 million Wayne County Jail.
Cultural facilities: symphony orchestra, International Institute, Meadow Brook music and drama programs, Institute of Arts, concert band, and the annual Freedom Festival, celebrating Canada's Dominion Day, July 1, and U.S. Independence Day, July 4.
Educational facilities: 13 colleges and universities in metro area including Wayne State Univ., Univ. of Detroit, and branches of the Univ. of Michigan and Michigan State.
Convention facilities: Cobo Hall and Convention Arena with 500,000 sq. ft. of exhibit space; Joe Louis Arena with 33,000 sq. ft. of exhibition space; more than 23,000 rooms in 350 hotels and motels in greater Detroit (Wayne, Oakland, Macomb counties).
Sports: Tigers baseball (American League), Express (NASL), NFL Lions, NHL Red Wings, NBA Pistons; 6 winter skiing areas within short driving distance.
Other attractions: Chrysler, Ford, American Motors, and General Motors auto plants; Henry Ford Museum and Greenfield Village, Cranbrook Institute (science museum and arts), Belle Isle (1,000 acre park), zoo, public library, historical museum, and Fort Wayne Military Museum.
History: founded 1701 by the Frenchman Cadillac as a strategic frontier fort and trading post, ceded to the British in 1763 and turned over to the U.S. in 1796 as a village of 2,500; reoccupied by the British for a year in the War of 1812. Completion of the Erie Canal in 1825 opened a cheap water transport route from New York to the Northwest and made Detroit an important commercial center. R. E. Olds built Detroit's first auto factory in 1899; and Henry Ford, who handbuilt his first car in 1896, formed his first company in 1899, and the present Ford Motor Co. in 1903. The area's industries made it the "Arsenal of Democracy" in World War II.
Further information: Greater Detroit Chamber of Commerce, 150 Michigan Avenue; and Detroit Public Information Dept., City-County Bldg., both Detroit, MI 48226; and Detroit Convention Bureau, 100 Renaissance Center, Detroit, MI 48243.

Dubuque, Iowa

The World Almanac is sponsored in the Dubuque area by the Dubuque Telegraph-Herald (eves. except Sat. and Sunday), P.O. Box 688, 8th and Bluff streets, Dubuque, IA 52001; phone (319) 588-5611; founded 1836; circulation 39,126 daily, 42,631 Sunday; executive editor Stephen Kent; publisher Norman McMullin; Adv. Dir. David Lewis.

Population: 64,336 city, 97,321 SMSA.
Area: 23.7 sq. mi. in Dubuque County on the Mississippi River on the eastern border of the state; Dubuque County seat.
Commerce: total retail sales in city $312 million (1979), median household income $19,817 (1979).
Medical facilities: 3 hospitals with over 700 beds; Iowa's 2d largest medical clinic.
Industry: meat processing, agriculture, manufacturing of industrial tractors, millwork, oil handling equipment, pumps, plumbing goods, furniture, paper containers, snow removal equipment, metal tanks and fittings, sheet metal goods, iron, copper, brass and aluminum castings, electrical furnaces, insulation board, packing house products, chemicals, insecticides, sulphuric acid, chemical fertilizer, publishing.
Transportation: Illinois Central Gulf, Milwaukee Road, Chicago Northwestern, and Burlington Northern railroads; Amtrak; 15 motor truck cos., 3 interstate bus lines, one taxicab co., radio-equipped; municipal intracity (Keyline) bus, barge transportation; airport served by Ozark and Mississippi Valley airlines, 2 charter services.
Communications: TV station, ABC affiliate with cable TV from Teleprompter; 2 AM, 3 FM radio stations; daily, weekly labor, and weekly Catholic newspapers.
Federal facilities: Federal Building houses post office, FBI and some federal agencies; gov't. lock and dam on river.
Cultural facilities: 9 art galleries, 2 art societies, symphony orchestra, community theater groups, public library.
Education: 15 public elementary, 3 junior and 2 senior high schools; 11 parochial elementary, one parochial high school; 3 private co-educational colleges; 3 theological seminaries, 2 vo-tech schools; nurses training school.
Recreation: 24 parks, YM-YWCA, city recreation programs; boating on the Mississippi; 6 golf courses in county; 3 public swimming pools, 2 nature preserves, ski area.
Convention facilities: 17 hotels and motels, 53 restaurants, 22 fast food services; 17 night clubs; new Five Flags Civic Center.
Sports: Dubuque Blues, Dubuque Merchants, and Dubuque Pilots, semi-pro baseball teams; racquetball, bowling; city league softball, basketball, volleyball, horseshoes, golf, ice hockey, tennis.
Other attractions: Fourth Street cable railway; Old Shot Tower from Civil War days; Farmers Market, held every Saturday May-October in streets; area-wide market selling homegrown and handmade products; Pickett's Brewery,

only one in Iowa; Trappist Monastery 12 miles southwest of Dubuque; riverboat museum; examples of architecture from 1870-1910 period, with many buildings listed on the National Register; mean annual temperature 46.6 degrees, annual precipitation 40.27 inches.
History: local government organized in 1837, city charter adopted 1841; council-manager-ward form of government adopted 1980; city named for Julien Dubuque, a French-Canadian fur trader who was permitted by Fox Indians to mine lead in the area in 1877.
Further information: Dubuque Area Chamber of Commerce, 880 Locust Street, Dubuque, IA 52001; phone (319) 583-8246. or Dubuque Information and Referral Service, 1358 Central Avenue, Dubuque, IA 52001, phone (319) 557-8800.

Edmonton, Alberta, Canada

The World Almanac is sponsored in central and northern Alberta by the Edmonton Journal, 10006 - 101 Street, Edmonton, Alberta, T5J 2S6; phone (403) 425-9120; founded November 11, 1903. A division of Southam Press Limited; circulation 185,000; publisher J. Patrick O'Callaghan; editor Andrew Snaddon; sponsor Learn to Ski, curl, play golf, tennis, and Shape Up Fitness programs; Literary Awards, Newspaper in Education.

Population: 516,000 city (1980 est.), 630,000 metro (1980 est.); capital of Alberta, largest Alberta city, 5th in Canada; total metro employed 310,000 (1978 est.).
Area: 123.34 sq. mi. on North Saskatchewan River.
Industry: 2d largest refining center in Canada, 7,000 producing wells; petrochemical facilities include plastics, fertilizers, man made fibers, steel tube mills, 2d largest meat processing center in Canada; serves 2 major oil sands plants to north; prosperous mixed farming area.
Commerce: major supply center for Northwest Territories, Yukon, northeastern B.C., and Canadian Arctic; origin and terminus of 5 oil and natural gas pipelines east and west; retail sales (metro, 1978) $4.4 billion, mfg. shipments (metro, 1978) $3.3 billion; trading area population (est.) 1.1 million.
Transportation: crossroads of Yellowhead, Alaska, and Mackenzie highways; Canadian National, Canadian Pacific; Northern Alberta, Great Slave, and Alberta Resources railroads; 4 airports, 6 airlines, 225,841 itinerant movements in 1978; Light Rapid Transit System.
Communications: 11 radio stations including one French station, 4 TV including one French station, 2 cable TV networks.
New construction: over $1 billion in building permits issued in metro area in 1979.
Medical facilities: 5 general and 5 auxiliary hospitals, 2 rehabilitation centers, 9 nursing homes.
Cultural facilities: Edmonton Symphony Orchestra, Edmonton Art Gallery, Centennial Library, Provincial Museum and Archives, Univ. of Alberta (Canada's 3d largest), Northern Alberta Institute of Technology (Canada's largest technical college), Grant McEwan Community College, Alberta and Edmonton ballet companies. Canada's most active professional theater, housed in the Citadel Theatre complex; Theatre Three, Northern Light professional theaters; Stage West dinner theater; Edmonton Opera, Northern Alberta Jubilee Auditorium, Queen Elizabeth Planetarium, Muttart Conservatory.
Other attractions: Klondike Days, annual celebration of the 1898 Yukon gold rush is held in mid-July; August Heritage Festival; Valley Zoo, Fort Edmonton, Capital City Recreation Park, Hawrelak Park; Alberta Game Farm, Elk Island Park, and many lakes nearby.
Sports: CFL Edmonton Eskimos, NHL Edmonton Oilers, NASL Drillers; 16,000 seat Coliseum; 45,000 seat sport complex and $8.5 million aquatic center built for the 1978 Commonwealth Games; Kinsmen Field House indoor track seats 4,000.
History: Fort Edmonton built in 1795, named after town now a borough of London, England; oil discovered at Leduc (20 miles south) in 1947 rocketed the city into prominence as one of the world's leading petrochemical centers.
Further information: Chamber of Commerce, 600 Sun Life Place, 10123 99 Street, Edmonton, Alta.

El Paso, Texas

The World Almanac is sponsored in the El Paso area by the El Paso Herald-Post, 401 Mills Avenue, El Paso, TX 79999; phone (915) 747-6700; Herald founded 1881, Post 1922, merged (under Scripps-Howard) 1931; circulation 36,135; Robert W. Lee editor, Robert McBrinn managing editor.

Population: 448,330 city, (Chamber of Commerce est.) with twin city Juarez, Mex., 544,195; total employed 147,933.
Area: 239 sq. mi., western tip of Texas where Rio Grande cuts boundaries of Texas, New Mexico, and Mexico at foot of the Rockies (including Franklin Mtns.); El Paso County seat.
Industry: manufacturing payroll $256.7 million in 1978; manufacturing employment 28,500; clothing largest employer, including Farah, Levi Straus, Mann, Hicks-Ponder, Billy the Kid; Juarez-El Paso border in-bond industries at 75 and 28,616 employed, including electronic and other, such as RCA, GTE, Sylvania, General Instruments, American Hospital Supply, and Allen Bradley; home of El Paso Natural Gas, ASARCO, Inc., Peyton Packing, Tony Lama Boots, Phelps Dodge, Standard and Texaco refineries, Old El Paso (pet foods), and Ashley's of Texas canned Mexican foods; nut processing, cattle, pecans, cotton and other agriculture.
Commerce: wholesale-retail center for west Texas, New Mexico, northern Mexico; retail sales (1978) $1.8 billion; 20 banks, 6 savings and loan associations. Value added (1978) $520.4 million including $229.9 million in labor; exports (1978) $630.9 million, with $783.9 million in imports.
Transportation: 5 major rail lines, Amtrak; 10 bus lines, 21 truck lines, 5 major highways; gateway to Mexico, busiest crossing point on the U.S. border with over 60 million crossings a year; International Airport, 6 airlines with 223,866 flights in 1978 and 912,656 passengers, 17,411 tons of freight.
Communications: 5 TV and 18 radio stations.
New construction: 1978 building permits totaled $219.1 million.
Medical facilities: 16 hospitals with 2,994 beds; area cancer treatment center; Univ. of Texas System School of Nursing, Texas Tech Univ. School of Medicine.
Federal facilities: Ft. Bliss (U.S. Army Air Defense center, Allied Students Missile Center, Sgts. Major Academy), William Beaumont Army Medical Center, and nearby McGregor Range, White Sands Missile Range, and Holloman AFB in New Mexico.
Cultural facilities: Univ. of Texas at El Paso, El Paso Community College, El Paso Symphony, Museum of Art with Kress Collection, Ballet El Paso, opera companies, theater groups, Chamizal National Memorial theater, and McKelligon Canyon Pavilion; civic-convention center, public libraries.
Other attractions: annual Sun Carnival and Sun Bowl football game; Tigua Indian community arts and crafts center, missions that pre-date those of the Californias, horse racing in nearby New Mexico, horse and dog racing in Juarez, zoo, Cavalry Museum, Wilderness Park Museum, Guadalupe Mountains and Big Bend National Parks within 300 miles; skiing in Ruidoso, N.M. and Carlsbad Caverns within 200 miles; exotic Juarez, Mexico and Pancho Villa country.
Further information: Convention and Visitors Bureau, Five Civic Center Plaza, El Paso, TX 79901.

Erie, Pennsylvania

The World Almanac is sponsored in the Erie area by The Erie Daily Times, 205 W. 12th Street, Erie, PA 16501; phone (814) 456-8531; founded in 1888; circulation 74,000 daily, 92,000 Sunday; Edward M. Mead, Michael Mead, co-publishers; executive editor Joseph Meagher, managing editor Len Kholos.

Population: 125,134 (city), 270,855 (county), 260,000 (metro area), 3d in state; total employed 52,440.
Area: 19.53 sq. mi. at tip of northwestern Pa.; Erie County seat.
Commerce: county produces $269 million in exports, highest per capita in Pennsylvania; Erie's retail sales total more than $855 million; tourism—5 miles of beaches, fishing, boating; winter sports with 6 county parks and Presque Isle State Park offering camping, hiking trails, tennis courts, picnic areas, and ball fields; seaport—60 or more oceangoing vessels each year, the only U.S. port of call for the Canadian passenger schooner Challenge; over 506 industrial plants produce machinery and parts, iron and steel forgings, hardware, meters, plastics, paper (Hammermill), furniture, toys; General Electric produces Amtrak passenger trains.
Special awards: Dept. of Housing and Urban Development award for 1,200 housing units for elderly and 400 family sites, AFL-CIO Community Service Award.
New construction: entering phase 2 of John E. Lampe marina, public facility which will provide 250 boat stalls, launching ramps, and include a 30 acre park; 10-story Southshore Apartments; tank pump house for Hammermill Paper Co.; $1.2 million Loblaws retail food store; $400,000 firehouse.
Transportation: 5 railroads, Boston-Chicago Amtrak line; airport; 35 trucking companies, 4 bus lines.
Cultural facilities: Penn State Univ. extension; Gannon, Mercyhurst, and Villa Maria colleges; Philharmonic Society, Council of the Arts; theater groups; Erie County Field House for plays, entertainment, and sports; work begun on $8 million Erie Civic Center.
Convention facilities: Erie Hilton, 2 Holiday Inns, 90 other hotels and motels with over 3,200 rooms.
Medical facilities: Hamot Medical Center, Saint Vincent Health Center, VA hospital, Medi-Center, Erie Osteopathic Hospital, Erie County Geriatric Center, Corry Memorial Hospital, Shriners' Hospital for Crippled Children, Union City Memorial Hospital, and Doctors' Osteopathic Hospital.
History: named after Eriez Indians; site of building of ship Niagara with which Oliver Hazard Perry defeated British in 1813 in Lake Erie battle.
Further information: Chamber of Commerce, 1006 State, Erie, PA 16501.

Evansville, Indiana

The World Almanac is sponsored in southwestern Indiana, western Kentucky, and southeastern Illinois by the Evansville Press, P.O. Box 454, Evansville, IN 47703; phone (812) 464-7600; founded July 2, 1906, by E.W. Scripps and J.C. Harper; circulation 45,600; editor William W. Sorrels, managing editor Tom Tuley.

Population: 133,566 (city), 286,700 (metro area), 4th in state.
Area: 47 sq. mi. at bend of Ohio River in southwest corner of state; Vanderburgh County seat.
Industry: Whirlpool Corp. plants (refrigeration and air conditioning); Mead Johnson & Co. (pharmaceutical division of Bristol-Myers Co.); Alcoa Warrick Operations (aluminum) just east of city; 283 manufacturing firms.
Commerce: retail sales $763 million (1979); effective buying income per household $14,290 (1979); home offices of Credi-Thrift of America, Inc.; 4 banks, 6 savings and loan.
Transportation: world headquarters of Atlas Van Lines; 4 railroads, 5 commercial barge lines, 4 interstate bus lines; Allegheny, Delta, Eastern air lines.
Communications: 2 daily newspapers; 4 TV and 6 radio stations.
New construction: more than $3 billion in commercial and industrial expansion underway including downtown Riverview Commerce Centre bank and hotel and Coal Exchange office building; major coal conversion plants across river at Henderson County, Ky.
Medical facilities: 4 general and mental hospitals; branch of Indiana University Medical School.
Cultural facilities: Philharmonic Orchestra, Museum of Arts and Science, Mesker Zoo, Univ. of Evansville, Indiana State Univ., Evansville; national headquarters of Phi Mu Alpha music fraternity; Abraham Lincoln boyhood home nearby.
Sports: Evansville Triplets baseball of American Assn. (AAA), farm team of Detroit Tigers.
Further information: Chamber of Commerce, Southern Securities Building, Evansville, IN 47708.

Fort Wayne, Indiana

The World Almanac is sponsored in the Fort Wayne area by the Journal-Gazette, 600 W. Main Street, Fort Wayne, IN 46802; phone (219) 461-8333; established June 14, 1899 by consolidation of The Journal and The Daily Gazette; circulation daily 61,018, Sundays 104,498; president-publisher Richard G. Inskeep; secretary-treasurer Naomi Erb; editor Larry W. Allen.

Population: 189,865 (city), 374,500 (metro area); total employed 178,000 (metro).
Area: 51.96 sq. mi. at confluence of St. Joseph, St. Mary's, and Maumee rivers in NE Ind.; Allen County seat. Allen County is largest of Indiana's 92 counties (671 sq. mi.), and has greatest number of farms in state, 2,011.
Industry: General Electric and International Harvester largest employers; Magnavox, Essex International, and Central Soya home offices; several firms manufacture about 85% of world's diamond wire dies.
Commerce: wholesale and retail center for northeastern Indiana, southeastern Michigan, northwestern Ohio; retail sales (metro) over $1.611 billion; bank deposits $2.096 billion; 5 banks, 4 savings-and-loan assns.; E. B. I. per household (metro) $22,810; 6 life insurance companies, including Lincoln National Life, based here.
Transportation: 2 major rail freight lines, Amtrak; 56 motor freight lines including home-based North American Van, Elway Express, Scott, and Transport Motor; I-69 connects city with Indianapolis and Indiana Toll Road; U.S. 30 dual lane to Chicago; municipal airport; hq. for 122d Tactical Fighter Wing, Indiana Air National Guard; United, Delta, Air Wisconsin airlines.
Communications: 10 radio, 4 TV stations.
Medical facilities: 4 hospitals including VA.
Cultural facilities: Philharmonic Orchestra; Fine Arts and Performing Arts complex; 9 universities and colleges; 3 museums; Foellinger outdoor theater.
Sports: Komet hockey team (IHL) plays at Allen Co. War Memorial Coliseum; annual Mad Anthony celebrities golf.
Other attractions: replica of 3d Fort Wayne (1815); children's zoo, 88 parks and playgrounds, 19 golf courses, 37 shopping centers.
History: first white settlement in Indiana (circa 1692).
Further information: Chamber of Commerce, 826 Ewing Street, Ft. Wayne, IN 46802.

Fort Worth, Texas

Population: city 426,400 (4th in state), county 860,450, Ft. Worth/Dallas metro area 2.79 million (1979 est.); work force 413,598.
Area: 861 sq. mi. on the Trinity River in north central Texas, about 50 miles from Oklahoma border; Tarrant County seat.
Commerce: diversified manufacturing, including aerospace, plants, food and beverage, mobile homes, autos, medical industries; 1,905 industrial plants in production; agribusiness related industry and services produces over $179.8 million in agriculture products a year.
Transportation: Dallas-Fort Worth regional airport 24 minutes driving time from downtown; 9 major railroads, Amtrak; 41 motor carriers; city-owned local bus service, 2 transcontinental, 2 intrastate bus lines.
Communications: one daily newspaper; 26 area radio stations, 6 area TV stations; weekly and monthly publications, including Fort Worth Magazine.
Medical facilities: 32 hospitals with 4,700 beds; 2 children's hospitals with 200 beds, 4 government hospitals.
Federal facilities: 14 federal agencies; Carswell AFB.
Cultural facilities: Casa Manana, America's first permanent musical arena theater; community theater; symphony, opera, ballet; Texas Boys Choir and Texas Girls Choir; Van Cliburn Piano Competition; Kimbell Art Museum, Amon Carter Museum of Western Art, Fort Worth Museum of Science & History, Fort Worth Art Center.
Education: 8 colleges and universities with more than 50,000 students; 28 other colleges and campuses within 50-mile radius with over 106,000 students; Texas Christian Univ., Univ. of Texas at Arlington; Texas Wesleyan College; Texas College of Osteopathic Medicine; 3 campuses of Tarrant County Junior College; Southwestern Baptist Theological Seminary.
Recreation: Forest Park, Heritage Park, Fort Worth Zoological Park, Trinity Park, Botanic Gardens, Japanese Garden, Water Garden Park, several other parks; 9 municipal golf courses.
Convention facilities: Tarrant County Convention Center; Will Rogers Memorial Center; 63 hotels and motels with 5,000 rooms.
Sports attractions: Dallas Cowboys football, Texas Rangers baseball, Fort Worth Texans hockey; Colonial National Golf Tournament; TCU football.
Other attractions: Six Flags Over Texas, Fat Stock Show and Rodeo, Miss Texas Pageant, Log Cabin Village, North Fort Worth western historical area; Cowtown Rodeo weekly; Pate Museum of Transportation.
History: Founded 1849 as a frontier Army post on the Chisholm Trail; later became major railhead.
Further information: Chamber of Commerce, 700 Throckmorton, Fort Worth, TX 76102.

Fresno, California

The World Almanac is sponsored in the Fresno area by The Fresno Bee, 1626 E Street, Fresno, CA 93786; phone (209) 441-6111; founded 1922; circulation daily 130,327, Sunday 151,766; president C. K. McClatchy, editor C. K. McClatchy, executive editor Frank McCulloch, managing editor George Gruner.

Population: 230,000 (city), 498,400 (county); total employed 272,600.
Area: one of largest counties in the state, 3,819,456 acres; located in geographical center of the state; Fresno County seat.
Agriculture: leading county in U.S. in farm production, number of farms, and annual value of agriculture production; state's leading county in production of field and seed crops, grapes, cantaloupes, barley, tomatoes, turkeys, peaches, boysenberries, figs, nectarines, potatoes, cotton seed, alfalfa seed, fruit, and nuts.
Industry: 600 diversified manufacturing establishments; food processing is major industry; 2d in importance is production of beverages, primarily wine, brandy, and spirits; metro retail sales over $1.7 billion.
Transportation: daily service by 9 airlines; Amtrak; freeways connect to all major metropolitan areas in California; served by 23 common truck carriers, one interstate bus line, and 2 mainline railroads with freight handling facilities; U.S. port of entry.
Communications: 7 commercial TV stations, 5 cable TV services, 18 commercial radio stations, and 2 public radio stations.
Medical facilities: 6 general hospitals including a VA installation; medical school under construction.
Cultural facilities: community philharmonic, opera, ballet and theater; Fresno Art Center, Meux Home Museum, Discovery Center, Kearney Museum, downtown malls with one of the best outdoor art displays in the West.
Recreation: Western Hockey League team, California Baseball League team; golf, tennis, swimming; Yosemite, Sequoia, and Kings Canyon national parks with groves of giant Sequoia trees plus facilities for boating, sailing, hunting, fishing, skiing, hiking, pack trips and camping.
Other attractions: Duncan Water Gardens, Underground Gardens; Roeding Park with city zoo and children's Storyland; nationally famous rodeo, county fair.
Convention facilities: Convention Center Theatre seats 2,361; Exhibit Hall facilities can accommodate up to 3,500 with banquet capacity of 2,400; 11 meeting rooms accommodate up to 390, exhibit space of 59,000 sq. ft; Selland Arena has capacity of 7,500, parking for 900 cars; 5,000 hotel and motel rooms.
History: area explored by the Spaniards in the early 1800s and visited by fur trappers before 1840; settlement began when gold miners came in the 1850s; county created Apr. 19, 1856, from parts of Mariposa, Merced, and Tulare counties.
Further information: Fresno City & County Chamber of Commerce, P.O. Box 1469, Fresno, CA 93786.

Greenville, South Carolina

The World Almanac is sponsored in the Greenville County area by The Greenville News and Greenville Piedmont (daily a.m. and p.m. and combined weekend editions), P.O. Box 1688, 305 S. Main Street, Greenville, SC 29602; phone (803) 298-4100; circulation 107,936 daily, 106,017 Sunday (Mar. 1979); chairman of the board and publisher J. Kelly Sisk, president and co-publisher Rhea T. Eskew, executive editor John S. Pittman.

Population: (1980 est.) 57,752 city, 289,401 county, 571,500 SMSA; 253,100 SMSA labor force, 5.1% SMSA unemployment.
Area: 789 sq. mi. in county; Greenville is county seat; in South Carolina's Piedmont area; county includes 7 incorporated areas.
Industry: textiles, apparel, tires, fiber production, chemicals, machinery, electronics, food.
Commerce: 1979 retail sales in SMSA $2.39 billion; 1979 bank debits in SMSA $23.8 billion; 1980 per capita income est. $7,344 county.
Transportation: 2 airports (one general aviation), 2 airlines, 2 bus lines, 3 railroads; Interstate 85, US highways 25, 29, 123, 276.
Communications: 5 TV, 15 radio stations, 2 cable TV services; 2 daily, 3 weekly newspapers.
New construction: $1.01 billion industrial development and expansion from 1960 to May 1980, creating more than 33,000 jobs in the county; $30 million downtown hotel-convention center under way.
Cultural facilities: Greenville County Museum of Art, Greenville Little Theatre, Warehouse Theatre, Bob Jones Univ. Classic Players, Furman Univ. Guild, Greenville Symphony Orchestra, Bob Jones Univ. Art Museum; 2 four-year

univs., two-year college, technical college; more than 400 churches representing 26 faiths.
Medical facilities: 9 hospitals in Greenville Hospital System, St. Francis Community Hospital, Shriners Hospital for Crippled Children.
Sports: Furman Univ. in Southern Conference, nearby Clemson Univ. in Atlantic Coast Conference; 3 stock car tracks in county; boating in upstate lakes.
History: county created by General Assembly 1786, city named Pleasantburg in 1797, Greenville in 1831.
Further information: Greater Greenville Chamber of Commerce, 24 Cleveland Street, P.O. Box 10048, Greenville, SC 29603; (803) 242-1050.

Halifax, Nova Scotia, Canada

The World Almanac is sponsored in Nova Scotia by The Chronicle-Herald and The Mail-Star, 1650 Argyle Street, Halifax, Nova Scotia; phone (902) 426-2811; circulation Chronicle (morning) 71,089, Mail-Star (aft.) 54,414; publisher Graham W. Dennis, president Fred G. Mounce, chairman of the board L. F. Daley, general manager Frank Huelin, managing editor Ken Foran, treasurer W.D. Coleman.

Population: 117,882 (1976); labor force 57,305, employed 53,170.
Area: 24.19 sq. mi. on the southeast coast of the province; capital city.
Industry: leading industrial area in Atlantic provinces; establishments include oil refineries, electronic equipment manufacturers, ship yards, car assembly plants, plastic fabricators, metal works, breweries, and fish processing; 3d largest and one of Canada's most diversified scientific research centers.
Commerce: financial center of region, regional head offices of all major banks; retail sales over $970 million, average per capita disposable income $7,217 Halifax County (1979); all 3 levels of government constitute employment for 18,000; armed forces have over 14,000 stationed in city.
Transportation: 2 major passenger-freight lines; 8 container lines call at easternmost commercial port on mainland North America; container port with 3 sea-shore cranes handled 233,000 20-foot equivalent containers with tonnage of 2.1 million (1979); about 533,000 tons break bulk cargo and 14.4 million tons bulk cargo; international airport.
Communications: 5 radio, 2 TV stations; 2 daily and one weekly newspapers.
New construction: building permits issued for $38.5 million worth of construction in 1979; new container port being built.
Education: 6 degree-granting universities; 48 common and 3 private schools, one technical institute.
Medical facilities: 9 hospitals (3 teaching).
Cultural facilities: Atlantic Symphony Orchestra; one professional live theater and 2 amateur; 2 public libraries.
Parks: 3 major parks (403 acres).
Sports: Halifax Voyageurs of the AHL.
History: founded in 1749; meeting place of first legislative assembly in Canada (1758).
Further information: Halifax Visitors and Convention Bureau, Suite 508, Market Mall, Scotia Square, Halifax, Nova Scotia; phone (902) 426-8736.

Hamilton, Ontario, Canada

The World Almanac is sponsored in Hamilton and the Niagara Peninsula by The Spectator (a division of Southam Inc.) 44 Frid Street, Hamilton, Ontario L8N 3G3; phone (416) 526-3333; founded in 1846; circulation 147,996; publisher John D. Muir; general manager Thomas J. McCarthy; executive editor John Doherty; managing editor Alex Beer.

Population: 306,538 (city), 407,758 (Hamilton-Wentworth region); 8th in Canada, 3d in province.
Area: 54.4 sq. mi. (city), 426 sq. mi. (region) at west end of Lake Ontario.
Industry: 58 per cent of Canada's steel is produced at the Steel Company of Canada Ltd., Dominion Foundries and Steel Ltd., and Slater Steel Ltd.; 757 plants in the metro area manufacturing iron and steel products, electrical appliances, agricultural equipment, tires, wire, food products, heavy machinery, chemicals, and textiles.
Commerce: retail sales (1979) $1.712 billion or 2.27 per cent of Canadian total sales; average weekly wage $300.66; disposable income per capita $7,710.
Transportation: Hamilton Street Railway, Canadian National and Canadian Pacific railways as well as Toronto, Hamilton, and Buffalo line; western terminus for GO transit (provincial rapid transit system); provincial highways to Toronto, Windsor, and Buffalo pass through region; city airport 9 miles south at Mount Hope.
Communications: TV station, community programming cable station, 4 radio stations.
New construction: $16 million convention center scheduled for completion in 1983; $60 million shopping mall scheduled for completion in 1981.
Medical facilities: 5 major hospitals including medical center at McMaster Univ., Hamilton Psychiatric Hospital, St. Peter's Center for chronically ill and geriatric patients.
Educational facilities: McMaster Univ., Mohawk College of Applied Arts and Technology.
Cultural facilities: Hamilton Place theater-auditorium; art gallery; Hamilton Philharmonic Orchestra; Hamilton Players' Guild; Theatre Aquarius; Multicultural Center; new $12.3 million public library.
Convention facilities: convention center under construction will have 17 meeting rooms, banquet space for 2,300 people in one room, topped by a 14-story office tower.
Other attractions: Dundurn Castle, restored prime minister's residence circa 1850; Whitehearn, restored Victorian home; Canadian Football Hall of Fame; Royal Botanical Gardens, one of the largest park systems per capita in Canada; Hess Village boutiques and restaurants in old restored homes; hiking on Bruce Trail, winding through region along Niagara Escarpment.
Sports: Hamilton Tiger-Cats football, 2 municipal golf courses, Royal Hamilton Yacht Club.
History: explorer Sieur de la Salle discovered Hamilton area in 1669; city takes name from George Hamilton, who laid out streets on part of the farm he bought in 1813.
Further information: Chamber of Commerce, 100 King Street W., Suite 830, Hamilton, Ont. L8P 1A2

Honolulu, Hawaii

The World Almanac is sponsored in Hawaii by The Honolulu Advertiser, P.O. Box 3110, Honolulu, HI 96802; phone (808) 537-2977; founded July 2, 1856, as Pacific Commercial Advertiser by Henry M. Whitney; circulation 76,196 mornings, 184,528 Sunday; president and publisher Thurston Twigg-Smith, editor-in-chief George Chaplin, executive editor Buck Buchwach, managing editor Mike Middlesworth; awards from American Political Science Assn., American Assn. for the Advancement of Science, others.

Population: 729,100 (metro); 80% of state population; total employed, 295,000.
Area: 595 sq. mi., encompassing Oahu Island; state capital.
Commerce: major destination for U.S., Japanese tourists; persons staying a night or more 3.9 million in 1979, up from 1.5 million a decade earlier; average daily visitor census 104,600 in 1979, up from 37,400 a decade earlier; tourist spending $2.6 billion in 1979, up from $550 million in 1969;

visitor dollars top military spending, $1.2 billion in 1979; sugarcane and pineapple major agriculture export crops; retail sales (statewide) $5.5 billion; total personal income $8.5 billion; per capita personal income $9,353; Pacific basin business and financial center.
Transportation: dependent on ships, planes for most goods; passengers arrive mostly by air; 19 airlines serve airport, 8 domestic carriers, 9 foreign, 2 inter-island.
Communications: 9 TV, 34 radio stations; 2 major daily newspapers.
Medical facilities: 22 civilian acute care hospitals, one military acute care hospital (Tripler Army Medical Center), 8 specialty long-term hospitals; Univ. of Hawaii School of Medicine.
Federal facilities: 7 major military bases, including Pearl Harbor Naval Base.
Cultural facilities: statewide public school system, 229 schools with 168,393 students in 1979; 140 private schools with 37,187 students in 1979; 9-campus Univ. of Hawaii with 43,375 students; main campus at Manoa in Honolulu 20,833 students in 1979; university stresses oceanography, tropical environment problems and resources, tsunami research, volcanology, inter-race relations; East-West Center, Inc., at Manoa is public education corp. funded by federal government, attracts international students and researchers; Bernice Pauahi Bishop Museum is center for studies of Pacific cultures, houses artifacts, maintains floating square-rigger Falls of Clyde; Polynesian Cultural Center showcases native dances, music, arts; Honolulu Academy of Arts, Iolani Palace.

Recreation: surfing, swimming, sailing, fishing, football, basketball, baseball.

Other attractions: Waikiki Beach, extinct volcano Diamond Head, Arizona Memorial, balmy weather, tradewinds, multi-racial population, cultural diversity, Polynesian heritage.

History: Honolulu ("sheltered bay" in Hawaiian) was a small village when first westerners called aboard 2 British ships in 1786, 8 years after Capt. James Cook became first known European to discover Hawaiian Islands.

Further information: Hawaii Visitors Bureau, 2270 Kalakaua Avenue, Honolulu, HI 96815.

Houston, Texas

The World Almanac is sponsored in the Southwest by The Houston Post, 4747 Southwest Freeway, Houston, TX 77001; phone (713) 621-7000; founded in 1836; circulation daily 325,085, Saturday 349,105, Sunday 386,640; Oveta Culp Hobby, chairman of the board and editor; William P. Hobby, president; awards include Pulitzer Prize, Grand Prix, Editor & Publisher; community events sponsored: Educational Services, Science Engineering Fair; Scholastic Art Awards, Scholastic Writing Awards, travel shows, Houston Post Family Night at the Shrine Circus, the Rodeo, the Ice Capades, the Harlem Globetrotters, and the Black Watch.

Population: (city) 1.7 million, 5th in nation; (SMSA) 2.9 million; total employed (SMSA) 1.4 million; total wages and salaries (SMSA) $25 billion.
Area: 556 sq. mi. (city) on upper center Gulf Coast prairies, 49 ft. above sea level; Harris County seat; connected to Gulf of Mexico by 50-mile inland waterway, the Ship Channel.
Industry: nation's leading manufacturer in petrochemicals, 5th in machinery manufacturing and first in chemicals and allied products; supplies nation with over 50% petrochemicals, 80% synthetic rubber; produces $73.4 million in agriculture, $14.9 million in soybeans; over 300 firms in underwater, offshore, and oceanographic markets; world's petroleum refining capital.
Commerce: Houston-Galveston SCSA leads south and southwest in retail sales volume; average spendable family income $22,960; 204 metro banks with resources of $27 billion and deposits of $22 billion; 44 foreign banks.
Transportation: Port of Houston (nation's 3d in tonnage) connects with 250 world ports by over 180 steamship lines, hosts 5,521 ships yearly; 16 major airlines, 2 airports; 6 major rail systems; 32 common-carrier truck lines; 209-mile freeway system; 875-mile bus transit system and expanding minibus fleet in downtown area.
Communications: 2 daily newspapers; 31 radio stations; 5 commercial, one educational TV station.
New construction: non-residential contracts awarded $2.6 billion, residential units completed value $2.2 billion (1979).
Medical facilities: Texas Medical Center includes 35 buildings on 235 acres; Harris County has 60 hospitals (including VA) with 16,017 beds, 30 ambulances, 3 emergency Life Flight helicopters.
Federal facilities: Lyndon B. Johnson Space Center, $202 million manned-spacecraft center; Ellington AFB.
Cultural facilities: $3 million Alley Theatre and Miller Outdoor Theatre; Houston Symphony Orchestra, Grand Opera Assn., Houston Ballet Foundation perform in $7.5 million Jones Hall for Performing Arts; 30 major art galleries including Museum of Fine Arts (permanent collection valued at $14 million) and Contemporary Arts Museum; Houston Public Library, 26 branches; Harris County Public Library, 17 branches, 2 bookmobiles.
Education: 29 major universities including Rice, Univ. of Houston, Texas Southern; 5 major medical schools including Baylor College of Medicine and Univ. of Texas Health Science Center (8 branches); Houston Independent School District, 7th largest in nation; total enrollment 193,409; 22 school districts in Harris County, total enrollment 469,213; private and parochial school enrollment 30,000.
Recreational facilities: 276 parks, 5 municipal golf courses, 42 municipal swimming pools, 3 tennis centers with 54 courts and 112 neighborhood courts; Astroworld 65-acre amusement park; botanical garden arboretum, Hermann Park and Zoo; 53 community centers, 58 county parks, 70 miles of Gulf beaches in one hour's drive.
Convention facilities: 465 major conventions held in Houston in 1979 with 666,771 delegates attending; hotels and motels have 23,000 rooms; the Astrodome can seat 60,000 for conventions; Astrohall has 550,000 sq. ft.; downtown locations include Albert Thomas Convention Center, 300,000 sq. ft.; Sam Houston Coliseum, 50,000 sq. ft.; Music Hall seats 3,036; Exposition Hall, 83,000 sq. ft. exhibit area.
Sports: Astros baseball, Oilers football, Rockets basketball, Angels women's basketball, Hurricanes soccer, Summit soccer; sports events centers are Astrodome and Summit.
Climate: temperature moderated by winds from Gulf of Mexico, abundant rainfall; average daily temp. 66.5, total precip. 58.97 inches (1979).
Scientific facilities: one of the top 10 science centers in the nation; over 80 research firms maintain facilities for study in petroleum, chemicals, medicine, earth sciences, aerospace, oceanography.
History: founded 1836 by J.K. and A.C. Allen, city eventually encompassed Old Harrisburg which was an 1826 townsite laid out by John Harris; named for Gen. Sam Houston, commander of the Texas Army, which won independence from Mexico for the Republic of Texas Apr. 21, 1836. Houston was first president of the Republic, later governor of the state of Texas; both Houston and Harrisburg were for brief periods capitals of the republic.
Further information: Houston Convention and Visitor Council, 1522 Main Street; Houston Chamber of Commerce, 1100 Milam, both Houston, TX 77002.

Huntington, West Virginia

The World Almanac is sponsored in the Huntington-Ashland-Ironton area by The Herald-Dispatch (morn.), Huntington Publishing Company, 946 Fifth Avenue, Huntington, WV 25701; member of the Gannett Group; circulation 50,149, Sunday 52,858; publisher and president Harold E. Burdick, controller Ed Burns, executive editor C. Donald Hatfield.

Population: 74,315 (city), 297,200 (5-county metro area); largest city in the state.
Area: 15.86 sq. mi., on Ohio River near where West Virginia, Ohio, and Kentucky meet; Cabell County seat.
Industry: center for coal transport and for hand-crafted glass; leading industries are Ashland Oil, Armco Steel Co., Huntington Alloys, Inc., division of International Nickel Co.
Commerce: largest port for inland vessels in U.S. handles nearly 20 million tons of materials per year, moved by 7 freight companies; 1978 total retail sales in metro area, $939.9 million.
Transportation: Tri-State Airport, with the longest runway in the state, is served by 2 airlines, 833 air movements a month; Amtrak; 18 truck lines; urban bus transport system; 2 interstate bus lines.
Communications: 4 TV and 14 radio stations.
Cultural facilities: Marshall Univ.; Ashland Community College (Univ. of Kentucky); The Huntington Galleries of Art.
Medical facilities: 6 general hospitals with 1,800 total beds; 3 specialty hospitals including a VA hospital.
New construction: $32 million renewal program includes downtown pedestrian shopping plaza, civic center and new city-county library; $18 million Henderson Center sports complex for Marshall Univ. and $125 million enclosed shopping mall under construction; riverfront marina and parkland development being planned.
Further information: Chamber of Commerce, 522 Ninth Street, Huntington, WV 25701.

Indianapolis, Indiana

The World Almanac is sponsored in the Indianapolis area by The Indianapolis Star, The Indianapolis News, 307 N. Pennsylvania Street, Indianapolis, IN 46204; phone (317) 633-1240. News founded 1869, Star 1903; circulation daily Star, 215,858, daily News, 143,499, Sunday Star, 357,694; publisher Eugene S. Pulliam; president William A. Dyer Jr; Star editor Lawrence S. Connor; News editor Dr. Harvey C. Jacobs; Pulitzer prizes-News, Star; Nat'l. Headliners first prize-Star.

Population: 745,739 (consolidated city 1970), 1,111,173 (metro 1970); total employed 560,000.
Area: 379.4 sq. mi.; geographic center of state; state capital and Marion County seat.
Industry: over 1,520 diversified manufacturers including plane and auto engines and parts, electronics, pharmaceuticals, machinery; 1979 manufacturing payroll over $2.1 billion.
Commerce: commercial center for Indiana; retail sales $5.7 billion; per capita personal income $8,342; 6 banks with resources over $6.7 billion; home offices of over 60 insurance companies.
Transportation; 6 airlines; Indianapolis International Airport; 5 rail freight lines; Amtrak; 3 interstate bus lines; 67 truck lines; 7 interstate freeway routes.
Communications: 6 TV stations and 18 radio stations.
New construction: projects totalling over $440.7 million under construction in 1980.
Medical facilities: 17 hospitals, over 6,800 beds.
Federal facilities: Fort Harrison incl. Army Finance and Accounting Center, U.S.A. Admin. Center.
Cultural facilities: Museum of Art and Oldfields Museum of Decorative Arts; Indiana State Museum; Indianapolis Zoo; Children's Museum; Conner Prairie Pioneer Settlement and Museum of Indiana Heritage; Clowes Hall, home of symphony orch.; Civic Theatre, oldest amateur theatrical group; repertory theater; Star-Light Musicals.
Education facilities: Butler Univ., Indiana Central Univ., Marian College, Christian Theological and St. Mauer's seminaries, Purdue-Indiana Univ. at Indianapolis, Indiana Univ. medical center, nation's largest.
Recreation facilities: 13,000 park acres, 16 municipal swimming pools, 12 public golf courses; 18,000-seat domed sports arena, Indianapolis Sports Center.
Convention facilities: Indiana Convention-Exposition Center, Indiana State Fairgrounds.
Sports: home of the Pacers NBA; minor league baseball, soccer, hockey.
Other attractions: Indianapolis 500; Hoosier 100; annual National Drag Racing championships; U.S. open Clay Court championships.
History: sesquicentennial in 1971; important before Civil War, with nation's first union railway station (1853); home of James Whitcomb Riley, Booth Tarkington, and President Benjamin Harrison.
Additional information: Indianapolis Chamber of Commerce, 320 N. Meridian Street, Indianapolis, IN 46204; phone (317) 635-4747.

Jacksonville, Florida

The World Almanac is sponsored in the Jacksonville area by The Florida Times-Union and the Jacksonville Journal, One Riverside Avenue, Jacksonville, FL 32202; phone (904) 358-4111; circulation, Times-Union 155,333, Journal 51,266, combined Saturday 176,719, combined Sunday 195,961; publisher J.J. Daniel, president John A. Tucker; Journal won Pulitzer Prize for photography in 1967.

Population: 566,420 (1979); total employment 225,200 (1978).
Area: 840 sq. mi., includes nearly all of Duval Co. in northeast Florida; under one consolidated government.
Industry: diversified economy; banking and insurance center.
Commerce: emphasis on finance distribution; home or regional headquarters for 34 insurance companies; 1979 retail sales $2.4 billion; effective buying income per household $18,974.
Transportation: 3 major railroads and Amtrak; over 40 truck lines; 8 airlines averaging 96 air movements daily; 2 interstate bus lines; port handled 15 million tons in 1977.
Communications: 5 TV and 26 radio stations.
New construction: $226.2 million in building permits issued in 1978.
Medical facilities: 11 general hospitals and one naval hospital with total of 3,358 beds.
Federal facilities: 3 naval stations add $580 million yearly to the economy.

Cultural facilities: Cummer Art Gallery, Jacksonville Art Museum, Jacksonville Museum of Arts and Sciences, Jacksonville Symphony, Ballet Guild, 6 community theaters.

Education: Univ. of North Florida, Jacksonville Univ., Edward Waters College, Florida Junior College, Jones College.

Sports: Gator Bowl, Tournament Players Championships golf tournament, $450,000 purse; professional baseball, Jacksonville basketball and baseball; semi-pro football.

Other attractions: civic auditorium, coliseum, Jacksonville Zoo, Fort Caroline, Kingsley Plantation, 8 miles of public beaches.

History. founded in 1822 by Isiah Hart, named for Andrew Jackson; fire in 1901 destroyed 2,368 buildings, left 10,000 homeless; city and county governments merged in 1968 after referendum.

Further information: Chamber of Commerce, 815 South Main Street, Suite 100, P.O. Drawer 329, Jacksonville, FL 32201; phone (904) 396-0100.

Kalamazoo, Michigan

The World Almanac is sponsored in the Kalamazoo area by The Kalamazoo Gazette, 401 S. Burdick, Kalamazoo, MI 49003; phone (616) 345-3511; founded 1833; circulation daily 58,802, Sunday 65,183; owned and operated by Booth Newspapers, Inc.; president Werner Veit, editor Daniel M. Ryan, manager Ralph H. Bastien Jr.

Population: 85,800 (city), 209,200 (county); total employed (Kalamazoo-Portage SMSA) 134,000.
Area: located equidistant to the 3d and 5th largest metro areas in nation — Chicago and Detroit, 140 miles away; Kalamazoo County seat.
Industry: paper-making is the traditional industry with 5 large plants; Checker Motors Corp. manufactures cars; Fisher Body Division body stamping plant; Upjohn Co., pharmaceuticals.
Commerce: shopping center for large part of southwestern Michigan; in 1959, city became first in country to close downtown streets and create a pedestrian mall, now known as "Mall City;" retail sales (1978) $998 million; 3 banks with combined assets in 1980 of $1 billion, 2 savings and loan assns. with assets over $600 million.
Communications: daily newspaper, one TV, 9 radio stations.

Transportation: 2 railroads provide freight service, Amtrak passenger service; 34 general carriers provide trucking services; airport with freight and passenger service; 3 bus lines.

Cultural facilities: 5 auditoriums offering music and theatrical performances; 5 live arts theaters, art center, symphony orchestra, Kalamazoo Civic Players.

Educational facilities: 3 colleges and one university with combined student enrollment over 30,000.

Other attractions: Kalamazoo Nature Center, 83 lakes (county), National Junior Tennis Championships, 2 major hospitals, Kalamazoo Hilton Convention Center, IHL Kalamazoo Wings (hockey).

Further information: Kalamazoo County Chamber of Commerce, 500 W. Crosstown, Kalamazoo, MI 49008, phone (616) 381-4000.

Kansas City, Missouri

Population: 458,251 (city), 1,281,300 (metro area); total employed, 683,700.
Area: 3,341 sq. mi., SMSA, at confluence of Missouri and Kansas rivers in Jackson, Clay, and Platte counties.
Industry: first in production of envelopes and greeting cards, farm equipment distribution, frozen food storage and distribution, foreign trade zone space, underground storage space, and hard winter wheat marketing. Top employers: U.S. government, General Motors, TWA, Bendix, Western Electric, Ford; city is a leading hard wheat center, stocker and feeder market, and is among the top 5 cities in flour production and grain elevator capacity.
Commerce: total retail sales in 1978, $5.968 billion; the center of a 7-county metro area: Jackson, Clay, Platte, Cass, and Ray counties in Missouri; Johnson and Wyandotte counties in Kansas.
Transportation: 9 airlines with 420 scheduled arrivals and departures daily at Kansas City International Airport; 169 truck lines and 4 barge companies; city is one of the nation's major rail centers.
New construction: $400 million Crown Center business and apartment complex covers 25 square blocks; new medical center of Univ. of Missouri and Univ. of Kansas; Mercantile Tower Building; United Missouri Bank headquarters; City Center Square, a 32-story office and retail building downtown; 27-story Mutual Benefit Life/IBM Plaza Bldg.; H. Roe Bartle exposition hall; Worlds of Fun recreation center; One Pershing Square office complex; Hyatt Regency Hotel; Bannister Mall Shopping Center.
Cultural facilities: Starlight Theater, nation's 2d largest outdoor theater; William Rockhill Nelson Gallery of Art, among the 10 top American museums with the 3d largest Oriental collection outside China; Performing Arts Foundation formed in 1965 to present festival events; Univ. of Missouri at Kansas City; Rockhurst College; Kansas City Art Institute; Univ. of Kansas Medical Center. Within commuting distance are Univ. of Kansas, Park College, William Jewell College, Truman Library in Independence. Linda Hall Library of Science and Technology is one of the largest privately endowed technical reference libraries in the nation.
Recreational facilities: more than 100 parks cover 5,345 acres, including Swope Park, 2d largest in nation, with zoo.
Sports: The American Royal Livestock and Horse Show each fall attracts entries from throughout the country; home of the NFL Chiefs, American League Royals, NBA Kings.
History: Kansas City's beginnings can be traced to a trading post of French fur trappers about 1826. It became an important trade and transportation center as the overland routes of the Oregon and Santa Fe trails spread westward. As agricultural production boomed, it became an important market and distribution center for crops from throughout the middle west.
Further information: Chamber of Commerce of Greater Kansas City, 920 Main, Kansas City, MO 64105.

Kitchener-Waterloo, Ontario, Canada

The World Almanac is sponsored in the Kitchener-Waterloo area by the Kitchener-Waterloo Record, 225 Fairway Road S., Kitchener, Ont.; phone (519) 894-2231; founded 1878; circulation 71,600; vice-president and publisher K. A. Baird.

Population: 136,091 (Kitchener), 51,795 (Waterloo), 300,719 (Waterloo region); total employed 167,000.
Area: 51.74 sq. mi. (Kitchener) and 25.47 sq. mi. (Waterloo), 65 miles west of Toronto.
Industry: highly diversified industry (500 companies), rubber, plastics, electronics, metal fabrication, brewing, distilling, meat packing, footwear, furniture, food processing, automotive components; Budd Canada Inc., largest autoframe manufacturer in Canada; Arrow Shirt Co., largest shirt making facility under one roof in Canada. Annual gross product exceeds $2.27 billion.
Agricultural: hog and dairy area; Waterloo Region's 1,588 farms (247,000 acres) accounted for $120 million production in 1978.
Commerce: wholesale and retail center for area; metro retail sales (1979) $1.27 billion; 8 banks, 60 branches; 15 trust companies, 25 branches; 41 life insurance offices, 29 other insurance offices; Waterloo, "The Hartford of Canada," head office for 6 insurance companies.
Transportation: 2 major rail lines, 34 truck lines, on Ontario's key highway 401; Waterloo-Wellington Airport; 45 mi. from Toronto International.

Communications: one TV and 4 radio stations; one daily, one weekly newspaper.

Medical facilities: 2 major hospitals.

Cultural facilities: symphony orchestra, Kitchener-Waterloo Art Gallery, Doon Pioneer Village; Centre in the Square, 28 mi. from Stratford, home of the Shakespearian Festival.

Educational facilities: Univ. of Waterloo, Wilfrid Laurier Univ., Conestoga College.

Other attractions: nationally-known farmers market; Canada's largest annual Oktoberfest celebration; Woodside, national historic park, boyhood home of W. L. Mackenzie King, Canadian prime minister 21 years.

History: founded 1807 by Pennsylvania German settlers; retains strong Germanic flavor.

Further information: Kitchener Chamber of Commerce, 67 King East; Waterloo Chamber of Commerce, 5 Bridgeport Road W.

Knoxville, Tennessee

The World Almanac is sponsored in the Knoxville area by The Knoxville News-Sentinel, 204 W. Church Avenue, Knoxville, TN 37901; Sentinel founded in 1886, News in 1921 by Scripps-Howard Newspapers; Sentinel purchased by Scripps-Howard in 1926 and combined with News; circulation 102,337 daily, 157,554 Sunday; president and business manager Roger A. Daley, editor Ralph L. Millett Jr., managing editor Harold E. Harlow.

Population: 181,918 (city), 335,298 (county), 487,898 (metro area), 3d in state; 191,200 total employed in metro area.
Area: city 77.6 sq. mi., county 528 sq. mi., located almost exact center of that portion of U.S. lying east of the Mississippi River and south of the Great Lakes; Knox County seat.
Industry: major manufacturing industries are chemicals and primary metals; nearly 300 plants representing 51 diversified major industries (coal and zinc mining, marble quarrying, meat packing, electronics, steel fabrication, industrial controls eqpt., furniture, auto safety eqpt., refuse eqpt., apparel), with Aluminum Co. of America, Union Carbide Corp. Nuclear Div. at Oak Ridge, headquarters for the Magnavox Consumer Electronics Corp., included in area market.
Commerce: wholesale and retail trade center of a multi-county area in east Tennessee, Virginia, Kentucky, and N. Carolina; county retail sales (1979) $81.9 billion.
Transportation: 5 airlines, one commuter airline, 2 interstate bus lines, 44 motor freight carriers; Interstate Highways I-40 and I-75 intersect in heart of city; Tennessee River Barges.
New construction: downtown renewal continues, $172 million expended since 1972; $225 million in Interstate improvements underway; Art and Architecture bldg. under construction; $24 million sewer plant; Neyland Stadium (football) enclosing north end to complete bowl and increase seating to 92,000; Magnavox Consumer Electronics Corp. national headquarters completed; Expo '82 World's Fair site preparation ($25 million) underway; London Fog plant underway ($24 million).
Cultural facilities: Univ. of Tennessee, Knoxville College, Knoxville Symphony Orchestra, 13 museums, art gallery, auditorium-coliseum, city-county library (616,753 volumes), Zoological Park, University community theater, choral society, opera workshop, Lamar House-Bijou Theater.

Sports: Univ. of Tennessee (all major collegiate sports), Knoxville College; Knoxville Blue Jays, Toronto farm club; Golden Gloves boxing arena; Ivy Glenn, training base for professional boxer John Tate.

Other attractions: Great Smoky Mountains National Park, 39 miles from Knoxville, offers year-round scenic beauty, skiing in season; within 30 miles of Knoxville, with 9 million visitations annually, 8 TVA lakes, 3,673 miles of shoreline providing fishing, boating, swimming; Oak Ridge, known for its nuclear developments, 22 miles from Knoxville; American Museum of Atomic Energy and Oak Ridge National Lab; Dogwood Arts Festival held each April; Expo '82 World's Fair.

Further information: Chamber of Commerce, 301 E. Church Avenue, or Knoxville Area Council for Conventions & Visitors, P.O. Box 15012, Knoxville, TN 37901.

Las Vegas, Nevada

The World Almanac is sponsored in the Las Vegas area by the Las Vegas Review-Journal, P.O. Box 70, 1111 W. Bonanza, Las Vegas, NV 89101; phone (702) 385-4241; founded as a weekly in 1909; purchased 1956 by Donald W. Reynolds, present publisher; member Donrey Media Group; circulation 79,292 weekdays, 87,956 Sundays; general manager William Wright; editor Don Digilio.

Population: (Oct., 1979) 165,049 (city), 435,970 (metro), 453,750 (county), first in state; labor force 195,800, total employment 184,500 (county, '79 annual avg.).
Area: 55 sq. mi. (city), 275 sq. mi. (metro), near center of broad desert valley in southern Nevada; 290 mi. NE of Los Angeles, 283 mi. NW of Phoenix, one of 8 joined cities and unincorporated towns (metro); Clark County seat.
Industry: 24 hr. tourism, manufacturing (stone, clay, glass, food, chemicals), warehousing, mining; employment (county, '79 annual avg.): mining 5,000; construction 15,500; transportation/utilities 12,500; wholesale/retail trade 43,300; finance/insurance/real estate 9,300; services 30,800; hotel/gaming/recreation 65,900; government (excluding military) 24,700.
Commerce: total taxable sales $3.5 billion (county, '79); average spendable family income $21,583; 6 commercial banks, 64 branches, $1.6 billion checking/saving deposits, 44% of state total (Dec. '79); 7 savings & loans, 37 branches, $8.8 million savings deposits, 54% of state total (Dec. '79).
Transportation: McCarran Int'l Airport 16th busiest in U.S., 10.5 million passengers in 1979; 18 major carriers, 6 commuter lines, 10 air freight carriers; Union Pacific RR; Amtrak; 17 truck lines; 6 major van lines; 9 bus lines; U.S. highways 93 & 95, Interstate 15; 372,217 vehicles—including 261,691 autos, 69,784 trucks, 27,912 trailers, 12,830 motorcycles (Dec. '79).
Communications: 5 TV stations (4 commercial, one PBS); 10 AM, 7 FM radio stations, one FM public; 3 daily newspapers.
Medical facilities: 8 hospitals, 1,679 beds; 20 convalescent and rest homes; 56 clinics.
Federal facilities: Nellis AFB, largest tactical fighter training base in world with 7.5 million acres combined air and ground area, home of Thunderbirds USAF Air Demonstration Squadron; 8,111 military, 908 civilian employees, $172 million payroll; Water & Power Resources Service, agency for Dept. of Interior, responsible for water in 17 western states.
Education: 79 elementary, 18 jr. high, 11 high schools, 4 spec. ed., one vo-tech, 32 private and church affiliated schools; one community college; Univ. of Nevada (UNLV); 91,313 K-12 enrollment, 18,568 college and univ.; Clark Co. School Dist., $149 million oper. budget ('79-'80).
Cultural facilities: libraries: 13 public, 19 special, 2 college, one univ.; Las Vegas Art League and Museum; Reed Whipple Cultural Arts Center; Judy Bayley Theatre; Artemus W. Ham Concert Hall; Las Vegas Civic Symphony; Nevada Dance Theatre; City Museum of Archeology; Southern Nevada Museum and Cultural Center; Las Vegas Valley Zoo.
Recreation: Lake Mead, Lake Mojave, Hoover Dam, Tule Springs, Valley of Fire, Red Rock Canyon area, Toiyabe National Forest (Mt. Charleston), Rogers Springs, Colorado River, skiing, boating, fishing, swimming, hiking, camping.
Sports: amateur and professional competition in tennis, golf, auto racing, bowling, basketball, boccie ball, boxing; UNLV sports competitions; Mint 400 Off Road race, Sahara Invitational golf tournament, Alan King tennis classic, WCT Challenge Cup, Pizza Hut basketball invitational, racquet ball.
History: first recorded group to enter the Las Vegas Valley was Antonio Armijo's party in early 1839. Las Vegas, Spanish for "The Meadows," first settled by Europeans in June 1855 by a 30-man Mormon group under William Bringhurst; city of Las Vegas founded May 15, 1905, as a result of public land auction by the railroad.
Further information: Las Vegas Chamber of Commerce, 2301 E. Sahara Avenue, Las Vegas, NV 89104, phone (702) 457-4664; Las Vegas Convention/Visitors Authority, 711 E. Desert Inn Road, Las Vegas, NV 89109, phone (702) 733-2323.

Lethbridge, Alberta, Canada

The World Almanac is sponsored in the Lethbridge area by The Lethbridge Herald, 504 7th Street S., Lethbridge, Alberta; phone (403) 328-4411; founded as a daily in 1907; circulation weekdays 28,702, Saturdays 30,687; editor Cleo W. Mowers, general manager Don Doram, managing editor Klaus Pohl.

Population: 53,135.
Area: 25 sq. mi.; located on Oldman River, 60 miles north of Montana border, 130 miles south of Calgary.
Industry: based on agriculture; 3 federally-inspected packing plants slaughtered 30% of the cattle slaughtered in Alberta in 1979; more than one million acres of irrigated farms produce sugar beets, market and processing vegetables, grains; much larger dryland area growing grains and rapeseed; vast ranching and cattle-feeding operations; brewery, distillery, flour mill, food processing plants, oilseed processing plants; foundry, recreation vehicle, mobile home, truck body, boat and farm machinery manufacturing.
Commerce: 1979 retail sales $400 million, 11% more than 1978; 6 banks, 6 trust companies, 3 credit unions, 11 finance companies: 4 major shopping malls; distributing center for area of 150,000 people.
Transportation: CP Rail, 2 bus lines, depots for 50 trucking firms, regional airline to major Alberta cities.
Communications: one newspaper; 2 TV, 3 radio stations.
New construction: building permits totalled $59.6 million in 1979, compared with $56.5 million in 1978.
Medical facilities: 2 general hospitals (plans for new 500-bed hospital), one long-term care hospital, 3 nursing homes, 4 senior citizens retirement lodges.
Education and culture: Lethbridge Agriculture Centre is Canada's 2d largest; Univ. of Lethbridge, Lethbridge Comm. College; Alexander Galt Museum, Nikka Yuko Centennial Japanese Garden, Fort Whoop-Up, replica of historic fort; Lethbridge Symphony Orchestra and Chorus, Bowman Arts Centre, Yates Memorial Centre.
Other attractions: 4 large parks, 5 artificial ice arenas, 3 golf courses, 3 indoor and 2 outdoor swim pools, Sportsplex (arena), exhibition grounds, Sick's Brewery Gardens.
Sports: Lethbridge Dodgers, farm team of L.A. Dodgers; Broncos, Western Canada Jr. Hockey League.
History: early coal-mining town; Coalbanks, renamed Lethbridge Oct. 16, 1885, after coal co. official; a whiskey-trader's depot, Fort Whoop-Up was booming 5 mi. southwest of Lethbridge in 1860s; first settlers came 15 years later, many from the U.S., others from Europe.
Further information: Lethbridge Chamber of Commerce, 309 Canada Trust Building, 304 7th Street S., Lethbridge, Alta. T1J 2G3; Travel and Convention Association of Southern Alberta, 2805 Scenic Drive, Lethbridge, Alta.

Lexington, Kentucky

The World Almanac is sponsored in central and eastern Kentucky by the Lexington Herald-Leader Co., publishers of the Lexington Leader (afternoon daily, circulation 34,105), the Lexington Herald (morning daily, circulation 70,790), and the Sunday Herald-Leader (circulation 104,895), all Knight-Ridder newspapers. Publisher and chairman Creed Black, president and general manager Ray Frazier, vice-president and Herald editor John Carroll, vice-president and Leader editor Steve Wilson, vice-president of marketing Lewis Owens, vice-president of production Phil Eaton.

Population: (1979) 193,193 city, 300,871 SMSA.
Area: 283 sq. mi.; 2d largest city in Kentucky, located in central Kentucky, 80 miles east of Louisville, 84 miles south of Cincinnati; Fayette County seat.
Industry: shipping and wholesale center for central and eastern Kentucky; livestock and general farming area; horse breeding and sales; loose leaf tobacco production and market.
Commerce: (1978) retail sales urban-county $950 million, retail sales SMSA $1.224 billion; effective buying income per household $20,116; 7 commercial banks with $1.093 billion in deposits; 5 savings and loan assns. with assets of $222 million; 8 mortgage companies.
Transportation: Chesapeake and Ohio, Southern, Louisville and Nashville railroads; 30 motor freight companies; Frontier, Delta, Piedmont, USAir, Air Kentucky airlines; Lex-Tran city bus service.
Communications: newspapers: Lexington Herald (morn.), Lexington Leader (eve.), Sunday Herald-Leader; 3 commercial TV stations, one state educational TV network; 4 AM, 3 FM radio stations.
New construction: (1979) 5,150 building permits totalling $130 million.
Medical facilities: 4 general hospitals (including the Univ. of Kentucky Medical Center), 1,505 beds; 5 specialized hospitals with 1,714 beds; 863 physicians, 2,619 registered nurses, 220 dentists, 15 optometrists, 250 pharmacists.
Cultural facilities: Lexington Council of the Arts; Lexington Philharmonic Orchestra; Kentucky Guild of Artists and Craftsmen; Lexington Ballet Co.; Studio Players; Univ. of Kentucky School of Fine Arts; Lexington Opera House; Ashland, home of Henry Clay; Blue Grass Trust for Historic Preservation.
Religion: 197 churches and synagogues representing 34 denominations.
Education: 34 elementary schools; 10 junior high schools, 5 senior high schools; 6 parochial schools; Univ. of Kentucky; Transylvania Univ.; Lexington Theological Seminary; Lexington Baptist College; Lexington Technical Institute; Episcopal Theological Seminary; 9 business and secretarial schools.
Sports and Recreation: Keeneland (thoroughbred racing), The Red Mile (harness racing), Kentucky Horse Park; Univ. of Kentucky basketball and football; 65 neighborhood playgrounds and community parks, 22 motion picture theaters, 8 private country clubs, 4 public golf courses.
Convention Facilities: Lexington Convention Center including 23,000-seat Rupp Arena; 28 hotels and motels with 3,919 rooms.
History: Incorporated as a township in May of 1781; one of the leading manufacturing centers of the early West for hemp goods, nails, and gunpowder; early site of cotton and furniture factories, breweries and distilleries; known as "Athens of the West" due to Transylvania Univ., first institution of higher learning west of the Allegheny Mountains.
Further information: Greater Lexington Chamber of Commerce, 421 North Broadway, Lexington, KY 40508.

Little Rock, Arkansas

The World Almanac is sponsored in the Little Rock area by the Arkansas Gazette, 112 West Third Street, Little Rock, AR 72203; phone (501) 371-3700; founded 1819 at Arkansas Post, A.T., by Wm. E. Woodruff, moved to Little Rock 1821; circulation 129,274 daily, 154,569 Sunday; Hugh B. Patterson Jr., publisher and president; Carrick H. Patterson, executive editor; J. O. Powell, editorial director; Robert R. Douglas, managing editor; J. R. Williamson, senior vice president; John T. Meriwether, vice president and general manager.

Population: 155,700 (city), 417,500 (metro); 183,800 employed (metro, May 1979).
Area: Little Rock, 51 sq. mi.; Pulaski County, 781.0 sq. mi.; State capital and Pulaski County seat.
Industry: (metro) 350 manufacturing plants, employing 30,000 persons, including Allis-Chalmers, Armstrong Rubber Co., Timex, AMF Cycle Div., Remington Arms, Jacuzzi Bros., Teletype, Westinghouse, CPC, International, and

General Electric.
Commerce: retail sales (est. 1979) $2.1 billion; bank resources (Jan. 1979) $2 billion; 11 banks, 6 building & loan associations, 4 old line insurance companies.
Transportation: 2 railroads, 6 federally certified airlines, 3 interstate bus lines, one inter-city line, 34 truck lines, 12 common carrier barge lines.
Communications: 3 commercial TV, one ETV, 14 radio stations; 2 daily, one weekly newspaper.
Medical facilities: 10 hospitals including UA Medical Sciences campus, 2 VA hospitals, and Ark. State Hospital for Nervous Diseases.
Federal facilities: Little Rock AFB, Tactical Airlift Wing; Camp Joseph T. Robinson, Arkansas National Guard headquarters and training center; U.S. National Guard Bureau's Non-Commissioned Officers Institute.
Education: Univ. of Arkansas at Little Rock with Schools of Law, Medicine, Nursing, and Pharmacy; UA Graduate Institute of Technology; Philander Smith, Shorter and Arkansas Baptist colleges; 112 public schools; 27 private and special schools.
Cultural facilities: Arkansas Symphony, Arkansas Arts Center, 3 major public libraries, convention center-auditorium-hotel; Arkansas Repertory Theatre; Arkansas Territorial Restoration and Museum of Science & Natural History.
History: French explorer Bernard de la Harpe noted "le petit roche" on his map of the Arkansas River Valley in 1722.
Further information: Metropolitan Chamber of Commerce, One Spring Street; Arkansas Parks & Tourist Dept., State Capitol; both Little Rock, AR 72201.

Los Angeles, California

The World Almanac is sponsored in Los Angeles by the Los Angeles Herald Examiner, 1111 S. Broadway, Los Angeles, CA 90015, phone (213) 748-1212; Los Angeles Examiner founded 1903 by Wm. R Hearst, merged Los Angeles Herald Express 1962; circulation 283,710 daily, 302,525 Sunday; Francis L. Dale publisher, James G. Bellows editor, Theodore P. Grassl general manager, David W. Feldman director of sales.

Population: 2.8 million (city), 7.1 million (county), (July '79); 5-county urban area 10.9 million (July '79); first in state, 2d county in nation, 3d urban area; total civilians employed 3.2 million (county, June '78); labor force 3.4 million (county, June '79).
Area: 463.7 sq. mi. on Pacific, 418 mi. south of San Francisco, 145 mi. north of Mexico; Los Angeles County seat; one of 81 cities in county.
Industry: leading aerospace industry with 7 of the top 10 defense contractors in the nation located in the area; center of entertainment industry with more than 600 firms in movie and television entertainment work. Women's clothing, sportswear, electronics, rubber tires, printing, furniture, paper, autos, auto parts, chemicals, manufacturing. Work force (county, Dec. '78): agriculture 12,500, oil and mining 11,300, construction 107,800, transport, utilities, and communication 190,400, trade 843,900 (263,300 wholesale, 580,700 retail.); finance, insurance, and real estate 215,900, services 787,300, government 494,300, manufacturing 911,700; 2d largest county in mfg. activity, $52.3 million in total shipments. Among top 20 counties in U.S. in agricultural production; farm income $219.3 million (county '79); livestock (dairy, eggs, meat) production $41.6 million; sea fish harvested 589.6 million pounds (county '76).
Commerce: total taxable retail sales $35.8 billion (county '78), $11.9 billion (city '78); median family income $16,933; personal income $54.7 billion (county '78); 81 banks, 1,131 branches, savings and loans with 614 branches; bank deposits $35.5 billion (June '78); S&L savings $29.9 billion (Sept. '78).
Transportation: Sante Fe, Union Pacific, Southern Pacific railroads; Amtrak; Continental, Greyhound bus lines; Southern California Rapid Transit District serving 4,150 mi. with 2,064 buses plus other local and intercity bus lines; Airport Transit Bus and Grey Line tours; 5.3 million vehicles (county, Dec. '79), one of largest concentrations in nation — 4.0 million autos, 756,970 trucks, 192,465 motorcycles, 398,198 trailers; 156.6 mi. freeway (city) 491.2 (county) (July '78); airlines (41 scheduled, 21 charter, 11 commuter) serving Los Angeles International airport, 542,976 takeoffs and landings, 34.9 million passengers, 1.8 billion pounds cargo ('79); 9 other airports; more than 46 miles of commercial waterfront in Los Angeles-Long Beach Harbor, 7,739 ships, 79.6 million tons cargo (Los Angeles 40.2 million, Long Beach 39.4 million) in '79.
Communications: 16 TV stations (7 UHF, 9 VHF), approx. 80 radio stations, 60 commercial; more than 45 newspapers in English and foreign languages, more than 25 publishing daily (county).
New construction: building permits $1.7 billion, including $189.3 million for 2,504 residential units (city, fiscal '79), plus $569 million in county building permits ('79).
Medical facilities: 813 hospitals and clinics with 76,086 beds, including 178 general care hospitals, 34,654 beds, 24 psychiatric, 2,497 beds, 410 nursing homes, 38,570 beds (county, June '77).
Educational facilities: 1,156 elementary, 190 jr. high, 153 sr. high, 77 continuation, 66 adult, approx. 800 private all levels (county '80); 61 libraries (city) plus 91 others in the county; UCLA, Univ. Southern Cal., California Institute of Technology; Loyola, Marymount, Pepperdine universities; Claremont, Woodbury, Occidental, Whittier, Mt. St. Mary colleges; 21 community colleges; campuses of California State University-Los Angeles, Long Beach, Northridge, Dominguez Hills.
Cultural facilities: 1,838 churches, Huntington Art Gallery and Library, Hollywood Bowl, Greek Theater, Music Center, Mark Taper Forum, Ahmanson Theater, Huntington Hartford Theater, Griffith Park Planetarium, Mt. Wilson and Mt. Palomar observatories; Los Angeles Museum, County Art Museum, UCLA Botanical Gardens, La Brea Tar Pits and natural history museum, Southwest Museum.
Recreational facilities: more than 300 city parks and recreation centers, plus 122 county parks; 14 public golf courses, 15 public beaches within 35 miles of city center; ocean, mountains, desert, lakes, forests; Disneyland, Marineland, Knott's Berry Farm, Lion County Safari, Universal Movie Studio tour.
Convention facilities: approx. 20,000 hotel rooms (city), 50,000 (county); large convention center.
Sports: collegiate sports including Rose Bowl; pro teams in baseball (Dodgers), basketball (Lakers), hockey (Kings), soccer (Aztecs).
History: discovered 1542 by Portuguese navigator Juan Rodriguez Cabrillo; Mission San Gabriel founded Sept., 1771; city formally founded Sept. 4, 1781 by Spanish colonial governor as El Pueblo de Nuestra Senora la Reina de los Angeles de Porciuncula; inc. April 4, 1850.
Further information: Chamber of Commerce, P.O. Box 3696, Terminal Annex, Los Angeles, CA 90051.

Louisville, Kentucky

The World Almanac is sponsored in Kentucky and Southern Indiana by The Courier-Journal and The Louisville Times, 525 West Broadway, Louisville, KY 40202; phone (502) 582-4011; Courier-Journal founded 1868, Times 1884; Courier circulation 190,942, Times 151,977, Sunday 331,103; chairman of the board Barry Bingham Sr., editor and publisher Barry Bingham Jr.; major awards include 8 Pulitzer prizes.

Population: 318,200 (city), 931,600 (metro area); first in state; total employed 395,400.
Area: 65.2 sq. mi. (city), 1,392 sq. mi. (metro); on southern bank of Ohio River.
Industry and Commerce: 10th in total industrial shipments; famous for baseball bats, cigarettes, railroad repair shops,

electrical appliances, farm machinery, motor vehicles, plumbing fixtures, and whiskey; 1,011 manufacturing firms in area; estimated retail sales (Jefferson County, 1979) $2,819 billion.
Transportation: 6 trunk-line railroads, one terminal railroad, 100 inter-city truck lines; 5 barge lines; 2 bus lines; 7 airlines, and 2 municipal airports.
Communications: 20 radio and 4 TV stations, 2 educational.
Medical facilities: 21 hospitals, 6,000 total beds.
Cultural facilities: Louisville Orchestra, Kentucky Opera Association, Art Center Association, J.B. Speed Art Museum; 20 private art galleries, Macauley Theatre, Actors Theatre, The Children's Theatre, Louisville Civic Ballet, Louisville-Jefferson County Youth Orchestra, The Louisville Free Public Library (24 branches); 700 churches, 40 denominations.
Education: 10 colleges and universities, 3 business colleges and technical schools in area.
Recreation: 158 public parks, covering more than 7,000 acres.
Convention facilities: Kentucky Fair & Exposition Center, largest ground-level exhibit hall and auditorium complex in North America with 650,000 sq. ft., 20,000-plus seating, parking for 27,000 cars; 100,000 sq. ft. Commonwealth Convention Center in downtown Louisville; Louisville Gardens, downtown, handles up to 7,000.
Sports: Kentucky Derby, held annually at Churchill Downs since 1875; Louisville Downs harness racing.
Other: Belle of Louisville excursion steamboat; Churchill Downs Museum; Louisville Zoo, American Printing House for the Blind; Kentucky Railway Museum; Museum of History and Science; Cave Hill Cemetery.
History: founded by explorer George Rogers Clark in 1778; named after King Louis XVI of France.
Further information: Louisville Area Chamber of Commerce, 300 West Liberty, Louisville, KY 40202.

Lubbock, Texas

The World Almanac is sponsored in the Lubbock area by the Lubbock Avalanche-Journal, 8th Street and Avenue J, Lubbock, TX 79408: phone (806) 762-8844; founded 1900 as Leader, became Avalanche 1908, daily 1921; Plains Journal weekly founded 1923; consolidated 1926: circulation (morn.) 56,932, (eve.) 15,055, (Sat.) 65,817, (Sun.) 78,327; member Southwestern Newspaper Corp.; general manager Robert Norris; editor Jay Harris.

Population: 175,250 (city), 195,250 (metro area); total employed 96,790.
Area: 82.2 sq. mi.; center of South Plains territory of northwest Texas; Lubbock County seat.
Industry: vegetable oils, cotton seed flour, grain sorghum, livestock, petroleum, sand and gravel; 250 manufacturing companies.
Commerce: wholesale and retail center for west Texas and eastern New Mexico; retail sales $629.8 million; bank resources $1.131 billion; 8 banks.
Transportation: 12 motor freight carriers; 2 major railroads, bus line; Lubbock Regional Airport, 4 major airlines averaging 62 flights per day; 2 intrastate airlines; 6 major federal and state highways.
Communications: 4 TV and 12 radio stations.
Medical facilities: 8 hospitals, Lubbock State School for Mentally Retarded; Texas Tech Medical School.
Federal facilities: Reese AFB, federal building, Federal Aviation Admin., and National Weather Service, U.S. Customs port of entry.
Cultural facilities: symphony orchestra, Theatre Centre; Museum of Texas Tech Univ., Moody Planetarium; Ranching Heritage Center (authentic ranch houses dating to 1835), Lubbock Christian College; Texas Tech Univ., Lubbock Cultural Affairs Council, Lubbock Garden & Arts Center.
Recreational facilities: 55 city parks, 3,000 acres, Mackenzie State Park, state's largest, with Prairie Dog Town; Buffalo Lakes, Canyon Lakes-Parks; Municipal Auditorium, 3,200 seats, Municipal Coliseum, 10,000 capacity; annual Panhandle South Plains Fair; Lubbock Memorial Civic Center, modern convention facility with 200,000 sq. ft. including 44,000 sq. ft. exhibit hall with banquet facilities for 1,500, auditorium seating 1,400.
Sports: Texas Tech, and Lubbock Christian college sports; Tech Jones Stadium, indoor rodeos.
Further information: Chamber of Commerce, P.O. Box 561, Lubbock, TX 79408.

Lynchburg, Virginia

The World Almanac is sponsored in the Lynchburg area by The News and the Daily Advance, PO Box 131, Lynchburg, VA 24505; phone (804) 237-2941; published by Carter Glass & Sons, Publishers, Inc.

Population: 67,000 (city), 72,470 (metro).
Area: 50 sq. mi.
Commerce: retail sales $339 million (1979).
Industry: Babcock and Wilcox, nuclear energy; General Electric, communications system; C. B. Fleet, pharmaceuticals; Meredith/Burda, rotogravure printing; Craddock-Terry, shoes; Lynchburg Foundry, metal castings.
Transportation: 17 trucking firms; airport served by 2 airlines, Piedmont and Cardinal Air Virginia; 3 railroads, Southern, N&W, and C&O; metropolitan transit system, bus fleet.
Communications: television, WSET; cablevision; 8 radio stations; newspapers, The News (morning) and The Daily Advance (afternoon).
New construction: $76.1 million in 1979.
Medical facilities: two hospitals, Virginia Baptist Hospital with 330 beds and Lynchburg General Hospital with 380 beds, and a 110 bed extended care facility; cooperative agreement between the hospitals prevents duplication of services.
Cultural facilities: Fine Arts Center which offers drama, music, and visual arts year round; Point of Honor Museum, Old Courthouse, Dabney Scott House, Adams House, Miller-Claytor House, Anne Spencer House, Monument Terrace, all historic landmarks; 100 churches representing some 27 faiths, including Thomas Road Baptist Church (17,000 members), one of the largest churches in the nation.
Education: 2 high schools, 3 junior high schools, 14 elementary schools with a 17/1 pupil-teacher ratio; Lynchburg, Randolph-Macon Woman's, and Liberty Baptist 4-year colleges.
Recreation: 8 parks covering 265 acres, Blackwater Creek Natural Area, 12 horseshoe pits, 2 public swimming pools, 35 tennis courts; city stadium with a seating capacity of 4,216, transportation museum, 8 playlots, public library with 100,000 items, 18 play areas, 6 senior citizen centers.
Sports: Lynchburg Mets baseball; interscholastic and intercollegiate sports including football, baseball, basketball, swimming, tennis, wrestling, and track; Lynchburg 10-miler for amateur runners is an annual event attracting over 4,000 runners from all over the country.
History: began as a tobacco trading center in the early 1800s; named after John Lynch.

Macon, Georgia

The World Almanac is sponsored in the Macon area by the Macon Telegraph & News, 120 Broadway, Macon, GA 31213; phone (912) 744-4200; acquired by Knight-Ridder Newspapers, Inc., 1969; circulation Telegraph (morn.) 51,753, News (eve.) 23,378, Sat. 65,370, Sun. 86,694; publisher and president Bert Struby, general manager Edmund E. Olson, Telegraph and executive editor Billy Watson, News editor Joe Parham.

Population: 129,300 (city), 245,300 (metro), 3d in state; civilian labor force 97,584 (metro).
Area: 52 sq. mi., 6 miles northwest of geographical center of Ga.; Bibb County seat.
Industry: Bibb Company, longtime textile industry leader and largest industrial employer, headquartered in area; textile-related are YKK Zipper Co. of Japan and Texprint; Armstrong Cork Co. acoustical tile plant is one of area's largest; Ga. Kraft container board manufacturer; Brown & Williamson Tobacco Corp.; Keebler Co. cracker manufacturing plant; Ga. Steel Inc., fabricated plate work and structural steel; Inland Container corrugated shipping containers; Levi Strauss & Co. clothing manufacturer. Kaolin deposits are mined in area and processed in numerous ways; Government Employees Insurance Co. regional office.
Transportation: City is served by Central of Georgia, Southern, Georgia, and Seaboard railroads; 28 motor freight carriers; Intercity Bus Lines; Trailways, Greyhound bus lines; Delta, Atlantic Southeast, Ocean Airways airlines.
Medical facilities: Bibb County has 4 hospitals located in Macon with 1,016 beds. The Macon-Bibb County Public Health Department serves Bibb, Jones, and Twiggs counties.
Federal facilities: Robins AFB including Warner Robins Air Logistics Center, 16 miles from Macon, is Georgia's largest employer.
Educational facilities: Wesleyan College, nation's oldest college for women, and Mercer Univ. with law school; Macon Jr. College.
Other attractions: Ocmulgee National Monument is largest archeological development east of the Mississippi disclosing 6 different Indian group occupancies and restored Indian mounds and lodges; $4.5 million coliseum seats 10,000.
History: settled when U. S. established Fort Hawkins in 1806; chartered in 1823, named for Nathaniel Macon of North Carolina.
Further information: Macon Chamber of Commerce, 305 Coliseum Drive, Macon, GA 31201; phone (912) 746-7601.

Madison, Wisconsin

The World Almanac is sponsored in Madison by Madison Newspapers, Inc., publisher of The Capital Times and the Wisconsin State Journal, 1901 Fish Hatchery Road, Madison, WI 53713; phone (608) 252-6100; circulation, Wisconsin State Journal (morn.) 78,967, The Capital Times (eve.) 35,353, combined daily 114,320, Sunday Wisconsin State Journal 131,678.

Population: 173,000 (city), 325,000 (metro/county), 2d in state; metro work force 176,000.
Area: 52 sq. mi. (city), 1,194 sq. mi. (metro/county) in south central Wisconsin; state capital and Dane County seat.
Commerce: home office of 29 insurance firms, 375 industrial firms, 28 banks, 10 savings and loans; 25 major shopping areas; 1980 retail sales $1.5 billion; average effective buying income $22,500; city has AAA financial rating.
Transportation: Dane County Regional Airport serving 700,000 passengers and 5 million lbs. of freight; 3 airlines, 3 railroads, 2 interstate highways (I-90, I-94); 4 bus lines, 30 common carriers, city owned bus system.
Communications: 3 commercial and one public TV stations, commercial (one AM and 3 FM) radio stations; 2 daily and 17 weekly newspapers (metro/county).
Medical facilities: 9 hospitals (5 general, 4 specialized) including Univ. of Wis. and VA; 20 major clinics, approx. 1,200 physicians.
Federal facilities: Forest Products Laboratory, National Fish and Wildlife Laboratory.
Cultural facilities: Dane County Coliseum, Madison Civic Center, 2 art centers, 2 museums, dinner playhouse, 11 drama groups, ballet company, symphony and 7 other music organizations; approx. 330 churches representing 45 denominations.
Education: Univ. of Wisconsin (approx. 39,000 enrollment), Edgewood, Madison Business, Madison Area Technical colleges; 35 elementary, 10 middle, 4 high schools, 14 parochial, one vocational-technical; 7 city and 32 university libraries.
Recreation: 5 lakes with total of 18,000 acres of water surface, approx. 4,700 acres of parks; Vilas Zoo, Univ. of Wis. Arboretum, 9 golf courses.
Convention facilities: Dane County Coliseum, 5 major convention size hotels, 55 supper clubs; Greater Madison Convention and Visitor's Bureau (425 W. Washington, Madison, WI 53703).
Sports: Univ. of Wisconsin in Big Ten, football, basketball, hockey and other major sports.
Other attractions: weekly Farmer's Market (May-Oct.), World Dairy Exposition headquarters, annual Winter Spirit Festival, numerous political organizations; All-American city.
Further information: Greater Madison Chamber of Commerce, 625 W. Washington Avenue, Madison, WI 53701; phone (608) 256-8348.

Memphis, Tennessee

The World Almanac is sponsored in the Memphis area by The Memphis Press-Scimitar, 495 Union Avenue, Memphis, TN 38101; phone (901) 529-2500; Scimitar founded 1880 by G.P.M. Turner; Press 1906 by Scripps-McRae League, predecessor of Scripps-Howard Newspapers; circulation 103,485; editor Milton R. Britten, managing editor Van Pritchartt Jr.

Population: 668,443 (city), 879,600 (metro area); first in state, 14th in nation; 367,700 employed.
Area: 290 sq. mi., Shelby County seat, on east bank of the Mississippi River.
Industry: extensive cotton marketing-warehousing and processing of cotton seed into vegetable oil products; headquarters of Holiday Inns Inc., Federal Express Co. (air freight), and Conwood Corp. (tobacco and food products); other large industries include Schering-Plough (drugs), International Harvester (cotton pickers, hay balers), and Firestone (tires).
Commerce: wholesale-retail center for large parts of Tennessee, Arkansas, and Mississippi; retail sales (1979) $3.5 billion; bank deposits $2.5 billion; 9 banks, 5 savings-loan assns.; per capita personal income $6,766.
Transportation: 14 airlines, 42 air freight companies, 6.3 million air passengers (1979); 7 trunk line railroads, 86 motor freight lines, 6 barge lines.
Communications: 6 TV and 24 radio stations, 2 daily newspapers.
Medical facilities: 18 hospitals housing 7,090 beds, 12 full-time clinics, 1,790 doctors, 527 dentists, 30 long-term care facilities housing 4,011 beds.
Federal facilities: Naval Air Station, Naval Air Technical Training Center, Defense Depot Memphis, and Air Force's 164th Air Transport Group.
Cultural facilities: Memphis Symphony Orchestra, opera theater, Theatre Memphis, Brooks Art Gallery, Chucalissa Indian Village & Museum, Memphis Museum; annual performances of Metropolitan Opera.
Educational facilities: Memphis State Univ., Southwestern, LeMoyne-Owen, Christian Brothers colleges; U-T Center for Health Sciences, Shelby State Comm. College, State Technical Institute, Southern College of Optometry, Mid-South Bible College; 166 public elementary-secondary schools, 100 private schools, 22 public library branches offer 1.3 million volumes.
Recreational facilities: Meeman-Shelby Forest state park, 190 other parks, 21 golf courses, 16 public swimming pools, 13 country clubs.

Convention facilities: Cook Convention Center, 1.3 million sq. ft, seating 17,000; 58 hotels & motels with 8,779 total rooms.
Sports: Liberty Bowl, home of Memphis State Univ. football, site of Liberty Bowl game; Mid-South Coliseum, home of MSU basketball team; Memphis Chicks, Southern League baseball; Danny Thomas Memphis Classic golf tournament; Memphis Rogues, professional indoor-outdoor soccer team; U. S. National Indoor Tennis Championships.
Other attractions: Cotton Carnival each May; Mid-South Fair each Sept., Libertyland theme park, Beale St., home of the blues where composer W. C. Handy lived; Mid-America Mall; Graceland, home and burial site of Elvis Presley.

History: DeSoto, exploring Mississippi River, stopped here in 1541; Ft. Adams est. in 1797; Memphis inc. in 1826; yellow fever in 1878 nearly depopulated city, but its population grew back to 64,589 in 1890.

Further information: Memphis Area Chamber of Commerce, 555 Beale Street, Memphis, TN 38103.

Mexico City (Ciudad de Mexico), Mexico

Population: 11,000,000 (govt. est. 1979).
Area: about 53 sq. mi. within the 573 sq. mi. Federal District (Distrito Federal; population, 1979 est. 14.2 million); in central Mexico at an altitude of 7,349 ft.
Industry and commerce: capital of Mexico; the political and economic hub of the nation; manufactures include steel, automobiles, appliances, textiles, rubber goods, furniture, and electrical equipment; marketing center of Mexico.
Transportation: center of modern highway and rail system; 25-mi. subway system is being extended and will eventually extend 40 to 50 miles; served by most international air lines, Mexico City is 4 hrs. by jet from New York and 3 hrs. from Los Angeles.
Communications: major media center for Mexico and parts of Latin America; major film center.
Cultural facilities: cultural capital of Latin America: Palace of Fine Arts and Ballet Folklorico; National Palace (Diego Rivera murals); National University with over 90,000 students; National Museum of Anthropology; Polyforum Cultural Siqueiros, containing world's largest mural; 4 symphony orchestras; city itself is an architectural exhibit of Aztec ruins, baroque cathedrals, and ultra-modern buildings.

Other attractions: Xochimilco with the "floating gardens" and gondolas; Chapultepec Castle, palace of the French-supported Emperor and Empress of Mexico, Maximilian and Carlota; 22-ton Aztec Calendar Stone; 2 volcanoes, Popocatepetl (17,887 ft.) and Iztaccihuatl (17,343 ft.); sports centers.

History: traditionally founded 1321 by Aztecs, city was called Tenochtitlan; captured by Spanish under Cortez in 1519 and again in 1521; occupied by the U.S. in 1847 and by the French from 1863 to 1867.

Further information: Mexican National Tourist Council, Mariano Escobedo 726, Mexico, D.F., or 405 Park Avenue, NY 10022; or 9701 Wilshire Boulevard, Beverly Hills, CA 90212.

Miami, Florida

The World Almanac is sponsored in the Miami area by The Miami Herald, 1 Herald Plaza, Miami, FL 33101; phone (305) 350-2111; founded Dec. 1, 1910, by Frank B. Shutts; circulation (1979) 413,177 daily, 546,318 Sunday; chairman James L. Knight, executive editor John McMullan, editor Jim Hampton, managing editor Bob Ingle; newspaper or staff writers have won or shared in 6 Pulitzer prizes, the latest in 1980, and numerous other honors.

Population: 354,000 (city), 1,500,000 (metro); first in state; total employed in metro area, 621,100 (1979 average).
Area: 53.8 sq. mi. land and water, on Biscayne Bay at mouth of Miami River in southeast Florida; largest of 28 municipalities in Dade County; Dade County seat.
Industry: 5,000 light manufacturing plants; tourism and aviation are mainstays of economy; 779 hotels and motels with 60,069 rooms handle 15 million visitors a year; aviation hub with Eastern (largest industrial employer) headquarter base; winter agriculture center.
Commerce: center of Pan-American finance and commerce with more than 100 banks, 16 savings and loan associations, new Federal Reserve branch to be built; annual retail sales total nearly $5 billion; Port of Miami busy in waterborne commerce and largest cruise center in world with 21 liners and 1.7 million passengers (1979).
Transportation: Miami International, served by 109 air carriers, handled more than 18.6 million travelers in 1979; Seaboard Coast Line, Amtrak, and all-freight Fla. East Coast Railroads operate in Miami, as do Greyhound and Trailways buses; 65 truck lines.
Communications: 6 commercial and 5 educational or closed-circuit TV stations; 31 radio stations.
New construction: $75 million Omni International Hotel with restaurants, shops, and theaters; $50 million restoration of Miami Beach beachfront under way; $5.7 million Amtrak station.
Medical facilities: 41 hospitals, 11,894 beds; 5,362 beds at 39 nursing homes in metro area; 2,975 members of Dade County Medical Association; VA hospital, Jackson Memorial Hospital one of area's leading research facilities.
Federal facilities: Homestead AFB south of Miami with 8,379 Air Force, Army, and Navy personnel; Federal Aviation Administration; Coast Guard bases; 2 federal hospitals; oceanographic center; 13,700 U.S. employees.
Cultural facilities: Philharmonic, Opera Guild, and other musical groups perform regularly; 18 auditoriums, resident and touring theatrical productions, 6 major art museums; 29 public libraries; 12 playhouses and 60 night clubs and theater restaurants, some in major hotels.
Educational facilities: 6 colleges and universities, plus 3 campuses of Miami-Dade Community College; total enrollment, 86,000; Univ. of Miami is largest independent institution of higher learning in southeast; Florida International Univ.; public school system has 229,858 students and is one of the largest in nation.
Recreational facilities: 14 miles of public beach on ocean and bay; 365 parks and playgrounds, 11 stadiums and grandstands, 45 golf courses, 57 marinas with 37,000 boats registered; 105 movie houses, 100 miles of bikeways, 28 bowling alleys.

Convention facilities: newly expanded Miami Beach convention hall can handle largest conventions; 300 conventions brought more than 86,000 delegates to Miami in 1979; 570 conventions brought 290,000 delegates to Miami Beach in same year.

Sports: pro football Miami Dolphins and Univ. of Miami play in Orange Bowl, which seats 75,000; stadium also hosts Orange Bowl game, Orange Blossom Classic; Miami Stadium is spring home of Baltimore Orioles; parimutuel wagering at 5 horse and greyhound tracks, jai-alai frontons.

Other attractions: balmy subtropical climate with mean annual temperature of 75.3 degrees; 600 Protestant churches; 53 Catholic churches, 55 synagogues; city is bilingual with over 500,000 Latin American residents; one of nation's largest Jewish communities; marine stadium features powerboat and regatta racing; Everglades National Park, 40 miles south of Miami, is virgin wilderness.

History: America's newest big city, Miami had only 3 houses in 1895 in a community called Fort Dallas. Julia Tuttle persuaded Henry Flagler to extend his railroad south from West Palm Beach to stimulate Miami development; city was incorporated in 1896, when railroad arrived.

Further information: Miami-Metro Department of Publicity and Tourism, 150 SE 2d Avenue, Suite 1250, Miami, FL 33131.

Milwaukee, Wisconsin

The World Almanac is sponsored in the Milwaukee area by The Milwaukee Journal, 333 W. State Street,). Box 661, Milwaukee, WI 53201; phone (414) 224-2000; founded 1882 by Lucius W. Nieman; circulation 2,932 daily, 515,108 Sunday; chairman of the board Donald B. Abert; publisher Warren J. Heyse; president The Journal Co. Thomas J. McCollow; editor Richard H. Leonard; major awards include 2 Pulitzer prizes to newspaper and 3 to staff members.

pulation: 638,890 (city), 1,442,900 (SMSA); city 16th and tro area 25th in U.S.; total employment 697,700 (metro a).

ea: 95.8 sq. mi. on shore of Lake Michigan, Milwaukee unty seat.

lustry: county 10th in U.S. in volume of industrial proction, $9 billion (1978); 30% of workers employed in mancturing; largest U.S. producer of diesel and gasoline enes, outboard motors, motorcycles, tractors, padlocks, er; 4th largest U.S. automaking center; major producer of ctrical equipment, mining, and construction machinery MSA); graphic arts and food processing are largest nonrable goods employers; location for 12 "Fortune 500" instries.

mmerce: wholesale and retail trade center for Wisconsin, per Michigan; total retail sales $5.8 billion (SMSA); olesale trade $9.7 billion (SMSA). Average household endable income $21,216 (SMSA); 97 banks with assets of billion; 49 savings and loan associations home offices in (SMSA), with deposits of over $3.3 billion.

ansportation: 5 major rail lines; Amtrak; 9 airlines prole direct service to East and West coasts, south, southeast, ithwest, and Florida for over 2.9 million users of Gen. tchell field which has international air arrivals facility; 30 S. and foreign-flag ship lines use Milwaukee's St. Lawice Seaway port, handling nearly 3.6 million tons annually luding 553,000 tons overseas cargo; port of Milwaukee teway for 350 cities in 31 states and overseas ports. Milwaukee SMSA 4th largest U.S. machinery exporter and 14th largest exporter all products; 4 inter-city bus lines, 70 motor freight carriers; I-94, I-43, 5 federal and 14 state highways intersect Milwaukee.

Communications: morning, evening, and Sunday metropolitan newspaper; 4 commercial, 2 educational TV stations; 28 AM and FM radio stations.

Medical facilities: 21 major hospitals and medical centers, including 600 bed VA hospital.

Cultural facilities: Milwaukee Symphony, Repertory Theater, opera and operetta companies; Mid-America Ballet; Milwaukee Art Center, Milwaukee museum, 4th largest in U.S.; Univ. of Wisconsin-Milwaukee, Marquette Univ., Medical College of Wisconsin, 8 other colleges and vocational schools; 3-theater Performing Arts Center; complete convention, exhibition arena-auditorium complex; Mitchell Park Conservatory, Milwaukee County Stadium, and Milwaukee County Zoo are parts of 13,000 acre Milwaukee County park system.

Sports: Brewers (American League), Bucks (NBA); Marquette Univ., Univ. Wisconsin-Milwaukee; Green Bay Packers (NFL) play 4 home games in Milwaukee.

History: founded by Solomon Juneau, (1818), one of many French trappers in area in early 1800s; incorporated as town 1837, as city 1846.

Further information: Metropolitan Milwaukee Association of Commerce, 756 N. Milwaukee Street, Milwaukee, WI 53202.

Minneapolis, Minnesota

pulation: 349,600 (city), 1,232,700 (metro); first in state, d in nation; total employed (city, 1979) 194,500.

ea: 59 sq. mi. (city), 4,000 sq. mi. (10-county metro area) ound St. Anthony Falls near junction of Minnesota and ississippi rivers; Hennepin County seat.

dustry: diverse; major electronics-computer manufacturg center including Honeywell, Control Data, Medtronics; adquarters for nation's 4 largest grain millers, including eneral Mills, Pillsbury, and International Multifoods.

mmerce: $20,700 median household income; $5.6 billion tal retail sales metro area (1979); 24 commercial banks, 6 vings and loan assns.; headquarters for Ninth Federal Reive District; world trade center, 12th among U.S. metro eas in exports; Mpls. Grain Exchange.

ansportation: 5 trunk railroads; 150 trucking firms; 5 mar barge lines headquartered in city; Mpls.-St. Paul Internanal Airport, averaging 600 flights daily.

mmunications: 4 commercial, 2 educational TV stations; radio stations.

edical facilities: 21 hospitals, including a leading heart spital at Univ. of Minn.

Federal facilities: Farm Credit Administration regional office; FBI regional office; EPA district office, area headquarters HUD.

Cultural facilities: Minnesota Orchestra, 7 art galleries-museums, Tyrone Guthrie Theatre, Walker Art Center, Univ. of Minnesota, Orchestra Hall, Inst. of Arts, Children's Theater.

Sports: Minnesota Twins (American League), Minnesota Vikings (NFL), Minnesota North Stars (NHL), Minnesota Kicks (NASL).

Other attractions: 153 parks, 22 lakes; 57-story IDS Tower; Minnehaha Falls; Mpls. Aquatennial celebration in July; average yearly snowfall, 41 inches.

History: first visited in 1680s by Fr. Louis Hennepin who discovered and named St. Anthony Falls on the Mississippi River; French fur traders used the area in 18th century; inc. 1871. Falls became power source for lumber and milling operations in 19th century.

Further information: Greater Minneapolis Chamber of Commerce Information, 15 S. 5th Street, Minneapolis, MN 55402.

Mobile, Alabama

The World Almanac is sponsored in the Mobile area by The Mobile Press Register, 304 Government Street, obile, AL 36630; phone (205) 433-1551; circulation, Register (morn.) 50,780, Press (eve.) 53,140, Sunday, 7,949; Register founded 1813, Press 1928. William J. Hearin publisher and president, Fallon Trotter execu-e editor, John Fay associate executive editor.

pulation: 205,000 (city), 428,000 (metro), 2d city in state; tal employed (metro) 164,900.

rea: 142 sq. mi. at head of Mobile Bay; Mobile County at.

dustry: $300 million-plus Alabama State Docks and the owing oil and natural gas fields in Mobile County have tracted varied industry to city; Mobile fields produced 2.8 illion barrels of oil, 3.8 million barrels of condensate and illions of cubic feet of natural gas in 1979; other industry cludes paper, timber, chemicals, alumina, paints, aircraft gines, shipbuilding, and metals.

ommerce: wholesale-retail center for large portion of uthwest Alabama and southeast Mississippi; county retail sales more than $1.8 billion (1979).

Transportation: served by 4 railroads; one of the great river systems; 4 major airlines, 55 truck lines, and 135 shipping lines.

Communications: 2 TV, 15 radio stations; cable TV.

Medical facilities: Univ. of South Alabama Medical Center, Cancer Research Center, and 5 modern hospitals.

Cultural facilities: Municipal Auditorium-Theater complex seats 16,000; art gallery, museum, amateur theater, public library and branches; Univ. of South Alabama, Spring Hill and Mobile colleges, and Bishop State Junior College.

Military facilities: Coast Guard base and Coast Guard aviation training center.

Annual attractions: Azalea Trail Run, America's Junior Miss, Senior Bowl football game, and Mardi Gras.
History: founded in 1702 by Jean Baptiste Le Moyne; 6 flags have flown over city since then.
Further information: Chamber of Commerce, Commer Guaranty Bank Building, Mobile, AL.

Montgomery, Alabama

The World Almanac is sponsored in the Montgomery area by the Advertiser-Journal, 200 Washing Street, Montgomery, AL 36102; phone (205) 262-1611; Advertiser founded 1828, Journal 1881; circulat Advertiser (morn) 47,823, Journal (eve) 25,013, combined Sunday 75,446; publisher Jim Martin.

Population: 157,581 (city), 277,954 (metro); 1980 annexation expected to increase population (city) to 179,268; total employed 108,000.
Area: 50.94 sq. mi. (city), 442 sq. mi. (county); 1980 annexation expected to increase city to 128.98 sq. mi.; state capital; Montgomery County seat.
Industry: machinery manufacture, glass products, textiles, refrigeration equipment, furniture, food products, paper, and fertilizers; industrial park in East Montgomery.
Commerce: wholesale retail center for 13 counties in central Alabama; SMSA retail sales $1.196 billion; average spendable income $17,201, per capita income $5,591; 7 banks, 5 savings and loan assns.; state docks, 42 trucking lines, 6 insurance co. home offices.
Transportation: 5 major railroads, 3 airlines, 2 national bus lines, one city bus line; interstates 65 and 85 intersect in the city; Alabama River navigable to the Gulf of Mexico.
Communications: 2 daily newspapers, one weekly newspaper; 4 TV, 14 radio stations; cable TV.
Medical facilities: 5 general hospitals, VA hospital, Air Force hospital, area mental health hospital, private hospital.
Federal facilities: Maxwell AFB, houses the Air Univ., Gunter Air Force station.
Cultural facilities: Art Guild, Civic Ballet, Little Theat Community Concert Series, Museum of Fine Arts, Tu bling Waters Flag Museum; 14 theaters, 19 recreational cilities, city zoo; 5 major colleges and universities; $14 n lion civic center.
Sports: Rebels, farm team of Detroit Tigers; Blue G. Football Classic; Southeastern Championship Rod George Lindsay Celebrity Golf Tournament, American press Tennis Tournament, Blue Gray Tennis Tournam Alabama River Run, Alabama River Raft Race.
Other attractions: river boat makes regularly scheduled cursions of the Alabama River; State Capitol housed C federate offices; White House of Confederacy, home of J ferson Davis; Hank Williams grave site, Dexter Aver Baptist Church; Fort Tolouse, antebellum town with ma colonial mansions and churches.
History: inc. 1819; site of inauguration of Jefferson Davis president of the Confederate States of America, Feb. 1861.
Further information: Chamber of Commerce, P.O. Box Montgomery, AL 36101.

Montreal, Quebec, Canada

The World Almanac is sponsored in Montreal area by The Gazette, a Southam newspaper, 250 St. Antoi Street, Montreal H2Y 1J7, Quebec, Canada; phone (514) 282-2222; founded 1778 by Fleury Mesplet; circu tion 220,000 daily; publisher Robert McConnell, editor Mark Harrison, managing editor Geoff Stevenson, e torial page editor Joan Fraser; sponsors Christmas fund; 14 National Newspaper awards in last 6 years.

Population: 1,214,300 (city), 2,761,000 (metro); after Paris, the 2d largest French-speaking city in the world, 67% French origin, 12% Anglo-Saxon, 21% other origins; Canada's largest urban center.
Area: 68 sq. mi. on an island of 190 sq. mi. in the St. Lawrence River where the Ottawa and Richelieu rivers flow into it at the head of the St. Lawrence Seaway; metro area extends over 1,000 sq. mi.; the 769 ft. Mount Royal dominates the Island which averages 100 ft. above sea level.
Industry: Canada's industrial hub ($7 billion, value of shipments of goods of own manufacturer).
Commerce: total effective buying income $15 billion, headquarters of many of Canada's largest financial institutions, home of the Montreal and Canadian stock exchanges; about 75% of countries have consulates or representatives in Montreal.
Transportation: $1 billion St. Lawrence Seaway, Port of Montreal; 14 miles long, 42 miles of harbor with 140 berths; $500 million Mirabel jetport with multi-million electric train link to downtown planned for early 1980's; existing Metro to expand to 46 miles by 1981; world headquarters of Air Canada, International Civil Aviation Organization, and International Air Transport Association serving 2 major airports; headquarters of Canadian National and Canadian Pacific railways.
Communications: 4 TV stations, 21 radio stations, 4 daily newspapers; headquarters for Bell Canada, CN-CP Telecommunications.
Educational facilities: Concordia University, McGill University, Universite de Montreal, Universite de Quebec; enrollment 78,000; faculty 5,500.
Cultural facilities: Place des Arts with 3,000 seat hall and 2 theaters, attracting the finest forms of artistic, cultural, a musical entertainment; the Montreal Museum of Fine A the Musee de l'Art Contemporain; some of the world's m beautiful churches, including the Mary Queen of The Wo Basilica, a half-size replica of St. Peter's in Rome.
Sports: Olympic complex including a 56,000 permanent s stadium, home of the National Baseball League Expos a the Canadian Football League Alouettes; 7,200 seat Ve drome, 2 50-meter pools, 25-meter diving pool, and a scu diving pool — 15-meter depth; the Montreal Forum, ho of the NHL Canadiens.
Recreational facilities: within an hour of the Laurentien a Eastern townships skiing, hunting, and fishing resort are over 5,000 restaurants of all lands; over 100 cinemas, 19 m seums, 13 city libraries, the Montreal Botanical Gardens, Helen's Island Park, Dow Planetarium, Montreal Munici Golf Course.
Convention facilities: over 15,000 hotel and motel roor full facilities for conventions; new Montreal Conventi Centre scheduled for completion in 1982.
Medical facilities: over 80 hospitals with 26,000 beds, cluding the renowned Montreal Neurological Institute, a the Montreal Children's Hospital.
History: Montreal was first visited by Jacques Cartier 1535; founded under the name of Ville Marie in 1642; C Montreal, some 1,000 acres in all, is the largest such resto tion in North America and retains the general atmosphere the 18th century.
Further information: Convention and Visitor's Bureau Greater Montreal, 1270 Sherbrooke Street W., H3G 1H The Montreal Tourist Bureau, 85 Notre Dame Street Ea Montreal, Quebec.

Nashville, Tennessee

The World Almanac is sponsored in Nashville by The Tennessean, 1100 Broadway, Nashville, TN 3720 phone (615) 255-1221; founded as The Tennessean in 1907 but incorporated publications date to 1812; circ lation daily 134,700, Sunday 236,400; president Amon Carter Evans, publisher John Seigenthaler; 3 Pulitz prizes, 8 Headliner awards, 3 Sigma Delta Chi awards.

›pulation: 486,000 ('77 est.) in unified metro government, in state; labor force 326,900.
ea: 533 sq. mi., straddling Cumberland River, in north ntral part of state; Davidson County seat.
dustry: music (over 50% of U.S. singles are recorded in 40 udio complexes); clothing, headquarters of Genesco, orld's largest and most diversified clothing and footwear anufacturer; insurance, 2 of largest U.S. companies located re; world's largest glass plant; chemicals, printing (espe-lly religious materials), aerostructures, tires, air condition-g, heating equipment.
mmerce: retail center for middle Tennessee, south Ken-cky; retail sales (1977) $2.2 billion; bank resources over $4 llion in 8 banks, 109 branches.
ansportation: 9 U.S. highways and 6 branches of the inter-ate system radiate from Nashville; 10 commercial airlines th 204 daily flights; 2 railroads, Amtrak; bus service, 73 otor freight lines.
mmunications: 5 TV stations (one public), and 22 AM d FM radio stations.
Medical facilities: 18 hospitals, 2 medical schools, VA hospital, speech-hearing center.
Cultural: symphony orchestra; replica of Parthenon with art gallery; public and state libraries; botanic garden and fine arts center, 3 community theaters.
Educational facilities: 17 colleges and universities; 137 public schools, 39 private schools.
Convention facilities: 10,000-seat auditorium; Opryland convention center.
Other attractions: Grand Ole Opry, Opryland U.S.A. (theme park featuring music); Country Music Hall of Fame; Hermitage (home of Andrew Jackson); Belle Meade antebellum mansion.
Recreation facilities: water sports, outdoor activity on Old Hickory and Percy Priest lakes.
History: settled in 1780 as a fort in then western North Carolina; incorporated, 1784, with first written charter west of Alleghenies.
Further information: Chamber of Commerce, 161 4th Avenue N., Nashville, TN 37219.

New Haven, Connecticut

The World Almanac is sponsored in the greater New Haven area by the New Haven Register (founded 312) and the New Haven Journal-Courier (founded 1755); circulation Register (eve.) 101,885, Sunday 11,167, Journal-Courier (morn.) 38,448; president, publisher, editor-in-chief Lionel S. Jackson; assistant pub-sher Lionel S. Jackson Jr.; vp and general manager Donald A. Spargo; vp and editor Robert J. Leeney.

opulation: 134,900 (city), 370,100 metro, 3d in state.
rea: 21.1 sq. mi. southern coast of Conn. on north shore of ong Island Sound; New Haven County seat.
dustry: 1,000 firms in immediate area; principal products e guns, hardware, rubber goods, paper products, machin-y, and tools.
ommerce: wholesale-retail center for southern Conn., total tail sales (1979) $2.9 billion; serves 850,000 people within radius of 25 miles; busy harbor, particularly oil tankers.
ansportation: Conrail, Amtrak Cosmopolitan turbotrain; major truck lines; 14 federal and state highways; Tweed-ew Haven Airport served by 3 commuter airlines, limo ser-ce to New York and Hartford airports; bus line.
ommunications: VHF, 2 UHF TV stations, and 6 radio ations.
ledical facilities: Yale Medical Center, Yale-New Haven ospital; Hospital of St. Raphael.
ultural facilities: Yale Univ. Library with over 6 million ooks, one of the world's largest collections; Yale's Peabody useum of Natural History, art gallery, and Beinecke Rare ook Library; The Yale Center for British Art, New Haven Colony Historical Society, cultural center, 3 legitimate theaters; New Haven Symphony, Woolsey Hall.
Educational facilities: Yale Univ. and graduate schools; Albertus Magnus, Southern Conn. State, South Central Community, Quinnipiac, Greater New Haven State Technical colleges; Univ. of New Haven.
Recreational facilities: Yale Bowl, Payne-Whitney Gym, Ingalls Rink, The Coliseum; 15 parks including Frederick Brewster's estate, West and East Rock scenic drives, West Rock Nature Center; 7 golf courses, 6 skating rinks.
Convention facilities: coliseum-convention center with 19-story hotel nearby.
Sports: AHL Nighthawks (hockey), West Haven Whitecaps (baseball).
History: founded 1638 by Puritans; named after Newhaven in England; incorporated 1638, became a part of Conn. 1662; first mayor was Roger Sherman, signer of Declaration of Independence.
Further information: Greater New Haven Chamber of Commerce, 195 Church Street, New Haven, CT. 06506.

New Orleans, Louisiana

The World Almanac is sponsored in New Orleans by The Times-Picayune-The States-Item, 3800 Howard venue, New Orleans, LA 70140; phone (504) 586-3560; founded 1837; editor Charles A. Ferguson; spon-ors the Crescent City Classic and City Park Fishing Rodeo.

opulation: 559,184 (city), 1,200,000 (metro area); first in ate; total employed, 480,200 (metro area as of May 1979).
rea: 363.5 sq. mi. of which 199.4 are land.
dustry: Port of New Orleans, 2d largest in nation handled) million tons domestic cargo and 64 million tons foreign 1977; foreign trade valued at $10 billion; tourist business 2d largest, with $1.1 billion spent in metro area in 1977.
ommerce: trade center for lower Mississippi Valley; metro ea bank deposits $4.7 billion as of Dec. 1978; savings and an associations, assets of $3.3 billion in Apr. 1979; average ousehold income 1976, $14,995; retail sales $3.9 billion in)78; per capita effective buying income $6,135.
ansportation: rail hub with direct lines north, east, and est; Amtrak passenger service to Chicago, Los Angeles; outhern railway to New York; New Orleans International irport serves airlines, Lakefront Airport commercial avia-on; cruise ships to Mexico and Caribbean.
ew construction: $300 million Canal Place and 27-story, 50 million Pan American Life Insurance Co. Bldg.; multi-illion dollar Louisiana Offshore Oil Port to handle 1.4 mil-on barrels of oil daily.
ommunications: 4 commercial TV stations and educational annel; 20 radio stations.
ledical facilities: major medical center with 2 schools of edicine; one dental school; Charity Hospital 2d largest in nation; Ochsner Medical Institutions.
Federal facilities: hdqtrs. 5th U. S. Circuit Court of Appeals and 8th Naval District; regional office U. S. Census Bureau, field office U. S. Dept. Agriculture Marketing Service.
Recreation: City Park, 1500 acres with golf, tennis, boating; Audubon Park, 250 acres with golf, tennis, and zoo; Pontchartrain Beach Amusement Park, large lakeside amusement center.
Convention facilities: 20,000 rooms in major hotels; 160,000 sq. ft. exhibition space in Superdome, 134,000 sq. ft. in Rivergate, and 32,500 sq. ft. Municipal Auditorium.
Cultural facilities: Theater for the Performing Arts seats 2,317 for operas, concerts; Municipal Auditorium seats up to 8,000 for special events; museums include New Orleans Museum of Art, Louisiana State Museum, Historic New Orleans Collection, and many small galleries.
Educational facilities: Tulane Univ., Univ. of New Orleans, Loyola Univ., Dillard, Southern Univ. in New Orleans, Xavier, St. Mary's Dominican.
Other attractions: Louisiana Superdome seats 75,000; French Quarter is historic tourist attraction.
Sports: Saints (NFL); Sugar Bowl game on New Year's day.
History: named after the Duke of Orleans, founded in swamp within crescent of the Mississippi River 100 miles from Gulf of Mexico by Jean Baptiste Le Moyne, Sieur de

Bienville, in 1718; became capital of Louisiana Territory in 1722, when Adrien de Pauger laid out what is now the French Quarter; became part of U.S. with Louisiana Purchase in 1803.

Further information: Chamber of Commerce of New C leans Area, 301 Camp Street; Greater New Orleans Tour and Convention Commission, 334 Royal Street, both N Orleans, LA 70130.

New York City, New York

The World Almanac is sponsored in the greater New York City metropolitan area by the New York Dai News, 220 E. 42d Street, New York, N.Y. 10017, phone (212) 949-1234. New York News Inc. founded Jur 26, 1919 by Joseph Medill Patterson; circulation daily 1,554,604; Sunday 2,202,601; president and publish Robert M. Hunt; executive vice president and general manager Joseph F. Barletta; editor and executive vic president Michael J. O'Neill; executive vice president and director of sales Henry K. Wurzer; managing edit and vice president William J. Brink; associate editor John J. Smee. Pulitzer Prizes for editorial writing, new photography, cartoon, international and local investigative reporting; sponsors Golden Gloves, National Spe ling Bee championships for New York City, Long Island, Westchester, and other major school athletic, cu tural, and educational events as community service programs.

Population: 7,149,300 (city), 10,716,300 (consolidated area, N.Y. City, Westchester, Nassau, Suffolk counties); first in state and nation; total employed 3,276,600 (1978); per capita personal income $8,288.
Area: 300 sq. mi. at mouth of Hudson River; embraces 5 boroughs — Manhattan, Bronx, Brooklyn, Queens, and Staten Island.
Industry: nation's leader in manufacturing and service industries; produces 25.2% of America's apparel, 15.7% of printing and publishing; 19,435 manufacturing establishments (June 1978).
Commerce: nation's richest port, handling annual 131,251 million pounds of maritime cargo; Wall Street, world's largest financial center, with New York and American stock exchanges; wholesale-retail center for New York, New Jersey and southwestern Connecticut, retail sales $16.1 billion (1977); 55 commercial banks, resources $164.4 billion (1978); 42 savings banks, resources $59.6 billion (1978); World Trade Center, twin 110-story towers.
Transportation: Kennedy International Airport handles 38.3% of nation's overseas air travel and 56.4% of export-import air tonnage, served by 66 scheduled air carriers; LaGuardia Airport served by 15 domestic airlines; 5 heliports. Penn Central Railroad, Amtrak; 2 major rail terminals, Penn and Grand Central stations; 40 interstate bus lines; subway network covers every borough except Staten Island; ferry and the 4,260-ft. Verrazano-Narrows Bridge (world's longest suspension span) link Staten Island to Manhattan and Brooklyn; 18 bridges connect Manhattan with other boroughs, George Washington Bridge over the Hudson to New Jersey; 4 tunnels under the Hudson and East rivers.
Communications: 17 TV stations (6 commercial, 4 educational, one municipal, 2 Spanish, 4 CATV); 58 AM and FM radio stations; WPIX-TV and WPIX-FM are broadcast affiliates of The News.
Medical facilities: over 100 hospitals, 5 major medical research centers specialize in cancer, heart diseases, sickle cell anemia, and other research; Sloan-Kettering Institute for Cancer Research; 4 VA hospitals.
Federal facilities: Fort Wadsworth, Staten Island; Governors Island, many federal agencies represented in buildin at Federal Plaza and 90 Church St.
Educational facilities: 29 universities and colleges includir medical colleges, law schools, colleges of pharmacy, colleg of dentistry, institutes of art and architecture; 993 schools i the public school system; more than 1,000 private school public libraries total 189.
Cultural facilities: Lincoln Center for the Performing Ar (Philharmonic, Ballet Company, Metropolitan Opera, an other theatrical arts), Carnegie Hall, Brooklyn Academy Music. Broadway and Off-Broadway alliance for varied th atrical productions; outdoor Delacorte Theatre in Centr Park; 65 museums including American Museum of Natur History, Metropolitan Museum of Art, Museum of the Pe forming Arts, Museum of Modern Art, Whitney Museun and South Street Seaport Museum.

Other attractions: United Nations; botanic gardens in th Bronx and Brooklyn; Central Park and Prospect Par Bronx Zoo and 4 other zoos; Hayden Planetarium; Th Cloisters; N.Y. Aquarium in Coney Island; 13 municip golf courses, 535 tennis courts, 37 outdoor swimming pools

Sports: NBA Knicks, NHL Rangers, Islanders; NL Me and NFL Jets play in Shea Stadium; AL Yankees play i Yankee Stadium; NFL Giants and NASL Cosmos play i Giants Stadium in nearby E. Rutherford, N.J. Thorougl bred racing at Belmont and Aqueduct; harness racing a Roosevelt, Yonkers, and the Meadowlands; area has of track betting.

History: discovered by Giovanni da Verrazano in 1524; i 1626 Peter Minuit bought the island from the Manhatta Indians for about $24 in goods and trinkets; settlemen named New Amsterdam. In 1664, British troops occupie city without resistance and named it New York in honor c the Duke of York, brother of the King. On Jan. 1, 189 Manhattan and large areas to the NE, E, and S were consol idated into one city of New York.

Further information: Department of Commerce and Indus try, 225 Broadway; Convention and Visitors Bureau, 9 East 42d Street, both New York, NY.

Newark, New Jersey

Population: 310,500, largest city in state; grows to 2 million with non-residents working, attending schools, and using state county and federal facilities.
Area: 24.14 sq. mi., 8 miles west of New York City; Essex County seat.
Industry: wide diversity of manufacturers, fine craftsmanship; major beer, chemicals, and plastics industries; more than 10,000 businesses; major banking and insurance center, headquarters for several national firms.
Transportation: International Airport; one of busiest port facilities on the East Coast; 6 railroads, largest privately owned bus system in the nation; shipping center.
Communications: 6 radio stations, one VHF public TV station and 2 UHF TV stations.
New construction: $64 million utilities tower housing the Public Service Electric and Gas Co. completed; ground broken for $39 million office complex.
Medical facilities: College of Medicine and Dentistry of New Jersey, Beth Israel Medical Center, 6 major hospitals.

Cultural facilities: museum, library; Symphony Hall; Ne Jersey Historical Society, New Jersey Opera, Garden Sta Ballet, Newark Community Center of the Arts, Cas Italiana, Newark Institute of Urban Programs, Rutger Univ. Institute of Jazz Studies, City Without Walls Urba Artist Collective.

Educational facilities: College of Medicine and Dentistry Rutgers Law School, Seton Hall Law School, New Jerse Institute of Technology, Essex County College.

Recreation: parks with over 870 acres; 7 pools, 74 play grounds, one ice rink, 2 lakes.

Conventions: large hotel, 3 motor inns.

Other attractions: annual Cherry Blossom Festival, 7 work of sculpture, including "John F. Kennedy" by Jacques Lip chitz and a seated Abraham Lincoln by Gutzon Borglum Sacred Heart, one of the largest Gothic cathedrals in th world; historic Plume House built in 1710, and Ballantin House built in 1885.

History: founded in 1666, incorporated 1836; British troops ravaged the town during the Revolution.

Further information: Greater Newark Chamber of Commerce, 50 Park Place, Newark, NJ 07102.

Norfolk, Virginia

Population: 284,033 (city), 790,300 (metro); first in state.
Area: 915 sq. mi. in SE Virginia.
Industry: General Electric, Ford Motor Co., Norfolk Shipbuilding & Drydock Corp., Royster Co., Smith-Douglas Div. of Borden Co.
Commerce: retail sales more than $2.5 billion (1979).
Transportation: Port of Hampton Roads, world's finest natural harbor, ranks first in export tonnage among Atlantic ports; biggest coal port in world; International Airport, 4 major airlines; Chesapeake Bay Bridge-Tunnel supplies direct highway route; 7 trunk line railroads, 50 trucking companies, 2 bus companies.
Communications: 5 TV, 13 AM, 12 FM radio stations.
Medical facilities: 12 hospitals including oldest and 2d largest naval hospital in U.S.
Federal facilities: greatest concentration of naval installations in world; approx. 36 major commands include Atlantic Fleet, Second Fleet, NATO Supreme Allied Command Atlantic (SACLANT), Armed Forces Staff College, and Commandant 5th Naval Dist.
Cultural facilities: symphony orchestra, Feldman Chamber Quartet, repertory theater, dinner and little theaters, civic and univ. ballet; Chrysler Museum collection; Va. Opera Assn.
Educational facilities: Old Dominion Univ., Norfolk State, Virginia Wesleyan, Tidewater Community colleges; Eastern Va. Medical School.
Recreational facilities: General Douglas MacArthur Memorial, Adam Thoroughgood House (1636), Gardens-by-the-sea; Dismal Swamp located in Chesapeake; Virginia Beach offers 38 mi. of swimming, fishing, and surfing; camping at Seashore State Park; Hermitage Foundation Museum.
Convention facilities: Scope, $30 million cultural and convention center.
Sports: Tidewater Tides, International League baseball.
Other attractions: Azalea Festival, Norfolk Harbor Fest, Va. Beach art show, Portsmouth Sewall art show.
Climate: Average temp. 70° to 52°.
Further information: Chamber of Commerce, 475 St. Paul Boulevard, Norfolk, VA 23501.

Oakland, California

Population: 333,055, employed in Oakland, 173,383.
Area: 53.4 sq. mi.; Alameda County seat.
Industry: food processing, fabricated metal products, transportation equipment, chemicals and paint; Port of Oakland is 2d in containerized cargo; home base for Kaiser Industries.
Commerce: 8,924 retail and wholesale outlets (1979) with taxable sales of $1.7 billion; median income for family, $11,997 per annum.
Transportation: western terminus for Southern Pacific, Santa Fe, and Western Pacific railroads; International Airport is major airfreight terminal and center for supplemental air carriers; headquarters for Bay Area Rapid Transit, underground, underwater 75-mile subway connecting 15 communities.
Medical facilities: 9 hospitals include Children's Hospital Medical Center, Kaiser Foundation, and the Veterans Administration.
New construction: Pacific Telephone Bldg., Wells Fargo Bldg., Clorox Bldg.; 16 square block city center project, and major downtown garage under construction.
Cultural facilities: museum, half garden, half gallery design, has divisions of natural science, history, and art; symphony, Chinese Community Cultural Center.
Educational facilities: Univ. of California at Berkeley, Mills College, College of Holy Names, Cal. State, Hayward; Chabot, California College of Arts and Crafts, Peralta Community College.
Recreational facilities: 26,000 acre regional park system serving the East Bay; zoo in 100-acre Knowland State Park has large collection of gibbons and aerial tram; Lake Merritt Park includes botanical garden, wildfowl refuge, natural science center, and Children's Fairyland.
Sports: Raiders (football), Athletics (baseball), Golden State Warriors (basketball).
Other attractions: Oakland Coliseum, over 50,000 capacity, for theatrical entertainment, exhibits, conventions, and circus; Jack London Square.
History: area explored in 1772, settled in 1850; incorporated as town in 1852, as city in 1854.
Further information: Chamber of Commerce, 1320 Webster Street, Oakland, CA 94612.

Oklahoma City, Oklahoma

The World Almanac is sponsored in the Oklahoma City area by The Daily Oklahoman and Oklahoma City Times, 500 N. Broadway, Oklahoma City, OK 73125; phone (405) 232-3311; morning Oklahoman founded 1894; evening Times in 1888; Oklahoma Publishing Co., acquired Oklahoman 1903, Times 1916; circulation Oklahoman 189,536, Times 87,696, Saturday Oklahoman and Times 277,232, Sunday Oklahoman 301,546; editor and publisher Edward L. Gaylord, managing editor Jim Standard.

Population: (1980 est.) 391,400 (city), 830,600 (metro); largest in state; labor force 408,000 (metro).
Area: city area, nation's 7th largest, 621 sq. mi., county 700 sq. mi., metro area 3,491 sq. mi.; located in state's center on Canadian River in Oklahoma, Cleveland, Canadian, McClain, and Pottawatomie counties; elev. 1,276 feet; state capital and Oklahoma County seat.
Industry: state's industry, finance, and government hub, chief market for state's livestock industry; General Motors assembly plant employs 5,400; oil, with 4,045 producing wells in metro area employs more than 13,000; Oklahoma City Air Logistics Center at Tinker AFB employs 17,200 civilians and 3,500 military; FAA Aeronautical Center and other aviation employ 30,000; home of Kerr-McGee, energy fuels; Hertz worldwide reservations center; IBM administrative, sales and service; Wilson Foods corporate offices and meat production plant; Haggar; Western Electric; ITT; Continental Baking; Rockwell International; Dayton Tire and Rubber; Westinghouse Electric; Star Manufacturing; Magnetic Peripherals; Oklahoma City Stockyards; 900 total manufacturing firms.
Commerce: regional, national, and international marketing center; average household income $16,102, effective buying income $5.5 billion (county), consumer retail sales $5.2 billion (metro); 37 banks with $5.5 billion resources, 7 savings and loans with $1.5 billion resources.
Transportation: 12 passenger airlines provide 230 flights daily at Will Rogers World Airport, Wiley Post and Clarence Page municipal airports; 2 private airparks; 4 interstates, 5 state highways and 6 U.S. highways with I-40 and I-35 intersecting city, Turner and H.E. Bailey turnpikes; fully planned urban expressway system; major bus and truck lines; intracity and commuter mass transit; rail service by Frisco, Katy, and Santa Fe railroads; Port of Muskogee on Arkansas River Navigation Channel 140 miles east of city.
Communications: 3 metropolitan daily newspapers, 4 suburban dailies; 23 radio stations, 5 commercial TV stations, one educational TV channel, cable TV construction underway.
New construction: building permits $422 million (city); One Galleria Place (first construction in downtown retail-office-hotel complex); downtown Mid-America Plaza office-hotel complex; Quail Springs regional shopping mall; Sycamore Square downtown condominium development; Myriad Gardens downtown recreation development.
Medical facilities: Oklahoma Health Center, including

Univ. of Oklahoma medical schools, VA and 3 other hospitals; Oklahoma Medical Research Foundation and Dean McGee Eye Institute; total 18 hospitals; 9 community health clinics, regional ambulance service.
Cultural facilities: National Cowboy Hall of Fame and Western Heritage Center; Oklahoma Art Center; Artsannex; Artsplace II, Oklahoma Museum of Art, Omniplex, Kirkpatrick Planetarium, Oklahoma Symphony Orchestra, Ballet Oklahoma, Oklahoma Heritage Center, National Softball Hall of Fame, Oklahoma Historical Society, 45th Infantry Division Museum, Firefighters Museum, Field Trial Hall of Fame, Lyric Theater, Oklahoma Theater Center, Oklahoma County Libraries with 11 branches and 5 bookmobiles.
Education: Univ. of Oklahoma Health Sciences Center, Oklahoma City Univ., Oklahoma Christian College, Oklahoma State Univ. Tech. Inst., South Oklahoma City Junior College, Southwestern College, Midwest Christian College (city); Oscar Rose Junior College, Central State Univ., Univ. of Oklahoma, Bethany Nazarene College, Hillsdale Free Will Baptist College, St. Gregory's College, Oklahoma Baptist Univ. (metro); 11 vo-tech schools, 20 public school districts with est. 100,000 pupils; 9 private high schools; many parochial schools and private academies.
Recreation: Hefner, Overholser, Stanley Draper, and Hiwassee lakes (city); Lake Thunderbird and Little River State Park (metro); 132 municipal parks, 11 gymnasiums, 24 recreation centers, Oklahoma City Zoo, Martin Park Nature Center, 28 golf courses, 84 public tennis courts, 60 public playgrounds, 12 municipal ball diamonds.
Convention facilities: Myriad Convention Center seats 26,700 in arena and exhibition halls; Civic Center Music Hall 3,200, State Fairgrounds complex 16,500; 84 hotels and motels with 8,750 rooms.

Sports: Univ. of Oklahoma Sooners in Big 8 Conference, '89ers baseball, Stars hockey, Dolls women's pro football.
Annual events: National Finals Rodeo, 7 major horse shows, Miss Rodeo America Pageant, Festival of the Arts, State Fair of Oklahoma, Heritage Hills and Mesta Park home tours, Oklahoma City Powwow, National Academy of Western Art Exhibition and Western Heritage Awards, Junior Livestock Show and Exposition.

History: settled by land run Apr. 22, 1889; became state capital in 1910.
Further information: Oklahoma City Chamber of Commerce, One Santa Fe Plaza, Oklahoma City, OK 73102.

Omaha, Nebraska

Population: (1980 est.) 320,000 city, 570,000 metro; first in state; 266,000 civilian labor force.
Area: eastern Nebraska, 92 sq. mi. of rolling hills on west bank of Missouri River; Douglas County seat.
Industry: $3.7 billion annual shipments; Western Electric, 600 others employ 36,000; food processing center; 4th largest livestock market in salable receipts.
Commerce: major trade center, $2.4 billion retail sales; 3,000 retail, 1,200 wholesale firms; $22,297 income per household; 42 banks, $2.5 billion deposits; 12 savings and loans, $3.4 billion assets; 4th largest insurance center in U.S., 44 principal admin. offices; headquarters Union Pacific, InterNorth, Northwestern Bell, ConAgra, Valmont, Peter Kiewit Sons, Hinky Dinky, Brandeis, Richman Gordman, Mutual of Omaha.
Transportation: 8 major airlines; 4th largest rail center, served by 8 major railroads, transcontinental Amtrak; 94 truck lines, Interstate highways 80 and 29, 2 intercity bus, 3 barge lines; 3.3 million tons carried on Missouri River annually; port of entry, foreign trade zone.
Communications: 6 TV channels, 17 radio stations, cable TV.
New Construction: 2 15-story office towers, parking garage, 18-story Northwestern Bell headquarters, Kiewit Conference Center, Central Park Mall.
Medical facilities: 14 hospitals, 4,400 acute care beds; medical schools (Nebraska U., Creighton U.), one dental, nursing schools, Eppley Institute for Cancer Research.
Federal facilities: Strategic Air Command's global headquarters, Army Corps of Engineers, Federal Reserve branch.
Cultural facilities: Orpheum performing arts center, symphony orchestra, opera, ballet, 17 theater groups, 15 museums, Joslyn Art Museum's $30 million collection.
Educational facilities: 3 universities, 6 colleges educate 32,000 students; 30 adult education schools.
Recreation: 6,000 acres of public parks include 140 tennis courts, 30 pools, 17 golf courses, 3 marinas, ice rinks.
Sports: Omaha Royals baseball, Ak-Sar-Ben horse racing, NCAA College World Series.
Other attractions: 1,300-acre Fontenelle Forest, Doorly Zoo, Boys Town, President Ford birthsite, Gen. Dodge House; Western Heritage and Aerospace museums; downtown's Old Market; unique 60,000-member Ak-Sar-Ben civic org., Schramm Aquarium. Ranked 10th among 50 largest U.S. cities in quality of life.
History: Lewis and Clark, 1804; Mormon settlement, 1846; capitol of Nebraska territory 1855-67.
Further information: Greater Omaha Chamber of Commerce, 1620 Dodge Street, Omaha, NE 68102.

Orange County, California

The World Almanac is sponsored in Orange County by The Register, 625 N. Grand Avenue, Santa Ana, CA 92711; phone (714) 835-1234; circulation combined daily morning and evening 230,533, Sunday 259,783; founded 1905, purchased in 1935 by the late R.C. Hoiles, founder of Freedom Newspapers Inc., a 30-daily newspaper group; R.D. Threshie Jr., publisher; Richard Wallace, general manager; Jim Dean, editor; Larry Burkhart, director of marketing.

Population: 1,938,800 (July 1980 est.) 2d most populous county in the state, compares with 212,364 in 1950, 2.5 million projected for 1990; county encompasses 26 cities.
Area: 511,040 acres in S. California from Pacific Ocean inland 25 miles to Cleveland National Forest; 42-mile coastline stretches from Long Beach past Huntington Beach surfing, Newport Beach yacht harbor, Laguna Beach art colony, Dana Point small-craft harbor, to San Clemente and Camp Pendleton.
Commerce and Industry: median income (1980) $25,900 (The Register's Consumer Attitude Survey) compared with (1978) $21,300; total personal income $19.4 billion (1979 est.); taxable retail sales (1979) $11.6 billion; automotive purchases led the retail sales category with $2.4 billion in taxable sales in 1979; general merchandise was 2d with $1.26 billion in sales, followed by eating and drinking places with $986 million. The unemployment rate average about 4.2 percent during 1979. Among the major employers in Orange County are Rockwell International, Hughes Aircraft, Alpha Beta Co., Beckman Instruments, and Disneyland.
New construction: 17,558 permits were issued for single and multiple family construction during 1979; the median price of a single family home was $130,000 (1979); vacancy factor was 3.4 percent during the year.
Transportation: 8 major freeways, including main Los Angeles-San Diego artery; transit district with countywide routes including freeway commuter buses and Dial-A-Ride in some areas; John Wayne Airport, nation's 2d busiest airport with 631,226 tower operations in 1979.
Communications: local UHF-TV station, 7 VHF-TV stations regionally, over 40 radio stations.
Federal facilities: Marine Corps Air Station at El Toro, Los Alamitos Naval Air Station, Seal Beach Naval Weapons Station, Santa Ana Marine Corps Lighter-Than-Air Station (now used for helicopters, once for dirigibles), federal building in Santa Ana, General Services Administration building-national archives center in Laguna Niguel, Cleveland National Forest, Marine Corps Camp Pendleton in nearby San Diego County.
Medical facilities: Univ. of Cal. medical school at Irvine, 6. hospitals and convalescent hospitals.
Recreation: 781 acres of beaches, more than 13,000 acres for regional parks, 141 scenic sea cliffs, 3 yacht basins, 3 fishing

lakes, wilderness campgrounds, 35 golf courses, 21-mile equestrian and bicycle trail along Santa Ana River.
Other attractions: Disneyland, Knott's Berry Farm amusement park, Lion Country Safari, Movieland Wax Museum, Los Alamitos Racetrack; motorcycle park, auto raceway, mid-summer Laguna Beach Art Festival-Pageant of Masters, Santa Ana Zoo, air and car museums, Anaheim Stadium.
Convention facilities: Anaheim Convention Center, Disneyland Convention Center, hotels in Anaheim, Buena Park, Costa Mesa, Irvine, Newport Beach, Santa Ana.
Sports: (AL) Cal. Angels, (NASL) Cal. Surf, (NFL) L.A. Rams; interscholastic sports.
Cultural-Educational facilities: 2 major public universities, one private liberal arts college, 7 community colleges, multiple trade and special interest schools, 507 public K-12 schools; 237 private and church K-12 schools; city and county libraries, symphony orchestra society; 2 master chorales, 6 ballet companies, 32 community theater groups, repertory theater, 4 art museums.

History: first Spanish expedition 1769 by Capt. Gaspar de Portola, who recorded first reported earthquake in the state; county formed March 11, 1889 from Los Angeles County; Glenn Martin tested his first plane near Santa Ana; Madame Modjeska resided in local forest hideaway; Toastmasters International founded in Santa Ana 1924; Howard Hughes set world's speed record in Santa Ana in 1935 with 351 mph airplane flight. Swallows traditionally return each year to Mission San Juan Capistrano on March 19.

Further information: Anaheim Visitor and Convention Center Bureau, 800 W. Katella Avenue, Anaheim, CA, Orange County Chamber of Commerce, One City Boulevard W., Orange, CA.

Orlando, Florida

The World Almanac is sponsored in the Orlando area by the Sentinel Star, 633 N. Orange Avenue, Orlando, FL 32802; phone (305) 420-5000; Sentinel and Evening Star founded as dailies in 1913; merged in 1931; acquired by Tribune Company of Chicago in 1965; combined to create "all day" newspaper in 1973; circulation (ABC Newspaper Publisher's Statement 6 months ending March 31, 1980) 201,383 weekdays, 194,348 Saturday, 243,704 Sunday; president and chief executive officer Charles T. Brumback, editor James D. Squires.

Population: (1979) 124,658 city, 640,475 metro; 289,922 employed (metro) average for 1979.
Area: 30.1 sq. mi. (city), 2,528 sq. mi. (metro) in east central Florida; 52 lakes inside city limits; av. temperature 72.5 degrees; Orange County seat.
Industry: center of citrus belt, heart of foliage industry; 8 regional and 9 national home insurance co. offices; 5 largest employers in manufacturing (metro): Martin Marietta, Stromberg Carlson, Piezo, Qwip, NCR; manufacturers opening or expanding (metro): Western Electric, Burroughs, Flintkote, Banner Distribution, Ingalls Iron Works, Jay Tool and Die, Marine Resources, Horian Engineering, Newtronics Corp. (Hustler Antenna Co.), Ozark Airlines regional office, Stone Container, Bremco, L. Luria and Sons distribution facility, Walgreen's Distribution Center, Spears Manufacturing, M. A. Bruder and Sons, DSMA, Midland Industries, Galley Matrick Ltd.; 25 industrial areas encompassing more than 18,000 acres; naval training center, 29 commands and activities, total impact $367.9 million (retirees, federal impact funds, services and materials, construction, payroll and other disbursements).
Commerce: 35 main commercial banks with 45 branches serving the tri-county metro area; total metro deposits (1979) close to $2 billion; 7 savings and loan assns. based in metro area with 63 branches; 30 major shopping centers with 4 regional malls; est. retail sales (metro) $3.2 billion in '78; est. average effective household buying income $17,279 in 1979.
Transportation: 12 major commercial airlines and 3 commuter airlines serving Orlando International Airport, 1979 passenger total (in and out) 6.5 million, 26% increase over 1978; 3 satellite airfields; Seaboard Coastline Railroad, Amtrak; 2 intercity bus lines, 33 common carrier truck lines, 8 freight forwarding companies (3 air, 4 surface, one export); Port Canaveral and Jacksonville, nearest ports of entry.
Communications: 11 AM and 11 FM radio stations; 5 television networks.
New construction: $300 million international airport terminal to open during 1980s; Sea World of Florida, continuing 5-year $100 million expansion plan; Walt Disney World EPCOT project grown to $800 million; $38 million convention center; $10.2 million Orlando Regional Medical Center improvement; $500 million Little England theme park; $600 million Plaza International; $38.8 million Sentinel Star production facility; $75 million Iron Bridge Sewage Treatment Plant, $65 million Royal Plaza; 12,697 residential permits (metro) in 1979.
Medical facilities: 15 hospitals (metro) including Orlando Regional Medical Center with 3 facilities; Florida Hospital with 2 satellite hospitals.
Cultural facilities: Florida Symphony Orchestra, Loch Haven Art Center, John Young Museum and Planetarium, Orange County Historical Museum, Central Florida Civic Theater, Central Florida Zoological Park, Orlando Public Library with 10 community libraries, 640,000 volumes; Rollins College, Univ. of Central Florida, Valencia (3 campuses) and Seminole community colleges, Jones Business College.

Other attractions: Walt Disney World, destination resort 18 miles from downtown Orlando, annual attendance 14 million; Sea World of Florida, entertainment, education and research facilities, annual attendance 2.8 million, $6 million shark exhibit just opened; Ringling Bros. and Barnum & Bailey Circus World; Church Street Station, renovated area in downtown Orlando; Six Flag's Stars Hall of Fame, wax museum; Wet 'n Wild; Mystery Fun House; Wings and Wheels, aviation and automotive museum.

Convention facilities: 32,000 rooms; 2,133 conventions attended by 440,867 in '79; first quarter '80, 713 conventions attended by 167,389; convention expenditures in 1979 totalled $66.3 million.

Sports: Minnesota Twins spring training site; Tangerine Sports Holiday (football bowl game, college invitational basketball tournament, swimming, soccer meets, minimarathon) each Dec.; Golden South Classic, annual AAU sanctioned post season track and field meet; PGA winter program at Walt Disney World; 3 major PGA tournaments: National PGA Team Championship at Walt Disney World, $300,000 Bay Hill Classic, Ladies' Citrus (LPGA) at Rio Pinar in April; Silver Spurs rodeos in Kissimmee each Feb. and July; Ben White Raceway, Seminole Harness Raceway, Sanford-Orlando Kennel Club, Jai Alai fronton.

Additional information: Orlando Area Chamber of Commerce, P.O. Box 1234, Orlando, FL 32802.

Ottawa, Ontario, Canada

Population: 313,000 (city), 738,600 (metro region including greater Ottawa 556,900 and Hull, Que. 181,700); Canada's 8th largest city, linked with neighboring city of Hull (pop. 76,000) by 5 bridges; labor force 243,000.
Area: 42.5 sq. mi. (city), 1,100 sq. mi. (region) on Ontario-Quebec border at the Chaudiere Falls on the Ottawa River; national capital.
National Capital Region: Ottawa and Hull, occupying 1,800 square miles of eastern Ontario and western Quebec, form the National Capital Region of Canada, administered by the National Capital Commission (NCC), created by Parliament in 1959, which deals directly with 2 provincial governments, 2 regional governments, and 57 municipal jurisdictions, all of which exercise their own proper authority.
Industry: major employer (87,400) is the federal government; tourism provides 12,000 jobs; E.B. Eddy Co. largest

private employer.
Commerce: 1977 retail sales total of $2.3 billion; 1977 per capita disposable income $7,250; 3d largest convention site in Canada with capacity for 5,000; 5,600 hotel-motel rooms in region; exhibit space 60,000 sq. ft. in 3 major hotels, 120,000 sq. ft. in the Civic Centre and 75,700 sq. ft. in the Nepean Sportsplex.
Transportation: Ottawa International Airport, 15 minutes from downtown, ranks as the nation's 10th busiest, more than 68 scheduled flights daily by 6 airlines; surface transportation provided by VIA rail and intercity bus service.
Communications: 3 daily (one in French), 4 weekly newspapers; 6 TV and 14 radio stations.
Education facilities: Carleton Univ., the bi-lingual Univ. of Ottawa, and Algonquin Community College.
Medical facilities: 11 hospitals, many include a public psychiatric unit; bed capacity over 4,000.
Cultural facilities: $45 million National Arts Centre with 2,300-seat opera house-concert hall, and an 800-seat theater; Ottawa Little Theatre.
National museums: National Gallery of Canada, Museum of Man, Museum of Natural Sciences, Museum of Science and Technology, Canadian War Museum, National Aeronautical Collection.
Sports: Ottawa Rough Riders, CFL; Ottawa 67's hockey.
Other attractions: gothic-style Parliament buildings, housing Canada's House of Commons and Senate; during the summer, Changing of the Guard ceremony 2 militia regiments; Peace Tower, memorial to Canada's war dead; Central Canada Exhibition; Ottawa's oldest building, the Bytown Museum; Royal Mint; Rideau Canal provides boating facilities in summer, the longest skating rink in the world; 5 miles of the Rideau Canal from downtown Ladies' to Carleton Univ.; the Experimental Farm, 1,200 working acres in the heart of Ottawa; Winter Fair; 80 camping and trailer parks, 7 regional beaches; mountain lake recreation facilities; Gatineau Park (88,218 acres).
History: founded 1827 as Bytown, inc. as Ottawa 1855; named after Outaouac (or Outaouais Indian tribe); chosen as Canada's capital in 1857 by Queen Victoria.
Further information: Canada's Capital Visitors Bureau, 7th Floor, 222 Queen Street, Ottawa, Ont. K1P 5V9.

Pensacola, Florida

The World Almanac is sponsored in the Pensacola area by the Pensacola News-Journal, One News Journal Plaza, Pensacola FL 32501; phone (904) 433-0041; predecessor The Floridian founded in 1821, first daily News 1899, Journal 1898, merged 1924; combined circulation daily 71,550, Sunday 71,699; member Gannett Group; publisher Clifford W. Barnhart, editor J. Earle Bowden.

Population: 66,800 (city), 230,800 (county), 281,400 (metro area).
Area: southern end of 759 sq. mi. Escambia County at westernmost edge of Florida panhandle.
Industry: Monsanto Corp., St. Regis Pulp & Paper Co., Vanity Fair, American Cyanamid, Armstrong Cork, Westinghouse, Air Products, Reichhold Chemicals.
Labor force: civilian 112,400, military 13,000.
Commerce: retail sales $1.2 billion; average family income $12,958; effective buying income over $1.4 billion.
Transportation: 3 airlines, 2 railroads, 2 bus lines, 16 truck lines, intercoastal waterway, interstate 10, 3 U.S. highways.
Communications: 3 TV, 13 radio stations.
New construction: interstate 110 spur, regional sewage plant, downtown mall, St. Regis Paper Co. expansion, port expansion, Bayfront Parkway.
Medical facilities: Baptist Hospital, University Hospital, West Florida Hospital, U.S. Naval Hospital, Sacred Heart Hospital.
Federal facilities: Naval Air Station, Corry Field, Saufley Field, Whiting Field, Ellyson Field, carrier USS Lexington.
Cultural facilities: public library, Historical Museum, T.T. Wentworth Museum, Hispanic Museum, Transportation Museum, Museum of Naval Aviation, Saenger Theater, Art Association, Arts Council, Inc., Oratorio Society.
Educational facilities: Univ. of West Florida, Pensacola Junior College.
Recreation facilities: Pensacola Beach, 6 golf courses.
Sports: Pensacola Open, American Amateur Golf Classic, Virginia Slims tennis, International Bill Fishing Tournament, Biggs Shark Rodeo; intercollegiate sports; pari-mutual greyhound racing; American Amateur Tennis Classic, Fiesta Road Run.
Events: Fiesta of Five Flags, Mardi Gras, Seafood Festival, Great Gulfcoast Art Festival, July 4th celebration.
Further information: Pensacola Area Chamber of Commerce, 117 West Garden Street, Pensacola, FL 32593; phone (904) 438-4081; Pensacola-Escambia Development Comm., 803 N. Palafox, Pensacola, FL 32501; phone (904) 433-3065.

Philadelphia, Pennsylvania

The World Almanac is sponsored in the Philadelphia area by The Philadelphia Inquirer, 400 N. Broad Street, Philadelphia, PA 19101; phone (215) 854-2000; est. 1829, lineage traced to Pennsylvania Packet, founded 1771; circulation 425,075 daily, 837,209 Sunday; Pulitzer prizes 1975, 1976, 1977, 1978, 1979, 1980; published by Philadelphia Newspapers, Inc.; president Sam S. McKeel; executive editor Eugene L. Roberts Jr.; editor Edwin Guthman; managing editor Gene Foreman; sponsors Delaware Valley Science Fair, Book & Author Luncheons, Old Newsboys' Day, Phila. Distance Run, Head of the Schuylkill Regatta. PNI also publishes the Philadelphia Daily News, afternoon tabloid, at same address; founded 1925; circulation 231,310; editor F. Gilman Spencer; executive editor Zachary Stalberg; managing editor Tom Livingston; sponsors Dragnet rewards program, high school all-star football game, Broad St. Run.

Population: 1.8 million (city/co.); 4.8 million (8-co. metro); 6.0 million (14-co. RTA); 7.0 million (20-co. ADI); employment 2.0 million (metro).
Area: 130 sq. mi. (city), 3,553 sq. mi. (metro); city located in southeastern Pa. on Delaware and Schuylkill rivers; 90 mi. from N.Y.C., 136 mi. from Wash., D.C., 60 mi. from Atlantic City; Phila. is county seat (city and co. coextensive).
Industry: over 90% of all U.S. basic industries represented; major center for textiles and apparel, food processing, petroleum (largest oil refining region on East Coast), printing and publishing, instruments, chemicals and pharmaceuticals, finance and insurance; companies headquartered in metro area include Sun Co., IU International, Campbell Soup, Scott Paper, Rohm & Haas, Crown Cork & Seal, Pennwalt, Certain-teed, SmithKline, Thiokol, Penn Mutual Life, INA, ARA Services, Alco Standard Bluebird.
Commerce: 62 comm. banks (metro), $21.7 billion deposits; 4 mutual savings banks, $10.8 billion; retail sales (metro) $17.4 billion; average household income (metro) $22,879.
Transportation: biggest fresh-water port in world (50 mi. waterfront); certified foreign trade zone; leader in intl. cargo among N. Atlantic U.S. ports (80.4 million tons in 1979); 2 modern marine terminals for containerized cargo; rail service by Conrail (Penn Central, Reading), Chessie System (B & O), and Amtrak; over 250 truck lines; vast highway network, 6 bridges in metro area between Pa. and N.J.; Phila. Intl. Airport handled 10.4 million passengers in 1979 and 133,598 tons of freight through Cargo City facility; area transit (SEPTA) conveyed 272.7 million passengers on subway, el, rail commuter, bus, and streetcar lines in 1979.
Communications: 4 daily newspapers: Inquirer, Bulletin, Daily News, and Journal; 24 AM, 21 FM, 6 comm. TV stations; cable TV.
New construction: $860 million under way in 1980, incl.

over $200 million in new center-city office bldgs. and $308 million center-city RR commuter tunnel (largest public bldg. project in Phila. history); Intl. Airport high-speed line; Franklin Town development (24-story SmithKline hdqtrs. bldg. and 30-story, 800-rm. Franklin Plaza Hotel completed in 1980).

Medical facilities: 102 hospitals (metro); 6 medical schools in Phila.

Federal facilities: Phila. Naval Base; Defense Industrial Supply Ctr.; Defense Personnel Support Ctr.; U.S. Navy Aviation Supply Office Compound; Veterans Adm. Ctr.; Internal Revenue Serv. Ctr.; U.S. Mint; Ft. Dix and McGuire AFB (metro).

Cultural facilities: Phila. Orchestra; Pa. Ballet; Opera Co. of Phila.; Acad. of Music; Museum of Art; Franklin Inst.; Pa. Acad. of the Fine Arts; Rodin Museum; University Museum; Acad. of Natural Sciences; Barnes Fdtn.; Robin Hood Dells (East and West); Walnut St. Theater (oldest in America); Shubert, Forrest, and New Locust theaters; community and summer theaters.

Educational facilities: 54 colleges and universities within 25 mi. of City Hall; University City Science Center (16-acre research complex).

Convention facilities: Civic Center with 383,000 sq. ft. of air-cond. exhibit space; 13,000-seat Convention Hall; over 500 motels/hotels (metro) with 20,000 first-class rooms.

Recreational facilities: over 8,600 acres of parks inc. 4,516-acre Fairmount Park (largest city park in U.S.); hundreds of playgrounds, swimming pools, golf courses, tennis courts, ice-skating rinks; close to seashore, mountains.

Sports: NL Phillies, NFL Eagles and NASL Fury (Veterans Stadium); NBA 76ers and NHL Flyers (Spectrum); Penn Relays (Franklin Fld.); Army-Navy football (Veterans Stadium); sculling races (Schuylkill R.); area horse racing (Keystone, Liberty Bell, Brandywine, Delaware Park).

Other attractions: old city district and Benjamin Franklin Parkway centers of interest; many historic bldgs. preserved, restored or reconstructed; Penn's Landing waterfront dev.; Afro-American Historical and Cultural Museum; City Hall; Elfreth's Alley; Franklin Court; Society Hill; Fairmount Park mansions; zoo (America's first); Mummers Parade (Jan. 1); Freedom Week (climaxed by July 4th celebration); Super Sunday festival (early Oct.); nearby attractions incl. Valley Forge, Longwood Gardens, Great Adventure.

History: Wm. Penn founded his "Greene Countrie Towne" as Quaker colony in 1682; gave it name that means "City of Brotherly Love"; national capital 1790-1800; historical shrines incl. Independence Hall, Liberty Bell, Carpenters' Hall, Franklin's grave, Betsy Ross House, Gloria Dei Church, Christ Church, USS Olympia, Fort Mifflin.

Further information: Victor Kendrick, Office of City Representative, 1660 Municipal Services Bldg., Phila., PA 19107, phone (215) 686-3655; Phila. Tourist Bureau, 1525 J.F. Kennedy Boulevard, Phila., PA 19102; phone (215) 864-1976.

Phoenix, Arizona

The World Almanac is sponsored in the Phoenix area by The Phoenix Gazette, 120 East Van Buren Street, Phoenix, AZ 85004; phone (602) 271-8000; founded Oct. 28, 1880, as Arizona Gazette by Charles H. McNeil; circulation 103,603; publisher emeritus Mason Walsh, publisher Darrow Tully, managing editor Alan D. Moyer; sponsors Christmas Fund Drive, Music Memory Programs, Family Symphony Concerts, Phoenix Giants' bat boy contest, tennis clinic, cactus show, and other events.

Population: 762,000 (city), 1,550,000 (metro); capital and largest city in state, 14th (city) in nation; total employed 668,300.

Area: 325 sq. mi. (city), 9,226 sq. mi. (metro), in south central Arizona.

Industry: electronic equipment manufacturers, Honeywell Information Systems, and Motorola, Inc. each employ more than 2,500; aircraft and parts manufacturers, AiResearch, a division of The Garrett Corp., and Sperry Flight Systems each employ more than 2,500; other major employers are Goodyear Aerospace, General Electric, Western Electric Cable, Reynolds Metals, Marathon Steel, Arizona Public Service, Salt River Project, Mountain Bell, Courier Terminal Systems, Spring City Knitting Co., Siemens Corp., Amerco, General Semi-conductor Industries, United-Metro, International Metal Products, Greyhound, American Express, and Phoenix Newspapers.

Commerce: wholesale-retail center for state; retail sales (1979) $6.9 billion; effective household buying income $18,925; bank and S&L assets $16.6 billion; 17 banks with 267 area offices, 7 S&Ls with 112 offices in metro area.

Transportation: transportation center of the Southwest; Sky Harbor International Airport served by 14 airlines, 7.0 million passengers (1979); 2 railroads; 2 transcontinental bus lines; 10 transcontinental truck lines; 25 transcontinental heavy equipment haulers; 34 interstate and 39 intrastate truck lines.

Communications: 6 TV and 32 radio stations.

New construction: In 1979, 34,045 new residential building units were permitted; total value all types of building permits, $2.6 billion.

Medical facilities: Barrow Neurological Institute; 21 general care hospitals, Veterans' Hospital; other special services.

Cultural facilities: art museum, public library, symphony orchestra, Indian museums, zoo, botanical gardens, community and professional theaters; Civic Plaza convention center; Gammage Auditorium.

Federal facilities: Luke AFB, Williams AFB.

Educational facilities: Arizona State Univ., American Graduate School of International Management; 4 community colleges; Maricopa Technical College (vocational); 67 public and parochial high schools.

Sports: 70 golf courses and $200,000 Phoenix Open; inland surfing beach; ice skating rinks; amusement park; pro basketball, baseball teams; auto, greyhound, and horse racing; annual Fiesta Bowl (holiday football game).

Other attractions: Frank Lloyd Wright's Taliesin West; Paolo Soleri's Arcosanti; Dons' Club guided tours of Arizona; full calendar of events including state and county fairs and rodeos, horse shows, regattas, polo tournaments.

History: founded 1870, on site of ancient Indian settlement; the Hohokam tribe, which flourished ca. 500-1200 A.D., developed an intricate system of irrigation canals which form the base of the canal system in use today.

Further information: Phoenix and Valley of the Sun Convention and Visitors Bureau, 2701 E. Camelback Road, Phoenix, AZ 85016; or Phoenix Metropolitan Chamber of Commerce, 34 W. Monroe, Suite 900, Phoenix, AZ 85003

Pittsburgh, Pennsylvania

The World Almanac is sponsored in the Pittsburgh area by The Pittsburgh Press, 34 Boulevard of the Allies, Pittsburgh, PA 15230; phone (412) 263-1100; founded June 23, 1884, as Evening Penny Press by Thomas J. Keenan; circulation 268,000 daily, 665,000 Sunday; editor John Troan, business manager Robert O'Connell, executive editor Leo Koeberlein, managing editor Ralph Brem; sponsors Press Old Newsboys Fund for Children's Hospital which raised $2.3 million in 1979.

Population: 421,760 (city), 2,277,326 (4-county metro area), 2d in state and 28th in nation; metro area labor force of 949,390 (Apr. 1980), unemployment was 5.9% (Apr. 1980).

Area: 55.5 sq. mi at juncture of Allegheny and Monongahela rivers which form Ohio River; Allegheny County seat; altitude, 702 feet.

Industry: one-fifth of nation's steelmaking capacity concentrated in metro area; western Pennsylvania mines produce 42.3 million tons of bituminous coal annually; 6,000 different products made in area; home of world's first full-scale

nuclear power plant; world's largest manufacturers of aluminum, steel rolls, rolling mill machinery, air brakes, plate and window glass, and safety equipment; 3d largest headquarters city in nation.
Commerce: retail sales (Allegheny County, 1979) $4.4 billion; exports abroad of products manufactured here totaled $393 million in 1978; average household effective buying income (Allegheny County) $20,000.
Transportation: 9 scheduled airlines handled 11,139,164 passengers on 346,775 flights at International Airport (1979); 7 railroads; Continental Trailways and Greyhound bus lines; over 400 common carriers; Port Authority Transit vehicles carried 110 million passengers (1979) over 176 routes, 5 trolley lines; 9 major highways serve the city; a 4.5 mile busway opened in 1977, and another 6.8 mile busway and $480 million 10.5 mile light rail trolley system, incl. a downtown subway, are under construction.
Communications: 2 daily newspapers; 6 TV (including country's first educational station) and 27 radio stations.
New construction: $32 million, 140,000 sq. ft. convention center set for completion in 1981.
Medical facilities: 21 hospitals include Univ. of Pittsburgh Health and Medical complex where Dr. Jonas Salk developed polio vaccine; VA installation.
Federal facilities: Federal Building contains scores of U.S. government offices (information center: 412/644-3456); Army base at Oakdale; Air Force base.
Cultural facilities: Heinz Hall is home of the opera co., ballet, civic light opera, youth symphony and symphony orchestra; 4 community theaters, one legitimate theater; Frick Art Museum; Carnegie Museum and Art Gallery, home of the Pittsburgh International series, a biennial one-man art show offering a $55,000 prize; American Wind Symphony.
Educational facilities: Univ. of Pittsburgh, Duquesne Univ., Point Park, Chatham, Carlow, Robert Morris, and La Roche colleges; Carnegie-Mellon Univ., Community College of Allegheny Co.; 18 Carnegie public libraries, 3 bookmobiles, community libraries.
Sports: World Series champion Pirates, Super Bowl champion Steelers; NHL Penquins, NSL Spirit.
Other attractions: Highland Park Zoo, children's zoo, Twilight Zoo, aquarium, aviary, Buhl Planetarium, Allegheny Observatory, Phipps Conservatory, Fort Pitt Museum; 2 amusement parks; 2 operating passenger inclines; folk festival; Three Rivers Arts Festival every June; harness racing; river cruises; Civic Arena; Three Rivers Stadium.
History: first hunters and trappers came through in 1714; city dates from Nov. 25, 1758, when English forces under Brig. Gen. John Forbes occupied the ruins of Fort Duquesne, which French soldiers had burned and abandoned, and built a new and bigger fortress called Fort Pitt. When incorporated in 1816, it already had a reputation as a "Smoky City" from factories and coal-burning homes. Massive "Renaissance Plan" has cleared the skies and rebuilt the heart of the city during the past 30 years.
Further information: Chamber of Commerce, 411 Seventh Avenue, Pittsburgh, PA 15219; Convention and Visitors Bureau, 200 Roosevelt Boulevard, Pittsburgh, PA 15222.

Portland, Maine

The World Almanac is sponsored in the Portland area by the Maine Sunday Telegram, 390 Congress, Portland, ME 04104; phone (207) 775-5811; published by Guy Gannett Publishing Co., founded 1921; circulation 116,055; publisher Jean Gannett Hawley, editor John K. Murphy; also publishes morning Press Herald, circulation 54,472, and Evening Express, 30,183.

Population: 62,000 (city), 209,000 (metro area), first in state; total employed 44,400.
Area: 21.6 sq. mi.; peninsula on Casco Bay; Cumberland County seat.
Industry: Atlantic Coast's 2d busiest oil shipping center, east terminus Montreal pipeline; fishing fleet base, seafood shipping center; landbased products: printed materials, clothing, metal, processed food, electronic parts.
Commerce: tourist center, regional retail-wholesale hub, large shopping complex, 1,485 retail, 350 wholesale, 600 service enterprises; retail sales (1979) $412.6 million; median family income (1979) $15,694.
Transportation: municipal jetport, Delta, Air New England, Bar Harbor Airlines; 3 rail freight lines, integrated bus system, Greyhound, Continental bus terminals, 25 truck lines; Maine Turnpike, Interstate 95 and 295 highways connect to all New England; deep water anchorage, auto cruise ferries year round to Yarmouth, Nova Scotia.
Communications: 3 TV, 5 AM, 6 FM stations.
New construction: 2 office bldgs., art museum, housing for elderly, fish processing complex, parking garage.
Medical facilities: medical center, 2 hospitals.
Cultural facilities: symphony orch., Kotzschmar organ, one of world's largest; public, historical libraries; Victorian, art museums; Henry Longfellow home (1785); branch Univ. of Maine, Westbrook College, art, vocational, and business schools; Portland Headlight, oldest lighthouse in country.
Recreation: 18-hole municipal golf course, 9 others in area; scenic cruises; swimming, tennis, fishing within easy travel; scenic parks.
Conventional facilities: civic center, 3 large assembly halls, meeting rooms in modern hotels and motels.
Sports: Maine Mariners hockey (AHL).
Further information: Tourist Bureau, 142 Free Street, Portland, ME.

Portland, Oregon

The World Almanac is sponsored in the Portland area by The Oregon Journal, 1320 SW Broadway, Portland, OR 97201; phone (503) 221-8275; founded Mar. 11, 1902; circulation 105,246; editor Donald J. Sterling Jr., managing editor Edward F. O'Meara.

Population: 378,200 (city), 1,156,200 (metro), first in state; total employed, 549,700.
Area: 80 sq. mi., at junction of Columbia and Willamette rivers; Multnomah County seat.
Industry: electrical and electronic industries along with lumber and wood products, food, and paper; ranks first in manufacture of logging, lumbering equipment; home of Georgia-Pacific, Louisiana-Pacific (forest products), Tektronix (oscilloscopes), Omark (saw cutting chain), Hyster (lifts, hoists, lumber handling), White Stag, Pendleton, Jantzen (clothing).
Commerce: wholesale-retail center for large part of Oregon, SW Washington; retail sales metro area (1978), $4.2 billion. There are 14 banks, 9 savings and loan associations.
Transportation: 3 major rail freight lines, Amtrak; Greyhound, Trailways buses; 10th largest freshwater port in U.S., with 27-mile frontage, 29 marine berths; 21 million tons of cargo pass over docks annually; more than 1,300 ships visit annually, most active harbor in U.S.; hub for 10 airlines, flights to all parts of world.
Communications: 5 TV and 29 radio stations.
Medical facilities: 17 major hospitals, Univ. of Oregon Health Sciences Center, VA hospital.
Cultural facilities: art museum, Oregon Symphony Orchestra, Opera Assn., Oregon Historical Society, Portland State Univ., Univ. of Portland, and Lewis & Clark, Reed, Warner Pacific, Judson Baptist, and Concordia colleges.
Other attractions: annual Rose Festival, Rose Show; park system includes Washington Park, Hoyt Arboretum International Rose Test Garden, Amer. Rhododendron Soc. Test Garden, Washington Park Zoo, Oregon Museum of Science and Industry, Forestry Center; Forest Park is largest forest area in a U.S. city's limits. Analysis of 243 population centers in mid-1970s named Portland as "America's Most Liveable City", based on "economic, political, environmental, health and education, and social components."
Sports: Trail Blazers of the NBA play at the Memorial Coliseum; Timbers (soccer) and Beavers (baseball) play at Civic Stadium.

History: chartered 1851 with population of 821; named after Portland, Me., rather than Boston, Mass., on flip of coin by 2 early citizens.

Further information: Chamber of Commerce, 824 SW 5th, Portland, OR 97204.

Providence, Rhode Island

The World Almanac is sponsored in the Providence area by The Providence Journal-Bulletin, 75 Fountain Street, Providence, RI 02902; phone (401) 277-7000; Journal founded 1829, Bulletin 1863, Sunday Journal 1883; circulation, Journal (morn.) 72,010, Bulletin (eve.) 142,525, Sunday Journal 222,016; chairman & chief executive officer John C. A. Watkins, publisher & president Michael P. Metcalf, senior v.p.-operations & admin. Charles P. O'Donnell, v.p. and exec. editor Charles McC Hauser.

Population: 162,300 (city), 851,200 (metro); total employed 111,272.

Area: 18.91 sq. mi., at the head of Narragansett Bay in Providence County; state capital.

Industry: jewelry, silverware, plated ware, costume jewelry are largest industries; Textron is based in Providence, 984 manufacturing companies in the city.

Commerce: wholesale-retail center for entire state; retail sales $2.9 billion (metro); median household effective buying income $16,644 (metro); home of Narragansett Capital, largest small business investment company in nation; 2 savings and loan assns., 2 mutual savings banks, one cooperative bank, 6 commercial banks.

Transportation: Amtrak, passenger service between Boston, Providence, New York, and Washington; 3 bus lines; 45 locally-based common carriers and contract truckers; 11 major highways link Providence to every corner of R.I.; 5 major airlines out of T. F. Green Airport in Warwick (15 min. away); port is 3d largest in New England with 25 wharves and docks, 10.5 miles of commercial waterfront on the bay.

Communications: 3 TV and 8 radio stations.

Medical facilities: 7 hospitals; one VA hospital.

Cultural facilities: Trinity Square Repertory Co., R. I. Philharmonic, R. I. School of Design Museum; R. I. Historical Society.

Education: Brown Univ., founded 1764, is 7th oldest college in nation; 7-year M.D. program inaugurated 1973; Providence and R. I. Colleges, and R. I. School of Design.

Recreation: one of America's most attractive recreational areas centers around Providence; 69 salt water beaches, 23 fresh water beaches, 50 golf and country clubs, 5 ski areas, 29 yacht clubs, 28 parks, all within 45 minutes of city.

Convention facilities: R.I. Civic Center (seats 12,000).

Sports: America's Cup races since 1930; Newport-Bermuda race starts at Newport every other year.

Other attractions: largest collection of original early American homes of any city; located along Benefit St., they have been preserved by the Providence Preservation Society.

History: founded 1636 by Roger Williams; incorporated 1832; official state name is "Rhode Island and Providence Plantations."

Further information: Chamber of Commerce, 10 Dorrance Street, Providence, RI 02903.

Quebec City, Quebec, Canada

Population: 186,088 (city), 480,500 (metro); oldest city in Canada (1608) and the capital city of the province of Quebec.

Area: 30 sq. mi.; natural citadel on north shore of St. Lawrence River at confluence with St. Charles River; 400 miles from Gulf of St. Lawrence; 167 miles east of Montreal; older part is built on a cliff 360 ft. above the St. Lawrence.

Industry: some 300 industrial firms, ranging from primary industry products to a variety of consumer products, employ over 16,000 people; food and beverage, leather footwear and leather products, textiles, apparel, wood products, pulp and paper, printing and publishing, iron and steel products, nonferrous metal and chemical products.

Commerce: total effective buying income $2.7 billion; Quebec harbor, one of the busiest seaports of Canada, accommodates the largest ocean-going vessels with year-round facilities, an important container terminal; Provincial Government, with more than 15,000 employees, is the largest single employer and consumer in the city.

Transportation: Canadian Pacific and Canadian National railroads; Air Canada, Quebecair, Nordair; major bus center.

Communications: 3 TV stations (2 French, one English); 6 radio stations (French), 2 newspapers (French).

Medical facilities: 5 large general hospitals, many smaller ones.

Cultural facilities: historic character, cultural appeal and natural beauty make tourism important area of economic activity; annual "Carnaval" in Feb. is internationally known; annual summer festival (July) changes the city into an open theater for numerous artistic events; Expo-Quebec, an annual provincial exhibition (industrial, commercial, and agricultural), draws over 500,000 people a year.

Educational facilities: Laval University, the first in North America; Quebec University; 3 colleges for general and vocational training, numerous private schools.

Sports: home of NHL Nordiques.

Other attractions: only walled city in North America with fortifications standing today as they were 125 years ago; the Citadel, built from 1823-1832, contains within its walls 25 buildings, including the summer residence of Governor-General of Canada, Parliament buildings (1886), Quebec Museum, Battlefield Park, Ursulines Museum, Seminary (1663), Talon cellars, Notre Dame des Victoires Church, and Tresor Street.

History: founded 1608 by French explorer Samuel de Champlain; cradle of French civilization in America; once the key to the interior of the North American continent.

Raleigh, North Carolina

The World Almanac is sponsored in eastern North Carolina by The News and Observer and The Raleigh Times, 215 S. McDowell Street, Raleigh, NC 27602; phone (919) 821-1234; circulation N&O (morn.) 134,000, Times (eve.) 34,200, N&0 Sunday 165,000; publisher Frank Daniels Jr., editorial director Claude Sitton, editor Times A.C. Snow, managing editor N&O Bob Brooks, Times Mike Yopp.

Population: 175,000 (city), 310,000 (county), 515,000 (metro); 3d in state; 284,000 employed (metro).

Area: 51.1 square miles in the geographical center of the state where Piedmont joins coastal plains; alt. 363 ft., temperate climate; state capital and Wake County seat.

Industry: major industry is government, employing 25% of work force.

Commerce: retail center of eastern N.C., retail sales $2.17 billion (1979); 16 banks and 6 savings and loans; average annual income per household $22,100.

Education: 11 colleges, N.C. State Univ. (Raleigh), Univ. of N.C. (Chapel Hill), and Duke Univ. (Durham) form Research Triangle; Triangle Park employs 11,000 in drug, fiber, biomedical, environmental, engineering, and humanities research; metro area has more Ph.Ds per capita than anywhere in world.

Transportation: 2 rail and 5 bus lines, Amtrak, 275 motor freight companies; airport has 10 airlines carrying 927,873 passengers per year; one interstate, 4 U.S., and 2 state highways into city; city mass transit bus system.

Communications: 4 TV and 14 radio stations; 2 daily newspapers, 10 weeklies.

New construction: $132 million (1979).
Medical facilities: 3 hospitals (1,000 beds); major state mental hospital; 285 doctors, 150 dentists.
Convention facilities: 38 motels, 4,900 rooms; Civic Center seats 10,000; Dorton Arena, 9,111; Memorial Auditorium, 3,000; Reynolds Coliseum, 12,000.
Cultural facilities: 3 museums, state fairgrounds, state symphony; community, college, and professional theater groups.
Recreation: 4,200-acre Umstead State Park, Carter Stadium, 100 city parks; first Green Survival City in U.S.
Sports: pro golf, pro tennis; annual powerboat regatta; college sports.
History: founded 1792; Andrew Johnson birthplace; Oakwood Historic District preserves large Victorian neighborhood.
Further information: Raleigh-Wake Chamber of Commerce, 411 S. Salisbury Street, Raleigh, NC 27602; phone (919) 833-3005.

Regina, Saskatchewan, Canada

The World Almanac is sponsored in southern Saskatchewan by The Leader-Post, 1964 Park Street, Regina, Sask., S4P 3GA, phone (306) 527-8511; founded 1883 by Nicholas Flood Davin; circulation 68,991; president Michael Sifton, Toronto; executive vice-president Max Macdonald; editor W. Ivor Williams; associate editor C.E.W. Bell; managing editor J.M.F. Swan; business manager William Duffus; advertising manager George Crawford; MacLaren Trophy for editorial page reproduction excellence.

Population: 155,211, first in province, 16th in nation; labor force, 76,000.
Area: 37.5 sq. mi., 100 miles north of Canada-U.S. border; provincial capital.
Industry: over 293 manufacturing industries; gross production value (1979) $560 million, 34% of Saskatchewan total.
Commerce: service center for oil, potash; grain production area; retail sales (1979) $757.5 million, 23.7% of province.
Transportation: 2 rail lines, 3 airlines, 3 bus lines, and 125 trucking companies; main Trans-Canada highway bisects; city-run transit system, including Telebus, hybrid system with demand/response taxi service and mass transit, provides to-and-from service to user's home.
Communications: 3 TV, 7 radio stations, cable television.
Medical facilities: 4 major hospitals, 1,442 beds.
Cultural facilities: Saskatchewan Centre of Arts, multi-purpose theater-convention center with: Jubilee theater (seats 450) stage, ballroom, reception hall and dining room; Centennial theater (seats 2,029); Hanbidge Hall convention area, 12,200 square feet, 9 meeting rooms, seats 1,600; Regina Symphony; Globe Repertory; Museum Natural History; Norman Mackenzie Art Gallery; RCMP Museum.
Educational facilities: Regina University; 14 collegiates; 97 elementary, 7 specialized schools; Wascana Institute of Applied Arts and Sciences.
Recreation facilities: Saskatchewan Roughriders (Canadian pro football); 154 parks and playgrounds; 8 golf courses; 6 swimming pools; 9 indoor ice rinks.
Other attractions: Wascana Centre, 2,300-acre development, with man-made lake, public buildings, parks, recreation in heart of city; home of Canadian Western Agribition, Canada's major international livestock show.
History: founded 1882, and since that time headquarters for RCMP training depot.
Further information: Regina Chamber of Commerce, 2145 Albert Street, Regina, Sask.

Reno, Nevada

The World Almanac is sponsored in the northern Nevada area by the Nevada State Journal and Reno Evening Gazette, 401 West Second Street, P.O. Box 280, Reno, NV 89520; phone (702) 786-8989; Journal founded 1870, Gazette founded 1876, combined daily circulation, 54,007, Sunday 47,069; publisher Warren L. Lerude.

Population: (1980 est.) 118,000 (city), 216,500 (county), including Sparks, 2d largest in the state; 1980 labor force 107,800.
Area: 36.8 sq. mi. (including Stead annexation) in northwestern part of the state at the eastern foot of the Sierra Nevadas; Washoe County seat.
Industry: gross gaming revenue for county $422.8 million (1979), netted state taxes of $33.4 million; warehousing continued to grow because of Nevada's liberal free port law with est. 24 million sq. ft. in the county; marriages (36,265) outnumbered divorces (3,708).
Commerce: taxable sales in SMSA (Washoe County) for 1979, $1.7 billion; assessed valuation (city) $847.8 million, median household income $24,000; bank resources $3.5 billion.
Transportation; 25 motor freight lines, 2 freight railroads, Amtrak, 3 commercial bus lines, 9 airlines; airport handled (1979) 2.7 million passengers; U.S. 395 and Interstate 80.
Communications: 3 TV, 12 radio stations, one CATV.
New construction: 97 commercial, 1,217 residential units totaling $107.5 million assessed valuation (1979, including county).
Medical facilities: 3 hospitals, including VA.
Educational facilities: Univ. of Nevada, Reno, 8,004 enrollment (1979); Truckee Meadow Comm. College 5,732, public schools 30,735, private/parochial schools 1,790.
Cultural facilities: 1,428 seat Pioneer Theater Auditorium, Atmospherium Planetarium, 8,000 seat Centennial Coliseum, and 300,000 volume library; national air races; Reno Rodeo ($140,000 purse); Nevada Historical Society, Nevada Opera Guild, Reno Philharmonic Orchestra; Sierra Nevada Museum of Art, Sierra Arts Foundation, Reno Little Theatre.
Recreation: 24-hour gambling; world's largest gambling casino; 21 ski resorts within a 1½ hour drive; Lake Tahoe and Pyramid Lake offering fishing, boating, swimming, sunbathing, medium game-hunting, camping; historic Virginia City mining town and tourist attraction within 1/2 hour drive.
Sports: Silver Sox minor league baseball.
History: established 1868 with public auction of land by Central Pacific Railroad Co., known prior as Lake's Crossing; named after Civil War hero General Jesse L. Reno.
Further information: Chamber of Commerce, P.O. Box 3499, Reno, NV 89505; Marketing Department, Reno Newspapers, Inc. P.O. Box 280, Reno, NV 89520.

Richmond, Virginia

The World Almanac is sponsored in the Richmond area by the Richmond Times-Dispatch and News Leader, 333 E. Grace Street, Richmond, VA 23213; phone (804) 649-6000; Times-Dispatch founded 1850 by James A Cowardin, circulation 134,880 daily, 214,825 Sunday; News Leader founded 1896 by Joseph Bryan, circulation 114,468; chairman D. Tennant Bryan; publisher J. Stewart Bryan III; president Alan S. Donnahoe; executive editor John E. Leard; Times-Dispatch managing editor Alf Goodykoontz; News Leader managing editor J.A. Finch.

Population: 215,000 (city), 589,900 (metro area), total employed (non-agricultural) 313,676.
Area: 62.5 sq. mi. (city), located at fall line of James River, 90 miles from Atlantic Ocean; independent city.
Industry: tobacco, with 11,900 workers, and chemicals, with 7,500 are leaders in employment; Philip Morris cigarette

plant is world's largest and most modern; printing, publishing, manufacture of paper and allied products, and food.
Commerce: wholesale-retail center for central Virginia; retail sales $2.52 billion in 1979, per capita income $9,369, median family buying income $19,738, total income $5.8 billion.
Transportation: 4 major railroads, 5 intercity bus lines, 4 commercial air lines, 2 commuter air lines, 69 motor truck lines; 3 interstate, 6 U.S., and 9 state highways; deepwater terminal accessible to ocean-going ships.
Communications: 4 TV, 20 radio stations; 2 cable TV stations.
Medical facilities: Medical College of Virginia known worldwide for heart and kidney transplants, medical research; 21 other hospitals, including McGuire VA Hospital.
Federal facilities: Defense General Supply Center, Fifth Federal Reserve Bank, U. S. Fourth Circuit Court, Ft. Lee (Quartermaster Corps).
Cultural facilities: Va. Museum and Theater with professional artists make city a center for dramatic, other performing arts; other drama groups; symphony orchestra.
Educational facilities: Virginia Commonwealth Univ. has state's largest enrollment; Univ. of Richmond, Virginia Union Univ., Union Theological Seminary (Presbyterian), Randolph-Macon College.
Recreational facilities: Coliseum for athletic, entertainment events; city-owned Mosque auditorium, Parker Field, City Stadium, numerous parks.
Convention facilities: large downtown hotels near Mosque and Coliseum.
Sports: Braves (IL baseball), Rifles (Eastern Hockey League); national ranked track and tennis events.
Other attractions: St. John's Church, scene of Patrick Henry's "Liberty or Death" speech; Virginia Capitol, designed by Thomas Jefferson; White House of the Confederacy; Civil War battlefields.
History: exploration here in 1607 by Capt. John Smith, first settlement 1609, incorporated as town 1742, made Va. capital 1779, Confederate Capital 1861-65; burned 1781 by Benedict Arnold, and 1865 when cotton, tobacco stockpiles fire set by fleeing Confederates spread to city; damaged by floods 1771, 1969, 1972.
Further information: Chamber of Commerce, 201 E. Franklin Street, Richmond, VA 23219.

Roanoke, Virginia

The World Almanac is sponsored in the Roanoke area by the Roanoke Times & World-News, 201-203 Campbell Avenue, Roanoke, VA 24010; phone (703) 981-3000; Times founded 1886, World-News founded 1889; Barton W. Morris Jr., president and publisher; circulation combined daily 113,812, Sunday 114,987.

Population: 101,300 (city, 1980), 223,200 (metro area); labor force 110,250.
Area: 43.25 sq. mi.; Metro SMSA includes Roanoke City, Salem City; Roanoke, Craig, Botetourt counties; located at southern extremity of Shenandoah Valley midway between Maryland and Tennessee.
Industry: 21.3% of work force in manufacturing. Leading firms are General Electric, Eaton Corp., ITT, Singer, Burlington Industries, Mohawk Rubber, Ingersoll Rand.
Commerce: headquarters Shenandoah Life Ins. Co., Estate Life Ins. Co., Appalachian Power Co., Advance Stores, Mick or Mack Groceries; Regional Allstate Ins. Co. offices; Kroger (central warehouse); retail sales metro area (1980) $1.088 billion; average household effective buying income $20,250 (metro area); retail center for 20 counties and parts of W. Va. and N.C.
Transportation: Norfolk & Western Railway Co. headquarters; 2 airlines; Trailways and Greyhound buses; Amtrak north-south Washington, D.C.-West Va.; 30 interstate trucking firms with terminals; Highways interstate 81, spur 581, US 11, 460, 220, 221, Blue Ridge Parkway.
Communications: 3 TV and 13 radio stations.
Medical facilities: 4 general, 4 specialty hospitals, VA facility; state hospital.
Cultural facilities: 2 civic centers with auditorium, coliseums and exhibit halls; symphony orchestra, art center, theaters; Roanoke, Hollins, Virginia Western Community, National Business colleges; Va. Polytechnic Inst. and State Univ.; concert and lecture series.
Other attractions: Mill Mt. Park rising 1,000 ft. in center of city; children's zoo; Transportation and Historical Museum, Smith Mt., Fairy Stone and Claytor Lakes state parks; Natural Bridge, Dixie Caverns, Peaks of Otter.
Sports: baseball; schools sports, winter skiing nearby; public recreation and parks programs.
History: formerly named Big Lick, Roanoke, an Indian word for shell money, became a city in 1884 with the linking of the Shenandoah Valley Railroad with Norfolk and Western Railroad.
Further information: Roanoke Valley Chamber of Commerce, 14 West Kirk Avenue, P.O. Box 20, Roanoke, VA 24001.

Rochester, New York

The World Almanac is sponsored in the Rochester area by Gannett Rochester Newspapers, 55 Exchange Street, Rochester, NY 14614; phone (716) 232-7100; circulation Democrat and Chronicle (morn.) 125,316, Times-Union (eve.) 121,897, Democrat and Chronicle (Sunday) 232,367; publisher Maurice Hickey, executive editor Robert Giles, director of advertising Peter Stegner. Times-Union reporters awarded a 1972 Pulitzer prize; Gannett News Service awarded 1980 Pulitzer prize.

Population: 5 county metro area 973,700 (est.); 438,900 employed; unemployment 5.8%.
Area: 675 sq. mi. (Monroe County), straddling Genesee River, on Lake Ontario, 2,966 sq. mi. (metro); Monroe County seat.
Industry: world leader in production of photographic, optical, and scientific instruments, with Eastman Kodak (55,800 employees), Xerox (14,000), and Bausch & Lomb (5,000), all founded in Rochester; other fields include machinery, food products, apparel, printing and publishing.
Commerce: retail sales (1979) $3.3 billion; 20 commercial and savings banks; 1978 average household effective buying income $20,352 (metro area).
Transportation: Monroe County Airport, with 3 major airlines and several freight companies; rail freight service by 4 lines, Amtrak; port of Rochester; over 75 motor freight firms.
Communications: 4 TV and 15 radio stations.
New construction: Eastman Kodak, 2 manufacturing plants; Strong Museum.
Medical facilities: one of the nation's most advanced health care centers; 8 general hospitals including Strong Memorial.
Cultural facilities: Eastman Theater, part of Univ. of Rochester's Eastman School of Music, and home of the Philharmonic Orchestra; Memorial Art Gallery; Museum and Science Center, including Strasenburgh Planetarium; George Eastman House of Photography; 3 theater companies.
Educational facilities: 8 private and 2 public 4-year colleges; 3 community colleges.
Recreational facilities: Finger Lakes area with 13 parks, summer and winter sports, golf, tennis, bowling; 16-park Monroe County System including Seneca Park Zoo, Highland Park, Lilac Festival.
Convention facilities: 2d largest used site in NY; War Memorial 7,500 cap., Dome Arena 5,000 cap.; 4,600 rms.
Sports: International League Red Wings, Baltimore Orioles farm team; AHL Amerks, NASL Lancers; thoroughbred racing and Finger Lake race track (Canandaigua).
Further information: Chamber of Commerce, 55 St. Paul Street, 14604; Convention and Publicity Bureau, 100 Exchange Street, 14614.

Rockford, Illinois

The World Almanac is sponsored in the Rockford area by the Rockford Newspapers, Inc., 99 E. State Street, Rockford, IL 61105; phone (815) 987-1200; publisher of the Rockford Register Star and Sunday Register Star, daily (a.m.) circulation 80,000; publisher Jerry Bean; member of the Gannett Group.

Population: 149,424 (city), 246,623 (county); 137,300 work force (county).
Area: 35.4 sq. mi. (city) on Rock River in extreme north central Illinois; Winnebago County seat; 519 sq. mi. (county).
Industry: more than 700 manufacturing establishments; products include machine tools (Sundstrand, Ingersoll Milling Machine, Barber-Colman, Greenlee Bros.), screws and bolts (Rockford Products, Elco, Camcar, National Lock), pharmaceuticals (Warner-Lambert, American Chicle), and paints (Valspar); Chrysler Corp. assembly plant is in nearby Belvidere.
Commerce: retail "magnet" for northern Ill. and southern Wis.; 21 shopping centers including Mall at CherryVale (105 stores); retail sales (1979) $955.2 million (city); 16 commercial banks, resources (1979) $1.008 billion; 4 savings and loan assns., resources (1979) $553.7 million.
Transportation: Amtrack Chicago connection; 4 rail freight lines, 3 bus lines, 50 truck lines; TWA and Ozark Air Lines with Chicago connection; Coleman Air Transport Co. (Detroit connection); U.S. 51 and 20, interstate 90, Ill. 70, 2 and 173.
Communications: 4 TV, 6 radio stations, one cable TV; 5 weekly newspapers, one daily newspaper.
Medical facilities: 3 hospitals, 2 public supported extended care facilities.
Cultural facilities: symphony orchestra, concert band, civic theater, 3 choral organizations, 6 legitimate theaters.
Education: (1979-80 school year) 69 public schools (K-12), 27 parochial and private schools (K-12); Rockford College, Rock Valley College (2 years, liberal arts), UI-Rockford School of Medicine, Rockford Business College (2 years).
Recreation: 23 forest preserves, over 100 parks totaling 3,000 acres; one state park, 4 public golf courses, 4 country club courses, 61 public tennis courts, 7 private tennis courts, 2 indoor tennis facilities, 2 private platform tennis facilities, 3 public swimming pools, 7 private swim clubs, 76 baseball diamonds; Riverview Ice House; 2 roller skating rinks.
Agriculture: 194,000 acres tilled farmland (est. value $679 million); 2,400 persons on 794 commercial farms.
Other attractions: Children's Farm, Time Museum, Tinker Swiss Cottage, Rockford Museum, John Erlander Home, Burpee Natural History Museum, Burpee Art Museum, Rockford Council for the Arts and Sciences.
New construction: metro center.
History: founded in 1834 by Germanicus Kent and Thatcher Blake beside fording place across Rock River; incorporated in 1852.
Further information: Rockford Area Chamber of Commerce: 815 E. State Street, Rockford, IL 61101.

Sacramento, California

The World Almanac is sponsored in the Sacramento area by The Sacramento Bee, 21st & Q, Sacramento, CA 95816; phone (916) 446-9211; founded 1857; circulation daily 203,779, Sunday 233,034; president C. K. McClatchy, editor C. K. McClatchy, executive editor Frank McCulloch, managing editor Mike Kidder.

Population: 274,400 (city), 770,200 (county), 996,700 (SMSA); total employed 429,400 (SMSA).
Area: 94 sq. mi. (city), 997 sq. mi. (county), 85 mi. northeast of San Francisco in Sacramento Valley, at junction of Sacramento and American rivers; state capital and Sacramento County seat.
Industry: 475 manufacturing plants including Campbell Soup, Procter & Gamble, Cal. Almond Growers Exchange, Del Monte, Teichert Construction, Aerojet-General, Hewlett-Packard, Computer Sciences Corp., and Cal. Farm Bureau Federation.
Commerce: wholesale-retail center for Sacramento Valley; total retail sales $4.6 billion in 1979.
Transportation: 3 county operated airports, including metropolitan airport, plus numerous private airports; $55 million Port of Sacramento gives access to Pacific; 2 mainline transcontinental rail carriers; junction 4 major highways.
Communications: 6 TV and 21 radio stations.
New construction: restoration of Old Sacramento as state and federal historical project, regional sewage treatment plant, major hotel, department store, Hewlett-Packard factory, Electron manufacturing plant.
Medical facilities: 10 major hospitals, Univ. of California Medical School in nearby Davis.
Federal facilities: 2 large air force bases, army depot, many regional federal offices.
Cultural facilities: Sacramento Community Center complex; symphony orchestra, ballet co., 10 live theaters (including the Music Circus, an in-the-round summer stock theater), the Crocker Art Gallery, and many art shows.
Education: California State Univ.-Sacramento, McGeorge College of Law, Lincoln Univ. Law School, the nearby Univ. of California-Davis, and 3 community colleges.
Recreation: zoo, 95 public parks, 74 playgrounds, 8 public and 4 private golf courses, fishing, hunting, boating, camping, hiking, and skiing in nearby high Sierras; Golden Bear harness racing, American River Parkway bicycle trail, nearby Lake Tahoe.
Other attractions: Sutter's fort, State Capitol, Governor's Mansion, Old Sacramento historical area, Railway Museum; annual events: Camellia Festival, Dixieland Jazz Festival, Golden West track & field meet, Pig Bowl.
History: first permanent settlement founded by John Augustus Sutter Sr. in 1839; James Marshall discovered gold at Sutter's Mill in 1848, 35 mi. northeast, gateway to the Mother Lode Country; Pony Express and Central Pacific Railroad were part of early history.
Further information: Sacramento Metropolitan Chamber of Commerce, 917 7th Street, P.O. Box 1017, Sacramento, CA 95805; phone (916) 443-3771.

St. Louis, Missouri

The World Almanac is sponsored in the St. Louis area by the Post-Dispatch, 900 N. Tucker Boulevard, St. Louis, MO 63101; phone (314) 622-7000; founded Dec. 12, 1878 by Joseph Pulitzer; circulation 255,340 daily, 433,116 Sunday; editor and publisher Joseph Pulitzer Jr., associate editor Michael E. Pulitzer, managing editor David Lipman, contributing editor, Evarts A. Graham Jr., sr. vice president Alex T. Primm, general manager of newspaper operations Glenn Christopher; major awards include 5 Pulitzer Prizes to the newspaper and 11 to staff members.

Population: 500,000 (city), 1,032,000 (county), 2,454,000 (metro), 12th in nation in payroll employment (991,000, first quarter of 1980).
Area: 4,935 sq. mi. (metro) just south of confluence of Missouri and Mississippi rivers.
Industry: 2d to Detroit in auto and truck assembly with Ford, GM, and Chrysler plants; McDonnell Douglas headquarters, aerospace manufacturer; other headquarters include nation's largest shoe company, Interco; Anheuser-Busch, world's largest brewer; Monsanto, General Dynamics, Ralston-Purina, Pet, Inc., Chromalloy American, Consolidated Aluminum, Emerson Electric, Brown Group; 3,215 manufacturing concerns employing 243,400 (first quarter of 1980); ranks 5th in nation in number of "Fortune

500" company headquarters.

Commerce: $8.9 billion retail sales (1979 metro); $18,185 median family income; more than 220 banking institutions, total deposits $11.78 billion (first quarter of 1980).

Transportation: 11 major airlines with 9.7 million passenger movements (1979); 2d largest rail center in nation, 17 trunk line railroads; largest inland river port in nation handled 22.5 millions tons of cargo in 1977; 9 major highways; 14 motor-bus lines; 350 motor freight lines, 14 barge lines.

Communications: 6 TV and 35 radio stations.

New construction: industrial and commercial contracts totaled $492 million and residential $499 million (1979); Lambert International Airport expansion; $40 million computer center for McDonnell-Douglas; $50 million IBM office project.

Medical facilities: 65 hospitals (metro) with 14,651 beds; Washington Univ. and St. Louis Univ. medical schools and affiliated hospitals provide treatment in many areas.

Federal facilities: Military Personnel Records Center, Defense Mapping Agency Aerospace Center, Army Troop Support and Aviation Material Readiness Command, Army Aviation Research & Development Command, Army Logistics Management Systems Agency, Postal Service Data Processing Center, Scott AFB.

Cultural facilities: Art Museum; Museum of Science and Natural History; restored historic homes; symphony orchestra; Mississippi River Festival near Edwardsville in summer; Loretto Hilton Repertory Theatre; St. Louis Opera Theater (3-week summer season,) American Theater; 4 dinner theaters; Laumeier Sculpture Garden; Municipal Theatre (Muny Opera) offers Broadway shows in big outdoor theater in Forest Park.

Educational facilities: 4 major universities: Washington, St. Louis, Univ. of Missouri at St. Louis, and Southern Illinois Univ. at Edwardsville; 26 colleges and seminaries with over 200 other private schools.

Convention facilities: 16,000 hotel rooms; 90,000 sq. ft. exhibit space in Kiel Auditorium; 240,000 sq. ft. exhibit space in Cervantes Convention Center.

Sports: Busch Stadium home of the Cardinal baseball and football teams; St. Louis Blues (NHL); horse racing at Fairmont Park; St. Louis Steammers, women's pro basketball; St. Louis Streak, indoor soccer.

Recreational facilities: Jefferson National Expansion Memorial with 630-foot Gateway Arch on riverfront; 1,326-acre Forest Park with 3 golf courses, ball fields, floral displays, zoo, McDonnell Planetarium, Steinberg skating arena, and Jefferson Memorial displaying Lindbergh trophies; National Museum of Transport; Six Flags Over Mid-America; Grant's Farm with President Grant's cabin and animal displays; Missouri Botanical Garden with floral displays, Japanese garden, and advanced research display greenhouse, the Climatron; excursion boats, show boat, minesweeper, Army Corps of Engineers museum on riverfront; Dental Health Theater with world's largest model teeth; Maryland Plaza/-Central West End, a collection of art galleries, shops, night spots, and entertainment; Westport Plaza, suburban night spots and entertainment; the Magic House, a 15-room mansion with scientific "magic."

Other attractions: climate has 4 distinct seasons; spring and autumn warm, winters mild, summers hot with 90-degree temperatures; average temperature 55.9 degrees; average precipitation 35.9 inches; downtown area contains significant architecture including Eads Bridge, Old Post Office, Union Station, Old Courthouse, Old Cathedral, Spanish International Pavilion which now contains a hotel tower; Louis Sullivan's Wainwright Building being refurbished, and restoration of Laclede's Landing area on riverfront adjoining Gateway Arch.

History: named for French King Louis IX by fur trapper Pierre Laclede whose trading post became major fur market and gateway to the West; starting point of Lewis and Clark expedition and other explorations.

Further information: Convention and Visitors Bureau, 500 N. Broadway, or Regional Commerce and Growth Assn., 10 S. Broadway, both St. Louis, Mo.

St. Paul, Minnesota

The World Almanac is sponsored in the St. Paul area by the St. Paul Dispatch and Pioneer Press, 55 E. 4th Street, St. Paul, MN 55101; phone (612) 222-5011; founded 1849 as Minnesota Pioneer by James Goodhue; circulation, Pioneer Press (morn M-F) 101,207; Dispatch (eve M-F) 119,258; Pioneer Press/Dispatch (morn Sat.) 176,551; Sunday Pioneer Press, 244,490; Bernard H. Ridder Jr., chairman, Knight-Ridder Newspapers, Inc.; publisher Thomas L. Carlin, executive editor John R. Finnegan, editor William G. Sumner. First newspaper published in Minnesota.

Population: 265,300 (city); 817,000 (metro), 2d in state; total employed (city, 1979) 142,300.

Area: 55 sq. mi. in eastern Minnesota on banks of Mississippi River close to Minnesota and Wisconsin vacationlands; state capital and Ramsey County seat.

Industry: West Publishing, world's largest law book publisher; international center for electronics and computer technology; Union Stockyards is largest livestock center in nation (2.7 million head in 1979). Headquarters 3M Co., Am. Hoist & Derrick Co., Burlington Northern RR, Univac, Brown & Bigelow, Whirlpool, Economics Laboratory, Hoerner-Waldorf Corp., St. Paul Companies (insurance).

Commerce: retail sales (1979) $2.9 billion; median household income, $18,700; 25 banks and 6 savings and loan associations.

Transportation: 5 major and 2 regional rail lines, Amtrak; 21 intercity truck firms, 37 terminals; 3 interstate bus lines; 730-mile public transit system; metropolitan airport, hub of 8 commercial airlines, headquarters for Northwest and Republic airlines, averages 600 air movements per day; Downtown Airport; 60 firms operate barges on Mississippi River using a 9-foot channel downtown.

Communications: 4 commercial and 2 educational TV stations; 29 radio stations.

Medical facilities: 12 private hospitals; a 611 bed community hospital and research center: St. Paul-Ramsey Hospital.

Federal facilities: Ft. Snelling; area headquarters for HEW; district headquarters for IRS, FCC, Immigration and Naturalization Service; U.S. District Court.

Cultural facilities: St. Paul Chamber Orchestra, St. Paul City Ballet, Science Museum of Minn. & Omnitheater. Univ. of Minnesota Institute of Agriculture, Hamline Univ., St. Thomas, St. Catherine, Bethel, Concordia, and Macalester colleges, and William Mitchell College of Law; city school system with 80 public schools and 61 private schools.

Recreational facilities: more than 900 lakes in metro area, 438 tennis courts, 148 swimming beaches, 513 parks, 50 golf courses, 27 ski centers; 52 neighborhood recreation centers, 35 miles of parkways, 100 miles of hiking and biking trails.

Convention facilities: Civic Center with 101,000 sq. ft. exhibit space, seating for 35,000 in 4 main buildings, 15 meeting halls; 50 hotels and motels.

Other attractions: Winter Carnival in Jan., Minnesota State Fair, Como Park Zoo and Conservatory; onyx statue of Indian God of Peace in City Hall, Minnesota Historical Society Museums, Arts & Science Center, Fort Snelling State Park, Minn. Zoological Garden nearby.

History: once called "Pig's Eye" for first settler, Pierre "Pig's Eye" Parrant; changed to St. Paul when Father Lucien Galtier built St. Paul's Chapel 1841; became town 1847, city 1854.

Further information: St. Paul Area Chamber of Commerce, Osborn Bldg., St. Paul, MN 55102.

St. Petersburg, Florida

The World Almanac is sponsored in Florida's Suncoast Area by The St. Petersburg Times and Evening Independent, 490 1st Avenue S., St. Petersburg, FL 33701; phone (813) 893-8111; Times founded 1884, Independent 1906; circulation Times (morn.) 209,781, Independent (evening) 39,887, Sunday Times 263,091; Eugene C. Patterson, editor of The Times and president of The Times Publishing Co.; Robert Stiff, editor, The Independent; John B. Lake, executive vice president and publisher, The Times Publishing Co.

Population: 240,427 (city), 725,457 (Pinellas County), 1,521,799 (metro); Pinellas County (March, 1980) employment 237,500, unemployment 4.8%.
Industry and Commerce: 3.6 million tourists visited county in 1979; industries include General Electric, Honeywell, Sperry, Milton Roy Co., Eckerd Drugs, Jim Walter Research, All-State Insurance regional office, GTE, Paradyne Corp., ECI, Aircraft Porous Media, VRN, Silor Optical; county (1979) retail sales $3.1 billion.
Transportation: U.S. 19, 41, and 98 link city to rest of Gulf Coast Florida; Interstates 175, 75, and 4 link St. Petersburg with Tampa, Orlando, and east coast; Tampa International Airport 25 miles from downtown; other airports are St. Petersburg-Clearwater International and Albert Whitted; Amtrak, Seaboard Coast Line railroads; Greyhound and Trailways bus lines.
Communications: 6 TV, 46 radio stations.
Convention and Tourist facilities: over 52,000 units house 160,000 visitors; Bayfront Center seats 8,250 in arena, 2,250 in auditorium; Pinellas restaurants can serve 116,500 people at one time; Disney World 2 hours away.
Medical facilities: 13 major hospitals; Bay Pines veterans complex to be greatly expanded adding 1,150 new beds; All Children's Hospital.
Cultural facilities: Museum of Fine Arts, Gulf Coast Symphony, Historical Museum, community theaters, Eckerd College Free Institutions Forums; varied musical, theatrical and dance events at Bayfront Center Complex.
Educational facilities: Univ. of South Florida's downtown Bayboro Campus to expand enrollment from 1,700 to 7,500, first building phase of $5 million is underway; Stetson College of Law, Eckerd College, St. Petersburg Junior College.
Recreational facilities: 76 parks on 1,800 acres, many with recreational buildings, pools, tennis courts, boat ramps, and picnic areas; municipal and private marinas; deep sea fishing, golf courses, baseball fields.
Sports: St. Louis Cardinals and New York Mets spring training site; greyhound racing, baseball, jai alai, horse racing, NFL football, basketball, pro tennis, boat racing, NASL soccer; LPGA-PGA team golf, LPGA S&H Green Stamps Golf Classic.
Additional information: St. Petersburg Chamber of Commerce, 225 4th Street S., St. Petersburg, FL 33701.

Salem, Oregon

The World Almanac is sponsored in the Salem area by the Statesman Journal Newspapers, 280 Church Street NE, P.O. Box 13009, Salem, OR 97309; phone (503) 399-6611; publisher of the morning Statesman-Journal; daily circulation 65,297, Sunday 62,161; John H. McMillan, publisher.

Population: 90,400 (city), 225,100 (metro).
Area: 32 sq. mi. on the Willamette River in the center of the bountiful Willamette Valley 50 miles south of Portland; 61 miles from Pacific Ocean; state capital, Marion County seat.
Industry: government (over 14,500 state employees), agriculture (over 100 crops), food processing — 2d in nation for fruit, berries, and vegetables; over 16 canneries produced over 10 million cases of canned goods and 260 million pounds of frozen foods; lumber and lumber products; manufacturing (batteries, radios, metal products, feeds, paints, textiles, food processing cans); pulp and paper mill.
Commerce: retail sales (1978) $710 million; med. household income (1978) $14,567; 7 commercial banks, deposits (1977) $416 million; 6 savings & loan associations, deposits (1977) $380 million.
Transportation: 2 rail freight lines, Amtrak; Greyhound, Trailways bus lines, 11 truck lines, Air Oregon.
Communications: one public TV, 6 radio stations, 2 daily newspapers, one farm weekly newspaper.
Medical facilities: hospital with 2 units, General and Memorial.
Cultural facilities: symphony orchestra, art association, little theater, Bush House museum, Deepwood, Mission Mill museum, Northwest History collection, Willamette Univ., Civic Center.
Education: metro area includes 108 public schools — 89 elementary, 12 junior highs, 20 high schools, and 15 parochial schools; State Schools for the Blind and Deaf, Chemeketa Community College, Willamette Univ., Western Baptist Bible College, and Oregon College of Education.
Recreation: back-packing, fishing, golf, snow and water skiing, camping, 44 parks in 5 mile radius; hunting for deer, elk, and fowl; Bush Pasture Park; within one hour drive Mt. Hood, Detroit Lake, Oregon Coast, Mt. Jefferson; 9 golf courses in 15 mile radius; 70 tennis courts in area.
Sports: Salem Senators baseball, Northwest League.
History: founded in 1842 by Methodist missionary, Jason Lee.
Further information: Chamber of Commerce, P.O. Box 231, Salem, OR 97308.

Salt Lake City, Utah

The World Almanac is sponsored in the Salt Lake City area by the Salt Lake Tribune, 143 S. Main Street, Salt Lake City, UT 84111; phone (801) 237-2045; founded Apr. 15, 1871; circulation, 114,629 daily, 189,311 Sunday; publisher, John W. Gallivan; executive editor, Arthur C. Deck; 1957 Pulitzer Prize; civic projects, statewide civic beautification awards; Sub for Santa program; Community Christmas Tree Plantings; Spring Garden Festival; Ski Race; No Champs Tennis and Golf tournaments, Newspaper in Education; Old Fashioned 4th of July.

Population: (1979 est.) 180,000 (city), 562,000 (county), 867,800 (metro); first in state; 77% of state pop. lives in Wasatch Front Counties of Salt Lake, Davis, Utah, and Weber; state capital and Salt Lake County seat.
Area: nestled in a vast valley (elev. 4,327 ft.) surrounded by Wasatch and Oquirrh mountains.
Industry: labor force (metro area, 1979 est.) 304,900; average unemployment rate 5%; effective buying income $3.4 billion (county, 1978); per family income (county, 1978) $17,177; total construction value (county, 1979) $521.2 million; major employers are Hill AFB (30 miles north), Univ. of Utah, Brigham Young Univ., Granite School District, Kennecott Copper Corp., local defense industries; county has over 900 manufacturing plants; metro area major center for electronics, apparel manufacturing, mining, smelting, refining, distribution, warehousing center of Mountain West; area becoming center for energy resources development operations.
Transportation: 11 air lines, customs office, free-trade zone, International Airport; 22 freight carriers maintain terminals in city; geographic center of 11 western states; hub of central transcontinental highway system; 3 railroads, all major western truck, bus lines.
Communications: 2 daily newspapers, 4 commercial TV sta-

tions, 3 cable TV, 2 public TV, Home Box Office TV; 18 radio stations.
New construction: more than 1.5 million sq. ft. of office space under construction in downtown area including Sheraton Hotel, $62 million, 170-store Crossroads Mall; $28 million, 480-room Marriott Hotel; $16.5 million expansion of Salt Palace convention, exhibit center.
Medical facilities: 10 hospitals, including Univ. of Utah Medical Center, major research in transplant surgery.
Educational facilities: Univ. of Utah; Westminster, Utah Technical, and LDS Business colleges.
Cultural facilities: Utah Symphony Orchestra, Mormon Tabernacle Choir, Ballet West, Utah Opera Co., Ririe-Woodbury Co., Repertory Dance Theatre, 2 cultural arts halls.
Other attractions: Temple Square, home of 4 million-member Church of Jesus Christ of Latter-Day Saints (Mormons); Salt Palace Civic Auditorium; 700 acres in 22 parks, 25 playgrounds, 10 golf courses, 100 tennis courts; near Great Salt Lake (7 times more salty than ocean); Hogle Zoological Gardens, Kennecott Copper's Bingham mine; 4 well-defined seasons, mean annual temperature 51.0 degrees F.
Sports: 9 major ski resorts; Golden Eagles (Central Hockey League), Salt Lake Gulls baseball; Bonneville Salt Flats, Salt Lake Stingers (International Volleyball Assn.), Univ. of Utah in major NCAA sports; Utah Jazz (NBA).
History: founded July 24, 1847 by Brigham Young and contingent of pioneers.
Further information: Chamber of Commerce, 19 E. 2d So.; Utah Travel Council, Council Hall; Salt Lake Valley Visitors and Convention Bureau, West Temple at First South, all Salt Lake City, UT.

San Antonio, Texas

The World Almanac is sponsored in the San Antonio area by the S. A. Express (morning) and S. A. News (evening), P.O. Box 2171, San Antonio, TX 78297; phone (512) 225-7411; circulation daily, Express 80,646, News 74,753, Sunday Express-News 181,598; chairman K. Rupert Murdoch, publisher and editor Charles O. Kilpatrick; Express-News Corp. is a division of News America, Inc.

Population: 860,000 city, 962,100 county, total employed 387,300.
Area: 1,247 sq. mi. (Bexar County); 2 1/2 hours from Gulf Coast and Mexican border.
Industry: 5 military bases include Kelly AFB, largest employer; fast-growing medical industry; diverse manufacturing, tourism, construction, trade, and service industries.
Commerce: center for 100 mile radius retail trade area, livestock production; retail sales (3d quarter, 1979) $2.6 billion.
Federal facilities: Kelly AFB, hq. AF Air Security Service; Randolph AFB, hq. Air Training Command & AF Personnel Center; Brooks AFB, hq. AF Aerospace Medical Division; Lackland AFB with Wilford Hall USAF Medical Center; Fort Sam Houston, hq. 5th Army, & Army Health Services Command, Brooke Army Medical Center.
Medical facilities: Univ. of Texas Medical, Dental, Nursing schools; Audie Murphy VA Hospital; Southwest Research Institute; Southwest Foundation of Res. and Educ.
Transportation: International Airport, Stinson air field, 12 major airlines; 3 rail freight, Amtrak; 6 bus lines; 44 common-carrier truck lines; 576 miles of freeway and state highways.
Educational facilities: Univ. of Texas at San Antonio; Trinity, St. Mary's, and Our Lady of the Lake universities; Incarnate Word College; 2 jr. colleges, San Antonio, St. Philip's; permanent extension of National Univ. of Mexico.
Convention facilities: Convention Center with large arena, theater, exhibit, meeting space.
Cultural facilities: symphony orchestra; Institute of Texan Cultures, Mexican Cultural Institute, Witte Museum, McNay Art Institute.
Other attractions: historic Alamo, old Spanish missions of San Jose, Concepcion, Capistrano, Espada; Hemis Fair Plaza with 750-foot observation tower-restaurant; downtown River Walk; zoo; annual events: Fiesta San Antonio, Livestock Show & Rodeo, Folklife Festival, Texas Open PGA Tournament, Avon Ladies Tennis Tournament; pro sports; Spurs (NBA); Dodgers minor league baseball, Charros minor league football.
Further information: Greater San Antonio Chamber of Commerce, 602 E. Commerce, P. O. Box 1628, San Antonio, TX 78296.

San Bernardino, California

The World Almanac is sponsored in the San Bernardino area by the Sun, 399 North D Street, San Bernardino, CA 92401; phone (714) 889-9666; Sun founded 1894; daily circulation 79,982, Sunday 87,187; member Gannett chain; publisher William Honeysett, advertising director William Ridenour, editor Wayne C. Sargent.

Population: 106,500 (city), 1,484,300 (2-county metro area).
Area: 47.22 sq. mi. at base of Cajon Pass, 58 miles east of Los Angeles; San Bernardino County seat.
Industry: business and industrial firms include Culligan, Edginton Oil, Fleetwood Enterprises, Hanford Foundry, Knudsen Dairy, Lifetime Foam, Mode O'Day, Pepsi Cola and Seven-Up bottling plants, Santa Fe Railway, TRW Systems, Monier Tile, and Terry Industries.
Commerce: trading center for 20,189 sq. mi. San Bernardino county, largest in the nation; retail sales (1979) $938 million; 7 banks, 22 branches; 12 savings and loan assns.; 2 major shopping center complexes, each parking over 5,000 cars.
Transportation: Santa Fe, Southern Pacific, and Union Pacific rail lines, Amtrak; Greyhound and Continental bus lines; major interstate highways leading from Mexico to Canada and West to East Coast; municipal airport and nearby Ontario International Airport, over 2 million passengers (1978).
Communications: 15 radio and one VHF educational TV station; access to 5 Los Angeles channels.
Medical facilities: 3 major hospitals with 995 beds; major research and training center for heart surgery and hip and knee replacement surgery.
Federal facilities: Norton Air Force Base.
Cultural facilities: symphony orchestra, Civic Light Opera, nearby Redlands Bowl (summer concerts); National Orange Show with orange festival every spring; Convention Center-Exhibit Hall complex.
Educational facilities: California State College, junior college, 3 major universities nearby.
New construction: 7 redevelopment project areas with commercial and industrial development sites.
Sports: Little League Western Regional Headquarters.
History: founded 1852 by Mormons who purchased land from Spanish grant holders.
Further information: Chamber of Commerce, 546 West 6th Street, San Bernardino, CA 92401.

San Diego, California

The World Almanac is sponsored in San Diego by The San Diego Union and The Evening Tribune (Copley Newspapers), P.O. Box 191, San Diego, CA 92112; phone (714) 299-3131; Union founded 1868 (pioneer daily of Southwest); circulation, Union (morn.) 203,839, Tribune (eve.) 130,702, Sunday Union 334,541; publisher Helen K. Copley, general manager Al De Bakcsy, Union editor Gerald L. Warren, Tribune editor Fred Kinne.

Population: 833,000 (1980 city), 1,829,600 (county); 11th in U.S. (official state estimate); total civilian employment, 663,000.
Area: (county) 4,255 sq. mi.; 70 mi. Pacific Coast, San Clemente to Mexican border.
Industry: tourism, manufacturing, military and agriculture; manufactured products earn $4.8 billion a year; non-military payroll $6.5 billion, military $1 billion; tourist spending over $923.9 million; corporations with bases or divisions include Bendix, Burroughs, Control Data, Cubic, General Dynamics, Gulf, Honeywell, International Harvester's Solar division, NCR Corp., Pacific Southwest Airlines, Rohr, Sea World, Teledyne Ryan, TraveLodge, Wickes, Van Camp sea food, Foodmaker (Jack-in-the-Box); aerospace, rapid transit design and manufacture, oceanography, nuclear energy, medicine important; also shipbuilding, tuna fishing, clothing, ocean shippping; among top 20 counties in farm products (avocados, cut flowers, eggs); Marine Corps Recruit Depot, Naval Training Center, North Island and Miramar Naval Air Stations, Naval Electronics Lab and Undersea Center, Marine Corps base at Camp Pendleton.
Transportation: freeway system is state's 2d largest; Amtrak, 11 airlines, bus lines; primary airport Lindbergh Field.
Communications: some 30 TV and radio stations.
Medical facilities: Salk Institute for Biological Studies, Scripps Clinic & Research Foundation; Naval Hospital; many hospitals.
Education and Cultural facilities: San Diego State Univ., U.S. International Univ., Univ. of San Diego, Univ. of California, San Diego (3 colleges and Scripps Institution of Oceanography), Point Loma College; symphony; Old Globe Theatre (functioning reproduction of Shakespeare's Globe Theatre); opera; ballet; Fine Arts and Timken galleries; La Jolla Museum of Contemporary Art.
Other attractions: world famous zoo and wild animal park; Balboa Park, central 1,400 acres containing museums, zoo, Fleet Space Theatre (computerized planetarium), many other attractions; Mission Bay Park includes Sea World; "Old San Diego" state historical park; "Star of India" ship-museum; visits to neighboring Mexico (Tijuana); 70 miles of beaches.
Sports: NFL Chargers; NL Padres; NBA Clippers; NASL Sockers; Holiday Bowl; Andy Williams Open golf tournament; racing at Del Mar, Caliente (Mexico).
Other attractions: climate sunny; summer and winter resort; average temp. 68° in summer, 57° in winter, rainfall mainly December to March; famous "place names" include La Jolla (part of city of San Diego); 70 golf courses including Torrey Pines; large convention facilities; off-shore "whale watching."
History: area discovered 1542 by Cabrillo, founded in 1769 by Father Junipero Serra.
Further information: San Diego Chamber of Commerce, 110 West "C", Suite 1600, San Diego, CA 92101.

San Francisco, California

The World Almanac is sponsored in the San Francisco-Oakland area by The San Francisco Examiner, P.O. Box 3100, Rincon Annex, San Francisco, CA 94119; phone (415) 777-2424; founded June 12, 1865; circulation daily Examiner, 156,083; Sunday Examiner & Chronicle, 668,550; president, R. A. Hearst; editor and publisher, Reg Murphy; major awards: Pulitzer Prize, Freedoms Foundation; Examiner sponsors Examiner Games, Golden Gloves, Bay to Breakers Race, Opera in the Park.

Population: 642,400, 3d in state, 13th in nation; total employed 530,100.
Area: 44.6 sq. mi. on the northern tip of a peninsula; San Francisco County seat.
Industry: food products, printing, publishing, fabricated metal products; west's financial capital and administrative center for many of the nation's leading corporations; West Coast operations' headquarters for a majority of the federal agencies; finance, insurance, and real estate; a major port of the Pacific Coast.
Commerce: wholesale-retail trade employment 103,100, services 137,300, manufacturing 48,600; total wholesale and retail outlets 25,725, taxable sales $4.5 billion; 40 banks with 157 branches; 25 savings and loans with 39 branches; total deposits in banks $32.4 billion.
Transportation: 40 major airlines serve the Bay Area; International Airport processed 24.1 million passengers, 765,497 tons of freight (1979); Municipal Railway (intra-city); AC-Transit and Bay Area Rapid Transit System (BART) to East Bay cities; Greyhound bus and Southern Pacific Railroad to Peninsula areas; Golden Gate Bridge District bus and ferry service to Marin County; Port of San Francisco services available: LASH, BULK, general cargo, containerization and barge service.
Communications: 2 major newspapers; 118 others serving the Bay Area; 45 radio stations, 7 TV channels received directly, one TV cable system.
Medical facilities: 24 general hospitals with over 7,406 beds, 5 specialty hospitals with over 1,935 beds; 3,033 physicians/surgeons and 772 dentists; Univ. of Cal. Medical Center, with 42 buildings, is a general teaching and research institute and is the largest kidney transplant center in the world.
Cultural facilities: San Francisco Opera, Spring Opera, Western Opera Theater, symphony, ballet, Civic Light Opera, American Conservatory Theater, Japanese Cultural Center, Chinese Cultural Center, International Film Festival; 3 museums, 29 libraries, 540 churches, and 136 theaters.
Educational facilities: 97 public elementary schools; 17 junior high, 11 high schools, and 965 special schools with a combined enrollment of 32,466; Univ. of California, San Francisco; California State Univ., Univ. of San Francisco, and City College of San Francisco.
Recreational facilities: 120 parks and many miniparks, 78 playgrounds, 6 golf courses, numerous tennis courts, 10 swimming pools, 5½ miles of ocean beach, one lake, one fishing pier, Marina small craft harbor and 3 yacht clubs.
Convention facilities: 102 hotels and motels with over 20,000 rooms.
Sports: Candlestick Park, home of the NL Giants and NFL 49ers; pro teams in all major sports.
Other attractions: zoo and 1,013-acre Golden Gate Park containing the California Academy of Sciences, De Young Museum, Japanese Tea Garden, and Arboretum; cable cars, Fisherman's Wharf, Chinatown, the Ferry Building.
History: San Francisco Bay discovered 1769 by Sgt. Jose Ortega; pueblo of Yerba Buena est. 1834, renamed San Francisco on January 3, 1847; inc. April 15, 1850.
Further information: Chamber of Commerce, 465 California Street, San Francisco, CA 94104; San Francisco Convention and Visitors Bureau, 1390 Market Street, San Francisco, CA 94102.

San Jose, California

The World Almanac is sponsored in the San Jose area by The Mercury and News, 750 Ridder Park Drive, San Jose, CA 95190; phone (408) 289-5000; Mercury founded June 20, 1851, News July 23, 1883; combined daily circulation 216,624, Sunday Mercury News 260,273; president and publisher P. Anthony Ridder, editor Larry Jinks.

Population: 610,400 (city), 1,265,200 (metro area coextensive with Santa Clara County); total employed 686,300 (metro, Mar. '80).
Area: broad alluvial 832,256-acre valley at south end of San Francisco Bay; Santa Clara County seat.
Industry: largest county in northern Cal. for manufacturing employment and total wages; called "Silicon Valley" due to high technology semiconductor and other electronics firms; IBM, Hewlett-Packard, Varian Assocs., Intel Corp., National Semiconductor, Memorex, Amdahl, Lockheed Mis-

siles & Space; diversity shown by Ford Motor Co., Spectra Physics, FMC Corp., Syntex; county a major producer of cut flowers; 50 wineries, many distributing world wide.
Commerce: leading retail trade center of northern Cal., $5.01 billion in sales; 137 shopping centers; 4th nationally in median household income among U.S. metro areas; 83% of households earn $10,000 plus annually, 73% earn $15,000 plus, 43% earn $25,000 plus (metro).
Transportation: Municipal Airport served by 11 airlines; highway system interconnected with inter-state in north-south, east-west directions; Southern Pacific and Western Pacific railroads; County transit buses link to Bay Area Rapid Transit.
Education: San Jose State, Santa Clara, and Stanford universities, plus several community colleges have total enrollments of 117,417, 47% of adult population is college educated (metro).
Cultural facilities: 100 year old Symphony, Civic Light Opera; California Actors, Actors Repertory, Dance and Children's Musical theaters; 2,700 seat Center for Performing Arts; Flint Center; First State Capital Museum; Rosicrucian Egyptian Museum, Planetarium, Art Gallery; De Saisset Gallery and Museum; Montalvo Center for the Arts; Triton Museum of Art; New Almaden Museum.
Sports: Earthquakes (soccer), Missions (minor league baseball), Diablos (pro volleyball), Rainbows (women's pro softball); 8 reservoirs with boat ramps, 2 with camping; outlet to S. F. Bay for ocean sports; Amer. and Nat. league football and baseball franchises.
Other attractions: Japanese Tea Gardens; Lick Observatory; Winchester Mystery House; Marriott's Great America.
History: founded 1777, first civil settlement in Cal.; county is one of original 27 in state; first public school in state, San Jose Granary, 1795; first state capitol, Dec. 15, 1849.
Further information: Chamber of Commerce Metro-San Jose, One Paseo de San Antonio, San Jose, CA 95113; phone (408) 998-7000.

San Juan, Puerto Rico

The World Almanac is sponsored in Puerto Rico by the San Juan Star, GPO Box 4187, San Juan, PR 00936; phone (809) 782-4200; founded Nov. 2, 1959; circulation 45,000 daily; 50,000 Sunday; president and general manager John A. Zerbe Jr.; vice president and editor Andrew T. Viglucci; major awards include 1961 Pulitzer Prize for editorial writing; APME citations 1960, 1965; staff awards include 1970 IAPA Mergenthaler Award, 1972 Overseas Press Club Award; National Spelling Bee 1975 champion.

Population: 535,000 (city), 1,200,000 (metro area), first in commonwealth.
Area: 47 sq. mi. in Caribbean, capital city.
Industry: seat of Puerto Rico's tourism industry with 19 luxury hotels and several dozen high rise condominiums. City is also the commercial and shipping hub of the island and is a major stop for cruise ships plying the Caribbean. Major industries are electronics, pharmaceuticals, and computers and computer components. Petrochemical industry represents $1.5 billion in investments. Center of island's rum industry with the Bacardi distillery on San Juan Bay, the largest in the world. More than 75 per cent of all rum sold in U.S. is Puerto Rican rum.
Transportation: San Juan International Airport handles more than 500,000 passengers monthly with 4 major U.S. airlines and 10 foreign lines; Isla Grande Airport handles small aircraft traffic.
Education: seat of the Rio Piedras campus of the Univ. of Puerto Rico, the public university system, InterAmerican Univ., College of the Sacred Heart, UPR Medical Sciences campus and UPR Law School, World Univ., and several junior and regional colleges.
Federal facilities: Ft. Buchanan army base with 9-hole golf course on grounds; Roosevelt Roads Naval Station.
Cultural facilities and events: The Casals Festival, guided for 18 years by the late Maestro Casals, is an annual June event bringing together some of the world's finest musicians; annual San Juan Carnival, last week in June; the Puerto Rico Institute of Culture is housed in a restored Dominican convent; El Morro, the Spanish-built fortress that guards the entrance to San Juan Harbor; numerous art museums in Old San Juan; the Puerto Rico Symphony Orchestra in concerts spread over the year; the capitol building and governor's mansion; Palace of Fine Arts opened in 1980.
Convention facilities: Condado Convention Center seats 5,000 for meetings, 3,000 for meals.
New construction: Old City restoration program, Ponce Art Museum; expansion of Plaza las Americas shopping center to house Sears Roebuck, Inc.; Banco de San Juan office bldg.; Carolina Plaza shopping mall 3 miles east of San Juan; expanded Condado Holiday Inn.
Sports: Hiram Bithorn Stadium, baseball, track, and outdoor events; Roberto Clemente Coliseum, basketball, boxing, and indoor events; soccer, cockfighting arenas (legal).
History: discovered by Columbus on his 2d voyage to the New World in 1493, colonized by Juan Ponce de Leon, Puerto Rico's first Spanish governor; since 1952 a commonwealth freely associated with the United States. Free market with U.S. and same currency, common citizenship.
Further information: Chamber of Commerce, 100 Tetuan Street, Old San Juan; Dept. of Tourism, Banco de Ponce Bldg., Hato Rey, PR.

Santa Ana, California

See Orange County, California

Saskatoon, Saskatchewan, Canada

The World Almanac is sponsored in northern Saskatchewan by the Saskatoon Star-Phoenix, 204 5th Avenue N., Saskatoon, Sask. S7K 2P1; phone (306) 652-9200; Daily Star and Phoenix founded in 1906 and 1902 respectively, merged in 1928 into the Star-Phoenix; circulation daily, 57,011; publisher Michael C. Sifton, executive vice president James K. Struthers.

Population: 145,000, 2d in province.
Area: 45.46 sq. mi. land, 1.5 sq. mi. water, on S. Sask. River, center of agricultural province.
Commerce: retail, wholesale, service, distribution hub for 400,000 in north central trading area; North America's potash capital; meat packing, grain handling dominant; electronics and research newest; base for billion dollar uranium mining, refining companies; retail sales (1979) $665 million.
Transportation: 2 railways, 3 airlines, air terminal, direct flight to U.K.; 3 bus lines, 55 transport firms; Yellowhead Highway, easiest access through Rockies from Prairies to Pacific.
Communications: One daily newspaper; 2 TV stations, cable, and 8 radio stations; one farm weekly, one community weekly.
Medical facilities: 3 major hospitals, 6 nursing homes; University Hospital known for kidney transplants, open-heart surgery.
Cultural facilities: 2,000-seat Centennial Auditorium, convention facilities for over 1,800; Mendel Art Gallery/Civic Conservatory; Western Development Museum houses N. America's largest display of antique cars, farm implements, and 1910 Pioneer Village; Pioneer Days, theme pavilion.
Education: Univ. of Sask. (17,500 students), famed for agriculture, space, Arctic, physics, medicine, veterinary college; Kelsey Institute for Applied Arts and Science (4,700 students); School For The Deaf.
Recreation: 2,494 acres parkland; wild animal farm; man-

made ski mountain; camping, fishing.
History: founded 1883 as temperance colony, incorporated 1906; battle sites of 1885 Riel Rebellion.
Further information: Board of Trade, Bessborough Hotel, Saskatoon, Sask. S7K 3G8.

Savannah, Georgia

The World Almanac is sponsored in the Savannah area by the Savannah News-Press, 111 West Bay Street, Savannah GA 31402; phone (912) 236-9511; publisher of the Savannah Morning News and Evening Press; combined circulation 77,020 daily, Sunday 72,556; Donald E. Harwood, general manager; Wallace M. Davis Jr., executive editor; Gene Stewart, advertising director.

Population: SMSA 227,400; Savannah-Chatham County 200,600; total SMSA civilian labor force 83,400.
Area: 50 sq. mi. on Savannah River, 18 mi. from Atlantic Ocean; Chatham County seat.
Industry: world's largest pulp-to-paper container plant owned by Union Camp Corp.; Savannah Sugar Refining Corp., nation's 3d largest seller; jet aircraft manufacturer (Gulf Stream American Aviation Corp.); tea packaging (Tetley); fertilizer materials, ship repair, titanium dioxide production (American Cyanamid).
Commerce: hub of "Coastal Empire" economic center of Ga. and 3 S. Carolina counties; the city is Georgia's gate to world trade; the Southeast's leading foreign trade port between Baltimore and New Orleans and a major container port; served by 100 steamship lines, 43 deep water terminals; retail sales (1979) $1.16 billion; 7 commercial banks, 4 savings and loan assns.
Transportation: 2 rail freight lines, Seaboard Coastline and Southern; Amtrak; Greyhound, Trailways bus lines, 74 truck lines; Delta, Eastern, Pan-American airlines; Intercoastal Waterway.
Communications: Savannah News-Press, Inc. (daily and Sunday), 3 weekly papers: The Herald, The Tribune, The Georgia Gazette; 5 TV and 14 radio stations.
New construction: Ga. Port Authority's port expansion, Hyatt Hotel on River Street, motel complex on Abercorn, shopping mall at Georgetown, Candler Hospital, Federal Bldg., shopping complexes at Dean Forest Road, Telfair Road extension, McAlpin Sq. shopping center.
Medical facilities: 6 hospitals, Medical Arts Center.
Federal facilities: U. S. Customs House, Ft. Stewart/Hunter assigned the 24th Infantry Division, 17,076 troops, 280,000 acres, 35 mi. so. of Savannah.
Cultural facilities: Savannah Art Assn., Savannah Symphony, Ballet Guild, Little Theatre, Telfair Academy of Arts and Sciences, Kennedy Fine Arts Center, SSC; Fine Arts Building, ASC; Maritime Museum, Fort Pulaski National Monument and Military Museum, civic center.
Education: Armstrong State and Savannah State colleges; units of the Univ. System of Ga.; 60 public, 3 vocational-tech, 18 parochial, 10 private, 3 business schools; Skidaway Inst. of Oceanography and Aquarium.
Recreation: 14 theaters; 6 golf courses, 33 public tennis courts; 71 squares, parks, and playgrounds; 3 sports fields, 2 recreation centers, 2 stadiums, 4 fishing piers, 12 boat ramps.
Convention facilities: 8,000 seat auditorium at civic center.
Sports: Savannah Braves, Southern League baseball; Savannah Speedway; SSC Tigers, ASC Pirates.
Annual events: St. Patrick's Day Parade, Oktober Festival, Blessing of the Fleet, Night in Olde Savannah, tour of homes, arts festival, farmer's market, Christmas Parade, garden club show.
Other attractions: museums include Savannah Science Museum, Ships of the Sea Museum, and Antique Car Museum; Fort Jackson, Fort Pulaski, Fort Screven and Tybee Museum, Fort McAllister; tours of downtown historic section; river cruises.
History: mother city of Ga.; Gen. James Oglethorpe and 120 followers settled last of 13 original colonies here; site of Revolutionary War battle, end of Gen. Sherman's Civil War "March to the Sea"; much of the old city is a national historic landmark, largest in the country.
Further information: Savannah Area Chamber of Commerce, Savannah Visitors Center, 301 W. Broad Street, Savannah, GA 31402; phone (912) 233-3069.

Seattle, Washington

The World Almanac is sponsored in the Seattle area by The Seattle Times, Fairview Avenue N. & John Street, P.O. Box 70, Seattle, WA 98111; phone (206) 464-2111; founded 1896 by Alden J. Blethen; circulation 260,762 daily, 348,678 Sunday; publisher John A. Blethen; president W.J. Pennington; senior vice president and general manager Harold G. Fuhrman.

Population: 498,000 (city), 1,526,800 (metro); first in state, 22d in nation; total employed (metro) 808,200.
Area: 91.6 sq. mi. between Puget Sound and Lake Washington; King County seat.
Industry: headquarters for Boeing, 79,000 employees, world's largest manufacturer of commercial jet aircraft; Port of Seattle has $800 million current value of properties and facilities including Seattle-Tacoma airport; nation's 4th largest containerized-shipping seaport; area has 39,424 employer units; major industries are transportation products, retail trade, shipbuilding, wood products, and food products.
Commerce: business center for western Wash. and Alaska; major import-export center for Far East; total retail sales (1979) $7.433 billion; per capita income (1979) $8,577; 41 commercial and savings banks incl. 310 branches.

Transportation: 3 transcontinental railroads, Amtrak; International Airport served by 19 scheduled airlines, 6 commuter airlines, handled 9.8 million passengers (1979); ferries serve Puget Sound, Canada, and Alaska.

Communications: 5 daily newspapers in metro area; 6 TV, 26 AM and 20 FM stations.
New construction: $346.1 million (city).

Medical facilities: 26 hospitals, including Univ. of Wash. Health Sciences Center, Northwest Kidney Center, and Fred Hutchinson Cancer Research Center.

Educational facilities: Four 4-year colleges: Univ. of Wash., Seattle Univ., Cornish Institute, and Seattle Pacific Univ.; 7 community colleges.
Federal facilities: 13th Naval Dist. Hdqts.; Pacific Marine center, National Oceanic & Atmospheric Admin.; 13th Coast Guard Dist. Hdqts.; many regional offices, 37-story federal office bldg.

Cultural facilities: symphony orchestra, opera association, art museum and 10 other museums, 6 professional theater companies.

Recreation: major boating center; salmon and trout fishing; several nearby ski areas; Mt. Rainier, North Cascades, and Olympic National parks within 2-hour drive.

Sports: IVA Smashers (volleyball); Kingdome, concrete-dome stadium, home of NFL Seahawks, AL Mariners, NBA SuperSonics and NASL Sounders.

Other attractions: $50 million Seattle Center, site of 1962 world's fair, has 14,000-seat coliseum, 3,100-seat opera house, playhouse, arena, Space Needle, and Pacific Science Center; Seattle Aquarium, Woodland Park Zoo.

History: settled 1851, named for an Indian chief who befriended the settlers; virtually destroyed by fire in 1889, quickly rebuilt; Alaska Gold Rush of 1897 spurred growth and propelled Seattle toward its status as the Northwest's principal city.

Further information: Chamber of Commerce, 215 Columbia Street, Seattle, WA 98104, or Convention and Visitors Bureau, 1815 7th Avenue, 98101.

Sioux Falls, South Dakota

The World Almanac is sponsored in the Sioux Falls area by the Argus Leader, 200 S. Minnesota Avenue, Sioux Falls, SD 57102; phone (605) 331-2200, a Gannett newspaper; founded in 1885; circulation 45,322 daily (A.M.), 54,952 Sunday; publisher and president Larry Fuller.

Population: 85,000 (city), 115,000 (metro); largest in state.
Area: 36 sq. mi. in southeastern South Dakota, located at junction of interstates 29 and 90; Minnehaha County seat.
Industry and Commerce: Sioux Falls stockyards are 3d largest in the U.S.; John Morrell & Co. is the largest employer with 2,845 employees; there are 24 banks, 5 savings and loan assns.; wholesale and retail center for South Dakota, parts of Minnesota and Iowa; yearly retail sales over $6.08 million.
Transportation: served by 5 major highways, 4 bus lines, and 3 rail lines; Joe Foss Field with modern terminal is within 2 miles of business district and has 3 major airlines.
Communication: daily and weekly newspaper, 3 TV and 12 radio stations; state headquarters for Northwestern Bell Telephone Co.
Medical facilities: 4 hospitals with over 1,040 beds, including the Royal C. Johnson Memorial Hospital for war veterans and Crippled Children's Hospital and School.
Federal facilities: Earth Resources Observation Systems Data Center of the U.S. Dept. of Interior.
Cultural and Educational facilities: public library, convention center, Civic Fine Arts Assn., Sioux Falls Symphony, Community Playhouse, Augustana College, Sioux Falls College, North American Baptist Seminary, the SD School for the Deaf, vocational school, 2 business schools, 2 nurses training schools, 28 public and 9 parochial schools; 96 churches.
Recreation: 52 parks, 4 swimming pools, 3 municipal golf courses, Great Plains Zoo, 10,000-seat Arena, 4,000-seat Coliseum, Packer Stadium.
Further information: Chamber of Commerce, 127 E. 10th Street, Sioux Falls, SD 57101.

Spokane, Washington

The World Almanac is sponsored in the Spokane area by the Spokane Daily Chronicle, P.O. Box 2168, Spokane, WA 99210; phone (509) 455-7121; founded 1881; circulation 63,500 daily; published by Cowles Pub. Co., William H. Cowles 3d president; John E. Smithmeyer general manager; Gordon Coe managing editor.

Population: 179,200 (city), 328,100 (county); 2d in state; total employed 139,500.
Area: 52.12 sq. mi. centrally located in eastern Washington 18 miles from the Idaho border; Spokane County seat.
Industry: heavily based on service industries and wholesale and retail trade with 462 manufacturing establishments, 2,544 retail, 717 wholesale, and 2,563 establishments dealing with services; annual payrolls in Spokane County $1.096 billion; effective buying income (1979) for Spokane County $2.5 billion; Kaiser Aluminum and Chemical Corp. has 2 plants, a reduction plant and a rolling mill; area industries include forest products, silver, lead, zinc, and other mining; agriculture, poultry, dairy and meat products, flour and cereals, livestock, processed foods, commercial truck trailer bodies, electrical fixtures, electronic keyboard manufacturing, and plastic products.
Commerce: retail, transportation, and medical center of an 80,000 sq. mi. inland market in eastern Washington, northern Idaho, and western Montana, known as the Inland Empire with a population of more than 1.3 million; retail sales in the Inland Empire $5.3 billion, metro area $1.3 billion; 12 commercial banks, 3 mutual savings banks, and 5 savings and loan assns.
Transportation: 2 transcontinental railroads, Amtrak; International Airport served by 4 major airlines and one commuter airline; 25 motor freight lines.
Communications: 2 daily newspapers; 3 commercial, one public, one cable TV; 12 AM, 6 FM radio stations.
Convention facilities: Riverpark Center, legacy of Expo '74, 2,700 seat opera house and 40,000 sq. ft. convention center; Spokane Coliseum capacity 8,000 with 45,000 sq. ft. exhibit space; hotels and motels have 3,000 guest rooms.
Medical facilities: 6 major hospitals, 7 specialized hospitals, and Fairchild AFB hospital.
Education facilities: one college, 2 universities, and 2 community colleges.
Federal facilities: Fairchild AFB, federal office bldg.
Cultural facilities: symphony orchestra, opera house, 2 museums, civic theater, arboretum, zoo, northwest Indian center; community concerts, music and allied arts festival.
Recreation: 76 lakes within a 50 mile radius of the city; 12 indoor and 7 outdoor theaters; 11 city swimming pools, 55 public tennis courts, 12 golf courses, 94 public parks; 12 national parks and 15 national forests within a day's drive; 2 snow ski resorts within 1½ hours drive; power and sail boating, hunting, and fishing.
Sports: Spokane Indians, farm club for Seattle Mariners; 35,000 seat Albi football stadium; Playfair horse race track; 8,000 seat Spokane Coliseum for basketball, hockey, and boxing; Spokane Flyers hockey.
Other attractions: city-center Riverfront Park, site of Expo '74 World's Fair, includes IMAX theater, ice rink, children's zoo, gondola ride over river falls, antique carousel, train ride, outdoor amphitheaters, popcorn wagons, and restaurant; average annual rainfall 17.19 inches.
History: Lewis and Clark expedition of 1804-06 passed through area; first permanent settlers in 1871 attracted to river and falls where they built a house and a sawmill; 2 sq. mi. city of 1,000 people inc. 1881 as Spokane Falls; after Washington gained statehood in 1890, city name changed to Spokane.
Further information: Spokane Area Chamber of Commerce, P.O. Box 2147, Spokane, WA 99210.

Springfield, Illinois

The World Almanac is sponsored in the Springfield area by the State Journal-Register (morning and evening), oldest newspaper in Illinois, 313 S. Sixth Street, P.O. Box 219, Springfield, IL 62705; phone (217) 788-8600; circulation 71,788; John P. Clarke publisher, Edward H. Armstrong editor, Patrick Coburn managing editor.

Population: 99,000 (city), 187,100 (metro), 4th in state; total employed (annual average) 89,774.
Area: 46.54 sq. mi. on Sangamon River in center of state; state capital and Sangamon County seat.
Commerce: state and federal offices; 11 banks, 10 savings and loan assns., 10 insurance co. home offices; 145 national, regional, and state assns.; 29 civic clubs, 68 social service organizations, 41 women's organizations; annual retail sales $760 million.
Transportation: 6 railroads, 54 truck carriers, one airport; nearby barge facilities.
Communications: 2 TV, 7 radio stations.
Medical facilities: 3 hospitals with 1,400 beds; 295 doctors, 110 dentists, 19 chiropractors; 36 clinics, 29 licensed nursing homes, the Springfield Regional Trauma Center.
Cultural facilities: municipal band, opera, symphony, chorus; Theatre Guild, state museum, Lincoln historical sites, New Salem State Park, Old State Capitol; art associations, summer theater, Springfield Ballet Co., Illinois Country Opry; Clayville renovated stagecoach stop, arts and

crafts festivals, Oliver Parks Telephone Museum, Lincoln Library, Lincoln Memorial Garden, Nelson Recreation Center, Henson Robinson Children's Zoo, civic convention center.
Education: Sangamon State Univ., Lincoln Land Community College, Springfield College in Ill., Southern Illinois Univ. School of Medicine, new Capital Area Vocational School.
Recreation: 40 parks; swimming, boating, water skiing on Lake Springfield; 4 public golf courses, tennis courts; 2,410 acres in parks.
Special events: Illinois State Fair, Old Capitol Art Fair, International Carillon Festival, Midwest Charity Horse Show, LPGA Rail Golf Classic, Springfield Redbirds baseball; Ethnic Festival, Autumnfest, Photo Fair, Old Capitol Sound and Light Show.
Further information: Greater Springfield Chamber of Commerce, 3 Old State Capitol Plaza, Springfield, IL.

Springfield, Massachusetts

The World Almanac is sponsored in the Springfield area by The Morning Union, the evening Daily News and The Sunday Republican, 1860 Main Street, Springfield, MA 01101, phone (413) 788-1000; Union founded 1864, Daily News 1880, Republican 1824; circulation Union 73,684, Daily News 76,706, Republican 143,782; publisher David Starr, Union-Republican editor Arnold S. Friedman, Daily News editor Richard C. Garvey.

Population: 168,785 (city), 536,898 (metro); 2d in state, 4th in New England; 76,081 employed in city.
Area: 33.1 sq. mi. in SW part of state; I-91 and I-90 cross near city; Hampden County seat.
Industry: 231 manufacturing plants produce boxes, children's games, wallets, handguns, plastics, envelopes, hair shampoo, chemicals, paper; among major employers: Monsanto, Milton Bradley, Smith & Wesson, Breck.
Commerce: metro retail sales $1.88 billion; avg. household spendable income $14,703; Mass. Mutual Life Ins. Co. is 10th largest in U.S.; Baystate West, a combined highrise shopping mall, office-hotel complex.
Transportation: Amtrak, 2 rail lines, 5 bus lines, Bradley International Airport (Hartford-Springfield) 18 miles south; major truck depot.
Communications: 3 TV, 9 radio stations.
Medical facilities: 6 major hospital complexes.
Educational facilities: 21 accredited colleges and universities include Amherst, American International, Hampshire, Mount Holyoke, Univ. of Massachusetts, Our Lady of the Elms, Smith, Springfield, Western New England (and Law School), Williams, Westfield State, North Adams State, Holyoke and Greenfield community colleges, Springfield Technical Community College.
Cultural facilities: State West Theater, Civic Center and Symphony Hall, quadrangle complex; 2 museums of art, library, natural history museum including planetarium; 145 churches and 7 synagogues; 155 parks; Eastern States Exposition, Tanglewood Music Festival.
Sports: Indians (AHL) hockey; Holyoke Millers baseball; Basketball Hall of Fame; Tip-Off Tourney opens college basketball season in U.S.
History: founded 1636 by William Pynchon; first U.S. musket developed at city's armory (now a U.S. landmark) 1795; Springfield rifle developed in 1903 and produced here (as was the Garand M-1 rifle.)
Further information: Chamber of Commerce, 1500 Main Street, Springfield, MA 01103.

Stockton, California

The World Almanac is sponsored in the San Joaquin County area by the Stockton Record (eves. and Saturday and Sunday mornings), 530 E. Market Street, Stockton, CA 95202; phone (209) 466-2652; founded in 1895; circulation 56,488 daily, 57,387 Sunday; president and publisher Robert P. Uecker, executive editor Philip Bookman, managing editor James S. Hushaw.

Population: 137,700 city, est. 185,000 metropolitan area, 325,100 county; total county employment 135,300 to 157,100 in 1979.
Area: 1,440 sq. mi. county, 35.13 sq. mi. city; located 80 mi. east of San Francisco; San Joaquin County seat.
Industry: agriculture, $684 million countywide in 1979; food processing, light manufacturing, Port of Stockton, Sharpe Army Depot, Rough and Ready Island Naval Station.
Commerce: $894 million taxable retail sales city, $1.8 billion county wide in 1979.
New construction: $186 million (city) in 1979
Medical facilities: San Joaquin General Hospital, Dameron, St. Joseph's, Oak Park Community, Stockton State (for mental and physically disabled).
Cultural facilities: 110 churches, Univ. of the Pacific (private), Delta College (2-year public), Humphreys College (private); Pioneer Museum and Haggin Galleries, city/county library, Stockton Civic Theater, Stockton Symphony, ballet troupe, 3 dinner theaters, Stockton Civic Auditorium.
Recreation: city-operated programs include softball leagues, soccer, 3 public golf courses, several private clubs offering golf, tennis, swimming, racquetball, boating facilities; access to 1,000 miles of San Joaquin-Sacramento River Delta waterways.
Convention facilities: Stockton Civic Auditorium, new Hilton Hotel.
History: founded 1844 by Capt. Charles M. Weber and inc. 1850; San Joaquin County established 1850; city was major transshipment point between San Francisco and the Central Sierra mines during Gold Rush era; most early commerce and industry centered around servicing mining activities; city later became the hub of a thriving agricultural community in the northern San Joaquin Valley and Delta areas.
Further information: Greater Stockton Chamber of Commerce, 1105 N. El Dorado Street, Stockton, CA 95202; phone (209) 466-7066.

Syracuse, New York

The World Almanac is sponsored in the Syracuse area by the Herald-Journal, Clinton Square, P.O. Box 4915, Syracuse, NY, 13221; phone (315) 473-7700; founded Jan. 15, 1877, by Arthur Jenkins; circulation 115,573 daily, 231,819 Sunday Herald-American Post Standard; publisher Stephen Rogers, editor William D. Cotter; sponsors Christmas toy fund.

Population: 197,297 (city), 636,507 (metro), 5th in state; 279,600 employed.
Area: 25.82 sq. mi. near center of state; interstate routes 90 and 81 intersect at Syracuse.
Industry: some 500 manufacturing plants produce electrical and non-electrical machinery, primary metals, food, transportation equipment, chemicals, pharmaceuticals, paper, candles, china; Schlitz brewery, world's largest ever built at one time, located in suburban Lysander; major Miller brewery north of city, sold to Anheuser-Busch in 1980; major employers: General Electric, Carrier Corp., Crucible Steel, Crouse-Hinds, Allied Chemical.
Commerce: retail sales (1980 est.) $2.3 billion; average household spendable income (1980 est.) $21,000.
Transportation: 2 rail freight lines, Amtrak; 3 bus lines, 160 truck lines; 5 airlines.
Communications: 4 TV, 15 radio stations.
Medical facilities: 4 major hospital complexes.
Cultural facilities: Syracuse Univ., State Univ. College of Environmental Science and Forestry, and Le Moyne, Maria

Regina, and Onondaga Community colleges; Everson Museum of Art; symphony; $22 million county center.
Sports: Syracuse Univ. football; Chiefs (baseball).
History: first explored 1615 by French; salt deposits led to area development, known as "Salt City;" "crossroads" since Indian days; became city 1847.
Further information: Chamber of Commerce, One MONY Plaza, Syracuse, NY 13202.

Tallahassee, Florida

The World Almanac is sponsored in the north Florida-south Georgia Panhandle area by The Tallahassee Democrat, 227 N. Magnolia Drive, Tallahassee, FL 32302; phone (904) 599-2100; founded 1905; circulation 46,485 (morn), 53,390 Sunday; member Knight-Ridder Newspapers, Inc., W. H. Harwell Jr. president and publisher; Walker Lundy, vice president and executive editor.

Population: 87,900 (city) 146,700 (metro); total employment 72,300.
Area: 26.14 sq. mi. between Gulf of Mexico and Georgia line; state capital and Leon County seat.
Commerce: 44% of economic base is state and local government; small manufacturers; agriculture only 1.1% of economic base; retail-wholesale center serving 17 county area; 5 shopping malls and 20 shopping centers; retail sales (1979) $634 million; effective buying income per household is $21,017, 3d highest in state; 16 commercial banks (resources, $433 million) and 5 savings & loan (resources $318 million).
Transportation: 3 major airlines, 2 commuter flight services, one railroad, 5 motor carriers.
Communications: 11 radio, 10 TV stations by cable.
Medical facilities: regional hospital, retardation hospital, university hospital, outpatient emergency hospital.
Recreational facilities: 6 recreation centers, 11 playgrounds, 51 ball fields, 31 tennis courts; salt water fishing in Gulf of Mexico, bass fishing in Lake Jackson; deer, dove, quail, duck, geese hunting; 4 golf courses, PGA Tallahassee Open Invitational.
Other attractions: civic center; college athletic events at Florida State Univ., and Florida A&M; symphony, ballet, repertory theater, opera, touring plays, and art exhibits; 1845 historic capitol and 22-story capitol tower; Apalachicola National Forest; Junior Museum; Wakulla Springs, Maclay Gardens State Park, LeMoyne Art Gallery, Natural Bridge State Historic Memorial, Florida State Univ. "Flying High" Circus.
History: established as state capital 1823; Tallahassee means "old town" or "deserted fields" in Creek; area prospered with large plantations and antebellum mansions, many still standing.
Further information: Chamber of Commerce, P.O. Box 1639, Tallahassee, FL 32302; phone (904) 224-8116.

Tampa, Florida

The World Almanac is sponsored in the Tampa Bay area by The Tampa Tribune and The Tampa Times, 202 S. Parker Street, Tampa, FL 33606; phone (813) 272-7711; Times founded 1893, Tribune 1894; combined circulation 210,924. D.T. Bryan, chairman of the board; A.S. Donnahoe, president; R.F. Pittman Jr., publisher; J.F. Urbanski, vice president/general manager; J. Clendinen, chairman of editorial board; P. Hogan, Tribune managing editor; B. Witwer, Times managing editor.

Population: 295,400 (city), 601,200 (county); total employed in county 267,500 (civilian, non-agricultural employment).
Area: 84.45 sq. mi. (city), 1,062.0 sq. mi. (county) on Gulf of Mexico, halfway between the northern edge and southern tip of Florida; Hillsborough County seat.
Industry: Port of Tampa is the closest U.S. deepwater port to the Panama Canal and the 7th largest in the nation; total tonnage for 1979 reached 49.8 million; principal export cargo, phosphate; Bone Valley Formation, 30% of world's phosphate production; cigar manufacturing, Cuesta-Rey, Fuenta Arturo, Hav-A-Tampa, Standard; strong shrimp industry, Singleton; beer breweries, Anheuser-Busch and Joseph Schlitz; Florida Steel Corp.; other industries include Jim Walter Corp., General Telephone, Florida Mining & Materials, and Lykes Bros.
Commerce: retail sales for the county (1978) $2.5 billion; 34 banks with total deposits (1979) of $2.4 billion; 10 savings and loans (1979) $1.2 billion.
Transportation: 25 freight lines; Amtrak; Seaboard Coast Line Railroad Co.; 5 bus lines, Greyhound, Trailways; city-owned bus system expanding into county; 46 trucking lines; junction of I-75 and I-4; Tampa International Airport, 7 million passengers in 1978, 14 major airlines and direct flights to Europe; Port of Tampa.
Communications: 7 TV and 27 radio stations, 2 daily newspapers.
Convention facilities: Curtis Hixon Hall, 8,000 capacity Main Hall, plus 10 other rooms; Tampa hotels and motels have over 10,000 guest rooms and over 125 meeting/banquet rooms with seating from 25 to 1,000.
New construction: Tampa City Center ($93 million), Westbank ($65 million), Metropolitan Tower ($25 million), Teco ($25 million), Paragon Plaza ($25 million), Saturn Condominium Project ($22 million), Seddon Island Development ($500 million); airport expansions ($51 million), harbor dredging ($150 million), Busch Gardens expansions and hotel ($59 million), Univ. of South Florida mass seating complex and business administration bldg. ($14 million); Marriot Hotel ($15 million), Austin Center ($15 million), Paragon Center ($10 million), Tampa Port construction projects ($43 million), extension of Crosstown Expressway.
Medical facilities: 6 major hospitals.
Federal facilities: MacDill AFB, Federal Bldg.
Cultural facilities: Florida Gulf Coast Symphony, The Tampa Museum, Tampa Theatre, Tampa Ballet Co.; $2.4 million library; Hillsborough County Museum of Science & Industry, community theater and theater companies, Gasparilla Art Fair.
Education: Univ. of S. Fla., Univ. of Tampa, Florida College, and Hillsborough Comm. College.
Other attractions: Busch Gardens (#2 attraction in attendance in Fla.), Lowry Park Zoo, Ybor City (Latin Quarter); 62 parks, 31 recreation areas, annual Gasparilla Pirate Invasion; site for Florida State Fair.
Sports: NFL Tampa Bay Buccaneers with 71,500 seat stadium; NASL (Soccer) Tampa Bay Rowdies, Tampa Tarpons (farm team for Cincinnati Reds), Cincinnati Reds spring training site; greyhound racing, jai-alai.
History: Fort Brooke est. 1824 on site of present Tampa; inc. 1885.
Further information: Greater Tampa Chamber of Commerce, 801 E. Kennedy Boulevard, Tampa, FL 33602; phone (813) 228-7777.

Toledo, Ohio

The World Almanac is sponsored in the Toledo area by The Blade, 541 Superior Street, Toledo, OH 43660; phone (419) 259-6000; founded 1835; circulation, 170,068 daily, 208,311 Sunday; publishers Paul Block Jr. and William Block; associate publisher John D. Willey; editor Bernard Judy; executive editor Robert Hartley; executive news editor Joseph O'Conor; managing editor William Rosenberg.

Population: 363,600 (city), 788,300 (metro), 5th in state; total employed 301,500.

Area: 85.3 sq. mi. at juncture of Maumee River and Lake Erie, in northwestern Ohio; Lucas County seat.
Industry: glass, headquarters for Owens-Illinois, Owens Corning & Libbey-Owens-Ford; automotive parts, largest producer in nation, home of American Motors Jeep, Toledo Scale, and Schindler Haughton Elevator; largest petroleum refining center between Chicago and the East Coast.
Commerce: Port of Toledo is one of the prime bulk shipping ports on the Great Lakes, handling vast quantities of grain, coal, iron ore, and petroleum products; ranks 3d on Great Lakes and 25th in U.S.; total retail sales $3.11 billion; spendable income per household $21,099.
Transportation: 7 railroads, 6 major airlines, 120 motor freight lines, 2 interstate bus lines; 13 major highways converge here, permitting the rapid flow of goods to almost 60% of the nation's consumers.
New construction: $94 million Owens-Illinois world headquarters, $10 million Toledo Trust Co. office bldg.
Communications: 4 TV, 13 radio stations and one cablevision company.
Medical facilities: 10 major hospital complexes, including the Medical College of Ohio Hospital.
Cultural facilities: Museum of Art with largest display of antique glass in the world; Peristyle used for the performing arts; symphony, opera company.
Education: Univ. of Toledo and its Community and Technical College; Michael J. Owens Technical College; Bowling Green State Univ.; Monroe Community College.
Other attractions: Municipal Zoo among top 10 in the nation; modern 2,500 seat Masonic Auditorium, Great Hall.
Sports: Mud Hens, farm club of the Minnesota Twins, at the Lucas County Recreation Center.
History: founded in 1837; took its name from sister city, Toledo, Spain.
Further information: Convention and Vistors Bureau, 218 Huron, Toledo, OH 43604.

Toronto, Ontario, Canada

The World Almanac is sponsored in the metropolitan Toronto area by The Toronto Star, One Yonge Street, Toronto, Ontario, M5E 1E6; phone (416) 367-2000; established 1892, Joseph E. Atkinson, publisher, 1899-1948; circulation daily 484,764, Saturday 780,677, Sunday 341,175; chairman and publisher Beland H. Honderich; president Martin Goodman; editor-in-chief Denis Harvey. Canada's largest newspaper in circulation, display, and classified advertising lineage; winner of 40 national newspaper awards and sponsor of the Santa Claus Fund and Fresh Air Fund.

Population: 595,291 (city), 2,131,159 (metro); largest city in Canada, 15th in North America; labor force 1.6 million.
Area: 241 sq. mi. on northwest shore of Lake Ontario; provincial capital.
Industry: Canada's leading commercial and industrial center; 6,050 manufacturing establishments; value of 1979 factory shipments $23.7 billion; principal industries: slaughtering and meat packing, clothing, printing and publishing, machinery, electrical goods, furniture, food products, rubber goods, sheet metal products.
Commerce: retail sales (1979) $9.8 billion; headquarters for Eaton's and Simpson's, Canada's largest department stores; head offices of 10 trust companies and 3 of 9 federally chartered banks; Toronto Stock Exchange, 3d in North America, traded shares worth $18.7 billion in 1979; per capita disposable income $8,777.
Transportation: 10 railway lines carry 350 freight and passenger trains daily; 12,000 trucks use 12 major highways; Transit Commission carries 346 million passengers annually on 722 miles of routes including 32 miles of subway; 2.5 million tons of cargo from 26 nations unloaded (1979) at this major Great Lakes port; 46 airlines handle 13.5 million passengers annually at International Airport.
Communications: 6 TV stations including educational and French-language channels; 10 AM and 8 FM radio stations; 3 daily newspapers, 42 foreign language newspapers.
New construction: value of building permits (1979) $983.5 million; $50-million expansion-renovation of Royal Ontario Museum; $70-million Bell Canada headquarters; $80-million downtown housing-commercial development will include 2,700-seat concert hall.
Medical facilities: 40 active-treatment hospitals including renowned Hospital for Sick Children; special treatment centers: Clark Institute for Psychiatry, Addiction Research Centre, Ontario Crippled Children's Centre, Ontario Centre for the Deaf (opened 1979).
Cultural facilities: 37 alternate and cabaret theater groups, including Canada's largest children's theater; National Ballet of Canada and Canadian Opera Company perform in 3,200-seat O'Keefe Centre; symphony orchestra and Mendelssohn Choir at Massey Hall; touring shows at Royal Alexandra Theatre; 82 public libraries, Henry Moore collection of sculptures and drawings in Art Gallery of Ontario.
Education: 2 universities, York and Toronto, Canada's largest (1979-80 enrollment: 48,900); Ryerson Polytechnical Institute, 4 colleges of applied arts and technology, 2 teachers' colleges, Royal Conservatory of Music, Ontario College of Art, Osgoode Hall Law School.
Recreation: Canadian National Exhibition, world's biggest annual fair; Ontario Place, 100 acres of offshore islands with restaurants, marina, and 1,000-seat Cinesphere for film showings; Toronto Islands have 3 yacht clubs, 560 acres of beaches and picnic grounds; Harborfront, 86-acre sports, arts, and entertainment park.
Convention facilities: Canada's top convention center; 249,750 visitors attended 490 conventions in 1979 and spent $75 million; total rooms 19,000.
Sports: 9 public golf courses; thoroughbred and harness racing; NHL Maple Leafs play in 16,435-seat Gardens; Blue Jays AL baseball, Argonauts CFL football, and Blizzard NASL soccer play in 54,000-seat Exhibition Stadium.
Other attractions: Ontario Science Centre, designed for participation and involvement; Black Creek Pioneer Village, living displays of Upper Canada; McMichael Conservation collection of paintings by Canada's famed Group of Seven; Metro Zoo has 500 species roaming 5 continental areas covering 700 acres; CN Tower, world's tallest free-standing structure; Eaton Centre downtown galleria contains 300 shops.
History: town of York founded 1793 on site of French fort as capital of British Colony of Upper Canada; incorporated as city 1834 and named Toronto from Indian word for meeting place.
Further information: Convention and Tourist Bureau, Toronto Eaton Centre, Toronto, Ontario M5B 2H1.

Tucson, Arizona

The World Almanac is sponsored in the Tucson area by The Arizona Daily Star, 4850 S. Park Avenue, PO Box 26807, Tucson, AZ 85726; phone (602) 294-4433; founded 1877 as a weekly; Michael E. Pulitzer, editor and publisher; William J. Woestendiek, executive editor; Frank E. Johnson, managing editor; Stephen E. Auslander, editorial page editor; Frank Delehanty, business manager; Sandra K. Hall, director, special services; Star sponsors Sportsmen's Fund for less-chance youngsters.

Population: 539,800 (1980 est.) in Pima County, 311,400 within city limits; 188,500 employed in county out of total civilian labor force of 198,700 (est.); data from Arizona Dept. of Economic Security.
Area: Sonoran Desert of southern Arizona, elev. 2,500 ft.; Santa Catalina Mts. immediately N and E reach 9,000 ft.; Pima County seat; 60 miles from Mexico.
Industry: Hughes Aircraft, IBM, Gates Learjet, Davis Monthan AFB, aircraft reclamation plants handling surplus craft from DM AFB; electronics, light manufacturing, tourism;

center of the "copper circle"—Anaconda, Duval, American Smelting and Refining, Kennecott, Magma, Pima, and other mining operations.
Transportation: International Airport with Cochise Airlines within Arizona, and AeroMexico and Hughes Airwest to and from Mexico; 3 smaller airports; 2 national, one local bus line; Southern Pacific Railroad; trucks.
Communications: 2 newspapers; 5 TV and 18 radio stations.
Medical facilities: 11 hospitals including Arizona Medical Center which has teaching hospital.
Climate: dry, mild; freezing temperatures are rare in winter; summer brings some rain and temperature of about 100 degrees F.
Culture: Univ. of Arizona, Pima Community College; Tucson Museum of Art, Tucson Symphony, Arizona Theater Co., Tucson Metropolitan Ballet; many musical, drama, and dance groups, dinner theaters; Ariz. Opera Co., Southern Arizona Light Opera Company, Tucson Boys Chorus; Los Changuitos Feos mariachi group provide local flavor, plus many ethnic groups.
Convention facilities: convention center accommodates 10,000 theater-style in arena, sit-down functions 5,000, meeting-rooms 1,000 theater-style, music hall 2,300; contiguous exhibit space 64,000 sq. ft. adjacent to hotel.
Sports: Toros, Pacific Coast League farm team of Houston Astros; Cleveland Indians spring training site; Tucson Open golf tournament; Tucson Sky, Internat. Volleyball League; various pro tennis tournaments; UA is a member of PAC 10 athletic conference.
Other attractions: Kitt Peak National Observatory is 60 miles from Tucson; UA Flandrau Planetarium, many other astronomical observatories; a nationally famous rodeo in Feb.
History: Presidio of Tucson est. 1775; Mission San Xavier del Bac founded nearby by Rev. Eusebio Francisco Kino SJ, who first visited area in 1692.
Further information: Tucson Metrop. Chamber of Commerce, PO Box 991, Tucson, AZ 85702; Tucson Convention and Visitors Bureau, 120 W. Broadway, PO Box 27210, Tucson, AZ 85726.

Tulsa, Oklahoma

The World Almanac is sponsored in the Tulsa area by The Tulsa Tribune, 318 S. Main, Tulsa, OK 74102; phone (918) 582-1101; founded in 1904 as The Tulsa Democrat (renamed the Tulsa Tribune in 1920); circulation 77,172; editor Jenkin Lloyd Jones, managing editor Gordon Fallis, executive editor Jenkin Lloyd Jones Jr.

Population: 366,300 (city), 635,800 (metro); 300,900 employed.
Area: 185.405 sq. mi. on Arkansas River at 96th meridian in Tulsa, Osage, and Rogers counties.
Industry: (1979) manufacturing, which includes aerospace, metal fabrication, and oil, provides jobs for 21% of the SMSA work force; 59,700 mfg. employees, including 41,000 production workers, total payroll $879 million; of these totals 42,536 worked in the city, earning $626 million; retail trade employs 17% SMSA workers, and the service industry employs 20%; top employers are American Airlines, Cities Service, Sun Oil, McDonnell Douglas, Rockwell International, The Williams Companies, and C-E Natco.
Commerce: retail sales (1979) $2.101 million; 27 banks, 5 savings and loan assns.; per capita income $9,373.
Transportation: (1979) Tulsa Port of Catoosa, nation's most inland port, head of Arkansas Verdigris navigation channel, barge tonnage, (1979) 1.5 million tons; 4 rail freight lines, 3 bus lines, 38 truck lines; 9 airlines with 2,121,174 passenger movements.
Communications: 2 daily newspapers, 4 TV, 14 radio stations.
New construction: (1979) building permits valued at $290 million.
Medical facilities: 5 hospitals, Osteopathic College, Univ. of Oklahoma medical school branch.
Federal facilities: District Corps of Engineers, hq. Southwestern Power Adm.
Cultural facilities: Univ. of Tulsa, Oral Roberts Univ., Tulsa junior college; Philharmonic, opera, civic ballet, 5 art museums, including Philbrook Art Center, Thomas Gilcrease Institute of American History and Art, World Museum Art Center, Rebecca and Gershon Fenster Gallery of Jewish Art, the Alexandre Hogue Gallery; American Theater Co.
Convention facilities: 402 conventions in 1979 with 222,469 attending.
Sports: Tulsa Roughnecks pro soccer; Tulsa Ice Oilers, pro hockey in the Central Hockey League; Tulsa team rodeo; Tulsa Drillers, farm team for Texas Rangers; intercollegiate athletics; 4 public and 7 country club golf courses.
Further information: Metropolitan Tulsa Chamber of Commerce, 616 S. Boston Avenue, Tulsa, OK 74119.

Vancouver, British Columbia, Canada

The World Almanac is sponsored in the Vancouver area by The Vancouver Sun, 2250 Granville Street, Vancouver, B.C., V6H 3G2; phone (604) 732-2111; founded 1886; circulation 140,000; publisher Clark Davey, director of marketing Michael J.B. Alexandor; sponsors world's largest free Salmon Derby, Sun Family Pops Concerts, Sun Tournament of Soccer Champions, and many other community services.

Population: 410,188 (city), 1,805,242 (metro area); first in province, 3d in Canada.
Area: 44 sq. mi. on the Pacific coast at the mouth of the north arm of the Fraser River; scenic beauty of the city accented by the towering, snowcapped Coast Mountains to the north and rich greenery of agricultural land to the east and south.
Industry: 98 miles of waterfront, stretching up Burrard Inlet, the largest cargo port on the Pacific and Canada's 2d busiest, with 45 million tons handled in 1979; major cargos: grain, lumber, coal, mineral ore, chemicals, and manufactured goods; tourism a major industry with an estimated 7.5 million visitors bringing in $825 million in 1979.
Commerce: retail sales $4.6 billion in 1979; value of shares traded on the Vancouver exchange $1.46 billion in 1979.
Transportation: western terminus of Canada's 2 national railways, Canadian National Railway and Canadian Pacific; headquarters of provincially operated British Columbia Railway, which is linked to the U.S. by Amtrak along the Burlington Northern Railway right-of-way; 3 major long-distance bus carriers, Provincial Stage Lines, Trailways, and Greyhound; International Airport served by 8 major airlines handled more than 6.7 million passengers in 1979.
Communications: 12 AM, 7 FM radio stations; 4 local TV stations; also U.S. network TV outlets.
Medical facilities: General and St. Paul's are largest hospitals; also Shaughnessy in Vancouver, Royal Columbian in New Westminster, Burnaby General, Lion's Gate in North Vancouver, and Riverview Psychiatric Hospital.
Cultural facilities: symphony orchestra, opera assn., several professional theater groups, Centennial and Maritime Museums and Art Gallery; Queen Elizabeth Theatre and The Orpheum are the major art facilities.
Other attractions: Pacific National Exhibition, Gastown, Chinatown, the H.R. MacMillan Planetarium, Bloedel Conservatory, Granville Island Public Market, aquarium; 1,000-acre Stanley Park, zoo, Capilano Suspension Bridge, VanDusen Botanical Garden, Park & Tilford Garden, Lynn Canyon Ecology Centre, Heritage Village; 18 golf courses, Grouse Mountain, Cypress Bowl, and Mount Seymour ski areas; Univ. of British Columbia, Simon Fraser Univ.; 18 beaches, fresh and salt water fishing.
Sports: B.C. Lions (CFL football); Canucks (NHL hockey); Whitecaps (NASL soccer); Vancouver Canadians (PCL baseball); Exhibition Park racetrack (thoroughbreds); Clo-

verdale Raceway (harness racing), and several amateur teams and sports activities.
History: discovered by Spaniards, first mapped 1791; taken possession by Capt. George Vancouver for British 1792; Hudson's Bay Co. post established early 1800s; city incorporated 1886.
Further information: Chamber of Commerce, 1177 West Hastings, Vancouver, B.C.

Washington, District of Columbia

The World Almanac is sponsored in the Washington, D.C., area by the Washington Star (a subsidiary of Time Inc.), 225 Virginia Avenue SE, Washington, DC 20061; phone (202) 484-5000; founded Dec. 16, 1852; chairman of the board James R. Shepley; publisher George W. Hoyt; editor Murray J. Gart; executive editor Sidney Epstein; awards received by newspaper and staff include 9 Pulitzer Prizes.

Population: (1979) 661,500 (city), 3,054,600 (metro area including D.C. and parts of Md. and Va.).
Area: 67 sq. mi. (city), 2,812 (metro) at head of tidewater of Potomac R., 30 miles from Chesapeake Bay, 130 miles from Atlantic Ocean, 240 miles from NYC.
Industry: U. S. Capital, federal government employs 362,100 civilian (April, 1980) and 55,916 military personnel (Sept., 1979), total employment 1,516,273 (1979); government related activity, law, journalism, professional and trade assns., unions, lobbying groups, and scientists provide another large portion of employment base; tourism a major industry.
Commerce: metro area average household spendable income, $27,200 (1979); area retail sales for 1979, $13.6 billion.
Transportation: circumferential highway; 100-mile rapid rail transit system to be completed 1990 with 33.6 miles in city and nearby suburbs now open; Metroliner to New York; long distance rail and bus service; National, Dulles, and Baltimore-Washington International airports; National Visitors Center at Union Station; Concorde service at Dulles.
Communications: several national magazines; news bureaus of major newspapers, wire services, and TV networks; 21 FM, 23 AM radio stations; 7 TV stations; 2 daily metropolitan newspapers, over 40 weekly newspapers.
Educational facilities: American, Catholic, District of Columbia, Georgetown, George Washington, and Howard universities, and Gallaudet College; nearby Univ. of Maryland and George Mason Univ.
Medical facilities: major medical research center; National Institutes of Health, Walter Reed Hospital, Bethesda Naval Medical Center; about 40 general and 3 teaching hospitals.
Cultural facilities: Kennedy Center with 3 performance halls and Wolf Trap Farm Park in nearby Vienna, Va., present major concerts, ballet, opera; Arena Stage, Ford's Theatre, National Theater, many community theater groups; Smithsonian Institution; Corcoran Gallery of Art, Library of Congress; D.C. Public Library with 24 branches.
Sports: pro sports include football (Redskins), basketball (Bullets), hockey (Capitals), soccer (Diplomats).
History: named for George Washington and Christopher Columbus; Georgetown in the District of Columbia first settled 1665, then annexed by the city when D.C. created as seat of federal government by Act of Congress 1790; governed by elected mayor and city council with budget controlled by Congress.
Further information: Convention and Visitors Bureau, 1129 20th Street NW, Washington, DC 20036.

West Palm Beach, Florida

The World Almanac is sponsored in Palm Beach County, Florida by Palm Beach Newspapers, Inc., 2751 S. Dixie Highway, West Palm Beach, FL 33405; phone (305) 833-7411; publisher of The Post and The Evening Times; combined daily circulation 124,136; Sunday, The Post 141,097.

Population: (1979) 66,170 (city), 564,950 (metro); total labor force 220,100.
Area: 43.5 sq. mi. (city), 2,023 sq. mi. (metro), in southeast top of Fla.'s "Gold Coast."
Industry: Pratt & Whitney Aircraft, IBM, U.S. Sugar Corp., Atlantic Sugar Assn., Gulf & Western Food Products Co., American Foods Inc. farms, Duda & Sons Coop, Assoc. farms, Rinker Materials Corp., Solitron Devices Inc., NCI Inc., Palm Beach Newspapers Inc., Perry Oceanographics Inc., Rel Reeves Inc., Southern Bell, Florida Power & Light, tourism. **Commerce:** 52 general service banks, 16 savings and loans, total assets $5.75 billion (1979); retail sales $2.68 billion (1979); per capita EBI $7,852 (1979).
Transportation: Palm Beach Intl. Airport; 2 rail freight lines, Amtrak; Greyhound, Trailways bus lines; Palm Beach County Transportation Authority (bus); Sunshine Lines 15 truck lines; Port of Palm Beach for freight shipping.
Communications: 2 TV, 13 radio stations, cable TV; 3 daily newspapers, one winter-season daily, 6 weeklies, society journal magazine, 7 special publications.
Medical facilities: 13 hospitals, 2,264 beds.
Cultural facilities: Society of Four Arts, Henry Morrison Flagler Museum, Norton Gallery & School of Art, Morikami Museum and Park; 4 community theaters, 2 legitimate theaters, 3 college theaters; West Palm Beach Auditorium, Lion Country Safari.
Education: Florida Atlantic Univ. (Jr. & Sr.), Palm Beach Jr. College, North & South Tech. Ed. centers, Palm Beach Atlantic College.
Sports: West Palm Beach Expos minor league baseball; Atlanta Braves spring training site; greyhound racing, jai-alai fronton, Gold Coast Barracudas semi-pro football team, 91 golf courses, 2 polo fields, county fairgrounds, auto race track; tennis, water sports, and hunting.
History: founded late 1800's by workers and business people associated with the construction of the Royal Poinciana Hotel in Palm Beach by Henry Morrison Flagler who set aside 48 homesites on the shore of Lake Worth; inc. 1894.
Further information: Area Planning Board of Palm Beach County, 2300 Palm Beach Lakes Boulevard, West Palm Beach, FL 33407; Chamber of Commerce, 501 N. Flagler Drive, West Palm Beach, FL 33401.

Wichita, Kansas

The World Almanac is sponsored in the Wichita area by the Wichita Eagle and Beacon Publishing Co., Inc., 825 East Douglas, Wichita, KS 67202; phone (316) 268-6000; founded 1872 as weeklies, became dailies 1884, consolidated 1961; circulation Eagle (morn.) 122,890, Beacon (eve.) 40,053, Sunday Eagle and Beacon 175,474; Norman Christiansen, president and publisher; Peter Ridder, general manager; Davis Merritt Jr., executive editor; Joe Harper, managing editor.

Population: Jan., 1980 (city) 261,001, first in state; (SMSA) 393,095; employment (1980) 218,900.
Area: (city) 101.5 sq. mi. at juncture of Arkansas and Little Arkansas rivers; Sedgwick County seat.
Industry: 60% of free world general aviation aircraft is manufactured in Wichita; aircraft employment in area: Beech 7,700, Cessna 15,700, Gates Learjet 2,700, Boeing 16,100; other fields: meat processing, flour milling, grain storage, petroleum refining, natural gas, chemicals; largest non-aero manufacturer employer, Coleman Co.
Commerce: wholesale-retail center for large part of Kansas and northern Oklahoma; metro (SMSA) retail sales (1979) $2.1 billion; bank resources $2.2 billion; median household income $17,000 (1979 est.).
Transportation: 3 major rail freight lines, Continental Trailways bus line, 63 truck lines, 8 major highways; Mid-

Continent Airport, Jabara Airport, 7 airlines, 64 flights daily, averages 720 air movements per day; National Flying Farmers headquarters.
Communications: 4 TV, 7 AM and 7 FM radio stations; cable TV.
Medical facilities: world's largest speech and hearing rehabilitation center (Institute of Logopedics); 5 hospital complexes including VA installation; 573 doctors.
Federal facilities: McConnell AFB, VA regional office.
Educational facilities: Wichita State Univ., Univ. of Kansas School of Medicine-Wichita, Friends Univ., Kansas Newman College, 91 elementary, 17 Jr. high, 10 high schools; 18 special, 17 vocational schools.
Cultural facilities: Wichita Symphony Orchestra; Omnisphere (planetarium); Wichita Art Museum, Wichita Art Assn. and Children's Theater, Wichita Music Theater, Crown Uptown Dinner Theater, Marple Theater; Ulrich Museum of Art; American Theatre League, Metropolitan Ballet Co., Mid-America Dance Co., Reportory Arts Assn., Wichita Choral Society; Century II auditorium and convention complex, Kansas Coliseum, community theater, city library; Mid-America All Indian Center; 436 churches.
Other attractions: Sedgwick County Zoo, Fanta Sea water amusement park; 69 city Parks (2,808 acres), 2 county parks, recreation lakes; Cow Town (restoration of 1872 Wichita); historical museum, National Junior Livestock Show, Wichita River Festival, Wichita Jazz Festival, Joyland Amusement Park; 11 golf courses, 5 tennis clubs.

Sports: Aeros, Chicago Cubs farm team; Wichita Wind hockey (Central Hockey League), Edmonton Oiler farm team; Wichita Wings professional soccer (Major Indoor Soccer League); National Baseball Congress (semi-pro) headquarters and tournaments; tennis and raquetball tournaments, auto racing, polo.

History: founded 1870, became railhead (shipping point) for cattle herds driven up Chisholm Trail; named after Wichita Indians.

Further information: Chamber of Commerce, 350 West Douglas, Wichita, KS 67202.

Wilmington, Delaware

The World Almanac is sponsored in Delaware by The News-Journal Company, Wilmington, DE 19899; phone (302) 573-2000; publisher of The Morning News, Evening Journal (combined circulation 133,754), The News Journal (Saturdays, circulation 117,257) and the Sunday News Journal (circulation 109,581), member Gannett Group; president and publisher, Joseph T. Lyons; vice president and executive editor, Frederick W. Hartmann; editor of the editorial page, J. Donald Brandt.

Population: 69,100 (Wilmington), 401,300 (New Castle County), 521,700 (metro); Wilmington is largest city in state.
Area: 15.1 sq. mi. at the confluence of the Brandywine, Christina, and Delaware rivers.
Industry: one of the largest chemical and petrochemical centers in the U.S.; autos, utilities, steel; about 400 manufacturing firms; many insurance firms and holding companies.
Commerce: port is major auto importing center; retail sales (SMSA 1979) $2.0 billion, est. 1979 income in SMSA $3.8 billion; state has 12 state-chartered commercial banks, 19 state-chartered savings and loans, 5 national banks, 2 mutual savings banks, 2 federally chartered savings and loans.
Transportation: 2 major railway lines, 3 bus lines, 35 motor freight carriers, airport.
Communications: one public TV station, 6 radio stations.
Medical facilities: Wilmington Medical Center (4 divisions); 2 private hospitals, Alfred I. duPont Institute for children with orthopedic handicaps.
Federal facilities: Dover AFB (Dover).
Cultural attractions: Grand Opera House, Winterthur Museum, Hagley Museum, Old Brandywine Village, Fort Christina Park; Wilmington Symphony Orchestra, Wilmington Opera Society, Wilmington Drama League, Museum of Natural History; Fort Delaware; Wilmington Institute Free Library.
Education: Univ. of Delaware (Newark); Delaware State College (Dover); Delaware Technical and Community College, Brandywine Junior College, Delaware Law School (Wilmington).
Sports: horse racing at Delaware Park, Brandywine Raceway, Dover Downs, Harrington Raceway (Harrington); auto racing at Dover Downs; Univ. of Delaware football.
Other attractions: Rehoboth Beach; Longwood Gardens and Brandywine River Museum (both in nearby PA); Delaware Art Museum (Wilmington); historic old New Castle; old Dover; Ashland Nature Center; several state parks and recreational areas.
Convention facilities: downtown Wilmington has 2 major hotels.
History: founded as Fort Christina in 1638; named for Queen of Sweden; name changed to Willington in 1731 and then to Wilmington in 1739 in honor of the Earl of Wilmington; it is the first city in the first state of the union.
Further information: Delaware State Chamber of Commerce, 1102 West Street, Wilmington, DE 19801; The News-Journal Co., Promotion/Public Service Dept., Wilmington, DE 19899.

Windsor, Ontario, Canada

The World Almanac is sponsored in Windsor and a large part of southwestern Ontario including Essex, Kent, and Lambton counties, by The Windsor Star, (ave. circ. 91,000), 167 Ferry Street, Windsor, Ontario, N9A 4M5; a division of Southam Inc.; published daily since 1890 (present name since 1957); publisher Gordon Bullock, general manager A.H. Fast, editor G.C. Morgan.

Population: 198,722 (city), 247,585 (metro), 314,102 (county of Essex), 545,002 (tri-county); total employed 112,000 (metro).

Area: 46.24 sq. mi. (city), 316.93 sq. mi. (metro), 718.97 sq. mi. (Essex County); one mile across Detroit River from Detroit, Mich.; largest Canadian city on U.S.-Canadian border.

Industry: (1979) private and public investment into Windsor's manufacturing sector was in excess of $361 million; over 840 manufacturers produced a diversity of products valued at $4.3 billion. Chrysler Canada has invested over $100 million in the past 2 years to retool its car assembly plant to produce smaller and lighter models; Ford Motor has 2 major plants under construction; General Motors is tripling the size of its transmission plant to 1.6 million sq. ft.; companies such as Kelsey Hayes, Gulf & Western, National Auto Rad, and Champion Spark Plug make the most of their location adjacent to Detroit to serve automotive markets in the U.S. and Canada. Windsor is the "home of Canadian Club" and a major food and beverage processing center; area processing companies include Green Giant, Chun-King, Dainty Rice, Windsor Packers, H.J. Heinz, and Holiday Juice; city is the machine tool center of Canada with 15% of Canada's tool and die makers; the chemical industry produces a wide range of paints and lacquers, metal working compounds, pharmaceuticals, and vitamin preparations.
Commerce: retail sales (metro) $789.5 million; ave. wkly. earnings $305.19; 5th largest manufacturing center in Canada; 10 banks, 82 branches; 15 trust companies; 26 finance companies; 34 credit unions.
Transportation: 6 major railways; 3 major airlines (Nordair, Air Canada, CP Air); 2 charter services (Southwest Air and Air Windsor); linked to Detroit by vehicular tunnel, rail tunnel, and suspension bridge; western terminus Highway 401; 20 motor freight carriers; deep water port; bonded

warehouse facilities; municipal bus line, 5 intercity bus lines.
Communications: daily and weekly newspaper; 6 radio stations; one TV outlet; access to Detroit's 50 radio and 6 TV outlets; monthly magazine.
New construction: (city) 2,509 dwelling units; (metro) 3,230 dwelling units; (Essex County) 4,032 dwelling units (1979); $598 million Ford expansion to be completed by 1983; $260 million G.M. expansion in construction phase; planned $9 million plant for Castec Foundries to manufacture small precision parts; Maple Leaf Monarch processing plant completed; 500,000 sq. ft. enclosed mall.
Medical facilities: 4 major hospitals; regional children's center; handicapped children's rehabilitation center.
Educational facilities: Univ. of Windsor, St. Clair College of Applied Arts & Technology.
Cultural facilities: Cleary Auditorium & Convention Centre; Art Gallery of Windsor; Windsor Symphony Orchestra; Multicultural Council of Windsor; Univ. of Windsor Players; Windsor Light Opera Assn.; Windsor Public Library; Essex Hall Theatre; Ontario Film Theatre.
Other attractions: Hiram Walker Historical Museum, Fort Malden Historic Park & Museum; Jackson Park Sunken Gardens; Dieppe Gardens; Coventry Gardens and Peace Fountain; Heritage Village; Windsor Raceway; Bob-Lo Island Amusement Park; Great Lakes resort areas; Ojibway Park; Point Pelee Provincial Park; site of International Freedom Festival and Multicultural Carousel of Nations Festival.

Sports: Windsor Spitfire Hockey Team, Windsor Minor Lacrosse Assn., Windsor Yacht Club, several marinas; 7 public golf courses, 2 public curling rinks, 96 parks and playgrounds.

History: originally established by Ottawa and Huron Indians; first permanent white settlement established around 1750; site of War of 1812 between Americans and the British; in 1836, citizens chose the name Windsor; became a city with a population of 11,000 in 1892; located at the crossroads of the most highly industrialized areas in Canada and the U.S., it is now the home of not only its original French and British settlers but of people representing every part of the world.

Further information: Chamber of Commerce, 500 Riverside Drive West, Tourist Information, 80 Chatham Street East, Windsor Essex County Development Commission, Place Goyeau, all Windsor, Ontario.

Winnipeg, Manitoba, Canada

The World Almanac is sponsored in the Winnipeg area by the Winnipeg Free Press, 300 Carlton Street, Winnipeg, Man., Canada; phone (204) 943-9331; founded 1872; daily circulation 146,300; publisher Don Nicol, editor John Dafoe, managing editor Murray Burt; the newspaper and its staff have received numerous journalism awards.

Population: 556,372.
Area: 235 sq. mi. surrounding the junction of Red and Assiniboine rivers, near center of North America; capital of the province of Manitoba.
Industry: manufacturing and agriculture are the largest source of jobs; 1,025 establishments, 53,000 employees; value of factory shipments $2.35 billion.
Commerce: retail sales over $1.9 billion in 1979; Winnipeg Commodity Exchange only gold futures market in Canada; headquarters Canada Grains Council, Canadian Grain Commission, Canadian Wheat Board.
Transportation: International Airport served by 10 airlines; 2 national railways, Via-Rail passenger service; one rail line to U.S.; 5 national and regional bus lines; major trucking hub.
Communications: 10 TV channels, 4 stations; 11 radio stations.
New construction: valued at $734.3 million in 1979, compared with $657.4 million in 1978.
Medical facilities: one of Canada's largest medical teaching centers; research in immunology, transplant-tissue rejection, cancer, blood diseases, respiratory diseases, endocrinology, neo-natal, pre-natal medicine; of Manitoba's 85 active treatment hospitals, 13 are in Winnipeg, including 2 major teaching centers plus Univ. of Manitoba Rh Inst.; 300-plus bed Seven Oaks Hospital opened in 1980.
Federal facilities: passport office, Canada mint.
Cultural facilities: art gallery, Royal Winnipeg Ballet, contemporary dancers, Winnipeg Symphony Orchestra, Manitoba Chamber Orchestra, Manitoba Opera Assn., Manitoba Theatre Center, Cercle Moliere, Museum of Man and Nature, summer Rainbow Stage, Manitoba theater workshop, over 12 amateur theater groups.
Educational facilities: Univ. of Manitoba with 4 affiliated colleges; Univ. of Winnipeg, Red River Community College.
Sports: Blue Bombers (Canadian Football League), Winnipeg Jets (National Hockey League), Assiniboia Downs.
Convention facilities: downtown Winnipeg Convention Center handles up to 5,000 delegates.
Other attractions: major zoo in Assiniboine Park; Red River exhibition, multi-cultural Folklorama festival each summer; folk festival in Birds Hill Park; French Canadian winter carnival in St. Boniface; planetarium.
History: first colony, Lord Selkirk Settlers, 1812; inc. Nov. 8, 1873; in 1972, amalgamation of city government replaced 7 cities, 4 urban municipalities, one town and a metropolitan government.
Additional information: Chamber of Commerce, 700-177 Lombard Avenue, Tourist Information, 101 Legislative Building, and Tourist and Convention Association of Manitoba, 226-375 York Avenue.

Winston-Salem, North Carolina

The World Almanac is sponsored in the Piedmont Triad area by the Winston-Salem Journal and The Sentinel, 418-420 N. Marshall Street, Winston-Salem, NC 27102; phone (919) 727-7211. Sentinel founded 1856; Journal 1897; brought under same ownership in 1926; now an affiliate of Media General Inc.; general manager Thomas E. Waldrop, publisher Joe Doster.

Population: (1979 est.) 145,000 (city), 235,000 (Forsyth County), work force in county 155,000.
Area: 61.34 sq. mi. (city), 419 sq. mi. (county), in north central N.C.; Forsyth County seat.
Industry: R. J. Reynolds Industries with diversified interests in tobacco, food, shipping, oil, and packaging; Western Electric Co., Westinghouse, Jos. Schlitz brewery, Hanes Corp., Hanes Dye and Finishing Co., Brenner Industries, Wachovia Corp., and Bahnson Co.
Commerce: total retail sales county (1978) $1.5 billion, part of the Piedmont Triad which with Greensboro and High Point comprise a rapidly growing part of the Piedmont part of N.C.
Transportation: headquarters for Piedmont Airlines at Smith Reynolds Airport; city also served by 4 airlines at Greensboro-High Point-Winston-Salem regional airport; 2 bus lines; 54 carriers of various types.
Communications: 4 TV, 10 radio stations; cable TV.
New construction: 18-story Integon insurance building occupied in 1980; 16-story Reynolds Plaza due for completion in 1981-82.
Medical facilities: Bowman Gray School of Medicine of Wake Forest Univ.; Baptist, Forsyth Memorial, and Medical Park hospitals; other treatment centers.
Cultural facilities: one of the nation's first arts councils formed in 1949; now building Winston Square, cultural center downtown; N.C. School of the Arts, Wake Forest Univ., Salem College, Winston-Salem State Univ.; Old Salem, restoration of town between 1766 and 1830.
Recreation: more than 50 public parks, 10 community cen-

ers, 10 public pools; boating and fishing at Winston and Salem lakes; 17 golf courses including Tanglewood where 1974 national PGA was played.
Convention facilities: Winston-Salem Hyatt hotel complex sits across street from Benton Convention Center; hotels and motels offer more than 2,400 rooms in area.
Sports: Red Sox, farm club of Boston Red Sox; stock car racing; Wake Forest football at Groves stadium; Winston-Salem State football at Bowman Gray Stadium; Atlantic Coast Conference baseball at Memorial Coliseum.
History: Salem founded 1766 by the Moravian Church; Winston founded in 1849 as industrial city; cities merged in 1913.
Further information: Chamber of Commerce, P.O. Box 1408, Winston-Salem, NC 27102.

Yakima, Washington

The World Almanac is sponsored in the Yakima SMSA by the Yakima Herald-Republic (published daily and Sunday), 114 North Fourth Street, Yakima, WA 98909; phone (509) 248-1251; founded 1903 as the Yakima Republic, given present name in 1970; circulation (May, 1980) daily 41,289, Sunday 43,001; publisher James E. Barnhill. The Yakima Herald-Republic is a division of Harte-Hanks Communications, Inc.

Population: (May, 1979) 52,900 city, 158,200 SMSA.
Area: 11.78 sq. mi. in south central Washington, 142 miles southeast of Seattle, 146 miles south of Canadian border; altitude 1,052 ft., Yakima County seat.
Industry: food processing, agriculture, timber; first in the nation in production of apples, hops, mint; first in number of fruit trees.
Commerce: (1979) retail sales $645.4 million (SMSA); E.B.I. per household (1979) $18,028; postal receipts (1979) $4 million.
Transportation: Republic Airlines and Cascade Airways; Burlington Northern, Union Pacific railroads, Amtrak; Greyhound; interstate 82, highways 12 and 97.
Communications: daily, weekly newspapers; 4 TV, 10 radio stations.
New construction: 843 building permits totalling over $34 million issued in 1979.
Medical facilities: 3 hospitals with 460 beds, 150 physicians, 11 osteopaths, 64 dentists, 13 optometrists; cardiac surgery at St. Elizabeth's Hospital.
Federal facilities: U.S. Army Firing Center, 409 permanent personnel, trains active and reserve units on 263,131 acres; U.S. Army, Marine, and Navy reserve facilities; U.S. Postal Service regional center.
Cultural facilities: Yakima Valley Museum, Yakima Valley Regional Library, Allied Arts Council, Yakima Symphony, Little Theater, Capitol Theater; over 95 churches.
Education: Yakima Valley College, J. M. Perry Institute, Yakima Business College; City College; 7 public school districts in and around city, 7 parochial schools, St. Elizabeth Health Sciences Library.
Sports and Recreation: 12 theaters, 5 drive-ins; historic trolleys; hunting and fishing; skiing in Cascade Mountains 45 minutes from city; 4 golf courses, 30 tennis courts, 9 swimming pools, 31 parks; auto racing, horse racing; youth baseball, softball; Central Washington State Fair, Washington State Open Horse Show.
Convention facilities: Yakima Convention Center, over 1,400 motel units.
History: founded Jan. 27, 1886 as North Yakima on route of Northern Pacific Railroad.
Further information: Greater Yakima Chamber of Commerce, P.O. Box 1490, or Yakima V&C Bureau, 10 North 8th Street, both Yakima, WA 98907.

Youngstown, Ohio

The World Almanac is sponsored in the Youngstown area by The Vindicator, Vindicator Square, Youngstown, OH 44501; phone (216) 747-1471; founded 1863 by J. H. Odell; Wm. F. Maag began daily Sept. 25, 1889; daily circulation 100,324, Sunday 156,657; president, publisher, general manager William J. Brown; advertising manager William Mittler; managing editor Ann N. Przelomski.

Population: 140,909 (city), Ohio's 7th largest; 536,836 (metro).
Area: 35 sq. mi. in northeastern Ohio at juncture of Ohio Turnpike, I-80, and Ohio Rt. 11; Mahoning County seat.
Industry: no longer a strong iron and steel center, still some production with Jones & Laughlin Steel Corp., Republic Steel; local steel supplied to big nearby plants of General Motors Packard Electric Div. in Warren and GMAD plant in Lordstown, where Chevrolet Monzas, vans, and other GM models are assembled; GF Business Equipment sells office furnishings world wide; Commercial Shearing does world-wide tunnel frame and hydraulics business; other fabricators use local steel, rubber.
Commerce: wholesale-retail center for large area of northeast Ohio, western Penna.; retail sales of metro area (est.) over $1.9 billion; (est.) value added by manufacturing $2.6 billion; average spendable family income $20,006.
Transportation: truck transport center with 95 motor freight terminals; rail lines; airport served by United Airlines, Dade Air Charter; headquarters for Beckett Aviation, largest fleet of executive aircraft in U.S.
Communications: 4 TV stations, all major networks and PBS; 9 radio stations.
Medical facilities: Northeastern Ohio Univ. College of Medicine, 6 large hospitals in area.
Federal facilities: U.S. Air Force Reserve base flying transports at airport; regional post office; army and navy reserve centers.
Cultural facilities: symphony orchestra with downtown bldg.; ballet guild, Youngstown Playhouse in own modern bldg., Butler Institute of American Art.
Educational facilities: Youngstown State Univ. with over 15,500 students and graduate program; Penn-Ohio Junior College; Youngstown College of Business and Professional Drafting; 55 public and parochial schools; branches of Kent State Univ. in nearby Warren, Salem, and East Liverpool.
Recreational facilities: 10 parks, 44 playgrounds, golf course, 6 swimming pools; Mill Creek Park with 2,383 acres; 4 large reservoirs in area for recreation, many golf courses.
Further information: Youngstown Area Chamber of Commerce, 200 Wick Bldg., Youngstown, OH 44503.

Washington, Capital of the U.S.

The Capitol

The United States Capitol has presented an entirely new east central front since 1961. That portion was extended 32 ft. 6 in. and reproduced in Georgia marble. The extension added 100 rooms and cost $11.4 million. The original wall of Virginia sandstone became an inner wall.

Dr. William Thornton, an amateur architect, submitted a plan for the Capitol in the spring of 1793 that won him $500 and a city lot. The design consisted of a center section topped with a low dome and on either side were wings to accomodate the House and Senate that measured about 126 ft. by 120 ft. George Washington laid the cornerstone Sept. 18, 1793 with Masonic ceremonies and in Nov. 1800 Congress met in that north or Senate wing. Also housed in that small wing were the Supreme Court, other local courts, and the Library of Congress.

The south, or House wing, was completed in 1807 under the direction of Benjamin H. Latrobe. At the time the Capitol was burned by the British in 1814 the Capitol consisted of these 2 wings joined by a wooden walkway. The interiors were gutted by the fire and nearly 5 laborious years were needed to rebuild the Capitol. It was occupied again in 1819 and the central portion with its low copper-covered wooden dome was completed in 1829 by the 3d architect of the Capitol, Charles Bulfinch.

The present Senate and House wings and the iron dome were designed and constructed by Thomas U. Walter, the 4th architect of the Capitol, between 1851-1863. The House moved into its chamber Dec. 16, 1857 and the Senate Jan. 4, 1859. These moves enabled the Supreme Court to occupy the Old Senate Chamber from 1860-1935 when it moved into its own building. The Old Hall of the House became Statuary Hall.

Recently those original chambers have been restored and are open to the public.

The present cast iron dome at its greatest exterior measures 135 ft. 5 in., and it is topped by the bronze Statue of Freedom that stands 19½ ft. and weighs 14,985 pounds. On its base are the words "E Pluribus Unum (Out of Many One). The sculptor was Thomas Crawford and the cost, including casting, $23,796. The Rotunda, covered by the huge dome, measures 96 ft. in diameter. Looking upward 180 ft. into the "eye" of the dome one sees the huge fresco, "Apotheosis of Washington," by Constantino Brumidi. Encircling the rotunda 58 ft. up is a frescoed frieze depicting scenes from the landing of Columbus in 1492 to Kitty Hawk in 1903. It measures 300 ft.

Inaugurations of presidents and vice presidents are usually held on a platform erected over the great steps on the east front. The oath of office of the president is usually given by the Chief Justice of the United States.

Prayer Room

A nondenominational room where members of Congress may pray and meditate is located off the rotunda. Dominating the room is a stained glass window of George Washington kneeling in prayer at Valley Forge. Beneath it is an altar of white oak on which stands an open Bible. Flanking either side is a floor candelabra, each with the traditional seven lights. The prayer room is not open to the public.

National Statuary Hall

Statuary Hall was created in 1864 and occupies the former Old Hall of the House. States were invited to contribute not more than 2 statues of distinguished deceased persons to the collection. Statues now number 92 and it has become necessary to display them throughout the Capitol. There remain only 8 states to contribute a 2d statue.

Office Buildings for Members

Members of Congress meet constituents and transact other business in five office buildings on Capitol Hill, two for the Senate and three for the House.

The original Senate building, the Richard Brevard Russell Office Building, was completed in 1909, enlarged in 1933; the second Senate building, the Everett McKinley Dirksen Office Building, was constructed in 1958. A subway connects both with the Capitol.

The original House building (1908) was named for former Speaker Joseph G. Cannon (R. Ill.), the second (1933) for former Speaker Nicholas Longworth (R. Oh.), and the third (1964) for former Speaker Sam Rayburn (D. Tex.). The Rayburn Building has underground transportation to the Capitol.

Also on Capitol Hill is the bell tower and statue memorial to Sen. Robert A. Taft of Ohio (1889-1953). It was erected by popular subscription and dedicated Apr. 14, 1959, by President Eisenhower.

Hours for Visiting

The Capitol is normally open from 9 a.m. to 4:30 p.m. daily. The Capitol is closed Christmas, New Year's Day, and Thanksgiving Day. Should either the House or the Senate remain in session beyond closing time, the wing of the Capitol in use stays open until the session closes.

Tours through the Capitol, including the House and Senate Galleries, are conducted from 9 a.m. to 4 p.m. without charge. It is not necessary to take a tour to see the Capitol. Visitors desiring to hear debate in either chamber for a longer period than the tour allows must obtain a visitor's card from their Senator or Representative.

The White House

The White House, the president's residence, stands on 18 acres on the south side of Pennsylvania Avenue, between the Treasury and the Executive Office Building. The main building 168 by 85-1/2 ft., has 6 floors, with the East Terrace, 135 by 35 ft., leading to the East Wing, a 3-story building, 139 by 82 ft., used for offices and as an entrance for official functions. The West Terrace, 174 by 35 ft., contains offices and press facilities, and leads to the West Wing, 3 stories high, 148 by 98 ft., erected in 1902 and enlarged several times since.

The White House was designed by James Hoban, an Irish-born architect, in a competition that paid $500. The main facade resembles the Duke of Leinster's house in Dublin. President Washington chose the site, which was included on the plan of the Federal City prepared by the French engineer, Major Pierre L'Enfant. The cornerstone was laid Oct. 13, 1792. President Washington never lived in the house. President John Adams entered in Nov. 1800, and Mrs. Adams hung her washing in the uncompleted East Room.

The walls are of sandstone, quarried at Aquia Creek, Va. The exterior walls were painted during the course of construction, causing the building to be termed the "White House." For many years, however, it was generally referred to as the "President's House" or the "President's Palace." Thomas Jefferson developed the east and west terraces and built one-story offices, woodsheds, and a wine cellar. On Aug. 24, 1814, during Madison's administration, the house was burned by the British. James Hoban completed rebuilding by Dec. 1817, and President Monroe moved in.

The south portico was added in 1824 and the north portico in 1829. In 1948 President Truman had a second-floor balcony built into the south portico. In 1948 he had Congress authorize complete rebuilding because the White House was unsafe. During its reconstruction he lived in Blair House, 1651 Pennsylvania Ave. Reconstruction cost $5,761,000. The interior was completely removed, new underpinning 24 ft. deep was placed under the outside walls and a steel frame was built to support the interior.

The Green Room is a Federal-style drawing room with most of the furniture made in New York about 1800-1820 by Duncan Phyfe or his contemporaries. The walls are covered with green silk moiré.

The Blue Room, an oval drawing room, is the main reception room. The parquet floor is covered by an oval Chinese rug; the walls are covered with wallpaper reproduced from a French document of 1800. Portraits of Washington, Adams, Jefferson, Monroe, Jackson, and Tyler decorate the walls. Seven chairs and a French clock from Monroe's original 1817 furnishings are used in the room.

The Red Room, used as a parlor, is furnished in the American Empire style, hung in red twill satin with gold scroll borders. The room has a Savonnerie carpet of the period and a marble-topped gueridon labeled by Charles-Honoré Lannuier. There are portraits of Pierce, Hayes, Van Buren, Dolley Madison, Angelica Van Buren, Audubon, and Alexander Hamilton in the room. There is also a marble bust of Martin Van Buren by Hiram Powers.

The State Dining Room has a large ornamental table on which is displayed a French bronze-doré plateau purchased by Monroe in 1817. For large dinners, small circular tables are brought in. The neo-classically carved oak wall paneling is painted ivory.

The Family Dining Room, used for breakfasts and luncheons, has a portrait of Mrs. Theodore Roosevelt by Theobold Chartran.

The President's Dining Room, on the second floor, is furnished with American Federal furniture, an 18th century chandelier, and blue silk window hangings. There is a mahogany sideboard once owned by Daniel Webster. It is used for private dining by the first family.

The Diplomatic Reception Room, an oval room on the ground floor, is used as the south entrance to the mansion at state functions. It has scenic wallpaper based on 1820 engravings, and an Aubusson style rug with seals of the 50 states.

The Library, on the ground floor, has the painted decor of an early 19th century American room. In Aug. 1963, 2,780 titles were selected by a distinguished committee to be placed in the library. All but a few are by American authors.

The Map Room, on the ground floor, a top-secret war room during World War II, was redecorated in 1970 in American Chippendale style. A portrait of Benjamin Franklin which was taken from Franklin's Philadelphia home by a British officer quartered there during the American Revolution hangs there.

The Lincoln Bedroom which contains an ornately carved bed and furniture of his period, is at the east end of the second floor. It served as Lincoln's cabinet room and in it he signed the Emancipation Proclamation of Jan. 1, 1863. A portrait of Jackson, admired by Lincoln, hangs there today. Seven pieces of furniture have Lincoln associations. The bed was used in the State Bedroom during the Lincoln administration. In the room is a copy of the **Gettysburg Address,** written out by Lincoln.

The Treaty Room was used as the cabinet room by Andrew Johnson and his successors until 1902. Here in 1899 was signed the peace protocol, a forerunner to the final treaty of peace with Spain. It is now a waiting or meeting room for the President and contains some of the original Victorian furniture. There are portraits of Presidents Andrew Johnson, Grant, and Taylor and paintings of McKinley observing the signing of the protocol, and of Lincoln and Grant in conference during the Civil War.

The Queen's Bedroom is assigned to distinguished women guests, and has sheltered five queens — Queen Mother Elizabeth and Queen Elizabeth II of Britain, Wilhelmina and Juliana of the Netherlands, Queen Mother Frederika of Greece. The English overmantel mirror was presented by Princess Elizabeth in 1951.

The Yellow Oval Room, directly above the Blue Room is used as a private sitting room by the president and first lady.

The President's Office, oval in form, is in the West Wing and looks out on the rose garden. The office was added in 1909 to the West Wing, which had been built 7 years earlier by Theodore Roosevelt. The West Wing also contains the Roosevelt Room and the Cabinet Room.

Visiting Hours

The White House is open from 10 a.m. to 12 noon, Tuesday through Friday, except on holidays. Also Saturdays, 10 a.m. to 2 p.m. Jun. 1 through Labor Day, and 10 a.m. to noon Labor Day through May 31. Only the public rooms on the ground floor and state floor may be visited.

President's Guest House

Blair House, the President's Guest House, fronts on Pennsylvania Ave., northwest of the White House grounds. It is supervised by the Dept. of State and is the official residence of heads of state who visit Washington. Built 1824, it was the home of Francis Preston Blair (1791-1876), political leader and Lincoln advisor. President Truman lived there 1948-1952 during rebuilding of the White House, and 2 Puerto Rican fanatics tried to shoot their way in Nov. 1, 1950, killing one guard and wounding 2 others.

Restoration and refurnishing began in 1963 and the house was reopened Jan. 14, 1964, on the occasion of the visit of President Antonio Segni of the Italian Republic. The Blair House Fine Arts Committee continues to provide for the house.

Other Centers of Interest

Arlington National Cemetery

Arlington National Cemetery, on the former Custis estate in Virginia, is the site of the **Tomb of the Unknown Soldier** and the final resting place of John Fitzgerald Kennedy, president of the United States, who was buried there Nov. 25, 1963. A torch burns day and night over his grave. The remains of his brother Sen. Robert F. Kennedy (N.Y.) were interred on June 8, 1968, in an area adjacent. Many other famous Americans are also buried at Arlington, as well as American soldiers from every major war.

Arlington National Cemetery, administered by the Department of the Army, was established June 15, 1864, on land originally the estate of George Washington Parke Custis. The land was part of the District of Columbia from 1791 until 1847, when Arlington County was returned to Virginia.

The Unknown Soldier of World War I was entombed on the east front of the Arlington Memorial Amphitheater Nov. 11, 1921, in the presence of President Warren G. Harding. The tomb is inscribed: *Here rests in honored glory an American solider known but to God.* The body had been chosen at Chalons-sur-Marne from unidentified dead in Europe. On Memorial Day, May 30, 1958, 2 unidentified servicemen, one of whom died in World War II and one in the Korean War, were placed in crypts beside the first, in ceremonies led by President Eisenhower and Vice President Nixon.

As of March 31, 1980, a total of 178,044 interments had been made in Arlington National Cemetery. Among the unknown dead are 2,111 who died on the battlefields of Virginia in the Civil War and 167 who lost their lives when the battleship Maine was blown up in Havana Harbor Feb. 15, 1898. The total of unknown dead interred in Arlington National Cemetery is 4,724.

Arlington House, The Robert E. Lee Memorial

On a hilltop above the cemetery, stands Arlington House, the Robert E. Lee Memorial, which from 1955 to 1972 was officially called the Custis-Lee Mansion. The house has a portico 60 ft. wide, with 8 Doric columns, and faces the Potomac. With its 2 wings the house extends 140 ft. It was built by George Washington Parke Custis, grandson of Martha Washington and father of Mary Ann Randolph Custis, who married Lee in this house in 1831. Here Lee wrote his resignation from the U.S. Army, Apr. 20, 1861. The house became a military headquarters and was confiscated by the government. The U.S. Supreme Court restored it to the legal heir, George Washington Custis Lee, grandson of the builder, who sold the entire estate (including the mansion) to the Government in 1883 for $150,000.

The mansion and grounds are administered by the National Park Service of the Dept. of the Interior.

U.S. Marine Corps War Memorial

North of the National Cemetery, approximately 350 yards, stands the bronze statue of the raising of the United States flag on Iwo Jima, executed by Felix de Weldon from the photograph by Joe Rosenthal, and presented to the nation by members and friends of the U.S. Marine Corps, at a cost of $850,000. It was dedicated Nov. 10, 1954, and is under the administration of the Dept. of the Interior, National Park Service.

Folger Shakespeare Library

The Folger Shakespeare Library on Capitol Hill, Washington, D. C., is a research institution devoted to the advancement of learning in the background of Anglo-American civilization in the 16th and 17th centuries and in most aspects of the continental Renaissance. It has the largest collection of Shakespeareana in the world with 79 copies of the First Folio. Its collection of English books printed before 1640 is the largest in the Western Hemisphere. It also has extensive source materials for the history of theater and drama from the Middle Ages to the end of the 19th century, both English and American. The library owns approximately 250,000 books and manuscripts, about half of them rare.

The library was founded and endowed by Henry Clay Folger, a former president of the Standard Oil Co. of New York, and his wife, Emily Jordan Folger. He left its administration to the trustees of his alma mater, Amherst College. The exhibition gallery and replica Elizabethan Theatre are open free 10 a.m. to 4 p.m. daily; closed federal holidays and on Sundays after Labor Day to April 15.

Library of Congress

Established by and for Congress in 1800, the Library of Congress has extended its services over the years to other Government agencies and other libraries, to scholars, and to the general public, and it now serves as the national library. Two buildings, an ornate Italian Renaissance structure, the Library of Congress Building, (1897) and a modern annex, the Thomas Jefferson Building, (1939), cover 6 acres of the 15⅔-acre library site and contain 35 acres of floor space. In addition the library occupies 10 other buildings dispersed through the Metropolitan area. In Oct. 1965 Congress passed a law authorizing construction of a third library building, the James Madison Memorial Building; completion is expected in 1980.

Dr. Daniel J. Boorstin became the 12th Librarian of Congress on November 12, 1975.

The library had over 3,000 volumes when it was destroyed in the burning of the Capitol, Aug. 24-25, 1814. In Jan. 1815 Congress bought Thomas Jefferson's library of some 6,000 volumes. In 1851 fire destroyed about half the collections. In 1866 the science library of the Smithsonian Institution was transferred to the library, and in 1870 the library became the repository for materials deposited for copyright. Today the library's collections contain more than 74 million items, including more than 18 million volumes and pamphlets.

In addition to providing a variety of reference and bibliographic services to other government agencies, the Library of Congress serves as a cataloging and bibliographic center for libraries throughout the country. Its cataloging data is available on printed cards (a service offered since 1901), on magnetic tapes for libraries using computers, and in book catalogs. A program called Cataloging in Publication makes cataloging information available in books themselves so that they can be processed and put into circulation almost immediately after their delivery to libraries.

The library's exhibit halls are open to the public. Guided tours are given every hour from 9 a.m. through 4 p.m. Monday through Friday. Arrangements for groups should be made in advance with the Tour Coordinator. Many of the library's treasures are on permanent exhibit and changing exhibits feature interesting selections from the library's collections of photographs, rare books, music, maps, and manuscipts. The library's resources are also made available to the public through publication of guides, bibliographies, catalogs, and facsimiles. An annual list of **Publications in Print** is available free of charge from Central Services Division, Library of Congress, Washington, DC 20540. A monthly **Calendar of Events** listing current exhibits and programs is also available from the same address. Information about the Library of Congress, publications, posters, color slides, and greeting and postal cards are available at the Information Counter, in the west entrance ground floor lobby of the Library of Congress Building.

Thomas Jefferson Memorial

The Thomas Jefferson Memorial stands on the south shore of the Tidal Basin in West Potomac park. It is a circular stone structure, with Vermont marble on the exterior and Georgia white marble inside and combines architectural elements of the dome of the Pantheon in Rome and the rotunda designed by Jefferson for the University of Virginia. The central circular chamber, 86¼ ft. in diameter, is dominated by a 19-ft. tall full-length figure of Thomas Jefferson by the American sculptor Rudulph Evans. The architects were John Russell Pope and his associates Otto R. Eggers and Daniel P. Higgins. The Memorial was dedicated by President F. D. Roosevelt Apr. 13, 1943, the 200th anniversary of Jefferson's birth.

On the pediment over the portico is a sculptured group by Adolph A. Weinman showing Jefferson standing before the committee appointed by the Continental Congress to draft the Declaration of Independence. On the interior walls are four panels with inscriptions from Jefferson's writings. On the frieze of the main entablature are Jefferson's lines: "I have sworn upon the altar of God eternal hostility against every form of tyranny over the mind of man."

The memorial is open daily from 8 a.m. to midnight, except Christmas Day. An elevator and curb ramps for the handicapped are in service.

John F. Kennedy Center

John F. Kennedy Center for the Performing Arts, designated by Congress as the National Cultural Center and the official memorial in Washington to President Kennedy, opened September 8, 1971. The white marble building, designed by Edward Durell Stone, houses a 2,300-seat Opera House, a 2,750-seat Concert Hall, the 1,150-seat Eisenhower Theater, the 513-seat Terrace Theater, the 224-seat American Film Institute Theater, a 100-seat laboratory theater, and 3 restaurants. All facilities are in full operation throughout the year. Tours are available daily, free of charge, between 10:00 a.m. and 1:15 p.m.

Lincoln Memorial

The Lincoln Memorial in West Potomac Park, on the axis of the Capitol and the Washington Monument, consists of a large marble hall enclosing a heroic statue of Abraham Lincoln in meditation sitting on a large armchair. It was dedicated on Memorial Day, May 30, 1922. The Memorial was designed by Henry Bacon. The statue was made by Daniel Chester French. Murals and ornamentation on the bronze ceiling beams are by Jules Guerin.

The memorial, built on bedrock, is of white Colorado-Yule marble. There are 2 Doric columns at the entrance and 36 others in the colonnade. The frieze above the 36 columns bears the names of the 36 states existing at the time of Lincoln's death. On the attic parapet are recorded names of the 48 states existing in 1922.

Inside are 3 memorials to Lincoln. The seated figure of Lincoln is 19 ft. from head to foot and the classic armchair is 12½ ft. tall. Over the back of the chair a flag is draped in marble. The statue was fashioned out of 28 blocks of Georgia white marble. On the north wall is inscribed the Second Inaugural Address. On the south wall is the Gettysburg Address.

The walls of the interior are Indiana limestone. The panels between the overhead girders are of Alabama marble saturated with melted beeswax to produce translucency. The interior floor and the wall base are of pink Tennessee marble. The cost of the Memorial was $2,957,000 and of the statue $88,400.

The memorial is open daily from 8 a.m. to midnight, except Christmas Day. A new elevator for the handicapped is in service.

Mount Vernon

Mount Vernon on the south bank of the Potomac, 16 miles below Washington, D. C., is part of a large tract of land in northern Virginia which was originally included in a royal grant made to Lord Culpepper, who in 1674 granted 5,000 acres to Nicholas Spencer and John Washington. The division between Spencer and Washington put John Washington's son Lawrence in possession of the Washington half in 1690. Later it became the property of Lawrence Washington's son Augustine, the father of George Washington.

The present house is an enlargement of one apparently built on the site of an earlier one by Augustine Washington, who lived there 1735-1738. His son Lawrence came there in 1743, when he renamed the plantation Mount Vernon in honor of Admiral Vernon under whom he had served in the West Indies. Lawrence Washington died in 1752 and was succeeded as proprietor of Mount Vernon by his half-brother, George Washington.

Washington brought his wife, Martha Dandridge Custis, to Mount Vernon in 1759, having previously enlarged the house from 1-½ to 2-½ stories. Just before the Revolution he planned additions, and when he was called away to war his kinsman Lund Washington supervised the work, which was completed after Washington returned in 1783. During the Revolution Washington visited Mount Vernon only twice, on the way to and from Yorktown in 1781. In 1789 he left to become president and lived in New York and Philadelphia, with brief visits to the plantation. He came back in 1797 and died in Mount Vernon Dec. 14, 1799. He was buried in the old family vault. He had made plans for a new burial vault and this was built in 1831. Both his remains and those of Martha, who died in 1802, were transferred there.

Mount Vernon was left to Washington's nephew, U.S. Supreme Court Justice Bushrod Washington, and by him to his nephew, John Augustine Washington, whose son, John A. Washington Jr., was the last private owner. In 1853 Miss Ann Pamela Cunningham of South Carolina organized the Mount Vernon Ladies' Assn., which bought the mansion and 200 acres, since extended to just under 500 acres. The Association reassembled original Washington furniture and repaired the buildings. It restored the kitchen garden, flower garden, and experimental botanical garden, reconstructed the greenhouse, and built a museum. Several trees planted by Washington still exist, and the boxwood dates from 1798.

The Association preserves house and tomb with the visitor's fee. The regent of the Mount Vernon Ladies' Association is Mrs. John H. Guy Jr. About 30 states are represented by vice regents. The Resident Director is John A. Castellani.

National Arboretum

The National Arboretum is one of Washington's great showplaces, occupying 444 acres in the northeastern section of the city. Collections of azaleas, magnolias, hollies, cherries, crabapples, conifers, and ferns and wildflowers are prime attractions. The National Herb Garden and National Bonsai Collection are special attractions in the nation's only federally-supported gardens.

The Arboretum is open every day of the year except Christmas. The visiting hours are 8 a.m. to 5 p.m. Monday through Friday and 10 a.m. to 5 p.m. on Saturday and Sunday.

National Archives

The Declaration of Independence, the Constitution of the United States, and the Bill of Rights are on permanent display in the National Archives Exhibition Hall. They are sealed in glass-and-bronze cases.

The National Archives holds the permanently valuable federal records of the United States government, 1774 to the present. As a research institution, it is designed to preserve these records and make them available to scholars, students, writers, and the general public.

The National Archives and Records Service is a part of the General Services Administration. Through the Office of Presidential Libraries it administers the Herbert Hoover Library at West Branch, Iowa, the Franklin D. Roosevelt Library at Hyde Park, N.Y., the Harry S. Truman Library at Independence, Mo., the Dwight D. Eisenhower Library at Abilene, Kan., the John Fitzgerald Kennedy Library at Boston, Mass., the Lyndon Baines Johnson Library at Austin, Tex., and the Gerald Ford Library to be built in Ann Arbor, Mich., and museum to stand in Grand Rapids.

James E. O'Neill is acting archivist of the United States, Pennsylvania Ave. and 8th St. N.W. For research information, call 202-523-3218. For visitor information, call 202-523-3000.

National Gallery of Art

The National Gallery of Art, situated in an area bounded by Constitution Avenue and the Mall, between Third and Seventh Streets, was established by Joint Resolution of Congress Mar. 24, 1937, and opened Mar. 17, 1941. Although technically a bureau of the Smithsonian Institution, the gallery is an autonomous organization governed by its own board of trustees. The chairman of the board is the chief justice of the United States. Other members are the secretaries of state and of the treasury, the secretary of the Smithsonian Institution, and 5 distinguished private citizens.

The collections comprise gifts of over 300 donors (none of the works were acquired with Government funds) and cover the American and various European schools of art from the 13th century to the present.

The building was erected with funds given by Andrew W. Mellon, who also gave his collection of 126 paintings and 26 pieces of sculpture, which included such masterpieces as Raphael's Alba Madonna, the Niccolini-Cowper Madonna, and St. George and the Dragon, van Eyck's Annunciation, Botticelli's Adoration of the Magi, and 9 Rembrandts. Twenty-one paintings came from the Hermitage in Leningrad. Also in this collection are the Vaughan Portrait of George Washington, by Gilbert Stuart, and The Washington Family, by Edward Savage.

The Samuel H. Kress Collection includes the great tondo of the Adoration of the Magi by Fra Angelico and Fra Filippo Lippi, the Laocoon by El Greco, and fine examples by Giorgione, Titian, Grunewald, Durer, Memling, Bosch, Juan de Flandes, Francois Clouet, Poussin, Watteau, Chardin, Boucher, Fragonard, David, and Ingres. Also included are a number of masterpieces of sculpture, especially of the Italian and French schools.

The Widener Collection of over 100 paintings includes 14 Rembrandts, 8 Van Dycks, 2 Vermeers, and examples of Italian, Spanish, English, and French painting, and Italian and French sculpture and decorative arts.

The Chester Dale collection includes masterpieces by Manet, Cézanne, Renoir, Toulouse-Lautrec, Monet, Modigliani, Pissarro, Degas, van Gogh, Gauguin, Matisse, Picasso, Braque, and such American artists as Gilbert Stuart, Childe Hassam, and George Bellows.

Several major works of art by some of the most important artists of the last hundred years, including Picasso, Cézanne, Gauguin, and the American painter Walt Kuhn, have been given to the gallery by the W. Averell Harriman Foundation in memory of Marie N. Harriman.

The Collection of Edgar William and Bernice Chrysler Garbisch includes more than 300 American naive paintings and watercolors covering the 18th and 19th centuries. Among them are Edward Hicks' Cornell Farm, Winthrop Chandler's portraits of Captain Samuel Chandler and Mrs. Samuel Chandler, and Linton Park's Flax Scutching Bee.

Pictures to round out the collection have been bought with funds provided by the late Ailsa Mellon Bruce, daughter of Andrew W. Mellon. Preeminent among them is the portrait of Ginevra de' Benci, the only generally acknowledged painting by Leonardo da Vinci outside Europe; Georges de la Tour's Repentant Magdalen, one of the rarest paintings of the 17th century; and Pablo Picasso's Nude Woman, the key work of the artist's analytical cubist period. Among others are: Rubens' Daniel in the Lions' Den; Claude Lorrain's Judgment of Paris; Saint George and the Dragon, attributed to van der Weyden; and a number of American paintings, including Cole's second set of The Voyage of Life.

Cézanne's great early portrait of his father and 351 paintings by George Catlin, mostly of North and South American Indians, are among recent acquisitions given by Paul Mellon, president of the gallery and son of Andrew Mellon. A fine collection of French impressionist pictures are on loan to the gallery from Mr. and Mrs. Mellon.

Among other works donated to the gallery's collection are Vermeer's A Lady Writing, given by Harry Waldron Havemeyer and Horace Havemeyer Jr., in memory of their father, Horace Havemeyer; Copley's Watson and the Shark, given by Ferdinand Lammot Belin; Goya's Victor Guye, given by William Nelson Cromwell; and Mondrian's Lozenge in Red, Yellow and Blue, given by Herbert and Nannette Rothschild.

The National Gallery's rapidly expanding graphic arts holdings number about 62,000 items and date from the 12th century to the present. Almost half of these works were the gift of Lessing J. Rosenwald, who had gathered one of the world's great collections of prints and drawings.

The Index of American Design contains over 17,000 watercolor renderings and 500 photographs of American crafts and folk arts from before 1700 until 1900.

The gallery's Education Department gives daily talks on the gallery's collection. The Extension Service lends films and slide programs to schools, colleges, and civic groups in more than 4,000 communities in the United States and Canada. Nearly all of the gallery's services are available to the public free of charge.

The National Gallery is in the process of moving into its new East Building, which adjoins the original West Building. Funds for the new construction have come from Mr. Paul Mellon, the late Ailsa Mellon Bruce, and The Andrew W. Mellon Foundation. The architect is I. M. Pei. The gallery segment of the East Building, which opened in 1978, provides space for temporary exhibitions and the gallery's growing collection. Alongside the gallery segment is the administrative and research segment, which will open in 1979 and will house the Center for Advanced Study in the Visual Arts together with a greatly expanded library, photographic archive, and office facilities. Already open to the public is an underground concourse connecting the East and West Buildings and containing a major new restaurant complex, the Cafe/Buffet.

Open daily except Christmas and New Year's, from 10 a.m. to 5 p.m. Monday through Saturday and noon to 9 p.m. Sunday. During the summer open Monday through Saturday 10 a.m. to 9 p.m., noon to 9 p.m. on Sunday.

The Pentagon

The Pentagon, headquarters of the Department of Defense, is the world's largest office building, with 3 times the floor space of the Empire State Building in New York. Situated in Arlington, Va., it houses more than 23,000 employees in offices that occupy 3,707,745 square feet.

The Pentagon was completed Jan. 15, 1943, at a cost of about $83 million. It covers 34 acres, is 5 stories high and consists of 5 rings of buildings connected by 10 corridors, with a 5-acre pentagonal court in the center. Each of the outermost sides of the building is 921 ft. long and the perimeter is $\frac{7}{8}$'s of a mile. Total length of the corridors is $17\frac{1}{2}$ miles.

Tours are available Monday through Friday (excluding federal holidays), and start every 30 minutes at the Concourse. The first tour begins at 9 a.m. and the last at 3:30 p.m. Walk-ins are welcome. During the summer tourist season, tours are conducted every 15 minutes.

Smithsonian Institution

The Smithsonian Institution is one of the world's great historical, scientific, educational, and cultural establishments. It comprises numerous facilities, mostly in the metropolitan Wash., D.C., area. It was founded by an Act of Congress in 1846, pursuant to a bequest of James Smithson, a British scholar-scientist, to the United States to found at Washington "an establishment for the increase and diffusion of knowledge among men." The Smithsonian, ever since its founding, has been a center for basic scientific research; it engages in programs of education and it is also the largest museum-gallery complex in the world. More than 24 million persons visit its halls annually. S. Dillon Ripley became the 8th secretary of the Smithsonian Feb. 1, 1964.

The Anacostia Neighborhood Museum, the first of its kind in the nation, opened in 1967 in a low-income urban community. The museum develops and presents exhibits on topics of interest to the residents of the community as well as the greater Washington area. The staff also conducts independent research in the areas of Afro-American history, minority and ethnic studies, and the history of the Anacostia community and Washington, D.C. Independent programs and activities, such as teacher workshops, seminars, and a lending library of children's books on African and Afro-American history serve the local school community.

The Arts and Industries Building reopened in May 1976 with an exhibit entitled "1876: A Centennial Exhibition" which displays actual items from the Centennial exhibition in Philadelphia as well as others of the same era. The 4 halls are devoted to various subjects including machinery, with a large number of the machines in operation; items from the military, U.S. Treasury and the Patent Office; manufactured articles; and displays from many of the 37 states in existence in 1876 and from the foreign countries represented in the Philadelphia exhibition.

The Freer Gallery of Art, the gift of Detroit industrialist Charles Lang Freer, is an outstanding museum and research center in art of the Far and Near East. The gallery also houses the Whistler Peacock Room and a fine collection of works by James A. McNeill Whistler.

The Hirshhorn Museum and Sculpture Garden opened in 1974 with a nucleus collection of more than 6,000 works of art donated to the nation by Joseph H. Hirshhorn. Primary emphasis is on art of the 20th century although the sculpture collection encompasses works from the 19th century as well and is international in scope.

The National Museum of History and Technology has exhibits illustrating American culture, civil and military history, and the history of science and technology. In the rotunda the visitor will find the original Star-Spangled Banner and a Foucault pendulum demonstrating the earth's rotation. "A Nation of Nations" is a museum within a museum tracing the peopling of America through 6,000 objects. Other major exhibits feature gowns of the first ladies, the Petroleum Hall, the history of transportation, American political and military history, numismatics, philately, ceramics and glass, musical instruments, timekeeping, physical and medical sciences, graphic arts, electricity, photography, and news reporting. National treasures on display include the desk on which Thomas Jefferson drafted the Declaration of Independence and Samuel Morse's first telegraph. A popular attraction is an authentic 19th century country store-post office where mail is hand-stamped with a "Smithsonian Station" postmark.

The National Museum of Natural History serves as a national and international center for the natural sciences. It maintains the largest reference collection in the nation and conducts a broad program of basic research on man, plants, animals, fossil organisms, rocks, minerals, and materials from outer space. Exhibits show aspects of life and cultures in Asia, Africa, the Pacific, and North and South America. Other exhibits include fossil plants and invertebrate animals, mammals, fishes, amphibians, dinosaurs, and primitive reptiles. There are halls of North American archeology, osteology, and physical anthropology; Western Civilization, Ice Age Mammals and the Emergence of Man, the Dynamics of Evolution, and the Splendors of Nature. Also on view are geology exhibits on the earth, the moon, and meteorites as well as a Hall of Minerals and Gems which includes the 45½-carat blue Hope diamond and the largest gem emerald on public exhibit, the 858-carat Gachala emerald. The World of Mammals, the Hall of Birds, the Fenykovi Elephant, and the Insect Zoo are additional major exhibits.

The National Air and Space Museum, which opened in a newly constructed building July 1, 1976, houses exhibits on space exploration, air travel and related scientific and technical topics. Its Milestones of Flight Gallery exhibits 'famous firsts' of air and space development such as the Wright Flyer, Lindbergh's "Spirit of St. Louis," John Glenn's Mercury capsule, the Friendship 7 craft, the Apollo 11 command module Columbia, and a moon rock. Aspects of space exploration and air travel are displayed in some galleries with others focusing on ballons and airships, flight technology, sea-air operations, and various kinds of military aviation. There is a giant screen theater with presentations related to air and space travel and the Albert Einstein Spacearium presents programs of sky and space simulation.

The National Collection of Fine Arts presents a panorama of American painting, sculpture, and graphic art from the 18th century to today with 18,000 works in its collections and approximately 25 special exhibitions each year. It is housed in the historic Old Patent Office Building; its Lincoln Gallery was the site of Abraham Lincoln's second inaugural reception. **The Renwick Gallery,** a curatorial department of the National Collection of Fine Arts, is a national showcase for American creativity in design, crafts, and the decorative arts. In addition to special temporary exhibitions, 2 rooms refurnished in the late 19th century period can be seen.

The National Portrait Gallery, also located in the Old Patent Office Bldg., exhibits the likenesses of persons who have made significant contributions to the history, development, and culture of the people of the United States. The gallery's temporary exhibitions are based on a variety of historical themes.

The National Zoological Park is noted for its outstanding collections including 2 giant pandas from China. Its research includes investigation in animal behavior, ecology, nutrition and reproduction physiology, pathology, and clinical medicine. Conservation-oriented studies cover maintenance of wild population and long-term captive breeding and care of endangered species.

The Smithsonian Associates was founded to stimulate interest and active participation in the Smithsonian's work. Its membership programs for adults and young people include seminars, lectures, workshops, demonstrations, concerts, theater, exhibition previews, dramas, films, tours, and field and camping trips. *Smithsonian,* a monthly magazine of the arts, sciences, and history, is available to members of the Associates.

The Smithsonian Institution Traveling Exhibition Service (SITES) organizes and circulates exhibitions for art and science museums, colleges, and other educational institutions around the United States and Canada. More than 175 exhibitions are on continuous tour, with about 65 openings of these shows occurring monthly across the country.

Washington Monument

The Washington Monument is a tapering shaft or obelisk of white marble, 555 ft., 5-⅛ inches in height and 55 ft., 1-½ inches square at base. Eight small windows, 2 on each side, are located at the 500-ft. level, where Washington points of interest are indicated.

The capstone weighs 3,300 lbs. and was placed Dec. 6, 1884. The monument was dedicated Feb. 21, 1885, and opened Oct. 9, 1888. It weighs 81,120 tons. It is dressed with white Maryland marble in 2-ft. courses. The first 150 ft. are backed by rubble masonry. From that point to 452 ft. Maine granite was used as backing, and above 452 ft. marble was used. The face of the monument is primarily marble from Maryland. Set into the interior wall are 190 memorial stones from states, foreign countries, and organizations. An iron stairway has 50 landings and 898 steps. A modern elevator takes sightseers to the 500-ft. level in one minute, compared with 12 "precarious minutes" in 1888.

The erection of the monument by the Washington National Monument society with funds obtained by popular subscription was authorized by Congress in 1848. The conerstone was laid July 4 of the same year. Work progressed slowly until 1854 when $300,000 had been subscribed and 152 ft. of the shaft erected. In that year the enterprise became controversial and contributions ceased. Work was resumed in 1880 at government expense by the Corps of Engineers.

The Monument is open 7 days a week, 9 a.m. to 5 p.m. Extended summer hours are 8 a.m. to 12 midnight. It is closed Christmas Day.

Famous Churches

The National Shrine of the Immaculate Conception, at Fourth St. and Michigan Ave. NE, Washington, D. C. is the largest Catholic church in the Western Hemisphere and the seventh largest in the world. Built by all the bishops and Catholics of the U.S., it honors the Blessed Virgin Mary as Patroness of the United States. The Shrine is impressive not only in size but in beauty. Its blue and gold dome and soaring bell-tower are prominent Washington landmarks. Open daily from 7 a.m. to 7 p.m., Sunday masses, 7:30, 9, 10:30 a.m., 12 noon, 1:30 and 4 p.m. (5:15 p.m. Sat. eve.). Free guided tours 9 a.m. to 5 p.m. daily; Sunday tours 2 p.m. to 5 p.m. Carillon concerts on Sundays and preceding organ and choral concerts. Organ recitals throughout the year.

Washington Cathedral, Massachusetts and Wisconsin Aves. NW, is atop Mt. Saint Alban. It is the seat of the Presiding Bishop of the Episcopal Church and of the Bishop of Washington. Started in 1907, the cathedral is nearly complete. The nave was finished and opened in 1976, with a festive dedicatory ceremony July 8, marking the visit of Queen Elizabeth to the nation's capital. It is the 6th largest cathedral in the world. Notables buried in the cathedral include Woodrow Wilson, Adm. George Dewey, Cordell Hull, and Frank B. Kellogg. The cathedral is considered one of the finest examples of Gothic architecture in the country.

Several Protestant churches commemorate the association of presidents with their congregations. **St. John's Episcopal Church,** across Lafayette Sq. from the White House, designed by Benj. Latrobe in 1815, has been attended by every president since Madison. **New York Ave. Presbyterian Church,** 1313 New York Ave. NW, established in 1803, retains the pew in which Lincoln sat, also an original manuscript of his first proposal to abolish slavery. The church was rebuilt on same site in 1950-51.

The National Presbyterian Church, on a 13-acre tract, at Nebraska Ave. and Van Ness St. NW, was dedicated on May 10, 1970. The Church traces its origin to a group of stonemasons who met in a carpenter's shop in the grounds of the White House in 1795, later becoming the First Presbyterian Church in the District of Columbia. The Church of the Covenant, founded in 1883, united with the original Presbyterian body in 1930 to become the congregation of the National Presbyterian Church. President Eisenhower was baptized by the pastor, at that time Dr. Edward L. R. Elson, and became a member of the Church on Feb. 1, 1953. He laid the cornerstone of the new Church on his 77th birthday, Oct. 14, 1967, and the Chapel of Presidents is dedicated to him. The Chapel of the Presidents contains the Eisenhower pew, and pews representing 16 additional presidents who worshipped with the congregation. The oldest president's pew, occupied by Jackson, Polk, Pierce, Buchanan, and Cleveland, is on view together with much historic memorabilia.

The Islamic Center, 2551 Massachusetts Ave. NW, a magnificent Islamic monument, institution for Islamic culture, and an outstanding landmark. Visitors welcome daily from 10 a.m. to 4 p.m.

Cherry Blossom Time

Cherry blossom time in Washington is looked upon as the opening of spring. The famous cherry trees encircle the Tidal Basin in West Potomac Park and for 2 miles line the roadside in East Potomac Park. A gift by the Mayor of Tokyo to the city of Washington, the original 3,000 trees were propagated from the trees on the Arawaka River in a suburb of Tokyo. The first trees were planted by Mrs. William Howard Taft, wife of the president, and by Viscountess Chinda, wife of the Japanese Ambassador, Mar. 27, 1912.

Today many of the 650 trees around the Tidal Basin have white blossoms, while some have pink; deep pink blossoms are in East Potomac Park. The trees usually are in full blossom the first week in April, but no precise date can be given earlier than 10 days prior to full blossom, which lasts about one week.

Other Points of Interest

Organization of American States Building, 17th St. and Constitution Ave., NW, houses the General Secretariat of the OAS, the oldest major international organization in the world, representing 26 countries of the western hemisphere. Of traditional Spanish architecture with a tropical garden courtyard, the building is one of the more gracious sights in Washington. It contains the Hall of the Americas assembly room, art exhibitions, the Columbus Memorial Library, and behind the building, the Aztec Gardens, and the Museum of Modern Art of Latin America.

National Society, Daughters of the American Revolution, established in 1890. Headquarters stands on a block bounded by 17th and 18th Sts., and C and D Sts. NW.

American Red Cross, 17th and D Sts. NW, occupies 3 white marble buildings of neoclassic design, embellished with a Corinthian portico, colonnades, and bronze doors. The Red Cross Museum is in the east building.

Federal Reserve Building, Constitution Ave., between 20th and 21st Sts. NW, is a 4-story white marble building of Georgian design, with formal gardens and fountains, and tasteful but relatively simple interiors, built 1937. An annex, the William McChesney Martin Building, was occupied in 1974.

The Corcoran Gallery of Art, 17th St. between New York Ave. and E St., NW. Permanent collections: 18th through 20th century American painting, sculpture; European painting, decorative arts. Contemporary exhibitions of painting, sculpture, photography. Open 10 a.m. to 4:30 p.m. Tuesday to Sunday; closed Mondays, major holidays. Free admission. May, 1980 through May, 1981: open Thurs. eve. 4:30 p.m. to 9 p.m.

N.Y. City Places of Interest

Museums, Zoos, Libraries, Churches, Historic Sites, Buildings, Other Attractions

See Index for Statue of Liberty

The New York Aquarium, in Coney Island, exhibits marine life from all climes, with over 12,000 live specimens including whales, sharks, seals, and sea lions.

The New York Botanical Garden, covering 250 acres in the Bronx, features the newly restored Enid A. Haupt Conservatory, specialized gardens, a botanical library, and a plant and book shop.

The Frick Collection, 1 E. 70th St., was founded by Henry Clay Frick (1849-1919). The principal part of the collection consists of 14th-19th century paintings. It also contains sculptures, furniture, porcelains, enamels, drawings and prints.

The Solomon R. Guggenheim Museum, 5th Ave. and 89th St.; permanent collection contains over 3,000 paintings, drawings, sculptures, and graphic works by 19th and 20th century artists. The museum's spiral building was designed by Frank Lloyd Wright.

The Hayden Planetarium, facing 81st St. near Central Park W., presents changing sky shows with a Zeiss projector under the world's most famous planetarium dome; "Astronomia," an exhibit of astronomy fact and fantasy throughout history; Guggenheim Space Theater shows, and a "Hall of the Sun."

The Jewish Museum, 5th Ave. at 92d St., offers exhibitions of Jewish art and ceremonial objects and exhibits of Jewish interest. The permanent collection of Judaica is considered the most comprehensive in the world.

The Metropolitan Museum of Art, 5th Ave. at 82d St. With over 1 million works of art, the museum's collection is the largest of its kind in the Western Hemisphere. Great masters of all the ages of art are included in the collections; Egyptian, Greek, Roman, Ancient Near Eastern, Islamic, Far Eastern, Medieval, Arms and Armor, European, Pre-Columbian, American, Contemporary Arts, Musical Instruments, Costume Institute.

The Cloisters, in Manhattan's Fort Tryon Park, is a branch of the Metropolitan devoted to Medieval art and architecture. Incorporated into its modern structure are 5 cloisters and other medieval European architectural elements.

The Museum of the American Indian, Heye Foundation, Broadway at 155th St., maintains the world's largest collection of American Indian materials, extensive archeological and ethnological displays from North, Central, and South America.

The Museum of Modern Art, 11 W. 53d St., presents 20th century painting, sculpture, drawings, prints, architectural and industrial design, photography, film, and video projects.

The American Museum of Natural History, Central Park W. between 77th and 81st Sts., has large exhibits of man and beast from the most primitive times to the present, with extensive reconstruction of fossilized remains, dinosaurs, birds, Indians, and Eskimos. The collections of gems, mollusks, meteorites, and ocean life are famous.

The Museum of the City of New York on 5th Ave. at 103d St., illustrates the history and life of the city with dioramas, paintings, prints, maps, photographs, portraits, ship models, silver, costumes, furniture, toys, and rare books.

The New-York Historical Society, founded 1804, is at 170 Central Park W. between 76th and 77th Sts. The society maintains a museum devoted to Americana; American portrait, landscape, and genre paintings; a reference library; manuscripts; maps, prints, broadsides, and photographs. Of special interest are the original watercolor drawings by John James Audubon for his *Birds of America.*

The New York Public Library: In 1979, its resources were placed at more than 34.5 million items of which over 9 million were books, over 10 million manuscripts, pamphlets, scrapbooks, and clippings. Of this total, 6 million books and the pictures are in the collections of the 83 branch libraries which are maintained by N.Y. City. The Research Libraries, based at 5th Ave. and 42d St., includes the Performing Arts Research Center at Lincoln Center, and the Schomburg Center for Research in Black Culture, 103 W. 135th St.

South Street Seaport Museum, on the East River waterfront in lower Manhattan, is a growing restoration of earlier eras of New York's port. At piers off South St. at Fulton, the museum has 5 ships, including two 4-masted, square-rigger barks, and the original Ambrose Lightship. Ashore on Fulton St. are museum galleries, a printing museum, and a bookshop.

Whitney Museum of American Art, Madison Ave. at 75th St., holds exhibitions of group and individual artists, historical and contemporary. Comprehensive permanent collection of American art. Has downtown branch at 55 Water St.

The New York Zoological Park (The Bronx Zoo), Pelham Parkway and Southern Boulevard, the Bronx, is one of the world's largest zoos. More than 3,000 mammals, birds, reptiles are displayed in its 252 acres.

Brooklyn Centers

Brooklyn Academy of Music, 30 Lafayette Ave., presents a Sept.-through-June program of music, dance, and theater.

Brooklyn Botanic Garden, Eastern Parkway, Washington and Flatbush Aves., has 50 acres of gardens, including rose, rock, wild flower, 3 Japanese, a fragrance garden for the blind, a Children's Garden, a Shakespeare Garden, and a conservatory housing its bonsai collection.

The Brooklyn Museum, Eastern Parkway and Washington Ave., estab. 1825, has comprehensive exhibitions in all major fields of art. An Outdoor Sculpture Garden contains ornaments from razed N.Y. area buildings.

Houses of Worship

Central Synagogue (Reform), Lexington Ave. at 55th St., is the oldest Jewish house of worship in N.Y. City (1872), and combines 2 earlier congregations founded in 1839 and 1846.

John Street United Methodist Church, 44 John St., erected 1841, on site of Wesley Chapel of 1768, "first Methodist preaching-house in America," houses oldest Methodist Society, formed 1766.

Marble Collegiate Church (Collegiate Reformed Protestant Dutch), 5th Ave. and W. 29th St., erected 1854, is headquarters for Dr. Norman Vincent Peale.

Plymouth Church of the Pilgrims (Congregational), Orange and Hicks Sts., Brooklyn, is a Nat'l. Historic Site, organized 1847, present structure 1849. Has windows illustrating Puritan influence on America and pew where Lincoln sat to hear Henry Ward Beecher, the first minister (1847-1887).

Riverside Church (Interdenominational), Riverside Drive and W. 122d St. The chief donor was John D. Rockefeller Jr. The tower, reminiscent of Chartres, is 100 ft. square, rises 392 ft.; it has the world's largest carillon, with 74 bells, and is open to public from 11 to 3.

Cathedral of St. John the Divine on Morningside Heights, Amsterdam Ave. and W. 112th St. (Episcopal), is the world's largest cathedral. It was begun 1892 as a Romanesque building; the design was changed to Gothic. The church is 603 ft. long, 146 ft. wide at nave, and will be 330 ft. wide at transept. Resumption of construction of its 2 front towers, which will rise to nearly 300 ft., began in June 1979.

St. Mark's-in-the-Bowery (Episcopal), 2d Ave. and E. 10th St., built in 1799 on the site of a chapel built on the farm of Director General Peter Stuyvesant in 1660. A statue of Stuyvesant in the churchyard was presented by Netherlands Queen Wilhelmina in 1915.

St. Patrick's Cathedral (Roman Catholic), 5th Ave. between E. 50th and E. 51st Sts., opposite Rockefeller Center, was begun in 1858 in granite and marble in a Gothic revival style designed by James Renwick. It was opened in part in 1877 and dedicated May 25, 1879. It has 2 spires, 330 ft. tall, and a 26-ft. rose window. St. Patrick's is the cathedral church of the Archdiocese of N.Y.

St. Paul's Chapel of Trinity Church (Episcopal), Broadway and Vesey St., is the oldest public building in continuous use in Manhattan. It was opened Oct. 30, 1766. Much of the interior decoration was by L'Enfant, who laid the plans for Washington, D.C.

St. Thomas Church (Episcopal), 5th Ave. at 53d St., is the 4th church building, consecrated 1916, of a parish founded in 1823. The limestone Gothic edifice was designed by architects Bertram G. Goodhue and Ralph Adams Cram.

Temple Emanu-El, 5th Ave. and 65th St., was erected 1929 by Congregation Emanu-El (Reform), which dates from 1845. It was built of limestone in early Romanesque style, its auditorium 77 ft. wide by 150 ft. long and 103 ft. high, one of the largest temples in the world. Noteworthy are the high arch at the entrance, the rose window, mosaics, and 6 bronze doors.

Trinity Church (Episcopal) faces Broadway at the head of Wall St. It was built 1841-46 of brown sandstone in perpendicular Gothic, designed by Richard Upjohn, is 78 ft. wide by 202 ft. long. The first church was completed in 1697. Alexander Hamilton and Robert Fulton are buried in the churchyard.

Historic Sites

Castle Clinton, Battery Park, lower Manhattan is an 1811 fort, restored 1975; historical exhibits.

Edgar Allan Poe Cottage, Grand Concourse and Kingsbridge Rd., Bronx, is a wood frame cottage, built 1812, was the final home of Poe from 1846-49 and where his wife, Virginia Clem, died in 1847.

Federal Hall National Memorial, Wall and Nassau Sts., is a Greek Revival structure of 1842, originally the Custom House, later the U.S. Sub-Treasury. The site was first occupied by the Colonial City Hall and next by Federal Hall, where the Stamp Act Congress, Continental, and U.S. Congresses met, and George Washington took the oath of office as president.

Fraunces Tavern, Broad and Pearl Sts., was erected 1719 as the DeLancey mansion, acquired 1762 by Samuel Fraunces and operated as the Queen's Head Tavern. The Long Room was the scene of Washington's Farewell to his officers, Dec. 4, 1783.

General Grant National Memorial (Grant's Tomb), Riverside Dr. and W. 122d St., is a formal Roman-style mausoleum, 165 ft. tall, where Gen. U.S. Grant, 18th president, and Mrs. Grant are interred.

The Morris-Jumel Mansion and Museum, W. 160th St. and Edgecombe Ave., is a 3-story Georgian mansion, the oldest residence remaining in Manhattan, with 4-pillared portico built in 1765 by retired British Lt. Col. Roger Morris. From Sept. 14-Oct. 18, 1776, it was the headquarters of Gen. George Washington. In 1810 Stephen Jumel bought 36 of the original 100 acres of the property. In 1833, the widowed Eliza Jumel married Aaron Burr in the mansion's front parlor.

Washington Square, at the foot of 5th Ave., is the best known landmark of **Greenwich Village,** a colorful community and tourist attraction. Facing the lower end of 5th Ave. is the marble **Washington Arch,** designed by Stanford White to mark the centennial of the first inauguration and completed in 1895.

Important Buildings

City Hall, headquarters of the mayor, the City Council, and the Board of Estimate of the City of New York, is in City Hall Park (the original Common), bounded by Broadway, Park Row, and Chambers St. Erected 1803-1812, it is an adaptation of French Renaissance with clock cupola surmounted by a figure of Justice.

Empire State Building, 5th Ave., between W. 33d and 34th Sts., is one of the world's tallest buildings (see also World Trade Center, below), 1,250 ft. high plus a 222-ft. television and FM radio transmitting tower. The building was opened May 1, 1931. Nearly 2 million persons annually visit the 86th and 102d floor observatories.

Lincoln Center for the Performing Arts opened 1962 with a concert in Philharmonic (later renamed Avery Fisher) Hall. The center lies between W. 62d and 66th Sts., Amsterdam and Columbus Aves. It is a private, nonprofit, tax-exempt corporation of 8 constituent organizations. The New York State Theater opened in 1964; the Vivian Beaumont Theater, which includes the Mitzi E. Newhouse Theater, and the New York Public Library at Lincoln Center, 1965; the Metropolitan Opera House, 1966; The Juilliard School including Alice Tully Hall, 1969.

Madison Square Garden Center, Pennsylvania Plaza (7th-8th Aves., 31st-33d Sts.). The huge sports and entertainment center, above the Pennsylvania Station, includes the Garden Arena seating over 20,000, the 4,500-seat Felt Forum, the Exposition Rotunda for trade and walk-around shows, and a 48-lane bowling facility.

Rockefeller Center, the largest privately-owned business and entertainment center in America was started Sept., 1931. Its surface area of 22 acres includes the 3 blocks from 48th to 51st Sts. between 5th Ave. and the Ave. of the Americas, a large portion of the 51st-52nd St. block and 4 blockfronts on the west side of the Ave. of the Americas between 47th and 51st Sts. There are 19 buildings. It has 175,000 daily visitors; over 66,000 work there.

The part of Rockefeller Center comprising theaters and radio and television studios is often referred to as Radio City. Studios of the National Broadcasting Co. are located in the 70-story RCA building (850 ft. tall). There is an observation roof on the 70th floor.

Radio City Music Hall Entertainment Center, Ave. of the Americas and W. 50th St., largest indoor theater of its kind in the world, seats 6,000 people. Its stage, 144 ft. wide by 67 ft. deep, has a proscenium arch 60 ft. high and 100 ft. wide. Has stage spectacles with the Rockettes, Symphony Orchestra, and guest artists, plus concerts and other special events.

New York Stock Exchange, visitors' entrance 20 Broad St., has visitors' center with gallery, exhibits, films and scheduled tours, Mon. through Fri., 10 a.m. to 4 p.m.

American Stock Exchange, visitors' entrance 78 Trinity Pl., has visitors' gallery, guides, multi-media shows, and other exhibits, Mon. through Fri., 9:45 a.m. to 4 p.m.

United Nations Headquarters occupies over 16 acres between 1st Ave. and F.D.R. (East River) Drive, E. 42d and E. 48th Sts. Most unusual is the Secretariat Bldg., 505 ft. high at front entrance, 286 ft. long and only 72 ft. wide. The 2 sides have 5,400 windows; the end walls are of 2,000 tons of Vermont marble. General Assembly Bldg. has a hall 165 ft. long, 115 ft. wide. Conference Bldg. houses 3 Council chambers, etc. There are guided tours daily.

World Trade Center, dedicated Apr. 4, 1973, on Manhattan's lower west side, has twin towers of 110 stories, 1,350 ft. each (2d in height to Chicago's Sears Tower) and 3 low-rise buildings, with total of more than 9 million sq. ft. of office space, plus a 22-story hotel.

Notable Tall Buildings in North American Cities

Height from sidewalk to roof, including penthouse and tower if enclosed as integral part of structure; actual number of stories beginning at street level. Asterisks (*) denote buildings still under construction Jan. 1981.

City	Hgt. ft.	Stories
Akron, Oh.		
First National Tower Bldg.	**330**	28
Akron Center	**321**	24
Ohio Edison, 76 S. Main St.	**275**	19
Albany, N.Y.		
Office Tower, So. Mall	**589**	44
State Office Building	**388**	34
Agency (4 bldgs.), So. Mall	**310**	23
University Towers	**286**	22
Atlanta, Ga.		
Peachtree Center Plaza Hotel	**721**	71
*Georgia Pacific Tower, 123 Peachtree	**697**	51
Southern Bell Telephone, 675 W. Peachtree	**677**	47
First National Bank, 2 Peachtree	**556**	44
Equitable Building, 100 Peachtree	**453**	34
101 Marietta Tower, 101 Marietta St.	**446**	36
National Bank of Georgia	**439**	32
Peachtree Summit No. 1	**406**	31
North Avenue Tower, 310 North Ave.	**403**	26
Tower Place, 3361 Piedmont Road	**401**	29
Richard B. Russell, Federal Bldg.	**383**	26
Atlanta Hilton Hotel	**383**	32
Peachtree Center Harris Bldg.	**382**	31
Southern Bell Telephone	**380**	...
Trust Company Bank	**377**	28
Coastal States Insurance	**377**	27
Peachtree Center Cain Building	**376**	30
Peachtree Center Building	**374**	31
Life of Georgia Tower	**371**	29
Georgia Power Tower, 333 Piedmont	**349**	24
Peachtree Center South	**332**	27
Gas Light Tower, 235 Peachtree	**331**	27
Hyatt Regency Hotel, 265 Peachtree	**330**	23
100 Colony Square, 1175 Peachtree	**328**	25
Georgia Power Building	**318**	22
Colony Square Hotel, 180 14th St.	**310**	28
400 Colony Square, 1201 Peachtree	**308**	23
Atlanta Center Building	**301**	23
Merchandise Mart, 240 Peachtree	**300**	22
Austin, Tex.		
Austin National Bank	**328**	26
American Bank	**313**	21
State Capitol	**309**	...
Univ. of Texas Admin. Bldg.	**307**	29
J. Frank Dobie Univ. Center	**299**	29
Baltimore, Md.		
U.S. Fidelity & Guaranty Co.	**529**	40
Maryland National Bank Bldg.	**509**	34
World Trade Center Bldg.	**405**	32
Saint-Paul Apartments Bldg.	**385**	37
Arlington Federal Savings and Loan Assn. Bldg.	**370**	28
Blaustein Bldg.	**370**	30
Charles Plaza Apts. So.	**350**	31
Charles Center South	**330**	26
Tower Bldg.	**330**	16
Baltimore Arts Tower	**319**	15
First National Bank of Maryland	**315**	22
Lord Baltimore Hotel	**315**	24
Mercantile-Safe Deposit and Trust Co.	**315**	21
Charles Plaza Apts. No.	**315**	28
Baltimore Hilton Hotel	**302**	29
One Charles Center Bldg.	**301**	24
Baltimore Gas and Electric Co. Bldg.	**300**	22
Chesapeake & Potomac Telephone Co.	**300**	16
Baton Rouge, La.		
State Capitol	**460**	34
American Bank Bldg.	**310**	25
Hilton Hotel	**290**	28
La. National Bank Bldg.	**277**	21
Birmingham, Ala.		
First Natl. Southern Natural Bldg.	**390**	30
South Central Bell Hdqts. Bldg.	**390**	30
City Federal Bldg.	**325**	27
Cabana Motel	**287**	21
Daniel Bldg.	**283**	20

City	Hgt. ft.	Stories
Boston, Mass.		
John Hancock Tower	**790**	60
Prudential Tower	**750**	52
Federal Reserve Bldg.	**604**	32
Boston Co. Bldg., Court St.	**601**	41
First National Bank of Boston	**591**	37
Shawmut Bank Bldg.	**520**	38
Sixty State St.	**509**	38
Employers Commercial Employees Bldg.	**507**	40
New England Merch. Bank Bldg.	**500**	40
Commercial Union	**500**	37
U.S. Custom House	**496**	32
John Hancock Bldg.	**495**	26
State St. Bank Bldg.	**477**	34
One Hundred Summer St.	**450**	33
McCormack Bldg.	**401**	22
Keystone Custodian Funds	**400**	32
Saltonstall Office Bldg.	**396**	22
Harbor Towers (2 bldgs.)	**396**	40
John F. Kennedy Bldg.	**387**	24
Longfellow Towers (2 bldgs.)	**380**	38
Federal Bldg. & Post Office	**345**	22
Suffolk County Courthouse	**330**	19
Jamaicaway Towers	**320**	30
Sheraton-Boston Hotel	**310**	29
Buffalo, N.Y.		
Marine Midland, Main St.	**529**	40
City Hall	**378**	32
Rand Bldg., not incl. 40-ft. beacon	**351**	29
Erie County Savings Bank, Main St.	**350**	26
Manuf. & Trades Trust Co.	**317**	21
Liberty Bank	**305**	23
Electric Tower	**294**	18
Calgary, Alta.		
Calgary Tower	**626**	...
Norcen Tower	**508**	33
Scotia Centre	**504**	38
Oxford Square North	**463**	34
Shell Tower	**460**	34
Oxford Square South	**449**	33
Three Bow Valley Square	**432**	35
Sun Oil Bldg.	**397**	34
Western Centre	**385**	40
Two Bow Valley Square	**380**	39
Mobil Tower	**369**	29
One Palliser Square	**350**	28
Mount Royal House	**330**	34
Standard Life Bldg.	**327**	25
Place Concorde (twin towers)	**321**	36
Charlotte, N.C.		
NCNB Plaza, 101 S. Tryon	**503**	40
First Union Plaza	**433**	32
Wachovia Center, 400 S. Tryon	**420**	32
Southern National Center, 200 S. College	**300**	22
City National Center, 200 S. Tryon	**299**	18
Chicago, Ill.		
Sears Tower (world's tallest)	**1,454**	110
Standard Oil (Indiana)	**1,136**	80
John Hancock Center	**1,127**	100
Water Tower Plaza (a)	**859**	74
First Natl. Bank	**850**	60
IBM Bldg.	**695**	52
Civic Center (city hall)	**662**	31
Lake Point Towers	**645**	70
Board of Trade, incl. 81 ft. statue	**605**	44
Prudential Bldg., 130 E. Randolph	**601**	41
Antenna tower, 311 ft., makes total	**912**	...
1000 Lake Shore Plaza Apts.	**590**	55
Marina City Apts., 2 buildings	**588**	61
Mid Continental Plaza	**580**	50
Pittsfield, 55 E. Washington St.	**557**	38
Kemper Insurance Bldg.	**555**	45
Newberry Plaza, State & Oak	**553**	56
Harbor Point	**550**	54
LaSalle Natl. Bank, 135 S. LaSalle St.	**535**	44
One LaSalle Street	**530**	49
111 E. Chestnut St.	**529**	56
River Plaza, Rush & Hubbard	**524**	56
Pure Oil, 35 E. Wacker Drive	**523**	40

City	Hgt. ft.	Stories
United Ins. Bldg., 1 E. Wacker Dr.	522	41
Lincoln Tower, 75 E. Wacker Dr.	519	42
Carbide & Carbon, 230 N. Mich.	503	37
Walton Colonnade	500	44
LaSalle-Wacker, 221 N. LaSalle St.	491	41
Amer. Nat'l. Bank, 33 N. LaSalle St.	479	40
Bankers, 105 W. Adams St.	476	41
Brunswick Bldg.	475	37
Continental Companies	475	45
American Furniture Mart	474	24
Sheraton Hotel, 505 N. Mich. Ave.	471	42
Playboy Bldg., 919 N. Mich. Ave.	468	37
188 Randolph Tower	465	45
Tribune Tower, 435 N. Mich. Ave.	462	36
Chicago Marriott, Mich. & Ohio Sts.	460	45
(a) World's tallest reinforced concrete bldg.		
Cincinnati, Oh.		
Carew Tower	574	48
First National Bank Center	545	28
Central Trust Tower	495	34
Dubois Tower, 5th & Walnut	423	32
Central Trust Center	364	27
Kroger Bldg.	345	25
Stouffer's Cincinnati Tower	324	33
Federated Bldg.	305	21
U. of Cinn., Sander Hall	297	27
Cleveland, Oh.		
Terminal Tower	708	52
Erieview Plaza Tower	529	40
Justice Center, 1250 Ontario	420	26
Federal Bldg.	419	32
Cleveland Trust Tower No. 1	383	29
Ohio-Bell Telephone	365	22
Cleveland State Univ. Towers	319	21
Central Natl. Bank Bldg.	305	23
Diamond Shamrock Bldg.	300	23
CEI Bldg.	300	22
National City Bank, 801 Euclid	289	35
Union Commerce Bldg.	289	21
Columbus, Oh.		
State Office Tower, 30 E. Broad	624	41
LeVeque-Lincoln Tower, 50 W. Broad	555	47
OneNationwide Plaza	485	40
Borden Bldg., 180 E. Broad	438	34
Franklin Cty. Municipal Courts Bldg.	357	19
Columbus Center, 100 E. Broad	357	20
Ohio Bell Bldg., 150 E. Gay St.	348	26
88 E. Broad St.	324	20
BancOhio Plaza, 155 E. Broad	317	25
Motorists Bldg., 471 E. Broad	297	21
Dallas, Tex.		
First International Bldg.	710	56
First National Bank	625	52
Republic Bank Tower	598	50
Reunion Tower	560	50
Southland Life Tower	550	42
Harwood Tower, 717 N. Harwood St.	550	34
2001 Bryan St.	512	40
Republic Bank Bldg., not incl. 150-ft. ornamental tower	452	36
One Main Place	445	34
Ling-Tempco-Vought Tower	434	31
Mercantile Natl. Bank Bldg., not incl. 115-ft. weather beacon	430	31
Mobil Bldg.	430	31
One Dallas Centre	400	30
Fidelity Union Tower	400	33
Southwestern Bell Toll Bldg.	372	22
Court House & Fedl. Office Bldg.	362	16
Mercantile Dallas Bldg.	360	22
Sheraton Hotel	352	38
Hyatt Hotel, 303 Reunion Blvd.	343	30
Elm Place, 1005-09 Elm St.	341	22
Main Tower	336	26
Park Central No. 3	327	20
Adolphus Tower	327	27
Bell Telephone Bldg.	326	23
Davis Bldg.	323	21
Manor House, Bank of Service & Trust	319	26
Preston Tower	316	29
Tower Petroleum Bldg.	315	23
Adolphus Hotel	312	25
Fairmont Hotel	308	24
Baptist Annuity Center	303	17
Life Bldg.	302	22

City	Hgt. ft.	Stories
Santa Fe Bldg. (1st unit)	300	23
Dayton, Oh.		
Winters Bank Bldg.	404	30
Mead Tower, 10 W. 2d St.	365	28
Centre City Office Bldg.	297	21
Hulman Bldg.	295	23
Grant-Deneau Bldg.	290	22
Denver, Col.		
*Argo Tower	600	42
Anaconda Tower	580	40
Amoco Bldg., 17th Ave. & Broadway	450	36
*One Denver Place	450	35
Brooks Towers, 1020 15th St.	420	42
First of Denver Plaza	415	32
Energy Center 1	404	29
Colorado Nat'l. Bank, 17th & Curtis	389	26
First National Bank	385	28
Security Life Bldg.	384	33
Energy Plaza, 1125 17th St.	370	28
Lincoln Center	366	30
Western Fed. Savings	357	27
Colorado State Bank	352	26
Executive Tower	350	30
410 Building	335	24
Mountain Bell, 17th & Curtis	330	21
D&F Tower	330	20
Great West Plaza (Twin Towers)	325	29
Prudential Tower Plaza	322	25
Des Moines, Ia.		
Ruan Center	457	36
Financial Center, 7th & Walnut	345	25
Equitable Bldg.	318	19
State Capitol	275	4
Detroit, Mich.		
Detroit Plaza Hotel	720	71
City Natl. Bank Bldg., 637 Griswold	557	47
Guardian, 500 Griswold	485	40
Renaissance Center (4 bldgs.)	479	39
Book Tower, 1227 Wash. Blvd.	472	35
Cadillac Tower, 51 Cadillac Sq.	437	40
David Stott, 1150 Griswold	436	38
Mich. Cons. Gas Co. Bldg.	430	32
Fisher, W. Grand Blvd. & 2d St.	420	28
J. L. Hudson Bldg.	397	28
McNamara Federal Office Bldg.	393	27
Detroit Bank & Trust Bldg.	370	28
Edison Plaza	365	25
Woodward Tower	358	34
Buhl, 535 Griswold	350	26
Michigan Bell Telephone	340	19
1st Federal Savings & Loan	338	23
Pontchartrain Motor Hotel	336	23
Commonwealth Bldg.	325	25
1300 Lafayette East	325	30
Edmonton, Alta.		
AGT Tower, 10020-100 St.	441	34
CN Tower, 1004-104 Ave.	365	26
Toronto Dominion Tower	325	27
Oxford Tower	325	29
Sun Life Bldg.	320	25
Edmonton House	315	34
Fort Wayne, Ind.		
One Summit Square, 911 S. Calhoun	442	27
Ft. Wayne Natl. Bank	339	26
Lincoln Natl. Bank	312	23
Fort Worth, Tex.		
Ft. Worth Natl. Bank	454	37
Continental Natl. Bank Bldg.	380	30
First National Bank, 500 W. 7th	300	21
Continental Life Ins. Bldg.	282	23
Hamilton, Ont.		
Century Twenty One	418	43
Stelco Tower	339	25
The Olympia	321	33
Harrisburg, Pa.		
State Office Tower #2	334	21
City Towers	291	25
State Capitol	272	6
Hartford, Conn.		
Travelers Ins. Co. Bldg.	527	34

City	Hgt. ft.	Stories
Hartford Plaza	420	22
Hartford Natl. Bank & Trust	360	26
One Financial Plaza, 755 Main	335	26

Honolulu, Ha.

City	Hgt. ft.	Stories
Ala Moana Hotel	390	38
Pacific Trade Center	360	30
Discovery Bay	350	42
Hyatt Regency Waikiki	350	39
Hemmeter Center	350	39
Mehelani Waikiki Lodge	350	43
Regency Tower, 2525 Date St.	350	42
Regency Tower #2	350	43
Yacht Harbor Towers	350	40
Canterbury Place	350	40
Iolani Towers	350	38
Diamond Head Tower	350	38
Ala Wai Sunset	350	44
Century Center	350	41
Pacific Beach Hotel	350	43
Waikiki Ala Wai Waterfront	350	43
Waikiki Lodge II	350	43
Chateau Waikiki	349	39
Rainbow Plaza	348	37
Waikiki Beach Tower	347	39
2121 Ala Wai Blvd.	347	41
Royal Kuhio	346	39
*Century Square	344	36
Waipuna	343	38
Ioloni Court Tower	341	40
Waikiki Banyon	341	36
Waikiki Sunset Makai	341	37
The Villa on Eaton Square	335	37
Kukui Plaza	333	33
The Skyrise	333	38
Grosvenor Center	330	30
Ke Aloha at Waikiki	330	35

Houston, Tex.

City	Hgt. ft.	Stories
Texas Commerce Tower	1,002	75
First International Plaza	744	55
One Shell Plaza (not incl. 285 ft. TV tower)	714	50
Capital Natl. Bank Plaza	685	50
One Houston Center	678	47
First City Tower	660	49
1100 Milam Bldg.	651	47
Exxon Bldg.	606	44
Two Houston Center	570	40
Dresser Tower	550	40
Pennzoil, 700 Milam	523	36
Two Allen Center	521	36
Entex Bldg.	518	35
Tenneco Bldg.	502	33
Conoco Tower	465	32
One Allen Center	452	34
Summit Tower West	441	31
Coastal Tower	441	31
Gulf Bldg.	428	37
First City Natl. Bank	410	32
Houston Lighting & Power	410	27
Neils Esperson Bldg.	409	31
Hyatt Regency Houston	401	34
Houston Natural Gas Bldg.	386	28
Bank of the Southwest	369	24
Sheraton-Lincoln Hotel	352	28
Two Shell Plaza	341	26
American General Life	337	25
Transco	333	25
Allied Chemical Bldg.	328	25
609 Fannin Bldg.	325	22
Holiday Inn	325	30
Post Oak Central 2	321	24
Capital Natl. Bank	320	21
Post Oak Central	318	25
St. Luke's Hospital	316	26
500 Jefferson Bldg.	316	21
Greenway 1 & 2	313	30
Marathon Manufacturing Co. Bldg.	313	21
Sterling Bldg.	312	22
Melrose Bldg.	308	21
Commerce Bldg.	306	22
Control Data Center	303	22
First National Life Bldg.	302	22

Indianapolis, Ind.

City	Hgt. ft.	Stories
*American United Life Ins. Co.	533	37
Indiana Natl. Bank Tower	504	37
City-County Bldg.	377	26
Indiana Bell Telephone	320	20
Blue Cross-Blue Shield Bldg.	302	18
Riley Towers (2 bldgs.)	294	30
Indiana Bell "220" Bldg.	284	20
Monument Circle	284	...
Market Square Office Bldg.	283	20

Jacksonville, Fla.

City	Hgt. ft.	Stories
Independent Life & Acccident Ins. Co.	535	37
Gulf Life Ins. Co. Bldg.	432	28
Prudential Ins. Co. of America	295	22
Blue Cross-Blue Shield	287	20
Atlantic National Bank	278	19

Jersey City, N.J.

Medical Center (5 bldgs.; 332 ft., 294 ft., 274 ft., (2) 273 ft.)

Kansas City, Mo.

City	Hgt. ft.	Stories
Kansas City Power and Light Bldg.	476	32
City Hall	443	29
Federal Office Bldg.	413	35
Commerce Tower	402	32
Southwest Bell Telephone Bldg.	394	27
Pershing Road Associates	352	28
A. T. & T. Long Line Bldg.	331	20
Bryant Bldg.	319	26
Federal Reserve Bldg.	311	21
City Center Square, 1100 Main	302	30
Holiday Inn	300	28

Las Vegas, Nev.

City	Hgt. ft.	Stories
*Sahara Hotel	376	37
Las Vegas Hilton	375	30
MGM Grand	362	26
Landmark Hotel	356	31
Sahara Hotel	294	24
Dunes Hotel	277	24

Little Rock, Ark.

City	Hgt. ft.	Stories
First National Bank	454	33
Worthen Bank & Trust	375	28
Union National Bank	331	24
Tower Bldg.	300	18

Los Angeles, Cal.

City	Hgt. ft.	Stories
United Cal. Bank	858	62
Security Pacific Natl. Bank	738	55
Atlantic Richfield Plaza (2 bldgs.)	699	52
Crocker-Citizen Plaza	620	42
*Jay Square, 444 S. Flower St.	597	48
Century Plaza Towers (2 bldgs.)	571	44
Union Bank Square	516	41
City Hall	454	28
Equitable Life Bldg.	454	34
Occidental Life Bldg.	452	32
Mutual Benefit Life Ins. Bldg.	435	31
Broadway Plaza	414	33
1900 Ave. of Stars	398	27
1 Wilshire Bldg.	395	28
Bonaventure Hotel, 404 S. Figueroa	367	34
Cal. Fed. Savings & Loan Bldg.	363	28
Century City Office Bldg.	363	24
Bunker Hill Towers	349	32
International Industries Plaza	347	24
City Natl. Bank Bldg.	344	24
Wilshire West Plaza	327	24

Louisville, Ky.

City	Hgt. ft.	Stories
First Natl. Bank	512	40
Citizen's Plaza	420	30
Galt House	325	25
Louisville Trust Bldg.	312	24
800 Apartments Bldg.	290	29

Memphis, Tenn.

City	Hgt. ft.	Stories
100 N. Main Bldg.	430	37
Commerce Square	396	31
Sterick Bldg.	365	31
Clark, 5100 Poplar	365	32
First Natl. Bank Bldg.	332	25
Hyatt Regency	329	28
Lowenstein's Towers	296	25
Lincoln American Life Tower	290	22

Miami, Fla.

City	Hgt. ft.	Stories
One Biscayne Corp.	456	40
First Federal Savings & Loan	375	32
Dade County Court House	357	28
New World Center	340	30
Plaza Venetia	332	33
Flagler Center Bldg.	318	25
Omni International Hotel	296	29

City	Hgt. ft.	Stories
Brickell Bay Club	286	29
Milwaukee, Wis.		
First Wis. Center & Office Tower	625	42
City Hall	350	9
Wisconsin Telephone Co.	313	19
Marine Plaza Bldg.	288	22
Allen-Bradley Co.	280	17
Minneapolis, Minn.		
IDS Center	772	57
Pillsbury Bldg., 200 S. 6th St.	529	40
Foshay Tower, not including 163-ft. antenna tower	447	32
Hennepin County Government Center	403	24
First Natl. Bank Bldg.	366	28
Municipal Building	355	14
North Western Bell Telephone	350	26
Cedar-Riverside	337	39
Dain Tower	311	26
Montreal, Que.		
Place Victoria	624	47
Place Ville Marie	616	42
Canadian Imperial Bank of Commerce	604	43
Le Complexe Desjardins		
La Tour du Sud	498	40
La Tour du L'Est	428	32
La Tour du Nord	355	27
La Tour Laurier	425	36
C.I.L. House	429	32
Chateau Champlain Hotel	420	38
Port Royal Apts.	400	33
Royal Bank Tower	397	22
Sun Life Bldg.	390	26
Banque Canadienne National	390	32
Place du Canada	372	33
Hydro Quebec	360	27
Alexis Nihon Plaza	331	33
Bell Telephone	324	22
Le Cartier Apts.	320	32
Nashville, Tenn.		
Natl. Life & Acc. Ins. Co.	452	31
Nashville Life & Casualty Tower	409	30
James K. Polk State Office Bldg.	383	32
First American Natl. Bank	354	28
Hyatt Regency	300	28
Third Natl. Bank Bldg.	292	20
Andrew Jackson State Office Bldg.	286	17
Newark, N.J.		
National Newark & Essex Bank	465	36
Raymond-Commerce	448	36
Prudential Corporate Bldg.	369	27
Prudential Ins. Co., 753 Broad St.	360	26
Western Electric Bldg.	359	31
Gateway 1	359	31
American Insurance Company	326	21
Raymond Plaza West	310	26
Prudential Ins. Co., 213 Washington St.	300	15
New Haven, Conn.		
Knights of Columbus Hqs.	319	23
New Orleans, La.		
One Shell Square	697	51
Plaza Tower	531	45
Marriott Hotel	450	42
Canal Place One	439	32
Bank of New Orleans	438	31
Int'l. Trade Mart Bldg.	407	33
225 Baronne St.	362	28
Hyatt-Regency Hotel, Poydras Plaza	360	25
Hibernia Bank Bldg.	355	23
1250 Poydras Plaza	341	24
New Orleans Hilton, Intl. River Center	340	29
American Bank Bldg.	330	23
Pan American Life Bldg.	323	27
Canal LaSalle Bldg.	288	24
New York, N.Y.		
World Trade Center (2 towers)	1,350	110
Empire State, 34th St. & 5th Ave.	1,250	102
TV tower, 222 ft., makes total	1,472	...
Chrysler, Lexington Ave. & 43d St.	1,046	77
American International Bldg., 70 Pine St.	950	67
40 Wall Tower	927	71
Citicorp Center	914	46
RCA, Rockefeller Center	850	70
1 Chase Manhattan Plaza	813	60
Pan Am Bldg., 200 Park Ave.	808	59
Woolworth, 233 Broadway	792	60
1 Penn Plaza	764	57
Exxon, 1251 Ave. of Americas	750	54
1 Liberty Plaza	743	50
Citibank	741	57
One Astor Plaza	730	54
Union Carbide Bldg., 270 Park Ave.	707	52
General Motors Bldg.	705	50
Metropolitan Life, 1 Madison Ave.	700	50
500 5th Ave.	697	60
9 W. 57th St.	688	50
Chem. Bank, N.Y. Trust Bldg.	687	50
55 Water St.	687	53
Chanin, Lexington Ave. & 42d St.	680	56
Gulf & Western Bldg.	679	44
Marine Midland Bldg., 140 Bway.	677	52
McGraw Hill, 1221 Ave. of Am.	674	51
Lincoln, 60 E. 52d Street	673	53
1633 Broadway	670	48
American Brands, 245 Park Ave.	648	47
*A. T. & T. Tower, 570 Madison Ave.	648	37
General Electric, 570 Lexington	640	50
Irving Trust, 1 Wall St.	640	50
345 Park Ave.	634	44
Grace Plaza, 1114 Ave. of Am.	630	50
1 New York Plaza	630	50
Home Insurance Co. Bldg.	630	44
N.Y. Telephone, 1095 Ave. of Am.	630	40
888 7th Ave.	628	42
1 Hammarskjold Plaza	628	50
Waldorf-Astoria, 301 Park Ave.	625	47
Burlington House, 1345 Ave. of Am.	625	50
Olympic Tower, 645 5th Ave.	620	51
10 E. 40th St.	620	48
New York Life, 51 Madison Ave.	615	40
Penney Bldg., 1301 Ave. of Am.	609	46
*IBM, 590 Madison Ave.	603	41
560 Lexington Ave.	600	46
Celanese Bldg., 1211 Ave. of Am.	592	45
U.S. Court House, 505 Pearl St.	590	37
Federal Bldg., Foley Square	587	41
Time & Life, 1271 Ave. of Am.	587	47
Cooper Bregstein Bldg., 1250 Bway.	580	40
1185 Ave. of Americas	580	42
Municipal, Park Row & Centre St.	580	34
1 Madison Square Plaza	576	42
Westvaco Bldg. 299 Park Ave.	574	42
Socony Mobil Bldg., East 42d St.	572	45
Sperry Rand Bldg., 1290 Ave. of Am.	570	43
600 3d Ave.	570	42
Helmsley Bldg., 230 Park Ave.	565	35
1 Bankers Trust Plaza	565	40
30 Broad St.	562	48
Sherry-Netherland, 5th Ave. & 59th St.	560	40
Continental Can, 633 3d Ave.	557	39
Sperry & Hutchinson, 330 Madison	555	39
Galleria, 117 E. 57th St.	552	57
Interchem Bldg., 1133 Ave. of Am.	552	45
N.Y. Telephone, 323 Bway.	550	45
919 3d Ave.	550	47
Burroughs Bldg., 605 3d Ave.	550	44
Bankers Trust, 33 E. 48 St.	547	41
Transportation Bldg., 225 Bway.	546	45
Equitable Life, 1285 Ave. of Am.	540	42
Ritz Tower, Park Ave. & 57th St.	540	41
Bankers Trust, 6 Wall St.	540	39
1166 Ave. of Americas	540	44
Equitable, 120 Broadway	538	42
1700 Broadway	533	41
Downtown Athletic Club, 19 West St.	530	45
Nelson Towers, 7th Ave. & 34th St.	525	45
Hotel Pierre, 5th Ave. & 61st St.	525	44
House of Seagram, 375 Park Ave.	525	38
Random House, 825 3d Ave.	522	40
3 Park Ave.	522	42
North American Plywood, 800 3d Ave.	520	41
Du Mont Bldg., 515 Madison Ave.	520	42
26 Broadway	520	31
Newsweek Bldg., 444 Madison Ave.	518	43
Sterling Drug Bldg., 90 Park Ave.	515	41
First National City Bank	515	41
Bank of New York, 48 Wall St.	513	32
Navarre, 512 7th Ave.	513	43
Williamsburg Savings Bank, Bklyn.	512	42
ITT—American, 437 Madison Ave.	512	40

City	Hgt. ft.	Stories
International, Rockefeller Center	512	41
1407 Broadway Realty Corp.	512	44
United Nations, 405 E. 42 St.	505	39
Park Vendome Tower	505	48
2 New York Plaza	504	40
22 E. 40th St.	503	43
60 Broad St.	503	39
Sheraton Centre	501	51
World Apparel Center, 1411 Bway.	501	42
Oakland, Cal.		
Ordway Bldg., 2150 Valdez St.	404	28
Kaiser Bldg.	390	28
Clorox Bldg.	330	24
City Hall	319	15
Tribune Tower	305	21
United Cal. Bank Bldg.	297	18
Blue Cross Bldg.	296	21
Telephone Bldg.	289	15
Oklahoma City, Okla.		
Liberty Tower	500	36
First National Bank	493	33
City National Bank Tower	440	32
Kerr-McGee Center	393	30
Fidelity Plaza	310	15
Southwestern Bell Telephone	303	15
The Regency Tower	288	25
Omaha, Neb.		
Woodmen Tower	469	30
Northwestern Bell Telephone Hdqrs.	334	16
Masonic Manor	320	22
First Natl. Bank	295	22
Ottawa, Ont.		
Place de Ville, Tower C	368	28
Skyline Hotel	315	23
Place Bell Canada	310	25
DBS Tower	308	26
Holiday Inn	300	25
Parliament Bldgs., Peace Tower	296	...
L'Esplanade Laurier (2 towers)	290	21
Philadelphia, Pa.		
City Hall Tower, incl. 37-ft. statue of Wm. Penn	548	7
1818 Market St.	500	40
Fidelity Mutual Life Ins. Bldg.	490	38
Phila. Saving Fund Society	490	39
Central Penn Natl. Bank	490	36
Centre Square	490	40
Industrial Valley Bank Bldg.	482	32
Philadelphia National Bank	475	25
2000 Market St. Bldg.	435	29
Atlantic Richfield Tower, Centre Square	412	33
Fidelity Bank Bldg.	410	30
Two Girard Plaza	404	30
Lewis Tower, 15th & Locust	397	33
Fifteen Hundred Locust	390	44
Philadelphia Electric Co.	384	27
INA Annex, 1600 Arch St.	383	27
Academy House, 1420 Locust St.	377	37
Penn Mutual Life	375	20
The Drake, 15th & Spruce	375	33
Medical Tower, 255 So. 17th	364	33
State Bldg., 1400 Spring Garden	351	18
United Engineers, 17th & Ludlow	344	20
Packard, 15th & Chestnut	340	25
Inquirer Building	340	18
Dorchester	339	32
Transportation Centre	336	18
Land Title, Broad & Chestnut	331	22
Suburban Station Bldg.	330	21
Phoenix, Ariz.		
Valley National Bank	483	40
Arizona Bank Downtown	407	31
First National Bank	372	27
United Bank Plaza, 3334 N. Central	356	27
First Federal Savings Bldg.	341	26
Regency Apts.	297	21
Hyatt-Regency Hotel	281	21
Del Webb Towne House	280	23
Pittsburgh, Pa.		
U.S. Steel Bldg.	841	64
Gulf, 7th Ave. and Grant St.	582	44
University of Pittsburgh	535	42
Mellon Bank Bldg.	520	41
1 Oliver Plaza	511	39
Grant, Grant St. at 3rd Ave.	485	40
Koppers, 7th Ave. and Grant	475	34
Equibank Bldg.	445	34
Pittsburgh National Bldg.	424	30
Alcoa Bldg., 425 Sixth Ave.	410	30
Westinghouse Bldg.	355	23
Oliver, 535 Smithfield St.	347	25
Gateway Bldg. No. 3	344	24
Centre City Tower	341	26
Federal Bldg., 1000 Liberty Ave.	340	23
Bell Telephone, 416 7th Ave.	339	21
Hilton Hotel	333	22
Frick, 437 Grant St.	330	20
Portland, Ore.		
First Natl. Bank of Oregon	538	41
Georgia Pacific Bldg.	367	27
Providence, R.I.		
Industrial National Bank	420	26
Rhode Island Hospital Trust Tower	410	30
40 Westminster Bldg.	301	24
Richmond, Va.		
Federal Reserve Bank	393	21
First & Merchants Natl. Bank	313	26
City Hall	310	18
One James River Plaza	302	21
Central National Bank Bldg.	282	24
Rochester, N.Y.		
Xerox Tower	443	30
Lincoln First Tower	390	26
Eastman Kodak Bldg.	360	19
First Federal Bank Plaza	305	22
Marine Midland Bank Bldg.	280	22
St. Louis, Mo.		
Gateway Arch	630	...
1st National Bank/IBM	560	40
Mercantile Trust Bldg.	485	35
Laclede Gas. Bldg., 8th & Olive	400	30
S.W. Bell Telephone Bldg.	398	31
Civil Courts	387	13
Queeny Tower	321	24
Counsil House Plaza	320	30
Park Plaza Hotel	310	30
Pierre Laclede Tower	309	24
Stauffer's Riverfront Inn, 3rd St.	301	22
Riverfront Holiday Inn	290	22
Mansion House	285	22
7777 Bonhomme Bldg.	285	22
500 Broadway	282	22
Marriott Hotel	280	22
Equitable Bldg.	280	21
St. Paul, Minn.		
First Natl. Bank Bldg., incl. 100-ft. sign	517	32
Osborn Bldg.	368	20
Kellogg Square Apts.	366	32
Northwestern Bell Telephone Bldg.	340	15
American National Bank Bldg.	335	25
North Central Tower	328	27
St. Paul Cathedral	307	...
Conwed Tower	305	25
U.S. Post Office Bldg.	274	12
St. Paul Radisson Hotel	273	24
Salt Lake City, Ut.		
L.D.S. Church Office Bldg.	420	30
Beneficial Life Tower	351	27
City & County Bldg.	290	...
State Capitol	285	...
Univ. Club Bldg.	277	24
San Antonio, Tex.		
Tower of the Americas	622	...
Tower Life	404	30
Nix Professional Bldg.	375	23
Natl. Bank of Commerce	310	24
First Natl. Bank Tower	302	20
Frost Bank Tower	300	21
Alamo National Bldg.	288	23
Milam Bldg.	280	20
San Diego, Cal.		
California First Bank	388	27
Wickes Bldg.	340	25

City	Hgt. ft.	Stories
Financial Square	339	24
Central Federal	320	22
Union Bank	320	22
Little America Westgate Hotel	303	19
San Diego Gas & Electric Bldg.	293	21
Chamber Bldg.	281	23
San Francisco, Cal.		
Transamerica Pyramid	853	48
Bank of America	778	52
Security Pacific Bank	569	45
One Market Plaza, Spear St.	565	43
Wells Fargo Bldg.	561	43
Standard Oil, 575 Market St.	551	39
Shaklee Bldg., 444 Market	537	38
Aetna Life	529	38
First & Market Bldg.	529	38
Metropolitan Life	524	38
Hilton Hotel	493	46
Pacific Gas & Electric	492	34
Union Bank	487	37
Pacific Insurance	476	34
Bechtel Bldg., Fremont St.	475	33
333 Market Bldg.	474	33
Hartford Bldg.	465	33
Mutual Benefit Life	438	32
Russ Bldg.	435	31
Pacific Telephone Bldg.	435	26
Embarcadero Center, No. 3	412	31
Levi Strauss	412	31
Cal. State Automobile Assn.	399	29
Alcoa Bldg.	398	27
St. Francis Hotel	395	32
Shell Bldg.	386	29
595 Market Bldg.	379	30
Del Monte	378	28
Great Western Savings	359	26
Union Square Hyatt House Hotel	355	35
Equitable Life Bldg.	355	25
Fox Plaza	354	29
International Bldg.	350	22
450 Sutter Street	343	26
Cathedral Apts.	340	21
Royal Towers	330	24
Fairmont Hotel	330	29
Seattle, Wash.		
Seattle-1st Natl. Bank Bldg.	609	50
Space Needle	605	...
*Seafirst 5th Ave. Plaza	543	42
Bank of Cal., 900 4th Ave.	536	42
Rainer Bank Tower, 4th & Univ.	514	42
Smith Tower	500	42
Federal Office Bldg.	487	37
Pacific Northwest Bell	466	33
One Union Square	456	38
1111 3d Ave. Bldg.	454	35
Washington Plaza	397	40
Financial Center	389	30
Fourth & Blanchard Bldg.	360	24
Park Hilton Hotel	352	33
Safeco Plaza	325	22
Norton Bldg.	310	21
Springfield, Mass.		
Valley Bank Tower	370	29
Chestnut Towers	290	34
Syracuse, N.Y.		
State Tower	315	22
Tampa, Fla.		
*Tampa City Center	496	39
First Financial Tower	458	36
Exchange Natl. Bldg.	280	22
Toledo, Oh.		
Owens-Corning Fiberglas Tower	400	30
Owens Illinois Bldg.	368	27
Toledo Trust Bldg.	288	21

City	Hgt. ft.	Stories
Toronto, Ont.		
CN Tower, World's tallest self-supporting structure	1,821	...
First Bank Tower, First Canadian Place.	952	72
Commerce Court West	784	57
Toronto-Dominion Tower (TD Centre).	758	56
Royal Trust Tower (TD Centre)	600	46
Royal Bank Plaza—South Tower	589	41
Manulife Centre	545	53
Two Bloor West	486	34
Commerce Court North	476	34
Simpson Tower	473	33
Sun Life Centre	470	35
*Continental Place	466	34
Palace Pier (2 bldgs.)	452	46
Continental Bank Bldg.	450	35
Cadillac-Fairview Bldg., 10 Queen St.	445	33
Sheraton Centre	443	43
Hudson's Bay Centre	442	35
Leaside Towers (2 bldgs.)	423	44
Commercial Union Tower (TD Centre)	420	32
Maple Leaf Mills Tower	419	30
Plaza 2 Hotel	415	41
Royal York Hotel	399	27
390 Bay St.	394	31
Royal Bank Plaza—North Tower	387	26
Eaton Tower	385	29
Harborside Apts.	380	39
Harbour Castle Hilton, East	374	35
Travellers Tower	369	27
York Centre	360	27
3 Massey Square	354	38
Harbour Castle Hilton, West	353	35
Mowat Block	349	24
Toronto Professional Tower	346	26
L'Apartel at Harbour Square	344	36
Sutton Place Hotel	340	32
Richmond-Adelaide Centre	340	26
50 Cordova Ave.	340	36
Tulsa, Okla.		
Bank of Oklahoma Tower	667	52
1st National Tower	516	41
4th Natl. Bank of Tulsa	412	33
320 South Boston Bldg.	400	24
Cities Service Bldg.	388	28
Univ. Club Tower	377	32
Philtower	343	24
Vancouver, B.C.		
Harbour Centre (incl. 100 ft. pylon)	581	32
Royal Bank Tower	468	37
Scotiabank Tower	451	36
T-D Bank Tower	410	31
200 Granville Square	403	30
Sheraton-Landmark Hotel	394	41
First Bank Tower	386	30
Hyatt Regency Vancouver	357	36
Hotel Vancouver	352	22
Oceanic Plaza	342	26
Board of Trade Tower	342	26
MacMillan-Bloedel Bldg.	340	28
Guinness Tower	328	23
Marine Bldg.	321	21
Four Seasons Hotel	311	30
Martello Tower	300	31
Wilmington, Del.		
Hercules Tower	287	23
American Life Ins. Co. Bldg.	282	21
Winnipeg, Man.		
Richardson Bldg., 1 Lombard Place	439	34
55 Nassau St.	354	39
North Star Inn	300	30
1 Evergreen Place	294	32
Winston-Salem, N.C.		
Wachovia Bldg.	410	30
Reynolds Bldg.	315	21

Tall Buildings in Other Cities

Figures denote number of stories. Height in feet is in parentheses.

Cape Canaveral, Fla., Vehicle Assembly Bldg., 40 (552); Albuquerque, N.M., National Bldg., 18 (272); Allentown, Pa., Power & Light Bldg., 23 (320); Amarillo, Tex., American Natl. Bank, 33 (374); Bethlehem, Pa., Martin Tower, 21 (332); Charleston, W. Va., Kanawha Valley Bldg., 20 (384); Cuyahoga Falls, Oh., Cathedral Tower Restaurant, 60 (554); Frankfort, Ky., Capital Plaza Office Tower, 28 (338); Galveston, Tex., American National Ins., 20 (358); Greenville, S.C., Daniel Bldg., 22 (305); Halifax, N.S., Fenwick Towers, 31 (300); Knoxville, Tenn., United American Bank, 30 (400); Lansing, Mich., Michigan Natl. Tower, 25 (300, not including antenna tower); Lexington, Ky., Kinkaid Tower, 22 (333); Lincoln, Neb., State Capitol (432); Mobile, Ala., First Natl. Bank, 33 (420); Niagara Falls, Ont., Skylon, (520); Norfolk, Va., Va. Natl. Bank, 23 (304); So. Bend Ind., American National Bank Bldg., 25 (312); Tacoma, Wash., Washington Plaza, 23 (290); Tallahassee, Fla., State Capitol Tower, 22 (345).

STATES AND OTHER AREAS OF THE U.S.

Sources: Population: Bureau of the Census (July 1, 1979 provisional estimates, including armed forces personnel in each state but excluding such personnel stationed overseas); area: Geography Division, Bureau of the Census; Value added by manufacture: Bureau of the Census; lumber production: Commerce Department; mineral production: Bureau of Mines; commercial fishlandings: Marine Fisheries Service; per capita income: Bureau of Economic Analysis, Commerce Department; forested land: Department of Agriculture, Forest Service; unemployment: Bureau of Labor Statistics; energy production: Energy Department; education: Education Department; construction valuation: Dodge Construction Potentials, McGraw-Hill Information Systems Company.

Alabama

Heart of Dixie, Cotton State

People. Population (1979): 3,769,000; **rank:** 22. **Pop. density:** 74.3 per sq. mi. **Urban** (1970): 58.4%. **Racial distrib. (1975):** 74.2% White; 25.4% Black; Hispanic (1970): 13,313. **Major ethnic groups:** German, English, Italian, Polish. **Net migration** (1970-79): +75,000.

Geography. Total area: 51,609 sq. mi.; **rank:** 29. **Land area:** 50,708 sq. mi. **Acres forested land:** 21,361,100. **Location:** in the east south central U.S., extending N-S from Tenn. to the Gulf of Mexico; east of the Mississippi River. **Climate:** long, hot summers; mild winters; generally abundant rainfall. **Topography:** coastal plains inc. Prairie Black Belt give way to hills, broken terrain; highest elevation, 2,407 ft. **Capital:** Montgomery.

Economy. Principal industries: apparel, textiles, primary metals, lumber and wood, food processing, fabricated metals, automotive tires. **Principal manufactured goods:** cast iron and plastic pipe, ships, paper products, chemicals, steel, mobile homes, fabrics, poultry processing. **Value added by manufacture** (1977): $8.4 bln. **Agriculture: Chief crops:** soybeans, cotton, peanuts, corn, hay, wheat, pecans, peaches, potatoes, tomatoes. **Livestock:** 1.73 mln. cattle; 880,000 hogs/pigs; 3,700 sheep; 22 mln. poultry. **Timber/lumber** (1978): pine, hardwoods; 1.3 bln. bd. ft. **Minerals** (1977): natural gas, bituminous coal, crude petroleum, accounting for 80% of the $1.3 bln. total mineral value for raw materials. Also, cement and stone. **Commercial fishing** (1979): $50 mln. **Chief ports:** Mobile. **Value of construction** (1979): $2.6 bln. **Employment distribution:** 25% manuf.; 18% trade; 13% serv. **Per capita income** (1979): $6,976. **Unemployment** (1979): 7.1% **Tourism** (1979): tourists spent $2.2 bln.

Finance (1977). **No. banks:** 312; **No. savings and loan assns.:** 60.

Federal government. No. federal civilian employees (Mar. 1979): 49,300. **Avg. salary:** $18,685. **Notable federal facilities:** George C. Marshall NASA Space Center, Huntsville; Maxwell AFB, Montgomery; Ft. Rucker, Ozark; Ft. McClellan, Anniston.

Energy. Electricity production (1979, mwh, by source): Hydroelectric: 11.8 mln. Mineral: 49.8 mln. Nuclear: 22.1 mln.

Education. No. schools: 1,557 elem. and second.; 56 higher ed. **Avg. salary, public school teachers** (1979): $12,600.

State data. Motto: We dare defend our rights. **Flower:** Camellia. **Bird:** Yellowhammer. **Tree:** Southern pine. **Song:** Alabama. **Entered union** Dec. 14, 1819; rank, 22d. **State fair** at: Birmingham; early Oct.

History. First Europeans were Spanish explorers in the early 1500s. The French made the first permanent settlement, on Mobile Bay, 1701-02; later, English settled in the northern areas. France ceded the entire region to England at the end of the French and Indian War, 1763, but Spanish Florida claimed the Mobile Bay area until U. S. troops took it, 1813. Gen. Andrew Jackson broke the power of the Creek Indians, 1814, and they were removed to Oklahoma. The Confederate States were organized Feb. 4, 1861, at Montgomery, the first capital.

Tourist attractions. Jefferson Davis' "first White House" of the Confederacy; Ivy Green, Helen Keller's birthplace at Tuscumbia; statue of Vulcan near Birmingham; George Washington Carver Museum at Tuskegee Institute.

At Russell Cave National Monument, near Bridgeport, may be seen a detailed record of occupancy by humans from about 7000 BC to 1650 AD.

Famous Alabamians include Hank Aaron, Tallulah Bankhead, Hugo L. Black, George Washington Carver, Nat King Cole, William C. Handy, Helen Keller, Harper Lee, Joe Louis, John Hunt Morgan, Jesse Owens, Booker T. Washington, Hank Williams.

Chamber of Commerce: 468 S. Perry St., P.O. Box 76, Montgomery, AL 36101.

Alaska

No official nickname

People. Population (1979): 406,000; **rank:** 50. **Pop. density:** 0.7 per sq. mi., **Urban** (1970): 48.4%. **Major ethnic groups:** Anglo-Saxons, Alaska natives (Eskimos, Aleuts and Indians). **Net migration** (1970-79): +47,000.

Geography. Total area: 589,757 sq. mi.; **rank:** 1. **Land area:** 569,600 sq. mi. **Acres forested land:** 119,114,900. **Location:** NW corner of North America, bordered on east by Canada. **Climate:** SE, SW, and central regions, moist and mild; far north extremely dry. Extended summer days, winter nights, throughout. **Topography:** includes Pacific and Arctic mountain systems, central plateau, and Arctic slope. Mt. McKinley, 20,320 ft., is the highest point in North America. **Capital:** Juneau.

Economy. Principal industries: oil, gas. **Principal manufactured goods:** fish products, lumber and pulp, furs. **Value added by manufacture** (1977): $479.3 mln. **Agriculture: Chief crops:** barley, hay, silage, potatoes, lettuce, milk, eggs. **Livestock:** 8,300 cattle; 800 hogs/-pigs; 6,500 sheep; 28,000 poultry. **Timber/lumber:** spruce, yellow cedar, hemlock. **Minerals** (1979): crude petroleum, natural gas, sand and gravel. Total mineral production valued at $5.7 bln. **Commercial fishing** (1979): $597 mln. **Chief ports:** Skagway, Juneau, Sitka, Valdez, Wrangell. **International airports at:** Anchorage, Fairbanks, Juneau. **Value of construction** (1979): $630 mln. **Employment distribution:** 27.9% gvt.; 16.1% serv. 9% transp. **Per capita income** (1979): $11,252 **Unemployment** (1979): 9.2% **Tourism** (1979): out-of-state visitors spent $650 mln.

Finance (1977). **No. banks:** 12; **No. savings and loan assns.:** 4.

Federal government. No. federal civilian employees (Mar. 1979): 12,633. **Avg. salary:** $21,439.

Energy. Electricity production (1979, mwh, by source): Hydroelectric: 458,548; Mineral: 2.6 mln.; Nuclear: 1.8 mln.

Education. No. schools: 402 elem. and second.; 9 higher ed. **Avg. salary, public school teachers** (1978): $22,397.

State data. Motto: North to the future. **Flower:** Forget-me-not. **Bird:** Willow ptarmigan. **Tree:** Sitka spruce. **Song:** Alaska's Flag. **Entered union:** Jan. 3, 1959; rank, 49th. **State fair at:** Palmer; late Aug.—early Sept.

History. Vitus Bering, a Danish explorer working for Russia, was the first European to land in Alaska, 1741. Alexander Baranov, first governor of Russian America, set up headquarters at Archangel, near present Sitka, in 1799. Secretary of State William H. Seward in 1867 bought Alaska from Russia for $7.2 million, a bargain some called "Seward's Folly." In 1896 gold was discovered and the famed Gold Rush was on.

Tourist attractions: Glacier Bay National Monument, Mt. McKinley National Park, one of North America's great wildlife sanctuaries, Pribilof Islands fur seal rookeries, restored St. Michael's Russian Orthodox Cathedral, Sitka.

Famous Alaskans include Carl Eielson, Ernest Gruening, Joe Juneau, Sydney Laurence, James Wickersham.

Chamber of Commerce: 200 N. Franklin St., Juneau, AK 99801.

Arizona

Grand Canyon State

People. Population (1979): 2,450,000; **rank:** 30. **Pop. density:** 21.6 per sq. mi. **Urban** (1970): 79.6%. **Racial distrib. (1975):** 90.7% White; 3.0% Black; 6.2% Other (includes American Indians); Hispanic (1970): 333,349. **Major ethnic groups:** Mexican, German, English, Italian. **Net migration** (1970-79): +464,000.

Geography. Total area: 113,909 sq. mi.; **rank:** 6. **Land area:** 113,417 sq. mi. **Acres forested land:** 18,493,900. **Location:** in the southwestern U.S. **Climate:** clear and dry in the southern regions and northern plateau; high central areas have heavy winter snows. **Topography:** Colorado plateau in the N, containing the Grand Canyon; Mexican Highlands running diagonally NW to SE; Sonoran Desert in the SW. **Capital:** Phoenix.

Economy: Principal industries: manufacturing, tourism, mining, agriculture. **Principal manufactured goods:** electronics, printing and publishing, foods, primary and fabricated metals, aircraft and missiles, apparel. **Value added by manufacture** (1977): $3.4 bln. **Agriculture: Chief crops:** cotton, sorghum, barley, corn, wheat, sugar beets, citrus fruits. **Livestock:** 1.14 mln. cattle; 99,000 hogs/pigs; 490,000 sheep; 565,000 poultry. **Timber/lumber** (1978): pine, fir, spruce; 383 mln. bd. ft. **Minerals** (1979): copper (prod. valued at $1.9 bln. 75% of total mineral production), gold, silver, molybdenum, sand and gravel, lime. **International airports at:** Phoenix, Tucson, Yuma. **Value of construction** (1979): $3.6 bln. **Employment distribution** (1979): 24.1% trade, 20.3% gvt., 19.5% serv., 14.7% manuf. **Per capita income** (1979): $8,305. **Unemployment** (1979): 5.1% **Tourism** (1979): tourists spent $4.0 bln.

Finance (1977). **No. banks:** 20; **No. savings and loan assns.:** 16.

Federal government: No. federal civilian employees Mar. 1979: 25,914. **Avg. salary:** $17,019. **Notable federal facilities:** Williams, Luke, Davis-Monthan AF bases; Ft. Huachuca Army Base; Yuma Proving Grounds.

Energy. Electricity production (1979, mwh, by source): Hydroelectric: 7.2 mln.; Mineral: 27.7 mln.; Nuclear: 4.7.

Education. No. schools: 1,009 elem. and second.; 22 higher ed. **Avg. salary, public school teachers** (1979): $14,682.

State data. Motto: Ditat Deus (God enriches). **Flower:** Blossom of the Seguaro cactus. **Bird:** Cactus wren. **Tree:** Paloverde. **Song:** Arizona. **Entered union** Feb. 14, 1912; rank, 48th. **State fair** at: Phoenix; late Oct.–early Nov.

History. Marcos de Niza, a Franciscan, and Estevan, a black slave, explored the area, 1539. Eusebio Francisco Kino, Jesuit missionary, taught Indians Christianity and farming, 1690-1711, left a chain of missions. Spain ceded Arizona to Mexico, 1821. The U. S. took over at the end of the Mexican War, 1848. The area below the Gila River was obtained from Mexico in the Gadsden Purchase, 1854. Long Apache wars did not end until 1886, with Geronimo's surrender.

Tourist attractions. The Grand Canyon of the Colorado, an immense, vari-colored fissure 217 mi. long, 4 to 13 mi. wide at the brim, 4,000 to 5,500 ft. deep; the Painted Desert, extending for 30 mi. along U.S. 66; the Petrified Forest; Canyon Diablo, 225 ft. deep and 500 ft. wide; Meteor Crater, 4,150 ft. across, 570 ft. deep, made by a prehistoric meteor. Also, London Bridge at Lake Havasu City.

Famous Arizonans include Cochise, Geronimo, Barry Goldwater, Zane Grey, George W. P. Hunt, Helen Jacobs, Percival Lowell, William H. Pickering, Morris Udall, Stewart Udall, Frank Lloyd Wright.

Chamber of Commerce: 2701 E. Camelback Rd. Phoenix, AZ 85016.

Arkansas

Land of Opportunity

People. Population (1979): 2,180,000; **rank:** 33. **Pop. density:** 42.0 per sq. mi. **Urban** (1970): 50%. **Racial distrib.** (1975): 81.6% White; 16.9% Black; Hispanic (1970): 9,333. **Major ethnic groups:** German, English, Italian, Polish. **Net migration** (1970-79): +136,000.

Geography. Total area: 53,104 sq. mi.; **rank:** 27. **Land area:** 51,945 sq. mi. **Acres forested land:** 18,281,500. **Location:** in the west south-central U.S. **Climate:** long, hot summers, mild winters; generally abundant rainfall. **Topography:** eastern delta and prairie, southern lowland forests, and the northwestern highlands, which include the Ozark Plateaus. **Capital:** Little Rock.

Economy. Principal industries: manufacturing, agriculture, tourism. **Principal manufactured goods:** poultry products, forestry products, aluminum, electric motors, transformers, garments, shoes, bricks, fertilizer, petroleum products. **Value added by manufacture** (1977): $4.9 bln. **Agriculture: Chief crops:** soybeans, rice, cotton, hay, wheat, sorghum, tomatoes, strawberries. **Livestock:** 2 mln. cattle; 400,000 hogs/pigs; 4,900 sheep; 40.3 mln. poultry. **Timber/lumber** (1978): oak, hickory, gum, cypress, pine; 1.6 bln. bd. ft. **Minerals** (1979): bauxite, bromine, and vanadium prod. 1st in U.S. Also natural gas, crude petroleum. Total mineral production valued at $667.9 mln. **Commercial fishing** (1979): $9.6 mln. **Chief ports:** Little Rock, Pine Bluff, Osceola, Helena, Fort Smith, Van Buren, Camden. **Value of construction** (1979): $1.8 mln. **Employment distribution:** 26.5% manuf.; 19.8% trade; 13.5% serv.; 8.9% agric. **Per capita income** (1979): $6,785. **Unemployment** (1979): 6.2% **Tourism** (1977): out-of state visitors spent $1.1 bln.

Finance (1977). **No. banks:** 259; **No. savings and loan assns.:** 71.

Federal government. No. federal civilian employees (Mar. 1979): 11,657. **Avg. salary:** $16,637. **Notable federal facilities:** Nat'l. Center for Toxicological Research, Jefferson; Pine Bluff Arsenal.

Energy. Electricity production (1979, mwh, by source): Hydroelectric: 3.4 mln.; Mineral: 9.6 mln.; Nuclear: 3.9 mln.

Education. No. schools: 1,264 elem. and second.; 29 higher ed. **Avg. salary, public school teachers** (1979): $11,447.

State data. Motto: Regnat Populus (The people rule). **Flower:** Apple Blossom. **Bird:** Mockingbird. **Tree:** Pine. **Song:** Arkansas. **Entered union:** June 15, 1836; rank, 25th. **State fair at:** Little Rock; late Sept.- early Oct.

History. First European explorers were de Soto, 1541, Jolliet, 1673; La Salle, 1682. First settlement was by the French under Henri de Tonty, 1686, at Arkansas Post. In 1762 the area was ceded by France to Spain, then back again in 1800, and was part of the Louisiana Purchase by the U.S. in 1803. Arkansas seceded from the Union in 1861, only after the Civil War began, and more than 10,000 Arkansans fought on the Union side.

Tourist attractions. Hot Springs National Park, water

ranging from 95° to 147°F; Blanchard Caverns, near Mountain View, are among the nation's largest; Crater of Diamonds, near Murfreesboro, only U.S. diamond mine.

Famous Arkansans include Hattie Caraway, "Dizzy" Dean, Orval Faubus, James W. Fulbright, Douglas MacArthur, John L. McClellan, Winthrop Rockefeller, Edward Durell Stone, Archibald Yell.

Chamber of Commerce: 911 Wallace Bldg., Little Rock, AR 72201.

California

Golden State

People. Population (1979): 22,694,000; **rank:** 1. **Pop. density:** 145.1 per sq. mi. **Urban** (1970): 90.9%. **Racial distrib. (1975):** 88.0% White; 7.6% Black; 4.4% Other (includes American Indians, Asian Americans, and Pacific Islanders); Hispanic (1970): 3,101,589. **Major ethnic groups:** English, German, Italian, Russian. **Net migration** (1970-79): +1,248,000.

Geography. Total area 158,693 sq. mi.; **rank:** 3. **Land area:** 156,361 sq. mi. **Acres forested land:** 40,152,100. **Location:** on western coast of the U.S. **Climate:** moderate temperatures and rainfall along the coast; extremes in the interior. **Topography:** long mountainous coastline; central valley; Sierra Nevada on the east; desert basins of the southern interior; rugged mountains of the north. **Capital:** Sacramento.

Economy. Principal industries: agriculture, aerospace, manufacturing, construction, recreation. **Principal manufactured goods:** foods, primary and fabricated metals, machinery, electric and electronic equipment, chemicals and allied products. **Value added by manufacture** (1977): $55.5 bln. **Agriculture: Chief crops:** cotton, grapes, dairy products, lettuce, eggs, tomatoes, nursery products, nuts, apricots, avocados, citrus fruits, barley, rice, olives. **Livestock** (1979): 4.7 mln. cattle; 190,000 hogs/pigs; 965,000 sheep; 83.2 mln. poultry. **Timber/-lumber** (1978): fir, pine, redwood, oak; 4.9 bln. bd. ft. **Minerals** (1977): crude petroleum, natural gas, and natural gas liquids 69% of to'al value mineral production, $4.1 bln. **Commercial fishing** (1979): $227.5 mln. **Chief ports:** Long Beach, San Diego, Oakland, San Francisco, Sacramento, Stockton. **International airports at:** Los Angeles, San Francisco. **Value of construction** (1979): $18 bln. **Employment distrubution** (1978): 22.3% trade; 20.8% serv.; 17.3% gvt. **Per capita income** (1979): $9,913 **Unemployment** (1979): 6.2% **Tourism** (1976): out-of-state visitors spent $12.4 bln.

Finance (1977). **Notable industries:** banking, insurance, real estate, investment. **No. banks:** 229; **No. savings and loan assns.:** 165.

Federal government. No. federal civilian employees (Mar. 1979): 204,790. **Avg. salary:** $18,319. **Notable federal facilities:** Vandenberg, Beale, Travis, McClellan AF bases, San Francisco Mint.

Energy. Electricity production (1979, mwh, by source): Hydroelectric: 34 mln.; Mineral: 106.5 mln.; Nuclear: 8.8 mln.

Education. No. schools: 8,684 elem. and second.; 252 higher ed. **Avg. salary, public school teachers** (1978): $17,149.

State Data. Motto: Eureka (I have found it). **Flower:** Golden poppy. **Bird:** California valley quail. **Tree:** California redwood. **Song:** I Love You, California. **Entered Union** Sept. 9, 1850; rank, 31st. **State fair** at: Sacramento; late Aug.—early Sept.

History. First European explorers were Cabrillo, 1542, and Drake, 1579. First settlement was the Spanish Alta California mission at San Diego, 1769, first in a string founded by Franciscan Father Junipero Serra. U. S. traders and settlers arrived in the 19th century and staged the abortive Bear Flag Revolt, 1846; the Mexican War began later in 1846 and U.S. forces occupied California; Mexico ceded the province to the U.S., 1848, the same year the Gold Rush began.

Tourist attractions. Scenic regions are Yosemite Valley; Lassen and Sequoia-Kings Canyon national parks; Lake Tahoe; the Mojave and Colorado deserts; San Francisco Bay; and Monterey Peninsula. Oldest living things on earth are believed to be a stand of Bristlecone pines in the Inyo National Forest, est. to be 4,600 years old. The world's tallest tree, the Howard Libbey redwood, 362 ft. with a girth of 44 ft., stands on Redwood Creek, Humboldt County.

Also, Palomar Observatory; Disneyland; J. Paul Getty Museum, Malibu; Tournament of Roses and Rose Bowl.

Famous Californians include Luther Burbank, John C. Fremont, Bret Harte, Wm. R. Hearst, Jack London, Aimee Semple McPherson, John Muir, William Saroyan, Junipero Serra, Leland Stanford, John Steinbeck, Earl Warren.

Chamber of Commerce: 455 Capitol Mall, Sacramento, CA 95814.

Colorado

Centennial State

People. Population (1979): 2,772,000; **rank:** 28. **Pop. density:** 26.7 per sq. mi. **Urban** (1970): 78.5%. **Racial distrib.** (1975): 95.3% White; 3.4% Black; Hispanic (1970): 286,467. **Major ethnic groups:** German, Russian, English, Italian. **Net migration** (1970-79): +350,000.

Geography. Total area: 104,247 sq. mi.; **rank:** 8. **Land area:** 103,766 sq. mi. **Acres forested land:** 22,271,000. **Location:** in west central U.S. **Climate:** low relative humidity, abundant sunshine, wide daily, seasonal temperatures ranges; alpine conditions in the high mountains. **Topography:** eastern dry high plains; hilly to mountainous central plateau; western Rocky Mountains of high ranges alternating with broad valleys and deep, narrow canyons. **Capital:** Denver.

Economy. Principal industries: manufacturing, government, mining, tourism, agriculture, aerospace. **Principal manufactured goods:** computer equipment, instruments, foods, machinery, aerospace products, rubber, steel. **Value added by manufacture** (1979): $6.14 bln. **Agriculture: Chief crops:** corn, wheat, hay, sugar beets, barley, potatoes, apples, peaches, pears, soy beans. **Livestock** (1979): 3.1 mln. cattle; 330,000 hogs/pigs; 795,000 sheep; 6,450,000 poultry. **Timber/lumber** (1979): oak, ponderosa pine, Douglas fir; 330.8 mln. bd. ft. **Minerals** (1979): molybdenum, uranium, coal, natural gas, petroleum. Total mineral production valued at $1.6 bln. **International airports at:** Denver. **Value of construction** (1979): $3.2 bln. **Employment distribution** (1979): 21.2% trade; 17.1% serv.; 16.7% gvt.; 12.8% manuf. **Per capita income** (1979): $8,945. **Unemployment** (1979): 4.8% **Tourism** (1979): out-of-state visitors spent $890 mln.

Finance (1977). **No. banks:** 299; **No. savings and loan assns.:** 46.

Federal government. No. federal civilian employees (Mar. 1979): 34,896. **Avg. salary:** $18,836. **Notable federal facilities:** U.S. Air Force Academy; U.S. Mint; Ft. Carson, Lowry AFB; Solar Energy Research Institute; U.S. Rail Transport. Test Center.

Energy. Electricity production (1979, mwh, by source): Hydroelectric: 1.6 mln.; Mineral: 20.7 mln.; Nuclear: 212,882.

Education. No. schools: 1,422 elem. and second.; 39 higher ed. **Avg. salary, public school teachers** (1979): $14,990.

State data. Motto: Nil Sine Numine (Nothing without Providence). **Flower:** Rocky Mountain columbine. **Bird:** Lark bunting. **Tree:** Colorado blue spruce. **Song:** Where the Columbines Grow. Entered union Aug. 1, 1876; rank 38th. **State fair** at: Pueblo; last week in Aug.

History. Early civilization centered around Mesa Verde 2,000 years ago. The U.S. acquired eastern Colorado in the Louisiana Purchase, 1803; Lt. Zebulon M. Pike explored the area, 1806, discovering the peak that bears his name. After the Mexican War, 1846-48, U.S. immigrants settled in the east, former Mexicans in the south.

Tourist attractions. Rocky Mountain National Park; Garden of the Gods; Great Sand Dunes and Dinosaur national monuments; Pikes Peak and Mt. Evans highways; Mesa Verde National Park (pre-historic cliff dwellings); 35 major ski areas. The Grand Mesa tableland comprises Grand Mesa Forest, 659,584 acres, with 200 lakes stocked with trout.

Famous Coloradans include Frederick Bonfils, William N. Byers, M. Scott Carpenter, Jack Dempsey, Douglas Fairbanks, Lowell Thomas, Byron R. White, Paul Whiteman.

Tourist information: Dept. of Local Affairs, 1313 Sherman St., Denver, CO 80203.

Connecticut

Constitution State, Nutmeg State

People. Population (1979): 3,115,000; **rank:** 24. **Pop. density:** 640.7 per sq. mi. **Urban** (1970): 77.4%. **Racial distrib. (1975):** 93.4% White; 6.1% Black; Hispanic (1970): 73,357. **Major ethnic groups:** Italian, Polish, English, Irish. **Net migration** (1970-79): −37,000.

Geography. Total area: 5,009 sq. mi.; **rank:** 48. **Land area:** 4,862 sq. mi. **Acres forested land:** 1,860,800. **Location:** New England state in the northeastern corner of the U.S. **Climate:** moderate; winters avg. slightly below freezing, warm, humid summers. **Topography:** western upland, the Berkshires, in the NW, highest elevations; narrow central lowland N-S; hilly eastern upland drained by rivers. **Capital:** Hartford.

Economy. Principal industries: manufacturing, retail trade, government, services. **Principal manufactured goods:** aircraft engines and parts, submarines, copper wire and tubing, silverware, helicopters, bearings, cutlery, machine tools. **Value added by manufacture** (1977): $11 bln. **Agriculture: Chief crops:** tobacco, hay, apples, potatoes, nursery stock. **Livestock:** 108,000 cattle; 9,000 hogs/pigs; 5,400 sheep; 5.3 mln. poultry. **Timber/lumber** (1977): oak, birch, beech, maple; 43 mln. bd. ft. **Minerals** (1978): stone, sand and gravel. Total mineral production valued at $46.1 mln. **Commercial fishing** (1979): $6.9 mln. **Chief ports:** New Haven, Bridgeport, New London. **International airports at:** Windsor Locks. **Value of construction** (1979): $1.6 bln. **Employment distribution:** 31% manuf.; 19% serv. **Per capita income** (1979): $9,959. **Unemployment** (1979): 5.1% **Tourism** (1976): out-of-state visitors spent $1 bln.

Finance (1977). **Notable industries:** insurance, finance, banking. **No. banks:** 65; **No. savings and loan assns.:** 37.

Federal Government. No. federal civilian employees (Mar. 1979): 9,327. **Avg. salary:** $18,714. **Notable federal facilities:** U.S. Coast Guard Academy.

Energy. Electricity production (1979, mwh, by source): Hydroelectric: 454,966; Mineral: 10.7 mln.; Nuclear: 12.7 mln.

Education. No. schools: 1,396 elem. and second.; 46 higher ed. **Avg. salary, public school teachers** (1979): $15,494.

State data. Motto: Qui Transtulit Sustinet (He who transplanted still sustains). **Flower:** Mountain laurel. **Bird:** American robin. **Tree:** White oak. **Song:** Yankee Doodle Dandy. **Fifth** of the 13 original states to ratify the Constitution, Jan. 9, 1788.

History. Adriaen Block, Dutch explorer, was the first European visitor, 1614. By 1634, settlers from Plymouth Bay started colonies along the Connecticut River and in 1637 defeated the Pequot Indians. In the Revolution, Connecticut men fought in most major campaigns and turned back British raids on Danbury and other towns, while Connecticut privateers captured British merchant ships.

Tourist attractions. Winchester Gun Museum, Yale University's Art Gallery, Peabody Museum, all in New Haven; Mystic Seaport, Mystic, a recreated 19th century seaport village; P.T. Barnum Museum, Bridgeport.

Famous "Nutmeggers" include Ethan Allen, Phineas T. Barnum, Samuel Colt, Jonathan Edwards, Nathan Hale, Katharine Hepburn, Isaac Hull, J. Pierpont Morgan, Israel Putnam, Harriet Beecher Stowe, Mark Twain, Noah Webster, Eli Whitney.

Chamber of Commerce: Suite 1202, 60 Washington St., Hartford, CT 06106.

Delaware

First State, Diamond State

People. Population (1979): 582,000; **rank:** 47. **Pop. density:** 296.2 per sq. mi. **Urban** (1970): 72.2%. **Racial distrib.** (1975): 84.8% White; 14.7% Black; Hispanic (1970): 6,267. **Major ethnic groups:** Italian, English, Polish, German. **Net migration** (1970-79): −2,000.

Geography. Total area: 2,057 sq. mi.; **rank:** 49. **Land area:** 1,982 sq. mi. **Acres forested land:** 391,800. **Location:** occupies the Delmarva Peninsula on the Atlantic coastal plain. **Climate:** moderate. **Topography:** Piedmont plateau to the N, sloping to a near sea-level plain. **Capital:** Dover.

Economy. Principal industries: chemistry, agriculture, poultry, shellfish, tourism, auto assembly, food processing, transportation equipment. **Principal manufactured goods:** nylon, apparel, luggage, foods, cash registers, autos, processed meats and vegetables, railroad and aircraft equipment. **Value added by manufacture** (1977): $1.62 bln. **Agriculture: Chief crops:** soybeans, corn, potatoes, mushrooms, greenhouse and dairy products, grain, hay. **Livestock:** 31,000 cattle; 50,000 hogs/pigs; 1,700 sheep; 850,000 poultry. **Minerals** (1978): Sand and gravel. Total mineral production valued at $2.2 mln. **Commercial fishing** (1979): $638,000. **Chief ports:** Wilmington. **International airports at:** Philadelphia/Wilmington. **Value of construction** (1979): $343 mln. **Employment distribution:** 71.4% serv.; 26.8% manuf. **Per capita income** (1979): $9,537. **Unemployment** (1979): 18.0%. **Tourism** (1977): out-of-state visitors spent $313 mln.

Finance (1977). **No. banks:** 17; **No. savings and loan assns.:** 19.

Federal government. No. federal civilian employees (Mar. 1979): 3,106. **Avg. salary:** $17,556. **Notable federal facilities:** Dover Air Force Base, Federal Wildlife Refuge, Bombay Hook.

Energy. Electricity production (1979, mwh, by source): Hydroelectric: —; Mineral: 7 mln.; Nuclear: —.

Education. No. schools: 241 elem. and second.; 10 higher ed. **Avg. salary, public school teachers** (1979): $13,736.

State data. Motto: Liberty and independence. **Flower:** Peach blossom. **Bird:** Blue hen chicken. **Tree:** American holly. **Song:** Our Delaware. **First** of original 13 states to ratify the Constitution, Dec. 7, 1787. **State fair** at: Harrington; end of July.

History. The Dutch first settled in Delaware near present Lewes, 1631, but were wiped out by Indians. Swedes settled at present Wilmington, 1638; Dutch settled anew, 1651, near New Castle and seized the Swedish settlement, 1655, only to lose all Delaware and New Netherland to the British, 1664.

Tourist attractions. Ft. Christina Monument, the site of founding of New Sweden; John Dickinson "Penman of the Revolution" home, Dover; Henry Francis du Pont Winterthur Museum; Hagley Museum, Wilmington; Old Swedes (Trinity Parish) Church, erected 1698, is the oldest Protestant church in the U.S. still in use.

Famous Delawareans include Thomas F. Bayard, Henry Seidel Canby, E. I. du Pont, John P. Marquand, Howard Pyle, Caesar Rodney.

Chamber of Commerce: 1102 West St., Wilmington, DE 19081.

Florida

Sunshine State

People. Population (1979): 8,860,000; **rank:** 8. **Pop. density:** 163.8 per sq. mi. **Urban** (1970): 80.5%. **Racial distrib. 1975:** 85.1% White; 14.2% Black; Hispanic (1970): 451,382. **Major ethnic groups:** German, English, Italian, Russian. **Net migration** (1970-79): +1,848,000.

Geography: Total area: 58,560 sq. mi.; **rank:** 22. **Land area:** 54,090 sq. mi. **Acres forested land:** 17,039,700. **Location:** peninsula jutting southward 500 mi. bet. the Atlantic and the Gulf of Mexico. **Climate:** subtropical N of Bradenton-Lake Okeechobee-Vero Beach line; tropical S of line. **Topography:** land is flat or rolling; highest point is 345 ft. in the NW. **Capital:** Tallahassee.

Economy. Principal industries: services, trade, gvt., agriculture, tourism, manufacturing, aerospace, food processing, chemical, finance, insurance, real estate, construction. **Principal manufactured goods:** metal products, paper, electrical and transportation equipment. **Value added by manufacture** (1979): $9.3 bln. **Agriculture: Chief crops:** citrus fruits, vegetables, sugarcane, avocados, watermelons, peanuts, cotton, tobacco, strawberries. **Livestock** (1978): 2.8 mln. cattle; 393,000 hogs/-pigs; 4,500 sheep; 17.3 mln. poultry. **Timber/lumber** (1979): pine, oak, cypress, palm; 472 mln. bd. ft. **Minerals** (1978): natural gas, petroleum, stone, Portland cement. Total mineral production valued at $1.9 bln. **Commercial fishing** (1979): $124.0 mln. **Chief ports:** Tampa, Jacksonville, Miami, Pensacola. **International airports at:** Miami, Tampa, Jacksonville, Orlando. **Value of construction** (1979): $12.2 bln. **Per capita income** (1979): $8,532. **Unemployment** (1979): 7.5%. **Tourism** (1976): out-of-state visitors spent $9.3 bln.

Finance (1977). **No. banks:** 613; **No. savings and loan assns.:** 122.

Federal government. No. federal civilian employees (Mar. 1979): 52,988. **Avg. salary:** $18,367. **Notable federal facilities:** John F. Kennedy Space Center, Cape Canaveral.

Energy. Electricity production (1979, mwh, by source): Hydroelectric: 240,784; Mineral: 78.4 mln.; Nuclear: 15.4 mln.

Education. No. schools: 2,486 elem. and second.; 73 higher ed. **Avg. salary, public school teachers** (1979): $13,545.

State data. Motto: In God we trust. **Flower:** Orange blossom. **Bird:** Mockingbird. **Tree:** Sabal palmetto palm. **Song:** Swanee River. **Entered union** Mar. 3, 1845; rank, 27th.

History. First European to see Florida was Ponce de Leon, 1513. France established a colony, Fort Caroline, on the St. Johns River, 1564; Spain settled St. Augustine, 1565, and Spanish troops massacred most of the French. Britain's Francis Drake burned St. Augustine, 1586. Britain held the area briefly, 1763-83, returning it to Spain. After Andrew Jackson led a U.S. invasion, 1818, Spain ceded Florida to the U.S., 1819. The Seminole War, 1835-42, resulted in removal of most Indians to Oklahoma. Florida seceded from the Union, 1861, was readmitted, 1868.

Tourist attractions. Miami, with the nation's greatest concentration of luxury hotels at Miami Beach; St. Augustine, oldest city in U.S.; Walt Disney World, an entertainment and vacation development near Orlando, Kennedy Space Center, Cape Canaveral.

Everglades National Park, 3d largest of U.S. national parks, preserves the beauty of the vast Everglades swamp. Castillo de San Marcos, St. Augustine, is a national monument. Also, the Ringling Museum of Art, the Ringling Museum of the Circus, and the Circus Hall of Fame, all in Sarasota.

Famous Floridians include Henry M. Flagler, James Weldon Johnson, MacKinlay Kantor, Henry B. Plant, Marjorie Kinnan Rawlings, Joseph W. Stilwell, Charles P. Summerall.

Chamber of Commerce: P.O. Box 5497, Tallahassee, FL 32301.

Georgia

Empire State of the South, Peach State

People. Population (1979): 5,117,000; **rank:** 13. **Pop. density:** 88.1 per sq. mi. **Urban** (1970): 60.3%. **Racial distrib.** (1975): 73.5% White; 26.1% Black; Hispanic (1970): 29,824. **Major ethnic groups:** German, English, Russian, Italian. **Net migration** (1970-79): +128,000.

Geography. Total area: 58,876 sq. mi.; **rank:** 21. **Land area:** 58,073 sq. mi. **Acres forested land:** 25,256,100. **Location:** South Atlantic state. **Climate:** maritime tropical air masses dominate in summer; continental polar air masses in winter; east central area drier. **Topography:** most southerly of the Blue Ridge Mtns. cover NE and N central; central Piedmont extends to the fall line of rivers; coastal plain levels to the coast flatlands. **Capital:** Atlanta.

Economy. Principal industries: manufacturing, forestry, agriculture, chemicals. **Principal manufactured goods:** textiles, transportation equipment, foods, clothing, paper and wood products, chemical products, cigarettes. **Value added by manufacture** (1977): $12.5 bln. **Agriculture: Chief crops:** cotton, peanuts, tobacco, pecans, peaches, rye, corn, soybeans. **Livestock** (1978): 1.85 mln. cattle; 1.59 mln. hogs/pigs; 3,200 sheep; 38.6 mln. poultry. **Timber/lumber** (1978): pine, hardwood; 1.3 bln. bd. ft. **Minerals** (1978): clay, crushed stone, and cement accounted for 91% of the total mineral production (valued at $577 mln.). **Commercial fishing** (1979): $27.7 mln. **Chief ports:** Savannah, Brunswick. **International airports at:** Atlanta. **Value of construction** (1979): $3.7 bln. **Employment distribution:** 25.2% manuf.; 22% trade; 14.2% serv. **Per capita income** (1979): $7,515. **Unemployment** (1979): 5.1% **Tourism** (1979): tourists spent $2.2 bln.

Finance (1977). **No. banks:** 440; **No. savings and loan assns.:** 96.

Federal government. No. federal civilian employees (Mar. 1979): 59,565. **Avg. salary:** $17,863. **Notable federal facilities:** Robins AFB; Fts. Benning, Gordon, McPherson; Nat'l. Law Enforcement Training Ctr., Glynco.

Energy. Electricity production (1979, mwh, by source): Hydroelectric: 4.4 mln.; Mineral: 46.7 mln.; Nuclear: 5.1 mln.

Education. No. schools: 1,998 elem. and second.; 67 higher ed. **Avg. salary, public school teachers** (1977): $9,911.

State data. Motto: Wisdom, justice and moderation. **Flower:** Cherokee rose. **Bird:** Brown thrasher. **Tree:** Live oak. **Song:** Georgia On My Mind. **Fourth** of the 13 original states to ratify the Constitution, Jan. 2, 1788.

History. Gen. James Oglethorpe established the first settlements, 1733, for poor and religiously-persecuted Englishmen. Oglethorpe defeated a Spanish army from Florida at Bloody Marsh, 1742. In the Revolution, Georgians seized the Savannah armory, 1775, and sent the munitions to the Continental Army; they fought seesaw campaigns with Cornwallis' British troops, twice liberating Augusta and forcing final evacuation by the British from Savannah, 1782.

Tourist attractions. The Little White House in Warm Springs where Pres. Franklin D. Roosevelt died Apr. 12, 1945, 2,500-acre Callaway Gardens, Jekyll Island State Park, the restored 1850s farming community of Westville; Dahlonega, site of America's first gold rush; Stone Mountain, and Six Flags Over Georgia.

Okefenokee in the SE is one of the largest swamps in the U.S., a wetland wilderness and peat bog covering 660 sq. mi. A large part of it is a National Wildlife Refuge, a home for wild birds, alligators, bear, deer.

Famous Georgians include James Bowie, Erskine Caldwell, Lucius D. Clay, Ty Cobb, John C. Fremont, Joel Chandler Harris, Martin Luther King Jr., Sidney Lanier, Margaret Mitchell, Joseph Wheeler.

Chamber of Commerce: 1200 Commerce Bldg., Atlanta, GA 30303.

Hawaii

Aloha State

People. Population (1979): 915,000; **rank:** 40. **Pop. density:** 142.4 per sq. mi. **Urban** (1970): 83.1%. **Racial distrib.** (1975): 36.5% White; —% Black; 62.2% Other (includes Asian Americans and Pacific Islanders); Hispanic (1970): 23,276. **Major ethnic groups:** Caucasian, part-Hawaiian, Japanese, Filipino, Chinese. **Net migration.** (1970-79): +36,000.

Geography. Total area: 6,450 sq. mi.; **rank:** 47. **Land area:** 6,425 sq. mi. **Acres forested land:** 1,986,000. **Location:** Hawaiian Islands lie in the North Pacific, 2,397 mi. SW from San Francisco. **Climate:** temperate, mountain regions cooler; Mt. Waialeale, on Kauai, wettest spot in the U.S. annual rainfall 486.1 in. **Topography:** islands are tops of a chain of submerged volcanic mountains; active volcanoes: Mauna Loa, Kilauea. **Capital:** Honolulu.

Economy. Principal industries: tourism, government, sugar refining, agriculture, aquaculture, fishing, motion pictures, manufacturing. **Principal manufactured goods:** sugar, canned pineapple, clothing, foods. **Value added by manufacture** (1977): $790.9 mln. **Agriculture: Chief crops:** sugar, pineapples, macadamia nuts, coffee, guava, vegetables and melons. **Livestock:** 213,000 cattle; 53,000 hogs/pigs; 1.3 mln. poultry. **Minerals** (1979): Portland cement, stone. Total mineral production valued at $55 mln. **Commercial fishing** (1979): $10.7 mln. **Chief ports:** Honolulu, Port Allen, Kahului, Hilo. **International airports at:** Honolulu. **Value of construction** (1979): $1.0 bln. **Employment distribution:** 66.7% among gvt., construct., trade; 23.9% serv. **Per capita income** (1979): $9,353. **Unemployment** (1979): 6.3%. **Tourism** (1979): visitors spent $3.9 bln.

Finance (1977). **No. banks:** 8; **No. savings and loan assns.:** 8.

Federal government. No. federal civilian employees (Mar. 1979): 22,129. **Avg. salary:** $19,234. **Notable federal facilities:** Pearl Harbor Naval Shipyard; Hickam AFB; Schofield Barracks.

Energy. Electricity production (1979, mwh, by source): Hydroelectric: 20,508; Mineral: 6.4 mln.; Nuclear: —.

Education. No. schools: 302 elem. and second.; 11 higher ed. **Avg. salary, public school teachers** (1979): $18,281.

State data. Motto: The life of the land is perpetuated in righteousness. **Flower:** Hibiscus. **Bird:** Hawaiian goose. **Tree:** Candlenut. **Song:** Hawaii Ponoi. **Entered union** Aug. 21, 1959; rank, 50th. **State fair** at: Honolulu; late May through mid-June.

History. Polynesians from islands 2,000 mi. to the south settled the Hawaiian Islands, probably about 700 A.D. First European visitor was British Capt. James Cook, 1778. Missionaries arrived, 1820, taught religion, reading and writing. King Kamehameha III and his chiefs created the first Constitution and a Legislature which set up a public school system. Sugar production began in 1835, it became the dominant industry. In 1893, Queen Liliuokalani was deposed, followed, 1894, by a republic headed by Sanford B. Dole. Annexation by the U.S. came in 1898.

Tourist attractions. Natl. Memorial Cemetery of the Pacific, USS Arizona Memorial, Pearl Harbor; Hawaii Volcanoes, Haleakala National Parks, Kilauea; Polynesian Cultural Center, Diamond Head, Waikiki Beach, Oahu.

Famous Islanders include John A. Burns, Father Joseph Damien, Sanford Dole, Hiram L. Fong, Daniel K. Inouye, Duke Kahanamoku, Queen Liliuokalani, Queen Kaahumanu, Bernice Pauahi Bishop, Bette Midler.

Chamber of Commerce: Dillingham Bldg., 735 Bishop St., Honolulu, HI 96813.

Idaho

Gem State

People. Population (1979): 905,000; **rank:** 41. **Pop. density:** 11.0 per sq. mi. **Urban** (1970): 54.1%. **Racial distrib.** (1975): 98.2% White; —% Black; Hispanic (1970): 18,476. **Major ethnic groups:** English, German, Swedish, Norwegian. **Net migration** (1970-79): +100,000.

Geography. Total area: 83,557 sq. mi.; **rank:** 13. **Land area:** 82,677 sq. mi. **Acres forested land:** 21,726,600. **Location:** Pacific Northwest-Mountain state bordering on British Columbia. **Climate:** tempered by Pacific westerly winds; drier, colder, continental clime in SE; altitude an important factor. **Topography:** Snake R. plains in the S; central region of mountains, canyons, gorges (Hells Canyon, 7,000 ft., deepest in N.A.); subalpine northern region. **Capital:** Boise.

Economy. Principal industries: agriculture, manufacturing, tourism, lumber, mining, electronics. **Principal manufactured goods:** processed foods, lumber and wood products, chemical products, primary metals, fabricated metal products, machinery. **Value added by manufacture** (1977): $1.4 bln. **Agriculture: Chief crops:** potatoes, peas, sugar beets, alfalfa seed, wheat, hops, barley, plums and prunes, mint, onions, corn, cherries, apples, trout. **Livestock:** 1.14 mln. cattle; 79,000 hogs/pigs; 486,000 sheep; 1.211 mln. poultry. **Timber/lumber** (1978): yellow, white pine; Douglas fir; white spruce; 2.0 bln. bd. ft. **Minerals** (1979): silver, phosphate rock, lead, zinc, sand and gravel. Total mineral production valued at $415 mln. **Commercial fishing** (1979): $35,000. **Chief ports:** Lewiston. **International airports at:** Boise. **Value of construction** (1979) $672 mln. **Employment distribution:** 20.3% trade; 18.1% agric.; 14.1% manuf.; 4.5% serv. **Per capita income** (1979): $7,446. **Unemployment** (1979): 5.7% **Tourism** (1976): out-of-state visitors spent $540 mln.

Finance (1977). **No. banks:** 24; **No. savings and loan assns.:** 11.

Federal government. No. federal civilian employees (Mar. 1979): 6,606. **Avg. salary:** $18,198. **Notable federal facilities:** Ida. Nat'l. Engineering Lab, Idaho Falls; Nat'l. Reactor Testing Sta., Upper Snake River Plains.

Energy. Electricity production (1979, mwh, by source): Hydroelectric: 9.2 mln.; Mineral: 40,789; Nuclear —.

Education: No. schools: 584 elem. and second.; 9 higher ed. **Avg. salary, public school teachers** (1979): $12,617.

State data. Motto: Esto Perpetua (It is perpetual). **Flower:** Syringa. **Bird:** Mountain bluebird. **Tree:** White pine. **Song:** Here We Have Idaho. **Entered union** July 3, 1890; rank, 43d. **State fair** at: Boise and Blackfoot; late Aug.—early Sept.

History. Exploration of the Idaho area began with Lewis and Clark, 1805-06. Next came fur traders, setting up posts, 1809-34, and missionaries, establishing missions, 1830s-1850s. Mormons made their first permanent settlement at Franklin, 1860. Idaho's Gold Rush began that same year, and brought thousands of permanent settlers. Strangest of the Indian Wars was the 1,300-mi. trek in 1877 of Chief Joseph and the Nez Perce tribe, pursued by troops that caught them a few miles short of the Canadian border. In 1890, Idaho adopted a progressive Constitution and became a state.

Tourist attractions. Hells Canyon, deepest gorge in N.A.; Craters of the Moon; Sun Valley, year-round resort in the Sawtooth Mtns.; Crystal Falls Cave; Shoshone Falls; Lava Hot Springs; Lake Pend Oreille; Lake Coeur d'Alene.

Famous Idahoans include William E. Borah, Fred T. Dubois, Chief Joseph, Sacagawea.

Chamber of Commerce: P.O. Box 389, Boise, ID 83701.

Illinois

The Inland Empire

People. Population (1979): 11,229,000; **rank:** 5. **Pop. density:** 201.4 per sq. mi. **Urban** (1970): 83%. **Racial distrib.** (1975): 85.3% White; 13.7% Black; Hispanic

(1970): 364,397. **Major ethnic groups:** German, Polish, Italian, English, Russian. **Net migration** (1970-79): −542,000.

Geography. Total area: 56,400 sq. mi.; **rank:** 24. **Land area:** 55,748 sq. mi. **Acres forested land:** 3,810,400. **Location:** east-north central state; western, southern, and eastern boundaries formed by Mississippi, Ohio, and Wabash Rivers, respectively. **Climate:** temperate; typically cold, snowy winters, hot summers. **Topography:** prairie and fertile plains throughout; open hills in the southern region. **Capital:** Springfield.

Economy. Principal industries: manufacturing, wholesale and retail trade, agriculture, finance, insurance, real estate, publishing. **Principal manufactured goods:** machinery, electric and electronic equipment, foods, primary and fabricated metals, chemical products, precision instruments. **Value added by manufacture** (1977): $40.3 bln. **Agriculture: Chief crops:** corn, soybeans, wheat, oats, hay. **Livestock** (1979): 2.85 mln. cattle; 6.55 mln. hogs/-pigs; 167,000 sheep; 17.6 mln. poultry. **Timber/lumber** (1978): cottonwood, gum, walnut; 221 mln. bd. ft. **Minerals** (1977): mineral fuels (coal, natural gas, petroleum) accounted for 75% of the total $1.7 bln. mineral production. Also stone, sand and gravel, cement. **Commercial fishing** (1979): $1.0 mln. **Chief ports:** Chicago. **International airports at:** Chicago. **Value of construction** (1979): $7.0 bln. **Employment distribution:** 24% manuf.; 17% serv.; 2% agric. **Per capita income** (1979): $9,823. **Unemployment** (1979) 5.5%. **Tourism** (1975): out-of-state visitors spent $3.7 bln.

Finance (1977). **Notable industries:** insurance, real estate. **No. banks:** 1,241; **No. savings and loan assns.:** 399.

Federal government. No. federal civilian employees (Mar. 1979): 54,813. **Avg. salary:** $18,353. **Notable federal facilities:** Fermi Nat'l. Accelerator Lab; Argonne Nat'l. Lab; Ft. Sheridan; Rock Island, Scott Field military installations, Great Lakes, Rantoul.

Energy. Electricity production (1979, mwh, by source): Hydroelectric: 112,192; Mineral: 77.1 mln.; Nuclear: 27.5 mln.

Education. No. schools: 5,571 elem. and second.; 149 higher ed. **Avg. salary, public school teachers** (1978): $15,518.

State data. Motto: State sovereignty—national union. **Flower:** Native violet. **Bird:** Cardinal. **Tree:** White oak. **Song:** Illinois. **Entered union** Dec. 3, 1818; rank, 21st. **State fair** at: Springfield; mid-Aug.

History. Fur traders were the first Europeans in Illinois, followed shortly, 1673, by Jolliet and Marquette, and, 1680, La Salle, who built a fort near present Peoria. First settlements were French, at Fort St. Louis on the Illinois River, 1692, and Kaskaskia, 1700. France ceded the area to Britain, 1763; Amer. Gen. George Rogers Clark, 1778, took Kaskaskia from the British without a shot. Defeat of Indian tribes in Black Hawk War, 1832, and railroads in 1850s, inspired immigration.

Tourist attractions: Lincoln shrines at Springfield, New Salem, Sangamon; Cahokia Mounds, E. St. Louis; Starved Rock State Park; Crab Orchard Wildlife Refuge; Mormon settlement at Nauvoo; Fts. Kaskaskia, Chartres, Massac (parks).

Famous Illinoisans include Jane Addams, William Jennings Bryan, Stephen A. Douglas, James T. Farrell, Ernest Hemingway, Edgar Lee Masters, Carl Sandburg, Adlai Stevenson, Frank Lloyd Wright.

Chamber of Commerce: 20 N. Wacker Dr., Chicago, IL 60606.

Indiana

Hoosier State

People. Population (1979): 5,400,000; **rank:** 12. **Pop. density:** 149.6 per sq. mi. **Urban** (1970): 64.9%. **Racial distrib. (1975):** 92.4% White; 7.3% Black; Hispanic (1970): 67,188. **Major ethnic groups:** German, Polish, English, Mexican. **Net migration** (1970-79): −150,000.

Geography. Total area: 36,291 sq. mi.; **rank:** 38. **Land area:** 36,097 sq. mi. **Acres forested land:** 3,942,900. **Location:** east north-central state; Lake Michigan on northern border. **Climate:** 4 distinct seasons with a temperate climate. **Topography:** hilly southern region; fertile rolling plains of central region; flat, heavily glaciated north; dunes along Lake Michigan shore. **Capital:** Indianapolis.

Economy: Principal industries: manufacturing, wholesale and retail trade, agriculture, government, services. **Principal manufactured goods:** primary and fabricated metals, transportation equipment, electrical and electronic equipment, non-electrical machinery, chemical products, foods. **Value added by manufacture** (1977): $23 bln. **Agriculture: Chief crops:** corn, oats, wheat, soybeans, hay. **Livestock:** 1.75 mln. cattle; 4.4 mln. hogs/pigs; 160,000 sheep; 20.9 mln. poultry. **Timber/lumber** (1977): oak, tulip, beech, sycamore; 166 mln. bd. ft. **Minerals** (1978): mineral fuels, esp. coal; sand, gravel, stone; total $741.4 mln. mineral production. **Commercial fishing** (1979): $66,000. **Chief ports:** Lake Michigan facility, east of Gary, Southwind Maritime Centre at Mt. Vernon. **International airports at:** Indianapolis. **Value of construction** (1979): $3.5 bln. **Employment distribution** (1979): 31.4% manuf.; 21.2% trade; 14.1% serv. **Per capita income** (1979): $8,686. **Unemployment** (1979). 6.4%. **Tourism** (1978): tourists spent $1.9 bln.

Finance (1977). **No. banks:** 404; **No. savings and loan assns.:** 166.

Federal government. No. federal civilian employees (Mar. 1979): 23,670. **Avg. salary:** $17,248. **Notable federal facilities:** Naval Avionics Ctr.; Ft. Benjamin Harrison; Grissom AFB; Navy Weapons Support Ctr., Crane.

Energy. Electricity production (1979, mwh, by source): Hydroelectric: 438,476; Mineral: 66.6 mln.; Nuclear: — .

Education. No. schools: 2,479 elem. and second.; 64 higher ed. **Avg. salary, public school teachers** (1979): $13,354.

State data. Motto: Crossroads of America. **Flower:** Peony. **Bird:** Cardinal. **Tree:** Tulip poplar. **Song:** On the Banks of the Wabash, Far Away. **Entered union** Dec. 11, 1816; rank, 19th. **State fair** at: Indianapolis; mid-Aug.

History: Pre-historic Indian Mound Builders of 1,000 years ago were the earliest known inhabitants. A French trading post was built, 1731-32, at Vincennes and La Salle visited the present South Bend area, 1679 and 1681. France ceded the area to Britain, 1763. During the Revolution, American Gen. George Rogers Clark captured Vincennes, 1778, and defeated British forces 1779; at war's end Britain ceded the area to the U.S. Miami Indians defeated U.S. troops twice, 1790, but were beaten, 1794, at Fallen Timbers by Gen. Anthony Wayne. At Tippecanoe, 1811, Gen. William H. Harrison defeated Tecumseh's Indian confederation.

Tourist attractions. Lincoln, George Rogers Clark memorials; Wyandotte Cave; Vincennes, Tippecanoe sites; Indiana Dunes; Hoosier Nat'l. Forest; Benjamin Harrison Home.

Famous "Hoosiers" include Ambrose Burnside, Hoagy Carmichael, Eugene V. Debs, Theodore Dreiser, Paul Dresser, Cole Porter, Gene Stratton Porter, Ernie Pyle, James Whitcomb Riley, Booth Tarkington, Lew Wallace, Wendell L. Willkie, Wilbur Wright.

Chamber of Commerce: Board of Trade Building, Indianapolis, IN 46204.

Iowa

Hawkeye State

People. Population (1979): 2,902,000; **rank:** 25. **Pop. density:** 51.9 per sq. mi. **Urban** (1970): 57.2%. **Racial distrib.** (1975): 98.4% White; 1.4% Black; Hispanic (1970): 17,448. **Major ethnic groups:** German, Scandinavian, English, Dutch. **Net migration** (1970-79): −56,000.

Geography. Total area: 56,290 sq. mi.; **rank:** 25. **Land**

area: 55,941 sq. mi. **Acres forested land:** 1,561,300. **Location:** Midwest state bordered by Mississippi R. on the E and Missouri R. on the W. **Climate:** humid, continental. **Topography:** Watershed from NW to SE; soil especially rich and land level in the N central counties. **Capital:** Des Moines.

Economy. Principal industries: manufacturing, agriculture. **Principal manufactured goods:** tires, farm machinery, electronic products, appliances, office furniture, chemicals, fertilizers, auto accessories. **Value added by manufacture** (1977): $8.7 bln. **Agriculture: Chief crops:** silage and grain corn, soybeans, oats, hay. **Livestock** (1978): 3.2 mln. cattle; 19.7 mln. hogs/pigs; 240,000 sheep; 8.4 mln. poultry. **Timber/lumber:** red cedar. **Minerals** (1978): cement, stone, and sand and gravel accounted for 93% of the total $263 mln. production. **Commercial fishing** (1979): $818,000. **Value of construction** (1979): $2.4 bln. **Per capita income** (1979): $8,589. **Unemployment** (1979): 4.1%. **Tourism** (1978): tourists spent $1.27 bln.

Finance (1977). **No. banks:** 650; **No. savings and loan assns.:** 78.

Federal government. No. federal civilian employees (Mar. 1979): 8,028. **Avg. salary:** $17,396.

Energy. Electricity production (1979, mwh, by source): Hydroelectric: 896,565; Mineral: 16.5 mln.; Nuclear: 2.9 mln.

Education. No. schools: 2,127 elem. and second.; 61 higher ed. **Avg. salary, public school teachers** (1979): $14,199.

State data. Motto: Our liberties we prize and our rights we will maintain. **Flower:** Wild rose. **Bird:** Eastern goldfinch. **Tree:** Oak. **Song:** The Song of Iowa. **Entered union** Dec. 28, 1846; rank, 29th. **State fair** at: Des Moines; mid-to-late Aug.

History. A thousand years ago several groups of prehistoric Indian Mound Builders dwelt on Iowa's fertile plains. Marquette and Jolliet gave France its claim to the area, 1673. It became U.S. territory through the 1803 Louisiana Purchase. Indian tribes were moved into the area from states further east, but by mid-19th century were forced to move on to Kansas. Before and during the Civil War, Iowans strongly supported Abraham Lincoln and became traditional Republicans.

Tourist attractions. Herbert Hoover birthplace and library, West Branch; Effigy Mounds Nat'l. Monument, Marquette, a pre-historic Indian burial site; Davenport Municipal Art Gallery's collection of Grant Wood's paintings and memorabilia.

Famous Iowans include James A. Van Allen, Marquis Childs, Buffalo Bill Cody, Susan Glaspell, James Norman Hall, Harry Hansen, Billy Sunday, Carl Van Vechten, Henry Wallace, Meredith Willson, Grant Wood.

Tourist information: Travel Development Council, 250 Jewett Bldg., Des Moines, IA 50319.

Kansas

Sunflower State

People. Population (1979): 2,369,000; **rank:** 32. **Pop. density:** 29.0 per sq. mi. **Urban** (1970): 66.1%. **Racial distrib.** (1975): 94.4% White; 4.7% Black; Hispanic (1970): 46,706. **Major ethnic groups:** German, Russian, English, Mexican. **Net migration** (1970-79): −4,000.

Geography. Total area: 82,264 sq. mi.; **rank:** 14. **Land area:** 81,787 sq. mi. **Acres forested land:** 1,344,400. **Location:** West North Central state, with Missouri R. on E. **Climate:** temperate but continental, with great extremes bet. summer and winter. **Topography:** hilly Osage Plains in the E; central region level prairie and hills; high plains in the W. **Capital:** Topeka.

Economy. Principal industries: agriculture, machinery, mining, aerospace. **Principal manufactured goods:** processed foods, aircraft, petroleum products, farm machinery. **Value added by manufacture** (1977): $5.4 bln. **Agriculture: Chief crops:** wheat, sorghum, corn, hay. **Livestock:** 6.1 mln. cattle; 1.93 mln. hogs/pigs; 235,000 sheep; 2.47 mln. poultry. **Timber/lumber:** oak, walnut. **Minerals** (1979): petroleum, natural gas liquids, cement salt, stone, sand and gravel. Total mineral production $2.4 bln. **Commercial fishing** (1979): $35,000. **Chief ports:** Kansas City. **International airports at:** Wichita. **Value of construction** (1979): $1.8 bln. **Employment distribution:** 18.8% trade; 16.4% manuf.; 15.1% gvt.; 13.7% serv. **Per capita income** (1979): $9,055. **Unemployment** (1979): 3.4% **Tourism** (1977): out-of-state visitors spent $1 bln.

Finance (1977). **No. banks:** 616; **No. savings and loan assns.:** 85.

Federal government. No. federal civilian employees (Mar. 1979): 13,856. **Avg. salary:** $17,400. **Notable federal facilities:** McConnell AFB; Fts. Riley, Leavenworth.

Energy. Electricity production (1979, mwh, by source): Hydroelectric: 3,654; Mineral: 23.6 mln.; Nuclear: —.

Education. No. schools: 1,794 elem. and second.; 52 higher ed. **Avg. salary, public school teachers** (1979): $13,278.

State data. Motto: Ad Astra per Aspera (To the stars through difficulties). **Flower:** Native sunflower. **Bird:** Western meadowlark. **Tree:** Cottonwood. **Song:** Home on the Range. **Entered union** Jan. 29, 1861; rank, 34th. **State fair** at: Hutchinson; 2d week of Sept.

History. Coronado marched through the Kansas area, 1541; French explorers came next. The U.S. took over in the Louisiana Purchase, 1803. In the pre-war North-South struggle over slavery, so much violence swept the area it was called Bleeding Kansas. Railroad construction after the war made Abilene and Dodge City terminals of large cattle drives from Texas.

Tourist attractions. Eisenhower Center and "Place of Meditation," Abilene; Agricultural Hall of Fame and National Ctr., Bonner Springs, displays farm equipment; Dodge City; Ft. Scott.

Famous Kansans include Thomas Hart Benton, John Brown, Walter P. Chrysler, Amelia Earhart, Cyrus Holliday, Gen. Hugh Johnson, Walter Johnson, Alf Landon, Brock Pemberton, Robert Stroud.

Chamber of Commerce: 500 First National Tower, One Townsite Plaza, Topeka, KS 66603.

Kentucky

Bluegrass State

People. Population (1979): 3,527,000 **rank:** 23. **Pop. density:** 89.0 per sq. mi. **Urban** (1970): 52.3%. **Racial Distrib. (1975):** 92.5% White; 7.2% Black; Hispanic (1970): 11,112. **Major ethnic groups:** German, English, Italian, Irish. **Net migration** (1970-79): +91,000.

Geography. Total area: 40,395 sq. mi.; **rank:** 37. **Land area:** 39,650 sq. mi. **Acres forested land:** 12,160,800. Location: east south central state, bordered on N by Illinois, Indiana, Ohio; on E by West Virginia and Virginia; in S by Tennessee; on W by Missouri. **Climate:** moderate, with plentiful rainfall. **Topography:** mountainous in E; rounded hills of the Knobs in the N; Bluegrass, heart of state; wooded rocky hillsides of the Pennyroyal; Western Coal Field; the fertile Purchase the SW. **Capital:** Frankfort.

Economy. Principal industries: tourism, agriculture, tobacco, manufacturing, mining, horse breeding. **Principal manufactured goods:** whiskey, textiles, cigarettes, steel products, trucks. **Value added by manufacture** (1977): $9.4 bln. **Agriculture: Chief crops:** tobacco, corn, hay, soybeans, wheat, fruit. **Livestock:** 2.6 mln. cattle; 1.15 mln. hogs/pigs; 22,000 sheep; 2.6 mln. chickens. **Timber/lumber** (1977): hardwoods, pines; 412 mln. bd. ft. **Minerals** (1978): fossil fuels accounted for 95% of the total $3.2 bln. mineral production. **Commercial fishing** (1978): $923,000. **Chief ports:** Paducah, Louisville, Covington, Owensboro, Ashland. **International airports at:** Covington. **Value of construction** (1979): $3.1 bln. **Per capita income** (1979): $7,342. **Unemployment** (1979):

5.6% **Tourism** (1978): tourists spent $1.4 bln.

Finance (1977). **No. banks:** 343; **No. savings and loan assns.:** 107.

Federal government. No. federal civilian employees (Mar. 1979): 25,673. **Avg. salary:** $16,155. **Notable federal facilities:** U.S. Gold Bullion Depository; Ft. Knox; Addiction Research Center and Federal Correction Institution, Lexington.

Energy. Electricity production (1979, mwh, by source): Hydroelectric: 3.9 mln.; Mineral: 50.8 mln.; Nuclear: —.

Education. No. schools: 1,640 elem. and second.; 38 higher ed. **Avg. salary, public school teachers** (1979): $13,130.

State data. Motto: United we stand, divided we fall. **Flower:** Goldenrod. **Bird:** Cardinal. **Tree:** Kentucky coffee tree. **Song:** My Old Kentucky Home. **Entered union** June 1, 1792; rank, 15th. **State fair** at: Louisville.

History. Kentucky was the first area west of the Alleghenies settled by American pioneers; first permanent settlement, Harrodsburg, 1774. Daniel Boone blazed the Wilderness Trail through the Cumberland Gap and founded Boonesboro, 1775. Indian attacks, spurred by the British, were unceasing until, during the Revolution, Gen. George Rogers Clark captured British forts in Indiana and Illinois, 1778. In 1792, after Virginia dropped its claims to the region, Kentucky became the 15th state.

Tourist attractions. Kentucky Derby and accompanying festivities, Louisville; Land Between the Lakes Nat'l. Recreation Area encompassing Kentucky Lake and Lake Barkley; Mammoth Cave with 150 mi. of passageways, 200-ft. high rooms, blind fish, and Echo River, 360 ft. below ground; Old Ft. Harrod State Park; Lincoln birthplace, Hodgenville; My Old Kentucky Home, Bardstown.

Famous Kentuckians include Alben Barkley, Daniel Boone, Louis D. Brandeis, Kit Carson, Henry Clay, Jefferson Davis, John Fox Jr., Thomas Hunt Morgan, Elizabeth Madox Roberts, Robert Penn Warren.

Chamber of Commerce: Versailles Rd., P.O. Box 817, Frankfort, KY 40601.

Louisiana

Pelican State

People. Population (1979): 4,018,000; **rank:** 20. **Pop. density:** 89.4 per sq. mi. **Urban** (1970): 66.1%. **Racial distrib.** (1975): 69.8% White; 29.8% Black; Hispanic (1970): 69,678. **Major ethnic groups:** Italian, German, English, French. **Net migration** (1970-79): +34,000.

Geography. Total area: 48,523 sq. mi.; **rank:** 31. **Land area:** 44,930 sq. mi. **Acres forested land:** 14,558,100. **Location:** south central Gulf Coast state. **Climate:** subtropical, affected by continental weather patterns. **Topography:** lowlands of marshes and Mississippi R. flood plain; Red R. Valley lowlands; upland hills in the Florida Parishes; average elevation, 100 ft. **Capital:** Baton Rouge.

Economy. Principal industries: wholesale and retail trade, government, manufacturing, construction, transportation, mining. **Principal manufactured goods:** chemical products, foods, transportation equipment, electronic equipment, apparel, petroleum products. **Value added by manufacture** (1977): $9.5 bln. **Agriculture: Chief crops:** soybean, sugarcane, rice, corn, cotton, sweet potatoes, melons, pecans. **Livestock:** 1.3 mln. cattle; 150,000 hogs/pigs; 13,000 sheep; 3.5 mln. poultry. **Timber/lumber** (1978): pines, hardwoods, oak; 756 mln. bd. ft. **Minerals** (1978): mineral fuels (natural gas, liquified petroleum gases, crude petroleum, natural gasoline and cycle products), sulfur, lime, salt, sand and gravel. Total mineral production valued at $12 bln. **Commercial fishing** (1979): $198.5 mln. **Chief ports:** New Orleans, Baton Rouge, Lake Charles, S. Louisiana Port Commission at La Place. **International airports at:** New Orleans. **Value of construction** (1979): $7.0 bln. **Employment distribution:** 24.1% trade; 18.2% gvt.; 16.8% serv.; 14.6% manuf.; 8.4% constr. **Per capita income** (1979): $7,477. **Unemployment** (1979): 6.7% **Tourism** (1978): out-of-state visitors spent $2.25 bln.

Finance (1977). **Notable industries:** finance, insurance, real estate. **No. banks:** 256; **No. savings and loan assn.:** 118.

Federal government. No. federal civilian employees (Mar. 1979): 20,200. **Avg. salary:** $16,728. **Notable federal facilities:** Barksdale, England, Ft. Polk military bases; Strategic Petroleum Reserve, New Orleans; Michood Assembly Plant, New Orleans; U.S. Public Service Hospital, Carville.

Energy. Electricity production (1979, mwh, by source): Hydroelectric: —; Mineral: 46.7 mln.; Nuclear: —.

Education. No. schools: 1,843 elem. and second.; 31 higher ed. **Avg. salary, public school teachers** (1979): $13,015.

State data. Motto: Union, justice and confidence. **Flower:** Magnolia. **Bird:** Eastern brown pelican. **Tree:** Cypress. **Song:** Give Me Louisiana. **Entered union** Apr. 30, 1812; rank, 18th. **State fair** at: Shreveport; Oct.

History. The area was first visited, 1530, by Cabeza de Vaca and Panfilo de Narvaez. The region was claimed for France by LaSalle, 1682. First permanent settlement was by French at Fort St. Jean Baptiste (now Natchitoches), 1717. France ceded the region to Spain, 1762, took it back, 1800, and sold it to the U.S., 1803, in the Louisiana Purchase. During the Revolution, Spanish Louisiana aided the Americans. Admitted to statehood, 1812, Louisiana was the scene of the Battle of New Orleans, 1815.

Louisiana Creoles are descendants of early French and/or Spanish settlers. About 4,000 Acadians, French settlers in Nova Scotia, Canada, were forcibly transported by the British to Louisiana in 1755 (an event commemorated in Longfellow's *Evangeline*) and settled near Bayou Teche; their descendants became known as Cajuns. Another group, the Islenos, were descendants of Canary Islanders brought to Louisiana by a Spanish governor in 1770. Traces of Spanish and French survive in local dialects.

Tourist attractions. Mardi Gras, French Quarter, Superdome, Dixieland Jazz, all New Orleans; Battle of New Orleans site; Longfellow-Evangeline Memorial Park.

Famous Louisianians include Louis Armstrong, Pierre Beauregard, Judah P. Benjamin, Braxton Bragg, Grace King, Huey Long, Leonidas K. Polk, Henry Miller Shreve, Edward D. White Jr.

Chamber of Commerce: P.O. Box 3988, Baton Rouge, LA 70821.

Maine

Pine Tree State

People. Population (1979): 1,097,000; **rank:** 38. **Pop. density:** 35.5 per sq. mi. **Urban** (1970): 50.8%. **Racial distrib.** (1975): 99.3% White; — % Black; Hispanic (1970): 3,730. **Major ethnic groups:** English, Irish, Italian, German. **Net migration** (1970-79): +52,000.

Geography. Total area: 33,215 sq. mi.; **rank:** 39. **Land area:** 30,920 sq. mi. **Acres forested land:** 17,718,300. **Location:** New England state at northeastern tip of U.S. **Climate:** Southern interior and coastal, influenced by air masses from the S and W; northern clime harsher, avg. +100 in. snow in winter. **Topography:** Appalachian Mtns. extend through state; western borders have rugged terrain; long sand beaches on southern coast; northern coast mainly rocky promontories, peninsulas, fjords. **Capital:** Augusta.

Economy. Principal industries: manufacturing, services, trade, government, agriculture, fisheries, forestry. **Principal manufactured goods:** paper and wood products, textiles, leather, processed foods. **Value added by manufacture** (1977): $2.4 bln. **Agriculture: Chief crops:** potatoes (80% of total farm income, $175 mln.), apples, blueberries, sweet corn, peas, beans. **Livestock:** 132,000 cattle; 7,100 hogs/pigs; 11,000 sheep; 10.1 mln. poultry. **Timber/lumber** (1978): pine, spruce, fir; 522 mln. bd. ft.

Minerals (1979): sand and gravel, cement, zinc, stone, copper. Total mineral production valued at $44.9 mln. **Commercial fishing** (1979): $80.3 mln. **Chief ports:** Searsport, Portland. **International airports at:** Portland, Bangor. **Value of construction** (1979): $479 mln. **Employment distribution** (1978): 27.5% manuf.; 21.9% trade; 20.6% gvt.; 17% serv. **Per capita income** (1979): $7,057. **Unemployment** (1979): 7.2% **Tourism** (1979): out-of-state visitors spent $478.6 mln.

Finance (1977). **No. banks:** 43; **No. savings and loan assns.:** 22.

Federal government. No. federal civilian employees (Mar. 1979): 4,885. **Avg. salary:** $16,819. **Notable federal facilities:** Kittery Naval Shipyard; Brunswick Naval Air Sta.

Energy. Electricity production (1979, mwh, by source): Hydroelectric: 1.8 mln. Mineral: 1.2 mln. Nuclear: 4.5 mln.

Education. No. schools: 826 elem. and second.; 25 higher ed. **Avg. salary, public school teachers** (1979): $12,275.

State data. Motto: Dirigo (I direct). **Flower:** White pine cone and tassel. **Bird:** Chickadee. **Tree:** Eastern white pine. **Song:** State of Maine Song. **Entered union** Mar. 15, 1820; rank, 23d.

History. Maine's rocky coast was explored by the Cabots, 1498-99. French settlers arrived, 1604, at the St. Croix River; English, 1607, on the Kennebec. In 1691, Maine was made part of Massachusetts. In the Revolution, a Maine regiment fought at Bunker Hill; a British fleet destroyed Falmouth (now Portland), 1775, but the British ship Margaretta was captured near Machiasport. In 1820, Maine broke off from Massachusetts, became a separate state.

Tourist attractions. Acadia Nat'l. Park, Bar Harbor, on Mt. Desert Is.; Bath Iron Works and Marine Museum; Boothbay (Harbor) Railway Museum; Sugarloaf/USA Ski Area; Ogunquit, Portland, York.

Famous "Down Easters" include James G. Blaine, Cyrus H.K. Curtis, Hannibal Hamlin, Longfellow, Sir Hiram and Hudson Maxim, Edna St. Vincent Millay, Kate Douglas Wiggin, Ben Ames Williams.

Chamber of Commerce: 477 Congress St., Portland, ME 04111.

Maryland

Old Line State, Free State

People. Population (1979): 4,148,000; rank: 18. **Pop. density:** 419.4 per sq. mi. **Urban** (1970): 76.6%. **Racial distrib.** (1975): 78.9% White; 20.1% Black; Hispanic (1970): 52,974. **Major ethnic groups:** German, Italian, Russian, English, Polish. **Net migration** (1970-79): +5,000.

Geography. Total area: 10,577 sq. mi.; **rank:** 42. **Land area:** 9,891 sq. mi. **Acres forested land:** 2,653,200. **Location:** Middle Atlantic state stretching from the Ocean to the Allegheny Mtns. **Climate:** continental in the west; humid subtropical in the east. **Topography:** Eastern Shore of coastal plain and Maryland Main of coastal plain, piedmont plateau, and the Blue Ridge, separated by the Chesapeake Bay. **Capital:** Annapolis.

Economy. Principal industries: government, manufacturing, fishing, services, publishing. **Principal manufactured goods:** food, kindred products, primary metals, electric and electronic equipment. **Value added by manufacture** (1977): $7.1 bln. **Agriculture: Chief crops:** tobacco, corn, soybeans. **Livestock:** 390,000 cattle; 190,000 hogs/pigs; 18,000 sheep; 1.87 mln. poultry. **Timber/lumber** (1977): hardwoods; 243 mln. bd. ft. **Minerals** (1977): coal, stone, sand and gravel. Total value of mineral production, $196 mln. **Commercial fishing** (1979): $37.0 mln. **Chief ports:** Baltimore. **International airports at:** Baltimore. **Value of construction** (1979): 2.6 bln. **Employment distribution:** 23.8% agric.; 19.9 mining; 15.2% serv. **Per capita income** (1979): $9,150. **Unemployment** (1979): 5.9% **Tourism** (1978): tourists spent $2 bln.

Finance (1977). **No. banks:** 106; **No. savings and loan assns.:** 206.

Federal government. No. federal civilian employees (Mar. 1979): 108,695. **Avg. salary:** $19,997. **Notable federal facilities:** U.S. Naval Academy, Annapolis.

Energy. Electricity production (1979, mwh, by source): Hydroelectric: 2.2 mln.; Mineral: 22.2 mln.; Nuclear: 9.7 mln.

Education. No. schools: 2,487 elem. and second.; 52 higher ed. **Avg. salary, public school teachers** (1979): $16,591.

State data. Motto. Fatti Maschii, Parole Femine (Manly deeds, womanly words). **Flower:** Black-eyed susan. **Bird:** Baltimore oriole. **Tree:** White oak. **Song:** Maryland, My Maryland. **Seventh** of the original 13 states to ratify Constitution, Apr. 28, 1788. **State fair** at: Timonium; end-Aug. to end-Sept.

History. Capt. John Smith first explored Maryland, 1608. William Claiborne set up a trading post on Kent Is. in Chesapeake Bay, 1631. Britain granted land to Cecilius Calvert, Lord Baltimore, 1632; his brother led 200 settlers to St. Marys River, 1634. The bravery of Maryland troops in the Revolution, as at the Battle of Long Island, won the state its nickname, The Old Line State. In the War of 1812, when a British fleet tried to take Fort McHenry, Marylander Francis Scott Key, 1814, wrote *The Star-Spangled Banner*.

Tourist Attractions. Racing events include the Preakness, at Pimlico track, Baltimore; the International at Laurel Race Course; the John B. Campbell Handicap at Bowie. Also Annapolis yacht races; Ocean City summer resort; restored Ft. McHenry, Baltimore, near which Francis Scott Key wrote *The Star-Spangled Banner;* Antietam Battlefield, 1862, near Hagerstown; South Mountain Battlefield, 1862; Edgar Allan Poe house, Baltimore; The State House, Annapolis, 1772, the oldest still in use in the U.S.

Famous Marylanders include Benjamin Banneker, Francis Scott Key, H.L. Mencken, William Pinkney, Upton Sinclair, Roger B. Taney, Charles Willson Peale.

Chamber of Commerce: 60 West St., Annapolis, MD 21401.

Massachusetts

Bay State, Old Colony

People. Population (1979): 5,769,000; **rank:** 10. **Pop. density:** 737.2 per sq. mi. **Urban** (1970): 84.6%. **Racial distrib.** (1975): 95.7% White; 3.6% Black; Hispanic (1970): 64,860. **Major ethnic groups:** Canadian, Italian, Irish, English, Polish. **Net migration** (1970-79): −92,000.

Geography. Total area: 8,257 sq. mi.; **rank:** 45. **Land area:** 7,826 sq. mi. **Acres forested land:** 2,952,300. **Location:** New England state along Atlantic seaboard. **Climate:** temperate, with colder and drier clime in western region. **Topography:** jagged indented coast from Rhode Island around Cape Cod; flat land yields to stony upland pastures near central region and gentle hilly country in west; except in west, land is rocky, sandy, and not fertile. **Capital:** Boston.

Economy. Principal industries: manufacturing, trade, services, construction, tourism. **Principal manufactured goods:** electronics, machinery, fabricated metals, instruments, printed material. **Value added by manufacture** (1977): $16.9 bln. **Agriculture: Chief crops:** corn, hay, cranberries, apples, tobacco, potatoes, peaches, maple syrup. **Livestock:** 95,000 cattle; 60,000 hogs/pigs; 6,700 sheep; 2.05 mln. poultry. **Timber/lumber** (1979): white pine, oak, other hard woods; 250 mln. bd. ft. **Minerals** (1978): sand and gravel, stone. Total value of mineral production $82.3 mln. **Commercial fishing** (1979): $175.5 mln. **Chief ports:** Boston, Fall River, Salem, New Bedford-Fairhaven. **International airport at:** Boston. **Value of construction** (1979): $2.6 bln. **Employment distribution** (1978): 31.4% manuf.; 26.3% trade; 26.0% serv. **Per**

capita income (1979): $8,844. **Unemployment** (1979): 5.5%. **Tourism** (1976): out-of-state visitors spent $2.6 bln.

Finance (1977). **No. banks:** 146; **No. savings and loan assns.:** 166.

Federal government. No. federal civilian employees (Mar. 1979): 32,699. **Avg. salary:** $18,217. **Notable federal facilities:** Ft. Devens; U.S. Custom House, Boston; Q.M. Laboratory, Natick.

Energy. Electricity production (1979, mwh, by source): Hydroelectric: 373,058; Mineral: 29.3 mln.; Nuclear: 6.1 mln.

Education. No. schools: 2,838 elem. and second.; 119 higher ed. **Avg. salary, public school teachers** (1979): $17,539.

State data. Motto: Ense Petit Placidam Sub Libertate Quietem (By the sword we seek peace, but peace only under liberty). **Flower:** Mayflower. **Bird:** Chickadee. **Tree:** American elm. **Song:** All Hail to Massachusetts. **Sixth** of the original 13 states to ratify Constitution, Feb. 6, 1788.

History. The Pilgrims, seeking religious freedom, made their first settlement at Plymouth, 1620; the following year they gave thanks for their survival with the first Thanksgiving Day. Indian opposition reached a high point in King Philip's War, 1675-76, won by the colonists. Demonstrations against British restrictions set off the "Boston Massacre," 1770, and Boston "tea party," 1773. First bloodshed of the Revolution was at Lexington, 1775.

Tourist attractions. Cape Cod with Provincetown artists' colony; Berkshire Music Festival, Tanglewood; Boston "Pops" concerts; Museum of Fine Arts, Arnold Arboretum, both Boston; Jacob's Pillow Dance Festival, West Becket; historical Shaker Village, Old Sturbridge, Lexington, Concord, Salem, Plymouth Rock.

Famous "Bay Staters" include Samuel Adams, Louisa May Alcott, Horatio Alger, Clara Barton, Emily Dickinson, Emerson, Hancock, Hawthorne, Oliver W. Holmes, Winslow Homer, Elias Howe, Samuel F.B. Morse, Poe, Revere, Sargent, Thoreau, Whistler, Whittier.

Chamber of Commerce: None.

Michigan

Great Lake State, Wolverine State

People. Population (1979): 9,207,000; **rank:** 7. **Pop. density:** 162.1 per sq. mi. **Urban** (1970): 73.8%. **Racial distrib. (1975):** 87.5% White; 11.9% Black; Hispanic (1970): 120,687. **Major ethnic groups:** Polish, German, English, Italian. **Net migration** (1970-79): −300,000.

Geography. Total area: 58,216 sq. mi.; **rank:** 23. **Land area:** 56,817 sq. mi. **Acres forested land:** 19,270,400. **Location:** east north central state bordering on 4 of the 5 Great Lakes, divided into an Upper and Lower Peninsula by the Straits of Mackinac, which link lakes Michigan and Huron. **Climate:** well-defined seasons tempered by the Great Lakes. **Topography:** low rolling hills give way to northern tableland of hilly belts in Lower Peninsula; Upper Peninsula is level in the east, with swampy areas; western region is higher and more rugged. **Capital:** Lansing.

Economy. Principal industries: manufacturing, mining, agriculture, food processing, tourism, fishing. **Principal manufactured goods:** automobiles, machine tools, chemicals, foods, primary metals and metal products, plastics. **Value added by manufacture** (1977): $37.5 bln. **Agriculture: Chief crops:** corn, winter wheat, soybeans, dry beans, oats, hay, sugar beets, honey, asparagus, sweet corn, apples, cherries, grapes, peaches, blueberries, flowers. **Livestock:** 1.31 mln. cattle; 960,000 hogs/pigs; 132,000 sheep; 8 mln. poultry. **Timber/lumber** (1977): hickory, ash, oak, hemlock; 350 mln. bd. ft. **Minerals** (1979): crude petroleum, iron ore, cement, natural gas, stone, sand and gravel. Total mineral production valued at $2.33 bln. **Commercial fishing** (1979): $3.6 mln. **Chief ports:** Detroit, Muskegon, Sault Ste. Marie. **International airports at:** Detroit. **Value of construction** (1979): $5.2 bln. **Employment distribution:** 32% manuf.; 17% serv.; **Per capita income** (1979): $9,269. **Unemployment** (1979): 7.8% **Tourism** (1976): out-of-state visitors spent $3.8 bln.

Finance (1977). **No. banks:** 364; **No. savings and loan assns.:** 66.

Federal government. No. federal civilian employees (Mar. 1979): 27,023. **Avg. salary:** $18,251. **Notable federal facilities:** Isle Royal, Sleeping Bear Dunes national parks.

Energy. Electricity production (1979, mwh, by source): Hydroelectric: 1.2 mln; Mineral: 62 mln.; Nuclear: 15.1 mln.

Education. No. schools: 4,690 elem. and second.; 94 higher ed. **Avg. salary, public school teachers** (1979): $17,596.

State data. Motto: Si Quaeris Peninsulam Amoenam Circumspice (If you seek a pleasant peninsula, look about you). **Flower:** Apple blossom. **Bird:** Robin. **Tree:** White pine. **Song:** Michigan, My Michigan. **Entered union** Jan. 26, 1837; rank, 26th. **State fair** at: Detroit; Aug.–early Sept.

History. French fur traders and missionaries visited the region, 1616, set up a mission at Sault Ste. Marie, 1641, and a settlement there, 1668. The whole region went to Britain, 1763. During the Revolution, the British led attacks from the area on American settlements to the south until Anthony Wayne defeated their Indian allies at Fallen Timbers, Ohio, 1794. The British returned, 1812, seized Ft. Mackinac and Detroit. Oliver H. Perry's Lake Erie victory and William H. Harrison's troops, who carried the war to the Thames River in Canada, 1813, freed Michigan once more.

Tourist attractions. Henry Ford Museum, Greenfield Village, reconstruction of a typical 19th cent. American village, both in Dearborn; Michigan Space Ctr., Jackson; Tahquamenon *(Hiawatha)* Falls; DeZwaan windmill and Tulip Festival, Holland; "Soo Locks," St. Marys Falls Ship Canal, Sault Ste. Marie.

Famous Michiganders include George Custer, Paul de Kruif, Thomas Dewey, Edna Ferber, Henry Ford, Edgar Guest, Betty Hutton, Robert Ingersoll, Will Kellogg, Danny Thomas, Stewart Edward White.

Chamber of Commerce: 501 S. Capitol Ave., Suite 500, Lansing, MI 48933.

Minnesota

North Star State, Gopher State

People. Population (1979): 4,060,000; **rank:** 19. **Pop. density:** 51.2 per sq. mi. **Urban** (1970): 66.4%. **Racial distrib. (1975):** 98.0% White; 1.0% Black; Hispanic (1970): 23,198. **Major ethnic groups:** German, Swedish, Norwegian. **Net migration** (1970-79): −16,000.

Geography. Total area: 84,068 sq. mi.; **rank:** 12. **Land area:** 79,289 sq. mi. **Acres forested land:** 16,709,200. **Location:** north central state bounded on the E by Wisconsin and Lake Superior, on the N by Canada, on the W by the Dakotas, and on the S by Iowa. **Climate:** northern part of state lies in the moist Great Lakes storm belt; the western border lies at the edge of the semi-arid Great Plains. **Topography:** central hill and lake region covering approx. half the state; to the NE, rocky ridges and deep lakes; to the NW, flat plain; to the S, rolling plains and deep river valleys. **Capital:** St. Paul.

Economy. Principal industries: agri business, forest products, mining, manufacturing, tourism. **Principal manufactured goods:** food processing, non-electrical machinery, chemicals, paper, electric and electronic equipment, printing and publishing, instruments, fabricated metal products. **Value added by manufacture** (1977): $9.3 bln. **Agriculture: Chief crops:** corn, soybeans, wheat, sugar beets, sunflowers, barley. **Livestock** (1980): 3.75 mln. cattle; 4.95 mln. hogs/pigs; 255,000 sheep; 37.2 mln. poultry. **Timber/lumber:** needle-leaves and hardwoods. **Minerals** (1979): iron ore (95% of the total $2.1 bln. of mineral production), sand and gravel, stone. **Commercial fishing** (1979): $2.0 mln. **Chief ports:** Duluth, St.

Paul, Minneapolis. **International airports at:** Minneapolis-St. Paul. **Value of construction** (1979): $3.3 bln. **Employment distribution** (1979): 21.5% trade; 18.6% manuf.; 17.3% serv.; 14.3% gvt. **Per capita income** (1979): $8,760. **Unemployment** (1979): 4.2%. **Tourism** (1976): out-of-state visitors spent $900 mln.

Finance (1977). **No. banks:** 758; **No. savings and loan assns.:** 65.

Federal government. No. federal civilian employees (1979): 14,167. **Avg. salary:** $18,272.

Energy. Electricity production (1979, mwh, by source): Hydroelectric: 766,116; Mineral: 18.7 mln.; Nuclear: 11.5 mln.

Education. No. schools: 2,136 elem. and second.; 65 higher ed. **Avg. salary, public school teachers** (1979): $15,504.

State data. Motto: L'Etoile du Nord (The star of the north). **Flower:** Pink and white lady's-slipper. **Bird:** Common loon. **Tree:** Red pine. **Song:** Hail! Minnesota. **Entered union** May 11, 1858; rank, 32d. **State fair** at: Saint Paul; end-Aug. to early Sept.

History. Fur traders and missionaries from French Canada opened the region in the 17th century. Britain took the area east of the Mississippi, 1763. The U.S. took over that portion after the Revolution and in 1803 bought the western area as part of the Louisiana Purchase. The U.S. built present Ft. Snelling, 1820, bought lands from the Indians, 1837. Sioux Indians staged a bloody uprising, 1862, and were driven from the state.

Tourist attractions. Minnehaha Falls, Minneapolis, inspiration for Longfellow's *Hiawatha;* Voyageurs Nat'l. Park, a water wilderness along the Canadian border; Mayo Clinic, Rochester; St. Paul Winter Carnival; the "land of 10,000 lakes" actually has 12,034 lakes over 10 acres in size; many water and winter sports and activities throughout the state.

Famous Minnesotans include F. Scott Fitzgerald, Cass Gilbert, Hubert Humphrey, Sinclair Lewis, Paul Manship, E. G. Marshall, William and Charles Mayo, Walter F. Mondale, Harold Stassen, Thorstein Veblen.

Chamber of Commerce: 200 Hanover Bldg., 480 Cedar St., St. Paul, MN 55101.

Mississippi

Magnolia State

People. Population (1979): 2,429,000; **rank:** 31. **Pop. density:** 51.4 per sq. mi. **Urban** (1970): 44.5%. **Racial distrib. (1975):** 63.6% White; 35.9% Black; Hispanic (1970): 8,182. **Major ethnic groups:** German, Italian, English. **Net migration** (1970-79): +7,000.

Geography. Total area: 47,716 sq. mi.; **rank:** 32. **Land area:** 47,296 sq. mi. **Acres forested land:** 16,715,600. **Location:** south central state bordered on the W by the Mississippi R. and on the S by the Gulf of Mexico. **Climate:** semi-tropical, with abundant rainfall, long growing season, and extreme temperatures unusual. **Topography:** low, fertile delta bet. the Yazoo and Mississippi rivers; loess bluffs stretching around delta border; sandy Gulf coastal terraces followed by piney woods and prairie; rugged, high sandy hills in extreme NE followed by black prairie belt. Pontotoc Ridge, and flatwoods into the north central highlands. **Capital:** Jackson.

Economy. Principal industries: manufacturing, food processing, seafood, government, wholesale and retail trade, agriculture. **Principal manufactured goods:** apparel, transportation equipment, lumber and wood products, foods, electrical machinery and equipment. **Value added by manufacture** (1977): $5.6 bln. **Agriculture: Chief crops:** soybeans, cotton, rice, pecans, sweet potatoes. **Livestock:** 1.79 mln. cattle; 410,000 hogs/pigs; 5,400 sheep; 11.5 mln. poultry. **Timber/lumber** (1978): pine, oak, hardwoods; 1.3 bln. bd. ft. **Minerals** (1977): crude petroleum and natural gas (85% of total $499 mln. value of mineral production), sand and gravel. **Commercial fishing** (1979): $33.3 mln. **Chief ports:** Pascagoula, Vicksburg, Gulfport, Natchez. **Value of construction** (1979): $3.9 bln. **Employment distribution:** 28.3% manuf.; 22.8% gvt.; 19.4% trade; 14.2% serv. **Per capita income** (1979): $6,167. **Unemployment** (1979): 5.8% **Tourism** (1976): out-of-state visitors spent $850.5 mln.

Finance (1977). **No. banks:** 184; **No. savings and loan assns.:** 60.

Federal government. No. federal civilian employees (Mar. 1979): 19,702. **Avg. salary:** $17,162. **Notable federal facilities:** Columbus, Kessler AF bases; Meridian Naval Air Station, NASA/NOAA International Earth Sciences Center.

Energy. Electricity production (1979, mwh, by source): Hydroelectric: —; Mineral 16.6 mln.; Nuclear: —.

Education. No. schools: 1,234 elem. and second.; 45 higher ed. **Avg. salary, public school teachers** (1979): $11,101.

State data. Motto: Virtute et Armis (By valor and arms). **Flower:** Magnolia. **Bird:** Mockingbird. **Tree:** Magnolia. **Song:** Go, Mississippi! **Entered union** Dec. 10, 1817; rank, 20th. **State fair** at: Jackson; Spring.

History. De Soto explored the area, 1540, discovered the Mississippi River, 1541. La Salle traced the river from Illinois to its mouth and claimed the entire valley for France, 1682. First settlement was the French Ft. Maurepas, near Ocean Springs, 1699. The area was ceded to Britain, 1763; American settlers followed. During the Revolution, Spain seized part of the area and refused to leave even after the U.S. acquired title at the end of the Revolution, finally moving out, 1798. Mississippi seceded 1861. Union forces captured Corinth and Vicksburg and destroyed Jackson and much of Meridian.

Tourist attractions. Vicksburg National Military Park and Cemetery, other Civil War sites; Natchez Trace; Indian mounds; estate pilgrimage at Natchez; Mardi Gras and blessing of the shrimp fleet, Aug., both in Biloxi.

Famous Mississippians include Dana Andrews, William Faulkner, Lucius O.C. Lamar, Elvis Presley, Leontyne Price, Hiram Revels, Eudora Welty.

Chamber of Commerce: P.O. Box 1849, Jackson, MS 39205.

Missouri

Show Me State

People. Population (1979): 4,867,000; **rank:** 15. **Pop. density:** 70.5 per sq. mi. **Urban** (1970): 70.1%. **Racial distrib. (1975):** 88.8% White; 10.6% Black; Hispanic (1970): 40,640. **Major ethnic groups:** German, Italian, English, Russian. **Net migration** (1970-79): −16,000.

Geography. Total area: 69,686 sq. mi.; **rank:** 19. **Land area:** 68,995 sq. mi. **Acres forested land:** 12,876,000. **Location:** West North central state near the geographic center of the conterminous U.S.; bordered on the E by the Mississippi R., on the NW by the Missouri R. **Climate:** continental, susceptible to cold Canadian air, moist, warm Gulf air, and drier SW air. **Topography:** Rolling hills, open, fertile plains, and well-watered prairie N of the Missouri R.; south of the river land is rough and hilly with deep, narrow valleys; alluvial plain in the SE; low elevation in the west. **Capital:** Jefferson City.

Economy. Principal industries: agriculture, manufacturing, aerospace, tourism. **Principal manufactured goods:** transportation equipment, food and related products, electrical and electronic equipment, chemicals. **Value added by manufacture** (1977): $12.8 bln. **Agriculture: Chief crops:** soybeans, corn, wheat, cotton. **Livestock:** 5.55 mln. cattle; 4.1 mln. hogs/pigs; 126,000 sheep; 18 mln. poultry. **Timber/lumber:** oak, hickory. **Minerals** (1979): lead, fire clay, zinc, barite, lime cement. Total value of mineral production $857 mln. **Commercial fishing** (1979) $203,000. **Chief ports:** St. Louis, Kansas City. **International airports at:** St. Louis, Kansas City. **Value of construction** (1979): $3.1 bln. **Employment distribution:** 24% trade; 23% manuf.; 18% serv.; 17% gvt.; 7% transp. **Per capita income** (1979): $8,132. **Un-**

employment (1979): 4.2%. **Tourism** (1977): out-of-state visitors spent $2.7 bln.

Finance (1977). **Notable industries:** banking. **No. banks:** 714; **No. savings and loan assns.:** 114.

Federal government: No. federal civilian employees (Mar. 1979): 44,489. **Avg. salary:** $17,525. **Notable federal facilities:** Federal Reserve banks, St. Louis, Kansas City; Ft. Leonard Wood, Rolla.

Energy. Electricity production (1979, mwh, by source): Hydroelectric: 1.1 mln.; Mineral: 46.0 mln.; Nuclear: —.

Education. No. schools: 2,707 elem. and second.; 83 higher ed. **Avg. salary, public school teachers** (1979): $12,920.

State data. Motto: Salus Populi Suprema Lex Esto (The welfare of the people shall be the supreme law). **Flower:** Hawthorn. **Bird:** Bluebird. **Tree:** Dogwood. **Song:** Missouri Waltz. **Entered union** Aug. 10, 1821; rank, 24th. **State fair** at: Sedalia; 3d week in Aug.

History. DeSoto visited the area, 1541. French hunters and lead miners made the first settlement, c. 1735, at Ste. Genevieve. The U.S. acquired Missouri as part of the Louisiana Purchase, 1803. The fur trade and the Santa Fe Trail provided prosperity; St. Louis became the "jump-off" point for pioneers on their way West. Pro- and anti-slavery forces battled each other there during the Civil War.

Tourist attractions. Mark Twain State Park, Florida; Tom Sawyer and Huckleberry Finn statues, Hannibal; Jesse James birthplace, Excelsior Springs; Pony Express Museum, St. Joseph. The Harry S. Truman Library, near Independence, contains presidential papers and memorabilia. Mr. Truman is buried in the library courtyard.

Famous Missourians include Zoe Akins, Thomas Hart Benton, Omar Bradley, George Washington Carver, Thomas Dooley, T. S. Eliot, Bernarr Macfadden, J. C. Penney; John J. Pershing, Joseph Pulitzer, Sara Teasdale, Mark Twain.

Chamber of Commerce: 400 E. High St., P.O. Box 149, Jefferson City, MO 65101.

Montana

Treasure State

People. Population (1979): 786,000; **rank:** 43. **Pop. density:** 5.4 per sq. mi. **Urban** (1970): 53.4%. **Racial distrib. (1975):** 95.2% White; —% Black; 4.5% Other (includes American Indians); Hispanic (1970): 7,771. **Major ethnic groups:** German, Norwegian, Russian, English. **Net migration** (1970-79): +38,000.

Geography. Total area: 147,138 sq. mi.; **rank:** 4. **Land area:** 145,587 sq. mi. **Acres forested land:** 22,559,300. **Location:** Mountain state bounded on the E by the Dakotas, on the S by Wyoming, on the S/SW by Idaho, and on the N by Canada. **Climate:** colder, continental climate with low humidity. **Topography:** Rocky Mtns. in western third of the state; eastern two-thirds gently rolling northern Great Plains. **Capital:** Helena.

Economy. Principal industries: agriculture, mining, manufacturing, tourism. **Principal manufactured goods:** petroleum products, primary metals and minerals, lumber and wood products, farm machinery, processed foods. **Value added by manufacture** (1977): $860 mln. **Agriculture: Chief crops:** wheat, cattle, barley, sheep, sugar beets, hay, flax, oats. **Livestock:** 2.65 mln. cattle; 209,000 hogs/pigs; 494,000 sheep; 890,000 poultry. **Timber/lumber** (1977): Douglas fir, pines, larch; 1.3 bln. bd. ft. **Minerals** (1978): mineral fuels (71% of the total $719 mln. mineral production), copper, silver. **International airports at:** Great Falls. **Value of construction** (1979): $569 mln. **Employment distribution:** 21.2% trade; 20% gvt.; 15.6% serv.; 9.2% agric.; 7.7% manuf. **Per capita income** (1979): $7,412. **Unemployment** (1979): 5.1%. **Tourism** (1979): out-of-state visitors spent $421.8 mln.

Finance (1977). **No. banks:** 160; **No. savings and loan assns.:** 15.

Federal government. No. federal civilian employees (Mar. 1979): 7,827. **Avg. salary:** $18,309. **Notable federal facilities:** Malmstrom AFB; Ft. Peck, Hungry Horse, Libby, Yellowtail dams.

Energy. Electricity production (1979, mwh, by source): Hydroelectric: 10.3 mln; Mineral: 5.4 mln.; Nuclear: —.

Education. No. schools: 856 elem. and second.; 12 higher ed. **Avg. salary, public school teachers** (1979): $13,540.

State data. Motto: Oro y Plata (Gold and silver). **Flower:** Bitterroot. **Bird:** Western meadowlark. **Tree:** Ponderosa pine. **Song:** Montana. **Entered union** Nov. 8, 1889; rank, 41st. **State fair** at: Great Falls; end July to early Aug.

History. French explorers visited the region, 1742. The U.S. acquired the area partly through the Louisiana Purchase, 1803, and partly through the explorations of Lewis and Clark, 1805-06. Fur traders and missionaries established posts in the early 19th century. Indian uprisings reached their peak with the Battle of the Little Big Horn, 1876. The coming of the Northern Pacific Railway, 1883, brought population growth.

Tourist attractions. Glacier National Park, on the Continental Divide, is a scenic and recreational wonderland, with 60 glaciers, 200 lakes, and many trout streams.

Also, Museum of the Plains Indian, Blackfeet Reservation near Browning; Custer Battlefield National Cemetery; Flathead Lake, in the NW, Lewis and Clark Cavern, Morrison Cave State Park, near Whitehall.

There are 7 Indian reservations, covering over 5 million acres; tribes are Blackfeet, Crow, Confederated Salish & Kootenai, Assiniboine, Gros Ventre, Sioux, Northern Cheyenne, Chippewa, Cree. Population of the reservations is approximately 25,500.

Famous Montanans include Gary Cooper, Marcus Daly, Chet Huntley, Will James, Myrna Loy, Mike Mansfield, Jeannette Rankin, Charles M. Russell, Brent Musberger.

Chamber of Commerce: 110 Neil Ave., P.O. Box 1730, Helena, MT 59601.

Nebraska

Cornhusker State

People. Population (1979): 1,562,000; **rank:** 35. **Pop. density:** 20.5 per sq. mi. **Urban** (1970): 61.5%. **Racial distrib. (1975):** 96.2% White; 3.0% Black; Hispanic (1970): 21,067. **Major ethnic groups:** German, Czechoslovakian, Swedish, Russian. **Net migration** (1970-79): −11,000.

Geography. Total area: 77,227 sq. mi.; **rank:** 15. **Land area:** 76,483 sq. mi. **Acres forested land:** 1,029,100. **Location:** West North Central state with the Missouri R. for a N/NE border. **Climate:** continental semi-arid. **Topography:** till plains of the central lowland in the eastern third rising to the Great Plains and hill country of the north central and NW. **Capital:** Lincoln.

Economy. Principal industries: agriculture, food processing, manufacturing. **Principal manufactured goods:** foods, machinery, electric and electronic equipment, chemicals, primary and fabricated metal products. **Value added by manufacture** (1977): $2.8 bln. **Agriculture: Chief crops:** corn, wheat, sorghum, hay, oats, beans, sugar beets, popcorn, potatoes, soybeans. **Livestock:** 6.4 mln. cattle; 4.15 mln. hogs/pigs; 210,000 sheep; 4.2 mln. poultry. **Minerals** (1979): cement, sand and gravel, natural gas liquids, petroleum. Total mineral production valued at $203.5 mln. **Commercial fishing** (1979): $25,000. **Chief ports:** Omaha, Sioux City, Brownsville, Blair, Plattsmouth. **Value of construction** (1979): $1.0 bln. **Employment distribution:** 22% trade; 17% gvt.; 15.3% serv.; 13.3% manuf. **Per capita income** (1979): $8,341. **Unemployment** (1979): 3.2%. **Tourism** (1976): out-of-state visitors spent $720.7 mln.

Finance (1977). **No. banks:** 452; **No. savings and loan assns.:** 44.

Federal government. No. federal civilian employees (Mar. 1979): 8,683 **Avg. salary:** $17,967. **Notable federal facilities:** Strategic Air Command Base, Omaha.

Energy. Electricity production (1979, mwh, by source): Hydroelectric: 1.3 mln.; Mineral: 7.5 mln.; Nuclear: 8.7 mln.

Education. No. schools: 1,994 elem. and second.; 29 higher ed. **Avg. salary, public school teachers** (1979): $12,936.

State data. Motto: Equality before the law. **Flower:** Goldenrod. **Bird:** Western meadowlark. **Tree:** Cottonwood. **Song:** Beautiful Nebraska. **Entered union** Mar. 1, 1867; rank, 37th. **State fair** at: Lincoln; Aug. 29 to Sept. 7.

History. Spanish and French explorers and fur traders visited the area prior to the Louisiana Purchase, 1803. Lewis and Clark passed through, 1804-06. First permanent settlement was Bellevue, near Omaha, 1823. Many Civil War veterans settled under free land terms of the 1862 Homestead Act; struggles followed between homesteaders and ranchers.

Tourist attractions. Boys Town, founded by Fr. Flanagan, west of Omaha, is a self-contained community of under-privileged and homeless boys. Arbor Lodge State Park, Nebraska City, is a memorial to J. Sterling Morton, founder of Arbor Day. Buffalo Bill Ranch State Historical Park, North Platte, contains Cody's home and memorabilia of his Wild West Show.

Also, Pioneer Village, Minden; Oregon Trail, landmarks, Scotts Bluff National Mountain and Chimney Rock Historic Site.

Famous Nebraskans include Fred Astaire, Charles W. and William Jennings Bryan, Willa Cather, Michael and Edward A. Cudahy, Loren Eiseley, Rev. Edward J. Flanagan, Henry Fonda, Rollin Kirby, Harold Lloyd, Malcolm X, Roscoe Pound.

Chamber of Commerce: 1008 Terminal Bldg., Lincoln, NE 68508.

Nevada

Sagebrush State, Battle Born State

People. Population (1979): 692,000; **rank:** 44. **Pop. density:** 6.3 per sq. mi. **Urban** (1970): 80.9%. **Racial distrib. (1975):** 91.7 White; 6.0% Black; Hispanic (1970): 27,142. **Major ethnic groups:** Italian, German, English, Mexican. **Net migration** (1970-80): +266,000.

Geography. Total area: 110,540 sq. mi.; **rank:** 7. **Land area:** 109,889 sq. mi. **Acres forested land:** 7,683,300. **Location:** Mountain state bordered on N by Oregon and Idaho, on E by Utah and Arizona, on SE by Arizona, and on SW/W by California. **Climate:** semi-arid. **Topography:** rugged N-S mountain ranges; southern area is within the Mojave Desert; lowest elevation, Colorado R. Canyon, 470 ft. **Capital:** Carson City.

Economy. Principal industries: tourism, mining, manufacturing, lumber, government, agriculture, warehousing, trucking. **Principal manufactured goods:** gaming devices, electronics, chemicals, forest products, stone-clay-glass products. **Value added by manufacture** (1977): $497.8 mln. **Agriculture: Chief crops:** alfalfa, barley, wheat, oats, cotton. **Livestock:** 570,000 cattle; 8,000 hogs/pigs; 133,000 sheep; 14,000 poultry. **Timber/lumber** (1977): pine, fir, spruce; 19 mln. bd. ft. **Minerals** (1979): gold (3d largest in U.S. with 26% of total output), copper, sand and gravel. Total mineral production valued at $251.2 mln. **International airports at** Las Vegas, Reno. **Value of construction** (1979): $1.2 bln. **Employment distribution:** 42% serv.; 20% trade; 14% gvt. **Per capita income** (1979): $10,204. **Unemployment** (1979): 5.1% **Tourism** (1976): out-of-state visitors spent $1.3 bln.

Finance (1977). **No banks:** 9; **No. savings and loan assns.:** 7.

Federal government. No. federal civilian employees (Mar. 1979): 6,721. **Avg. salary:** $18,482. **Notable federal facilities:** Nevada Test Site.

Energy. Electricity production (1979, mwh, by source): Hydroelectric: 1.7 mln.; Mineral: 13 mln. Nuclear: —.

Education. No. schools: 273 elem. and second.; 6 higher ed. **Avg. salary, public school teachers** (1979): $15,206.

State data. Motto: All for our country. **Flower:** Sagebrush. **Bird:** Mountain bluebird. **Tree:** Single-leaf pinon. **Song:** Home Means Nevada. **Entered union** Oct. 31, 1864; rank, 36th. **State fair** at Reno; early Sept.

History. Nevada was first explored by Spaniards in 1776. Hudson's Bay Co. trappers explored the north and central region, 1825; trader Jedediah Smith crossed the state, 1826 and 1827. The area was acquired by the U.S., in 1848, at the end of the Mexican War. First settlement, Mormon Station, now Genoa, was est. 1849. In the early 20th century, Nevada adopted progressive measures such as the initiative, referendum, recall, and woman suffrage.

Tourist attractions. Legalized gambling provided the impetus for the development of resort areas Lake Tahoe, Reno, and Las Vegas. Ghost towns, rodeos, trout fishing, water sports and hunting important.

Notable are Helldorado Week in May, Las Vegas; Basque Festival, Elko; Reno Rodeo, 4th of July; Valley of Fire State Park, Overton; Death Valley, on the California border; Lehman Caves National Monument.

Famous Nevadans include Walter Van Tilburg Clark, Sarah Winnemucca Hopkins, Dr. Robert C. Lynch, Pat McCarran, William Morris Stewart.

Chamber of Commerce: P.O. Box 3499, Reno, NV 89505.

New Hampshire

Granite State

People. Population (1979): 883,000; **rank:** 42. **Pop. density:** 97.8 per sq. mi. **Urban** (1970): 56.4%. **Racial distrib. (1975):** 99.3% White; — % Black; Hispanic (1970): 2,681. **Major ethnic groups:** English, Irish, French, Polish, Italian, German. **Net migration** (1970-79): +101,000.

Geography. Total area: 9,304 sq. mi.; **rank:** 44. **Land area:** 9,027 sq. mi. **Acres forested land:** 5,013,500. **Location:** New England state bounded on S by Massachusetts, on W by Vermont, on N/NW by Canada, on E by Maine and the Atlantic O. **Climate:** highly varied, due to its nearness to high mountains and ocean. **Topography:** low, rolling coast followed by countless hills and mountains rising out of a central plateau. **Capital:** Concord.

Economy. Principal industries: manufacturing, communications, trade, agriculture, mining. **Principal manufactured goods:** leather products, wood and paper products, electrical equipment, machinery, minerals, fabricated metal products. **Value added by manufacture** (1977): $2.2 bln. **Agriculture: Chief crops:** vegetables, dairy products, greenhouse products, hay, apples. **Livestock:** 74,000 cattle; 8,400 hogs/pigs; 6,900 sheep; 1.36 mln. poultry. **Timber/lumber** (1977): white pine, hemlock, oak, birch; 177 mln. bd. ft. **Minerals** (1978): sand and gravel. Total mineral production valued at $20.7 mln. **Commercial fishing** (1979): $3.3 mln. **Chief ports:** Portsmouth. **Value of construction** (1979): $547 mln. **Employment distribution:** 30% manuf.; 31% trade; 7% serv. **Per capita income** (1979): $8,231. **Unemployment** (1979): 3.1%. **Tourism** (1976): out-of-state visitors spent $690.6 mln.

Finance (1977). **Notable industries:** insurance, banking. **No. banks:** 78; **No. savings and loan assns.:** 17.

Federal government. No. federal civilian employees (Mar. 1979): 11,574. **Avg. salary:** $17,410. **Notable federal facilities:** Pease Air Base, Newington.

Energy. Electricity production (1979, mwh, by source): Hydroelectric: 1.1 mln.; Mineral: 5.1 mln.; Nuclear: —.

Education: No. schools: 555 elem. and second.; 24

higher ed. **Avg. salary, public school teachers** (1979): $11,692.

State data. Motto: Live free or die. **Flower:** Purple lilac. **Bird:** Purple finch. **Tree:** White birch. **Song:** Old New Hampshire. **Ninth** of the original 13 states to ratify the Constitution, June 21, 1788.

History. First explorers to visit the New Hampshire area were England's Martin Pring, 1603, and Champlain, 1605. First settlement was Little Harbor, near Rye, 1623. Indian raids were halted, 1759, by Robert Rogers' Rangers. Before the Revolution, New Hampshire men seized a British fort at Portsmouth, 1774, and drove the royal governor out, 1775. Three regiments served in the Continental Army and scores of privateers raided British shipping.

Tourist attractions. Mt. Washington, highest peak in Northeast, hub of network of trails; Lake Winnipesaukee; White Mt. Natl. Forest; Crawford, Franconia, Pinkham notches in White Mt. region—Franconia famous for the Old Man of the Mountain, described by Hawthorne as the Great Stone Face; the Flume, a spectacular gorge; the aerial tramway on Cannon Mt; the MacDowell Colony, Peterborough, summer haven for writers, composers, artists.

Famous New Hampshirites include Salmon P. Chase, Ralph Adams Cram, Mary Baker Eddy, Daniel Chester French, Robert Frost, Horace Greeley, Sarah Buell Hale, Augustus Saint-Gaudens, Daniel Webster.

Chamber of Commerce: 57 Market St., Manchester, NH 03101.

New Jersey

Garden State

People. Population (1979): 7,306,000; **rank:** 9. **Pop. density:** 971.4 per sq. mi. **Urban** (1970): 88.9%. **Racial distrib. (1975):** 87.2% White; 11.9% Black; Hispanic (1970): 135,677. **Major ethnic groups:** Italian, German, Polish. **Net migration** (1970-79): −129,000.

Geography. Total area: 7,836 sq. mi.; **rank:** 46. **Land area:** 7,521 sq. mi. **Acres forested land:** 1,928,400. **Location:** Middle Atlantic state bounded on the N and E by New York and the Atlantic O., on the S and W by Delaware and Pennsylvania. **Climate:** moderate, with marked difference bet. NW and SE extremities. **Topography:** Appalachian Valley in the NW also has highest elevation, High Pt., 1,801 ft.; Appalachian Highlands, flat-topped NE-SW mountain ranges; Piedmont Plateau, low plains broken by high ridges (Palisades) rising 400-500 ft.; Coastal Plain, covering three-fifths of state in SE, gradually rises from sea level to gentle slopes. **Capital:** Trenton.

Economy. Principal industries: manufacturing, tourism, finance, transportation, communication, public utilities, construction. **Principal manufactured goods:** pharmaceuticals, textiles, clothing, plastics, petroleum products, electronic equipment, glassware, processed foods. **Value added by manufacture** (1977): $23.2 bln. **Agriculture: Chief crops:** tomatoes, cranberries, blueberries, corn, peaches, soybeans, asparagus, potatoes, onions, strawberries, cabbage, apples, wheat, barley. **Livestock:** 114,000 cattle; 75,000 hogs/pigs; 8,300 sheep; 2.12 mln. poultry. **Timber/lumber** (1977): pine, white cedar, oak, elm; 16 mln. bd. ft. **Minerals** (1978): sand and gravel, stone, zinc. Total value of mineral production, $118 mln. **Commercial fishing** (1979): $53.0 mln. **Chief ports:** Newark, Elizabeth, Hoboken, Ameri-Port (Delaware R.). **International airports at:** Newark. **Value of construction** (1979): $3.6 bln. **Employment distribution:** 1.0% agric.; 25.4% manuf.; 17.8% serv.; 16.7% gvt.; 22.6% trade. **Per capita income** (1979): $9,702. **Unemployment** (1979): 6.9%. **Tourism** (1978): tourists spent $4.0 bln.

Finance (1977). **Notable industries:** banking, insurance. **No. banks:** 184; **No. savings and loan assns.:** 222.

Federal government. No. federal civilian employees (Mar. 1979): 39,111. **Avg. salary:** $19,105. **Notable federal facilities:** McGuire AFB Fort Dix; Fort Monmouth; Picatinny Arsenal; Lakewood Naval Air Station, Lakehurst Naval Air Engineering Center.

Energy. Electricity production (1979, mwh, by source): Hydroelectric: —; Mineral: 20.2 mln.; Nuclear: 6.6 mln.

Education. No. schools: 3,144 elem. and second.; 65 higher ed. **Avg. salary, public school teachers** (1979): $16,325.

State Data. Motto: Liberty and prosperity. **Flower:** Purple violet. **Bird:** Eastern goldfinch. **Tree:** Red oak. **Third** of the original 13 states to ratify the Constitution, Dec. 18, 1787. **State fair** at: Hamilton Twp., Mercer Co.; 2d week of Sept.

History. The Lenni Lenape (Delaware) Indians had mostly peaceful relations with European colonists who arrived after the explorers Verrazano, 1524, and Hudson, 1609. The Dutch were first; when the British took New Netherland, 1664, the area between the Delaware and Hudson Rivers was given to Lord John Berkeley and Sir George Carteret. New Jersey was the scene of nearly 100 battles, large and small, during the Revolution, including Trenton, 1776, Princeton, 1777, Monmouth, 1778.

Tourist attractions. Grover Cleveland birthplace, Caldwell; Walt Whitman Poetry Center, Camden; Edison Lab National Monument, West Orange; numerous Revolutionary historic sites; Great Adventure amusement park; 127 miles of Atlantic Ocean beaches; Miss America Pageant, Atlantic City; legalized casino gambling, inaugurated 1978, in Atlantic City.

Famous New Jerseyites include Aaron Burr, James Fenimore Cooper, Stephen Crane, Thomas Edison, Alexander Hamilton, Joyce Kilmer, Gen. George McClellan, Thomas Paine, Molly Pitcher, Paul Robeson, Walt Whitman, Alexander Woolcott.

Chamber of Commerce: 5 Commerce St., Newark, NJ 07102.

New Mexico

Land of Enchantment

People. Population (1979): 1,225,000; **rank:** 37. **Pop. density:** 10.1 per sq. mi. **Urban** (1970): 69.8%. **Racial distrib. (1975):** 90.2% White; —% Black; 8.0% Other (includes American Indians); Hispanic (1970); 407,286. **Major ethnic groups:** Mexican, German, English. **Net migration** (1970-79): +90,000.

Geography. Total area: 121,666 sq. mi.; **rank:** 5. **Land area:** 121,412 sq. mi. **Acres forested land:** 18,059,800. **Location:** southwestern state bounded by Colorado on the N, Oklahoma, Texas, and Mexico on the E and S, and Arizona on the W. **Climate:** dry, with temperatures rising or falling 5°F with every 1,000 ft. elevation. **Topography:** eastern third, Great Plains; central third Rocky Mtns. (85% of the state is over 4,000 ft. elevation); western third high plateau. **Capital:** Santa Fe.

Economy. Principal industries: government, mining, tourism. **Principal manufactured goods:** foods, electrical machinery, apparel, lumber, printing, transportation equipment. **Value added by manufacture** (1977): $790 mln. **Agriculture: Chief crops:** wheat, hay, sorghum, grain, onions, cotton, corn. **Livestock:** 1.72 mln. cattle; 72,000 hogs/pigs; 578,000 sheep; 1.21 mln. poultry. **Timber/-lumber** (1978): Ponderosa pine, Douglas fir; 199 mln. bd. ft. **Minerals** (1978): perlite, potassium salts, uranium each ranked first in U.S. production. Also copper, molybdenum, natural gas, natural gas liquids, pumice, crude petroleum. Total value of mineral production, $3.4 bln. **International airports at:** Albuquerque. **Value of construction** (1979): $1.1 bln. **Employment distribution:** 23.0% serv.; 18.0% agric.; 10% manuf.; 8.9% gvt. **Per capita income** (1979): $7,294. **Unemployment** (1979): 6.6% **Tourism** (1978): out-of-state visitors spent $912 mln.

Finance (1977). **No. banks:** 86; **No. savings and loan assns.:** 34.

Federal government. No. federal civilian employees (Mar. 1979): 22,248. **Avg. salary:** $17,556. **Notable federal facilities:** Kirtland, Cannon, Hollomon AF bases; Los Alamos Scientific Laboratory; White Sands Missile Range.

Energy. Electricity production (1979, mwh, by source): Hydroelectric: 67,813; Mineral: 20.4 mln.; Nuclear: —.

Education. No. schools: 681 elem. and second.; 17 higher ed. **Avg. salary, public school teachers** (1979): $14,198.

State data. Motto: Crescit Eundo (It grows as it goes). **Flower:** Yucca. **Bird:** Roadrunner. **Tree:** Pinon. **Song:** O, Fair New Mexico, Asi Es Nuevo Mexico. **Entered union** Jan. 6, 1912; rank, 47th. **State fair** at: Albuquerque; mid-Sept.

History. Franciscan Marcos de Niza and a black slave Estevan explored the area, 1539, seeking gold. First settlements were at San Juan Pueblo, 1598, and Santa Fe, 1610. Settlers alternately traded and fought with the Apaches, Comanches, and Navajos. Trade on the Santa Fe Trail to Missouri started 1821. The Mexican War was declared May, 1846, Gen. Stephen Kearny took Santa Fe, August. In the 1870s, cattlemen staged the famed Lincoln County War in which Billy (the Kid) Bonney played a leading role. Pancho Villa raided Columbus, 1916.

Tourist Attractions. Carlsbad Caverns, a national park, has caverns on 3 levels and the largest natural cave "room" in the world, 1,500 by 300 ft., 300 ft. high; White Sands Natl. Monument, the largest gypsum deposit in the world.

Pueblo ruin from 100 AD, Chaco Canyon; Acoma, the "sky city," built atop a 357-ft. mesa; 19 Pueblo, 4 Navajo, and 2 Apache reservations. Also, ghost towns, dude ranches, skiing, hunting, and fishing.

Famous New Mexicans include Billy (the Kid) Bonney, Kit Carson, Peter Hurd, Archbishop Jean Baptiste Lamy, Bill Mauldin, Georgia O'Keeffe, Kim Stanley, Lew Wallace.

Tourist information: New Mexico Travel Division, Bataan Bldg., Sante Fe, N.M. 87503 (800-545-2040).

New York

Empire State

People. Population (1979): 17,623,000; **rank:** 2. **Pop. density:** 341.0 per sq. mi. **Urban** (1970): 88.9%. **Racial distrib. (1975):** 85.4% White; 13.2% Black; Hispanic (1970): 872,471. **Major ethnic groups:** Italian, Russian, Polish, German. **Net migration** (1970-79): −1,352,000.

Geography. Total area: 49,576 sq. mi.; **rank:** 30. **Land area:** 47,831 sq. mi. **Acres forested land:** 17,218,400. **Location:** Middle Atlantic state, bordered by the New England states, Atlantic Ocean, New Jersey and Pennsylvania, Lakes Ontario and Erie, and Canada. **Climate:** variable; the SE region moderated by the ocean. **Topography:** highest and most rugged mountains in the NE Adirondack upland; St. Lawrence-Champlain lowlands extend from Lake Ontario NE along the Canadian border; Hudson-Mohawk lowland follows the flows of the rivers N and W, 10-30 mi. wide; Atlantic coastal plain in the SE; Appalachian Highlands, covering half the state westward from the Hudson Valley, include the Catskill Mtns., Finger Lakes; plateau of Erie-Ontario lowlands. **Capital:** Albany.

Economy. Principal industries: manufacturing, finance, communications, tourism, transportation. **Principal manufactured goods:** books and periodicals, clothing and apparel, pharmaceuticals, machinery, instruments, toys and sporting goods, electronic equipment, automotive and aircraft components. **Value added by manufacture** (1977): $44.7 bln. **Agriculture: Chief crops:** potatoes, apples, corn, grapes, onions, hay. **Products:** milk, eggs, nursery products, poultry, wines. **Livestock:** 1.71 mln. cattle; 140,000 hogs/pigs; 63,000 sheep; 12.7 mln. poultry. **Timber/lumber** (1978): evergreens, maples, red cedar; 311 mln. bd. ft. **Minerals** (1978): natural gas, sand and gravel, stone, peat, clay. First in garnet, talc, ilmenite production. Total value mineral production, $438 mln. **Commercial fishing** (1979): $39.0 mln. **Chief ports:** New York, Buffalo, Albany. **International airports at:** New York, Buffalo, Syracuse, Niagara Falls, Ogdensburg, Sullivan County. **Value of construction** (1979): $5.4 bln. **Employment distribution:** 1.3% agric.; 24% manuf.; 29% serv.; 20% trade. **Per capita income** (1979): $9,098. **Unemployment** (1979): 7.1%. **Tourism** (1979): tourists spent $7 bln.

Finance (1977). **Notable industries:** banking, trade, security and commodity brokerage and exchange, insurance, real estate. **No. banks:** 225; **No. savings and loan assns.:** 134.

Federal government. No. federal civilian employees (Mar. 1979): 78,123. **Avg. salary:** $17,663. **Notable federal facilities:** West Point Military Academy; Merchant Marine Academy; Ft. Drum; Griffiss, Plattsburgh AF bases; Watervliet Arsenal.

Energy. Electricity production (1979, mwh, by source): Hydroelectric: 26.2 mln.; Mineral: 60.5 mln.; Nuclear: 18.5 mln.

Education: No. schools: 5,965 elem. and second.; 287 higher ed. **Avg. salary, public school teachers** (1979): $18,600.

State data. Motto: Excelsior (Ever upward). **Flower:** Rose. **Bird:** Bluebird. **Tree:** Sugar maple. **Eleventh** of the original 13 states to ratify the Constitution, July 26, 1788. **State fair** at: Syracuse, end-Aug. to early Sept.

History. In 1609 Henry Hudson discovered the river that bears his name and Champlain explored the lake, far upstate, which was named for him. Dutch built posts near Albany 1614 and 1624; in 1626 they settled Manhattan. A British fleet seized New Netherland, 1664. Ninety-two of the 300 or more engagements of the Revolution were fought in New York, including the Battle of Bemis Heights-Saratoga, a turning point of the war.

Tourist attractions. New York City; Adirondack and Catskill mtns.; Finger Lakes, Great Lakes; Thousand Islands; Niagara Falls; Saratoga Springs racing and spas; Philipsburg Manor, Sunnyside, the restored home of Washington Irving, The Dutch Church of Sleepy Hollow, all in North Tarrytown; Corning Glass Center and Steuben factory, Corning; Fenimore House, National Baseball Hall of Fame and Museum, both in Cooperstown; Ft. Ticonderoga overlooking lakes George and Champlain.

The Franklin D. Roosevelt National Historic Site, Hyde Park, includes the graves of Pres. and Mrs. Roosevelt, the family home since 1867, the Roosevelt Library. Sagamore Hill, Oyster Bay, the Theodore Roosevelt estate, includes his home.

Famous New Yorkers include Peter Cooper, George Eastman, Julia Ward Howe, Charles Evans Hughes, Henry and William James, Herman Melville, Alfred E. Smith, Elizabeth Cady Stanton, Walt Whitman.

Chamber of Commerce: 150 State St., Albany, NY 12207.

North Carolina

Tar Heel State, Old North State

People. Population (1979): 5,511,000; **rank:** 11. **Pop. density:** 112.9 per sq. mi. **Urban** (1970): 45%. **Racial distrib. (1975):** 76.9% White; 21.9% Black; Hispanic (1970): 22,611. **Major ethnic groups:** German, English. **Net migration** (1970-79): +151,000.

Geography. Total area: 52,586 sq. mi.; **rank:** 28. **Land area:** 48,798 sq. mi. **Acres forested land:** 20,043,300. **Location:** South Atlantic state bounded by Virginia, South Carolina, Georgia, Tennessee, and the Atlantic O. **Climate:** sub-tropical in SE, medium-continental in mountain region; tempered by the Gulf Stream and the mountains in W. **Topography:** coastal plain and tidewater, two-fifths of state, extending to the fall line of the rivers; piedmont plateau, another two-fifths, 200 mi. wide of gentle to rugged hills; southern Appalachian Mtns. contains the Blue Ridge and Great Smoky mtns. **Capital:** Raleigh.

Economy. Principal industries: manufacturing, agriculture, tobacco. **Principal manufactured goods:** textiles, tobacco products, food products, chemicals, furniture, electrical and non-electrical machinery. **Value added by manufacture** (1977): $18.1 bln. **Agriculture: Chief crops:** tobacco, soybeans, corn, peanuts, small sweet potatoes, grains. **Livestock:** 1.08 mln. cattle; 2.6

mln. hogs/pigs; 7,500 sheep; 20.8 mln. poultry. **Timber/-lumber** (1978): yellow pine, oak, hickory, poplar, maple. 1.2 bln. bd. ft. **Minerals** (1979): stone, phosphate rock, sand and gravel, cement, lithium compounds. Total mineral production valued at $296 mln. **Commercial fishing** (1979): $58.5 mln. **Chief ports:** Morehead City, Wilmington. **Value of construction** (1979): $5.9 bln. **Employment distribution:** 31.6% manuf.; 16.8% trade; 14.0% gvt.; 12.2% serv. **Per capita income** (1979): $7,359. **Unemployment** (1979): 4.8%. **Tourism** (1976): out-of-state visitors spent $2.2 bln.

Finance (1977). **No. banks: 89; No. savings and loan assns.:** 182.

Federal government. No. federal civilian employees (Mar. 1979): 26,336. **Avg. salary:** $16,727. **Notable federal facilities:** Ft. Bragg; Camp LeJeune Marine Base; U.S. EPA Research and Development Labs, Cherry Point Marine Corps Air Station.

Energy. Electricity production (1979, mwh, by source): Hydroelectric: 7.9 mln.; Mineral: 53.4 mln.; Nuclear: 6.8 mln.

Education. No. schools: 2,240 elem. and second.; 116 higher ed. **Avg. salary, public school teachers** (1979): $13,537.

State data. Motto: Esse Quam Videri (To be rather than to seem). **Flower:** Dogwood. **Bird:** Cardinal. **Tree:** Pine. **Song:** The Old North State. **Twelfth** of the original 13 states to ratify the Constitution, Nov. 21, 1789. **State fair** at: Raleigh; mid-Oct.

History. The first English colony in America was the first of 2 established by Sir Walter Raleigh on Roanoke Is., 1585 and 1587. The first group returned to England; the second, the "Lost Colony," disappeared without trace. Permanent settlers came from Virginia, c. 1660. Roused by British repressions, the colonists drove out the royal governor, 1775; the province's congress was the first to vote for independence; ten regiments were furnished to the Continental Army. Cornwallis' forces were defeated at Kings Mountain, 1780, and forced out after Guilford Courthouse, 1781.

Tourist attractions. Cape Hatteras and Cape Lookout national seashores; Great Smoky Mtns. (half in Tennessee); Guilford Courthouse and Moore's Creek parks, Revolutionary battle sites; Bennett Place, NW of Durham, where Gen. Joseph Johnston surrendered the last Confederate army to Gen. Wm. Sherman; Ft. Raleigh, Roanoke Is., where Virginia Dare, first child of English parents in the New World, was born Aug. 18, 1587; Wright Brothers National Memorial, Kitty Hawk.

Famous North Carolinians include Richard J. Gatling, Billy Graham, Wm. Rufus King, Dolley Madison, Edward R. Murrow, Enos Slaughter, Moses Waddel.

Tourist information: Division of Travel & Tourism Development, P.O. Box 25249, Raleigh, NC 27611.

North Dakota

Sioux State, Flickertail State

People. Population (1979): 646,000; **rank:** 46. **Pop. density:** 9.3 per sq. mi. **Urban** (1970): 44.3%. **Racial distrib. (1975):** 96.7% White; —% Black; Hispanic (1970): 2,007. **Major ethnic groups** Norwegian, Russian, German. **Net migration** (1970-79): −14,000.

Geography. Total area: 70,665 sq. mi.; **rank:** 17. **Land area:** 69,273 sq. mi. **Acres forested land:** 421,800. **Location:** West North Central state, situated exactly in the middle of North America, bounded on the N by Canada, on the E by Minnesota, on the S by South Dakota, on the W by Montana. **Climate:** continental, with a wide range of temperature and moderate rainfall. **Topography:** Central Lowland in the E comprises the flat Red River Valley and the Rolling Drift Prairie; Missouri Plateau of the Great Plains on the W. **Capital:** Bismarck.

Economy. Principal industries: agriculture, manufacturing. **Principal manufactured goods:** farm equipment, processed foods. **Value added by manufacture** (1977): $475 mln. **Agriculture: Chief crops:** spring wheat, durum, barley, rye, flaxseed, oats, potatoes, soybeans, sugarbeets, sunflowers, hay. **Livestock:** 2 mln. cattle; 335,000 hogs/pigs; 236,000 sheep; 1.5 mln. poultry. **Minerals** (1977): petroleum (70% of the total $277.3 mln. output value), natural gas, natural gas liquids, lignite, salt, lime. **Commercial fishing** (1979): $101,000. **International airports at:** Fargo, Grand Forks, Bismarck, Minot. **Value of construction** (1979): $597 mln. **Employment distribution:** 19.4% agric.; 13.9% serv.; 5.4% manuf. **Per capita income** (1979): $7,774. **Unemployment** (1979): 3.7% **Tourism** (1979): out-of-state visitors spent $196 mln.

Finance (1977). **No. banks:** 171; **No. savings and loan assns.:** 12.

Federal government. No. federal civilian employees (Mar. 1979): 5,080. **Avg. salary:** $16,899. **Notable federal facilities:** Strategic Air Command bases at Minot, Grand Forks; Northern Prairie Wildlife Research Center; Garrison Dam; Theodore Roosevelt Natl. Park; Grand Forks Energy Research Center.

Energy. Electricity production (1979, mwh, by source): Hydroelectric: 2.7 mln.; Mineral: 11.1 mln.; Nuclear: —.

Education. No. schools: 825 elem. and second.; 15 higher ed. **Avg. salary, public school teachers** (1979): $12,060.

State data. Motto: Liberty and union, now and forever, one and inseparable. **Flower:** Wild prairie rose. **Bird:** Western Meadowlark. **Tree:** American elm. **Song:** North Dakota Hymn. **Entered union** Nov. 2, 1889; rank, 39th. **State fair** at: Minot; 3d week in July.

History. Pierre La Verendrye was the first French fur trader in the area, 1738, followed later by the English. The U.S. acquired half the territory in the Louisiana Purchase, 1803. Lewis and Clark built Ft. Mandan, spent the winter of 1804-05 there. In 1818, American ownership of the other half was confirmed by agreement with Britain. First permanent settlement was at Pembina, 1812. Missouri River steamboats reached the area, 1832; the first railroad, 1873, bringing many homesteaders. The state was first to hold a presidential primary, 1912.

Tourist attractions. International Peace Garden, a 2,200-acre tract extending across the border into Manitoba, commemorates the friendly relations between the U.S. and Canada; 65,000-acre Theodore Roosevelt National Memorial Park, Badlands, contains the president's Elkhorn Ranch; Ft. Abraham Lincoln State Park and Museum, S of Mandan.

Famous North Dakotans include Maxwell Anderson, Angie Dickinson, John Bernard Flannagan; Louis L'Amour, Peggy Lee, Eric Sevareid, Vilhjalmur Stefansson, Lawrence Welk.

Chamber of Commerce: P.O. Box 2467, Fargo, ND 58102.

Ohio

Buckeye State

People. Population (1979): 10,718,000; **rank:** 6. **Pop. density:** 261.6 per sq. mi. **Urban** (1970): 75.3%. **Racial distrib. (1975):** 89.9% White; 9.6% Black; Hispanic (1970): 95,128. **Major ethnic groups:** German, Italian, Polish, English. **Net migration** (1970-79): −624,000.

Geography. Total area: 41,222 sq. mi.; **rank:** 35. **Land area:** 40,975 sq. mi. **Acres forested land:** 6,146,600. **Location:** East North Central state bounded on the N by Michigan and Lake Erie; on the E and S by Pennsylvania, West Virginia; and Kentucky; on the W by Indiana. **Climate:** temperate but variable; weather subject to much precipitation. **Topography:** generally rolling plain; Allegheny plateau in E; Lake [Erie] plains extend southward; central plains in the W. **Capital:** Columbus.

Economy. Principal industries: manufacturing, tourism, government, trade. **Principal manufactured goods:** transportation equipment, machinery, primary and fabricated metal products. **Value added by manufacture** (1977): $43.3 bln. **Agriculture: Chief crops:** corn, hay, winter wheat, oats, soybeans. **Livestock** (1979): 1.85 mln. cattle; 2.1 mln. hogs/pigs; 320,000 sheep; 12.3 mln. poultry. **Timber/lumber** (1977): oak, ash, maple, walnut, beech; 181 mln. bd. ft. **Minerals** (1978): mineral fuels (79% of the total $1.48 bln. value of mineral production), clays, sand and gravel, stone, gypsum. **Commercial fishing** (1979): $3.5 mln. **Chief ports:** Cleveland, Toledo, Cincinnati, Ashtabula. **International airports at:** Cleveland, Columbus, Dayton. **Value of construction** (1979): $6.3 bln. **Employment distribution:** 29.1% manuf.; 20.7% trade; 17.1% serv.; 14.2% gvt. **Per capita income** (1979): $8,775. **Unemployment** (1979): 5.9%. **Tourism** (1976): out-of-state visitors spent $3.18 bln.

Finance (1977). **Notable industries:** banking, insurance. **No. banks:** 481; **No. savings and loan assns.:** 405.

Federal government. No. federal civilian employees (Mar. 1979): 54,688. **Avg. salary:** $19,440. **Notable federal facilities:** Wright Paterson, Rickenbacker AF bases; Lewis Research Ctr.; Portsmouth Gaseous Diffusion Plant; Mound Laboratory.

Energy. Electricity production (1979, mwh, by source): Hydroelectric: 4,451; Mineral: 134 mln.; Nuclear: 3.2 mln.

Education. No. schools: 4,912 elem. and second.; 131 higher ed. **Avg. salary, public school teachers** (1979): $14,200.

State data. Motto: With God, all things are possible. **Flower:** Scarlet carnation. **Bird:** Cardinal. **Tree:** Buckeye. **Song:** Beautiful Ohio. **Entered union** Mar. 1, 1803; rank, 17th. **State fair** at: Columbus; mid-Aug.

History. LaSalle visited the Ohio area, 1669. American fur-traders arrived, beginning 1685; the French and Indians sought to drive them out. During the Revolution, Virginians defeated the Indians, 1774, but hostilities were renewed, 1777. The region became U.S. territory after the Revolution. First organized settlement was at Marietta, 1788. Indian warfare ended with Anthony Wayne's victory at Fallen Timbers, 1794. In the War of 1812, Oliver H. Perry's victory on Lake Erie and William H. Harrison's invasion of Canada, 1813, ended British incursions.

Tourist attractions. Memorial City Group National Monuments, a group of 24 prehistoric Indian burial mounds; Neil Armstrong Air and Space Museum, Wapakoneta; Air Force Museum, Dayton; Pro Football Hall of Fame, Canton; birthplaces, homes, and memorials to Ohio's 6 U.S. presidents: Wm. Henry Harrison, U.S. Grant, Garfield, Hayes, McKinley, Harding.

Famous Ohioans include Sherwood Anderson, George Bellows, Ambrose Bierce, Paul Laurence Dunbar, Thomas Edison, John Glenn, Bob Hope, Eddie Rickenbacker, John D. Rockefeller Sr. and Jr., Gen. Wm. Sherman, Orville Wright.

Chamber of Commerce: 17 S. High St., 8th Fl., Columbus, OH 43215.

Oklahoma

Sooner State

People. Population (1979): 2,862,000; **rank:** 27. **Pop. density:** 41.6 per sq. mi. **Urban** (1970): 68%. **Racial distrib. (1977):** 88.7% White; 7.0% Black; 3.9% Amer. Ind. **Major ethnic groups:** German, English, Mexican. **Net migration** (1970-79): +160,000.

Geography. Total area: 69,919 sq. mi.; **rank:** 18. **Land area:** 68,782 sq. mi. **Acres forested land:** 8,513,300. **Location:** West South Central state bounded on the N by Colorado and Kansas; on the E by Missouri and Arkansas; on the S and W by Texas and New Mexico. **Climate:** temperate; southern humid belt merging with colder northern continental; humid eastern and dry western zones. **Topography:** high plains predominate the W, hills and small mountains in the E; the east central region is dominated by the Arkansas R. Basin, and the Red R. Plains, in the S. **Capital:** Oklahoma City.

Economy. Principal industries: manufacturing, agriculture, mining. **Principal manufactured goods:** nonelectrical machinery, fabricated metal products, transportation equipment. **Value added by manufacture** (1977): $4.7 bln. **Agriculture: Chief crops:** wheat, cotton lint, sorghum grain, peanuts, hay, soybeans, cotton seed, barley, oats, pecans. **Livestock:** 5.3 mln. cattle; 315,000 hogs/pigs; 89,000 sheep; 4.5 mln. poultry. **Timber/lumber** (1978): pine, oaks, hickory; 288 mln. bd. ft. **Minerals** (1978): mineral fuels (96% of the total $3.8 bln. mineral production), gypsum, sand and gravel, stone, feldspar, pumice. **Commercial fishing** (1979): $2.8 mln. **Chief ports:** Catoosa, Muskogee. **International airports at:** Oklahoma City, Tulsa. **Value of construction** (1979): $2.9 bln. **Employment distribution:** 20.8% trade; 18.2% gvt.; 14.6% manuf.; 14.5% serv. **Per capita income** (1979): $8,226. **Unemployment** (1979): 3.4%. **Tourism** (1977): tourists spent $1.4 bln.

Finance (1977). **No. banks:** 478; **No. savings and loan assns.:** 59.

Federal government. No. federal civilian employees (Mar. 1979): 36,570. **Avg. salary:** $17,421. **Notable federal facilities:** Federal Aviation Agency and Tinker AFB, both Oklahoma City; Ft. Sill, Lawton; Altus AFB, Altus; Vance AFB, Enid.

Energy. Electricity production (1979, mwh, by source): Hydroelectric: 2.3 mln.; Mineral: 39.3 mln.; Nuclear: —.

Education. No. schools: 1,913 elem. and second.; 44 higher ed. **Avg. salary, public school teachers** (1979): $12,500.

State data. Motto: Labor Omnia Vincit (Labor conquers all things). **Flower:** Mistletoe. **Bird:** Scissortailed flycatcher. **Tree:** Redbud. **Song:** Oklahoma! **Entered union** Nov. 16, 1907; rank, 46th. **State fair** at: Oklahoma City; last week of Sept.

History. Part of the Louisiana Purchase, 1803, Oklahoma was known as Indian Territory (but was not given territorial government) after it became the home of the "Five Civilized Tribes"—Cherokee, Choctaw, Chickasaw, Creek, and Seminole—1828-1846. The land was also used by Comanche, Osage, and other Plains Indians. As white settlers pressed west, land was opened for homesteading by runs and lottery, the first run taking place Apr. 22, 1889. The most famous run was to the Cherokee Outlet, 1893.

Tourist attraction. Will Rogers Memorial, Claremore, contains his collections of saddles, ropes, trophies; his tomb is there. Also, National Cowboy Hall of Fame, Oklahoma City; restored Ft. Gibson Stockade, near Muskogee, the Army's largest outpost in Indian lands; Indian powwows; rodeos; fishing; hunting; Ouachita National Forest.

Famous Oklahomans include Carl Albert, Woody Guthrie, Gen. Patrick J. Hurley, Karl Jansky, Mickey Mantle, Wiley Post, Oral Roberts, Will Rogers, Maria Tallchief, Jim Thorpe.

Chamber of Commerce: 4020 N. Lincoln Blvd., Oklahoma City, OK 73105.

Oregon

Beaver State

People. Population (1979): 2,524,000; **rank:** 29. **Pop. density:** 26.2 per sq. mi. **Urban** (1970): 67.1%. **Racial distrib. (1975):** 97.0% White; 1.3% Black; Hispanic (1970): 34,577. **Major ethnic groups:** German, Scandinavian, English, Russian. **Net migration** (1970-79): +293,000.

Geography. Total area: 96,981 sq. mi.; **rank:** 10. **Land area:** 96,184 sq. mi. **Acres forested land:** 29,810,000. **Location:** Pacific state, bounded on N by Washington; on E by Idaho; on S by Nevada and California; on W by the Pacific. **Climate:** coastal mild and humid climate; continental dryness and extreme temperatures in the interior. **Topography:** Coast Range of rugged mountains; fertile Willamette R. Valley to E and S; Cascade Mtn. Range of volcanic peaks E of the valley; plateau E of Cascades, remaining two-thirds of state. **Capital:** Salem.

Economy. Principal industries: manufacturing, mining, forestry, food processing, tourism, agriculture. **Principal manufactured goods:** furniture, lumber, paper, foods, transportation equipment, fabricated metal. **Value added by manufacture** (1977): $6.3 bln. **Agriculture: Chief crops:** wheat, oats, potatoes, berries, pears, cherries, filberts, walnuts, vegetables. **Livestock:** 1.5 mln. cattle; 115,000 hogs/pigs; 460,000 sheep; 5.18 mln. poultry. **Timber/lumber** (1978): Douglas fir, hemlock, ponderosa pine; 7.5 bln. bd. ft. **Minerals** (1978): nickel, stone, sand and gravel, cement, clays, diatomite, lime, pumice, talc. Total mineral production valued at $122.7 mln. **Commercial fishing** (1979): $65.2 mln. **Chief ports:** Portland, Astoria, Newport, Coos Bay. **International Airports at:** Portland. **Value of construction** (1979): $2.5 bln. **Employment distribution:** 23.6% trade; 20.9% manuf.; 16.9% serv. **Per capita income** (1979): $8,842. **Unemployment** (1979): 6.8%. **Tourism** (1979): out-of-state visitors spent $1.1 bln.

Finance (1977). **No. banks:** 60; **No. savings and loan assns.:** 28.

Federal government. No. federal civilian employees (Mar. 1979): 17,085. **Avg. salary:** $18,664. **Notable federal facilities:** Bonneville Power Administration.

Energy: Electricity production (1979, mwh, by source): Hydroelectric: 29.8 mln.; Mineral: 784,138; Nuclear: 4.5 mln.

Education. No. schools: 1,414 elem. and second.; 43 higher ed. **Avg. salary, public school teachers** (1979): $14,570.

State data. Motto: The union. **Flower:** Oregon grape. **Bird:** Western meadowlark. **Tree:** Douglas fir. **Song:** Oregon, My Oregon. **Entered union** Feb. 14, 1859; rank, 33d. **State fair** at: Salem; end-Aug. to early Sept.

History. American Capt. Robert Gray discovered and sailed into the Columbia River, 1792; Lewis and Clark, traveling overland, wintered at its mouth 1805-06; fur traders followed. Settlers arrived in the Willamette Valley, 1834. In 1843 the first large wave of settlers arrived via the Oregon Trail. Early in the 20th century, the "Oregon System," reforms which included the initiative, referendum, recall, direct primary, and woman suffrage, was adopted.

Tourist attractions. Crater Lake National Park, deepest lake in the U.S. (1,932 ft.) in a former volcano, 6 mi. in diameter; Oregon Dunes National Recreation Area; Ft. Clatsop National Memorial includes a replica of the fort in which Lewis and Clark spent the winter of 1805-06. Oregon Caves National Monument contains stone waterfalls. Also skiing, annual Pendleton Round-Up.

Famous Oregonians include Ernest Bloch, Childe Hassam, Ernest Haycox, Chief Joseph, Edwin Markham, Dr. John McLoughlin, Joaquin Miller, Linus Pauling, John Reed, William Simon U'Ren.

Chamber of Commerce: 220 Cottage St., N.E., Salem, OR 97301.

Pennsylvania

Keystone State

People. Population (1979): 11,721,000; **rank:** 4. **Pop. density:** 260.7 per sq. mi. **Urban** (1970): 71.5%. **Racial distrib. (1975):** 90.6% White; 8.8% Black; Hispanic (1970): 44,535. **Major ethnic groups:** Italian, Polish, German, English. **Net migration** (1970-79): −478,000.

Geography. Total area: 45,333 sq. mi.; **rank:** 33. **Land area:** 44,966 sq. mi. **Acres forested land:** 16,825,900. **Location:** Middle Atlantic state, bordered on the E by the Delaware R., on the S by the Mason-Dixon Line; on the W by West Virginia and Ohio; on the N/NE by Lake Erie and New York. **Climate:** continental with wide fluctuations in seasonal temperatures. **Topography:** Allegheny Mtns. run SW to NE, with Piedmont and Coast Plain in the SE triangle; Allegheny Front a diagonal spine across the state's center; N and W rugged plateau falls to Lake Erie Lowland. **Capital:** Harrisburg.

Economy. Principal industries: steel, travel, health, apparel, machinery, food & agriculture. **Principal manufactured goods:** primary metals, foods, fabricated metal products, non-electrical machinery, electrical machinery. **Value added by manufacture** (1978): $39.1 bln. **Agriculture: Chief crops:** corn, hay, mushrooms, apples, potatoes, winter wheat, oats, vegetables, tobacco, grapes. **Livestock:** 1.9 mln. cattle; 820,000 hogs/pigs; 85,000 sheep; 20.9 mln. poultry. **Timber/lumber** (1978): pine, spruce, oak, maple; 558 mln. bd. ft. **Minerals** (1978): bituminous coal, anthracite, sand & gravel, limestone. **Commercial fishing** (1979): $251,000. **Chief ports:** Philadelphia, Pittsburgh, Erie. **International airports at:** Philadelphia, Pittsburgh, Erie, Harrisburg. **Value of construction** (1979): $4.5 bln. **Employment distribution:** 28.8% manuf.; 20.5% trades; 18.7% serv.; 15.2% gvt. **Per capita income** (1979): $8,559. **Unemployment** (1979): 6.9%. **Tourism** (1978): out-of-state visitors spent $5 bln.

Finance (1977). **No. banks:** 370; **No. savings and loan assns.:** 417.

Federal government. No. federal civilian employees (Mar. 1979): 85,252. **Avg. salary.** $17,034. **Notable federal facilities:** Army War College, Carlisle; Ships Control Ctr., Mechanicsburg; New Cumberland Army Depot.

Energy. Electricity production (1979, mwh, by source): Hydroelectric: 1.2; Mineral: 107.8 mln. Nuclear: 18.8 mln.

Education. No. schools: 5,286 elem. and second.; 179 higher ed. **Avg. salary, public school teachers** (1979): $15,300.

State data. Motto: Virtue, liberty and independence. **Flower:** Mountain laurel. **Bird:** Ruffed grouse. **Tree:** Hemlock. **Second** of the original 13 states to ratify the Constitution, Dec. 12, 1787. **State fair** at: Harrisburg; 2d week in Jan.

History. First settlers were Swedish, 1643, on Tinicum Is. In 1655 the Dutch seized the settlement but lost it to the British, 1664. The region was given by Charles II to William Penn, 1681, Philadelphia (brotherly love) was the capital of the colonies during most of the Revolution, and of the U.S., 1790-1800. Philadelphia was taken by the British, 1777; Washington's troops encamped at Valley Forge in the bitter winter of 1777-78. The Declaration of Independence, 1776, and the Constitution, 1787, were signed in Philadelphia.

Tourist attractions. Independence Hall, Liberty Bell, Carpenters Hall, all in Philadelphia; Valley Forge; Gettysburg battlefield; Amish festivals, Lancaster Cty., Hershey Chocolate World; Pocono Mtns.; Delaware Water Gap; Longwood Gardens, near Kennett Square; Pine Creek Gorge; hunting, fishing, winter sports.

Famous Pennsylvanians include Marian Anderson, Maxwell Anderson, Andrew Carnegie, Stephen Foster, Benjamin Franklin, George C. Marshall, Andrew W. Mellon; Robert E. Peary, Mary Roberts Rinehart, Betsy Ross.

Chamber of Commerce: 222 N. 3d St., Harrisburg, PA 17101.

Rhode Island

Little Rhody, Ocean State

People. Population (1979): 924,000; **rank:** 39. **Pop. density:** 880.8 per sq. mi. **Urban** (1970): 87.1% **Racial distrib. (1975):** 96.3% White; 3.0% Black; Hispanic (1975): 6,961. **Major ethnic groups:** Italian, English, Irish. **Net migration** (1970-79): −27,000.

Geography. Total area: 1,214 sq. mi.; **rank:** 50. **Land area:** 1,049 sq. mi. **Acres forested land:** 404,200. **Location:** New England state. **Climate:** invigorating and changeable. **Topography:** eastern lowlands of Narragansett Basin; western uplands of flat and rolling hills. **Capital:** Providence.

Economy. Principal industries: manufacturing, services. **Principal manufactured goods:** costume jewelry, machinery, textiles, electronics, silverware. **Value added**

by manufacture (1977): $2.8 bln. **Agriculture: Chief crops:** potatoes, apples, corn. **Livestock:** 10,000 cattle; 8,700 hogs/pigs; 2,100 sheep; 260,000 poultry. **Timber/-lumber:** oak, chestnut. **Minerals** (1979): gem stones, sand and gravel, stone. Total value mineral production, $7.6 mln. **Commercial fishing** (1979): $36.0 mln. **Chief ports:** Providence, Newport, Tiverton. **Value of construction** (1979): $392 mln. **Employment distribution:** 33.1% manuf.; 20.3% trade; 19.7% serv. **Per capita income** (1979): $8,266. **Unemployment** (1979): 6.6% **Tourism** (1979): out-of-state visitors spent $250 mln.

Finance (1977). **Notable industries:** banking, insurance. **No. banks:** 14; **No. savings and loan assns.:** 6.

Federal government. No. federal civilian employees (Mar. 1979): 5,887. **Avg. salary:** $18,323. **Notable federal facilities:** Naval War College.

Energy. Electricity production (1979, mwh, by source): Hydroelectric: 3,343; Mineral: 686,904; Nuclear: —.

Education. No. schools: 428 elem. and second.; 12 higher ed. **Avg. salary, public school teachers** (1979): $16,568.

State data. Motto: Hope. **Flower:** Violet. **Bird:** Rhode Island red. **Tree:** Red maple. **Song:** Rhode Island. **Thirteenth** of original 13 states to ratify the Constitution, May 29, 1790. **State fair** at: E. Greenwich; mid-Aug.

History. Rhode Island is distinguished for its battle for freedom of conscience and action, begun by Roger Williams, founder of Providence, who was exiled from Massachusetts Bay Colony in 1636, and Anne Hutchinson, exiled in 1638. Rhode Island gave protection to Quakers in 1657 and to Jews from Holland in 1658.

The colonists broke the power of the Narragansett Indians in the Great Swamp Fight, 1675, the decisive battle in King Philip's War. British trade restrictions angered the colonists and they burned the British revenue cutter Gaspee, 1772. The colony declared its independence May 4, 1776. Gen. John Sullivan and Lafayette won a partial victory, 1778, but failed to oust the British.

Tourist attractions. Newport mansions; summer resorts and water sports; Touro Synagogue, Newport, 1763; first Baptist Church in America, Providence, 1638; Gilbert Stuart birthplace, Saunderstown; Narragansett Indian Fall Festival.

Famous Rhode Islanders include Ambrose Burnside, George M. Cohan, Nelson Eddy, Jabez Gorham, Nathanael Greene, Christopher and Oliver La Farge, Matthew C. and Oliver Perry, Gilbert Stuart.

Chamber of Commerce: 206 Smith St., Providence, RI 02908.

South Carolina

Palmetto State

People. Population (1979): 2,866,000; **rank:** 26. **Pop. density:** 94.8 per sq. mi. **Urban** (1970): 47.6%. **Racial distrib. (1975):** 68.8% White; 30.8% Black; Hispanic (1970): 10,999. **Major ethnic groups:** German, English. **Net migration** (1970-79): +95,000.

Geography. Total area: 31,055 sq. mi.; **rank:** 40. **Land area:** 30,225 sq. mi. **Acres forested land:** 12,249,400. **Location:** south Atlantic coast state, bordering North Carolina on the N; Georgia on the SW and W; the Atlantic O. on the E, SE and S. **Climate:** humid sub-tropical. **Topography:** Blue Ridge province in NW has highest peaks; piedmont lies between the mountains and the fall line; coastal plain covers two-thirds of the state. **Capital:** Columbia.

Economy: Principal industries: tourism, textiles, apparel, chemical, agriculture, manufacturing. **Principal manufactured goods:** textiles, chemicals and allied products, non-electrical machinery, apparel and related products. **Value added by manufacture** (1977): $8.1 bln. **Agriculture: Chief crops:** tobacco, soybeans, corn, cotton, peaches, hay, vegetables. **Livestock** (1978): 960,000 cattle; 525,000 hogs/pigs; 1,300 sheep; 8.05 mln. poultry. **Timber/lumber** (1978): pine, oak; 1.0 bln. bd. ft. **Minerals** (1978): cement, stone, limestone, granite, sand and gravel, clays; vermiculite, kaolin, both 2d in U.S. production. Total mineral production valued at $176 mln. **Commercial fishing** (1979): $25.8 mln. **Chief ports:** Charleston, Georgetown. **International airports at:** Charleston, Greenville-Spartanburg. **Value of construction** (1979): $4.8 bln. **Employment distribution:** 34% manuf.; 20% gvt.; 13% serv. **Per capita income** (1979): $7,027. **Unemployment** (1979): 5%. **Tourism** (1979): out-of-state visitors spent $1.8 bln.

Finance (1977). **No. banks:** 87; **No. savings and loan assns.:** 74.

Federal government: No. federal civilian employees (Mar. 1978): 23,900. **Avg. Salary:** $16,777. **Notable federal facilities:** Polaris Submarine Base; Barnwell Nuclear Power Plant; Ft. Jackson.

Energy. Electricity production (1979, mwh, by source): Hydroelectric: 3.9 mln.; Mineral: 19.5 mln.; Nuclear: 18.2 mln.

Education. No. schools: 1,100 elem. and second.; 56 higher ed. **Avg. salary, public school teachers** (1979): $12,206.

State data. Motto: Dum Spiro Spero (While I breathe, I hope). **Flower:** Carolina jessamine. **Bird:** Carolina wren. **Tree:** Palmetto. **Song:** Carolina. **Eighth** of the original 13 states to ratify the Constitution, May 23, 1788. **State fair** at: Columbia; 3d week in Oct.

History. The first English colonists settled, 1670, on the Ashley River, moved to the site of Charleston, 1680. The colonists seized the government, 1775, and the royal governor fled. The British took Charleston, 1780, but were defeated at Kings Mountain that year, and at Cowpens and Eutaw Springs, 1781. In the 1830s, South Carolinians, angered by federal protective tariffs, adopted the Nullification Doctrine, holding a state can void an act of Congress. The state was the first to secede and, in 1861, Confederate troops fired on and forced the surrender of U. S. troops at Ft. Sumter, in Charleston Harbor, launching the Civil War.

Tourist attractions. Restored historic Charleston harbor area and Charleston gardens: Middleton Place, Magnolia, Cypress; other gardens at Brookgreen, Edisto, Glencairn; state parks; coastal islands; shore resorts such as Myrtle Beach; fishing and quail hunting; Ft. Sumter National Monument, in Charleston Harbor; Charleston Museum, est. 1773, is the oldest museum in the U.S..

Famous South Carolinians include James F. Byrnes, John C. Calhoun, DuBose Heyward, James Longstreet, Francis Marion, Charles Pinckney, John Rutledge, Thomas Sumter.

Chamber of Commerce: 1002 Calhoun St., Columbia, SC 29201.

South Dakota

Coyote State, Sunshine State

People. Population (1979): 683,000; **rank:** 45. **Pop. density:** 9.1 per sq. mi. **Urban** (1970): 44.6%. **Racial distrib. (1975):** 93.9% White; —% Black; 5.8% Other (includes American Indians); Hispanic (1970): 2,954. **Major ethnic groups:** German, Norwegian, Russian. **Net migration** (1970-79): −30,000.

Geography. Total area: 77,047 sq. mi.; **rank:** 16. **Land area:** 75,955 sq. mi. **Acres forested land:** 1,702,000. **Location:** West North Central state bounded on the N by North Dakota; on the E by Minnesota and Iowa; on the S by Nebraska; on the W by Wyoming and Montana. **Climate:** characterized by extremes of temperature, persistent winds, low precipitation and humidity. **Topography:** Prairie Plains in the E; rolling hills of the Great Plains in the W; the Black Hills, rising 3,500 ft. in the SW corner. **Capital:** Pierre.

Economy: Principal industries: mining, manufacturing, agriculture. **Principal manufactured goods:** processed meats, electrical appliances, occupational health and safety products, computer sub-assemblies. **Value added**

by manufacture (1977): $608.5 mln. **Agriculture: Chief crops:** rye, flaxseed, oats, durum, wheat, honey, alfalfa. **Livestock** (1979): 4.01 mln. cattle; 1.62 mln. hogs/pigs; 740,000 sheep; 2.97 mln. poultry. **Timber/lumber** (1978): ponderosa pine; 119 mln. bd. ft. **Minerals** (1978): gold (1st in U.S.), crude oil, stone, sand and gravel. Total value mineral production, $112.1 mln. **Commercial fishing** (1979): $309,000. **Value of construction** (1979): $542 mln. **Employment distribution:** 15% serv.; 13.2% agric.; 8.2% manuf. **Per capita income** (1979): $7,334. **Unemployment** (1979): 3.5%. **Tourism** (1979): out-of-state visitors spent $415 mln.

Finance (1977). **No. banks:** 155; **No. savings and loan assns.:** 18.

Federal government. No. federal civilian employees (Mar. 1979): 6,489. **Avg. salary:** $16,737. **Notable federal facilities:** Bureau of Indian Affairs.

Energy. Electricity production (1979, mwh, by source): Hydroelectric: 6.3 mln.; Mineral: 2.9 mln.; Nuclear: —.

Education: No. schools: 858 elem. and second.; 17 higher ed. **Avg. salary, public school teachers** (1979): $11,750.

State data. Motto: Under God, the people rule. **Flower:** Pasque flower. **Bird:** Ringnecked pheasant. **Tree:** Black Hills spruce. **Song:** Hail, South Dakota. **Entered union** Nov. 2, 1889; rank, 40th. **State fair** at: Huron; late Aug.-early Sept.

History. La Verendrye explored the region, 1742-43. Lewis and Clark passed through the area, 1804 and 1806. First American settlement was at Sioux Falls, 1859. Gold was discovered, 1874, on the Sioux Reservation; miners rushed in. The U.S. first tried to stop them, then relaxed its opposition. Custer's defeat by the Sioux followed; the Sioux relinquished the land, 1877 and the "great Dakota Boom" began. A new Indian uprising came in 1890, climaxed by the massacre of Indian families at Wounded Knee.

Tourist attractions. Needles Highway through the Black Hills; Badlands National Monument "moonscape"; Custer State Park's bison and burro herds; Ft. Sisson, a restored army frontier post of 1864; the "Great Lakes of South Dakota," reservoirs created behind Oahe, Big Bend, Ft. Randall, and Gavins Point dams on the Missouri R.

Mount Rushmore, in the Black Hills, has an altitude of 6,200 ft. Sculptured on its granite face are the heads of Washington, Jefferson, Lincoln, and Theodore Roosevelt. These busts by Gutzon Borglum are proportionate to men 465 ft. tall. Rushmore is visited by about 2 million persons annually.

Famous South Dakotans include Crazy Horse, Alvin H. Hansen, Dr. Ernest O. Lawrence, Sacagawea, Sitting Bull.

Chamber of Commerce: P.O. Box 190, Pierre, SD 57501.

Tennessee

Volunteer State

People. Population (1979): 4,359,000; **rank:** 17. **Pop. density:** 105.5 per sq. mi. **Urban** (1970): 58.7%. **Racial distrib. (1975):** 84.1% White; 15.6% Black; Hispanic (1970): 13,873. **Major ethnic groups:** German, English, Italian. **Net migration** (1970-79): +176,000.

Geography. Total area: 42,244 sq. mi.; **rank:** 34. **Land area:** 41,328 sq. mi. **Acres forested land:** 13,160,500. **Location:** East South Central state bounded on the N by Kentucky and Virginia; on the E by North Carolina; on the S by Georgia, Alabama, and Mississippi; on the W by Arkansas and Missouri. **Climate:** humid continental to the N; humid sub-tropical to the S. **Topography:** rugged country in the E; the Great Smoky Mtns. of the Unakas; low ridges of the Appalachian Valley; the flat Cumberland Plateau; slightly rolling terrain and knobs of the Interior Low Plateau, the largest region; Eastern Gulf Coastal Plain to the W, is laced with meandering streams; Mississippi Alluvial Plain, a narrow strip of swamp and flood plain in the extreme W. **Capital:** Nashville.

Economy. Principal industries: manufacturing, agriculture, publishing, music. **Principal manufactured goods:** primary and fabricated metals, foods, electrical and electronic machinery, transportation equipment, apparel. **Value added by manufacture** (1977): $12.7 bln. **Agriculture: Chief crops:** soybeans, tobacco, cotton, corn, nursery stock, hay. **Livestock:** 2.35 mln. cattle; 1.3 mln. hogs/pigs; 13,000 sheep; 5.35 mln. poultry. **Timber/-lumber** (1978): locust, poplar, maple, oak; 624 mln. bd. ft. **Minerals** (1978): bituminous coal, stone, zinc, cement. Total value mineral production, $347.5 mln. **Commercial fishing** (1978): $2.4 mln. **Chief ports:** Memphis, Nashville, Knoxville, Chattanooga. **International airports at:** Memphis, Nashville, Knoxville, Chattanooga. **Value of construction** (1979): $4.9 bln. **Employment distribution:** 31.1% manuf.; 15.4% serv.; 8.3% agric. **Per capita income** (1979): $7,299. **Unemployment** (1979): 5.8%. **Tourism** (1978): out-of-state visitors spent $1.3 mln.

Finance (1977). **Notable industries:** insurance. **No. banks:** 348; **No. savings and loan assns.:** 97.

Federal government. No. federal civilian employees (Mar. 1979): 55,476. **Avg. salary:** $17,828. **Notable federal facilities:** Tennessee Valley Authority; Oak Ridge Nat'l. Laboratories.

Energy: Electricity production (1979, mwh, by source): Hydroelectric: 12.3 mln.; Mineral: 46.4 mln.; Nuclear: —.

Education. No. schools: 1,831 elem. and second.; 67 higher ed. **Avg. salary, public school teachers** (1979): $12,272.

State data. Motto: Agriculture and commerce. **Flower:** Iris. **Bird:** Mockingbird. **Tree:** Tulip poplar. **Song:** The Tennessee Waltz. **Entered union** June 1, 1796; rank, 16th. **State fair** at: Nashville; 3d week of Sept.

History. Spanish explorers first visited the area, 1541. English traders crossed the Great Smokies from the east while France's Marquette and Jolliet sailed down the Mississippi on the west, 1673. First permanent settlement was by Virginians on the Watauga River, 1769. During the Revolution, the colonists helped win the Battle of Kings Mountain, N.C., 1780, and joined other eastern campaigns. The state seceded from the Union 1861, and saw many engagements of the Civil War, but 30,000 soldiers fought for the Union.

Tourist attractions. Natural wonders include Reelfoot Lake, the reservoir basin of the Mississippi R. formed by the 1811 earthquake; Lookout Mountain, Chattanooga; Fall Creek Falls, 256 ft. high; Great Smoky Mountains National Park.

Also, the Hermitage, 13 mi. E of Nashville, home of Andrew Jackson; the homes of presidents Polk and Andrew Johnson; the Parthenon, Nashville, a replica of the Parthenon of Athens; the Grand Old Opry, Nashville.

Famous Tennesseans include Davy Crockett, David Farragut, William C. Handy, Sam Houston, Cordell Hull, Grace Moore, Dinah Shore, Alvin York.

Chamber of Commerce: 505 Fesslers La., Nashville, TN 37210.

Texas

Lone Star State

People. Population (1979): 13,241,000; **rank:** 3. **Pop. density:** 50.5 per sq. mi. **Urban** (1970): 79.7%. **Racial distrib. (1975):** 86.9% White; 12.5% Black; Hispanic (1970): 2,059,671. **Major ethnic groups:** Mexican, German. **Net migration** (1970-79): +1,025,000.

Geography: Total area: 267,338 sq. mi.; **rank:** 2. **Land area:** 262,134 sq. mi. **Acres forested land:** 23,279,300. **Location:** Southwestern state, bounded on the SE by the Gulf of Mexico; on the SW by Mexico, separated by the Rio Grande; surrounding states are Louisiana, Arkansas, Oklahoma, New Mexico. **Climate:** extremely varied; driest region is the Trans-Pecos; wettest is the NE. **Topogra-**

phy: Gulf Coast Plain in the S and SE; North Central Plains slope upward with some hills; the Great Plains extend over the Panhandle, are broken by low mountains; the Trans-Pecos is the southern extension of the Rockies. **Capital:** Austin.

Economy. Principal industries: agriculture, petroleum, manufacturing, construction. **Principal manufactured goods:** machinery, transportation equipment, foods, refined petroleum, apparel. **Value added by manufacture** (1977): $32.9 bln. **Agriculture: Chief crops:** cotton, grain sorghum, grains, vegetables, citrus and other fruits, pecans, peanuts. **Livestock:** 13.4 mln. cattle; 800,000 hogs/pigs; 2.46 mln. sheep; 17.3 mln. poultry. **Timber/lumber** (1978): pine, cypress; 950 mln. bd. ft. **Minerals** (1978): petroleum, natural gas, natural gas liquids, cement, sulfur, stone, sand and gravel, lime, salt; total $19.6 bln. **Commercial fishing** (1979): $160 mln. **Chief ports:** Houston, Galveston, Brownsville, Beaumont, Port Arthur, Corpus Christi. **Major International airports at:** Houston, Dallas/Ft. Worth, San Antonio. **Value of construction** (1979): $13.1 bln. **Employment distribution:** 18% manuf.; 17% serv.; 6% transp. **Per capita income** (1979): $8,649. **Unemployment** (1979): 4.2%. **Tourism** (1979): out-of-state visitors spent $4.8 bln.

Finance (1977). **No. banks:** 1,395; **No. savings and loan assns.:** 330.

Federal government. No. federal civilian employees (Mar. 1979): 106,913. **Avg. salary:** $17,281. **Notable federal facilities:** Fort Hood (Killeen).

Energy. Electricity production (1979, mwh, by source): Hydroelectric: 1.2 mln. Mineral: 186.3 mln.; Nuclear: —.

Education. No. schools: 5,922 elem. and second.; 146 higher ed. **Avg. salary, public school teachers** (1979): $13,059.

State data. Motto: Friendship. **Flower:** Bluebonnet. **Bird:** Mockingbird. **Tree:** Pecan. **Song:** Texas, Our Texas. **Entered union** Dec. 29, 1845; rank, 28th. **State fair** at: Dallas; mid-Oct.

History. Pineda sailed along the Texas coast, 1519; Cabeza de Vaca and Coronado visited the interior, 1541. Spaniards made the first settlement at Ysleta, near El Paso, 1682. Americans moved into the land early in the 19th century. Mexico, of which Texas was a part, won independence from Spain, 1821; Santa Anna became dictator, 1835. Texans rebelled; Santa Anna wiped out defenders of the Alamo, 1836. Sam Houston's Texans defeated Santa Anna at San Jacinto and independence was proclaimed the same year. In 1845, Texas was admitted to the Union.

Tourist attractions. Padre Island National Seashore; Big Bend, Guadalupe Mtns. national parks; The Alamo; Ft. Davis; Six Flags Amusement Park. Named for Pres. Lyndon B. Johnson are a state park, a natl. historic site marking his birthplace, boyhood home, and ranch, all near Johnson City, and a library in Austin.

Famous Texans include Stephen Austin, James Bowie, Carol Burnett, J. Frank Dobie, Sam Houston, Howard Hughes, Mary Martin, Chester Nimitz, Katharine Ann Porter, Sam Rayburn.

Chamber of Commerce: 1004 International Life Bldg., Austin, TX 78701.

Utah

Beehive State

People. Population (1979): 1,362,000; **rank:** 36. **Pop. density:** 16.6 per sq. mi. **Urban** (1970): 80.4%. **Racial distrib. (1975):** 97.5% White; —% Black; Hispanic (1970): 43,550. **Major ethnic groups:** English, German, Danish. **Net migration** (1970-79): +70,000.

Geography. Total area: 84,916 sq. mi.; **rank:** 11. **Land area:** 82,096 sq. mi. **Acres forested land:** 15,557,400. **Location:** Middle Rocky Mountain state; its southeastern corner touches Colorado, New Mexico, and Arizona, and is the only spot in the U.S. where 4 states join. **Climate:** arid; yet the SW has a semitropical climate. **Topography:** high Colorado plateau is cut by brilliantly-colored canyons of the SE; broad, flat, desert-like Great Basin of the W; the Great Salt Lake and Bonneville Salt Flats to the NW; Middle Rockies in the NE run E-W; valleys and plateaus of the Wasatch Front. **Capital:** Salt Lake City.

Economy. Principal industries: mining, manufacturing, tourism, trade, services, transportation. **Principal manufactured goods:** guided missiles and parts, electronic components, apparel, lumber and wood products, primary metals, electrical and transportation equipment. **Value added by manufacture** (1980 est.): $2.8 bln. **Agriculture: Chief crops:** wheat, hay, apples, peaches, barley, potatoes. **Livestock:** 810,000 cattle; 49,000 hogs/pigs; 486,000 sheep; 4,944,000 poultry. **Timber/lumber:** aspen, spruce, pine. **Minerals** (1978): crude oil, copper, coal, uranium, gold, natural gas, vanadium, silver, zinc, lead, iron ore, lime, salt. Total value of mineral production valued at $1.3 bln. **International airports at:** Salt Lake City. **Value of construction** (1979): $1.5 bln. **Employment distribution:** 22.6% trade; 16.4% serv.; 14.7% manuf. **Per capita income** (1979): $7,185. **Unemployment** (1979): 4.5%. **Tourism** (1978): out-of-state visitors spent $220 mln.

Finance (1977). **No. banks:** 66; **No. savings and loan assns.:** 16.

Federal government. No. federal civilian employees (Mar. 1979): 31,166. **Avg. salary:** $16,958. **Notable federal facilities:** Hill AFB; Tooele Army Depot, IRS Western Service Center.

Energy. Electricity production (1979, mwh, by source): Hydroelectric: 801,952; Mineral: 10 mln.; Nuclear: —.

Education. No. schools: 572 elem. and second.; 14 higher ed. **Avg. salary, public school teachers** (1979): $13,910.

State data. Motto: Industry. **Flower:** Sego lily. **Bird:** Seagull. **Tree:** Blue spruce. **Song:** Utah, We Love Thee. **Entered union** Jan. 4, 1896; rank, 45th. **State fair** at: Salt Lake City; Sept.

History. Spanish Franciscans visited the area, 1776, the first white men to do so. American fur traders followed. Permanent settlement began with the arrival of the Mormons, 1847. They made the arid land bloom and created a prosperous economy, organized the State of Deseret, 1849, and asked admission to the Union. This was not achieved until 1896, after a long period of controversy over the Mormon Church's doctrine of polygamy, which it discontinued in 1890.

Tourist attractions. Temple Square, Mormon Church hdqtrs., Salt Lake City; Great Salt Lake; fishing streams; lakes and reservoirs, numerous winter sports; campgrounds. Natural wonders may be seen at Zion, Canyonlands, Bryce Canyon, Arches, and Capitol Reef national parks; Dinosaur, Rainbow Bridge, Timpanogas Cave, and Natural Bridges national monuments. Also Lake Powell and Flaming Gorge Dam.

Famous Utahans include Maude Adams, Ezra Taft Benson, John Moses Browning, Philo Farnsworth, Osmond Family, Ivy Baker Priest, George Romney, Brigham Young, Loretta Young.

Tourist information: Division of Travel Development, Council Hall, Salt Lake City, UT 84114.

Vermont

Green Mountain State

People. Population (1979): 493,000; **rank:** 48. **Pop. density:** 53.2 per sq. mi. **Urban** (1970): 32.2%. **Racial distrib. (1975):** 99.2% White; —% Black; Hispanic (1970): 2,469. **Major ethnic groups:** English, Italian, German. **Net migration** (1970-79): +21,000.

Geography. Total area: 9,609 sq. mi.; **rank:** 43. **Land area:** 9,267 sq. mi. **Acres forested land:** 4,511,700. **Location:** northern New England state. **Climate:** temperate, with considerable temperature extremes; heavy snowfall in mountains. **Topography:** Green Mtns. N-S backbone 20-36 mi. wide; avg. altitude 1,000 ft. **Capital:** Montpelier.

Economy. Principal industries: manufacturing, tourism, agriculture, mining, government. **Principal manufactured goods:** machine tools, furniture, scales, books, computer components, skis, fishing rods. **Value added by manufacture** (1977): $1.05 bln. **Agriculture: Chief crops:** apples, maple syrup, hay; also, dairy products. **Livestock:** 320,000 cattle; 6,300 hogs/pigs; 8,000 sheep; 570,000 poultry. **Timber/lumber:** pine, spruce, fir, hemlock. **Minerals** (1979): stone; asbestos (2d in U.S.); talc (1st in U.S.); sand and gravel; gemstones; dimension granite, marble, and slate (2d in U.S.). Total value mineral production, $49.5 mln. **International airports at:** Burlington. **Value of construction** (1979): $303.3 mln. **Employment distribution:** 22% manuf.; 19% serv.; 14% retail trade. **Per capita income** (1979): $7,280. **Unemployment** (1979): 5.1% **Tourism** (1979): out-of-state visitors spent $430 mln.

Finance (1977). **No. banks:** 29; **No. savings and loan assns.:** 7.

Federal government. No. federal civilian employees (Mar. 1979): 2,185. **Avg. salary:** $17,312.

Energy. Electricity production (1979, mwh, by source): Hydroelectric: 856,626; Mineral: 64,842; Nuclear: 3.5 mln.

Education. No. schools: 435 elem. and second.; 23 higher ed. **Avg. salary, public school teachers** (1979): $11,787.

State data. Motto: Freedom and unity. **Flower:** Red clover. **Bird:** Hermit thrush. **Tree:** Sugar maple. **Song:** Hail, Vermont. **Entered union** Mar. 4, 1791; rank, 14th. **State fair** at: Rutland; early Sept.

History. Champlain explored the lake that bears his name, 1609. First American settlement was Ft. Dummer, 1724, near Brattleboro. Ethan Allen and the Green Mountain Boys captured Ft. Ticonderoga, 1775; John Stark defeated part of Burgoyne's forces near Bennington, 1777. In the War of 1812, Thomas MacDonough defeated a British fleet on Champlain off Plattsburgh, 1814.

Tourist attractions. Year-round outdoor sports, esp. hiking, camping and skiing; there are over 56 ski areas in the state. Popular are the Shelburne Museum; Rock of Ages Tourist Center, Graniteville; Vermont Marble Exhibit, Proctor; Bennington Battleground; Pres. Coolidge homestead, Plymouth.

Famous Vermonters include Ethan Allen, Adm. George Dewey, John Dewey, Stephen A. Douglas, Dorothy Canfield Fisher, James Fisk.

Chamber of Commerce: P.O. Box 37, Montpelier, VT 05602.

Virginia

Old Dominion

People. Population (1979): 5,045,000; **rank:** 14. **Pop. density:** 126.9 per sq. mi. **Urban** (1970): 63.1%. **Racial distrib. (1975):** 80.5% White; 18.7% Black; Hispanic (1970): 48,742. **Major ethnic groups:** English, German, Italian. **Net migration** (1970-79): +248,000.

Geography. Total area: 40,817 sq. mi.; **rank:** 36. **Land area:** 39,780 sq. mi. **Acres forested land:** 16,417,400. **Location:** South Atlantic state bounded by the Atlantic O. on the E and surrounded by North Carolina, Tennessee, Kentucky, West Virginia, and Maryland. **Climate:** mild and equable. **Topography:** mountain and valley region in the W, including the Blue Ridge Mtns.; rolling piedmont plateau; tidewater, or coastal plain, including the eastern shore. **Capital:** Richmond.

Economy. Principal industries: government, manufacturing, agriculture, tourism, trade. **Principal manufactured goods:** textiles, food processing, apparel, transportation equipment, chemicals. **Value added by manufacture** (1977): $10.8 bln. **Agriculture: Chief crops:** tobacco, hay, corn, peanuts. **Livestock:** 1.62 mln. cattle; 670,000 hogs/pigs; 172,000 sheep; 104 mln. poultry. **Timber/lumber** (1977): pine and hardwoods; 957 mln. bd. ft. **Minerals** (1977): bituminous coal, stone, cement, lime, sand and gravel, zinc. Total value mineral production, $1.3 bln. **Commercial fishing** (1979): $84.6 mln. **Chief ports:** Hampton Roads, Chesapeake Bay. **International airports at:** Norfolk, Dulles, Richmond, Newport News. **Value of construction** (1979): $4.0 bln. **Employment distribution:** 30% agric.; 20.9% manuf.; 17% serv. **Per capita income** (1979): $8,605. **Unemployment** (1979): 4.7%. **Tourism** (1978): out-of-state visitors spent $2.4 bln.

Finance (1977). **No. banks:** 262; **No. savings and loan assns.:** 82.

Federal government. No. federal civilian employees (Mar. 1979): 124,717. **Avg. salary:** $19,405. **Notable federal facilities:** Pentagon; Naval Sta., Norfolk; Naval Air Sta., Norfolk, Virginia Beach; Naval Shipyard, Portsmouth; Marine Corps Base, Quantico; Langley AFB; NASA at Langley.

Energy. Electricity production (1979, mwh, by source): Hydroelectric: 1.5 mln.; Mineral: 26.4 mln.; Nuclear: 7.1 mln.

Education. No. schools: 2,021 elem. and second.; 72 higher ed. **Avg. salary, public school teachers** (1979): $13,200.

State data. Motto: Sic Semper Tyrannis (Thus always to tyrants). **Flower:** Dogwood. **Bird:** Cardinal. **Tree:** Dogwood. **Song:** Carry Me Back to Old Virginia. **Tenth** of the original 13 states to ratify the Constitution, June 26, 1788. **State fair** at: Richmond; late Sept.-early Oct.

History. English settlers founded Jamestown, 1607. Virginians took over much of the government from royal Gov. Dunmore in 1775, forcing him to flee. Virginians under George Rogers Clark freed the Ohio-Indiana-Illinois area of British forces. Benedict Arnold burned Richmond and Petersburg for the British, 1781. That same year, Britain's Cornwallis was trapped at Yorktown and surrendered.

Tourist attractions. Colonial Williamsburg; Busch Gardens; Wolf Trap Farm, near Falls Church; Arlington National Cemetery; Mt. Vernon, home of George Washington; Jamestown Festival Park; Yorktown; Jefferson's Monticello, Charlottesville; Robert E. Lee's birthplace, Stratford Hall, and grave, at Lexington; Appomattox; Shenandoah National Park; Blue Ridge Parkway; Virginia Beach.

Famous Virginians include Richard E. Byrd, James B. Cabell, Patrick Henry, Joseph E. Johnston, Robert E. Lee, Meriwether Lewis and William Clark, John Marshall, Edgar Allan Poe, Walter Reed, Booker T. Washington.

Chamber of Commerce: 611 E. Franklin St., Richmond, VA 23219.

Washington

Evergreen State

People. Population (1979): 3,876,000; **rank:** 21. **Pop. density:** 58.2 per sq. mi. **Urban** (1970): 72.6%. **Racial distrib.** (1970): 94.9% White; 2.3% Black; Hispanic (1970): 70,734. **Major ethnic groups:** German, English, Norwegian. **Net migration** (1970-79): +296,000.

Geography. Total area: 68,192 sq. mi.; **rank:** 20. **Land area:** 66,570 sq. mi. **Acres forested land:** 23,181,000. **Location:** northwestern coastal state bordered by Canada on the N; Idaho on the E; Oregon on the S; and the Pacific O. on the W. **Climate:** mild, dominated by the Pacific O. and protected by the Rockies. **Topography:** Olympic Mtns. on NW peninsula; open land along coast to Columbia R.; flat terrain of Puget Sound Lowland; Cascade Mtns. region's high peaks to the E; Columbia Basin in central portion; highlands to the NE; mountains to the SE. **Capital:** Olympia.

Economy. Principal industries: aerospace, agriculture, aluminum, lumber, trade. **Principal manufactured 46.8%.** transportation equipment, electronics, machinery, fabricated metals, foods. **Value added by manufacture**

(1977): $8.7 bln. **Agriculture: Chief crops:** Wheat, apples, hay, potatoes, sugar beets, pears, corn, sweet cherries. **Livestock:** 1,375,000 cattle; 64,000 hogs/pigs; 50,000 sheep; 6,234,000 poultry. **Timber/lumber** (1978): Douglas fir, cedar, Sitka spruce; 4.4 bln. bd. ft. **Minerals** (1978): sand and gravel, stone, coal, cement. Total value mineral production, $174 mln. **Commercial fishing** (1979): $116.0 mln. **Chief ports:** Seattle, Tacoma, Vancouver, Kelso-Longview. **International airports at:** Seattle/Tacoma, Spokane, Yakima, Pasco. **Value of construction** (1979): $4.5 bln. **Employment distribution:** 23.6% trade; 18.3% serv.; 17.4% manuf. **Per capita income** (1979): $9,435. **Unemployment** (1979): 6.8%. **Tourism** (1976): out-of-state visitors spent $2.1 bln.

Finance (1977). **No. banks:** 93; **No. savings and loan assns.:** 49.

Federal government. No. federal civilian employees (Mar. 1979): 44,965. **Avg. salary:** $18,649. **Notable federal facilities:** Bonneville Power Admin.; Ft. Lewis; McChord AFB; Hanford Nuclear Reservation; Bremerton Naval Shipyards.

Energy. Electricity production (1979, mwh, by source): Hydroelectric: 79.4 mln.; Mineral: 7.9 mln.; Nuclear: 3.6 mln.

Education. No. schools: 1,837 elem. and second.; 48 higher ed. **Avg. salary, public school teachers** (1979): $17,358.

State data. Motto. Alki (By and by). **Flower:** Western rhododendron. **Bird:** Willow goldfinch. **Tree:** Western hemlock. **Song:** Washington, My Home. **Entered union** Nov. 11, 1889; rank, 42d.

History. Spain's Bruno Hezeta sailed the coast, 1775. American Capt. Robert Gray sailed up the Columbia River, 1792. Canadian fur traders set up Spokane House, 1810; Americans under John Jacob Astor established a post at Fort Okanogan, 1811. Missionary Marcus Whitman settled near Walla Walla, 1836. Final agreement on the border of Washington and Canada was made with Britain, 1846, and gold was discovered in the state's northeast, 1855, bringing new settlers.

Tourist attractions. Mt. Rainier, Olympic, North Cascades national parks; Pacific beaches; outdoor year-round sports; rodeos; Indian reservations.

Famous Washingtonians include Chester Carlson, Bing Crosby, Mary McCarthy, Marcus Whitman, Minoru Yamasaki.

Chamber of Commerce: P.O. Box 658, Olympia, WA 98507.

West Virginia

Mountain State

People. Population (1979): 1,877,000; **rank:** 34. **Pop. density:** 78.0 per sq. mi. **Urban** (1970): 39%. **Racial distrib. (1975):** 96.1% White; 3.6% Black; Hispanic (1970): 6,261. **Major ethnic groups:** Italian, English, German. **Net migration** (1970-79): +28,000.

Geography. Total area: 24,181 sq. mi.; **rank:** 41. **Land area:** 24,070 sq. mi. **Acres forested land:** 11,668,600. **Location:** South Atlantic state bounded on the N by Ohio, Pennsylvania, Maryland; on the S and W by Virginia, Kentucky, Ohio; on the E by Maryland and Virginia. **Climate:** humid continental climate except for marine modification in the lower panhandle. **Topography:** rugged, ranging from hilly to mountainous; Allegheny Plateau in the W, covers two-thirds of the state; mountains here are the highest in the state, over 4,000 ft. **Capital:** Charleston.

Economy. Principal industries: mining, mineral and chemical production, agriculture. **Principal manufactured goods:** synthetic fibers, plastics. **Value added by manufacture** (1977): $3.9 bln. **Agriculture: Chief crops:** apples, peaches, dairy, tobacco, corn meal. **Chief products:** dairy products. **Livestock:** 545,000 cattle; 56,000 hogs/pigs; 113,000 sheep; 3.1 mln. poultry. **Timber/lumber:** oak, yellow poplar, hickory. **Minerals** (1977): bituminous coal, natural gas, crude petroleum, clay, cement, lime. Total value mineral production $3.7 billion. **Commercial fishing** (1979): $14,000. **Chief port:** Huntington. **Value of construction** (1979): $1.2 bln. **Per capita income** (1979): $7,470. **Unemployment** (1979): 6.7%. **Tourism** (1976): out-of-state visitors spent $771 mln.

Finance (1977). **No. banks:** 231; **No. savings and loan assns.:** 38.

Federal government. No. federal civilian employees (Mar. 1979): 9,884. **Avg. salary:** $16,964. **Notable federal facilities:** National Radio Astronomy Observatory, Green Bank.

Energy. Electricity production (1979, mwh, by source): Hydroelectric: 513,054; Mineral: 67.3 mln.; Nuclear: —.

Education. No. schools: 1,303 elem. and second.; 28 higher ed. **Avg. salary, public school teachers** (1979): $12,675.

State Data. Motto: Montani Semper Liberi (Mountaineers are always free) **Flower:** Big rhododendron. **Bird:** Cardinal. **Tree:** Sugar maple. **Songs:** The West Virginia Hills; This Is My West Virginia; West Virginia, My Home, Sweet Home. **Entered union** June 20, 1863; rank, 35th. **State fair** at: Lewisburg; 3d week in Aug.

History. Early explorers included George Washington, 1753, and Daniel Boone. The area became part of Virginia and often objected to rule by the eastern part of the state. When Virginia seceded, 1861, the Wheeling Conventions repudiated the act and created a new state, Kanawha, subsequently changed to West Virginia. It was admitted to the Union as such, 1863.

Tourist attractions. Harpers Ferry National Historic Park has been restored to its condition in 1859, when John Brown seized the U.S. Armory. Still standing is the fire-engine house in which Brown and a score of followers were besieged and captured by a force of U.S. Marines under Col. Robert E. Lee.

Also Science and Cultural Center, Charleston; White Sulphur and Berkeley Springs mineral water resorts; state parks and forests; trout fishing; turkey, deer, and bear hunting.

Famous West Virginians include Newton D. Baker, Pearl Buck, John W. Davis, Thomas "Stonewall" Jackson, Dwight Whitney Morrow, Michael Owens.

Chamber of Commerce: P.O. Box 2789, Charleston, WV 25330.

Wisconsin

Badger State

People. Population (1979): 4,718,000; **rank:** 16. **Pop. density:** 86.6 per sq. mi. **Urban** (1970): 65.9%. **Racial distrib. (1975):** 96.1% White; 3.1% Black; Hispanic (1970): 41,402. **Major ethnic groups:** German, Norwegian, Italian. **Net migration** (1970-79): +26,000.

Geography. Total area: 56,154 sq. mi.; **rank:** 26. **Land area:** 54,464 sq. mi. **Acres forested land:** 14,907,700. **Location:** North central state, bounded on the N by Lake Superior and Upper Michigan; on the E by Lake Michigan; on the S by Illinois; on the W by the St. Croix and Mississippi rivers. **Climate:** long, cold winters and short, warm summers tempered by the Great Lakes. **Topography:** narrow Lake Superior Lowland plain met by Northern Highland which slopes gently to the sandy crescent Central Plain; Western Upland in the SW; 3 broad parallel limestone ridges running N-S are separated by wide and shallow lowlands in the SE. **Capital:** Madison.

Economy. Principal industries: manufacturing, trade, services, government, transportation, communications, agriculture, tourism. **Principal manufactured goods:** machinery, foods, fabricated metals, transportation equipment, paper and wood products. **Value added by manufacture** (1979): $16.7 bln. **Agriculture: Chief crops:** corn, beans, beets, peas, hay, oats, cabbage, cranberries. **Chief products:** milk, cheese. **Livestock:** 1.8 mln. milk cows; 1.65 mln. hogs/pigs; 95,000 sheep; 11.1 mln. poultry. **Timber/lumber:** maple, birch, oak, evergreens. **Min-**

erals (1978): sand and gravel and crushed stone, dimension stone, taconite, lime. Total value mineral production $152.1 mln. **Commercial fishing** (1979): $4.9 mln. **Chief ports:** Superior, Milwaukee, Green Bay, La Crosse, Kenosha. **International airports at:** Milwaukee. **Value of construction** (1979): $3.0 bln. **Employment distribution** (1978): 28.4% manuf.; 21.6% trade; 16.9% serv.; 14.8% gvt. **Per capita income** (1979): $8,419. **Unemployment** (1979): 4.5% **Tourism** (1976): out-of-state visitors spent $2.4 bln.

Finance (1977). **Notable industries:** insurance. **No. banks:** 628; **No. savings and loan assns.:** 118.

Federal government. No. federal civilian employees (Mar. 1979): 12,234. **Avg. salary:** $17,345. **Notable federal facilities:** Ft. McCoy.

Energy. Electricity production (1979, mwh, by source): Hydroelectric: 2 mln.; Mineral: 25.6 mln.; Nuclear: 10.4 mln.;

Education. No. schools: 3,009 elem and second.; 58 higher ed. **Avg. salary, public school teachers** (1978): $15,995.

State data. Motto: Forward. **Flower:** Wood violet. **Bird:** Robin. **Tree:** Sugar maple. **Song:** On, Wisconsin! **Entered union** May 29, 1848; rank, 30th. **State fair** at: West Allis; mid-Aug.

History. Jean Nicolet was the first European to see the Wisconsin area, arriving in Green Bay, 1634; French missionaries and fur traders followed. The British took over, 1763. The U.S. won the land after the Revolution but the British were not ousted until after the War of 1812. Lead miners came next, then farmers. Railroads were started in 1851, serving growing wheat harvests and iron mines.

Tourist attractions. Old Wade House and Carriage Museum, Greenbush; Villa Louis, Prairie du Chien; Circus World Museum, Baraboo; Wisconsin Dells; Door County peninsula; Chequamegon and Nicolet national forests; Lake Winnebago; numerous lakes for water sports, ice boating and fishing; skiing and hunting.

Famous Wisconsinites include Edna Ferber, King Camp Gillette, Harry Houdini, Robert LaFollette, Alfred Lunt, Joseph R. McCarthy, Spencer Tracy, Thorstein Veblen, Orson Welles, Thornton Wilder, Frank Lloyd Wright.

Tourist information: Wisconsin Assn. of Manufacturers and Commerce, 111 E. Wisconsin Ave., Milwaukee, WI 53202.

Wyoming

Equality State

People. Population (1979): 446,000; **rank:** 49. **Pop. density:** 4.6 per sq. mi. **Urban** (1970): 60.5%. **Racial distrib.** (1975): 96.9% White; —% Black; Hispanic (1970): 18,551. **Major ethnic groups:** German, English, Russian. **Net migration** (1970-79): +77,000.

Geography. Total area: 97,914 sq. mi.; **rank:** 9. **Land area:** 97,203 sq. mi. **Acres forested land:** 10,028,300. **Location:** Mountain state lying in the high western plateaus of the Great Plains. **Climate:** semi-desert conditions throughout; true desert in the Big Horn and Great Divide basins. **Topography:** the eastern Great Plains rise to the foothills of the Rocky Mtns.; the Continental Divide crossed the state from the NW to the SE. **Capital:** Cheyenne.

Economy. Principal industries: mining, agriculture, forestry, tourism. **Principal manufactured goods:** refined petroleum products, foods, wood products, stone, clay and glass products. **Value added by manufacture** (1977) $380.7 mln. **Agriculture: Chief crops:** wheat, barley, oats, sugar beets, hay. **Livestock:** 1.30 mln. cattle; 30,000 hogs/pigs; 1.11 mln. sheep; 90,000 poultry. **Timber/lumber** (1978): aspen, yellow pine; 217 mln. bd. ft. **Minerals** (1978): petroleum, sodium carbonate, coal, uranium, natural gas; total $2.6 bln. value of mineral production. **International airports at:** Casper. **Value of construction** (1979): $595 mln. **Employment distribution:** 16% trade; 14% serv.; 12% mining. **Per capita income** (1979): $9,657. **Unemployment** (1979): 2.8%. **Tourism** (1979): out-of-state visitors spent $531 mln.

Finance (1977). **No. banks:** 88; **No. savings and loan assns.:** 13.

Federal government. No. federal civilian employees (Mar. 1979): 4,453. **Avg. salary:** $17,751. **Notable federal facilities:** Warren AFB; Laramie Energy Research Ctr.

Energy. Electricity production (1979, mwh, by source): Hydroelectric: 1.1 mln., Mineral: 21 mln.; Nuclear: —.

Education. No. schools: 401 elem. and second.; 8 higher ed. **Avg. salary, public school teachers** (1979): $14,469.

State data. Motto: Equal Rights. **Flower:** Indian paintbrush. **Bird:** Meadowlark. **Tree:** Cottonwood. **Song:** Wyoming. **Entered union** July 10, 1890; rank, 44th. **State fair** at: Douglas; end of Aug.

History. Francês Francois and Louis Verendrye were the first Europeans, 1743. John Colter, American, was first to traverse Yellowstone Park, 1807-08. Trappers and fur traders followed in the 1820s. Forts Laramie and Bridger became important stops on the pioneer trail to the West Coast. Indian wars followed massacres of army detachments in 1854 and 1866. Population grew after the Union Pacific crossed the state, 1869. Women won the vote, for the first time in the U.S., from the Territorial Legislature, 1869.

Tourist attractions. Yellowstone National Park, 3,472 sq. mi. in the NW corner of Wyoming and the adjoining edges of Montana and Idaho, the oldest U.S. national park, est. 1872, has some 10,000 geysers, hot springs, mud volcanoes, fossil forests, a volcanic glass (obsidian) mountain, the 1,000-ft.-deep canyon and 308-ft.-high waterfall of the Yellowstone River, and a wide variety of animals living free in their natural habitat.

Also, Grand Teton National Park, with mountains 13,000 ft. high; National Elk Refuge, covering 25,000 acres; Devils Tower, a cluster of rock columns 865 ft. high; Fort Laramie and surrounding areas of pioneer trails; Buffalo Bill Museum, Cody; Cheyenne Frontier Days Celebration, last full week in July, the state's largest rodeo, and world's largest purse.

Famous Wyomingites include James Bridger, Buffalo Bill Cody, Nellie Tayloe Ross.

Tourist information: Travel Commission, Etchepare Circle, Cheyenne, WY 82002.

District of Columbia

Area: 67 sq. mi. **Population:** (1979): 648,000. **Motto:** Justitia omnibus, Justice for all. **Flower:** American beauty rose. **Tree:** Scarlet oak. **Bird:** Wood thrush. The city of Washington is coextensive with the District of Columbia.

The District of Columbia is the seat of the federal government of the United States. It lies on the west central edge of Maryland on the Potomac River, opposite Virginia. Its area was originally 100 sq. mi. taken from the sovereignty of Maryland and Virginia. Virginia's portion south of the Potomac was given back to that state in 1846.

The 23d Amendment, ratified in 1961, granted residents the right to vote for president and vice president for the first time and gave them 3 members in the Electoral College. The first such votes were cast in Nov. 1964.

Congress, which has legislative authority over the District under the Constitution, established in 1878 a government of 3 commissioners appointed by the president. The Reorganization Plan of 1967 substituted a single commissioner (also called mayor), assistant, and 9-member City Council. Funds were still appropriated by Congress; residents had no vote in local government, except to elect school board members.

In Sept. 1970, Congress approved legislation giving the District one delegate to the House of Representatives. The delegate could vote in committee but not on the House floor. The first was elected 1971.

In May 1974 voters approved a charter giving them the right to elect their own mayor and a 13-member city council; the first took office Jan. 2, 1975. The district won the right to levy its own taxes but Congress retained power to veto council actions, and approve the city's annual budget.

Proposals for a "federal town" for the deliberations of the Continental Congress were made in 1783, 4 years before the adoption of the Constitution that gave the Confederation a national government. Rivalry between northern and southern delegates over the site appeared in the First Congress, 1789. John Adams, presiding officer of the Senate, cast the deciding vote of that body for Germantown, Pa. In 1790 Congress compromised by making Philadelphia the temporary capital for 10 years. The Virginia members of the House wanted a capital on the eastern bank of the Potomac; they were defeated by the Northerners, while the Southerners defeated the Northern attempt to have the nation assume the war debts of the 13 original states, the Assumption Bill fathered by Alexander Hamilton. Hamilton and Jefferson arranged a compromise: the Virginia men voted for the Assumption Bill, and the Northerners conceded the capital to the Potomac. President Washington chose the site in Oct. 1790 and persuaded landowners to sell their holdings to the government at £25, then about $66, an acre. The capital was named Washington.

Washington appointed Pierre Charles L'Enfant, a French engineer who had come over with Lafayette, to plan the capital on an area not over 10 mi. square. The L'Enfant plan, for streets 100 to 110 feet wide and one avenue 400 feet wide and a mile long, seemed grandiose and foolhardy. But Washington endorsed it. When L'Enfant ordered a wealthy landowner to remove his new manor house because it obstructed a vista, and demolished it when the owner refused, Washington stepped in and dismissed the architect. The official map and design of the city was completed by Benjamin Banneker, a distinguished black architect and astronomer, and Andrew Ellicott.

On Sept. 18, 1793, Pres. Washington laid the cornerstone of the north wing of the Capitol. On June 3, 1800, Pres. John Adams moved to Washington and on June 10, Philadelphia ceased to be the temporary capital. The City of Washington was incorporated in 1802; the District of Columbia was created as a municipal corporation in 1871, embracing Washington, Georgetown, and Washington County.

Outlying U.S. Areas

Commonwealth of Puerto Rico

(Estado Libre Asociado de Puerto Rico)

People. Population (1979): 3,410,000. **Pop. density:** 996.7 per sq. mi. **Urban** (1975): 61.8%. **Racial distribution:** 99% Hispanic. **Net migration** (1979): +6,078.

Geography. Total area: 3,435 sq. mi. **Land area:** 3,421 sq. mi. **Location:** island lying between the Atlantic to the N and the Caribbean to the S; it is easternmost of the West Indies group called the Greater Antilles, of which Cuba, Hispaniola, and Jamaica are the larger units. **Climate:** mild, with a mean temperature of 76°. **Topography:** mountainous throughout three-fourths of its rectangular area, surrounded by a broken coastal plain; highest peak is Cerro de Punta, 4,389 ft. **Capital:** San Juan.

Economy. Principal industries: manufacturing. **Principal manufactured goods:** apparel; petrochemicals; pharmaceuticals; scientific instruments; medical supplies; food products. **Value added by manufacture:** $3.3 bln. **Agriculture: Chief crops:** sugar; plantains; coffee; bananas; yams; taniers; pineapples; pidgeon peas; peppers; tomatoes; pumpkins; coriander; lettuce; tobacco. **Livestock** (1978): 563,000 cattle; 269,000 pigs; 5,544,000 poultry. **Minerals** (1979): cement, crushed stone, sand and gravel, lime. Total value mineral production, $142 mln. **Commercial fishing:** $6.4 million. **Chief ports/river shipping:** San Juan, Ponce, Mayaguez, Guayanilla, Yabucoa, Aguirre. **International airports at:** San Juan; Aguadilla. **Value of construction** (1979): $1.2 bln. **Employment distribution:** 23% gvt.; 20% manuf.; 19% trade; 18% serv. **Per capita income** (1979): $2,934. **Unemployment** (1979): 17.5%. **Tourism** (1977): No. out-of-area visitors: 1,376,000; $424 mln. spent.

Finance. Notable industries: life insurance, mortgage banks, credit unions, retirement fund systems. **Financial institutions:** No. banks: 143; No. savings and loan assns.: 12; Other: 4 retirement fund systems; over 100 credit unions.

Federal government. No. federal civilian employees (Mar. 1977): 8,558. **Federal payroll** (1977): $117.5 mln. **Notable federal facilities:** U.S. Naval Station at Roosevelt Roads; U.S. Army Salinas Training Area and Ft. Allen; Sabana SECA Communications Center (U.S. Navy).

Energy. Production (1979): Hydroelectric: 11,443 Kwh.

Education. No. schools: 1,767 elem.; 118 second.; 30 higher ed. **Avg. salary, public school teachers** (1978): $8,100.

Misc. Data. Motto. Joannes Est Nomen Ejus (John is his name). **Flower:** Maga. **Bird:** Reinita. **Tree:** Ceiba. **Song:** La Borinquena.

History: Puerto Rico (or Borinquen, after the original Arawak Indian name Boriquen), was discovered by Columbus, Nov. 19, 1493. Ponce de Leon conquered it for Spain, 1509, and established the first settlement at Caparra, across the bay from San Juan.

Sugar cane was introduced, 1515, and slaves were imported 3 years later. Gold mining petered out, 1570. Spaniards fought off a series of British and Dutch attacks; slavery was abolished, 1873. The U.S. took the island during the Spanish-American War, 1898, without any major battle.

General tourist attractions: Ponce Museum of Art; forts El Morro and San Cristobal; Old Walled City of San Juan; Arecibo Observatory; Cordillera Central and state parks; El Yungue Rain Forest; San Juan Cathedral; Porta Coeli Chapel and Museum of Religious Art, San German; Condado Convention Center; Casa Blanca, Ponce de Leon family home, now the Puerto Rican Family Museum of 16th and 17 centuries.

Cultural facilities, festivals, etc.: Festival Casals classical music concerts, mid-June; Puerto Rico Symphony Orchestra at Music Conservatory; Botanical Garden and Museum of Anthropology, Art, and History at the University of Puerto Rico; Institute of Puerto Rican Culture, at the Dominican Convent.

The Commonwealth of Puerto Rico is a self-governing part of the U.S. with a primary Hispanic culture. Puerto Ricans are U.S. citizens and about 1.5 million now live in the continental U.S., although since 1974, a reverse migration flow has resulted in net immigration to the island.

The current commonwealth political status of Puerto Rico gives the island's citizens virtually the same control over their internal affairs as the fifty states of the U.S. However, they do not vote in national elections, although they do vote in national primary elections.

Puerto Rico is represented in Congress solely by a resident commissioner who has a voice but no vote, except in committees.

Most federal taxes are not levied in Puerto Rico, except those, such as Social Security, which are imposed by mutual consent. No federal income tax is collected from residents on income earned from local sources in Puerto Rico.

Puerto Rico's famous "Operation Bootstrap" begun in the late 1940s succeeded in changing the island from "The Poorhouse of the Caribbean" to an area with the highest per capita income in Latin America. This pioneering program encouraged manufacturing and the development of the tourist trade by selective tax exemption, low-interest loans, and other incentives. Despite the marked success of Puerto Rico's development efforts over an extended period of time, per capita income in Puerto Rico is low in comparison to that of the U.S. In calendar year 1977, net transfer payments from the U.S. government to individuals and governments in Puerto Rico totalled $2.183 bln., or 22.5% of the Gross Domestic Product of $9.717 bln.

Famous Puerto Ricans include: Pablo Casals, Orlando Cepeda, Roberto Clemente, Jose Feliciano, Jose

Ferrer, Dona Felisa Rincon de Gautier, Luis Munoz Marin, Rita Moreno, Adm. Horacio Rivero.

Chamber of Commerce: 100 Tetuan P.O.B. S3789, San Juan, PR 00904.

Guam

Pearl of the Pacific

The World Almanac is sponsored on Guam by the Pacific Daily News, 90 O'Hara St., Agana, GU 96910; phone 777-9711; successor in 1970 to Guam Daily News; circulation throughout Micronesia, 18,344; a Gannett newspaper; president and publisher, Robert E. Udick; editor Joseph Murphy, managing editor, John Simpson.

People. Population (1978): 109,000. **Pop. density:** 521.5 per sq. mi. **Urban** (1970): 25.5%. Native Guamanians, ethnically called chamorros, are basically of Indonesian stock, with a mixture of Spanish and Filipino. In addition to the offical language, they speak the native Chamorros.

Geography. Total area: 212 sq. mi. land, 30 mi. long and 4 to 8.5 mi. wide. **Location:** largest and southernmost of the Mariana Islands in the West Pacific, 3,000 mi. W of Hawaii. **Climate:** tropical, with temperatures from 70° to 90°F; avg. annual rainfall, about 70 in. **Topography:** coralline limestone plateau in the N; southern chain of low volcanic mountains sloping gently to the W, more steeply to coastal cliffs on the E; general elevation, 500 ft.; highest pt., Mt. Lamlam, 1,334 ft. **Capital:** Agana.

Economy. Principal industries: contruction, manufacturing, tourism, petroleum refining, watch assembly, banking. **Principal manufactured goods:** textiles, foods, petroleum products. **Value added by manufacture:** $187.5 million/yr. **Agriculture: Chief crops:** cabbages, eggplants, cucumber, taro, bananas, coconuts, watermelon, yams, avocados, papayas, maize, sweet potatoes, sugar cane. **Livestock:** 1,493 cattle; 10,637 hogs/pigs; 147,875 poultry. **Commercial fishing:** $187,000. **Chief ports:** Apra Harbor. **International airports at:** Tamuning. **Value of construction** (1978): $111.2 mln. **Employment distribution:** 45% gvt.; 13% construct.; 3% manufacturing; 12% services; 18% trade. **Per capita income** (1974): $3,333. **Unemployment** (1978): 26% **Tourism** (1978): No. out-of-area visitors: 232,000.

Finance (1977).**Notable industries:** insurance, real estate, finance. **No. banks:** 16; **No. savings and loan assns.:** 2.

Federal government. No. federal employees (1976): 6,014. **Notable federal facilities:** Andersen AFB; other naval and air bases, including a nuclear submarine installation and a large ship-repair yard.

Education. No. public schools: 27 elementary; 9 secondary; 1 higher education. **Avg. salary, public school teachers** (1979): $12,684.

Misc. Data. Flower: Puti Tai Nobio (Bougainvillea). **Bird:** Toto (Fruit dove). **Tree:** Ifit (Intsiabijuga). **Song:** Stand Ye Guamanians.

History. Magellan arrived in the Marianas Mar. 6, 1521, and called them the Ladrones (thieves). They were colonized in 1668 by Spanish missionaries who renamed them the Mariana Islands in honor of Maria Anna, queen of Spain. When Spain ceded Guam to the U.S., it sold the other Marianas to Germany. Japan obtained a League of Nations mandate over the German islands in 1919; in Dec. 1941 it seized Guam; the island was retaken by the U.S. in July 1944.

Guam is under the jurisdiction of the Interior Department. It is administered under the Organic Act of 1950, which provides for a governor and a 21-member unicameral legislature, elected biennially by the residents who are American citizens but do not vote for president.

Beginning in Nov., 1970, Guamanians elected their own governor, previously appointed by the U.S. president. He took office in Jan. 1971. In 1972 a U.S. law gave Guam one delegate to the U.S. House of Representatives; the delegate may vote in committee but not on the House floor.

General tourist attractions. annual mid-Aug. Merizo Water Festival; Tarzan Falls; beaches; water sports, duty-free port shopping.

Virgin Islands

St. John, St. Croix, St. Thomas

People. Population (1978): 100,000. **Pop. density:** 757.6 per sq. mi. **Urban** (1970): 25%. **Racial distribution:** 15% White; 85% Black. **Major ethnic groups:** West Indian, Chachas. **Net migration** (1977): +9,000.

Geography. Total area: 133 sq. mi.; **Land area:** 132 sq. mi. **Location:** 3 larger and 50 smaller islands and cays in the S and W of the V.I. group (British V.I. colony to the N and E) which is situated 70 mi. E of Puerto Rico, located W of the Anegada Passage, a major channel connecting the Atlantic O. and the Caribbean Sea. **Climate:** subtropical; the sun tempered by gentle trade winds; humidity is low; average temperature, 78° F. **Topography:** St. Thomas is mainly a ridge of hills running E and W, and has little tillable land; St. Croix rises abruptly in the N but slopes to the S to flatlands and lagoons; St. John has steep, lofty hills and valleys with little level tillable land. **Capital:** Charlotte Amalie, St. Thomas.

Economy. Principal industries: tourism, rum, petroleum refining, bauxite processing, watch assembly, textiles. **Principal manufactured goods:** rum, textiles, pharmaceuticals, perfumes. **Gross Domestic Product** (1977): $500 million. **Agriculture: Chief crops:** truck garden produce. **Minerals:** sand, gravel. **Chief ports:** Cruz Bay, St. John; Frederiksted and Christiansted, St. Croix; Charlotte Amalie, St. Thomas. **International airports on:** St. Thomas, St. Croix. **Value of construction** (1976): $42,303,000. **Per capita income** (1977): $5,000. **Unemployment** (1977): 7.9%. **Tourism** (1977): No. out-of-area visitors: 1,119,726; $152.2 million spent. **No. banks:** 8.

Education: No. public schools: 33 elem. and second.; 1 higher education. **Avg. salary, public school teachers** (1979): $12,331.

Misc. data. Flower: Yellow elder or yellow cedar. **Bird:** Yellow breast. **Song:** Virgin Islands March.

History. The islands were discovered by Columbus in 1493, who named them for the virgins of St. Ursula, the sailor's patron saint. Spanish forces, 1555, defeated the Caribes and claimed the territory; by 1596 the native population was annihilated. First permanent settlement in the U.S. territory, 1672, by the Danes; U.S. purchased the islands, 1917, for defense purposes.

The inhabitants have been citizens of the U.S. since 1927. Legislation originates in a unicameral house of 15 senators, elected for 2 years. The governor, formerly appointed by the U.S. president, was popularly elected for the first time in Nov. 1970. In 1972 a U.S. law gave the Virgin Islands one delegate to the U.S. House of Representatives; the delegate may vote in committee but not in the House.

General tourist attractions. Megen Bay, St. Thomas; duty-free shopping; Virgin Islands National Park, 14,488 acres on St. John of lush growth, beaches, Indian relics, and evidence of colonial Danes.

Chamber of Commerce: for St. Thomas and St. John: P.O. Box 324, St. Thomas, VI 00801; for St. Croix: 17 Church St., Christiansted, St. Croix, VI 00820.

American Samoa

Capital: Fagotogo, Island of Tutuila. **Area:** 76 sq. mi. **Population:** (1978 est.) 31,171. **Motto:** Samoa Muamua le Atua (In Samoa, God Is First). **Song:** Amerika Samoa. **Flower:** Paogo (Ula-fala). **Plant:** Ava.

Blessed with spectacular scenery and delightful South Seas climate, American Samoa is the most southerly of all lands under U. S. ownership. It is an unincorporated territory consisting of 6 small islands of the Samoan group: **Tutuila, Aunu'u, Manu'a Group (Ta'u, Olosega and Ofu),** and **Rose.** Also administered as part of American Samoa is **Swain's Island,** 210 mi. to the NW, acquired by the U.S. in 1925. The islands are 2,600 mi. SW of Honolulu.

American Samoa became U. S. territory by a treaty with the United Kingdom and Germany in 1899. The islands were ceded by local chiefs in 1900 and 1904.

Samoa (Western), comprising the larger islands of the

Samoan group, was a New Zealand mandate and UN Trusteeship until it became an independent nation Jan. 1, 1962 *(see Index.)*

Tutuila and Annu'u have an area of 52 sq. mi. Ta'u has an area of 17 sq. mi., and the islets of Ofu and Olosega, 5 sq. mi. with a population of a few thousand. Swain's Island has nearly 2 sq. mi. and a population of about 100.

About 70% of the land is bush. Chief products and exports are fish products, copra, and handicrafts. Taro, bread-fruit, yams, coconuts, pineapples, oranges, and bananas are also produced.

Formerly under jurisdiction of the Navy, since July 1, 1951, it has been under the Interior Dept. On Jan. 3, 1978, the first popularly elected Samoan governor and lieutenant governor were inaugurated. Previously, the governor was appointed by the Secretary of the Interior. American Samoa has a bicameral legislature and an elected delegate to appear before U.S. agencies in Washington. In 1980 the Territory will elect a non-voting delegate to Congress.

The American Samoans are of Polynesian origin. They are nationals of the U.S.; there are more than 15,000 in Hawaii and 90,000 on the U.S. west coast.

Minor Caribbean Islands

Quita Sueño Bank, Roncador and Serrana, lie in the Caribbean between Nicaragua and Jamaica. They are uninhabited. They were to be turned over to Colombia under a 1972 agreement, but this still awaits U.S. Senate action.

Navassa lies between Jamaica and Haiti, covers about 2 sq. mi., is reserved by the U.S. for a lighthouse and is uninhabited.

Wake, Midway, Other Islands

Wake Island, and its sister islands, **Wilkes** and **Peale,** lie in the Pacific Ocean on the direct route from Hawaii to Hong Kong, about 2,000 mi. W of Hawaii and 1,290 mi. E of Guam. The group is 4.5 mi. long, 1.5 mi. wide, and totals less than 3 sq. mi. Population (1970) was 1,647.

The U.S. flag was hoisted over Wake Island, July 4, 1898, formal possession taken Jan. 17, 1899; Wake has been administered by the U.S. Air Force since 1972. Population (1978) was 200.

The **Midway Islands,** acquired in 1867, consist of 2, **Sand** and **Eastern,** in the North Pacific 1,150 mi. NW of Hawaii, with area of about 2 sq. mi., administered by the Navy Dept. Population (1975 est.) was 2,256.

Johnston Atoll, SW of Hawaii, area 1 sq. mi., pop. 300 (1978), is under Air Force control, and **Kingman Reef,** S of Hawaii, is under Navy control.

Howland, Jarvis, and **Baker Islands** south of the Hawaiian group, uninhabited since World War II, are under the Interior Dept.

Palmyra is an atoll SW of Hawaii, 4 sq. mi. Privately owned, it is under the Interior Dept.

Islands Under Trusteeship

The U. S Trust Territory of the Pacific Islands, also called Micronesia, includes 3 major archipelagoes: the **Caroline Islands, Marshall Islands,** and **Mariana Islands** (except **Guam:** see above). There are 2,141 islands, 98 of them inhabited. Total land area is 687 sq. mi., but the islands are scattered over 3 million sq. mi. in the western Pacific N of the equator and E of the Philippines. Population (1978 est.): 136,810.

The Marianas

In process of becoming a U.S. commonwealth were the Northern Mariana Islands, which since 1947 had been part of the Trust Territory of the Pacific Islands, assigned to U.S. administration by the United Nations. The Northern Marianas comprise all the Marianas except Guam, stretching N-S in a 500-mi. arc of tropical islands east of the Philippines and southeast of Japan.

Residents of the islands on June 17, 1975, voted 78% in favor of becoming a commonwealth of the U.S. rather than continuing with the Carolines and Marshalls in the U.S.-UN Trusteeship. On Mar. 24, 1976, U.S. Pres. Ford signed a congressionally-approved commonwealth covenant giving the Marianas control of domestic affairs and giving the U.S. control of foreign relations and defense, and the right to maintain military bases on the islands.

Pres. Carter, on Oct. 24, 1977, approved the Constitution of the Northern Mariana Islands with the effective date of Jan. 9, 1978. In December 1977, the voters of the Northern Marianas elected a governor, lieutenant governor, and members of a bicameral legislature for the new government.

Ferdinand Magellan was the first European to visit the Marianas, 1521. Spain, Germany, and Japan held the islands in turn until World War II when the U.S. seized them in bitter battles on 2 of the main islands, Saipan and Tinian.

Population in 1980 was estimated at 16,600, mostly on Saipan. English is the official language, Roman Catholicism the major religion. The people are descendants of the early Chamorros, Spanish, Japanese, Filipinos, and Mexicans. Land area is 181.9 sq. mi.

Tourism is an important industry; visitors are mostly from Japan. Crops include coconuts, breadfruit, melons and tomatoes.

The Carolines and Marshalls

In 1885, many of the Carolines, Marshalls, and Marianas were claimed by Germany. Others, held by Spain, were sold to Germany at the time of the Spanish-American War, 1898. After the outbreak of World War I, Japan took over the 3 archipelagoes; following that war, League of Nations mandates over them were awarded to Japan.

After World War II, the United Nations assigned them, 1947, as a Trust Territory to be administered by the U.S. They were placed, 1951, under administration of the U.S. Interior Dept.

There is a high commissioner, appointed by the U.S. president. Saipan is the headquarters of the administration. The Congress of Micronesia, an elected legislature with limited powers, held its first meeting, 1965.

In 1969, a commission of the Congress of Micronesia recommended that Micronesia be given internal self-government in free association with the U.S.

A U.S. offer of commonwealth status was rejected by Micronesian leaders in 1970.

In May of 1977, Pres. Carter announced his administration's intention to take steps to terminate the trusteeship by 1981. The U.S. and three Trust Territory negotiating commissions representing, respectively, the Marshall Islands, Palau, and the Federated States of Micronesia, comprised of Truk, Yap, Ponape and Kosrae, are negotiating a free association arrangement: the three Micronesian areas would enjoy full self-government; the U.S. would retain responsibility for defense.

Among the noted islands are the former Japanese strongholds of **Palau, Peleliu, Truk,** and **Yap** in the Carolines; **Bikini** and **Eniwetok,** where U.S. nuclear tests were staged, and **Kwajalein,** another World War II battle scene, all in the Marshalls.

Many of the islands are volcanic with luxuriant vegetation; others are of coral formation. Only a few are self-sustaining. Principal exports are copra, trochus shells, fish products, handicrafts, and vegetables.

Disputed Pacific Islands

In the central Pacific, S and SW of Hawaii lie 25 islands that were claimed by the U.S.; 14 of them were also claimed by the United Kingdom. Kiribati achieved its independence from the U.K. in July, 1979; conflicting U.S.-Great Britain claims to islands were thereafter resolved by a U.S.-Kiribati Treaty, Sept. 1979, relinquishing U.S. claims. The treaty is still pending U.S. Senate ratification.

The **Tuvalu (Ellice) Islands,** including Funafuti, Nukufetau, Nukulailai, and Nurakita, became independent of the UK, Oct. 1, 1978; treaty relinquishing U.S. claim still pending U.S. Senate ratification (*See Index*).

The islands claimed by New Zealand are: The **Tokelau (Union) Islands,** including Nukunono, Atafu, and Fakaofu. All are inhabited and administered as part of a New Zealand territory.

Also, the **Cook Islands,** including Danger, Manahiki, Rakahanga, and Penrhyn (Tongareva), are a state in free association with New Zealand.

HISTORY

Memorable Dates in U.S. History

1492

Christopher Columbus and crew sighted land **Oct. 12** in the Caribbean.

1497

John Cabot explored northeast coast to Delaware.

1513

Juan Ponce de Leon explored Florida coast.

1524

Giovanni da Verrazano led French expedition along coast from Carolina north to Nova Scotia; entered New York harbor.

1539

Hernando de Soto landed in Florida **May 28;** crossed Mississippi River, **1541.**

1540

Francisco Vazquez de Coronado explored Southwest north of Rio Grande. Hernando de Alarcon reached Colorado River, Don Garcia Lopez de Cardenas reached Grand Canyon. Others explored California coast.

1565

St. Augustine, Fla. founded by Pedro Menendez. Razed by Francis Drake **1586.**

1579

Francis Drake claimed California for Britain. Metal plate, found **1936,** thought to be left by Drake, termed probable hoax **1979.**

1607

Capt. John Smith and 105 cavaliers in 3 ships landed on Virginia coast, started first permanent English settlement in New World at **Jamestown, May 13.**

1609

Henry Hudson, English explorer of Northwest Passage, employed by Dutch, sailed into New York harbor in **Sept.,** and up Hudson to Albany. The same year, **Samuel de Champlain** explored Lake Champlain just to the north.

Spaniards settled **Santa Fe., N.M.**

1619

House of Burgesses, first representative assembly in New World, elected **July 30** at Jamestown, Va.

First Negro laborers — indentured servants — in English N. American colonies, landed by Dutch at Jamestown in **Aug.** Chattel slavery legally recognized, **1650.**

1620

Plymouth Pilgrims, Puritan separatists from Church of England, some living in Holland, left Plymouth, England **Sept. 15** on Mayflower. Original destination Virginia, they reached Cape Cod **Nov. 19,** explored coast; 103 passengers landed **Dec. 21** (Dec. 11 Old Style) at Plymouth. Mayflower Compact was agreement to form a government and abide by its laws. Half of colony died during harsh winter.

1624

Dutch left 8 men from ship New Netherland on **Manhattan Island** in **May.** Rest sailed to Albany.

1626

Peter Minuit bought Manhattan for Dutch from Man-a-hat-a Indians **May 6** for trinkets valued at $24.

1634

Maryland founded as Catholic colony with religious tolerance.

1636

Harvard College founded **Oct. 28,** now oldest in U.S., Grammar school, compulsory education established at Boston.

Roger Williams founded Providence, R.I., **June,** as a democratically ruled colony with separation of church and state. Charter was granted, **1644.**

1654

First Jews arrived in New Amsterdam.

1660

British Parliament passed **Navigation Act,** regulating colonial commerce to suit English needs.

1664

Three hundred **British troops Sept. 8 seized New Netherland** from Dutch, who yield peacefully. Charles II granted province of New Netherland and city of New Amsterdam to brother, Duke of York; both renamed New York. The Dutch recaptured the colony **Aug. 9, 1673,** but ceded it to Britain **Nov. 10, 1674.**

1676

Nathaniel Bacon led planters against autocratic British Gov. Berkeley, burned Jamestown, Va. Bacon died, 23 followers executed.

Bloody **Indian war** in New England ended **Aug. 12.** King Philip, Wampanoag chief, and many Narragansett Indians killed.

1682

Robert Cavelier, Sieur de La Salle, claimed lower Mississippi River country for France, called it Louisiana **Apr. 9.** Had French outposts built in Illinois and Texas, **1684.** Killed during mutiny **Mar. 19, 1687.**

1683

William Penn signed treaty with Delaware Indians and made payment for Pennsylvania lands.

1692

Witchcraft delusion at Salem (now Danvers) Mass. inspired by preaching; 19 persons executed.

1696

Capt. William Kidd, American hired by British to fight pirates and take booty, becomes pirate. Arrested and sent to England, where he was hanged **1701.**

1699

French settlements made in Mississippi, Louisiana.

1704

Indians attacked Deerfield, Mass. **Feb. 28-29,** killed 40, carried off 100.

Boston News Letter, first regular newspaper, started by John Campbell, postmaster. (*Publick Occurences* was suppressed after one issue **1690.**)

1709

British-Colonial troops captured French fort, Port Royal, Nova Scotia, in **Queen Anne's War 1701-13.** France yielded Nova Scotia by treaty **1713.**

1712

Slaves revolted in New York **Apr. 6.** Six committed suicide, 21 were executed. Second rising, **1741;** 13 slaves hanged, 13 burned, 71 deported.

1716

First theater in colonies opened in Williamsburg, Va.

1728

Pennsylvania Gazette founded by Samuel Keimer in Philadelphia. Benjamin Franklin bought interest **1729.**

1732

Benjamin Franklin published first *Poor Richard's Almanac;* published annually to 1757.

1735

Freedom of the press recognized in New York by acquittal of John Peter Zenger, editor of *Weekly Journal,* on charge of libeling British Gov. Cosby by criticizing his conduct in office.

1740-41

Capt. Vitus Bering, Dane employed by Russians, reached Alaska.

1744

King George's War pitted British and colonials vs. French. Colonials captured Louisburg, Cape Breton Is. **June 17, 1745.** Returned to France **1748** by Treaty of Aix-la-Chapelle.

1752

Benjamin Franklin, flying kite in thunderstorm, proved

lightning is electricity **June 15;** invented lightning rod.

1754

French and Indian War (in Europe called 7 Years War, started 1756) began when French occupied Ft. Duquesne (Pittsburgh). British moved Acadian French from Nova Scotia to Louisiana **Oct. 1755.** British captured Quebec **Sept. 18, 1759** in battles in which French Gen. Montcalm and British Gen. Wolfe were killed. Peace signed **Feb. 10 1763.** French lost Canada and American Midwest. British tightened colonial administration in North America.

1764

Sugar Act placed duties on lumber, foodstuffs, molasses and rum in colonies.

1765

Stamp Act required revenue stamps to help defray cost of royal troops. Nine colonies, led by New York and Massachusetts at Stamp Act Congress in New York **Oct. 7-25, 1765,** adopted Declaration of Rights opposing taxation without representation in Parliament and trial without jury by admiralty courts. Stamp Act **repealed Mar. 17, 1766.**

1767

Townshend Acts levied taxes on glass, painter's lead, paper, and tea. In **1770** all duties except on tea were repealed.

1770

British troops fired **Mar. 5** into Boston mob, killed 5 including **Crispus Attucks,** a Negro, reportedly leader of group; later called **Boston Massacre.**

1773

East India Co. tea ships turned back at Boston, New York, Philadelphia in **May.** Cargo ship burned at Annapolis **Oct. 14,** cargo thrown overboard at **Boston Tea Party Dec. 16.**

1774

"Intolerable Acts" of Parliament curtailed Massachusetts self-rule; barred use of Boston harbor till tea was paid for.

First Continental Congress held in Philadelphia **Sept. 5-Oct. 26;** protested British measures, called for civil disobedience.

Rhode Island abolished slavery.

1775

Patrick Henry addressed Virginia convention, **Mar. 23** said "Give me liberty or give me death."

Paul Revere and William Dawes on night of **Apr. 18** rode to alert patriots that British were on way to Concord to destroy arms. At Lexington, Mass. **Apr. 19** Minutemen lost 8 killed. On return from Concord British took 273 casualties.

Col. Ethan Allen (joined by Col. Benedict Arnold) captured Ft. **Ticonderoga, N.Y. May 10;** also Crown Point. Colonials headed for **Bunker Hill,** fortified Breed's Hill, Charlestown, Mass., repulsed British under Gen. William Howe twice before retreating **June 17;** British casualties 1,000; called Battle of Bunker Hill. Continental Congress **June 15** named **George Washington** commander-in-chief.

1776

France and Spain each agreed **May 2** to provide one million livres in arms to Americans.

In Continental Congress **June 7,** Richard Henry Lee (Va.) moved "that these united colonies are and of right ought to be free and independent states." Resolution adopted July 2. **Declaration of Independence** approved **July 4.**

Col. Moultrie's batteries at **Charleston, S.C.** repulsed British sea attack **June 28.**

Washington, with 10,000 men, lost **Battle of Long Island Aug. 27,** evacuated New York.

Nathan Hale executed as spy by British **Sept. 22.**

Brig. Gen. Arnold's **Lake Champlain** fleet was defeated at Valcour **Oct. 11,** but British returned to Canada. Howe failed to destroy Washington's army at **White Plains Oct. 28.** Hessians captured Ft. Washington, Manhattan, and 3,000 men **Nov. 16;** Ft. Lee, N.J. **Nov. 18.**

Washington in Pennsylvania, recrossed **Delaware River Dec. 25-26,** defeated 1,400 Hessians at Trenton, N.J. **Dec. 26.**

1777

Washington defeated Lord Cornwallis at **Princeton Jan. 3.** Continental Congress adopted Stars and Stripes. *See Flag article.*

Maj. Gen. John Burgoyne with 8,000 from Canada captured **Ft. Ticonderoga July 6.** Americans beat back Burgoyne at Bemis Heights **Oct. 7** and cut off British escape route. Burgoyne surrendered 5,000 men at **Saratoga N.Y. Oct. 17.**

Marquis de Lafayette, aged 20, made major general.

Articles of Confederation and Perpetual Union adopted by Continental Congress **Nov. 15**

France recognized independence of 13 colonies **Dec. 17.**

1778

France signed treaty of aid with U.S. **Feb. 6.** Sent fleet; British evacuated Philadelphia in consequence **June 18.**

1779

John Paul Jones on the *Bonhomme Richard* defeated *Serapis* in British North Sea waters **Sept. 23.**

1780

Charleston, S.C. fell to the British **May 12,** but a British force was defeated near **Kings Mountain, N.C. Oct. 7** by militiamen.

Benedict Arnold found to be a traitor **Sept. 23.** Arnold escaped, made brigadier general in British army.

1781

Bank of North America incorporated in Philadelphia **May 26.**

Cornwallis, harrassed by U.S. troops, retired to **Yorktown, Va.** Adm. De Grasse landed 3,000 French and stopped British fleet in Hampton Roads. Washington and Rochambeau joined forces, arrived near Williamsburg **Sept. 26.** When siege of Cornwallis began **Oct. 6,** British had 6,000, Americans 8,846, French 7,800. **Cornwallis surrendered Oct. 19.**

1782

New **British** cabinet agreed **in March** to **recognize U.S.** independence. Preliminary agreement signed in Paris **Nov. 30.**

1783

Massachusetts Supreme Court **outlawed slavery** in that state, noting the words in the state Bill of Rights "all men are born free and equal."

Britain, U.S. signed **peace treaty Sept. 3** (Congress ratified it **Jan. 14, 1784).**

Washington ordered army disbanded Nov. 3, bade farewell to his officers at Fraunces Tavern, N.Y. City **Dec. 4.**

Noah Webster published *American Spelling Book,* great bestseller.

1784

First successful daily newspaper, **Pennsylvania Packet & General Advertiser,** published **Sept. 21.**

1786

Delegates from 5 states at **Annapolis, Md. Sept. 11-14** asked Congress to call convention in Philadelphia to write practical constitution for the 13 states.

1787

Shays's Rebellion, of debt-ridden farmers in Massachusetts, failed **Jan. 25.**

Northwest Ordinance adopted **July 13** by Continental Congress. Determined government of Northwest Territory north of Ohio River, west of New York; 60,000 inhabitants could get statehood. Guaranteed freedom of religion, support for schools, no slavery.

Constitutional convention opened at Philadelphia **May 25** with George Washington presiding. Constitution adopted by delegates **Sept. 17;** ratification by 9th state, New Hampshire, **June 21, 1788,** meant adoption; declared in effect **Mar. 4, 1789.**

1789

George Washington chosen president by all electors voting (73 eligible, 69 voting, 4 absent); John Adams, vice president, 34 votes. **Feb. 4.** First Congress met at Federal Hall, N.Y. City; regular sessions began **Apr. 6.** Washington inaugurated there **Apr. 30.** Supreme Court created by Federal Judiciary Act **Sept. 24.**

1790

Congress met in Philadelphia **Dec. 6,** new temporary Capital.

1791

Bill of Rights went into effect **Dec. 15.**

1792

Gen. **"Mad" Anthony Wayne** made commander in Ohio-Indiana area, trained "American Legion"; established string of forts. Routed Indians at Fallen Timbers on Maumee River **Aug. 20, 1794,** checked British at Fort Miami, Ohio.

1793

Eli Whitney invented **cotton gin,** reviving southern slavery.

1794

Whiskey Rebellion, west Pennsylvania farmers protesting liquor tax of **1791,** was suppressed by 15,000 militiamen **Sept. 1794.** Alexander Hamilton used incident to establish authority of the new federal government in enforcing its laws.

1795

U.S. bought peace from **Algiers and Tunis** by paying $800,000, supplying a frigate and annual tribute of $25,000 **Nov. 28.**

Gen. Wayne signed peace with Indians at Fort Greenville.

Univ. of North Carolina became first operating state university.

1796

Washington's Farewell Address as president delivered **Sept. 19.** Gave strong warnings against permanent alliances with foreign powers, big public debt, large military establishment and devices of "small, artful, enterprising minority" to control or change government.

1797

U.S. **frigate United States** launched at Philadelphia **July 10;** Constellation at Baltimore **Sept. 7;** Constitution (Old Ironsides) at Boston **Sept. 20.**

1798

War with France threatened over French raids on U.S. shipping and rejection of U.S. diplomats. Congress voided all treaties with France, ordered Navy to capture French armed ships. Navy (45 ships) and 365 privateers captured 84 French ships. USS Constellation took French warship Insurgente **1799.** Napoleon stopped French raids after becoming First Consul.

1801

Tripoli declared war June 10 against U.S., which refused added tribute to commerce-raiding Arab corsairs. Land and naval campaigns forced Tripoli to conclude **peace June 4, 1805.**

1803

Supreme Court, in **Marbury v. Madison** case, for the first time overturned a U.S. law **Feb. 24.**

Napoleon, who had recovered Louisiana from Spain by secret treaty, sold all of **Louisiana,** stretching to Canadian border, to U.S., for $11,250,000 in bonds, plus $3,750,000 indemnities to American citizens with claims against France. U.S. took title **Dec. 20.** Purchases doubled U.S. area.

1804

Lewis and Clark expedition ordered by Pres. Jefferson to explore what is now northwest U.S. Started from St. Louis **May 14;** ended **Sept. 23, 1806.** Sacajawea, an Indian woman, served as guide.

Vice Pres. **Aaron Burr,** after long political rivalry, **shot Alexander Hamilton** in a duel **July 11** in Weehawken, N.J.; Hamilton died the next day.

1807

Robert Fulton made first practical steamboat trip; left N.Y. City **Aug. 17,** reached Albany, 150 mi., in 32 hrs.

1808

Slave importation outlawed. Some 250,000 slaves were illegally imported **1808-1860.**

1811

William Henry Harrison, governor of Indiana, defeated Indians under the Prophet, in battle of Tippecanoe **Nov. 7.**

Cumberland Road begun at Cumberland, Md.; became important route to West.

1812

War of 1812 had 3 main causes: Britain seized U.S. ships trading with France; Britain seized 4,000 naturalized U.S. sailors by **1810;** Britain armed Indians who raided western border. U.S. stopped trade with Europe **1807** and **1809.** Trade with Britain only was stopped, **1810.**

Unaware that Britain had raised the blockade 2 days before, **Congress declared war June 18** by a small majority. The West favored war, New England opposed it. The British were handicapped by war with France.

U.S. naval victories in **1812** included: USS Essex captured Alert **Aug. 13;** USS Constitution destroyed Guerriere **Aug. 19;** USS Wasp took Frolic **Oct. 18;** USS United States defeated Macedonian off Azores **Oct. 25;** Constitution beat Java **Dec. 29.** British captured Detroit **Aug. 16.**

1813

Commodore **Oliver H. Perry** defeated British fleet at Battle of Lake Erie, **Sept. 10.** U.S. victory at Battle of the Thames, Ont., **Oct. 5,** broke Indian allies of Britain, and made Detroit frontier safe for U.S. But Americans failed in Canadian invasion attempts. York (Toronto) and Buffalo were burned.

1814

British landed in Maryland in August, defeated U.S. force **Aug. 24, burned Capitol** and White House. Maryland militia stopped British advance **Sept. 12.** Bombardment of Ft. McHenry, Baltimore, for 25 hours, **Sept. 13-14,** by British fleet failed; Francis Scott Key wrote words to **Star Spangled Banner.**

U.S. won naval Battle of **Lake Champlain Sept. 11.** Peace treaty signed at Ghent **Dec. 24.**

1815

Some 5,300 British, unaware of peace treaty, attacked U.S. entrenchments near **New Orleans, Jan. 1.** British had over 2,000 casualties, Americans lost 71.

U.S. flotilla finally ended piracy by **Algiers, Tunis, Tripoli** by **Aug. 6.**

1816

Second Bank of the U.S. chartered.

1817

Rush-Bagot treaty signed **Apr. 28-29;** limited U.S., British armaments on the Great Lakes.

1819

Spain cedes **Florida** to U.S. **Feb. 22.**

American steamship Savannah made first part steam-powered, part sail-powered crossing of Atlantic, Savannah, Ga. to Liverpool, Eng., 29 days.

1820

Henry Clay's **Missouri Compromise** bill passed by Congress **May 3.** Slavery was allowed in Missouri, but not elsewhere west of the Mississippi River north of 36° 30′ latitude (the southern line of Missouri). Repealed **1854.**

1821

Emma Willard founded Troy Female Seminary, first U.S. women's college.

1823

Monroe Doctrine enunciated **Dec. 2,** opposing European intervention in the Americas.

1824

Pawtucket, R.I. **weavers strike** in first such action by women.

1825

Erie Canal opened; first boat left Buffalo **Oct. 26,** reached N.Y. City **Nov. 4.** Canal cost $7 million but cut travel time one-third, shipping costs nine-tenths; opened Great Lakes area, made N.Y. City chief Atlantic port.

John Stevens, of Hoboken, N.J., built and operated first experimental **steam locomotive** in U.S.

1828

South Carolina **Dec. 19** declared the right of state **nullification of federal laws,** opposing the "Tariff of Abominations."

Noah Webster published his *American Dictionary of the English Language.*

Baltimore & Ohio first U.S. passenger railroad, was begun **July 4.**

1830

Mormon church organized by Joseph Smith in Fayette, N.Y. **Apr. 6.**

1831

Nat Turner, Negro slave in Virginia, led local slave rebellion, killed 57 whites in **Aug.** Army called in, Turner captured, tried, and hanged.

1832

Black Hawk War (Ill.-Wis.) **Apr.-Sept.** pushed Sauk and Fox Indians west across Mississippi.

South Carolina convention passed **Ordinance of Nullification in Nov.** against permanent tariff, threatening to withdraw from the Union. Congress **Feb. 1833** passed a compromise tariff act, whereupon South Carolina repealed its act.

1833

Oberlin College, first in U.S. to adopt coeducation; refused to bar students on account of race, **1835.**

1835

Texas proclaimed right to secede from Mexico; Sam Houston put in command of Texas army, **Nov. 2-4.**

Gold discovered on **Cherokee land** in Georgia. Indians forced to cede lands **Dec. 20** and to cross Mississippi.

1836

Texans besieged in Alamo in San Antonio by Mexicans under Santa Anna **Feb. 23-Mar. 6;** entire garrison killed. Texas independence declared, **Mar. 2.** At San Jacinto **Apr. 21** Sam Houston and Texans defeated Mexicans.

Marcus Whitman, H.H. Spaulding and wives reached Fort Walla Walla on Columbia River, Oregon. **First white women to cross plains.**

Seminole Indians in Florida under Osceola began attacks **Nov. 1,** protesting forced removal. The unpopular 8-year war ended **Aug. 14, 1842;** Indians were sent to Oklahoma. War cost the U.S. 1,500 soldiers.

1841

First emigrant **wagon train for California,** 47 persons, left Independence, Mo. **May 1,** reached Cal. **Nov. 4.**

Brook Farm commune set up by New England transcendentalist intellectuals. Lasts to **1846.**

1842

Webster-Ashburton Treaty signed **Aug. 9,** fixing the U.S.-Canada border in Maine and Minnesota.

First use of **anesthetic** (sulphuric ether gas).

Settlement of Oregon begins via **Oregon Trail.**

1844

First message over first **telegraph line** sent **May 24** by inventor Samuel F.B. Morse from Washington to Baltimore: "What hath God wrought!"

1845

Texas Congress **voted for annexation** to U.S. **July 4.** U.S. Congress admits Texas to Union **Dec. 29.**

1846

Mexican War. Pres. James K. Polk ordered Gen. Zachary Taylor to seize disputed Texan land settled by Mexicans. After border clash, U.S. declared war **May 13;** Mexico **May 23.** Northern Whigs opposed war, southerners backed it.

Bear flag of Republic of California raised by American settlers at Sonoma **June 14.**

About 12,000 U.S. troops took Vera Cruz Mar. 27, 1847, Mexico City Sept. 14, 1947. By **treaty, Feb. 1848,** Mexico ceded claims to Texas, California, Arizona, New Mexico, Nevada, Utah, part of Colorado. U.S. assumed $3 million American claims and paid Mexico $15 million.

Treaty with Great Britain **June 15** set **boundary in Oregon** territory at 49th parallel (extension of existing line). Expansionists had used slogan "54° 40' or fight."

Mormons, after violent clashes with settlers over polygamy, left Nauvoo, Ill. for West under Brigham Young, settled **July 1847 at Salt Lake City, Utah.**

Elias Howe invented **sewing machine.**

1847

First **adhesive U.S. postage stamps** on sale **July 1;** Benjamin Franklin 5¢, Washington 10¢.

Ralph Waldo Emerson published first book of poems; **Henry Wadsworth Longfellow** published *Evangeline.*

1848

Gold discovered Jan. 24 in California; 80,000 prospectors emigrate in **1849.**

Lucretia Mott and Elizabeth Cady Stanton lead **Seneca Falls, N.Y. Women's Rights Convention July 19-20.**

1850

Sen. Henry Clay's **Compromise of 1850** admitted California as 31st state **Sept. 9,** slavery forbidden; made Utah and New Mexico territories without decision on slavery; made Fugitive Slave Law more harsh; ended District of Columbia slave trade.

1851

Herman Melville's *Moby Dick,* **Nathaniel Hawthorne's** *House of the Seven Gables* published.

1852

Uncle Tom's Cabin, by **Harriet Beecher Stowe,** published.

1853

Commodore Matthew C. Perry, U.S.N., received by Lord of Toda, Japan **July 14; negotiated treaty to open Japan** to U.S. ships.

1854

Republican party formed at Ripon, Wis. **Feb. 28.** Opposed Kansas-Nebraska Act (became law **May 30**) which left issue of slavery to vote of settlers.

Henry David Thoreau published *Walden.*

1855

Walt Whitman published *Leaves of Grass.*

First railroad train crossed Mississippi on the river's first bridge, Rock Island, Ill.-Davenport, Ia. **Apr. 21.**

1856

Republican party's first nominee for president, **John C. Fremont,** defeated. Abraham Lincoln made 50 speeches for him.

Lawrence, Kan. sacked **May 21** by slavery party; abolitionist **John Brown** led anti-slavery men against Missourians at **Osawatomie, Kan. Aug. 30**

1857

Dred Scott decision by U.S. Supreme Court **Mar. 6** held, 6-3, that a Negro slave did not become free when taken into a free state, Congress could not bar slavery from a territory, and Negroes could not be citizens.

1858

First **Atlantic cable** completed by Cyrus W. Field **Aug. 5;** cable failed **Sept. 1.**

Lincoln-Douglas debates in Illinois **Aug. 21-Oct. 15.**

1859

First commercially productive **oil well,** drilled near Titusville, Pa., by Edwin L. Drake **Aug. 27.**

Abolitionist **John Brown** with 21 men seized U.S. Armory at **Harpers Ferry (then Va.) Oct. 16.** U.S. Marines captured raiders, killing several. Brown was hanged for treason by Virginia **Dec. 2.**

1860

New England shoe-workers, 20,000, strike, win higher wages.

Abraham Lincoln, Republican, elected president in 4-way race.

First **Pony Express** between Sacramento, Cal. and St. Joseph, Mo. started **Apr. 3;** service ended **Oct. 24, 1861** when first transcontinental telegraph line was completed.

1861

Seven southern states set up **Confederate States of America Feb. 8,** with Jefferson Davis as president. Confederates fired on **Ft. Sumter** in Charleston, S.C. **Apr. 12,** captured it **Apr. 14.**

President **Lincoln called for 75,000 volunteers Apr. 15.** By **May,** 11 states had seceded. Lincoln blockaded southern ports **Apr. 19,** cutting off vital exports, aid.

Confederates repelled Union forces at first **Battle of Bull Run July 21.**

First **transcontinental telegraph** was put in operation.

1862

Homestead Act was approved **May 20;** it granted free

family farms to settlers.

Land Grant Act approved **July 7,** providing for public land sale to benefit agricultural education; eventually led to establishment of state university systems.

Union forces were victorious in western campaigns, took **New Orleans.** Battles in East were inconclusive.

1863

Lincoln issued **Emancipation Proclamation Jan. 1,** freeing "all slaves in areas still in rebellion."

The entire **Mississippi River** was in Union hands by **July 4.** Union forces won a major victory at **Gettysburg, Pa. July 1-July 4.** Lincoln read his **Gettysburg Address Nov. 19.**

Draft riots in N.Y. City killed about 1,000, including Negroes who were hung by mobs **July 13-16.** Rioters protested provision allowing money payment in place of service. Such payments were ended 1864.

1864

Gen. Sherman marched through Georgia, taking Atlanta **Sept. 1,** Savannah **Dec. 22.**

Sand Creek massacre of Cheyenne and Arapaho Indians **Nov. 29** in a raid by 900 cavalrymen who killed 150-500 men, women, and children; 9 soldiers died. The tribes were awaiting surrender terms when attacked.

1865

Robert E. Lee surrendered 27,800 Confederate troops to Grant at Appomattox Court House, Va. **Apr. 9.** J.E. Johnston surrendered 31,200 to Sherman at Durham Station, N.C. **Apr. 18.** Last rebel troops surrendered **May 26.**

President **Lincoln was shot Apr. 14** by John Wilkes Booth in Ford's Theater, Washington; died the following morning. Booth was reported dead **Apr. 26.** Four co-conspirators were hung **July 7.**

Thirteenth Amendment, abolishing slavery, took effect **Dec. 18.**

1866

First post of the **Grand Army of the Republic** formed **Apr. 6;** was a major national political force for years. Last encampment, **Aug. 31, 1949,** attended by 6 of the 16 surviving veterans.

Ku Klux Klan formed secretly in South to terrorize Negros who voted. Disbanded **1869-71.** A second Klan was organized **1915.**

Congress took control of southern Reconstruction, backed freedmen's rights.

1867

Alaska sold to U.S. by Russia for $7.2 million **Mar. 30** through efforts of Sec. of State William H. Seward.

Horatio Alger published first book, *Ragged Dick.*

The **Grange** was organized **Dec 4,** to protect farmer interests.

1868

The World Almanac, a publication of the *New York World,* appeared for the first time.

Pres. **Andrew Johnson** tried to remove Edwin M. Stanton, secretary of war; was impeached by House **Feb. 24** for violation of Tenure of Office Act; acquitted by Senate **March-May.** Stanton resigned.

1869

Financial "**Black Friday**" in New York **Sept. 24;** caused by attempt to "corner" gold.

Transcontinental railroad completed; golden spike driven at Promontory, Utah **May 10** marking the junction of Central Pacific and Union Pacific.

Knights of Labor formed in Philadelphia. By **1886,** it had 700,000 members nationally.

Woman suffrage law passed in Territory of Wyoming **Dec. 10.**

1871

Great fire destroyed Chicago Oct. 8-11; loss est. at $196 million.

1872

Amnesty Act restored civil rights to citizens of the South **May 22** except for 500 Confederate leaders.

Congress founded first national park — **Yellowstone** in Wyoming.

1873

First U.S. **postal card** issued **May 1.**

Banks failed, panic began in **Sept.** Depression lasted 5 years.

"Boss" William Tweed of N.Y. City convicted of stealing public funds. He died in jail in **1878.**

Bellevue Hospital in N.Y. City started the first **school of nursing.**

1875

Congress passed **Civil Rights Act Mar. 1** giving equal rights to Negroes in public accommodations and jury duty. Act invalidated in **1883** by Supreme Court.

First **Kentucky Derby** held **May 17** at Churchill Downs, Louisville, Ky.

1876

Samuel J. Tilden, Democrat, received majority of popular votes for president over **Rutherford B. Hayes,** Republican, but 22 electoral votes were in dispute; issue left to Congress. Hayes given presidency **in Feb., 1877** after Republicans agree to end Reconstruction of South.

Col. **George A. Custer** and 264 soldiers of the 7th Cavalry killed **June 25** in "last stand," Battle of the Little Big Horn, Mont., in Sioux Indian War.

Mark Twain published *Tom Sawyer.*

1877

Molly Maguires, Irish terrorist society in Scranton, Pa. mining areas, broken up by hanging of 11 leaders for murders of mine officials and police.

Pres. Hayes sent troops in violent national **railroad strike.**

1878

First commercial **telephone** exchange opened, New Haven, Conn. **Jan. 28.**

1879

F.W. Woolworth opened his first five-and-ten store in Utica, N.Y. **Feb. 22.**

Henry George published *Progress & Poverty,* advocating single tax on land.

1881

Pres. **James A. Garfield shot** in Washington, D.C. **July 2;** died **Sept. 19.**

Booker T. Washington founded Tuskegee Institute for Negroes.

Helen Hunt Jackson published *A Century of Dishonor* about mistreatment of Indians.

1883

Pendleton Act, passed **Jan. 16,** reformed federal civil service.

Brooklyn Bridge opened **May 24.**

1886

Haymarket riot and bombing, evening of **May 4,** followed bitter labor battles for 8-hour day in Chicago; 7 police and 4 workers died, 66 wounded. Eight anarchists found guilty. Gov. John P. Altgeld denounced trial as unfair.

Geronimo, Apache Indian, finally surrendered **Sept. 4.**

American Federation of Labor (AFL) formed **Dec. 8** by 25 craft unions.

1888

Great blizzard in eastern U.S. **Mar. 11-14;** 400 deaths.

1889

Johnstown, Pa. flood May 31; 2,200 lives lost.

1890

First execution by **electrocution:** William Kemmler **Aug. 6** at Auburn Prison, Auburn, N.Y., for murder.

Battle of **Wounded Knee, S.D. Dec. 29,** the last major conflict between Indians and U.S. troops. About 200 Indian men, women, and children, and 29 soldiers were killed.

Castle Garden closed as N.Y. immigration depot; **Ellis Island** opened **Dec. 31,** closed **1954.**

Sherman Antitrust Act begins federal effort to curb monopolies.

Jacob Riis published *How the Other Half Lives,* about city slums.

1892

Homestead, Pa., strike at Carnegie steel mills; 7 guards and 11 strikers and spectators shot to death **July 6;** setback for unions.

1893

Financial panic began, led to 4-year depression.

1894

Thomas A. **Edison's kinetoscope** (motion pictures) (invented **1887**) given first public showing **Apr. 14** in N.Y. City.

Jacob S. Coxey led 500 unemployed from the Midwest into Washington, D.C. **Apr. 29.** Coxey was arrested for trespassing on Capitol grounds.

1896

William Jennings Bryan delivered "Cross of Gold" speech at Democratic National Convention in Chicago **July 8.**

Supreme Court, in **Plessy v. Ferguson,** approved racial segregation under the "separate but equal" doctrine.

1898

U.S. **battleship Maine** blown up **Feb. 15** at Havana, 260 killed.

U.S. blockaded Cuba Apr. 22 in aid of independence forces. Spain declared **war Apr. 24.** U.S. destroyed Spanish fleet in Philippines **May 1,** took Guam **June 20.**

Puerto Rico taken by U.S. **July 25-Aug. 12.** Spain agreed **Dec. 10** to cede Philippines, Puerto Rico, and Guam, and approved independence for Cuba.

U.S. annexed independent republic of **Hawaii.**

1899

Filipino insurgents, unable to get recognition of independence from U.S., started guerrilla war **Feb. 4.** Crushed with capture **May 23, 1901** of leader, Emilio Aguinaldo.

U.S. declared **Open Door Policy** to make China an open international market and to preserve its integrity as a nation.

John Dewey published *School and Society,* backing progressive education.

1900

Carry Nation, Kansas anti-saloon agitator, began raiding with hatchet.

U.S. helped suppress **"Boxers"** in Peking.

1901

Pres. William **McKinley was shot Sept. 6** by an anarchist, Leon Czolgosz; died **Sept. 14.**

1903

Treaty between U.S. and Colombia to have U.S. dig **Panama Canal** signed **Jan. 22,** rejected by Colombia. Panama declared independence with U.S. support **Nov. 3;** recognized by Pres. Theodore Roosevelt **Nov. 6.** U.S., Panama signed canal treaty **Nov. 18.**

Wisconsin set first **direct primary** voting system **May 23.**

First **automobile trip** across U.S. from San Francisco to New York **May 23-Aug. 1.**

First successful flight in heavier-than-air mechanically propelled airplane by **Orville Wright Dec. 17** near Kitty Hawk, N.C., 120 ft. in 12 seconds. Fourth flight same day by **Wilbur Wright,** 852 ft. in 59 seconds. Improved plane patented **May 22, 1906.**

Jack London published *Call of the Wild.*

Great Train Robbery, pioneering film, produced.

1904

Ida Tarbell published muckraking *History of Standard Oil.*

1905

First **Rotary Club** of local businessmen founded in Chicago.

1906

San Francisco earthquake and fire **Apr. 18-19** left 452 dead, $350 million damages.

Pure Food and Drug Act and Meat Inspection Act both passed **June 30.**

1907

Financial panic and depression started **Mar. 13.**

First round-world cruise of U.S. **"Great White Fleet";** 16 battleships, 12,000 men.

1909

Adm. Robert E. Peary reached **North Pole Apr. 6** on 6th attempt, accompanied by Matthew Henson, a black, and 4 Eskimos.

National Conference on the Negro convened **May 30,** leading to founding of the National Association for the Advancement of Colored People.

1910

Boy Scouts of America founded **Feb. 8.**

1911

Supreme Court dissolved **Standard Oil Co.**

First **transcontinental airplane flight** (with numerous stops) by C.P. Rodgers, New York to Pasadena, **Sept. 17-Nov. 5;** time in air 82 hrs., 4 min.

1912

U.S. sent marines **Aug. 14** to **Nicaragua,** which was in default of loans to U.S. and Europe.

1913

N.Y. Armory Show introduced modern art to U.S. public **Feb. 17.**

U.S. blockaded Mexico in support of revolutionaries.

Charles Beard published his *Economic Interpretation of the Constitution.*

Federal Reserve System was authorized **Dec. 23,** in a major reform of U.S. banking and finance.

1914

Ford Motor Co. raised basic wage rates from $2.40 for 9-hr. day to $5 for 8-hr. day **Jan. 5.**

When U.S. sailors were arrested at Tampico **Apr. 9,** Atlantic fleet was sent to **Veracruz,** occupied city.

Pres. Wilson proclaimed **U.S. neutrality** in the European war **Aug. 4.**

The **Clayton Antitrust Act** was passed **Oct. 15,** strengthening federal anti-monopoly powers.

1915

First **telephone talk,** New York to San Francisco, **Jan. 25** by Alexander Graham Bell and Thomas A. Watson.

British ship **Lusitania** sunk **May 7** by German submarine; 128 American passengers lost (Germany had warned passengers in advance). As a result of U.S. campaign, Germany issued apology and promise of payments **Oct. 5.** Pres. Wilson asked for a military fund increase **Dec. 7.**

U.S. troops landed in **Haiti July 28.** Haiti became a virtual U.S. protectorate under **Sept. 16** treaty.

1916

Gen. John J. **Pershing entered Mexico** to pursue Francisco (Pancho) Villa, who had raided U.S. border areas. Forces withdrawn **Feb. 5, 1917.**

Rural Credits Act passed **July 17,** followed by Warehouse Act. **Aug. 11;** both provided financial aid to farmers.

Bomb exploded during **San Francisco** Preparedness Day parade **July 22,** killed 10. Thomas J. Mooney, labor organizer, and Warren K. Billings, shoe worker, were convicted; both pardoned in **1939.**

U.S. bought **Virgin Islands** from Denmark **Aug. 4.**

U.S. established military government in the **Dominican Republic Nov. 29.**

Trade and loans to **European Allies** soared during the year.

John Dewey published *Democracy in Education.*

Carl Sandburg published *Chicago Poems.*

1917

Germany, suffering from British blockade, declared almost unrestricted **submarine warfare Jan. 31.** U.S. cut diplomatic ties with Germany **Feb. 3,** and formally declared war **Apr. 6.**

Conscription law was passed **May 18.** First U.S. troops arrived in Europe **June 26.**

The 18th **(Prohibition)** Amendment to the Constitution was submitted to the states by Congress **Dec. 18.** On **Jan. 16, 1919,** the 36th state (Nebraska) ratified it. Franklin D. Roosevelt, as 1932 presidential candidate, endorsed repeal; 21st Amendment repealed 18th; ratification completed **Dec. 5, 1933.**

1918

Over one million **American troops** were in Europe by **July.** War ended **Nov. 11.**

Influenza epidemic killed an estimated 20 million worldwide, 548,000 in U.S.

1919

First **transatlantic flight,** by U.S. Navy seaplane, left Rockaway, N.Y. **May 8,** stopped at Newfoundland, Azores, Lisbon **May 27.**

Boston police strike Sept. 9; National Guard breaks strike.

Sherwood Anderson published *Winesburg, Ohio.*

About 250 **alien radicals** were deported **Dec. 22.**

1920

In national **Red Scare,** some 2,700 Communists, anarchists, and other radicals were arrested **Jan.-May.**

Senate refused **Mar. 19** to ratify the **League of Nations Covenant.**

Nicola Sacco, 29, shoe factory employee and radical agitator, and **Bartolomeo Vanzetti,** 32, fish peddler and anarchist, accused of killing 2 men in Mass. payroll holdup **Apr. 15.** Found guilty **1921.** A 6-year worldwide campaign for release on grounds of want of conclusive evidence and prejudice failed. Both were executed **Aug. 23, 1927.** Vindicated July 19, 1977 by proclamation of Mass. Gov. Dukakis.

First regular licensed **radio broadcasting** begun **Aug. 20.**

Wall St., N.Y. City, **bomb** explosion killed 30, injured 100, did $2 million damage **Sept. 16.**

Sinclair Lewis' *Main Street,* **F. Scott Fitzgerald's** *This side of Paradise* published.

1921

Congress sharply curbed **immigration,** set national quota system **May 19.**

Joint Congressional resolution declaring **peace with Germany, Austria, and Hungary** signed **July 2** by Pres. Harding; treaties were signed in **Aug.**

Limitation of Armaments Conference met in Washington **Nov. 12 to Feb. 6, 1922.** Major powers agreed to curtail naval construction, outlaw poison gas, restrict submarine attack on merchantmen, respect integrity of China. Ratified **Aug. 5, 1925.**

Ku Klux Klan began revival with violence against blacks in North, South, and Midwest.

1922

Violence during **coal-mine strike** at Herrin, Ill., **June 22-23** cost 36 lives, 21 of them non-union miners.

Reader's Digest founded.

1923

First **sound-on-film motion picture,** "Phonofilm" was shown by Lee de Forest at Rivoli Theater, N.Y. City, beginning in **April.**

1924

Law approved by Congress **June 15** making all **Indians citizens.**

Nellie Tayloe Ross elected governor of Wyoming **Nov. 9** after death of her husband **Oct. 2;** installed **Jan. 5, 1925,** first woman governor. **Miriam (Ma) Ferguson** was elected governor of Texas **Nov. 9;** installed **Jan. 20, 1925.**

George Gershwin wrote *Rhapsody in Blue.*

1925

John T. Scopes found guilty of having taught evolution in Dayton, Tenn. high school, fined $100 and costs **July 24.**

1926

Dr. Robert H. Goddard demonstrated practicality of **rockets Mar. 16** at Auburn, Mass. with first liquid fuel rocket; rocket traveled 184 ft. in 2.5 secs.

Air Commerce Act passed, providing federal aid for airlines and airports.

1927

About 1,000 **marines landed in China Mar. 5** to protect property in civil war. U.S. and British consulates looted by nationalists **Mar. 24.**

Capt. **Charles A. Lindbergh** left Roosevelt Field, N.Y. **May 20** alone in plane Spirit of St. Louis on first New York-Paris nonstop flight. Reached Le Bourget airfield **May 21,** 3,610 miles in 33 1/2 hours.

The Jazz Singer, with **Al Jolson,** demonstrated part-talking pictures in N.Y. City **Oct. 6.**

Show Boat opened in New York **Dec. 27.**

O. E. Rolvaag published *Giants in the Earth.*

1929

"St. Valentine's Day massacre" in Chicago **Feb. 14;** gangsters killed 7 rivals.

Farm price stability aided by **Agricultural Marketing Act,** passed **June 15.**

Albert B. Fall, former sec. of the interior, was convicted of accepting a bribe of $100,000 in the leasing of the **Elk Hills (Teapot Dome)** naval oil reserve; sentenced **Nov. 1** to $100,000 fine and year in prison.

Stock Market crash Oct. 29 marked end of postwar prosperity as stock prices plummeted. Stock losses for 1929-31 estimated at $50 billion; worst American depression began.

Thomas Wolfe published *Look Homeward, Angel.* **William Faulkner** published *The Sound and the Fury.*

1930

London **Naval Reduction Treaty** signed by U.S., Britain, Italy, France, and Japan **Apr. 22;** in effect **Jan. 1, 1931;** expired **Dec. 31, 1936.**

Hawley-Smoot Tariff signed; rate hikes slash world trade.

1931

Empire State Building opened in N.Y. City **May 1.**

Pearl Buck published *The Good Earth.*

1932

Reconstruction Finance Corp. established **Jan. 22** to stimulate banking and business. Unemployment stood at 12 million.

Charles Lindbergh Jr. kidnaped Mar. 1, found dead **May 12.**

Bonus March on Washington **May 29** by World War I veterans demanding Congress pay their bonus in full. Army, under Gen. Douglas MacArthur, disbanded the marchers on Pres. Hoover's orders.

1933

All **banks in the U.S. were ordered closed** by Pres. Roosevelt **Mar. 6.**

In the "100 days" special session, **Mar. 9—June 16,** Congress passed **New Deal** social and economic measures.

Gold standard dropped by U.S.; announced by Pres. Roosevelt **Apr. 19,** ratified by Congress **June 5.**

Prohibition ended in the U.S. as 36th state ratified 21st Amendment **Dec. 5.**

U.S. foreswore armed intervention in **Western Hemisphere** nations **Dec. 26.**

1934

U.S. troops pull out of **Haiti Aug. 6.**

1935

Comedian **Will Rogers** and aviator Wiley Post **killed Aug. 15** in Alaska plane crash.

Social Security Act passed by Congress **Aug. 14.**

Huey Long, Senator from Louisiana and national political leader, was **assassinated Sept. 8.**

Porgy and Bess, **George Gershwin** opera on American Negro theme, opened **Oct. 10** in N.Y. City.

Committee for Industrial Organization (CIO) formed to expand industrial unionism **Nov. 9.**

1936

Boulder Dam completed.

Margaret Mitchell published *Gone With the Wind.*

1937

Amelia Earhart Putnam, aviator, and co-pilot Fred Noonan lost **July 2** near Howland Is. in the Pacific.

Pres. Roosevelt asked for 6 additional Supreme Court justices; **"packing" plan** defeated.

Auto, steel labor unions won first big contracts.

1938

Naval Expansion Act passed **May 17.**

National minimum wage enacted **June 28.**

Orson Welles radio dramatization of *War of the Worlds* caused nationwide scare **Oct. 30.**

1939

Pres. Roosevelt asked **defense budget hike Jan. 5, 12.**

N.Y. World's Fair opened **Apr. 30,** closed **Oct. 31;** reopened **May 11, 1940,** and finally closed **Oct. 21.**

Einstein alerts FDR to **A-bomb** opportunity in **Aug. 2** letter.

U.S. declares its neutrality in European war **Sept. 5.**

Roosevelt proclaimed a limited **national emergency Sept. 8,** an unlimited emergency **May 27, 1941.** Both ended by Pres. Truman **Apr. 28, 1952.**

John Steinbeck published *Grapes of Wrath.*

1940

U.S. authorized sale of **surplus war material** to Britain **June 3;** announced transfer of 50 overaged destroyers **Sept. 3.**

First **peacetime draft** approved **Sept. 14.**

Richard Wright published *Native Son.*

1941

The **Four Freedoms** termed essential by Pres. Roosevelt in speech to Congress **Jan. 6;** freedom of speech and religion, freedom from want and fear.

Lend-Lease Act signed **Mar. 11,** providing $7 billion in military credits for Britain. Lend-Lease for USSR approved in **Nov.**

U.S. occupied **Iceland July 7.**

The **Atlantic Charter,** 8-point declaration of principles, issued by Roosevelt and Winston Churchill **Aug. 14.**

Japan attacked **Pearl Harbor,** Hawaii, 7:55 a.m. **Dec. 7,** 19 ships sunk or damaged, 2,300 dead. U.S. declared war on Japan **Dec. 8,** on Germany and Italy **Dec. 11** after those countries declared war.

1942

Federal government forcibly moved 110,000 **Japanese-Americans** (including 75,000 U.S. citizens) from West Coast to detention camps. Exclusion lasted 3 years.

Battle of **Midway June 3-6** was Japan's first major defeat.

Marines landed on **Guadalcanal Aug. 7;** last Japanese not expelled until **Feb. 9, 1943.**

U.S., Britain invaded North Africa **Nov. 8.**

First **nuclear chain reaction** (fission of uranium isotope U-235) produced at Univ. of Chicago, under physicists Arthur Compton, Enrico Fermi, others **Dec. 2.**

1943

All war contractors barred from **racial discrimination May 27.**

Pres. Roosevelt signed **June 10** the pay-as-you-go income tax bill. Starting **July 1** wage and salary earners were subject to a **paycheck withholding** tax.

Race riot in Detroit June 21; 34 dead, 700 injured. Riot in Harlem section of N.Y. City; 6 killed.

U.S. troops invaded Italy **Sept. 9.**

Marines advanced in **Gilbert Is. in Nov.**

1944

U.S., Allied forces invaded Europe at **Normandy June 6.**

G.I. Bill of Rights signed **June 22,** providing veterans benefits.

U.S. forces landed on **Leyte,** Philippines **Oct. 20.**

1945

Yalta Conference met in the Crimea, USSR, **Feb. 3-11.** Roosevelt, Churchill, and Stalin agreed Russia would enter war against Japan.

Marines landed on **Iwo Jima Feb. 19;** U.S. forces invaded **Okinawa Apr. 1.**

Pres. Roosevelt, 63, died of cerebral hemorrhage in Warm Springs, Ga. **Apr. 12.**

Germany surrendered May 7.

First **atomic bomb,** produced at Los Alamos, N.M., exploded at Alamogordo, N.M. **July 16.** Bomb dropped on **Hiroshima Aug. 6,** on **Nagasaki Aug. 9.** Japan surrendered **Aug. 15.**

U.S. forces entered **Korea** south of 38th parallel to displace Japanese **Sept. 8.**

Gen. Douglas MacArthur took over supervision of Japan **Sept. 9.**

1946

Strike by 400,000 **mine workers** began **Apr. 1;** other industries followed.

Philippines given independence by U.S. **July 4.**

1947

Truman Doctrine: Pres. Truman asked Congress to aid Greece and Turkey to combat Communist terrorism **Mar. 12.** Approved **May 15.**

United Nations Security Council voted unanimously **Apr. 2** to place under **U.S. trusteeship** the Pacific islands formerly mandated to Japan.

Jackie Robinson on Brooklyn Dodgers **Apr. 11,** the first black to play in major league baseball.

Taft-Hartley Labor Act curbing strikes was vetoed by Truman **June 20;** Congress overrode the veto.

Proposals later known as the **Marshall Plan,** under which the U.S. would extend aid to European countries, were made by Sec. of State George C. Marshall **June 5.** Congress authorized some $12 billion in next 4 years.

1948

USSR began a land **blockade of Berlin's** Allied sectors **Apr. 1.** This blockade and Western counter-blockade were lifted **Sept. 30, 1949,** after British and U.S. planes had lifted 2,343,315 tons of food and coal into the city.

Organization of American States founded **Apr. 30.**

Alger Hiss, former State Dept. official, indicted Dec. 15 for perjury, after denying he had passed secret documents to Whittaker Chambers for transmission to a communist spy ring. His second trial ended in conviction **Jan. 21, 1950,** and a sentence of 5 years in prison.

Kinsey Report on Sexuality in the Human Male published.

1949

U.S. troops withdrawn from **Korea June 29.**

North Atlantic Treaty Organization **(NATO)** established **Aug. 24** by U.S., Canada, and 10 West European nations, agreeing that "an armed attack against one or more of them in Europe and North America shall be considered an attack against all."

Mrs. I. Toguri D'Aquino **(Tokyo Rose** of Japanese wartime broadcasts) was sentenced **Oct. 7** to 10 years in prison for treason. Paroled **1956,** pardoned **1977.**

Eleven leaders of **U.S. Communist party** convicted **Oct. 14,** after 9-month trial in N.Y. City, of advocating violent overthrow of U.S. government. Ten defendants sentenced to 5 years in prison each and the 11th, to 3 years. Supreme Court upheld the convictions **June 4, 1951.**

1950

U.S. **Jan 14** recalled all consular officials from **China** after the latter seized the American consulate general in Peking.

Masked bandits robbed **Brink's Inc.,** Boston express office, **Jan. 17** of $2.8 million, of which $1.2 million was in cash. Case solved **1956,** 8 sentenced to life.

Pres. Truman authorized production of **H-bomb Jan. 31.**

United Nations asked for troops to restore Korea peace **June 25.**

Truman ordered Air Force and Navy to Korea **June 27** after North Korea invaded South. Truman approved ground forces, air strikes against North **June 30.**

U.S. sent 35 military advisers to **South Vietnam June 27,** and agreed to provide military and economic aid to anti-Communist government.

Army seized all railroads Aug. 27 on Truman's order to prevent a general strike; roads returned to owners in **1952.**

U.S. forces landed at Inchon Sept. 15; UN force took Pyongyang **Oct. 20,** reached China border **Nov. 20,** China sent troops across border **Nov. 26.**

Two members of a **Puerto Rican nationalist** movement tried to kill Pres. Truman **Nov. 1.** (see Assassinations)

U.S. **Dec. 8** banned shipments to **Communist China** and to Asiatic ports trading with it.

1951

Sen. **Estes Kefauver** led Senate investigation into organized crime. Preliminary report **Feb. 28** said gambling take was over $20 billion a year.

Julius Rosenberg, his wife, Ethel, and Morton Sobell, all U.S. citizens, were found guilty **Mar. 29** of conspiracy to commit wartime espionage. Rosenbergs sentenced to death, Sobell to 30 years. Rosenbergs **executed June 19, 1953.** Sobell released **Jan. 14, 1969.**

Gen. Douglas MacArthur was removed from his Korea command **Apr. 11** for making unauthorized policy statements.

Korea cease-fire talks began in July; lasted 2 years. **Fighting ended July 27, 1953.**

Tariff concessions by the U.S. to the Soviet Union, Communist China, and all communist-dominated lands were suspended **Aug. 1.**

The U.S., **Australia,** and **New Zealand** signed a mutual security pact **Sept. 1.**

Transcontinental television inaugurated **Sept. 4** with Pres. Truman's address at the Japanese Peace Treaty Conference in San Francisco.

Japanese Peace Treaty signed in San Francisco **Sept. 8** by U.S., Japan, and 47 other nations.

J.D. Salinger published *Catcher in the Rye.*

1952

U.S. **seizure of nation's steel mills** was ordered by Pres. Truman **Apr. 8** to avert a strike. Ruled illegal by Supreme Court **June 2.**

Peace contract between West Germany, U.S., Great Britain, and France was signed **May 26.**

The last racial and ethnic barriers to naturalization were removed, **June 26-27,** with the passage of the **Immigration and Naturalization Act of 1952.**

First **hydrogen device** explosion **Nov. 1** at Eniwetok Atoll in Pacific.

1953

Pres. Eisenhower announced **May 8** that U.S. had given France $60 million for **Indochina War.** More aid was announced in **Sept.** In **1954** it was reported that three fourths of the war's costs were met by U.S.

1954

Nautilus, first atomic-powered submarine, was launched at Groton, Conn. **Jan. 21.**

Five members of Congress were wounded in the House **Mar. 1** by 4 **Puerto Rican independence supporters** who fired at random from a spectators' gallery.

Sen. Joseph McCarthy led televised hearings **Apr. 22-June 17** into alleged Communist influence in the Army.

Racial segregation in public schools was unanimously ruled unconstitutional by the Supreme Court **May 17,** as a violation of the 14th Amendment clause guaranteeing equal protection of the laws.

Southeast Asia Treaty Organization (**SEATO**) formed by collective defense pact signed in Manila **Sept. 8** by the U.S., Britain, France, Australia, New Zealand, Philippines, Pakistan, and Thailand.

Condemnation of **Sen. Joseph R. McCarthy** (R., Wis.) voted by Senate, 67-22 **Dec. 2** for contempt of a Senate elections subcommittee, for abuse of its members, and for insults to the Senate during his Army investigation hearings.

1955

U.S. agreed **Feb. 12** to help train **South Vietnamese** army.

Supreme Court ordered **"all deliberate speed"** in integration of public schools **May 31.**

A **summit meeting** of leaders of U.S., Britain, France, and USSR took place **July 18-23** in Geneva, Switzerland.

Rosa Parks refused **Dec. 1** to give her seat to a white man on a bus in Montgomery, Ala. Bus segregation ordinance declared unconstitutional by a federal court following boycott and NAACP protest.

Merger of America's 2 largest labor organizations was effected **Dec. 5** under the name American Federation of Labor and Congress of Industrial Organizations. The merged **AFL-CIO** had a membership estimated at 15 million.

1956

Massive resistance to Supreme Court desegregation rulings was called for **Mar. 12** by 101 Southern congressmen.

Federal-Aid **Highway Act** signed **June 29,** inaugurating interstate highway system.

First transatlantic **telephone cable** went into operation **Sept. 25.**

1957

Congress approved first **civil rights bill** for Negroes since Reconstruction **Apr. 29,** to protect voting rights.

National Guardsmen, called out by Arkansas Gov. Orval Faubus **Sept. 4,** barred 9 Negro students from entering previously all-white Central High School in **Little Rock.** Faubus complied **Sept. 21** with a federal court order to remove the National Guardsmen. The Negroes entered school **Sept. 23** but were ordered to withdraw by local authorities because of fear of mob violence. Pres. Eisenhower sent federal troops **Sept. 24** to enforce the court's order.

Jack Kerouac published *On the Road,* beatnik journal.

1958

First U.S. earth satellite to go into orbit, **Explorer I,** launched by Army **Jan. 31** at Cape Canaveral, Fla.; discovered Van Allen radiation belt.

Five thousand U.S. Marines sent to **Lebanon** to protect elected government from threatened overthrow **July-Oct.**

First domestic **jet airline** passenger service in U.S. opened by National Airlines **Dec. 10** between New York and Miami.

1959

Alaska admitted as 49th state **Jan. 3; Hawaii** admitted **Aug. 21.**

St. Lawrence Seaway opened **Apr. 25.**

The George Washington, first U.S. ballistic-missile submarine, launched at Groton, Conn. **June 9.**

N.S. Savannah, world's first atomic-powered merchant ship, launched **July 21** at Camden, N.J.

Soviet Premier **Khrushchev** paid unprecedented visit to U.S. **Sept. 15-27,** made transcontinental tour.

1960

A wave of **sit-ins** began **Feb. 1** when 4 Negro college students in Greensboro, N.C. refused to move from a Woolworth lunch counter when they were denied service. By **Sept. 1961** more than 70,000 students, whites and blacks, had participated in sit-ins.

U.S. launched first **weather satellite,** Tiros I, **Apr. 1.**

Congress approved a strong **voting rights act Apr. 21.**

A **U-2 reconnaisance plane** of the U.S. was shot down in the Soviet Union **May 1.** The incident led to cancellation of an imminent Paris summit conference.

Mobs attacked U.S. embassy in **Panama Sept. 17** in dispute over flying of U.S. and Panamanian flags.

U.S. announced **Dec. 15** it backed rightist group in **Laos,** which took power the next day.

1961

The U.S. severed diplomatic and consular relations with **Cuba Jan. 3,** after disputes over nationalizations of U.S. firms, U.S. military presence at Guantanamo base, etc.

Invasion of Cuba's **"Bay of Pigs" Apr. 17** by Cuban exiles trained, armed, and directed by the U.S., attempting to overthrow the regime of Premier Fidel Castro, was repulsed.

Commander Alan B. Shepard Jr. was rocketed from Cape Canaveral, Fla., 116.5 mi. above the earth in a Mercury capsule **May 5** in the first U.S. manned sub-orbital space flight.

1962

Lt. Col. John H. Glenn Jr. became the first American in orbit **Feb. 20** when he circled the earth 3 times in the Mercury capsule **Friendship 7.**

Pres. Kennedy said **Feb. 14** U.S. military advisers in Vietnam would fire if fired upon.

Supreme Court **Mar. 26** backed **one-man one-vote** apportionment of seats in state legislatures.

First U.S. **communications satellite** launched in **July.**

The **largest cash robbery** to date in U.S. history occurred **Aug. 14** when a gang held up a U.S. mail truck near Plymouth, Mass., and stole $1,551,277.

James Meredith became first black student at Univ. of Mississippi **Oct. 1** after 3,000 troops put down riots.

A Soviet **offensive missile buildup in Cuba** was revealed **Oct. 22** by Pres. Kennedy, who ordered a naval and air quarantine on shipment of offensive military equipment to the island. Kennedy and Soviet Premier Khrushchev reached agreement **Oct. 28** on a formula to end the crisis. Kennedy announced **Nov. 2** that Soviet missile bases in Cuba were being dismantled.

Rachel Carson's *Silent Spring* launched environmentalist movement.

1963

Supreme Court ruled **Mar. 18** that all **criminal defendants** must have counsel and that illegally acquired evidence was not admissible in state as well as federal courts.

Supreme Court ruled, 8-1, **June 17** that laws requiring **recitation of the Lord's Prayer** or Bible verses in public schools were unconstitutional.

A limited **nuclear test-ban treaty** was agreed upon **July 25** by the U.S., Soviet Union and Britain, barring all nuclear tests except underground.

Washington demonstration by 200,000 persons **Aug. 28** in support of **Negro demands** for equal rights. Highlight was speech in which Dr. Martin Luther King said: "I have a dream that this nation will rise up and live out the true meaning of its creed, 'We hold these truths to be self-evident: that all men are created equal.' "

South Vietnam Pres. **Ngo Dinh Diem assassinated Nov. 2;** U.S. had earlier withdrawn support.

Pres. John F. Kennedy was shot and fatally wounded by an assassin **Nov. 22** as he rode in a motorcade through downtown Dallas, Tex. Vice Pres. Lyndon B. Johnson was inaugurated president shortly after in Dallas. Lee Harvey Oswald was arrested and charged with the murder. Oswald was shot and fatally wounded **Nov. 24** by Jack Ruby, 52, a Dallas nightclub owner, who was convicted of murder **Mar. 14, 1964** and sentenced to death. Ruby died of natural causes **Jan. 3, 1967** while awaiting retrial.

U.S. troops in **Vietnam** totalled over 15,000 by year-end; aid to South Vietnam was over $500 million in **1963.**

1964

Panama suspended relations with U.S. **Jan. 9** after riots. U.S. offered **Dec. 18** to negotiate a new canal treaty.

Supreme Court ordered **Feb. 17** that **congressional districts** have equal populations.

U.S. reported **May 27** it was sending military planes to **Laos.**

Omnibus **civil rights bill** passed **June 29** banning discrimination in voting, jobs, public accommodations, etc.

Three **civil rights workers** were reported missing in Mississippi **June 22;** found buried **Aug. 4.** Twenty-one white men were arrested. On **Oct. 20, 1967,** an all-white federal jury convicted 7 of conspiracy in the slayings.

U.S. Congress **Aug. 7** passed **Tonkin Resolution,** authorizing presidential action in Vietnam, after North Vietnam boats reportedly attacked 2 U.S. destroyers **Aug. 2.**

Congress approved War on Poverty bill **Aug. 11.**

The **Warren Commission** released **Sept. 27** a report concluding that Lee Harvey Oswald was solely responsible for the Kennedy assassination.

1965

Pres. Johnson in **Feb.** ordered continuous **bombing of North Vietnam** below 20th parallel.

Some 14,000 U.S. troops sent to **Dominican Republic** during civil war **Apr. 28.** All troops withdrawn by following year.

New **Voting Rights Act** signed **Aug. 6.**

Los Angeles riot by blacks living in **Watts** area resulted in death of 35 persons and property damage est. at $200 million **Aug. 11-16.**

Water Quality Act passed **Sept. 21** to meet pollution, shortage problems.

National origins quota system of **immigration** abolished **Oct. 3.**

Massive **electric power failure** blacked out most of northeastern U.S, parts of 2 Canadian provinces the night of **Nov. 9-10.**

U.S. forces in **South Vietnam** reached 184,300 by year-end.

1966

U.S. forces began firing into **Cambodia May 1.**

Bombing of Hanoi area of North Vietnam by U.S. planes began **June 29.** By **Dec. 31,** 385,300 U.S. troops were stationed in South Vietnam, plus 60,000 offshore and 33,000 in Thailand.

Medicare, government program to pay part of the medical expenses of citizens over 65, began **July 1.**

Edward Brooke (R, Mass.) elected **Nov. 8** as first Negro U.S. senator in 85 years.

1967

Black representative **Adam Clayton Powell** (D, N.Y.) was denied **Mar. 1** his seat in Congress because of charges he misused government funds. Reelected in 1968, he was seated, but fined $25,000 and stripped of his 22 years' seniority.

Massive **tariff cuts** were approved **May 15** by 53 countries.

Pres. Johnson and Soviet Premier Aleksei Kosygin met **June 23 and 25** at **Glassboro State College** in N.J.; agreed not to let any crisis push them into war.

Black riots in **Newark, N.J. July 12-17** killed some 26, injured 1,500; over 1,000 arrested. In Detroit, Mich., **July 23-30** at least 40 died; 2,000 injured, and 5,000 left homeless by rioting, looting, burning in city's black ghetto. Quelled by 4,700 federal paratroopers and 8,000 National Guardsmen.

Thurgood Marshall sworn in **Oct. 2** as first black U.S. Supreme Court Justice. Carl B. Stokes (D, Cleveland) and Richard G. Hatcher (D, Gary, Ind.) were elected first black mayors of major U.S. cities **Nov. 7.**

By **December** 475,000 U.S. troops were in **South Vietnam,** all North Vietnam was subject to bombing. Protests against the war mounted in U.S. during year.

1968

USS Pueblo and 83-man crew seized in Sea of Japan **Jan. 23** by North Koreans; 82 men released **Dec. 22.**

"Tet offensive": Communist troops attacked Saigon, 30 province capitals **Jan. 30,** suffer heavy casualties.

Pres. Johnson **curbed bombing** of North Vietnam **Mar. 31.** Peace talks began in Paris **May 10.** All bombing of North is halted **Oct. 31.**

Martin Luther King Jr., 39, assassinated Apr. 4 in Memphis, Tenn. James Earl Ray, an escaped convict, pleaded guilty to the slaying, was sentenced to 99 years.

Sen. Robert F. Kennedy (D, N.Y.) 42, **shot June 5** in Hotel Ambassador, Los Angeles, after celebrating presidential primary victories. Died **June 6.** Sirhan Bishara Sirhan, Jordanian, convicted of murder.

1969

Expanded four-party **Vietnam peace talks** began **Jan. 18.** U.S. force peaked at 543,400 in April. Withdrawal started **July 8.** Pres. Nixon set Vietnamization policy **Nov. 3.**

Unarmed **U.S. reconnaissance plane,** with 31 aboard, shot down by North Korean jets **Apr. 15** in the Sea of Japan about 100 mi. from the mainland. No survivors found.

A car driven by **Sen. Edward M. Kennedy** (D, Mass.) plunged off a bridge into a tidal pool on Chappaquiddick Is., Martha's Vineyard, Mass. **July 18.** The body of Mary Jo Kopechne, a 28-year-old secretary, was found drowned in the car.

U.S. astronaut **Neil A. Armstrong,** 38, commander of the Apollo 11 mission, became the first man to **set foot on the moon July 20.** Air Force Col. Edwin E. Aldrin Jr. accompanied Armstrong.

Anti-Vietnam War **demonstrations reached peak** in U.S.; some 250,000 marched in Washington, D.C. **Nov. 15.**

Massacre of hundreds of civilians at **Mylai, South Vietnam** in 1968 incident was reported **Nov. 16.**

1970

United Mine Workers official **Joseph A. Yablonski,** his wife, and their daughter were found shot **Jan. 5** in their Clarksville, Pa. home. UMW chief W. A. (Tony) Boyle was later convicted of the killing.

A federal jury **Feb. 18** found the defendants in the **"Chicago 7"** trial innocent of conspiring to incite riots during the 1968 Democratic National Convention. However, 5 were convicted of crossing state lines with intent to incite riots.

Millions of Americans participated in anti-pollution demonstrations **Apr. 22** to mark the first **Earth Day.**

U.S. and South Vietnamese forces crossed **Cambodian** borders **Apr. 30** to get at enemy bases. Four students were killed **May 4** at **Kent St.** Univ. in Ohio by National Guardsmen during a protest against the war.

Two **women generals,** the first in U.S. history, were named by Pres. Nixon **May 15.**

A **postal reform** measure was signed **Aug. 12,** creating an independent U.S. Postal Service, thus relinquishing governmental control of the U.S. mails after almost 2 centuries.

1971

Charles Manson, 36, and 3 of his followers were found guilty **Jan. 26** of first-degree murder in the 1969 slaying of actress Sharon Tate and 6 others.

U.S. air and artillery forces aided a 44-day incursion by South Vietnam forces into **Laos** starting **Feb. 8.**

A treaty prohibiting installation of **nuclear weapons on the seabed** beyond any nation's 12-mi. coastal zone was signed by 63 nations **Feb. 11.**

A Constitutional Amendment lowering the **voting age to 18** in all elections was approved in the Senate by a vote of 94-0 **Mar. 10.** The proposed 26th Amendment got House approval by a 400-19 vote **Mar. 23.** Thirty-eighth state ratified **June 30.**

A court-martial jury of 6 officers Mar. 29, after 13 days deliberation, convicted **Lt. William L. Calley Jr.** of premeditated murder of 22 South Vietnamese at Mylai on **Mar. 16, 1968.** He was sentenced to life imprisonment **Mar. 31.** Sentence was reduced to 20 years **Aug. 20.**

Publication of classified **Pentagon papers** on the U.S. involvement in Vietnam was begun **June 13** by the New York Times. In a 6-3 vote, the U.S. Supreme Court **June 30** upheld the right of the Times and the Washington Post to publish the documents under the protection of the First Amendment.

U.S., Japan signed treaty **June 17** for return of **Okinawa I.,** seized during World War II.

Pres. Nixon began a sweeping new economic program **Aug. 15** imposing a 90-day **wage, price, and rent freeze.** He also devalued the dollar by cutting its tie with gold.

More than 1,000 N.Y. State troopers and police stormed the **Attica State Correctional Facility** where 1,200 inmates held 38 guards hostage **Sept. 13,** ending a 4-day rebellion in the maximum-security prison; 9 hostages, 28 convicts killed in the assault.

U.S. bombers struck massively in North Vietnam for 5 days starting **Dec. 26,** in retaliation for alleged violations of agreements reached prior to the 1968 bombing halt. U.S. forces at year-end were down to 140,000.

1972

Pres. Nixon arrived in **Peking Feb. 21** for an 8-day visit to China, which he called a "journey for peace." The unprecedented visit ended with a joint communique pledging that both powers would work for "a normalization of relations."

By a vote of 84 to 8, the Senate approved **Mar. 22** a Constitutional Amendment banning **discrimination against women** because of their sex and sent the measure to the states for ratification.

North Vietnamese forces launched the biggest attacks in 4 years across the demilitarized zone **Mar. 30.** The U.S. responded **Apr. 15** by resumption of bombing of Hanoi and Haiphong after a 4-year lull.

Nixon announced **May 8** the mining of **North Vietnam ports.** Last U.S. combat troops left **Aug. 11.**

Alabama Gov. George C. Wallace, campaigning at a Laurel, Md. shopping center **May 15, was shot** and seriously wounded as he greeted a large crowd. Arthur H. Bremer, 21, was sentenced Aug. 4 to 63 years for shooting Wallace and 3 bystanders.

In the first visit of a U.S. president to Moscow, Nixon arrived **May 22** for a week of summit talks with Kremlin leaders which culminated in a landmark **strategic arms pact.**

The Environmental Protection Agency announced **June 14** a near-total ban on agricultural and other uses of the pesticide **DDT,** to be effective **Dec. 31.**

Five men were arrested **June 17** for breaking into the offices of the Democratic National Committee in the **Watergate** office complex in Washington, D.C.

The White House announced **July 8** that the U.S. would sell to the USSR at least $750 million of **American wheat,** corn, and other grains over a period of 3 years. But the USSR bought most of it in 1st year.

Less than 2 weeks after **Sen. Thomas F. Eagleton** received the Democratic vice-presidential nomination, he confirmed **July 25** reports that he had undergone electroshock therapy on 2 occasions years before. He withdrew as the nominee **July 31.**

Life ended publication with its **Dec. 29** issue after 36 years as the leading weekly pictorial magazine.

1973

Five of seven defendants in the **Watergate** break-in trial pleaded guilty **Jan. 11 and 15,** and the other 2 were convicted **Jan. 30.**

All state laws that limited a woman's right to an **abortion** during the first 3 months of pregnancy were overturned **Jan. 22** by the U.S. Supreme Court 7-2.

Four-party **Vietnam peace pacts** were signed in Paris **Jan. 27,** and North Vietnam released some 590 U.S. prisoners by **Apr. 1.** Last U.S. troops left **Mar. 29.**

The **end of the military draft** was announced **Jan. 27** by Defense Sec. Melvin R. Laird.

China and the U.S. agreed **Feb. 22** to set up permanent liaison offices in each other's country.

Some 200-300 members of the militant American Indian Movement **Feb. 27** seized the trading post and church at historic **Wounded Knee** on the Oglala Sioux Reservation in South Dakota. The insurgents demanded that the U.S. Senate Foreign Relations Committee hold hearings on treaties made with Indians, and that the Senate start a "full-scale investigation" of government treatment of Indians. The hamlet was evacuated **May 8.**

Top **Nixon aides** H.R. Haldeman, John D. Ehrlichman, and John W. Dean, and Attorney General Richard Kleindienst **resigned Apr. 30** amid charges of White House efforts to obstruct justice in the Watergate case.

Soviet leader Leonid **Brezhnev visited the U.S. June 16-25,** and signed 9 cooperation agreements with the U.S.

The Federal Trade Commission **July 9** charged 8 of the largest U.S. **oil companies** with conspiracy to monopolize the refining of petroleum products. The commission said the conspiracy had led to shortages of gasoline and higher prices, and caused some independent marketers to close down.

The Senate Armed Services Committee **July 16** began a probe into allegations that the U.S. Air Force had made 3,500 secret **B-52 raids into Cambodia** in **1969** and **1970.**

John Dean, former Nixon counsel, told Senate hearings **June 25** that Nixon, his staff and campaign aides, and the Justice Department all had conspired to cover up Watergate facts. Nixon refused July 23 to release **tapes** of relevant White House conversations. Some tapes were turned over to the court **Nov. 26.**

The U.S. officially ceased bombing in **Cambodia** at midnight **Aug. 14** in accord with a June Congressional action.

Vice Pres. Spiro T. Agnew Oct. 10 resigned and pleaded "nolo contendere" (no contest) to charges of tax evasion on payments made to him by Maryland contractors. Agnew was sentenced to 3 years probation and fined $10,000. Gerald Rudolph Ford **Oct. 12** became first appointed vice president under the 25th Amendment; sworn in **Dec. 6.**

A total ban on **oil exports** to the U.S. was imposed by Arab oil-producing nations **Oct. 19-21** after the outbreak of an Arab-Israeli war. The ban was lifted **Mar. 18, 1974.**

Atty. Gen. Elliot Richardson resigned, and his deputy William D. Ruckelshaus and Watergate Special Prosecutor Archibald Cox were fired by Pres. Nixon **Oct. 20** when Cox threatened to secure a judicial ruling that Nixon was violating a court order to turn tapes over to Watergate case Judge John Sirica.

Leon Jaworski, conservative Texas Democrat, was named **Nov. 1** by the Nixon administration to be special prosecutor to succeed Archibald Cox.

Congress overrode **Nov. 7** Nixon's veto of the **war powers** bill which curbed the president's power to commit armed forces to hostilities abroad without Congressional approval.

1974

Herbert W. Kalmbach, Pres. Nixon's personal lawyer and fundraiser, pleaded guilty **Feb. 25** to promising a contributor an ambassadorship for a $100,000 contribution.

Impeachment hearings were opened **May 9** against Nixon by the House Judiciary Committee.

Ex-Atty. Gen. **Richard G. Kleindienst** pleaded guilty May 16 to a misdemeaner charge that he did not testify accurately and fully before a Congressional committee probing handling of an ITT anti-trust settlement.

John D. Ehrlichman and 3 **White House "plumbers"** were found guilty **July 12** of conspiring to violate the civil rights of Dr. Lewis Fielding, formerly psychiatrist to Pentagon Papers leaker Daniel Ellsberg, by breaking into his Beverly Hills, Cal. office.

The U.S. Supreme Court ruled, 8-0, **July 24** that Nixon had to turn over **64 tapes** of White House conversations sought by Watergate Special Prosecutor Leon Jaworski.

The House Judiciary Committee, in televised hearings **July 24-30,** recommended 3 **articles of impeachment** against Nixon. The first, voted 27-11 **July 27,** charged Nixon with taking part in a criminal conspiracy to obstruct justice in the Watergate cover-up. The second, voted 28-10 **July 29,** charged he "repeatedly" failed to carry out his constitutional oath in a series of alleged abuses of power. The third, voted 27-17 **July 30,** accused him of unconstitutional defiance of committee subpoenas. The House of Representatives voted without debate **Aug. 20,** by 412-3, to accept the committee report, which included the recommended impeachment articles.

Ex-presidential counsel **John W. Dean 3d** was sentenced **Aug. 2** to 1-3 years, on his plea of guilty of conspiring to obstruct justice.

Nixon resigned Aug. 9. His support began eroding **Aug. 5** when he released 3 tapes, admitting he originated plans to have the FBI stop its probe of the Watergate break-in for political as well as national security reasons.

An **unconditional pardon** to ex-Pres. Nixon for all federal crimes that he "committed or may have committed" while president was issued by Pres. Gerald Ford **Sept. 8.**

Charges that the Central Intelligence Agency **(CIA)** abused its powers by massive domestic operations were published **Dec. 21.**

1975

Found guilty of **Watergate** cover-up charges **Jan. 1** were ex-Atty. Gen. John N. Mitchell, ex-presidential advisers H.R. Haldeman and John D. Ehrlichman.

U.S. civilians were evacuated from **Saigon Apr. 29** as communist forces completed takeover of South Vietnam.

U.S. merchant ship **Mayaguez** and crew of 39 seized by Cambodian forces in Gulf of Siam **May 12.** In rescue operation, U.S. Marines attacked Tang Is., planes bombed air base; Cambodia surrendered ship and crew; U.S. losses were 15 killed in battle and 23 dead in a helicopter crash.

Congress voted $405 million for South **Vietnam refugees May 16;** 140,000 were flown to the U.S.

Illegal **CIA operations,** including records on 300,000 persons and groups, infiltration of agents into black, anti-war and political movements, monitoring of overseas phone calls, mail surveillance, and drug-testing, were described by a "blue-ribbon" panel headed by Vice Pres. Rockefeller **June 10.** Information on assassination plots against foreign leaders was ordered withheld by Pres. Ford.

A U.S. **Apollo** and a USSR **Soyuz** linked together 140 mi. above the Atlantic **July 17.** The crews exchanged visits and shared meals in the 2 crafts.

Two **assassination attempts** against Pres. Ford, by women in California, failed **Sept. 5 and 22.**

William L. Calley's court-martial conviction for the murder of 22 Vietnamese, overturned in lower courts, was reinstated by the U.S. Court of Appeals in New Orleans **Sept. 10.**

FBI agents captured **Patricia (Patty) Hearst,** kidnaped **Feb. 4, 1974,** in San Francisco **Sept. 18** with others. She was indicted for bank robbery; a San Francisco jury convicted her **Mar. 20, 1976.**

1976

Payments abroad of $22 million in bribes by Lockheed Aircraft Corp. to sell its planes were revealed **Feb. 4** by a Senate subcommittee. Lockheed admitted payments in Japan, Turkey, Italy, and Holland.

A mechanical respirator that had been keeping **Karen Anne Quinlan,** 22, alive for 11 months could be turned off, the New Jersey Supreme Court ruled **Mar. 31;** her parents had asked the ruling so that Karen might die "with grace and dignity." The respirator was disconnected but Karen did not die.

The U.S. celebrated its **Bicentennial July 4,** marking the 200th anniversary of its independence with festivals, parades, and N.Y. City's Operation Sail, a gathering of tall ships from around the world viewed by 6 million persons.

A mystery ailment **"legionnaire's disease"** killed 29 persons who attended an American Legion convention **July 21-24** in Philadelphia. The cause was found to be a bacterium, it was reported **June 18, 1977.**

The Viking II lander set down on **Mars'** Utopia Plains **Sept. 3,** following the successful landing by Viking I **July 20.** Photographs and other reports sent to earth by the unmanned craft showed rocks, reddish soil, light blue skies; there was evidence of possibly biological activity, and it appeared that Mars' north polar cap was frozen water.

1977

Pres. Jimmy Carter **Jan. 27** pardoned most Vietnam War **draft evaders,** who numbered some 10,000.

A **natural gas shortage** caused by severe winter weather led Congress **Feb. 2** to approve an emergency federal allocation program.

Convicted murderer **Gary Gilmore** was executed by a Utah firing squad **Jan. 17,** in the first exercise of capital punishment anywhere in the U.S. since **1967.** Gilmore had opposed all attempts to delay the execution.

Carter signed an act **Aug. 4** creating a new Cabinet-level **Energy Department.**

Carter announced **Sept. 21** that budget director **Bert Lance,** a personal friend, had resigned due to pressure over his disputed private financial practices.

A 25-point plan for action on women's rights was approved by 1,422 delegates to the first National Women's Conference in Houston, Tex., **Nov. 21.**

The FBI released, **Dec. 7,** some 40,000 pages of previously secret files on the investigation of the 1963 assassination of Pres. John F. Kennedy.

1978

Sen. Hubert H. Humphrey (D., Minn.), 66, lost a battle with cancer **Jan. 13,** after 32 years of public service, including 4 years as vice-president of the United States.

A crippling 105-day strike by the 160,000-member **United Mineworker's Union** ended **Apr. 4** with final ratification of a new contract; Pres. Carter had invoked the Taft-Hartley Act, **Mar. 6,** to attempt to end the strike, but the miners ignored the order and began going back to work **Mar. 25,** only after a contract agreement was announced.

Pres. Carter's decision, announced **Apr. 7,** to "defer production" of the controversial **neutron bomb,** drew criticism and the resignation from the Army **Apr. 28** of Maj. Gen. John K. Singlaub, who called the decision "ridiculous" and "militarily unsound."

U.S. Senate voted **Apr. 18** to turn over the **Panama Canal** to Panama on Dec. 31, 1999, by a vote of 68-32, ending several months of heated debate; an earlier vote (**Mar. 16**) had given approval to a treaty guaranteeing the area's neutrality after the year 2000.

California voters **June 6** approved (by a 65% majority) the **Proposition 13** initiative to cut property taxes in the state by 57%, thus severely limiting government spending.

The U.S. Supreme Court **June 28** voted 5-4 not to allow a firm quota system in affirmative action plans and ordered that **Alan Bakke** be admitted to a California medical school; Bakke, a white, had contended that he was a victim of "reverse discrimination"; the Court did uphold affirmative action programs that were more "flexible" in nature.

Conservative U.S. Rep. **Philip M. Crane** (R., Ill.) became first announced Republican candidate for President in 1980, **Aug. 6.**

The **House Select Committee on Assassinations** opened hearings **Sept. 6** into assassinations of Pres. Kennedy and Martin Luther King Jr.; the committee recessed **Dec. 30** after concluding conspiracies likely in both cases, but with no further hard evidence for further prosecutions.

Congress passed the **Humphrey-Hawkins "full employment" Bill Oct. 15,** which set national goal of reducing unemployment to 4% by 1983, while reducing inflation to 3% in same period; Pres. Carter signed bill, **Oct. 27.**

1979

The **last Watergate prisoner,** former Attorney General John Mitchell, was released **Jan. 19.** A total of 25 men served terms ranging from 25 days to 52½ months for Watergate crimes.

A major accident occurred, **Mar. 28,** at a nuclear reactor on **Three Mile Island** near Middletown, Pa. Radioactive gases escaped through the plant's venting system and a large hydrogen gas bubble formed in the top of the reactor containment vessel. Although the reactor cooled and the crisis was declared over **Apr. 9,** the clean-up was estimated to take 4 years.

In the worst disaster in U.S. aviation history, an American Airlines **DC-10 jetliner** lost its left engine and crashed shortly after takeoff in Chicago, **May 25,** killing 275 people.

A new **mobile intercontinental missile system,** called MX, was approved, **June 7,** by Pres. Carter. The $30-billion weapons system was designed to counter the ability of the Soviet Union's weapons to eliminate American land-based Minutemen missiles. On **Sept. 7,** Carter approved a "race-track" scheme of circular roadways for the deployment of the missiles.

Pope John Paul II, Oct. 1-6, visited the U.S. and reaffirmed traditional Roman Catholic teachings.

The federal government announced, **Nov. 1,** a $1.5 billion loan-guarantee plan to aid the nation's 3d largest automaker, **Chrysler Corp.,** which had reported a loss of $460.6 million for the 3d quarter of 1979.

Some 90 people, including 63 Americans, were taken hostage, **Nov. 3,** at the **American embassy in Teheran,** Iran, by militant students who demanded the return of former Shah Mohammad Reza Pahlavi, who was undergoing medical treatment in New York City. Pres. Carter, **Nov. 12,** suspended all Iranian oil imports to the U.S. and, **Nov. 14,** froze all official Iranian assets in American banks. After some of the hostages were released, 50 Americans at the embassy and 3 U.S. diplomats at the Iranian Foreign Ministry remained in captivity.

For events of 1980 and late 1979, See Chronology

Paleontology: The History of Life

All dates are approximate, and are subject to change based on new fossil finds or new dating techniques; but the sequence of events is generally accepted. Dates are in years before the present.

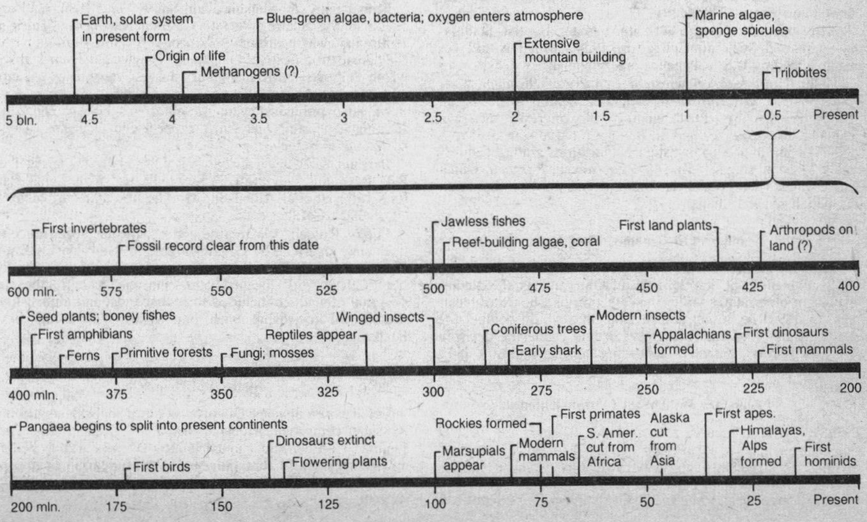

100 Years Ago

Two world leaders were assassinated in 1881. On March 1, the Russian emperor Alexander II, called the "Czar Liberator" for abolishing serfdom, was killed by a bomb thrown by members of a revolutionary terrorist organization. The son who succeeded him as Alexander III would pursue a reactionary domestic policy that included the restriction of the autonomy of peasant communes, the Russification of national minorities, and the persecution of Jews and non-Orthodox Christians. "Pogroms"—violent attacks on Jews throughout Russia—would multiply during Alexander's reign. Possibly organized by the government, certainly encouraged by official anti-Semitism, and often not interfered with by soldiers or police, the attacks would spur the emigration of millions of Jews from Russia to the U.S. during the next 30 years.

Four months after Alexander II's assassination, U.S. President James A. Garfield, in office just four months, was shot by Charles J. Guiteau, a disappointed office seeker. Garfield lingered between life and death for 80 days, which raised the constitutional question of whether Vice President Chester A. Arthur should serve as acting president, or should displace Garfield and become president. The problem remained unresolved when Garfield succumbed on September 19. Arthur became the 21st president.

Clara Barton Founds American Red Cross

Clara Barton, inspired by her work with the International Red Cross in Europe, founded the American National Red Cross in 1881. She would serve as its president until 1904. She would also campaign successfully for a U.S. signature on the Geneva treaty, which deals with the care of war wounded and prisoners of war, and would author an amendment to the International Red Cross constitution enlarging its role to include relief in times of disasters other than war.

Also in 1881, Andrew Carnegie donated funds for a Pittsburgh library, the first of his 2,800 public library donations. In all, the Pittsburgh steel tycoon's philanthropies would eventually total some $350 million.

First Black Colleges

Two pioneer schools for blacks were established in 1881. Forty students and two unequipped buildings made up the Tuskegee Normal and Industrial School in Tuskegee, Alabama, founded and headed by Booker T. Washington, then 25. Thirty-four years later at the educator's death, he would be the most prominent black in the U.S., and the school would have more than 100 buildings, more than 1,500 students, and almost 200 faculty.

Also opened was the Atlanta Female Baptist Seminary—renamed Spelman College in 1924—which would become a leading U.S. college for black women.

Helen Hunt Jackson wrote *A Century of Dishonor,* a report on U.S. government injustices in dealing with Indian tribes. She distributed it to members of Congress at her own expense. Mrs. Jackson would be appointed a year later to a federal commission to investigate conditions among California's Mission Indians. In 1884, her novel, *Ramona,* which came out of this experience, would arouse public indignation on behalf of the Indians.

Standard Oil Becomes First Trust

The first modern "trust" was created in 1881, when John D. Rockefeller put Standard Oil of Ohio and its allied companies in other states under the direction of a board of trustees. In 1892 the Supreme Court of Ohio would compel the trust to dissolve, but Rockefeller would evade the decision by transferring control to a holding company until a 1911 Supreme Court decision declared this illegal.

Legendary Wild West Outlaw Killed

Billy the Kid, reputed to have killed 21 men—the first at age 12—escaped in April from a New Mexico jail, and remained at large until gunned down July 15 by a former friend turned lawman, Pat Garrett.

That same year, Marshall Virgil Earp, his deputized brothers Wyatt and Morgan, and "Doc" Holliday, killed a gang headed by Ike Clanton in the "shootout at the O.K. Corral," outside Tombstone, in Arizona Territory. Virgil lost his marshall's job in the controversy over whether the Earps and Holliday were the good guys or the bad. After Wyatt's death in 1929 his legend as a fearless lawman would grow, although evidence to the contrary remained.

Scientific Advances

Louis Pasteur developed a vaccine to prevent anthrax in sheep and hogs; Scottish bacteriologist Jaime Ferran discovered a cholera serum; Cuban physician Carlos Finlay published a paper suggesting that yellow fever may be spread by mosquitos. Also, California judge James Harvey Logan crossed the red raspberry with a California wild blackberry: the result was named in his honor.

French Take Tunis

The French occupied Tunis, No. Africa, and established a protectorate with the Treaty of Bardo. French prime minister Jules Ferry's ardent colonialism also would be largely responsible for the acquisition of Tonkin, Madagascar, and the French Congo in 1884-1885.

Austria-Hungary joined Germany and Russia in the Three Emperors' League. The original alliance of 1873 was devised by German chancellor Otto von Bismark. Among the provisions of the 1881 treaty: no territorial changes should take place in the Balkans without prior agreement; in the event of war between one nation and another outside the treaty, the other two nations should maintain friendly neutrality. The treaty would be renewed in 1884, but end in 1887 because of continued conflicts of interest between Austria-Hungary and Russia in the Balkans.

With a victory at the Battle of Majuba Hill, the Boers, or Afrikaners—South Africans of Dutch or French Huguenot descent—regained independence from Britain in the Transvaal. In 1857 the British had officially proclaimed the area the South African Republic, but 20 years later they had annexed it. In August, 1881, the Treaty of Pretoria granted the Transvaal internal self-government, giving the British control over external relations. The Treaty would break down within a year, and the South African War between Boers and British would erupt in 1899.

Achievements in the Arts

Monet painted "Sunshine and Snow," and Renoir, "Luncheon of the Boating Party." Offenbach's opera, "Tales of Hoffman," was posthumously produced, and Brahms wrote the "Academic Festival Overture." Playwright Henrik Ibsen wrote "Ghosts," novelist Henry James, *Portrait of a Lady,* and novelist Anatole France, *The Crime of Sylvestre Bonnard.* Also published were the children's books, *Heidi,* by Johann Spyri, and *Five Little Peppers and How They Grew,* by Margaret Sidney.

Barnum & Bailey's Circus was formed by the merger of P.T. Barnum's "Greatest Show on Earth" with James Bailey's International Allied Shows. The first Parisian cabaret, "The Black Cat," opened.

Lillian Russell, 19, became a star with her appearance in the comic opera "The Great Mogul" at New York's Bijou Opera House. She would be famous for nearly 40 years for her "Gibson girl" beauty, clear soprano, and flamboyant personal life, which included four husbands, and almost four decades of friendship with bon vivant "Diamond Jim" Brady.

Births and Deaths

The Russian novelist Dostoyevsky died in 1881, as did the Russian composer Moussorgsky, the English historian Thomas Carlyle, and English statesman and writer Benjamin Disraeli. Born that year were the Hungarian composer Bela Bartok, the Austrian author Stefan Zweig, and Pablo Picasso.

WORLD HISTORY

by Barry Youngerman

Prehistory: Our Ancestors Take Over

Homo sapiens. The precise origins of *homo sapiens,* the species to which all humans belong, are subject to broad speculation based on a small number of fossils, genetic and anatomical studies, and the geological record. But nearly all scientists agree that we evolved from ape-like primate ancestors in a process that began millions of years ago.

Current theories say the first hominid (human-like primate) was *Ramapithecus,* who emerged 12 million years ago. Its remains have been found in Asia, Europe, and Africa. Further development was apparently limited to Africa, where 2 lines of hominids appeared some 5 or 6 million years ago. One was *Australopithecus,* a tool-maker and social animal, who lived from perhaps 4 to 3 million years ago, and then apparently became extinct.

The 2nd was a human line, *Homo habillus,* a large-brained specimen that walked upright and had a dextrous hand. *Homo habillus* lived in semi-permanent camps and had a food-gathering and sharing economy.

Homo erectus, our nearest ancestor, appeared in Africa perhaps 1.75 million years ago, and began spreading into Asia and Europe soon after. It had a fairly large brain and a skeletal structure similar to ours. *Homo erectus* learned to control fire, and probably had primitive language skills. The final brain development to *Homo sapiens* and then to our sub-species *Homo sapiens sapiens* occurred between 500,000 and 50,000 years ago, over a wide geographic area and in many different steps and recombinations. All humans of all races belong to this sub-species.

The spread of mankind into the remaining habitable continents probably took place during the last ice age up to 100,000 years ago: to the Americas across a land bridge from Asia, and to Australia across the Timor Straits.

Earliest cultures. A variety of cultural modes — in tool-making, diet, shelter, and possibly social arrangements and spiritual expression, arose as early mankind adapted to different geographic and climatic zones.

Three basic tool-making traditions are recognized by archeologists as arising and often coexisting from one million years ago to the near past: the *chopper tradition,* found largely in E. Asia, with crude chopping tools and simple flake tools; the *flake tradition,* found in Africa and W. Europe, with a variety of small cutting and flaking tools, and the *biface tradition,* found in all of Africa, W. and S. Europe, and S. Asia, producing pointed hand axes chipped on both faces. Later biface sites yield more refined axes and a variety of other tools, weapons, and ornaments using bone, antler, and wood as well as stone.

Only sketchy evidence remains for the different stages in man's increasing control over the environment. Traces of 400,000-year-old covered wood shelters have been found at Nice, France. Scraping tools at Neanderthal sites (200,000-30,000 BC in Europe, N. Africa, the Middle East and Central Asia) suggest the treatment of skins for clothing. Sites from all parts of the world show seasonal migration patterns and exploitation of a wide range of plant and animal food sources.

Painting and decoration, for which there is evidence at the Nice site, flourished along with stone and ivory sculpture after 30,000 years ago; 60 caves in France and 30 in Spain show remarkable examples of wall painting. Other examples have been found in Africa. Proto-religious rites are suggested by these works, and by evidence of ritual cannibalism by Peking Man, 500,000 BC, and of ritual burial with medicinal plants and flowers by Neanderthals at Shanidar in Iraq.

The Neolithic Revolution. Sometime after 10,000 BC, among widely separated human communities, a series of dramatic technological and social changes occurred that are summed up as the Neolithic Revolution. The cultivation of previously wild plants encouraged the growth of permanent settlements. Animals were domesticated as a work force and food source. The manufacture of pottery and cloth began. These techniques permitted a huge increase in world population and in human control over the earth.

No region can safely claim priority as the "inventor" of these techniques. Dispersed sites in Cen. and S. America, S.E. Europe, and the Middle East show roughly contemporaneous (10-8,000 BC) evidence of one or another "neolithic" trait. Dates near 6-3,000 BC have been given for E. and S. Asian, W. European, and sub-Saharan African neolithic remains. The variety of crops — field grains, rice, maize, and roots, and the varying mix of other traits suggest that the revolution occurred independently in all these regions.

History Begins: 4000 - 1000 BC

Near Eastern cradle. If history began with writing, the first chapter opened in Mesopotamia, the Tigris-Euphrates river valley. Clay tablets with pictographs were used by the Sumerians to keep records after 4000 BC. A **cuneiform** (wedge shaped) script evolved by 3000 BC as a full syllabic alphabet. Neighboring peoples adapted the script to their own language.

Sumerian life centered, from 4000 BC, on large cities (Eridu, Ur, Uruk, Nippur, Kish, Lagash) organized around temples and priestly bureaucracies, with the surrounding plains watered by vast irrigation works and worked with traction plows. Sailboats, wheeled vehicles, potters wheels, and kilns were used. Copper was smelted and tempered in Sumeria from c4000 BC and bronze was produced not long after. Ores, as well as precious stones and metals were obtained through long-distance ship and caravan trade. Iron was used from c2000 BC. Improved ironworking, developed partly by the **Hittites,** became widespread by 1200 BC.

Sumerian political primacy passed among cities and their kingly dynasties. Semitic-speaking peoples, with cultures derived from the Sumerian, founded a succession of dynasties that ruled in Mesopotamia and neighboring areas for most of 1800 years; among them the **Akkadians** (first under Sargon c2350 BC), the Amorites (whose laws, codified by **Hammurabi,** c1792-1750 BC, have Biblical parallels), and the Assyrians, with interludes of rule by the Hittites, Kassites, and Mitanni, all possibly Indo-Europeans. The political and cultural center of gravity shifted northwest with each successive empire.

Mesopotamian learning, maintained by scribes and preserved by successive rulers in vast libraries, was not abstract or theoretical. Algebraic and geometric problems could be solved on a practical basis in construction, commerce, or administration. Systematic lists of astronomical phenomena, plants, animals and stones were kept; medical texts listed ailments and their herbal cures.

The Sumerians worshipped anthropomorphic gods representing natural forces — Anu, god of heaven; Enlil (Ea), god of water. Epic poetry related these and other gods in a hierarchy. Sacrifices were made at **ziggurats** — huge stepped temples. Gods were thought to control all events, which could be foretold using oracular materials. This religious pattern persisted into the first millenium BC.

The Syria-Palestine area, site of some of the earliest urban remains (Jericho, 7000 BC), and of the recently uncovered **Ebla** civilization (fl. 2500 BC), experienced Egyptian cultural and political influence along with Mesopotamian. The **Phoenician** coast was an active commercial center. A phonetic alphabet was invented here before 1600 BC. It became the ancestor of all European, Middle Eastern, Indian, S.E.

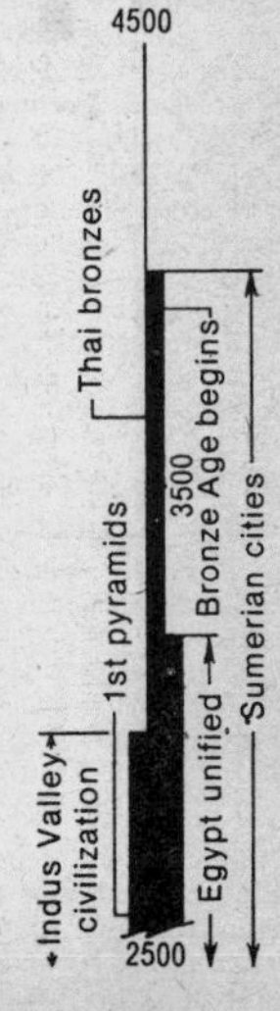

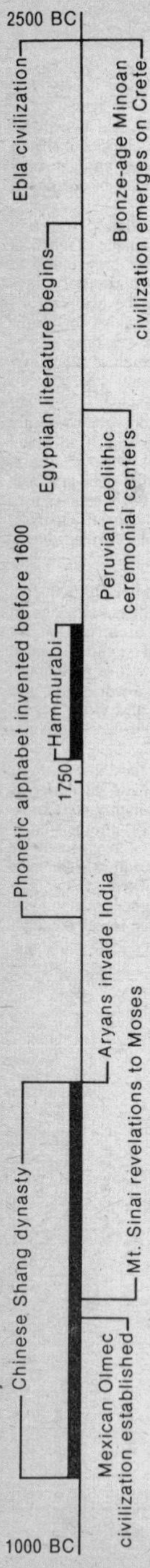

Asian, Ethiopian, and Korean alphabets.

Regional commerce and diplomacy were aided by the use of Akkadian as a *lingua franca,* later replaced by Aramaic.

Egypt. Agricultural villages along the Nile were united by 3300 BC into two kingdoms, Upper and Lower Egypt, unified under the Pharaoh Menes c3100 BC; Nubia to the south was added 2600 BC. A national bureaucracy supervised construction of canals and monuments (**pyramids** starting 2700 BC). Brilliant First Dynasty achievements in architecture, sculpture and painting, set the standards and forms for all subsequent Egyptian civilization and are still admired. **Hieroglyphic writing** appeared by 3400 BC, recording a sophisticated literature including romantic and philosophical modes after 2300 BC.

An ordered hierarchy of gods, including totemistic animal elements, was served by a powerful priesthood in Memphis. The pharaoh was identified with the falcon god Horus. Later trends were the belief in an afterlife, and the quasi-monotheistic reforms of **Akhenaton** (c1379-1362 BC).

After a period of conquest by Semitic Hyksos from Asia (c1700-1500 BC), the New Kingdom established an empire in Syria. Egypt became increasingly embroiled in Asiatic wars and diplomacy. Eventually it was conquered by Persia in 525 BC, and it faded away as an independent culture.

India. An urban civilization with a so-far-undeciphered writing system stretched across the Indus Valley and along the Arabian Sea c3000-1500 BC. Major sites are Harappa and **Mohenjo-Daro** in Pakistan, well-planned geometric cities with underground sewers and vast granaries. The entire region (600,000 sq. mi.) may have been ruled as a single state. Bronze was used, and arts and crafts were highly developed. Religious life apparently took the form of fertility cults.

Indus civilization was probably in decline when it was destroyed by **Aryan invaders** from the northwest, speaking an Indo-European language from which all the languages of Pakistan, north India and Bangladesh descend. Led by a warrior aristocracy whose legendary deeds are recorded in the **Rig Veda,** the Aryans spread east and south, bringing their pantheon of sky gods, elaborate priestly (Brahmin) ritual, and the beginnings of the caste system; local customs and beliefs were assimilated by the conquerors.

Europe. On Crete, the bronze-age **Minoan civilization** emerged c2500 BC. A prosperous economy and richly decorative art (e.g. at Knossos palace) was supported by seaborne commerce. Mycenae and other cities in Greece and Asia Minor (e.g. **Troy**) preserved elements of the culture to c1100 BC. Cretan Linear A script, c2000-1700 BC, is undeciphered; Linear B, c1300-1200 BC, records a Greek dialect.

Possible connection between Minoan-Mycenaean monumental stonework, and the great megalithic monuments and tombs of W. Europe, Iberia, and Malta (c4000-1500 BC) is unclear.

China. Proto-Chinese neolithic cultures had long covered northern and southeastern China when the first large political state was organized in the north by the **Shang dynasty** c1500 BC. Shang kings called themselves Sons of Heaven, and presided over a cult of human and animal sacrifice to ancestors and nature gods. The Chou dynasty, starting c1100 BC, expanded the area of the Son of Heaven's dominion, but feudal states exercised most temporal power.

A writing system with 2,000 different characters was already in use under the Shang, with **pictographs** later supplemented by phonetic characters. The system, with modifications, is still in use, despite changes in spoken Chinese.

Technical advances allowed urban specialists to create fine ceramic and jade products, and bronze casting after 1500 BC was the most advanced in the world.

Bronze artifacts have recently been discovered in northern Thailand dating to 3600 BC, hundreds of years before similar Middle Eastern finds.

Americas. Olmecs settled on the Gulf coast of Mexico, 1500 BC, and soon developed the first civilization in the Western Hemisphere. Temple cities and huge stone sculpture date to 1200 BC. A rudimentary calendar and writing system existed. Olmec religion, centering on a jaguar god, and art forms influenced all later Meso-American cultures.

Neolithic ceremonial centers were built on the Peruvian desert coast, c2000 BC.

Classical Era of Old World Civilizations

Greece. After a period of decline during the Dorian Greek invasions (1200-1000 BC), Greece and the Aegean area developed a unique civilization. Drawing upon Mycenaean traditions, Mesopotamian learning (weights and measures, lunisolar calendar, astronomy, musical scales), the Phoenician alphabet (modified for Greek), and Egyptian art, the revived **Greek city-states** saw a rich elaboration of intellectual life. Long-range commerce was aided by metal coinage (introduced by the Lydians in Asia Minor before 700 BC); colonies were founded around the Mediterranean and Black Sea shores (Cumae in Italy 760 BC, Massalia in France c600 BC).

Philosophy, starting with Ionian speculation on the nature of matter and the universe (Thales c634-546), and including mathematical speculation (Pythagoras c580-c500), culminated in Athens in the rationalist idealism of **Plato** (c428-347) and **Socrates** (c470-399); the latter was executed for alleged impiety. Aristotle (384-322) united all fields of study in his system. The arts were highly valued. Architecture culminated in the **Parthenon** in Athens (438, sculpture by Phidias); poetry and drama (Aeschylus 525-456) thrived. Male beauty and strength, a chief artistic theme, were enhanced at the gymnasium and the national games at Olympia.

Ruled by local tyrants or oligarchies, the Greeks were never politically united, but managed to resist inclusion in the Persian Empire (Darius defeated at Marathon 490 BC, Xerxes at Salamis, Plataea 479 BC). Local warfare was common; the **Peloponnesian Wars,** 431-404 BC, ended in Sparta's victory over Athens. Greek political power waned, but classical Greek cultural forms spread thoughout the ancient world from the Atlantic to India.

Hebrews. Nomadic Hebrew tribes entered Canaan before 1200 BC, settling among other Semitic peoples speaking the same language. They brought from the desert a **monotheistic faith** said to have been revealed to Abraham in Canaan c1800 BC and to Moses at Mt. Sinai c1250 BC, after the Hebrews' escape from bondage in Egypt. David (ruled 1000-961 BC) and Solomon (ruled 961-922 BC) united the Hebrews in a kingdom that briefly dominated the area. Phoenicians to the north established colonies

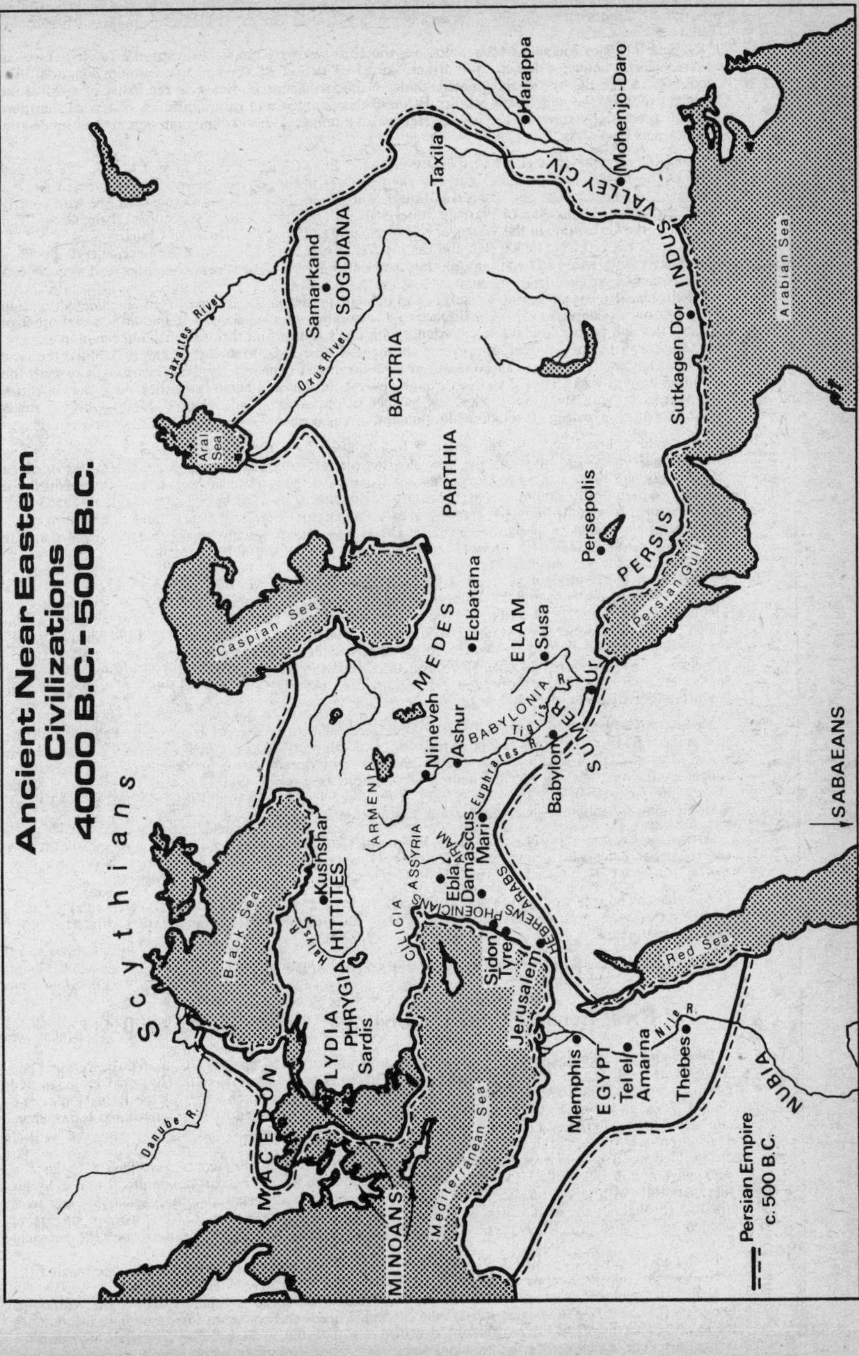
Ancient Near Eastern
Civilizations
4000 B.C.-500 B.C.
Scythians
MACEDON
MINOANS
LYDIA
PHRYGIA
Sardis
HITTITES
Kushshar
Halys R.
Black Sea
Caspian Sea
Aral Sea
Danube R.
Mediterranean Sea
CILICIA
PHOENICIANS
ASSYRIA
ARMENIA
ARAM
Ebla
Damascus
Mari
Sidon
Tyre
HEBREWS
ARABS
Jerusalem
Memphis
EGYPT
Tel el Amarna
Thebes
Nile R.
NUBIA
Red Sea
SABAEANS
Nineveh
Ashur
BABYLONIA
Tigris R.
Euphrates R.
Babylon
SUMER
Ur
MEDES
Ecbatana
ELAM
Susa
PERSIS
Persepolis
Persian Gulf
PARTHIA
BACTRIA
Oxus River
Jaxartes River
Samarkand
SOGDIANA
Taxila
Harappa
Mohenjo-Daro
INDUS VALLEY CIV.
Sutkagen Dor
Arabian Sea
Persian Empire c. 500 B.C.

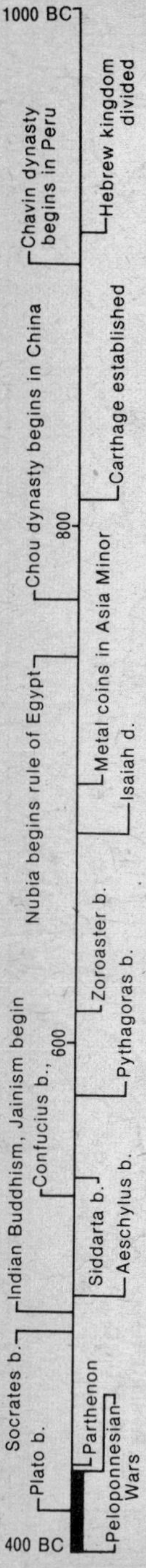

around the E. and W. Mediterranean (**Carthage** c814 BC) and sailed into the Atlantic.

A temple in Jerusalem became the national religious center, with sacrifices performed by a hereditary priesthood. Polytheistic influences, especially of the fertility cult of Baal, were opposed by **prophets** (Elijah, Amos, Isaiah).

Divided into **two kingdoms** after Solomon, the Hebrews were unable to resist the revived Assyrian empire, which conquered Israel, the northern kingdom in 722 BC. Judah, the southern kingdom, was conquered in 586 BC by the Babylonians under Nebuchadnezzar II. But with the fixing of most of the Biblical canon by the mid-fourth century BC, and the emergence of rabbis, arbiters of law and custom, Judaism successfully survived the loss of Hebrew autonomy. A Jewish kingdom was revived under the Hasmoneans (168-42 BC).

China. During the **Eastern Chou** dynasty (770-256 BC), Chinese culture spread east to the sea and south to the Yangtze. Large feudal states on the periphery of the empire contended for pre-eminence, but continued to recognize the Son of Heaven (king), who retained a purely ritual role enriched with courtly music and dance. In the Age of Warring States (403-221 BC), when the first sections of the **Great Wall** were built, the Ch'in state in the West gained supremacy, and finally united all of China.

Iron tools entered China c500 BC, and casting techniques were advanced, aiding agriculture. Peasants owned their land, and owed civil and military service to nobles. Cities grew in number and size, though barter remained the chief trade medium.

Intellectual ferment among noble scribes and officials produced the Classical Age of Chinese literature and philosophy. **Confucius** (551-479 BC) urged a restoration of a supposedly harmonious social order of the past through proper conduct in accordance with one's station and through filial and ceremonial piety. The *Analects*, attributed to him, are revered throughout East Asia. **Mencius** (d. 289 BC) added the view that the Mandate of Heaven can be removed from an unjust dynasty. The Legalists sought to curb the supposed natural wickedness of people through new institutions and harsh laws; they aided the Ch'in rise to power. The Naturalists emphasized the balance of opposites — yin, yang — in the world. **Taoists** sought mystical knowledge through meditation and disengagement.

India. The political and cultural center of India shifted from the Indus to the Ganges River Valley. Buddhism, Jainism, and mystical revisions of orthodox Vedism all developed around 500-300 BC. The *Upanishads*, last part of the *Veda*, urged escape from the illusory physical world. Vedism remained the preserve of the priestly Brahmin caste. In contrast, **Buddhism,** founded by Siddarta Gautama (c563-c483 BC), appealed to merchants in the growing urban centers, and took hold at first (and most lastingly) on the geographic fringes of Indian civilization. The classic Indian epics were composed in this era: The *Ramayana* around 300 BC, the *Mahabharata* over a period starting 400 BC.

Northern India was divided into a large number of monarchies and aristocratic republics, probably derived from tribal groupings, when the Magadha kingdom was formed in Bihar c542 BC. It soon became the dominant power. The **Maurya dynasty,** founded by Chandragupta c321 BC, expanded the kingdom, uniting most of N. India in a centralized bureaucratic empire. The third Mauryan king, **Asoka** (ruled c274-236) conquered most of the subcontinent: he converted to Buddhism, and inscribed its tenets on pillars throughout India. He downplayed the caste system and tried to end expensive sacrificial rites.

Before its final decline in India, Buddhism developed the popular worship of heavenly Bodhisatvas (enlightened beings), and produced a refined architecture (stupa—shrine—at Sanchi 100 AD) and sculpture (Gandhara reliefs 1-400 AD).

Persia. Aryan peoples (Persians, Medes) dominated the area of present Iran by the beginning of the first millenium BC. The prophet **Zoroaster** (born c628 BC) introduced a dualistic religion in which the forces of good (Ahura Mazda, Lord of Wisdom) and evil (Ahiram) battle for dominance; individuals are judged by their actions and earn damnation or salvation. Zoroaster's hymns (*Gathas*) are included in the *Avesta*, the Zoroastrian scriptures. A version of this faith became the established religion of the Persian Empire, and probably influenced later monotheistic religions.

Africa. Nubia, periodically occupied by Egypt since the third millenium, ruled Egypt c750-661, and survived as an independent Egyptianized kingdom (**Kush;** capital Meroe) for 1,000 years.

The Iron Age Nok culture flourished c500 BC-200 AD on the Benue Plateau of **Nigeria.**

Americas. The Chavin culture controlled north Peru from 900-200 BC. Its ceremonial centers, featuring the jaguar god, survived long after. Chavin architecture, ceramics, and textiles influenced other Peruvian cultures.

Mayan civilization began to develop in Central America in the 5th century BC.

Great Empires Unite the Civilized World: 400 BC - 400 AD

Persia and Alexander. Cyrus, ruler of a small kingdom in Persia from 559 BC, united the Persians and Medes within 10 years, conquered Asia Minor and Babylonia in another 10. His son Cambyses and grandson **Darius** (ruled 522-486) added vast lands to the east and north as far as the Indus Valley and Central Asia, as well as Egypt and Thrace. The whole empire was ruled by an international bureaucracy and army, with Persians holding the chief positions. The resources and styles of all the subject civilizations were exploited to create a rich syncretic art.

The Hellenized kingdom of Macedon, which under Phillip II dominated Greece, passed to his son **Alexander** in 336 BC. Within 13 years, Alexander conquered all the Persian dominions. Imbued by his tutor Aristotle with Greek ideals, Alexander encouraged Greek colonization, and Greek-style cities were founded throughout the empire (e.g. Alexandria, Egypt). After his death in 323 BC, wars of succession divided the empire into three parts — **Macedon,** Egypt (ruled by the **Ptolemies**), and the **Seleucid** Empire.

In the ensuing 300 years (the **Hellenistic Era),** a cosmopolitan Greek-oriented culture permeated the ancient world from W. Europe to the borders of India, absorbing native elites everywhere.

Hellenistic philosophy stressed the private individual's search for happiness. The Cynics followed Diogenes (c372-287), who stressed satisfaction of animal needs and contempt for social convention. Zeno (c335-c263) and the Stoics exalted reason, identified it with virtue, and counseled an ascetic disregard for misfortune. The Epicureans tried to build lives of moderate pleasure without political or emotional

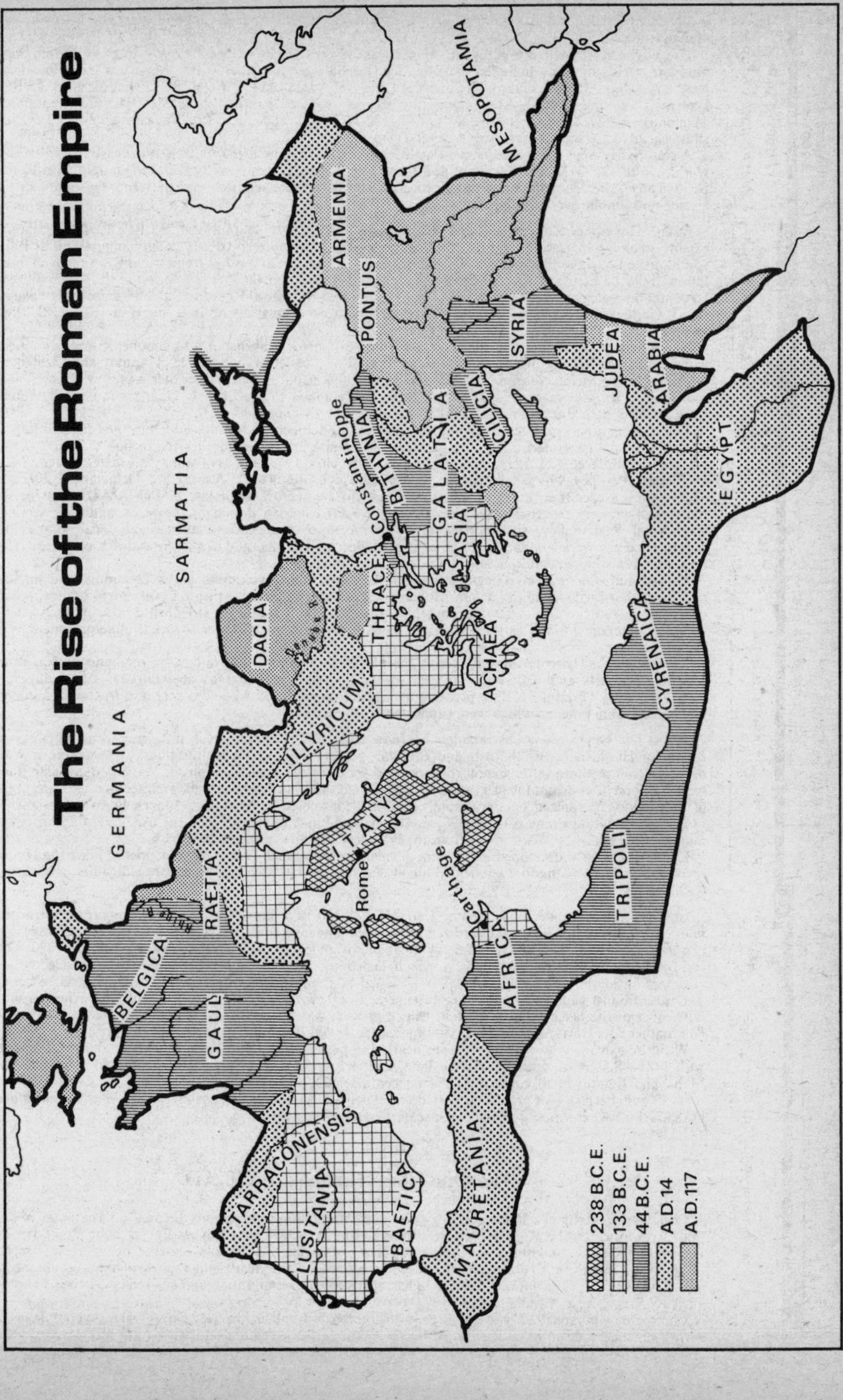
The Rise of the Roman Empire
GERMANIA
SARMATIA
DACIA
ARMENIA
MESOPOTAMIA
PONTUS
SYRIA
JUDEA
ARABIA
CILICIA
GALATIA
BITHYNIA
Constantinople
ASIA
THRACE
ACHAEA
ILLYRICUM
ITALY
Rome
Carthage
RAETIA
BELGICA
GAUL
AFRICA
TRIPOLI
CYRENAICA
EGYPT
TARRACONENSIS
LUSITANIA
BAETICA
MAURETANIA
238 B.C.E.
133 B.C.E.
44 B.C.E.
A.D. 14
A.D. 117

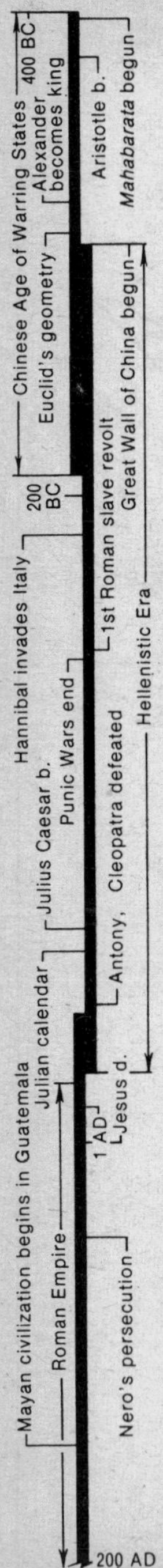

involvement. Hellenistic arts imitated life realistically, especially in sculpture and literature (comedies of Menander, 342-292).

The sciences thrived, especially at Alexandria, where the Ptolemies financed a great library and museum. Fields of study included mathematics (**Euclid's** geometry, c300 BC; Menelaus' non-Euclidean geometry, c100 AD); astronomy (heliocentric theory of Aristarchus, 310-230 BC; Julian calendar 45 BC; Ptolemy's *Almagest,* c150 AD); geography (world map of Eratosthenes, 276-194 BC); hydraulics (**Archimedes,** 287-212 BC); medicine (Galen, 130-200 AD), and chemistry. Inventors refined uses for siphons, valves, gears, springs, screws, levers, cams, and pulleys.

A restored Persian empire under the **Parthians** (N. Iranian tribesmen) controlled the eastern Hellenistic world 250 BC-229 AD. The Parthians and the succeeding Sassanian dynasty (229-651) fought with Rome periodically. The **Sassanians** revived Zoroastrianism as a state religion, and patronized a nationalistic artistic and scholarly renaissance.

Rome. The city of Rome was founded, according to legend, by Romulus in 753 BC. Through military expansion and colonization, and by granting citizenship to conquered tribes, the city annexed all of Italy south of the Po in the 100-year period before 268 BC. The Latin and other Italic tribes were annexed first, followed by the Etruscans (a civilized people north of Rome) and the Greek colonies in the south. With a large standing army and reserve forces of several hundred thousand, Rome was able to defeat Carthage in the 3 **Punic Wars,** 264-241, 218-201, 149-146 (despite the invasion of Italy by Hannibal, 218), thus gaining Sicily and territory in Spain and North Africa.

New provinces were added in the East, as Rome exploited local disputes to conquer Greece and Asia Minor in the 2d century BC, and Egypt in the first (after the defeat and suicide of **Antony and Cleopatra,** 30 BC). All the Mediterranean civilized world up to the disputed Parthian border was now Roman, and remained so for 500 years. Less civilized regions were added to the Empire: Gaul (conquered by Julius Caesar, 56-49 BC), Britain (43 AD) and Dacia NE of the Danube (117 AD).

The original aristocratic republican government, with democratic features added in the fifth and fourth centuries BC, deteriorated under the pressures of empire and class conflict (**Gracchus** brothers, social reformers, murdered 133, 121; slave revolts 135, 73). After a series of civil wars (Marius vs. Sulla 88-82, Caesar vs. Pompey 49-45, triumvirate vs. Caesar's assassins 44-43, Antony vs. Octavian 32-30), the empire came under the rule of a deified monarch (first emperor, **Augustus,** 27 BC-14 AD). Provincials (nearly all granted citizenship by Caracalla, 212 AD) came to dominate the army and civil service. Traditional Roman law, systematized and interpreted by independent jurists, and local self-rule in provincial cities were supplanted by a vast tax-collecting bureaucracy in the 3d and 4th centuries. The legal rights of women, children, and slaves were strengthened.

Roman innovations in **civil engineering** included water mills, windmills, and rotary mills, and the use of cement that hardened under water. Monumental architecture (baths, theaters, apartment houses) relied on the arch and the dome. The network of roads (some still standing) stretched 53,000 miles, passing through mountain tunnels as long as 3.5 miles. Aqueducts brought water to cities, underground sewers removed waste.

Roman art and literature were derivative of Greek models. Innovations were made in sculpture (naturalistic busts and equestrian statues), decorative wall painting (as at Pompeii), satire (Juvenal, 60-127), history (Tacitus 56-120), prose romance (Petronius, d. 66 AD). Violence and torture dominated mass public amusements, which were supported by the state.

India. The **Gupta** monarchs reunited N. India c320 AD. Their peaceful and prosperous reign saw a revival of Hindu religious thought and Brahmin power. The old Vedic traditions were combined with devotion to a plethora of indigenous deities (who were seen as manifestations of Vedic gods). **Caste lines** were reinforced, and Buddhism gradually disappeared. The art (often erotic), architecture, and literature of the period, patronized by the Gupta court, are considered to be among India's finest achievements (Kalidasa, poet and dramatist, fl. c400). Mathematical innovations included the use of zero and decimal numbers. Invasions by White Huns from the NW destroyed the empire c550.

Rich cultures also developed in S. India in this era. Emotional Tamil religious poetry aided the Hindu revival. The Pallava kingdom controlled much of S. India c350-880, and helped spread Indian civilization to S.E. Asia.

China. The Ch'in ruler Shih Huang Ti (ruled 221-210 BC), known as the First Emperor, centralized political authority in China, standardized the written language, laws, weights, measures, and coinage, and conducted a census, but tried to destroy most philosophical texts. The **Han dynasty** (206 BC-220 AD) instituted the Mandarin bureaucracy, which lasted for 2,000 years. Local officials were selected by examination in the Confucian classics and trained at the imperial university and at provincial schools. The invention of **paper** facilitated this bureaucratic system. Agriculture was promoted, but the peasants bore most of the tax burden. Irrigation was improved; water clocks and sundials were used; astronomy and mathematics thrived; landscape painting was perfected.

With the expansion south and west (to nearly the present borders of today's China), trade was opened with India, S.E. Asia, and the Middle East, over sea and caravan routes. Indian missionaries brought Mahayana Buddhism to China by the first century AD, and spawned a variety of sects. Taoism was revived, and merged with popular superstitions. Taoist and Buddhist monasteries and convents multiplied in the turbulent centuries after the collapse of the Han dynasty.

The One God Triumphs: 1-750 AD

Christianity. Religions indigenous to particular Middle Eastern nations became international in the first 3 centuries of the Roman Empire. Roman citizens worshipped **Isis** of Egypt, **Mithras** of Persia, **Demeter** of Greece, and the great mother **Cybele** of Phrygia. Their cults centered on mysteries (secret ceremonies) and the promise of an afterlife, symbolized by the death and rebirth of the god. Judaism, which had begun as the national cult of Judea, also spread by emigration and conversion. It was the only ancient religion west of India to survive.

Christians, who emerged as a distinct sect in the second half of the 1st century AD, revered **Jesus,** a Jewish preacher said to have been killed by the Romans at the request of Jewish authorities in Jerusalem c30 AD. They considered him the Savior (Messiah, or Christ) who rose from the dead and could grant eternal life to the faithful, despite their sinfulness. They believed he was an incarnation of the one god worshipped by the Jews, and that he would return soon to pass final judgment on the world. The missionary activities of such early leaders as **Paul of Tarsus** spread the faith, at first mostly among Jews or among quasi-Jews attracted by the Pauline rejection of such difficult Jewish laws as circumcision. Intermittent persecution, as in Rome under Nero in 64 AD, on grounds of suspected disloyalty, failed to disrupt the Christian communities. Each congregation, generally urban and of plebeian character, was tightly organized under a leader (bishop) elders (presbyters or priests), and assistants (deacons). Stories about Jesus (the Gospels) and the early church (Acts) were written down in the late first and early 2d centuries, and circulated along with letters of Paul. An authoritative canon of these writings was not fixed until the 4th century.

A school for priests was established at Alexandria in the second century. Its teachers (**Origen** c182-251) helped define Christian doctrine and promote the faith in Greek-style philosophical works. Pagan Neoplatonism was given Christian coloration in the works of Church Fathers such as Augustine (354-430). Christian hermits, often drawn from the lower classes, began to associate in monasteries, first in Egypt (St. Pachomius c290-345), then in other eastern lands, then in the West (**St. Benedict's rule,** 529). Popular adoration of saints, especially Mary, mother of Jesus, spread.

Under **Constantine** (ruled 306-337), Christianity became in effect the established religion of the Empire. Pagan temples were expropriated, state funds were used to build huge churches and support the hierarchy, and laws were adjusted in accordance with Christian notions. Pagan worship was banned by the end of the fourth century, and severe restrictions were placed on Judaism.

The newly established church was rocked by doctrinal disputes, often exacerbated by regional rivalries both within and outside the Empire. Chief heresies (as defined by church councils backed by imperial authority) were **Arianism,** which denied the divinity of Jesus; **Donatism,** which rejected the convergence of church and state and denied the validity of sacraments performed by sinful clergy; and the **Monophysite** position denying the dual nature of Christ.

Judaism. First century Judaism embraced several sects, including: the **Sadducees,** mostly drawn from the Temple priesthood, who were culturally Hellenized; the **Pharisees,** who upheld the full range of traditional customs and practices as of equal weight to literal scriptural law, and elaborated synagogue worship; and the **Essenes,** an ascetic, millenarian sect. Messianic fervor led to repeated, unsuccessful rebellions against Rome (66-70, 135). As a result, the Temple was destroyed, and the population decimated.

To avoid the dissolution of the faith, a program of codification of law was begun at the academy of Yavneh. The work continued for some 500 years in Palestine and Babylonia, ending in the final redaction of the **Talmud** (c600), a huge collection of legal and moral debates, rulings, liturgy, Biblical exegesis, and legendary materials.

Islam. The earliest Arab civilization emerged by the end of the 2d millenium BC in the watered highlands of Yemen. Seaborne and caravan trade in frankincense and myrrh connected the area with the Nile and Fertile Crescent. The Minaean, Sabean (Sheba), and Himyarite states successively held sway. By Mohammed's time (7th century AD), the region was a province of Sassanian Persia. In the North, the **Nabataean kingdom** at Petra and the kingdom of Palmyra were first Aramaicized and then Romanized, and finally absorbed like neighboring Judea into the Roman Empire. Nomads shared the central region with a few trading towns and oases. Wars between tribes and raids on settled communities were common, and were celebrated in a poetic tradition that by the 6th century helped establish a classic literary Arabic.

In 611 **Mohammed,** a wealthy 40-year-old Arab of Mecca, had a revelation from Allah, the one true god, calling on him to repudiate pagan idolatry. Drawing on elements of Judaism and Christianity, and eventually incorporating some Arab pagan traditions (such as reverence for the black stone at the kaaba shrine in Mecca), Mohammed's teachings, recorded in the **Koran,** forged a new religion, Islam (submission to Allah). Opposed by the leaders of Mecca, Mohammed made a *hejira* (migration) to Medina to the north in 622, the beginning of the Moslem lunar calendar. He and his followers defeated the Meccans in 624 in the first *jihad* (holy war), and by his death (632), nearly all the Arabian peninsula accepted his religious and secular leadership.

Under the first two **caliphs** (successors) Abu Bakr (632-34) and Oman (634-44), Moslem rule was confirmed over Arabia. Raiding parties into Byzantine and Persian border areas developed into campaigns of conquest against the two empires, which had been weakened by wars and by disaffection among subject peoples (including Coptic and Syriac Christians opposed to the Byzantine orthodox church). Syria, Palestine, Egypt, Iraq, and Persia all fell to the inspired Arab armies. The Arabs at first remained a distinct minority, using non-Moslems in the new administrative system, and tolerating Christians, Jews, and Zoroastrians as self-governing "Peoples of the Book," whose taxes supported the empire.

Disputes over the succession, and puritan reaction to the wealth and refinement that empire brought to the ruling strata, led to the growth of schismatic movements. The followers of Mohammed's son-in-law Ali (assassinated 661) and his descendants became the founders of the more mystical **Shi'ite** sect, still the largest non-orthodox Moslem sect. The Karijites, puritanical, militant, and egalitarian, persist as a minor sect to the present.

Under the **Ummayad** caliphs (661-750), the boundaries of Islam were extended across N. Africa and into Spain. Arab armies in the West were stopped at Tours in 732 by the Frank **Charles Martel.** Asia Minor, the Indus Valley, and Transoxiana were conquered in the East. The vast majority of the subject population gradually converted to Islam, encouraged by tax and career privileges. The Arab language supplanted the local tongues in the central and western areas, but Arab soldiers and rulers in the East eventually became assimilated to the indigenous languages.

New Peoples Enter History: 400-900

Barbarian invasions. Germanic tribes infiltrated S and E from their Baltic homeland during the 1st millenium BC, reaching S. Germany by 100 BC and the Black Sea by 214 AD. Organized into large federated tribes under elected kings, most resisted Roman domination and raided the empire in time of civil war (Goths took Dacia 214, raided Thrace 251-269). German troops and commanders came to dominate the Roman armies by the end of the 4th century. **Huns,** invaders from Asia, entered Europe 372, driving more Germans into the western empire. Emperor Valens allowed Visigoths to cross

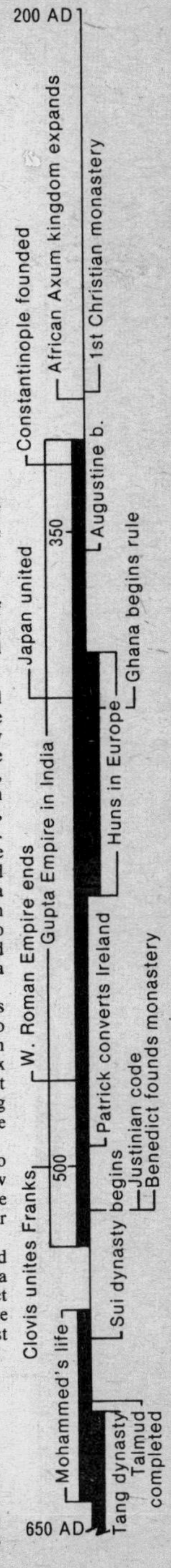

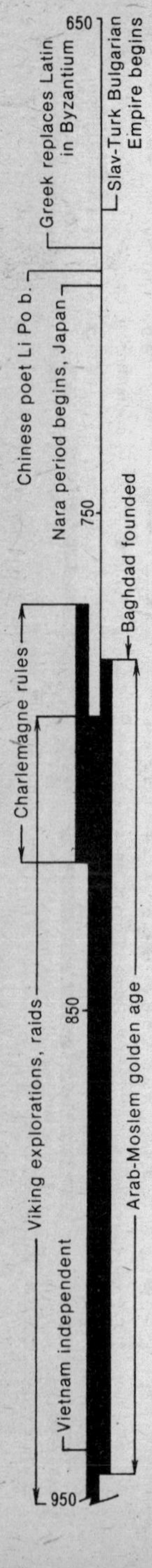

the Danube 376. Huns under Attila (d. 453) raided Gaul, Italy, Balkans. The western empire, weakened by overtaxation and social stagnation, was overrun in the 5th century. Gaul was effectively lost 406-7, Spain 409, Britain 410, Africa 429-39. Rome itself was sacked 410 by Visigoths under Alaric, 455 by Vandals. The last western emperor, Romulus Augustulus, was deposed 476 by the Germanic chief Odoacer.

Celts. Celtic cultures, which in pre-Roman times covered most of W. Europe, were confined almost entirely to the British Isles after the Germanic invasions. **St. Patrick** completed the conversion of Ireland (c457-92). A strong monastic tradition took hold. Irish monastic missionaries in Scotland, England, and the continent (Columba c521-597; Columban c543-615) helped restore Christianity after the Germanic invasions. The monasteries became renowned centers of classic and Christian learning, and presided over the recording of a Christianized Celtic mythology, elaborated by secular writers and bards. An intricate decorative art style developed, especially in book illumination (Lindisfarne Gospels, c700, Book of Kells, 8th century).

Successor states. The Visigoth kingdom in Spain (from 419) and much of France (to 507) saw a continuation of much Roman administration, language, and law (Breviary of Alaric 506), until its destruction by the Moslems, 711. The Vandal kingdom in Africa, from 429, was conquered by the Byzantines, 533. Italy was ruled in succession by an Ostrogothic kingdom under Byzantine suzerainty 489-554, direct Byzantine government, and the German Lombards (568-774). The latter divided the peninsula with the Byzantines and the papacy under the dynamic reformer Pope Gregory the Great (590-604) and his successors.

King Clovis (ruled 481-511) united the Franks on both sides of the Rhine, and after his conversion to orthodox Christianity, defeated the Arian Burgundians (after 500) and Visigoths (507) with the support of the native clergy and the papacy. Under the **Merovingian** kings a feudal system emerged: power was fragmented among hierarchies of military landowners. Social stratification, which in late Roman times had acquired legal, hereditary sanction, was reinforced. The Carolingians (747-987) expanded the kingdom and restored central power. **Charlemagne** (ruled 768-814) conquered nearly all the Germanic lands, including Lombard Italy, and was crowned Emperor by Pope Leo III in Rome in 800. A centuries-long decline in commerce and the arts was reversed under Charlemagne's patronage. He welcomed Jews to his kingdom, which became a center of Jewish learning (Rashi 1040-1105). He sponsored the "Carolingian Renaissance" of learning under the Anglo-Latin scholar Alcuin (c732-804), who reformed church liturgy.

Byzantine Empire. Under Diocletian (ruled 284-305) the empire had been divided into 2 parts to facilitate administration and defense. Constantine founded **Constantinople,** 330, (at old Byzantium) as a fully Christian city. Commerce and taxation financed a sumptuous, orientalized court, a class of hereditary bureaucratic families, and magnificent urban construction (Hagia Sophia, 532-37). The city's fortifications and naval innovations (Greek fire) repelled assaults by Goths, Huns, Slavs, Bulgars, Avars, Arabs, and Scandinavians. Greek replaced Latin as the official language by c700. Byzantine art, a solemn, sacral, and stylized variation of late classical styles (mosaics at S. Vitale, Ravenna, 526-48) was a starting point for medieval art in E. and W. Europe.

Justinian (ruled 527-65) reconquered parts of Spain, N. Africa, and Italy, codified Roman law (*codex Justinianus,* 529, was medieval Europe's chief legal text), closed the Platonic Academy at Athens and ordered all pagans to convert. Lombards in Italy, Arabs in Africa retook most of his conquests. The Isaurian dynasty from Anatolia (from 717) and the Macedonian dynasty (867-1054) restored military and commercial power. The Iconoclast controversy (726-843) over the permissibility of images, helped alienate the Eastern Church from the papacy.

Arab Empire. Baghdad, founded 762, became the seat of the **Abbasid** Caliphate (founded 750), while Ummayads continued to rule in Spain. A brilliant cosmopolitan civilization emerged, inaugurating an Arab-Moslem golden age. Arab lyric poetry revived; Greek, Syriac, Persian, and Sanskrit books were translated into Arabic, often by Syriac Christians and Jews, whose theology and Talmudic law, respectively, influenced Islam. The arts and music flourished at the court of **Harun al-Rashid** (786-809), celebrated in *The Arabian Nights.* The sciences, medicine, and mathematics were pursued at Baghdad, Cordova, and Cairo (founded 969). Science and Aristotelian philosophy culminated in the systems of Avicenna (980-1037), Averroes (1126-98), and Maimonides (1135-1204), a Jew; all influenced later Christian scholarship and theology. The Islamic ban on images encouraged a sinuous, geometric decorative tradition, applied to architecture and illumination. A gradual loss of Arab control in Persia (from 874) led to the capture of Baghdad by Persians, 945. By the next century, Spain and N. Africa were ruled by Berbers, while Turks prevailed in Asia Minor and the Levant. The loss of political power by the caliphs allowed for the growth of non-orthodox trends, especially the mystical **Sufi** tradition (theologian Ghazali, 1058-1111).

Africa. Immigrants from Saba in S. Arabia helped set up the **Axum** kingdom in Ethiopia in the 2d century (their language, Ge'ez, is preserved by the Ethiopian Church). In the 4th century, when the kingdom became Christianized, it defeated Kushite Meroe and expanded into Yemen. Axum was the center of a vast ivory trade; it controlled the Red Sea coast until c1100. Arab conquest in Egypt cut Axum's political and economic ties with Byzantium.

The Iron Age entered W. Africa by the end of the 1st millenium BC. **Ghana,** the first known sub-Saharan state, ruled in the upper Senegal-Niger region c400-1240, controlling the trade of gold from mines in the S to trans-Sahara caravan routes to the N. The **Bantu** peoples, probably of W. African origin, began to spread E and S perhaps 2000 years ago, displacing the Pygmies and Bushmen of central and southern Africa over a 1,500-year period.

Japan. The advanced Neolithic Yayoi period, when irrigation, rice farming, and iron and bronze casting techniques were introduced from China or Korea, persisted to c400 AD. The myriad Japanese states were then united by the **Yamato** clan, under an emperor who acted as the chief priest of the animistic **Shinto** cult. Japanese political and military intervention in Korea by the 6th century quickened a Chinese cultural invasion, bringing Buddhism, the Chinese language (which long remained a literary and governmental medium), Chinese ideographs and Buddhist styles in painting, sculpture, literature, and architecture (7th c. Horyu-ji temple at Nara). The Taika Reforms, 646, tried to centralize Japan according to Chinese bureaucratic and Buddhist philosophical values, but failed to curb traditional Japanese decentralization. A nativist reaction against the Buddhist **Nara period** (710-94) ushered in the

Heian period (794-1185) centered at the new capital, Kyoto. Japanese elegance and simplicity modified Chinese styles in architecture, scroll painting, and literature; the writing system was also simplified. The courtly novel *Tale of Genji* (1010-20) testifies to the enhanced role of women.

Southeast Asia. The historic peoples of southeast Asia began arriving some 2500 years ago from China and Tibet, displacing scattered aborigines. Their agriculture relied on rice and tubers (yams), which they may have introduced to Africa. Indian cultural influences were strongest; literacy and Hindu and Buddhist ideas followed the southern India-China trade route. From the southern tip of Indochina, the kingdom of **Funan** (1st-7th centuries) traded as far west as Persia. It was absorbed by Chenla, itself conquered by the **Khmer Empire** (600-1300). The Khmers, under Hindu god-kings (Suryavarman II, 1113-c1150), built the monumental Angkor Wat temple center for the royal phallic cult. The **Nam-Viet** kingdom in Annam, dominated by China and Chinese culture for 1,000 years, emerged in the 10th century, growing at the expense of the Khmers, who also lost ground in the NW to the new, highly-organized **Thai** kingdom. On Sumatra, the **Srivijaya** Empire at Palembang controlled vital sea lanes (7th to 10th centuries). A Buddhist dynasty, the Sailendras, ruled central **Java** (8th-9th centuries), building at Borobudur one of the largest stupas in the world.

China. The short-lived Sui dynasty (581-618) ushered in a period of commercial, artistic, and scientific achievement in China, continuing under the **T'ang** dynasty (618-906). Such inventions as the magnetic compass, gunpowder, the abacus, and printing were introduced or perfected. Medical innovations included cataract surgery. The state, from the cosmopolitan capital, Ch'ang-an, supervised foreign trade which exchanged Chinese silks, porcelains, and art works for spices, ivory, etc., over Central Asian caravan routes and sea routes reaching Africa. A golden age of poetry bequeathed tens of thousands of works to later generations (Tu Fu 712-70, Li Po 701-62). Landscape painting flourished. Commercial and industrial expansion continued under the **Northern Sung** dynasty (960-1126), facilitated by paper money and credit notes. But commerce never achieved respectability; government monopolies expropriated successful merchants. The population, long stable at 50 million, doubled in 200 years with the introduction of early-ripening rice and the double harvest. In art, native Chinese styles were revived.

Americas. An Indian empire stretched from the Valley of Mexico to Guatemala, 300-600, centering on the huge city **Teotihuacan** (founded 100 BC). To the S, in Guatemala, a high **Mayan** civilization developed, 150-900, around hundreds of rural ceremonial centers. The Mayans improved on Olmec writing and the calendar, and pursued astronomy and mathematics (using the idea of zero). In S. America, a widespread pre-Inca culture grew from **Tiahuanaco** near Lake Titicaca (Gateway of the Sun, c700).

Christian Europe Regroups and Expands: 900-1300

Scandinavians. Pagan Danish and Norse (**Viking**) adventurers, traders, and pirates raided the coasts of the British Isles (Dublin founded c831), France, and even the Mediterranean for over 200 years beginning in the late 8th century. Inland settlement in the W was limited to Great Britain (King Canute, 994-1035) and Normandy, settled under Rollo, 911, as a fief of France. Other Vikings reached Iceland (874), Greenland (c986), and probably N. America (Leif Eriksson c1000). Norse traders (**Varangians**) developed Russian river commerce from the 8th-11th centuries, and helped set up a state at Kiev in the late 9th century. Conversion to Christianity occurred during the 10th century, reaching Sweden 100 years later. Eleventh century Norman bands conquered S. Italy and Sicily. Duke **William of Normandy** conquered England, 1066, bringing continental feudalism and the French language, essential elements in later English civilization.

East Europe. Slavs inhabited areas of E. Central Europe in prehistoric times, and reached most of their present limits by c850. The first Slavic states were in the Balkans (Slav-Turk **Bulgarian Empire,** 680-1018) and Moravia (628). Missions of St. Cyril (whose Greek-based Cyrillic alphabet is still used by S. and E. Slavs) converted Moravia, 863. The Eastern Slavs, part-civilized under the overlordship of the Turkish-Jewish **Khazar** trading empire (7th-10th centuries), gravitated toward Constantinople by the 9th century. The **Kievan state** adopted Eastern Christianity under Prince Vladimir, 989. King Boleslav I (992-1025) began **Poland's** long history of eastern conquest. The Magyars (**Hungarians**) in Europe since 896, accepted Latin Christianity, 1001.

Germany. The German kingdom that emerged after the breakup of Charlemagne's Empire remained a confederation of largely autonomous states. The Saxon Otto I, king from 936, established the **Holy Roman Empire** of Germany and Italy in alliance with Pope John XII, who crowned him emperor, 962; he defeated the Magyars, 955. Imperial power was greatest under the **Hohenstaufens** (1138-1254), despite the growing opposition of the papacy, which ruled central Italy, and the Lombard League cities. Frederick II (1194-1250) improved administration, patronized the arts; after his death German influence was removed from Italy.

Christian Spain. From its northern mountain redoubts, Christian rule slowly migrated south through the 11th century, when Moslem unity collapsed. After the capture of **Toledo** (1085), the kingdoms of Portugal, Castile, and Aragon undertook repeated crusades of reconquest, finally completed in 1492. Elements of Islamic civilization persisted in recaptured areas, influencing all W. Europe.

Crusades. Pope Urban II called, 1095, for a crusade to restore Asia Minor to Byzantium and conquer the Holy Land from the Turks. Some 10 crusades (to 1291) succeeded only in founding 4 temporary Frankish states in the Levant. The 4th crusade sacked Constantinople, 1204. In Rhineland (1096), England (1290), France (1306), Jews were massacred or expelled, and wars were launched against Christian heretics (**Albigensian** crusade in France, 1229). Trade in eastern luxuries expanded, led by the Venetian naval empire.

Economy. The agricultural base of European life benefitted from improvements in **plow design** c1000, and by draining of lowlands and clearing of forests, leading to a rural population increase. Towns grew in N. Italy, Flanders, and N. Germany (Hanseatic League). Improvements in **loom design** permitted factory textile production. **Guilds** dominated urban trades from the 12th century. Banking (centered in Italy, 12th-15th century) facilitated long-distance trade.

The Church. The split between the Eastern and Western churches was formalized in 1054. W. and

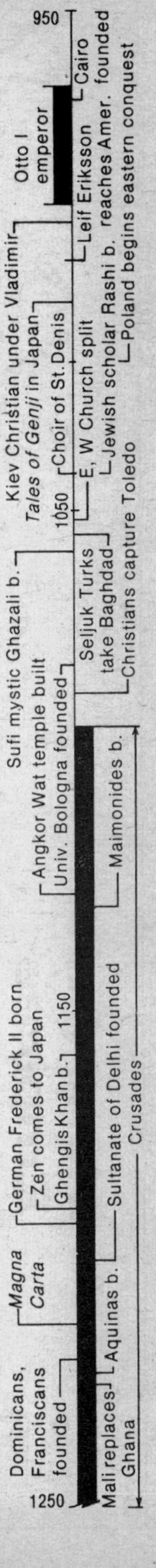

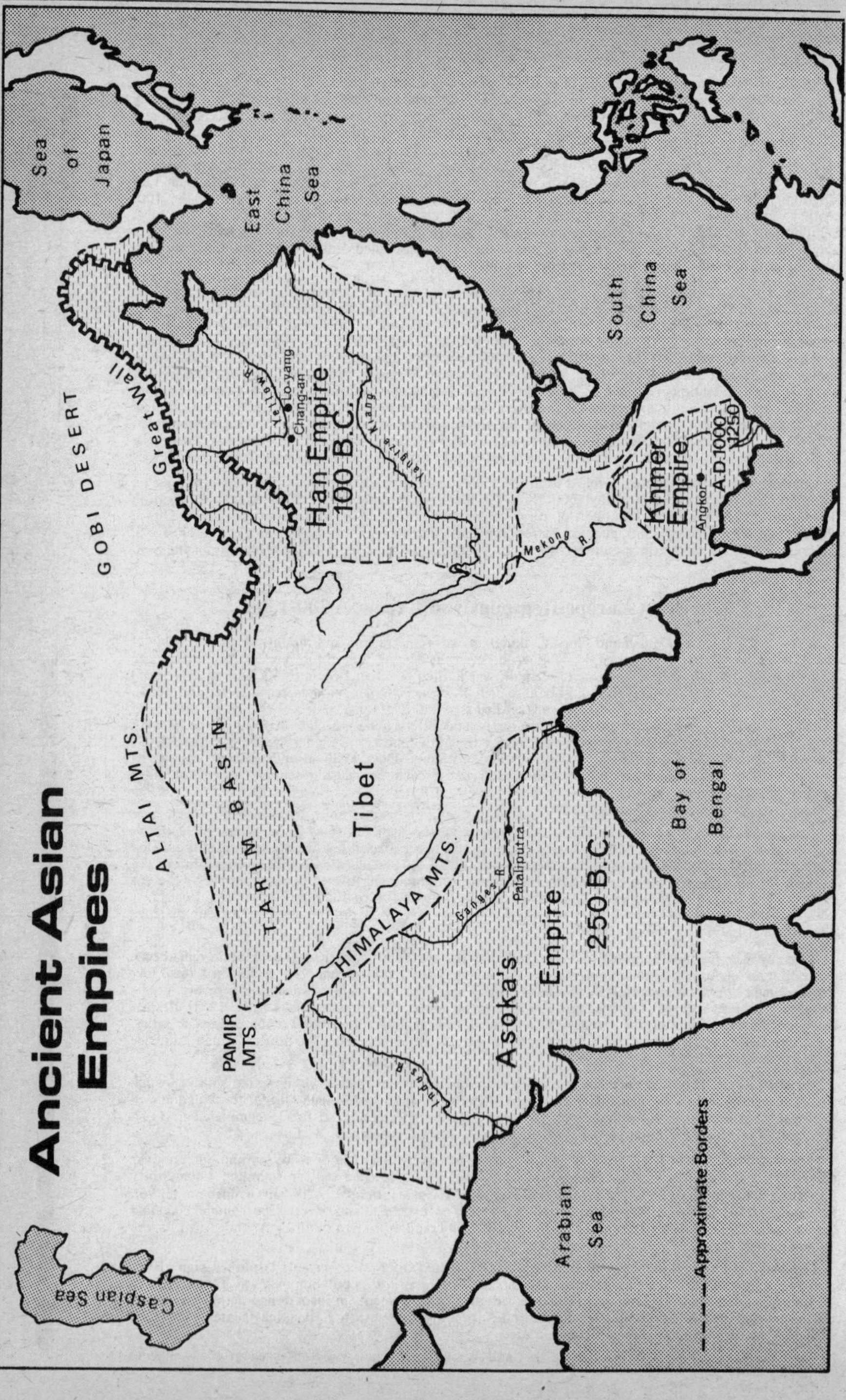
Ancient Asian Empires
Sea of Japan
East China Sea
South China Sea
Bay of Bengal
Arabian Sea
Caspian Sea
GOBI DESERT
Great Wall
Yellow R.
Lo-yang
Chang-an
Han Empire 100 B.C.
Yangtze Kiang
Mekong R.
Khmer Empire A.D.1000-1250
Angkor
ALTAI MTS.
TARIM BASIN
Tibet
HIMALAYA MTS.
Ganges R.
Pataliputra
Asoka's Empire 250 B.C.
PAMIR MTS.
Indus R.
Approximate Borders

Central Europe was divided into 500 bishoprics under one united hierarchy, but conflicts between secular and church authorities were frequent (German **Investiture Controversy,** 1075-1122). Clerical power was first strengthened through the international monastic reform begun at Cluny, 910. Popular religious enthusiasm often expressed itself in heretical movements (Waldensians from 1173), but was channelled by the **Dominican** (1215) and **Franciscan** (1223) friars into the religious mainstream.

Arts. Romanesque architecture (11th-12th centuries) expanded on late Roman models, using the rounded arch and massed stone to support enlarged basilicas. Painting and sculpture followed Byzantine models. The literature of **chivalry** was exemplified by the epic (Chanson de Roland, c1100) and by courtly love poems of the troubadours of Provence and minnesingers of Germany. **Gothic architecture** emerged in France (choir of St. Denis, c1040) and spread as French cultural influence predominated in Europe. Rib vaulting and pointed arches were used to combine soaring heights with delicacy, and freed walls for display of stained glass. Exteriors were covered with painted relief sculpture and elaborate architectural detail.

Learning. Law, medicine, and philosophy were advanced at independent **universities** (Bologna, late 11th century), originally corporations of students and masters. Twelfth century translations of Greek classics, especially Aristotle, encouraged an analytic approach. Scholastic philosophy, from Anselm (1033-1109) to Aquinas (1225-74) attempted to reconcile reason and revelation.

Apogee of Central Asian Power; Islam Grows: 1250-1500

Turks. Turkic peoples, of Central Asian ancestry, were a military threat to the Byzantine and Persian Empires from the 6th century. After several waves of invasions, during which most of the Turks adopted Islam, the **Seljuk Turks** took Baghdad, 1055. They ruled Persia, Iraq, and, after 1071, Asia Minor, where massive numbers of Turks settled. The empire was divided in the 12th century into smaller states ruled by Seljuks, Kurds (**Saladin** c1137-93), and Mamelukes (a military caste of former Turk, Kurd, and Circassian slaves), which governed Egypt and the Middle East until the Ottoman era (c1290-1922).

Osman I (ruled c1290-1326) and succeeding sultans united Anatolian Turkish warriors in a militaristic state that waged holy war against Byzantium and Balkan Christians. Most of the Balkans had been subdued, and Anatolia united, when **Constantinople fell,** 1453. By the mid-16th century, Hungary, the Middle East, and North Africa had been conquered. The Turkish advance was stopped at Vienna, 1529, and at the naval battle of Lepanto, 1571, by Spain, Venice, and the papacy.

The Ottoman state was governed in accordance with orthodox Moslem law. Greek, Armenian, and Jewish communities were segregated, and ruled by religious leaders responsible for taxation; they dominated trade. State offices and most army ranks were filled by slaves through a system of child conscription among Christians.

India. Mahmud of Ghazni (971-1030) led repeated Turkish raids into N. India. Turkish power was consolidated in 1206 with the start of the **Sultanate at Delhi.** Centralization of state power under the early Delhi sultans went far beyond traditional Indian practice. Moslem rule of most of the subcontinent lasted until the British conquest some 600 years later.

Mongols. Genghis Khan (c1162-1227) first united the feuding Mongol tribes, and built their armies into an effective offensive force around a core of highly mobile cavalry. He and his immediate successors created the largest land empire in history; by 1279 it stretched from the east coast of Asia to the Danube, from the Siberian steppes to the Arabian Sea. East-West trade and contacts were facilitated (Marco Polo c1254-1324). The western Mongols were Islamized by 1295; successor states soon lost their Mongol character by assimilation. They were briefly reunited under the Turk Tamerlane (1336-1405).

Kublai Khan ruled China from his new capital Peking (founded 1264). Naval campaigns against Japan (1274, 1281) and Java (1293) were defeated, the latter by the Hindu-Buddhist maritime kingdom of Majapahit. The **Yuan** dynasty made use of Mongols and other foreigners (including Europeans) in official posts, and tolerated the return of Nestorian Christianity (suppressed 841-45) and the spread of Islam in the South and West. A native reaction expelled the Mongols, 1367-68.

Russia. The Kievan state in Russia, weakened by the decline of Byzantium and the rise of the Catholic Polish-Lithuanian state, was overrun by the Mongols, 1238-40. Only the northern trading republic of Novgorod remained independent. The grand dukes of Moscow emerged as leaders of a coalition of princes that eventually defeated the Mongols, by 1481. With the fall of Constantinople, the **Tsars** (Caesars) at Moscow (from Ivan III, ruled 1462-1505) set up an independent Russian Orthodox Church. Commerce failed to revive. The isolated Russian state remained agrarian, with the peasant class falling into serfdom.

Persia. A revival of Persian literature, using the Arab alphabet and literary forms, began in the 10th century (epic of Firdausi, 935-1020). An art revival, influenced by Chinese styles, began in the 12th. Persian cultural and political forms, and often the Persian language, were used for centuries by Turkish and Mongol elites from the Balkans to India. Persian mystics from Rumi (1207-73) to Jami (1414-92) promoted **Sufism** in their poetry.

Africa. Two Berber dynasties, imbued with Islamic militance, emerged from the Sahara to carve out empires from the Sahel to central Spain — the **Almoravids,** c1050-1140, and the fanatical **Almohads,** c1125-1269. The Ghanaian empire was replaced in the upper Niger by Mali, c1230-c1340, whose Moslem rulers imported Egyptians to help make **Timbuktu** a center of commerce (in gold, leather, slaves) and learning. The Songhay empire (to 1590) replaced Mali. To the S, forest kingdoms produced refined art works (Ife terra cotta, **Benin** bronzes). Other Moslem states in Nigeria (Hausas) and Chad originated in the 11th century, and continued in some form until the 19th century European conquest. Less developed Bantu kingdoms existed across central Africa.

Some 40 Moslem Arab-Persian trading colonies and city-states were established all along the E. African coast from the 10th century (Kilwa, Mogadishu). The interchange with Bantu peoples produced the **Swahili** language and culture. Gold, palm oil, and slaves were brought from the interior, stimulating the growth of the Monamatapa kingdom of the Zambezi (15th century). The Christian Ethiopian empire (from 13th century) continued the traditions of Axum.

Southeast Asia. Islam was introduced into Malaya and the Indonesian islands by Arab, Persian, and

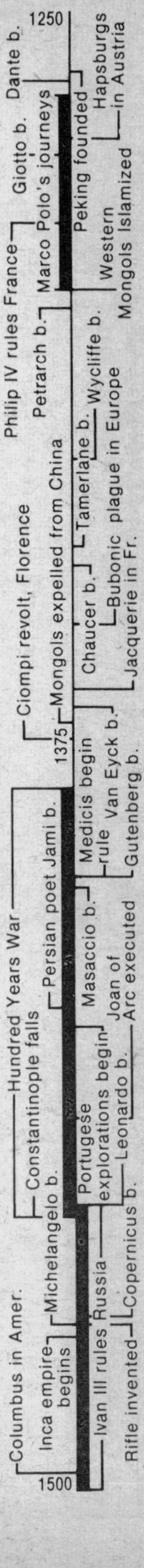

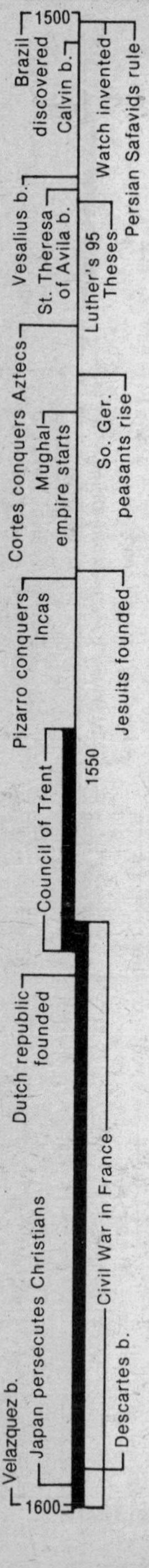

Indian traders. Coastal Moslem cities and states (starting before 1300), enriched by trade, soon dominated the interior. Chief among these was the **Malacca** state, on the Malay peninsula, c1400-1511.

Arts and Statecraft Thrive in Europe: 1350-1600

Italian Renaissance & humanism. Distinctive Italian achievements in the arts in the late Middle Ages (Dante, 1265-1321, Giotto, 1276-1337) led to the vigorous new styles of the Renaissance (14th-16th centuries). Patronized by the rulers of the quarreling petty states of Italy (Medicis in Florence and the papacy, c1400-1737), the plastic arts perfected realistic techniques, including **perspective** (Masaccio, 1401-28, Leonardo 1452-1519). Classical motifs were used in architecture and increased talent and expense were put into secular buildings. The Florentine dialect was refined as a national literary language (Petrarch, 1304-74). Greek refugees from the E strengthened the respect of humanist scholars for the classic sources (Bruni 1370-1444). Soon an international movement aided by the spread of **printing** (Gutenberg c1400-1468), **humanism** was optimistic about the power of human reason (Erasmus of Rotterdam, 1466-1536, Thomas More's *Utopia,* 1516) and valued individual effort in the arts and in politics (Machiavelli, 1469-1527).

France. The French monarchy, strengthened in its repeated struggles with powerful nobles (Burgundy, Flanders, Aquitaine) by alliances with the growing commercial towns, consolidated bureaucratic control under Philip IV (ruled 1285-1314) and extended French influence into Germany and Italy (popes at Avignon, France, 1309-1417). The **Hundred Years War,** 1338-1453, ended English dynastic claims in France (battles of Crécy, 1346, Poitiers, 1356; Joan of Arc executed, 1431). A French Renaissance, dating from royal invasions of Italy, 1494, 1499, was encouraged at the court of Francis I (ruled 1515-47), who centralized taxation and law. French vernacular literature consciously asserted its independence (La Pleiade, 1549).

England. The evolution of England's unique political institutions began with the Magna Carta, 1215, by which King John guaranteed the privileges of nobles and church against the monarchy and assured jury trial. After the Wars of the Roses (1455-85), the **Tudor dynasty** reasserted royal prerogatives (Henry VIII, ruled 1509-47), but the trend toward independent departments and ministerial government also continued. English trade (wool exports from c1340) was protected by the nation's growing maritime power (**Spanish Armada** destroyed, 1588).

English replaced French and Latin in the late 14th century in law and literature (Chaucer, 1340-1400) and English translation of the Bible began (Wycliffe, 1380s). Elizabeth I (ruled 1558-1603) presided over a confident flowering of poetry (Spenser, 1552-99), drama (**Shakespeare,** 1552-1616), and music.

German Empire. From among a welter of minor feudal states, church lands, and independent cities, the **Hapsburgs** assembled a far-flung territorial domain, based in Austria from 1276. The family held the title Holy Roman Emperor from 1452 to the Empire's dissolution in 1806, but failed to centralize its domains, leaving Germany disunited for centuries. Resistance to Turkish expansion brought Hungary under Austrian control from the 16th century. The Netherlands, Luxembourg, and Burgundy were added in 1477, curbing French expansion.

The Flemish painting tradition of naturalism, technical proficiency, and bourgeois subject matter began in the 15th century (Jan Van Eyck, 1366-1440), the earliest northern manifestation of the Renaissance. **Durer** (1471-1528) typified the merging of late Gothic and Italian trends in 16th century German art. Imposing civic architecture flourished in the prosperous commercial cities.

Spain. Despite the unification of Castile and Aragon in 1479, the 2 countries retained separate governments, and the nobility, especially in Aragon and Catalonia, retained many privileges. Spanish lands in Italy (Naples, Sicily) and the Netherlands entangled the country in European wars through the mid-17th century, while explorers, traders, and conquerors built up a Spanish empire in the Americas and the Philippines.

From the late 15th century, a **golden age** of literature and art produced works of social satire (plays of Lope de Vega, 1562-1635; Cervantes, 1547-1616), as well as spiritual intensity (El Greco, 1541-1614; Velazquez, 1599-1660).

Black Death. The bubonic plague reached Europe from the E in 1348, killing as much as half the population by 1350. Labor scarcity forced a rise in wages and brought greater freedom to the peasantry, making possible **peasant uprisings** (Jacquerie in France, 1358, Wat Tyler's rebellion in England, 1381). In the *ciompi* revolt, 1378, Florentine wage earners demanded a say in economic and political power.

Explorations. Organized European maritime exploration began, seeking to evade the Venice-Ottoman monopoly of eastern trade and to promote Christianity. Expeditions from Portugal beginning 1418 explored the west coast of Africa, until **Vasco da Gama** rounded the Cape of Good Hope in 1497 and reached India. A Portuguese trading empire was consolidated by the seizure of Goa, 1510, and Malacca, 1551. Japan was reached in 1542. Spanish voyages (**Columbus,** 1492-1504) uncovered a new world, which Spain hastened to subdue. Navigation schools in Spain and Portugal, the development of large sailing ships (carracks), and the invention of the rifle, c1475, aided European penetration.

Mughals and Safavids. East of the Ottoman empire, two Moslem dynasties ruled unchallenged in the 16th and 17th centuries. The Mughal empire in India, founded by Persianized Turkish invaders from the NW under Babur, dates from their 1526 conquest of Delhi. The dynasty ruled most of India for over 200 years, surviving nominally until 1857. **Akbar** (ruled 1556-1605) consolidated administration at his glorious court, where Urdu (Persian-influenced Hindi) developed. Trade relations with Europe increased. Under Shah Jahan (1629-58), a secularized art fusing Hindu and Moslem elements flourished in miniature painting and architecture (**Taj Mahal**). Sikhism, founded c1519, combined elements of both faiths. Suppression of Hindus and Shi'ite Moslems in S India in the late 17th century weakened the empire.

Fanatical devotion to the Shi'ite sect characterized the Safavids of Persia, 1502-1736, and led to hostilities with the Sunni Ottomans for over a century. The prosperity and strength of the empire are evidenced by the mosques at its capital, **Isfahan.** The dynasty enhanced Iranian national consciousness.

China. The Ming emperors, 1368-1644, the last native dynasty in China, wielded unprecedented personal power, while the Confucian bureaucracy began to suffer from inertia. European trade (Portugese monopoly through **Macao** from 1557) was strictly controlled. Jesuit scholars and scientists (Matteo Ricci 1552-1610) introduced some Western science; their writings familiarized the West with China. Chinese technological inventiveness declined from this era, but the arts thrived, especially painting and ceramics.

Japan. After the decline of the first hereditary shogunate (chief generalship) at **Kamakura** (1185-1333), fragmentation of power accelerated, as did the consequent social mobility. Under Kamakura and the Ashikaga shogunate, 1338-1573, the daimyos (lords) and samurai (warriors) grew more powerful and promoted a martial ideology. Japanese pirates and traders plied the China coast. Popular Buddhist movements included the nationalist Nichiren sect (from c1250) and **Zen** (brought from China, 1191), which stressed meditation and a disciplined esthetic (tea ceremony, landscape gardening, judo, Noh drama).

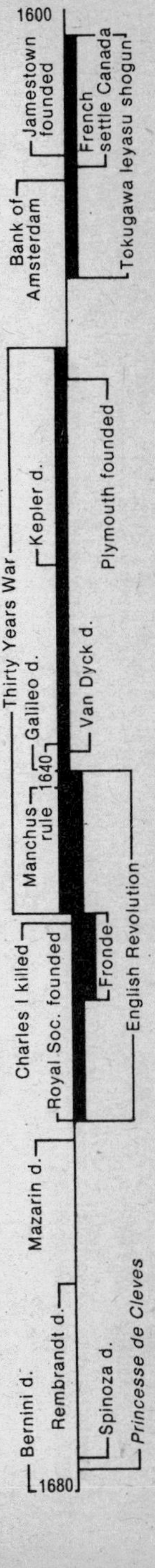

Reformed Europe Expands Overseas: 1500-1700

Reformation begun. Theological debate and protests against real and perceived clerical corruption existed in the medieval Christian world, expressed by such dissenters as Wycliffe (c1320-84) and his followers, the Lollards, in England, and **Huss** (burned as a heretic, 1415) in Bohemia.

Luther (1483-1546) preached that only faith could lead to salvation, without the mediation of clergy or good works. He attacked the authority of the Pope, rejected priestly celibacy, and recommended individual study of the Bible (which he translated, c1525). His 95 Theses (1517) led to his excommunication (1520). **Calvin** (1509-64) said God's elect were predestined for salvation; good conduct and success were signs of election. Calvin in Geneva and Knox (1505-72) in Scotland erected theocratic states.

Henry VIII asserted English national authority and secular power by breaking away from the Catholic church, 1534. Monastic property was confiscated, and some Protestant doctrines given official sanction.

Religious wars. A century and a half of religious wars began with a South German peasant uprising, 1524, repressed with Luther's support. Radical sects—democratic, pacifist, milennarian—arose (Anabaptists ruled Muenster, 1534-35), and were suppressed violently. Civil war in France from 1562 between **Huguenots** (Protestant nobles and merchants) and Catholics ended with the 1598 Edict of Nantes tolerating Protestants (revoked 1685). Hapsburg attempts to restore Catholicism in Germany were resisted in 25 years of fighting; the 1555 Peace of Augsburg guarantee of religious independence to local princes and cities was confirmed only after the **Thirty Years War,** 1618-48, when much of Germany was devastated by local and foreign armies (Sweden, France).

A Catholic Reformation, or **counter-reformation,** met the Protestant challenge, clearly defining an official theology at the Council of Trent, 1545-63. The **Jesuit** order, founded 1534 by Loyola (1491-1556), helped reconvert large areas of Poland, Hungary, and S. Germany and sent missionaries to the New World, India, and China, while the Inquisition helped suppress heresy in Catholic countries. A revival of piety appeared in the devotional literature (Theresa of Avila, 1515-82) and the grandiose Baroque art (Bernini, 1598-1680) of Roman Catholic countries.

Scientific Revolution. The late nominalist thinkers (Ockham, c1300-49) of Paris and Oxford challenged Aristotelian orthodoxy, allowing for a freer scientific approach. But metaphysical values, such as the Neoplatonic faith in an orderly, mathematical cosmos, still motivated and directed subsequent inquiry. **Copernicus** (1473-1543) promoted the heliocentric theory, which was confirmed when Kepler (1571-1630) discovered the mathematical laws describing the orbits of the planets. The Christian-Aristotelian belief that heavens and earth were fundamentally different collapsed when **Galileo** (1564-1642) discovered moving sunspots, irregular moon topography, and moons around Jupiter. He and **Newton** (1642-1727) developed a mechanics that unified cosmic and earthly phenomena. To meet the needs of the new physics, Newton and Leibnitz (1646-1716) invented calculus, Descartes (1596-1650) invented analytic geometry.

An explosion of observational science included the discovery of blood circulation (Harvey, 1578-1657) and microscopic life (Leeuwenhoek, 1632-1723), and advances in anatomy (Vesalius, 1514-64, dissected corpses) and chemistry (Boyle, 1627-91). Scientific research institutes were founded: Florence, 1657, London **(Royal Society),** 1660, Paris, 1666. Inventions proliferated (Savery's steam engine, 1696).

Arts. Mannerist trends of the high Renaissance (**Michelangelo,** 1475-1564) exploited virtuosity, grace, novelty, and exotic subjects and poses. The notion of artistic genius was promoted, in contrast to the anonymous medieval artisan. Private connoisseurs entered the art market. These trends were elaborated in the 17th century **Baroque** era, on a grander scale. Dynamic movement in painting and sculpture was emphasized by sharp lighting effects, use of rich materials (colored marble, gilt), realistic details. Curved facades, broken lines, rich, deep-cut detail, and ceiling decoration characterized Baroque architecture, especially in Germany. Monarchs, princes, and prelates, usually Catholic, used Baroque art to enhance and embellish their authority, as in royal portraits by Velazquez (1599-1660) and Van Dyck (1599-1641).

National styles emerged. In France, a taste for rectilinear order and serenity (Poussin, 1594-1665), linked to the new rational philosophy, was expressed in classical forms. The influence of **classical values** in French literature (tragedies of Racine, 1639-99) gave rise to the "battle of the Ancients and Moderns." New forms included the essay (Montaigne, 1533-92) and novel (*Princesse de Cleves,* La Fayette, 1678).

Dutch painting of the 17th century was unique in its wide social distribution. The Flemish tradition of undemonstrative realism reached its peak in **Rembrandt** (1606-69) and Vermeer (1632-75).

Economy. European economic expansion was stimulated by the new trade with the East, New World gold and silver, and a doubling of population (50 mln. in 1450, 100 mln. in 1600). New business and financial techniques were developed and refined, such as joint-stock companies, insurance, and letters of credit and exchange. The Bank of Amsterdam, 1609, and the Bank of England, 1694, broke the old monopoly of private banking families. The rise of a business mentality was typified by the spread of clock towers in cities in the 14th century. By the mid-15th century, portable clocks were available; the first watch was invented in 1502.

By 1650, most governments had adopted the **mercantile system,** in which they sought to amass metallic wealth by protecting their merchants' foreign and colonial trade monopolies. The rise in prices and the new coin-based economy undermined the craft guild and feudal manorial systems. Expanding industries, such as clothweaving and mining, benefitted from technical advances. Coal replaced disappearing wood as the chief fuel; it was used to fuel new 16th century blast furnaces making cast iron.

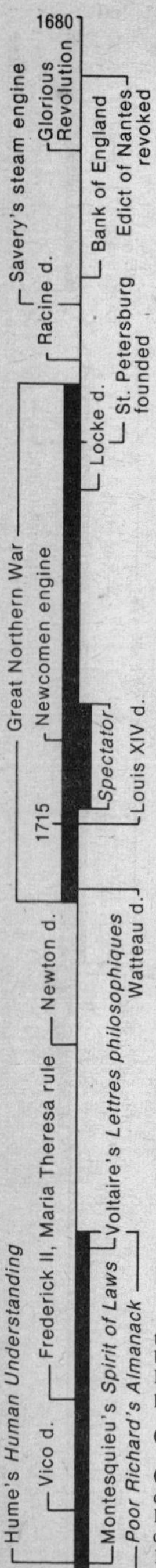

New World. The **Aztecs** united much of the Mesoamerican culture area in a militarist empire by 1519, from their capital, Tenochtitlan (pop. 300,000), which was the center of a cult requiring enormous levels of ritual human sacrifice. Most of the civilized areas of S. America were ruled by the centralized **Inca Empire** (1476-1534), stretching 2,000 miles from Ecuador to N.W. Argentina. Lavish and sophisticated traditions in pottery, weaving, sculpture, and architecture were maintained in both regions.

These empires, beset by revolts, fell in 2 short campaigns to gold-seeking Spanish forces based in the Antilles and Panama. **Cortes** took Mexico, 1519-21; **Pizarro** Peru, 1531-35. From these centers, land and sea expeditions claimed most of N. and S. America for Spain. The Indian high cultures did not survive the impact of Christian missionaries and the new upper class of whites and mestizos. In turn, New World silver, and such Indian products as potatoes, tobacco, corn, peanuts, chocolate, and rubber exercised a major economic influence on Europe. While the Spanish administration intermittently concerned itself with the welfare of Indians, the population remained impoverished at most levels, despite the growth of a distinct South American civilization. European diseases reduced the native population.

Brazil, which the Portuguese discovered in 1500 and settled after 1530, and the Caribbean colonies of several European nations developed a plantation economy where sugar cane, tobacco, cotton, coffee, rice, indigo, and lumber were grown commercially by slaves. From the early 16th to the late 19th centuries, some 10 million Africans were transported to **slavery** in the New World.

Netherlands. The urban, Calvinist northern provinces of the Netherlands rebelled against Hapsburg Spain, 1568, and founded an oligarchic mercantile republic. Their strategic control of the Baltic grain market enabled them to exploit Mediterranean food shortages. Religious refugees — French and Belgian Protestants, Iberian Jews — added to the cosmopolitan commercial talent pool. After Spain absorbed Portugal in 1580, the Dutch seized Portuguese possessions and created a vast, though generally short-lived commercial empire in Brazil, the Antilles, Africa, India, Ceylon, Malacca, Indonesia, and Taiwan, and challenged or supplanted Portuguese traders in China and Japan.

England. Anglicanism became firmly established under Elizabeth I after a brief Catholic interlude under "Bloody Mary," 1553-58. But religious and political conflicts led to a rebellion by Parliament, 1642. Roundheads (Puritans) defeated Cavaliers (Royalists); Charles I was beheaded, 1649. The new **Commonwealth** was ruled as a military dictatorship by Cromwell, who also brutally crushed an Irish rebellion, 1649-51. Conflicts within the Puritan camp (democratic Levelers defeated 1649) aided the Stuart restoration, 1660, but Parliament was permanently strengthened and the peaceful **"Glorious Revolution"**, 1688, advanced political and religious liberties (writings of Locke, 1632-1704). British privateers (Drake, 1540-96) challenged Spanish control of the New World, and penetrated Asian trade routes (Madras taken, 1639). N. American colonies (Jamestown, 1607, Plymouth, 1620) provided an outlet for religious dissenters.

France. Emerging from the religious civil wars in 1628, France regained military and commercial great power status under the ministries of **Richelieu** (1624-42), Mazarin (1643-61), and Colbert (1662-83). Under Louis XIV (ruled 1643-1715) royal absolutism triumphed over nobles and local *parlements* (defeat of Fronde, 1648-53). Permanent colonies were founded in Canada (1608), the Caribbean (1626), and India (1674).

Sweden. Sweden seceded from the Scandinavian Union in 1523. The thinly-populated agrarian state (with copper, iron, and timber exports) was united by the Vasa kings, whose conquests by the mid-17th century made Sweden the dominant Baltic power. The empire collapsed in the Great Northern War (1700-21).

Poland. After the union with Lithuania in 1447, Poland ruled vast territories from the Baltic to the Black Sea, resisting German and Turkish incursions. Catholic nobles failed to gain the loyalty of the Orthodox Christian peasantry in the East; commerce and trades were practiced by German and Jewish immigrants. The bloody 1648-49 cossack uprising began the kingdom's dismemberment.

China. A new dynasty, the **Manchus,** invaded from the NE and seized power in 1644, and expanded Chinese control to its greatest extent in Central and Southeast Asia. Trade and diplomatic contact with Europe grew, carefully controlled by China. New crops (sweet potato, maize, peanut) allowed an economic and population growth (300 million pop. in 1800). Traditional arts and literature were pursued with increased sophistication (*Dream of the Red Chamber,* novel, mid-18th century).

Japan. Tokugawa Ieyasu, shogun from 1603, finally unified and pacified feudal Japan. Hereditary daimyos and samurai monopolized government office and the professions. An urban merchant class grew, literacy spread, and a cultural renaissance occurred (haiku of Basho, 1644-94). Fear of European domination led to persecution of Christian converts from 1597, and stringent isolation from outside contact from 1640.

Philosophy, Industry, and Revolution: 1700-1800

Science and Reason. Faith in human reason and science as the source of truth and a means to improve the physical and social environment, espoused since the Renaissance (Francis Bacon, 1561-1626), was bolstered by scientific discoveries in spite of theological opposition (**Galileo's forced retraction,** 1633). Descartes applied the logical method of mathematics to discover "self-evident" scientific and philosophical truths, while Newton emphasized induction from experimental observation.

The challenge of reason to traditional religious and political values and institutions began with **Spinoza** (1632-77), who interpreted the Bible historically and called for political and intellectual freedom.

French philosophes assumed leadership of the **"Enlightenment"** in the 18th century. Montesquieu (1689-1755) used British history to support his notions of limited government. Voltaire's (1694-1778) diaries and novels of exotic travel illustrated the intellectual trends toward secular ethics and relativism. Rousseau's (1712-1778) radical concepts of the **social contract** and of the inherent goodness of the common man gave impetus to anti-monarchical republicanism. The *Encyclopedia,* 1751-72, edited by Diderot and d'Alembert, designed as a monument to reason, was largely devoted to practical technology.

In England, ideals of political and religious liberty were connected with empiricist philosophy and science in the followers of Locke. But the extreme **empiricism of Hume** (1711-76) and Berkeley

(1685-1753) posed limits to the identification of reason with absolute truth, as did the evolutionary approach to law and politics of Burke (1729-97) and the utilitarianism of Bentham (1748-1832). Adam Smith (1723-90) and other **physiocrats** called for a rationalization of economic activity by removing artificial barriers to a supposedly natural free exchange of goods.

Despite the political disunity and backwardness of most of Germany, German writers participated in the new philosophical trends popularized by Wolff (1679-1754). **Kant's** (1724-1804) **idealism,** unifying an empirical epistemology with *a priori* moral and logical concepts, directed German thought away from skepticism. Italian contributions included work on electricity by Galvani (1737-98) and Volta (1745-1827), the pioneer **historiography of Vico** (1668-1744), and writings on penal reform by Beccaria (1738-94). The American Franklin (1706-90) was celebrated in Europe for his varied achievements.

The growth of the **press** (*Spectator,* 1711-14) and the wide distribution of realistic but sentimental **novels** attested to the increase of a large bourgeois public.

Arts. Rococo art, characterized by extravagant decorative effects, asymmetries copied from organic models, and artificial pastoral subjects, was favored by the continental aristocracy for most of the century (Watteau, 1684-1721), and had musical analogies in the ornamentalized polyphony of late Baroque. The **Neoclassical** art after 1750, associated with the new scientific archeology, was more streamlined, and infused with the supposed moral and geometric rectitude of the Roman Republic (David, 1748-1825). In England, **town planning** on a grand scale began (Edinburgh, 1767).

Industrial Revolution in England. Agricultural improvements, such as the sowing drill (1701) and livestock breeding, were implemented on the large fields provided by enclosure of common lands by private owners. Profits from agriculture and from colonial and foreign trade (1800 volume, £ 54 million) were channelled through hundreds of banks and the **Stock Exchange** (founded 1773) into new industrial processes.

The Newcomen steam pump (1712) aided coal mining. Coal fueled the new efficient steam engines patented by Watt in 1769, and coke-smelting produced cheap, sturdy iron for machinery by the 1730s. The **flying shuttle** (1733) and **spinning jenny** (1764) were used in the large new cotton textile factories, where women and children were much of the work force. Goods were transported cheaply over **canals** (2,000 miles built 1760-1800).

Central and East Europe. The monarchs of the three states that dominated eastern Europe — Austria, Prussia, and Russia — accepted the advice and legitimation of philosophes in creating more modern, centralized institutions in their kingdoms, enlarged by the division of Poland (1772-95).

Under **Frederick II** (ruled 1740-86) Prussia, with its efficient modern army, doubled in size. State monopolies and tariff protection fostered industry, and some legal reforms were introduced. Austria's heterogeneous realms were legally unified under **Maria Theresa** (ruled 1740-80) and **Joseph II** (1780-90). Reforms in education, law, and religion were enacted, and the Austrian serfs were freed (1781). With its defeat in the Seven Years' War in 1763, Austria lost Silesia and ceased its active role in Germany, but was compensated by expansion to the E and S (Hungary, Croatia, 1699, Galicia, 1772).

Russia, whose borders continued to expand in all directions, adopted some Western bureaucratic and economic policies under **Peter I** (ruled 1682-1725) and Catherine II (ruled 1762-96). Trade and cultural contacts with the West multiplied from the new Baltic Sea capital, **St. Petersburg** (founded 1703).

American Revolution. The British colonies in N. America attracted a mass immigration of religious dissenters and poor people throughout the 17th and 18th centuries, coming from all parts of the British Isles, Germany, the Netherlands, and other countries. The population reached 3 million whites and blacks by the 1770s. The small native population was decimated by European diseases and wars with and between the various colonies. British attempts to control colonial trade, and to tax the colonists to pay for the costs of colonial administration and defense clashed with traditions of local self government, and eventually provoked the colonies to rebellion. (*See American Revolution in Index.*)

French Revolution. The growing French middle class lacked political power, and resented aristocratic tax privileges, especially in light of liberal political ideals popularized by the American Revolution. Peasants lacked adequate land and were burdened with feudal obligations to nobles. Wars with Britain drained the treasury, finally forcing the king to call the **Estates-General** in 1789 (first time since 1614), in an atmosphere of food riots (poor crop in 1788).

Aristocratic resistance to absolutism was soon overshadowed by the reformist Third Estate (middle class), which proclaimed itself the **National Constituent Assembly** June 17 and took the "Tennis Court oath" on June 20 to secure a constitution. The storming of the **Bastille** July 14 by Parisian artisans was followed by looting and seizure of aristocratic property throughout France. Assembly reforms included abolition of class and regional privileges, a Declaration of Rights, suffrage by taxpayers (75% of males), and the **Civil Constitution of the Clergy** providing for election and loyalty oaths for priests. A republic was declared Sept. 22, 1792, in spite of royalist pressure from Austria and Prussia, which had declared war in April (joined by Britain the next year). Louis XVI was beheaded Jan. 21, 1793, Queen Marie Antoinette was beheaded Oct. 16, 1793.

Royalist uprisings in La Vendee and the S and military reverses led to a **reign of terror** in which tens of thousands of opponents of the Revolution and criminals were executed. Radical reforms in the **Convention** period (Sept. 1793-Oct. 1795) included the abolition of colonial slavery, economic measures to aid the poor, support of public education, and a short-lived de-Christianization.

Division among radicals (execution of Hebert, March 1794, Danton, April, and Robespierre, July) aided the ascendance of a moderate **Directory,** which consolidated military victories. **Napoleon Bonaparte** (1769-1821), a popular young general, exploited political divisions and participated in a coup Nov. 9, 1799, making himself first consul (dictator).

India. Sikh and Hindu rebels (Rajputs, Marathas) and Afghans destroyed the power of the Mughals during the 18th century. After France's defeat in the Seven Years War, 1763, Britain was the chief European trade power in India. Its control of inland **Bengal and Bihar** was recognized by the Mughal shah in 1765, who granted the **British East India Co.** (under Clive, 1727-74) the right to collect land revenue there. Despite objections from Parliament (1784 India Act) the company's involvement in local wars and politics led to repeated acquisitions of new territory. The company exported Indian textiles, sugar, and indigo.

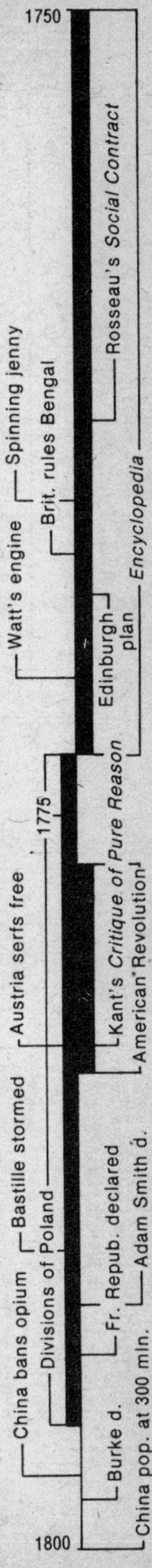

19th Century Railroad Growth
in Selected Countries

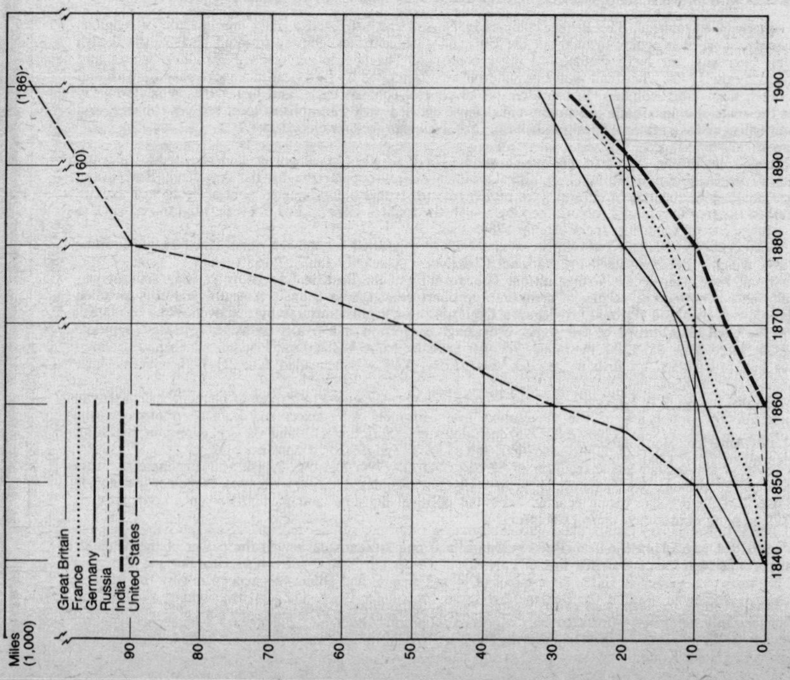

World Population Growth 10,000 BC to 1978

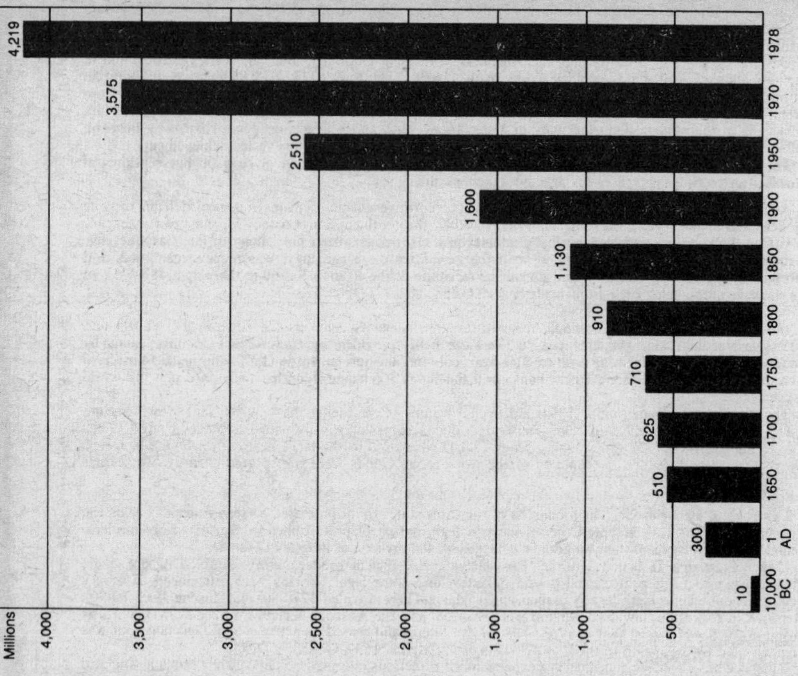

Change Gathers Steam: 1800-1840

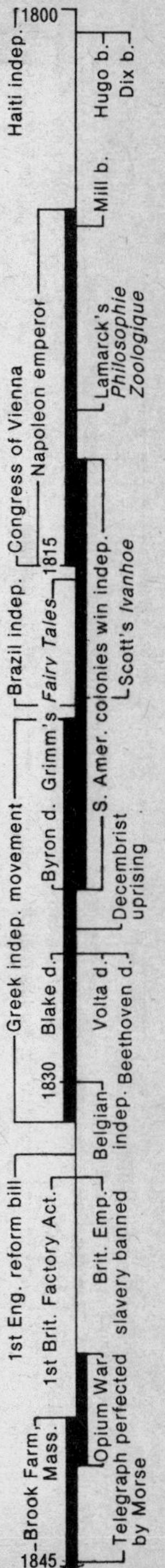

French ideals and empire spread. Inspired by the ideals of the French Revolution, and supported by the expanding French armies, new republican regimes arose near France: the **Batavian** Republic in the Netherlands (1795-1806), the **Helvetic** Republic in Switzerland (1798-1803), the **Cisalpine** Republic in N. Italy (1797-1805), the **Ligurian** Republic in Genoa (1797-1805), and the **Parthenopean** Republic in S. Italy (1799). A Roman Republic existed briefly in 1798 after Pope Pius VI was arrested by French troops. In Italy and Germany, new nationalist sentiments were stimulated both in imitation of and reaction to France (anti-French and anti-Jacobin peasant uprisings in Italy, 1796-9).

From 1804, when Napoleon declared himself emperor, to 1812, a succession of military victories (Austerlitz, 1805, Jena, 1806) extended his control over most of Europe, through puppet states (**Confederation of the Rhine** united W. German states for the first time and **Grand Duchy of Warsaw** revived Polish national hopes), expansion of the empire, and alliances.

Among the lasting reforms initiated under Napoleon's absolutist reign were: establishment of the Bank of France, centralization of tax collection, codification of law along Roman models (*Code Napoleon*), and reform and extension of secondary and university education. In an 1801 concordat, the papacy recognized the effective autonomy of the French Catholic Church. Some 400,000 French soldiers were killed in the Napoleonic Wars, along with 600,000 foreign troops.

Last gasp of old regime. France's coastal blockade of Europe (**Continental System**) failed to neutralize Britain. The disastrous 1812 invasion of Russia exposed Napoleon's overextension. After an 1814 exile at Elba, Napoleon's armies were defeated at **Waterloo,** 1815, by British and Prussian troops.

At the **Congress of Vienna,** the monarchs and princes of Europe redrew their boundaries, to the advantage of Prussia (in Saxony and the Ruhr), Austria (in Illyria and Venetia), and Russia (in Poland and Finland). British conquest of Dutch and French colonies (S. Africa, Ceylon, Mauritius) was recognized, and France, under the restored Bourbons, retained its expanded 1792 borders. The settlement brought 50 years of international peace to Europe.

But the Congress was unable to check the advance of liberal ideals and of nationalism among the smaller European nations. The 1825 **Decembrist uprising** by liberal officers in Russia was easily suppressed. But an independence movement in **Greece,** stirred by commercial prosperity and a cultural revival, succeeded in expelling Ottoman rule by 1831, with the aid of Britain, France, and Russia.

A constitutional monarchy was secured in France by an **1830 revolution;** Louis Philippe became king. The revolutionary contagion spread to **Belgium,** which gained its independence from the Dutch monarchy, 1830; to **Poland,** whose rebellion was defeated by Russia, 1830-31; and to Germany.

Romanticism. A new style in intellectual and artistic life began to replace Neo-classicism and Rococo after the mid-18th century. By the early 19th, this style, Romanticism, had prevailed in the European world.

Rousseau had begun the reaction against excessive rationalism and skepticism; in education (*Emile,* 1762) he stressed subjective spontaneity over regularized instruction. In Germany, Lessing (1729-81) and Herder (1744-1803) favorably compared the German folk song to classical forms, and began a cult of Shakespeare, whose passion and "natural" wisdom was a model for the Romantic *Sturm und Drang* (storm and stress) movement. **Goethe's** *Sorrows of Young Werther* (1774) set the model for the tragic, passionate genius.

A new interest in **Gothic architecture** in England after 1760 (Walpole, 1717-97) spread through Europe, associated with an aesthetic Christian and mystic revival (Blake, 1757-1827). Celtic, Norse, and German mythology and folk tales were revived or imitated (Macpherson's Ossian translation, 1762, Grimm's *Fairy Tales,* 1812-22). The medieval revival (Scott's *Ivanhoe,* 1819) led to a new interest in history, stressing national differences and organic growth (Carlyle, 1795-1881; Michelet, 1798-1874), corresponding to theories of natural evolution (Lamarck's *Philosophie zoologique,* 1809, Lyell's *Geology,* 1830-33).

Revolution and war fed an obsession with freedom and conflict, expressed by poets (**Byron,** 1788-1824, **Hugo,** 1802-85) and philosophers (**Hegel,** 1770-1831).

Wild gardens replaced the formal French variety, and painters favored rural, stormy, and mountainous landscapes (**Turner,** 1775-1851; **Constable,** 1776-1837). Clothing became freer, with wigs, hoops, and ruffles discarded. Originality and genius were expected in the life as well as the work of inspired artists (Murger's *Scenes from Bohemian Life,* 1847-49). Exotic locales and themes (as in "Gothic" horror stories) were used in art and literature (Delacroix, 1798-1863, **Poe,** 1809-49).

Music exhibited the new dramatic style and a breakdown of classical forms (Beethoven, 1770-1827). The use of folk melodies and modes aided the growth of distinct national traditions (Glinka in Russia, 1804-57).

Latin America. Haiti, under the former slave **Toussaint L'Ouverture,** was the first Latin American independent state, 1800. All the mainland Spanish colonies won their independence 1810-24, under such leaders as **Bolivar** (1783-1830). Brazil became an independent empire under the Portuguese prince regent, 1822. A new class of military officers divided power with large landholders and the church.

United States. Heavy immigration and exploitation of ample natural resources fueled rapid economic growth. The spread of the franchise, public education, and antislavery sentiment were signs of a widespread democratic ethic.

China. Failure to keep pace with Western arms technology exposed China to greater European influence, and hampered efforts to bar imports of opium, which had damaged Chinese society and drained wealth overseas. In the **Opium War,** 1839-42, Britain forced China to expand trade opportunities and to cede Hong Kong.

Triumph of Progress: 1840-80

Idea of Progress. As a result of the cumulative scientific, economic, and political changes of the preceding eras, the idea took hold among literate people in the West that continuing growth and improvement was the usual state of human and natural life.

Darwin's statement of the **theory of evolution** and survival of the fittest (*Origin of Species,* 1859), defended by intellectuals and scientists against theological objections, was taken as confirmation that progress was the natural direction of life. The controversy helped define popular ideas of the dedicated scientist and ever-expanding human knowledge of and control over the world (Foucault's demonstration of earth's rotation, 1851, Pasteur's germ theory, 1861).

Liberals following Ricardo (1772-1823) in their faith that unrestrained competition would bring continuous economic expansion sought to adjust political life to the new social realities, and believed that unregulated competition of ideas would yield truth (Mill, 1806-73). In England, successive reform bills (1832, 1867, 1884) gave representation to the new industrial towns, and extended the franchise to the middle and lower classes and to Catholics, Dissenters, and Jews. On both sides of the Atlantic, reformists tried to improve conditions for the mentally ill (Dix, 1802-87), women (Anthony, 1820-1906), and prisoners. Slavery was barred in the British Empire, 1833; the United States, 1865; and Brazil, 1888.

Socialist theories based on ideas of human perfectibility or historical progress were widely disseminated. Utopian socialists like Saint-Simon (1760-1825) envisaged an orderly, just society directed by a technocratic elite. A model factory town, New Lanark, Scotland, was set up by utopian Robert Owen (1771-1858), and utopian communal experiments were tried in the U.S. (Brook Farm, Mass., 1841-7). Bakunin's (1814-76) anarchism represented the opposite utopian extreme of total freedom. Marx (1818-83) posited the inevitable triumph of socialism in the industrial countries through a historical process of class conflict.

Spread of industry. The technical processes and managerial innovations of the English industrial revolution spread to Europe (especially Germany) and the U.S., causing an explosion of industrial production, demand for raw materials, and competition for markets. Inventors, both trained and self-educated, provided the means for larger-scale production (Bessemer steel, 1856, sewing machine, 1846). Many inventions were shown at the 1851 London Great Exhibition at the Crystal Palace, whose theme was universal prosperity.

Local specialization and long-distance trade were aided by a revolution in transportation and communication. Railroads were first introduced in the 1820s in England and the U.S. Over 150,000 miles of track had been laid worldwide by 1880, with another 100,000 miles laid in the next decade. Steamships were improved (*Savannah* crossed Atlantic, 1819). The telegraph, perfected by 1844 (Morse), connected the Old and New Worlds by cable in 1866, and quickened the pace of international commerce and politics. The first commercial telephone exchange went into operation in the U.S. in 1878.

The new class of industrial workers, uprooted from their rural homes, lacked job security, and suffered from dangerous overcrowded conditions at work and at home. Many responded by organizing trade unions (legalized in England, 1824; France, 1884). The U.S. Knights of Labor had 700,000 members by 1886. The First International, 1864-76, tried to unite workers internationally around a Marxist program. The quasi-Socialist Paris Commune uprising, 1871, was violently suppressed. Factory Acts to reduce child labor and regulate conditions were passed (1833-50 in England). Social security measures were introduced by the Bismarck regime in Germany, 1883-89.

Revolutions of 1848. Among the causes of the continent-wide revolutions were an international collapse of credit and resulting unemployment, bad harvests in 1845-7, and a cholera epidemic. The new urban proletariat and expanding bourgeoisie demanded a greater political role. Republics were proclaimed in France, Rome, and Venice. Nationalist feelings reached fever pitch in the Hapsburg empire, as Hungary declared independence under Kossuth, a Slav Congress demanded equality, and Piedmont tried to drive Austria from Lombardy. A national liberal assembly at Frankfurt called for German unification.

But riots fueled bourgeois fears of socialism (Marx and Engels' 1848 *Communist Manifesto*) and peasants remained conservative. The old establishment — The Papacy, the Hapsburgs (using Croats and Romanians against Hungary), the Prussian army — was able to rout the revolutionaries by 1849. The French Republic succumbed to a renewed monarchy by 1852 (Emperor Napoleon III).

Great nations unified. Using the "blood and iron" tactics of Bismarck from 1862, Prussia controlled N. Germany by 1867 (war with Denmark, 1864, Austria, 1866). After defeating France in 1870 (loss of Alsace-Lorraine), it won the allegiance of S. German states. A new **German Empire** was proclaimed, 1871. **Italy,** inspired by Mazzini (1805-72) and Garibaldi (1807-82), was unified by the reformed Piedmont kingdom through uprisings, plebiscites, and war.

The **U.S.,** its area expanded after the 1846-47 Mexican War, defeated a secession attempt by slave states, 1861-65. The Canadian provinces were united in an autonomous **Dominion of Canada,** 1867. Control in **India** was removed from the East India Co. and centralized under British administration after the 1857-58 Sepoy rebellion, laying the groundwork for the modern Indian State. Queen Victoria was named Empress of India, 1876.

Europe dominates Asia. The Ottoman Empire began to collapse in the face of Balkan nationalisms and European imperial incursions in N. Africa (Suez Canal, 1869). The Turks had lost control of most of both regions by 1882. Russia completed its expansion south by 1884 (despite the temporary setback of the Crimean War with Turkey, Britain, and France, 1853-56) taking Turkestan, all the Caucasus, and Chinese areas in the East and sponsoring Balkan Slavs against the Turks. A succession of reformist and reactionary regimes presided over a slow modernization (serfs freed, 1861). Persian independence suffered as Russia and British India competed for influence.

China was forced to sign a series of unequal treaties with European powers and Japan. Overpopulation and an inefficient dynasty brought misery and caused rebellions (Taiping, Moslems) leaving tens of millions dead. Japan was forced by the U.S. (Commodore Perry's visits, 1853-54) and Europe to end its isolation. The Meiji restoration, 1868, gave power to a Westernizing oligarchy. Intensified empire-building gave Burma to Britain, 1824-86, and Indo-China to France, 1862-95. Christian missionary activity followed imperial and trade expansion in Asia.

Respectability. The fine arts were expected to reflect and encourage the progress of morals and

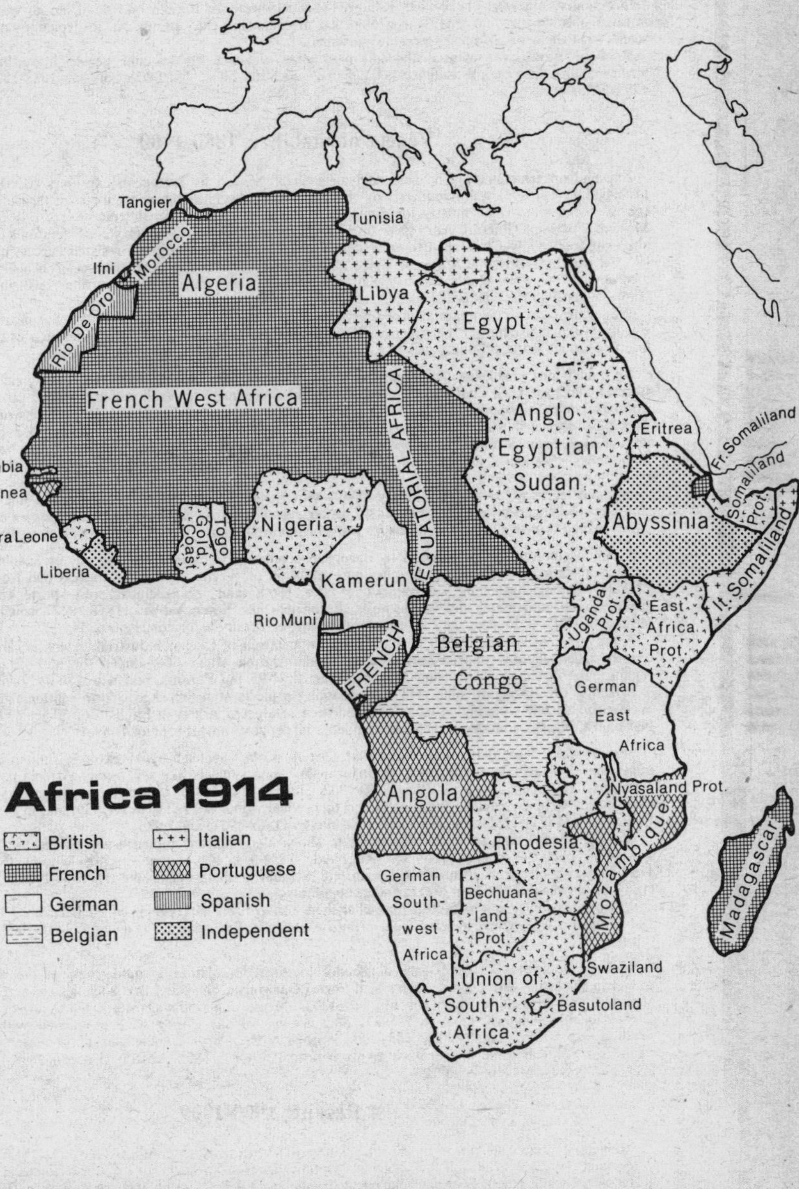
Africa 1914
British
French
German
Belgian
Italian
Portuguese
Spanish
Independent
Tangier
Tunisia
Morocco
Ifni
Algeria
Rio De Oro
Libya
Egypt
French West Africa
EQUATORIAL AFRICA
Anglo Egyptian Sudan
Eritrea
Fr. Somaliland
Somaliland Prot.
Abyssinia
It. Somaliland
Gambia
Port. Guinea
Sierra Leone
Liberia
Gold Coast
Togo
Nigeria
Kamerun
Rio Muni
FRENCH
Belgian Congo
Uganda Prot.
East Africa Prot.
German East Africa
Angola
Nyasaland Prot.
Rhodesia
Mozambique
Madagascar
German South-west Africa
Bechuana-land Prot.
Swaziland
Union of South Africa
Basutoland

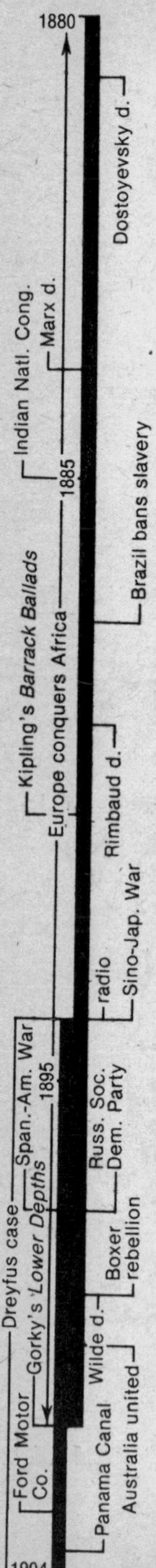

manners among the different classes. "Victorian" prudery, exaggerated delicacy, and familial piety were heralded by **Bowdler's** expurgated edition of Shakespeare (1818). Government-supported mass education inculcated a work ethic as a means to escape poverty (Horatio Alger, 1832-99).

The official **Beaux Arts** school in Paris set an international style of imposing public buildings (Paris Opera, 1861-74, Vienna Opera, 1861-69) and uplifting statues (Bartholdi's *Statue of Liberty,* 1885). Realist painting, influenced by photography (Daguerre, 1837), appealed to a new mass audience with social or historical narrative (Wilkie, 1785-1841, Poynter, 1836-1919) or with serious religious, moral, or social messages (pre-Raphaelites, Millet's Angelus, 1858) often drawn from ordinary life. The **Impressionists** (Pissarro, 1830-1903, Renoir, 1841-1919) rejected the central role of serious subject matter in favor of a colorful and sensual depiction of a moment, but their sunny, placid depictions of bourgeois scenes kept them within the respectable consensus.

Realistic **novelists** presented the full panorama of social classes and personalities, but retained sentimentality and moral judgment (Dickens, 1812-70, Eliot, 1819-80, Tolstoy, 1828-1910, Balzac, 1799-1850).

Veneer of Stability: 1880-1900

Imperialism triumphant. The vast **African** interior, visited by European explorers (Barth, 1821-65, Livingstone, 1813-73) was conquered by the European powers in rapid, competitive thrusts from their coastal bases after 1880, mostly for domestic political and international strategic reasons. W. African Moslem kingdoms (Fulani), Arab slave traders (Zanzibar), and Bantu military confederations (Zulu) were alike subdued. Only Christian Ethiopia (defeat of Italy, 1896) and Liberia resisted successfully. France (W. Africa) and Britain ("Cape to Cairo," Boer War, 1899-1902) were the major beneficiaries. The ideology of "the white man's burden" (Kipling, *Barrack Room Ballads,* 1892) or of a "civilizing mission" (France) justified the conquests.

West European foreign capital investments soared to nearly $40 billion by 1914, but most was in E. Europe (France, Germany) the Americas (Britain) and the white colonies. The foundation of the modern interdependent world economy was laid, with cartels dominating raw material trade.

An industrious world. Industrial and technological proficiency characterized the 2 new great powers — **Germany** and the **U.S.** Coal and iron deposits enabled Germany to reach second or third place status in iron, steel, and shipbuilding by the 1900s. German electrical and chemical industries were world leaders. The U.S. post-civil war boom (interrupted by "panics," 1884, 1893, 1896) was shaped by massive immigration from S. and E. Europe from 1880, government subsidy of railroads, and huge private monopolies (Standard Oil, 1870, U.S. Steel, 1901). The **Spanish-American War,** 1898 (Phillipine rebellion, 1899-1901) and the Open Door policy in China (1899) made the U.S. a world power.

England led in **urbanization** (72% by 1890), with **London** the world capital of finance, insurance, and shipping. Electric subways (London, 1890), sewer systems (Paris, 1850s), parks, and bargain department stores helped improve living standards for most of the urban population of the industrial world.

Asians assimilate. Asian reaction to European economic, military, and religious incursions took the form of imitation of Western techniques and adoption of Western ideas of progress and freedom. The Chinese "self-strengthening" movement of the 1860s and 70s included rail, port, and arsenal improvements and metal and textile mills. Reformers like **K'ang Yu-wei** (1858-1927) won liberalizing reforms in 1898, right after the European and Japanese "scramble for concessions."

A universal education system in Japan and importation of foreign industrial, scientific, and military experts aided Japan's unprecedented rapid modernization after 1868, under the authoritarian Meiji regime. Japan's victory in the **Sino-Japanese War,** 1894-95, put Formosa and Korea in its power.

In India, the British alliance with the remaining princely states masked reform sentiment among the Westernized urban elite; higher education had been conducted largely in English for 50 years. The **Indian National Congress,** founded in 1885, demanded a larger government role for Indians.

"Fin-de-siecle" sophistication. Naturalist writers pushed realism to its extreme limits, adopting a quasi-scientific attitude and writing about formerly taboo subjects like sex, crime, extreme poverty, and corruption (Flaubert, 1821-80, Zola, 1840-1902, Hardy, 1840-1928). Unseen or repressed psychological motivations were explored in the clinical and theoretical works of **Freud** (1856-1939) and in the fiction of Dostoevsky (1821-81), James (1843-1916), Schnitzler (1862-1931) and others.

A contempt for bourgeois life or a desire to shock a complacent audience was shared by the French **symbolist** poets (Verlaine, 1844-96, Rimbaud, 1854-91), neo-pagan English writers (Swinburne, 1837-1909), continental dramatists (Ibsen, 1828-1906) and satirists (Wilde, 1854-1900). **Nietzsche** (1844-1900) was influential in his elitism and pessimism.

Post-impressionist art neglected long-cherished conventions of representation (Cezanne, 1839-1906) and showed a willingness to learn from primitive and non-European art (Gauguin, 1848-1903, Japanese prints).

Racism. Gobineau (1816-82) gave a pseudo-biological foundation to modern racist theories, which spread in the latter 19th century along with **Social Darwinism,** the belief that societies are and should be organized as a struggle for survival of the fittest. The Medieval period was interpreted as an era of natural Germanic rule (Chamberlain, 1855-1927) and notions of superiority were associated with German national aspirations (Treitschke, 1834-96). **Anti-Semitism,** with a new racist rationale, became a significant political force in Germany (Anti-Semitic Petition, 1880), Austria (Lueger, 1844-1910), and France (Dreyfus case, 1894-1906).

Last Respite: 1900-1909

Alliances. While the peace of Europe (and its dependencies) continued to hold (1907 **Hague Conference** extended the rules of war and international arbitration procedures), imperial rivalries, protectionist trade practices (in Germany and France), and the escalating arms race (British *Dreadnought* battleship launched, Germany widens Kiel canal, 1906) exacerbated minor disputes (German-French Moroccan "crises", 1905, 1911).

Security was sought through alliances: **Triple Alliance** (Germany, Austria-Hungary, Italy) renewed

1902, 1907; Anglo-Japanese Alliance, 1902; Franco-Russian Alliance, 1899; **Entente Cordiale** (Britain, France) 1904; Anglo-Russian Treaty, 1907; German-Ottoman friendship.

Ottomans decline. The inefficient, corrupt Ottoman government was unable to resist further loss of territory. Nearly all European lands were lost in 1912 to Serbia, Greece, Montenegro, and Bulgaria. Italy took Libya and the Dodecanese islands the same year, and Britain took Kuwait, 1899, and the Sinai, 1906. The **Young Turk** revolution in 1908 forced the sultan to restore a constitution, introduced some social reform, industrialization, and secularization.

British Empire. British trade and cultural influence remained dominant in the empire, but constitutional reforms presaged its eventual dissolution: the colonies of **Australia** were united in 1901 under a self-governing commonwealth. **New Zealand** acquired dominion status in 1907. The old Boer republics joined Cape Colony and Natal in the self-governing **Union of South Africa** in 1910.

The 1909 Indian Councils Act enhanced the role of elected province legislatures in **India.** The Moslem League, founded 1906, sought separate communal representation.

East Asia. Japan exploited its growing industrial power to expand its empire. Victory in the 1904-05 war against Russia (naval battle of Tsushima, 1905) assured Japan's domination of **Korea** (annexed 1910) and Manchuria (took Port Arthur 1905).

In China, central authority began to crumble (empress died, 1908). Reforms (Confucian exam system ended 1905, modernization of the army, building of railroads) were inadequate and secret societies of reformers and nationalists, inspired by the Westernized **Sun Yat-sen** (1866-1925) fomented periodic uprisings in the south.

Siam, whose independence had been guaranteed by Britain and France in 1896, was split into spheres of influence by those countries in 1907.

Russia. The population of the Russian Empire approached 150 million in 1900. Reforms in education, law, and local institutions (*zemstvos*), and an industrial boom starting in the 1880s (oil, railroads) created the beginnings of a modern state, despite the autocratic tsarist regime. Liberals (1903 Union of Liberation), Socialists (Social Democrats founded 1898, Bolsheviks split off 1903), and populists (Social Revolutionaries founded 1901) were periodically repressed, and national minorities persecuted (anti-Jewish pogroms, 1903, 1905-6).

An industrial crisis after 1900 and harvest failures aggravated poverty in the urban proletariat, and the 1904-05 defeat by Japan (which checked Russia's Asian expansion) sparked the revolution of 1905-06. A **Duma** (parliament) was created, and an agricultural reform (under Stolypin, prime minister 1906-11) created a large class of landowning peasants (kulaks).

The world shrinks. Developments in transportation and communication and mass population movements helped create an awareness of an interdependent world. Early **automobiles** (Daimler, Benz, 1885) were experimental, or designed as luxuries. Assembly-line mass production (Ford Motor Co., 1903) made the invention practicable, and by 1910 nearly 500,000 motor vehicles were registered in the U.S. alone. **Heavier-than-air flights** began in 1903 in the U.S. (Wright brothers), preceded by glider, balloon, and model plane advances in several countries. Trade was advanced by improvements in **ship design** (gyrocompass, 1907), speed (Lusitania crossed Atlantic in 5 days, 1907), and reach (Panama Canal begun, 1904).

The first transatlantic **radio** telegraphic transmission occurred in 1901, 6 years after Marconi discovered radio. Radio transmission of human speech had been made in 1900. Telegraphic transmission of photos was achieved in 1904, lending immediacy to news reports. **Phonographs,** popularized by Caruso's recordings (starting 1902) made for quick international spread of musical styles (ragtime). **Motion pictures,** perfected in the 1890s (Dickson, Lumiere brothers), became a popular and artistic medium after 1900; newsreels appeared in 1909.

Emigration from crowded European centers soared in the decade: 9 million migrated to the U.S., and millions more went to Siberia, Canada, Argentina, Australia, South Africa, and Algeria. Some 70 million Europeans emigrated in the century before 1914. Several million Chinese, Indians, and Japanese migrated to Southeast Asia, where their urban skills often enabled them to take a predominant economic role.

Social reform. The social and economic problems of the poor were kept in the public eye by realist fiction writers (Dreiser's *Sister Carrie,* 1900; Gorky's *Lower Depths,* 1902; Sinclair's *Jungle,* 1906), journalists (U.S. **muckrakers** — Steffens, Tarbell) and artists (Ashcan school). Frequent labor strikes and occasional assassinations by anarchists or radicals (Austrian Empress, 1898; King Umberto I of Italy, 1900; U.S. Pres. McKinley, 1901; Russian Interior Minister Plehve, 1904; Portugal's King Carlos, 1908) added to social tension and fear of revolution.

But democratic reformism prevailed. In Germany, Bernstein's (1850-1932) **revisionist Marxism,** downgrading revolution, was accepted by the powerful Social Democrats and trade unions. The British Fabian Society (the Webbs, Shaw) and the Labour Party (founded 1906) worked for reforms such as social security and union rights (1906), while women's suffragists grew more militant. U.S. **progressives** fought big business (Pure Food and Drug Act, 1906). In France, the 10-hour work day (1904) and separation of church and state (1905) were reform victories, as was universal suffrage in Austria (1907).

Arts. An unprecedented period of experimentation, centered in France, produced several new **painting** styles: fauvism exploited bold color areas (Matisse, *Woman with Hat,* 1905); expressionism reflected powerful inner emotions (the Brücke group, 1905); cubism combined several views of an object on one flat surface (Picasso's *Demoiselles,* 1906-07); futurism tried to depict speed and motion (Italian Futurist Manifesto, 1910). **Architects** explored new uses of steel structures, with facades either neo-classical (Adler and Sullivan in U.S.); curvilinear Art Nouveau (Gaudi's Casa Mila, 1905-10); or functionally streamlined (Wright's Robie House, 1909).

Music and **Dance** shared the experimental spirit. Ruth St. Denis (1877-1968) and Isadora Duncan (1878-1927) pioneered modern dance, while Diaghilev in Paris revitalized classic ballet from 1909. Composers explored atonal music (Debussy, 1862-1918) and dissonance (Schönberg, 1874-1951), or revolutionized classical forms (Stravinsky, 1882-71), often showing jazz or folk music influences.

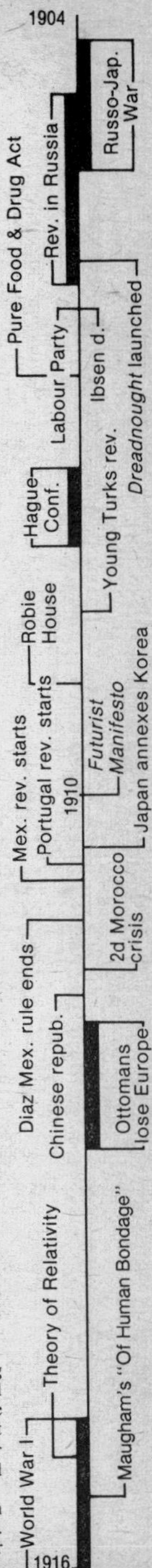

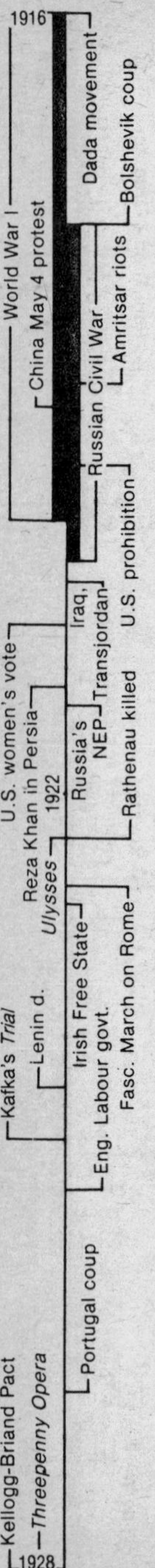

War and Revolution: 1910-1919

War threatens. Germany under Wilhelm II sought a political and imperial role consonant with its industrial strength, challenging Britain's world supremacy and threatening France, still resenting the loss of Alsace-Lorraine. Austria wanted to curb an expanded Serbia (after 1912) and the threat it posed to its own Slav lands. Russia feared Austrian and German political and economic aims in the Balkans and Turkey. An accelerated arms race resulted: the German standing army rose to over 2 million men by 1914. Russia and France had over a million each, Austria and the British Empire nearly a million each. Dozens of enormous battleships were built by the powers after 1906.

The **assassination of Austrian Archduke Ferdinand** by a Serbian, June 28, 1914, was the pretext for war. The system of alliances made the conflict Europe-wide; Germany's invasion of Belgium to outflank France forced Britain to enter the war. Patriotic fervor was nearly unanimous among all classes in most countries.

World War I. German forces were stopped in France in one month. The rival armies dug **trench networks.** Artillery and improved machine guns prevented either side from any lasting advance despite repeated assaults (600,000 dead at **Verdun,** Feb.-July 1916). Poison gas, used by Germany in 1915, proved ineffective. Over one million U.S. troops tipped the balance after mid-1917, forcing Germany to sue for peace.

In the East, the Russian armies were thrown back (battle of **Tannenberg,** Aug. 20, 1914) and the war grew unpopular. An allied attempt to relieve Russia through Turkey failed (**Gallipoli** 1916). The new Bolshevik regime signed the capitulatory Brest-Litovsk peace in March, 1918. Italy entered the war on the allied side, Apr. 1915, but was pushed back by Oct. 1917. A renewed offensive with Allied aid in Oct.-Nov. 1918 forced Austria to surrender.

The British Navy successfully blockaded Germany, which responded with submarine U-boat attacks; **unrestricted submarine warfare** against neutrals after Jan. 1917 helped bring the U.S. into the war. Other battlefields included Palestine and Mesopotamia, both of which Britain wrested from the Turks in 1917, and the African and Pacific colonies of Germany, most of which fell to Britain, France, Australia, Japan, and South Africa.

From 1916, the civilian population and economy of both sides were mobilized to an unprecedented degree. Over 10 million soldiers died (May 1917 French mutiny crushed). *For further details, see 1978 and earlier editions of The World Almanac.*

Settlement. At the **Versailles conference** (Jan.-June 1919) and in subsequent negotiations and local wars (Russian-Polish War 1920), the map of Europe was redrawn with a nod to U.S. Pres. Wilson's principle of self-determination. Austria and Hungary were separated and much of their land was given to Yugoslavia (formerly Serbia), Romania, Italy, and the newly independent Poland and Czechoslovakia. Germany lost territory in the West, North, and East, while Finland and the Baltic states were detached from Russia. Turkey lost nearly all its Arab lands to British-sponsored Arab states or to direct French and British rule.

A huge **reparations** burden and partial demilitarization were imposed on Germany. Wilson obtained approval for a League of Nations, but the U.S. Senate refused to allow the U.S. to join.

Russian revolution. Military defeats and high casualties caused a contagious lack of confidence in Tsar Nicholas, who was forced to abdicate, Mar. 1917. A liberal provisional government failed to end the war, and massive desertions, riots, and fighting between factions followed. A moderate socialist government under Kerensky was overthrown in a violent **coup by the Bolsheviks** in Petrograd under Lenin, who disbanded the elected Constituent Assembly, Nov. 1917.

The Bolsheviks brutally suppressed all opposition and ended the war with Germany, Mar. 1918. **Civil war** broke out in the summer between the Red Army, including the Bolsheviks and their supporters, and monarchists, anarchists, nationalities (Ukrainians, Georgians, Poles) and others. Small U.S., British, French and Japanese units also opposed the Bolsheviks, 1918-19 (Japan in Vladivostok to 1922). The civil war, anarchy, and pogroms devastated the country until the 1920 Red Army victory. The wartime total monopoly of political, economic, and police power by the Communist Party leadership was retained.

Other European revolutions. An unpopular monarchy in **Portugal** was overthrown in 1910. The new republic took severe anti-clerical measures, 1911.

After a century of Home Rule agitation, during which **Ireland** was devastated by famine (one million dead, 1846-47) and emigration, republican militants staged an unsuccessful uprising in Dublin, Easter 1916. The execution of the leaders and mass arrests by the British won popular support for the rebels. The Irish Free State, comprising all but the 6 northern counties, achieved dominion status in 1922.

In the aftermath of the world war, radical revolutions were attempted in Germany (**Spartacist** uprising Jan. 1919), **Hungary** (Kun regime 1919), and elsewhere. All were suppressed or failed for lack of support.

Chinese revolution. The Manchu Dynasty was overthrown and a republic proclaimed, Oct. 1911. First president Sun Yat-sen resigned in favor of strongman Yuan Shih-k'ai. Sun organized the parliamentarian **Kuomintang** party.

Students launched protests May 4, 1919 against League of Nations concessions in China to Japan. Nationalist, liberal, and socialist ideas and political groups spread. The **Communist Party** was founded 1921. A communist regime took power in Mongolia with Soviet support in 1921.

India restive. Indian objections to British rule erupted in nationalist riots as well as in the non-violent tactics of Gandhi (1869-1948). Nearly 400 unarmed demonstrators were shot at **Amritsar,** Apr. 1919. Britain approved limited self-rule that year.

Mexican revolution. Under the long Diaz dictatorship (1876-1911) the economy advanced, but Indian and mestizo lands were confiscated, and concessions to foreigners (mostly U.S.) damaged the middle class. A **revolution in 1910** led to civil wars and U.S. intervention (1914, 1916-17). Land reform and a more democratic constitution (1917) were achieved.

The Aftermath of War: 1920-29

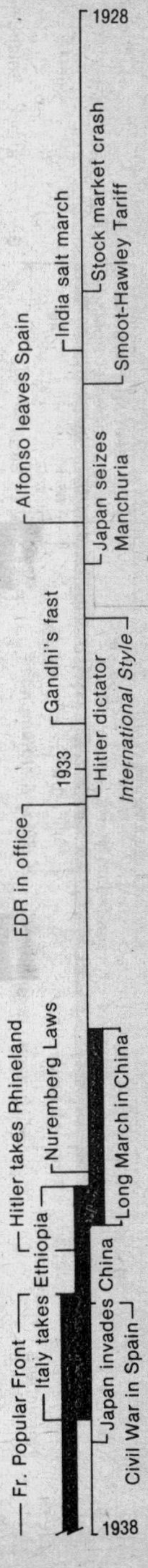

U.S. Easy credit, technological ingenuity, and war-related industrial decline in Europe caused a long economic boom, in which ownership of the new products — autos, phones, radios — became democratized. Prosperity, an increase in women workers, women's suffrage (1920) and drastic change in fashion (flappers, mannish bob for women, clean-shaven men), created a wide perception of social change, despite prohibition of alcoholic beverages (1919-33). Union membership and strikes increased. Fear of radicals led to Palmer raids (1919-20) and Sacco/Vanzetti case (1921-27).

Europe sorts itself out. Germany's liberal **Weimar constitution** (1919) could not guarantee a stable government in the face of rightist violence (Rathenau assassinated 1922) and Communist refusal to cooperate with Socialists. Reparations and allied occupation of the Rhineland caused staggering inflation which destroyed middle class savings, but economic expansion resumed after mid-decade, aided by U.S. loans. A sophisticated, innovative culture developed in architecture and design (Bauhaus, 1919-28), film (Lang, *M*, 1931), painting (Grosz), music (Weill, *Threepenny Opera*, 1928), theater (Brecht, *A Man's a Man*, 1926), criticism (Benjamin), philosophy (Jung), and fashion. This culture was considered decadent and socially disruptive by rightists.

England elected its first labor governments (Jan. 1924, June 1929). A 10-day general strike in support of coal miners failed, May 1926. In **Italy,** strikes, political chaos and violence by small Fascist bands culminated in the Oct. 1922 Fascist March on Rome, which established Mussolini's dictatorship. Strikes were outlawed (1926), and Italian influence was pressed in the Balkans (Albania a protectorate 1926). A conservative dictatorship was also established in **Portugal** in a 1926 military coup.

Czechoslovakia, the only stable democracy to emerge from the war in Central or East Europe, faced opposition from Germans (in the Sudetenland), Ruthenians, and some Slovaks. As the industrial heartland of the old Hapsburg empire, it remained fairly prosperous. With French backing, it formed the Little Entente with Yugoslavia (1920) and **Romania** (1921) to block Austrian or Hungarian irredentism. **Hungary** remained dominated by the landholding classes and expansionist feeling. Croats and Slovenes in **Yugoslavia** demanded a federal state until King Alexander proclaimed a dictatorship (1929). Poland faced nationality problems as well (Germans, Ukrainians, Jews); Pilsudski ruled as dictator from 1926. The Baltic states were threatened by traditionally dominant ethnic Germans and by Soviet-supported communists.

An economic collapse and famine in **Russia,** 1921-22, claimed 5 million lives. The New Economic Policy (1921) allowed land ownership by peasants and some private commerce and industry. Stalin was absolute ruler within 4 years of Lenin's 1924 death. He inaugurated a brutal collectivization program 1929-32, and used foreign communist parties for Soviet state advantage.

Internationalism. Revulsion against World War I led to pacifist agitation, the Kellogg-Briand Pact renouncing aggressive war (1928), and **naval disarmament** pacts (Washington, 1922, London, 1930). But the League of Nations was able to arbitrate only minor disputes (Greece-Bulgaria, 1925).

Middle East. Mustafa Kemal (Ataturk) led **Turkish** nationalists in resisting Italian, French, and Greek military advances, 1919-23. The sultanate was abolished 1922, and elaborate reforms passed, including secularization of law and adoption of the Latin alphabet. Ethnic conflict led to persecution of **Armenians** (over 1 million dead in 1915, 1 million expelled), Greeks (forced Greek-Turk population exchange, 1923), and Kurds (1925 uprising).

With evacuation of the Turks from **Arab** lands, the puritanical Wahabi dynasty of eastern Arabia conquered present Saudi Arabia, 1919-25. British, French, and Arab dynastic and nationalist maneuvering resulted in the creation of two more Arab monarchies in 1921: Iraq and Transjordan (both under British control), and two French mandates: Syria and Lebanon. Jewish immigration into British-mandated **Palestine,** inspired by the Zionist movement, was resisted by Arabs, at times violently (1921, 1929 massacres).

Reza Khan ruled **Persia** after his 1921 coup (shah from 1925), centralized control, and created the trappings of a modern state.

China. The Kuomintang under **Chiang Kai-shek** (1887-1975) subdued the warlords by 1928. The Communists were brutally suppressed after their alliance with the Kuomintang was broken in 1927. Relative peace thereafter allowed for industrial and financial improvements, with some Russian, British, and U.S. cooperation.

Arts. Nearly all bounds of subject matter, style, and attitude were broken in the arts of the period. **Abstract** art first took inspiration from natural forms or narrative themes (Kandinsky from 1911), then worked free of any representational aims (Malevich's suprematism, 1915-19, Mondrian's geometric style from 1917). The **Dada** movement from 1916 mocked artistic pretension with absurd collages and constructions (Arp, Tzara, from 1916). Paradox, illusion, and psychological taboos were exploited by **surrealists** by the latter 1920s (Dali, Magritte). Architectural schools celebrated industrial values, whether vigorous abstract constructivism (Tatlin, *Monument to 3rd International*, 1919) or the machined, streamlined **Bauhaus** style, which was extended to many design fields (Helvetica type face).

Prose writers explored revolutionary narrative modes related to dreams (Kafka's *Trial*, 1925), internal monologue (Joyce's *Ulysses*, 1922), and word play (Stein's *Making of Americans*, 1925). Poets and novelists wrote of modern alienation (Eliot's *Waste Land*, 1922) and aimlessness (Lost Generation).

Sciences. Scientific specialization prevailed by the 20th century. Advances in knowledge and technological aptitude increased with the geometric increase in the number of practitioners. Physicists challenged common-sense views of causality, observation, and a mechanistic universe, putting science further beyond popular grasp (Einstein's general theory of relativity, 1915; Bohr's quantum mechanics, 1913; Heisinger's uncertainty principle, 1927).

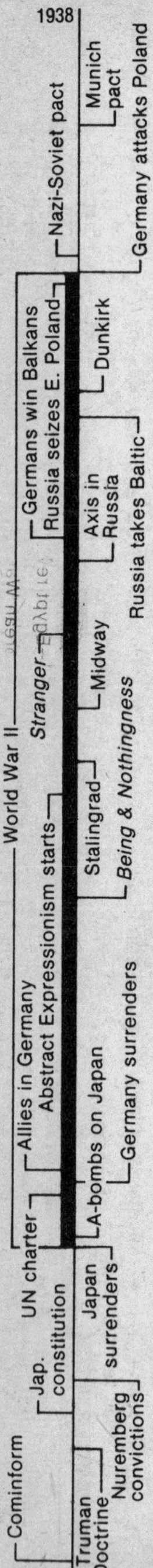

Rise of the Totalitarians: 1930-39

Depression. A worldwide financial panic and economic depression began with the Oct. 1929 U.S. stock market crash and the May 1931 failure of the Austrian Credit-Anstalt. A credit crunch caused international bankruptcies and **unemployment:** 12 million jobless by 1932 in the U.S., 5.6 million in Germany, 2.7 million in England. Governments responded with **tariff restrictions** (Smoot-Hawley Act 1930; Ottawa Imperial Conference, 1932) which dried up world trade. Government public works programs were vitiated by deflationary budget balancing.

Germany. Years of agitation by violent extremists was brought to a head by the Depression. Nazi leader **Hitler** was named chancellor by Pres. Hindenburg Jan. 1933, and given dictatorial power by the Reichstag in Mar. Opposition parties were disbanded, strikes banned, and all aspects of economic, cultural, and religious life brought under central government and Nazi party control and manipulated by sophisticated propaganda. Severe persecution of Jews began (**Nuremberg Laws** Sept. 1935). Many Jews, political opponents and others were sent to concentration camps (Dachau, 1933) where thousands died or were killed. Public works, renewed conscription (1935), arms production, and a 4-year plan (1936) ended unemployment.

Hitler's expansionism started with reincorporation of the Saar (1935), occupation of the **Rhineland** (Mar. 1936), and annexation of Austria (Mar. 1938). At **Munich,** Sept. 1938, an indecisive Britain and France sanctioned German dismemberment of Czechoslovakia.

Russia. Urbanization and education advanced. Rapid industrialization was achieved through successive **5-year-plans** starting 1928, using severe labor discipline and mass forced labor. Industry was financed by a decline in living standards and exploitation of agriculture, which was almost totally collectivized by the early 1930s (*kolkhoz,* collective farm; *sovkhoz,* state farm, often in newly-worked lands). Successive **purges** increased the role of professionals and management at the expense of workers. Millions perished in a series of man-made disasters: elimination of kulaks (peasant land-owners), 1929-34; severe famine, 1932-33; party purges (Great Purge, 1936-38); suppression of nationalities; and poor conditions in labor camps.

Spain. An industrial revolution during World War I created an urban proletariat, which was attracted to socialism and anarchism; Catalan nationalists challenged central authority. The 5 years after King Alfonso left Spain, Apr. 1931, were dominated by tension between intermittent leftist and anti-clerical governments and clericals, monarchists and other rightists. Anarchist and communist rebellions were crushed, but a July, 1936, extreme right rebellion led by Gen. Francisco Franco and aided by Nazi Germany and Fascist Italy succeeded, after a 3-year **civil war** (over 1 million dead in battles and atrocities). The war polarized international public opinion.

Italy. Despite propaganda for the ideal of the Corporate State, few domestic reforms were attempted. An entente with Hungary and Austria, Mar. 1934, a pact with Germany and Japan, Nov. 1937, and intervention by 50-75,000 troops in Spain, 1936-39, sealed Italy's identification with the fascist bloc (anti-Semitic laws after Mar. 1938). Ethiopia was conquered, 1935-37, and **Albania** annexed, Jan. 1939, in conscious imitation of ancient Rome.

East Europe. Repressive regimes fought for power against an active opposition (liberals, socialists, communists, peasants, Nazis). Minority groups and Jews were restricted within national boundaries that did not coincide with ethnic population patterns. In the destruction of **Czechoslovakia, Hungary** occupied southern Slovakia (Mar. 1938) and Ruthenia (Mar. 1939), and a pro-Nazi regime took power in the rest of Slovakia. Other boundary disputes (e.g. Poland-Lithuania, Yugoslavia-Bulgaria, Romania-Hungary) doomed attempts to build joint fronts against Germany or Russia. Economic depression was severe.

East Asia. After a period of liberalism in **Japan,** nativist militarists dominated the government with peasant support. Manchuria was seized, Sept. 1931-Feb. 1932, and a puppet state set up (Manchukuo). Adjacent Jehol (inner Mongolia) was occupied in 1933. China proper was invaded July 1937; large areas were conquered by Oct. 1938.

In **China** Communist forces left Kuomintang-besieged strongholds in the South in a Long March (1934-35) to the North. The Kuomintang-Communist civil war was suspended Jan. 1937 in the face of threatening Japan.

The democracies. The Roosevelt Administration, in office Mar. 1933, embarked on an extensive program of social reform and economic stimulation, including protection for labor unions (heavy industries organized), social security, public works, wages and hours laws, assistance to farmers. Isolationist sentiment (1937 Neutrality Act) prevented U.S. intervention in Europe, but military expenditures were increased in 1939.

French political instability and polarization prevented resolution of economic and international security questions. The **Popular Front** government under Blum (June 1936-Apr. 1938) passed social reforms (40-hour week) and raised arms spending. National coalition governments ruled Britain from Aug. 1931, brought some economic recovery, but failed to define a consistent foreign policy until Chamberlain's government (from May 1937), which practiced deliberate **appeasement** of Germany and Italy.

India. Twenty years of agitation for autonomy and then for independence (Gandhi's **salt march,** 1930) achieved some constitutional reform (extended provincial powers, 1935) despite Moslem-Hindu strife. Social issues assumed prominence with peasant uprisings (1921), strikes (1928), Gandhi's efforts for untouchables (1932 "fast unto death"), and social and agrarian reform by the provinces after 1937.

Arts. The streamlined, geometric design motifs of Art Deco (from 1925) prevailed through the 1930s. Abstract art flourished (Moore sculptures from 1931) alongside a new realism related to social and political concerns (**Socialist Realism** the official Soviet style from 1934; Mexican muralists Rivera, 1886-1957, and Orozco, 1883-1949), which was also expressed in fiction and poetry (Steinbeck's *Grapes of Wrath,* 1939; Sandburg's *The People, Yes,* 1936). Modern architecture (*International Style,* 1932) was unchallenged in its use of man-made materials (concrete, glass), lack of decoration, and monumentality (Rockefeller Center, 1929-40). U.S.-made films captured a world-wide audience with their larger-than-life fantasies (*Gone with the Wind,* 1939).

War, Hot and Cold: 1940-49

War in Europe. The Nazi-Soviet non-agression pact (Aug. '39) freed Germany to attack Poland (Sept.). Britain and France, who had guaranteed Polish independence, declared war on Germany. Russia seized East Poland (Sept.), attacked Finland (Nov.) and took the Baltic states (July '40). Mobile German forces staged **"blitzkrieg"** attacks Apr.-June, '40, conquering neutral Denmark, Norway, and the low countries and defeating France; 350,000 British and French troops were evacuated at **Dunkirk** (May). The Battle of Britain, June-Dec. '40, denied Germany air superiority, German-Italian campaigns won the Balkans by Apr. '41. Three million Axis troops **invaded Russia** June '41, marching through the Ukraine to the Caucasus, and through White Russia and the Baltic republics to Moscow and Leningrad.

Russian winter counterthrusts, '41-'42 and '42-'43 stopped the German advance (Stalingrad Sept. '42-Feb. '43). With British and U.S. Lend-Lease aid and sustaining great casualties, the Russians drove the Axis from all E. Europe and the Balkans in the next 2 years. Invasions of N. Africa (Nov. '42), Italy (Sept. '43), and Normandy (June '44) brought U.S., British, Free French and allied troops to Germany by spring '45. Germany surrendered May 7, 1945.

War in Asia-Pacific. Japan occupied Indochina Sept. '40, dominated Thailand Dec. '41, attacked Hawaii, the Philippines, Hong Kong, Malaya Dec. 7, 1941. Indonesia was attacked Jan. '42, Burma conquered Mar. 42. Battle of **Midway** (June '42) turned back the Japanese advance. "Island-hopping" battles (Guadalcanal Aug. '42-Jan. '43, **Leyte Gulf** Oct. '44, Iwo Jima Feb.-Mar. '45, Okinawa Apr. '45) and massive bombing raids on Japan from June '44 wore out Japanese defenses. Two U.S. atom bombs, dropped Aug. 6 and 9, forced Japan to surrender Aug. 14, 1945. *For further details, see 1978 and earlier editions of The World Almanac.*

Atrocities. The war brought 20th-century cruelty to its peak. Nazi murder camps (Auschwitz) systematically killed 6 million Jews. Gypsies, political opponents, sick and retarded people, and others deemed undesirable were murdered by the Nazis, as were vast numbers of Slavs, especially leaders. German bombs killed 70,000 English civilians. Some 100,000 Chinese civilians were killed by Japanese forces in the capture of Nanking. Severe retaliation by the Soviet army, E. European partisans, Free French and others took a heavy toll. U.S. and British bombing of Germany killed hundreds of thousands, as did U.S. bombing of Japan (80-200,000 at Hiroshima alone). Some 45 million people lost their lives in the war.

Home front. All industries were reoriented to war production and support, and rationing was universal. Science was harnessed for the war effort, yielding such innovations as radar, jet planes, and synthetic materials. Unscathed U.S. industry, partly staffed by women, helped decide the war.

Settlement. The United Nations charter was signed in San Francisco June 26, 1945 by 50 nations. The International Tribunal at Nuremberg convicted 22 German leaders for war crimes Sept. '46, 23 Japanese leaders were convicted Nov. '48. Postwar border changes included large gains in territory for the USSR, losses for Germany, a shift westward in Polish borders, and minor losses for Italy. Communist regimes, supported by Soviet troops, took power in most of E. Europe, including Soviet-occupied Germany (GDR proclaimed Oct. '49). Japan lost all overseas lands.

Recovery. Basic political and social changes were imposed on Japan and W. Germany by the western allies (Japan constitution Nov. '46, W. German basic law May '49). U.S. Marshall Plan aid ($12 billion '47-'51) spurred W. European economic recovery after a period of severe inflation and strikes in Europe and the U.S. The British Labour Party introduced a national health service and nationalized basic industries in 1946.

Cold War. Western fears of further Soviet advances (Cominform formed Oct. '47, Czechoslovakia coup, Feb. '48, Berlin blockade Apr.'48-Sept. '49) led to formation of NATO. Civil War in Greece and Soviet pressure on Turkey led to U.S. aid under the Truman Doctrine (Mar. '47). Other anti-communist security pacts were the Org. of American States (Apr. '48) and Southeast Asia Treaty Org. (Sept. '54). A new wave of Soviet purges and repression intensified in the last years of Stalin's rule, extending to E. Europe (Slansky trial in Czechoslovakia, 1951). Only Yugoslavia resisted Soviet control (expelled by Cominform, June '48; U.S. aid, June '49).

China, Korea. Communist forces emerged from World War II strengthened by the Soviet takeover of industrial Manchuria. In 4 years of fighting, the Kuomintang was driven from the mainland; the People's Republic was proclaimed Oct. 1, 1949. Korea was divided by Russian and U.S. occupation forces. Separate republics were proclaimed in the 2 zones Aug.-Sept. '48.

India. India and Pakistan became independent dominions Aug. 15, 1947. Millions of Hindu and Moslem refugees were created by the partition; riots, 1946-47, took hundreds of thousands of lives; Gandhi himself was assassinated Jan. '48. Burma became completely independent Jan. '48; Ceylon took dominion status in Feb.

Middle East. The UN approved partition of Palestine into Jewish and Arab states. Israel was proclaimed May 14, 1948. Arabs rejected partition, but failed to defeat Israel in war, May '48-July '49. Immigration from Europe and the Middle East swelled Israel's Jewish population. British and French forces left Lebanon and Syria, 1946. Transjordan occupied most of Arab Palestine.

Southeast Asia. Communists and others fought against restoration of French rule in Indochina from 1946; a non-communist government was recognized by France Mar. '49, but fighting continued. Both Indonesia and the Philippines became independent, the former in 1949 after 4 years of war with Netherlands, the latter in 1946. Philippine economic and military ties with the U.S. remained strong; a communist-led peasant rising was checked in '48.

Arts. New York became the center of the world art market; abstract expressionism was the chief mode (Pollock from '43, de Kooning from '47). Literature and philosophy explored existentialism (Camus' *Stranger*, 1942, Sartre's *Being and Nothingness*, 1943). Non-western attempts to revive or create regional styles (Senghor's Negritude, Mishima's novels) only confirmed the emergence of a universal culture. Radio and phonograph records spread American popular music (swing, bebop) around the world.

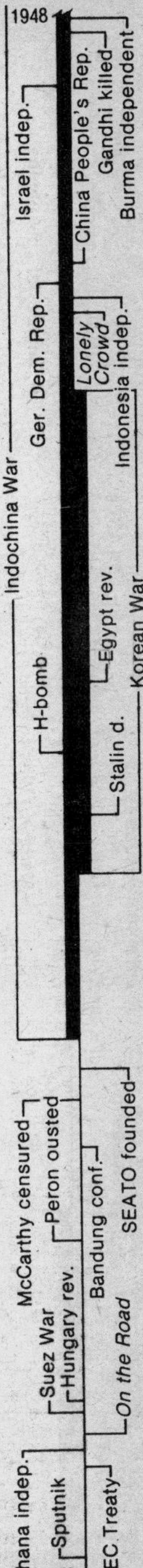

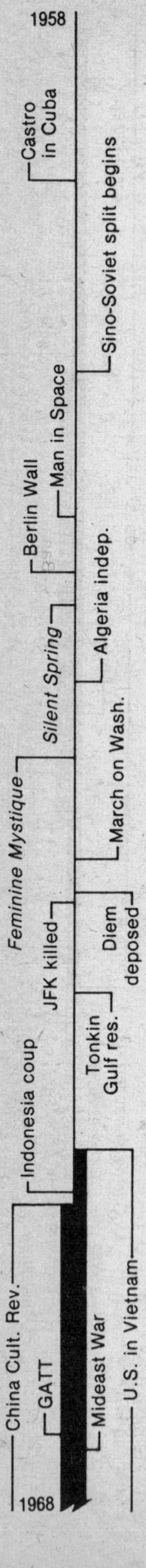

The American Decade: 1950-59

Polite decolonization. The peaceful decline of European political and military power in Asia and Africa accelerated in the 1950s. Nearly all of **N. Africa** was freed by 1956, but France fought a bitter war to retain Algeria, with its large European minority, until 1962. **Ghana,** independent 1957, led a parade of new black African nations (over 2 dozen by 1962) which altered the political character of the UN. Ethnic disputes often exploded in the new nations after decolonization (UN troops in Cyprus 1964; **Nigeria** civil war 1967-70). Leaders of the new states, mostly sharing socialist ideologies, tried to create an Afro-Asian bloc (Bandung Conf. 1955), but Western economic influence and U.S. political ties remained strong (Baghdad Pact, 1955).

Trade. World trade volume soared, in an atmosphere of monetary stability assured by international accords (**Bretton Woods** 1944). In Europe, economic integration advanced (**European Economic Community** 1957, European Free Trade Association 1960). Comecon (1949) coordinated the economies of Soviet-bloc countries.

U.S. Economic growth produced an abundance of consumer goods (9.3 million motor vehicles sold, 1955). Suburban housing tracts changed life patterns for middle and working classes (Levittown 1946-51). **Eisenhower's** landside election victories (1952, 1956) reflected consensus politics. Censure of McCarthy (Dec. '54) curbed the political abuse of anti-communism. A system of alliances and military bases bolstered U.S. influence on all continents. Trade and payments surpluses were balanced by overseas investments and foreign aid ($50 billion, 1950-59).

USSR. In the "thaw" after Stalin's death in 1953, relations with the West improved (evacuation of Vienna, Geneva summit conf., both 1955). Repression of scientific and cultural life eased, and many prisoners were freed or rehabilitated culminating in **de-Stalinization** (1956). Khrushchev's leadership aimed at consumer sector growth, but farm production lagged, despite the virgin lands program (from 1954). The 1956 Hungarian revolution, the 1960 U-2 spy plane episode, and other incidents renewed East-West tension and domestic curbs.

East Europe. Resentment of Russian domination and Stalinist repression combined with nationalist, economic and religious factors to produce periodic violence. East Berlin workers rioted in 1953, Polish workers rioted in Poznan, June 1956, and a broad-based revolution broke out in Hungary, Oct. 1956. All were suppressed by Soviet force or threats (at least 7,000 dead in Hungary). But Poland was allowed to restore private ownership of farms, and a degree of personal and economic freedom returned to Hungary. Yugoslavia experimented with worker self-management and a market economy.

Korea. The 1945 division of Korea left industry in the North, which was organized into a militant regime and armed by Russia. The South was politically disunited. Over 60,000 North Korean troops invaded the South June 25, 1950. The U.S., backed by the UN Security Council, sent troops. UN troops reached the Chinese border in Nov. Some 200,000 Chinese troops crossed the Yalu River and drove back UN forces. Cease-fire in July 1951 found the opposing forces near the original 38th parallel border. After 2 years of sporadic fighting, an armistice was signed July 27, 1953. U.S. troops remained in the South, and U.S. economic and military aid continued. The war stimulated rapid economic recovery in Japan. *For details, see 1978 and earlier editions of The World Almanac.*

China. Starting in 1952, industry, agriculture, and social institutions were forcibly collectivized. As many as several million people were executed as Kuomintang supporters or as class and political enemies. The Great Leap Forward, 1958-60, unsuccessfully tried to force the pace of development by substituting labor for investment.

Indochina. Ho's forces, aided by Russia and the new Chinese Communist government, fought French and pro-French Vietnamese forces to a standstill, and captured the strategic Dienbienphu camp in May, 1954. The Geneva Agreements divided Vietnam in half pending elections (never held), and recognized Laos and Cambodia as independent. The U.S. aided the anti-Communist Republic of Vietnam in the South.

Middle East. Arab revolutions placed leftist, militantly nationalist regimes in power in Egypt (1952) and Iraq (1958). But Arab unity attempts failed (United Arab Republic joined Egypt, Syria, Yemen 1958-61). Arab refusal to recognize Israel (Arab League economic blockade began Sept. 1951) led to a permanent state of war, with repeated incidents (Gaza, 1955). Israel occupied Sinai, Britain and France took the Suez Canal, Oct. 1956, but were replaced by the UN Emergency Force. The Mossadegh government in Iran nationalized the British-owned oil industry May 1951, but was overthrown in a U.S.-aided coup Aug. 1953.

Latin America. Dictator Juan Peron, in office 1946, enforced land reform, some nationalization, welfare state measures, and curbs on the Roman Catholic Church, but crushed opposition. A Sept. 1955 coup deposed Peron. The 1952 revolution in Bolivia brought land reform, nationalization of tin mines, and improvement in the status of Indians, who nevertheless remained poor. The Batista regime in Cuba was overthrown, Jan. 1959, by Fidel Castro, who imposed a communist dictatorship, aligned Cuba with Russia, improved education and health care. A U.S.-backed anti-Castro invasion (Bay of Pigs, Apr. 1961) was crushed. Self-government advanced in the British Caribbean.

Technology. Large outlays on research and development in the U.S. and USSR focussed on military applications (H-bomb in U.S. 1952, USSR 1953, Britain 1957, intercontinental missiles late 1950s). Soviet launching of the Sputnik satellite, Oct. 1957, spurred increases in U.S. science education funds (National Defense Education Act).

Literature and letters. Alienation from social and literary conventions reached an extreme in the theater of the absurd (Beckett's *Waiting for Godot* 1952), the "new novel" (Robbe-Grillet's *Voyeur* 1955), and avant-garde film (Antonioni's *L'Avventura* 1960). U.S. Beatniks (Kerouac's *On the Road* 1957) and others rejected the supposed conformism of Americans (Riesman's *Lonely Crowd* 1950).

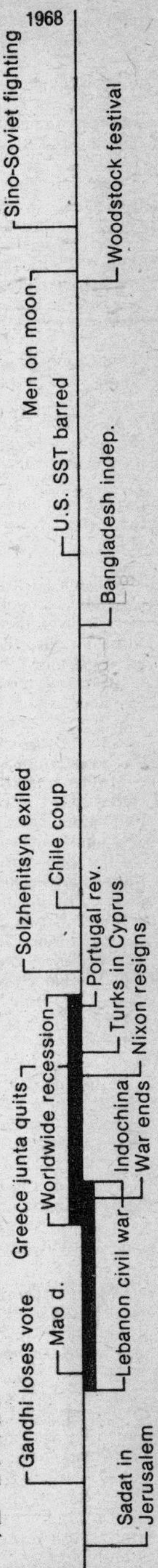

Rising Expectations: 1960-69

Economic boom. The longest sustained economic boom on record spanned almost the entire decade in the capitalist world; the closely-watched GNP figure doubled in the U.S. 1960-70, fueled by Vietnam War-related budget deficits. The **General Agreement on Tariffs and Trade,** 1967, stimulated West European prosperity, which spread to peripheral areas (Spain, Italy, E. Germany). Japan became a top economic power ($20 billion exports 1970). Foreign investment aided the industrialization of Brazil. Soviet 1965 economic reform attempts (decentralization, material incentives) were limited; but growth continued.

Reform and radicalization. A series of political and social reform movements took root in the U.S., later spreading to other countries with the help of ubiquitous U.S. film and television programs and heavy overseas travel (2.2 million U.S. passports issued 1970). Blacks agitated peaceably and with partial success against segregation and poverty (1963 March on Washington, 1964 **Civil Rights Act**); but some urban ghettos erupted in extensive riots (Watts, 1965; Detroit, 1967; King assassination, Apr. 4, 1968). New concern for the poor (Harrington's *Other America,* 1963) led to Pres. Johnson's **"Great Society"** programs (Medicare, Water Quality Act, Higher Education Act, all 1965). Concern with the **environment** surged (Carson's *Silent Spring,* 1962). **Feminism** revived as a cultural and political movement (Friedan's *Feminine Mystique,* 1963, National Organization for Women founded 1966) and a movement for homosexual rights emerged (Stonewall riot, in NYC, 1969).

Opposition to U.S. involvement in Vietnam, especially among university students (**Moratorium** protest Nov. '69) turned violent (Weatherman Chicago riots Oct. '69). New Left and Marxist theories became popular, and membership in radical groups swelled (Students for a Democratic Society, Black Panthers). Maoist groups, especially in Europe, called for total transformation of society. In France, students sparked a nationwide strike affecting 10 million workers May-June '68, but an electoral reaction barred revolutionary change.

Arts and styles. The boundary between fine and popular arts were blurred by Pop Art (Warhol) and rock musicals (Hair, 1968). Informality and exaggeration prevailed in fashion (beards, miniskirts). A non-political "counterculture" developed, rejecting traditional bourgeois life goals and personal habits, and use of marijuana and hallucinogens spread (Woodstock festival Aug. '68). Indian influence was felt in music (Beatles), religion (Ram Dass), and fashion.

Science. Achievements in space (men on moon July '69) and electronics (lasers, integrated circuits) encouraged a faith in scientific solutions to problems in agriculture ("green revolution"), medicine (heart transplants 1967) and other areas. The harmful effects of science, it was believed, could be controlled (1963 nuclear weapon test ban treaty, 1968 non-proliferation treaty).

China. Mao's revolutionary militance caused disputes with Russia under "revisionist" Khrushchev, starting 1960. The two powers exchanged fire in 1969 border disputes. China used force to capture areas disputed with India, 1962. The "Great Proletarian Cultural Revolution" tried to impose a utopian egalitarian program in China and spread revolution abroad; political struggle, often violent, convulsed China 1965-68.

Indochina. Communist-led guerrillas aided by N. Vietnam fought from 1960 against the S. Vietnam government of Ngo Dinh Diem (killed 1963). The U.S. military role increased after the 1964 Tonkin Gulf incident. U.S. forces peaked at 543,400, Apr. '69. Massive numbers of N. Viet troops also fought. Laotian and Cambodian neutrality were threatened by communist insurgencies, with N. Vietnamese aid, and U.S. intrigues. *For details, see 1978 and earlier editions of The World Almanac.*

Third World. A bloc of authoritarian leftist regimes among the newly independent nations emerged in political opposition to the U.S.-led Western alliance, and came to dominate the conference of nonaligned nations (Belgrade 1961, Cairo 1964, Lusaka 1970). Soviet political ties and military bases were established in Cuba, Egypt, Algeria, Guinea, and other countries, whose leaders were regarded as revolutionary heros by opposition groups in pro-Western or colonial countries. Some leaders were ousted in coups by pro-Western groups—Zaire's Lumumba (killed 1961), Ghana's Nkrumah (exiled 1966), and Indonesia's Sukarno (effectively ousted 1965 after a Communist coup failed).

Middle East. Arab-Israeli tension erupted into a brief war June 1967. Israel emerged as a major regional power. Military shipments before and after the war brought much of the Arab world into the Soviet political sphere. Most Arab states broke U.S. diplomatic ties, while Communist countries cut their ties to Israel. Intra-Arab disputes continued: Egypt and Saudi Arabia supported rival factions in a bloody Yemen civil war 1962-70; Lebanese troops fought Palestinian commandos in 1969.

East Europe. To stop the large-scale exodus of citizens, E. German authorities built a fortified wall across Berlin Aug. '61. Soviet sway in the Balkans was weakened by Albania's support of China (USSR broke ties Dec. '61) and Romania's assertion of industrial and foreign policy autonomy in 1964. Liberalization in Czechoslovakia, spring 1968, was crushed by troops of 5 Warsaw Pact countries. West German treaties with Russia and Poland, 1970, facilitated the transfer of German technology and confirmed post-war boundaries.

Disillusionment: 1970-79

U.S.: Caution and neoconservatism. A relatively sluggish economy, energy and resource shortages (natural gas crunch 1975, gasoline shortage 1979), and environmental problems contributed to a **"limits of growth"** philosophy that affected politics (Cal. Gov. Brown). Suspicion of science and technology killed or delayed major projects (supersonic transport dropped 1971, DNA recombination curbed 1976, Seabrook A-plant protests 1977-78) and was fed by the Three Mile Island nuclear reactor accident in Mar. '79.

Mistrust of big government weakened support for government reform plans among liberals. School busing and racial quotas were opposed (**Bakke decision** June '78); the Equal Rights Amendment for women languished; civil rights for homosexuals were opposed (Dade County referendum June '77).

U.S. defeat in **Indochina** (evacuation Apr. '75), revelations of Central Intelligence Agency misdeeds (Rockefeller Commission report June '75), and the **Watergate** scandals (Nixon quit Aug. '74) reduced faith in U.S. moral and material capacity to influence world affairs. Revelations of Soviet crimes (Solzhenitsyn's *Gulag Archipelago* from 1974) and Russian intervention in Africa aided a revival of anti-Communist sentiment.

Economy sluggish. The 1960s boom faltered in the 1970s; a severe recession in the U.S. and Europe 1974-75 followed a huge oil price hike Dec. '73. Monetary instability (U.S. cut ties to gold Aug. '71), the decline of the dollar, and **protectionist** moves by industrial countries (1977-78) threatened trade. Business investment and spending for research declined. Severe inflation plagued many countries (25% in Britain, 1975; 18% in U.S., 1979).

China picks up pieces. After the 1976 deaths of Mao and Chou, a power struggle for the leadership succession was won by pragmatists. A nationwide purge of orthodox Maoists was carried out, and the "**Gang of Four**", led by Mao's widow Chiang Ching, was arrested.

The new leaders freed over 100,000 political prisoners, and reduced public adulation of Mao. Political and trade ties were expanded with Japan, Europe, and the U.S. in the late 1970's, as relations worsened with Russia, Cuba, and Vietnam (4-week invasion by China in 1979). Ideological guidelines in industry, science, education, and the armed forces, which the ruling faction said had caused chaos and decline, were reversed (bonuses to workers, Dec. '77; exams for college entrance, Oct. '77). Severe restrictions on cultural expression were eased (Beethoven ban lifted Mar. '77).

Europe. European unity moves (EEC-EFTA trade accord 1972) faltered as economic problems appeared (Britain floated pound 1972; France floated franc 1974). Germany and Switzerland curbed guest workers from S. Europe. Greece and Turkey quarreled over Cyprus (Turks intervened 1974) and Aegean oil rights.

All of non-Communist Europe was under democratic rule after free elections were held in **Spain** June '76, 7 months after the death of Franco. The conservative, colonialist regime in **Portugal** was overthrown Apr. '74. In **Greece,** the 7-year-old military dictatorship yielded power in 1974. Northern Europe, though ruled mostly by Socialists (**Swedish** Socialists unseated 1976, after 44 years in power), turned conservative. The **British** Labour government imposed wage curbs 1975, and suspended nationalization schemes. Terrorism in **Germany** (1972 Munich Olympics killings) led to laws curbing some civil liberties. **French** "new philosophers" rejected leftist ideologies, and the shaky Socialist-Communist coalition lost a 1978 election bid.

Religion back in politics. The improvement in Moslem countries' political fortunes by the 1950s (with the exception of Central Asia under Soviet and Chinese rule), and the growth of Arab oil wealth, was followed by a resurgence of traditional piety. **Libyan** dictator Qaddafi mixed strict Islamic laws with socialism in his militant ideology and called for an eventual Moslem return to Spain and Sicily. The illegal Moslem Brotherhood in **Egypt** was accused of violence, while extreme Moslem groups bombed theaters, 1977, to protest secular values.

In **Turkey,** the National Salvation Party was the first Islamic group to share power (1974) since secularization in the 1920s. Religious authorities, such as Ayatollah Ruholla Khomeini, led the **Iranian** revolution and religiously motivated Moslems took part in the insurrection in Saudi Arabia that briefly seized the Grand Mosque in Mecca in 1979. Moslem puritan opposition to **Pakistan** Pres. Bhutto helped lead to his overthrow July '77. However, Moslem solidarity could not prevent Pakistan's eastern province (**Bangladesh**) from declaring independence, Dec. '71, after a bloody civil war.

Moslem and Hindu resentment against coerced sterilization in **India** helped defeat the Gandhi government, which was replaced Mar. '77 by a coalition including religious Hindu parties and led by devout Hindu Desai. Moslems in the southern **Philippines,** aided by Libya, conducted a long rebellion against central rule from 1973.

Evangelical Protestant groups grew in numbers and prosperity in the U.S. ("**born again**" Pres. Carter elected 1976), and the Catholic charismatic movement obtained respectability. A revival of interest in Orthodox Christianity occurred among **Russian** intellectuals (Solzhenitsyn). The secularist **Israeli** Labor party, after decades of rule, was ousted in 1977 by conservatives led by Begin, an observant Jew; religious militants founded settlements on the disputed West Bank, part of Biblically-promised Israel. U.S. Reform Judaism revived many previously discarded traditional practices.

The Buddhist Soka Gakkai movement launched the Komeito party in Japan, 1964, which became a major opposition party in 1972 and 1976 elections.

Old-fashioned religious wars raged intermittently in **N. Ireland** (Catholic vs. Protestant, 1969-) and **Lebanon** (Christian vs. Moslem, 1975-), while religious militancy complicated the Israel-Arab dispute (1973 Israel-Arab war. In spite of a **1979 peace treaty between Egypt and Israel** which looked forward to a resolution of the Palestinian issue, increased religious militancy on the West Bank made such a resolution seem unlikely.

Latin America. Repressive conservative regimes strengthened their hold on most of the continent, with the violent coup against the elected Allende government in **Chile,** Sept. '73, the 1976 military coup in **Argentina,** and coups against reformist regimes in **Bolivia,** 1971 and 1979, and **Peru,** 1976. In Central America, increasing liberal and leftist militancy led to the ouster of the Somoza regime of Nicaragua in 1979 and civil conflict in El Salvador.

Indochina. Communist victory in Vietnam, Cambodia, and Laos by May '75 did not bring peace. Attempts at radical social reorganization left over one million dead in Cambodia during 1975-78 and caused hundreds of thousands of ethnic Chinese and others to flee Vietnam ("boat people," 1979). The Vietnamese invasion of Cambodia swelled the refugee population and contributed to widespread starvation in that devastated country.

Russian expansion. Soviet influence, checked in some countries (troops ousted by Egypt 1972) was projected further afield, often with the use of Cuban troops (Angola 1975- , Ethiopia 1977-), and aided by a growing navy, merchant fleet, and international banking ability. Detente with the West — 1972 Berlin pact, 1970 strategic arms pact (**SALT**) — gave way to a more antagonistic relationship in the late 1970s, exacerbated by the Soviet invasion of Afghanistan in 1979.

Africa. The last remaining European colonies were granted independence (**Spanish Sahara** 1976, **Djibouti** 1977) and, after 10 years of civil war and many negotiation sessions, a black government took over Zimbabwe (Rhodesia) in 1979; white domination remained in **S. Africa.** Great power involvement in local wars (Russia in **Angola, Ethiopia;** France in **Chad, Zaire, Mauritania**) and the use of tens of thousands of Cuban troops was denounced by some African leaders as neocolonialism. Ethnic or tribal clashes made Africa the chief world locus of sustained warfare in the late 1970s.

Arts. Traditional modes in painting, architecture, and music, pursued in relative obscurity for much of the 20th century, returned to popular and critical attention in the 1970s. The pictorial emphasis in neorealist and photorealist painting, the return of many architects to detail, decoration, and traditional natural materials, and the concern with ordered structure in musical composition were, ironically, novel experiences for artistic consumers after the exhaustion of experimental possibilities. However, these more conservative styles coexisted with modernist works in an atmosphere of variety and tolerance.

Some Notable Marine Disasters Since 1850

(Figures indicate estimated lives lost)

1854, Mar.—City of Glasgow; British steamer missing in North Atlantic; 480.

1854, Sept. 27—Arctic; U.S. (Collins Line) steamer sunk in collision with French steamer Vesta near Cape Race; 285-351.

1856, Jan. 23—Pacific; U.S. (Collins Line) steamer missing in North Atlantic; 186-286.

1858, Sept. 23—Austria; German steamer destroyed by fire in North Atlantic; 471.

1860, Feb. 19—Hungarian; British steamer wrecked at Cape Sable; 237.

1863, Apr. 27—Anglo-Saxon; British steamer wrecked at Cape Race; 238.

1865, Apr. 27—Sultana; a Mississippi River steamer blew up near Memphis, Tenn; 1,400.

1869, Oct. 27—Stonewall; steamer burned on Mississippi River below Cairo, Ill.; 200.

1870, Jan. 25—City of Boston; British (Inman Line) steamer vanished between New York and Liverpool; 177.

1870, Oct 19—Cambria; British steamer wrecked off northern Ireland; 196.

1872, Nov. 7—Mary Celeste; U.S. half-brig sailed from New York for Genoa; found abandoned in Atlantic 4 weeks later in mystery of sea; crew never heard from; loss of life unknown.

1873, Jan. 22—Northfleet; British steamer foundered off Dungeness, England; 300.

1873, Apr. 1—Atlantic; British (White Star) steamer wrecked off Nova Scotia; 585.

1873, Nov. 23—Ville du Havre; French steamer, sunk after collision with British sailing ship Loch Earn; 226.

1875, May 7—Schiller; German steamer wrecked off Scilly Isles; 312.

1875, Nov. 4—Pacific; U.S. steamer sunk after collision off Cape Flattery; 236.

1878, Sept. 3—Princess Alice; British steamer sank after collision in Thames; 700.

1878, Dec. 18—Byzantin; French steamer sank after Dardanelles collision; 210.

1880, Nov. 24—Uncle Joseph; French steamer sank in collision off Spezzia, Greece; 250.

1881, May 24—Victoria; steamer capsized in Thames River, Canada; 200.

1883, Jan. 19—Cimbria; German steamer sunk in collision with British steamer Sultan in North Sea; 389.

1887, Nov. 15—Wah Yeung; British steamer burned at sea; 400.

1890, Feb. 17—Duburg; British steamer wrecked, China Sea; 400.

1890, Sept. 19—Ertogrul; Turkish frigate foundered off Japan; 540.

1891, Mar. 17—Utopia; British steamer sank in collision with British ironclad Anson off Gibraltar; 562.

1895, Jan. 30—Elbe; German steamer sank in collision with British steamer Craithie in North Sea; 332.

1895, Mar. 11—Reina Regenta; Spanish cruiser foundered near Gibraltar; 400.

1898, Feb. 15—Maine; U.S. battleship blown up in Havana Harbor; 266.

1898, July 4—La Bourgogne; French steamer sunk in collision with British sailing ship Cromartyshire off Nova Scotia; 549.

1904, June 15—General Slocum; excursion steamer burned in East River, New York City; 1,030.

1904, June 28—Norge; Danish steamer wrecked on Rockall Island, Scotland; 620.

1906, Aug. 4—Sirio; Italian steamer wrecked off Cape Palos, Spain; 350.

1908, Mar. 23—Matsu Maru; Japanese steamer sank in collision near Hakodate, Japan; 300.

1909, Aug. 1—Waratah; British steamer, Sydney to London, vanished; 300.

1910, Feb. 9—General Chanzy; French steamer wrecked off Minorca, Spain; 200.

1911, Sept. 25—Liberté; French battleship exploded at Toulon; 285.

1912, Apr. 14-15—Titanic; British (White Star) steamer hit iceberg in North Atlantic; 1,503.

1912, Sept. 28—Kichemaru; Japanese steamer sank off Japanese coast; 1,000.

1914, May 29—Empress of Ireland; British (Canadian Pacific) steamer sunk in collision with Norwegian collier in St. Lawrence River; 1,014.

1915, May 7—Lusitania; British (Cunard Line) steamer torpedoed and sunk by German submarine U. 20 off Ireland; 1,198.

1915, July 24—Eastland; excursion steamer capsized in Chicago River; 812.

1916, Feb. 26—Provence; French cruiser sank in Mediterranean; 3,100.

1916, Mar. 3—Principe de Asturias; Spanish steamer wrecked near Santos, Brazil; 558.

1916, Aug. 29—Hsin Yu; Chinese steamer sank off Chinese coast; 1,000.

1917, Dec. 6—Mont Blanc, Imo; French ammunition ship and Belgian steamer collided in Halifax Harbor; 1,600.

1918, Apr. 25—Kiang-Kwan Chinese steamer sank in collision off Hankow; 500.

1918, July 12—Kawachi; Japanese battleship blew up in Tokayama Bay; 500.

1918, Oct. 25—Princess Sophia; Canadian steamer sank off Alaskan coast; 398.

1919, Jan. 17—Chaonia; French steamer lost in Straits of Messina, Italy; 460.

1919, Sept. 9—Valbanera; Spanish steamer lost off Florida coast; 500.

1921, Mar. 18—Hong Kong; steamer wrecked in South China Sea; 1,000.

1922, Aug. 26—Niitaka; Japanese cruiser sank in storm off Kamchatka, USSR; 300.

1927, Oct. 25—Principessa Mafalda; Italian steamer blew up, sank off Porto Seguro, Brazil; 314.

1934, Sept. 8—Morro Castle; U.S. steamer, Havana to New York, burned off Asbury Park, N.J.; 125.

1939, May 23—Squalus; U.S. submarine sank off Portsmouth, N.H.; 26.

1939, June 1—Thetis; British submarine, sank in Liverpool Bay; 99.

1942, Feb. 18—Truxton and Pollux; U.S. destroyer and cargo ship ran aground, sank off Newfoundland; 204.

1942, Oct. 2—Curacao; British cruiser sank after collision with liner Queen Mary; 335.

1947, Jan. 19—Himera; Greek steamer hit a mine off Athens; 392.

1947, Apr. 16—Grandcamp; French freighter exploded in Texas City, Tex., Harbor, starting fires; 510.

1952, Apr. 26—Hobson and Wasp; U.S. destroyer and aircraft carrier collided in Atlantic; 176.

1953, Jan. 31—Princess Victoria; British ferry foundered off northern Irish coast; 134.

1954, Sept. 26—Toya Maru; Japanese ferry sank in Tsugaru Strait, Japan; 1,172.

1956, July 26—Andrea Doria and Stockholm; Italian liner and Swedish liner collided off Nantucket; 51.

1957, July 14—Eshghabad; Soviet ship ran aground in Caspian Sea; 270.

1961, Apr. 8—Dara; British liner burned in Persian Gulf; 212.

1961, July 8—Save; Portuguese ship ran aground off Mozambique; 259.

1963, Apr. 10—Thresher; U.S. Navy atomic submarine sank in North Atlantic; 129.

1964, Feb. 10—Voyager, Melbourne; Australian destroyer sank after collision with Australian aircraft carrier Melbourne off New South Wales; 82.

1968, Jan. 25—Dakar; Israeli submarine vanished in Mediterranean; 69.

1968, Jan. 27—Minerve; French submarine vanished in Mediterranean; 52.

1968, May 21—Scorpion; U.S. nuclear submarine sank in Atlantic near Azores; 99.

1969, June 2—Evans; U.S. destroyer cut in half by Australian carrier Melbourne, S. China Sea; 74.

1970, Mar. 4—Eurydice; French submarine sank in Mediterranean near Toulon; 57.

1970, Dec. 15—Namyong-Ho; South Korean ferry sank in Korea Strait; 308.

1974, May 1— Motor launch capsized off Bangladesh; 250.

1974, Sept. 26— Soviet destroyer burned and sank in Black Sea; est. 200.

1975, Aug. 9— Two Chinese riverboats collided and sank near Canton; c.500.

1976, Oct. 20—George Prince and Frosta; ferryboat and Norwegian tanker collided on Mississippi R. at Luling, La.; 77.

1976, Dec. 25—Patria; Egyptian liner caught fire and sank in the Red Sea; c. 100.

1977, Jan. 11—Grand Zenith; Panamanian-registered tanker sank off Cape Cod, Mass.; 38.

1977, Jan. 17—Spanish freighter collided with launch in Barcelona, Spain harbor; 46.

1979, Jan. 8—Betelgeuse; French oil tanker exploded in Bantry Bay, Ire.; 50.

1979, Aug. 14—23 yachts competing in Fastnet yacht race sunk or abandoned during storm in S. Irish Sea; 18.

1980, Jan. 28—Blackthorn; U.S. Coast Guard vessel sunk in collision with oil tanker in Tampa Bay; 23.

Major Earthquakes

Sources: National Earthquake Information Service, U.S. Geological Survey, and historical records

Magnitude of earthquakes (Mag.), distinct from deaths or damage caused, is measured on the Richter scale, on which each higher number represents a tenfold increase in energy measured in ground motion. Adopted in 1935, the scale has been applied in the following table to earthquakes as far back as reliable seismograms are available.

	Date	Place	Deaths	Mag.
526	May 20	Syria, Antioch.	250,000	N.A.
856	....	Greece, Corinth	45,000	"
1057	....	China, Chihli	25,000	"
1268	....	Asia Minor, Cilicia	60,000	"
1290	Sept. 27	China, Chihli	100,000	"
1293	May 20	Japan, Kamakura	30,000	"
1531	Jan. 26	Portugal, Lisbon	30,000	"
1556	Jan. 24	China, Shaanxi	830,000	"
1667	Nov.	Caucasia, Shemaka	80,000	"
1693	Jan. 11	Italy, Catania	60,000	"
1730	Dec. 30	Japan, Hokkaido	137,000	"
1737	Oct. 11	India, Calcutta	300,000	"
1755	June 7	Northern Persia	40,000	"
1755	Nov. 1	Portugal, Lisbon	60,000	8.75*
1783	Feb. 4	Italy, Calabria.	30,000	N.A.
1797	Feb. 4	Ecuador, Quito	41,000	N.A.
1822	Sept. 5	Asia Minor, Aleppo.	22,000	N.A.
1828	Dec. 28	Japan, Echigo	30,000	"
1868	Aug. 13-15	Peru and Ecuador	40,000	"
1875	May 16	Venezuela, Colombia	16,000	"
1896	June 15	Japan, sea wave.	27,120	"
1906	Apr. 18-19	Cal., San Francisco	452	8.3
1906	Aug. 16	Chile, Valparaiso.	20,000	8.6
1908	Dec. 28	Italy, Messina.	83,000	7.5
1915	Jan. 13	Italy, Avezzano.	29,980	7.5
1920	Dec. 16	China, Gansu.	100,000	8.6
1923	Sept. 1	Japan, Tokyo.	99,330	8.3
1927	May 22	China, Nan-Shan.	200,000	8.3
1932	Dec. 26	China, Gansu.	70,000	7.6
1933	Mar. 2	Japan	2,990	8.9
1934	Jan. 15	India, Bihar-Nepal	10,700	8.4
1935	May 31	India, Quetta	30,000	7.5
1939	Jan. 24	Chile, Chillan	28,000	8.3
1939	Dec. 26	Turkey, Erzincan.	30,000	7.9
1946	Dec. 21	Japan, Honshu.	2,000	8.4
1948	June 28	Japan, Fukui	5,131	7.3
1949	Aug. 5	Ecuador, Pelileo	6,000	6.8
1950	Aug. 15	India, Assam	1,530	8.7
1953	Mar. 18	NW Turkey	1,200	7.2
1956	June 10-17	N. Afghanistan	2,000	7.7
1957	July 2	Northern Iran	2,500	7.4
1957	Dec. 13	Western Iran	2,000	7.1
1960	Feb. 29	Morocco, Agadir	12,000	5.8
1960	May 21-30	Southern Chile	5,000	8.3
1962	Sept. 1	Northwestern Iran	12,230	7.1
1963	July 26	Yugoslavia, Skopje	1,100	6.0
1964	Mar. 27	Alaska.	114	8.5
1966	Aug. 19	Eastern Turkey.	2,520	6.9
1968	Aug. 31	Northeastern Iran	12,000	7.4
1970	Mar. 28	Western Turkey	1,086	7.4
1970	May 31	Northern Peru	66,794	7.7
1971	Feb. 9	Cal., San Fernando Valley.	65	6.5
1972	Apr. 10	Southern Iran.	5,057	6.9
1972	Dec. 23	Nicaragua.	5,000	6.2
1974	Dec. 28	Pakistan (9 towns)	5,200	6.3
1975	Sept. 6	Turkey (Lice, etc.)	2,312	6.8
1976	Feb. 4	Guatemala	22,778	7.5
1976	May 6	Northeast Italy	946	6.5
1976	June 26	New Guinea, Irian Jaya	443	7.1
1976	July 28	China, Tangshan.	800,000	8.2
1976	Aug. 17	Philippines, Mindanao	8,000	7.8
1976	Nov. 24	Eastern Turkey.	4,000	7.9
1977	Mar. 4	Romania, Bucharest, etc.	1,541	7.5
1977	Aug. 19	Indonesia	200	8.0
1977	Nov. 23	Northwestern Argentina.	100	8.2
1978	June 12	Japan, Sendai	21	7.5
1978	Sept. 16	Northeast Iran	25,000	7.7
1979	Sept. 12	Indonesia	100	8.1
1979	Dec. 12	Colombia, Equador	800	7.9

(*) estimated from earthquake intensity. (N.A.) not available.

Floods, Tidal Waves

Date		Location	Deaths
1887	....	Huang He River, China	900,000
1889	May 31	Johnstown, Pa.	2,200
1900	Sept. 8	Galveston, Tex.	5,000
1903	June 15	Heppner, Ore.	325
1911	....	Chang Jiang River, China.	100,000
1913	Mar. 25-27	Ohio, Indiana.	732
1915	Aug. 17	Galveston, Tex.	275
1928	Mar. 13	Collapse of St. Francis Dam, Santa Paula, Cal.	450
1928	Sept. 13	Lake Okeechobee, Fla.	2,000
1931	Aug.	Huang He River, China	3,700,000
1937	Jan. 22	Ohio, Miss. Valleys	250
1939	....	Northern China	200,000
1947	....	Honshu Island, Japan.	1,900
1951	Aug.	Manchuria	1,800
1953	Jan. 31	Western Europe	2,000
1954	Aug. 17	Farahzad, Iran	2,000
1955	Oct. 7-12	India, Pakistan	1,700
1959	Nov. 1	Western Mexico	2,000
1959	Dec. 2	Frejus, France	412
1960	Oct. 10	Bangladesh	6,000
1960	Oct. 31	Bangladesh	4,000
1962	Feb. 17	German North Sea coast	343
1962	Sept. 27	Barcelona, Spain	445
1963	Oct. 9	Dam collapse, Vaiont, Italy	1,800
1966	Nov. 4-6	Florence, Venice, Italy	113
1967	Jan. 18-24	Eastern Brazil	894
1967	Mar. 19	Rio de Janeiro, Brazil	436
1968	Aug. 7-14	Gujarat State, India	1,000
1968	Oct. 7	Northeastern India.	780
1969	Mar. 17	Mundau Valley, Alagoas, Brazil	218
1969	Aug. 25	Western Virginia	189
1969	Sept. 15	South Korea	250
1969	Oct. 1-8	Tunisia	500
1970	May 20	Central Romania	160
1970	July 22	Himalayas, India.	500
1971	Feb. 26	Rio de Janeiro, Brazil	130
1972	Feb. 26	Buffalo Creek, W. Va.	118
1972	June 9	Rapid City, S.D.	236
1972	Aug. 7	Luzon Is., Philippines	454
1974	Mar. 29	Tubaro, Brazil	1,000
1974	Aug. 12	Monty-Long, Bangladesh	2,500
1975	Jan. 11	Southern Thailand.	131
1976	June 5	Teton Dam collapse, Ida.	11
1976	July 31	Big Thompson Canyon, Col.	130
1976	Nov. 17	East Java, Indonesia	136
1977	July 19-20	Johnstown, Pa.	68
1978	June-Sept.	Northern India	1,200
1979	Jan.-Feb.	Brazil	204
1979	July	Lomblem Is., Indonesia	539
1979	Aug. 11	Morvi, India	5,000-15,000
1980	Feb. 13-22	So. Cal., Ariz.	26

Some Major Tornadoes Since 1925

Source: National Climatic Center, NOAA, U.S. Commerce Department

Date			Place	Deaths
1925	Mar.	18	Mo., Ill. Ind.	689
1926	Nov.	25	Belleville to Portland, Ark.	53
1927	Apr.	12	Rock Springs, Tex.	74
1927	May	9	Arkansas, Poplar Bluff, Mo.	92
1927	Sept.	29	St. Louis, Mo.	72
1929	Apr.	25	SE-Central Ga.	40
1930	May	6	Hill & Ellis Co., Tex.	41
1932	Mar.	21	Ala. (series of tornadoes)	268
1936	Apr.	5	Tupelo, Miss.	216
1936	Apr.	6	Gainesville, Ga.	203
1938	Sept.	29	Charleston, S.C.	32
1942	Mar.	16	Central to NE Miss.	75

Date			Place	Deaths
1942	Apr.	27	Rogers & Mayes Co., Okla.	52
1944	June	23	Oh., Pa., W. Va., Md.	150
1945	Apr.	12	Okla.-Ark.	102
1947	Apr.	9	Tex., Okla. & Kan.	169
1948	Mar.	19	Bunker Hill & Gillespie, Ill.	33
1949	Jan.	3	La. & Ark.	58
1952	Mar.	21	Ark., Mo., Tenn. (series)	208
1953	May	11	Waco, Tex.	114
1953	June	8	Flint to Lakeport, Mich.	116
1953	June	9	Worcester and vicinity, Mass.	90
1953	Dec.	5	Vicksburg, Miss.	38
1955	May	25	Udall, Kan.	80
1957	May	20	Kan., Mo.	48
1958	June	4	Northwestern Wisconsin	30
1959	Feb.	10	St. Louis, Mo.	21
1960	May	5, 6	SE Oklahoma, Arkansas	30
1965	Apr.	11	Ind., Ill., Oh., Mich., Wis.	271
1966	Mar.	3	Jackson, Miss.	57
1966	Mar.	3	Mississippi, Alabama	61
1967	Apr.	21	Illinois	33
1968	May	15	Arkansas	34
1969	Jan.	23	Mississippi	32
1971	Feb.	21	Mississippi delta	110
1973	May	26-7	South, Midwest (series)	47
1974	Apr.	3-4	Ala., Ga., Tenn., Ky., Oh.	350
1977	Apr.	1	Southeast Bangladesh	600
1977	Apr.	4	Ala., Miss., Ga.	22
1978	Apr.	16	Orissa, India	500
1979	Apr.	10	Tex., Okla.	60

Number of U. S. Tornadoes Since 1937, Deaths

Year	No.	Deaths
1937	147	29
1938	213	183
1939	152	91
1940	124	65
1941	118	53
1942	167	384
1943	152	58
1944	169	275
1945	121	210
1946	106	78
1947	165	313
1948	183	139
1949	249	211
1950	199	70
1951	264	34
1952	240	229
1953	421	515
1954	550	36
1955	595	126
1956	504	83
1957	856	192
1958	564	66
1959	604	58
1960	616	46
1961	697	51
1962	657	28
1963	464	31
1964	704	73
1965	906	296
1966	585	98
1967	926	114
1968	660	131
1969	608	66
1970	653	72
1971	888	156
1972	741	*27
1973	†1102	87
1974	947	361
1975	920	60
1976	835	44
1977	852	43
1978	788	53
1979	852	84

*Record low, †Record high.

Hurricanes, Typhoons, Blizzards, Other Storms

Names of hurricanes and typhoons in italics—H.—hurricane; T.—typhoon

Date	Location	Deaths
1888 Mar. 11-14	Blizzard, Eastern U.S.	400
1900 Sept. 8	H., Galveston, Tex.	6,000
1926 Sept. 16-22	H., Fla., Ala.	372
1926 Oct. 20	H., Cuba	600
1928 Sept. 12-17	H., W. Indies, Fla.	4,000
1930 Sept. 3	H., San Domingo	2,000
1938 Sept. 21	H., New England	600
1942 Oct. 15-16	H., Bengal, India	11,000
1944 Sept. 12-16	H., N.C. to New Eng.	389
1953 Sept. 25-27	T., Vietnam, Japan	1,300
1954 Aug. 30	H. *Carol*, Northeast U.S.	68
1954 Oct. 12-13	H. *Hazel*, Eastern, U.S., Haiti	347
1955 Aug. 12-13	H. *Connie*, Carolinas, Va., Md.	43
1955 Aug. 18-19	H. *Diane*, Eastern U.S.	400
1955 Sept. 19	H. *Hilda*, Mexico	200
1955 Sept. 22-28	H. *Janet*, Caribbean	500
1956 Feb. 1-29	Blizzard, Western Europe	1,000
1957 June 27-30	H. *Audrey*, La., Tex.	430
1958 Feb. 15-16	Blizzard, NE U.S.	171
1959 Sept. 17-19	T. *Sarah*, Far East	2,000
1959 Sept. 26-27	T. *Vera*, Honshu, Japan	4,466
1960 Sept. 4-12	H. *Donna*, Caribbean, E. U.S.	148
1961 Oct. 31	H. *Hattie*, Br. Honduras	400
1962 Feb. 17	Flooding, German Coast	343
1962 Sept. 27	Flooding, Barcelona, Spain	445
1963 May 28-29	Windstorm, Bangladesh	22,000
1963 Oct. 4-8	H. *Flora*, Cuba, Haiti	6,000
1964 Oct. 4-7	H. *Hilda*, La., Miss., Ga.	38
1964 June 30	T. *Winnie*, N. Philippines	107
1964 Sept. 5	T. *Ruby*, Hong Kong and China	735
1964 Sept. 14	Flooding, central S. Korea	563
1964 Nov. 12	Flooding, S. Vietnam	7,000
1965 May 11-12	Windstorm, Bangladesh	17,000
1965 June 1-2	Windstorm, Bangladesh	30,000
1965 Sept. 7-10	H. *Betsy*, Fla., Miss., La.	74
1965 Dec. 15	Windstorm, Bangladesh	10,000
1966 June 4-10	H. *Alma*, Honduras, SE U.S.	51
1966 Sept. 24-30	H. *Inez*, Carib., Fla., Mex.	293
1967 July 9	T. *Billie*, Japan	347
1967 Sept. 5-23	H. *Beulah*, Carib., Mex., Tex.	54
1967 Dec. 12-20	Blizzard, Southwest, U.S.	51
1968 Nov. 18-28	T. *Nina*, Philippines	63
1969 Aug. 17-18	H. *Camille*, Miss., La.	256
1970 July 30-Aug. 5	H. *Celia*, Cuba, Fla., Tex.	31
1970 Aug. 20-21	H. *Dorothy*, Martinique	42
1970 Sept. 15	T. *Georgia*, Philippines	300
1970 Oct. 14	T. *Sening*, Philippines	583
1970 Oct. 15	T. *Titang*, Philippines	526
1970 Nov. 13	Cyclone, Bangladesh (est.)	300,000
1971 Aug. 1	T. *Rose*, Hong Kong	130
1972 June 19-29	H. *Agnes*, Fla. to N.Y.	118
1972 Dec. 3	T. *Theresa*, Philippines	169
1973 June-Aug.	Monsoon rains in India	1,217
1974 June 11	Storm *Dinah*, Luzon Is., Philip.	71
1974 July 11	T. *Gilda*, Japan, S. Korea	108
1974 Sept. 19-20	H. *Fifi*, Honduras	2,000
1974 Dec. 25	Cyclone leveled Darwin, Aus.	50
1975 Sept. 13-27	H. *Eloise*, Caribbean, NE U.S.	71
1976 May 20	T. *Olga*, floods, Philippines	215
1977 July 25, 31	T. *Thelma*, T. *Vera*, Taiwan	39
1978 Oct. 27	T. *Rita*, Philippines	c. 400
1979 Aug. 30-Sept. 7	H. *David*, Caribbean, E US	1,100

Record Oil Spills

Name, place	Date	Cause	Tons
Ixtoc I oil well, southern Gulf of Mexico	June 3, 1979	Blowout	600,000
Atlantic Empress & Aegean Captain, off Trinidad & Tobago	July 19, 1979	Collision	300,000
Amoco Cadiz, near Portsall, France	March 16, 1978	Grounding	223,000
Torrey Canyon, off Land's End, England	March 18, 1967	Grounding	119,000
Sea Star, Gulf of Oman	Dec. 19, 1972	Collision	115,000
Urquiola, La Coruna, Spain	May 12, 1976	Grounding	100,000
Hawaiian Patriot, northern Pacific	Feb. 25, 1977	Fire	99,000
Othello, Tralhavet Bay, Sweden	March 20, 1970	Collision	60,000-100,000
Jacob Maersk, Porto do Leixoes, Portugal	Jan. 29, 1975	Grounding	84,000
Wafra, Cape Agulhas, South Africa	Feb. 27, 1971	Grounding	63,000
Epic Colacotroni, Caribbean	May, 1975	Grounding	57,000

Other Notable Oil Spills

Source: Conservation Division, U.S. Geological Survey, U.S. Interior Department

Name, place	Date	Cause	Gallons
World Glory, off South Africa	June 13, 1968	Hull failure	13,524,000
Keo, off Massachusetts	Nov. 5, 1969	Hull failure	8,820,000

Name, place	Date	Cause	Gallons
Storage tank, Sewaren, N.J.	Nov. 4, 1969	Tank rupture	8,400,000
Ekofisk oil field, North Sea	Apr. 22, 1977	Well blowout	8,200,000
Argo Merchant, Nantucket, Mass.	Dec. 15, 1976	Grounding	7,700,000
Pipeline, West Delta, La.	Oct. 15, 1967	Dragging anchor	6,720,000
Tanker off Japan	Nov. 30, 1971	Ship broke in half	6,258,000

Explosions

Date			Location	Deaths
1910	Oct.	1	Los Angeles Times Bldg.,	21
1913	Mar.	7	Dynamite, Baltimore harbor	55
1915	Sept.	27	Gasoline tank car, Ardmore, Okla.	47
1917	Apr.	10	Munitions plant, Eddystone, Pa.	133
1917	Dec.	6	Halifax Harbor, Canada	1,654
1918	May	18	Chemical Plant, Oakdale, Pa.	193
1918	July	2	Explosives, Split Rock, N.Y.	50
1918	Oct.	4	Shell plant, Morgan Station, N.J.	64
1919	May	22	Food plant, Cedar Rapids, Ia.	44
1920	Sept.	16	Wall Street, New York, bomb	30
1924	Jan.	3	Food plant, Pekin, Ill.	42
1928	April	13	Dance hall, West Plains, Mo.	40
1937	Mar.	18	New London, Tex., school	294
1940	Sept.	11	Hercules Powder, Kenvil, N.J.	51
1942	June	5	Ordnance plant, Elwood, Ill.	49
1944	Apr.	14	Bombay, India, harbor	700
1944	July	17	Port Chicago, Cal., pier	322
1944	Oct.	21	Liquid gas tank, Cleveland	135
1947	Apr.	16	Texas City, Tex., pier	561
1948	July	28	Farben works, Ludwigshafen, Ger.	184
1950	May	19	Munitions barges, S. Amboy, N. J.	30
1956	Aug.	7	Dynamite trucks, Cali, Colombia	1,100
1958	Apr.	18	Sunken munitions ship, Okinawa	40
1958	May	22	Nike missiles, Leonardo, N.J.	10
1959	Apr.	10	World War II bomb, Philippines	38
1959	June	28	Rail tank cars, Meldrin, Ga.	25
1959	Aug.	7	Dynamite truck, Roseburg, Ore.	13
1959	Nov.	2	Jamuri Bazar, India, explosives	46
1959	Dec.	13	Dortmund, Ger., 2 apt. bldgs.	26
1960	Mar.	4	Belgian munitions ship, Havana	100
1960	Oct.	25	Gas, Windsor, Ont., store	11
1962	Jan.	16	Gas pipeline, Alberta, Canada	19
1962	Mar.	3	Gasoline truck, Syria	31
1962	Oct.	3	Telephone Co. office, N. Y. City	23
1963	Jan.	2	Packing plant, Terre Haute, Ind.	16
1963	Mar.	9	Dynamite plant, S. Africa	45
1963	Mar.	9	Steel plant, Belecke, W. Germany	19
1963	Aug.	13	Explosives dump, Gauhiti, India	32
1963	Oct.	31	State Fair Coliseum, Indianapolis	73
1964	July	23	Bone, Algeria, harbor munitions	100
1965	Mar.	4	Gas pipeline, Natchitoches, La.	17
1965	Aug.	9	Missile silo, Searcy, Ark.	53
1965	Oct.	21	Bridge, Tila Bund, Pakistan	80
1965	Oct.	30	Cartagena, Colombia	48
1965	Nov.	24	Armory, Keokuk, Ia.	20
1966	Oct.	13	Chemical plant, La Salle, Que.	11
1967	Feb.	17	Chemical plant, Hawthorne, N.J.	11
1967	Dec.	25	Apartment bldg., Moscow	20
1968	Apr.	6	Sports store, Richmond, Ind.	43
1970	Apr.	8	Subway construction, Osaka, Japan	73
1971	June	24	Tunnel, Sylmar, Cal.	17
1971	June	28	School, fireworks, Pueblo, Mex.	13
1971	Oct.	21	Shopping center, Glasgow, Scot.	20
1973	Feb.	10	Liquified gas tank, Staten Is., N.Y.	40
1975	Dec.	27	Chasnala, India, mine	431
1976	Apr.	13	Lapua, Finland, munitions works	45
1977	Nov.	11	Freight train, Iri, S. Korea	57
1977	Dec.	22	Grain elevator, Westwego, La.	35
1978	Feb.	24	Derailed tank car, Waverly, Tenn.	12
1978	July	11	Propylene tank truck, Spanish coastal campsite	150

Fires

Date			Location	Deaths
1845	May		Theater, Canton, China	1,670
1871	Oct.	8	Chicago, $196 million loss	250
1871	Oct.	8	Peshtigo, Wis., forest fire	1,182
1876	Dec.	5	Brooklyn (N.Y.), theater	295
1877	June	20	St. John, N. B., Canada	100
1881	Dec.	8	Ring Theater, Vienna	850
1887	May	25	Opera Comique, Paris	200
1887	Sept.	4	Exeter, England, theater	200
1894	Sept.	1	Hinckley, Minn., forest fire	413
1897	May	4	Charity bazaar, Paris	150
1900	June	30	Hoboken, N. J., docks	326
1902	Sept.	20	Church, Birmingham, Ala.	115
1903	Dec.	30	Iroquois Theater, Chicago	602
1908	Jan.	13	Rhoads Thea., Boyertown, Pa.	170
1908	Mar.	4	School, Collinwood, Oh.	176
1911	Mar.	25	Triangle factory, N. Y. City	145
1913	Oct.	14	Colliery, Mid Glamorgan, Wales	439
1918	Apr.	13	Norman Okla., state hospital	38
1918	Oct.	12	Cloquet, Minn., forest fire	400
1919	June	20	Mayaguez Theater, San Juan	150
1923	May	17	School, Camden, S. C.	76
1924	Dec.	24	School, Hobart, Okla.	35
1929	May	15	Clinic, Cleveland, Oh.	125
1930	Apr.	21	Penitentiary, Columbus, Oh.	320
1931	July	24	Pittsburgh, Pa., home for aged	48
1938	May	16	Atlanta, Ga., Terminal Hotel	35
1940	Apr.	23	Dance hall, Natchez, Miss.	198
1942	Nov.	28	Cocoanut Grove, Boston	491
1942			Hostel, St. John's, Newfoundland	100
1943	Sept.	7	Gulf Hotel, Houston	55
1944	July	6	Ringling Circus, Hartford	168
1946	June	5	LaSalle Hotel, Chicago	61
1946	Dec.	7	Winecoff Hotel, Atlanta	119
1946	Dec.	12	New York, ice plant, tenement	37
1949	Apr.	5	Hospital, Effingham, Ill.	77
1950	Jan.	7	Davenport, Ia., Mercy Hospital	41
1953	Mar.	29	Largo, Fla., nursing home	35
1953	Apr.	16	Chicago, metalworking plant	35
1957	Feb.	17	Home for aged, Warrenton, Mo.	72
1958	Mar.	19	New York City loft building	24
1958	Dec.	1	Parochial school, Chicago	95
1958	Dec.	16	Store, Bogota, Colombia	83
1959	June	23	Resort hotel, Stalheim, Norway	34
1960	Mar.	12	Pusan, Korea, chemical plant	68
1960	July	14	Mental hospital, Guatemala City	225
1960	Nov.	13	Movie theater, Amude, Syria	152
1961	Jan.	6	Thomas Hotel, San Francisco	20
1961	May	15	Tenement, Hong Kong	25
1961	Dec.	8	Hospital, Hartford, Conn.	16
1961	Dec.	17	Circus, Niteroi, Brazil	323
1963	May	4	Theater, Diourbel, Senegal	64
1963	Nov.	18	Surfside Hotel, Atlantic City, N.J.	25
1963	Nov.	23	Rest home, Fitchville, Oh.	63
1963	Dec.	29	Roosevelt Hotel, Jacksonville, Fla.	22
1964	May	8	Apartment building, Manila	30
1964	Dec.	18	Nursing home, Fountaintown, Ind.	20
1965	Mar.	1	Apartment, LaSalle, Canada	28
1966	Mar.	11	Numata, Japan, 2 ski resorts	31
1966	Aug.	13	Melbourne, Australia, hotel	29
1966	Sept.	12	Anchorage, Alaska, hotel	14
1966	Oct.	17	N. Y. City bldg. (firemen)	12
1966	Dec.	7	Erzurum, Turkey, barracks	68
1967	Feb.	7	Restaurant, Montgomery, Ala.	25
1967	May	22	Store, Brussels, Belgium	322
1967	July	16	State prison, Jay, Fla.	37
1968	Jan.	9	Brooklyn, N. Y., tenement	13
1968	Feb.	26	Shrewsbury, England, hospital	22
1968	May	11	Vijayawada, India, wedding hall	58
1968	Nov.	18	Glasgow, Scotland, factory	24
1969	Jan.	26	Victoria Hotel, Dunnville, Ont.	13
1969	Dec.	2	Nursing home, Notre Dame, Can.	54
1970	Jan.	9	Nursing home, Marietta, Oh.	27
1970	Mar.	20	Hotel, Seattle, Wash.	19
1970	Nov.	1	Dance hall, Grenoble, France	145
1970	Nov.	5	Nursing home, Pointe-aux-Trembles, Que.	17
1970	Dec.	20	Hotel, Tucson, Arizona	28
1971	Mar.	6	Psychiatric clinic, Burghoezli, Switzerland	28
1971	Apr.	20	Hotel, Bangkok, Thailand	24
1971	Oct.	19	Nursing home, Honesdale, Pa.	15
1971	Dec.	25	Hotel, Seoul, So. Korea	162

Date			Location	Deaths
1972	May	13	Osaka, Japan, nightclub	116
1972	July	5	Sherborne, England, hospital	30
1973	Feb.	6	Paris, France, school	21
1973	Nov.	6	Fukui, Japan, train	28
1973	Nov.	29	Kumamoto, Japan, department store	107
1973	Dec.	2	Seoul, Korea, theater	50
1974	Feb.	1	Sao Paulo, Brazil, bank building	189
1974	June	30	Port Chester, N. Y., discotheque	24
1974	Nov.	3	Seoul, So. Korea, hotel discotheque	88
1975	Dec.	12	Mina, Saudi Arabia, Tent City	138
1976	Oct.	24	Bronx, N.Y., social club	25
1977	Feb.	25	Rossiya Hotel, Moscow	45
1977	May	28	Southgate, Ky., nightclub	164
1977	June	9	Abidjan, Ivory Coast nightclub	41
1977	June	26	Columbia, Tenn., jail	42
1977	Nov.	14	Manila, Pl, hotel	47
1978	Jan.	28	Kansas City, Coates House Hotel	16
1979	Dec.	31	Chapais, Quebec, social club	44

Major U.S. Railroad Wrecks

Source: Office of Safety, Federal Railroad Administration

Date			Location	Deaths
1876	Dec.	29	Ashtabula, Oh.	92
1880	Aug.	11	Mays Landing, N. J.	40
1887	Aug.	10	Chatsworth, Ill.	81
1888	Oct.	10	Mud Run, Pa.	55
1896	July	30	Atlantic City, N. J.	60
1903	Dec.	23	Laurel Run, Pa.	53
1904	Aug.	7	Eden, Col.	96
1904	Sept.	24	New Market Tenn.	56
1906	Mar.	16	Florence, Col.	35
1906	Oct.	28	Atlantic City, N. J.	40
1906	Dec.	30	Washington, D. C.	53
1907	Jan.	2	Volland, Kan.	33
1907	Jan.	19	Fowler, Ind.	29
1907	Feb.	16	New York City	22
1907	Feb.	23	Colton, Cal.	26
1907	July	20	Salem, Mich.	33
1910	Mar.	1	Wellington, Wash.	96
1910	Mar.	21	Green Mountain, Ia.	55
1911	Aug.	25	Manchester, N. Y.	29
1912	July	4	East Corning, N. Y.	39
1912	July	5	Ligonier, Pa.	23
1914	Aug.	5	Tipton Ford, Mo.	43
1914	Sept.	15	Lebanon, Mo.	28
1916	Mar.	29	Amherst, Oh.	27
1917	Feb.	27	Mount Union, Pa.	20
1917	Sept.	28	Kellyville, Okla.	23
1917	Dec.	20	Shepherdsville, Ky.	46
1918	June	22	Ivanhoe, Ind.	68
1918	July	9	Nashville, Tenn.	101
1918	Nov.	2	Brooklyn, N. Y., Malbone St. Tunnel	97
1919	Jan.	12	South Byron, N. Y.	22
1919	July	1	Dunkirk, N. Y.	12
1919	Dec.	20	Onawa, Maine	23
1921	Feb.	27	Porter, Ind.	37
1921	Dec.	5	Woodmont, Pa.	27
1922	Aug.	5	Sulphur Spring, Mo.	34
1922	Dec.	13	Humble, Tex.	22
1923	Sept.	27	Lockett, Wy.	31
1925	June	16	Hackettstown, N. J.	50
1925	Oct.	27	Victoria, Miss.	21
1926	Sept.	5	Waco, Col.	30
1928	Aug.	24	I.R.T. subway, Times Sq., N. Y.	18
1938	June	19	Saugus, Mont.	47
1939	Aug.	12	Harney, Nev.	24
1940	Aug.	19	Little Falls, N. Y.	31
1940	July	31	Cuyahoga Falls, Oh.	43
1943	Aug.	29	Wayland, N. Y.	27
1943	Sept.	6	Frankford Junction, Philadelphia, Pa.	79
1943	Dec.	16	Between Rennert and Buie, N. C.	72
1944	July	6	High Bluff, Tenn.	35
1944	Aug.	4	Near Stockton, Ga.	47
1944	Sept.	14	Dewey, Ind.	29
1944	Dec.	31	Bagley, Utah	50
1945	Aug.	9	Michigan, N. D.	34
1946	Apr.	25	Naperville, Ill.	45
1947	Feb.	18	Gallitzin, Pa.	24
1950	Feb.	17	Rockville Centre, N. Y.	31
1950	Sept.	11	Coshocton, Oh.	33
1950	Nov.	22	Richmond Hill, N. Y.	79
1951	Feb.	6	Woodbridge, N. J.	84
1951	Nov.	12	Wyuta, Wyo.	17
1951	Nov.	25	Woodstock, Ala.	17
1953	Mar.	27	Conneaut, Oh.	21
1956	Jan.	22	Los Angeles, Cal.	30
1956	Feb.	28	Swampscott, Mass.	13
1956	Sept.	5	Springer, N. M.	20
1957	June	11	Vroman, Col.	12
1958	Sept.	15	Elizabethport, N. J.	48
1960	Mar.	14	Bakersfield, Cal.	14
1962	July	28	Steelton, Pa.	19
1966	Dec.	28	Everett, Mass.	13
1971	June	10	Salem, Ill.	11
1972	Oct.	30	Chicago, Ill.	45
1977	Jan.	4	Chicago, Ill., elevated train	11

World's worst train wreck occurred Dec. 12, 1917, Modane, France, passenger train derailed, 543 killed.

Some Notable Aircraft Disasters Since 1937

Date			Aircraft	Site of accident	Deaths
1937	May	6	German zeppelin Hindenburg	Burned at mooring, Lakehurst, N.J.	36
1944	Aug.	23	U.S. Air Force B-24	Hit school, Freckelton, England	76[1]
1945	July	28	U.S. Army B-25	Hit Empire State bldg., N.Y.C.	14[1]
1947	May	30	Eastern Air Lines DC-4	Crashed near Ft. Deposit, Md.	53
1952	Dec.	20	U.S. Air Force C-124	Fell, burned, Moses Lake, Wash.	87
1953	Mar.	3	Canadian Pacific Comet Jet	Karachi, Pakistan	11[2]
1953	June	18	U.S. Air Force C-124	Crashed, burned near Tokyo	129
1955	Nov.	1	United Air Lines DC-6B	Exploded, crashed near Longmont, Col.	44[3]
1956	June	20	Venezuelan Super-Constellation	Crashed in Atlantic off Asbury Park, N.J.	74
1956	June	30	TWA Super-Const., United DC-7	Collided over Grand Canyon, Arizona	128
1960	Dec.	16	United DC-8 jet, TWA Super-Const.	Collided over N.Y. City	134[4]
1962	Mar.	4	Br. Caledonian Airlines DC-7C	Crashed near Douala, Cameroon	111
1962	Mar.	16	Flying Tiger Super-Const.	Vanished in Western Pacific	107
1962	June	3	Air France Boeing 707 jet	Crashed on takeoff from Paris	130
1962	June	22	Air France Boeing 707 jet	Crashed in storm, Guadeloupe, W.I.	113
1963	June	3	Chartered Northw. Airlines DC-7	Crashed in Pacific off British Columbia	101
1963	Nov.	29	Trans-Canada Airlines DC-8F	Crashed after takeoff from Montreal	118
1965	May	20	Pakistani Boeing 720-B	Crashed at Cairo, Egypt, airport	121
1966	Jan.	24	Air India Boeing 707 jetliner	Crashed on Mont Blanc, France-Italy	117
1966	Feb.	4	All-Nippon Boeing 727	Plunged into Tokyo Bay	133
1966	Mar.	5	BOAC Boeing 707 jetliner	Crashed on Mount Fuji, Japan	124
1966	Dec.	24	U.S. military-chartered CL-44	Crashed into village in So. Vietnam	129[1]
1967	Apr.	20	Swiss Britannia turboprop	Crashed at Nicosia, Cyprus	126
1967	July	19	Piedmont Boeing 727, Cessna 310	Collided in air, Hendersonville, N.C.	82
1968	Apr.	20	S. African Airways Boeing 707	Crashed on takeoff, Windhoek, SW Africa	122
1968	May	3	Braniff International Electra	Crashed in storm near Dawson, Tex.	85
1969	Mar.	16	Venezuelan DC-9	Crashed after takeoff from Maracaibo, Venezuela	155[5]
1969	Mar.	20	United Arab Ilyushin-18	Crashed at Aswan airport, Egypt	87
1969	June	4	Mexican Boeing 727	Rammed into mountain near Monterrey, Mexico	79

Date			Aircraft	Site of accident	Deaths
1969	Dec.	8	Olympia Airways DC-6B	Crashed near Athens in storm	93
1970	Feb.	15	Dominican DC-9	Crashed into sea on takeoff from Santo Domingo	102
1970	July	3	British chartered jetliner	Crashed near Barcelona, Spain.	112
1970	July	5	Air Canada DC-8	Crashed near Toronto International Airport	108
1970	Aug.	9	Peruvian turbojet	Crashed after takeoff from Cuzco, Peru	101[1]
1970	Nov.	14	Southern Airways DC-9	Crashed in mountains near Huntington, W. Va.	75[6]
1971	July	30	All-Nippon Boeing 727 and Japanese Air Force F-86	Collided over Morioka, Japan	162[7]
1971	Aug.	11	Soviet Aeroflot Tupolev-104	Crashed at Irkutsk airport, USSR	97
1971	Sept.	4	Alaska Airlines Boeing 727	Crashed into mountain near Juneau, Alaska	111
1972	Mar.	14	Danish Airliner	Crashed near Dubai, United Arab Emirates	112
1972	Aug.	14	E. German Ilyushin-62	Crashed on take-off East Berlin	156
1972	Oct.	13	Aeroflot Ilyushin-62	E. German airline crashed near Moscow	176
1972	Dec.	3	Chartered Spanish airliner	Crashed on take-off, Canary Islands	155
1972	Dec.	29	Eastern Airlines Lockheed Tristar	Crashed on approach to Miami Int'l. Airport	101
1973	Jan.	22	Chartered Boeing 707	Burst into flames during landing, Kano Airport, Nigeria	176
1973	Apr.	10	British Vanguard turboprop	Crashed during snowstorm at Basel, Switzerland	104
1973	June	3	Soviet Supersonic TU-144	Exploded in air near Goussainville, France	14[8]
1973	July	11	Brazilian Boeing 707	Crashed on approach to Orly Airport, Paris	122
1973	July	31	Delta Airlines jetliner	Crashed, landing in fog at Logan Airport, Boston	89
1973	Dec.	23	French Caravelle jet	Crashed in Morocco	106
1974	Jan.	31	Pan American Boeing 707 jet	Crashed in Pago Pago, American Samoa	96
1974	Mar.	3	Turkish DC-10 jet	Crashed at Ermenonville near Paris	346
1974	Apr.	23	Pan American 707 jet	Crashed in Bali, Indonesia	107
1974	Sept.	8	TWA 707 jet	Crashed in Ionian Sea off Greece, after bomb explosion Arab guerrilla group claimed responsibility	80
1974	Dec.	1	TWA-727	Crashed in storm, Upperville, Va.	92
1974	Dec.	4	Dutch-chartered DC-8	Crashed in storm near Colombo, Sri Lanka	191
1975	Apr.	4	Air Force Galaxy C-58	Crashed near Saigon, So. Vietnam, after takeoff with load of orphans	172
1975	June	24	Eastern Airlines 727 jet	Crashed in storm, JFK Airport, N.Y. City	113
1975	Aug.	3	Chartered 707	Hit mountainside, Agadir, Morocco	168
1976	Sept.	10	British Airways Trident, Yugoslav DC-9	Collided near Zagreb, Yugoslavia	176
1976	Sept.	19	Turkish 727	Hit mountain, southern Turkey	155
1976	Oct.	6	Cuban DC-8	Crashed near Barbados after bomb explosion	73
1976	Oct.	12	Indian Caravelle jet	Crashed after takeoff, Bombay airport	95
1976	Oct.	13	Bolivian 707 cargo jet	Crashed in Santa Cruz, Bolivia	100[9]
1976	Dec.	28	Aeroflot TU-104	Crashed at Moscow's Sheremetyevo airport	72
1977	Jan.	13	Aeroflot TU-104	Exploded and crashed at Alma-Ata, Central Asia	90
1977	Mar.	27	KLM 747, Pan American 747	Collided on runway, Tenerife, Canary Islands	581
1977	Nov.	19	TAP Boeing 727	Crashed on Madeira	130
1977	Dec.	4	Malaysian Boeing 737	Hijacked, then exploded in mid-air over Straits of Johore	100
1977	Dec.	13	U.S. DC-3	Crashed after takeoff at Evansville, Ind.	29[10]
1978	Jan.	1	Air India 747	Exploded, crashed into sea off Bombay	213
1978	Mar.	16	Bulgarian TU-134	Crashed at Vratsa, Bulgaria	73
1978	Sept.	25	Boeing 727, Cessna 172	Collided in air, San Diego, Cal.	150
1978	Nov.	15	Chartered DC-8	Crashed near Colombo, Sri Lanka	183
1979	May	25	American Airlines DC-10	Crashed after takeoff at O'Hare Intl. Airport, Chicago	275[11]
1979	Aug.	17	Two Soviet Aeroflot jetliners	Collided over Ukraine	173
1979	Oct.	31	Western Airlines DC-10	Mexico City Airport	74
1979	Nov.	26	Pakistani Boeing 707	Crashed near Jeddah, Saudi Arabia	156
1979	Nov.	28	New Zealand DC-10	Crashed into mountain in Antarctica	257
1980	Mar.	14	Polish Ilyushin 62	Crashed making emergency landing, Warsaw	87[12]

(1) Including those on the ground and in buildings. (2) First fatal crash of commercial jet plane. (3) Caused by bomb planted by John G. Graham in insurance plot to kill his mother, a passenger. (4) Including all 128 aboard the planes and 6 on ground. (5) Killed 84 on plane and 71 on ground. (6) Including 43 Marshall U. football players and coaches. (7) Airliner-fighter crash, pilot of fighter parachuted to safety, was arrested for negligence. (8) First supersonic plane crash killed 6 crewmen and 8 on the ground; there were no passengers. (9) Crew of 3 killed; 97, mostly children, killed on ground. (10) Including U. of Evansville basketball team. (11) Highest death toll in U.S. aviation history. (12) Including 22 members of U.S. boxing team.

Principal U.S. Mine Disasters

Source: Bureau of Mines, U.S. Interior Department

Note: Prior to 1968, only disasters with losses of 50 or more lives are listed; since 1968, all disasters in which 5 or more people were killed are listed. Only fatalities to mining company employees are included. All Bituminous-coal mines unless otherwise noted.

Date	Location	Deaths
1855 Mar.	Coalfield, Va.	55
1867 Apr. 3	Winterpock, Va.	69
1869[1] Sept. 6	Plymouth, Pa.	110
1883 Feb. 16	Braidwood, Ill.	69
1884 Jan. 24	Crested Butte, Col.	59
1884 Mar. 13	Pocahontas, Va.	112
1891 Jan. 27	Mount Pleasant, Pa.	109
1892 Jan. 7	Krebs, Okla.	100
1895 Mar. 20	Red Canyon, Wy.	60
1896[1] June 28	Pittston, Pa.	58
1900 Jan. 1	Scofield, Ut.	200
1902 May 19	Coal Creek, Tenn.	184
1902 July 10	Johnstown, Pa.	112
1903 June 30	Hanna, Wy.	169
1904 Jan. 25	Cheswick, Pa.	179
1905 Feb. 20	Virginia City, Ala.	112
1907 Jan. 29	Stuart W. Va.	84
1907 Dec. 6	Monongah, W. Va.	361
1907 Dec. 16	Yolande, Ala.	57
1907 Dec. 19	Jacobs Creek, Pa.	239
1908 Mar. 28	Hanna, Wy.	59
1908 Nov. 28	Marianna, Pa.	154
1908 Dec. 29	Switchback, W. Va.	50
1909 Jan. 12	Switchback, W. Va.	67
1909 Nov. 13	Cherry, Ill.	259
1910 Jan. 31	Primero, Col.	75
1910 May 5	Palos, Ala.	90
1910 Oct. 8	Starkville, Col.	56
1910 Nov. 8	Delagua, Col.	79
1911 Apr. 7	Throop, Pa.	72
1911 Apr. 8	Littleton, Ala.	128
1911 Dec. 9	Briceville, Tenn.	84
1912 Mar. 20	McCurtain, Okla.	73
1912 Mar. 26	Jed, W. Va.	83
1913 Apr. 23	Finleyville, Pa.	96
1913 Oct. 22	Dawson, N.M.	263
1914 Apr. 28	Eccles, W. Va.	181
1914 Oct. 27	Royalton, Ill.	52
1915 Mar. 2	Layland, W. Va.	112
1917 Apr. 27	Hastings, Col.	121
1917[2] June 8	Butte, Mon.	163
1917 Aug. 4	Clay, Ky.	62

Date	Location	Deaths	Date	Location	Deaths
1919[1] June 5	Wilkes-Barre, Pa.	92	1930 Nov. 5	Millfield, Oh.	79
1922 Nov. 6	Spangler, Pa.	77	1932 Dec. 23	Moweagua, Ill.	54
1922 Nov. 22	Dolomite, Ala.	90	1940 Jan. 10	Bartley, W. Va.	91
1923 Feb. 8	Dawson, N.M.	120	1940 Mar. 16	St. Clairsville, Oh.	72
1923 Aug. 14	Kemmerer, Wy.	99	1940 July 15	Portage, Pa.	63
1924 Mar. 8	Castle Gate, Ut.	171	1942 May 12	Osage, W. Va.	56
1924 Apr. 28	Benwood, W. Va.	119	1943 Feb. 27	Washoe, Mon.	74
1925 Feb. 20	Sullivan, Ind.	52	1944 July 5	Belmont, Oh.	66
1925 May 27	Coal Glen, N.C.	53	1947 Mar. 25	Centralia, Ill.	111
1925 Dec. 10	Acmar, Ala.	53	1951 Dec. 21	West Frankfort, Ill.	119
1926 Jan. 13	Wilburton, Okla.	91	1968[3] Mar. 6	Calumet, La.	21
1926[2] Nov. 3	Ishpeming, Mich.	51	1968 Nov. 20	Farmington, W. Va.	78
1927 Apr. 30	Everettville, W. Va.	97	1970 Dec. 30	Hyden, Ky.	38
1928 May 19	Mather, Pa.	195	1972[2] May 2	Kellogg, Ida	91
1929 Dec. 17	McAlester, Okla.	61	1976 Mar. 9, 11	Oven Fork, Ky.	26
			1977 Mar. 1	Tower City, Pa.	9

(1) Anthracite mine. (2) Metal mine. (3) Nonmetal mine.

World's worst mine disaster killed 1,549 workers in Honkeiko Colliery in Manchuria Apr. 25, 1942.

Historic Assassinations Since 1865

1865—Apr. 14. U. S. Pres. Abraham Lincoln, shot in Washington, D. C.; died Apr. 15.

1881—Mar. 13. Alexander II, of Russia—July 2. U. S. Pres. James A. Garfield, Washington; died Sept. 19.

1900—July 29. Umberto I, king of Italy.

1901—Sept. 6. U. S. Pres. William McKinley in Buffalo, N. Y., died Sept. 14. Leon Czolgosz executed for the crime Oct. 29.

1913—Feb. 23. Mexican Pres. Francisco, I, Madero and Vice Pres. Jose Pino Suarez.—Mar. 18. George, king of Greece.

1914—June 28. Archduke Francis Ferdinand of Austria-Hungary and his wife in Sarajevo, Bosnia (later part of Yugoslavia), by Gavrillo Princip.

1916—Dec. 30. Grigori Rasputin, politically powerful Russian monk.

1918—July 12. Grand Duke Michael of Russia, at Perm.—July 16. Nicholas II, abdicated as czar of Russia; his wife, the Czarina Alexandra, their son, Czarevitch Alexis, and their daughters, Grand Duchesses Olga, Tatiana, Marie, Anastasia, and 4 members of their household were executed by Bolsheviks at Ekaterinburg.

1920—May 20. Mexican Pres. Gen. Venustiano Carranza in Tlaxcalantongo.

1922—Aug. 22. Michael Collins, Irish revolutionary.

1923—July 20. Gen. Francisco "Pancho" Villa, ex-rebel leader, in Parral, Mexico.

1928—July 17. Gen. Alvaro Obregon, president-elect of Mexico, in San Angel, Mexico.

1933—Feb. 15. In Miami, Fla. Joseph Zangara, anarchist, shot at Pres.-elect Franklin D. Roosevelt, but a woman seized his arm, and the bullet fatally wounded Mayor Anton J. Cermak, of Chicago, who died Mar. 6. Zangara was electrocuted on Mar. 20, 1933.

1934—July 25. In Vienna, Austrian Chancellor Engelbert Dollfuss by Nazis.

1935—Sept. 8. U. S. Sen. Huey P. Long, shot in Baton Rouge, La., by Dr. Carl Austin Weiss, who was slain by Long's bodyguards.

1940—Aug. 20. Leon Trotsky (Lev Bronstein), 63, exiled Russian war minister, near Mexico City. Killer identified as Ramon Mercador del Rio, a Spaniard, served 20 years in Mexican prison.

1948—Jan. 30. Mohandas K. Gandhi, 78, shot in New Delhi, India, by Nathuran Vinayak Godse.—Sept. 17. Count Folke Bernadotte, UN mediator for Palestine, ambushed in Jerusalem.

1951—July 20. King Abdullah ibn Hussein of Jordan.

1956—Sept. 21. Pres. Anastasio Somoza of Nicaragua, in Leon; died Sept. 29.

1957—July 26. Pres. Carlos Castillo Armas of Guatemala, in Guatemala City by one of his own guards.

1958—July 14. King Faisal of Iraq; his uncle, Crown Prince Abdul Illah, and July 15, Premier Nuri as-Said, by rebels in Baghdad.

1959—Sept. 25. Prime Minister Solomon Bandaranaike of Ceylon, by Buddhist monk in Colombo.

1961—Jan. 17. Ex-Premier Patrice Lumumba of the Congo, in Katanga Province—May 30. Dominican dictator Rafael Leonidas Trujillo Molina shot to death by assassins near Ciudad Trujillo.

1963—June 12. Medgar W. Evers, NAACP's Mississippi field secretary, in Jackson, Miss.—Nov. 2. Pres. Ngo Dinh Diem of the Republic of Vietnam and his brother, Ngo Dinh Nhu, in a military coup.—Nov. 22. U. S. Pres. John F. Kennedy fatally shot in Dallas, Tex.; accused Lee Harvey Oswald murdered while awaiting trial.

1965—Jan. 21. Iranian premier Hassan Ali Mansour fatally wounded by assassin in Teheran; 4 executed.—Feb. 21. Malcolm X, black nationalist, fatally shot in N. Y. City; 3 sentenced to life.

1966—Sept. 6. Prime Minister Hendrik F. Verwoerd of South Africa stabbed to death in parliament at Capetown by drifter later ruled insane.

1968—Apr. 4. Rev. Dr. Martin Luther King Jr. fatally shot in Memphis, Tenn.; James Earl Ray sentenced to 99 years.—June 5. Sen. Robert F. Kennedy (D-N. Y.) fatally shot in Los Angeles; Sirhan Sirhan, resident alien, convicted of murder.

1969—July 5. Tom Mboya, Kenya's minister of economic planning and development, in Nairobi.

1971—Nov. 28. Jordan Prime Minister Wasfi Tal, in Cairo, by Palestinian guerrillas.

1973—Mar. 2. U. S. Ambassador Cleo A. Noel Jr., U. S. Charge d'Affaires George C. Moore and Belgian Charge d'Affaires Guy Eid tortured and killed by Palestinian guerrillas in Khartoum, Sudan.

1974—Aug. 15. Mrs. Park Chung Hee, wife of president of So. Korea, hit by bullet meant for her husband.—Aug. 19. U. S. Ambassador to Cyprus, Rodger P. Davies, killed by sniper's bullet in Nicosia.

1975—Feb. 11. Pres. Richard Ratsimandrava, of Madagascar, machine-gunned in Tananarive.—Mar. 25. King Faisal of Saudi Arabia shot by nephew Prince Musad Abdel Aziz, in royal palace, Riyadh.

1975—Aug. 15. Bangladesh Pres. Sheik Mujibur Rahman and wife and son killed in army coup.

1976—Feb. 13. Nigerian head of state, Gen. Murtala Ramat Mohammed, slain by self-styled "young revolutionaries."

1977—Mar. 16. Kamal Jumblat, Lebanese Druse chieftain, was shot and killed on a mountain road near Beirut.

1977—Mar. 18. Congo Pres. Marien Ngouabi shot in Brazzaville.

1978—July 9. Former Iraqi Premier Abdul Razak Al-Naif shot in London.

1979—Feb. 14. U.S. Ambassador Adolph Dubs shot and killed by Afghan Moslem extremists in Kabul.

1979—Mar. 30. British Tory MP Airey Neave killed when bomb in his car exploded. IRA claimed responsibility.

1979—Aug. 27. Lord Mountbatten, WW2 hero, and 2 others were killed when a bomb exploded on his fishing boat off the coast of Co. Sligo, Ire. The IRA claimed responsibility.

1979—Oct. 26. So. Korean President Park Chung Hee and 6 bodyguards fatally shot by Kim Jae Kyu, head of Korean CIA, and 5 aides in Seoul.

1980—Apr. 12. Liberian President William R. Tolbert slain in military coup.

Assassination Attempts

1910—Aug. 6. N. Y. City Mayor William J. Gaynor shot and seriously wounded by discharged city employee.

1912—Oct. 14. Former U. S. President Theodore Roosevelt shot and seriously wounded by demented man in Milwaukee.

1950—Nov. 1. In an attempt to assassinate President Truman, 2 men identified as members of a Puerto Rican nationalist movement—Griselio Torresola and Oscar Collazo—tried to shoot their way into Blair House. Torresola was killed, and a guard, Pvt. Leslie Coffelt was fatally shot. Collazo, wounded, recovered and was tried and convicted Mar. 7. 1951 for the murder of Coffelt. His death sentence was commuted to life imprisonment by President Truman; sentence commuted by Pres. Carter, Sept. 1979.

1970—Nov. 27. Pope Paul VI unharmed by knife-wielding assailant dressed as priest who attempted to attack him in Manila airport.

1972—May 15. Alabama Gov. George Wallace shot in Laurel,

Md. by Arthur Bremer; seriously crippled.

1972—Dec. 7. Mrs. Ferdinand E. Marcos, wife of the Philippine president, was stabbed and seriously injured in Pasay City, Philippines.

1975—Sept. 5. Pres. Gerald R. Ford was unharmed when a Secret Service agent grabbed a pistol aimed at him by Lynette (Squeaky) Fromme, a Charles Manson follower, in Sacramento.

1975—Sept. 22. Pres. Gerald R. Ford escaped unharmed when Sara Jane Moore, a political activist, fired a revolver at him.

1980—Apr. 14. Indian Prime Minister Indira Gandhi was unharmed when a man threw a knife at her in New Delhi.

Major Kidnapings

Edward A. Cudahy Jr., 16, in Omaha, Neb., **Dec. 18, 1900.** Returned Dec. 20 after $25,000 paid. Pat Crowe confessed.

Robert Franks, 13, in Chicago, **May 22, 1924,** by 2 youths, Richard Loeb and Nathan Leopold, who killed boy. Demand for $10,000 ignored. Loeb died in prison, Leopold paroled 1958, freed 1963.

Charles A. Lindbergh Jr., 20 mos. old, in Hopewell, N.J., **Mar. 1, 1932;** found dead May 12. Ransom of $50,000 was paid to man identified as Bruno Richard Hauptmann, 35, paroled German convict who entered U.S. illegally. Hauptmann passed ransom bill and $14,000 marked money was found in his garage. He was convicted after spectactular trial at Flemington, and electrocuted in Trenton, N.J., prison, Apr. 3. 1936.

William A. Hamm Jr., 39, in St. Paul, **June 15, 1933.** $100,000 paid. Alvin Karpis given life, paroled in 1969.

Charles F. Urschel, in Oklahoma City, **July 22, 1933.** Released July 31 after $200,000 paid. George (Machine Gun) Kelly and 5 others given life.

George Weyerhaeuser, 9, in Tacoma, Wash., **May 24, 1935.** Returned home June 1 after $200,000 paid. Kidnappers given 20 to 60 years.

Charles Mattson, 10, in Tacoma, Wash., **Dec. 27, 1936.** Found dead Jan. 11, 1937. Kidnaper asked $28,000, failed to contact.

Arthur Fried, in White Plains, N.Y., **Dec. 4, 1937.** Body not found. Two kidnapers executed.

Robert C. Greenlease, 6, son of a Kansas City, Mo. motor car dealer, taken from school **Sept. 28, 1953,** and held for $600,000. Body found Oct. 7, when Mrs. Bonnie Brown Heady and Carl A. Hall were arrested. They pleaded guilty and were executed.

Peter Weinberger, 32 days old, Westbury, N.Y., **July 4, 1956,** for $2,000 ransom, not paid. Child found dead. Angelo John LaMarca, 31, convicted, executed.

Cynthia Ruotolo, 6 wks old, taken from carriage in front of Hamden, Conn. store **Sept. 1, 1956.** Body found in lake.

Lee Crary, 8 in Everett, Wash., **Sept. 22, 1957,** $10,000 ransom, not paid. He escaped after 3 days, led police to George E. Collins, who was convicted.

Eric Peugeot, 4, taken from playground at St. Cloud golf course, Paris, **Apr. 12, 1960.** Released unharmed 3 days later after payment of undisclosed sum. Two sentenced to prison.

Frank Sinatra Jr., 19, from hotel room in Lake Tahoe, Cal., **Dec. 8, 1963.** Released **Dec. 11** after his father paid $240,000 ransom. John W. Irwin, Barry W. Keenan and Joseph C. Amsler sentenced to prison; most of ransom recovered.

Barbara Jane Mackle, 20, abducted **Dec. 17, 1968,** from Atlanta, Ga., motel, was found unharmed 3 days later, buried in a coffin-like wooden box 18 inches underground, after her father had paid $500,000 ransom; Gary Steven Krist sentenced to life, Ruth Eisenmann-Schier to 7 years; most of ransom recovered.

Anne Katherine Jenkins, 22, abducted **May 10, 1969,** from her Baltimore apartment, freed 3 days later after her father paid $10,000 ransom.

Mrs. Roy Fuchs, 35, and 3 children held hostage 2 hours, **May 14, 1969,** in Long Island, N. Y., released after her husband, a bank manager, paid kidnapers $129,000 in bank funds; 4 men arrested, ransom recovered.

C. Burke Elbrick, U.S. ambassador to Brazil, kidnaped by revolutionaries in Rio de Janeiro **Sept. 4, 1969;** released 3 days later after Brazil yielded to kidnaper's demands to publish manifesto and release 15 political prisoners.

Patrick Dolan, 18, found shot to death near Sao Paulo, Brazil, **Nov. 5, 1969,** after he was kidnaped and $12,500 paid.

Sean M. Holly, U.S. diplomat, in Guatemala **Mar. 6, 1970;** freed 2 days later upon release of 3 terrorists from prison.

Lt. Col. Donald J. Crowley, U.S. air attache, in Dominican Republic **Mar. 24, 1970;** released after government allowed 20 prisoners to leave the country.

Count Karl von Spreti, W. German ambassador to Guatemala, **Mar. 31, 1970;** slain after Guatemala refused demands for $700,000 and release of 22 prisoners.

Pedro Eugenio Arambaru, former Argentine president, by terrorists **May 29, 1970;** body found July 17.

Rudy W. Martinez, Guatemalan coffee exporter, by terrorists **Apr. 23, 1970;** released on payment of large ransom.

Ehrenfried von Holleben, W. German ambassador to Brazil, by terrorists **June 11, 1970;** freed after release of 40 prisoners.

Daniel A. Mitrione, U.S. diplomat, **July 31, 1970,** by terrorists in Montevideo, Uruguay; body found Aug. 10 after government rejected demands for release of all political prisoners.

Aloysio Dias Gomide, Brazilian vice counsul, in Montevideo, **July 31, 1970;** released Feb. 1, 1971, after wife paid ransom estimated at over $250,000.

James R. Cross, British trade commissioner, **Oct. 5, 1970,** by French Canadian separatists in Quebec; freed Dec. 3 after 3 kidnapers and relatives flown to Cuba by government.

Pierre Laporte, Quebec Labor Minister, by separatists **Oct. 10, 1970;** body found Oct. 18.

Giovanni E. Bucher, Swiss ambassador **Dec. 7, 1970,** by revolutionaries in Rio de Janeiro; freed Jan. 16, 1971, after Brazil released 70 political prisoners.

Geoffrey Jackson, British ambassador, in Montevideo, **Jan. 8, 1971,** by Tupamaro terrorists. Held as ransom for release of imprisoned terrorists, he was released Sept. 9, after the prisoners escaped.

Ephraim Elrom, Israel consul general in Istanbul, **May 17, 1971.** Held as ransom for imprisoned terrorists, he was found dead May 23.

Mrs. Virginia Piper, 49 abducted **July 27, 1972,** from her home in suburban Minneapolis; found unharmed near Duluth 2 days later after her husband paid $1 million ransom to the kidnapers.

Victor E. Samuelson, Exxon executive, **Dec. 6, 1973,** in Campana, Argentina, by Marxist guerrillas, freed Apr. 29, 1974, after payment of record $14.2 million ransom.

J. Paul Getty 3d, 17, grandson of the U.S. oil mogul, released by kidnapers **Dec. 15, 1973,** in southern Italy after family paid $2.8 million ransom.

Patricia (Patty) Hearst, 19, taken from her Berkeley, Cal., apartment **Feb. 4, 1974.** Symbionese Liberation Army demanded her father, Randolph A. Hearst, publisher, give millions to poor. Hearst offered $2 million in food; the Hearst Corp. offered $4 million worth. Kidnapers objected to way food was distributed. Patricia, in message, said she had joined SLA; she was identified by FBI as taking part in a San Francisco bank holdup, **Apr. 15;** she claimed, in message, she had been coerced. Again identified by FBI in a store holdup, **May 16,** she was classified by FBI as "an armed, dangerous fugitive." FBI, **Sept. 18, 1975,** captured Patricia and others in San Francisco; they were indicted on various charges. Patricia for bank robbery. A San Francisco jury convicted her, **Mar. 20, 1976.** She was released from prison under executive clemency, **Feb. 1, 1979.** In 1978, William and Emily Harris were sentenced to 10 years to life for the Hearst kidnaping.

J. Reginald Murphy, 40, an editor of *Atlanta* (Ga.) *Constitution*, kidnaped **Feb. 20, 1974,** freed **Feb. 22** after payment of $700,000 ransom by the newspaper. Police arrested William A. H. Williams, a contractor; most of the money was recovered.

J. Guadalupe Zuno Hernandez, 83, father-in-law of Mexican President Luis Echeverria Alvarez, seized by 4 terrorists **Aug. 28, 1974;** government refused to negotiate; he was released **Sept. 8.**

E. B. Reville, Hepzibah, Ga., banker, and wife Jean, kidnaped **Sept. 30, 1974.** Ransom of $30,000 paid. He was found alive; Mrs. Reville was found dead of carbon monoxide fumes in car trunk **Oct. 2.**

Jack Teich, Kings Point, N.Y., steel executive, seized **Nov. 12, 1974;** released **Nov. 19** after payment of $750,000.

Samuel Bronfman, 21, heir to Seagram liquor fortune, abducted **Aug. 9, 1975,** in Purchase, N.Y.; $2.3 million ransom paid by father, Edgar. FBI and N.Y.C. police rescued Samuel **Aug. 17** in Brooklyn, N.Y., apartment, recovered ransom, and arrested Mel Patrick Lynch, a city fireman, and Dominic Byrne, a limousine operator. Two found not guilty of kidnap, but convicted of extortion after they claimed young Bronfman masterminded ransom plot.

Hanns-Martin Schleyer, a West German industrialist, was kidnaped in Cologne, **Sept. 5, 1977** by armed terrorists. His driver and 3 of his police guards were killed in the terrorist action. Schleyer was found dead, **Oct. 19,** in an abandoned car shortly after 3 jailed terrorist leaders of the Baader-Meinhof gang were found dead in their prison cells near Stuttgart, West Germany.

Aldo Moro, former Italian premier, kidnaped in Rome, **Mar. 16, 1978,** by left-wing terrorists. Five of his bodyguards killed during abduction. Moro's bullet-ridden body was found in a parked car, **May 9,** in Rome. Six members of the Red Brigades arrested, charged, June 5, with complicity in the kidnaping.

ASTRONOMY AND CALENDAR

Edited by Dr. Kenneth L. Franklin, Astronomer
American Museum-Hayden Planetarium

Celestial Events Highlights, 1981

(All times are Greenwich Mean Time)

Planets and meteor showers will put on a show for us this year. Jupiter and Saturn give us a rare triple conjunction, the events occurring in January, February, and July. Venus and Jupiter, both bright, will be less than 1° apart in August, and Venus and the crescent moon will be a beautiful sight each summer month in the evening twilight. Venus will be at its brightest in December, giving us a fine evening star for the holiday season.

Around April 1, a rare multiple alignment of planets will occur. Very nearly on a line for a few days are Mars, Venus, Sun, Earth, Jupiter, Saturn, and Pluto, in that order. Mercury, Uranus, and Neptune are nowhere near this line at this time, but Mercury will be in superior conjunction late this month. Pluto is off the line by about 13° and should not really be included, but it is close.

As mentioned in the last two years, the Perseid meteor shower may give us a good show, especially a few surprising fireballs. The comet of 1862 discovered by Swift and Tuttle is due back shortly. Perhaps fragments from its last solar visit are harbingers of its return.

Halley's comet is awaited for late 1985 and early 1986. Two meteor showers may be related to it: the Eta Aquarids in May and the Orionids in October. Although these are not spectacular showers, they should be observed for several years before and after Halley's return to see if their activity is altered by the comet's return.

There is a 2-minute total eclipse of the sun on July 31. Siberia, anyone?

January

Mercury, in superior conjunction New Year's Eve, is not visible until late this month in the evening sky.

Venus is 3° south of the waning crescent moon on the 4th, increasingly difficult to see in the morning twilight.

Mars, looking like a reddish star of +1.4 magnitude, is not at all obvious in the evening twilight; it is 1°.6 south of the nearly 2-day old moon on the 7th.

Jupiter, in Virgo throughout the year, is 1°.1 south of Saturn on the 14th, the first of 3 such conjunctions, and begins its retrograde motion on the 25th when it will be 3° south of the moon.

Saturn, also in Virgo all year, is 1°.1 north of Jupiter on the 14th, the first of 3 such conjunctions this year, begins its retrograde motion on the 19th, and is 2° south of the moon on the 25th.

Moon is at perigee on the 15th, 229,800 miles away, and at apogee on the 27th, 251,400 miles away, passes Venus on the 4th, Mars on the 7th, occults Aldebaran on the 16th, is in penumbral eclipse on the 20th, and passes Saturn and Jupiter on the 25th.

Jan. 2—Earth at perihelion, 91.4 million miles from the sun.

Jan. 3—Quadrantid meteor shower is not affected by the moon.

Jan. 14—Jupiter and Saturn in conjunction, 1°.1 apart.

Jan. 16—Moon occults Aldebaran.

Jan. 19—Saturn begins its retrograde motion; Sun enters Capricornus.

Jan. 20—Penumbral lunar eclipse.

Jan. 25—Jupiter begins its retrograde motion.

February

Mercury is at greatest eastern elongation, 18° from the sun, on the 2nd, not especially favorable for viewing, and at inferior conjunction on the 17th.

Venus is still visible in the morning twilight, but by month's end it will be lost in the sun's glare.

Mars is too close to the sun to be seen.

Jupiter is again in conjunction with Saturn, 1°.1 south of the latter on the 19th, the second of the triple conjunction.

Saturn is 1°.1 north of Jupiter on the 19th, in the second of the triple conjunction.

Moon passes Venus on the 3rd, causes an annular solar eclipse on the 4th, occults Mars on the 5th, passes Mercury on the 6th, is at perigee on the 8th, 228,900 miles away, occults Aldebaran on the 12th, passes Jupiter and Saturn on the 22nd, and is at apogee on the 24th, 251,700 miles away.

Feb. 2—Mercury at greatest eastern elongation.

Feb. 4—Annular solar eclipse.

Feb. 12—Occultation of Aldebaran.

Feb. 16—Sun enters Aquarius.

Feb. 17—Mercury in inferior conjunction.

Feb. 19—Jupiter in conjunction with Saturn.

March

Mercury is stationary on the 1st, and at greatest western elongation on the 16th, 28° from the sun, worth an attempt at viewing before dawn.

Venus is lost in the sun's glare.

Mars is also lost in the sun.

Jupiter is at opposition on the 26th and at its brightest, -2.0 magnitude.

Saturn is at opposition on the 27th, also at its brightest, but only +0.6 magnitude because its rings are still quite narrow.

Moon passes Mercury on the 4th, is at perigee on the 8th, 225,500 miles away, occults Aldebaran on the 12th, passes Jupiter and Saturn on the 21st, and is at apogee on the 24th, 252,300 miles away.

Mar. 1—Mercury ends its retrograde motion.

Mar. 11—Sun enters Pisces.

Mar. 12—Occultation of Aldebaran.

Mar. 16—Mercury at greatest western elongation.

Mar. 20—Vernal Equinox; Spring begins in the Northern Hemisphere.

Mar. 26—Jupiter at opposition.

Mar. 27—Saturn at opposition.

April

Mercury, in superior conjunction on the 27th, is too close to the sun to be seen.

Venus, in superior conjunction on the 7th, is lost in the sun's glare.

Mars, in conjunction on the 2nd, joins Mercury and Venus beyond the sun.

Jupiter is still in retrograde motion in Virgo.

Saturn is still in retrograde motion in Virgo.

Moon passes Mercury on the 3rd, is at perigee on the 5th, 222,900 miles away, passes Jupiter and Saturn on the 17th, and is at apogee on the 20th, 252,600 miles away.

Apr. 2—Mars in conjunction.

Apr. 7—Venus in superior conjunction.

Apr. 18—Sun enters Aries.

Apr. 22—Lyrid meteor shower disturbed by bright waning gibbous moon.

Apr. 27—Mercury in superior conjunction.

May

Mercury is 8° north of Aldebaran on the 14th, and is at greatest eastern elongation on the 27th, 28° from the sun. This will be a good time to look for it in the evening twilight.

Venus may be seen by month's end in the evening twilight.

Mars is still lost in the sun's glare.

Jupiter, still in Virgo, ends its retrograde motion on the 28th.

Saturn, still in its retrograde motion, becomes slightly fainter by the end of the month.

Moon is at perigee on the 4th, 222,000 miles away, passes Jupiter and Saturn on the 14th, and is at apogee on the 17th, 252,700 miles away.

May 5—Eta Aquarids, a weak shower of swift meteors, is free of moonlight. This shower may be associated with Halley's comet and should be observed for several years ahead of the comet's return in 1986 to see if its activity is altered.

May 13—Sun enters Taurus.

May 27—Mercury at greatest eastern elongation.

May 28—Jupiter stationary.

June

Mercury begins its retrograde motion and passes 1°.7 south of Venus on the 9th, and is at inferior conjunction on the 22nd.

Venus is becoming increasingly easy to see in the evening twilight, passing 1°.7 north of Mercury on the 9th.

Mars resembles a +1.7 magnitude reddish star in Taurus passing 6° north of Aldebaran on the 19th.

Jupiter is still the brightest object in Virgo.

Saturn resumes its direct (eastward) motion on the 6th.

Moon is at perigee on the 1st, 222,900 miles away, passes Mercury and Venus on the 3rd, Jupiter and Saturn on the 10th, is at apogee on the 14th, 252,300 miles away, at perigee the second time this month on the 29th, 225,300 miles away, and passes Mars on the 30th.

June 6—Saturn stationary.

June 9—Mercury stationary; in conjunction with Venus, 1°.7 away.

June 19—Mars 6° north of Aldebaran.

June 20—Sun enters Gemini.

June 21—Summer Solstice; Summer begins in the Northern Hemisphere.

June 22—Mercury in inferior conjunction.

July

Mercury ends its retrograde motion on the 3rd, is at greatest western elongation, 21° from the sun on the 14th, and is 6° south of Pollux on the 29th.

Venus is 1°.3 north of the 2-day-old crescent moon on the 3rd, a beautiful sight, and 1°.2 north of Regulus on the 23rd.

Mars moves into Gemini by month's end.

Jupiter is 1°.2 south of Saturn on the 30th, the 3rd event of the triple conjunction.

Saturn is 1°.2 north of Jupiter on the 30th, completing the triple conjunction.

Moon passes Venus on the 3rd, Jupiter and Saturn on the 7th, is at apogee on the 11th, 251,700 miles away, in partial eclipse on the 17th, at perigee on the 27th, 228,400 miles away, passes Mars on the 29th, and totally eclipses the sun on the 31st.

July 3—Venus and the crescent moon is an attractive sight this evening; Mercury stationary. Earth at aphelion, 94.6 million miles from the sun.

July 14—Mercury at greatest western elongation.

July 17—Partial lunar eclipse.

July 20—Sun enters Cancer.

July 23—Venus 1°.2 north of Regulus.

July 29—Delta Aquarid meteor shower reaches its midpoint of activity without much interference from the moon, perhaps 20 an hour may be expected.

July 31—Total solar eclipse.

August

Mercury is in superior conjunction on the 10th.

Venus and the crescent moon are 2° apart on the 2nd, is 2° south of Saturn on the 25th, and 0°.9 south of Jupiter on the 28th. This is a good picture opportunity.

Mars is 6° south of Pollux on the 23rd, and 1°.4 north of the moon on the 26th.

Jupiter, still close to Saturn, is 0°.9 north of Venus on the 28th.

Saturn is 2° north of Venus on the 25th, and remains close to Jupiter.

Moon passes Venus on the 2nd, Jupiter and Saturn on the 4th, is at apogee on the 8th, 251,400 miles away, at perigee on the 21st, 229,842 miles away, passes Mars on the 26th, and Mercury on the 30th.

Aug. 2—Venus and the crescent moon are beautiful again.

Aug. 10—Mercury in superior conjunction; Sun enters Leo.

Aug. 12—Perseid meteor shower deserves attention for at least 3 nights, centered on the 12th, even though the moon may interfere. It has been showing fireballs recently. Expect 30-50 meteors an hour after the moon sets.

Aug. 28—Venus in conjunction with Jupiter.

September

Mercury is in the evening sky all month, passing 4° south of Saturn on the 10th, 3° south of Jupiter on the 13th, 0°.4 south of Spica on the 20th, and at greatest eastern elongation, 26°, on the 23rd.

Venus is 5° south of the crescent moon on the 1st, and 1°.9 north of Spica on the 6th.

Mars moves into Cancer this month and is occulted by the moon on the 24th.

Jupiter by month's end will be too close to the sun to be seen.

Saturn by mid-month will be too close to the sun to be seen.

Moon passes Saturn and Jupiter on the 1st, is at apogee on the 5th, 251,500 miles away, at perigee on the 17th, 227,300 miles away, occults Mars on the 24th, and passes Mercury on the 30th.

Sept. 6—Venus is 1°.9 north of Spica.
Sept. 16—Sun enters Virgo.
Sept. 23—Autumnal Equinox; Autumn begins in the Northern Hemisphere; Mercury at greatest eastern elongation.
Sept. 24—Occultation of Mars.

October

Mercury begins retrograde motion on the 6th, is in inferior conjunction on the 18th, and is in direct motion after the 26th.

Venus, increasingly bright, is 1°.9 north of Antares on the 17th.

Mars enters Leo this month and passes 1°.1 north of Regulus on the 19th, and 1°.4 south of the moon on the 22nd.

Jupiter is in conjunction with the sun on the 14th.

Saturn is in conjunction with the sun on the 6th.

Moon passes Venus on the 1st, is at apogee on the 3rd, 252,000 miles away, at perigee on the 15th, 224,100 miles away, passes Mars on the 22nd, Saturn on the 26th, and is at apogee again on the 30th, 252,600 miles away.

Oct. 6—Saturn in conjunction; Mercury stationary.
Oct. 14—Jupiter in conjunction.
Oct. 17—Venus 1°.9 north of Antares.
Oct. 18—Mercury in inferior conjunction.
Oct. 19—Mars 1°.1 north of Regulus.
Oct. 21—Orionid meteor shower deserves careful attention from now on, as it may be associated with Halley's comet, due back in 1986. If so, the shower's activity may change.
Oct. 26—Mercury stationary.
Oct. 30—Sun entering Libra.

November

Mercury is 5° north of Spica and at its greatest western elongation, 19°, on the 3rd, and is 1°.2 north of Jupiter on the 6th.

Venus is at greatest eastern elongation on the 11th, 47° from the sun, and 3° south of the moon on the 30th.

Mars, still in Leo, is 2° south of the moon on the 20th, and is becoming brighter during the month.

Jupiter is rapidly becoming more visible in the dawn sky, and is 4° south of the moon on the 23rd.

Saturn, seemingly only a +1.0 magnitude star, is 3° south of the moon on the 22nd.

Moon passes Venus on the 1st, is at perigee on the 12th, 222,000 miles away, passes Mars on the 20th, Saturn on the 22nd, Jupiter on the 23rd, is at apogee on the 26th, 252,800 miles away, and passes Venus again on the 30th.

Nov. 3—Mercury at greatest western elongation.
Nov. 4—Taurids, a weak meteor shower, should not be troubled by the moon.
Nov. 6—Mercury 1°.2 north of Jupiter.
Nov. 11—Venus at greatest eastern elongation.
Nov. 22—Sun enters Scorpius.
Nov. 29—Sun enters Ophiuchus.

December

Mercury is in superior conjunction on the 10th, and lost all month in the sun.

Venus is a perfect Christmas Star, attaining greatest brilliance on the 16th, then beginning its retrograde motion on the 30th. A telescope or good binoculars show Venus as a crescent at this time, getting thinner and thinner all month and into the new year.

Mars is 3° south of the last quarter moon on the 18th, getting noticeably brighter during the month as it moves into Virgo.

Jupiter is 4° south of the moon on the 21st.

Saturn is 3° south of the moon on the 20th.

Moon is at perigee on the 11th, 221,800 miles away, passes Mars on the 18th, Saturn on the 20th, Jupiter on the 21st, is at apogee on the 23rd, 252,700 miles away, and passes Venus on the 29th.

Dec. 10—Mercury in superior conjunction.
Dec. 13—Geminid meteor shower, a good shower of up to 50 meteors an hour in a dark sky, noted for a fireball every hour or two. Waning gibbous moon may interfere with the fainter streaks.
Dec. 16—Venus at greatest brilliance; Sun enters Sagittarius.
Dec. 21—Winter Solstice; Winter begins in the Northern Hemisphere.
Dec. 30—Venus stationary.

Astronomical Signs and Symbols

☉	The Sun	⊕	The Earth	♅	Uranus	□	Quadrature
☾	The Moon	♂	Mars	♆	Neptune	☍	Opposition
☿	Mercury	♃	Jupiter	♇	Pluto	☊	Ascending Node
♀	Venus	♄	Saturn	☌	Conjunction	☋	Descending Node

Two heavenly bodies are in "conjunction" (☌) when they are due north and south of each other, either in Right Ascension (with respect to the north celestial pole) or in Celestial Longitude (with respect to the north ecliptic pole). If the bodies are seen near each other, they will rise and set at nearly the same time. They are in "opposition" (☍) when their Right Ascensions differ by exactly 12 hours, or their Celestial Longitudes differ by 180°. One of the two objects in opposition will rise while the other is setting. "Quadrature" (□) refers to the arrangement when the coordinates of two bodies differ by exactly 90°. These terms may refer to the relative positions of any two bodies as seen from the earth, but one of the bodies is so frequently the sun that mention of the sun is omitted; otherwise both bodies are named. The geocentric angular separation between sun and object is termed "elongation." Elongation is limited only for Mercury and Venus; the "greatest elongation" for each of these bodies is noted in the appropriate tables and is approximately the time for longest observation. When a planet is in its "ascending" (☊) or "descending" (☋) node, it is passing northward or southward, respectively, through the plane of the earth's orbit, across the celestial circle called the ecliptic. The term "perihelion" means nearest to the sun, and "aphelion," farthest from the sun. An "occultation" of a planet or star is an eclipse of it by some other body, usually the moon.

Planets and the Sun

The planets of the solar system, in order of their distance from the sun, are Mercury, Venus, Earth, Mars, Jupiter, Saturn, Uranus, Neptune and Pluto. Uranus, Neptune and Pluto are not included in the celestial list because they are too faint to be seen without optical aid. Both Uranus and Neptune are visible through good field glasses, but Pluto is so distant and so small that only large telescopes or long exposure photographs can make it visible.

Since Mercury and Venus are nearer to the sun than is the earth, their motions about the sun are seen from the earth as wide swings first to one side of the sun and then to the other, although they are both passing continuously around the sun in orbits that are almost circular. When their passage takes them either between the earth and the sun, or beyond the sun as seen from the earth, they are invisible to us. Because of the laws which govern the motions of planets about the sun, both Mercury and Venus require much less time to pass between the earth and the sun than around the far side of the sun, so their periods of visibility and invisibility are unequal.

The planets that lie farther from the sun than does the earth may be seen for longer periods of time and are invisible only when they are so located in our sky that they rise and set about the same time as the sun when, of course, they are overwhelmed by the sun's great brilliance. None of the planets has any light or radiant heat of its own but each shines only by reflecting sunlight from its surface. Mercury and Venus, because they are between the earth and the sun, show phases very much as the moon does. The planets farther from the sun are always seen as full, although Mars does occasionally present a slightly gibbous phase — like the moon when not quite full.

The planets move rapidly among the stars because they are very much nearer to us. The stars are also in motion, some of them at tremendous speeds, but they are so far away that their motion does not change their apparent positions in the heavens sufficiently for anyone to perceive that change in a single lifetime. The very nearest star is about 7,000 times as far away as the most distant planet.

Visible Planets of the Solar System

Mercury, Venus, Mars, Jupiter and Saturn

Mercury

Mercury, nearest planet to the sun, is the second smallest of the nine planets known to be orbiting the sun. Its diameter is 3,100 miles and its mean distance from the sun is 36,000,000 miles.

Mercury moves with great speed in its journey about the sun, averaging about 30 miles a second to complete its circuit in 88 of our days. Mercury rotates upon its axis over a period of nearly 59 days, thus exposing all of its surface periodically to the sun. It is believed that the surface passing before the sun may have a temperature of about 800° F., while the temperature on the side turned temporarily away from the sun does not fall as low as might be expected. This night temperature has been described by Russian astronomers as "room temperature" — possibly about 70°. This would contradict the former belief that Mercury did not possess an atmosphere, for some sort of atmosphere would be needed to retain the fierce solar radiation that strikes Mercury. A shallow but dense layer of carbon dioxide would produce the "greenhouse" effect, in which heat accumulated during exposure to the sun would not completely escape at night. The actual presence of a carbon dioxide atmosphere is in dispute.

This uncertainty about conditions upon Mercury and its motion arise from its shorter angular distance from the sun as seen from the earth, for Mercury is always too much in line with the sun to be observed against a dark sky, but is always seen during either morning or evening twilight.

Mariner 10 made 3 passes by Mercury in 1974 and 1975. A large fraction of the surface was photographed from varying distances, revealing a degree of cratering similar to that of the moon. An atmosphere of hydrogen and helium may be made up of gases of the solar wind temporarily concentrated by the presence of Mercury. The discovery of a weak but permanent magnetic field was a surprise. It has been held that both a fluid core and rapid rotation were necessary for the generation of a planetary magnetic field. Mercury may demonstrate these conditions to be unnecessary, or the field may reveal something about the history of Mercury.

Venus

Venus, slightly smaller than the earth, moves about the sun at a mean distance of 67,000,000 miles in 225 of our days. Its synodical revolution — its return to the same relationship with the earth and the sun, which is a result of the combination of its own motion and that of the earth — is 584 days. Every 19 months, then, Venus will be nearer to the earth than any other planet of the solar system. The planet is covered with a dense, white, cloudy atmosphere that conceals whatever is below it. This same cloud reflects sunlight efficiently so that when Venus is favorably situated, it is the third brightest object in the sky, exceeded only by the sun and the moon.

Spectral analysis of sunlight reflected from Venus' cloud tops has shown features that can best be explained by identifying the material of the clouds as sulphuric acid (oil of vitriol). Infrared spectroscopy from a balloon-borne telescope nearly 20 miles above the earth's surface gave indications of a small amount of water vapor present in the same region of the atmosphere of Venus. In 1956, radio astronomers at the Naval Research Laboratories in Washington, D. C., found a temperature for Venus of about 600° F., in marked contrast to minus 125° F., previously found at the cloud tops. Subsequent radio work confirmed a high temperature and produced evidence for this temperature to be associated with the solid body of Venus. With this peculiarity in mind, space scientists devised experiments for the U.S. space probe Mariner 2 to perform when it flew by in 1962. Mariner 2 confirmed the high temperature and the fact that it pertained to the ground rather than to some special activity of the atmosphere. In addition, Mariner 2 was unable to detect any radiation belts similar to the earth's so-called Van Allen belts. Nor was it able to detect the existence of a magnetic field even as weak as 1/100,000 of that of the earth.

In 1967, a Russian space probe, Venera 4, and the American Mariner 5 arrived at Venus within a few hours of each other. Venera 4 was designed to allow an instrument package to land gently on the planet's surface via parachute. It ceased transmission of information in about 75 minutes when the temperature it read went above 500° F. After considerable controversy, it was agreed that it still had 20 miles to go to reach the surface. The U.S. probe, Mariner 5, went around the dark side of Venus at a distance of about 6,000 miles. Again, it detected no significant magnetic field but its radio signals passed to earth through Venus' atmosphere twice — once on the night side and once on the day side. The results are startling. Venus' atmosphere is nearly all carbon dioxide and must exert a pressure at the planet's surface of up to 100 times the earth's normal sea-level pressure of one atmosphere. Since the earth and Venus are about the same size, and were presumably formed at the same time by the same general process from the same mixture of chemical elements, one is faced with the question: which is the planet with the unusual history — earth or Venus?

Radar astronomers using powerful transmitters as well as sensitive receivers and computers have succeeded in determining the rotation period of Venus. It turns out to be 243 days clockwise — in other words, contrary to the spin of most of the other planets and to its own motion around the sun. If it were exactly 243.16 days, Venus would always present the same face toward the earth at every inferior conjunction. This rate and sense of rotation allows a "day" on Venus of 117.4 earth days. Any part of Venus will receive sunlight on its clouds for over 58 days and will be in darkness for 58 days. Recent radar observations have shown surface features below the clouds. Large craters have been identified.

Mariner 10 passed Venus before traveling on to Mercury in 1974. The carbon dioxide molecule found in such abundance in the atmosphere is rather opaque to certain ultraviolet wavelengths, enabling sensitive television cameras to take pictures of the Venusian cloud cover. Photos radioed to earth show a spiral pattern in the clouds from equator to the poles.

In December, 1978, two U. S. Pioneer probes arrived at Venus. One went into orbit about Venus, the other split into 5 separate probes targeted for widely-spaced entry points to sample different conditions. The instrumentation ensemble was selected on the basis of previous missions that had shown the range of conditions to be studied. The probes confirmed expected high surface temperatures and high winds aloft. Winds of about 200 miles per hour, there, may account for the transfer of heat into the night side in spite of the low rotation speed of the planet. Surface winds were light at the time, however. Atmosphere and cloud chemistries were examined in detail, providing much data for continued analysis. The probes detected 4 layers of clouds and more light on the surface than expected solely from sunlight. This light allowed Russian scientists to obtain at least two photos showing rocks on the surface. Sulphur seems to play a large role in the chemistry of Venus, and reactions involving sulphur may be responsible for the glow. To learn more about the weather and atmospheric circulation on Venus, the orbiter takes daily photos of the daylight side cloud cover. It confirms the cloud pattern and its circulation shown by Mariner 10. The ionosphere shows large variability. The orbiter's radar operates in 2 modes: one, for ground elevation variability, and the second for ground reflectivity in 2 dimensions, thus "imaging" the surface. Radar maps of the entire planet have been produced.

Mars

Mars is the first planet beyond the earth, away from the sun. Mars' diameter is about 4,200 miles, although a determination of the radius and mass of Mars by the space-probe, Mariner 4, which flew by Mars on July 14, 1965 at a distance of less than 6,000 miles, indicated that these dimensions were slightly larger than had been previously estimated. While Mars' orbit is also nearly circular, it is somewhat more eccentric than the orbits of many of the other planets, and Mars is more than 30 million miles farther from the sun in some parts of its year than it is at others. Mars takes 687 of our days to make one circuit of the sun, traveling at about 15 miles a second. Mars rotates upon its axis in almost the same period of time that the earth does — 24 hours and 37 minutes. Mars' mean distance from the sun is 141 million miles, so that the temperature on Mars would be lower than that on the earth even if Mars' atmosphere were about the same as ours. The atmosphere is not, however, for Mariner 4 reported that atmospheric pressure on Mars is between 1% and 2% of the earth's atmospheric pressure. This thin atmosphere appears to be largely carbon dioxide. No evidence of free water was found.

There appears to be no magnetic field about Mars. This would eliminate the previous conception of a dangerous radiation belt around Mars. The same lack of a magnetic field would expose the surface of Mars to an influx of cosmic radiation about 100 times as intense as that on earth.

Deductions from years of telescopic observation indicate that 5/8ths of the surface of Mars is a desert of reddish rock, sand, and soil. The rest of Mars is covered by irregular patches that appear generally green in hues that change through the Martian year. These were formerly held to be some sort of primitive vegetation, but with the findings of Mariner 4 of a complete lack of water and oxygen, such growth does not appear possible. The nature of the green areas is now unknown. They may be regions covered with volcanic salts whose color changes with changing temperatures and atmospheric conditions, or they may be gray, rather than green. When large gray areas are placed beside large red areas, the gray areas will appear green to the eye.

Mars' axis of rotation is inclined from a vertical to the plane of its orbit about the sun by about 25° and therefore has seasons as does the earth, except that the Martian seasons are longer because Mars' year is longer. White caps form about the winter pole of Mars, growing through the winter and shrinking in summer. These polar caps are now believed to be both water ice and carbon dioxide ice. It is the carbon dioxide that is seen to come and go with the seasons. The water ice is apparently in many layers with dust between them, indicating climatic cycles.

The canals of Mars have become more of a mystery than they were before the voyage of Mariner 4. Markings forming a network of fine lines crossing much of the surface of Mars have been seen there by men who have devoted much time to the study of the planet, but no canals have shown clearly enough in previous photographs to be universally accepted. A few of the 21 photographs sent back to earth by Mariner 4 covered areas crossed by canals. The pictures show faint, ill-defined, broad, dark markings, but no positive identification of the nature of the markings.

Mariners 6 & 7 in 1969 sent back many more photographs of higher quality than those of the pioneering Mariner 4. These pictures showed cratering similar to the earlier views, but in addition showed 2 other types of terrain. Some regions seemed featureless for many square miles, but others were chaotic, showing high relief without apparent organization into mountain chains or craters.

Mariner 9, the first artificial body to be placed in an orbit about Mars, has transmitted over 10,000 photographs covering 100% of the planet's surface. Preliminary study of these photos and other data shows that Mars resembles no other planet we know. Using terrestrial terms, however, scientists describe features that seem to be clearly of volcanic origin. One of these features is Nix Olympica, apparently a caldera whose outer slopes are over 300 miles in diameter. Some features may have been produced by cracking (faulting) of the surface and the sliding of one region over or past another. Many craters seem to have been produced by impacting bodies such as may have come from the nearby asteroid belt. Features near the south pole may have been produced by glaciers that are no longer present. Flowing water, nonexistent on Mars at the present time, probably carved canyons, one 10 times longer and 3 times deeper than the Grand Canyon.

Although the Russians landed a probe on Martian surface, it transmitted for only 20 seconds. In 1976, the U.S. landed 2 Viking spacecraft on the Martian surface. The landers have devices aboard to perform chemical analyses of the soil in search of evidence of life. So far, the results have been inconclusive. The 2 Viking orbiters have returned the best pictures yet of Martian topographic features. Many features can be explained only if Mars once had large quantities of flowing water.

Mars' position in its orbit and its speed around that orbit in relation to the earth's position and speed bring Mars fairly close to the earth on occasions about two years apart and then move Mars and the earth too far apart for accurate observation and photography. Every 15-17 years, the close approaches are especially favorable to close observation.

Mars has 2 satellites, discovered in 1877 by Asaph Hall. The outer satellite, Deimos, revolves around Mars in about 31 hours. The inner satellite, Phobos, whips around Mars in a little more than 7 hours, making 3 trips around the planet each Martian day. Mariner and Viking photos show these bodies to be irregularly shaped and pitted with numerous craters. Phobos also shows a system of linear grooves, each about 1/3-mile across and roughly parallel. Phobos measures about 8 by 12 miles and Deimos about 5 by 7.5 miles in size.

Jupiter

Jupiter is the largest of the planets. Its equatorial diameter is 88,000 miles, 11 times the diameter of the earth. Its polar diameter is about 6,000 miles shorter. This is an equilibrium condition resulting from the liquidity of the planet and its extremely rapid rate of rotation: a Jupiter day is only 10 earth hours long. For a planet this size, this rotational speed is amazing, and it moves a point on Jupiter's equator at a speed of 22,000 miles an hour, as compared with 1,000 miles an hour for a point on the earth's equator. Jupiter is at an average distance of 480 million miles from the sun and takes almost 12 of our years to make one complete circuit of the sun.

The only directly observable chemical constituents of Jupiter's atmosphere are methane (CH_4) and ammonia (NH_3), but it is reasonable to assume the same mixture of elements available to make Jupiter as to make the sun. This would mean a large fraction of hydrogen and helium must be present also, as well as water (H_2O). The temperature at the tops of the clouds may be about minus 260° F. The clouds are probably ammonia ice crystals, becoming ammonia droplets lower down. There may be a space before water ice crystals show up as clouds: in turn, these become water droplets near the bottom of the entire cloud layer. The total atmosphere may be only a few hundred miles in depth, pulled down by the surface gravity (= 2.64 times earth's) to a relatively thin layer. Of course, the gases become denser with depth until they may turn into a slush or a slurry. Perhaps there is no surface — no real interface between the gaseous atmosphere and the body of Jupiter. Pioneers 10 and 11 provided evidence for considering Jupiter to be almost entirely liquid hydrogen. Long before a rocky core about the size of the earth is reached, hydrogen mixed with helium becomes a liquid metal at very high temperature. Jupiter's cloudy atmosphere is a fairly good reflector of sunlight and makes it appear far brighter than any of the stars.

Jupiter has 14 known satellites, although the last one discovered by Kowal at the Hale Observatory is so faint that it has been lost. Four of the moons are large and bright, rivaling our own moon and the planet Mercury in diameter, and may be seen through a field glass. They move rapidly around Jupiter and their change of position from night to night is extremely interesting to watch. The other satellites are much smaller and in all but one instance much farther from Jupiter and cannot be seen except through powerful telescopes. The 4 outermost satellites are revolving around Jupiter clockwise as seen from the north, contrary to the motions of the great majority of the satellites in the solar system and to the direction of revolution of the planets around the sun. The reason for this retrograde motion is not known, but one theory is that Jupiter's tremendous gravitational power may have captured 4 of the minor planets or asteroids that move about the sun between Mars and Jupiter, and that these would necessarily revolve backward. At the great distance of these bodies from Jupiter — some 14 million miles — direct motion would result in decay of the orbits, while retrograde orbits would be stable. Jupiter's mass is more than twice the mass of all the other planets put together, and accounts for Jupiter's tremendous gravitational field and so, probably, for its numerous satellites and its dense atmosphere.

In December, 1973, Pioneer 10 passed about 80,000 miles from the equator of Jupiter and was whipped into a path taking it out of our solar system in about 50 years. In December, 1974, Pioneer 11 passed within 30,000 miles of Jupiter, moving roughly from south to north, over the poles.

Photographs from both encounters were useful at the time but were far surpassed by those of Voyagers I and II. Thousands of high resolution multi-color pictures show rapid variations of features both large and small. The Great Red Spot exhibits internal counterclockwise rotation. Much turbulence is seen in adjacent material passing north or south of it. The satellites Amalthea, Io, Europa, Ganymede, and Callisto were photographed, some in great detail. Each is individual and unique, with no similarities to other known planets or satellites. Io has active volcanoes that probably have ejected material into a doughnut-shaped ring enveloping its orbit about Jupiter.

Saturn

Saturn, last of the planets visible to the unaided eye, is almost twice as far from the sun as Jupiter, almost 900 million miles. It is second in size to Jupiter but its mass is much smaller. Saturn's specific gravity is less than that of water. Its diameter is about 71,000 miles at the equator; its rotational speed spins it completely around in a little more than 10 hours, and its atmosphere is much like that of Jupiter, except that its temperature at the top of its cloud layer is at least 100° colder. At about 300° F. below zero, the ammonia would be frozen out of Saturn's clouds. The theoretical construction of Saturn resembles that of Jupiter; it is either all gas, or it has a small dense center surrounded by a layer of liquid and a deep atmosphere.

Until Pioneer 11 passed Saturn in September 1979 only 10 satellites of Saturn were known. Since that time, the situation is quite confused. Added to data interpretations from the fly-by are earth-based observations using new techniques while the rings are edge-on and virtually invisible. It is hoped that the Voyager I fly-by in November 1980 will help sort out the system.

Because of Saturn's inclination, as stated above, there are 2 periods during Saturn's journey around the sun when the rings are presented to us edge-on. At these times, the rings disappear. Nothing that is only 10 miles wide can be seen from a distance of nearly 900 million miles. The rings are receding from a favorable position to be seen. They were edge-on in 1966, reached maximum visibility in 1973, and will be edge-on twice in 1980.

Saturn's ring system begins about 7,000 miles above the visible disk of Saturn, lying above its equator and extending about 35,000 miles into space. The diameter of the ring system, including Saturn itself, is about 170,000 miles; the rings are estimated to be no thicker than 10 miles. In 1973, radar observation showed the ring particles to be large chunks of material averaging a meter on a side.

Pioneer 11 was guided to pass Jupiter in such a way that Jupiter swung Pioneer 11 into an orbit that brought it near Saturn in Sept. 1979. If the space craft is functioning adequately at that time, it will send us the photos and physical data possible only from a close fly-by. Voyager 1 will inspect Saturn, its rings, and some satellites in November 1980; Voyager 2 will visit in 1981.

Greenwich Sidereal Time for 0^h GMT, 1981

(Add 12 hours to obtain Right Ascension of Mean Sun)

Date		h	m	Date		h	m	Date		h	m	Date		h	m
Jan.	1	06	47.2		11	13	16.5	July	10	19	11.3		18	01	45.6
	11	07	21.6		21	13	55.9		20	19	50.7		28	02	25.0
	21	07	01.1	May	1	14	35.3		30	20	30.2	Nov.	7	03	04.4
	31	08	40.5		11	15	14.8	Aug.	9	21	09.6		17	03	43.8
Feb.	10	09	19.9		21	15	54.2		19	21	49.0		27	04	23.2
	20	09	59.3		31	16	33.6		29	22	28.4	Dec.	7	05	02.7
Mar.	2	10	38.8	June	10	17	13.0	Sept.	8	23	07.8		17	05	42.1
	12	11	18.2		20	17	52.4		18	23	47.2		27	06	21.5
	22	11	57.6		30	18	31.8		28	00	26.7				
Apr.	1	12	37.0					Oct.	8	01	06.1				

Planetary Configurations, 1981

Greenwich Mean Time (0 designates midnight; 12 designates noon)

Mo D. h. m.		
Jan. 2 02	-	⊕ at perihelion
4 09	- ☌ ♀ ☽	♀ 3° S
7 21	- ☌ ♂ ☽	♂ 1°.6 S
14 08	- ☌ ♃ ♄	♃ 1°.1 S
16 17	- ☌ * ☽	Aldebaran 0°.9 S; occultation
20 08	- ☍ ☽ ⊙	Penumbral eclipse
23 22	- ☌ ☿ ♂	☿ 0°.3 S
25 17	- ☌ ♄ ☽	♄ 2° S
25 18	- ☌ ♃ ☽	♃ 3° S
Feb. 02 01	-	☿ Greatest eastern elongation; 18°
3 17	- ☌ ♀ ☽	♀ 1°.6 S
4 22	- ☌ ☽ ⊙	Annular eclipse
5 20	- ☌ ♂ ☽	♂ 0°.6 S; occultation
6 04	- ☌ ☿ ☽	☿ 4° N
10 18	- ☌ ☿ ♂	☿ 4° N
12 22	- ☌ * ☽	Aldebaran 0°.9 S; occultation
17 11	- ☌ ☿ ⊙	Inferior
19 07	- ☌ ♃ ♄	♃ 1°.1 S
22 00	- ☌ ♃ ☽	♃ 3° S
22 00	- ☌ ♄ ☽	♄ 2° S
22 01	- ☌ ☿ ♀	☿ 5° N
Mar. 4 14	- ☌ ☿ ☽	☿ 2° N
12 04	- ☌ * ☽	Aldebaran 1°.0 S; occultation
16 01	-	☿ Greatest western elongation; 28°
20 17 03		**Vernal equinox; Spring begins**
21 01	- ☌ ♃ ☽	♃ 3° S
21 04	- ☌ ♄ ☽	♄ 1°.7 S
26 06	- ☍ ♃ ⊙	
27 05	- ☍ ♄ ⊙	
Apr. 2 14	- ☌ ♂ ⊙	
3 06	- ☌ ☿ ☽	☿ 1°.1 N
7 09	- ☌ ♀ ⊙	Superior
17 01	- ☌ ♃ ☽	♃ 3° S
17 06	- ☌ ♄ ☽	♄ 1°.7 S
27 16	- ☌ ♀ ⊙	Superior
May 14 01	- ☌ * ☿	☿ 8° N of Aldebaran
14 03	- ☌ ♃ ☽	♃ 3° S
14 09	- ☌ ♄ ☽	♄ 1°.8 S
20 06	- ☌ * ♀	♀ 6° N of Aldebaran
27 04	-	☿ Greatest eastern elongation; 23°
June 3 13	- ☌ ♀ ☽	♀ 4° N
3 23	- ☌ ☿ ☽	☿ 3° N
9 11	- ☌ ☿ ♀	☿ 1°.7 S
10 09	- ☌ ♃ ☽	♃ 3° S
10 14	- ☌ ♄ ☽	♄ 2° S
19 20	- ☌ * ♂	♂ 6° N of Aldebaran
21 11 45		**Summer solstice; Summer begins**
22 01	- ☌ ☿ ⊙	Inferior
30 06	- ☌ ♂ ☽	♂ 4° N
July 3 13	- ☌ ♀ ☽	♀ 1°.3 N
3 23	-	⊕ at aphelion
7 20	- ☌ ♃ ☽	♃ 4° S
7 23	- ☌ ♄ ☽	♄ 2° S
14 14	-	☿ Greatest western elongation; 21°
17 05	- ☍ ☽ ⊙	Partial eclipse
23 21	- ☌ * ♀	♀ 1°.2 N of Regulus
29 00	- ☌ ♂ ☽	♂ 3° N
29 19	- ☌ * ☿	☿ 6° S of Pollux
30 22	- ☌ ♃ ♄	♃ 1°.2 S
31 04	- ☌ ☽ ⊙	Total eclipse
Aug. 2 13	- ☌ ♀ ☽	♀ 2° S
4 12	- ☌ ♃ ☽	♃ 4° S
4 12	- ☌ ♄ ☽	♄ 3° S
10 06	- ☌ ☿ ⊙	Superior
23 17	- ☌ * ♂	♂ 6° S of Pollux
25 22	- ☌ ♀ ♄	♀ 2° S
26 15	- ☌ ♂ ☽	♂ 1°.4 N
28 01	- ☌ ♀ ♃	♀ 0°.9 S
30 23	- ☌ ☿ ☽	☿ 4° S
Sept. 1 01	- ☌ ♄ ☽	♄ 3° S
1 06	- ☌ ♃ ☽	♃ 4° S
1 15	- ☌ ♀ ☽	♀ 5° S
6 21	- ☌ * ♀	♀ 1°.9 N of Spica
10 15	- ☌ ☿ ♄	☿ 4° S
13 19	- ☌ ♀ ♃	♀ 3° S
20 19	- ☌ * ☿	☿ 0°.4 S
23 03 05		**Autumnal equinox; Autumn begins**
23 16	-	☿ Greatest eastern elongation; 26°
24 05	- ☌ ♂ ☽	♂ 0°.04 S; occultation
30 02	- ☌ ☿ ☽	☿ 9° S
Oct. 1 21	- ☌ ♀ ☽	♀ 7° S
6 04	- ☌ ♄ ⊙	
14 05	- ☌ ♃ ⊙	
17 06	- ☌ * ♀	♀ 1°.9 N of Antares
18 11	- ☌ ☿ ⊙	Inferior
19 11	- ☌ * ♂	♂ 1°.1 N of Regulus
22 17	- ☌ ♂ ☽	♂ 1°.4 S
26 04	- ☌ ♄ ☽	♄ 3° S
Nov. 1 03	- ☌ ♀ ☽	♀ 6° S
3 01	- ☌ * ☿	☿ 5° N of Spica
3 04	-	☿ Greatest western elongation; 19°
6 00	- ☌ ☿ ♃	☿ 1°.2 N
11 02	-	♀ Greatest eastern elongation; 47°
20 04	- ☌ ♂ ☽	♂ 2° S
22 16	- ☌ ♄ ☽	♄ 3° S
23 13	- ☌ ♃ ☽	♃ 4° S
30 20	- ☌ ♀ ☽	♀ 3° S
Dec. 10 15	- ♀ ☿ ⊙	Superior
16 19	-	♀ Greatest brilliancy
18 13	- ☌ ♂ ☽	♂ 3° S
20 03	- ☌ ♄ ☽	♄ 3° S
21 06	- ☌ ♃ ☽	♃ 4° S
21 22 51		**Winter solstice; Winter begins**
29 05	- ☌ ♀ ☽	♀ 2° N

Planetary Configurations 1982

Jan. 4 12	-	⊕ at perihelion
8 06	- ☌ * ♄	♄ 5° N of Spica
9 14	- ☌ ☿ ♀	☿ 5° S
9 20	- ☍ ☽ ⊙	Eclipse
15 19	- ☌ ♂ ☽	♂ 3° S
16 12	-	☿ Greatest eastern elongation; 19°
16 13	- ☌ ♄ ☽	♄ 3° S
17 20	- ☌ ♃ ☽	♃ 4° S
21 10	- ☌ ♀ ⊙	Inferior
25 05	- ☌ ☽ ⊙	Partial eclipse
Feb. 1 04	- ☌ ☿ ⊙	Inferior
12 16	- ☌ ♂ ☽	♂ 2° S
12 22	- ☌ ♄ ☽	♄ 3° S
14 09	- ☌ ♃ ☽	♃ 4° S
20 16	- ☌ ♀ ☽	♀ 7° N
25 01	-	♀ Greatest brilliancy
25 08	- ☌ * ♄	♄ 5° N of Spica
26 11	-	♀ Greatest western elongation; 27°
Mar. 11 12	☌ ♂ ☽	♂ 2° S
12 05	- ☌ ♄ ☽	♄ 3° S
13 17	- ☌ ♃ ☽	♃ 4° S
20 22 56		**Vernal equinox; Spring begins**

Rising and Setting of Planets, 1981

Greenwich Mean Time (0 designates midnight)

Venus, 1981

1981	20° N. Latitude Rise	20° N. Latitude Set	30° N. Latitude Rise	30° N. Latitude Set	40° N. Latitude Rise	40° N. Latitude Set	50° N. Latitude Rise	50° N. Latitude Set	60° N. Latitude Rise	60° N. Latitude Set
Jan. 6	5:02	15:58	5:23	15:37	5:48	15:12	6:25	14:35	7:28	13:32
16	5:18	16:12	5:39	15:51	6:05	15:24	6:43	14:47	7:48	13:42
26	5:32	16:28	5:52	16:08	6:18	15:42	6:54	15:06	7:56	14:04
Feb. 5	5:43	16:45	6:01	16:27	6:24	16:04	6:56	15:32	7:51	14:37
15	5:50	17:02	6:06	16:46	6:25	16:27	6:52	16:00	7:36	15:16
25	5:55	17:17	6:07	17:05	6:22	16:50	6:42	16:30	7:14	15:58
Mar. 7	5:56	17:32	6:04	17:24	6:14	17:14	6:28	17:00	6:49	16:39
17	5:56	17:46	6:00	17:42	6:05	17:37	6:12	17:30	6:22	17:20
27	5:55	17:59	5:55	17:59	5:54	18:00	5:54	18:00	5:53	18:01
Apr. 6	5:54	18:14	5:50	18:18	5:45	18:23	5:37	18:31	5:25	18:43
16	5:53	18:27	5:45	18:35	5:34	18:46	5:19	19:01	4:56	19:24
26	5:54	18:42	5:42	18:54	5:26	19:10	5:04	19:32	4:29	20:07
May 6	5:58	18:58	5:42	19:14	5:21	19:35	4:52	20:03	4:05	20:51
16	6:04	19:14	5:44	19:34	5:20	19:58	4:45	20:33	3:44	21:34
26	6:13	19:31	5:52	19:52	5:24	20:20	4:44	21:00	3:32	22:12
June 5	6:27	19:45	6:06	20:06	6:18	19:54	4:58	21:14	3:46	22:26
15	6:40	20:00	6:17	20:23	6:31	20:09	5:06	21:34	3:48	22:52
25	6:56	20:12	6:35	20:33	6:48	20:20	5:29	21:39	4:20	22:48
July 5	7:11	20:19	6:53	20:37	7:04	20:26	5:56	21:34	4:59	22:31
15	7:27	20:23	7:12	20:38	7:21	20:29	6:26	21:24	5:42	22:08
25	7:40	20:24	7:29	20:35	7:36	20:28	6:55	21:09	6:24	21:40
Aug. 4	7:53	20:23	7:46	20:30	7:37	20:39	7:25	20:51	7:05	21:11
14	8:01	20:15	7:58	20:18	7:54	20:22	7:49	20:27	7:41	20:35
24	8:16	20:16	8:18	20:14	8:19	20:13	8:22	20:10	8:25	20:07
Sept. 3	8:28	20:12	8:34	20:06	8:41	19:59	8:50	19:50	9:05	19:35
13	8:39	20:09	8:49	19:59	9:02	19:46	9:19	19:29	9:45	19:03
23	8:51	20:07	9:05	19:53	9:23	19:35	9:47	19:11	10:26	18:32
Oct. 3	9:03	20:07	9:21	19:48	9:44	19:26	10:15	18:54	11:08	18:02
13	9:17	20:09	9:38	19:48	10:05	19:21	10:43	18:43	11:50	17:36
23	9:28	20:14	9:52	19:50	10:22	19:20	11:05	18:33	12:26	17:16
Nov. 2	9:38	20:20	10:04	19:54	10:35	19:23	11:22	18:36	12:52	17:06
12	9:46	20:26	10:11	20:01	10:43	19:29	11:29	18:43	13:00	17:12
22	9:47	20:31	10:11	20:07	10:41	19:37	11:25	18:53	12:48	17:30
Dec. 2	9:41	20:31	10:03	20:09	10:31	19:41	11:10	19:02	12:21	17:51
12	9:27	20:25	9:46	20:06	10:11	19:41	10:45	19:07	11:44	18:08
22	9:01	20:09	9:18	19:52	9:39	19:31	10:09	19:01	10:57	18:13

Mars, 1981

1981	20° N. Latitude Rise	20° N. Latitude Set	30° N. Latitude Rise	30° N. Latitude Set	40° N. Latitude Rise	40° N. Latitude Set	50° N. Latitude Rise	50° N. Latitude Set	60° N. Latitude Rise	60° N. Latitude Set
Jan. 6	7:55	18:59	8:13	18:41	8:36	18:18	9:07	17:47	10:00	16:54
16	7:45	18:55	8:01	18:39	8:21	18:19	8:48	17:52	9:33	17:07
26	7:33	18:51	7:47	18:37	8:04	18:20	8:27	17:57	9:04	17:20
Feb. 5	7:20	18:46	7:31	18:35	7:45	18:21	8:04	18:02	8:33	17:33
15	7:07	18:41	7:15	18:33	7:26	18:22	7:40	18:08	8:02	17:46
25	6:52	18:36	6:58	18:30	7:05	18:23	7:15	18:13	7:30	17:58
Mar. 7	6:37	18:29	6:40	18:26	6:44	18:22	6:49	18:17	6:57	18:09
17	6:21	18:23	6:22	18:22	6:22	18:22	6:23	18:21	6:24	18:20
27	6:05	18:17	6:03	18:19	6:01	18:21	5:57	18:25	5:51	18:31
Apr. 6	5:50	18:10	5:45	18:15	5:39	18:21	5:31	18:29	5:18	18:42
16	5:34	18:04	5:27	18:11	5:18	18:20	5:05	18:33	4:46	18:52
26	5:19	17:57	5:09	18:07	4:57	18:19	4:40	18:36	4:13	19:03
May 6	5:04	17:50	4:52	18:02	4:37	18:17	4:15	18:39	3:42	19:12
16	4:50	17:44	4:36	17:58	4:18	18:16	3:52	18:42	3:11	19:23
26	4:37	17:37	4:20	17:54	4:00	18:14	3:30	18:44	2:42	19:32
June 5	4:24	17:30	4:06	17:48	3:42	18:12	3:10	18:44	2:14	19:40
15	4:11	17:23	3:51	17:43	3:26	18:08	2:51	18:43	1:48	19:46
25	4:00	17:16	3:39	17:37	3:13	18:03	2:34	18:42	1:26	19:50
July 5	3:49	17:07	3:27	17:29	2:59	17:57	2:19	18:37	1:06	19:50
15	3:39	16:59	3:17	17:21	2:48	17:50	2:07	18:31	0:51	19:47
25	3:29	16:49	3:07	17:11	2:38	17:40	1:57	18:21	0:40	19:38
Aug. 4	3:19	16:37	2:56	17:00	2:28	17:28	1:48	18:08	0:33	19:23
14	3:09	16:25	2:47	16:47	2:20	17:14	1:40	17:54	0:29	19:05
24	2:59	16:13	2:38	16:33	2:12	17:00	1:35	17:37	0:29	18:43
Sept. 3	2:48	15:58	2:29	16:17	2:04	16:42	1:29	17:17	0:29	18:17
13	2:37	15:43	2:19	16:01	1:57	16:23	1:25	16:55	0:31	17:49
23	2:26	15:26	2:10	15:42	1:49	16:03	1:20	16:32	0:32	17:20
Oct. 3	2:14	15:08	1:59	15:23	1:41	15:41	1:15	16:07	0:33	16:49
13	2:02	14:50	1:49	15:03	1:33	15:19	1:10	15:42	0:34	16:18
23	1:48	14.30	1:37	14:41	1:23	14:55	1:03	15:15	0:33	15:45
Nov. 2	1:34	14:10	1:24	14:20	1:13	14:31	0:57	14:47	0:31	15:13
12	1:18	13:48	1:10	13:56	1:01	14:05	0:48	14:18	0:27	14:39
22	1:02	13:26	0:56	13:32	0:49	13:39	0:39	13:49	0:23	14:05
Dec. 2	0:45	13:03	0:41	13:07	0:35	13:13	0:28	13:20	0:17	13:31
12	0:26	12:40	0:24	12:42	0:21	12:45	0:16	12:50	0:09	12:57
22	0:07	12:15	0:06	12:16	0:04	12:18	0:02	12:20	23:59*	12:23

*Previous Day

Jupiter, 1981

1981	20° N. Latitude Rise	20° N. Latitude Set	30° N. Latitude Rise	30° N. Latitude Set	40° N. Latitude Rise	40° N. Latitude Set	50° N. Latitude Rise	50° N. Latitude Set	60° N. Latitude Rise	60° N. Latitude Set
Jan. 6	23:36*	11:34	23:38*	11:32	23:40*	11:30	23:43*	11:27	23:48*	11:22
26	22:20*	10:18	22:22*	10:16	22:25*	10:13	22:28*	10:10	22:33*	10:05
Feb. 15	20:59*	8:57	21:01*	8:55	21:03*	8:53	21:05*	8:51	21:09	8:47
Mar. 7	19:33*	7:33	19:34*	7:32	19:35*	7:31	19:37*	7:29	19:39	7:27

	20° N. Latitude Rise	Set	30° N. Latitude Rise	Set	40° N. Latitude Rise	Set	50° N. Latitude Rise	Set	60° N. Latitude Rise	Set
27	18:03*	6:07	18:04*	6:06	18:04*	6:06	18:04*	6:06	18:04*	6:06
Apr. 16	16:30	4:36**	16:29	4:37**	16:29	4:37**	16:27	4:39**	16:25	4:41**
May 6	15:06	3:10**	15:03	3:13**	15:01	3:15**	14:59	3:17**	14:56	3:20**
26	13:45	1:49**	13:41	1:53**	13:40	1:54**	13:37	1:57**	13:33	2:01**
June 15	12:26	0:34**	12:25	0:35**	12:24	0:36**	12:21	0:39**	12:18	0:42**
July 5	11:14	23:20	11:14	23:20	11:13	23:21	11:12	23:22	11:10	23:24
25	10:07	22:09	10:07	22:09	10:07	22:09	10:08	22:08	10:08	22:08
Aug. 14	9:02	21:00	9:03	20:59	9:05	20:57	9:07	20:55	9:11	20:51
Sept. 3	7:59	19:53	8:02	19:50	8:05	19:47	8:10	19:42	8:16	19:36
23	6:58	18:48	7:02	18:44	7:08	18:38	7:14	18:32	7:25	18:21
Oct. 13	5:58	17:42	6:03	17:37	6:10	17:30	6:04	17:36	6:33	17:07
Nov. 2	4:57	16:37	5:04	16:30	5:13	16:21	5:24	16:10	5:42	15:52
22	3:57	15:33	4:06	15:24	4:16	15:14	4:30	15:00	4:51	14:39
Dec. 12	2:54	14:26	3:04	14:16	3:15	14:05	3:31	13:49	3:56	13:24

*Previous Day **Next Day

Saturn, 1981

	20° N. Rise	Set	30° N. Rise	Set	40° N. Rise	Set	50° N. Rise	Set	60° N. Rise	Set
Jan. 6	23:36*	11:36	23:37*	11:35	23:38*	11:34	23:39*	11:33	23:41*	11:31
26	22:18*	10:18	22:19*	10:17	22:20*	10:16	22:21*	10:15	22:23*	10:13
Feb. 15	20:56*	8:58	20:57*	8:57	20:58*	8:56	20:59*	8:55	21:00*	8:54
Mar. 7	19:33*	7:37	19:34*	7:36	19:34*	7:36	22:19*	6:51	19:34*	7:36
27	18:09*	6:13	18:08*	6:14	18:08*	6:14	18:07*	6:15	18:06*	6:16
Apr. 16	16:39	4:45**	16:38	4:46**	16:37	4:47**	16:35	4:49**	16:33	4:51**
Mar. 6	15:15	3:23**	15:14	3:24**	15:12	3:26**	15:10	3:28**	15:07	3:31**
26	13:54	2:02**	13:52	2:04**	13:50	2:05**	13:48	2:08	13:45	2:11
June 15	12:35	0:43**	12:34	0:44**	12:32	0:46**	12:30	0:48**	12:26	0:52**
July 5	11:19	23:27	11:18	23:28	11:17	23:29	11:15	23:31	11:12	23:34
25	10:06	22:12	10:06	22:12	10:05	22:13	10:04	22:14	10:02	22:16
Aug. 14	8:55	20:59	8:55	20:59	8:55	20:59	8:56	20:58	8:55	20:59
Sept. 3	7:45	19:47	7:46	19:46	7:47	19:45	7:49	19:43	7:50	19:42
23	6:37	18:35	6:39	18:33	6:41	18:31	6:43	18:29	6:47	18:25
Oct. 13	5:28	17:24	5:31	17:21	5:34	17:18	5:38	17:14	5:44	17:08
Nov. 2	4:20	16:12	4:23	16:09	4:27	16:05	4:32	16:00	4:40	15:52
22	3:11	15:01	3:15	14:57	3:19	14:53	3:26	14:46	3:35	14:37
Dec. 12	2:00	13:48	2:04	13:44	2:10	13:38	2:17	13:31	2:28	13:20

*Previous Day **Next Day

The Planets and the Solar System

Planet	Mean daily motion "	Orbital velocity miles per sec.	Sidereal revolution days	Synodical revolution days	Dist. from sun in millions of mi. Max.	Min.	Dist. from Earth in millions of mi. Max.	Min.	Light at[1] perihelion	aphelion
Mercury . .	14732.420	29.75	87.9693	115.9	43.403	28.597	136	50	10.58	4.59
Venus . . .	5767.668	21.76	224.7009	583.9	67.726	66.813	161	25	1.94	1.89
Earth	3548.192	18.51	365.2564	—	94.555	91.445	—	—	1.03	0.97
Mars	1886.519	14.99	686.9796	779.9	154.936	128.471	248	35	0.524	0.360
Jupiter . . .	298.993	8.12	4332.1248	398.9	507.046	460.595	600	368	0.0408	0.0336
Saturn . . .	119.718	5.99	10825.863	378.1	937.541	838.425	1031	745	0.01230	0.00984
Uranus . . .	41.978	4.23	30676.15	369.7	1859.748	1699.331	1953	1606	0.00300	0.00250
Neptune . .	21.493	3.38	59911.13	367.5	2821.686	2760.386	2915	2667	0.00114	0.00109
Pluto	14.116	2.95	90824.2	366.7	4551.386	2756.427	4644	2663	0.00114	0.00042

Light at perihelion and aphelion is solar illumination in units of mean illumination at Earth.

Planet	Mean longitude of:* ascending node °	′	″	perihelion °	′	″	Inclination* of orbit to ecliptic °	′	″	Mean distance**	Eccentricity of orbit	Mean longitude at the epoch* °	′	″
Mercury	48	05	58	77	09	04	7	00	16	0.387099	0.205631	133	20	21
Venus	76	30	13	131	17	45	3	23	40	0.723332	0.006783	239	15	48
Earth				102	36	14				1.000000	0.016718	248	39	09
Mars	49	24	24	335	41	56	1	50	59	1.523691	0.093387	205	58	50
Jupiter	100	14	41	14	35	05	1	18	20	5.204377	0.0478063	160	33	28
Saturn.	113	30	41	95	28	15	2	29	11	9.577971	0.0554680	170	25	57
Uranus	74	00	19	172	55	20	0	46	18	19.26020	0.0503139	224	56	18
Neptune . . .	131	31	22	58	30	43	1	46	23	30.09421	0.0066466	261	34	19
Pluto	109	57	57	223	00	51	17	08	14	39.82984	0.2547843	210	06	59

*Consistent for the standard Epoch: 1980 June 10.0 Ephemeris Time **Astronomical units

Sun and planets	Semi-diameter at unit distance ′ ″	at mean least dist. ′ ″	in miles mean s.d.	Volume ⊕=1.	Mass. ⊕=1.	Density ⊕=1.	Axial rotation d.	h.	m.	s.	Gravity at surface ⊕=1.	Reflecting power Pct.	Probable temperature °F.
Sun	15 59.62	___	432560	1303730	332830	0.26	24	16	48		27.9	___	+10,000
Mercury . . .	3.37	5.45	1505	0.054	0.0554	0.98	59				0.37	0.06	+ 620
Venus	8.46	30.50	3762	0.880	0.8150	0.94	244.3	(R)			0.88	0.72	+ 900
Earth	___	___	3960	1.000	1.000	1.00		23	56	4	1.00	0.39	+ 72
Moon	2.40	16 43.00	1080	0.020	0.0123	0.61	27	7	43	12	0.17	0.07	− 10
Mars	4.68	8.94	2107	0.149	0.1075	0.72		24	37	23	0.38	0.16	− 10
Jupiter	98.37	23.43	44270	1316.	317.84	0.24		9	50	30	2.64	0.70	− 240
Saturn	82.80	9.76	37300	755.	95.147	0.13		10	14		1.15	0.75	− 300
Uranus	32.90	1.80	15200	52.	14.54	0.29		10	49	(R)	1.15	0.90	− 340
Neptune . . .	31.10	1.06	15600	57.	17.23	0.30		15	48		1.12	0.82	− 370
Pluto*.	1.80	0.06	800	0.008	0.0016	0.19	6	9			0.04	0.14	? ?

*Much of this information is too new to be verified, but observers at the U.S. Naval Observatory have derived values similar to these after having discovered that Pluto has a satellite. It apparently revolves about Pluto in a period equal to Pluto's rotation period. (R) retrograde of Venus and Uranus.

Four Eclipses in 1981

Greenwich Mean Time

First Eclipse

A penumbral eclipse of the moon, January 20. In a penumbral lunar eclipse, no part of the moon is in complete shadow. In this eclipse, the northern limb of the moon will appear to be somewhat darker than the rest near mid-eclipse. All of North America will be able to see the moon during the entire event.

Circumstances of the Eclipse

Moon enters penumbra . . .	Jan. 20, 5:36.9
Middle of Eclipse	20, 7:49.9
Moon leaves penumbra . . .	20, 10:03.9
Penumbral Magnitude . . .	1.039

Second Eclipse

An annular eclipse of the sun, February 4-5. This eclipse begins the day before it ends, crossing the dateline in the Pacific Ocean. The only large land mass the central path touches is southern Tasmania. The moon appearing too small to hide the sun completely, an annulus, or ring of solar surface, is formed. Since this surface is sufficiently bright to interfere with observation of the faint corona, an annular eclipse is of limited scientific value.

Circumstances of the Eclipse

Eclipse begins	Feb. 4, 19:27.8
Central eclipse begins	4, 20:33.3
Central eclipse at local apparent noon	4, 21:57.6
Central eclipse ends	4, 23:43.9
Eclipse ends	5, 00:49.2
Duration at mid eclipse . . .	00m 34s

Third Eclipse

A partial eclipse of the moon, July 17. A little more than half the moon will pass into the umbral shadow of the earth. It may be seen from any place the moon has risen. Thus, most of North America can view this event.

Circumstances of the Eclipse

Moon enters penumbra . . .	July 17, 2:05.2
Moon enters umbra	17, 3:24.8
Middle of eclipse	17, 4:46.8
Moon leaves umbra	17, 6:08.9
Moon leaves penumbra . . .	17, 7:28.4
Magnitude of the eclipse . .	0.554

Fourth Eclipse

A total eclipse of the sun, July 31. The path of totality begins at dawn at the southern end of the Black Sea, passes over the northern Caspian Sea, touches the northern tip of Lake Baikal, passes into the Pacific Ocean from the center of the Sakhalin Islands, ending at sunset north of the Hawaiian Islands.

Circumstances of the Eclipse

Eclipse begins	July 31, 1:11.3
Central eclipse begins	31, 2:17.8
Central eclipse at local apparent noon . . .	31, 3:35.6
Central eclipse ends	31, 5:13.8
Eclipse ends	31, 6:20.4
Duration at mid-eclipse . . .	2m 3s

Morning and Evening Stars 1981

Greenwich Mean Time

	Morning	Evening
Jan.	Venus Jupiter Saturn	Mercury Mars
Feb.	Mercury (from Feb. 17) Venus Jupiter Saturn	Mercury (to Feb. 17) Mars
Mar.	Mercury Venus Jupiter (to Mar. 26) Saturn (to Mar. 27)	Mars Jupiter (from Mar. 26) Saturn (from Mar. 27)
Apr.	Mercury (to Apr. 27) Venus (to Apr. 7) Mars (from Apr. 2)	Mercury (from Apr. 27) Venus (from Apr. 7) Mars (to Apr. 2) Jupiter Saturn
May	Mars	Mercury Venus Jupiter Saturn
June	Mercury (from June 22) Mars	Mercury (to June 22) Venus Jupiter
July	Mercury Mars	Saturn Venus Jupiter Saturn
Aug.	Mercury (to Aug. 10) Mars	Mercury (from Aug. 10) Venus Jupiter Saturn
Sept.	Mars	Mercury Venus Jupiter Saturn
Oct.	Mercury (from Oct. 18) Mars Jupiter (from Oct. 14) Saturn (from Oct. 6)	Mercury (to Oct. 18) Venus Jupiter (to Oct. 14) Saturn (to Oct. 6)
Nov.	Mercury Mars Jupiter Saturn	Venus
Dec.	Mercury (to Dec. 10) Mars Jupiter Saturn	Mercury (from Dec. 10) Venus

Aurora Borealis and Aurora Australis

The Aurora Borealis, also called the Northern Lights, is a broad display of rather faint light in the northern skies at night. The Aurora Australis, a similar phenomenon, appears at the same time in southern skies. The aurora appears in a wide variety of forms. Sometimes it is seen as a quiet glow, almost foglike in character; sometimes as vertical streamers in which there may be considerable motion; sometimes as a series of luminous expanding arcs. There are many colors, with white, yellow, and red predominating.

The auroras are most vivid and most frequently seen at about 20 degrees from the magnetic poles, along the northern coast of the North American continent and the eastern part of the northern coast of Europe. They have been seen as far south as Key West and as far north as Australia and New Zealand, but such occasions are rare.

While the cause of the auroras is not known beyond question, there does seem to be a definite correlation between auroral displays and sun-spot activity. It is thought that atomic particles expelled from the sun by the forces that cause solar flares speed through space at velocities of 400 to 600 miles per second. These particles are entrapped by the earth's magnetic field, forming what are termed the Van Allen belts. The encounter of these clouds of the solar wind with the earth's magnetic field weakens the field so that previously trapped particles are allowed to impact the upper atmosphere. The collisions between solar and terrestrial atoms result in the glow in the upper atmosphere called the aurora. The glow may be vivid where the lines of magnetic force converge near the magnetic poles.

The auroral displays appear at heights ranging from 50 to about 600 miles and have given us a means of estimating the extent of the earth's atmosphere.

The auroras are often accompanied by magnetic storms whose forces, also guided by the lines of force of the earth's magnetic field, disrupt electrical communication.

Star Tables, 1981

These tables include stars of visual magnitude 2.5 and brighter. Co-ordinates are for the epoch Jan. 0.432, 1981. Where no parallax figures are given, the trigonometric parallax figure is smaller than the margin for error and the distance given is obtained by indirect methods. Stars of variable magnitude designated by v.

To find the time when the star is on meridian, subtract R.A.M.S. of the sun table on page 760 from the star's right ascension, first adding 24h to the latter, if necessary. Mark this result P.M., if less than 12h; but if greater than 12, subtract 12h and mark the remainder A.M.

Star	Magnitude	Parallax ″	Light yrs.	Right ascen. h. m.	Declination ° ′
α Andromedae (Alpheratz)	2.06	0.02	90	0 07.4	+28 59
β Cassiopeiae	2.26v	0.07	45	0 08.2	+59 03
α Phoenicis	2.39	0.04	93	0 25.3	−42 25
α Cassiopeiae (Schedir)	2.22	0.01	150	0 39.4	+56 26
β Ceti	2.02	0.06	57	0 42.6	−18 05
γ Cassiopeiae	2.13v	0.03	96	0 55.6	+60 37
β Andromedae	2.02	0.04	76	1 08.7	+35 31
α Eridani (Achernar)	0.51	0.02	118	1 37.0	−57 20
γ Andromedae	2.14		260	2 02.7	+42 14
α Arietis	2.00	0.04	76	2 06.1	+23 22
α Ursae Min. (Pole Star)	1.99v		680	2 12.7	+89 11
o Ceti	2.00v	0.01	103	2 18.4	−3 04
β Persei (Algol)	2.06v	0.03	105	3 06.9	+40 53
α Persei	1.80	0.03	570	3 23.0	+49 48
α Tauri (Aldebaran)	0.86v	0.05	68	4 34.8	+16 28
β Orionis (Rigel)	0.14v		900	5 13.6	−8 13
α Aurigae (Capella)	0.05	0.07	45	5 15.3	+45 59
γ Orionis (Bellatrix)	1.64	0.03	470	5 24.1	+6 20
β Tauri (El Nath)	1.65	0.02	300	5 25.1	+28 36
δ Orionis	2.20v		1500	5 31.0	−0 19
ε Orionis	1.70		1600	5 35.2	−1 13
ζ Orionis	1.79	0.02	1600	5 39.8	−1 57
κ Orionis	2.06	0.01	2100	5 46.9	−9 41
α Orionis (Betelgeuse)	0.41v		520	5 54.1	+7 24
β Aurigae	1.86	0.04	88	5 58.1	+44 57
β Canis Majoris	1.96	0.01	750	6 21.9	−17 57
α Carinae (Canopus)	−0.72	0.02	98	6 23.5	−52 41
γ Geminorum	1.93	0.03	105	6 36.6	+16 25
α Canis Majoris (Sirius)	−1.47	0.38	8.7	6 44.3	−16 41
ε Canis Majoris	1.48		680	6 57.9	−28 57
δ Canis Majoris	1.85		2100	7 07.6	−26 22
η Canis Majoris	2.46		2700	7 23.3	−29 16
α Geminorum (Castor)	1.97	0.07	45	7 33.4	+31 56
α Canis Minoris (Procyon)	0.37	0.29	11.3	7 38.3	+5 16
β Geminorum (Pollux)	1.16	0.09	35	7 44.2	+28 04
ζ Puppis	2.23		2400	8 02.9	−39 57
γ Velorum	1.88		520	8 08.9	−47 17
ε Carinae	1.90		340	8 22.1	−59 27
δ Velorum	1.95	0.04	76	8 44.2	−54 38
λ Velorum	2.24	0.02	750	9 07.3	−43 21
β Carinae	1.67	0.04	86	9 13.0	−69 38
ι Carinae	2.25		750	9 16.6	−59 12
κ Velorum	2.49	0.01	470	9 21.5	−54 56
α Hydrae	1.98	0.02	94	9 26.7	−8 35
α Leonis (Regulus)	1.36	0.04	84	10 07.4	+12 04
γ Leonis	1.99	0.02	90	10 18.9	+19 56
β Ursae Majoris (Merak)	2.37	0.04	78	11 00.7	+56 29
α Ursae Majoris (Dubhe)	1.81	0.03	105	11 02.6	+61 51
β Leonis (Denebola)	2.14	0.08	43	11 48.1	+14 41
γ Ursae Majoris (Phecda)	2.44	0.02	90	11 52.8	+53 48
α Crucis	1.39		370	12 25.5	−63 00
γ Crucis	1.69		220	12 30.1	−57 00
γ Centauri	2.17		160	12 40.5	−48 51
β Crucis	1.28v		490	12 46.5	−59 35
ε Ursae Majoris (Alioth)	1.79v	0.01	68	12 53.2	+56 04
ζ Ursae Majoris (Mizar)	2.26	0.04	88	13 23.2	+55 01
α Virginis (Spica)	0.91v	0.02	220	13 24.2	−11 04
ε Centauri	2.33v		570	13 38.7	−53 22
η Ursae Majoris (Alkaid)	1.87		210	13 46.8	+49 24
β Centauri	0.63v	0.02	490	14 02.5	−60 17
θ Centauri	2.04	0.06	55	14 05.6	−36 17
α Bootis (Arcturus)	−0.06	0.09	36	14 14.8	+19 17
η Centauri	2.39v		390	14 34.3	−42 04
α Centauri	0.01	0.75	4.3	14 38.3	−60 45
α Lupi	2.32v		430	14 40.7	−47 18
ε Bootis	2.37	0.01	103	14 44.2	+27 09
β Ursae Minoris	2.07	0.03	105	14 50.7	+74 14
α Coronae Borealis	2.23v	0.04	76	15 33.9	+26 47
δ Scorpii	2.34		590	15 59.2	−22 34
α Scorpii (Antares)	0.92v	0.02	520	16 28.2	−26 23
α Trianguli Australis	1.93	0.02	82	16 46.6	−69 00
ε Scorpii	2.28	0.05	66	16 48.9	−34 16
η Ophiuchi	2.43	0.05	69	17 09.3	−15 42
λ Scorpii	1.60v		310	17 32.3	−37 05
α Ophiuchi	2.09	0.06	58	17 34.0	+12 34
θ Scorpii	1.86	0.02	650	17 36.0	−42 59
κ Scorpii	2.39v		470	17 41.2	−39 01
γ Draconis	2.21	0.02	108	17 56.2	+51 29
ε Sagittarii	1.81	0.02	124	18 22.9	−34 24
α Lyrae (Vega)	0.04	0.12	26.5	18 36.3	+38 46
σ Sagittarii	2.12		300	18 54.1	−26 19
α Aquilae (Altair)	0.77	0.20	16.5	19 49.9	+8 49
γ Cygni	2.22		750	20 21.5	+40 12
α Pavonis	1.95		310	20 24.2	−56 48
α Cygni (Deneb)	1.26		1600	20 40.8	+45 13
ε Cygni	2.46	0.04	74	20 45.3	+33 54
α Cephei	2.44	0.06	52	21 18.1	+62 30
ε Pegasi	2.38		780	21 43.3	+9 47
α Gruis	1.76	0.05	64	22 07.0	−47 03
β Gruis	2.17v		280	22 41.5	−46 59
α Piscis Austrinis (Fomalhaut)	1.15	0.14	22.6	22 56.6	−29 43
β Pegasi	2.50v	0.02	210	23 02.8	+27 59
α Pegasi	2.50	0.03	109	23 03.8	+15 06

Comet Table 1980-1986

Name	Year of first known perihelion	Due to return	Period in years	Perihelion dist.	Aphelion dist.	Inclination to ecliptic degree	Long. of ascend. node degree	From asc. node to perihelion degree
Brooks II	1889	Nov. 1980	6.88	1.84	5.39	6	176	198
Harrington	1953	Nov. 1980	6.80	1.58	5.59	9	119	233
Reinmuth I	1928	Nov. 1980	7.63	2.00	5.75	8	121	9
Encke	1786	Dec. 1980	3.30	0.34	4.02	12	334	186
Tuttle	1790	Jan. 1981	13.77	1.02	10.47	54	270	207
Reinmuth II	1947	Feb. 1981	6.74	1.94	5.20	7	296	45
Borrelly	1905	Feb. 1981	6.76	1.32	5.84	30	75	353
Schwassmann-Wachmann II	1929	Feb. 1981	6.51	2.14	4.83	4	126	357
West-Kohoutek-Ikemara*	1975	Mar. 1981	6.11	1.40	5.29	30	85	358
Neujmin II	1916	May 1981	5.43	1.34	4.84	11	328	194
Finlay	1886	June 1981	6.95	1.10	6.19	4	42	322
Stephan-Oterma	1867	Oct. 1981	38.84	1.60	21.34	18	79	358
Swift-Gehrels	1889	Nov. 1981	9.23	1.35	7.44	9	314	84
Slaughter-Burnham	1958	Nov. 1981	11.62	2.54	7.72	8	346	44
Gehrels II*	1973	Nov. 1981	7.94	2.35	5.61	7	216	183
Kearns-Kwee	1963	Dec. 1981	9.01	2.23	6.43	9	315	131
Oterma	1942	Jan. 1982	7.88	3.39	4.53	4	155	355
Perrine-Mrkos	1896	Apr. 1982	6.72	1.27	5.85	18	240	166
Gale	1927	June 1982	10.99	1.18	8.70	12	67	209
Swift-Tuttle*	1862	Aug. 1982	119.98	0.96	47.69	114	139	153
Gunn	1969	Nov. 1982	6.80	2.45	4.74	10	68	198
Arend	1951	Dec. 1982	7.76	1.82	6.02	22	358	45
Neujmin III	1929	Dec. 1982	10.57	1.98	7.66	4	150	147
Vaisala I	1939	Dec. 1982	11.28	1.87	8.19	12	135	50
Kojima*	1970	Feb. 1983	6.19	1.63	5.11	4	291	178
Pons-Winneke	1819	Mar. 1983	6.34	1.25	5.60	22	93	172
Harrington-Abell	1954	Sept. 1983	7.19	1.77	5.68	17	146	338
Kohoutek	1975	Apr. 1986	5.67	1.56	4.80	5	274	169
Halley	240 B.C.	May 1986	76.1	0.59	35.3	162	58	112

*One appearance only.

Most of the comets in the table will not be seen except by professional astronomers or by well-equipped amateurs. At any given time, these observers may be able to follow about a half dozen comets of which the public is unaware. An easily seen comet is rare, one or two every ten to fifteen years.

Comets are named for their discoverers, up to three independent observers being so honored. If a comet becomes unusual, it may be well-known by these names. Usually, however, a preliminary designation is used: the year followed by a letter of the alphabet assigned in the order of discovery during that year. About two years later after any likely late discoveries, comets are given their permanent designation which states the year of their perihelion passage and a Roman numeral giving the order of passage during that year. Well-known periodic comets receive these designations at each appearance, but the literature and the Comet Table will continue to identify them by their discoverers' names.

Astronomical Constants; Speed of Light

The following astronomical constants were adopted in 1968, in accordance with the resolutions and recommendations of the International Astronomical Union (Hamburg 1964): Velocity of light, 299,792.5 kilometers per second, or about 186,282.3976 statute miles per second: solar parallax, 8′.794: constant of nutation, 9′.210; and constant of aberration, 20′.496.

Moon's Perigee and Apogee, 1981

Perigee Day	Hour GMT	Hour EST	Perigee Day	Hour GMT	Hour EST	Apogee Day	Hour GMT	Hour EST	Apogee Day	Hour GMT	Hour EST
Jan. 15	04	23*	July 27	09	04	Jan. 27	20	15	Aug. 8	12	07
Feb. 8	23	18	Aug. 21	21	16	Feb. 24	17	12	Sept. 5	07	02
Mar. 8	12	07	Sept. 17	04	23*	Mar. 24	09	04	Oct. 3	01	20*
Apr. 5	19	14	Oct. 15	02	21*	Apr. 20	16	11	Oct. 30	16	11
May 4	05	00	Nov. 12	11	06	May 17	18	13	Nov. 26	21	16
June 1	14	09	Dec. 11	00	19*	June 14	03	22*	Dec. 23	23	18
June 29	19	14	.....			July 11	18	13	.....		

*Previous day

Largest Telescopes Are in Northern Hemisphere

Most of the world's major astronomical installations are in the northern hemisphere, while many of astronomy's major problems are found in the southern sky. This imbalance has long been recognized and is being remedied.

In the northern hemisphere the largest reflector is the 236-inch mirror at the Special Astrophysical Observatory in the Caucasus in the Soviet Union. The largest reflectors in the U.S. include 3 in California: at Palomar Mtn., 200 inches; at Lick Observatory, Mt. Hamilton, 120 inches; and at Mt. Wilson Observatory, 100 inches. Also in the U.S. are a 158 inch reflector at Kitt Peak, Arizona, dedicated in June 1973, and a 107-inch telescope at the McDonald Observatory on Mt. Locke in Texas. A telescope at the Crimean Astrophysical Observatory in the Soviet Union has a 104-inch mirror.

Placed in service in 1975 were three large reflectors for the southern hemisphere. Associated Universities for Research in Astronomy (AURA), the operating organization of Kitt Peak National Observatory, dedicated the 158-inch reflector (twin of the telescope on Kitt Peak) at Cerro Tololo International Observatory, Chile; the European Southern Observatory has a 141-inch reflector at La Silla, Chile; and the Anglo-Australian telescope, 152 inches in diameter, is at Siding

Spring Observatory in Australia.

Optical Telescopes

Optical astronomical telescopes are of two kinds, refracting and reflecting. In the first, light passes through a lens which brings the light rays into focus, where the image may be examined after being magnified by a second lens, the eyepiece, or directly photographed.

The reflector consists of a concave parabolic mirror, generally of Pyrex or now of a relatively heat insensitive material, cervit, coated with silver or aluminum, which reflects the light rays back toward the upper end of the telescope, where they are either magnified and observed by the eyepiece or, as in the case of the refractors, photographed. In most reflecting telescopes, the light is reflected again by a secondary mirror and comes to a focus after passing through a hole in the side of the telescope, where the eye-piece or camera is located, or after passing through a hole in the center of the primary mirror.

World's Largest Refractors

Location and diameter in inches

Yerkes Obs., Williams Bay, Wis.	40
Lick Obs., Mt. Hamilton, Cal.	36
Astrophys. Obs., Potsdam, E. Germany	32
Paris Observatory, Meuden, France	32
Allegheny Obs., Pittsburgh, Pa.	30
Univ. of Paris, Nice, France	30
Royal Greenwich Obs., Herstmonceux, England	28
Union Obs., Johannesburg, South Africa	26.5
Universitats-Sternwarte, Vienna, Austria	26.5
University of Virginia	26
Obs., Academy of Sciences, Pulkova, USSR	26
Astronomical Obs., Belgrade, Yugoslavia	26
Leander McCormick Obs., Charlottesville, Va.	26
Obs. Mitaka, Tokyo-to, Japan	26
US Naval Obs., Washington, D.C.	26
Mt. Stromlo Obs., Canberra, Australia	26

World's Largest Reflectors

Special Astrophysical Obs., Zelenchukskaya, USSR	236
Hale Obs., Palomar Mtn., Cal.	200, 100, 60
Mt. Hopkins (SAO), Ariz.	176*, 60
Kitt Peak National Obs., Tucson, Ariz.	158, 84, 60
Cerro Tololo, Chile	158, 60
Siding Spring, Australia	153
La Silla, Chile	141, 60
Lick Obs., Mt. Hamilton, Cal.	120
McDonald Obs., Fort Davis, Tex.	107, 82
Crimean Astrophys. Obs., Nauchny, USSR	104
Byurakan Obs., Armenia S.S.R.	102
Royal Greenwich Obs., Herstmonceux, England	98
Steward Obs., Tucson, Ariz.	90
Mauna Kea Obs., Univ. of Hawaii, Ha.	88, 84
Shemakha Astroph. Obs., Azerbaijan S.S.R.	79
Saint Michel l'Observatoire, (Basses Alpes), Fr.	77
Haute Provence, France	76, 60
Tokyo Obs., Japan	74
Mt. Stromlo, Australia	74
David Dunlap Obs., Ont., Canada	74
Helwan Obs., Helwan, Egypt	74
Astrophys. Obs., Kamogata, Okayama-ken, Japan	74
Sutherland, South Africa	74
Dominion Astrophys. Obs., Victoria, B.C.	73
Perkins Obs., Flagstaff, Ariz.	72
Obs., Padua Univ., Asiago, Italy	72
Agassiz Station Harvard Obs., Cambridge, Mass.	61
National Obs., Bosque Alegre Sta., Argentina	61
U.S. Naval Obs., Flagstaff, Ariz.	61
Catalina Mtn., Ariz.	61
Arizona Univ. Obs., Tucson, Ariz.	60
Boyden Obs., Bloemfontein, South Africa	60
Mt. Haleakala, Ha.	60
Figl Astroph. Obs., Vienna, Austria	60
Mt. Wilson Obs., Pasadena, Cal.	60

*Multiple mirror telescope, equivalent aperture.

Major U.S. Planetariums

Academy Planetarium, U.S. Air Force Academy
Adler Planetarium, Chicago, Ill.
American Museum-Hayden Planetarium, N.Y.C.
Buhl Planetarium, Pittsburgh, Pa.
Charles Hayden Planetarium, Boston, Mass.
Einstein Spacearium, Washington, D.C.
Fels Planetarium, Philadelphia, Pa.
Fernbank Science Center Planetarium, Altanta, Ga.
Griffith Planetarium, Los Angeles, Cal.
La. Arts and Science Planetarium, Baton Rouge, La.
McDonnell Planetarium, St. Louis, Mo.
Morehead Planetarium, Chapel Hill, N.C.
Morrison Planetarium, San Francisco, Cal.
Robert T. Longway Planetarium, Flint, Mich.
Strassenburgh Planetarium, Rochester, N.Y.

The Sun

The sun, the controlling body of our solar system, is a star whose dimensions cause it to be classified among stars as average in size, temperature, and brightness. Its proximity to the earth makes it appear to us as tremendously large and bright. A series of thermo-nuclear reactions involving the atoms of the elements of which it is composed produces the heat and light that make life possible on earth.

The sun has a diameter of 864,000 miles and is distant, on the average, 92,900,000 miles from the earth. It is 1.41 times as dense as water. The light of the sun reaches the earth in 499.012 seconds or slightly more than 8 minutes. The average solar surface temperature has been measured by several indirect methods which agree closely on a value of 6,000° Kelvin or about 10,000° F. The interior temperature of the sun is about 35,000,000 F.°.

When sunlight is analyzed with a spectroscope, it is found to consist of a continuous spectrum composed of all the colors of the rainbow in order, crossed by many dark lines. The "absorption lines" are produced by gaseous materials in the atmosphere of the sun. More than 60 of the natural terrestrial elements have been identified in the sun, all in gaseous form because of the intense heat of the sun.

Spheres and Corona

The radiating surface of the sun is called the **photosphere,** and just above it is the **chromosphere.** The chromosphere is visible to the naked eye only at times of total solar eclipses, appearing then to be a pinkish-violet layer with occasional great prominences projecting above its general level. With proper instruments the chromosphere can be seen or photographed whenever the sun is visible without waiting for a total eclipse. Above the chromosphere is the **corona,** also visible to the naked eye only at times of total eclipse. Instruments also permit the brighter portions of the corona to be studied whenever conditions are favorable. The pearly light of the corona surges millions of miles from the sun. Iron, nickel, and calcium are believed to be principal contributors to the composition of the corona, all in a state of extreme attenuation and high ionization that indicates temperatures on the order of a million degrees Fahrenheit.

Sunspots

There is an intimate connection between sunspots and the corona. At times of low sunspot activity, the fine streamers of the corona will be much longer above the sun's equator than over the polar regions of the sun, while during high sunspot activity, the corona extends fairly evenly outward from all regions of the sun, but to a much greater distance in space. Sunspots are dark, irregularly-shaped regions whose diameters may reach tens of thousands of miles. The average life of a sunspot group is from two to three weeks, but there have been groups that have lasted for more than a year, being carried repeatedly around as the sun rotated upon its axis. The record for the duration of a sunspot is 18 months. Sunspots reach a low point every 11.3 years, with a peak of activity occurring irregularly between two successive minima.

The sun is 400,000 times as bright as the full moon and gives the earth 6 million times as much light as do all the other stars put together. Actually, most of the stars that can be easily seen on any clear night are brighter than the sun.

The Moon

The moon completes a circuit around the earth in a period whose mean or average duration is 27 days 7 hours 43.2 minutes. This is the moon's sidereal period. Because of the motion of the moon in common with the earth around the sun, the mean duration of the lunar month — the period from one new moon to the next new moon — is 29 days 12 hours 44.05 minutes. This is the moon's synodical period.

The mean distance of the moon from the earth according to the American Ephemeris is 238,857 miles. Because the orbit of the moon about the earth is not circular but elliptical, however, the maximum distance from the earth that the moon may reach is 252,710 miles and the least distance is 221,463 miles. All distances are from the center of one object to the center of the other.

The moon's diameter is 2,160 miles. If we deduct the radius of the moon, 1,080 miles, and the radius of the earth, 3,963 miles from the minimum distance or perigee, given above, we shall have for the nearest approach of the bodies' surfaces 216,420 miles.

The moon rotates on its axis in a period of time exactly equal to its sidereal revolution about the earth — 27.321666 days. The moon's revolution about the earth is irregular because of its elliptical orbit. The moon's rotation, however, is regular and this, together with the irregular revolution, produces what is called "libration in longitude" which permits us to see first farther around the east side and then farther around the west side of the moon. The moon's variation north or south of the ecliptic permits us to see farther over first one pole and then the other of the moon and this is "libration in latitude." These two libration effects permit us to see a total of about 60% of the moon's surface over a period of time. The hidden side of the moon was photographed in 1959 by the Soviet space vehicle Lunik III. Since then many excellent pictures of nearly all of the moon's surface have been transmitted to earth by Lunar Orbiters launched by the U.S.

The tides are caused mainly by the moon, because of its proximity to the earth. The ratio of the tide-raising power of the moon to that of the sun is 11 to 5.

Harvest Moon and Hunter's Moon

The Harvest Moon, the full moon nearest the Autumnal Equinox, ushers in a period of several successive days when the moon rises soon after sunset. This phenomenon gives farmers in temperate latitudes extra hours of light in which to harvest their crops before frost and winter come. The 1981 Harvest Moon falls on Sept. 14. Harvest moon in the south temperate latitudes falls on Apr. 20.

The next full moon after Harvest Moon is called the Hunter's Moon, accompanied by a similar phenomenon but less marked; — Oct. 13, northern hemisphere; Apr. 20, southern hemisphere.

The Zodiac

The sun's apparent yearly path among the stars is known as the **ecliptic.** The zone 16° wide, 8° on each side of the ecliptic, is known as the **zodiac.** Inside of this zone are the apparent paths of the sun, moon, earth, and major planets. Beginning at the point on the ecliptic which marks the position of the sun at the vernal equinox, and thence proceeding eastward, the zodiac is divided into twelve signs of 30° each, as shown herewith.

These signs are named from the twelve constellations of the zodiac with which the signs coincided in the time of the astronomer Hipparchus, about 2,000 years ago. Owing to the precession of the equinoxes, that is to say, to the retrograde motion of the equinoxes along the ecliptic, each sign in the zodiac has, in the course of 2,000 years, moved backward 30° into the constellation west of it; so that the sign Aries is now in the constellation Pisces, and so on. The vernal equinox will move from Pisces into Aquarius about the middle of the 26th century. The signs of the zodiac with their Latin and English names are as follows:

Spring	1.	♈ Aries.	The Ram.
	2.	♉ Taurus.	The Bull.
	3.	♊ Gemini.	The Twins.
Summer	4.	♋ Cancer.	The Crab.
	5.	♌ Leo.	The Lion.
	6.	♍ Virgo.	The Virgin.
Autumn	7.	♎ Libra.	The Balance.
	8.	♏ Scorpio.	The Scorpion.
	9.	♐ Sagittarius.	The Archer.
Winter	10.	♑ Capricorn.	The Goat.
	11.	♒ Aquarius.	The Water Bearer.
	12.	♓ Pisces.	The Fishes.

The Earth: Size, Computation of Time, Seasons

Size and Dimensions

The earth is the fifth largest planet and the third from the sun. Its mass is 6 sextillion, 588 quintillion short tons. Using the parameters of an ellipsoid adopted by the International Astronomical Union in 1964 and recognized by the International Union of Geodesy and Geophysics in 1967, the length of the equator is 24,901.55 miles, the length of a meridian is 24,859.82 miles, the equatorial diameter is 7,926.41 miles, and the area of this reference ellipsoid is approximately 196,938,800 square miles.

The earth is considered a solid, rigid mass with a dense core of magnetic, probably metallic material. The outer part of the core is probably liquid. Around the core is a thick shell or mantle of heavy crystalline rock which in turn is covered by a thin crust forming the solid granite and basalt base of the continents and ocean basins. Over broad areas of the earth's surface the crust has a thin cover of sedimentary rock such as sandstone, shale, and limestone formed by weathering of the earth's surface and deposition of sands, clays, and plant and animal remains.

The temperature in the earth increases about 1°F. with every 100 to 200 feet in depth, in the upper 100 kilometers of the earth, and the temperature near the core is believed to be near the melting point of the core materials under the conditions at that depth. The heat of the earth is believed to be derived from radioactivity in the rocks, pressures developed within the earth, and original heat (if the earth in fact was formed at high temperatures).

Atmosphere of the Earth

The earth's atmosphere is a blanket composed of nitrogen, oxygen, and argon, in amounts of about 78, 21, and 1% by volume. Also present in minute quantities are carbon dioxide, hydrogen, neon, helium, krypton, and xenon.

Water vapor displaces other gases and varies from nearly zero to about 4% by volume. The height of the **ozone** layer varies from approximately 12 to 21 miles above the earth. Traces exist as low as 6 miles and as high as 35 miles. Traces of methane have been found.

The atmosphere rests on the earth's surface with the weight equivalent to a layer of water 34 ft. deep. For about 300,000 ft. upward the gases remain in the proportions stated. Gravity holds the gases to the earth. The weight of the air compresses it at the bottom, so that the greatest density is at the earth's surface. Pressure, as well as density, decreases as height increases because the weight pressing upon any layer is always less than that pressing upon the layers below.

The temperature of the air drops with increased height until the **tropopause** is reached. This may vary from 25,000 to 60,000 ft. The atmosphere below the tropopause is the **troposphere;** the atmosphere for about twenty miles above the tropopause is the **stratosphere,** where the temperature generally increases with height except at high latitudes in winter. A temperature maximum near the 30-mile level is called the **stratopause.** Above this boundary is the **mesosphere** where the temperature decreases with height to a minimum, the **mesopause,** at a height of 50 miles. Extending above the mesosphere to the outer fringes of the atmosphere is the **thermosphere,** a region where temperature increases with height to a value measured in thousands of degrees Fahrenheit. The lower portion of this region, extending from 50 to about 400 miles in altitude, is characterized by a high ion density, and is thus called the **ionosphere.** The outer region is called **exosphere;** this is the region where gas molecules traveling at high speed may escape into outer space, above 600 miles.

Latitude, Longitude

Position on the globe is measured by means of meridians and parallels. Meridians, which are imaginary lines drawn around the earth through the poles, determine **longitude.** The meridian running through Greenwich, England, is the **prime meridian of longitude,** and all others are either east or west. Parallels, which are imaginary circles parallel with the equator, determine **latitude.** The length of a degree of longitude varies as the cosine of the latitude. At the equator a degree is 69.171 statute miles; this is gradually reduced toward the poles. Value of a longitude degree at the poles is zero.

Latitude is reckoned by the number of degrees north or south of the equator, an imaginary circle on the earth's surface everywhere equidistant between the two poles. According to the IAU Ellipsoid of 1964, the length of a degree of latitude is 68.708 statute miles at the equator and varies slightly north and south because of the oblate form of the globe; at the poles it is 69.403 statute miles.

Computation of Time

The earth rotates on its axis and follows an elliptical orbit around the sun. The rotation makes the sun appear to move across the sky from East to West. It determines day and night and the complete rotation, in relation to the sun, is called the **apparent** or **true solar day.** This varies but an average determines the **mean solar day** of 24 hours.

The mean solar day is in universal use for civil purposes. It may be obtained from apparent solar time by correcting observations of the sun for the equation of time, but when high precision is required, the mean solar time is calculated from its relation to sidereal time. These relations are extremely complicated, but for most practical uses, they may be considered as follows:

Sidereal time is the measure of time defined by the diurnal motion of the vernal equinox, and is determined from observation of the meridian transits of stars. One complete rotation of the earth relative to the equinox is called the **sidereal day.** The **mean sidereal day** is 23 hours, 56 minutes, 4,091 seconds of mean solar time.

The **Calendar Year** begins at 12 o'clock precisely local clock time, on the night of Dec. 31-Jan. 1. The day and the calendar month also begin at midnight by the clock. The interval required for the earth to make one absolute revolution around the sun is a **sidereal year;** it consisted of 365 days, 6 hours, 9 minutes, and 9.5 seconds of mean solar time (approximately 24 hours per day) in 1900, and is increasing at the rate of 0.0001-second annually.

The **Tropical Year,** on which the return of the seasons depends, is the interval between two consecutive returns of the sun to the vernal equinox. The tropical year consists of 365 days, 5 hours, 48 minutes, and 46 seconds in 1900. It is decreasing at the rate of 0.530 seconds per century.

In 1956 the unit of time interval was defined to be identical with the second of **Ephemeris Time,** 1/31,556,925.9747 of the tropical year for 1900 January Od 12th hour E.T. A physical definition of the second based on a quantum transition of cesium (atomic second) was adopted in 1964. The atomic second is equal to 9,192,631,770 cycles of the emitted radiation. In 1967 this atomic second was adopted as the unit of time interval for the Intern'l System of Units.

The Zones and Seasons

The five zones of the earth's surface are Torrid, lying between the Tropics of Cancer and Capricorn; North Temperate, between Cancer and the Arctic Circle; South Temperate, between Capricorn and the Antarctic Circle; The Frigid Zones, between the polar Circles and the Poles.

The inclination or tilt of the earth's axis with respect to the sun determines the seasons. These are commonly marked in the North Temperate Zone, where spring begins at the vernal equinox, summer at the summer solstice, autumn at the autumnal equinox and winter at the winter solstice.

In the South Temperate Zone, the seasons are reversed. Spring begins at the autumnal equinox, summer at the winter solstice, etc.

If the earth's axis were perpendicular to the plane of the earth's orbit around the sun there would be no change of seasons. Day and night would be of nearly constant length and there would be equable conditions of temperature. But the axis is tilted 23° 27′ away from a perpendicular to the orbit and only in March and September is the axis at right angles to the sun.

The points at which the sun crosses the equator are the equinoxes, when day and night are most nearly equal. The points at which the sun is at a maximum distance from the equator are the solstices. Days and nights are then most unequal.

In June the North Pole is tilted 23° 27′ toward the sun and the days in the northern hemisphere are longer than the nights, while the days in the southern hemisphere are shorter than the nights. In December the North Pole is tilted 23° 27′ away from the sun and the situation is reversed.

The Seasons in 1981

In 1981 the 4 seasons will begin as follows: add one hour to EST for Atlantic Time; subtract one hour for Central, two hours for Mountain, 3 hours for Pacific, 4 hours for Yukon, 5 hours for Alaska-Hawaii and six hours for Bering Time. Also shown in Greenwich Mean Time.

		Date	GMT	EST
Vernal Equinox	**Spring**	Mar. 20	17:03	12:03
Summer Solstice	**Summer**	June 21	11:45	06:45
Autumnal Equinox	**Autumn**	Sept. 23	03:05	22:05*
Winter Solstice	**Winter**	Dec. 21	22:51	17:51

*Previous day

Poles of The Earth

The geographic (rotation) poles, or points where the earth's axis of rotation cuts the surface, are not absolutely fixed in the body of the earth. The pole of rotation describes an irregular curve about its mean position.

Two periods have been detected in this motion: (1) an annual period due to seasonal changes in barometric pressure, load of ice and snow on the surface and to other phenomena of seasonal character; (2) a period of about 14 months due to the shape and constitution of the earth.

In addition there are small but as yet unpredictable irregularities. The whole motion is so small that the actual pole at any time remains within a circle of 30 or 40 feet in radius centered at the mean position of the pole.

The pole of rotation for the time being is of course the pole having a latitude of 90° and an indeterminate longitude.

Magnetic Poles

The **north magnetic pole** of the earth is that region where the magnetic force is vertically downward and the **south magnetic pole** that region where the magnetic force is vertically upward. A compass placed at the magnetic poles experiences no directive force.

There are slow changes in the distribution of the earth's magnetic field. These changes were at one time attributed in part to a periodic movement of the magnetic poles around the geographical poles, but later evidence refutes this theory and points, rather, to a slow migration of "disturbance" foci over the earth.

There appear shifts in position of the magnetic poles due to the changes in the earth's magnetic field. The center of the area designated as the north magnetic pole was estimated to be in about latitude 70.5° N and longitude 96° W in 1905; from recent nearby measurements and studies of the secular changes, the position in 1970 is estimated as latitude 76.2° N and longitude 101° W. Improved data rather than actual motion account for at least part of the change.

The position of the south magnetic pole in 1912 was near 71° S and longitude 150° E; the position in 1970 is estimated at latitude 66° S and longitude 139.1° E.

The direction of the horizontal components of the magnetic field at any point is known as magnetic north at that point, and the angle by which it deviates east or west of true north is known as the magnetic declination, or in the mariner's terminology, the **variation of the compass.**

A compass without error points in the direction of magnetic north. (In general this is *not* the direction of the magnetic north pole.) If one follows the direction indicated by the north end of the compass, he will travel along a rather irregular curve which eventually reaches the north magnetic pole (though not usually by a great-circle route). However, the action of the compass should not be thought of as due to any influence of the distant pole, but simply as an indication of the distribution of the earth's magnetism at the place of observation.

Rotation of The Earth

The speed of rotation of the earth about its axis has been found to be slightly variable. The variations may be classified as:

(A) **Secular.** Tidal friction acts as a brake on the rotation and causes a slow secular increase in the length of the day, about 1 millisecond per century.

(B) **Irregular.** The speed of rotation may increase for a number of years, about 5 to 10, and then start decreasing. The maximum difference from the mean in the length of the day during a century is about 5 milliseconds. The accumulated difference in time has amounted to approximately 44 seconds since 1900. The cause is probably motion in the interior of the earth.

(C) **Periodic.** Seasonal variations exist with periods of one year and six months. The cumulative effect is such that each year the earth is late about 30 milliseconds near June 1 and is ahead about 30 milliseconds near Oct. 1. The maximum seasonal variation in the length of the day is about 0.5 millisecond. It is believed that the principal cause of the annual variation is the seasonal change in the wind patterns of the Northern and Southern Hemispheres. The semiannual variation is due chiefly to tidal action of the sun, which distorts the shape of the earth slightly.

The secular and irregular variations were discovered by comparing time based on the rotation of the earth with time based on the orbital motion of the moon about the earth and of the planets about the sun. The periodic variation was determined largely with the aid of quartz-crystal clocks. The introduction of the cesium-beam atomic clock in 1955 made it possible to determine in greater detail than before the nature of the irregular and periodic variations.

Astronomical Twilight—Meridian of Greenwich

Date 1981	20° Begin	20° End	30° Begin	30° End	40° Begin	40° End	50° Begin	50° End	60° Begin	60° End
	h m	h m	h m	h m	h m	h m	h m	h m	h m	h m
Jan. 1	5 16	**6 50**	5 30	**6 35**	5 45	**6 21**	6 00	**6 07**	6 18	**5 49**
11	5 19	**6 56**	5 33	**6 43**	5 46	**6 30**	6 00	**6 17**	6 15	**6 01**
21	5 21	**7 01**	5 32	**6 51**	5 43	**6 40**	5 55	**6 30**	6 06	**6 18**
Feb. 1	5 21	**7 07**	5 29	**6 58**	5 38	**6 51**	5 45	**6 44**	5 51	**6 38**
11	5 18	**7 11**	5 24	**7 05**	5 29	**7 01**	5 32	**6 59**	5 32	**7 01**
21	5 13	**7 15**	5 17	**7 12**	5 17	**7 12**	5 16	**7 14**	5 09	**7 23**
Mar. 1	5 08	**7 18**	5 08	**7 19**	5 06	**7 21**	4 59	**7 29**	4 44	**7 45**
11	5 00	**7 21**	4 58	**7 24**	4 50	**7 32**	4 38	**7 46**	4 12	**8 12**
21	4 52	**7 24**	4 45	**7 32**	4 33	**7 44**	4 14	**8 04**	3 37	**8 43**
Apr. 1	4 42	**7 28**	4 31	**7 39**	4 14	**7 57**	3 47	**8 25**	2 53	**9 21**
11	4 32	**7 32**	4 18	**7 47**	3 56	**8 09**	3 20	**8 47**	2 03	**10 10**
21	4 23	**7 36**	4 04	**7 54**	3 37	**8 23**	2 52	**9 11**	0 37	**11 47**
May 1	4 14	**7 41**	3 52	**8 04**	3 19	**8 37**	2 22	**9 39**		
11	4 08	**7 46**	3 41	**8 13**	3 03	**8 53**	1 49	**10 09**		
21	4 02	**7 52**	3 32	**8 22**	2 48	**9 07**	1 13	**10 46**		
June 1	3 58	**7 58**	3 26	**8 30**	2 36	**9 20**	0 21	**11 52**		
11	3 56	**8 03**	3 22	**8 36**	2 29	**9 30**				
21	3 57	**8 06**	3 22	**8 40**	2 28	**9 35**				
July 1	3 59	**8 07**	3 25	**8 41**	2 30	**9 35**				
11	4 03	**8 06**	3 30	**8 39**	2 40	**9 30**				
21	4 08	**8 03**	3 39	**8 33**	2 52	**9 18**	1 12	**11 23**		
Aug. 1	4 15	**7 56**	3 48	**8 23**	3 09	**9 01**	1 49	**10 20**		
11	4 20	**7 50**	3 56	**8 13**	3 22	**8 46**	2 21	**9 46**		
21	4 24	**7 41**	4 05	**8 01**	3 34	**8 27**	2 47	**9 15**		
Sept. 1	4 29	**7 31**	4 14	**7 46**	3 51	**8 08**	3 13	**8 43**	1 40	**10 02**
11	4 32	**7 20**	4 20	**7 33**	4 02	**7 50**	3 33	**8 16**	2 36	**9 12**
21	4 35	**7 11**	4 26	**7 19**	4 14	**7 31**	3 52	**7 52**	3 11	**8 31**
Oct. 1	4 38	**7 02**	4 33	**7 05**	4 25	**7 13**	4 10	**7 28**	3 41	**7 54**
11	4 40	**6 53**	4 40	**6 53**	4 35	**6 58**	4 26	**7 05**	4 07	**7 23**
21	4 43	**6 47**	4 45	**6 44**	4 45	**6 43**	4 41	**6 46**	4 32	**6 55**
Nov. 1	4 46	**6 41**	4 52	**6 34**	4 56	**6 30**	4 58	**6 27**	4 56	**6 27**
11	4 50	**6 38**	4 59	**6 28**	5 06	**6 21**	5 13	**6 14**	5 17	**6 08**
21	4 55	**6 36**	5 06	**6 25**	5 16	**6 15**	5 26	**6 04**	5 37	**5 52**
Dec. 1	5 00	**6 37**	5 13	**6 24**	5 25	**6 11**	5 38	**5 58**	5 53	**5 42**
11	5 06	**6 40**	5 20	**6 26**	5 34	**6 12**	5 48	**5 57**	6 06	**5 38**
21	5 11	**6 45**	5 25	**6 30**	5 39	**6 16**	5 55	**6 00**	6 15	**5 40**
31	5 15	**6 50**	5 30	**6 35**	5 44	**6 21**	6 00	**6 06**	6 18	**5 48**

Latitude, Longitude, and Altitude of North American Cities

Source: National Oceanic and Atmospheric Administration, U.S. Commerce Department for geographic positions.
Source for Canadian cities: Geodetic Survey of Canada, Dept. of Energy, Mines, and Resources.
Altitudes U.S. Geological Survey and various sources. *Approx. altitude at downtown business area U.S.; in Canada at tower of major airport.

City	Lat. N °	'	"	Long. W °	'	"	Alt.* feet
Abilene, Tex.	32	27	05	99	43	51	1710
Akron, Oh.	41	05	00	81	30	44	874
Albany, N.Y.	42	39	01	73	45	01	20
Albuquerque, N.M.	35	05	01	106	39	05	4,945
Allentown, Pa.	40	36	11	75	28	06	255
Alert, N.W.T.	82	29	50	62	21	15	95
Altoona, Pa.	40	30	55	78	24	03	1,180
Amarillo, Tex.	35	12	27	101	50	04	3,685
Anchorage, Alas.	61	10	00	149	59	00	118
Ann Arbor, Mich.	42	16	59	83	44	52	880
Asheville, N.C.	35	35	42	82	33	26	1,985
Ashland, Ky.	38	28	36	82	38	23	536
Atlanta, Ga.	33	45	10	84	23	37	1,050
Atlantic City, N.J.	39	21	32	74	25	53	10
Augusta, Ga.	33	28	20	81	58	00	143
Augusta, Me.	44	18	53	69	46	29	45
Austin, Tex.	30	16	09	97	44	37	505
Bakersfield, Cal.	35	22	31	119	01	18	400
Baltimore, Md.	39	17	26	76	36	45	20
Bangor, Me.	44	48	13	68	46	18	20
Baton Rouge, La.	30	26	58	91	11	00	57
Battle Creek, Mich.	42	18	58	85	10	48	820
Bay City, Mich.	43	36	04	83	53	15	595
Beaumont, Tex.	30	05	20	94	06	09	20
Belleville, Ont.	44	09	30	77	22	30	280
Bellingham, Wash.	48	45	34	122	28	36	60
Berkeley, Cal.	37	52	10	122	16	17	40
Bethlehem, Pa.	40	37	16	75	22	34	235
Billings, Mon.	45	47	00	108	30	04	3,120
Biloxi, Miss.	30	23	48	88	53	00	20
Binghamton, N.Y.	42	06	03	75	54	47	865
Birmingham, Ala.	33	31	01	86	48	36	600
Bismarck, N.D.	46	48	23	100	47	17	1,674
Bloomington, Ill.	40	28	58	88	59	36	800
Boise, Ida.	43	37	07	116	11	58	2,704
Boston, Mass.	42	21	24	71	03	25	21
Bowling Green, Ky.	36	59	41	86	26	33	510
Brandon, Man.	49	51	00	99	57	00	1,265
Brantford, Ont.	43	07	30	80	15	30	705
Brattleboro, Vt.	42	51	06	72	33	48	300
Bridgeport, Conn.	41	10	49	73	11	22	10
Brockton, Mass.	42	05	02	71	01	25	130
Brownsville, Tex.	25	54	07	97	29	58	35
Buffalo, N.Y.	42	52	52	78	52	21	585
Burlington, Ont.	43	18	30	79	46	30	875
Burlington, Vt.	44	28	34	73	12	46	110
Butte, Mon.	46	01	06	112	32	11	5,765
Calgary, Alta.	51	02	46	114	03	24	3,557
Cambridge, Mass.	42	22	01	71	06	22	20
Camden, N.J.	39	56	41	75	07	14	30
Canton, Oh.	40	47	50	81	22	37	1,030
Carson City, Nev.	39	10	00	119	46	00	4,680
Cedar Rapids, Ia.	41	58	01	91	39	53	730
Central Islip, N.Y.	40	47	24	73	12	00	80
Champaign, Ill.	40	07	05	88	14	48	740
Charleston, S.C.	32	46	35	79	55	53	9
Charleston, W.Va.	38	21	01	81	37	52	601
Charlotte, N.C.	35	13	44	80	50	45	720
Charlottetown, P.E.I.	46	14	00	63	07	45	181
Chattanooga, Tenn.	35	02	41	85	18	32	675
Cheyenne, Wy.	41	08	09	104	49	07	6,100
Chicago, Ill.	41	52	28	87	38	22	595
Churchill, Man.	58	45	15	94	10	00	94
Cincinnati, Oh.	39	06	07	84	30	35	550
Cleveland, Oh.	41	29	51	81	41	50	660
Colorado Springs	38	50	07	104	49	16	5,980
Columbia, Mo.	38	57	03	92	19	46	730
Columbia, S.C.	34	00	02	81	02	00	190
Columbus, Ga.	32	28	07	84	59	24	265
Columbus, Oh.	39	57	47	83	00	17	780
Concord, N.H.	43	12	22	71	32	25	290
Corpus Christi, Tex.	27	47	51	97	23	45	35
Dallas, Tex.	32	47	09	96	47	37	435
Dartmouth, N.S.	44	38	39	63	34	34	476
Davenport, Ia.	41	31	19	90	34	33	590
Dawson, Yukon	64	03	30	139	26	00	1,211
Dayton, Oh.	39	45	32	84	11	43	574
Daytona Beach, Fla.	29	12	44	81	01	10	7
Decatur, Ill.	39	50	42	88	56	47	682
Denver, Col.	39	44	58	104	59	22	5,280
Des Moines, Ia.	41	35	14	93	37	00	805
Detroit, Mich.	42	19	48	83	02	57	585
Dodge City, Kan.	37	45	17	100	01	09	2,480
Dubuque, Ia.	42	29	55	90	40	08	620
Duluth, Minn.	46	46	56	92	06	24	610
Durham, N.C.	36	00	00	78	54	45	405
Eau Claire, Wis.	44	48	31	91	29	49	790
Edmonton, Alta.	53	32	45	113	29	15	2,373
El Paso, Tex.	31	45	36	106	29	11	3,695
Elizabeth, N.J.	40	39	43	74	12	59	21
Enid, Okla.	36	23	40	97	52	35	1,240
Erie, Pa.	42	07	15	80	04	57	685
Eugene, Ore.	44	03	16	123	05	30	422
Eureka, Cal.	40	48	08	124	09	46	45
Evansville, Ind.	37	58	20	87	34	21	385
Fairbanks, Alas.	64	48	00	147	51	00	448
Fall River, Mass.	41	42	06	71	09	18	40
Fargo, N.D.	46	52	30	96	47	18	900
Flagstaff, Ariz.	35	11	36	111	39	06	6,900
Flint, Mich.	43	00	50	83	41	33	750
Ft. Smith, Ark.	35	23	10	94	25	36	440
Fort Wayne, Ind.	41	04	21	85	08	26	790
Fort Worth, Tex.	32	44	55	97	19	44	670
Fredericton, N.B.	45	57	40	66	38	30	67
Fresno, Cal.	36	44	12	119	47	11	285
Gadsden, Ala.	34	00	57	86	00	41	555
Gainesville, Fla.	29	38	56	82	19	19	175
Gallup, N.M.	35	31	30	108	44	30	6,540
Galveston, Tex.	29	18	10	94	47	43	5
Gary, Ind.	41	36	12	87	20	19	590
Grand Junction, Col.	39	04	06	108	33	54	4,590
Grand Rapids, Mich.	42	58	03	85	40	13	610
Great Falls, Mon.	47	29	33	111	18	23	3,340
Green Bay, Wis.	44	30	48	88	00	50	590
Greensboro, N.C.	36	04	17	79	47	25	839
Greenville, S.C.	34	50	50	82	24	01	966
Guelph, Ont.	43	32	30	80	15	30	1,075
Gulfport, Miss.	30	22	04	89	05	36	20
Halifax, N.S.	44	38	39	63	34	34	476
Hamilton, Ont.	43	15	17	79	52	28	776
Hamilton, Oh.	39	23	59	84	33	47	600
Harrisburg, Pa.	40	15	43	76	52	59	365
Hartford, Conn.	41	46	12	72	40	49	40
Helena, Mon.	46	35	33	112	02	24	4,155
Hilo, Hawaii	19	43	30	155	05	24	40
Holyoke, Mass.	42	12	29	72	36	36	115
Honolulu, Ha.	21	18	22	157	51	35	21
Houston, Tex.	29	45	26	95	21	37	40
Hull, Que.	45	26	00	75	44	00	225
Huntington, W.Va.	38	25	12	82	26	33	565
Huntsville, Ala.	34	44	18	86	35	19	640
Indianapolis, Ind.	39	46	07	86	09	46	710
Iowa City, Ia.	41	39	37	91	31	53	685
Jackson, Mich.	42	14	43	84	24	22	940
Jackson, Miss.	32	17	56	90	11	06	298
Jacksonville, Fla.	30	19	44	81	39	42	20
Jersey City, N.J.	40	43	50	74	03	56	20
Johnstown, Pa.	40	19	35	78	55	03	1,185
Joplin, Mo.	37	05	26	90	42	11	990
Juneau, Alas.	58	18	12	134	24	30	50
Kalamazoo, Mich.	42	17	29	85	35	14	755
Kansas City, Kan.	39	07	04	94	38	24	750
Kansas City, Mo.	39	04	56	94	35	20	750
Kenosha, Wis.	42	35	43	87	50	11	610
Key West, Fla.	24	33	30	81	48	12	5
Kingston, Ont.	44	13	30	76	30	00	310
Kitchener, Ont.	43	26	59	80	29	17	1,031
Knoxville, Tenn.	35	57	39	83	55	07	890
Lafayette, Ind.	40	25	11	86	53	39	550
Lancaster, Pa.	40	02	25	76	18	29	355
Lansing, Mich.	42	44	01	84	33	15	830
Laredo, Tex.	27	30	22	99	30	30	440
La Salle, Que.	45	25	30	73	38	30	100
Las Vegas, Nev.	36	10	20	115	08	37	2,030
Laval, Que.	45	35	30	73	45	30	100
Lawrence, Mass.	42	42	16	71	10	08	65
Lethbridge, Alta.	49	41	30	112	49	00	2,990
Lexington, Ky.	38	02	50	84	29	46	955
Lihue, Ha.	21	58	48	159	22	30	210
Lima, Oh.	40	44	35	84	06	20	865
Lincoln, Neb.	40	48	59	96	42	15	1,150
Little Rock, Ark.	34	44	42	92	16	37	286
London, Ont.	42	59	00	81	15	00	912
Long Beach, Cal.	33	46	14	118	11	18	35
Lorain, Oh.	41	28	05	82	10	49	610
Los Angeles, Cal.	34	03	15	118	14	28	340
Louisville, Ky.	38	14	47	85	45	49	450
Lowell, Mass.	42	38	25	71	19	14	100
Lubbock, Tex.	33	35	05	101	50	33	3,195
Macon, Ga.	32	50	12	83	37	36	335
Madison, Wis.	43	04	23	89	22	55	860

City	Lat. N °	'	"	Long. W °	'	"	Alt.* Feet
Manchester, N.H.	42	59	28	71	27	41	175
Marshall, Tex.	32	33	00	94	23	00	410
Memphis, Tenn.	35	08	46	90	03	13	275
Meriden, Conn.	41	32	06	72	47	30	190
Mexico City, Mexico	19	25	45	99	07	00	7,347
Miami, Fla.	25	46	37	80	11	32	10
Milwaukee, Wis.	43	02	19	87	54	15	635
Minneapolis, Minn.	44	58	57	93	15	43	815
Minot, N.D.	48	14	09	101	17	38	1,550
Mississauga, Ont.	43	33	00	79	35	00	260
Mobile, Ala.	30	41	36	88	02	33	5
Moline, Ill.	41	30	31	90	30	49	585
Moncton, N.B.	46	05	30	64	47	30	75
Montgomery, Ala.	32	22	33	86	18	31	160
Montpelier, Vt.	44	15	36	72	34	41	485
Montreal, Que.	45	30	30	73	33	20	117
Moose Jaw, Sask.	50	23	30	105	32	30	1,810
Muncie, Ind.	40	11	28	85	23	16	950
Nashville, Tenn.	36	09	33	86	46	55	450
Natchez, Miss.	31	33	48	91	23	30	210
Newark, N.J.	40	44	14	74	10	19	55
New Bedford, Mass.	41	38	13	70	55	41	15
New Britain, Conn.	41	40	08	72	46	59	200
New Haven, Conn.	41	18	25	72	55	30	40
New Orleans, La.	29	56	53	90	04	10	5
New York, N.Y.	40	45	06	73	59	39	55
Niagara Falls, N.Y.	43	05	34	79	03	26	570
Niagara Falls, Ont.	43	05	30	79	03	30	585
Nome, Alas.	64	30	00	165	25	00	25
Norfolk, Va.	36	51	10	76	17	21	10
North Bay, Ont.	46	18	30	79	27	30	925
Oakland, Cal.	37	48	03	122	15	54	25
Ogden, Ut.	41	13	31	111	58	21	4,295
Oklahoma City	35	28	26	97	31	04	1,195
Omaha, Neb.	41	15	42	95	56	14	1,040
Orlando, Fla.	28	32	42	81	22	38	70
Oshawa, Ont.	43	54	00	78	52	00	350
Ottawa, Ont.	45	25	40	75	42	45	374
Paducah, Ky.	37	05	13	88	35	56	345
Pasadena, Cal.	34	08	44	118	08	41	830
Paterson, N.J.	40	55	01	74	10	21	100
Pensacola, Fla.	30	24	51	87	12	56	15
Peoria, Ill.	40	41	42	89	35	33	470
Peterborough, Ont.	44	18	00	78	19	30	685
Philadelphia, Pa.	39	56	58	75	09	21	100
Phoenix, Ariz.	33	27	12	112	04	28	1,090
Pierre, S.D.	44	22	18	100	20	54	1,480
Pittsburgh, Pa.	40	26	19	80	00	00	745
Pittsfield, Mass.	42	26	53	73	15	14	1,015
Pocatello, Ida.	42	51	38	112	27	01	4,460
Port Arthur, Tex.	29	52	30	93	56	15	10
Portland, Me.	43	39	33	70	15	19	25
Portland, Ore.	45	31	06	122	40	35	77
Portsmouth, N.H.	43	04	30	70	45	24	20
Portsmouth, Va.	36	50	07	76	18	14	10
Prince Rupert, B.C.	54	19	00	130	19	00	125
Providence, R.I.	41	49	32	71	24	41	80
Provo, Ut.	40	14	06	111	39	24	4,550
Pueblo, Col.	38	16	17	104	36	33	4,690
Quebec City, Que.	46	48	46	71	12	20	239
Racine, Wis.	42	43	49	87	47	12	630
Rapid City, S.D.	44	04	52	103	13	11	3,230
Raleigh, N.C.	35	46	38	78	38	21	365
Reading, Pa.	40	20	09	75	55	40	265
Regina, Sask.	50	27	02	104	36	30	1,894
Reno, Nev.	39	31	27	119	48	40	4,490
Richmond, Va.	37	32	15	77	26	09	160
Roanoke, Va.	37	16	13	79	56	44	905
Rochester, Minn.	44	01	21	92	28	03	990
Rochester, N.Y.	43	09	41	77	36	21	515
Rockford, Ill.	42	16	07	89	05	48	715
Sacramento, Cal.	38	34	57	121	29	41	30
Saginaw, Mich.	43	25	52	83	56	05	595
St. Catharines, Ont.	43	09	30	79	14	30	362
St. Cloud, Minn.	45	34	00	94	10	24	1,040
Saint John, N.B.	45	16	00	66	04	30	80
St. John's, Nfld.	47	34	00	52	43	30	200
St. Joseph, Mo.	39	45	57	94	51	02	850
St. Louis, Mo.	38	37	45	90	12	22	455
St. Paul, Minn.	44	57	19	93	06	07	780
St. Petersburg, Fla.	27	46	18	82	38	19	20
Salem, Ore.	44	56	24	123	01	59	155

City	Lat. N °	'	"	Long. W °	'	"	Alt.* Feet
Salina, Kan.	38	50	36	97	36	46	1,229
Salt Lake City, Ut.	40	45	23	111	53	26	4,390
San Angelo, Tex.	31	27	39	100	26	03	1,845
San Antonio, Tex.	29	25	37	98	29	06	650
San Bernardino, Cal.	34	06	30	117	17	28	1,080
San Diego, Cal.	32	42	53	117	09	21	20
San Francisco, Cal.	37	46	39	122	24	40	65
San Jose, Cal.	37	20	16	121	53	24	90
San Juan, P.R.	18	27	00	66	04	15	35
Santa Barbara, Cal.	34	25	18	119	41	55	100
Santa Cruz, Cal.	36	58	18	122	01	18	20
Santa Fe, N.M.	35	41	11	105	56	10	6,950
Sarasota, Fla.	27	20	05	82	32	30	20
Saskatoon, Sask.	52	07	50	106	39	41	1,653
Sault Ste. Marie, Ont.	46	31	30	84	20	00	650
Savannah, Ga.	32	04	42	81	05	37	20
Schenectady, N.Y.	42	48	42	73	55	42	245
Scranton, Pa.	41	24	32	75	39	46	725
Seattle, Wash.	47	36	32	122	20	12	10
Sheboygan, Wis.	43	45	03	87	42	52	630
Sherbrooke, Que.	45	24	00	71	53	30	625
Sheridan, Wy.	44	47	55	106	57	10	3,740
Shreveport, La.	32	30	46	93	44	58	204
Sioux City, Ia.	42	29	46	96	24	30	1,110
Sioux Falls, S.D.	43	32	35	96	43	35	1,395
Somerville, Mass.	42	23	15	71	06	07	13
South Bend, Ind.	41	40	33	86	15	01	710
Spartanburg, S.C.	34	57	03	81	56	06	875
Spokane, Wash.	47	39	32	117	25	33	1,890
Springfield, Ill.	39	47	58	89	38	51	610
Springfield, Mass.	42	06	21	72	35	32	85
Springfield, Mo.	37	13	03	93	17	32	1,300
Springfield, Oh.	39	55	38	83	48	29	980
Stamford, Conn.	41	03	09	73	32	24	35
Steubenville, Oh.	40	21	42	80	36	53	660
Stockton, Cal.	37	57	30	121	17	16	20
Sudbury, Ont.	46	28	30	80	58	30	917
Superior, Wis.	46	43	14	92	06	07	630
Sydney, N.S.	46	08	30	60	11	00	50
Syracuse, N.Y.	43	03	04	76	09	14	400
Tacoma, Wash.	47	14	59	122	26	15	110
Tallahassee, Fla.	30	26	30	84	16	56	150
Tampa, Fla.	27	56	58	82	27	25	15
Terre Haute, Ind.	39	28	03	87	24	26	496
Texarkana, Tex.	33	25	48	94	02	30	324
Thunder Bay, Ont.	48	25	00	89	14	00	650
Toledo, Oh.	41	39	14	83	32	39	585
Topeka, Kan.	39	03	16	95	40	23	930
Toronto, Ont.	43	39	12	79	23	00	532
Trenton, N.J.	40	13	14	74	46	13	35
Trois-Rivieres, Que.	46	21	00	72	33	00	115
Troy, N.Y.	42	43	45	73	40	58	35
Tucson, Ariz.	32	13	15	110	58	08	2,390
Tulsa, Okla.	36	09	12	95	59	34	804
Urbana, Ill.	40	06	42	88	12	06	...
Utica, N.Y.	43	06	12	75	13	33	415
Vancouver, B.C.	49	16	30	123	07	30	388
Victoria, B.C.	48	25	40	123	21	45	...
Waco, Tex.	31	33	12	97	08	00	405
Walla Walla, Wash.	46	04	08	118	20	24	936
Washington, D.C.	38	53	51	77	00	33	25
Waterbury, Conn.	41	33	13	73	02	31	260
Waterloo, Ia.	42	29	40	92	20	20	850
West Palm Beach, Fla.	26	42	36	80	03	07	15
Wheeling, W. Va.	40	04	03	80	43	20	650
Whitehorse, Yukon	60	43	15	135	03	15	2,305
White Plains, N.Y.	41	02	00	73	45	48	220
Wichita, Kan.	37	41	30	97	20	16	1,290
Wichita Falls, Tex.	33	54	34	98	29	28	945
Wilkes-Barre, Pa.	41	14	32	75	53	17	640
Wilmington, Del.	39	44	46	75	32	51	135
Wilmington, N.C.	34	14	14	77	56	58	35
Windsor, Ont.	42	19	50	83	03	00	590
Winnipeg, Man.	49	53	56	97	08	20	765
Winston-Salem, N.C.	36	05	52	80	14	42	860
Worcester, Mass.	42	15	37	71	48	17	475
Yakima, Wash.	46	36	09	120	30	39	1,060
Yellowknife, N.W.T.	62	28	15	114	22	00	674
Yonkers, N.Y.	40	55	55	73	53	54	10
York, Pa.	39	57	35	76	43	36	370
Youngstown, Oh.	41	05	57	80	39	02	840
Yuma, Ariz.	32	42	54	114	37	24	160
Zanesville, Oh.	39	56	18	82	00	30	720

World Cities

City	Lat.			Long.			Alt.
London, UK (Greenwich)	51	30	00N	0	0	0	245
Paris, France	48	50	14N	2	20	14E	300
Berlin, Germany	52	32	00N	13	25	00E	110
Rome, Italy	41	53	00N	12	30	00E	95
Warsaw, Poland	52	15	00N	21	00	00E	360
Moscow, USSR	55	45	00N	37	42	00E	394
Athens, Greece	37	58	00N	23	44	00E	300
Jerusalem, Israel	31	47	00N	35	13	00E	2,500
Johannesburg, So. Afr.	26	10	00S	28	02	00E	5,740
New Delhi, India	28	38	00N	77	12	00E	770
Peking, China	39	54	00N	116	28	00E	600
Rio de Janeiro, Brazil	22	53	43S	43	13	22W	30
Tokyo, Japan	35	45	00N	139	45	00E	30
Sydney, Australia	33	52	00S	151	12	00E	25

Calendar Adjustment Tables

These tables enable you to determine sun and moon rise and set times at your specific location. To find sunrise and sunset times, use steps A and C only; use all 3 steps for moonrise and moonset times.

A. Find your latitude and longitude or that of a nearby city on pages 771-772. Strike off the figure in the tens column from your latitude, find the remainder at the left of Table A, and mark it. Find the nearest longitude at the left of Table B and mark it. Now, for the day you wish, find the times of the event in the calendar tables in the columns for the latitude to your south and to your north. Subtract the southern time from the northern time. Find the nearest tens of minutes to your answer in a column head in Table A. Run down the column to the latitude row you have marked. Add the number you find there (or subtract, if your answer is negative) to the southern time.

B. Find the time of the event for the next day at the southern latitude. Subtract the time for the present day from the time for the next day. In Table B find the column headed by the nearest tens of this answer. Run down the column to the proper longitude row. Add this number to the step A answer.

C. To determine actual clock time, subtract the nearest time zone meridian used in your area from your longitude. (These are: Atlantic, 60°; Eastern, 75°; Central, 90°; Mountain, 105°; Pacific, 120°; Alaska-Hawaii, 150°.) Change this to degrees and decimals of a degree (divide the minutes by 60 and add this decimal to the degrees) and multiply by 4. Write this number on this page for future use and add it (or subtract it, if minus) to the step B answer. If you are on Daylight Time, add one hour.

Example: Find the approximate time of moonset for Jan. 9, 1981 in Raleigh, latitude 35°46′, longitude 78°38′ or 78.6°. A resident there should mark row 5°40′ in Table A and row 80° in Table B.

A. Calendar time for 40°	20:24	
Calendar time for 30°	20:38	20:38
Difference: North minus South	−14 min.	−:06
		20:32
Table A for 5°40′ and 10 min.	6	
B. Calendar time for 30°, Jan. 10	21.40	
Calendar time for 30°, Jan. 9	20:38	20:32
Difference: Jan. 10 − Jan. 9=	+:62	+:13
Table B for 80° and 60 min.	13	20:45
C. Raleigh longitude	78.6	20:45
EST meridian	75.0	+:14
−3.6° × 4 min. per degree=	+14.4 min.	20:59

Table A: Latitude Adjustment

Diff in. Min. / Lat.	10	20	30	40	50	60	70	80	90	100	110	120
0° 20	0	1	1	1	2	2	2	3	3	3	4	4
40	1	1	2	3	3	4	5	5	6	7	7	8
1 00	1	2	3	4	5	6	7	8	9	10	11	12
20	1	3	4	5	7	8	9	11	12	13	15	16
40	2	3	5	7	8	10	12	13	15	17	18	20
2 00	2	4	6	8	10	12	14	16	18	20	22	24
20	2	5	7	9	12	14	16	19	21	23	26	28
40	3	5	8	11	13	16	19	21	24	27	29	32
3 00	3	6	9	12	15	18	21	24	27	30	33	36
20	3	7	10	13	17	20	23	27	30	33	37	40
40	4	7	11	15	18	22	26	29	33	37	40	44
4 00	4	8	12	16	20	24	28	32	36	40	44	48
20	4	9	13	17	22	26	30	35	39	43	48	52
40	5	9	14	19	23	28	33	37	42	47	51	56
5 00	5	10	15	20	25	30	35	40	45	50	55	60
20	5	11	16	21	27	32	37	43	48	53	59	64
40	6	11	17	23	28	34	40	45	51	57	62	68
6 00	6	12	18	24	30	36	42	48	54	60	66	72
20	6	13	19	25	32	38	44	51	57	63	70	76
40	7	13	20	27	33	40	47	53	60	67	73	80
7 00	7	14	21	28	35	42	49	56	63	70	77	84
20	7	15	22	29	37	44	51	59	66	73	81	88
40	8	15	23	31	38	46	54	61	69	77	84	92
8 00	8	16	24	32	40	48	56	64	72	80	88	96
20	8	17	25	33	42	50	58	67	75	83	92	100
40	9	17	26	35	43	52	61	69	78	87	95	104
9 00	9	18	27	36	45	54	63	72	81	90	99	108
20	9	19	28	37	47	56	65	75	84	93	103	112
40	10	19	29	39	48	58	68	77	87	97	106	116

Table B: Longitude Adjustment

Diff. in Min. / Long.	10	20	30	40	50	60	70	80	90	100	110	120
50°	1	3	4	6	7	8	10	11	12	14	15	17
55	2	3	5	6	8	9	11	12	14	15	17	18
60	2	3	5	7	8	10	12	13	15	17	18	20
65	2	4	5	7	9	11	13	14	16	18	20	22
70	2	4	6	8	10	12	14	16	18	19	21	23
75	2	4	6	8	10	12	15	17	19	21	23	25
80	2	4	7	9	11	13	16	18	20	22	24	27
85	2	5	7	9	12	14	16	19	21	24	26	28
90	2	5	8	10	12	15	18	20	22	25	28	30
95	3	5	8	11	13	16	18	21	24	26	29	32
100	3	6	8	11	14	17	19	22	25	28	31	33
105	3	6	9	12	15	18	20	23	26	29	32	35
110	3	6	9	12	15	18	21	24	28	31	34	37
115	3	6	10	13	16	19	22	26	29	32	35	38
120	3	7	10	13	17	20	23	27	30	33	37	40
125	4	7	10	14	17	21	24	28	31	35	38	42
130	4	7	11	14	18	22	25	29	32	36	40	43
135	4	8	11	15	19	22	26	30	34	38	41	45
140	4	8	12	16	19	23	27	31	35	39	43	47
145	4	8	12	16	20	24	28	32	36	40	44	48
150	4	8	12	17	21	25	29	33	38	42	46	50
155	4	9	13	17	22	26	30	34	39	43	47	52
160	4	9	13	18	22	27	31	36	40	44	49	53
165	5	9	14	18	23	28	32	37	41	46	50	55
170	5	9	14	19	24	28	33	38	42	47	52	57

1st Month **January, 1981** 31 days

Greenwich Mean Time

NOTE: Light figures indicate Sun. **Dark** figures indicate **Moon.** *Degrees are North Latitude.*

CAUTION: Must be converted to local time. For instruction see page 773.

Day of month week year	Sun on meridian **Moon phase**	20° Rise Sun **Moon**	20° Set Sun **Moon**	30° Rise Sun **Moon**	30° Set Sun **Moon**	40° Rise Sun **Moon**	40° Set Sun **Moon**	50° Rise Sun **Moon**	50° Set Sun **Moon**	60° Rise Sun **Moon**	60° Set Sun **Moon**
	h m s	h m	h m	h m	h m	h m	h m	h m	h m	h m	h m
1 Th	12 03 24	06 36	17 32	06 56	17 11	07 22	16 45	07 59	16 09	09 02	15 06
1		**02 15**	**14 02**	**02 24**	**13 51**	**02 35**	**13 38**	**02 51**	**13 20**	**03 16**	**12 52**
2 Fr	12 03 52	06 36	17 33	06 56	17 12	07 22	16 46	07 59	16 10	09 02	15 07
2		**03 04**	**14 42**	**03 17**	**14 28**	**03 33**	**14 11**	**03 54**	**13 48**	**04 29**	**13 10**
3 Sa	12 04 20	06 36	17 34	06 56	17 13	07 22	16 47	07 59	16 11	09 01	15 08
3		**03 56**	**15 25**	**04 11**	**15 09**	**04 30**	**14 48**	**04 57**	**14 20**	**05 41**	**13 34**
4 Su	12 04 48	06 36	17 34	06 56	17 14	07 22	16 48	07 58	16 12	09 00	15 10
4		**04 48**	**16 12**	**05 06**	**15 54**	**05 28**	**15 31**	**05 59**	**14 59**	**06 51**	**14 06**
5 Mo	12 05 15	06 37	17 34	06 57	17 14	07 22	16 49	07 58	16 13	09 00	15 12
5		**05 41**	**17 02**	**06 00**	**16 43**	**06 24**	**16 19**	**06 57**	**15 46**	**07 54**	**14 48**
6 Tu	12 05 42	06 37	17 35	06 57	17 15	07 22	16 50	07 58	16 14	08 59	15 13
6	**07 24** ●	**06 34**	**17 56**	**06 54**	**17 38**	**07 17**	**17 14**	**07 51**	**16 41**	**08 48**	**15 44**
7 We	12 06 08	06 37	17 36	06 57	17 16	07 22	16 51	07 58	16 16	08 58	15 15
7		**07 26**	**18 53**	**07 44**	**18 36**	**08 07**	**18 14**	**08 38**	**17 44**	**09 30**	**16 53**
8 Th	12 06 34	06 37	17 36	06 57	17 16	07 22	16 52	07 57	16 17	08 57	15 17
8		**08 17**	**19 51**	**08 32**	**19 36**	**08 52**	**19 18**	**09 19**	**18 53**	**10 03**	**18 11**
9 Fr	12 07 00	06 37	17 37	06 57	17 17	07 22	16 53	07 56	16 18	08 56	15 19
9		**09 04**	**20 49**	**09 17**	**20 38**	**09 32**	**20 24**	**09 54**	**20 05**	**10 27**	**19 35**
10 Sa	12 07 24	06 37	17 38	06 57	17 18	07 22	16 54	07 56	16 20	08 55	15 21
10		**09 50**	**21 47**	**09 58**	**21 40**	**10 09**	**21 31**	**10 24**	**21 20**	**10 47**	**21 01**
11 Su	12 07 49	06 37	17 39	06 57	17 19	07 22	16 55	07 56	16 21	08 54	15 23
11		**10 33**	**22 45**	**10 38**	**22 42**	**10 44**	**22 39**	**10 51**	**22 35**	**11 03**	**22 28**
12 Mo	12 08 12	06 38	17 40	06 57	17 20	07 22	16 56	07 55	16 22	08 52	15 25
12		**11 16**	**23 43**	**11 17**	**23 45**	**11 17**	**23 47**	**11 18**	**23 51**	**11 18**	**23 55**
13 Tu	12 08 35	06 38	17 40	06 57	17 21	07 21	16 57	07 54	16 24	08 50	15 27
13	**10 10** ☽	**11 59**		**11 55**		**11 50**		**11 44**		**11 34**	
14 We	12 08 58	06 38	17 41	06 57	17 22	07 21	16 58	07 54	16 25	08 49	15 29
14		**12 44**	**00 42**	**12 36**	**00 48**	**12 25**	**00 56**	**12 12**	**01 07**	**11 51**	**01 24**
15 Th	12 09 19	06 38	17 42	06 57	17 23	07 20	16 59	07 53	16 26	08 48	15 32
15		**13 31**	**01 42**	**13 18**	**01 52**	**13 03**	**02 05**	**12 43**	**02 23**	**12 11**	**02 52**
16 Fr	12 09 40	06 38	17 42	06 56	17 24	07 20	17 00	07 52	16 28	08 46	15 34
16		**14 21**	**02 42**	**14 05**	**02 57**	**13 46**	**03 14**	**13 19**	**03 39**	**12 37**	**04 19**
17 Sa	12 10 00	06 38	17 42	06 56	17 24	07 20	17 01	07 51	16 30	08 44	15 36
17		**15 14**	**03 43**	**14 56**	**04 01**	**14 34**	**04 22**	**14 03**	**04 52**	**13 11**	**05 42**
18 Su	12 10 20	06 38	17 43	06 56	17 25	07 19	17 02	07 50	16 31	08 43	15 39
18		**16 10**	**04 44**	**15 51**	**05 03**	**15 27**	**05 26**	**14 54**	**05 59**	**13 58**	**06 55**
19 Mo	12 10 39	06 38	17 44	06 56	17 26	07 19	17 03	07 49	16 32	08 41	15 41
19		**17 08**	**05 42**	**16 49**	**06 01**	**16 26**	**06 25**	**15 53**	**06 58**	**14 58**	**07 54**
20 Tu	12 10 57	06 38	17 44	06 56	17 26	07 18	17 04	07 48	16 34	08 40	15 44
20	**07 39** ○	**18 06**	**06 36**	**17 49**	**06 54**	**17 28**	**07 16**	**16 58**	**07 47**	**16 08**	**08 38**
21 We	12 11 14	06 38	17 45	06 55	17 27	07 18	17 06	07 47	16 36	08 38	15 46
21		**19 03**	**07 27**	**18 48**	**07 42**	**18 30**	**08 01**	**18 06**	**08 28**	**17 25**	**09 10**
22 Th	12 11 31	06 38	17 46	06 55	17 28	07 17	17 07	07 46	16 37	08 36	15 48
22		**19 57**	**08 12**	**19 46**	**08 25**	**19 33**	**08 40**	**19 14**	**09 01**	**18 44**	**09 34**
23 Fr	12 11 47	06 38	17 46	06 55	17 29	07 16	17 08	07 45	16 39	08 34	15 50
23		**20 50**	**08 54**	**20 43**	**09 03**	**20 34**	**09 14**	**20 21**	**09 29**	**20 02**	**09 52**
24 Sa	12 12 02	06 38	17 47	06 54	17 30	07 16	17 10	07 44	16 40	08 32	15 53
24		**21 40**	**09 33**	**21 37**	**09 38**	**21 33**	**09 45**	**21 27**	**09 54**	**21 18**	**10 07**
25 Su	12 12 16	06 37	17 48	06 54	17 31	07 15	17 11	07 43	16 42	08 30	15 56
25		**22 30**	**10 10**	**22 30**	**10 12**	**22 30**	**10 13**	**22 31**	**10 16**	**22 32**	**10 20**
26 Mo	12 12 30	06 37	17 48	06 54	17 32	07 14	17 12	07 42	16 44	08 28	15 58
26		**23 18**	**10 46**	**23 22**	**10 44**	**23 27**	**10 41**	**23 34**	**10 37**	**23 45**	**10 32**
27 Tu	12 12 42	06 37	17 49	06 54	17 33	07 13	17 13	07 41	16 46	08 26	16 01
27			**11 22**		**11 16**		**11 09**		**10 59**		**10 45**
28 We	12 12 54	06 36	17 50	06 53	17 34	07 12	17 14	07 41	16 48	08 24	16 04
28	**04 19** ☾	**00 06**	**11 58**	**00 14**	**11 49**	**00 24**	**11 38**	**00 37**	**11 22**	**00 57**	**10 59**
29 Th	12 13 06	06 36	17 50	06 52	17 34	07 12	17 16	07 38	16 49	08 21	16 06
29		**00 55**	**12 37**	**01 06**	**12 24**	**01 20**	**12 09**	**01 39**	**11 48**	**02 10**	**11 15**
30 Fr	12 13 16	06 36	17 51	06 52	17 35	07 11	17 17	07 37	16 51	08 19	16 09
30		**01 45**	**13 18**	**02 00**	**13 03**	**02 17**	**12 44**	**02 42**	**12 18**	**03 22**	**11 36**
31 Sa	12 13 25	06 36	17 52	06 51	17 36	07 10	17 18	07 36	16 53	08 16	16 12
31		**02 37**	**14 03**	**02 54**	**13 45**	**03 15**	**13 24**	**03 44**	**12 53**	**04 32**	**12 03**

2nd Month — February, 1981 — 28 Days

Greenwich Mean Time

NOTE: Light figures indicate Sun. **Dark** figures indicate **Moon.** *Degrees are North Latitude.*

CAUTION: Must be converted to local time. For instruction see page 773.

Day of month week year	Sun on meridian **Moon phase** h m s	20° Rise Sun **Moon** h m	20° Set Sun **Moon** h m	30° Rise Sun **Moon** h m	30° Set Sun **Moon** h m	40° Rise Sun **Moon** h m	40° Set Sun **Moon** h m	50° Rise Sun **Moon** h m	50° Set Sun **Moon** h m	60° Rise Sun **Moon** h m	60° Set Sun **Moon** h m
1 Su	12 13 34	06 36	17 52	06 50	17 37	07 09	17 19	07 34	16 54	08 14	16 14
32		**03 30**	**14 51**	**03 48**	**14 33**	**04 11**	**14 09**	**04 44**	**13 36**	**05 39**	**12 40**
2 Mo	12 13 42	06 35	17 52	06 50	17 38	07 08	17 20	07 32	16 56	08 12	16 16
33		**04 23**	**15 44**	**04 42**	**15 25**	**05 06**	**15 01**	**05 40**	**14 27**	**06 37**	**13 30**
3 Tu	12 13 49	06 35	17 53	06 49	17 39	07 07	17 21	07 31	16 58	08 09	16 19
34		**05 16**	**16 40**	**05 34**	**16 22**	**05 58**	**15 59**	**06 30**	**15 27**	**07 25**	**14 34**
4 We	12 13 56	06 34	17 53	06 49	17 40	07 06	17 22	07 30	17 00	08 06	16 22
35	**22 14 ●**	**06 07**	**17 38**	**06 24**	**17 23**	**06 45**	**17 03**	**07 14**	**16 35**	**08 02**	**15 49**
5 Th	12 14 01	06 34	17 54	06 48	17 40	07 05	17 24	07 28	17 01	08 04	16 24
36		**06 57**	**18 38**	**07 11**	**18 25**	**07 29**	**18 10**	**07 52**	**17 48**	**08 30**	**17 13**
6 Fr	12 14 06	06 34	17 54	06 48	17 41	07 04	17 25	07 26	17 02	08 02	16 27
37		**07 45**	**19 38**	**07 55**	**19 29**	**08 08**	**19 19**	**08 25**	**19 04**	**08 52**	**18 41**
7 Sa	12 14 10	06 33	17 55	06 47	17 42	07 03	17 26	07 25	17 04	07 59	16 30
38		**08 30**	**20 38**	**08 37**	**20 34**	**08 44**	**20 28**	**08 55**	**20 21**	**09 10**	**20 10**
8 Su	12 14 13	06 33	17 55	06 46	17 43	07 02	17 27	07 23	17 06	07 56	16 32
39		**09 15**	**21 37**	**09 17**	**21 38**	**09 19**	**21 38**	**09 22**	**21 39**	**09 26**	**21 40**
9 Mo	12 14 15	06 32	17 56	06 45	17 44	07 00	17 28	07 22	17 08	07 54	16 35
40		**09 59**	**22 37**	**09 56**	**22 42**	**09 53**	**22 48**	**09 48**	**22 56**	**09 42**	**23 10**
10 Tu	12 14 17	06 32	17 56	06 44	17 44	06 59	17 30	07 20	17 09	07 52	16 38
41		**10 43**	**23 36**	**10 36**	**23 46**	**10 27**	**23 57**	**10 16**		**09 58**	
11 We	12 14 17	06 31	17 57	06 43	17 45	06 58	17 31	07 18	17 11	07 49	16 40
42	**17 49 ☽**	**11 29**		**11 18**		**11 04**		**10 46**	**00 13**	**10 17**	**00 38**
12 Th	12 14 17	06 31	17 57	06 42	17 46	06 57	17 32	07 16	17 13	07 47	16 43
43		**12 18**	**00 36**	**12 03**	**00 50**	**11 45**	**01 06**	**11 20**	**01 29**	**10 40**	**02 06**
13 Fr	12 14 16	06 30	17 58	06 42	17 47	06 56	17 34	07 14	17 14	07 44	16 46
44		**13 09**	**01 37**	**12 51**	**01 53**	**12 30**	**02 13**	**12 00**	**02 42**	**11 11**	**03 29**
14 Sa	12 14 15	06 30	17 58	06 41	17 48	06 54	17 35	07 13	17 16	07 42	16 48
45		**14 02**	**02 36**	**13 44**	**02 54**	**13 20**	**03 17**	**12 47**	**03 50**	**11 52**	**04 44**
15 Su	12 14 12	06 29	17 59	06 40	17 49	06 53	17 36	07 11	17 18	07 38	16 51
46		**14 58**	**03 33**	**14 39**	**03 52**	**14 16**	**04 16**	**13 42**	**04 50**	**12 46**	**05 46**
16 Mo	12 14 09	06 29	17 59	06 39	17 50	06 52	17 37	07 09	17 20	07 35	16 54
47		**15 55**	**04 28**	**15 37**	**04 46**	**15 15**	**05 09**	**14 44**	**05 41**	**13 51**	**06 35**
17 Tu	12 14 05	06 28	18 00	06 38	17 50	06 50	17 38	07 07	17 22	07 32	16 56
48		**16 51**	**05 19**	**16 36**	**05 35**	**16 16**	**05 56**	**15 49**	**06 24**	**15 05**	**07 11**
18 We	12 14 01	06 28	18 00	06 37	17 51	06 49	17 39	07 05	17 23	07 30	16 58
49	**22 58 ○**	**17 46**	**06 05**	**17 34**	**06 19**	**17 18**	**06 36**	**16 57**	**07 00**	**16 23**	**07 37**
19 Th	12 13 56	06 27	18 01	06 36	17 52	06 48	17 40	07 03	17 25	07 27	17 01
50		**18 40**	**06 49**	**18 31**	**06 59**	**18 20**	**07 12**	**18 04**	**07 30**	**17 41**	**07 57**
20 Fr	12 13 50	06 26	18 01	06 35	17 53	06 46	17 41	07 01	17 27	07 24	17 04
51		**19 31**	**07 29**	**19 26**	**07 36**	**19 20**	**07 44**	**19 11**	**07 55**	**18 58**	**08 13**
21 Sa	12 13 43	06 26	18 02	06 34	17 54	06 45	17 42	07 00	17 28	07 22	17 06
52		**20 21**	**08 06**	**20 20**	**08 10**	**20 18**	**08 13**	**20 16**	**08 19**	**20 13**	**08 26**
22 Su	12 13 36	06 25	18 02	06 33	17 54	06 44	17 44	06 58	17 30	07 19	17 09
53		**21 10**	**08 43**	**21 13**	**08 42**	**21 16**	**08 41**	**21 20**	**08 40**	**21 27**	**08 39**
23 Mo	12 13 28	06 24	18 03	06 32	17 55	06 42	17 45	06 56	17 32	07 16	17 12
54		**21 59**	**09 19**	**22 05**	**09 14**	**22 13**	**09 09**	**22 23**	**09 02**	**22 40**	**08 51**
24 Tu	12 13 19	06 23	18 03	06 31	17 56	06 41	17 46	06 54	17 34	07 13	17 14
55		**22 47**	**09 55**	**22 57**	**09 47**	**23 09**	**09 38**	**23 26**	**09 24**	**23 52**	**09 04**
25 We	12 13 10	06 23	18 04	06 30	17 56	06 40	17 47	06 52	17 36	07 10	17 17
56		**23 37**	**10 33**	**23 50**	**10 21**		**10 08**		**09 49**		**09 19**
26 Th	12 13 01	06 22	18 04	06 29	17 57	06 38	17 48	06 50	17 37	07 08	17 20
57			**11 12**		**10 58**	**00 06**	**10 41**	**00 28**	**10 16**	**01 04**	**09 38**
27 Fr	12 12 51	06 21	18 04	06 28	17 58	06 37	17 49	06 48	17 39	07 05	17 22
58	**01 14 ☾**	**00 27**	**11 55**	**00 43**	**11 38**	**01 02**	**11 17**	**01 30**	**10 49**	**02 15**	**10 02**
28 Sa	12 12 40	06 20	18 05	06 27	17 58	06 36	17 50	06 46	17 40	07 02	17 24
59		**01 18**	**12 41**	**01 36**	**12 23**	**01 58**	**12 00**	**02 30**	**11 27**	**03 23**	**10 33**

3rd Month — March, 1981 — 31 Days

Greenwich Mean Time

NOTE: Light figures indicate Sun. **Dark** figures indicate **Moon.** *Degrees are North Latitude.*

CAUTION: Must be converted to local time. For instruction see page 773.

Day of month week year	Sun on meridian **Moon phase**	20° Rise Sun **Moon**	20° Set Sun **Moon**	30° Rise Sun **Moon**	30° Set Sun **Moon**	40° Rise Sun **Moon**	40° Set Sun **Moon**	50° Rise Sun **Moon**	50° Set Sun **Moon**	60° Rise Sun **Moon**	60° Set Sun **Moon**
	h m s	h m	h m	h m	h m	h m	h m	h m	h m	h m	h m
1 Su	12 12 29	06 20	18 05	06 26	17 59	06 34	17 52	06 44	17 42	06 59	17 27
60		**02 10**	**13 31**	**02 29**	**13 12**	**02 53**	**12 48**	**03 27**	**12 14**	**04 24**	**11 16**
2 Mo	12 12 17	06 19	18 06	06 25	18 00	06 32	17 53	06 42	17 44	06 56	17 30
61		**03 03**	**14 24**	**03 22**	**14 06**	**03 46**	**13 42**	**04 19**	**13 09**	**05 16**	**12 13**
3 Tu	12 12 05	06 18	18 06	06 24	18 00	06 31	17 54	06 40	17 45	06 53	17 32
62		**03 54**	**15 21**	**04 12**	**15 04**	**04 35**	**14 43**	**05 06**	**14 13**	**05 58**	**13 22**
4 We	12 11 52	06 17	18 06	06 23	18 01	06 30	17 55	06 38	17 47	06 50	17 34
63	**10 31** ●	**04 45**	**16 21**	**05 01**	**16 06**	**05 20**	**15 48**	**05 46**	**15 24**	**06 29**	**14 43**
5 Th	12 11 39	06 16	18 06	06 22	18 02	06 28	17 56	06 36	17 48	06 47	17 37
64		**05 34**	**17 21**	**05 46**	**17 11**	**06 01**	**16 57**	**06 22**	**16 39**	**06 54**	**16 10**
6 Fr	12 11 25	06 16	18 07	06 21	18 02	06 26	17 57	06 33	17 50	06 44	17 40
65		**06 21**	**18 22**	**06 29**	**18 16**	**06 39**	**18 08**	**06 53**	**17 58**	**07 14**	**17 41**
7 Sa	12 11 11	06 15	18 07	06 20	18 03	06 25	17 58	06 31	17 52	06 41	17 42
66		**07 07**	**19 24**	**07 11**	**19 22**	**07 16**	**19 20**	**07 22**	**19 18**	**07 31**	**19 14**
8 Su	12 10 57	06 14	18 07	06 19	18 04	06 23	17 59	06 29	17 54	06 38	17 44
67		**07 53**	**20 25**	**07 52**	**20 29**	**07 51**	**20 33**	**07 49**	**20 38**	**07 47**	**20 47**
9 Mo	12 10 42	06 14	18 08	06 18	18 04	06 22	18 00	06 27	17 55	06 35	17 47
68		**08 38**	**21 27**	**08 33**	**21 35**	**08 26**	**21 45**	**08 17**	**21 59**	**08 03**	**22 20**
10 Tu	12 10 27	06 13	18 08	06 16	18 05	06 20	18 01	06 25	17 56	06 32	17 50
69		**09 25**	**22 29**	**09 15**	**22 41**	**09 03**	**22 56**	**08 47**	**23 17**	**08 22**	**23 51**
11 We	12 10 12	06 12	18 08	06 15	18 06	06 18	18 02	06 23	17 58	06 29	17 52
70		**10 14**	**23 31**	**10 00**	**23 46**	**09 43**		**09 20**		**08 44**	
12 Th	12 09 56	06 11	18 08	06 14	18 06	06 16	18 03	06 21	18 00	06 26	17 54
71		**11 05**		**10 48**		**10 28**	**00 06**	**09 59**	**00 33**	**09 12**	**01 18**
13 Fr	12 09 40	06 10	18 09	06 12	18 07	06 15	18 04	06 18	18 02	06 23	17 57
72	**01 50** ☽	**11 59**	**00 31**	**11 40**	**00 49**	**11 17**	**01 12**	**10 44**	**01 43**	**09 50**	**02 36**
14 Sa	12 09 23	06 10	18 10	06 11	18 08	06 14	18 06	06 16	18 03	06 20	18 00
73		**12 54**	**01 29**	**12 34**	**01 48**	**12 10**	**02 12**	**11 37**	**02 46**	**10 40**	**03 43**
15 Su	12 09 07	06 09	18 10	06 10	18 08	06 12	18 07	06 14	18 05	06 17	18 02
74		**13 50**	**02 24**	**13 31**	**02 43**	**13 08**	**03 07**	**12 36**	**03 40**	**11 41**	**04 35**
16 Mo	12 08 50	06 08	18 10	06 09	18 09	06 10	18 08	06 12	18 06	06 14	18 04
75		**14 45**	**03 16**	**14 29**	**03 33**	**14 08**	**03 54**	**13 40**	**04 24**	**12 52**	**05 14**
17 Tu	12 08 32	06 07	18 10	06 08	18 10	06 08	18 09	06 10	18 08	06 11	18 07
76		**15 40**	**04 03**	**15 26**	**04 18**	**15 09**	**04 36**	**14 46**	**05 01**	**14 08**	**05 42**
18 We	12 08 15	06 06	18 11	06 06	18 10	06 07	18 10	06 07	18 10	06 08	18 10
77		**16 33**	**04 46**	**16 23**	**04 58**	**16 10**	**05 12**	**15 52**	**05 32**	**15 25**	**06 03**
19 Th	12 07 57	06 05	18 11	06 05	18 11	06 05	18 11	06 05	18 11	06 05	18 12
78		**17 24**	**05 27**	**17 18**	**05 35**	**17 10**	**05 45**	**16 59**	**05 59**	**16 41**	**06 20**
20 Fr	12 07 40	06 04	18 11	06 04	18 11	06 04	18 12	06 03	18 12	06 02	18 14
79	**15 22** ○	**18 15**	**06 05**	**18 12**	**06 09**	**18 09**	**06 15**	**18 04**	**06 22**	**17 57**	**06 33**
21 Sa	12 07 22	06 04	18 12	06 03	18 12	06 02	18 13	06 02	18 14	05 59	18 17
80		**19 04**	**06 41**	**19 05**	**06 42**	**19 06**	**06 43**	**19 08**	**06 44**	**19 11**	**06 46**
22 Su	12 07 04	06 03	18 12	06 02	18 12	06 00	18 14	05 59	18 16	05 56	18 20
81		**19 53**	**07 17**	**19 57**	**07 14**	**20 04**	**07 10**	**20 12**	**07 06**	**20 25**	**06 58**
23 Mo	12 06 46	06 02	18 12	06 01	18 13	05 59	18 15	05 57	18 17	05 53	18 22
82		**20 41**	**07 53**	**20 50**	**07 47**	**21 00**	**07 38**	**21 15**	**07 27**	**21 38**	**07 11**
24 Tu	12 06 27	06 01	18 12	06 00	18 14	05 57	18 16	05 55	18 19	05 50	18 24
83		**21 30**	**08 30**	**21 42**	**08 20**	**21 57**	**08 08**	**22 18**	**07 51**	**22 51**	**07 25**
25 We	12 06 09	06 00	18 12	05 58	18 14	05 56	18 17	05 52	18 20	05 47	18 26
84		**22 20**	**09 09**	**22 35**	**08 56**	**22 54**	**08 39**	**23 20**	**08 17**		**07 41**
26 Th	12 05 51	05 59	18 13	05 57	18 15	05 54	18 18	05 50	18 22	05 44	18 29
85		**23 10**	**09 50**	**23 28**	**09 34**	**23 49**	**09 14**		**08 47**	**00 02**	**08 02**
27 Fr	12 05 33	05 58	18 13	05 56	18 16	05 52	18 19	05 48	18 24	05 41	18 31
86			**10 34**		**10 16**		**09 54**	**00 20**	**09 22**	**01 11**	**08 30**
28 Sa	12 05 14	05 57	18 13	05 55	18 16	05 50	18 20	05 46	18 26	05 38	18 34
87	**19 34** ☾	**00 01**	**11 21**	**00 20**	**11 02**	**00 44**	**10 38**	**01 17**	**10 04**	**02 14**	**09 07**
29 Su	12 04 56	05 56	18 14	05 54	18 17	05 49	18 21	05 44	18 27	05 35	18 36
88		**00 53**	**12 12**	**01 12**	**11 53**	**01 36**	**11 29**	**02 11**	**10 55**	**03 09**	**09 56**
30 Mo	12 04 38	05 56	18 14	05 52	18 18	05 48	18 22	05 41	18 28	05 32	18 38
89		**01 43**	**13 06**	**02 02**	**12 48**	**02 26**	**12 25**	**02 58**	**11 53**	**03 54**	**10 59**
31 Tu	12 04 20	05 55	18 14	05 51	18 18	05 46	18 23	05 39	18 30	05 29	18 41
90		**02 33**	**14 03**	**02 50**	**13 47**	**03 11**	**13 27**	**03 41**	**12 59**	**04 29**	**12 13**

4th Month **April, 1981** 30 Days

Greenwich Mean Time

NOTE: Light figures indicate Sun. **Dark** figures indicate **Moon.** *Degrees are North Latitude.*

CAUTION: Must be converted to local time. For instruction see page 773.

Day of month week year	Sun on meridian **Moon phase**	20° Rise Sun **Moon**	20° Set Sun **Moon**	30° Rise Sun **Moon**	30° Set Sun **Moon**	40° Rise Sun **Moon**	40° Set Sun **Moon**	50° Rise Sun **Moon**	50° Set Sun **Moon**	60° Rise Sun **Moon**	60° Set Sun **Moon**
	h m s	h m	h m	h m	h m	h m	h m	h m	h m	h m	h m
1 We	12 04 02	05 54	18 14	05 50	18 18	05 44	18 24	05 37	18 32	05 26	18 44
91		**03 22**	**15 02**	**03 36**	**14 49**	**03 53**	**14 34**	**04 17**	**14 12**	**04 55**	**13 36**
2 Th	12 03 44	05 53	18 14	05 48	18 19	05 43	18 25	05 35	18 33	05 23	18 46
92		**04 09**	**16 02**	**04 19**	**15 54**	**04 32**	**15 43**	**04 50**	**15 28**	**05 17**	**15 05**
3 Fr	12 03 27	05 52	18 14	05 47	18 20	05 42	18 26	05 33	18 34	05 20	18 48
93		**04 55**	**17 04**	**05 01**	**17 00**	**05 09**	**16 55**	**05 19**	**16 48**	**05 35**	**16 38**
4 Sa	12 03 09	05 51	18 15	05 46	18 20	05 40	18 27	05 31	18 36	05 17	18 51
94	**20 19** ●	**05 41**	**18 06**	**05 43**	**18 07**	**05 44**	**18 08**	**05 47**	**18 10**	**05 51**	**18 12**
5 Su	12 02 52	05 50	18 15	05 45	18 21	05 38	18 28	05 29	18 38	05 14	18 54
95		**06 27**	**19 09**	**06 24**	**19 15**	**06 20**	**19 23**	**06 15**	**19 32**	**06 07**	**19 48**
6 Mo	12 02 34	05 50	18 16	05 44	18 22	05 36	18 29	05 26	18 40	05 11	18 56
96		**07 15**	**20 14**	**07 07**	**20 24**	**06 57**	**20 37**	**06 44**	**20 55**	**06 24**	**21 23**
7 Tu	12 02 17	05 49	18 16	05 42	18 22	05 35	18 30	05 24	18 41	05 08	18 58
97		**08 05**	**21 18**	**07 52**	**21 32**	**07 37**	**21 50**	**07 17**	**22 16**	**06 44**	**22 57**
8 We	12 02 00	05 48	18 16	05 41	18 23	05 33	18 31	05 22	18 43	05 05	19 01
98		**08 57**	**22 21**	**08 41**	**22 39**	**08 21**	**23 01**	**07 54**	**23 31**	**07 11**	
9 Th	12 01 44	05 47	18 16	05 40	18 24	05 32	18 32	05 20	18 44	05 02	19 03
99		**09 51**	**23 23**	**09 33**	**23 42**	**09 10**		**08 38**		**07 45**	**00 23**
10 Fr	12 01 27	05 46	18 16	05 39	18 24	05 30	18 33	05 18	18 46	04 59	19 06
100		**10 48**		**10 28**		**10 04**	**00 06**	**09 30**	**00 39**	**08 32**	**01 37**
11 Sa	12 01 11	05 46	18 17	05 38	18 24	05 28	18 34	05 16	18 48	04 56	19 08
101	**11 11** ☽	**11 44**	**00 20**	**11 25**	**00 40**	**11 02**	**01 04**	**10 28**	**01 38**	**09 31**	**02 35**
12 Su	12 00 56	05 45	18 17	05 37	18 25	05 27	18 35	05 14	18 49	04 53	19 10
102		**12 41**	**01 13**	**12 24**	**01 32**	**12 02**	**01 54**	**11 31**	**02 26**	**10 41**	**03 18**
13 Mo	12 00 40	05 44	18 17	05 36	18 26	05 26	18 36	05 12	18 50	04 50	19 12
103		**13 36**	**02 02**	**13 21**	**02 18**	**13 03**	**02 38**	**12 37**	**03 05**	**11 56**	**03 49**
14 Tu	12 00 25	05 43	18 18	05 34	18 26	05 24	18 37	05 10	18 52	04 47	19 15
104		**14 29**	**02 46**	**14 18**	**02 59**	**14 04**	**03 15**	**13 44**	**03 37**	**13 13**	**04 11**
15 We	12 00 10	05 42	18 18	05 33	18 27	05 22	18 38	05 07	18 54	04 44	19 18
105		**15 21**	**03 27**	**15 13**	**03 37**	**15 03**	**03 48**	**14 50**	**04 04**	**14 29**	**04 28**
16 Th	11 59 55	05 41	18 18	05 32	18 28	05 21	18 39	05 05	18 55	04 41	19 20
106		**16 11**	**04 05**	**16 07**	**04 11**	**16 02**	**04 18**	**15 55**	**04 28**	**15 45**	**04 42**
17 Fr	11 59 41	05 40	18 18	05 31	18 28	05 20	18 40	05 03	18 56	04 38	19 22
107		**17 00**	**04 42**	**17 00**	**04 44**	**17 00**	**04 46**	**16 59**	**04 50**	**16 59**	**04 55**
18 Sa	11 59 27	05 40	18 19	05 30	18 29	05 18	18 41	05 01	18 58	04 35	19 25
108		**17 48**	**05 18**	**17 52**	**05 16**	**17 57**	**05 14**	**18 03**	**05 11**	**18 13**	**05 06**
19 Su	11 59 13	05 39	18 20	05 29	18 30	05 16	18 42	04 59	19 00	04 32	19 28
109	**07 59** ○	**18 37**	**05 53**	**18 44**	**05 48**	**18 54**	**05 41**	**19 06**	**05 32**	**19 26**	**05 18**
20 Mo	11 59 00	05 38	18 20	05 28	18 30	05 15	18 43	04 57	19 01	04 29	19 30
110		**19 26**	**06 30**	**19 37**	**06 21**	**19 51**	**06 09**	**20 09**	**05 54**	**20 39**	**05 31**
21 Tu	11 58 47	05 37	18 20	05 27	18 31	05 14	18 44	04 55	19 03	04 26	19 32
111		**20 16**	**07 08**	**20 30**	**06 55**	**20 47**	**06 40**	**21 12**	**06 19**	**21 52**	**05 46**
22 We	11 58 35	05 37	18 20	05 26	18 32	05 12	18 45	04 54	19 05	04 24	19 35
112		**21 06**	**07 48**	**21 23**	**07 32**	**21 44**	**07 13**	**22 13**	**06 47**	**23 02**	**06 05**
23 Th	11 58 23	05 36	18 21	05 25	18 32	05 11	18 46	04 52	19 06	04 21	19 38
113		**21 57**	**08 31**	**22 15**	**08 13**	**22 39**	**07 51**	**23 12**	**07 20**		**06 30**
24 Fr	11 58 12	05 35	18 21	05 24	18 33	05 10	18 47	04 50	19 08	04 18	19 40
114		**22 47**	**09 16**	**23 07**	**08 57**	**23 31**	**08 33**		**08 00**	**00 08**	**07 03**
25 Sa	11 58 01	05 34	18 21	05 23	18 34	05 08	18 48	04 48	19 10	04 15	19 42
115		**23 37**	**10 05**	**23 57**	**09 46**		**09 21**	**00 06**	**08 46**	**01 05**	**07 47**
26 Su	11 57 51	05 34	18 22	05 22	18 34	05 07	18 49	04 46	19 11	04 12	19 45
116			**10 57**		**10 38**	**00 21**	**10 14**	**00 55**	**09 41**	**01 53**	**08 43**
27 Mo	11 57 41	05 34	18 22	05 21	18 34	05 06	18 50	04 44	19 12	04 10	19 48
117	**10 14** ☾	**00 26**	**11 52**	**00 44**	**11 34**	**01 07**	**11 13**	**01 38**	**10 42**	**02 31**	**09 52**
28 Tu	11 57 32	05 33	18 22	05 20	18 35	05 04	18 51	04 42	19 14	04 07	19 50
118		**01 14**	**12 48**	**01 30**	**12 33**	**01 49**	**12 15**	**02 16**	**11 50**	**02 59**	**11 10**
29 We	11 57 23	05 32	18 22	05 19	18 36	05 03	18 52	04 40	19 16	04 04	19 52
119		**02 00**	**13 46**	**02 13**	**13 35**	**02 28**	**13 22**	**02 49**	**13 03**	**03 21**	**12 34**
30 Th	11 57 15	05 32	18 22	05 18	18 36	05 02	18 53	04 38	19 17	04 02	19 55
120		**02 45**	**14 45**	**02 54**	**14 38**	**03 04**	**14 30**	**03 18**	**14 19**	**03 39**	**14 02**

5th Month — May, 1981 — 31 days

Greenwich Mean Time

NOTE: Light figures indicate Sun. **Dark** figures indicate **Moon.** *Degrees are North Latitude.*

CAUTION: Must be converted to local time. For instruction see page 773.

Day of month week year	Sun on meridian **Moon phase**	20° Rise Sun **Moon**	20° Set Sun **Moon**	30° Rise Sun **Moon**	30° Set Sun **Moon**	40° Rise Sun **Moon**	40° Set Sun **Moon**	50° Rise Sun **Moon**	50° Set Sun **Moon**	60° Rise Sun **Moon**	60° Set Sun **Moon**
	h m s	h m	h m	h m	h m	h m	h m	h m	h m	h m	h m
1 Fr	11 57 07	05 31	18 24	05 17	18 37	05 00	18 54	04 37	19 18	03 59	19 58
121		**03 30**	**15 45**	**03 34**	**15 44**	**03 39**	**15 42**	**03 45**	**15 39**	**03 55**	**15 34**
2 Sa	11 57 00	05 30	18 24	05 16	18 38	04 59	18 55	04 35	19 20	03 56	20 00
122		**04 15**	**16 48**	**04 14**	**16 51**	**04 13**	**16 55**	**04 12**	**17 00**	**04 10**	**17 09**
3 Su	11 56 53	05 30	18 24	05 15	18 38	04 58	18 56	04 33	19 22	03 53	20 02
123		**05 01**	**17 51**	**04 56**	**18 00**	**04 49**	**18 10**	**04 40**	**18 23**	**04 26**	**18 45**
4 Mo	11 56 47	05 29	18 24	05 14	18 39	04 56	18 57	04 32	19 23	03 51	20 05
124	**04 19** ●	**05 50**	**18 57**	**05 40**	**19 09**	**05 27**	**19 25**	**05 11**	**19 47**	**04 45**	**20 22**
5 Tu	11 56 41	05 28	18 25	05 14	18 40	04 55	18 58	04 30	19 24	03 48	20 08
125		**06 42**	**20 03**	**06 28**	**20 19**	**06 10**	**20 40**	**05 46**	**21 08**	**05 07**	**21 56**
6 We	11 56 37	05 28	18 25	05 13	18 40	04 54	18 59	04 28	19 26	03 45	20 10
126		**07 37**	**21 08**	**07 19**	**21 26**	**06 58**	**21 50**	**06 27**	**22 23**	**05 38**	**23 20**
7 Th	11 56 32	05 28	18 26	05 12	18 41	04 53	19 00	04 26	19 28	03 42	20 12
127		**08 35**	**22 09**	**08 15**	**22 29**	**07 51**	**22 54**	**07 17**	**23 29**	**06 20**	
8 Fr	11 56 28	05 27	18 26	05 12	18 42	04 52	19 01	04 25	19 29	03 40	20 15
128		**09 34**	**23 07**	**09 14**	**23 26**	**08 50**	**23 49**	**08 15**		**07 16**	**00 28**
9 Sa	11 56 25	05 26	18 26	05 11	18 42	04 51	19 02	04 24	19 30	03 38	20 18
129		**10 33**	**23 58**	**10 14**		**09 51**		**09 19**	**00 23**	**08 24**	**01 18**
10 Su	11 56 22	05 26	18 27	05 10	18 43	04 50	19 03	04 22	19 32	03 35	20 20
130	**22 22** ☽	**11 30**		**11 14**	**00 16**	**10 54**	**00 37**	**10 26**	**01 06**	**09 40**	**01 54**
11 Mo	11 56 20	05 26	18 27	05 09	18 44	04 49	19 04	04 20	19 34	03 32	20 22
131		**12 25**	**00 45**	**12 12**	**01 00**	**11 56**	**01 17**	**11 34**	**01 41**	**10 58**	**02 19**
12 Tu	11 56 18	05 25	18 28	05 08	18 44	04 48	19 05	04 19	19 35	03 30	20 24
132		**13 17**	**01 28**	**13 08**	**01 39**	**12 57**	**01 52**	**12 41**	**02 10**	**12 16**	**02 38**
13 We	11 56 17	05 24	18 28	05 08	18 45	04 47	19 06	04 18	19 36	03 28	20 27
133		**14 08**	**02 07**	**14 02**	**02 14**	**13 56**	**02 23**	**13 47**	**02 35**	**13 33**	**02 53**
14 Th	11 56 17	05 24	18 28	05 07	18 46	04 46	19 07	04 16	19 38	03 25	20 29
134		**14 57**	**02 44**	**14 56**	**02 47**	**14 54**	**02 51**	**14 51**	**02 57**	**14 47**	**03 05**
15 Fr	11 56 17	05 24	18 28	05 06	18 46	04 45	19 08	04 14	19 39	03 23	20 32
135		**15 46**	**03 19**	**15 48**	**03 19**	**15 51**	**03 18**	**15 55**	**03 17**	**16 01**	**03 16**
16 Sa	11 56 17	05 24	18 29	05 06	18 47	04 44	19 09	04 13	19 40	03 20	20 34
136		**16 34**	**03 54**	**16 40**	**03 50**	**16 48**	**03 45**	**16 58**	**03 38**	**17 15**	**03 28**
17 Su	11 56 18	05 23	18 30	05 06	18 48	04 43	19 10	04 12	19 42	03 18	20 36
137		**17 23**	**04 30**	**17 32**	**04 22**	**17 45**	**04 13**	**18 01**	**04 00**	**18 28**	**03 40**
18 Mo	11 56 18	05 23	18 30	05 05	18 48	04 42	19 11	04 10	19 43	03 16	20 39
138		**18 12**	**05 08**	**18 25**	**04 56**	**18 42**	**04 42**	**19 04**	**04 23**	**19 41**	**03 54**
19 Tu	11 56 20	05 23	18 30	05 04	18 49	04 41	19 12	04 09	19 44	03 14	20 41
139	**00 04** ○	**19 02**	**05 47**	**19 18**	**05 32**	**19 38**	**05 14**	**20 07**	**04 50**	**20 53**	**04 11**
20 We	11 56 25	05 22	18 31	05 04	18 50	04 40	19 13	04 08	19 46	03 12	20 43
140		**19 53**	**06 29**	**20 11**	**06 12**	**20 34**	**05 51**	**21 07**	**05 21**	**22 01**	**04 33**
21 Th	11 56 29	05 22	18 32	05 04	18 50	04 40	19 14	04 06	19 48	03 09	20 45
141		**20 44**	**07 14**	**21 04**	**06 55**	**21 28**	**06 31**	**22 03**	**05 58**	**23 03**	**05 02**
22 Fr	11 56 32	05 22	18 32	05 03	18 51	04 39	19 15	04 05	19 49	03 07	20 47
142		**21 35**	**08 02**	**21 54**	**07 42**	**22 19**	**07 17**	**22 54**	**06 42**	**23 54**	**05 42**
23 Sa	11 56 37	05 22	18 32	05 02	18 52	04 38	19 16	04 04	19 50	03 05	20 49
143		**22 24**	**08 53**	**22 43**	**08 33**	**23 06**	**08 09**	**23 39**	**07 34**		**06 34**
24 Su	11 56 42	05 22	18 32	05 02	18 52	04 38	19 16	04 03	19 52	03 03	20 52
144		**23 11**	**09 46**	**23 28**	**09 28**	**23 49**	**09 05**		**08 33**	**00 35**	**07 39**
25 Mo	11 56 47	05 21	18 33	05 02	18 53	04 37	19 17	04 02	19 53	03 02	20 54
145		**23 57**	**10 40**		**10 25**		**10 05**	**00 18**	**09 38**	**01 05**	**08 52**
26 Tu	11 56 53	05 21	18 33	05 01	18 53	04 36	19 18	04 01	19 54	02 59	20 56
146	**21 00** ☾		**11 36**	**00 11**	**11 24**	**00 28**	**11 08**	**00 51**	**10 47**	**01 29**	**10 13**
27 We	11 56 00	05 21	18 34	05 00	18 54	04 36	19 19	04 00	19 55	02 58	20 58
147		**00 41**	**12 33**	**00 51**	**12 25**	**01 04**	**12 14**	**01 21**	**12 00**	**01 47**	**11 37**
28 Th	11 57 07	05 20	18 34	05 00	18 54	04 35	19 20	03 59	19 56	02 56	21 00
148		**01 24**	**13 31**	**01 30**	**13 27**	**01 37**	**13 22**	**01 47**	**13 15**	**02 03**	**13 05**
29 Fr	11 57 14	05 20	18 34	05 00	18 55	04 35	19 20	03 58	19 57	02 54	21 02
149		**02 07**	**14 30**	**02 08**	**14 31**	**02 10**	**14 32**	**02 13**	**14 33**	**02 17**	**14 35**
30 Sa	11 57 22	05 20	18 35	05 00	18 55	04 34	19 21	03 57	19 58	02 53	21 04
150		**02 51**	**15 31**	**02 48**	**15 37**	**02 44**	**15 44**	**02 39**	**15 53**	**02 31**	**16 08**
31 Su	11 57 31	05 20	18 35	05 00	18 56	04 34	19 22	03 56	19 59	02 52	21 06
151		**03 37**	**16 35**	**03 29**	**16 45**	**03 20**	**16 58**	**03 07**	**17 16**	**02 47**	**17 44**

6th Month — June, 1981 — 30 days

Greenwich Mean Time

NOTE: Light figures indicate Sun. **Dark** figures indicate **Moon.** *Degrees are North Latitude.*

CAUTION: Must be converted to local time. For instruction see page 773.

Day of month week year	Sun on meridian **Moon phase**	20° Rise Sun **Moon**	20° Set Sun **Moon**	30° Rise Sun **Moon**	30° Set Sun **Moon**	40° Rise Sun **Moon**	40° Set Sun **Moon**	50° Rise Sun **Moon**	50° Set Sun **Moon**	60° Rise Sun **Moon**	60° Set Sun **Moon**
	h m s	h m	h m	h m	h m	h m	h m	h m	h m	h m	h m
1 Mo	11 57 39	05 20	18 36	05 00	18 56	04 33	19 22	03 56	20 00	02 50	21 08
152		**04 26**	**17 40**	**04 14**	**17 55**	**03 59**	**18 13**	**03 39**	**18 38**	**03 07**	**19 19**
2 Tu	11 57 49	05 20	18 36	04 59	18 56	04 32	19 23	03 56	20 01	02 48	21 09
153	**11 32** ●	**05 19**	**18 46**	**05 03**	**19 04**	**04 44**	**19 26**	**04 16**	**19 57**	**03 32**	**20 50**
3 We	11 57 58	05 20	18 36	04 59	18 57	04 32	19 24	03 55	20 02	02 47	21 11
154		**06 16**	**19 51**	**05 58**	**20 10**	**05 34**	**20 35**	**05 02**	**21 10**	**04 08**	**22 09**
4 Th	11 58 08	05 20	18 36	04 59	18 58	04 32	19 24	03 54	20 03	02 46	21 12
155		**07 16**	**20 52**	**06 56**	**21 12**	**06 32**	**21 37**	**05 57**	**22 11**	**04 57**	**23 10**
5 Fr	11 58 19	05 20	18 37	04 58	18 58	04 32	19 25	03 54	20 04	02 44	21 14
156		**08 17**	**21 48**	**07 58**	**22 07**	**07 34**	**22 30**	**06 59**	**23 01**	**06 01**	**23 54**
6 Sa	11 58 29	05 20	18 38	04 58	18 58	04 31	19 26	03 53	20 05	02 43	21 16
157		**09 17**	**22 39**	**09 00**	**22 55**	**08 38**	**23 14**	**08 08**	**23 41**	**07 17**	
7 Su	11 58 40	05 20	18 38	04 58	18 59	04 31	19 26	03 52	20 06	02 42	21 17
158		**10 15**	**23 25**	**10 01**	**23 37**	**09 43**	**23 52**	**09 18**		**08 37**	**00 24**
8 Mo	11 58 51	05 20	18 38	04 58	19 00	04 31	19 27	03 52	20 07	02 41	21 18
159		**11 10**		**10 59**		**10 46**		**10 27**	**00 13**	**09 58**	**00 46**
9 Tu	11 59 03	05 20	18 38	04 58	19 00	04 31	19 28	03 52	20 08	02 40	21 19
160	**11 33** ☽	**12 03**	**00 06**	**11 56**	**00 15**	**11 47**	**00 25**	**11 35**	**00 40**	**11 17**	**01 02**
10 We	11 59 15	05 20	18 39	04 58	19 00	04 31	19 28	03 51	20 08	02 39	21 20
161		**12 53**	**00 44**	**12 50**	**00 49**	**12 46**	**00 55**	**12 41**	**01 03**	**12 33**	**01 15**
11 Th	11 59 27	05 20	18 39	04 58	19 01	04 31	19 29	03 51	20 09	02 38	21 21
162		**13 42**	**01 20**	**13 43**	**01 21**	**13 44**	**01 22**	**13 45**	**01 24**	**13 48**	**01 26**
12 Fr	11 59 39	05 20	18 39	04 58	19 01	04 31	19 29	03 51	20 10	02 38	21 22
163		**14 30**	**01 56**	**14 35**	**01 53**	**14 41**	**01 49**	**14 49**	**01 45**	**15 02**	**01 38**
13 Sa	11 59 51	05 20	18 40	04 58	19 02	04 30	19 30	03 50	20 10	02 37	21 23
164		**15 19**	**02 31**	**15 27**	**02 24**	**15 38**	**02 16**	**15 52**	**02 06**	**16 15**	**01 49**
14 Su	12 00 03	05 20	18 40	04 58	19 02	04 30	19 30	03 50	20 10	02 36	21 24
165		**16 08**	**03 08**	**16 20**	**02 57**	**16 35**	**02 45**	**16 55**	**02 28**	**17 29**	**02 02**
15 Mo	12 00 16	05 20	18 40	04 58	19 02	04 30	19 30	03 50	20 11	02 36	21 25
166		**16 58**	**03 46**	**17 13**	**03 33**	**17 32**	**03 16**	**17 58**	**02 53**	**18 42**	**02 17**
16 Tu	12 00 29	05 20	18 40	04 58	19 02	04 30	19 30	03 50	20 11	02 36	21 26
167		**17 49**	**04 27**	**18 06**	**04 11**	**18 29**	**03 51**	**19 00**	**03 23**	**19 52**	**02 37**
17 We	12 00 42	05 20	18 41	04 58	19 03	04 30	19 31	03 50	20 12	02 36	21 26
168	**15 04** ○	**18 40**	**05 11**	**18 59**	**04 53**	**19 24**	**04 30**	**19 58**	**03 58**	**20 57**	**03 04**
18 Th	12 00 54	05 21	18 42	04 59	19 04	04 31	19 32	03 50	20 12	02 35	21 27
169		**19 31**	**05 59**	**19 51**	**05 39**	**20 16**	**05 14**	**20 52**	**04 39**	**21 53**	**03 40**
19 Fr	12 01 07	05 21	18 42	04 59	19 04	04 31	19 32	03 50	20 12	02 35	21 27
170		**20 21**	**06 49**	**20 41**	**06 29**	**21 05**	**06 04**	**21 39**	**05 29**	**22 37**	**04 28**
20 Sa	12 01 20	05 21	18 42	04 59	19 04	04 31	19 32	03 50	20 12	02 35	21 27
171		**21 10**	**07 42**	**21 28**	**07 23**	**21 50**	**06 59**	**22 20**	**06 26**	**23 11**	**05 29**
21 Su	12 01 33	05 22	18 42	05 00	19 04	04 32	19 32	03 50	20 12	02 36	21 28
172		**21 56**	**08 36**	**22 11**	**08 20**	**22 30**	**07 59**	**22 55**	**07 29**	**23 36**	**06 40**
22 Mo	12 01 46	05 22	18 42	05 00	19 04	04 32	19 33	03 51	20 13	02 36	21 28
173		**22 40**	**09 32**	**22 52**	**09 18**	**23 06**	**09 01**	**23 25**	**08 37**	**23 56**	**07 59**
23 Tu	12 01 59	05 22	18 42	05 00	19 04	04 32	19 33	03 51	20 13	02 36	21 28
174		**23 23**	**10 28**	**23 31**	**10 18**	**23 40**	**10 05**	**23 52**	**09 48**		**09 22**
24 We	12 02 12	05 22	18 42	05 00	19 04	04 32	19 33	03 52	20 13	02 36	21 28
175			**11 24**		**11 18**		**11 11**		**11 02**	**00 12**	**10 47**
25 Th	12 02 25	05 22	18 42	05 00	19 04	04 32	19 33	03 52	20 13	02 37	21 28
176	**04 25** ☾	**00 05**	**12 21**	**00 08**	**12 20**	**00 12**	**12 18**	**00 18**	**12 16**	**00 26**	**12 13**
26 Fr	12 02 38	05 23	18 43	05 01	19 05	04 33	19 33	03 52	20 13	02 38	21 27
177		**00 47**	**13 19**	**00 46**	**13 23**	**00 44**	**13 27**	**00 42**	**13 33**	**00 39**	**13 42**
27 Sa	12 02 50	05 23	18 43	05 01	19 05	04 33	19 33	03 53	20 13	02 38	21 27
178		**01 30**	**14 19**	**01 24**	**14 28**	**01 17**	**14 38**	**01 08**	**14 52**	**00 54**	**15 14**
28 Su	12 03 03	05 23	18 43	05 01	19 05	04 34	19 33	03 54	20 13	02 39	21 26
179		**02 16**	**15 22**	**02 06**	**15 34**	**01 53**	**15 50**	**01 37**	**16 12**	**01 10**	**16 47**
29 Mo	12 03 15	05 24	18 43	05 02	19 05	04 34	19 33	03 54	20 12	02 40	21 26
180		**03 06**	**16 26**	**02 52**	**16 42**	**02 34**	**17 03**	**02 10**	**17 31**	**01 32**	**18 18**
30 Tu	12 03 27	05 24	18 43	05 02	19 05	04 34	19 33	03 54	20 12	02 41	21 26
181		**04 00**	**17 30**	**03 42**	**17 49**	**03 20**	**18 13**	**02 50**	**18 46**	**02 01**	**19 43**

7th Month — July, 1981 — 31 Days

Greenwich Mean Time

NOTE: Light figures indicate Sun. **Dark** figures indicate **Moon.** *Degrees are North Latitude.*

CAUTION: Must be converted to local time. For instruction see page 773.

Day of month week year	Sun on meridian **Moon phase**	20° Rise Sun **Moon**	20° Set Sun **Moon**	30° Rise Sun **Moon**	30° Set Sun **Moon**	40° Rise Sun **Moon**	40° Set Sun **Moon**	50° Rise Sun **Moon**	50° Set Sun **Moon**	60° Rise Sun **Moon**	60° Set Sun **Moon**
	h m s	h m	h m	h m	h m	h m	h m	h m	h m	h m	h m
1 We	12 03 39	05 24	18 43	05 02	19 05	04 35	19 33	03 55	20 12	02 42	21 25
182	**19 03** ●	**04 58**	**18 34**	**04 38**	**18 54**	**04 14**	**19 19**	**03 40**	**19 54**	**02 42**	**20 54**
2 Th	12 03 51	05 24	18 43	05 02	19 05	04 36	19 33	03 56	20 12	02 43	21 24
183		**05 58**	**19 33**	**05 38**	**19 52**	**05 13**	**20 16**	**04 38**	**20 50**	**03 38**	**21 47**
3 Fr	12 04 02	05 24	18 44	05 03	19 05	04 36	19 32	03 56	20 12	02 44	21 23
184		**07 00**	**20 27**	**06 41**	**20 45**	**06 18**	**21 06**	**05 45**	**21 36**	**04 50**	**22 24**
4 Sa	12 04 13	05 25	18 44	05 04	19 05	04 36	19 32	03 57	20 11	02 46	21 22
185		**08 00**	**21 17**	**07 44**	**21 31**	**07 24**	**21 48**	**06 56**	**22 12**	**06 10**	**22 50**
5 Su	12 04 24	05 25	18 44	05 04	19 05	04 37	19 32	03 58	20 11	02 47	21 21
186		**08 58**	**22 01**	**08 45**	**22 11**	**08 29**	**22 24**	**08 08**	**22 41**	**07 33**	**23 08**
6 Mo	12 04 34	05 26	18 44	05 04	19 05	04 38	19 32	03 59	20 10	02 48	21 20
187		**09 53**	**22 41**	**09 44**	**22 48**	**09 33**	**22 56**	**09 18**	**23 07**	**08 55**	**23 23**
7 Tu	12 04 44	05 26	18 44	05 05	19 05	04 38	19 32	04 00	20 10	02 50	21 19
188		**10 45**	**23 19**	**10 40**	**23 21**	**10 34**	**23 25**	**10 26**	**23 29**	**10 14**	**23 35**
8 We	12 04 54	05 26	18 43	05 06	19 04	04 38	19 31	04 00	20 10	02 52	21 18
189		**11 35**	**23 55**	**11 35**	**23 54**	**11 34**	**23 52**	**11 33**	**23 50**	**11 31**	**23 47**
9 Th	12 05 03	05 27	18 43	05 06	19 04	04 39	19 31	04 01	20 09	02 53	21 17
190	**02 39** ☽	**12 24**		**12 28**		**12 32**		**12 37**		**12 46**	**23 58**
10 Fr	12 05 12	05 27	18 43	05 06	19 04	04 40	19 30	04 02	20 08	02 54	21 16
191		**13 13**	**00 30**	**13 20**	**00 25**	**13 29**	**00 19**	**13 41**	**00 11**	**14 00**	
11 Sa	12 05 21	05 28	18 43	05 07	19 04	04 40	19 30	04 03	20 08	02 56	21 14
192		**14 02**	**01 07**	**14 13**	**00 58**	**14 26**	**00 47**	**14 44**	**00 33**	**15 13**	**00 10**
12 Su	12 05 28	05 28	18 43	05 08	19 03	04 41	19 30	04 04	20 07	02 58	21 12
193		**14 52**	**01 44**	**15 06**	**01 32**	**15 23**	**01 17**	**15 47**	**00 57**	**16 27**	**00 24**
13 Mo	12 05 36	05 28	18 43	05 08	19 03	04 42	19 29	04 05	20 06	02 59	21 11
194		**15 42**	**02 24**	**15 59**	**02 09**	**16 20**	**01 50**	**16 49**	**01 24**	**17 38**	**00 42**
14 Tu	12 05 43	05 28	18 43	05 08	19 03	04 43	19 28	04 06	20 05	03 01	21 09
195		**16 34**	**03 07**	**16 52**	**02 49**	**17 16**	**02 27**	**17 49**	**01 57**	**18 46**	**01 06**
15 We	12 05 49	05 29	18 42	05 09	19 02	04 44	19 28	04 07	20 04	03 03	21 08
196		**17 25**	**03 53**	**17 45**	**03 34**	**18 10**	**03 10**	**18 45**	**02 36**	**19 46**	**01 38**
16 Th	12 05 55	05 30	18 42	05 10	19 02	04 44	19 28	04 08	20 03	03 05	21 06
197		**18 16**	**04 43**	**18 36**	**04 23**	**19 01**	**03 58**	**19 36**	**03 23**	**20 35**	**02 22**
17 Fr	12 06 01	05 30	18 42	05 10	19 02	04 45	19 27	04 09	20 02	03 07	21 04
198	**04 39** ○	**19 06**	**05 36**	**19 25**	**05 16**	**19 48**	**04 52**	**20 20**	**04 18**	**21 13**	**03 19**
18 Sa	12 06 06	05 30	18 42	05 10	19 02	04 46	19 26	04 10	20 01	03 09	21 02
199		**19 54**	**06 30**	**20 10**	**06 13**	**20 30**	**05 51**	**20 57**	**05 20**	**21 42**	**04 28**
19 Su	12 06 10	05 30	18 42	05 11	19 01	04 46	19 26	04 12	20 00	03 11	21 00
200		**20 39**	**07 26**	**20 52**	**07 12**	**21 08**	**06 53**	**21 29**	**06 28**	**22 03**	**05 46**
20 Mo	12 06 14	05 31	18 41	05 12	19 00	04 47	19 25	04 13	19 59	03 13	20 58
201		**21 23**	**08 23**	**21 32**	**08 12**	**21 43**	**07 58**	**21 58**	**07 39**	**22 20**	**07 08**
21 Tu	12 06 17	05 31	18 41	05 12	19 00	04 48	19 24	04 14	19 58	03 15	20 56
202		**22 05**	**09 20**	**22 10**	**09 13**	**22 15**	**09 04**	**22 23**	**08 52**	**22 35**	**08 33**
22 We	12 06 20	05 32	18 41	05 13	19 00	04 49	19 23	04 15	19 57	03 17	20 54
203		**22 47**	**10 10**	**22 47**	**10 14**	**22 47**	**10 11**	**22 48**	**10 06**	**22 48**	**09 59**
23 Th	12 06 22	05 32	18 40	05 14	18 59	04 50	19 22	04 16	19 56	03 20	20 52
204		**23 29**	**11 13**	**23 25**	**11 16**	**23 19**	**11 18**	**23 12**	**11 22**	**23 02**	**11 27**
24 Fr	12 06 24	05 32	18 40	05 14	18 58	04 51	19 22	04 18	19 54	03 22	20 49
205	**09 40** ☾		**12 12**		**12 19**	**23 53**	**12 27**	**23 39**	**12 38**	**23 17**	**12 56**
25 Sa	12 06 25	05 33	18 40	05 15	18 58	04 52	19 21	04 19	19 53	03 24	20 47
206		**00 13**	**13 12**	**00 04**	**13 23**		**13 37**		**13 55**	**23 36**	**14 26**
26 Su	12 06 26	05 33	18 40	05 16	18 57	04 53	19 20	04 20	19 52	03 26	20 45
207		**01 00**	**14 13**	**00 47**	**14 28**	**00 31**	**14 47**	**00 10**	**15 13**		**15 55**
27 Mo	12 06 26	05 34	18 39	05 16	18 56	04 54	19 19	04 22	19 50	03 28	20 42
208		**01 50**	**15 16**	**01 34**	**15 34**	**01 13**	**15 56**	**00 46**	**16 28**	**00 01**	**17 21**
28 Tu	12 06 25	05 34	18 38	05 17	18 56	04 54	19 18	04 24	19 48	03 31	20 40
209		**02 45**	**16 18**	**02 26**	**16 38**	**02 02**	**17 02**	**01 29**	**17 37**	**00 35**	**18 37**
29 We	12 06 24	05 34	18 38	05 17	18 55	04 55	19 17	04 25	19 47	03 33	20 38
210		**03 43**	**17 18**	**03 23**	**17 38**	**02 58**	**18 03**	**02 23**	**18 37**	**01 23**	**19 36**
30 Th	12 06 22	05 34	18 38	05 18	18 55	04 56	19 16	04 26	19 46	03 35	20 36
211		**04 43**	**18 14**	**04 24**	**18 33**	**03 59**	**18 56**	**03 25**	**19 27**	**02 27**	**20 20**
31 Fr	12 06 20	05 35	18 38	05 18	18 54	04 57	19 15	04 28	19 44	03 38	20 33
212	**03 52** ●	**05 44**	**19 06**	**05 26**	**19 22**	**05 04**	**19 41**	**04 34**	**20 08**	**03 43**	**20 50**

8th Month August, 1981 31 Days

Greenwich Mean Time

NOTE: Light figures indicate Sun. **Dark** figures indicate **Moon.** *Degrees are North Latitude.*

CAUTION: Must be converted to local time. For instruction see page 773.

Day of month week year	Sun on meridian **Moon phase**	20° Rise Sun **Moon**	20° Set Sun **Moon**	30° Rise Sun **Moon**	30° Set Sun **Moon**	40° Rise Sun **Moon**	40° Set Sun **Moon**	50° Rise Sun **Moon**	50° Set Sun **Moon**	60° Rise Sun **Moon**	60° Set Sun **Moon**
	h m s	h m	h m	h m	h m	h m	h m	h m	h m	h m	h m
1 Sa	12 06 17	05 36	18 37	05 18	18 54	04 58	19 14	04 29	19 42	03 39	20 30
213		**06 43**	**19 53**	**06 28**	**20 05**	**06 11**	**20 20**	**05 46**	**20 40**	**05 06**	**21 12**
2 Su	12 06 13	05 36	18 37	05 19	18 53	04 59	19 13	04 30	19 41	03 42	20 28
214		**07 40**	**20 35**	**07 29**	**20 44**	**07 16**	**20 54**	**06 58**	**21 08**	**06 29**	**21 29**
3 Mo	12 06 09	05 36	18 36	05 20	18 52	05 00	19 12	04 32	19 40	03 44	20 26
215		**08 34**	**21 14**	**08 27**	**21 19**	**08 19**	**21 24**	**08 08**	**21 31**	**07 51**	**21 42**
4 Tu	12 06 04	05 36	18 36	05 20	18 51	05 01	19 10	04 33	19 38	03 47	20 23
216		**09 26**	**21 52**	**09 23**	**21 52**	**09 20**	**21 53**	**09 16**	**21 53**	**09 10**	**21 54**
5 We	12 05 59	05 37	18 35	05 21	18 50	05 02	19 09	04 34	19 36	03 50	20 20
217		**10 16**	**22 28**	**10 18**	**22 24**	**10 20**	**22 20**	**10 23**	**22 14**	**10 27**	**22 05**
6 Th	12 05 52	05 37	18 34	05 22	18 49	05 03	19 08	04 36	19 35	03 52	20 18
218		**11 05**	**23 04**	**11 11**	**22 57**	**11 18**	**22 48**	**11 27**	**22 36**	**11 42**	**22 17**
7 Fr	12 05 46	05 37	18 34	05 22	18 48	05 04	19 07	04 38	19 33	03 54	20 15
219	**19 26** ☽	**11 55**	**23 41**	**12 04**	**23 30**	**12 15**	**23 17**	**12 31**	**22 59**	**12 56**	**22 31**
8 Sa	12 05 39	05 38	18 33	05 23	18 48	05 04	19 06	04 39	19 32	03 57	20 12
220		**12 44**		**12 57**		**13 13**	**23 49**	**13 34**	**23 25**	**14 10**	**22 47**
9 Su	12 05 31	05 38	18 32	05 24	18 47	05 05	19 04	04 40	19 30	04 00	20 10
221		**13 34**	**00 20**	**13 50**	**00 06**	**14 09**		**14 37**	**23 55**	**15 22**	**23 08**
10 Mo	12 05 22	05 38	18 32	05 24	18 46	05 06	19 03	04 42	19 28	04 02	20 07
222		**14 25**	**01 02**	**14 43**	**00 45**	**15 06**	**00 24**	**15 38**		**16 32**	**23 36**
11 Tu	12 05 13	05 38	18 31	05 25	18 45	05 07	19 02	04 44	19 26	04 04	20 04
223		**15 16**	**01 46**	**15 36**	**01 27**	**16 01**	**01 04**	**16 35**	**00 31**	**17 35**	
12 We	12 05 03	05 39	18 30	05 26	18 44	05 08	19 00	04 45	19 24	04 06	20 02
224		**16 08**	**02 34**	**16 28**	**02 15**	**16 53**	**01 50**	**17 28**	**01 15**	**18 29**	**00 14**
13 Th	12 04 53	05 40	18 30	05 26	18 43	05 09	18 59	04 46	19 22	04 09	19 59
225		**16 58**	**03 26**	**17 18**	**03 06**	**17 41**	**02 41**	**18 15**	**02 06**	**19 12**	**01 06**
14 Fr	12 04 42	05 40	18 29	05 27	18 42	05 10	18 58	04 48	19 20	04 11	19 56
226		**17 48**	**04 20**	**18 05**	**04 02**	**18 26**	**03 39**	**18 55**	**03 06**	**19 44**	**02 11**
15 Sa	12 04 31	05 40	18 28	05 28	18 41	05 11	18 57	04 50	19 18	04 14	19 53
227	**16 37** ○	**18 35**	**05 17**	**18 49**	**05 01**	**19 06**	**04 41**	**19 30**	**04 13**	**20 08**	**03 27**
16 Su	12 04 19	05 40	18 28	05 28	18 40	05 12	18 56	04 51	19 16	04 16	19 50
228		**19 20**	**06 14**	**19 30**	**06 02**	**19 43**	**05 46**	**20 00**	**05 24**	**20 27**	**04 49**
17 Mo	12 04 07	05 41	18 28	05 28	18 39	05 13	18 54	04 52	19 15	04 18	19 48
229		**20 03**	**07 12**	**20 09**	**07 04**	**20 17**	**06 53**	**20 27**	**06 39**	**20 42**	**06 16**
18 Tu	12 03 54	05 41	18 27	05 29	18 38	05 14	18 53	04 54	19 13	04 21	19 45
230		**20 46**	**08 10**	**20 47**	**08 06**	**20 49**	**08 01**	**20 52**	**07 54**	**20 56**	**07 44**
19 We	12 03 40	05 41	18 26	05 30	18 37	05 15	18 52	04 56	19 11	04 24	19 42
231		**21 28**	**09 08**	**21 25**	**09 09**	**21 22**	**09 10**	**21 17**	**09 11**	**21 10**	**09 12**
20 Th	12 03 26	05 42	18 26	05 30	18 36	05 16	18 50	04 57	19 09	04 26	19 39
232		**22 12**	**10 07**	**22 04**	**10 12**	**21 55**	**10 19**	**21 43**	**10 28**	**21 25**	**10 42**
21 Fr	12 03 12	05 42	18 25	05 30	18 35	05 17	18 48	04 58	19 07	04 28	19 36
233		**22 58**	**11 06**	**22 46**	**11 16**	**22 32**	**11 28**	**22 12**	**11 45**	**21 42**	**12 12**
22 Sa	12 02 57	05 42	18 24	05 31	18 34	05 18	18 47	05 00	19 05	04 31	19 33
234	**14 16** ☾	**23 46**	**12 07**	**23 31**	**12 21**	**23 12**	**12 38**	**22 46**	**13 02**	**22 04**	**13 41**
23 Su	12 02 42	05 42	18 23	05 32	18 33	05 19	18 46	05 02	19 03	04 33	19 30
235			**13 08**		**13 25**	**23 57**	**13 47**	**23 26**	**14 17**	**22 34**	**15 07**
24 Mo	12 02 26	05 42	18 22	05 32	18 32	05 20	18 44	05 03	19 01	04 36	19 28
236		**00 38**	**14 09**	**00 20**	**14 29**		**14 53**		**15 27**	**23 16**	**16 25**
25 Tu	12 02 10	05 43	18 21	05 32	18 31	05 21	18 42	05 04	18 59	04 38	19 25
237		**01 34**	**15 09**	**01 14**	**15 29**	**00 49**	**15 54**	**00 15**	**16 29**		**17 29**
26 We	12 01 54	05 43	18 20	05 33	18 30	05 22	18 41	05 06	18 57	04 40	19 22
238		**02 32**	**16 05**	**02 12**	**16 24**	**01 47**	**16 48**	**01 12**	**17 21**	**00 12**	**18 17**
27 Th	12 01 37	05 43	18 19	05 34	18 29	05 23	18 40	05 08	18 55	04 42	19 19
239		**03 31**	**16 57**	**03 13**	**17 14**	**02 50**	**17 35**	**02 18**	**18 04**	**01 23**	**18 51**
28 Fr	12 01 20	05 44	18 18	05 34	18 28	05 24	18 38	05 09	18 53	04 45	19 16
240		**04 30**	**17 45**	**04 14**	**17 59**	**03 55**	**18 16**	**03 27**	**18 39**	**02 42**	**19 16**
29 Sa	12 01 02	05 44	18 18	05 35	18 26	05 25	18 36	05 10	18 51	04 48	19 13
241	**14 43** ●	**05 27**	**18 29**	**05 15**	**18 39**	**05 00**	**18 51**	**04 39**	**19 08**	**04 05**	**19 34**
30 Su	12 00 44	05 44	18 17	05 36	18 25	05 26	18 35	05 12	18 49	04 50	19 10
242		**06 23**	**19 10**	**06 14**	**19 16**	**06 04**	**19 23**	**05 50**	**19 33**	**05 28**	**19 48**
31 Mo	12 00 26	05 44	18 16	05 36	18 24	05 27	18 34	05 14	18 47	04 52	19 07
243		**07 16**	**19 48**	**07 11**	**19 50**	**07 06**	**19 52**	**06 59**	**19 56**	**06 48**	**20 01**

9th Month — September, 1981 — 30 Days

Greenwich Mean Time

NOTE: Light figures indicate Sun. **Dark** figures indicate **Moon.** *Degrees are North Latitude.*

CAUTION: Must be converted to local time. For instruction see page 773.

Day of month week year	Sun on meridian **Moon phase**	20° Rise Sun **Moon**	20° Set Sun **Moon**	30° Rise Sun **Moon**	30° Set Sun **Moon**	40° Rise Sun **Moon**	40° Set Sun **Moon**	50° Rise Sun **Moon**	50° Set Sun **Moon**	60° Rise Sun **Moon**	60° Set Sun **Moon**
	h m s	h m	h m	h m	h m	h m	h m	h m	h m	h m	h m
1 Tu	12 00 07	05 44	18 16	05 37	18 22	05 28	18 32	05 15	18 44	04 54	19 04
244		**08 07**	**20 25**	**08 07**	**20 23**	**08 07**	**20 20**	**08 07**	**20 17**	**08 07**	**20 12**
2 We	11 59 48	05 45	18 15	05 38	18 21	05 28	18 30	05 16	18 42	04 57	19 01
245		**08 57**	**21 01**	**09 01**	**20 55**	**09 06**	**20 48**	**09 13**	**20 38**	**09 23**	**20 24**
3 Th	11 59 29	05 45	18 14	05 38	18 20	05 29	18 29	05 18	18 40	04 59	18 58
246		**09 46**	**21 38**	**09 54**	**21 28**	**10 04**	**21 16**	**10 18**	**21 01**	**10 39**	**20 36**
4 Fr	11 59 10	05 45	18 13	05 38	18 19	05 30	18 27	05 20	18 38	05 02	18 55
247		**10 36**	**22 16**	**10 47**	**22 03**	**11 02**	**21 47**	**11 21**	**21 25**	**11 53**	**20 51**
5 Sa	11 58 50	05 46	18 12	05 39	18 18	05 31	18 26	05 21	18 36	05 04	18 52
248		**11 26**	**22 56**	**11 40**	**22 40**	**11 59**	**22 21**	**12 24**	**21 53**	**13 06**	**21 09**
6 Su	11 58 30	05 46	18 11	05 40	18 16	05 32	18 24	05 22	18 33	05 06	18 48
249	**13 26** ☽	**12 16**	**23 39**	**12 33**	**23 21**	**12 55**	**22 58**	**13 26**	**22 27**	**14 17**	**21 34**
7 Mo	11 58 10	05 46	18 10	05 40	18 15	05 33	18 22	05 24	18 31	05 09	18 46
250		**13 07**		**13 26**		**13 50**	**23 41**	**14 24**	**23 06**	**15 22**	**22 07**
8 Tu	11 57 49	05 46	18 09	05 40	18 14	05 34	18 20	05 26	18 29	05 11	18 43
251		**13 58**	**00 25**	**14 18**	**00 06**	**14 43**		**15 19**	**23 54**	**16 20**	**22 53**
9 We	11 57 29	05 46	18 08	05 41	18 13	05 35	18 19	05 27	18 27	05 14	18 40
252		**14 48**	**01 15**	**15 08**	**00 55**	**15 33**	**00 30**	**16 08**		**17 07**	**23 51**
10 Th	11 57 08	05 46	18 07	05 42	18 12	05 36	18 18	05 28	18 25	05 16	18 37
253		**15 38**	**02 08**	**15 56**	**01 48**	**16 19**	**01 24**	**16 50**	**00 50**	**17 43**	
11 Fr	11 56 47	05 46	18 06	05 42	18 11	05 37	18 16	05 30	18 23	05 18	18 34
254		**16 26**	**03 03**	**16 41**	**02 46**	**17 01**	**02 24**	**17 27**	**01 54**	**18 10**	**01 03**
12 Sa	11 56 26	05 46	18 05	05 42	18 10	05 38	18 14	05 31	18 21	05 20	18 31
255		**17 12**	**04 00**	**17 24**	**03 46**	**17 39**	**03 28**	**17 59**	**03 03**	**18 31**	**02 23**
13 Su	11 56 05	05 46	18 04	05 43	18 08	05 39	18 12	05 32	18 18	05 22	18 28
256		**17 57**	**04 59**	**18 05**	**04 48**	**18 14**	**04 35**	**18 28**	**04 18**	**18 48**	**03 49**
14 Mo	11 55 43	05 47	18 04	05 44	18 07	05 40	18 11	05 34	18 16	05 25	18 25
257	**03 09** ○	**18 40**	**05 58**	**18 44**	**05 52**	**18 48**	**05 44**	**18 54**	**05 34**	**19 02**	**05 18**
15 Tu	11 55 22	05 47	18 03	05 44	18 06	05 41	18 09	05 35	18 14	05 27	18 22
258		**19 24**	**06 57**	**19 23**	**06 56**	**19 21**	**06 55**	**19 19**	**06 53**	**19 16**	**06 49**
16 We	11 55 00	05 47	18 02	05 45	18 05	05 42	18 07	05 36	18 12	05 30	18 19
259		**20 08**	**07 57**	**20 02**	**08 01**	**19 55**	**08 06**	**19 45**	**08 12**	**19 31**	**08 21**
17 Th	11 54 39	05 48	18 01	05 46	18 04	05 42	18 06	05 38	18 10	05 32	18 16
260		**20 54**	**08 58**	**20 44**	**09 07**	**20 31**	**09 17**	**20 14**	**09 32**	**19 47**	**09 54**
18 Fr	11 54 18	05 48	18 00	05 46	18 02	05 43	18 04	05 40	18 07	05 34	18 12
261		**21 43**	**10 00**	**21 28**	**10 13**	**21 11**	**10 29**	**20 46**	**10 51**	**20 07**	**11 27**
19 Sa	11 53 56	05 48	17 59	05 47	18 01	05 44	18 02	05 41	18 05	05 37	18 09
262		**22 35**	**11 02**	**22 17**	**11 19**	**21 55**	**11 39**	**21 25**	**12 08**	**20 35**	**12 56**
20 Su	11 53 35	05 48	17 58	05 48	18 00	05 45	18 00	05 42	18 03	05 39	18 06
263	**19 47** ☾	**23 29**	**12 04**	**23 10**	**12 23**	**22 45**	**12 47**	**22 11**	**13 20**	**21 13**	**14 18**
21 Mo	11 53 14	05 48	17 57	05 48	17 58	05 46	17 59	05 44	18 00	05 42	18 03
264			**13 04**		**13 24**	**23 41**	**13 49**	**23 06**	**14 25**	**22 04**	**15 26**
22 Tu	11 52 53	05 49	17 56	05 48	17 57	05 47	17 58	05 46	17 58	05 44	18 00
265		**00 26**	**14 01**	**00 06**	**14 20**		**14 45**		**15 19**	**23 10**	**16 18**
23 We	11 52 31	05 49	17 55	05 49	17 56	05 48	17 56	05 47	17 56	05 46	17 57
266		**01 25**	**14 53**	**01 05**	**15 11**	**00 42**	**15 33**	**00 08**	**16 04**		**16 55**
24 Th	11 52 11	05 49	17 54	05 50	17 55	05 49	17 54	05 49	17 54	05 48	17 54
267		**02 23**	**15 42**	**02 06**	**15 57**	**01 45**	**16 15**	**01 15**	**16 41**	**00 26**	**17 21**
25 Fr	11 51 50	05 50	17 54	05 50	17 54	05 50	17 52	05 50	17 52	05 50	17 51
268		**03 19**	**16 26**	**03 06**	**16 37**	**02 49**	**16 52**	**02 25**	**17 11**	**01 47**	**17 41**
26 Sa	11 51 29	05 50	17 53	05 50	17 52	05 51	17 51	05 52	17 50	05 53	17 48
269		**04 14**	**17 07**	**04 05**	**17 14**	**03 52**	**17 24**	**03 36**	**17 36**	**03 09**	**17 56**
27 Su	11 51 09	05 50	17 52	05 51	17 51	05 52	17 49	05 54	17 48	05 56	17 45
270		**05 07**	**17 45**	**05 02**	**17 49**	**04 55**	**17 53**	**04 45**	**17 59**	**04 30**	**18 08**
28 Mo	11 50 49	05 50	17 51	05 52	17 50	05 53	17 47	05 56	17 46	05 58	17 42
271	**04 07** ●	**05 59**	**18 22**	**05 57**	**18 22**	**05 55**	**18 21**	**05 53**	**18 20**	**05 49**	**18 19**
29 Tu	11 50 29	05 50	17 50	05 52	17 48	05 54	17 46	05 57	17 44	06 00	17 39
272		**06 49**	**18 58**	**06 52**	**18 54**	**06 55**	**18 49**	**06 59**	**18 41**	**07 06**	**18 30**
30 We	11 50 09	05 51	17 49	05 52	17 47	05 55	17 44	05 58	17 41	06 03	17 36
273		**07 39**	**19 35**	**07 46**	**19 27**	**07 54**	**19 17**	**08 05**	**19 03**	**08 22**	**18 42**

10th Month — October, 1981 — 31 Days

Greenwich Mean Time

NOTE: Light figures indicate Sun. **Dark** figures indicate **Moon.** *Degrees are North Latitude.*

CAUTION: Must be converted to local time. For instruction see page 773.

Day of month week year	Sun on meridian **Moon phase**	20° Rise Sun **Moon**	20° Set Sun **Moon**	30° Rise Sun **Moon**	30° Set Sun **Moon**	40° Rise Sun **Moon**	40° Set Sun **Moon**	50° Rise Sun **Moon**	50° Set Sun **Moon**	60° Rise Sun **Moon**	60° Set Sun **Moon**
	h m s	h m	h m	h m	h m	h m	h m	h m	h m	h m	h m
1 Th	11 49 50	05 51	17 48	05 53	17 46	05 56	17 43	06 00	17 39	06 05	17 33
274		**08 29**	**20 13**	**08 39**	**20 10**	**08 52**	**19 46**	**09 09**	**19 26**	**09 37**	**18 55**
2 Fr	11 49 30	05 51	17 47	05 54	17 45	05 57	17 41	06 02	17 37	06 08	17 30
275		**09 19**	**20 52**	**09 32**	**20 37**	**09 49**	**20 18**	**10 13**	**19 53**	**10 51**	**19 12**
3 Sa	11 49 11	05 52	17 46	05 54	17 44	05 58	17 40	06 03	17 34	06 10	17 27
276		**10 09**	**21 34**	**10 25**	**21 16**	**10 46**	**20 54**	**11 15**	**20 24**	**12 04**	**19 34**
4 Su	11 48 53	05 52	17 46	05 55	17 42	05 59	17 38	06 04	17 32	06 12	17 24
277		**10 59**	**22 18**	**11 18**	**21 59**	**11 41**	**21 34**	**12 15**	**21 00**	**13 11**	**20 02**
5 Mo	11 48 35	05 52	17 45	05 56	17 41	06 00	17 36	06 06	17 30	06 15	17 21
278		**11 49**	**23 06**	**12 10**	**22 45**	**12 35**	**22 20**	**13 10**	**21 44**	**14 12**	**20 42**
6 Tu	11 48 17	05 52	17 44	05 56	17 40	06 01	17 34	06 08	17 28	06 17	17 18
279	**07 45** ☽	**12 39**	**23 56**	**13 00**	**23 36**	**13 25**	**23 11**	**14 01**	**22 35**	**15 03**	**21 34**
7 We	11 47 59	05 52	17 43	05 57	17 38	06 02	17 33	06 09	17 26	06 20	17 15
280		**13 28**		**13 48**		**14 12**		**14 45**	**23 35**	**15 42**	**22 39**
8 Th	11 47 42	05 53	17 42	05 58	17 37	06 03	17 32	06 10	17 24	06 22	17 12
281		**14 16**	**00 49**	**14 33**	**00 31**	**14 54**	**00 08**	**15 24**		**16 12**	**23 55**
9 Fr	11 47 25	05 53	17 41	05 58	17 36	06 04	17 30	06 12	17 22	06 24	17 09
282		**15 02**	**01 45**	**15 16**	**01 29**	**15 33**	**01 09**	**15 57**	**00 41**	**16 35**	
10 Sa	11 47 09	05 53	17 40	05 58	17 35	06 05	17 28	06 14	17 20	06 26	17 06
283		**15 47**	**02 42**	**15 57**	**02 29**	**16 10**	**02 14**	**16 26**	**01 52**	**16 53**	**01 17**
11 Su	11 46 53	05 54	17 40	05 59	17 34	06 06	17 27	06 15	17 18	06 29	17 03
284		**16 31**	**03 40**	**16 37**	**03 32**	**16 44**	**03 21**	**16 53**	**03 07**	**17 08**	**02 45**
12 Mo	11 46 37	05 54	17 39	06 00	17 33	06 07	17 26	06 16	17 15	06 32	17 00
285		**17 15**	**04 39**	**17 16**	**04 36**	**17 17**	**04 31**	**17 19**	**04 25**	**17 21**	**04 16**
13 Tu	11 46 22	05 54	17 38	06 00	17 32	06 08	17 24	06 18	17 13	06 34	16 57
286	**12 49** ○	**17 59**	**05 40**	**17 55**	**05 42**	**17 51**	**05 43**	**17 45**	**05 46**	**17 35**	**05 49**
14 We	11 46 08	05 54	17 37	06 01	17 31	06 09	17 22	06 20	17 11	06 36	16 54
287		**18 45**	**06 42**	**18 37**	**06 49**	**18 26**	**06 57**	**18 12**	**07 07**	**17 51**	**07 24**
15 Th	11 45 54	05 54	17 36	06 02	17 30	06 10	17 21	06 22	17 09	06 39	16 52
288		**19 35**	**07 46**	**19 21**	**07 57**	**19 05**	**08 11**	**18 44**	**08 30**	**18 09**	**09 01**
16 Fr	11 45 41	05 55	17 36	06 02	17 28	06 11	17 20	06 23	17 07	06 42	16 49
289		**20 27**	**08 51**	**20 10**	**09 06**	**19 49**	**09 25**	**19 20**	**09 52**	**18 34**	**10 36**
17 Sa	11 45 28	05 55	17 35	06 03	17 27	06 12	17 18	06 25	17 05	06 44	16 46
290		**21 22**	**09 55**	**21 03**	**10 13**	**20 39**	**10 37**	**20 05**	**11 09**	**19 08**	**12 05**
18 Su	11 45 16	05 56	17 34	06 04	17 26	06 13	17 16	06 26	17 03	06 46	16 43
291		**22 20**	**10 58**	**22 00**	**11 18**	**21 34**	**11 43**	**20 58**	**12 19**	**19 56**	**13 21**
19 Mo	11 45 04	05 56	17 34	06 04	17 25	06 14	17 15	06 28	17 01	06 49	16 40
292		**23 19**	**11 57**	**22 59**	**12 17**	**22 35**	**12 42**	**21 59**	**13 18**	**20 59**	**14 19**
20 Tu	11 44 54	05 56	17 33	06 05	17 24	06 16	17 14	06 30	16 59	06 52	16 37
293	**03 40** ☾		**12 51**		**13 10**	**23 38**	**13 33**	**23 06**	**14 06**	**22 14**	**15 01**
21 We	11 44 44	05 57	17 32	06 06	17 23	06 17	17 12	06 31	16 57	06 54	16 34
294		**00 18**	**13 41**	**00 00**	**13 57**		**14 17**		**14 45**	**23 34**	**15 29**
22 Th	11 44 34	05 57	17 32	06 07	17 22	06 18	17 11	06 33	16 55	06 56	16 31
295		**01 15**	**14 26**	**01 00**	**14 39**	**00 42**	**14 54**	**00 16**	**15 16**		**15 50**
23 Fr	11 44 25	05 58	17 31	06 08	17 21	06 19	17 10	06 34	16 54	06 59	16 28
296		**02 10**	**15 07**	**01 59**	**15 16**	**01 45**	**15 27**	**01 26**	**15 42**	**00 55**	**16 05**
24 Sa	11 44 17	05 58	17 30	06 08	17 20	06 20	17 08	06 36	16 52	07 02	16 26
297		**03 03**	**15 45**	**02 56**	**15 51**	**02 47**	**15 57**	**02 35**	**16 05**	**02 16**	**16 17**
25 Su	11 44 09	05 58	17 30	06 09	17 19	06 21	17 07	06 38	16 50	07 04	16 23
298		**03 54**	**16 22**	**03 51**	**16 23**	**03 47**	**16 24**	**03 42**	**16 26**	**03 34**	**16 28**
26 Mo	11 44 03	05 58	17 29	06 10	17 18	06 22	17 06	06 40	16 48	07 06	16 20
299		**04 44**	**16 58**	**04 45**	**16 55**	**04 47**	**16 51**	**04 49**	**16 46**	**04 51**	**16 39**
27 Tu	11 43 57	05 59	17 28	06 10	17 18	06 23	17 04	06 41	16 46	07 09	16 18
300	**20 13** ●	**05 34**	**17 34**	**05 39**	**17 27**	**05 45**	**17 19**	**05 54**	**17 07**	**06 08**	**16 50**
28 We	11 43 51	06 00	17 28	06 10	17 17	06 24	17 03	06 42	16 44	07 12	16 15
301		**06 23**	**18 11**	**06 32**	**18 00**	**06 44**	**17 47**	**06 59**	**17 30**	**07 23**	**17 02**
29 Th	11 43 47	06 00	17 27	06 11	17 16	06 25	17 02	06 44	16 42	07 14	16 12
302		**07 13**	**18 50**	**07 26**	**18 36**	**07 42**	**18 18**	**08 03**	**17 54**	**08 38**	**17 17**
30 Fr	11 43 43	06 00	17 26	06 12	17 15	06 26	17 01	06 46	16 40	07 16	16 10
303		**08 03**	**19 30**	**08 19**	**19 13**	**08 39**	**18 52**	**09 06**	**18 23**	**09 52**	**17 36**
31 Sa	11 43 40	06 01	17 26	06 13	17 14	06 28	17 00	06 47	16 38	07 19	16 07
304		**08 54**	**20 14**	**09 12**	**19 55**	**09 35**	**19 31**	**10 07**	**18 57**	**11 02**	**18 01**

11th Month November, 1981 30 Days

Greenwich Mean Time

NOTE: Light figures indicate Sun. **Dark** figures indicate **Moon.** *Degrees are North Latitude.*

CAUTION: Must be converted to local time. For instruction see page 773.

Day of month week year	Sun on meridian **Moon phase**	20° Rise Sun **Moon**	20° Set Sun **Moon**	30° Rise Sun **Moon**	30° Set Sun **Moon**	40° Rise Sun **Moon**	40° Set Sun **Moon**	50° Rise Sun **Moon**	50° Set Sun **Moon**	60° Rise Sun **Moon**	60° Set Sun **Moon**
	h m s	h m	h m	h m	h m	h m	h m	h m	h m	h m	h m
1 Su	11 43 38	06 02	17 26	06 14	17 13	06 29	16 58	06 49	16 37	07 22	16 04
305		**09 44**	**21 00**	**10 04**	**20 39**	**10 29**	**20 14**	**11 05**	**19 38**	**12 06**	**18 36**
2 Mo	11 43 37	06 02	17 25	06 15	17 12	06 30	16 57	06 51	16 35	07 24	16 02
306		**10 34**	**21 49**	**10 54**	**21 28**	**11 20**	**21 02**	**11 57**	**20 26**	**13 01**	**19 22**
3 Tu	11 43 36	06 02	17 24	06 16	17 11	06 31	16 56	06 53	16 34	07 27	16 00
307		**11 22**	**22 40**	**11 42**	**22 20**	**12 08**	**21 56**	**12 43**	**21 21**	**13 44**	**20 21**
4 We	11 43 36	06 03	17 24	06 16	17 10	06 32	16 54	06 54	16 32	07 30	15 57
308		**12 09**	**23 33**	**12 28**	**23 16**	**12 51**	**22 54**	**13 23**	**22 23**	**14 16**	**21 32**
5 Th	11 43 37	06 04	17 24	06 17	17 10	06 34	16 53	06 56	16 30	07 32	15 54
309	**01 09** ☽	**12 55**		**13 11**		**13 30**	**23 56**	**13 57**	**23 31**	**14 40**	**22 50**
6 Fr	11 43 39	06 04	17 23	06 18	17 09	06 35	16 52	06 58	16 29	07 35	15 52
310		**13 39**	**00 28**	**13 51**	**00 13**	**14 06**		**14 27**		**14 59**	
7 Sa	11 43 42	06 04	17 23	06 19	17 08	06 36	16 51	07 00	16 28	07 38	15 50
311		**14 21**	**01 24**	**14 30**	**01 13**	**14 40**	**01 00**	**14 53**	**00 42**	**15 14**	**00 13**
8 Su	11 43 45	06 05	17 22	06 20	17 08	06 37	16 50	07 01	16 26	07 40	15 47
312		**15 04**	**02 21**	**15 08**	**02 15**	**15 12**	**02 07**	**15 18**	**01 57**	**15 27**	**01 40**
9 Mo	11 43 49	06 06	17 22	06 20	17 08	06 38	16 49	07 02	16 24	07 42	15 44
313		**15 47**	**03 20**	**15 46**	**03 19**	**15 45**	**03 17**	**15 43**	**03 15**	**15 40**	**03 11**
10 Tu	11 43 54	06 06	17 22	06 21	17 07	06 39	16 48	07 04	16 23	07 45	15 42
314		**16 32**	**04 21**	**16 26**	**04 24**	**16 19**	**04 29**	**16 09**	**04 35**	**15 54**	**04 45**
11 We	11 44 00	06 06	17 22	06 22	17 06	06 40	16 47	07 06	16 22	07 48	15 40
315	**22 26** ○	**17 20**	**05 24**	**17 09**	**05 33**	**16 56**	**05 43**	**16 38**	**05 58**	**16 10**	**06 21**
12 Th	11 44 07	06 07	17 22	06 22	17 06	06 42	16 46	07 08	16 20	07 50	15 38
316		**18 12**	**06 29**	**17 57**	**06 43**	**17 38**	**06 59**	**17 12**	**07 22**	**16 31**	**08 00**
13 Fr	11 44 15	06 08	17 21	06 23	17 06	06 43	16 46	07 09	16 18	07 52	15 35
317		**19 08**	**07 36**	**18 49**	**07 53**	**18 26**	**08 15**	**17 54**	**08 45**	**17 01**	**09 36**
14 Sa	11 44 23	06 08	17 21	06 24	17 05	06 44	16 45	07 11	16 17	07 55	15 33
318		**20 07**	**08 42**	**19 47**	**09 02**	**19 21**	**09 27**	**18 45**	**10 02**	**17 43**	**11 03**
15 Su	11 44 32	06 09	17 21	06 25	17 04	06 45	16 44	07 12	16 16	07 58	15 31
319		**21 08**	**09 46**	**20 48**	**10 06**	**20 22**	**10 32**	**19 45**	**11 09**	**18 42**	**12 12**
16 Mo	11 44 43	06 10	17 20	06 26	17 04	06 46	16 44	07 14	16 15	08 00	15 29
320		**22 09**	**10 45**	**21 50**	**11 04**	**21 27**	**11 29**	**20 53**	**12 04**	**19 56**	**13 02**
17 Tu	11 44 54	06 10	17 20	06 26	17 04	06 47	16 43	07 16	16 14	08 02	15 27
321		**23 09**	**11 38**	**22 53**	**11 55**	**22 32**	**12 17**	**22 04**	**12 47**	**21 17**	**13 36**
18 We	11 45 05	06 11	17 20	06 27	17 03	06 48	16 42	07 17	16 13	08 05	15 25
322	**14 54** ☾		**12 25**	**23 53**	**12 39**	**23 37**	**12 57**	**23 15**	**13 21**	**22 41**	**13 59**
19 Th	11 45 18	06 12	17 20	06 28	17 02	06 49	16 41	07 19	16 12	08 08	15 23
323		**00 06**	**13 08**		**13 18**		**13 31**		**13 48**		**14 15**
20 Fr	11 45 32	06 12	17 20	06 29	17 02	06 50	16 40	07 20	16 10	08 10	15 21
324		**01 00**	**13 47**	**00 51**	**13 54**	**00 40**	**14 02**	**00 26**	**14 12**	**00 02**	**14 28**
21 Sa	11 45 46	06 12	17 19	06 30	17 02	06 52	16 40	07 22	16 09	08 12	15 19
325		**01 51**	**14 24**	**01 47**	**14 26**	**01 41**	**14 29**	**01 34**	**14 33**	**01 22**	**14 39**
22 Su	11 46 01	06 13	17 19	06 31	17 01	06 53	16 39	07 24	16 08	08 15	15 17
326		**02 42**	**15 00**	**02 41**	**14 58**	**02 41**	**14 56**	**02 40**	**14 53**	**02 39**	**14 49**
23 Mo	11 46 18	06 14	17 19	06 32	17 01	06 54	16 38	07 26	16 07	08 17	15 15
327		**03 31**	**15 35**	**03 35**	**15 30**	**03 39**	**15 23**	**03 45**	**15 13**	**03 55**	**14 59**
24 Tu	11 46 34	06 14	17 19	06 32	17 00	06 55	16 38	07 27	16 06	08 20	15 14
328		**04 20**	**16 11**	**04 28**	**16 02**	**04 37**	**15 50**	**04 50**	**15 35**	**05 11**	**15 11**
25 We	11 46 52	06 14	17 19	06 33	17 00	06 56	16 38	07 28	16 06	08 22	15 12
329		**05 09**	**16 49**	**05 21**	**16 36**	**05 35**	**16 20**	**05 55**	**15 58**	**06 26**	**15 24**
26 Th	11 47 10	06 15	17 19	06 34	17 00	06 57	16 37	07 30	16 05	08 24	15 10
330	**14 38** ●	**05 59**	**17 29**	**06 14**	**17 13**	**06 32**	**16 53**	**06 58**	**16 25**	**07 41**	**15 41**
27 Fr	11 47 30	06 16	17 19	06 35	17 00	06 58	16 37	07 31	16 04	08 26	15 08
331		**06 50**	**18 11**	**07 07**	**17 53**	**07 29**	**17 30**	**08 00**	**16 57**	**08 53**	**16 03**
28 Sa	11 47 49	06 16	17 19	06 36	17 00	06 59	16 36	07 32	16 04	08 28	15 07
332		**07 40**	**18 57**	**08 00**	**18 36**	**08 25**	**18 11**	**09 00**	**17 35**	**10 00**	**16 34**
29 Su	11 48 10	06 17	17 19	06 36	17 00	07 00	16 36	07 34	16 03	08 31	15 06
333		**08 30**	**19 45**	**08 51**	**19 24**	**09 17**	**18 58**	**09 54**	**18 21**	**10 58**	**17 16**
30 Mo	11 48 31	06 18	17 19	06 37	17 00	07 01	16 36	07 35	16 02	08 33	15 04
334		**09 19**	**20 35**	**09 40**	**20 15**	**10 06**	**19 49**	**10 42**	**19 13**	**11 45**	**18 11**

12th Month December, 1981 31 days

Greenwich Mean Time

NOTE: Light figures indicate Sun. **Dark** figures indicate **Moon.** *Degrees are North Latitude.*

CAUTION: Must be converted to local time. For instruction see page 773.

Day of month week year	Sun on meridian **Moon phase**	20° Rise Sun **Moon**	20° Set Sun **Moon**	30° Rise Sun **Moon**	30° Set Sun **Moon**	40° Rise Sun **Moon**	40° Set Sun **Moon**	50° Rise Sun **Moon**	50° Set Sun **Moon**	60° Rise Sun **Moon**	60° Set Sun **Moon**
	h m s	h m	h m	h m	h m	h m	h m	h m	h m	h m	h m
1 Tu	11 48 53	06 19	17 19	06 38	17 00	07 02	16 36	07 36	16 02	08 35	15 03
335		**10 07**	**21 27**	**10 26**	**21 09**	**10 50**	**20 45**	**11 24**	**20 13**	**12 21**	**19 17**
2 We	11 49 16	06 20	17 20	06 38	17 00	07 03	16 36	07 38	16 01	08 37	15 02
336		**10 52**	**22 20**	**11 09**	**22 04**	**11 30**	**21 45**	**11 59**	**21 17**	**12 47**	**20 31**
3 Th	11 49 39	06 20	17 20	06 39	17 00	07 04	16 35	07 39	16 00	08 39	15 00
337		**11 35**	**23 14**	**11 49**	**23 02**	**12 06**	**22 47**	**12 30**	**22 25**	**13 07**	**21 51**
4 Fr	11 50 03	06 21	17 20	06 40	17 00	07 05	16 35	07 40	16 00	08 41	14 59
338	**16 22** ☽	**12 17**		**12 27**		**12 40**	**23 50**	**12 56**	**23 36**	**13 22**	**23 14**
5 Sa	11 50 27	06 22	17 20	06 41	17 00	07 06	16 35	07 41	16 00	08 43	14 58
339		**12 58**	**00 09**	**13 04**	**00 01**	**13 11**		**13 21**		**13 35**	
6 Su	11 50 52	06 22	17 20	06 42	17 00	07 07	16 35	07 42	15 59	08 44	14 58
340		**13 39**	**01 05**	**13 40**	**01 01**	**13 42**	**00 56**	**13 44**	**00 50**	**13 47**	**00 40**
7 Mo	11 51 17	06 22	17 21	06 42	17 00	07 08	16 35	07 44	15 58	08 46	14 57
341		**14 21**	**02 02**	**14 18**	**02 03**	**14 14**	**02 05**	**14 08**	**02 06**	**14 00**	**02 09**
8 Tu	11 51 43	06 23	17 21	06 43	17 00	07 09	16 35	07 45	15 58	08 48	14 56
342		**15 06**	**03 02**	**14 58**	**03 08**	**14 48**	**03 16**	**14 34**	**03 26**	**14 14**	**03 41**
9 We	11 52 09	06 24	17 21	06 44	17 00	07 10	16 35	07 46	15 58	08 50	14 56
343		**15 55**	**04 05**	**15 42**	**04 16**	**15 26**	**04 29**	**15 05**	**04 48**	**14 31**	**05 17**
10 Th	11 52 36	06 24	17 22	06 44	17 00	07 10	16 35	07 47	15 58	08 51	14 55
344		**16 48**	**05 10**	**16 31**	**05 26**	**16 10**	**05 45**	**15 41**	**06 11**	**14 55**	**06 55**
11 Fr	11 53 03	06 24	17 22	06 45	17 01	07 11	16 35	07 48	15 58	08 52	14 54
345	**08 41** ○	**17 46**	**06 18**	**17 26**	**06 36**	**17 02**	**07 00**	**16 27**	**07 33**	**15 29**	**08 29**
12 Sa	11 53 31	06 25	17 22	06 46	17 01	07 12	16 35	07 49	15 58	08 54	14 54
346		**18 48**	**07 24**	**18 27**	**07 45**	**18 01**	**08 11**	**17 24**	**08 48**	**16 20**	**09 51**
13 Su	11 53 59	06 26	17 22	06 47	17 01	07 13	16 35	07 50	15 58	08 55	14 54
347		**19 52**	**08 28**	**19 32**	**08 49**	**19 06**	**09 14**	**18 31**	**09 51**	**17 29**	**10 53**
14 Mo	11 54 27	06 26	17 23	06 48	17 02	07 14	16 36	07 51	15 58	08 56	14 54
348		**20 55**	**09 26**	**20 37**	**09 45**	**20 15**	**10 08**	**19 43**	**10 41**	**18 51**	**11 36**
15 Tu	11 54 56	06 27	17 24	06 48	17 02	07 14	16 36	07 52	15 59	08 57	14 53
349		**21 55**	**10 18**	**21 41**	**10 34**	**21 23**	**10 54**	**20 58**	**11 21**	**20 17**	**12 04**
16 We	11 55 25	06 28	17 24	06 49	17 02	07 15	16 36	07 53	15 59	08 58	14 53
350		**22 52**	**11 05**	**22 42**	**11 17**	**22 29**	**11 32**	**22 11**	**11 52**	**21 43**	**12 23**
17 Th	11 55 54	06 28	17 24	06 50	17 02	07 16	16 36	07 54	15 59	08 59	14 53
351		**23 46**	**11 46**	**23 40**	**11 54**	**23 32**	**12 04**	**23 22**	**12 17**	**23 06**	**12 38**
18 Fr	11 56 23	06 29	17 24	06 50	17 03	07 16	16 36	07 54	16 00	09 00	14 54
352	**05 47** ☾		**12 25**		**12 29**		**12 33**		**12 40**		**12 49**
19 Sa	11 56 53	06 30	17 25	06 50	17 04	07 17	16 37	07 54	16 00	09 00	14 54
353		**00 37**	**13 01**	**00 36**	**13 01**	**00 33**	**13 01**	**00 30**	**13 00**	**00 25**	**13 00**
20 Su	11 57 22	06 30	17 25	06 51	17 04	07 18	16 37	07 55	16 00	09 01	14 54
354		**01 27**	**13 37**	**01 30**	**13 32**	**01 32**	**13 27**	**01 36**	**13 20**	**01 42**	**13 10**
21 Mo	11 57 52	06 30	17 26	06 52	17 04	07 18	16 38	07 56	16 00	09 02	14 54
355		**02 16**	**14 12**	**02 23**	**14 04**	**02 31**	**13 54**	**02 41**	**13 41**	**02 58**	**13 20**
22 Tu	11 58 22	06 31	17 26	06 52	17 05	07 19	16 38	07 56	16 01	09 02	14 55
356		**03 05**	**14 49**	**03 16**	**14 37**	**03 28**	**14 23**	**03 46**	**14 03**	**04 13**	**13 32**
23 We	11 58 52	06 32	17 26	06 52	17 06	07 20	16 39	07 56	16 02	09 02	14 56
357		**03 55**	**15 28**	**04 09**	**15 13**	**04 26**	**14 54**	**04 50**	**14 29**	**05 28**	**13 48**
24 Th	11 59 22	06 32	17 27	06 53	17 06	07 20	16 40	07 57	16 02	09 03	14 56
358		**04 45**	**16 09**	**05 02**	**15 52**	**05 23**	**15 29**	**05 52**	**14 59**	**06 41**	**14 08**
25 Fr	11 59 52	06 32	17 28	06 54	17 07	07 20	16 40	07 57	16 03	09 03	14 57
359		**05 36**	**16 54**	**05 55**	**16 34**	**06 19**	**16 09**	**06 53**	**15 35**	**07 51**	**14 35**
26 Sa	12 00 22	06 33	17 28	06 54	17 08	07 20	16 41	07 58	16 04	09 04	14 58
360	**10 10** ●	**06 27**	**17 41**	**06 47**	**17 20**	**07 13**	**16 54**	**07 49**	**16 17**	**08 53**	**15 13**
27 Su	12 00 52	06 34	17 29	06 54	17 08	07 21	16 42	07 58	16 04	09 04	14 59
361		**07 19**	**18 31**	**07 37**	**18 11**	**08 03**	**17 45**	**08 40**	**17 08**	**09 45**	**16 04**
28 Mo	12 01 21	06 34	17 30	06 55	17 09	07 21	16 42	07 58	16 05	09 04	15 00
362		**08 05**	**19 23**	**08 25**	**19 04**	**08 50**	**18 40**	**09 25**	**18 06**	**10 24**	**17 07**
29 Tu	12 01 51	06 34	17 30	06 55	17 10	07 21	16 43	07 58	16 06	09 04	15 01
363		**08 51**	**20 16**	**09 09**	**19 59**	**09 31**	**19 38**	**10 02**	**19 09**	**10 53**	**18 20**
30 We	12 02 20	06 34	17 31	06 56	17 10	07 22	16 44	07 58	16 07	09 04	15 02
364		**09 35**	**21 10**	**09 50**	**20 56**	**10 09**	**20 39**	**10 34**	**20 16**	**11 15**	**19 38**
31 Th	12 02 49	06 35	17 32	06 56	17 10	07 22	16 44	07 59	16 08	09 03	15 04
365		**10 17**	**22 04**	**10 28**	**21 54**	**10 42**	**21 42**	**11 01**	**21 25**	**11 31**	**20 59**

Julian and Gregorian Calendars; Leap Year

Calendars based on the movements of sun and moon have been used since ancient times, but none has been perfect. The Julian calendar, under which western nations measured time until 1582 A.D., was authorized by Julius Caesar in 46 B.C., the year 709 of Rome. His expert was a Greek, Sosigenes. The Julian calendar, on the assumption that the true year was 365 1/4 days long, gave every fourth year 366 days. The Venerable Bede, an Anglo-Saxon monk, announced in 730 A.D. that the 365 1/4-day Julian year was 11 min., 14 sec. too long, making a cumulative error of about a day every 128 years, but nothing was done about it for over 800 years.

By 1582 the accumulated error was estimated to have amounted to 10 days. In that year Pope Gregory XIII decreed that the day following Oct. 4, 1582, should be called Oct. 15, thus dropping 10 days.

However, with common years 365 days and a 366-day leap year every fourth year, the error in the length of the year would have recurred at the rate of a little more than 3 days every 400 years. So 3 of every 4 centesimal years (ending in 00) were made common years, not leap years. Thus 1600 was a leap year, 1700, 1800 and 1900 were not, but 2000 will be. Leap years are those divisible by 4 except centesimal years, which are common unless divisible by 400.

The Gregorian calendar was adopted at once by France, Italy, Spain, Portugal and Luxembourg. Within 2 years most German Catholic states, Belgium and parts of Switzerland and the Netherlands were brought under the new calendar, and Hungary followed in 1587. The rest of the Netherlands, along with Denmark and the German Protestant states made the change in 1699-1700 (German Protestants retained the old reckoning of Easter until 1776).

The British Government imposed the Gregorian calendar on all its possessions, including the American colonies, in 1752. The British decreed that the day following Sept. 2, 1752, should be called Sept. 14, a loss of 11 days. All dates preceding were marked O.S., for Old Style. In addition New Year's Day was moved to Jan. 1 from Mar. 25. (e.g., under the old reckoning, Mar. 24, 1700 had been followed by Mar. 25, 1701.) George Washington's birth date, which was Feb. 11, 1731, O.S., became Feb. 22, 1732, N.S. In 1753 Sweden too went Gregorian, retaining the old Easter rules until 1844.

In 1793 the French Revolutionary Government adopted a calendar of 12 months of 30 days each with 5 extra days in September of each common year and a 6th extra day every 4th year. Napoleon reinstated the Gregorian calendar in 1806.

The Gregorian system later spread to non-European regions, first in the European colonies, then in the independent countries, replacing traditional calendars at least for official purposes. Japan in 1873, Egypt in 1875, China in 1912 and Turkey in 1917 made the change, usually in conjunction with political upheavals. In China, the republican government began reckoning years from its 1911 founding — e.g., 1948 was designated the year 37. After 1949, the Communists adopted the Common, or Christian Era year count, even for the traditional lunar calendar.

In 1918 the revolutionary government in Russia decreed that the day after Jan. 31, 1918, Old Style, would become Feb. 13, 1918, New Style. Greece followed in 1923. (In Russia the Orthodox Church has retained the Julian calendar, as have various Middle Eastern Christian sects.) For the first time in history, all major cultures have been brought under one calendar.

To change from the Julian to the Gregorian calendar, add 10 days to dates Oct. 5, 1582, through Feb. 28, 1700; after that date add 11 days through Feb. 28, 1800; 12 days through Feb. 28, 1900; and 13 days through Feb. 28, 2100.

Julian Calendar

To find which of the 14 calendars printed on pages 788-789 applies to any year under the Julian system, find the century for the desired year in the three left-hand columns below; read across. Then find the year in the four top rows; read down. The number in the intersection is the calendar designation for that year.

Year (last two figures of desired year)

				01	02	03	04	05	06	07	08	09	10	11	12	13	14	15	16	17	18	19	20	21	22	23	24	25	26	27	28
				29	30	31	32	33	34	35	36	37	38	39	40	41	42	43	44	45	46	47	48	49	50	51	52	53	54	55	56
				57	58	59	60	61	62	63	64	65	66	67	68	69	70	71	72	73	74	75	76	77	78	79	80	81	82	83	84
Century			00	85	86	87	88	89	90	91	92	93	94	95	96	97	98	99													
0	700	1400	12	7	1	2	10	5	6	7	8	3	4	5	13	1	2	3	11	6	7	1	9	4	5	6	14	2	3	4	12
100	800	1500	11	6	7	1	9	4	5	6	14	2	3	4	12	7	1	2	10	5	6	7	8	3	4	5	13	1	2	3	11
200	900	1600	10	5	6	7	8	3	4	5	13	1	2	3	11	6	7	1	9	4	5	6	14	2	3	4	12	7	1	2	10
300	1000	1700	9	4	5	6	14	2	3	4	12	7	1	2	10	5	6	7	8	3	4	5	13	1	2	3	11	6	7	1	9
400	1100	1800	8	3	4	5	13	1	2	3	11	6	7	1	9	4	5	6	14	2	3	4	12	7	1	2	10	5	6	7	8
500	1200	1900	14	2	3	4	12	7	1	2	10	5	6	7	8	3	4	5	13	1	2	3	11	6	7	1	9	4	5	6	14
600	1300	2000	13	1	2	3	11	6	7	1	9	4	5	6	14	2	3	4	12	7	1	2	10	5	6	7	8	3	4	5	13

Gregorian Calendar

Pick desired year from table below or on page 788 (for years 1800 to 2059). The number shown with each year shows which calendar to use for that year, as shown on pages 788-789 (The Gregorian calendar was inaugurated Oct. 15, 1582. From that date to Dec. 31, 1582, use calendar 6.)

1583-1802

1583 . . 7	1603 . . 4	1623 . . 1	1643 . . 5	1663 . . 2	1683 . . 6	1703 . . 2	1723 . . 6	1743 . . 3	1763 . . 7	1783 . . 4
1584 . . 8	1604 . 12	1624 . . 9	1644 . 13	1664 . 10	1684 . 14	1704 . 10	1724 . 14	1744 . 11	1764 . . 8	1784 . 12
1585 . . 3	1605 . . 7	1625 . . 4	1645 . . 1	1665 . . 5	1685 . . 2	1705 . . 5	1725 . . 2	1745 . . 6	1765 . . 3	1785 . . 7
1586 . . 4	1606 . . 1	1626 . . 5	1646 . . 2	1666 . . 6	1686 . . 3	1706 . . 6	1726 . . 3	1746 . . 7	1766 . . 4	1786 . . 1
1587 . . 5	1607 . . 2	1627 . . 6	1647 . . 3	1667 . . 7	1687 . . 4	1707 . . 7	1727 . . 4	1747 . . 1	1767 . . 5	1787 . . 2
1588 . 13	1608 . 10	1628 . 14	1648 . 11	1668 . . 8	1688 . 12	1708 . . 8	1728 . 12	1748 . . 9	1768 . 13	1788 . 10
1589 . . 1	1609 . . 5	1629 . . 2	1649 . . 6	1669 . . 3	1689 . . 7	1709 . . 3	1729 . . 7	1749 . . 4	1769 . . 1	1789 . . 5
1590 . . 2	1610 . . 6	1630 . . 3	1650 . . 7	1670 . . 4	1690 . . 1	1710 . . 4	1730 . . 1	1750 . . 5	1770 . . 2	1790 . . 6
1591 . . 3	1611 . . 7	1631 . . 4	1651 . . 1	1671 . . 5	1691 . . 2	1711 . . 5	1731 . . 2	1751 . . 6	1771 . . 3	1791 . . 7
1592 . 11	1612 . . 8	1632 . 12	1652 . . 9	1672 . 13	1692 . 10	1712 . 13	1732 . 10	1752 . 14	1772 . 11	1792 . . 8
1593 . . 6	1613 . . 3	1633 . . 7	1653 . . 4	1673 . . 1	1693 . . 5	1713 . . 1	1733 . . 5	1753 . . 2	1773 . . 6	1793 . . 3
1594 . . 7	1614 . . 4	1634 . . 1	1654 . . 5	1674 . . 2	1694 . . 6	1714 . . 2	1734 . . 6	1754 . . 3	1774 . . 7	1794 . . 4
1595 . . 1	1615 . . 5	1635 . . 2	1655 . . 6	1675 . . 3	1695 . . 7	1715 . . 3	1735 . . 7	1755 . . 4	1775 . . 1	1795 . . 5
1596 . . 9	1616 . 13	1636 . 10	1656 . 14	1676 . 11	1696 . . 8	1716 . 11	1736 . . 8	1756 . 12	1776 . . 9	1796 . 13
1597 . . 4	1617 . . 1	1637 . . 5	1657 . . 2	1677 . . 6	1697 . . 3	1717 . . 6	1737 . . 3	1757 . . 7	1777 . . 4	1797 . . 1
1598 . . 5	1618 . . 2	1638 . . 6	1658 . . 3	1678 . . 7	1698 . . 4	1718 . . 7	1738 . . 4	1758 . . 1	1778 . . 5	1798 . . 2
1599 . . 6	1619 . . 3	1639 . . 7	1659 . . 4	1679 . . 1	1699 . . 5	1719 . . 1	1739 . . 5	1759 . . 2	1779 . . 6	1799 . . 3
1600 . 14	1620 . 11	1640 . . 8	1660 . 12	1680 . . 9	1700 . . 6	1720 . . 9	1740 . 13	1760 . 10	1780 . 14	1800 . . 4
1601 . . 2	1621 . . 6	1641 . . 3	1661 . . 7	1681 . . 4	1701 . . 7	1721 . . 4	1741 . . 1	1761 . . 5	1781 . . 2	1801 . . 5
1602 . . 3	1622 . . 7	1642 . . 4	1662 . . 1	1682 . . 5	1702 . . 1	1722 . . 5	1742 . . 2	1762 . . 6	1782 . . 3	1802 . . 6

The Julian Period

How many days have you lived? To determine this, you must multiply your age by 365, add the number of days since your last birthday until today, and account for all leap years. Chances are your answer would be wrong. Astronomers, however, find it convenient to express dates and long time intervals in days rather than in years, months and days. This is done by placing events within the Julian period.

The Julian period was devised in 1582 by Joseph Scaliger and named after his father Julius (not after the Julian calendar). Scaliger had Julian Day (JD) #1 begin at noon, Jan. 1, 4713 B. C., the most recent time that three major chronological cycles began on the same day — 1) the 28-year solar cycle, after which dates in the Julian calendar (e.g., Feb. 11) return to the same days of the week (e.g., Monday); 2) the 19-year lunar cycle, after which the phases of the moon return to the same dates of the year; and 3) the 15-year indiction cycle, used in ancient Rome to regulate taxes. It will take 7980 years to complete the period, the product of 28, 19, and 15.

Noon of Dec. 31, 1980, marks the beginning of JD 2,444,605; that many days will have passed since the start of the Julian period. The JD at noon of any date in 1981 may be found by adding to this figure the day of the year for that date, which is given in the left hand column in the chart below. Simple JD conversion tables are used by astronomers.

Days Between Two Dates

Table covers period of two ordinary years. Example—Days between Feb. 10, 1979 and Dec. 15, 1980; subtract 41 from 714; answer is 673 days. For leap year, such as 1980, one day must be added: final answer 674.

Date	Jan.	Feb.	Mar.	April	May	June	July	Aug.	Sept.	Oct.	Nov.	Dec.
1	1	32	60	91	121	152	182	213	244	274	305	335
2	2	33	61	92	122	153	183	214	245	275	306	336
3	3	34	62	93	123	154	184	215	246	276	307	337
4	4	35	63	94	124	155	185	216	247	277	308	338
5	5	36	64	95	125	156	186	217	248	278	309	339
6	6	37	65	96	126	157	187	218	249	279	310	340
7	7	38	66	97	127	158	188	219	250	280	311	341
8	8	39	67	98	128	159	189	220	251	281	312	342
9	9	40	68	99	129	160	190	221	252	282	313	343
10	10	41	69	100	130	161	191	222	253	283	314	344
11	11	42	70	101	131	162	192	223	254	284	315	345
12	12	43	71	102	132	163	193	224	255	285	316	346
13	13	44	72	103	133	164	194	225	256	286	317	347
14	14	45	73	104	134	165	195	226	257	287	318	348
15	15	46	74	105	135	166	196	227	258	288	319	349
16	16	47	75	106	136	167	197	228	259	289	320	350
17	17	48	76	107	137	168	198	229	260	290	321	351
18	18	49	77	108	138	169	199	230	261	291	322	352
19	19	50	78	109	139	170	200	231	262	292	323	353
20	20	51	79	110	140	171	201	232	263	293	324	354
21	21	52	80	111	141	172	202	233	264	294	325	355
22	22	53	81	112	142	173	203	234	265	295	326	356
23	23	54	82	113	143	174	204	235	266	296	327	357
24	24	55	83	114	144	175	205	236	267	297	328	358
25	25	56	84	115	145	176	206	237	268	298	329	359
26	26	57	85	116	146	177	207	238	269	299	330	360
27	27	58	86	117	147	178	208	239	270	300	331	361
28	28	59	87	118	148	179	209	240	271	301	332	362
29	29	—	88	119	149	180	210	241	272	302	333	363
30	30	—	89	120	150	181	211	242	273	303	334	364
31	31	—	90	—	151	—	212	243	—	304	—	365

Date	Jan.	Feb.	Mar.	April	May	June	July	Aug.	Sept.	Oct.	Nov.	Dec.
1	366	397	425	456	486	517	547	578	609	639	670	700
2	367	398	426	457	487	518	548	579	610	640	671	701
3	368	399	427	458	488	519	549	580	611	641	672	702
4	369	400	428	459	489	520	550	581	612	642	673	703
5	370	401	429	460	490	521	551	582	613	643	674	704
6	371	402	430	461	491	522	552	583	614	644	675	705
7	372	403	431	462	492	523	553	584	615	645	676	706
8	373	404	432	463	493	524	554	585	616	646	677	707
9	374	405	433	464	494	525	555	586	617	647	678	708
10	375	406	434	465	495	526	556	587	618	648	679	709
11	376	407	435	466	496	527	557	588	619	649	680	710
12	377	408	436	467	497	528	558	589	620	650	681	711
13	378	409	437	468	498	529	559	590	621	651	682	712
14	379	410	438	469	499	530	560	591	622	652	683	713
15	380	411	439	470	500	531	561	592	623	653	684	714
16	381	412	440	471	501	532	562	593	624	654	685	715
17	382	413	441	472	502	533	563	594	625	655	686	716
18	383	414	442	473	503	534	564	595	626	656	687	717
19	384	415	443	474	504	535	565	596	627	657	688	718
20	385	416	444	475	505	536	566	597	628	658	689	719
21	386	417	445	476	506	537	567	598	629	659	690	720
22	387	418	446	477	507	538	568	599	630	660	691	721
23	388	419	447	478	508	539	569	600	631	661	692	722
24	389	420	448	479	509	540	570	601	632	662	693	723
25	390	421	449	480	510	541	571	602	633	663	694	724
26	391	422	450	481	511	542	572	603	634	664	695	725
27	392	423	451	482	512	543	573	604	635	665	696	726
28	393	424	452	483	513	544	574	605	636	666	697	727
29	394	—	453	484	514	545	575	606	637	667	698	728
30	395	—	454	485	515	546	576	607	638	668	699	729
31	396	—	455	—	516	—	577	608	—	669	—	730

Lunar Calendar, Chinese New Year, Vietnamese Tet

The ancient Chinese lunar calendar is divided into 12 months of either 29 or 30 days (compensating for the fact that the mean duration of the lunar month is 29 days, 12 hours, 44.05 minutes). The calendar is synchronized with the solar year by the addition of extra months at fixed intervals.

The Chinese calendar runs on a sexagenary cycle, i.e., 60 years. The cycles 1876-1935 and 1936-1995, with the years grouped under their twelve animal designations, are printed below. The Year 1981 is found in the tenth column, under Rooster, and is known as a "Year of the Rooster." Readers can find the animal name for the year of their birth, marriage, etc., in the same chart. (Note: the first 3-7 weeks of each of the western years belong to the previous Chinese year and animal designation.)

Both the western (Gregorian) and traditional lunar calendars are used publicly in China, and two New Year's celebrations are held. On Taiwan, in overseas Chinese communities, and in Vietnam, the lunar calendar has been used only to set the dates for traditional festivals, with the Gregorian system in general use.

The four-day Chinese New Year, Hsin Nien, and the three-day Vietnamese New Year festival, Tet, begin at the first new moon after the sun enters Aquarius. The day may fall, therefore, between Jan. 21 and Feb. 19 of the Gregorian calendar. Feb. 5, 1981 marks the start of the new Chinese year. The date is fixed according to the date of the new moon in the Far East. Since this is west of the International Date Line the date may be one day later than that of the new moon in the United States.

Rat	Ox	Tiger	Hare (Rabbit)	Dragon	Snake	Horse	Sheep (Goat)	Monkey	Rooster	Dog	Pig
1876	1877	1878	1879	1880	1881	1882	1883	1884	1885	1886	1887
1888	1889	1890	1891	1892	1893	1894	1895	1896	1897	1898	1899
1900	1901	1902	1903	1904	1905	1906	1907	1908	1909	1910	1911
1912	1913	1914	1915	1916	1917	1918	1919	1920	1921	1922	1923
1924	1925	1926	1927	1928	1929	1930	1931	1932	1933	1934	1935
1936	1937	1938	1939	1940	1941	1942	1943	1944	1945	1946	1947
1948	1949	1950	1951	1952	1953	1954	1955	1956	1957	1958	1959
1960	1961	1962	1963	1964	1965	1966	1967	1968	1969	1970	1971
1972	1973	1974	1975	1976	1977	1978	1979	1980	1981	1982	1983
1984	1985	1986	1987	1988	1989	1990	1991	1992	1993	1994	1995

Perpetual Calendar

The number shown for each year indicates which Gregorian calendar to use. For 1583-1802, or for Julian calendar, see page 786. For years 1803-1820, use numbers for 1983-2000, respectively.

1821....2	1847....6	1873....4	1899....1	1925....5	1951....2	1977....7	2003....4	2029....2	2055....6
1822....3	1848...14	1874....5	1900....2	1926....6	1952...10	1978....1	2004...12	2030....3	2056...14
1823....4	1849....2	1875....6	1901....3	1927....7	1953....5	1979....2	2005....7	2031....4	2057....2
1824...12	1850....3	1876...14	1902....4	1928....8	1954....6	1980...10	2006....1	2032...12	2058....3
1825....7	1851....4	1877....2	1903....5	1929....3	1955....7	1981....5	2007....2	2033....7	2059....4
1826....1	1852...12	1878....3	1904...13	1930....4	1956....8	1982....6	2008...10	2034....1	2060..12
1827....2	1853....7	1879....4	1905....1	1931....5	1957....3	1983....7	2009....5	2035....2	2061..7
1828...10	1854....1	1880...12	1906....2	1932...13	1958....4	1984....8	2010....6	2036...10	2062..1
1829....5	1855....2	1881....7	1907....3	1933....1	1959....5	1985....3	2011....7	2037....5	2063..2
1830....6	1856...10	1882....1	1908...11	1934....2	1960...13	1986....4	2012....8	2038....6	2064..10
1831....7	1857....5	1883....2	1909....6	1935....3	1961....1	1987....5	2013....3	2039....7	2065..5
1832....8	1858....6	1884...10	1910....7	1936...11	1962....2	1988...13	2014....4	2040....8	2066..6
1833....3	1859....7	1885....5	1911....1	1937....6	1963....3	1989....1	2015....5	2041....3	2067..7
1834....4	1860....8	1886....6	1912....9	1938....7	1964...11	1990....2	2016...13	2042....4	2068..8
1835....5	1861....3	1887....7	1913....4	1939....1	1965....6	1991....3	2017....1	2043....5	2069..3
1836...13	1862....4	1888....8	1914....5	1940....9	1966....7	1992...11	2018....2	2044...13	2070..4
1837....1	1863....5	1889....3	1915....6	1941....4	1967....1	1993....6	2019....3	2045....1	2071..5
1838....2	1864...13	1890....4	1916...14	1942....5	1968....9	1994....7	2020...11	2046....2	2072..13
1839....3	1865....1	1891....5	1917....2	1943....6	1969....4	1995....1	2021....6	2047....3	2073..1
1840...11	1866....2	1892...13	1918....3	1944...14	1970....5	1996....9	2022....7	2048...11	2074..2
1841....6	1867....3	1893....1	1919....4	1945....2	1971....6	1997....4	2023....1	2049....6	2075..3
1842....7	1868...11	1894....2	1920...12	1946....3	1972...14	1998....5	2024....9	2050....7	2076..11
1843....1	1869....6	1895....3	1921....7	1947....4	1973....2	1999....6	2025....4	2051....1	2077..6
1844....9	1870....7	1896...11	1922....1	1948...12	1974....3	2000...14	2026....5	2052....9	2078..7
1845....4	1871....1	1897....6	1923....2	1949....7	1975....4	2001....2	2027....6	2053....4	2079..1
1846....5	1872....9	1898....7	1924...10	1950....1	1976...12	2002....3	2028...14	2054....5	2080..9

1

JANUARY

S	M	T	W	T	F	S
1	2	3	4	5	6	7
8	9	10	11	12	13	14
15	16	17	18	19	20	21
22	23	24	25	26	27	28
29	30	31				

FEBRUARY

S	M	T	W	T	F	S
			1	2	3	4
5	6	7	8	9	10	11
12	13	14	15	16	17	18
19	20	21	22	23	24	25
26	27	28				

MARCH

S	M	T	W	T	F	S
			1	2	3	4
5	6	7	8	9	10	11
12	13	14	15	16	17	18
19	20	21	22	23	24	25
26	27	28	29	30	31	

APRIL

S	M	T	W	T	F	S
						1
2	3	4	5	6	7	8
9	10	11	12	13	14	15
16	17	18	19	20	21	22
23	24	25	26	27	28	29
30						

MAY

S	M	T	W	T	F	S
	1	2	3	4	5	6
7	8	9	10	11	12	13
14	15	16	17	18	19	20
21	22	23	24	25	26	27
28	29	30	31			

JUNE

S	M	T	W	T	F	S
				1	2	3
4	5	6	7	8	9	10
11	12	13	14	15	16	17
18	19	20	21	22	23	24
25	26	27	28	29	30	

JULY

S	M	T	W	T	F	S
						1
2	3	4	5	6	7	8
9	10	11	12	13	14	15
16	17	18	19	20	21	22
23	24	25	26	27	28	29
30	31					

AUGUST

S	M	T	W	T	F	S
		1	2	3	4	5
6	7	8	9	10	11	12
13	14	15	16	17	18	19
20	21	22	23	24	25	26
27	28	29	30	31		

SEPTEMBER

S	M	T	W	T	F	S
					1	2
3	4	5	6	7	8	9
10	11	12	13	14	15	16
17	18	19	20	21	22	23
24	25	26	27	28	29	30

OCTOBER

S	M	T	W	T	F	S
1	2	3	4	5	6	7
8	9	10	11	12	13	14
15	16	17	18	19	20	21
22	23	24	25	26	27	28
29	30	31				

NOVEMBER

S	M	T	W	T	F	S
			1	2	3	4
5	6	7	8	9	10	11
12	13	14	15	16	17	18
19	20	21	22	23	24	25
26	27	28	29	30		

DECEMBER

S	M	T	W	T	F	S
					1	2
3	4	5	6	7	8	9
10	11	12	13	14	15	16
17	18	19	20	21	22	23
24	25	26	27	28	29	30
31						

2

JANUARY

S	M	T	W	T	F	S
	1	2	3	4	5	6
7	8	9	10	11	12	13
14	15	16	17	18	19	20
21	22	23	24	25	26	27
28	29	30	31			

FEBRUARY

S	M	T	W	T	F	S
				1	2	3
4	5	6	7	8	9	10
11	12	13	14	15	16	17
18	19	20	21	22	23	24
25	26	27	28			

MARCH

S	M	T	W	T	F	S
				1	2	3
4	5	6	7	8	9	10
11	12	13	14	15	16	17
18	19	20	21	22	23	24
25	26	27	28	29	30	31

APRIL

S	M	T	W	T	F	S
1	2	3	4	5	6	7
8	9	10	11	12	13	14
15	16	17	18	19	20	21
22	23	24	25	26	27	28
29	30					

MAY

S	M	T	W	T	F	S
		1	2	3	4	5
6	7	8	9	10	11	12
13	14	15	16	17	18	19
20	21	22	23	24	25	26
27	28	29	30	31		

JUNE

S	M	T	W	T	F	S
					1	2
3	4	5	6	7	8	9
10	11	12	13	14	15	16
17	18	19	20	21	22	23
24	25	26	27	28	29	30

JULY

S	M	T	W	T	F	S
1	2	3	4	5	6	7
8	9	10	11	12	13	14
15	16	17	18	19	20	21
22	23	24	25	26	27	28
29	30	31				

AUGUST

S	M	T	W	T	F	S
			1	2	3	4
5	6	7	8	9	10	11
12	13	14	15	16	17	18
19	20	21	22	23	24	25
26	27	28	29	30	31	

SEPTEMBER

S	M	T	W	T	F	S
						1
2	3	4	5	6	7	8
9	10	11	12	13	14	15
16	17	18	19	20	21	22
23	24	25	26	27	28	29
30						

OCTOBER

S	M	T	W	T	F	S
	1	2	3	4	5	6
7	8	9	10	11	12	13
14	15	16	17	18	19	20
21	22	23	24	25	26	27
28	29	30	31			

NOVEMBER

S	M	T	W	T	F	S
				1	2	3
4	5	6	7	8	9	10
11	12	13	14	15	16	17
18	19	20	21	22	23	24
25	26	27	28	29	30	

DECEMBER

S	M	T	W	T	F	S
						1
2	3	4	5	6	7	8
9	10	11	12	13	14	15
16	17	18	19	20	21	22
23	24	25	26	27	28	29
30	31					

3

JANUARY

S	M	T	W	T	F	S
		1	2	3	4	5
6	7	8	9	10	11	12
13	14	15	16	17	18	19
20	21	22	23	24	25	26
27	28	29	30	31		

FEBRUARY

S	M	T	W	T	F	S
					1	2
3	4	5	6	7	8	9
10	11	12	13	14	15	16
17	18	19	20	21	22	23
24	25	26	27	28		

MARCH

S	M	T	W	T	F	S
					1	2
3	4	5	6	7	8	9
10	11	12	13	14	15	16
17	18	19	20	21	22	23
24	25	26	27	28	29	30
31						

APRIL

S	M	T	W	T	F	S
	1	2	3	4	5	6
7	8	9	10	11	12	13
14	15	16	17	18	19	20
21	22	23	24	25	26	27
28	29	30				

MAY

S	M	T	W	T	F	S
			1	2	3	4
5	6	7	8	9	10	11
12	13	14	15	16	17	18
19	20	21	22	23	24	25
26	27	28	29	30	31	

JUNE

S	M	T	W	T	F	S
						1
2	3	4	5	6	7	8
9	10	11	12	13	14	15
16	17	18	19	20	21	22
23	24	25	26	27	28	29
30						

JULY

S	M	T	W	T	F	S
	1	2	3	4	5	6
7	8	9	10	11	12	13
14	15	16	17	18	19	20
21	22	23	24	25	26	27
28	29	30	31			

AUGUST

S	M	T	W	T	F	S
				1	2	3
4	5	6	7	8	9	10
11	12	13	14	15	16	17
18	19	20	21	22	23	24
25	26	27	28	29	30	31

SEPTEMBER

S	M	T	W	T	F	S
1	2	3	4	5	6	7
8	9	10	11	12	13	14
15	16	17	18	19	20	21
22	23	24	25	26	27	28
29	30					

OCTOBER

S	M	T	W	T	F	S
		1	2	3	4	5
6	7	8	9	10	11	12
13	14	15	16	17	18	19
20	21	22	23	24	25	26
27	28	29	30	31		

NOVEMBER

S	M	T	W	T	F	S
					1	2
3	4	5	6	7	8	9
10	11	12	13	14	15	16
17	18	19	20	21	22	23
24	25	26	27	28	29	30

DECEMBER

S	M	T	W	T	F	S
1	2	3	4	5	6	7
8	9	10	11	12	13	14
15	16	17	18	19	20	21
22	23	24	25	26	27	28
29	30	31				

4

JANUARY

S	M	T	W	T	F	S
			1	2	3	4
5	6	7	8	9	10	11
12	13	14	15	16	17	18
19	20	21	22	23	24	25
26	27	28	29	30	31	

FEBRUARY

S	M	T	W	T	F	S
						1
2	3	4	5	6	7	8
9	10	11	12	13	14	15
16	17	18	19	20	21	22
23	24	25	26	27	28	

MARCH

S	M	T	W	T	F	S
						1
2	3	4	5	6	7	8
9	10	11	12	13	14	15
16	17	18	19	20	21	22
23	24	25	26	27	28	29
30	31					

APRIL

S	M	T	W	T	F	S
		1	2	3	4	5
6	7	8	9	10	11	12
13	14	15	16	17	18	19
20	21	22	23	24	25	26
27	28	29	30			

MAY

S	M	T	W	T	F	S
				1	2	3
4	5	6	7	8	9	10
11	12	13	14	15	16	17
18	19	20	21	22	23	24
25	26	27	28	29	30	31

JUNE

S	M	T	W	T	F	S
1	2	3	4	5	6	7
8	9	10	11	12	13	14
15	16	17	18	19	20	21
22	23	24	25	26	27	28
29	30					

JULY

S	M	T	W	T	F	S
		1	2	3	4	5
6	7	8	9	10	11	12
13	14	15	16	17	18	19
20	21	22	23	24	25	26
27	28	29	30	31		

AUGUST

S	M	T	W	T	F	S
					1	2
3	4	5	6	7	8	9
10	11	12	13	14	15	16
17	18	19	20	21	22	23
24	25	26	27	28	29	30
31						

SEPTEMBER

S	M	T	W	T	F	S
	1	2	3	4	5	6
7	8	9	10	11	12	13
14	15	16	17	18	19	20
21	22	23	24	25	26	27
28	29	30				

OCTOBER

S	M	T	W	T	F	S
			1	2	3	4
5	6	7	8	9	10	11
12	13	14	15	16	17	18
19	20	21	22	23	24	25
26	27	28	29	30	31	

NOVEMBER

S	M	T	W	T	F	S
						1
2	3	4	5	6	7	8
9	10	11	12	13	14	15
16	17	18	19	20	21	22
23	24	25	26	27	28	29
30						

DECEMBER

S	M	T	W	T	F	S
	1	2	3	4	5	6
7	8	9	10	11	12	13
14	15	16	17	18	19	20
21	22	23	24	25	26	27
28	29	30	31			

5 1981

JANUARY

S	M	T	W	T	F	S
				1	2	3
4	5	6	7	8	9	10
11	12	13	14	15	16	17
18	19	20	21	22	23	24
25	26	27	28	29	30	31

FEBRUARY

S	M	T	W	T	F	S
1	2	3	4	5	6	7
8	9	10	11	12	13	14
15	16	17	18	19	20	21
22	23	24	25	26	27	28

MARCH

S	M	T	W	T	F	S
1	2	3	4	5	6	7
8	9	10	11	12	13	14
15	16	17	18	19	20	21
22	23	24	25	26	27	28
29	30	31				

APRIL

S	M	T	W	T	F	S
			1	2	3	4
5	6	7	8	9	10	11
12	13	14	15	16	17	18
19	20	21	22	23	24	25
26	27	28	29	30		

MAY

S	M	T	W	T	F	S
					1	2
3	4	5	6	7	8	9
10	11	12	13	14	15	16
17	18	19	20	21	22	23
24	25	26	27	28	29	30
31						

JUNE

S	M	T	W	T	F	S
	1	2	3	4	5	6
7	8	9	10	11	12	13
14	15	16	17	18	19	20
21	22	23	24	25	26	27
28	29	30				

JULY

S	M	T	W	T	F	S
			1	2	3	4
5	6	7	8	9	10	11
12	13	14	15	16	17	18
19	20	21	22	23	24	25
26	27	28	29	30	31	

AUGUST

S	M	T	W	T	F	S
						1
2	3	4	5	6	7	8
9	10	11	12	13	14	15
16	17	18	19	20	21	22
23	24	25	26	27	28	29
30	31					

SEPTEMBER

S	M	T	W	T	F	S
		1	2	3	4	5
6	7	8	9	10	11	12
13	14	15	16	17	18	19
20	21	22	23	24	25	26
27	28	29	30			

OCTOBER

S	M	T	W	T	F	S
				1	2	3
4	5	6	7	8	9	10
11	12	13	14	15	16	17
18	19	20	21	22	23	24
25	26	27	28	29	30	31

NOVEMBER

S	M	T	W	T	F	S
1	2	3	4	5	6	7
8	9	10	11	12	13	14
15	16	17	18	19	20	21
22	23	24	25	26	27	28
29	30					

DECEMBER

S	M	T	W	T	F	S
		1	2	3	4	5
6	7	8	9	10	11	12
13	14	15	16	17	18	19
20	21	22	23	24	25	26
27	28	29	30	31		

6 1982

JANUARY

S	M	T	W	T	F	S
					1	2
3	4	5	6	7	8	9
10	11	12	13	14	15	16
17	18	19	20	21	22	23
24	25	26	27	28	29	30
31						

FEBRUARY

S	M	T	W	T	F	S
	1	2	3	4	5	6
7	8	9	10	11	12	13
14	15	16	17	18	19	20
21	22	23	24	25	26	27
28						

MARCH

S	M	T	W	T	F	S
	1	2	3	4	5	6
7	8	9	10	11	12	13
14	15	16	17	18	19	20
21	22	23	24	25	26	27
28	29	30	31			

APRIL

S	M	T	W	T	F	S
				1	2	3
4	5	6	7	8	9	10
11	12	13	14	15	16	17
18	19	20	21	22	23	24
25	26	27	28	29	30	

MAY

S	M	T	W	T	F	S
						1
2	3	4	5	6	7	8
9	10	11	12	13	14	15
16	17	18	19	20	21	22
23	24	25	26	27	28	29
30	31					

JUNE

S	M	T	W	T	F	S
		1	2	3	4	5
6	7	8	9	10	11	12
13	14	15	16	17	18	19
20	21	22	23	24	25	26
27	28	29	30			

JULY

S	M	T	W	T	F	S
				1	2	3
4	5	6	7	8	9	10
11	12	13	14	15	16	17
18	19	20	21	22	23	24
25	26	27	28	29	30	31

AUGUST

S	M	T	W	T	F	S
1	2	3	4	5	6	7
8	9	10	11	12	13	14
15	16	17	18	19	20	21
22	23	24	25	26	27	28
29	30	31				

SEPTEMBER

S	M	T	W	T	F	S
			1	2	3	4
5	6	7	8	9	10	11
12	13	14	15	16	17	18
19	20	21	22	23	24	25
26	27	28	29	30		

OCTOBER

S	M	T	W	T	F	S
					1	2
3	4	5	6	7	8	9
10	11	12	13	14	15	16
17	18	19	20	21	22	23
24	25	26	27	28	29	30
31						

NOVEMBER

S	M	T	W	T	F	S
	1	2	3	4	5	6
7	8	9	10	11	12	13
14	15	16	17	18	19	20
21	22	23	24	25	26	27
28	29	30				

DECEMBER

S	M	T	W	T	F	S
			1	2	3	4
5	6	7	8	9	10	11
12	13	14	15	16	17	18
19	20	21	22	23	24	25
26	27	28	29	30	31	

7

JANUARY

S	M	T	W	T	F	S
						1
2	3	4	5	6	7	8
9	10	11	12	13	14	15
16	17	18	19	20	21	22
23	24	25	26	27	28	29
30	31					

FEBRUARY

S	M	T	W	T	F	S
		1	2	3	4	5
6	7	8	9	10	11	12
13	14	15	16	17	18	19
20	21	22	23	24	25	26
27	28					

MARCH

S	M	T	W	T	F	S
		1	2	3	4	5
6	7	8	9	10	11	12
13	14	15	16	17	18	19
20	21	22	23	24	25	26
27	28	29	30	31		

APRIL

S	M	T	W	T	F	S
					1	2
3	4	5	6	7	8	9
10	11	12	13	14	15	16
17	18	19	20	21	22	23
24	25	26	27	28	29	30

MAY

S	M	T	W	T	F	S
1	2	3	4	5	6	7
8	9	10	11	12	13	14
15	16	17	18	19	20	21
22	23	24	25	26	27	28
29	30	31				

JUNE

S	M	T	W	T	F	S
			1	2	3	4
5	6	7	8	9	10	11
12	13	14	15	16	17	18
19	20	21	22	23	24	25
26	27	28	29	30		

JULY

S	M	T	W	T	F	S
					1	2
3	4	5	6	7	8	9
10	11	12	13	14	15	16
17	18	19	20	21	22	23
24	25	26	27	28	29	30
31						

AUGUST

S	M	T	W	T	F	S
	1	2	3	4	5	6
7	8	9	10	11	12	13
14	15	16	17	18	19	20
21	22	23	24	25	26	27
28	29	30	31			

SEPTEMBER

S	M	T	W	T	F	S
				1	2	3
4	5	6	7	8	9	10
11	12	13	14	15	16	17
18	19	20	21	22	23	24
25	26	27	28	29	30	

OCTOBER

S	M	T	W	T	F	S
						1
2	3	4	5	6	7	8
9	10	11	12	13	14	15
16	17	18	19	20	21	22
23	24	25	26	27	28	29
30	31					

NOVEMBER

S	M	T	W	T	F	S
		1	2	3	4	5
6	7	8	9	10	11	12
13	14	15	16	17	18	19
20	21	22	23	24	25	26
27	28	29	30			

DECEMBER

S	M	T	W	T	F	S
				1	2	3
4	5	6	7	8	9	10
11	12	13	14	15	16	17
18	19	20	21	22	23	24
25	26	27	28	29	30	31

8

JANUARY

S	M	T	W	T	F	S
1	2	3	4	5	6	7
8	9	10	11	12	13	14
15	16	17	18	19	20	21
22	23	24	25	26	27	28
29	30	31				

FEBRUARY

S	M	T	W	T	F	S
			1	2	3	4
5	6	7	8	9	10	11
12	13	14	15	16	17	18
19	20	21	22	23	24	25
26	27	28	29			

MARCH

S	M	T	W	T	F	S
				1	2	3
4	5	6	7	8	9	10
11	12	13	14	15	16	17
18	19	20	21	22	23	24
25	26	27	28	29	30	31

APRIL

S	M	T	W	T	F	S
1	2	3	4	5	6	7
8	9	10	11	12	13	14
15	16	17	18	19	20	21
22	23	24	25	26	27	28
29	30					

MAY

S	M	T	W	T	F	S
		1	2	3	4	5
6	7	8	9	10	11	12
13	14	15	16	17	18	19
20	21	22	23	24	25	26
27	28	29	30	31		

JUNE

S	M	T	W	T	F	S
					1	2
3	4	5	6	7	8	9
10	11	12	13	14	15	16
17	18	19	20	21	22	23
24	25	26	27	28	29	30

JULY

S	M	T	W	T	F	S
1	2	3	4	5	6	7
8	9	10	11	12	13	14
15	16	17	18	19	20	21
22	23	24	25	26	27	28
29	30	31				

AUGUST

S	M	T	W	T	F	S
			1	2	3	4
5	6	7	8	9	10	11
12	13	14	15	16	17	18
19	20	21	22	23	24	25
26	27	28	29	30	31	

SEPTEMBER

S	M	T	W	T	F	S
						1
2	3	4	5	6	7	8
9	10	11	12	13	14	15
16	17	18	19	20	21	22
23	24	25	26	27	28	29
30						

OCTOBER

S	M	T	W	T	F	S
	1	2	3	4	5	6
7	8	9	10	11	12	13
14	15	16	17	18	19	20
21	22	23	24	25	26	27
28	29	30	31			

NOVEMBER

S	M	T	W	T	F	S
				1	2	3
4	5	6	7	8	9	10
11	12	13	14	15	16	17
18	19	20	21	22	23	24
25	26	27	28	29	30	

DECEMBER

S	M	T	W	T	F	S
						1
2	3	4	5	6	7	8
9	10	11	12	13	14	15
16	17	18	19	20	21	22
23	24	25	26	27	28	29
30	31					

9

JANUARY

S	M	T	W	T	F	S
	1	2	3	4	5	6
7	8	9	10	11	12	13
14	15	16	17	18	19	20
21	22	23	24	25	26	27
28	29	30	31			

FEBRUARY

S	M	T	W	T	F	S
				1	2	3
4	5	6	7	8	9	10
11	12	13	14	15	16	17
18	19	20	21	22	23	24
25	26	27	28	29		

MARCH

S	M	T	W	T	F	S
					1	2
3	4	5	6	7	8	9
10	11	12	13	14	15	16
17	18	19	20	21	22	23
24	25	26	27	28	29	30
31						

APRIL

S	M	T	W	T	F	S
	1	2	3	4	5	6
7	8	9	10	11	12	13
14	15	16	17	18	19	20
21	22	23	24	25	26	27
28	29	30				

MAY

S	M	T	W	T	F	S
			1	2	3	4
5	6	7	8	9	10	11
12	13	14	15	16	17	18
19	20	21	22	23	24	25
26	27	28	29	30	31	

JUNE

S	M	T	W	T	F	S
						1
2	3	4	5	6	7	8
9	10	11	12	13	14	15
16	17	18	19	20	21	22
23	24	25	26	27	28	29
30						

JULY

S	M	T	W	T	F	S
	1	2	3	4	5	6
7	8	9	10	11	12	13
14	15	16	17	18	19	20
21	22	23	24	25	26	27
28	29	30	31			

AUGUST

S	M	T	W	T	F	S
				1	2	3
4	5	6	7	8	9	10
11	12	13	14	15	16	17
18	19	20	21	22	23	24
25	26	27	28	29	30	31

SEPTEMBER

S	M	T	W	T	F	S
1	2	3	4	5	6	7
8	9	10	11	12	13	14
15	16	17	18	19	20	21
22	23	24	25	26	27	28
29	30					

OCTOBER

S	M	T	W	T	F	S
		1	2	3	4	5
6	7	8	9	10	11	12
13	14	15	16	17	18	19
20	21	22	23	24	25	26
27	28	29	30	31		

NOVEMBER

S	M	T	W	T	F	S
					1	2
3	4	5	6	7	8	9
10	11	12	13	14	15	16
17	18	19	20	21	22	23
24	25	26	27	28	29	30

DECEMBER

S	M	T	W	T	F	S
1	2	3	4	5	6	7
8	9	10	11	12	13	14
15	16	17	18	19	20	21
22	23	24	25	26	27	28
29	30	31				

10 1980

JANUARY

S	M	T	W	T	F	S
		1	2	3	4	5
6	7	8	9	10	11	12
13	14	15	16	17	18	19
20	21	22	23	24	25	26
27	28	29	30	31		

FEBRUARY

S	M	T	W	T	F	S
					1	2
3	4	5	6	7	8	9
10	11	12	13	14	15	16
17	18	19	20	21	22	23
24	25	26	27	28	29	

MARCH

S	M	T	W	T	F	S
						1
2	3	4	5	6	7	8
9	10	11	12	13	14	15
16	17	18	19	20	21	22
23	24	25	26	27	28	29
30	31					

APRIL

S	M	T	W	T	F	S
		1	2	3	4	5
6	7	8	9	10	11	12
13	14	15	16	17	18	19
20	21	22	23	24	25	26
27	28	29	30			

MAY

S	M	T	W	T	F	S
				1	2	3
4	5	6	7	8	9	10
11	12	13	14	15	16	17
18	19	20	21	22	23	24
25	26	27	28	29	30	31

JUNE

S	M	T	W	T	F	S
1	2	3	4	5	6	7
8	9	10	11	12	13	14
15	16	17	18	19	20	21
22	23	24	25	26	27	28
29	30					

JULY

S	M	T	W	T	F	S
		1	2	3	4	5
6	7	8	9	10	11	12
13	14	15	16	17	18	19
20	21	22	23	24	25	26
27	28	29	30	31		

AUGUST

S	M	T	W	T	F	S
					1	2
3	4	5	6	7	8	9
10	11	12	13	14	15	16
17	18	19	20	21	22	23
24	25	26	27	28	29	30
31						

SEPTEMBER

S	M	T	W	T	F	S
	1	2	3	4	5	6
7	8	9	10	11	12	13
14	15	16	17	18	19	20
21	22	23	24	25	26	27
28	29	30				

OCTOBER

S	M	T	W	T	F	S
			1	2	3	4
5	6	7	8	9	10	11
12	13	14	15	16	17	18
19	20	21	22	23	24	25
26	27	28	29	30	31	

NOVEMBER

S	M	T	W	T	F	S
						1
2	3	4	5	6	7	8
9	10	11	12	13	14	15
16	17	18	19	20	21	22
23	24	25	26	27	28	29
30						

DECEMBER

S	M	T	W	T	F	S
	1	2	3	4	5	6
7	8	9	10	11	12	13
14	15	16	17	18	19	20
21	22	23	24	25	26	27
28	29	30	31			

11

JANUARY

S	M	T	W	T	F	S
			1	2	3	4
5	6	7	8	9	10	11
12	13	14	15	16	17	18
19	20	21	22	23	24	25
26	27	28	29	30	31	

FEBRUARY

S	M	T	W	T	F	S
						1
2	3	4	5	6	7	8
9	10	11	12	13	14	15
16	17	18	19	20	21	22
23	24	25	26	27	28	29

MARCH

S	M	T	W	T	F	S
1	2	3	4	5	6	7
8	9	10	11	12	13	14
15	16	17	18	19	20	21
22	23	24	25	26	27	28
29	30	31				

APRIL

S	M	T	W	T	F	S
			1	2	3	4
5	6	7	8	9	10	11
12	13	14	15	16	17	18
19	20	21	22	23	24	25
26	27	28	29	30		

MAY

S	M	T	W	T	F	S
					1	2
3	4	5	6	7	8	9
10	11	12	13	14	15	16
17	18	19	20	21	22	23
24	25	26	27	28	29	30
31						

JUNE

S	M	T	W	T	F	S
	1	2	3	4	5	6
7	8	9	10	11	12	13
14	15	16	17	18	19	20
21	22	23	24	25	26	27
28	29	30				

JULY

S	M	T	W	T	F	S
			1	2	3	4
5	6	7	8	9	10	11
12	13	14	15	16	17	18
19	20	21	22	23	24	25
26	27	28	29	30	31	

AUGUST

S	M	T	W	T	F	S
						1
2	3	4	5	6	7	8
9	10	11	12	13	14	15
16	17	18	19	20	21	22
23	24	25	26	27	28	29
30	31					

SEPTEMBER

S	M	T	W	T	F	S
		1	2	3	4	5
6	7	8	9	10	11	12
13	14	15	16	17	18	19
20	21	22	23	24	25	26
27	28	29	30			

OCTOBER

S	M	T	W	T	F	S
				1	2	3
4	5	6	7	8	9	10
11	12	13	14	15	16	17
18	19	20	21	22	23	24
25	26	27	28	29	30	31

NOVEMBER

S	M	T	W	T	F	S
1	2	3	4	5	6	7
8	9	10	11	12	13	14
15	16	17	18	19	20	21
22	23	24	25	26	27	28
29	30					

DECEMBER

S	M	T	W	T	F	S
		1	2	3	4	5
6	7	8	9	10	11	12
13	14	15	16	17	18	19
20	21	22	23	24	25	26
27	28	29	30	31		

12

JANUARY

S	M	T	W	T	F	S
				1	2	3
4	5	6	7	8	9	10
11	12	13	14	15	16	17
18	19	20	21	22	23	24
25	26	27	28	29	30	31

FEBRUARY

S	M	T	W	T	F	S
1	2	3	4	5	6	7
8	9	10	11	12	13	14
15	16	17	18	19	20	21
22	23	24	25	26	27	28
29						

MARCH

S	M	T	W	T	F	S
	1	2	3	4	5	6
7	8	9	10	11	12	13
14	15	16	17	18	19	20
21	22	23	24	25	26	27
28	29	30	31			

APRIL

S	M	T	W	T	F	S
				1	2	3
4	5	6	7	8	9	10
11	12	13	14	15	16	17
18	19	20	21	22	23	24
25	26	27	28	29	30	

MAY

S	M	T	W	T	F	S
						1
2	3	4	5	6	7	8
9	10	11	12	13	14	15
16	17	18	19	20	21	22
23	24	25	26	27	28	29
30	31					

JUNE

S	M	T	W	T	F	S
		1	2	3	4	5
6	7	8	9	10	11	12
13	14	15	16	17	18	19
20	21	22	23	24	25	26
27	28	29	30			

JULY

S	M	T	W	T	F	S
				1	2	3
4	5	6	7	8	9	10
11	12	13	14	15	16	17
18	19	20	21	22	23	24
25	26	27	28	29	30	31

AUGUST

S	M	T	W	T	F	S
1	2	3	4	5	6	7
8	9	10	11	12	13	14
15	16	17	18	19	20	21
22	23	24	25	26	27	28
29	30	31				

SEPTEMBER

S	M	T	W	T	F	S
			1	2	3	4
5	6	7	8	9	10	11
12	13	14	15	16	17	18
19	20	21	22	23	24	25
26	27	28	29	30		

OCTOBER

S	M	T	W	T	F	S
					1	2
3	4	5	6	7	8	9
10	11	12	13	14	15	16
17	18	19	20	21	22	23
24	25	26	27	28	29	30
31						

NOVEMBER

S	M	T	W	T	F	S
	1	2	3	4	5	6
7	8	9	10	11	12	13
14	15	16	17	18	19	20
21	22	23	24	25	26	27
28	29	30				

DECEMBER

S	M	T	W	T	F	S
			1	2	3	4
5	6	7	8	9	10	11
12	13	14	15	16	17	18
19	20	21	22	23	24	25
26	27	28	29	30	31	

13

JANUARY

S	M	T	W	T	F	S
					1	2
3	4	5	6	7	8	9
10	11	12	13	14	15	16
17	18	19	20	21	22	23
24	25	26	27	28	29	30
31						

FEBRUARY

S	M	T	W	T	F	S
	1	2	3	4	5	6
7	8	9	10	11	12	13
14	15	16	17	18	19	20
21	22	23	24	25	26	27
28	29					

MARCH

S	M	T	W	T	F	S
		1	2	3	4	5
6	7	8	9	10	11	12
13	14	15	16	17	18	19
20	21	22	23	24	25	26
27	28	29	30	31		

APRIL

S	M	T	W	T	F	S
					1	2
3	4	5	6	7	8	9
10	11	12	13	14	15	16
17	18	19	20	21	22	23
24	25	26	27	28	29	30

MAY

S	M	T	W	T	F	S
1	2	3	4	5	6	7
8	9	10	11	12	13	14
15	16	17	18	19	20	21
22	23	24	25	26	27	28
29	30	31				

JUNE

S	M	T	W	T	F	S
			1	2	3	4
5	6	7	8	9	10	11
12	13	14	15	16	17	18
19	20	21	22	23	24	25
26	27	28	29	30		

JULY

S	M	T	W	T	F	S
					1	2
3	4	5	6	7	8	9
10	11	12	13	14	15	16
17	18	19	20	21	22	23
24	25	26	27	28	29	30
31						

AUGUST

S	M	T	W	T	F	S
	1	2	3	4	5	6
7	8	9	10	11	12	13
14	15	16	17	18	19	20
21	22	23	24	25	26	27
28	29	30	31			

SEPTEMBER

S	M	T	W	T	F	S
				1	2	3
4	5	6	7	8	9	10
11	12	13	14	15	16	17
18	19	20	21	22	23	24
25	26	27	28	29	30	

OCTOBER

S	M	T	W	T	F	S
						1
2	3	4	5	6	7	8
9	10	11	12	13	14	15
16	17	18	19	20	21	22
23	24	25	26	27	28	29
30	31					

NOVEMBER

S	M	T	W	T	F	S
		1	2	3	4	5
6	7	8	9	10	11	12
13	14	15	16	17	18	19
20	21	22	23	24	25	26
27	28	29	30			

DECEMBER

S	M	T	W	T	F	S
				1	2	3
4	5	6	7	8	9	10
11	12	13	14	15	16	17
18	19	20	21	22	23	24
25	26	27	28	29	30	31

14

JANUARY

S	M	T	W	T	F	S
						1
2	3	4	5	6	7	8
9	10	11	12	13	14	15
16	17	18	19	20	21	22
23	24	25	26	27	28	29
30	31					

FEBRUARY

S	M	T	W	T	F	S
		1	2	3	4	5
6	7	8	9	10	11	12
13	14	15	16	17	18	19
20	21	22	23	24	25	26
27	28	29				

MARCH

S	M	T	W	T	F	S
			1	2	3	4
5	6	7	8	9	10	11
12	13	14	15	16	17	18
19	20	21	22	23	24	25
26	27	28	29	30	31	

APRIL

S	M	T	W	T	F	S
						1
2	3	4	5	6	7	8
9	10	11	12	13	14	15
16	17	18	19	20	21	22
23	24	25	26	27	28	29
30						

MAY

S	M	T	W	T	F	S
	1	2	3	4	5	6
7	8	9	10	11	12	13
14	15	16	17	18	19	20
21	22	23	24	25	26	27
28	29	30	31			

JUNE

S	M	T	W	T	F	S
				1	2	3
4	5	6	7	8	9	10
11	12	13	14	15	16	17
18	19	20	21	22	23	24
25	26	27	28	29	30	

JULY

S	M	T	W	T	F	S
						1
2	3	4	5	6	7	8
9	10	11	12	13	14	15
16	17	18	19	20	21	22
23	24	25	26	27	28	29
30	31					

AUGUST

S	M	T	W	T	F	S
		1	2	3	4	5
6	7	8	9	10	11	12
13	14	15	16	17	18	19
20	21	22	23	24	25	26
27	28	29	30	31		

SEPTEMBER

S	M	T	W	T	F	S
					1	2
3	4	5	6	7	8	9
10	11	12	13	14	15	16
17	18	19	20	21	22	23
24	25	26	27	28	29	30

OCTOBER

S	M	T	W	T	F	S
1	2	3	4	5	6	7
8	9	10	11	12	13	14
15	16	17	18	19	20	21
22	23	24	25	26	27	28
29	30	31				

NOVEMBER

S	M	T	W	T	F	S
			1	2	3	4
5	6	7	8	9	10	11
12	13	14	15	16	17	18
19	20	21	22	23	24	25
26	27	28	29	30		

DECEMBER

S	M	T	W	T	F	S
					1	2
3	4	5	6	7	8	9
10	11	12	13	14	15	16
17	18	19	20	21	22	23
24	25	26	27	28	29	30
31						

Chronological Eras, 1981

The year 1981 of the Christian Era comprises the latter part of the 205th and the beginning of the 206th year of the independence of the United States of America.

Era	Year	Begins in 1981
Byzantine	7490	Sept. 14
Jewish	5742	Sept. 29 (sunset)
Olympiads (First year of Olympiad 690)	2757	July 1
Roman (Ab Urbe Condita)	2734	Jan. 14
Nabonassar (Babylonian)	2730	Apr. 28
Japanese	2641	Jan. 1
Grecian (Seleucidae)	2293	Sept. 14 or Oct. 14
Diocletian	1698	Sept. 11
Indian (Saka)	1903	Mar. 22
Mohammedan (Hegira)	1402	Oct. 30

Chronological Cycles, 1981

Dominical Letter	D	Golden Number (Lunar Cycle)	VI	Roman Indiction	4
Epact	24	Solar Cycle	2	Julian Period (year of)	6694

Standard Time Differences — North American Cities

At 12 o'clock noon, Eastern Standard Time, the standard time in N.A. cities is as follows:

Akron, Oh.	12.00 Noon	Frankfort, Ky.	12.00 Noon	Pierre, S.D.	11.00 A.M.
Albuquerque, N.M.	10.00 A.M.	Galveston, Tex.	11.00 A.M.	Pittsburgh, Pa.	12.00 Noon
Atlanta, Ga.	12.00 Noon	Grand Rapids, Mich.	12.00 Noon	Portland, Me.	12.00 Noon
Austin, Tex.	11.00 A.M.	Halifax, N.S.	1.00 P.M.	Portland, Ore.	9.00 A.M.
Baltimore, Md.	12.00 Noon	Hartford, Conn.	12.00 Noon	Providence, R.I.	12.00 Noon
Birmingham, Ala.	11.00 A.M.	Helena, Mon.	10.00 A.M.	*Regina, Sask.	11.00 A.M.
Bismarck, N.D.	11.00 A.M.	*Honolulu, Ha.	7.00 A.M.	Reno, Nev.	9.00 A.M.
Boise, Ida.	10.00 A.M.	Houston, Tex.	11.00 A.M.	Richmond, Va.	12.00 Noon
Boston, Mass.	12.00 Noon	*Indianapolis, Ind.	12.00 Noon	Rochester, N.Y.	12.00 Noon
Buffalo, N.Y.	12.00 Noon	Jacksonville, Fla.	12.00 Noon	Sacramento, Cal.	9.00 A.M.
Butte, Mon.	10.00 A.M.	Juneau, Alas.	9.00 A.M.	St. John's, Nfld.	1.30 P.M.
Calgary, Alta.	10.00 A.M.	Kansas City, Mo.	11.00 A.M.	St. Louis, Mo.	11.00 A.M.
Charleston, S.C.	12.00 Noon	Knoxville, Tenn.	12.00 Noon	St. Paul, Minn.	11.00 A.M.
Charleston, W.Va.	12.00 Noon	Lexington, Ky.	12.00 Noon	Salt Lake City, Ut.	10.00 A.M.
Charlotte, N.C.	12.00 Noon	Lincoln, Neb.	11.00 A.M.	San Antonio, Tex.	11.00 A.M.
Charlottetown, P.E.I.	1.00 P.M.	Little Rock, Ark.	11.00 A.M.	San Diego, Cal.	9.00 A.M.
Chattanooga, Tenn.	12.00 Noon	Los Angeles, Cal.	9.00 A.M.	San Francisco, Cal.	9.00 A.M.
Cheyenne, Wy.	10.00 A.M.	Louisville, Ky.	12.00 Noon	Santa Fe, N.M.	10.00 A.M.
Chicago, Ill.	11.00 A.M.	*Mexico City	11.00 A.M.	Savannah, Ga.	12.00 Noon
Cleveland, Oh.	12.00 Noon	Memphis, Tenn.	11.00 A.M.	Seattle, Wash.	9.00 A.M.
Colorado Spr., Col.	10.00 A.M.	Miami, Fla.	12.00 Noon	Shreveport, La.	11.00 A.M.
Columbus, Oh.	12.00 Noon	Milwaukee, Wis.	11.00 A.M.	Sioux Falls, S.D.	11.00 A.M.
Dallas, Tex.	11.00 A.M.	Minneapolis, Minn.	11.00 A.M.	Spokane, Wash.	9.00 A.M.
*Dawson, Yuk.	9.00 A.M.	Mobile, Ala.	11.00 A.M.	Tampa, Fla.	12.00 Noon
Dayton, Oh.	12.00 Noon	Montreal, Que.	12.00 Noon	Toledo, Oh.	12.00 Noon
Denver, Col.	10.00 A.M.	Nashville, Tenn.	11.00 A.M.	Topeka, Kan.	11.00 A.M.
Des Moines, Ia.	11.00 A.M.	New Haven, Conn.	12.00 Noon	Toronto, Ont.	12.00 Noon
Detroit, Mich.	12.00 Noon	New Orleans, La.	11.00 A.M.	*Tuscon, Ariz.	10.00 A.M.
Duluth, Minn.	11.00 A.M.	New York, N.Y.	12.00 Noon	Tulsa, Okla.	11.00 A.M.
El Paso, Tex.	10.00 A.M.	Nome, Alas.	6.00 A.M.	Vancouver, B.C.	9.00 A.M.
Erie, Pa.	12.00 Noon	Norfolk, Va.	12.00 Noon	Washington, D.C.	12.00 Noon
Evansville, Ind.	11.00 A.M.	Okla. City, Okla.	11.00 A.M.	Wichita, Kan.	11.00 A.M.
Fairbanks, Alas.	7.00 A.M.	Omaha, Neb.	11.00 A.M.	Wilmington, Del.	12.00 Noon
Flint, Mich.	12.00 Noon	Peoria, Ill.	11.00 A.M.	Winnipeg, Man.	11.00 A.M.
*Fort Wayne, Ind.	12.00 Noon	Philadelphia, Pa.	12.00 Noon		
Fort Worth, Tex.	11.00 A.M.	*Phoenix, Ariz.	10.00 A.M.		

*Cities with an asterisk do not observe daylight savings time. During much of the year, it is necessary to add one hour to the cities which do observe daylight savings time to get the proper time relation.

Standard Time Differences—World Cities

The time indicated in the table is fixed by law and is called the legal time, or, more generally, Standard Time. Use of Daylight Saving Time varies widely. *Indicates morning of the following day. At 12.00, Eastern Standard Time, the standard time (in 24-hour time) in foreign cities is as follows:

Alexandria	19 00	Caracas	13 00	Leningrad	20 00	Rome	18 00
Amsterdam	18 00	Copenhagen	18 00	Lima	12 00	Santiago (Chile)	13 00
Athens	19 00	Dacca	23 00	Lisbon	18 00	Seoul	2 00*
Auckland	5 00*	Delhi	22 30	Liverpool	17 00	Shanghai	1 00*
Baghdad	20 00	Dublin	17 00	London	17 00	Singapore	12 30*
Bangkok	0 00	Gdansk	18 00	Madrid	18 00	Stockholm	18 00
Belfast	17 00	Geneva	18 00	Manila	1 00*	Sydney (Australia)	3 00*
Berlin	18 00	Havana	12 00	Melbourne	3 00*	Tashkent	23 00
Bogota	12 00	Helsinki	19 00	Montevideo	14 00	Teheran	20 30
Bombay	22 30	Ho Chi Minh City	1 00*	Moscow	20 00	Tel Aviv	19 00
Bremen	18 00	Hong Kong	1 00*	Nagasaki	2 00*	Tokyo	2 00*
Brussels	18 00	Istanbul	19 00	Oslo	18 00	Valparaiso	13 00
Bucharest	19 00	Jakarta	0 00	Paris	18 00	Vladivostok	3 00*
Budapest	18 00	Jerusalem	19 00	Peking	1 00*	Vienna	18 00
Buenos Aires	14 00	Johannesburg	19 00	Prague	18 00	Warsaw	18 00
Calcutta	22 30	Karachi	22 00	Rangoon	23 30	Wellington (N.Z.)	5 00*
Cape Town	19 00	Le Havre	18 00	Rio De Janeiro	14 00	Yokohama	2 00*
						Zurich	18 00

Standard Time, Daylight Saving Time, and Others

Source: Defense Mapping Agency Hydrographic Center; Department of Transportation; National Bureau of Standards; U.S. Naval Observatory

Standard Time

Standard time is reckoned from Greenwich, England, recognized as the Prime Meridian of Longitude. The world is divided into 24 zones, each 15° of arc, or one hour in time apart. The Greenwich meridian (0°) extends through the center of the initial zone, and the zones to the east are numbered from 1 to 12 with the prefix "minus" indicating the number of hours to be subtracted to obtain Greenwich Time.

Westward zones are similarly numbered, but prefixed "plus" showing the number of hours that must be added to get Greenwich Time. While these zones apply generally to sea areas, it should be noted that the Standard Time maintained in many countries does not coincide with zone time. A graphical representation of the zones is shown on the Standard Time Zone Chart of the World published by the Defense Mapping Agency Hydrographic Center, Washington, DC 20390.

The United States and possessions are divided into eight Standard Time zones, as set forth by the Uniform Time Act of 1966, which also provides for the use of Daylight Saving Time therein. Each zone is approximately 15° of longitude in width. All places in each zone use, instead of their own local time, the time counted from the transit of the "mean sun" across the Standard Time meridian which passes near the middle of that zone.

These time zones are designated as Atlantic, Eastern, Central, Mountain, Pacific, Yukon, Alaska-Hawaii, and Bering, and the time in these zones is basically reckoned from the 60th, 75th, 90th, 105th, 120th, 135th, 150th, 165th meridians west of Greenwich. The line wanders to conform to local geographical regions. The time in the various zones is earlier than Greenwich Time by 4, 5, 6, 7, 8, 9, 10, and 11 hours respectively.

24-Hour Time

24-hour time is widely used in scientific work throughout the world. In the United States it is used also in operations of the Armed Forces. In Europe it is used in preference to the 12-hour a.m. and p.m. system. With the 24-hour system the day begins at midnight and hours are numbered 0 through 23.

International Date Line

The Date Line is a zig-zag line that approximately coincides with the 180th meridian, and it is where each calendar day begins. The date must be advanced one day when crossing in a westerly direction and set back one day when crossing in an easterly direction.

The line is deflected between north latitude 48° and 75°, so that all Asia lies to the west of it.

Daylight Saving Time

Daylight Saving Time is achieved by advancing the clock one hour. Under the Uniform Time Act, which became effective in 1967, all states, the District of Columbia, and U.S. possessions were to observe Daylight Saving Time beginning at 2 a.m. on the last Sunday in April and ending at 2 a.m. on the last Sunday in October. Any state could, by law, exempt itself; a 1972 amendment to the act authorized states split by time zones to take that into consideration in exempting themselves. Arizona, Hawaii, Puerto Rico, the Virgin Islands, American Samoa, and part of Indiana are now exempt. Some local zone boundaries in Kansas, Texas, Florida, Michigan, and Alaska have been modified in the last several years by the Dept. of Transportation, which oversees the act. To conserve energy Congress put most of the nation on year-round Daylight Saving Time for two years effective Jan. 6, 1974 through Oct. 26, 1975; but a further bill, signed in October, 1974, restored Standard Time from the last Sunday in that month to the last Sunday in February, 1975. At the end of 1975, Congress failed to renew this temporary legislation and the nation returned to the older end-of April to end-of October DST system.

Legal or Public Holidays, 1981

Technically there are no national holidays in the United States; each state has jurisdiction over its holidays, which are designated by leglislative enactment or executive proclamation. In practice, however, most states observe the federal legal public holidays, even though the President and Congress can legally designate holidays only for the District of Columbia and for federal employees.

Federal legal public holidays are: New Year's Day, Washington's Birthday, Memorial Day, Independence Day, Labor Day, Columbus Day, Veterans Day, Thanksgiving, and Christmas.

Chief Legal or Public Holidays

When a holiday falls on a Sunday or a Saturday it is usually observed on the following Monday or preceding Friday. For some holidays, government and business closing practices vary. In most states, the office of the Secretary of State can provide details of holiday closings.

Jan. 1 (Thursday) — New Year's Day. All the states.

Feb. 12 (Thursday) — Lincoln's Birthday. Alaska, Cal., Col., Conn., Ill., Ind., Ia., Kan., Md., Mich., Mo., Mon., N.C., N.J., N.Y., Okla., Pa., Vt., Wash., W.Va. In Ariz., Feb. 9; Del., Ore., celebrated Feb. 2 in 1981.

Feb. 16 (3d Monday in Feb.) — Washington's Birthday. All the states except Fla. and Wyo. In several states, the holiday is called Presidents' Day or Washington-Lincoln Day. In Mo., Ut., celebrated Feb. 23, 1981.

Apr. 17 — Good Friday. Observed in all the states. A legal or public holiday in Conn., Del., Ha., Ind., Ky., La., Md., N.J., N.D., Okla., Tenn., W.Va., P.R. Partial holiday in Wis.

May 25 (last Monday in May) — Memorial Day. All the states except Ala., Miss., S.C., (Confederate Memorial Day in Va., Decoration Day in Tenn.). Observed May 29 in Del., Md., N.H., Ut., Vt.

July 4 (Saturday) — Independence Day. All the states.

Sept. 7 (1st Monday in Sept.) — Labor Day. All the states.

Oct. 12 (2d Monday in Oct.) — Columbus Day. Ala., Ariz., Cal., Col., Conn., Del., D.C., Ga., Ha., Ida., Ill., Ind., Kan., La., Me., Mass., Mich., Mo., Mont., Neb., N.H., N.J., N.M., N.Y., N.C., Oh., Okla., Pa., R.I., S.D., Tenn., Tex., Ut., Vt., Va., W.Va., Wis., Wy., P.R.

Nov. 3 (1st Tuesday after 1st Monday in Nov.) — General Election Day. Col., Mo., Mon., N.J., N.Y., N.C., Okla., Pa., R.I., S.C., Va., Wyo. Primary election days are observed as holidays or part holidays in some states.

Nov. 11 (Wednesday) — Armistice Day (Veterans Day). All the states; N.C. celebrates Oct. 26.

Nov. 26 (4th Thursday in Nov.) — Thanksgiving Day. All the states. The day after Thanksgiving is observed as a full or partial holiday in several states.

Dec. 25 (Friday) — Christmas. All the states.

Other Legal or Public Holidays

Dates are for 1981 observance, when known.

Jan. 8 — Battle of New Orleans. In La.

Jan. 15 — Martin Luther King's Birthday. Conn., D.C., Ill., La., Md., Mass., N.J., Pa., S.C. Observed Jan. 19 by Mich., Oh. Many schools and black groups in other states also observe the day.

Jan. 19 — Robert E. Lee's Birthday. Al., Ga., La., Miss., S.C.; Lee-Jackson Day in Va., Confederate Heroes Day in Tex.

Feb. 6 — Arbor Day. In Ariz. (most counties).

Feb. 14 — Admission Day. In Ariz.

Mar. 2 — Texas Independence Day. In that state.

Mar. 3 — Mardi Gras (Shrove Tuesday). Ala., La.; Town Meeting Day (1st Tuesday in Mar.) In Vt.

Mar. 17 — Evacuation Day. In Boston and Suffolk County, Mass.

Mar. 25 — Maryland Day. In that state.

Mar. 26 — Kuhio Day. In Ha.

Mar. 30 — Seward's Day. In Alas.

Apr. 3 — Arbor Day. In Ariz. (5 counties).

Apr. 9 — Patriot's Day. In Me.

Apr. 13 — Thomas Jefferson's Birthday. In Ala.

Apr. 20 — Patriot's Day. In Mass., Me. Easter Monday in N.C.

Apr. 21 — San Jacinto Day. In Tex.

Apr. 22 — Arbor Day. In Neb.

Apr. 24 — Arbor Day (last Friday in Apr.). In Ut.

Apr. 25 — Confederate Memorial Day. Fla.

Apr. 27 — Confederate Memorial Day. In Ala., Ga., Miss. Fast Day (4th Monday in Apr.). In N.H.

May 4 — Rhode Island Independence Day. In that state.

May 8 — Harry Truman's Birthday. In Mo.

May 11 — Confederate Memorial Day. In S.C.

May 19 — Primary Election Day. In Pa.

May 28 — Confederate Memorial Day. In Va. Decoration Day in Tenn.

June 1 — Birthday of Jefferson Davis. Ala., Ga. (June 3), Miss., S.C. (June 3).

June 3 — Confederate Memorial Day. In La.

June 11 — Kamehameha Day. In Ha.

June 14 — Flag Day. Observed in all states; a legal holiday in Pa. (June 15).

June 17 — Bunker Hill Day. In Boston and Suffolk County, Mass.

June 19 — Emancipation Day. In Texas.

June 20 — West Virginia Day. In that state.

July 24 — Pioneer Day. In Ut.

Aug. 2 — American Family Day. In Ariz.

Aug. 3 — Colorado Day. In that state.

Aug. 10 — Victory Day (2d Monday in Aug.). In R.I.

Aug. 16 — Bennington Battle Day. In Vt.

Aug. 21 — Admission Day (3d Friday in Aug.). In Ha.

Aug. 27 — Lyndon Johnson's Birthday. In Tex.

Aug. 30 — Huey Long's Birthday. In La.

Sept. 9 — Admission Day. In Cal.

Sept. 11 — Defenders' Day. In Md.

Oct. 18 — Alaska Day. In that state.

Oct. 31 — Nevada Day. In that state.

Nov. 1 — All Saints' Day. In La.

Nov. 27 — Day after Thanksgiving. Fl., Me., Minn., Neb., Wash.

Dec. 24 — Christmas Eve. In Ark.

Dec. 26 — Day after Christmas. In S.C.

Days Usually Observed

All Saints' Day, Nov. 1. A public holiday in Louisiana.

American Indian Day (Sept. 25 in 1981). Always fourth Friday in September.

Arbor Day. Tree-planting day. First observed April 10, 1872, in Nebraska. Now observed in every state in the Union except Alaska (often on the last Friday in April). A legal holiday in Utah (always last Friday in April), and in Nebraska (April 22).

Armed Forces Day (May 16 in 1981). Always third Saturday in that month, by presidential proclamation. Replaced Army, Navy, and Air Force Days.

Bill of Rights Day, Dec. 15. By Act of Congress. Bill of Rights took effect Dec. 15, 1791.

Bird Day. Often observed with Arbor Day.

Child Health Day (Oct. 5 in 1981). Always first Monday in October, by presidential proclamation.

Citizenship Day, Sept. 17. President Truman, Feb. 29, 1952, signed bill designating Sept. 17 as annual Citizenship Day. It replaced I Am An American Day, formerly 3rd Sunday in May and Constitution Day, formerly Sept. 17.

Easter Monday (Apr. 20 in 1981). A statutory day in Canada and in N.C.

Easter Sunday (Apr. 19 in 1981).

Elizabeth Cady Stanton Day, Nov. 12. Birthday of pioneer leader for equal rights for women.

Father's Day (June 21, in 1981). Always third Sunday in that month.

Flag Day, June 14. By presidential proclamation. It is a legal holiday in Pennsylvania.

Forefathers' Day, Dec. 21. Landing on Plymouth Rock, in 1620. Is celebrated with dinners by New England societies especially "Down East."

Nathan Bedford Forrest's Birthday, July 13. Observed in Tennessee to honor the Civil War general.

Four Chaplains Memorial Day, Feb. 3.

Gen. Douglas MacArthur Day, Jan. 26. A memorial day in Arkansas.

Gen. Pulaski Memorial Day, Oct. 11. Native of Poland and Revolutionary War hero; died (Oct. 11, 1779) from wounds received at the seige of Savannah, Ga. Observed officially in Indiana.

Gen. von Steuben Memorial Day, Sept. 17. By presidential proclamation.

Georgia Day, Feb. 12. Observed in that state. Commemorates landing of first colonists in 1733.

Grandparent's Day (Sept. 13 in 1981). Always first Sunday after Labor Day. Legislated in 1979.

Groundhog Day, Feb. 2. A popular belief is that if the groundhog sees his shadow this day, he returns to his burrow and winter continues 6 weeks longer.

Halloween, Oct. 31. The evening before All Saints or All-Hallows Day. Informally observed in the U.S. with masquerading and pumpkin-decorations. Traditionally an occasion for children to play pranks.

Leif Ericsson Day, Oct. 9. Observed in Minnesota, Wisconsin.

Loyalty Day, May 1. By act of Congress.

May Day. Name popularly given to May 1st. Celebrated as Labor Day in most of the world, and by some groups in the U.S. Observed in many schools as a Spring Festival.

Minnesota Day, May 11. In that state.

Mother's Day (May 10 in 1981). Always second Sunday in that month. First celebrated in Philadelphia in 1908. Mother's Day has become an international holiday.

National Aviation Day, Aug. 19. By presidential proclamation.

National Day of Prayer. By presidential proclamation each year on a day other than a Sunday.

National Freedom Day, Feb. 1. To commemorate the signing of the Thirteenth Amendment, abolishing slavery, Feb. 1, 1865. By presidential proclamation.

National Maritime Day, May 22. First proclaimed 1935 in commemoration of the departure of the SS Savannah, from Savannah, Ga., on May 22, 1819, on the first successful transatlantic voyage under steam propulsion. By presidential proclamation.

Pan American Day, Apr. 14. In 1890 the First International Conference of American States, meeting in Washington, was held on that date. A resolution was adopted which resulted in the creation of the organization known today as the Pan American Union. By presidential proclamation.

Primary Election Day. Observed usually only when presidential or general elections are held.

Reformation Day, Oct. 31. Observed by Protestant groups.

Sadie Hawkins Day (Nov. 14 in 1981). First Saturday after November 11.

St. Patrick's Day, Mar. 17. Observed by Irish Societies, especially with parades.

St. Valentine's Day, Feb. 14. Festival of a martyr beheaded at Rome under Emperor Claudius. Association of this day with lovers has no connection with the saint and probably had its origin in an old belief that on this day birds begin to choose their mates.

Senior Citizens' Day (Sept. 27 in 1981). Celebrated in Indiana on the fourth Sunday in September.

Susan B. Anthony Day, Feb. 15. Birthday of a pioneer crusader for equal rights for women.

United Nations Day, Oct. 24. By presidential proclamation, to commemorate founding of United Nations.

Verrazano Day, Apr. 7. Observed by New York State, to commemorate the probable discovery of New York harbor by Giovanni da Verrazano in April, 1524.

Victoria Day (May 18 in 1981). Birthday of Queen Victoria, a statutory day in Canada, celebrated the first Monday before May 25.

Francis Willard Day, Sept. 28. Observed in Minnesota to honor the educator and temperance leader.

Will Rogers Day, Nov. 4. In Oklahoma.

World Poetry Day, Oct. 15.

Wright Brothers Day, Dec. 17. By presidential designation, to commemorate first successful flight by Orville and Wilbur Wright, Dec. 17, 1903.

Youth Honor Day, Oct. 31. Iowa day of observance.

Other Holidays, Anniversaries, Events — 1981

Jan. 25 (Sun.)	— Superbowl game.
Feb. 11 (Wed.)	— National Inventors Day.
Feb. 14 (Sat.)	— St. Valentine's Day.
Feb. 20 (Fri.)	— John Glenn Day.
Mar. 1, 1781	— Articles of Confederation adopted by 13 colonies.
Mar. 13, 1881	— Russia's Aleksandr II is assassinated.
Mar. 13, 1906	— Susan B. Anthony dies.
Mar. 20 (Fri.)	— Spring begins, 12:03 P.M. EST.
Mar. 29 (Sun.)	— Vietnam Veterans' Day.
Apr. 1 (Wed.)	— April Fool's Day.
Apr. 18, 1906	— San Francisco earthquake occurs.
Apr. 20 (Mon.)	— Boston Marathon.
Apr. 22 (Wed.)	— Earth Day.
Apr. 24 (Fri.)	— Secretaries' Day.
May 2 (Sat.)	— Kentucky Derby.
May 4 (Mon.)	— Students' Memorial Day.
May 8 (Fri.)	— V-E Day.
May 16 (Sat.)	— Armed Forces Day.
May 24 (Sun.)	— Indianapolis 500 auto race.
June 21 (Sun.)	— Summer begins, 6:45 A.M. EST.
June 24 (Wed.)	— San Juan Day, in Puerto Rico, St. Jean Day in Quebec.
June 26 (Fri.)	— United Nations Charter Day.
July 1 (Wed.)	— Dominion Day, or Canada Day.
July 2, 1881	— Pres. Garfield is mortally wounded.
July 14 (Tues.)	— Bastille Day in France.
July 15, 1881	— Billy the Kid is shot dead.
July 18, 1936	— Spanish Civil War begins.
July 26, 1956	— Egypt seized Suez Canal.
Aug. 6 (Thurs.)	— Hiroshima Day.
Aug. 13, 1906	— Race riot in Brownsville, Tex., occurs.
Aug. 19 (Wed.)	— National Aviation Day.
Sept. 4, 1781	— The city of Los Angeles was founded.
Sept. 16 (Wed.)	— Mexican Independence Day.
Sept. 22 (Tues.)	— Autumn begins, 10:05 P.M. EST.
Oct. 19, 1781	— American Revol. ends as Cornwallis surrenders.
Oct. 24 (Sat.)	— UN Day.
Nov. 4, 1956	— Hungarian revolt crushed by Soviets.
Nov. 5 (Thurs.)	— Guy Fawkes Day in Britain.
Nov. 23, 1936	— Life magazine begins publication.
Dec. 12 (Sat.)	— Fiesta of Our Lady of Guadalupe in Mexico.
Dec. 21 (Mon.)	— Winter begins, 5:51 P.M. EST.
Dec. 26 (Sat.)	— Boxing Day in the British Commonwealth of Nations.

The Meaning of "One Inch of Rain"

An acre of ground contains 43,560 square feet. Consequently, a rainfall of 1 inch over 1 acre of ground would mean a total of 6,272,640 cubic inches of water. This is equivalent of 3,630 cubic feet.

As a cubic foot of pure water weights about 62.4 pounds, the exact amount varying with the density, it follows that the weight of a uniform coating of 1 inch of rain over 1 acre of surface would be 226,512 pounds, or about 113 short tons. The weight of 1 U.S. gallon of pure water is about 8.345 pounds. Consequently a rainfall of 1 inch over 1 acre of ground would mean 27,143 gallons of water.

Temperature-Humidity (Discomfort) Index

The temperature-humidity index, THI, is a measure of summertime human discomfort resulting from the combined effects of temperature and humidity. (The THI may be calculated by adding wet-bulb and dry-bulb temperatures, multiplying the sum by 0.4 and adding 15.)

The following chart shows the combinations of temperature degrees and humidity percentages which produce discomfort for most persons (the equivalent of a THI value of 75) and those which produce acute discomfort for almost everyone (equivalent to a THI of 80).

Discomfort temp.-humid.	Acute discomfort temp.-humid.	Discomfort temp.-humid.	Acute discomfort temp.-humid.	Discomfort temp.-humid.	Acute discomfort temp.-humid.
75°—100%	81°—100%	82°—49%	88°—54%	90°—14%	96°—20%
76°— 91%	82°— 93%	83°—43%	89°—49%	91°—10%	97°—16%
77°— 82%	83°— 86%	84°—38%	90°—43%	92°— 7%	98°—13%
78°— 75%	84°— 78%	85°—33%	91°—38%	93°— 5%	99°—11%
79°— 68%	85°— 71%	86°—29%	92°—34%	94°— 3%	100°— 8%
80°— 61%	86°— 65%	87°—25%	93°—30%	95°— 1%	101°— 6%
81°— 55%	87°— 59%	88°—20%	94°—26%	96°— 1%	102°— 3%
		89°—17%	95°—23%	97°— 1%	103°— 1%

From 95 degrees up there is discomfort at any humidity. When the temperature is over 102 degrees there is acute discomfort at any humidity.

Chemical Elements, Discoverers, Atomic Weights

Atomic weights, based on the exact number 12 as the assigned atomic mass of the principal isotope of carbon, carbon 12, are provided through the courtesy of the International Union of Pure and Applied Chemistry and Butterworth Scientific Publications.

For the radioactive elements, with the exception of uranium and thorium, the mass number of either the isotope of longest half-life (*) or the better known isotope (**) is given.

Chemical element	Symbol	Atomic number	Atomic weight	Year discov.	Discoverer
Actinium	Ac	89	227*	1899	Debierne
Aluminum	Al	13	26.9815	1825	Oersted
Americium	Am	95	243*	1944	Seaborg, et al.
Antimony	Sb	51	121.75	1450	Valentine
Argon	Ar	18	39.948	1894	Rayleigh, Ramsay
Arsenic	As	33	74.9216	13th c.	Albertus Magnus
Astatine	At	85	210*	1940	Corson, et al.
Barium	Ba	56	137.34	1808	Davy
Berkelium	Bk	97	249**	1949	Thompson, Ghiorso, Seaborg
Beryllium	Be	4	9.0122	1798	Vauquelin
Bismuth	Bi	83	208.980	15th c.	Valentine
Boron	B	5	10.811a	1808	Gay-Lussac, Thenard
Bromine	Br	35	79.904b	1826	Balard
Cadmium	Cd	48	112.40	1817	Stromeyer
Calcium	Ca	20	40.08	1808	Davy
Californium	Cf	98	251**	1950	Thompson, et al.
Carbon	C	6	12.01115a	B.C.	
Cerium	Ce	58	140.12	1803	Klaproth
Cesium	Cs	55	132.905	1860	Bunsen, Kirchhoff
Chlorine	Cl	17	35.453b	1774	Scheele
Chromium	Cr	24	51.996b	1797	Vauquelin
Cobalt	Co	27	58.9332	1735	Brandt
Copper	Cu	29	63.546b	B.C.	
Curium	Cm	96	247*	1944	Seaborg, James, Ghiorso
Dysprosium	Dy	66	162.50	1886	Boisbaudran
Einsteinium	Es	99	254*	1952	Ghiorso, et al.
Erbium	Er	68	167.26	1843	Mosander
Europium	Eu	63	151.96	1901	Demarcay
Fermium	Fm	100	257*	1953	Ghiorso, et al.
Fluorine	F	9	18.9984	1771	Scheele
Francium	Fr	87	223*	1939	Perey
Gadolinium	Gd	64	157.25	1886	Marignac
Gallium	Ga	31	69.72	1875	Boisbaudran
Germanium	Ge	32	72.59	1886	Winkler
Gold	Au	79	196.967	B.C.	
Hafnium	Hf	72	178.49	1923	Coster, Hevesy
Hahnium	Ha	105	262*	1970	Ghiorso, et al.
Helium	He	2	4.0026	1868	Janssen, Lockyer
Holmium	Ho	67	164.930	1878	Soret, Delafontaine
Hydrogen	H	1	1.00797a	1766	Cavendish
Indium	In	49	114.82	1863	Reich, Richter
Iodine	I	53	126.9044	1811	Courtois
Iridium	Ir	77	192.2	1804	Tennant
Iron	Fe	26	55.847b	B.C.	
Krypton	Kr	36	83.80	1898	Ramsay, Travers
Lanthanum	La	57	138.91	1839	Mosander
Lawrencium	Lr	103	256*	1961	Ghiorso, T. Sikkeland, A.E. Larsh, and R.M. Latimer
Lead	Pb	82	207.19	B.C.	
Lithium	Li	3	6.939	1817	Arfvedson
Lutetium	Lu	71	174.97	1907	Welsbach, Urbain
Magnesium	Mg	12	24.312	1829	Bussy
Manganese	Mn	25	54.9380	1774	Gahn
Mendelevium	Md	101	258*	1955	Ghiorso, et al.
Mercury	Hg	80	200.59	B.C.	
Molybdenum	Mo	42	95.94	1782	Hjelm
Neodymium	Nd	60	144.24	1885	Welsbach
Neon	Ne	10	20.183	1898	Ramsay, Travers
Neptunium	Np	93	237*	1940	McMillan, Abelson
Nickel	Ni	28	58.71	1751	Cronstedt
Niobium'	Nb	41	92.906	1801	Hatchett
Nitrogen	N	7	14.0067	1772	Rutherford
Nobelium	No	102	255*	1958	Ghiorso, et al.
Osmium	Os	76	190.2	1804	Tennant
Oxygen	O	8	15.9994a	1774	Priestley, Scheele
Palladium	Pd	46	106.4	1803	Wollaston
Phosphorus	P	15	30.9738	1669	Brand
Platinum	Pt	78	195.09	1735	Ulloa
Plutonium	Pu	94	242**	1940	Seaborg, et al.
Polonium	Po	84	210**	1898	P. and M. Curie
Potassium	K	19	39.102	1807	Davy
Praseodymium	Pr	59	140.907	1885	Welsbach
Promethium	Pm	61	147**	1945	Glendenin, Marinsky, Coryell
Protactinium	Pa	91	231*	1917	Hahn, Meitner
Radium	Ra	88	226*	1898	P. & M. Curie, Bemont
Radon	Rn	86	222*	1900	Dorn
Rhenium	Re	75	186.2	1925	Noddack, Tacke, Berg
Rhodium	Rh	45	102.905	1803	Wollaston
Rubidium	Rb	37	85.47	1861	Bunsen, Kirchhoff
Ruthenium	Ru	44	101.07	1845	Klaus
Rutherfordium	Rf	104	261*	1969	Ghiorso, et al.

Chemical element	Symbol	Atomic number	Atomic weight	Year discov.	Discoverer
Samarium	Sm.	62	150.35	1879	Boisbaudran
Scandium	Sc	21	44.956	1879	Nilson
Selenium	Se	34	78.96	1817	Berzelius
Silicon	Si	14	28.086a	1823	Berzelius
Silver	Ag	47	107.868b	B.C.	
Sodium	Na	11	22.9898	1807	Davy
Strontium	Sr	38	87.62	1790	Crawford
Sulfur	S.	16	32.064a	B.C.	
Tantalum	Ta	73	180.948	1802	Ekeberg
Technetium	Tc	43	99**	1937	Perrier and Segre
Tellurium	Te	52	127.60	1782	Von Reichenstein
Terbium	Tb	65	158.924	1843	Mosander
Thallium	Tl	81	204.37	1861	Crookes
Thorium	Th	90	232.038	1828	Berzelius
Thulium	Tm	69	168.934	1879	Cleve
Tin	Sn	50	118.69	B.C.	
Titanium	Ti	22	47.90	1791	Gregor
Tungsten (Wolfram)	W	74	183.85	1783	d'Elhujar
Uranium	U.	92	238.03	1789	Klaproth
Vanadium	V.	23	50.942	1830	Sefstrom
Xenon	Xe	54	131.30	1898	Ramsay, Travers
Ytterbium	Yb	70	173.04	1878	Marignac
Yttrium	Y.	39	88.905	1794	Gadolin
Zinc	Zn	30	65.37	B.C.	
Zirconium	Zr	40	91.22	1789	Klaproth

(1) Formerly Columbium. (a) Atomic weights so designated are known to be variable because of natural variations in isotopic composition. The observed ranges are: hydrogen±0.0001; boron±0.003; carbon±0.005; oxygen±0.0001; silicon±0.001; sulfur±0.003. (b) Atomic weights so designated are believed to have the following experimental uncertainties: chlorine±0.001; chromium±0.001; iron±0.003; bromine±0.001; silver±0.001; copper±0.001.

Inventions and Scientific Discoveries

Invention	Date	Inventor	Nation.
Adding machine	1642	Pascal	French
Adding machine	1885	Burroughs	U.S.
Addressograph	1892	Duncan	U.S.
Aerosol spray	1941	Goodhue	U.S.
Air brake	1868	Westinghouse	U.S.
Air conditioning	1911	Carrier	U.S.
Air pump	1650	Guericke	German
Airplane, automatic pilot	1929	Green	U.S.
Airplane, experimental	1896	Langley	U.S.
Airplane jet engine	1939	Ohain	German
Airplane with motor	1903	Wright bros.	U.S.
Airplane, hydro	1911	Curtiss	U.S.
Airship	1852	Giffard	French
Airship, rigid dirigible	1900	Zeppelin	German
Arc tube	1923	Alexanderson	U.S.
Autogyro	1920	de la Cierva	Spanish
Automobile, differential gear	1885	Benz	German
Automobile, electric	1892	Morrison	U.S.
Automobile, exp'mtl	1875	Marcus	Austrian
Automobile, gasoline	1887	Daimler	German
Automobile, gasoline	1892	Duryea	U.S.
Automobile magneto	1897	Bosch	German
Automobile muffler	...	Maxim, H.P.	U.S.
Automobile self-starter	1911	Kettering	U.S.
Automobile, steam	1889	Roper	U.S.
Babbitt metal	1839	Babbitt	U.S.
Bakelite	1907	Baekeland	Belg., U.S.
Balloon	1783	Montgolfier	French
Barometer	1643	Torricelli	Italian
Bicycle, modern	1884	Starley	English
Bifocal lens	1780	Franklin	U.S.
Block signals, railway	1867	Hall	U.S.
Bomb, depth	1916	Tait	U.S.
Bottle machine	1903	Owens	U.S.
Braille printing	1829	Braille	French
Burner, gas	1855	Bunsen	German
Calculating machine	1823	Babbage	English
Camera—see also Photography			
Camera, Kodak	1888	Eastman, Walker	U.S.
Camera, Polaroid Land	1948	Land	U.S.
Car coupler	1873	Janney	U.S.
Carburetor, gasoline	1876	Daimler	German
Card time recorder	1894	Cooper	U.S.
Carding machine	1797	Whittemore	U.S.
Carpet sweeper	1876	Bissell	U.S.
Cash register	1879	Ritty	U.S.
Cathode ray tube	1878	Crookes	English
Cellophane	1911	Brandenberger	Swiss
Celluloid	1870	Hyatt	U.S.
Cement, Portland	1845	Aspdin	English
Chronometer	1735	Harrison	English
Circuit breaker	1925	Hilliard	U.S.
Clock, pendulum	1657	Huygens	Dutch
Coaxial cable system	1929	Affel, Espensched	U.S.
Coke oven	1893	Hoffman	Austrian
Compressed air rock drill	1871	Ingersoll	U.S.
Comptometer	1887	Felt	U.S.
Computer, automatic sequence	1939	Aiken et al.	U.S.
Condenser microphone (telephone)	1920	Wente	U.S.
Corn, hybrid	1917	Jones	U.S.
Cotton gin	1793	Whitney	U.S.
Cream separator	1880	DeLaval	Swedish
Cultivator, disc	1878	Mallon	U.S.
Cystoscope	1877	Nitze	German
Dental plate, rubber	1855	Goodyear	U.S.
Diesel engine	1895	Diesel	German
Dynamite	1866	Nobel	Swedish
Dynamo, continuous current	1860	Picinotti	Italian
Dynamo, hydrogen cooled	1915	Schuler	U.S.
Electric battery	1800	Volta	Italian
Electric fan	1882	Wheeler	U.S.
Electrocardiograph	1903	Einthoven	Dutch
Electroencephalograph	1929	Berger	German
Electromagnet	1824	Sturgeon	English
Electron spectrometer	1944	Deutsch, Elliott, Evans	U.S.
Electron tube multigrid	1913	Langmuir	U.S.
Electroplating	1805	Brugnatelli	Italian
Electrostatic generator	1929	Van de Graaff	U.S.
Elevator brake	1852	Otis	U.S.
Elevator, push button	1922	Larson	U.S.
Engine, automobile	1879	Benz	German
Engine, coal-gas 4-cycle	1877	Otto	German
Engine, compression ignition	1883	Daimler	German
Engine, electric ignition	1880	Benz	German
Engine, gas, compound	1926	Eickemeyer	U.S.
Engine, gasoline	1872	Brayton, Geo.	U.S.
Engine, gasoline	1886	Daimler	German
Engine, steam, piston	1705	Newcomen	English
Engine, steam, piston	1769	Watt	Scottish
Engraving, half-tone	1893	Ives	U.S.

Invention	Date	Inventor	Nation.
Filament, tungsten	**1915**	Langmuir	U.S.
Flanged rail	**1831**	Stevens	U.S.
Flatiron, electric	**1882**	Seeley	U.S.
Furnace (for steel)	**1861**	Siemens	German
Galvanometer	**1820**	Sweigger	German
Gas discharge tube	**1922**	Hull	U.S.
Gas lighting	**1792**	Murdoch	Scottish
Gas mantle	**1885**	Welsbach	Austrian
Gasoline (lead ethyl)	**1922**	Midgley	U.S.
Gasoline, cracked	**1913**	Burton	U.S.
Gasoline, high octane	**1930**	Ipatieff	Russian
Geiger counter	**1913**	Geiger	German
Glass, laminated safety	**1909**	Benedictus	French
Glider	**1853**	Cayley	English
Gun, breechloader	**1811**	Thornton	U.S.
Gun, Browning	**1916**	Browning	U.S.
Gun, magazine	**1875**	Hotchkiss	U.S.
Gun, silencer	**1909**	Maxim, H.P.	U.S.
Guncotton	**1846**	Schoenbein	German
Gyrocompass	**1911**	Sperry	U.S.
Gyroscope	**1852**	Foucault	French
Harvester-thresher	**1888**	Matteson	U.S.
Helicopter	**1939**	Sikorsky	U.S.
Hydrometer	**1768**	Baume	French
Ice-making machine	**1851**	Gorrie	U.S.
Iron lung	**1928**	Drinker, Slaw	U.S.
Kaleidoscope	**1817**	Brewster	English
Kinetoscope	**1887**	Edison	U.S.
Lacquer, nitrocellulose	**1921**	Flaherty	U.S.
Lamp, arc	**1879**	Brush	U.S.
Lamp, incandescent	**1879**	Edison	U.S.
Lamp, incand., frosted	**1924**	Pipkin	U.S.
Lamp, incand., gas	**1916**	Langmuir	U.S.
Lamp, Klieg	**1911**	Kliegl, A.&J.	U.S.
Lamp, mercury vapor	**1912**	Hewitt	U.S.
Lamp, miner's safety	**1816**	Davy	English
Lamp, neon	**1915**	Claude	French
Lathe, turret	**1845**	Fitch	U.S.
Launderette	**1934**	Cantrell	U.S.
Lens, achromatic	**1758**	Dollond	English
Lens, fused bifocal	**1908**	Borsch	U.S.
Leydenjar (condenser)	**1745**	von Kleist	German
Lightning rod	**1752**	Franklin	U.S.
Linoleum	**1860**	Walton	English
Linotype	**1885**	Mergenthaler	U.S.
Lock, cylinder	**1865**	Yale	U.S.
Locomotive, electric	**1851**	Vail	U.S.
Locomotive, exp'mtl	**1801**	Trevithick	English
Locomotive, exp'mtl	**1812**	Fenton et al.	English
Locomotive, exp'mtl	**1813**	Hedley	English
Locomotive, exp'mtl	**1814**	Stephenson	English
Locomotive practical	**1829**	Stephenson	English
Locomotive, 1st U.S.	**1830**	Cooper, P.	U.S.
Loom, power	**1785**	Cartwright	English
Loudspeaker, dynamic	**1924**	Rice, Kellogg	U.S.
Machine gun	**1861**	Gatling	U.S.
Machine gun, improved	**1872**	Hotchkiss	U.S.
Machine gun (Maxim)	**1883**	Maxim, H.S.	U.S., Eng.
Magnet, electro	**1828**	Henry	U.S.
Mantle, gas	**1885**	Welsbach	Austrian
Mason jar	**1858**	Mason, J.	U.S.
Match, friction	**1827**	John Walker	English
Mercerized textiles	**1843**	Mercer, J.	English
Meter, induction	**1888**	Shallenberger	U.S.
Metronome	**1816**	Malzel	Austrian
Micrometer	**1636**	Gascoigne	English
Microphone	**1877**	Berliner	U.S.
Microscope, compound	**1590**	Janssen	Dutch
Microscope, electronic	**1931**	Knoll, Ruska	German
Microscope, field ion	**1951**	Mueller	Germany
Monitor, warship	**1861**	Ericsson	U.S.
Monotype	**1887**	Lanston	U.S.
Motor, AC	**1892**	Tesla	U.S.
Motor, induction	**1887**	Tesla	U.S.
Motorcycle	**1885**	Daimler	German
Movie machine	**1894**	Jenkins	U.S.
Movie, panoramic	**1952**	Waller	U.S.
Movie, talking	**1927**	Warner Bros.	U.S.
Mower, lawn	**1868**	Hills	U.S.
Mowing machine	**1831**	Manning	U.S.
Neoprene	**1930**	Carothers	U.S.
Nylon synthetic	**1930**	Carothers	U.S.
Nylon	**1937**	Du Pont lab	U.S.
Oil cracking furnace	**1891**	Gavrilov	Russian
Oil filled power cable	**1921**	Emanueli	Italian
Oleomargarine	**1868**	Mege-Mouries	French
Ophthalmoscope	**1851**	Helmholtz	German
Paper machine	**1809**	Dickinson	U.S.
Parachute	**1785**	Blanchard	French
Pen, ballpoint	**1888**	Loud	U.S.
Pen, fountain	**1884**	Waterman	U.S.
Pen, steel	**1780**	Harrison	English
Pendulum	**1581**	Galileo	Italian
Percussion cap	**1814**	Shaw	U.S.
Phonograph	**1877**	Edison	U.S.
Photo, color	**1892**	Ives	U.S.
Photo film, celluloid	**1887**	Goodwin	U.S.
Photo film, transparent	**1878**	Eastman, Goodwin	U.S.
Photoelectric cell	**1895**	Elster	German
Photographic paper	**1898**	Baekeland	U.S.
Photography	**1835**	Talbot	English
Photography	**1837**	Daguerre	French
Photography	**1839**	Niepce	French
Photophone	**1880**	Bell	U.S.
Phototelegraphy	**1925**	Bell Labs	U.S.
Piano	**1709**	Cristofori	Italian
Piano, player	**1863**	Fourneaux	French
Pin, safety	**1849**	Hunt	U.S.
Pistol (revolver)	**1835**	Colt	U.S.
Plow, cast iron	**1797**	Newbold	U.S.
Plow, disc	**1896**	Hardy	U.S.
Pneumatic hammer	**1890**	King	U.S.
Powder, smokeless	**1863**	Schultze	German
Printing press, rotary	**1846**	Hoe	U.S.
Printing press, web	**1865**	Bullock	U.S.
Propeller, screw	**1804**	Stevens	U.S.
Propeller, screw	**1837**	Ericsson	Swedish
Punch card accounting	**1884**	Hollerith	U.S.
Radar	**1922**	Taylor, Young	U.S.
Radio amplifier	**1907**	De Forest	U.S.
Radio beacon	**1928**	Donovan	U.S.
Radio crystal oscillator	**1918**	Nicolson	U.S.
Radio receiver, cascade tuning	**1913**	Alexanderson,	U.S.
Radio receiver, heterodyne	**1913**	Fessenden	U.S.
Radio transmitter triode modulation	**1914**	Alexanderson	U.S.
Radio tube-diode	**1905**	Fleming	English
Radio tube oscillator	**1915**	De Forest	U.S.
Radio tube triode	**1907**	De Forest	U.S.
Radio, signals	**1895**	Marconi	Italian
Radio, magnetic detector	**1902**	Marconi	Italian
Radio FM 2-path	**1929**	Armstrong	U.S.
Rayon	**1883**	Swan	English
Razor, electric	**1931**	Schick	U.S.
Razor, safety	**1895**	Gillette	U.S.
Reaper	**1834**	McCormick	U.S.
Record, cylinder	**1887**	Bell, Tainter	U.S.
Record, disc	**1887**	Berliner	U.S.
Record, long playing	**1948**	Goldmark	U.S.
Record, wax cylinder	**1888**	Edison	U.S.
Refrigerants, low-boiling fluorine compound	**1930**	Midgely and co-workers	U.S.
Refrigerator car	**1868**	David	U.S.
Resin, synthetic	**1931**	Hill	English
Rifle, repeating	**1860**	Spencer	U.S.
Rocket engine	**1929**	Goddard	U.S.
Rubber, vulcanized	**1839**	Goodyear	U.S.
Saw, band	**1808**	Newberry	English
Saw, circular	**1777**	Miller	English
Searchlight, arc	**1915**	Sperry	U.S.
Sewing machine	**1846**	Howe	U.S.
Shoe-sewing machine	**1860**	McKay	U.S.
Shrapnel shell	**1784**	Shrapnel	English
Shuttle, flying	**1733**	Kay	English
Sleeping-car	**1858**	Pullman	U.S.
Slide rule	**1620**	Oughtred	English
Soap, hardwater	**1928**	Bertsch	German
Spectroscope	**1859**	Kirchoff, Bunsen	German
Spectroscope (mass)	**1918**	Dempster	U.S.
Spinning jenny	**1767**	Hargreaves	English
Spinning mule	**1779**	Crompton	English
Steamboat, exp'mtl	**1783**	Jouffroy	French

Invention	Date	Inventor	Nation.
Steamboat, exp'mtl	1785	Fitch	U.S.
Steamboat, exp'mtl	1787	Rumsey	U.S.
Steamboat, exp'mtl	1788	Miller	Scottish
Steamboat, exp'mtl	1803	Fulton	U.S.
Steamboat, exp'mtl	1804	Stevens	U.S.
Steamboat, practical	1802	Symington	Scottish
Steamboat, practical	1807	Fulton	U.S.
Steam car	1770	Cugnot	French
Steam turbine	1884	Parsons	English
Steel	1856	Bessemer	English
Steel alloy	1891	Harvey	U.S.
Steel alloy, high-speed	1901	Taylor, White	U.S.
Steel, electric	1900	Heroult	French
Steel, manganese	1884	Hadfield	English
Steel, stainless	1916	Brearley	English
Stereoscope	1838	Wheatstone	English
Stethoscope	1819	Laennec	French
Stethoscope, binaural	1840	Cammann	U.S.
Stock ticker	1870	Edison	U.S.
Storage battery, rechargeable	1859	Plante	French
Stove, electric	1896	Hadaway	U.S.
Submarine	1891	Holland	U.S.
Submarine, even keel	1894	Lake	U.S.
Submarine, torpedo	1776	Bushnell	U.S.
Tank, military	1914	Swinton	English
Tape recorder, magnetic	1899	Poulsen	Danish
Telegraph, magnetic	1837	Morse	U.S.
Telegraph, quadruplex	1874	Edison	U.S.
Telegraph, railroad	1887	Woods	U.S.
Telegraph, wireless high frequency	1896	Marconi	Italian
Telephone	1876	Bell	U.S.-Can.
Telephone amplifier	1912	De Forest	U.S.
Telephone, automatic	1891	Stowger	U.S.
Telephone, radio	1902	Poulsen, Fessenden	U.S.
Telephone, radio	1906	De Forest	U.S.
Telephone, radio, l. d	1915	AT&T	U.S.
Telephone, recording	1898	Poulseon	Danish
Telephone, wireless	1899	Collins	U.S.
Telescope	1608	Lippershey	Neth.
Telescope	1609	Galileo	Italian
Telescope, astronomical	1611	Kepler	German
Teletype	1928	Morkrum, Kleinschmidt	U.S.
Television, iconoscope	1923	Zworykin	U.S.
Television, electronic	1927	Farnsworth	U.S.
Television, (mech. scanner)	1926	Baird	Scottish
Thermometer	1593	Galileo	Italian
Thermometer	1710	Reaumur	French
Thermometer, mercury	1714	Fahrenheit	German
Time recorder	1890	Bundy	U.S.
Time, self-regulator	1918	Bryce	U.S.
Tire, double-tube	1845	Thomson	English
Tire, pneumatic	1888	Dunlop	Irish
Toaster, automatic	1918	Strite	U.S.
Tool, pneumatic	1865	Law	English
Torpedo, marine	1804	Fulton	U.S.
Tractor, crawler	1900	Holt	U.S.
Transformer A.C.	1885	Stanley	U.S.
Transistor	1947	Shockley, Brattain, Bardeen	U.S.
Trolley car, electric	1884 -87	Van DePoele, Sprague	U.S.
Tungsten, ductile	1912	Coolidge	U.S.
Turbine, gas	1899	Curtis, C.G.	U.S.
Turbine, hydraulic	1849	Francis	U.S.
Turbine, steam	1896	Curtis, C.G.	U.S.
Type, movable	1450	Gutenberg	German
Typewriter	1868	Soule, Glidden	U.S.
Vacuum cleaner, electric	1907	Spangler	U.S.
Washer, electric	1907	Hurley Co.	U.S.
Welding, atomic hydrogen	1924	Langmuir, Palmer	U.S.
Welding, electric	1877	Thomson	U.S.
Wind tunnel	1923	Munk	U.S.
Wire, barbed	1874	Glidden	U.S.
Wire, barbed	1875	Haisn	U.S.
X-ray tube	1913	Coolidge	U.S.
Zipper	1891	Judson	U.S.

Discoveries and Innovations: Chemistry, Physics, Biology, Medicine

	Date	Discoverer	Nation.
Acetylene gas	1892	Wilson	U.S.
ACTH	1949	Armour & Co.	U.S.
Adrenalin	1901	Takamine	Japanese
Aluminum, electrolytic process	1886	Hall	U.S.
Aluminum, isolated	1825	Oersted	Danish
Analine dye	1856	Perkin	English
Anesthesia, ether	1842	Long	U.S.
Anesthesia, local	1885	Koller	Austrian
Anesthesia, spinal	1898	Bier	German
Anti-rabies	1885	Pasteur	French
Antiseptic surgery	1867	Lister	English
Antitoxin, diphtheria	1891	Von Behring	German
Argyrol	1901	Barnes	U.S.
Arsphenamine	1910	Ehrlich	German
Aspirin	1889	Dresser	German
Atabrine	...	Mietzsch, et al.	German
Atomic numbers	1913	Moseley	English
Atomic theory	1803	Dalton	English
Atomic time clock	1947	Libby	U.S.
Atom-smashing theory	1919	Rutherford	English
Aureomycin	1948	Duggar	U.S.
Bacitracin	1945	Johnson, et al.	U.S.
Bacteria (described)	1676	Leeuwenhoek	Dutch
Barbital	1903	Fischer	German
Bleaching powder	1798	Tennant	English
Blood, circulation	1628	Harvey	English
Bordeaux mixture	1885	Millardet	French
Bromine from sea	1924	Edgar Kramer	U.S.
Calcium carbide	1888	Wilson	U.S.
Calculus	1670	Newton	English
Camphor synthetic	1896	Haller	French
Canning (food)	1804	Appert	French
Carbomycin	1952	Tanner	U.S.
Carbon oxides	1925	Fisher	German
Chlorine	1810	Davy	English
Chloroform	1831	Guthrie, S.	U.S.
Chloromycetin	1947	Burkholder	U.S.
Classification of plants and animals	1735	Linnaeus	Swedish
Cocaine	1860	Niermann	German
Combustion explained	1777	Lavoisier	French
Conditioned reflex	1914	Pavlov	Russian
Conteben	1950	Belmisch, Mietzsch, Domagk	German
Cortisone	1936	Kendall	U.S.
Cortisone, synthesis	1946	Sarett	U.S.
Cosmic rays	1910	Gockel	Swiss
Cyanimide	1905	Frank, Caro	German
Cyclotron	1930	Lawrence	U.S.
DDT (not applied as insecticide until 1939)	1874	Zeidler	German
Deuterium	1932	Urey, Brickwedde, Murphy	U.S.
DNA (structure)	1951	Crick	English
		Watson	U.S.
		Wilkins	English
Electric resistance (law)	1827	Ohm	German
Electric waves	1888	Hertz	German
Electrolysis	1852	Faraday	English
Electromagnetism	1819	Oersted	Danish
Electron	1897	Thomson, J.	English
Electron diffraction	1936	Thomson, G.	English
		Davisson	U.S.
Electroshock treatment	1938	Cerletti, Bini	Italian
Erythromycin	1952	McGuire	U.S.
Evolution, natural selection	1858	Darwin	English
Falling bodies, law	1590	Galileo	Italian

	Date	Discoverer	Nation.
Gases, law of combining volumes	1808	Gay-Lussac	French
Geometry, analytic	1619	Descartes	French
Gold (cyanide process for extraction)	1887	MacArthur, Forest	British
Gravitation, law	1687	Newton	English
Holograph	1948	Gabor	British
Human heart transplant	1967	Barnard	S. African
Indigo, synthesis of	1880	Baeyer	German
Induction, electric	1830	Henry	U.S.
Insulin	1922	Banting, Best, Macleod	Canadian
Intelligence testing	1905	Binet, Simon	French
Isinazid	1952	Hoffman-La-Roche	U.S.
		Domagk	German
Isotopes, theory	1912	Soddy	English
Laser (light amplification by stimulated emission of radiation)	1958	Townes, Schawlow	U.S.
Light, velocity	1675	Roemer	Danish
Light, wave theory	1690	Huygens	Dutch
Lithography	1796	Senefelder	Bohemian
Lobotomy	1935	Egas Moniz	Portuguese
LSD-25	1943	Hoffman	Swiss
Mendelian laws	1866	Mendel	Austrian
Mercator projection (map)	1568	Mercator (Kremer)	Flemish
Methanol	1925	Patard	French
Milk condensation	1853	Borden	U.S.
Molecular hypothesis	1811	Avogadro	Italian
Motion, laws of	1687	Newton	English
Neomycin	1949	Waksman, Lechevalier	U.S.
Neutron	1932	Chadwick	English
Nitric acid	1648	Glauber	German
Nitric oxide	1772	Priestley	English
Nitroglycerin	1846	Sobrero	Italian
Oil cracking process	1891	Dewar	U.S.
Oxygen	1774	Priestley	English
Ozone	1840	Schonbein	German
Paper, sulfite process	1867	Tilghman	U.S.
Paper, wood pulp, sulfate process	1884	Dahl	German
Penicillin	1929	Fleming	English
practical use	1941	Florey, Chain	English
Periodic law and table of elements	1869	Mendeleyev	Russian
Planetary motion, laws	1609	Kepler	German
Plutonium fission	1940	Kennedy, Wahl, Seaborg, Segre	U.S.

	Date	Discoverer	Nation.
Polymixin	1947	Ainsworth	English
Positron	1932	Anderson	U.S.
Proton	1919	Rutherford	English
Psychoanalysis	1900	Freud	Austrian
Quantum theory	1900	Planck	German
Quasars	1963	Matthews, Sandage	U.S.
Quinine synthetic	1918	Rabe	German
Radioactivity	1896	Becquerel	French
Radium	1898	Curie, Pierre	French
		Curie, Marie	Pol.-Fr.
Relativity theory	1905	Einstein	German
Reserpine	1949	Jal Vaikl	Indian
Salvarsan (606)	1910	Ehrlich	German
Schick test	1913	Schick	U.S.
Silicon	1823	Berzelius	Swedish
Streptomycin	1945	Waksman	U.S.
Sulfadiazine	1940	Roblin	U.S.
Sulfanilamide	1934	Domagk	German
Sulfanilamide theory	1908	Gelmo	German
Sulfapyridine	1938	Ewins, Phelps	English
Sulfathiazole	...	Fosbinder, Walter	U.S.
Sulfuric acid	1831	Phillips	English
Sulfuric acid, lead	1746	Roebuck	English
Terramycin	1950	Finlay, et al.	U.S.
Tuberculin	1890	Koch	German
Uranium fission (theory)	1939	Hahn, Meitner, Strassmann	German
		Bohr	Danish
		Fermi	Italian
		Einstein, Pegran, Wheeler	U.S.
Uranium fission, atomic reactor	1942	Fermi, Szilard	U.S.
Vaccine, measles	1954	Enders, Peebles	U.S.
Vaccine, polio	1953	Salk	U.S.
Vaccine, polio, oral	1955	Sabin	U.S.
Vaccine, rabies	1885	Pasteur	French
Vaccine, smallpox	1796	Jenner	English
Vaccine, typhus	1909	Nicolle	French
Van Allen belts, radiation	1958	Van Allen	U.S.
Vitamin A	1913	McCollum, Davis	U.S.
Vitamin B	1916	McCollum	U.S.
Vitamin C	1912	Holst, Froelich	Norwegian
Vitamin D	1922	McCollum	U.S.
Wassermann test	1906	Wassermann	German
Xerography	1938	Carlson	U.S.
X-ray	1895	Roentgen	German

Copyright Law of The United States

Source: Copyright Office, Library of Congress

Original works of authorship fixed in any tangible medium of expression are entitled to protection under the copyright law (Title 17 of the United States Code) in accordance with a complete revision of the statute which was signed by President Gerald R. Ford on Oct. 19, 1976 (Public Law 94-553, 90 Stat. 2541). The new law came into effect on Jan. 1, 1978; it supersedes the copyright act of 1909, as amended. Prior to the 1976 Act, there had been only three general revisions of the original copyright law of 1790, namely those of 1831, 1870, and 1909.

Categories of Works

Copyright protection under the new law extends to original works of authorship fixed in any tangible medium of expression, now known or later developed, from which they can be perceived, reproduced, or otherwise communicated, either directly or with the aid of a machine or device. Works of authorship include books, periodicals and other literary works, musical compositions with accompanying lyrics, dramas and dramatico-musical compositions, pantomimes and choreographic works, motion pictures and other audiovisual works, and sound recordings.

The owner of a copyright is given the exclusive right to reproduce the copyrighted work in copies or phonorecords and distribute them to the public by sale, rental, lease, or lending. The owner of a copyright also enjoys the exclusive right to make derivative works based upon the copyrighted work, to perform the work publicly if it be a literary, musical, dramatic, or choreographic work, a pantomime, motion picture, or other audiovisual work, and in the case of literary, musical, dramatic, and choreographic works, pantomimes, and pictorial, graphic, or sculptural works, including the individual images of a motion picture or other audiovisual work, to display the copyrighted work publicly. All of these rights are subject to certain specified exceptions, including the so-called judicial doctrine of "fair use," which is included in the law for the first time.

The new act also provides special provisions permitting compulsory licensing for the recording and distribution of phonorecords of nondramatic musical compositions, noncommercial transmissions by public broadcasters of published musical, pictorial, sculptural, and graphic works, performances of copyrighted nondramatic music by means of jukeboxes, and the secondary transmission of copyrighted works on cable television systems.

Single National System

The new law establishes a single national system of statutory protection for all copyrightable works fixed in tangible form, whether published or unpublished. Prior to Jan. 1, 1978 unpublished works were entitled to protection under the common law of the various states while published works came under the Federal statute.

Registration of a claim to copyright in any work, whether published or unpublished, may be made voluntarily at any time during the copyright term by the owner of the copyright or of any exclusive right in the work. Registration will not be a condition of copyright protection, but will be a prerequisite to an infringement suit. Subject to certain exceptions, the remedies of statutory damages and attorney's fees will not be available for those infringements occurring before registration. Even if registration is not made, copies or phonorecords of works published in the U.S. with notice of copyrights are required to be deposited for the collections of the Library of Congress. This deposit requirement is not a condition of protection, but does render the copyright owner subject to penalties for failure to deposit after a demand by the Register of Copyrights.

Duration of Copyright

For works created on or after Jan. 1, 1978, copyright subsists from their creation for a term consisting of the life of the author and 50 years after the author's death. For works made for hire, and for anonymous and pseudonymous works (unless the author's identity is revealed in Copyright Office records), the term is 100 years from creation or 75 years from first publication, whichever is shorter.

The new law retains for works already under statutory protection, the present term of copyright of 28 years from first publication (or from registration in some cases), renewable by certain persons for a second term of protection, but it increases the length of the second or renewal period to 47 years. Copyrights in their first 28-year term on Jan. 1, 1978, will still have to be renewed in order to be protected for the full new maximum term of 75 years. Copyrights in their second term on Jan. 1, 1978 were automatically extended to last for a total term of 75 years.

For works that had been created before the new law came into effect but had neither been published nor registered for copyright before Jan. 1, 1978, the term of copyright will generally be computed in the same way as for new works: the life-plus-50 or 75/100-year terms will apply. However, all works in this category are guaranteed at least 25 years of statutory protection. The law specifies that copyright in a work of this kind will not expire before Dec. 31, 2002, and if the work is published before that date the term is extended by another 25 years, through the end of the year 2027.

Notice of Copyright

Under the 1909 copyright law the copyright notice was the most important requirement for obtaining copyright protection for a published work. For published works, all copies had to bear the prescribed notice from the time of first publication. If a work was published before Jan. 1, 1978 without the required notice, copyright protection was lost permanently and cannot be regained.

The new copyright law requires a notice on copies or phonorecords of sound recordings that are distributed to the public. Errors and omissions, however, will not immediately result in forfeiture of the copyright and can be corrected within prescribed time limits. Innocent infringers misled by an omission or error in the notice will generally be shielded from liability.

The notice of copyright required on all visually perceptible copies published in the U.S. or elsewhere under the 1976 Act consists of the symbol © (the letter C in a circle), the word "Copyright," or the abbreviation "Copr.," and the year of first publication, and the name of the owner of copyright in the work. Example: © 1980 JOHN DOE

The notice must be affixed in such manner and location as to give reasonable notice of the claim of copyright.

The notice of copyright prescribed for all published phonorecords of sound recordings consists of the symbol ℗ (the letter P in a circle), the year of first publication of the sound recording, and the name of the owner of copyright in the sound recording, placed on the surface of the phonorecord, or on the phonorecord label or container in such manner and location as to give reasonable notice of the claim of copyright. Example: ℗ 1980 DOE RECORDS, INC.

Manufacturing Requirements

Under the 1909 Act certain works had to be manufactured in the U.S. to receive copyright protection. The new law does not make manufacture in the U.S. a condition of protection; additionally, it narrows the coverage of the manufacturing provisions, permits the importation of 2,000 copies manufactured abroad instead of the previous limit of 1,500 copies, and equates manufacture in Canada with manufacture in the U.S. Even the narrower requirement is scheduled to terminate on July 1, 1982.

The manufacturing requirements of the new law apply as a general rule only to the copies of a work that consists "preponderantly of a nondramatic literary material that is in the English language." They do not extend to dramatic, musical, pictorial, or graphic works; foreign language, bilingual, or multilingual works; public domain material; or works consistng preponderantly of material not subject to the manufacturing provision.

Under the new statute, compliance with the manufacturing requirements will no longer constitute a condition of copyright, but, in cases where the requirements are not satisfied, the rights with respect to reproduction and the distribution of copies are limited as against certain infringers. Even if copies are imported or distributed in violation of the new law, there would be no effect on the copyright owner's right to make and distribute phonorecords of the work, to make derivative works including dramatizations and motion pictures, and to perform or display the work publicly.

International Protection

The U.S. has copyright relations with more than 70 countries, under which works of American authors are protected in those countries, and the works of their authors are protected in the U.S. The basic feature of this protection is "national treatment," under which the alien author is treated by a country in the same manner that it treats its own authors. Relations exist by virtue of bilateral agreements or through the Buenos Aires Convention or the Universal Copyright Convention. U.S. legislation implementing the latter convention, which became effective Sept. 16, 1955, gives the works of foreign authors the benefit of exemptions from the manufacturing requirements of the U.S. copyright law, provided the works are first published abroad with a copyright notice including the symbol © , the name of the copyright owner and the year date of first publication, and that the work either is by an "author" who is a citizen or subject of a foreign country which belongs to the Convention or is first published in a foreign member country. Conversely, works of U.S. authors are exempt from certain burdensome requirements in particular foreign member countries.

Works published on or after Jan. 1, 1978, are subject to protection under the new copyrights statute if, on the date of first publication, one or more of the authors is a national or domiciliary of the U.S., or is a national, domiciliary, or sovereign authority of a foreign nation that is a party to a copyright treaty to which the United States is also a party, or is a stateless person, regardless of domicile, or if the work is first published either in the U.S. or in a foreign nation that, on the date of first publication is a party to the Universal Copyright Convention. All unpublished works are protected here regardless of the citizenship or domicile of the author.

A U.S. author may obtain copyright protection in all countries that are members of the Universal Copyright Convention (UCC). In member countries, where no formalities are required, the works of U.S. authors are protected automatically. Member countries whose laws impose formalities protect U.S. works if all published copies bear a convention notice which consists of the symbol ©, together with the name of the copyright owner and the year date of publication. Example: © JOHN DOE 1980

Further information and application forms may be obtained free of charge by writing to the Copyright Office, The Library of Congress, Washington, D.C. 20559.

Off-Beat News Stories of 1980

What me guilty? Many off-beat news stories pop up when the law tries to impose order. With this in mind, the quarterly news magazine of the Georgia State Lodge of the Fraternal Order of Police decided to survey its readers to find "the most creative excuse" offered by the state's traffic violators. Officer Steve Rose of the Shamblee Police Department, near Atlanta, reported on a close encounter of a different kind. After he had pulled aside a speeding driver, he approached the driver's window. As soon as he got close, Rose said, the driver "flipped open his wallet and spoke to it, saying 'Kirk to Enterprise, Kirk to Enterprise, beam me out of here fast.' " Then there was the man stopped by Officer Gary Roberson. Pulled over for following an ambulance too closely at high speed, the driver said that his uncle was in the ambulance. "Wouldn't you follow your kin to the hospital?" the man entreated. Roberson escorted the man to the hospital and watched attendants bring an elderly woman out of the ambulance.

Don't tell Greyhound bus driver Wayne Thompson that the law doesn't miss a beat. Wayne foiled a hijacker on his Chicago-Cleveland bus last year by summoning the police with the CB radio under his seat. But the man arrested wasn't the only one in hot water. Wayne's CB radio was against company rules and he was suspended for 10 days, losing $700 in pay.

Party rivalries go a long way. That's what the police blotter in Detroit, the week after the Republican National Convention, would lead you to believe. That week Richard Nixon arrested Jimmy Carter. Officer Nixon, that is, collared 25-year-old Jimmy Carter when he allegedly broke into an advertising specialties company.

Hunter Warren Stovall had to duck when he opened his freezer door. Out flew a mallard he had shot that morning and put into the freezer. Stovall's wife, Charlotte, reported that Stovall started screaming. "I think he thought the dead bird had come back to get him," she said. Stovall had wrapped separately in tin foil and sealed with tape 2 ducks he had shot that morning. He then put them into the freezer until a busy taxidermist could stuff them. One of the ducks had worked his way out of the foil and when the freezer door opened, the half-frozen bird with buckshot wounds in the neck and wing flapped out of the refrigerator and flew around the room. A weeping Mrs. Stovall wrapped the bird in a blanket and rocked it like a baby. She nursed it through the weekend and took it to the veterinarian, who said that the stunned bird had survived in the freezer because of its natural insulation.

Isn't God's work supposed to be virtuous in itself? Two employees at the American Bible Society in New York City have even more evidence of their moral value than what their vocation provides. The society's new special secretary for literature for 1980 is named John Duguid (pronounced do-good) and the society's new public relations spokesman is named David Virtue.

One man's response to an ever unpopular figure, the collection attorney, was to mix animosity with his alimony. When the attorney came after his wife's $17,500 divorce settlement, Bob Taylor of Tulsa, Okla., paid it off in an unusual way. He hired a security company to go to the bank and pick up the money in quarters, nickels, and dimes. He also made sure the 30-odd bags of coins, weighing about a ton, were delivered to the lawyer's office after regular banking hours. "Paying it all in coins is sure getting me out of the blues," Mr. Taylor said.

A house divided doesn't necessarily cause problems. The dividing line between the cities of Pawtucket and Central Falls, R.I., cuts straight through some houses, giving their residents a choice on tax bills, police and fire protection, schools, and trash collection. But there still is some confusion. Two title searches were necessary when Ernest Mowry bought his house. Although Martin Tarpy was born on the Pawtucket side of his parents' home, the doctor thought it was closer to go to Central Falls to record the birth. Consequently, Martin had some difficulty getting a copy of his birth certificate. But what God has joined, no human-made boundary can break asunder. Edward Gnys and his wife sleep in different towns, but, since the city line runs through their bedroom, said Mr. Gnys, my wife "still speaks to me."

America's streets are still paved with gold, at least for Melina Chica de Zapata from Colombia. She was visiting her relatives in Queens, N.Y., when she found a dollar bill on the street. That isn't much of a discovery these days. But, deciding that the dollar was a lucky omen, Mrs. Zapata used it to buy a New York State Lotto ticket, choosing some combinations from the dollar's serial number to play the ticket. She won $391,000, which will be payable over a 10-year period.

Many people have walked a mile for charity, but few have sat in soup for 2 days. Disc Jockey Joe Thomas of station WNAB in Bridgeport, Conn., did just that. He eased himself into a hot tub containing 700 gallons of chicken soup in order to raise $15,000 for the Easter Seals Rehabilitation Center of Eastern Fairfield County. Other people joined Mr. Thomas, in order to collect donations of pledged support for each minute they paddled about in the soup. "It's nice and warm, the soup's 90 degrees," said Mr. Thomas at the start of the weekend. "We're going to throw in a couple of rubber chickens to give it atmosphere. The way I look at it, chicken soup's supposed to be so good for colds, I shouldn't catch one for 10 years."

The United States Monopoly Championship this year unleashed the forces of competition. A 10-year-old Staten Island boy, Angelo Repole, took on defending champion Dana Terman of Maryland, and he didn't hide his disappointment when some real estate deals went against him. At one point, Angelo ran sobbing to the men's room when he could not raise the $1,300 in rent he owed for landing on Mr. Terman's Park Place property. After admitting bankruptcy and defeat, Angelo needed 10 minutes in the men's room to wash his face and regain his composure, before returning to the Monopoly table to shake hands with Mr. Terman. "Angelo can't stand losing," his mother confided.

"I say, do you chaps know anything about selling stars?" asked a telephone caller of the staff of the Smithsonian Astrophysical Observatory in Cambridge, Mass. He had seen one of several advertisements offering to name a specific star after someone for $25. An organization calling itself Name a Star Immortality Inc. had placed an add in The National Enquirer that read: "The Smithsonian Astrophysical Observatory catalog lists some 250,000 stars that are as yet unnamed. Name a Star is offering 250,000 people the opportunity to have a specific star named after them or after a loved one . . . and to have that star and its new name identified by number permanently . . . and . . . registered in the Library of Congress." Well, it's not that easy to attach your name to a star. The Smithsonian Institution issued a statement condemning such sky-high selling. "In fact," said the statement, "stars are not named for individuals but are numbered and all official star designations are made by the International Astronomical Union, a scientific organization."

If you can't sell stars, then how about potholes. Mayor John McGee of the rural town of Falls City, Ore. (pop. 752) didn't have the money to pave the town's potholes. Instead, he came up with a program of selling them as Christmas gifts "for people who have everything." The charge was $10 for a regular repaving job, while the $20 deluxe job came with the recipient's name embossed in fluorescent orange paint on top of the patch. Purchasers were given a certificate describing their pothole sites, the date each was filled, and written assurance the purchase price was used only for the pothole. At the end of 1979, the city recorder, Velta Mack, said: "We have sold almost all the potholes."

Out in the wild west, everyone helps out, even if the cause is the rebuilding of a bordello that was destroyed by fire. A fire on Nov. 20, 1979, nearly destroyed Fran's Star Ranch, about 3 miles outside Beatty, Nevada. Never ones to neglect a needy neighbor, the local Veterans of Foreign Wars post and its Women's Auxiliary held a "fire dance" and raised more than $5,000. Said the president of the Women's Auxiliary: "We do this for anybody who needs help. We aren't doing this to restore a brothel. We're doing this for Fran. She's one of a kind." Fran, who runs one of 5 legal brothels in Nye County, makes regular donations to the Beatty Volunteer Fire Department and once purchased uniforms for the local softball team. Until the new bordello would be built, she was using a trailer to conduct business.

SPORTS OF 1980

Olympic Games Records

The modern Olympic Games, first held in Athens, Greece, in 1896, were the result of efforts by Baron Pierre de Coubertin, a French educator, to promote interest in education and culture, also to foster better international understanding through the universal medium of youth's love of athletics.

His source of inspiration for the Olympic Games was the ancient Greek Olympic Games, most notable of the four Panhellenic celebrations. The games were combined patriotic, religious, and athletic festivals held every four years. The first such recorded festival was that held in 776 B.C., the date from which the Greeks began to keep their calendar by "Olympiads," or four-year spans between the games.

The first Olympiad is said to have consisted merely of a 200-yard foot race near the small city of Olympia, but the games gained in scope and became demonstrations of national pride. Only Greek citizens — amateurs — were permitted to participate. Winners received laurel, wild olive, and palm wreaths and were accorded many special privileges. Under the Roman emperors, the games deteriorated into professional carnivals and circuses. Emperor Theodosius banned them in 394 A.D.

Baron de Coubertin enlisted 9 nations to send athletes to the first modern Olympics in 1896; now more than 100 nations compete. Winter Olympic Games were started in 1924.

In 1980, 62 nations, including the United States, Canada, W. Germany, and Japan, refused to participate in the games in protest against the Soviet invasion of Afghanistan.

Sites and Unofficial Winners of Games

1896 Athens (U.S.)
1900 Paris (U.S.)
1904 St. Louis (U.S.)
1906 Athens (U.S.)*
1908 London (U.S.)
1912 Stockholm (U.S.)
1920 Antwerp (U.S.)
1924 Paris (U.S.)
1928 Amsterdam (U.S.)
1932 Los Angeles (U.S.)
1936 Berlin (Germany)
1948 London (U.S.)
1952 Helsinki (U.S.)
1956 Melbourne (USSR)
1960 Rome (USSR)
1964 Tokyo (U.S.)
1968 Mexico City (U.S.)
1972 Munich (USSR)
1976 Montreal (USSR)
1980 Moscow (USSR)
1984 Los Angeles (scheduled)

*Games not recognized by International Olympic Committee. Games 6 (1916), 12 (1940), and 13 (1944) were not celebrated. East and West Germany began competing separately in 1968.

Olympic Games Champions, 1896—1980

(*Indicates Olympic Records)

Track and Field — Men

60-Meter Run

1900	Alvin Kraenzlein, United States	7s*
1904	Archie Hahn, United States	7s*

100-Meter Run

1896	Thomas Burke, United States	12s
1900	Francis W. Jarvis, United States	10.8s
1904	Archie Hahn, United States	11s
1908	Reginald Walker, South Africa	10.8s
1912	Ralph Craig, United States	10.8s
1920	Charles Paddock, United States	10.8s
1924	Harold Abrahams, Great Britain	10.6s
1928	Percy Williams, Canada	10.8s
1932	Eddie Tolan, United States	10.3s
1936	Jesse Owens, United States	10.3s
1948	Harrison Dillard, United States	10.3s
1952	Lindy Remigino, United States	10.4s
1956	Bobby Morrow, United States	10.5s
1960	Armin Hary, Germany	10.2s
1964	Bob Hayes, United States	10.0s
1968	Jim Hines, United States	9.9s*
1972	Valeri Borzov, USSR	10.14s
1976	Hasely Crawford, Trinidad	10.06s
1980	Allan Wells, Great Britain	10.25s

200-Meter Run

1900	Walter Tewksbury, United States	22.2s
1904	Archie Hahn, United States	21.6s
1908	Robert Kerr, Canada	22.4s
1912	Ralph Craig, United States	21.7s
1920	Allan Woodring, United States	22s
1924	Jackson Scholz, United States	21.6s
1928	Percy Williams, Canada	21.8s
1932	Eddie Tolan, United States	21.2s
1936	Jesse Owens, United States	20.7s
1948	Mel Patton, United States	21.1s
1952	Andrew Stanfield, United States	20.7s
1956	Bobby Morrow, United States	20.6s
1960	Livio Berruti, Italy	20.5s
1964	Henry Carr, United States	20.3s
1968	Tommie Smith, United States	19.8s*
1972	Valeri Borzov, USSR	20.00s
1976	Donald Quarrie, Jamaica	20.23s
1980	Pietro Mennea, Italy	20.19s

400-Meter Run

1896	Thomas Burke, United States	54.2s
1900	Maxey Long, United States	49.4s
1904	Harry Hillman, United States	49.2s
1908	Wyndham Halswelle, Great Britain, walkover	50s
1912	Charles Reidpath, United States	48.2s
1920	Bevil Rudd, South Africa	49.6s
1924	Eric Liddell, Great Britain	47.6s
1928	Ray Barbuti, United States	47.8s
1932	William Carr, United States	46.2s
1936	Archie Williams, United States	46.5s
1948	Arthur Wint, Jamaica, B W I	46.2s
1952	George Rhoden, Jamaica, B W I	45.9s
1956	Charles Jenkins, United States	46.7s
1960	Otis Davis, United States	44.9s
1964	Michael Larrabee, United States	45.1s
1968	Lee Evans, United States	43.8s*
1972	Vincent Matthews, United States	44.66s
1976	Alberto Juantorena, Cuba	44.26s
1980	Viktor Markin, USSR	44.60s

800-Meter Run

1896	Edwin Flack, Great Britain	2m. 11s
1900	Alfred Tysoe, Great Britain	2m. 1.4s
1904	James Lightbody, United States	1m. 56s
1908	Mel Sheppard, United States	1m. 52.8s
1912	James Meredith, United States	1m. 51.9s
1920	Albert Hill, Great Britain	1m. 53.4s
1924	Douglas Lowe, Great Britain	1m. 52.4s
1928	Douglas Lowe, Great Britain	1m. 51.8s
1932	Thomas Hampson, Great Britain	1m. 49.8s
1936	John Woodruff, United States	1m. 52.9s
1948	Mal Whitfield, United States	1m. 49.2s
1952	Mal Whitfield, United States	1m. 49.2s
1956	Thomas Courtney, United States	1m. 47.7s
1960	Peter Snell, New Zealand	1m. 46.3s
1964	Peter Snell, New Zealand	1m. 45.1s
1968	Ralph Doubell, Australia	1m. 44.3s
1972	Dave Wottle, United States	1m. 45.9s
1976	Alberto Juantorena, Cuba	1m. 43.50s*
1980	Steve Ovett, Great Britain	1m. 45.40s

1,500-Meter Run

1896	Edwin Flack, Great Britain	4m. 33.2s
1900	Charles Bennett, Great Britain	4m. 6s

1904	James Lightbody, United States	4m. 5.4s
1908	Mel Sheppard, United States	4m. 3.4s
1912	Arnold Jackson, Great Britain	3m. 56.8s
1920	Albert Hill, Great Britain	4m. 1.8s
1924	Paavo Nurmi, Finland	3m. 53.6s
1928	Harry Larva, Finland	3m. 53.2s
1932	Luigi Beccali, Italy	3m. 51.2s
1936	Jack Lovelock, New Zealand	3m. 47.8s
1948	Henri Eriksson, Sweden	3m. 49.8s
1952	Joseph Barthel, Luxemburg	3m. 45.2s
1956	Ron Delany, Ireland	3m. 41.2s
1960	Herb Elliott, Australia	3m. 35.6s
1964	Peter Snell, New Zealand	3m. 38.1s
1968	Kipchoge Keino, Kenya	3m. 34.9s*
1972	Pekka Vasala, Finland	3m. 36.3s
1976	John Walker, New Zealand	3m. 39.17s
1980	Sebastian Coe, Great Britain	3m. 38.4s

3,000-Meter Steeplechase

1920	Percy Hodge, Great Britain	10m. 0.4s
1924	Willie Ritola, Finland	9m. 33.6s
1928	Toivo Loukola, Finland	9m. 21.8s
1932	Volmari Iso-Hollo, Finland (About 3,450 mtrs. extra lap by error)	10m. 33.4s
1936	Volmari Iso-Hollo, Finland	9m. 3.8s
1948	Thure Sjoestrand, Sweden	9m. 4.6s
1952	Horace Ashenfelter, United States	8m. 45.4s
1956	Chris Brasher, Great Britain	8m. 41.2s
1960	Zdzislaw Krzyszkowiak, Poland	8m. 34.2s
1964	Gaston Roelants, Belgium	8m. 30.8s
1968	Amos Biwott, Kenya	8m. 51s
1972	Kipchoge Keino, Kenya	8m. 23.6s
1976	Anders Garderud, Sweden	8m. 08.2s*
1980	Bronislaw Malinowski, Poland	8m. 09.7s

5,000-Meter Run

1912	Hannes Kolehmainen, Finland	14m. 36.6s
1920	Joseph Guillemot, France	14m. 55.6s
1924	Paavo Nurmi, Finland	14m. 31.2s
1928	Willie Ritola, Finland	14m. 38s
1932	Lauri Lehtinen, Finland	14m. 30s
1936	Gunnar Hockert, Finland	14m. 22.2s
1948	Gaston Reiff, Belgium	14m. 17.6s
1952	Emil Zatopek, Czechoslovakia	14m. 6.6s
1956	Vladimir Kuts, USSR	13m. 39.6s
1960	Murray Halberg, New Zealand	13m. 43.4s
1964	Bob Schul, United States	13m. 48.8s
1968	Mohamed Gammoudi, Tunisia	14m. 05.0s
1972	Lasse Viren, Finland	13m. 26.4s
1976	Lasse Viren, Finland	13m. 24.76s
1980	Miruts Yifter, Ethiopia	13m. 21.0s*

10,000-Meter Run

1912	Hannes Kolehmainen, Finland	31m. 20.8s
1920	Paavo Nurmi, Finland	31m. 45.8s
1924	Willie Ritola, Finland	30m. 23.2s
1928	Paavo Nurmi, Finland	30m. 18.8s
1932	Janusz Kusocinski, Poland	30m. 11.4s
1936	Ilmari Salminen, Finland	30m. 15.4s
1948	Emil Zatopek, Czechoslovakia	29m. 59.6s
1952	Emil Zatopek, Czechoslovakia	29m. 17.0s
1956	Vladimir Kuts, USSR	28m. 45.6s
1960	Pytor Bolotnikov, USSR	28m. 32.2s
1964	Billy Mills, United States	28m. 24.4s
1968	Naftali Temu, Kenya	29m. 27.4s
1972	Lasse Viren, Finland	27m. 38.4s*
1976	Lasse Viren, Finland	27m. 40.38s
1980	Miruts Yifter, Ethiopia	27m. 42.7s

Marathon

1896	Spiridon Loues, Greece	2h. 58m. 50s
1900	Michel Teato, France	2h. 59m. 45s
1904	Thomas Hicks, United States	3h. 28m. 53s
1908	John J. Hayes, United States	2h. 55m. 18.4s
1912	Kenneth McArthur, South Africa	2h. 36m. 54.8s
1920	Hannes Kolehmainen, Finland	2h. 32m. 35.8s
1924	Albin Stenroos, Finland	2h. 41m. 22.6s
1928	A.B. El Ouafi, France	2h. 32m. 57s
1932	Juan Zabala, Argentina	2h. 31m. 36s
1936	Kitei Son, Japan	2h. 29m. 19.2s
1948	Delfo Cabrera, Argentina	2h. 34m. 51.6s
1952	Emil Zatopek, Czechoslovakia	2h. 23m. 03.2s
1956	Alain Mimoun, France	2h. 25m.
1960	Abebe Bikila, Ethiopia	2h. 15m. 16.2s
1964	Abebe Bikila, Ethiopia	2h. 12m. 11.2s
1968	Mamo Wolde, Ethiopia	2h. 20m. 26.4s
1972	Frank Shorter, United States	2h. 12m. 19.8s
1976	Waldemar Cierpinski, E. Germany	2h. 09m. 55s*
1980	Waldemar Cierpinski, E. Germany	2h. 11m. 03s

10,000-Meter Cross-Country

1920	Paavo Nurmi, Finland	27m. 15s*
1924	Paavo Nurmi, Finland	32m. 54.8s

20-Kilometer Walk

1956	Leonid Spirine, USSR	1h. 31m. 27.4s
1960	Vladimir Golubnichy, USSR	1h. 34m. 7.2s
1964	Kenneth Mathews, Great Britain	1h. 29m. 34.0s
1968	Vladimir Golubnichy, USSR	1h. 35m. 58.4s
1972	Peter Frenkel, E. Germany	1h. 26m. 42.4s
1976	Daniel Bautista, Mexico	1h. 24m. 40.6s
1980	Maurizio Damilano, Italy	1h. 23m. 35.5s*

50-Kilometer Walk

1932	Thomas W. Green, Great Britain	4h. 50m. 10s
1936	Harold Whitlock, Great Britain	4h. 30m. 41.4s
1948	John Ljunggren, Sweden	4h. 41m. 52s
1952	Giuseppe Dordoni, Italy	4h. 28m. 07.8s
1956	Norman Read, New Zealand	4h. 30m. 42.8s
1960	Donald Thompson, Great Britain	4h. 25m. 30s
1964	Abdon Pamich, Italy	4h. 11m. 11.4s
1968	Christoph Hohne, E. Germany	4h. 20m. 13.6s
1972	Bern Kannenberg, W. Germany	3h. 56m. 11.6s
1980	Hartwig Gauder, E. Germany	3h. 49m. 24.0s*

110-Meter Hurdles

1896	Thomas Curtis, United States	17.6s
1900	Alvin Kraenzlein, United States	15.4s
1904	Frederick Schule, United States	16s
1908	Forrest Smithson, United States	15s
1912	Frederick Kelly, United States	15.1s
1920	Earl Thomson, Canada	14.8s
1924	Daniel Kinsey, United States	15s
1928	Sydney Atkinson, South Africa	14.8s
1932	George Saling, United States	14.6s
1936	Forrest Towns, United States	14.2s
1948	William Porter, United States	13.9s
1952	Harrison Dillard, United States	13.7s
1956	Lee Calhoun, United States	13.5s
1960	Lee Calhoun, United States	13.8s
1964	Hayes Jones, United States	13.6s
1968	Willie Davenport, United States	13.3s
1972	Rod Milburn, United States	13.24s*
1976	Guy Drut, France	13.30s
1980	Thomas Munkelt, E. Germany	13. 39s

200-Meter Hurdles

1900	Alvin Kraenzlein, United States	25.4s
1904	Harry Hillman, United States	24.6s*

400-Meter Hurdles

1900	J.W.B. Tewksbury, United States	57.6s
1904	Harry Hillman, United States	53s
1908	Charles Bacon, United States	55s
1920	Frank Loomis, United States	54s
1924	F. Morgan Taylor, United States	52.6s
1928	Lord Burghley, Great Britain	53.4s
1932	Robert Tisdall, Ireland	51.8s
1936	Glenn Hardin, United States	52.4s
1948	Roy Cochran, United States	51.1s
1952	Charles Moore, United States	50.8s
1956	Glenn Davis, United States	50.1s
1960	Glenn Davis, United States	49.3s
1964	Rex Cawley, United States	49.6s
1968	Dave Hemery, Great Britain	48.1s
1972	John Akii-Bua, Uganda	47.82s
1976	Edwin Moses, United States	47.64s*
1980	Volker Beck, E. Germany	48.70s

Standing High Jump

1900	Ray Ewry, United States	5ft. 5 in.
1904	Ray Ewry, United States	4ft. 11 in.
1908	Ray Ewry, United States	5ft. 2 in.
1912	Platt Adams, United States	5ft. 4 1-4 in.*

Running High Jump

1896	Ellery Clark, United States	5ft. 11 1-4 in.
1900	Irving Baxter, United States	6ft. 2 4-5 in.
1904	Samuel Jones, United States	5ft. 11 in.
1908	Harry Porter, United States	6ft. 3 in.
1912	Alma Richards, United States	6ft. 4 in.
1920	Richard Landon, United States	6ft. 4 1-4 in.
1924	Harold Osborn, United States	6ft. 6 in.
1928	Robert W. King, United States	6ft. 4 3-8 in.
1932	Duncan McNaughton, Canada	6ft. 5 5-8 in.
1936	Cornelius Johnson, United States	6ft. 7 15-16 in.
1948	John L. Winter, Australia	6ft. 6 in.
1952	Walter Davis, United States	6ft. 8.32 in.
1956	Charles Dumas, United States	6ft. 11 1-4 in.
1960	Robert Shavlakadze, USSR	7ft. 1 in.

1964	Valery Brumel, USSR	7ft. 1 3-4 in.
1968	Dick Fosbury, United States	7ft. 4 1-4 in.
1972	Yuri Tarmak, USSR	7ft. 3 3-4 in.
1976	Jacek Wszola, Poland	7ft. 4 1-2 in.
1980	Gerd Wessig, E. Germany	7ft. 9 in.*

Standing Broad Jump

1900	Ray Ewry, United States	10ft. 6 2-5 in.
1904	Ray Ewry, United States	11ft. 4 7-8 in.*
1908	Ray Ewry, United States	10ft. 11 1-4 in.
1912	Constantin Tsicilitras, Greece	11ft. 3-4 in.

Long Jump

1896	Ellery Clark, United States	20ft. 9 3-4 in.
1900	Alvin Kraenzlein, United States	23ft. 6 7-8 in.
1904	Myer Prinstein, United States	24ft. 1 in.
1908	Frank Irons, United States	24ft. 6 1-2 in.
1912	Albert Gutterson, United States	24ft. 11 1-4 in.
1920	William Petterssen, Sweden	23ft. 5 1-2 in.
1924	DeHart Hubbard, United States	24ft. 5 1-8 in.
1928	Edward B. Hamm, United States	25ft. 4 3-4 in
1932	Edward Gordon, United States	25ft. 3-4 in.
1936	Jesse Owens, United States	26ft. 5 5-16 in.
1948	William Steele, United States	25ft. 8 in.
1952	Jerome Biffle, United States	24ft. 10 in.
1956	Gregory Bell, United States	25ft. 8 1-4 in.
1960	Ralph Boston, United States	26ft. 7 3-4 in.
1964	Lynn Davies, Great Britain	26ft. 5 3-4 in.
1968	Bob Beamon, United States	29ft. 2 1-2 in.*
1972	Randy Williams, United States	27ft. 1-2 in.
1976	Arnie Robinson, United States	27ft. 4 1-2 in.
1980	Lutz Dombrowski, E. Germany	28ft. 1-4 in.

400-Meter Relay

1912	Great Britain	42.4s
1920	United States	42.2s
1924	United States	41s
1928	United States	41s
1932	United States	40s
1936	United States	39.8s
1948	United States	40.6s
1952	United States	40.1s
1956	United States	39.5s
1960	Germany (U.S. disqualified)	39.5s
1964	United States	39.0s
1968	United States	38.2s
1972	United States	38.19s*
1976	United States	38.33s
1980	USSR	38.26s

1,600-Meter Relay

1908	United States	3m. 27.2s
1912	United States	3m. 16.6s
1920	Great Britain	3m. 22.2s
1924	United States	3m. 16s
1928	United States	3m. 14.2s
1932	United States	3m. 8.2s
1936	Great Britain	3m. 9s
1948	United States	3m. 10.4s
1952	Jamaica, B.W.I.	3m. 03.9s
1956	United States	3m. 04.8s
1960	United States	3m. 02.2s
1964	United States	3m. 00.7s
1968	United States	2m. 56.1s*
1972	Kenya	2m. 59.8s
1976	United States	2m. 59.52s
1980	USSR	3m. 01.1s

Pole Vault

1896	William Hoyt, United States	10ft. 9 3-4 in.
1900	Irving Baxter, United States	10ft. 9 7-8 in.
1904	Charles Dvorak, United States	11ft. 6 in.
1908	A. C. Gilbert, United States Edward Cook Jr., United States	12ft. 2 in.
1912	Harry Babcock, United States	12ft. 11 1-2 in.
1920	Frank Foss, United States	13ft. 5 in.
1924	Lee Barnes, United States	12ft. 11 1-2 in.
1928	Sabin W. Carr, United States	13ft. 9 3-8 in.
1932	William Miller, United States	14ft. 1 7-8 in.
1936	Earle Meadows, United States	14ft. 3 1-4 in.
1948	Guinn Smith, United States	14ft. 1 1-4 in.
1952	Robert Richards, United States	14ft. 11 1-8 in.
1956	Robert Richards, United States	14ft. 11 1-2 in.
1960	Don Bragg, United States	15ft. 5 1-8 in.
1964	Fred Hansen, United States	16ft. 8 3-4 in.
1968	Bob Seagren, United States	17ft. 8 1-2 in.
1972	Wolfgang Nordwig, E. Germany	18ft. 1-2 in.
1976	Tadeusz Slusarski, Poland	18ft. 1-2 in.
1980	Wladyslaw Kozakiewicz, Poland	18ft. 11 1-2 in.*

16-lb. Hammer Throw

1900	John Flanagan, United States	167ft. 4 in.
1904	John Flanagan, United States	168ft. 1 in.
1908	John Flanagan, United States	170ft. 4 1-4 in.
1912	Matt McGrath, United States	179ft. 7 1-8 in.
1920	Pat Ryan, United States	173ft. 5 5-8 in.
1924	Fred Tootell, United States	174ft. 10 1-8 in.
1928	Patrick O'Callaghan, Ireland	168ft. 7 1-2 in.
1932	Patrick O'Callaghan, Ireland	176ft. 11 1-8 in.
1936	Karl Hein, Germany	185ft. 4 in.
1948	Imre Nemeth, Hungary	183ft. 11 1-2 in.
1952	Jozsef Csermak, Hungary	197ft. 11 9-16 in.
1956	Harold Connolly, United States	207ft. 3 1-2 in.
1960	Vasily Rudenkov, USSR	220ft. 1 5-8 in.
1964	Romuald Klim, USSR	228ft. 9 1-2 in.
1968	Gyula Zsivotsky, Hungary	240ft. 8 in.
1972	Anatoli Bondarchuk, USSR	248ft. 8 in.
1976	Yuri Sedykh, USSR	254ft. 4 in.
1980	Yuri Sedykh, USSR	268ft. 4 1-2 in.*

Discus Throw

1896	Robert Garrett, United States	95ft. 7 1-2 in.
1900	Rudolf Bauer, Hungary	118ft. 2.9-10 in.
1904	Martin Sheridan, United States	128ft. 10 1-2 in.
1908	Martin Sheridan, United States	134ft. 2 in.
1912	Armas Taipale, Finland	148ft. 4 in.
	Both hands—Armas Taipale, Finland	271ft. 10 1-4 in.
1920	Elmer Niklander, Finland	146ft. 7 1-4 in.
1924	Clarence Houser, United States	151ft. 5 1-8 in.
1928	Clarence Houser, United States	155ft. 3 in.
1932	John Anderson, United States	162ft. 4 7-8 in.
1936	Ken Carpenter, United States	165ft. 7 3-8 in.
1948	Adolfo Consolini, Italy	173ft. 2 in.
1952	Sim Iness, United States	180ft. 6.85 in.
1956	Al Oerter, United States	184ft. 10 1-2 in.
1960	Al Oerter, United States	194ft. 2 in.
1964	Al Oerter, United States	200ft. 1 1-2 in.
1968	Al Oerter, United States	212ft. 6 1-2 in.
1972	Ludvik Danek, Czechoslovakia	211ft. 3 in.
1976	Mac Wilkins, United States	221ft. 5.4 in.*
1980	Viktor Rashchupkin, USSR	218ft. 8 in.

Standing Hop, Step, and Jump

1900	Ray Ewry, United States	34ft. 8 1-2 in.*
1904	Ray Ewry, United States	34ft. 7 1-4 in.

Triple Jump

1896	James Connolly, United States	45ft.
1900	Myer Prinstein, United States	47ft. 4 1-4 in.
1904	Myer Prinstein, United States	47 ft.
1908	Timothy Aheame, Great Britain	48ft. 11 1-4 in.
1912	Gustaf Lindblom, Sweden	48ft. 5 1-8 in.
1920	Vilho Tuulos, Finland	47ft. 6 7-8 in.
1924	Archie Winter, Australia	50ft. 11 1-4 in.
1928	Mikio Oda, Japan	49ft. 11 in.
1932	Chuhei Nambu, Japan	51ft. 7 in.
1936	Naoto Tajima, Japan	52ft. 5 7-8 in.
1948	Arne Ahman, Sweden	50ft. 6 1-4 in.
1952	Adhemar de Silva, Brazil	53ft. 2 9-16 in.
1956	Adhemar de Silva, Brazil	53ft. 7 1-2 in.
1960	Jozef Schmidt, Poland	55ft. 1 3-4 in.
1964	Jozef Schmidt, Poland	55ft. 3 1-4 in.
1968	Viktor Saneev, USSR	57ft. 3-4 in.*
1972	Viktor Saneev, USSR	56ft. 11 in.
1976	Viktor Saneev, USSR	56ft. 8 3-4 in.
1980	Jaak Uudmae, USSR	56ft. 11 1-8 in.

16-lb. Shot Put

1896	Robert Garrett, United States	36ft. 9 3-4 in.
1900	Robert Sheldon, United States	46ft. 3 1-8 in.
1904	Ralph Rose, United States	48ft. 7 in.
1908	Ralph Rose, United States	46ft. 7 1-2 in.
1912	Pat McDonald, United States	50ft. 4 in.
	Both hands—Ralph Rose, United States	90ft. 5 1-2 in.
1920	Ville Porhola, Finland	48ft. 7 1-8 in.
1924	Clarence Houser, United States	49ft. 2 1-2 in.
1928	John Kuck, United States	52ft. 3-4 in.
1932	Leo Sexton, United States	52ft. 6 3-16 in.
1936	Hans Woellke, Germany	53ft. 1 3-4 in.
1948	Wilbur Thompson, United States	56ft. 2 in.
1952	Parry O'Brien, United States	57ft. 1 7-16 in.
1956	Parry O'Brien, United States	60ft. 11 in.
1960	William Nieder, United States	64ft. 6 3-4 in.
1964	Dallas Long, United States	66ft. 8 1-4 in.
1968	Randy Matson, United States	67ft. 4 3-4 in.
1972	Wladyslaw Komar, Poland	69ft. 6 in.
1976	Udo Beyer, E. Germany	69ft. 3-4 in.
1980	Vladimir Kiselyov, USSR	70ft. 1-2 in.*

Javelin Throw

1908	Erik Lemming, Sweden	178ft. 7 1-2 in.
	Held in middle—Erik Lemming, Sweden	179ft. 10 1-2 in.
1912	Erik Lemming, Sweden	198ft. 11 1-4 in.
	Both hands, Julius Saaristo, Finland	358ft. 11 7-8 in.
1920	Jonni Myrra, Finland	215ft. 9 3-4 in.
1924	Jonni Myrra, Finland	206ft. 6 3-4 in.
1928	Eric Lundquist, Sweden	218ft. 6 1-8 in.
1932	Matti Jarvinen, Finland	238ft. 7 in.
1936	Gerhard Stoeck, Germany	235ft. 8 5-16 in.
1948	Kaj Rautavaara, Finland	228ft. 10 1-2 in.
1952	Cy Young, United States	242ft. 0.79 in.
1956	Egil Danielsen, Norway	281ft. 2 1-4 in.
1960	Viktor Tsibulenko, USSR	277ft. 8 3-8 in.
1964	Pauli Nevala, Finland	271ft. 2 1-2 in.
1968	Janis Lusis, USSR	295ft. 7 1-4 in.
1972	Klaus Wolfermann, W. Germany	296ft. 10 in.
1976	Miklos Nemeth, Hungary	310ft. 4 in.*
1980	Dainis Kula, USSR	299ft. 2 3-8 in.

Decathlon

1912	Hugo Wieslander, Sweden	7,724.49 pts.
1920	Helge Lovland, Norway	6,804.35 pts.
1924	Harold Osborn, United States	7,710.77 pts.
1928	Paavo Yrjola, Finland	8,053.29 pts.
1932	James Bausch, United States	8,462.23 pts.
1936	Glenn Morris, United States	7,900 pts.
1948	Robert Mathias, United States	7,139 pts.
1952	Robert Mathias, United States	7,887 pts.
1956	Milton Campbell, United States	7,937 pts.
1960	Rafer Johnson, United States	8,392 pts.
1964	Willi Holdorf, Germany	7,887 pts.
1968	Bill Toomey, United States	8,193 pts.
1972	Nikola Avilov, USSR	8,454 pts.
1976	Bruce Jenner, United States	8,618 pts.*
1980	Daley Thompson, Great Britain	8,495pts.

Former point systems used prior to 1964.

Track and Field—Women

100-Meter Run

1928	Elizabeth Robinson, United States	12.2s
1932	Stella Walsh, Poland	11.9s
1936	Helen Stephens, United States	11.5s
1948	Francina Blankers-Koen, Netherlands	11.9s
1952	Marjorie Jackson, Australia	11.5s
1956	Betty Cuthbert, Australia	11.5s
1960	Wilma Rudolph, United States	11.0s*
1964	Wyomia Tyus, United States	11.4s
1968	Wyomia Tyus, United States	11.0s*
1972	Renate Stecher, E. Germany	11.07s
1976	Annegret Richter, W. Germany	11.08s*
1980	Ludmila Kondratyeva, USSR	11.6s

200-Meter Run

1948	Francina Blankers-Koen, Netherlands	24.4s
1952	Marjorie Jackson, Australia	23.7s
1956	Betty Cuthbert, Australia	23.4s
1960	Wilma Rudolph, United States	24.0s
1964	Edith McGuire, United States	23.0s
1968	Irena Szewinska, Poland	22.5s
1972	Renate Stecher, E. Germany	22.40s
1976	Barbel Eckert, E. Germany	22.37s
1980	Barbel Wockel, E. Germany	22.03*

400-Meter Run

1964	Betty Cuthbert, Australia	52s
1968	Colette Besson, France	52s
1972	Monika Zehrt, E. Germany	51.08s
1976	Irena Szewinska, Poland	49.29s
1980	Marita Koch, E. Germany	48.88s*

800-Meter Run

1928	Lina Radke, Germany	2m. 16.8s
1960	Ludmila Shevcova, USSR	2m. 4.3s
1964	Ann Packer, Great Britain	2m. 1.1s
1968	Madeline Manning, United States	2m. 0.9s
1972	Hildegard Flack, W. Germany	1m. 58.6s
1976	Tatyana Kazankina, USSR	1m. 54.94
1980	Nadezhda Olizarenko, USSR	1m. 53.5s*

1,500-Meter Run

1972	Ludmila Bragina, USSR	4m. 01.4s
1976	Tatyana Kazankina, USSR	4m. 05.48s
1980	Tatyana Kazankina, USSR	3m. 56.6s*

400-Meter Relay

1928	Canada	48.4s
1932	United States	47.0s
1936	United States	46.9s
1948	Netherlands	47.5s
1952	United States	45.9s
1956	Australia	44.5s
1960	United States	44.5s
1964	Poland	43.6s
1968	United States	42.8s
1972	West Germany	42.81s
1976	East Germany	42.55s
1980	East Germany	41.60s*

1,600-Meter Relay

1972	East Germany	3m. 23s
1976	East Germany	3m. 19.23s*
1980	USSR	3m. 20.02s

80-Meter Hurdles

1932	Mildred Didrikson, United States	11.7s
1936	Trebisonda Villa, Italy	11.7s
1948	Francina Blankers-Koen, Netherlands	11.2s
1952	Shirley Strickland de la Hunty, Australia	10.9s
1956	Shirley Strickland de la Hunty, Australia	10.7s
1960	Irina Press, USSR	10.8s
1964	Karen Balzer, Germany	10.5s
1968	Maureen Caird, Australia	10.3s*

100-Meter Hurdles

1972	Annelie Ehrhardt, E. Germany	12.59
1976	Johanna Schaller, E. Germany	12.77s
1980	Vera Komisova, USSR	12.56s*

High Jump

1928	Ethel Catherwood, Canada	5ft. 3 in.
1932	Jean Shiley, United States	5ft. 5 1-4 in.
1936	Ibolya Csak, Hungary	5ft. 3 in.
1948	Alice Coachman, United States	5ft. 6 1-8 in.
1952	Esther Brand, South Africa	5ft. 5 3-4 in.
1956	Mildred L. McDaniel, United States	5ft. 9 1-4 in.
1960	Iolanda Balas, Romania	6ft. 3-4 in.
1964	Iolanda Balas, Romania	6ft. 2 3-4 in.
1968	Miloslava Reskova, Czechoslovakia	5ft. 11 3-4 in.
1972	Ulrike Meyfarth, W. Germany	6ft. 3 1-4 in.
1976	Rosemarie Ackermann, E. Germany	6ft. 3 3-4 in.
1980	Sara Simeoni, Italy	6ft. 5 1-2 in.*

Discus Throw

1928	Helena Konopacka, Poland	129ft. 11 7-8 in.
1932	Lillian Copeland, United States	133ft. 2 in.
1936	Gisela Mauermayer, Germany	156ft. 3 3-16 in.
1948	Micheline Ostermeyer, France	137ft. 6 1-2 in.
1952	Nina Romaschkova, USSR	168ft. 8 1-2 in.
1956	Olga Fikotova, Czechoslovakia	176ft. 1 1-2 in.
1960	Nina Ponomareva, USSR	180ft. 8 1-4 in.
1964	Tamara Press, USSR	187ft. 10 1-2 in.
1968	Lia Manoliu, Romania	191ft. 2 1-2 in.
1972	Faina Melnik, USSR	218ft. 7 in.
1976	Evelin Schlaak, E. Germany	226ft. 4 1-2 in.
1980	Evelin Jahl, E. Germany	229ft. 6 1-4 in.*

Javelin Throw

1932	Mildred Didrikson, United States	143ft. 4 in.
1936	Tilly Fleischer, Germany	148ft. 2 3-4 in.
1948	Herma Bauma, Austria	149ft. 6 in.
1952	Dana Zatopkova, Czechoslovakia	165ft. 7 in.
1956	Inessa Janzeme, USSR	176ft. 8 in.
1960	Elvira Ozolina, USSR	183ft. 8 in.
1964	Mihaela Penes, Romania	198ft. 7 1-2 in.
1968	Angela Nemeth, Hungary	198ft. 1-2 in.
1972	Ruth Fuchs, E. Germany	209ft. 7 in.
1976	Ruth Fuchs, E. Germany	216ft. 4 in.
1980	Maria Colon, Cuba	224ft. 4 3-4 in.*

Shot Put (8lb., 13oz.)

1948	Micheline Ostermeyer, France	45ft. 1 1-2 in.
1952	Galina Zybina, USSR	50ft. 1 1-2 in.
1956	Tamara Tishkyevich, USSR	54ft. 5 in.
1960	Tamara Press, USSR	56ft. 9 7-8 in.
1964	Tamara Press, USSR	59ft. 6 1-4 in.
1968	Margitta Gummel, E. Germany	64ft. 4 in.
1972	Nadezhda Chizova, USSR	69ft.

1976	Ivanka Christova, Bulgaria	69ft. 5 in.
1980	Ilona Słupianek, E. Germany	73ft. 11 in.*

Long Jump

1948	Olga Gyarmati, Hungary	18ft. 8 1-4 in.
1952	Yvette Williams, New Zealand	20ft. 5 3-4 in.
1956	Elzbieta Krzeskinska, Poland	20ft. 9 3-4 in.
1960	Vyera Krepkina, USSR	20ft. 10 3-4 in.
1964	Mary Rand, Great Britain	22ft. 2 1-4 in.
1968	Viorica Viscopoleanu, Romania	22ft. 4 1-2 in.
1972	Heidemarie Rosendahl, W. Germany	22ft. 3 in.
1976	Angela Voigt, E. Germany	22ft. 2 1-2 in.
1980	Tatiana Kolpakova, USSR	23ft. 2 in.*

Pentathlon

1964	Irina Press, USSR	5,246 pts.
1968	Ingrid Becker, W. Germany	5,098 pts.
1972	Mary Peters, England	4,801 pts.
1976	Sigrun Siegl, E. Germany	4,745 pts.
1980	Nadyezhda Tkachenko, USSR	5,083pts.*

Former point system, 1964–1968

Swimming—Men

100-Meter Freestyle

1896	Alfred Hajos, Hungary	1:22.2
1904	Zoltan de Halmay, Hungary (100 yards)	1:02.8
1908	Charles Daniels, U.S.	1:05.6
1912	Duke P. Kahanamoku, U.S.	1:03.4
1920	Duke P. Kahanamoku, U.S.	1:01.4
1924	John Weissmuller, U.S.	59.0
1928	John Weissmuller, U.S.	58.6
1932	Yasuji Miyazaki, Japan	58.2
1936	Ferenc Csik, Hungary	57.6
1948	Wally Ris, U.S.	57.3
1952	Clark Scholes, U.S.	57.4
1956	Jon Henricks, Australia	55.4
1960	John Devitt, Australia	55.2
1964	Don Schollander, U.S.	53.4
1968	Mike Wenden, Australia	52.2
1972	Mark Spitz, U.S.	51.22
1976	Jim Montgomery, U.S.	49.99*
1980	Jorg Woithe, E. Germany	50.40

200-Meter Freestyle

1968	Mike Wenden, Australia	1:55.2
1972	Mark Spitz, U.S.	1:52.78
1976	Bruce Furniss, U.S.	1:50.29
1980	Sergei Kopliakov, USSR	1:49.81*

400-Meter Freestyle

1904	C. M. Daniels, U.S. (440 yards)	6:16.2
1908	Henry Taylor, Great Britain	5:36.8
1912	George Hodgson, Canada	5:24.4
1920	Norman Ross, U.S.	5:26.8
1924	John Weissmuller, U.S.	5:04.2
1928	Albert Zorilla, Argentina	5:01.6
1932	Clarence Crabbe, U.S.	4:48.4
1936	Jack Medica, U.S.	4:44.5
1948	William Smith, U.S.	4:41.0
1952	Jean Boiteux, France	4:30.7
1956	Murray Rose, Australia	4:27.3
1960	Murray Rose, Australia	4:18.3
1964	Don Schollander, U.S.	4:12.2
1968	Mike Burton, U.S.	4:09.0
1972	Brad Cooper, Australia	4:00.27
1976	Brian Goodell, U.S.	3:51.93
1980	Vladimir Salnikov, USSR	3:51.31*

1,500-Meter Freestyle

1908	Henry Taylor, Great Britain	22:48.4
1912	George Hodgson, Canada	22:00.0
1920	Norman Ross, U.S.	22:23.2
1924	Andrew Charlton, Australia	20:06.6
1928	Arne Borg, Sweden	19:51.8
1932	Kusuo Kitamura, Japan	19:12.4
1936	Noboru Terada, Japan	19:13.7
1948	James McLane, U.S.	19:18.5
1952	Ford Konno, U.S.	18:30.0
1956	Murray Rose, Australia	17:58.9
1960	Jon Konrads, Australia	17:19.6
1964	Robert Windle, Australia	17:01.7
1968	Mike Burton, U.S.	16:38.9
1972	Mike Burton, U.S.	15:52.58
1976	Brian Goodell, U.S.	15:02.40
1980	Vladimir Salnikov, USSR	14:58.27*

400-Meter Medley Relay

1960	United States	4:05.4
1964	United States	3:58.4
1968	United States	3:54.9
1972	United States	3:48.16
1976	United States	3:42.22*
1980	Australia	3:45.70

400-Meter Freestyle Relay

1964	United States	3:33.2
1968	United States	3:31.7
1972	United States	3:26.42*

800-Meter Freestyle Relay

1908	Great Britain	10:55.6
1912	Australia	10:11.6
1920	United States	10:04.4
1924	United States	9:53.4
1928	United States	9:36.2
1932	Japan	8:58.4
1936	Japan	8:51.5
1948	United States	8:46.0
1952	United States	8:31.1
1956	Australia	8:23.6
1960	United States	8:10.2
1964	United States	7:52.1
1968	United States	7:52.3
1972	United States	7:35.78
1976	United States	7:23.22*
1980	USSR	7:23.50

100-Meter Backstroke

1904	Walter Brack, Germany (100 yds.)	1:16.8
1908	Arno Bieberstein, Germany	1:24.6
1912	Harry Hebner, U.S.	1:21.2
1920	Warren Kealoha, U.S.	1:15.2
1924	Warren Kealoha, U.S.	1:13.2
1928	George Kojac, U.S.	1:08.2
1932	Masaji Kiyokawa, Japan	1:08.6
1936	Adolph Kiefer, U.S.	1:05.9
1948	Allen Stack, U.S.	1:06.4
1952	Yoshi Oyakawa, U.S.	1:05.4
1956	David Thiele, Australia	1:02.2
1960	David Thiele, Australia	1:01.9
1968	Roland Matthes, E. Germany	58.7
1972	Roland Matthes, E. Germany	56.58
1976	John Naber, U.S.	55.49*
1980	Bengt Baron, Sweden	56.53

200-Meter Backstroke

1964	Jed Graef, U.S.	2:10.3
1968	Roland Matthes, E. Germany	2:09.6
1972	Roland Matthes, E. Germany	2:02.82
1976	John Naber, U.S.	1:59.19*
1980	Sandor Wladar, Hungary	2:01.93

100-Meter Breaststroke

1968	Don McKenzie, U.S.	1:07.7
1972	Nobutaka Taguchi, Japan	1:04.94
1976	John Hencken, U.S.	1:03.11*
1980	Duncan Goodhew, Great Britain	1:03.34

200-Meter Breaststroke

1908	Frederick Holman, Great Britain	3:09.2
1912	Walter Bathe, Germany	3:01.8
1920	Haken Malmroth, Sweden	3:04.4
1924	Robert Skelton, U.S.	2:56.6
1928	Yoshiyuki Tsuruta, Japan	2:48.8
1932	Yoshiyuki Tsuruta, Japan	2:45.4
1936	Tetsuo Hamuro, Japan	2:42.5
1948	Joseph Verdeur, U.S.	2:39.3
1952	John Davies, Australia	2:34.4
1956	Masura Furukawa, Japan	2:34.7
1960	William Mulliken, U.S.	2:37.4
1964	Ian O'Brien, Australia	2:27.8
1968	Felipe Munoz, Mexico	2:28.7
1972	John Hencken, U.S.	2:21.55

1976	David Wilkie, Great Britain	2:15.11*
1980	Robertas Zulpa, USSR	2:15.85

100-Meter Butterfly

1968	Doug Russell, U.S.	55.9
1972	Mark Spitz, U.S.	54.27*
1976	Matt Vogel, U.S.	54.35
1980	Par Arvidsson, Sweden	54.92

200-Meter Butterfly

1956	William Yorzyk, U.S.	2:19.3
1960	Michael Troy, U.S.	2:12.8
1964	Kevin J. Berry, Australia	2:06.6
1968	Carl Robie, U.S.	2:08.7
1972	Mark Spitz, U.S.	2:00.70
1976	Mike Bruner, U.S.	1:59.23*
1980	Sergei Fesenko, USSR	1:59.76

200-Meter Individual Medley

1968	Charles Hickcox, U.S.	2:12.0
1972	Gunnar Larsson, Sweden	2:07.17*

400-Meter Individual Medley

1964	Dick Roth, U.S.	4:45.4
1968	Charles Hickcox, U.S.	4:48.4
1972	Gunnar Larsson, Sweden	4:31.98
1976	Rod Strachan, U.S.	4:23.68
1980	Aleksandr Sidorenko, USSR	4:22.89*

Springboard Diving

		Points
1908	Albert Zurner, Germany	85.5
1912	Paul Guenther, Germany	79.23
1920	Louis Kuehn, U.S.	675.00
1924	Albert White, U.S.	696.40
1928	Pete Desjardins, U.S.	185.04
1932	Michael Galitzen, U.S.	161.38
1936	Richard Degener, U.S.	161.57
1948	Bruce Harlan, U.S.	163.64
1952	David Browning, U.S.	205.29
1956	Robert Clotworthy, U.S.	159.56
1960	Gary Tobian, U.S.	170.00
1964	Kenneth Sitzberger, U.S.	159.90
1968	Bernie Wrightson, U.S.	170.15
1972	Vladimir Vasin, USSR	594.09
1976	Phil Boggs, U.S.	619.52
1980	Aleksandr Portnov, USSR	905.02

Platform Diving

		Points
1904	Dr. G.E. Sheldon, U.S.	12.75
1908	Hjalmar Johansson, Sweden	83.75
1912	Erik Adlerz, Sweden	73.94
1920	Clarence Pinkston, U.S.	100.67
1924	Albert White, U.S.	487.30
1928	Pete Desjardins, U.S.	98.74
1932	Harold Smith, U.S.	124.80
1936	Marshall Wayne, U.S.	113.58
1948	Sammy Lee, U.S.	130.05
1952	Sammy Lee, U.S.	156.28
1956	Joaquin Capilla, Mexico	152.44
1960	Robert Webster, U.S.	165.56
1964	Robert Webster, U.S.	148.58
1968	Klaus Dibiasi, Italy	164.18
1972	Klaus Dibiasi, Italy	504.12
1976	Klaus Dibiasi, Italy	600.51
1980	Falk Hoffman, E. Germany	835.65

Swimming—Women

100-Meter Freestyle

1912	Fanny Durack, Australia	1:22.2
1920	Ethelda Bleibtrey, U.S.	1:13.6
1924	Ethel Lackie, U.S.	1:12.4
1928	Albina Osipowich, U.S.	1:11.0
1932	Helene Madison, U.S.	1:06.8
1936	Hendrika Mastenbroek, Holland	1:05.9
1948	Greta Anderson, Denmark	1:06.3
1952	Katalin Szoke, Hungary	1:06.3
1956	Dawn Fraser, Australia	1:02.0
1960	Dawn Fraser, Australia	1:01.2
1964	Dawn Fraser, Australia	59.5
1968	Jan Henne, U.S.	1:00.0
1972	Sandra Neilson, U.S.	58.59
1976	Kornelia Ender, E. Germany	55.65
1980	Barbara Krause, E. Germany	54.79*

200-Meter Freestyle

1968	Debbie Meyer, U.S.	2:10.5
1972	Shane Gould, Australia	2:03.56
1976	Kornelia Ender, E. Germany	1:59.26
1980	Barbara Krause, E. Germany	1:58.33*

400-Meter Freestyle

1924	Martha Norelius, U.S.	6:02.2
1928	Martha Norelius, U.S.	5:42.8
1932	Helene Madison, U.S.	5:28.5
1936	Hendrika Mastenbroek, Netherlands	5:26.4
1948	Ann Curtis, U.S.	5:17.8
1952	Valerie Gyenge, Hungary	5:12.1
1956	Lorraine Crapp, Australia	4:54.6
1960	Susan Chris von Saltza, U.S.	4:50.6
1964	Virginia Duenkel, U.S.	4:43.3
1968	Debbie Meyer, U.S.	4:31.8
1972	Shane Gould, Australia	4:19.04
1976	Petra Thuemer E. Germany	4:09.89
1980	Ines Diers, E. Germany	4:08.76*

800-Meter Freestyle

1968	Debbie Meyer, U.S.	9:24.0
1972	Keena Rothhammer, U.S.	8:53.68
1976	Petra Thuemer, E. Germany	8:37.14
1980	Michelle Ford, Australia	8:28.90*

100-Meter Backstroke

1924	Sybil Bauer, U.S.	1:23.3
1928	Marie Braun, Netherlands	1:22.0
1932	Eleanor Holm, U.S.	1:19.4
1936	Dina Senff, Netherlands	1:18.9
1948	Karen Harup, Denmark	1:14.4
1952	Joan Harrison, South Africa	1:14.3
1956	Judy Grinham, Great Britain	1:12.9
1960	Lynn Burke, U.S.	1:09.3
1964	Cathy Ferguson, U.S.	1:07.7
1968	Kaye Hall, U.S.	1:06.2
1972	Melissa Belote, U.S.	1:05.78
1976	Ulrike Richter, E. Germany	1:01.83
1980	Rica Reinisch, E. Germany	1:00.86*

200-Meter Backstroke

1968	Pokey Watson, U.S.	2:24.8
1972	Melissa Belote, U.S.	2:19.19
1976	Ulrike Richter, E. Germany	2:13.43
1980	Rica Reinisch, E. Germany	2:11.77*

100-Meter Breaststroke

1968	Djurdjica Bjedov, Yugoslavia	1:15.8
1972	Cathy Carr, U.S.	1:13.58
1976	Hannelore Anke, E. Germany	1:11:16
1980	Ute Geweniger, E. Germany	1:10.22*

200-Meter Breaststroke

1924	Lucy Morton, Great Britain	3:32.2
1928	Hilde Schrader, Germany	3:12.6
1932	Clare Dennis, Australia	3:06.3
1936	Hideko Maehata, Japan	3:03.6
1948	Nelly Van Vliet, Netherlands	2:57.2
1952	Eva Szekely, Hungary	2:51.7
1956	Ursula Happe, Germany	2:53.1
1960	Anita Lonsbrough, Great Britain	2:49.5
1964	Galina Prozumenschikova, USSR	2:46.4
1968	Sharon Wichman, U.S.	2:44.4
1972	Beverly Whitfield, Australia	2:41.71
1976	Marina Koshevaia, USSR	2:33.35
1980	Lina Kachushite, USSR	2:29.54*

200-Meter Individual Medley

1968	Claudia Kolb, U.S.	2:24.7
1972	Shane Gould, Australia	2:23.07*

400-Meter Individual Medley

1964	Donna de Varona, U.S.	5:18.7
1968	Claudia Kolb, U.S.	5:08.5
1972	Gail Neall, Australia	5:02.97
1976	Ulrike Tauber, E. Germany	4:42.77
1980	Petra Schneider, E. Germany	4:36.29*

100-Meter Butterfly

1956	Shelley Mann, U.S.	1:11.0
1960	Carolyn Schuler, U.S.	1:09.5
1964	Sharon Stouder, U.S.	1:04.7
1968	Lynn McClements, Australia	1:05.5
1972	Mayumi Aoki, Japan	1:03.34
1976	Kornelia Ender, E. Germany	1:00.13*
1980	Caren Metschuck, E. Germany	1:00.42

200-Meter Butterfly

1968	Ada Kok, Netherlands	2:24.7
1972	Karen Moe, U.S.	2:15.57
1976	Andrea Pollack, E. Germany	2:11.41
1980	Ines Geissler, E. Germany	2:10.44*

400-Meter Medley Relay

1960	United States	4:41.1
1960	United States	4:33.9
1968	United States	4:28.3
1972	United States	4:20.75
1976	East Germany	4:07.95
1980	East Germany	4:06.67*

400-Meter Freestyle Relay

1912	Great Britain	5:52.8
1920	United States	5:11.6
1924	United States	4:58.8
1928	United States	4:47.6
1932	United States	4:38.0
1936	Netherlands	4:36.0
1948	United States	4:29.2
1952	Hungary	4:24.4
1956	Australia	4:17.1
1960	United States	4:08.9
1964	United States	4:03.8
1968	United States	4:02.5
1972	United States	3:55.19
1976	United States	3:44.82
1980	East Germany	3:42.71*

	Springboard Diving	Points
1920	Aileen Riggin, U.S.	539.90
1924	Elizabeth Becker, U.S.	474.50
1928	Helen Meany, U.S.	78.62
1932	Georgia Coleman U.S.	87.52
1936	Marjorie Gestring, U.S.	89.27
1948	Victoria M. Draves, U.S.	108.74
1952	Patricia McCormick, U.S.	147.30
1956	Patricia McCormick, U.S.	142.36
1960	Ingrid Kramer, Germany	155.81
1964	Ingrid Engel-Kramer, Germany	145.00
1968	Sue Gossick, U.S.	150.77
1972	Micki King, U.S.	450.03
1976	Jenni Chandler, U.S.	506.19
1980	Irina Kalinina, USSR	725.91

	Platform Diving	Points
1912	Greta Johansson, Sweden	39.90
1920	Stefani Fryland-Clausen, Denmark	34.60
1924	Caroline Smith, U.S.	166.00
1928	Elizabeth B. Pinkston, U.S.	31.60
1932	Dorothy Poynton, U.S.	40.26
1936	Dorothy Poynton Hill, U.S.	33.93
1948	Victoria M. Draves, U.S.	68.87
1952	Patricia McCormick, U.S.	79.37
1956	Patricia McCormick, U.S.	84.85
1960	Ingrid Kramer, Germany	91.28
1964	Lesley Bush, U.S.	99.80
1968	Milena Duchkova, Czech.	109.59
1972	Ulrika Knape, Sweden	390.00
1976	Elena Vaytsekhouskaya, USSR	406.59
1980	Martina Jaschke, USSR	596.25

22d Summer Olympics

Moscow, USSR, July 19-Aug. 3, 1980

Final Medal Standings

(nations in alphabetical order)

	Gold	Silver	Bronze	Total
Australia	2	2	5	9
Austria	1	3	1	5
Belgium	1	0	0	1
Brazil	2	0	2	4
Britain	5	7	9	21
Bulgaria	8	16	16	40
Cuba	8	7	5	20
Czechoslovakia	2	2	9	13
Denmark	2	1	2	5
Ethiopia	2	0	2	4
Finland	3	1	4	8
France	6	5	3	14
Germany, East	47	36	43	126
Greece	1	0	2	3
Guyana	0	0	1	1
Holland	0	1	3	4
Hungary	7	10	15	32
India	1	0	0	1
Ireland	0	1	1	2
Italy	8	3	4	15
Jamaica	0	0	3	3
Korea, North	0	3	2	5
Lebanon	0	0	1	1
Mexico	0	1	3	4
Mongolia	0	2	2	4
Poland	3	14	14	31
Romania	6	6	13	25
Spain	1	3	2	6
Sweden	3	3	6	12
Switzerland	2	0	0	2
Tanzania	0	2	0	2
USSR	80	70	47	197
Uganda	0	1	0	1
Venezuela	0	1	0	1
Yugoslavia	2	3	4	9
Zimbabwe	1	0	0	1

Duplicate medals awarded in some events

Olympic Gold Medal Winners

Gold Medal Winners

Archery

Men—Tomi Poikolainen, Finland.
Women—Keto Losaberidze, USSR.

Basketball

Men—Yugoslavia.
Women—USSR.

Boxing

106 lbs.—Shamil Sabyrov, USSR.
112 lbs.—Petar Lessov, Bulgaria.
119 lbs.—Juan Hernandez, Cuba.
126 lbs.—Rudl Fink, E. Germany.
132 lbs.—Angel Herrera, Cuba.
140 lbs.—Patrizio Oliva, Italy.
148 lbs.—Andres Aidama, Cuba.
157 lbs.—Armando Martinez, Cuba.
165 lbs.—Jose Gomez, Cuba.
179 lbs.—Slobodan Kacar, Yugoslavia.
Over 179 lbs.—Teofilo Stevenson, Cuba.

Canoeing—Men

500-Meter Single Canoe—Sergei Postrekhin, USSR.
500-Meter Canoe Pairs—Laszio Foitan, Istvan Vaskut, Hungary.
1,000-Meter Single Canoe—Ludomir Lubenov, Bulgaria.
1,000-Meter Double Canoe—Ivan Potzaichin, Toma Simionov, Romania.
500-Meter Single Kayak—Vladimir Parfenovich, USSR.
500-Meter Kayak Pairs—Vladimir Parfenovich, Sergei Chukhrai, USSR.

1,000-Meter Kayak Singles—Rudiger Helm, E. Germany.
1,000-Meter Double Kayak—Vladimir Parfenovich, Sergei Chukhrai, USSR.
1,000-Meter 4-Man Kayak—E. Germany
500-Meter Single Canoe (Woman)—Birgit Fischer, E. Germany.

Cycling

Individual Pursuit—Robert Dill-Bundi, Switzerland.
189-Kilometer Road Race—Sergei Soukhoroutchenkov, USSR.
1,000-Meter Time Trials—Lothar Thoms, E. Germany.
Individual Sprint—Lutz Hesslich, E. Germany.
4,000-Meter Team Pursuit—USSR.

Equestrian

3-Day Individual Event—Federico Euro Roman, Italy.
Individual Dressage—Elisabeth Theurer, Austria.
Grand Prix Individual Jumping—Jan Kowalczyk, Poland.
Team Jumping—USSR.
Team Dressage—USSR.
Team Competition—USSR.

Fencing—Men

Individual Foil—Vladimir Smirnov, USSR.
Individual Sabre—Viktor Krovopuskov, USSR.
Individual Epee—Johan Harmenberg, Sweden.
Team Foil—France.
Team Sabre—USSR.
Team Epee—France.

Women

Individual Foil—Pascale Triquet, France.
Team Foil—France.

Field Hockey

Men—India.
Women—Zimbabwe.

Gymnastics—Men

Team—USSR.
All Around—Alexandr Dityatin, USSR.
Side Horse—Zoltan Magyar, Hungary.
Floor Exercise—Roland Bruckner, E. Germany.
Vault—Nikolai Andrianov, USSR.
Rings—Alexandr Dityatin, USSR.
Parallel Bars—Alexandr Tkachyov, USSR.
Horizontal Bar—Stoyan Deltchev, Bulgaria.

Women

Team—USSR.
All-Around—Yelena Davydova, USSR.
Vault—Natallya Shaposhnikova, USSR.
Uneven Bars—Maxi Gnauck, E. Germany.
Balance Beam—Nadia Comaneci, Romania.
Floor Exercise—(tie) Nelli Kim, USSR & Nadia Comaneci, Romania.

Handball

Men—E. Germany.
Women—USSR.

Judo

132 lbs.—Thierry Rey, France.
143 lbs.—Nikolay Solodukhin, USSR.
157 lbs.—Ezio Gamba, Italy.
172 lbs.—Shota Khabarell, USSR.
190 lbs.—Juerg Roethisberger, Switzerland.
209 lbs.—Robert Van De Walle, Belgium.
209 lbs and Over—Angelo Parisi, France.
Open Weight—Dietmar Lorenz, E. Germany.

Modern Pentathlon

Team—USSR.

Rowing—Men

Pair with coxswain—E. Germany.
Four with coxswain—E. Germany.
Eight with coxswain—E. Germany.
Single Sculls—Pertti Karppinen, Finland.
Double Sculls—E. Germany.
Four Sculls—E. Germany.
Pair without coxswain—E. Germany.
Four without coxswain—E. Germany.

Women

Four with coxswain—E. Germany.
Eight with coxswain—E. Germany.
Pairs without coxswain—E. Germany.
Single Sculls—Sanda Toma, Romania.
Double Sculls—USSR.
Four Sculls with coxswain—E. Germany.

Shooting

50-Meter Free Pistol—Aleksandr Melentev, USSR.
Small Bore Rifle, prone position—Karoly Varga, Hungary.
Small Bore Rifle, 3 positions—Viktor Vlasov, USSR.
Clay Target Trap—Luciano Giovannetti, Italy.
Running Boar Target—Igor Sokolov, USSR.
Rapid Fire Pistol—Corneliu Ion, Romania.
Clay Target Skeet—Hans Kjeld Rasmussen, Denmark.

Soccer

Team—Czechoslovakia.

Volleyball

Men—USSR.
Women—USSR.

Water Polo

Team—USSR.

Weightlifting

115 lbs.—Kanibek Osmanoliev, USSR.
123 lbs.—Daniel Nunez, Cuba.
132 lbs.—Viktor Mazin, USSR.
149 lbs.—Vanko Roussev, Bulgaria.
165 lbs.—Assen Ziatev, Bulgaria.
182 lbs.—Yurik Vardanyan, USSR.
198 lbs.—Peter Baczako, Hungary.
220 lbs.—Ota Zaremba, Czechlosovakia.
242 lbs.—Leonid Taranenko, USSR.
Over 242 lbs.—Sultan Rakhmanov, USSR.

Wrestling—Freestyle

106 lbs.—Claudio Pollio, Italy.
115 lbs.—Anatoly Belogiazov, USSR.
126 lbs.—Sergei Belogiazov, USSR.
137 lbs.—Magomedgasan Anushev, USSR.
149 lbs.—Salpulla Absaidov, USSR.
163 lbs.—Valentin Raitchev, Bulgaria.
181 lbs.—Ismail Abilov, Bulgaria.
198 lbs.—Sanasar Oganesyan, USSR.
220 lbs.—Ilya Mate, USSR.
Over 220 lbs.—Sosian Andiev, USSR.

Wrestling—Greco-Roman

106 lbs.—Saksylik Ushkempirov, USSR.
114 lbs.—Vakhtang Biagidze, USSR.
125 lbs.—Sahmil Serikov, USSR.
136 lbs.—Stillanos Migakis, Greece.
150 lbs.—Stefan Rusu, Romania.
163 lbs.—Ferenc Kocsis, Hungary.
180 lbs.—Gennady Korban, USSR.
198 lbs.—Norbert Nottny, Hungary.
220 lbs.—Gheorghi Raidov, Bulgaria.
Over 220 lbs.—Alexandr Koichinsky, USSR.

Yachting

Soling Class—Denmark.
Finn Dinghy—Finland.
Flying Dutchman—Spain.
470 Class—Brazil.
Star—USSR.
Tornado—Brazil.

Winter Olympic Games Champions, 1924-1980

Sites and Unofficial Winners of Games

1924 Chamonix, France (Norway)
1928 St. Moritz, Switzerland (Norway)
1932 Lake Placid, N.Y. (U.S.)
1936 Garmisch-Partenkirchen (Norway)
1948 St. Moritz (Sweden)
1952 Oslo, Norway (Norway)
1956 Cortina d'Ampezzo, Italy (USSR)
1960 Squaw Valley, Cal. (USSR)
1964 Innsbruck, Austria (USSR)
1968 Grenoble, France (Norway)
1972 Sapporo, Japan (USSR)
1976 Innsbruck, Austria (USSR)
1980 Lake Placid, N.Y. (E. Germany)

Biathlon

10 Kilometers	Time
1980 Frank Ulrich, E. Germany	32:10.69

20 Kilometers	Time
1960 Klas Lestander, Sweden	1:33:21.6
1964 Vladimir Melanin, USSR	1:20:26.8
1968 Magnar Solberg, Norway	1:13:45.9
1972 Magnar Solberg, Norway	1:15:55.50
1976 Nikolai Kruglov, USSR	1:14:12.26
1980 Anatoly Alabyev, USSR	1:08:16.31

40-Kilometer Relay	Time
1968 USSR, Norway, Sweden	2:13:02
1972 USSR, Finland, E. Germany	1:51:44
1976 USSR, Finland, E. Germany	1:57:55.64
1980 USSR, E. Germany, W. Germany (30 km.)	1:34:03.27

Bobsledding

4-Man Bob

(Driver in parentheses)	Time
1924 Switzerland (Edward Scherrer)	5:45.54
1928 United States (William Fiske) (5-man)	3:20.50
1932 United States (William Fiske)	7:53.68
1936 Switzerland (Pierre Musy)	5:19.85
1948 United States (Edward Rimkus)	5:20.10
1952 Germany (Andreas Ostler)	5:07.84
1956 Switzerland (Frank Kapus)	5:10.44
1964 Canada (Victor Emery)	4:14.46
1968 Italy (Eugenio Monti) (2 races)	2:17.39
1972 Switzerland (Jean Wicki)	4:43.07
1976 E. Germany (Meinhard Nehmer)	3:40.43
1980 E. Germany (Mainhard Nehmer)	3:59.92

2-Man Bob	Time
1932 United States (Hubert Stevens)	8:14.74
1936 United States (Ivan Brown)	5:29.29
1948 Switzerland (F. Endrich)	5:29.20
1952 Germany (Andreas Ostler)	5:24.54
1956 Italy (Dalla Costa)	5:30.14
1964 Great Britain (Antony Nash)	4:21.90
1968 Italy (Eugenio Monti)	4:41.54
1972 W. Germany (Wolfgang Zimmerer)	4:47.07
1976 E. Germany (Meinhard Nehmer)	3:40.43
1980 Switzerland (Erich Schaerer)	4:09.36

Figure Skating

Men's Singles

1908 Ulrich Sachow, Sweden
1920 Gillis Grafstrom, Sweden
1924 Gillis Grafstrom, Sweden
1928 Gillis Grafstrom, Sweden
1932 Karl Schaefer, Austria
1936 Karl Schaefer, Austria
1948 Richard Button, U.S.
1952 Richard Button, U.S.
1956 Hayes Alan Jenkins, U.S.
1960 David W. Jenkins, U.S.
1964 Manfred Schnelldorfer, Germany
1968 Wolfgang Schwartz, Austria
1972 Ondrej Nepela, Czechoslovakia
1976 John Curry, Great Britain
1980 Robin Cousins, Great Britain

Women's Singles

1908 Madge Syers, Great Britain
1920 Magda Julin-Mauroy, Sweden
1924 Heima von Szabo-Planck, Austria
1928 Sonja Henie, Norway
1932 Sonja Henie, Norway
1936 Sonja Henie, Norway
1948 Barbara Ann Scott, Canada
1952 Jeanette Altwegg, Great Britain
1956 Tenley Albright, U.S.
1960 Carol Heiss, U.S.
1964 Sjoukje Dijkstra, Netherlands
1968 Peggy Fleming, U.S.
1972 Beatrix Schuba, Austria
1976 Dorothy Hamill, U.S.
1980 Anett Poetzsch, E. Germany

Pairs

1908 Anna Hubler & Heinrich Burger, Germany
1920 Ludovika & Walter Jakobsson, Finland
1924 Helene Engelman & Alfred Berger, Austria
1928 Andree Joly & Pierre Brunet, France
1932 Andree Joly & Pierre Brunet, France
1936 Maxie Herber & Ernest Baier, Germany
1948 Micheline Lannoy & Pierre Baugniet, Belgium
1952 Ria and Paul Falk, Germany
1956 Elisabeth Schwarz & Kurt Oppelt, Austria
1960 Barbara Wagner & Robert Paul, Canada
1964 Ludmila Beloussova & Oleg Protopopov, USSR
1968 Ludmila Beloussova & Oleg Protopopov, USSR
1972 Irina Rodnina & Alexei Ulanov, USSR
1976 Irina Rodnina & Aleksandr Zaitzev, USSR
1980 Irina Rodnina & Aleksandr Zaitzev, USSR

Ice Dancing

1976 Ludmila Pakhomova & Aleksandr Gorschkov, USSR
1980 Natalya Linichuk & Gennadi Karponosov, USSR

Alpine Skiing

Men's Downhill	Time
1948 Henri Oreiller, France	2:55.0
1952 Zeno Colo, Italy	2:30.8
1956 Anton Sailer, Austria	2:52.2
1960 Jean Vuarnet, France	2:06.0
1964 Egon Zimmermann, Austria	2:18.16
1968 Jean Claude Killy, France	1:59.85
1972 Bernhard Russi, Switzerland	1:51.43
1976 Franz Klammer, Austria	1:45.73
1980 Leonhard Stock, Austria	1:45.50

Men's Giant Slalom	Time
1952 Stein Eriksen, Norway	2:25.0
1956 Anton Sailer, Austria	3:00.1
1960 Roger Staub, Switzerland	1:48.3
1964 Francois Bonlieu, France	1:46.71
1968 Jean Claude Killy, France	3:29.28
1972 Gustavo Thoeni, Italy	3:09.62
1976 Heini Hemmi, Switzerland	3:26.97
1980 Ingemar Stenmark, Sweden	2:40.74

Men's Slalom	Time
1948 Edi Reinalter, Switzerland	2:10.3
1952 Othmar Schneider, Austria	2:00.0
1956 Anton Sailer, Austria	194.7 pts.
1960 Ernst Hinterseer, Austria	2:08.9
1964 Josef Stiegler, Austria	2:11.13
1968 Jean Claude Killy, France	1:39.73
1972 Francesco Fernandez Ochoa, Spain	1:49.27
1976 Piero Gros, Italy	2:03.29
1980 Ingemar Stenmark, Sweden	1:44.23

Women's Downhill	Time
1948 Heidi Schlunegger, Switzerland	2:28.3
1952 Trude Jochum-Beiser, Austria	1:47.1
1956 Madeline Berthod, Switzerland	1:40.7
1960 Heidi Biebl, Germany	1:37.6
1964 Christi Haas, Austria	1:55.39
1968 Olga Pall, Austria	1:40.87
1972 Marie Therese Nadig, Switzerland	1:36.68
1976 Rosi Mittermaier, W. Germany	1:46.16
1980 Annemarie Proell Moser, Austria	1:37.52

Women's Giant Slalom	Time
1952 Andrea Mead Lawrence, U.S.	2:06.8
1956 Ossi Reichert, Germany	1:56.5
1960 Yvonne Ruegg, Switzerland	1:39.9
1964 Marielle Goitschel, France	1:52.24

1968	Nancy Greene, Canada	1:51.97
1972	Marie Therese Nadig, Switzerland	1:29.90
1976	Kathy Kreiner, Canada	1:29.13
1980	Hanni Wenzel, Liechtenstein	2:41.66

	Women's Slalom	Time
1948	Gretchen Fraser, U.S.	1:57.2
1952	Andrea Mead Lawrence, U.S.	2:10.6
1956	Renee Colliard, Switzerland	112.3 pts.
1960	Anne Heggtveigt, Canada	1:49.6
1964	Christine Goitschel, France	1:29.86
1968	Marielle Goitschel, France	1:25.86
1972	Barbara Cochran, U.S.	1:31.24
1976	Rosi Mittermaier, W. Germany	1:30.54
1980	Hanni Wenzel, Liechtenstein	1:25.09

Nordic Skiing

Men's Cross-Country Events

	15 kilometers (9.3 miles)	Time
1924	Thorleif Haug, Norway	1:14:31
1928	Johan Grottumsbraaten, Norway	1:37:01
1932	Sven Utterstrom, Sweden	1:23:07
1936	Erik-August Larsson, Sweden	1:14:38
1948	Martin Lundstrom, Sweden	1:13:50
1952	Hallgeir Brenden, Norway	1:01:34
1956	Hallgeir Brenden, Norway	49:39.0
1960	Haakon Brusveen, Norway	51:55.0
1964	Eero Maentyranta, Finland	50:54.1
1968	Harald Groenningen, Norway	47:54.2
1972	Sven-Ake Lundback, Sweden	45:28.24
1976	Nikolai Bajukov, USSR	43:58.47
1980	Thomas Wassberg, Sweden	41:57.63

(Note: approx. 18-km. course 1924-1952)

	30 kilometers (18.6 miles)	Time
1956	Veikko Hakulinen, Finland	1:44:06.0
1960	Sixten Jernberg, Sweden	1:51:03.9
1964	Eero Maentyranta, Finland	1:30:50.7
1968	Franco Nones, Italy	1:35:39.2
1972	Vyacheslav Vedenin, USSR	1:36:31.15
1976	Sergei Savaliev, USSR	1:30:29.38
1980	Nikolai Zimyatov, USSR	1:27:02.80

	50 kilometers (31 miles)	Time
1924	Thorleif Haug, Norway	3:44:32.0
1928	Per Erik Hedlund, Sweden	4:52:03.0
1932	Veli Saarinen, Finland	4:28:00.0
1936	Elis Viklund, Sweden	3:30:11.0
1948	Nils Karlsson, Sweden	3:47:48.0
1952	Veikko Hakulinen, Finland	3:33:33.0
1956	Sixten Jernberg, Sweden	2:50:27.0
1960	Kalevi Hamalainen, Finland	2:59:06.3
1964	Sixten Jernberg, Sweden	2:43:52.6
1968	Ole Ellefsaeter, Norway	2:28:45.8
1972	Paal Tyldum, Norway	2:43:14.75
1976	Ivar Formo, Norway	2:37:30.05
1980	Nikolai Zimyatov, USSR	2:27:24.60

	40-km. Cross-Country Relay	Time
1936	Finland, Norway, Sweden	2:41:33.0
1948	Sweden, Finland, Norway	2:32:08.0
1952	Finland, Norway, Sweden	2:20:16.0
1956	USSR, Finland, Sweden	2:15:30.0
1960	Finland, Norway, USSR	2:18:45.6
1964	Sweden, Finland, USSR	2:18:34.6
1968	Norway, Sweden, Finland	2:08:33.5
1972	USSR, Norway, Switzerland	2:04:47.94
1976	Finland, Norway, USSR	2:07:59.72
1980	USSR, Norway, Finland	1:57:03.46

	15-km. Cross-Country & Jumping	Points
1924	Thorleif Haug, Norway	453.800
1928	Johan Grottumsbraaten, Norway	427.800
1932	Johan Grottumsbraaten, Norway	446.200
1936	Oddbjorn Hagen, Norway	430.300
1948	Heikki Hasu, Finland	448.800
1952	Simon Slattvik, Norway	451.621
1956	Sverre Stenersen, Norway	455.000
1960	Georg Thoma, Germany	457.952
1964	Tormod Knutsen, Norway	469.280
1968	Franz Keller, W. Germany	449.040
1972	Ulrich Wehling, E. Germany	413.340
1976	Ulrich Wehling, E. Germany	423.390
1980	Ulrich Wehling, E. Germany	432.200

	Ski Jumping (90 meters)	Points
1924	Jacob Thams, Norway	227.5
1928	Alfred Andersen, Norway	230.5
1932	Birger Ruud, Norway	228.0
1936	Birger Ruud, Norway	232.0
1948	Petter Hugsted, Norway	228.1
1952	Anders Bergmann, Norway	226.0
1956	Antti Hyvarinen, Finland	227.0
1960	Helmut Recknagel, Germany	227.2
1964	Toralf Engan, Norway	230.7
1968	Vladimir Beloussov, USSR	231.3
1972	Wojiech Fortuna, Poland	219.9
1976	Karl Schnabl, Austria	234.8
1980	Jouko Tormanen, Finland	231.5

	Ski Jumping (70 meters)	Points
1964	Veikko Kankkonen, Finland	229.9
1968	Jiri Raska, Czechoslovakia	216.5
1972	Yukio Kasaya, Japan	244.2
1976	Hans Aschenbach, E. Germany	252.0
1980	Anton Innauer, Austria	266.3

Women's Events

	5 kilometers (approx. 3.1 miles)	Time
1964	Claudia Boyarskikh, USSR	17:50.5
1968	Toini Gustafsson, Sweden	16:45.2
1972	Galina Koulacova, USSR	17:00.50
1976	Helena Takalo, Finland	15:48.69
1980	Raisa Smetanina, USSR	15:06.92

	10 kilometers	Time
1952	Lydia Wideman, Finland	41:40.0
1956	Lyubov Kosyreva, USSR	38:11.0
1960	Maria Gusakova, USSR	39:46.6
1964	Claudia Boyarskikh, USSR	40:24.3
1968	Toini Gustafsson, Sweden	36:46.5
1972	Galina Koulacova, USSR	34:17.82
1976	Raisa Smetanina, USSR	30:13.41
1980	Barbara Petzold, E. Germany	30:31.54

	15-km. Cross-Country Relay	Time
1956	Finland, USSR, Sweden	1:09:01.0
1960	Sweden, USSR, Finland	1:04:21.4
1964	USSR, Sweden, Finland	59:20.2
1968	Norway, Sweden, USSR	57:30.0
1972	USSR, Finland, Norway	48:46.1
1976	USSR, Finland, E. Germany (20 km.)	1:07:49.75
1980	E. Germany, USSR, Norway (20 km.)	1:02:11.10

Ice Hockey

1920	Canada, U.S., Czechoslovakia
1924	Canada, U.S., Great Britain
1928	Canada, Sweden, Switzerland
1932	Canada, U.S., Germany
1936	Great Britain, Canada, U.S.
1948	Canada, Czechoslovakia, Switzerland
1952	Canada, U.S., Sweden
1956	USSR, U.S., Canada
1960	U.S., Canada, USSR
1964	USSR, Sweden, Czechoslovakia
1968	USSR, Czechoslovakia, Canada
1972	USSR, U.S., Czechoslovakia,
1976	USSR, Czechoslovakia, W. Germany
1980	U.S., USSR, Sweden

Luge

	Men's Singles	Time
1964	Thomas Keohler, Germany	3:26.77
1968	Manfred Schmid, Austria	2:52.48
1972	Wolfgang Scheidel, E. Germany	3:27.58
1976	Detlef Guenther, E. Germany	3:27.688
1980	Bernhard Glass, E. Germany	2:54.796

	Men's Doubles	Time
1964	Austria	1:41.62
1968	E. Germany	1:35.85
1972	Italy, E. Germany (tie)	1:28.35
1976	E. Germany	1:25.604
1980	E. Germany	1:19.331

	Women's Singles	Time
1964	Ortun Enderlein, Germany	3:24.67
1968	Erica Lechner, Italy	2:28.66
1972	Anna M. Muller, E. Germany	2:59.18
1976	Margit Schumann, E. Germany	2:50.621
1980	Vera Zozulya, USSR	2:36.537

Speed Skating

Men's Events

500 meters (approx. 547 yds.) — **Time**

		Time
1924	Charles Jewtraw, U.S.	0:44.0
1928	Clas Thunberg, Finland & Bernt Evensen, Norway (tie)	0:43.4
1932	John A. Shea, U.S.	0:43.4
1936	Ivar Ballangrud, Norway	0:43.4
1948	Finn Helgesen, Norway	0:43.1
1952	Kenneth Henry, U.S.	0:43.2
1956	Evgeniy Grishin, USSR	0:40.2
1960	Evgeniy Grishin, USSR	0:40.2
1964	Terry McDermott, U.S.	0:40.1
1968	Erhard Keller, W. Germany	0:40.3
1972	Erhard Keller, W. Germany	0:39.44
1976	Evgeny Kulikov, USSR	0:39.17
1980	Eric Heiden, U.S.	0:38.03

1,000 meters

		Time
1976	Peter Mueller, U.S.	1:19.32
1980	Eric Heiden, U.S.	1:15.18

1,500 meters

		Time
1924	Clas Thunberg, Finland	2:20.8
1928	Clas Thunberg, Finland	2:21.1
1932	John A. Shea, U.S.	2:57.2
1936	Charles Mathiesen, Norway	2:19.2
1948	Sverre Farstad, Norway	2:17.6
1952	Hjalmar Andersen, Norway	2:20.4
1956	Evgeniy Grishin, & Yuri Mikhailov, both USSR (tie)	2:08.6
1960	Roald Edgar Aas, Norway & Evgeniy Grishin, USSR (tie)	2:10.4
1964	Ants Anston, USSR	2:10.3
1968	Cornetis Verkerk, Netherlands	2:03.4
1972	Ard Schenk, Netherlands	2:02.96
1976	Jan Egil Storholt, Norway	1:59.38
1980	Eric Heiden, U.S.	1:55.44

5,000 meters

		Time
1924	Clas Thunberg, Finland	8:39.0
1928	Ivar Ballangrud, Norway	8:50.5
1932	Irving Jaffee, U.S.	9:40.8
1936	Ivar Ballangrud, Norway	8:19.6
1948	Reidar Liaklev, Norway	8:29.4
1952	Hjalmar Andersen, Norway	8:10.6
1956	Boris Shilkov, USSR	7:48.7
1960	Viktor Kosichkin, USSR	7:51.3
1964	Knut Johannesen, Norway	7:38.4
1968	F. Anton Maier, Norway	7:22.4
1972	Ard Schenk, Netherlands	7:23.61
1976	Sten Stensen, Norway	7:24.48
1980	Eric Heiden, U.S.	7:02.29

10,000 meters

		Time
1924	Julius Skutnabb, Finland	18:04.8
1928	Event not held, thawing of ice	
1932	Irving Jaffee, U.S.	19:13.6
1936	Ivar Ballangrud, Norway	17:24.3
1948	Ake Seyffarth, Norway	17:26.3
1952	Hjalmar Andersen, Norway	16:45.8
1956	Sigvard Ericsson, Sweden	16:35.9
1960	Knut Johannesen, Norway	15:46.6
1964	Jonny Nilsson, Sweden	15:50.1
1968	Jonny Hoeglin, Sweden	15:23.6
1972	Ard Schenk, Netherlands	15:01.3
1976	Piet Kleine, Netherlands	14:50.59
1980	Eric Heiden, U.S.	14:28.13

Women's Events

500 meters

		Time
1960	Helga Haase, Germany	0:45.9
1964	Lydia Skoblikova, USSR	0:45.0
1968	Ludmila Titova, USSR	0:46.1
1972	Anne Henning, U.S.	0:43.44
1976	Sheila Young, U.S.	0:42.76
1980	Karin Enke, E. Germany	0:41.78

1,000 meters

		Time
1960	Klara Guseva, USSR	1:34.1
1964	Lydia Skoblikova, USSR	1:33.2
1968	Caroline Geijssen, Netherlands	1:32.6
1972	Monika Pflug, W. Germany	1:31.40
1976	Tatiana Averina, USSR	1:28.43
1980	Natalya Petruseva, USSR	1:24.10

1,500 meters

		Time
1960	Lydia Skoblikova, USSR	2:52.2
1964	Lydia Skoblikova, USSR	2:22.6
1968	Kaija Mustonen, Finland	2:22.4
1972	Dianne Holum, U.S.	2:20.85
1976	Galina Stepanskaya, USSR	2:16.58
1980	Anne Borckink, Netherlands	2:10.95

3,000 meters

		Time
1960	Lydia Skoblikova, USSR	5:14.3
1964	Lydia Skoblikova, USSR	5:14.9
1968	Johanna Schut, Netherlands	4:56.2
1972	Stien Baas-Kaiser, Netherlands	4:52.14
1976	Tatiana Averina, USSR	4:45.19
1980	Bjoerg Eva Jensen, Norway	4:32.13

Winter Olympic Medal Winners in 1980

1980 Final Medal Standing

Lake Placid, N.Y., Feb. 12-24

	Gold	Silver	Bronze	Total
Austria	3	2	2	7
Bulgaria	0	0	1	1
Canada	0	1	1	2
Czechoslovakia	0	0	1	1
Finland	1	5	3	9
France	0	0	1	1
Germany, East	9	7	7	23
Germany, West	0	2	3	5
Great Britain	1	0	0	1
Hungary	0	1	0	1
Italy	0	2	0	2
Japan	0	1	0	1
Liechtenstein	2	2	0	4
Netherlands	1	2	1	4
Norway	1	3	6	10
Sweden	3	0	1	4
Switzerland	1	1	3	5
USSR	10	6	6	22
United States	6	4	2	12

Individual Medals

Alpine Skiing

Men's Downhill—1. Leonhard Stock, Austria; 2. Peter Wirnsberger, Austria; 3. Stephen Podborski, Canada.

Men's Giant Slalom—1. Ingemar Stenmark, Sweden; 2. Andreas Wenzel, Liechtenstein; 3. Hans Enn, Austria.

Men's Slalom—1. Ingemar Stenmark; 2. Phil Mahre, U.S.; 3. Jacques Luethy, Switzerland.

Women's Downhill—1. Annemarie Proell Moser, Austria; 2. Hanni Wenzel, Liechtenstein; 3. Marie-Theres Nadig, Switzerland.

Women's Giant Slalom—1. Hanni Wenzel; 2. Irene Epple, W. Germany; 3. Perrine Pelen, France.

Women's Slalom—1. Hanni Wenzel; 2. Christa Kinhofer, W. Germany; 3. Erika Hess, Switzerland.

Nordic Skiing

Men's 15 km.—1. Thomas Wassberg, Sweden; 2. Juha Mieto, Finland; 3. Ove Aunli, Norway.

Men's 30 km.—1. Nikolai Zimyatov, USSR; 2. Vasily Rochev, USSR; 3. Ivan Lebanov, Bulgaria.

Men's 50 km.—1. Nikolai Zimyatov; 2. Juha Mieto; 3. Alexander Zavalov.

Men's Combined—1. Ulrich Wehling, E. Germany; 2. Jouko Karjalainen, Finland; 3. Konrad Winkler, E. Germany.

Women's 5 km.—1. Raisa Smetanina, USSR; 2. Hilkka Riihivuori, Finland; 3. Kveta Jeriova, Czech.

Women's 10 km.—1. Barbara Petzold, E. Germany; 2. Hilkka Riihivuori; 3. Helena Takalo, Finland.

Ski Jumping

70 meters—1. Anton Annauer, Austria; 2. (tie) Hirokazu Yagi, Japan & Manfred Deckert, E. Germany.
90 meters—1. Jouko Tormanen, Finland; 2. Hubert Neuper, Austria; 3. Jari Puikkonen, Finland.

Biathlon

10 km.—1. Frank Ulrich, E. Germany; 2. Vladimir Aliken, USSR; 3. Anatoly Alabyev, USSR.
20 km.—1. Anatoly Alabyev; 2. Frank Ulrich; 3. Eberhard Rosch, E. Germany.

Figure Skating

Men—1. Robin Cousins, Great Britain; 2. Jan Hoffmann, E. Germany; 3. Charles Tickner, U.S.
Women—1. Anett Poetzsch, E. Germany; 2. Linda Fratianne, U.S.; 3. Dagmar Lurz, W. Germany.
Pairs—1. Irina Rodnina & Aleksandr Zaitsev, USSR; 2. Marina Chersekova & Sergei Shakrai, USSR; 3. Manuela Mager & Uwe Bewersdorf, E. Germany.
Ice Dancing—1. Natalya Linichuk & Gennadi Karponosov, USSR; 2. Krisztina Regozzy & Andras Sallay, Hungary; 3. Irina Moiseeva & Andrei Minenkov, USSR.

Speed Skating

Men's 500 meters—1. Eric Heiden, U.S.; 2. Yevgeny Kulikov, USSR; 3. Lieuwe DeBoer, Netherlands.
Men's 1,000 meters—1. Eric Heiden; 2. Gaetan Boucher, Canada; 3. (tie) Froede Roenning, Norway & Vladimir Lobanov, USSR.
Men's 1,500 meters—1. Eric Heiden; 2. Kai Arne Stenshjemmet, Norway; 3. Terje Andersen, Norway.
Men's 5,000 meters—1. Eric Heiden; 2. Kai Arne Stenshjemmet; 3. Tom Erik Oxholm, Norway.
Men's 10,000 meters—1. Eric Heiden; 2. Piet Kleine, Netherlands; 3. Tom Erik Oxholm.
Women's 500 meters—1. Karin Enke, E. Germany; 2. Leah Mueller, U.S.; 3. Natalya Petruseva, USSR.
Women's 1,000 meters—1. Natalya Petruseva; 2. Leah Mueller; 3. Silvia Albrecht, E. Germany.
Women's 1,500 meters—1. Anne Borckink, Netherlands; 2. Ria Visser, Netherlands; 3. Sabine Becker, E. Germany.
Women's 3,000 meters—1. Bjoerg Eva Jensen, Norway; 2. Sabine Becker; 3. Beth Heiden, U.S.

Luge

Men—1. Bernhard Glass, E. Germany; 2. Paul Hildgartner, Italy; 3. Anton Winkler, W. Germany.
Women—1. Vera Zozulya, USSR; 2. Mellita Sollmann, E. Germany; 3. Ingrida Amantova, USSR.

Olympic Information

Symbol: Five rings or circles, linked together to represent the sporting friendship of all peoples. The rings also symbolize the 5 continents—Europe, Asia, Africa, Australia, and America. Each ring is a different color—blue, yellow, black, green, and red.

Flag: The symbol of the 5 rings on a plain white background.

Motto: "Citius, Altius, Fortius." Latin meaning "faster, higher, braver," or the modern interpretation "swifter, higher, stronger". The motto was coined by Father Didon, a French educator, in 1895.

Creed: "The most important thing in the Olympic Games is not to win but to take part, just as the most important thing in life is not the triumph but the struggle. The essential thing is not to have conquered but to have fought well."

Oath: An athlete of the host country recites the following at the opening ceremony. "In the name of all competitors I promise that we will take part in these Olympic Games, respecting and abiding by the rules which govern them, in the true spirit of sportsmanship for the glory of sport and the honor of our teams." Both the oath and the creed were composed by Pierre de Coubertin, the founder of the modern Games.

Flame: Symbolizes the continuity between the ancient and modern Games. The modern version of the flame was adopted in 1936. The torch used to kindle the flame is first lit by the sun's rays at Olympia, Greece, and then carried to the site of the Games by relays of runners. Ships and planes are used when necessary.

Power Boat Racing Champions

APBA Gold Cup Race

Year	Boat	Owner	Driver	Winner's fastest heat MPH	Site
1967	Miss Bardahl	Ole Bardahl	Bill Schumacher	**104.691**	Seattle, Wash.
1968	Miss Bardahl	Ole Bardahl	Bill Schumacher	**111.248**	Detroit, Mich.
1969	Miss Budweiser	Bernard Little & Tom Friedkin	Bill Sterett	**103.587**	San Diego, Cal.
1970	Miss Budweiser	Hydroplanes, Inc.	Dean Chenoweth	**101.848**	San Diego, Cal.
1971	Miss Madison	Miss Madison, Inc.	Jim McCormick	**101.522**	Madison, Ind.
1972	Atlas Van Lines	Atlas Van Lines	Bill Muncey	**103.547**	Detroit, Mich.
1973	Miss Budweiser	Hydroplanes, Inc.	Dean Chenoweth	**104.046**	Tri-Cities, Wash.
1974	Pay'N Pak	David J. Heerensperger	George Henley	**112.056**	Seattle, Wash.
1975	Pay 'N Pak	David J. Heerensperger	George Henley	**113.350**	Tri-Cities, Wash.
1976	Miss U.S.	U.S. Racing Team, Inc.	Tom D'Eath	**108.021**	Detroit, Mich.
1977	Atlas Van Lines	Bill Muncey Industries, Inc.	Bill Muncey	**114.869**	Tri-Cities, Wash.
1978	Atlas Van Lines	Bill Muncey Industries, Inc.	Bill Muncey	**104.448**	Owensboro, Ky.
1979	Atlas Van Lines	Bill Muncey Industries, Inc.	Bill Muncey	**107.892**	Madison, Ind.
1980	Miss Budweiser	Hydroplanes, Inc.	Dean Chenoweth	**117.391**	Madison, Ind.

National AAU Senior Weightlifting Championships in 1980

Philadelphia, Pa., May 31-June 1, 1980

(Note: lifts are in kilograms; one kilogram = 2.2 lbs.)

114 lbs.—Leslie Sewall, unattached. **182.5 kg.**
123 lbs.—Joe Widdel, unattached. **210 kg.**
132 lbs.—Philip Sanderson, York Barbell. **242.5 kg.**
148¾ lbs.—Cal Schake, Butler YMCA. **290 kg.**
165¼ lbs.—Myron Davis, N.W. Co. YMCA. **297.5 kg.**
181¾ lbs.—Michael Karchut, Sayre Park. **327.5 kg.**
198¼ lbs.—James Curry Jr., Sports Palace. **337.5 kg.**
220 lbs.—Brian Derwin, Belleville. **362.5 kg.**
242 lbs.—Mark Cameron, York Barbell. **372.5 kg.**
Super heavyweight—Tom Stock, York Barbell. **392.5 kg.**

Sports Arenas

The seating capacity of sports arenas can vary depending on the event being presented. The figures below are the normal seating capacity for basketball. (*) indicates hockey seating capacity.

Name, location	Capacity
Allen County Memorial, Ft. Wayne	*8,022
Arizona Veteran's Memorial Coliseum, Phoenix	12,660-*12,474
Astrohall, Houston	10,000
Baltimore Civic Center	13,043-*10,200
Bismarck Coliseum, N.D.	7,000
Boston Garden	15,276-*14,673
Buffalo Memorial Auditorium	17,900-*16,433(a)
Capital Centre, Landover, Md.	19,035-*18,130
Charlotte Coliseum	11,666-*9,575
Checkerdome, St. Louis	20,000-*17,797
Chicago Stadium	17,374-*17,100
Cincinnati Gardens	11,650-*10,606
Cobo Hall, Detroit	11,147
The Coliseum, Richfield Township, Oh.	19,548
Convention Center, San Antonio	10,146
Convention Hall, Philadelphia	9,200-*9,500
Cow Palace, San Francisco	14,500-*12,195
Denver Coliseum	*9,038
Dorton Arena, Raleigh, N.C.	8,058
Fair Park Coliseum, Dallas	*7,593
Fairgrounds Coliseum, Indianapolis	9,479
Freedom Hall, Louisville, Ky.	16,613
Greensboro Coliseum	15,500-*13,280
Halifax Metro Centre	*9,549
Hampton Roads Coliseum, Va.	10,000-*8,200
Hartford Civic Center	*14,600
HemisFair Arena, San Antonio	16,000
Hersheypark Arena, Pa.	*7,286
Hofheinz Pavilion, Houston	10,218
International Amphitheatre, Chicago	9,000
Jefferson County Civic Center, Birmingham, Ala.	*16,753
Joe Louis Sports Arena, Detroit	*19,275
Kemper Memorial Arena, Kansas City	16,348-*16,999
Kiel Auditorium, St. Louis	10,574
Kingdome, Seattle	27,894
Las Vegas Convention Center	9,000
Long Beach Arena, Cal.	11,168
Los Angeles Forum	17,505-*16,005
Los Angeles Sports Arena	15,333-*11,325
Louisiana Superdome	47,284
Lubbock Municipal Coliseum, Tex.	10,400
Madison Square Garden, New York	19,571-*17,500
Maple Leaf Gardens, Toronto	17,000-*16,485(a)
Market Square Arena, Indianapolis	16,926-15,861
McNichols Sports Arena, Denver	17,387-*16,399
Met. Sports Center, Bloomington, Minn.	*15,184
Mid-South Coliseum, Memphis	11,065
Milwaukee Arena	10,938-*8,000
Mobile Municipal Auditorium	13,100
Montreal Forum	*16,074
Moody Coliseum, Dallas	9,500
Myriad, Oklahoma City	*13,263
Nashville Municipal Auditorium	8,000
Nassau Coliseum, Uniondale, N.Y.	*15,317
New Orleans Municipal Auditorium	9,100
Norfolk Scope, Va.	10,600-*9,364
Northlands Coliseum, Edmonton	*15,246
Oakland Coliseum Arena	13,237
Olympia Stadium, Detroit	*16,673
Olympic Auditorium, Los Angeles	10,500
Omaha Civic Auditorium	9,144
The Omni, Atlanta	15,600-*15,191
Ottawa Civic Center	*9,355
Pacific Coliseum, Vancouver, B.C.	*15,613
Penn Palestra, Philadelphia	9,200
Philadelphia Civic Center	*8,055
Pittsburgh Civic Arena	*16,033
Portland Memorial Coliseum	12,666-*10,500
Providence Civic Center	11,619-*10,730
Quebec Coliseum	*10,484
Reynolds Coliseum, Raleigh, N.C.	12,400
Richmond Coliseum, Va.	10,700-*8,400
Riverfront Coliseum, Cincinnati	*15,794
Roanoke Civic Center, Va.	10,000-*8,372
St. Paul Civic Center, Minn.	*15,594
Salt Palace, Salt Lake City	12,201-*10,640
San Diego Sports Arena	13,703-*13,039
Seattle Center Coliseum	14,098
Silverdome, Pontiac, Mich.	22,366
Spectrum, Philadelphia	18,276-*17,077
Springfield Civic Center, Mass.	*7,625
The Summit, Houston	15,676-*15,256
Tarrant County Convention Center, Ft. Worth	13,500
Tingley Coliseum, Albuquerque	*12,000
Uline Arena, Washington, D. C.	11,000
Veterans Memorial Audit., Des Moines	15,000
Veterans Memorial Coliseum, New Haven	*8,765
Winnipeg Arena	*10,151
Winston-Salem Memorial Coliseum	9,020

(a) includes standees

James E. Sullivan Memorial Trophy Winners

The James E. Sullivan Memorial Trophy, named after the former president of the AAU and inaugurated in 1930, is awarded annually by the AAU to the athlete who "by his or her performance, example and influence as an amateur, has done the most during the year to advance the cause of sportmanship."

Year	Winner	Sport
1930	Bobby Jones	Golf
1931	Barney Berlinger	Track
1932	Jim Bausch	Track
1933	Glen Cunningham	Track
1934	Bill Bonthron	Track
1935	Lawson Little	Golf
1936	Glenn Morris	Track
1937	Don Budge	Tennis
1938	Don Lash	Track
1939	Joe Burk	Rowing
1940	Greg Rice	Track
1941	Leslie MacMitchell	Track
1942	Cornelius Warmerdam	Track
1943	Gilbert Dodds	Track
1944	Ann Curtis	Swimming
1945	Doc Blanchard	Football
1946	Arnold Tucker	Football
1947	John Kelly Jr.	Rowing
1948	Robert Mathias	Track
1949	Dick Button	Skating
1950	Fred Wilt	Track
1951	Rev. Robert Richards	Track
1952	Horace Ashenfelter	Track
1953	Dr. Sammy Lee	Diving
1954	Mal Whitfield	Track
1955	Harrison Dillard	Track
1956	Patricia McCormick	Diving
1957	Bobby Joe Morrow	Track
1958	Glen Davis	Track
1959	Parry O'Brien	Track
1960	Rafer Johnson	Track
1961	Wilma Rudolph Ward	Track
1962	James Beatty	Track
1963	John Pennel	Track
1964	Don Schollander	Swimming
1965	Bill Bradley	Basketball
1966	Jim Ryun	Track
1967	Randy Matson	Track
1968	Debbie Meyer	Swimming
1969	Bill Toomey	Track
1970	John Kinsella	Swimming
1971	Mark Spitz	Swimming
1972	Frank Shorter	Track
1973	Bill Walton	Basketball
1974	Rick Wohlhuter	Track
1975	Tim Shaw	Swimming
1976	Bruce Jenner	Track
1977	John Naber	Swimming
1978	Tracy Caulkins	Swimming
1979	Kurt Thomas	Gymnastics

National AAU Judo Championships in 1980

E. Lansing, Mich., Apr. 24-26, 1980

Senior Men

132 lbs.—Maurice De La Torriente, Arlington Heights, Ill.
143 lbs.—Fred Glock, Minnesota.
156 lbs.—Steve Seck, Los Angeles, Cal.
172 lbs.—Brett Barron, San Mateo, Cal.
189 lbs.—Tommy Martin, Stockton, Cal.
Under 209 lbs.—Miguel Tudela, Los Angeles, Cal.
Over 209 lbs.—John Saylor, Westfield, N.Y.
Open—Dewey Mitchell, Seven Springs, Fla.

Senior Women

106 lbs.—Jan Zakarzeci, E. Lansing, Mich.
114 lbs.—Eve Aronoff, unattached.
123 lbs.—Geri Bindell, New Milford, N.J.
134 lbs.—Sandra Coons, Rochelle, Ill.
145 lbs.—Christine Penick, San Jose, Cal.
158 lbs.—Amy Kublin, Boston, Mass.
Heavyweight—Margie Castro, New York, N.Y.

NCAA Basketball Championships in 1980

East

First round—Villanova 77, Marquette 59; Iowa 86, Virginia Commonwealth 72; Iona 84, Holy Cross 78; Tennessee 80, Furman 69.

Second round—Syracuse 97, Villanova 83; Iowa 77, North Carolina State 64; Georgetown 74, Iona 71; Maryland 86, Tennessee 75.

Semifinals—Iowa 88, Syracuse 77; Georgetown 74, Maryland 68.

Championship—Iowa 81, Georgetown 80.

Midwest

First round—Alcorn State 70, South Alabama 62; Missouri 61, San Jose State 51; Texas A & M 55, Bradley 53; Kansas State 71, Arkansas 53.

Second round—Louisiana State 98, Alcorn State 88; Missouri 87, Notre Dame 84; Texas A & M 78, North Carolina 61; Louisville 71, Kansas State 69.

Semifinals—Louisiana State 68, Missouri 63; Louisville 66, Texas A & M 55.

Championship—Louisville 86, Louisiana State 66.

Mideast

First round—Florida State 94, Toledo 91; Penn 62, Washington State 55; Purdue 90, La Salle 82; Virginia Tech 89, Western Kentucky 85.

Second round—Kentucky 97, Florida State 78; Duke 52, Penn 42; Purdue 87, St. John's 72; Indiana 68, Virginia Tech 59.

Semifinals—Duke 55, Kentucky 54; Purdue 76, Indiana 69.

Championship—Purdue 68, Duke 60.

West

First round—UCLA 87, Old Dominion 74; Arizona State 99, Loyola (Cal.) 71; Clemson 76, Utah State 73; Lamar 87, Weber State 86.

Second round—UCLA 77, De Paul 71; Ohio State 89, Arizona State 75; Clemson 71, Brigham Young 66; Lamar 81, Oregon State 77.

Semifinals—UCLA 72, Ohio State 68; Clemson 74, Lamar 66.

Championship—UCLA 85, Clemson 74.

National Semifinals

Louisville 80, Iowa 72; UCLA 67, Purdue 62.

National Championship

Louisville 59, UCLA 64.

NCAA Division I Champions

Year	Champion	Year	Champion	Year	Champion	Year	Champion
1939	Oregon	1950	CCNY	1961	Cincinnati	1971	UCLA
1940	Indiana	1951	Kentucky	1962	Cincinnati	1972	UCLA
1941	Wisconsin	1952	Kansas	1963	Loyola (Chi.)	1973	UCLA
1942	Stanford	1953	Indiana	1964	UCLA	1974	No. Carolina State
1943	Wyoming	1954	La Salle	1965	UCLA	1975	UCLA
1944	Utah	1955	San Francisco	1966	Texas Western	1976	Indiana
1945	Oklahoma A&M	1956	San Francisco	1967	UCLA	1977	Marquette
1946	Oklahoma A&M	1957	North Carolina	1968	UCLA	1978	Kentucky
1947	Holy Cross	1958	Kentucky	1969	UCLA	1979	Michigan State
1948	Kentucky	1959	California	1970	UCLA	1980	Louisville
1949	Kentucky	1960	Ohio State				

National Invitation Tournament Champions

Year	Champion	Year	Champion	Year	Champion	Year	Champion
1938	Temple	1949	San Francisco	1960	Bradley	1971	North Carolina
1939	Long Island Univ.	1950	CCNY	1961	Providence	1972	Maryland
1940	Colorado	1951	Brigham Young	1962	Dayton	1973	Virginia Tech
1941	Long Island Univ.	1952	LaSalle	1963	Providence	1974	Purdue
1942	West Virginia	1953	Seton Hall	1964	Bradley	1975	Princeton
1943	St. John's	1954	Holy Cross	1965	St. John's	1976	Kentucky
1944	St. John's	1955	Duquesne	1966	Brigham Young	1977	St. Bonaventure
1945	De Paul	1956	Louisville	1967	Southern Illinois	1978	Texas
1946	Kentucky	1957	Bradley	1968	Dayton	1979	Indiana
1947	Utah	1958	Xavier (Ohio)	1969	Temple	1980	Virginia
1948	St. Louis	1959	St. John's	1970	Marquette		

NCAA Division II Champions

Year	Champion	Year	Champion	Year	Champion	Year	Champion
1965	Evansville	1969	Kentucky Wesleyan	1973	Kentucky Wesleyan	1977	Tennessee-Chattanooga
1966	Kentucky Wesleyan	1970	Philadelphia Textile	1974	Morgan State	1978	Cheyney State
1967	Winston-Salem	1971	Evansville	1975	Old Dominion	1979	North Alabama
1968	Kentucky Wesleyan	1972	Roanoke	1976	Puget Sound	1980	Virginia Union

Curling Champions

Source: North American Curling News

World Champions

Year	Country, skip	Year	Country, skip	Year	Country, skip
1966	Canada, Ron Northcott	1971	Canada, Don Duguid	1976	United States, Bruce Roberts
1967	Scotland, Chuck Hay	1972	Canada, Crest Melesnuk	1977	Sweden, Ragnar Kamp
1968	Canada, Ron Northcott	1973	Sweden, Kjell Oscarius	1978	United States, Bob Nichols
1969	Canada, Ron Northcott	1974	United States, Bud Somerville	1979	Norway, Kristian Soerum
1970	Canada, Don Duguid	1975	Switzerland, Otto Danieli	1980	Canada, Rich Folk

U.S. Men's Champions

Year	State, skip	Year	State, skip	Year	State, skip
1966	North Dakota, Joe Zbacnik	1971	North Dakota, Dale Dalziel	1976	Minnesota, Bruce Roberts
1967	Washington, Bruce Roberts	1972	North Dakota, Bob LaBonte	1977	Minnesota, Bruce Roberts
1968	Wisconsin, Bud Somerville	1973	Massachusetts, Barry Blanchard	1978	Wisconsin, Bob Nichols
1969	Wisconsin, Bud Somerville	1974	Wisconsin, Bud Somerville	1979	Minnesota, Scotty Baird
1970	North Dakota, Art Tallackson	1975	Washington, Ed Risling	1980	Minnesota, Paul Pustover

U.S. Ladies Champions

Year	State, skip	Year	State, skip	Year	State, skip
1978	Wisconsin, Sandy Robarge	1979	Washington, Nancy Langley	1980	Washington, Sharon Kozai

Notable Sports Personalities

Henry Aaron, b. 1934: Milwaukee-Atlanta outfielder hit record 755 home runs; led NL 4 times.
Kareem Abdul-Jabbar, b. 1947: Milwaukee, L.A. Lakers center; MVP 5 times; leading scorer twice.
Grover Cleveland Alexander, (1887-1950): pitcher won 374 NL games; pitched 16 shutouts, 1916.
Muhammad Ali, b. 1942; 3-time heavyweight champion.
Mario Andretti, b. 1940; U.S. Auto Club national champ 3 times: won Indy 500, 1969; Grand Prix champ, 1978.
Eddie Arcaro, b. 1916: jockey rode 4,779 winners including the Kentucky Derby 5 times; the Preakness and Belmont Stakes 6 times each.
Henry Armstrong, b. 1912: boxer held feather-, welter-, lightweight titles simultaneously, 1937-38.
Arthur Ashe, b. 1943: U.S. singles champ, 1968, Wimbledon champ, 1975.
Red Auerbach, b. 1917: coached Boston Celtics to 9 NBA championships.
Ernie Banks, b. 1931: Chicago Cubs slugger hit 512 NL homers: twice MVP.
Roger Bannister, b. 1929: Briton ran first sub 4-minute mile, May 6, 1954.
Rick Barry, b. 1944: NBA scoring leader, 1967; ABA, 1969.
Sammy Baugh, b. 1914: Washington Redskins quarterback held numerous records upon retirement after 16 pro seasons.
Elgin Baylor, b. 1934: L.A. Lakers forward; 1st team all-star 10 times.
Bob Beamon, b. 1946: long jumper won 1968 Olympic gold medal with record 29 ft. 2½ in.
Jean Beliveau, b. 1931: Montreal Canadiens center scored 507 goals; twice MVP.
Johnny Bench, b. 1947: Cincinnati Reds catcher; MVP twice; led league in home runs twice, RBIs 3 times.
Patty Berg, b. 1918: won over 80 golf tournaments: AP Woman Athlete-of-the-Year 3 times.
Yogi Berra, b. 1925: N.Y. Yankees catcher; MVP 3 times; played in 14 World Series.
Raymond Berry, b. 1933: Baltimore Colts receiver caught 631 passes.
George Blanda, b. 1927: quarterback, kicker; 26 years as active player, scoring record 2,002 points.
Fanny Blankers-Koen, b. 1918: Dutch track star won 4 1948 Olympic gold medals.
Bjorn Borg, b. 1956: led Sweden to first Davis Cup, 1975; Wimbledon champion, 5 times.
Julius Boros, b. 1920: won U.S. Open, 1952, 1963; PGA champ, 1968.
Jack Brabham, b. 1926: Grand Prix champ 3 times.
Lou Brock, b. 1939: St. Louis Cardinals outfielder stole record 118 bases, 1974; record 937 career; led NL 8 times.
Jimmy Brown, b. 1936: Cleveland Browns fullback ran for record 12,312 career yards; MVP 3 times.
Don Budge, b. 1915: won numerous amateur and pro tennis titles, "grand slam," 1938.
Maria Bueno, b. 1939: U.S. singles champ 4 times; Wimbledon champ 3 times.
Mike Burton, b. 1947: swimmer won 1968, 1972 Olympic 1,500 meter freestyle.
Dick Butkus, b. 1942: Chicago Bears linebacker twice chosen best NFL defensive player.
Dick Button, b. 1929: figure skater won 1948, 1952 Olympic gold medals; world titlist, 1948-52.
Walter Camp, (1859-1925): Yale football player, coach, athletic director; established many rules; promoted All-America designations.
Roy Campanella, b. 1921: Brooklyn Dodgers catcher; MVP 3 times.
Earl Campbell, b. 1955: Houston Oilers running back; NFL MVP 1978, 1979.
Rod Carew, b. 1945: Minnesota Twins infielder won 7 batting titles; MVP, 1977.
Steve Carlton, b. 1944: NL pitcher won 20 games 4 times, Cy Young award twice.
Billy Casper, b. 1931: PGA Player-of-the-Year 3 times; U.S. Open champ twice.
Steve Cauthen, b. 1960: jockey; rode triple crown winner Affirmed, 1978.
Wilt Chamberlain, b. 1936: center scored NBA career record 31,419 points; MVP 4 times.
Jim Clark, (1936-1968): world driving champ twice; won Indy 500, 1965.
Bobby Clarke, b. 1949: Philadelphia Flyers center led team to 2 Stanley Cup championships: MVP 3 times.
Roberto Clemente, (1934-1972): Pittsburgh Pirates outfielder won 4 batting titles; MVP, 1966.
Ty Cobb, (1886-1961): Detroit Tigers outfielder had record .367 lifetime batting average, 4,191 hits, 12 batting titles.
Sebastian Coe, b. 1956: Briton set record in 800 meters, 1,500 meters, and mile, 1979.
Nadia Comaneci, b. 1961: Romanian gymnast won 3 gold medals, achieved 7 perfect scores, 1976 Olympics.
Maureen Connolly, (1934-1969): won tennis "grand slam," 1953; AP Woman-Athlete-of-the-Year 3 times.
Jimmy Connors, b. 1952: U.S. singles champ 3 times.
James J. Corbett, (1866-1933): heavyweight champion, 1892-97; credited with being the first "scientific" boxer.
Margaret Smith Court, b. 1942: Australian won U.S. singles championship 5 times; Wimbledon champ 3 times.
Bob Cousy, b. 1928: Boston Celtics guard led team to 6 NBA championships: MVP, 1957.
Dave Cowens, b. 1948: Boston Celtics center chosen MVP, 1973.
Stanley Dancer, b. 1927: harness racing driver drove Hambletonian winner 3 times, Little Brown Jug winner 4 times.
Dizzy Dean, (1911-1974): colorful pitcher for St. Louis Cardinals "Gashouse Gang" in the 30s; MVP, 1934.
Jack Dempsey, b. 1895: heavyweight champion, 1919-26.
Joe DiMaggio, b. 1914: N.Y. Yankees outfielder hit safely in record 56 consecutive games, 1941; MVP 3 times.
Leo Durocher, b. 1906: colorful manager of Dodgers, Giants, and Cubs; won 3 NL pennants.
Gertrude Ederle, b. 1906: first woman to swim English Channel, broke existing men's record, 1926.
Kornelia Ender, b. 1958: E. German swimmer broke 23 world records; won 4 1976 Olympic gold medals.
Julius Erving, b. 1950: MVP and leading scorer in ABA 3 times.
Phil Esposito, b. 1942: scored record 76 goals and 152 points in 1970-71; NHL scoring leader 5 times.
Chris Evert-Lloyd, b. 1954: U.S. singles champ 4 times, Wimbledon champ twice.
Ray Ewry, (1873-1937): track and field star won 8 gold medals, 1900, 1904, and 1908 Olympics.
Juan Fangio, b. 1911: Argentine World Grand Prix champion 5 times.
Bob Feller, b. 1918: Cleveland Indians pitcher won 266 games; pitched 3 no-hitters, 12 one-hitters.
Peggy Fleming, b. 1948: world figure skating champion, 1966-68; gold medalist 1968 Olympics.
Whitey Ford, b. 1928: N.Y. Yankees pitcher won record 10 World Series games.
Dick Fosbury, b. 1947: high jumper won 1968 Olympic gold medal; developed the "Fosbury Flop."
George Foster, b. 1951: Cincinnati Reds outfielder hit 52 home runs, selected MVP, 1977; led NL RBI's, 1976-78.
Jimmy Foxx, (1907-1967): Red Sox, Athletics slugger; MVP 3 times; triple crown, 1933.
A.J. Foyt, b. 1935: won Indy 500 4 times; U.S. Auto Club champ 6 times.
Dawn Fraser, b. 1937: Australian swimmer won Olympics 100-meter freestyle 3 times.
Joe Frazier, b. 1944: heavyweight champion, 1970-73.
Walt Frazier, b. 1945: New York-Cleveland guard; first team all-star 4 times.
Lou Gehrig, (1903-1941): N.Y. Yankees 1st baseman played record 2,130 consecutive games, MVP, 1936.
George Gervin, b. 1952: leading NBA scorer, 1978-80.
Althea Gibson, b. 1927: twice U.S. and Wimbledon singles champ.
Bob Gibson, b. 1935: St. Louis Cardinals pitcher won Cy Young award twice; struck out NL record 3,117 batters.
Frank Gifford, b. 1930: N.Y. Giants back; MVP 1956.
Pancho Gonzalez, b. 1928: World professional tennis champ, 8 years.
Otto Graham, b. 1921: Cleveland Browns quarterback; all-pro 4 times.
Red Grange, b 1903: All-America at Univ. of Illinois; played for Chicago Bears, 1925-35.
Joe Greene, b. 1946: Pittsburgh Steelers lineman; twice NFL outstanding defensive player.
Lefty Grove, (1900-1975): pitcher won 300 AL games; 20-game winner 8 times.
Walter Hagen, (1892-1969): won PGA championship 5 times. British Open 4 times.
George Halas, b. 1895: founder-coach of Chicago Bears; won 5 NFL championships.
Bill Hartack, b. 1932: jockey rode 5 Kentucky Derby winners.
Doug Harvey, b. 1930: Montreal Canadiens defenseman; Norris Trophy 7 times.
Bill Haughton, b. 1923: harness racing driver won Little Brown Jug 4 times, Hambletonian 3 times.
John Havlicek, b. 1940: Boston Celtics forward scored over 26,000 NBA points.
Eric Heiden, b. 1958: speed skater won 5 1980 Olympic gold medals.

Carol Heiss, b. 1940: world champion figure skater 5 consecutive years, 1956-60; won 1960 Olympic gold medal.
Sonja Henie, (1912-1969): world champion figure skater, 1927-36; Olympic gold medalist, 1928, 1932, 1936.
Graham Hill, (1929-1975): twice World Grand Prix champ.
Ben Hogan, b. 1912: won 4 U.S. Open championships, 2 PGA, 2 Masters.
Willie Hoppe, (1887-1959): won some 50 world billiard titles.
Rogers Hornsby, (1896-1963): NL 2d baseman batted record .424 in 1924; twice won triple crown; batting leader 6 consecutive years, 1920-25.
Paul Hornung, b. 1935: Green Bay Packers runner-placekicker scored record 176 points, 1960.
Gordie Howe, b. 1928: hockey forward holds NHL career records in goals, assists, and points; NHL MVP 6 times, leading scorer 6 times.
Carl Hubbell, b. 1903: N.Y. Giants pitcher; 20-game winner 5 consecutive years, 1933-37.
Bobby Hull, b. 1939: NHL all-star 10 times, WHA all-star 4 times.
Catfish Hunter, b 1946: pitched perfect game, 1968; 20-game winner 5 times.
Don Hutson, b. 1913: Green Bay Packers receiver caught NFL record 99 touchdown passes.
Reggie Jackson, b. 1946; slugger twice led AL in home runs; MVP, 1973; hit 5 World Series home runs, 1977.
Bruce Jenner, b. 1949: decathlon gold medalist, 1976.
Jack Johnson, (1878-1946): heavyweight champion, 1910-15.
Rafer Johnson, b. 1935: decathlon gold medalist, 1960.
Walter Johnson, (1887-1946): Washington Senators pitcher won 414 games.
Bert Jones, b. 1951: Baltimore Colts quarterback; MVP, 1976.
Bobby Jones, (1902-1971); won "grand slam of golf" 1930; U.S. Amateur champ 5 times, U.S. Open champ 4 times.
Deacon Jones, b. 1938: L.A. Rams lineman; twice NFL outstanding defensive player.
Sonny Jurgensen, b. 1934: quarterback named all-pro 5 times; completed record 288 passes, 1967.
Duke Kahanamoku, (1890-1968): swimmer won 1912, 1920 Olympic gold medals in 100-meter freestyle.
Harmon Killebrew, b. 1936: Minnesota Twins slugger led AL in home runs 6 times.
Jean Claude Killy, b. 1943: French skier won 3 1968 Olympic gold medals.
Ralph Kiner, b. 1922: Pittsburgh Pirates slugger led NL in home runs 7 consecutive years, 1946-52.
Billie Jean King, b. 1943: U.S. singles champ 4 times; Wimbledon champ 6 times.
Olga Korbut, b. 1956: Soviet gymnast won 3 1972 Olympic gold medals.
Sandy Koufax, b. 1935: Dodgers pitcher won Cy Young award 3 times; lowest ERA in NL, 1962-66; pitched 4 no-hitters, one a perfect game.
Jack Kramer, b. 1921: twice U.S. singles champ.
Guy Lafleur, b. 1951: Montreal Canadiens forward led NHL in scoring 3 times; MVP, 1977, 1978.
Tom Landry, b. 1924: Dallas Cowboys head coach since 1960.
Rod Laver, b. 1938: Australian won tennis "grand slam," 1962, 1969; Wimbledon champ 4 times.
Sugar Ray Leonard, b. 1956: WBC welterweight champ, 1979-80.
Vince Lombardi, (1913-1970): Green Bay Packers coach led, team to 5 NFL championships and 2 Super Bowl victories.
Johnny Longden, b. 1907: jockey rode 6,032 winners.
Joe Louis, b. 1914: heavyweight champion, 1937-49.
Sid Luckman, b. 1916: Chicago Bears quarterback led team to 4 NFL championships; MVP, 1943.
Connie Mack, (1892-1956): Philadelphia Athletics manager, 1901-50; won 9 pennants, 5 championships.
Bill Madlock, b. 1951: NL batting leader, 1975 and 1976.
Mickey Mantle, b. 1931: N.Y. Yankees outfielder; triple crown, 1956; 18 World Series home runs.
Pete Maravich, b. 1948: averaged 44.2 ppg at LSU; led NBA in scoring, 1977.
Alice Marble, b. 1913: U.S. singles champ 4 times.
Rocky Marciano, (1923-1969): heavyweight champion, 1952-56; retired undefeated.
Roger Maris, b. 1934: N.Y. Yankees outfielder hit record 61 home runs, 1961; MVP, 1960 and 1961.
Billy Martin, b. 1928: baseball manager led N.Y. Yankees to World Series title, 1977.
Eddie Mathews, b. 1931: Milwaukee-Atlanta 3d baseman hit 512 career home runs.
Christy Mathewson, (1880-1925): N.Y. Giants pitcher won 373 games.
Bob Mathias, b. 1930: decathlon gold medalist, 1948, 1952.
Willie Mays, b. 1931: N.Y.-S.F. Giants center fielder hit 660 home runs; twice MVP.
Bob McAdoo, b. 1951: leading NBA scorer, 1974-76; MVP, 1975.
John McGraw, (1873-1934): N.Y. Giants manager led team to 10 pennants, 3 championships.
Debbie Meyer, b. 1952: swimmer won 200-, 400-, and 800- meter freestyle events, 1968 Olympics.
George Mikan, b. 1924: Minneapolis Lakers center selected in a 1950 AP poll as the greatest basketball player of the first half of the 20th century.
Stan Mikita, b. 1940: Chicago Black Hawks center led NHL in scoring 4 times; MVP twice.
Archie Moore, b. 1913: world light-heavyweight champion, 1952-62.
Howie Morenz, (1902-1937): Montreal Canadiens forward chosen in a 1950 Canadian press poll as the outstanding hockey player of the first half of the 20th century.
Joe Morgan, b. 1943: National League MVP, 1975, 1976.
Thurman Munson, (1947-1979): N.Y. Yankees catcher; MVP, 1976.
Isaac Murphy, (1856-1896): jockey rode 3 Kentucky Derby winners.
Stan Musial, b. 1920: St. Louis Cardinals star won 7 NL batting titles; MVP 3 times; NL record 3,630 hits.
Bronko Nagurski, b. 1908: Chicago Bears fullback and tackle; gained over 4,000 yds. rushing.
Joe Namath, b. 1943: quarterback passed for record 4,007 yds., 1967.
Byron Nelson, b. 1912: won 11 consecutive golf tournaments in 1945, ending the year with record 19 victories; twice Masters and PGA titlist.
Ernie Nevers, (1903-1976): Stanford star selected the best college fullback to play between 1919-1969, in a poll of the Football Writers Assn.; played pro football and baseball.
John Newcombe, b. 1943: Australian twice U.S. singles champ; Wimbledon titlist 3 times.
Jack Nicklaus, b. 1940: PGA Player-of-the-Year, 1967, 1972; leading money winner 7 times.
Chuck Noll, b. 1931: Pittsburgh Steelers coach led team to 4 Super Bowl titles.
Paavo Nurmi, (1897-1973): Finnish distance runner won 6 Olympic gold medals, 1920, 1924, 1928.
Al Oerter, b. 1936: discus thrower won gold medal at 4 consecutive Olympics, 1956-68.
Barney Oldfield, (1878-1946): turn-of-the-century auto racer.
Bobby Orr, b. 1948: Boston Bruins defenseman; Norris Trophy 8 times; led NHL in scoring twice, assists 5 times.
Mel Ott, (1909-1958): N.Y. Giants outfielder hit 511 home runs; led NL 6 times.
Jesse Owens, (1913-1980): track and field star won 4 1936 Olympic gold medals.
Satchel Paige, b. 1906: pitcher starred in Negro leagues, 1924-48; entered major leagues at age 42.
Arnold Palmer, b. 1929: golf's first $1 million winner; won 4 Masters, 2 British Opens.
Jim Palmer, b. 1945: Baltimore Orioles pitcher; Cy Young award 3 times; 20-game winner 7 times.
Dave Parker, b. 1951: Pittsburgh Pirates outfielder led NL in batting, 1977, 1978; MVP, 1978.
Floyd Patterson, b. 1935: twice heavyweight champion.
Walter Payton, 1954: Chicago Bears running back ran for game record 275 yards, 1977; leading NFC rusher, 1976-79.
Pele, b. 1940: Brazilian soccer star scored 1,281 goals during 22-year career.
Bob Pettit, b. 1932: Milwaukee-St. Louis Hawks forward was first NBA player to score 20,000 points; twice NBA scoring leader.
Richard Petty, b. 1937: NASCAR national champ 6 times; 6-times Daytona 500 winner.
Laffit Pincay Jr., b. 1946: leading money-winning jockey, 1970-74, 1979.
Jacques Plante, b. 1929: goalie, 7 Vezina trophies; first goalie to wear a mask in a game.
Gary Player, b. 1935: South African won the Masters, U.S. Open, PGA, and twice the British Open.
Annemarie Proell Moser, b. 1953: Austrian skier won the World Cup championship 5 times; 1980 Olympic gold medalist.
Willis Reed, b. 1942: N.Y. Knicks center; MVP, 1970; playoff MVP, 1970, 1973.
Jim Rice, b. 1953: Boston Red Sox outfielder led AL in home runs, 1977-78; MVP 1978.
Maurice Richard, b. 1924: Montreal Canadiens forward scored 544 regular season goals, 82 playoff goals.
Branch Rickey, (1881-1965): executive instrumental in breaking baseball's color barrier, 1947; initiated farm system, 1919.
Oscar Robertson, b. 1938: guard averaged career 25.7 points per game; record 9,887 career assist; MVP, 1964.
Brooks Robinson, b. 1937: Baltimore Orioles 3d baseman played in 4 World Series; MVP, 1964.
Frank Robinson, b. 1935: slugger MVP in both NL and AL; triple crown winner, 1966; first black manager in majors.

Jackie Robinson, (1919-1972): broke baseball's color barrier with Brooklyn Dodgers, 1947; MVP, 1949.
Sugar Ray Robinson, b. 1920: middleweight champion 5 times, welterweight champion.
Knute Rockne, (1883-1931): Notre Dame football coach, 1918-31; revolutionized game by stressing forward pass.
Pete Rose, b. 1942: won 3 NL batting titles; has over 3,300 hits; hit safely in 44 consecutive games, 1978.
Ken Rosewall, b. 1934: Australian twice U.S. singles champ.
Wilma Rudolph, b. 1940: sprinter won 3 1960 Olympic gold medals.
Bill Russell, b. 1934: Boston Celtics center led team to 11 NBA titles; MVP 5 times; first black coach of major pro sports team.
Babe Ruth, (1895-1948): N.Y. Yankees outfielder hit 60 home runs, 1927; 714 lifetime; led AL 11 times.
Nolan Ryan, b. 1947: pitcher struck out record 383 batters, 1973; pitched 4 no-hitters.
Jim Ryun, b. 1947: runner set records for the mile and 1,500 meters, 1967.
Gene Sarazen, b. 1902: won PGA championship 3 times, U.S. Open twice; developer of sand wedge.
Gale Sayers, b. 1943: Chicago Bears back twice led NFC in rushing.
Mike Schmidt, b. 1949: Phillies 3d baseman led NL in home runs, 1974-76.
Tom Seaver, b. 1944: NL pitcher won Cy Young award 3 times.
Willie Shoemaker, b. 1931: jockey rode 3 Kentucky Derby and 5 Belmont Stakes winners; leading career money winner.
Eddie Shore, b. 1902; Boston Bruins defenseman; MVP 4 times, first-team all-star 7 times.
Al Simmons, (1902-1956): AL outfielder had lifetime .334 batting average.
O.J. Simpson, b. 1947: running back rushed for record 2,003 yds., 1973; AFC leading rusher 4 times.
George Sisler, (1893-1973): St. Louis Browns 1st baseman had record 257 hits, 1920; batted .340 lifetime.
Sam Snead, b. 1912: PGA and Masters champ 3 times each.
Peter Snell, b. 1938: New Zealand runner won 800-meter race, 1960, 1964 Olympics.
Warren Spahn, b. 1921: pitcher won 363 NL games; 20-game winner 13 times; Cy Young award, 1957.
Tris Speaker, (1885-1958): AL outfielder batted .344 over 22 seasons; hit record 793 career doubles.
Mark Spitz, b. 1950: swimmer won 7 1972 Olympic gold medals.
Amos Alonzo Stagg, (1862-1965): coached Univ. of Chicago football team for 41 years, including 5 undefeated seasons; introduced huddle, man-in-motion, and end-around play.
Willie Stargell, b. 1941: Pittsburgh Pirate slugger chosen NL, World Series MVP, 1979.
Bart Starr, b. 1934: Green Bay Packers quarterback led team to 5 NFL titles and 2 Super Bowl victories.
Roger Staubach, b. 1942: Dallas Cowboys quarterback; leading NFC passer 5 times.
Casey Stengel, (1890-1975): managed Yankees to 10 pennants, 7 championships, 1949-60.
Jackie Stewart, b. 1939: Scot auto racer retired with record 27 Grand Prix victories.
John L. Sullivan, (1858-1918): last bareknuckle heavyweight champion, 1882-1892.
Fran Tarkenton, b. 1940: quarterback holds career passing records for touchdowns, completions, yardage.
Gustave Thoeni, b. 1951: Italian 4-time world alpine ski champ.
Jim Thorpe, (1888-1953): football All-America, 1911, 1912; won pentathlon and decathlon, 1912 Olympics; played major league baseball for 6 seasons.
Bill Tilden, (1893-1953): U.S. singles champ 7 times; played on 11 Davis Cup teams.
Y.A. Tittle, b. 1926: N.Y. Giants quarterback; MVP, 1961, 1963.
Lee Trevino, b. 1939: won the U.S. and British Open championships twice.
Gene Tunney, (1897-1978): heavyweight champion, 1926-28.
Wyomia Tyus, b. 1945: sprinter won 1964, 1968 Olympic 100-meter dash.
Johnny Unitas, b. 1933: Baltimore Colts quarterback passed for over 40,000 yds.; MVP, 1957, 1967.
Al Unser, b. 1939: Indy 500 winner, 3 times.
Bobby Unser, b. 1934: Indy 500 winner, 1968, twice U.S. Auto Club national champ.
Norm Van Brocklin, b. 1926: quarterback passed for game record 554 yds., 1951; MVP, 1960.
Honus Wagner, (1874-1955): Pittsburgh Pirates shortstop won 8 NL batting titles.
Joe Walcott, b. 1914: heavyweight champion, 1951-52.
Mickey Walker, b. 1901: colorful welter- and middleweight champion of the 20s and 30s.
Bill Walton b. 1952: led Portland Trail Blazers to NBA championship, 1977; MVP, 1978.
Tom Watson, b. 1949: leading money-winning golfer, 1977-79.
Johnny Weissmuller, b. 1903: swimmer won 52 national championships, 5 Olympic gold medals; set 67 world records.
Jerry West, b. 1938: L.A. Lakers guard had career average 27 points per game; first team all-star 10 times.
Kathy Whitworth, b. 1939: women's golf leading money winner 4 times: first woman to earn over $300,000.
Ted Williams, b. 1918: Boston Red Sox outfielder won 6 batting titles; last major leaguer to hit over .400: .406 in 1941: .344 lifetime batting average.
Helen Wills, b. 1906: winner of 7 U.S., 8 British, 4 French women's singles titles.
John Wooden, b. 1910: coached UCLA basketball team to 10 national championships.
Mickey Wright, b. 1935: won LPGA championship 4 times, Vare Trophy 5 times; twice AP Woman-Athlete-of-the-Year.
Carl Yastrzemski, b. 1939: Boston Red Sox slugger won 3 batting titles, triple crown, 1967.
Cy Young, (1867-1955): pitcher won record 511 major league games.
Babe Didrikson Zaharias, (1914-1956): track star won 2 1932 Olympic gold medals; won numerous golf tournaments.
Emil Zatopek, b. 1922: Czech distance runner won 5,000- and 10,000-meter and marathon, 1952 Olympics.

Westminster Kennel Club

Year	Best-in-show	Breed	Owner
1969	Ch. Glamoor Good News	Skye terrier	Walter & Mrs. Adele F. Goodman
1970	Ch. Arriba's Prima Donna	Boxer	Dr. & Mrs. P. J. Pagano & Dr. Theodore S. Fickles
1971	Ch. Chinoe's Adamant James	English springer spaniel	Dr. Milton Prickett
1972	Ch. Chinoe's Adamant James	English springer spaniel	Dr. Milton Prickett
1973	Ch. Acadia Command Performance	Poodle	Mrs. Jo Ann Sering & Edward B. Jenner
1974	Ch. Gretchenhof Columbia River	German pointer	Dr. Richard Smith
1975	Ch. Sir Lancelot of Barvan	Old English sheepdog	Mr. & Mrs. Ronald Vanword
1976	Ch. Jo-Ni's Red Baron of Crofton	Lakeland terrier	Virginia Dickson
1977	Ch. Dersade Bobby's Girl	Sealyham	Dorothy Wymer
1978	Ch. Cede Higgens	Yorkshire terrier	Barbara & Charles Switzer
1979	Ch. Oak Tree's Irishtocrat	Irish water spaniel	Anne E. Snelling
1980	Ch. Sierra Cinnar	Siberian husky	Kathleen Kanzler

Leonard Brumby Sr. Memorial Trophy

Junior Winner at Westminster Kennel Club

1970 Pat Hardy, Cincinnati, Oh. **Breed**—Golden Retriever.
1971 Heidi Shellenbarger, Costa Mesa, Cal. **Breed**—Whippet.
1972 Deborah Dagny Von Aherns, Edison Township, N. J. **Breed**—Afghan.
1973 Teresa Nail, Ft. Worth, Tex. **Breed**—Doberman Pinscher.
1974 Leslie Church, St. Louis, Mo. **Breed**—Min. Schnauzer.
1975 Virginia Westfield, Huntington, N.Y. **Breed**—Bulldog.
1976 Cathy Hritzo, Hubbard, Oh. **Breed**—Samoyed.
1977 Randy McAteer, Ocala, Fla. **Breed**—Irish Setter.
1978 Sonna Peterson, San Diego, Cal. **Breed**—Boxer.
1979 Susan Schneider, Lorton, Pa. **Breed**—English Springer Spaniel.
1980 Laura Mazzaro, Huntington, Conn. **Breed**—Norwegian Elkhound.

World Record Fish Caught by Rod and Reel

Source: International Game Fish Association.
Records confirmed to June, 1980

Saltwater Fish

The International Game Fish Assn. revised its standards for world records, effective July 1, 1970. Line samples and line tests are now required in order for a world record application to be recognized. Records listed below are based on the new standards.

Species	Weight	Where Caught	Date	Angler
Albacore	88 lbs. 2 oz.	Pt. Mogan, Canary Islands	Nov. 19, 1977	Siegried Dickemann
Amberjack	149 lbs.	Bermuda	June 21, 1964	Peter Simons
Barracuda, great	83 lbs.	Lagos, Nigeria	Jan. 13, 1952	K.J.W. Hackett
Bass, black sea	8 lbs. 12 oz.	Oregon Inlet, N.C.	Apr. 21, 1979	Joe W. Mizelle Sr.
Bass, giant sea	563 lbs. 8 oz.	Anacaba Island, Cal.	Aug. 20, 1968	James D. McAdam Jr.
Bass, striped	72 lbs.	Cuttyhunk, Mass.	Oct. 10, 1969	Edward J. Kirker
Bluefish	31 lbs. 12 oz.	Hatteras Inlet, N.C.	Jan. 30, 1972	James M. Hussey
Bonefish	19 lbs.	Zululand, S. Africa	May 26, 1962	Brian W. Batchelor
Bonito, Atlantic	13 lbs. 3 oz.	Canary Islands	Aug. 22, 1979	Renate Reichel
Bonito, Pacific	23 lbs. 8 oz.	Victoria, Mahe Seychelles	Feb. 19, 1975	Anne Cochain
Cobia	110 lbs. 5 oz.	Mombasa, Kenya	Sept. 8, 1964	Eric Tinworth
Cod	98 lbs. 12 oz.	Isle of Shoals, N.H.	June 8, 1969	Alphonse Bielevich
Dolphin	87 lbs.	Papagallo Gulf, Costa Rica	Sept. 25, 1976	Manual Salazar
Drum, black	113 lbs. 1 oz.	Lewes, Del.	Sept. 15, 1975	Gerald Townsend
Drum, red	90 lbs.	Rodanthe, N.C.	Nov. 7, 1973	Elvin Hooper
Flounder, summer	22 lb. 7 oz.	Montauk, N.Y.	Sept. 15, 1975	Charles Nappi
Halibut, California	37 lbs. 8 oz.	San Diego, Cal.	July 22, 1979	William E. Williams
Jack, crevalle	51 lbs.	Lake Worth, Fla.	June 20, 1978	Stephen Schwenk
Jack, horse-eye	21 lbs. 5 oz.	Arcus Bank, Bermuda	June 24, 1979	Tom Smith
Jewfish	680 lbs.	Fernandina Beach, Fla.	May 20, 1961	Lynn Joyner
Kawakawa	21 lbs.	Kauai, Ha.	Aug. 21, 1975	E. John O'Dell
Mackerel, king	90 lbs.	Key West, Fla.	Feb. 16, 1976	Norton Thomton
Marlin, Atlantic blue	1,282 lbs.	St. Thomas, Virgin Islands	Aug. 6, 1977	Larry Martin
Marlin, black	1,560 lbs.	Cabo Blanco, Peru	Aug. 4, 1953	A. C. Glassell Jr.
Marlin, Pacific blue	1,153 lbs.	Guam	Aug. 21, 1969	Greg Perez
Marlin, striped	417 lb. 8 oz.	Cavalli Islands, N.Z.	Jan. 14, 1977	Phillip Bryers
Marlin, white	181 lbs. 14 oz.	Vitoria, Brazil	Dec. 8, 1979	Evandro Luiz Caser
Permit	51 lbs. 8 oz.	Lake Worth, Fla.	Apr. 28, 1978	William M. Kenney
Pollock	46 lbs. 7 oz.	Brielle, N.J.	May 26, 1975	John Tomes Holton
Pompano, African	41 lbs. 8 oz.	Ft. Lauderdale, Fla.	Feb. 15, 1978	Wayne Sommers
Roosterfish	114 lbs.	La Paz, Mexico	June 1, 1960	Abe Sackheim
Runner, rainbow	33 lbs. 10 oz.	Clarion Is., Mexico	Mar. 14, 1976	Ralph A. Mikkelsen
Sailfish, Atlantic	128 lbs. 1 oz.	Luanda, Angola	Mar. 27, 1974	Harm Steyn
Sailfish, Pacific	221 lbs.	Santa Cruz Is., Ecuador	Feb. 12, 1947	C. W. Stewart
Seabass, white	83 lbs. 12 oz.	San Felipe, Mexico	Mar. 31, 1953	L.C. Baumgardner
Seatrout, spotted	16 lbs.	Mason's Beach, Va.	May 28, 1977	William Katko
Shark, blue	437 lbs.	Catherine Bay, N.S.W. Australia	Oct. 2, 1976	Peter Hyde
Shark, hammerhead	703 lbs.	Jacksonville Beach, Fla.	July 5, 1975	H.B. Reasor
Shark, man-eater or white	2,664 lbs.	Ceduna, Australia	Apr. 21, 1959	Alfred Dean
Shark, porbeagle	465 lbs.	Cornwall, England	July 23, 1976	Jorge Potier
Shark, shortfin mako	1,080 lbs.	Montauk, N.Y.	Aug. 26, 1979	James Melanson
Shark, thresher	739 lbs.	Tutukaka, N.Z.	Feb. 17, 1975	Brian Galvin
Shark, tiger	1,780 lbs.	Cherry Grove, S.C.	June 14, 1964	Walter Maxwell
Skipjack, black	14 lbs. 8 oz.	Baja, Mexico	May 24, 1977	Lorraine Carlton
Snook	53 lbs. 10 oz.	Costa Rica	Oct. 18, 1978	Gilbert Ponzi
Spearfish	79 lbs. 5 oz.	Madeira Islands	May 25, 1979	Ronald Eckert
Swordfish	1,182 lbs.	Iquique, Chile	May 7, 1953	L. Marron
Tanguigue	85 lbs. 6 oz.	Rottnest Is., W. Australia	May 5, 1978	Barry Wrightson
Tarpon	283 lbs.	L. Maracaibo, Venezuela	Mar. 19, 1956	M. Salazar
Tautog	21 lbs. 6 oz.	Cape May, N.J.	June 12, 1954	R.N. Sheafer
Trevally, lowly	116 lbs.	Pago Pago, Amer. Samoa	Feb. 20, 1978	William G. Foster
Tuna, Atlantic bigeye	375 lbs. 8 oz.	Ocean City, Md.	Aug. 26, 1977	Cecil Browne
Tuna, blackfin	42 lbs.	Bermuda	June 2, 1978	Alan J. Card
Tuna, bluefin	1,496 lbs.	Aulds Cove, Nova Scotia	Oct. 26, 1979	Ken Fraser
Tuna, dog-tooth	189 lbs. 2 oz.	Tanzania	Nov. 12, 1978	Luke J. Samaras
Tuna, longtail	65 lbs.	Pt. Stephens, N.S.W., Australia	Apr. 20, 1978	Michael James
Tuna, Pacific bigeye	435 lbs.	Cabo Blanco, Peru	Apr. 17, 1957	Dr. Russel Lee
Tuna, skipjack	39 lbs. 15 oz.	Walker Cay, Bahamas	Jan. 21, 1952	F. Drowley
	40 lbs.	Mauritius	Apr. 19, 1971	Joseph Caboche Jr.
Tuna, southern bluefin	256 lbs. 13 oz.	Tasmania, Australia	May 29, 1979	Rodney J. Beard
Tuna, yellowfin	388 lbs. 12 oz.	San Benedicto Island, Mexico	Apr. 1, 1977	Curt Wiesenhutter
Tunny, little	27 lbs.	Key Largo, Fla.	Apr. 20, 1976	William E. Allison
Wahoo	149 lbs.	Cay Cay, Bahamas	June 15, 1962	John Pirovano
Weakfish	19 lbs. 8 oz.	Trinidad, W. Indies	Apr. 13, 1962	Dennis Hall
Yellowtail, California	71 lbs. 15 oz.	Alijos Rocks, Mexico	June 24, 1979	Michael Carpenter
Yellowtail, southern	111 lbs.	Bay of Islands, N.Z.	June 11, 1961	A.F. Plim

Freshwater Fish

Species	Weight	Where caught	Date	Angler
Bass, largemouth	22 lbs. 4 oz.	Montgomery Lake, Ga.	June 2, 1932	George W. Perry
Bass, redeye	8 lbs. 3 oz.	Flint River, Ga.	Oct. 23, 1977	David A. Hubbard
Bass rock	3 lbs.	York River, Ont.	Aug. 1, 1974	Peter Gulgin

Species	Weight	Where caught	Date	Angler
Bass, smallmouth	11 lbs. 15 oz.	Dale Hollow Lake, Ky.	July 9, 1955	David L. Hayes
Bass, spotted	8 lbs. 15 oz.	Lewis Smith Lake, Ala.	Mar. 18, 1978	Philip Terry Jr.
Bass, white	5 lbs. 5 oz.	Ferguson Lake, Cal.	Mar. 8, 1972	Norman W. Mize
	5 lbs. 6 oz.	Grenada, Miss.	Apr. 21, 1979	William Mulvihill
Bass, whiterock	20 lbs.	Savannah River, Ga.	May 5, 1977	Don Raley
Bass, yellow	2 lbs. 4 oz.	L. Monroe, Ind.	Mar. 27, 1977	Donald L. Stalker
Black bullhead	8 lbs.	Lake Waccabuc, N.Y.	Aug. 1, 1951	Kani Evans
Bluegill	4 lbs. 12 oz.	Ketona Lake, Ala.	Apr. 9, 1950	T.S. Hudson
Bowfin	19 lbs. 12 oz.	Lake Marion, S.C.	Nov. 5, 1972	M.R. Webster
Buffalo, bigmouth	56 lbs.	Lock Loma L., Mo.	Aug. 19, 1976	W. J. Long
Buffalo, smallmouth	51 lbs.	Lawrence, Kan.	May 2, 1979	Scott Butler
Carp	55 lbs. 5 oz.	Clearwater Lake, Minn.	July 10, 1952	Frank J. Ledwein
Catfish, blue	97 lbs.	Missouri River, S.D.	Sept. 16, 1959	E.B. Elliott
Catfish, channel	58 lbs.	Santee-Cooper Res., S.C.	July 7, 1964	W.B. Whaley
Catfish, flathead	79 lbs. 8 oz.	White River, Ind.	Aug. 13, 1955	Glenn T. Simpson
Catfish, white	10 lbs. 5 oz.	Raritan R., N.J.	June 23, 1976	Lewis W. Lomerson
Char, Arctic	29 lbs. 11 oz.	Arctic River, N.W.T.	Aug. 21, 1968	Jeanne P. Branson
Crappie, black	5 lbs.	Santee-Cooper Res., S.C.	Mar. 15, 1957	Paul E. Foust
Crappie, white	5 lbs. 3 oz.	Enid Dam, Miss.	July 31, 1957	Fred L. Bright
Dolly Varden	32 lbs.	L. Pend Oreille, Ida.	Oct. 27, 1949	N.L. Higgins
Drum, freshwater	54 lbs. 8 oz.	Nickajack Lake, Tenn.	Apr. 20, 1972	Benny E. Hull
Gar, alligator	279 lbs.	Rio Grande R., Tex.	Dec. 2, 1951	Bill Valverde
Gar, longnose	50 lbs. 5 oz.	Trinity River, Tex.	July 30, 1954	Townsend Miller
Grayling, American	5 lbs. 15 oz.	Katseyedie R., N.W.T.	Aug. 16, 1967	Jeanne P. Branson
Kokanee	6 lbs. 9 oz.	Priest Lake, Ida.	June 9, 1975	Jerry Verge
Muskellunge	69 lbs. 15 oz.	St. Lawrence R., N.Y.	Sept. 22, 1957	Arthur Lawton
Perch, white	4 lbs. 12 oz.	Messalonskee Lake, Me.	June 4, 1949	Mrs. Earl Small
Perch, yellow	4 lbs. 3 oz.	Bordentown, N.J.	May, 1865	Dr. C.C. Abbot
Pickerel, chain	9 lbs. 6 oz.	Homerville, Ga.	Feb. 17, 1961	Baxley McQuaig Jr.
Pike, northern	46 lbs. 2 oz.	Sacandaga Res., N.Y.	Sept. 15, 1940	Peter Dubuc
Redhorse, silver	4 lbs. 2 oz.	Gasconade River, Mo.	Oct. 5, 1974	C. Larry McKinney
Salmon, Atlantic	79 lbs. 2 oz.	Tana R., Norway	1928	Henrik Henriksen
Salmon, chinook	93 lbs.	Kelp Bay, Alas.	June 24, 1977	Howard C. Rider
Salmon, chum	27 lbs. 3 oz.	Raymond Cove, Alas.	June 11, 1977	Robert A. Jahnke
Salmon, landlocked	22 lbs. 8 oz.	Sebago Lake, Me.	Aug. 1, 1907	Edward Blakely
Salmon, silver	31 lbs.	Cowichan Bay, B.C.	Oct. 11, 1947	Mrs. Lee Hallberg
Sauger	8 lbs. 12 oz.	Lake Sakakawea, N.D.	Oct. 6, 1971	Mike Fischer
Shad, American	9 lbs. 4 oz.	Delaware R., Pa.	Apr. 26, 1979	J. Edward Whitman
Sturgeon, white	360 lbs.	Snake River, Ida.	Apr. 24, 1956	Willard Cravens
Sunfish, green	2 lbs. 2 oz.	Stockton Lake, Mo.	June 18, 1971	Paul M. Dilley
Sunfish, redbreast	1 lb. 8 oz.	Suwannee River, Fla.	Apr. 30, 1977	Tommy D. Cason Jr.
Sunfish, redear	4 lbs. 8 oz.	Chase City, Va.	June 19, 1970	Maurice E. Ball
Trout, brook	14 lbs. 8 oz.	Nipigon R., Ont.	July, 1916	Dr. W.J. Cook
Trout, brown	35 lbs. 15 oz.	Nahuel Huapi, Argentina	Dec. 16, 1952	Eugenio Cavaglia
Trout, cutthroat	41 lbs.	Pyramid Lake, Nev.	Dec., 1925	J. Skimmerhorn
Trout, golden	11 lbs.	Cook's Lake, Wyo.	Aug. 5, 1948	Charles S. Reed
Trout, lake	65 lbs.	Great Bear Lake, N.W.T.	Aug. 8, 1970	Larry Daunis
Trout, rainbow steelhead or kamloops	42 lbs. 2 oz.	Bell Island, Alas.	June 22, 1970	David Robert White
Trout sunapee	11 lbs. 8 oz.	Lake Sunapee, N.H.	Aug. 1, 1954	Ernest Theoharis
Trout, tiger	17 lbs.	Lake Michigan, Wis.	Aug. 2, 1977	Edward Rudnicki
Walleye	25 lbs.	Old Hickory Lake, Tenn.	Aug. 1, 1960	Mabry Harper
Warmouth	2 lbs.	Sylvania, Ga.	May 4, 1974	Carlton Robbins
Whitefish, lake	13 lbs.	Great Bear Lake, N.W.T.	July 14, 1974	Robert L. Stintsman
Whitefish, mountain	5 lbs.	Athabasca R., Alta.	June 3, 1963	Orville Welch

Canadian Interuniversity Athletic Union Champions

	Basketball	Football	Hockey	Soccer	Swimming, Diving	Volleyball	Wrestling
1966	Windsor	St. Francis Xavier	Toronto	—	Toronto	—	—
1967	Windsor	Alberta	Toronto	—	Toronto	British Columbia	—
1968	Waterloo Lutheran	Queen's	Alberta	—	Toronto	Ottawa	—
1969	Windsor	Manitoba	Toronto	—	Toronto	Winnipeg	—
1970	British Columbia	Manitoba	Toronto	—	Toronto	Montreal	Alberta
1971	Acadia	Western Ontario	Toronto	—	Toronto	Winnipeg	Alberta
1972	British Columbia	Alberta	Toronto	Alberta	McGill	Winnipeg	Alberta
1973	St. Mary's	St. Mary's	Toronto	Loyola	Toronto	Winnipeg	O.U.A.A.
1974	Guelph	Western Ontario	Waterloo	British Columbia	Toronto	Winnipeg	O.U.A.A.
1975	Waterloo	Ottawa	Alberta	Victoria	Toronto	Sherbrooke	O.U.A.A.
1976	Manitoba	Western Ontario	Toronto	Concordia	Toronto	British Columbia	O.U.A.A.
1977	Acadia	Western Ontario	Toronto	York	Waterloo	Winnipeg	O.U.A.A.
1978	St. Mary's	Queen's	Alberta	Manitoba	Waterloo	Manitoba	O.U.A.A.
1979	St. Mary's	Acadia	Alberta	Alberta	Waterloo	Saskatchewan	O.U.A.A.
1980	Victoria		Alberta		Toronto	Manitoba	Lakehead

NCAA Wrestling Champions

Year	Champion	Year	Champion	Year	Champion	Year	Champion	Year	Champion
1961	Oklahoma State	1965	Iowa State	1969	Iowa State	1973	Iowa State	1977	Iowa State
1962	Oklahoma State	1966	Oklahoma State	1970	Iowa State	1974	Iowa State	1978	Iowa
1963	Oklahoma	1967	Michigan State	1971	Oklahoma State	1975	Iowa	1979	Iowa
1964	Oklahoma State	1968	Oklahoma State	1972	Iowa State	1976	Iowa	1980	Iowa

Kentucky Derby

Churchill Downs, Louisville, Ky.

Inaugurated 1875; distance 1-1/4 miles; 1-1/2 miles until 1896. 3-year olds. Times—seconds in fifths.

Year	Winner	Jockey	Trainer	Wt.	Second	Winner's share	Time
1907	Pink Star	A. Minder	W. H. Fizer	117	Zal	$4,850	2:12.3
1908	Stone Street	A. Pickens	J. W. Hall	117	Sir Cleges	4,850	2:15.1
1909	Wintergreen	V. Powers	C. Mack	117	Miami	4,850	2:08.1
1910	Donau	F. Herbert	G. Ham	117	Joe Morris	4,850	2:06.2
1911	Meridian	G. Archibald	A. Ewing	117	Governor Gray	4,850	2:05.
1912	Worth	C. H. Shilling	F. M. Taylor	117	Duval	4,850	2:09.2
1913	Donerail	R. Goose	T. P. Hayes	117	Ten Point	5,475	2:04.4
1914	Old Rosebud	J. McCabe	F. D. Weir	114	Hodge	9,125	2:03.2
1915	Regret*	J. Notter	J. Rowe Sr.	112	Pebbles	11,450	2:05.2
1916	George Smith	J. Loftus	H. Hughes	117	Star Hawk	16,600	2:04.3
1917	Omar Khayyam	C. Borel	C. T. Patterson	117	Ticket	9,750	2:04.
1918	Exterminator	W. Knapp	H. McDaniel	114	Escoba	14,700	2:10.4
1919	Sir Barton	J. Loftus	H. G. Bedwell	112	Billy Kelly	20,825	2:09.4
1920	Paul Jones	T. Rice	W. Garth	126	Upset	30,375	2:09.
1921	Behave Yourself	C. Thompson	H. J. Thompson	126	Black Servant	38,450	2:04.1
1922	Morvich	A. Johnson	F. Burlew	126	Bet Mosie	46,775	2:04.3
1923	Zev	E. Sande	D. J. Leary	126	Martingale	53,600	2:05.2
1924	Black Gold	J. D. Mooney	H. Webb	126	Chilhowee	52,775	2:05.1
1925	Flying Ebony	E. Sande	W. B. Duke	126	Captain Hal	52,950	2:07.3
1926	Bubbling Over	A. Johnson	H. J. Thompson	126	Bagenbaggage	50,075	2:03.4
1927	Whiskery	L. McAtee	F. Hopkins	126	Osmand	51,000	2:06.
1928	Reigh Count	C. Lang	B. S. Michell	126	Misstep	55,375	2:10.2
1929	Clyde Van Dusen	L. McAtee	C. Van Dusen	126	Naishapur	53,950	2:10.4
1930	Gallant Fox	E. Sande	J. Fitzsimmons	126	Gallant Knight	50,725	2:07.3
1931	Twenty Grand	C. Kurtsinger	J. Rowe Jr.	126	Sweep All	48,725	2:01.4
1932	Burgoo King	E. James	H. J. Thompson	126	Economic	52,350	2:05.1
1933	Brokers Tip	D. Meade	H. J. Thompson	126	Head Play	48,925	2:06.4
1934	Cavalcade	M. Garner	R. A. Smith	126	Discovery	28,175	2:04.
1935	Omaha	W. Saunders	J. Fitzsimmons	126	Roman Soldier	39,525	2:05.
1936	Bold Venture	I. Hanford	M. Hirsch	126	Brevity	37,725	2:03.3
1937	War Admiral	C. Kurtsinger	G. Conway	126	Pompoon	52,050	2:03.1
1938	Lawrin	E. Arcaro	B. A. Jones	126	Dauber	47,050	2:04.4
1939	Johnstown	J. Stout	J. Fitzsimmons	126	Challedon	46,350	2:03.2
1940	Gallahadion	C. Bierman	R. Waldron	126	Bimelech	60,150	2:05.
1941	Whirlaway	E. Arcaro	B. A. Jones	126	Staretor	61,275	2:01.2
1942	Shut Out	W. D. Wright	J. M. Gaver	126	Alsab	64,225	2:04.2
1943	Count Fleet	J. Longden	G. D. Cameron	126	Blue Swords	60,275	2:04.
1944	Pensive	C. McCreary	B. A. Jones	126	Broadcloth	64,675	2:04.1
1945	Hoop, Jr.	E. Arcaro	I. H. Parke	126	Pot o'Luck	64,850	2:07.
1946	Assault	W. Mehrtens	M. Hirsch	126	Spy Song	96,400	2:06.3
1947	Jet Pilot	E. Guerin	T. Smith	126	Phalanx	92,160	2:06.3
1948	Citation	E. Arcaro	B. A. Jones	126	Coaltown	83,400	2:05.2
1949	Ponder	S. Brooks	B. A. Jones	126	Capot	91,600	2:04.1
1950	Middleground	W. Boland	M. Hirsch	126	Hill Prince	92,650	2:01.3
1951	Count Turf	C. McCreary	S. Rutchick	126	Royal Mustang	98,050	2:02.3
1952	Hill Gail	E. Arcaro	B. A. Jones	126	Sub Fleet	96,300	2:01.3
1953	Dark Star	H. Moreno	E. Hayward	126	Native Dancer	90,050	2:02.
1954	Determine	R. York	W. Molter	126	Hasty Road	102,050	2:03.
1955	Swaps	W. Shoemaker	M. A. Tenney	126	Nashua	108,400	2:01.4
1956	Needles	D. Erb	H. L. Fontaine	126	Fabius	123,450	2:03.2
1957	Iron Liege	W. Hartack	H. A. Jones	126	Gallant Man	107,950	2:02.1
1958	Tim Tam	I. Valenzuela	H. A. Jones	126	Lincoln Road	116,400	2:05.
1959	Tomy Lee	W. Shoemaker	F. Childs	126	Sword Dancer	119,650	2:02.1
1960	Venetian Way	W. Hartack	V. Sovinski	126	Bally Ache	114,850	2:02.2
1961	Carry Back	J. Sellers	J. A. Price	126	Crozier	120,500	2:04.
1962	Decidedly	W. Hartack	H. Luro	126	Roman Line	119,650	2:00.2
1963	Chateaugay	B. Baeza	J. Conway	126	Never Bend	108,900	2:01.4
1964	Northern Dancer	W. Hartack	H. Luro	126	Hill Rise	114,300	2:00.
1965	Lucky Debonair	W. Shoemaker	F. Catrone	126	Dapper Dan	112,000	2:01.1
1966	Kauai King	D. Brumfield	H. Forrest	126	Advocator	120,500	2:02.
1967	Proud Clarion	R. Ussery	L. Gentry	126	Barbs Delight	119,700	2:00.3
1968	Dancer's Image (a)	R. Ussery	H. Forrest	126	Forward Pass	122,600	2:02.1
1969	Majestic Prince	W. Hartack	J. Longden	126	Arts and Letters	113,200	2:01.4
1970	Dust Commander	M. Manganello	D. Combs	126	My Dad George	127,800	2:03.2
1971	Canonero II	G. Avila	J. Arias	126	Jim French	145,500	2:03.1
1972	Riva Ridge	R. Turcotte	L. Laurin	126	No Le Hace	140,300	2:01.4
1973	Secretariat	R. Turcotte	L. Laurin	126	Sham	155,050	1:59.2
1974	Cannonade	A. Cordero	W. C. Stephens	126	Hudson County	274,000	2:04.
1975	Foolish Pleasure	J. Vasquez	L. Jolley	126	Avatar	209,611	2:02.
1976	Bold Forbes	A. Cordero	L. Barrea	126	Honest Pleasure	165,200	2:01.3
1977	Seattle Slew	J. Cruquet	W. H. Turner Jr.	126	Run Dusty Run	214,700	2:02.1
1978	Affirmed	S. Cauthen	L. Barrera	126	Alydar	186,900	2:01.1
1979	Spectacular Bid	R. Franklin	G. Delp	126	General Assembly	228,650	2:02.2
1980	Genuine Risk*	J. Vasquez	L. Jolley	126	Rumbo	250,550	2:02

(a) Dancer's Image was disqualified from purse money after tests disclosed that he had run with a pain-killing drug, phenylbutazone, in his system. All wagers were paid on Dancer's Image. Forward Pass was awarded first place money.

The Kentucky Derby has been won five times by two jockeys, Eddie Arcaro, 1938, 1941, 1945, 1948 and 1952; and Bill Hartack, 1957, 1960, 1962, 1964 and 1969; and three times by each of three jockeys, Isaac Murphy, 1884, 1890, and 1891; Earle Sande, 1923, 1925 and 1930, and Willie Shoemaker, 1955, 1959, 1965. *Regret and Genuine Risk are the only fillies to win the Derby.

Preakness

Pimlico, Baltimore, Md.; inaugurated 1873; 1 3-16 miles, 3 yr. olds. Time—seconds in fifths.

Year	Winner	Jockey	Trainer	Wt.	Second	Winner's share	Time
1941	Whirlaway	E. Arcaro	B.A. Jones	126	King Cole	$49,365	1:58.4
1942	Alsab	B. James	A. Swenke	126	Requested, Sun Again (tie).	58,175	1:57
1943	Count Fleet	J. Longden	G.D. Cameron	126	Blue Swords	43,190	1:57.2
1944	Pensive	C. McCreary	B.A. Jones	126	Platter	60,075	1:59.1
1945	Polynesian	W.D. Wright	M. Dixon	126	Hoop Jr.	66,170	1:58.4
1946	Assault	W. Mehrtens	M. Hirsch	126	Lord Boswell	96,620	2:01.2
1947	Faultless	D. Dodson	H.A. Jones	126	On Trust	98,005	1:59
1948	Citation	E. Arcaro	H.A. Jones	126	Vulcan's Forge	91,870	2:02.2
1949	Capot	T. Atkinson	J.M. Gaver	126	Palestinian	79,985	1:56
1950	Hill Prince	E. Arcaro	J.H. Hayes	126	Middleground	56,115	1:59.1
1951	Bold	E. Arcaro	P.M. Burch	126	Counterpoint	83,110	1:56.2
1952	Blue Man	C. McCreary	W.C. Stephens	126	Jampol	86,135	1:57.2
1953	Native Dancer	E. Guerin	W.C. Winfrey	126	Jamie K	65,200	1:57.4
1954	Hasty Road	J. Adams	H. Trotsek	126	Correlation	91,600	1:57.2
1955	Nashua	E. Arcaro	J. Fitzsimmons	126	Saratoga	67,550	1:54.3
1956	Fabius	W. Hartack	H.A. Jones	126	Needles	84,250	1:58.2
1957	Bold Ruler	E. Arcaro	J. Fitzsimmons	126	Iron Liege	65,250	1:56.1
1958	Tim Tam	I. Valenzuela	H.A. Jones	126	Lincoln Road	97,900	1:57.1
1959	Royal Orbit	W. Harmatz	R. Cornell	126	Sword Dancer	136,200	1:57
1960	Bally Ache	R. Ussery	H.J. Pitt	126	Victoria Park	121,000	1:57.3
1961	Carry Back	J. Sellers	J.A. Price	126	Globemaster	126,200	1:57.3
1962	Greek Money	J.L. Rotz	V.W. Raines	126	Ridan	135,800	1:56.1
1963	Candy Spots	W. Shoemaker	M.A. Tenney	126	Chateaugay	127,500	1:56.1
1964	Northern Dancer	W. Hartack	H. Luro	126	The Scoundrel	124,200	1:56.4
1965	Tom Rolfe	R. Turcotte	F.Y. Whiteley Jr.	126	Dapper Dan	128,100	1:56.1
1966	Kauai King	D. Brumfield	H. Forrest	126	Stupendous	129,000	1:55.2
1967	Damascus	W. Shoemaker	F.Y. Whiteley Jr.	126	In Reality	141,500	1:55.1
1968	Forward Pass	I. Valenzuela	H. Forrest	126	Out of the Way	142,700	1:56.4
1969	Majestic Prince	W. Hartack	J. Longden	126	Arts and Letters	129,500	1:55.3
1970	Personality	E. Belmonte	J.W. Jacobs	126	My Dad George	151,300	1:56.1
1971	Canonero II	G. Avila	J. Arias	126	Eastern Fleet	137,400	1:54
1972	Bee Bee Bee	E. Nelson	D.W. Carroll	126	No Le Hace	135,300	1:55.3
1973	Secretariat	R. Turcotte	L. Laurin	126	Sham	129,900	1:54.2
1974	Little Current	M. Rivera	L. Rondinello	126	Neopolitan Way	156,000	1:56.3
1975	Master Derby	D. McHargue	W.E. Adams	126	Foolish Pleasure	158,100	1:56.2
1976	Elocutionist	J. Lively	P.T. Adwell	126	Play The Red	129,700	1:55
1977	Seattle Slew	J. Cruquet	W.H. Turner Jr.	126	Iron Constitution	138,600	1:54.2
1978	Affirmed	S. Cauthen	L. Barrera	126	Alydar	136,200	1:54.2
1979	Spectacular Bid	R. Franklin	G. Delp	126	Golden Act	165,300	1:54.1
1980	Codex	A. Cordero	D.W. Lucas	126	Genuine Risk	180,600	1:54.1

Belmont Stakes

Elmont, N.Y.; inaugurated 1867; 1 ½ miles, 3 year olds. Time—seconds in fifths.

Year	Winner	Jockey	Trainer	Wt.	Second	Winner's share	Time
1941	Whirlaway	E. Arcaro	B.A. Jones	126	Robert Morris	$39,770	2:31
1942	Shut Out	E. Arcaro	J.M. Garver	126	Alsab	44,520	2:29.1
1943	Count Fleet	J. Longden	G.D. Cameron	126	Fairy Manhurst	35,340	2:28.1
1944	Bounding Home	G.L. Smith	M. Brady	126	Pensive	55,000	2:32.1
1945	Pavot	E. Arcaro	O. White	126	Wildlife	52,675	2:30.1
1946	Assault	W. Mehrtens	M. Hirsch	126	Natchez	75,400	2:30.4
1947	Phalanx	R. Donoso	S. Veitch	126	Tide Rips	78,900	2:29.2
1948	Citation	E. Arcaro	H.A. Jones	126	Better Self	77,700	2:28.1
1949	Capot	T. Atkinson	J.M. Gaver	126	Ponder	60,900	2:30.1
1950	Middleground	W. Boland	M. Hirsch	126	Lights Up	61,350	2:28.3
1951	Counterpoint	D. Gorman	S. Veitch	125	Battlefield	82,000	2:29
1952	One Count	E. Arcaro	O. White	126	Blue Man	82,400	2:30.1
1953	Native Dancer	E. Guerin	W.C. Winfrey	126	Jamie K.	82,500	2:28.3
1954	High Gun	E. Guerin	M. Hirsch	126	Fisherman	89,000	2:30.4
1955	Nashua	E. Arcaro	J. Fitzsimmons	126	Blazing Count	83,700	2:29
1956	Needles	D. Erb	H. Fontaine	126	Career Boy	83,600	2:29.4
1957	Gallant Man	W. Shoemaker	J. Nerud	126	Inside Tract	77,300	2:26.3
1958	Cavan	P. Anderson	T.J. Barry	126	Tim Tam	73,440	2:30.1
1959	Sword Dancer	W. Shoemaker	J.E. Burch	126	Bagdad	93,525	2:28.2
1960	Celtic Ash	W. Hartack	T.J. Barry	126	Venetian Way	96,785	2:29.3
1961	Sherluck	B. Baeza	H. Young	126	Globemaster	104,900	2:29.1
1962	Jaipur	W. Shoemaker	W.F. Mulholland	126	Admiral's Voyage	109,550	2:28.4
1963	Chateaugay	B. Baeza	J.P. Conway	126	Candy Spots	101,700	2:30.1
1964	Quadrangle	M. Ycaza	J.E. Burch	126	Roman Brother	110,850	2:28.2
1965	Hail to All	J. Sellers	E. Yowell	126	Tom Rolfe	104,150	2:28.2
1966	Amberoid	W. Boland	L. Laurin	126	Buffle	117,700	2:29.3
1967	Damascus	W. Shoemaker	F.Y. Whiteley Jr.	126	Cool Reception	104,950	2:28.4
1968	Stage Door Johnny	H. Gustines	J.M. Gaver	126	Forward Pass	117,700	2:27.1
1969	Arts and Letters	B. Baeza	J.E. Burch	126	Majestic Prince	104,050	2:28.4
1970	High Echelon	J.L. Rotz	J.W. Jacobs	126	Needles N Pens	115,000	2:34
1971	Pass Catcher	W. Blum	E. Yowell	126	Jim French	97,710	2:30.2
1972	Riva Ridge	R. Turcotte	L. Laurin	126	Ruritania	93,950	2:28
1973	Secretariat	R. Turcotte	L. Laurin	126	Twice A Prince	90,120	2:24
1974	Little Current	M. Rivera	L. Rondinello	126	Jolly Johu	101,970	2:29.1
1975	Avatar	W. Shoemaker	A.T. Doyle	126	Foolish Pleasure	116,160	2:28.1
1976	Bold Forbes	A. Cordero	L.S. Barrera	126	McKenzie Bridge	116,850	2:29
1977	Seattle Slew	J. Cruquet	W.H. Turner Jr.	126	Run Dusty Run	109,080	2:29.3
1978	Affirmed	S. Cauthen	L.S. Barrera	126	Alydar	110,580	2:26.4
1979	Coastal	R. Hernandez	D.A. Whiteley	126	Golden Act	161,400	2:28.3
1980	Temperence Hill	E. Maple	J. Cantey	126	Genuine Risk	176,220	2:29.4

Triple Crown Turf Winners, Jockeys, and Trainers

(Kentucky Derby, Preakness, and Belmont Stakes)

Year	Horse	Jockey	Trainer
1919	Sir Barton	J. Loftus	H. G. Bedwell
1930	Gallant Fox	E. Sande	J. Fitzsimmons
1935	Omaha	W. Sanders	J. Fitzsimmons
1937	War Admiral	C. Kurtsinger	G. Conway
1941	Whirlaway	E. Arcaro	B.A. Jones
1943	Count Fleet	J. Longden	G.D. Cameron
1946	Assault	Mehrtens	M. Hirsch
1948	Citation	E. Arcaro	H.A. Jones
1973	Secretariat	R. Turcotte	L. Laurin
1977	Seattle Slew	J. Cruquet	W.H. Turner Jr.
1978	Affirmed	S. Cauthen	L.S. Barrera

U.S. Thoroughbred Records

Furlongs	Horse, age, weight	Track, state	Date	Time
3	El Macho	Gulfstream, Fla.	Feb. 26, 1974	0:32.1
4 (½ mile)	Norgor, 9, 118	Ruidoso Downs, N.M.	Aug. 14, 1976	0:44.3
4½	Kathryn's Doll, 2, 111	Turf Paradise, Ariz.	Apr. 9, 1967	0:50.2
	Dear Ethel, 2, 114	Miles Park, Ky.	July 4, 1967	0:50.2
	Bold Liz, 2, 118	Sunland Park, N.M.	Mar. 19, 1972	0:50.2
	Scott's Poppy, 2, 118	Turf Paradise, Ariz.	Feb. 22, 1975	0:50.2
5	Zip Pocket, 3, 122	Turf Paradise, Ariz.	Apr. 22, 1967	0:55.2
5½	Zip Pocket, 3, 129	Turf Paradise, Ariz.	Nov. 19, 1967	1:01.2
6 (¾ mile)	Grey Papa, 6, 116	Longacres, Wash.	Sept. 4, 1972	1:07.1
6½	Best Hitter, 4, 114	Longacres, Wash.	Aug. 24, 1973	1:13.4
7	Triple Bend, 4, 123	Hollywood, Cal.	May 6, 1972	1:19.4
8 (1 mile)	Dr. Fager, 4, 134	Arlington, Ill.	Aug. 24, 1968	1:32.1
8½	Swaps, 4, 130	Hollywood, Cal.	June 23, 1956	1:39
9	Secretariat, 3, 124	Belmont, N.Y.	Sept. 15, 1973	1:45.2
9½	Riva Ridge, 4, 127	Aqueduct, N.Y.	July 4, 1973	1:52.2
10	Spectacular Bid, 4, 126	Santa Anita, Cal.	Feb. 3, 1980	1:57.4
10½	Tempted, 4, 128	Aqueduct, N.Y.	Oct. 12, 1959	2:09
11	Man o' War, 3, 126	Belmont, N.Y.	June 12, 1920	2:14.1
12 (1½ miles)	Secretariat, 3, 126	Belmont, N.Y.	June 9, 1973	2:24
13	Swaps, 4, 130	Hollywood, Cal.	July 25, 1956	2:38.1
14	Noor, 5, 117	Santa Anita, Cal.	Mar. 4, 1950	2:52.4
16 (2 miles)	Kelso, 7, 124	Aqueduct, N.Y.	Oct. 31, 1964	3:19.1
18	Fenelon, 4, 119	Belmont, N.Y.	Oct. 4, 1941	3:47
20	Miss Grillo, 6, 118	Pimlico, Md.	Nov. 12, 1948	4:14.3

Annual Leading Money-Winning Horses

Year	Horse	Dollars
1944	Pavot	179,040
1945	Busher	273,735
1946	Assault	424,195
1947	Armed	376,325
1948	Citation	709,470
1949	Ponder	321,825
1950	Noor	346,940
1951	Counterpoint	250,525
1952	Crafty Admiral	277,255
1953	Native Dancer	513,425
1954	Determine	328,700
1955	Nashua	752,550
1956	Needles	440,850
1957	Round Table	600,383
1958	Round Table	662,780
1959	Sword Dancer	537,004
1960	Bally Ache	455,045
1961	Carry Back	565,349
1962	Never Bend	402,969
1963	Candy Spots	604,481
1964	Gun Bow	580,100
1965	Buckpasser	568,096
1966	Buckpasser	669,078
1967	Damascus	817,941
1968	Forward Pass	546,674
1969	Arts and Letters	555,604
1970	Personality	444,049
1971	Riva Ridge	503,263
1972	Droll Roll	471,633
1973	Secretariat	860,404
1974	Chris Evert	551,063
1975	Foolish Pleasure	716,278
1976	Forego	491,701
1977	Seattle Slew	641,370
1978	Affirmed	901,541
1979	Spectacular Bid	1,279,334

Annual Leading Jockey—Money Won

Year	Jockey	Dollars
1950	Eddie Arcaro	1,410,160
1951	Willie Shoemaker	1,329,890
1952	Eddie Arcaro	1,859,591
1953	Willie Shoemaker	1,784,187
1954	Willie Shoemaker	1,876,760
1955	Eddie Arcaro	1,864,796
1956	Bill Hartack	2,343,955
1957	Bill Hartack	3,060,501
1958	Willie Shoemaker	2,961,693
1959	Willie Shoemaker	2,843,133
1960	Willie Shoemaker	2,123,961
1961	Willie Shoemaker	2,690,819
1962	Willie Shoemaker	2,916,844
1963	Willie Shoemaker	2,526,925
1964	Willie Shoemaker	2,649,553
1965	Braulio Baeza	2,582,702
1966	Braulio Baeza	2,951,022
1967	Braulio Baeza	3,088,888
1968	Braulio Baeza	2,835,108
1969	Jorge Velasquez	2,542,315
1970	Laffit Pincay Jr.	2,626,526
1971	Laffit Pincay Jr.	3,784,377
1972	Laffit Pincay Jr.	3,225,827
1973	Laffit Pincay Jr.	4,093,492
1974	Laffit Pincay Jr.	4,251,060
1975	Braulio Baeza	3,695,198
1976	Angel Cordero Jr.	4,709,500
1977	Steve Cauthen	6,151,750
1978	Darrel McHargue	6,029,885
1979	Laffit Pincay Jr.	8,193,535

Leading Money-Winning Horses

As of June 15, 1980

Horse, year foaled	Sts.	1st	2d	3d	Dollars
Spectacular Bid, 1976	27	23	2	1	2,394,268
Affirmed, 1975	29	22	5	1	2,393,818
Kelso, 1957	63	39	12	2	1,977,896
Forego, 1970	57	34	9	7	1,938,957
Round Table, 1954	66	43	8	5	1,749,869
Excellor, 1973	33	15	5	6	1,654,002
Dahlia, 1970	48	15	3	7	1,543,139
Buckpasser, 1963	31	25	4	1	1,462,014
Allez France, 1970	21	13	3	1	1,386,146
Secretariat, 1970	21	16	3	1	1,316,808
Nashua, 1952	30	22	4	1	1,288,565
Ancient Title, 1970	57	24	11	9	1,252,791
Susan's Girl, 1969	63	29	14	11	1,251,667
Carry Back, 1958	62	21	11	11	1,241,165
Foolish Pleasure, 1972	26	16	4	3	1,216,705
Seattle Slew, 1974	17	14	2	0	1,208,726
Damascus, 1964	32	21	7	3	1,176,781

Eclipse Awards in 1979

Sponsored by the Thoroughbred Racing Assn., Daily Racing Form, and the National Turf Writers Assn.

Horse of the Year—Affirmed
Best 2-year-old colt—Rockhill Native
Best 2-year-old filly—Smart Angle
Best 3-year-old colt—Spectacular Bid
Best 3-year-old filly—Davona Dale
Best colt, horse, or gelding (4-year-olds & up)—Affirmed
Best filly or mare (4-year-olds & up)—Waya
Best turf horse—Bowl Game
Best sprinter—Star De Naskra
Best steeplechase horse—Martie's Anger
Outstanding trainer—Laz Barrera
Outstanding jockey—Lafitt Pincay Jr.
Outstanding apprentice jockey—Cash Asmussen
Leading breeder—Claiborne Farms

Figure Skating Champions

National Champions			World Champions	
Men	**Women**	**Year**	**Men**	**Women**
Richard Button	Tenley Albright	**1952**	Richard Button, U.S.	Jacqueline du Bief, France
Hayes Jenkins	Tenley Albright	**1953**	Hayes Jenkins, U.S.	Tenley Albright, U.S.
Hayes Jenkins	Tenley Albright	**1954**	Hayes Jenkins, U.S.	Gundi Busch, W. Germany
Hayes Jenkins	Tenley Albright	**1955**	Hayes Jenkins, U.S.	Tenley Albright, U.S.
Hayes Jenkins	Tenley Albright	**1956**	Hayes Jenkins, U.S.	Carol Heiss, U.S.
Dave Jenkins	Carol Heiss	**1957**	Dave Jenkins, U.S.	Carol Heiss, U.S.
Dave Jenkins	Carol Heiss	**1958**	Dave Jenkins, U.S.	Carol Heiss, U.S.
Dave Jenkins	Carol Heiss	**1959**	Dave Jenkins, U.S.	Carol Heiss, U.S.
Dave Jenkins	Carol Heiss	**1960**	Alain Giletti, France	Carol Heiss, U.S.
Bradley Lord	Laurence Owen	**1961**	none	none
Monty Hoyt	Barbara Roles Pursley	**1962**	Don Jackson, Canada	Sjoukje Dijkstra, Neth.
Tommy Litz	Lorraine Hanlon	**1963**	Don McPherson, Canada	Sjoukje Dijkstra, Neth.
Scott Allen	Peggy Fleming	**1964**	Manfred Schnelldorfer, W. Germany	Sjoukje Dijkstra, Neth.
Gary Visconti	Peggy Fleming	**1965**	Alain Calmat, France	Petra Burka, Canada
Scott Allen	Peggy Fleming	**1966**	Emmerich Danzer, Austria	Peggy Fleming, U.S.
Gary Visconti	Peggy Fleming	**1967**	Emmerich Danzer, Austria	Peggy Fleming, U.S.
Tim Wood	Peggy Fleming	**1968**	Emmerich Danzer, Austria	Peggy Fleming, U.S.
Tim Wood	Janet Lynn	**1969**	Tim Wood, U.S.	Gabriele Seyfert, E. Germany
Tim Wood	Janet Lynn	**1970**	Tim Wood, U.S.	Gabriele Seyfert, E. Germany
John Misha Petkevich	Janet Lynn	**1971**	Ondrej Nepela, Czech.	Beatrix Schuba, Austria
Ken Shelley	Janet Lynn	**1972**	Ondrej Nepela, Czech.	Beatrix Schuba, Austria
Gordon McKellen Jr.	Janet Lynn	**1973**	Ondrej Nepela, Czech.	Karen Magnussen, Canada
Gordon McKellen Jr.	Dorothy Hamill	**1974**	Jan Hoffmann, E. Germany	Christine Errath, E. Germany
Gordon McKellen Jr.	Dorothy Hamill	**1975**	Sergei Volkov, USSR	Dianne de Leeuw, Neth.-U.S.
Terry Kubicka	Dorothy Hamill	**1976**	John Curry, Gt. Britain	Dorothy Hamill, U.S.
Charles Tickner	Linda Fratianne	**1977**	Vladimir Kovalev, USSR	Linda Fratianne, U.S.
Charles Tickner	Linda Fratianne	**1978**	Charles Tickner, U.S.	Anett Potzsch, E. Germany
Charles Tickner	Linda Fratianne	**1979**	Vladimir Kovalev, USSR	Linda Fratianne, U.S.
Charles Tickner	Linda Fratianne	**1980**	Jan Hoffmann, E. Germany	Anett Potzsch, E. Germany

World Pairs Championship in 1980

Marina Chersekova and Sergei Shakhrai of the Soviet Union won the 1980 world pairs figure skating championship in Dortmund, W. Germany on Mar. 12.

Canadian National Figure Skating Champions

Year	Men	Women
1963	Donald McPherson	Wendy Griner
1964	Charles Snelling	Petra Burka
1965	Donald Knight	Petra Burka
1966	Donald Knight	Petra Burka
1967	Donald Knight	Valerie Jones
1968	Jay Humphrey	Karen Magnussen
1969	Jay Humphrey	Linda Carbonetto
1970	David McGillivray	Karen Magnussen
1971	Toller Cranston	Karen Magnussen
1972	Toller Cranston	Karen Magnussen
1973	Toller Cranston	Karen Magnussen
1974	Toller Cranston	Lynn Nightingale
1975	Toller Cranston	Lynn Nightingale
1976	Toller Cranston	Lynn Nightingale
1977	Ron Shaver	Lynn Nightingale
1978	Brian Pockar	Heather Kemkaran
1979	Brian Pockar	Janet Morissey
1980	Brian Pockar	Heather Kemkaren

Pro Rodeo Championship Standings in 1979

Event	Winner	Money won
All Around	Tom Ferguson, Miami, Okla.	$96,272
Saddle Bronc	Bobby Berger, Lexington, Okla.	41,709
Bareback	Bruce Ford, Kersey, Col.	80,260
Bull Riding	Don Gay, Mexquite, Tex.	59,999
Calf Roping	Paul Tierney, Rapid City, S.C.	$59,294
Steer Wrestling	Stan Williamson, Kellyville, Okla.	44,865
Team Roping	Allen Bach, Queen Creek, Ariz.	27,887

Pro Rodeo Cowboy All Around Champions

Year	Winner	Money won
1962	Tom Nesmith, Bethel, Oklahoma	$32,611
1963	Dean Oliver, Boise, Idaho	31,329
1964	Dean Oliver, Boise, Idaho	31,150
1965	Dean Oliver, Boise, Idaho	33,163
1966	Larry Mahan, Brooks, Oregon	40,358
1967	Larry Mahan, Brooks, Oregon	51,996
1968	Larry Mahan, Salem, Oregon	49,129
1969	Larry Mahan, Brooks, Oregon	57,726
1970	Larry Mahan, Brooks, Oregon	41,493
1971	Phil Lyne, George West, Texas	$49,245
1972	Phil Lyne, George West, Texas	60,852
1973	Larry Mahan, Dallas, Texas	64,447
1974	Tom Ferguson, Miami, Oklahoma	66,929
1975	Leo Camarillo, Oakdale, California	50,830
1976	Tom Ferguson, Miami, Oklahoma	87,908
1977	Tom Ferguson, Miami, Oklahoma	100,080
1978	Tom Ferguson, Miami, Oklahoma	131,233
1979	Tom Ferguson, Miami, Oklahoma	117,222*

*Including bonuses.

National Hockey League, 1979-80

Final Standings

Lester Patrick Division

Club	W	L	T	Pts	GF	GA
Philadelphia	48	12	20	116	327	254
N.Y. Islanders	39	28	13	91	281	247
N.Y. Rangers	38	32	10	86	308	284
Atlanta	35	32	13	83	282	269
Washington	27	40	13	67	261	293

Charles F. Adams Division

Club	W	L	T	Pts	GF	GA
Buffalo	47	17	16	110	318	201
Boston	46	21	13	105	310	234
Minnesota	36	28	16	88	311	253
Toronto	35	40	5	75	304	327
Quebec	25	44	11	61	248	313

Conn Smythe Division

Club	W	L	T	Pts	GF	GA
Chicago	34	27	19	87	241	250
St. Louis	34	34	12	80	266	278
Vancouver	27	37	16	70	256	281
Edmonton	28	39	13	69	301	322
Winnipeg	20	49	11	51	214	314
Colorado	19	48	13	51	234	308

James Norris Division

Club	W	L	T	Pts	GF	GA
Montreal	47	20	13	107	328	240
Los Angeles	30	36	14	74	290	313
Pittsburgh	30	37	13	73	251	303
Hartford	27	34	19	73	301	312
Detroit	26	43	11	63	268	306

Stanley Cup Playoff Results

Philadelphia defeated Edmonton 3 games to 0.
Montreal defeated Hartford 3 games to 0.
Buffalo defeated Vancouver 3 games to 1.
N.Y. Islanders defeated Los Angeles 3 games to 1.
N.Y. Rangers defeated Atlanta 3 games to 1.
Chicago defeated St. Louis 3 games to 0.
Minnesota defeated Toronto 3 games to 0.
Boston defeated Pittsburgh 3 games to 2.
Buffalo defeated Chicago 4 games to 0.
Philadephia defeated N.Y. Rangers 4 games to 1.
N.Y. Islanders defeated Boston 4 games to 1.
Minnesota defeated Montreal 4 games to 3.
Philadelphia defeated Minnesota 4 games to 1.
N.Y. Islanders defeated Buffalo 4 games to 2.
N.Y. Islanders defeated Philadelphia 4 games to 2.

Leading Scorers

Player, Club	GP	G	A	Pts
Dionne, Los Angeles	80	53	84	137
Gretzky, Edmonton	79	51	86	137
Lafleur, Montreal	75	50	75	125
Perreault, Buffalo	80	40	66	106
Rogers, Hartford	80	44	61	105
Trottier, Islanders	78	42	62	104
Simmer, Los Angeles	64	56	44	100
Stoughton, Hartford	80	56	44	100
Sittler, Toronto	73	40	57	97
MacDonald, Edmonton	80	46	48	94
Federko, St. Louis	79	38	56	94
MacAdam, Minnesota	80	42	51	93
Nilsson, Atlanta	80	40	53	93
Bossy, Islanders	75	51	41	92
Middleton, Boston	80	40	52	92
Larouche, Montreal	73	50	41	91
Taylor, Los Angeles	61	37	53	90
Gare, Buffalo	76	56	33	89
Shutt, Montreal	77	47	42	89
Cloutier, Quebec	67	42	46	88
Payne, Minnesota	80	42	43	85
Smith, Minnesota	61	27	56	83
McCourt, Detroit	80	30	51	81
M. Howe, Hartford	74	24	56	80

Leading Goalies

(25 or more games)

Goalie, Club	G	GA	ShO	Avg
Sauve, Buffalo	32	74	4	2.36
Herron, Montreal	34	80	0	2.51
Edwards, Buffalo	49	125	2	2.57
Peeters, Philadelphia	40	108	1	2.73
Gilbert, Boston	33	88	1	2.73
Cheevers, Boston	42	116	4	2.81
Smith, Islanders	38	104	2	2.95
Esposito, Chicago	69	205	6	2.97
Resch, Islanders	45	132	3	3.04
Meloche, Minnesota	54	160	1	3.06
Liut, St. Louis	64	194	2	3.18
Bouchard, Atlanta	53	163	2	3.18
Edwards, Minnesota	26	82	0	3.20
Riggin, Atlanta	25	73	2	3.20
Davidson, Rangers	41	123	2	3.29
Larocque, Montreal	39	125	3	3.32

Stanley Cup Champions

1928	New York
1929	Boston
1930	Montreal
1931	Montreal
1932	Toronto
1933	New York
1934	Chicago
1935	Montreal Maroons
1936	Detroit
1937	Detroit
1938	Chicago
1939	Boston
1940	New York
1941	Boston
1942	Toronto
1943	Detroit
1944	Montreal
1945	Toronto
1946	Montreal
1947	Toronto
1948	Toronto
1949	Toronto
1950	Detroit
1951	Toronto
1952	Detroit
1953	Montreal
1954	Detroit
1955	Detroit
1956	Montreal
1957	Montreal
1958	Montreal
1959	Montreal
1960	Montreal
1961	Chicago
1962	Toronto
1963	Toronto
1964	Toronto
1965	Montreal
1966	Montreal
1967	Toronto
1968	Montreal
1969	Montreal
1970	Boston
1971	Montreal
1972	Boston
1973	Montreal
1974	Philadelphia
1975	Philadelphia
1976	Montreal
1977	Montreal
1978	Montreal
1979	Montreal
1980	N.Y. Islanders

Conn Smythe Trophy (MVP in Playoffs)

1965	Jean Beliveau, Montreal
1966	Roger Crozier, Detroit
1967	Dave Keon, Toronto
1968	Glenn Hall, St. Louis
1969	Serge Sevard, Montreal
1970	Bobby Orr, Boston
1971	Ken Dryden, Montreal
1972	Bobby Orr, Boston
1973	Yvan Cournoyer, Montreal
1974	Bernie Parent, Philadelphia
1975	Bernie Parent, Philadelphia
1976	Reg Leach, Philadelphia
1977	Guy Lafleur, Montreal
1978	Larry Robinson, Montreal
1979	Bob Gainey, Montreal
1980	Bryan Trottier, N.Y. Islanders

NHL Trophy Winners

Ross Trophy
Leading scorer

1980	Marcel Dionne, Los Angeles
1979	Bryan Trottier, N.Y. Islanders
1978	Guy Lafleur, Montreal
1977	Guy Lafleur, Montreal
1976	Guy Lafleur, Montreal
1975	Bobby Orr, Boston
1974	Phil Esposito, Boston
1973	Phil Esposito, Boston
1972	Phil Esposito, Boston
1971	Phil Esposito, Boston
1970	Bobby Orr, Boston
1969	Phil Esposito, Boston
1968	Stan Mikita, Chicago
1967	Stan Mikita, Chicago
1966	Bobby Hull, Chicago
1965	Stan Mikita, Chicago
1964	Stan Mikita, Chicago

Norris Trophy
Best defenseman

1980	Larry Robinson, Montreal
1979	Denis Potvin, N.Y. Islanders
1978	Denis Potvin, N.Y. Islanders
1977	Larry Robinson, Montreal
1976	Denis Potvin, N.Y. Islanders
1975	Bobby Orr, Boston
1974	Bobby Orr, Boston
1973	Bobby Orr, Boston
1972	Bobby Orr, Boston
1971	Bobby Orr, Boston
1970	Bobby Orr, Boston
1969	Bobby Orr, Boston
1968	Bobby Orr, Boston
1967	Harry Howell, N.Y. Rangers
1966	Jacques Laperriere, Montreal
1965	Pierre Pilote, Chicago
1964	Pierre Pilote, Chicago

Calder Trophy
Best rookie

1980	Ray Bourque, Boston
1979	Bob Smith, Minnesota
1978	Mike Bossy, N.Y. Islanders
1977	Willi Plett, Atlanta
1976	Bryan Trottier N.Y. Islanders
1975	Eric Vail, Atlanta
1974	Denis Potvin, N.Y. Islanders
1973	Steve Vickers, N.Y. Rangers
1972	Ken Dryden, Montreal
1971	Gil Perreault, Buffalo
1970	Tony Esposito, Chicago
1969	Danny Grant, Minnesota
1968	Derek Sanderson, Boston
1967	Bobby Orr, Boston
1966	Brit Selby, Toronto
1965	Roger Crozier, Detroit
1964	Jacques Laperriere, Montreal

Hart Trophy
MVP

1980	Wayne Gretzky, Edmonton
1979	Bryan Trottier, N.Y. Islanders
1978	Guy Lafleur, Montreal
1977	Guy Lafleur, Montreal
1976	Bobby Clarke, Philadelphia
1975	Bobby Clarke, Philadelphia
1974	Phil Esposito, Boston
1973	Bobby Clarke, Philadelphia
1972	Bobby Orr, Boston
1971	Bobby Orr, Boston
1970	Bobby Orr, Boston
1969	Phil Esposito, Boston
1968	Stan Mikita, Chicago
1967	Stan Mikita, Chicago
1966	Bobby Hull, Chicago
1965	Bobby Hull, Chicago
1964	Jean Beliveau, Montreal

Vezina Trophy
Leading goalie

1980	Edwards, Sauve, Buffalo
1979	Dryden, Larocque, Montreal
1978	Dryden, Larocque, Montreal
1977	Dryden, Larocque, Montreal
1976	Ken Dryden, Montreal
1975	Bernie Parent, Philadelphia
1974	Tony Esposito, Chicago Bernie Parent, Philadelphia
1973	Ken Dryden, Montreal
1972	Esposito, Smith, Chicago
1971	Giacomin, Villemure, N.Y. Rangers
1970	Tony Esposito, Chicago
1969	Hall, Plante, St. Louis
1968	Worsley, Vachon, Montreal
1967	Hall, De Jordy, Chicago
1966	Hodge, Worsley, Montreal
1965	Sawchuck, Bower, Toronto
1964	Charlie Hodge, Montreal

Lady Byng Trophy
Sportsmanship

1980	Wayne Gretzky, Edmonton
1979	Bob MacMillan, Atlanta
1978	Butch Goring, Los Angeles
1977	Marcel Dionne, Los Angeles
1976	Jean Ratelle, Boston
1975	Marcel Dionne, Detroit
1974	John Bucyk, Boston
1973	Gilbert Perreault, Buffalo
1972	Jean Ratelle, N.Y. Rangers
1971	John Bucyk, Boston
1970	Phil Goyette, St. Louis
1969	Alex Devecchio, Detroit
1968	Stan Mikita, Chicago
1967	Stan Mikita, Chicago
1966	Alex Devecchio, Detroit
1965	Bobby Hull, Chicago
1964	Ken Wharram, Chicago

Frank Selke Trophy (best defensive forward)—1978-80, Bob Gainey, Montreal.

Players in the Hockey Hall of Fame

Exhibition Place, Toronto, Ont.

Abel, Sid
Adams, Jack
Apps, Syl
Armstrong, George
Bailey, Ace
Bain, Donald
Baker, Hobey
Barry, Marty
Bathgate, Andy
Beliveau, Jean
Benedict, Benny
Bentley, Doug
Bentley, Max
Blake, Toe
Boon, Dickie
Bouchard, Butch
Boucher, Frank
Boucher, Buck
Bower, John
Bowie, Russell
Brimsek, Frank
Broadbent, Punch
Broda, Turk
Burch, Billy
Cameron, Harry
Clancy, King
Clapper, Dit
Cleghorn, Sprague
Colville, Neil
Conacher, Charlie
Connell, Alex
Cook, Bill
Coulter, Art
Cowley, Bill
Crawford, Rusty
Darragh, Jack
Davidson, Scotty
Day, Hap
Delvecchio, Alex
Denneny, Cy
Drillon, Gordon
Drinkwater, Charles
Dunderdale, Tommy
Durnan, Bill
Dutton, Red
Dye, Babe
Farrell, Arthur
Foyston, Frank
Fredrickson, Frank
Gadsby, Bill
Gardiner, Chuck
Gardiner, Herb
Gardner, Jimmy
Geoffrion, Boom Boom
Gerard, Eddie
Gilmour, Billy
Goodfellow, Ebbie
Goheen, Moose
Grant, Mike
Green, Shorty
Griffis, Silas
Hainsworth, George
Hall, Glenn
Hall, Joe
Harvey, Doug
Hay, George
Hern, Riley
Hextall, Bryan
Holmes, Hap
Hooper, Tom
Horner, Red
Horton, Tim
Howe, Gordie
Howe, Syd
Howell, Harry
Hutton, John
Hyland, Harry
Irvin, James
Jackson, Busher
Johnson, Moose
Johnson, Ching
Johnson, Tom
Joliat, Aurel
Keats, Gordon
Kelly, Red
Kennedy, Ted
Lach, Elmer
Lalonde, Newsy
Laviolette, Jack
Lehman, Hugh
LeSueur, Percy
Lindsay, Ted
Lumley, Harry
Mackay, Duncan
Mantha, Sylvio
Malone, Joe
Marshall, Jack
Maxwell, Fred
McGee, Frank
McGimsie, Billy
McNamara, George
Moore, Dickie
Moran, Patrick
Morenz, Howie
Mosienko, Bill
Nighbor, Frank
Noble, Reginald
Oliver, Harry
Orr, Bobby
Patrick, Lester
Patrick, Lynn
Phillips, Tom
Pilote, Pierre
Pitre, Pit
Plante, Jacques
Pratt, Babe
Primeau, Joe
Pronovost, Marcel
Pulford, Harvey
Quakenbush, Bill
Rankin, Frank
Rayner, Chuck
Reardon, Ken
Richard, Henri
Richard, Rocket
Richardson, George
Roberts, Gordon
Ross, Arthur
Russell, Blair
Russell, Ernie
Ruttan, Jack
Sawchuck, Terry
Scanlan, Fred
Schmidt, Milt
Schriner, Sweeney
Seibert, Earl
Seibert, Oliver
Shore, Eddie
Siebert, Babe
Simpson, Joe
Smith, Alf
Smith, Hooley
Smith, Tommy
Stanley, Barney
Stewart, Jack
Stewart, Nels
Stuart, Bruce
Stuart, Hod
Taylor, Cyclone
Trihey, Harry
Thompson, Tiny
Vezina, Georges
Walsh, Martin
Walker, Jack
Watson, Harry
Westwick, Harry
Weiland, Cooney
Whitcroft, Fred
Wilson, Phat
Worsley, Gump
Worters, Roy

NHL Leaders, 1979–80

Goals

Charlie Simmer, Los Angeles	56
Danny Gare, Buffalo	56
Blaine Stoughton, Hartford	56
Marcel Dionne, Los Angeles	53
Wayne Gretzky, Edmonton	51
Mike Bossy, N.Y. Islanders	51
Guy Lafleur, Montreal	50
Pierre Larouche, Montreal	50
Reg Leach, Philadelphia	50
Steve Shutt, Montreal	47

Assists

Wayne Gretzky, Edmonton	86
Marcel Dionne, Los Angeles	84
Guy Lafleur, Montreal	75
Gil Perreault, Buffalo	66
Bryan Trottier, N.Y. Islanders	62
Mike Rogers, Hartford	61
Ken Linseman, Philadelphia	57
Darryl Sittler, Toronto	57
Bernie Federko, St. Louis	56
Bobby Smith, Minnesota	56
Mark Howe, Hartford	56

Power Play Goals

Charlie Simmer, Los Angeles	21
Marcel Dionne, Los Angeles	17
Danny Gare, Buffalo	17
Steve Shutt, Montreal	17
Darryl Sittler, Toronto	17
Blaine Stoughton, Hartford	16
Mike Bossy, N.Y. Islanders	16
Steve Payne, Minnesota	16

Shorthanded Goals

Anders Kallur, N.Y. Islanders	4
Reg Leach, Philadelphia	4
Bob MacMillan, Atlanta	3
Mike Murphy, Los Angeles	3
Ron Duguay, N.Y. Rangers	3
Rick MacLeish, Philadelphia	3
George Ferguson, Pittsburgh	3

Game Winning Goals

Danny Gare, Buffalo	11
Blaine Stoughton, Hartford	9
Peter McNab, Boston	9
Charlie Simmer, Los Angeles	8
Mike Bossy, N.Y. Islanders	8

Penalty Minutes

Jimmy Mann, Winnipeg	287
Tiger Williams, Vancouver	278
Paul Holmgren, Philadelphia	267
Terry O'Reilly, Boston	265
Terry Ruskowski, Chicago	252
Paul Mulvey, Washington	240
Willi Plett, Atlanta	231
Garry Howatt, N.Y. Islanders	219
Behn Wilson, Philadelphia	212
Stan Jonathan, Boston	208

Rookie Point Scorers

Brian Propp., Philadelphia	75
Mike Foligno, Detroit	71
Ray Bourque, Boston	65
Bengt Gustafsson, Washington	60
Dave Lumley, Edmonton	58
Ron Wilson, Winnipeg	57
Anders Kallur, N.Y. Islanders	52
Laurie Boschman, Toronto	48

NHL All Star Team, 1980

First team	Position	Second team
Tony Esposito, Chicago	Goalie	Don Edwards, Buffalo
Larry Robinson, Montreal	Defense	Borje Salming, Toronto
Ray Bourque, Boston	Defense	Jim Schoenfeld, Buffalo
Marcel Dionne, Los Angeles	Center	Wayne Gretzky, Edmonton
Guy Lafleur, Montreal	Right Wing	Danny Gare, Buffalo
Charlie Simmer, Los Angeles	Left Wing	Steve Shutt, Montreal

WHA Champions and Trophy Winners

Avco World Trophy — Playoff winner

1973	New England Whalers
1974	Houston Aeros
1975	Houston Aeros
1976	Winnipeg Jets
1977	Quebec Nordiques
1978	Winnipeg Jets
1979	Winnipeg Jets

Gordie Howe Trophy — MVP

1973	Bobby Hull, Winnipeg
1974	Gordie Howe, Houston
1975	Bobby Hull, Winnipeg
1976	Marc Tardif, Quebec
1977	Robbie Ftorek, Phoenix
1978	Marc Tardif, Quebec
1979	Dave Dryden, Edmonton

Hunter Trophy — Leading scorer

1973	Andre Lacroix, Philadelphia
1974	Mike Walton, Minnesota
1975	Andre Lacroix, San Diego
1976	Marc Tardif, Quebec
1977	Real Cloutier, Quebec
1978	Marc Tardif, Quebec
1979	Real Cloutier, Quebec

NCAA Hockey Champions

1951	Michigan
1952	Michigan
1953	Michigan
1954	Rensselaer Poly
1955	Michigan
1956	Michigan
1957	Colorado College
1958	Denver
1959	North Dakota
1960	Denver
1961	Denver
1962	Michigan Tech
1963	North Dakota
1964	Michigan
1965	Michigan Tech
1966	Michigan State
1967	Cornell
1968	Denver
1969	Denver
1970	Cornell
1971	Boston Univ.
1972	Boston Univ
1973	Wisconsin
1974	Minnesota
1975	Michigan Tech
1976	Minnesota
1977	Wisconsin
1978	Boston Univ.
1979	Minnesota
1980	North Dakota

U.S. National Alpine Championships in 1980

Men's Downhill—Dave Irwin, Canada
Men's Slalom—Steve Mahre, U.S.
Men's Giant Slalom—Peter Monod, Canada

Women's Downhill—Cindy Nelson, U.S.
Women's Slalom—Christin Cooper, U.S.
Women's Giant Slalom—Christin Cooper.

The World Cup Winners

Men

1967	Jean Claude Killy, France
1968	Jean Claude Killy, France
1969	Karl Schranz, Austria
1970	Karl Schranz, Austria
1971	Gustavo Thoeni, Italy
1972	Gustavo Thoeni, Italy
1973	Gustavo Thoeni, Italy
1974	Piero Gros, Italy
1975	Gustavo Thoeni, Italy
1976	Ingemar Stenmark, Sweden
1977	Ingemar Stenmark, Sweden
1978	Ingemar Stenmark, Sweden
1979	Peter Luescher, Switzerland
1980	Andreas Wenzel, Liechtenstein

Women

1967	Nancy Greene, Canada
1968	Nancy Greene, Canada
1969	Gertrud Gabl, Austria
1970	Michele Jacot, France
1971	Annemarie Proell, Austria
1972	Annemarie Proell, Austria
1973	Annemarie Proell, Austria
1974	Annemarie Proell, Austria
1975	Annemarie Proell, Austria
1976	Rose Mittermaier, W. Germany
1977	Lise-Marie Morerod, Austria
1978	Hanni Wenzel, Liechtenstein
1979	Annemarie Proell Moser, Austria
1980	Hanni Wenzel, Liechtenstein

Nation's Cup

1967	France
1968	France
1969	Austria
1970	France
1971	France
1972	France
1973	Austria
1974	Austria
1975	Austria
1976	Italy
1977	Austria
1978	Austria
1979	Austria
1980	Austria

National Basketball Association, 1979-80

Final Standings

Eastern Conference

Atlantic Division

Club	W	L	Pct	GB
Boston	61	21	.744	.....
Philadelphia	59	23	.720	2
Washington	39	43	.476	22
New York	39	43	.476	22
New Jersey	34	48	.415	27

Central Division

Club	W	L	Pct	GB
Atlanta	50	32	.610	.....
Houston	41	41	.500	9
San Antonio	41	41	.500	9
Cleveland	37	45	.451	13
Indiana	37	45	.451	13
Detroit	16	66	.195	34

Western Conference

Midwest Division

Club	W	L	Pct	GB
Milwaukee	49	33	.598	.....
Kansas City	47	35	.573	2
Chicago	30	52	.366	19
Denver	30	52	.366	19
Utah	24	58	.293	25

Pacific Division

Club	W	L	Pct	GB
Los Angeles	60	22	.732	.....
Seattle	56	26	.683	4
Phoenix	55	27	.671	5
Portland	38	44	.463	22
San Diego	35	47	.427	25
Golden State	24	58	.293	36

NBA Playoff Results

Philadelphia defeated Washington 2 games to 0.
Houston defeated San Antonio 2 games to 1.
Seattle defeated Portland 2 games to 1.
Phoenix defeated Kansas City 2 games to 1.
Boston defeated Houston 4 games to 0.
Philadelphia defeated Atlanta 4 games to 1.
Los Angeles defeated Phoenix 4 games to 1.
Seattle defeated Milwaukee 4 games to 3.
Philadelphia defeated Boston 4 games to 1.
Los Angeles defeated Seattle 4 games to 1.
Los Angeles defeated Philadelphia 4 games to 2.

NBA Champions 1947-1980

	Regular season		Playoffs	
Year	Eastern Conference	Western Conference	Winner	Runner-up
1947	Washington	Chicago	Philadelphia	Chicago
1948	Philadelphia	St. Louis	Baltimore	Philadelphia
1949	Washington	Rochester	Minneapolis	Washington
1950	Syracuse	Minneapolis	Minneapolis	Syracuse
1951	Philadelphia	Minneapolis	Rochester	New York
1952	Syracuse	Rochester	Minneapolis	New York
1953	New York	Minneapolis	Minneapolis	New York
1954	New York	Minneapolis	Minneapolis	Syracuse
1955	Syracuse	Ft. Wayne	Syracuse	Ft. Wayne
1956	Philadelphia	Ft. Wayne	Philadelphia	Ft. Wayne
1957	Boston	St. Louis	Boston	St. Louis
1958	Boston	St. Louis	St. Louis	Boston
1959	Boston	St. Louis	Boston	Minneapolis
1960	Boston	St. Louis	Boston	St. Louis
1961	Boston	St. Louis	Boston	St. Louis
1962	Boston	Los Angeles	Boston	Los Angeles
1963	Boston	Los Angeles	Boston	Los Angeles
1964	Boston	San Francisco	Boston	San Francisco
1965	Boston	Los Angeles	Boston	Los Angeles
1966	Philadelphia	Los Angeles	Boston	Los Angeles
1967	Philadelphia	San Francisco	Philadelphia	San Francisco
1968	Philadelphia	St. Louis	Boston	Los Angeles
1969	Baltimore	Los Angeles	Boston	Los Angeles
1970	New York	Atlanta	New York	Los Angeles

Year	Atlantic	Central	Midwest	Pacific	Winner	Runner-up
1971	New York	Baltimore	Milwaukee	Los Angeles	Milwaukee	Baltimore
1972	Boston	Baltimore	Milwaukee	Los Angeles	Los Angeles	New York
1973	Boston	Baltimore	Milwaukee	Los Angeles	New York	Los Angeles
1974	Boston	Capital	Milwaukee	Los Angeles	Boston	Milwaukee
1975	Boston	Washington	Chicago	Golden State	Golden State	Washington
1976	Boston	Cleveland	Milwaukee	Golden State	Boston	Phoenix
1977	Philadelphia	Houston	Denver	Los Angeles	Portland	Philadelphia
1978	Philadelphia	San Antonio	Denver	Portland	Washington	Seattle
1979	Washington	San Antonio	Kansas City	Seattle	Seattle	Washington
1980	Boston	Atlanta	Milwaukee	Los Angeles	Los Angeles	Philadelphia

NBA All League Team in 1980

First team	Position	Second team
Julius Erving, Philadelphia	Forward	Marquis Johnson, Milwaukee
Larry Bird, Boston	Forward	Dan Roundfield, Atlanta
Kareem Abdul-Jabbar, Los Angeles	Center	Moses Malone, Houston
Paul Westphal, Phoenix	Guard	Dennis Johnson, Seattle
George Gervin, San Antonio	Guard	Gus Williams, Seattle

Final Statistics

Individual Scoring Leaders

(Minimum: 70 games played or 1400 points)

	G	FG	FT	Pts	Avg
Gervin, San Antonio	78	1024	505	2585	33.1
Free, San Diego	68	737	572	2055	30.2
Dantley, Utah	68	730	443	1903	28.0
Erving, Philadelphia	78	838	420	2100	26.9
Malone, Houston	82	778	563	2119	25.8
Abdul-Jabbar, Los Angeles	82	835	364	2034	24.8
Issel, Denver	82	715	517	1951	23.8
Hayes, Washington	81	761	334	1859	23.0
Birdsong, Kansas City	82	781	286	1858	22.7
Mitchell, Cleveland	82	775	270	1820	22.2
Williams, Seattle	82	739	331	1816	22.1
Westphal, Phoenix	82	692	382	1792	21.9
Cartwright, New York	82	665	451	1781	21.7
Johnson, Milwaukee	77	689	291	1671	21.7
Davis, Phoenix	75	657	299	1613	21.5
Bird, Boston	82	693	301	1745	21.3
Newlin, New Jersey	78	611	367	1634	20.9
R. Williams, New York	82	687	333	1714	20.9

Field Goal Leaders

(Minimum: 300 FG made)

	FGM	FGA	Pct
Maxwell, Boston	457	750	.609
Abdul-Jabbar, Los Angeles	835	1383	.604
Gilmore, Chicago	305	513	.595
Dantley, Utah	730	1267	.576
Boswell, Utah	346	613	.564
Davis, Phoenix	657	1166	.563
Nater, San Diego	443	799	.554
Washington, Portland	421	761	.553
Cartwright, New York	665	1215	.547
Johnson, Milwaukee	689	1267	.544

Free Throw Leaders

(Minimum: 125 FT made)

	FTM	FTA	Pct
Barry, Houston	143	153	.935
Murphy, Houston	271	302	.897
Boone, Utah	175	196	.893
Silas, San Antonio	339	382	.887
Newlin, New Jersey	367	415	.884
Furlow, Utah	171	196	.872
Phegley, New Jersey	177	203	.872
Bratz, Phoenix	141	162	.870
Grevey, Washington	216	249	.867

3-Pt. Field Goals

	FG	FGA	Pct
Brown, Seattle	39	88	.443
Ford, Boston	70	164	.427
Bird, Boston	58	143	.406
Roche, Denver	49	129	.380
Taylor, San Diego	90	239	.377

Assists Leaders

(Minimum: 70 games or 400 assists)

	G	No	Avg
Richardson, New York	82	832	10.1
Archibald, Boston	80	671	8.4
Walker, Cleveland	76	607	8.0
Nixon, Los Angeles	82	642	7.8
Lucas, Golden State	80	602	7.5
Ford, Kansas City	82	610	7.4
Johnson, Los Angeles	77	563	7.3
Cheeks, Philadelphia	79	556	7.0
Porter, Washington	70	457	6.5

Rebound Leaders

(Minimum: 70 games or 800 rebounds)

	G	Off	Def	Tot	Avg
Nater, San Diego	81	352	864	1216	15.0
Malone, Houston	82	573	617	1190	14.5
Unseld, Washington	82	334	760	1094	13.3
C. Jones, Philadelphia	80	219	713	950	11.9
Sikma, Seattle	82	198	710	908	11.1
Hayes, Washington	81	269	627	896	11.1
Parish, Golden State	72	247	536	783	10.9
Abdul-Jabbar, Los Angeles	82	190	696	886	10.8
Washington, Portland	80	325	517	842	10.5
Bird, Boston	82	216	636	852	10.4

Steals Leaders

(Minimum: 70 games or 125 steals)

	G	No	Avg
Richardson, New York	82	265	3.23
Jordan, New Jersey	82	223	2.72
Bradley, Indiana	82	211	2.57
Williams, Seattle	82	200	2.44
Johnson, Los Angeles	77	187	2.43
Cheeks, Philadelphia	79	183	2.32
Erving, Philadelphia	78	170	2.18
Parker, Golden State	82	173	2.11
Walker, Cleveland	76	155	2.04
R. Williams, New York	82	167	2.04

Blocked Shots Leaders

(Minimum: 70 games or 100 blocked shots)

	G	No	Avg
Abdul-Jabbar, Los Angeles	82	280	3.41
Johnson, New Jersey	81	258	3.19
Rollins, Atlanta	82	244	2.98
Tyler, Detroit	82	220	2.68
Hayes, Washington	81	189	2.33
Catchings, Milwaukee	72	162	2.25
C. Jones, Philadelphia	80	162	2.03
Poquette, Utah	82	162	1.98
Meriweather, New York	65	120	1.85
Erving, Philadelphia	78	140	1.79

NBA Scoring Leaders

Year	Scoring champion	Pts	Avg
1947	Joe Fulks, Philadelphia	1,389	23.2
1948	Max Zaslofsky, Chicago	1,007	21.0
1949	George Mikan, Minneapolis	1,698	28.3
1950	George Mikan, Minneapolis	1,865	27.4
1951	George Mikan, Minneapolis	1,932	28.4
1952	Paul Arizin, Philadelphia	1,674	25.4
1953	Neil Johnston, Philadelphia	1,564	22.3
1954	Neil Johnston, Philadelphia	1,759	24.4
1955	Neil Johnston, Philadelphia	1,631	22.7
1956	Bob Pettit, St. Louis	1,849	25.7
1957	Paul Arizin, Philadelphia	1,817	25.6
1958	George Yardley, Detroit	2,001	27.8
1959	Bob Pettit, St. Louis	2,105	29.2
1960	Wilt Chamberlain, Philadelphia	2,707	37.9
1961	Wilt Chamberlain, Philadelphia	3,033	38.4
1962	Wilt Chamberlain, Philadelphia	4,029	50.4
1963	Wilt Chamberlain, San Francisco	3,586	44.8
1964	Wilt Chamberlain, San Francisco	2,948	36.5
1965	Wilt Chamberlain, San Fran., Phila.	2,534	34.7
1966	Wilt Chamberlain, Philadelphia	2,649	33.5
1967	Rick Barry, San Francisco	2,775	35.6
1968	Dave Bing, Detroit	2,142	27.1
1969	Elvin Hayes, San Diego	2,327	28.4
1970	Jerry West, Los Angeles	2,309	31.2
1971	Lew Alcindor, Milwaukee	2,596	31.7
1972	Kareem Abdul-Jabar (Alcindor), Milwaukee	2,822	34.8
1973	Nate Archibald, Kansas City-Omaha	2,719	34.0
1974	Bob McAdoo, Buffalo	2,261	30.6
1975	Bob McAdoo, Buffalo	2,831	34.5
1976	Bob McAdoo, Buffalo	2,427	31.1
1977	Pete Maravich, New Orleans	2,273	31.1
1978	George Gervin, San Antonio	2,232	27.2
1979	George Gervin, San Antonio	2,365	29.6
1980	George Gervin, San Antonio	2,585	33.1

NBA Team Statistics in 1979-80

Offense

	Field Goals			Free Throws			Rebounds			Scoring	
Team	Made	Att	Pct	Made	Att	Pct	Off	Def	Tot	Pts	Avg
San Antonio	3856	7738	.498	2024	2528	.801	1153	2515	3668	9788	119.4
Los Angeles	3898	7368	.529	1622	2092	.775	1085	2653	3738	9438	115.1
Cleveland	3811	8041	.474	1702	2205	.772	1307	2381	3688	9360	114.1
New York	3802	7672	.496	1698	2274	.747	1236	2303	3539	9344	114.0
Boston	3617	7387	.490	1907	2449	.779	1227	2457	3684	9303	113.5
Indiana	3639	7689	.473	1753	2333	.751	1398	2326	3724	9119	111.2
Phoenix	3570	7235	.493	1906	2466	.773	1071	2458	3529	9114	111.1
Houston	3599	7496	.480	1782	2326	.766	1394	2217	3611	9084	110.8
Milwaukee	3685	7553	.488	1605	2102	.764	1245	2396	3641	9025	110.1
Philadelphia	3523	7156	.492	1876	2431	.772	1187	2635	3822	8949	109.1
Detroit	3643	7596	.480	1590	2149	.740	1226	2415	3641	8933	108.9
Seattle	3554	7565	.470	1730	2253	.768	1380	2550	3930	8897	108.5
New Jersey	3456	7504	.461	1882	2406	.782	1229	2535	3764	8879	108.3
Denver	3462	7470	.463	1871	2539	.737	1311	2524	3835	8878	108.3
Kansas City	3582	7489	.478	1671	2250	.743	1187	2429	3616	8860	108.0
San Diego	3524	7494	.470	1595	2167	.736	1294	2308	3602	8820	107.6
Chicago	3362	6943	.484	2019	2592	.779	1115	2465	3580	8813	107.5
Washington	3574	7796	.458	1552	2048	.758	1334	2723	4057	8773	107.0
Atlanta	3261	7027	.464	2038	2645	.771	1369	2406	3775	8573	104.5
Golden State	3527	7318	.482	1412	1914	.738	1155	2437	3592	8493	103.6
Portland	3408	7167	.476	1560	2100	.743	1295	2408	3703	8402	102.5
Utah	3382	6817	.496	1571	1943	.809	967	2359	3326	8394	102.4

Defense

	Field Goals			Free Throws			Rebounds			Scoring		
Allowed by	Made	Att	Pct	Made	Att	Pct	Off	Def	Tot	Pts	Avg	Dif
Atlanta	3144	6872	.458	2000	2616	.765	1261	2339	3600	8334	101.6	+2.9
Portland	3349	7008	.478	1716	2281	.752	1138	2358	3496	8469	103.3	−0.8
Seattle	3408	7424	.459	1640	2147	.764	1203	2409	3612	8515	103.8	+4.7
Kansas City	3328	6992	.476	1906	2497	.763	1140	2644	3784	8603	104.9	+3.1
Philadelphia	3444	7561	.455	1640	2145	.765	1318	2352	3670	8603	104.9	+4.2
Boston	3439	7313	.470	1712	2222	.770	1168	2294	3462	8664	105.7	+7.8
Milwaukee	3456	7487	.462	1714	2275	.753	1360	2293	3653	8702	106.1	+4.0
Phoenix	3563	7480	.476	1593	2119	.752	1216	2447	3663	8819	107.5	+3.6
Golden State	3438	6975	.493	1905	2544	.749	1056	2564	3620	8853	108.0	−4.4
Utah	3559	7182	.496	1702	2205	.772	1159	2288	3447	8887	108.4	−6.0
Los Angeles	3723	7921	.470	1430	1884	.759	1312	2242	3554	8954	109.2	+5.9
New Jersey	3480	7427	.469	1957	2572	.761	1285	2596	3881	8975	109.5	−1.2
Washington	3615	7771	.465	1696	2184	.777	1197	2672	3869	8982	109.5	−2.5
Chicago	3585	7222	.496	1811	2358	.768	1159	2345	3504	9035	110.2	−2.7
Houston	3658	7382	.496	1696	2153	.788	1290	2317	3607	9070	110.6	+0.2
San Diego	3752	7508	.500	1613	2086	.773	1222	2487	3709	9160	111.7	−4.1
Indiana	3693	7545	.489	1734	2295	.756	1394	2552	3946	9176	111.9	−0.7
Denver	3736	7591	.492	1698	2235	.760	1197	2587	3784	9240	112.7	−4.4
Cleveland	3811	7610	.501	1645	2150	.765	1230	2638	3868	9332	113.8	+0.3
New York	3707	7492	.495	1969	2556	.770	1293	2432	3725	9439	115.0	−1.1
Detroit	3847	7761	.496	1858	2405	.773	1319	2572	3891	9609	117.2	−8.3
San Antonio	4000	7997	.500	1731	2283	.758	1248	2472	3720	9819	119.7	−0.3

NBA Most Valuable Player

Kareem Abdul-Jabbar of the Los Angeles Lakers was selected as the winner of the Maurice Podoloff Trophy (named after the former league commissioner) for Most Valuable Player in the NBA for the 1979-80 season.

1956 Bob Pettit, St. Louis
1957 Bob Cousy, Boston
1958 Bill Russell, Boston
1959 Bob Pettit, St. Louis
1960 Wilt Chamberlain, Philadelphia
1961 Bill Russell, Boston
1962 Bill Russell, Boston
1963 Bill Russell, Boston
1964 Oscar Robertson, Cincinnati
1965 Bill Russell, Boston
1966 Wilt Chamberlain, Philadelphia
1967 Wilt Chamberlain, Philadelphia
1968 Wilt Chamberlain, Philadelphia
1969 Wes Unseld, Baltimore
1970 Willis Reed, New York
1971 Lew Alcindor, Milwaukee
1972 Kareem Abdul-Jabbar (Alcindor), Milwaukee
1973 Dave Cowens, Boston
1974 Kareem Abdul-Jabbar, Milwaukee
1975 Bob McAdoo, Buffalo
1976 Kareem Abdul-Jabbar, Los Angeles
1977 Kareem Abdul-Jabbar, Los Angeles
1978 Bill Walton, Portland
1979 Moses Malone, Houston
1980 Kareem Abdul-Jabbar, Los Angeles

NBA Rookie of the Year

1954 Don Meineke, Ft. Wayne
1955 Ray Felix, Baltimore
1956 Maurice Stokes, Rochester
1957 Tom Heinsohn, Boston
1958 Woody Sauldsberry, Philadelphia
1959 Elgin Baylor, Minnesota
1960 Wilt Chamberlain, Philadelphia
1961 Oscar Robertson, Cincinnati
1962 Walt Bellamy, Chicago
1963 Terry Dischinger, Chicago
1964 Jerry Lucas, Cincinnati
1965 Willis Reed, New York
1966 Rick Barry, San Francisco
1967 Dave Bing, Detroit
1968 Earl Monroe, Baltimore
1969 Wes Unseld, Baltimore
1970 Lew Alcindor, Milwaukee
1971 Dave Cowens, Boston;
Geoff Petrie, Portland (tie)
1972 Sidney Wicks, Portland
1973 Bob McAdoo, Buffalo
1974 Ernie DiGregorio, Buffalo
1975 Keith Wilkes, Golden State
1976 Alvan Adams, Phoenix
1977 Adrian Dantley, Buffalo
1978 Walter Davis, Phoenix
1979 Phil Ford, Kansas City
1980 Larry Bird, Boston

NBA All-Defensive Team in 1980

First team	Position	Second team
Bobby Jones, Philadelphia	Forward	Scott Wedman, Kansas City
Dan Roundfield, Atlanta	Forward	Kermit Washington, Portland
Kareem Abdul-Jabbar, Los Angeles	Center	David Cowens, Boston
Dennis Johnson, Seattle	Guard	Quinn Buckner, Milwaukee
(tie) Don Buse, Phoenix	Guard	Eddie Johnson, Atlanta
Michael Ray Richardson, New York		

1980 NBA Player Draft

The following are the first round picks of the National Basketball Assn.

Golden State—Joe Barry Carroll, Purdue
Utah—Darrell Griffith, Louisville
Boston—Kevin McHale, Minnesota
Chicago—Kelvin Ransey, Ohio State
Denver—James Ray, Jacksonville
New Jersey—Mike O'Koren, North Carolina
New Jersey—Mike Gminski, Duke
Philadelphia—Andrew Toney, Southwestern Louisiana
San Diego—Michael Brooks, La Salle
Portland—Ronnie Lester, Iowa
Dallas—Kiki Vanderweghe, UCLA
New York—Mike Woodson, Indiana
Golden State—Rickey Brown, Mississippi State
Washington—Wes Matthews, Wisconsin
San Antonio—Reggie Johnson, Tennessee
Kansas City—Charles Whitney, North Carolina State
Detroit—Larry Drew, Missouri
Atlanta—Don Collins, Washington State
Utah—John Duren, Georgetown
Seattle—Bill Hanzlik, Notre Dame
Philadelphia—Monte Davis, Tennessee State
Cleveland—Chad Kinch, N.C.-Charlotte
Denver—Carl Nicks, Indiana State

Basketball Hall of Fame

Springfield, Mass.

Players

Arizin, Paul
Baylor, Elgin
Beckman, John
Borgmann, Bennie
Brennan, Joseph
Chamberlain, Wilt
Cooper, Charles
Cousy, Bob
Davies, Bob
DeBernardi, Forrest
Dehnert, Dutch
Endacott, Paul
Foster, Bud
Friedman, Max
Fulks, Joe
Gale, Lauren
Gola, Tom
Gruenig, Ace
Hagan, Cliff
Hanson, Victor
Holman, Nat
Hyatt, Chuck
Johnson, William
Krause, Moose
Kurland, Bob
Lapchick, Joe
Lucas, Jerry
Luisetti, Hank
McCracken, Branch
McCracken, Jack
Macauley, Ed
Mikan, George
Murphy, Stretch
Page, Pat
Pettit, Bob
Phillip, Andy
Pollard, Jim
Robertson, Oscar
Roosma, John S.
Russell, Honey
Russell, Bill
Schayes, Adolph
Schmidt, Ernest
Schommer, John
Sedran, Barney
Sharman, Bill
Steinmetz, Christian
Thompson, Cat
Vandivier, Fuzzy
Wachter, Edward
West, Jerry
Wooden, John

Coaches

Auerbach, Red
Barry, Sam
Blood, Ernest
Cann, Howard
Carlson, Dr. H. C.
Carnevale, Ben
Dean, Everett
Diddle, Edgar
Drake, Bruce
Gill, Slats
Hickey, Edgar
Hobson, Howard
Iba, Hank
Julian, Alvin
Keaney, Frank
Keogan, George
Lambert, Ward
Litwack, Harry
Loeffler, Kenneth
Lonborg, Dutch
McGuire, Frank
McLendon, John
Meyer, Ray
Meanwell, Dr. W. E.
Newell, Pete
Rupp, Adolph
Sachs, Leonard
Shelton, Everett
Wooden, John

Referees

Enright, James
Hepbron, George
Hoyt, George
Kennedy, Matthew
Nucatola, John
Quigley, Ernest
Shirley, J. Dallas
Tobey, David
Walsh, David

Contributors

Allen, Phog
Bee, Clair
Brown, Walter
Bunn, John
Douglas, Bob
Fisher, Harry
Gottlieb, Edward
Gulick, Dr. L. H.
Harrison, Lester
Hickox, Edward
Hinkle, Tony
Irish, Ned
Jones, R. W.
Liston, Emil
Mokray, Bill
Morgan, Ralph
Morgenweck, Frank
Naismith, Dr. James
O'Brien, John
Olsen, Harold
Podoloff, Maurice
Porter, H. V.
Reid, William
Ripley, Elmer
St. John, Lynn
Saperstein, Abe
Schabinger, Arthur
Stagg, Amos Alonzo
Taylor, Chuck
Tower, Oswald
Trester, Arthur
Wells, Clifford

Teams

First Team
Original Celtics
Buffalo Germans
Renaissance

American Basketball Association, 1968-1976

Champions

	Regular season		Playoffs	
Year	Eastern division	Western division	Winner	Runner-up
1968	Pittsburgh	New Orleans	Pittsburgh	New Orleans
1969	Indiana	Oakland	Oakland	Indiana
1970	Indiana	Denver	Indiana	Los Angeles
1971	Virginia	Indiana	Utah	Kentucky
1972	Kentucky	Utah	Indiana	New York
1973	Carolina	Utah	Indiana	Kentucky
1974	New York	Utah	New York	Utah
1975	Kentucky	Denver	Kentucky	Indiana
1976	Denver		New York	Denver

Scoring Leaders

Year	Leader	Pts	Avg
1968	Connie Hawkins, Pittsburgh	1,875	26.7
1969	Rick Barry, Oakland	1,190	34.0
1970	Spencer Haywood, Denver	2,519	29.9
1971	Dan Issel, Kentucky	2,480	29.8
1972	Charlie Scott, Virginia	2,524	34.5
1973	Julius Erving, Virginia	2,268	31.9
1974	Julius Erving, New York	2,299	27.3
1975	George McGinnis, Indiana	2,353	29.7
1976	Julius Erving, New York	2,462	29.3

Annual Results of Major Bowl Games

Rose Bowl, Pasadena

1902 Michigan 49, Stanford 0
1916 Wash. State 14, Brown 0
1917 Oregon 14, Pennsylvania 0
1918-19 Service teams
1920 Harvard 7, Oregon 6
1921 California 28, Ohio State 0
1922 Wash. & Jeff. 0, California 0
1923 So. California 14, Penn State 3
1924 Navy 14, Washington 14
1925 Notre Dame 27, Stanford 10
1926 Alabama 20, Washington 19
1927 Alabama 7, Stanford 7
1928 Stanford 7, Pittsburgh 6
1929 Georgia Tech 8, California 7
1930 So. California 47, Pittsburgh 14
1931 Alabama 24, Wash. State 0
1932 So. California 21, Tulane 12
1933 So. California 35, Pittsburgh 0
1934 Columbia 7, Stanford 0
1935 Alabama 29, Stanford 13
1936 Stanford 7, So. Methodist 0
1937 Pittsburgh 21, Washington 0
1938 California 13, Alabama 0
1939 So. California 7, Duke 3
1940 So. California 14, Tennessee 0
1941 Stanford 21, Nebraska 13
1942 Oregon St. 20, Duke 16 (at Durham)
1943 Georgia 9, UCLA 0
1944 So. California 29, Washington 0
1945 So. California 25, Tennessee 0
1946 Alabama 34, So. California 14
1947 Illinois 45, UCLA 14
1948 Michigan 49, So. California 0
1949 Northwestern 20, California 14
1950 Ohio State 17, California 14
1951 Michigan 14, California 6
1952 Illinois 40, Stanford 7
1953 So. California 7, Wisconsin 0
1954 Mich. State 28, UCLA 20
1955 Ohio State 20, So. California 7
1956 Mich. State 17, UCLA 14
1957 Iowa 35, Oregon St. 19
1958 Ohio State 10, Oregon 7
1959 Iowa 38, California 12
1960 Washington 44, Wisconsin 8
1961 Washington 17, Minnesota 7
1962 Minnesota 21, UCLA 3
1963 So. California 42, Wisconsin 37
1964 Illinois 17, Washington 7
1965 Michigan 34, Oregon St. 7
1966 UCLA 14, Mich. State 12
1967 Purdue 14, So. California 13
1968 Southern Cal. 14, Indiana 3
1969 Ohio State 27, Southern Cal 16
1970 Southern Cal 10, Michigan 3
1971 Stanford 27, Ohio State 17
1972 Stanford 13, Michigan 12
1973 So. California 42, Ohio State 17
1974 Ohio State 42, So. California 21
1975 So. California 18, Ohio State 17
1976 UCLA 23, Ohio State 10
1977 So. California 14, Michigan 6
1978 Washington 27, Michigan 20
1979 So. California 17, Michigan 10
1980 So. California 17, Ohio State 16

Orange Bowl, Miami

1933 Miami (Fla.) 7, Manhattan 0
1934 Duquesne 33, Miami (Fla.) 7
1935 Bucknell 26, Miami (Fla.) 0
1936 Catholic U. 20, Mississippi 19
1937 Duquesne 13, Miss. State 12
1938 Auburn 6, Mich. State 0
1939 Tennessee 17, Oklahoma 0
1940 Georgia Tech 21, Missouri 7
1941 Miss. State 14, Georgetown 7
1942 Georgia 40, TCU 26
1943 Alabama 37, Boston Col. 21
1944 LSU 19, Texas A&M 14
1945 Tulsa 26, Georgia Tech 12
1946 Miami (Fla.) 13, Holy Cross 6
1947 Rice 8, Tennessee 0
1948 Georgia Tech 20, Kansas 14
1949 Texas 41, Georgia 28
1950 Santa Clara 21, Kentucky 13
1951 Clemson 15, Miami (Fla.) 14
1952 Georgia Tech 17, Baylor 14
1953 Alabama 61, Syracuse 6
1954 Oklahoma 7, Maryland 0
1955 Duke 34, Nebraska 7
1956 Oklahoma 20, Maryland 6
1957 Colorado 27, Clemson 21
1958 Oklahoma 48, Duke 21
1959 Oklahoma 21, Syracuse 6
1960 Georgia 14, Missouri 0
1961 Missouri 21, Navy 14
1962 LSU 25, Colorado 7
1963 Alabama 17, Oklahoma 0
1964 Nebraska 13, Auburn 7
1965 Texas 21, Alabama 17
1966 Alabama 39, Nebraska 28
1967 Florida 27, Georgia Tech 12
1968 Oklahoma 26, Tennessee 24
1969 Penn State 15, Kansas 14
1970 Penn State 10, Missouri 3
1971 Nebraska 17, Louisiana St. 12
1972 Nebraska 38, Alabama 6
1973 Nebraska 40, Notre Dame 6
1974 Penn State 16, Louisiana St. 9
1975 Notre Dame 13, Alabama 11
1976 Oklahoma 14, Michigan 6
1977 Ohio State 27, Colorado 10
1978 Arkansas 31, Oklahoma 6
1979 Oklahoma 31, Nebraska 24
1980 Oklahoma 24, Florida St. 7

Sugar Bowl, New Orleans

1935 Tulane 20, Temple 14
1936 TCU 3, LSU 2
1937 Santa Clara 21, LSU 14
1938 Santa Clara 6, LSU 0
1939 TCU 15, Carnegie Tech 7
1940 Texas A&M 14, Tulane 13
1941 Boston Col. 19, Tennessee 13
1942 Fordham 2, Missouri 0
1943 Tennessee 14, Tulsa 7
1944 Georgia Tech 20, Tulsa 18
1945 Duke 29, Alabama 26
1946 Oklahoma A&M 33, St. Mary's 13
1947 Georgia 20, No. Carolina 10
1948 Texas 27, Alabama 7
1949 Oklahoma 14, No. Carolina 6
1950 Oklahoma 35, LSU 0
1951 Kentucky 13, Oklahoma 7
1952 Maryland 28, Tennessee 13
1953 Georgia Tech. 24, Mississippi 7
1954 Georgia Tech 42, West Virginia 19
1955 Navy 21, Mississippi 0
1956 Georgia Tech 7, Pittsburgh 0
1957 Baylor 13, Tennessee 7
1958 Mississippi 39, Texas 7
1959 LSU 7, Clemson 0
1960 Mississippi 21, LSU 0
1961 Mississippi 14, Rice 6
1962 Alabama 10, Arkansas 3
1963 Mississippi 17, Arkansas 13
1964 Alabama 12, Mississippi 7
1965 LSU 13, Syracuse 10
1966 Missouri 20, Florida 18
1967 Alabama 34, Nebraska 7
1968 LSU 20, Wyoming 13
1969 Arkansas 16, Georgia 2
1970 Mississippi 27, Arkansas 22
1971 Tennessee 34, Air Force 13
1972 Oklahoma 40, Auburn 22
*1972 (Dec.) Oklahoma 14, Penn State 0
1973 Notre Dame 24, Alabama 23
1974 Nebraska 13, Florida 10
1975 Alabama 13, Penn State 6
1977 (Jan.) Pittsburgh 27, Georgia 3
1978 Alabama 35, Ohio State 6
1979 Alabama 14, Penn State 7
1980 Alabama 24, Arkansas 9

*Penn St. awarded game by forfeit

Cotton Bowl, Dallas

1937 TCU 16, Marquette 6
1938 Rice 28, Colorado 14
1939 St. Mary's 20, Texas Tech 13
1940 Clemson 6, Boston Col. 3
1941 Texas A&M 13, Fordham 12
1942 Alabama 29, Texas A&M 21
1943 Texas 14, Georgia Tech 7
1944 Randolph Field 7, Texas 7
1945 Oklahoma A&M 34, TCU 0
1946 Texas 40, Missouri 27
1947 Arkansas 0, LSU 0
1948 So. Methodist 13, Penn State 13
1949 So. Methodist 21, Oregon 13
1950 Rice 27, No. Carolina 13
1951 Tennessee 20, Texas 14
1952 Kentucky 20, TCU 7
1953 Texas 16, Tennessee 0
1954 Rice 28, Alabama 6
1955 Georgia Tech 14, Arkansas 6
1956 Mississippi 14, TCU 13
1957 TCU 28, Syracuse 27
1958 Navy 20, Rice 7
1959 TCU 0, Air Force 0
1960 Syracuse 23, Texas 14
1961 Duke 7, Arkansas 6
1962 Texas 12, Mississippi 7
1963 LSU 13, Texas 0
1964 Texas 28, Navy 6
1965 Arkansas 10, Nebraska 7
1966 LSU 14, Arkansas 7
1967 Georgia 24, So. Methodist 9
1968 Texas A&M 20, Alabama 16
1969 Texas 36, Tennessee 13
1970 Texas 21, Notre Dame 17
1971 Notre Dame 24, Texas 11
1972 Penn State 30, Texas 6
1973 Texas 17, Alabama 13
1974 Nebraska 19, Texas 3
1975 Penn State 41, Baylor 20
1976 Arkansas 31, Georgia 10
1977 Houston 30, Maryland 21
1978 Notre Dame 38, Texas 10
1979 Notre Dame 35, Houston 34
1980 Houston 17, Nebraska 14

Fiesta Bowl, Phoenix

1971 Arizona St. 45, Flordia St. 38
1972 Arizona St. 49, Missouri 35
1973 Arizona St. 28, Pittsburgh 7
1974 Okla. St. 16, Brigham Young 6
1975 Arizona St. 17, Nebraska 14
1976 Oklahoma 41, Wyoming 7
1977 Penn St. 42, Arizona St. 30
1978 UCLA 10, Arkansas 10
1979 Pittsburgh 16, Arizona 10

Liberty Bowl, Memphis

1959 Penn State 7, Alabama 0
1960 Penn State 41, Oregon 12
1961 Syracuse 15, Miami 14
1962 Oregon State 6, Villanova 0
1963 Miss. State 16, N.C. State 12
1964 Utah 32, West Virginia 6
1965 Mississippi 13, Auburn 7
1966 Miami (Fla.) 14, Va. Tech 7
1967 N.C. State 14, Georgia 7
1968 Mississippi 34, Va. Tech 17
1969 Colorado 47, Alabama 33
1970 Tulane 17, Colorado 3
1971 Tennessee 14, Arkansas 13
1972 Georgia Tech 31, Iowa State 30
1973 No. Carolina St. 31, Kansas 18
1974 Tennessee 7, Maryland 3
1975 USC 20, Texas A&M 0
1976 Alabama 36, UCLA 6
1977 Nebraska 27, N. Carolina 17
1978 Missouri 20, Louisiana St. 15
1979 Penn St. 9, Tulane 6

Sun Bowl, El Paso

1936 Hardin Simmons 14, New Mex. St. 14
1937 Hardin-Simmons 34, Texas Mines 6
1938 West Virginia 7, Texas Tech 6
1939 Utah 26, New Mexico 0
1940 Catholic U. 0, Arizona St. 0
1941 Western Reserve 26, Arizona St. 13
1942 Tulsa 6, Texas Tech 0
1943 2d Air Force 13, Hardin-Simmons 7
1944 Southwestern (Tex.) 7, New Mexico 0
1945 Southwestern (Tex.) 35, U. of Mex. 0
1946 New Mexico 34, Denver 24
1947 Cincinnati 38, Virginia Tech 6
1948 Miami (O.) 13, Texas Tech 12
1949 West Virginia 21, Texas Mines 12
1950 Texas Western 33, Georgetown 20
1951 West Texas St. 14, Cincinnati 13
1952 Texas Tech 25, Col. Pacific 14
1953 Col. Pacific 26, Miss. Southern 7
1954 Texas Western 37, Miss. Southern 14
1955 Texas Western 47, Florida St. 20
1956 Wyoming 21, Texas Tech 14
1957 Geo. Washington 13, Tex. Western 0
1958 Louisville 34, Drake 20
1959 Wyoming 14, Hardin-Simmons 6
1960 New Mexico St. 28, No. Texas St. 8
1961 New Mexico St. 20, Utah State 13
1962 Villanova 17, Wichita 9
1963 West Texas St. 15, Ohio U. 14
1964 Oregon 21, So. Methodist 14
1965 Georgia 7, Texas Tech 0
1966 Texas Western 13, TCU 12
1967 Wyoming 28, Florida St. 20
1968 UTex El Paso 14, Mississippi 7
1969 Auburn 34, Arizona 10
1969 (Dec.) Nebraska 45, Georgia 6
1970 Georgia Tech. 17, Texas Tech. 9
1971 LSU 33, Iowa State 15
1972 North Carolina 32, Texas Tech 28
1973 Missouri 34, Auburn 17
1974 Mississippi St. 26, No. Carolina 24
1975 Pittsburgh 33, Kansas 19
1977 (Jan.) Texas A&M 37, Florida 14
1977 Stanford 24, Louisiana St. 14
1978 Texas 42, Maryland 0
1979 Washington 14, Texas 7

Gator Bowl, Jacksonville

1946 Wake Forest 26, So. Carolina 14
1947 Oklahoma 34, N.C. State 13
1948 Maryland 20, Georgia 20
1949 Clemson 24, Missouri 23
1950 Maryland 20, Missouri 7
1951 Wyoming 20, Wash. & Lee 7
1952 Miami (Fla.) 14, Clemson 0
1953 Florida 14, Tulsa 13
1954 Texas Tech 35, Auburn 13
1955 Auburn 33, Baylor 13
1956 Vanderbilt 25, Auburn 13
1957 Georgia Tech 21, Pittsburgh 14
1958 Tennessee 3, Texas A&M 0
1959 Mississippi 7, Florida 3
1960 Arkansas 14, Georgia Tech 7
1961 Florida 13, Baylor 12
1962 Penn State 30, Georgia Tech 15
1963 Florida 17, Penn State 7
1964 No. Carolina 35, Air Force 0
1965 Florida St. 36, Oklahoma 19
1966 Georgia Tech 31, Texas Tech 21
1967 Tennessee 18, Syracuse 12
1968 Penn State 17, Florida St. 17
1969 Missouri 35, Alabama 10
1969 (Dec.) Florida 14, Tenn. 13
1971 Auburn 35, Mississippi 28
1972 Georgia 7, N. Carolina 3
1973 Auburn 24, Colorado 3
1973 (Dec.) Tex. Tech. 28, Tenn. 19
1974 Auburn 27, Texas 3
1975 Maryland 13, Florida 0
1976 Notre Dame 20, Penn State 9
1977 Pittsburgh 34, Clemson 3
1978 Clemson 17, Ohio State 15
1979 No. Carolina 17, Michigan 15

Bluebonnet Bowl, Houston

1959 Clemson 23, TCU 7
1960 Texas 3, Alabama 3
1961 Kansas 33, Rice 7
1962 Missouri 14, Georgia Tech 10
1963 Baylor 14, LSU 7
1964 Tulsa 14, Mississippi 7
1965 Tennessee 27, Tulsa 6
1966 Texas 19, Mississippi 0
1967 Colorado 31, Miami (Fla.) 21
1968 SMU 28, Oklahoma 27
1969 Houston 36, Auburn 7
1970 Oklahoma 24, Alabama 24
1971 Colorado 29, Houston 17
1972 Tennessee 24, Louisiana St. 17
1973 Houston 47, Tulane 7
1974 N. Carolina St. 31, Houston 31
1975 Texas 38, Colorado 21
1976 Nebraska 27, Texas Tech 24
1977 USC 47, Texas A&M 28
1978 Stanford 25, Georgia 22
1979 Purdue 27, Tennessee 22

Peach Bowl, Atlanta

1968 LSU 31, Florida St. 27
1969 West Virginia 14, S. Carolina 3
1970 Arizona St. 48, N. Carolina 26
1971 Mississippi 41, Georgia Tech. 18
1972 N. Carolina St. 49, W. Va. 13
1973 Georgia 17, Maryland 16
1974 Vanderbilt 6, Texas Tech. 6
1975 W. Virginia 13, No. Carolina St. 10
1976 Kentucky 21, North Carolina 0
1977 N. Carolina St. 24, Iowa St. 14
1978 Purdue 41, Georgia Tech. 21
1979 Baylor 24, Clemson 18

Tangerine Bowl, Orlando

1968 Richmond 49, Ohio 42
1969 Toledo 56, Davidson 33
1970 Toledo 40, William & Mary 12
1971 Toledo 28, Richmond 3
1972 Tampa 21, Kent State 18
1973 Miami, Ohio 16, Florida 7
1974 Miami, Ohio 21, Georgia 10
1975 Miami, Ohio 20, South Carolina 7
1976 Okla. St. 49, Brigham Young 21
1977 Florida St. 40, Texas Tech 17
1978 N. Carolina St. 30, Pittsburgh 17
1979 Louisiana St. 34, Wake Forest 10

Heisman Trophy Winners

Awarded annually to the nation's outstanding college football player.

1935 Jay Berwanger, Chicago, HB
1936 Larry Kelley, Yale, E
1937 Clinton Frank, Yale, QB
1938 David O'Brien, Tex. Christian, QB
1939 Nile Kinnick, Iowa, QB
1940 Tom Harmon, Michigan, HB
1941 Bruce Smith, Minnesota, HB
1942 Frank Sinkwich, Georgia, HB
1943 Angelo Bertelli, Notre Dame, QB
1944 Leslie Horvath, Ohio State, QB
1945 Felix Blanchard, Army, FB
1946 Glenn Davis, Army, HB
1947 John Lujack, Notre Dame, QB
1948 Doak Walker, SMU, HB
1949 Leon Hart, Notre Dame, E
1950 Vic Janowicz, Ohio State, HB
1951 Richard Kazmaier, Princeton, HB
1952 Billy Vessels, Oklahoma, HB
1953 John Lattner, Notre Dame, HB
1954 Alan Ameche, Wisconsin, FB
1955 Howard Cassady, Ohio St., HB
1956 Paul Hornung, Notre Dame, QB
1957 John Crow, Texas A & M, HB
1958 Pete Dawkins, Army, HB
1959 Billy Cannon, La. State, HB
1960 Joe Bellino, Navy, HB
1961 Ernest Davis, Syracuse, HB
1962 Terry Baker, Oregon State, QB
1963 Roger Staubach, Navy, QB
1964 John Huarte, Notre Dame, QB
1965 Mike Garrett, USC, HB
1966 Steve Spurrier, Florida, QB
1967 Gary Beban, UCLA, QB
1968 O. J. Simpson, USC, RB
1969 Steve Owens, Oklahoma, RB
1970 Jim Plunkett, Stanford, QB
1971 Pat Sullivan, Auburn, QB
1972 Johnny Rodgers, Nebraska, RB-R
1973 John Cappelletti, Penn State, RB
1974 Archie Griffin, Ohio State, RB
1975 Archie Griffin, Ohio State, RB
1976 Tony Dorsett, Pittsburgh, RB
1977 Earl Campbell, Texas, RB
1978 Billy Sims, Oklahoma, RB
1979 Charles White, USC, RB

College Football Conference Champions

Atlantic Coast

1966	Clemson
1967	Clemson
1968	No. Carolina St.
1969	So. Carolina
1970	Wake Forest
1971	North Carolina
1972	North Carolina
1973	No. Carolina St.
1974	Maryland
1975	Maryland
1976	Maryland
1977	North Carolina
1978	Clemson
1979	No. Carolina St.

Ivy League

1966	Dartmouth, Harvard, Princeton
1967	Yale
1968	Yale, Harvard
1969	Princeton, Dartmouth, Yale
1970	Dartmouth
1971	Dartmouth, Cornell
1972	Dartmouth
1973	Dartmouth
1974	Yale, Harvard
1975	Harvard
1976	Yale, Brown
1977	Yale
1978	Dartmouth
1979	Yale

Big Eight

1966	Nebraska
1967	Oklahoma
1968	Kansas, Oklahoma
1969	Missouri, Nebraska
1970	Nebraska
1971	Nebraska
1972	Nebraska
1973	Oklahoma
1974	Oklahoma
1975	Oklahoma, Nebraska
1976	Oklahoma, Colorado, Oklahoma State
1977	Oklahoma
1978	Nebraska, Oklahoma
1979	Oklahoma

Big Ten

1966	Michigan State
1967	Indiana, Purdue, Minn.
1968	Ohio State
1969	Michigan, Ohio State
1970	Ohio State
1971	Michigan
1972	Ohio State, Michigan
1973	Ohio State, Michigan
1974	Ohio State, Michigan
1975	Ohio State
1976	Michigan, Ohio State
1977	Michigan, Ohio State
1978	Michigan St., Michigan
1979	Ohio State

Mid-America

1966	Miami, Western Mich.
1967	Toledo, Ohio Univ.
1968	Ohio Univ.
1969	Toledo
1970	Toledo
1971	Toledo
1972	Kent State
1973	Miami
1974	Miami
1975	Miami
1976	Ball State
1977	Miami
1978	Ball State
1979	Central Michigan

Missouri Valley

1966	No. Texas, Tulsa
1967	North Texas
1968	Memphis State
1969	Memphis State
1970	Louisville
1971	Memphis State
1972	Louisville, W. Texas, Drake
1973	No. Texas St., Tulsa
1974	Tulsa
1975	Tulsa
1976	Tulsa, N. Mexico St.
1977	W. Texas St.
1978	N. Mexico St.
1979	W. Texas St.

Southeastern

1966	Alabama, Georgia
1967	Tennessee
1968	Georgia
1969	Tennessee
1970	Louisiana State
1971	Alabama
1972	Alabama
1973	Alabama
1974	Alabama
1975	Alabama
1976	Georgia
1977	Alabama
1978	Alabama
1979	Alabama

Southwest

1966	Southern Methodist
1967	Texas A & M
1968	Texas, Arkansas
1969	Texas
1970	Texas
1971	Texas
1972	Texas
1973	Texas
1974	Baylor
1975	Texas A&M, Texas, Arkansas
1976	Houston
1977	Texas
1978	Houston
1979	Houston, Arkansas

Pacific Ten

1966	USC
1967	USC
1968	USC
1969	USC
1970	Stanford
1971	Stanford
1972	USC
1973	USC
1974	USC
1975	UCLA, Cal.
1976	USC
1977	Washington
1978	USC
1979	USC

Southern

1966	East Carolina, William & Mary
1967	West Virginia
1968	Richmond
1969	Richmond, Davidson
1970	William & Mary
1971	Richmond
1972	East Carolina
1973	East Carolina
1974	VMI
1975	Richmond
1976	East Carolina
1977	Tenn.-Chattanooga
1978	Tenn.-Chattanooga, Furman
1979	Tenn.-Chattanooga

Western Athletic

1966	Wyoming
1967	Wyoming
1968	Wyoming
1969	Arizona State
1970	Arizona State
1971	Arizona State
1972	Arizona State
1973	Arizona State, Arizona
1974	Brigham Young
1975	Arizona State
1976	Wyoming, Brigham Young
1977	Brigham Young, Arizona St.
1978	Brigham Young
1979	Brigham Young

Pacific Coast

1969	San Diego State
1970	Long Beach State
1971	Long Beach State
1972	San Diego State
1973	San Diego State
1974	San Diego State
1975	San Jose State
1976	San Diego State
1977	Fresno State
1978	Utah St., San Jose St.
1979	San Jose St.

Outland Awards

Honoring the outstanding interior lineman selected by the Football Writers' Association of America.

1946	George Connor, Notre Dame, T
1947	Joe Steffy, Army, G
1948	Bill Fischer, Notre Dame, G
1949	Ed Bagdon, Michigan St., G
1950	Bob Gain, Kentucky, T
1951	Jim Weatherall, Oklahoma, T
1952	Dick Modzelewski, Maryland, T
1953	J. D. Roberts, Oklahoma, G
1954	Bill Brooks, Arkansas, G
1955	Calvin Jones, Iowa, G
1956	Jim Parker, Ohio State, G
1957	Alex Karras, Iowa, T
1958	Zeke Smith, Auburn, G
1959	Mike McGee, Duke, T
1960	Tom Brown, Minnesota, G
1961	Merlin Olsen, Utah State, T
1962	Bobby Bell, Minnesota, T
1963	Scott Appleton, Texas, T
1964	Steve Delong, Tennessee, T
1965	Tommy Nobis, Texas, G
1966	Loyd Phillips, Arkansas, T
1967	Ron Yary, Southern Cal, T
1968	Bill Stanfill, Georgia, T
1969	Mike Reid, Penn State, DT
1970	Jim Stillwagon, Ohio State, LB
1971	Larry Jacobson, Nebraska, DT
1972	Rich Glover, Nebraska, MG
1973	John Hicks, Ohio State, G
1974	Randy White, Maryland, DE
1975	Leroy Selmon, Oklahoma, DT
1976	Ross Browner, Notre Dame, DE
1977	Brad Shearer, Texas, DT
1978	Greg Roberts, Oklahoma, G
1979	Jim Ritcher, No. Carolina St., C

National College Football Champions

The NCAA recognizes as unofficial national champion the team selected each year by the AP (poll of writers) and the UPI (poll of coaches). When the polls disagree both teams are listed. The AP poll originated in 1936 and the UPI poll in 1950.

1936	Minnesota
1937	Pittsburgh
1938	Texas Christian
1939	Texas A&M
1940	Minnesota
1941	Minnesota
1942	Ohio State
1943	Notre Dame
1944	Army
1945	Army
1946	Notre Dame
1947	Notre Dame
1948	Michigan
1949	Notre Dame
1950	Oklahoma
1951	Tennessee
1952	Michigan State
1953	Maryland
1954	Ohio State, UCLA
1955	Oklahoma
1956	Oklahoma
1957	Auburn, Ohio State
1958	Louisiana State
1959	Syracuse
1960	Minnesota
1961	Alabama
1962	Southern Cal.
1963	Texas
1964	Alabama
1965	Alabama, Mich. State
1966	Notre Dame
1967	Southern Cal.
1968	Ohio State
1969	Texas
1970	Nebraska, Texas
1971	Nebraska,
1972	Southern Cal.
1973	Notre Dame, Alabama
1974	Oklahoma, So. Cal.
1975	Oklahoma
1976	Pittsburgh
1977	Notre Dame
1978	Alabama, So. Cal.
1979	Alabama

College Football Teams

Division I Teams

Team	Nickname	Team colors	Conference	Coach	1979 record (W-L-T)
Air Force	Falcons	Blue & silver	Western Athletic	Ken Hatfield	2-9-0
Akron	Zips	Blue & Gold	Mid-Continent	Jim Dennison	6-5-0
Alabama	Crimson Tide	Crimson & white	Southeastern	Paul Bryant	12-0-0
Alcorn State	Braves	Purple & gold	Southwestern	Marino Casem	8-2-0
Appalachian State	Mountaineers	Black & gold	Southern	Mike Working	3-8-0
Arizona	Wildcats	Red & blue	Pacific Ten	Larry Smith	6-5-1
Arizona State	Sun Devils	Maroon & gold	Pacific Ten	Darryl Rogers	6-6-0
Arkansas	Razorbacks	Cardinal & white	Southwest	Lou Holtz	10-2-0
Arkansas State	Indians	Scarlet & black	Southland	Lawrence Lacewell	4-7-0
Army	Cadets	Black, gold, gray	Independent	Lou Saban	2-8-1
Auburn	Tigers	Orange & blue	Southeastern	Doug Barfield	8-3-0
Austin Peay State	Governors	Scarlet & white	Ohio Valley	Watson Brown	7-4-0
Ball State	Cardinals	Cardinal & white	Mid-American	Dwight Wallace	6-5-0
Baylor	Bears	Green & gold	Southwest	Grant Teaff	8-4-0
Bethune-Cookman	Wildcats	Maroon & gold	Southern	Bobby Frazier	5-6-0
Boise State	Broncos	Orange & Blue	Big Sky	Jim Criner	10-1-0
Boston College	Eagles	Maroon & gold	Independent	Ed Chiebek	5-6-0
Boston Univ.	Terriers	Scarlet & white	Yankee	Rick Taylor	8-1-1
Bowling Green St.	Falcons	Orange & brown	Mid-American	Denny Stolz	4-7-0
Brigham Young	Cougars	Royal blue & white	Western Athletic	LaVell Edwards	11-1-0
Brown	Bruins, Bears	Brown, cardinal, white	Ivy	John Anderson	6-3-0
Bucknell	Bisons	Orange & blue	Independent	Bob Curtis	4-4-2
California	Golden Bears	Blue & gold	Pacific Ten	Roger Theder	6-6-0
Central Michigan	Chippewas	Maroon & gold	Mid-American	Herb Deromedi	10-0-1
Cincinnati	Bearcats	Red & black	Independent	Ralph Staub	2-9-0
Citadel	Cadets	Blue & white	Southern	Art Baker	6-5-0
Clemson	Tigers	Purple & orange	Atlantic Coast	Danny Ford	8-4-0
Colgate	Red Raiders	Maroon	Independent	Fred Dunlap	5-4-1
Colorado State	Rams	Green & gold	Western Athletic	Sarkis Arslanian	4-7-1
Colorado	Buffaloes	Silver & gold	Big Eight	Chuck Fairbanks	3-8-0
Columbia	Lions	Blue & white	Ivy	Bob Naso	1-8-0
Connecticut	Huskies	Blue & white	Yankee	Walt Nadzak	3-6-2
Cornell	Big Red	Carnelian & white	Ivy	Bob Blackman	5-4-0
Dartmouth	Big Green	Dartmouth green	Ivy	Joe Yukica	4-4-1
Davidson	Wildcats	Red & black	Independent	Ed Farrell	6-4-0
Delaware	Fightin' Blue Hens	Blue & gold	Independent	Harold Raymond	13-1-0
Delaware State	Hornets	Red & blue	Mid-Eastern	Charles Henderson	4-5-1
Drake	Bulldogs	Blue & white	Missouri Valley	Chuck Shelton	3-8-0
Duke	Blue Devils	Royal blue & white	Atlantic Coast	Red Wilson	2-8-1
East Carolina	Pirates	Purple & gold	Independent	Ed Emory	7-3-1
East Tennessee St.	Buccaneers	Blue & gold	Southern	Jack Carlisle	7-4-0
Eastern Kentucky	Colonels	Maroon & white	Ohio Valley	Roy Kidd	11-2-0
Eastern Michigan	Hurons	Green & white	Mid-American	Mike Stock	2-8-1
Florida	Gators	Orange & blue	Southeastern	Charley Pell	0-10-1
Florida A&M	Rattlers	Orange & green	Mid-Eastern	Rudy Hubbard	7-4-0
Florida State	Seminoles	Garnet & gold	Independent	Bobby Bowden	11-1-0
Fresno State	Bulldogs	Cardinal & blue	Pacific Coast	Jim Sweeney	4-7-0
Fullerton, Cal. State	Titans	Blue, orange, white	Pacific Coast	Gene Murphy	3-8-0
Furman	Palidans	Purple & white	Southern	Dick Sheridan	5-6-0
Georgia	Bulldogs	Red & black	Southeastern	Vince Dooley	6-5-0
Georgia Tech	Yellow Jackets	Old gold & white	Independent	Bill Curry	4-6-1
Grambling State	Tigers	Black & gold	Southwestern	Eddie Robinson	8-3-0
Harvard	Crimson	Crimson	Ivy	Joe Restic	3-6-0
Hawaii	Rainbow Warriors	Green & white	Western Athletic	Dick Tomey	6-5-0
Holy Cross	Crusaders	Royal purple	Independent	Neil Wheelwright	5-6-0
Houston	Cougars	Scarlet & white	Southwest	Bill Yeoman	12-1-0
Howard	Bison	Blue & white	Mid-Eastern	Floyd Keith	5-6-0
Idaho	Vandals	Silver & gold	Big Sky	Jerry Davitch	4-7-0
Idaho State	Bengals	Orange & black	Big Sky	Dave Kragthorpe	0-11-0
Illinois	Fighting Illini	Orange & blue	Big Ten	Mike White	2-8-1
Illinois State	Redbirds	Red & white	Independent	Charley Cowdrey	3-8-0
Indiana	Fightin' Hoosiers	Cream & crimson	Big Ten	Lee Corso	8-4-0
Indiana State	Sycamores	Blue & white	Missouri Valley	Dennis Raetz	8-3-0
Iowa	Hawkeyes	Old gold & black	Big Ten	Hayden Fry	5-6-0
Iowa State	Cyclones	Cardinal & gold	Big Eight	Donnie Duncan	3-8-0
Jackson State	Tigers	Blue & white	Southwestern	W.C. Gorden	8-3-0
James Madison	Dukes	Purple & gold	Independent	Challace McMillin	4-6-0
Kansas	Jayhawks	Crimson & blue	Big Eight	Don Fambrough	3-8-0
Kansas State	Wildcats	Purple & white	Big Eight	Jim Dickey	3-8-0
Kent State	Golden Flashes	Blue & gold	Mid-American	Ron Blackledge	1-10-0
Kentucky	Wildcats	Blue & white	Southeastern	Fran Curci	5-6-0
Lafayette	Leopards	Maroon & white	Independent	Neil Putnam	5-3-2
Lamar	Cardinals	Red & white	Southland	Larry Kennan	6-3-2
Lehigh	Engineers	Brown & white	Independent	John Whitehead	10-3-0
Long Beach, Cal. State	Forty Niners	Brown & gold	Pacific Coast	Dave Currey	7-4-0
Louisiana State	Fighting Tigers	Purple & gold	Southeastern	Jerry Stoval	7-5-0
Louisiana Tech	Bulldogs	Red & blue	Southland	Billy Brewer	2-9-0
Louisville	Cardinals, Red Rage	Red, black, white	Independent	Bob Weber	4-6-1
Maine	Black Bears	Blue & white	Yankee	Jack Bicknell	2-9-0
Marshall	Thundering Herd	Green & white	Southern	Sonny Randle	1-10-0
Maryland	Terps	Red & white	Atlantic Coast	Jerry Claiborne	7-4-0

Team	Nickname	Team colors	Conference	Coach	1979 record (W-L-T)
Massachusetts	Minutemen	Maroon & white	Yankee	Robert Pickett	6-4-0
McNeese State	Cowboys	Blue & gold	Southland	Ernie Duplechin	11-1-0
Memphis State	Tigers	Blue & gray	Independent	Richard Williamson	5-6-0
Miami (Fla.)	Hurricanes	Orange, green, white	Independent	Howard Schnellenberger	5-6-0
Miami (Ohio)	Redskins	Red & white	Mid-American	Tom Reed	6-5-0
Michigan	Wolverines	Maize & blue	Big Ten	Bo Schembechler	8-4-0
Michigan State	Spartans	Green & white	Big Ten	Frank Waters	5-6-0
Middle Tennessee St.	Blue Raiders	Blue & white	Ohio Valley	Boots Donnelly	1-9-0
Minnesota	Gophers	Maroon & gold	Big Ten	Joe Salem	4-6-1
Mississippi	Rebels	Red & blue	Southeastern	Steve Sloan	4-7-0
Mississippi State	Bulldogs	Maroon & white	Southeastern	Emory Bellard	3-8-0
Miss. Valley State	Delta Devils	Green & white	Southwestern	Archie Cooley	4-5-0
Missouri	Tigers	Old gold & black	Big Eight	Warren Powers	7-5-0
Montana	Grizzlies	Copper, silver, gold	Big Sky	Larry Donovan	3-7-0
Montana State	Bobcats	Blue & gold	Big Sky	Sonny Lubick	6-4-0
Morehead State	Eagles	Blue & gold	Ohio Valley	Tom Lichtenberg	5-4-1
Murray State	Racers	Blue & gold	Ohio Valley	Mike Gottfried	9-2-1
Navy	Midshipmen	Navy blue & gold	Independent	George Welsh	7-4-0
Nebraska	Cornhuskers	Scarlet & cream	Big Eight	Tom Osborne	10-2-0
Nevada-Las Vegas	Rebels	Scarlet & gray	Independent	Tony Knap	9-1-2
Nevada-Reno	Wolf Pack	Silver & blue	Big Sky	Chris Ault	8-4-0
New Hampshire	Wildcats	Blue & white	Yankee	Bill Bowes	5-4-2
New Mexico	Lobos	Cherry, silver & turquoise	Western Athletic	Joe Morrison	6-6-0
New Mexico State	Aggies	Crimson & white	Missouri Valley	Gil Krueger	2-9-0
Nicholls St.	Colonels	Red & grey	Independent	Michael Vendetti	8-3-0
North Carolina	Tar Heels	Blue & white	Atlantic Coast	Dick Crum	8-3-1
North Carolina A & T	Aggies	Blue & gold	Mid-Eastern	Jim McKinley	4-6-1
North Carolina State	Wolfpack	Red & white	Atlantic Coast	Monte Kiffin	7-4-0
North Texas State	Mean Green, Eagles	Green & white	Independent	Jerry Moore	5-6-0
Northeast Louisiana	Indians	Maroon & gold	Independent	John David Crow	3-8-0
Northeastern	Huskies	Red & black	Independent	Robert Lyons	3-7-0
Northern Arizona	Lumberjacks	Blue & gold	Big Sky	Dwain Painter	7-4-0
Northern Illinois	Huskies	Cardinal & black	Mid-American	Bill Mallory	5-5-1
Northwestern	Wildcats	Purple & white	Big Ten	Rick Venturi	1-10-1
Northwestern State	Demons	Burnt orange, purple, white	Independent	A.L. Williams	3-6-0
Notre Dame	Fighting Irish	Gold & blue	Independent	Dan Devine	7-4-0
Ohio State	Buckeyes	Scarlet & gray	Big Ten	Earl Bruce	11-1-0
Ohio Univ	Bobcats	Green & white	Mid-American	Brian Burke	6-5-0
Oklahoma	Sooners	Crimsom & cream	Big Eight	Barry Switzer	11-1-0
Oklahoma State	Cowboys	Orange & black	Big Eight	Jimmy Johnson	7-4-0
Oregon	Ducks	Green & yellow	Pacific Ten	Rich Brooks	6-5-0
Oregon State	Beavers	Orange & black	Pacific Ten	Joe Avezzano	1-10-0
Pacific	Tigers	Orange & black	Pacific Coast	Bob Toledo	3-7-0
Penn State	Nittany Lions	Blue & white	Independent	Joe Paterno	8-4-0
Pennsylvania	Red & Blue, Quakers	Red & blue	Ivy	Harry Gamble	0-9-0
Pittsburgh	Panthers	Gold & blue	Independent	Jackie Sherrill	11-1-0
Portland State	Vikings	Green & white	Independent	Darrel Davis	6-5-0
Prairie View A & M	Panthers	Purple & gold	Southwestern	Cornelius Cooper	0-11-0
Princeton	Tigers	Orange & black	Ivy	Frank Navarro	5-4-0
Purdue	Boilermakers	Old gold & black	Big Ten	Jim Young	10-2-0
Rhode Island	Rams	Blue & white	Yankee	Bob Griffin	1-9-1
Rice	Owls	Blue & gray	Southwest	Ray Alborn	1-10-0
Richmond	Spiders	Red & blue	Independent	Dal Shealy	0-11-0
Rutgers	Scarlet Knights	Scarlet	Independent	Frank Burns	8-3-0
San Diego State	Aztecs	Scarlet & black	Western Athletic	Claude Gilbert	8-3-0
San Jose State	Spartans	Blue, gold & white	Pacific Coast	Jack Elway	6-4-1
South Carolina	Fighting Gamecocks	Garnet & black	Independent	Jim Carlen	8-4-0
South Carolina State	Bulldogs	Garnet & blue	Mid-Eastern	Bill Davis	8-3-0
Southeastern La.	Lions	Green & gold	Independent	Oscar Lofton	6-5-0
Southern	Jaguars	Blue & gold	Southwestern	Cass Jackson	7-4-0
Southern California	Trojans	Cardinal & gold	Pacific Ten	John Robinson	11-0-1
Southern Illinois	Salukis	Maroon & white	Missouri Valley	Rey Dempsey	8-3-0
Southern Methodist	Mustangs	Red & blue	Southwest	Ron Meyer	5-6-0
Southern Mississippi	Golden Eagles	Black & gold	Independent	Bobby Collins	6-4-1
Southwestern La.	Ragin' Cajuns	Vermillion & white	Southland	Sam Robertson	4-7-0
Stanford	Cardinals	Cardinal & white	Pacific Ten	Paul Wiggin	5-5-1
Syracuse	Orangemen	Orange	Independent	Frank Maloney	7-5-0
Temple	Owls	Cherry & white	Independent	Wayne Hardin	10-2-0
Tennessee	Volunteers	Orange & white	Southeastern	John Majors	7-5-0
Tenn.-Chattanooga	Moccasins	Navy blue & gold	Southern	Bill Oliver	9-2-0
Tennessee State	Tigers	Blue & white	Independent	John A. Merritt	8-3-0
Tennessee Tech	Golden Eagles	Purple & gold	Ohio Valley	Don Wade	1-8-2
Texas	Longhorns	Orange & white	Southwest	Fred Akers	9-3-0
Texas-Arlington	Mavericks	Royal blue & white	Southland	Bud Elliott	9-2-0
Texas-El Paso	Miners	Orange & white	Western Athletic	Bill Michael	2-9-0
Texas A & M	Aggies	Maroon & white	Southwest	Tom Wilson	6-5-0
Texas Christian	Horned Frogs	Purple & white	Southwest	F.A. Dry	2-8-1
Texas Southern	Tigers	Maroon & gray	Southwestern	James Sorey	3-8-0
Texas Tech	Red Raiders	Scarlet & black	Southwest	Rex Dockery	3-6-2
Toledo	Rockets	Blue & gold	Mid-American	Chuck Stobart	7-3-1
Tulane	Green Wave	Olive green & sky blue	Independent	Vince Gibson	9-3-0
Tulsa	Golden Hurricane	Blue, red, gold	Missouri Valley	John Cooper	6-5-0
UCLA	Bruins	Navy blue & gold	Pacific Ten	Terry Donahue	5-6-0
Utah State	Aggies	Navy blue & white	Pacific Coast	Bruce Snyder	7-3-1

Team	Nickname	Team colors	Conference	Coach	1979 record (W-L-T)
Utah	Utes	Crimson & white	Western Athletic	Wayne Howard	6-6-0
Vanderbilt	Commodores	Black & gold	Southeastern	George MacIntyre	1-10-0
Villanova	Wildcats	Blue & white	Independent	Dick Bedesem	5-6-0
Virginia	Cavaliers	Orange & blue	Atlantic Coast	Dick Bestwick	6-5-0
VMI	Keydets	Red, white & yellow	Southern	Bob Thalman	6-4-1
Virginia Tech	Gobblers	Orange & marroon	Independent	Bill Dooley	5-6-0
Wake Forest	Demon Deacons	Old gold & black	Atlantic Coast	John Mackovic	8-4-0
Washington	Huskies	Purple & gold	Pacific Ten	Don James	9-3-0
Washington State	Cougars	Crimson & gray	Pacific Ten	Jim Walden	3-8-0
Weber State	Wildcats	Purple & white	Big Sky	Pete Riehlman	3-8-0
West Texas State	Buffaloes	Maroon & white	Missouri Valley	Bill Yung	5-5-1
West Virginia	Mountaineers	Old gold & blue	Independent	Don Nehlen	5-6-0
Western Carolina	Catamounts	Purple & gold	Southern	Bob Waters	6-5-0
Western Kentucky	Hilltoppers	Red & white	Ohio Valley	Jimmy Feix	5-5-0
Western Michigan	Broncos	Brown & gold	Mid-American	Elliot Uzelac	6-5-0
Wichita State	Shockers	Gold & black	Missouri Valley	Willie Jeffries	1-10-0
William & Mary	Indians	Green, gold, silver	Independent	Jimmye Laycock	4-7-0
Wisconsin	Badgers	Cardinal & white	Big Ten	Dave McClain	4-7-0
Wyoming	Cowboys	Brown & yellow	Western Athletic	Pat Dye	4-8-0
Yale	Bulldogs, Elis	Yale blue	Ivy	Carmen Cozza	8-1-0

Selected Division 2 and 3 Teams

Alma	Scots	Maroon & cream	Michigan	Phil Brooks	3-6-0
Amherst	Lord Jeffs	Purple & white	Little Three	James Ostendarp	3-5-0
Baldwin-Wallace	Yellow Jackets	Brown & gold	Ohio	Lee J. Tressel	9-2-0
Beloit	Buccaneers	Gold & blue	Midwest	Ed DeGeorge	4-4-0
Butler	Bulldogs	Blue & white	Heartland	Bill Sylvester	5-5-0
Carleton	Knights	Maize & blue	Midwest	Bob Sullivan	4-5-0
Cheyney State	Wolves	Blue & white	Pennsylvania	Andy Hinson	9-2-0
Chico, Cal. St.	Wildcats	Cardinal & white	Far Western	Dick Trimmer	5-6-0
Coast Guard	Cadets, Bears	Blue & white	Independent	Bill Hickey	1-8-1
Coe	Kohawks	Crimson & gold	Midwest	Roger Schlegel	4-5-0
Dayton	Flyers	Red & blue	Independent	Rick Carter	8-2-1
Denison	Big Red	Red & white	Ohio	Keith Piper	7-2-0
Emory & Henry	Wasps	Blue & gold	Old Dominion	Larry Bales	3-7-0
Evansville	Purple Aces	Purple & white	Heartland	Randy Rodgers	3-7-0
John Carroll	Blue Streaks	Blue & gold	Presidents	Don Stupica	3-6-0
Kalamazoo	Hornets	Orange & black	Michigan	Ed Baker	5-3-0
Kenyon	Lords	Purple & white	Ohio	Tom McHugh	2-7-0
Knox	Siwash	Purple & gold	Midwest	Joe Campanelli	4-4-0
Lawrence	Vikings	Navy & white	Midwest	Ron Roberts	9-1-0
Michigan Tech	Huskies	Silver & gold	Northern	Jim Kapp	4-6-0
Middlebury	Panthers	Blue & white	Independent	Mickey Heinecken	5-3-0
Morgan State	Bears	Blue & orange	Mid-Eastern	Clarence Thomas	9-2-0
Mt. Union	Purple Raiders	Purple & white	Ohio	Ken Wable	7-2-0
Muhlenberg	Mules	Cardinal & gray	Middle Atlantic	Frank Marino	5-3-1
North Dakota State	Bison	Yellow & green	North Central	Don Morton	6-4-0
North Dakota	Sioux	Green & white	North Central	Pat Behrns	10-2-0
Northern Iowa	Panthers	Purple & old gold	Mid-Continent	Stan Sheriff	6-5-0
Northern Michigan	Wildcats	Old gold & green	Mid-Continent	Bill Rademacher	4-6-0
Ohio Northern	Polar Bears	Orange & black	Ohio	A. Wallace Hood	5-3-1
Ohio Wesleyan	Battling Bishops	Red & black	Ohio	Jack Fouts	1-8-0
Olivet	Comets	Red & white	Michigan	Ron Lynch	4-5-0
Puget Sound	Loggers	Green & gold	Independent	Ron Simonson	7-4-0
Ripon	Redmen	Crimson & white	Midwest	Bob Giesey	4-5-0
Rochester	Yellow Jackets	Yellow & blue	Independent	Pat Stark	5-4-0
St. Cloud State	Huskies	Red & black	Northern	Mike Simpson	5-6-0
St. Lawrence	Saints	Scarlet & brown	ICAC	Andy Talley	3-6-0
St. Norbert	Green Knights	Green & gold	Independent	Larry Van Alstine	1-9-0
St. Olaf	Oles	Black & gold	Minn. IAC	Tom Porter	7-3-0
Santa Clara	Broncos	Cardinal & white	Independent	Pat Malley	6-3-0
Slippery Rock	Rockets, The Rock	Green & white	Pennsylvania	Bob DeSpirito	3-6-0
So. Dakota State	Jackrabbits	Yellow & blue	North Central	John Gregory	8-4-0
South Dakota	Coyotes	Vermilion & white	North Central	Dave Triplett	5-6-0
Southern Oregon	Red Raiders	Red & black	Evergreen	Chuck Mills	2-7-0
Swarthmore	Little Quakers	Garnet	Middle Atlantic	Tom Lapinski	4-4-1
Thiel	Tomcats	Blue & gold	President's Athletic	Wayne Petrarca	6-3-0
Trenton State	Lions	Blue & gold	New Jersey State	Eric Hamilton	7-3-0
Tufts	Jumbos	Blue & brown	Independent	Vic Gatto	8-0-0
Upsala	Vikings	Blue & gray	Middle Atlantic	Pat Briante	8-1-1
Valparaiso	Crusaders	Brown & gold	Heartland	Bill Koch	5-4-0
Wash. & Jeff.	Presidents	Red & black	Presidents Athletic	Pat Mondock	1-8-0
Wash. & Lee	Generals	Royal blue, white	Old Dominion	Gary Fallon	3-7-0
Wayne State	Tartars	Green & gold	Great Lakes	Steve Fickert	3-5-1
Wesleyan	Cardinals	Red & black	Little Three	Bill MacDermott	5-3-0
Western Illinois	Leathernecks	Purple & gold	Mid-Continent	Pete Rodriguez	3-8-0
Wilkes	Colonels	Navy & gold	Middle Atlantic	Roland Schmidt	4-4-0
Williams	Ephmen	Purple	Little Three	Robert Odell	4-4-0
Wittenberg	Tigers	Red & white	Ohio	Dave Maurer	11-1-0
Wooster	Fighting Scots	Black & gold	Ohio	Tom Hollman	6-3-0
Youngstown State	Penguins	Red & white	Mid-Continent	Bill Narduzzi	11-2-0

Tour de France in 1980

Joop Zoetemelk of the Netherlands won the 1980 Tour de France, the world's most prestigious bicycle endurance race, for the first time after finishing 2d in the event 5 times. The race covered 2,436 miles from Frankfurt, Germany to Paris.

College Football Stadiums

School	Capacity
Alabama, Univ. of (Denny Stad.), University, Ala.	59,000
Arizona State Univ. (Sun Devil), Tempe	70,311
Arizona, Univ. of (Arizona Stad.), Tucson	57,000
Arkansas, Univ. of (Razorback Stad.) Fayetteville	43,500
Auburn Univ. (Jordan Hare Stad.), Auburn, Ala.	61,291
Baylor Univ. Stad., Waco, Tex.	48,000
Boston Coll. (Alumni Stad.), Boston, Mass.	32,000
Bowling Green State Univ. (Doyt Perry Field)	23,272
Brigham Young Univ. Stad., Provo, Ut.	30,000
Cal., Univ. of (Memorial Stad.), Berkeley	76,780
Central Mich. Univ. (Shorts Stad.), Mt. Pleasant	20,000
Cincinnati, Univ. of (Nippert), Oh.	25,692
Citadel (Johnson Hagood Stad.), Charleston, S.C.	22,500
Clemson Univ. (Memorial Stad.), S.C.	53,306
Colorado St. Univ. (Hughes Stad.), Ft. Collins	30,000
Colorado, Univ. of (Folsom Field), Boulder	52,005
Columbia Univ. (Baker Field), N.Y., N.Y.	32,000
Cornell (Schoellkopf Crescent), Ithaca, N.Y.	27,000
Dartmouth Coll. (Memorial Field), Hanover, N.H.	20,416
Delaware, Univ. of (Delaware Stad.), Newark	21,919
Duke Univ., (Wade Stad.), Durham, N.C.	40,078
E. Carolina Univ. (Ficklen Stad.), Greenville, N.C.	35,000
Eastern Kentucky (Hanger Field), Richmond	20,000
Florida State, (Campbell Stad.), Tallahassee	47,413
Florida, Univ. of (Florida Field), Gainesville	62,000
Georgia Inst. of Tech. (Grant Field), Atlanta	58,121
Georgia, Univ. of (Sanford Stad.), Athens	59,200
Harvard Stad., Boston, Mass.	37,289
Hawaii, Univ. of (Aloha Stad.), Honolulu	50,000
Holy Cross (Fitton Field), Worcester, Mass.	25,000
Illinois, Univ. of (Memorial Stad.), Urbana	71,229
Indiana St. (Memorial Stad.), Terre Haute	20,500
Indiana Univ. (Memorial Stad.), Bloomington	52,354
Iowa State Univ. (Cyclone Stad.), Ames	50,000
Iowa, Univ. of (Kinnick Stad.), Iowa City	60,200
Kansas State Univ. Stad., Manhattan	42,000
Kansas, Univ. of (Memorial Stad.), Lawrence	51,500
Kent State Univ. (Dix Stad.), Kent, Oh.	28,883
Kentucky, Univ. of (Commonwealth), Lexington	58,000
La. State Univ. (Tiger Stad.), Baton Rouge	76,050
Louisiana Tech. Univ. (Joe Aillet Stad.), Ruston	22,500
Maryland, Univ. of (Byrd), College Park	45,000
McNeese St. Univ. (Cowboy Stad.), Lake Charles, La.	20,000
Memphis State (Liberty Bowl)	50,180
Michigan State Univ. (Spartan Stad.), E. Lansing	76,000
Michigan, Univ. of (Mich. Stad.), Ann Arbor	101,701
Minnesota, Univ. of (Memorial Stad.), Minneapolis	56,725
Mississippi St. Univ. (Scott Field)	35,000
Mississippi, Univ. of (Hemingway Stad.)	35,000
Missouri, Univ. of (Faurot Field), Columbia	60,000
Nebraska, Univ. of (Memorial Stad.), Lincoln	76,400
Nevada-Las Vegas, Univ. of (Silver Bowl)	32,000
New Mexico State Univ. (Memorial Stad.), Las Cruces	30,000
New Mexico, Univ. Stad., Albuquerque	30,646
North Carolina St. U. (Carter Stad.), Raleigh	45,600
North Carolina, Univ. of (Kenan Stad.)	48,000
North Texas St. Univ. (Fouts Field), Denton	20,000
Northern Illinois Univ. (Huskie Stad.), DeKalb	20,257
Northwestern Univ. (Dyche Stad.), Evanston, Ill.	48,500
Notre Dame Stad., South Bend, Ind.	59,075
Ohio State Univ. (Ohio Stad.), Columbus	83,112
Oklahoma State (Lewis Stad.), Stillwater	50,588
Oklahoma, Univ. of (Owen Field), Norman	71,186
Oregon St. Univ. (Parker Stad.), Corvallis	40,593
Oregon, Univ. of (Autzen Stad.), Eugene	42,000
Pacific, Univ. of the (Pacific Memorial), Stockton, Cal.	30,000
Penn. State Univ. (Beaver Stad.)	76,639
Penn., Univ. of (Franklin Field), Phila.	60,546
Pittsburgh, Univ. of (Pitt. Stad.), Pa.	56,500
Princeton, (Palmer Stad.), Princeton, N.J.	45,725
Purdue, (Ross-Ade Stad.), Lafayette, Ind.	69,250
Rice Stad., Houston, Texas	70,000
Rutgers Stad., New Brunswick, N.J.	23,000
So. Carolina, Univ. of (Williams-Brice), Columbia	54,406
So. Illinois Univ. (McAndrew Stad.), Carbondale	20,100
So. Miss., Univ. of (Roberts Stad.), Hattiesburg	33,000
Southwestern La., Univ. of (Cajun Field), Lafayette	24,610
Stanford Stad., Stanford, Cal.	86,933
Syracuse Univ., N.Y.	50,000
Tenn., Univ. of (Neyland Stad.), Knoxville	80,250
Texas A. & M. Univ. (Kyle Field), College Station	71,600
Texas Christian Univ. (TCU-Amon Carter Stad.)	46,000
Texas-El Paso (Sun Bowl)	30,000
Texas Tech. Univ. (Jones Stad.), Lubbock	47,000
Texas, Univ. of (Memorial Stad.), Austin	80,000
Tulsa, Univ. of (Skelly Stad.), Okla.	40,235
U.S. Air Force Acad. (Falcon Stad.), Col.	49,668
U.S. Military Academy (Michie Stad.), West Point, N.Y.	39,514
U.S. Naval Academy (Navy-Marine Corps Mem. Stad.) Annapolis, Md.	28,000
Utah State Univ. (Romney Stad.), Logan	20,000
Utah, Univ. of (Robert Rice Stad.), Salt Lake City	30,000
Vanderbilt (Dudley Stad.), Nashville	34,694
Virginia Tech. (Lane Stad.), Blacksburg	40,000
Virginia, Univ. of (Scott Stad.), Charlottesville	36,000
Wake Forest (Groves Stad.), Winston-Salem, N.C.	31,000
Washington State Univ. (Clarence D. Martin)	39,000
Washington, Univ. of (Husky Stad.), Seattle	58,946
West Texas State Univ. (Kimbrough Stad.), Canyon	20,000
West Virginia Univ. (Mountaineer Field)	34,000
Western Mich. Univ. (Waldo Stad.), Kalamazoo	24,500
Wichita State Univ. (Cessna Stad.)	31,500
Wisconsin, Univ. of (Camp Randall), Madison	77,280
Wyoming, Univ. of (Memorial), Laramie	32,000
Yale Bowl, New Haven, Conn.	70,874

Badminton Championships in 1980

World Championships

Jakarta, Indonesia, May 27-June 1, 1980

Men's Singles—Rudy Hartono, Indonesia def. Liem Swie King, Indonesia, 15-9, 15-9.

Women's Singles—Wiharjo Verawaty, Indonesia def. Lie Ivana, Indonesia, 11-1, 11-3.

Men's Doubles—Ade Chandra & Christian Hadinata, Indonesia def. Kartono & Haryanto, Indonesia, 5-15, 15-5, 15-7.

Women's Doubles—Nora Perry & Jane Webster, England def. Wiharjo Verawaty & Imelda Wigoeno, Indonesia, 15-12, 15-3.

Mixed Doubles—Christian Hadinata & Imelda Wigoeno, Indonesia def. Mike Tredgett & Nora Perry, England, 15-12, 15-4.

U.S. Championships

Offutt AFB, Neb., Apr. 16-19, 1980

Men's Singles—Gary Higgins, Alhambra, Cal. def. Chris Kinard, Pasadena, Cal., 15-5, 15-8.

Women's Singles—Cheryl Carton, San Diego, Cal. def. Judianne Kelly, Costa Mesa, Cal., 11-4, 8-11, 11-8.

Men's Doubles—Matt Fogarty, Duxbury, Mass. & Mike Walker, Manhattan Beach, Cal. def. John Britton, Redondo Beach, Cal. & Gary Higgins, Alhambra, Cal., 8-15, 15-8, 15-12.

Women's Doubles—Pam Brady, Flint, Mich. & Judianne Kelly, Costa Mesa, Cal., def. Cheryl Carton, San Diego, Cal. & Vicki Toutz, Los Alamitos, Cal., 15-9, 15-8.

Mixed Doubles—Mike Walker, Manhattan Beach, Cal. & Judianne Kelly, Costa Mesa, Cal. def. Danny Brady, Flint, Mich. & Pam Brady, Flint, Mich., 15-12, 14-18, 18-16.

Senior Men's Singles—Jim Poole, Westminster, Cal. def. Tom Carmichael, Ortonville, Mich., 18-16, 15-6.

Senior Men's Doubles—Don Paup, Washington, D.C. & Jim Poole, Westminster, Cal. def. Jim Bell, Ypsilanti, Mich. & Tom Carmichael, Ortonville, Mich., 15-4, 15-6.

Senior Women's Doubles—Claire Bowyer, Canada & Ethel Marshall, Williamsville, N.Y. def. Sondra Fogarty, Duxbury, Mass. & Sandy Norton, Madison, Wis., 15-2, 15-1.

Senior Mixed Doubles—Don Paup, Washington, D.C. & Sondra Fogarty, Duxbury, Mass. def. Tom Carmichael, Ortonville, Mich. & Gloria Eli, Swartz Creek, Mich., 15-7, 15-7.

National Football League

Final 1979 Standings

National Conference

Eastern Division

Club	W.	L.	T.	Pct.	Pts.	Opp.
Dallas	11	5	0	.688	371	313
Philadelphia	11	5	0	.688	339	282
Washington	10	6	0	.625	348	295
New York Giants	6	10	0	.375	237	323
St. Louis	5	11	0	.313	307	358

Central Division

Club	W.	L.	T.	Pct.	Pts.	Opp.
Tampa Bay	10	6	0	.625	273	237
Chicago	10	6	0	.625	306	249
Minnesota	7	9	0	.438	259	337
Green Bay	5	11	0	.313	246	316
Detroit	2	14	0	.125	219	365

Western Division

Club	W.	L.	T.	Pct.	Pts.	Opp.
Los Angeles	9	7	0	.563	323	309
New Orleans	8	8	0	.500	370	360
Atlanta	6	10	0	.375	300	388
San Francisco	2	14	0	.125	308	416

American Conference

Eastern Division

Club	W.	L.	T.	Pct.	Pts.	Opp.
Miami	10	6	0	.625	341	257
New England	9	7	0	.563	411	326
New York Jets	8	8	0	.500	337	383
Buffalo	7	9	0	.438	268	279
Baltimore	5	11	0	.313	271	351

Central Division

Club	W.	L.	T.	Pct.	Pts.	Opp.
Pittsburgh	12	4	0	.750	416	262
Houston	11	5	0	.688	362	331
Cleveland	9	7	0	.563	359	352
Cincinnati	4	12	0	.250	337	421

Western Division

Club	W.	L.	T.	Pct.	Pts.	Opp.
San Diego	12	4	0	.733	411	246
Denver	10	6	0	.667	289	262
Oakland	9	7	0	.563	365	337
Seattle	9	7	0	.563	378	372
Kansas City	7	9	0	.438	238	262

NFC Playoffs—Philadelphia 27, Chicago 17; Tampa Bay 24, Philadelphia 17; Los Angeles 21, Dallas 19; Los Angeles 9, Tampa Bay 0.
AFC Playoffs—Houston 13, Denver 7; Houston 17, San Diego 14; Pittsburgh 34, Miami 14; Pittsburgh 27, Houston 13.
Championship game—Pittsburgh 31, Los Angeles 19.

Pittsburgh Defeats Los Angeles in Super Bowl

The Pittsburgh Steelers won the fourth Super Bowl championship by defeating the Los Angeles Rams 31-19 on Jan. 20, 1980 at the Rose Bowl in Pasadena, Cal. Terry Bradshaw of the Steelers was chosen the game's most valuable player.

Score by Periods

Los Angeles	7	6	6	0—19
Pittsburgh	3	7	7	14—31

Scoring

Pittsburgh—Field goal Bahr 41.
Los Angeles—Bryant 1 run (Corral kick).
Pittsburgh—Harris 1 run (Bahr kick).
Los Angeles—Field goal Corral 31.
Los Angeles—Field goal Corral 45.
Pittsburgh—Swann 47 pass from Bradshaw (Bahr kick).
Los Angeles—Smith 24 pass from McCutcheon (kick failed).
Pittsburgh—Stallworth 73 pass from Bradshaw (Bahr kick).
Pittsburgh—Harris 1 run (Bahr kick).

Team Statistics

	Los Angeles	Pittsburgh
Total first downs	16	19
By rushing	6	8
By passing	9	10
By penalty	1	1
Third down efficiency	6-16	9-14
Total net yards	301	393
Total offensive plays	59	58
Average gain per play	5.1	6.8
Net yards rushing	107	84
Total rushing plays	29	37
Avg. gain per rush	3.7	2.3
Net yards passing	194	309
Yds. lost attempting to pass	4-42	0-0
Gross yards passing	236	309
Passes	16-26-1	14-21-3
Avg. gain per pass	6.5	14.7
Punts	5-44.0	2-42.5
Had blocked	0	0
Total ret. yards	104	209
Punt returns	1-4	4-31
Kickoff returns	6-79	5-162
Interception returns	3-21	1-16
Penalties/yards	2-26	6-65
Fumbles/lost	0-0	0-0
Time of possession	29:30	30:30

Attendance—103,985.

Individual Statistics

Rushing—Los Angeles, Tyler 17-60, McCutcheon 5-10, Bryant 6-30, Ferragamo 1-7; Pittsburgh, Harris 20-46, Bleier 10-25, Bradshaw 3-9, Thornton 4-4.

Passing—Los Angeles, Ferragamo 15-21-1—212, McCutcheon 1-1-0—24; Pittsburgh, Bradshaw 14-21-3—309.

Receiving—Los Angeles, Bryant 3-21, Tyler 3-20, McCutcheon 1-16, Nelson 2-20, Waddy 3-75, Smith 1-24, Dennard 2-32, D. Hill 1-28; Pittsburgh, Harris 3-66, Cunningham 2-21, Swann 5-79, Stallworth 3-121, Thornton 1-22.

Kickoff Returns—Los Angeles, Jodat 2-32, Andrews 1-0, E. Hill 3-47; Pittsburgh, L. Anderson 5-162.

Punt Returns—Los Angeles, Brown 1-4; Pittsburgh, Bell 2-17, Smith 2-14.

Interceptions—Los Angeles, Elmendorf 1-10, Brown 1-6, Thomas 0-6, Perry 1-minus 1; Pittsburgh, Lambert 1-16.

Punting—Los Angeles, Clark 5-44.0; Pittsburgh, Colquitt 2-42.5.

Field Goals—Los Angeles, Corral 2-2; Pittsburgh, Bahr 1-1.

Fumbles—None.

Super Bowl

Year	Winner	Loser	Site
1967	Green Bay Packers, 35	Kansas City Chiefs, 10	Los Angeles Coliseum
1968	Green Bay Packers, 33	Oakland Raiders, 14	Orange Bowl, Miami
1969	New York Jets, 16	Baltimore Colts, 7	Orange Bowl, Miami
1970	Kansas City Chiefs, 23	Minnesota Vikings, 7	Tulane Stadium, New Orleans
1971	Baltimore Colts, 16	Dallas Cowboys, 13	Orange Bowl, Miami
1972	Dallas Cowboys, 24	Miami Dolphins, 3	Tulane Stadium, New Orleans
1973	Miami Dolphins, 14	Washington Redskins, 7	Los Angeles Coliseum
1974	Miami Dolphins, 24	Minnesota Vikings, 7	Rice Stadium, Houston
1975	Pittsburgh Steelers, 16	Minnesota Vikings, 6	Tulane Stadium, New Orleans
1976	Pittsburgh Steelers, 21	Dallas Cowboys, 17	Orange Bowl, Miami
1977	Oakland Raiders, 32	Minnesota Vikings, 14	Rose Bowl, Pasadena
1978	Dallas Cowboys, 27	Denver Broncos, 10	Louisiana Superdome, New Orleans
1979	Pittsburgh Steelers, 35	Dallas Cowboys, 31	Orange Bowl, Miami
1980	Pittsburgh Steelers, 31	Los Angeles Rams, 19	Rose Bowl, Pasadena

National Football League Champions

Year	East Winner (W.L.T.)	West Winner (W.L.T.)	Playoff
1933	New York Giants (11-3-0)	Chicago Bears (10-2-1)	Chicago Bears 23, New York 21
1934	New York Giants (8-5-0)	Chicago Bears (13-0-0)	New York 30, Chicago Bears 13
1935	New York Giants (9-3-0)	Detroit Lions (7-3-2)	Detroit 26, New York 7
1936	Boston Redskins (7-5-0)	Green Bay Packers (10-1-1)	Green Bay 21, Boston 6
1937	Washington Redskins (8-3-0)	Chicago Bears (9-1-1)	Washington 28, Chicago Bears 21
1938	New York Giants (8-2-1)	Green Bay Packers (8-3-0)	New York 23, Green Bay 17
1939	New York Giants (9-1-1)	Green Bay Packers (9-2-0)	Green Bay 27, New York 0
1940	Washington Redskins (9-2-0)	Chicago Bears (8-3-0)	Chicago Bears 73, Washington 0
1941	New York Giants (8-3-0)	Chicago Bears (10-1-1)(a)	Chicago Bears 37, New York 9
1942	Wash. Redskins (10-1-1)	Chicago Bears (11-0-0)	Washington 14, Chicago Bears 6
1943	Wash. Redskins (6-3-1)(a)	Chicago Bears (8-1-1)	Chicago Bears, 41, Washington 21
1944	New York Giants (8-1-1)	Green Bay Packers (8-2-0)	Green Bay 14, New York 7
1945	Wash. Redskins (8-2-0)	Cleveland Rams (9-1-0)	Cleveland 15, Washington 14
1946	New York Giants (7-3-1)	Chicago Bears (8-2-1)	Chicago Bears 24, New York 14
1947	Philadelphia Eagles (8-4-0)(a)	Chicago Cardinals (9-3-0)	Chicago Cardinals 28, Philadelphia 21
1948	Philadelphia Eagles (9-2-1)	Chicago Cardinals (11-1-0)	Philadelphia 7, Chicago Cardinals 0
1949	Philadelphia Eagles (11-1-0)	Los Angeles Rams (8-2-2)	Philadelphia 14, Los Angeles 0
1950	Cleveland Browns (10-2-0)(a)	Los Angeles Rams (9-3-0)(a)	Cleveland 30, Los Angeles 28
1951	Cleveland Browns (11-1-0)	Los Angeles Rams (8-4-0)	Los Angeles 24, Cleveland 17
1952	Cleveland Browns (8-4-0)	Detroit Lions (9-3-0)(a)	Detroit 17, Cleveland 7
1953	Cleveland Browns (11-1-0)	Detroit Lions (10-2-0)	Detroit 17, Cleveland 16
1954	Cleveland Browns (9-3-0)	Detroit Lions (9-2-1)	Cleveland 56, Detroit 10
1955	Cleveland Browns (9-2-1)	Los Angeles Rams (8-3-1)	Cleveland 38, Los Angeles 14
1956	New York Giants (8-3-1)	Chicago Bears (9-2-1)	New York 47, Chicago Bears 7
1957	Cleveland Browns (9-2-1)	Detroit Lions (8-4-0)(a)	Detroit 59, Cleveland 14
1958	New York Giants (9-3-0)(a)	Baltimore Colts (9-3-0)	Baltimore 23, New York 17(b)
1959	New York Giants (10-2-0)	Baltimore Colts (9-3-0)	Baltimore 31, New York 16
1960	Philadelphia Eagles (10-2-0)	Green Bay Packers (8-4-0)	Philadelphia 17, Green Bay 13
1961	New York Giants (10-3-1)	Green Bay Packers (11-3-0)	Green Bay 37, New York 0
1962	New York Giants (12-2-0)	Green Bay Packers (13-1-0)	Green Bay 16, New York 7
1963	New York Giants (11-3-0)	Chicago Bears (11-1-2)	Chicago 14, New York 10
1964	Cleveland Browns (10-3-1)	Baltimore Colts (12-2-0)	Cleveland 27, Baltimore 0
1965	Cleveland Browns (11-3-0)	Green Bay Packers (10-3-1)(a)	Green Bay 23, Cleveland 12
1966	Dallas Cowboys (10-3-1)	Green Bay Packers (12-2-0)	Green Bay 34, Dallas 27

(a) Won divisional playoff. (b) Won at 8:15 sudden death overtime period.

Year	Conference	Division	Winner (W-L-T)	Playoff
1967	East	Century	Cleveland (9-5-0)	Dallas 52, Cleveland 14
		Capitol	Dallas (9-5-0)	
	West	Central	Green Bay (9-4-1)	Green Bay 28, Los Angeles 7
		Coastal	Los Angeles (11-1-2)(a)	Green Bay 21, Dallas 17
1968	East	Century	Cleveland (10-4-0)	Cleveland 31, Dallas 20
		Capitol	Dallas (12-2-0)	
	West	Central	Minnesota (8-6-0)	Baltimore 24, Minnesota 14
		Coastal	Baltimore (13-1-0)	Baltimore 34, Cleveland 0
1969	East	Century	Cleveland (10-3-1)	Cleveland 38, Dallas 14
		Capitol	Dallas (11-2-1)	
	West	Central	Minnesota (12-2-0)	Minnesota 23, Los Angeles 20
		Coastal	Los Angeles (11-3-0)	Minnesota 27, Cleveland 7
1970	American	Eastern	Baltimore (11-2-1)	Baltimore 17, Cincinnati 0
		Central	Cincinnati (8-6-0)	Oakland 21, Miami 14
		Western	Oakland (8-4-2)	Baltimore 27, Oakland 17
	National	Eastern	Dallas (10-4-0)	Dallas 5, Detroit 0
		Central	Minnesota (12-2-0)	San Francisco 17, Minnesota 14
		Western	San Francisco (10-3-1)	Dallas 17, San Francisco 10
1971	American	Eastern	Miami (10-3-1)	Miami 27, Kansas City 24
		Central	Cleveland (9-5-0)	Baltimore 20, Cleveland 3
		Western	Kansas City (10-3-1)	Miami 21, Baltimore 0
	National	Eastern	Dallas (11-3-0)	Dallas 20, Minnesota 12
		Central	Minnesota (11-3-0)	San Francisco 24, Washington 20
		Western	San Francisco (9-5-0)	Dallas 14, San Francisco 3
1972	American	Eastern	Miami (14-0-0)	Miami 20, Cleveland 14
		Central	Pittsburgh (11-3-0)	Pittsburgh 13, Oakland 7
		Western	Oakland (10-3-1)	Miami 21, Pittsburgh 17
	National	Eastern	Washington (11-3-0)	Washington 16, Green Bay 3
		Central	Green Bay (10-4-0)	Dallas 30, San Francisco 28
		Western	San Francisco (8-5-1)	Washington 26, Dallas 3
1973	American	Eastern	Miami (12-2-0)	Miami 34, Cincinnati 16
		Central	Cincinnati (10-4-0)	Oakland 33, Pittsburgh 14
		Western	Oakland (9-4-1)	Miami 27, Oakland 10
	National	Eastern	Dallas (10-4-0)	Dallas 27, Los Angeles 16
		Central	Minnesota (12-2-0)	Minnesota 27, Washington 20
		Western	Los Angeles (12-2-0)	Minnesota 27, Dallas 10
1974	American	Eastern	Miami (11-3-0)	Oakland 28, Miami 26
		Central	Pittsburgh (10-3-1)	Pittsburgh 32, Buffalo 14
		Western	Oakland (12-2-0)	Pittsburgh 24, Oakland 13
	National	Eastern	St. Louis (10-4-0)	Minnesota 30, St. Louis 14
		Central	Minnesota (10-4-0)	Los Angeles 19, Washington 10
		Western	Los Angeles (10-4-0)	Minnesota 14, Los Angeles 10
1975	American	Eastern	Baltimore (10-4-0)	Pittsburgh 28, Baltimore 10
		Central	Pittsburgh (12-2-0)	Oakland 31, Cincinnati 28
		Western	Oakland (11-3-0)	Pittsburgh 16, Oakland 10
	National	Eastern	St. Louis (11-3-0)	Dallas 17, Minnesota 14

(continued)

(continued)

Year	Conference	Division	Winner (W-L-T)	Playoff
		Central	Minnesota (12-2-0)	Los Angeles 35, St. Louis 23
		Western	Los Angeles (12-2-0)	Dallas 37, Los Angeles 7
1976	American	Eastern	Baltimore (11-3-0)	Pittsburgh 40, Baltimore 14
		Central	Pittsburgh (10-4-0)	Oakland 24, New England 21
		Western	Oakland (13-1-0)	Oakland 24, Pittsburgh 12
	National	Eastern	Dallas (11-3-0)	Minnesota 35, Washington 20
		Central	Minnesota (11-2-1)	Los Angeles 14, Dallas 12
		Western	Los Angeles (10-3-1)	Minnesota 24, Los Angeles 13
1977	American	Eastern	Baltimore (10-4-0)	Oakland 37, Baltimore 31
		Central	Pittsburgh (9-5-0)	Denver 34, Pittsburgh 21
		Western	Denver (12-2-0)	Dallas 37, Chicago 7
	National	Eastern	Dallas (12-2-0)	Minnesota 14, Los Angeles 7
		Central	Minnesota (9-5-0)	Denver 20, Oakland 17
		Western	Los Angeles (10-4-0)	Dallas 23, Minnesota 6
1978	American	Eastern	New England (11-5-0)	Pittsburgh 33, Denver 10
		Central	Pittsburgh (14-2-0)	Houston 31, New England 14
		Western	Denver (10-6-0)	Pittsburgh 34, Houston 5
	National	Eastern	Dallas (12-4-0)	Dallas 27, Atlanta 20
		Central	Minnesota (8-7-1)	Los Angeles 34, Minnesota 10
		Western	Los Angeles (12-4-0)	Dallas 28, Los Angeles 0
1979	American	Eastern	Miami (10-6-0)	Houston 17, San Diego 14
		Central	Pittsburgh (12-4-0)	Pittsburgh 34, Miami 14
		Western	San Diego (12-4-0)	Pittsburgh 27, Houston 13
	National	Eastern	Dallas (11-5-0)	Tampa Bay 24, Philadelphia 17
		Central	Tampa Bay (10-6-0)	Los Angeles 21, Dallas 19
		Western	Los Angeles (9-7-0)	Los Angeles 9, Tampa Bay 0

1979 NFL Individual Leaders

National Football Conference

Passing[1]

	Att	Comp	Pct Comp	Yards Gained	Avg Yd Gained	TD Pass	Pct TD	Int	Rating
Staubach, Dallas	461	267	57.9	3586	7.78	27	5.9	11	92.4
Theismann, Washington	395	233	59.0	2797	7.08	20	5.1	13	84.0
Jaworski, Philadelphia	374	190	50.8	2669	7.14	18	4.8	12	76.8
Manning, New Orleans	420	252	60.0	3169	7.55	15	3.6	20	75.6
DeBerg, San Francisco	578	347	60.0	3652	6.32	17	2.9	21	73.1
Kramer, Minnesota	566	315	55.7	3397	6.00	23	4.1	24	69.7
Phipps, Chicago	255	134	52.5	1535	6.02	9	3.5	8	69.7
Haden, Los Angeles	290	163	56.2	1854	6.39	11	3.8	14	68.2
Bartkowski, Atlanta	380	204	53.7	2505	6.59	17	4.5	20	67.2
Simms, New York	265	134	50.6	1743	6.58	13	4.9	14	65.9
Whitehurst, Green Bay	322	179	55.6	2247	6.98	10	3.1	18	64.5
Hart, St. Louis	378	194	51.3	2218	5.87	9	2.4	20	55.2
Komlo, Detroit	368	183	49.7	2238	6.08	11	3.0	23	52.6
Williams, Tampa Bay	397	166	41.8	2448	6.17	18	4.5	24	52.6

Rushing

	Att	Yds	Avg	TDs
Payton, Chicago	369	1610	4.4	14
Anderson, St. Louis	331	1605	4.8	8
Montgomery, Phila.	338	1512	4.5	9
Bell, Tampa Bay	283	1263	4.5	7
Muncie, New Orleans	238	1198	5.0	11
Riggins, Washington	260	1153	4.4	9
Tyler, Los Angeles	218	1109	5.1	9
Dorsett, Dallas	250	1107	4.4	6
Andrews, Atlanta	239	1023	4.3	3
Young, Minnesota	188	708	3.8	3

Punt Returns

	No	Yds	Avg	TDs
Sciarra, Philadelphia	16	182	11.4	0
Schubert, Chicago	25	238	9.5	1
Henry, Philadelphia	35	320	9.1	0
Hardeman, Washington	24	207	8.6	0
Arnold, Detroit	19	164	8.6	0
Mauti, New Orleans	27	218	8.1	0
Wilson, Dallas	35	236	6.7	0
Harrell, St. Louis	32	205	6.4	0
Reece, Tampa Bay	70	431	6.2	0
Solomon, San Francisco	23	142	6.2	0

Receiving

	No	Yds	Avg	TDs
Rashad, Minnesota	80	1156	14.5	9
Francis, Atlanta	74	1013	13.7	8
Young, Minnesota	72	519	7.2	4
Chandler, New Orleans	65	1069	16.4	6
Scott, Detroit	62	929	15.0	5
Hill, Dallas	60	1062	17.7	10
Hofer, San Francisco	58	662	11.4	2
Galbreath, New Orleans	58	484	8.3	1
Tilley, St. Louis	57	938	16.5	6
Solomon, San Francisco	57	807	14.2	7

Kickoff Returns

	No	Yds	Avg	TDs
Edwards, Minnesota	44	1103	25.1	0
Green, St. Louis	41	1005	24.5	1
Owens, San Francisco	41	1002	24.4	1
Henry, Philadelphia	28	668	23.9	0
Arnold, Detroit	23	539	23.4	0
Harrell, St. Louis	22	497	22.6	0
Walterscheid, Chicago	19	427	22.5	0
Mauti, New Orleans	36	801	22.3	0
Hammond, Washington	25	544	21.8	0
Odom, New York	44	949	21.6	0

Interceptions

	No	Yds	TDs
Parrish, Washington	9	65	0
Myers, New Orleans	7	127	1
Lawrence, Atlanta	6	120	0
Lavender, Washington	6	77	0
Stone, St. Louis	6	70	0
Schmidt, Chicago	6	44	1
Fencik, Chicago	6	31	0

Scoring-Kicking

	XP-XPA	FG-FGA	Pts
Moseley, Washington	39-39	25-33	114
Franklin, Philadelphia	36-39	23-31	105
Septien, Dallas	40-44	19-29	97
Wersching, San Fran.	32-35	20-24	92
Thomas, Chicago	34-37	16-27	82
Corral, Los Angeles	36-39	13-25	75
Yepremian, New Orleans	39-40	12-16	75

Punting

	No	Yds	Avg
Jennings, New York	104	4445	42.7
D. White, Dallas	76	3168	41.7
Partridge, New Orleans	57	2330	40.9
Beverly, Green Bay	69	2785	40.4
Clark, Los Angeles	93	3731	40.1
Swider, Detroit	88	3523	40.0
James, Atlanta	83	3296	39.7
Blanchard, Tampa Bay	93	3679	39.6
Runager, Philadelphia	74	2927	39.6

Scoring-Touchdowns

	Tot	Rush	Pass	Pts
Payton, Chicago	16	14	2	96
Montgomery, Philadelphia	14	9	5	84
Riggins, Washington	12	9	3	72
Carmichael, Philadelphia	11	0	11	66
Muncie, New Orleans	11	11	0	66
Taylor, New York	11	7	4	66
Anderson, St. Louis	10	8	2	60
Galbreath, New Orleans	10	9	1	60
Hill, Dallas	10	0	10	60
Tyler, Los Angeles	10	9	1	60

Team Rushing

	Off Avg		Def Avg
St. Louis	161.4	Tampa Bay	117.1
Chicago	155.4	Chicago	123.6
New Orleans	154.8	Los Angeles	124.8
Los Angeles	153.8	Dallas	132.2
Tampa Bay	152.3	Washington	134.4
Philadelphia	151.3	Atlanta	135.2
Dallas	148.2	St. Louis	137.8
Washington	145.5	San Francisco	138.3
Atlanta	137.5	Philadelphia	141.9
San Francisco	120.8	New York	153.3
Green Bay	116.3	New Orleans	154.3
New York	113.8	Detroit	157.2
Minnesota	110.3	Minnesota	157.9
Detroit	104.8	Green Bay	180.3

Team Passing

	Off Avg		Def Avg
San Francisco	227.6	Tampa Bay	129.8
Dallas	224.8	Detroit	152.6
New Orleans	196.9	Dallas	154.4
Minnesota	196.2	Philadelphia	154.6
Atlanta	170.6	Chicago	158.0
Green Bay	167.6	Los Angeles	159.8
Los Angeles	167.0	Minnesota	168.6
Tampa Bay	163.3	Green Bay	172.6
Philadelphia	163.1	St. Louis	179.6
St. Louis	162.6	New York	182.9
Washington	161.0	Washington	187.3
Detroit	146.0	New Orleans	191.6
Chicago	134.4	San Francisco	198.8
New York	122.1	Atlanta	224.8

American Conference

Passing[1]

	Att	Comp	Pct Comp	Yards Gained	Avg Yd Gained	TD Pass	Pct TD	Int	Rating
Fouts, San Diego	530	332	62.6	4082	7.70	24	4.5	24	82.6
Stabler, Oakland	498	304	61.0	3615	7.26	26	5.2	22	82.2
Anderson, Cincinnati	339	189	55.8	2340	6.90	16	4.7	10	80.9
Zorn, Seattle	505	285	56.4	3661	7.25	20	4.0	18	77.6
Grogan, New England	423	206	48.7	3286	7.77	28	6.6	20	77.5
Bradshaw, Pittsburgh	472	259	54.9	3724	7.89	26	5.5	25	77.0
Landry, Baltimore	457	270	59.1	2932	6.42	15	3.3	15	75.3
Ferguson, Buffalo	458	238	52.0	3572	7.80	14	3.1	15	74.5
Sipe, Cleveland	535	286	53.5	3793	7.09	28	5.2	26	73.1
Griese, Miami	310	176	56.8	2160	6.97	14	4.5	16	71.8
Morton, Denver	370	204	55.1	2626	7.10	16	4.3	19	70.7
Todd, New York	334	171	51.2	2660	7.96	16	4.8	22	66.4
Pastorini, Houston	324	163	50.3	2090	6.45	14	4.3	18	61.9
Fuller, Kansas City	270	146	54.1	1484	5.50	6	2.2	14	55.8

(1) At least 192 passes needed to qualify. Leader based on percentage of completions, touchdown passes, interceptions, and average yards.

Rushing

	Att	Yds	Avg	TDs
Campbell, Houston	368	1697	4.6	19
M. Pruitt, Cleveland	264	1294	4.9	9
Harris, Pittsburgh	267	1186	4.4	11
Gaines, New York	186	905	4.9	0
Washington, Baltimore	242	884	3.7	4
P. Johnson, Cincinnati	243	865	3.6	14
Csonka, Miami	220	837	3.8	12
van Eeghen, Oakland	223	818	3.7	7
Smith, Seattle	194	775	4.0	11
Dierking, New York	186	767	4.1	3

Receiving

	No	Yds	Avg	TDs
Washington, Baltimore	82	750	9.1	3
Joiner, San Diego	72	1008	14.0	4
Stallworth, Pittsburgh	70	1183	16.9	8
Largent, Seattle	66	1237	18.7	9
Upchurch, Denver	64	937	14.6	7
Jefferson, San Diego	61	1090	17.9	10
Logan, Cleveland	59	982	16.6	7
Branch, Oakland	59	844	14.3	6
Bass, Cincinnati	58	724	12.5	3
Chester, Oakland	58	712	12.3	8

Punt Returns

	No	Yds	Avg	TDs
Nathan, Miami	28	306	10.9	1
Smith, Kansas City	58	612	10.6	2
D. Hall, Cleveland	29	295	10.2	0
Upchurch, Denver	30	304	10.1	0
Morgan, New England	29	289	10.0	1
Fuller, San Diego	46	448	9.7	0
Smith, Pittsburgh	16	146	9.1	0
Harper, New York	33	290	8.8	0
Bell, Pittsburgh	45	378	8.4	0
Moody, Buffalo	38	318	8.4	0

Kickoff Returns

	No	Yds	Avg	TDs
Brunson, Oakland	17	441	25.9	0
Matthews, Oakland	35	873	24.9	1
Owens, San Diego	35	791	22.6	0
Nathan, Miami	45	1016	22.6	0
Glasgow, Baltimore	50	1126	22.5	0
Clark, New England	37	816	22.1	0
L. Anderson, Pittsburgh	34	732	21.5	0
Ellender, Houston	24	514	21.4	0
Harper, New York	55	1158	21.1	0

Interceptions

	No	Yds	TDs
Reinfeldt, Houston	12	205	0
Barbaro, Kansas City	7	142	1
Hayes, Oakland	7	100	2

Scoring-Kicking

	XP-XPA	FG-FGA	Pts
Smith, New England	46-49	23-33	115
Bahr, Pittsburgh	50-52	18-30	104
Fritsch, Houston	41-43	21-25	104
Herrera, Seattle	43-46	19-23	100
von Schamann, Miami	36-40	21-29	99

Punting

	No	Yds	Avg
Grupp, Kansas City	89	3883	43.6
Guy, Oakland	69	2939	42.6
McInally, Cincinnati	89	3678	41.3
Evans, Cleveland	69	2844	41.2
Ramsey, New York	73	2979	40.8
Parsley, Houston	93	3777	40.6
Roberts, Miami	69	2772	40.2
Colquitt, Pittsburgh	68	2733	40.2
Weaver, Seattle	66	2651	40.2

Scoring-Touchdowns

	Tot	Rush	Pass	Pts
Campbell, Houston	19	19	0	114
P. Johnson, Cincinnati	15	14	1	90
Smith, Seattle	15	11	4	90
Csonka, Miami	13	12	1	78
Morgan, New England	13	0	12	78
Harris, Pittsburgh	12	11	1	72
C. Williams, San Diego	12	12	0	72
M. Pruitt, Cleveland	11	9	2	66
Jefferson, San Diego	10	0	10	60
Thornton, Pittsburgh	10	6	4	60

Team Rushing

	Off Avg		Def Avg
New York	165.4	Denver	105.8
Pittsburgh	162.7	Miami	106.4
Houston	160.7	New York	106.6
Cincinnati	145.6	Pittsburgh	106.8
Kansas City	144.8	New England	111.3
Cleveland	142.6	Kansas City	115.4
New England	140.8	San Diego	119.2
Miami	136.7	Cincinnati	138.7
Denver	127.3	Houston	139.1
Seattle	122.9	Baltimore	144.1
Oakland	110.2	Seattle	148.4
Baltimore	104.6	Oakland	148.4
San Diego	104.3	Buffalo	155.1
Buffalo	102.0	Cleveland	162.8

Team Passing

	Off Avg		Def Avg
San Diego	244.7	Buffalo	158.1
Pittsburgh	228.4	San Diego	159.3
Seattle	224.4	New England	159.6
Cleveland	218.2	Pittsburgh	160.1
Oakland	213.2	Miami	171.1
New England	201.1	Houston	172.8
Buffalo	201.0	Baltimore	173.0
Baltimore	198.3	Cleveland	190.4
Denver	194.1	Oakland	194.5
Miami	172.7	Kansas City	195.3
New York	162.4	Denver	197.4
Cincinnati	144.4	Seattle	216.2
Houston	141.0	Cincinnati	230.8
Kansas City	103.8	New York	257.2

NEA All-NFL Team in 1979

Chosen by team captains, team representatives, and coaches of the 28 NFL teams in a poll conducted by Newspaper Enterprise Assn.

First team	Offense	Second team
John Stallworth, Pittsburgh	Wide receiver	Ahmad Rashad, Minnesota
John Jefferson, San Diego	Wide receiver	Wes Chandler, New Orleans
Raymond Chester, Oakland	Tight end	Dave Casper, Oakland
Jon Kolb, Pittsburgh	Tackle	Russ Washington, San Diego
Leon Gray, Houston	Tackle	Marvin Powell, New York Jets
John Hannah, New England	Guard	Doug Wilkerson, San Diego
Joe DeLamielleure, Buffalo	Guard	Gerry Mullins, Pittsburgh
Mike Webster, Pittsburgh	Center	Jack Rudnay, Kansas City
Dan Fouts, San Diego	Quarterback	Terry Bradshaw, Pittsburgh
Walter Payton, Chicago	Running back	Ottis Anderson, St. Louis
Earl Campbell, Houston	Running back	Franco Harris, Pittsburgh
Toni Fritsch, Houston	Placekicker	Mark Moseley, Washington

First team	Defense	Second team
Jack Youngblood, Los Angeles	End	Harvey Martin, Dallas
Lee Roy Selmon, Tampa Bay	End	Al Baker, Detroit
Randy White, Dallas	Tackle	Joe Greene, Pittsburgh
Charles Johnson, Philadelphia	Tackle	Gary Johnson, San Diego
Jack Lambert, Pittsburgh	Middle linebacker	Randy Gradishar, Denver
Jack Ham, Pittsburgh	Linebacker	Dave Lewis, Tampa Bay
Robert Brazile, Houston	Linebacker	Tom Jackson, Denver
Louis Wright, Denver	Corner back	Mike Haynes, New England
Lemar Parrish, Washington	Corner back	Mel Blount, Pittsburgh
Donnie Shell, Pittsburgh	Strong safety	Bill Thompson, Denver
Mike Reinfeldt, Houston	Free safety	Tim Foley, Miami
Bob Grupp, Kansas City	Punter	Ray Guy, Oakland

Jim Thorpe Trophy Winners

The winner of the Jim Thorpe Trophy, named after the athletic great, is picked by Murray Olderman of Newspaper Enterprise Assn. in a poll of players from the 28 NFL teams. It goes to the most valuable NFL player and is the oldest and highest professional football award.

Year	Player, team
1955	Harlon Hill, Chicago Bears
1956	Frank Gifford, N.Y. Giants
1957	John Unitas, Baltimore Colts
1958	Jim Brown, Cleveland Browns
1959	Charley Conerly, N.Y. Giants
1960	Norm Van Brocklin, Philadelphia Eagles
1961	Y.A. Tittle, N.Y. Giants
1962	Jim Taylor, Green Bay Packers
1963	(tie) Jim Brown, Cleveland Browns, and Y.A. Tittle, N.Y. Giants
1964	Lenny Moore, Baltimore Colts
1965	Jim Brown, Cleveland Browns
1966	Bart Starr, Green Bay Packers

Year	Player, team
1967	John Unitas, Baltimore Colts
1968	Earl Morrall, Baltimore Colts
1969	Roman Gabriel, Los Angeles Rams
1970	John Brodie, San Francisco 49ers
1971	Bob Griese, Miami Dolphins
1972	Larry Brown, Washington Redskins
1973	O.J. Simpson, Buffalo Bills
1974	Ken Stabler, Oakland Raiders
1975	Fran Tarkenton, Minnesota Vikings
1976	Bert Jones, Baltimore Colts
1977	Walter Payton, Chicago Bears
1978	Earl Campbell, Houston Oilers
1979	Earl Campbell, Houston Oilers

National Football Conference Leaders

(National Football League prior to 1970)

Passing

Player, team	Atts	Com	YG	TD	Year
Bart Starr, Green Bay	272	163	2,144	4	**1964**
Rudy Bukich, Chicago	312	176	2,641	9	**1965**
Bart Starr, Green Bay	251	156	2,257	3	**1966**
Sonny Jurgensen, Washington	508	288	3,747	16	**1967**
Earl Morrall, Baltimore	317	182	2,909	17	**1968**
Sonny Jurgensen, Washington	422	274	3,102	15	**1969**
John Brodie, San Francisco	378	223	2,941	24	**1970**
Roger Staubach, Dallas	211	126	1,882	15	**1971**
Norm Snead, N.Y. Giants	325	196	2,307	17	**1972**
Roger Staubach, Dallas	286	179	2,428	23	**1973**
Sonny Jurgensen, Washington	167	107	1,185	11	**1974**
Fran Tarkenton, Minnesota	425	273	2,294	25	**1975**
James Harris, Los Angeles	158	91	1,460	8	**1976**
Roger Staubach, Dallas	361	210	2,620	18	**1977**
Roger Staubach, Dallas	413	231	3,190	25	**1978**
Roger Staubach, Dallas	461	267	3,586	27	**1979**

Pass-Receiving

Player, team	Ct	YG	TD
Johnny Morris, Chicago	93	1,200	10
Dave Parks, San Francisco	80	1,344	12
Charlie Taylor, Washington	72	1,119	12
Charlie Taylor, Washington	70	990	9
Clifton McNeil, San Francisco	71	944	7
Dan Abramowicz, New Orleans	73	1,015	7
Dick Gordon, Chicago	71	1,026	13
Bob Tucker, Giants	59	791	4
Harold Jackson, Philadelphia	62	1,048	4
Harold Carmichael, Philadelphia	67	1,116	9
Charles Young, Philadelphia	63	696	3
Chuck Foreman, Minnesota	73	691	9
Drew Pearson, Dallas	58	806	6
Ahmad Rashad, Minnesota	51	681	2
Rickey Young, Minnesota	88	704	5
Ahmad Rashad, Minnesota	80	1,156	9

Scoring

Player, team	TD	PAT	FG	Pts	Year
Lenny Moore, Baltimore	20	0	0	120	**1964**
Gale Sayers, Chicago	22	0	0	132	**1965**
Bruce Gossett, Los Angeles	0	29	28	113	**1966**
Jim Bakken, St. Louis	0	36	27	117	**1967**
Leroy Kelly, Cleveland	20	0	0	120	**1968**
Fred Cox, Minnesota	0	43	26	121	**1969**
Fred Cox, Minnesota	0	35	30	125	**1970**
Curt Knight, Washington	0	27	29	114	**1971**
Chester Marcol, Green Bay	0	29	33	128	**1972**
David Ray, Los Angeles	0	40	30	130	**1973**
Chester Marcol, Green Bay	0	19	25	94	**1974**
Chuck Foreman, Minnesota	22	0	0	132	**1975**
Mark Moseley, Washington	0	31	22	97	**1976**
Walter Payton, Chicago	16	0	0	96	**1977**
Frank Corrall, Los Angeles	0	31	29	118	**1978**
Mark Moseley, Washington	0	39	25	114	**1979**

Rushing

Player, team	Yds	Atts	TD
Jimmy Brown, Cleveland	1,446	280	7
Jimmy Brown, Cleveland	1,544	289	17
Gale Sayers, Chicago	1,231	229	8
Leroy Kelly, Cleveland	1,205	235	11
Leroy Kelly, Cleveland	1,239	248	16
Gayle Sayers, Chicago	1,032	236	8
Larry Brown, Washington	1,125	237	5
John Brockington, Green Bay	1,105	216	4
Larry Brown, Washington	1,216	285	8
John Brockington, Green Bay	1,144	265	3
Larry McCutcheon, Los Angeles	1,109	236	3
Jim Otis, St. Louis	1,076	269	5
Walter Payton, Chicago	1,390	311	13
Walter Payton, Chicago	1,852	339	14
Walter Payton, Chicago	1,395	333	11
Walter Payton, Chicago	1,610	369	14

American Football Conference Leaders

(American Football League prior to 1970)

Passing

Player, team	Atts	Com	YG	TD	Year
Len Dawson, Kansas City	354	199	2,879	18	**1964**
Jack Hadl, San Diego	348	174	2,798	21	**1965**
Len Dawson, Kansas City	284	159	2,527	10	**1966**
Daryle Lamonica, Oakland	425	220	3,228	20	**1967**
Len Dawson, Kansas City	224	131	2,109	9	**1968**
Greg Cook, Cincinnati	197	106	1,845	11	**1969**
Daryle Lamonica, Oakland	356	179	2,516	22	**1970**
Bob Griese, Miami	263	145	2,089	19	**1971**
Earl Morrall, Miami	150	83	1,360	11	**1972**
Ken Stabler, Oakland	260	163	1,997	14	**1973**
Ken Anderson, Cincinnati	328	213	2,667	18	**1974**
Ken Anderson, Cincinnati	377	228	3,169	21	**1975**
Ken Stabler, Oakland	291	194	2,737	27	**1976**
Bob Griese, Miami	307	180	2,252	22	**1977**
Terry Bradshaw, Pittsburgh	368	207	2,915	28	**1978**
Dan Fouts, San Diego	530	332	4,082	24	**1979**

Pass-Receiving

Player, team	Ct	YG	TD
Charlie Hennigan, Houston	101	1,561	8
Lionel Taylor, Denver	85	1,131	6
Lance Alworth, San Diego	73	1,383	13
George Sauer, N.Y. Jets	75	1,189	6
Lance Alworth, San Diego	68	1,312	10
Lance Alworth, San Diego	64	1,003	4
Marlin Briscoe, Buffalo	57	1,036	8
Fred Biletnikoff, Oakland	61	929	9
Fred Biletnikoff, Oakland	58	802	7
Fred Willis, Houston	57	371	1
Lydell Mitchell, Baltimore	72	544	2
Reggie Rucker, Cleveland	60	770	3
Lydell Mitchell, Baltimore	60	554	4
MacArthur Lane, Kansas City	66	686	1
Lydell Mitchell, Baltimore	71	620	4
Steve Largent, Seattle	71	1,168	8
Joe Washington, Baltimore	82	750	3

Scoring

Player, team	TD	PAT	FG	Pts	Year
Gino Cappelletti, Boston	7	36	25	155	**1964**
Gino Cappelletti, Boston	9	27	17	132	**1965**
Gino Cappelletti, Boston	6	35	16	119	**1966**
George Blanda, Oakland	0	56	20	116	**1967**
Jim Turner, N.Y. Jets	0	43	34	145	**1968**
Jim Turner, N.Y. Jets	0	33	32	129	**1969**
Jan Stenerud, Kansas City	0	26	30	116	**1970**
Garo Yepremian, Miami	0	33	28	117	**1971**
Bobby Howfield, N.Y. Jets	0	40	27	121	**1972**
Roy Gerela, Pittsburgh	0	36	29	123	**1973**
Roy Gerela, Pittsburgh	0	33	20	93	**1974**
O.J. Simpson, Buffalo	23	0	0	138	**1975**
Toni Linhart, Baltimore	0	49	20	109	**1976**
Errol Mann, Oakland	0	39	20	99	**1977**
Pat Leahy, N.Y. Jets	0	41	22	107	**1978**
John Smith, New England	0	46	23	115	**1979**

Rushing

Player, team	Yds	Atts	TD
Cookie Gilchrist, Buffalo	981	230	6
Paul Lowe, San Diego	1,121	222	7
Jim Nance, Boston	1,458	299	11
Jim Nance, Boston	1,216	269	7
Paul Robinson, Cincinnati	1,023	238	8
Dick Post, San Diego	873	182	6
Floyd Little, Denver	901	209	3
Floyd Little, Denver	1,133	284	6
O.J. Simpson, Buffalo	1,251	292	6
O.J. Simpson, Buffalo	2,003	332	12
Otis Armstrong, Denver	1,407	263	9
O.J. Simpson, Buffalo	1,817	329	16
O.J. Simpson, Buffalo	1,503	290	8
Mark van Eeghen, Oakland	1,273	324	7
Earl Campbell, Houston	1,450	302	13
Earl Campbell, Houston	1,697	368	19

1980 NFL Player Draft

The following are the first round picks of the National Football League

Team	Player	Pos.	College	Team	Player	Pos.	College
1—Detroit	Billy Sims	RB	Oklahoma	15—Los Angeles	Johnnie Johnson	DB	Texas
2—New York Jets	Lam Jones	WR	Texas	16—Oakland	Marc Wilson	QB	Brigham Young
3—Cincinnati	Anthony Munoz	OT	USC	17—Buffalo	Jim Ritcher	C	No. Carolina St.
4—Green Bay	Bruce Clark	DT	Penn State	18—Washington	Art Monk	WR	Syracuse
5—Baltimore	Curtis Dickey	RB	Texas A&M	19—Chicago	Otis Wilson	LB	Louisville
6—St. Louis	Curtis Greer	DE	Michigan	20—San Francisco	Jim Stuckey	DE	Clemson
7—Atlanta	Junior Miller	TE	Nebraska	21—Miami	Don McNeal	DB	Alabama
8—N. Y. Giants	Mark Haynes	DB	Colorado	22—Tampa Bay	Ray Snell	OG	Wisconsin
9—Minnesota	Doug Martin	DE	Washington	23—Philadelphia	Roynell Young	DB	Alcorn State
10—Seattle	Jacob Green	DE	Texas A&M	24—Baltimore	Derrick Hatchett	DB	Texas
11—Kansas City	Brad Budde	OG	USC	25—New England	Vagas Ferguson	RB	Notre Dame
12—New Orleans	Stan Brock	OT	Colorado	26—Green Bay	George Cumby	LB	Oklahoma
13—San Francisco	Earl Cooper	RB	Rice	27—Cleveland	Charles White	RB	USC
14—New England	Roland Jones	DB	Tennessee	28—Pittsburgh	Mark Malone	QB	Arizona State

Pro Football Hall of Fame

Canton, Ohio

Herb Adderley
Lance Alworth
Cliff Battles
Sammy Baugh
Chuck Bednarik
Bert Bell
Raymond Berry
Charles Bidwell
Jim Brown
Paul Brown
Roosevelt Brown
Dick Butkus
Tony Canadeo
Joe Carr
Guy Chamberlin
Jack Christiansen
Dutch Clark
George Connor
Jim Conzelman
Art Donovan
Paddy Driscoll
Bill Dudley
Turk Edwards
Weeb Ewbank
Tom Fears
Ray Flaherty
Len Ford
Dr. Daniel Fortmann
Bill George
Frank Gifford
Otto Graham
Red Grange
Forrest Gregg
Lou Groza
Joe Guyon
George Halas
Ed Healey
Mel Hein
Pete Henry
Arnold Herber
Bill Hewitt
Clarke Hinkle
Elroy Hirsch
Cal Hubbard
Lamar Hunt
Don Hutson
Deacon Jones
Walt Kiesling
Frank (Bruiser) Kinard
Curly Lambeau
Dick (Night Train) Lane
Yale Lary
Dante Lavelli
Bobby Layne
Tuffy Leemans
Bob Lilly
Vince Lombardi
Sid Luckman
Link Lyman
Tim Mara
Gino Marchetti
George Marshall
Ollie Matson
George McAfee
Hugh McElhenny
John (Blood) McNally
Mike Michalske
Wayne Millner
Ron Mix
Lenny Moore
Marion Motley
Bronko Nagurski
Greasy Neale
Ernie Nevers
Ray Nitschke
Leo Nomellini
Jim Otto
Steve Owen
Clarence (Ace) Parker
Jim Parker
Joe Perry
Pete Pihos
Hugh (Shorty) Ray
Dan Reeves
Andy Robustelli
Art Rooney
Gale Sayers
Joe Schmidt
Bart Starr
Ernie Stautner
Ken Strong
Joe Stydahar
Jim Taylor
Jim Thorpe
Y. A. Tittle
George Trafton
Charlie Trippi
Emlen Tunnell
Clyde (Bulldog) Turner
Norm Van Brocklin
Steve Van Buren
Johnny Unitas
Bob Waterfield
Bill Willis
Larry Wilson
Alex Wojciechowicz

Canadian Football League

Final 1979 Standings

Eastern Conference

	W	L	T	PF	PA	Pts
Montreal Alouettes	11	4	1	351	284	23
Ottawa Rough Riders	8	6	2	349	315	18
Hamilton Tiger-Cats	6	10	0	280	338	12
Toronto Argonauts	5	11	0	234	352	10

Western Conference

	W	L	T	PF	PA	Pts
Edmonton Eskimos	12	2	2	495	219	26
Calgary Stampeders	12	4	0	382	278	24
B.C. Lions	9	6	1	328	333	19
Winnipeg Blue Bombers	4	12	0	283	340	8
Saskatchewan Roughriders	2	14	0	194	437	4

East semifinal—Ottawa 29, Hamilton 26.
West semifinal—Calgary 37, B.C. 2.
East final—Montreal 17, Ottawa 6.
West final—Edmonton 19, Calgary 7.
Championship (Grey Cup)—Edmonton 17, Montreal 9.

Canadian Football League (Grey Cup)

Winners of Eastern and Western divisions meet in championship game for Grey Cup (donated by Governor-General Earl Grey in 1909). Canadian football features 3 downs, 110-yard field, and each team can have 12 players on field at one time.

1948 Calgary Stampeders 12, Ottawa Rough Riders 7
1949 Montreal Alouettes 28, Calgary Stampeders 15
1950 Toronto Argonauts 13, Winnipeg Blue Bombers 0
1951 Ottawa Rough Riders 21, Saskatchewan Roughriders 14
1952 Toronto Argonauts 21, Edmonton Eskimos 11
1953 Hamilton Tiger-Cats 12, Winnipeg Blue Bombers 6
1954 Edmonton Eskimos 26, Montreal Alouettes 25
1955 Edmonton Eskimos 34, Montreal Alouettes 19
1956 Edmonton Eskimos 50, Montreal Alouettes 27
1957 Hamilton Tiger-Cats 32, Winnipeg Blue Bombers 7
1958 Winnipeg Blue Bombers 35, Hamilton Tiger-Cats 28
1959 Winnipeg Blue Bombers 21, Hamilton Tiger-Cats 7
1960 Ottawa Rough Riders 16, Edmonton Eskimos 6
1961 Winnipeg Blue Bombers 21, Hamilton Tiger-Cats 14
1962 Winnipeg Blue Bombers 28, Hamilton Tiger-Cats 27
1963 Hamilton Tiger-Cats 21, British Columbia Lions 10
1964 British Columbia Lions 34, Hamilton Tiger-Cats 24
1965 Hamilton Tiger-Cats 22, Winnipeg Blue Bombers 16
1966 Saskatchewan Roughriders 29, Ottawa Rough Riders 14
1967 Hamilton Tiger-Cats 24, Saskatchewan Roughriders 1
1968 Ottawa Rough Riders 24, Calgary Stampeders 21
1969 Ottawa Rough Riders 29, Saskatchewan Roughriders 11
1970 Montreal Alouettes 23, Calgary Stampeders 10
1971 Calgary Stampeders 14, Toronto Argonauts 11
1972 Hamilton Tiger-Cats 13, Saskatchewan Roughriders 10
1973 Ottawa Rough Riders 22, Edmonton Eskimos 18
1974 Montreal Alouettes 20, Edmonton Eskimos 7
1975 Edmonton Eskimos 9, Montreal Alouettes 8
1976 Ottawa Rough Riders 23, Saskatchewan Roughriders 20
1977 Montreal Alouettes 41, Edmonton Eskimos 6
1978 Edmonton Eskimos 20, Montreal Alouettes 13
1979 Edmonton Eskimos 17, Montreal Alouettes 9

All-Time Pro Football Records

NFL, AFL, and All-American Football Conference

(as of Sept. 6, 1980)

Leading Lifetime Rushers

Player	League	Yrs	Att	Yards	Avg	Player	League	Yrs	Att	Yards	Avg
Jim Brown	NFL	9	2,359	12,312	5.2	Lydell Mitchell	NFL	8	1,668	6,518	3.9
O.J. Simpson	AFL-NFL	11	2,404	11,236	4.7	Floyd Little	AFL-NFL	9	1,641	6,323	3.8
Joe Perry	AAFC-NFL	16	1,929	9,723	5.0	Don Perkins	NFL	8	1,500	6,217	4.1
Jim Taylor	NFL	10	1,941	8,597	4.4	Lawrence McCutcheon	NFL	8	1,435	6,186	4.3
Franco Harris	NFL	8	2,012	8,563	4.3	Ken Willard	NFL	10	1,622	6,105	3.8
Larry Csonka	AFL-NFL	11	1,891	8,081	4.3	Calvin Hill	NFL	10	1,447	6,049	4.2
Leroy Kelly	NFL	10	1,727	7,274	4.2	Chuck Foreman	NFL	7	1,529	5,879	3.8
Walter Payton	NFL	5	1,548	6,926	4.5	Larry Brown	NFL	8	1,530	5,875	3.8
John Riggins	NFL	9	1,666	6,822	4.1	Steve Van Buren	NFL	8	1,320	5,860	4.3
John Henry Johnson	NFL-AFL	13	1,571	6,803	4.3	Bill Brown	NFL	14	1,649	5,838	3.4

Most Yards Gained, Season — 2,003, O.J. Simpson, Buffalo Bills, 1973.
Most Yards Gained, Game — 275, Walter Payton, Chicago Bears vs. Minnesota Vikings, Nov. 20, 1977.
Most Games, 100 Yards or more, Season — 11, O.J. Simpson, Buffalo Bills, 1973.
Most Games, 100 Yards or more, Career — 58, Jim Brown, Cleveland Browns, 1957-1965.
Most Games, 200 Yards or more, Career — 6, O.J. Simpson, Buffalo Bills, 1969-1977; San Francisco 49ers, 1978.
Most Touchdowns Rushing,, Career — 106, Jim Brown, Cleveland Browns, 1957-1965.
Most Touchdowns Rushing, Season — 19, Jim Taylor, Green Bay Packers, 1962.
Most Touchdowns Rushing, Game — 6, Ernie Nevers, Chicago Cardinals vs. Chicago Bears, Nov. 8, 1929.
Most Rushing Attempts, Season — 369, Walter Payton, Chicago Bears, 1979.
Most Rushing Attempts, Game — 41, Franco Harris, Pittsburgh vs. Cincinnati, Oct. 17, 1976.
Longest run from Scrimmage — 97 yds., Andy Uram, Green Bay vs. Chicago Cardinals, Oct. 8, 1939; Bob Gage, Pittsburgh vs. Chicago Bears, Dec. 4, 1949. (Both scored touchdown).

Leading Lifetime Passers

(Minimum 1,500 attempts)

Player	League	Yrs	Att	Comp	Yds	Pts*	Player	League	Yrs	Att	Comp	Yds	Pts*
Otto Graham	AAFC-NFL	10	2,626	1,464	23,584	86.8	Frank Ryan	NFL	13	2,133	1,090	16,042	77.7
Roger Staubach	NFL	11	2,958	1,685	22,700	83.5	Bob Griese	AFL-NFL	13	3,329	1,865	24,302	77.0
Sonny Jurgensen	NFL	18	4,262	2,433	32,224	82.8	Norm Van Brocklin	NFL	12	2,895	1,553	23,611	75.3
Len Dawson	NFL-AFL	19	3,741	2,136	28,711	82.6	Sid Luckman	NFL	12	1,744	904	14,686	75.0
Fran Tarkenton	NFL	18	6,467	3,686	47,003	80.5	Don Meredith	NFL	9	2,308	1,170	17,199	74.7
Bert Jones	NFL	7	1,592	890	11,435	80.3	Roman Gabriel	NFL	15	4,495	2,365	29,429	74.5
Bart Starr	NFL	16	3,149	1,808	24,718	80.3	Y.A. Tittle	AAFC-NFL	17	4,395	2,427	33,070	74.4
Ken Stabler	AFL-NFL	10	2,481	1,486	19,078	79.9	Earl Morrall	NFL	21	2,689	1,379	20,809	74.2
Ken Anderson	NFL	9	2,785	1,570	20,030	79.1	Greg Landry	NFL	12	2,204	1,227	15,383	73.6
Johnny Unitas	NFL	18	5,186	2,830	40,239	78.2	Frank Albert	AAFC-NFL	7	1,564	831	10,795	73.5

*Rating points based on performances in the following categories: Percentage of completions, percentage of touchdown passes, percentage of interceptions, and average gain per pass attempt.

Most Yards Gained, Season — 4,082, Dan Fouts, San Diego Chargers, 1979.
Most Yards Gained, Game — 554, Norm Van Brocklin, Los Angeles Rams vs. New York Yankees, Sept. 18, 1951 (27 completions in 41 attempts).
Most Touchdowns Passing, Career — 342, Fran Tarkenton, Minnesota Vikings, 1961-65; N.Y. Giants, 1967-71; Minnesota Vikings, 1972-78.
Most Touchdown Passing, Season — 36, George Blanda, Houston Oilers, 1961 and Y.A. Tittle, N.Y. Giants, 1963.
Most Touchdown Passing, Game — 7, Sid Luckman, Chicago Bears vs. New York Giants, Nov. 14, 1943; Adrian Burk, Philadelphia Eagles vs. Washington Redskins, Oct. 17, 1954; George Blanda, Houston Oilers vs. New York Titans, Nov. 19, 1961; Y.A. Tittle, New York Giants vs. Washington Redskins, Oct. 28, 1962; Joe Kapp, Minnesota Vikings vs. Baltimore Colts, Sept. 28, 1969.
Most Passing Attempts, Season — 578, Steve DeBerg, San Francisco 49ers, 1979.
Most Passing Attempts, Game — 68, George Blanda, Houston Oilers vs. Buffalo Bills, Nov. 1, 1964 (37 completions).
Most Passes Completed, Season — 347, Steve DeBerg, San Francisco 49ers, 1979 (578 attempts).
Most Passes Completed, Game — 37, George Blanda, Houston Oilers vs. Buffalo Bills, Nov. 1, 1964 (68 attempts).
Most Consecutive Passes Completed — 17, Bert Jones, Baltimore Colts vs. N.Y. Jets, Dec. 15, 1974.

Leading Lifetime Receivers

Player	League	Yrs	No	Yds	Avg	Player	League	Yrs	No	Yds	Avg
Charley Taylor	NFL	13	649	9,110	14.0	Don Hutson	NFL	11	488	7,991	16.4
Don Maynard	AFL-NFL	15	633	11,834	18.7	Jackie Smith	NFL	16	488	7,991	16.4
Ray Berry	NFL	13	631	9,275	14.7	Art Powell	AFL-NFL	10	479	8,046	16.8
Fred Biletnikoff	AFL-NFL	14	589	8,974	15.2	Boyd Dowler	NFL	12	474	7,270	15.4
Lionel Taylor	AFL	10	567	7,195	12.7	Pete Retzlaff	NFL	11	452	7,412	16.4
Lance Alworth	AFL-NFL	11	542	10,266	18.9	Roy Jefferson	NFL	12	451	7,539	16.7
Bobby Mitchell	NFL	11	521	7,954	15.3	Carroll Dale	NFL	14	438	8,271	18.9
Billy Howton	NFL	12	503	8,459	16.8	Paul Warfield	NFL	13	427	8,565	20.1
Harold Jackson	NFL	12	497	8,840	17.8	Mike Ditka	NFL	12	427	5,812	13.6
Tommy McDonald	NFL	12	495	8,410	17.0	Bobby Joe Conrad	NFL	12	422	5,902	14.0

Most Yards Gained, Season — 1,746, Charley Hennigan, Houston Oilers, 1961.
Most Yards Gained, Game — 303, Jim Benton, Cleveland Rams vs. Detroit Lions, Nov. 22, 1945 (10 receptions).
Most Pass Receptions, Season — 101, Charley Hennigan, Houston Oilers, 1964.
Most Pass Receptions, Game — 18, Tom Fears, Los Angeles Rams vs. Green Bay Packers, Dec. 3, 1950 (189 yards).
Most Consecutive Games, Pass Receptions — 105, Dan Abramowicz, New Orleans Saints, 1967-1973; San Francisco 49ers, 1973-1974.
Most Touchdown Passes, Career — 99, Don Hutson, Green Bay Packers, 1935-1945.
Most Touchdown Passes, Season — 17, Don Hutson, Green Bay Packers, 1942; Elroy Hirsch, Los Angeles Rams, 1951; Bill Groman, Houston Oilers, 1961.
Most Touchdown Passes, Game — 5, Bob Shaw, Chicago Cardinals vs. Baltimore Colts, Oct. 2, 1950.
Most Consecutive Games, Touchdown Passes — 11, Elroy Hirsch, Los Angeles Rams, 1950-1951; Buddy Dial, Pittsburgh, 1959-1960.

Leading Lifetime Scorers

Player	League	Yrs	TD	PAT	FG	Total
George Blanda	NFL-AFL	26	9	943	335	2,002
Lou Groza	AAFC-NFL	21	1	810	264	1,608
Jim Turner	AFL-NFL	16	1	521	304	1,439
Jim Bakken	NFL	17	0	534	282	1,380
Fred Cox	NFL	15	0	519	282	1,365
Jan Stenerud	AFL-NFL	13	0	394	279	1,231
Gino Cappelletti	AFL	11	42	350	176	1,130
Bruce Gossett	NFL	11	0	374	219	1,031
Don Cockroft	NFL	12	0	393	200	993
Garo Yepremian	AFL-NFL	12	0	407	192	983
Sam Baker	NFL	15	2	428	179	977
Lou Michaels	NFL	13	1	386	187	955*
Roy Gerela	AFL-NFL	11	0	351	184	903
Bobby Walston	NFL	12	46	365	80	881
Pete Gogolak	AFL-NFL	10	0	344	173	863
Errol Mann	NFL	11	0	315	177	846
Don Hutson	NFL	11	105	172	7	823
Paul Hornung	NFL	9	62	190	66	760
Jim Brown	NFL	9	126	0	0	756
Tom Davis	NFL	11	0	348	130	738

*Includes safety.

Most Points, Season — 176, Paul Hornung, Green Bay Packers, 1960 (15 TD's, 41 PAT's, 15 FG's).
Most Points, Game — 40, Ernie Nevers, Chicago Cardinals vs. Chicago Bears, Nov. 28, 1929 (6 TD's, 4 PAT's).
Most Touchdowns, Season — 23, O.J. Simpson, Buffalo Bills, 1975 (16 rushing, 9 pass receptions).
Most Touchdowns, Game — 6, Ernie Nevers, Chicago Cardinals vs. Chicago Bears, Nov. 28, 1929 (6 rushing); Dub Jones, Cleveland Browns vs. Chicago Bears, Nov. 25, 1951 (4 rushing, 2 pass receptions); Gale Sayers, Chicago Bears vs. San Francisco 49ers, Dec. 12, 1965 (4 rushing, 1 pass reception, 1 punt return).
Most Points After Touchdown, Season — 64, George Blanda, Houston Oilers, 1961 (65 attempts).
Most Consecutive Points After Touchdown — 234, Tommy Davis, San Francisco 49ers, 1959-1965.
Most Field Goals, Game — 7, Jim Bakken, St. Louis Cardinals vs. Pittsburgh Steelers, Sept. 24, 1967.
Most Field Goals, Season — 34, Jim Turner, New York Jets, 1968 and 1969.
Most Field Goals Attempted, Season — 49, Bruce Gossett, Los Angeles Rams, 1966; Curt Knight, Washington Redskins, 1971.
Most Field Goals Attempted, Game — 9, Jim Bakken, St. Louis Cardinals vs. Pittsburgh Steelers, Sept. 24, 1967 (7 successful).
Most Consecutive Field Goals — 16, Jan Stenerud, Kansas City Chiefs, 1969; Don Cockroft, Cleveland Browns, 1974-75.
Most Consecutive Games, Field Goal — 31, Fred Cox, Minnesota Vikings, 1968-1970.
Longest Field Goal — 63 yds., Tom Dempsey, New Orleans Saints vs. Detroit Lions, Nov. 8, 1970.
Highest Field Goal Completion Percentage, Season (14 attempts) — 88.46, Lou Groza, Cleveland Browns, 1953 (23 FG's in 26 attempts).

Pass Interceptions

Most Passes Had Intercepted, Game — 8, Jim Hardy, Chicago Cardinals vs. Philadelphia Eagles, Sept. 24, 1950 (39 attempts)
Most Passes Had Intercepted, Season — 42, George Blanda, Houston Oilers, 1962 (418 attempts).
Most Passes Had Intercepted, Career — 277, George Blanda, Chicago Bears, 1949-1958; Houston Oilers, 1960-1966; Oakland Raiders, 1967-1975 (4,000 attempts).
Most Consecutive Passes Attempted Without Interception — 294, Bart Starr, Green Bay Packers, 1964-1965.
Most Interceptions By, Season — 14, Dick Lane, Los Angeles Rams, 1952.
Most Interceptions By, Career — 81, Paul Krause, Washington Redskins, 1964-67; Minnesota Vikings, 1968-79.
Most Consecutive Games, Passes Intercepted By — 8, Tom Morrow, Oakland Raiders, 1962 (4), 1963 (4).
Most Touchdowns Scored via Pass Interceptions, Lifetime — 9, Ken Houston, Houston Oilers, 1967 (2); 1968 (2); 1969; 71 (4).

Punting

Highest Punting Average, Career (300 punts) — 45.10, Sam Baugh, Washington Redskins, 1937-1952 (338 punts).
Highest Punting Average, Season (20 punts) — 51.3, Sam Baugh, Washington Redskins, 1940 (35 punts).
Longest Punt — 98 yds., Steve O'Neal, New York Jets vs. Denver Broncos, Sept. 21, 1969.

Kickoff Returns

Most Yardage Returning Kickoffs, Career — 6,922, Ron Smith, Chicago Bears, 1965; Atlanta Falcons, 1966-67; Los Angeles Rams, 1968-69; Chicago Bears, 1970-72; San Diego Chargers, 1973; Oakland Raiders, 1974.
Most Yardage Returning Kickoffs, Season — 1,317, Bobby Jancik, Houston Oilers, 1963.
Most Yardage Ruturning Kickoffs, Game — 294, Wally Triplett, Detroit Lions vs. Los Angeles Rams, Oct. 29, 1950 (4 returns).
Most Touchdowns Scored via Kickoff Returns, Career — 6, Ollie Matson, Chicago Cardinals, 1952 (2), 1954, 1956, 1958 (2); Gale Sayers, Chicago Bears, 1965, 1966 (2), 1967 (3); Travis Williams, Green Bay Packers, 1967 (4), 1969; Los Angeles Rams, 1971.
Most Touchdowns Scored via Kickoff Returns, Season — 4, Travis Williams, Green Bay Packers, 1967; Cecil Turner, Chicago Bears, 1970.
Most Touchdowns Scored via Kickoff Returns, Game — 2, Tim Brown, Philadelphia Eagles vs. Dallas Cowboys, Nov. 6, 1966; Travis Williams, Green Bay Packers vs. Cleveland Browns, Nov. 12, 1967.
Most Kickoff Returns, Career — 275, Ron Smith, Chicago Bears, 1965; Atlanta Falcons, 1966-67; Los Angeles Rams, 1968-69; Chicago Bears, 1970-72; San Diego Chargers, 1973; Oakland Raiders, 1974.
Most Kickoff Returns, Season — 55, Bruce Harper, New York Jets, 1978, 1979; David Turner, Cincinnati Bengals, 1979.
Longest Kickoff Return — 106 yds., Al Carmichael, Green Bay Packers vs. Chicago Bears, October 7, 1956 (scored touchdown); Noland Smith, Kansas City vs. Denver, Dec. 17, 1967 (scored touchdown).

Punt Returns

Most Yardage Returning Punts, Career — 2,209, Emlen Tunnell, New York Giants, 1948-1958; Green Bay Packers, 1959-1961.
Most Yardage Returning Punts, Season — 655, Neal Colzie, Oakland Raiders, 1975.
Most Yardage Returning Punts, Game — 205, George Atkinson, Oakland Raiders vs. Buffalo Bills, Sept. 15, 1968.
Most Touchdowns Scored via Punt Returns, Career — 8, Jack Christiansen, Detroit Lions, 1951 (4), 1952 (2), 1954, 1956.
Most Punt Returns, Career — 258, Emlen Tunnell, New York Giants, 1948-1958; Green Bay Packers, 1959-1961.
Most Punt Returns, Season — 57, Eddie Brown, Washington Redskins, 1977.
Longest Punt Return — 98, Gil LeFebvre, Cincinnati Reds vs. Brooklyn Dodgers, Dec. 3, 1933 (scored touchdown); Charles West, Minnesota Vikings vs. Washington Redskins, Nov. 3, 1968 (scored touchdown).

Miscellaneous Records

Most Fumbles, Season — 17, Dan Pastorini, Houston Oilers, 1973.
Most Fumbles, Game — 7, Len Dawson, Kansas City Chiefs vs. San Diego Chargers, Nov. 15, 1964.
Longest Run with Recovered Fumble — 104 yds., Jack Tatum, Oakland Raiders vs. Green Bay Packers, Sept. 24, 1972.
Longest Winning Streak (regular season) — 17 games, Chicago Bears, 1933-1934.
Longest Undefeated Streak (includes tie games) — 29 games, Cleveland Browns, 1947-1949 (won 27, tied 2).
Most Seasons, Active Player — 26, George Blanda, Chicago Bears, 1949-1958; Houston Oilers, 1960-1966 and Oakland, 67-75.

George Halas Trophy Winners

The Halas Trophy, named after football coach George Halas, is awarded annually to the outstanding defensive player in football in a poll conducted by Murray Olderman of Newspaper Enterprise Assn.

1966	Larry Wilson, St. Louis	1971	Carl Eller, Minnesota	1976	Jerry Sherk, Cleveland
1967	Deacon Jones, Los Angeles	1972	Joe Greene, Pittsburgh	1977	Harvey Martin, Dallas
1968	Deacon Jones, Los Angeles	1973	Alan Page, Minnesota	1978	Randy Gradishar, Denver
1969	Dick Butkus, Chicago	1974	Joe Greene, Pittsburgh	1979	Lee Roy Selmon, Tampa Bay
1970	Dick Butkus, Chicago	1975	Curley Culp, Houston		

Bert Bell Memorial Trophy Winners

The Bert Bell Memorial Trophy, named after the former NFL commissioner, is awarded annually to the outstanding rookies in a poll conducted by Murray Olderman of Newspaper Enterprise Assn.

1964	Charlie Taylor, Washington, WR
1965	Gale Sayers, Chicago, RB
1966	Tommy Nobis, Atlanta, LB
1967	Mel Farr, Detroit, RB
1968	Earl McCullouch, Detroit, WR
1969	Calvin Hill, Dallas, RB
1970	Raymond Chester, Oakland, TE
1971	AFC: Jim Plunkett, New England, QB
	NFC: John Brockington, Green Bay, RB
1972	AFC: Franco Harris, Pittsburgh, RB
	NFC: Willie Buchanon, Green Bay, DB
1973	AFC: Boobie Clark, Cincinnati, RB
	NFC: Chuck Foreman, Minnesota, RB
1974	Don Woods, San Diego, RB
1975	AFC: Robert Brazile, Houston, LB
	NFC: Steve Bartkowski, Atlanta, QB
1976	AFC: Mike Haynes, New England, CB
	NFC: Sammy White, Minnesota, WR
1977	Tony Dorsett, Dallas, RB
1978	Earl Campbell, Houston, RB
1979	Ottis Anderson, St. Louis, RB

American Football League

Year	Eastern Division	Western Division	Playoff
1960	Houston Oilers (10-4-0)	L. A. Chargers (10-4-0)	Houston 24, Los Angeles 16
1961	Houston Oilers (10-3-1)	San Diego Chargers (12-2-0)	Houston 10, San Diego 3
1962	Houston Oilers (11-3-0)	Dallas Texans (11-3-0)	Dallas 20, Houston 17(b)
1963	Boston Patriots (8-6-1)(a)	San Diego Chargers (11-3-0)	San Diego 51, Boston 10
1964	Buffalo Bills (12-2-0)	San Diego Chargers (8-5-1)	Buffalo 20, San Diego 7
1965	Buffalo Bills (10-3-1)	San Diego Chargers (9-2-3)	Buffalo 23, San Diego 0
1966	Buffalo Bills (9-4-1)	Kansas City Chiefs (11-2-1)	Kansas City 31, Buffalo 7
1967	Houston Oilers (9-4-1)	Oakland Raiders (13-1-0)	Oakland 40, Houston 7
1968	New York Jets (11-3-0)	Oakland Raiders (12-2-0)(a)	New York 27, Oakland 23
1969	New York Jets (10-4-0)	Oakland Raiders (12-1-1)	Kansas City 17, Oakland 7(c)

(a) won divisional playoff (b) won at 2:45 of second overtime. (c) Kansas City defeated Jets to make playoffs.

Football Stadiums

See index for major league baseball seating capacity, and college stadiums.

Name, location	Capacity
Anaheim Stadium, Anaheim, Cal.	43,000
Arrowhead Stadium, Kansas City, Mo.	78,094
Atlanta-Fulton County Stadium	60,489
Astrodome, Houston, Tex.	50,000
Baltimore Memorial Stadium	60,020
Buffalo War Memorial Stadium	46,206
Busch Memorial Stadium, St. Louis	51,392
Candlestick Park, San Francisco, Cal.	61,246
Cleveland Municipal Stadium	80,385
Columbus (Ga.) Memorial Stadium	35,000
Cotton Bowl, Dallas, Tex.	72,000
Franklin Field, Philadelphia, Pa.	60,658
Gator Bowl, Jacksonville, Fla.	70,000
Giants Stadium, E. Rutherford, N.J.	76,500
John F. Kennedy Stadium, Philadelphia, Pa.	105,000
Robert F. Kennedy Memorial Stadium, Wash., D.C.	55,004
Kezar Stadium, San Francisco, Cal.	59,636
Kingdome, Seattle, Wash.	64,752
Ladd Memorial Stadium, Mobile, Ala.	40,605
Lambeau Field, Green Bay, Wis.	56,267
Legion Field, Birmingham, Ala.	72,000
Liberty Bowl, Memphis, Tenn.	50,180
Los Angeles Memorial Coliseum	90,000
Louisiana Superdome, New Orleans	71,330
Metropolitan Stadium, Bloomington, Minn.	48,446
Mile High Stadium, Denver, Col.	75,086
Milwaukee County Stadium	55,958
Mississippi Memorial Stadium, Jackson	46,000
Oakland-Alameda County Coliseum	54,615
Orange Bowl, Miami, Fla.	76,114
Pontiac Silverdome, Mich.	80,638
Rich Stadium, Buffalo, N.Y.	80,020
Riverfront Stadium, Cincinnati, Oh.	56,200
Rose Bowl, Pasadena, Cal.	106,721
Rubber Bowl, Akron, Oh.	35,007
San Diego Stadium	52,552
Schaefer Stadium, Foxboro, Mass.	61,279
Shea Stadium, New York, N.Y.	60,000
Soldier Field, Chicago, Ill.	58,064
Sugar Bowl, New Orleans, La.	80,982
Tampa Stadium, Tampa, Fla.	72,112
Texas Stadium, Dallas, Tex.	65,101
Three Rivers Stadium, Pittsburgh, Pa.	50,350
Veterans Stadium, Philadelphia, Pa.	66,052

Intercollegiate Rowing Association Championship

Onondaga Lake, Syracuse, N.Y. (3 miles)

Year	Winner	Time
1960	California	15:57.0
1961	California	16:49.2
1962	Cornell	17:02.9
1963	Cornell	17:24.0
1964	California (a)	6:31.1
1965	Navy	16:51.3
1966	Wisconsin	16:03.4
1967	Penn	16:15.9
1968	Penn (a)	6:15.6
1969	Penn (a)	6:30.4
1970	Washington (a)	6:39.3
1971	Cornell (a)	6:06.0
1972	Penn (a)	6:22.6
1973	Wisconsin (a)	6:21.0
1974	Wisconsin (a)	6:33.0
1975	Wisconsin (a)	6:08.2
1976	California (a)	6:31.0
1977	Cornell (a)	6:32.4
1978	Syracuse (a)	6:39.5
1979	Brown (a)	6:26.4
1980	Navy (a)	6:46.0

(a) race at 2,000 meters

Professional Sports Directory

Baseball

Commissioner's Office
75 Rockefeller Plaza
New York, NY 10019

National League

National League Office
1 Rockefeller Plaza
New York, NY 10020

Atlanta Braves
PO Box 4064
Atlanta, GA 30302

Chicago Cubs
Wrigley Field
Chicago, IL 60613

Cincinnati Reds
100 Riverfront Stadium
Cincinnati, OH 45202

Houston Astros
Astrodome
P.O. Box 288
Houston, TX 77001

Los Angeles Dodgers
Dodger Stadium
1000 Elysian Park Ave.
Los Angeles, CA 90012

Montreal Expos
PO Box 500, Station M
Montreal, Quebec H1V 3P2

New York Mets
William A. Shea Stadium
Roosevelt Ave. & 126th St.
Flushing, NY 11368

Philadelphia Phillies
PO Box 7575
Philadelphia, PA 19101

Pittsburgh Pirates
600 Stadium Circle
Pittsburgh, PA 15212

St. Louis Cardinals
Busch Memorial Stadium
250 Stadium Plaza
St. Louis, MO 63102

San Diego Padres
PO Box 2000
San Diego, CA 92120

San Francisco Giants
Candlestick Park
San Francisco, CA 94124

American League

American League Office
280 Park Ave.
New York, NY 10017

Baltimore Orioles
Memorial Stadium
Baltimore, MD 21218

Boston Red Sox
24 Yawkey Way
Boston, MA 02215

California Angels
Anaheim Stadium
2000 State College Blvd.
Anaheim, CA 92806

Chicago White Sox
Comiskey Park
Dan Ryan & 35th St.
Chicago, IL 60616

Cleveland Indians
Cleveland Stadium
Cleveland, OH 44114

Detroit Tigers
Tiger Stadium
Detroit, MI 48216

Kansas City Royals
Harry S. Truman Sports Complex
PO Box 1969
Kansas City, MO 64141

Milwaukee Brewers
Milwaukee County Stadium
Milwaukee, WI 53214

Minnesota Twins
Metropolitan Stadium
8001 Cedar Ave.
Bloomington, MN 55420

New York Yankees
Yankee Stadium
Bronx, NY 10451

Oakland A's
Oakland-Alameda County Coliseum
Oakland, CA 94621

Seattle Mariners
PO Box 4100
Seattle, WA 98104

Texas Rangers
Arlington Stadium
PO Box 1111
Arlington, TX 76010

Toronto Blue Jays
Box 7777
Adelaide St. PO
Toronto, Ont. M5C 2K7

National Basketball Association

League Office
Olympic Tower
645 5th Ave.
New York, NY 10022

Atlanta Hawks
100 Techwood Drive NW
Atlanta, GA 30303

Boston Celtics
Boston Garden
North Station
Boston, MA 02114

Chicago Bulls
333 North Michigan Ave.
Chicago, IL 60601

Cleveland Cavaliers
The Coliseum
2923 Streetsboro Rd.
Richfield, OH 44286

Dallas Mavericks
6830 Dartbrook
Dallas, TX 75240

Denver Nuggets
PO Box 4286
Denver, CO 80204

Detroit Pistons
Pontiac Silverdome
1200 Featherstone
Pontiac, MI 48057

Golden State Warriors
Oakland Coliseum Arena
Oakland, CA 94621

Houston Rockets
The Summit
Houston, TX 77046

Indiana Pacers
Market Square Center
151 N. Delaware
Indianapolis, IN 46204

Kansas City Kings
1800 Genessee
Kansas City, MO 64102

Portland Trail Blazers
Lloyd Bldg.
700 NE Multnomah St.
Portland, OR 97232

San Antonio Spurs
HemisFair Arena
P.O. Box 530
San Antonio, TX 78292

San Diego Clippers
San Diego Sports Arena
3500 Sports Arena Blvd.
San Diego, CA 92110

Seattle SuperSonics
419 Occidental South
Seattle, WA 98104

Utah Jazz
Salt Palace
100 SW Temple
Salt Lake City, UT 84101

Washington Bullets
1 Harry S. Truman Dr.
Landover, MD 20786

Los Angeles Lakers
The Forum
3900 W. Manchester Blvd.
or PO Box 10
Inglewood, CA 90306

Milwaukee Bucks
901 North 4th St.
Milwaukee, WI 53203

New Jersey Nets
185 E. Union Ave.
E. Rutherford, NJ 07073

New York Knickerbockers
Madison Square Garden Center
4 Pennsylvania Plaza
New York, NY 10001

Philadelphia 76ers
Veterans Stadium
PO Box 25040
Philadelphia, PA 19147

Phoenix Suns
PO Box 1369
Phoenix, AZ 85001

National Hockey League

League Headquarters
960 Sun Life Bldg.
Montreal, Quebec H3B 2W2

Boston Bruins
150 Causeway St.
Boston, MA 02114

Buffalo Sabres
Memorial Auditorium
Buffalo, NY 14202

Calgary Flames
1500 Home Oil Tower
Calgary, Alta. T2P 2Z2

Chicago Black Hawks
1800 W. Madison St.
Chicago, IL 60612

Colorado Rockies
McNichols Sports Arena
Denver, CO 80204

Detroit Red Wings
5920 Grand River Ave.
Detroit, MI 48208

Edmonton Oilers
Edmonton Coliseum
Edmonton, Alta. T5B 4M9

Hartford Whalers
One Civic Center Plaza
Hartford, CT 06103

Los Angeles Kings
PO Box 10
Inglewood, CA 90306

Minnesota North Stars
7901 Cedar Ave. S.
Bloomington, MN 55420

Montreal Canadiens
2313 St. Catherine St., West
Montreal, Quebec H3H 1N2

New York Islanders
Nassau Coliseum
Uniondale, NY 11553

New York Rangers
Madison Square Garden
4 Pennsylvania Plaza
New York, NY 10001

Philadelphia Flyers
The Spectrum
Pattison Place
Philadelphia, PA 19148

Pittsburgh Penguins
Civic Arena
Pittsburgh, PA 15219

Quebec Nordiques
5555 3ieme Ave. Ouest
Charlesbourg, Quebec G1H 6R1

St. Louis Blues
5700 Oakland Ave.
St. Louis, MO 63110

Toronto Maple Leafs
60 Carlton St.
Toronto, Ont. M5B 1L1

Vancouver Canucks
100 North Renfrew St.
Vancouver, B.C. V5K 3N7

Washington Capitals
Capital Centre
Landover, MD 20786

Winnipeg Jets
15-1430 Maroons Road
Winnipeg, Man. R3G 0L5

National Football League

League Office
410 Park Avenue
New York, NY 10022

Atlanta Falcons
Suwanee Road
Suwanee, GA 30174

Baltimore Colts
Executive Plaza
Hunt Valley, MD 21031

Buffalo Bills
1 Bills Drive
Orchard Park, NY 14127

Chicago Bears
55 E. Jackson Blvd.
Chicago, IL 60604

Cincinnati Bengals
200 Riverfront Stadium
Cincinnati, OH 45202

Cleveland Browns
Cleveland Stadium
Cleveland, OH 44114

Dallas Cowboys
6116 North Central Expressway
Dallas, TX 75206

Denver Broncos
5700 Logan St.
Denver, CO 80216

Detroit Lions
1200 Featherstone Rd.
Box 4200
Pontiac, MI 48507

Green Bay Packers
1265 Lombardi Ave.
Green Bay, WI 54303

Houston Oilers
P.O. Box 1516
Houston, TX 77001

Kansas City Chiefs
1 Arrowhead Drive
Kansas City, MO 64129

Los Angeles Rams
10271 W. Pico Blvd.
Los Angeles, CA 90064

Miami Dolphins
330 Biscayne Blvd.
Miami, FL 33132

Minnesota Vikings
7110 France Ave. So.
Edina, MN 55435

New England Patriots
Schaefer Stadium
Foxboro, MA 02035

New Orleans Saints
1500 Poydras St.
New Orleans, LA 70112

New York Giants
Giants Stadium
E. Rutherford, NJ 07073

New York Jets
598 Madison Ave.
New York, NY 10022

Oakland Raiders
7811 Oakport St.
Oakland, CA 94621

Philadelphia Eagles
Veterans Stadium
Philadelphia, PA 19148

Pittsburgh Steelers
Three Rivers Stadium
Pittsburgh, PA 15212

St. Louis Cardinals
200 Stadium Plaza
St. Louis, MO 63102

San Diego Chargers
San Diego Stadium
P.O. Box 20666
San Diego, CA 92120

San Francisco 49ers
711 Nevada St.
Redwood City, CA 94061

Seattle Seahawks
5305 Lake Washington Blvd.
Kirkland, WA 98033

Tampa Bay Buccaneers
1 Buccaneer Place
Tampa, FL 33607

Washington Redskins
PO Box 17247
Dulles Intl. Airport
Washington, DC 20041

North American Soccer League

League Office
1133 Ave. of the Americas
Suite 3500
New York, NY 10036

Atlanta Chiefs
PO Box 5015
Atlanta, GA 30302

California Surf
PO Box 4449
Anaheim, CA 92803

Chicago Sting
Suite 1525
333 N. Michigan Ave.
Chicago, IL 60601

Dallas Tornado
6116 N. Central Expwy.
Dallas, TX 75206

Detroit Express
Pontiac Silverdome
1200 Featherstone Road
Pontiac, MI 48057

Edmonton Drillers
10039 Jasper Ave.
Edmonton, Alta. T5J 1T4

Ft. Lauderdale Strikers
1350 North East 56th St.
Ft. Lauderdale, FL 33334

Houston Hurricane
PO Box 27229
Houston, TX 77042

Los Angeles Aztecs
777 Rose Bowl Drive
Pasadena, CA 91103

Memphis Rogues
2200 Union Ave.
Memphis, TN 38104

Minnesota Kicks
7200 France Ave. So.
Minneapolis, MN 55435

New England Tea Men
34 Mechanic St.
Foxboro, MA 02035

New York Cosmos
75 Rockefeller Plaza
New York, NY 10019

Philadelphia Fury
Veterans Stadium
Broad St. & Pattison Ave.
Philadelphia, PA 19148

Portland Timbers
910 Southwest 18th
Portland, OR 97205

Rochester Lancers
812 Wilder Bldg.
Rochester, NY 14614

San Diego Sockers
San Diego Stadium
9449 Friars Road
San Diego, CA 92108

San Jose Earthquakes
Suite 272
2025 Gateway Place
San Jose, CA 95110

Seattle Sounders
419 Occidental South
Seattle, WA 98104

Tampa Bay Rowdies
Suite 109
1311 N. West Shore Blvd.
Tampa, FL 33607

Toronto Blizzard
Exhibition Stadium
Toronto, Ont. M6K 3C3

Tulsa Roughnecks
PO Box 35190
Tulsa, OK 75135

Vancouver Whitecaps
3683 E. Hastings St.
Vancouver, B.C. V5K 2B1

Washington Diplomats
RFK Stadium
E. Capitol Sts. & 22d NE
Washington, DC 20003

National AAU Senior Boxing Championships in 1980

Las Vegas, Nev., May 5-11, 1980

106 lbs.—Robert Shannon, Edmonds, Wash.
112 lbs.—Richard Sandoval, Pomona, Cal.
119 lbs.—Jackie Beard, Jackson, Tenn.
125 lbs.—Clifford Gray, Boynton Beach, Fla.
132 lbs.—Melvin Paul, New Orleans, La.
139 lbs.—Johnny Bumphus, Houston, Tex.
147 lbs.—Ronald Hatcher, Ft. Worth, Tex.
156 lbs.—Don Bowers, Jackson, Tenn.
165 lbs.—Martin Pierce, Flint, Mich.
178 lbs.—Jeff Lampkin, Youngstown, Oh.
Heavyweight—Marvis Frazier, Philadelphia, Pa.

American Bowling Congress Championships in 1980

77th Tournament, Louisville, Ky.

Regular Division

Individual

1. Mike Eaton, Grand Rapids, Mich. 245, 258, 279 — 782.
2. Tim Rogers, Newark, Oh., 256, 254, 258 — 768.
3. Roger Dodson, Newark, Oh., 245, 267, 243 — 755.

Runners-up — John Megna, Milwaukee, Wis., 747; Tom Greenwis, Cleveland, Oh., 744; Tom Eder, North Vernon, Ind., 740; David Causey, Louisville, Ky., 738; John Matus Jr., Allentown, Pa., 736; Randy Walters, Dover, Oh., 734; Rick Sajek, Portage, Ind., 733.

All Events

1. Steve Fehr, Cincinnati, Oh., 673, 710, 693 — 2,076.
2. Matts Karlsson, Stockholm, Sweden, 693, 695, 685 — 2,073.
3. Bob Bures, Cleveland, Oh., 607, 761, 664 — 2,032.

Runners-up — Joe Vito Buenrostro, San Antonio, Tex., 2,025; Jerry Edwards, Chicago, Ill., 2,007; Gordy Baer, Chicago, Ill., 2,005; Chris Neidert, Akron, Oh., 2,003; Bob Goike, Detroit, Mich., 2,003; Bob Freehauf, San Antonio, Tex., 1,998; Jack Calhoun, Columbus, Oh., 1,998.

Doubles

1. Ron Thacker, Cleveland, Oh., 188, 201, 228 — 617; Bob Bures, Cleveland, Oh., 246, 267, 248 — 761. Aggregate — 1,378.
2. Dave Howlett, Louisville, Ky., 224, 215, 234 — 673; Jim Kirchner, Louisville, Ky., 201, 231, 267 — 699. Aggregate — 1,372.
3. Carlos Castanada, San Antonio, Tex., 215, 220, 224 — 659; Joe Vito Buenrostro. San Antonio, Tex., 216, 247, 236 — 699. Aggregate — 1,358.

Team

1. Stroh's Beer, Detroit, Mich. — Dennis Graziani 179, 204, 173 — 556; Bob Basacchi 167, 235, 212 — 614; Harry Campbell 227, 190, 214 — 631; Bob Chamberlain 198, 267, 178 — 643; Edwin Peart 210, 279, 186 — 675. Aggregate —3,119.
2. Spectrum East Bowling Supply, Tulsa, Okla. — Billy Young Jr. 204, 230, 226 — 660; Wally Cummings 200, 186, 208 — 594; Rick Majors 169, 203, 214 — 586; Bill Ryan 235, 213, 216 — 664; Trach Patterson 200, 194, 216 — 610. Aggregate —3,114.

Booster Division

Team

1. Aqua Lanes, Edgerton, Minn. — Dave Van Stelten 184, 191, 158 — 533; Don Post 264, 211, 177 — 652; Rick Fey 158, 167, 199 — 524; Clyde DeBoer 176, 242, 205 — 623; Virg Van Hulzen 156, 185, 164 — 505. Aggregate — 2,837.
2. Lefty's Lounge, Chicago, Ill. — Don Costello 226, 181, 147 — 554; Mike Nicholas 156, 171, 193 — 520; Jerry Silman 224, 237, 159 — 620; Mike Kurszak 158, 180, 223 — 563; Tom Baker 186, 191, 191 — 568. Aggregate — 2,825.

Other Bowling Championships in 1980

U.S. Open — Men — Windsor Locks, Conn., Mar. 16-22: Steve Martin, Kingsport, Tenn., average 218, prize $21,000. Women — Rockford, Ill., Apr. 21-26: Pat Costello, Union City, Cal., average 201, prize $8,000.

National Intercollegiate Championships — Men — Louisville, Ky., Apr. 1-2; doubles (tie) — Marty Schram, San Jose State and Mike Fegel, Santa Clara; Tim Tyler, Univ. of Wis.-La Crosse and Bob Worrall, Northern Arizona; singles, Don Garrett, Univ. of Tenn.; all events, Bob Worrall, Northern Arizona. Women — Seattle, Wash., Apr. 7; doubles, Terry Yoshihara, Hillsborough C.C. and Michele Sullivan, West Texas State; singles, Terry Yoshihara; all events, Terry Yoshihara.

National Collegiate Team Championship — Milwaukee, Wis., May 1-3; Men — Wichita State. Women — Erie C.C.

Masters Bowling Tournament Champions

Year	Winner	Runner-up	W-L	Avg
1970	Don Glover, Bakersfield, Cal.	Bob Strampe, Detroit	9-1	215
1971	Jim Godman, Lorain, Oh.	Don Johnson, Akron	9-1	229
1972	Bill Beach, Sharon, Pa.	Jim Godman, Lorain, Oh.	8-1	220
1973	Dave Soutar, Gilroy, Cal.	Dick Ritger, Hartford, Wis.	7-0	218
1974	Paul Colwell, Tucson	Steve Neff, Sarasota, Fla.	7-0	234
1975	Ed Ressler Jr., Allentown, Pa.	Sam Flanagan, Parkersburg, W. Va.	9-1	213
1976	Nelson Burton Jr., St. Louis	Steve Carson, Oklahoma City	7-0	220
1977	Earl Anthony, Tacoma, Wash.	Jim Godman, Lorain, Oh.	7-0	218
1978	Frank Ellenburg, Mesa, Ariz.	Earl Anthony, Tacoma, Wash.	8-1	200
1979	Doug Myers, El Toro, Cal.	Bill Spigner, Hamden, Conn.	7-1	202
1980	Neil Burton, St. Louis, Mo.	Mark Roth, North Arlington, N.J.	7-1	206

All-Time Records for League and Tournament Play

Type of record	Holder of record	Year	Score	Competition
High team total	Budweiser Beer, St. Louis	1958	3,858	League
High team game	V. Loria & Sons, Paramus, N.J.	1979	1,350	League
High doubles total	Nelson Burton Jr., Billy Walden, St. Louis	1970	1,614	Tournament
High doubles game	Jesse Foley and Wendell Cromer, Shreveport, La.	1976	598*	League
High individual total	Albert Brandt, Lockport, N.Y.	1939	886	League
High all events score	Denny Campbell, Chicago	1976	2,314	Tournament

* In 4-person league.

Record Averages for Consecutive Tournaments

No. in row	Holder of record	Span	Games	Average
Two	Jim Godman, Lorain, Oh.	1974-75	18	228.78
Three	Jim Godman, Lorain, Oh.	1974-76	27	223.96
Four	Jim Godman, Lorain, Oh.	1974-77	36	219.44
Five	Jim Godman, Lorain, Oh.	1973-77	45	216.33
Ten	Bob Strampe, Detroit	1961-70	111	211.10

Official Records of Annual ABC Tournaments

Type of record	Holder of record	Year	Score
High team total	Ace Mitchell Shur-Hooks, Akron	1966	3,357
High team game	Falstaff Beer, San Antonio	1958	1,226
High doubles score	John Klares-Steve Nagy, Cleveland	1952	1,453
High doubles game	Tommy Hudson, Akron, Ohio-Les Zikes, Chicago	1976	558
High singles total	Mickey Higham, Kansas City, Mo.	1977	801
High all events score	Jim Godman, Lorain, Oh.	1974	2,184
High team all events	Chadwick Studio, Houston, Tex.	1980	9,628
High life-time pin total	Bill Doehrman, Ft. Wayne	1908-1980	108,741

Bowlers with 6 or More Sanctioned 300 Games

Elvin Mesger, Sullivan, Mo. 27
George Billick, Old Forge, Pa. 17
Dick Weber, St. Louis 17
Don Johnson, Las Vegas 16
Dave Soutar, Gilroy, Cal. 15
Ron Graham, Louisville 15
Al Faragalli, Wayne, N.J. 14
Don Carter, Miami, Fla. 13
Ray Bluth, St. Louis 12
Walter Ward, Cleveland 12
Casey Jones, Plymouth, Wis. 12
Dennis Soper, Tustin, Cal. 12
John Wilcox Jr., Shavertown, Pa. . . . 12
Dave Williams, Sebastopol, Cal. 12
*Hank Marino, Milwaukee 11
Frank Clause, Old Forge, Pa. 11
Ed Lubanski, Detroit 11
Pat Patterson, St. Louis 11
Norm Meyers, St. Louis, Mo. 11
Jim Ewald, Louisville, Ky. 11
Mike Durbin, Lorain, Oh. 10
George Pappas, Charlotte, N.C. 10
Boss Bosco, Akron 9
Mickey Higham, Kansas City, Mo. . . . 9
Al Savas, Milwaukee 9
Lou Foxie, Paterson, N.J. 9
Jerry Woji, Stockton, Cal. 9
Tom Hennessey, St. Louis 9
Russell Field, San Jose, Cal. 9
Roger Fink, Lodi, Cal. 9
Howard Holmes, Los Angeles 8
Dennis Wright, Milwaukee 8
Ray Eklund, Milwaukee. 8
Walter King, Detroit 8
Junie McMahon, Lodi, N.J. 8
Bud Horn, Los Angeles. 8
Jim Godman, Lorain, Oh. 8
Don Dubro, St. Louis 8
Joe Donato, Schenectady, N.Y. 7
Eddie Botten, Union City, N.J. 7
Dick Hoover, Akron 7
Ken McKenzie, Dallas 7
Ray Schanen, Milwaukee 7
Wayne Pinkalla, Milwaukee 7
Bob Ramirez, Los Angeles. 7
Don McCune, Munster, Ind. 7
Don Glover, Rosenberg, Tex. 7
Mark Sutter, St. Louis. 7
Salvatore Bivona, Paterson, N.J. 6
Lou Campi, Dumont, N.J. 6
Ed Davis, Milford, N.J. 6
*Bill Flynn, Cleveland. 6
Sam Garofalo, St. Louis 6
Joe Joseph, Lansing, Mich. 6
Pete Kozloski, Plains, Pa. 6
Vince Lucci, Trenton, N.J. 6
Steve Nagy, Cleveland. 6
Frank Pollak, Pittsburgh 6
Robert Pinkalla, Milwaukee 6
Harold Schaeffer, St. Louis 6
Harry Smith, Rochester, N.Y. 6
Bob Strampe, Detroit 6
Jerry Tharp, St. Louis. 6
George Tomek, Plymouth, Pa. 6
Stephen Tomek, Plymouth, Pa. 6
William Capleton, Prospect Park, N.J. . 6

*Bowled two 300 games in official 3-game series.

Women's International Bowling Congress Champions

Individual	All events	Year	2-woman teams	5-woman teams
Shirley Garms, Island Lake, Ill. . . . 702	Judy Soutar, Kansas City, Mo. . . . 1,944	1974	Jane Leszczynski, Milwaukee-Carol Miller, Waukesha, Wis. 1,313	Kalicak International Construction, Kansas City, Mo. . . 2,973
Barbara Leicht, Albany, N.Y. 689	Virginia Norton South Gate, Cal. . . . 1,821	1975	Jennette James, Oyster Bay, Dawn Raddatz, Northport, N.Y. 1,234	Atlanta Bowling Center (Ga.) Buffalo, N.Y. 2,836
Beverly Shonk, Canton, Oh. 686	Betty Morris, Stockton, Cal. 1,866	1976	Georgene Cordes-Shirley Sjostrom, Bloomington, Minn.; Eloise Vacco-Debbie Rainone, Cleveland Hts., Oh. (tie). . . 1,232	PWBA 1, Oklahoma City, Okla. 2,839
Akiko Yamaga, Tokyo 714	Akiko Yamaga 1,895	1977	Ozella Houston-Dorothy Jackson, Detroit, Mich. 1,234	Allgauer's Restaurant Chicago, Ill. 2,818
Mae Bolt, Berwyn, Ill. 709	Annese Keily, Brooklyn, N.Y. 1,896	1978	Barbara Shelton, Annese Kelly, New York, N.Y. 1,211	Cook County Vending, Chicago, Ill. 2,956
Betty Morris, Stockton, Cal. . . . 699	Betty Morris, Stockton, Cal. 1,945	1979	Mary Ann Deptula, Geri Beattie, Warren, Dearborn Hts., Mich. . 1,314	Alpine Lanes, Euless, Tex. 3,096
Bobbie Soldan, Costa Mesa, Cal. . 706	Toni Starin, Midwest City, Okla. . . 1,910	1980	Dorothy Gothergill, N. Attleboro, Mass. & Mildred Martorella, Rochester, N.Y. 1,238	Walker's Body Shop, Aurora, Ill. 2,703

Most Sanctioned 300 Games

Betty Morris, Stockton, Cal. 5
Beverly Ortner, Tuscon, Ariz. 4
Sylvia Wene Martin, Philadelphia, Pa. . 3
Donna Adamek, Durate, Cal. 2
Mary Altmeyer, St. Louis, Mo. 2
Shirley Anderson, Anaheim, Cal. 2
Sandra Bigley, Ventura, Cal. 2
Marjorie Caruso, Hayward, Cal. 2
Velda Gooden, Richmond, Cal. 2
Regi Jonak, St. Louis, Mo. 2
Kathy LeCroy, Fort Worth, Tex. 2
Jeanne Maiden, Willowick, Oh. 2
Joan McRae, Northridge, Cal. 2
Gail Menke, St. Louis, Mo. 2
Betty Mivelaz, Tujunga, Cal. 2
Vickie Myers, Sunland, Cal. 2
Edie Jo (Neal) Norman, Miami, Fla. . . 2
Virginia Norton, South Gate, Cal. 2
Pat Petersohn, San Jose, Cal. 2
Connie Pick, N. Hollywood, Cal. 2
Carol Pike, Cypress, Cal. 2
Joli Pollard, Lee's Summit, Mo. 2
Norma Rittelmeyer, Dallas, Tex. 2
Patricia Robinette, Louisville, Ky. . . . 2
Janet Rohrbaugh, Santa Barbara, Cal. 2
Ruby Thomas, Abilene, Tex. 2
Dina Wheeler, Independence, Mo. . . . 2
Jean Worthy, Norwalk, Cal. 2

Sanctioned 300 Games During 1979-80 Season

Gloria Alderman, Fort Worth, Tex.; Sandra Alexander, Huntington Beach, Cal.; Shirley Anderson, Anaheim, Cal.; Jayne Attanasio, Philadelphia, Pa.; Terry Ayers, Fountain Valley, Cal.; Patti Balcomb, Levittown, Pa.; Cathy Barthle, Hialeah, Fla.; Debbie Bennett, Akron, Oh.; Sandra Bigley, Ventura, Cal.; Carol Blum, Fort Pierce, Fla.; Mary Boucher, Deerfield Beach, Fla.; Paula Carter, Miami, Fla.; Sally Casale, Beaverton, Ore.; Cindy Coburn, Buffalo, N.Y.; Karen Crowther, Northridge, Cal.; Edwina Dempsey, Wilmington, Del.; Ruth Dozier, Dayton, Oh.; Geneva Duvall, St. Louis, Mo.; Ruth Farris, Hurst, Tex.; Gloria Fenske, Mukwonago, Wis.; Cindy Fournier, West Linn, Ore.; Kay Hollenbeck, Belleville, Mich.; Gail Holmes, Rockville Centre, N.Y.; Dee Hughes, Maryville, Tenn.; Ruby Jacobsen, Fort Dodge, Ia.; Virginia Johnson, Broken Arrow, Okla.; Regi Jonak, St. Louis, Mo.; Nancy Koester, Saginaw, Mich.; Rose Kotnik, Brook Park, Oh.; Wilma LaGris, Portland, Ore.; Kathy LeCroy, Fort Worth, Tex.; Mary Lightner, South Bend, Ind.; Jean Miens, Duluth, Minn.; Kathy Miguel, Chico, Cal.; Theresa Monaco, Independence, Mo.; Lyn Nelson, Roseville, Minn.; Carol Norman, Ardmore, Okla.; Beverly Perry, Arcata, Cal.; Connie Pick, N. Hollywood, Cal.; Carol Pike, Cypress, Cal.; Bev Riley, Independence, Mo.; Sheila Rosenblatt, Hallandale, Fla.; Ruby Thomas, Dayton, Oh.; Margaret Walker, Richardson, Tex.; Delores Ward, Jacksonville, Fla.; Dina Wheeler, Independence, Mo.; Rita Williams, South Elgin, Ill.; Linda Wilson, Lyndhurst, N.J.

PBA Winter Tour, 1980

Date	Event	Winner	Winner's share
Jan. 5	ARC Alameda Open, Alameda, Cal.	Warren Nelson	$10,000
Jan. 12	Showboat Invitational, Las Vegas	Wayne Webb	21,000
Jan. 19	Miller High Life Classic, Anaheim, Cal.	Gary Dickinson	21,000
Jan. 26	Quaker State Open, Grand Prairie, Tex.	Hugh Miller	15,000
Feb. 2	Rolaids Open, Florissant, Mo.	Alvin Lou	15,000
Feb. 9	Midas Open, Palatine, Ill.	Mike Aulby	20,000
Feb. 16	AMF MagicScore Open, Peoria, Ill.	Joe Hutchinson	20,000
Feb. 23	Ford Open, No. Olmsted, Oh.	Kyle Shedd	15,000
Mar. 1	True Value Open, Miami, Fla.	Palmer Fallgren	20,000
Mar. 8	Fair Lanes Open, Adelphi, Md.	Nelson Burton Jr.	11,000
Mar. 15	Long Island Open, Garden City, N.Y.	Earl Anthony	10,000
Mar. 22	BPAA U.S. Open, Windsor Locks, Conn.	Steve Martin	21,000
Mar. 29	PBA Championship, Sterling Heights, Mich.	Johnny Petraglia	15,000
Apr. 5	Miller High Life Open, Milwaukee	Alvin Lou	21,000
Apr. 12	King Louie Open, Overland Park, Kan.	Ernie Schlegel	11,000
Apr. 19	Firestone Tournament of Champions, Akron	Wayne Webb	30,000

Leading Averages in 1979

(16 or More Tournaments)

Pos.	Name, City	Tournaments	Games	Pinfall	Average
1.	Mark Roth, North Arlington, N.J.	26	977	216564	221.662
2.	Earl Anthony, Kent, Wash.	27	925	203067	219.532
3.	Marshall Holman, Medford, Ore.	29	1096	238000	217.153
4.	Ed Ressler Jr., Bethlehem, Pa.	34	1086	235548	216.895
5.	Tom Baker, Buffalo, N.Y.	28	799	172865	216.352
6.	Dennis Lane, Kingsport, Tenn.	25	741	160073	216.023
7.	Gary Dickinson, Ft. Worth, Tex.	29	800	172608	215.760
8.	Dick Ritger, River Falls, Wis.	16	559	120426	215.431
9.	George Pappas, Charlotte, N.C.	29	826	177803	215.258
10.	Joe Berardi, Pearl River, N.Y.	31	977	210271	215.221
11.	Gil Sliker, Washington, N.J.	32	999	214668	214.883
12.	Mike Durbin, Chagrin Falls, Oh.	32	881	189046	214.581
13.	Butch Soper, Whittier, Cal.	31	916	196365	214.372
14.	Cliff McNealy, San Lorenzo, Cal.	25	700	150018	214.311
15.	Nelson Burton Jr., St. Louis, Mo.	22	688	147282	214.073

Firestone Tournament of Champions

This is professional bowling's richest tournament and has been held each year since its inception in 1965, in Akron, Oh., the home of the Professional Bowlers Association. First prize is $30,000.

Year	Winner	Year	Winner	Year	Winner	Year	Winner
1965	Billy Hardwick	1969	Jim Godman	1973	Jim Godman	1977	Mike Berlin
1966	Wayne Zahn	1970	Don Johnson	1974	Earl Anthony	1978	Earl Anthony
1967	Jim Stefanich	1971	Johnny Petraglia	1975	Dave Davis	1979	George Pappas
1968	Dave Davis	1972	Mike Durbin	1976	Marshall Holman	1980	Wayne Webb

Leading PBA Averages by Year

Year	Bowler	Tournaments	Average	Year	Bowler	Tournaments	Average
1962	Don Carter, St. Louis, Mo.	25	212.844	1971	Don Johnson, Akron, Oh.	31	213.977
1963	Billy Hardwick, Louisville, Ky.	26	210.346	1972	Don Johnson, Akron, Oh.	30	215.290
1964	Ray Bluth, St. Louis, Mo.	27	210.512	1973	Earl Anthony, Tacoma, Wash.	29	215.799
1965	Dick Weber, St. Louis, Mo.	19	211.895	1974	Earl Anthony, Tacoma, Wash.	28	219.394
1966	Wayne Zahn, Atlanta, Ga.	27	208.663	1975	Earl Anthony, Tacoma, Wash.	30	219.060
1967	Wayne Zahn, Atlanta, Ga.	29	212.342	1976	Mark Roth, New York, N.Y.	28	215.970
1968	Jim Stefanich, Joliet, Ill.	33	211.895	1977	Mark Roth, New York, N.Y.	28	218.174
1969	Bill Hardwick, Louisville, Ky.	33	212.957	1978	Mark Roth, North Arlington, N.J.	25	219.834
1970	Nelson Burton Jr., St. Louis, Mo.	32	214.908	1979	Mark Roth, North Arlington, N.J.	26	221.662

PBA Leading Money Winners

Total winnings are from PBA, ABC Masters, and BPAA All-Star tournaments only, and do not include numerous other tournaments or earnings from special television shows and matches.

Year	Bowler	Dollars	Year	Bowler	Dollars	Year	Bowler	Dollars
1960	Don Carter	22,525	1967	Dave Davis	54,165	1974	Earl Anthony	99,585
1961	Dick Weber	26,280	1968	Jim Stefanich	67,377	1975	Earl Anthony	107,585
1962	Don Carter	49,972	1969	Billy Hardwick	64,160	1976	Earl Anthony	110,833
1963	Dick Weber	46,333	1970	Mike McGrath	52,049	1977	Mark Roth	105,583
1964	Bob Strampe	33,592	1971	Johnny Petraglia	85,065	1978	Mark Roth	134,500
1965	Dick Weber	47,674	1972	Don Johnson	56,648	1979	Mark Roth	124,517
1966	Wayne Zahn	54,720	1973	Don McCune	69,000			

Boxing Champions by Classes

As of Aug., 1980 the only universally accepted title holder was in the middleweight division. The following are the recognized champions of the World Boxing Association and the World Boxing Council.

	WBA	WBC
Heavyweight	Mike Weaver, Los Angeles, Cal.	Larry Holmes, Easton, Pa.
Light Heavyweight	Eddie Mustava Muhammad, Brooklyn, N.Y.	Matthew Saad Muhammad, Philadelphia, Pa.
Middleweight	Alan Minter, England	Alan Minter, England
Jr. Middleweight	Alub Kalule, Denmark	Maurice Hope, England
Welterweight	Thomas Hearns, Detroit, Mich.	Roberto Duran, Panama
Jr. Welterweight	Aaron Pryor, Cincinnati, Oh.	Saoul Mamby, New York, N.Y.
Lightweight	Hilmer Kenty, Detroit, Mich.	Jim Watt, Scotland
Jr. Lightweight	Sammy Serrano, Puerto Rico	Alexis Arguello, Nicaragua
Featherweight	Eusebio Pedroza, Panama	Salvadore Sanchez, Mexico
Jr. Featherweight	Leo Randolph, Tacoma, Wash.	Wilfredo Gomez, Puerto Rico
Bantamweight	Jorge Lujan, Panama	Lupe Pintor, Mexico
Flyweight	Tae-Shik Kim, So. Korea	Shoji Oguma, Japan

Ring Champions by Years

*Abandoned title

Heavyweights

1882-1892	John L. Sullivan (a)
1892-1897	James J. Corbett (b)
1897-1899	Robert Fitzsimmons
1899-1905	James J. Jeffries (c)
1905-1906	Marvin Hart
1906-1908	Tommy Burns
1908-1915	Jack Johnson
1915-1919	Jess Willard
1919-1926	Jack Dempsey
1926-1928	Gene Tunney*
1928-1930	vacant
1930-1932	Max Schmeling
1932-1933	Jack Sharkey
1933-1934	Primo Carnera
1934-1935	Max Baer
1935-1937	James J. Braddock
1937-1949	Joe Louis*
1949-1951	Ezzard Charles
1951-1952	Joe Walcott
1952-1956	Rocky Marciano*
1956-1959	Floyd Patterson
1959-1960	Ingemar Johansson
1960-1962	Floyd Patterson
1962-1964	Sonny Liston
1964-1967	Cassius Clay* (Muhammad Ali) (d)
1970-1973	Joe Frazier
1973-1974	George Foreman
1974-1978	Muhammad Ali
1978-1979	Leon Spinks (e), Muhammad Ali*
1978	Ken Norton (WBC), Larry Holmes (WBC)
1979	John Tate (WBA)
1980	Mike Weaver (WBA)

(a) London Prize Ring (bare knuckle champion).
(b) First Marquis of Queensberry champion.
(c) Jeffries abandoned the title (1905) and designated Marvin Hart and Jack Root as logical contenders and agreed to referee a fight between them, the winner to be declared champion. Hart defeated Root in 12 rounds (1905) and in turn was defeated by Tommy Burns (1906) who immediately laid claim to the title. Jack Johnson defeated Burns (1908) and was recognized as champion. He clinched the title by defeating Jeffries in an attempted comeback (1910).
(d) Title declared vacant by the World Boxing Assn. and other groups in 1967 after Clay's refusal to fulfill his military obligation.
(e) After Spinks defeated Ali, the WBC recognized Ken Norton as champion. Norton subsequently lost his title to Larry Holmes.

Light Heavyweights

1903	Jack Root, George Gardner
1903-1905	Bob Fitzsimmons
1905-1912	Philadelphia Jack O'Brien*
1912-1916	Jack Dillon
1916-1920	Battling Levinsky
1920-1922	George Carpentier
1922-1923	Battling Siki
1923-1925	Mike McTigue
1925-1926	Paul Berlenbach
1926-1927	Jack Delaney*
1927-1929	Tommy Loughran*
1930-1934	Maxey Rosenbloom
1934-1935	Bob Olin
1935-1939	John Henry Lewis*
1939	Melio Bettina
1939-1941	Billy Conn*
1941	Anton Christoforidis (won NBA title)
1941-1948	Gus Lesnevich, Freddie Mills
1948-1950	Freddie Mills
1950-1952	Joey Maxim
1952-1960	Archie Moore
1961-1962	vacant
1962-1963	Harold Johnson
1963-1965	Willie Pastrano
1965-1966	Jose Torres
1966-1968	Dick Tiger
1968-1974	Bob Foster*, John Conteh (WBA)
1975-1977	John Conteh (WBC), Miguel Cuello (WBC), Victor Galindez (WBA)
1978	Mike Rossman (WBA), Mate Parlov (WBC), Marvin Johnson (WBC)
1979	Victor Galindez (WBA), Matthew Saad Muhammad (WBC)
1980	Eddie Mustava Muhammad (WBA)

Middleweights

1884-1891	Jack "Nonpareil" Dempsey
1891-1897	Bob Fitzsimmons*
1897-1907	Tommy Ryan*
1907-1908	Stanley Ketchel, Billy Papke
1908-1910	Stanley Ketchel
1911-1913	vacant
1913	Frank Klaus, George Chip
1914-1917	Al McCoy
1917-1920	Mike O'Dowd
1920-1923	Johnny Wilson
1923-1926	Harry Greb
1926-1931	Tiger Flowers, Mickey Walker
1931-1932	Gorilla Jones (NBA)
1932-1937	Marcel Thil
1938	Al Hostak (NBA), Solly Krieger (NBA)
1939-1940	Al Hostak (NBA)
1941-1947	Tony Zale
1947-1948	Rocky Graziano
1948	Tony Zale, Marcel Cerdan
1949-1951	Jake LaMotta
1951	Ray Robinson, Randy Turpin, Ray Robinson*
1953-1955	Carl (Bobo) Olson
1955-1957	Ray Robinson
1957	Gene Fullmer, Ray Robinson, Carmen Basilio
1958	Ray Robinson
1959	Gene Fullmer (NBA); Ray Robinson (N.Y.)
1960	Gene Fullmer (NBA); Paul Pender (New York and Mass.)
1961	Gene Fullmer (NBA); Terry Downes (New York, Mass., Europe)
1962	Gene Fullmer, Dick Tiger (NBA), Paul Pender (New York and Mass.)*
1963	Dick Tiger (universal).
1963-1965	Joey Giardello
1965-1966	Dick Tiger
1966-1967	Emile Griffith
1967	Nino Benvenuti
1967-1968	Emile Griffith
1968-1970	Nino Benvenuti
1970-1977	Carlos Monzon*

1977-1978	Rodrigo Valdez
1978-1979	Hugo Corro
1979-1980	Vito Antuofermo
1980	Alan Minter

Welterweights

1892-1894	Mysterious Billy Smith
1894-1896	Tommy Ryan
1896	Kid McCoy*
1900	Rube Ferns, Matty Matthews
1901	Rube Ferns
1901-1904	Joe Walcott
1904-1906	Dixie Kid, Joe Walcott, Honey Mellody
1907-1911	Mike Sullivan
1911-1915	vacant
1915-1919	Ted Lewis
1919-1922	Jack Britton
1922-1926	Mickey Walker
1926	Pete Latzo
1927-1929	Joe Dundee
1929	Jackie Fields
1930	Jack Thompson, Tommy Freeman
1931	Freeman, Thompson, Lou Brouillard
1932	Jackie Fields
1933	Young Corbett, Jimmy McLarnin
1934	Barney Ross, Jimmy McLarnin
1935-1938	Barney Ross
1938-1940	Henry Armstrong
1940-1941	Fritzie Zivic
1941-1946	Fred Cochrane
1946-1946	Marty Servo*; Ray Robinson (a)
1946-1950	Ray Robinson*
1951	Johnny Bratton (NBA)
1951-1954	Kid Gavilan
1954-1955	Johnny Saxton
1955	Tony De Marco, Carmen Basilio
1956	Carmen Basilio, Johnny Saxton, Carmen Basilio
1957	Carmen Basilio*
1958-1960	Virgil Akins, Don Jordan
1960	Benny Paret
1961	Emile Griffith, Benny Paret
1962	Emile Griffith
1963	Luis Rodriguez, Emile Griffith
1964-1966	Emile Griffith*
1966-1969	Curtis Cokes
1969-1970	Jose Napoles, Billy Backus
1971-1975	Jose Napoles
1975-1976	John Stracey (WBC), Angel Espada (WBA)
1976-1979	Carlos Palomino (WBC), Jose Cuevas (WBA)
1979	Wilfredo Benitez (WBC), Sugar Ray Leonard (WBC)
1980	Roberto Duran (WBC), Thomas Hearns (WBA)

(a) Robinson gained the title by defeating Tommy Bell in an elimination agreed to by the NY Commission and the NBA. Both claimed Robinson waived his title when he won the middleweight crown from LaMotta in 1951, Gavilan defeated Bratton in an elimination to find a successor.

Lightweights

1896-1899	Kid Lavigne
1899-1902	Frank Erne
1902-1908	Joe Gans
1908-1910	Battling Nelson
1910-1912	Ad Wolgast
1912-1914	Willie Ritchie
1914-1917	Freddie Welsh
1917-1925	Benny Leonard*
1925	Jimmy Goodrich, Rocky Kansas
1926-1930	Sammy Mandell
1930	Al Singer, Tony Canzoneri
1930-1933	Tony Canzoneri
1933-1935	Barney Ross*
1935-1936	Tony Canzoneri
1936-1938	Lou Ambers
1938	Henry Armstrong
1939	Lou Ambers
1940	Lew Jenkins
1941-1943	Sammy Angott
1944	S. Angott (NBA), J. Zurita (NBA)
1945-1951	Ike Williams (NBA: later universal)
1951-1952	James Carter
1952	Lauro Salas, James Carter
1953-1954	James Carter
1954	Paddy De Marco; James Carter
1955	James Carter; Bud Smith
1956	Bud Smith, Joe Brown
1956-1962	Joe Brown
1962-1965	Carlos Ortiz
1965	Ismael Laguna
1965-1968	Carlos Ortiz
1968-1969	Teo Cruz
1969-1970	Mando Ramos
1970	Ismael Laguna, Ken Buchanan (WBA)
1971	Mando Ramos (WBC), Pedro Carrasco (WBC)
1972-1979	Roberto Duran* (WBA)
1972	Pedro Carrasco (WBC), Mando Ramos (WBC), Chango Carmona (WBC), Rodolfo Gonzalez (WBC)
1974-1976	Guts Ishimatsu (WBC)
1976-1977	Esteban De Jesus (WBC)
1979	Jim Watt (WBC), Ernesto Espana (WBA)
1980	Hilmer Kenty (WBA)

Featherweights

1892-1900	George Dixon (disputed)
1900-1901	Terry McGovern, Young Corbett*
1901-1912	Abe Attell
1912-1923	Johnny Kilbane
1923	Eugene Criqui, Johnny Dundee
1923-1925	Johnny Dundee*
1925-1927	Kid Kaplan*
1927-1928	Benny Bass, Tony Canzoneri
1928-1929	Andre Routis
1929-1932	Battling Battalino*
1932-1934	Tommy Paul (NBA)
1933-1936	Freddie Miller
1936-1937	Petey Sarron
1937-1938	Henry Armstrong*
1938-1940	Joey Archibald (b)
1942-1948	Willie Pep
1948-1949	Sandy Saddler
1949-1950	Willie Pep
1950-1957	Sandy Saddler*
1957-1959	Hogan (Kid) Bassey
1959-1963	Davey Moore
1963-1964	Sugar Ramos
1964-1967	Vicente Saldivar*
1968-1971	Paul Rojas (WBA), Sho Saijo (WBA)
1971	Antonio Gomez (WBA), Kuniaki Shibada (WBC)
1972	Ernesto Marcel* (WBA), Clemente Sanchez* (WBC), Jose Legra (WBC)
1973	Eder Jofre (WBC)
1974	Ruben Olivares (WBA), Alexis Arguello (WBA), Bobby Chacon (WBC)
1975	Ruben Olivares (WBC), David Kotey (WBC)
1976	Danny Lopez (WBC)
1977	Rafael Ortega (WBA)
1978	Cecilio Lastra (WBA), Eusebio Pedrosa (WBA)
1980	Hilmer Kenty (WBA), Salvador Sanchez (WBC)

(b) After Petey Scalzo knocked out Archibald (Dec. 5, 1938) in an overweight match and was refused a title bout, the NBA named Scalzo champion. The NBA title succession was: Petey Scalzo, 1938-1941; Richard Lemos, 1941; Jackie Wilson, 1941-1943; Jackie Callura, 1943; Phil Terranova, 1943-1944; Sal Bartolo, 1944-1946.

History of Heavyweight Championship Bouts

*Title Changed Hands

1889—July 8—John L. Sullivan def. Jake Kilrain, 75, Richburg, Miss. Last championship bare knuckles bout.

***1892**—Sept. 7—James J. Corbett def. John L. Sullivan, 21, New Orleans. Big gloves used for first time.

1894—Jan. 25—James J. Corbett KOd Charley Mitchell, 3, Jacksonville, Fla.

***1897**—Bob Fitzsimmons def. James J. Corbett, 14, Carson City, Nev.

***1899**—June 9—James J. Jeffries def. Bob Fitzsimmons, 11, Coney Island, N.Y.

1899—Nov. 3—James J. Jeffries def. Tom Sharkey, 25, Coney Island, N.Y.

1900—May 11—James J. Jeffries KOd James J. Corbett, 23, Coney Island, N.Y.

1901—Nov. 15—James J. Jeffries KOd Gus Ruhlin, 5, San Francisco.

1902—July 25—James J. Jeffries KOd Bob Fitzsimmons, 8, San Francisco.

1903—Aug. 14—James J. Jeffries KOd James J. Corbett, 10, San Francisco.

1904—Aug. 26—James J. Jeffries KOd Jack Monroe, 2, San Francisco.

***1905**—James J. Jeffries retired, July 3—Marvin Hart KOd Jack Root, 12, Reno. Jeffries refereed and presented the title to the victor. Jack O'Brien also claimed the title.

***1906**—Feb. 23—Tommy Burns def. Marvin Hart, 20, Los Angeles.

1906—Nov. 28—Philadelphia Jack O'Brien and Tommy Burns, 20, draw, Los Angeles.

1907—May 8—Tommy Burns def. Jack O'Brien, 20, Los Angeles.

1907—July 4—Tommy Burns KOd Bill Squires, 1, Colma, Cal.

1907—Dec. 2—Tommy Burns KOd Gunner Moir, 10, London.

1908—Feb. 10—Tommy Burns KOd Jack Palmer, 4, London.

1908—March 17—Tommy Burns KOd Jem Roche, 1, Dublin.

1908—April 18—Tommy Burns KOd Jewey Smith, 5, Paris.

1908—June 13—Tommy Burns KOd Bill Squires, 8, Paris.

1908—Aug. 24—Tommy Burns KOd Bill Squires, 13, Sydney, New South Wales.

1908—Sept. 2—Tommy Burns KOd Bill Lang, 2, Melbourne, Australia.

***1908**—Dec. 26—Jack Johnson KOd Tommy Burns, 14, Sydney, Australia. Police halted contest.

1909—May 19—Jack Johnson and Jack O'Brien, 6, draw, Philadelphia.

1909—June 30—Jack Johnson and Tony Ross, 6, draw, Pittsburgh.

1909—Sept. 9—Jack Johnson and Al Kaufman, 10, draw, San Francisco.

1909—Oct. 16—Jack Johnson KOd Stanley Ketchel, 12, Colma, Cal.

1910—July 4—Jack Johnson KOd Jim Jeffries, 15, Reno, Nev. Jeffries came back from retirement.

1912—July 4—Jack Johnson def. Jim Flynn, 9, Las Vegas, N.M. Contest stopped by police.

1913—Nov. 28—Jack Johnson KOd Andre Spaul, 2, Paris.

1913—Dec. 9—Jack Johnson and Jim Johnson, 10, draw, Paris. Bout called a draw when Jack Johnson declared he had broken his arm.

1914—June 27—Jack Johnson def. Frank Moran, 20, Paris.

***1915**—April 5—Jess Willard KOd Jack Johnson, 26, Havana. Cuba.

1916—March 25—Jess Willard and Frank Moran, 10, draw, New York.

***1919**—July 4—Jack Dempsey KOd Jess Willard, Toledo, Oh. Willard failed to answer bell for 4th round.

1920—Sept. 6—Jack Dempsey KOd Billy Miske, 3, Benton Harbor, Mich.

1920—Dec. 14—Jack Dempsey KOd Bill Brennan, 12, New York.

1921—July 2—Jack Dempsey KOd George Carpentier, 4, Boyle's Thirty Acres, Jersey City, N.J. Carpentier had held the so-called white heavyweight title since July 16, 1914, in a series established in 1913, after Jack Johnson's exile in Europe late in 1912.

1923—July 4—Jack Dempsey def. Tom Gibbons, 15, Shelby, Mont.

1923—Sept. 14—Jack Dempsey KOd Luis Firpo, 2, New York.

***1926**—Sept. 23—Gene Tunney def. Jack Dempsey, 10, Philadelphia.

1927—Sept. 22—Gene Tunney def. Jack Dempsey, 10, Chicago.

1928—July 26—Gene Tunney KOd Tom Heeney, 11, New York; soon afterward he announced his retirement.

***1930**—June 12—Max Schmeling def. Jack Sharkey, 4, New York. Sharkey fouled Schmeling in a bout which was generally considered to have resulted in the election of a successor to Gene Tunney, New York.

1931—July 3—Max Schmeling KOd Young Stribling, 15, Cleveland.

***1932**—June 21—Jack Sharkey def. Max Schmeling, 15, New York.

***1933**—June 29—Primo Carnera KOd Jack Sharkey, 6, New York.

1933—Oct. 22—Primo Carnera def. Paulino Uzcudun, 15, Rome.

1934—March 1—Primo Carnera def. Tommy Loughran, 15, Miami.

***1934**—June 14—Max Baer KOd Primo Carnera, 11, New York.

***1935**—June 13—James J. Braddock def. Max Baer, 15, New York.

***1937**—June 22—Joe Louis KOd James J. Braddock, 8, Chicago.

1937—Aug. 30—Joe Louis def. Tommy Farr, 15, New York.

1938—Feb. 23—Joe Louis KOd Nathan Mann, 3, New York.

1938—April 1—Joe Louis KOd Harry Thomas, 5, New York.

1938—June 22—Joe Louis KOd Max Schmeling, 1, New York.

1939—Jan. 25—Joe Louis KOd John H. Lewis, 1, New York.

1939—April 17—Joe Louis KOd Jack Roper, 1, Los Angeles.

1939—June 28—Joe Louis KOd Tony Galento, 4, New York.

1939—Sept. 20—Joe Louis KOd Bob Pastor, 11, Detroit.

1940—February 9—Joe Louis def. Arturo Godoy, 15, New York.

1940—March 29—Joe Louis KOd Johnny Paycheck, 2, New York.

1940—June 20—Joe Louis KOd Arturo Godoy, 8, New York.

1940—Dec. 16—Joe Louis KOd Al McCoy, 6, Boston.

1941—Jan. 31—Joe Louis KOd Red Burman, 5, New York.

1941—Feb. 17—Joe Louis KOd Gus Dorzaio, 2, Philadelphia.

1941—March 21—Joe Louis KOd Abe Simon, 13, Detroit.

1941—April 8—Joe Louis KOd Tony Musto, 9, St. Louis.

1941—May 23—Joe Louis def. Buddy Baer, 7, Washington, D.C., on a disqualification.

1941—June 18—Joe Louis KOd Billy Conn, 13, New York.

1941—Sept. 29—Joe Louis KOd Lou Nova, 6, New York.

1942—Jan. 9—Joe Louis KOd Buddy Baer, 1, New York.

1942—March 27—Joe Louis KOd Abe Simon, 6, New York.

1946—June 19—Joe Louis KOd Billy Conn, 8, New York.

1946—Sept. 18—Joe Louis KOd Tami Mauriello, 1, New York.

1947—Dec. 5—Joe Louis def. Joe Walcott, 15, New York.

1948—June 25—Joe Louis KOd Joe Walcott, 11, New York.

***1949**—June 22—Following Joe Louis' retirement Ezzard Charles def. Joe Walcott, 15, Chicago, NBA recognition only.

1949—Aug. 10—Ezzard Charles KOd Gus Lesnevich, 7, New York.

1949—Oct. 14—Ezzard Charles KOd Pat Valentino, 8, San Francisco; clinched American title.

1950—Aug. 15—Ezzard Charles KOd Freddy Beshore, 14, Buffalo.

1950—Sept. 27—Ezzard Charles def. Joe Louis in latter's attempted comeback, 15, New York; universal recognition.

1950—Dec. 5—Ezzard Charles KOd Nick Barone, 11, Cincinnati.

1951—Jan. 12—Ezzard Charles KOd Lee Oma, 10, New York.

1951—March 7—Ezzard Charles def. Joe Walcott, 15, Detroit.

1951—May 30—Ezzard Charles def. Joey Maxim, light heavyweight champion, 15, Chicago.

***1951**—July 18—Joe Walcott KOd Ezzard Charles, 7, Pittsburgh.

1952—June 5—Joe Walcott def. Ezzard Charles, 15, Philadelphia.

***1952**—Sept. 23—Rocky Marciano KOd Joe Walcott, 13, Philadelphia.

1953—May 15—Rocky Marciano KOd Joe Walcott, 1, Chicago.

1953—Sept. 24—Rocky Marciano KOd Roland LaStarza, 11, New York.

1954—June 17—Rocky Marciano def. Ezzard Charles, 15, New York.

1954—Sept. 17—Rocky Marciano KOd Ezzard Charles, 8, New York.

1955—May 16—Rocky Marciano KOd Don Cockell, 9, San Francisco.

1955—Sept. 21—Rocky Marciano KOd Archie Moore, 9, New York. Marciano retired undefeated, Apr. 27, 1956.

***1956**—Nov. 30—Floyd Patterson KOd Archie Moore, 5, Chicago.

1957—July 29—Floyd Patterson KOd Hurricane Jackson, 10, New York.

1957—Aug. 22—Floyd Patterson KOd Pete Rademacher, 6, Seattle.

1958—Aug. 18—Floyd Patterson KOd Roy Harris, 12, Los Angeles.

1959—May 1—Floyd Patterson KOd Brian London, 11, Indianapolis.

***1959**—June 26—Ingemar Johansson KOd Floyd Patterson, 3, New York.

***1960**—June 20—Floyd Patterson KOd Ingemar Johansson, 5, New York. First heavyweight in boxing history to regain title.

1961—Mar. 13—Floyd Patterson KOd Ingemar Johansson, 6, Miami Beach.

1961—Dec. 4—Floyd Patterson KOd Tom McNeeley, 4, Toronto.

***1962**—Sept. 25—Sonny Liston KOd Floyd Patterson, 1, Chicago.

1963—July 22—Sonny Liston KOd Floyd Patterson, 1, Las Vegas.

***1964**—Feb. 25—Cassius Clay KOd Sonny Liston, 7, Miami Beach.

1965—May 25—Cassius Clay KOd Sonny Liston, 1, Lewiston, Maine.
1965—Nov. 11—Cassius Clay KOd Floyd Patterson, 12, Las Vegas.
1966—Mar. 29—Cassius Clay def. George Chuvalo, 15, Toronto.
1966—May 21—Cassius Clay KOd Henry Cooper, 6, London.
1966—Aug. 6—Cassius Clay KOd Brian London, 3, London.
1966—Sept. 10—Cassius Clay KOd Karl Mildenberger, 12, Frankfurt, Germany.
1966—Nov. 14—Cassius Clay KOd Cleveland Williams, 3, Houston.
1967—Feb. 6—Cassius Clay def. Ernie Terrell, 15, Houston.
1967—Mar. 22—Cassius Clay KOd Zora Folley, 7, New York. Clay was stripped of his title by the WBA and others for refusing military service.
***1970**—Feb. 16—Joe Frazier KOd Jimmy Ellis, 5, New York.
1970—Nov. 18—Joe Frazier KOd Bob Foster, 2, Detroit.
1971—Mar. 8—Joe Frazier def. Cassius Clay (Muhammad Ali), 15, New York.
1972—Jan. 15—Joe Frazier KOd Terry Daniels, 4, New Orleans.
1972—May 25—Joe Frazier KOd Ron Stander, 5, Omaha.
***1973**—Jan. 22—George Foreman KOd Joe Frazier, 2, Kingston, Jamaica.
1973—Sept. 1—George Foreman KOd Joe Roman, 1, Tokyo.
1974—Mar. 3—George Foreman KOd Ken Norton, 2, Caracas.
***1974**—Oct. 30—Muhammad Ali KOd George Foreman, 8, Zaire.
1975—Mar. 24—Muhammad Ali KOd Chuck Wepner, 15, Cleveland.
1975—May 16—Muhammad Ali KOd Ron Lyle, 11, Las Vegas.
1975—June 30—Muhammad Ali def. Joe Bugner, 15, Malaysia.
1975—Oct. 1—Muhammad Ali KOd Joe Frazier, 14, Manila.
1976—Feb. 20—Muhammad Ali KOd Jean-Pierre Coopman, 5, San Juan.
1976—Apr. 30—Muhammad Ali def. Jimmy Young, 15, Landover, Md.
1976—May 25—Muhammad Ali KOd Richard Dunn, 5, Munich.
1976—Sept. 28—Muhammad Ali def. Ken Norton, 15, New York.
1977—May 16—Muhammad Ali def. Alfredo Evangelista, 15, Landover, Md.
1977—Sept. 29—Muhammad Ali def. Earnie Shavers, 15, New York.
***1978**—Feb. 15—Leon Spinks def. Muhammad Ali, 15, Las Vegas.
***1978**—Sept. 15—Muhammad Ali def. Leon Spinks, 15, New Orleans. Ali retired in 1979.

(Bouts when title changed hands only)

***1978**—June 9—(WBC) Larry Holmes def. Ken Norton, 15, Las Vegas.
***1980**—Mar. 31—(WBA) Mike Weaver KOd John Tate, 15, Knoxville.

Earnings of Athletes

The actual amount of money paid by a club to an athlete is known only to the club, the athlete, his agent, and the IRS. The following salary and earnings figures have been taken from published sources, reliable, but not official. The figures do not include outside income, such as fees for personal appearances and commercial endorsements. The earnings of boxers are difficult to determine. As much as 1/3 of their earnings may go to their managers. They also have large training expenses. It is estimated that boxers such as Larry Holmes, Ray Leonard, and Wilfredo Benitez earned between $1 million to $2.5 million in purses in 1979.

Estimated Earnings of Athletes

Athlete	Dollars
Bjorn Borg, tennis (1979)	1,019,345
John McEnroe, tennis (1979)	1,005,238
Nolan Ryan, baseball	1,000,000
Phil Niekro, baseball (mostly deferred payments)	1,000,000
Moses Malone, basketball	1,000,000
George Brett, baseball	1,000,000
Dave Parker, baseball	900,000
Rod Carew, baseball	900,000
Kareem Abdul-Jabbar, basketball	700,000-825,000
Lafitt Pincay, horse racing (1979)	819,000
Bill Walton, basketball	800,000
Martina Navratilova, tennis (1979)	747,548
Pete Rose, baseball	745,000
David Thompson, basketball	650,000-750,000
Jimmy Connors, tennis (1979)	701,341
Bruce Sutter, baseball	700,000
Jim Rice, baseball	700,000
Vida Blue, baseball	700,000
George Foster, baseball	700,000
Julius Erving, basketball	500,000-700,000
Ted Simmons, baseball	665,000
Larry Bird, basketball	650,000
Keith Hernandez, baseball	600,000
Craig Swan, baseball	600,000
Marcel Dionne, hockey	600,000
Magic Johnson, basketball	600,000
Reggie Jackson, baseball	580,000
Chris Evert-Lloyd, tennis (1979)	564,398
Angel Cordero, horse racing (1979)	563,000
Mike Schmidt, baseball	560,000
Tracy Austin, tennis (1979)	541,676
Richard Petty, auto racing (1979)	531,292
Larry Hisle, baseball	530,000
Jorge Velesquez, horse racing (1979)	530,000
Darrell Waltrip, auto racing (1979)	523,691
Bert Blyleven, baseball	500,000
Johan Cruyff, soccer	500,000
Bob McAdoo, basketball	500,000
Chris McCarron, horse racing (1979)	492,000
Bobby Bonds, baseball	480,000
Sparky Lyle, baseball	480,000
Oscar Gamble, baseball	475,000
Jeffrey Fell, horse racing (1979)	474,000
Tommy John, baseball	470,000
Robin Yount, baseball	470,000
Tom Watson, golf (1979)	462,636
Bob Lanier, basketball	450,000
Walter Payton, football	450,000
George McGinnis, basketball	450,000
Rich Gossage, baseball	450,000
Bill Shoemaker, horse racing (1979)	442,000
Joe Rudi, baseball	440,000
Cale Yarborough, auto racing (1979)	431,842
Dave Goltz, baseball	425,000
Vitas Gerulaitas, tennis (1979)	424,515
Johnny Bench, baseball	420,000
Rennie Stennett, baseball	400,000
Bob Griese, football	400,000

Other noteworthy earnings

Athlete	Dollars
Archie Manning, football	379,000
Dan Pastorini, football	358,000
Gil Perreault, hockey	350,000
Wendy Turnbull, tennis (1979)	317,463
Chuck Foreman, football	300,000
John Riggins, football	300,000
Phil Esposito, hockey	250,000-295,000
Giorgio Chinaglia, soccer	283,000
Larry Nelson, golf (1979)	281,022
Bert Jones, football	275,000
Brad Park, hockey	265,000
Franz Beckenbauer, soccer	250,000
Jack Ham, football	230,000
Lee Roy Selmon, football	218,000
Nancy Lopez, golf (1979)	215,987
Mark Roth, bowling (1979)	124,517

Little League World Series in 1980

Taiwan won the 1980 Little League World Series by defeating Tampa (Fla.) 4-3 at Williamsport, Pa. on Aug. 27. The victory was Taiwan's 9th world title in the past 12 years.

World Track and Field Records

As of Aug. 4, 1980

*Indicates pending record; a number of new records await confirmation. The International Amateur Athletic Federation, the world body of track and field, announced July 27, 1976, a plan to overhaul the track and field record book. Eliminated are all records in yards except for the mile. Also eliminated are all hand-timed records for distances up to and including 400 meters. The records below meet the new standards except where noted. Records in yards and miles are included although they are no longer officially considered world records.

Men's Records

Running

Event	Record	Holder	Country	Date	Where made
100 yds.	**9.0 s.**	Ivory Crockett	U.S.	May 11, 1974	Knoxville, Tenn.
		Houston McTear	U.S.	May 9, 1975	Winter Park, Fla.
220 yds.	**19.5 s.**	Tommie Smith	U.S.	May 7, 1966	San Jose, Cal.
220 yds.	**19.9 s**(turn)	Don Quarrie	Jamaica	June 7, 1975	Eugene, Ore.
		Steve Williams	U.S.	June 7, 1975	Eugene, Ore.
440 yds.	**44.5 s.**	John Smith	U.S.	June 26, 1972	Eugene, Ore.
880 yds.	**1 m., 44.1 s.**	Rick Wohlhuter	U.S.	June 8, 1974	Eugene, Ore.
1 mile	***3m., 48.8 s.**	Steve Ovett	Gr. Britain	July 1, 1980	Oslo
3 miles	**12 m., 47.8 s.**	Emiel Puttemans	Belgium	Sept. 20, 1972	Brussels
6 miles	**26 m., 47.0 s.**	Ron Clarke	Australia	July 14, 1965	Oslo
10 miles	**45 m., 57.2 s.**	Jos Hermens	Netherlands	Sept. 14, 1975	Netherlands
15 miles	**1 hr., 11 min., 52.6 s.**	Pekka Paivarinta	Finland	May 15, 1975	Oulu, Finland

Running — Metric Distances

Event	Record	Holder	Country	Date	Where made
100 meters	**9.95 s.**	Jim Hines	U.S.	Oct. 14, 1968	Mexico City
200 meters	**19.72 s.**	Pietro Mennea	Italy	Sept. 12, 1979	Mexico City
400 meters	**43.86 s.**	Lee Evans	U.S.	Oct. 18, 1968	Mexico City
800 meters	**1 m., 42.4 s.**	Sebastian Coe	Gr. Britain	July 5, 1979	Oslo
1,000 meters	***2 m., 13.4 s.**	Sebastian Coe	Gr. Britain	July, 1980	Oslo
1,500 meters	**3 m., 32.1 s.**	Sebastian Coe	Gr. Britain	Aug. 15, 1979	Zurich
		Steve Ovett	Gr. Britain	July 15, 1980	Oslo
2,000 meters	**4 m., 51.4 s.**	John Walker	New Zealand	June 30, 1976	Oslo
3,000 meters	**7 m., 32.1 s.**	Henry Rono	Kenya	June 27, 1978	Oslo
5,000 meters	**13 m., 08.4 s.**	Henry Rono	Kenya	Apr. 8, 1978	Berkeley, Cal.
10,000 meters	**27 m., 22.47 s.**	Henry Rono	Kenya	June 11, 1978	Vienna
20,000 meters	**57 m., 24.2 s.**	Jos Hermens	Netherlands	May 1, 1976	Netherlands
25,000 meters	**1 hr., 14 m., 12 s.**	Bill Rodgers	U.S.	Feb. 21, 1979	Saratoga, Cal.
30,000 meters	**1 hr., 31 m., 30.4 s.**	Jim Adler	Gr. Britain	Sept. 5, 1970	London
3,000 meter stpl	**8 m., 05.4 s.**	Henry Rono	Kenya	May 13, 1978	Seattle

Hurdles

Event	Record	Holder	Country	Date	Where made
120 yards	**13.0 s.**	Rod Milburn	U.S.	June 25, 1971	Eugene, Ore.
		Rod Milburn	U.S.	June 20, 1973	Eugene, Ore.
		Guy Drut	France	Aug. 22, 1975	Berlin, W. Ger.
220 yards	**21.9 s.**	Don Styron	U.S.	Apr. 2, 1960	Baton Rouge
440 yards	**48.7 s.**	Jim Bolding	U.S.	July 24, 1974	Turin, Italy
110 meters	**13 s.**	Renaldo Nehemiah	U.S.	May 6, 1979	Los Angeles
200 meters	**21.9 s. (not ET)**	Don Styron	U.S.	Apr. 2, 1960	Baton Rouge
200 meters	**22.5 s. (not ET)** (turn)	Martin Lauer	W. Germany	July 7, 1959	Zurich
	(not ET)	Glenn Davis	U.S.	Aug. 20, 1960	Bern
400 meters	***47.13 s.**	Edwin Moses	U.S.	July 3, 1980	Milan, Italy

Relay Races

Event	Record	Holder	Country	Date	Where made
440 yds. (4×110) (2 turns)	**38.6 s.**	USC (McCullouch, Kuller, Simpson, Miller)	U.S.	June 17, 1967	Provo, Utah
830 yds. (4×220)	**1 m., 21.7 s.**	Texas A&M (Rogers, Woods, M. Mills, C. Mills)	U.S.	Apr. 24, 1970	Des Moines
1 mile (4×440)	**3 m., 02.4 s.**	National team (Ray, Taylor, Peoples, Vinson)	U.S.	July 18, 1975	Durham, N.C.
2 miles (4×880)	**7 m., 10.4 s.**	Chicago TC (Bach, Sparks, Paul, Wohlhuter)	U.S.	May 12, 1973	Durham, N.C.
4 miles (4×1) (mile)	**16 m., 02.8 s.**	National team (Ross, Polhill, Tayler, Quax)	New Zealand	Feb. 3, 1972	Auckland, N.Z.

Relay Races — Metric Distances

Event	Record	Holder	Country	Date	Where made
400 mtrs.	**38.03 s.**	National team (Collins, Riddick, Wiley, Williams)	U.S.	Sept. 3, 1977	Dusseldorf
800 mtrs. (4×200)	**1 m., 20.3 s.**	USC	U.S.	May 27, 1978	Tempe, Ariz.
1,600 mtrs. (4×400)	**2 m., 56.1 s.**	National team (Matthews, Freeman, James, Evans)	U.S.	Oct. 20, 1968	Mexico City
3,200 mtrs. (4×800)	**7 m., 08.1 s.**	National team	USSR	Aug. 12, 1978	USSR

Walking

Event	Record	Holder	Country	Date	Where made
2 hours	**17 mi., 881 yds.**	Jose Marin	Spain	Apr. 8, 1979	Barcelona
30 km.	**2 h., 8 min.**	Jose Marin	Spain	Apr. 8, 1979	Barcelona
50 km.	**3 hr., 41 m., 39 s.**	Raul Gonzales	Mexico	May 25, 1978	Norway

Field Events

Event	Record	Holder	Country	Date	Where made
High jump	***7 ft., 9 in.**	Gerd Wessig	E. Germany	Aug. 1, 1980	Moscow
Long jump	**29 ft., 2½ in.**	Bob Beamon	U.S.	Oct. 18,1968	Mexico City
Triple jump	**58 ft., 8¼ in.**	Joao de Oliveira	Brazil	Oct. 15, 1975	Mexico City
Pole vault	***18 ft., 11½ in.**	Wladyslaw Kozakiewicz	Poland	July 30, 1980	Moscow
16 lb. shot put	**72 ft., 8 in.**	Udo Beyer	E. Germany	July 6, 1978	Sweden
Discus throw	**233 ft., 5 in.**	Wolfgang Schmidt	E. Germany	Aug. 9, 1978	E. Berlin
Javelin throw	**310 ft., 4 in.**	Miklos Nemeth	Hungary	July 26, 1976	Montreal
16 lb. hammer throw	***268 ft., 4½ in.**	Yuri Sedykh	USSR	July 31, 1980	Moscow
Decathlon	***8,649 pts.**	Guido Kratschmer	W. Germany	June, 1980	W. Germany

Women's Records

Running

100 yards	**10.0 s.**	Chi Cheng	Taiwan	June 13, 1970	Portland, Ore.
220 yards	**22.6 s.**	Chi Cheng	Taiwan	July 3, 1970	Los Angeles
440 yards	**52.2 s.**	Kathy Hammond	U.S.	Aug. 12, 1972	Urbana, Ill.
		Debra Sapenter	U.S.	June 29, 1974	Bakersfield, Cal.
880 yards	**2 m., 02.0 s.**	Judy Pollock	Australia	July 5, 1967	Sweden
		Dixie Willis	Australia	Mar. 3, 1962	Perth, Australia
1 mile	***4 m., 21.7 s.**	Mary Decker	U.S.	Jan. 26, 1980	Auckland, N.Z.
100 meters	***10.87 s.**	Lyudmila Kondratyeva	USSR	June 3, 1980	Moscow
200 meters	**21.71 s.**	Marita Koch	E. Germany	June 10, 1979	E. Berlin
400 meters	**48.60 s.**	Marita Koch	E. Germany	Aug. 4, 1979	Turin, Italy
800 meters	***1 m., 53.5 s.**	Nadezhda Olizarenko	USSR	July, 1980	Moscow
1,500 meters	***3 m., 55 s.**	Tatyana Kazankina	USSR	July 6, 1980	Moscow
3,000 meters	**8 m., 27.1 s.**	Ludmila Bragina	USSR	Aug. 7, 1976	College Park, Md.

Hurdles

100 meters	***12.36 s.**	Grazyna Rabsztyn	Poland	June, 1980	Warsaw
400 meters	***54.28 s.**	Karin Rossley	E. Germany	May, 1980	E. Germany

Field Events

High jump	**6 ft., 7 in.**	Sara Simeoni	Italy	Aug. 31, 1978	Prague
Shot put	**73 ft., 2¾ in.**	Helena Fibigerova	Czech.	Aug. 20, 1977	Czech.
Long jump	**23 ft., 3¼ in.**	Vilma Bardauskiene	USSR	Aug. 29, 1978	Prague
Discus throw	***235 ft., 7 in.**	Maria Vergova-Petkova	Bulgaria	July, 1980	Sofia
Javelin	***229 ft., 11 in.**	Tatyana Biryulina	USSR	July, 1980	Podolsk, USSR
Pentathlon	***5,083 pts.**	Nadyezhda Tkachenko	USSR	July, 1980	Moscow

Relay Races

400 mtrs. (4×100)	***41.60 s.**	National team	E. Germany	July, 1980	Moscow
800 mtrs. (4×200)	**1 m., 20.3 s.**	National team	U.S.	May, 1978	Tempe, Ariz.
1,600 mtrs. (4×400)	**3 m., 19.2 s.**	National team	E. Germany	July 31, 1976	Montreal
1 mile (4×440)	**3 m., 30.3 s.**	National team (Krause, Jost, Weinstein, Barth)	W. Germany	July 19, 1975	Durham, N.C.

Evolution of the World Record for the One-Mile Run

The table below shows how the world record for the one-mile has been lowered in the past 116 years.

Year	Individual, country	Time	Year	Individual, country	Time
1864	Charles Lawes, Britain	**4:56**	1937	Sydney Wooderson, Britain	**4:06.4**
1865	Richard Webster, Britain	**4:36.5**	1942	Gunder Haegg, Sweden	**4:06.2**
1868	William Chinnery, Britain	**4:29**	1942	Arne Andersson, Sweden	**4:06.2**
1868	W. C. Gibbs, Britain	**4:28.8**	1942	Gunder Haegg, Sweden	**4:04.6**
1874	Walter Slade, Britain	**4:26**	1943	Arne Andersson, Sweden	**4:02.6**
1875	Walter Slade, Britain	**4:24.5**	1944	Arne Andersson, Sweden	**4:01.6**
1880	Walter George, Britain	**4:23.2**	1945	Gunder Haegg, Sweden	**4:01.4**
1882	Walter George, Britain	**4:21.4**	1954	Roger Bannister, Britain	**3:59.4**
1882	Walter George, Britain	**4:19.4**	1954	John Landy, Australia	**3:58**
1884	Walter George, Britain	**4:18.4**	1957	Derek Ibbotson, Britain	**3:57.2**
1894	Fred Bacon, Scotland	**4:18.2**	1958	Herb Elliott, Australia	**3:54.5**
1895	Fred Bacon, Scotland	**4:17**	1962	Peter Snell, New Zealand	**3:54.4**
1895	Thomas Conneff, U.S.	**4:15.6**	1964	Peter Snell, New Zealand	**3:54.1**
1911	John Paul Jones, U.S.	**4:15.4**	1965	Michel Jazy, France	**3:53.6**
1913	John Paul Jones, U.S.	**4:14.6**	1966	Jim Ryun, U.S.	**3:51.3**
1915	Norman Taber, U.S.	**4:12.6**	1967	Jim Ryun, U.S.	**3:51.1**
1923	Paavo Nurmi, Finland	**4:10.4**	1975	Filbert Bayi, Tanzania	**3:51**
1931	Jules Ladoumegue, France	**4:09.2**	1975	John Walker, New Zealand	**3:49.4**
1933	Jack Lovelock, New Zealand	**4:07.6**	1979	Sebastian Coe, Britain	**3:49**
1934	Glenn Cunningham, U.S.	**4:06.8**	1980	Steve Overt, Britain	**3:48.8**

U.S. National Open Table Tennis Championships

Ft. Worth, Tex., June 26-29, 1980

Men's Singles — Mikael Appelgren, Sweden.
Women's Singles — Kayoko Kawahigashi, Japan.
Mixed Doubles — Si-Hung Yoo & Soo-Ja Lee, South Korea.
Women's Doubles — Kyung-Ja Kim & Soo-Ja Lee, South Korea.
Men's Doubles — Dan & Rick Seemiller, Pittsburgh, Pa.
Men's Team — United States.
Women's Team — South Korea.

Track and Field Events in 1980

73d Annual Millrose Games

New York, N.Y., Feb. 8, 1980

Men

60 Yds.—Houston McTear, Muhammad Ali TC. **Time—0:06.17.**
60-Yd. High Hurdles—Greg Foster, Muhammad Ali TC. **Time—0:07.05.**
400 Meters—Tony Darden, Philadelphia Pioneers. **Time—0:48.25.**
500 Yds.—Bert Cameron, Texas, El Paso. **Time—0:56.0.**
600 Yds.—Chris Person, Univ. of Maryland. **Time—1:09.4.**
800 Meters—Peter Lemashon, Texas, El Paso. **Time—1:48.4**
1,000 Yds.—Bill Martin, Iona. **Time—2:06.8.**
One Mile—Eamonn Coghlan, New York AC. **Time—3:58.2.**
5,000 Meters—Suleiman Nyambui, Texas, El Paso. **Time—13:39.2.**
One-Mile Walk—Todd Scully, Shore AC. **Time—6:09.6.**
High Jump—Franklin Jacobs, Fairleigh Dickinson. **7 ft. 5 in.**
Pole Vault—Earl Bell, unattached. **18 ft.**

Women

60 Yds.—Brenda Morehead, Tenn. State. **Time—0:06.78.**
60-Yd. High Hurdles—Stephanie Hightower, Ohio State. **Time—0:07.47.**
400 Meters—(tie) Gwen Gardner, Los Angeles Mercurettes & June Griffith, Adelphi. **Time—0:53.31.**
800 Meters—Madeline Manning, Oral Roberts TC. **Time—2:05.6.**
1,500 Meters—Mary Decker, Athletics West. **Time—4:00.8.**
High Jump—Joni Huntley, Pacific Coast Club. **6 ft. 4¹⁄₄ in.**

Toronto Star — Maple Leaf Indoor Games

Toronto, Ont., Feb. 1, 1980

Men

50 Yds.—Emmit King, Jefferson State. **Time—0:05.38.**
50-Yd. Hurdles—James Walker, Auburn. **Time—0:06.22.**
600 Yds.—Fred Sowerby, D.C. International. **Time—1:10.9.**
1,000 Yds.—Mike Boit, Kenya. **Time—2:09.4.**
One Mile—Eamonn Coghlan, Ireland. **Time—3:58.2.**
3 Miles—Suleiman Nyambui, Texas. **Time—13:11.7.**
Pole Vault—Earl Bell, Sacramento, Cal. **17 ft. 8¹⁄₂ in.**

Women

50 Yds.—Evelyn Ashford, Los Angeles, Cal. **Time—0:05.86.**
50-Yd. Hurdles—Candy Young, Beaver Falls, Pa. **Time—0:06.44.**
600 Meters—June Griffith, Adelphi. **Time—1:31.6.**
1,500 Meters—Jan Merrill, Age Class AA. **Time—4:17.4.**
High Jump—Debbie Brill, Pacific Coast Club. **6 ft. 2³⁄₄ in.**

National AAU Indoor Track and Field Championships

New York, N.Y., Feb. 29, 1980

Men

60 Yds.—Curtis Dickey, Texas A & M. **Time—0:06.09.**
60-Yd. High Hurdles—Rod Milburn, Houston TC. **Time—0:07.09.**
600-Yds.—Mark Enyeart, unattached. **Time—1:09.2.**
1,000 Yds.—Bill Martin, Iona. **Time—2:07.7.**
One Mile—Craig Masback, New York Pioneer Club. **Time—4:02.2.**
3 Miles—Eamonn Coghlan, New York AC. **Time—13:02.8.**
2-Mile Walk—Todd Scully, Shore AC. **Time—12:35.1**
35-lb. Weight Throw—Ed Kania, unattached. **72 ft. 8 in.**
Triple Jump—Ron Livers, unattached. **55 ft. 1¹⁄₂ in.**
Long Jump—Larry Myricks, Athletic Attic TC. **26 ft. 11¹⁄₄ in.**
Shot Put—Jessie Stuart, Univ. of Chicago TC. **66 ft. 5 in.**
Pole Vault—Earl Bell, New York AC. **18 ft. 2¹⁄₄ in.**
High Jump—Franklin Jacobs, Fairleigh Dickinson. **7 ft. 4¹⁄₂ in.**

Women

60 Yds.—Evelyn Ashford, American Council of Athletes. **Time—0:06.76.**
60-Yd. High Hurdles—Stephanie Hightower, Ohio State. **Time—0:07.4.**
220 Yds.—Wanda Hooker, Memphis State. **Time—0:24.0.**
440 Yds.—Rosalyn Bryant, Muhammad Ali TC. **Time—0:53.92.**
880 Yds.—Madeline Manning, Oral Roberts TC. **Time—2:04.5.**
One Mile—Maggie Keyes, Maccabi Union TC. **Time—4:39.3.**
2 Miles—Cindy Bremser, Wisconsin-United TC. **Time—9:45.0.**
Long Jump—Pat Johnson, Univ. of Wisconsin. **20 ft. 11¹⁄₂ in.**
Shot Put—Maren Seidler, San Jose Stars. **57 ft. ¹⁄₄ in.**
High Jump—Louise Ritter, Texas Woman's Univ. **6 ft. 3 in.**

NCAA Indoor Track and Field Championships

Detroit, Mich., Mar. 14, 1980

60 Yds.—Curtis Dickey, Texas A & M. **Time—0:06.12.**
60-Yd. Hurdles—Rodney Wilson, Villanova. **Time—0:07.15.**
600 Yds.—Mike Ricks, Kansas. **Time—1:10.06.**
1,000 Yds.—Don Paige, Villanova. **Time—2:05.80.**
One Mile—Suleiman Nyambui, Texas, El Paso. **Time—4:05.26.**
2 Miles—Suleiman Nyambui. **Time—8:36.82.**
3 Miles—Solomon Chebor, Fairleigh Dickinson. **Time—13:20.94.**
Pole Vault—Randy Hall, Texas A & M. **17 ft. 9¹⁄₂ in.**
High Jump—Franklin Jacobs, Fairleigh Dickinson. **7 ft. 4¹⁄₄ in.**
35-Lb. Weight Throw—David Pellegrini, Princeton. **69 ft. 3¹⁄₄ in.**
Shot Put—Mike Carter, Southern Methodist. **67 ft. 7¹⁄₂ in.**
Long Jump—Carl Lewis, Houston. **26 ft. 4¹⁄₂ in.**
Triple Jump—Sanya Owolabi, Kansas. **54 ft. 3³⁄₄ in.**
Team champion—Texas, El Paso.

NCAA Outdoor Track and Field Championships

Austin, Tex., June 5-7, 1980

100 Meters—Stanley Floyd, Auburn. **Time—0:10.10.**
110-Meter Hurdles—Greg Foster, UCLA. **Time—0:13.43.**
200 Meters—Mike Roberson, Florida State. **Time—0:19.96.**
400 Meters—Bert Cameron, Texas-El Paso. **Time—0:45.23.**
400-Meter Hurdles—David Lee, Southern Illinois. **Time—0:48.87.**
800 Meters—Don Paige, Villanova. **Time—1:45.81.**
1,500 Meters—Sydney Maree, Villanova. **Time—3:38.64.**
3,000-Meter Steeplechase—Randy Jackson, Wisconsin. **Time—8:22.81.**
5,000 Meters—Suleiman Nyambui, Texas-El Paso. **Time—13:44.43.**
10,000 Meters—Suleiman Nyambui. **Time—29:21.85.**
400-Meter Relay—Southern California. **Time—0:39.16.**
1,600-Meter Relay—Tennessee. **Time—3:03.94.**
Hammer Throw—Thommie Sjoholm, Texas-El Paso. **225 ft.**
Javelin Throw—Curt Ransford, San Jose State. **269 ft. 3 in.**
Discus Throw—Goran Svensson, Brigham Young. **202 ft. 6 in.**
Pole Vault—Randy Hall, Texas A & M. **18 ft. 2 in.**
Triple Jump—Steve Hanna, Texas-El Paso. **55 ft. 1 in.**
High Jump—Jeff Woodard, Alabama. **7 ft. 7¹⁄₄ in.**
Shot Put—Mike Carter, Southern Methodist. **66 ft. 11¹⁄₄ in.**
Long Jump—Carl Lewis, Houston. **27 ft. 4³⁄₄ in.**
Team champion—Texas-El Paso.

The Athletics Congress National Championship

Walnut, Cal., June 15-16, 1980

Men

100 Meters—Stanley Floyd, Auburn. **Time—0:10.19.**
110-Meter Hurdles—Renaldo Nehemiah, D.C. International. **Time—0:13.49.**
200 Meters—LaMonte King, Stars and Stripes TC. **Time—0:20.08.**
400 Meters—Willie Smith, Auburn, **Time—0:45.36.**
400-Meter Hurdles—David Lee, Southern Illinois. **Time—0:49.38.**
800 Meters—James Robinson, Inner City AC. **Time—1:46.2.**
1,500 Meters—Steve Lacy, Southern California Striders, **Time—4:40.86.**
3,000-Meter Steeplechase—Doug Brown, Athletics West. **Time—8:26.2.**
10,000 Meters—Rodolfo Gomez, Mexico, **Time—28:44.0.**
Pole Vault—Tom Hintnaus, Southern California Striders. **18 ft. 2 in.**
Shot Put—Brian Oldfield, Univ. of Chicago TC. **71 ft. 7 in.**
Triple Jump—Willie Banks, American Council of Athletics. **56 ft. 11½ in.**
Javelin—Duncan Atwood, Athletics West. **273 ft. 10 in.**
Hammer Throw—Gian Paolo Urlando, Italy. **251 ft. 3 in.**
High Jump—Franklin Jacobs, Athletic Attic. **7 ft. 4¼ in.**
Long Jump—Larry Myricks, Athletic Attic. **27 ft. 1¼ in.**

Women

100 Meters—Alice Brown, L.A. Naturite. **Time—0:11.21.**
100-Meter Hurdles—Stephanie Hightower, Ohio State. **Time 0:13.14.**
200 Meters—Karen Hawkins, Texas Southern. **Time—0:22.80.**
400 Meters—Sherri Howard, Muhammad Ali TC. **Time—0:51.51.**
400-Meter Hurdles—Esther Mahr, KCQB TC. **Time—0:56.3.**
800 Meters—Madeline Manning Mims, Oral Roberts TC. **Time—1:58.75.**
1,500 Meters—Francie Larrieu, Pacific Coast Club. **Time—4:12.72.**
10,000-Meter Walk—Sue Brodock, Southern California Road Runners. **Time—51:01.0.**
Javelin—Karin Smith, American Council of Athletics. **199 ft. 1 in.**
Long Jump—Jodi Anderson, L.A. Naturite. **21 ft 9¾ in.**
High Jump—Coleen Rienstra, Sun Devils Sports. **6 ft. 4 in.**
Shot Put—Maren Seidler, San Jose Stars. **59 ft. 1 in.**

U.S. Amateur Roller Skating Championship in 1980

American Senior Dance—Harvey White-Beth Wahlig, Newark, Del.
American Free Dance—Scott Oakley-Gladys Smith, East Meadow, N.Y.
International Senior Dance—Charles Kirchner-Linda Todd, Cherry Hill, N.J.
International Junior Dance—Robert DeMarco-Kathy Cavazzi, East Meadow, N.Y.
Senior Men's Figures—Tony St. Jacques, Virginia Beach, Va.
Senior Ladies Figures—Anna Conklin, Bakersfield, Cal.
Senior Men's Singles—Michael Glatz, San Diego, Cal.
Senior Ladies Singles—Kathleen DiFelice, Delanco, N.J.
Junior Men's Figures—Dallas Oskey, Flint, Mich.
Junior Ladies Figures—Tammy DeWulf, Brighton, Mich.
Junior Men's Singles—Rick Monturo, Cleveland, Oh.
Junior Ladies Singles—Gerry Goodman, Chula Vista, Cal.
Senior Pairs—Paul Price-Tina Kneisley, Brighton, Mich.
Junior Pairs—Rick Monturo-Valerie Acree, Cleveland, Oh.

Speed Skating

Senior Men—Robb Dunn, Farmington Hills, Mich.
Senior Ladies—Linda Swaim, High Point, N.C.
Junior Men—Greg Collins, Franklin, Ind.
Junior Ladies—Darlene Kessinger, Franklin, Ind.
Senior Four-Man Relay—Chris Snyder, Mark Sutton, Marty Sutton, Mike Vouklizas, Irving, Tex.
Senior Four-Lady Relay—Kathy Katovich, Denise McLeod, Tammy Griffith, Sue Dooley, Farmington Hills, Mich.

Sports on Television

Source: Sports 1979, A.C. Nielsen Co.

	Household rating %	% Viewing audience			
		Men	Women	Teens	Children
Football					
NFL Superbowl	46.3	48	34	10	8
ABC-NFL (Monday evening)	19.6	58	29	8	5
CBS-NFL	15.0	57	27	9	7
NBC-NFL	14.0	55	28	9	8
College bowl games	16.2	51	31	7	11
College All-Star games	8.9	48	32	11	9
NCAA regular season	11.4	57	28	8	7
Baseball					
World Series	28.5	50	37	7	6
All-Star game	23.4	51	32	10	7
Regular season	6.5	55	28	9	8
Horse racing					
Average all	7.4	46	41	7	6
Basketball					
NBA average	5.5	52	31	10	7
NCAA average	6.9	51	29	10	10
Bowling					
Pro tour	8.8	43	37	10	10
Auto racing	8.3	48	32	10	10
Golf					
Tournaments	5.2	52	37	5	6
Tennis					
Wimbledon	5.0	46	31	10	13
Tournament average	4.5	45	39	6	10
Multi-sports series					
ABC Wide World of Sports	10.7	44	34	9	13
CBS Sports Spectacular	6.2	44	34	10	12
Sportsworld	5.6	50	28	11	11

Golf Records

United States Open

Year	Winner	Year	Winner	Year	Winner	Year	Winner
1897	Joe Lloyd	1917-18	(Not played)	1938	Ralph Guldahl	1961	Gene Littler
1898	Fred Herd	1919	Walter Hagen	1939	Byron Nelson	1962	Jack Nicklaus
1899	Willie Smith	1920	Edward Ray	1940	Lawson Little	1963	Julius Boros
1900	Harry Vardon	1921	Jim Barnes	1941	Craig Wood	1964	Ken Venturi
1901	Willie Anderson	1922	Gene Sarazen	1942-45	(Not played)	1965	Gary Player
1902	L. Auchterlonie	1923	Bobby Jones*	1946	Lloyd Mangrum	1966	Billy Casper
1903	Willie Anderson	1924	Cyril Walker	1947	L. Worsham	1967	Jack Nicklaus
1904	Willie Anderson	1925	Willie MacFarlane	1948	Ben Hogan	1968	Lee Trevino
1905	Willie Anderson	1926	Bobby Jones*	1949	Cary Middlecoff	1969	Orville Moody
1906	Alex Smith	1927	Tommy Armour	1950	Ben Hogan	1970	Tony Jacklin
1907	Alex Ross	1928	John Farrell	1951	Ben Hogan	1971	Lee Trevino
1908	Fred McLeod	1929	Bobby Jones*	1952	Julius Boros	1972	Jack Nicklaus
1909	George Sargent	1930	Bobby Jones*	1953	Ben Hogan	1973	Johnny Miller
1910	Alex Smith	1931	Wm. Burke	1954	Ed Furgol	1974	Hale Irwin
1911	John McDermott	1932	Gene Sarazen	1955	Jack Fleck	1975	Lou Graham
1912	John McDermott	1933	John Goodman*	1956	Cary Middlecoff	1976	Jerry Pate
1913	Francis Ouimet*	1934	Olin Dutra	1957	Dick Mayer	1977	Hubert Green
1914	Walter Hagen	1935	Sam Parks Jr.	1958	Tommy Bolt	1978	Andy North
1915	Jerome Travers*	1936	Tony Manero	1959	Billy Casper	1979	Hale Irwin
1916	Chick Evans*	1937	Ralph Guldahl	1960	Arnold Palmer	1980	Jack Nicklaus

*Amateur

U.S. Women's Open Golf Champions

Year	Winner	Year	Winner	Year	Winner	Year	Winner
1948	"Babe" Zaharias	1956	Mrs. K. Cornelius	1964	Mickey Wright	1972	Susie Maxwell Berning
1949	Louise Suggs	1957	Betsy Rawls	1965	Carol Mann	1973	Susie Maxwell Berning
1950	"Babe" Zaharias	1958	Mickey Wright	1966	Sandra Spuzich	1974	Sandra Haynie
1951	Betsy Rawls	1959	Mickey Wright	1967	Catherine Lacoste*	1975	Sandra Palmer
1952	Louise Suggs	1960	Betsy Rawls	1968	Susie Maxwell Berning	1976	JoAnne Carner
1953	Betsy Rawls	1961	Mickey Wright	1969	Donna Caponi	1977	Hollis Stacy
1954	"Babe" Zaharias	1962	Marie Lindstrom	1970	Donna Caponi	1978	Hollis Stacy
1955	Fay Crocker	1963	Mary Mills	1971	JoAnne Carner	1979	Jerilyn Britz
						1980	Amy Alcott

*Amateur

Masters Golf Tournament Champions

Year	Winner	Year	Winner	Year	Winner	Year	Winner
1934	Horton Smith	1948	Claude Harmon	1959	Art Wall Jr.	1970	Billy Casper
1935	Gene Sarazen	1949	Sam Snead	1960	Arnold Palmer	1971	Charles Coody
1936	Horton Smith	1950	Jimmy Demaret	1961	Gary Player	1972	Jack Nicklaus
1937	Byron Nelson	1951	Ben Hogan	1962	Arnold Palmer	1973	Tommy Aaron
1938	Henry Picard	1952	Sam Snead	1963	Jack Nicklaus	1974	Gary Player
1939	Ralph Guldahl	1953	Ben Hogan	1964	Arnold Palmer	1975	Jack Nicklaus
1940	Jimmy Demaret	1954	Sam Snead	1965	Jack Nicklaus	1976	Ray Floyd
1941	Craig Wood	1955	Cary Middlecoff	1966	Jack Nicklaus	1977	Tom Watson
1942	Byron Nelson	1956	Jack Burke	1967	Gay Brewer Jr.	1978	Gary Player
1943-1945	(Not played)	1957	Doug Ford	1968	Bob Goalby	1979	Fuzzy Zoeller
1946	Herman Keiser	1958	Arnold Palmer	1969	George Archer	1980	Severiano Ballesteros
1947	Jimmy Demaret						

Professional Golfer's Association Championships

Year	Winner	Year	Winner	Year	Winner	Year	Winner
1920	Jock Hutchison	1935	Johnny Revolta	1951	Sam Snead	1966	Al Geiberger
1921	Walter Hagen	1936	Denny Shute	1952	James Turnesa	1967	Don January
1922	Gene Sarazen	1937	Denny Shute	1953	Walter Burkemo	1968	Julius Boros
1923	Gene Sarazen	1938	Paul Runyan	1954	Melvin Harbert	1969	Ray Floyd
1924	Walter Hagen	1939	Henry Picard	1955	Doug Ford	1970	Dave Stockton
1925	Walter Hagen	1940	Byron Nelson	1956	Jack Burke	1971	Jack Nicklaus
1926	Walter Hagen	1941	Victor Ghezzi	1957	Lionel Hebert	1972	Gary Player
1927	Walter Hagen	1942	Sam Snead	1958	Dow Finsterwald	1973	Jack Nicklaus
1928	Leo Diegel	1944	Bob Hamilton	1959	Bob Rosburg	1974	Lee Trevino
1929	Leo Diegel	1945	Byron Nelson	1960	Jay Hebert	1975	Jack Nicklaus
1930	Tommy Armour	1946	Ben Hogan	1961	Jerry Barber	1976	Dave Stockton
1931	Tom Creavy	1947	Jim Ferrier	1962	Gary Player	1977	Lanny Wadkins
1932	Olin Dutra	1948	Ben Hogan	1963	Jack Nicklaus	1978	John Mahaffey
1933	Gene Sarazen	1949	Sam Snead	1964	Bob Nichols	1979	David Graham
1934	Paul Runyan	1950	Chandler Harper	1965	Dave Marr	1980	Jack Nicklaus

Canadian Open Golf Champions

Year	Winner	Year	Winner	Year	Winner	Year	Winner
1945	Byron Nelson	1954	Pat Fletcher	1963	Doug Ford	1972	Gay Brewer
1946	George Fazio	1955	Arnold Palmer	1964	Kel Nagle	1973	Tom Weiskopf
1947	Bobby Locke	1956	Doug Sanders	1965	Gene Littler	1974	Bobby Nichols
1948	C.W. Congdon	1957	George Bayer	1966	Don Massengale	1975	Tom Weiskopf
1949	E.J. Harrison	1958	Wes Ellis Jr.	1967	Billy Casper	1976	Jerry Pate
1950	Jim Ferrier	1959	Doug Ford	1968	Bob Charles	1977	Lee Trevino
1951	Jim Ferrier	1960	Art Wall, Jr.	1969	Tommy Aaron	1978	Bruce Lietzke
1952	John Palmer	1961	Jacky Cupit	1970	Kermit Zarley	1979	Lee Trevino
1953	Dave Douglas	1962	Ted Kroll	1971	Lee Trevino	1980	Bob Gilder

Professional Golf Tournaments in 1980

Date	Event	Winner	Score	Prize
Jan. 14	Bob Hope Desert Classic, Palm Springs, Cal.	Craig Stadler	343	$50,000
Jan. 20	Phoenix Open	Jeff Mitchell	272	54,000
Jan. 27	Andy Williams-San Diego Open	Tom Watson	*275	45,000
Feb. 3	Bing Crosby National Pro-Am, Pebble Beach, Cal.	George Burns	280	54,000
Feb. 10	Hawaiian Open, Honolulu	Andy Bean	266	58,000
Feb. 19	Tucson Open	Jim Colbert	270	54,000
Feb. 24	Glenn Campbell-Los Angeles Open	Tom Watson	276	45,000
Mar. 2	Bay Hill Classic, Orlando, Fla.	Dave Eichelberger	279	54,000
Mar. 9	Inverrary Classic, Lauderhill, Fla.	Johnny Miller	274	54,000
Mar. 16	Doral-Eastern Open, Miami, Fla.	Ray Floyd	*279	45,000
Mar. 23	Tournament Players Championship, Ponte Vedra Beach, Fla.	Lee Trevino	278	72,000
Mar. 31	Sea Pines Heritage Classic, Hilton Head, S.C.	Doug Tewell	*280	54,000
Apr. 6	Greater Greensboro Open, N.C.	Craig Stadler	275	45,000
Apr. 13	Masters Tournament, Augusta, Ga.	Severiano Ballesteros	275	55,000
Apr. 20	Tournament of Champions, Rancho La Costa, Cal.	Tom Watson	276	54,000
Apr. 27	New Orleans Open	Tom Watson	273	45,000
May 4	Houston Open	Curtis Strange	*266	63,000
May 13	Byron Nelson Classic, Dallas, Tex.	Tom Watson	275	54,000
May 18	Colonial National Tournament, Ft. Worth, Tex.	Bruce Lietzke	271	54,000
May 25	Memorial Tournament, Dublin, Oh.	David Graham	280	54,000
June 1	Kemper Open, Bethesda, Md.	John Mahaffey	275	72,000
June 8	Atlanta Classic	Larry Nelson	270	50,000
June 15	U.S. Open, Springfield, N.J.	Jack Nicklaus	272	55,000
June 22	Canadian Open, Ile Bizard, Que.	Bob Gilder	274	63,000
June 29	Danny Thomas-Memphis Classic	Lee Trevino	285	54,000
July 6	Western Open, Oak Brook, Ill.	Scott Simpson	281	54,000
July 13	Milwaukee Open	Bill Kratzert	266	36,000
July 20	Quad Cities Open, Coal City, Ill.	Scott Hoch	266	36,000
July 27	Greater Hartford Open	Howard Twitty	*266	54,000
Aug. 4	Philadelphia Classic	Doug Tewell	272	45,000
Aug. 10	PGA Championship, Rochester, N.Y.	Jack Nicklaus	274	60,000
Aug. 17	Westchester Classic, Harrison, N.Y.	Curtis Strange	273	72,000
Aug. 24	World Series of Golf, Akron, Oh.	Tom Watson	270	100,000
Aug. 31	B.C. Open, Endicott, N.Y.	Don Pooley	271	49,500
Sept. 7	Pleasant Valley Classic, Sutton, Mass.	Wayne Levi	273	54,000

Women

Date	Event	Winner	Score	Prize
Feb. 3	Deer Creek Championship, Deerfield, Fla.	JoAnne Carner	282	$15,000
Feb. 24	Bent Tree Classic, Sarasota, Fla.	JoAnne Carner	280	15,000
Mar. 2	Sun City Classic, Sun City, Ariz.	Jan Stephenson	275	15,000
Mar. 9	Sunstar Classic, Los Angeles, Cal.	JoAnne Carner	207	18,750
Mar. 23	National Pro-Am, Las Vegas, Nev.	Donna Caponi Young	286	30,000
Mar. 30	Women's Kemper Open, Costa Mesa, Cal.	Nancy Lopez Melton	284	22,500
Apr. 6	Colgate-Dinah Shore Winners Circle, Palm Springs, Cal.	Donna Caponi Young	275	37,500
Apr. 20	Lady Citrus, Orlando, Fla.	Donna White	283	15,000
Apr. 27	Birmingham Classic, Birmingham, Ala.	Barbara Barrow	210	15,000
May 4	Women's International, Hilton Head, S.C.	Hollis Stacy	*279	15,000
May 18	Coca-Cola Classic, Clifton, N.J.	Donna White	*217	18,000
May 25	Corning Classic, Corning, N.Y.	Donna Caponi Young	281	15,000
June 1	Golden Lights Classic, New Rochelle, N.Y.	Beth Daniel	287	18,750
June 18	LPGA Championship, Mason, Oh.	Sally Little	285	22,500
June 22	Lady Keystone Open, Hershey, Pa.	JoAnne Carner	207	15,000
July 6	Mayflower Classic, Noblesville, Ind.	Amy Alcott	275	22,500
July 13	U.S. Women's Open, Nashville, Tenn.	Amy Alcott	280	19,000
July 20	Greater Baltimore Golf Classic	Pat Bradley	206	15,000
July 27	WUI Classic, Jericho, N.Y.	Sally Little	284	18,750
Aug. 4	West Virginia Classic, Wheeling, W. Va.	Sandra Post	*211	15,000
Aug. 10	Peter Jackson Classic, Toronto, Ont.	Pat Bradley	277	22,500
Aug. 17	Patty Berg Classic, St. Paul, Minn.	Beth Daniel	210	15,000
Aug. 24	Denver Ladies Classic, Denver, Col.	Beth Daniel	276	22,500
Sept. 7	World Series of Women's Golf, Cleveland, Oh.	Beth Daniel	282	50,000

*Won playoff.

British Open Golf Champions

Year	Winner	Year	Winner	Year	Winner	Year	Winner
1913	J.H. Taylor	1932	Gene Sarazen	1952	Bobby Locke	1967	Roberto de Vicenzo
1914	Harry Vardon	1933	Denny Shute	1953	Ben Hogan	1968	Gary Player
1915-19	(Not played)	1934	Henry Cotton	1954	Peter Thomson	1969	Tony Jacklin
1920	George Duncan	1935	Alf Perry	1955	Peter Thomson	1970	Jack Nicklaus
1921	Jock Hutchison	1936	Alf Padgham	1956	Peter Thomson	1971	Lee Trevino
1922	Walter Hagen	1937	T.H. Cotton	1957	Bobby Locke	1972	Lee Trevino
1923	Arthur Havers	1938	R.A. Whitcombe	1958	Peter Thomson	1973	Tom Weiskopf
1924	Walter Hagen	1939	Richard Burton	1959	Gary Player	1974	Gary Player
1925	Jim Barnes	1940-45	(Not played)	1960	Ken Nagle	1975	Tom Watson
1926	Bobby Jones	1946	Sam Snead	1961	Arnold Palmer	1976	Johnny Miller
1927	Bobby Jones	1947	Fred Daly	1962	Arnold Palmer	1977	Tom Watson
1928	Walter Hagen	1948	Henry Cotton	1963	Bob Charles	1978	Jack Nicklaus
1929	Walter Hagen	1949	Bobby Locke	1964	Tony Lema	1979	Severiano Ballesteros
1930	Bobby Jones	1950	Bobby Locke	1965	Peter Thomson		
1931	Tommy Armour	1951	Max Faulkner	1966	Jack Nicklaus	1980	Tom Watson

U.S. Amateur

Year	Winner	Year	Winner	Year	Winner	Year	Winner
1913	Jerome Travers	1930	Bobby Jones	1949	Charles Coe	1965	Robert Murphy Jr.
1914	Francis Ouimet	1931	Francis Ouimet	1950	Sam Urzetta	1966	Gary Cowan
1915	Robert Gardner	1932	Ross Somerville	1951	Billy Maxwell	1967	Bob Dickson
1916	Chick Evans Jr.	1933	George Dunlap Jr.	1952	Jack Westland	1968	Bruce Fleisher
1917-18	(not played)	1934	Lawson Little	1953	Gene Littler	1969	Steve Melnyk
1919	Davidson Herron	1935	Lawson Little	1954	Arnold Palmer	1970	Lanny Wadkins
1920	Chick Evans Jr.	1936	John Fischer	1955	Harvie Ward	1971	Gary Cowan
1921	Jesse Guilford	1937	John Goodman	1956	Harvie Ward	1972	Vinnie Giles
1922	Jess Sweetser	1938	Willie Turnesa	1957	Hillman Robbins	1973	Craig Stadler
1923	Max Marston	1939	Bud Ward	1958	Charles Coe	1974	Jerry Pate
1924	Bobby Jones	1940	Dick Chapman	1959	Jack Nicklaus	1975	Fred Ridley
1925	Bobby Jones	1941	Bud Ward	1960	Deane Beman	1976	Bill Sander
1926	George Von Elm	1942-45	(not played)	1961	Jack Nicklaus	1977	John Fought
1927	Bobby Jones	1946	Ted Bishop	1962	Labron Harris Jr.	1978	John Cook
1928	Bobby Jones	1947	Skee Riegel	1963	Deane Beman	1979	Mark O'Meara
1929	Harrison Johnston	1948	Willie Turnesa	1964	Bill Campbell	1980	Hal Sutton

Women's U.S. Amateur

Year	Winner	Year	Winner	Year	Winner	Year	Winner
1913	Gladys Raven Scroft	1930	Glenna Collett	1949	Dorothy Porter	1965	Jean Ashley
1914	Mrs. H. A. Jackson	1931	Helen Hicks	1950	Beverly Hanson	1966	JoAnne Carner
1915	Mrs. C. H. Vanderbeck	1932	Virginia Van Wie	1951	Dorothy Kirby	1967	Lou Dill
1916	Alexa Stirling	1933	Virginia Van Wie	1952	Jackie Pung	1968	JoAnn Carner
1917-18	(not played)	1934	Virginia Van Wie	1953	Mary Faulk	1969	Catherine Lacoste
1919	Alexa Stirling	1935	Glenna C. Vare	1954	Barbara Romack	1970	Martha Wilkinson
1920	Alexa Stirling	1936	Pamela Barton	1955	Pat Lesser	1971	Laura Baugh
1921	Marion Hollins	1937	Mrs. J. A. Page	1956	Marlene Stewart	1972	Mary Budke
1922	Glenna Collett	1938	Patty Berg	1957	JoAnne Gunderson	1973	Carol Semple
1923	Edith Cummings	1939	Betty Jameson	1958	Anne Quast	1974	Cynthia Hill
1924	Mrs. D.C. Hurd	1940	Betty Jameson	1959	Barbara McIntire	1975	Beth Daniel
1925	Glenna Collett	1941	Mrs. Frank New	1960	JoAnne Gunderson	1976	Donna Horton
1926	Mrs. G. Stetson	1942-45	(not played)	1961	Anne Q. Decker	1977	Beth Daniel
1927	Mrs. M. Horn	1946	"Babe" Zaharias	1962	JoAnne Gunderson	1978	Cathy Sherk
1928	Glenna Collett	1947	Louise Suggs	1963	Anne Q. Welts	1979	Carolyn Hill
1929	Glenna Collett	1948	Grace Lenczyk	1964	Barbara McIntire	1980	Julie Simpson Inkster

PGA Hall of Fame

Established in 1940 to honor those who have made outstanding contributions to the game by their lifetime playing ability.

Anderson, Willie
Armour, Tommy
Barnes, Jim
Berg, Patty
Boros, Julius
Brady, Mike
Burke, Billy
Burke Jr., Jack
Cooper, Harry
Cruickshank, Bobby
Demaret, Jimmy
Diegel, Leo
Dudley, Edward
Dutra, Olin
Evans, Chick
Farrell, Johnny
Ford, Doug
Ghezzi, Vic
Guldahl, Ralph
Hagen, Walter
Harbert, M. R. (Chick)
Harper, Chandler
Harrison, E. J.
Hogan, Ben
Hutchison Sr., Jock
Jones, Bob
Little, W. Lawson
Mangrum, Lloyd
McDermott, John
McLeod, Fred
Middlecoff, Cary
Nelson, Byron
Ouimet, Francis
Picard, Henry
Revolta, Johnny
Runyan, Paul
Sarazen, Gene
Shute, Denny
Smith, Alex
Smith, Horton
Smith, MacDonald
Snead, Sam
Travers, Jerry
Travis, Walter
de Vicenzo, Roberto
Wood, Craig
Zaharias, Mildred (Babe)

PGA Leading Money Winners

Year	Player	Dollars	Year	Player	Dollars	Year	Player	Dollars
1945	Byron Nelson	52,511	1957	Dick Mayer	65,835	1969	Frank Beard	175,223
1946	Ben Hogan	42,556	1958	Arnold Palmer	42,407	1970	Lee Trevino	157,037
1947	Jimmy Demaret	27,936	1959	Art Wall Jr.	53,167	1971	Jack Nicklaus	244,490
1948	Ben Hogan	36,812	1960	Arnold Palmer	75,262	1972	Jack Nicklaus	320,542
1949	Sam Snead	31,593	1961	Gary Player	64,540	1973	Jack Nicklaus	308,362
1950	Sam Snead	35,758	1962	Arnold Palmer	81,448	1974	Johnny Miller	353,201
1951	Lloyd Mangrum	26,088	1963	Arnold Palmer	128,230	1975	Jack Nicklaus	323,149
1952	Julius Boros	37,032	1964	Jack Nicklaus	113,284	1976	Jack Nicklaus	266,438
1953	Lew Worsham	34,002	1965	Jack Nicklaus	140,752	1977	Tom Watson	310,653
1954	Bob Toski	65,819	1966	Billy Casper	121,944	1978	Tom Watson	362,429
1955	Julius Boros	65,121	1967	Jack Nicklaus	188,988	1979	Tom Watson	462,636
1956	Ted Kroll	72,835	1968	Billy Casper	205,168			

LPGA Leading Money Winners

Year	Winner	Dollars	Year	Winner	Dollars	Year	Winner	Dollars
1953	Louise Suggs	19,816	1962	Mickey Wright	21,641	1971	Kathy Whitworth	41,181
1954	Patty Berg	16,011	1963	Mickey Wright	31,269	1972	Kathy Whitworth	65,063
1955	Patty Berg	16,492	1964	Mickey Wright	29,800	1973	Kathy Whitworth	82,854
1956	Marlene Hagge	20,235	1965	Kathy Whitworth	28,658	1974	JoAnne Carner	87,094
1957	Patty Berg	16,272	1966	Kathy Whitworth	33,517	1975	Sandra Palmer	94,805
1958	Beverly Hanson	12,629	1967	Kathy Whitworth	32,937	1976	Judy Rankin	150,734
1959	Betsy Rawls	26,774	1968	Kathy Whitworth	48,379	1977	Judy Rankin	122,890
1960	Louise Suggs	16,892	1969	Carol Mann	49,152	1978	Nancy Lopez	189,813
1961	Mickey Wright	22,236	1970	Kathy Whitworth	30,235	1979	Nancy Lopez	215,987

Ryder Cup Matches

United States vs. Great Britain — Professional (biennial)
Series standing — United States 19, Great Britain 3, 1 tie

Series record

1955 United States 8; Great Britain 4
1957 Great Britain 7; United States 4
1959 United States 8½; Great Britain 3½
1961 United States 14½; Great Britain 9½
1963 United States 23; Great Britain 9
1965 United States 19½; Great Britain 12½
1967 United States 23½; Great Britain 8½

Series record

1969 United States 16; Great Britain 16
1971 United States 18½; Great Britain 13½
1973 Great Britain 13; United States 10
1975 United States 21; Great Britain 11
1977 United States 12½; Great Britain 7½
1979 United States 17; Great Britain-Ireland 11

International Walker Cup Golf Match

United States vs. Great Britain — Men's Amateur (biennial)
Series standing — United States, 24, Great Britain 2, 1 tie

Series record

1955 United States 10; Great Britain 2
1957 United States 10; Great Britain 2
1959 United States 9; Great Britain 3
1961 United States 11; Great Britain 1
1963 United States 9; Great Britain 3
1965 United States 11; Great Britain 11
1967 United States 13; Great Britain 7

Series record

1969 United States 10; Great Britain 8
1971 Great Britain 13; United States 11
1973 United States 14; Great Britain 10
1975 United States 15½; Great Britain 8½
1977 United States 16; Great Britain 8
1979 United States 15½; Great Britain-Ireland 8½

International Curtis Cup Golf Match

United States vs. Great Britain (plus Ireland) — Women's Amateur (biennial)
Series standing — United States 17, Great Britain 2, 2 ties

Series record

1954 United States 6; Great Britain 3
1957 Great Britain 5; United States 4
1959 Great Britain 4½; United States 4½
1960 United States 6½; Great Britain 2½
1962 United States 8; Great Britain 1
1964 United States 10½; Great Britain 7½
1966 United States 13; Great Britain 5

Series record

1968 United States 10½; Great Britain 7½
1970 United States 11½; Great Britain 6½
1972 United States 10; Great Britain 8
1974 United States 13; Great Britain 5
1976 United States 11½; Great Britain 6½
1978 United States 12; Great Britain 6
1980 United States 13; Great Britain 5

Contract Bridge Championships in 1979-80

Source: American Contract Bridge League, Memphis, Tenn.

Fall Championships

Cincinnati, Oh., Nov. 16-25, 1979

Open Teams (Board-A-Match) Reisinger Trophy — A. E. (Bud) Reinhold, Northbrook, Ill.; Robert Levin, N. Miami Beach, Fla.; Russ Arnold, Miami, Fla.; Jeff Meckstroth, Reynoldsburg, Oh.; Eric Rodwell, West Lafayette, Ind.

North American Swiss Teams — Jim Robison, Hermine Baron, Los Angeles, Cal.; Paul Ivaska, Las Vegas, Nev.; R. J. Becker, Boston, Mass.

Blue Ribbon Pairs — Robert Levin, N. Miami Beach, Ron Smith, Miami, Fla.

Life Master Men's Pairs — Eric Rodwell, West Lafayette, Ind.; Jeff Meckstroth, Reynoldsburg, Oh.

Life Master Women's Pairs — Edith Kemp, Miami Beach, Fla.; Nancy Gruver, Ellicott City, Md.

Mixed Pairs — Mike Smolen, Juanita Skelton, Marina del Rey, Cal.

Most master points for tournament — Robert Levin, N. Miami Beach, Fla.

Spring Championships

Fresno, Cal. Mar. 14-23, 1980

Vanderbilt Trophy Teams — A. E. (Bud) Reinhold, Russ Arnold, Miami, Fla.; Robert Levin, N. Miami Beach, Fla.; Jeff Meckstroth, Reynoldsburg, Oh.; Eric Rodwell, West Lafayette, Ind.

Men's Board-A-Match Teams — Sam Stayman, Palm Beach, Fla.; Ross Grabel, East Providence, R.I.; Milton Rosenberg, Lombard, Ill.; William Rosen, Highland Park, Ill.; Bart Bramley, Avon, Conn.; George Tornay, New York, N.Y.

Women's Knockout Teams — Leo Spivack (non-playing captain) Chicago, Ill.; Kathie Wei, Judi Radin, New York, N.Y.; Carol Sanders, Nashville, Tenn.; Betty Ann Kennedy, Shreveport, La.; Edith Kemp, Miami Beach, Fla.; Nancy Gruver, Ellicott City, Md.

North American Open Pairs — Michael Schreiber, Thousand Oaks, Cal.; Paul Lewis, Berkeley, Cal.

Men's Pairs — Peter Weichsel, Flushing, N.Y.; Neil Silverman, New York, N.Y.

Grand National Pairs — Bob Feller, Albany, N.Y.; Jeffrey Hall, Clifton Park, N.Y.

Women's Pairs — Mildred Boyce, Barbara Norwood, Austin, Tex.

Most master points for tournament — (tie) Jeff Meckstroth, Reynoldsburg, Oh.; Eric Rodwell, West Lafayette, Ind.

Summer Championships

Chicago, Ill., July 18-27, 1980

Spingold Knockout Teams — Mike Becker, New York, N.Y.; Kyle Larsen, Walnut Creek, Cal.; Ron Rubin, Livingston, N.J.; Alan Sontag, New York, N.Y.; Ron von derPorten, San Francisco, Cal.; Peter Weichsel, Flushing, N.Y.

Grand National Teams — Craig and Jan Janitschke, Dick Lesko, Jack Bitman, Denver, Col.

Master Mixed Teams — Barry Crane, Studio City, Cal.; Kerri Shuman, Los Angeles, Cal.; Jose John Hamui, Elias Konstantnovsky, Laura Mariscal, Mexico City, Mexico.

Life Master Pairs — Robert Hamman, Dallas, Tex.; Eric Rodwell, West Lafayette, Ind.

Most master points for tournament — Peter Weichsel, Flushing, N.Y.

Trotting and Pacing Records

Source: Martin J. Evans, U.S. Trotting Assn.; records to Sept., 1980

Trotting Records

Asterisk (*) denotes record was made against the clock. Times—seconds in fifths.

One mile records (mile track)

All-age — *1:54.4 — Nevele Pride, Indianapolis, Ind., Aug. 31, 1969.

Two-year-old — 1:57 — Brisco Hanover, Du Quoin, Ill., Sept. 2, 1977.

Three-year-old — 1:55 — Speedy Somolli and Florida Pro, Du Quoin, Ill., Sept. 2, 1978.

(Half-mile track)

All-age — 1:56.4 — Nevele Pride, Saratoga Springs, N.Y., Sept. 6, 1969.

Two-year-old — 2:00.1 — Ayres, Delaware, Oh., 1963.

Three-year-old — 1:58.3 — Songcan, Delaware, Oh., 1972.

(Five Eighth-mile track)

All-Age — 1:57.1 — Lindy's Crown, Wilmington, Del., July 27, 1980.

Two-year-old — 2:01 — Starlark Hanover, Wilkes-Barre, Pa., Aug. 30, 1973; Green Speed, Philadelphia, Pa., Oct. 19, 1976.

Three-year old — 1:58.1 — Speedy Somolli, Meadow Lands, Pa., Aug. 4, 1978.

Pacing Records

One mile records (mile track)

All-age — *1:52 — Steady Star, Lexington, Ky., Oct. 1, 1971.

Two-year-old — 1:54.1 — Jade Prince, Lexington, Ky., Oct. 5, 1976.

Three-year-old — *1:52.2 — Falcon Almahurst, Lexington, Ky., Sept. 29, 1978.

(Half-mile track)

All-age — 1:55.2 — Falcon Almahurst, Delaware, Oh., Sept. 21, 1978.

Two-year-old — 1:57.4 — Whamo, Louisville, Ky., Aug. 31, 1979.

Three-year-old — 1:55.2 — Falcon Almahurst, Delaware, Oh., Sept. 21, 1978.

(Five Eighth-mile track)

All-Age — 1:53.2 — Storm Damage, Washington, Pa., Aug. 6, 1980.

Two-year-old — 1:57 — Wellwood Hanover, Philadephia, Pa., Oct. 11, 1977.

Three-year-old — 1:53.2 — Storm Damage, Washington, Pa., Aug. 6, 1980.

The Hambletonian (3-year-old trotters)

Year	Winner	Driver	Purse	Year	Winner	Driver	Purse
1947	Hoot Mon	S.F. Palin	$46,267	1964	Ayres	John Simpson Sr.	$115,281
1948	Demon Hanover	Harrison Hoyt	59,941	1965	Egyptian Candor	Del Cameron	122,245
1949	Miss Tilly	Fred Egan	69,791	1966	Kerry Way	Frank Ervin	122,540
1950	Lusty Song	Del Miller	75,209	1967	Speedy Streak	Del Cameron	122,650
1951	Mainliner	Guy Crippen	95,263	1968	Nevele Pride	Stanley Dancer	116,190
1952	Sharp Note	Bion Shively	87,637	1969	Lindy's Pride	Howard Beissinger	124,910
1953	Helicopter	Harry Harvey	117,118	1970	Timothy T	John Simpson Sr.	143,630
1954	Newport Dream	Del Cameron	106,830	1971	Speedy Crown	Howard Beissinger	128,770
1955	Scott Frost	Joe O'Brien	86,863	1972	Super Bowl	Stanley Dancer	119,090
1956	The Intruder	Ned Bower	98,591	1973	Flirth	Ralph Baldwin	144,710
1957	Hickory Smoke	John Simpson Sr.	111,126	1974	Christopher T	Bill Haughton	160,150
1958	Emily's Pride	Flave Nipe	106,719	1975	Bonefish	Stanley Dancer	232,192
1959	Diller Hanover	Frank Ervin	125,284	1976	Steve Lobell	Bill Haughton	263,524
1960	Blaze Hanover	Joe O'Brien	144,590	1977	Green Speed	Bill Haughton	284,131
1961	Harlan Dean	James Arthur	131,573	1978	Speedy Somolli	Howard Beissinger	241,280
1962	A.C. Os Viking	Sanders Russell	116,312	1979	Legend Hanover	George Sholty	300,000
1963	Speedy Scot	Ralph Baldwin	115,549	1980	Burgomeister	Bill Haughton	293,570

Annual Leading Money-Winning Horses

Trotters

Year	Horse	Dollars	Year	Horse	Dollars	Year	Horse	Dollars
1953	Newport Dream	94,933	1962	Duke Rodney	206,113	1971	Fresh Yankee	293,960
1954	Katie Key	84,867	1963	Speedy Scot	144,403	1972	Super Bowl	437,108
1955	Scott Frost	186,101	1964	Speedy Scot	235,710	1973	Spartan Hanover	262,023
1956	Scott Frost	85,851	1965	Dartmouth	252,348	1974	Delmonica Hanover	252,165
1957	Hoot Song	114,877	1966	Noble Victory	210,696	1975	Savoir	351,385
1958	Emily's Pride	118,830	1967	Carlisle	231,243	1976	Steve Lobell	338,770
1959	Diller Hanover	149,897	1968	Nevele Pride	427,440	1977	Green Speed	584,405
1960	Su Mac Lad	159,662	1969	Lindy's Pride	323,997	1978	Speedy Somolli	362,404
1961	Su Mac Lad	245,750	1970	Fresh Yankee	359,002	1979	Chiola Hanover	553,058

Pacers

Year	Horse	Dollars	Year	Horse	Dollars	Year	Horse	Dollars
1953	Keystoner	59,131	1962	Henry T. Adios	220,302	1971	Albatross	558,009
1954	Red Sails	66,615	1963	Overtrick	208,833	1972	Albatross	459,921
1955	Adios Harry	98,900	1964	Race Time	199,292	1973	Sir Dalrae	307,354
1956	Adios Harry	129,912	1965	Bret Hanover	341,784	1974	Armbro Omaha	345,146
1957	Torpid	113,982	1966	Bret Hanover	407,534	1975	Silk Stockings	336,312
1958	Belle Action	167,887	1967	Romulus Hanover	277,636	1976	Keystone Ore	539,762
1959	Bye Bye Byrd	199,933	1968	Rum Customer	355,618	1977	Governor Skipper	522,148
1960	Bye Bye Byrd	187,612	1969	Overcall	373,150	1978	Abercrombie	703,260
1961	Adios Butler	180,250	1970	Most Happy Fella	387,239	1979	Hot Hitter	826,542

Leading Money-Winning Horses

(As of Sept. 18, 1980)

Trotters				Pacers			
Bellino II	$1,960,945	Keystone Pioneer	$1,071,927	Niatross	$1,738,796	Rum Customer	$1,001,548
Une de Mai	1,660,627	Roquepine	956,161	Rambling Willie	1,699,647	Cardigan Bay	1,000,837
Savoir	1,365,145	Green Speed	953,013	Albatross	1,201,470	Abercrombie	984,391
Fresh Yankee	1,294,252	Wayne Eden	925,000	Governor Skipper	1,039,756	Hot Hitter	963,574
Eleazer	1,290,194	Cold Comfort	897,396	Land Grant	1,026,510	Bret Hanover	922,616

Harness Horse of the Year

(Chosen by the U.S. Trotting Assn. and the U.S. Harness Writers Assn.)

1948	Rodney	1956	Scott Frost	1964	Bret Hanover	1972	Albatross
1949	Good Time	1957	Torpid	1965	Bret Hanover	1973	Sir Dalrae
1950	Proximity	1958	Emily's Pride	1966	Bret Hanover	1974	Delmonica Hanover
1951	Pronto Don	1959	Bye Bye Byrd	1967	Nevele Pride	1975	Savior
1952	Good Time	1960	Adios Butler	1968	Nevele Pride	1976	Keystone Ore
1953	Hi Lo's Forbes	1961	Adios Butler	1969	Nevele Pride	1977	Green Speed
1954	Stenographer	1962	Su Mac Lad	1970	Fresh Yankee	1978	Abercrombie
1955	Scott Frost	1963	Speedy Scot	1971	Albatross	1979	Niatross

Leading Drivers

Races Won

Year	Driver		Year	Driver		Year	Driver		Year	Driver	
1958	Bill Haughton	176	1964	Bob Farrington	312	1970	Herve Filion	486	1975	Daryl Buse	360
1959	William Gilmour	165	1965	Bob Farrington	310	1971	Herve Filion	543	1976	Herve Filion	445
1960	Del Insko	156	1966	Bob Farrington	283	1972	Herve Filion	605	1977	Herve Filion	441
1961	Bob Farrington	201	1967	Bob Farrington	277	1973	Herve Filion	445	1978	Herve Filion	423
1962	Bob Farrington	203	1968	Herve Filion	407	1974	Herve Filion	637	1979	Ron Waples	443
1963	Donald Busse	201	1969	Herve Filion	394						

Money Won

Year	Driver	Dollars	Year	Driver	Dollars	Year	Driver	Dollars
1957	Bill Haughton	586,950	1965	Bill Haughton	889,943	1973	Herve Filion	2,233,302
1958	Bill Haughton	816,659	1966	Stanley Dancer	1,218,403	1974	Herve Filion	3,474,315
1959	Bill Haughton	711,435	1967	Bill Haughton	1,305,773	1975	Carmine Abbatiello	2,275,093
1960	Del Miller	567,282	1968	Bill Haughton	1,654,172	1976	Herve Filion	2,241,045
1961	Stanley Dancer	674,723	1969	Del Insko	1,635,463	1977	Herve Filion	2,551,058
1962	Stanley Dancer	760,343	1970	Herve Filion	1,647,837	1978	Carmine Abbatiello	3,344,457
1963	Bill Haughton	790,086	1971	Herve Filion	1,915,945	1979	John Campbell	3,308,984
1964	Stanley Dancer	1,051,538	1972	Herve Filion	2,473,265			

Little Brown Jug (3-year-old pacers)

Delaware, Oh.

Year	Winner	Driver	Purse	Year	Winner	Driver	Purse
1957	Torpid	John Simpson Sr.	$73,528	1969	Laverne Hanover	Billy Haughton	$109,731
1958	Shadow Wave	Joe O'Brien	65,252	1970	Most Happy Fella	Stanley Dancer	100,110
1959	Adios Butler	Clint Hodgins	76,582	1971	Nansemond	Herve Filion	102,944
1960	Bullet Hanover	John Simpson Sr.	66,510	1972	Strike Out	Keith Waples	104,916
1961	Henry T. Adios	Stanley Dancer	70,069	1973	Melvin's Woe	Joe O'Brien	120,000
1962	Lehigh Hanover	Stanley Dancer	75,038	1974	Ambro Omaha	Billy Haughton	132,630
1963	Overtrick	John Patterson Sr.	68,294	1975	Seatrain	Ben Webster	147,813
1964	Vicar Hanover	Billy Haughton	66,590	1976	Keystone Ore	Stanley Dancer	153,799
1965	Bret Hanover	Frank Ervin	71,447	1977	Gov. Skipper	John Chapman	150,000
1966	Romeo Hanover	George Sholty	74,616	1978	Happy Escort	Bill Popfinger	186,760
1967	Best of All	James Hackett	84,778	1979	Hot Hitter	Herve Filion	226,455
1968	Rum Customer	Billy Haughton	104,226	1980	Niatross	Clint Galbraith	207,000

Polo Records

U.S. Open

1971	Oak Brook 8, Green Hill Farm 7.
1972	Milwaukee 9, Tulsa 5.
1973	Oak Brook 9, Willow Bend 4.
1974	Milwaukee 7, Houston 6.
1975	Milwaukee 14, Tulsa-Dallas 6.
1976	Willow Bend 10, Tulsa 5.
1977	Retama 11, Wilson Ranch 7.
1978	Abercrombie & Kent 7, Tulsa 6.
1979	Retama 6, Huisache 5.

Silver Cup

1971	Green Hill Farm 8, Milwaukee 6.
1972	Red Doors Farm 10, Sun Ranch 6.
1973	Houston 6, Willow Bend 4.
1974	Houston 7, Willow Bend 6.
1975	Lone Oak-Bunntyco 8, Tulsa 5.
1976	Wilson Ranch 10, Tulsa 8.
1977	Boca Raton 6, Houston 5.
1978	Wilson Ranch 7, Ft. Lauderdale 6.
1979	Retama 7, Willow Bend 6.
1980	Retama 9, Houston 8.

Other tournaments in 1980

Delegate's Cup—Tennessee 9, Mobile 4.
America Cup—Macondo, 6, Mallet Hill 5.
North American Cup—Kingsville 9, Retama 8.
Michelob World Cup—Hallal (Nigeria) 13, Retama 8.
Cup of the Americas—Argentina 10, U.S. 6.

U.S. Squash Racquets Association Amateur Champions

1961	Henri R. Salaun	1966	Victor Niederhoffer	1971	Colin Adair	1976	Peter Briggs
1962	Samuel P. Howe 3d	1967	Samuel P. Howe 3d	1972	Victor Niederhoffer	1977	Thomas E. Page
1963	Benjamin H. Heckscher	1968	Colin Adair	1973	Victor Niederhoffer	1978	Michael Desaulniers
1964	Ralph E. Howe	1969	Anil Nayar	1974	Victor Niederhoffer	1979	Mario Sanchez
1965	Stephen T. Vehslage	1970	Anil Nayar	1975	Victor Niederhoffer	1980	Michael Desaulniers

World Swimming Records

As of Aug. 4, 1980

Effective June 1, 1969, FINA recognizes only records made over a 50-meter course.

Men's Records

Freestyle

Distance	Time	Holder	Country	Where made	Date
100 Meters	**0:49.44**	Jonty Skinner	So. Africa	Philadelphia	Aug. 14, 1976
200 Meters	**1:49.16**	Rowdy Gaines	U.S.	Austin, Tex.	Apr. 11, 1980
400 Meters	**3:50.49**	Peter Szmidt	Canada	Ontario, Canada	July, 1980
800 Meters	**7:56.43**	Vladimir Salnikov	USSR	Minsk	Mar., 1979
1,500 Meters	**14:58.27**	Vladimir Salnikov	USSR	Moscow	July, 1980

Breaststroke

100 Meters	**1:02.86**	Gerald Moerken	W. Germany	Jonkoping, Sweden	Aug. 17, 1977
200 Meters	**2:15.11**	David Wilkie	Gt. Britain	Montreal	July 24, 1976

Butterfly

100 Meters	**0:54.15**	Per Arvidsson	Sweden	Austin, Tex.	Apr. 11, 1980
200 Meters	**1:58.46**	Craig Beardsley	U.S.	Irvine, Cal.	Aug. 2, 1980

Backstroke

100 Meters	**0:55.49**	John Naber	U.S.	Montreal	July 19, 1976
200 Meters	**1:59.19**	John Naber	U.S.	Montreal	July 24, 1976

Individual Medley

200 Meters	**2:03.24**	Bill Barrett	U.S.	Irvine, Cal.	Aug. 2, 1980
400 Meters	**4:20.05**	Jesse Vassallo	U.S., Puerto Rico	W. Berlin	Aug. 22, 1978

Freestyle Relays

400 M. (4×100)	**3:19.74**	Babashoff, Gaines, McCagg, Montgomery	U.S.	W. Berlin	Aug. 22, 1978
800 M. (4×200)	**7:20.83**	Forrester, Furniss, Gaines, Hackett	U.S.	W. Berlin	Aug., 1978

Medley Relays

400 M. (4×100)	**3:42.22**	Hencken, Naber, Montgomery, Vogel	U.S.	Montreal	July 22, 1976

Women's Records

Freestyle

100 Meters	**0:54.79**	Barbara Krause	E. Germany	Moscow	July, 1980
200 Meters	**1:58.43**	Cynthia Woodhead	U.S.	San Juan, P.R.	Aug., 1979
400 Meters	**4:06.28**	Tracey Wickham	Australia	W. Berlin	Aug. 24, 1978
800 Meters	**8:18.77**	Cynthia Woodhead	U.S.	Paris	Feb. 8, 1980
1,500 Meters	**16:04.49**	Kim Linehan	U.S.	Ft. Lauderdale, Fla.	Aug. 19, 1979

Breaststroke

100 Meters	**1:10.11**	Ute Geweniger	E. Germany	Moscow	July, 1980
200 Meters	**2:28.36**	Lina Kachushite	USSR	Potsdam	Mar. 6, 1979

Butterfly

100 Meters	**0:59.26**	Mary T. Meagher	U.S.	Austin, Tex.	Apr. 11, 1980
200 Meters	**2:06.37**	Mary T. Meagher	U.S.	Irvine, Cal.	Aug. 2, 1980

Backstroke

100 Meters	**1:00.86**	Rica Reinisch	E. Germany	Moscow	July, 1980
200 Meters	**2:11.77**	Rica Reinisch	E. Germany	Moscow	July, 1980

Individual Medley

200 Meters	**2:13.00**	Petra Schneider	E. Germany	E. Germany	May, 1980
400 Meters	**4:36.29**	Petra Schneider	E. Germany	Moscow	July, 1980

Freestyle Relays

400 M. (4×100)	**3:42.71**	National Team	E. Germany	Moscow	July, 1980

Medley Relays

400 M. (4×100)	**4:06.67**	National Team	E. Germany	Moscow	July, 1980

U.S. Outdoor Swimming Championships

Irvine, Cal., July 29-31, 1980

Men

50-Meter Freestyle—Joe Bottom, Walnut Creek, Cal. **Time—0:23.07.**
100-Meter Freestyle—Rowdy Gaines, Gainesville, Ga. **Time—0:50.19.**
200-Meter Freestyle—Rowdy Gaines. **Time—1:50.02.**
400-Meter Freestyle—Mike Bruner, Mesa, Ariz. **Time—3:52.19.**
800-Meter Freestyle—Brian Goodell, Mission Viejo, Cal. **Time—7:59.66.**
1,500-Meter Freestyle—Mike Bruner. **Time—15:19.80.**
100-Meter Breaststroke—Steve Lundquist, Jonesboro, Ga. **Time—1:02.88.**
200-Meter Breaststroke—Glenn Mills, Cincinnati, Oh. **Time—2:18.78.**
100-Meter Backstroke—Peter Rocca, Pleasant Hill, Cal. **Time—0:56.64.**
200-Meter Backstroke—Steve Barnicoat, Mission Viejo, Cal. **Time—2:01.06.**
100-Meter Butterfly—William Paulus, Austin, Tex. **Time—0:54.34.**
200-Meter Butterfly—Craig Beardsley, Gainesville, Fla. **Time—1:58.46.**
200-Meter Individual Medley—Bill Barrett, Alpharetta, Ga. **Time—2:03.24.**
400-Meter Individual Medley—Jesse Vassallo, Mission Viejo, Cal. **Time—4:21.51.**
400-Meter Freestyle Relay—Florida Aquatic. **Time—3:22.24.**
800-Meter Freestyle Relay—Florida Aquatic. **Time—7:26.67.**
400-Meter Medley Relay—Dr Pepper, Dallas. **Time—3:47.13.**

Women

50-Meter Freestyle—Jill Sterkel, Austin, Tex. **Time—0:26.21.**
100-Meter Freestyle—Cynthia Woodhead, Cupertino, Cal. **Time—0:56.57.**
200-Meter Freestyle—Cynthia Woodhead. **Time—1:59.44.**
400-Meter Freestyle—Kim Linehan, Austin, Tex. **Time—4:07.77.**
800-Meter Freestyle—Kim Linehan. **Time—8:27.86.**
1,500-Meter Freestyle—Kim Linehan. **Time—16:21.74.**
100-Meter Breaststroke—Tracy Caukins, Nashville, Tenn. **Time—1:10.40.**
200-Meter Breaststroke—(tie) Tracy Caukins & Terri Baxter, Menlo Park, Cal. **Time—2:34.66.**
100-Meter Backstroke—Linda Jezek, Stanford, Cal. **Time—1:03.16.**
200-Meter Backstroke—Linda Jezek. **Time—2:14.52.**
100-Meter Butterfly—Mary T. Meagher, Cincinnati, Oh. **Time—0:59.41.**
200-Meter Butterfly—Mary T. Meagher. **Time—2:06.37.**
200-Meter Individual Medley—Tracy Caukins. **Time—2:14.64.**
400-Meter Individual Medley—Tracy Caukins. **Time—4:40.61.**
400-Meter Freestyle Relay—Cincinnati Pepsi Marlins. **Time—3:48.83.**
800-Meter Freestyle Relay—Cincinnati Pepsi Marlins. **Time—8:13.07.**
400-Meter Medley Relay—Cincinnati Pepsi Marlins. **Time—4:17.81.**

Lacrosse Champions in 1980

Source: Jack Kelly, U.S. Lacrosse Information

U.S. Intercollegiate Assn. National Champion—Johns Hopkins
Atlantic Coast Conference—Virginia, Maryland (tie).
Colonial League (New England)—Babson.
East Coast League—Delaware.
Independent College Athletic Conference—Hobart.
Ivy League—Cornell, Harvard (tie).
Knickerbocker League—Kean.
Middle Atlantic League—Franklin & Marshall.
Mideast League—Montclair State (N.J.).
Midwest League—Denison.
Northeast League—Massachusetts.
Rocky Mountain League—Air Force Academy.
Snivley League—Middlebury.
SUNY—Cortland State.
Tri-State League—William & Mary.

NCAA Division I Championship

At Ithaca, N.Y., May 31—Johns Hopkins 9, Virginia 8.

Semi-finals

Johns Hopkins 16, Syracuse 11; Virginia 11, North Carolina 10.

Quarter-finals

Johns Hopkins 16, Harvard 12; Syracuse 12, W & L 4; Virginia 9, Cornell 8; North Carolina 18, Navy 11.

NCAA Division II Championship

At Catonsville, Md., May 18—UMBC 23, Adelphi 14.

NCAA Division III Championship

At Geneva, N.Y., May 25—Hobart 11, Cortland 9.

All-Star College game

At Lexington, Va., June 14—North 9, South 8.

U.S. Club Lacrosse Association Championship

At Catonsville, Md., June 15—Long Island L.C. 15, Maryland L.C. 10.

U.S. Junior College Lacrosse Championship

At Hempstead, N.Y., May 11—Nassau (L.I.) C.C. 20, Cobleskill A & T 5.

Coach of the Year

Division I—Roy Simmons, Syracuse Univ.
Division II—Dick Watts, UMBC.
Division III—Dave Urich, Hobart.

USILA Division I All America Team

Attack: Mike Buzzell (Navy), Tim O'Hara (Syracuse), Stan Cockerton (N.C. State).
Midfield: Brendan Schneck (Hopkins), John Driscoll (Virginia), Kevin Griswold (North Carolina), Peter Worstell (Maryland).
Defense: Mark Greenberg (Hopkins), Kevin O'Shea (Virginia), Mike McLaughlin (Navy).
Goalie: Mike Federico (Hopkins), Bob Clements (W & L).
Note: 4 midfielders selected for the 3 midfield positions; 2 goalies named.

National Collegiate Women Lacrosse Championship Division I

1—Penn State Univ.
2—Univ. of Maryland
3—Univ. of Pennsylvania
4—Univ. of Massachusetts
5—Princeton Univ.
6—William & Mary

All-Championship Team

Lynn Thompson,	Penn State
Candy Finn,	Penn State
Pixie Hamilton,	William & Mary
Laurie Hoke,	Penn State
Cinnie Klein,	Pennsylvania
Sandy Lanahan,	Maryland
Laura O'Neil,	Massachusetts
Jane Koffenberger,	Penn State
Laura Le Mire,	Maryland
Tracy Vause,	Pennsylvania
Sharon Watson,	Maryland
Denise Wescott,	Maryland

Rifle and Pistol Individual Championships in 1980

Source: National Rifle Assn.

National Outdoor Rifle and Pistol Championships

Pistol — SFC Joseph J. Pascarella, Las Cruces, N.M., 2657-139X.
Civilian pistol — Guigno D. Carapellotti, Darby, Pa., 2633-111X.
Regular service — MSG Bonnie D. Harmon, Ft. Benning, Ga., 2635-133X.
Police pistol — John L. Farley, Americus, Ga., 2604-85X.
Woman pistol — SP4 Ruby E. Fox, Parker, Ariz., 2597-82X.
Senior pistol — Gil Hebard, Knoxville, Ill., 2571-80X.
Collegiate pistol — Russell L. May, Sarasota, Fla., 2539-73X.
Junior pistol — Kenneth O. Swanson, Birmingham, Ala., 2539-72X.
Smallbore rifle prone — CPT Ernest Vande Zande, Ft. Benning, Ga., 6396-571.
Civilian smallbore rifle prone — Carl C. Jooss, New Albany, Oh., 6396-530X.
Woman smallbore rifle prone — SP5 Mary E. Stidworthy, Prescott, Ariz., 6394-571X.
Senior smallbore rifle prone — Ransford D. Triggs, Madison, N.J., 6390-510X.
Collegiate smallbore rifle prone — SP5 Mary E. Stidworthy, Prescott, Ariz., 6394-571X.
Smallbore rifle position — LTC Lones W. Wigger Jr., Ft. Benning, Ga., 1745.
Civilian smallbore rifle position — John R. Foster, Bozeman, Mont., 1693.
Woman smallbore rifle position — Lt. Denise J. Cannella, Ft. Benning, Ga., 1674.
Senior smallbore rifle position — Donald W. Burtis, Levittown, Pa., 1509.
Collegiate smallbore rifle position — Kurt H. Fitz-Randolph, Palm Bay, Fla., 1691.
High power rifle — Carl R. Bernosky, Gordon, Pa., 2374-120X.
High power civilian — Carl R. Bernosky, 2374-120X.
High power service — CW4 Robert L. Goller, Quantico, Va., 2363-95X.
High power woman — SSG Anne Joseph, Blue Ridge, Ga., 2312-66X.
High power junior — Mark R. Liebetrau, Black Earth, Wis., 2346-77X.
High power senior — Gerritt H. Stekeur, Latham, N.Y., 2319-69X.
High power collegiate — LT David B. Erickson, Bellevue, Wash. 2353-70X.

U.S. NRA International Shooting Championships

English match — David Kimes, Monterey Park, Cal., 1785.
Smallbore three position — Lones Wigger, Ft. Benning, Ga., 3475.
Air rifle — Lones Wigger, 1164.
Ladies air rifle — Karen Monez, Ft. Benning, Ga., 1161.
Woman standard rifle prone — Wanda Jewell, Ft. Benning, Ga., 1767.
Woman standard rifle three position — Sue Ann Sandusky, Brooklyn, N.Y., 1721.
Free pistol — Steve F. Reiter, Daly City, Cal., 1653.
Air pistol — Erich Buljung, Ft. Benning, Ga., 1159.
Woman air pistol — Ruby Fox, Parker, Ariz., 1106.
Center fire pistol — Frank M. Goza, Lookout Mountain, Tenn., 591.
Rapid fire pistol — Darius R. Young, Winterburn, Canada, 1757.
Standard pistol — John Kailer, Ft. Benning, Ga., 578.
Woman smallbore pistol — Ruby Fox, 575.

National Indoor Rifle and Pistol Championships

Conventional rifle — Karen E. Monez, Ft. Benning, Ga., 799.
International rifle — Ronald F. Butterman, Ft. Benning, Ga., 1179.
Woman international rifle — Karen E. Monez, 1171.
NRA 3-position rifle — John Duus, Johnson City, Tenn. 587.
Conventional pistol — Donald L. Hamilton, Kingston, Mass., 891.
Woman conventional pistol — Madeline B. Thompson, Lewistown, Pa., 838.
International standard pistol — Erich Buljung, Ft. Benning, Ga., 575.
Woman international standard pistol — Patricia A. Olsowsky, York, N.Y., 536.
International free pistol — Jack D. Elliott, Dothan, Ala., 555.
Woman international free pistol — Patricia A. Olsowsky, 509.

National Skeet Shooting Assn. Championships in 1980

Savannah, Ga., July 24 - Aug. 1, 1980

High Overall - 550 targets

Champion — Al Magyar, Allen Park, Mich., 549.
Women — Carla Brundage, San Antonio, Tex., 544.
Industry — Jimmy Prall, Tulsa, Okla., 547.
Veteran — L. Barbee Ponder, Amite, La., 541.
Sub-senior — Gus Sanderson, Ottawa, Ont., Canada, 546.
Senior — Jesse L. Vint, Tulsa, Okla., 541.
Junior — Bobby Wrenn, Punta Gorda, Fla., 544.
Collegiate — John Shima, San Antonio, Tex., 547.

12 Gauge - 250 targets

Champion — Tito Killian, San Antonio, Tex., 250.
Women — Barbara Thomas, Brooklyn, N.Y., 250.
Industry — Tony Rosetti, Hagerstown, Md., 250.
Veteran — L. Barbee Ponder, Amite, La., 247.
Sub-senior — Doug C. Burdett, Downsville, Ont., Canada, 250.
Senior — Eliot Farley Jr., Mattapoisett, Mass., 250.
Junior — Tal Sprinkles, Roundrock, Tex., 249.
Collegiate — Robbie Purser, Macon, Ga., 250.

20 Gauge - 100 targets

Champion — Bruce Evans, Burnet, Tex., 100.
Women — Sandra McCurley, Mobile, Ala., 100.
Industry — Tony Rosetti, Hagerstown, Md., 100.
Veteran — L. Barbee Ponder, Amite, La., 98.
Sub-senior — Gus Sanderson, Ottawa, Ont., Canada, 100.
Senior — A. S. Beard, Fairfax, Va., 100.
Junior — Bobby Wrenn, Punta Gorda, Fla., 100.
Collegiate — Robert Morrison, San Antonio, Tex., 100.

28 Gauge - 100 targets

Champion — George Desatoff, Hacienda Heights, Cal., 100.
Women — Ila Hill, Birmingham, Mich., 98.
Industry — John Hancock, Stone Mountain, Ga., 100.
Veteran — L. Barbee Ponder, Amite, La., 100.
Sub-senior — Tom Foley, Staffordville, Conn., 100.
Senior — Les McAlister, Huntsville, Ala., 100.
Junior — Donnie Park, Clemmons, N.C., 100.
Collegiate — Chip Youngblood, Ft. Lauderdale, Fla., 100.

.410 Bore - 100 targets

Champion — Wayne Mayes, Hixson, Tenn., 100.
Women — Carla Brundage, San Antonio, Tex., 99.
Industry — Jimmy Prall, Tulsa, Okla., 99.
Veteran — L. Barbee Ponder, Amite, La., 96.
Sub-senior — T. J. Maddox, Macon, Ga., 100.
Senior — Jesse L. Vint, Tulsa, Okla., 98.
Junior — Bobby Wrenn, Punta Gorda, Fla., 100.
Collegiate — Maxie Wright, New Albany, Oh., 99.

Champion of Champions - 100 targets

Champion — Todd Bender, San Antonio, Tex., 100.
Women — Cheri Confer, Warren, Mich., 98.
Veteran — Chesley Crites, Detroit, Mich., 94.
Sub-senior — Boyd Wickman, W. Des Moines, Ia., 100.
Senior — Jesse L. Vint, Tulsa, Okla., 99.
Junior — J. C. Martin IV, Laredo, Tex., 99.
Collegiate — Todd Bender, San Antonio, Tex., 100.

Auto Racing

Indianapolis 500 Winners

Year	Winner	Chassis	Engine	MPH	Purse	Runner up
1948	Mauri Rose	Deidt	Offenhauser	119.814	$171,075	Bill Holland
1949	Bill Holland	Deidt	Offenhauser	121.327	179,050	Johnnie Parsons
1950	Johnnie Parsons	Kurtis Kraft	Offenhauser	124.002(a)	201,135	Bill Holland
1951	Lee Wallard	Kurtis Kraft	Offenhauser	126.244	207,650	Mike Nazaruk
1952	Troy Ruttman	Kuzma	Offenhauser	128.922	230,100	Jim Rathmann
1953	Bill Vukovich	Kurtis Kraft 500A	Offenhauser	128.740	246,300	Art Cross
1954	Bill Vukovich	Kurtis Kraft 500A	Offenhauser	130.840	269,375	Jim Bryan
1955	Bob Sweikert	Kurtis Kraft 500C	Offenhauser	128.209	270,400	Tony Bettenhausen
1956	Pat Flaherty	Watson	Offenhauser	128.490	282,052	Sam Hanks
1957	Sam Hanks	Epperly	Offenhauser	135.601	300,252	Jim Rathmann
1958	Jimmy Bryan	Epperly	Offenhauser	133.791	305,217	George Amick
1959	Rodger Ward	Watson	Offenhauser	135.857	338,100	Jim Rathmann
1960	Jim Rathmann	Watson	Offenhauser	138.767	369,150	Rodger Ward
1961	A.J. Foyt	Watson	Offenhauser	139.130	400,000	Eddie Sachs
1962	Rodger Ward	Watson	Offenhauser	140.293	426,152	Len Sutton
1963	Parnelli Jones	Watson	Offenhauser	143.137	494,031	Jim Clark
1964	A.J. Foyt	Watson	Offenhauser	147.350	506,625	Rodger Ward
1965	Jim Clark	Lotus	Ford	151.388	628,399	Parnelli Jones
1966	Graham Hill	Lola	Ford	144.317	691,809	Jim Clark
1967	A.J. Foyt	Coyote	Ford	151.207	737,109	Al Unser
1968	Bobby Unser	Eagle	Offenhauser	152.882	809,627	Dan Gurney
1969	Mario Andretti	Hawk	Ford	156.867	805,127	Dan Gurney
1970	Al Unser	P.J. Colt	Ford	155.749	1,000,002	Mark Donohue
1971	Al Unser	P.J. Colt	Ford	157.735	1,001,604	Peter Revson
1972	Mark Donohue	McLaren	Offenhauser	163.465	1,011,846	Al Unser
1973	Gordon Johncock	Eagle	Offenhauser	159.014(b)	1,011,846	Billy Vukovich
1974	Johnny Rutherford	McLaren	Offenhauser	158.589	1,015,686	Bobby Unser
1975	Bobby Unser	Eagle	Offenhauser	149.213(c)	1,101,322	Johnny Rutherford
1976	Johnny Rutherford	McLaren	Offenhauser	148.725(d)	1,037,775	A.J. Foyt
1977	A.J. Foyt	Coyote	Ford	161.331	1,116,807	Tom Sneva
1978	Al Unser	Lola	Cosworth	161.363	1,145,225	Tom Sneva
1979	Rick Mears	Penske	Cosworth	158.899	1,271,954	A.J. Foyt
1980	Johnny Rutherford	Chaparral	Cosworth	142.862	1,502,425	Tom Sneva

(a) 345 miles. (b) 332.5 miles. (c) 435 miles. (d) 255 miles. Race record—163.465 MPH, Mark Donohue, 1972.

1980 Indianapolis 500 Final Standings

1—Johnny Rutherford, Ft. Worth, Tex., Chaparral-Cosworth.
2—Tom Sneva, Spokane, Wash., McLaren-Cosworth.
3—Gary Bettenhausen,, Monrovia, Ind., Wildcat-DGS.
4—Gordon Johncock, Phoenix, Ariz., Penske-Cosworth.
5—Rick Mears, Bakersfield, Cal., Penske-Cosworth.
6—Pancho Carter, Brownsburg, Ind., Penske-Cosworth.
7—Danny Ongais, Costa Mesa, Cal., Parnelli-Cosworth.
8—Tom Bigelow, Whitewater, Wis., Lola-Cosworth.
9—Tim Richmond, Ashland, Oh., Penske-Cosworth.
10—Greg Leffler, Winchester, Ind., Lola-Cosworth.

Notable One-Mile Speed Records

Date	Driver	Car	MPH
1/26/06	Marriott	Stanley (Steam)	127.659
3/16/10	Oldfield	Benz	131.724
4/23/11	Burman	Benz	141.732
2/12/19	DePalma	Packard	149.875
4/27/20	Milton	Dusenberg	155.046
4/28/26	Parry-Thomas	Thomas Spl.	170.624
3/29/27	Seagrave	Sunbeam	203.790
4/22/28	Keech	White Triplex	207.552
3/11/29	Seagrave	Irving-Napier	231.446
2/ 5/31	Campbell	Napier-Campbell	246.086
2/24/32	Campbell	Napier-Campbell	253.96
2/22/33	Campbell	Napier-Campbell	272.109
9/ 3/35	Campbell	Bluebird Special	301.13
11/19/37	Eyston	Thunderbolt 1	311.42
9/16/38	Eyston	Thunderbolt 1	357.5
8/23/39	Cobb	Railton	368.9
9/16/47	Cobb	Railton-Mobil	394.2
8/ 5/63	Breedlove	Spirit of America	407.45
10/27/64	Arfons	Green Monster	536.71
11/15/65	Breedlove	Spirit of America	600.601
10/23/70	Gabélich	Blue Flame	622.407
10/9/79	Barrett	Budweiser Rocket	638.637*

*not recognized as official by sanctioning bodies.

World Grand Prix Champions

Year	Driver
1950	Nino Farina, Italy
1951	Juan Fangio, Argentina
1952	Alberto Ascari, Italy
1953	Alberto Ascari, Italy
1954	Juan Fangio, Argentina
1955	Juan Fangio, Argentina
1956	Juan Fangio, Argentina
1957	Juan Fangio, Argentina
1958	Mike Hawthorne, England
1959	Jack Brabham, Australia
1960	Jack Brabham, Australia
1961	Phil Hill, United States
1962	Graham Hill, England
1963	Jim Clark, Scotland
1964	John Surtees, England
1965	Jim Clark, Scotland
1966	Jack Brabham, Australia
1967	Denis Hulme, New Zealand
1968	Graham Hill, England
1969	Jackie Stewart, Scotland
1970	Jochen Rindt, Austria
1971	Jackie Stewart, Scotland
1972	Emerson Fittipaldi, Brazil
1973	Jackie Stewart, Scotland
1974	Emerson Fittipaldi, Brazil
1975	Nicki Lauda, Austria
1976	James Hunt, England
1977	Nikki Lauda, Austria
1978	Mario Andretti, U.S.
1979	Jody Scheckter, So. Africa

United States Auto Club National Champions

Year	Driver	Year	Driver	Year	Driver	Year	Driver
1956	Jimmy Bryan	1962	Rodger Ward	1968	Bobby Unser	1974	Bobby Unser
1957	Jimmy Bryan	1963	A. J. Foyt	1969	Mario Andretti	1975	A. J. Foyt
1958	Tony Bettenhausen	1964	A. J. Foyt	1970	Al Unser	1976	Gordon Johncock
1959	Rodger Ward	1965	Mario Andretti	1971	Joe Leonard	1977	Tom Sneva
1960	A.J. Foyt	1966	Mario Andretti	1972	Joe Leonard	1978	Tom Sneva
1961	A. J. Foyt	1967	A. J. Foyt	1973	Roger McCluskey	1979	A. J. Foyt

Grand Prix for Formula 1 Cars in 1980

Grand Prix	Winner, car	Grand Prix	Winner, car
Argentine	Alan Jones, Williams	French	Alan Jones, Williams
Austrian	Jean-Pierre Jabouille, Renault	German	Jacques Laffite, Ligier
Belgian	Didier Pironi, Ligier	Italian	Nelson Piquet, Brabham
British	Alan Jones, Williams	Long Beach	Nelson Piquet, Brabham
Brazilian	Rene Arnoux, Renault	Monaco	Carlos Reutemann, Williams
Canadian	Alan Jones, Williams	South African	Rene Arnoux, Renault
Dutch	Nelson Piquet, Brabham	Spanish	Alan Jones, Williams
		United States	Alan Jones, Williams

NASCAR Racing in 1980

Winston Cup Grand National Races

Date	Race, site	Winner	Car	Winnings
Jan. 19	Winston Western 500, Riverside, Cal.	Darrell Waltrip	Chevrolet	$24,700
Feb. 17	Daytona 500, Daytona Beach, Fla.	Buddy Baker	Oldsmobile	102,175
Mar. 16	Atlanta 500, Atlanta, Ga.	Dale Earnhardt	Chevrolet	36,200
Mar. 30	Valleydale Southeastern 500, Bristol, Tenn.	Dale Earnhardt	Chevrolet	20,625
Apr. 13	CRC Chemicals Rebel 500, Darlington, S.C.	David Pearson	Chevrolet	21,430
Apr. 20	Northwestern Bank 400, N. Wilkesboro, N.C.	Richard Petty	Chevrolet	18,925
Apr. 27	Virginia 500, Martinsville, Va.	Darrell Waltrip	Chevrolet	26,850
May 4	Winston 500, Talladega, Ala.	Buddy Baker	Oldsmobile	32,150
May 10	Music City 420, Nashville, Tenn.	Richard Petty	Chevrolet	15,350
May 18	Mason-Dixon 500, Dover, Del.	Bobby Allison	Ford	21,900
May 25	World 600, Charlotte, N.C.	Benny Parsons	Chevrolet	44,850
June 1	Nascar 400, College Station, Tex.	Cale Yarborough	Chevrolet	21,000
June 8	Warner W. Hodgdon 400, Riverside, Cal.	Darrell Waltrip	Chevrolet	22,100
June 15	Gabriel 400, Brooklyn, Mich.	Benny Parsons	Chevrolet	24,800
July 4	Firecracker 400, Daytona Beach, Fla.	Bobby Allison	Mercury	24,805
July 12	Busch Nashville 420, Nashville, Tenn.	Dale Earnhardt	Chevrolet	14,600
July 27	Coca-Cola 500, Pocono, Pa.	Neil Bonnett	Mercury	19,915
Aug. 3	Talladega 500, Talladega, Ala.	Neil Bonnett	Mercury	35,675
Aug. 17	Champion Spark Plug 400, Brooklyn, Mich.	Cale Yarborough	Chevrolet	19,700
Aug. 23	Volunteer 500, Bristol, Tenn.	Cale Yarborough	Chevrolet	16,550
Sept. 1	Southern 500, Darlington, S.C.	Terry Labonte	Chevrolet	27,325
Sept. 7	Capital City 400, Richmond, Va.	Bobby Allison	Ford	17,175
Sept. 14	CRC Chemicals 500, Dover, Del.	Darrell Waltrip	Chevrolet	22,900
Sept. 21	Holly Farms 400, N. Wilkesboro, N.C.	Bobby Allison	Ford	17,725

Daytona 500 Winners

Year	Driver, car	Avg. MPH	Year	Driver, car	Avg. MPH
1961	Marvin Panch, Pontiac	149.601	1971	Richard Petty, Plymouth	144.456
1962	Fireball Roberts, Pontiac	152.529	1972	A. J. Foyt, Mercury	161.550
1963	Tiny Lund, Ford	151.566	1973	Richard Petty, Dodge	157.205
1964	Richard Petty, Plymouth	154.334	1974	Richard Petty, Dodge (c)	140.894
1965	Fred Lorenzen, Ford (a)	141.539	1975	Benny Parsons, Chevrolet	153.649
1966	Richard Petty, Plymouth (b)	160.627	1976	David Pearson, Mercury	152.181
1967	Mario Andretti, Ford	146.926	1977	Cale Yarborough, Chevrolet	153.218
1968	Cale Yarborough, Mercury	143.251	1978	Bobby Allison, Ford	159.730
1969	Lee Roy Yarborough, Ford	160.875	1979	Richard Petty, Oldsmobile	143.977
1970	Pete Hamilton, Plymouth	149.601	1980	Buddy Baker, Oldsmobile	177.602

(a) 322.5 miles because of rain. (b) 495 miles because of rain. (c) 450 miles.

Leading Daytona 500 Finishers in 1980

	Driver, car	Laps	Winnings		Driver, car	Laps	Winnings
1	Buddy Baker, Oldsmobile	200	$102,175	6	Terry Labonte, Oldsmobile	197	$26,475
2	Bobby Allison, Mercury	200	54,450	7	Donnie Allison, Oldsmobile	195	35,160
3	Neil Bonnett, Mercury	199	51,100	8	Sterling Marlin, Chevrolet	194	17,810
4	Dale Earnhardt, Oldsmobile	199	36,350	9	Lennie Pond, Buick	194	18,000
5	Benny Parsons, Oldsmobile	197	32,375	10	Jody Ridley, Mercury	194	20,305

Grand National Champions (NASCAR)

Year	Driver	Year	Driver	Year	Driver	Year	Driver
1952	Tim Flock	1959	Lee Petty	1966	David Pearson	1973	Benny Parson
1953	Herb Thomas	1960	Rex White	1967	Richard Petty	1974	Richard Petty
1954	Lee Petty	1961	Ned Jarrett	1968	David Pearson	1975	Richard Petty
1955	Tim Flock	1962	Joe Weatherly	1969	David Pearson	1976	Cale Yarborough
1956	Buck Baker	1963	Joe Weatherly	1970	Bobby Isaac	1977	Cale Yarborough
1957	Buck Baker	1964	Richard Petty	1971	Richard Petty	1978	Cale Yarborough
1958	Lee Petty	1965	Ned Jarrett	1972	Richard Petty	1979	Richard Petty

Tennis

USTA National Champions

Men's Singles

Year	Champion	Final opponent	Year	Champion	Final opponent
1920	Bill Tilden	William Johnston	1951	Frank Sedgman	E. Victor Seixas Jr.
1921	Bill Tilden	Wallace Johnston	1952	Frank Sedgman	Gardnar Mulloy
1922	Bill Tilden	William Johnston	1953	Tony Trabert	E. Victor Seixas Jr.
1923	Bill Tilden	William Johnston	1954	E. Victor Seixas Jr.	Rex Hartwig
1924	Bill Tilden	William Johnston	1955	Tony Trabert	Ken Rosewall
1925	Bill Tilden	William Johnston	1956	Ken Rosewall	Lewis Hoad
1926	Rene Lacoste	Jean Borotra	1957	Malcolm Anderson	Ashley Cooper
1927	Rene Lacoste	Bill Tilden	1958	Ashley Cooper	Malcolm Anderson
1928	Henri Cochet	Francis Hunter	1959	Neale A. Fraser	Alejandro Olmedo
1929	Bill Tilden	Francis Hunter	1960	Neale A. Fraser	Rod Laver
1930	John Doeg	Francis Shields	1961	Roy Emerson	Rod Laver
1931	H. Ellsworth Vines	George Lott	1962	Rod Laver	Roy Emerson
1932	H. Ellsworth Vines	Henri Cochet	1963	Rafael Osuna	F. A. Froehling 3d
1933	Fred Perry	John Crawford	1964	Roy Emerson	Fred Stolle
1934	Fred Perry	Wilmer Allison	1965	Manuel Santana	Cliff Drysdale
1935	Wilmer Allison	Sidney Wood	1966	Fred Stolle	John Newcombe
1936	Fred Perry	Don Budge	1967	John Newcombe	Clark Graebner
1937	Don Budge	Baron G. von Cramm	1968	Arthur Ashe	Tom Okker
1938	Don Budge	C. Gene Mako	1969	Rod Laver	Tony Roche
1939	Robert Riggs	S. Welby Van Horn	1970	Ken Rosewall	Tony Roche
1940	Don McNeill	Robert Riggs	1971	Stan Smith	Jan Kodes
1941	Robert Riggs	F. L. Kovacs	1972	Ilie Nastase	Arthur Ashe
1942	F. R. Schroeder Jr.	Frank Parker	1973	John Newcombe	Jan Kodes
1943	Joseph Hunt	Jack Kramer	1974	Jimmy Connors	Ken Rosewall
1944	Frank Parker	William Talbert	1975	Manuel Orantes	Jimmy Connors
1945	Frank Parker	William Talbert	1976	Jimmy Connors	Bjorn Borg
1946	Jack Kramer	Thomas Brown Jr.	1977	Guillermo Vilas	Jimmy Connors
1947	Jack Kramer	Frank Parker	1978	Jimmy Connors	Bjorn Borg
1948	Pancho Gonzales	Eric Sturgess	1979	John McEnroe	Vitas Gerulaitis
1949	Pancho Gonzales	F. R. Schroeder Jr.	1980	John McEnroe	Bjorn Borg
1950	Arthur Larsen	Herbert Flam			

Men's Doubles

Year	Champions	Year	Champions
1925	R. Norris Williams—Vincent Richards	1954	E. Victor Seixas Jr.—Tony Trabert
1926	R. Norris Williams—Vincent Richards	1955	Kosei Kamo—Atsushi Miyagi
1927	Bill Tilden—Francis Hunter	1956	Lewis Hoad—Ken Rosewall
1928	George Lott—John Hennessey	1957	Ashley Cooper—Neale Fraser
1929	George Lott—John Doeg	1958	Hamilton Richardson—Alejandro Olmedo
1930	George Lott—John Doeg	1959	Neale A. Fraser—Roy Emerson
1931	Wilmer Allison—John Van Ryn	1960	Neale A. Fraser—Roy Emerson
1932	H. Ellsworth Vines—Keith Gledhill	1961	Dennis Ralston—Chuck McKinley
1933	George Lott—Lester Stoefen	1962	Rafael Osuna—Antonio Palafox
1934	George Lott—Lester Stoefen	1963	Dennis Ralston—Chuck McKinley
1935	Wilmer Allison—John Van Ryn	1964	Dennis Ralston—Chuck McKinley
1936	Don Budge—C. Gene Mako	1965	Roy Emerson—Fred Stolle
1937	Baron G. von Cramm—Henner Henkel	1966	Roy Emerson—Fred Stolle
1938	Don Budge—C. Gene Mako	1967	John Newcombe—Tony Roche
1939	Adrian Quist—John Bromwich	1968	Robert Lutz—Stan Smith
1940	Jack Kramer—Frederick Schroeder Jr.	1969	Fred Stolle—Ken Rosewall
1941	Jack Kramer—Frederick Schroeder Jr.	1970	Pierre Barthes—Nicki Pilic
1942	Gardnar Mulloy—William Talbert	1971	John Newcombe—Roger Taylor
1943	Jack Kramer—Frank Parker	1972	Cliff Drysdale—Roger Taylor
1944	Don McNeill—Robert Falkenburg	1973	John Newcombe—Owen Davidson
1945	Gardnar Mulloy—William Talbert	1974	Bob Lutz—Stan Smith
1946	Gardnar Mulloy—William Talbert	1975	Jimmy Connors—Ilie Nastase
1947	Jack Kramer—Frederick Schroeder Jr.	1976	Marty Riessen—Tom Okker
1948	Gardnar Mulloy—William Talbert	1977	Bob Hewitt—Frew McMillan
1949	John Bromwich—William Sidwell	1978	Stan Smith—Bob Lutz
1950	John Bromwich—Frank Sedgman	1979	John McEnroe—Peter Fleming
1951	Frank Sedgman—Kenneth McGregor	1980	Bob Lutz—Stan Smith
1952	Mervyn Rose—E. Victor Seixas Jr.		
1953	Rex Hartwig—Mervyn Rose		

Women's Singles

Year	Champion	Year	Champion	Year	Champion	Year	Champion
1935	Helen Jacobs	1947	A. Louise Brough	1959	Maria Bueno	1970	Margaret Smith Court
1936	Alice Marble	1948	Mrs. Margaret O. du Pont	1960	Darlene Hard	1971	Billie Jean King
1937	Anita Lizana	1949	Mrs. Margaret O. du Pont	1961	Darlene Hard	1972	Billie Jean King
1938	Alice Marble	1950	Mrs. Margaret O. du Pont	1962	Margaret Smith	1973	Margaret Smith Court
1939	Alice Marble	1951	Maureen Connolly	1963	Maria Bueno	1974	Billie Jean King
1940	Alice Marble	1952	Maureen Connolly	1964	Maria Bueno	1975	Chris Evert
1941	Mrs. Sarah P. Cooke	1953	Maureen Connolly	1965	Margaret Smith	1976	Chris Evert
1942	Pauline Betz	1954	Doris Hart	1966	Maria Bueno	1977	Chris Evert
1943	Pauline Betz	1955	Doris Hart	1967	Billie Jean King	1978	Chris Evert
1944	Pauline Betz	1956	Shirley J. Fry	1968	Virginia Wade	1979	Tracy Austin
1945	Sarah P. Cooke	1957	Althea Gibson	1969	Margaret Smith Court	1980	Chris Evert Lloyd
1946	Pauline Betz	1958	Althea Gibson				

Women's Doubles

Year	Champions	Year	Champions
1937	Mrs. Sarah P. Fabyan—Alice Marble	1959	Darlene Hard—Jeanne Arth
1938	Alice Marble—Mrs. Sarah P. Fabyan	1960	Darlene Hard—Maria Bueno
1939	Alice Marble—Mrs. Sarah P. Fabyan	1961	Darlene Hard—Lesley Turner
1940	Alice Marble—Mrs. Sarah P. Fabyan	1962	Maria Bueno—Darlene Hard
1941	Mrs. S. P. Cooke—Margaret Osborne	1963	Margaret Smith—Robyn Ebbern
1942	A. Louise Brough—Margaret Osborne	1964	Billie Jean Moffitt—Karen Susman
1943	A. Louise Brough—Margaret Osborne	1965	Carole C. Graebner—Nancy Richey
1944	A. Louise Brough—Margaret Osborne	1966	Maria Bueno—Nancy Richey
1945	A. Louise Brough—Margaret Osborne	1967	Rosemary Casals—Billie Jean King
1946	A. Louise Brough—Margaret Osborne	1968	Maria Bueno—Margaret S. Court
1947	A. Louise Brough—Margaret Osborne	1969	Francoise Durr—Darlene Hard
1948	A. Louise Brough—Mrs. M. O. du Pont	1970	M. S. Court—Judy Tegart Dalton
1949	A. Louise Brough—Mrs. M. O. du Pont	1971	Rosemary Casals—Judy Tegart Dalton
1950	A. Louise Brough—Mrs. M. O. du Pont	1972	Francoise Durr—Betty Stove
1951	Doris Hart—Shirley Fry	1973	Margaret S. Court—Virginia Wade
1952	Doris Hart—Shirley Fry	1974	Billie Jean King—Rosemary Casals
1953	Doris Hart—Shirley Fry	1975	Margaret Court—Virginia Wade
1954	Doris Hart—Shirley Fry	1976	Linky Boshoff—Ilana Kloss
1955	A. Louise Brough—Mrs. M. O. du Pont	1977	Betty Stove—Martina Navratilova
1956	A. Louise Brough—Mrs. M. O. du Pont	1978	Martina Navratilova—Billie Jean King
1957	A. Louise Brough—Mrs. M. O. du Pont	1979	Betty Stove—Wendy Turnbull
1958	Darlene Hard—Jeanne Arth	1980	Billie Jean King—Martina Navratilova

Mixed Doubles

Year	Champions	Year	Champions
1950	Mrs. M. O. duPont—Kenneth MacGregor	1966	Donna Floyd Fales—Owen Davidson
1951	Doris Hart—Frank Sedgman	1967	Billie Jean King—Owen Davidson
1952	Doris Hart—Frank Sedgman	1968	Mary Ann Eisel—Peter Curtis
1953	Doris Hart—E. Victor Seixas Jr.	1969	Margaret S. Court—Marty Riessen
1954	Doris Hart—E. Victor Seixas Jr.	1970	Margaret S. Court—Marty Riessen
1955	Doris Hart—E. Victor Seixas Jr.	1971	Billie Jean King—Owen Davidson
1956	Mrs. M. O. duPont—Ken Rosewall	1972	Margaret S. Court—Marty Riessen
1957	Althea Gibson—Kurt Nielsen	1973	Billie Jean King—Owen Davidson
1958	Mrs. M. O. duPont—Neale Fraser	1974	Pam Teeguarden—Geoff Masters
1959	Mrs. M. O. duPont—Neale Fraser	1975	Rosemary Casals—Dick Stockton
1960	Mrs. M. O. duPont—Neale Fraser	1976	Billie Jean King—Phil Dent
1961	Margaret Smith—Robert Mark	1977	Betty Stove—Frew McMillan
1962	Margaret Smith—Fred Stolle	1978	Betty Stove—Frew McMillan
1963	Margaret Smith—Kenneth Fletcher	1979	Greer Stevens—Bob Hewitt
1964	Margaret Smith—John Newcombe	1980	Wendy Turnbull—Marty Riessen
1965	Margaret Smith—Fred Stolle		

British Champions, Wimbledon

Inaugurated 1877

Year	Men's singles	Women's singles	Year	Men's singles	Women's singles
1947	Jack Kramer	Margaret Osborne	1965	Roy Emerson	Margaret Smith
1948	Bob Falkenburg	A. Louise Brough	1966	Manuel Santana	Billie Jean King
1949	Fred R. Schroeder	A. Louise Brough	1967	John Newcombe	Billie Jean King
1950	Budge Patty	A. Louise Brough	1968	Rod Laver	Billie Jean King
1951	Dick Savitt	Doris Hart	1969	Rod Laver	Ann Jones
1952	Frank Sedgman	Maureen Connolly	1970	John Newcombe	Margaret S. Court
1953	Victor Seixas	Maureen Connolly	1971	John Newcombe	Evonne Goolagong
1954	Jaroslav Drobny	Maureen Connolly	1972	Stan Smith	Billie Jean King
1955	Tony Trabert	A. Louise Brough	1973	Jan Kodes	Billie Jean King
1956	Lewis Hoad	Shirley Fry	1974	Jimmy Connors	Chris Evert
1957	Lewis Hoad	Althea Gibson	1975	Arthur Ashe	Billie Jean King
1958	Ashley Cooper	Althea Gibson	1976	Bjorn Borg	Chris Evert
1959	Alex Olmedo	Maria Bueno	1977	Bjorn Borg	Virginia Wade
1960	Neale Fraser	Maria Bueno	1978	Bjorn Borg	Martina Navratilova
1961	Rod Laver	Angela Mortimer	1979	Bjorn Borg	Martina Navratilova
1962	Rod Laver	Karen Hantze Susman	1980	Bjorn Borg	Evonne Goolagong Cawley
1963	Chuck McKinley	Margaret Smith			
1964	Roy Emerson	Maria Bueno			

Leading Tennis Money Winners in 1979

Men		Women	
Bjorn Borg	$1,019,345	Martina Navratilova	$747,548
John McEnroe	1,005,238	Chris Evert Lloyd	564,398
Jimmy Connors	701,341	Tracy Austin	541,676
Vitas Gerulaitis	424,515	Wendy Turnbull	317,463
Guillermo Vilas	374,195	Dianne Fromholtz	266,990
Peter Fleming	353,315	Billie Jean King	185,804
Roscoe Tanner	263,433	Betty Stove	182,006
Eddie Dibbs	249,293	Sue Barker	175,452
Wojtek Fibak	234,452	Evonne Goolagong	171,573
Harold Solomon	222,078	Virginia Wade	146,283

WCT World Series of Tennis in 1980

Dates	Event, city	Singles winner	Doubles winners
Jan. 14-20	Birmingham International Indoor Tournament, Birmingham, Ala.	Jimmy Connors	Wojtek Fibak-Tom Okker
Jan. 21-27	U.S. Pro Indoor Championships, Philadelphia, Pa.	Jimmy Connors	John McEnroe-Peter Fleming
Jan. 28-Feb. 3	United Virginia Bank Classic, Richmond, Va.	John McEnroe	Fritz Buehning-Johan Kriek
Mar. 10-16	ABN Wereldtennis Tournament, Rotterdam, The Netherlands	Heinz Gunthardt	Vijay Amritraj-Stan Smith
Mar. 17-23	WCT Trevira Cup '80, Frankfurt, Germany	Stan Smith	Vijay Amritraj-Stan Smith
Mar. 24-30	The Ramazzotti Cup, Milan, Italy	John McEnroe	John McEnroe-Peter Fleming
Mar. 31-Apr. 6	WCT Monte Carlo Volvo Open, Monte Carlo, Monaco	Bjorn Borg	Paolo Bertolucci-Adriano Panatta
Apr. 7-13	River Oaks/Houston National Bank Tournament, Houston, Tex.	Ivan Lendl	Peter McNamara-Paul McNamee

WCT Finals

Dallas, Tex., Apr. 28-May 4, 1980

Quarterfinals

John McEnroe def. Heinz Gunthardt 6-2, 6-1, 6-0.
Johan Kriek def. John Sadri 7-5, 6-4, 7-5.
Ivan Lendl def. Vijay Amritraj 6-4, 6-1, 6-3.
Jimmy Connors def. Bill Scanlon 7-6, 7-6, 6-4.

Semifinals

McEnroe def. Kriek 6-4, 4-6, 7-6, 6-3.
Connors def. Lendl 6-4, 7-5, 6-3.

Final

Connors def. McEnroe 2-6, 7-6, 6-1, 6-2.

Aetna World Cup

Hartford, Conn., Mar. 6-9, 1980

Singles

Tom Gorman (U.S.) def. Ken Rosewall (Aust.) 5-7, 6-2, 6-4.
Marty Riessen (U.S.) def. John Newcombe (Aust.) 6-1, 2-6, 6-4.
Marty Riessen (U.S.) def. Ken Rosewall (Aust.) 6-4, 6-1.
Jim Osborne (U.S.) def. John Newcombe (Aust.) 7-5, 6-7, 6-3.

Doubles

Fred Stolle-Roy Emerson (Aust.) def. Dennis Ralston-Marty Riessen (U.S.) 4-6, 6-2, 7-6.
Rod Laver-John Newcombe (Aust.) def. Charlie Pasarell-Tom Gorman (U.S.) 6-1, 5-7, 7-6.
Dennis Ralston-Charlie Pasarell (U.S.) def. Roy Emerson-Rod Laver (Aust.) 3-6, 7-5, 6-2.

Tournament of Champions

Forest Hills, N.Y., May 5-11, 1980

First round

McEnroe def. Walts 6-2, 6-1.
Moor def. McNamee 6-4, 6-2.
Fleming def. Schoenfield 6-1, 4-6, 6-2.
Dibbs def. Glickstein 6-2, 6-2.
Ramirez def. Okker 5-7, 6-1, 6-1.
Fibak def. Amaya 6-2, 3-6, 7-5.
Taroczy def. Teltscher 2-6, 7-6, 6-3.
McNamara def. Scanlon 5-7, 7-6, 6-3.
Gerulaitis def. Sadri 4-6, 7-6, 7-6.
Pecci def. Feigl 4-6, 7-5, 6-0.
Pattison def. Warwick 6-0, 6-4.
V. Amritraj def. Gunthardt 3-6, 7-5, 7-5.

Second round

McEnroe def. Moor 6-1, 6-2.
Teacher def. Fleming 2-6, 7-5, 6-2.
Ramirez def. Dibbs 6-4, 6-3.
Fibak def. Gottfried 6-4, 6-0.
Taroczy def. Gildemeister 6-0, 6-2.
Gerulaitis def. McNamara 6-4, 7-6.
Pecci def. Pattison 6-1, 6-4.
V. Amritraj def. Connors 6-4, 4-6, 6-3.

Quarterfinals

McEnroe def. Teacher 6-1, 6-2.
Ramirez def. Fibak 6-2, 2-6, 6-4.
Gerulaitis def. Taroczy 6-4, 7-6.
V. Amritraj def. Pecci 6-4, 7-6.

Semifinals

McEnroe def. Ramirez 6-3, 6-4.
Gerulaitis def. V. Amritraj 7-6, 4-6, 6-3.

Final

Gerulaitis def. McEnroe 2-6, 6-2, 6-0.

NCAA Tennis Champions

Year	Singles	College	Doubles	College
1968	Stan Smith	USC	Stan Smith—Bob Lutz	USC
1969	Joaquin Loyo Mayo	USC	Joaquin Loyo Mayo—Marcelo Lara	USC
1970	Jeff Borowiak	UCLA	Pat Cramer—Luis Garcia	Miami (Fla.)
1971	Jimmy Connors	UCLA	Jeff Borowiak—Haroon Rahim	UCLA
1972	Dick Stockton	Trinity (Tex.)	Sandy Mayer—Roscoe Tanner	Stanford
1973	Sandy Mayer	Stanford	Sandy Mayer—Jim Delaney	Stanford
1974	John Whitlinger	Stanford	John Whitlinger—Jim Delaney	Stanford
1975	Billy Martin	UCLA	Butch Walts—Bruce Manson	USC
1976	Bill Scanlon	Trinity	Peter Fleming—Ferdi Taygan	UCLA
1977	Matt Mitchell	Stanford	Bruce Manson—Chris Lewis	USC
1978	John McEnroe	Stanford	Bruce Nichols—John Austin	UCLA
1979	Kevin Curren	Texas	Erick Iskersky—Ben McKown	Trinity
1980	Robert Van't Hof	USC	Mel Purcell—Rodney Harman	Tennessee

Clay Court Champions

Year	Champion	Year	Champion	Year	Champion	Year	Champion
1956	Herbert Flam	1963	Chuck McKinley	1969	Zeljko Franulovic	1975	Manuel Orantes
1957	E. Victor Seixas, Jr.	1964	Dennis Ralston	1970	Cliff Richey	1976	Jimmy Connors
1958	Bernard Bartzen	1965	Dennis Ralston	1971	Zeljko Franulovic	1977	Manuel Orantes
1959	Bernard Bartzen	1966	Cliff Richey	1972	Bob Hewitt	1978	Jimmy Connors
1960	Barry MacKay	1967	Arthur Ashe	1973	Manuel Orantes	1979	Jimmy Connors
1961	Bernard Bartzen	1968	Clark Graebner	1974	Jimmy Connors	1980	Jose-Luis Clerc
1962	Chuck McKinley						

Davis Cup Challenge Round

Year	Result	Year	Result	Year	Result
1900	United States 5, British Isles 0	1928	France 4, United States 1	1958	United States 3, Australia 2
1901	(not played)	1929	France 3, United States 2	1959	Australia 3, United States 2
1902	United States 3, British Isles 2	1930	France 4, United States 1	1960	Australia 4, Italy 1
1903	British Isles 4, United States 1	1931	France 3, Great Britain 2	1961	Australia 5, Italy 0
1904	British Isles 5, Belgium 0	1932	France 3, United States 2	1962	Australia 5, Mexico 0
1905	British Isles 5, United States 0	1933	Great Britain 3, France 2	1963	United States 3, Australia 2
1906	British Isles 5, United States 0	1934	Great Britain 4, United States 1	1964	Australia 3, United States 2
1907	Australia 3, British Isles 2	1935	Great Britain 5, United States 0	1965	Australia 4, Spain 1
1908	Australasia 3, United States 2	1936	Great Britain 3, Australia 2	1966	Australia 4, India 1
1909	Australasia 5, United States 0	1937	United States 4, Great Britain 1	1967	Australia 4, Spain 1
1910	(not played)	1938	United States 3, Australia 2	1968	United States 4, Australia 1
1911	Australasia 5, United States 0	1939	Australia 3, United States 2	1969	United States 5, Romania 0
1912	British Isles 3, Australasia 2	1940-45	(not played)	1970	United States 5, W. Germany 0
1913	United States 3, British Isles 2	1946	United States 5, Australia 0	1971	United States 3, Romania 2
1914	Australasia 3, United States 2	1947	United States 4, Australia 1	1972	United States 3, Romania 2
1915-18	(not played)	1948	United States 5, Australia 0	1973	Australia 5, United States 0
1919	Australasia 4, British Isles 1	1949	United States 4, Australia 1	1974	South Africa (default by India)
1920	United States 5, Australasia 0	1950	Australia 4, United States 1	1975	Sweden 3, Czech. 2
1921	United States 5, Japan 0	1951	Australia 3, United States 2	1976	Italy 4, Chile 1
1922	United States 4, Australasia 1	1952	Australia 4, United States 1	1977	Australia 3, Italy 1
1923	United States 4, Australasia 1	1953	Australia 3, United States 2	1978	United States 4, Great Britain 1
1924	United States 5, Australasia 0	1954	United States 3, Australia 2	1979	United States 5, Italy 0
1925	United States 5, France 0	1955	Australia 5, United States 0		
1926	United States 4, France 1	1956	Australia 5, United States 0		
1927	France 3, United States 2	1957	Australia 3, United States 2		

National Junior Tennis Champions

Boys' 18 singles

1973 Billy Martin
1974 Ferd Taygan
1975 Howard Schoenfield
1976 Larry Gottfried
1977 Van Winitsky
1978 David Dowlen
1979 Scott Davis

Boys' 18 doubles

1973 Billy Martin and Trey Waitke
1974 Francisco Gonzalez and Rocky Maguire
1975 Larry Gottfried and John McEnroe
1976 Larry Gottfried and John McEnroe
1977 Robert Van'tHov and Van Winitsky
1978 Scott Bondurant and Blaine Willenborg
1979 Rodney Harmon and Mike DePalmer

Boys' 16 singles

1973 Ben McKnown
1974 Walter Redondo
1975 Larry Gottfried
1976 Tim Wilkison
1977 Ramesh Krishnan
1978 Ben Testerman
1979 Matt Auger

Boys' 16 doubles

1973 Nial Brash and Matt Mitchell
1974 Jeff Robbins and Van Winitsky
1975 Tony Giammalva and Billy Scanlon
1976 Murray Robinson and Tim Wilkison
1977 Sean Brawley and David Siegler
1978 Scott Davis and Ben Testerman
1979 Sam Giammalva and Billy Quigley

Girls' 18 singles

1973 Carrie Fleming
1974 Rayni Fox
1975 Beth Norton
1976 Lynn Epstein
1977 Tracy Austin
1978 Tracy Austin
1979 Andrea Jaeger

Girls' 18 doubles

1973 Susan Boyle and Kathy May
1974 Anne Bruning and Barbara Hallquist
1975 Lea Antonoplis and Berta McCallum
1976 Sherry Acker and Anne Smith
1977 Lea Antonoplis and Kathy Jordan
1978 Tracy Austin and Maria Fernandez
1979 Andrea and Susy Jaeger

Girls' 16 singles

1973 Betsy Nagelson
1974 Zenda Leiss
1975 Lea Antonoplis
1976 Peanut Louie
1977 Linda Siegel
1978 Tracy Austin
1979 Kathy Horvath

Girls' 16 doubles

1973 Susan Mehmedbasich and Robin Tenney
1974 Sherry Acker and Anne Smith
1975 Lea Antonoplis and Berta McCallum
1976 Lucia Fernandez and Trey Lewis
1977 Tracy Austin and Maria Fernandez
1978 Pam Shriver and Barbara Potter
1979 Kathy Horvath and Pilar Vasquez

Women's Indoor Champions

Year	Singles	Doubles
1964	Mary Ann Eisel	Mary Ann Eisel—Katherine Hubbell
1965	Nancy Richey	Carol Hanks Aucamp—Mary Ann Eisel
1966	Billie Jean King	Billie Jean King—Rosemary Casals
1967	Billie Jean King	Carol Hanks Aucamp—Mary Ann Eisel
1968	Billie Jean King	Billie Jean King—Rosemary Casals
1969	Mary Ann Eisel	Mary Ann Eisel—Valerie Ziegenfuss
1970	Mary Ann E. Curtis	Peaches Bartkowicz—Nancy Richey
1971	Billie Jean King	Billie Jean King—Rosemary Casals
1972	Virginia Wade	Rosemary Casals—Virginia Wade
1973	Evonne Goolagong	Olga Morozova—Marina Kroskina
1974	Billie Jean King	none
1975	Martina Navratilova	Billie Jean King—Rosemary Casals
1976	Virginia Wade	Francoise Durr—Rosemary Casals
1977	Chris Evert	Martina Navratilova—Betty Stove
1978	Chris Evert	Kerry Reid—Wendy Turnbull
1979	Chris Evert Lloyd	Kerry Reid—Wendy Turnbull
1980	Tracy Austin	Kiyomora—Reynolds

Men's Indoor Champions

Year	Singles	Doubles
1967	Charles Pasarell	Arthur Ashe—Charles Pasarell
1968	Cliff Richey	Thomas Koch—Tom Okker
1969	Stan Smith	Stan Smith—Robert Lutz
1970	Ilie Nastase	Stan Smith—Arthur Ashe
1971	Clark Graebner	Juan Gisbert—Manuel Orantes
1972	Stan Smith	Andres Gimeno—Manuel Orantes
1973	Jimmy Connors	Juan Gisbert—Jurgen Fassbender
1974	Jimmy Connors	Jimmy Connors—Frew McMillan
1975	Jimmy Connors	Jimmy Connors—Ilie Nastase
1976	Ilie Nastase	Sherwood Stewart—Fred McNair
1977	Bjorn Borg	Sherwood Stewart—Fred McNair
1978	Jimmy Connors	Brian Gottfried—Raul Ramirez
1979	Jimmy Connors	Wojtek Fibak—Tom Okker
1980	John McEnroe	John McEnroe—Brian Gottfried

Tennis Championships in 1980

Australian Open (Melbourne) — Men's Singles: Guillermo Vilas def. John Sadri 7-6, 6-3, 6-2. Women's Singles: Barbara Jordan def. Sharon Walsh 6-3, 6-3.

Italian Open — Men's Singles: Guillermo Vilas def. Yannich Noah 6-0, 6-4, 6-4. Women's Singles: Chris Evert Lloyd def. Virginia Ruzici 5-7, 6-2, 6-2.

French Open — Men's Singles: Bjorn Borg def. Vitas Gerulaitis 6-4, 6-1, 6-2; Men's Doubles: Amaya-Pfister def. Gottfried-Ramirez 1-6, 6-4, 6-4, 6-3. Women's Singles: Chris Evert Lloyd def. Virginia Ruzici 6-0, 6-3; Women's Doubles: Jordan-Smith def. Madruga-Villagran 6-1, 6-0.

The America's Cup

Competition for the America's Cup grew out of the first contest to establish a world yachting championship, one of the carnival features of the London Exposition of 1851. The race, open to all classes of yachts from all over the world, covered a 60-mile course around the Isle of Wight; the prize was a cup worth about $500, donated by the Royal Yacht Squadron of England, known as the "America's Cup" because it was first won by the United States yacht America. Successive efforts of British and Australian yachtsmen have failed to win the famous trophy, which remains in the United States.

On Sept. 25, 1980, the yacht Freedom defeated the Australian challenger, Australia, for the 4th time in 5 races to keep the symbol of world sailing supremacy in the United States. Freedom was skippered by Dennis Connor of San Diego, Cal.

Winners of the America's Cup

1851	America
1870	Magic defeated Cambria, England, (1-0)
1871	Columbia (first three races) and Sappho (last two races) defeated Livonia, England, (4-1)
1876	Madeline defeated Countess of Dufferin, Canada, (2-0)
1881	Mischief defeated Atalanta, Canada, (2-0)
1885	Puritan defeated Genesta, England, (2-0)
1886	Mayflower defeated Galatea, England, (2-0)
1887	Volunteer defeated Thistle, Scotland, (2-0)
1893	Vigilant defeated Valkyrie II, England, (3-0)
1895	Defender defeated Valkyrie III, England, (3-0)
1899	Columbia defeated Shamrock, England, (3-0)
1901	Columbia defeated Shamrock II, England, (3-0)
1903	Reliance defeated Shamrock III, England, (3-0)
1920	Resolute defeated Shamrock IV, England, (3-2)
1930	Enterprise defeated Shamrock V, England, (4-0)
1934	Rainbow defeated Endeavour, England, (4-2)
1937	Ranger defeated Endeavour II, England, (4-0)
1958	Columbia defeated Sceptre, England, (4-0)
1962	Weatherly defeated Gretel, Australia, (4-1)
1964	Constellation defeated Sovereign, England, (4-0)
1967	Intrepid defeated Dame Pattie, Australia, (4-0)
1970	Intrepid defeated Gretel II, Australia, (4-1)
1974	Courageous defeated Southern Cross, Australia, (4-0)
1977	Courageous defeated Australia, Australia, (4-0)
1980	Freedom defeated Australia, Australia, (4-1)

Chess

Chess dates back to antiquity. Its exact origin is unknown. The strongest players of their time, and therefore regarded by later generations as world champions, were Francois Philidor, France; Alexandre Deschappelles, France; Louis de la Bourdonnais, France; Howard Staunton, England; Adolph Anderssen, Germany and Paul Morphy, United States. In 1866 Wilhelm Steinitz of Czechoslovakia defeated Adolph Anderssen and claimed the title of world champion. The official world champions, since the title was first used follow:

1866-1894 Wilhelm Steinitz, Czech.
1894-1921 Dr. Emanuel Lasker, Germany
1921-1927 Jose R. Capablanca, Cuba
1927-1935 Dr. Alexander A. Alekhine, USSR
1935-1937 Dr. Max Euwe, Netherlands
1937-1946 Dr. Alexander A. Alekhine, USSR
1948-1957 Mikhail Botvinnik, USSR
1957-1958 Vassily Smysolv, USSR
1958-1959 Mikhail Botvinnik, USSR
1960-1961 Mikhail Tal, USSR
1961-1963 Mikhail Botvinnik, USSR
1963-1969 Tigran Petrosian, USSR
1969-1972 Boris Spassky, USSR
1972-1975 Bobby Fischer, U.S. (a)
1975 Anatoly Karpov, USSR

(a) Defaulted championship after refusal to accept International Chess Federation rules for a championship match, April 1975.

United States Champions

Unofficial champions

1857-1871 Paul Morphy
1871-1876 George Mackenzie
1876-1880 James Mason
1880-1889 George Mackenzie
1889-1890 S. Lipschutz
1890 Jackson Showalter
1890-1891 Max Judd
1891-1892 Jackson Showalter
1892-1894 S. Lipschutz

Official champions

1894 Jackson Showalter
1894-1895 Albert Hodges
1895-1897 Jackson Showalter
1897-1909 Harry Pillsbury
1909-1936 Frank Marshall
1936-1944 Samuel Reshevsky
1944-1946 Arnold Denker
1946-1948 Samuel Reshevsky
1948-1951 Herman Steiner
1951-1954 Larry Evans
1954-1957 Arthur Bisguier
1957-1961 Bobby Fischer
1961-1962 Larry Evans
1962-1968 Bobby Fischer
1968-1969 Larry Evans
1969-1972 Samuel Reshevsky
1972-1973 Robert Byrne
1973-1974 Lubomir Kavalek, John Grefe
1974-1977 Walter Browne
1978-1980 Lubomir Kavalek
1980 (tie) Larry Evans, Larry Christiansen, Walter Browne

Motorcycle Racing Grand National Champion

Year	Champion	Year	Champion	Year	Champion	Year	Champion
1956	Joe Leonard	1962	Bart Markel	1968	Gary Nixon	1974	Ken Roberts
1957	Joe Leonard	1963	Dick Mann	1969	Mert Lawwill	1975	Gary Scott
1958	Carroll Resweber	1964	Roger Reiman	1970	Gene Romero	1976	Jay Springsteen
1959	Carroll Resweber	1965	Bart Markel	1971	Dick Mann	1977	Jay Springsteen
1960	Carroll Resweber	1966	Bart Markel	1972	Mark Brelsford	1978	Jay Springsteen
1961	Carroll Resweber	1967	Gary Nixon	1973	Ken Roberts	1979	Steve Eklund

Baseball

Members of National Baseball Hall of Fame and Museum

The shrine of organized baseball, dedicated June 12, 1939, is located in Cooperstown, N. Y.

Alexander, Grover Cleveland
Anson, Cap
Averill, Earl
Appling, Luke
Baker, Home Run
Bancroft, Dave
Banks, Ernie
Barrow, Edward G.
Beckley, Jake
Bell, Cool Papa
Bender, Chief
Berra, Yogi
Bottomley, Jim
Boudreau, Lou
Bresnahan, Roger
Brouthers, Dan
Brown (Three Finger), Mordecai
Bulkeley, Morgan C.
Burkett, Jesse C.
Campanella, Roy
Carey, Max
Cartwright, Alexander
Chadwick, Henry
Chance, Frank
Charleston, Oscar
Chesbro, John
Clarke, Fred
Clarkson, John
Clemente, Roberto
Cobb, Ty
Cochrane, Mickey
Collins, Eddie
Collins, James
Combs, Earle
Comiskey, Charles A.
Conlan, Jocko
Connolly, Thomas H.
Connor, Roger
Coveleski, Stan
Crawford, Sam
Cronin, Joe
Cummings, Candy
Cuyler, Kiki
Dean, Dizzy
Delahanty, Ed
Dickey, Bill
DiHigo, Martin
DiMaggio, Joe
Duffy, Hugh
Evans, Billy
Evers, John
Ewing, Buck
Faber, Urban
Feller, Bob
Flick, Elmer H.
Ford, Whitey
Foxx, Jimmy
Frick, Ford
Frisch, Frank
Galvin, Pud
Gehrig, Lou
Gehringer, Charles
Gibson, Josh
Giles, Warren
Gomez, Lefty
Goslin, Goose
Greenberg, Hank
Griffith, Clark
Grimes, Burleigh
Grove, Lefty
Hafey, Chick
Haines, Jesee
Hamilton, Bill
Harridge, Will
Harris, Bucky
Hartnett, Gabby
Heilmann, Harry
Herman, Billy
Hooper, Harry
Hornsby, Rogers
Hoyt, Waite
Hubbard, Cal
Hubbell, Carl
Huggins, Miller
Irvin, Monte
Jennings, Hugh
Johnson, Byron
Johnson, William (Rudy)
Johnson, Walter
Joss, Addie
Kaline, Al
Keefe, Timothy
Keeler, William
Kelley, Joe
Kelly, George
Kelly, King
Kiner, Ralph
Klein, Chuck
Klem, Bill
Koufax, Sandy
Lajoie, Napoleon
Landis, Kenesaw M.
Lemon, Bob
Leonard, Buck
Lindstrom, Fred
Lloyd, Pop
Lopez, Al
Lyons, Ted
Mack, Connie
MacPhail, Larry
Mantle, Mickey
Manush, Henry
Maranville, Rabbit
Marquard, Rube
Mathews, Eddie
Mathewson, Christy
Mays, Willie
McCarthy, Joe
McCarthy, Thomas
McGinnity, Joe
McGraw, John
McKechnie, Bill
Medwick, Joe
Musial, Stan
Nichols, Kid
O'Rourke, James
Ott, Mel
Paige, Satchel
Pennock, Herb
Plank, Ed
Radbourne, Charlie
Rice, Sam
Rickey, Branch
Rixey, Eppa
Roberts, Robin
Robinson, Jackie
Robinson, Wilbert
Roush, Edd
Ruffing, Red
Rusie, Amos
Ruth, Babe
Schalk, Ray
Sewell, Joe
Simmons, Al
Sisler, George
Snider, Duke
Spahn, Warren
Spalding, Albert
Speaker, Tris
Stengel, Casey
Terry, Bill
Thompson, Sam
Tinker, Joe
Traynor, Pie
Vance, Dazzy
Waddell, Rube
Wagner, Honus
Wallace, Roderick
Walsh, Ed.
Waner, Lloyd
Waner, Paul
Ward, John
Weiss, George
Welch, Mickey
Wheat, Zach
Williams, Ted
Wilson, Hack
Wright, George
Wright, Harry
Wynn, Early
Yawkey, Tom
Young, Cy
Youngs, Ross

All-Star Baseball Games, 1933-1980

Year	Winner	Score	Location
1933	American	**4-2**	Chicago
1934	American	**9-7**	New York
1935	American	**4-1**	Cleveland
1936	National	**4-3**	Boston
1937	American	**8-3**	Washington
1938	National	**4-1**	Cincinnati
1939	American	**3-1**	New York
1940	National	**4-0**	St. Louis
1941	American	**7-5**	Detroit
1942	American	**3-1**	New York
1943*	American	**5-3**	Philadelphia
1944*	National	**7-1**	Pittsburgh
1945	(not played)		
1946	American	**12-0**	Boston
1947	American	**2-1**	Chicago
1948	American	**5-2**	St. Louis
1949	American	**11-7**	New York
1950	National (1)	**4-3**	Chicago
1951	National	**8-3**	Detroit
1952	National	**3-2**	Philadelphia
1953	National	**5-1**	Cincinnati
1954	American	**11-9**	Cleveland
1955	National (2)	**6-5**	Milwaukee
1956	National	**7-3**	Washington
1957	American	**6-5**	St. Louis
1958	American	**4-3**	Baltimore
1959	National	**5-4**	Pittsburgh
1959	American	**5-3**	Los Angeles
1960	National	**5-3**	Kansas City
1960	National	**6-0**	New York
1961	National (3)	**5-4**	San Francisco
1961	Called-Rain	**1-1**	Boston
1962	National (3)	**3-1**	Washington
1962	American	**9-4**	Chicago
1963	National	**5-3**	Cleveland
1964	National	**7-4**	New York
1965	National	**6-5**	Minnesota
1966	National (3)	**2-1**	St. Louis
1967	National (4)	**2-1**	Anaheim
1968*	National	**1-0**	Houston
1969	National	**9-3**	Washington
1970*	National (2)	**5-4**	Cincinnati
1971*	American	**6-4**	Detroit
1972*	National	**4-3**	Atlanta
1973*	National	**7-1**	Kansas City
1974*	National	**7-2**	Pittsburgh
1975*	National	**6-3**	Milwaukee
1976*	National	**7-1**	Philadelphia
1977*	National	**7-5**	New York
1978*	National	**7-3**	San Diego
1979*	National	**7-6**	Seattle
1980*	National	**4-2**	Los Angeles

(1) 14 innings, (2) 12 innings, (3) 10 innings, (4) 15 innings *Night game.

Major League Perfect Games Since 1900

Year	Player	Clubs	Score
1904	Cy Young	Boston vs. Phil. (AL)	3-0
1908	Addie Joss	Cleveland vs. Chicago (AL)	1-0
1917	Ernie Shore (a)	Boston vs. Wash. (AL)	4-0
1922	Charles Robertson	Chicago vs. Detroit (AL)	2-0
1956	Don Larson (b)	N.Y. Yankees vs. Brooklyn	2-0
1964	Jim Bunning	Phil. vs. N.Y. Mets (NL)	6-0
1965	Sandy Koufax	Los Angeles vs. Chic. (NL)	1-0
1968	Jim Hunter	Oakland vs. Minn. (AL)	4-0

(a) Babe Ruth, the starting pitcher, was ejected from the game after walking the first batter. Shore replaced him and the base-runner was out stealing. Shore retired the next 26 batters. (b) World Series.

Major League Pennant Winners, 1901–1980

National League

Year	Winner	Won	Lost	Pct	Manager
1901	Pittsburgh	90	49	**.647**	Clarke
1902	Pittsburgh	103	36	**.741**	Clarke
1903	Pittsburgh	91	49	**.650**	Clarke
1904	New York	106	47	**.693**	McGraw
1905	New York	105	48	**.686**	McGraw
1906	Chicago	116	36	**.763**	Chance
1907	Chicago	107	45	**.704**	Chance
1908	Chicago	99	55	**.643**	Chance
1909	Pittsburgh	110	42	**.724**	Clarke
1910	Chicago	104	50	**.675**	Chance
1911	New York	99	54	**.647**	McGraw
1912	New York	103	48	**.682**	McGraw
1913	New York	101	51	**.664**	McGraw
1914	Boston	94	59	**.614**	Stallings
1915	Philadelphia	90	62	**.592**	Moran
1916	Brooklyn	94	60	**.610**	Robinson
1917	New York	98	56	**.636**	McGraw
1918	Chicago	84	45	**.651**	Mitchell
1919	Cincinnati	96	44	**.686**	Moran
1920	Brooklyn	93	60	**.604**	Robinson
1921	New York	94	56	**.614**	McGraw
1922	New York	93	61	**.604**	McGraw
1923	New York	95	58	**.621**	McGraw
1924	New York	93	60	**.608**	McGraw
1925	Pittsburgh	95	58	**.621**	McKechnie
1926	St. Louis	89	65	**.578**	Hornsby
1927	Pittsburgh	94	60	**.610**	Bush
1928	St. Louis	95	59	**.617**	McKechnie
1929	Chicago	98	54	**.645**	McCarthy
1930	St. Louis	92	62	**.597**	Street
1931	St. Louis	101	53	**.656**	Street
1932	Chicago	90	64	**.584**	Grimm
1933	New York	91	61	**.599**	Terry
1934	St. Louis	95	58	**.621**	Frisch
1935	Chicago	100	54	**.649**	Grimm
1936	New York	91	62	**.597**	Terry
1937	New York	95	57	**.625**	Terry
1938	Chicago	89	63	**.586**	Hartnett
1939	Cincinnati	97	57	**.630**	McKechnie
1940	Cincinnati	100	53	**.654**	McKechnie
1941	Brooklyn	100	54	**.649**	Durocher
1942	St. Louis	106	48	**.688**	Southworth
1943	St. Louis	105	49	**.682**	Southworth
1944	St. Louis	105	49	**.682**	Southworth
1945	Chicago	98	56	**.636**	Grimm
1946	St. Louis	98	58	**.628**	Dyer
1947	Brooklyn	94	60	**.610**	Shotton
1948	Boston	91	62	**.595**	Southworth
1949	Brooklyn	97	57	**.630**	Shotton
1950	Philadelphia	91	63	**.591**	Sawyer
1951	New York	98	59	**.624**	Durocher
1952	Brooklyn	96	57	**.627**	Dressen
1953	Brooklyn	105	49	**.682**	Dressen
1954	New York	97	57	**.630**	Durocher
1955	Brooklyn	98	55	**.641**	Alston
1956	Brooklyn	93	61	**.604**	Alston
1957	Milwaukee	95	59	**.617**	Haney
1958	Milwaukee	92	62	**.597**	Haney
1959	Los Angeles	88	68	**.564**	Alston
1960	Pittsburgh	95	59	**.617**	Murtaugh
1961	Cincinnati	93	61	**.604**	Hutchinson
1962	San Francisco	103	62	**.624**	Dark
1963	Los Angeles	99	63	**.611**	Alston
1964	St. Louis	93	69	**.574**	Keane
1965	Los Angeles	97	65	**.599**	Alston
1966	Los Angeles	95	67	**.586**	Alston
1967	St. Louis	101	60	**.627**	Schoendienst
1968	St. Louis	97	65	**.599**	Schoendienst

American League

Year	Winner	Won	Lost	Pct	Manager
1901	Chicago	83	53	**.610**	Griffith
1902	Philadelphia	83	53	**.610**	Mack
1903	Boston	91	47	**.659**	Collins
1904	Boston	95	59	**.617**	Collins
1905	Philadelphia	92	56	**.622**	Mack
1906	Chicago	93	58	**.616**	Jones
1907	Detroit	92	58	**.613**	Jennings
1908	Detroit	90	63	**.588**	Jennings
1909	Detroit	98	54	**.645**	Jennings
1910	Philadelphia	102	48	**.680**	Mack
1911	Philadelphia	101	50	**.669**	Mack
1912	Boston	105	47	**.691**	Stahl
1913	Philadelphia	96	57	**.627**	Mack
1914	Philadelphia	99	53	**.651**	Mack
1915	Boston	101	50	**.669**	Carrigan
1916	Boston	91	63	**.591**	Carrigan
1917	Chicago	100	54	**.649**	Rowland
1918	Boston	75	51	**.595**	Barrow
1919	Chicago	88	52	**.629**	Gleason
1920	Cleveland	98	56	**.636**	Speaker
1921	New York	98	55	**.641**	Huggins
1922	New York	94	60	**.610**	Huggins
1923	New York	98	54	**.645**	Huggins
1924	Washington	92	62	**.597**	Harris
1925	Washington	96	55	**.636**	Harris
1926	New York	91	63	**.591**	Huggins
1927	New York	110	44	**.714**	Huggins
1928	New York	101	53	**.656**	Huggins
1929	Philadelphia	104	46	**.693**	Mack
1930	Philadelphia	102	52	**.622**	Mack
1931	Philadelphia	107	45	**.704**	Mack
1932	New York	107	47	**.695**	McCarthy
1933	Washington	99	53	**.651**	Cronin
1934	Detroit	101	53	**.656**	Cochrane
1935	Detroit	93	58	**.616**	Cochrane
1936	New York	102	51	**.667**	McCarthy
1937	New York	102	52	**.662**	McCarthy
1938	New York	99	53	**.651**	McCarthy
1939	New York	106	45	**.702**	McCarthy
1940	Detroit	90	64	**.584**	Baker
1941	New York	101	53	**.656**	McCarthy
1942	New York	103	51	**.669**	McCarthy
1943	New York	98	56	**.636**	McCarthy
1944	St. Louis	89	65	**.578**	Sewell
1945	Detroit	88	65	**.575**	O'Neill
1946	Boston	104	50	**.675**	Cronin
1947	New York	97	57	**.630**	Harris
1948	Cleveland	97	58	**.626**	Boudreau
1949	New York	97	57	**.630**	Stengel
1950	New York	98	56	**.636**	Stengel
1951	New York	98	56	**.636**	Stengel
1952	New York	95	59	**.617**	Stengel
1953	New York	99	52	**.656**	Stengel
1954	Cleveland	111	43	**.721**	Lopez
1955	New York	96	58	**.623**	Stengel
1956	New York	97	57	**.630**	Stengel
1957	New York	98	56	**.636**	Stengel
1958	New York	92	62	**.597**	Stengel
1959	Chicago	94	60	**.610**	Lopez
1960	New York	97	57	**.630**	Stengel
1961	New York	109	53	**.673**	Houk
1962	New York	96	66	**.593**	Houk
1963	New York	104	57	**.646**	Houk
1964	New York	99	63	**.611**	Berra
1965	Minnesota	102	60	**.630**	Mele
1966	Baltimore	97	63	**.606**	Bauer
1967	Boston	92	70	**.568**	Williams
1968	Detroit	103	59	**.636**	Smith

National League

Year	East Winner	W	L	Pct	Manager	West Winner	W	L	Pct	Manager	Playoff winner
1969	N.Y. Mets	100	62	**.617**	Hodges	Atlanta	93	69	**.574**	Harris	New York
1970	Pittsburgh	89	73	**.549**	Murtaugh	Cincinnati	102	60	**.630**	Anderson	Cincinnati
1971	Pittsburgh	97	65	**.599**	Murtaugh	San Francisco	90	72	**.556**	Fox	Pittsburgh
1972	Pittsburgh	96	59	**.619**	Virdon	Cincinnati	95	59	**.617**	Anderson	Cincinnati
1973	N.Y. Mets	82	79	**.509**	Berra	Cincinnati	99	63	**.611**	Anderson	New York
1974	Pittsburgh	88	82	**.543**	Murtaugh	Los Angeles	102	60	**.630**	Alston	Los Angeles
1975	Pittsburgh	92	69	**.571**	Murtaugh	Cincinnati	108	54	**.667**	Anderson	Cincinnati
1976	Philadelphia	101	61	**.623**	Ozark	Cincinnati	102	60	**.630**	Anderson	Cincinnati
1977	Philadelphia	100	61	**.621**	Ozark	Los Angeles	98	64	**.605**	Lasorda	Los Angeles

Year	Winner	East W	L	Pct	Manager	Winner	West W	L	Pct	Manager	Playoff winner
1978	Philadelphia . . .	90	72	**.556**	Ozark	Los Angeles . . .	95	67	**.586**	Lasorda	Los Angeles
1979	Pittsburgh	98	64	**.605**	Tanner	Cincinnati.	90	71	**.559**	McNamara	Pittsburgh
1980	Philadelphia	91	71	**.562**	Green	Houston	93	70	**.571**	Virdon	Philadelphia

American League

Year	Winner	East W	L	Pct	Manager	Winner	West W	L	Pct	Manager	Playoff winner
1969	Baltimore.	109	53	**.673**	Weaver	Minnesota	97	65	**.599**	Martin	Baltimore
1970	Baltimore.	108	54	**.667**	Weaver	Minnesota	98	64	**.605**	Rigney	Baltimore
1971	Baltimore.	101	57	**.639**	Weaver	Oakland	101	60	**.627**	Williams	Baltimore
1972	Detroit	86	70	**.551**	Martin	Oakland	93	72	**.600**	Williams	Oakland
1973	Baltimore.	97	65	**.599**	Weaver	Oakland	94	68	**.580**	Williams	Oakland
1974	Baltimore.	91	71	**.562**	Weaver	Oakland	90	72	**.556**	Dark	Oakland
1975	Boston	95	65	**.594**	Johnson	Oakland	98	64	**.605**	Dark	Boston
1976	New York	97	62	**.610**	Martin	Kansas City	90	72	**.556**	Herzog	New York
1977	New York	100	62	**.617**	Martin	Kansas City	102	60	**.630**	Herzog	New York
1978	New York	100	63	**.613**	Martin, Lemon	Kansas City	92	70	**.568**	Herzog	New York
1979	Baltimore.	102	57	**.642**	Weaver	California.	88	74	**.543**	Fregosi	Baltimore
1980	New York	103	59	**.636**	Howser	Kansas City	97	65	**.599**	Frey	Kansas City

Baseball Stadiums

National League

Team	Stadium	Home run distances (ft.) LF	Center	RF	Seating capacity
Atlanta Braves.	Atlanta-Fulton County Stadium	330	402	330	52,194
Chicago Cubs	Wrigley Field.	355	400	353	37,741
Cincinnati Reds	Riverfront Stadium	330	404	330	51,786
Houston Astros	Astrodome.	330	406	330	45,000
Los Angeles Dodgers.	Dodger Stadium.	330	395	330	56,000
Montreal Expos	Olympic Stadium	330	404	330	59,511
New York Mets	Shea Stadium	341	410	341	55,300
Philadelphia Phillies.	Veterans Stadium.	330	408	330	58,651
Pittsburgh Pirates	Three Rivers Stadium	335	400	335	50,230
St. Louis Cardinals	Busch Memorial Stadium.	330	404	330	50,222
San Diego Padres.	San Diego Stadium	330	410	330	48,443
San Francisco Giants.	Candlestick Park	335	410	335	58,000

American League

Team	Stadium	LF	Center	RF	Seating capacity
Baltimore Orioles	Memorial Stadium.	309	405	309	52,862
Boston Red Sox.	Fenway Park	315	420	302	33,538
California Angels	Anaheim Stadium	333	404	333	43,250
Chicago White Sox	Comiskey Park	352	440	352	44,492
Cleveland Indians	Cleveland Stadium	320	400	320	76,713
Detroit Tigers	Tiger Stadium	340	440	325	53,676
Kansas City Royals.	Royals Stadium	330	410	330	40,760
Milwaukee Brewers.	Milwaukee County Stadium	320	402	315	54,187
Minnesota Twins	Metropolitan Stadium.	330	410	330	45,919
New York Yankees	Yankee Stadium	312	417	310	57,545
Oakland A's	Oakland-Alameda County Coliseum	330	400	330	49,649
Seattle Mariners.	Kingdome	316	405	316	59,059
Texas Rangers	Arlington Stadium.	330	400	330	41,097
Toronto Blue Jays.	Exhibition Stadium	330	400	330	43,737

Cy Young Award Winners

Year	Player, club
1956	Don Newcombe, Dodgers
1957	Warren Spahn, Braves
1958	Bob Turley, Yankees
1959	Early Wynn, White Sox
1960	Vernon Law, Pirates
1961	Whitey Ford, Yankees
1962	Don Drysdale, Dodgers
1963	Sandy Koufax, Dodgers
1964	Dean Chance, Angels
1965	Sandy Koufax, Dodgers
1966	Sandy Koufax, Dodgers
1967	(NL) Mike McCormick, Giants
	(AL) Jim Lonborg, Red Sox
1968	(NL) Bob Gibson, Cardinals
	(AL) Dennis McLain, Tigers
1969	(NL) Tom Seaver, Mets
	(AL) (tie) Dennis McLain, Tigers
	Mike Cuellar, Orioles
1970	(NL) Bob Gibson, Cardinals
	(AL) Jim Perry, Twins
1971	(NL) Ferguson Jenkins, Cubs
	(AL) Vida Blue, A's
1972	(NL) Steve Carlton, Phillies
	(AL) Gaylord Perry, Indians
1973	(NL) Tom Seaver, Mets
	(AL) Jim Palmer, Orioles
1974	(NL) Mike Marshall, Dodgers
	(AL) Jim (Catfish) Hunter, A's
1975	(NL) Tom Seaver, Mets
	(AL) Jim Palmer, Orioles
1976	(NL) Randy Jones, Padres
	(AL) Jim Palmer, Orioles
1977	(NL) Steve Carlton, Phillies
	(AL) Sparky Lyle, Yankees
1978	(NL) Gaylord Perry, Padres
	(AL) Ron Guidry, Yankees
1979	(NL) Bruce Sutter, Cubs
	(AL) Mike Flanagan, Orioles

College World Series in 1980

The Univ. of Arizona won the 1980 College World Series by defeating the Univ. of Hawaii 5-3 in the final game at Omaha, Neb.

Home Run Leaders

National League

Year		HR
1921	George Kelly, New York	23
1922	Rogers Hornsby, St. Louis	42
1923	Cy Williams, Philadelphia	41
1924	Jacques Fournier, Brooklyn	27
1925	Rogers Hornsby, St. Louis	39
1926	Hack Wilson, Chicago	21
1927	Hack Wilson, Chicago; Cy Williams, Philadelphia	30
1928	Hack Wilson, Chicago; Jim Bottomley, St. Louis	31
1929	Charles Klein, Philadelphia	43
1930	Hack Wilson, Chicago	56
1931	Charles Klein, Philadelphia	31
1932	Charles Klein, Philadelphia, Mel Ott, New York	38
1933	Charles Klein, Philadelphia	28
1934	Collins, St. Louis; Mel Ott, New York	35
1935	Walter Berger, Boston	34
1936	Mel Ott, New York	33
1937	Mel Ott, New York; Joe Medwick, St. Louis	31
1938	Mel Ott, New York	36
1939	John Mize, St. Louis	28
1940	John Mize, St. Louis	43
1941	Dolph Camilli, Brooklyn	34
1942	Mel Ott, New York	30
1943	Bill Nicholson, Chicago	29
1944	Bill Nicholson, Chicago	33
1945	Tommy Holmes, Boston	28
1946	Ralph Kiner, Pittsburgh	23
1947	Ralph Kiner, Pittsburgh; John Mize, New York	51
1948	Ralph Kiner, Pittsburgh; John Mize, New York	40
1949	Ralph Kiner, Pittsburgh	54
1950	Ralph Kiner, Pittsburgh	47
1951	Ralph Kiner, Pittsburgh	42
1952	Ralph Kiner, Pittsburgh; Hank Sauer, Chicago	37
1953	Ed Mathews, Milwaukee	47
1954	Ted Kluszewski, Cincinnati	49
1955	Willie Mays, New York	51
1956	Duke Snider, Brooklyn	43
1957	Hank Aaron, Milwaukee	44
1958	Ernie Banks, Chicago	47
1959	Ed Mathews, Milwaukee	46
1960	Ernie Banks, Chicago	41
1961	Orlando Cepeda, San Francisco	46
1962	Willie Mays, San Francisco	49
1963	Hank Aaron, Milwaukee, Willie McCovey, San Francisco	44
1964	Willie Mays, San Francisco	47
1965	Willie Mays, San Francisco	52
1966	Hank Aaron, Atlanta	44
1967	Hank Aaron, Atlanta	39
1968	Willie McCovey, San Francisco	36
1969	Willie McCovey, San Francisco	45
1970	Johnny Bench, Cincinnati	45
1971	Willie Stargell, Pittsburgh	48
1972	Johnny Bench, Cincinnati	40
1973	Willie Stargell, Pittsburgh	44
1974	Mike Schmidt, Philadelphia	36
1975	Mike Schmidt, Philadelphia	38
1976	Mike Schmidt, Philadelphia	38
1977	George Foster, Cincinnati	52
1978	George Foster, Cincinnati	40
1979	Dave Kingman, Chicago	48
1980	Mike Schmidt, Philadelphia	48

American League

Year		HR
1921	Babe Ruth, New York	59
1922	Ken Williams, St. Louis	39
1923	Babe Ruth, New York	41
1924	Babe Ruth, New York	46
1925	Bob Meusel, New York	33
1926	Babe Ruth, New York	47
1927	Babe Ruth, New York	60
1928	Babe Ruth, New York	54
1929	Babe Ruth, New York	46
1930	Babe Ruth, New York	49
1931	Babe Ruth, Lou Gehrig, New York	46
1932	Jimmy Foxx, Philadelphia	58
1933	Jimmy Foxx, Philadelphia	48
1934	Lou Gehrig, New York	49
1935	Jimmy Foxx, Philadelphia, Hank Greenberg, Detroit	36
1936	Lou Gehrig, New York	49
1937	Joe DiMaggio, New York	46
1938	Hank Greenberg, Detroit	58
1939	Jimmy Foxx, Boston	35
1940	Hank Greenberg, Detroit	41
1941	Ted Williams, Boston	37
1942	Ted Williams, Boston	36
1943	Rudy York, Detroit	34
1944	Nick Etten, New York	22
1945	Vern Stephens, St. Louis	24
1946	Hank Greenberg, Detroit	44
1947	Ted Williams, Boston	32
1948	Joe DiMaggio, New York	39
1949	Ted Williams, Boston	43
1950	Al Rosen, Cleveland	37
1951	Gus Zernial, Chicago-Philadelphia	33
1952	Larry Doby, Cleveland	32
1953	Al Rosen, Cleveland	43
1954	Larry Doby, Cleveland	32
1955	Mickey Mantle, New York	37
1956	Mickey Mantle, New York	52
1957	Roy Sievers, Washington	42
1958	Mickey Mantle, New York	42
1959	Rocky Colavito, Cleveland, Harmon Killebrew, Washington	42
1960	Mickey Mantle, New York	40
1961	Roger Maris, New York	61
1962	Harmon Killebrew, Minnesota	48
1963	Harmon Killebrew, Minnesota	45
1964	Harmon Killebrew, Minnesota	49
1965	Tony Conigliaro, Boston	32
1966	Frank Robinson, Baltimore	49
1967	Carl Yastrzemski, Boston, Harmon Killebrew, Minn.	44
1968	Frank Howard, Washington	44
1969	Harmon Killebrew, Minnesota	49
1970	Frank Howard, Washington	44
1971	Bill Melton, Chicago	33
1972	Dick Allen, Chicago	37
1973	Reggie Jackson, Oakland	32
1974	Dick Allen, Chicago	32
1975	George Scott, Milwaukee; Reggie Jackson, Oakland	36
1976	Graig Nettles, New York	32
1977	Jim Rice, Boston	39
1978	Jim Rice, Boston	46
1979	Gorman Thomas, Milwaukee	45
1980	Reggie Jackson, New York; Ben Oglivie, Milwaukee	41

All-time Major League Record (154-game Season)—60—Babe Ruth, New York Yankees (A), 1927. **(162-game Season)—61—**Roger Maris, New York Yankees, 1961. Prior to the 1931 season a batted ball that bounced into the stands was a home run (now a ground-rule double). None of Babe Ruth's record 60 homers bounced into the stands.

Runs Batted In Leaders

National League

Year		RBI
1944	Bill Nicholson, Chicago	122
1945	Dixie Walker, Brooklyn	124
1946	Enos Slaughter, St. Louis	130
1947	John Mize, New York	138
1948	Stan Musial, St. Louis	131
1949	Ralph Kiner, Pittsburgh	127
1950	Del Ennis, Philadelphia	126
1951	Monte Irvin, New York	121
1952	Hank Sauer, Chicago	121
1953	Roy Campanella, Brooklyn	142
1954	Ted Kluszewski, Cincinnati	141
1955	Duke Snider, Brooklyn	136
1956	Stan Musial, St. Louis	109
1957	Hank Aaron, Milwaukee	132
1958	Ernie Banks, Chicago	129
1959	Ernie Banks, Chicago	143
1960	Hank Aaron, Milwaukee	126

American League

Year		RBI
1944	Vern Stephens, St. Louis	109
1945	Nick Etten, New York	111
1946	Hank Greenberg, Detroit	127
1947	Ted Williams, Boston	114
1948	Joe DiMaggio, New York	155
1949	Ted Williams, Vern Stephens, Boston	159
1950	Walt Dropo, Vern Stephens, Boston	144
1951	Gus Zernial, Chicago-Philadelphia	129
1952	Al Rosen, Cleveland	105
1953	Al Rosen, Cleveland	145
1954	Larry Doby, Cleveland	126
1955	Ray Boone, Detroit, Jack Jensen, Boston	116
1956	Mickey Mantle, New York	130
1957	Roy Sievers, Washington	114
1958	Jack Jensen, Boston	122
1959	Jack Jensen, Boston	112
1960	Roger Maris, New York	112

Year		RBI
1961	Orlando Cepeda, San Francisco	142
1962	Tommy Davis, Los Angeles	153
1963	Hank Aaron, Milwaukee	130
1964	Ken Boyer, St. Louis	119
1965	Deron Johnson, Cincinnati	130
1966	Hank Aaron, Atlanta	127
1967	Orlando Cepeda, St. Louis	111
1968	Willie McCovey, San Francisco	105
1969	Willie McCovey, San Francisco	126
1970	Johnny Bench, Cincinnati	148
1971	Joe Torre, St. Louis	137
1972	Johnny Bench, Cincinnati	125
1973	Willie Stargell, Pittsburgh	119
1974	Johnny Bench, Cincinnati	129
1975	Greg Luzinski, Philadelphia	120
1976	George Foster, Cincinnati	121
1977	George Foster, Cincinnati	149
1978	George Foster, Cincinnati	120
1979	Dave Winfield, San Diego	118
1980	Mike Schmidt, Philadelphia	121

Year		RBI
1961	Roger Maris, New York	142
1962	Harmon Killebrew, Minnesota	126
1963	Dick Stuart, Boston	118
1964	Brooks Robinson, Baltimore	118
1965	Rocky Colavito, Cleveland	108
1966	Frank Robinson, Baltimore	122
1967	Carl Yastrzemski, Boston	121
1968	Ken Harrelson, Boston	109
1969	Harmon Killebrew, Minnesota	140
1970	Frank Howard, Washington	126
1971	Harmon Killebrew, Minnesota	119
1972	Dick Allen, Chicago	113
1973	Reggie Jackson, Oakland	117
1974	Jeff Burroughs, Texas	118
1975	George Scott, Milwaukee	109
1976	Lee May, Baltimore	109
1977	Larry Hisle, Minnesota	119
1978	Jim Rice, Boston	139
1979	Don Baylor, California	139
1980	Cecil Cooper, Milwaukee	122

Batting Champions

National League

Year	Player	Club	Pct.
1917	Edd Rousch	Cincinnati	**.341**
1918	Zack Wheat	Brooklyn	**.335**
1919	Edd Roush	Cincinnati	**.321**
1920	Rogers Hornsby	St. Louis	**.370**
1921	Rogers Hornsby	St. Louis	**.397**
1922	Rogers Hornsby	St. Louis	**.401**
1923	Rogers Hornsby	St. Louis	**.384**
1924	Rogers Hornsby	St. Louis	**.424**
1925	Rogers Hornsby	St. Louis	**.403**
1926	Eugene Hargrave	Cincinnati	**.353**
1927	Paul Waner	Pittsburgh	**.380**
1928	Rogers Hornsby	Boston	**.387**
1929	Lefty O'Doul	Philadelphia	**.398**
1930	Bill Terry	New York	**.401**
1931	Chick Hafey	St. Louis	**.349**
1932	Lefty O'Doul	Brooklyn	**.368**
1933	Charles Klein	Philadelphia	**.368**
1934	Paul Waner	Pittsburgh	**.362**
1935	Arky Vaughan	Pittsburgh	**.385**
1936	Paul Waner	Pittsburgh	**.373**
1937	Joe Medwick	St. Louis	**.374**
1938	Ernie Lombardi	Cincinnati	**.342**
1939	John Mize	St. Louis	**.349**
1940	Debs Garms	Pittsburgh	**.355**
1941	Pete Reiser	Brooklyn	**.343**
1942	Ernie Lombardi	Boston	**.330**
1943	Stan Musial	St. Louis	**.357**
1944	Dixie Walker	Brooklyn	**.357**
1945	Phil Cavarretta	Chicago	**.355**
1946	Stan Musial	St. Louis	**.365**
1947	Harry Walker	Philadelphia	**.363**
1948	Stan Musial	St. Louis	**.376**
1949	Jackie Robinson	Brooklyn	**.342**
1950	Stan Musial	St. Louis	**.346**
1951	Stan Musial	St. Louis	**.355**
1952	Stan Musial	St. Louis	**.336**
1953	Carl Furillo	Brooklyn	**.344**
1954	Willie Mays	New York	**.345**
1955	Richie Ashburn	Philadelphia	**.338**
1956	Hank Aaron	Milwaukee	**.328**
1957	Stan Musial	St. Louis	**.351**
1958	Richie Ashburn	Philadelphia	**.350**
1959	Hank Aaron	Milwaukee	**.355**
1960	Dick Groat	Pittsburgh	**.325**
1961	Roberto Clemente	Pittsburgh	**.351**
1962	Tommy Davis	Los Angeles	**.346**
1963	Tommy Davis	Los Angeles	**.326**
1964	Roberto Clemente	Pittsburgh	**.339**
1965	Roberto Clemente	Pittsburgh	**.329**
1966	Matty Alou	Pittsburgh	**.342**
1967	Roberto Clemente	Pittsburgh	**.357**
1968	Pete Rose	Cincinnati	**.335**
1969	Pete Rose	Cincinnati	**.348**
1970	Rico Carty	Atlanta	**.366**
1971	Joe Torre	St. Louis	**.363**
1972	Billy Williams	Chicago	**.333**
1973	Pete Rose	Cincinnati	**.338**
1974	Ralph Garr	Atlanta	**.353**
1975	Bill Madlock	Chicago	**.354**
1976	Bill Madlock	Chicago	**.339**
1977	Dave Parker	Pittsburgh	**.338**
1978	Dave Parker	Pittsburgh	**.334**
1979	Keith Hernandez	St. Louis	**.344**
1980	Bill Buckner	Chicago	**.324**

American League

Year	Player	Club	Pct.
1917	Ty Cobb	Detroit	**.383**
1918	Ty Cobb	Detroit	**.382**
1919	Ty Cobb	Detroit	**.384**
1920	George Sisler	St. Louis	**.407**
1921	Harry Heilmann	Detroit	**.394**
1922	George Sisler	St. Louis	**.420**
1923	Harry Heilmann	Detroit	**.403**
1924	Babe Ruth	New York	**.378**
1925	Harry Heilmann	Detroit	**.393**
1926	Henry Manush	Detroit	**.378**
1927	Harry Heilmann	Detroit	**.398**
1928	Goose Goslin	Washington	**.379**
1929	Lew Fonseca	Cleveland	**.369**
1930	Al Simmons	Philadelphia	**.381**
1931	Al Simmons	Philadelphia	**.390**
1932	Dale Alexander	Detroit-Boston	**.367**
1933	Jimmy Foxx	Philadelphia	**.356**
1934	Lou Gehrig	New York	**.363**
1935	Buddy Myer	Washington	**.349**
1936	Luke Appling	Chicago	**.388**
1937	Charlie Gehringer	Detroit	**.371**
1938	Jimmy Foxx	Boston	**.349**
1939	Joe DiMaggio	New York	**.381**
1940	Joe DiMaggio	New York	**.352**
1941	Ted Williams	Boston	**.406**
1942	Ted Williams	Boston	**.356**
1943	Luke Appling	Chicago	**.328**
1944	Lou Boudreau	Cleveland	**.327**
1945	George Stirnweiss	New York	**.309**
1946	Mickey Vernon	Washington	**.353**
1947	Ted Williams	Boston	**.343**
1948	Ted Williams	Boston	**.369**
1949	George Kell	Detroit	**.343**
1950	Billy Goodman	Boston	**.354**
1951	Ferris Fain	Philadelphia	**.344**
1952	Ferris Fain	Philadelphia	**.327**
1953	Mickey Vernon	Washington	**.337**
1954	Roberto Avila	Cleveland	**.341**
1955	Al Kaline	Detroit	**.340**
1956	Mickey Mantle	New York	**.353**
1957	Ted Williams	Boston	**.388**
1958	Ted Williams	Boston	**.328**
1959	Harvey Kuenn	Detroit	**.353**
1960	Pete Runnels	Boston	**.320**
1961	Norm Cash	Detroit	**.361**
1962	Pete Runnels	Boston	**.326**
1963	Carl Yastrzemski	Boston	**.321**
1964	Tony Oliva	Minnesota	**.323**
1965	Tony Oliva	Minnesota	**.321**
1966	Frank Robinson	Baltimore	**.316**
1967	Carl Yastrzemski	Boston	**.326**
1968	Carl Yastrzemski	Boston	**.301**
1969	Rod Carew	Minnesota	**.332**
1970	Alex Johnson	California	**.328**
1971	Tony Oliva	Minnesota	**.337**
1972	Rod Carew	Minnesota	**.318**
1973	Rod Carew	Minnesota	**.350**
1974	Rod Carew	Minnesota	**.364**
1975	Rod Carew	Minnesota	**.359**
1976	George Brett	Kansas City	**.333**
1977	Rod Carew	Minnesota	**.388**
1978	Rod Carew	Minnesota	**.333**
1979	Fred Lynn	Boston	**.333**
1980	George Brett	Kansas City	**.390**

National League Records in 1980

Final standings

Eastern Division

Club	W	L	Pct	GB
Philadelphia	91	71	.562	...
Montreal	90	72	.556	1
Pittsburgh	83	79	.512	8
St. Louis	74	88	.457	17
New York	67	95	.414	24
Chicago	64	98	.395	27

Western Division

Club	W	L	Pct	GB
*Houston	93	70	.571	...
*Los Angeles	92	71	.564	1
Cincinnati	89	73	.549	3½
Atlanta	81	80	.503	11
San Francisco	75	86	.466	17
San Diego	73	89	.451	19½

*Houston defeated Los Angeles, 7-1 in playoff for West Division championship.

National League Playoffs

First game — Philadelphia 3, Houston 1
Second game — Houston 7, Philadelphia 4
Third game — Houston 1, Philadelphia 0
Fourth game — Philadelphia 5, Houston 3
Fifth game — Philadelphia 8, Houston 7

Club Batting

Club	Pct.	AB	R	H	HR	SB
St. Louis	**.275**	5608	738	1541	101	117
Philadelphia	**.270**	5625	728	1517	117	140
Pittsburgh	**.266**	5517	666	1469	116	209
Los Angeles	**.263**	5568	663	1462	148	123
Cincinnati	**.262**	5516	707	1445	113	156
Houston	**.261**	5566	637	1455	75	194
Montreal	**.257**	5465	694	1407	114	237
New York	**.257**	5478	611	1407	61	158
San Diego	**.255**	5541	591	1410	67	239
Chicago	**.251**	5619	614	1411	107	93
Atlanta	**.250**	5402	630	1352	144	73
San Francisco	**.244**	5368	573	1310	80	100

Club Pitching

Club	ERA	CG	IP	H	R	BB	SO
Houston	**3.10**	31	1483	1367	589	466	929
Los Angeles	**3.24**	24	1473	1358	591	480	835
Philadelphia	**3.43**	25	1480	1419	639	530	889
San Francisco	**3.46**	27	1448	1446	634	492	811
Montreal	**3.48**	33	1457	1447	629	460	823
Pittsburgh	**3.58**	25	1458	1422	646	451	832
San Diego	**3.65**	19	1466	1474	654	536	728
Atlanta	**3.77**	29	1428	1397	660	454	696
Cincinnati	**3.85**	30	1459	1404	670	506	833
New York	**3.85**	17	1451	1473	702	510	886
Chicago	**3.89**	13	1480	1525	728	589	923
St. Louis	**3.93**	34	1447	1454	710	495	664

Individual Batting

Leaders—440 or more at bats

Player, club	Pct.	AB	R	H	HR	RBI	SB
Buckner, Chicago†	**.324**	578	69	187	10	68	1
Hernandez, St. Louis†	**.321**	595	111	191	16	99	14
Templeton, St. Louis‡	**.319**	504	83	161	4	43	31
McBride, Philadelphia†	**.309**	554	68	171	9	87	13
Cedeno, Houston	**.309**	499	71	154	10	73	48
Dawson, Montreal	**.308**	577	96	178	17	87	34
Garvey, Los Angeles	**.304**	658	77	200	26	106	6
Collins, Cincinnati‡	**.303**	551	94	167	3	35	79
Simmons, St. Louis‡	**.303**	495	84	150	21	98	1
Hendrick, St. Louis	**.302**	572	73	173	25	109	6
Cruz, Houston†	**.302**	612	79	185	11	91	36

Individual Pitching

Leaders—162 or more innings

Pitcher, club	W	L	ERA	G	IP	H	BB	SO
Sutton, Los Angeles	13	5	**2.21**	32	212	163	47	128
Carlton, Philadelphia†	24	9	**2.34**	38	304	243	90	286
Reuss, Los Angeles†	18	6	**2.52**	37	229	193	40	111
Blue, San Francisco†	14	10	**2.97**	31	224	202	61	129
Rogers, Montreal	16	11	**2.98**	37	281	247	85	147
Zachry, New York	6	10	**3.00**	28	165	145	58	88
Soto, Cincinnati	10	8	**3.08**	53	190	126	84	182
Whitson, San Francisco	11	13	**3.10**	34	212	222	56	90
Sanderson, Montreal	16	11	**3.11**	33	211	206	56	125
Forsch, Houston	12	13	**3.20**	32	222	230	41	84

*Rookie †Bats or pitches lefthanded ‡Switch hitter

Individual Batting (at least 100 at-bats); Individual Pitching (at least 50 innings)

Atlanta Braves

Batting	Pct.	G	AB	R	H	HR	RBI	SB
Asselstine†	**.284**	87	218	18	62	3	25	1
Chambliss†	**.282**	158	602	83	170	18	72	7
Murphy	**.281**	156	569	98	160	33	89	9
Matthews	**.278**	155	571	79	159	19	75	11
Horner	**.268**	124	463	81	124	35	89	3
*Ramirez	**.267**	50	165	17	44	2	11	2
Burroughs	**.263**	99	278	35	73	13	51	1
Benedict	**.253**	120	359	18	91	2	34	3
Hubbard	**.248**	117	431	55	107	9	43	7
Royster	**.242**	123	392	42	95	1	20	22
Nahorodny	**.242**	59	157	14	38	5	18	0
Blanks	**.204**	88	221	23	45	2	12	1
Gomez	**.191**	121	278	18	53	0	24	0

Pitching	W	L	ERA	G	IP	H	BB	SO
Camp	6	4	**1.92**	77	108	92	29	33
Bradford†	3	4	**2.45**	56	55	49	22	32
Hanna	2	0	**3.19**	32	79	63	44	35
Boggs	12	9	**3.42**	32	192	180	46	84
Hrabosky†	4	2	**3.60**	45	60	50	31	31
Niekro	15	18	**3.63**	40	275	256	85	176
Garber	5	5	**3.84**	68	82	95	24	51
Alexander	14	11	**4.19**	35	232	227	74	114
Matula	11	13	**4.58**	33	177	195	60	62
McWilliams†	9	14	**4.94**	30	164	188	39	77

Chicago Cubs

Batting	Pct.	G	AB	R	H	HR	RBI	SB
Buckner†	**.324**	145	578	69	187	10	68	1
Vail	**.298**	114	312	30	93	6	47	2
Kingman	**.278**	81	255	31	71	18	57	2
Randle‡	**.276**	130	489	67	135	5	39	19
Blackwell‡	**.272**	103	320	24	87	5	30	0
DeJesus	**.259**	157	618	78	160	3	33	44
*Tracy†	**.254**	42	122	12	31	3	9	2
*Figueroa†	**.253**	115	198	20	50	1	11	2
Rittner†	**.249**	127	273	21	68	1	34	1
Foote	**.238**	63	202	16	48	6	28	1
Tyson	**.238**	123	341	34	81	3	23	1
Johnson	**.235**	68	196	28	46	10	34	0
Martin	**.227**	141	494	57	112	23	73	8
Dillard	**.225**	100	244	31	55	4	27	2
Thompson†	**.212**	102	226	26	48	2	13	6
Kelleher	**.146**	105	96	12	14	0	4	1

Pitching	W	L	ERA	G	IP	H	BB	SO
Caudill	4	6	**2.18**	72	128	100	59	112
Sutter	5	8	**2.65**	60	102	90	34	76
Tidrow	6	5	**2.79**	84	116	97	53	97
Reuschel	11	13	**3.40**	38	257	281	76	140
Capilla†	2	8	**4.10**	39	90	82	51	51
Krukow	10	15	**4.39**	34	205	200	80	130
Hernandez†	1	9	**4.42**	53	108	115	45	75
McGlothen	12	14	**4.80**	39	182	211	64	119
Lamp	10	13	**5.19**	41	203	259	82	83

Cincinnati Reds

Batting	Pct.	G	AB	R	H	HR	RBI	SB
Nolan†	**.307**	70	176	16	54	3	26	0
Collins‡	**.303**	144	551	94	167	3	35	79
Griffey†	**.294**	146	544	89	160	13	85	23
Mejias	**.278**	71	108	16	30	1	10	4
*Oester	**.277**	100	303	40	84	2	20	6
Foster	**.273**	144	528	79	144	25	93	1
Spilman†	**.267**	65	101	14	27	4	19	0
Driessen†	**.265**	154	524	81	139	14	74	19
Knight	**.264**	162	618	71	163	14	78	1
Kennedy	**.261**	104	337	31	88	1	34	3
Concepcion	**.260**	156	622	72	162	5	77	12
Geronimo†	**.255**	103	145	16	37	2	9	2
Bench	**.250**	114	360	52	90	24	68	4

Pitching	W	L	ERA	G	IP	H	BB	SO
Hume	9	10	**2.56**	78	137	121	38	68
Soto	10	8	**3.08**	53	190	126	84	182
Pastore	13	7	**3.26**	27	185	161	42	110
*Price†	7	3	**3.57**	24	111	95	37	44
Seaver	10	8	**3.64**	26	168	140	59	101
Moskau	9	7	**4.00**	33	153	147	41	94
Bair	3	6	**4.24**	61	85	91	39	62
*Leibrandt†	10	9	**4.24**	36	174	200	54	62
LaCoss	10	12	**4.63**	34	169	207	68	59

Houston Astros

Batting	Pct	G	AB	R	H	HR	RBI	SB
Cedeno	**.309**	137	499	71	154	10	73	48
Cruz†	**.302**	160	612	79	185	11	91	36
Walling†	**.299**	100	284	30	85	3	29	4
Howe	**.283**	110	321	34	91	10	46	1
Puhl†	**.282**	141	535	75	151	13	55	27
Cabell	**.276**	152	604	69	167	2	55	21
Ashby‡	**.256**	116	352	30	90	3	48	0
Landestoy‡	**.247**	149	393	42	97	1	27	23
Morgan†	**.243**	141	461	66	112	11	49	24
Reynolds†	**.226**	137	381	34	86	3	28	2
Leonard	**.213**	88	216	29	46	3	20	4
Pujols	**.199**	78	221	15	44	0	20	0

Pitching	W	L	ERA	G	IP	H	BB	SO
Richard	10	4	**1.89**	17	114	65	40	119
*Smith	7	5	**1.92**	57	103	90	32	85
Sambito†	8	4	**2.20**	64	90	65	22	75
Ruhle	12	4	**2.38**	28	159	148	29	55
LaCorte	8	5	**2.82**	55	83	61	43	66
Forsch	12	13	**3.20**	32	222	230	41	84
Ryan	11	10	**3.35**	35	234	205	98	200
Niekro	20	12	**3.55**	37	256	268	79	127
Andujar	3	8	**3.91**	35	122	132	43	75

Los Angeles Dodgers

Batting	Pct	G	AB	R	H	HR	RBI	SB
*Guerrero	**.322**	75	183	27	59	7	31	2
Smith‡	**.322**	92	311	47	100	15	55	5
Johnstone†	**.307**	109	251	31	77	2	20	3
Garvey	**.304**	163	658	77	200	26	106	6
Baker	**.294**	153	579	80	170	29	97	12
Monday†	**.268**	96	194	35	52	10	25	2
Thomas‡	**.266**	117	297	32	79	1	22	7
Russell	**.264**	130	466	38	123	3	34	13
*Law†	**.260**	128	388	55	101	1	23	40
Cey	**.254**	157	551	81	140	28	77	2
*Scioscia†	**.254**	54	134	8	34	1	8	1
Lopes	**.251**	141	553	79	139	10	49	23
Ferguson	**.238**	77	172	20	41	8	29	2
Thomasson†	**.216**	80	111	6	24	1	12	0
Yeager	**.211**	96	227	20	48	2	20	2

Pitching	W	L	ERA	G	IP	H	BB	SO
*Beckwith	3	3	**1.95**	38	60	60	23	40
Sutton	13	5	**2.21**	32	212	163	47	128
Reuss†	18	6	**2.52**	37	229	193	40	111
*Howe†	7	9	**2.65**	59	85	83	22	39
Castillo	8	6	**2.76**	61	98	70	45	60
Welch	14	9	**3.28**	32	214	190	79	141
Hooton	14	8	**3.65**	34	207	194	64	118
Goltz	7	11	**4.32**	35	171	198	59	91
Sutcliffe	3	9	**5.56**	42	110	122	55	59

Montreal Expos

Batting	Pct.	G	AB	R	H	HR	RBI	SB
Valentine	**.315**	86	311	40	98	13	67	5
Dawson	**.308**	151	577	96	178	17	87	34
Macha	**.290**	49	107	10	31	1	8	0
Cromartie†	**.288**	162	597	74	172	14	70	8
Montanez†	**.272**	142	500	40	136	6	64	3
Office†	**.267**	116	292	36	78	6	30	3
Speier	**.265**	128	388	35	103	1	32	0
Carter	**.264**	154	549	76	145	29	101	3
White‡	**.262**	110	214	22	56	7	23	8
LeFlore	**.257**	139	521	95	134	4	39	97
Parrish	**.254**	126	452	55	115	15	72	2
*Bernazard‡	**.224**	82	183	26	41	5	18	9
Scott‡	**.224**	154	567	84	127	0	46	63

Pitching	W	L	ERA	G	IP	H	BB	SO
Fryman†	7	4	**2.25**	61	80	61	30	59
Palmer	8	6	**2.98**	24	130	124	30	73
Rogers	16	11	**2.98**	37	281	247	85	147
*Gullickson	10	5	**3.00**	24	141	127	50	120
Sosa	9	6	**3.06**	67	94	104	19	58
Bahnsen	7	6	**3.07**	57	91	80	33	48
Sanderson	16	11	**3.11**	33	211	206	56	125
D'Acquisto	2	5	**3.38**	50	88	81	45	59
*Lea	7	5	**3.72**	21	104	103	55	56
Norman†	4	4	**4.13**	48	98	96	40	58
Lee†	4	6	**4.96**	24	118	156	22	34

New York Mets

Batting	Pct.	G	AB	R	H	HR	RBI	SB
Henderson	**.290**	143	513	75	149	8	58	23
Stearns	**.285**	91	319	42	91	0	45	7
Mazzilli‡	**.280**	152	578	82	162	16	76	41
Taveras	**.279**	141	562	65	157	0	25	32
Youngblood	**.276**	146	514	58	142	8	69	14
Washington†	**.275**	79	284	38	78	10	42	17
Trevino	**.256**	106	355	26	91	0	37	0
Jorgensen†	**.255**	119	321	43	82	7	43	0
Flynn	**.255**	128	443	46	113	0	24	2
Morales	**.254**	94	193	19	49	3	30	2
*Wilson	**.248**	27	105	16	26	0	4	7
Maddox	**.246**	130	411	35	101	4	34	1
Almon	**.193**	66	150	15	29	0	7	2

Pitching	W	L	ERA	G	IP	H	BB	SO
*Reardon	8	7	**2.62**	61	110	96	47	101
Zachry	6	10	**3.00**	28	165	145	58	88
Swan	5	9	**3.59**	21	128	117	30	79
Allen	7	10	**3.71**	59	97	87	40	79
Hausman	6	5	**3.98**	55	122	125	26	53
Burris	7	13	**4.02**	29	170	181	54	83
*Bomback	10	8	**4.09**	36	163	191	49	68
Glynn†	3	3	**4.15**	38	52	49	23	32
Jackson	1	7	**4.18**	24	71	78	20	58
Falcone†	7	10	**4.53**	37	157	163	58	109
*Pacella	3	4	**5.14**	32	84	89	59	68

Philadelphia Phillies

Batting	Pct.	G	AB	R	H	HR	RBI	SB
*Smith	**.339**	100	298	69	101	3	20	33
*Moreland	**.314**	62	159	13	50	4	29	3
McBride†	**.309**	137	554	68	171	9	87	13
Trillo	**.292**	141	531	68	155	7	43	8
Schmidt	**.286**	150	548	104	157	48	121	12
Rose‡	**.282**	162	655	96	185	1	64	12
Aviles	**.277**	51	101	12	28	2	9	0
Bowa‡	**.268**	147	538	57	144	2	39	21
Unser†	**.264**	96	110	15	29	0	10	0
Maddox	**.259**	143	549	59	142	11	73	25
Gross†	**.240**	127	154	19	37	0	12	1
Boone	**.229**	141	480	34	110	9	55	3
Luzinski	**.228**	106	368	44	84	19	56	3

Pitching	W	L	ERA	G	IP	H	BB	SO
McGraw†	5	4	**1.47**	57	92	62	23	75
Carlton†	24	9	**2.34**	38	304	243	90	286
Saucier†	7	3	**3.42**	40	50	50	20	25
Ruthven	17	10	**3.55**	33	223	241	74	86
Espinosa	3	5	**3.79**	12	76	73	19	13
Noles	1	4	**3.89**	48	81	80	42	57
Christenson	5	1	**4.01**	14	74	62	27	49
Reed	7	5	**4.05**	55	91	88	30	54
*Walk	11	7	**4.56**	27	152	163	71	94
Lerch†	4	14	**5.16**	30	150	178	55	57

Pittsburgh Pirates

Batting	Pct.	G	AB	R	H	HR	RBI	SB
Easler†	**.338**	132	393	66	133	21	74	5
Lacy	**.335**	109	278	45	93	7	33	18
Parker†	**.295**	139	518	71	153	17	79	10
B. Robinson	**.287**	100	272	28	78	12	36	1
Madlock	**.277**	137	494	62	137	10	53	16
Foli	**.265**	127	495	61	131	3	38	11
Stargell†	**.262**	67	202	28	53	11	38	0
Ott†	**.260**	120	392	35	102	8	41	1
Garner	**.259**	151	548	62	142	5	58	32
Moreno†	**.249**	162	676	87	168	2	36	96
Milner†	**.244**	114	238	31	58	8	34	2
Bevacqua	**.228**	84	114	5	26	0	16	1
Berra	**.220**	93	245	21	54	6	31	2
Nicosia	**.216**	60	176	16	38	1	22	0

Pitching	W	L	ERA	G	IP	H	BB	SO
Solomon	7	3	**2.70**	26	100	96	37	35
Jackson†	8	4	**2.92**	61	71	71	20	31
Romo	5	5	**3.27**	74	124	117	28	32
Bibby	19	6	**3.33**	35	238	210	88	144
Tekulve	8	12	**3.39**	78	93	96	40	47
Blyleven	8	13	**3.82**	34	217	219	59	168
Rhoden	7	5	**3.83**	20	127	133	40	70
D. Robinson	7	10	**3.99**	29	160	157	45	103
Candelaria†	11	14	**4.02**	35	233	246	50	97

St. Louis Cardinals

Batting	Pct.	G	AB	R	H	HR	RBI	SB
Hernandez†	**.321**	159	595	111	191	16	99	14
Templeton†	**.319**	118	504	83	161	4	43	31
Oberkfell†	**.303**	116	422	58	128	3	46	4
Simmons‡	**.303**	145	495	84	150	21	98	1
Iorg†	**.303**	105	251	33	76	3	36	1
Hendrick	**.302**	150	572	73	173	25	109	6
Durham†	**.271**	96	303	42	82	8	42	8
Reitz	**.270**	151	523	39	141	8	58	0
*Ramsey‡	**.262**	59	126	11	33	0	8	0
Kennedy†	**.254**	84	248	28	63	4	34	0
Scott‡	**.251**	143	415	51	104	0	28	22
*Herr‡	**.248**	76	222	29	55	0	15	9
Phillips†	**.234**	63	128	13	30	0	7	0
Bonds	**.203**	86	231	37	47	5	24	15

Pitching	W	L	ERA	G	IP	H	BB	SO
*Littlefield	5	5	**3.14**	52	66	71	20	22
Fulgham	4	6	**3.39**	15	85	66	32	48
Hood†	4	6	**3.40**	33	82	90	34	35
Vuckovich	12	9	**3.41**	32	222	203	68	132
Urrea	4	1	**3.46**	30	65	57	41	36
Forsch	11	10	**3.77**	31	215	225	33	87
Kaat†	8	7	**3.81**	49	130	140	33	36
Sykes†	6	10	**4.64**	27	126	134	54	50
Thomas	2	3	**4.75**	24	55	59	25	22
Martinez	5	10	**4.80**	25	120	127	48	39
Otten	0	5	**5.56**	31	55	71	26	38

San Diego Padres

Batting	Pct.	G	AB	R	H	HR	RBI	SB
Perkins†	**.370**	43	100	18	37	2	14	2
*Salazar	**.337**	44	169	28	57	1	25	11
Richards†	**.301**	158	642	91	193	4	41	61
Mumphrey‡	**.298**	160	564	61	168	4	59	52
Turner†	**.288**	85	153	22	44	3	18	8
Winfield	**.276**	162	558	89	154	20	87	23
Fahey†	**.257**	93	241	18	62	1	22	2
*Flannery†	**.240**	95	292	15	70	0	25	2
Evans	**.232**	73	125	11	29	1	14	1
Smith‡	**.230**	158	609	67	140	0	35	57
Cash	**.227**	130	397	25	90	1	23	6
Tenace	**.222**	133	316	46	70	16	50	4
Rodriguez	**.200**	89	175	7	35	2	13	1

Pitching	W	L	ERA	G	IP	H	BB	SO
Fingers	11	9	**2.80**	66	103	101	32	69
*Lucas†	5	8	**3.24**	46	150	138	43	85
Curtis†	10	8	**3.51**	30	187	184	67	71
Shirley†	11	12	**3.55**	59	137	143	54	67
*Eichelberger	4	2	**3.64**	15	89	73	55	43
Mura	8	7	**3.67**	37	169	149	86	109
Wise	6	8	**3.68**	27	154	172	37	59
Jones†	5	13	**3.92**	24	154	165	29	53
Kinney†	4	6	**4.23**	50	83	79	37	40
Rasmussen	4	11	**4.38**	40	111	130	33	50

San Francisco Giants

Batting	Pct.	G	AB	R	H	HR	RBI	SB
Whitfield	**.296**	118	321	38	95	4	26	4
Strain	**.286**	77	189	26	54	0	16	1
Clark	**.284**	127	437	77	124	22	82	2
Wohlford	**.280**	91	193	17	54	1	24	1
Venable†	**.268**	64	138	13	37	0	10	8
Evans†	**.264**	154	556	69	147	20	78	17
May†	**.260**	111	358	27	93	6	50	0
Herndon	**.258**	139	493	54	127	8	49	8
Sadek	**.252**	64	151	14	38	1	16	0
North‡	**.251**	128	415	73	104	1	19	45
Stennett	**.244**	120	397	34	97	2	37	4
Ivie	**.241**	79	286	21	69	4	25	1
*Pettini	**.232**	63	190	19	44	1	9	5
*Murray	**.216**	53	194	19	42	4	24	2
LeMaster	**.215**	135	405	33	87	3	31	0
McCovey†	**.204**	48	113	8	23	1	16	0

Pitching	W	L	ERA	G	IP	H	BB	SO
*Holland†	5	3	**1.76**	54	82	71	34	65
Minton	4	6	**2.47**	68	91	81	34	42
Griffin	5	1	**2.75**	42	108	80	49	79
Blue†	14	10	**2.97**	31	224	202	61	129
Whitson	11	13	**3.10**	34	212	222	56	90
Lavelle†	6	8	**3.42**	62	100	106	36	66
Knepper†	9	16	**4.10**	35	215	242	61	103
Ripley	9	10	**4.14**	23	113	119	36	65
*Hargesheimer	4	6	**4.32**	15	75	82	32	40
Montefusco	4	8	**4.38**	22	113	120	39	85

Leading Pitchers, Earned-Run Average

National League

Year	Player, club	G	IP	ERA
1963	Sandy Koufax, Los Angeles	40	311	**1.88**
1964	Sandy Koufax, Los Angeles	29	223	**1.74**
1965	Sandy Koufax, Los Angeles	43	336	**2.04**
1966	Sandy Koufax, Los Angeles	41	323	**1.73**
1967	Phil Niekro, Atlanta	46	207	**1.87**
1968	Bob Gibson, St. Louis	34	305	**1.12**
1969	Juan Marichal, San Francisco	37	300	**2.10**
1970	Tom Seaver, New York	37	291	**2.81**
1971	Tom Seaver, New York	36	286	**1.76**
1972	Steve Carlton, Philadelphia	41	346	**1.98**
1973	Tom Seaver, New York	36	290	**2.07**
1974	Buzz Capra, Atlanta	39	217	**2.28**
1975	Randy Jones, San Diego	37	285	**2.24**
1976	John Denny, St. Louis	30	207	**2.52**
1977	John Candelaria, Pittsburgh	33	231	**2.34**
1978	Craig Swan, New York	29	207	**2.43**
1979	J. R. Richard, Houston	38	292	**2.71**
1980	Don Sutton, Los Angeles	32	212	**2.21**

American League

Year	Player, club	G	IP	ERA
1963	Gary Peters, Chicago	41	243	**2.33**
1964	Dean Chance, Los Angeles	46	278	**1.56**
1965	Sam McDowell, Cleveland	42	274	**2.17**
1966	Gary Peters, Chicago	29	204	**2.03**
1967	Joe Horlen, Chicago	35	258	**2.06**
1968	Luis Tiant, Cleveland	34	258	**1.60**
1969	Dick Bosman, Washington	31	193	**2.19**
1970	Diego Segui, Oakland	47	162	**2.56**
1971	Vida Blue, Oakland	39	312	**1.82**
1972	Luis Tiant, Boston	43	179	**1.91**
1973	Jim Palmer, Baltimore	38	296	**2.40**
1974	Catfish Hunter, Oakland	41	318	**2.49**
1975	Jim Palmer, Baltimore	39	323	**2.09**
1976	Mark Fidrych, Detroit	31	250	**2.34**
1977	Frank Tanana, California	31	241	**2.54**
1978	Ron Guidry, New York	35	274	**1.74**
1979	Ron Guidry, New York	33	236	**2.78**
1980	Rudy May, New York	41	175	**2.47**

ERA is computed by multiplying earned runs allowed by 9, then dividing by innings pitched.

Most Valuable Player

Baseball Writers' Association

National League

Year	Player, team
1931	Frank Frisch, St. Louis
1932	Charles Klein, Philadelpha
1933	Carl Hubbell, New York
1934	Dizzy Dean, St. Louis
1935	Gabby Hartnett, Chicago
1936	Carl Hubbell, New York
1937	Joe Medwick, St. Louis
1938	Ernie Lombardi, Cincinnati
1939	Bucky Walters, Cincinnati
1940	Frank McCormick, Cincinnati
1941	Dolph Camilli, Brooklyn
1942	Mort Cooper, St. Louis
1943	Stan Musial, St. Louis
1944	Martin Marion, St. Louis
1945	Phil Cavarretta, Chicago
1946	Stan Musial, St. Louis
1947	Bob Elliott, Boston
1948	Stan Musial, St. Louis
1949	Jackie Robinson, Brooklyn
1950	Jim Konstanty, Philadelphia
1951	Roy Campanella, Brooklyn
1952	Hank Sauer, Chicago
1953	Roy Campanella, Brooklyn
1954	Willie Mays, New York
1955	Roy Campenella, Brooklyn
1956	Don Newcombe, Brooklyn
1957	Henry Aaron, Milwaukee
1958	Ernie Banks, Chicago
1959	Ernie Banks, Chicago
1960	Dick Groat, Pittsburgh
1961	Frank Robinson, Cincinnati
1962	Maury Wills, Los Angeles
1963	Sandy Koufax, Los Angeles
1964	Ken Boyer, St. Louis
1965	Willie Mays, San Francisco
1966	Roberto Clemente, Pittsburgh
1967	Orlando Cepeda, St. Louis
1968	Bob Gibson, St. Louis
1969	Willie McCovey, San Francisco
1970	Johnny Bench, Cincinnati
1971	Joe Torre, St. Louis
1972	Johnny Bench, Cincinnati
1973	Pete Rose, Cincinnati
1974	Steve Garvey, Los Angeles
1975	Joe Morgan, Cincinnati
1976	Joe Morgan, Cincinnati
1977	George Foster, Cincinnati
1978	Dave Parker, Pittsburgh
1979	(tie) Willie Stargell, Pittsburgh Keith Hernandez, St. Louis

American League

Year	Player, team
1931	Lefty Grove, Philadelphia
1932	Jimmy Foxx, Philadelphia
1933	Jimmy Foxx, Philadelphia
1934	Mickey Cochrane, Detroit
1935	Henry Greenberg, Detroit
1936	Lou Gehrig, New York
1937	Charley Gehringer, Detroit
1938	Jimmy Foxx, Boston
1939	Joe DiMaggio, New York
1940	Hank Greenberg, Detroit
1941	Joe DiMaggio, New York
1942	Joe Gordon, New York
1943	Spurgeon Chandler, New York
1944	Hal Newhouser, Detroit
1945	Hal Newhouser, Detroit
1946	Ted Williams, Boston
1947	Joe DiMaggio, New York
1948	Lou Boudreau, Cleveland
1949	Ted Williams, Boston
1950	Phil Rizzuto, New York
1951	Yogi Berra, New York
1952	Bobby Shantz, Philadelphia
1953	Al Rosen, Cleveland
1954	Yogi Berra, New York
1955	Yogi Berra, New York
1956	Mickey Mantle, New York
1957	Mickey Mantle, New York
1958	Jackie Jensen, Boston
1959	Nellie Fox, Chicago
1960	Roger Maris, New York
1961	Roger Maris, New York
1962	Mickey Mantle, New York
1963	Elston Howard, New York
1964	Brooks Robinson, Baltimore
1965	Zoilo Versalles, Minnesota
1966	Frank Robinson, Baltimore
1967	Carl Yastrzemski, Boston
1968	Denny McLain, Detroit
1969	Harmon Killebrew, Minnesota
1970	John (Boog) Powell, Baltimore
1971	Vida Blue, Oakland
1972	Dick Allen, Chicago
1973	Reggie Jackson, Oakland
1974	Jeff Burroughs, Texas
1975	Fred Lynn, Boston
1976	Thurman Munson, New York
1977	Rod Carew, Minnesota
1978	Jim Rice, Boston
1979	Don Baylor, California

Rookie of the Year

Baseball Writers' Association

1947—Combined selection—Jackie Robinson, Brooklyn, 1b
1948—Combined selection—Alvin Dark, Boston, N.L. ss

National League

Year	Player, team
1949	Don Newcombe, Brooklyn, p
1950	Sam Jethroe, Boston, of
1951	Willie Mays, New York, of
1952	Joe Black, Brooklyn, p
1953	Jim Gilliam, Brooklyn, 2b
1954	Wally Moon, St. Louis, of
1955	Bill Virdon, St. Louis, of
1956	Frank Robinson, Cincinnati, of
1957	Jack Sanford, Philadelphia, p
1958	Orlando Cepeda, S.F., 1b
1959	Willie McCovey, S.F., 1b
1960	Frank Howard, Los Angeles, of
1961	Billy Williams, Chicago, of
1962	Ken Hubbs, Chicago, 2b
1963	Pete Rose, Cincinnati, 2b
1964	Richie Allen, Philadelphia, 3b
1965	Jim Lefebvre, Los Angeles, 2b
1966	Tommy Helms, Cincinnati, 2b
1967	Tom Seaver, New York, p
1968	Johnny Bench, Cincinnati c
1969	Ted Sizemore, Los Angeles, 2b
1970	Carl Morton, Montreal, p
1971	Earl Williams, Atlanta, c
1972	Jon Matlack, New York, p
1973	Gary Matthews, S.F., of
1974	Bake McBride, St. Louis, of
1975	John Montefusco, S.F., p
1976	(tie) Butch Metzger, San Diego, p Pat Zachry, Cincinnati, p
1977	Andre Dawson, Montreal, of
1978	Bob Horner, Atlanta, 3b
1979	Rick Sutcliffe, Los Angeles, p

American League

Year	Player, team
1949	Roy Sievers, St. Louis, of
1950	Walt Dropo, Boston, 1b
1951	Gil McDougald, New York, 3b
1952	Harry Byrd, Philadelphia, p
1953	Harvey Kuenn, Detroit, ss
1954	Bob Grim, New York, p
1955	Herb Score, Cleveland, p
1956	Luis Aparicio, Chicago, ss
1957	Tony Kubek, New York, if-of
1958	Albie Pearson, Washington, of
1959	Bob Allison, Washington, of
1960	Ron Hansen, Baltimore, ss
1961	Don Schwall, Boston, p
1962	Tom Tresh, New York, if-of
1963	Gary Peters, Chicago, p
1964	Tony Oliva, Minnesota, of
1965	Curt Blefary, Baltimore, of
1966	Tommie Agee, Chicago, of
1967	Rod Carew, Minnesota, 2b
1968	Stan Bahnsen, New York, p
1969	Lou Piniella, Kansas City, of
1970	Thurman Munson, New York, c
1971	Chris Chambliss, Cleveland, 1b
1972	Carlton Fisk, Boston, c
1973	Al Bumbry, Baltimore, of
1974	Mike Hargrove, Texas, 1b
1975	Fred Lynn, Boston, of
1976	Mark Fidrych, Detroit, p
1977	Eddie Murray, Baltimore, dh
1978	Lou Whitaker, Detroit, 2b
1979	(tie) John Castino, Minnesota, 3b Alfredo Griffin, Toronto, ss

Triple Crown Winners

Players leading league in batting, runs batted in, and homers in a single season

Year	Player, team
1909	Ty Cobb, Detroit Tigers
1922	Rogers Hornsby, St. Louis Cardinals
1925	Rogers Hornsby, St. Louis Cardinals
1933	Jimmy Foxx, Philadelphia Athletics
1933	Chuck Klein, Philadelphia Phillies
1934	Lou Gehrig, New York Yankees
1937	Joe Medwick, St. Louis Cardinals
1942	Ted Williams, Boston Red Sox
1947	Ted Williams, Boston Red Sox
1956	Mickey Mantle, New York Yankees
1966	Frank Robinson, Baltimore Orioles
1967	Carl Yastrzemski, Boston Red Sox

American League Records in 1980

Final standings

Eastern Division

Club	W	L	Pct.	GB
New York	103	59	.636	...
Baltimore	100	62	.617	3
Milwaukee	86	76	.531	17
Boston	83	77	.519	19
Detroit	84	78	.519	19
Cleveland	79	81	.494	23
Toronto	67	95	.414	36

Western Division

Club	W	L	Pct.	GB
Kansas City	97	65	.599	...
Oakland	83	79	.512	14
Minnesota	77	84	.478	19½
Texas	76	85	.472	20½
Chicago	70	90	.438	26
California	65	95	.406	31
Seattle	59	103	.364	38

American League Playoffs

First game — Kansas City 7, New York 2
Second game — Kansas City 3, New York 2
Third game — Kansas City 4, New York 2

Club Batting

Club	Pct	AB	R	H	HR	SB
Kansas City	**.286**	5714	809	1633	115	185
Texas	**.284**	5690	756	1616	124	91
Boston	**.283**	5603	757	1588	162	79
Cleveland	**.277**	5470	738	1517	89	118
Milwaukee	**.275**	5653	811	1555	203	131
Detroit	**.273**	5648	830	1543	143	75
Baltimore	**.273**	5585	805	1523	156	111
New York	**.267**	5553	820	1484	189	86
Minnesota	**.265**	5530	670	1468	99	62
California	**.265**	5443	698	1442	106	91
Oakland	**.259**	5495	686	1424	137	175
Chicago	**.259**	5444	587	1408	91	68
Toronto	**.251**	5571	624	1398	126	67
Seattle	**.248**	5489	610	1359	104	116

Club Pitching

Club	ERA	CG	IP	H	R	BB	SO
Oakland	**3.46**	94	1472	1347	642	521	769
New York	**3.59**	29	1464	1433	662	463	845
Baltimore	**3.64**	42	1460	1438	640	507	789
Milwaukee	**3.71**	48	1450	1530	682	420	575
Kansas City	**3.83**	37	1459	1496	694	465	614
Chicago	**3.92**	32	1435	1434	722	563	724
Minnesota	**3.93**	35	1451	1502	724	468	744
Texas	**4.02**	35	1452	1561	752	519	890
Toronto	**4.19**	39	1466	1523	762	635	705
Detroit	**4.25**	40	1467	1505	757	558	741
Boston	**4.38**	30	1441	1557	767	481	696
Seattle	**4.38**	31	1457	1565	793	540	703
California	**4.52**	22	1428	1548	797	529	725
Cleveland	**4.68**	35	1428	1519	807	552	843

Individual Batting

Leaders—440 or more at bats

Player, club	Pct	AB	R	H	HR	RBI	SB
G. Brett, Kansas City†	**.390**	449	87	175	24	118	15
Cooper, Milwaukee†	**.352**	622	96	219	25	122	17
Dilone, Cleveland‡	**341**	528	82	180	0	40	61
Rivers, Texas†	**.333**	630	96	210	7	60	18
Carew, California†	**.331**	540	74	179	3	59	23
Bell, Texas	**.329**	490	76	161	17	83	3
Wilson, Kansas City‡	**.326**	705	133	230	3	49	79
*Stapleton, Boston	**.321**	449	61	144	7	45	3
Oliver, Texas†	**.319**	656	96	209	19	117	5
Bumbry, Baltimore†	**.318**	645	118	205	9	53	44

Individual Pitching

Leaders—162 or more innings

Pitcher, club	W	L	ERA	G	IP	H	BB	SO
May, New York†	15	5	**2.47**	41	175	144	39	133
Norris, Oakland	22	9	**2.54**	33	284	215	83	180
*Burns, Chicago†	15	13	**2.84**	34	238	213	63	133
Keough, Oakland	16	13	**2.92**	34	250	218	94	121
Gura, Kansas City†	18	10	**2.96**	36	283	272	76	113
Haas, Milwaukee	16	15	**3.11**	33	252	246	56	146
Stone, Baltimore	25	7	**3.23**	37	251	224	101	149
Erickson, Minnesota	7	13	**3.25**	32	191	198	56	97
Langford, Oakland	19	12	**3.26**	35	290	276	64	102
Clancy, Toronto	13	16	**3.30**	34	251	217	128	152

*Rookie †Bats or pitches lefthanded ‡Switch hitter

Individual Batting (at least 115 at-bats); Individual Pitching (at least 50 innings)

Baltimore Orioles

Batting	Pct	G	AB	R	H	HR	RBI	SB
Bumbry†	**.318**	160	645	118	205	9	53	44
Lowenstein†	**.311**	104	196	38	61	4	27	7
Singleton‡	**.304**	156	583	85	177	24	104	0
Murray‡	**.300**	158	621	100	186	32	116	7
Crowley†	**.288**	92	233	33	67	12	50	0
Dauer	**.284**	152	557	71	158	2	63	3
*Graham†	**.278**	86	266	32	74	15	54	0
Ayala	**.265**	76	170	28	45	10	33	0
Dempsey	**.262**	119	362	51	95	9	40	3
Kelly†	**.260**	89	200	38	52	3	26	16
DeCinces	**.249**	145	489	64	122	16	64	11
May	**.243**	78	222	20	54	7	31	2
Roenicke	**.239**	118	297	40	71	10	28	2
Belanger	**.228**	113	268	37	61	0	22	6
Garcia	**.199**	111	311	27	62	1	27	8

Pitching	W	L	ERA	G	IP	H	BB	SO
Stoddard	5	3	**2.51**	64	86	72	38	64
T. Martinez†	4	4	**3.00**	53	81	69	34	68
Stone	25	7	**3.23**	37	251	224	101	149
McGregor†	20	8	**3.32**	36	252	254	58	119
Stewart	7	7	**3.55**	33	119	103	60	78
D. Martinez	6	4	**3.96**	25	100	103	44	42
Palmer	16	10	**3.98**	34	224	238	74	109
Flanagan†	16	13	**4.12**	37	251	278	71	128
*Ford	1	3	**4.24**	25	70	66	13	22

Boston Red Sox

Batting	Pct	G	AB	R	H	HR	RBI	SB
Rader†	**.328**	50	137	14	45	3	17	1
*Stapleton	**.321**	106	449	61	144	7	45	3
Remy†	**.313**	63	230	24	72	0	9	14
Lynn†	**.301**	110	415	67	125	12	61	12
Rice	**.294**	124	504	81	148	24	86	8
Fisk	**.289**	131	478	73	138	18	62	11
Hancock†	**.287**	46	115	9	33	4	19	0
*Hoffman	**.285**	114	312	37	89	4	42	2
Dwyer†	**.285**	93	260	41	74	9	38	3
Burleston	**.278**	155	644	89	179	8	51	12
Perez	**.275**	151	585	73	161	25	105	1
Yastrzemski†	**.275**	105	364	49	100	15	50	0
Evans	**.266**	148	463	72	123	18	60	3
Hobson	**.228**	93	324	35	74	11	39	1

Pitching	W	L	ERA	G	IP	H	BB	SO
Burgmeier†	5	4	**2.00**	62	99	87	20	54
*Tudor†	8	5	**3.03**	16	92	81	31	45
Stanley	10	8	**3.39**	52	175	186	52	71
Drago	7	7	**4.13**	43	133	127	44	63
Renko	9	9	**4.20**	32	165	180	56	90
Eckersley	12	14	**4.27**	30	198	188	44	121
Rainey	8	3	**4.86**	16	87	92	41	43
Torrez	9	16	**5.09**	36	207	256	75	97

California Angels

Batting	Pct	G	AB	R	H	HR	RBI	SB
Carew†	**.331**	144	540	74	179	3	59	23
Thompson†	**.288**	138	438	69	126	21	90	2
Ford	**.279**	65	226	22	63	7	26	0
Harlow†	**.276**	109	301	47	83	4	27	3
Miller†	**.274**	129	412	52	113	2	38	7
Grich	**.271**	150	498	60	135	14	62	3
Patek	**.264**	86	273	41	72	5	34	7
Lansford	**.261**	151	602	87	157	15	80	14
Thon	**.255**	80	267	32	68	0	15	7
Campaneris	**.252**	77	210	32	53	2	18	10
Baylor	**.250**	90	340	39	85	5	51	6
Rudi	**.237**	104	372	42	88	16	53	1
*Clark	**.230**	78	261	26	60	5	23	0
Donohue	**.188**	84	218	18	41	2	14	5

Pitching	W	L	ERA	G	IP	H	BB	SO
Hassler†	5	1	**2.49**	41	83	67	37	75
Clear	11	11	**3.31**	58	106	82	65	105
Aase	8	13	**4.06**	40	175	193	66	74
LaRoche†	3	5	**4.08**	52	128	122	39	89
Tanana†	11	12	**4.15**	32	204	223	45	113
*Martinez	7	9	**4.53**	30	149	150	59	57
Lemanczyk	4	9	**4.75**	31	110	138	42	29
Kison	3	6	**4.93**	13	73	73	32	28
Montague	4	2	**5.11**	37	74	97	21	22
Frost	4	8	**5.31**	15	78	97	21	28
Barr	1	4	**5.56**	24	68	90	23	22
Knapp	2	11	**6.15**	32	117	133	51	46

Chicago White Sox

Batting	Pct	G	AB	R	H	HR	RBI	SB
Lemon	**.292**	147	514	76	150	11	51	6
Molinaro†	**.291**	119	344	48	100	5	36	18
Squires†	**.283**	131	343	38	97	2	33	8
Morrison	**.283**	162	604	66	171	15	57	9
L.Johnson	**.277**	147	541	51	150	13	81	2
Nordhagen	**.277**	123	415	45	115	15	59	0
Moore	**.256**	45	121	9	31	1	10	0
*Baines†	**.255**	141	491	55	125	13	49	2
Kimm	**.243**	100	251	20	61	0	19	1
Pryor	**.240**	122	338	32	81	1	29	2
Cruz	**.237**	108	333	28	79	3	23	2
Bosley†	**.224**	70	147	12	33	2	14	3
Foley†	**.212**	68	137	14	29	4	15	0
Bell	**.178**	92	191	16	34	1	11	0

Pitching	W	L	ERA	G	IP	H	BB	SO
*Burns†	15	13	**2.84**	34	238	213	63	133
Proly	5	10	**3.06**	62	147	136	58	56
Farmer	7	9	**3.33**	64	100	92	56	54
Baumgarten†	2	12	**3.44**	24	136	127	52	66
Trout†	9	16	**3.69**	32	200	229	49	89
*Dotson	12	10	**4.27**	33	198	185	87	109
*Hoyt	9	3	**4.58**	24	112	123	41	55
Wortham†	4	7	**5.97**	41	92	102	58	45
Kravec†	3	6	**6.91**	20	82	100	44	37

Cleveland Indians

Batting	Pct	G	AB	R	H	HR	RBI	SB
Dilone‡	**.341**	132	528	82	180	0	40	61
Hassey†	**.318**	130	390	43	124	8	65	0
Hargrove†	**.304**	160	589	86	179	11	85	4
Orta†	**.291**	129	481	78	140	10	64	6
*Charboneau	**.289**	131	453	76	131	23	87	2
Bannister	**.283**	126	392	57	111	1	41	14
Kuiper†	**.282**	42	149	10	42	0	9	0
Veryzer	**.271**	109	358	28	97	2	28	0
Harrah	**.267**	160	561	100	150	11	72	17
Brohamer†	**.251**	74	199	18	50	2	21	0
Rosello	**.248**	71	117	16	29	2	12	0
Manning†	**.234**	140	471	55	110	3	52	12
*Dybzinski	**.230**	114	248	32	57	1	23	4
Johnson	**.230**	54	174	25	40	6	28	0
Diaz	**.227**	76	207	15	47	3	32	1
Alexander	**.225**	76	178	22	40	5	31	0

Pitching	W	L	ERA	G	IP	H	BB	SO
Cruz	6	7	**3.45**	55	86	71	27	88
Monge†	3	5	**3.54**	67	94	80	40	61
Barker	19	12	**4.17**	36	246	237	92	187
Denny	8	6	**4.38**	16	109	116	47	59
Waits†	13	14	**4.46**	33	224	231	82	109
Garland	6	9	**4.62**	25	150	163	48	55
Spillner	16	11	**5.29**	34	194	225	74	100
Owchinko†	2	9	**5.29**	29	114	138	47	66
*Stanton	1	3	**5.44**	51	86	98	44	74
Grimsley†	4	5	**6.72**	14	75	103	24	18

Detroit Tigers

Batting	Pct	G	AB	R	H	HR	RBI	SB
Trammell	**.300**	146	560	107	168	9	65	12
Summers†	**.297**	120	347	61	103	17	60	4
Kemp†	**.293**	135	508	88	149	21	101	5
*Peters‡	**.291**	133	477	79	139	2	42	13
Hebner†	**.290**	104	341	48	99	12	82	0
Corcoran†	**.288**	84	153	20	44	3	18	0
Parrish	**.286**	144	553	79	158	24	82	6
Brookens	**.275**	151	509	64	140	10	66	13
Wockenfuss	**.274**	126	372	56	102	16	65	1
Cowens	**.268**	142	522	69	140	6	59	6
*Gibson†	**.263**	51	175	23	46	9	16	4
*Lentine	**.261**	67	161	19	42	1	17	2
Whitaker†	**.233**	145	477	68	111	1	45	8
*Stegman	**.177**	65	130	12	23	2	9	1

Pitching	W	L	ERA	G	IP	H	BB	SO
Underwood†	3	6	**3.58**	49	113	121	35	60
Lopez	13	6	**3.77**	67	124	125	45	97
Rozema	6	9	**3.91**	42	145	152	49	49
Petry	10	9	**3.93**	27	165	156	83	88
Tobik	1	0	**3.98**	17	61	61	21	34
Schatzeder†	11	13	**4.01**	32	193	178	58	94
*Weaver	3	4	**4.08**	19	64	56	34	42
Morris	16	15	**4.18**	36	250	252	87	112
Wilcox	13	11	**4.48**	32	199	201	68	97
*Robbins†	4	2	**6.58**	15	52	60	28	23

Kansas City Royals

Batting	Pct	G	AB	R	H	HR	RBI	SB
G. Brett	**.390**	117	449	87	175	24	118	15
Wilson‡	**.326**	161	705	133	230	3	49	79
Wathan	**.305**	126	453	57	138	6	58	17
McRae	**.297**	124	489	73	145	14	83	10
Hurdle†	**.294**	130	395	50	116	10	60	0
Aikens†	**.278**	151	543	70	151	20	98	1
Quirk†	**.276**	62	163	13	45	5	21	3
Washington‡	**.273**	153	549	79	150	6	53	20
White	**.264**	154	560	70	148	7	60	19
Otis	**.251**	107	394	56	99	10	53	16
Chalk	**.251**	69	167	19	42	1	20	1
Porter†	**.249**	118	418	51	104	7	51	1
LaCock†	**.205**	114	156	14	32	1	18	1

Pitching	W	L	ERA	G	IP	H	BB	SO
Gura†	18	10	**2.96**	36	283	272	76	113
Quisenberry	12	7	**3.09**	75	128	129	27	37
Pattin	4	0	**3.64**	37	89	97	23	40
Leonard	20	11	**3.79**	38	280	271	80	155
Gale	13	9	**3.91**	32	191	169	78	97
Splittorff†	14	11	**4.15**	34	204	236	43	53
*Martin	10	10	**4.40**	32	137	133	70	68

Milwaukee Brewers

Batting	Pct	G	AB	R	H	HR	RBI	SB
Cooper†	**.352**	153	622	96	219	25	122	17
Oglivie†	**.304**	156	592	94	180	41	118	11
Molitor	**.304**	111	450	81	137	9	37	34
Yount	**.293**	143	611	121	179	23	87	20
Moore	**.291**	111	320	42	93	2	30	10
Gantner†	**.282**	132	415	47	117	4	40	11
Davis	**.271**	106	365	50	99	4	30	5
Money	**.256**	86	289	39	74	17	46	0
Thomas	**.239**	162	628	78	150	38	105	8
*Brouhard	**.232**	45	125	17	29	5	16	1
Lezcano	**.229**	112	411	51	94	18	55	1
Martinez	**.224**	76	219	16	49	3	17	1
Bando	**.197**	78	254	28	50	5	31	5

Pitching	W	L	ERA	G	IP	H	BB	SO
Castro	2	4	**2.79**	56	84	89	17	32
McClure†	5	8	**3.07**	52	91	83	37	47
Haas	16	15	**3.11**	33	252	246	56	146
Mitchell	5	5	**3.54**	17	89	92	15	29
Sorensen	12	10	**3.67**	35	196	242	45	54
Cleveland	11	9	**3.74**	45	154	150	49	54
Travers†	12	6	**3.92**	29	154	147	47	62
Caldwell†	13	11	**4.04**	34	225	248	56	74
Augustine†	4	3	**4.50**	39	70	83	36	22

Minnesota Twins

Batting	Pct	G	AB	R	H	HR	RBI	SB
Morales	**.303**	97	241	36	73	8	36	0
Castino	**.302**	150	546	67	165	13	64	7
Adams†	**.286**	99	262	32	75	6	38	2

Batting	Pct	G	AB	R	H	HR	RBI	SB
Landreaux†	**.281**	129	484	56	136	7	62	8
Smalley†	**.278**	133	486	64	135	12	63	3
Mackanin	**.266**	108	319	31	85	4	35	6
Jackson	**.265**	131	396	48	105	5	42	1
Powell†	**.262**	137	485	58	127	6	35	14
Wynegar†	**.255**	146	486	61	124	5	57	3
Edwards	**.250**	81	200	26	50	2	20	2
Wilfong†	**.248**	131	416	55	103	8	45	10
*Sofield†	**.247**	131	417	52	103	9	49	4
Cubbage†	**.246**	103	285	29	70	8	42	0
Goodwin†	**.200**	55	115	12	23	1	11	0

Pitching	W	L	ERA	G	IP	H	BB	SO
*Corbett	8	6	**1.99**	73	136	102	42	89
Erickson	7	13	**3.25**	32	191	198	56	97
*Williams	6	2	**3.51**	18	77	73	30	35
Jackson†	9	9	**3.87**	32	172	161	69	90
Verhoeven	3	4	**3.96**	44	100	109	29	42
Koosman†	16	13	**4.04**	38	243	252	69	149
Zahn†	14	18	**4.40**	38	233	273	66	96
Redfern	7	7	**4.54**	23	105	117	33	73
Arroyo	6	6	**4.70**	21	92	97	32	27

New York Yankees

Batting	Pct	G	AB	R	H	HR	RBI	SB
Watson	**.307**	130	469	62	144	13	68	2
Jackson†	**.300**	143	514	94	154	41	111	1
Randolph	**.294**	138	513	99	151	7	46	30
Piniella	**.287**	116	321	39	92	2	27	0
Soderholm	**.287**	95	275	38	79	11	35	0
Gamble†	**.278**	78	194	40	54	14	50	2
Cerone	**.277**	147	519	70	144	14	85	1
Murcer†	**.269**	100	297	41	80	13	57	2
Dent	**.262**	141	489	57	128	5	52	0
Brown†	**.260**	137	412	65	107	14	47	27
Nettles†	**.244**	89	324	52	79	16	45	0
Spencer†	**.236**	97	259	38	61	13	43	1
*Lefebvre†	**.227**	74	150	26	34	8	21	0
Jones†	**.223**	83	328	38	73	9	42	18
Rodriguez	**.220**	52	164	14	36	3	14	0

Pitching	W	L	ERA	G	IP	H	BB	SO
Gossage	6	2	**2.27**	64	99	74	37	103
May†	15	5	**2.47**	41	175	144	39	133
Bird	3	0	**2.65**	22	51	47	14	17
Davis	9	3	**2.95**	53	131	121	32	65
John†	22	9	**3.43**	36	265	270	56	78
Guidry†	17	10	**3.56**	37	220	215	80	166
Underwood†	13	9	**3.66**	38	187	163	66	116
Perry	10	13	**3.67**	34	206	224	64	135
*Griffin	2	4	**4.83**	13	54	64	23	25
Tiant	8	9	**4.90**	25	136	139	50	84

Oakland A's

Batting	Pct	G	AB	R	H	HR	RBI	SB
Henderson	**.303**	158	591	111	179	9	53	100
Revering†	**.290**	106	376	48	109	15	62	1
Gross†	**.281**	113	366	45	103	14	61	5
Armas	**.279**	158	628	87	175	35	109	5
Murphy†	**.274**	159	573	86	157	13	68	26
Klutts	**.269**	75	197	20	53	4	21	1
Page†	**.244**	110	348	58	85	17	51	14
McKay‡	**.244**	123	295	29	72	1	29	1
Heath	**.243**	92	305	27	74	1	33	3
Picciolo	**.240**	95	271	32	65	5	18	1
Guerrero	**.239**	116	381	32	91	2	23	3
Newman	**.233**	127	438	37	102	15	56	3
Essian	**.232**	87	285	19	66	5	29	1
*Cox	**.213**	59	169	20	36	0	9	8

Pitching	W	L	ERA	G	IP	H	BB	SO
Norris	22	9	**2.54**	33	284	215	83	180
Keough	16	13	**2.92**	34	250	218	94	12
Lacey†	3	2	**2.93**	47	80	68	21	45
Langford	19	12	**3.26**	35	290	276	64	102
Kingman	8	20	**3.84**	32	211	209	82	116
McCatty	14	14	**3.85**	33	222	202	99	114

Seattle Mariners

Batting	Pct	G	AB	R	H	HR	RBI	SB
Bochte†	**.300**	148	520	62	156	13	78	2
Meyer†	**.275**	146	531	56	146	11	71	8
Paciorek	**.273**	126	418	44	114	15	59	3
Stein	**.268**	67	198	16	53	5	27	1
Milbourne‡	**.264**	106	258	31	68	0	26	7
L. Roberts	**.251**	119	374	48	94	10	33	8
Simpson†	**.249**	129	365	42	91	3	34	17
Mendoza	**.245**	114	277	27	68	2	14	3
T. Cox	**.243**	83	247	17	60	2	23	0
*Craig‡	**.238**	70	240	30	57	3	20	3
Beniquez	**.228**	70	237	26	54	6	21	2
Anderson	**.227**	116	317	46	72	8	30	2
Horton	**.221**	97	335	32	74	8	36	0
Cruz‡	**.209**	119	422	66	88	2	16	45
L. Cox	**.202**	105	243	18	49	4	20	1

Pitching	W	L	ERA	G	IP	H	BB	SO
Rawley†	7	7	**3.32**	59	114	103	63	68
Bannister†	9	13	**3.47**	32	218	200	66	155
Heaverlo	6	3	**3.87**	60	79	75	35	42
Honeycutt†	10	17	**3.95**	30	203	221	60	79
Dressler	4	10	**3.99**	30	149	161	33	50
Abbott	12	12	**4.10**	31	215	228	49	78
D. Roberts†	2	3	**4.39**	37	80	86	27	47
Beattie	5	15	**4.86**	33	187	205	98	67
McLaughlin	3	6	**6.82**	45	91	124	50	41
Parrott	1	16	**7.28**	27	94	136	42	53

Texas Rangers

Batting	Pct	G	AB	R	H	HR	RBI	SB
Rivers†	**.333**	147	630	96	210	7	60	18
Bell	**.329**	129	490	76	161	17	83	3
Oliver†	**.319**	163	656	96	209	19	117	5
Staub†	**.300**	109	340	42	102	9	55	1
Zisk	**.290**	135	448	48	130	19	77	0
Grubb†	**.277**	110	274	40	76	9	32	2
Sundberg	**.273**	151	505	59	138	10	63	2
Harrelson‡	**.272**	87	180	26	49	1	9	4
Wills‡	**.263**	146	578	102	152	5	58	34
Putnam†	**.263**	147	410	42	108	13	55	0
Sample	**.260**	99	204	29	53	4	19	8
Norris†	**.247**	119	174	23	43	0	16	6
Frias	**.242**	116	227	27	55	0	10	5
Roberts	**.238**	101	235	27	56	10	30	0
Ellis	**.236**	73	182	12	43	1	23	3

Pitching	W	L	ERA	G	IP	H	BB	SO
Darwin	13	4	**2.62**	53	110	98	50	104
Matlack†	10	10	**3.68**	35	235	265	48	142
Jenkins	12	12	**3.77**	29	198	190	52	129
Medich	14	11	**3.93**	34	204	230	56	91
Hough	2	2	**3.98**	16	61	54	37	47
Lyle†	3	2	**4.67**	49	81	97	28	43
Kern	3	11	**4.86**	38	63	65	45	40
Figueroa	3	10	**6.52**	23	98	152	36	25

Toronto Blue Jays

Batting	Pct	G	AB	R	H	HR	RBI	SB
Woods†	**.300**	109	373	54	112	15	47	4
*Garcia	**.278**	140	543	50	151	4	46	13
Howell†	**.269**	142	528	51	142	10	57	0
Velez	**.269**	104	357	54	96	20	62	0
Bonnell	**.268**	130	463	55	124	13	56	3
Griffin‡	**.254**	155	653	63	166	2	41	18
Mayberry†	**.248**	149	501	62	124	30	82	0
*Iorg	**.248**	80	222	24	55	2	14	2
Ainge	**.243**	38	111	11	27	0	4	3
Whitt†	**.237**	106	295	23	70	6	34	1
Bailor	**.236**	117	347	44	82	1	16	12
*Moseby†	**.229**	114	389	44	89	9	46	4
Davis	**.216**	91	218	18	47	4	19	0
Bosetti	**.213**	53	188	24	40	4	18	4
Ault	**.194**	64	144	12	28	3	15	0

Pitching	W	L	ERA	G	IP	H	BB	SO
Garvin	4	7	**2.28**	61	83	70	27	52
Clancy	13	16	**3.30**	34	251	217	128	152
Stieb	12	15	**3.70**	34	243	232	83	108
Todd	5	2	**4.02**	12	85	90	30	44
Barlow	3	1	**4.09**	40	55	57	21	19
Mirabella†	5	12	**4.33**	33	131	151	66	53
Buskey	3	1	**4.43**	33	67	68	26	34
McLaughlin	6	9	**4.50**	55	136	159	53	70
*Leal	3	4	**4.50**	13	60	72	31	26
Moore†	1	1	**5.26**	31	65	76	31	22
Jefferson	4	13	**5.46**	29	122	130	52	53
Kucek	3	8	**6.75**	23	68	83	41	35

Major League Leaders in 1980

National League

Runs

Hernandez, St. Louis, 111; Schmidt, Philadelphia, 104; Murphy, Atlanta, 98; Dawson, Montreal, 96; Rose, Philadelphia, 96.

RBIs

Schmidt, Philadelphia, 121; Hendrick, St. Louis, 109; Garvey, Los Angeles, 106; Carter, Montreal, 101; Hernandez, St. Louis 99.

Hits

Garvey, Los Angeles, 199; Richards, San Diego, 193; Hernandez, St. Louis, 191; Buckner, Chicago, 187; Rose, Philadelphia, 185.

Doubles

Rose, Philadelphia, 42; Dawson, Montreal, 41; Buckner, Chicago, 40; Hernandez, St. Louis, 39; Knight, Cincinnati, 39.

Triples

Scott, Montreal, 13; Moreno, Pittsburgh, 13; LeFlore, Montreal, 11; McBride, Philadelphia, 10; Griffey, Cincinnati, 10; Herndon, San Francisco, 10.

Home Runs

Schmidt, Philadelphia, 48; Horner, Atlanta, 35; Murphy, Atlanta, 33; Carter, Montreal, 29; Baker, Los Angeles, 29.

Stolen Bases

LeFlore, Montreal, 97; Moreno, Pittsburgh 96; Collins, Cincinnati, 79; Scott, Montreal, 63; Richards, San Diego, 60.

Pitching (16 Decisions)

Bibby, Pittsburgh, 19-6, .760, 3.29; Reuss, Los Angeles, 18-6, .750, 2.51; Ruhle, Houston, 12-4, .750, 2.42; Carlton, Philadelphia, 24-9, .727, 2.34; Sutton, Los Angeles, 13-5, .722, 2.21; Pastore, Cincinnati, 13-7, .650, 3.27; Hooton, Los Angeles, 14-8, .636, 3.63; Ruthven, Philadelphia, 17-10, .630, 3.63.

Strikeouts

Carlton, Philadelphia, 286; Ryan, Houston, 200; Soto, Cincinnati, 181; P. Niekro, Atlanta, 176; Blyleven, Pittsburgh, 168.

American League

Runs

Wilson, Kansas City, 134; Yount, Milwaukee, 121; Bumbry, Baltimore, 117; Henderson, Oakland, 111; Trammell, Detroit, 106.

RBIs

Cooper, Milwaukee, 122; Brett, Kansas City, 118; Oglivie, Milwaukee, 117; Oliver, Texas, 117; Murray, Baltimore, 115.

Hits

Wilson, Kansas City, 230; Cooper, Milwaukee, 219; Rivers, Texas, 210; Oliver, Texas, 209; Bumbry, Baltimore, 205.

Doubles

Yount, Milwaukee, 49; Oliver, Texas, 43; Morrison, Chicago, 40; McRae, Kansas City, 39; Evans, Boston, 37.

Triples

Griffin, Toronto, 15; Wilson, Kansas City, 15; Washington, Kansas City, 11; Landreaux, Minnesota, 11; Yount, Milwaukee, 10.

Home Runs

Oglivie, Milwaukee, 41; Jackson, Yankees, 41; Thomas, Milwaukee, 38; Armas, Oakland, 35; Murray, Baltimore, 32.

Stolen Bases

Henderson, Oakland, 100; Wilson, Kansas City, 79; Dilone, Cleveland, 61; Cruz, Seattle, 45; Bumbry, Baltimore, 44.

Pitching (16 Decisions)

Stone, Baltimore, 25-7, .781, 3.23; Darwin, Texas, 13-4, .765, 2.63; May, Yankees, 15-5, .750, 2.46; McGregor, Baltimore, 20-8, .714, 3.32; John, Yankees, 22-9, .710, 3.43; Norris, Oakland, 22-9, .710, 2.53; Lopez, Detroit, 13-6, .684, 3.77; Travers, Milwaukee, 12-6, .667, 3.97.

Strikeouts

Barker, Cleveland, 188; Norris, Oakland, 181; Guidry, Yankees, 166; Leonard, Kansas City, 155; Bannister, Seattle, 154.

Leading Relief Pitchers in 1980

National League

Pitcher, club	Saves	Relief wins	Total points
Hume, Cincinnati	25	9	34
Fingers, San Diego	23	11	34
Sutter, Chicago	28	5	33
Allen, New York	22	7	29
Tekulve, Pittsburgh	21	8	29
Camp, Atlanta	22	6	28
McGraw, Philadelphia	20	5	25
Sambito, Houston	17	8	25
Howe, Los Angeles	17	7	24
Fryman, Montreal	17	7	24
Minton, San Francisco	19	4	23
LaCorte, Houston	11	8	19
Sosa, Montreal	9	9	18

American League

Pitcher, club	Saves	Relief wins	Total points
Quisenberry, Kansas City	33	12	45
Gossage, New York	33	6	39
Farmer, Chicago	30	7	37
Lopez, Detroit	21	13	34
Corbett, Minnesota	23	8	31
Stoddard, Baltimore	26	5	31
Burgmeier, Boston	24	5	29
Clear, California	9	11	20
Darwin, Texas	8	12	20
Rawley, Seattle	13	7	20
Cruz, Cleveland	12	6	18
Stanley, Boston	14	4	18
Monge, Cleveland	14	3	17

Most Home Runs in One Season

Homers	Player, team	Year
61	Roger Maris, New York (AL)	1961
60	Babe Ruth, New York (AL)	1927
59	Babe Ruth, New York (AL)	1921
58	Jimmy Foxx, Philadelphia (AL)	1932
58	Hank Greenberg, Detroit (AL)	1938
56	Hack Wilson, Chicago (NL)	1930
54	Babe Ruth, New York (AL)	1920
54	Babe Ruth, New York (AL)	1928
54	Ralph Kiner, Pittsburgh (NL)	1949
54	Mickey Mantle, New York (AL)	1961
52	Mickey Mantle, New York (AL)	1956
52	Willie Mays, San Francisco (NL)	1965
52	George Foster, Cincinnati (NL)	1977
51	Ralph Kiner, Pittsburgh (NL)	1947
51	John Mize, New York (NL)	1947
51	Willie Mays, New York (NL)	1955
50	Jimmy Foxx, Boston (AL)	1938
49	Babe Ruth, New York (AL)	1930
49	Lou Gehrig, New York (AL)	1934
49	Lou Gehrig, New York (AL)	1936
49	Ted Kluszewski, Cincinnati (NL)	1954
49	Willie Mays, San Francisco (NL)	1962
49	Harmon Killebrew, Minnesota (AL)	1964
49	Frank Robinson, Baltimore (AL)	1966
49	Harmon Killebrew, Minnesota (AL)	1969

World Series, 1980

Composite Box Score

Kansas City Royals

	g	ab	r	h	2b	3b	hr	rbi	so	bb	avg	po	a	e	pct
Willie Wilson, lf	6	26	3	4	1	0	0	0	12	4	.154	15	1	0	1.000
Hal McRae, dh	6	24	3	9	3	0	0	1	2	2	.375	0	0	0	.000
George Brett, 3b	6	24	3	9	2	1	1	3	4	2	.375	4	17	1	.955
Dave Chalk, 3b	1	0	1	0	0	0	0	0	0	1	.000	0	1	0	1.000
Willie Aikens, 1b	6	20	5	8	0	1	4	8	8	6	.400	55	2	2	.966
Pete LaCock, 1b	1	0	0	0	0	0	0	0	0	0	.000	2	0	0	1.000
Darrell Porter, c-ph	5	14	1	2	0	0	0	0	4	3	.143	13	2	0	1.000
Amos Otis, cf	6	23	4	11	2	0	3	7	3	3	.478	21	0	0	1.000
Clint Hurdle, rf	4	12	1	5	1	0	0	0	1	2	.417	8	0	0	1.000
Onix Concepcion, pr	3	0	0	0	0	0	0	0	0	0	.000	0	0	0	.000
Jose Cardenal, rf	4	10	0	2	0	0	0	0	3	0	.200	7	0	0	1.000
John Wathan, rf-c	3	7	1	2	0	0	0	1	1	2	.286	7	1	0	1.000
Frank White, 2b	6	25	0	2	0	0	0	0	5	1	.080	13	21	2	.944
U.L. Washington, ss	6	22	1	6	0	0	0	2	6	0	.273	8	20	1	.966
Dennis Leonard, p	2	0	0	0	0	0	0	0	0	0	.000	0	0	1	.000
Renie Martin, p	3	0	0	0	0	0	0	0	0	0	.000	0	0	0	.000
Dan Quisenberry, p	6	0	0	0	0	0	0	0	0	0	.000	1	1	0	1.000
Larry Gura, p	2	0	0	0	0	0	0	0	0	0	.000	2	4	0	1.000
Rich Gale, p	2	0	0	0	0	0	0	0	0	0	.000	0	1	0	1.000
Paul Splittorff, p	1	0	0	0	0	0	0	0	0	0	.000	0	1	0	1.000
Marty Pattin, p	1	0	0	0	0	0	0	0	0	0	.000	0	0	0	.000
Totals	**6**	**207**	**23**	**60**	**9**	**2**	**8**	**22**	**49**	**26**	**.290**	**156**	**72**	**7**	**.970**

Philadelphia Phillies

	g	ab	r	h	2b	3b	hr	rbi	so	bb	avg	po	a	e	pct
Lonnie Smith, lf-dh	6	19	2	5	1	0	0	1	1	1	.263	4	1	0	1.000
Del Unser, cf	3	6	2	3	2	0	0	2	1	0	.500	1	0	0	1.000
Greg Gross, lf	4	2	0	0	0	0	0	0	0	0	.000	1	0	0	1.000
Pete Rose, 1b	6	23	2	6	1	0	0	1	2	2	.261	49	6	0	1.000
Mike Schmidt, 3b	6	21	6	8	1	0	2	7	3	4	.381	9	9	0	1.000
Keith Moreland, dh	3	12	1	4	0	0	0	1	1	0	.333	0	0	0	.000
Bake McBride, rf	6	23	3	7	1	0	1	5	1	2	.304	13	1	0	1.000
Greg Luzinski, dh-lf	3	9	0	0	0	0	0	0	5	1	.000	1	0	0	1.000
Garry Maddox, cf	6	22	1	5	2	0	0	1	3	1	.227	11	1	0	1.000
Manny Trillo, 2b	6	23	4	5	2	0	0	2	0	0	.217	14	25	1	.975
Larry Bowa, ss	6	24	3	9	1	0	0	2	0	0	.375	5	17	0	1.000
Bob Boone, c	6	17	3	7	2	0	0	4	0	4	.412	49	3	0	1.000
Bob Walk, p	1	0	0	0	0	0	0	0	0	0	.000	2	0	0	1.000
Tug McGraw, p	4	0	0	0	0	0	0	0	0	0	.000	0	1	0	1.000
Steve Carlton, p	2	0	0	0	0	0	0	0	0	0	.000	0	3	0	1.000
Ron Reed, p	2	0	0	0	0	0	0	0	0	0	.000	0	0	0	.000
Dick Ruthven, p	1	0	0	0	0	0	0	0	0	0	.000	0	0	0	.000
Larry Christenson, p	1	0	0	0	0	0	0	0	0	0	.000	0	0	1	.000
Dickie Noles, p	1	0	0	0	0	0	0	0	0	0	.000	1	0	0	1.000
Kevin Saucier, p	1	0	0	0	0	0	0	0	0	0	.000	0	0	0	.000
Warren Brusstar, p	1	0	0	0	0	0	0	0	0	0	.000	0	0	0	.000
Marty Bystrom, p	1	0	0	0	0	0	0	0	0	0	.000	1	1	0	1.000
Totals	**6**	**201**	**27**	**59**	**13**	**0**	**3**	**26**	**17**	**15**	**.294**	**161**	**68**	**2**	**.991**

Pitching Summary

Kansas City

	g	cg	ip	h	r	bb	so	hb	wp	w	l	pct	er	era
Dennis Leonard	2	0	10⅔	15	9	2	5	1	1	1	1	.500	8	6.75
Renie Martin	3	0	9⅔	11	3	3	2	1	0	0	0	.000	3	2.79
Dan Quisenberry	6	0	10⅓	10	6	3	0	0	0	1	2	.333	6	5.23
Larry Gura	2	0	12⅓	8	4	3	4	0	0	0	0	.000	3	2.43
Rich Gale	2	0	6⅓	11	4	4	4	0	0	0	1	.000	3	4.26
Paul Splittorff	1	0	1⅔	4	1	0	0	0	0	0	0	.000	1	5.40
Marty Pattin	1	0	1	0	0	0	2	0	0	0	0	.000	0	0.000
Totals	**6**	**0**	**52**	**59**	**27**	**15**	**17**	**2**	**1**	**2**	**4**	**.333**	**24**	**4.15**

Philadelphia

	g	cg	ip	h	r	bb	so	hb	wp	w	l	pct	er	era
Bob Walk	1	0	7	8	6	3	3	0	1	1	0	1.000	6	6.75
Tug McGraw	4	0	7⅔	7	1	8	10	0	0	1	1	.500	1	1.17
Steve Carlton	2	0	15	14	5	9	17	0	1	2	0	1.000	4	2.40
Ron Reed	2	0	2	2	0	0	2	0	0	0	0	.000	0	0.00
Dick Ruthven	1	0	9	9	3	0	7	0	0	0	0	.000	3	3.00
Larry Christenson	1	0	⅓	5	4	0	0	0	0	0	1	.000	4	108.00
Dickie Noles	1	0	4⅔	5	1	2	6	0	0	0	0	.000	1	1.93
Kevin Saucier	1	0	⅔	0	0	2	0	0	1	0	0	.000	0	0.00
Warren Brusstar	1	0	2⅓	0	0	1	0	0	0	0	0	.000	0	0.00
Marty Bystrom	1	0	5	10	3	1	4	0	0	0	0	.000	3	5.40
Totals	**6**	**0**	**53⅔**	**60**	**23**	**26**	**49**	**0**	**3**	**4**	**2**	**.667**	**22**	**3.70**

First Game

Veterans Stadium, Philadelphia, Pa., Oct. 14

Kansas City	ab	r	h	bi	Philadelphia	ab	r	h	bi
Wilson lf	5	0	0	0	Smith lf	4	0	2	0
McRae dh	3	1	1	0	Gross lf	1	0	0	0
Brett 3b	4	1	1	0	Rose 1b	3	1	0	0
Aikens 1b	4	2	2	4	Schmidt 3b	2	2	1	0
Porter c	2	1	0	0	McBride rf	4	1	3	3
Otis cf	4	1	3	2	Luzinski dh	3	0	0	0
Hurdle rf	3	0	1	0	Maddox cf	3	0	0	1
Wathan rf	1	0	0	0	Trillo 2b	4	1	1	0
White 2b	4	0	1	0	Bowa ss	4	1	1	0
Washington ss	4	0	0	0	Boone c	4	1	3	2
Totals	**34**	**6**	**9**	**6**	**Totals**	**32**	**7**	**11**	**6**

Kansas City	0 2 2	0 0 0	0 2 0—6
Philadelphia	0 0 5	1 1 0	0 0 x—7

E - Leonard, DP - Philadelphia 1. LOB - Kansas City 4, Philadelphia 6. 2B - Boone 2, Brett. HRs - Otis (1), Aikens 2 (2), McBride (1). SB - Bowa, White. SF - Maddox.

	ip	h	r	er	bb	so
Kansas City						
Leonard L,0-1	3 2/3	6	6	6	1	3
Martin	4	5	1	1	1	1
Quisenberry	1/3	0	0	0	0	0
Philadelphia						
Walk W, 1-0	7	8	6	6	3	3
McGraw S, 1	2	1	0	0	0	2

HBP - by Leonard (Rose), by Martin (Luzinski). Wild pitch - Walk. T - 3:01.

How runs were scored—Two in Royals second: Porter walked. Otis hit a home run.

Two in Royals third: McRae singled. Aikens hit a home run.

Five in Phillies third: Bowa singled. Boone doubled scoring Bowa. Smith singled scoring Boone. Rose was hit by a pitch. Schmidt walked. McBride hit a home run.

One in Phillies fourth: Trillo singled. Boone doubled scoring Trillo.

One in Phillies fifth: Schmidt walked. McBride singled. Luzinski was hit by a pitch. Maddox hit a sacrifice fly scoring Schmidt.

Two in Royals eighth: Brett doubled. Aikens hit a home run.

Second Game

Veterans Stadium, Philadelphia, Pa., Oct. 15

Kansas City	ab	r	h	bi	Philadelphia	ab	r	h	bi
Wilson lf	4	1	1	0	Smith lf	3	0	0	0
Washington ss	4	0	1	0	Unser cf	1	1	1	1
Brett 3b	2	0	2	0	Rose 1b	4	0	0	0
Chalk 3b	0	1	0	0	McBride rf	3	1	1	1
Porter ph	1	0	0	0	Schmidt 3b	4	1	2	1
McRae dh	4	1	3	0	Moreland dh	4	1	2	1
Otis cf	5	1	2	2	Maddox cf	3	1	1	0
Wathan c	3	0	0	1	Gross lf	1	0	0	0
Aikens 1b	3	0	1	0	Trillo 2b	2	0	0	1
LaCock 1b	0	0	0	0	Bowa ss	3	0	1	1
Cardenal rf	4	0	0	0	Boone C	1	1	0	0
White 2b	4	0	1	0					
Totals	**34**	**4**	**11**	**3**	**Totals**	**29**	**6**	**8**	**6**

Kansas City	0 0 0	0 0 1	3 0 0—4
Philadelphia	0 0 0	0 2 0	0 4 x—6

E - Trillo. DP - Kansas City 2, Philadelphia 4. LOB - Kansas City 11, Philadelphia 3. 2B - Maddox, Otis, Unser, Schmidt. SB - Wilson, Chalk. S - Washington. SF - Trillo, Wathan.

	ip	h	r	er	bb	so
Kansas City						
Gura	6	4	2	2	2	2
Quisenberry L,0-1	2	4	4	4	1	0
Philadelphia						
Carlton W,1-0	8	10	4	3	6	10
Reed S,1	1	1	0	0	0	2

Wild pitch - Carlton. T - 3:01. A - 65,775.

How runs were scored—Two in Phillies fifth: Moreland singled. Maddox doubled. Trillo hit a sacrifice fly scoring Moreland. Bowa singled scoring Maddox.

One in Royals sixth: Otis singled. Wathan walked. Otis scored on an infield error.

Three in Royals seventh: Wilson, Chalk, and McRae walked. Otis doubled scoring Wilson and Chalk. Wathan hit a sacrifice fly scoring McRae.

Four in Phillies eighth: Boone walked. Unser doubled scoring Boone. McBride singled scoring Unser. Schmidt doubled scoring McBride. Moreland singled scoring Schmidt.

Third Game

Royals Stadium, Kansas City, Oct. 17

Philadelphia	ab	r	h	bi	Kansas City	ab	r	h	bi
L.Smith lf	4	0	2	1	Wilson lf	4	1	0	0
Gross lf	0	0	0	0	White 2b	5	0	0	0
Rose 1b	4	0	1	1	G.Brett 3b	4	1	2	1
Schmidt 3b	5	1	1	1	Aikens 1b	5	1	2	1
McBride rf	5	0	2	0	McRae dh	4	0	2	1
Moreland dh	5	0	1	0	Otis cf	4	1	2	1
Maddox cf	4	0	1	0	Hurdle rf	4	0	2	0
Trillo 2b	5	1	2	0	Concepcion pr	0	0	0	0
Bowa ss	5	1	3	0	Cardenal rf	0	0	0	0
Boone c	4	0	1	0	Porter c	4	0	0	0
					Washington ss	4	0	1	0
Totals	**41**	**3**	**14**	**3**	**Totals**	**38**	**4**	**11**	**4**

Philadelphia	0 1 0	0 1 0	0 1 0	0—3
Kansas City	1 0 0	1 0 0	1 0 0	1—4

DP—Philadelphia 1, Kansas City 2. LOB—Philadelphia 15, Kansas City 7. 2B—Trillo, G. Brett. 3B—Aikens, HRs—G. Brett (1), Schmidt (1), Otis (2). SB—Hurdle, Bowa, Wilson. S—Gross.

	ip	h	r	er	bb	so
Philadelphia						
Ruthven	9	9	3	3	0	7
McGraw L, 0-1	*2/3	2	1	1	2	1
Kansas City						
Gale	4 1/3	7	2	2	3	3
Martin	3 1/3	5	1	1	1	1
Quisenberry W, 1-1	2 1/3	2	0	0	2	0

*Two outs when winning run scored. T—3:19.

How runs were scored—One in Royals first: Brett hit a home run.

One in Phillies second: Trillo and Bowa singled. Smith walked. Trillo scored on an infield grounder.

One in Royals fourth: Aikens tripled. McRae singled scoring Aikens.

One in Phillies fifth: Schmidt hit a home run.

One in Royals seventh: Otis hit a home run.

One in Phillies eighth: Bowa singled. Smith walked. Rose singled scoring Bowa.

One in Royals tenth: Wilson walked and stole second base. Aikens singled scoring Wilson.

Fourth Game

Royals Stadium, Kansas City, Oct. 18

Philadelphia	ab	r	h	bi	Kansas City	ab	r	h	bi
Smith dh	4	0	0	0	Wilson lf	4	1	1	0
Rose 1b	4	1	2	0	White 2b	5	0	0	0
McBride rf	3	0	1	0	GBrett 3b	5	1	1	1
Schmidt 3b	3	0	1	1	Aikens 1b	3	2	2	3
Unser lf	4	0	1	0	McRae dh	4	1	2	0
Maddox cf	4	0	1	0	Otis cf	4	0	2	1
Trillo 2b	4	2	1	0	Hurdle rf	2	0	1	0
Bowa ss	4	0	2	1	Porter c	3	0	0	0
Boone c	3	0	1	1	Washington ss	4	0	1	0
Totals	**33**	**3**	**10**	**3**	**Totals**	**34**	**5**	**10**	**5**

Philadelphia	0 1 0	0 0 0	1 1 0—3
Kansas City	4 1 0	0 0 0	0 0 x—5

E—White, Christenson, Washington. DP—Kansas City 1. LOB—Philadelphia 5, Kansas City 10. 2B—McRae 2, Otis, Hurdle, McBride, Trillo, Rose. 3B—G. Brett. HR—Aikens 2 (4). SB—Bowa. SF—Schmidt.

	ip	h	r	er	bb	so
Philadelphia						
Christenson L,0-1	1/3	5	4	4	0	0
Noles	4 2/3	5	1	1	2	6
Saucier	2/3	0	0	0	2	0
Brusstar	2 1/3	0	0	0	1	0
Kansas City						
Leonard W, 1-1	7	9	3	2	1	2
Quisenberry S, 1	2	1	0	0	0	0

How runs were scored—Four in Royals first: Wilson singled. Brett tripled scoring Wilson. Aikens hit a home run. McRae doubled. Otis doubled scoring McRae.

One in Phillies second: Trillo reached second on an error. Bowa singled scoring Trillo.

One in Royals second: Aikens hit a home run.

One in Phillies seventh: Trillo doubled. Bowa singled. Boone hit a sacrifice fly scoring Trillo.

One in Phillies eighth: Rose doubled and went to third on an infield out. Schmidt hit a sacrifice fly scoring Rose.

Fifth Game

Royals Stadium, Kansas City, Oct. 19

Philadelphia	ab	r	h	bi	Kansas City	ab	r	h	bi
Rose 1b	4	0	0	0	Wilson lf	5	0	2	0
McBride rf . . .	4	1	0	0	White 2b	3	0	0	0
Schmidt 3b. . .	4	2	2	2	G.Brett 3b . . .	5	0	1	1
Luzinski lf . . .	2	0	0	0	Aikens 1b . . .	3	0	1	0
L.Smith lf. . . .	0	0	0	0	Concepcion pr.	0	0	0	0
Unser lf.	1	1	1	1	McRae dh . . .	5	0	1	0
Moreland dh . .	3	0	1	0	Otis cf	3	1	2	1
Maddox cf . . .	4	0	0	0	Hurdle rf	3	1	1	0
Trillo 2b	4	0	1	1	Cardenal rf. . .	2	0	0	0
Bowa ss	4	0	1	0	Porter c	4	0	2	0
Boone c	3	0	1	0	Washington ss.	3	1	2	1
Totals	**33**	**4**	**7**	**4**	**Totals . . . .**	**36**	**3**	**12**	**2**

Philadelphia.	0	0	0	2	0	0	0	0	2	—4
Kansas City.	0	0	0	0	1	2	0	0	0	—3

E—Aikens, G. Brett. DP—Kansas City 2. LOB—Philadelphia 4, Kansas City 13. 2B—Wilson, McRae, Unser. HRs—Schmidt (2), Otis (3). SB—G. Brett. S—White, Moreland. SF—Washington.

	ip	h	r	er	bb	so
Philadelphia						
Bystrom	5	10	3	3	1	4
Reed.	1	1	0	0	0	0
McGraw W, 1-1. . . .	3	1	0	0	4	5
Kansas City						
Gura	$6\frac{1}{3}$	4	2	1	1	2
Quisenberry L, 1-2 . .	$2\frac{2}{3}$	3	2	2	0	0

T—2:51.

How runs were scored—Two in Phillies fourth: McBride reached first on an error. Schmidt hit a home run.

One in Royals fifth: Washington and Wilson singled. Brett grounded out scoring Washington.

Two in Royals sixth: Otis hit a home run. Hurdle and Porter singled. Washington hit a sacrifice fly scoring Hurdle.

Two in Phillies ninth: Schmidt singled. Unser doubled scoring Schmidt. Trillo singled scoring Unser.

Sixth Game

Veterans Stadium, Philadelphia, Oct. 21

Kansas City	ab	r	h	bi	Philadelphia	ab	r	h	bi
Wilson lf	4	0	0	0	L. Smith lf . . .	4	2	1	0
Washington ss.	3	0	1	1	Gross lf.	0	0	0	0
G. Brett 3b. . .	4	0	2	0	Rose 1b	4	0	3	0
McRae dh . . .	4	0	0	0	Schmidt 3b. . .	3	0	1	2
Otis cf	3	0	0	0	McBride rf . . .	4	0	0	1
Aikens 1b . . .	2	0	0	0	Luzinski dh. . .	4	0	0	0
Concepcion pr.	0	0	0	0	Maddox cf . . .	4	0	2	0
Wathan c. . . .	3	1	2	0	Trillo 2b	4	0	0	0
Cardenal rf. . .	4	0	2	0	Bowa ss	4	1	1	0
White 2b	4	0	0	0	Boone c	2	1	1	1
Totals	**31**	**1**	**7**	**1**	**Totals . . . .**	**33**	**4**	**9**	**4**

Kansas City.	0	0	0	0	0	0	0	1	0	—1
Philadelphia.	0	0	2	0	1	1	0	0	x	—4

E—White, Aikens. DP—Kansas City 1, Philadelphia 2. LOB—Kansas City 9, Philadelphia 7. 2B—Maddox, L. Smith, Bowa. SF—Washington.

	ip	h	r	er	bb	so
Kansas City						
Gale L, 0-1	2	4	2	1	1	1
Martin	$2\frac{1}{3}$	1	1	1	1	0
Splittorff	$1\frac{2}{3}$	4	1	1	0	0
Pattin.	1	0	0	0	0	2
Quisenberry.	1	0	0	0	0	0
Philadelphia						
Carlton W, 2-0	7	4	1	1	3	7
McGraw S,2.	2	3	0	0	2	2

T—3:00

How runs were scored—Two in Phillies third: Boone walked. Smith reached first on an infield error. Rose singled. Schmidt singled scoring Boone and Smith.

One in Phillies fifth: Smith doubled. McBride grounded out scoring Smith.

One in Phillies sixth: Bowa doubled. Boone singled scoring Bowa.

One in Royals eighth: Wathan walked. Cardenal singled. Wilson walked. Washington hit a sacrifice fly scoring Wathan.

World Series Results, 1903-1980

1903 Boston AL 5, Pittsburgh NL 3
1904 No series
1905 New York NL 4, Philadelphia AL 1
1906 Chicago AL 4, Chicago NL 2
1907 Chicago NL 4, Detroit AL 0, 1 tie
1908 Chicago NL 4, Detroit AL 1
1909 Pittsburgh NL 4, Detroit AL 3
1910 Philadelphia AL 4, Chicago NL 1
1911 Philadelphia AL 4, New York NL 2
1912 Boston AL 4, New York NL 3, 1 tie
1913 Philadelphia AL 4, New York NL 1
1914 Boston NL 4, Philadelphia AL 0
1915 Boston AL 4, Philadelphia NL 1
1916 Boston AL 4, Brooklyn NL 1
1917 Chicago AL 4, New York NL 2
1918 Boston AL 4, Chicago NL 2
1919 Cincinnati NL 5, Chicago AL 3
1920 Cleveland AL 5, Brooklyn NL 2
1921 New York NL 5, New York AL 3
1922 New York NL 4, New York AL 0, 1 tie
1923 New York AL 4, New York NL 2
1924 Washington AL 4, New York NL 3
1925 Pittsburgh NL 4, Washington AL 3
1926 St. Louis NL 4, New York AL 3
1927 New York AL 4, Pittsburgh NL 0
1928 New York AL 4, St. Louis NL 0
1929 Philadelphia AL 4, Chicago NL 1
1930 Philadelphia AL 4, St. Louis NL 2
1931 St. Louis NL 4, Philadelphia AL 3
1932 New York AL 4, Chicago NL 0
1933 New York NL 4, Washington AL 1
1934 St. Louis NL 4, Detroit AL 3
1935 Detroit AL 4, Chicago NL 2
1936 New York AL 4, New York NL 2
1937 New York AL 4, New York NL 1
1938 New York AL 4, Chicago NL 0
1939 New York AL 4, Cincinnati NL 0
1940 Cincinnati NL 4, Detroit AL 3
1941 New York AL 4, Brooklyn NL 1
1942 St. Louis NL 4, New York AL 1
1943 New York AL 4, St. Louis NL 1
1944 St. Louis NL 4, St. Louis AL 2
1945 Detroit AL 4, Chicago NL 3
1946 St. Louis NL 4, Boston AL 3
1947 New York AL 4, Brooklyn NL 3
1948 Cleveland AL 4, Boston NL 2
1949 New York AL 4, Brooklyn NL 1
1950 New York AL 4, Philadelphia NL 0
1951 New York AL 4, New York NL 2
1952 New York AL 4, Brooklyn NL 3
1953 New York AL 4, Brooklyn NL 2
1954 New York NL 4, Cleveland AL 0
1955 Brooklyn NL 4, New York AL 3
1956 New York AL 4, Brooklyn NL 3
1957 Milwaukee NL 4, New York AL 3
1958 New York AL 4, Milwaukee NL 3
1959 Los Angeles NL 4, Chicago AL 2
1960 Pittsburgh NL 4, New York AL 3
1961 New York AL 4, Cincinnati NL 1
1962 New York AL 4, San Francisco NL 3
1963 Los Angeles NL 4, New York AL 0
1964 St. Louis NL 4, New York AL 3
1965 Los Angeles NL 4, Minnesota AL 3
1966 Baltimore AL 4, Los Angeles NL 0
1967 St. Louis NL 4, Boston AL 3
1968 Detroit AL 4, St. Louis NL 3
1969 New York NL 4, Baltimore AL 1
1970 Baltimore AL 4, Cincinnati NL 1
1971 Pittsburgh NL 4, Baltimore AL 3
1972 Oakland AL 4, Cincinnati NL 3
1973 Oakland AL 4, New York NL 3
1974 Oakland AL 4, Los Angeles NL 1
1975 Cincinnati NL 4, Boston AL 3
1976 Cincinnati NL 4, New York AL 0
1977 New York AL 4, Los Angeles NL 2
1978 New York AL 4, Los Angeles NL 2
1979 Pittsburgh NL 4, Baltimore AL 3
1980 Philadelphia NL 4, Kansas City AL 2

All-American Derby in 1980

Native Gambler won the $1.4 million All-American Derby, the richest event in quarterhorse racing, on Aug. 24, 1980, at Ruidoso Downs, New Mexico.

The colt, owned by Gary Benton of Lubbock, Texas, earned $501,147 for his first place finish. Pea Jay Jet, a filly, finished second, and Charge It Poppa finished third.

Major League Baseball Attendance

National League

Club	1980	1979		Change
Atlanta	1,044,412	769,465	+	274,947
Chicago	1,192,070	1,648,587	–	456,517
Cincinnati	2,022,450	2,356,933	–	334,483
Houston	2,281,217	1,900,312	+	380,905
Los Angeles	3,249,287	2,860,954	+	388,333
Montreal	2,226,059	2,102,173	+	123,886
New York	1,185,203	788,905	+	396,298
Philadelphia	2,651,681	2,775,011	–	123,330
Pittsburgh	1,646,757	1,435,454	+	211,303
St. Louis	1,395,397	1,627,256	–	231,859
San Diego	1,139,026	1,456,967	–	317,941
San Francisco	1,096,167	1,456,402	–	360,235
Totals	**21,129,726**	**21,178,419**	–	**48,693**

American League

Club	1980	1979		Change
Baltimore	1,802,088	1,681,009	+	121,079
Boston	1,922,251	2,353,114	–	430,863
California	2,296,827	2,523,575	–	226,748
Chicago	1,200,364	1,280,702	–	80,338
Cleveland	1,033,827	1,011,644	+	22,183
Detroit	1,780,293	1,630,929	+	149,364
Kansas City	2,288,714	2,261,845	+	26,869
Milwaukee	1,857,408	1,918,343	–	60,935
Minnesota	769,206	1,070,521	–	301,315
New York	2,627,417	2,537,765	+	89,652
Oakland	842,259	306,763	+	535,496
Seattle	836,205	844,447	–	8,242
Texas	1,198,175	1,519,671	–	321,496
Toronto	1,414,362	1,431,651	–	17,289
Totals	**21,869,396**	**22,371,979**	–	**502,583**

Major League Attendance Records

Season, both leagues—43,548,450 in 1979.
Season, one club—3,347,776—Los Angeles Dodgers,1978.
World Series—420,784—1959 Series between Los Angeles Dodgers and Chicago White Sox.
World Series game—92,706—fifth game, 1959, Los Angeles.
Regular season game—84,587—Municipal Stadium, Cleveland, Sept. 12, 1954, in doubleheader between the Indians and Yankees. (Not including pass list of 1,976).
Regular season single game—78,672—Los Angeles Memorial Coliseum, April 18, 1958, in opening game between Los Angeles Dodgers and San Francisco Giants.

All-Time Home Run Leaders

Player	HR	Player	HR	Player	HR	Player	HR	Player	HR
Hank Aaron	755	Lou Gehrig	493	Gil Hodges	370	Hank Greenberg	331	Frank Thomas	286
Babe Ruth	714	Stan Musial	475	Ralph Kiner	369	Bobby Bonds	326	Mike Schmidt	283
Willie Mays	660	Willie Stargell	472	Joe DiMaggio	361	Willie Horton	325	Ken Boyer	282
Frank Robinson	586	Billy Williams	426	John Mize	359	Roy Sievers	318	Graig Nettles	280
Harmon Killebrew	573	Carl Yastrzemski	419	Yogi Berra	358	Al Simmons	307	Ted Kluszewski	279
Mickey Mantle	536	Reggie Jackson	410	Johnny Bench	356	Rogers Hornsby	302	Rusty Staub	279
Jimmy Foxx	534	Duke Snider	407	Dick Allen	351	Chuck Klein	300	Rudy York	277
Ted Williams	521	Al Kaline	399	Lee May	351	Reggie Smith	295	Roger Maris	275
Willie McCovey	521	Frank Howard	382	Tony Perez	348	Jim Wynn	291	George Scott	271
Ed Mathews	512	Orlando Cepeda	379	Ron Santo	342	Robert Johnson	288	Dave Kingman	270
Ernie Banks	512	Norm Cash	377	John (Boog) Powell	339	Hank Sauer	288	Brooks Robinson	268
Mel Ott	511	Rocky Colavito	374	Joe Adcock	336	Del Ennis	288	Vic Wertz	266

Major League Franchise Shifts and Additions

1953—Boston Braves (N. L.) became Milwaukee Braves. Home attendance, last season in Boston (1952), 281,278; first season in Milwaukee (1953), 1,826,397.

1954—St. Louis Browns (A. L.) became Baltimore Orioles. Home attendance, last season in St. Louis (1953), 297,238; first season in Baltimore (1954), 1,060,910.

1955—Philadelphia Athletics (A. L.) became Kansas City Athletics. Home attendance, last season in Phila. (1954), 627,100; first season in K.C. (1955), 1,393,054.

1958—New York Giants (N. L.) became San Francisco Giants. Home attendance, last season in New York (1957), 653,923; first season in San Francisco (1958), 1,272,625.

1958—Brooklyn Dodgers (N. L.) became Los Angeles Dodgers. Home attendance, last season in Brooklyn (1957), 1,028,258; first season in Los Angeles (1958), 1,845,556.

1961—Washington Senators (A. L.) became Minnesota Twins. Home attendance, last season in Washington (1960), 743,404; first season in Minneapolis-St. Paul (1961), 1,256,722.

1961—Los Angeles Angels (later renamed the California Angels) enfranchised by the American League.

1961—Washington Senators enfranchised by the American League (a new team, replacing the former Washington club, whose franchise was moved to Minneapolis-St. Paul).

1962—Houston Colt .45's (later renamed the Houston Astros) enfranchised by the National League.

1962—New York Mets enfranchised by the National League.

1966—Milwaukee Braves (N. L.) became Atlanta Braves. Home attendance, last season in Milwaukee (1965), 555,584; first season in Atlanta (1966), 1,539,801.

1968—Kansas City Athletics (A. L.) became Oakland Athletics. Home attendance, last season in Kansas City (1967), 652,246; first season in Oakland (1968), 838,501.

1969—Two major leagues each added two teams for totals of 12 and split into two divisions. American League additions: Kansas City Royals and Seattle Pilots; National League additions: Montreal Expos and San Diego Padres.

1970—Seattle franchise shifted to Milwaukee. Club was renamed Milwaukee Brewers.

1971—Washington franchise to Dallas-Fort Worth, with field at Arlington, Tex.

1977—Toronto and Seattle enfranchised by the American League.

Softball Tournament Champions in 1980

Source: Amateur Softball Assn.

Men

Major Slow Pitch — Campbell's Carpets, Concord, Cal.
Major Ind. Slow Pitch — Sikorsky, Stratford, Conn.
"A" Slow Pitch — Houston Wreckers, Houston, Tex.
"A" Ind. Slow Pitch — Local 761, Louisville, Ky.
Church — West End Baptist, Houston, Tex.
"A" Fast Pitch — S.H. Good, Narvon, Pa.
Major Fast Pitch — Peterbilt Western, Seattle, Wash.

Women

Major Fast Pitch — Reybestos Brakettes, Stratford, Conn.
Major Slow Pitch — Howard Rubi-Otts, Graham, N.C.
"A" Fast Pitch — San Diego Astro's, San Diego, Cal.
"A" Slow Pitch — Encore, Prince George Co., metro Washington, D.C.
Church — Rock Creek Methodist, Snow Camp, N.C.

Water Ski Champions in 1980

Source: American Water Ski Association

38th Annual National Water Ski Championships

Tyler, Tex., Aug. 20-24, 1980

Men's Open Overall—Carl Roberge, Orlando, Fla., 3,159 points.
Men's Open Slalom—Carl Roberge, 58 buoys.
Men's Open Tricks—Cory Pickos, Eagle Lake, Fla., 7,600 points.
Men's Open Jumping—Bob LaPoint, Castro Valley, Cal., 179 feet.
Women's Open Overall—Karin Roberge, Orlando, Fla., 3,379 points.
Women's Open Slalom—Cyndi Benzel, Newberry Springs, Cal., 57 buoys.
Women's Open Tricks—Karin Roberge, 6,040 points.
Women's Open Jumping—Linda Giddens, Eastman, Ga., 120 feet.
Senior Men's Overall—Dr. J. D. Morgan, Lake Wales, Fla., 2,985 points.
Senior Men's Slalom—Dr. J. D. Morgan, 52 buoys.
Senior Men's Tricks—Robert Hurm, St. Marys, Oh., 4,410 points.
Senior Men's Jumping—Dr. J. D. Morgan, 124 feet.
Senior Women's Overall—Thelma Salmas, Lake Worth, Fla., 3,200 points.
Senior Women's Slalom—Gun Evans, Hollywood, Fla., 46½ buoys.
Senior Women's Tricks—Thelma Salmas, 4,260 points.
Senior Women's Jumping—Gun Evans, 109 feet.
Boys' Overall—Dennis Cooper, San Diego, Cal., 2,335 points.
Boys' Slalom—Chris Swann, Winter Park, Fla., 47 buoys.
Boys' Tricks—Ned Kwasniewski, W. Brookfield, Mass., 3,780 points.
Boys' Jumping—Dan Zeisler, Sandy Hook, Conn., 132 feet.
Girls' Overall—Kristi Hill, Shawnee Mission, Kan., 2,754 points.
Girls' Slalom—Jennifer Leachman, Hockingport, Oh., 50 buoys.
Girls' Tricks—Nathalie Roberge, Orlando, Fla., 4,140 points.
Girls' Jumping—Kristi Hill, Shawnee Mission, Kan., 108 feet.

22d Annual Masters Tournament

Callaway Gardens, Ga., July 12-13, 1980

Men's Overall—Mike Hazelwood, London, England, 2,798 points.
Men's Slalom—Bob LaPoint, Castro Valley, Cal., 53 buoys.
Men's Tricks—Cory Pickos, Eagle Lake, Fla., 8,190 points.
Men's Jumping—Sammy Duvall, Greenville, S. C., 183 feet.
Women's Overall—Karin Roberge, Orlando, Fla., 2,661 points.
Women's Slalom—Karin Roberge, 49 buoys.
Women's Tricks—Ana Marie Carrasco, Caracas, Venezuela, 5,070 points.
Women's Jumping—Linda Giddens, Eastman, Ga., 117 feet.

Ten Most Dramatic Sports Events, Nov. 1979—Oct. 1980

Selected by The World Almanac sports staff

—The United States hockey team winning the gold medal at the Winter Olympics in Lake Placid, N.Y. They upset the Soviet Union and Finland in the final 2 games to win the gold medal.

—The Philadelphia Phillies winning the World Series for the first time in their 98-year history. They defeated the American League champion Kansas City Royals in 6 games.

—Roberto Duran winning a 15-round decision over champion Sugar Ray Leonard to become the World Boxing Council's welterweight champion.

—Eric Heiden becoming the first athlete to win 5 gold medals for individual events during a single Olympics. He won all 5 men's speed skating competitions in record time.

—Genuine Risk becoming the first filly to win the Kentucky Derby in 65 years and only the 2d in the race's history.

—Larry Holmes retaining his World Boxing Council heavyweight title when Muhammad Ali was unable to answer the bell for the 11th round. Ali was attempting to become the first 4-time heavyweight champion.

—George Brett attempting to become the first major leaguer to bat .400 since Ted Williams hit .406 in 1941. The Kansas City Royals 3d baseman finished the season with a .390 batting average.

—The Pittsburgh Steelers winning their 2d consecutive Super Bowl and their 4th in the past 6 years. The Steelers defeated the Los Angeles Rams 31-19.

—Charles White of the Univ. of Southern California rushing for 247 yards and scoring a touchdown with less than 2 minutes to play to give USC a 17-16 victory over Ohio State in the Rose Bowl.

—The Philadelphia Flyers setting a National Hockey League record by playing 35 consecutive games without a loss. During the streak, the Flyers won 25 games and tied 10.

Marathons in 1980

Boston Marathon

Bill Rodgers covered the traditional distance of 26 miles 385 yards in 2 hours 12 minutes 11 seconds to win the 84th annual Boston Marathon on April 21, 1980. It was the third consecutive victory in the event for the Boston-area native and his fourth in the last six years. He became the second man in the history of the Boston Marathon to win four times overall, and the second to win three consecutive years. Marco Marchei of Italy finished second, and Ron Tabb of Houston finished third.

Rosie Ruiz of New York City was declared the women's winner following the race and given the victor's wreath and medal. On April 29, officials declared the Ruiz victory invalid, claiming that she had not actually run the race. Jacqueline Garreau of Canada was awarded the women's title. Garreau's time was 2 hours 34 minutes 26 seconds.

New York Marathon

Alberto Salazar, 22-year old senior at the Univ. of Oregon, covered the 26-mile-385-yard course in a course record 2 hours 9 minutes 41 seconds to win the New York Marathon on Oct. 26, 1980. Salazar, who was born in Cuba and now lives in Wayland, Mass., defeated 14,011 challengers from 44 countries. Rodolfo Gomez of Mexico finished second, and John Graham of England finished third. Bill Rodgers, who had won the event the last four years, finished fifth.

Grete Waitz of Norway was the women's champion for the third consecutive year. She ran the race in 2 hours 25 minutes 41 seconds to finish 74th overall. Patti Catalano of Boston finished second, and Ingred Christensen of Norway finished third.

North American Soccer League in 1980

National Conference

Eastern Division

	W	L	GF	GA	Bonus points	Total points
New York	24	8	87	41	69	213
Washington	17	15	72	61	57	159
Toronto	14	18	49	65	44	128
Rochester	12	20	42	67	37	109

Central Division

	W	L	GF	GA	Bonus points	Total points
Dallas	18	14	57	58	49	157
Minnesota	16	16	66	56	51	147
Tulsa	15	17	56	62	49	139
Atlanta	7	25	34	84	32	74

Western Division

	W	L	GF	GA	Bonus points	Total points
Seattle	25	7	74	31	57	207
Los Angeles	20	12	61	52	54	174
Vancouver	16	16	52	47	43	139
Portland	15	17	50	53	43	133

American Conference

Eastern Division

	W	L	GF	GA	Bonus points	Total points
Tampa Bay	19	13	61	50	54	168
Ft. Lauderdale	18	14	61	55	55	163
New England	18	14	54	56	46	154
Philadelphia	10	22	42	68	38	98

Central Division

	W	L	GF	GA	Bonus points	Total points
Chicago	21	11	80	50	61	187
Houston	14	18	56	69	46	130
Detroit	14	18	51	52	45	129
Memphis	14	18	49	57	42	126

Western Division

	W	L	GF	GA	Bonus points	Total points
Edmonton	17	15	58	51	47	149
California	15	17	61	67	54	144
San Diego	16	16	53	51	44	140
San Jose	9	23	45	68	41	95

Total points: Win - 6 points, Loss - 0 points. Bonus points: one point is awarded for each goal scored up to a maximum of 3 per team per game. No bonus points are given for goals scored in overtime or the Shootout.

Playoffs

National Conference

Quarter finals

Seattle 2, Vancouver 1.
Seattle 3, Vancouver 1.
Washington 1, Los Angeles 0.
Los Angeles 2, Washington 1.
Los Angeles 2, Washington 0.
Dallas 1, Minnesota 0.
Dallas 2, Minnesota 0.
New York 3, Tulsa 1.
New York 8, Tulsa 1.

Semi-finals

Los Angeles 3, Seattle 0.
Seattle 4, Los Angeles 0.
Los Angeles 2, Seattle 1.
New York 3, Dallas 2.
Dallas 3, New York 0.
New York 3, Dallas 0.

Finals

New York 2, Los Angeles 1.
New York 3, Los Angeles 1.

American Conference

Quarter finals

San Diego 2, Chicago 1.
Chicago 3, San Diego 2.
San Diego 2, Chicago 1.
Tampa Bay 1, New England 0.
Tampa Bay 4, New England 0.
Edmonton 2, Houston 1.
Houston 1, Edmonton 0.
Edmonton 1, Houston 0.
Ft. Lauderdale 2, California 1.
California 2, Ft. Lauderdale 0.
Ft. Lauderdale 1, California 0.

Semi-finals

San Diego 6, Tampa Bay 3.
Tampa Bay 6, San Diego 0.
San Diego 2, Tampa Bay 1.
Ft. Lauderdale 1, Edmonton 0.
Edmonton 3, Ft. Lauderdale 2.
Ft. Lauderdale 2, Edmonton 0.

Finals

Ft. Lauderdale 2, San Diego 1.
San Diego 4, Ft. Lauderdale 2.
Ft. Lauderdale 2, San Diego 0.

Championship

New York 3, Ft. Lauderdale 0.

Leading Scorers

Player, team	Goals	Assists	Points
Giorgio Chinaglia, New York	32	13	77
Karl-Heinz Granitza, Chicago	19	26	64
Roger Davies, Seattle	25	11	61
Luis Fernando, Los Angeles	28	4	60
Alan Green, Washington	25	9	59
Laurie Abrahams, California	17	15	49
Julio Romero, New York	14	19	47
Arno Steffenhagen, Chicago	15	15	45
Ace Ntsoelengoe, Minnesota	13	17	43
Edi Kirschner, Edmonton	15	12	42
Teofilo Cubillas, Ft. Lauderdale	14	14	42

Leading Goalkeepers

Player, team	*Minutes	Goals against	Average
Jack Brand, Seattle	2,975	30	0.91
Hubert Birkenmeier, New York	2,993	38	1.14
Bruce Grobbelaar, Vancouver	2,117	28	1.19
Alfredo Anhielo, Los Angeles	2,715	40	1.32
Volkmar Gross, San Diego	2,810	43	1.38
Phil Parkes, Chicago	2,784	43	1.39
Jim Brown, Detroit	3,005	47	1.407
Tino Lettieri, Minnesota	2,806	44	1.411
Winston DuBose, Tampa Bay	2,845	47	1.49
Bob Stetler, Memphis	2,481	42	1.52

*At least 1,440 minutes needed to qualify

NASL Leading Scorers

Year	Player, team	G	A	Pts
1967	Yanko Daucik, Toronto	20	8	48
1968	John Kowalik, Chicago	30	9	69
1969	Kaizer Motaung, Atlanta	16	4	36
1970	Kirk Apostolidis, Dallas	16	3	35
	Carlos Metidieri, Rochester	14	7	35
1971	Carlos Metidieri, Rochester	19	8	46
1972	Randy Horton, New York	9	4	22
1973	Kyle Rote, Jr., Dallas	10	10	30
1974	Paul Child, San Jose	15	6	36
1975	Steven David, Miami	23	6	52
1976	Giorgio Chinaglia, New York	19	11	49
1977	Steven David, Los Angeles	26	6	58
1978	Giorgio Chinaglia, New York	34	11	79
1979	Oscar Fabbiani, Tampa Bay	25	8	58
1980	Giorgio Chinaglia, New York	32	13	77

NASL Leading Goalkeepers

Year	Player, team	GP	G	Avg
1967	Mirko Stojanovic, Oakland	29	29	1.00
1968	Ataulfo Sanchez, San Diego	22	19	0.93
1969	Manfred Kammerer, Atlanta	14	15	1.07
1970	Lincoln Phillips, Washington	22	21	0.95
		Minutes		
1971	Mirko Stojanovic, Dallas	1,359	11	0.79
1972	Ken Cooper, Dallas	1,260	12	0.86
1973	Bob Rigby, Philadelphia	1,157	8	0.62

Year	Player, team	Minutes	G	Avg
1974	Barry Watling, Seattle	1,800	16	0.80
1975	Shep Messing, Boston	1,639	17	0.93
1976	Tony Chursky, Seattle	1,981	20	0.91
1977	Ken Cooper, Dallas	2,100	21	0.90
1978	Phil Parkes, Vancouver	2,650	28	0.95
1979	Phil Parkes, Vancouver	2,705	29	0.96
1980	Jack Brand, Seattle	2,975	30	0.91

NASL Champions

Year Champion

1967—Oakland Clippers (NPSL)
1967—Los Angeles Wolves (USA)
1968—Atlanta Chiefs
1969—Kansas City Spurs
1970—Rochester Lancers
1971—Dallas Tornado
1972—New York Cosmos
1973—Philadelphia Atoms
1974—Los Angeles Aztecs
1975—Tampa Bay Rowdies
1976—Toronto Metros
1977—New York Cosmos
1978—New York Cosmos
1979—Vancouver Whitecaps
1980—New York Cosmos

NASL All-Star Team in 1980

First team	Position	Second team
Phil Parkes, Chicago	Goalkeeper	Jack Brand, Seattle
Carlos Alberto, New York	Defender	Mihalj Keri, Los Angeles
Mike Connell, Tampa Bay	Defender	Peter Nogly, Edmonton
Rudi Krol, Vancouver	Defender	Wim Rijsbergen, New York
Bruce Rioch, Seattle	Defender	John Ryan, Seattle
Franz Beckenbauer, New York	Midfielder	Alan Hudson, Seattle
Vladislav Bogicevic, New York	Midfielder	Johan Neeskens, New York
Teofilo Cubillas, Ft. Lauderdale	Midfielder	Arno Steffenhagen, Chicago
Giorgio Chinaglia, New York	Forward	Luis Fernando, Los Angeles
Johan Cruyff, Washington	Forward	Karl-Heinz Granitza, Chicago
Roger Davies, Seattle	Forward	Steve Wegerle, Tampa Bay

The World Cup

The World Cup, emblematic of International soccer supremacy, was won by Argentina on June 25, 1978, with a 3-1 overtime victory over the Netherlands. By winning the championship, Argentina became the fifth host country to emerge as champion since the competition began in 1930. Winners and sites of previous World Cup play follow:

Year	Winner	Site
1930	Uruguay	Uruguay
1934	Italy	Italy
1938	Italy	France
1950	Uruguay	Brazil
1954	W. Germany	Switzerland
1958	Brazil	Sweden
1962	Brazil	Chile
1966	England	England
1970	Brazil	Mexico City
1974	W. Germany	W. Germany
1978	Argentina	Argentina

World Pocket Billiards Champions

1931	Ralph Greenleaf
1932	Ralph Greenleaf
1933	Erwin Rudolph
1934	Erwin Rudolph
1935	Andrew Ponzi
1936	James Caras
1937	Ralph Greenleaf
1938	James Caras
1939	James Caras
1940	Andrew Ponzi
1941	Willie Mosconi, Erwin Rudolph
1942	Irving Crane
1943	Andrew Ponzi
1944	Willie Mosconi
1945	Willie Mosconi
1946	Irving Crane
1947	Willie Mosconi
1948	Willie Mosconi
1949	James Caras
1950	Willie Mosconi
1951	Willie Mosconi
1952	Willie Mosconi
1953	Willie Mosconi
1954	none
1955	Irving Crane, Willie Mosconi
1956-62	none
1963	Luther Lassiter
1964	Luther Lassiter, Arthur Cranfield
1965	Joe Balsis
1966	Luther Lassiter
1967	Luther Lassiter
1968	Irving Crane
1969	Ed Kelly
1970	Irving Crane
1971	Ray Martin
1972	Irving Crane
1973	Lou Butera
1974	Ray Martin
1975	none
1976	Larry Lisciotti
1977	Allen Hopkins
1978	Ray Martin
1979	Mike Sigel
1980	Nick Varner

Balukas Wins Women's Title

Jean Balukas of Brooklyn, N.Y. won the women's world's open pocket billiards championship by defeating Billie Billing on Aug. 24, 1980 in New York City. Miss Balukas has lost only 2 games to women in the past 8 years.

U.S. Outdoor Diving Championships in 1980

Greg Louganis won the men's one-meter, 3-meter, and 10-meter titles at the U.S. outdoor championships in Bartlesville, Okla. He is the first diver to sweep the 3 titles in successive years.

The women's titles were won by Kelly McCormick (one-meter), Chris Seufert (3-meter), and Barb Weinstein (10-meter).

CHRONOLOGY OF THE YEAR'S EVENTS

Reported Month by Month in 3 Categories: National, International, and General — Nov. 1, 1979, to Nov. 1, 1980

NOVEMBER

National

Carter Rescue Plan for Chrysler Proposed — The Carter Administration, **Nov. 1,** proposed a $1.5 billion federal loan guarantee plan for Chrysler Corp. The proposal was for double the amount that Chrysler had requested **Oct. 17.** Treasury Secretary G. William Miller said the proposed aid was greater than requested because of Chrysler's record 3d quarter losses (reported **Oct. 30** as $460.6 million) and because of the "reduced level of activity in the (automobile) industry." Even though the government was opposed to direct intervention in private enterprise, Miller said, the Administration supported the aid because of the economic importance of Chrysler and the automobile industry. The proposal would require Chrysler to raise an additional $1.5 billion from new private loans without Federal guarantees. In addition, the company had to provide the government with a 4-year plan showing in detail how it would return to profitability in that period. Chrysler would have until Dec. 31, 1990, to repay the guaranteed loans completely. A final version of the Chrysler aid bill passed both the House and the Senate **Dec. 21.** The bill offered federal loan guarantees only on the condition that banks, unions, suppliers, dealers, and state and local governments which had a stake in the company first provided "adequate assurances" that they would contribute $2 billion in loans or in wage and other concessions to help Chrysler survive. On **Jan. 7,** Pres. Carter signed the bill.

Candidates for Presidential Nomination — Four more candidates entered the races for nomination as candidates in the 1980 presidential election. Sen. Howard Baker Jr., the Senate Republican leader since 1977, formally declared his presidential candidacy **Nov. 1** and stressed that his 13 years in Congress made him the one who "knows Washington enough to change Washington." After declining appeals to run for the presidency in the last 3 campaigns, Sen. Edward Kennedy entered the 1980 race **Nov. 7.** As a challenger to Pres. Carter within the Democratic Party, Kennedy said that he felt "compelled by events and my commitment to public life" to enter the race and he asserted that the contest would strengthen rather than divide the party. Democratic Gov. Edmund Brown Jr. of Cal. formally announced his candidacy, **Nov. 8,** with a statement charging a lack of presidential leadership. The Republican front-runner in the polls, former Cal. Governor Ronald Reagan, opened his campaign, **Nov. 13,** with a nationally televised speech in New York City. Reagan called for a new North American economic and military partnership with Mexico and Canada to take full advantage of the assets of the continent. On **Nov. 17,** Reagan received 36 percent of the vote in a presidential straw poll at the Florida Republican Convention to John Connally's 27 percent and George Bush's 21 percent.

5 Killed at Anti-Klan Rally — Ku Klux Klan members, **Nov. 3,** shot 4 demonstrators to death at an anti-Klan march in Greensboro, N.C. A 5th person died of gunshot wounds the next day; 8 others were wounded in the gunfight. The shooting occurred when carloads of Klansmen arrived at a racially mixed anti-Klan rally of about 100 persons sponsored by the Workers' Viewpoint Organization, also known as the Communist Workers Party, U.S.A. The Klansmen shouted obscenities and racial epithets at the protesters and the marchers responded by beating on the Klansmen's cars with sticks. About a dozen persons jumped from their cars and started shooting into the crowd. The demonstrators returned the fire; the battle lasted about 2 minutes until the police arrived. Fourteen Klansmen charged in the shooting were held without bond **Nov. 5.** A national organizer of the Workers' Viewpoint group was also charged with inciting to riot based on the flyers advertising the march that invited the Klan to a showdown. Police considered the Klan motive for the killings to be vengeance for a July 8, 1979, raid on a Klan rally in China Grove, N.C. for which the Workers' Viewpoint group had claimed responsibility.

Carter Hospital Cost Plan Rejected — Pres. Carter's plan for standby mandatory controls on hospital cost increases, one of his top domestic priorities, was rejected, **Nov. 15,** by the House of Representatives. The House adopted, by a vote of 234-166, an amendment by Rep. Richard Gephardt (D, Mo.) which replaced mandatory controls with a purely voluntary attempt to hold down hospital costs. Opponents of Carter's plan claimed that Federal controls would impair the quality of health care and burden hospitals with more bureaucracy. They also questioned whether the plan would effectively reduce costs.

Meany Bids Farewell to AFL-CIO — George Meany, **Nov. 15,** bade farewell to the American Federation of Labor and Congress of Industrial Organizations after leading the 13.6 million-member labor federation since its inception in 1955. At the federation's 13th biennial convention in Washington, the 85-year-old labor leader warned the union delegates to beware of the status quo and urged them to "look constantly to the future." Lane Kirkland, **Nov. 19,** was elected as the 2d president of the AFL-CIO. Secretary-treasurer of the organization for the past 10 years, Kirkland implored unions outside the federation to rejoin the fold. On **Jan. 11,** Meany died.

Troops Exposed to Herbicide — Thousands of U.S. troops were deployed in areas of South Vietnam that had been sprayed with Agent Orange herbicide, the General Accounting Office reported **Nov. 24.** The Defense Department had previously denied such assertions. The report claimed that at least 5,900 marines were within one-third of a mile of the sprayed areas during and shortly after defoliation missions during the Vietnam war. The Defense Department's contention that no U.S. troops were in the sprayed areas until at least a month had passed and the herbicide had decomposed, was labeled "inaccurate" by the GAO study. About 4,800 former Vietnam servicemen had asked the Veterans Administration for treatment of what the veterans believed were health problems, such as cancer, impotence, and personality changes, that were related to contact with the herbicide. Agent Orange contains dioxin, a highly toxic chemical. The Defense Department, Veterans Administration, and Dow Chemical Co., which manufactured the herbicide, denied that there was any firm evidence linking Agent Orange to illnesses. On **Dec. 12,** Dr. Lyndon Lee of the Veterans Administration disclosed the results of laboratory tests that for the first time found traces of dioxin in veterans exposed to Agent Orange. The amounts ranged from 3 to 57 parts per trillion, amounts so small, said Dr. Lee, that it was impossible to place any significance on the findings.

Prices Up, Jobs Down — The Labor Department announced, **Nov. 27,** that consumer prices rose by 1 percent in Oct. or 13.2 percent at an adjusted annual rate. Leading the increase was housing costs which climbed 1.5 percent in Oct. after the **Oct. 6** austerity moves of the Federal Reserve System. The Bureau of Labor Statistics, **Nov. 2,** had reported that unemployment had only risen .2 percent to 6 percent in Oct.

International

Coup in Bolivia — Bolivia's 3-month-old civilian government, the first in a decade, was overthrown, **Nov. 1,** by troops loyal to Col. Alberto Natusch Busch. The soldiers surrounded the Presidential Palace and killed 6 persons in a crowd of protesters. A labor federation, **Nov. 2,** called for a general strike, which closed down the country's crucial tin mines and most of the stores in the cities. The same day, the U.S. cut off all assistance to the country, except for its Food for Peace aid. When Bolivia's political parties refused to support Col. Natusch, the military leader closed the Congress. By **Nov. 16,** over 200 persons were killed in continuing street battles. Natusch, **Nov. 14,** was forced to close the banks to halt the flow of money out of the country. After gaining assurances that ousted President Walter Guevara Arze would not be reinstated, Natusch resigned. The Bolivian Congress, **Nov. 16,** elected Lidia Gueiler Tejada as interim president until elections scheduled for May 4. The struggle between military and civilian authority resumed, **Nov. 23,** when the new president ordered the army commander to step down and he refused. The commander acquiesced to the order only after securing the right to name his successor.

Japanese Premier Reelected — Masayoshi Ohira, **Nov. 6,** was reelected premier of Japan by 138 votes to 121 for former Prime Minister Takeo Fukuda at a special session of the House of Representatives, the lower house of the Diet. It was the first time in Japanese parliamentary history that 2 candidates of the same party had contested the premiership.

Palestinian Mayor Arrested by Israel — Israeli military authorities, **Nov. 11,** arrested Mayor Bassam Shaka of the West Bank city of Nablus on charges of supporting terrorism. The incident began the week before when the Israeli newspaper Haaretz published an account of a private conversation between Shaka and the Israeli military governor, Maj. Gen. Danny Matt. The account quoted the Mayor as having justified the terrorist raid on Israel in Mar. 1978 in which 35 civilians were killed. Another newspaper quoted Shaka as saying: "Operations like these, if they occur, are only a reaction to other [Israeli] acts. As long as there is occupation and killing, you can expect many operations of this type." At the time of his arrest, Shaka was served with a deportation order, but the Israeli Supreme Court stayed the execution of the order temporarily. All 25 Arab mayors in the occupied territories of the West Bank and the Gaza Strip submitted their resignations, **Nov. 14,** when the Ministerial Defense Committee of Israel ruled that the expulsion of the Nablus mayor should go ahead as ordered. Fearing that the incident might inflict damage on attempts to include Palestinian leaders in the autonomy plan being negotiated under the Egyptian-Israeli peace treaty, the U.S. and Egypt urged Israel to drop the case. On **Dec. 5,** the Israeli Cabinet voted to release the mayor.

British Art Historian Named as Spy — Prime Minister Margaret Thatcher notified the House of Commons, **Nov. 15,** that Anthony Blunt, a former curator of Queen Elizabeth's art collection who was knighted in 1956, had been a Soviet agent, the long-sought "fourth man" in the Burgess-Maclean spy case of the 1950's and 1960's. The disclosure came after the publication of a book, *The Climate of Treason* by Andrew Boyle, which contended that there had been 4th and 5th members of a famous spy ring of upper-class Britons. Although the book did not name Blunt as part of the ring, it provided information which aroused suspicions about the distinguished art historian that led to the disclosure. Blunt was stripped of his knighthood the day of the announcement. A political uproar racked Britain after the announcement when it was revealed that Blunt had been warned by the government, as a "common courtesy" according to a spokesman, that his secret past was going to be made public and he went into hiding. Government officials maintained that Blunt was not a fugitive since he had been granted immunity from prosecution in 1964 in exchange for his confession and other information about Soviet espionage activities. On **Nov. 20,** Blunt emerged from hiding and admitted that he had made "an appalling mistake" in agreeing to spy for the Soviet Union 40 years ago.

Cambodia Famine — Thailand, **Nov. 18,** agreed to open its borders to a large flow of Cambodian refugees from among as many as 560,000 camped on the Cambodian side of the border. Political obstacles continued to foil attempts to remedy the food and refugee problem with Cambodia. Three U.S. Senators, **Oct. 21-23,** had toured the Thai camps and, **Oct. 24,** met with Cambodian officials. They proposed to the Cambodians that food be trucked from Thailand to starving people in Cambodia. Calling the American bid a "maneuver by the imperialists and international reactionaries" to provide assistance to the guerrilla Pol Pot forces, the Vietnamese-backed People's Revolutionary Council of Cambodia rejected the proposal **Oct. 27.** Rosalynn Carter, wife of U.S. Pres. Carter, visited Thailand, **Nov. 8-9,** to inspect refugee camps. A report from Bangkok, **Nov. 25,** said that food reaching Cambodia was still far below the level

Iranian Militants Seize U.S. Embassy and Hold Hostages

About 500 Iranian militants seized the U.S. embassy, **Nov. 4,** and took about 90 hostages including some 65 Americans. The students vowed to stay in the embassy and not release their captives until deposed Shah Mohammed Riza Pahlevi, who was undergoing medical treatment in New York, was returned to Iran by the U.S. to stand trial for alleged torture, murder, and robbery.

The shah had flown to New York from his exile in Mexico, **Oct. 22,** for treatment of cancer of the lymph nodes and a gallstone ailment. For the past 8 months former Secretary of State Henry Kissinger and David Rockefeller, the chairman of the Chase Manhattan Bank, had been periodically pressing the U.S. government to admit the shah as an old friend of the country. As reports of the shah's deteriorating health filtered back to Washington from Mexico, the shah's place of asylum, the Carter Administration decided to temporarily admit the shah for humanitarian reasons. U.S. officials involved in the decision thought that the shah would die within a few days, according to the *New York Times,* and had assurances from Iranian Foreign Minister Ibrahim Yazdi that the Iranian government would protect the U.S. embassy as it had last February when the embassy was attacked.

On **Nov. 1,** the inspirational leader of the Iranian revolution and leading religious figure, Ayatollah Khomeini, had appealed to students over the radio to observe the anniversary of student protests that occurred Nov. 4, 1978, and "expand with all their might their attacks against the United States and Israel, so they may force the United States to return the deposed and cruel shah." The militants responded with the takeover.

Iran's civil government under Prime Minister Mehdi Bazargan initially promised to help in negotiating the hostages' release but, after Khomeini's advisers supported the occupation of the embassy, Bazargan and his cabinet decided to resign, **Nov. 6.**

The U.S. took a series of steps to respond to the crisis. On **Nov. 7,** U.S. emissaries with known sympathies for the Iranian revolution were sent to Iran with a personal letter from Pres. Carter, but Khomeini refused to receive them. Fearing clashes between American and Iranian demonstrators in the U.S., Carter, **Nov. 10,** ordered the deportation of Iranian students illegally in the U.S. Carter, **Nov. 12,** suspended all Iranian oil imports to the U.S. and, **Nov. 14,** froze all official Iranian assets in American banks. Thirteen women and black hostages were released, 3 on **Nov. 19** and 10 on **Nov. 20,** and the last 5 non-American hostages were released **Nov. 22.** The U.S., **Nov. 20,** warned that it might take military action if the remaining American hostages were not released. A 6-ship U.S. task force was ordered to join another 8-ship group in the Indian Ocean to reinforce the American presence in the region.

On **Nov. 18,** Khomeini threatened that some of the embassy personnel would be tried as spies. On **Nov. 22,** he said that he took "great joy" in the sacking of the U.S. embassy in Pakistan the previous day.

Citing a "serious threat to international peace and security," UN Secretary General Kurt Waldheim, **Nov. 25,** requested an "urgent meeting" of the Security Council to deal with the Iranian crisis. Iranian Acting Foreign Minister Abolhassan Bani-Sadr had been attempting to find an international forum to publicly investigate the charges against the shah, but hopes for a diplomatic solution were dashed when Khomeini, **Nov. 27,** attacked plans for a UN Security Council meeting as being part of a U.S. plan with a predetermined conclusion. Bani-Sadr was dismissed, **Nov. 28,** and replaced by Sadegh Ghotbzadeh.

The shah had a gallstone removed from his bile duct **Nov. 26.** Mexico unexpectedly announced, **Nov. 29,** that he would not be allowed to return there. The U.S., **Nov. 30,** said that the shah was expected to leave when his treatment was completed and a behind-the-scenes search was begun to find the deposed ruler another refuge.

needed to effectively combat starvation.

Mecca Mosque Seized, U.S. Embassy in Pakistan Stormed — In an apparent attempt to overthrow the Saudi Arabian government, several hundred members of an ultra-conservative Islamic tribe, **Nov. 20,** seized the Grand Mosque in Mecca, the holiest site in the Moslem world. It was dawn when they attacked and 50,000 worshippers had assembled for prayers on the first day of Muharram, the opening month of the Islamic new year, and the start of the Islamic 15th century. Contrary to early reports that some of them had been taken as hostages, the worshippers managed to scramble to freedom before the fanatics barricaded themselves inside the huge mosque. The insurgents demanded the abolition of television, an end to women working in public and a ban on soccer, all recent developments in the modernizing country of Saudi Arabia. A wave of anti-American feeling jolted the Moslem world in the wake of the Nov. 4 seizure of U.S. hostages in Iran and inaccurate reports, disseminated by Iran, about U.S. involvement in the mosque seizure. A mob of Pakistanis, **Nov. 21,** stormed the U.S. embassy in Islamabad, burned it partially, and killed 2 U.S. servicemen and 2 Parkistani clerks. The 90 other members of the embassy staff were rescued from the roof by Pakistani helicopters after being trapped for hours in a vault which had been used as a refuge. Four other U.S. missions in Pakistan were damaged by demonstrators and protests were staged in Turkey, India, and Bangladesh. On **Nov. 26,** the U.S. told its embassies in about 10 Moslem countries to evacuate "voluntarily" dependents, nonessential diplomats and private businessmen. After suspending a news blackout it had imposed, Saudi Arabia identified the occupants of the mosque as mostly members of the Oteiba tribe from the southern part of the country, although non-Saudis also participated in the attack. Fierce fighting between Saudi Arabian troops and the Islamic militants continued sporadically until complete control of the mosque was regained **Dec. 4.** More than 130 people were reported killed in the battles. On **Jan. 9,** 63 men involved in the seizure were executed.

Mountbatten Killer Convicted — A 31-year-old Irishman, Thomas McMahon, was found guilty, **Nov. 23,** of the murder of Earl Mountbatten of Burma on Aug. 27, 1979, and was sentenced to life in prison. McMahon, according to police, was the leading expert in remote-controlled bombs in the provisional wing of the Irish Republican Army.

General

Emory Univ. Given $100 Million — In a gift that was believed to be the largest single donation in the history of U.S. philanthropy, Robert Woodruff, the retired chairman of Coca-Cola Corp., gave Emory Univ. $100 million, it was announced **Nov. 8.** The gift made Emory's endowment, $270 million, the nation's 11th largest.

Chlorine Gas Forces Evacuation in Canada — Almost 250,000 people were forced to evacuate Mississauga, Ontario, Canada's 10th largest city, when a train laden with toxic chemicals derailed **Nov. 11.** A tank car carrying chlorine gas was ruptured, releasing tons of the deadly gas into the air. Other cars filled with propane gas exploded and burned, causing officials to speed the evacuation out of fear that the intense heat from the fire might crack the chlorine tank car and release the gas all at once. "It's been an absolute miracle," commented Hazel McCallion, Mississauga's Mayor, on the lack of fatalities or serious injuries.

Airlines Fined for Improper Maintenance — The Federal Aviation Administration, **Nov. 16,** announced that American Airlines had paid a $500,000 fine for improper maintenance of DC-10 jumbo jets. An American Airlines DC-10 had crashed May 25, 1979 in Chicago and killed 273 people due to the loss of an engine-pylon assembly that had been improperly installed. Announced simultaneously was the payment of a $100,000 fine by Continental Airlines for some of the same violations. On **Nov. 7,** the F.A.A. imposed a record fine of $1.5 million against Braniff International Airways for conducting hundreds of flights with planes that were allegedly "unairworthy".

Footprints by Ancestor of Man Found — Along the northeast shore of Lake Turkana, Kenya, 7 footprints that might be the oldest made by a direct ancestor of man were found by a scientific team led by Drs. Anna Behrensmeyer and Leo LaPorte, it was announced **Nov. 18.** The 1.5 million-year-old prints were the oldest recorded from the period when the genus of modern man, Homo erectus, existed.

Scientists Explain Color Vision — The 100-year-old mystery of color vision was reported solved, **Nov. 28,** by Prof. Koji Nakanishi and co-workers at Columbia University. According to the scientists, retinal, the basic substance of vision, attaches itself to cone cells or rod cells in the retina of the eye. The three kinds of cone cells are sensitive to red, blue, or green; the rod cells are sensitive to black and white. All other colors and tones are combinations of these. Each type of cell binds the retinal with a different protein, each of which surrounds the retinal with a different pattern of electrical charges. Retinal's sensitivity to different wavelengths of light is explained by the number and location of those electrical charges. The wave length of blue light, for example, disrupts the specific pattern of charges in the blue cone cells and causes the cells to send a signal to the brain. The researchers suggested it was theoretically possible now to find a cure for color blindness.

Pope Visits Turkey — Pope John Paul II flew to Turkey, **Nov. 28,** to work toward the reconciliation of the Roman Catholic and Eastern Orthodox churches. On **Nov. 30,** the pope and Dimitrios I, the Orthodox Ecumenical Patriarch, celebrated together the feast day of St. Andrew, the Patron of the Orthodox Church, and announced the formation of a joint commission consisting of prelates and theologians of the 2 churches to discuss the remaining theological disagreements between them. The pope also made an appeal to Christians for greater understanding of Islam as a monotheistic religion that shared many beliefs and moral values with Christianity.

Air Crash in Antarctica — In the 4th worst disaster in aviation history, a New Zealand DC-10 on a sightseeing flight over Antarctica crashed, **Nov. 29,** into a 12,400-foot mountain near McMurdo Station, killing all 257 people on board. The 3d fatal DC-10 crash in 1979 was apparently caused by a navigational error by the pilot who steered the plane around the side of the mountain that was notorious for high winds.

Disasters — At least 15 crewmen from the Liberian tanker Burmah Agate were reported dead and 17 reported missing, after the tanker was rammed by a freighter, **Nov. 1,** about 5 miles south of Galveston, Texas . . . A fire swept through a boarding home for the elderly and retarded in Pioneer, Ohio, **Nov. 11,** killing at least 14 persons . . . Mudbrick villages near Meshed, Iran, were struck, **Nov. 14,** by a powerful earthquake and at least 248 persons were killed . . . A strong earthquake, measuring 6.4 on the Richter scale, rocked Pereira, Colombia, **Nov. 23,** and killed 60 persons . . . A Pakistani jetliner carrying Moslem pilgrims returning to Pakistan from Mecca crashed, **Nov. 26,** about 30 miles north of Jeddah, Saudi Arabia, killing at least 156 persons . . .

DECEMBER

National

Terrorists Ambush Navy Bus — Two U.S. sailors were killed and 10 others wounded, **Dec. 3,** when a group of men ambushed a Navy bus carrying 18 sailors to work at the Sabana Secca Navy Communications Center near San Juan, Puerto Rico. Three Puerto Rican nationalist groups claimed responsibility for the attack. The last fatal attack by terrorists against U.S. military personnel in Puerto Rico was in 1970. The attack began when a pickup truck forced the bus to the side of the road. A group of men jumped out of a nearby van and opened fire in a barrage that left the bus with more than 40 bullet holes. A communique found later in the day said that the attack was in retaliation for the deaths of 3 Puerto Rican nationalists, one found hanged in his prison cell in Florida, **Nov. 11,** and 2 killed by the Puerto Rican police July 25, 1978.

Carter Declares Candidacy — Pres. Carter, **Dec. 4,** officially declared himself a candidate for re-election. In a paid political announcement broadcast on TV, Carter said that he would have deferred his announcement if it had not been for the filing deadlines set by the election laws. Due to the Iranian crisis, Carter said, he would continue to postpone his campaign travels in order to deal with "an ever-changing situation of the greatest sensitivity and importance." On **Dec. 2,** Sen. Edward Kennedy, Carter's major rival for the

Democratic nomination, said in a TV interview that the deposed Shah Mohammed Riza Pahlevi "ran one of the most violent regimes in the history of mankind" and had stolen "umpteen billions of dollars from his country." Political opponents criticized Kennedy for making the remarks which they thought might endanger the 50 Americans held hostage. In a dramatic turnaround, a Gallup poll reported, **Dec. 11,** that, for the first time in 2 years, Carter led Kennedy in a nationwide survey of Democrats. Out of the sample of 530 Democrats, 48 percent chose Carter and 40 percent chose Kennedy for presidential nominee. On **Dec. 28,** Carter withdrew from a forum with his political rivals for the Democratic presidential nomination that had been scheduled for **Jan. 7** in Des Moines prior to the Iowa precinct caucus on **Jan. 21.** The President said the hostage crisis in Iran made an appearance at a partisan political event inappropriate. Gov. Edmund Brown Jr. (Cal., D.) and Kennedy charged that Carter had withdrawn in order to keep attention away from them and away from economic issues.

Cambodian Food Aid Delayed — The U.S., **Dec. 6,** accused the Phnom Penh government and Vietnam of deliberately blocking the distribution of relief supplies in Cambodia. UN relief official Henry Labouisse, **Dec. 13,** said that supplies were piling up in warehouses in Cambodia, but blamed delays on lack of transport within the country. The International Red Cross, **Dec. 17,** reported that little of the 33,000 tons of supplies that it had delivered had been distributed and warned that it would discontinue its relief if the delay did not end. The director of Oxfam's relief program said, **Dec. 20,** that he did not see any lack of will on the part of the government there, but that food distribution was hindered by technical and logistical problems.

Carter Dismisses NRC Chief — Pres. Carter, **Dec. 7,** dismissed Joseph Hendrie as chairman of the Nuclear Regulatory Commission in response to the report of the President's Commission on the Accident at Three Mile Island which was released **Oct. 30.** Among the recommendations of the President's Commission was the abolishment of the NRC and its replacement by an agency within the executive branch headed by one executive rather than a 5-man commission. Carter decided to retain the NRC, but he promised to send to Congress early next year a reorganization plan to strengthen the role of its chairman. Carter said that he would create a 5-member advisory committee to monitor the NRC, order a federal inspector at every reactor site as quickly as possible, and ask Congress to add about $50 million to the NRC's budget. Carter reaffirmed his support of nuclear power and called upon the NRC to end in at least 6 months its temporary ban on licensing the construction and operation of atomic reactors. On **Dec. 26,** a report by a group investigating the Three Mile Island accident for the NRC tentatively recommended that serious consideration be given to closing any reactor whose operator is unable to develop plans to evacuate everybody living within a 30-mile radius of the reactor.

Carter Calls for 5-Year Increase in Defense Budget — Pres. Carter, **Dec. 12,** proposed a 4.5 percent annual increase in the military budget over the next 5 years, compared with the 3 percent "real" annual increases that he had sought for the previous 3 years. He said that he would seek Congressional approval of a military budget of $157 billion in appropriations for fiscal 1981. To explain his request, Carter cited recent events in Iran as a "vivid reminder" of America's need for military strength. In addition, Carter mentioned that the Soviet Union had been increasing its real military spending by 3 or 4 percent a year for nearly 20 years while U.S. military spending had "declined in real terms every year from 1968 through 1976."

Senate Passes 'Windfall' Oil Tax — The Senate, **Dec. 17,** approved a tax on the "windfall" profits of the oil industry that would channel $178 billion from the oil industry to the government in the next 11 years. Designed to tax profits resulting from oil price decontrol, the 38% average tax was believed to be the largest single tax ever imposed on an industry. On **June 28,** the House had passed a similar bill that set an average tax rate of about 60% on windfall profits.

Prices Up, Economic Activity Declines — The Bureau of Labor Statistics, **Dec. 21,** reported that the Consumer Price Index increased 1 percent in Nov., the 11th consecutive monthly rise of about 1 percent. Housing, cars, and public transportation price rises were considered the driving forces behind the Nov. rise in the index, according to the *New York Times.* On **Dec. 31,** the Commerce Department reported that the composite index of leading indicators dropped 1.3 percent in November. After a 1.4 percent decline in Oct., the Nov. figure made the 2-month decline the most severe since the 1974-75 recession. On **Dec. 7,** the Labor Department reported that the unemployment rate for November was 5.8 percent, down only slightly from the month before.

International

S. Korean Martial Law Head Arrested by Army Rebels — Gen. Chung Seung Hwa, Martial Law Commander and Army Chief of Staff of South Korea, was arrested, **Dec. 12,** along with at least 16 other top officers, by a group of generals led by Maj. Gen. Chon Too Hwan, the chief of the Army Security Command and the head of the investigation into the assassination of President Park Chung Hee on Oct. 26. At least 5 persons, including 4 of Chung's guards, were killed in a shootout before the arrest. Official South Korean accounts said that Chung was suspected of taking part in Park's assassination. On **Dec. 15,** the confessed assassin of Park, Kim Jae Kyu, said in court that he had planned the killing alone. On **Dec. 20,** Kim and 6 other men were sentenced to death for the assassination. Chung Seung Hwa was found guilty of having willfully delayed the arrest of Kim Jae Kyu and was sentenced, **Mar. 13,** to a 10-year prison term.

NATO Agrees to Install Missiles — The members of the North Atlantic Treaty Alliance, with the exception of France and Greece, agreed, **Dec. 12,** to install 572 medium-range nuclear missiles in Europe by 1983. The Netherlands and Belgium said that they would not agree to accept their quotas of 48 missiles each until negotiations for arms control were tried again and there was no progress. The missiles would be the first nuclear weapons in Europe capable of hitting targets within the Soviet Union. Accompanying the decision was an offer from the allies to limit their missiles' installation if the Russians agreed to negotiate limits on Soviet missiles targeted on Western Europe. The move was in response to a continuing Soviet buildup that most recently had deployed highly accurate and mobile SS-20 missiles capable of delivering 600 to 700 warheads on Western Europe. In a "peace offensive" prior to the NATO decision, a Soviet tank unit consisting of 18 T-62 tanks and 150 soldiers left East Germany, **Dec. 5,** for the Soviet Union as part of a unilateral withdrawal from East Europe announced **Oct. 6.** After NATO decided to modernize its nuclear force, Tass, the Soviet press agency, said, **Dec. 14,** that the decision "killed the basis for talks on medium-range weapons" in the area and that the Soviet Union was withdrawing its offer to remove some of its forces in East Germany. On **Dec. 13,** NATO's foreign ministers offered to withdraw 13,000 U.S. troops from Central Europe in return for the withdrawal of 30,000 Soviet troops. The new proposal was an attempt by the foreign ministers at the meeting to show that they were as interested in arms limitation as in rearmament, according to the *New York Times.*

Canadian Government Defeated — After only 6 1/2 months in office, the Progressive Conservative government of Prime Minister Joe Clark in Canada ended, **Dec. 14,** after its budget proposal was defeated in the House of Commons. The Social Credit party refused to support the budget because it contained a proposal for an immediate increase in the excise tax on gasoline. Other taxes and a proposed decrease in government spending made the budget unpopular in a political environment that favored a tax cut and the stimulation of the economy. Prime Minister Joe Clark announced immediately that he considered the defeat a vote of no confidence. Observers said that the budget sought to put Canada on the road to self-sufficiency in energy and to reduce the country's budgetary and payments deficits. On **Dec. 18,** the Liberal party drafted former Prime Minister Pierre Elliott Trudeau to lead it in the election scheduled for **Feb. 18.**

OPEC Price Rise — To bring their oil prices into line with other members of the Organization of Petroleum Exporting Countries (OPEC), Saudi Arabia, Venezuela, the United Arab Emirates and Qatar raised their prices by as much as 33 percent **Dec. 13.** The 4 producers had been on the low end of the spectrum of prices and made the change in preparation for the meeting of the cartel's ministers **Dec. 17.** The 4-day meeting in Caracas, Venezuela, was the longest and most divisive in OPEC's history and ended without the members agreeing on prices. OPEC's newly elected president Humberto Calderon Berti said, "Every country will be free to set its own price." Several countries, such as Venezuela, Libya, Indonesia and Iraq, **Dec. 28,** announced price rises of 10 to 15 percent. Experts estimated the aggregate increase in prices for the month at about 8 percent, making the increase for the year of 1979 approximately 80 percent.

Shah Leaves U.S., Iranian Crisis Continues — Former Iranian Shah Mohammed Riza Pahlevi, **Dec. 15,** left the U.S. for Panama, while militant Iranian students continued to hold American hostages in hopes of having the deposed ruler brought to trial. On **Dec. 2,** the shah had flown to a military hospital in Texas to recuperate from his medical treatment in New York. Iranian Foreign Minister Sadegh Ghotbzadeh, **Dec. 16,** said the shah's departure from the U.S. showed that the U.S. had "retreated one step and we have shown the whole world that a dictator and criminal like the shah comes to the point that there is no place for him to live." The student militants holding the hostages had been concentrating on showing how their captives were "spies" unworthy of diplomatic immunity. On **Dec. 1,** they charged 2 of the captive diplomats with being undercover operatives for the Central Intelligence Agency based on a State Dept. cable they said they found in the embassy. Another embassy hostage was accused, **Dec. 6,** of carrying a false Belgian passport. In yet another bid to influence world opinion, the students allowed a hostage U.S. Marine to be interviewed on television **Dec. 10.** International bodies, however, condemned the seizure. A unanimously approved resolution by the UN Security Council, **Dec. 4,** demanded the immediate release of the 50 hostages and their deliverance from Iran. On **Dec. 15,** the International Court of Justice also unanimously demanded the release of the hostages and rejected the Iranian position that the case could not be considered in isolation from the activities of the U.S. in Iran since 1953. Meanwhile, the U.S. pursued its own strategies and attempted to apply increments of pressure on Iran. On **Dec. 11-12,** U.S. Secretary of State Cyrus Vance flew to several major European capitals asking allies to take joint economic action against Iran. In an act of retaliation, Carter, **Dec. 21,** ordered most of the Iranian diplomats in the U.S. to leave the country. Pres. Carter also announced, **Dec. 21,** that he had decided to ask the UN Security Council to impose economic sanctions against Iran. There was opposition to the Iranian government from within the country as well. After a nationwide plebiscite approved, **Dec. 2-3,** a new Islamic constitution, Iran's Kurdistan and Azerbaijan provinces erupted in violence, **Dec. 5-13,** and at least 12 persons were killed and 80 wounded in the Baluchistan-Seistan province **Dec. 20-22.** Other ripples of violence from the continuing crisis included a mob attack on the U.S. Embassy in Libya, **Dec. 2,** and the assassination of the shah's nephew in Paris **Dec. 7.** Ayatollah Khomeini, after the hostages had endured 50 days of confinement, allowed 3 U.S. clergymen to visit the hostages **Dec. 24-25.** In a diplomatic triumph for

Soviet Union Invades Afghanistan

The Soviet Union airlifted, **Dec. 25-26,** at least 5,000 troops to Kabul, Afghanistan, in an effort to shore up that country's Marxist government against increasingly effective Islamic resistance.

Following 4 hours of heavy street fighting in Kabul and the death of President Hafizullah Amin, a new government led by Babrak Karmal was installed, **Dec. 27.** Amin, a Marxist opposed to excessive Soviet influence, had come to power in a coup **Sept. 16,** as had his Marxist predecessor, Nur Mohammad Taraki, on Apr. 27, 1978. Karmal, a former deputy to Taraki in 1978, had been in exile in East Germany and Czechoslovakia after his pro-Moscow faction had been purged from the Afghan government.

Another 15,000 Soviet troops entered the country, **Dec. 28,** following the coup. Two overland routes were used by several mechanized Soviet divisions to cross the border. A brief gun battle broke out in Kabul, **Dec. 31,** between dissident elements of the Afghan army and the Soviets, but the country's capital stayed firmly under Soviet control. Islamic rebels, who had been fighting the Afghan government for 2 years and were thought to control perhaps two-thirds of the countryside, fought skirmishes with Soviet troops at scattered points throughout the country. They were aided and often armed by Afghan army deserters.

On **Dec. 30,** Pravda, the Communist Party newspaper, said the USSR had sent a "limited" military contingent to Afghanistan due to "imperialist interference" in Afghan affairs that was "taking form and acquiring a scale that placed the very existence of the republic in danger."

The Soviet Union justified the intervention on the basis of its defense treaty with Kabul and Article 51 of the UN Charter, which grants any country the right to provide military aid to a member state that appeals for such help. On **Jan. 1,** the Soviet Union said that it had sent the troops to help repel "reactionary bands" armed, trained, and directed by the U.S. and China.

To explain the first Soviet use of ground troops outside Eastern Europe, Western analysts cited the deteriorating situation within Afghanistan and Soviet fears that the Islamic insurrection might spread to its own large Moslem population in Central Asia. Foreign policy reversals, such as the **Dec. 12**th approval of new missile deployments by NATO and the dim prospects for the SALT treaty, were also noted as possible factors inclining the Soviets to accept the risk of the invasion.

In his first public appearance since the coup, Karmal, **Jan. 2,** appealed for public support of the change of governments. He reportedly released 2,000 political prisoners in a conciliatory move **Jan. 6.**

The international repercussions of the invasion were prolonged and widespread. On **Dec. 31,** Pres. Carter accused Soviet Pres. Leonid Brezhnev of "not telling the facts accurately" in a **Dec. 28** cable in which he had told Carter that Afghanistan had invited the Soviets to intervene. Brezhnev's explanation was "obviously false, because the person he claimed invited him in, President Amin, was murdered or assassinated after the Soviets pulled their coup," Carter said. On **Jan. 2,** Carter recalled the U.S. Ambassador in Moscow and said he would ask the Senate to delay consideration of the SALT treaty. Warning that "aggression unopposed becomes a contagious disease," Carter, **Jan. 4,** announced a cutoff of high technology sales to the Soviet Union, a limitation of fishing privileges, a grain embargo, and a deferral of any new cultural and economic exchanges between the U.S. and the Soviet Union.

In a major policy change linked to the Afghan crisis, the U.S. announced, **Jan. 24,** that it was willing to sell military equipment to China for the first time. In the first visit by a U.S. Secretary of Defense to China since 1949, Harold Brown held talks with Chinese military officials, **Jan. 6-9,** and announced, **Jan. 8,** that the U.S. would sell China a ground station for receiving information from the Landsat Earth Resources Satellite, a move with possible military applications.

On **Jan. 7,** the UN Security Council voted 13-2 to condemn the Soviet Union for its invasion and demanded that it withdraw its forces immediately. Widespread disapproval of the Soviet invasion by the Third World was demonstrated, **Jan. 14,** when 78 Third World nations joined a 104-18 vote for a similar resolution in the UN General Assembly. A Conference of Islamic States passed an analogous resolution, **Jan. 29,** and the leaders of France and West Germany issued a statement, **Feb. 5,** calling for the withdrawal of Soviet forces "without delay."

By Jan. 16, an estimated 85,000 Soviet troops were in Afghanistan and international concern was aroused by reports that many of them were in western Afghanistan near the border of Iran.

On **Jan. 20,** Carter stated that if the 1980 Summer Olympics were held in Moscow, the U.S. would boycott them unless the Soviet Union withdrew its troops from Afghanistan by **Feb. 20.** As a clear response to the geopolitical shift that resulted from the Soviet invasion, Carter warned, **Jan. 23,** in his State of the Union address to Congress, that the U.S. was prepared to go to war if necessary to protect the oil-supply routes of the Persian Gulf region.

the U.S., the UN Security Council voted 11-0, **Dec. 31,** to give Iran one week to let the hostages go before deciding on economic sanctions. UN Secretary General Kurt Waldheim left for Teheran the same day in an effort to negotiate the release of the hostages.

Zimbabwe Rhodesia Peace Pacts Signed — The parties to the 7-year Rhodesian civil war signed, **Dec. 21,** a peace agreement in London that participants hoped would end a conflict which had killed over 20,000 people. A tentative agreement on a cease-fire had been reached **Nov. 5** but the difficult negotiations between the embittered parties remained precarious until the signing. The country had returned, **Dec. 12,** to the colonial status under Britain from which it had unilaterally withdrawn in 1965. Lord Soames, the son-in-law of Winston Churchill, became the British governor general of Rhodesia, commissioned to guide the nation to black majority rule. The economic sanctions against the country were ended by Britain **Dec. 12,** the U.S. **Dec. 15,** and the UN Security Council **Dec. 21.** Fears about the difficulty of maintaining a cease-fire were fueled when, on **Dec. 22,** gunmen in a speeding car fired shots at a former home of Robert Mugabe, the Rhodesian guerrilla leader, wounding 2 of his nephews. On **Dec. 28,** Soames set elections for February.

Khmer Rouge Leader Resigns — Khmer Rouge chief Pol Pot, architect of policies which had resulted in the deaths of hundreds of thousands of Cambodians, resigned **Dec. 22** in favor of Khieu Samphan, in an attempt to gain popular and international support for the Khmer Rouge's continuing resistance to the Hanoi-backed regime of Heng Samrin.

General

Youths Killed at Cincinnati Rock Concert — Eleven youths were killed and dozens of others were injured, **Dec. 3,** when thousands of people rushed the doors of the Riverfront Coliseum in Cincinnati to get unreserved seats at a concert given by The Who, a British rock group. According to Cincinnati Mayor John Blackwell, the doors of the coliseum opened an hour later than usual for holders of "first-come, first-served" general admission tickets and the band began final checks on its equipment late, leading some of the crowd to believe that the concert had started without them. Some of the doors that were still closed sprang open after several of their windows were broken by the impatient crowd and in the ensuing stampede to get inside, several people were trampled underfoot. An off-duty police detail of 22 officers and 3 supervisors had been hired to handle the crowd of 18,000. The concert was allowed to proceed as scheduled in order to prevent another panic situation from arising.

Liberal Theologian Censured — The Rev. Hans Kung, a Swiss Roman Catholic theologian, was censured, **Dec. 18,** by the Vatican and barred from teaching. Kung, professor of theology at the University of Tubingen in West Germany and head of its Institute of Ecumenical Research, was the author of *Infallible?—An Inquiry, On Being Christian* and many other works. The condemnation was issued by the Vatican's Sacred Congregation for the Doctrine of the Faith, which said that it had issued on Feb. 15, 1975 a public document stating that some of Prof. Kung's views were "opposed in different degrees to the doctrine of the church" and that Kung had not changed his opinions in the intervening years. The Congregation declared that, since Kung had departed from the "integral truth of Catholic faith" in his writings, he "can no longer be considered a Catholic theologian nor function as such in a teaching role." In addition to being charged with placing the infallibility of the church in doubt, Kung was accused of questioning the Virgin Birth of Jesus and of saying that Jesus never said he believed he was the Son of God. Father Kung, who could continue to be a priest, said that he was "deeply ashamed of my church" which "has now begun to defend human rights" while it "defames and discredits its own theologians." Kung announced that he would fight the censure and liberal theologians organized themselves on his behalf. On **Dec. 30,** the Vatican announced that the pope and 5 West German prelates summoned to Rome, upheld the censure. On **Jan. 2,** Kung's bishop ordered him to leave the theology department of Tubingen University under a 1933 concordat with West Germany that required a Roman Catholic theologian at a state university to have church authorization to teach. Kung, however, continued to teach at the university, drawing even larger audiences.

Pain Control Brain Chemical Found — A brain chemical 200 times more powerful in action than morphine was discovered by scientists at Stanford and Cal Tech, it was reported **Dec. 20.** The chemical, dynorphin, was so potent, specific, and selective in its action on nerve cells that it was thought by the scientists to hold the key to pain control. The chemical was a member of the endorphin group of brain chemicals, first discovered 5 years ago.

Disasters — After rolling out of a station down a steep grade, a runaway train without a crew ran into a stationary passenger train at high speed near Barcelona, Spain, **Dec. 6,** killing at least 14 people and injuring 60 . . . A powerful earthquake struck the Colombia-Ecuador border area, **Dec. 12,** and killed at least 133 persons and injured as many as 2,000 . . . The island of Bali was rocked by an earthquake measuring 6.1 on the Richter scale, **Dec. 18,** killing 19 people and injuring more than 160 . . . At least 43 people were killed, **Dec. 21,** when a bus packed with people going home for Christmas was driven onto a collapsed bridge and crashed into a river in Ilagan, Philippines . . . A fire broke out, **Dec. 27,** in a 150-year old jail in Lancaster County, South Carolina, killing 10 inmates and injuring 8 other persons . . .

JANUARY

National

Govt. Buys Grain to Soften Embargo's Effect — In order to prevent the dumping of large quantities of grain on the market at disastrous prices, the federal government announced, **Jan. 7,** it would buy the contracts for an estimated 14.5 million tons of wheat, corn, and soybeans that were embargoed, **Jan. 4,** from delivery to the Soviet Union. The government's purchase of 2.5 to 3 billion dollars worth of grain would be made with Commodity Credit Corporation funds. Due to the possible market disruption resulting from the grain embargo, the trading in grains for future delivery was suspended **Jan. 7-8.** When the market reopened **Jan. 9,** prices dropped immediately to the daily trading limit. After the International Longshoremen's Association told its members, **Jan. 8,** to stop handling Soviet ships, the government agreed, **Jan. 19,** to buy another 2.5 million tons of undelivered grain not affected by the embargo decision since it was contracted under a separate 1976 agreement to deliver 8 million tons a year to the Soviets for 5 years. With the first contest in the 1980 presidential election taking place in the agricultural state of Iowa **Jan. 21** at its precinct caucuses, the Carter Administration sent Secretary of Agriculture Robert Bergland and Vice President Walter Mondale across the state, **Jan. 9-13,** to defend the government's embargo. "We're being tested by the Russians to find out what we're made of," Bergland told the farmers. He also mentioned the possible use of surplus grain from the embargo in the production of alcohol for use in a fuel mixture—gasohol. By **Jan. 19,** price levels of corn had returned to what they were before the announcement of the embargo, soybean prices were higher, and wheat prices were rapidly recovering.

Supreme Court Justice William Douglas Dies — The longest-serving justice in the history of the Supreme Court, William O. Douglas, died **Jan. 18.** An ardent champion of the right to dissent during his years on the court from 1939 to 1975, he wrote more than 1,200 opinions during his tenure. Douglas was also a well-known conservationist, world traveler, and author.

Carter and Bush Win in Iowa — Precinct caucuses in Iowa, **Jan. 21,** gave Pres. Carter 59 percent of the Democratic vote to Sen. Edward Kennedy's 31 percent. In the Republican party, George Bush won with 32 percent of the votes, Ronald Reagan gained 29 percent, and Sen. Howard Baker came in 3d with 16 percent. The votes represented the presidential preferences of delegates chosen for the next stage of the delegate selection process, the county caucuses. The results were an unexpected blow to Kennedy and a boost to Bush. At the beginning of the election year, the Republicans had ended their moratorium on partisan attacks on Pres. Carter during the hostage crisis in Iran. Republican National Chairman Bill Brock lashed out at Carter, **Jan. 1,** for a "policy of deception" in attempting to use national unity on the hostages in Iran to divert attention from foreign policy weaknesses. Carter's foreign policy came under more attack at a televised debate of 6 Republican presidential candidates in Des Moines, Iowa, **Jan. 5.** Sen. Kennedy, **Jan. 7,** charged Pres. Carter with "lurching" from crisis to crisis in domestic and foreign policy. Kennedy suggested, **Jan. 20,** that Carter's reversal of policy over a Soviet combat brigade in Cuba in Sept. 1979 may have influenced Moscow's decision to intervene in Afghanistan. After his damaging defeat at the Iowa caucus, Kennedy withdrew to reconsider his strategy and emerged, **Jan. 28,** to propose: an immediate 6-month wage-price freeze followed by mandatory wage-price controls, immediate gasoline rationing to help free the nation from dependence on Middle East oil, and the immediate establishment of a UN commission to investigate Iranian grievances against the deposed Shah, to begin work as soon as the U.S. hostages are freed.

Carter Delivers State of the Union Address — "It has never been more clear that the state of our union depends on the state of the world," Pres. Carter said, **Jan. 23,** in a State of the Union address preoccupied with foreign affairs. The crises in Iran and Afghanistan dramatized, according to Carter, how "our excessive dependence on foreign oil is a clear and present danger to our nation's security." Carter said he would soon submit legislation providing incentives for electric utilities to convert from oil and natural gas to other fuels, especially coal. In preparation for an emergency, an improved standby program for gasoline rationing would also be proposed. Carter warned that the U.S. was prepared to go to war if necessary to protect the oil-supply routes of the Persian Gulf region. To improve the country's readiness for international action, Carter asked Congress to remove "unwarranted restraints" on U.S. intelligence-gathering capabilities and said that he would seek the authority to resume Selective Service registration to insure that the nation can "meet future mobilization needs rapidly if they arise." Few new domestic goals were outlined in the message. "Restraining inflation remains my highest domestic priority," Carter said. However, Carter did propose spending an additional $2 billion over the next 2 years to provide job training for out-of-work young people. He said he would propose extending general revenue sharing at the current levels for another 5 years. Carter also said he would ask Congress to reorganize the Nuclear Regulatory Commission and would press for a "comprehensive program" for safe disposal of nuclear waste.

Largest Increase in Inflation in 33 Years Reported — The Labor Dept. reported, **Jan. 25,** that consumer prices rose 13.3 percent in 1979, the largest annual increase in 33 years. Only 1946 and 1917-19 had shown greater increases in prices since the government began compiling statistics in 1913. The December increase in the Consumer Price Index was 1.2 percent, the highest in nearly a year. Large increases in the cost of energy and housing led the increases for both the month and the year. The purchasing power of workers for the year declined by 5.3 percent, it was reported. On **Jan. 11,** the Labor Dept. reported that the rate of unemployment remained virtually the same during December, rising only 0.1 percent to 5.9 percent. Continued predictions of a recession were proved wrong, **Jan. 18,** when the government announced that the economy had grown a moderate 1.4 percent during the last quarter of 1979, making the growth rate 2.3 percent for the year.

Chicago Teachers Strike — The nation's 3d largest school system shut down, **Jan. 28,** as Chicago teachers struck to protest proposed layoffs and delinquent paychecks. The fiscal crisis of the Chicago school board had been apparent since **Nov. 13** when its credit rating had plummeted. It was estimated that the board needed 500 to 700 million dollars to avoid bankruptcy. In addition, the board was unable to account for some $44.2 million of employee payroll deductions. In hearings on the situation, a representative of the school board's outside auditors said that accountants had repeatedly warned the board that its financial practices could lead to serious problems. The accounting company had found that at 4 different times the school board's deficit was almost double the amount that school officials had reported in public statements. Chicago Mayor Byrne charged, **Dec. 5,** that there had been a "10-year cover-up by school and business officials" who made it appear that the system was financially sound when it was not. The school board was given a Feb. 1 deadline for making $60 million in mandatory budget cuts under the terms of a 3-part $875 million rescue agreement. The board decided to lay off 1,600 teachers. It was the threatened layoff and the failure of the board to pay its employees for 2 weeks that precipitated the teacher's strike. A compromise was reached and the strike ended, **Feb. 11,** when the school board agreed to lay off only 1,375 teachers.

International

Gandhi Wins Landslide Victory — Capping a dramatic political comeback, Indira Gandhi and her Congress-I Party, **Jan. 3** and **6,** won an overwhelming victory in India's parliamentary elections. Out of the 542 seats in the parliament, 350 of them went to candidates supporting Gandhi and her party. Indira Gandhi had been Prime Minister from 1966 to 1977, when she was not only turned out of office but indicted for official corruption. As recently as Dec. 19, 1978, she had been taken from Parliament and jailed for a short period, after a majority in the chamber voted to expel and imprison her for having harassed officials while she was prime minister in 1975. A division of opposition votes among the Janata, Lok Dal, and Congress Parties—which respectively won 32, 41, and 13 seats—was held responsible for Gandhi's victory. Although her party won nearly 70 percent of the seats, Gandhi's Congress-I Party got only 42 percent of the total votes. Her winning candidates polled only a third of the votes cast in at least 100 districts. Gandhi's controversial son, Sanjay, also won a seat. During the campaign, Gandhi had stressed the need to cut inflation and restore law and order within India and called for recognition of the new Vietnamese-backed Heng Samrin government in Cambodia and closer relations with Third World countries. It was expected that she would crack down on hoarders of sugar and kerosene, important commodities in India. On **Jan. 14,** Gandhi was sworn in as prime minister and her 14-member Cabinet, which had little previous ministerial experience, also assumed office. On **Jan. 15,** a New Delhi court judge dismissed 2 cases against Gandhi arising from her rule in 1975.

Russians Secure New Bases, Clash with Afghan Army — Soviet military units in Afghanistan, according to the *New York Times* **Jan. 10,** appeared to be concentrating on securing newly established bases and staging areas. Soviet military transports loaded with troops and equipment were reported landing in Kabul at a rate of a dozen a day. The U.S. State Department, **Jan. 13,** announced that there had been heavy fighting between Soviet forces and Afghan Army units, on **Jan. 1,** at the town of Bala Zhar. Soviet forces killed or interned 700 soldiers of the Afghan Army's 26th Parachute Regiment when they refused a Soviet request to disarm. There were also reports of massive defections from the Afghan Army, which had dwindled to less than 60,000 soldiers from more than 100,000 during the past year. Many army defectors joined the insurgent Afghan Moslems. Despite persistent rebel disunity, with at least 7 groups competing for supremacy, Islamic leader Zia Khan Nassary, chairman of the Afghan Islamic and Revolutionary Party, **Jan. 25,** proclaimed a "Free Islamic Republic" in 3 Afghan provinces (Paktia, Ghazni, Logar), claiming that Moslem forces were in control of these eastern provinces, and appealed for foreign arms to fight the Soviet troops. On **Jan. 16,** Chinese officials said that they were ready to increase a covert flow of Chinese small arms to the insurgents.

U.S. Offers Aid to Pakistan — In order to help strengthen Pakistan's security after the Soviet invasion of Afghanistan, the U.S., **Jan. 12,** offered the South Asian country $400 million in economic and military aid over the next 2 years. U.S. aid to Pakistan had been cut off Apr. 6, 1979, after it was learned that Pakistan was constructing a uranium enrichment facility that could produce atomic bomb material. Half of the proferred aid would be military credits and would be limited to defensive arms, such as anti-tank weapons, antiaircraft systems, infantry weapons and artillery and armor. President Mohammed Zia ul-Haq of Pakistan appealed, **Jan. 15,** for international aid and support. The Soviet Union, **Jan. 1,** had accused Pakistan of training officers to command Afghan Moslem groups to fight in Afghanistan. The UN had reported, **Jan. 6,** that 15,000 Afghan refugees had fled to Pakistan in the last 2 weeks of December 1979, bringing to 402,000 the number of

Afghan refugees in Pakistan. Lord Carrington, the British Foreign Secretary, **Jan. 16**, visited Pakistan and its border with Afghanistan to dramatize Britain's support of the country. On **Jan. 17**, President Zia dismissed the $400 million U.S. offer as "peanuts" and said that his country needed much more than that amount. Pres. Carter reaffirmed the U.S. offer of aid in his State of the Union message, **Jan. 23.**

Zimbabwe Leaders Return from Exile — Patriotic Front leader Joshua Nkomo returned, **Jan. 13**, to Zimbabwe Rhodesia after more than 3 years of exile, greeted by a crowd of more than 100,000 people. The leader returned under the recently negotiated peace accord in order to campaign in the up-coming election. In the peace accord, the Salisbury army and the 2 Patriotic Front forces had agreed to disengage and gather at specified camps. On **Jan. 7**, it was reported that 20,000 guerrillas had gathered at 16 designated assembly places in the bush where they were to be monitored by a Commonwealth force during the election campaign. But at least 2,000 guerrillas were thought to still be at large. Most of the guerrillas that remained outside the camps were thought to be followers of Patriotic Front leader Robert Mugabe. On **Jan. 7**, a confrontation had been averted when 450 of Mugabe's Zimbabwe African National Union (ZANU) guerrillas were persuaded to surrender and report to assembly points. On **Jan. 18**, British governor general Lord Soames extended the state of emergency in the country until the installation of a new government. Meanwhile, Britain quickly moved to reestablish Zimbabwe's links with neighboring black nations in trade, transportation and communication in order to make it difficult to reverse the transition to black rule. After acquiescing to British demands to release 71 ZANU dissidents held by his party in Mozambique, Mugabe, **Jan. 27**, was allowed to return to Zimbabwe and a jubilant welcome. Mugabe had criticized Soames for allowing South African troops to remain in the country to guard the road and rail bridge between the 2 countries. On **Jan. 30** the troops left after an agreement between the Patriotic Front and the British had been reached.

Gold Soars Above $800 — Gold bullion prices, **Jan. 18**, soared to $835 an ounce on the London market. The meteoric rise began **Jan. 2** when the International Monetary Fund held its monthly gold auction and sold its gold at $562.85 an ounce, $136.48 an ounce higher than at its previous auction Dec. 5, 1979. The price in Hong Kong reached a high of $660, **Jan. 3.** After a lull, gold prices took off again during the week of **Jan. 14-18.** The $700 mark was passed **Jan. 15**, and the closing price of $802 in New York, **Jan. 18**, was $159 higher than the price at the beginning of the week. Most dealers attributed the wild trading in gold to Middle Eastern investors worried about recent developments in the Middle East, Iran, and Afghanistan, as well as the failing health of Yugoslavian President Tito.

Tito Loses Leg — With international tensions at their peak after the Soviet invasion of Afghanistan, the deteriorating health of longtime Yugoslav President Josip Broz Tito aroused widespread concern over the future of a country which had broken with the Soviet block in 1948. The left leg of the 87-year-old leader was amputated **Jan. 20**, after an unsuccessful operation, **Jan. 12**, for the removal of a blocked artery in his leg. On **Jan. 15**, Yugoslavia placed its army on partial alert and, on **Jan. 18**, the U.S. government reaffirmed American support for "the unity, independence and territorial integrity of Yugoslavia." Doctors said, **Jan. 21**, that Tito was in good condition after the amputation.

Soviet Union's Foremost Dissident Arrested — Andrei Sakharov, a physicist who had received the Nobel Peace Prize in 1975 for his work on the behalf of human rights, was arrested, **Jan. 22**, and sent from Moscow into internal exile in Gorky, an industrial city 250 miles east of the Russian capital. He was also stripped of his title Hero of Socialist Labor and all other Soviet awards. In an interview on **Jan. 2**, Sakharov had called on the UN to put pressure on the Soviet Union to withdraw its forces from Afghanistan and had come out in support of boycotting the summer Olympic Games slated for Moscow. Tass, the Soviet news agency, charged that Sakharov "has been conducting subversive activities against the Soviet state for a number of years" and "lately embarked on the road of open calls to reactionary circles of imperialist states to interfere in the USSR's internal affairs." On **Jan. 23**, Izvestia, the government newspaper, charged the physicist with divulging state secrets to foreign diplomats and journalists and slandering the Soviet Union. Sakharov had been removed from Soviet nuclear weapons work in 1968 after he wrote an essay in which he denounced censorship, intellectual restraints, and Soviet pressure against liberal Communist rule in Czechoslovakia. On **Jan. 25**, Tass reported that, "for humane considerations and taking Sakharov's previous services into account," Sakharov would not be put on trial. In a written statement his wife brought from his exile in Gorky, **Jan. 28**, Sakharov said that he wanted a public and open trial and did not need a "gilded cage." The *New York Times* reported, **Jan. 28**, that Sakharov was under police supervision and had been forbidden to communicate by mail or phone with foreigners or even relatives abroad. He was forbidden to leave the city limits of Gorky. A leading Soviet poet, Bella Akhmadulina, **Jan. 31**, spoke out on Sakharov's behalf as Soviet intellectuals grappled with the banishment of one of the 231 full members of the Soviet Academy of Sciences, a distinguished body relatively immune from politics. On **Feb. 9**, Yelena Bonner, Sakharov's wife, called on members of the Academy of Sciences and other Soviet scientists to come to the physicist's defense. His wife had continued to transmit messages from Sakharov to foreign reporters even though Soviet authorities had warned her not to. On **Feb. 4**, Sakharov said that he had been threatened with a pistol and had been warned that he faced harsher exile or commitment to a psychiatric hospital if his wife continued to carry his written statements to Moscow.

Canada Helps U.S. Diplomats Escape Iran — As U.S. efforts to gain the release of American citizens held hostage in Iran continued to meet frustration, U.S. and Canadian officials announced, **Jan. 29**, that 6 U.S. Embassy employees not among the 50 known U.S. hostages in Teheran had flown out of Iran the previous day with the help of Canadian diplomats. After hiding for 3 months in diplomatic residences in Teheran, the Americans posed as Canadian diplomats and carried forged Iranian visas when they boarded regular commercial flights out of Iran. Five of the employees had escaped the U.S. embassy through a back door when it was taken over, **Nov. 4**, by Iranian student militants. On **Nov. 8**, they called the Canadian embassy to ask for sanctuary, which was granted. A 6th American, who had been with friends when the embassy was attacked, called the Canadians, **Nov. 22**, and joined the other 5 that day. A tight web of secrecy was woven around the Americans out of fear that Iranian militants might try to capture them. As a precautionary measure, the small Canadian embassy staff remaining in Teheran also left the country. Meanwhile, UN and American strategies to release the hostages remained unsuccessful. UN Secretary General Kurt Waldheim had conferred, **Jan. 1-3**, with Iranian officials in Teheran in an attempt to increase Iranian confidence in the UN as a mediator in the crisis. Although Waldheim was not allowed to visit the hostages or Ayatollah Khomeini during his stay, he did meet with the Revolutionary Council. Upon returning to New York, Waldheim, **Jan. 7**, told the UN Security Council that Iran's student militants "make their decisions independently" and were a power center independent of the Revolutionary Council. Pres. Carter, **Jan. 9**, warned the American public that it could take months to gain the hostages' release. "There is no legitimate political bargaining leverage that can be exerted on" the Iranian militants, Carter warned, and "there is no entity there with whom one can negotiate." Two weeks after a UN Security Council resolution called for economic sanctions against Iran if the hostages were not released in a week, the Soviet Union, **Jan. 13**, vetoed a UN Security Council resolution to impose economic sanctions upon the recalcitrant country. The U.S. and some of its allies vowed to continue to seek sanctions. Accusing newsmen of excessive coverage of the hostages and Iran's domestic turmoil and a neglect of the shah's past crimes, Iran, **Jan. 14**, ousted all U.S. journalists from the country, after they had filed reports about domestic unrest in Tabriz that killed at least 43 **Jan. 4-6.** Some hope for resolution of the crisis emerged after the election, **Jan. 25**, of Finance Minister Abolhassan Bani-Sadr as president of Iran with 75 percent of the votes. Bani-Sadr had been the only revolutionary leader to openly criticize the militants who had taken over the U.S. embassy. But he took a tough stance, **Jan. 27**, when he charged the U.S. with the major responsibility for ending the crisis.

General

Lung Cancer in Women Increases — In the first report by the U.S. Surgeon General to deal exclusively with the health risks of cigarette smoking for women, Surgeon General Julius Richmond warned, **Jan. 14,** that lung cancer among women was increasing dramatically and that within 3 years it could overtake breast cancer as the leading cancer killer of women. In 1978, the lung cancer death rate for women was 15 per 100,000, about 25,000 deaths a year. This was a 3-fold increase over the rate of 5 deaths per 100,000 in the early 1960's. Scientists projected that by 1983 the rate would approach 25 deaths per 100,000. Most previous studies on smoking had concentrated on men, since women began smoking in great numbers only after World War II. As the women grew older and continued to smoke, doctors were able to trace the same symptoms and problems as those suffered by men. "This report points out that the first signs of an epidemic of smoking-related disease among women are now appearing," the report said. The report also said that pregnant women who smoke run an increased risk of problems before, during, and after childbirth.

Virus-Fighting Substance Made by Gene Splicing — Scientists and officers of Biogen, S.A., an international genetic research concern, **Jan. 16,** announced that human interferon, a natural disease-fighting substance, had been made successfully in the laboratory by gene-splicing techniques. Scarce and prohibitively expensive, interferon was thought to hold great potential for curing a wide variety of virus diseases and some forms of cancer. Further improvements in the gene-splicing technique would enable the large-scale commercial production of the substance. Also known as recombinant DNA research, gene splicing involves taking genetic material from cells and growing it in bacteria. The genes are then reproduced and naturally make the hormone or other product characteristic of the gene. Human insulin and human growth hormone had also been produced using the technique, which might produce a new scientific-industrial revolution based on the cheap, large-scale production of biological substances.

Colombia Bullring Collapses, Killing 222 People — While 40,000 fans wildly cheered scores of men in a bullring who were running from several bulls, 5 sections of crowded wooden bleachers collapsed, **Jan. 20,** killing at least 222 persons and injuring more than 500 others in Sincelejo, Colombia. Heavy rains had softened the ground beneath the overcrowded bleachers until their wooden supports slipped under the weight of 3,000 spectators. "In 30 seconds the stands crashed down like a castle of cards," a newsman at the scene reported.

Disasters — An earthquake registering 7.0 on the Richter scale hit Portugal's Azores Islands in the Mid-Atlantic, **Jan. 1,** crumbling buildings, killing at least 52 persons, and leaving more than 300 persons injured . . . A fire swept through a crowded social club in Chapais, Quebec, at a 1979 New Year's Eve party, killing 44 persons, it was reported **Jan. 1** . . . An Iranian jetliner on a domestic flight from the eastern city of Meshed to Teheran crashed, **Jan. 21,** about 20 miles northeast of Teheran, killing all 128 persons aboard . . . In the worst peacetime disaster in Coast Guard history, Coast Guard vessel *Blackthorn* collided, **Jan. 29,** with the oil tanker *Capricorn* in Tampa Bay, off Florida, killing 23 seamen . . .

FEBRUARY

National

Congressmen Investigated in Bribery Scandal — In the most sweeping inquiry into suspected political corruption undertaken by the Federal Bureau of Investigation in at least 25 years, 31 public officials, including a U.S. Senator and 7 Representatives, were subjects of a 2-year undercover operation by the FBI, it was reported **Feb. 3.** Called Operation Abscam (for Arab Scam), the investigation had surreptitiously videotaped and recorded meetings between undercover agents, posing as businessmen and Arab sheiks willing to pay bribes, and public officials who were paid hundreds of thousands of dollars in cash for political "favors." It began on Feb. 17, 1978, when the Arab cover story was successfully used by the FBI in the recovery of two 17th-century paintings stolen 14 years ago from a New York art dealer. With the help of the informer who provided information for this investigation, the agents moved into an investigation of political corruption using the same successful method. During 1979, undercover FBI agents pretended to be working for an invented Arab sheik and sought help from the targets in making investments, building hotels and gaining a casino license in Atlantic City, N.J., and obtaining permission for Arab businessmen to reside in the U.S. Meetings were held in New York hotels, a rented townhouse in Washington, a yacht off the coast of Florida and several other locations. According to law enforcement authorities, Mayor Angelo Errichetti of Camden, N.J., was a central figure in several early deals and introduced the agents to other politicians and their associates. Among those named by law enforcement authorities as subjects of the investigation were: Sen. Harrison Williams Jr. (D, N.J.), Rep. John Murphy (D, N.Y.), Rep. Frank Thompson Jr. (D, N.J.), Rep. Michael Myers (D, Pa.), Rep. John Murtha (D, Pa.), Rep. Raymond Lederer (D, Pa.), Rep. John Jenrette (D, S.C.), and Rep. Richard Kelly (R, Fla.). Sen Larry Pressler (R, S.D.) had met with the FBI agents posing as Arab businessmen, but spurned the offer of a campaign contribution in exchange for political favors. Said Pressler upon hearing about the investigation: "I'm a little upset because I'm clean. My campaign records are kept perfectly. Why would they want to test me out?" In explaining how the investigation snowballed, Philip Heymann of the Justice Department said: "No one associated with the United States ever picked any politician for the investigation. The middlemen did all of that." The middlemen, who introduced the undercover agents to the public officials, did not know that the men posing as wealthy Arabs and their representatives were law-enforcement officials. The ethics committees of both houses of Congress immediately began investigations of the bribery allegations despite objections by Attorney General Benjamin Civiletti, made public **Feb. 5,** that Congressional inquiries could jeopardize criminal cases that the government might bring. Consumer activist Ralph Nader, **Feb. 8,** called the leaks to the press of information prior to its presentation to a grand jury "damned offensive." "In the mind of millions of people these guys are guilty, and they haven't even been charged," Nader said. On **Feb. 11,** Civiletti appointed Richard Blumenthal, U.S. Attorney for Connecticut, to investigate how news organizations obtained confidential information about Abscam. Rep. Richard Kelley, the only Congressman to admit taking a bribe from one of the undercover agents, resigned **Feb. 21** from the House Republican Conference to avoid a possible vote to expel him for his alleged involvement in the Abscam scandal. Two other corruption investigations by the FBI which used bogus business operations as a front were reported during the month. It was reported **Feb. 8** that a 9-month undercover investigation, named Brilab for "bribery-labor," had recorded several southwestern politicians and labor leaders taking bribes. A phony insurance company paid the bribes in order to obtain city and state employee insurance programs. On **Feb. 14,** it was reported that indictments against 55 persons in 10 states had been handed down after a 2½-year undercover investigation of pornography distribution and film piracy, called Miporn for "Miami pornography."

Chrysler Reports '79 Loss — Chrysler Corp., **Feb. 7,** reported for the year 1979 a loss of $1.1 billion, believed to be the largest yearly loss in American corporate history. During 1978, the ailing automaker had lost $204.6 million. Chrysler's 1979 car and truck sales fell 18.8 percent as buyers switched to smaller, more fuel-efficient models. The company said that it could return to profitability when the 1981 model cars were introduced.

Monthly Inflation at 5-Year High — Producer prices, the ones retailers and manufacturers pay for goods, increased 1.6 percent in January, it was reported **Feb. 15.** This was the largest monthly rise in 5 years and led the Federal Reserve System the same day to tighten credit by increasing its discount rate a full percentage-point to a record 13 percent. The bad economic news continued, **Feb. 22,** when the Labor Department announced that the Consumer Price Index increased 1.4 percent in January, pushed by a 7.4 percent increase in gasoline prices. On **Feb. 25,** Pres. Carter said that inflation had "reached a crisis stage" and pointed to the failure of Congress to adopt a comprehensive energy policy as a major cause of the situation. Energy Department officials, **Feb. 26,** said that they forsaw $1.50-a-gallon gasoline by the end of the year. Strong sentiment for balancing the 1981 Federal budget was reported, **Feb. 29,** in Congress. Rep. Robert Giaimo, chairman of the House Budget Committee, said: "This place is panicked—the House, the Senate, the Administration. They have realized we have got to take drastic steps." On **Feb. 1,** the Labor Department reported that the unemployment rate had jumped up to 6.2 percent in January, the highest level in 18 months.

FBI Cover-Up Reported in 60's Klan Attacks — After obtaining the report of the Rowe Task Force of the Justice Department, the *New York Times* revealed, **Feb. 17,** that the FBI had known about and covered up involvement in violent attacks on blacks and civil rights activists by Gary Thomas Rowe Jr., its chief paid informer inside the Ku Klux Klan in the early 1960's. The 302-page report also claimed that FBI head J. Edgar Hoover had twice blocked prosecution of 4 Ku Klux Klansmen identified by FBI agents as the bombers who, in 1963, killed 4 black children at the 16th Street Baptist Church in Birmingham, Alabama. There was no reported evidence that Rowe was involved in the bombing. The 2 times that Hoover foiled attempts to pass information on the bombing to officials in the Justice Department, he had said that "the chance of prosecution in state or Federal Court is very remote." One of the Klansmen, Robert Chambliss, was convicted of murder 14 years later, in 1977, when less direct evidence was available to the trial jury than there was to Hoover in 1964 when he halted the prosecution. The task force concluded that the church bombing case did not reach a grand jury until 1977 because Hoover's Justice Department superiors were never given the full account of what the FBI knew about the case. The report also said that the bureau did not investigate information that Rowe was involved in a series of racial killings between 1960 and 1965 when he was on the bureau payroll. "As long as he was providing good intelligence, the Birmingham field office appeared willing to overlook Rowe's own involvement" in Klan violence, the task force said. Rules prohibiting violence were imposed on FBI informers in 1975. The *New York Times* said that the task force report had been withheld for 7 months and there was some speculation within the Justice Department that the refusal to release it was due to Senate Judiciary Committee deliberations over a new FBI charter that could impose stricter rules on the use of informers. A Justice Department official explained that its release could prejudice an impending trial of Rowe, who was under indictment for murder in the 1965 death of Viola Gregg Liuzzo, a white civil rights marcher from Detroit.

Reagan, Carter Win N.H. Primary; Campaign Heats Up — In a confirmation of pollsters' designation of him as front-runner, Ronald Reagan, **Feb. 26,** scored a large victory over his Republican opponents in the New Hampshire primary. Fifty percent of the New Hampshire voters supported the candidate after he intensified his campaigning and renewed his tough conservative positions. George Bush trailed with 24 percent and Howard Baker and John Anderson polled 13 percent and 10 percent of the vote, respectively. Reagan received 15 delegates, while Bush won 5. In the Democratic primary, Carter won a clear victory with 49 percent of the vote and 10 delegates to Edward Kennedy's 38 percent and 9 delegates and Edmund Brown's 10 percent. The loss was a serious one for Kennedy on his home turf in New England, but Carter's victory margin was not 2 to 1, as pre-election polls had predicted. Carter had defeated Kennedy by another modest margin, **Feb. 10,** in the Maine caucuses with 46 percent of the vote to Kennedy's 40 percent and Brown's 13 percent. As the campaigns heated up during the month, candidates in both parties exchanged angry words. Carter and Kennedy, **Feb. 12-13,** argued over the formation of an international commission as part of the process to gain release of the American hostages held in Teheran. Kennedy said that the Carter Administration had "stubbornly resisted this solution until I and others made the proposal and broke the silence on Iran." Kennedy had proposed it in a speech **Jan. 28** and the Administration's endorsement of it was announced **Feb. 13.** Administration officials claimed that the proposal had been under consideration before Kennedy proposed it. In a televised news conference, Carter said of Kennedy's statements: "They've not been accurate. And they have not been responsible, and they have not helped our country. . . . [His criticism] is very damaging to our country." The Republican bloodbath occurred **Feb. 23** over a debate in Nashua, N.H. Reagan, with 4 other Republican candidates in tow, argued dramatically for an open debate, rather than one between only him and Bush—as the sponsor, the Nashua Telegraph, had stipulated. Bush weakly defended the sponsor's rules. The debate went on as planned, but the television cameras, barred from the debate itself, followed the 4 uninvited candidates into another room where they denounced Bush. Reagan, **Feb. 26,** fired his campaign chief, John Sears, who was opposed by conservatives in Reagan's campaign for his attempts to moderate Reagan's conservative image in order to broaden his support.

International

Trudeau Reelected Canada's Head — Former Canadian Prime Minister Pierre Elliott Trudeau and his Liberal Party, **Feb. 18,** captured a clear majority of 146 seats in the 282-member House of Commons. Before being turned out of office on May 22, 1979, Trudeau had been Prime Minister since 1968. The Progressive Conservatives lost 33 seats in the election, reducing their total in the Parliament to 103 seats. The New Democratic Party increased its standing to 32 seats, while the Social Credit Party lost all of its 5 seats. More than 70% of the Canadian electorate braved the winter to vote. The campaign had come to be known popularly as "the 18-cent election," because of the Progressive Conservative plan to increase the excise tax on gasoline by 18 cents Canadian. The 6 eastern provinces gave the victory to the Liberals over the west and oil and gas producing provinces of Alberta and Saskatchewan.

Afghans Resist Soviet Occupation — The commercial life of Kabul, Afghanistan's capital city of 1 million people, halted, **Feb. 21,** as almost every merchant in the city closed his business to protest the Soviet military presence in the country. Clandestine anti-Soviet leaflets, produced by anti-Communist insurgents, had urged the shopkeepers to show their "unanimous condemnation" of the 2-month-old Soviet intervention by striking. The Soviets, **Feb. 22,** imposed martial law as at least 3 large street protests were staged in the city. Chants of "God is great" and "Death to the Russians" were heard along with erratic gun shots. The strike spread to civil servants and laborers and to the cities of Herat, Kandahar and Jalabad. At least 300 civilians were reported killed in the first few days of the strike. Soviet MIG fighters and helicopters buzzed Kabul **Feb. 22-23** to discourage the anti-Soviet demonstrations. Nevertheless, the demonstrations and strikes continued until there were widespread arrests, **Feb. 26,** of Shiite Moslems suspected of having instigated the anti-Soviet disturbances. On **Feb. 27,** Kabul was reported back to normal. The civilian resistance occurred just as there had been an increase in military clashes with insurgents in northeast provinces of the mountainous country. On **Feb. 23,** Afghan troops loyal to the regime closed off the Kabul-Peshawar highway, ending all road traffic to and from Pakistan for the first time. Internationally, the U.S. persisted in its attempt to make the Soviet Union pay a price for its aggression. France and West Germany, through their foreign ministers, had called, **Feb. 5,** for a Soviet withdrawal, but France announced, **Feb. 8,** that because it was not "of a nature to reduce international tension," France would not attend a scheduled allied conference on the Afghan problem. As it tried to coordinate the West's response to the invasion, the U.S., **Feb. 9,** criticized France for "rapid shifts" in policy. Tensions between the U.S. and its European allies worsened as the U.S. pressured Europe to give up some of the benefits of detente with the Soviets by cutting exports, and European governments criticized the erratic character of recent U.S. policy and the U.S. failure to consult with European nations. To back up his extension of the U.S. military umbrella over the Persian Gulf, Carter ordered, **Feb. 12,** a 1,800-man Marine assault battalion to the Arabian Sea in March to exhibit the U.S. ability to project its military power. On **Feb. 15,** the U.S. admitted that it had begun supplying light infantry weapons to Afghan insurgent groups in mid-January, the first covert mission of this sort by the Central Intelligence Agency since 1976 during the Angolan civil war. With the military situation both within and outside Afghanistan becoming more threatening, Britain, **Feb. 29,** formally presented to the Soviet Union a proposal for the neutralization of Afghanistan backed with a Western guarantee in exchange for the Soviet withdrawal of its troops.

Diplomats Held Hostage in Colombia — A reception marking the Dominican Republic's national independence holiday, was invaded by leftist guerrillas who seized that country's embassy in Bogota, Colombia, **Feb. 27.** Dressed in joggers' warmup suits with their weapons in gym bags, 17 guerrillas of the Movement of April 19 ran into the embassy. In the ensuing shootout with security guards, 4 people were wounded and one guerrilla killed. A large portion of Bogota's diplomatic corps, including the U.S. Ambassador and the papal nuncio, were taken hostage, as was the embassy staff. The guerrillas, subject along with other leftist groups to an intensive crackdown the last 18 months in which nearly 2,000 guerrilla suspects were seized, made the following demands: the release of political prisoners, including 311 from their movement; the publication of an April 19 manifesto in the main newspapers of the hostages' countries; and payment of a $50 million ransom to be raised from the hostages' countries. The April 19 Movement, also known as M-19, was a radical leftist group that broke away from the youth movement of the National Popular Alliance of Gen. Gustavo Rojas Pinilla after Pinilla was defeated in an election for president on April 19, 1970; some of Pinilla's followers charged fraud and turned to terrorism. The Colombian government refused to release prisoners or pay a ransom as negotiations began **Mar. 2** in a van parked about 40 yards from the embassy. In exchange for food and supplies, 13 hostages were freed **Feb. 28** and the last 5 female hostages were freed **Feb. 29.** On **Mar. 6,** Austrian ambassador Edgar Karl Selzer was released so that he could return to his sick wife in Vienna. On **Mar. 17,** Uruguayan Ambassador Fernando Gomez jumped from a 2d-story window of the embassy in the early morning darkness and scrambled to freedom. The negotiations deadlocked over the release of prisoners, which the guerrillas initially called a nonnegotiable demand and which the Colombian govern-

UN Commission Visits Iran

A 5-member UN commission on the rule of the deposed Shah Mohammed Reza Pahlavi arrived in Teheran, **Feb. 23,** in an attempt to take advantage of the election of a new Iranian president, who appeared to want to end the American hostage crisis in order to consolidate his power.

The new president, Abolhassan Bani-Sadr, had been named head of Iran's Revolutionary Council **Feb. 7** and supreme commander of the armed forces **Feb. 19** by Ayatollah Ruhollah Khomeini. On **Feb. 6,** Bani-Sadr had denounced the militants holding the hostages as "self-centered children" who were behaving like a "government within a government." On the same day, the Revolutionary Council ordered the state broadcasting system to stop granting the militants automatic air time to publicize their allegations.

As the internal political situation in Iran appeared to improve the chances for the hostages' release, Pres. Carter, **Feb. 13,** gave public approval for the first time of a "carefully defined" international commission of inquiry into Iranian grievances as a step toward freeing the hostages. The U.S. opposed questioning of the hostages during the proposed inquiry. Previously, the U.S. had insisted that such a body could be formed only after the hostages were released.

In announcing the establishment of the commission on **Feb. 20,** UN Secretary General Kurt Waldheim was careful to describe it as a "fact-finding" body, not a judicial one. He said that the group of 5 lawyers from Sri Lanka, France, Venezuela, Syria, and Algeria had a 2-part mission: "to hear Iran's grievances and to allow for an early solution of the crisis between Iran and the United States." Iranian leaders continued to disavow any linkage between the commission and the release of the hostages but Waldheim told U.S. officials that Iran stood by the agreed twofold mandate for the commission. Waldheim had additional assurances from Bani-Sadr, according to the *New York Times,* that Khomeini welcomed the commission.

However, when the commission arrived, **Feb. 23,** in Teheran, Khomeini announced that the hostages could only be released by a parliament that was to be elected in March and meet in April. The announcement jolted U.S. officials, according to the *New York Times,* and over the next few days the officials expressed frustration and confusion over what they saw as the undermining of the commission's twofold mission by Iranian leaders. One U.S. official said that the Carter Administration had been assured by Waldheim that the hostages would be freed during the period mandated for the commission's work. "This was more than a gentlemen's agreement," he said. "But it was not a commitment in writing." Another diplomat, once stationed in Teheran, said: "You never get anything cut and dried with Iranians before you enter a negotiation."

The Iranian leaders and militants had different positions on what conditions had to be fulfilled for the hostages to be released. Bani-Sadr had stressed in interviews that Iran no longer demanded the return of the shah as a condition for the release of the hostages, although he made it clear that Iran expected it to happen via the work of the international commission. On television **Feb. 16,** Bani-Sadr insisted that Iran was making 3 demands: U.S. self-criticism of its past role in Iran, a guarantee that the U.S. would not interfere in Iranian affairs in the future and would not try to prevent Iran's prosecution of the deposed shah. Although the U.S. had always refused to apologize for its involvement in Iran, some compromise language might be used, according to officials, that would satisfy the Iranians. The militants, however, continued to insist on the return of the shah or a direct order from Khomeini as a prior condition for the hostages' release. Having arrived in Teheran, the commission proceeded with its inquiry after meeting, **Feb. 24,** with Bani-Sadr and Foreign Minister Sadegh Ghotbzadeh and being promised their cooperation. U.S. and UN officials and Bani-Sadr hoped that a sympathetic hearing of grievances against the shah by the commission might produce a climate conducive to a visit with the hostages or their possible release. On **Feb. 26,** the commission took testimony from 5 Iranian jurists and more than 140 invalids who said they were the victims of the shah's regime. The governor of Iran's central bank, Ali Reza Nobari, testified that "we have documents showing that the total amount of money plundered by the former imperial family was 500 billion rials," equivalent to $7.14 billion. On **Feb. 28,** the group met with about 1,500 Iranians, most of whom had been injured during demonstrations shortly before the shah was deposed. The commission's co-chairman, Mohammed Bedjaoui of Algeria, said to the crowd: "We will fulfill our mandate and . . . the international community will know to what unimaginable lengths the violations of human rights were carried in this land."

Meanwhile, the commission members attempted to visit the hostages. The militants insisted that they could see only some of the hostages at this stage and only to ask them about embassy documents that were said to show the hostages were spies. Waldheim said that he had written permission from the Iranian government that the commission could visit all of the hostages to check on their health. The details of a possible visit became the subject of a diplomatic tug-of-war in the next few days. On **Mar. 3,** the Revolutionary Council promised that "the commission will see all the hostages," after an aide to Khomeini, **Feb. 29,** said that the meeting could go ahead. The commission was still refused entry to the U.S. compound, however, and were preparing to leave Iran when the militants, **Mar. 6,** announced that they would turn the hostages over to the Revolutionary Council due to "intolerable pressures" exerted on them by Iranian authorities. The commissioners stayed in Teheran, but a plan to transfer the hostages **Mar. 8** failed when the militants balked at giving them up to Foreign Minister Ghotbzadeh. Ghotbzadeh and the militants spent the day accusing each other of lying over whether Khomeini had approved a plan allowing the commission to visit the captives. The final blow to hopes that the commission would visit the hostages was dealt by Khomeini, **Mar. 10,** when he fully backed the militants and placed stringent conditions on any visit by the commission to the captives. As a consequence, the 5-member panel left the country and suspended issuing a report of its investigation.

ment insisted was illegal under its 94-year-old constitution. The guerrillas reduced to 10 the number of prisoners it wanted released and the government agreed to speed up the trials of its political prisoners. A breakthrough, however, did not occur until the end of April when the Cuban government offered its services, and "private" negotiators and the Human Rights Commission, an organ of the Organization of American States, entered the talks. The guerrillas settled for a commitment from the Colombian government that observers from the Inter-American Human Rights Commission would monitor prison conditions and attend trials. Private sources provided a ransom (smaller than the guerrillas' initial demand) and the terrorists, with 12 of the remaining 18 hostages, left for Havana, **Apr. 27,** on a Cuban commercial airliner. The hostages were released in Cuba and both sides in the extended crisis claimed victory.

General

33 Killed in New Mexico Prison Riot — In one of the worst prison uprisings in U.S. history, inmates at the New Mexico state penitentiary in Santa Fe, rioted **Feb. 2-3,** in a 36-hour rampage of murder and vandalism. During the night of **Feb. 2,** 2 prisoners overpowered a guard who had discovered them drinking homemade whisky. Then 400 inmates took over the 5 wings of the main building of the prison and the rioters turned on fellow inmates. All of the dead were prison inmates. Witnesses said that execution squads of prisoners armed with axes and blowtorches had tortured and murdered fellow prisoners, particularly those purported to be informers. Some of the inmate deaths, however, were from overdoses of drugs obtained from the prison infirmary and smoke inhalation from the fires that were set. About 600 of the prison's 1,136 inmates eventually fled the building, but remained in the prison yard. The 11 hostages seized when the takeover began were released one by one until only 3 remained when police entered the prison. More than 250 state police and National Guardsmen, **Feb. 3,** recaptured the prison without firing a shot. N.M. Gov. Bruce King had spoken with the inmates over the phone. According to officials, this act and negotiations with prison spokesmen had helped make possible the peaceful retaking of the prison. Prison officials made public 11 demands by inmates, among which were less crowding, better food, and improved recreation and education facilities. Two years previously, the American Civil Liberties Union filed a class action lawsuit in Federal District Court in Albuquerque demanding an improvement in conditions at the penitentiary. The prison held one-third more prisoners than it was designed for. On **Dec. 9,** 11 prisoners had escaped from the prison. By **Feb. 11,** 482 of the prisoners had been sent out of state and 538 remained in the prison. Gov. King estimated that $60 million might be needed to replace the ruined prison, which had undergone extensive physical damage.

Common Ancestor of Man and Apes Found — A Duke University scientist, Elwyn Simons, **Feb. 6,** announced the discovery of the oldest primate fossils in the chain of human hereditary lineage found to date. In the last 3 years, more than 2 dozen skeletal fossils of monkey-like primates the size of a house cat were found at the edge of the windswept Sahara in Egypt. The primate, a common ancestor of both apes and humans, was named Aegyptopithecus. It was thought to have roamed Africa 30 million years ago and to have had a complex social structure defended by males.

Spaceship To Study Sun Flares Launched — An unmanned U.S. spacecraft was launched, **Feb. 14,** into an orbit of earth. The 5,100-pound craft was designed to study sun flares, violent eruptions near the sun's surface that send gusts of radiation and gases into space and cause radio and TV disruptions and auroral displays. Sunspots and related solar flares were expected to reach the peak of their 11-year cycle from April to June. The spacecraft, named Solar Maximum Mission or Solar Max, was tentatively scheduled to be retrieved by the space shuttle on its 15th mission in late 1982 or early 1983.

Most Cars Fail U.S. Safety Test — The Dept. of Transportation announced, **Feb. 28,** that all the 1979 foreign cars and most domestic cars subjected to 35-mile-an-hour crash tests had failed to protect occupants. The test was only 5 miles an hour over the speed specified in the minimum safety standards and its purpose "was to see who tried to provide an extra measure of safety," said David Umansky, an agency spokesman. The Chevrolet Citation, the Plymouth Horizon and the redesigned Ford Mustang were praised for doing well on the test. The Citation almost passed the test at 40 miles an hour. "Failure" in the crash test meant that a passenger would have been killed or very seriously injured in a similar crash. Joan Claybrook, chief of the National Highway Traffic Safety Administration, said: "This information becomes even more vital since the fuel economy crunch and the trend toward smaller cars."

Disasters — At least 26 people were killed and thousands lost their homes when torrential rains and gale-force winds resulted in flash-floods in Southern California **Feb. 13-22.** Nearly 13 inches of rain were dumped on the region. Central Arizona and the Mexican border areas were also hard hit by the storms that came from the Pacific ocean. On **Feb. 21,** Pres. Carter declared 6 California counties federal disaster areas and, on **Feb. 20,** he similarly designated 3 Arizona counties.

MARCH

National

Carter, Reagan Accumulate Delegates in Primaries — In a critical month of primaries, Pres. Carter and Ronald Reagan built up strong leads in the number of delegates committed to them at the party conventions, even though they lost some of the contests. Sen. Edward Kennedy, **Mar. 4,** won impressively in his home state of Massachusetts with 65 percent of the vote and 77 delegates to Carter's 26 percent and 34 delegates. The surprise in the Republican contest in that state was the emergence of Rep. John Anderson (R, Ill.) as a serious contender with 31 percent of the vote and 13 delegates. George Bush won the race with 31 percent of the vote and 14 delegates. Reagan came in 3d with 29 percent of the vote and 13 delegates, and Howard Baker came in 4th with 5 percent of the vote and 2 delegates. In the Vermont primary, Carter, **Mar. 4,** swamped Kennedy with 74 percent of the vote to Kennedy's 26 percent. Reagan won 31 percent of the vote, Anderson 30 percent, Bush 23 percent, and Baker 13 percent. Baker withdrew from the race **Mar. 5.** Reagan defeated John Connally's determined challenge in South Carolina, **Mar. 8,** with a resounding 54 percent of the vote to Connally's 30 percent. Bush trailed with 15 percent of the vote. On **Mar. 9,** Connally withdrew from the race. Carter and Reagan, **Mar. 11,** spurted out ahead of the pack by sweeping 3 southern states. In Florida, Carter won 61 percent of the vote and 74 delegates, while Kennedy won only 23 percent of the vote and 25 delegates. Reagan tallied 57 percent of the vote and received all 51 delegates. Bush won 30 percent of the vote and Anderson won 9 percent. In Georgia, the president's home state, Carter won 88 percent of the vote and 62 delegates. Kennedy won 9 percent of the vote and 1 delegate. Reagan trounced Bush with 73 percent of the vote and 36 delegates to Bush's 13 percent of the vote and Anderson's 9 percent. Reagan maintained another huge margin of victory in Alabama, where he garnered 70 percent of the vote and 18 delegates to Bush's 26 percent of the vote and 9 delegates. Carter, the first president from the deep south in over a century, handily won 82 percent of the vote and 43 delegates while Kennedy finished with only 13 percent of the vote and 2 delegates. Former President Gerald Ford, **Mar. 15,** announced his decision not to enter the 1980 presidential race. On **Mar. 1,** Ford had declared that Reagan could not win the general election and had invited the Republican party to ask him to run again for president. The party did not respond. Also on **Mar. 15,** Sen. Bob Dole (R, Kan.) withdrew from the Republican race, citing a lack of money, management, and manpower. On the eve of the Democratic Puerto Rican primary, armed terrorists of the pro-independence Puerto Rican group FALN (Armed Forces of National Liberation), **Mar. 15,** invaded the Carter-Mondale headquarters in Chicago and the Bush headquarters in New York, gagged staff members and spray-painted the offices' walls with anti-statehood slogans. No injuries were reported in either raid; each lasted no more than a half hour. After campaigning for the island's statehood, Bush had won the Republican primary in Puerto Rico, **Feb. 17,** with 61 percent of the vote and 14 delegates to Howard Baker's 37 percent. On **Mar. 16,** Carter, backed by the pro-statehood New Progressive party, won the Puerto Rican Democratic primary with 52 percent of the vote and 21 delegates. Kennedy came in a close 2d with 48 percent of the vote and 20 delegates. Despite the endorsement of Chicago Mayor Jane Byrne, Kennedy went down to a stunning defeat in the Illinois primary with 30 percent of the vote and 14 delegates. Carter won 65 percent of the vote and 165 delegates. Gov. Edmund Brown, Jr. of California received 5 percent of the vote. In the Republican contest, Reagan won 39 delegates with 48 percent of the vote. Anderson, in his home state, won a respectable 37 percent of the vote and 26 delegates, aided by a large crossover vote by Independents and Democrats. Bush won 2 delegates, and Rep. Phillip Crane, another native son, won 4. Kennedy's crumbling campaign received a lift, **Mar. 25,** when he decisively beat Carter in both the New York and Connecticut primaries. In New York, Kennedy won 59 percent of the vote and 164 delegates to Carter's 41 percent of the vote and 118 delegates. Polls indicated that dissatisfaction with the economy and foreign policy had led many people to vote against the president. Reagan crushed Bush with 75 percent of the vote and 73 delegates to Bush's 6 percent and 6 delegates. Thirty-five Republican delegates were uncommitted. In Connecticut, Kennedy once again beat Carter by 47 percent to 41 percent, and gained 29 delegates. Carter won 25. Bush, in the state where he grew up and which his father represented as a U.S. senator, came in 1st with 39 percent of the vote and 15 delegates. Reagan was a strong 2d with 34 percent of the vote and 14 delegates and Anderson continued to siphon off votes with 22 percent of the tally and 6 delegates.

Chicago Firemen Strike Ends — A 23-day strike by Chicago's firefighters ended, **Mar. 8,** after the city and union agreed to turn the dispute over to a fact-finding panel and, if necessary, binding arbitration. The strike, the first ever by Chicago firefighters, began **Feb. 14** when talks broke down on a written contract, which the firefighters were fighting to obtain for the first time. Chicago Mayor Jane Byrne insisted on having a no-strike clause in a contract. "I refuse to play Russian roulette with the safety of Chicago citizens by granting firemen the right to strike," said Byrne. The firemen wanted the right to strike if no contract was in force. On **Feb. 18,** Byrne said that she would never again negotiate with the Chicago Fire Fighters Union or its president, Frank Muscare. The same day, the city assigned hundreds of men to the fire stations to replace the strikers. Muscare was jailed **Feb. 21** for contempt of a state court order to the strikers to return to work. Negotiations resumed **Mar. 6** after Rev. Jesse Jackson, the civil rights activist, intervened. Muscare was released **Mar. 13** pending an appeal. The interim agreement stipulated a no-strike, no-lockout status until Dec. 31. A 3-member fact-finding board would make recommendations for a settlement and, if negotiations on the board's proposals were unsuccessful, the issues would be submitted for binding arbitration. Twenty-two people died from fires during the 23 days of the strike, about the same as in the same period the year before.

Ford Corp. Cleared in 3 Deaths — In the first criminal prosecution of an American corporation in a case involving alleged product defects that led to a death, the Ford Motor Corp., **Mar. 13,** was found not guilty on 3 charges of reckless homicide. Only monetary penalties would have been levied if the verdict had been guilty. The case involved the death of 3 young women whose 1973 Pinto burst into flames after it was struck from the rear by a van near Winamac, Indiana in August 1978. The prosecution charged that Ford officials knew that the Pinto's gasoline tanks tended to explode when struck from behind and that they did nothing to correct the defect after manufacture. Ford denied the charges and said that the car was as safe as its competitors. Upon hearing the verdict, Philip Caldwell, Ford's chairman, said that "the principal that came out of this was that there must be responsibility on the part of those who use products as well as for those who design and build them." Pulaski County Circuit Judge Harold Staffeldt had restricted the scope of the trial, allowing the state to show the jury only about 24 of the more than 200 documents it wanted to introduce. Due to the national controversy over the safety of the fuel tank in rear-end collisions, Ford had voluntarily recalled 1.9 million Pintos in June 1978 to improve the safety of the tanks.

Carter Announces Anti-Inflation Program Based on Budget Cuts — After a 3-week review of economic policies, Pres. Carter, **Mar. 14,** announced a 5-point anti-inflation package. The 5 major elements were: $13 billion in federal spending cuts to balance the 1981 budget combined with $2 billion in cuts for the current year; controls on unsecured loans and other forms of consumer credit, as well as restraints on banks and money market mutual funds; a new voluntary pay standard of 7 1/2 to 9 1/2 percent, and an expansion of the staff monitoring wages and prices; a $4.62 fee on each barrel of imported oil, translating to a 10-cent-a-gallon increase in gasoline prices; and measures to encourage productivity, savings, and research. Separately, the Federal Reserve announced the same day an additional surcharge of 3 percentage points on the discount rate to large banks borrowing from the Fed on a frequent basis; this move raised the total rate to 16 percent. On **Mar. 7,** the government announced that the producer price index soared 1.5 percent in February, pushed by energy prices that rose 7.5 percent during the month, the greatest energy price rise in 6 years. The unemployment rate dropped to 6 percent in February, indicating that the economy was still not entering a recession. On **Mar. 25,** the government announced that the average American worker lost 1.4 percent of his purchasing power in February, which meant that for the first 2 months of 1980, the quantity of goods and services the worker could buy was declining at a staggering annual rate of 17.3 percent. In his Mar. 14 speech, Carter said that inflation was a dangerous situation that called for "urgent measures." "They involve pain," Carter admitted. "But the cost of acting is far less than the cost of not acting." On **Mar. 31,** Carter sent Congress a revised budget for fiscal 1981, which contained $15 billion in proposed spending cuts, some $2 billion more than expected. The revised budget projected receipts of $628 billion and outlays of $611.5 billion. Carter's first fiscal 1981 budget had projected revenues of $600 billion. The revised budget's big increase in projected revenues ($28 billion) came from inflation-produced tax receipts of $11.6 billion and 2 new tax proposals, one of which, the import fee on petroleum, would net some $12.6 billion. The principal cuts in the revised budget focused on aid to states and cities and the disadvantaged but did not include benefit programs like Social Security. The Defense Department, which accounted for a quarter of all federal spending, was asked to absorb only $1.4 billion of the $15 billion in cuts and accounted for the greatest share, $5.7 billion, of the projected increases since January in federal spending for 1981. The Council of Economic Advisors estimated that the revised fiscal 1980 and 1981 budgets taken together represented a swing of $70 billion in the direction of restraint on the economy.

Silver Drop Shakes Hunts' Empire — The price of silver plummeted, **Mar. 27,** to $10.80 an ounce, down $5 during the day, causing huge losses for speculators and threatening the collapse of the $2 billion silver empire of Nelson Bunker Hunt and W. Herbert Hunt of Dallas, Texas. A sharp fall in silver futures prices, **Mar. 26,** led brokerage houses to make margin calls for more cash from investors to maintain their equity in holdings of commodities bought on credit. The investment house of Bache Halsey Stuart Shields Inc. announced, **Mar. 27,** that the Hunt brothers had failed to meet $100 million of margin calls on their silver accounts, which caused panic in the silver market. The Hunts had built up silver holdings estimated at more than 200 million ounces since the summer of 1979 and had helped drive the price of an ounce of silver up to its January high of $50.05. The call had put a severe cash squeeze on the Hunts, given the size of their holdings, and they had been either unable or unwilling to raise the cash. Bache had begun to sell out its holdings of the Hunts' silver-futures and stock positions, **Mar. 26.** Bache itself, 5.6 percent owned by the Hunts, announced, **Mar. 31,** that it had incurred $50 million in potential losses in connection with the Hunts' silver accounts and that the Hunts had paid the firm $17 million that day. On **Mar. 31,** the Hunts signed a preliminary agreement to cover another $400 million in losses that resulted from their silver trading activities. The brothers agreed to turn over Canadian oil and gas properties and silver holdings to Engelhard Minerals and Chemicals Corp. in exchange for Engelhard's agreement to let the Hunts out of a contract to buy 19 million ounces of silver at $35 an ounce. The contract came due Mar. 31, but silver that day had closed in New York at $14.20 an ounce. Engelhard would keep its 19 million ounces of silver, receive another 8.5 million ounces fron the Hunts, and acquire oil holdings worth an estimated $500 million.

International

Soviets Attack Afghan Rebels — In the first major Soviet military move against the Afghanistan rebels, Soviet and Afghan troops, backed by at least 50 helicopter gunships and 200 tanks, attacked, **Mar. 1,** rebel strongholds in the eastern Province of Kunar. The Soviet offensive came during early spring in the area, which melted the heavy cover of snow in the valleys of the mountainous region. A rebel report, **Mar. 4,** said the insurgents in the area were routed by the attack: "There is no one left in the Kunar Valley now except Russian soldiers and Afghan troops." The spokesman, representing the Mujahedeen Moslem Fighters of Kunar and Nuristan, estimated civilian and insurgent casualties at more than 1,000 killed and attributed many of the casualties to several days of artillery and air strikes which had leveled several villages between Chagasarei and Asmar prior to the attack. The spokesman accused Soviet troops of having used napalm, incendiary devices and poison gas. Thousands of villagers reportedly fled the area, crossing the mountains into Pakistan. Pakistani military sources, **Mar. 11,** said that Soviet troops were continuing their drive to oust rebels in Kunar, after gaining control of the road along the Kunar River Valley. These sources reported, however, that insurgents remained in control of every mountain pass leading from Kunar Province into northern Pakistan. On **Mar. 29,** the *New York Times* reported that rebel activity in Kunar Valley and the northeastern province of Badakshan had been virtually wiped out. According to the newspaper, estimates that about 1,500 Soviet soldiers had been killed since Dec. were called conservative by travelers who had heard about the situation in military and civilian hospitals. Only 35,000 soldiers were reported left in the Afghan army after recent desertions and defections.

U.S. Disavows Its UN Vote Against Israeli West Bank Settlements — In an extraordinary statement issued **Mar. 3,** Pres. Carter disavowed an American vote in favor of a UN Security Council resolution calling on Israel to dismantle its settlements in the West Bank and Gaza Strip. The resolution had passed unanimously **Mar. 1.** Carter said that the U.S. vote, the first time that the U.S. had voted against Israel on the issue of settlements in the Council, had been cast in error and had resulted from a communication failure between the U.S. delegation to the UN and the White House. "The United States vote in the United Nations was approved with the understanding that all references to Jerusalem would be deleted," Carter explained. "The failure to communicate this clearly resulted in a vote in favor of the resolution rather than in an abstention." Donald McHenry, chief U.S. delegate to the UN, said that he had been told by Secretary of State Cyrus Vance to vote for the resolution if one particularly objectionable paragraph, paragraph 7 which implied criticism of Israel's administration of the holy places in Jerusalem, and the language on dismantling the settlements had been deleted. Paragraph 7 was deleted and McHenry suggested to Vance that he could deal with the other issue by making a statement about the language on dismantling the settlements. Believing that the resolution was in conformity with U.S. policy since the 2 issues were dealt with, Vance advised Carter that it conformed to U.S. policy and Carter authorized the vote without reading the text of the proposed resolution himself. On **Mar. 1,** McHenry voted for the resolution and read a statement that described the call for dismantling the existing settlements as "impractical." According to the *New York Times,* the U.S. had wanted to send Israel a signal of American unhappiness over Israel's **Feb. 10** decision to allow Jews to settle in the West Bank city of Hebron. Israel and Egypt were negotiating autonomy for Arabs on the West Bank when Israel made the decision to allow the Jewish settlement. When Carter returned to the White House from Camp David the morning of **Mar. 3,** he reviewed the text of the UN resolution for the first time and reportedly became angry when he discovered that the text still contained many references to Jerusalem, a sensitive subject for Israel which had annexed the eastern side of the city in 1967 and intended to keep the undivided city as its capital. Carter said in his Mar. 3 statement that the fate of Jerusalem should be left to the current Israeli-Egyptian negotiations. Carter decided to issue a statement disavowing the vote. On **Mar. 4,** Vance accepted the blame for the "failure in communication." The U.S. reversal provoked a furor both domestically and internationally. Diplomats claimed that the move placed U.S. credibility in question and McHenry, **Mar. 5,** conceded: "Obviously, my job is going to be made more difficult." Mondale claimed that pressure from Israel on American Jewish groups had "nothing to do" with Carter's decision to reverse his position. Before the House Foreign Affairs Committee **Mar. 21,** Vance testified that Carter disavowed the vote because "in the present phase of the [Palestinian] autonomy negotiations it would not be helpful to raise the issue of Jerusalem in a United Nations resolution concerning settlements." The Carter Administration, Vance said, still supported parts of the resolution and considered the Jewish settlements to be illegal and impediments to peace. On **Mar. 19,** Carter invited Egyptian President Anwar Sadat and Israeli Prime Minister Menahem Begin to meet with him in order to explore ways in which to move the talks on Palestinian autonomy forward.

Mugabe Wins Zimbabwe Election — By a surprising large margin, Robert Mugabe, the Marxist leader of the Zimbabwe African National Union (ZANU) guerrilla force, won the election for a new black government in Zimbabwe Rhodesia, it was announced **Mar. 4.** Mugabe's ZANU-Patriotic Front party received 62.9 percent of the popular vote and 57 of the 80 seats reserved for blacks in the future 100-member parliament (20 seats were reserved for whites). Joshua Nkomo, Mugabe's former guerrilla colleague, won 24.1 percent of the vote and 20 seats. Bishop Abel Muzorewa, prime minister of the former black-led government, won 8.2 percent of the vote and 3 seats. The election gave Mugabe an unexpected black majority, which led the leader to reassure the country's 230,000 whites that their interests would be taken into consideration in his government. Land would not be confiscated nor would other retributions against whites be permitted, said Mugabe. Mugabe outlined a moderate course for the future of the country: "We recognize that the economic structure is based on capitalism and that whatever ideas we have must build on that." In order to incorporate groups that were at war just a few months before, Mugabe pledged to have a coalition government and include "people of all races" in his cabinet. Mugabe asked Lt. Gen. Peter Walls, a white officer who led Rhodesian forces against the black guerrillas for 7 years, to head the new Zimbabwe army. Mugabe, **Mar. 10,** appointed Joshua Nkomo, a rival black leader and partner in the Patriotic Front guerrilla alliance, to be Minister of Home Affairs. The cabinet sworn in **Apr, 19** included 21 blacks and 2 whites. The election had been marred by allegations of voter intimidation by Mugabe's followers and others. A Commonwealth observation team, composed of 63 members from 11 Commonwealth countries, concluded, **Mar. 2,** that the election had been basically free and fair and accused Britain of bias against Mugabe. The voter turnout was 93.6 percent, much higher than the 64 percent turnout in the 1979 elections from which the guerrillas were excluded. Martial law in the country ended **Mar. 20.** On **Apr. 17,** 90 years of white rule ended as Zimbabwe Rhodesia officially became the independent nation of Zimbabwe.

Pakistan Turns Down U.S. Aid Offer — Foreign Minister Agha Shahi of Pakistan, **Mar. 5,** rejected a $400 million U.S. aid package, saying that it would detract from rather than enhance Pakistan's security. Instead, Shahi said, Pakistan would base its foreign policy on close ties to Islamic and nonaligned nations. The U.S. had offered the aid to Pakistan **Jan. 12** in the wake of the Soviet invasion of Afghanistan. Some officials described the Pakistani rejection of the aid as an embarrassing setback of the American policy of strengthening ties with nations in the Persian Gulf area.

Shah Leaves Panama for Egypt — The day before Iran's revolutionary government was due to present Panamanian authorities with a formal request for his extradition, deposed Iranian Shah Mohammed Reza Pahlavi, **Mar. 23,** left Panama and arrived the following day in Cairo, where Egyptian President Anwar Sadat granted him permanent asylum. Egypt was the 6th country in which the shah had sought refuge since he fled Iran on Jan. 16, 1979. Earlier the shah had been found to have an enlarged spleen and the required surgery had also been mired in controversy. White House

Chief of Staff Hamilton Jordan had flown to Panama **Mar. 21** to persuade the shah not to leave the country. He attempted to assure him that a dispute between American and Panamanian doctors over treatment of his medical problems had been resolved, and that it was doubtful that Panama would grant Iran its request for extradition. Panama President Aristides Royo had stated that no extradition request would be granted, since it was made from political motives and the deportee would face the death penalty. But the shah was thought to have been alarmed that Panama was willing to accept a formal petition from Iran. The shah's departure was considered a blow to U.S. attempts to release the American hostages since it could be seen in Iran as evidence of an American plot for the shah to evade extradition. The U.S. renewed a previous strategy to gain the release of the hostages after the failure of the UN Commission when it appealed to the International Court of Justice in The Hague, **Mar. 18-20,** to make a final judgment on Iran's violation of international law. Ayatollah Ruhollah Khomeini had authorized Iran's new parliament to make decisions on the hostages, but after the 1st round of voting, further parliamentary elections were delayed indefinitely, **Mar. 26.** The U.S. delivered an ultimatum to Iran, **Mar. 30,** demanding that the government take control of the hostages by Mar. 31 or face new sanctions. Iranian President Abolhassan Bani-Sadr asked for a 24-hour postponement of the deadline, conferred with the Revolutionary Council, and, on **Apr. 1,** announced that the Iranian government would take control of the hostages if the U.S. pledged not to make threats against Iran. Carter responded by deciding that same day to postpone putting additional economic sanctions on Iran. Meanwhile, the shah's spleen was removed, **Mar. 28,** by U.S. surgeon Michael DeBakey in Cairo and there were demonstrations against the ex-shah's presence in Egypt by university students in Asyut **Mar. 28** and **31.**

Swedes in a Referendum Back A-Power — Swedish voters, **Mar. 23,** supported the limited expansion of nuclear energy in a nonbinding referendum. The 2 proposals that backed the use of nuclear power won 58.1 percent of the vote. One proposal, which won 39.4 percent of the vote, called for operating at most 12 nuclear plants, and phasing out nuclear power after 25 years. The other pro-nuclear proposal, which won 18.7 percent of the vote, supported the use of 12 power plants for 25 years—their estimated service life—without specifying what nuclear policy Sweden would follow later. The proposal to dismantle the country's 6 operating reactors over 10 years received 38.6 percent. Support for the expansion of nuclear power was strongest in areas where there were reactors, which caused some observers to note that the concern that jobs would be lost overcame the fear of a major nuclear accident. Sweden obtains 25 percent of its electricity from nuclear energy and imports more oil per capita than any other Western country. Premier Thorbjorn Falldin, who opposed nuclear power, said that he would respect the wishes of the voters.

Archbishop Assassinated in El Salvador — Roman Catholic Archbishop Oscar Arnulfo Romero, one of the most respected church leaders in El Salvador, was assassinated, **Mar. 24,** as he officiated at a mass in San Salvador. A sniper stood just inside the door of the chapel of the Divine Providence Hospital, fired a single shot at the prelate, and escaped. No group claimed responsibility for the killing of the outspoken priest, who had often backed aid for the poor and called for peace in the strife-torn country. In the last 2 years, at least 6 priests had been killed by right-wing terrorists and some observers attributed this killing to these same terrorists. Hours after the murder, at least 30 bombs were detonated in several cities, damaging stores, banks, and other businesses. During the funeral for Romero, on **Mar. 30,** more than 30,000 people were jammed into the plaza before the Metropolitan Cathedral where the funeral was taking place. After an explosion, panic swept the crowd, which surged into the cathedral and side streets. Observers witnessed snipers firing guns from building tops for the next hour. At least 26 people were killed and about 200 injured. Many people, including U.S. Ambassador Robert White, blamed leftist groups for starting the violence, but some eyewitnesses blamed rightist organizations. "First one extreme tries to create panic by shooting one person," White said, referring to the archbishop. "Then the others try to take political advantage of his death and kill more people in the process." The *New York Times* estimated, **Mar. 31,** that political extremists in El Salvador had been killing each other at the rate of 10 a day for the last 3 months.

General

'Scarsdale Diet' Doctor Slain — Dr. Herman Tarnower, a prominent physician and author of the best-selling *The Complete Scarsdale Medical Diet,* was shot and killed, **Mar. 10,** in his home in Purchase, N.Y. Jean Harris, a long-time friend of Tarnower's and headmistress of the Madeira School, a prestigious school in Virginia, was charged, **Mar. 11,** with second-degree murder. Tarnower was found unconscious on the floor of his bedroom bleeding profusely from 3 bullet wounds and was pronounced dead an hour later at a hospital. Harris was seen driving away from Tarnower's house as police arrived to investigate a reported disturbance. She turned over a .32-caliber revolver and later admitted that she had shot Tarnower. On **Mar. 28,** she pleaded not guilty to a 3-count indictment charging that she had intended to kill Tarnower. She claimed that she had gone to see the doctor with the intention of having Tarnower kill her, but that she had had an argument with the cardiologist and he began to push her saying, "Get out of here, you're crazy." Harris had visible bruises around her mouth after the incident.

Man Found Guilty of Killing 33 — John Gacy was found guilty, **Mar. 12,** of committing 33 murders, more than any other mass killer in U.S. history. Gacy was also convicted of taking indecent liberties with a minor and of deviant sexual assault. The trial had centered on the issue of whether Gacy was a cold-blooded murderer who had planned the killings or a mentally diseased man who was incapable of understanding his actions. Gacy had been arrested Dec. 22, 1978, and charged with murdering a 15-year-old youth, Robert Piest. Gacy subsequently told police of committing 32 other murders of boys and young men whom he lured to his home with the promise of jobs between 1972 and 1978. The bodies of 28 victims were found in the crawlspace under his house in Des Plaines, Ill., 3 were found in his garage and 4 more were found in a nearby river. On **Mar. 13,** Gacy was sentenced to die in the electric chair. The last execution in Illinois was in 1962.

Political Activist Slain — Former U.S. Rep. Allard Lowenstein was shot and killed, **Mar. 14,** in his New York City law office. Lowenstein had been the main architect of the 1968 anti-Vietnam War movement to block the Democratic renomination of President Lyndon Johnson and had spent a term as a New York Congressman. The gunman was identified by police as Dennis Sweeney, a former associate of Lowenstein in the civil rights movement in the south in the 1960's. Sweeney and Lowenstein talked in the activist's law office briefly, shots were heard and Sweeney walked out of the inner office, placed a semi-automatic pistol on a secretary's desk and waited until the police arrived. Lowenstein died 6 hours later after doctors operated to close bullet wounds in his heart and to remove an injured lung. Sweeney, who had a history of treatment for mental disorders, was indicted **Mar. 18** on a charge of second-degree murder in the slaying. Police said that Sweeney had blamed Lowenstein for family problems that had led to the death of his stepfather after a heart attack in Oregon in February.

Mexico Caps Oil Well, Stopping Worst Spill — After a 9-month fight against the world's worst oil spill, Mexican officials, **Mar. 24,** said that engineers had successfully capped the Ixtoc I oil well that had spilled more than 3.1 billion barrels of crude oil since blowing up June 3, 1979. The spill was twice as bad as the worst previous one when the tanker Amoco Cadiz ran aground and sank near Portsall, France, on Mar. 16, 1978.

North Sea Oil Platform Capsizes, Killing 123 — A North Sea floating oil field platform with more than 200 persons aboard capsized, **Mar. 27,** in a gale. The French-built platform had been mounted on 5 columns that rode on pontoons in the water. When one of the legs snapped, the platform listed 45 degrees in a matter of moments, then capsized within 20 minutes. Eighty-nine persons were saved, 40 were known dead, and 83 were officially listed as "missing, presumed dead." Officials of the Phillips Petroleum Co., which operated the platform in the Ekofisk oil field in the Norwegian sector of the North Sea, were reported to believe that

that metal fatigue caused a break in a welded joint in the leg.

Disasters — A severe snowstorm, **Mar. 2-3,** over the eastern half of the U.S. killed at least 20 persons. . .A Polish jetliner, carrying a 22-member American amateur boxing team, crashed, **Mar. 14,** killing all 87 people on board, after an engine failed minutes before landing at Warsaw. . .Thirty-one South African miners were killed, **Mar. 27,** when the cable of a mineshaft elevator snapped, plunging the miners more than a mile to their deaths in the Vaal Reefs mine. . .

APRIL

National

Carter, Reagan Increase Delegate Leads — The relentless buildup of the convention delegate leads of Pres. Carter and Ronald Reagan, the frontrunners in the party races for the presidential nomination, mounted in the April primaries. On **April 1** in Wisconsin, Reagan picked up 28 delegates and won 40 percent of the vote, while George Bush won only 31 percent of the vote and no delegates (because they were allotted on a winner-take-all basis by congressional district). John Anderson came in 3d with 28 percent of the vote and 6 delegates. The Republicans had attracted a remarkable turnout, 52 percent higher than the 1976 Republican vote. In the Democratic race, Carter regained momentum after his loss of 2 primaries the previous week by overwhelming Kennedy to win 56 percent of the vote and 49 delegates to the Massachusetts senator's 30 percent of the vote and 26 delegates. California Gov. Edmund "Jerry" Brown Jr. withdrew from the race after receiving only 12 percent of the vote. Carter then received 62 delegates and Reagan 49 when they handily won the Kansas and Louisiana primaries **Apr. 1** and **5.** Both Kennedy and Bush mounted intense campaigns in Pennsylvania to re-ignite their faltering campaigns. Both had previously done well in urban, industrial states. Kennedy concentrated on economic issues as layoffs spread in the auto industry. Bush worked the state for 14 days, deriding Reagan for his "simplistic solutions." Although Kennedy and Bush did win the **Apr. 22** race in Pennsylvania, they were not able to slow down the frontrunners' rush to the delegate count necessary for nomination. Kennedy beat Carter by only about 10,000 votes out of more than 1.5 million cast and won only one delegate more than the 92 that Carter picked up. Bush won 53 percent of the vote to Regan's 46 percent but, in the separate delegate contest, Reagan's supporters managed to gain 35 delegates for him, while Bush received only 17. By the end of the month, Reagan had 607 of the 990 needed to be nominated and Carter had 1,137 of the 1,666 delegates he needed to be nominated.

"Windfall Profits" Oil Tax Bill Signed — Pres. Carter, **Apr. 2,** signed into law the Crude Oil Windfall Profit Tax Act of 1980, which was believed to be the largest single tax ever imposed on an industry. The tax was expected to bring in at least $227.3 billion in revenue over the next 10 years, and more if the price of oil continued to increase. Carter had proposed the tax in April 1979 to accompany the decontrol of oil prices that was expected to bring oil producers an extra $1 trillion by the end of the decade. Other federal, state and local taxes and royalties would take about $552 billion of the producers' increase in income during the decade, which would leave producers with $221 billion after more than $227 billion was collected by the "windfall profits" measure. Although it was called a "windfall profits" tax, the legislation actually applied to price increases above the 1979 controlled levels, not to profits. By a 302-107 vote, the House, **Mar. 13,** had passed a version of the bill; the Senate had passed the compromise conference committee version of the bill on **Mar. 27** by a 66-31 vote.

Phone Industry Computer Curb Lifted — The Federal Communications Commission, **Apr. 7,** authorized by a vote of 5-2 an extensive deregulation of the telecommunications industry. Under the ruling, which would go into effect Mar. 1, 1982, basic phone service and rates would continue to be regulated by the commission, but the phone companies would be allowed to enter the growing business of linking computer to computer for data transmission. Under the ruling, the sale of phone equipment would also be allowed on the free market. The giant American Telephone and Telegraph Company had been barred from offering data-processing services by a 1956 Federal Court consent decree. Commerce Department officials said that they hoped that the entry of A.T. & T. and other U.S. enterprises into the booming telecommunications field would help the U.S. meet the intensified competition of Japanese and Western European firms in the field.

New York Transit Strike Ends — The New York City transit strike ended, **Apr. 11,** after union leaders approved a tentative agreement on a new contract. The five million people who normally ride the nation's largest mass transit system had been walking, biking, and car-pooling to work during the 11-day walkout. The settlement called for a 17 percent pay increase over 2 years for the 33,000 bus and subway workers that would rise to about 20.7 percent in the final 6 months with a cost-of-living adjustment. New York State Gov. Hugh Carey approved the settlement and said that he would work to obtain funds to save the existing 50 cents transit fare. New York City Mayor Edward Koch, who faced negotiations in the next few months with all the city's major unions, said that the settlement would raise the expectations of city workers "way beyond what we can possibly afford to pay."

Carter Says Recession Has Begun — After the automobile industry announced a sharp drop in sales and a 22 percent decline in March in the construction of new homes was announced, Pres. Carter, **Apr. 17,** admitted that a "short" recession had probably begun. Some economists predicted that even a deeper recession than that forecasted by Carter might be beginning when the Commerce Department, **Apr. 30,** announced a 2.6 percent decline in the index of leading indicators for March. One of the indicators was the increase in the March unemployment rate to 6.2 percent, which had been announced **Apr. 4.** A contributor to the slowdown was the government's tight money policy, which was supposed to halt the recent acceleration of inflation by reducing business expansion. On **Apr. 3,** banks had lifted their prime lending rate to a record 20 percent. Prices, however, continued to rise. Increases in the cost of food, clothing, and housing pushed consumer prices up 1.4 percent in March, the Labor Department reported **Apr. 22.**

Anderson Announces Independent Bid for Presidency — Rep. John Anderson announced, **Apr. 24,** that he would run for the presidency as an independent because the nation needed a choice in the November election. "Too many people in our nation are disillusioned with the prospective choices our party structures are offering," Anderson said. An **April 17** New York Times/CBS News poll had reported that half of the American public found Carter and Reagan an unsatisfactory choice for president and that Anderson was drawing 18 to 21 percent of the national vote from the 2 frontrunners. Admitting that Reagan had the Republican nomination all but locked up with 607 of the needed 998 delegates so early in the race, Anderson released the 59 delegates that he had won in 6 previous primaries. He began immediately to accumulate signatures on petitions, the first step to have his name placed on various state ballots as an independent.

Lance Cleared of Bank Fraud — After a 16-week trial, former U.S. Budget Director Bert Lance was acquitted, **Apr. 30,** by a federal jury in Atlanta, Ga., of 9 counts of bank fraud. A mistrial was declared on 3 remaining counts against Lance because the jury wasn't able to reach a verdict. Lance, a friend of Pres. Carter, had resigned in Sept. 1977 as director of the Office of Management and Budget in the midst of a controversy over his banking practices when he served as president and chief executive officer of both the National Bank of Georgia and the Calhoun First National Bank. When the trial began **Jan. 14,** Lance and 3 of his business associates had been charged with 33 counts. On **Apr. 9,** Federal District Judge Charles Moye Jr. dismissed a banking conspiracy charge and 12 other counts, due to insufficient evidence. The jury acquitted Lance of 9 remaining charges which claimed that he misused the funds of the 2 Georgia banks that he headed by making about $1 million in questionable loans to his wife, his son, and 3 friends. The jury deadlocked over 2 charges involving false financial statements pertaining to his debts and net worth, and one involving a $12,000 loan to one of his friends. After spending nearly $1 million in legal fees and battling with the government for 3 years, Lance said that he was not "bitter" about the experience, just "changed." The Lance case had been instrumental in the passage of the Financial Institutions Regulatory and Interest Rate Control Act of 1978, which curbed insider dealings that benefit bank officers, their families, and friends.

International

Cubans Seeks Asylum in Peru's Embassy — Some 10,800 Cubans jammed into the grounds of the Peruvian embassy in Havana, **Apr. 5-6,** after Cuba had withdrawn its guards from outside the compound and word spread that those inside the compound could leave the island if they could obtain visas from another country. The football field-size compound of the Peruvian embassy was packed so tightly with people that some were pressed against the chain-link fence surrounding the compound. Cubans at the embassy said in interviews that they wanted to leave their country in order to better their lives economically. Some of them said that they wished to escape the constant surveillance in Cuba. Cuba had removed its guards from the embassy after Peru had refused to return 6 men who, **Apr. 1,** had successfully crashed through the gates of the embassy in a bus to reach asylum and had killed a Cuban guard in the process. Cuban President Fidel Castro, **Apr. 7,** personally went to the embassy to assure the refugees inside that they would be granted safe passage out of Cuba when another country agreed to take them. To relieve the crowding in the compound, the Cuban government, **Apr. 7,** offered safe-conduct passes to those wishing to return to their homes before emigrating, but only 1,730 persons reportedly accepted the offer. The rest refused out of fear that they would not be al-

U.S. Aborts Mission To Rescue Hostages, Vance Resigns in Disagreement

After several diplomatic initiatives had failed to resolve the crisis in Iran, the U.S., **Apr. 24,** attempted to rescue the Americans held hostage in the U.S. Embassy in Teheran, but the mission was called off due to equipment failure. Eight Americans were killed and 5 were injured during the pullout in a collision between a helicopter and a transport plane.

On **Apr. 28,** Secretary of State Cyrus Vance resigned because he could not support Pres. Carter's decision to undertake a military mission to rescue the hostages. Vance argued that it was possible to obtain release of the hostages through diplomatic channels, augmented by economic and political sanctions. In addition, it was reported that Vance had considered the rescue plan unfeasible and too risky. On **Apr. 29,** Sen. Edward Muskie (D, Me.) was named by Carter to succeed Vance at the State Department.

The rescue attempt began with the take-off of 8 RH-53D Sea Stallion helicopters from the U.S.S. Nimitz in the Gulf of Oman and 6 C-130 Hercules transport planes from Egypt. The transports carried 90 commandos, equipment, and additional fuel for the helicopters. All 6 C-130s, but, due to mechanical problems, only 6 of the 8 helicopters landed at the designated rendezvous at Dasht-i-Kavir (the Great Salt Desert), 200 miles southeast of Teheran. One of the helicopters that landed at the rendezvous had a cracked nut which had caused a leak in its 2d-stage hydraulic pump during flight and it was unable to take off again.

The rescue plan called for a minimum of 6 helicopters to carry out the rescue and only 5 remained operational. On the recommendation of the mission commander and his military advisers, Pres. Carter canceled the operation and ordered the U.S. force to leave Iran.

During the pullout, one helicopter collided with a C-130 transport, resulting in the death of 8 men and injury to 5 others. All surviving members of the mission then boarded the remaining 5 C-130s and left; the remaining 5 helicopters were left behind as were the 8 dead.

The Iranian state radio announced, **Apr. 26,** that the American hostages had been removed from the U.S. Embassy in Teheran to other cities in the country to prevent further rescue attempts. On **Apr. 25,** Iran's revolutionary leader Ayatollah Ruhollah Khomeini, denounced the rescue attempt as a "stupid act" by Pres. Carter and warned that another attempt would endanger the lives of the U.S. hostages. Iranian authorities, **Apr. 27,** displayed the bodies of the Americans killed and claimed that 9 U.S. servicemen had been killed. The bodies were returned to the U.S. **May 6.**

Pres. Carter defended the mission, **Apr. 29,** by insisting that it had a good chance of success and would have ended the crisis. "There is a deeper failure than that of incomplete success," he said. "That is the failure to attempt a worthy effort—a failure to try." Carter visited the wounded at the Brooke Army Medical Center hospital in San Antonio, Tex., **Apr. 27,** where he described the Iranian display of the bodies of the dead as "inhumane" and "ghoulish."

The rescue attempt occurred after a flurry of diplomatic activity had failed to gain the release of the hostages and as the American public's frustration over the situation continued to mount. A New York Times/CBS News poll reported, **Apr. 17,** that only 39 percent of the public approved of Carter's handling of the hostage situation, down from 49 percent in March and 63 percent in February.

After Khomeini's refusal to order the transfer of the hostages from the militants to the Iranian government, the U.S., **Apr. 7,** had severed diplomatic relations with Iran, imposed a formal embargo on its exports to that country, and ordered the ouster of Iranian diplomats from the U.S. More than 50 Iranian diplomats and their families had left for Teheran **Apr. 8** and the Iranian Embassy in Washington and consulate offices in 5 other cities were closed.

In an attempt to further isolate Iran internationally, the U.S., **Apr. 8,** had appealed to its allies to join Washington in retaliatory action against Iran. The governments of Canada, Japan, Australia, New Zealand, and the Western European nations, **Apr. 9,** had received messages from Secretary of State Vance asking them to halt their non-food exports to Iran and to withdraw their ambassadors as a show of support for the latest American actions against Iran. Meeting in Lisbon, **Apr. 10,** the foreign ministers of the 9 Common Market countries had declined to impose sanctions or cut back ties to Iran. Instead, they had issued a conventional diplomatic demand for the release of the hostages, which Japan endorsed **Apr. 11.** Many European diplomats feared that sanctions might undercut the moderates in Teheran and increase Soviet influence in Southwest Asia. Europe and Japan rely heavily on imported Middle Eastern oil as well and were reported wary of provoking the wrath of oil producing states in the area. In a television interview broadcast in Europe **Apr. 13,** Carter had said that the U.S. wanted its allies to impose economic sanctions against Iran later in April and then break diplomatic ties with Teheran by mid-May if there was no progress in releasing the hostages. If the latest economic and political moves did not produce success, Carter had stated, "we will be required to take additional action which may very well involve military means." The press had reported that Britain and West Germany were the leaders in pressing for sanctions against Iran, while France had blocked such moves, not wanting to be "stampeded into economic warfare with Iran," as one French official put it, simply because Carter had decided it was time to get tough.

Carter had escalated the pressure on Iran, **Apr. 17,** when he announced new U.S. sanctions: a ban on all imports from Iran, a ban on financial transfers to Iran, and a ban on travel to Iran by Americans. Carter had also announced that all U.S. military equipment previously purchased by Iran and subsequently impounded, would be made available to U.S. military forces or sold to other countries.

Goaded by fear of a possible American military action against Iran and a desire to prevent a disruption of the Atlantic alliance, the foreign ministers of the 9-member European Community, **Apr. 22,** had voted unanimously to impose economic and diplomatic sanctions against Iran on May 17 unless "decisive progress" was made to gain release of the U.S. hostages held in Teheran. A total embargo of all exports to Iran except food and medicine would be imposed on that date. Until that time, the 9 countries would reduce embassy staffs in Teheran and Iranian representation in Europe, introduce a visa system for Iranians traveling to their countries, and withhold permission for all military sales to Iran. Canada, **Apr. 23,** and Japan, **Apr. 24,** had taken similar measures.

lowed back in if they left the embassy. Overcome by the heat, poor sanitation, and lack of food, about 6,000 of the Cubans left the Peruvian embassy a few days later to wait for evacuation at home, after they had obtained passports and exit visas from Cuban officials. On **Apr. 16,** more than 230 of the Cubans who had sought asylum at the Peruvian embassy were flown to Costa Rica and, on **Apr. 17,** another plane carrying 252 arrived there. However, on **Apr. 18,** the flights to Costa Rica were halted when the Cuban government demanded that the refugees be flown directly to the countries where they were to settle. The U.S., **Apr. 14,** had agreed to admit up to 3,500 of the Cubans, after they were processed in Costa Rica, and 10 other countries agreed to take at least 2,500 more. Some Cubans from south Florida's large Cuban exile community succeeded in retrieving relatives and embassy refugees by boat and the news raced through the Cuban-American community that Castro was allowing boats to enter the port of Mariel, 27 miles west of Havana, to pick up refugees. Most importment to the exiles, the news spread that any Cuban, not only squatters at the Peruvian embassy, could be issued an exit permit. On **Apr. 21,** about 50 small fishing boats set sail from Florida for Mariel and, by **Apr. 24,** some 600 Cuban-American boat owners had reached Key West in order to set sail for Cuba. To stem the tide of immigration, the U.S. Justice Department warned, **Apr. 23,** that boat owners faced stiff penalties and fines of up to $1,000 for every Cuban citizen they ferried to the U.S. The Cuban-Americans took off for the Cuban port anyway, clogging it with hundreds of vessels. Boats had to wait several days in the port to pick anyone up and then were allowed to take friends and relatives as only a small fraction of their passenger load. As the number of boats making the 110-mile trip between Key West and Mariel increased, a storm with 100 mile-an-hour winds hit the area, **Apr. 25-28.** At least a dozen of the boats making runs to Cuba capsized, killing at least 4 persons. By **May 1,** an estimated 3,000 boats were waiting to pick up people at Mariel and 6,000 refugees had been processed in Key West.

Terrorists Raid Israeli Nursery — Five members of the Arab Liberation Front, an Iraqi-supported group belonging to the Palestinian Liberation Organization, attacked, **Apr. 7,** the children's dormitory of the Israeli kibbutz Misgav Am, near the Lebanese border, and took children hostage. In return for the hostages, the terriorists demanded the release of Palestinian guerrillas held in Israeli prisons. About an hour after the raid, armed kibbutz dwellers attempted to storm the dormitory but were repulsed. Eight hours later, Israeli soldiers successfully retook the building, killing all 5 terrorists. A 2½-year old Israeli boy, an Israeli soldier, and a kibbutz secretary were also killed during the 9-hour siege. In an attempt to retaliate for the PLO raid, on **Apr. 9,** 350 Israeli soldiers penetrated 5 miles into southern Lebanon but encountered no opposition from Lebanese troops. An Israeli spokesman said that the soldiers carried out "patrols in southern Lebanon as a precaution against possible terrorist activity." After a 5-day occupation they withdrew.

Liberian President Killed in Coup — Liberian Army enlisted men, **Apr. 12,** killed President William Tolbert Jr. and 27 others, and then took over the government and vowed to end corruption. Master Sgt. Samuel Doe assumed leadership of the country. Shooting was reported before dawn at the executive mansion and at several military installations. Doe said, in a radio broadcast, that "the rampant corruption and continuous failure by the government to effectively handle the affairs of the Liberian people left the enlisted men no alternative." Doe immediately released imprisoned members of the opposition Progressive People's Party, who were arrested **Mar. 9** after calling for a general strike to force Tolbert out of office. According to the human rights organization, Amnesty International, Tolbert's True Whig Party, **Apr. 9,** had offered rewards of up to $2,000 for the capture-dead or alive-of opposition leaders still at large. Four of the released men were appointed, **Apr. 13,** as members of the new 15-man cabinet, which included 5 military officers. Sporadic looting was reported in the capital city of Monrovia until **Apr. 15,** when the city was reported calm after stringent security measures were put into effect. On **Apr. 22,** 13 ministers and other top officials of the former government were executed by firing squad.

Zimbabwe Gains Independence — Ninety years of white rule ended officially, **Apr. 17,** for the country of Zimbabwe Rhodesia as it became the independent nation of Zimbabwe. The British flag, which had flown over the country during the transitional period of the previous 4 months and for some 70 years prior to 1965, was lowered over Salisbury in ceremonies presided over by Prince Charles of Britain. A new flag, emblazoned with the Zimbabwe bird, symbol of the country's ancient culture, was raised while a 21-gun salute marked the occasion. Robert Mugabe, the black leader who had been elected in March by a landslide to lead the new country, was sworn in as prime minister. In a speech, Mugabe reiterated the theme of reconciliation that had been the overriding message of his statements after his election victory to a country racked by 10 years of civil war.

Troops Make Arrests in Assam — The Indian government, **Apr. 19,** called out troops to quell the unrest in the northeastern state of Assam, which had been the site of protests for 10 months. After hundreds of protesters were arrested, tens of thousands of people poured into the streets of Gauhati, the state capital, in open defiance of a curfew. The protests had been staged by a student-led movement which demanded deportation of several million Bengalis who had settled in the area over the last 3 decades and competed for jobs and land with the natives. Leaders of the movement had demanded that all immigrants since 1950 be identified and removed from the electoral rolls and then dispersed into other Indian states. The movement had attempted to shut down the activities of the central government with protests and had blocked with picketing the flow of crude oil from Assam to refineries elsewhere in India for over 100 days.

Students Demonstrate in Afghanistan — Protests against the Soviet occupation of Afghanistan broke out in Kabul, **Apr. 21,** when the Soviet-backed government unveiled a new flag that resembled the flag flown under the monarchy before pro-Soviet factions came to power 2 years ago. There were sporadic protests at schools where the flags were distributed. On **Apr. 28,** students at the Omar Shaheed School for boys and at the Habibia High School began burning the old and new flags and throwing stones at troops. The troops fired back, killed at least 13 students, and arrested 200. On **Apr. 30,** the protests spread to the University of Kabul where groups gathered and shouted anti-Soviet slogans. Witnesses claimed that machine guns were fired by soldiers into the crowd and at least 60 people were killed.

U.S. Olympic Committee Backs Boycott of Moscow Games — The House of Delegates of the U.S. Olympic Committee voted 1,604 to 797, **Apr. 22,** in favor of a resolution to boycott the 1980 Summer Olympics in Moscow. The vote was considered a major victory for the Carter Administration, which had been urging the U.S. committee to back its decision to boycott the games and had been pressuring the governments of other nations to also protest the Soviet invasion of Afghanistan by not participating in the games. Many athletes, however, opposed the boycott, which they saw as an intrusion of politics into sports. After the vote, Bill Rodgers, the world's top marathon runner, said that the Olympic Committee officials should be forced to quit because "they've given up what their jobs stood for, which was not to allow any racial, religious or political pressures to affect them." Speaking to the committee prior to its vote, Vice President Walter Mondale claimed that the Soviet Union had long ago erased the line between politics and sports. According to Mondale, the Kremlin had been building up the Olympics for propaganda purposes and purging cities of dissidents prior to the games. Mondale reminded his audience of the 1936 Olympics in Berlin and said that they had ratified the policies of Hitler. Mondale also promised the committee that the government would increase its financial contributions to the committee's lagging fund-raising drive. On **Apr. 23,** a class action suit was filed in the U.S. District Court in Washington, challenging the committee's authority to ban the athletes' participation in the games. Eighteen amateur athletes, a coach, and a member of the committee's executive board brought the suit. The suit was dismissed **May 16** by U.S. District Judge John Pratt, who cited the Amateur Sports Act of 1978 as an upholder of the committee's authority.

Beatrix Assumes Dutch Throne — Queen Beatrix of the Netherlands, **Apr. 30,** was invested as the 6th Dutch monarch, succeeding her mother, Queen Juliana, who abdicated on her 71st birthday. The 42-year-old woman appealed to her people to build stronger links with the developing countries because "we can no longer disassociate our domestic polity from the distress in the world." Squatters in Amsterdam staged a demonstration to coincide with the investiture to protest the housing shortage. Fighting between the police and demonstrators left at least 125 persons injured.

General

Little Health Impact by 3 Mile Island Accident Found — Dr. George Tokuhata, director of epidemiology in the Pennsylvania Health Department, **Apr. 2,** said that there had been no significant change in the infant and perinatal death rates among people living near Three Mile Island both before and after the nation's worst commercial nuclear accident occurred there Mar. 28, 1979. He said that from April 1 to Sept. 30, 1979, there were 15.7 infant deaths for every 1,000 live births for those living within 10 miles of the reactor. In the 6 months from Oct. 1, 1978 to Mar. 31, 1979, there had been 17.2 infant deaths per 1,000 births. "The differences in these rates are so small, they are statistically insignificant—that is, they could be the result of chance," Dr. Tokuhata said. A 70-page report by the House Science and Technology Committee concluded, **Apr. 3,** that the accident was not a major nuclear disaster and that experts still considered one unlikely. Rep. Mike McCormack (D, Wash.), whose subcommittee prepared the report, said: "Three Mile Island was a serious accident, but not a serious threat to human health." On **Apr. 17,** the State Health Department of Pennsylvania released a study of the psychological effects of the accident which noted a "surprising" persistence of anxiety among a large part of population near the reactor. The study said that there were increases of 113 percent in the number of persons using sleeping pills and 88 percent in those using tranquilizers. The survey also found that nearly 13 percent of the 37,000 people living within a 5-mile radius of Three Mile Island had become antinuclear activists.

Record Set in Simulated Sea Dive — Three volunteers at Duke University in Durham, N.C., emerged, **Apr. 2,** from a pressure tank after a 28-day test in which they set a world record simulating a dive to 2,132 feet beneath the sea. The test used a novel mixture of breathing gases, combining helium and oxygen with 10 percent nitrogen. The use of nitrogen was innovative since most deep divers omit nitrogen entirely from their breathing mixtures due to its ability to cause "the bends" when divers are decompressed. In this case, the nitrogen was believed to act as a narcotic, which countered the effects, such as convulsions, which extreme pressures can have on the nervous system. Some specialists in deep-diving physiology believed that the test results could open large, previously restricted areas of the sea floor to relatively unencumbered human activity.

Neutrinos Found To Have Mass — Physicist Frederick Reines of the University of California at Irvine told a meeting of the American Physical Society in Washington, **Apr. 30,** that recent experiments indicated that the subatomic particle known as the "neutrino" appears to have mass. Experiments by Reines and his coworkers showed that the neutrino oscillates between different states, an instability that is associated, in theory, with mass. According to Harvard physicist Carlo Rubbia, "the cosmological consequences" of the finding "are absolutely fantastic." Physicists think that the universe is filled with the particles, heretofore conceived as having neither mass nor charge. Neutrinos would be the dominant material of the universe if they have mass and might be able to explain the nature of the invisible "stuff" whose gravity holds together the galaxies and clusters of galaxies.

Disasters — A bus attempting to pass a truck on a narrow bridge went over the edge and crashed into a shallow ditch near Culiacan, Mexico, **Apr. 7,** killing 48 persons and injuring 36 others. . . . A chartered British jetliner carrying vacationers crashed, **Apr. 25,** into a mountain on the Canary Island of Tenerife, killing all 146 persons aboard. . . .

MAY

National

Recession Deepens — The government announced, **May 16,** that industrial output declined 1.9 percent in April, the largest drop in more than 5 years. Additional news of the recession came **May 2,** when the Labor Department announced a rise in the unemployment level to 7 percent in April, the highest level since Aug. 1977. Much of the increase came from the automobile and housing industries. However, there was also some encouraging news indicating that inflation was slowing. On **May 9,** the Bureau of Labor Statistics reported that the prices paid by retailers rose by only 0.5 percent in April; they had risen by 1.4 percent in March. On **May 23,** it was announced that the Consumer Price Index had increased by only 0.9 percent in April and that the month was the first one in 2 years in which gasoline prices did not rise. The Carter Administration's chief inflation fighter, Alfred Kahn, said that some of the decline in the Consumer Price Index was "clearly attributable to the recession, which can hardly be a source of satisfaction."

18 Die in Miami Riot — Racial rioting in Miami, Fla., **May 17-19,** left 18 persons dead, injured more than 300 people, and caused an estimated $100 million in damage to property, making it the costliest urban disorder in the nation's history. The rioting started only hours after an all-white jury in Tampa had acquitted 4 Miami police officers who had been charged in the fatal beating of Arthur McDuffie, a black Miami insurance executive whom they had chased and stopped for a traffic violation. When news of the acquittal spread through black neighborhoods, rock and bottle throwing began, and the violence quickly escalated into arson, looting, beatings, and shootings. Most of the trouble occurred in a black neighborhood called Liberty City in northwest Miami, where dozens of fires were reported. Florida Gov. Bob Graham quickly ordered the National Guard into the neighborhood and imposed a dawn-to-dusk curfew in an area several miles square. The area was closed off from traffic and police withdrew, entering the area only to escort fire trucks or stem outbreaks of looting. More than 50 fires broke out **May 18** and a black man was shot as he attacked police officers with a knife. By **May 19,** most of the violence had ended and many of the fires had burned out, leaving large sections of the area gutted and smoldering. By **May 20,** 3,600 guardsmen were patrolling the area and 1,267 people had been arrested. Attorney General Benjamin Civiletti arrived, **May 19,** in an effort to calm the outrage of the black community over the freeing of the 4 white police officers. On **May 21,** the National Guard began pulling out, the curfew was lifted, and a federal grand jury convened to consider possible civil rights violations in the Arthur McDuffie case. In an attempt to explain the 3 days of black rage, Florida officials said that the anger of the black community in Miami had been building during the past year when at least 4 widely publicized cases of alleged brutality by white policemen against blacks had taken place. The recent influx of Cuban refugees was reported to also anger blacks who resented the additional competition for jobs. On **June 7,** Pres. Carter visited the riot-torn area of Miami and talked to local leaders, telling them that the rebuilding initiative "must come from the community" itself but that he would meet private industry "at least halfway" to help rebuild the area. An angry crowd of several hundred demonstrators booed the president as he left the meeting and several bottles were thrown at his motorcade.

Love Canal Aid Ordered — Pres. Carter declared a state of emergency at the Love Canal in Niagara Falls, N.Y., **May 21,** which authorized the government to pay for the relocation of families away from an area contaminated by toxic wastes. About 710 families would be temporarily housed by the government until it could be determined whether the area was safe for their return. The Love Canal had been used as a chemical dump site for many years by the Hooker Chemicals and Plastics Corp. and, in 1978, 239 families abandoned homes in the area because of the existence and threat of health problems from the leaking toxic chemicals. According to Barbara Blum, deputy administrator of the Environmental Protection Agency, the federal government did not declare a state of emergency until 2 sets of findings gave it sufficient evidence. On **May 16,** the Environmental Protection Agency released the findings of a study which claimed that some residents in the area had incurred chromosome damage from the toxic chemicals buried there. Out of a sample of 36 persons tested on **Jan. 18** and **19,** 11, or 30 percent, had suffered chromosome damage that was frequently linked to cancer and birth defects, and could lead to genetic damage in offspring. Another study's findings, released **May 20,** suggested peripheral nerve damage among residents of the area. About 80 percent of the residents tested had diminished nerve sensitivity. After release of the first set of findings, residents in the area were reportedly angry and bitter over the government's unwillingness to pay for their evacuation and, on **May 19,** several homeowners held 2 Federal environmental officials captive for 5 hours to protest government inaction. Many homeowners insisted that the government purchase their houses, but the White House claimed that such purchases were not provided for under federal law. By **May 26,** 220 families had registered for the move, while many others contended that they would not leave until the government bought their houses.

Reagan Locks Up Nomination, Carter Is Just 28 Delegates Short — Ronald Reagan was assured of the nomination for president by the Republican party when he won, **May 27,** 3 primaries that pushed his total number of delegates over the total of 998 that constituted a majority at the party's convention. In another boost to his campaign, his major rival, George Bush, had ceased active campaigning **May 26.** Pres. Carter came close to the same goal when he swept the Arkansas, Kentucky, and Nevada primaries, **May 27,** bringing his total to 1,638 delegates, according to a tally of the *New York Times.* The Texas primary was won by frontrunners, Reagan and Carter on **May 4.** In a non-binding preference vote, Carter trounced Kennedy, 56 percent to 22, and seemed bound to get most of the state's 152 Democratic delegates in the precinct caucuses that ended June 21. A surprising 19 percent of the Texas Democrats were "uncommitted" in preference. Reagan defeated Bush in his home state, 51 percent to 47, and added another 61 delegates to his total. Tennessee, Indiana, and North Carolina, **May 6,** gave Carter 161 delegates and Edward Kennedy only 62. Reagan likewise gained numerous delegates, totaling 108, in the 3 contests to George Bush's mere 32. Kennedy and Bush, however, did manage to win the District of Columbia primary the same day, but they only reaped 11 and 14 delegates, respectively. One more primary hurdle was easily passed by the frontrunners, **May 13,** when they won the presidential preference votes in Maryland and Nebraska, leaving Carter with 92 percent of the delegates he needed and Reagan with 94 percent, according to the *New York Times.* After making a strong effort in the state, Bush bounced back to victory in the Michigan primary, **May 20,** winning 57 percent of the vote to Reagan's 32 percent. However, just as Bush was demonstrating strength, the declaration by 2 broadcast networks, ABC and CBS, that Reagan had passed the total number of delegates necessary for the nomination with 29 Michigan delegates and 18 in Oregon, knocked the wind out of Bush's campaign. He quit active campaigning and ended his 2-year quest for the nomination **May 26** when campaign financing dried up after the television pronouncement and when, according to Bush, "a widespread perception that the campaign is over" spread. According to the tabulation of the *New York Times,* Reagan still needed 5 more delegates at that time. Kennedy fought to keep his candidacy alive even though he suffered a string of defeats in Arkansas, Kentucky, and Nevada, **May 27,** in primaries that attracted small turnouts with the nomination almost clinched by the president. Kennedy declared that a strong showing by him on June 3 in the several big states slated for primaries would throw the Carter nomination into doubt.

Jordan Cleared of Cocaine Charges — Arthur Christy, the special federal prosecutor appointed to investigate allegations that White House chief of staff Hamilton Jordan had used cocaine, announced, **May 28,** that a special grand jury concluded that there was "insufficient evidence" for an indictment of Jordan. Jordan had been accused of cocaine use during a 1978 visit to New York's Studio 54 discotheque. The original allegations had been made by Steve Rubell, a co-owner of Studio 54, who said he observed Jordan using cocaine at his club. The report by Christy noted that the allegations against Jordan were made after Rubell and another Studio 54 owner were indicted on charges of tax evasion. Christy also reported that he had looked into allegations that Jordan used cocaine during a 1977 visit to Los Angeles and had found "no evidence whatsoever" that that had occurred.

Black Leader Wounded by Sniper — Black civil rights leader Vernon Jordan Jr., president of the National Urban League, was shot and critically injured in a motel parking lot in Fort Wayne, Ind., **May 29.** The 44-year-old leader underwent a four-and-a-half-hour operation and was listed in "very serious" condition. Jordan had addressed the local Urban League's annual dinner in the evening. After the dinner, he had struck up a conversation with Martha Coleman, a white member of the board of directors of the Ft. Wayne Urban League chapter. Coleman then drove Jordan to her home, where they had coffee. Then, at about 2 a.m., she drove him to his motel. Jordan was shot twice in the back in the parking lot as he walked from her car towards his room. Black leaders, including Mayor Richard Hatcher of Gary, Ind., the Rev. Jesse Jackson, president of Operation People United to Save Humanity, and Benjamin Hooks, executive director of the National Association for the Advancement of Colored People, arrived in Ft. Wayne a few hours after the shooting to monitor the investigation. Sen. Edward Kennedy visited Jordan in the hospital on **May 29** and Pres. Carter, who called the attack an "assassination," visited Jordan **June 1.** Police had few facts and leads to go on in the investigation. They found a 30.06-caliber shell lying in a grassy area near the motel and also a padded-down section of grass in the same area that could have been made by a gunman lying in ambush. Coleman cooperated with the police and was not considered a suspect. She told police that, a few minutes before reaching the motel, 3 white men in a car alongside hers at a stop light had shouted racial slurs at her and Jordan. Police determined that there probably would not have been enough time for the 3 to get to the motel in order to commit the crime. Two women employees of a telephone company across the interstate highway from the motel, reported that they saw a car parked along the exit ramp of the highway at the time of the shooting. However, several weeks later, police and the F.B.I., who had been taking part in the investigation, still had no suspects. On **June 12,** Jordan was transferred to a New York hospital and his condition was described as "still serious but stable and improving."

International

Palestinians Kill 6 Jews in West Bank — Palestinian terrorists, **May 2,** fired automatic rifles and threw hand grenades into a crowd of Jewish worshippers returning from Sabbath prayers, killing 5 people and wounding 17. One of the wounded died later. The assault took place near the former Jewish-owned Hadassah clinic in the Arab city of Hebron. The victims were Jewish settlers, members of Gush Emunim, an Israeli ultranationalist group. Responsibility for the attack was claimed by Al Fatah, the main group of the Palestinian Liberation Organization (PLO). In response to the attack, Israel, **May 3,** deported 3 prominent West Bank leaders to Lebanon—Hebron Mayor Fahad Kawasmeh, Mohammed Milhem, mayor of nearby Halhul, and Sheik Raja Bayud Tamimi, the Moslem judge of Hebron. Maj. Gen. Danny Matt, coordinator for the occupied areas, said all three had made inflammatory statements that constituted incitement. PLO leader Yasir Arafat met with the 3 deported West Bank leaders in Beirut, **May 7,** and said the attack in Hebron was an act of "resistance by those who are under occupation."

Yugoslav President Tito Dies — After a 4-month illness, Josip Broz Tito, president of Yugoslavia since the end of World War II, died **May 4.** The longtime leader was known most for his rift with the Soviet Union in 1948, which ended an era of monolithic Communism when Yugoslavia withdrew from the Soviet bloc. He also led the guerrilla movement in his country during World War II and was a founder of the "nonalignment" movement among nations. His funeral attracted a large number of world leaders, with the notable exception of Pres. Carter, who sent Vice President Walter Mondale. The attendance of Soviet President Leonid Brezhnev at the funeral caused widespread speculation that the Soviet Union would try to bring the country into its orbit once again. In 1974, Tito had created 2 collective leadership bodies to take over after his death: the State Presidency and the Presidium of the Communist Party. A rotating system of succession for the leadership of those bodies was put into operation upon Tito's death.

British Commandos Storm Iran's London Embassy, Freeing 19 Hostages — A British commando team stormed the Iranian Embassy in London, **May 5,** and freed 19 people who had been held hostage since **Apr. 30.** The assault was ordered after the Arab Iranians holding the building killed a hostage and threw his body out onto the street. Members of the British army's antiterrorist unit, the Special Air Service regiment, moved in as 2 explosions rocked the embassy. Unleashing a hail of gunfire, the commandos entered the building, which was in flames. Five of the terrorists were killed in the assault. One surviving terrorist and the remaining hostages were evacuated as the building continued to burn. On **May 7,** another hostage, who was killed by the terrorists just prior to the assault, was found in the debris of the building. The Iranian embassy had been seized by the terrorists, **Apr. 30.** The armed men had identified themselves as Iranian Arabs who wanted autonomy for the Iranian province of Khuzistan and the release of 91 Arab prisoners they claimed were imprisoned in Iran. One hostage was released **May 1,** 2 more **May 3,** and a last one **May 4.** British police said that negotiations with the terrorists were going well and the situation remained calm, until **May 5,** when the terrorists suddenly announced that they would kill one of their hostages every 30 minutes until the Iranian government met their demands. Surviving hostages said that the terrorists had started to fire on the hostages with machine guns in the last minutes of the commandos' assault. On **May 6,** British Prime Minister Margaret Thatcher said that she hoped that the successful raid on the Iranian Embassy would "have an effect on the future position with regard to the American hostages in Iran." Thatcher said that it is the responsibility of "each and every government to look after the safety of diplomats on their territory."

Soviet Auto Workers Strike — More than 250,000 workers at the Soviet Union's 2 largest automobile factories went on separate 2-day walkouts in early May, according to unofficial Soviet sources cited in the Western press **June 13.** The strikes occurred at the Togliatti motor works, 650 miles southeast of Moscow on the Volga River, **May 6,** and at the Gorky auto and truck plant **May 8-9.** Both were reportedly protests against prolonged shortages of meat and dairy products in the Volga region. Worsened by the U.S. grain embargo, the shortages were caused by the 1979 Soviet grain harvest failure and by stockpiling for the 1980 Moscow Summer Olympics. Soviet authorities quickly transported large quantities of fresh food and supplies to the 2 industrial complexes and labor peace resumed. The strikes were never officially reported by the Soviet press.

Swedish Labor Dispute Settled — A labor dispute which had idled 800,000 workers in Sweden, a nation with a reputation for labor peace, ended, **May 11,** when unions agreed to wage increases of about 7 percent. The country had been crippled by the labor crisis, which had begun **May 2** when employers had locked out 770,000 workers and labor unions had responded with strikes involving more than 100,000 other workers. About one fifth of the country's workers were involved in the dispute. "Labor and capital can no longer cooperate in the fine old spirit," commented Gunnar Nilsson, chairman of the union confederation.

Military Ousts Uganda President — Soldiers loyal to the Army Chief of Staff, Brig. David Oyite Ojok, ousted Pres. Godfrey Binaisa of Uganda, **May 11,** after Binaisa dismissed Ojok, **May 10,** from the National Consultative Council, the country's interim ruling body. The military commission that took over the government criticized Binaisa for corruption and incompetence. Ojok had reportedly been dismissed because of his close ties to former President Milton Obote, who was ousted by Idi Amin in 1971. Tribal conflicts also played a role in the coup: Ojok and Obote are Langos from the north while Binaisa is a Baganda from the south. On **May 14,** the military junta announced that it was lifting Binaisa's ban on political parties. Obote returned to Uganda, **May 27,** from 9 years' exile in Tanzania and was reported to be readying a campaign to regain the presidency.

Carter Halts Flotilla From Cuba — Just 9 days after he had welcomed the illegal Cuban refugees streaming into Key West, Fla., with "open heart and open arms," Pres. Carter, **May 14,** changed his policy and opposed the private flotilla that had transported an estimated 46,000 Cubans into the U.S. by **May 15.** Instead, Carter offered to start an airlift to transport the Cubans to the U.S. in a safe, orderly fashion. Cuban President Fidel Castro did not respond to the proposal. The policy reversal came after at least 18 persons had died while traveling on the overcrowded boats in the tricky waters between the U.S. and Cuba, and after hundreds of refugees with criminal records and serious medical problems had disembarked. A backlash against the incoming Cubans was growing as well. A *Newsweek* poll in the 2d week of May reported that 59 percent of those questioned felt the influx was bad for the U.S. Following Carter's new order, the Coast Guard prohibited any boats from leaving Key West for Mariel, Cuba, and began seizing boats returning with refugees. By **May 16,** 119 boats had been seized. On **May 17,** the Coast Guard set a 200-mile patrol zone stretching from Key West to Miami to enforce the new policy. The same day, a heavily-overloaded 36-foot cabin cruiser sank 25 miles off Cuba, killing 14 of its 52 refugees. Refugees continued to be transported to Florida, however, by the hundreds of boats that had been waiting in the harbor of Mariel to pick up refugees. Some boat captains said that they were prevented from leaving the port without carrying refugees. The huge numbers of Cubans disembarking at Key West were processed in 4 centers around the country: Elgin Air Force Base in the Florida panhandle, Fort Chaffee in Arkansas, Fort Indiantown Gap in Pennsylvania, and Fort McCoy in Wisconsin. On **May 24,** several hundred Cuban refugees at Elgin Air Force Base threw stones and scuffled with military police out of anger and frustration over the delays in their processing. Most of the 8,475 Cubans at the base had been there for at least 3 weeks and the camp had been resettling the refugees at the rate of about 100 to 200 a day. Between 20 and 100 of the refugees fled during the disturbance, but most of them had been returned by the next day. On **June 1,** refugees at the Fort Chaffee processing center also rioted out of anger and frustration over delays. Some 200 Cubans burst through the front gate at the fort, but they were forced back inside by police officers and soldiers who used tear gas and clubs in an attempt to subdue them. Once back inside, the refugees went on a rampage, setting fire to some barracks. Thirty-five Cubans were arrested for instigating the riot. Forty persons were injured in the disturbance and 4 buildings were burned to the ground. Officials said that, as of **June 1,** a total of 94,710 Cubans had arrived in the U.S. and 48 percent of them had been resettled. However, relatively few of the refugees in the camps had been resettled because they had no relatives in the country. Pres. Carter, **June 7,** ordered the Justice Department to expel any Cuban refugee who had committed "serious crimes" in Cuba and to prosecute or expel those responsible for the rioting at Fort Chaffee. About 450 of all the refugees who had arrived were described as "hardened criminals." On **June 5,** the Coast Guard estimated that only 20 to 80 boats remained in the Cuban port of Mariel and that the refugee count in the 48-day exodus had topped 110,000. The cost of resettlement of the refugees was put at $300 million, **May 25,** by James McIntyre Jr., director of the Office of Management and Budget.

NATO Condemns Afghan Invasion — Foreign and defense ministers of the North Atlantic Treaty Organization, **May 14,** denounced the Soviet invasion of Afghanistan and agreed that the organization had to strengthen its military preparedness in view of the Soviet action. The declaration marked a shift in NATO policy on Afghanistan, which previously had concluded that Afghanistan was not crucial to the alliance. The ministers also adopted a series of recommendations to improve Europe's NATO capability if U.S. forces were engaged elsewhere in the world, such as the Persian Gulf. The participants agreed to increase ammunition stocks, improve defenses against chemical warfare, and bolster the alliance along its southern flank.

Reduced Sanctions Against Iran Approved By EEC — The European Economic Community (EEC), in support of American efforts to release the U.S. hostages in Iran, canceled, **May 18,** all trade contracts signed with Iran since Nov. 4, 1979, when the U.S. embassy in Iran was seized. The final approval of sanctions by the EEC fell short of its original pledge, made **Apr. 22,** to cancel all trade with Iran except food and medicine. Britain, **May 19,** broke with the other EEC members and limited the trade ban to new contracts. The U.S. publicly criticized Britain, **May 20,** for not fulfilling a commitment to block exports to Iran under earlier contracts. Britain, **May 29,** further weakened its sanctions until only businesses which had been in the process of negotiating contracts with Iran would be affected. A British official explained that his government was not prepared "to issue an order that was going to hurt British businessmen more than it hurt Iran."

Quebec Voters Reject Separation From Canada — In a **May 20** referendum, voters of the predominately French-speaking province of Quebec rejected by an overwhelming margin a request by the province for a mandate to negotiate sovereignty for Quebec together with a new and equal association with the rest of Canada. Only 42 percent of the voters were for the proposal, while 58 percent voted against it. An estimated 54 percent of French-speaking Quebecers joined 80 percent of the English Canadians and other ethnic groups to vote against it. The election attracted one of the heaviest turnouts in Quebec's history, about 80 percent of the 4.3 million registered voters. Quebec Premier Rene Levesque called the results "the last gasp of the old Quebec" and urged his supporters to hope for the "next time." Canadian Prime Minister Pierre Elliott Trudeau called for a period of national healing and, **May 21,** announced a new round of talks with provincial and territorial leaders on rewriting the Canadian Constitution to make the 113-year-old document more adequately meet the modern needs of the country.

World Court Demands Iran Free American Hostages — The International Court of Justice, **May 24,** ordered the immediate release of all American hostages held in Iran, warned the Iranians to not put any of them on trial, and ruled that Iran was liable for reparations. The rulings of the court, which is a part of the United Nations, would enable the U.S. to request the Security Council to take new measures against Iran if it fails to comply with the court's rulings. The ruling on reparations would apply to the Iranian deposits frozen in U.S. banks. The U.S. had asked the court on Nov. 29, 1979, to order Iran to free the hostages. The Iranian government was repeatedly asked to present its case to the court but it only sent 2 telex messages. The messages were that Iranian grievances against the United States, which primarily had to do with the continued support that the U.S. gave to the deposed shah, must also be considered and that the court had no jurisdiction in the case. The court ruled that it had the right to hear the U.S. case against Iran under the 1961 and 1963 Vienna conventions on diplomatic and consular relations. Those agreements prohibit any form of arrest or detention of diplomats "regardless of any grievance the state may believe that it has against any diplomat."

Committee Counts 85 Nations Going to Moscow Olympics — The International Olympic Committee announced, **May 27,** that at least 85 nations would compete in the 1980 Summer Olympics in Moscow, despite the U.S. campaign for a boycott of the games in protest of the Soviet invasion of Afghanistan. The committee said that 85 countries had accepted invitations to compete, 29 nations had rejected invitations and another 27 countries had not responded by the May 24 deadline. Every Western European country except West Germany, Liechtenstein, Norway, and Monaco accepted. Canada, China, Japan, Israel, and Turkey had rejected the invitation. At the 1976 Summer Olympics at Montreal, 88 nations took part when some 29 African nations boycotted the games. Both the Soviet Union and the U.S. disputed the committee's list and claimed victory for their respective positions. The U.S. had been reported displeased with the vote of the French Olympic Committee, **May 13,** to go to the Olympic games in Moscow, after the French government declined to take a public position on the issue.

S. Korean Troops Recapture Rebellious City — After the city had been held by rebels for 6 days, South Korean troops, **May 27,** regained full control of Kwangju, the South Cholla province capital of 800,000 people, in a predawn strike that met with little rebel resistance. In less than 2 hours, nearly 300 dissidents were arrested, and 19 were killed in the military operation which ended the worst outbreak of violence in South Korea since the Korean War. Rebels had taken over the city during 3 days of rioting, **May 18-21,** over the imposition of martial law, in which at least 100 people were killed and many more were injured. The main military strongman in the country, Lieut. Gen. Chun Doo Hwan, the head of the Korean Central Intelligence Agency and the Defense Security Command, had imposed a comprehensive martial law on **May 17** in order to end 2 weeks of bloody demonstrations in several cities by students who were demanding a concrete timetable for the democratization of the country. A politician who was a native of South Cholla province and popular there, Kim Dae Jung, was immediately arrested. Soldiers, **May 18,** entered Chonnam National University in Kwangju to enforce the martial-law decree, which closed all universities. Rumors of troop brutality towards the students ignited the city residents. Demonstrators demanded the resignation of Chun and the release of Kim Dae Jung, and repeatedly clashed with troops. On **May 21,** demonstrators stormed an arms warehouse and seized about 6,000 rifles, as well as armored personnel carriers, trucks, and jeeps. Government forces were quickly driven out of the city by 200,000 insurgents and disturbances spread to 15 other towns in the province. South Korean troops surrounded the city and negotiations began. The discussions became deadlocked when student leaders of the insurrection insisted on the immediate end to martial law and progress toward democratic rule. The Martial Law Command said it had used all possible peaceful means to end the strife before deciding to suppress the rebellion by force.

General

Catholic Priest Barred From Politics — The Rev. Robert Drinan, a Democratic U.S. Representative from Massachusetts and the only priest in Congress, was barred from seeking a new term, **May 5,** by the Very Rev. Pedro Arrupe, superior general of the Society of Jesus (Jesuits) in Rome. The order was reportedly issued on the request of Pope John Paul II. Drinan said that he accepted the order with "regret and pain." In announcing his compliance with the order, Drinan said of his 10 years in Congress, where he was rated one of its most liberal members, "I can think of no other activities more worthy of the involvement of a priest and a Jesuit." On **May 4,** in Kinshasa, Zaire, during his African tour, John Paul told African priests: "Leave political responsibility to those who are entrusted with it. The role that is expected of you is another one, a magnificent one. You are leaders in another jurisdiction as priests of Christ."

First Balloon Trip Across Continent Accomplished — Two men in a 75-foot-high helium-filled balloon named Kitty Hawk, **May 15,** completed a 4-day voyage across North America, landing on the Gaspé Penninsula of eastern Canada. It was the first nonstop transcontinental balloon flight and the longest overland voyage in a balloon, more than 3,100 miles. One of the balloonists, Maxie Anderson, had taken part in the first trans-Atlantic balloon voyage in 1978. Anderson was accompanied by his son, Kris, on this flight. Anderson described this flight as more difficult, although perhaps less dangerous, that the Atlantic crossing, since weather overland can be more unpredictable. The 2 men landed more than 1,000 miles north of their original destination.

Mt. St. Helens Erupts, Devastating a 120-Mile Area — Mt. St. Helens, a volcano located in southwestern Washington state, erupted, **May 18,** in a giant blast that hurled ash and steam some 60,000 feet into the sky. The top of the mountain was blown off, leaving the 9,677-foot peak only 8,300 feet high. A 2-mile-long crater was also formed. Scientists calculated that the explosion released 500 times more energy than the atomic bomb that destroyed Hiroshima in World War II. Its shock waves leveled some 44,000 acres of fir trees. The intense heat emitted by the blast killed millions of salmon and trout in rivers and streams, started huge forest fires, and melted snow, which resulted in floods and superhot mudslides. Propelled up to 50 miles an hour by the gases, the mudflows smashed at least 10 bridges and swallowed homes. Drifting volcanic ash up to 7 inches deep blanketed many communities in eastern Washington, northern Idaho, and western Montana in the next few days. An aerial search was begun for survivors and, several days later, there were 26 persons known dead and at least 46 others were missing. Pres. Carter helicoptered around the mountain, **May 22,** and said: "The moon looks like a golf course compared to what's up there." He had declared the state a major disaster area the day before. There had been some geological activity prior to the blast. On **Mar. 20,** a series of earthquakes began to shake the mountain and, on **Mar. 27,** a 20,000-foot plume of steam and ash erupted from the crater on the mountain's top. On the morning of the big blast, a pair of earthquakes shook the mountain and an avalanche of earth began to descend down the mountain's north face. The pressure on the molten material within the mountain was reduced suddenly by the avalanche and gasses that had been dissolved in the material expanded in a gigantic explosion. There was no lava flow. On **May 25,** St. Helens erupted again with much less force, spewing forth another cloud of ash which covered some of the most populous areas of coastal Oregon and Washington. It was estimated, **June 10,** that the volcano had caused $2.7 billion worth of damage. Another major eruption occurred **June 12,** once again covering the area with ash.

Report Discourages Cutback in Cholesterol Intake — The Food and Nutrition Board of the National Research Council, **May 27,** said that it had found no evidence to recommend that healthy persons reduce consumption of cholesterol or fat. In the past decade, 18 major organizations involved with health and nutrition issues had advised a reduction in the intake of fat and cholesterol as a means of lessening the risk of heart disease and other fatal diseases. This report, called "Toward Healthful Diets," cited 7 large-scale studies in which diets were modified to alter the incidence of heart disease and there was only a "marginal decrease" in the rate of heart attacks "but no effect on overall mortality." According to Dr. Norman Spritz, a recognized expert on nutrition, "it turns out that our bodies manufacture much of our cholesterol" and the effect of diet is "relatively small." "People should not be afraid of food and what they eat," said Dr. Alfred Harper, chairman of the Food and Nutrition Board. The report did recommend a substantial reduction in salt intake to help prevent high blood pressure and emphasized the importance of controlling body weight.

Disasters — In the 3d worst bridge disaster in the nation's history, a 35,000-ton phosphate freighter, the Summit Venture, **May 9,** struck the Sunshine Skyway Bridge over Tampa Bay in Florida during a driving rainstorm and tore away a 1,000-foot section of the span, killing at least 35 persons . . .A pre-dawn fire swept through a 2-story wooden home for poor and elderly women in Kingston, Jamaica, **May 20,** killing at least 157 people . . .

JUNE

National

Carter Gains Convention Delegate Majority — On the final day of the primary season, Pres. Carter, **June 3,** won 3 of the 8 primaries and gained 321 delegates, which catapulted his total number of delegates to 1,964, 298 over the majority needed for the nomination. Carter beat Edward Kennedy in the populous state of Ohio by 51 percent of the vote to 44 percent. Kennedy, however, had his best day of the primary season as he won the other 5 contests, taking California with 45 percent of the vote to Carter's 38 percent and amassing 56 percent of the vote in New Jersey to Carter's 37 percent. Heartened by the victories, Kennedy said that June 3 was "the first night of the rest of the campaign" and he continued to argue that the Democrats should nominate someone who can carry major industrial states, as he did when he won primaries in California, New Jersey, New York, Pennsylvania, and Michigan. Ronald Reagan won all 9 Republican primaries on June 3; his major challenger, George Bush, had dropped out of the race at the end of May. A poll by the *New York Times* and CBS News taken of voters as they left election booths on June 3 indicated that the long primary season had left considerable discontent with the candidates among the electorate.

Computer Errors Trigger 2 False Nuclear Alarms — Errors in the U.S. defense network's computer system in Colorado Springs, Colo., sent out false signals that Soviet land-based and submarine-based nuclear missiles had been launched against the U.S. **June 3** and **6.** At each alarm, the engines of 100 B-52 bombers were started, communications with U.S. missile crews were intensified, and Pres. Carter's "airborne command post" was prepared for take-off. Within 3 minutes of each alarm, officers in Washington, Omaha, Neb., and Cheyenne Mountain, Colo., discovered that the warnings were false by checking other sensors and ended the alarms. Officials insisted that, during the alarms, the U.S. had not been close to launching a nuclear strike, which required a direct order from the President. They also pointed to the quick cancellation of the alarms as a demonstration that human judgment played a critical role in the Pentagon's alert system.

Lance, Talmadge Cases Dropped — The Justice Department, **June 6,** said that it would not retry Pres. Carter's former Budget Director, Bert Lance, and 2 co-defendants on 3 banking charges. After a long trial, which ended **Apr. 30,** 9 bank fraud charges had been dismissed against Lance and a mistrial had been declared on 3 remaining counts. The Justice Department said that it had balanced the expenditure of resources that would be required for multiple retrials against the interests to be served by further prosecution in making its decision. On **May 30,** the Justice Department had announced that it would not prosecute Sen. Herman Talmadge (D, Ga.), who had been denounced, Oct. 11, 1979, for mishandling his office and campaign finances. Officials said that after reviewing the evidence, they decided that they would probably not obtain a conviction.

Jobless Rate Soars, Inflation Eases — The Labor Department announced, **June 6,** that the unemployment rate increased to 7.8 percent in May. The jobless rate had jumped 0.8 percent in each of the last 2 months, one of the biggest 2-month increases since such records were first kept early in this century. On the same day, the Bureau of Labor Statistics announced that the prices charged by producers and wholesalers rose by only 0.3 percent in May, the smallest one-month rise in 32 months. Treasury Secretary G. William Miller called the economic signals "mixed" and said that no change in policy was being considered. On **June 18,** the Commerce Department estimated that the gross national product had plunged at an annual rate of 8.5 percent in the 2d quarter of the year, one of the sharpest declines of any quarter. Unlike the 1975 recession, the decline was attributed to a lack of consumer demand, rather than a reduction of inventories by businesses. Further evidence of the moderation of inflation came in an announcement, **June 24,** by the Bureau of Labor Statistics that the Consumer Price Index had only risen by 0.9 percent in May, the same as in April. The figure put the projected annual inflation rate based on the last 2 months at about 11 percent, compared with an 18.1 percent rate in the first 3 months of 1980.

Congress Overrides Carter Veto, Bars Oil Import Fee — The Senate, **June 6,** by a vote of 68 to 10, and the House, **June 5,** by a vote of 335 to 34, overrode Pres. Carter's veto of a resolution that rejected his proposed oil import fee. The override of the veto was the first by a Congress controlled by the president's own party since 1952. The proposal would have imposed a levy of $4.62 on each barrel of imported oil. This levy would have been transferred to the consumer in a 10-cent-a-gallon duty at the gasoline pump to discourage energy consumption. Congressional opponents of the measure had argued that it would conserve little energy and hurt those consumers least able to pay. Other congressmen had felt that the tax would be politically difficult to back in an election year.

Congress Approves 1981 Budget — Congress **June 12,** approved a budget resolution for 1981 that called for $613.6 billion in spending and a surplus of $200 million. The vote was considered to be a test of the 6-year-old budget process in which Congress has committed itself to fiscal discipline. The yearly budget's figures change with changing economic conditions but the budget does set legislative spending priorities. Congress fought fiercely over priorities in 1980 and approved the June 12 compromise bill only after cutting $800 million from the Defense Department's future-year spending authority, which won it the support of many House Democrats who had earlier rejected the bill. The House approved the bill 205 to 195.

Congressmen Indicted in Abscam Scandal — A Washington, D.C. federal grand jury, **June 13,** indicted Rep. John Jenrette Jr. (D, S.C.) on charges of bribery and conspiracy arising from the Abscam (for "Arab scam") investigation. On **June 18,** a federal grand jury in Brooklyn, N.Y., indicted Rep. Frank Thompson Jr. (D, N.J.) and Rep. John Murphy (D, N.Y.) on charges of bribery and conspiracy arising from the same investigation. Abscam figures Rep. Michael Meyers (D, N.Y.) and Camden, N.J., Mayor Angelo Errichetti had been indicted **May 27** and Rep. Raymond Lederer (D, Pa.) on **May 28.**

Draft Registration Bill Signed — Pres. Carter, **June 27,** signed a funding bill for a peacetime draft registration, 6 months after he had said, in the wake of the Soviet invasion of Afghanistan, that a revival of the registration would demonstrate a national resolve to resist aggression. The U.S. had suspended draft registration in 1975 and actual conscription in 1973. In January, Carter had asked Congress to provide the Selective Service with $20 million to pay for registering 19- and 20-year-old women as well as men, but both houses of Congress had rejected the inclusion of women. In the Senate, which passed the final bill by a 58-34 vote on **June 12,** there had been a week-long filibuster to kill the bill. After the Senate voted 63-32 on **June 10** to invoke cloture, which limited debate on the bill to 100 hours, Sen. Mark Hatfield (R, Ore.), who was leading the opposition to the bill, continued to use delaying tactics, but finally agreed to end the filibuster in exchange for a vote on a final amendment. The amendment, which attempted to get the Senate to vote for funds to set up registration machinery but not for actual registration, was defeated, 59-35. On **July 2,** Carter signed a proclamation that required 4 million young men to register later in July for possible military conscription.

Synthetic Fuels Bill Signed — Saying that the scope of the program "will dwarf the combined programs that led us to the moon and built our interstate highway system," Pres. Carter, **June 30,** signed legislation authorizing a program to develop synthetic energy sources. The bill created the United States Synthetic Fuels Corporation, authorized $20 billion to be used by the corporation over the next 5 years, and made another $68 billion available for the following 7 years, subject to Congressional appropriation. The bill, aimed at reducing U.S. dependence on imported oil, set a goal of the production of the equivalent of 500,000 barrels of oil a day by 1987 and 2 million barrels a day by 1992 from alternative sources. Coal would be turned into gasoline and oil would be extracted from shale. The bill also created a solar-energy bank and authorized a $1.45 billion alcohol fuel production program.

International

2 South African Petroleum Plants and a Refinery Bombed — Two synthetic petroleum plants and one of South Africa's largest oil refineries were bombed, **June 1,** in the most successful guerrilla action to date against the country's white minority government. One of the oil-from-coal plants and the refinery were located at Sasolburg, 55 miles southwest of Johannesburg, and the other petroleum plant was located at Secunda, 75 miles southeast of Johannesburg. More than $7 million worth of damage resulted from the blasts and the subsequent fires. Officials said that production at the 3 plants was not affected, since most of the damage was at storage tanks. The London-based African National Congress, a black nationalist group banned in South Africa, claimed responsibility for the bombings. The African National Congress had stepped up its guerrilla activity during the last 18 months, mostly by attacking police stations.

2 West Bank Mayors Injured By Bombs — In a coordinated terrorist attack, 2 mayors on the Israeli-occupied West Bank were maimed, **June 2,** by bombs in or near their cars and an Israeli explosives expert was blinded by a bomb rigged to a 3d mayor's garage door. Mayor Bassam al-Shaka of Nablus lost both legs above the knees and Mayor Karim Khalef of Ramallah lost part of his left foot and suffered injuries to his right leg. Israeli Jewish extremists were believed to be responsible for the bombings. West Bank shopkeepers began a general protest strike **June 3** but Israeli soldiers, **June 4,** forced the merchants to reopen their stores. The UN Security Council, **June 5,** voted 14 to 0 to condemn Israel for failing to protect Arab lives in the West Bank.

Bengalis Massacred in India — Indigenous tribal residents in the Indian state of Tripura killed at least 350 Bengali immigrants in the village of Mandai, **June 7-8.** An Indian army unit that arrived at the village **June 9** found bodies stacked in heaps along the road and no survivors. Many of the dead had been shot with arrows. The incident was the worst occurrence of violence in the conflict between Bengali immigrants and native tribal people in the Indian states of Assam and Tripura. Nearly 200,000 people in Tripura had fled their homes due to the strife and were housed in about 100 camps set up by the Indian government. The Mandai massacre brought the number of deaths in Tripura to at least 700. The Chief Minister of Tripura, Nripen Chakravarti, **June 16** blamed the Indian government for the massacre. He asserted that if the Indian government had heeded his pleas to put down the current tribal insurgency, the massacre at Mandai would not have taken place.

OPEC Quarrels Over Prices — The Organization of Petroleum Exporting Countries (OPEC) held a 2-day ministerial meeting in Algiers, **June 9-10,** in which they increased the base price of their crude oil by $4 to $32 a barrel, set a ceiling price of $37 a barrel, and attempted to give the impression of unity despite the intense quarreling that the price issue evoked. Saudi Arabia and the United Arab Emirates voted against the price base because they found it excessive. Members heralded the assent of the 11 other OPEC members to the accord as a first step toward price unification. The cartel of nations was reported to want price unanimity before their Nov. meeting when the group would observe its 20th anniversary.

Americans Attend Anti-U.S. Conference in Iran — A 10-member American group led by former Attorney General Ramsey Clark attended, **June 2-5,** an Iranian-sponsored conference in Teheran on U.S. "intervention in Iran" in defiance of Pres. Carter's ban on travel to the country. The conference was also attended by some 300 nongovernmental delegates from what were described as "anti-imperialist" organizations in about 60 countries. "Our reason for coming here," Clark told reporters, **June 2,** "is the belief that dialogue between all people is essential for understanding and respect." Clark, in a speech **June 3,** called on Iran to free the 53 U.S. hostages and volunteered to take the place of any of them if it would help resolve the crisis. Iranian Foreign Minister Sadegh Ghotbzadeh said that the conference had no connection to the hostages, although, on June 5, he admitted that the hostage issue could be "clarified" if the U.S. acknowledged what it had done to the "oppressed people of Iran within the last 25 years." The final declaration of the conference, issued **June 6,** denounced Clark as a possible secret agent of Pres. Carter. The declaration, which contained 12 points, denounced the U.S. for what it said was its continued interference in Iran over 27 years and did not mention the 53 American hostages. The American delegation had tried to add the hostage issue to the final document. Carter, **June 10,** told reporters that he favored taking legal action against Clark and the other 9 Americans who had defied his travel ban to Iran. Clark, **June 11,** said: "I was disappointed and sad that President Carter would be commenting publicly on what may become a criminal case because it shows insensitivity to the rule of law."

Japanese Premier Dies, His Party Wins Election — Japanese Premier Masayoshi Ohira, 70, died of a heart attack in a Tokyo hospital **June 12.** His death came at an uneasy time in Japanese politics. Ohira had lost a vote of confidence **May 16** and had been campaigning for the upcoming election when he entered the hospital, **May 31,** suffering from exhaustion and a heart ailment. After his death, chief Cabinet secretary, Masayoshi Ito, became acting premier in accordance with Japan's cabinet law. The uneasy period ended when the ruling Liberal Democratic Party, **June 22,** won firm majorities in both houses of the Japanese parliament. The party won 284 seats in the 511-member lower House of Representatives and 135 seats in the 252-member upper House of Councilors. In the previous Diet, or parliament, the party had had only slim working majorities with the aid of independents. The Liberal Democratic Party members of both houses of the parliament elected, **July 15,** Zenko Suzuki as president of the party. Suzuki was then elected premier of Japan, **July 17,** making him Ohira's successor.

Europeans Urge PLO Peace Role — The European Economic Community (EEC), **June 13,** backed the self-determination of the Palestinian people and suggested that the Palestine Liberation Organization (PLO) be "associated with" negotiations for a peaceful settlement of the Arab-Israeli conflict. The U.S. and Israel had refused to accept the PLO as a negotiating partner in the talks on the future of the Israeli-occupied West Bank and Gaza. The European initiative reflected the continuing concern of the Europeans over the tension in the Middle Eastand a lack of confidence by the Europeans in the negotiations over Palestinian autonomy that came out of the Camp David peace treaty of

1979 between Israel and Egypt. The negotiations had left the ultimate status of Palestinian residents of the occupied West Bank and Gaza Strip undecided. The EEC issued an 11-point declaration, **June 14,** after its 2-day meeting in Venice. Included in the points was the declaration that Israel must "put an end to the terrorist occupation" of the West Bank and Gaza Strip and that the EEC would not accept any unilateral initiative to change the status of Jerusalem.

30 Killed In Capetown Riots — Clashes between police and mixed-race demonstrators in areas around Capetown, South Africa, **June 16-18,** killed at least 30 persons and injured 174. The violence was the worst in the country since the Soweto race riots of 1976. Crowds in the Elsie's River and Ravensmead areas defied, **June 16,** a ban on all political and commemorative meetings marking the 4th anniversary of the Soweto incident. Demonstrators stoned police cars and other vehicles and blocked roads. Looting and arson followed. Police were reported to have fired into the crowds on 3 successive days. Unrest among the mixed-race people in these areas had begun in April with a student boycott protesting alleged racial discrimination in the school system. The *New York Times* reported, **June 18,** that South African whites were surprised by the intensity of the riots because they had considered the mixed-race people to be their natural ally against the blacks.

Carter Approves Uranium Sale To India — Pres. Carter, **June 19,** signed an executive order approving the sale of 38 tons of enriched uranium to India. The order overruled a **May 16** decision by the Nuclear Regulatory Commission denying 2 export licenses for the shipment of the nuclear fuel. Under law, Congress had 60 days to overturn Carter's action. Many congressmen opposed the sale because it ran counter to the nation's policy of nuclear nonproliferation. India had refused to accept international safeguards and inspections of its nuclear facilities. Carter Administration officials argued that the U.S. had an obligation to continue to honor the 1963 contract under which the nation supplied uranium for India's nuclear plant at Tarapur.

7 Western Industrial Nations Meet At Conference — At the 6th of an annual series of economic conferences by the leaders of the largest non-Communist industrial countries in Venice, the 7 leaders, **June 22-23,** discussed their dependence on oil imports and the Soviet invasion of Afghanistan. The conference's final declaration, agreed upon by the 7 nations, vowed that the participants would switch from oil to alternative fuels by 1990. "We must break the existing link between economic growth and consumption of oil and we mean to do so in this decade," said the document. The leaders said that the supply of these alternatives to oil would be increased by the equivalent of 15-20 million barrels of oil a day by 1990. At the beginning of the conference, the Soviet Union, **June 22,** issued a statement that some Soviet troops would be withdrawn from Afghanistan. The Western leaders responded in a joint statement later in the day, saying the withdrawal would have to be permanent and continued until the complete withdrawal of Soviet troops.

Vietnamese Troops Raid Thailand — Vietnamese troops in Cambodia, **June 23,** crossed the border into Thailand and fought with Thai troops for 2 days. More than 60 Thai soldiers and, according to Thailand, more than 100 Vietnamese soldiers were killed in the clashes. The Vietnamese attack occurred near the Thai village of Non Mak Mun in an area that serves as a temporary home for some 200,000 Cambodian refugees loosely controlled by anti-Communist Cambodian guerrillas. The Vietnamese attack, which penetrated at least a mile into Thai territory, was reportedly made in order to halt the repatriation of Cambodian refugees, many of whom joined the fight against the Vietnamese occupation army when they returned. Border villages were set aflame in the attack and an estimated 400 refugees were killed. Vietnamese troops were supported by tanks and artillery and Thai forces used helicopter gunships and bombers. On **June 24,** a Thai spotter plane and a helicopter were shot down by antiaircraft fire coming from inside Cambodia. The Vietnamese were forced to withdraw from 2 Thai villages and 2 large refugee camps by the Thai bombing. Thailand, **June 24,** formally protested the attack to Vietnam and cited Vietnam's repeated pledges not to violate Thai territory. Vietnamese Foreign Minister Nguyen Co Thack, **June 26,** denied that Thai territorial integrity had been violated and claimed that Vietnamese troops attacked only after Thai soldiers had "escorted" insurgents 4 miles inside Cambodian territory. Thai Foreign Minister Siddhi Savetsila said, **June 26,** that the attack had driven more than 100,000 Cambodian refugees into Thailand.

Sanjay Gandhi Killed in Plane Crash — Indian Prime Minister Indira Gandhi's son, Sanjay, died **June 23** when the small light plane he was flying crashed in New Delhi. Sanjay was one of the most powerful figures in India. On **June 6,** the ruling Congress-I Party in Uttar Pradesh had elected him as its leader. He had been known to be his mother's closest adviser and had been believed to be her heir apparent.

Pope Visits France — Pope John Paul II, **June 2,** ended the first papal visit to France since 1814 by visiting the shrine of St. Therese and a Carmelite convent in Lisieux, Normandy. The major theme of the pope's 4-day visit had been the "spiritual fatigue" of the French church, which had seen its practicing participants decline to 15 percent of its professed membership. John Paul II arrived in Paris **May 30,** where he addressed a crowd at the Place de la Concorde on the issue of religious drift. The next day he met with French President Valery Giscard d'Estaing and discussed world problems. Later in the day, he met with 15,000 Polish immigrants and descendants at the Eiffel Tower and said mass for 2,500 workers at the Basilica of St. Denis in a working-class industrial suburb of Paris. In gusts of driving rain, the pope, **June 1,** said an outdoor mass for a half-million persons at Le Bourget airport.

Oldest Biological Cells Found — Paleobiologist J. William Schopf of the University of California at Los Angeles, announced, **June 19,** that an international team of scientists headed by him, had discovered fossils in northwestern Australia that contained the oldest biological cells ever found on earth. The cells, of 5 different types and almost identical in structure to several modern-day bacteria, are 3.5 billion years old, about 1.2 billion years older than previous finds and three-quarters of the age of the earth. Scientists believe that, as living cells, they once formed matlike sheets on the floors of lagoons and saline lakes. According to Schopf, the discovery "says that the origin of life occurred quite a lot earlier than we had expected, and that evolution had proceeded to an advanced level in the first billion years of the history of the planet."

Disasters — A series of 7 tornadoes, **June 3,** struck Grand Island, Neb., killing 4 persons and injuring nearly 200 . . . The wreckage of an Italian jetliner, which had apparently exploded in midair, was found, **June 28,** in the Tyrrhenian Sea, 90 miles southwest of Naples; bodies of 42 of the 81 people on board were also found, but no survivors were discovered . . .

JULY

National

13 Smuggled Aliens Die in Arizona — U.S. Border Patrol agents, **July 6,** found the bodies of 13 illegal aliens from El Salvador in Arizona's Organ Pipe National Monument. The aliens had died of dehydration in 115-degree temperatures. On **July 5,** 14 illegal aliens, from the same group, had been rescued near death. Border Patrol agents had first learned of the aliens' distress on **July 4** when agents found 2 other Salvadorans and a Mexican smuggler, who had separated from the group. On **July 5,** a woman flagged down a passing Border Patrol vehicle on a desert highway near the town of Ajo, Ariz., and told agents where her companions could be found. Investigators said that the Salvadorans had entered Mexico as a part of a group of 45 late in June and had split into 2 groups in San Luis Rio Colorado, south of the Arizona border. The group which attempted to cross the Organ Pipe Desert carried only 20 gallons of water when it set out, according to one account. The Salvadorans had paid the smugglers $1,200 each for their illicit passage. Three women survivors said that they were raped by a Salvadoran smuggler, who perished in the heat. Three Mexicans and another Salvadoran were charged with the smuggling.

Inflation Continues, Recession Eases — The Bureau of

Labor Statistics, **July 8,** reported that the producers price index, the prices that retailers pay for finished goods, rose 0.8 percent in June. "It shows you inflation isn't over," said Robert Russell, director of the Council on Wage and Price Stability. Amid fears that the summer drought would further increase food prices in the future, the government announced, **July 23,** that the consumer price index had risen by 1 percent in June, despite the 2d monthly drop in gasoline prices. However, on a more positive note, the government announced the biggest monthly increase since June 1975 in its index of leading economic indicators. They rose 2.5 percent in June, the Commerce Department reported **July 30.** Many economists indicated that this index figure was evidence that the worst of the recession was over.

Reagan, Bush Nominated — The 32d Republican National Convention, meeting in Detroit, **July 14–17,** nominated former Calif. Gov. Ronald Reagan as its presidential candidate and former CIA Director and former UN Ambassador George Bush as its vice-presidential candidate in the 1980 national election. (see Convention coverage, p. 39).

Racial Disorders in Chattanooga — After 2 Ku Klux Klan members were acquitted of shooting and wounding 4 black women, racial disorders erupted in Chattanooga, Tenn., **July 22–24.** A 3d Ku Klux Klansman was convicted in the case on the reduced charges of assault. Shortly after the verdicts, firebombings, and stone and bottle throwing erupted in black neighborhoods and lasted 3 nights. Seven police officers were wounded by birdshot fired from ambush **July 24.** By **July 25,** more than 50 persons had been arrested. On **July 24,** Mayor Charles Rose, a white, imposed a curfew. Calm was restored **July 25** after the police had been withdrawn from the troubled neighborhoods and replaced by volunteer "peace patrols" of black leaders. There were also racial disorders in Miami, **July 15–17,** and Orlando, Fla., **July 29–31.**

Car Makers Report Record Losses — The General Motors Corporation, **July 24,** reported a record $412-million loss for the 2d quarter of 1980, its first loss since the Depression in a quarter in which there was no strike. The 2d largest U.S. auto maker, Ford Motor Company, **July 29,**

President's Brother Registers as an Agent of Libya; Senate Investigates the White House's Role in the Case

With the Democratic National Convention only a month away, Billy Carter, the brother of Pres. Carter, registered, **July 14,** with the Justice Department as an agent of the government of Libya and revealed that he had received $20,000 in December and $200,000 in April in loans from the African country. He registered in return for a Justice Department agreement to not file criminal charges against him for failing to report services that he had rendered to the Libyan government since Sept. 1978.

Billy had taken 2 trips to Libya and was host to a 5-week visit by Libyans in the U.S. He had also made a deal with the Charter Oil Company to receive a commission of up to 50 cents a barrel if he helped the company obtain more Libyan oil.

Billy, **July 15,** said that he had never discussed his Libyan ties with the President, who said, **July 17,** that he had not known the details of his brother's relationship with Libya until "just a few days ago." The White House had repeatedly denied that it had any ties with Billy Carter regarding Libya. However, on **July 17,** Carter Administration officials admitted that in 1978 a foreign-policy specialist on the staff of the National Security Council had briefed Billy on U.S.-Libyan relations prior to his first trip there. The White House revealed, **July 24,** that Pres. Carter's wife, Rosalynn, had suggested to Billy that he use his ties to Libya to help try to free the American hostages in Iran. The White House further revealed that National Security Adviser Zbigniew Brzezinski, Billy Carter, and Ali el-Houderi, Libya's chief representative to the U.S., had met on Nov. 19, 1979, to discuss the hostage situation. After the meeting, Libya sent a letter to Iranian leader Ayatollah Ruhollah Khomeini urging the hostages' release. These disclosures, which contradicted previous White House disavowals of any ties with the Billy Carter-Libya connection, spurred the Senate, **July 24,** to set up a special panel to investigate Billy Carter's role as a paid agent for Libya.

Further disclosures included the admission, **July 25,** by Attorney General Benjamin Civiletti that he and Pres. Carter had discussed the Billy Carter investigation on June 17, although he asserted that he had not discussed the details of the investigation with the President. Previously, Civiletti had denied that he had any contact with the White House on the case and the White House, **July 22,** had stated that "at no time" did it have any contact with the Justice Department on the conduct of the department's investigation of Billy's relations with Libya.

On **July 30,** Pres. Carter admitted that he had discussed with his brother classified State Department cables on Billy's initial trip to Libya in Sept. 1978. The cables were from the U.S. embassy in Libya and had a low-level classification. The cables, copies of which were released **July 31,** said that Billy had agreed to not make any political comments during the trip and had rated the impact of the visit favorably.

Hoping to quickly end the controversy over his brother's ties to Libya, Carter sent a 13,000-word report on the matter to the Senate panel investigating the controversy, **Aug. 4,** and fielded questions from reporters for an hour in a televised news conference. Carter declared "categorically" that his brother had in no way influenced American policy toward Libya and denied that he had committed any impropriety in his dealings with his brother. Carter said that he had tried repeatedly to convince Billy to reduce his contacts with the Libyans and had opposed Billy's 2d trip there. Entries from Carter's diary, which were included in his report to the Senate, indicated that, between Feb. 1979 and July 1980, Carter had at least 8 discussions and exchanged 2 letters with Billy about his relations with Libya. Carter admitted that it "may have been bad judgment" to use Billy to set up a meeting with a Libyan representative to help gain release of the American hostages in Iran since it "may have enhanced Billy's stature in the minds of the Libyans." But, he added, "I did what I thought was best for our country and best for the hostages." According to Carter, his conversation with Civiletti on June 17 did not compromise the Justice Department's investigation of Billy. It never went beyond Civiletti's labeling of Billy as "foolish" for not registering as a foreign agent. Carter said that he had asked his counsel to draft a rule that would bar employees of the executive branch from dealing with any member of the President's family under any circumstances that "create either the reality or appearance of improper favor or influence."

On **Aug. 21,** Billy testified under oath before the Senate panel investigating the case that he did not ask the U.S. to assist Libya. He said that he had taken the $220,000 loan from Libya, which was an advance on $500,000 he was hoping to receive, in order to solve some financial difficulties that his brother's presidency had placed him in. He planned to repay the loan with the future proceeds of his share of a deal between the Charter Oil Co. and Libya.

The tremendous interest that the Billy Carter case initially aroused, with its possible similarities to the Watergate case and its timing before an election, subsided as the 9-week investigation by the special Senate subcommittee failed to find any data that disagreed with Pres. Carter's Aug. 4 statements. In its report, released **Oct. 2,** the committee concluded that Pres. Carter and high officials of his administration had exercised poor judgment in the way they handled Billy Carter's relationship with Libya. The President, according to the report, should have explicitly dissociated himself from his brother's activities in behalf of Libya and should not have permitted his brother to act in a diplomatic role in setting up a meeting with a Libyan representative. However, the subcommittee found no evidence that Billy Carter had influenced the policies of the U.S. and no evidence of illegal actions by government officials. It did conclude that Attorney General Benjamin Civiletti, National Security Adviser Zbigniew Brzezinski, and CIA Director Stansfield Turner had dealt with information available to them in an unprofessional manner. Due to their handling of information, the target of a Justice Department investigation, Billy Carter, was given information that was withheld from his investigators.

reported a record $467.9 million loss for the 2d quarter of 1980. On **July 31,** the Chrysler Corporation reported the largest loss ever by a U.S. car maker; it lost $536.1 million in the 2d quarter of 1980. The industry slump was attributed to poor U.S. sales as Japanese-made fuel-efficient imports made inroads into the American market. The sales of the 3 largest auto-makers were down nearly 27 percent in the first half of 1980 in comparison with the same period in 1979. The 4 largest auto makers had laid off 300,000 workers because of losses and sales drops. The major auto manufacturers expect to spend $80 billion by 1985 to develop and produce cars that will average at least 27.5 miles per gallon of gasoline—twice the 1975 average—and will improve their competitive position in the market.

International

Iran Frees One U.S. Hostage — One of the 53 American hostages held in Iran since the takeover of the U.S. embassy in Teheran in Nov. of 1979, was released due to deteriorating health at the order of Ayatollah Ruhollah Khomeini. Richard Queen, 28, vice council at the embassy, was flown to Zurich, Switzerland, **July 12,** for medical treatment. The same day he was transferred to a U.S. Air Force base hospital in Wiesbaden, West Germany. On **July 15,** it was announced that he was suffering from multiple sclerosis. He left for the U.S. **July 18.** According to the Iranian militants who had held Queen for 250 days, he was well until **July 8,** when he began vomiting and stumbling. When doctors in a Teheran hospital concluded that he could receive better treatment outside Iran, Ayatollah Khomeini approved Queen's release on "humanitarian grounds." A State Department physician, Dr. Jerome Korcak, who participated in the diagnosis of Queen's multiple sclerosis, said that stress was a recognized factor in the disease's clinical development, but he added that it was impossible to prove that conditions in Iran influenced the progression of the disease.

Bolivia's Military Stages Coup — Bolivia's armed forces, **July 17,** seized control of the government to prevent Herman Siles Zuazo, a leftist, from being chosen president by the Congress. The military uprising began in the city of Trinidad and quickly spread to La Paz, where the government Palace was seized and the interim chief of state, Pres. Lydia Gueler Tejada, was captured. Gueiler resigned, turning power over to a junta consisting of the chiefs of the 3 armed services. The junta ordered the disbanding of Congress, which was to have met Aug. 4 to choose a new president among the top vote getters in the June 29 election. Siles Zuazo had won a plurality in the elections and was expected to win the Congressional election with the votes of his left-wing coalition in the legislature. The junta broadcast a statement that it had taken over the country "for the dignity of Bolivia, to reject the results of the general elections and to declare the Congress and its actions unconstitutional." Resistance to the takeover sprang up, **July 20,** in the tin and zinc mining district of Santa Ana, some 400 miles southeast of La Paz, when troops and miners clashed in several skirmishes.

Former Iranian Attache Slain — Ali Akbar Tabatabai, a former press attache at the Iranian Embassy in Washington, was shot to death, **July 22,** at his home in Bethesda, Md., by a gunman disguised as a postal worker. Notified that there was special-delivery mail for him, Tabatabai came to his door and was shot several times in the abdomen. Within an hour of the shooting, investigators found a U.S. Postal Service jeep abandoned 2 blocks from Tabatabai's home. The postal carrier driving the vehicle said he had been approached by 3 men who forced him to surrender the jeep. After further investigation, police, **July 23,** arrested 2 suspects in the case: the mail carrier, Tyrone Frazier, and Horace Butler. A 3d person, believed to have fired the shots and identified as David Belfield, was charged with 1st degree murder and was still at large. Belfield was a member of a small group of American black Muslims who had adopted Ayatollah Ruhollah Khomeini's brand of Islamic fundamentalism. One of the most outspoken and highly visible opponents of Kohomeini, Tabatabai was president of the Iran Freedom Foundation, a group dedicated to the creation of a "secular democracy" in Iran. Another Iranian exile, former Premier Shahpur Bakhtiar, escaped an assassination attempt in Paris **July 18.** Three men burst into his home and 2 persons were killed and 4 were wounded in a shootout.

Canadian Oil Talks Fail — Primer Minister Pierre Trudeau and Alberta Premier Peter Lougheed, **July 25,** failed to reach agreement on oil-pricing and revenue-sharing after 2 days of intense negotiations. The province of Alberta which accounts for 85 percent of Canada's energy production was in dispute with the national government over the distribution of the benefits of this energy production. Trudeau refused to drop a federal proposal for a tax on natural gas exported to the U.S. which would have transferred revenue from Alberta to the federal treasury. Alberta's Lougheed said, "The tax is a serious encroachment on our ownership rights." The discussions involved the political question of federal and provincial responsibility and the failure of the talks, observers said, would have serious consequences for the nation's efforts to devise a new constitution.

Shah of Iran Dies in Egypt — Deposed Shah Mohammed Riza Pahlevi died, **July 27,** in an Egyptian military hospital near Cairo, when his circulatory system collapsed. The 60-year-old former ruler had been suffering from lymphatic cancer for 7 years and side effects of the cancer resulted in his death. A state funeral for the shah was held in Cairo on **July 29.** Former President Richard Nixon and former King Constantine of Greece were the only prominent foreigners to attend. A spokesman for Iranian President Abolhassan Bani-Sadr said that the death of the shah would have no effect on the fate of the 52 American hostages held in Teheran. "Since the shah's death was predictable, it won't change anything," said another Iranian official.

Israel Reaffirms Jerusalem Claim — The Israeli Knesset, **July 30,** approved by a vote of 69 to 15 a bill affirming all of Jerusalem as the capital of Israel and rebuffing Arab claims to East Jerusalem. The legislation did not alter the city's de facto status. Israel had annexed Arab East Jerusalem in the 1967 war and has regarded the entire city as its capital ever since. The passage of the bill was aided by Israeli resentment over the approval, **July 29,** by the UN General Assembly of an Arab-sponsored resolution calling for the establishment of a Palestinian state and Israeli withdrawal from all the occupied lands, including East Jerusalem, by Nov. 15. Observers feared that the Israeli action would make it more difficult to resume the deadlocked negotiations between Israel and Egypt on the issue of self-rule for Palestinians in the occupied West Bank and Gaza. The talks had been suspended on **May 15** by Egyptian President Anwar Sadat when it became clear for the first time that Israeli Premier Menahem Begin's government was determined to push the bill on Jerusalem through parliament. On **July 13,** talks resumed at the committee level in a gesture of good will by Sadat to Pres. Carter, who had a great deal of personal prestige at stake, during an election year, in talks that he had originally set up. The talks were to resume at a higher level Aug. 3 but Sadat sent a letter to Begin on **Aug. 3** asking for at least a temporary delay in the talks on Palestinian autonomy until Begin responded to Sadat's protest of the Israeli legislation. Egyptian Foreign Minister Kamal Hassan Ali said that in his protest, Sadat told Begin that Egypt "totally rejected" the law on Jerusalem and urged Begin to repeat earlier statements that all issues, including Jerusalem, were negotiable. Begin's reply, made public **Aug. 11,** said that during his meetings with Sadat, he had never misrepresented Israel's claim to an undivided Jerusalem. Begin called Egypt's vote for the July 29 UN resolution in favor of a Palestinian state "a flagrant contradiction of the Camp David agreement." Citing Egypt's 4 suspensions of the autonomy talks, Begin urged an end to unilateral suspensions and a renewal to negotiations.

General

Pope Ends 12-Day Visit to Brazil — Pope John Paul II ended the longest papal trip outside Italy in modern times **July 11,** after spending 12 days in Brazil, the world's most populous Catholic country. In stops at 13 cities on his 17,500-mile journey, the pope had continued to stress a prominent theme of his papacy, the need for the church to return to its traditional task of spreading the gospel, but he had also addressed the controversial new role of the church in social change in Brazil. The pope endorsed the work of the activist clergy in behalf of the poor, but he cautioned that the improvement of the lot of the poor must be without class violence and in accordance with Christian, not Marxist concepts.

Heat-Wave Strikes 15 States — Pres. Carter, **July 16,** ordered that nearly $7 million in emergency funds be made available to Texas, Oklahoma, Missouri, Kansas, and Lousiana to aid victims of the vicious heat wave that had held that area in its grip since late June. On **June 22,** a heat wave had struck states in the mid-Mississippi Valley, the Southwest, and the South. Some areas had suffered temperatures above 100 degrees for several weeks in a row. An extraordinarily strong and stationary high-pressure system caused high temperatures, the hottest weather in decades in the region. The nation-wide death toll from the heat surpassed 700 on **July 16** and was placed at 1,265 by the end of the heat-wave. A severe drought also afflicted Texas, Oklahoma, Kansas, Arkansas, Missouri, and Colorado, causing extensive agricultural damage to crops and livestock. Losses were expected to exceed $12 billion. The drought strained the region's water supply, already heavily taxed by the burgeoning population of the rapidly growing area. The alignment of high-pressure systems began to break up at the end of July and cloud-bearing, low-pressure systems, bringing their precipitation and cooling winds, were allowed into the area.

Synanon Founder Convicted of Snake Attack — Charles Dederich, the founder of the Synanon drug rehabilitation organization, and 2 members of the group's security force pleaded no contest, **July 15,** to charges that they had conspired to commit murder with a rattlesnake. Judge William Hogoboom of California's Superior Court, declaring that the effect of the no-contest pleas was identical to that of guilty pleas, found Dederich and the others guilty of charges stemming from a 1978 attack on Paul Morantz, a lawyer. Morantz had sued Synanon on behalf of former members and relatives of members who contended that they were being kept in the group against their will. The lawyer was bitten by a rattlesnake placed in his mailbox in Oct. 1978 and was hospitalized for 6 days. Dederich had been the subject of international publicity in the 1960's for his success in rehabilitating drug addicts. In the 1970's, members of the Synanon organization complained that the group was being transformed into a profit-making authoritarian cult centered around Dederich. The California Attorney General's office investigated the organization and found a large cache of weapons in the group's possession and improper usage by the group of its tax-exempt status. Dederich agreed not to participate in the management of Synanon as his part of his no-contest plea bargain. Prosecutors agreed to not pursue a prison term for Dederich, who was 67 and suffering from heart and circulatory problems.

Cells Creating Human Antibodies Developed — Dr. Henry Kaplan and Dr. Lennart Olsson announced, **July 29,** that they had produced a pure hybrid cell line that makes pure human antibodies like "tiny little factories." Antibodies are the body's first line of defense against disease and the development might lead to the production of antibodies to help diagnose and treat a number of diseases. The researchers at Stanford University Medical School fused bone-marrow cancer cells with specially prepared human spleen cells to make the antibody-producing cells. Previously, researchers had succeeded in artificially producing only pure mouse antibodies, which the human body naturally fights against.

Disasters — The collapse during a storm of a Chinese offshore oil drilling rig in the Bo Hai Gulf killed 70 persons, it was reported **July 6.** . . . A fire swept through a 4-story wood and stucco hotel for the elderly and mentally retarded in Bradley Beach, N.J., **July 26,** killing 23 persons. . . . On **July 29,** a collision between the U.S. aircraft carrier, U.S.S. *Midway,* and the Panamanian-registered merchant ship *Cactus* in a passage between Palawan Island in the Philippines and North Borneo, killed 2 U.S. sailors and injured 3 others. . . .

AUGUST

National

Jobless Rate Holds Steady — For the 3d consecutive month, the unemployment rate remained steady in July, the Labor Department reported **Aug. 1.** The unemployment rate had undergone steep increases in early spring. The July rate was 7.8 percent, up a "statistically insignificant" .1 percentage point from June's 7.7 percent. Treasury Secretary G. William Miller said that the labor market results and other recent indicators suggested the recession might be "bottoming out." The price indexes, however, gave mixed signals during the month. Although the Labor Department announced **Aug. 15** that the producers price index had risen 1.7 percent in July, it reported **Aug. 22** that the consumer price index registered no increase in July, the first time since March 1967 that the index had not risen. Economists warned that the stable figure was misleading, since it was due primarily to a 5.7 percent monthly decline in mortgage interest rates. Prices in other consumer categories continued to rise.

New U.S. Nuclear Strategy Announced — Carter Administration officials announced, **Aug. 5,** that the U.S. had adopted a new strategy for nuclear war that would give priority to attacking military and political targets in the Soviet Union rather than to destroying cities and industrial complexes. The change in policy came in response to the Soviet Union's mounting effort to threaten U.S. land-based missiles, which had led U.S. officials to believe that the Soviets did not accept the American concept of mutual deterence based on the quick, massive destruction of civilian targets. Instead, according to U.S. officials, the Soviet Union was ready to fight a prolonged, but limited, nuclear war centered on military targets. The new U.S. policy, contained in a document known as Presidential Directive 59, was designed to deter such a war by increasing the ability of the U.S. to destroy vital Soviet military forces with highly accurate missiles, such as the MX rocket, which had just been developed. This capability, known as "counterforce," was designed to threaten "the targets the Soviet leadership values most: its military forces and its own ability to maintain control after a war starts," according to U.S. officials. Critics of the new U.S. policy maintained that, in fact, the capability enabled a "first strike" which could eliminate the enemies' military forces and that such capability pressured both sides to launch their missiles in a severe crisis. On **Aug. 8,** Secretary of State Edmund Muskie announced that he had first learned of the change in nuclear strategy in the newspapers. Muskie said that he was concerned primarily with his being "frozen out of discussions" of the policy, rather than with the policy revision itself. Pentagon spokesmen, **Aug. 10,** said that the State Department had fully participated in the review of nuclear policy which lasted until early 1980, before Muskie was appointed Secretary of State.

Carter, Mondale Nominated — The 38th Democratic National Convention, meeting in New York City, **Aug. 11-14,** nominated Pres. Jimmy Carter and Vice President Walter Mondale as its presidential and vice-presidential candidates in the 1980 national elections. (See Convention, page 37.)

Jets Hijacked by Cuban Refugees — Cuban refugees, reportedly unhappy with life in the U.S. and eager to reunite with their families, hijacked several planes to Cuba. On **Aug. 10,** a man, saying that he had a bomb in a box, diverted an Air Florida shuttle from its route from Miami to Key West and took it to Cuba. On **Aug. 13,** 7 Cuban refugees took over an Air Florida jetliner and directed it to Cuba by threatening to ignite a bottle of gasoline. On **Aug. 14,** 2 men commandeered a National Airlines DC-10 flying from Miami to San Juan, P.R., and forced it to land in Havana. The Federal Aviation Administration announced, **Aug. 15,** that it was increasing the number of sky marshals on commercial flights and tightening boarding procedures in an effort to stop further hijackings. On **Aug. 16,** there were 3 more hijackings to Cuba: an Eastern Air Lines jet on a flight to Orlando from Miami was seized by 6 men; a Republic Airlines jet on the same route was taken over by 3 men; and a Delta Air Lines jet from San Juan, P.R., was forced to Cuba by a single man. The Cuban government reported, **Aug. 17,** that it was prosecuting the people involved in 5 of the 6 hijackings. On **Aug. 17,** authorities at Miami International Airport caught 2 Cuban refugees carrying gasoline-filled bottles as they were attempting to board a flight to Key West and 4 men were arrested in Tampa after 4 plastic bottles filled with gasoline were found in their luggage at the airport. In another indication of discontent, Cuban refugees, frustrated by the lack of sponsors to help them settle in the U.S., rioted at the Fort Indiantown Gap, Pa., camp 5 times during

Aug., killing one Cuban, and at the Fort McCoy, Wisc., camp, **Aug. 13.** As of **Aug. 29,** some 14,000 Cuban refugees were still in the 4 camps in the U.S.

Anderson Chooses Running Mate — Independent presidential candidate John Anderson, **Aug. 25,** announced that he had selected Patrick J. Lucey, a Democrat, as his running mate. Lucey served as governor of Wisconsin from 1971 to 1977 and as ambassador to Mexico from 1977 to 1979. He was also a former deputy manager of Sen. Edward Kennedy's presidential campaign and his selection was designed to attract supporters of the Senator who could not accept Pres. Carter as the Democratic nominee.

International

Bologna Blast Kills 76 — An explosion in the central train station of Bologna, Italy, killed 76 people and injured 160, **Aug. 2.** The station was crowded with travelers departing for their August vacations and the blast collapsed an entire 150-foot wing of the structure, flattening a crowded restaurant, 2 packed waiting rooms, and a train platform. Investigators found tiny pieces of metal that could have been part of a bomb near the apparent site of the explosion in the floor of the 2d-class waiting room. Experts said the extent of the damage indicated an explosive equivalent to 90 pounds of TNT. The city police chief, **Aug. 3,** said that he was "95%

Strikes in Poland Force Government to Allow Independent Trade Unions; Security Affairs Chief Replaces Gierek as Party Head

After 2 months of labor turmoil had crippled Poland, the Polish government, **Aug. 30,** granted striking workers at the Lenin Shipyard in the Baltic city of Gdansk the right to form independent trade unions, an unprecedented political development in the Soviet bloc, where the workers' interests are supposedly identical with those of the communist governments. All 21 demands of the strike committee at the shipyards were granted, although many of the specific economic issues were only partly resolved. The workers were also granted the right to strike, the release of all political prisoners, the abolition of government censorship, free access for all religious groups to the mass media, and salary increases of an average of $66 a month for everyone as compensation for higher prices. In the accord with the government, the strike committee agreed that the new unions would "fulfill all constitutional principles, and recognize the leading role of the party, the state and all of Poland's alliances and international obligations." The signing of the accord was broadcast, **Aug. 31,** on national television.

After granting these concessions to Poland's workers, Edward Gierek, the leader of the Polish Communist Party, was replaced, **Sept. 6,** by Stanislaw Kania, a Politburo member in charge of security affairs. Gierek was reportedly dismissed because of a heart ailment. His predecessor, Wladyslaw Gomulka, had been toppled in 1970 by strikes after he had used force to crush them in the cities of Gdansk and Szczecin and 45 workers were killed.

The labor unrest had begun on **July 2** after Prime Minister Edward Babiuch had announced that the government would end its annual subsidy of meat prices, which was costing it $3.3 billion a year. The price of a pound of boneless beef rose immediately to $1.03 from 64 cents. Workers staged work stoppages in major factories across the country, including the city of Ursus where strikes protesting food price increases had begun in 1976. The workers demanded pay increases and, although Gierek warned that such increases were inflationary, several pay increases were announced, **July 21,** as scattered strikes continued to spread. By mid-August, there had been at least 150 protest strikes in various cities, including walkouts by Warsaw transit and garbage workers.

The crisis intensified, **Aug. 14,** when 16,000 workers in Gdansk seized the Lenin Shipyard and went beyond the economic demands of the previous strikes to make political demands, chiefly the disbanding of the official party-controlled trade unions in favor of independent unions run by the workers. The government, **Aug. 14,** granted the workers in Gdansk their demands for reinstatement of 3 dismissed workers, including strike leader Lech Walesa, and the building of a monument for the workers killed by police in the 1970 riots, but it rejected the demand for independent unions. On **Aug. 15,** strikes spread throughout the Baltic industrial region, to cities such as Gdynia and Sopot. By the end of the week the strikes involved more than 100,000 workers and idled more than 200 enterprises. On **Aug. 16,** telephone lines to Gdansk were cut by authorities and an Interfactory Strike Committee was formed by strikers in 3 Baltic cities to consolidate their efforts.

After an emergency meeting of the Politburo of the Communist Party, Gierek, **Aug. 18,** in a television speech, made promises of pay increases but rejected the demands for political reform. "Only a socialist Poland can be a free and independent state with inviolable borders," he said, in a statement that many observers considered an allusion to the threat of Soviet intervention. Soviet intervention, however, was considered unlikely by many diplomats, since the U.S.S.R. was bogged down in the occupation of Afghanistan.

Dissident sources, **Aug. 19,** said that strikes had spread in the past day from 130 to 174 factories in the Baltic industrial region in defiance of Gierek's speech. The government attempted to break the solidarity of the strikers, **Aug. 20-21,** by arresting 24 leaders of the Social Self Defense Committee (KOR), a dissident group that had supported the strikes, and offering wage settlements to striking factories on an individual basis. Meanwhile, the unrest spread outside the Baltic region until more than 300,000 workers were involved.

Gierek granted his first major concession on **Aug. 23** when the government agreed to negotiate directly with the strikers' representatives, whom the government had previously called "illegal." In a further concession, Gierek, **Aug. 24,** purged some hardliners, including Prime Minister Babiuch, 3 full members of the Politburo, and 11 other top officials, from the party. He also pledged the allowance of an "unlimited number of candidates" in union elections, to replace the current practice of having outgoing representatives propose almost all of the candidates, which enabled them to hold onto their power. Vowing that the strikes would continue, strike leader Walesa said of Gierek's concessions: "It's a patching up of holes. We want something new."

On **Aug. 25,** 800 delegates representing 200,000 strikers voted to break off negotiations until telephone links between Gdansk and the rest of the country were restored. In a few hours, the telephones were working. Stefan Cardinal Wyszynski, the Roman Catholic Primate of the country, went on television **Aug. 26** in an unprecedented appearance and urged "peace, calm, reason, prudence, and responsibility for the Polish nation."

The labor crisis spread for the first time to the important mining and industrial region of Silesia in southern Poland, **Aug. 29.** At least 20,000 coal miners walked out around Katowice, an area that had been Gierek's political base and produced much of the country's chief export, coal.

The spread of the strikes to a new, critical industry and the deterioration of an already ailing economy, led the government, **Aug. 30,** to grant the strike committee at the Lenin Shipyard its 21 demands. Allowed to form independent trade unions and access to documents used in economic decisions, the strikers agreed to not form a political party out of the new unions and to allow the existence of the present party-controlled unions alongside the new bodies.

The Silesian miners reached an accord with the government on **Sept. 3** which included many of the points of the Gdansk agreement and some added safety measures and work cycle improvements. Most of the Silesian miners returned to work the next day but some stayed out for further demands.

The new unions called for a one-hour nationwide protest strike on **Oct. 3** and hundreds of thousands of workers responded. The strike, which was covered on national television, was a protest against the government's failure to keep to a timetable in honoring provisions for wage rises and other aspects of the Aug. 31 agreement.

or even more sure" that the explosion was the work of terrorists. The bombing bore characteristics of earlier neo-fascist terrorist attacks—random bombings in public places calculated to cause maximum terror. On **Aug. 6,** French police arrested in Nice as a suspect an Italian fugitive, Marco Affatigato, who answered the description of a man seen shortly before the blast in the 2d-class waiting room.

Controversy Arises Over Iranians Imprisoned in U.S. — As a controversy over their treatment was growing, 171 Iranian men held without charge in a federal prison in Otisville, N.Y., and 20 Iranian women held in a New York City detention facility were released, **Aug. 5,** after they had identified themselves. One Iranian continued to be held in custody since he faced charges of assaulting a police officer. On **Aug. 3,** Iran's revolutionary leader Ayatollah Ruhollah Khomeini had claimed that the prisoners were being tortured and the speaker of the Iranian Parliament, **Aug. 4,** had said that debate on the 52 American hostages in Iran had been postponed because of the mistreatment of the prisoners in the U.S. On **Aug. 5** before the release of the prisoners, 6 Moslem and Christian clergymen visited the Iranian prisoners in Otisville and reported that their condition was good and that they had no complaints about their treatment. Prison authorities, however, admitted that, on **Aug. 4,** at least 18 prisoners had been forcibly given nutritional supplements to counter the effects of a hunger strike. The prisoners had gone on a hunger strike to protest their "illegal arrest." They had been arrested, **July 27,** outside the White House on charges of disorderly conduct for scuffling with police and anti-Khomeini demonstrators. The charges were dropped **Aug. 2,** but they were still detained while immigration officials attempted to identify them and determine whether they were illegal aliens. After their arrest, the Iranians had refused to give their names. The quick release of the prisoners after they identified themselves prompted a protest on the part of several U.S. immigration officers, who said, **Aug. 6,** that the Iranians had been released prematurely, before their names and legal status could be verified. Verne Jervis, a spokesman for the immigration service, said that the service had checked with some, but not all of the schools where the Iranians were said to be enrolled. When most of the Iranians were discovered to be in compliance with their visas, Jervis said, it was considered less important to verify the information given by the others.

Moslems and Hindus Riot in India — The worst communal violence in India in 11 years broke out in the city of Moradabad **Aug. 13.** After a rumor had spread among Moslem worshipers that the police were allowing pigs, a ritually unclean animal, to graze near a mosque, the worshipers turned on the police, who fired into the crowd. As the crowd panicked, many victims were trampled to death. Eighty-six people were killed in the riot. The killings heightened tension between the Moslems and Hindus and violence between the 2 groups broke out in the city and spread throughout the northern state of Uttar Pradesh. The army was called out in the cities of Ranpur, Kanpur, and Meerut. The death toll reached 142 in Uttar Pradesh by **Aug. 17.** On **Aug. 17,** the violence spread to the state of Kashmir, India's northernmost state. Deaths had also occurred in clashes between police and demonstrators protesting high prices in the southern state of Gujarat. Curfews, strictly enforced by police and para-military units, ended the violence. On **Sept. 23,** a new national security law was put into effect, giving the government of Prime Minister Indira Gandhi the power to jail anyone for a year without a trial. The law, proclaimed as an executive fiat, was deemed necessary to contain the spreading violence between Hindus and Moslems and to deal with persons "acting in any manner prejudicial to the defense of India or the security of India."

U.S. Republican Candidates Offend China — Chinese officials, the *New York Times* reported **Aug. 23,** said that they were insulted by pro-Taiwan statements made by Republican candidate Ronald Reagan even as his vice presidential running mate, George Bush, was visiting China, **Aug. 20-22,** and telling the Chinese leadership that Reagan would not renew official U.S. ties with Taiwan. China does not recognize Taiwan as a sovereign country, but rather considers it to be a province of China. The U.S. has held the same view since it established full diplomatic relations with China on Jan. 1, 1979. Because it considers Taiwan a Chinese province, the U.S. has only unofficial relations with the island. Just before Bush left for China on a trip that was intended to show the Republican ticket's concern for foreign affairs, Reagan, **Aug. 16,** said that he favored an "official governmental relationship" with Taiwan. Chinese officials greeted Bush coolly, according to *Time* magazine. During Bush's 3-day visit, Reagan, in the U.S., stood by his original statement. However, in a news conference on **Aug. 25,** Reagan said that he had abandoned his proposal to convert the Amerian liaison office on Taiwan into an official U.S. government office and had "misstated" on previous occasions. He did go on to say, however, that he "would not pretend, as Carter does, that the relationship we now have with Taiwan, enacted by our Congress, is not official." On **Aug. 26,** Leonard Woodcock, the U.S. Ambassador to China, said that Reagan's assertions on Taiwan endangered U.S. links with China.

Chun Becomes South Korean President — South Korea's military strongman, Gen. Chun Doo Hwan, took control of the civilian government when he was elected president, **Aug. 27,** by the country's National Conference of Unification. He replaced Choi Kyu Ha, who had resigned **Aug. 16.** The only candidate for the post, Chun received 2,524 out of 2,525 votes in the electoral college, with one ballot declared invalid. Chun, who had staged a coup within the military on Dec. 12, 1979, said that his immediate aim was to achieve stability under a revised constitution to be announced in late September and submitted to a national referendum in October. He promised new presidential and National Assembly elections. Observers, however, questioned the government's tolerance of democratic opposition when it pressed charges of sedition, which were called "farfetched" by the U.S., against veteran opposition politician Kim Dae Jung. Kim was convicted by military judges and sentenced, **Sept. 17,** to death.

General

Cars Fail U.S. Crash Test — In a 2d series of 35-mile-an-hour crash tests, the Department of Transportation announced, **Aug. 19,** that only 2 out of 12 1980-model small cars succeeded in protecting passengers. All the others—2 German and 8 Japanese cars—failed. The 2 cars were the Chevrolet Chevette and the Fiat Strada. According to the Department of Transportation, during 1979, when small cars represented about 38 percent of the cars on the road, passengers in small cars accounted for 55 percent of deaths in accidents.

Acoustic Microscope Developed — Prof. Calvin Quate of Stanford University announced, **Aug. 23,** the development of a new microscope that uses very short sound waves. The tool would enable scientists to examine alloys, computer components, and living cells in new ways. With an acoustic microscope, the image depends on the elastic properties of the material being scanned, and not on its reactions to light, as in the case of an optical microscope. Quate noted that much of the material of living cells is transparent to light, but reacts to acoustic scanning in revealing ways. The new microscope would also have the ability to examine the properties of specimens a short way below their surface. When the sound waves hit the specimen at a certain "critical" angle, they cause internal vibrations which result in observable effects on the image.

Disasters — Hurricane Allen, the 2d-strongest Atlantic storm of the century, killed at least 272 persons between **Aug. 4** and **11** as it tore a path of destruction across the eastern Caribbean, Mexico's Yucatan Peninsula, and the Texas Gulf Coast. . .Floodwaters of the Ganges river killed at least 500 people in northern India, it was reported **Aug. 9.** . .In the worst rail disaster in Polish history, a freight train missed a stop signal, headed down the wrong track, and collided head on with a crowded passenger train, **Aug. 19,** near the city of Torun, killing 62 and injuring 50. . .In the 2d worst disaster involving a single plane in aviation history, a Saudi Arabian Airlines Lockheed Tristar landed in flames at Riyadh, **Aug. 19,** and all 301 people on board were killed. Later reports said that the fire had started in the passenger cabin, but the inability of the victims to use the emergency exits was not explained. . . .

SEPTEMBER

National

Carter Declines to Debate 2 Rivals — After the League of Women Voters, **Sept. 9,** invited independent candidate John Anderson to participate in its first presidential debate, President Carter declined to attend the event. Carter insisted that the first debate of the presidential campaign should be a 2-man encounter between himself and Republican candidate Ronald Reagen. Carter strategists, observers said, thought that the inclusion of Anderson in an initial 3-way debate would help Anderson's candidacy and increase the likelihood that he would draw votes away from Carter and perhaps tip the election to Reagan. The League of Women Voters said it had invited Anderson because he had "clearly demonstrated significant voter interest and support" by gaining 15 percent support in several recent public opinion polls. Anderson's candidacy had recently received several boosts: the **Aug. 30** unveiling of his party's platform; the **Sept. 4** ruling by the Federal Election Commission that he could receive Federal funds; and the **Sept. 6** endorsement by New York State's Liberal party. Carter, **Sept. 10,** rejected 2 compromise proposals for 3-man debates. On **Sept. 21,** the Reagan-Anderson debate took place in Baltimore before a television audience estimated at 50 million people. The 2 candidates disagreed on almost all issues, including abortion, tax cuts, the MX missile system, and energy. According to a New York Times/CBS News Poll, reported **Sept. 28,** Reagan was the only candidate to benefit from the debate. Reagan went from 4 percentage points behind Carter in the poll before the debate to 5 points ahead of him after the debate, when 40 percent of the electorate supported Reagan and 35 percent supported Carter. Anderson held steady with 9 percent of the electorate before and after the debate.

Nuclear Missile Silo Explodes — A fuel explosion in an underground Titan 2 nuclear missile silo near Damascus, Ark., **Sept. 19,** killed one Air Force employee and injured 21 others. The blast shattered the 750-ton concrete door on top of the silo and left a crater 250 feet wide. The state police immediately evacuated for 12 hours 1,400 people within a 5-mile radius of the blast, as concern mounted over possible radioactive leaks from the 9-megaton warhead that had been attached to the missile. The warhead was designed to detonate only after it is launched and a series of events has occurred. Air Force officials refused to tell the public of the whereabouts and condition of the warhead, which angered local officials and residents. Finally, on **Sept. 21,** officials stated that the warhead had been ejected from the silo and had landed within the secured area of the missile site. On **Sept. 22,** the 6,000-pound warhead, which Defense Department officials said had suffered a few dents but had not developed any radioactive leaks, was moved to Little Rock Air Force Base and then flown to the Pantex Nuclear Weapons Assembly Plant near Amarillo, Tex. On **Oct. 1,** the Air Force reported that tests taken since the explosion indicated that the accident had caused no significant environmental contamination.

Maine Votes to Keep Nuclear Plant — In the first plebiscite in the nation on nuclear energy since the accident at Three Mile Island in 1979, voters in Maine, **Sept. 23,** defeated a referendum proposal to shut down the state's only nuclear power plant, the Maine Yankee facility near Wiscasset. Fifty nine percent of the vote was in favor of keeping the plant open, while 41 percent was in favor of closing it, with more than half of the electorate casting ballots. The 8-year-old plant produces about one-third of the electricity consumed in the state. The pro-nuclear coalition had argued that consumers would pay an increase of $140 million a year in electric rates if Maine Yankee was shut down. The pro-nuclear group had spent nearly $800,000 advertising its message while the anti-nuclear group had spent $130,000. The anti-nuclear coalition had formed after the Maine plant had been closed for 3 months last year when it was discovered that calculations used to determine its ability to withstand earthquakes had been incorrectly performed. While the plant was closed, a minor earthquake shook the area and the plant withstood it.

Senate Approves Uranium Sale to India — The Senate, **Sept. 24,** voted, 48-46, to defeat a resolution that would have blocked the sale of 38 tons of enriched uranium to India. Both houses of Congress had to pass the resolution in order to block the execution order that Pres. Carter signed **June 19** approving the sale. Therefore, the sale would go through even though the House **Sept. 19,** had voted, 298-98, to block the sale.

Cuban Refugee Boatlift Ends — The Cuban government, **Sept. 26,** closed the harbor at Mariel, ending the 5-month-long boatlift of Cubans to the U.S. The exodus had brought 125,000 refugees to the country since Apr. 21.

Recession Believed To Be Ending — At the end of the year's 3d quarter, the Commerce Department, **Sept. 30,** reported that the index of leading indicators rose by 1.9 percent in August, the 3d monthly rise in a row and a possible indication that the recession was coming to an end. The Commerce Department, **Sept. 19,** had released a preliminary report on the year's 3d quarter which had said that the gross national product (GNP) was unchanged from the previous quarter, another signal of economic strength since the GNP had declined at a 9.6 percent annual rate in the 2d quarter. Economists attributed the abrupt turnaround, in part, to a rebound by the housing and auto industries and to the reaction by consumers to the end of credit controls. However, the continuation of a high rate of inflation during an economic comeback was a bad sign for efforts to control price rises, economists warned. The country had never come out of a recession, which generally lessens price increases, with a rate of inflation as high as it was in August. On **Sept. 23,** the Bureau of Labor Statistics reported that the Consumer Price Index, pushed by food costs, rose by 0.7 percent in August. From January through August, the Bureau also reported the index rose at what would be an annual rate of 12.1 percent.

International

Egypt and Israel Agree to Resume Talks — A month after Egypt had withdrawn from talks with Israel on Palestinian autonomy following Israel's declaration that all of Jerusalem was its capital, the 2 nations, **Sept. 3,** agreed to resume the talks. The talks would be resumed in the next few weeks and both nations would join the U.S. in a summit meeting after the U.S. presidential election in November. The announcement was made by Sol Linowitz, the special U.S. envoy to the Middle East, who had met with Egyptian Pres. Anwar Sadat on **Sept. 3** and with Israeli Premier Menachem Begin on **Sept. 1-2.** Linowitz said that his current mission was not a politically motivated attempt by the Carter Administration to score a foreign policy success before the fall elections. "I'm here because the situation was deteriorating. The tone had become quite sharp, and tension had increased," Linowitz said. It was revealed, **Sept. 8,** that Israel had told the U.S. and Egypt that it would limit itself to 4 more new settlements on the West Bank. The assurance reportedly had a role in Egypt's decision to resume the autonomy talks.

New Chinese Leaders Installed — In the most sweeping peaceful change of Chinese leadership since Mao Tse-tung took over in 1949, Premier Hua Guofeng resigned, **Sept. 7,** during the National People's Congress, as did 5 vice premiers and a number of ministerial appointees. Zhao Ziyang, the former Communist Party chief of Sichuan Province who was credited with boosting the economic performance of the province, took over as premier. The change of leadership was part of a campaign to end the practice of granting lifelong posts to leading officials. Many of those who resigned were at least 80 years old. Another important change in China was the launching of a major program to change China's financial and economic practices, which had been announced **Aug. 31** by Finance Minister Wang Bingqain. The program emphasized profits and local control in order to promote economic growth. The changes in leadership and economic policy represented victories for China's supreme ruler, Deputy Premier Deng Xiaoping, a known pragmatist and proponent of modernization.

Armed Forces Take Over Turkey — Turkey's armed forces, **Sept. 12,** ousted Prime Minister Suleyman Demirel in a bloodless, predawn coup and vowed to bring stability to the nation. The military had warned the civilian government several times during the year that the political parties in the country were failing to deal with Turkey's economic problems and political terrorism. Political violence had reportedly already taken 1,800 lives in 1980 and continued to escalate: some 220 persons died from political conflicts in the first 11 days in September. For the past 5 months, the parliament had not been able to choose a president, a largely symbolic role, due to the inability of any political party to command a majority. After the coup, the leaders of the 3 major political groups and 95 members of parliament were placed in protective custody. The military leaders, under Chief of Staff Gen. Kenan Evren, abolished the country's 19-year-old constitution, dissolved parliament, and extended martial law to all 67 provinces. On **Sept. 14,** right-wing leader Alparslan Turkes, a figure behind much of the political violence, surrendered to the military authorities. On **Sept. 21,** a new 26-member civilian cabinet which included 7 retired generals was announced. Prime Minister Bulent Ulusu, **Sept. 27,** promised a quick return to civilian rule as soon as the National Assembly would write a new constitution. According to Ulusu, the separation of powers introduced by the present constitution "degenerated in effect into a conflict of powers." Observers expected the new constitution to strengthen the leading political parties and discourage the splintering into minority parties that had paralyzed parliamentary action.

Ousted Nicaraguan Ruler Slain — Anastasio Somoza Debayle, the former president of Nicaragua who had been ousted in July, 1979 and gone into exile in Paraguay in August 1979, was assassinated in Asuncion, Paraguay, **Sept. 17,** by gunmen firing machine guns and a bazooka. His driver and a business associate were also killed. A stolen pickup truck sped alongside Somoza's car as it was traveling about 10 blocks from his residence. The truck cut in front of the car, stopping it, and at least 3 men jumped out, firing automatic weapons into the car. Two others emerged from a rented house across the street, firing at the car, and another man from the house fired a projectile from a rocket-launcher, which blew off the 2 front doors and roof of the car. Firing at the bodyguards in the 2 cars which were following Somoza's car, the attackers fled. An alleged Argentine terrorist who was a suspect in the slaying was shot and killed by police, **Sept. 18.** Police held 60 people for questioning and traced the weapons used in the ambush to Nicaragua.

General

Foreign Genes Transplanted into Mice — Genes from the Herpes simplex and SV-40 viruses were successfully transplanted into mouse embryos, Dr. Francis Ruddle of Yale University reported **Sept. 3.** The experiment's success in altering an animal's fundamental genetic composition was heralded as an important advance in genetic research. After injecting the genetic material from the viruses into newly fertilized mouse egg cells, Ruddle and his colleagues implanted the egg cells into female mice, allowed the 21-day pregnancy to occur, then killed the mice after birth, and made tests to discover whether the foreign genetic material had become a permanent part of the animals. Successful transplants occurred in 2 out of 150 cases. Successful "gene-splicing" with foreign genes had previously been done in bacteria but not in animals.

Vaccine for Hepatitis B Developed — Researchers at the New York Blood Center, **Sept. 29,** reported that an experimental vaccine against hepatitis B has been shown to give virtually complete protection against the viral liver infection, which is common throughout the world. The vaccine, made by Merck, Sharpe & Dohme of West Point, Pa., reduced the incidence of hepatitis B in 92 percent of a group that took the vaccine. The vaccine resulted from research on hepatitis which had been carried out for the past 25 years.

Disasters — Wagons loaded with coal went out of control on underground tracks, killing 8 coal miners and injuring 18 **Sept. 1,** near Katowice, Poland. . .At least 24 people drowned when a dam high above the Mexican town of Arandas broke, rescue officials reported **Sept. 2** . . .Floods that surged through Ibadan, Nigeria, killed at least 240 people, the Nigerian News Agency reported **Sept. 3** . . .It was reported **Sept. 6,** that torrential monsoon rains had triggered the collapse of 11 buildings in Sargodha, Pakistan, killing 11 people and injuring 25. . .Huge boulders and tons of earth, **Sept. 8,** swept down the Himalayas near Darjeeling, India, killing 250 people and trapping 30,000. . .A burst dam and flash floods killed at least 100 people and marooned more than 55,000, **Sept. 18,** in the state of Orissa in India. . .After a week of rains, flooding and mudslides in Caracas, Venezuela, **Sept. 25,** killed 20 people and left 1,000 homeless. . .A bomb exploded at the Oktoberfest in Munich, West Germany, **Sept. 26,** and killed 10 people and injured at last 67. . .

OCTOBER

National

Abscam Congressman Ousted From the House — For the first time since 1861, the House of 5Representatives, **Oct. 2,** expelled a member, Rep. Michael J. Myers (D, Pa.). Myers had been convicted of bribery and conspiracy, **Aug. 30,** charges that had come out of the Abscam investigation in which FBI agents posed as representatives of Arab sheiks and offered cash in exchange for the promise of legislative favors. A videotape, which Congressmen had observed, showed Myers taking a $50,000 bribe from undercover agents in return for assurances by the Congressman that he would introduce private immigration bills and take other steps to allow the fictitious Arab sheiks to enter and remain in the U.S. Myers said of the tapes: "What you see on the film is strictly play-acting, which I was instructed to do prior to going to those meetings. I was set up from the word 'go.'" Another congressman, Rep. John Jenrette Jr. (D, S.C.), was convicted of conspiracy and taking a $50,000 bribe by a Federal District Court in Washington, D.C., **Oct. 7.** On **Oct. 30,** Sen. Harrison Williams Jr. (D, N.J.), the only senator which the Abscam investigation had caught on videotape allegedly taking a bribe, was indicted by a federal grand jury in Brooklyn, N.Y., on charges of bribery and conspiracy.

J. P. Stevens Co. and Union Reach Accord — After 17 years of feuding, the J. P. Stevens Company and the Amalgamated Clothing and Textile Workers Union, **Oct. 19,** announced a collective bargaining agreement for 10 plants. For many years the textile company had been a symbol of resistance to unionization in southern states. The contract provided an 8.5 percent pay raise in the first year, back pay to bring workers in line with employees at non-union Stevens plants that received increases in the past 2 years, the right to check off union dues, health and safety provisions, and 3d party arbitration of contract disputes. Stevens also agreed to extend the terms of the contract to any of the company's 150 non-union plants that might be organized by the union. The union agreed to drop its boycott of Stevens products and its campaign to isolate Stevens from other companies. One observer who had followed the dispute for many years said that the breakthrough came because "both sides realized after all those years of acrimony that de-energized both company and union that a fair conclusion would let them spend their time in far better ways."

Recession Ends — The Commerce Department reported, **Oct. 17,** that the gross national product rose at an annual rate of 1 percent in the 3d quarter of the year, indicating that the 1980 recession was over and thus the shortest in modern times. The Commerce Department had also reported, **Oct. 16,** that industrial production at U.S. factories and mines was up 1 percent in September, the largest increase since May 1979. Other signals of an economic comeback, reported on **Oct. 3,** were a 0.1 percent decline in unemployment to 7.5 percent in Sept., and a 0.2 percent decline in the producer price index, the first decline in that index in 4½ years. The most encouraging sign of the month was an increase in the rate of productivity in the private sector of the economy at a 1.4 percent annual rate in the 3d quarter, reported by the Labor Department on **Oct. 27.** It was the first quarterly rise in productivity in 1½ years and an important indication of the strength of the economy and its ability to withstand inflationary pressures. However, in the last inflation report before the election, the Labor Department reported, **Oct. 24,** that consumer prices rose 1 percent in September, showing that the economy continued to be susceptible to inflation. The meager nature of the economic comeback had been underscored, **Oct. 10,** by a group of the nation's leading business executives who were members of the Business Council. Although they had agreed that there was little chance that the economy would soon dip downward again, they had contended that any recovery would probably be extremely sluggish.

International

Canada Seeks Constitutional Changes — Despite opposition from the country's provinces, Canada's federal government, **Oct. 2,** introduced a resolution into parliament that would seek an end to the British North America Act of 1867, which has served as the Constitution, and create a new charter that for the first time would impose a bill of rights on the provinces. Discussions between the 10 provinces and Prime Minister Pierre Elliott Trudeau on a constitution had broken off, **Sept. 13,** when they had failed to resolve disputes on power-sharing between the central government and the provinces. Many provinces opposed placing a bill of rights in the constitution, which would remove such rights from the control of their legislatures. On **Oct. 14,** 5 of the provincial premiers decided to bring a legal challenge against the federal government's plan to act alone in obtaining a new constitution. Trudeau responded by sending 14 members of his cabinet to the western provinces to win their public opinion and he personally traveled to the hostile province of Quebec, **Oct. 22,** to defend his plan. On **Oct. 28,** the federal government once again asserted its power over the provinces by announcing tax and energy policies that will increase national ownership, restrain energy costs, and make the country energy self-sufficient by 1990. However, the announced policies also granted concessions to the energy-rich western provinces by abandoning a proposal to tax gas exports to the U.S., which would have cut directly into provincial revenues.

Paris Synagogue Bombed — A terrorist bomb exploded, **Oct. 3,** in front of a Jewish temple in Paris, France, killing 4 people and injuring 12. The explosion occurred outside a Reform temple as 300 worshipers attended holy day services within. There was little damage inside the temple but the force of the explosion outside the temple overturned several cars. Two of the dead and a number of the injured were non-Jewish Parisians who happened to be passing by when the bomb went off. Two demonstrations of several thousand people each, **Oct. 4,** protested the bombing and, on **Oct. 7,** a crowd of at least 100,000 people marched for 4 hours to protest the incident. The bombing provoked a unanimous chorus of condemnation by France's newspapers and political parties, as the nation reacted in anger to an incident that also awoke fears of a resurgent anti-semitism in the country. French President Valery Giscard d'Estaing went on television, **Oct. 8,** and said that the government would ban neo-Nazi meetings, dissolve "racist organizations," and increase police protection to those under threat. The police had few clues in its investigation and no group admitted responsibility for the bombing. An extreme right-wing group, the Revolutionary Nationalist Movement, did admit to the bombing of a Dutch automobile on **Oct. 5** in Paris after the protest march. Several incidents of violence against members of right-wing groups were reported during the following weeks.

West German Chancellor Schmidt's Coalition Wins Election — In national parliamentary elections **Oct. 5,** Chancellor Helmut Schmidt's ruling coalition of Social Democrats and Free Democrats won an increased majority of seats in the lower house of parliament, which assured Schmidt of another 4 years in office. The new coalition's majority was 45 seats, up from 10. "We can govern very nicely with that and I'm satisfied," said Schmidt of the greater margin. The biggest gains went to the junior partner in the coalition, the Free Democrats, who gained 14 seats, giving them 53, while the Social Democrats gained 4 seats, giving them 218. Observers attributed the Free Democrat's advance to its lack of involvement in the invective which had marked the campaign. Both the major parties, the Social Democrats and the Christian Democrats, had harshly criticized the opposing candidate for chancellor. Agriculture Minister Joseph Ertl, a member of the Free Democrats, said that his party's gains showed "a clear rejection of verbal radicalism in this country." In the overall election, the incumbent parties received 53.5 percent of the total vote and the opposition parties received 44.5 percent, with 88.7 percent of the eligible electorate participating.

General

Quake Strikes Algerian City — A double earthquake struck the Algerian city of Al Asnam, **Oct. 10,** with shocks measured at 7.5 and 6.5 on the Richter scale. Many of the city's principal buildings, including its mosque and main department store, were destroyed and at least 4,500 people were killed. Soldiers with dogs and foreign rescue teams searched for survivors in the wreckage. The first of the shocks lasted for 2 minutes and, according to a French resident, the center of the city was in ruins within 30 seconds. Some officials estimated that as many as 200,000 people lost their homes and livelihoods in the earthquake.

Disasters — An outbreak of encephalitis killed at least 194 people in northern India in the previous 5 weeks, an Indian news agency reported **Oct. 7.** . .Ammonia gas, which escaped from a ruptured pipe at a railroad loading platform **Oct. 8,** killed 9 people and hospitalized 28 in Mexico City. . .In the northwest section of Atlanta, Ga., the explosion of a gas-fired boiler in a day-care nursery, **Oct. 13,** killed 4 preschool children and one adult. . .Officials said, **Oct. 14,** that monsoon floods had killed 28 people and submerged 44 out of Thailand's 74 provinces. . .On a highway 25 miles north of Oaxaca, Mexico, a bus, **Oct. 15,** plunged off a highway and fell to the bottom of a 750-foot gorge, killing 23 people and injuring 18. . .A powerful explosion, **Oct. 23,** destroyed an elementary school in Ortuella, Spain, killing at least 64 people and injuring more than 100. . .An earthquake, registering 6.5 on the Richter scale, struck southern Mexico near Huajuapan de Leon, **Oct. 24,** killing at least 29 people and injuring hundreds more. . .

Iraq Attacks Iran, Lays Siege to Its Southwestern Cities —

After skirmishing intermittently for 10 months over the sovereignty of the disputed Shatt al-Arab waterway that divides both countries, Iraq and Iran, **Sept. 22,** entered into open warfare when Iraqi fighter-bombers attacked 10 Iranian airfields, including the Teheran airport, and Iranian planes retaliated with strikes on 2 Iraqi bases. On **Sept. 23,** Iraqi planes attacked Iran's huge oil refineries at Abadan and Iraqi troops crossed into Iran at several points. Iranian planes attacked the center of Baghdad 3 times, bombing military and civilian airports, and struck at the northern Iraqi oil centers of Kirkuk and Mosul and petrochemical complexes near Basra and at Zubair. At Zubair, at least 29 people were killed, including 2 British and 4 U.S. workers at the facility.

Attempting to cripple each other's economies, the 2 countries again attacked each other's oil facilities on **Sept. 24,** and both countries halted their oil shipments from the Persian Gulf region, which total some 2.7 million barrels of oil a day. Iraq reported that it had seized a 10-mile-deep strip of Iranian territory 200 to 300 miles north of Abadan.

In the next few days, there was heavy ground fighting around Abadan and the adjacent port of Khurramshahr as Iraq pressed its attack on Iran's oil-rich province of Khuzistan. Iraqi forces surrounded and pummeled with its artillery the province's major cities of Abadan, Ahwaz, and Dizful.

After reaching about 50 miles inside Iran with its initial surprise attack, Iraq encountered stiff resistance from zealous Iranian revolutionary guards and effective Iranian air strikes. Because Iraq avoided frontal assaults that would risk heavy casualties, the military situation quickly became stalemated. Iraqi tactics were to cut oil supplies by attacking refineries and pipelines and apply military pressure with continuous artillery barrages in the hope that Iran would negotiate. Reporters were rarely allowed close to the front to independently verify conflicting battle reports and there were no reports of the size of the military forces in combat.

Despite prior false claims by Iraq that it had taken the port city of Khurramshahr, most observers believed Iraq's claim, **Oct. 24,** that it had eliminated the last pocket of resistance in the city. Tanks and supplies had already moved on to Abadan over pontoon bridges on the Karun River early in October and the fighting at the refinery center intensified after the port city was taken. The siege of Ahwaz and Dizful continued, with Teheran radio reporting, **Oct. 26,** that an Iraqi missile attack had killed 100 at Dizful.

On **Oct. 21,** Iraqi First Deputy Prime Minister Taha Yasin Ramadan said that his country intended to seize the cities and the oil fields of the Iranian oil province of Khuzistan and then wanted to negotiate with Iran for the disputed territory. Iraq has made territorial claims upon the entire Shatt al-Arab waterway, 3 islands in the Strait of Hormuz, and the Musian area in Iran.

Analysts speculated that the Iraqi attack was motivated by the belief that Iran's armed forces had been considerably weakened by the country's revolution and subsequent turmoil. Iraqi President Saddam Hussein's ambitions to be the leader of the Arab world and his desire to counter Ayatollah Ruhollah Khomeini's calls for revolution among the Shiite sect of Islam in Iraq, who constitute a majority of the country's population and are ruled by a secular government composed of Moslems of the Sunni sect, were also cited as possible motivations for the Iraqi attack.

At the outbreak of warfare, international concern centered on the Strait of Hormuz through which 60 percent of the world's oil trade passes. President Carter, **Sept. 24,** said the U.S. was consulting with other nations on plans to assure the continued shipment of oil through the strait. Aiding the country that it imports the most oil from, the U.S., **Sept. 30,** sent 4 Air Force radar command planes called AWACS (Airborne Warning and Control Systems) and 300 personnel to Saudi Arabia to strengthen that country's defense.

Pakistani President Muhammad Zia ul-Haq attempted an unsuccessful peace mission, **Sept. 27-30,** sponsored by the Conference of Islamic States. The mission failed, Zia reported, **Oct. 1,** to a meeting of the conference's foreign ministers, because Iraq wanted to negotiate its territorial claims and Iran refused to do so as long as Iraqi troops were on its land.

On **Oct. 7,** Iranian forces defending Khurramshahr opened fire at a number of foreign ships anchored in the Shatt al-Arab, sinking 3 and setting at least 5 ablaze. Although the flow of oil tankers continued, some set anchor to wait out the war due to the high insurance rates they were being charged for passage through the Strait of Hormuz.

Further international concern waxed when Middle Eastern countries threw their support to the opposing countries, raising the possibility of a wider war. On **Oct. 6,** Jordan declared its support for Iraq, while, on **Oct. 10,** Libya declared its support for Iran.

Deaths, Nov. 1, 1979—Oct. 31, 1980

A

Adamson, Joy, 69; naturalist and author, *Born Free;* Kenya, Jan. 3.

Adler, Samuel, 81; abstract painter, sculptor, and educator; New York City, Nov. 12.

Alsop, Mary O'Hara, 95; novelist, *My Friend Flicka;* Chevy Chase, Md., Oct. 15.

Anson, Jay, 58; author of *The Amityville Horror;* Palo Alto, Cal., Mar. 12.

Ardizzone, Edward, 79; British author and illustrator of "Little Tim" series; London, Nov. 8.

Arnold, Elliot, 67; author of some 25 novels; New York, May 13.

Ashford, Emmett, 66; first black umpire in major league baseball; Los Angeles, Mar. 1.

Avery, Fred, 72; cartoon animator created "Daffy Duck" and "Droopy the Dog"; Burbank, Cal., Sept. 1.

B

Bailey, Jack, 72; radio and television host, "Queen for a Day"; Santa Monica, Cal., Feb. 1.

Barry, Don "Red", 69; film actor in numerous westerns in the 1940s; Los Angeles, July 17.

Barth, Alan, 73; author and editorial writer for *The Washington Post* for 30 years; Washington, D.C., Nov. 20.

Beaton, Cecil, 76; British photographer, designer, and author; Wiltshire, England, Jan. 18.

Belcher, Page, 81; U.S. representative from Oklahoma, 1950-72; Midwest City, Okla., Aug. 2.

Bernays, Doris Fleischman, 88; pioneer public relations counsel; Cambridge, Mass., July 10.

Bible, Dana X., 88; former college football coach whose teams won 14 major conference titles; Austin, Tex., Jan. 19.

Blondell, Joan, 70; actress since the 1930s in films and later television; Santa Monica, Cal., Dec. 26.

Bonelli, Richard, 91; operatic baritone; Los Angeles, June 7.

Bonham, John, 32; drummer for the Led Zeppelin rock group; Windsor England, Sept. 25.

Bostwick, A.C., 79; thoroughbred breeder and owner; steeplechase rider, Old Westbury, N.Y., Sept. 26

Bowman, Lee, 64, film leading man in the 1940s; Brentwood, Cal., Dec. 25.

Britton, Barbara, 59; film and television actress; New York, Jan. 17.

Browne, Virgil, 102; business innovator who helped pioneer six-pack cartons, vending machines, and parking meters; Oklahoma City, Dec. 31.

Burpee, David, 87; headed mail-order seed catalogue company; Doylestown, Pa., June 24.

Burrows, Dr. Millar, 91; author of several books on the Dead Sea Scrolls; Ann Arbor, Mich., Apr. 29.

Byrd, Henry, 61; singer and pianist who helped pioneer rock-and-roll; New Orleans, Jan. 30.

C

Caetano, Marcello, 74; former prime minister of Portugal; Rio de Janeiro, Oct. 26.

Capp, Al, 70; cartoonist created "Li'l Abner" comic strip; Cambridge, Mass., Nov. 5.

Carpenter, Rhys, 90; archeologist and classical scholar who authored some 20 books; Devon, Pa., Jan. 2.

Cavanagh, Jerome P., 51; mayor of Detroit, 1962-67; Lexington, Ky., Nov. 27.

Cavanaugh, Rev. John Joseph, 80; president of Notre Dame Univ., 1946-52; South Bend, Ind., Dec. 28.

Chalfen, Morris, 72; impresario who participated in U.S.-Soviet cultural exchange programs; Minneapolis, Nov. 4.

Champion, Gower, 61; dancer, musical director, and choreographer; New York, Aug. 25.

Chang Kuo-tao, 82; a founder of the Chinese Communist Party; Toronto, Dec. 4.

Chapman, John, 51; harness racing driver who won over 3,900 races; Westbury, N.Y., May 2.

Clurman, Harold, 78; stage director, drama critic, and author; New York, Sept. 9.

Cochran, Jacqueline, 70; aviator who set over 200 records; first woman to fly faster than the speed of sound; Indio, Cal., Aug. 8.

Colean, Miles L., 82; economist helped create the Federal Housing Admin.; coined the phrase "urban renewal"; Washington, D.C., Sept. 16.

Collier, John, 78; British author of novels, short stories, and films; Pacific Palisades, Cal., Apr. 6.

Comer, William, 90; U.S. representative from Mississippi, 1933-73; Pascagoula, Miss., Sept. 9.

Crittenberger, Gen. Willis D., 89; World War II commander of Allied troops in Italy; Chevy Chase, Md., Aug. 8.

D

Davis, Benny, 84; vaudeville performer, songwriter, "Margie", "Baby Face"; No. Miami, Fla., Dec. 20.

Delaunay, Sonia, 94; artist influenced 1920s fabric design; Paris, Dec. 5.

Deutsch, Adolph, 82; composer won 3 Academy Awards for film scores; Palm Desert, Cal., Jan. 1.

Dionne, Oliva, 76; father of the world famous quintuplets; North Bay, Ont., Nov. 15.

Donovan, Arthur, 89; boxing referee worked 14 heavyweight title bouts; New York, Sept. 1.

Douglas, Helen Gahagan, 79; actress, U.S. representative, 1945-51; lost U.S. Senate race to Richard Nixon, 1950; New York, June 28.

Douglas, William O., 81; associate justice of the U.S. Supreme Court for 36 years, 1939-75; Washington, D.C., Jan. 19.

Dragonette, Jessica, ?; soprano popular on radio in the 1930s; New York, Mar. 18.

Durante, Jimmy, 86; comedian with raspy voice and large nose who was a popular and beloved entertainer for some 60 years; Santa Monica, Cal., Jan. 29.

Dvorak, Ann, 67; actress who appeared in some 50 films in the 1930s and 1940s; Honolulu, Dec. 10.

E

Eisenhower, Mamie, 82; widow of the 34th president of the United States, Dwight D. Eisenhower; Washington, D.C., Nov. 1.

Eliot, Ray, 74, football coach at Univ. of Illinois whose teams won 2 Rose Bowl games; Urbana, Ill., Feb. 24.

Emory, Katherine, 73; actress starred in the original Broadway production of *The Children's Hour,* 1934; Portland, Me., Feb. 8.

Enlow, Grayson, 63; actor was radio

voice of "The Shadow" in 1940s and 1950s; Mission, Kan., May 18.

Etchebaster, Pierre, 86; court tennis champion for 26 years, 1928-54; St. Jean-de-Luz, France, Mar. 24.

Evans, Bill, 51; jazz pianist; New York, Sept. 15.

Evans, Charles, 89; a leading amateur golfer from 1907 to mid-1950s; Chicago, Nov. 6.

F

Fallis, Barbara, 56; ballet dancer and teacher; New York, Sept. 5.

Fallon, George, 77; U.S. representative from Maryland, 1945-71; Baltimore, Mar. 21.

Farago, Ladislas, 74; author of books on war, world affairs, and espionage, *The Game of the Foxes;* New York, Oct. 15.

Fernandez, Royce, 50; ballet dancer renowned for classical style; New York, Mar. 3.

Finletter, Thomas K., 86; secretary of the Air Force, 1950-53; ambassador to NATO, 1961-65; New York, Apr. 24.

Fitzsimmons, Freddie, 78; baseball pitcher for the Giants and Dodgers who won 217 major league games; Yucca Valley, Cal., Nov. 18.

Fogarty, Anne, 60; fashion designer identified with the American look of the 1950s; New York, Jan. 15.

Fouche, Jacobus J., 82; president of South Africa, 1968-75; Cape Town, Sept. 23.

Fox, Virgil, 68; organist who played hundreds of concerts during 55-year career; W. Palm Beach, Fla., Oct. 25.

Froman, Jane, 72; singer whose comeback from injuries suffered in a plane crash was basis for 1952 film, *With a Song in My Heart;* Columbia, Mo., Apr. 23.

Fromm, Erich, 79; psychoanalyst, social philosopher, and author, *The Art of Loving;* Maralto, Switzerland, Mar. 18.

Furlow, Terry, 25; basketball player for the Utah Jazz of the NBA; Linndale, Oh., May 23.

G

Galindez, Victor, 31; Argentine boxer who held light-heavyweight title between 1974 and 1979; Argentina, Oct. 26.

Gantt, Dr. William H., 87; behavioral psychiatrist; Baltimore, Feb. 26.

Gardiner, Dorothy, 85; author of historical and mystery novels; Buffalo, N.Y., Dec. 4.

Gardiner, Reginald, 77; British actor who appeared in some 100 films, usually in comic roles; Westwood, Cal., July 7.

de Gaulle, Yvonne, 79; widow of French president, Charles de Gaulle; Paris, Nov. 8.

Gorman, Patrick E., 87; labor leader who headed Amalgamated Meat Cutters and Butcher Workmen of North America, 1942-76; Chicago, Sept. 3.

Gottlieb, Eddie, 81; basketball coach and owner who helped found the National Basketball Assn.; Philadelphia, Dec. 7.

Gottlieb, Michael, 79; contract bridge player who won 9 major national titles, 1929-36; Burlingame, Cal., Apr. 8.

Green, Sihugo, 47; basketball player with several NBA teams in the 1950s and 1960s; Pittsburgh, Oct. 4.

Grenfell, Joyce, 69; British stage and screen actress; London, Nov. 30.

Griffin, John Howard, 60; author, *Black Like Me;* Ft. Worth, Tex., Sept. 9.

Griffith, Hugh, 67; Welsh character actor, *Tom Jones;* London, May 14.

Gimbel, Bruce A., 67; business executive who headed department store chain; Greenwich, Conn., Oct. 7.

Grubb, David, 61; novelist, *The Night of the Hunter;* New York, July 24.

Gruen, Victor, 76; architect who pioneered development of suburban shopping centers in the 1950s; Vienna, Feb. 14.

Guggenheim, Peggy, 81; millionaire famed for modern art collection; Venice, Italy, Dec. 23.

H

Hall, Jon, 66; actor in action films in the 1930s and 1940s; North Hollywood, Cal., Dec. 13.

Hall, Paul, 65; labor leader who helped build the Seafarers International Union in the 1930s; New York, June 22.

Harmon, Gen. Ernest N., 85; commanded "Hell on Wheels" 2d Armored Division in Battle of the Bulge; White River Junction, Vt., Nov. 13.

Harris, Jed, 79; Broadway producer and director in the 1920s and 30s; New York, Nov. 15.

Hass, Eric, 75; 4-time U.S. presidential candidate for the Socialist Labor Party; Santa Rosa, Cal., Oct. 2.

Haymes, Dick, 61; singer popular during the Big Band era; Los Angeles, Mar. 28.

Hays, H.R., 76; poet, novelist, critic, and playwright; Southampton, N.Y., Oct. 17.

Heindorf, Ray, 71; film score composer who won 3 Academy Awards; Los Angeles, Feb. 2.

Herbert, F. Edward, 78; Democratic representative from Louisiana, 1941-77; New Orleans, Dec. 29.

Hicks, Sue Kerr, 84; asst. prosecutor in 1925 "Scopes monkey trial"; name inspired hit song, "A Boy Named Sue"; Sweetwater, Tenn., June 27.

Hitchcock, Alfred, 80; director of psychological thrillers and suspense films for over 50 years; Los Angeles, Apr. 29.

Hurley, Ruby, 70; black leader of the civil rights movement in the South in the 1950s and 1960s; Atlanta, Aug. 9.

I

Iturbi, Jose, 84; Spanish-born pianist and conductor who appeared in several films; Hollywood, Cal., May 28.

J

Jackson, Eddie, 84; entertainer, longtime partner of Jimmy Durante; Los Angeles, July 16.

Janssen, David, 49; actor who starred in films, television, "The Fugitive"; Malibu, Cal., Feb. 13.

Johnson, Gerald W., 89; author, journalist, and historian; Baltimore, Mar. 23.

Jones, Howard Mumford, 88; historian who won 1965 Pulitzer Prize for general nonfiction; Cambridge, Mass., May 11.

K

Kaminska, Ida, 80; actress, director, and producer in the Yiddish theater; New York, May 21.

Kean, Robert W., 86; U.S. representative from New Jersey, 1938-58; Livingston, N.J., Sept. 21.

Kenney, Douglas, 33; co-founder of National Lampoon magazine; co-author of the film, *Animal House;* Kauai, Ha., reported Sept. 1.

Khama, Sir Seretse, 59; president of Botswana since 1966; Botswana, July 13.

Kirkus, Virginia, 86; founder of the influential book-review service; Danbury, Conn., Sept. 10.

Kokoschka, Oskar, 93; Austrian expressionist painter; Montreux, Switzerland, Feb. 22.

Korjus, Miliza, 68?; coloratura soprano; Los Angeles, Aug. 26.

Kostelanetz, Andre, 78; conductor of symphonic and popular music; Port-au-Prince, Haiti, Jan. 13.

Kroneberger, Louis, 75; critic, essayist, anthologist, and author; Brookline, Mass., Apr. 30.

Kuter, Gen. Laurence, 74; U.S. Air Force general who helped plan air power strategy during World War II; Naples, Fla., Nov. 30.

L

Lauck, Chester, 78; actor played "Lum" on popular Lum and Abner radio program, 1931-55; Hot Springs, Ark., Feb. 21.

Lesser, Sol, 90; film pioneer produced over 100 motion pictures; Hollywood, Cal., Sept. 19.

Levenson, Sam, 68; television humorist and author; New York, Aug. 27.

Libby, Dr. Willard, 71; atomic scientist who won 1960 Nobel Prize in chemistry; Los Angeles, Sept. 8.

Loden, Barbara, 48; actress, screenwriter, and director; New York, Sept. 7.

Longley, James B., 56; governor of Maine, 1975-79; Lewiston, Me., Aug. 16.

Longworth, Alice Roosevelt, 96; last surviving child of President Theodore Roosevelt; Washington, D.C., Feb. 20.

Lowenstein, Allard K., 51; antiwar, civil rights leader who led "dump Johnson" movement in 1968; New York, Mar. 14.

M

Malik, Yakov, 73; Soviet diplomat, UN ambassador, 1948-52, 1968-76; Moscow, Feb. 11.

Mantovani, Annunzio, 74; conductor of string-filled orchestras popular for "easy listening" sound; Kent, England, Mar. 29.

Marshall, Dr. John L., 44; orthopedic surgeon and sports-medicine expert; in a plane crash near Saranac Lake, N.Y., Feb. 12.

Marquard, Rube, 90; baseball pitcher who won 19 consecutive games for N.Y. Giants in 1912; Baltimore, Md., June 1.

Martin, Pete, 79; writer for *The Saturday Evening Post* famed for interviews with Hollywood personalities; Birchrunville, Pa., Oct. 13.

Martin, Strother, 61; character actor in films and television; Thousand Oaks, Cal., Aug. 1.

Marx, Zeppo, 78; member of Marx Brothers comedy team until 1934; theatrical agent; Palm Springs, Cal., Nov. 30.

Mauchley, John W., 72; co-inventor of first electronic computer, 1946; Ambler, Pa., Jan. 8.

McCarty, Mary, 56; stage and screen actress, often in comic supporting roles; Los Angeles, Apr. 5.

McClatchy, Eleanor, 85; former chairman of McClatchy newspapers; Sacramento, Cal., Oct. 18.

McCulloch, William M., 78; Republican representative from Ohio, 1946-73; instrumental in passage of major civil rights legislation; Washington, D.C., Feb. 22.

McDonnell, James S., 81; aviation and spacecraft pioneer who headed McDonnell Douglas Corp.; Ladue, Mo., Aug. 22.

McGraw, Charles, 66; actor in numerous films, usually in tough-guy roles; Studio City, Cal., July 29.

McWilliams, Carey, 74; editor of *The Nation,* 1955-75; New York, June 27.

Meany, George, 85; labor leader who headed the AFL-CIO, 1955-79; Washington, D.C., Jan. 11.

Medford, Kay, 59; comic actress of stage and films; New York, Apr. 10.

Mercer, David, 52; British playwright and screenwriter, *Morgan;* Haifa, Israel, Aug. 8.

Milestone, Lewis, 84; Hollywood film director for over 40 years; won 2 Oscars; Los Angeles, Sept. 25.

Miller, Henry, 88; writer, *Tropic of Cancer;* Pacific Palisades, Cal., June 7.

Mingo, Norman, 84; magazine illustrator who created Alfred E. Neuman as the trademark of Mad magazine; White Plains, N.Y., May 24.

Monroney, A.S. "Mike," 77; U.S. senator from Oklahoma, 1951-69; Rockville, Md., Feb. 13.

Morgenthau, Hans J., 76; political scientist, author, and teacher; leading Vietnam War critic; New York, July 19.

Munoz Marin, Luis, 82; first elected governor of Puerto Rico; 1948-64; San Juan, Apr. 30.

N

Nenni, Pietro, 88; Italian socialist leader; Rome, Jan. 1.

Nielsen, Arthur C., 83; market researcher who devised system that rates TV programs; Chicago, June 1.

Nolan, Bob, 72; singer and songwriter with the "Sons of the Pioneers" musical group in over 150 Western films; Costa Mesa, Cal., June 16.

Nugent, Elliott, 83; actor, writer, director in the theater and films; New York, Aug. 9.

O

Oberon, Merle, 68; film leading lady of the 1930s and 40s, *Wuthering Heights;* Los Angeles, Nov. 22.

Ohira, Masayoshi, 70; Japanese prime minister; Tokyo, June 12.

Okun, Arthur, 51; economist who headed the Council of Economic Advisors, 1968; Washington, D.C., Mar. 23.

Owens, Jesse, 66; track and field star who won 4 gold medals at the 1936 Olympics; Tucson, Ariz., Mar. 31.

P

Pahlevi, Mohammad Riza, "Shah of Iran," 60; deposed Iranian monarch who led that country for 40 years; nr. Cairo, Egypt, July 27.

Pal, George, 72; film producer and director known for "Puppetoons" and science-fiction films; Beverly Hills, Cal., May 2.

Patrick, Gail, 69; film actress and TV producer, "Perry Mason" series; Hollywood, Cal., July 6.

Patrick, Lynn, 67; National Hockey League player, coach, and general manager; St. Louis, Jan. 26.

Patterson, William A., 80; aviation pioneer who headed United Airlines, 1934-66; Glenview, Ill., June 13.

Piaget, Jean, 84; Swiss psychologist noted for his studies of child development; Geneva, Sept. 16.

Porter, Katherine Anne, 90; short-story writer and novelist, *Ship of Fools;* Silver Springs, Md., Sept. 18.

Potter, Charles E., 63; former U.S. senator and representative from Michigan; Washington, D.C., Nov. 23.

Powers, John "Shorty", 57; the "voice of the astronauts" in the 1960s; Phoenix, Ariz., Jan. 1.

Pownall, Harry, 77; harness racing driver and trainer; Honolulu, Dec. 31.

Page, Joe, 62; ace relief pitcher for the N.Y. Yankees in the 1940s; Latrobe, Pa., Apr. 21.

R

Reed, Stanley F., 95, associate justice of the U.S. Supreme Court, 1938-57; Huntington, N.Y., Apr. 3.

Randolph, Lillian, 65; actress in radio, television, and films for some 40 years; Arcadia, Cal., Sept. 12.

Renaldo, Duncan, 76; actor who played the "Cisco Kid" on television in the 1950s; Santa Barbara, Cal., Sept. 3.

Rhine, Joseph B., 84; psychologist who pioneered experiments in ESP; Hillsborough, N.C., Feb. 20.

Robbins, Gale, 58; actress and singer; a popular World War II pin-up girl; Los Angeles, Feb. 18.

Robinson, Francis, 70; executive, media personality long associated with the Metropolitan Opera; New York, May 14.

Rodgers, Richard, 77; composer of musicals including *Oklahoma, Pal Joey, South Pacific,* and *The Sound of Music;* New York, Dec. 30.

Romero, Oscar Arnulfo, 62; archbishop of El Salvador; San Salvador, Mar. 24.

Ronne, Finn, 80; explorer who led several expeditions to Antarctica; Bethesda, Md., Jan. 12.

Rosenstein, Nettie, 90; designer who popularized the "little black dress"; New York, Mar. 13.

Roth, Lillian, 69; singer and actress whose autobiography, *I'll Cry Tomorrow,* was made into a successful film; New York, May 12.

Rukeyser, Muriel, 66; poet of social protest whose work spanned 4 decades; New York, Feb. 12.

Runnels, Rep. Harold, 56; Democratic representative from New Mexico from 1971; New York, Aug. 5.

S

Saltzer, Louis B., 82; editor of *The Cleveland Press,* 1937-66; Spencer, Oh., Apr. 2.

Sands, Dorothy, 87; stage actress for nearly 50 years; noted for one-woman shows; Croton-on-Hudson, N.Y., Sept. 11.

Sartre, Jean-Paul, 74; existentialist philosopher and writer who influenced 2 generations of thinkers and writers; Paris, Apr. 15.

Sauer, Dr. Louis W., 94; pediatrician who helped develop vaccines against whooping cough, diphtheria, and tetanus; Coral Gables, Fla., Feb. 10.

Schary, Dore, 74; film producer and playwright, *Sunrise at Campobello;* New York, July 7.

Schwab, Jack, 75; founder of the famed Hollywood drug store; Hollywood, Cal., Mar. 17.

Sellers, Peter, 54; British actor known for his zany comic roles; starred in the "Pink Panther" series; London, July 24.

Sharaf, Abdul Hamid, 41; premier of Jordan; Amman, Jordan, July 3.

Sheen, Archbishop Fulton J., 84; Roman Catholic author and preacher; best known for "Life Is Worth Living" TV series in the 1950s; New York, Dec. 9.

Sherrill, Bishop Henry Knox, 89; Episcopal church leader; Boxford, Mass., May 11.

Shields, Warren, 82; pathologist, pioneer in radiation effects; Mashpee, Mass., July 1.

Short, Dewey, 82; U.S. representative from Missouri, 1935-57; Washington, D.C., Nov. 19;

Silverheels, Jay, 62; actor played Tonto in "The Lone Ranger" television series; Woodland Hills, Cal., Mar. 5.

Slack, Rep. John M., 64; West Virginia Democrat who served in the House from 1959; Alexandria, Va., Mar. 17.

Snow, C.P., 74; British scientist, novelist, and playwright; London, July 1.

Somoza Debayle, Anastasio, 55; ousted Nicaraguan ruler; Asuncion, Paraguay, Sept. 17.

Stein, Dr. William H., 68; biochemist who shared 1972 Nobel Prize in chemistry; New York, Feb. 2.

Stevens, Dr. Mal, 79; orthopedic surgeon; football coach at Yale, New York Univ.; New York, Dec. 6.

Stewart, George R., 85; scholar and novelist; San Francisco, Aug. 22.

Still, Clyfford, 75; artist who helped found "abstract expressionist" school of painting; Baltimore, June 23.

Stone, Milburn, 75; actor who played Doc Adams in the long-running TV series "Gunsmoke"; La Jolla, Cal., June 12.

Summerskill, Baroness Edith, 78; British politician who campaigned for women's rights and social welfare; London, Feb. 4.

T

Tarnower, Dr. Herman, 69; physician who wrote the bestseller *The Complete Scarsdale Medical Diet;* Purchase, N.Y., Mar. 10.

Teale, Edwin Way, 81; naturalist, illustrator, photographer, and writer who won 1966 Pulitzer Prize for general nonfiction; Norwich, Conn., Oct. 18.

Tiomkin, Dimitri, 85; Russian-born composer who won 4 Oscars for his film scores; London, Nov. 11.

Tito, Josip Broz, 87; president of Yugoslavia and leader of the League of Communists, its ruling party; Ljubljana, Yugoslavia, May 4.

Tobias, George, 78; character actor in numerous films, mostly as genial tough guy; Hollywood, Cal., Feb. 27.

Tolbert, William R., 66; president of Liberia; Monrovia, Liberia, Apr. 12.

Ton Duc Thang, 91; president of Vietnam from 1969; Hanoi, Mar. 30.

Travis, Robert, 73; union organizer who led 1936 strike against General Motors that led to recognition of UAW union; Los Angeles, Nov. 19.

Tuckner, Howard, 48; newspaper and television journalist; New York, Aug. 12.

Tynan, Kenneth, 53; British drama critic; Santa Monica, Cal., July 26.

Tyrer, Jim, 41; pro-football offensive tackle for 14 years, mostly with the Kansas City Chiefs; Kansas City, Mo., Sept. 15.

V

Van, Bobby, 47; actor, comedian, and dancer; Los Angeles, July 31.

Velikovsky, Immanuel, 84; Russian-born psychoanalyst and author, *Worlds in Collision,* Princeton, N.J., Nov. 17.

Vysotsky, Vladimir, 46; Soviet actor and balladeer; Moscow, July 24.

W

Wilhemina (Behmenburg), 40; Dutch-born model who appeared on 28 Vogue magazine covers; headed own modeling agency; Greenwich, Conn., Mar. 1.

Wright, James, 52; poet who won 1972 Pulitzer Prize; New York, Mar. 25.

Z

Zanuck, Darryl F., 77; film producer who headed Twentieth Century-Fox; Palm Springs, Cal., Dec. 22.

U.S. Places of 5,000 or More Population—With ZIP and Area Codes

Source: U.S. Bureau of the Census; U.S. Postal Service; N.Y. Telephone Co.

The listings below show the official urban population of the United States. "Urban population" is defined as all persons living in (a) places of 5,000 inhabitants or more, incorporated as cities, villages, boroughs (except Alaska), and towns (except in New England, New York, New Jersey, Pennsylvania and Wisconsin), but excluding those persons living in the rural portions of extended cities; (b) unincorporated places of 5,000 inhabitants or more; and (c) other territory, incorporated or unincorporated, included in urbanized areas.

The non-urban portion of an extended city contains one or more areas, each at least 5 square miles in extent and with a population density of less than 100 persons per square mile. The area or areas constitute at least 25 percent of the legal city's land area of a total of 25 square miles or more.

The 1980 population figures listed below in roman type are preliminary totals in the 1980 census, conducted on Apr. 1, 1980, for all places released by the Census Bureau as of Oct. 15, 1980. Population figures listed in italics are 1978 Census Bureau estimates.

In New England, New York, New Jersey, Pennsylvania, and Wisconsin, minor civil divisions called "towns" often include rural areas and one or more urban areas. Only the urban areas of these "towns" are included here, except in the case of New England where entire town populations, which may include some rural population, are shown; these towns are indicated by italics. Boroughs in Alaska may contain one or more urban areas which are included here.

(u) means place is unincorporated.

The ZIP Code of each place appears before the name of that place, if it is obtainable. Telephone Area Code appears in parentheses after the name of the state or, if a state has more than one number, after the name of the place.

CAUTION—Where an asterisk (*) appears before the ZIP Code, ask your local postmaster for the correct ZIP Code for a specific address within the place listed.

Alabama (205)

ZIP code	Place	1980	1970
35007	Alabaster	*6,367*	4,286
35950	Albertville	12,039	9,963
35010	Alexander City	*12,828*	12,358
36420	Andalusia	*9,788*	10,092
36201	Anniston	*31,264*	31,533
.....	Anniston Northwest(u)	NA	6,609
35016	Arab	*5,389*	5,159
35611	Athens	14,524	14,360
36502	Atmore	*8,735*	8,293
35954	Attalla	*7,223*	7,510
36830	Auburn	*25,180*	22,767
36507	Bay Minette	*7,080*	6,727
35020	Bessemer	*31,294*	33,663
*35203	Birmingham	*280,413*	300,910
35226	Bluff Park(u)	NA	12,372
35957	Boaz	*6,216*	5,635
36426	Brewton	*6,895*	6,747
35215	Center Point(u)	NA	15,675
36611	Chickasaw	*7,741*	8,447
35044	Childersburg	*5,162*	4,831
35045	Clanton	*6,643*	5,868
35055	Cullman	13,069	12,601
35601	Decatur	41,927	38,044
36732	Demopolis	*7,699*	7,651
36301	Dothan	*46,868*	36,733
36330	Enterprise	*16,670*	15,591
36027	Eufaula	*10,890*	9,102
35064	Fairfield	*12,402*	14,369
36532	Fairhope	*6,268*	5,720
35630	Florence	36,825	34,031
35214	Forestdale(u)	NA	6,091
36201	Fort McClellan(u)	NA	5,334
35967	Fort Payne	*8,771*	8,435
36360	Fort Rucker(u)	NA	14,242
35068	Fultondale	*7,090*	5,163
*35901	Gadsden	*48,693*	53,928
35071	Gardendale	*14,091*	6,537
36037	Greenville	*7,540*	8,033
35976	Guntersville	*7,396*	6,491
35640	Hartselle	*8,698*	7,355
35209	Homewood	*22,445*	21,137
35020	Hueytown	*12,745*	7,095
*35804	Huntsville	142,238	139,282
35210	Irondale	*5,460*	3,166
36545	Jackson	*6,401*	5,957
36265	Jacksonville	*8,790*	7,715
35501	Jasper	*12,256*	10,798
36863	Lanett	*6,924*	6,908
35094	Leeds	*9,235*	6,991
35228	Midfield	*6,523*	6,340
*36601	Mobile	*207,741*	190,026
36460	Monroeville	*5,715*	4,846
*36104	Montgomery	*158,724*	133,386
35223	Mountain Brook	*21,230*	19,509
35660	Muscle Shoals	*8,275*	6,907
35476	Northport	*15,353*	9,435
36801	Opelika	*21,875*	19,027
36467	Opp	*6,701*	6,493
36360	Ozark	*14,580*	13,555
36203	Oxford	*11,249*	7,056
35124	Pelham	*7,514*	2,443
35125	Pell City	*6,417*	5,602
36867	Phenix City	*27,210*	25,281
36272	Piedmont	*5,213*	5,063
36067	Prattville	*17,607*	13,116
36610	Prichard	*40,265*	41,578
35901	Rainbow City	*6,023*	3,107
36274	Roanoke	*5,372*	5,251
35653	Russellville	*7,790*	7,814
36571	Saraland	*10,114*	7,840
35768	Scottsboro	14,752	9,324
36701	Selma	*24,278*	27,379
35660	Sheffield	11,816	13,115
35150	Sylacauga	*12,283*	12,255
35160	Talladega	*18,271*	17,662
35217	Tarrant City	*7,683*	6,835
36081	Troy	*12,248*	11,482
35401	Tuscaloosa	*69,263*	65,773
35674	Tuscumbia	*8,485*	8,828
36083	Tuskegee	*12,437*	11,028
35216	Vestavia Hills	*16,878*	8,311
36201	West End-Cobb(u)	NA	5,515

Alaska (907)

ZIP code	Place	1980	1970
*99502	Anchorage	NA	48,081
99702	Eielson(u)	NA	6,149
99506	Elmendorf(u)	NA	6,018
99701	Fairbanks	*31,994*	14,771
99505	Fort Richardson(u)	NA	8,960
99703	Fort Wainwright(u)	NA	9,097
99801	Juneau, city and borough	*19,249*	13,556
99611	Kenai Peninsula borough	*26,670*	16,586
99901	Ketchikan	*7,500*	6,994
99503	Spenard(u)	NA	18,089

Arizona (602)

ZIP code	Place	1980	1970
85321	Ajo(u)	NA	5,881
85220	Apache Junction	*7,514*	2,443
85323	Avondale	*6,512*	6,626
85603	Bisbee	*10,325*	8,328
85222	Casa Grande	*13,713*	10,536
85224	Chandler	*21,453*	13,763
85533	Clifton	*5,318*	5,087
85228	Coolidge	*6,587*	5,314
85607	Douglas	13,148	12,462
85231	Eloy	*6,193*	5,381
86001	Flagstaff	34,821	26,117
85613	Fort Huachuca(u)	NA	6,659
*85301	Glendale	*78,188*	36,228
85501	Globe	*6,237*	7,333
86025	Holbrook	*5,270*	4,759
86401	Kingman	*8,383*	7,312
86403	Lake Havasu	11,972	4,111
85301	Luke(u)	NA	5,047
*85201	Mesa	*117,840*	62,853
85621	Nogales	13,968	8,946
86040	Page(u)	NA	1,439
85253	Paradise Valley	*10,969*	7,155
85345	Peoria	*10,184*	4,792
*85026	Phoenix	*681,355*	582,500
86301	Prescott	*18,446*	13,283
85546	Safford	*6,760*	5,333
*85251	Scottsdale	*82,297*	67,823
85635	Sierra Vista	24,901	6,689
85713	South Tucson	*6,425*	6,620
85351	Sun City(u)	NA	13,670
85273	Superior	*6,182*	4,975
*85282	Tempe	*99,194*	63,550
*85726	Tucson	331,506	262,933
85364	West Yuma(u)	NA	5,552
86047	Winslow	*7,517*	8,066
85364	Yuma	*32,638*	29,007

Arkansas (501)

ZIP code	Place	1980	1970
71923	Arkadelphia	9,761	9,841
72501	Batesville	8,269	7,209
72015	Benton	18,172	16,499
72712	Bentonville	7,869	5,508
72315	Blytheville	24,247	24,752
72021	Brinkley	5,090	5,275
71701	Camden	15,372	15,147
72830	Clarksville	5,313	4,616
72032	Conway	20,109	15,510
71635	Crossett	6,908	6,191
71639	Dumas	5,241	4,600
71730	El Dorado	24,574	25,283
72701	Fayetteville	35,349	30,729
71742	Fordyce	5,035	4,837
72335	Forrest City	12,692	12,521
72901	Fort Smith	68,432	68,802
72601	Harrison	9,368	7,239
72342	Helena	8,789	10,415
71801	Hope	9,260	8,810
71901	Hot Springs	40,602	35,631
72076	Jacksonville	25,546	19,832
72401	Jonesboro	31,076	27,050
*72201	Little Rock	151,756	132,483
71753	Magnolia	11,656	11,303
72104	Malvern	10,566	8,739
72360	Marianna	5,704	6,196
71654	McGehee	5,771	4,683
71655	Monticello	7,324	5,085
72110	Morrilton	6,462	6,814
72653	Mountain Home	6,839	3,936
72112	Newport	7,634	7,725
*72114	North Little Rock	62,823	60,040
72370	Osceola	8,293	7,204
72450	Paragould	15,199	10,639
72455	Pocahontas	5,845	4,544
71601	Pine Bluff	55,857	57,389
72756	Rogers	16,800	11,050
72801	Russellville	14,753	11,750
72143	Searcy	11,221	9,040
72116	Sherwood	9,748	2,754
72761	Siloam Springs	7,605	6,009
72204	Southwest Little Rock(u)	NA	13,231
72764	Springdale	21,039	16,783
72160	Stuttgart	10,399	10,477
75501	Texarkana	19,822	21,682
72472	Trumann	6,776	6,023
72956	Van Buren	10,796	8,373
71671	Warren	7,773	6,433
72390	West Helena	10,458	11,007
72301	West Memphis	27,128	25,892
72396	Wynne	7,605	6,696

California

ZIP code	Place	Area code	1980	1970
94501	Alameda	(415)	63,700	70,968
94507	Alamo-Danville(u)	(415)	15,101	14,059
94706	Albany	(415)	15,101	14,674
*91802	Alhambra	(213)	60,363	62,125
90249	Alondra Park(u)	(213)	NA	12,193
91001	Altadena(u)	(213)	NA	42,415
95116	Alum Rock(u)	(408)	NA	18,355
*92803	Anaheim	(714)	207,007	166,408
96007	Anderson	(916)	6,861	5,492
94509	Antioch	(415)	37,760	28,060
92307	Apple Valley(u)	(714)	NA	6,702
95003	Aptos(u)	(408)	NA	8,704
91006	Arcadia	(213)	46,587	45,138
95521	Arcata	(707)	12,465	8,985
95825	Arden-Arcade(u)	(916)	NA	82,492
93420	Arroyo Grande	(805)	10,384	7,454
90701	Artesia	(213)	14,679	14,757
93203	Arvin	(805)	6,141	5,090
94577	Ashland(u)	(415)	NA	14,810
93422	Atascadero(u)	(805)	12,611	10,290
94025	Atherton	(415)	7,824	8,085
95301	Atwater	(209)	15,515	11,640
95603	Auburn	(916)	7,301	6,570
92505	August School Area(u)	(209)	NA	6,293
91746	Avocado Heights(u)	(213)	NA	9,810
91702	Azusa	(213)	27,928	25,217
*93302	Bakersfield	(805)	86,800	69,515
91706	Baldwin Park	(213)	50,538	47,285
92220	Banning	(714)	12,595	12,034
92311	Barstow	(714)	17,020	17,442
95903	Beale East(u)	(916)	NA	7,029
92223	Beaumont	(714)	6,624	5,484
90201	Bell	(213)	22,385	21,836
90706	Bellflower	(213)	50,510	51,454
90201	Bell Gardens	(213)	31,496	29,308
94002	Belmont	(415)	25,929	23,538
94510	Benicia	(707)	12,957	7,349
*94704	Berkeley	(415)	103,134	116,716
*90213	Beverly Hills	(213)	25,867	33,416
92314	Big Bear(u)	(714)	NA	5,268
92316	Bloomington(u)	(714)	NA	11,957
92225	Blythe	(714)	7,301	7,047
92227	Brawley	(714)	14,299	13,746
92621	Brea	(714)	26,651	18,447
95605	Broderick-Bryte(u)	(916)	NA	12,782
*90620	Buena Park	(714)	63,391	63,646
*91505	Burbank	(213)	83,781	88,871
94010	Burlingame	(415)	27,466	27,320
92231	Calexico	(714)	13,890	10,625
93010	Camarillo	(805)	37,437	19,219
93010	Camarillo Heights(u)	(805)	NA	5,892
95124	Cambrian Park(u)	(408)	NA	5,316
95008	Campbell	(408)	25,144	23,797
95010	Capitola	(408)	8,577	5,080
92007	Cardiff-by-the-Sea(u)	(714)	NA	5,724
92008	Carlsbad	(714)	29,985	14,944
95608	Carmichael(u)	(916)	NA	37,625
93013	Carpinteria	(805)	10,769	6,982
90744	Carson	(213)	79,934	71,150
94546	Castro Valley(u)	(415)	NA	44,760
95307	Ceres	(209)	10,880	6,029
90701	Cerritos	(213)	50,302	15,856
94541	Cherryland(u)	(415)	NA	9,969
95926	Chico	(916)	25,619	19,580
95926	Chico North(u)	(916)	NA	6,656
93555	China Lake(u)	(714)	NA	11,105
91710	Chino	(714)	37,106	20,411
*92010	Chula Vista	(714)	81,192	67,901
95610	Citrus Heights(u)	(916)	NA	21,760
91711	Claremont	(714)	30,950	23,998
93612	Clovis	(209)	28,451	13,856
92236	Coachella	(714)	8,668	8,353
93210	Coalinga	(209)	6,253	6,161
92324	Colton	(714)	19,215	20,016
90022	Commerce	(213)	10,006	10,635
*90220	Compton	(213)	74,193	78,547
*94520	Concord	(415)	98,974	85,164
93212	Corcoran	(209)	5,854	5,249
91720	Corona	(714)	36,560	27,519
92118	Coronado	(714)	20,969	20,020
94925	Corte Madera	(415)	7,934	8,464
*92626	Costa Mesa	(714)	79,191	72,660
*91722	Covina	(213)	34,859	30,395
91730	Cucamonga(u)	(714)	NA	5,796
90201	Cudahy	(213)	16,612	16,998
90230	Culver City	(213)	38,378	34,451
95014	Cupertino	(408)	23,205	17,895
90630	Cypress	(714)	40,976	31,569
*94017	Daly City	(415)	73,838	66,922
95616	Davis	(916)	35,263	23,488
90250	Del Aire(u)	(213)	NA	11,930
93215	Delano	(805)	15,393	14,559
92014	Del Mar	(714)	5,262	3,956
91765	Diamond Bar(u)	(714)	NA	10,576
93618	Dinuba	(209)	9,631	7,917
95620	Dixon	(916)	6,284	4,432
90810	Dominguez(u)	(213)	NA	5,980
*90241	Downey	(213)	85,158	88,573
91010	Duarte	(213)	14,942	14,981
94566	Dublin(u)	(415)	NA	13,641
90220	East Compton(u)	(213)	NA	5,853
90638	East La Mirada(u)	(213)	NA	12,339
90022	East Los Angeles(u)	(213)	NA	104,881
94303	East Palo Alto(u)	(415)	NA	18,727
93523	Edwards(u)	(805)	NA	10,331
*92020	El Cajon	(714)	69,741	52,273
92243	El Centro	(714)	23,856	19,272
94530	El Cerrito	(415)	22,689	25,190
93017	El Encanto Heights(u)	(213)	NA	6,225
*91734	El Monte	(213)	66,597	68,892
93446	El Paso de Robles	(213)	8,473	7,168
93030	El Rio(u)	(805)	NA	6,173
90245	El Segundo	(213)	13,757	15,620
92630	El Toro(u)	(714)	NA	8,654
92709	El Toro Station(u)	(714)	NA	6,970
92024	Encinitas(u)	(714)	NA	5,375
96001	Enterprise(u)	(916)	NA	11,486
92025	Escondido	(714)	59,273	36,792
95501	Eureka	(707)	24,147	24,337
93221	Exeter	(209)	5,386	4,475
94930	Fairfax	(415)	7,659	7,661
94533	Fairfield	(707)	54,605	44,146
95628	Fair Oaks(u)	(916)	NA	11,256
92028	Fallbrook(u)	(714)	NA	6,945
93015	Fillmore	(805)	8,684	6,285
90001	Florence-Graham(u)	(213)	NA	42,900
95828	Florin(u)	(916)	NA	9,646
95630	Folsom	(916)	10,983	5,810
92335	Fontana	(714)	28,103	20,673
95437	Fort Brass	(707)	5,329	4,455
95540	Fortuna	(707)	7,974	7,210
94404	Foster City	(415)	22,986	9,522
92708	Fountain Valley	(714)	55,367	31,886
95019	Freedom(u)	(408)	NA	5,563
*94536	Fremont	(415)	122,028	100,869
*93706	Fresno	(209)	199,273	165,665
*92631	Fullerton	(714)	100,844	85,987
95632	Galt	(209)	5,208	3,200
*90247	Gardena	(213)	46,919	41,021
95205	Garden Acres(u)	(213)	NA	7,870
*92640	Garden Grove	(714)	122,749	121,155
92392	George(u)	(714)	NA	7,404
95020	Gilroy	(408)	18,790	12,684
92509	Glen Avon(u)	(714)	NA	5,759

ZIP code	Place		1980	1970
*91209	Glendale	(213)	137,279	132,664
91740	Glendora	(213)	35,439	31,349
92324	Grand Terrace(u)	(714)	*6,785*	5,901
95945	Grass Valley	(916)	*6,689*	5,149
92041	Grossmont-Mt.Helix(u)	(714)	NA	8,723
93433	Grover City	(805)	*8,003*	5,939
91745	Hacienda Heights	(213)	NA	35,969
94019	Half Moon Bay	(415)	*7,136*	4,023
93230	Hanford	(209)	*19,130*	15,179
90716	Hawaiian Gardens	(213)	*9,473*	9,052
90250	Hawthorne	(213)	56,101	53,304
*94544	Hayward	(415)	*95,802*	93,058
95448	Healdsburg	(707)	*6,726*	5,438
92343	Hemet	(714)	*20,538*	12,252
92343	Hemet East(u)	(714)	NA	8,598
90254	Hermosa Beach	(213)	17,963	17,412
92346	Highland(u)	(714)	NA	12,669
94010	Hillsborough	(415)	*10,171*	8,753
95023	Hollister	(408)	*9,620*	7,663
91720	Home Gardens(u)	(714)	NA	5,116
*92647	Huntington Beach	(714)	*167,897*	115,960
90255	Huntington Park	(213)	*38,546*	33,744
92032	Imperial Beach	(714)	*20,197*	20,244
92201	Indio	(714)	*19,351*	14,459
*90306	Inglewood	(213)	94,148	89,985
*92711	Irvine	(714)	*48,556*	7,381
93017	Isla Vista(u)	(408)	NA	13,441
94707	Kensington(u)	(415)	NA	5,823
93930	King City	(408)	*5,354*	3,717
91011	La Canada-Flintridge	(213)	*19,551*	20,714
91214	La Crescenta-Montrose(u)	(213)	NA	19,620
90045	Ladera Heights(u)	(213)	NA	6,079
94549	Lafayette	(415)	*19,572*	20,484
*92651	Laguna Beach	(714)	*18,188*	14,550
92653	Laguna Hills(u)	(714)	NA	13,676
90631	La Habra	(213)	*44,075*	41,350
92040	Lakeside(u)	(714)	NA	11,991
92330	Lake Elsinore	(714)	*5,654*	3,530
*90714	Lakewood	(213)	*79,520*	83,025
92041	La Mesa	(714)	*50,006*	39,178
90638	La Mirada	(714)	*44,890*	30,808
93241	Lamont(u)	(805)	NA	7,007
93534	Lancaster	(805)	*41,929*	32,728
90624	La Palma	(714)	*15,246*	9,687
91747	La Puente	(213)	30,893	31,092
94939	Larkspur	(415)	*12,552*	10,487
91750	La Verne	(714)	23,416	12,965
90260	Lawndale	(213)	23,331	24,825
92045	Lemon Grove	(209)	*21,086*	19,794
93245	Lemoore Station(u)	(209)	NA	9,210
90304	Lennox(u)	(213)	NA	16,121
95207	Lincoln Village(u)	(916)	NA	6,112
95901	Linda(u)	(916)	NA	7,112
93247	Lindsay	(209)	*6,745*	5,206
95062	Live Oak(u) (Santa Cruz)	(408)	NA	6,443
94550	Livermore	(415)	*49,688*	37,703
95240	Lodi	(209)	*32,464*	32,065
92354	Loma Linda	(714)	*9,129*	7,651
90717	Lomita	(213)	18,337	19,784
93436	Lompoc	(805)	26,167	25,284
*90801	Long Beach	(213)	*339,629*	358,879
90720	Los Alamitos	(213)	*11,347*	11,346
94022	Los Altos	(415)	*27,366*	25,062
94022	Los Altos Hills	(415)	*7,364*	6,865
*90052	Los Angeles	(213)	*2,787,176*	2,811,801
93635	Los Banos	(209)	*9,347*	9,188
95030	Los Gatos	(408)	*25,452*	22,613
90262	Lynwood	(213)	*39,819*	43,354
93637	Madera	(209)	21,675	16,044
90266	Manhattan Beach	(213)	31,544	35,352
95336	Manteca	(209)	*20,762*	13,845
93933	Marina	(408)	*21,070*	8,343
94553	Martinez	(415)	*20,975*	16,506
95901	Marysville	(916)	*9,760*	9,353
95655	Mather(u)	(916)	NA	7,027
90270	Maywood	(213)	*17,828*	16,996
93023	Meiners Oaks-Mira Monte(u)	(805)	NA	7,025
94025	Menlo Park	(415)	*26,100*	26,826
95340	Merced	(209)	*33,602*	22,670
94030	Millbrae	(415)	*20,187*	20,920
94941	Mill Valley	(415)	*13,486*	12,942
95035	Milpitas	(408)	*33,885*	26,561
91752	Mira Loma(u)	(714)	NA	8,482
92675	Mission Viejo(u)	(714)	NA	11,933
*95350	Modesto	(209)	*97,538*	61,712
91016	Monrovia	(213)	*29,361*	30,562
91763	Montclair	(714)	*20,899*	22,546
90640	Montebello	(213)	*49,271*	42,807
93940	Monterey	(408)	*27,626*	26,302
91754	Monterey Park	(213)	*51,125*	49,166
94556	Moraga	(415)	*15,148*	14,205
95037	Morgan Hill	(408)	*15,272*	5,579
93442	Morro Bay	(805)	*8,759*	7,109
*94042	Mountain View	(415)	*55,727*	54,132
92405	Muscoy(u)	(714)	NA	7,091
94558	Napa	(707)	*49,398*	35,978
92050	National City	(714)	46,936	43,184
94560	Newark	(415)	*31,176*	27,153
91321	Newhall(u)	(805)	NA	9,651
*92660	Newport Beach	(714)	*67,113*	49,582
91760	Norco	(714)	*19,207*	14,511
94025	North Fair Oaks(u)	(415)	NA	9,740
95660	North Highlands(u)	(916)	NA	31,854
92135	North Island(u)	(714)	NA	6,892
90650	Norwalk	(213)	*83,262*	91,827
94947	Novato	(415)	*39,195*	31,006
95361	Oakdale	(209)	*8,375*	6,594
*94615	Oakland	(415)	338,721	361,561
92054	Oceanside	(714)	*68,626*	40,494
93308	Oildale(u)	(805)	NA	20,879
93023	Ojai	(805)	*6,253*	5,591
95961	Olivehurst(u)	(916)	NA	8,100
*91761	Ontario	(714)	*72,534*	64,118
95060	Opal Cliffs(u)	(408)	NA	5,425
*92667	Orange	(714)	*86,359*	77,365
95662	Orangevale(u)	(916)	NA	16,493
93454	Orcutt(u)	(805)	NA	8,500
94563	Orinda Village	(415)	NA	6,790
95965	Oroville	(916)	*7,961*	7,536
92010	Otay-Castle Park(u)	(714)	NA	15,445
93030	Oxnard	(805)	115,692	71,225
94044	Pacifica	(415)	*37,242*	36,020
93950	Pacific Grove	(408)	*16,431*	13,505
93550	Palmdale	(805)	*11,116*	8,511
92260	Palm Desert	(714)	*11,120*	6,171
92262	Palm Springs	(714)	*32,627*	20,936
94302	Palo Alto	(415)	*54,293*	56,040
90274	Palos Verdes Estates	(213)	14,303	13,631
95969	Paradise(u)	(916)	NA	14,539
90723	Paramount	(213)	*31,026*	34,734
95823	Parkway-Sacramento So.(u)	(916)	NA	28,574
*91109	Pasadena	(213)	*106,208*	112,951
92055	Pendleton North(u)	(714)	NA	11,803
92055	Pendleton South(u)	(714)	NA	13,692
92370	Perris	(714)	*6,251*	4,228
94952	Petaluma	(707)	*32,394*	24,870
90660	Pico Rivera	(213)	*50,549*	54,170
94611	Piedmont	(415)	10,505	10,917
94564	Pinole	(415)	*15,164*	13,266
93449	Pismo Beach	(805)	*5,035*	4,043
94565	Pittsburg	(415)	*27,859*	20,651
92670	Placentia	(714)	*33,876*	21,948
95667	Placerville	(916)	*6,918*	5,416
94523	Pleasant Hill	(415)	*24,724*	24,610
94566	Pleasanton	(415)	*35,134*	18,328
91766	Pomona	(714)	92,636	87,384
93257	Porterville	(209)	*16,920*	12,602
93257	Porterville West(u)	(209)	NA	6,200
93041	Port Hueneme	(805)	17,683	14,295
94025	Portola Valley	(415)	*5,152*	4,996
92064	Poway(u)	(714)	NA	9,422
95670	Rancho Cordova(u)	(916)	NA	30,451
91730	Rancho Cucamonga	(714)	*46,968*	19,484
92270	Rancho Mirage	(714)	*6,459*	2,767
90274	Rancho Palos Verdes	(213)	36,510	33,285
95014	Rancho Rinconada(u)	(408)	NA	5,149
96080	Red Bluff	(916)	*9,082*	7,676
96001	Redding	(916)	41,963	16,659
92373	Redlands	(714)	*36,566*	36,355
*90277	Redondo Beach	(213)	59,935	57,451
*94064	Redwood City	(415)	*54,858*	55,686
93654	Reedley	(209)	*10,106*	8,131
92376	Rialto	(714)	*32,104*	28,370
*94802	Richmond	(415)	74,217	79,043
93555	Ridgecrest	(714)	*15,220*	7,629
95673	Rio Linda(u)	(916)	NA	7,524
95367	Riverbank	(209)	*5,112*	3,949
*92502	Riverside	(714)	*157,087*	140,089
95677	Rocklin	(916)	*5,713*	3,039
94572	Rodeo(u)	(415)	NA	5,356
94928	Rohnert Park	(707)	*19,429*	6,133
90274	Rolling Hills Estates	(213)	*7,604*	6,735
95401	Roseland(u)	(707)	NA	5,105
91770	Rosemead	(213)	*40,165*	40,972
95678	Roseville	(916)	*22,752*	18,221
90720	Rossmoor(u)	(213)	NA	12,922
91745	Rowland Heights(u)	(213)	NA	16,881
92509	Rubidoux(u)	(714)	NA	13,969
*95813	Sacramento	(916)	274,488	257,105
93901	Salinas	(408)	*78,999*	58,896
94960	San Anselmo	(415)	*12,616*	13,031
*92403	San Bernardino	(714)	*103,982*	106,869
94066	San Bruno	(415)	*37,894*	36,254
...	San Buenaventura (*see Ventura*)	(805)		
94070	San Carlos	(415)	*27,091*	26,053
92672	San Clemente	(714)	*25,813*	17,063
*92109	San Diego	(714)	*816,659*	697,027
91773	San Dimas	(714)	23,887	15,692
*91340	San Fernando	(213)	17,516	16,571
*94101	San Francisco	(415)	*649,315*	715,674
91776	San Gabriel	(213)	*29,902*	29,336
93657	Sanger	(209)	*11,080*	10,088
92383	San Jacinto	(714)	*7,313*	4,859
92375	San Juan Capistrano	(714)	*17,254*	3,781
95101	San Jose	(408)	*592,773*	459,913
94577	San Leandro	(415)	*67,829*	68,698
94580	San Lorenzo(u)	(415)	NA	24,633
93401	San Luis Obispo	(805)	*33,901*	28,036
92069	San Marcos	(714)	*14,714*	4,243
91108	San Marino	(213)	*13,465*	14,177

ZIP code	Place		1980	1970
*94402	San Mateo	(415)	79,150	78,991
94806	San Pablo	(415)	19,737	21,461
*94901	San Rafael	(415)	45,153	38,977
*92711	Santa Ana	(714)	185,155	155,710
*93102	Santa Barbara	(805)	74,810	70,215
*95050	Santa Clara	(408)	84,217	87,717
95060	Santa Cruz	(408)	39,160	32,076
90670	Santa Fe Springs	(213)	15,380	14,750
93454	Santa Maria	(805)	39,448	32,749
93454	Santa Maria South(u)	(805)	NA	7,129
*90406	Santa Monica	(213)	88,122	88,289
93060	Santa Paula	(805)	20,180	18,001
*95402	Santa Rosa	(707)	74,419	50,006
92071	Santee(u)	(714)	NA	21,107
95070	Saratoga	(408)	29,905	26,810
94965	Sausalito	(415)	6,530	6,158
95066	Scotts Valley	(408)	6,615	3,924
90740	Seal Beach	(213)	26,927	24,441
93955	Seaside	(408)	33,067	35,935
93662	Selma	(209)	9,162	7,459
93263	Shafter	(805)	6,350	5,327
91024	Sierra Madre	(213)	11,767	12,140
90806	Signal Hill	(213)	5,909	5,588
93065	Simi Valley	(805)	77,185	56,464
92075	Solana Beach(u)	(714)	NA	5,023
93960	Soledad	(408)	5,719	4,222
95476	Sonoma	(707)	5,796	4,579
95073	Soquel(u)	(408)	NA	5,795
91733	South El Monte	(213)	14,053	13,443
90280	South Gate	(213)	60,171	56,909
95705	South Lake Tahoe	(916)	21,191	12,921
95350	South Modesto(u)	(209)	NA	7,889
91030	South Pasadena	(213)	22,992	22,979
94080	South San Francisco	(415)	49,142	46,646
91770	South San Gabriel(u)	(213)	NA	5,051
91744	South San Jose Hills(u)	(213)	NA	12,386
90605	South Whittier(u)	(213)	NA	46,641
95991	South Yuba(u)	(916)	NA	5,352
*92077	Spring Valley(u)	(714)	NA	29,742
94305	Stanford(u)	(415)	NA	8,691
90680	Stanton	(714)	23,486	18,186
*95204	Stockton	(209)	125,526	109,963
94585	Suisun City	(707)	7,576	2,917
92381	Sun City	(714)	NA	5,519
92388	Sunnymead(u)	(714)	NA	6,708
*94086	Sunnyvale	(408)	106,162	95,976
96130	Susanville	(916)	7,192	6,608
91780	Temple City	(213)	29,682	31,034
*91360	Thousand Oaks	(805)	82,109	35,873
94920	Tiburon	(415)	7,172	6,209
*90510	Torrance	(213)	129,511	134,968
95396	Tracy	(209)	16,306	14,724
93274	Tulare	(209)	20,128	16,235
95380	Turlock	(209)	21,561	13,992
92680	Tustin	(714)	NA	21,099
92705	Tustin-Foothills(u)	(714)	NA	26,699
92277	Twentynine Palms(u)	(714)	NA	5,667
92278	Twentynine Palms Base(u)	(714)	NA	5,647
95482	Ukiah	(707)	12,067	10,095
94587	Union City	(415)	34,985	14,724
91786	Upland	(714)	42,133	32,551
95688	Vacaville	(707)	37,686	21,690
91744	Valinda(u)	(213)	NA	18,837
94590	Vallejo	(707)	71,692	71,710
93437	Vandenburg(u)	(805)	NA	13,193
*93001	Ventura	(805)	83,012	10,845
92392	Victorville	(714)	13,211	12,268
90043	View Park-Windsor Hills(u)	(213)	NA	12,268
92667	Villa Park	(714)	7,417	2,723
93277	Visalia	(209)	42,717	27,268
92083	Vista	(714)	32,932	24,688
91789	Walnut	(714)	NA	5,992
*94596	Walnut Creek	(415)	10,299	39,844
94596	Walnut Creek West(u)	(415)	49,704	8,330
90255	Walnut Park(u)	(213)	NA	8,925
93280	Wasco	(805)	8,926	8,269
95076	Watsonville	(408)	20,823	14,569
90044	West Athens(u)	(213)	NA	13,311
90502	West Carson(u)	(213)	NA	15,501
90247	West Compton(u)	(213)	NA	5,748
*91793	West Covina	(213)	79,256	68,034
90069	West Hollywood(u)	(213)	NA	34,622
92683	Westminster	(714)	70,238	60,076
95351	West Modesto(u)	(209)	NA	6,135
90047	Westmont(u)	(213)	NA	29,310
94565	West Pittsburg(u)	(415)	NA	5,969
91746	West Puente Valley(u)	(213)	NA	20,733
95691	West Sacramento(u)	(916)	NA	12,002
*90606	West Whittier-Los Nietos(u)	(213)	NA	20,845
*90605	Whittier	(213)	69,039	72,863
90222	Willowbrook(u)	(213)	NA	28,705
95695	Woodland	(916)	27,485	20,677
94062	Woodside	(415)	5,392	4,734
92686	Yorba Linda	(714)	26,411	11,856
96097	Yreka City	(916)	5,496	5,394
95991	Yuba City	(916)	16,523	13,986
92399	Yucaipa(u)	(714)	NA	19,284

Colorado (303)

ZIP code	Place	1980	1970
81101	Alamosa	8,148	6,985
80401	Applewood(u)	NA	8,214
*80001	Arvada	83,901	49,083
80010	Aurora	141,548	74,974
*80302	Boulder	76,289	66,870
80601	Brighton	11,888	8,309
80020	Broomfield	23,701	7,261
81212	Canon City	13,115	9,206
80110	Cherry Hills	6,450	4,605
*80901	Colorado Springs	206,939	135,060
80022	Commerce City	15,846	17,407
81321	Cortez	6,730	4,205
81625	Craig	7,323	6,677
*80202	Denver	474,595	514,678
80022	Derby(u)	NA	10,206
81301	Durango	12,555	10,333
80214	Edgewater	5,338	4,910
80110	Englewood	42,529	33,695
80221	Federal Heights	6,659	1,502
80913	Fort Carson(u)	NA	19,399
80521	Fort Collins	66,725	43,337
80701	Fort Morgan	8,873	7,594
80017	Fountain	9,040	2,306
80401	Golden	14,924	9,817
81501	Grand Junction	28,135	20,170
80631	Greeley	50,472	38,902
81230	Gunnison	5,245	5,111
80026	Lafayette	5,416	3,498
81050	La Junta	8,303	7,938
80215	Lakewood	126,469	92,743
81052	Lamar	8,015	7,797
80120	Littleton	NA	26,466
80120	Littleton Southeast(u)	33,029	22,899
80501	Longmont	36,958	23,209
80537	Loveland	30,231	16,220
81401	Montrose	7,860	6,496
80233	North Glenn	37,589	27,748
81501	Orchard Mesa(u)	NA	5,824
*81003	Pueblo	101,504	97,453
81201	Salida	5,275	4,355
80911	Security-Widefield(u)	NA	15,297
80110	Sheridan	6,454	5,108
80221	Sherrelwood(u)	NA	18,868
80751	Sterling	11,299	10,636
80906	Stratton Meadows(u)	NA	6,223
80229	Thornton	29,928	13,326
81082	Trinidad	9,793	9,901
80229	Welby(u)	NA	6,875
80030	Westminster	27,105	19,432
80221	Westminster East(u)	NA	7,576
80033	Wheat Ridge	33,048	29,778

Connecticut (203)

See Note on Page 933

ZIP code	Place	1980	1970
06401	Ansonia	18,841	21,160
06001	*Avon*	11,226	8,352
06037	*Berlin*	15,141	14,149
06801	*Bethel*	15,730	10,945
06002	*Bloomfield*	18,595	18,301
06405	*Branford*	22,847	20,444
*06602	Bridgeport	142,459	156,542
06010	Bristol	57,177	55,487
06804	*Brookfield*	12,647	9,688
06019	*Canton*	NA	6,868
06410	*Cheshire*	21,545	19,051
06413	*Clinton*	11,224	10,267
06413	Clinton Center(u)	NA	5,957
06415	*Colchester*	NA	6,603
06340	Conning Towers-Nautilus Park(u)	NA	9,791
06238	*Coventry*	NA	8,140
06416	*Cromwell*	10,268	7,400
06810	Danbury	59,303	50,781
06820	Darien	18,808	20,336
06418	Derby	12,184	12,599
06424	*East Hampton*	NA	7,078
06108	*East Hartford*	52,554	57,583
06512	*East Haven*	24,978	25,120
06333	*East Lyme*	13,935	11,399
06016	*East Windsor*	NA	8,513
06029	*Ellington*	NA	7,707
06082	*Enfield*	42,709	46,189
06430	*Fairfield*	54,699	56,487
06032	*Farmington*	16,410	14,390
06033	*Glastonbury*	24,276	20,651
06035	*Granby*	NA	6,150
06830	*Greenwich*	58,667	59,755
06351	*Griswold*	NA	7,763
06340	*Groton*	40,995	38,244
06340	Groton Borough	10,091	8,933
06437	*Guilford*	17,729	12,033
06514	*Hamden*	51,015	49,357
*06101	Hartford	136,319	158,017
06239	*Killingly*	14,529	13,573
06339	*Ledyard*	13,700	14,837
06759	*Litchfield*	NA	7,399
06443	*Madison*	13,925	9,768
06040	*Manchester*	49,802	47,994
06250	*Mansfield*	20,747	19,994
06450	Meriden	56,506	55,959

ZIP code	Place	1980	1970
06762	*Middlebury*	NA	5,542
06457	Middletown	39,030	36,924
06460	Milford	49,103	50,858
06468	*Monroe*	13,952	12,047
06353	*Montville*	16,459	15,662
06770	Naugatuck	26,157	23,034
*06050	New Britain	73,674	83,441
06840	*New Canaan*	17,845	17,451
06810	*New Fairfield*	11,041	6,991
*06510	New Haven	125,787	137,707
06111	*Newington*	28,839	26,037
06320	New London	28,907	31,630
06776	*New Milford*	19,316	14,601
06470	*Newtown*	18,794	16,942
06471	*North Branford*	11,474	10,778
06473	*North Haven*	22,031	22,194
06856	Norwalk	76,730	79,113
06360	Norwich	38,052	41,433
06475	*Old Saybrook*	NA	8,468
06477	*Orange*	13,225	13,524
02891	Pawcatuck(u)	NA	5,255
06374	*Plainfield*	12,794	11,957
06062	*Plainville*	16,429	16,733
06782	*Plymouth*	10,745	10,321
06480	*Portland*	NA	8,812
06712	*Prospect*	NA	6,543
06260	Putnam	*6,722*	6,918
.....	*Putnam*	NA	8,598
06875	*Redding*	NA	5,590
06877	Ridgefield Center(u)	NA	5,878
.....	*Ridgefield*	20,035	18,188
06067	*Rocky Hill*	14,569	11,103
06483	*Seymour*	13,343	12,776
06484	Shelton	31,401	27,165
06070	*Simsbury*	21,084	17,475
06071	Somers	NA	6,893
06488	*Southbury*	13,955	7,852
06489	*Southington*	36,747	30,946
06074	*South Windsor*	17,204	15,553
06075	*Stafford*	NA	8,680
*06904	Stamford	101,636	108,798
06378	*Stonington*	16,242	15,940
06268	Storrs(u)	NA	10,691
06497	*Stratford*	50,533	49,775
06078	*Suffield*	NA	8,634
06787	*Thomaston*	NA	6,233
06277	*Thompson*	NA	7,580
06084	*Tolland*	NA	7,857
06790	Torrington	30,982	31,952
06611	*Trumbull*	33,011	31,394
06060	*Vernon*	28,007	27,237
06492	*Wallingford*	36,704	35,714
*06701	Waterbury	102,230	108,033
06385	*Waterford*	17,809	17,227
06795	*Watertown*	19,485	18,610
06107	*West Hartford*	61,342	68,031
06516	West Haven	53,128	52,851
06880	*Weston*	NA	7,417
06880	*Westport*	25,317	27,318
06109	*Wethersfield*	26,029	26,662
06226	Willimantic	14,636	14,402
06897	*Wilton*	15,169	13,572
06094	*Winchester*	10,850	11,106
06280	*Windham*	21,068	19,626
06095	*Windsor*	25,171	22,502
06096	*Windsor Locks*	12,132	15,080
06098	Winsted	NA	8,954
06716	*Wolcott*	12,949	12,495
06525	*Woodbridge*	NA	7,673
06798	*Woodbury*	NA	5,869

Delaware (302)

ZIP code	Place	1980	1970
19711	Brookside Park(u)	NA	7,856
19703	Claymont(u)	NA	6,584
19901	Dover	*23,460*	17,488
19901	Dover Base(u)	NA	8,106
19805	Elsmere	*8,838*	8,415
19963	Milford	*5,623*	5,314
19711	Newark	25,260	21,298
19973	Seaford	*5,443*	5,537
19899	Wilmington	70,363	80,386
19720	Wilmington Manor —Chelsea—Leedom	NA	10,134

District of Columbia (202)

ZIP code	Place	1980	1970
*20013	Washington	635,185	756,510

Florida

ZIP code	Place	Area code	1980	1970
32701	Altamonte Springs	(305)	*20,661*	4,711
32703	Apopka	(305)	*5,726*	4,045
33821	Arcadia	(813)	*5,910*	5,658
32233	Atlantic Beach	(904)	*7,889*	6,132
33825	Avon Park	(813)	*7,203*	6,712
32807	Azalea Park(u)	(305)	NA	7,367
33830	Bartow	(813)	*14,518*	12,891
33505	Bayshore Gardens(u)	(813)	NA	9,255
33430	Belle Glade	(305)	*15,823*	15,949
33432	Boca Raton	(305)	*46,580*	28,506
33435	Boynton Beach	(305)	*32,665*	18,115
*33506	Bradenton	(813)	*27,615*	21,040
33511	Brandon(u)	(813)	NA	12,749
33314	Broadview Park-Rock Hill(u)	(305)	NA	6,049
33512	Brooksville	(904)	*5,846*	4,387
33311	Browardale(u)	(305)	NA	17,444
33142	Browns Village(u)	(305)	NA	23,442
33054	Bunche Park(u)	(305)	NA	5,773
32401	Callaway	(904)	*6,358*	3,702
32920	Cape Canaveral	(305)	*5,108*	4,258
33904	Cape Coral	(813)	*24,378*	11,470
33055	Carol City(u)	(305)	NA	27,361
33023	Carver Ranch Estates(u)	(305)	NA	5,515
32707	Casselberry	(305)	*16,517*	9,438
33505	Cedar Hammock-Bradenton South(u)	(813)	NA	10,820
32324	Chattahoochee	(904)	NA	7,944
*33515	Clearwater	(813)	*77,598*	52,074
32711	Clermont	(904)	*5,129*	3,661
32922	Cocoa	(305)	*15,679*	16,110
32931	Cocoa Beach	(305)	*11,312*	9,952
32922	Cocoa West(u)	(305)	NA	5,779
33064	Collier Manor-Cresthaven(u)	(305)	NA	7,202
32809	Conway(u)	(305)	NA	8,642
33134	Coral Gables	(305)	*42,550*	42,494
33065	Coral Springs	(305)	*23,072*	1,489
32536	Crestview	(904)	*8,996*	7,952
33157	Cutler Ridge(u)	(305)	NA	17,441
33004	Dania	(305)	*12,041*	9,013
33314	Davie	(305)	*16,188*	5,859
*32015	Daytona Beach	(904)	*48,880*	45,327
33441	Deerfield Beach	(305)	*33,103*	16,662
32720	De Land	(904)	*13,592*	11,641
33444	Delray Beach	(305)	*32,253*	19,915
33528	Dunedin	(813)	*27,563*	17,639
33610	East Lake-Orient Park (u)	(813)	NA	5,697
33940	East Naples(u)	(813)	NA	6,152
32032	Edgewater	(904)	*5,439*	3,348
32542	Eglin(u)	(904)	NA	7,769
33614	Egypt Lake(u)	(813)	NA	7,556
33533	Englewood(u)	(813)	NA	5,108
32726	Eustis	(904)	*7,949*	6,722
32034	Fernandina Beach	(904)	*8,513*	6,955
33030	Florida City	(305)	*5,145*	5,133
*33310	Fort Lauderdale	(305)	*149,408*	139,590
*33920	Fort Myers	(813)	*36,206*	27,351
33901	Fort Myers Southwest(u)	(813)	NA	5,086
33450	Fort Pierce	(305)	*32,538*	29,721
32548	Fort Walton Beach	(904)	*22,760*	19,994
*32601	Gainesville	(904)	*71,590*	64,510
32960	Gifford(u)	(305)	NA	5,772
33170	Goulds(u)	(305)	NA	6,690
33463	Greenacres City	(305)	*5,011*	1,731
32561	Gulf Breeze	(904)	*6,273*	4,190
33581	Gulf Gate Estates(u)	(813)	NA	5,874
33737	Gulfport	(813)	*11,436*	9,976
33844	Haines City	(813)	*10,233*	8,956
33009	Hallandale	(305)	*33,225*	23,849
*33010	Hialeah	(305)	*125,365*	102,452
32805	Holden Heights(u)	(305)	NA	6,206
32017	Holly Hill	(904)	*8,692*	8,191
*33022	Hollywood	(305)	*114,943*	106,873
33030	Homestead	(305)	*20,810*	13,674
33030	Homestead Base(u)	(305)	NA	8,257
32937	Indian Harbour Beach	(305)	*6,148*	5,371
*32201	Jacksonville	(904)	*592,787*	528,865
32250	Jacksonville Beach	(904)	*14,961*	12,779
33458	Jupiter	(305)	*7,101*	3,136
33156	Kendall(u)	(305)	NA	35,497
33040	Key West	(305)	*22,763*	29,312
32741	Kissimmee	(305)	*12,774*	7,119
33618	Lake Carroll(u)	(305)	NA	5,577
32055	Lake City	(904)	*10,537*	10,575
32208	Lake Forest(u)	(904)	NA	5,216
33803	Lake Holloway(u)	(305)	NA	6,227
*33802	Lakeland	(813)	*50,368*	42,803
33612	Lake Magdalene(u)	(813)	NA	9,266
33403	Lake Park	(305)	*8,296*	6,993
33853	Lake Wales	(813)	*9,235*	8,240
33460	Lake Worth	(305)	*26,223*	23,714
33460	Lantana	(305)	*8,117*	7,126
33540	Largo	(813)	*52,556*	22,031
33313	Lauderdale Lakes	(305)	*23,610*	10,577
33313	Lauderhill	(305)	*33,288*	8,465
32748	Leesburg	(904)	*14,477*	11,869
33614	Leto(u)	(904)	NA	8,458
33064	Lighthouse Point	(305)	*12,281*	9,071
32060	Live Oak	(904)	*7,130*	6,830
32810	Lockhart(u)	(305)	NA	5,809
33548	Longboat Key	(813)	*8,221*	2,850
32750	Longwood	(305)	*7,754*	3,203
32444	Lynn Haven	(904)	*5,588*	4,044
32751	Maitland	(305)	*8,706*	7,157
33063	Margate	(305)	*30,016*	8,867
32446	Marianna	(904)	*7,013*	6,741
*32901	Melbourne	(305)	*42,307*	40,236
33314	Melrose Park(u)	(904)	NA	6,111
32952	Merritt Island(u)	(305)	NA	29,233
*33152	Miami	(305)	*347,862*	334,859
33139	Miami Beach	(305)	*88,466*	87,072
33153	Miami Shores	(305)	*8,855*	9,425

ZIP code	Place	Area code	1980	1970
33166	Miami Springs	(305)	*12,282*	13,279
32570	Milton	(904)	*7,702*	5,360
32754	Mims(u)	(305)	NA	8,309
33023	Miramar	(305)	*29,772*	23,997
32757	Mount Dora	(904)	*6,465*	4,729
32506	Myrtle Grove(u)	(904)	NA	16,186
33940	Naples	(813)	*15,869*	12,042
33552	New Port Richey	(813)	*9,532*	6,098
32069	New Smyrna Beach	(904)	*15,338*	10,580
32578	Niceville	(904)	*7,322*	5,059
33308	North Andrews Terrace(u)	(305)	NA	7,082
33903	North Fort Myers(u)	(813)	NA	8,798
33314	North Lauderdale	(305)	*15,377*	1,213
33161	North Miami	(305)	*42,407*	34,767
33160	North Miami Beach	(305)	*35,991*	30,544
33408	North Palm Beach	(305)	*11,679*	9,035
33169	Norwood(u)	(305)	NA	14,973
33308	Oakland Park	(305)	*21,852*	16,261
32670	Ocala	(904)	*35,030*	22,583
32548	Ocean City(u)	(904)	NA	5,267
32761	Ocoee	(813)	*5,914*	3,937
33054	Opa-Locka	(305)	*13,869*	11,902
32073	Orange Park	(904)	*9,042*	7,619
*32802	Orlando	(305)	*120,181*	99,006
32074	Ormond Beach	(904)	*18,653*	14,063
32074	Ormond By-The-Sea(u)	(904)	NA	6,002
33476	Pahokee	(305)	*5,690*	5,663
32077	Palatka	(904)	*9,409*	9,444
32905	Palm Bay	(305)	*12,394*	7,176
33480	Palm Beach	(305)	*9,652*	9,086
33403	Palm Beach Gardens	(305)	*11,165*	6,102
33561	Palmetto	(813)	*8,311*	7,422
33619	Palm River-Clair Mel(u)	(813)	NA	8,536
33460	Palm Springs	(305)	*8,505*	4,340
32401	Panama City	(904)	*40,918*	32,096
33023	Pembroke Pines	(305)	*29,466*	15,496
32502	Pensacola	(904)	*66,539*	59,507
33157	Perrine(u)	(305)	NA	10,257
32347	Perry	(904)	*7,782*	7,701
32808	Pine Hills(u)	(305)	NA	13,882
33565	Pinellas Park	(813)	*29,703*	22,287
33566	Plant City	(813)	*15,548*	15,451
33314	Plantation	(813)	*42,069*	23,523
*33060	Pompano Beach	(305)	*52,629*	38,587
33064	Pompano Beach Highlands(u)	(305)	NA	5,014
33950	Port Charlotte(u)	(813)	NA	10,769
32019	Port Orange	(904)	*13,633*	3,781
33452	Port St. Lucie	(305)	*5,862*	330
*33950	Punta Gorda	(813)	*6,904*	3,879
32351	Quincy	(904)	*7,887*	8,334
33156	Richmond Heights(u)	(305)	NA	6,663
33312	Riverland Vil.-Lauderdale Is.(u)	(305)	NA	5,512
33404	Riviera Beach	(305)	*26,430*	21,401
32955	Rockledge	(305)	*10,776*	10,523
32084	St. Augustine	(904)	*12,662*	12,352
32769	St. Cloud	(305)	*6,710*	5,041
*33730	St. Petersburg	(813)	*230,965*	216,159
33706	St. Petersburg Beach	(813)	*10,214*	8,024
32771	Sanford	(305)	*23,129*	17,393
*33578	Sarasota	(813)	*50,814*	40,237
33579	Sarasota Southeast(u)	(813)	NA	6,885
32937	Satellite Beach	(305)	*7,839*	6,558
33870	Sebring	(813)	*8,855*	7,223
32021	South Daytona	(904)	*11,569*	6,988
33143	South Miami	(305)	*11,314*	11,780
33157	South Miami Heights(u)	(305)	NA	10,395
32937	South Patrick Shores(u)	(305)	NA	10,313
32401	Springfield	(904)	*6,755*	5,949
32091	Starke	(904)	*5,222*	4,848
33494	Stuart	(305)	*9,245*	4,820
33304	Sunrise	(305)	*32,905*	7,403
33144	Sweetwater	(305)	*7,268*	3,357
33614	Sweetwater Creek(u)	(813)	NA	19,453
*32303	Tallahassee	(904)	*86,121*	72,624
33313	Tamarac	(305)	*24,609*	5,078
*33602	Tampa	(813)	*264,325*	277,714
33589	Tarpon Springs	(813)	*12,166*	7,118
33617	Temple Terrace	(813)	*10,705*	7,347
33905	Tice(u)	(813)	NA	7,254
32780	Titusville	(305)	*31,494*	30,515
33740	Treasure Island	(813)	*7,272*	6,120
33620	University (Hillsborough)(u)	(813)	NA	10,039
32580	Valparaiso	(904)	*5,598*	6,504
33595	Venice	(813)	*12,223*	6,648
32960	Vero Beach	(305)	*16,318*	11,908
32960	Vero Beach South(u)	(305)	NA	7,330
32507	Warrington(u)	(904)	NA	15,848
33505	West Bradenton(u)	(813)	NA	6,162
32446	West End(u)	(904)	NA	5,289
33144	West Miami	(305)	*5,646*	5,494
*33401	West Palm Beach	(305)	*59,125*	57,375
32505	West Pensacola(u)	(904)	NA	20,924
33880	West Winter Haven(u)	(813)	NA	7,716
33165	Westwood Lakes(u)	(305)	NA	12,811
33305	Wilton Manors	(305)	*13,756*	10,948
32787	Winter Garden	(305)	*6,277*	5,153
33880	Winter Haven	(813)	*19,647*	16,136
32789	Winter Park	(305)	*22,056*	21,895
32707	Winter Springs	(305)	*6,140*	1,161

Georgia

ZIP code	Place	Area code	1980	1970
30101	Acworth	(404)	*7,720*	3,929
31620	Adel	(912)	*5,306*	4,972
*31701	Albany	(912)	*77,011*	72,623
30201	Alpharetta	(404)	*5,422*	2,455
31709	Americus	(912)	*15,185*	16,091
*30601	Athens	(404)	*49,185*	44,342
*30304	Atlanta	(404)	*405,437*	495,039
*30901	Augusta	(404)	*50,526*	59,864
31717	Bainbridge	(912)	*10,547*	10,887
31723	Blakely	(912)	*5,224*	5,267
31520	Brunswick	(912)	*18,557*	19,585
30518	Buford	(404)	*9,083*	4,640
31728	Cairo	(912)	*8,398*	8,061
30701	Calhoun	(404)	*5,446*	4,748
30117	Carrollton	(404)	14,062	13,520
30120	Cartersville	(404)	*10,730*	10,138
30125	Cedartown	(404)	*8,649*	9,253
30341	Chamblee	(404)	*7,963*	9,127
30021	Clarkston	(404)	*5,784*	3,127
30337	College Park	(404)	*24,744*	18,203
*31902	Columbus	(404)	*163,837*	155,028
30207	Conyers	(404)	*13,146*	4,809
31015	Cordele	(912)	*10,689*	10,733
30209	Covington	(404)	*11,184*	10,267
30720	Dalton	(404)	*20,765*	18,872
*30030	Decatur	(404)	*19,809*	21,943
31520	Dock Junction(u)	(912)	NA	6,009
30340	Doraville	(404)	*9,114*	9,157
31533	Douglas	(912)	*10,273*	10,195
30134	Douglasville	(404)	*12,275*	5,472
31021	Dublin	(912)	*15,490*	15,143
31023	Eastman	(912)	*5,396*	5,416
30344	East Point	(404)	*34,855*	39,315
30635	Elberton	(404)	*6,596*	6,438
30213	Fairburn	(404)	*5,301*	3,143
30214	Fayetteville	(404)	*5,078*	2,160
31750	Fitzgerald	(912)	*8,100*	8,187
30050	Forest Park	(404)	*19,179*	19,994
31905	Fort Benning(u)	(404)	NA	27,495
30905	Fort Gordon(u)	(404)	NA	15,589
30741	Fort Oglethorpe	(404)	*5,689*	3,869
31030	Fort Valley	(912)	*9,593*	9,251
30501	Gainesville	(404)	*21,126*	15,459
31408	Garden City	(404)	*7,703*	5,790
30223	Griffin	(404)	*24,625*	22,734
30354	Hapeville	(404)	*6,614*	9,567
30643	Hartwell	(404)	*5,199*	4,865
31313	Hinesville	(912)	*8,589*	6,160
31545	Jesup	(912)	*8,945*	9,091
30236	Jonesboro	(404)	*6,167*	4,105
30144	Kennesaw	(404)	*7,068*	3,548
30728	La Fayette	(404)	*5,955*	6,044
30240	La Grange	(404)	*23,933*	23,301
30245	Lawrenceville	(404)	*18,198*	5,115
30247	Lilburn	(404)	*5,499*	1,688
*31201	Macon	(912)	*121,122*	122,423
30060	Marietta	(404)	*33,690*	27,216
31034	Midway-Hardwick(u)	(912)	NA	14,047
31061	Milledgeville	(912)	*12,652*	11,601
30655	Monroe	(404)	*9,173*	8,071
30260	Morrow	(404)	*5,633*	3,708
31768	Moultrie	(912)	*14,109*	14,400
30263	Newnan	(404)	11,446	11,205
30269	Peachtree City	(404)	*5,024*	793
31069	Perry	(912)	*8,425*	7,771
30073	Powder Springs	(404)	*5,535*	2,559
*30274	Riverdale	(404)	*8,540*	2,521
30161	Rome	(404)	29,717	30,759
30075	Roswell	(404)	*24,149*	5,430
31522	St. Simons(u)	(912)	NA	5,346
31082	Sandersville	(912)	*5,191*	5,546
*31401	Savannah	(912)	*135,896*	118,349
30080	Smyrna	(404)	*21,233*	19,157
30278	Snellville	(404)	*12,705*	1,990
30458	Statesboro	(912)	*16,579*	14,616
30747	Summerville	(404)	*5,019*	5,043
30401	Swainsboro	(912)	*7,847*	7,325
31791	Sylvester	(912)	*5,517*	4,492
30286	Thomaston	(404)	*10,945*	10,024
31792	Thomasville	(912)	*18,288*	18,155
30824	Thomson	(404)	*7,479*	6,503
31794	Tifton	(912)	*12,727*	12,179
30577	Toccoa	(404)	*8,495*	6,971
31601	Valdosta	(912)	*35,836*	32,303
30474	Vidalia	(912)	*10,518*	9,507
31093	Warner Robins	(912)	*40,534*	33,491
31501	Waycross	(912)	*19,323*	18,996
30830	Waynesboro	(404)	*5,324*	5,530
30680	Winder	(404)	*6,592*	6,605
31406	Windsor Forest(u)	(912)	NA	7,288

Hawaii (808)

ZIP code	Place	1980	1970
96701	Aiea	*NA*	12,560
96706	Ewa Beach	*NA*	7,765
96701	Halawa Heights	*NA*	5,809
96824	Hickam Housing	*NA*	7,352
96720	Hilo	*NA*	26,353
*96813	Honolulu	*722,689*	324,871

ZIP code	Place		1980	1970
96732	Kahului		*NA*	8,280
96734	Kailua		*NA*	33,783
96744	Kaneohe		*NA*	29,903
96734	Maunawili		*NA*	5,303
96734	Mokapu		*NA*	7,860
96792	Nanakuli		*NA*	6,506
96782	Pacific Palisades		*NA*	7,846
96782	Pearl City		*NA*	19,552
96786	Schofield Barracks		*NA*	13,516
96786	Wahiawa		*NA*	17,598
96793	Wailuku		*NA*	7,979
96797	Waipahu		*NA*	24,150

Idaho (208)

ZIP code	Place	1980	1970
83221	Blackfoot	10,054	8,716
*83708	Boise City	*114,033*	74,990
83318	Burley	*8,883*	8,279
83605	Caldwell	*16,572*	14,219
83201	Chubbuck	*6,608*	2,924
83814	Coeur D'Alene	20,019	16,228
83401	Idaho Falls	39,198	35,776
83338	Jerome	*6,049*	4,183
83501	Lewiston	27,972	26,068
83642	Meridian	*5,713*	2,885
83843	Moscow	16,431	14,146
83647	Mountain Home	*8,111*	6,451
83648	Mountain Home Base(u)	NA	6,038
83651	Nampa	*28,062*	20,768
83661	Payette	*5,180*	4,521
83201	Pocatello	46,341	40,036
83440	Rexburg	11,573	8,727
83350	Rupert	*5,798*	4,563
83301	Twin Falls	*24,129*	21,914

Illinois

ZIP code	Place	Area code	1980	1970
60101	Addison	(312)	*29,213*	24,482
60658	Alsip	(312)	*15,685*	11,279
62002	Alton	(618)	*33,862*	39,700
*60004	Arlington Heights	(312)	*71,277*	64,884
*60507	Aurora	(312)	*80,671*	74,182
60010	Barrington	(312)	*10,053*	8,674
60103	Bartlett	(312)	*10,465*	3,604
61607	Bartonville	(309)	*6,102*	7,221
60510	Batavia	(312)	*12,011*	8,994
62618	Beardstown	(217)	*5,827*	6,222
*62220	Belleville	(618)	*45,081*	41,699
60104	Bellwood	(312)	*19,537*	22,096
61008	Belvidere	(815)	*16,856*	14,061
60106	Bensenville	(312)	*14,019*	12,956
62812	Benton	(618)	*7,203*	6,833
60162	Berkeley	(312)	*5,554*	6,152
60402	Berwyn	(312)	*46,561*	52,502
62010	Bethalto	(618)	*8,372*	7,074
60108	Bloomingdale	(312)	*10,606*	2,974
61701	Bloomington	(309)	*41,632*	39,992
60406	Blue Island	(312)	*20,181*	22,958
60439	Bolingbrook	(312)	*35,326*	7,651
60914	Bourbonnais	(815)	*12,500*	5,909
60915	Bradley	(815)	*10,828*	9,881
60455	Bridgeview	(312)	*14,086*	12,522
60153	Broadview	(312)	*8,445*	9,623
60513	Brookfield	(312)	*19,742*	20,284
60090	Buffalo Grove	(312)	*20,712*	11,799
60459	Burbank	(312)	*29,025*	26,726
62206	Cahokia	(618)	*21,091*	20,649
62914	Cairo	(618)	*5,056*	6,277
60409	Calumet City	(312)	*38,938*	33,107
60643	Calumet Park	(312)	*10,948*	10,069
61520	Canton	(309)	*13,961*	14,217
62901	Carbondale	(815)	*23,596*	22,816
62626	Carlinville	(217)	*5,600*	5,675
62821	Carmi	(618)	*5,508*	6,033
60187	Carol Stream	(312)	*11,767*	4,434
60110	Carpentersville	(312)	*26,313*	24,059
60013	Cary	(312)	*5,579*	4,358
62801	Centralia	(618)	*15,629*	15,217
62206	Centreville	(618)	*11,647*	11,378
61820	Champaign	(217)	*57,982*	56,837
60410	Channahon	(815)	*5,494*	2,600
61920	Charleston	(217)	*18,123*	16,421
62629	Chatham	(217)	*5,349*	2,788
62233	Chester	(618)	*5,296*	5,310
*60607	Chicago	(312)	*3,049,479*	3,369,357
60411	Chicago Heights	(312)	*38,530*	40,900
60415	Chicago Ridge	(312)	*13,082*	9,187
61523	Chillicothe	(309)	*6,072*	6,052
60650	Cicero	(312)	*58,873*	67,058
60514	Clarendon Hills	(312)	*7,970*	6,750
61727	Clinton	(217)	*7,647*	7,570
62234	Collinsville	(618)	*18,753*	17,992
60477	Country Club Hills	(312)	*14,412*	6,920
60525	Countryside	(312)	*5,612*	2,864
60435	Crest Hill	(815)	*9,106*	7,460
60445	Crestwood	(312)	*9,377*	5,770
60417	Crete	(312)	*5,144*	4,656
61611	Creve Coeur	(309)	*7,079*	6,440
60014	Crystal Lake	(815)	*20,018*	14,541
61832	Danville	(217)	*40,763*	42,570
60559	Darien	(312)	*12,865*	7,789
*62521	Decatur	(217)	*89,585*	90,397
60015	Deerfield	(312)	*19,557*	18,876
60115	De Kalb	(815)	*32,830*	32,949
*60016	Des Plaines	(312)	*56,317*	57,239
61021	Dixon	(815)	*15,413*	18,147
60419	Dolton	(312)	*25,122*	25,990
60515	Downers Grove	(312)	*41,050*	32,751
62832	Du Quoin	(618)	*6,299*	6,691
62024	East Alton	(618)	*7,549*	7,309
60411	East Chicago Heights	(312)	*5,833*	5,000
61244	East Moline	(309)	*20,502*	20,832
61611	East Peoria	(309)	*21,697*	18,455
*62201	East St. Louis	(618)	*51,399*	69,996
62025	Edwardsville	(618)	*13,081*	11,070
62401	Effingham	(217)	*11,060*	9,458
60120	Elgin	(312)	*63,132*	55,691
60007	Elk Grove Village	(312)	NA	20,346
60126	Elmhurst	(312)	*44,249*	48,887
60635	Elmwood Park	(312)	*24,216*	26,160
*60204	Evanston	(312)	*70,326*	80,113
60642	Evergreen Park	(312)	*23,320*	25,921
62837	Fairfield	(618)	*5,786*	5,897
62208	Fairview Heights	(618)	*18,139*	8,625
60422	Flossmoor	(312)	*8,232*	7,846
60130	Forest Park	(312)	*14,383*	15,472
60020	Fox Lake	(312)	*5,938*	4,511
60131	Franklin Park	(312)	*17,744*	20,348
61032	Freeport	(815)	*24,580*	27,736
60030	Gages Lake-Wildwood(u)	(312)	NA	5,337
61401	Galesburg	(309)	*32,778*	36,290
61254	Geneseo	(309)	*6,302*	5,840
60134	Geneva	(312)	*10,020*	9,115
60022	Glencoe	(312)	*9,622*	10,542
60137	Glendale Heights	(618)	*21,660*	11,406
60137	Glen Ellyn	(312)	*24,852*	21,909
60025	Glenview	(312)	*31,868*	24,880
60425	Glenwood	(312)	*10,507*	7,416
62040	Granite City	(618)	*38,699*	40,685
60030	Grayslake	(312)	*5,916*	4,907
62246	Greenville	(618)	*5,099*	4,785
60103	Hanover Park	(312)	*25,863*	11,916
62946	Harrisburg	(618)	*9,471*	9,535
60033	Harvard	(815)	*5,230*	5,177
60426	Harvey	(312)	*32,156*	34,636
60656	Harwood Heights	(312)	*8,742*	9,060
60429	Hazel Crest	(312)	*13,043*	10,329
62948	Herrin	(618)	*10,096*	9,623
60457	Hickory Hills	(312)	*14,822*	13,176
62249	Highland	(618)	*6,708*	5,981
60035	Highland Park	(312)	*32,487*	32,263
60162	Hillside	(312)	*8,061*	8,888
60521	Hinsdale	(312)	*17,015*	15,918
60172	Hoffman Estates	(312)	*34,016*	22,238
60456	Hometown	(312)	*5,846*	6,729
60430	Homewood	(312)	*19,244*	18,871
60942	Hoopeston	(217)	*6,717*	6,461
60143	Itasca	(312)	*6,395*	4,638
62650	Jacksonville	(217)	*18,234*	20,553
62052	Jerseyville	(618)	*7,252*	7,446
*60431	Joliet	(815)	*72,372*	78,887
60458	Justice	(312)	*9,215*	9,473
60901	Kankakee	(815)	*27,988*	30,944
61109	Ken Rock(u)	(815)	NA	5,945
61443	Kewanee	(309)	*15,194*	15,762
60525	La Grange	(312)	*16,029*	17,814
60525	La Grange Highlands(u)	(312)	NA	6,842
60525	La Grange Park	(312)	*13,205*	15,459
60044	Lake Bluff	(312)	*5,120*	5,008
60045	Lake Forest	(312)	*15,408*	15,642
60102	Lake in the Hills	(312)	*5,735*	3,240
60047	Lake Zurich	(312)	*7,759*	4,082
60438	Lansing	(312)	*27,609*	28,805
61301	La Salle	(815)	*9,814*	10,736
62439	Lawrenceville	(618)	*5,434*	5,863
60439	Lemont	(312)	*5,141*	5,080
60048	Libertyville	(312)	*16,228*	11,684
62656	Lincoln	(217)	*14,565*	17,582
60645	Lincolnwood	(312)	*13,031*	12,929
60046	Lindenhurst	(312)	*5,731*	3,141
60532	Lisle	(312)	*11,570*	5,329
62056	Litchfield	(217)	*6,804*	7,190
60441	Lockport	(815)	*10,424*	9,985
60148	Lombard	(312)	*36,242*	34,043
61111	Loves Park	(815)	*12,091*	12,390
60534	Lyons	(312)	*10,066*	11,124
61455	Macomb	(309)	*22,084*	19,643
62060	Madison	(618)	*5,371*	7,042
62959	Marion	(618)	*14,058*	11,724
60426	Markham	(312)	*15,830*	15,987
62258	Mascoutah	(618)	*5,437*	5,045
60443	Matteson	(312)	*8,916*	4,741
61938	Mattoon	(217)	*17,884*	19,681
60153	Maywood	(312)	*26,128*	29,019
60050	McHenry	(815)	*10,059*	6,772
*60160	Melrose Park	(312)	*19,702*	22,716
61342	Mendota	(815)	*6,874*	6,902
62960	Metropolis	(618)	*6,439*	6,940
60445	Midlothian	(312)	*13,951*	15,939
61264	Milan	(309)	*6,778*	4,873

ZIP code	Place		1980	1970
61265	Moline	(309)	43,323	46,237
61462	Monmouth	(309)	10,193	11,022
60450	Morris	(815)	9,021	8,194
61550	Morton	(309)	15,306	10,419
60053	Morton Grove	(312)	25,300	26,369
62863	Mount Carmel	(618)	8,155	8,096
60056	Mount Prospect	(312)	52,955	34,995
62864	Mount Vernon	(618)	17,208	16,382
60060	Mundelein	(312)	18,760	16,128
62966	Murphysboro	(618)	9,863	10,013
60540	Naperville	(312)	37,360	22,617
60451	New Lenox	(815)	5,172	2,855
60648	Niles	(312)	28,686	31,432
61761	Normal	(309)	35,230	26,396
60656	Norridge	(312)	15,761	17,113
60542	North Aurora	(312)	5,579	4,833
60062	Northbrook	(312)	30,215	25,422
60064	North Chicago	(312)	41,436	47,275
60164	Northlake	(312)	12,098	14,191
61111	North Park(u)	(815)	NA	15,679
60546	North Riverside	(312)	7,090	8,097
60521	Oak Brook	(312)	5,234	4,164
60452	Oak Forest	(312)	24,429	17,870
*60454	Oak Lawn	(312)	61,206	60,305
*60301	Oak Park	(312)	55,151	62,511
62269	O'Fallon	(618)	12,080	7,268
62450	Olney	(618)	8,715	8,974
60462	Orland Park	(312)	18,266	6,391
61350	Ottawa	(815)	17,519	18,716
60067	Palatine	(312)	32,003	26,050
60463	Palos Heights	(312)	10,812	9,915
60465	Palos Hills	(312)	16,171	6,629
62557	Pana	(217)	5,929	6,326
61944	Paris	(217)	9,614	9,971
60466	Park Forest	(312)	33,331	30,638
60466	Park Forest South	(312)	6,350	1,748
60068	Park Ridge	(312)	40,387	42,614
61554	Pekin	(309)	32,281	31,375
*61601	Peoria	(309)	122,981	126,963
61614	Peoria Heights	(309)	7,921	7,943
61354	Peru	(815)	11,041	11,772
61764	Pontiac	(815)	11,035	10,595
60469	Posen	(312)	5,188	5,498
60070	Prospect Heights(u)	(312)	NA	13,333
62301	Quincy	(217)	41,226	45,288
61866	Rantoul	(217)	23,106	25,562
60471	Richton Park	(312)	8,564	2,558
60627	Riverdale	(312)	13,888	15,806
60305	River Forest	(312)	12,749	13,402
60171	River Grove	(312)	10,598	11,465
60546	Riverside	(312)	9,371	10,432
60472	Robbins	(312)	8,840	9,641
62454	Robinson	(618)	6,914	7,178
61068	Rochelle	(815)	9,305	8,594
61071	Rock Falls	(815)	10,560	10,287
*61125	Rockford	(815)	139,999	147,370
61201	Rock Island	(309)	45,992	50,166
60008	Rolling Meadows	(312)	20,176	19,178
60441	Romeoville	(312)	20,826	12,674
60172	Roselle	(312)	12,520	6,207
60073	Round Lake Beach	(312)	12,148	5,717
60174	St. Charles	(312)	16,407	12,945
62881	Salem	(618)	7,510	6,187
60548	Sandwich	(815)	5,683	5,056
60411	Sauk Village	(312)	10,544	7,479
60172	Schaumburg	(312)	50,184	18,730
60176	Schiller Park	(312)	11,483	12,712
62225	Scott(u)	(618)	NA	7,871
61282	Silvis	(309)	6,894	5,907
60076	Skokie	(312)	64,696	68,322
60177	South Elgin	(312)	5,508	4,289
60473	South Holland	(312)	24,822	23,931
60459	South Stickney(u) (see Burbank)	(312)	NA	
*62703	Springfield	(217)	86,159	91,753
61362	Spring Valley	(815)	5,528	5,605
60475	Steger	(312)	9,417	8,104
61081	Sterling	(815)	17,489	16,113
60402	Stickney	(312)	6,497	6,601
60103	Streamwood	(312)	23,077	18,176
61364	Streator	(815)	14,734	15,600
60501	Summit	(312)	9,999	11,569
62221	Swansea	(618)	5,449	5,432
60178	Sycamore	(815)	8,942	7,843
62568	Taylorville	(217)	11,142	10,927
60477	Tinley Park	(312)	26,190	12,382
61801	Urbana	(217)	34,827	33,739
60061	Vernon Hills	(312)	6,903	1,056
60181	Villa Park	(312)	22,004	25,891
60555	Warrenville	(312)	8,257	4,564
61571	Washington	(309)	10,174	6,790
62204	Washington Park	(618)	8,313	9,524
60970	Watseka	(815)	5,075	5,294
60084	Wauconda	(312)	6,054	5,460
60085	Waukegan	(312)	63,948	65,134
60153	Westchester	(312)	17,813	20,033
60185	West Chicago	(312)	16,273	10,111
61120	West End(u)	(815)	NA	7,554
60558	Western Springs	(312)	13,005	13,029
62896	West Frankfort	(618)	8,953	8,854
60559	Westmont	(312)	14,376	8,920
61604	West Peoria(u)	(309)	NA	6,873
60187	Wheaton	(312)	40,652	31,138
60090	Wheeling	(312)	19,555	14,751
60091	Wilmette	(312)	30,793	32,134
60093	Winnetka	(312)	13,800	14,131
60096	Winthrop Harbor	(312)	5,172	2,850
60191	Wood Dale	(312)	11,311	8,831
60515	Woodridge	(312)	19,926	11,028
62095	Wood River	(618)	12,247	13,186
60098	Woodstock	(815)	11,512	10,226
60482	Worth	(312)	12,125	11,999
60099	Zion	(312)	18,953	17,268

Indiana

ZIP code	Place		1980	1970
46001	Alexandria	(317)	5,814	5,600
46011	Anderson	(317)	68,556	70,787
46706	Auburn	(219)	7,936	7,388
47421	Bedford	(812)	14,166	13,087
46107	Beech Grove	(317)	14,198	13,559
46408	Black Oak(u)	(219)	NA	9,624
47401	Bloomington	(812)	50,344	43,262
46714	Bluffton	(219)	8,459	8,297
47601	Boonville	(812)	5,958	5,736
47834	Brazil	(812)	7,613	8,163
46112	Brownsburg	(317)	9,228	6,568
46032	Carmel	(317)	18,050	15,181
46303	Cedar Lake	(219)	8,652	7,589
47111	Charlestown	(812)	6,182	5,933
46304	Chesterton	(219)	7,464	6,177
47130	Clarksville	(812)	16,369	13,806
47842	Clinton	(317)	5,077	5,340
46725	Columbia City	(219)	5,106	4,911
47201	Columbus	(812)	29,222	27,141
47331	Connersville	(317)	16,959	17,604
47933	Crawfordsville	(317)	14,153	13,842
46307	Crown Point	(219)	15,456	12,061
46122	Danville	(317)	5,688	3,771
46733	Decatur	(219)	8,089	8,445
46311	Dyer	(219)	10,294	4,906
46312	East Chicago	(219)	39,656	46,982
46405	East Gary	(219)	NA	9,858
46124	Edinburg	(812)	5,436	2,569
46514	Elkhart	(219)	48,267	43,152
46036	Elwood	(317)	10,334	11,196
*47708	Evansville	(812)	134,388	138,764
*46802	Fort Wayne	(219)	181,066	178,021
46041	Frankfort	(317)	13,835	14,956
46131	Franklin	(317)	13,517	11,477
*46401	Gary	(219)	156,056	175,415
46933	Gas City	(317)	6,336	5,742
46526	Goshen	(219)	19,448	17,171
46135	Greencastle	(317)	8,372	8,852
46140	Greenfield	(317)	12,117	9,886
47240	Greensburg	(812)	8,901	8,620
46142	Greenwood	(317)	19,112	11,408
46319	Griffith	(219)	17,075	18,168
*46320	Hammond	(219)	93,440	107,983
47348	Hartford City	(317)	7,721	8,207
46322	Highland	(219)	26,086	24,947
46342	Hobart	(219)	22,483	21,485
47542	Huntingburg	(812)	5,112	4,794
46750	Huntington	(219)	15,314	16,217
*46206	Indianapolis	(317)	704,045	746,021
47546	Jasper	(812)	10,031	8,641
47130	Jeffersonville	(812)	22,841	20,008
46755	Kendallville	(219)	6,547	6,838
46901	Kokomo	(317)	52,153	44,042
*47901	Lafayette	(317)	49,561	44,955
46405	Lake Station	(219)	14,085	15,218
46350	La Porte	(219)	22,208	22,140
46226	Lawrence	(317)	25,955	16,917
46052	Lebanon	(317)	10,112	9,766
47441	Linton	(812)	5,148	5,450
46947	Logansport	(219)	17,563	19,255
46356	Lowell	(219)	5,804	3,839
47250	Madison	(812)	12,737	13,081
46952	Marion	(317)	39,710	39,607
46151	Martinsville	(317)	11,198	9,723
46410	Merrillville	(219)	27,224	15,918
46360	Michigan City	(219)	41,467	39,369
46544	Mishawaka	(219)	39,517	35,517
47960	Monticello	(219)	6,257	3,025
46158	Mooresville	(317)	7,336	5,800
47620	Mount Vernon	(812)	7,275	6,770
*47302	Muncie	(317)	81,076	69,082
46321	Munster	(219)	19,984	16,514
47150	New Albany	(812)	37,863	38,402
47362	New Castle	(317)	20,187	21,215
46774	New Haven	(219)	6,650	5,728
46060	Noblesville	(317)	11,680	7,548
46962	North Manchester	(219)	5,565	5,791
46970	Peru	(317)	13,397	14,139
46168	Plainfield	(317)	8,730	8,211
46563	Plymouth	(219)	7,870	7,661
46368	Portage	(219)	25,495	19,127
47371	Portland	(219)	6,811	7,115
47670	Princeton	(812)	9,175	7,431
47374	Richmond	(317)	43,440	43,999

ZIP code	Place		1980	1970
46173	Rushville	(317)	7,014	6,686
47167	Salem	(812)	5,465	5,041
46375	Schererville	(219)	9,562	3,663
47274	Seymour	(812)	13,952	13,352
46176	Shelbyville	(317)	13,968	15,094
*46624	South Bend	(219)	113,147	125,580
46224	Speedway	(317)	14,612	14,523
47586	Tell City	(812)	8,301	7,933
*47808	Terre Haute	(812)	63,817	70,335
46383	Valparaiso	(219)	23,783	20,020
47591	Vincennes	(812)	18,871	19,867
46992	Wabash	(219)	13,025	13,379
46580	Warsaw	(219)	10,320	7,506
47501	Washington	(812)	10,533	11,358
46408	West Glen Park(u)	(219)	NA	5,940
47906	West Lafayette	(317)	21,166	19,157
46394	Whiting	(219)	6,919	7,054

Iowa

ZIP code	Place		1980	1970
50511	Algona	(515)	6,603	6,032
50009	Altoona	(515)	5,454	2,883
50010	Ames	(515)	45,820	39,505
50021	Ankeny	(515)	15,410	9,151
50022	Atlantic	(712)	7,600	7,306
52722	Bettendorf	(319)	27,461	22,126
50036	Boone	(515)	12,578	12,468
52601	Burlington	(319)	29,448	32,366
51401	Carroll	(712)	9,411	8,716
50613	Cedar Falls	(319)	35,275	29,597
*52401	Cedar Rapids	(319)	107,071	110,642
52544	Centerville	(515)	6,269	6,531
50616	Charles City	(515)	8,847	9,268
51012	Cherokee	(712)	6,772	7,272
51632	Clarinda	(712)	5,305	5,420
50428	Clear Lake City	(515)	7,116	6,430
52732	Clinton	(319)	33,342	34,719
52240	Coralville	(319)	7,069	6,130
51501	Council Bluffs	(712)	58,429	60,348
50801	Creston	(515)	8,106	8,234
*52802	Davenport	(319)	101,478	98,469
52101	Decorah	(319)	7,493	7,458
51442	Denison	(712)	6,417	5,882
*50318	Des Moines	(515)	190,910	200,587
52001	Dubuque	(319)	60,794	62,309
51334	Estherville	(712)	7,790	8,108
50707	Evansdale	(319)	5,472	5,038
52556	Fairfield	(515)	7,794	8,715
50501	Fort Dodge	(515)	29,744	31,263
52627	Fort Madison	(319)	13,400	13,996
51534	Glenwood	(712)	5,252	4,195
50112	Grinnell	(515)	8,791	8,402
51537	Harlan	(712)	5,283	5,409
50644	Independence	(319)	6,134	5,910
50125	Indianola	(515)	10,822	8,852
52240	Iowa City	(319)	48,587	46,850
50126	Iowa Falls	(515)	6,043	6,454
52632	Keokuk	(319)	13,862	14,631
50138	Knoxville	(515)	7,724	7,755
51031	Le Mars	(712)	8,041	8,159
52060	Maquoketa	(319)	5,885	5,677
52302	Marion	(319)	19,333	18,028
50158	Marshalltown	(515)	27,007	26,219
50401	Mason City	(515)	30,165	30,379
52641	Mount Pleasant	(319)	6,822	7,007
52761	Muscatine	(319)	23,545	22,405
50201	Nevada	(515)	5,333	4,952
50208	Newton	(515)	15,164	15,619
50662	Oelwein	(319)	7,577	7,735
52577	Oskaloosa	(515)	10,837	11,224
52501	Ottumwa	(515)	27,285	29,610
50219	Pella	(515)	7,827	6,668
50220	Perry	(515)	6,551	6,906
51566	Red Oak	(712)	6,583	6,210
51601	Shenandoah	(712)	6,318	5,968
*51101	Sioux City	(712)	84,394	85,925
51301	Spencer	(712)	11,488	10,278
50588	Storm Lake	(712)	8,631	8,591
50322	Urbandale	(515)	17,854	14,434
52349	Vinton	(319)	5,004	4,962
52353	Washington	(319)	5,960	6,317
*50701	Waterloo	(319)	79,613	75,533
50677	Waverly	(319)	7,333	7,205
50595	Webster City	(515)	8,274	8,488
50265	West Des Moines	(515)	21,892	16,441
50311	Windsor Heights	(515)	7,051	6,303

Kansas

ZIP code	Place		1980	1970
67410	Abilene	(913)	6,430	6,661
67005	Arkansas City	(316)	12,736	13,216
66002	Atchison	(913)	10,694	12,565
67010	Augusta	(316)	6,594	5,977
66012	Bonner Springs	(913)	7,044	5,361
66720	Chanute	(316)	10,058	10,341
67432	Clay Center	(913)	5,046	4,963
67337	Coffeyville	(316)	14,295	15,116
67701	Colby	(913)	5,370	4,658
66901	Concordia	(913)	6,651	7,221
67037	Derby	(316)	9,132	7,947
67801	Dodge City	(316)	15,626	14,127
67042	El Dorado	(316)	12,209	12,308
66801	Emporia	(316)	24,347	23,327
66205	Fairway	(913)	6,262	5,133
66027	Fort Leavenworth(u)	(913)	NA	8,060
66701	Fort Scott	(316)	8,707	8,967
67846	Garden City	(316)	18,653	14,790
67735	Goodland	(913)	5,678	5,510
67530	Great Bend	(316)	16,262	16,133
67601	Hays	(913)	17,596	15,396
67060	Haysville	(316)	8,538	6,483
67501	Hutchinson	(316)	41,831	36,885
67301	Independence	(316)	10,394	10,347
66749	Iola	(316)	6,813	6,493
66441	Junction City	(913)	18,684	19,018
*66110	Kansas City	(913)	164,250	168,213
66044	Lawrence	(913)	50,780	45,698
66048	Leavenworth	(913)	35,540	25,147
66206	Leawood	(913)	12,845	10,645
66215	Lenexa	(913)	13,937	5,549
67901	Liberal	(316)	15,114	13,471
67460	McPherson	(316)	11,114	10,851
66502	Manhattan	(913)	34,741	27,575
66203	Merriam	(913)	11,682	10,955
66222	Mission	(913)	8,555	8,125
67114	Newton	(316)	15,634	15,439
66442	North Fort Riley(u)	(913)	NA	12,469
66061	Olathe	(913)	32,323	17,917
66067	Ottawa	(913)	10,399	11,036
66204	Overland Park	(913)	82,917	77,934
67357	Parsons	(316)	12,223	13,015
66762	Pittsburg	(316)	18,521	20,171
66208	Prairie Village	(913)	25,775	28,378
67124	Pratt	(316)	6,811	6,736
66203	Roeland Park	(913)	12,506	9,760
67665	Russell	(913)	5,458	5,371
67401	Salina	(913)	38,798	37,714
*66203	Shawnee	(913)	25,653	20,946
*66603	Topeka	(913)	122,100	125,011
67152	Wellington	(316)	7,739	8,072
*67202	Wichita	(316)	267,748	276,554
67156	Winfield	(316)	11,067	11,405

Kentucky

ZIP code	Place		1980	1970
41101	Ashland	(606)	26,972	29,245
40004	Bardstown	(502)	7,199	5,816
41073	Bellevue	(606)	7,791	8,847
40403	Berea	(606)	7,868	6,956
42101	Bowling Green	(502)	38,709	38,705
40218	Buechel(u)	(502)	NA	5,359
42718	Campbellsville	(502)	7,426	7,598
42330	Central City	(502)	5,763	3,455
40701	Corbin	(606)	9,324	7,317
*41011	Covington	(606)	45,756	52,535
41031	Cynthiana	(606)	5,921	6,356
40422	Danville	(606)	11,774	11,542
41074	Dayton	(606)	7,401	8,751
41017	Edgewood	(606)	7,947	4,139
42701	Elizabethtown	(502)	15,343	11,748
41018	Elsmere	(606)	6,158	5,161
41018	Erlanger	(606)	14,480	12,676
41139	Flatwoods	(606)	9,808	7,380
41042	Florence	(606)	16,365	11,661
42223	Fort Campbell North(u)	(502)	NA	13,616
40121	Fort Knox(u)	(502)	NA	37,608
41017	Fort Mitchell	(606)	7,114	6,982
41075	Fort Thomas	(606)	16,121	16,338
41011	Fort Wright	(606)	5,528	5,297
40601	Frankfort	(502)	24,831	21,902
42134	Franklin	(502)	8,019	6,553
40324	Georgetown	(502)	9,515	8,629
42141	Glasgow	(502)	11,616	11,301
40330	Harrodsburg	(606)	6,682	6,741
41701	Hazard	(606)	5,843	5,459
42420	Henderson	(502)	23,532	22,976
42240	Hopkinsville	(502)	26,519	21,250
41051	Independence	(606)	6,386	4,851
40299	Jeffersontown	(502)	11,580	9,701
40033	Lebanon	(502)	5,945	5,528
*40511	Lexington-Fayette	(606)	190,686	108,137
*40201	Louisville	(502)	317,503	361,706
42431	Madisonville	(502)	17,913	15,332
42066	Mayfield	(502)	9,882	10,724
41056	Maysville	(606)	6,864	7,411
40965	Middlesborough	(606)	11,774	11,844
40351	Morehead	(606)	7,034	7,191
40353	Mount Sterling	(606)	6,149	5,083
42071	Murray	(502)	13,747	13,537
*41071	Newport	(606)	21,142	25,998
40356	Nicholasville	(606)	10,561	5,829
40219	Okolona(u)	(502)	NA	17,643
42301	Owensboro	(502)	50,612	50,329
42001	Paducah	(502)	33,253	31,627
40361	Paris	(606)	7,068	7,823
41501	Pikeville	(606)	6,259	5,205
40258	Pleasure Ridge Park(u)	(502)	NA	28,566
42445	Princeton	(502)	6,954	6,292

ZIP code	Place		1980	1970
40160	Radcliff	(502)	*14,945*	7,881
40475	Richmond	(606)	*19,586*	16,861
42276	Russellville	(502)	*6,793*	6,456
40207	St. Matthews	(502)	*14,248*	13,152
40216	Shively	(502)	*18,207*	19,139
42501	Somerset	(606)	*13,280*	10,436
40272	Valley Station(u)	(502)	NA	24,471
40383	Versailles	(606)	*7,511*	5,679
40391	Winchester	(606)	*16,438*	13,402

Louisiana

ZIP code	Place		1980	1970
70510	Abbeville	(318)	*13,018*	10,996
71301	Alexandria	(318)	*49,816*	41,557
70714	Baker	(504)	*13,324*	8,281
71220	Bastrop	(318)	*14,680*	14,713
*70821	Baton Rouge	(504)	*311,053*[1]	165,963
70360	Bayou Cane(u)	(504)	NA	9,077
70380	Bayou Vista(u)	(504)	NA	5,121
70427	Bogalusa	(504)	*17,534*	18,412
71010	Bossier City	(318)	*48,182*	41,595
71322	Bunkie	(318)	*5,063*	5,395
71101	Cooper Road(u)	(318)	NA	9,034
70433	Covington	(504)	*9,206*	7,170
70526	Crowley	(318)	*16,019*	16,104
70726	Denham Springs	(504)	*8,997*	6,752
70634	De Ridder	(318)	*11,010*	8,030
70346	Donaldsonville	(504)	*7,850*	7,367
70535	Eunice	(318)	*11,917*	11,390
70538	Franklin	(318)	*8,847*	9,325
70737	Gonzales	(504)	*7,253*	5,725
70053	Gretna	(504)	*30,461*	24,875
70401	Hammond	(504)	*15,420*	12,487
70123	Harahan	(504)	*13,858*	13,037
70058	Harvey(u)	(504)	NA	6,347
70360	Houma	(504)	*31,184*	30,922
70544	Jeanerette	(318)	*6,782*	6,322
70121	Jefferson Heights(u)	(504)	NA	16,489
70546	Jennings	(318)	*12,311*	11,783
71251	Jonesboro	(318)	*5,072*	5,072
70548	Kaplan	(318)	*5,172*	5,540
70062	Kenner	(504)	*54,616*	29,858
70501	Lafayette	(318)	*81,127*	68,908
70601	Lake Charles	(318)	*79,276*	77,998
71254	Lake Providence	(318)	*5,447*	6,183
70068	Laplace(u)	(504)	NA	5,953
71446	Leesville	(318)	*9,156*	8,928
70123	Little Farms(u)	(504)	NA	15,713
71052	Mansfield	(318)	*7,119*	6,432
70072	Marrero(u)	(504)	NA	29,015
*70004	Metairie(u)	(504)	NA	136,477
71055	Minden	(318)	*14,265*	13,996
71201	Monroe	(318)	*64,036*	56,374
70380	Morgan City	(504)	*16,294*	16,586
71457	Natchitoches	(318)	*17,793*	15,974
70560	New Iberia	(318)	*34,260*	30,147
*70113	New Orleans	(504)	556,913	593,471
71459	North Fort Polk(u)	(318)	NA	7,955
71463	Oakdale	(318)	*6,749*	7,301
70570	Opelousas	(318)	*19,965*	20,387
71360	Pineville	(318)	*12,381*	8,951
70764	Plaquemine	(504)	*7,598*	7,739
70767	Port Allen	(504)	*6,009*	5,728
70578	Rayne	(318)	*9,698*	9,510
70084	Reserve(u)	(504)	NA	6,381
71270	Ruston	(318)	*19,528*	17,365
70582	St. Martinville	(318)	*7,416*	7,153
70807	Scotlandville(u)	(504)	NA	22,599
*71102	Shreveport	(318)	*201,920*	182,064
70458	Slidell	(504)	*29,394*	16,101
71459	South Fort Polk(u)	(318)	NA	15,600
71075	Springhill	(318)	*6,343*	6,496
70663	Sulphur	(318)	*18,894*	14,959
71282	Tallulah	(318)	*9,360*	9,643
71285	Terry(u)	(318)	NA	13,382
70301	Thibodaux	(504)	*18,276*	15,038
71373	Vidalia	(318)	*5,804*	5,538
70586	Ville Platte	(318)	*9,608*	9,692
71291	West Monroe	(318)	*16,269*	14,868
70094	Westwego	(504)	*13,396*	11,402
71483	Winnfield	(318)	*6,767*	7,142
71295	Winnsboro	(318)	*5,578*	5,349
70791	Zachary	(504)	*7,664*	6,039

[1] Baton Rouge Metro

Maine (207)

See Note Page 933

ZIP code	Place	1980	1970
04210	Auburn	23,130	24,151
04330	Augusta	21,712	21,945
04401	Bangor	31,645	33,168
04530	Bath	10,222	9,679
04915	Belfast	*6,514*	5,957
04005	Biddeford	19,624	19,983
04412	Brewer	*9,090*	9,300
04011	Brunswick Center(u)	NA	10,867
.....	*Brunswick*	NA	16,195
04107	*Cape Elizabeth*	NA	7,873
04736	Caribou	*11,119*	10,419
04605	Ellsworth	*5,253*	4,603
.....	*Fairfield*	NA	5,684
04105	*Falmouth*	NA	6,291
.....	*Farmington*	NA	5,657
04345	Gardiner	*6,805*	6,685
.....	*Gorham*	NA	7,839
04730	Houlton Center(u)	NA	6,760
.....	*Houlton*	NA	8,111
.....	*Kennebunk*	NA	5,646
03904	Kittery Center(u)	NA	7,363
.....	*Kittery*	NA	11,028
04240	Lewiston	40,534	41,779
04750	*Limestone*	NA	10,360
04250	*Lisbon*	NA	6,544
04750	Loring(u)	NA	7,881
.....	*Madawaska*	NA	5,585
04462	Millinocket Center(u)	NA	7,558
.....	*Millinocket*	NA	7,742
04064	Old Orchard Beach Ctr.(u)	NA	5,273
.....	*Old Orchard Beach*	NA	5,404
04468	Old Town	*8,335*	9,057
04473	Orono Center(u)	NA	9,146
.....	*Orono*	*7,096*	9,989
*04101	Portland	*61,530*	65,116
04769	Presque Isle	11,171	11,452
04841	Rockland	*7,736*	8,505
04276	Rumford Compact(u)	NA	6,198
.....	*Rumford*	NA	9,363
04072	Saco	12,933	11,678
04073	Sanford Center(u)	NA	10,457
.....	*Sanford*	NA	15,812
04074	*Scarborough*	NA	7,845
04976	Skowhegan Center(u)	NA	6,571
.....	*Skowhegan*	NA	7,601
04106	South Portland	22,599	23,267
.....	*Topsham*	NA	5,022
04901	Waterville	17,748	18,192
04092	Westbrook	14,955	14,444
04082	*Windham*	NA	6,593
04901	Winslow Center(u)	NA	5,389
.....	*Winslow*	NA	7,299
03909	*York*	NA	5,690

Maryland (301)

ZIP code	Place	1980	1970
21001	Aberdeen	*14,120*	12,375
21005	Aberdeen Proving Ground(u)	NA	7,403
20331	Andrews(u)	NA	6,418
*21401	Annapolis	31,426	30,095
21227	Arbutus(u)	NA	22,745
20853	Aspen Hill(u)	NA	16,887
20783	Avenel-Hillandale(u)	NA	19,520
21905	Bainbridge Center(u)	NA	5,257
*21233	Baltimore	*791,857*	905,759
21014	Bel Air	*9,658*	6,307
20705	Beltsville(u)	NA	8,912
20014	Bethesda(u)	NA	71,621
20021	Birchwood City(u)	NA	13,514
20710	Bladensburg	*7,217*	7,488
20715	Bowie	*37,072*	35,028
21225	Brooklyn(u)	NA	13,896
20705	Calverton(u)	NA	6,543
21613	Cambridge	*11,681*	11,595
20031	Camp Springs(u)	NA	22,776
20027	Carmody Hills-Pepper Mill(u)	NA	6,245
21228	Catonsville(u)	NA	54,812
20027	Chapel Oaks-Cedar Heights(u)	NA	6,049
20785	Cheverly(u)	*5,444*	6,808
20015	Chevy Chase(u)	NA	16,424
20783	Chillum(u)	NA	35,656
20904	Colesville(u)	NA	9,455
20740	College Park	*26,579*	26,156
21043	Columbia(u)	NA	8,815
20027	Coral Hills(u)	NA	9,058
21502	Cumberland	*26,002*	29,724
21222	Defense Heights(u)	NA	6,775
20028	District Heights	*7,200*	7,659
21222	Dundalk(u)	NA	85,377
21601	Easton	*7,335*	6,809
21219	Edgemere(u)	NA	10,352
21040	Edgewood	NA	8,551
21921	Elkton	*6,178*	5,362
*21043	Ellicott(u)	NA	9,435
21221	Essex(u)	NA	38,193
21061	Ferndale(u)	NA	9,929
20028	Forestville(u)	NA	16,188
20755	Fort Meade(u)	NA	16,699
21701	Frederick	*27,686*	23,641
21532	Frostburg	*7,572*	7,327
20760	Gaithersburg	22,462	8,344
21061	Glen Burnie(u)	NA	38,608
20801	Good Luck(u)	NA	10,584
20770	Greenbelt	*15,775*	18,199
21740	Hagerstown	*36,957*	35,862
21740	Halfway(u)	NA	6,106
20852	Halpine(u)	NA	6,118
21078	Havre De Grace	*11,325*	9,791

ZIP code	Place	1980	1970
20031	Hillcrest Heights	NA	24,037
*20780	Hyattsville	*12,273*	14,998
21085	Joppatowne(u)	NA	9,092
20904	Kemp Mill(u)	NA	10,037
20785	Kentland(u)	NA	9,649
20785	Landover(u)	NA	5,597
20787	Langley Park(u)	NA	11,564
20801	Lanham-Seabrook(u)	NA	13,244
21227	Lansdowne-Baltimore Highlands(u)	NA	17,770
20810	Laurel	*9,679*	10,525
20653	Lexington Pk.-Patuxent R.(u)	NA	9,136
21090	Linthicum(u)	NA	9,775
21093	Lutherville-Timonium(u)	NA	24,055
20810	Maryland City(u)	NA	7,102
21220	Middle River(u)	NA	19,935
20852	Montrose(u)	NA	5,902
20822	Mount Rainier	*6,829*	8,180
20784	New Carrollton	*12,431*	14,870
20854	North Potomac(u)	NA	12,784
20012	North Takoma Park(u)	NA	7,373
21113	Odenton(u)	NA	5,989
21206	Overlea(u)	NA	13,124
21117	Owings Mills(u)	NA	7,360
20021	Oxon Hill(u)	NA	11,974
20785	Palmer Park(u)	NA	8,172
21234	Parkville	NA	33,589
21128	Perry Hall(u)	NA	5,446
21208	Pikesville(u)	NA	25,395
20016	Potomac Valley(u)	NA	5,122
21227	Pumphrey(u)	NA	6,425
21133	Randallstown(u)	NA	33,683
20853	Randolph(u)	NA	13,215
21136	Reisterstown(u)	NA	12,568
20840	Riverdale	NA	5,724
20840	Riverdale Hgts.-E. Pines(u)	NA	8,941
21122	Riviera Beach(u)	NA	7,464
*20850	Rockville	43,622	41,821
21237	Rosedale(u)	NA	19,417
21801	Salisbury	*16,526*	15,252
20027	Seat Pleasant	*7,088*	7,217
21146	Severna Park	NA	16,358
*20907	Silver Spring(u)	NA	77,411
21061	South Gate(u)	NA	9,356
20795	South Kensington(u)	NA	10,289
20810	South Laurel(u)	NA	13,345
20023	Suitland-Silver Hills(u)	NA	30,355
20012	Takoma Park	*15,476*	18,507
21204	Towson(u)	NA	77,768
20601	Waldorf(u)	NA	7,368
20028	Walker Mill(u)	NA	7,103
21157	Westminster	*10,174*	7,207
20902	Wheaton(u)	NA	66,280
20903	White Oak(u)	NA	19,769
21207	Woodlawn-Woodmoor(u)	NA	28,821

Massachusetts

See Note on Page 933

ZIP code	Place	Area code	1980	1970
02351	*Abington*	(617)	13,522	12,334
01720	*Acton*	(617)	17,558	14,770
02743	*Acushnet*	(617)	NA	7,767
01220	Adams Center(u)	(413)	NA	11,256
.....	*Adams*	(413)	10,385	11,772
01001	*Agawam*	(413)	26,281	21,717
01913	Amesbury Center(u)	(617)	NA	10,088
.....	*Amesbury*	(617)	13,961	11,388
01002	Amherst Center	(413)	NA	17,926
.....	*Amherst*	(413)	39,210	26,331
01810	*Andover*	(617)	26,365	23,695
02174	*Arlington*	(617)	48,263	53,534
01721	*Ashland*	(617)	NA	8,882
01331	Athol Center(u)	(617)	NA	9,723
.....	*Athol*	(617)	10,619	11,185
02703	Attleboro	(617)	34,221	32,907
01501	*Auburn*	(617)	14,832	15,347
02322	*Avon*	(617)	NA	5,295
*01432	*Ayer*	(617)	NA	8,325
02630	*Barnstable*	(617)	30,780	19,842
01730	*Bedford*	(617)	13,026	13,513
01007	*Belchertown*	(413)	NA	5,936
02019	*Bellingham*	(617)	14,179	13,967
02178	*Belmont*	(617)	26,082	28,285
01915	Beverly	(617)	37,038	38,348
01821	*Billerica*	(617)	36,719	31,648
01504	*Blackstone*	(617)	NA	6,566
*02109	Boston	(617)	562,118	641,071
02532	*Bourne*	(617)	13,948	12,636
02184	*Braintree*	(617)	36,243	35,050
02324	*Bridgewater*	(617)	17,124	11,829
*02403	Brockton	(617)	94,990	89,040
02145	*Brookline*	(617)	54,675	58,886
01803	*Burlington*	(617)	23,493	21,980
*02138	Cambridge	(617)	95,351	100,361
02021	*Canton*	(617)	18,143	17,100
01824	*Chelmsford*	(617)	31,145	31,432
02150	Chelsea	(617)	25,420	30,625
*01021	Chicopee	(413)	55,048	66,676
01510	*Clinton*	(617)	12,665	13,383
02025	*Cohasset*	(617)	NA	6,954
01742	*Concord*	(617)	16,295	16,148
01226	*Dalton*	(413)	NA	7,505
01923	*Danvers*	(617)	24,069	26,151
02714	*Dartmouth*	(617)	23,978	18,800
02026	*Dedham*	(617)	25,121	25,938
02638	*Dennis*	(617)	12,341	6,454
01826	*Dracut*	(617)	21,176	18,214
01570	*Dudley*	(617)	NA	8,087
02332	*Duxbury*	(617)	11,808	7,636
02333	*East Bridgewater*	(617)	NA	8,347
01027	*Easthampton*	(413)	15,548	13,012
01028	*East Longmeadow*	(413)	12,898	13,029
02334	*Easton*	(617)	16,606	12,157
01249	Everett	(617)	37,121	42,485
02719	*Fairhaven*	(617)	15,793	16,332
*02722	Fall River	(617)	92,240	96,898
*02540	Falmouth Center(u)	(617)	NA	5,806
.....	*Falmouth*	(617)	23,640	15,942
01420	Fitchburg	(617)	39,332	43,343
01433	Fort Devens(u)	(617)	NA	12,915
02035	*Foxborough*	(617)	14,063	14,218
01701	*Framingham*	(617)	64,616	64,048
02038	Franklin Center(u)	(617)	NA	8,863
.....	*Franklin*	(617)	18,165	17,830
01440	Gardner	(617)	17,837	19,748
01833	*Georgetown*	(617)	NA	5,290
01930	Gloucester	(617)	27,712	27,941
01519	*Grafton*	(617)	11,221	11,659
01033	*Granby*	(413)	NA	5,473
01230	*Great Barrington*	(413)	NA	7,537
01301	Greenfield Center(u)	(413)	NA	14,642
.....	*Greenfield*	(413)	18,415	18,116
01450	*Groton*	(617)	NA	5,109
01834	*Groveland*	(617)	NA	5,382
01936	*Hamilton*	(617)	NA	6,373
02339	*Hanover*	(617)	11,364	10,107
02341	*Hanson*	(617)	NA	7,148
01451	*Harvard*	(617)	12,163	13,426
02645	*Harwich*	(617)	NA	5,892
01830	Haverhill	(617)	46,815	46,120
02043	*Hingham*	(617)	20,292	18,845
02343	*Holbrook*	(617)	11,036	11,775
01520	*Holden*	(617)	13,272	12,564
01746	*Holliston*	(617)	12,659	12,069
01040	Holyoke	(413)	44,819	50,112
01748	*Hopkinton*	(617)	NA	5,981
01749	Hudson Center(u)	(617)	NA	14,283
.....	*Hudson*	(617)	16,448	16,084
02045	*Hull*	(617)	NA	9,961
02601	Hyannis(u)	(617)	NA	6,847
01938	Ipswich(u)	(617)	NA	5,022
.....	*Ipswich*	(617)	11,131	10,750
02364	*Kingston*	(617)	NA	5,999
01523	*Lancaster*	(617)	NA	6,095
*01842	Lawrence	(617)	62,770	66,915
01238	*Lee*	(413)	NA	6,426
01524	*Leicester*	(617)	NA	9,140
01240	*Lenox*	(413)	NA	5,804
01453	Leominster	(617)	34,318	32,939
01273	*Lexington*	(617)	29,550	31,886
01773	*Lincoln*	(617)	NA	7,567
01460	*Littleton*	(617)	NA	6,380
01106	*Longmeadow*	(413)	16,309	15,630
*01853	Lowell	(617)	92,160	94,239
01056	*Ludlow*	(413)	18,182	17,580
01462	*Lunenburg*	(617)	NA	7,419
*01901	Lynn	(617)	78,299	90,294
01940	*Lynnfield*	(617)	11,248	10,826
02148	Malden	(617)	53,431	56,127
01944	*Manchester*	(617)	NA	5,151
02048	*Mansfield*	(617)	13,452	9,939
01945	*Marblehead*	(617)	20,085	21,295
01752	Marlborough	(617)	30,709	27,936
02050	*Marshfield*	(617)	20,944	15,223
01754	*Maynard*	(617)	NA	9,710
02052	*Medfield*	(617)	58,303	9,821
02155	Medford	(617)	NA	64,397
02053	*Medway*	(617)	NA	7,938
02176	Melrose	(617)	29,926	33,180
01844	*Methuen*	(617)	36,616	35,456
02346	Middleborough Center(u)	(617)	NA	6,259
.....	*Middleborough*	(617)	16,377	13,607
01757	Milford Center(u)	(617)	NA	13,740
.....	*Milford*	(617)	23,350	19,352
01527	*Millbury*	(617)	11,781	11,987
02054	*Millis*	(617)	NA	5,686
02186	*Milton*	(617)	NA	27,190
01057	*Monson*	(413)	NA	7,355
01351	*Montague*	(413)	NA	8,451
01760	*Natick*	(617)	29,422	31,057
02192	*Needham*	(617)	NA	29,748
*02741	New Bedford	(617)	98,397	101,777
01950	Newburyport	(617)	15,910	15,807
02158	Newton	(617)	83,586	91,066
01247	North Adams	(413)	17,874	19,195
01060	Northampton	(413)	29,128	29,664
01845	*North Andover*	(617)	20,072	16,284
*02760	*North Attleborough*	(617)	21,071	18,665
01532	*Northborough*	(617)	10,540	9,218
01534	*Northbridge*	(617)	12,206	11,795

ZIP code	Place		1980	1980
01864	*North Reading*	(617)	11,447	11,264
02060	North Scituate(u)	(617)	NA	5,507
02766	*Norton*	(617)	12,736	9,487
02061	*Norwell*	(617)	NA	7,796
02062	*Norwood*	(617)	NA	30,815
01364	*Orange*	(617)	NA	6,104
01253	Otis(u)	(413)	NA	5,596
01540	Oxford Center(u)	(617)	NA	6,109
.....	*Oxford*	(617)	11,648	10,345
01069	*Palmer*	(413)	11,410	11,680
01960	Peabody	(617)	45,664	48,080
02359	*Pembroke*	(617)	13,453	11,193
01463	*Pepperell*	(617)	NA	5,887
01866	Pinehurst	(617)	NA	5,681
01201	Pittsfield	(413)	51,942	57,020
*02360	Plymouth Center(u)	(617)	NA	6,940
.....	*Plymouth*	(617)	35,761	18,606
02169	Quincy	(617)	83,907	87,966
02368	*Randolph*	(617)	NA	27,035
02767	*Raynham*	(617)	NA	6,705
01867	*Reading*	(617)	22,710	22,539
02769	*Rehoboth*	(617)	NA	6,512
02151	Revere	(617)	42,256	43,159
02370	*Rockland*	(617)	15,655	15,674
01966	*Rockport*	(617)	NA	5,636
01970	Salem	(617)	38,302	40,556
02563	*Sandwich*	(617)	NA	5,239
01906	*Saugus*	(617)	24,664	25,110
02066	*Scituate*	(617)	17,316	16,973
02771	*Seekonk*	(617)	12,259	11,116
02067	*Sharon*	(617)	NA	12,367
01545	*Shrewsbury*	(617)	22,577	19,196
02725	*Somerset*	(617)	18,826	18,088
02143	Somerville	(617)	77,393	88,779
01772	*Southborough*	(617)	16,625	5,798
01550	Southbridge Center(u)	(617)	NA	14,261
.....	*Southbridge*	(617)	NA	17,057
01075	*South Hadley*	(413)	16,463	17,033
01077	*Southwick*	(413)	NA	6,330
02664	South Yarmouth(u)	(617)	NA	5,380
01562	Spencer Center	(617)	NA	5,895
.....	*Spencer*	(617)	10,689	8,779
*01101	Springfield	(413)	152,212	163,905
02180	*Stoneham*	(617)	21,419	20,725
02072	*Stoughton*	(617)	NA	23,459
01776	*Sudbury*	(617)	14,030	13,506
01907	*Swampscott*	(617)	13,877	13,578
02777	*Swansea*	(617)	15,349	12,640
02780	Taunton	(617)	44,675	43,756
01468	*Templeton*	(617)	NA	5,863
01876	*Tewksbury*	(617)	24,478	22,755
01983	*Topsfield*	(617)	NA	5,225
01376	Turners Falls(u)	(413)	NA	5,168
01569	*Uxbridge*	(617)	NA	8,253
01880	*Wakefield*	(617)	24,871	25,402
02081	*Walpole*	(617)	NA	18,149
02154	Waltham	(617)	58,298	61,582
01082	Ware Center(u)	(413)	NA	6,509
.....	*Ware*	(413)	NA	8,187
02571	*Wareham*	(617)	18,443	11,492
02172	*Watertown*	(617)	34,399	39,307
01778	*Wayland*	(617)	12,196	13,461
01570	Webster Center(u)	(617)	NA	12,432
.....	*Webster*	(617)	14,371	14,917
02181	*Wellesley*	(617)	NA	28,051
01581	*Westborough*	(617)	13,610	12,594
01583	*West Boylston*	(617)	NA	6,369
02379	*West Bridgewater*	(617)	NA	7,152
01085	Westfield	(413)	36,356	31,433
01886	*Westford*	(617)	13,438	10,368
02193	*Weston*	(617)	11,175	10,870
02790	*Westport*	(617)	13,756	9,791
01089	*West Springfield*	(413)	26,960	28,461
02090	*Westwood*	(617)	NA	12,570
02188	*Weymouth*	(617)	NA	54,610
01588	Whitinsville(u)	(617)	NA	5,210
02382	*Whitman*	(617)	13,557	13,059
01095	*Wilbraham*	(413)	12,062	11,984
01267	*Williamstown*	(413)	NA	8,454
01887	*Wilmington*	(617)	17,495	17,102
01475	*Winchendon*	(617)	NA	6,635
01890	*Winchester*	(617)	20,694	22,269
02152	*Winthrop*	(617)	19,307	20,335
01801	Woburn	(617)	36,533	37,406
*01613	Worcester	(617)	161,384	176,572
02093	*Wrentham*	(617)	NA	7,315
02675	*Yarmouth*	(617)	18,294	12,033

Michigan

ZIP code	Place		1980	1980
49221	Adrian	(517)	*20,046*	20,382
49224	Albion	(517)	*13,347*	12,112
48101	Allen Park	(313)	34,166	40,747
49010	Allegan	(616)	*5,807*	4,516
48801	Alma	(517)	*9,969*	9,611
49707	Alpena	(517)	12,192	13,805
*48106	Ann Arbor	(313)	*105,213*	100,035
*49016	Battle Creek	(616)	*41,328*	38,931
48706	Bay City	(517)	41,588	49,449
48809	Belding	(616)	*5,644*	5,121
49022	Benton Central(u)	(616)	NA	8,067
49022	Benton Harbor	(616)	*15,353*	16,481
48072	Berkley	(313)	18,658	21,879
48009	Beverly Hills	(313)	*11,749*	13,598
49307	Big Rapids	(616)	*15,075*	11,995
*48012	Birmingham	(313)	21,654	26,170
*48502	Burton	(313)	30,021	32,540
49601	Cadillac	(616)	*10,659*	9,990
48724	Carrollton(u)	(517)	NA	7,300
48015	Center Line	(313)	*9,159*	10,379
48813	Charlotte	(517)	*9,907*	8,244
49721	Cheboygan	(616)	*5,518*	5,553
48017	Clawson	(313)	15,090	17,617
49036	Coldwater	(517)	*10,289*	9,155
49041	Comstock(u)	(616)	NA	5,003
49321	Comstock Park(u)	(616)	NA	5,766
49508	Cutlerville(u)	(616)	NA	6,267
48423	Davison	(313)	*6,388*	5,259
*48120	Dearborn	(313)	90,589	104,199
48127	Dearborn Heights	(313)	67,680	80,069
*48233	Detroit	(313)	*1,257,879*	1,514,063
49047	Dowagiac	(616)	*6,472*	6,583
48020	Drayton Plains(u)	(313)	NA	16,462
48021	East Detroit	(313)	38,309	45,920
49506	East Grand Rapids	(616)	10,880	12,565
48823	East Lansing	(517)	*50,164*	47,540
49001	Eastwood(u)	(517)	NA	9,682
48827	Eaton Rapids	(517)	*5,615*	4,494
48229	Ecorse	(313)	14,443	17,515
49829	Escanaba	(906)	14,359	15,368
48732	Essexville	(517)	*5,782*	4,990
48024	Farmington	(313)	11,035	10,329
48024	Farmington Hills	(313)	57,922	48,694
48430	Fenton	(313)	*10,474*	8,284
48220	Ferndale	(313)	26,202	30,850
48134	Flat Rock	(313)	*6,580*	5,643
*48502	Flint	(313)	159,576	193,317
48433	Flushing	(313)	*8,422*	7,190
48026	Fraser	(313)	*14,067*	11,868
49412	Fremont	(616)	*5,204*	3,465
48135	Garden City	(313)	35,667	41,864
49837	Gladstone	(906)	NA	5,237
48439	Grand Blanc	(313)	*5,601*	5,132
49417	Grand Haven	(616)	11,860	11,844
48837	Grand Ledge	(517)	*7,674*	6,032
*49501	Grand Rapids	(616)	181,602	197,649
49418	Grandville	(616)	12,417	10,764
48838	Greenville	(616)	*8,707*	7,493
48138	Grosse Ile(u)	(313)	NA	8,306
48236	Grosse Pointe	(313)	*5,971*	6,637
48236	Grosse Pointe Farms	(313)	10,556	11,701
48236	Grosse Pointe Park	(313)	13,297	15,641
48236	Grosse Pointe Woods	(313)	18,812	21,878
48212	Hamtramck	(313)	*22,289*	27,245
48236	Harper Woods	(313)	16,570	20,186
49058	Hastings	(616)	*7,580*	6,501
48030	Hazel Park	(313)	20,919	23,784
48203	Highland Park	(313)	*28,882*	35,444
49242	Hillsdale	(517)	*8,578*	7,728
49423	Holland	(616)	21,615	26,479
48442	Holly	(313)	*5,239*	4,355
48842	Holt(u)	(517)	NA	6,980
49931	Houghton	(906)	*6,849*	6,067
48843	Howell	(517)	*8,281*	5,224
48070	Huntington Woods	(313)	*7,522*	8,536
48141	Inkster	(313)	35,245	38,595
48846	Ionia	(616)	*6,580*	6,361
49801	Iron Mountain	(906)	*8,622*	8,702
49938	Ironwood	(906)	*7,969*	8,711
49849	Ishpeming	(906)	*8,375*	8,245
*49201	Jackson	(517)	*43,057*	45,484
49428	Jenison(u)	(616)	NA	11,266
*49001	Kalamazoo	(616)	*78,279*	85,555
49508	Kentwood	(616)	30,449	20,310
49788	Kincheloe(u)	(906)	NA	6,331
49801	Kingsford	(906)	*5,406*	5,276
49843	K.I. Sawyer(u)	(906)	NA	8,224
49015	Lakeview(u)	(517)	NA	11,391
48144	Lambertville(u)	(313)	NA	5,711
*48924	Lansing	(517)	*125,229*	131,403
48446	Lapeer	(313)	*5,619*	6,314
48503	Lapeer Heights(u)	(313)	NA	7,130
48146	Lincoln Park	(313)	*45,008*	52,984
*48150	Livonia	(313)	104,660	110,109
49431	Ludington	(616)	*10,355*	9,021
48071	Madison Heights	(313)	35,211	38,599
49660	Manistee	(616)	*8,098*	7,723
48039	Marine City	(313)	*5,331*	4,567
49855	Marquette	(906)	23,336	21,967
49068	Marshall	(616)	*7,449*	7,253
48040	Marysville	(313)	*7,026*	5,610
48854	Mason	(517)	*6,451*	5,468
48122	Melvindale	(313)	12,313	13,862
49858	Menominee	(906)	10,088	10,748
48640	Midland	(517)	37,290	35,176
48161	Monroe	(313)	*24,782*	23,894
48043	Mount Clemens	(313)	*23,830*	20,476
48858	Mount Pleasant	(517)	*24,521*	20,524

ZIP code	Place		1980	1970
*49440	Muskegon	(616)	40,518	44,631
49444	Muskegon Heights	(616)	14,587	17,304
49866	Negaunee	(906)	5,568	5,248
48047	New Baltimore	(313)	5,395	4,132
49120	Niles	(616)	13,440	12,988
48167	Northville	(313)	7,472	5,400
49441	Norton Shores	(616)	21,995	22,271
48050	Novi	(313)	17,693	9,668
48237	Oak Park	(313)	31,561	36,762
48864	Okemos(u)	(517)	NA	7,770
48867	Owosso	(517)	16,457	17,179
49770	Petoskey	(616)	6,055	6,342
48170	Plymouth	(313)	10,219	11,758
*48053	Pontiac	(313)	78,501	85,279
49081	Portage	(616)	36,974	36,590
48060	Port Huron	(313)	33,901	35,794
48024	Quakertown North(u)	(313)	NA	7,101
49959	Ramsey	(906)	7,475	2,336
48218	River Rouge	(313)	12,770	15,947
48192	Riverview	(313)	14,534	11,342
48063	Rochester	(313)	9,511	7,054
48174	Romulus	(313)	24,802	22,879
48066	Roseville	(313)	54,376	60,529
*48068	Royal Oak	(313)	70,795	88,238
*48605	Saginaw	(517)	77,529	91,849
*48083	St. Clair Shores	(313)	76,227	88,093
48879	St. Johns	(517)	8,458	6,672
49085	St. Joseph	(616)	10,718	11,042
48176	Saline	(313)	7,018	4,811
49793	Sault Ste. Marie	(906)	14,418	15,136
*48075	Southfield	(313)	75,492	69,285
48198	Southgate	(313)	32,000	33,909
49090	South Haven	(616)	5,919	6,471
49015	Springfield	(616)	5,607	3,994
*48078	Sterling Heights	(313)	108,998	61,365
49091	Sturgis	(616)	9,212	9,295
48473	Swartz Creek	(313)	7,089	4,928
48180	Taylor	(313)	77,454	70,020
49286	Tecumseh	(517)	8,234	7,120
49093	Three Rivers	(616)	6,456	7,355
49684	Traverse City	(616)	15,393	18,048
48183	Trenton	(313)	22,734	24,127
48084	Troy	(313)	67,003	39,419
49504	Walker	(616)	15,097	11,492
*48089	Warren	(313)	161,173	179,260
48184	Wayne	(313)	21,140	21,054
48185	Westland	(313)	43,278	86,749
49007	Westwood(u)	(616)	41,343	9,143
48096	Wixom	(313)	5,346	2,010
49799	Wolverine Lake	(313)	5,593	4,301
48183	Woodhaven	(313)	10,890	3,566
48753	Wurtsmith(u)	(517)	NA	6,932
*48192	Wyandotte	(313)	33,961	41,061
49509	Wyoming	(616)	59,589	56,560
48197	Ypsilanti	(313)	27,618	29,538
49464	Zeeland	(616)	5,966	4,734

Minnesota

ZIP code	Place		1980	1970
56007	Albert Lea	(507)	19,089	19,418
56308	Alexandria	(612)	7,470	6,973
55303	Anoka	(612)	16,219	13,298
55068	Apple Valley	(612)	19,919	8,502
55112	Arden Hills	(612)	7,968	5,149
55912	Austin	(507)	22,889	26,210
56601	Bemidji	(218)	10,868	11,490
55433	Blaine	(612)	32,439	20,570
55420	Bloomington	(612)	78,624	81,970
56401	Brainerd	(218)	10,424	11,667
55429	Brooklyn Center	(612)	30,969	35,173
55429	Brooklyn Park	(612)	40,203	26,230
55337	Burnsville	(612)	33,890	19,940
55317	Chanhassen	(612)	5,487	4,879
55318	Chaska	(612)	7,990	4,352
55719	Chisholm	(218)	5,885	5,913
55720	Cloquet	(218)	11,184	8,699
55421	Columbia Heights	(612)	23,966	23,997
55433	Coon Rapids	(612)	32,061	30,505
55016	Cottage Grove	(612)	17,972	13,419
56716	Crookston	(218)	8,240	8,312
55428	Crystal	(612)	26,832	30,925
56501	Detroit Lakes	(218)	6,799	5,797
*55806	Duluth	(218)	92,789	100,578
55121	Eagan	(612)	19,734	10,398
55005	East Bethel	(612)	5,819	2,586
56721	East Grand Forks	(218)	8,849	7,607
55343	Eden Prairie	(612)	10,473	6,938
55424	Edina	(612)	48,791	44,046
56031	Fairmont	(507)	11,481	10,751
55113	Falcon Heights	(507)	5,523	5,530
55021	Fairbault	(507)	15,659	16,595
55024	Farmington	(612)	5,666	3,464
56537	Fergus Falls	(218)	11,726	12,443
55421	Fridley	(612)	36,594	29,233
55427	Golden Valley	(612)	22,525	24,246
55744	Grand Rapids	(218)	9,550	7,247
55303	Ham Lake	(612)	5,387	3,327
55033	Hastings	(612)	16,612	12,195
55811	Hermantown	(218)	6,735	6,737
55746	Hibbing	(218)	15,812	16,104
55343	Hopkins	(612)	15,874	13,428
55350	Hutchinson	(612)	8,643	8,031
56649	International Falls	(218)	5,674	6,439
55075	Inver Grove Heights	(612)	18,512	12,148
55044	Lakeville	(612)	11,584	7,556
55355	Litchfield	(612)	5,294	5,262
55110	Little Canada	(612)	6,483	3,481
56345	Little Falls	(612)	7,614	7,467
56001	Mankato	(507)	27,200	30,895
55369	Maple Grove	(612)	16,324	6,275
55109	Maplewood	(612)	26,606	25,186
56258	Marshall	(507)	9,962	9,866
55118	Mendota Heights	(612)	8,401	6,565
*55401	Minneapolis	(612)	353,992	434,400
55343	Minnetonka	(612)	45,390	35,776
56265	Montevideo	(612)	5,385	5,661
56560	Moorhead	(218)	28,901	29,687
56267	Morris	(612)	5,178	5,366
55364	Mound	(612)	10,117	7,572
55112	Mounds View	(612)	14,498	10,599
55112	New Brighton	(612)	19,780	19,507
54428	New Hope	(612)	22,335	23,180
56073	New Ulm	(507)	14,024	13,051
55057	Northfield	(507)	11,703	10,235
56001	North Mankato	(507)	8,402	7,347
55109	North St. Paul	(612)	11,351	11,950
55119	Oakdale	(612)	11,058	7,795
55060	Owatonna	(507)	18,128	15,341
55427	Plymouth	(612)	25,700	18,077
55066	Red Wing	(612)	13,483	10,441
56283	Redwood Falls	(507)	5,017	4,774
55423	Richfield	(612)	40,465	47,231
55422	Robbinsdale	(612)	14,228	16,845
55901	Rochester	(507)	56,732	53,766
55068	Rosemount	(612)	5,227	4,034
55113	Roseville	(612)	39,331	34,438
55418	St. Anthony	(612)	9,372	9,239
56301	St. Cloud	(612)	41,404	39,691
55426	St. Louis Park	(612)	44,778	48,883
*55101	St. Paul	(612)	263,147	309,866
55071	St. Paul Park	(612)	5,861	5,587
56082	St. Peter	(507)	8,214	8,339
56379	Sauk Rapids	(612)	5,117	5,051
55379	Shakopee	(612)	8,959	6,876
55112	Shoreview	(612)	17,723	10,978
55075	South St. Paul	(612)	20,560	25,016
55432	Spring Lake Park	(612)	9,020	6,417
55082	Stillwater	(612)	16,372	10,191
56701	Thief River Falls	(218)	8,926	8,618
55792	Virginia	(218)	11,053	12,450
56093	Waseca	(507)	7,938	6,789
55118	West St. Paul	(612)	18,046	18,802
55110	White Bear Lake	(612)	23,814	23,313
56201	Willmar	(612)	13,889	12,869
55987	Winona	(507)	25,078	26,438
55119	Woodbury	(612)	12,857	6,184
56187	Worthington	(507)	10,385	9,916

Mississippi (601)

ZIP code	Place	1980	1970
39730	Aberdeen	7,123	6,157
38821	Amory	7,476	7,236
39520	Bay St. Louis	7,081	6,752
*39530	Biloxi	43,927	48,486
39042	Brandon	9,843	3,379
38829	Booneville	5,857	5,895
39601	Brookhaven	10,636	10,700
39046	Canton	11,632	10,503
38614	Clarksdale	21,034	21,673
38732	Cleveland	14,487	7,289
39056	Clinton	13,379	13,327
39429	Columbia	7,017	7,587
39701	Columbus	26,799	25,795
38834	Corinth	11,329	11,581
39532	D'Iberville(u)	NA	7,288
39437	Ellisville	5,362	4,643
38701	Greenville	40,444	39,648
38930	Greenwood	20,151	22,400
38901	Grenada	11,167	9,944
39501	Gulfport	44,666	40,791
39401	Hattiesburg	41,397	38,277
38635	Holly Springs	5,918	5,728
38751	Indianola	8,905	8,947
*39205	Jackson	190,791	153,968
39090	Kosciusko	6,652	7,266
39440	Laurel	23,681	24,145
38756	Leland	5,896	6,000
39560	Long Beach	8,265	6,170
39339	Louisville	6,365	6,626
39648	McComb	12,364	11,969
39301	Meridian	44,027	45,083
39563	Moss Point	20,379	19,321
39120	Natchez	23,368	19,704
38652	New Albany	6,769	6,426
39564	Ocean Springs	15,612	9,580
38655	Oxford City	11,408	13,846
39567	Pascagoula	31,170	27,264
39571	Pass Christian	5,259	2,979
39208	Pearl	19,419	9,623
39465	Petal	9,245	6,986

ZIP code	Place	Area code	1980	1970
39350	Philadelphia		*6,263*	6,274
39466	Picayune		*10,297*	10,467
38668	Senatobia		*5,246*	4,247
38671	Southaven(u)		NA	8,931
39759	Starkville		*14,128*	11,369
38801	Tupelo		*23,934*	20,471
39180	Vicksburg		*31,016*	25,478
39501	West Gulfport(u)		NA	6,996
39773	West Point		*8,336*	8,714
38967	Winona		*5,591*	5,521
39194	Yazoo City		12,098	11,688

Missouri

ZIP code	Place	Area code	1980	1970
63123	Affton(u)	(314)	NA	24,264
63010	Arnold	(314)	*21,503*	17,381
65605	Aurora	(417)	*6,086*	5,359
63011	Ballwin	(314)	*15,655*	10,656
63137	Bellefontaine Neighbors	(314)	*12,510*	14,084
63133	Bel-Ridge	(314)	*5,302*	5,346
64012	Belton	(816)	*14,098*	12,179
63134	Berkeley	(314)	*16,228*	19,743
63031	Black Jack	(314)	*5,817*	4,145
64015	Blue Springs	(816)	*19,146*	6,779
65613	Bolivar	(417)	*5,259*	5,029
65233	Boonville	(816)	*7,178*	7,514
63114	Breckenridge Hills	(816)	*7,320*	7,011
63144	Brentwood	(314)	*9,493*	11,248
63044	Bridgeton	(314)	*17,792*	19,992
64628	Brookfield	(816)	*5,066*	5,491
63701	Cape Girardeau	(314)	*33,473*	31,282
64836	Carthage	(417)	*10,610*	11,035
63830	Caruthersville	(314)	*7,245*	7,350
63834	Charleston	(314)	NA	5,131
64601	Chillicothe	(816)	*9,491*	9,519
63105	Clayton	(314)	*15,007*	16,100
64735	Clinton	(816)	*7,476*	7,504
65201	Columbia	(314)	*65,781*	58,812
63128	Concord(u)	(314)	NA	21,217
63126	Crestwood	(314)	*15,305*	15,123
63141	Creve Coeur	(314)	*10,937*	8,967
63136	Dellwood	(314)	*6,955*	7,137
63020	De Soto	(314)	*5,625*	5,984
63131	Des Peres	(314)	*8,355*	5,333
63841	Dexter	(314)	*6,257*	6,024
63011	Ellisville	(314)	*5,152*	4,681
64024	Excelsior Springs	(816)	*11,311*	9,411
63640	Farmington	(314)	*7,486*	6,590
63135	Ferguson	(314)	*25,850*	28,759
63028	Festus	(314)	*7,925*	7,530
*63033	Florissant	(314)	*70,387*	65,908
65473	Fort Leonard Wood(u)	(314)	NA	33,799
65251	Fulton	(314)	*11,418*	12,248
64118	Gladstone	(816)	*31,745*	23,422
63122	Glendale	(314)	*6,690*	6,981
64030	Grandview	(816)	*23,669*	17,456
63401	Hannibal	(314)	*17,709*	18,609
64701	Harrisonville	(816)	*6,166*	5,052
*63042	Hazelwood	(314)	*13,807*	14,082
*64051	Independence	(816)	*112,544*	111,630
63755	Jackson	(314)	*7,120*	5,896
65101	Jefferson City	(314)	*37,749*	32,407
63136	Jennings	(314)	*16,724*	19,379
64801	Joplin	(417)	*41,061*	39,256
*64108	Kansas City	(816)	*456,907*	507,330
63857	Kennett	(314)	*10,187*	10,090
63140	Kinloch	(314)	*5,654*	5,629
63501	Kirksville	(816)	*15,392*	15,560
63122	Kirkwood	(314)	*30,535*	31,679
63124	Ladue	(314)	*10,867*	10,359
65536	Lebanon	(417)	*8,276*	8,616
64063	Lee's Summit	(816)	*24,401*	16,230
63125	Lemay(u)	(314)	NA	40,529
64068	Liberty	(816)	*15,944*	13,704
63552	Macon	(816)	*5,467*	5,301
63863	Malden	(314)	*6,448*	5,374
63011	Manchester	(314)	*9,629*	5,031
63143	Maplewood	(314)	*10,540*	12,785
65340	Marshall	(816)	*11,370*	12,051
63043	Maryland Heights(u)	(314)	NA	8,805
64468	Maryville	(816)	*9,193*	9,970
65265	Mexico	(314)	*11,847*	11,807
65270	Moberly	(816)	*12,917*	12,988
65708	Monett	(417)	*5,885*	5,937
64850	Neosho	(417)	*8,690*	7,517
64772	Nevada	(417)	*9,027*	9,736
63121	Normandy	(314)	*6,089*	6,236
64116	North Kansas City	(816)	NA	5,183
63121	North Woods	(314)	*6,902*	6,047
63366	O'Fallon	(314)	*9,540*	7,018
63124	Olivette	(314)	*8,598*	9,156
63114	Overland	(314)	*21,667*	24,819
63775	Perryville	(314)	*6,397*	5,149
63120	Pine Lawn	(314)	*5,867*	5,745
63901	Poplar Bluff	(314)	*17,189*	16,653
64133	Raytown	(816)	*32,513*	33,306
63117	Richmond Heights	(314)	*12,345*	13,802
63124	Rock Hill	(314)	*6,506*	6,815
65401	Rolla	(314)	*15,563*	13,571
63074	St. Ann	(314)	*16,652*	18,215
63301	St. Charles	(314)	*41,724*	31,834
63114	St. John	(314)	*8,712*	8,960
*64501	St. Joseph	(816)	NA	72,748
*63155	St. Louis	(314)	*508,496*	622,236
63126	Sappington(u)	(314)	NA	10,603
65301	Sedalia	(816)	*22,169*	22,847
63119	Shrewsbury	(314)	*5,597*	5,896
63801	Sikeston	(314)	*17,251*	14,699
63138	Spanish Lake(u)	(314)	NA	15,647
*65801	Springfield	(417)	*138,833*	120,096
63080	Sullivan	(314)	*5,067*	5,111
64683	Trenton	(816)	*6,405*	6,063
63084	Union	(314)	*6,097*	5,183
63130	University City	(314)	*44,159*	47,527
64093	Warrensburg	(816)	*15,342*	13,125
63090	Washington	(314)	*9,356*	8,499
64870	Webb City	(417)	*6,753*	6,811
63119	Webster Groves	(314)	*24,262*	27,457
63112	Wellston	(314)	*6,271*	7,050
65775	West Plains	(417)	*7,764*	6,893
63134	Woodson Terrace	(314)	*5,473*	5,880

Montana (406)

ZIP code	Place	Area code	1980	1970
59711	Anaconda-Deer Lodge		*13,976*	15,652
*59101	Billings		68,317	61,581
59715	Bozeman		21,611	18,670
59701	Butte-Silver Bow		37,044	41,981
59701	Floral Park(u)		NA	5,113
59330	Glendive		*5,872*	6,305
*59401	Great Falls		56,568	60,091
59501	Havre		10,842	10,558
59601	Helena		23,818	22,730
59901	Kalispell		10,299	10,526
59044	Laurel		*5,450*	4,454
59457	Lewistown		*7,037*	6,437
59047	Livingston		*7,164*	6,883
59402	Malmstrom(u)		NA	8,374
59301	Miles City		*9,574*	9,023
59801	Missoula		33,027	29,497
59801	Missoula West(u)		NA	9,148
59270	Sidney		*5,085*	4,543

Nebraska

ZIP code	Place	Area code	1980	1970
69301	Alliance	(308)	*8,860*	6,862
68310	Beatrice	(402)	*11,260*	12,389
68005	Bellevue	(402)	*23,510*	21,953
68008	Blair	(402)	*6,352*	6,106
69337	Chadron	(308)	*5,210*	5,921
68601	Columbus	(402)	17,317	15,471
68025	Fremont	(402)	*23,626*	22,962
69341	Gering	(308)	*7,288*	5,639
68801	Grand Island	(308)	33,159	32,358
68901	Hastings	(402)	23,019	23,580
68949	Holdrege	(308)	*5,778*	5,635
68847	Kearney	(308)	21,149	19,181
68128	La Vista	(402)	*11,489*	4,807
68850	Lexington	(308)	*6,711*	5,654
*68501	Lincoln	(402)	*166,311*	149,518
69001	McCook	(308)	*8,428*	8,285
68410	Nebraska City	(402)	*7,160*	7,441
68701	Norfolk	(402)	*18,077*	16,607
69101	North Platte	(308)	24,475	19,447
68113	Offutt East(u)	(402)	NA	5,195
68113	Offutt West(u)	(402)	NA	8,445
69153	Ogallala	(308)	*5,764*	4,976
*68108	Omaha	(402)	*368,347*	346,929
68046	Papillion	(402)	*7,941*	5,606
68048	Plattsmouth	(402)	*7,096*	6,371
69361	Scottsbluff	(308)	14,136	14,507
68434	Seward	(402)	*5,492*	5,294
69162	Sidney	(308)	*6,060*	6,403
68776	South Sioux City	(402)	*8,836*	7,920
68467	York	(402)	*7,412*	6,778

Nevada (702)

ZIP code	Place	Area code	1980	1970
89005	Boulder City		*7,247*	5,223
89701	Carson City		*29,694*	15,468
89112	East Las Vegas(u)		NA	6,501
89801	Elko		*8,907*	7,621
89301	Ely		*5,479*	6,216
89015	Henderson		22,001	16,395
*89114	Las Vegas		164,275	125,787
89110	Nellis(u)		NA	6,449
89030	North Las Vegas		42,668	45,542
89109	Paradise(u)		NA	24,477
*89501	Reno		*91,986*	72,863
89431	Sparks		*36,953*	24,187
89110	Sunrise Manor(u)		NA	9,684
89109	Vegas Creek(u)		NA	8,970
89101	Winchester(u)		NA	13,981

New Hampshire (603)

See note on page 933

ZIP code	Place	Area code	1980	1970
03102	*Bedford*		NA	5,859
03570	Berlin		13,090	15,256
03743	Claremont		*13,740*	14,221

ZIP code	Place	1980	1970
03301	Concord	30,360	30,022
03038	Derry Compact(u)	NA	6,090
.....	*Derry*	18,799	11,712
03820	Dover	22,265	20,850
03824	Durham Compact(u)	NA	7,221
.....	*Durham*	10,657	8,869
03833	Exeter Compact(u)	NA	6,439
.....	*Exeter*	10,983	8,892
03235	Franklin	*7,460*	7,292
03045	*Goffstown*	11,319	9,284
03842	Hampton Compact(u)	NA	5,407
.....	*Hampton*	10,437	8,011
03755	Hanover Compact(u)	NA	6,147
.....	*Hanover*	NA	8,494
03106	*Hooksett*	NA	5,564
03061	*Hudson*	13,977	10,638
03431	Keene	21,385	20,467
03246	Laconia	15,579	14,888
03766	Lebanon	11,052	9,725
03516	*Littleton*	NA	5,290
03053	*Londonderry*	13,522	5,346
*03101	Manchester	90,757	87,754
03054	*Merrimack*	15,437	8,595
03055	*Milford*	NA	6,622
03060	Nashua	67,817	55,820
03773	*Newport*	*64,226*	5,899
03076	*Pelham*	NA	5,408
03801	Portsmouth	26,214	25,717
03867	Rochester	21,579	17,938
03079	*Salem*	24,100	20,142
03874	*Seabrook*	NA	3,053
03878	Somersworth	10,313	9,026

New Jersey

ZIP code	Place	Area code	1980	1970
08201	Absecon	(609)	*6,892*	6,094
07401	Allendale	(201)	*6,078*	6,240
07712	Asbury Park	(201)	*15,112*	16,533
*08401	Atlantic City	(609)	*41,978*	47,859
08106	Audubon	(609)	*9,750*	10,802
08007	Barrington	(609)	*7,820*	8,409
07002	Bayonne	(201)	64,982	72,743
08722	Beachwood	(201)	*7,166*	4,390
07109	Belleville	(201)	*36,428*	37,629
08030	Bellmawr	(609)	13,658	15,618
07719	Belmar	(201)	*6,023*	5,782
07621	Bergenfield	(201)	*26,516*	29,000
07922	Berkeley Hts. Twp.	(201)	12,496	13,078
08009	Berlin	(609)	*5,583*	4,997
07924	Bernardsville	(201)	*6,639*	6,652
07003	Bloomfield	(201)	*49,318*	52,029
07403	Bloomingdale	(201)	*7,927*	7,797
07603	Bogota	(201)	*8,151*	8,960
07005	Boonton	(201)	*8,697*	9,261
08805	Bound Brook	(201)	*9,607*	10,450
08723	Brick Twp	(201)	NA	35,057
08302	Bridgeton	(609)	*19,664*	20,435
08203	Brigantine	(609)	*8,501*	6,741
08015	Browns Mills(u)	(609)	NA	7,144
08016	Burlington	(609)	*11,479*	12,010
07405	Butler	(201)	*7,697*	7,051
07006	Caldwell	(201)	*7,896*	8,677
*08101	Camden	(609)	84,763	102,551
08701	Candlewood(u)	(201)	NA	5,629
07072	Carlstadt	(201)	*6,268*	6,724
07008	Carteret	(201)	*20,870*	23,137
07009	Cedar Grove Twp.	(201)	NA	15,582
07928	Chatham	(201)	*8,962*	9,566
*08002	Cherry Hill Twp.	(609)	68,706	64,395
08077	Cinaminson Twp.	(609)	NA	16,962
07066	Clark Twp.	(201)	16,647	18,829
08312	Clayton	(609)	*5,947*	5,193
08021	Clementon	(609)	*5,874*	4,492
07010	Cliffside Park	(201)	21,425	18,891
07721	Cliffwood-Cliffwood Beach(u)	(201)	NA	7,056
*07015	Clifton	(201)	*74,427*	82,437
07624	Closter	(201)	*8,331*	8,604
08108	Collingswood	(609)	15,897	17,422
07016	Cranford Twp.	(201)	24,505	27,391
07626	Cresskill	(201)	*7,801*	8,298
08075	Delran Twp.	(609)	NA	10,065
07627	Demarest	(201)	*5,017*	5,133
07834	Denville Twp.	(201)	NA	14,045
08096	Deptford Twp.	(609)	NA	24,232
07801	Dover	(201)	*13,933*	15,039
07628	Dumont	(201)	*18,535*	20,155
08812	Dunellen	(201)	*6,513*	7,072
08816	East Brunswick Twp.	(201)	NA	34,166
*07019	East Orange	(201)	*70,499*	75,471
07073	East Rutherford	(201)	*8,147*	8,536
08520	East Windsor Twp.	(609)	NA	11,736
07724	Eatontown	(201)	*12,638*	14,619
08817	Edison Twp.	(201)	NA	67,120
07020	Edgewater	(201)	*5,111*	4,987
*07201	Elizabeth	(201)	105,384	112,654
07407	Elmwood Park	(201)	*19,205*	20,511
07630	Emerson	(201)	*7,948*	8,428
*07631	Englewood	(201)	*23,383*	24,985
07632	Englewood Cliffs	(201)	*5,996*	5,938
08053	Evesham Twp.	(609)	NA	13,477
08618	Ewing Twp.	(609)	NA	32,831
07701	Fair Haven	(201)	*5,854*	6,142
07410	Fair Lawn	(201)	*34,951*	37,975
07022	Fairview	(201)	10,511	10,698
07023	Fanwood	(201)	*8,284*	8,920
08518	Florence-Roebling(u)	(609)	NA	7,551
07932	Florham Park	(201)	*9,244*	8,094
08640	Fort Dix(u)	(609)	NA	26,290
07024	Fort Lee	(201)	*33,848*	30,631
07417	Franklin Lakes	(201)	*8,363*	7,550
07728	Freehold	(201)	*10,856*	10,545
07026	Garfield	(201)	*27,920*	30,797
08028	Glassboro	(609)	*14,392*	12,938
07028	Glen Ridge	(201)	*7,951*	8,518
07452	Glen Rock	(201)	*11,923*	13,011
08030	Gloucester City	(609)	13,103	14,707
07093	Guttenberg	(201)	*7,975*	5,754
*07602	Hackensack	(201)	*37,207*	36,008
07840	Hackettstown	(201)	*9,742*	9,472
08108	Haddon Twp.	(609)	15,879	18,192
08033	Haddonfield	(609)	12,345	13,118
08035	Haddon Heights	(609)	*8,828*	9,365
07508	Haledon	(201)	*5,963*	6,767
08037	Hammonton	(609)	*11,838*	11,464
07981	Hanover Twp.	(201)	NA	10,700
07029	Harrison	(201)	12,205	11,811
07604	Hasbrouck Heights	(201)	*12,515*	13,651
07506	Hawthorne	(201)	*17,428*	19,173
07730	Hazlet Twp.	(201)	NA	22,239
08904	Highland Park	(609)	*13,474*	14,385
08520	Hightstown	(609)	*5,183*	5,431
07642	Hillsdale	(201)	*11,259*	11,768
07205	Hillside Twp.	(201)	21,433	21,636
07030	Hoboken	(201)	42,378	45,380
07843	Hopatcong	(201)	*13,713*	9,052
08560	Hopewell Twp. (Mercer)	(609)	NA	10,030
07111	Irvington	(201)	*54,986*	59,743
08527	Jackson Twp.	(201)	NA	18,276
*07303	Jersey City	(201)	222,764	260,350
07734	Keansburg	(201)	*9,599*	9,720
07032	Kearny	(201)	35,716	37,585
08824	Kendall Park(u)	(201)	NA	7,412
07033	Kenilworth	(201)	*8,592*	9,165
07735	Keyport	(201)	*7,174*	7,205
07405	Kinnelon	(201)	*8,040*	7,600
07034	Lake Hiawatha(u)	(201)	NA	11,389
07871	Lake Mohawk(u)	(201)	NA	6,262
07054	Lake Parsippany(u)	(201)	NA	7,488
08701	Lakewood(u)	(201)	NA	17,874
08879	Laurence Harbor(u)	(201)	NA	6,715
07605	Leonia	(201)	*8,064*	8,847
07035	Lincoln Park	(201)	*8,579*	9,034
07036	Linden	(201)	37,761	41,409
08021	Lindenwold	(609)	*18,377*	12,199
08221	Linwood	(609)	*6,464*	6,159
07424	Little Falls Twp.	(201)	NA	11,727
07643	Little Ferry	(201)	*9,256*	9,064
07739	Little Silver	(201)	*5,827*	6,010
07039	Livingston Twp.	(201)	NA	30,127
07644	Lodi	(201)	*24,323*	25,163
07740	Long Branch	(201)	*31,829*	31,774
07071	Lyndhurst Twp.	(201)	20,308	22,729
07940	Madison	(201)	*16,039*	16,710
08049	Magnolia	(609)	*5,617*	5,893
07430	Mahwah Twp.	(201)	NA	10,800
08736	Manasquan	(201)	*5,187*	4,971
08835	Manville	(201)	*12,012*	13,029
08052	Maple Shade Twp.	(609)	NA	16,464
07040	Maplewood Twp.	(201)	NA	24,932
08402	Margate City	(609)	*10,660*	10,576
07746	Marlboro Twp.	(201)	NA	12,273
08053	Marlton(u)	(609)	NA	10,180
07747	Matawan	(201)	*9,350*	9,136
07607	Maywood	(201)	*10,093*	11,087
07641	McGuire(u)	(609)	NA	10,933
08055	Medford Lakes	(609)	*5,881*	4,792
08619	Mercerville-Hamilton Sq.(u)	(609)	NA	24,465
08840	Metuchen	(201)	*14,583*	16,031
08846	Middlesex	(201)	*13,956*	15,038
07748	Middletown Twp.	(201)	NA	54,623
07432	Midland park	(201)	*7,701*	8,159
07041	Milburn Twp.	(201)	NA	21,089
08850	Milltown	(201)	*6,741*	6,470
08332	Millville	(609)	*24,391*	21,366
07434	Monroe Twp. (Gloucester)	(201)	NA	14,071
*07042	Montclair	(201)	*39,736*	44,043
07645	Montvale	(201)	*7,453*	7,327
07045	Montville Twp.	(201)	NA	11,846
08057	Moorestown-Lenola(u)	(609)	NA	14,179
07950	Morris Plains	(201)	*5,338*	5,540
07960	Morristown	(201)	*16,396*	17,662
07092	Mountainside	(201)	*7,068*	7,520
08059	Mount Ephraim	(609)	*5,025*	5,625
08060	Mount Holly Twp.	(609)	NA	12,713
07753	Neptune Twp.	(201)	NA	27,863
07753	Neptune City	(201)	*5,866*	5,502
*07102	Newark	(201)	*314,412*	381,930
*08901	New Brunswick	(201)	*41,713*	41,885
08511	New Hanover	(201)	NA	27,410

ZIP code	Place		1980	1970
07646	New Milford	(201)	17,423	19,149
07974	New Providence	(201)	12,415	13,796
07724	New Shrewsbury	(201)	NA	8,395
07860	Newton	(201)	8,966	7,297
07032	North Arlington	(201)	16,525	18,096
07047	North Bergen Twp.	(201)	47,606	47,751
08902	North Brunswick Twp.	(201)	NA	16,691
07006	North Caldwell	(201)	6,647	6,733
08225	Northfield	(609)	7,928	8,646
07508	North Haledon	(201)	7,159	7,614
07060	North Plainfield	(201)	19,534	21,796
07647	Northvale	(201)	5,117	5,177
07110	Nutley	(201)	29,938	31,913
07755	Oakhurst(u)	(201)	NA	5,558
07436	Oakland	(201)	13,686	14,420
08226	Ocean City	(609)	12,513	10,575
07757	Oceanport	(201)	5,924	7,503
08857	Old Bridge(u)	(201)	NA	25,176
07649	Oradell	(201)	8,584	8,903
*07050	Orange	(201)	29,846	32,566
07650	Palisades Park	(201)	13,133	13,351
08065	Palmyra	(609)	7,696	6,969
07625	Paramus	(201)	27,388	28,381
07656	Park Ridge	(201)	8,998	8,709
*07055	Passaic	(201)	48,193	55,124
*07510	Paterson	(201)	145,426	144,824
08066	Paulsboro	(609)	7,204	8,084
08110	Pennsauken Twp.	(609)	33,750	36,394
08069	Penns Grove	(609)	5,270	5,727
08070	Pennsville Center(u)	(609)	NA	11,014
07440	Pequannock Twp.	(201)	NA	14,350
*08861	Perth Amboy	(201)	35,244	38,798
08865	Phillipsburg	(201)	17,438	17,849
08021	Pine Hill	(201)	8,241	5,132
08854	Piscataway Twp.	(201)	NA	36,418
08071	Pitman	(609)	9,420	10,257
*07061	Plainfield	(201)	45,368	46,862
08232	Pleasantville	(609)	13,791	14,007
08742	Point Pleasant	(201)	17,380	15,968
07442	Pompton Lakes	(201)	10,787	11,397
08540	Princeton	(609)	12,423	12,311
08540	Princeton North(u)	(609)	NA	5,488
*07065	Rahway	(201)	26,639	29,114
08057	Ramblewood(u)	(609)	NA	5,556
07446	Ramsey	(201)	12,398	12,571
07970	Randolph Twp.	(201)	NA	13,296
08869	Raritan	(201)	6,091	6,691
07701	Red Bank	(201)	12,067	12,847
07657	Ridgefield	(201)	10,293	11,308
07660	Ridgefield Park	(201)	12,854	13,990
*07451	Ridgewood	(201)	25,580	27,547
07456	Ringwood	(201)	12,497	10,393
07661	River Edge	(201)	11,579	12,850
08075	Riverside Twp.	(609)	NA	8,591
07662	Rochell Park Twp.	(201)	NA	6,380
07866	Rockaway	(201)	6,669	6,383
07068	Roseland	(201)	5,171	4,453
07203	Roselle	(201)	20,677	22,585
07204	Roselle Park	(201)	13,363	14,227
07760	Rumson	(201)	7,466	7,421
08078	Runnemede	(609)	9,740	10,475
*07070	Rutherford	(201)	19,011	20,802
07662	Saddle Brook Twp.	(201)	NA	15,975
08079	Salem	(609)	7,142	7,648
08872	Sayreville	(201)	31,130	32,508
07076	Scotch Plains Twp.	(201)	20,752	22,279
07094	Secaucus	(201)	13,677	13,228
08083	Somerdale	(609)	6,474	6,510
08244	Somers Point	(609)	9,786	7,919
08876	Somerville	(201)	13,104	13,652
08879	South Amboy	(201)	8,587	9,338
07079	South Orange	(201)	NA	16,971
07080	South Plainfield	(201)	20,679	21,142
08882	South River	(201)	14,765	15,428
07871	Sparta Twp.	(201)	NA	10,819
08884	Spotswood	(201)	8,060	7,891
07081	Springfield Twp.	(201)	13,927	15,740
07762	Spring Lake Heights	(201)	5,520	4,602
08084	Stratford	(609)	8,885	9,801
07747	Strathmore(u)	(609)	NA	7,674
07901	Summit	(201)	21,033	23,620
07666	Teaneck Twp.	(201)	NA	42,355
07670	Tenafly	(201)	13,807	14,827
07724	Tinton Falls	(201)	8,076	8,395
08753	Toms River	(201)	NA	7,303
07512	Totowa	(201)	11,022	11,580
*08608	Trenton	(609)	94,772	104,786
07083	Union Twp.	(201)	50,148	53,077
07735	Union Beach	(201)	6,195	6,472
07087	Union City	(201)	55,360	57,305
07458	Upper Saddle River	(201)	8,366	7,949
08406	Ventnor City	(609)	11,252	10,385
07044	Verona	(201)	14,675	15,067
08360	Vineland	(609)	52,701	46,050
07463	Waldwick	(201)	11,766	12,313
07057	Wallington	(201)	10,371	10,284
07465	Wanaque	(201)	8,984	8,636
07882	Washington	(201)	6,576	5,943
07675	Washington Twp. (Bergen)	(201)	NA	10,577
07060	Watchung	(201)	5,203	4,750
07470	Wayne Twp.	(201)	NA	49,141
07087	Weehawken Twp.	(201)	13,131	13,383
07006	West Caldwell	(201)	11,451	11,913
*07091	Westfield	(201)	30,324	33,720
07764	West Long Branch	(201)	7,108	6,845
07480	West Milford Twp.	(201)	NA	17,304
07093	West New York	(201)	39,101	40,627
07052	West Orange	(201)	41,053	43,715
07424	West Paterson	(201)	10,603	11,692
07675	Westwood	(201)	10,847	11,105
07885	Wharton	(201)	5,605	5,535
08610	White Horse-Yardville(u)	(609)	NA	18,680
07886	White Meadow Lake(u)	(201)	NA	8,499
08046	Willingboro Twp.	(609)	NA	43,386
08095	Winslow Twp.	(609)	NA	11,202
07095	Woodbridge Twp.	(201)	NA	98,944
08096	Woodbury	(609)	11,386	12,408
07675	Woodcliff Lake	(201)	5,719	5,506
07075	Wood-Ridge	(201)	8,055	8,311
07481	Wyckoff Twp.	(201)	NA	16,039

New Mexico (505)

ZIP code	Place	1980	1970
88310	Alamogordo	24,018	23,035
*87101	Albuquerque	295,150	243,751
88210	Artesia	10,430	10,315
87410	Aztec	5,201	3,354
87002	Belen	6,317	4,823
88101	Cannon(u)	NA	5,461
88220	Carlsbad	25,592	21,297
88101	Clovis	30,474	28,495
88030	Deming	10,038	8,343
87532	Espanola	7,769	5,934
87401	Farmington	31,792	21,979
87301	Gallup	18,293	14,596
87020	Grants	11,854	8,768
88240	Hobbs	28,708	26,025
88330	Holloman(u)	NA	8,001
88001	Las Cruces	44,902	37,857
87701	Las Vegas	14,727	14,320
87544	Los Alamos(u)	NA	11,310
88260	Lovington	9,392	8,915
87107	North Valley(u)	NA	10,366
88130	Portales	10,408	10,554
87740	Raton	7,658	6,962
88201	Roswell	39,698	33,908
87115	Sandia(u)	NA	6,867
87501	Santa Fe	46,162	41,167
88061	Silver City	9,858	8,557
87801	Socorro	6,481	5,849
87105	South Valley(u)	NA	29,389
87901	Truth or Consequences	5,467	4,656
88401	Tucumcari	7,229	7,189

New York

ZIP code	Place		1980	1970
*12207	Albany	(518)	115,781	115,781
11507	Albertson(u)	(516)	NA	6,825
14411	Albion	(716)	5,683	5,122
14802	Alfred	(607)	5,118	3,804
11701	Amityville	(516)	8,426	9,794
12010	Amsterdam	(518)	23,344	25,524
12603	Arlington(u)	(914)	NA	11,203
13021	Auburn	(315)	32,020	34,599
*11702	Babylon	(516)	14,119	12,897
11510	Baldwin(u)	(516)	NA	34,525
13027	Baldwinsville	(315)	7,625	6,298
12020	Balston Spa	(518)	5,694	4,968
14020	Batavia	(716)	16,667	17,338
14810	Bath	(607)	6,255	6,053
11705	Bayport(u)	(516)	NA	8,232
11706	Bay Shore(u)	(516)	NA	11,119
11709	Bayville	(516)	6,735	6,147
12508	Beacon	(914)	11,945	13,255
11710	Bellmore(u)	(516)	NA	18,431
11714	Bethpage(u)	(516)	NA	18,555
*13902	Binghamton	(607)	55,745	64,123
10913	Blauvelt(u)	(914)	NA	5,426
11716	Bohemia(u)	(516)	NA	8,926
11717	Brentwood(u)	(516)	NA	28,327
10510	Briarcliff Manor	(914)	5,917	6,521
14420	Brockport	(716)	12,361	7,878
10708	Bronxville	(914)	6,260	6,674
*14240	Buffalo	(716)	357,002	462,768
14424	Canandaigua	(716)	12,508	10,488
13032	Canastota	(315)	5,039	5,033
13617	Canton	(315)	7,363	6,398
11514	Carle Place(u)	(516)	NA	6,326
12414	Catskill	(518)	5,563	5,317
11516	Cedarhurst	(516)	6,889	6,941
11720	Centereach(u)	(516)	NA	9,427
11722	Central Islip(u)	(516)	NA	36,391
12065	Clifton Knolls(u)	(518)	NA	5,771
12043	Cobleskill	(518)	5,056	6,277
12047	Cohoes	(518)	17,592	18,653
12205	Colonie	(518)	8,870	8,701
11725	Commack(u)	(516)	NA	24,138
10920	Congers(u)	(914)	NA	5,928
11726	Copiague(u)	(516)	NA	19,632
14830	Corning	(607)	13,997	15,792
13045	Cortland	(607)	20,094	19,621

ZIP code	Place		1980	1970
10520	Croton-on-Hudson	(914)	*8,597*	7,523
14437	Dansville	(716)	*5,148*	5,436
11729	Deer Park(u)	(516)	NA	32,274
14043	Depew	(716)	*19,819*	22,158
13214	DeWitt(u)	(315)	NA	10,032
11746	Dix Hills(u)	(516)	NA	10,050
10522	Dobbs Ferry	(914)	*11,459*	10,353
14048	Dunkirk	(716)	*15,663*	16,855
14052	East Aurora	(716)	*7,757*	7,033
10709	Eastchester(u)	(914)	NA	23,750
12302	East Glenville(u)	(518)	NA	5,898
11746	East Half Hollow Hills(u)	(516)	NA	9,691
11576	East Hills	(516)	*8,540*	8,624
11730	East Islip(u)	(516)	NA	6,861
11758	East Massapequa(u)	(516)	NA	15,926
11554	East Meadow(u)	(516)	NA	46,290
11743	East Neck(u)	(516)	NA	5,221
11731	East Northport(u)	(516)	NA	12,392
11772	East Patchogue(u)	(516)	NA	8,092
14445	East Rochester	(716)	*8,524*	8,347
11518	East Rockaway	(516)	*11,546*	11,795
13902	East Vestal(u)	(607)	NA	10,472
*14901	Elmira	(607)	35,363	39,945
11003	Elmont(u)	(516)	NA	29,363
11731	Elwood(u)	(516)	NA	15,031
13760	Endicott	(607)	14,457	16,556
13760	Endwell(u)	(607)	NA	15,999
13219	Fairmount(u)	(315)	NA	15,317
14450	Fairport	(716)	*7,399*	6,474
12601	Fairview(u)	(914)	NA	8,517
11735	Farmingdale	(516)	*8,764*	9,297
13066	Fayetteville	(315)	*5,320*	4,996
*11001	Floral Park	(516)	*18,192*	18,466
11010	Franklin Square(u)	(516)	NA	32,156
14063	Fredonia	(716)	*11,194*	10,326
11520	Freeport	(516)	*39,818*	40,374
13069	Fulton	(315)	*13,381*	14,003
11530	Garden City	(516)	*26,904*	25,373
11040	Garden City Park(u)	(516)	NA	7,488
14454	Geneseo	(716)	*6,655*	5,714
14456	Geneva	(315)	*15,728*	16,793
11542	Glen Cove	(516)	*25,305*	25,770
12801	Glens Falls	(518)	*17,088*	17,222
12078	Gloversville	(518)	*18,322*	19,677
10924	Goshen	(914)	*5,374*	4,342
*11022	Great Neck	(516)	*6,011*	10,798
11740	Greenlawn(u)	(516)	NA	8,493
11746	Half Hollow Hills(u)	(516)	NA	12,081
14075	Hamburg	(716)	10,591	10,215
10528	Harrison	(914)	*21,878*	21,544
10530	Hartsdale(u)	(914)	NA	12,226
10706	Hastings-on-Hudson	(914)	*8,580*	9,479
11787	Hauppauge(u)	(516)	NA	13,957
10927	Haverstraw	(914)	*8,930*	8,198
*11551	Hempstead	(516)	*40,245*	39,411
13350	Herkimer	(315)	*7,983*	8,960
11040	Herricks(u)	(516)	NA	9,112
11557	Hewlett(u)	(516)	NA	6,796
*11802	Hicksville(u)	(516)	NA	49,820
10977	Hillcrest(u)	(914)	NA	5,357
11741	Holbrook-Holtsville(u)	(516)	NA	12,103
14843	Hornell	(607)	*10,451*	12,144
14845	Horseheads	(607)	*8,158*	7,989
12534	Hudson	(518)	*7,725*	8,940
12839	Hudson Falls	(518)	*7,586*	7,917
11743	Huntington(u)	(516)	NA	12,601
11746	Huntington Station(u)	(516)	NA	28,817
13357	Ilion	(315)	*9,311*	9,808
11696	Inwood(u)	(516)	NA	8,433
10533	Irvington	(914)	*5,817*	5,878
11558	Island Park	(516)	*5,246*	5,396
11751	Islip(u)	(516)	NA	7,692
14850	Ithaca	(607)	23,560	26,226
14701	Jamestown	(716)	*35,634*	39,795
10535	Jefferson Valley-Yorktown(u)	(914)	NA	9,008
11753	Jericho(u)	(516)	NA	14,010
13790	Johnson City	(607)	17,115	18,025
12095	Johnstown	(518)	*9,634*	10,045
14217	Kenmore	(716)	18,475	20,980
11754	Kings Park(u)	(516)	NA	5,555
11024	Kings Point	(516)	*5,915*	5,614
12401	Kingston	(914)	*23,382*	25,544
14218	Lackawanna	(716)	*22,730*	28,657
11755	Lake Grove	(516)	*10,164*	8,133
14086	Lancaster	(716)	13,049	13,365
10538	Larchmont	(914)	*6,955*	7,203
12110	Latham(u)	(914)	NA	9,661
11559	Lawrence	(516)	*6,643*	6,566
14482	Le Roy	(716)	*5,330*	5,118
11756	Levittown(u)	(516)	NA	65,440
11757	Lindenhurst	(516)	*29,855*	28,359
13365	Little Falls	(315)	*6,848*	7,629
14094	Lockport	(716)	*24,857*	25,399
11791	Locust Grove(u)	(516)	NA	11,626
11561	Long Beach(u)	(516)	*32,559*	33,127
12211	Loudonville(u)	(518)	NA	9,299
11563	Lynbrook	(516)	*22,964*	23,151
10541	Mahopac(u)	(914)	NA	5,265
12953	Malone	(518)	*7,524*	8,048
11565	Malverne	(516)	*9,955*	10,036
10543	Mamaroneck	(914)	*18,031*	18,909
11030	Manhasset(u)	(516)	NA	8,541
13104	Manlius	(315)	*5,050*	4,295
11050	Manorhaven	(516)	*5,697*	5,488
11758	Massapequa(u)	(516)	NA	26,821
11762	Massapequa Park	(516)	20,847	22,112
13662	Massena	(315)	*12,835*	14,042
13211	Mattydale(u)	(315)	NA	8,292
12118	Mechanicville	(518)	*5,671*	6,247
14103	Medina	(716)	*6,441*	6,415
11746	Melville(u)	(516)	NA	6,641
11566	Merrick(u)	(516)	NA	25,904
10940	Middletown	(914)	*26,277*	22,607
11501	Mineola	(516)	*20,625*	21,845
10950	Monroe	(914)	*5,177*	4,439
10952	Monsey(u)	(914)	NA	8,797
12701	Monticello	(914)	*6,420*	5,991
10549	Mt. Kisco	(914)	*8,245*	8,172
*10551	Mount Vernon	(914)	*73,654*	72,788
10954	Nanuet(u)	(914)	NA	10,447
11767	Nesconset(u)	(516)	NA	10,048
14513	Newark	(315)	NA	11,644
12550	Newburgh	(914)	*27,607*	26,219
11590	New Cassel(u)	(516)	NA	8,721
10956	New City(u)	(914)	NA	27,344
11040	New Hyde Park	(516)	*9,688*	10,116
12561	New Paltz	(914)	*6,642*	6,058
*10802	New Rochelle	(914)	*70,861*	75,385
*12550	New Windsor Center(u)	(914)	NA	8,803
*10001	New York	(212)	*7,134,542*	7,895,563
*10451	Bronx	(212)	NA	1,471,701
*11201	Brooklyn	(212)	NA	2,602,102
*10001	Manhattan	(212)	NA	1,539,233
*(Q)	Queens	(212)	NA	1,987,174

(Q) There are 4 P.O.s for Queens: 11101 for L.I. City; 11690 Far Rockaway; 11351 Flushing; and 11431 Jamaica.

ZIP code	Place		1980	1970
*10314	Staten Island	(212)	NA	295,443
*14302	Niagara Falls	(716)	71,344	85,615
13745	Nimmonsburg-Chenango Br.(u)	(607)	NA	5,059
12309	Niskayuna(u)	(518)	NA	6,186
11701	North Amityville(u)	(516)	NA	11,936
11703	North Babylon(u)	(516)	NA	39,526
11710	North Bellmore(u)	(516)	NA	22,893
11713	North Bellport(u)	(516)	NA	5,903
11752	North Great River(u)	(516)	NA	12,080
11757	North Lindenhurst(u)	(516)	NA	11,117
11758	North Massapequa(u)	(516)	NA	23,123
11566	North Merrick(u)	(516)	NA	13,650
11040	North New Hyde Park(u)	(516)	NA	18,154
11772	North Patchogue(u)	(516)	NA	5,232
11768	Northport	(516)	*8,272*	7,494
13212	North Syracuse	(315)	*8,956*	8,687
10591	North Tarrytown	(914)	*8,041*	8,334
14120	North Tonawanda	(716)	35,717	36,012
11580	North Valley Stream(u)	(516)	NA	14,881
11793	North Wantagh(u)	(516)	NA	15,053
13815	Norwich	(607)	*8,238*	8,843
10960	Nyack	(914)	*6,185*	6,659
11769	Oakdale(u)	(516)	NA	7,334
11572	Oceanside(u)	(516)	NA	35,372
13669	Ogdensburg	(315)	*12,641*	14,554
11804	Old Bethpage(u)	(516)	NA	7,084
14760	Olean	(716)	*17,766*	19,169
13421	Oneida	(315)	*11,035*	11,658
13820	Oneonta	(607)	*14,982*	16,030
10562	Ossining	(914)	*20,127*	21,659
13126	Oswego	(315)	*20,951*	20,923
11771	Oyster Bay(u)	(516)	NA	6,822
11772	Patchogue	(516)	*11,714*	11,582
10965	Pearl River(u)	(914)	NA	17,146
10566	Peekskill	(914)	*20,463*	19,283
10803	Pelham	(914)	*7,079*	7,260
10803	Pelham Manor	(914)	*6,407*	6,673
14527	Penn Yan	(315)	*5,119*	5,293
11714	Plainedge(u)	(516)	NA	10,759
11803	Plainview(u)	(516)	NA	31,695
12901	Plattsburg	(518)	*20,681*	18,715
12903	Plattsburgh Base(u)	(518)	NA	7,078
10570	Pleasantville	(914)	*7,241*	7,110
10573	Port Chester	(914)	*22,903*	25,803
11777	Port Jefferson	(516)	*6,122*	5,515
11776	Port Jefferson Station(u)	(516)	NA	7,403
12771	Port Jervis	(914)	*8,483*	8,852
11050	Port Washington(u)	(516)	NA	15,923
13676	Potsdam	(315)	*11,430*	10,303
*12601	Poughkeepsie	(914)	*31,200*	32,029
12144	Rensselaer	(518)	*9,035*	10,136
11901	Riverhead(u)	(516)	NA	7,585
*14603	Rochester	(716)	241,539	295,011
*11570	Rockville Centre	(516)	*27,108*	27,444
12205	Roessleville(u)	(518)	NA	5,476
13440	Rome	(315)	*46,314*	50,148
11779	Ronkonkoma(u)	(516)	NA	7,284
11575	Roosevelt(u)	(516)	NA	15,008
11577	Roslyn Heights(u)	(516)	NA	7,242
12303	Rotterdam(u)	(518)	NA	25,214
10580	Rye	(914)	*15,639*	15,869
11780	St. James(u)	(516)	NA	10,500
14779	Salamanca	(716)	*7,034*	7,877

ZIP code	Place		1980	1970
11754	San Remo(u)	(516)	NA	8,302
12983	Saranac Lake	(518)	5,158	6,086
12866	Saratoga Springs	(518)	23,477	18,845
11782	Sayville(u)	(516)	NA	11,680
10583	Scarsdale	(914)	18,969	19,229
*12301	Schenectady	(518)	71,676	77,958
12302	Scotia	(518)	6,939	7,370
11579	Sea Cliff	(516)	5,561	5,890
11783	Seaford(u)	(516)	NA	17,379
11784	Selden(u)	(516)	NA	11,613
13148	Seneca Falls	(315)	7,200	7,794
11733	Setauket-South Setauket(u)	(516)	NA	6,857
11967	Shirley(u)	(516)	NA	6,280
13209	Solvay	(315)	7,462	8,280
11735	South Farmingdale(u)	(516)	NA	20,464
11968	Southampton	(516)	5,438	4,904
11741	South Holbrook(u)	(516)	NA	6,700
11746	South Huntington(u)	(516)	NA	9,115
14904	Southport(u)	(607)	NA	8,685
11790	South Stony Brook(u)	(516)	NA	15,329
11581	South Valley Stream(u)	(516)	NA	6,595
11590	South Westbury(u)	(516)	NA	10,978
10977	Spring Valley	(914)	21,378	18,112
11790	Stony Brook(u)	(516)	NA	6,391
10980	Stony Point(u)	(914)	NA	8,270
10901	Suffern	(914)	10,110	8,273
11791	Syosset(u)	(516)	NA	10,084
*13201	Syracuse	(315)	174,899	197,297
10983	Tappan(u)	(914)	NA	7,424
10591	Tarrytown	(914)	11,555	11,115
10594	Thornwood(u)	(914)	NA	6,874
14150	Tonawanda	(716)	18,701	21,898
*12180	Troy	(518)	58,209	62,918
10707	Tuckahoe	(914)	5,880	6,236
11553	Uniondale(u)	(516)	NA	22,077
*13503	Utica	(315)	78,718	91,340
10989	Valley Cottage(u)	(914)	NA	6,007
*11580	Valley Stream	(516)	38,924	40,413
11731	Vernon Valley(u)	(516)	NA	7,925
13850	Vestal-Twin Orchards(u)	(607)	NA	8,303
10901	Viola(u)	(914)	NA	5,136
12586	Walden	(914)	5,596	5,277
11793	Wantagh(u)	(516)	NA	21,783
12590	Wappingers Falls	(914)	6,469	5,607
13165	Waterloo	(315)	5,446	5,418
13601	Watertown	(315)	27,726	30,787
12189	Watervliet	(518)	11,693	12,404
14580	Webster	(716)	5,610	5,037
14895	Wellsville	(716)	5,568	5,815
11758	West Amityville(u)	(516)	NA	6,424
11704	West Babylon(u)	(516)	NA	12,893
11590	Westbury	(516)	14,666	15,362
14905	West Elmira(u)	(607)	NA	5,901
10993	West Haverstraw	(914)	10,054	8,558
11552	West Hempstead(u)	(516)	NA	20,375
11795	West Islip(u)	(516)	NA	17,374
12203	Westmere(u)	(518)	NA	6,364
10994	West Nyack(u)	(914)	NA	5,510
11796	West Sayville(u)	(516)	NA	7,386
13219	Westvale(u)	(315)	NA	7,253
*10602	White Plains	(914)	47,196	50,346
14221	Williamsville	(716)	7,334	6,835
11596	Williston Park	(516)	9,011	9,154
11598	Woodmere(u)	(516)	NA	19,831
11798	Wyandach(u)	(516)	NA	15,716
11980	Yaphank(u)	(516)	NA	5,460
*10701	Yonkers	(914)	190,240	204,297
10598	Yorktown Heights(u)	(914)	NA	6,805

North Carolina

ZIP code	Place		1980	1970
27910	Ahoskie	(919)	5,181	5,105
28001	Albemarle	(704)	10,361	11,126
27263	Archdale	(919)	6,057	4,874
27203	Asheboro	(919)	16,112	15,351
*28801	Asheville	(704)	58,551	57,681
28012	Belmont	(704)	5,560	5,054
28016	Bessemer City	(704)	5,370	4,991
28607	Boone	(704)	11,905	8,754
28712	Brevard	(704)	5,807	5,243
27215	Burlington	(919)	36,853	35,930
28542	Camp Le Jeune Central(u)	(919)	NA	34,549
27510	Carrboro	(919)	9,031	5,058
27511	Cary	(919)	19,032	7,435
27514	Chapel Hill	(919)	36,020	25,537
*28202	Charlotte	(704)	299,444	241,178
28533	Cherry Point(u)	(919)	NA	12,029
28328	Clinton	(919)	8,644	7,157
28025	Concord	(704)	18,999	18,464
28334	Dunn	(919)	9,149	8,302
*27701	Durham	(919)	105,060	95,438
27288	Eden	(919)	15,460	15,871
27932	Edenton	(919)	5,477	4,956
27909	Elizabeth City	(919)	14,337	14,381
*28302	Fayetteville	(919)	59,476	53,510
28043	Forest City	(704)	7,365	7,179
28307	Fort Bragg(u)	(919)	NA	46,995
27529	Garner	(919)	11,550	6,921
28052	Gastonia	(704)	48,844	47,142
27530	Goldsboro	(919)	31,752	26,810
27253	Graham	(919)	9,475	8,172
*27420	Greensboro	(919)	163,493	144,076
27834	Greenville	(919)	32,960	29,063
27536	Henderson	(919)	13,276	13,896
28739	Hendersonville	(704)	8,232	6,443
28601	Hickory	(704)	20,459	20,569
*27260	High Point	(919)	68,339	63,229
28540	Jacksonville	(919)	17,580	16,289
28081	Kannapolis(u)	(704)	NA	36,293
27284	Kernersville	(919)	6,948	4,815
28086	Kings Mountain	(704)	8,286	8,465
28501	Kinston	(919)	25,110	23,020
28352	Laurinburg	(919)	11,479	8,859
28645	Lenoir	(704)	15,447	14,705
27292	Lexington	(704)	16,501	17,205
28092	Lincolnton	(704)	5,378	5,293
28358	Lumberton	(919)	18,187	16,961
28110	Monroe	(704)	11,328	11,282
28115	Moorsville	(704)	9,045	8,808
28557	Morehead City	(919)	5,942	5,233
28655	Morganton	(704)	13,745	13,625
27030	Mount Airy	(919)	7,864	7,325
28120	Mount Holly	(704)	5,262	5,107
28560	New Bern	(919)	14,545	14,660
28540	New River Gieger(u)	(919)	NA	8,699
28658	Newton	(704)	8,417	7,857
28012	North Belmont(u)	(704)	NA	10,672
27565	Oxford	(919)	7,222	7,178
*27611	Raleigh	(919)	138,410	123,793
27320	Reidsville	(919)	12,576	13,636
27870	Roanoke Rapids	(919)	14,296	13,508
28379	Rockingham	(919)	7,680	5,852
27801	Rocky Mount	(919)	40,627	34,284
27573	Roxboro	(919)	8,581	5,370
28144	Salisbury	(704)	24,923	22,515
27330	Sanford	(919)	15,822	11,716
27530	Seymour-Johnson(u)	(919)	NA	8,172
28150	Shelby	(704)	16,448	16,328
27344	Siler City	(919)	5,340	4,689
27577	Smithfield	(919)	7,675	6,677
28387	Southern Pines	(919)	8,205	5,937
28390	Spring Lake	(919)	5,921	5,279
28677	Statesville	(704)	21,555	20,007
27886	Tarboro	(919)	10,948	9,425
27360	Thomasville	(919)	15,245	15,230
27889	Washington	(919)	8,766	8,961
28786	Waynesville	(704)	8,171	6,488
28025	West Concord(u)	(704)	NA	5,347
28472	Whiteville	(919)	5,065	5,292
27892	Williamston	(919)	6,101	6,570
28401	Wilmington	(919)	41,848	46,169
27893	Wilson	(919)	34,038	29,347
*27102	Winston-Salem	(919)	140,438	133,683

North Dakota (701)

ZIP code	Place	1980	1970
58501	Bismarck	44,447	34,703
58301	Devils Lake	7,309	7,078
58601	Dickinson	15,893	12,405
58102	Fargo	61,281	53,365
58237	Grafton	5,636	5,946
58201	Grand Forks(u)	43,760	39,008
58201	Grand Forks Base(u)	NA	10,474
58401	Jamestown	16,281	15,385
58554	Mandan	15,378	11,093
58701	Minot	32,886	32,290
58701	Minot Base(u)	NA	12,077
58072	Valley City	6,991	7,843
58075	Wahpeton	8,799	7,076
58078	West Fargo	8,514	5,161
58801	Williston	13,354	11,280

Ohio

ZIP code	Place		1980	1970
45810	Ada	(419)	5,830	5,309
*44309	Akron	(216)	239,229	275,425
44601	Alliance	(216)	25,746	26,547
44001	Amherst	(216)	10,620	9,902
44805	Ashland	(419)	20,252	19,872
44004	Ashtabula	(216)	22,971	24,313
45701	Athens	(614)	21,341	23,310
44202	Aurora	(216)	9,159	6,549
44515	Austintown(u)	(216)	NA	29,393
44011	Avon	(216)	7,150	7,214
45404	Avondale(u)	(513)	NA	5,240
44012	Avon Lake	(216)	13,184	12,261
44203	Barberton	(216)	26,819	33,052
44140	Bay Village	(216)	17,889	18,163
44122	Beachwood	(216)	10,892	9,631
45305	Bellbrook	(513)	5,555	6,139
44146	Bedford	(216)	15,600	17,552
44146	Bedford Heights	(216)	13,187	13,063
43906	Bellaire	(614)	8,542	9,655
43311	Bellefontaine	(513)	11,003	11,255
44811	Bellevue	(419)	9,323	8,604
45714	Belpre	(614)	7,408	7,189
44017	Berea	(216)	19,686	22,465
43209	Bexley	(614)	14,734	14,888
43004	Blacklick Estates(u)	(614)	NA	8,351
45242	Blue Ash	(513)	10,485	8,324

ZIP code	Place		1980	1970
44512	Boardman(u)	(216)	NA	30,852
43402	Bowling Green	(419)	25,903	21,760
44141	Brecksville	(216)	10,188	9,137
45211	Bridgetown(u)	(513)	NA	13,352
44141	Broadview Heights	(216)	10,909	11,463
44144	Brooklyn	(216)	13,257	13,142
44142	Brook Park	(216)	26,195	30,774
44212	Brunswick	(216)	27,645	15,852
43506	Bryan	(419)	6,965	7,008
44820	Bucyrus	(419)	13,557	13,111
43725	Cambridge	(614)	12,660	13,656
44405	Campbell	(216)	11,591	12,577
44406	Canfield	(216)	6,850	5,459
*44711	Canton	(216)	96,339	110,053
45822	Celina	(419)	9,493	8,072
45459	Centerville	(513)	16,990	10,333
45211	Cheviot	(513)	9,583	11,135
45601	Chillicothe	(614)	23,384	24,842
44505	Churchill(u)	(216)	NA	7,457
*45234	Cincinnati	(513)	399,072	451,410
43113	Circleville	(614)	11,682	11,687
*44101	Cleveland	(216)	594,529	750,879
44118	Cleveland Heights	(216)	55,563	60,767
43410	Clyde	(419)	6,094	5,503
44408	Columbiana	(216)	5,607	4,959
*43216	Columbus	(614)	524,304	540,025
44030	Conneaut	(216)	13,839	14,552
43812	Coshocton	(614)	13,409	13,747
45238	Covedale(u)	(513)	NA	6,639
44827	Crestline	(419)	5,928	5,947
45341	Crystal Lakes(u)	(513)	NA	5,851
*44222	Cuyahoga Falls	(216)	44,293	49,678
*45401	Dayton	(513)	190,564	242,917
45236	Deer Park	(513)	6,456	7,415
43512	Defiance	(419)	16,084	16,281
43015	Delaware	(614)	19,924	15,008
45833	Delphos	(419)	7,431	7,608
44622	Dover	(216)	11,318	11,516
44112	East Cleveland	(216)	36,915	39,600
44094	Eastlake	(216)	21,954	19,690
43920	East Liverpool	(216)	21,587	20,020
43920	East Liverpool North(u)	(216)	NA	6,223
44413	East Palestine	(216)	6,110	5,604
45320	Eaton	(513)	6,838	6,020
*44035	Elyria	(216)	57,039	53,427
45322	Englewood	(513)	11,047	7,885
44117	Euclid	(216)	59,641	71,552
45324	Fairborn	(513)	33,259	32,267
45014	Fairfield	(513)	26,983	14,680
44313	Fairlawn	(216)	6,763	6,102
44126	Fairview Park	(216)	19,283	21,699
45840	Findlay	(419)	37,570	35,800
45405	Forest Park	(513)	20,240	15,139
45426	Fort McKinley(u)	(513)	NA	11,536
44830	Fostoria	(419)	11,232	16,037
45005	Franklin	(513)	11,228	10,075
43420	Fremont	(419)	17,887	18,490
43230	Gahanna	(614)	15,543	12,400
44833	Galion	(419)	13,325	13,123
45631	Gallipolis	(614)	7,153	7,490
44125	Garfield Heights	(216)	34,956	41,417
44041	Geneva	(216)	7,275	6,449
44420	Girard	(216)	12,506	14,119
45237	Golf Manor	(513)	5,111	5,170
43212	Grandview Heights	(614)	9,191	8,460
45218	Greenhills	(513)	5,427	6,092
45331	Greenville	(513)	12,863	12,380
43123	Grove City	(614)	17,993	13,911
*45012	Hamilton	(513)	67,535	67,865
45030	Harrison	(513)	5,769	5,731
43055	Heath	(614)	8,319	6,768
44124	Highland Heights	(216)	7,050	5,926
43026	Hilliard	(614)	8,946	8,369
45133	Hillsboro	(513)	6,070	5,584
44425	Hubbard	(216)	9,191	8,583
45424	Huber Heights(u)	(513)	NA	18,943
44839	Huron	(419)	7,604	6,896
44131	Independence	(216)	6,630	7,034
45243	Indian Hill	(513)	5,247	5,651
45638	Ironton	(614)	14,081	15,030
45640	Jackson	(614)	7,000	6,843
44240	Kent	(216)	26,323	28,183
43326	Kenton	(419)	8,102	8,315
45236	Kenwood(u)	(513)	NA	15,789
45429	Kettering	(513)	61,223	71,864
44094	Kirtland	(216)	6,327	5,530
45432	Knollwood(u)	(513)	NA	5,353
44107	Lakewood	(216)	61,921	70,173
43130	Lancaster	(614)	34,911	32,911
45036	Lebanon	(513)	8,438	7,934
*45802	Lima	(419)	50,602	53,734
45215	Lincoln Heights	(513)	6,233	6,099
43228	Lincoln Village(u)	(614)	NA	11,215
45215	Lockland	(513)	5,840	5,288
43138	Logan	(614)	6,131	6,269
43140	London	(614)	8,573	6,481
*44052	Lorain	(216)	73,743	78,185
44641	Louisville	(216)	6,913	6,298
45140	Loveland	(513)	9,039	7,144
44124	Lyndhurst	(216)	18,093	19,749
44056	Macedonia	(216)	6,207	6,375
45243	Madeira	(513)	10,186	6,713
44057	Madison North(u)	(216)	NA	6,882
*44901	Mansfield	(419)	56,704	55,047
44137	Maple Heights	(216)	29,731	34,093
45750	Marietta	(614)	16,400	16,861
43302	Marion	(614)	38,725	38,646
43935	Martins Ferry	(614)	9,837	10,757
43040	Marysville	(513)	8,374	5,744
45040	Mason	(513)	7,387	5,677
44646	Massillon	(216)	35,214	32,539
43537	Maumee	(419)	17,910	15,937
44124	Mayfield Heights	(216)	21,383	22,139
44256	Medina	(216)	15,309	10,913
44060	Mentor	(216)	41,903	36,912
44060	Mentor-on-the-Lake	(216)	8,231	6,517
45342	Miamisburg	(513)	15,896	14,797
44130	Middleburg Heights	(216)	16,228	12,367
45042	Middletown	(513)	47,958	48,767
44657	Minerva	(216)	6,014	4,614
44260	Mogadore	(216)	5,845	4,825
45242	Montgomery	(513)	6,106	5,683
45231	Mount Healthy	(513)	7,135	7,446
43050	Mount Vernon	(614)	15,615	13,373
43545	Napoleon	(419)	8,173	7,791
45764	Nelsonville	(614)	5,087	4,812
43055	Newark	(614)	39,947	41,836
45344	New Carlisle	(513)	6,480	6,112
44663	New Philadelphia	(216)	15,357	15,184
44444	Newton Falls	(216)	5,795	5,378
44446	Niles	(216)	25,676	21,581
44720	North Canton	(216)	17,390	15,228
45239	North College Hill	(513)	11,906	12,363
44070	North Olmsted	(216)	36,480	34,861
45414	Northridge(u)	(513)	NA	10,084
44039	North Ridgeville	(216)	21,240	13,152
44133	North Royalton	(216)	17,705	12,807
43619	Northwood	(419)	5,211	4,222
44203	Norton	(216)	13,820	12,308
44857	Norwalk	(419)	14,348	13,386
45212	Norwood	(513)	25,226	30,420
45419	Oakwood	(513)	8,692	10,095
44074	Oberlin	(216)	8,353	8,761
44138	Olmsted Falls	(216)	5,775	5,027
43616	Oregon	(419)	18,180	16,563
44667	Orrville	(216)	8,316	7,408
45431	Overlook-Page Manor(u)	(513)	NA	19,719
45056	Oxford	(513)	20,524	15,868
44077	Painesville	(216)	16,351	16,536
44077	Painesville Southwest(u)	(216)	NA	5,461
44129	Parma	(216)	92,578	100,219
44130	Parma Heights	(216)	23,054	27,192
44124	Pepper Pike	(216)	6,371	5,382
43551	Perrysburg	(419)	9,292	7,693
45356	Piqua	(513)	20,030	20,741
43452	Port Clinton	(419)	7,266	7,202
45662	Portsmouth	(614)	25,993	27,633
44266	Ravenna	(216)	11,898	11,780
45215	Reading	(513)	12,968	14,617
43068	Reynoldsburg	(614)	19,095	13,921
44143	Richmond Heights	(213)	10,234	9,220
43217	Rickenbacker Base(u)	(614)	NA	5,623
44270	Rittman	(216)	6,986	6,308
44116	Rocky River	(216)	21,070	22,958
43460	Rossford	(419)	6,070	5,302
45217	St. Bernard	(513)	5,183	6,131
43950	St. Clairsville	(614)	5,211	4,222
45885	St. Marys	(419)	8,132	7,699
44460	Salem	(216)	15,694	14,186
44870	Sandusky	(419)	31,303	32,674
44870	Sandusky South(u)	(419)	NA	8,501
44131	Seven Hills	(216)	13,614	12,700
44120	Shaker Heights	(216)	31,225	36,306
45241	Sharonville	(513)	11,911	11,393
44054	Sheffield Lake	(216)	10,498	8,734
44875	Shelby	(419)	9,346	9,847
45415	Shiloh(u)	(419)	NA	11,368
45365	Sidney	(513)	18,297	16,332
45236	Silverton	(513)	5,965	6,588
44139	Solon	(216)	13,950	11,147
44121	South Euclid	(216)	25,721	29,579
45246	Springdale	(216)	9,933	8,127
*45501	Springfield	(513)	73,376	81,941
43952	Steubenville	(614)	27,056	30,771
44224	Stow	(216)	25,354	19,847
44240	Streetsboro	(216)	8,264	7,966
44136	Strongsville	(216)	28,525	15,182
44471	Struthers	(216)	13,609	15,343
43560	Sylvania	(419)	15,094	12,031
44278	Tallmadge	(216)	15,600	15,274
44883	Tiffin	(419)	19,567	21,596
45371	Tipp City	(513)	6,192	5,090
*43601	Toledo	(419)	351,686	383,105
43964	Toronto	(614)	7,689	7,705
45067	Trenton	(513)	6,498	5,278
45426	Trotwood	(513)	7,921	6,997
45373	Troy	(513)	18,514	17,186
44087	Twinsburg	(216)	7,211	6,432
44683	Uhrichsville	(614)	5,771	5,731
45322	Union	(513)	5,324	3,654

ZIP code	Place		1980	1970
44118	University Heights	(216)	15,369	17,055
43221	Upper Arlington	(614)	*37,101*	38,727
43351	Upper Sandusky	(419)	*5,526*	5,645
43078	Urbana	(513)	*11,967*	11,237
45377	Vandalia	(513)	*11,894*	10,796
45891	Van Wert	(419)	*11,180*	11,320
44089	Vermilion	(216)	11,011	9,872
44281	Wadsworth	(216)	*15,420*	13,142
45895	Wapakoneta	(419)	15,187	7,324
*44481	Warren	(216)	55,456	63,494
44122	Warrensville Heights	(216)	16,352	18,925
43160	Washington	(513)	12,648	12,495
43567	Wausem	(419)	*5,877*	4,932
45692	Wellston	(614)	*5,613*	5,410
43968	Wellsville	(216)	*6,211*	5,891
45449	West Carrollton	(513)	*13,134*	10,748
43081	Westerville	(614)	*20,104*	12,530
44145	Westlake	(216)	19,475	15,689
43213	Whitehall	(614)	*25,544*	25,263
44092	Wickliffe	(216)	17,022	21,354
44890	Willard	(419)	*5,416*	5,510
44094	Willoughby	(216)	19,135	18,634
44094	Willoughby Hills	(216)	*6,826*	5,247
44094	Willowick	(216)	17,669	21,237
45177	Wilmington	(513)	10,106	10,051
43952	Wintersville	(614)	*5,387*	4,921
44691	Wooster	(216)	*20,124*	18,703
43085	Worthington	(614)	*17,470*	15,326
45433	Wright-Patterson(u)	(513)	NA	10,151
45215	Wyoming	(513)	*8,555*	9,089
45385	Xenia	(513)	*30,889*	25,373
*44501	Youngstown	(216)	115,429	140,909
43701	Zanesville	(614)	*38,292*	33,045

Oklahoma

ZIP code	Place		1980	1970
74820	Ada	(405)	*14,661*	14,859
73521	Altus	(405)	*25,007*	23,302
73717	Alva	(405)	*5,848*	7,440
73005	Anadarko	(405)	*6,482*	6,682
73401	Ardmore	(405)	*24,700*	20,881
74003	Bartlesville	(918)	*30,329*	29,683
73008	Bethany	(405)	*21,679*	22,694
74008	Bixby	(918)	*6,352*	4,957
74631	Blackwell	(405)	*8,158*	8,645
74012	Broken Arrow	(918)	*30,727*	11,787
73018	Chickasha	(405)	*15,033*	14,194
73020	Choctaw	(405)	*7,786*	4,750
74017	Claremore	(918)	*10,601*	9,084
73601	Clinton	(405)	*7,895*	8,513
74023	Cushing	(918)	*7,350*	7,529
73115	Del City	(405)	*29,625*	27,133
73533	Duncan	(405)	*20,724*	19,718
74701	Durant	(405)	*10,607*	11,118
73034	Edmond	(405)	*24,340*	16,633
73644	Elk City	(405)	*8,373*	7,323
73036	El Reno	(405)	*15,990*	14,510
73701	Enid	(405)	*50,166*	44,986
73503	Fort Sill(u)	(405)	NA	21,217
73542	Frederick	(405)	*5,778*	6,132
73044	Guthrie	(405)	*10,122*	9,575
73942	Guymon	(405)	*8,846*	7,674
74437	Henryetta	(918)	*6,167*	6,430
74848	Holdenville	(405)	*5,457*	5,181
74743	Hugo	(405)	*6,196*	6,585
74745	Idabel	(405)	*7,164*	5,946
74037	Jenks	(918)	*5,187*	3,096
73501	Lawton	(918)	*85,073*	74,470
73055	Marlow	(405)	*5,075*	3,995
74501	McAlester	(918)	*16,556*	18,802
74354	Miami	(918)	*13,966*	13,880
73110	Midwest City	(405)	*50,430*	48,212
73060	Moore	(405)	*30,086*	18,761
74401	Muskogee	(918)	*41,325*	37,331
73064	Mustang	(405)	*6,821*	2,637
73069	Norman	(405)	*63,382*	52,117
*73125	Oklahoma City	(405)	*372,690*	368,164
74447	Okmulgee	(918)	*15,487*	15,180
74055	Owasso	(918)	*5,711*	3,491
73075	Pauls Valley	(405)	*5,366*	5,769
73077	Perry	(405)	*5,610*	5,341
74601	Ponca City	(405)	*26,511*	25,940
74953	Poteau	(918)	*6,200*	5,500
74361	Pryor	(918)	*7,815*	7,057
74955	Sallisaw	(918)	*6,008*	5,153
74063	Sand Springs	(918)	*12,780*	10,565
74066	Sapulpa	(918)	*16,480*	15,159
74868	Seminole	(405)	*8,024*	7,878
74801	Shawnee	(405)	*26,234*	25,075
74074	Stillwater	(405)	*34,846*	31,126
74464	Tahlequah	(918)	*8,771*	9,254
74873	Tecumseh	(405)	*5,870*	4,451
73120	The Village	(405)	*12,920*	13,695
*74101	Tulsa	(918)	*328,684*	330,350
74467	Wagoner	(918)	*6,958*	4,959
73132	Warr Acres	(405)	*12,723*	9,887
73096	Weatherford	(405)	*8,756*	7,959
73801	Woodward	(405)	*12,273*	9,412
73099	Yukon	(405)	*19,019*	8,411

Oregon (503)

ZIP code	Place	1980	1970
97321	Albany	NA	18,181
97601	Altamont(u)	NA	15,746
97520	Ashland	*15,000*	12,342
97103	Astoria	*10,483*	10,244
97814	Baker	*9,556*	9,354
97005	Beaverton	*26,140*	18,577
97701	Bend	17,121	13,710
97013	Canby	*7,089*	3,813
97502	Central Point	*6,267*	4,843
97420	Coos Bay	*14,609*	13,466
97330	Corvallis	*38,823*	35,056
97424	Cottage Grove	*7,389*	6,004
97338	Dallas	*9,800*	6,361
*97401	Eugene	*102,591*	79,028
97116	Forest Grove	*11,012*	8,275
97301	Four Corners(u)	NA	5,823
97027	Gladstone	*9,607*	6,254
97526	Grants Pass	*15,117*	12,455
97030	Gresham	*29,728*	10,030
97303	Hayesville(u)	NA	5,518
97838	Hermiston	*8,226*	4,893
97123	Hillsboro	*24,797*	14,675
97031	Hood River	*5,612*	3,991
97303	Keizer(u)	NA	11,405
97601	Klamath Falls	*18,228*	15,775
97850	La Grande	*10,970*	9,645
97034	Lake Oswego	*21,963*	14,615
97355	Lebanon	*9,805*	6,636
97128	McMinnville	*14,579*	10,125
97501	Medford	*38,072*	28,454
97222	Milwaukie	*19,208*	16,444
97361	Monmouth	*7,917*	5,237
97132	Newberg	*9,744*	6,507
97365	Newport	*6,984*	5,188
97459	North Bend	*9,965*	8,553
97914	Ontario	*8,395*	6,523
97045	Oregon City	*15,176*	9,176
97801	Pendleton	*14,858*	13,197
*97208	Portland	*364,735*	379,967
97754	Prineville	*5,914*	3,937
97756	Redmond	*7,964*	4,639
97467	Reedsport	*5,231*	4,031
97470	Roseburg	*19,137*	14,461
97051	St. Helens	*7,484*	6,212
*97301	Salem	*89,770*	68,480
97381	Silverton	*5,396*	4,301
97477	Springfield	*40,913*	26,874
97386	Sweet Home	*11,316*	6,365
97058	The Dalles	10,802	10,423
97223	Tigard	*13,756*	5,302
97068	West Linn	*11,929*	7,091
97071	Woodburn	*11,287*	7,495

Pennsylvania

ZIP code	Place		1980	1970
19001	Abington(u)	(215)	NA	8,391
19018	Aldan	(215)	*5,060*	5,001
15001	Aliquippa	(412)	*20,097*	22,277
*18101	Allentown	(215)	*102,077*	109,871
*16603	Altoona	(814)	*68,043*	63,115
19002	Ambler	(215)	*7,718*	7,800
15003	Ambridge	(412)	*9,352*	11,324
18403	Archbald	(717)	*6,334*	6,118
19003	Ardmore(u)	(215)	NA	5,131
15068	Arnold	(412)	*6,795*	8,174
15202	Avalon	(412)	*6,486*	7,010
15005	Baden	(412)	*5,777*	5,536
19004	Bala-Cynwyd(u)	(215)	NA	6,483
15234	Baldwin	(412)	*25,268*	26,729
18013	Bangor	(215)	*5,211*	5,425
15009	Beaver	(412)	*5,711*	6,100
15010	Beaver Falls	(412)	*13,670*	14,375
16823	Bellefonte	(814)	*5,813*	6,828
15202	Bellevue	(412)	*9,958*	11,586
18603	Berwick	(717)	*11,808*	12,274
15102	Bethel Park	(412)	*38,362*	34,758
*18016	Bethlehem	(215)	*72,550*	72,686
18447	Blakely	(717)	*6,960*	6,391
17815	Bloomsburg	(717)	*13,177*	11,652
15104	Braddock	(412)	*5,641*	8,795
16701	Bradford	(814)	*11,232*	12,672
19406	Brandywine Village(u)	(215)	NA	11,411
15227	Brentwood	(412)	*12,919*	13,732
15017	Bridgeville	(412)	*6,282*	6,717
19007	Bristol	(215)	*11,224*	12,085
19015	Brookhaven	(215)	*7,696*	7,370
19010	Bryn Mawr(u)	(215)	NA	5,815
16001	Butler	(412)	*20,818*	18,691
15419	California	(412)	*5,294*	6,635
17011	Camp Hill	(717)	*9,185*	9,931
15317	Canonsburg	(412)	*11,084*	11,439
18407	Carbondale	(717)	*11,746*	12,478
17013	Carlisle	(717)	*19,972*	18,079
15106	Carnegie	(412)	*9,815*	10,864
15108	Carnot-Moon(u)	(412)	NA	13,093
15234	Castle Shannon	(412)	*10,627*	12,036
18032	Catasauqua	(215)	*6,171*	5,702
19095	Cedarbrook-Melrose Park(u)	(215)	NA	9,990
19428	Cedar Heights(u)	(215)	NA	6,326

ZIP code	Place		1980	1970
17201	Chambersburg	(717)	16,541	17,315
15022	Charleroi	(412)	6,377	6,723
19380	Chatwood(u)	(215)	NA	7,168
*19003	Chester	(215)	44,173	56,331
15025	Clairton	(412)	13,257	15,051
16214	Clarion	(814)	7,116	6,095
18411	Clarks Summit	(717)	6,560	5,376
16830	Clearfield	(814)	7,722	8,176
19018	Clifton Heights	(215)	7,368	8,348
19320	Coatesville	(215)	12,204	12,331
19023	Collingdale	(215)	10,111	10,605
17512	Columbia	(717)	10,794	11,237
15425	Connellsville	(412)	11,297	11,643
19428	Conshohocken	(215)	8,498	10,195
15108	Coraopolis	(412)	7,995	8,435
16407	Corry	(814)	6,820	7,435
15205	Crafton	(412)	7,621	8,233
17821	Danville	(717)	6,153	6,176
19023	Darby	(215)	11,989	13,729
18519	Dickson City	(717)	7,119	7,698
15033	Donora	(412)	7,404	8,825
15216	Dormont	(412)	10,099	12,856
19335	Downingtown	(215)	7,890	7,437
18901	Doylestown	(215)	11,557	8,270
15801	Du Bois	(814)	9,447	10,112
18512	Dunmore	(717)	17,166	18,168
15110	Duquesne	(412)	9,770	11,410
18042	Easton	(215)	28,515	29,450
18301	East Stroudsburg	(717)	9,155	7,894
15005	Economy	(412)	8,599	7,176
16412	Edinboro	(814)	5,489	4,817
18704	Edwardsville	(717)	5,403	5,633
17022	Elizabethtown	(717)	8,643	8,072
16117	Ellwood City	(412)	10,605	10,857
18049	Emmaus	(215)	11,880	11,511
17522	Ephrata	(717)	10,115	9,662
*16501	Erie	(814)	122,152	129,231
15223	Etna	(412)	5,214	5,819
16121	Farrell	(412)	8,734	11,000
19031	Flourtown(u)	(215)	NA	9,149
19032	Folcroft	(215)	9,195	9,610
15221	Forest Hills	(412)	8,491	9,561
18704	Forty Fort	(717)	5,314	6,114
18015	Fountain Hill	(215)	5,549	5,384
17931	Frackville	(215)	5,108	5,445
16323	Franklin	(814)	7,818	8,629
15143	Franklin Park	(412)	5,547	5,310
18052	Fullerton(u)	(215)	NA	7,908
19004	General Wayne(u)	(215)	NA	5,368
17325	Gettysburg	(717)	7,310	7,275
15045	Glassport	(412)	6,394	7,450
19036	Glenolden	(215)	8,119	8,697
19038	Glenside(u)	(215)	NA	17,353
15601	Greensburg	(412)	17,472	17,077
15220	Green Tree	(412)	5,787	6,441
16125	Greenville	(412)	9,400	8,704
16127	Grove City	(412)	8,018	8,312
17331	Hanover	(717)	14,313	15,623
*17105	Harrisburg	(717)	55,027	68,061
19040	Hatboro	(215)	8,880	8,880
19044	Hatboro West(u)	(215)	NA	14,278
18201	Hazelton	(717)	28,227	30,426
18055	Hellertown	(215)	6,716	6,615
17033	Hershey(u)	(717)	NA	7,407
18042	Highland Park (Northampton)(u)	(717)	NA	5,500
16648	Hollidaysburg	(814)	6,016	6,262
16001	Homeacre-Lyndora(u)	(412)	NA	8,415
18431	Honesdale	(717)	5,367	5,224
17036	Hummelstown	(717)	6,159	4,723
16552	Huntingdon	(814)	7,019	6,987
15701	Indiana	(412)	17,480	16,100
15644	Jeannette	(412)	13,081	15,209
15344	Jefferson	(412)	7,634	8,512
19401	Jefferson-Trooper(u)	(215)	NA	13,901
18229	Jim Thorpe	(717)	5,332	5,456
*15901	Johnstown	(814)	35,417	42,476
19348	Kennett Square	(215)	5,357	4,876
18704	Kingston	(717)	15,905	18,325
16201	Kittanning	(412)	6,203	6,231
19444	Lafayette Hills-Plymouth Meeting(u)	(215)	NA	8,275
*17604	Lancaster	(717)	56,996	57,690
19446	Lansdale	(215)	20,430	18,451
19050	Lansdowne	(215)	13,548	14,090
15650	Latrobe	(412)	10,813	11,749
17042	Lebanon	(717)	29,462	28,572
18235	Lehighton	(215)	5,978	6,095
17837	Lewisburg	(717)	6,056	6,376
17044	Lewistown	(717)	9,699	11,098
17543	Lititz	(717)	9,501	7,072
17745	Lock Haven	(717)	9,305	11,427
15068	Lower Burrell	(412)	13,244	13,654
15237	McCandless	(412)	NA	22,404
*15134	McKeesport	(412)	31,902	37,977
15136	McKees Rocks	(412)	10,630	11,901
17948	Mahanoy City	(717)	6,026	7,257
17545	Manheim	(717)	5,858	5,434
16335	Meadville	(814)	15,656	16,573
17055	Mechanicsburg	(717)	12,397	9,385
*19063	Media	(215)	6,221	6,444
19066	Merion(u)	(215)	NA	5,686
17057	Middletown	(717)	9,653	9,080
17551	Millersville	(717)	7,208	6,396
15209	Millvale	(412)	5,237	5,815
17847	Milton	(717)	7,095	7,723
17954	Minersville	(717)	5,504	6,012
15061	Monaca	(412)	7,486	7,486
15062	Monessen	(412)	11,929	15,216
15063	Monogahela	(412)	6,098	7,113
15146	Monroeville	(412)	31,439	29,011
17754	Montoursville	(717)	5,910	5,985
18507	Moosic	(717)	5,412	4,646
19067	Morrisville	(215)	10,719	11,309
17851	Mount Carmel	(717)	8,149	9,317
17552	Mount Joy	(717)	5,625	5,041
15666	Mount Pleasant	(412)	5,424	5,895
15120	Munhall	(412)	14,670	16,574
15668	Murrysville	(412)	16,055	12,661
18634	Nanticoke	(717)	13,573	14,638
18064	Nazareth	(215)	6,605	5,815
15066	New Brighton	(412)	7,663	7,637
*16101	New Castle	(412)	35,187	38,559
17070	New Cumberland	(717)	10,661	9,803
15068	New Kensington	(412)	17,653	20,312
*19401	Norristown	(215)	34,626	38,169
18067	Northampton	(215)	8,765	8,389
19003	North Ardmore(u)	(215)	NA	5,856
15104	North Braddock	(412)	8,527	10,838
16428	North East	(814)	6,358	3,846
19038	North Hills-Ardsley(u)	(215)	NA	13,096
19074	Norwood	(215)	7,007	7,229
19126	Oak Lane(u)	(215)	NA	6,182
15139	Oakmont	(412)	6,789	7,550
19117	Ogontz(u)	(215)	NA	5,242
16301	Oil City	(814)	13,996	15,033
18518	Old Forge	(717)	9,806	9,522
18447	Olyphant	(717)	5,340	5,422
19075	Oreland(u)	(215)	NA	9,349
18071	Palmerton	(215)	5,270	5,620
17078	Palmyra	(717)	8,073	7,615
19301	Paoli(u)	(215)	NA	5,835
17331	Parkville(u)	(717)	NA	5,120
19004	Pencoyd(u)	(215)	NA	6,650
19401	Penn Sq.-Plymouth Valley(u)	(215)	NA	20,255
19151	Penn Wynne(u)	(215)	NA	6,038
18944	Perkasie	(215)	7,488	5,451
*19104	Philadelphia	(215)	1,680,235	1,949,996
19460	Phoenixville	(215)	14,823	14,823
*15219	Pittsburgh	(412)	423,962	520,089
*18640	Pittston	(717)	11,038	11,113
18705	Plains(u)	(717)	NA	6,606
15236	Pleasant Hills	(412)	10,440	10,409
15239	Plum	(412)	25,099	21,932
18651	Plymouth	(717)	7,659	9,536
19464	Pottstown	(215)	26,144	25,355
17901	Pottsville	(717)	17,873	19,715
19076	Prospect Park	(215)	6,653	7,250
15767	Punxsutawney	(814)	7,464	7,792
18951	Quakertown	(215)	8,989	7,276
*19603	Reading	(215)	76,742	87,643
17356	Red Lion	(717)	5,684	5,645
15853	Ridgway	(814)	5,475	6,022
19078	Ridley Park	(215)	8,379	9,025
19001	Roslyn(u)	(215)	NA	18,811
19046	Rydal(u)	(215)	NA	5,826
15857	St. Marys	(814)	7,040	7,470
18840	Sayre	(717)	6,803	7,473
17972	Schuylkill Haven	(717)	6,095	6,125
15683	Scottdale	(412)	5,730	5,818
*18503	Scranton	(717)	89,890	102,696
17870	Selinsgrove	(717)	5.120	5,116
15143	Sewickley	(412)	6,029	5,660
17872	Shamokin	(717)	10,440	11,719
16146	Sharon	(412)	20,974	22,653
19079	Sharon Hill	(215)	7,276	7,464
16150	Sharpsville	(412)	5,416	6,126
17976	Shenandoah	(717)	7,179	8,287
19607	Shillington	(215)	6,583	6,249
17257	Shippensburg	(717)	7,992	6,536
16057	Slippery Rock	(412)	5,872	4,949
15501	Somerset	(814)	6,266	6,269
18964	Souderton	(215)	6,539	6,366
17701	South Williamsport	(717)	6,589	7,153
16801	State College	(814)	38,369	33,778
17113	Steelton	(717)	6,839	8,556
18360	Stroudsburg	(717)	5,213	5,451
16323	Sugar Creek	(717)	6,104	5,944
17801	Sunbury	(717)	11,857	13,025
19081	Swarthmore	(215)	6,281	6,156
15218	Swissvale	(412)	11,660	13,819
18704	Swoyersville	(717)	5,963	6,786
18252	Tamaqua	(717)	8,918	9,246
15084	Tarentum	(412)	6,494	7,379
18517	Taylor	(717)	7,775	6,977
16354	Titusville	(814)	6,653	7,331
15145	Turtle Creek	(412)	7,093	8,308
16686	Tyrone	(814)	6,051	7,072
15401	Uniontown	(814)	15,061	16,282
15690	Vandergrift	(412)	7,008	7,889

ZIP code	Place		1980	1970
16365	Warren	(814)	*12,054*	12,998
15301	Washington	(412)	*19,851*	19,827
17268	Waynesboro	(717)	*9,288*	10,011
19380	West Chester	(215)	*20,721*	19,301
18201	West Hazelton	(717)	*5,210*	6,059
15122	West Mifflin	(412)	*26,577*	28,070
15905	Westmont	(814)	*5,986*	6,673
18643	West Pittston	(717)	*6,481*	7,074
15229	West View	(412)	*7,958*	8,312
18052	Whitehall	(412)	*15,984*	16,450
15131	White Oak	(717)	*10,055*	9,304
*18701	Wilkes-Barre	(717)	*53,832*	58,856
15221	Wilkinsburg	(412)	*22,907*	26,780
17701	Williamsport	(717)	*33,904*	37,918
19090	Willow Grove(u)	(717)	NA	16,194
15025	Wilson	(412)	*8,320*	8,406
15963	Windber	(814)	*6,907*	6,332
19610	Wyomissing	(215)	*8,337*	7,136
19050	Yeadon	(215)	*11,658*	12,136
*17405	York	(717)	*45,622*	50,335

Rhode Island (401)

See Note on Page 933

ZIP code	Place	1980	1970
02806	*Barrington*	16,181	17,554
02809	*Bristol*	20,165	17,860
02830	*Burrillville*	13,098	10,087
02863	Central Falls	16,901	18,716
02816	*Coventry*	26,985	22,947
02910	Cranston	72,034	74,287
02864	*Cumberland*	27,009	26,605
02818	*East Greenwich*	10,208	9,577
02914	East Providence	50,960	48,207
02833	*Hopkinton*	NA	5,392
02919	*Johnston*	24,835	22,037
02881	Kingston(u)	NA	5,601
02865	*Lincoln*	16,904	16,182
02840	*Middletown*	17,251	29,290
02882	*Narragansett*	12,097	7,138
02840	Newport	29,266	34,562
02843	Newport East(u)	NA	10,285
02852	*North Kingstown*	21,855	29,793
02908	*North Providence*	NA	24,337
02876	*North Smithfield*	NA	9,349
*02860	Pawtucket	71,033	76,984
02871	*Portsmouth*	14,256	12,521
*02904	Providence	156,421	179,116
02857	*Scituate*	NA	7,489
02917	*Smithfield*	16,869	13,468
02879	*South Kingstown*	20,411	16,913
02878	*Tiverton*	13,484	12,559
*02880	Wakefield-Peacedale(u)	NA	6,331
02885	*Warren*	10,609	10,523
*02887	Warwick	87,064	83,694
02891	*Westerly*	18,507	17,248
02891	Westerly Center(u)	NA	13,654
02893	*West Warwick*	26,975	24,323
02895	Woonsocket	45,876	46,820

South Carolina (803)

ZIP code	Place	1980	1970
29620	Abbeville	*5,597*	5,515
29801	Aiken	*14,630*	13,436
29621	Anderson	*30,420*	27,556
29407	Avondale-Moorland(u)	NA	5,236
29902	Beaufort	*8,808*	9,434
29627	Belton	*5,340*	5,257
29512	Bennettsville	*8,146*	7,468
29611	Berea(u)	NA	7,186
29020	Camden	*8,392*	8,532
29033	Cayce	*10,461*	9,967
*29401	Charleston	*59,280*	66,945
29404	Charleston Base(u)	NA	6,238
29408	Charleston Yard(u)	NA	13,565
29520	Cheraw	*5,309*	5,627
29706	Chester	*7,148*	7,045
29631	Clemson	*6,933*	5,578
29325	Clinton	*7,687*	8,138
*29201	Columbia	*108,216*	113,542
29526	Conway	*9,134*	8,151
29532	Darlington	*7,199*	6,990
29536	Dillon	*6,231*	6,391
29640	Easley	*13,088*	11,175
29501	Florence	*32,577*	25,997
29206	Forest Acres	*6,755*	6,808
29340	Gaffney	*16,054*	13,253
29605	Gantt(u)	NA	11,386
29440	Georgetown	*11,833*	10,449
29445	Goose Creek	*16,471*	10,774
*29602	Greenville	*55,407*	61,436
29646	Greenwood	*25,720*	21,069
29651	Greer	*12,239*	10,642
29410	Hanahan	*9,656*	9,118
29550	Hartsville	*7,895*	8,017
29560	Lake City	*6,578*	6,247
29720	Lancaster	*10,135*	9,186
29360	Laurens	*10,010*	10,298
29571	Marion	*7,839*	7,435
29464	Mount Pleasant	*10,523*	6,879
29574	Mullins	*6,042*	6,006
29577	Myrtle Beach	*20,529*	14,568
29108	Newberry	*9,177*	9,218
29841	North Augusta	*14,251*	12,883
29406	North Charleston	*61,402*	21,211
29115	Orangeburg	*17,184*	13,252
29905	Parris Island(u)	NA	8,868
29730	Rock Hill	*37,684*	33,846
29407	St. Andrews(u)	NA	9,202
29678	Seneca	*8,214*	6,382
29150	Shannontown(u)	NA	7,491
29152	Shaw(u)	NA	5,819
*29301	Spartanburg	*46,279*	44,546
29483	Summerville	*7,471*	4,603
29150	Sumter	*25,086*	24,555
29687	Taylors(u)	NA	6,831
29379	Union	*10,237*	10,775
29607	Wade-Hampton(u)	NA	17,152
29488	Walterboro	*6,598*	6,257
29169	West Columbia	*14,612*	10,433
29745	York	*6,427*	5,081

South Dakota (605)

ZIP code	Place	1980	1970
57401	Aberdeen	25,937	26,476
57006	Brookings	14,915	13,717
57706	Ellsworth(u)	NA	6,207
57350	Huron	13,000	14,299
57042	Madison	*5,508*	6,315
57301	Mitchell	13,917	13,425
57501	Pierre	11,966	9,699
57701	Rapid City	46,340	43,836
*57101	Sioux Falls	80,747	72,488
57069	Vermillion	10,140	9,128
57201	Watertown	15,632	13,388
57078	Yankton	11,992	11,919

Tennessee

ZIP code	Place		1980	1970
37701	Alcoa	(615)	*6,879*	7,739
37303	Athens	(615)	*12,337*	11,790
38134	Bartlett	(901)	*14,358*	5,222
38008	Bolivar	(901)	*5,705*	6,674
37027	Brentwood	(615)	*8,862*	4,099
37620	Bristol	(615)	23,937	20,064
38012	Brownsville	(901)	*8,487*	7,011
*37401	Chattanooga	(615)	*162,778*	119,923
37040	Clarksville	(615)	*56,644*	44,380
37311	Cleveland	(615)	*31,009*	20,651
38017	Collierville	(901)	*3,651*	6,983
38401	Columbia	(615)	*23,258*	21,471
38501	Cookeville	(615)	*18,526*	15,847
38019	Covington	(901)	*6,275*	5,801
38555	Crossville	(615)	*6,183*	5,381
37055	Dickson	(615)	*7,022*	5,665
38024	Dyersburg	(901)	*15,768*	14,523
37801	Eagleton Village(u)	(615)	NA	5,345
37412	East Ridge	(615)	*22,761*	21,799
37643	Elizabethton	(615)	12,410	12,269
37334	Fayetteville	(615)	*7,114*	7,030
42223	Fort Campbell South(u)	(615)	NA	9,279
37064	Franklin	(615)	*11,356*	9,497
37066	Gallatin	(615)	NA	13,253
38138	Germantown	(901)	*16,065*	3,899
37072	Goodlettsville	(615)	*8,151*	6,979
37075	Greater Hendersonville(u)	(615)	*25,029*	11,996
37743	Greeneville	(615)	13,987	13,722
37748	Harriman	(615)	*9,050*	8,734
37343	Hixson(u)	(615)	NA	6,188
38343	Humboldt	(901)	*10,100*	10,066
38301	Jackson	(901)	*47,532*	43,417
37760	Jefferson City	(615)	*5,210*	5,124
37601	Johnson City	(615)	39,763	33,770
*37662	Kingsport	(615)	31,737	31,938
37665	Kingsport North(u)	(615)	NA	13,118
*37901	Knoxville	(615)	*185,236*	174,587
37766	La Follette	(615)	*8,980*	6,902
37416	Lake Hills-Murray Hills(u)	(615)	NA	7,806
37086	LaVergne	(615)	*3,714*	5,220
38464	Lawrenceburg	(615)	*10,438*	8,889
37087	Lebanon	(615)	*13,582*	12,492
37771	Lenoir City	(615)	*5,300*	5,324
37091	Lewisburg	(615)	*8,513*	7,207
38351	Lexington	(901)	*5,831*	5,024
37110	McMinnville	(615)	*10,916*	10,662
37355	Manchester	(615)	*7,343*	6,208
38237	Martin	(901)	*7,804*	7,781
37801	Maryville	(615)	*20,529*	13,808
*38101	Memphis	(901)	*663,769*	623,530
38358	Milan	(901)	*6,666*	7,313
38053	Millington	(901)	*20,848*	21,177
37814	Morristown	(615)	19,318	20,318
37130	Murfreesboro	(615)	*33,400*	26,360
*37202	Nashville-Davidson	(615)	*425,424*	**447,877
37821	Newport	(615)	*7,369*	7,328
37830	Oak Ridge	(615)	*28,896*	28,319
38242	Paris	(901)	*10,506*	9,892
38478	Pulaski	(615)	*7,355*	6,989

ZIP code	Place		1980	1970
37415	Red Bank White Oak	(615)	15,043	12,715
37854	Rockwood	(615)	5,352	5,259
38372	Savannah	(901)	6,462	5,576
37160	Shelbyville	(615)	11,845	12,262
37377	Signal Mountain	(615)	6,833	5,397
37167	Smyrna	(615)	8,196	5,698
37379	Soddy-Daisy	(615)	11,011	7,569
38583	Sparta	(615)	5,249	4,930
37172	Springfield	(615)	10,309	9,720
37388	Tullahoma	(615)	15,176	15,311
38261	Union City	(901)	12,997	11,925
37398	Winchester	(615)	5,208	5,256

***Comprises the Metropolitan Government of Nashville and Davidson County.*

Texas

ZIP code	Place		1980	1970
*79604	Abilene	(915)	96,573	89,653
78209	Alamo Heights	(512)	6,979	6,933
78332	Alice	(512)	20,318	20,121
79830	Alpine	(915)	5,814	5,971
77511	Alvin	(713)	15,980	10,671
*79105	Amarillo	(806)	143,665	127,010
79714	Andrews	(915)	10,332	8,625
77515	Angleton	(713)	14,451	9,770
78336	Aransas Pass	(512)	6,565	5,813
*76010	Arlington	(817)	132,932	90,032
75751	Athens	(214)	9,243	9,582
75551	Atlanta	(214)	5,783	5,007
*78710	Austin	(512)	319,194	251,808
75149	Balch Springs	(214)	12,938	10,464
77414	Bay City	(713)	16,011	13,445
77520	Baytown	(713)	53,024	43,980
*77704	Beaumont	(713)	117,764	117,548
76021	Bedford	(817)	17,265	10,049
78102	Beeville	(512)	13,323	13,506
77401	Bellaire	(713)	17,492	19,009
76704	Bellmead	(817)	9,047	7,698
76513	Belton	(817)	11,302	8,696
76126	Benbrook	(817)	11,649	8,169
79720	Big Spring	(915)	25,113	28,735
75418	Bonham	(214)	6,810	7,698
79007	Borger	(806)	14,458	14,195
76230	Bowie	(817)	5,489	5,185
76825	Brady	(915)	5,862	5,557
76024	Breckenridge	(817)	6,144	5,944
77833	Brenham	(713)	10,530	8,922
77611	Bridge City(u)	(713)	8,058	8,164
79316	Brownfield	(806)	9,704	9,647
78520	Brownsville	(512)	71,554	52,522
76801	Brownwood	(915)	19,246	17,368
77801	Bryan	(713)	37,402	33,719
76354	Burkburnett	(817)	10,413	9,230
76028	Burleson	(817)	12,751	7,713
76520	Cameron	(817)	5,185	5,546
79015	Canyon	(806)	8,976	8,333
78834	Carrizo Springs	(512)	6,699	5,374
75006	Carrolton	(214)	29,877	13,860
75633	Carthage	(214)	5,954	5,392
78213	Castle Hills	(512)	5,151	5,311
79201	Childress	(817)	5,453	5,408
76031	Cleburne	(817)	15,866	16,015
77327	Cleveland	(713)	6,785	5,627
77531	Clute City	(713)	7,578	6,023
76834	Coleman	(915)	5,598	5,608
77840	College Station	(713)	30,539	17,676
79512	Colorado City	(915)	5,027	5,227
75428	Commerce	(214)	7,480	9,534
77301	Conroe	(713)	25,741	11,969
76522	Copperas Cove	(817)	22,715	10,818
*78408	Corpus Christi	(512)	214,647	204,525
75110	Corsicana	(214)	19,630	19,972
75835	Crockett	(713)	6,392	6,616
76036	Crowley	(817)	6,358	2,662
78839	Crystal City	(512)	7,794	8,104
77954	Cuero	(512)	7,049	6,956
79022	Dalhart	(806)	6,442	5,705
*75260	Dallas	(214)	847,420	844,401
77536	Deer Park	(713)	22,059	12,773
78840	Del Rio	(512)	29,866	21,330
75020	Denison	(214)	23,727	24,923
76201	Denton	(817)	43,571	39,874
75115	De Soto	(214)	14,349	6,617
77539	Dickinson(u)	(713)	8,411	10,776
78537	Donna	(512)	8,948	7,365
79029	Dumas	(806)	10,665	9,771
75116	Duncanville	(214)	26,729	14,105
78852	Eagle Pass	(512)	20,799	15,364
78539	Edinburg	(512)	20,666	17,163
77957	Edna	(512)	5,680	5,332
77437	El Campo	(713)	9,383	9,332
79910	El Paso	(915)	424,522	322,261
75119	Ennis	(214)	11,516	11,046
76039	Euless	(817)	22,601	19,316
76140	Everman	(817)	6,230	4,570
78355	Falfurrias	(512)	5,965	6,355
75234	Farmers Branch	(214)	34,761	27,492
76119	Forest Hill	(817)	10,225	8,236
79906	Fort Bliss(u)	(915)	NA	13,288
76544	Fort Hood(u)	(817)	NA	32,597
78234	Fort Sam Houston(u)	(512)	NA	10,553
79735	Fort Stockton	(915)	8,883	8,283
76101	Fort Worth	(817)	367,432	393,476
78624	Fredericksburg	(512)	5,734	5,326
77541	Freeport	(713)	12,737	11,997
77546	Friendswood	(713)	16,045	5,675
76240	Gainesville	(817)	12,882	13,830
77547	Galena Park	(713)	9,748	10,479
77550	Galveston	(713)	59,407	61,809
*75040	Garland	(214)	131,263	81,437
76528	Gatesville	(817)	5,604	5,290
78626	Georgetown	(512)	10,457	6,395
75647	Gladewater	(214)	6,353	5,574
78629	Gonzales	(512)	6,318	5,854
76046	Graham	(817)	8,164	7,477
75050	Grand Prairie	(214)	62,855	50,904
76051	Grapevine	(817)	10,804	7,023
75401	Greenville	(214)	22,665	22,043
77619	Groves	(713)	17,700	18,067
76117	Haltom City	(817)	29,423	28,127
76541	Harker Heights	(817)	9,096	4,216
78550	Harlingen	(512)	41,897	33,503
75652	Henderson	(214)	11,544	10,187
79045	Hereford	(806)	14,874	13,414
75205	Highland Park	(214)	9,158	10,133
76645	Hillsboro	(817)	6,484	7,224
77563	Hitchcock	(713)	6,824	5,565
78861	Hondo	(512)	5,748	5,487
*77013	Houston	(713)	1,572,981	1,233,535
77338	Humb	(713)	6,641	3,272
77340	Huntsville	(713)	21,746	17,610
76053	Hurst	(817)	30,393	27,215
76367	Iowa Park	(817)	6,580	5,796
*75061	Irving	(214)	105,101	97,260
77029	Jacinto City	(713)	11,726	9,563
75766	Jacksonville	(214)	10,650	9,734
75951	Jasper	(713)	7,040	6,251
77450	Katy	(713)	11,912	2,923
79745	Kermit	(915)	7,892	7,884
78028	Kerrville	(512)	15,189	12,672
75662	Kilgore	(214)	11,183	9,495
76541	Killeen	(817)	52,236	35,507
78363	Kingsville	(512)	28,833	28,915
78236	Lackland(u)	(512)	NA	19,141
77566	Lake Jackson	(713)	17,872	13,376
77568	La Marque	(713)	16,109	16,131
79631	Lamesa	(806)	11,074	11,559
76550	Lampasas	(512)	6,641	5,922
75146	Lancaster	(214)	13,601	10,522
77571	La Porte	(713)	9,760	7,149
78040	Laredo	(512)	81,383	69,024
77573	League City	(713)	15,794	10,818
78238	Leon Valley	(512)	6,327	2,487
79336	Levelland	(806)	12,482	11,445
75067	Lewisville	(214)	29,192	10,049
77575	Liberty	(713)	6,785	5,591
79339	Littlefield	(806)	6,962	6,738
78233	Live Oak	(512)	6,784	2,779
77351	Livingston	(713)	6,275	3,965
78644	Lockhart	(512)	7,189	6,489
75601	Longview	(214)	56,231	49,627
*79408	Lubbock	(806)	168,127	149,101
75901	Lufkin	(713)	30,204	25,504
78501	McAllen	(512)	53,604	37,636
75069	McKinney	(214)	13,126	15,193
76063	Mansfield	(817)	7,729	4,269
76661	Marlin	(817)	5,651	6,351
75670	Marshall	(214)	27,773	25,263
78368	Mathis	(512)	5,658	5,351
78570	Mercedes	(512)	10,219	9,355
75149	Mesquite	(214)	63,060	55,131
76667	Mexia	(214)	6,107	5,943
79701	Midland	(915)	67,251	59,463
76067	Mineral Wells	(817)	17,533	18,411
78572	Mission	(512)	18,839	13,043
77459	Missouri City	(713)	10,870	4,136
79756	Monahans	(915)	8,220	8,333
75455	Mount Pleasant	(214)	10,471	9,459
75961	Nacogdoches	(713)	26,668	22,544
77058	Nassau Bay	(713)	7,011	4,462
77627	Nederland	(713)	18,359	16,810
78130	New Braunfels	(512)	20,647	17,859
76118	North Richland Hills	(817)	24,127	16,514
*79760	Odessa	(915)	90,366	78,380
77630	Orange	(713)	26,601	24,457
75801	Palestine	(214)	15,432	14,525
79065	Pampa	(806)	20,512	21,726
75460	Paris	(214)	22,159	23,441
*77501	Pasadena	(713)	104,385	89,957
77581	Pearland	(713)	12,799	6,444
78061	Pearsall	(512)	6,726	5,545
79772	Pecos	(915)	12,844	12,682
79070	Perryton	(806)	7,636	7,810
78577	Pharr	(512)	19,767	15,829
79072	Plainview	(806)	19,921	19,096
75074	Plano	(214)	53,021	17,872
78064	Pleasanton	(512)	6,405	5,407
77640	Port Arthur	(713)	61,439	65,158
78374	Portland	(512)	10,896	7,302
77979	Port Lavaca	(512)	11,009	10,491

ZIP code	Place		1980	1970
77651	Port Neches	(713)	*14,479*	10,894
78580	Raymondville	(512)	*9,075*	7,987
75080	Richardson	(214)	*67,518*	48,582
76118	Richland Hills	[illegible]	*9,635*	8,865
77469	Richmond	(713)	*10,043*	5,777
78582	Rio Grande City(u)	(512)	NA	5,676
77019	River Oaks	(817)	*10,017*	8,193
78380	Robstown	(512)	*10,726*	11,217
77471	Rosenberg	(713)	*17,408*	12,098
78664	Round Rock	(512)	*11,033*	3,286
76901	San Angelo	(915)	*68,626*	63,884
*78284	San Antonio	(512)	*798,195*	654,153
78586	San Benito	(512)	*17,293*	15,176
78589	San Juan	(512)	*7,157*	5,070
78666	San Marcos	(512)	*22,712*	18,860
76114	Sansom Park Village	(817)	*5,729*	4,771
78154	Schertz	(512)	*7,820*	4,550
77586	Seabrook	(713)	*5,888*	3,811
75159	Seagoville	(214)	*6,003*	4,390
78155	Sequin	(512)	*17,365*	15,934
75090	Sherman	(214)	*27,357*	29,061
77656	Silsbee	(713)	*9,759*	7,271
78387	Sinton	(512)	*5,430*	5,563
79364	Slaton	(806)	*6,931*	6,583
79549	Snyder	(915)	*12,521*	11,171
77587	South Houston	(713)	*12,193*	11,527
76401	Stephenville	(214)	*9,995*	9,277
75482	Sulphur Springs	(214)	*11,134*	10,642
79556	Sweetwater	(915)	*11,916*	12,020
76574	Taylor	(512)	*10,073*	9,616
76501	Temple	(817)	*39,672*	33,431
75160	Terrell	(214)	*11,864*	14,182
75501	Texarkana	(214)	*36,335*	30,497
77590	Texas City	(713)	*42,748*	38,908
77375	Tomball	(713)	*6,489*	2,734
79088	Tulia	(806)	*5,323*	5,294
75701	Tyler	(214)	*66,741*	57,770
78148	Universal City	(512)	*12,198*	7,613
76308	University Park	(214)	*23,183*	23,498
78801	Uvalde	(512)	*13,035*	10,764
76384	Vernon	(817)	*11,162*	11,454
77901	Victoria	(512)	*49,394*	41,349
77662	Vidor	(713)	*12,003*	9,738
*76701	Waco	(817)	*103,768*	95,326
76148	Watauga	(817)	*9,535*	3,778
75165	Waxahachie	(214)	*13,802*	13,452
76086	Weatherford	(817)	*13,217*	11,750
78596	Weslaco	(512)	*19,823*	15,313
77005	West University Place	(713)	*15,665*	13,317
76114	Westworth	(817)	*5,858*	4,578
77488	Wharton	(713)	*8,601*	7,881
76108	White Settlement	(817)	*16,914*	13,449
*76307	Wichita Falls	(817)	*94,875*	96,265
78239	Windcrest	(512)	*7,737*	3,371
76710	Woodway	(817)	*5,823*	4,819
77995	Yoakum	(512)	*5,934*	5,755

Utah (801)

84003	American Fork	12,076	7,713
84010	Bountiful	32,978	27,751
84302	Brigham City	15,573	14,007
84720	Cedar City	10,947	8,946
84014	Centerville	*6,921*	3,557
84015	Clearfield	17,937	13,316
84121	Cottonwood(u)	NA	8,431
84109	East Millcreek(u)	NA	26,579
84119	Granger-Hunter(u)	NA	9,029
84106	Granite Park(u)	NA	9,573
84117	Holladay(u)	NA	23,014
84037	Kaysville	*8,894*	6,192
84118	Kearns(u)	NA	17,247
84041	Layton	22,585	13,603
84043	Lehi	*6,675*	4,659
84321	Logan	26,871	22,333
84044	Magna(u)	NA	5,509
84047	Midvale	10,142	7,840
84532	Moab	*5,576*	4,793
84117	Mount Olympus(u)	NA	5,909
84107	Murray	25,502	21,206
84404	North Ogden	*7,453*	5,257
*84401	Ogden	64,444	69,478
84057	Orem	52,474	25,729
84651	Payson	*8,338*	2,226
84062	Pleasant Grove	10,684	5,327
84501	Price	*9,518*	6,218
84601	Provo	74,007	53,131
84701	Richfield	*5,492*	4,471
84403	Riverdale	*5,488*	3,704
84067	Roy	19,718	14,356
84770	St. George	11,330	7,097
*84101	Salt Lake City	162,960	175,885
84070	Sandy City	52,128	6,438
84065	South Jordan	*5,822*	2,942
84403	South Ogden	11,250	9,991
84115	South Salt Lake	*9,405*	7,810
84660	Spanish Fork	*9,373*	7,284
84663	Springfield	11,995	8,790
84015	Sunset	*6,278*	6,268
84074	Tooele	14,331	12,539
84078	Vernal	*7,501*	4,477
84403	Washington Terrace	*8,024*	7,241
84084	West Jordan	26,688	4,221
74070	White City(u)	NA	6,402

Vermont (802)

See Note on Page 933

05641	Barre	*10,004*	10,209
.....	*Barre*	NA	6,509
05201	*Bennington*	15,772	14,586
.....	Bennington	NA	7,950
05301	Brattleboro Center(u)	NA	9,055
.....	*Brattleboro*	11,880	12,239
05401	Burlington	37,135	38,633
05446	*Colchester*	12,624	8,776
05451	*Essex*	14,418	10,951
05452	Essex Junction	*7,770*	6,511
05047	*Hartford*	NA	6,477
05753	*Middlebury*	NA	6,532
05602	Montpelier	*8,059*	8,609
05701	Rutland	18,427	19,293
05478	St. Albans	*7,392*	8,082
05819	*St. Johnsbury*	NA	8,409
05401	*South Burlington*	10,690	10,032
05156	Springfield Center(u)	NA	5,632
.....	*Springfield*	10,180	10,063
05404	Winooski	*7,300*	7,309

Virginia

*22313	Alexandria	(703)	*104,085*	110,927
22003	Annandale(u)	(703)	NA	27,405
*22210	Arlington(u)	(703)	NA	174,284
22041	Bailey's Crossroads(u)	(703)	NA	7,295
24523	Bedford	(703)	*6,313*	6,011
22307	Belleview(u)	(703)	NA	8,299
24060	Blacksburg	(703)	*29,727*	9,384
24605	Bluefield	(703)	*5,946*	5,286
23235	Bon Air(u)	(804)	NA	10,771
24201	Bristol	(703)	*20,845*	14,857
24416	Buena Vista	(703)	*6,724*	6,425
*22906	Charlottesville	(804)	*39,245*	38,880
*23320	Chesapeake	(804)	*113,965*	89,580
23831	Chester(u)	(804)	NA	5,556
24073	Christiansburg	(703)	*10,032*	7,857
24078	Collinsville(u)	(703)	NA	6,015
23834	Colonial Heights	(804)	*17,317*	15,097
24426	Covington	(703)	*8,987*	10,060
22701	Culpeper	(703)	*8,124*	6,056
22191	Dale City(u)	(703)	*NA*	13,857
24541	Danville	(804)	45,832	46,391
23847	Emporia	(804)	*5,194*	5,300
22030	Fairfax	(703)	19,404	22,009
*22046	Falls Church	(703)	*9,016*	10,772
23901	Farmville	(804)	*6,087*	5,674
22060	Fort Belvoir(u)	(703)	NA	14,591
22308	Fort Hunt(u)	(703)	NA	10,415
23801	Fort Lee(u)	(804)	NA	12,435
23851	Franklin	(804)	*7,037*	6,880
22401	Fredericksburg	(703)	*17,896*	14,450
22630	Front Royal	(703)	*10,830*	8,211
24333	Galax	(703)	*6,693*	6,278
22306	Groveton(u)	(703)	NA	11,761
*23360	Hampton	(804)	*125,116*	120,779
22801	Harrisonburg	(703)	*18,981*	14,605
22070	Herndon	(703)	*12,835*	4,301
23075	Highland Springs(u)	(804)	NA	7,345
23860	Hopewell	(804)	23,364	23,471
22303	Huntington(u)	(703)	NA	5,559
22042	Jefferson(u)	(804)	NA	25,432
22041	Lake Barcroft(u)	(703)	NA	11,605
23228	Lakeside(u)	(804)	NA	11,137
22075	Leesburg	(703)	*8,134*	4,821
24450	Lexington	(703)	*7,661*	7,597
22312	Lincoln(u)	(703)	NA	10,761
22030	Long Branch(u)	(703)	NA	21,634
*24505	Lynchburg	(804)	*64,466*	54,083
22110	Manassas	(703)	*12,950*	9,164
22110	Manassas Park	(703)	8,969	6,844
22030	Mantua(u)	(703)	NA	6,911
24354	Marion	(703)	*7,373*	8,158
24112	Martinsville	(703)	17,929	19,653
22101	McLean(u)	(703)	NA	17,698
23111	Merchanicsville(u)	(804)	NA	5,189
*23607	Newport News	(804)	*144,023*	138,177
*23501	Norfolk	(804)	*280,568*	307,951
22151	North Springfield(u)	(703)	NA	8,631
23803	Petersburg	(804)	40,885	36,103
23662	Poquoson	(804)	*9,336*	5,441
*23705	Portsmouth	(804)	*108,297*	110,963
24301	Pulaski	(703)	*10,373*	10,279
22134	Quantico Station(u)	(703)	NA	6,213
24141	Radford	(703)	*12,558*	11,596
22070	Reston(u)	(703)	NA	5,723
24641	Richlands	(703)	*6,267*	4,843
*23232	Richmond	(804)	219,429	249,431
*24001	Roanoke	(703)	*98,074*	92,115

ZIP code	Place		1980	1970
22310	Rose Hill(u)	(703)	NA	14,492
24153	Salem	(703)	24,102	21,982
22044	Seven Corners(u)	(703)	NA	5,590
24592	South Boston	(804)	7,308	6,889
*22150	Springfield	(703)	NA	11,613
24401	Staunton	(703)	21,523	24,504
22170	Sterling Park(u)	(703)	NA	8,321
23434	Suffolk	(804)	46,851	9,858
22180	Vienna	(703)	20,387	17,146
24179	Vinton	(703)	8,171	6,347
*23458	Virginia Beach	(804)	245,076	172,106
22980	Waynesboro	(703)	16,244	16,707
22152	West Springfield(u)	(703)	NA	14,143
23185	Williamsburg	(804)	11,438	9,069
22601	Winchester	(703)	23,061	14,643
22191	Woodbridge-Marumsco(u)	(703)	NA	25,412
24382	Wytheville	(703)	7,027	6,069

Washington

ZIP code	Place		1980	1970
98520	Aberdeen	(206)	19,342	18,489
98221	Anacortes	(206)	9,008	7,701
98002	Auburn	(206)	24,559	21,653
*98009	Bellevue	(206)	71,471	61,196
98225	Bellingham	(206)	44,205	39,375
98011	Bothell	(206)	6,816	5,420
98310	Bremerton	(206)	41,652	35,307
98607	Camas	(206)	6,179	5,790
98531	Centralia	(206)	10,990	10,054
98532	Chehalis	(206)	6,581	5,727
99004	Cheney	(509)	7,164	6,358
99403	Clarkston	(509)	7,688	6,312
99324	College Place	(509)	5,444	4,817
99213	Dishman(u)	(509)	NA	9,079
98020	Edmonds	(206)	28,111	23,998
98926	Ellensburg	(509)	12,609	13,568
98823	Ephrata	(509)	5,456	5,255
*98201	Everett	(206)	52,690	53,622
99011	Fairchild(u)	(509)	NA	6,754
98466	Fircrest	(206)	5,903	5,651
98433	Fort Lewis(u)	(206)	NA	38,054
98550	Hoquiam	(206)	10,616	10,466
98626	Kelso	(206)	10,659	10,296
99336	Kennewick	(509)	28,418	15,212
98031	Kent	(206)	21,119	16,596
98033	Kirkland	(206)	16,712	14,970
98503	Lacey	(206)	13,382	9,696
98499	Lakes District(u)	(206)	NA	48,195
98632	Longview	(206)	30,037	28,373
98036	Lynwood	(206)	24,044	16,919
98438	McChord(u)	(206)	NA	6,515
98040	Mercer Island	(206)	21,318	19,047
98837	Moses Lake	(509)	10,893	10,310
98043	Mountlake Terrace	(206)	16,857	16,600
98273	Mount Vernon	(206)	12,274	8,804
98277	Oak Harbor	(206)	11,901	9,167
*98501	Olympia	(206)	29,696	23,296
99214	Opportunity(u)	(509)	NA	16,604
98444	Parkland(u)	(206)	NA	21,012
99301	Pasco	(509)	15,822	13,920
98362	Port Angeles	(206)	17,844	16,367
98368	Port Townsend	(206)	6,004	5,241
99163	Pullman	(509)	23,768	20,509
98371	Puyallup	(206)	16,799	14,742
98052	Redmond	(206)	20,217	11,020
98055	Renton	(206)	28,949	25,878
99352	Richland	(509)	33,516	26,290
*98109	Seattle	(206)	485,487	530,831
98284	Sedro Woolley	(206)	5,985	4,598
98584	Shelton	(206)	6,958	6,515
98290	Snohomish	(206)	5,242	5,174
98387	Spanaway(u)	(206)	NA	5,768
*99210	Spokane	(509)	170,993	170,516
98944	Sunnyside	(509)	7,688	6,751
*98402	Tacoma	(206)	156,625	154,407
98948	Toppenish	(509)	6,015	5,744
99268	Town and Country(u)	(509)	NA	6,484
98502	Tumwater	(206)	6,540	5,373
98406	University Place(u)	(206)	NA	13,230
*98660	Vancouver	(206)	48,438	41,859
99362	Walla Walla	(509)	24,337	23,619
98801	Wenatchee	(509)	18,136	16,912
*98901	Yakima	(509)	53,820	45,588

West Virginia (304)

ZIP code	Place	1980	1970
25801	Beckley	20,347	19,884
24701	Bluefield	15,882	15,921
26201	Buckhannon	8,119	7,261
*25301	Charleston	66,811	71,505
26301	Clarksburg	22,122	24,864
25064	Dunbar	8,881	9,151
26241	Elkins	8,324	8,287
26554	Fairmont	23,881	26,093
26354	Grafton	6,464	6,433
*25701	Huntington	68,261	74,315
26726	Keyser	6,642	6,586
25401	Martinsburg	13,075	14,626
26505	Morgantown	27,565	29,431
26041	Moundsville	12,405	13,560
26155	New Martinsville	6,889	6,528
25143	Nitro	8,252	8,019
25901	Oak Hill	7,921	6,123
26101	Parkersburg	38,827	44,208
25550	Point Pleasant	5,859	6,122
24740	Princeton	7,669	7,253
25177	St. Albans	14,485	14,356
25303	South Charleston	16,530	16,333
26105	Vienna	11,036	11,549
26062	Weirton	25,073	27,131
26452	Weston	6,144	7,323
26003	Wheeling	42,237	48,188

Wisconsin

ZIP code	Place		1980	1970
54301	Allouez(u)	(414)	NA	13,753
54409	Antigo	(715)	8,394	9,005
59411	Appleton	(414)	61,017	56,377
54806	Ashland	(715)	9,490	9,615
54304	Ashwaubenon	(414)	14,992	9,323
53913	Baraboo	(608)	7,787	7,931
53916	Beaver Dam	(414)	14,482	14,265
53511	Beloit	(608)	33,602	35,729
54923	Berlin	(414)	5,286	5,338
53005	Brookfield	(414)	35,203	32,140
53209	Brown Deer	(414)	12,929	12,582
53105	Burlington	(414)	9,244	7,479
53012	Cedarburg	(414)	10,371	7,697
54729	Chippewa Falls	(715)	12,545	12,351
53110	Cudahy	(414)	19,524	22,078
53115	Delavan	(414)	5,691	5,526
54115	De Pere	(414)	15,105	13,309
54701	Eau Claire	(715)	49,336	44,619
53122	Elm Grove	(414)	7,877	7,201
54935	Fond Du Lac	(414)	36,506	35,515
53538	Fort Atkinson	(414)	9,990	9,164
53217	Fox Point	(414)	8,135	7,939
53132	Franklin	(414)	16,750	12,247
53022	Germantown	(414)	9,886	6,974
53209	Glendale	(414)	13,842	13,426
53024	Grafton	(414)	8,751	5,998
*54305	Green Bay	(414)	91,347	87,809
53129	Greendale	(414)	16,836	15,089
53220	Greenfield	(414)	31,075	24,424
53130	Hales Corners	(414)	8,992	7,771
53027	Hartford	(414)	7,620	6,499
54303	Howard	(414)	7,418	4,911
54016	Hudson	(715)	5,855	5,049
53545	Janesville	(608)	50,372	46,426
53549	Jefferson	(414)	5,857	5,429
54130	Kaukauna	(414)	11,617	11,308
53140	Kenosha	(414)	78,949	78,805
54136	Kimberly	(414)	6,155	6,131
54601	La Crosse	(608)	49,231	51,153
53147	Lake Geneva	(414)	5,455	4,890
54140	Little Chute	(414)	6,956	5,522
*53701	Madison	(608)	170,382	171,769
54220	Manitowoc	(414)	33,208	33,430
54143	Marinette	(715)	12,128	12,696
54449	Marshfield	(715)	17,258	15,619
54952	Menasha	(414)	15,064	14,863
53051	Menomonee Falls	(414)	31,816	31,697
54751	Menomonie	(414)	11,556	11,112
53092	Mequon	(414)	16,032	12,150
54452	Merrill	(715)	9,313	9,502
53562	Middleton	(608)	11,583	8,286
*53203	Milwaukee	(414)	633,220	717,372
53716	Monona	(608)	9,512	10,420
53566	Monroe	(608)	9,658	8,654
53150	Muskego	(414)	15,165	11,573
54956	Neenah	(414)	23,897	22,902
53151	New Berlin	(414)	32,758	26,910
54961	New London	(414)	6,271	5,801
53154	Oak Creek	(414)	16,896	13,928
53066	Oconomowoc	(414)	10,687	8,741
54650	Onalaska	(608)	9,193	4,909
54901	Oshkosh	(414)	49,828	53,082
53511	Perry Go Place(u)	(608)	NA	5,912
53818	Platteville	(608)	9,133	9,599
53073	Plymouth	(414)	6,127	5,810
53901	Portage	(608)	7,652	7,821
53074	Port Washington	(414)	8,481	8,752
53821	Prairie du Chien	(608)	5,884	5,540
*53401	Racine	(414)	92,718	95,162
54501	Rhinelander	(715)	8,385	8,218
54868	Rice Lake	(715)	7,822	7,278
54971	Ripon	(414)	7,000	7,053
54022	River Falls	(715)	8,381	7,238
53207	St. Francis	(414)	10,384	10,489
54166	Shawano	(715)	6,929	6,488
53081	Sheboygan	(414)	48,815	48,484
53085	Sheboygan Falls	(414)	5,273	4,771
53211	Shorewood	(414)	14,342	15,576
53172	South Milwaukee	(414)	21,096	23,297
54656	Sparta	(608)	6,679	6,258
54481	Stevens Point	(715)	23,708	23,479
53589	Stoughton	(608)	7,972	6,096
54235	Sturgeon Bay	(414)	8,241	6,776
53590	Sun Prairie	(608)	13,757	9,935
54880	Superior	(715)	29,479	32,237

ZIP code	Place		1980	1970
54660	Tomah	(608)	*6,954*	5,647
54241	Two Rivers	(414)	*12,962*	13,553
53094	Watertown	(414)	*17,510*	15,683
53186	Waukesha	(414)	*50,252*	39,695
53963	Waupun	(414)	*7,935*	7,946
54401	Wausau	(715)	*32,601*	32,806
54401	Wausau West(u)	(715)	NA	6,399
53213	Wauwatosa	(414)	51,173	58,676
53214	West Allis	(414)	63,678	71,649
53095	West Bend	(414)	*22,904*	16,555
53217	Whitefish Bay	(414)	14,942	17,402
53190	Whitewater	(414)	*10,807*	12,038
54494	Wisconsin Rapids	(715)	*18,503*	18,587

Wyoming (307)

ZIP code	Place	1980	1970
82601	Casper	50,704	39,361
82001	Cheyenne	47,207	40,914
82414	Cody	*7,265*	5,161
82633	Douglas	*6,297*	2,677
82716	Gillette	12,125	7,194
82335	Green River	12,785	4,196
82520	Lander	*7,881*	7,125
82070	Laramie	24,339	23,143
82301	Rawlins	11,488	7,855
82501	Riverton	*9,597*	7,995
82901	Rock Springs	19,415	11,657
82801	Sheridan	15,136	10,856
82401	Worland	*5,756*	5,055

Census and Areas of Counties and States

Source: U.S. Bureau of the Census
With names of county seats or court houses

Population figures listed below are preliminary totals in the 1980 census, conducted on Apr. 1, 1980, for all counties and states released by the Census Bureau as of Oct. 15, 1980. Population figures listed in italics are 1978 Census Bureau population estimates. County figures do not add up to state totals in all cases.

Alabama

(67 counties, 50,708 sq. mi. land; pop., *3,742,000*)

County	Pop.	County Seat or court house	Land area sq. mi.
Autauga	*29,200*	Prattville	599
Baldwin	*73,900*	Bay Minette	1,578
Barbour	*25,100*	Clayton	891
Bibb	*14,700*	Centreville	625
Blount	*33,600*	Oneonta	639
Bullock	*11,700*	Union Springs	615
Butler	*21,700*	Greenville	773
Calhoun	*116,700*	Anniston	611
Chambers	*37,600*	Lafayete	597
Cherokee	*18,100*	Centre	556
Chilton	*29,100*	Clanton	699
Choctaw	*17,000*	Butler	911
Clarke	*28,000*	Grove Hill	1,232
Clay	*13,900*	Ashland	603
Cleburne	*11,900*	Heflin	574
Coffee	*35,800*	Elba	677
Colbert	54,324	Tuscumbia	596
Conecuh	*15,900*	Evergreen	850
Coosa	*11,300*	Rockford	650
Covington	*35,100*	Andalusia	984
Crenshaw	*14,200*	Luverne	611
Cullman	61,592	Cullman	730
Dale	*46,200*	Ozark	559
Dallas	*53,100*	Selma	976
De Kalb	*50,600*	Fort Payne	778
Elmore	*41,400*	Wetumpka	624
Escambia	*35,700*	Brewton	962
Etowah	*98,600*	Gadsden	555
Fayette	*16,800*	Fayette	627
Franklin	28,280	Russellville	644
Geneva	*24,200*	Geneva	577
Greene	*10,500*	Eutaw	627
Hale	*15,400*	Greensboro	662
Henry	*15,500*	Abbeville	554
Houston	*71,500*	Dothan	575
Jackson	51,326	Scottsboro	1,079
Jefferson	*657,200*	Birmingham	1,115
Lamar	*15,600*	Vernon	605
Lauderdale	80,218	Florence	662
Lawrence	30,141	Moulton	685
Lee	*70,600*	Opelika	612
Limestone	45,992	Athens	546
Lowndes	*13,800*	Hayneville	715
Macon	*26,800*	Tuskegee	616
Madison	196,716	Huntsville	803
Marengo	*23,700*	Linden	978
Marion	*26,900*	Hamilton	743
Marshall	65,499	Guntersville	571
Mobile	*361,500*	Mobile	1,240
Monroe	*22,900*	Monroeville	1,032
Montgomery	*187,700*	Montgomery	790
Morgan	89,871	Decatur	570
Perry	*13,600*	Marion	734
Pickens	*21,800*	Carrollton	887
Pike	*26,900*	Troy	673
Randolph	*18,900*	Wedowee	581
Russell	*46,600*	Phenix City	627
St. Clair	*36,700*	Ashville & Pell City	640
Shelby	*58,000*	Columbiana	798
Sumter	*16,800*	Livingston	915
Talladega	*69,200*	Talladega	750
Tallapoosa	*36,200*	Dadeville	704
Tuscaloosa	*126,300*	Tuscaloosa	1,333
Walker	*66,300*	Jasper	805
Washington	*17,700*	Chatom	1,066
Wilcox	*14,500*	Camden	899
Winston	*19,800*	Double Springs	615

Alaska

(29 divisions, 566,432 sq. mi. land; pop., *403,000*)

Census division	Pop.	Land area sq. mi.
Aleutian Islands	*7,400*	14,583
Anchorage	*179,800*	927
Angoon	*900*	2,825
Barrow	*4,400*	57,587
Bethel	*9,200*	19,642
Bristol Bay Borough	*1,300*	531
Bristol Bay	*4,100*	36,565
Cordova-McCarthy	*2,300*	15,481
Fairbanks	*52,600*	7,074
Haines	*1,700*	2,128
Juneau	*18,800*	1,286
Kenai-Cook Inlet	*22,300*	12,474
Ketchikan	*10,400*	1,345
Kobuk	*4,600*	42,978
Kodiak	*9,300*	5,375
Kuskokwim	*3,000*	56,562
Matanuska-Susitna	*16,100*	25,730
Nome	*6,700*	24,968
Outer Ketchikan	*1,400*	3,762
Prince of Wales	*3,200*	3,485
Seward	*3,100*	3,727
Sitka	*7,500*	2,296
Skagway-Yakutat	*3,100*	8,646
Southeast Fairbanks	*4,900*	17,713
Upper Yukon	*1,400*	84,142
Valdez-Chitina-Whittier	*7,400*	18,619
Wade Hampton	*4,700*	16,770
Wrangell-Petersburg	*5,700*	6,178
Yukon-Koyukuk	*5,400*	73,053

Arizona

(14 counties, 113,417 sq. mi. land; pop. *2,354,000*)

County	Pop.	County seat or court house	Land area sq. mi.
Apache	51,990	Saint Johns	11,171
Cochise	85,870	Bisbee	6,256
Coconino	75,122	Flagstaff	18,540
Gila	37,098	Globe	4,748
Graham	22,855	Safford	4,618
Greenlee	11,428	Clifton	1,879
Maricopa	*1,293,200*	Phoenix	9,155
Mohave	*41,400*	Kingman	13,217
Navajo	67,307	Holbrook	9,910
Pima	531,896	Tucson	9,240
Pinal	*87,500*	Florence	5,364
Santa Cruz	18,731	Nogales	1,246
Yavapai	*58,300*	Prescott	8,091
Yuma	*73,600*	Yuma	9,983

Arkansas

(75 counties, 51,945 sq. mi. land; pop. *2,186,000*)

County	Pop.	County seat or court house	Land area sq. mi.
Arkansas	*24,400*	DeWitt & Stuttgart	1,015
Ashley	*26,400*	Hamburg	928
Baxter	*25,300*	Mountain Home	537
Benton	*66,400*	Bentonville	851
Boone	*24,500*	Harrison	586
Bradley	*12,700*	Warren	651
Calhoun	*5,600*	Hampton	629

County	Pop.	County seat or court house	Land area sq. mi.
Carroll	*14,900*	Berryville and Eureka Sp.	626
Chicot	*16,800*	Lake Village	643
Clark	*21,400*	Arkadelphia	878
Clay	*19,800*	Corning; Piggott	639
Cleburne	*15,800*	Heber Springs	554
Cleveland	*7,000*	Rison	601
Columbia	*26,500*	Magnolia	768
Conway	*18,600*	Morrilton	561
Craighead	*62,100*	Jonesboro and Lake City	716
Crawford	*33,400*	Van Buren	596
Crittenden	*50,200*	Marion	608
Cross	*20,400*	Wynne	625
Dallas	*10,000*	Fordyce	672
Desha	*19,200*	Arkansas City	736
Drew	*16,800*	Monticello	832
Faulkner	*41,400*	Conway	641
Franklin	*13,700*	Charleston and Ozark	613
Fulton	*9,500*	Salem	608
Garland	*65,600*	Hot Spgs. Nat'l Pk.	658
Grant	*13,400*	Sheridan	631
Greene	*30,700*	Paragould	579
Hempstead	*20,700*	Hope	726
Hot Spring	*24,800*	Malvern	621
Howard	*13,400*	Nashville	569
Independence	*23,600*	Batesville	752
Izard	*10,000*	Melbourne	574
Jackson	*21,100*	Newport	629
Jefferson	*85,900*	Pine Bluff	873
Johnson	*17,100*	Clarksville	673
Lafayette	*9,600*	Lewisville	523
Lawrence	*19,100*	Walnut Ridge	590
Lee	*17,100*	Marianna	608
Lincoln	*13,100*	Star City	563
Little River	*12,000*	Ashdown	486
Logan	*19,200*	Booneville & Paris	718
Lonoke	*35,200*	Lonoke	796
Madison	*11,200*	Huntsville	832
Marion	*12,100*	Yellville	584
Miller	*33,100*	Texarkana	623
Mississippi	*65,000*	Blytheville and Osceola	904
Monroe	*14,400*	Clarendon	607
Montgomery	*6,500*	Mount Ida	775
Nevada	*10,700*	Prescott	616
Newton	*7,100*	Jasper	822
Ouachita	*29,000*	Camden	736
Perry	*7,300*	Perryville	551
Phillips	*37,900*	Helena	686
Pike	*9,600*	Murfreesboro	600
Poinsett	*28,100*	Harrisburg	760
Polk	*15,300*	Mena	859
Pope	*36,100*	Russellville	812
Prairie	*10,200*	Des Arc and De Valls Bluff	661
Pulaski	*329,300*	Little Rock	765
Randolph	*17,800*	Pocahontas	647
St. Francis	*31,500*	Forest City	635
Saline	*47,000*	Benton	724
Scott	*8,300*	Waldron	898
Searcy	*8,600*	Marshall	664
Sebastian	*90,600*	Fort Smith; Greenwood	527
Sevier	*12,000*	De Queen	522
Sharp	*12,800*	Ash Flat	581
Stone	*8,900*	Mountain View	608
Union	*45,800*	El Dorado	1,050
Van Buren	*11,800*	Clinton	699
Washington	*94,100*	Fayetteville	958
White	*47,600*	Searcy	1,041
Woodruff	*11,300*	Augusta	591
Yell	*16,300*	Danville and Dardanelle	929

California

(58 counties, 156,361 sq. mi. land; pop. *22,294,000*)

County	Pop.	County seat or court house	Land area sq. mi.
Alameda	*1,102,600*	Oakland	733
Alpine	1,093	Markleeville	727
Amador	19,261	Jackson	583
Butte	*133,600*	Oroville	1,645
Calaveras	20,442	San Andreas	1,024
Colusa	*12,800*	Colusa	1,152
Contra Costa	*622,500*	Martinez	735
Del Norte	18,210	Crescent City	1,007
El Dorado	*75,800*	Placerville	1,715
Fresno	*479,000*	Fresno	5,966
Glenn	*20,700*	Willows	1,314
Humboldt	108,486	Eureka	3,586
Imperial	*91,100*	El Centro	4,241
Inyo	17,871	Independence	10,130
Kern	*365,300*	Bakersfield	8,152
Kings	*71,400*	Hanford	1,396
Lake	36,507	Lakeport	1,261
Lassen	21,674	Susanville	4,561
Los Angeles	*7,080,900*	Los Angeles	4,069
Madera	63,078	Madera	2,145
Marin	*223,600*	San Rafael	520
Mariposa	11,055	Mariposa	1,453
Mendocino	66,751	Ukiah	3,511
Merced	*125,300*	Merced	1,958
Modoc	8,618	Alturas	4,097
Mono	8,589	Bridgeport	3,027
Monterey	*275,800*	Salinas	3,324
Napa	*93,300*	Napa	787
Nevada	51,751	Nevada City	973
Orange	*1,833,000*	Santa Ana	782
Placer	*107,100*	Auburn	1,431
Plumas	17,365	Quincy	2,566
Riverside	*606,700*	Riverside	7,176
Sacramento	780,391	Sacramento	975
San Benito	*21,600*	Hollister	1,396
San Bernardino	*778,700*	San Bernardino	20,117
San Diego	*1,743,600*	San Diego	4,261
San Francisco	*647,500*	San Francisco	45
San Joaquin	*313,100*	Stockton	1,412
San Luis Obispo	*141,500*	San Luis Obispo	3,183
San Mateo	*587,600*	Redwood City	447
Santa Barbara	296,996	Santa Barbara	2,737
Santa Clara	*1,232,200*	San Jose	1,300
Santa Cruz	*173,300*	Santa Cruz	440
Shasta	114,779	Redding	3,788
Sierra	3,069	Downieville	958
Siskiyou	39,715	Yreka	6,262
Solano	*207,700*	Fairfield	823
Sonoma	*274,200*	Santa Rosa	1,604
Stanislaus	*246,100*	Modesto	1,511
Sutter	*48,800*	Yuba City	603
Tehama	38,876	Red Bluff	2,982
Trinity	11,849	Weaverville	3,173
Tulare	*225,200*	Visalia	4,812
Tuolumne	33,921	Sonora	2,252
Ventura	527,942	Ventura	1,863
Yolo	*107,800*	Woodland	1,028
Yuba	*48,300*	Marysville	639

Colorado

(63 counties, 103,766 sq. mi. land; pop. *2,670,000*)

County	Pop.	County seat or court house	Land area sq. mi.
Adams	*234,000*	Brighton	1,237
Alamosa	*11,600*	Alamosa	719
Arapahoe	*254,000*	Littleton	797
Archuleta	*3,700*	Pagosa Springs	1,364
Baca	*5,600*	Springfield	2,563
Bent	*6,200*	Las Animas	1,519
Boulder	*174,700*	Boulder	748
Chaffee	*12,100*	Salida	1,038
Cheyenne	*2,200*	Cheyenne Wells	1,772
Clear Creek	7,264	Georgetown	394
Conejos	*8,000*	Conejos	1,268
Costilla	*3,300*	San Luis	1,213
Crowley	*2,800*	Ordway	802
Custer	*1,400*	Westcliffe	737
Delta	*19,600*	Delta	1,154
Denver	*468,600*	Denver	95
Dolores	*1,700*	Dove Creek	1,026
Douglas	25,138	Castle Rock	843
Eagle	12,707	Eagle	1,681
Elbert	*6,200*	Kiowa	1,864
El Paso	308,920	Colorado Springs	2,157
Fremont	*26,200*	Canon City	1,561
Garfield	22,483	Glenwood Springs	2,996
Gilpin	2,441	Central City	148
Grand	7,453	Hot Sulphur Springs	1,854
Gunnison	*8,500*	Gunnison	3,220
Hinsdale	*500*	Lake City	1,054
Huerfano	*6,400*	Walsenburg	1,574
Jackson	1,865	Walden	1,622
Jefferson	*348,700*	Golden	783
Kiowa	*1,800*	Eads	1,767
Kit Carson	*7,600*	Burlington	2,171
Lake	*8,000*	Leadville	379
La Plata	*25,400*	Durango	1,683
Larimer	149,205	Fort Collins	2,611
Las Animas	*15,200*	Trinidad	4,794
Lincoln	*4,400*	Hugo	2,593
Logan	19,696	Sterling	1,822
Mesa	81,482	Grand Junction	3,301
Mineral	*800*	Creede	921
Moffat	13,129	Craig	4,743
Montezuma	*15,400*	Cortez	2,094
Montrose	*22,200*	Montrose	2,238
Morgan	21,977	Fort Morgan	1,278
Otero	*22,900*	LaJunta	1,254
Ouray	*1,900*	Ouray	540
Park	*5,000*	Fairplay	2,162
Phillips	4,526	Holyoke	680
Pitkin	10,222	Aspen	973
Prowers	*13,300*	Lamar	1,621
Pueblo	125,737	Pueblo	2,405
Rio Blanco	6,294	Meeker	3,263
Rio Grande	*10,700*	Del Norte	915
Routt	13,374	Steamboat Springs	2,330
Saguache	*4,200*	Saguache	3,144
San Juan	*800*	Silverton	391
San Miguel	*2,900*	Telluride	1,283
Sedgwick	3,264	Julesburg	544
Summit	8,704	Breckenridge	604
Teller	8,019	Cripple Creek	553
Washington	5,301	Akron	2,526
Weld	*110,300*	Greeley	4,002
Yuma	9,658	Wray	2,379

Connecticut

(8 counties, 4,862 sq. mi. land; pop. 3,096,951)

County	Pop.	County seat or court house	Land area sq. mi.
Fairfield	*808,400*	Bridgeport	626
Hartford	807,153	Hartford	739
Litchfield	156,564	Litchfield	925
Middlesex	129,191	Middletown	372
New Haven	*754,600*	New Haven	604
New London	238,383	Norwich	667
Tolland	115,052	Rockville	416
Windham	92,353	Putnam	514

Delaware

(3 counties, 1,982 sq. mi. land; pop. 594,711)

County	Pop.	County seat or court house	Land area sq. mi.
Kent	98,592	Dover	594
New Castle	398,626	Wilmington	438
Sussex	97,493	Georgetown	950

District of Columbia

(61 sq. mi. land; pop. 635,185)

Florida

(67 counties, 54,090 sq. mi. land; pop. *8,594,000*)

County	Pop.	County seat or court house	Land area sq. mi.
Alachua	*129,700*	Gainesville	916
Baker	*13,400*	Macclenny	585
Bay	*92,100*	Panama City	747
Bradford	*17,500*	Starke	294
Brevard	*234,400*	Titusville	1,011
Broward	*881,900*	Fort Lauderdale	1,219
Calhoun	*8,900*	Blountstown	561
Charlotte	*46,800*	Punta Gorda	703
Citrus	*43,500*	Inverness	560
Clay	*59,400*	Green Cove Spgs.	593
Collier	*70,100*	Naples	2,006
Columbia	*30,500*	Lake City	784
Dade	*1,451,200*	Miami	2,042
De Soto	*16,900*	Arcadia	648
Dixie	*6,900*	Cross City	692
Duval	*554,900*	Jacksonville	766
Escambia	*225,600*	Pensacola	665
Flagler	*8,400*	Bunnell	487
Franklin	*8,000*	Apalachicola	536
Gadsden	*36,400*	Quincy	512
Gilchrist	*5,700*	Trenton	346
Glades	*5,700*	Moore Haven	753
Gulf	*10,300*	Port St. Joe	565
Hamilton	*8,500*	Jasper	514
Hardee	*17,000*	Wauchula	629
Hendry	*16,200*	La Belle	1,187
Hernando	*32,600*	Brooksville	484
Highlands	*39,800*	Sebring	997
Hillsborough	*584,300*	Tampa	1,038
Holmes	*14,200*	Bonifay	482
Indian River	*48,800*	Vero Beach	506
Jackson	*36,700*	Marianna	935
Jefferson	*10,300*	Monticello	605
Lafayette	*3,800*	Mayo	549
Lake	*93,300*	Tavares	961
Lee	*183,400*	Fort Myers	785
Leon	*130,500*	Tallahassee	670
Levy	*16,600*	Bronson	1,083
Liberty	*3,900*	Bristol	839
Madison	*14,500*	Madison	703
Manatee	*129,200*	Bradenton	739
Marion	*105,000*	Ocala	1,600
Martin	*49,800*	Stuart	556
Monroe	*47,700*	Key West	1,034
Nassau	*31,200*	Fernandina Beach	650
Okaloosa	*104,500*	Crestview	944
Okeechobee	*18,400*	Okeechobee	777
Orange	*420,000*	Orlando	910
Osceola	*39,100*	Kissimmee	1,313
Palm Beach	*486,700*	West Palm Beach	2,023
Pasco	*152,500*	Dade City	742
Pinellas	*659,400*	Clearwater	265
Polk	*278,200*	Bartow	1,858
Putnam	*45,100*	Palatka	779
St. Johns	*42,500*	Saint Augustine	605
St. Lucie	*72,200*	Fort Pierce	584
Santa Rosa	*49,900*	Milton	1,032
Sarasota	*174,400*	Sarasota	587
Seminole	*150,800*	Sanford	305
Sumter	*21,200*	Bushnell	555
Suwannee	*19,400*	Live Oak	686
Taylor	*14,300*	Perry	1,051
Union	*10,800*	Lake Butler	241
Volusia	*217,900*	De Land	1,062
Wakulla	*9,500*	Crawfordville	601
Walton	*18,100*	De Funiak Springs	1,053
Washington	*13,500*	Chipley	585

Georgia

(158 cos., 1 Con. govt., 58,073 sq. mi. land; pop. *5,084,000*)

County	Pop.	County seat or court house	Land area sq. mi.
Appling	*14,900*	Baxley	513
Atkinson	*6,100*	Pearson	318
Bacon	*9,500*	Alma	293
Baker	*3,900*	Newton	355
Baldwin	*32,500*	Milledgeville	255
Banks	*7,300*	Homer	231
Barrow	*19,800*	Winder	171
Bartow	40,697	Cartersville	461
Ben Hill	*15,000*	Fitzgerald	255
Berrien	*13,400*	Nashville	468
Bibb	*143,500*	Macon	254
Bleckley	*10,500*	Cochran	219
Brantley	*8,000*	Nahunta	447
Brooks	*13,500*	Quitman	491
Bryan	*8,400*	Pembroke	443
Bulloch	*35,900*	Statesboro	685
Burke	*18,700*	Waynesboro	831
Butts	*12,600*	Jackson	185
Calhoun	*6,600*	Morgan	289
Camden	*12,000*	Woodbine	653
Candler	*6,900*	Metter	250
Carroll	56,163	Carrollton	495
Catoosa	36,998	Ringgold	167
Charlton	*6,800*	Folkston	796
Chatham	*192,200*	Savannah	445
Chattahoochee	*16,600*	Cusseta	253
Chattooga	21,825	Summerville	317
Cherokee	51,748	Canton	415
Clarke	*69,100*	Athens	116
Clay	*3,500*	Fort Gaines	200
Clayton	*137,400*	Jonesboro	149
Clinch	*6,500*	Homerville	797
Cobb	*258,600*	Marietta	343
Coffee	*25,100*	Douglas	612
Colquitt	*34,100*	Moultrie	563
Columbia	*33,800*	Appling	290
Cook	*12,400*	Adel	233
Coweta	39,186	Newnan	442
Crawford	*7,000*	Knoxville	315
Crisp	*19,200*	Cordele	292
Dade	12,347	Trenton	168
Dawson	*4,800*	Dawsonville	211
Decatur	*24,900*	Bainbridge	575
De Kalb	*459,600*	Decatur	269
Dodge	*16,800*	Eastman	498
Dooly	*11,100*	Vienna	395
Dougherty	*95,000*	Albany	324
Douglas	*49,400*	Douglasville	202
Early	*13,200*	Blakely	524
Echols	*2,200*	Statenville	425
Effingham	*17,900*	Springfield	480
Elbert	*18,500*	Elberton	358
Emanuel	*20,300*	Swainsboro	686
Evans	*8,600*	Claxton	186
Fannin	14,787	Blue Ridge	394
Fayette	*23,700*	Fayetteville	199
Floyd	79,839	Rome	514
Forsyth	*23,000*	Cumming	219
Franklin	*13,900*	Carnesville	263
Fulton	*561,200*	Atlanta	530
Gilmer	11,126	Ellijay	439
Glascock	*2,700*	Gibson	143
Glynn	*49,600*	Brunswick	412
Gordon	29,921	Calhoun	358
Grady	*19,300*	Cairo	466
Greene	*10,900*	Greensboro	403
Gwinnett	*136,900*	Lawrenceville	437
Habersham	*24,700*	Clarkesville	282
Hall	*69,900*	Gainesville	378
Hancock	*9,300*	Sparta	478
Haralson	18,467	Buchanan	285
Harris	*13,000*	Hamilton	465
Hart	*16,900*	Hartwell	231
Heard	6,513	Franklin	297
Henry	*30,400*	McDonough	331
Houston	*75,300*	Perry	380
Irwin	*8,900*	Ocilla	372
Jackson	*23,900*	Jefferson	346
Jasper	*6,900*	Monticello	373
Jeff Davis	*10,400*	Hazlehurst	331
Jefferson	*17,400*	Louisville	530
Jenkins	*8,500*	Millen	351
Johnson	*7,500*	Wrightsville	313
Jones	*16,100*	Gray	402
Lamar	*11,700*	Barnesville	181
Lanier	*5,100*	Lakeland	177
Laurens	*35,500*	Dublin	810
Lee	*10,300*	Leesburg	355
Liberty	*30,200*	Hinesville	514
Lincoln	*6,200*	Lincolnton	193
Long	*3,700*	Ludowici	402
Lowndes	*63,000*	Valdosta	508
Lumpkin	*10,000*	Dahlonega	292
McDuffie	*17,800*	Thomson	253
McIntosh	*8,900*	Darien	426

County	Pop.	County seat or court house	Land area sq. mi.
Macon	*11,900*	Oglethorpe	403
Madison	*16,500*	Danielsville	281
Marion	*5,600*	Buena Vista	365
Meriwether	*20,800*	Greenville	499
Miller	*6,400*	Colquitt	287
Mitchell	*19,600*	Camilla	510
Monroe	*13,700*	Forsyth	398
Montgomery	*6,700*	Mount Vernon	237
Morgan	*10,200*	Madison	356
Murray	19,654	Chatsworth	342
Newton	*32,900*	Covington	271
Oconee	*12,000*	Watkinsville	186
Oglethorpe	*8,300*	Lexington	435
Paulding	26,086	Dallas	318
Peach	*19,700*	Fort Valley	151
Pickens	11,700	Jasper	225
Pierce	*11,100*	Blackshear	342
Pike	*8,900*	Zebulon	230
Polk	32,081	Cedartown	312
Pulaski	*8,300*	Hawkinsville	253
Putnam	*9,600*	Eatonton	339
Quitman	*2,000*	Georgetown	156
Rabun	*9,100*	Clayton	368
Randolph	*8,900*	Cuthbert	436
Richmond	*157,900*	Augusta	323
Rockdale	*31,900*	Conyers	128
Schley	*3,300*	Ellaville	162
Screven	*13,200*	Sylvania	651
Seminole	*8,000*	Donalsonville	246
Spalding	*45,700*	Griffin	201
Stephens	*22,800*	Toccoa	173
Stewart	*5,200*	Lumpkin	452
Sumter	*27,600*	Americus	488
Talbot	*6,400*	Talbotton	390
Taliaferro	*2,100*	Crawfordville	195
Tattnall	*17,100*	Reidsville	490
Taylor	*7,800*	Butler	403
Telfair	*11,700*	MacRae	440
Terrell	*10,700*	Dawson	329
Thomas	*37,700*	Thomasville	541
Tift	*31,600*	Tifton	266
Toombs	*21,400*	Lyons	368
Towns	*5,000*	Hiawassee	166
Treutlen	*6,200*	Soperton	194
Troup	*45,700*	La Grange	415
Turner	*8,900*	Ashburn	293
Twiggs	*8,100*	Jeffersonville	364
Union	*8,200*	Blairsville	309
Upson	*24,900*	Thomaston	334
Walker	56,826	La Fayette	445
Walton	*29,400*	Monroe	330
Ware	*36,500*	Waycross	912
Warren	*6,200*	Warrenton	284
Washington	*16,700*	Sandersville	674
Wayne	*19,400*	Jesup	645
Webster	*2,400*	Preston	195
Wheeler	*4,900*	Alamo	306
White	*8,900*	Cleveland	243
Whitfield	65,725	Dalton	281
Wilcox	*7,300*	Abbeville	383
Wilkes	*10,400*	Washington	468
Wilkinson	*9,900*	Irwinton	458
Worth	*16,500*	Sylvester	579
Consolidated government			
Columbus	*164,900*		220

Hawaii

(4 counties, 6,425 sq. mi. land; pop. *897,000*)

Hawaii	92,206	Hilo	4,037
Honolulu	*719,600*	Honolulu	596
Kauai	39,117	Lihue	619
Maui*	71,191	Wailuku	1,173

*Includes population of Kalawao County (146).

Idaho

(44 counties, 82,677 sq. mi. land; pop. *878,000*)

Ada	172,915	Boise	1,043
Adams	3,347	Council	1,371
Bannock	65,430	Pocatello	1,122
Bear Lake	6,946	Paris	984
Benewah	8,295	Saint Maries	788
Bingham	36,473	Blackfoot	2,084
Blaine	9,825	Hailey	2,647
Boise	2,998	Idaho City	1,910
Bonner	24,155	Sandpoint	1,733
Bonneville	65,565	Idaho Falls	1,836
Boundary	7,302	Bonners Ferry	1,275
Butte	3,351	Arco	2,239
Camas	809	Fairfield	1,054
Canyon	83,661	Caldwell	578
Caribou	8,689	Soda Springs	1,746
Cassia	19,476	Burley	2,544
Clark	798	Dubois	1,751
Clearwater	10,383	Orofino	2,521
Custer	3,392	Challis	4,929
Elmore	21,502	Mountain Home	3,048
Franklin	8,892	Preston	664
Fremont	10,806	Saint Anthony	1,864
Gem	11,967	Emmett	555
Gooding	11,845	Gooding	720
Idaho	14,724	Grangeville	8,516
Jefferson	15,316	Rigby	1,096
Jerome	14,804	Jerome	595
Kootenai	59,785	Coeur d'Alene	1,249
Latah	28,667	Moscow	1,090
Lemhi	7,444	Salmon	4,580
Lewis	4,084	Nezperce	476
Lincoln	3,439	Shoshone	1,203
Madison	19,502	Rexberg	473
Minidoka	19,693	Rupert	750
Nez Perce	33,218	Lewiston	844
Oneida	3,233	Malad City	1,191
Owyhee	8,239	Murphy	7,641
Payette	15,827	Payette	402
Power	6,879	American Falls	1,413
Shoshone	19,234	Wallace	2,609
Teton	2,907	Driggs	457
Twin Falls	52,869	Twin Falls	1,947
Valley	5,633	Cascade	3,676
Washington	8,815	Weiser	1,462

Illinois

(102 counties, 55,748 sq. mi. land; pop. *11,243,000*)

Adams	*68,300*	Quincy	862
Alexander	*11,200*	Cairo	229
Bond	*14,300*	Greenville	378
Boone	*27,000*	Belvidere	283
Brown	*5,200*	Mount Sterling	306
Bureau	*37,300*	Princeton	866
Calhoun	*5,400*	Hardin	247
Carroll	*18,400*	Mount Carroll	456
Cass	*13,500*	Virginia	371
Champaign	*164,200*	Urbana	1,000
Christian	*36,500*	Taylorville	709
Clark	*16,600*	Marshall	505
Clay	*14,500*	Louisville	464
Clinton	*31,100*	Carlyle	434
Coles	*49,000*	Charleston	506
Cook	*5,269,700*	Chicago	954
Crawford	*20,100*	Robinson	443
Cumberland	*10,600*	Toledo	347
De Kalb	*71,000*	Sycamore	636
De Witt	*17,000*	Clinton	399
Douglas	*19,600*	Tuscola	420
Du Page	*599,100*	Wheaton	331
Edgar	*21,300*	Paris	628
Edwards	*78,000*	Albion	225
Effingham	*29,400*	Effingham	481
Fayette	*21,300*	Vandalia	703
Ford	*14,900*	Paxton	488
Franklin	*41,400*	Benton	434
Fulton	*43,100*	Lewiston	877
Gallatin	*6,900*	Shawneetown	328
Greene	*16,400*	Carrollton	543
Grundy	*30,000*	Morris	432
Hamilton	*9,100*	McLeansboro	435
Hancock	*22,700*	Carthage	797
Hardin	*5,300*	Elizabethtown	183
Henderson	*8,400*	Oquawka	376
Henry	*56,900*	Cambridge	826
Iroquois	*32,700*	Watseka	1,122
Jackson	*55,800*	Murphysboro	605
Jasper	*11,300*	Newton	495
Jefferson	*36,400*	Mount Vernon	573
Jersey	*20,200*	Jerseyville	376
Jo Daviess	*22,700*	Galena	606
Johnson	*9,000*	Vienna	345
Kane	*276,800*	Geneva	520
Kankakee	*96,600*	Kankakee	678
Kendall	*34,900*	Yorkville	320
Knox	*60,500*	Galesburg	728
Lake	*429,200*	Waukegan	457
La Salle	*107,400*	Ottawa	1,150
Lawrence	*17,900*	Lawrenceville	374
Lee	*35,500*	Dixon	728
Livingston	*40,800*	Pontiac	1,043
Logan	*29,900*	Lincoln	622
McDonough	*36,900*	Macomb	582
McHenry	*140,000*	Woodstock	610
McLean	*118,600*	Bloomington	1,173
Macon	*127,800*	Decatur	578
Macoupin	*47,000*	Carlinville	872
Madison	*245,800*	Edwardsville	733
Marion	*41,900*	Salem	579
Marshall	*13,600*	Lacon	391
Mason	*19,800*	Havana	541
Massac	*15,000*	Metropolis	245
Menard	*11,200*	Petersburg	312
Mercer	*18,200*	Aledo	556
Monroe	*19,200*	Waterloo	382
Montgomery	*31,000*	Hillsboro	705
Morgan	*35,300*	Jacksonville	561
Moultrie	*13,500*	Sullivan	326

County	Pop.	County seat or court house	Land area sq. mi.
Ogle	42,600	Oregon	758
Peoria	199,500	Peoria	623
Perry	21,000	Pickneyville	439
Piatt	16,000	Monticello	437
Pike	18,800	Pittsfield	828
Pope	4,500	Golconda	381
Pulaski	8,600	Mound City	204
Putnam	5,600	Hennepin	160
Randolph	34,300	Chester	594
Richland	17,100	Olney	364
Rock Island	161,600	Rock Island	424
St. Clair	279,900	Belleville	673
Saline	27,400	Harrisburg	383
Sangamon	173,300	Springfield	879
Schuyler	8,100	Rushville	434
Scott	5,900	Winchester	251
Shelby	22,800	Shelbyville	752
Stark	7,200	Toulon	291
Stephenson	46,700	Freeport	568
Tazewell	129,000	Pekin	652
Union	16,900	Jonesboro	416
Vermilion	97,100	Danville	899
Wabash	13,600	Mt. Carmel	222
Warren	21,300	Monmouth	541
Washington	15,400	Nashville	564
Wayne	17,300	Fairfield	715
White	17,200	Carmi	502
Whiteside	63,200	Morrison	687
Will	314,900	Joliet	847
Williamson	54,500	Marion	429
Winnebago	242,400	Rockford	519
Woodford	32,100	Eureka	528

Indiana

(92 counties, 36,097 sq. mi. land; pop. *5,374,000*)

Adams	27,800	Decatur	345
Allen	291,200	Fort Wayne	671
Bartholomew	60,800	Columbus	402
Benton	10,700	Fowler	409
Blackford	15,200	Hartford City	167
Boone	34,400	Lebanon	427
Brown	10,300	Nashville	319
Carroll	18,100	Delphi	374
Cass	39,300	Logansport	415
Clark	87,900	Jeffersonville	384
Clay	25,000	Brazil	364
Clinton	29,800	Frankfort	407
Crawford	8,800	English	312
Daviess	25,800	Washington	430
Dearborn	33,200	Lawrenceburg	306
Decatur	23,800	Greensburg	370
DeKalb	31,900	Auburn	366
Delaware	127,700	Muncie	396
Dubois	32,700	Jasper	433
Elkhart	135,700	Goshen	468
Fayette	26,900	Connersville	215
Floyd	58,500	New Albany	149
Fountain	18,300	Covington	397
Franklin	18,800	Brookville	394
Fulton	18,000	Rochester	368
Gibson	32,100	Princeton	498
Grant	82,800	Marion	421
Greene	28,100	Bloomfield	549
Hamilton	79,400	Noblesville	401
Hancock	42,200	Greenfield	305
Harrison	25,300	Corydon	479
Hendricks	66,000	Danville	417
Henry	53,500	New Castle	400
Howard	87,900	Kokomo	293
Huntington	35,200	Huntington	369
Jackson	34,700	Brownstown	520
Jasper	24,300	Rensselaer	562
Jay	23,300	Portland	386
Jefferson	28,200	Madison	366
Jennings	21,000	Vernon	377
Johnson	75,900	Franklin	315
Knox	39,300	Vincennes	516
Kosciusko	55,300	Warsaw	540
Lagrange	24,200	Lagrange	381
Lake	539,400	Crown Point	513
La Porte	106,300	La Porte	607
Lawrence	40,500	Bedford	459
Madison	138,100	Anderson	453
Marion	768,300	Indianapolis	392
Marshall	39,100	Plymouth	443
Martin	11,000	Shoals	345
Miami	39,100	Peru	377
Monroe	92,200	Bloomington	386
Montgomery	34,300	Crawfordsville	507
Morgan	51,100	Martinsville	406
Newton	13,700	Kentland	413
Noble	33,300	Albion	412
Ohio	5,100	Rising Sun	87
Orange	17,400	Paoli	405
Owen	14,100	Spencer	390
Parke	15,800	Rockville	445
Perry	18,300	Cannelton	384
Pike	12,500	Petersburg	335
Porter	109,100	Valparaiso	425
Posey	23,600	Mount Vernon	412
Pulaski	12,900	Winamac	433
Putnam	29,100	Greencastle	490
Randolph	28,400	Winchester	457
Ripley	22,300	Versailles	442
Rush	20,100	Rushville	409
St. Joseph	241,700	South Bend	466
Scott	19,500	Scottsburg	193
Shelby	38,800	Shelbyville	409
Spencer	17,900	Rockport	396
Starke	20,900	Knox	310
Steuben	23,400	Angola	309
Sullivan	19,800	Sullivan	457
Switzerland	6,800	Vevay	221
Tippecanoe	115,000	Lafayette	500
Tipton	15,800	Tipton	261
Union	7,100	Liberty	168
Vanderburgh	162,500	Evansville	241
Vermillion	16,900	Newport	263
Vigo	112,200	Terre Haute	415
Wabash	36,200	Wabash	398
Warren	8,400	Williamsport	368
Warrick	37,900	Boonville	391
Washington	21,000	Salem	516
Wayne	75,700	Richmond	405
Wells	24,800	Bluffton	368
White	22,600	Monticello	497
Whitely	25,300	Columbia City	337

Iowa

(99 counties; 55,941 sq. mi. land; pop. *2,896,000*)

Adair	9,515	Greenfield	569
Adams	5,729	Corning	426
Allamakee	15,800	Waukon	636
Appanoose	15,300	Centerville	523
Audubon	9,300	Audubon	448
Benton	24,100	Vinton	718
Black Hawk	138,800	Waterloo	568
Boone	26,169	Boone	573
Bremer	24,400	Waverly	439
Buchanan	22,900	Independence	568
Buena Vista	20,600	Storm Lake	572
Butler	17,300	Allison	582
Calhoun	13,600	Rockwell City	571
Carroll	23,500	Carroll	574
Cass	17,100	Atlantic	559
Cedar	18,100	Tipton	585
Cerro Gordo	48,000	Mason City	575
Cherokee	16,500	Cherokee	573
Chickasaw	15,600	New Hampton	505
Clarke	8,623	Oscea	429
Clay	19,600	Spencer	580
Clayton	20,600	Elkader	779
Clinton	58,200	Clinton	693
Crawford	18,800	Denison	716
Dallas	29,580	Adel	597
Davis	8,800	Bloomfield	509
Decatur	9,786	Leon	530
Delaware	19,300	Manchester	572
Des Moines	45,900	Burlington	408
Dickinson	14,400	Spirit Lake	380
Dubuque	92,900	Dubuque	612
Emmet	13,800	Estherville	394
Fayette	25,500	West Union	728
Floyd	20,100	Charles City	503
Franklin	13,300	Hampton	586
Fremont	9,100	Sidney	524
Greene	12,110	Jefferson	569
Grundy	14,300	Grundy Center	501
Guthrie	11,978	Guthrie Center	596
Hamilton	17,700	Webster City	577
Hancock	13,700	Garner	570
Hardin	21,400	Eldora	574
Harrison	16,300	Logan	696
Henry	18,100	Mount Pleasant	440
Howard	11,100	Cresco	471
Humboldt	12,500	Dakota City	435
Ida	8,800	Ida Grove	431
Iowa	15,000	Marengo	584
Jackson	22,700	Maquoketa	644
Jasper	36,600	Newton	731
Jefferson	15,100	Fairfield	436
Johnson	78,000	Iowa City	619
Jones	19,800	Anamosa	585
Keokuk	13,200	Sigourney	579
Kossuth	22,800	Algona	979
Lee	42,400	Fort Madison and Keokuk	527
Linn	166,500	Cedar Rapids	717
Louisa	11,600	Wapello	403
Lucas	10,326	Chariton	434
Lyon	13,400	Rock Rapids	588
Madison	12,611	Winterset	564
Mahaska	22,700	Oskaloosa	572
Marion	28,900	Knoxville	498
Marshall	42,300	Marshalltown	574
Mills	13,100	Glenwood	447

County	Pop.	County seat or court house	Land area sq. mi.
Mitchell	12,600	Osage	467
Monona	11,900	Onawa	699
Monroe	9,400	Albia	435
Montgomery	13,000	Red Oak	422
Muscatine	39,500	Muscatine	443
O'Brien	17,400	Primghar	575
Osceola	8,000	Sibley	398
Page	19,000	Clarinda	535
Palo Alto	13,200	Emmetsburg	561
Plymouth	24,700	Le Mars	863
Pocahontas	11,600	Pocahontas	581
Polk	301,879	Des Moines	578
Pottawattamie	86,000	Council Bluffs	963
Poweshiek	19,400	Montezuma	589
Ringgold	6,106	Mount Ayr	538
Sac	14,700	Sac City	578
Scott	155,700	Davenport	454
Shelby	15,200	Harlan	587
Sioux	30,100	Orange City	766
Story	72,324	Nevada	568
Tama	20,000	Toledo	720
Taylor	8,370	Bedford	528
Union	13,882	Creston	425
Van Buren	8,700	Keosauqua	487
Wapello	40,400	Ottumwa	437
Warren	34,857	Indianola	558
Washington	18,900	Washington	568
Wayne	8,179	Corydon	532
Webster	47,000	Fort Dodge	718
Winnebago	13,900	Forest City	401
Winneshiek	21,900	Decorah	688
Woodbury	102,700	Sioux City	871
Worth	9,100	Northwood	400
Wright	16,800	Clarion	577

Kansas

(105 counties, 81,787 sq. mi. land; pop. *2,348,000*)

Allen	16,000	Iola	505
Anderson	8,600	Garnett	577
Atchison	17,700	Atchison	427
Barber	6,400	Medicine Lodge	1,146
Barton	31,600	Great Bend	894
Bourbon	15,900	Fort Scott	639
Brown	11,700	Hiawatha	577
Butler	43,500	El Dorado	1,442
Chase	3,400	Cottonwood Falls	774
Chautauqua	4,400	Sedan	647
Cherokee	21,600	Columbus	586
Cheyenne	3,900	Saint Francis	1,027
Clark	2,800	Ashland	983
Clay	10,100	Clay Center	635
Cloud	13,000	Concordia	711
Coffey	8,900	Burlington	617
Comanche	2,700	Coldwater	800
Cowley	35,300	Winfield	1,136
Crawford	37,600	Girard	598
Decatur	5,100	Oberlin	899
Dickinson	20,500	Abilene	855
Doniphan	8,900	Troy	388
Douglas	65,200	Lawrence	471
Edwards	4,500	Kinsley	617
Elk	3,900	Howard	647
Ellis	27,400	Hays	900
Ellsworth	6,200	Ellsworth	717
Finney	23,700	Garden City	1,301
Ford	24,000	Dodge City	1,091
Franklin	21,000	Ottawa	577
Geary	28,600	Junction City	374
Gove	3,900	Gove	1,070
Graham	4,400	Hill City	891
Grant	7,400	Ulysses	571
Gray	5,200	Cimarron	872
Greeley	1,800	Tribune	783
Greenwood	9,200	Eureka	1,133
Hamilton	2,900	Syracuse	992
Harper	7,900	Anthony	801
Harvey	29,100	Newton	540
Haskell	4,400	Sublette	580
Hodgeman	2,500	Jetmore	860
Jackson	12,100	Holton	656
Jefferson	14,600	Oskaloosa	510
Jewell	5,800	Mankato	910
Johnson	262,600	Olathe	476
Kearny	3,700	Lakin	855
Kingman	8,900	Kingman	864
Kiowa	4,100	Greensburg	720
Labette	25,900	Oswego	654
Lane	2,600	Dighton	720
Leavenworth	55,100	Leavenworth	466
Lincoln	4,500	Lincoln	725
Linn	8,600	Mound City	606
Logan	3,600	Oakley	1,073
Lyon	34,900	Emporia	841
McPherson	26,300	McPherson	896
Marion	13,400	Marion	945
Marshall	13,300	Marysville	883
Meade	5,100	Meade	979
Miami	21,800	Paola	592
Mitchell	8,100	Beloit	714
Montgomery	40,500	Independence	628
Morris	6,800	Council Grove	697
Morton	3,700	Elkhart	728
Nemaha	11,400	Seneca	708
Neosho	18,800	Erie	587
Ness	4,700	Ness City	1,081
Norton	6,700	Norton	872
Osage	14,800	Lyndon	707
Osborne	6,400	Osborne	886
Ottawa	6,400	Minneapolis	723
Pawnee	8,400	Larned	755
Phillips	7,600	Phillipsburg	897
Pottawatomie	14,100	Westmoreland	820
Pratt	10,100	Pratt	729
Rawlins	4,300	Atwood	1,078
Reno	63,700	Hutchinson	1,260
Republic	7,700	Belleville	718
Rice	12,300	Lyons	725
Riley	66,100	Manhattan	597
Rooks	7,300	Stockton	886
Rush	4,800	LaCrosse	724
Russell	9,100	Russell	867
Saline	48,900	Salina	720
Scott	6,100	Scott City	724
Sedgwick	354,000	Wichita	1,007
Seward	16,900	Liberal	646
Shawnee	157,100	Topeka	548
Sheridan	3,900	Hoxie	893
Sherman	7,900	Goodland	1,055
Smith	6,400	Smith Center	893
Stafford	6,200	Saint John	795
Stanton	2,600	Johnson	676
Stevens	4,800	Hugoton	731
Sumner	24,500	Wellington	1,186
Thomas	8,500	Colby	1,070
Trego	4,400	Wakeeney	901
Wabaunsee	7,000	Alma	792
Wallace	2,200	Sharon Springs	911
Washington	9,000	Washington	891
Wichita	3,300	Leoti	724
Wilson	12,000	Fredonia	574
Woodson	4,400	Yates Center	497
Wyandotte	174,200	Kansas City	152

Kentucky

(120 counties, 39,650 sq. mi. land; pop. *3,489,000*)

Adair	14,200	Columbia	370
Allen	13,300	Scottsville	351
Anderson	11,400	Lawrenceburg	206
Ballard	9,000	Wickliffe	259
Barren	30,900	Glasgow	468
Bath	9,400	Owingsville	287
Bell	33,500	Pineville	370
Boone	41,800	Burlington	249
Bourbon	19,700	Paris	300
Boyd	54,900	Catlettsburg	159
Boyle	23,900	Danville	183
Bracken	7,700	Brooksville	204
Breathitt	17,100	Jackson	494
Breckinridge	16,000	Hardinsburg	554
Bullitt	39,100	Shepherdsville	300
Butler	10,600	Morgantown	443
Caldwell	13,200	Princeton	357
Calloway	28,900	Murray	384
Campbell	83,800	Alexandria	149
Carlisle	6,300	Bardwell	195
Carroll	8,800	Carrollton	130
Carter	23,300	Grayson	397
Casey	14,600	Liberty	435
Christian	67,600	Hopkinsville	725
Clark	26,900	Winchester	259
Clay	21,800	Manchester	474
Clinton	8,900	Albany	190
Crittenden	9,200	Marion	365
Cumberland	7,200	Burkesville	310
Daviess	81,100	Owensboro	462
Edmonson	9,500	Brownsville	298
Elliott	6,400	Sandy Hook	240
Estill	13,600	Irvine	260
Fayette	191,600	Lexington	280
Fleming	11,700	Flemingsburg	350
Floyd	43,500	Prestonsburg	399
Franklin	39,200	Frankfort	211
Fulton	9,100	Hickman	203
Gallatin	4,600	Warsaw	100
Garrard	10,100	Lancaster	236
Grant	12,300	Williamstown	249
Graves	33,100	Mayfield	60
Grayson	19,500	Leitchfield	496
Green	11,000	Greensburg	282
Greenup	37,000	Greenup	351
Hancock	7,400	Hawesville	187
Hardin	78,300	Elizabeth	616
Harlan	40,900	Harlan	469
Harrison	14,800	Cynthiana	308
Hart	15,300	Munfordville	420

Parish	Pop.	Parish seat or court house	Land area sq. mi.
Henderson	38,700	Henderson	433
Henry	11,700	New Castle	289
Hickman	6,200	Clinton	246
Hopkins	45,400	Madisonville	553
Jackson	10,600	McKee	337
Jefferson	678,200	Louisville	375
Jessamine	24,300	Nicholasville	177
Johnson	22,700	Paintsville	264
Kenton	132,000	Independence	165
Knott	18,200	Hindman	356
Knox	28,700	Barbourville	373
Larue	11,600	Hodgenville	260
Laurel	35,200	London	446
Lawrence	12,800	Louisa	425
Lee	7,400	Beattyville	210
Leslie	13,700	Hyden	409
Letcher	27,800	Whitesburg	339
Lewis	13,900	Vanceburg	486
Lincoln	18,300	Stanford	340
Livingston	9,500	Smithland	311
Logan	22,300	Russellville	563
Lyon	6,200	Eddyville	216
McCracken	62,700	Paducah	250
McCreary	15,200	Whitley City	418
McLean	10,800	Calhoun	257
Madison	49,500	Richmond	446
Magoffin	12,300	Salyersville	303
Marion	17,000	Lebanon	343
Marshall	24,400	Benton	303
Martin	12,500	Inez	231
Mason	17,200	Maysville	238
Meade	21,100	Brandenburg	305
Menifee	4,700	Frenchburg	210
Mercer	18,100	Harrodsburg	256
Metcalfe	8,700	Edmonton	296
Monroe	12,000	Tompkinsville	334
Montgomery	18,000	Mount Sterling	204
Morgan	11,200	West Liberty	369
Muhlenberg	32,000	Greenville	481
Nelson	26,400	Bardstown	437
Nicholas	7,000	Carlisle	204
Ohio	21,900	Hartford	596
Oldham	23,600	La Grange	184
Owen	8,300	Owenton	351
Owsley	5,500	Booneville	197
Pendleton	10,900	Falmouth	279
Perry	29,500	Hazard	341
Pike	73,800	Pikeville	782
Powell	9,600	Stanton	173
Pulaski	43,400	Somerset	653
Robertson	2,100	Mount Olivet	101
Rockcastle	13,400	Mount Vernon	311
Rowan	17,500	Morehead	290
Russell	12,200	Jamestown	238
Scott	20,200	Georgetown	284
Shelby	21,300	Shelbyville	383
Simpson	14,500	Franklin	239
Spencer	5,800	Taylorsville	193
Taylor	18,900	Campbellsville	277
Todd	12,100	Elkton	376
Trigg	10,000	Cadiz	408
Trimble	5,900	Bedford	146
Union	18,000	Morganfield	340
Warren	64,400	Bowling Green	546
Washington	10,400	Springfield	307
Wayne	16,400	Monticello	440
Webster	15,200	Dixon	339
Whitley	30,900	Williamsburg	459
Wolfe	6,400	Campton	227
Woodford	17,000	Versailles	193

Louisiana

(64 parishes, 44,930 sq. mi. land; pop. *3,966,000*)

Acadia	54,300	Crowley	663
Allen	20,700	Oberlin	774
Ascension	44,400	Donaldsville	301
Assumption	20,800	Napoleonville	356
Avoyelles	39,200	Marksville	832
Beauregard	27,600	De Ridder	1,181
Bienville	17,200	Arcadia	832
Bossier	71,700	Benton	849
Caddo	242,400	Shreveport	899
Calcasieu	157,700	Lake Charles	1,105
Caldwell	10,200	Columbia	551
Cameron	9,500	Cameron	1,441
Catahoula	11,700	Harrisonburg	742
Claiborne	16,700	Homer	763
Concordia	22,200	Vidalia	718
De Soto	23,700	Mansfield	894
East Baton Rouge	332,300	Baton Rouge	459
East Carroll	11,700	Lake Providence	436
East Feliciana	16,500	Clinton	454
Evangeline	33,300	Ville Platte	669
Franklin	24,000	Winnsboro	648
Grant	15,200	Colfax	670
Iberia	64,600	New Iberia	589
Iberville	30,800	Plaquemine	627
Jackson	16,900	Jonesboro	582
Jefferson	427,000	Gretna	369
Jefferson Davis	31,500	Jennings	658
Lafayette	134,200	Lafayette	283
Lafourche	76,900	Thibodaux	1,141
La Salle	15,200	Jena	643
Lincoln	37,200	Ruston	469
Livingston	49,900	Livingston	654
Madison	14,600	Tallulah	661
Morehouse	33,700	Bastrop	804
Natchitoches	36,200	Natchitoches	1,292
Orleans	556,913	New Orleans	197
Ouachita	130,700	Monroe	638
Plaquemines	26,700	Pointe a la Hacke	1,030
Pointe Coupee	22,600	New Roads	563
Rapides	124,900	Alexandria	1,318
Red River	9,300	Coushatta	406
Richland	21,500	Rayville	576
Sabine	20,100	Many	873
St. Bernard	62,300	Chalmette	514
St. Charles	34,700	Hahnville	294
St. Helena	9,900	Greensburg	420
St. James	19,900	Convent	253
St. John The Baptist	28,600	Edgard	227
St. Landry	83,200	Opelousas	932
St. Martin	36,000	Saint Martinville	736
St. Mary	61,700	Franklin	624
St. Tammany	92,600	Covington	887
Tangipahoa	76,400	Amite	808
Tensas	8,400	Saint Joseph	626
Terrebonne	89,400	Houma	1,368
Union	20,100	Farmerville	885
Vermilion	47,000	Abbeville	1,205
Vernon	45,900	Leesville	1,351
Washington	43,100	Franklinton	665
Webster	42,100	Minden	615
West Baton Rouge	18,100	Port Allen	203
West Carroll	12,800	Oak Grove	356
West Feliciana	9,900	Saint Francisville	405
Winn	17,200	Winnfield	950

Maine

(16 counties, 30,920 sq. mi. land; pop. 1,123,562)

Androscoggin	99,682	Auburn	474
Aroostook	91,256	Houlton	6,821
Cumberland	215,521	Portland	879
Franklin	27,003	Farmington	1,709
Hancock	41,735	Ellsworth	1,536
Kennebec	109,721	Augusta	872
Knox	32,952	Rockland	369
Lincoln	25,600	Wiscasset	454
Oxford	48,949	South Paris	2,080
Penobscot	137,018	Bangor	3,390
Piscataquis	17,612	Dover-Foxcroft	3,892
Sagadahoc	28,763	Bath	257
Somerset	44,989	Skowhegan	3,894
Waldo	28,418	Belfast	737
Washington	34,921	Machias	2,554
York	139,420	Alfred	1,001

Maryland

(23 cos., 1 ind. city, 9,891 sq. mi. land; pop. *4,143,000*)

Allegany	79,600	Cumberland	428
Anne Arundel	369,914	Annapolis	423
Baltimore	638,900	Towson	598
Calvert	34,308	Prince Frederick	217
Caroline	22,500	Denton	321
Carroll	92,500	Westminster	456
Cecil	56,400	Elkton	362
Charles	72,343	La Plata	459
Dorchester	30,600	Cambridge	594
Frederick	107,900	Frederick	665
Garrett	25,900	Oakland	659
Harford	146,200	Bel Air	453
Howard	116,600	Ellicott City	251
Kent	16,200	Chestertown	281
Montgomery	574,106	Rockville	495
Prince Georges	662,200	Upper Marlboro	485
Queen Annes	23,800	Centreville	375
St. Marys	59,799	Leonardtown	373
Somerset	19,100	Princess Anne	339
Talbot	26,800	Easton	261
Washington	109,600	Hagerstown	459
Wicomico	60,600	Salisbury	381
Worcester	27,800	Snow Hill	479
Independent City			
Baltimore	789,700		78

Massachusetts

(14 counties; 7,826 sq. mi. land; pop. 5,725,983)

Barnstable	147,591	Barnstable	393
Berkshire	144,892	Pittsfield	941
Bristol	473,902	Taunton	554
Dukes	8,878	Edgartown	104

County	Pop.	County seat or court house	Land area sq. mi.
Essex	631,265	Salem	494
Franklin	64,333	Greenfield	708
Hampden	442,884	Springfield	619
Hampshire	138,630	Northampton	529
Middlesex	1,366,969	Cambridge	825
Nantucket	5,072	Nantucket	46
Norfolk	603,281	Dedham	394
Plymouth	404,921	Plymouth	654
Suffolk	649,101	Boston	56
Worcester	643,968	Worcester	1,509

Michigan

(83 counties; 56,817 sq. mi. land; pop. *9,189,000*)

Alcona	9,719	Harrisville	678
Alger	9,220	Munising	905
Allegan	*74,000*	Allegan	826
Alpena	32,238	Alpena	565
Antrim	16,166	Bellaire	476
Arenac	*13,500*	Standish	367
Baraga	8,480	L'Anse	901
Barry	*42,900*	Hastings	554
Bay	119,849	Bay City	447
Benzie	11,165	Beulah	316
Berrien	*167,300*	Saint Joseph	580
Branch	*38,900*	Coldwater	506
Calhoun	*140,700*	Marshall	709
Cass	*45,400*	Cassopolis	491
Charlevoix	19,892	Charlevoix	414
Cheboygan	20,605	Cheboygan	721
Chippewa	28,964	Sault Sainte Marie	1,590
Clare	*23,800*	Harrison	571
Clinton	*55,000*	Saint Johns	572
Crawford	9,475	Grayling	561
Delta	38,963	Escanaba	1,177
Dickinson	25,777	Iron Mountain	757
Eaton	*82,100*	Charlotte	571
Emmet	22,792	Petoskey	461
Genesee	450,343	Flint	642
Gladwin	*18,300*	Gladwin	503
Gogebic	19,617	Bessemer	1,107
Grand Traverse	54,698	Traverse City	462
Gratiot	*39,300*	Ithaca	566
Hillsdale	*41,200*	Hillsdale	600
Houghton	37,839	Houghton	1,017
Huron	36,422	Bad Axe	819
Ingham	*271,000*	Mason	559
Ionia	*49,700*	Ionia	575
Iosco	28,273	Iawas City	544
Iron	13,607	Crystal Falls	1,171
Isabella	*52,100*	Mount Pleasant	572
Jackson	*150,200*	Jackson	698
Kalamazoo	*208,000*	Kalamazoo	562
Kalkaska	10,926	Kalkaska	566
Kent	444,030	Grand Rapids	857
Keweenaw	1,964	Eagle River	538
Lake	*7,000*	Baldwin	571
Lapeer	69,992	Lapeer	658
Leelanau	13,986	Leland	345
Lenawee	*87,300*	Adrian	753
Livingston	*92,300*	Howell	572
Luce	6,659	Newberry	906
Mackinac	10,193	Saint Ignace	1,014
Macomb	*693,400*	Mount Clemens	480
Manistee	*22,500*	Manistee	553
Marquette	74,115	Marquette	1,828
Mason	*24,700*	Ludington	490
Mecosta	*34,800*	Big Rapids	560
Menominee	26,224	Menominee	1,038
Midland	73,672	Midland	520
Missaukee	9,997	Lake City	565
Monroe	*131,800*	Monroe	557
Montcalm	*45,400*	Stanton	712
Montmorency	7,467	Atlanta	555
Muskegon	157,103	Muskegon	501
Newaygo	*33,400*	White Cloud	849
Oakland	*1,009,400*	Pontiac	867
Oceana	*21,000*	Hart	536
Ogemaw	16,439	West Branch	571
Ontonagon	9,832	Ontonagon	1,316
Osceola	*18,200*	Reed City	581
Oscoda	6,843	Mio	563
Otsego	14,983	Gaylord	527
Ottawa	156,975	Grand Haven	563
Presque Isle	14,217	Rogers City	648
Roscommon	16,324	Roscommon	521
Saginaw	227,862	Saginaw	814
St. Clair	138,685	Port Huron	734
St. Joseph	*51,800*	Centreville	506
Sanilac	40,729	Sandusky	961
Schoolcraft	8,574	Manistique	1,181
Shiawassee	71,136	Corunna	540
Tuscola	56,843	Caro	815
Van Buren	*62,300*	Paw Paw	603
Washtenaw	*254,500*	Ann Arbor	711
Wayne	*2,390,600*	Detroit	605
Wexford	*22,800*	Cadillac	559

Minnesota

(87 counties; 79,289 sq. mi. land; pop., *4,008,000*)

Aitkin	13,395	Aitkin	1,828
Anoka	*199,500*	Anoka	424
Becker	*28,400*	Detroit Lakes	1,297
Beltrami	30,815	Bemidji	2,507
Benton	*22,800*	Foley	402
Big Stone	*7,700*	Ortonville	490
Blue Earth	*50,400*	Mankato	737
Brown	*30,100*	New Ulm	610
Carlton	*30,200*	Carlton	862
Carver	*35,600*	Chaska	359
Cass	21,104	Walker	1,998
Chippewa	*15,700*	Montevideo	582
Chisago	*24,000*	Center City	419
Clay	*47,900*	Moorhead	1,045
Clearwater	8,700	Bagley	1,000
Cook	*4,300*	Grand Marais	1,346
Cottonwood	*15,300*	Windom	636
Crow Wing	*40,100*	Brainerd	995
Dakota	*190,200*	Hastings	576
Dodge	*14,000*	Mantorville	435
Douglas	*25,900*	Alexandria	647
Faribault	*19,800*	Blue Earth	711
Fillmore	*21,800*	Preston	859
Freeborn	*36,900*	Albert Lea	701
Goodhue	*38,400*	Red Wind	753
Grant	*7,500*	Elbow Lake	546
Hennepin	*909,900*	Minneapolis	567
Houston	*18,200*	Caledonia	565
Hubbard	14,072	Park Rapids	932
Isanti	*21,500*	Cambridge	438
Itasca	43,178	Grand Rapids	2,633
Jackson	*14,200*	Jackson	696
Kanabec	*11,500*	Mora	524
Kandiyohi	*34,200*	Willmar	783
Kittson	6,679	Hallock	1,123
Koochiching	17,477	International Falls	3,127
Lac Qui Parle	*11,200*	Madison	768
Lake	*13,200*	Two Harbors	2,062
Lake of the Woods	3,764	Baudette	1,311
Le Sueur	*22,100*	Le Center	440
Lincoln	*8,200*	Ivanhoe	531
Lyon	*24,600*	Marshall	709
McLeod	*29,600*	Glencoe	488
Mahnomen	5,536	Mahnomen	563
Marshall	13,013	Warren	1,789
Martin	*24,800*	Fairmont	703
Meeker	*20,400*	Litchfield	619
Mille Lacs	*18,900*	Milaca	571
Morrison	*28,100*	Falls	1,127
Mower	*41,300*	Austin	703
Murray	*12,300*	Slayton	703
Nicollet	*25,500*	Saint Peter	432
Nobles	*22,700*	Worthington	712
Norman	9,346	Ada	885
Olmstead	*92,300*	Rochester	656
Otter Tail	*50,100*	Fergus Falls	1,962
Pennington	15,212	Thief River Falls	622
Pine	*18,900*	Pine City	1,414
Pipestone	*11,700*	Pipestone	464
Polk	34,565	Crookston	2,013
Pope	*11,500*	Glenwood	669
Ramsey	*451,900*	Saint Paul	155
Red Lake	5,471	Red Lake Falls	432
Redwood	*19,700*	Redwood Falls	874
Renville	*20,400*	Olivia	979
Rice	*44,300*	Faribault	496
Rock	*11,400*	Luverne	485
Roseau	12,550	Roseau	1,676
St. Louis	*220,500*	Duluth	6,092
Scott	*43,200*	Shakopee	353
Sherburne	*30,900*	Elk River	431
Sibley	*15,400*	Gaylord	583
Stearns	*106,700*	Saint Cloud	1,342
Steele	*30,700*	Owatonna	425
Stevens	*11,200*	Morris	558
Swift	*13,200*	Benson	739
Todd	*23,900*	Long Prairie	942
Traverse	*6,100*	Wheaton	568
Wabasha	*19,200*	Wabasha	522
Wadena	*14,100*	Wadena	536
Waseca	*18,400*	Waseca	415
Washington	*115,300*	Stillwater	386
Watonwan	*12,300*	Saint James	433
Wilkin	*8,600*	Breckenridge	752
Winona	*45,900*	Winona	620
Wright	*52,100*	Buffalo	674
Yellow Medicine	*13,900*	Granite Falls	753

Mississippi

(82 counties, 47,296 sq. mi. land; pop. *2,404,000*)

Adams	*38,100*	Natchez	449
Alcorn	*30,700*	Corinth	405
Amite	*13,200*	Liberty	729
Attala	*19,200*	Kosciusko	724
Benton	*8,100*	Ashland	412

County	Pop.	County seat or court house	Land area sq. mi.
Bolivar	45,900	Cleveland & Rosedale	923
Calhoun	15,200	Pittsboro	575
Carroll	9,666	Carrollton & Vaiden	637
Chickasaw	17,600	Houston & Okolona	506
Choctaw	9,300	Ackerman	417
Claiborne	11,200	Port Gibson	489
Clarke	16,200	Quitman	697
Clay	20,700	West Point	414
Coahoma	36,613	Clarksdale	569
Copiah	26,300	Hazlehurst	780
Covington	14,900	Collins	416
De Soto	53,740	Hernando	476
Forrest	63,300	Hattiesburg	468
Franklin	8,400	Meadville	568
George	15,000	Lucedale	481
Greene	9,200	Leakesville	728
Grenada	20,546	Grenada	431
Hancock	19,600	Bay Saint Louis	482
Harrison	147,700	Gulfport	585
Hinds	236,300	Jackson & Raymond	876
Holmes	22,783	Lexington	769
Humphreys	13,910	Belzoni	421
Issaquena	2,518	Mayersville	414
Itawamba	18,400	Fulton	541
Jackson	117,800	Pascagoula	736
Jasper	16,900	Bat Springs & Paulding	683
Jefferson	9,500	Fayette	521
Jefferson Davis	13,000	Prentiss	414
Jones	59,900	Ellisville & Laurel	702
Kemper	10,100	De Kalb	757
Lafayette	28,400	Oxford	668
Lamar	19,200	Purvis	500
Lauderdale	69,700	Meridian	708
Lawrence	11,800	Monticello	433
Leake	17,400	Carthage	586
Lee	53,200	Tupelo	455
Leflore	41,550	Greenwood	592
Lincoln	27,000	Brookhaven	586
Lowndes	54,700	Columbus	508
Madison	34,800	Canton	727
Marion	24,400	Columbia	550
Marshall	26,800	Holly Springs	710
Monroe	34,900	Aberdeen	769
Montgomery	13,000	Winona	403
Neshoba	21,600	Philadelphia	568
Newton	19,500	Decatur	580
Noxubee	13,100	Macon	695
Oktibbeha	33,800	Starkville	454
Panola	27,579	Batesville & Sardis	693
Pearl River	29,600	Poplarville	828
Perry	10,200	New Augusta	653
Pike	35,300	Magnolia	409
Pontotoc	19,500	Pontotoc	501
Prentiss	21,200	Booneville	418
Quitman	12,597	Marks	412
Rankin	62,400	Brandon	775
Scott	22,400	Forest	615
Sharkey	7,976	Rolling Fork	436
Simpson	20,900	Mendenhall	587
Smith	14,700	Raleigh	642
Stone	8,300	Wiggins	448
Sunflower	34,807	Indianola	694
Tallahatchie	17,014	Charleston & Sumner	644
Tate	20,084	Senatobia	405
Tippah	18,000	Ripley	464
Tishomingo	16,400	Iuka	443
Tunica	9,626	Tunica	458
Union	21,100	New Albany	422
Walthall	13,400	Tylertown	403
Warren	49,600	Vicksburg	581
Washington	71,850	Greenville	734
Wayne	18,600	Waynesboro	827
Webster	10,400	Walthall	416
Wilkinson	10,400	Woodville	674
Winston	19,400	Louisville	606
Yalobusha	13,133	Coffeeville & Water Valley	488
Yazoo	27,387	Yazoo City	938

Missouri

(114 cos., 1 ind. city, 68,995 sq. mi. land; pop. 4,860,000)

County	Pop.	County seat or court house	Land area sq. mi.
Adair	23,300	Kirksville	572
Andrew	14,000	Savannah	436
Atchison	8,600	Rockport	549
Audrain	25,600	Mexico	692
Barry	23,300	Cassville	783
Barton	11,100	Lamar	594
Bates	15,500	Butler	841
Benton	12,100	Warsaw	735
Bollinger	10,100	Marble Hill	621
Boone	90,600	Columbia	685
Buchanan	86,100	Saint Joseph	404
Butler	37,400	Poplar Buff	715
Caldwell	9,100	Kingston	430
Callaway	29,500	Fulton	835
Camden	18,200	Camdenton	640
Cape Girardeau	55,300	Jackson	574
Carroll	11,800	Carrollton	697
Carter	4,800	Van Buren	506
Cass	48,800	Harrisonville	698
Cedar	11,000	Stockton	496
Chariton	10,400	Keytesville	754
Christian	21,100	Ozark	567
Clark	8,100	Kahoka	506
Clay	137,000	Liberty	412
Clinton	14,700	Plattsburg	420
Cole	54,200	Jefferson City	384
Cooper	14,900	Boonville	566
Crawford	17,100	Steelville	760
Dade	7,800	Greenfield	504
Dallas	11,900	Buffalo	537
Daviess	8,500	Gallatin	563
De Kalb	7,900	Maysville	423
Dent	12,900	Salem	756
Douglas	10,800	Ava	809
Dunklin	36,000	Kennett	543
Franklin	67,000	Union	934
Gasconade	13,100	Hermann	519
Gentry	7,700	Albany	488
Greene	183,700	Springfield	677
Grundy	11,200	Trenton	435
Harrison	9,700	Bethany	720
Henry	18,800	Clinton	734
Hickory	6,400	Hermitage	377
Holt	6,800	Oregon	458
Howard	10,000	Fayette	472
Howell	27,500	West Plains	920
Iron	10,600	Ironton	554
Jackson	639,500	Independence	603
Jasper	83,800	Carthage	642
Jefferson	129,400	Hillsboro	668
Johnson	35,800	Warrensburg	826
Knox	5,800	Edina	512
Laclede	23,200	Lebanon	770
Lafayette	28,800	Lexington	632
Lawrence	28,100	Mount Vernon	619
Lewis	10,700	Monticello	508
Lincoln	20,400	Troy	625
Linn	14,900	Linneus	622
Livingston	16,400	Chillicothe	530
McDonald	15,400	Pineville	540
Macon	16,000	Macon	798
Madison	9,300	Fredericktown	496
Maries	7,100	Vienna	525
Marion	27,500	Palmyra	438
Mercer	4,600	Princeton	455
Miller	17,800	Tuscumbia	600
Mississippi	16,100	Charleston	415
Moniteau	11,600	California	419
Monroe	10,000	Paris	669
Montgomery	11,000	Montgomery City	534
Morgan	12,800	Versailles	592
New Madrid	24,000	New Madrid	679
Newton	37,300	Neosho	629
Nodaway	21,400	Maryville	877
Oregon	10,300	Alton	784
Osage	11,800	Linn	608
Ozark	7,900	Gainesville	732
Pemiscot	25,100	Caruthersville	493
Perry	15,600	Perryville	471
Pettis	36,500	Sedalia	679
Phelps	31,800	Rolla	677
Pike	17,500	Bowling Green	681
Platte	43,100	Platte City	427
Polk	17,800	Bolivar	637
Pulaski	41,200	Waynesville	551
Putnam	6,400	Unionville	518
Ralls	8,500	New London	478
Randolph	24,200	Huntsville	473
Ray	19,400	Richmond	573
Reynolds	6,700	Centerville	817
Ripley	12,900	Doniphan	639
St. Charles	129,200	St. Charles	551
St. Clair	9,200	Osceola	697
St. Francois	39,300	Farmington	457
St. Louis	979,700	Clayton	499
Ste. Genevieve	14,600	Ste. Genevieve	499
Saline	23,400	Marshall	757
Schuyler	4,800	Lancaster	306
Scotland	5,600	Memphis	441
Scott	37,500	Benton	421
Shannon	7,600	Eminence	999
Shelby	7,400	Shelbyville	501
Stoddard	29,000	Bloomfield	823
Stone	14,200	Galena	449
Sullivan	7,300	Milan	654
Taney	19,400	Forsyth	615
Texas	20,500	Houston	1,183
Vernon	19,500	Nevada	838
Warren	13,200	Warrenton	426
Washington	17,300	Potosi	760
Wayne	10,700	Greenville	766
Webster	19,500	Marshfield	590
Worth	3,200	Grant City	267
Wright	15,700	Hartville	684
Independent City			
St. Louis	504,600		61

Montana

(57 counties, 145,587 sq. mi. land; pop., 783,674)

County	Pop.	County seat or court house	Land area sq. mi.
Beaverhead	8,204	Dillon	5,551
Big Horn	11,083	Hardin	5,023
Blaine	6,990	Chinook	4,275
Broadwater	3,263	Townsend	1,193
Carbon	8,081	Red Lodge	2,066
Carter	1,800	Ekalaka	3,313
Cascade	80,639	Great Falls	2,661
Chouteau	6,090	Fort Benton	3,927
Custer	13,070	Miles City	3,756
Daniels	2,826	Scobey	1,443
Dawson	11,850	Glendive	2,370
Deer Lodge	12,507	Anaconda	740
Fallon	3,769	Baker	1,633
Fergus	13,052	Lewistown	4,242
Flathead	51,462	Kalispell	5,137
Gallatin	42,821	Bozeman	2,517
Garfield	1,649	Jordan	4,455
Glacier	9,662	Cut Bank	2,964
Golden Valley	1,017	Ryegate	1,176
Granite	2,691	Philipsburg	1,733
Hill	17,931	Havre	2,927
Jefferson	7,040	Boulder	1,652
Judith Basin	2,636	Stanford	1,880
Lake	19,098	Polson	1,494
Lewis & Clark	43,053	Helena	3,476
Liberty	2,322	Chester	1,439
Lincoln	17,731	Libby	3,714
McCone	2,707	Circle	2,607
Madison	5,437	Virginia City	3,528
Meagher	2,145	White Sulphur Springs	2,354
Mineral	3,674	Superior	1,222
Missoula	75,432	Missoula	2,612
Musselshell	4,417	Roundup	1,887
Park	12,682	Livingston	2,626
Petroleum	657	Winnett	1,655
Phillips	5,357	Malta	5,213
Pondera	6,135	Conrad	1,645
Powder River	2,523	Broadus	3,288
Powell	6,939	Deer Lodge	2,336
Prairie	1,833	Terry	1,730
Ravalli	22,427	Hamilton	2,382
Richland	12,225	Sidney	2,079
Rossevelt	10,446	Wolf Point	2,385
Rosebud	9,965	Forsyth	5,037
Sanders	8,859	Thompson Falls	2,778
Sheridan	5,391	Plentywood	1,694
Silver Bow	37,930	Butte	715
Stillwater	5,597	Columbus	1,794
Sweet Grass	3,211	Big Timber	1,840
Teton	6,485	Choteau	2,294
Toole	5,568	Shelby	1,950
Treasure	981	Hysham	985
Valley	10,249	Glasgow	4,974
Wheatland	2,359	Harlowton	1,420
Wibaux	1,479	Wibaux	890
Yellowstone	107,659	Billings	2,642
Yellowstone Nat. Park	275		269

Nebraska

(93 counties, 76,483 sq. mi. land; pop., *1,565,000*)

County	Pop.	County seat or court house	Land area sq. mi.
Adams	30,643	Hastings	562
Antelope	8,688	Neligh	853
Arthur	509	Arthur	704
Banner	918	Harrisburg	738
Blaine	859	Brewster	710
Boone	7,383	Albion	683
Box Butte	13,688	Alliance	1,065
Boyd	3,321	Butte	538
Brown	4,351	Ainsworth	1,216
Buffalo	34,757	Kearney	949
Burt	*8,700*	Tekamah	483
Butler	*9,100*	David City	582
Cass	*20,000*	Plattsmouth	555
Cedar	*11,300*	Hartington	742
Chase	4,749	Imperial	890
Cherry	6,753	Valentine	5,966
Cheyenne	10,024	Sidney	1,186
Clay	8,124	Clay Center	570
Colfax	*9,600*	Schuyler	406
Cuming	*11,900*	West Point	571
Custer	13,827	Broken Bow	2,558
Dakota	*16,800*	Dakota City	255
Dawes	9,639	Chadron	1,386
Dawson	22,138	Lexington	975
Deuel	2,452	Chappell	436
Dixon	*7,100*	Ponca	475
Dodge	*35,700*	Fremont	528
Douglas	*410,400*	Omaha	335
Dundy	2,830	Benkelman	921
Fillmore	*7,900*	Geneva	577
Franklin	4,366	Franklin	578
Frontier	3,645	Stockville	962
Furnas	6,476	Beaver City	722
Gage	*23,400*	Beatrice	858
Garden	2,806	Oshkosh	1,678
Garfield	2,359	Burwell	569
Gosper	2,136	Elwood	464
Grant	882	Hyannis	764
Greeley	3,448	Greeley	570
Hall	47,651	Grand Island	537
Hamilton	9,226	Aurora	537
Harlan	4,268	Alma	556
Hayes	1,370	Hayes Center	711
Hitchcock	4,079	Trenton	712
Holt	13,543	O'Neil	2,405
Hooker	985	Mullen	722
Howard	6,719	Saint Paul	564
Jefferson	*9,900*	Fairbury	577
Johnson	*5,500*	Tecumseh	377
Kearney	7,013	Minden	512
Keith	9,339	Ogallala	1,032
Keya Paha	1,296	Springview	768
Kimball	4,880	Kimball	953
Knox	*11,100*	Center	1,107
Lancaster	*186,200*	Lincoln	845
Lincoln	36,422	North Platte	2,522
Logan	979	Stapleton	570
Loup	853	Taylor	574
McPherson	593	Tryon	856
Madison	*29,600*	Madison	572
Merrick	8,946	Central City	480
Morrill	6,132	Bridgeport	1,402
Nance	4,746	Fullerton	439
Nemaha	*8,100*	Auburn	400
Nuckolls	6,738	Nelson	579
Otoe	*15,100*	Nebraska City	619
Pawnee	*3,900*	Pawnee City	433
Perkins	3,626	Grant	885
Phelps	9,713	Holdrege	544
Pierce	*8,500*	Pierce	573
Platte	28,842	Columbus	667
Polk	6,338	Osceola	432
Red Willow	12,611	McCook	686
Richardson	*11,200*	Falls City	550
Rock	2,357	Bassett	1,009
Saline	*13,000*	Wilber	575
Sarpy	*85,300*	Papillion	239
Saunders	*18,200*	Wahoo	759
Scotts Bluff	38,150	Gering	726
Seward	*15,300*	Seward	571
Sheridan	7,563	Rushville	2,462
Sherman	4,219	Loup City	567
Sioux	1,839	Harrison	2,063
Stanton	*6,100*	Stanton	431
Thayer	*7,900*	Hebron	577
Thomas	972	Thedford	716
Thurston	*7,100*	Pender	388
Valley	5,631	Ord	569
Washington	*15,200*	Blair	386
Wayne	*9,400*	Wayne	443
Webster	4,862	Red Cloud	575
Wheeler	1,056	Bartlett	576
York	*14,600*	York	577

Nevada

(16 cos., 1 ind. city, 109,889 sq. mi. land; pop., *663,000*)

County	Pop.	County seat or court house	Land area sq. mi.
Churchill	13,873	Fallon	4,883
Clark	462,012	Las Vegas	7,874
Douglas	*14,300*	Minden	703
Elko	17,409	Elko	17,162
Esmeralda	773	Goldfield	3,570
Eureka	1,183	Eureka	4,182
Humboldt	9,487	Winnemucca	9,702
Lander	4,183	Austin	5,621
Lincoln	3,697	Pioche	10,649
Lyon	*11,100*	Yerington	2,030
Mineral	6,141	Hawthorne	3,765
Nye	9,096	Tonopah	18,064
Pershing	3,396	Lovelock	6,001
Storey	*1,200*	Virginia City	262
Washoe	*163,200*	Reno	6,366
White Pine	8,184	Ely	8,904
Independent City			
Carson City	*29,500*	Carson City	150

New Hampshire

(10 counties, 9,027 sq. mi. land; pop., 918,959)

County	Pop.	County seat or court house	Land area sq. mi.
Belknap	43,806	Laconia	400
Carroll	27,730	Ossipee	938
Cheshire	61,939	Keene	715
Coos	35,061	Lancaster	1,820
Grafton	65,628	Woodsville	1,732
Hillsborough	276,341	Nashua	887
Merrimack	98,038	Concord	930
Rockingham	190,047	Exeter	691
Strafford	85,272	Dover	376
Sullivan	36,097	Newport	539

New Jersey

(21 counties, 7,521 sq. mi. land; pop., *7,327,000*)

County	Pop.	County seat or court house	Land area sq. mi.
Atlantic	*190,000*	Mays Landing	569
Bergen	727,549	Hackensack	234
Burlington	*363,500*	Mount Holly	819
Camden	*471,600*	Camden	221
Cape May	*77,000*	Cape May Court House	267
Cumberland	*130,200*	Bridgeton	500
Essex	*829,900*	Newark	130
Gloucester	*200,000*	Woodbury	329
Hudson	555,478	Jersey City	47
Hunterdon	*84,200*	Flemington	423
Mercer	*317,200*	Trenton	228
Middlesex	*591,100*	New Brunswick	312
Monmouth	*499,900*	Freehold	476
Morris	*404,000*	Morristown	468
Ocean	*331,500*	Toms River	642
Passaic	*444,700*	Paterson	192
Salem	*62,400*	Salem	365
Somerset	*207,800*	Somerville	307
Sussex	*109,200*	Newton	527
Union	502,464	Elizabeth	103
Warren	*84,000*	Belvidere	362

New Mexico

(32 counties, 121,412 sq. mi. land; pop., *1,212,000*)

County	Pop.	County seat or court house	Land area sq. mi.
Bernalillo	*384,200*	Albuquerque	1,169
Catron	2,735	Reserve	6,897
Chaves	51,099	Roswell	6,084
Colfax	*12,800*	Raton	3,764
Curry	*41,300*	Clovis	1,403
De Baca	*2,800*	Fort Sumner	2,356
Dona Ana	95,861	Las Cruces	3,804
Eddy	47,971	Carlsbad	4,167
Grant	26,269	Silver City	3,970
Guadalupe	*4,600*	Santa Rosa	2,998
Harding	*1,200*	Mosquero	2,134
Hidalgo	6,046	Lordsburg	3,447
Lea	55,564	Lovington	4,393
Lincoln	10,993	Carrizozo	4,858
Los Alamos	*18,000*	Los Alamos	108
Luna	15,653	Deming	2,957
McKinley	*55,500*	Gallup	5,454
Mora	*4,700*	Mora	1,940
Otero	44,638	Alamogordo	6,638
Quay	*11,100*	Tucumcari	2,875
Rio Arriba	*28,200*	Tierra Amarilla	5,843
Roosevelt	*16,400*	Portales	2,454
Sandoval	*24,600*	Bernalillo	3,714
San Juan	*74,800*	Aztec	5,500
San Miguel	*22,500*	Las Vegas	4,741
Santa Fe	*65,600*	Santa Fe	1,902
Sierra	8,447	Truth or Consequences	4,166
Socorro	12,237	Socorro	6,603
Taos	*19,900*	Taos	2,256
Torrance	*7,400*	Estancia	3,346
Union	*5,200*	Clayton	3,816
Valencia	*53,800*	Los Lunas	5,656

New York

(62 counties, 47,831 sq. mi. land; pop., *17,748,000*)

County	Pop.	County seat or court house	Land area sq. mi.
Albany	285,666	Albany	526
Allegany	*49,700*	Belmon	1,047
Bronx	*1,235,400*	Bronx	41
Broome	213,346	Binghamton	714
Cattaraugus	*85,400*	Little Valley	1,318
Cayuga	*77,800*	Auburn	698
Chautauqua	*144,000*	Mayville	1,081
Chemung	97,586	Elmira	415
Chenango	49,309	Norwich	903
Clinton	*82,300*	Plattsburgh	1,059
Columbia	*56,000*	Hudson	645
Cortland	48,839	Cortland	502
Delaware	47,177	Delhi	1,443
Dutchess	*233,300*	Poughkeepsie	813
Erie	1,013,373	Buffalo	1,058
Essex	*35,100*	Elizabethtown	1,823
Franklin	*44,700*	Malone	1,674
Fulton	*54,500*	Johnstown	498
Genesee	59,336	Batavia	501
Greene	*38,300*	Catskill	653
Hamilton	*5,000*	Lake Pleasant	1,735
Herkimer	*65,200*	Herkimer	1,435
Jefferson	*89,500*	Watertown	1,294
Kings	*2,276,400*	Brooklyn	70
Lewis	*25,600*	Lowville	1,291
Livingston	56,955	Geneseo	638
Madison	*66,000*	Wampsville	661
Monroe	701,145	Rochester	675
Montgomery	*54,500*	Fonda	408
Nassau	*1,392,700*	Mineola	289
New York	*1,357,700*	New York	23
Niagara	226,449	Lockport	532
Oneida	*260,300*	Utica	1,223
Onondaga	*473,500*	Syracuse	794
Ontario	*87,100*	Canandaigua	651
Orange	*252,600*	Goshen	833
Orleans	38,473	Albion	396
Oswego	*110,100*	Oswego	964
Otsego	*57,700*	Cooperstown	1,013
Putnam	*71,600*	Carmel	231
Queens	*1,941,600*	Jamaica	108
Rensselaer	151,699	Troy	665
Richmond	*338,200*	Saint George	58
Rockland	*258,700*	New City	176
St. Lawrence	*116,000*	Canton	2,768
Saratoga	153,693	Ballston Spa	818
Schenectady	149,766	Schenectady	207
Schoharie	*27,600*	Schoharie	624
Schuyler	*17,400*	Watkins Glen	330
Seneca	*33,900*	Ovid & Waterloo	330
Steuben	*100,700*	Bath	1,410
Suffolk	*1,297,300*	Riverhead	929
Sillivan	64,937	Monticello	980
Tioga	49,724	Owego	524
Tompkins	87,046	Ithaca	482
Ulster	*154,300*	Kingston	1,141
Warren	*52,000*	Lake George	887
Washington	*55,200*	Hudson Falls	836
Wayne	*81,900*	Lyons	606
Westchester	*877,000*	White Plains	443
Wyoming	39,795	Warsaw	598
Yates	*21,400*	Penn Yan	343

North Carolina

(100 counties, 48,798 sq. mi. land; pop., *5,577,000*)

County	Pop.	County seat or court house	Land area sq. mi.
Alamance	*98,000*	Graham	428
Alexander	*22,600*	Taylorsville	259
Alleghany	*8,800*	Sparta	225
Anson	25,360	Wadesboro	533
Ashe	*20,800*	Jefferson	426
Avery	*13,800*	Newland	245
Beaufort	*40,000*	Washington	826
Bertie	*21,200*	Windsor	698
Bladen	30,069	Elizabethtown	883
Brunswick	35,349	Southport	856
Buncombe	*154,400*	Asheville	657
Burke	*63,800*	Morganton	511
Cabarrus	*79,700*	Concord	363
Caldwell	*60,900*	Lenoir	469
Camden	*5,700*	Camden	239
Carteret	40,794	Beaufort	536
Caswell	*19,600*	Yanceyville	428
Catawba	*100,900*	Newton	394
Chatham	*31,000*	Pittsboro	709
Cherokee	*17,700*	Murphy	452
Chowan	*12,300*	Edenton	173
Clay	*6,000*	Hayesville	209
Cleveland	*78,300*	Shelby	468
Columbus	51,015	Whiteville	945
Craven	70,631	New Bern	699
Cumberland	246,522	Fayetteville	654
Currituck	*10,600*	Currituck	246
Dare	*10,600*	Manteo	391
Davidson	112,618	Lexington	549
Davie	24,451	Mocksville	265
Duplin	40,658	Kenansville	815
Durham	*145,600*	Durham	295
Edgecombe	*55,500*	Tarboro	510
Forsyth	242,581	Winston-Salem	419
Franklin	*28,100*	Louisburg	491
Gaston	*156,000*	Gastonia	356
Gates	*8,300*	Gatesville	337
Graham	*7,000*	Robbinsville	292
Granville	*32,900*	Oxford	537
Greene	15,898	Snow Hill	267
Guilford	*305,400*	Greensboro	655
Halifax	*55,500*	Halifax	734
Harnett	*55,700*	Lillington	603
Haywood	*44,600*	Waynesville	551
Henderson	*51,600*	Hendersonville	378
Hertford	*25,000*	Winton	353
Hoke	20,293	Raeford	389
Hyde	*5,500*	Swanquarter	613
Iredell	*79,300*	Statesville	572
Jackson	*25,400*	Sylva	491
Johnston	*66,700*	Smithfield	797
Jones	9,673	Trenton	467
Lee	*35,100*	Sanford	256
Lenoir	59,391	Kinston	400
Lincoln	*38,900*	Lincolnton	297
McDowell	*34,100*	Marion	436
Macon	*19,200*	Franklin	513
Madison	*17,200*	Marshall	450
Martin	*25,400*	Williamston	455
Mecklenburg	*384,700*	Charlotte	530
Mitchell	*14,100*	Bakersville	215
Montgomery	22,355	Troy	488
Moore	50,374	Carthage	704
Nash	*67,400*	Nashville	544
New Hanover	97,926	Wilmington	185
Northampton	*23,400*	Jackson	536
Onslow	112,165	Jacksonville	765

County	Pop.	County seat or court house	Land area sq. mi.
Orange	*69,600*	Hillsboro	400
Pamlico	*10,000*	Bayboro	338
Pasquotank	*28,800*	Elizabeth City	228
Pender	22,107	Burgaw	871
Perquimans	*8,800*	Hertford	246
Person	*27,100*	Roxboro	401
Pitt	*81,600*	Greenville	655
Polk	*12,400*	Columbus	239
Randolph	*84,700*	Asheboro	798
Richmond	45,383	Rockingham	475
Robeson	101,401	Lumberton	949
Rockingham	*76,600*	Wentworth	569
Rowan	98,829	Salisbury	523
Rutherford	*51,600*	Rutherfordton	563
Sampson	49,243	Clinton	945
Scotland	32,244	Laurinburg	319
Stanly	*45,200*	Albemarle	398
Stokes	32,968	Danbury	457
Surry	59,330	Dobson	536
Swain	*10,200*	Bryson City	524
Transylvania	*22,000*	Brevard	382
Tyrrell	*4,000*	Columbia	390
Union	*65,300*	Monroe	639
Vance	*34,300*	Henderson	249
Wake	*278,500*	Raleigh	858
Warren	*17,100*	Warrenton	424
Washington	*15,100*	Plymouth	343
Watauga	*28,700*	Boone	317
Wayne	96,513	Goldsboro	557
Wilkes	*55,700*	Wilkesboro	757
Wilson	*60,800*	Wilson	375
Yadkin	28,367	Yadkinville	336
Yancey	*14,600*	Burnsville	312

North Dakota

(53 counties, 69,273 sq. mi. land; pop., *652,000*)

County	Pop.	County seat or court house	Land area sq. mi.
Adams	3,312	Hettinger	989
Barnes	13,949	Valley City	1,479
Benson	7,949	Minnewaukan	1,403
Billings	1,132	Medora	1,139
Bottineau	9,243	Bottineau	1,677
Bowman	4,241	Bowman	1,170
Burke	3,794	Bowbells	1,119
Burleigh	54,784	Bismarck	1,625
Cass	88,434	Fargo	1,749
Cavalier	7,621	Langdon	1,512
Dickey	7,206	Ellendale	1,143
Divide	3,483	Crosby	1,300
Dunn	4,626	Manning	1,992
Eddy	3,554	New Rockford	635
Emmons	3,838	Linton	1,503
Foster	4,616	Carrington	645
Golden Valley	2,401	Beach	1,014
Grand Forks	66,088	Grand Forks	1,438
Grant	4,282	Carson	1,666
Griggs	3,719	Cooperstown	710
Hettinger	4,275	Mott	1,134
Kidder	3,871	Steele	1,358
La Moure	6,476	La Moure	1,136
Logan	3,474	Napoleon	1,001
McHenry	7,850	Towner	1,879
McIntosh	4,791	Ashley	992
McKenzie	7,137	Watford City	2,735
McLean	12,359	Washburn	2,065
Mercer	9,421	Stanton	1,042
Morton	24,951	Mandan	1,920
Mountrail	7,663	Stanley	1,819
Nelson	5,218	Lakota	995
Oliver	2,504	Center	721
Pembina	10,386	Cavalier	1,124
Pierce	6,175	Rugby	1,038
Ramsey	13,026	Devils Lake	1,248
Ransom	6,714	Lisbon	861
Renville	3,591	Mohall	886
Richland	19,197	Wahpeton	1,449
Rolette	12,199	Rolla	913
Sargent	5,512	Forman	853
Sheridan	2,812	McClusky	989
Sioux	3,633	Fort Yates	1,103
Slope	1,171	Amidon	1,225
Stark	23,703	Dickinson	1,316
Steele	3,112	Finley	710
Stutsman	24,159	Jamestown	2,264
Towner	4,048	Cando	1,043
Traill	9,629	Hillsboro	861
Walsh	15,381	Grafton	1,286
Ward	58,266	Minot	2,044
Wells	6,983	Fessenden	1,299
Williams	22,263	Williston	2,064

Ohio

(88 counties, 40,975 sq. mi. land; pop., *10,749,000*)

County	Pop.	County seat or court house	Land area sq. mi.
Adams	24,328	West Union	587
Allen	112,018	Lima	410
Ashland	46,082	Ashland	424
Ashtabula	103,922	Jefferson	700
Athens	*54,900*	Athens	504
Auglaize	42,461	Wapakoneta	400
Belmont	*81,700*	Saint Clairsville	534
Brown	*31,100*	Georgetown	490
Butler	*256,400*	Hamilton	471
Carroll	*26,100*	Carrollton	390
Champaign	33,641	Urbana	432
Clark	*150,600*	Springfield	402
Clermont	*120,100*	Batavia	458
Clinton	34,629	Wilmington	410
Columbiana	*114,200*	Lisbon	534
Coshocton	*34,700*	Coshocton	562
Crawford	50,067	Bucyrus	404
Cuyahoga	*1,542,100*	Cleveland	456
Darke	*53,600*	Greenville	605
Defiance	39,825	Defiance	412
Delaware	*53,100*	Delaware	450
Erie	79,452	Sandusky	264
Fairfield	93,549	Lancaster	505
Fayette	27,430	Washington C. H.	404
Franklin	*870,600*	Columbus	538
Fulton	37,750	Wauseon	407
Gallia	30,152	Gallipolis	471
Geauga	74,279	Chardon	407
Greene	*129,000*	Xenia	415
Guernsey	*39,100*	Cambridge	528
Hamilton	*885,300*	Cincinnati	414
Hancock	64,158	Findlay	532
Hardin	32,684	Kenton	467
Harrison	*17,600*	Cadiz	401
Henry	28,371	Napoleon	416
Highland	33,403	Hillsboro	549
Hocking	24,346	Logan	421
Holmes	*26,000*	Millersburg	424
Huron	54,490	Norwalk	497
Jackson	30,601	Jackson	419
Jefferson	*93,100*	Steubenville	411
Knox	46,267	Mount Vernon	531
Lake	212,145	Painesville	231
Lawrence	63,778	Ironton	456
Licking	120,857	Newark	686
Logan	39,051	Bellefontaine	460
Lorain	273,983	Elyria	495
Lucas	471,280	Toledo	343
Madison	*32,200*	London	463
Mahoning	289,629	Youngstown	415
Marion	68,062	Marion	405
Medina	113,008	Medina	425
Meigs	*22,200*	Pomeroy	436
Mercer	38,242	Celina	444
Miami	*88,100*	Troy	407
Monroe	*16,400*	Woodsfield	456
Montgomery	*580,000*	Dayton	459
Morgan	*13,500*	McConnelsville	420
Morrow	26,476	Mount Gilead	403
Muskingum	*81,900*	Zanesville	651
Noble	*11,100*	Caldwell	398
Ottawa	40,034	Port Clinton	261
Paulding	21,313	Paulding	417
Perry	*30,100*	New Lexington	410
Pickaway	43,694	Circleville	504
Pike	22,751	Waverly	443
Portage	*133,300*	Ravenna	495
Preble	*37,100*	Eaton	427
Putnam	32,938	Ottawa	486
Richland	131,310	Mansfield	496
Ross	64,940	Chillicothe	687
Sandusky	63,332	Fremont	409
Scioto	84,571	Portsmouth	608
Seneca	61,871	Tiffin	551
Shelby	43,101	Sidney	408
Stark	*377,700*	Canton	576
Summit	*523,700*	Akron	408
Trumbull	238,105	Warren	608
Tuscarawas	*80,100*	New Philadelphia	569
Union	29,540	Marysville	434
Van Wert	30,339	Van Wert	409
Vinton	11,590	McArthur	411
Warren	*92,900*	Lebanon	408
Washington	*61,400*	Marietta	641
Wayne	*96,300*	Wooster	561
Williams	36,306	Bryan	421
Wood	107,280	Bowling Green	619
Wyandot	22,666	Upper Sandusky	406

Oklahoma

(77 counties, 68,782 sq. mi. land; pop., *2,880,000*)

County	Pop.	County seat or court house	Land area sq. mi.
Adair	*17,700*	Stillwell	570
Alfalfa	*8,000*	Cherokee	868
Atoka	*11,600*	Atoka	991
Beaver	*7,000*	Beaver	1,790
Beckham	*16,700*	Sayre	907
Blaine	*13,200*	Watonga	917
Bryan	*28,100*	Durant	889
Caddo	*33,200*	Anadarko	1,272
Canadian	*51,000*	El Reno	897
Carter	*43,800*	Ardmore	830

County	Pop.	County seat or court house	Land area sq. mi.
Cherokee	27,000	Tahlequah	756
Choctaw	14,800	Hugo	778
Cimarron	3,700	Boise City	1,843
Cleveland	110,900	Norman	527
Coal	6,100	Coalgate	526
Comanche	119,900	Lawton	1,084
Cotton	7,400	Walters	651
Craig	15,700	Vinita	764
Creek	55,200	Sapulpa	936
Custer	23,200	Arapaho	980
Delaware	21,500	Jay	707
Dewey	6,500	Taloga	1,018
Ellis	5,400	Arnett	1,242
Garfield	63,200	Enid	1,054
Garvin	27,900	Pauls Valley	814
Grady	37,100	Chickasha	1,096
Grant	7,700	Medford	1,007
Greer	8,000	Mangum	633
Harmon	4,700	Hollis	545
Harper	5,000	Buffalo	1,041
Haskell	10,600	Stigler	602
Hughes	14,300	Holdenville	807
Jackson	33,900	Altus	810
Jefferson	8,500	Waurika	780
Johnston	9,000	Tishomingo	638
Kay	50,800	Newkirk	950
Kingfisher	14,700	Kingfisher	904
Kiowa	12,600	Hobart	1,027
Latimer	9,800	Wilburton	737
Le Flore	37,800	Poteau	1,560
Lincoln	22,700	Chandler	973
Logan	23,000	Guthrie	751
Love	6,800	Marietta	513
McClain	20,600	Purcell	573
McCurtain	33,900	Idabel	1,800
McIntosh	14,700	Eufaula	608
Major	8,300	Fairview	963
Marshall	9,300	Madill	366
Mayes	29,500	Pryor	648
Murray	10,900	Sulphur	423
Muskogee	67,200	Muskogee	818
Noble	11,200	Perry	743
Nowata	10,800	Nowata	537
Okfuskee	11,600	Okemah	637
Oklahoma	554,400	Oklahoma City	700
Okmulgee	38,400	Okmulgee	700
Osage	35,000	Pawhuska	2,272
Ottawa	33,200	Miami	464
Pawnee	14,400	Pawnee	61
Payne	57,800	Stillwater	694
Pittsburg	38,600	McAlester	1,241
Pontotoc	32,000	Ada	714
Pottawatomie	52,600	Shawnee	794
Pushmataha	11,100	Antlers	1,420
Roger Mills	4,600	Cheyenne	1,140
Rogers	37,700	Claremore	685
Seminole	28,300	Wewoka	630
Sequoyah	28,600	Sallisaw	696
Stephens	41,100	Duncan	891
Texas	18,700	Guymon	2,062
Tillman	12,300	Frederick	901
Tulsa	440,500	Tulsa	573
Wagoner	30,700	Wagoner	563
Washington	44,500	Bartlesville	424
Washita	13,300	Cordell	1,009
Woods	10,100	Alva	1,298
Woodward	19,100	Woodward	1,251

Oregon

(36 counties, 96,184 sq. mi. land; pop., 2,444,000)

Baker	16,127	Baker	3,068
Benton	65,800	Corvallis	668
Clackamas	228,800	Oregon City	1,884
Clatsop	30,500	Astoria	805
Columbia	32,600	Saint Helens	639
Coos	62,400	Coquille	1,604
Crook	13,097	Prineville	2,975
Curry	15,600	Gold Beach	1,627
Deschutes	61,918	Bend	3,031
Douglas	89,100	Roseburg	5,063
Gilliam	2,061	Condon	1,208
Grant	8,216	Canyon City	4,530
Harney	8,306	Burns	10,166
Hood River	15,810	Hood River	523
Jackson	123,100	Medford	2,812
Jefferson	11,556	Madras	1,793
Josephine	53,700	Grants Pass	1,625
Klamath	59,002	Klamath Falls	5,970
Lake	7,523	Lakeview	8,231
Lane	257,700	Eugene	4,552
Lincoln	31,300	Newport	986
Linn	85,700	Albany	2,283
Malheur	26,891	Vale	9,859
Marion	182,200	Salem	1,166
Morrow	7,525	Heppner	2,060
Multnomah	523,700	Portland	423
Polk	43,700	Dallas	736
Sherman	2,177	Moro	830
Tillamook	19,900	Tillamook	1,115
Umatilla	58,840	Pendleton	3,227
Union	23,935	La Grande	2,032
Wallowa	7,269	Enterprise	3,178
Wasco	21,711	The Dalles	2,381
Washington	216,100	Hillsboro	716
Wheeler	1,511	Fossil	1,707
Yamhill	49,700	McMinnville	711

Pennsylvania

(67 counties, 44,966 sq. mi. land; pop., 11,750,000)

Adams	63,300	Gettysburg	526
Allegheny	1,476,800	Pittsburgh	728
Armstrong	76,600	Kittanning	652
Beaver	207,700	Beaver	440
Bedford	44,000	Bedford	1,018
Berks	305,500	Reading	862
Blair	134,100	Hollidaysburg	530
Bradford	59,500	Towanda	1,148
Bucks	471,800	Doylestown	614
Butler	143,100	Butler	794
Cambria	182,974	Ebensburg	692
Cameron	6,700	Emporium	401
Carbon	52,400	Jim Thorpe	404
Centre	109,700	Bellefonte	1,115
Chester	301,900	West Chester	761
Clarion	41,800	Clarion	597
Clearfield	79,600	Clearfield	1,139
Clinton	37,800	Lock Haven	899
Columbia	59,700	Bloomsburg	484
Crawford	85,300	Meadville	1,012
Cumberland	173,900	Carlisle	555
Dauphin	222,100	Harrisburg	518
Delaware	551,967	Media	184
Elk	36,200	Ridgeway	807
Erie	269,400	Erie	813
Fayette	155,900	Uniontown	802
Forest	5,300	Tionesta	419
Franklin	107,200	Chambersburg	754
Fulton	12,100	McConnellsburg	435
Greene	39,400	Waynesburg	578
Huntingdon	39,200	Huntingdon	895
Indiana	88,100	Indiana	825
Jefferson	47,200	Brookville	652
Juniata	18,600	Mifflintown	386
Lackawanna	232,200	Scranton	454
Lancaster	351,200	Lancaster	946
Lawrence	105,500	New Castle	367
Lebanon	106,500	Lebanon	363
Lehigh	263,800	Allentown	348
Luzerne	337,800	Wilkes-Barre	886
Lycoming	113,300	Williamsport	1,216
McKean	50,700	Smethport	992
Mercer	125,100	Mercer	670
Mifflin	44,000	Lewistown	431
Monroe	59,300	Stroudsburg	611
Montgomery	627,600	Norristown	496
Montour	16,600	Danville	130
Northampton	225,600	Easton	376
Northumberland	99,200	Sunbury	453
Perry	33,800	New Bloomfield	551
Philadelphia	1,680,235	Philadelphia	129
Pike	14,700	Milford	542
Potter	16,900	Coudersport	1,092
Schuylkill	157,100	Pottsville	784
Snyder	31,400	Middleburg	327
Somerset	81,267	Somerset	1,078
Sullivan	5,800	Laporte	478
Susquehanna	36,300	Montrose	833
Tioga	41,300	Wellsboro	1,146
Union	31,200	Lewisburg	318
Venango	62,400	Franklin	678
Warren	45,800	Warren	905
Washington	212,400	Washington	857
Wayne	35,300	Honesdale	741
Westmoreland	372,296	Greensburg	1,024
Wyoming	23,800	Tunkhannock	398
York	292,300	York	909

Rhode Island

(5 counties, 1,049 sq. mi. land; pop., 945,761)

Bristol	46,955	Bristol	25
Kent	153,957	East Greenwich	173
Newport	81,371	Newport	115
Providence	567,000	Providence	416
Washington	93,171	West Kingston	321

South Carolina

(46 counties, 30,225 sq. mi. land; pop., 2,918,000)

Abbeville	22,200	Abbeville	506
Aiken	99,200	Aiken	1,087
Allendale	10,200	Allendale	418
Anderson	120,300	Anderson	749
Bamberg	16,500	Bamberg	395

County	Pop.	County seat or court house	Land area sq. mi.
Barnwell	*19,600*	Barnwell	553
Beaufort	*57,800*	Beaufort	579
Berkeley	*76,000*	Moncks Corner	1,110
Calhoun	*11,400*	Saint Matthews	377
Charleston	*260,600*	Charleston	939
Cherokee	*41,700*	Gaffney	394
Chester	*30,700*	Chester	584
Chesterfield	38,292	Chesterfield	790
Clarendon	27,467	Manning	599
Colleton	*29,900*	Walterboro	1,049
Darlington	62,743	Darlington	543
Dillon	31,102	Dillon	407
Dorchester	*52,300*	Saint George	569
Edgefield	*16,700*	Edgefield	482
Fairfield	*20,300*	Winnsboro	696
Florence	110,024	Florence	805
Georgetown	42,396	Georgetown	812
Greenville	*271,800*	Greenville	792
Greenwood	*53,600*	Greenwood	446
Hampton	*17,400*	Hampton	562
Horry	101,040	Conway	1,154
Jasper	*14,700*	Ridgeland	652
Kershaw	52,908	Camden	781
Lancaster	*48,300*	Lancaster	502
Laurens	*51,200*	Laurens	711
Lee	18,862	Bishopville	409
Lexington	*130,500*	Lexington	717
McCormick	*8,000*	McCormick	360
Marion	34,012	Marion	487
Marlboro	31,685	Bennettsville	483
Newberry	*30,800*	Newberry	635
Oconee	*44,800*	Walhalla	654
Orangeburg	*79,000*	Orangeburg	1,106
Pickens	*72,500*	Pickens	492
Richland	*249,500*	Columbia	748
Saluda	*14,800*	Saluda	458
Spartanburg	*196,800*	Spartanburg	831
Sumter	*83,800*	Sumter	672
Union	*30,200*	Union	514
Williamsburg	38,165	Kingstree	935
York	*98,700*	York	684

South Dakota

(67 counties, 75,955 sq. mi. land; pop., 687,643)

Aurora	3,614	Plankinton	709
Beadle	19,210	Huron	1,259
Bennett	3,031	Martin	1,181
Bon Homme	8,061	Tyndall	560
Brookings	24,263	Brookings	800
Brown	36,901	Aberdeen	1,674
Brule	5,169	Chamberlain	818
Buffalo	1,795	Gannvalley	482
Butte	8,373	Belle Fourche	2,250
Campbell	2,237	Mound City	732
Charles Mi	9,693	Lake Andes	1,097
Clark	4,889	Clark	964
Clay	13,693	Vermillion	405
Codington	20,898	Watertown	687
Corson	5,125	McIntosh	2,470
Custer	5,868	Custer	1,557
Davison	17,811	Mitchell	432
Day	8,106	Webster	1,030
Deuel	5,271	Clear Lake	639
Dewey	5,350	Timber Lake	2,351
Douglas	4,179	Armour	435
Edmunds	5,174	Ipswich	1,154
Fall River	8,431	Hot Springs	1,743
Faulk	3,298	Faulkton	996
Grant	8,999	Milbank	681
Gregory	5,995	Burke	997
Haakon	2,781	Philip	1,816
Hamlin	5,248	Hayti	511
Hand	4,956	Miller	1,432
Hanson	3,385	Alexandria	430
Harding	1,691	Buffalo	2,682
Hughes	14,211	Pierre	748
Hutchinson	9,357	Olivet	815
Hyde	2,084	Highmore	863
Jackson	3,189	Kadoka	808
Jerauld	2,921	Wessington Spgs	527
Jones	1,454	Murdo	973
Kingsbury	6,684	De Smet	818
Lake	10,766	Madison	567
Lawrence	18,386	Deadwood	800
Lincoln	13,965	Canton	576
Lyman	3,853	Kennebec	1,683
McCook	6,455	Salem	575
McPherson	4,029	Leola	1,147
Marshall	5,410	Britton	848
Meade	20,684	Sturgis	3,465
Mellette	2,211	White River	1,306
Miner	3,741	Howard	570
Minnehaha	109,490	Sioux Falls	813
Moody	6,682	Flandreau	523
Pennington	70,253	Rapid City	2,779
Perkins	4,570	Bison	2,860
Potter	3,686	Gettysburg	869
Roberts	10,897	Sisseton	1,108
Sanborn	3,206	Woonsocket	570
Shannon	9,407	(Attached to Fall River)	2,100
Spink	9,207	Redfield	1,505
Stanley	2,542	Fort Pierce	1,414
Sully	1,991	Onida	1,004
Todd	7,329	(Attached to Tripp)	1,388
Tripp	7,266	Winner	1,620
Turner	9,260	Parker	612
Union	10,745	Elk Point	452
Walworth	7,006	Selby	718
Washabaugh	—	(Attached to Jackson)	1,061
Yankton	18,933	Yankton	519
Zeibach	2,288	Dupree	1,981

Tennessee

(95 counties, 41,328 sq. mi. land; pop., *4,357,000*)

Anderson	*65,900*	Clinton	335
Bedford	*26,800*	Shelbyville	482
Benton	*13,400*	Camden	392
Bledsoe	*8,500*	Pikeville	404
Blount	*75,500*	Maryville	575
Bradley	*62,800*	Cleveland	334
Campbell	*32,100*	Jacksboro	451
Cannon	*9,400*	Woodbury	271
Carroll	*27,400*	Huntingdon	596
Carter	50,051	Elizabethton	348
Cheatham	*18,900*	Ashland City	305
Chester	*12,100*	Henderson	285
Claiborne	24,516	Tazewell	444
Clay	*6,900*	Celina	233
cocke	28,711	Newport	424
Coffee	*35,300*	Manchester	434
Crockett	*14,600*	Alamo	269
Cumberland	*27,200*	Crossville	678
Davidson	*451,200*	Nashville	508
Decatur	*10,000*	Decaturville	337
De Kalb	*12,800*	Smithville	278
Dickson	*28,300*	Charlotte	485
Dyer	*33,800*	Dyersburg	529
Fayette	*25,000*	Somerville	704
Fentress	*14,600*	Jamestown	498
Franklin	*30,400*	Winchester	553
Gibson	*47,800*	Trenton	607
Giles	*23,400*	Pulaski	619
Grainger	16,676	Rutledge	282
Greene	54,157	Greeneville	613
Grundy	*12,400*	Altamont	358
Hamblen	48,911	Morristown	155
Hamilton	*269,600*	Chattanooga	550
Hancock	6,873	Sneedville	230
Hardeman	*23,100*	Bolivar	656
Hardin	*20,900*	Savannah	587
Hawkins	43,662	Rogersville	480
Haywood	*21,600*	Brownsville	519
Henderson	*20,000*	Lexington	515
Henry	*26,400*	Paris	567
Hickman	*14,200*	Centerville	610
Houston	*6,700*	Erin	201
Humphreys	*15,200*	Waverly	530
Jackson	*8,800*	Gainesboro	323
Jefferson	31,176	Dandridge	274
Johnson	13,753	Mountain City	293
Knox	*302,400*	Knoxville	508
Lake	*7,100*	Tiptonville	167
Lauderdale	*23,100*	Ripley	477
Lawrence	*33,900*	Lawrenceburg	634
Lewis	*8,700*	Hohenwald	285
Lincoln	*25,300*	Fayetteville	580
Loudon	*27,300*	Loudon	237
McMinn	*39,700*	Athens	432
McNairy	*21,600*	Selmer	569
Macon	*15,000*	Lafayette	304
Madison	*71,300*	Jackson	560
Marion	*23,400*	Jasper	506
Marshall	*18,300*	Lewisburg	377
Maury	*48,300*	Columbia	614
Meigs	*7,000*	Decatur	191
Monroe	*27,200*	Madisonville	660
Montgomery	*80,100*	Clarksville	539
Moore	*4,000*	Lynchburg	124
Morgan	*15,900*	Wartburg	539
Obion	*34,000*	Union City	556
Overton	*17,200*	Livingston	441
Perry	*6,200*	Linden	411
Pickett	*4,400*	Byrdstown	158
Polk	*13,200*	Benton	434
Putnam	*41,900*	Cookeville	405
Rhea	*22,700*	Dayton	312
Roane	*44,700*	Kingston	350
Robertson	*32,900*	Springfield	476
Rutherford	*76,600*	Murfreesboro	612
Scott	*17,800*	Huntsville	544
Sequatchie	*7,700*	Dunlap	273
Sevier	41,293	Sevierville	597
Shelby	*754,500*	Memphis	755
Smith	*14,100*	Carthage	323
Stewart	*9,300*	Dover	470

County	Pop.	County seat or court house	Land area sq. mi.
Sullivan	143,178	Blountville	413
Sumner	*78,000*	Gallatin	534
Tipton	*32,100*	Covington	459
Trousdale	*5,600*	Hartsville	114
Unicoi	16,341	Erwin	185
Union	*11,900*	Maynardville	212
Van Buren	*4,300*	Spencer	254
Warren	*31,300*	McMinnville	439
Washington	88,635	Jonesboro	323
Wayne	*13,500*	Waynesboro	739
Weakley	*30,900*	Dresden	576
White	*19,700*	Sparta	382
Williamson	*50,500*	Franklin	593
Wilson	*49,600*	Lebanon	567

Texas

(254 counties, 262,134 sq. mi. land; pop., *13,014,000*)

County	Pop.	County seat or court house	Land area sq. mi.
Anderson	*34,900*	Palestine	1,072
Andrews	*11,600*	Andrews	1,504
Angelina	*57,800*	Lufkin	738
Aransas	*11,900*	Rockport	275
Archer	*6,500*	Archer City	913
Armstrong	*2,000*	Claude	907
Atascosa	*20,700*	Jourdanton	1,206
Austin	*15,700*	Bellville	663
Bailey	*7,700*	Muleshoe	835
Bandera	*6,700*	Bandera	763
Bastrop	*20,100*	Bastrop	890
Baylor	*4,700*	Seymour	845
Bee	*22,900*	Beeville	842
Bell	*162,200*	Belton	1,047
Bexar	*965,700*	San Antonio	1,246
Blanco	*3,900*	Johnson City	719
Borden	*900*	Gail	907
Bosque	*12,700*	Meridian	990
Bowie	*73,600*	Boston	891
Brazoria	*143,900*	Angleton	1,423
Brazos	*76,100*	Bryan	586
Brewster	7,578	Alpine	6,204
Briscoe	*2,600*	Silverton	874
Brooks	*7,400*	Falfurrias	904
Brown	*29,200*	Brownwood	938
Burleson	*10,600*	Caldwell	670
Burnet	*16,300*	Burnet	996
Caldwell	*22,300*	Lockhart	544
Calhoun	*17,900*	Port Lavanca	527
Callahan	*10,200*	Baird	856
Cameron	*177,400*	Brownsville	896
Camp	*8,600*	Pittsburg	192
Carson	*6,600*	Panhandle	900
Cass	*26,900*	Linden	941
Castro	*10,600*	Dimmitt	880
Chambers	*14,500*	Anahuac	616
Cherokee	*32,300*	Rusk	1,049
Childress	*6,400*	Childress	699
Clay	*9,100*	Henrietta	1,102
Cochran	*4,700*	Morton	783
Coke	3,200	Robert Lee	911
Coleman	*10,200*	Coleman	1,280
Collin	*110,100*	McKinney	836
Collingsworth	*4,300*	Wellington	894
Colorado	*17,400*	Columbus	949
Comal	*31,900*	New Braunfels	567
Comanche	*12,100*	Comanche	944
Concho	*2,800*	Paint Rock	1,004
Cooke	*24,700*	Gainesville	985
Coryell	*46,900*	Gatesville	1,043
Cottle	*3,100*	Paducah	900
Crane	4,597	Crane	795
Crockett	4,588	Ozona	2,794
Crosby	*8,400*	Crosbyton	911
Culberson	3,319	Van Horn	3,851
Dallam	*6,700*	Dalhart	1,494
Dallas	*1,483,500*	Dallas	859
Dawson	*15,700*	Lamesa	902
Deaf Smith	*20,100*	Hereford	1,510
Delta	*4,500*	Cooper	276
Denton	*103,900*	Denton	911
Dewitt	*18,500*	Cuero	910
Dickens	*3,600*	Dickens	931
Dimmit	*11,200*	Carrizo Springs	1,344
Donley	*3,800*	Clarendon	905
Duval	*11,800*	San Diego	1,814
Eastland	*18,300*	Eastland	952
Ector	*105,500*	Odessa	907
Edwards	2,048	Rocksprings	2,076
Ellis	*53,800*	Waxahachie	940
El Paso	478,834	El Paso	1,057
Erath	*19,800*	Stephenville	1,085
Falls	*16,100*	Marlin	764
Fannin	*23,000*	Bonham	905
Fayette	*17,700*	La Grange	934
Fisher	*5,900*	Roby	904
Floyd	*10,100*	Floydada	993
Foard	*2,200*	Crowell	676
Fort Bend	*95,100*	Richmond	869
Franklin	*6,600*	Mount Vernon	293
Freestone	*12,300*	Fairfield	865
Frio	*13,100*	Pearsall	1,116
Gaines	*11,100*	Seminole	1,489
Galveston	*198,000*	Galveston	399
Garza	*5,200*	Post	914
Gillespie	*11,700*	Fredericksburg	1,055
Glasscock	1,308	Garden City	863
Goliad	*4,800*	Goliad	871
Gonzales	*15,600*	Gonzales	1,056
Gray	*25,100*	Pampa	934
Grayson	*84,500*	Sherman	940
Gregg	*87,000*	Longview	282
Grimes	*12,500*	Anderson	801
Guadalupe	*40,100*	Seguin	714
Hale	*35,000*	Plainview	979
Hall	*5,600*	Memphis	885
Hamilton	*7,500*	Hamilton	844
Hansford	*6,100*	Spearman	907
Hardeman	*6,100*	Quanah	687
Hardin	*38,300*	Kountze	897
Harris	*2,194,000*	Houston	1,723
Harrison	*46,500*	Marshall	894
Hartley	*3,300*	Channing	1,488
Haskell	*7,600*	Haskell	877
Hays	*35,000*	San Marcos	650
Hemphill	*4,000*	Canadian	904
Henderson	*34,600*	Athens	943
Hidalgo	*235,800*	Edinburg	1,543
Hill	*22,300*	Hillsboro	1,010
Hockley	*21,500*	Levelland	908
Hood	*12,400*	Granbury	426
Hopkins	*22,700*	Sulphur Springs	793
Houston	*19,300*	Crockett	1,237
Howard	*34,800*	Big Spring	911
Hudspeth	2,748	Sierra Blanca	4,554
Hunt	*50,100*	Greenville	826
Hutchinson	*25,700*	Stinnett	875
Irion	1,397	Mertzon	1,073
Jack	*7,000*	Jacksboro	945
Jackson	*13,100*	Edna	850
Jasper	*28,500*	Jasper	907
Jeff Davis	1,648	Fort Davis	2,259
Jefferson	*245,300*	Beaumont	951
Jim Hogg	*4,800*	Hebbronville	1,143
Jim Wells	*34,500*	Alice	845
Johnson	*60,100*	Cleburne	740
Jones	*16,300*	Anson	956
Karnes	*12,600*	Karnes City	758
Kaufman	*36,100*	Kaufman	815
Kendall	*9,100*	Boerne	670
Kenedy	*600*	Sarita	1,394
Kent	*1,206*	Jayton	880
Kerr	*23,300*	Kerrville	1,101
Kimble	4,063	Junction	1,274
King	*400*	Guthrie	944
Kinney	*2,200*	Brackettville	1,393
Kleberg	*32,700*	Kingsville	851
Knox	*5,600*	Benjamin	851
Lamar	*37,700*	Paris	984
Lamb	*17,400*	Littlefield	1,022
Lampasas	*11,600*	Lampasas	726
La Salle	*5,600*	Cotulla	1,500
Lavaca	*17,500*	Hallettsville	975
Lee	*9,100*	Giddings	637
Leon	*9,100*	Centerville	1,102
Liberty	*41,500*	Liberty	1,180
Limestone	*18,000*	Groesbeck	931
Lipscomb	*3,700*	Lipscomb	934
Live Oak	*6,900*	George West	1,055
Llano	*9,100*	Llano	941
Loving	91	Mentone	648
Lubbock	*200,000*	Lubbock	893
Lynn	*8,700*	Tahoka	915
McCulloch	*8,300*	Brady	1,066
McLennan	*160,900*	Waco	1,000
McMullen	*800*	Tilden	1,159
Madison	*9,300*	Madisonville	480
Marion	*8,900*	Jefferson	380
Martin	*5,000*	Staton	911
Mason	*3,300*	Mason	935
Matagorda	*32,300*	Bay City	1,157
Maverick	*24,600*	Eagle Pass	1,289
Medina	*21,600*	Hondo	1,352
Menard	2,342	Menard	914
Midland	*73,900*	Midland	939
Milam	*20,000*	Cameron	1,028
Mills	*4,100*	Goldthwaite	734
Mitchell	*8,900*	Colorado City	920
Montague	*16,500*	Montague	932
Montgomery	*104,600*	Conroe	1,090
Moore	*15,000*	Dumas	909
Morris	*13,600*	Daingerfield	260
Motley	*1,800*	Matador	980
Nacogdoches	*42,500*	Nacogdoches	902
Navarro	*31,600*	Corsicana	1,070
Newton	*12,600*	Newton	949
Nolan	*16,600*	Sweetwater	922
Nueces	*249,100*	Corpus Christi	841
Ochiltree	*9,400*	Perryton	907
Oldham	*2,600*	Vega	1,478

County	Pop.	County seat or court house	Land area sq. mi.
Orange	80,700	Orange	359
Palo Pinto	24,300	Palo Pinto	948
Panola	18,400	Carthage	869
Parker	37,100	Weatherford	903
Parmer	10,100	Farwell	859
Pecos	14,641	Fort Stockton	4,740
Polk	19,600	Livingston	1,100
Potter	91,800	Amarillo	898
Presidio	5,169	Marfa	3,892
Rains	4,500	Emory	210
Randall	66,300	Canyon	914
Reagan	4,126	Big Lake	1,132
Real	2,200	Leakey	622
Red River	14,200	Clarksville	1,033
Reeves	15,682	Pecos	2,608
Refugio	9,100	Refugio	774
Roberts	1,100	Miami	899
Robertson	13,900	Franklin	877
Rockwall	10,600	Rockwall	147
Runnels	11,300	Ballinger	1,058
Rusk	37,800	Henderson	939
Sabine	7,400	Hemphill	456
San Augustine	8,600	San Augustine	473
San Jacinto	9,700	Coldspring	624
San Patricio	53,000	Sinton	685
San Saba	5,300	San Saba	1,120
Schleicher	2,795	Eldorado	1,331
Scurry	17,600	Snyder	904
Shackelford	3,400	Albany	887
Shelby	20,300	Center	778
Sherman	3,700	Stratford	916
Smith	113,800	Tyler	934
Somervell	3,900	Glen Rose	197
Starr	22,300	Rio Grande City	1,211
Stephens	9,100	Breckenridge	899
Sterling	1,209	Sterling City	914
Stonewall	2,200	Aspermont	926
Sutton	5,120	Sonora	1,493
Swisher	10,100	Tulia	896
Tarrant	789,600	Fort Worth	861
Taylor	105,100	Abilene	912
Terrell	1,605	Sanderson	2,391
Terry	13,600	Brownfield	899
Throckmorton	2,200	Throckmorton	920
Titus	19,000	Mount Pleasant	418
Tom Green	77,300	San Angelo	1,500
Travis	384,700	Austin	1,012
Trinity	7,800	Groveton	707
Tyler	15,000	Woodville	919
Upshur	25,300	Gilmer	584
Upton	4,464	Rankin	1,312
Uvalde	20,300	Uvalde	1,588
Val Verde	35,722	Del Rio	3,241
Van Zandt	27,600	Canton	845
Victoria	62,500	Victoria	892
Walker	35,200	Huntsville	790
Waller	16,300	Hempstead	509
Ward	14,024	Monahans	827
Washington	20,100	Brenham	594
Webb	85,800	Laredo	3,306
Wharton	37,200	Wharton	1,076
Wheeler	6,200	Wheeler	914
Wichita	119,900	Wichita Falls	611
Wilbarger	14,900	Vernon	952
Willacy	16,300	Raymondville	591
Williamson	58,200	Georgetown	1,104
Wilson	14,200	Floresville	802
Winkler	9,961	Kermit	887
Wise	22,600	Decatur	922
Wood	21,900	Quitman	721
Yoakum	7,400	Plains	830
Young	17,700	Graham	888
Zapata	5,600	Zapata	957
Zavala	11,300	Crystal City	1,291

Utah

(29 counties, 82,096 sq. mi. land; pop. 1,454,630)

Beaver	4,377	Beaver	2,584
Box Elder	33,212	Brigham City	5,603
Cache	57,220	Logan	1,174
Carbon	22,101	Price	1,476
Daggett	765	Manila	682
Davis	146,242	Farmington	297
Duchesne	12,537	Duchesne	3,255
Emery	11,455	Castle Dale	4,439
Garfield	3,660	Panguitch	5,158
Grand	8,312	Moab	3,682
Iron	17,304	Parowan	3,300
Juab	5,516	Nephi	3,412
Kane	4,003	Kanab	3,904
Millard	8,736	Fillmore	6,793
Morgan	4,914	Morgan	603
Piute	1,328	Junction	754
Rich	2,115	Randolph	1,023
Salt Lake	615,586	Salt Lake City	764
San Juan	12,270	Monticello	7,707
Sanpete	14,615	Manti	1,597
Sevier	14,742	Richfield	1,929
Summit	10,227	Coalville	1,849
Tooele	26,012	Tooele	6,923
Uintah	20,479	Vernal	4,487
Utah	217,281	Provo	2,014
Wasatch	8,531	Heber City	1,191
Washington	26,002	Saint George	2,427
Wayne	1,918	Loa	2,486
Weber	143,170	Ogden	581

Vermont

(14 counties, 9,267 sq. mi. land; pop. 511,297)

Addison	29,420	Middlebury	784
Bennington	33,310	Bennington	672
Calendonia	25,814	Saint Johnsbury	612
Chittenden	115,002	Burlington	533
Essex	6,300	Guildhall	663
Franklin	34,800	Saint Albans	660
Grand Isle	4,593	North Hero	83
Lamoille	16,769	Hyde Park	474
Orange	22,763	Chelsea	690
Orleans	23,455	Newport	715
Rutland	58,332	Rutland	927
Washington	52,391	Montpelier	707
Windham	36,880	Newfane	784
Windsor	50,882	Woodstock	962

Virginia

(95 cos., 41 ind. cities, 39,780 sq. mi. land; pop. *5,148,000*)

Accomack	31,900	Accomac	476
Albemarle	49,400	Charlottesville	740
Alleghany	12,900	Covington	444
Amelia	8,344	Amelia, C.H.	366
Amherst	27,500	Amherst	470
Appomattox	11,500	Appomattox	345
Arlington	149,400	Arlington	26
Augusta	51,900	Staunton	986
Bath	5,500	Warm Springs	540
Bedford	31,100	Bedford	727
Bland	6,400	Bland	369
Botetourt	21,500	Fincastle	548
Brunswick	15,594	Lawrenceville	579
Buchanan	36,000	Grundy	508
Buckingham	11,700	Buckingham	582
Campbell	44,300	Rustburg	529
Caroline	17,000	Bowling Green	545
Carroll	23,800	Hillsville	494
Charles City	6,600	Charles City	181
Charlotte	12,187	Charlotte Courthouse	470
Chesterfield	141,140	Chesterfield	442
Clarke	9,200	Berryville	174
Craig	4,100	New Castle	336
Culpeper	21,900	Culpeper	389
Cumberland	7,782	Cumberland	291
Dickenson	20,000	Clintwood	332
Dinwiddie	22,285	Dinwiddie	507
Essex	8,100	Tappahannock	250
Fairfax	545,500	Fairfax	399
Fauquier	31,300	Warrenton	660
Floyd	10,700	Floyd	383
Fluvanna	10,100	Palmyra	288
Franklin	32,600	Rocky Mount	716
Frederick	28,300	Winchester	405
Giles	16,700	Pearisburg	363
Gloucester	18,000	Gloucester	228
Goochland	11,400	Goochland	289
Grayson	15,600	Independence	452
Greene	7,300	Stanardsville	153
Greensville	10,000	Emporia	299
Halifax	30,321	Halifax	796
Hanover	52,100	Hanover	465
Henrico	180,315	Richmond	229
Henry	57,407	Martinsville	381
Highland	2,800	Monterey	416
Isle of Wight	20,400	Isle of Wight	317
James City	21,000	Williamsburg	152
King and Queen	6,100	King and Queen	318
King George	9,800	King George	176
King William	8,600	King William	278
Lancaster	10,200	Lancaster	137
Lee	25,300	Jonesville	438
Loudoun	53,200	Leesburg	517
Louisa	17,700	Louisa	517
Lunenburg	11,998	Lunenburg	442
Madison	9,900	Madison	327
Mathews	8,200	Mathews	89
Mecklenburg	29,257	Boydton	612
Middlesex	7,400	Saluda	130
Montgomery	59,800	Christiansburg	394
Nelson	11,700	Lovingston	471
New Kent	7,800	New Kent	210
Northampton	15,400	Eastville	220
Northumberland	9,500	Heathsville	190
Nottoway	15,222	Nottoway	308
Orange	17,000	Orange	355
Page	18,900	Luray	316
Patrick	16,200	Stuart	464

County	Pop.	County seat or court house	Land area sq. mi.
Pittsylvania	65,615	Chatham	1,001
Powhatan	12,854	Powhatan	269
Prince Edward	16,200	Farmville	357
Prince George	25,646	Prince George	276
Prince William	*134,700*	Manassas	347
Pulaski	*33,000*	Pulaski	328
Rappahannock	*5,900*	Washington	267
Richmond	*6,800*	Warsaw	190
Roanoke	*63,200*	Salem	262
Rockbridge	*16,700*	Lexington	601
Rockingham	*54,500*	Harrisonburg	865
Russell	*28,600*	Lebanon	483
Scott	*24,700*	Gate City	539
Shenandoah	*27,000*	Woodstock	507
Smyth	*32,400*	Marion	435
Southampton	*19,600*	Courtland	602
Spotsylvania	*29,600*	Spotsylvania	409
Stafford	*37,100*	Stafford	270
Surry	*5,700*	Surry	277
Sussex	*10,800*	Sussex	494
Tazewell	*49,500*	Tazewell	522
Warren	*19,800*	Front Royal	219
Washington	*41,500*	Abingdon	574
Westmoreland	*13,700*	Montross	229
Wise	*44,300*	Wise	412
Wythe	*24,300*	Wytheville	460
York	*33,700*	Yorktown	129
Independent cities			
Alexandria	*104,700*		15
Bedford	*6,200*		7
Bristol	*20,900*		4
Buena Vista	*6,700*		3
Charlottesville	*39,000*		10
Chesapeake	*112,500*		341
Clifton Forge	*4,800*		4
Colonial Heights	*17,300*		8
Covington	*9,000*		4
Danville	*44,200*		17
Emporia	*5,100*		2
Fairfax	*20,400*		6
Falls Church	*8,900*		2
Franklin	*7,100*		4
Fredericksburg	*17,100*		6
Galax	*6,600*		7
Hampton	*124,300*		55
Harrisonburg	*18,900*		6
Hopewell	*23,900*		9
Lexington	*7,600*		3
Lynchburg	*64,700*		25
Manassas	*12,800*		—
Manassas Park	*8,500*		—
Martinsville	*17,700*		11
Newport News	*143,700*		69
Norfolk	*280,200*		53
Norton	*4,300*		4
Petersburg	*43,100*		8
Poquoson	*9,300*		—
Portsmouth	*107,900*		29
Radford	*12,400*		5
Richmond	*219,600*		60
Roanoke	*98,700*		27
Salem	*23,300*		14
South Boston	*7,200*		5
Staunton	*21,300*		9
Suffolk	*46,900*		2
Virginia Beach	*242,000*		259
Waynesboro	*16,300*		7
Williamsburg	*11,300*		5
Winchester	*23,100*		3

Washington

(39 counties, 66,570 sq. mi. land; pop., *3,774,000*)

Adams	13,322	Ritzville	1,894
Asotin	16,822	Asotin	633
Benton	*96,800*	Prosser	1,722
Chelan	*43,000*	Wenatchee	2,918
Clallam	*45,200*	Port Angeles	1,753
Clark	*171,500*	Vancouver	627
Columbia	4,098	Dayton	853
Cowlitz	*74,100*	Kelso	1,144
Douglas	22,156	Waterville	1,831
Ferry	5,748	Republic	2,202
Franklin	*31,200*	Pasco	1,253
Garfield	2,483	Pomeroy	709
Grant	*49,000*	Ephrata	2,675
Grays Harbor	*63,300*	Montesano	1,910
Island	*39,400*	Coupeville	212
Jefferson	*14,000*	Port Townsend	1,805
King	*1,177,600*	Seattle	2,128
Kitsap	*127,300*	Port Orchard	393
Kittitas	*25,000*	Ellensburg	2,317
Klickitat	*14,400*	Goldendale	1,908
Lewis	*51,900*	Chehalis	2,423
Lincoln	9,597	Davenport	2,306
Mason	*25,800*	Shelton	962
Okanogan	30,654	Okanogan	5,301
Pacific	*16,200*	South Bend	908
Pend Oreille	8,561	Newport	1,402
Pierce	*436,900*	Tacoma	1,676
San Juan	*6,900*	Friday Harbor	179
Skagit	*58,600*	Mount Vernon	1,735
Skamania	*6,000*	Stevenson	1,672
Snohomish	*290,000*	Everett	2,098
Spokane	341,058	Spokane	1,758
Stevens	29,008	Colville	2,481
Thurston	*112,800*	Olympia	714
Wahkiakum	*3,800*	Cathlamet	261
Walla Walla	*43,400*	Walla Walla	1,262
Whatcom	*96,800*	Bellingham	2,126
Whitman	40,321	Colfax	2,153
Yakima	*159,300*	Yakima	4,268

West Virginia

(55 counties, 24,070 sq. mi. land; pop., *1,860,000*)

Barbour	16,623	Philippi	341
Berkeley	46,846	Martinsburg	316
Boone	30,235	Madison	501
Braxton	13,880	Sutton	511
Brooke	30,116	Wellsburg	88
Cabell	104,798	Huntington	279
Calhoun	8,181	Grantsville	281
Clay	11,221	Clay	343
Doddridge	7,421	West Union	319
Fayette	57,033	Fayetteville	663
Gilmer	8,321	Glenville	339
Grant	10,218	Petersburg	478
Greenbrier	37,334	Lewisburg	1,026
Hampshire	14,864	Romney	639
Hancock	40,809	New Cumberland	83
Hardy	10,051	Moorefield	585
Harrison	77,488	Clarksburg	418
Jackson	25,597	Ripley	461
Jefferson	30,311	Charles Town	211
Kanawha	223,114	Charleston	907
Lewis	18,894	Weston	392
Lincoln	22,860	Hamlin	438
Logan	50,511	Logan	456
McDowell	49,550	Welch	533
Marion	65,525	Fairmont	311
Marshall	41,391	Moundsville	304
Mason	26,763	Point Pleasant	433
Mercer	73,363	Princeton	417
Mineral	27,159	Keyser	330
Mingo	37,052	Williamson	423
Monongalia	75,240	Morgantown	365
Monroe	12,857	Union	473
Morgan	10,696	Berkeley Springs	233
Nicholas	28,071	Summersville	642
Ohio	61,560	Wheeling	106
Pendleton	7,935	Franklin	695
Pleasants	8,245	St. Marys	129
Pocahontas	9,930	Marlinton	943
Preston	30,468	Kingwood	645
Putnam	36,754	Winfield	348
Raleigh	85,942	Beckley	605
Randolph	28,784	Elkins	1,036
Ritchie	11,415	Harrisville	452
Roane	15,799	Spencer	486
Summers	15,314	Hinton	350
Taylor	16,616	Grafton	174
Tucker	8,657	Parsons	421
Tyler	11,306	Middlebourne	256
Upshur	23,541	Buckhannon	352
Wayne	45,095	Wayne	513
Webster	12,306	Webster Springs	551
Wetzel	21,908	New Martinsville	363
Wirt	4,652	Elizabeth	235
Wood	92,043	Parkersburg	368
Wyoming	35,850	Pineville	504

Wisconsin

(72 counties, 54,464 sq. mi. land; pop., *4,679,000*)

Adams	*11,500*	Friendship	646
Ashland	*17,400*	Ashland	1,038
Barron	*37,500*	Barron	864
Bayfield	*13,400*	Washburn	1,460
Brown	*178,000*	Green Bay	524
Buffalo	*14,600*	Alma	711
Burnett	*11,600*	Grantsburg	840
Calumet	*29,000*	Chilton	322
Chippewa	*50,700*	Chippewa Falls	1,018
Clark	*32,800*	Neillsville	1,221
Columbia	*42,500*	Portage	776
Crawford	*16,500*	Prairie du Chien	568
Dane	*319,000*	Madison	1,198
Dodge	*73,900*	Juneau	889
Door	*24,400*	Sturgeon Bay	492
Douglas	*45,200*	Superior	1,305
Dunn	*33,100*	Menomonie	853
Eau Claire	*74,900*	Eau Claire	647
Florence	*4,300*	Florence	487
Fond Du Lac	*89,500*	Fond du Lac	725
Forest	*8,900*	Crandon	1,007

County	Pop.	County seat or court house	Land area sq. mi.
Grant	51,700	Lancaster	1,147
Green	29,400	Monroe	585
Green Lake	17,600	Green Lake	354
Iowa	19,400	Dodgeville	762
Iron	6,800	Hurley	747
Jackson	16,100	Black River Falls	999
Jefferson	65,400	Jefferson	564
Juneau	19,200	Mauston	774
Kenosha	123,600	Kenosha	272
Kewaunee	19,800	Kewaunee	330
La Crosse	89,800	La Crosse	451
Lafayette	18,000	Darlington	643
Langlade	19,300	Antigo	856
Lincoln	26,000	Merrill	892
Manitowoc	83,100	Manitowoc	590
Marathon	108,500	Wausau	1,586
Marinette	39,100	Marinette	1,378
Marquette	11,200	Montello	455
Menominee	3,200	Keshena	360
Milwaukee	960,573	Milwaukee	237
Monroe	33,900	Sparta	915
Oconto	28,500	Oconto	1,001
Oneida	30,400	Rhinelander	1,112
Outagamie	129,000	Appleton	634
Ozaukee	65,277	Port Washington	236
Pepin	7,500	Durand	235
Pierce	30,200	Ellsworth	590
Polk	31,300	Balsam Lake	931
Portage	55,200	Stevens Point	806
Price	15,400	Phillips	1,260
Racine	177,100	Racine	337
Richland	16,900	Richland Center	583
Rock	134,400	Janesville	721
Rusk	15,100	Ladysmith	906
St. Croix	41,400	Hudson	734
Sauk	40,600	Baraboo	841
Sawyer	11,700	Hayward	1,259
Shawano	35,800	Shawano	919
Sheboygan	101,300	Sheboygan	505
Taylor	19,500	Medford	975
Trempealeau	24,700	Whitehall	735
Vernon	25,300	Viroqua	802
Vilas	15,600	Eagle River	867
Walworth	69,500	Elkhorn	557
Washburn	13,100	Shell Lake	817
Washington	83,800	West Bend	429
Waukesha	282,000	Waukesha	554
Waupaca	41,600	Waupaca	751
Waushara	16,600	Wautoma	627
Winnebago	132,500	Oshkosh	448
Wood	71,000	Wisconsin Rapids	807

Wyoming

(23 counties, 97,203 sq. mi. land; pop., 468,909)

County	Pop.	County seat or court house	Land area sq. mi.
Albany	28,974	Laramie	4,248
Big Horn	11,901	Basin	3,157
Campbell	24,363	Gillette	4,756
Carbon	21,823	Rawlins	7,905
Converse	14,025	Douglas	4,281
Crook	5,303	Sundance	2,882
Fremont	39,074	Lander	9,106
Goshen	12,022	Torrington	2,228
Hot Springs	5,712	Thermopolis	2,022
Johnson	6,714	Buffalo	4,175
Laramie	68,604	Cheyenne	2,703
Lincoln	12,177	Kemmerer	4,085
Natrona	71,589	Casper	5,342
Niobrara	2,928	Lusk	2,614
Park	21,504	Cody	6,959
Platte	11,991	Wheatland	2,086
Sheridan	25,025	Sheridan	2,532
Sublette	4,545	Pinedale	4,851
Sweetwater	41,662	Green River	10,429
Teton	9,354	Jackson	4,000
Uinta	13,021	Evanston	2,086
Washakie	9,493	Worland	2,262
Weston	7,105	Newcastle	2,407

Population of Outlying Areas

Source: U.S. Bureau of the Census

Population figures are preliminary figures from the 1980 census conducted on Apr. 1, 1980.

Puerto Rico

ZIP code	Municipios	Pop.	Land area sq. mile
00601	Adjuntas	18,617	66
00602	Aguada	31,521	30
00603	Aguadilla	52,627	36
00607	Aguas Buenas	22,431	30
00609	Aibonito	22,230	31
00610	Anasco	22,945	40
00612	Arecibo	86,660	127
00615	Arroyo	17,055	15
00617	Barceloneta	18,869	24
00618	Barranquitas	21,690	33
00619	Bayamon	195,965	44
00623	Cabo Rojo	33,909	72
00625	Caguas	118,020	58
00627	Camuy	24,886	46
00629	Canovanas	31,934	28
00630	Carolina	165,207	48
00632	Catano	26,318	5
00633	Cayey	40,927	50
00635	Ceiba	14,781	27
00638	Ciales	16,014	66
00639	Cidra	28,135	36
00640	Coamo	30,752	77
00642	Comerio	18,212	28
00643	Corozal	28,218	42
00645	Culebra	1,265	10
00646	Dorado	25,515	23
00648	Fajardo	32,011	31
00650	Florida	7,193	10
00653	Guanica	18,784	37
00654	Guayama	40,137	65
00656	Guayanilla	21,012	42
00657	Guaynabo	80,857	27
00658	Gurabo	23,576	28
00659	Hatillo	28,973	42
00660	Hormigueros	13,983	11
00661	Humacao	45,916	45
00662	Isabela	37,451	56
00664	Jayuya	14,720	39
00665	Juana Diaz	43,464	61
00666	Juncos	25,433	26
00667	Lajas	21,190	60
00669	Lares	26,742	62
00670	Las Marias	8,606	44
00671	Las Piedras	22,425	33
00672	Loiza	20,902	25
00673	Luquillo	14,924	26
00701	Manati	36,480	46
00706	Maricao	6,617	37
00707	Maunabo	11,785	21
00708	Mayaguez	95,886	77
00716	Moca	29,309	51
00717	Morovis	21,145	39
00718	Naguabo	20,633	52
00719	Naranjito	23,613	28
00720	Orocovis	19,304	63
00723	Patillas	17,820	48
00724	Penuelas	18,489	44
00731	Ponce	188,219	116
00742	Quebradillas	19,775	23
00743	Rincon	11,770	14
00745	Rio Grande	34,326	61
00747	Sabana Grande	20,164	37
00751	Salinas	26,494	69
00753	San German	32,941	54
*00936	San Juan	432,973	47
00754	San Lorenzo	32,333	53
00755	San Sebastian	35,877	71
00757	Santa Isabel	19,832	34
00758	Toa Alta	31,946	27
00759	Toa Baja	78,119	24
00760	Trujillo Alto	51,389	21
00761	Utuado	34,384	115
00762	Vega Alta	28,225	28
00763	Vega Baja	46,841	47
00765	Vieques	7,628	52
00766	Villalba	20,737	37
00767	Yabucoa	30,589	55
00768	Yauco	37,682	68
Total		**3,187,570**	**3,421**

ZIP code	Area	Pop.	Land area sq. mile
	American Samoa		
96799	American Samoa	32,395	76
	Guam		
	Guam	**105,816**	**209**
96910	Agana	881	1
	Agana Hts.	3,284	1
96915	Agat	3,979	10
	Asan	2,012	6
96913	Barrigada	7,762	9
	Chalan-Pago-Ordot	3,135	6
96912	Dededo	23,659	30
96916	Inarajan	2,062	19
	Mangilao	6,822	10
96916	Merizo	1,658	6
	Mongmong-Too-Maite	5,280	2
	Piti	1,521	7
96915	Santa Rita	10,408	17
	Sinajana	2,471	1
	Talofofo	2,016	17
96911	Tamuning	13,527	6
	Umatac	732	6
	Yigo	10,424	35
96914	Yona	4,237	20
	Virgin Islands		
	St. Croix	48,916	80
	St. John	2,470	20
	St. Thomas	43,828	32
00801	Charlotte Amalie	NA	
00820	Christiansted	NA	
00840	Frederiksted	NA	
Total		**95,214**	**132**
	Trust Territory of Pacific Islands		
	Mariana district	NA	184
	Marshall district	NA	70
	Palau district	NA	192
	Ponape district	NA	176
	Truk district	NA	49
	Yap district	NA	46
Total		**NA**	**717**

QUICK REFERENCE INDEX

First Class Postal Rates in Brief

U.S. Domestic (in effect Sept. 1, 1980)

Letters—15¢ first ounce, 13¢ each additional ounce.
Postal cards—10¢ each (up to 4½ × 6 in.). Double cards, 20¢. Private cards, 10¢; double 20¢.

U.S. International (in effect Sept. 1, 1980)

Letters—(1) Canada (max. weight 60 lbs.) and Mexico (max. weight 4 lbs.), 15¢ first ounce, 13¢ each addl. ounce to 12 ounces; over 12 ounces to 1 pound, $2.25; over 1 pound to 1½ pounds, $2.50; over 1½ to 2 pounds, $2.83; over 2 to 2½ pounds, $3.16; over 2½ to 3 pounds, $3.50; over 3 to 3½ pounds, $3.83; over 3½ to 4 pounds, $4.16; over 4 to 4½ pounds, $4.50; over 4½ to 5 pounds, $4.83; over 5 pounds, $1.33 each additional 2 pounds. (2) Countries other than Canada and Mexico, 1 ounce, 20¢; over 1 to 2 ounces, 36¢; over 2 to 4 ounces, 48¢; over 4 to 8 ounces, 96¢; over 8 ounces to 1 pound, $1.84; over 1 to 2 pounds, $3.20; and over 2 to 4 pounds, $5.20.
Air mail letters—(1) Canada, and Mexico, same as domestic surface rates. (2) Cen. America, Colombia, Venezuela, the Caribbean Is., Bahamas, Bermuda, and St. Pierre and Miquelon, 25¢ per half ounce through 2 ounces; 21¢ each addl. ½ oz. (3) All other countries, 31¢ per half ounce through 2 ounces; 26¢ each addl. ½ oz.

Aerogrammes—to all countries, 22¢ each.
Postal cards—to Canada and Mexico 10¢ each. To all other countries, 14¢ each.
Air mail postcards—to Canada and Mexico 10¢ each, to other countries 21¢ each.

Canada (in effect July 1, 1980)

Letter mail and postcards—Up to 30g 17¢, 31-50g 26¢, 51-100g 38¢, 101-150g 56¢, 151-200g 74¢, 201-250g 91¢, 251-300g $1.09, 301-350g $1.27, 351-400g $1.44, 401-450g $1.62, 451-500g $1.80.
To U.S.A. territories and possessions—(1) **Airmail letters and postcards,** up to and including 30g 17¢, 30-50g 30¢ plus approx. 25¢ for each additional 50g up to 500g. Over 500g up to and including 1kg $3.90 with increases up to $52.69 for a maximum of 30kg. (2) **Surface parcel post.** Up to and including 1kg $1.90 plus 55¢ for each additional 500g up to a maximum of 16g.